THE CAMBRIDGE
GUIDE TO
THEATRE
Martin Banham

CAMBRIDGE
UNIVERSITY PRESS

Published by the Press Syndicate of the University of Cambridge
The Pitt Building, Trumpington Street, Cambridge CB2 1RP
40 West Street, New York, NY 10011–4211, USA
10 Stamford Road, Oakleigh, Melbourne 3166, Australia

First published 1988 as *The Cambridge Guide to World Theatre*
Revised paperback edition first published 1992
This edition first published 1995

Printed in Great Britain at the University Press, Cambridge

A catalogue record is available from the British Library

Library of Congress cataloging in publication data

Banham, Martin.
The Cambridge guide to theatre / Martin Banham. – New ed.
1248 p. 25.3 cm.
Rev. ed. of: The Cambridge guide to world theatre. 1988.
Includes bibliographical references.
1. Theater–Dictionaries.
I. Banham, Martin. Cambridge guide to world theatre.
II. Title.
PN2035.C27 1995
792'.03–dc20 95–1011

ISBN 0 521 434378 hardback

THE
CAMBRIDGE
GUIDE TO

THEATRE

Martin Banham

Editor's Introduction

This new edition of *The Cambridge Guide to Theatre* offers a comprehensive updating and revision of *The Cambridge Guide to World Theatre* first published in 1988, and of the paperback edition published in 1992. In the introduction to that edition I noted that, in the four years since the publication of the first edition, startling changes had taken place – for instance, in 1988 Václav Havel was to be noted as a dissident Czech playwright and by 1989 he was President of his country. In 1988 we wrote of South African theatre reflecting that country's unique social problems. Today we can record a theatre contributing to a people's understanding of a post-apartheid society. Old stars have been rediscovered, through the archaeological excavations in London of the Elizabethan playhouses, the Rose and the Globe, and new stars have established themselves.

This second edition contains over two hundred entirely new entries, and major reworkings of many other substantial entries. For instance, John Conteh-Morgan offers a total reconsideration of the lively francophone theatre of Africa; John Emigh and James Brandon contribute a major contextualizing essay on Asian influences in Western drama; Les du S. Read looks at the history and language of costume from a truly international standpoint. New entries are offered on masks, liturgical drama, miracle and mystery plays, on actors, directors and playwrights, and from Laurence Senelick we have a splendid exploration of stage food. Leonard Conolly has overseen revisions of English-language Canadian theatre materials and Phyllis Zatlin has been responsible for reconsideration of the Spanish entries. The *Guide* is fortunate in the authority and enterprise of its individual contributors, themselves drawn from over twenty-five countries worldwide. As editor my thanks are due to them all. I have also been greatly helped by correspondents' and reviewers' reactions – always constructive and helpful – to the previous editions of the *Guide*. I give particular thanks to Girish Karnad for a valuable addition to our material on India. The editorial board of the *Guide* is alert and rigorous, though in no way responsible for the editor's quirks and preferences! New board members are Professor Eldred Durosimi Jones from Sierra Leone, Dr Anuradha Kapur from Delhi and Professor Yasunari Takahashi from Japan.

Our original intentions in publishing the *Guide* were, and remain, to offer a comprehensive view of the history and present practice of theatre in all parts of the world, thus pointing to the dynamic interaction of performance traditions from all cultures in present day theatre. We also aim to celebrate the vitality and importance of popular theatre and popular entertainment, and the constructive relationship between 'high' and 'low' art in the theatre – the fusion that brings together the eccentric comedian Max Wall and Samuel Beckett's Vladimir, and which gives us equal interest in Shakespeare's famous clown Will Kempe and in his mastery of the jig.

As editor my aim is to offer both students of the theatre and the general theatregoer information, assessment and entertainment, and a base from which they may explore particular interests. Although a large number of the entries are concerned with theatrical practitioners, we also offer substantial coverage of national traditions of theatre, from Russia to Ecuador, Canada to Nigeria. We are concerned, too, with a range of other important topics, such as dramatic theory, criticism, censorship, lighting, sound, design, theatre buildings, as well as puppets and performing animals, fireworks, waxworks, acrobatics, carnival and cabaret. The *Guide* has been recognized as 'the single most useful volume on theatre in the language'. I'm pleased that we can now, through the initiative of Cambridge Reference, offer the full new edition at an accessible price.

Editing a work of reference such as this is rather like painting the Forth Bridge – no sooner completed than it is necessary to start again. One also suffers from a morbid interest in obituaries. I am helped by readers who draw errors or omissions to my attention, or who dispute, as King Lear says, 'who's in, who's out'. I hope readers will continue to write c/o Cambridge University Press, in the confidence that opinions and information are greatly valued. I owe special thanks to colleagues and friends who have helped me in an impressive variety of ways, especially the staff and students from the Workshop Theatre of the School of English at the University of Leeds, my indispensable secretary Mrs Nicola Wildman, and Judith Greenwood.

The first edition recorded thanks to many who had assisted in the birth of the *Guide* or given special help to individual contributors, and those thanks are reiterated here. At Cambridge University Press Sarah Stanton has to take credit for the initiative that led to the *Guide* in the first place, and she continues to support our work (with her own concised edition complementing this volume). At Cambridge Reference Adrian du Plessis has shown great confidence in the future of the *Guide* and Caroline Bundy has been the most impressive and helpful of press editors. Without her support, dedication, friendship and sheer professional hard work this volume would probably never have appeared. In Sue Phillpott I have had the advantage of the most expert of copyeditors. Her work has been meticulous and constructively creative, and I thank her for it.

Finally, my warm thanks to my wife, Kate, and my family for their support. The dedication of the volume remains to the memory of my mother Mary Winifred (Molly) Banham and to my grandchildren Tom and Lucy Lopez.

MARTIN BANHAM
Leeds, 1995

Contributors

KAM KAMAL ABDEL-MALEK
Brown University

MA MICHAEL ANDERSON
University of Kent at Canterbury

SMA STEPHEN M ARCHER
University of Missouri-Columbia

GSA GORDON S ARMSTRONG
University of Rhode Island

AA ARNOLD ARONSON
Columbia University

MB MARTIN BANHAM
University of Leeds

RKB ROSEMARY K BANK
Kent State University

AB ALEC BARON†

WOB WILLIAM O BEEMAN
Brown University

EBen EUGENE BENSON
University of Guelph

MBer MISHA BERSON
critic, Seattle Times

RPB RICHARD BOON
University of Leeds

DB DAVID BRADBY
Royal Holloway, University of London

JRB JAMES R BRANDON
University of Hawai'i at Manoa

GWB GEORGE W BRANDT
University of Bristol, emeritus

EB EUGENE BROGYÁNYI
*Dramaturge, Threshold Theatre Company,
NYC*

ALB ANDREW BROWN
Independent scholar

ElB ELAINE BUNN
Drew University

JMB JARKA M BURIAN
State University of New York, Albany

FB FRANCES BZOWSKI
Independent scholar, State of Rhode Island

SC STEPHEN CHIFUNYISE
Independent scholar

OkC OH-KON CHO
State University of New York, Brockport

LDC LARRY D CLARK
University of Missouri-Columbia

RC RUBY COHN
University of California, Davis

DC DAVID COLLISON
Adventure Projects, Hampton, UK

TC THOMAS CONNOLLY
Suffolk University

JCM JOHN CONTEH-MORGAN
*University of Sierra Leone/Ohio State University,
Columbus*

JD JILL DAVIS
University of Kent at Canterbury

JDo JILL DOLAN
*Graduate Center, City University of
New York*

LED LEONARD DOUCETTE
*University of Toronto,
Scarborough Campus*

CD CHRIS DUNTON
University of Lesotho

WD WELDON DURHAM
University of Missouri-Columbia

JE JOHN ELSOM
City University, London

JEm JOHN EMIGH
Brown University

RE RONALD ENGLE
University of North Dakota

ME	**MICHAEL ETHERTON** *Oxfam, Oxford*	**GH**	**GEORGE HAUGER** *University of Leeds*
AF	**ANGELIKA FESTA** *Independent scholar, New York City*	**MCH**	**MARY C HENDERSON** *Independent scholar/writer, New York*
GF	**GERALD FITZGIBBON** *University College, Cork*	**PHe**	**PAUL HERNARDI** *University of California,* *Santa Barbara*
KFl	**KATHY FLETCHER** *University of Nebraska, Lincoln*	**WH**	**WIL HILDEBRAND** *Utrecht University*
KF	**KATHY FOLEY** *University of California, Santa Cruz*	**EGH**	**ERROL G. HILL** *Dartmouth College, emeritus*
SF	**SCOTT FOSDICK** *Independent scholar/critic, Chicago*	**FH**	**FOSTER HIRSCH** *Brooklyn College*
LF	**LISA FUSILLO** *University of Nebraska, Lincoln*	**PH**	**PETER HOLLAND** *University of Cambridge*
KG	**KIMANI GECAU** *Independent scholar*	**MPH**	**MARION P HOLT** *Graduate Center, City University of* *New York*
DG	**DANIEL GEROULD** *Graduate Center, City University of* *New York*	**AH**	**ANDREW HORN** *University of the South Pacific*
MG	**MARTIN VAN GINKEL** *Utrecht University*	**EH**	**ERIN HURLEY** *City University of New York*
SG	**SPENCER GOLUB** *Brown University*	**AI**	**ARNI IBSEN** *Independent scholar, Reykjavík*
DGG	**DAVID G GOODMAN** *University of Illinois at* *Urbana-Champaign*	**PI**	**PETRIT IMAMI** *University of Arts, Belgrade*
FG	**FRANCES GRAY** *University of Sheffield*	**CI**	**CHRISTOPHER INNES** *York University, Ontario*
AEG	**A E GREEN** *University College, Bretton Hall*	**AJ**	**ANTHONY JACKSON** *University of Manchester*
WG	**WILLIAM GREEN** *Queen's College, City University of NewYork*	**CLJ**	**C LEE JENNER** *Independent scholar/critic,* *New York City*
JG	**JUDITH GREENWOOD** *Independent scholar*	**KJ**	**KRISHEN JIT** *University of Malaya*
DAH	**DOROTHY A HADFIELD** *University of Western Ontario*	**CK**	**CHRISTOPHER KAMLONGERA** *University of Malawi*
RAH	**ROGER A HALL** *James Madison University*	**NK**	**NICOLÁS KANELLOS** *University of Houston*
MH	**MARTHA T HALSEY** *Pennsylvania State University*	**GK**	**GIRISH KARNAD** *Actor, Director, Playwright*
FHa	**FRANCES HARDING** *School of Oriental and African Studies,* *University of London*	**RK**	**ROBERT KAVANAGH** *University of Zimbabwe*
TH-S	**TORI HARING-SMITH** *Brown University*	**LK**	**LAURENCE KEATES** *University of Leeds*

DK **DRAGAN KLAIC**
Theater Instituut, The Netherlands

MK **MARGARET M KNAPP**
Arizona State University

PK **PHILIP KOLIN**
University of Southern Mississippi

JK-D **JAMES KOTSILIBAS-DAVIS**
Independent writer, New York City

REK **RICHARD E KRAMER**
Independent scholar, New York City

HL **HARRY LANE**
University of Guelph

SL **STEPHEN LANGLEY**
Brooklyn College

BL **BISTRA LANKOVA**
Independent scholar

TL **THOMAS LEABHART**
Pomona College

CL **C I LEWIS**
Independent scholar

PL **PETER LEWIS**
University of Durham

FHL **FELICIA HARDISON LONDRÉ**
University of Missouri, Kansas City

BMCC **BRUCE A MCCONACHIE**
William & Mary College

JMCC **JOHN MCCORMICK**
Samuel Beckett Centre for Drama, Dublin

DMCD **DOUGLAS MCDERMOTT**
California State University, Stanislaus

LM **LINDA MACKENNEY**
Independent scholar

CPM **COLIN MACKERRAS**
Griffith University

BMCN **BROOKS MCNAMARA**
New York University

HDMCN **HOWARD MCNAUGHTON**
University of Canterbury, Christchurch

MMac **MARGARET MACPHERSON**
Makerere University, emeritus

DMa **DOROTHY MANDEL**
Independent scholar, Boulder, Colorado

LMa **LAURENCE MASLON**
Arena Stage, Washington DC

JDM **JEFFREY D MASON**
California State University, Bakersfield

DM **DESMOND MAXWELL**
York University, Ontario

PM **PETER MEREDITH**
University of Leeds

WJM **WALTER J MESERVE**
Graduate Center, City University of New York, emeritus

TM **TOM MIKOWICZ**
University of Maine

TLM **TICE L MILLER**
University of Nebraska, Lincoln

NWaM **NGUGI WA MIRII**
University of Zimbabwe

BM **BOGDAN MISCHIU**
Independent scholar

PMM **PENINA MLAMA**
University of Dar Es Salaam

RM **RICHARD MOODY**
Indiana University, emeritus

LRM **LYNETTE MUIR**
University of Leeds

DMW **DICKSON MWANSA**
Independent scholar

KN **KENT NEELY**
Boise State University

PN **PENNY NEWMAN**
University of Leeds

IN **IRMELI NIEMI**
Department of Culture, Ministry of Education, Finland

AJN **ANDREA J NOURYEH**
St Lawrence University

BO **BOBBI OWEN**
University of North Carolina, Chapel Hill

RP **RICHARD PILBROW**
Theatre Projects, Connecticut

DP **DANIEL PIRES**
Independent scholar

JP **JØRGEN PJETTURSON**
Independent scholar

JPl **JANE PLASTOW**
University of Leeds

AP	**ADRIANA POPESCU** *National Theatre, Bucharest*		**JS**	**JULIUS SPENCER** *Fourah Bay College,* *University of Sierra Leone*
TP	**THOMAS POSTLEWAIT** *Ohio State University*		**SS**	**SARAH STANTON** *Cambridge University Press*
APr	**AMANDA PRICE** *University of Leeds*		**IS**	**IAN STEADMAN** *University of the Witwatersrand*
LSR	**LESLIE DU S READ** *University of Exeter*		**JRS**	**J R STEPHENS** *University of Swansea*
FR	**FRANCIS REID** *Theatre Consultant, Norwich*		**ES**	**ELSA STRIETMAN** *University of Cambridge*
MR	**MARTIN REILINGH** *McNeese State University*		**JET**	**JOHN E TAILBY** *University of Leeds*
KR	**KENNETH RICHARDS** *University of Manchester*		**GT**	**G THANIEL** *Independent scholar*
LR	**LAURA RICHARDS** *Salford University*		**PT**	**PETER THOMSON** *University of Exeter*
FaR	**FARLEY RICHMOND** *State University of New York, Stony Brook*		**DV**	**DEV VIRAHSAWMY** *L'Express-Culture and Research,* *Mauritius*
HR	**HUGH RORRISON** *University of Leeds*		**CW**	**CLIVE WAKE** *Independent scholar*
DR	**DONALD ROY** *University of Hull*		**AW**	**ANTON WAGNER** *York University, Canada*
GAR	**GRAHAM RUNNALLS** *University of Edinburgh*		**RHW**	**RONALD H WAINSCOTT** *University of Nebraska, Lincoln*
NS	**NAHMA SANDROW** *Bronx Community College*		**DJW**	**DANIEL J WATERMEIER** *University of Toledo*
CS	**CHRISTOPHER SCARLES** *Cambridge University Press*		**MW**	**MARGARET WILLIAMS** *University of New South Wales*
RAS	**ROBERT A SCHANKE** *Central College, Iowa*		**SW**	**SIMON WILLIAMS** *University of California,* *Santa Barbara*
HS	**HENRI SCHOENMAKERS** *Utrecht University*		**DBW**	**DON B WILMETH** *Brown University*
ClS	**CLAUDE SCHUMACHER** *University of Glasgow*		**BBW**	**BARRY B WITHAM** *University of Washington, Seattle*
HaS	**HANNA SCOLNICOV** *Hebrew University of Jerusalem*		**GW**	**GEORGE WOODYARD** *University of Kansas, Lawrence*
ACS	**A C SCOTT†**		**DSPY**	**DANIEL S P YANG** *Hong Kong Repertory Theatre*
MS	**MAXINE S SELLER** *State University of New York, Buffalo*		**MY**	**MASAKO YUASA** *University of Leeds*
LS	**LAURENCE SENELICK** *Tufts University*		**PZ**	**PHYLLIS ZATLIN** *Rutgers University*
LSh	**LOUIS SHEAFFER†**			
AS	**ALISA SOLOMON** *critic, Village Voice*			

A note on less obvious entries

The list below, while not intended to be in any way exhaustive, is intended to point the reader to entries in various categories, and to indicate the range of topics that we aim to cover in the *Guide* beyond those one would normally expect.

animal impersonation
animals as performers
Aquarium
Asian influences on
    Western theatre
baiting
ballad opera
Barnum's American Museum
below
book-holder
book-keeper
boulevard
breeches part
burlesque
cabaret
carnival
castrato
censorship
circus
citizen comedy
claque
closure of the theatres
clown
collective theatre groups
    (USA)
comedy of humours
copyright
costume
Crazy Gang
criticism
directing
discovery space
dramatic theory
epic theatre
ethnic theatre (USA)
expressionism
Federal Street Theatre
female impersonation
feminist theatre
fireworks
flyting

folk theatre, Asian
fringe theatre (Britain)
frontier theatre
futurism
gag
gay theatre
gracioso
grand opera
Hanswurst
Harlequin
heavens
hero-combat play
hippodrama
hunger artist
inns as playhouses
interlude
juggler
Krio theatre
laterna magika
Leipzig style
lesbian theatre
liturgical drama
living newspaper
magic
male impersonation
Maori theatre
marionette
masks
medicine show
Mickery-theater
mime, pantomime
minstrel show
nudity
nurseries
Nuyorican theatre
opera
parody
pastoral
penny theatres
Pepper's ghost
Pierrot

play
pornographic theatre
producer
resident non-professional
    theatre (USA)
revue
rite of passage
ritual
Sami theatre
satire
shadow puppets
shaman
showboats
sound in the theatre
Soviet children's theatre
stage food
stage lighting
Stainless Stephen
surrealism
symbolism
television drama
tent show
theatre design
theatre-in-education
theatrical monopoly
Theatrical Syndicate
Third World popular theatre
tireman
Toby
toy theatre
travesty role
Uncle Tom's Cabin
university and school drama
    (16th–18th centuries)
war of the theatres
waxworks
well made play
Wild West exhibition
Women's Project and
    Productions
Yankee theatre

Note to the Reader

Entries are listed in alphabetical word-by-word order, ignoring hyphens and apostrophes. Thus La Grange will precede Laberge or L'Arronge; De Rojas will precede DeMille. Names beginning with Mc have been put with those beginning with Mac. St has been ordered as Saint.

A name or part of a name which is unused is put in round brackets: e.g. Barrie, J(ames) M(atthew). Where a person (or genre) is known by more than one name, or started life with a different one, the alternative name appears in square brackets after the more familiar one: e.g. Astaire [Austerlitz], Fred.

The appearance of SMALL CAPITALS or *SMALL ITALIC CAPITALS* in the course of an entry indicates that the topic receives an entry of its own elsewhere in the *Guide*.

The break-up of the USSR has been dealt with as follows: individuals whose careers preceded 1917 or extend beyond 1991 are called Russian. Those whose careers coincided with the period 1917–91 are called Soviet. Persons whose careers spanned the 1917 marker are referred to as Russian-Soviet. The exceptions are those individuals whose republican nationality (Lithuanian, Ukrainian, Georgian) is a significant factor in their careers.

Abbey, Henry E(dwin) 1846–96 American impresario known early in his career for presenting costly entertainments to audiences outside major US theatre centres and, from 1880, for his success in booking the best European actors, actresses and opera singers for US engagements, for which he became known as 'the Napoleon of the Managers'. The partnership of Abbey, John B. Schoeffel and Maurice Grau managed theatres in New York, Boston and Philadelphia, as well as the tours of domestic and international stars. At the Park Theatre, New York (1877), he brought together WILLIAM H. CRANE and STUART ROBSON, a starring tandem that flourished until 1889. The partnership took over the Metropolitan Opera House, New York (1883), and until Abbey's death in 1896 the management was distinctive for the great stars they hired. WD

Abbey Theatre The Dublin theatre by whose name the Irish National Theatre Society Ltd is popularly known. The Society's predecessors were the Irish Literary Theatre (1899–1901), founded by W. B. YEATS, AUGUSTA LADY GREGORY and Edward Martyn to create an indigenous Irish dramatic literature; and the Irish National Dramatic Company of Frank and Willie Fay. The Society, formed by the Fays, Yeats, Lady Gregory and J. M. SYNGE, aimed to encourage new writers, in Synge's words, to 'work in English that is perfectly Irish in essence'. The 1904 Abbey Street theatre – a converted morgue – was the gift of an English admirer of Yeats, ANNIE HORNIMAN.

The Fay brothers were experienced amateurs, whose emphasis on simplicity of design and clarity of vocal presentation Yeats found compatible, but the demanding patronage of Miss Horniman and the embattled relationship with contemporary cultural nationalism generated many disputes. Maude Gonne and Arthur Griffith took the Fays' rejection of PADRAIC COLUM'S *The Saxon Shillin'* as censorship of patriotic art, and resigned. When Miss Horniman's subsidy turned the players into salaried employees without voting rights, more left, some, with Padraic Colum and Edward Martyn, to set up the rival Theatre of Ireland (1906–12). By 1911 the Fays had gone, Synge had died and the Horniman subsidy had ceased; the Abbey was being run by the inexperienced LENNOX ROBINSON under the direction of Yeats and Gregory.

In the early years the theatre's political difficulties fastened themselves on Synge, whose disreputable peasant characters provoked riotous nationalist demonstrations, especially against *The Playboy of the Western World* (1907). Yeats showed his courage in outfacing the demonstrators, but the Abbey audience's taste was more inclined to Lady Gregory's low-key and undisturbing folk dramas. Synge's mantle passed to SEAN O'CASEY and his synthesis of poetic vernacular and urban REALISM. His irreverent treatment of the patriotic myths of Easter 1916 in *The Plough and the Stars* (1926) caused more riots. 'You have disgraced yourselves again,' Yeats told the audience. Sadly, O'Casey abandoned the Abbey when in 1928 Yeats rejected his part-expressionistic (see EXPRESSIONISM) *The Silver Tassie*.

Despite Yeats's poetic intentions, however, the Abbey had consolidated a line of essentially realist drama on local themes – the characteristic work of Colum, Robinson and T. C. MURRAY. Robinson (play director 1909–14, 1919–35) was receptive to this kind of play, but also inaugurated the DUBLIN DRAMA LEAGUE (1919–29), opening the Abbey stage to experimental European and American drama.

A series of American tours and in 1925 an annual government subsidy – largely due to government minister Ernest Blythe (board of directors 1935–41, managing director 1941–72) – mitigated the Abbey's chronic penury and enabled the directors to develop a little theatre, the Peacock. Their better-known players – Sarah Allgood,

The first production of *The Plough and the Stars* by Sean O'Casey, Abbey Theatre, 1926.

Barry Fitzgerald, CYRIL CUSACK, Siobhan McKenna – remained at risk to the rewards of London and Hollywood. Under Blythe's autocratic rule, with Yeats now infrequently present, the Abbey languished but survived. In the 1930s and 40s the discipline of acting and direction slackened, vulgarizing perhaps its best writer of the period, GEORGE SHIELS. A few substantial new playwrights – including PAUL VINCENT CARROLL and M. J. MOLLOY – emerged. HUGH HUNT's tenure (play director 1935–8) was too brief to establish reform.

The fire which destroyed the old Abbey in 1951 exiled the company for 15 years to the decrepit Queen's Theatre, a larger house requiring runs longer than the Abbey's practice, until it returned to its new home – a 628-seat modern theatre on the old site with, like the 167-seat new Peacock, sophisticated stage and lighting facilities. After an indecisive start, the new Abbey found its confidence, enlivened by the considerable talents of the directors Tomas MacAnna, Alan Simpson, Joe Dowling, and a permanent company. However, recent times have seen both trouble and triumph. On the one hand there have been five artistic directors in about eight years, and the Abbey's primacy has been challenged by a resurgent GATE THEATRE. Garry Hynes (1990–3) bravely attempted to recreate a sense of distinctive and radical directorial style – her productions of *The Plough and the Stars* and McGahern's *The Power of Darkness* provoked major controversy – but departed after three years of struggle with an unwieldy structure and a critical public. It remains to be seen whether Patrick Mason, her successor, will fare better. On the other hand there have been successful European and American tours, both of classics and of new work like BRIAN FRIEL's *Dancing at Lughnasa*; the theatre has had the stimulus of distinguished guest directors; and it has established SHAKESPEARE, CHEKHOV and BRECHT in its programming.

The Abbey remains essentially a writers' theatre – despite some aberrant rejections – and was an important instrument in the dramatic revival which began in the 1960s. Among the contemporary Irish writers mainly associated with it are Brian Friel, Bernard Farrell, TOM MURPHY, TOM KILROY, TOM MACINTYRE, FRANK MCGUINNESS and SEBASTIAN BARRY. So, despite its recent turbulent history, the Abbey continues to be at the centre of Irish theatre and a major force in Irish cultural life.   DM GF

Abbott, George 1887–1995 American director, playwright and actor. In his 1963 autobiography (*Mister Abbott*), Abbott praises his Harvard drama teacher GEORGE PIERCE BAKER in a way that defines his own theatrical creed: 'Professor Baker gave you no nonsense about inner meanings and symbolism; he turned your whole thoughts and energies into the practical matter of how to make a show.' Taking Baker's lessons to heart, Abbott became the most practical showman in BROADWAY history. As performer, co-author, play doctor, and director of over 130 productions, Abbott entertained audiences more often and over a longer period of time than anyone else, garnering six Tonys and a Pulitzer. He first acted on a Broadway stage in 1913; in the autumn of 1989 he directed a workshop production of a new MUSICAL called *Frankie*. As both director and co-author his specialities were racy contem-

porary MELODRAMA (*Broadway*, 1926); split-second FARCE (*Three Men on a Horse*, 1935); and peppy musicals with vigorous choreography (*On Your Toes*, 1936; *Damn Yankees*, 1955). Gangsters, bookies, gold diggers, politicians, baseball heroes, hoofers and hookers populate his work, providing colourful slices of Americana. Despite the occasional suggestion of sexual daring (as in *Coquette* (1927) and *New Girl in Town* (1957), his musical version of *Anna Christie*) and of political conflict (*The Pajama Game*, 1954; *Fiorello!*, 1959), the typical Abbott show was archly conservative. The famed 'Abbott touch' always kept his shows spinning at a brisk clip, but Abbott downplayed his technique, claiming that all he did was to make actors 'say their final syllables'. At age 106 he was still active, revising *Damn Yankees* for a 1994 production.   FH

Abell, Kjeld 1901–61 Danish playwright. Abell began his career designing Balanchine ballets at the KONGELIGE TEATER, before writing his own ballet scenario *The Widow in the Mirror* (1934), which explored the alienating effects of social convention. Ballet influenced the visual, non-realistic elements in his plays, beginning with *The Melody that Got Lost* (1935), produced at the Riddersalen cabaret theatre, which Abell admired. More substantial than CABARETS, his early expressionistic plays (see EXPRESSIONISM), *The Melody* and *Eve Does Her Duty* (1936), sharply depict the suffocating effect of bourgeois values. During and after the Second World War, plays like *Anna Sophie Hedvig* (1939), *Judith* (1940), *The Queen on Tour* (1943), *Silkeborg* (1946) and *Days on a Cloud* (1947) identify activism as self-liberation, and escapism as self-annihilation. After protesting against the murder of KAJ MUNK, Abell spent part of the war in hiding. His subsequent plays increased in complexity, exploring in a cinematic style the spiritual linking of minds through time and space, and the despair of those who resist such bonds: the deceased David in *Vetsera Doesn't Bloom for Everyone* (1950), Tordis in *The Blue Pekingese* (1954) and the organist Dan in his last play, *The Scream*.   HL

Abington, Frances 1737–1815 English actress. Born into a poor family, she worked as a flower-seller and for a milliner before she began acting, though she still managed to learn French and Italian. By 1755 she was working with THEOPHILUS CIBBER at the HAYMARKET Theatre and the following year joined DRURY LANE on the recommendation of SAMUEL FOOTE. After a period acting in Ireland she returned to London to join GARRICK's company at Drury Lane. Garrick always admired her acting though, irritated by her temperament, he called her 'the worst of bad women'. In 1776 she made the first announcement of her retirement but continued to act, playing Lady Teazle in SHERIDAN's *The School for Scandal* (1777). Though very highly paid she retired on a whim in 1790, making an unsuccessful return in 1799, by which time she was overweight and 'her elegance somewhat unfashionable'. For much of her career she was a leader of fashion, popularizing hairstyles and hats named after her.   PH

above A term much used in the often enigmatic stage directions of Elizabethan plays, the 'above' was a practical upper level, equally important in the public and private theatres of London. It is generally assumed that the gallery over the stage of the SWAN, clearly visible in De Witt's drawing of that theatre, represents the kind of fixture normally used by actors entering 'above', although there are occasions on which a free-standing two-tier structure would have proved more satisfactory. There is precedent for such structures in medieval staging, which often calls for an upper level for the accommodation of God and angels. (See also BELOW.) PT

absurd, theatre of the see THEATRE OF THE ABSURD

Accesi Two acting companies of the Italian COMMEDIA DELL'ARTE, both begun under the patronage of Vincenzo I Gonzaga, Duke of Mantua. The first may have been founded about 1595, the other around 1600, by Tristano Martinelli and Pier Maria Cecchini, who eventually took over its management. The troupe toured Italy and appeared several times in France with such players as Flaminio Scala and Drusiano Martinelli. They merged with GIOVAN BATTISTA ANDREINI's troupe, the FEDELI, for a brief period, before dissolving about 1626, at which time SILVIO FIORILLO was the company's outstanding player in his role as Captain Matamoros. LS

Accius, Lucius 170–c.86 BC A prolific and popular Roman tragedian, apparently the last Roman tragedian to write regularly for the stage. About 700 lines survive, revealing a flamboyant and melodramatic style. He also wrote works of scholarship, including literary history. ALB

Achurch, Janet 1864–1916 British actress whose career is identified with IBSEN and SHAW. As a member of F. R. BENSON's company in the 1880s, she established a reputation as a tragedian. On taking over the management of London's Novelty Theatre in 1889 she played Nora in the first British production of *A Doll's House*, returning to play Mrs Linde as her final stage appearance in 1911. In 1900 she starred in the premieres of *Candida* and *Captain Brassbound's Conversion*, and her correspondence with Shaw was made the basis for a play in 1978. CI

Ackermann family The most important family of German actors in the 18th century. After a career in the military, in 1740 **Konrad (Ernst)** (1712–71) joined the SCHÖNEMANN troupe. He soon left to set up his own troupe, along with SOPHIE SCHRÖDER (1714–92), who was shortly to be the mother of FRIEDRICH SCHRÖDER. After Sophie's husband died, Konrad married her. The Ackermann troupe toured widely in Central and Eastern Europe, acquiring a considerable name for itself, above all for introducing to the German stage the genre of the BÜRGERLICHES TRAUERSPIEL. In particular, after EKHOF joined the company in 1764, it became widely known for the comparative realism of its acting. In 1767, temporarily without the leadership of Ackermann, the troupe formed the Hamburg National Theatre company. When that project foundered, they returned to the road. After Ackermann's death, Friedrich Schröder took over the leadership, eventually settling permanently in the Hamburg Town Theatre. Ackermann's two daughters, **Dorothea**

(1752–1821) and **Charlotte** (1757–74), promised, by their talent and beauty, to be among the greatest actresses of the German stage, but Dorothea disliked acting and left the profession for marriage in 1778. Charlotte, a great favourite with the Hamburg audiences, was driven too hard by her stepbrother Friedrich; she died, possibly by her own hand, before she was 18. SW

Acquart, André 1922– French stage designer. Educated in Algiers at the École Nationale des Beaux Arts, Acquart moved to Paris in 1951. Since then he has designed in Germany and France but is known primarily for his work in the 1960s for leading French directors. Such productions include *The Blacks* (1959), directed by ROGER BLIN, *The Resistible Rise of Arturo Ui* (1961), co-directed by JEAN VILAR and Georges Wilson, and *Biedermann and the Firebugs* (1960), directed by JEAN-MARIE SERREAU. His designs are abstract, utilizing skeletal structures such as tubes or movable flats and multiple playing levels. This style is best exemplified in his pivoting and folding flats designed for ROGER PLANCHON's *Troilus and Cressida* (1964), and in his use of steps and mobile paper screens for Roger Blin's version of GENET's *The Screens* (1966). AJN

acrobatics One of the most ancient and prevalent forms of physical entertainment. Egyptian and Etruscan murals depict leapers and vaulters, who often performed at feasts, and the springboard itself was known to antiquity. The earliest work devoted to the subject is Arcangelo Tuccaro's *Trois dialogues de l'exercice de sauter et voltiger en l'air* (1599), which applied to the architectonics of the leap and the mastery of mind over body the same attention to physicality that was creating ritualistic etiquette at the court of Charles IX. In 1641 Tommaso Garzoni drew up a list of distinguished acrobats.

The most basic move is the *salto* or leap into the air, in which neither hands nor feet must move. All sorts of combinations are possible – backwards, forwards, sideways (the Arab jump), the flip-flop (a backward somersault from a standing position), and from trampolines and flying trapezes. The *salto mortale* or death-defying leap is so called from its dangerousness. A double *salto mortale* was first performed by an Englishman named Tomkinson in 1840; a triple, two years later, at Van Amburgh's CIRCUS resulted in a fatal accident. The first successful triple from a high springboard was made by the American Billy Dutton in 1860 and later Alfredo Codona mastered it on the flying trapeze.

Other forms of acrobatics include the antipodean, in which one acrobat lies on his back and juggles the other performer with his feet; and its offshoot, the Icarian games, invented by the Englishman Cottrelly c.1850, in which performers are tossed, balanced and caught by the feet of their partners, lying on specially constructed cushions. The most outstanding exponents were the Schäffers and the Kremos: Sylvester Schäffer (1860–1931) created a six-man column, balanced on the feet of the low man. Risley stunts, named after Professor Richard Risley (Carlisle), involve somersaults performed by two children, from foot to foot of the recumbent partner.

In popular amusements like the COMMEDIA DELL'ARTE and the harlequinade, acrobatics is at a premium, but it is

The Three Emersons, a clown acrobatic act active in European variety in the early 20th century.

neglected by the dramatic stage, except in actors' training. TOM STOPPARD in *Jumpers* (1972) used acrobatics as a metaphor for mental gymnastics, and the 12th-century fabliau of *The Tumbler of Our Lady* has been made into an OPERA (Massenet, 1902), a ballet (D. Howes, 1936) and several plays. LS

acting The impulse to make-believe and PLAY is common to humanity. To act is both to do and to pretend to do. For both actor and spectator, the uncanny power of any performance springs from an ambiguous tension between what is actual and what is fictional. This ambiguity is present in all acting however much a particular society or individual may wish to resolve it. In the 20th century many Western theories of acting have stressed the integrity of the doing, while in the 18th century, for example, Europeans were more concerned with the authentic nature of the pretence, its style and social aptness.

Throughout history, the unease aroused by this ambiguity has been reflected in the status of the actor. Even in classical Greece (see GREECE, ANCIENT), where acting had religious and political importance, there is evidence from the 4th century BC onwards that the *technitai* of Dionysus were viewed with ambivalence. Certainly in ROME acting was felt to be the work of slaves and aliens; while in modern Europe players long existed on the margins of law and religion (MOLIÈRE could not be buried in consecrated ground).

In Asia, outside the confines of local prestige, religious purpose or court patronage, performers were, and often still are, equated with wanderers and beggars. Although in ancient India, actors were believed to trace their ancestry to a member of the highest caste, the priestly Bharata, sacred myths tell how they were soon condemned to the lowest caste for their satire and mockery of the sages. Only through the intervention of kings could this ambivalence be somewhat allayed. In China, decrees dating from as

early as 1369 banned actors from entering for state examinations; while in Japan, support from the shogun and nobility for some *sarugaku* players became in time a rigorously circumscribed privilege which excluded the majority of popular performers. (When, in the early 17th century, *nō* actors were given samurai rank only their sons could continue the tradition and act in *nō*.)

The social assimilation of the acting profession in the West, around the beginning of the 20th century, was paralleled by sustained and serious evaluation of its art. In England, for example, IRVING's knighthood in 1895, the first to be bestowed on an actor, was followed not only by further theatrical knighthoods (six before 1914) but also by the founding of the Academy of Dramatic Art (later RADA). Similar developments are evident throughout Europe, most notably in Russia where for STANISLAVSKY training combined with a radical analysis of the art. Stanislavsky's accounts of his psycho-physical method constitute the first systematic examination of acting, in the West, written from the viewpoint of the actor. Earlier writings are either anecdotal or, as with DIDEROT, written from the perspective of the auditorium.

In the East, such approaches to practice can be found in works like the *Natyasastra* (c.200 BC) and ZEAMI's treatises on the *nō* (c.1402–30). The systematic encoding of traditional acting genres found in such manuals emphasizes a performer's obligation to embody the received wisdom and aesthetics of particular styles and techniques. Training in the genre rather than rehearsal for the individual play is paramount. In Asian theatre, the master–pupil relationship is ubiquitous. Imparting the traditional form through example, through long apprenticeship and disciplined physical preparation and practice, establishes the importance of performance over text, of the transmitted skill in its present-tense embodiment over individual expression.

The art of acting lies in showing and sharing an action,

image, character or story. It is rooted in the present-tense encounter of actor with actor, and/or actor with audience. The material of the art is the body, voice and being of the performer. Different styles demand different skills of this material. Bodily skills may range from the acrobatic and pantoMIME, as in traditional Chinese theatre, through schematic languages of dance and gesture, as found in *KUTIYATTAM* or *KATHAKALI*, to the faithful reproduction of everyday motions, as in Western NATURALISM. Vocal skills likewise may range from song, through chant or declamation, to conversational speech. As for being, individual and group accomplishment may be openly celebrated or hidden. This is not simply a contrast between a presentational mode of acting with its emphasis on display and a representational mode with its stress on verisimilitude. It relates to human identity and human energies, to a range of percepts of which MASK and trance are an ambiguous part. Acting works with living presence. This is of utmost importance in performances and of the utmost contention in discussion. Contraries abound – inspiration versus technique, talent versus training. KEAN or KEMBLE, Irving or COQUELIN, DUSE or BERNHARDT? Theatre is a social art, and attitudes to being and social relationships inform any idea or style of acting. LSR

Acting Company (USA) JOHN HOUSEMAN and Margot Harley organized the first graduating class of the Drama Division of the Juilliard School into a permanent repertory troupe (originally, City Center Acting Company), which began performing at the City Center in New York in 1972. Since 1980 it has functioned as the touring arm of the JOHN F. KENNEDY CENTER FOR THE PERFORMING ARTS in Washington, DC; headquartered in New York, it continues primarily as a touring company with members selected nationally by auditions and moulded into an ensemble. Actors perform a variety of roles, classical and modern. The 1988–9 repertoire included: *Boy Meets Girl, The Phantom Tollbooth* and *Love's Labour's Lost.* By 1991 the Acting Company had performed over 67 plays in 46 states before 2 million people. Alumni of the company include KEVIN KLINE, PATTI LUPONE, WILLIAM HURT and Christopher Reeve. ZELDA FICHANDLER served as artistic director from 1991 to May 1994, replaced by Harley as producing director. TLM

Actors Studio, The (USA) Founded in 1947 by GROUP THEATRE alumni ELIA KAZAN, CHERYL CRAWFORD and ROBERT LEWIS, the Actors Studio is a unique workshop for professional actors. It is not a school; it charges no tuition; and once an actor is accepted (by a rigorous audition process) he or she becomes a member for life, for the Studio's basic assumption is that there is no terminal degree for an actor. Under LEE STRASBERG, who joined the Studio in 1949 and who from 1951 until his death in February 1982 was its strong-willed artistic director, the Studio became renowned as the high temple of the Method. The popular notion of the Studio as a place where the mumble, scratch and slouch are tokens of integrity derives from films directed by Elia Kazan (*A Streetcar Named Desire*, 1951; *On the Waterfront*, 1954; *East of Eden*, 1955) which feature moody, verbally inarticulate, spectacularly neurotic performances by such Studio members as MARLON BRANDO and James Dean.

Those who admire the Studio's naturalistic style (see NATURALISM) praise it for psychological revelation. Opponents attack the Studio as a place where self-indulgence, mannerism and inaudibility are encouraged, as actors examine their own emotions at the expense of the character or the play. Even Studio detractors, however, admit that the Method is a useful technique for the requirements of realistic film acting (see REALISM). The Studio's achievements continue to be hotly debated but its influence is undeniable; its Method has come to be identified as the quintessential American style. In 1963, after years of hesitation, the Studio formed its own short-lived theatre on BROADWAY; but its enduring legacy is the films directed by Kazan and the vibrant film performances of its many illustrious members, from Brando, Dean and Montgomery Clift to DUSTIN HOFFMAN, Robert de Niro, AL PACINO, Shelley Winters, GERALDINE PAGE and Frank Corsaro, who is the Studio's present artistic director. FH

Actors Theatre of Louisville One of the leading American regional theatres, located in Louisville, Kentucky, most noted for encouraging and producing original scripts. Richard Block and Ewel Cornett founded the Actors Theatre in 1964. Although successful, Block was replaced at his request in 1969 by Jon Jory, who had previously worked at the CLEVELAND PLAY HOUSE and had co-founded New Haven's LONG WHARF THEATRE. Jory's appointment and leadership proved beneficial. By 1970–1, season tickets accounted for 95 per cent of the house's capacity. In 1972 the company moved to their present location, the old Bank of Louisville Building. A $1.7 million conversion of the building resulted in the Pamela Brown Theatre (capacity 641) and the Victor Jory Theatre (capacity 160). A new 320-seat venue (Bingham Theatre) opened in autumn 1994.

In 1977 the Actors Theatre achieved international acclaim by initiating the Humana Festival of New American Plays. Scripts such as *The Gin Game* and *Crimes of the Heart* premiered at the Actors Theatre, moved to BROADWAY, and won Pulitzer Prizes for Drama. Other new plays produced included *Extremities* and *Execution of Justice*. In 1986 ATL initiated the Classics in Context Festival, which presents works from world literature supported by films, lectures and exhibits. The Bingham Signature Shakespeare Project and Flying Solo are recent innovations.

Jory and the Actors Theatre have received numerous awards and prizes as a result of their work. In 1978 they received the MARGO JONES Award for achievement in regional theatres; the next year the SHUBERT Foundation's James N. Vaughn Award for encouraging new scripts. In 1980 they received a special Tony. SMA

Adamov, Arthur 1908–70 French playwright of Armenian origins who grew up speaking French as his first language, as was common in wealthy Russian families. Because of his father's passion for gambling, as well as Revolution and exile, the family passed from riches to rags, and settled in Paris in 1924. Adamov's 20s and 30s were marked by loneliness and neurosis, chronicled in *L'Aveu* (*The Confession*, 1946) and *L'Homme et l'enfant*

(*Man and Child*, 1968). After the Second World War he began writing plays, completing seven between 1947 and 1953. Influenced by STRINDBERG, to whom he devoted a monograph, these plays depict a world of terror and persecution stemming from Adamov's own dreams and neuroses, but with a remarkable feel for the telling stage image that can embody, in literal form, a whole state of mind. The masterpiece of this period is *Professor Taranne* (1953). In 1955, when the THEATRE OF THE ABSURD, with which he had been linked, was becoming well known, Adamov's *Ping-Pong* heralded a move towards a more politicized theatre. His *Paolo Paoli* (directed by PLANCHON, 1957) was praised as the first successful BRECHTian play in France. Dogged by illness for ten years, Adamov did not achieve further success until *Off Limits* (directed by Garran and Grüber, 1969) and *Si l'été revenait* (*If Summer Returned*), published in 1970. His plays are complex and have not always been successful when performed, though his early work was championed by such as VILAR, BLIN and SERREAU. His move towards political theatre was made in tandem with Planchon, whose productions have shown how powerful Adamov's work can be, given sufficiently imaginative direction, notably in *A. A. Théâtres d'Adamov*, a posthumous tribute performed at the THÉÂTRE NATIONAL POPULAIRE in 1975.   DB

Adams, Edwin 1834–77 American actor. He made his debut in Boston in 1853, and after almost a decade of acting in support of such stars as JOSEPH JEFFERSON III and E. A. SOTHERN, he had his first important New York engagement in 1863 with KATE BATEMAN's company. During the Civil War, he established himself as a travelling star especially distinguished for his playing of romantic or light COMEDY characters in such vehicles as *The Lady of Lyons* and *Narcisse*. In 1869, EDWIN BOOTH selected him to play Mercutio opposite his Romeo for the opening of BOOTH'S THEATRE. He was subsequently featured at Booth's Theatre in several roles, including the dual roles of Phidias and Raphael in *The Marble Heart* and most notably the title role in a dramatization of Tennyson's *Enoch Arden*, perhaps his favourite characterization. In 1876, following a starring tour of Australia, Adams returned to the USA gravely ill. He made his last appearance at the California Theatre in San Francisco on 27 May 1876.   DJW

Adams [née Kiskadden], **Maude** 1872–1953 American actress, daughter of Salt Lake City star Annie Adams. At five Maude was starring as Little Schneider in *Fritz, Our Cousin German* in San Francisco. Her adult career began at 16 with a New York debut at the Star Theatre in *The Paymaster*. In 1890 she began an association with producer CHARLES FROHMAN that lasted until 1915. A box-office favourite until 1932 (despite an early retirement during 1918–31), she emerged in 1897 as a star, capitalizing on her eternal youthfulness and whimsy, as Lady Babbie in *The Little Minister*, a character rewritten for her by J. M. BARRIE. She also starred in US productions of his *Quality Street* (1901), *Peter Pan* (1905), *What Every Woman Knows* (1908), *The Legend of Leonora* (1914) and *A Kiss for Cinderella* (1916). Other parts included the title role in ROSTAND's *L'Aiglon*, the strutting hero in his *Chantecler*, and SHAKESPEARE's Viola, Juliet and Rosalind. In the 1920s

she was a lighting consultant for General Electric. In 1931 she toured with OTIS SKINNER in *The Merchant of Venice*. During 1937–50 she taught theatre at Stephens College, Missouri.   DBW

Addison, Joseph 1672–1719 English playwright. He wrote only two plays in the middle of a busy career as essayist and politician. In his collaborations with SIR RICHARD STEELE on the periodicals the *Tatler* and the *Spectator* he frequently wrote about drama and the practice of the theatres, often admiringly but frequently with a sharp mockery. His play *Cato* (1713) was the subject of an energetic controversy, partly over its alleged political allegory and partly over its success as a controlled neoclassical TRAGEDY of dignity and grief. Cato, who will weep for Rome but not for the death of his son, is offered as an exemplar of political duty. Addison's comedy *The Drummer or the Haunted House* (1716) was not a success.   PH

Ade, George 1866–1944 American playwright and librettist. Born and educated in Indiana, Ade made a name for himself as a reporter in Chicago before turning his talents to the theatre. His most popular librettos, *The Sultan of Sulu* (1902) and *The Sho-Gun* (1904), were influenced by GILBERT and Sullivan, but he is best remembered for two dramatic comedies of small-town life, *The County Chairman* (1903) and *The College Widow* (1904). The latter introduced the subject of collegiate adventures and the game of college football to the American stage. Because he had an outstanding ear for current slang and a keen eye for characterizing the everyday residents of his native mid-America, his more than a dozen plays and librettos, although seldom revived, illuminate the social record of the turn of the 20th century.   LDC

Adejumo, Moses Olaiya [Baba Sala] 1936– Nigerian actor-manager and founder-owner of the Alawada Theatre ('theatre of the one who entertains'). Olaiya, whose stage name is Baba Sala, is one of the most popular comedians in Nigeria today and his company (both acting and trading) is the most commercially successful, despite performances being almost entirely in Yoruba. The fact that the company is licensed to produce plays, run musical groups and hotels, and produce records and magazines is a clear indicator of Olaiya's vigorous business sense.

He started his first theatre group in 1963, and developed what is now his unique comic format in 1965, when he won first prize (a tour of West Germany) in a Nigerian TELEVISION DRAMA competition. He was denied the prize as his company was considered too coarse to represent Nigeria – its membership, being non-literate in English, might blemish the image of Nigeria abroad! He was, however, compensated with a permanent slot on local television. Ironically, this made his name and ensured the future success of his travelling theatre. Since 1965 he has performed continuously all over Nigeria and coastal West Africa.

Olaiya is a religious syncretist who, though Christian, has many wives and children. The strength of his hardworking company resides in its use of an aspect of Yoruba traditional theatrical heritage, the *yeye* (fun-making, also called *efe*), to treat diverse areas of human experience. Unlike his predecessors in the genre, HUBERT OGUNDE and

DURO LADIPO, Baba Sala does not take any noble roles in his plays, which always centre on the comic escapades and misadventures of one Lamidi Sani (Baba Sala himself). His comedies are improvised, witty and extremely funny, ensuring the popularity and the huge commercial returns that sustain his travelling theatre. The critic B. Jeyifo contends that, despite the plays' debunking of all social pretensions, Olaiya's potential for social protest is neutralized by the 'amoral, cynical social posture of this great satirist and parodist'.

Like Ogunde and Ade Afolayan, Baba Sala has branched into film-making, in which since the late 1970s he has been increasingly involved. In common with many practitioners in the YORUBA TRAVELLING THEATRE, by 1990 he had virtually abandoned live performance. He began using film by projecting shorts – often film material culled from other sources – as inserts in plays such as *Kunkusi*, *De Director* and *Tokunbo*, then turned to producing full-length films such as *Orun Mooru* (*Heaven Is Heated*). Subsequently he has turned to video as a medium. His videos are designed for projection before an audience, not for distribution as cassettes for sale to the public. Recent video productions include *Ore Adisa* (*Friend of Adisa*) and *Ashale Gege* (*Pamperer of Prostitutes*). He continues also to film for television. CD

Adelphi Theatre (London) Of four theatres on the same site in the Strand, the first was built in 1806 and called the Sans Pareil. It was renamed the Adelphi in 1819 and attracted sudden attention in 1821 with the successful run – the first to exceed 100 performances – of W. T. MONCRIEFF's *Tom and Jerry*. Under the management of Frederick Yates and Daniel Terry (1825–8), the Adelphi became known for its adaptations of Scott's novels and for nautical MELODRAMAS starring T. P. COOKE. During the long management (1844–74) of BENJAMIN WEBSTER, the theatre was rebuilt to accommodate 1500 (1858). It was well attended for most of this time, and the description 'Adelphi dramas' was familiarly attached to strong melodramas, well staged (the 'sinking stage' had been used at the Adelphi in 1834, for the first time in England) and powerfully acted by such as Cooke, Webster himself, his mistress MME CÉLESTE and O'Smith. BUCKSTONE and BOUCICAULT were among the featured dramatists. At the end of the century 'Adelphi dramas' still predominated, with WILLIAM TERRISS as swashbuckling hero. Terriss's murder at the stage door of the Adelphi in 1897 brought the great years of the theatre to an abrupt end. It was subsequently twice rebuilt, in 1901 and in 1930. PT

Adler, Jacob 1855–1926 YIDDISH actor, who began his career in theatre as a young man with a small company in Riga, Latvia, and by the 1880s became, in London and then New York, one of its stars. As actor and producer (especially at New York's Grand Theatre), he identified himself with serious emotional roles and with JACOB GORDIN's *The Jewish King Lear* (1892). Also famous for love affairs, for most of his career he was married to Sara Adler and often co-starred with her. Of their seven children, six became actors. Especially talented were Celia, famous on the Yiddish stage, and Luther and STELLA, famous on the English-language stage. NS

Adler, Stella 1903–92 American actress and teacher. Daughter of the YIDDISH actor-producer JACOB ADLER, Stella grew up surrounded by great plays and bravura acting. Always interested in the technique of acting, she studied with RICHARD BOLESLAVSKI at the AMERICAN LABORATORY THEATRE in the 1920s even after she had become an established performer. She joined the GROUP THEATRE in 1931 because she believed in its founder, HAROLD CLURMAN, whom she married. A tall, statuesque blonde with imperial carriage and mid-Atlantic diction, Adler ironically had her greatest theatrical success playing downtrodden Depression-era housewives in the Group's productions of CLIFFORD ODETS's *Awake and Sing!* (1935) and *Paradise Lost* (1935).

Her last appearance on a New York stage was in 1945 in *He Who Gets Slapped*, but from 1949, when she founded the Stella Adler Conservatory, she had served the theatre as a teacher. Reminiscing about her famous acting family and her husband, recalling her experiences studying with STANISLAVSKY in Paris in 1934, rising from her throne-like chair to demonstrate an action, continuing to flay the memory of her arch-rival LEE STRASBERG, issuing threats and portents, and regaling students with advice about life as well as art, Adler was a witty, exhilarating teacher. Countering Strasberg's Method with its focus on self, she urged students to transcend their own experiences by developing their imaginations and by investigating the play's circumstances rather than their own – an approach developed in her book *The Technique of Acting* (1988). FH

Admiral's Men This English company took its name from its patron, Lord Howard, who was created Lord High Admiral in 1585, the year in which the Admiral's Men first appeared at Queen Elizabeth's court. We do not know at which London theatre they performed in their early years. Probably they alternated between the THEATRE, the CURTAIN and Newington Butts. But the emergence of the Admiral's Men as a distinct and distinguished company is properly associated with three men, PHILIP HENSLOWE, EDWARD ALLEYN and CHRISTOPHER MARLOWE. It was Alleyn's acting in Marlowe's plays at Henslowe's ROSE that established the company's reputation. It was only the formation of the LORD CHAMBERLAIN'S MEN in 1594 that nudged the Admiral's Men into second place in the Elizabethan theatrical hierarchy. Henslowe's financial involvement may not, in the long run, have been an advantage, although it provided a greater security than was common, and helped the company to evade the general prohibition of plays after the *Isle of Dogs* affair in 1597. The opportunistic Henslowe was quick to obtain for the Admiral's Men the services of several leading members of Pembroke's Men, jobless because of their involvement in the performance of *The Isle of Dogs*. His shrewdness was certainly an asset and his wealth a comfort in times of hardship. But Henslowe was not himself a member of the Admiral's Men. He was the owner of their theatre.

When, in 1599, the Lord Chamberlain's Men opened the GLOBE, very close to the Rose, the Admiral's Men suffered in the competition for audiences. Unlike their rivals, they did not own their own theatre. Partly as a result, perhaps, they did not command the same loyalty from their actors.

Alleyn's increasing involvement in his business partnership with Henslowe deprived them of a star. The move north of the Thames, to the FORTUNE, in 1600 brought a new audience and sufficient prosperity. As London's acknowledged second company, they were granted royal patronage and the title of Prince Henry's Men after the accession of James I. Regular writers included DEKKER, MUNDAY, CHETTLE and a host of lesser names, but the regular revival of Marlowe's plays and the sinking reputation of the Fortune during the second decade of the 17th century announced the company's creative impoverishment. As the Palsgrave's Men, they continued their occupation of the Fortune, rebuilt in 1623 after destruction by fire in 1621, without much success. By 1631, when some of the Fortune actors joined a newly formed Prince Charles's Men at SALISBURY COURT, the long tradition of the Admiral's Men had been broken. PT

Adriani, Placido d. c.1740 Italian Benedictine monk, residing in Naples, who specialized in the role of Pulcinella (see PUNCH) in monastery recitals and staged sacred performances, such as *S. Francesco di Paola* (1719). His importance lies in his manuscript collection, *Selva, overo Zibaldone di concetti comici* (1734), which was discovered by Benedetto Croce in the public library of Perugia in the 1890s. It is a rich repository of COMMEDIA DELL'ARTE scenarios, plots and *lazzi* (see LAZZO). LS

Aeschylus 525/4–456/5 BC Greek tragic playwright. A native of Eleusis, Aeschylus is said to have produced tragedies as early as 499, and won his first victory at the Great Dionysia (see GREECE, ANCIENT) in 484. He fought against the Persians at the Battle of Marathon (490), and probably also at Salamis (480). He became the most popular tragedian of his day, winning a total of 13 victories at Athens and also visiting Sicily to produce plays for the tyrant Hieron I of Syracuse. It was on a later visit to Sicily that he died. Already by the time of ARISTOPHANES, who affectionately parodies his style in *Frogs*, he was regarded as the first of the great tragedians (*Frogs* 1004–5).

For at least part of his career he played the leading role in his own plays, as was normal until the time of SOPHOCLES. He is said to have been responsible for reducing the role of the Chorus and for introducing the second actor – clearly a momentous innovation. Many, perhaps most, of his plays belonged to connected tetralogies, but it is uncertain whether these were a speciality of his or were standard in the early 5th century.

Aeschylus is said to have written 90 plays; we know the titles of over 70; seven survive under his name. *Persians* (472), which depicts the despair of the Persian court on hearing of the Greek victory at Salamis, is the earliest drama we possess and the only surviving Greek tragedy on a historical subject. It did not belong to a connected tetralogy. *Seven against Thebes* (467) was the third play of a tetralogy about Oedipus and his family, the others being *Laius*, *Oedipus* and the satyr play *Sphinx*. *Suppliant Women* (once thought to be the earliest play but now dated between 466 and 459) almost certainly belonged to a connected tetralogy about the daughters of Danaus. *Agamemnon*, *Choephori* (*Libation-Bearers*) and *Eumenides* together form the *Oresteia* (458), the only connected trilogy that survives (the lost satyr play *Proteus* completed the tetralogy).

The seventh play, *Prometheus Bound*, was until recently accepted as authentic by most scholars, but detailed examination of its language, metre and stagecraft has made it very probable that it is post-Aeschylean, perhaps datable to the 440s BC. It was accompanied by the lost *Prometheus Unbound*, in which Prometheus was released from his torment by Heracles. The surviving play combines an extraordinary boldness of overall conception (the reason for its popularity among 19th-century romantics) with a distinct clumsiness of detailed execution. Like the *Oresteia*, it employs three actors.

Fragments also survive, not extensive but providing valuable evidence for Aeschylus' satyr plays, as well as for lost tragedies.

The authentic surviving plays, though so few in number, are so diverse that it is difficult to generalize about them. Each is fairly simple in plot, though those of the *Oresteia*, perhaps influenced by Sophocles, are more complex than the others. Each, except *Suppliant Women* and *Eumenides*, invests a single public event (such as the Persian defeat or the murder of Agamemnon by his wife Clytemnestra) with great moral and religious significance. Before it occurs, or is announced, the event is foreshadowed with foreboding or (in *Choephori*) with illusory hope, and we become more and more aware of the network of forces making it inevitable; afterwards its ethical implications are explored and its future consequences predicted. We can see in the *Oresteia*, and glimpse in *Seven against Thebes*, how the significance of this central event could be further enriched through its relation to others in the same trilogy. Characterization tends to be subordinate to the deeds which the characters perform rather than being pursued for its own sake; but this does not prevent those characters from being fully intelligible in human terms.

The Chorus is constantly exploited throughout the authentic plays. Its songs, often longer and more elaborate than any in Sophocles or EURIPIDES, carry much of the moral and emotional weight of the drama. It can also be seen as a counterpart, within the play, of the audience outside it, making the characters aware that their deeds are on public view and enabling them to project their speeches outward to that public. This may have been usual in Aeschylus' day; what can never have been usual, and was probably a bold experiment, was the use of the Chorus as a major party to the action, which we see in *Suppliant Women* and *Eumenides*.

An unusual richness of language, and boldness – often obscurity – of verbal imagery is apparent both in the choral songs and in much of the spoken dialogue. Powerful use is made of sustained image patterns, especially in the *Oresteia*, where some images (such as the net, the hunt, the light seen in darkness) recur throughout the trilogy. Visual effects are also exploited, sometimes in symbolic ways, the classic examples being the so-called carpet in *Agamemnon* and the robe in *Choephori*. The impression given by some ancient (and modern) critics, however, that Aeschylus was addicted to grandiose spectacle for its own sake, is not to be trusted.

Divine and human causation work together (see e.g.

Persians 472, *Agamemnon* 1505–8), so that events are intelligible in purely human terms (except in *Eumenides*, where the gods themselves take the stage) but the influence of divine forces can always be seen in them. The supremacy of Zeus is frequently stressed; but it is no longer fashionable to see Aeschylus as a champion of an 'advanced', almost monotheist religion. Zeus and the other gods ensure that crime is punished and are to that extent 'just', but they are less concerned to see innocence rewarded; indeed, in some plays it seems that the punishment of crime must always involve further crime, creating an unbreakable cycle (*Seven* 742–65, *Agamemnon* 757–71). In *Eumenides*, however, Aeschylus expresses an emotional faith that the cycle can be broken, linking this to his faith in the future of Athens.

Aeschylus does not, any more than the other tragedians, fill his plays with contemporary political allusions. *Persians* cannot help making an appeal to Greek patriotic pride, but this is not allowed to detract from the sombre tragedy of Xerxes, ruined by his own folly. *Eumenides* is exceptional among Greek tragedies in not only having broadly political implications but appearing to be a reaction to a particular event – Ephialtes' democratic reform of the Council of the Areopagus in 462/1. Even here, however, Aeschylus does not take any clear stance for or against the reform. ALB

Afinogenov, Aleksandr (Nikolaevich) 1904–41 Soviet playwright. One of GORKY's would-be heirs apparent, Afinogenov searched for a new Soviet psychological drama in the post-revolutionary years of transition from primitive AGIT-PROP to doctrinaire socialist realism. Raised by revolutionary parents, a Communist Party member from 1922 and a graduate of the Moscow School of Journalism (1924), this author of 26 plays seemed to be well equipped for the task. His early plays – *Robert Tim* (1923), *The Other Side of the Slot* (adapted from Jack London, 1926), *At the Breaking Point* (1927), *Keep Your Eyes Peeled* (1927) and *Raspberry Jam* (1928) – were produced by the civic-minded Proletkult Theatre, where Afinogenov served as literary manager and director, and reflected the group's single-minded proletarian bias. Afinogenov tired of the schematic, predictable plots, the superficial character-typing and telegraphic language which characterized the Proletkult dramatic style. He formally broke with the organization in 1928, joining the Russian Association of Proletarian Writers (RAPP), whose dialectical-materialist approach to art he helped to define in his *The Creative Method of the Theatre: The Dialectics of the Creative Process* (1931).

However, RAPP, which was dissolved by Stalin in 1932, proved to be equally unsympathetic to his artistic goals, which had become clearer from 1929 with his drama *The Eccentric*. In this character study of a romantic non-communist dreamer set against the backdrop of First Five-Year Plan ideological enthusiasm the author had the temerity to cast communists as villains, in counterpoint to his unallied hero. His best play, *Fear* (1931), further defined the nature and scope of the social-psychological drama, separating it from the MOSCOW ART THEATRE's individualistic 'biological psychologism' and bringing some subtlety and humanity to a basically dialectic confrontation between a good communist and an unenlightened but salvageable elder scientist who is surrounded by the usual opportunistic and decadent types. Considered pivotal in the Soviet dramatic canon, *Fear* was successfully staged by STANISLAVSKY at MAT.

Afinogenov's remaining plays include *Distant Point* (1935), a Soviet philosophical drama; *Hail, Spain!* (1936), a heroically scaled popular romantic piece; and *Mashenka* (1940), a very popular amalgam of personal and patriotic dramas. Afinogenov was criticized throughout the 1930s for his insistence on psychological REALISM at the expense of ideological concerns, was charged with being a Trotskyite agent and lost his Party membership in 1937. His membership was restored in 1938, and he was made head of the Literary Department of the Soviet Information Bureau. SG

Africa, English-speaking see under individual countries

Africa (North), French-speaking see FRENCH-SPEAKING NORTH AFRICA

Africa, Portuguese-speaking see PORTUGUESE-SPEAKING AFRICA

Africa (south of the Sahara) see FRENCH-SPEAKING AFRICA SOUTH OF THE SAHARA

African Theatre (New York City) This first African-American company was founded on 21 September 1821 by WILLIAM HENRY BROWN at his African Grove apartments located behind City Hospital, lower Broadway. The company opened with a cut version of *Richard III*. In the succeeding two years it moved to two locations on Mercer Street before being forced to disband by the police. In its repertoire was Brown's *The Drama of King Shotoway*, the earliest known play by a black writer, which dealt with the insurrection of the Caribs of St Vincent. From this company came the internationally acclaimed actor IRA ALDRIDGE. EGH

African-American theatre Of dual origin. First came the indigenous theatre consisting of folk tales, songs, music, dance and mimicry that blacks performed in cabins, at camp meetings, and in open parks like Congo Square in New Orleans. African in spirit, these expressions were transformed by the American environment. Then came the AFRICAN THEATRE in imitation of white playhouses and scripted dramas that WILLIAM HENRY BROWN established in 1821. Though Brown began with SHAKESPEARE, he also staged a sketch on slavery and his own play *The Drama of King Shotaway* (1823). His theatre produced two notable Shakespearian actors in James Hewlett and IRA ALDRIDGE.

The African Theatre had no successors in ante-bellum America, except for two plays written by the ex-slave William Wells Brown and read by him on abolitionist platforms. One, *The Escape; or, A Leap for Freedom* (1858), survives. Black indigenous expressions, however, were by the 1840s adopted by white comedians and fashioned into blackface minstrelsy that caricatured blacks on Southern plantations. Ironically, the now-disdained MINSTREL SHOW opened the professional stage to African Americans. Billed as authentic Negroes, black minstrels inherited the burnt-cork stereotype characters created by whites and gave them validity. At the same time, black performers were polishing acting skills in short FARCES that were added to their shows. Ernest Hogan, Billy Kersands and Sam Lucas were three leading black minstrels, while noteworthy black troupes included Charles B. Hicks's Georgia Minstrels (1865), Callender's Original Georgia Minstrels (1872) and Haverly's Colored Minstrels (1878). Since black playgoers were segregated in an upper gallery section in most theatres, these shows played primarily to white audiences; yet their success ensured perpetuation of the genre into the first decades of the 20th century.

Vying for popularity with the minstrels were the ubiquitous 'Tom shows' based on the dramatization of UNCLE TOM'S CABIN (1852). Despite the novel's intent to eradicate slavery, stage versions seen throughout the land for 80 years reinforced the theatrical image of blacks as ignorant, submissive, happy-go-lucky creatures. Tom shows also began to employ blacks as slave characters and in plantation choruses, but eventually the play was denounced by black leaders.

Black companies of higher calibre emerged after the Civil War. Anna and Emma Hyers, classically trained prodigies from Sacramento, California, toured the country in OPÉRA BOUFFE and original MUSICALS such as Out of Bondage (1877). The Astor Place Company of Colored Tragedians under J. A. ARNEAUX came into being in 1884 with a Shakespearian repertoire, and in 1889 Theodore Drury gave the first performance of his Opera Company. Professional concert artists and solo readers like HENRIETTA VINTON DAVIS appeared across the country.

In the popular theatre a shift in the minstrel pattern occurred with white-produced shows. Sam Jack's Creole Show (1891–7) introduced women in the line-up and as a dancing chorus. John W. Isham added a story line to olio specialities in The Octoroons (1895) and operatic selections for the finale of Oriental America (1896). This last production prepared BROADWAY for the invasion of original black musicals such as A Trip to Coontown (1898) by the multi-talented BOB COLE and Billy Johnson and In Dahomey (1902) by BERT WILLIAMS and George Walker. Teamed with these star performers were the composer Will Marion Cook, who wrote the OPERETTA Clorindy; or, The Origin of the Cake Walk (1898), the playwright Jesse Shipp, and the versatile brothers James W. and J. Rosamond Johnson. Also prominent at this time were long-lasting road companies in VAUDEVILLE, notably Sissieretta Jones's Black Patti Troubadours and Gus Hill's the Smart Set, which was later acquired by brothers Salem Tutt Whitney and J. Homer Tutt.

In straight drama, William Edgar Easton wrote two historical plays on the Haitian revolution: Dessalines (1893) and Christophe (1911), which were produced by Henrietta Vinton Davis. Scott Joplin composed his opera Treemonisha (1911), but it remained unproduced for decades. In 1897 Bob Cole organized a STOCK COMPANY and training school at Worth's Museum in New York. Others followed, urged on by black critics Sylvester Russell of the Freeman (Indianapolis) and Lester Walton of the New York

Age, who felt that resident companies in African-American theatres would encourage dramatic plays, provide regular employment to black actors, and permit open seating. In 1906 Robert Motts of Chicago started the Pekin Stock Company, whose success spawned other Pekins in Cincinnati, Ohio, and Savannah, Georgia. In New York the Negro Players were formed in 1912, and the LAFAYETTE PLAYERS in 1915. Some of these companies staged original musicals and dramas; others contented themselves with popular Broadway revivals.

Blacks first appeared on Broadway in dramatic roles in Three Plays for a Negro Theatre (1917) by the white writer Ridgely Torrence. This auspicious start, cut short by America's imminent entry into the First World War, was confirmed by CHARLES GILPIN's stunning performance for the PROVINCETOWN PLAYERS in The Emperor Jones (1920). However, the commercial success of Shuffle Along (1921) brought a resurgence of black musicals that stirred critics to rail against the pervasive image of black song-and-dance clowns on the professional stage. W. E. B. Du Bois, editor of The Crisis, urged formation of a nationwide movement of little theatres presenting plays 'about us, by us, for us, and near us'. His magazine and Opportunity sponsored playwriting competitions and published prize-winning entries. W. Richardson's one-act The Chip Woman's Fortune (1923) was the earliest non-musical black play seen on Broadway. In the years ahead, black college drama professors like Randolph Edmonds, Owen Dodson and Thomas D. Pawley would begin writing and directing original plays with their students.

Three dramas by white playwrights demonstrated the reach of black histrionic talent. PAUL GREEN's In Abraham's Bosom (1926) shared Pulitzer Prize honours with an experienced cast including the gifted ROSE McCLENDON; DOROTHY AND DUBOSE HEYWARD's 1927 hit Porgy inspired the operatic version by GEORGE GERSHWIN (Porgy and Bess); and MARC CONNELLY's The Green Pastures (1930) with De Lawd magnificently played by Richard B. Harrison earned a Pulitzer Prize and a five-year run. The 1930s witnessed an upsurge of socially relevant plays like Hall Johnson's Run Little Chillun (1933), LANGSTON HUGHES's Mulatto (1935) and Stevedore (1934) by white authors Paul Peters and George Sklar. The short-lived FEDERAL THEATRE PROJECT, through its Negro units in 22 cities, sponsored black playwrights and productions including Theodore Browne's Natural Man (1937) in Seattle, Theodore Ward's Big White Fog (1938) in Chicago, and ORSON WELLES's production of the 'voodoo' Macbeth (1936) in Harlem.

In the 1940s the American Negro Theatre made steady progress in training and production at its Harlem-based Library Theatre, until its successful Anna Lucasta (1944) transferred to Broadway and caused the break-up of the company. Richard Wright's Native Son (1941), imaginatively staged by Orson Welles, revealed the driving, versatile talent of CANADA LEE as Bigger Thomas, and Theodore Ward's Our Lan' (1946), a moving historical drama about newly freed slaves seeking a homestead, showed well OFF-BROADWAY but lost its appeal when altered for a bigger house. PAUL ROBESON's record-breaking Othello (1943) belongs to this decade.

After the Second World War the civil rights movement

gained momentum. Plays such as Louis Peterson's *Take a Giant Step* (1953) on Broadway, William Branch's *In Splendid Error* (1954), ALICE CHILDRESS's *Trouble in Mind* (1955) and LOFTEN MITCHELL's *A Land beyond the River* (1957) at the Greenwich Mews Theatre Off-Broadway dealt unambiguously with the racial problem and used racially mixed casts. Companies like JOSEPH PAPP's NEW YORK SHAKESPEARE FESTIVAL began to cast black actors in traditionally white roles. The trend towards integration was reflected in LORRAINE HANSBERRY's award-winning drama *A Raisin in the Sun* (1959) and OSSIE DAVIS's satiric COMEDY *Purlie Victorious* (1961). Nevertheless, the slow pace of social reform, coupled with a controversial Vietnam War, triggered unrest on college campuses and in black urban communities. African-American theatre revealed this frustration in a series of revolutionary dramas led by AMIRI BARAKA's *Dutchman* (1964). As government and foundation funds were hurriedly released to ameliorate conditions in inner cities, black theatres mushroomed nationwide, generating a crop of new playwrights and productions and opening opportunities for directors, designers and technicians. The search for a black identity led to experimentation with new dramatic forms. In 1969 LONNE ELDER's *Ceremonies in Dark Old Men* just missed, and Charles Gordone's *No Place to Be Somebody* captured, the Pulitzer Prize. Other significant playwrights of the period were ED BULLINS, Phillip Hayes Dean, ADRIENNE KENNEDY, Ron Milner, Charlie Russell, Joseph Walker and Richard Wesley.

Among the few theatre groups to survive when funding was withdrawn were the NEGRO ENSEMBLE COMPANY of New York and the Inner City Cultural Center in Los Angeles. African-American theatre had gained immeasurably from this period of upheaval but had made little headway in the Broadway commercial theatre, which responded by staging a number of extravagant revivals and adaptations of white musicals with black casts, such as *Hello, Dolly!* (1967), *The Wiz* (1975) and *Timbuktu!* (1978). Only *The Great White Hope* (1968) by white playwright Howard Sackler, with a bravura performance by JAMES EARL JONES as prizefighter Jack Jefferson, merits attention. Both Sackler and Jones received top awards for their work. Important black productions of the 1970s and early 80s include NTOZAKE SHANGE's *For Colored Girls ...* (1976), Vinnette Carroll's *Your Arms Too Short to Box with God* (1976), Phillip Hayes Dean's monodrama *Paul Robeson* (1978) and CHARLES FULLER's Pulitzer Prize-winning *A Soldier's Play* (1981). The most important voice to emerge in the 1980s was that of AUGUST WILSON, who, in close collaboration with director LLOYD RICHARDS, has written and staged a series of plays chronicling black life in the decades of the 20th century. Six plays have so far been produced, with two of them, *Fences* (1983) and *The Piano Lesson* (Broadway, 1990), winning Pulitzer Prizes. EGH

Agate, James (Evershed) 1877–1947 British drama critic, born and brought up in Manchester, where his boyhood love of theatre and French literature was nurtured. He began writing reviews for the *Manchester Guardian* while working as a cotton merchant, but it was his appointment as drama critic of *The Sunday Times* in 1923 that brought him to prominence. Determined above all to write well, Agate was an unreliable judge of plays and a partisan promoter of his favourite actors. His natural conservatism was a discouragement to dramatic innovation, and his delight in flamboyant actors, from SARAH BERNHARDT to DONALD WOLFIT, however stylishly expressed, was perilously nostalgic. As his notoriety grew, he became over-conscious of his own personality, a self-regard expressed in the very title of his nine-volume selection from his diary, *Ego* (1932–47). Agate published well over 20 volumes of his essays and reviews, from *Buzz, Buzz!* (1918) to *Immoment Toys* (1945), as well as three indifferent novels and a biography of the French actress, RACHEL. PT

Agathon c.447–c.401 BC Greek tragedian who produced plays at Athens for some years before departing c.407, like EURIPIDES, for the court of Archelaus of Macedon. ARISTOTLE mentions a TRAGEDY of his (*Antheus*) in which plot and characters were entirely invented (not drawn from myth), and another which contained enough material for an epic. He also says that Agathon was the first to write choral odes which were mere interludes irrelevant to the play's action. A few fragments survive. ALB

Ager Fikir (Patriotic Theatre Association) The first Ethiopian professional theatre company. Established in 1935 by a prominent government official, Makonnen Hapte-Wold, the Ager Fikir was formed from a group of azmaris who performed music, dance and short propaganda plays in Menelik II Square to inspire the citizens of Addis Ababa to resist Italian invasion. The company was reformed in 1942 after the restoration of the monarchy, and for many years functioned as a traditional craft centre as well as a performance arts group. Early performances comprised short plays followed by popular music and dance. The Ager Fikir acquired its present home in 1953, when Emperor Haile Selassie donated a hall originally built to display photographs of a tour to America. Nowadays the Ager Fikir presents plays three times a week in repertory, and puts on a weekly Sunday VARIETY show. As with all theatres in Ethiopia, the building is also used as a cinema. JPl

agit-prop Term used to describe theatre pieces devised to ferment political action (agitation) and propaganda. MB

Aguilera Malta, Demetrio 1909–79 Ecuadorian dramatist, poet, novelist, short story writer and diplomat. Born in Guayaquil, he was one-fifth of the famous literary Grupo de Guayaquil, a leftist literary group dedicated to social change but committed as well to literary excellence. His early reputation was based on *Don Goyo*, a vanguard novel published in 1933. In the early period his full-length plays, such as *España leal* (*Loyal Spain*, 1938), *Lázaro* (*Lazarus*, 1941), *Sangre azul* (*Blue Blood*, 1954) and *No bastan los átomos* (*Atoms Aren't Enough*, 1954), are realistic presentations with social denunciations and commitments. Aguilera Malta's best efforts clearly belong to his expressionistic period (see EXPRESSIONISM), with *El tigre* (*The Tiger*, 1955), a play of magical realism in the supernatural tropics, *Dientes blancos* (*White Teeth*, 1955) and *Honorarios* (*Fees*, 1957). He served his country in various capacities – in Ecuador, in the diplomatic corps in Santiago, in the Pan American Union in Washington, and for the last years of his life as Ecuador's ambassador to Mexico. During this period he wrote *Infierno negro* (*Black Hell*, 1967) and *Muerte, S. A.* (*Death, Inc.*, 1970), both continuing the expressionistic tendencies but with mordant SATIRE and the denunciation of discrimination. GW

Agustín, José 1944– Mexican playwright and novelist, who combines novelistic and dramatic techniques into interesting compositions. *Abolición de la propiedad* (*Abolition of Property*) was published in 1969, but first staged in 1979 because of the complexities of a text that relies on closed circuit TV, recordings and projections in dealing with an almost psychopathic perception of reality. *Círculo vicioso* (*Vicious Circle*, 1972) is an exposé of corruption in the Mexican penal system (using Lecumberri as an example). The play was censored by the Mexican authorities for its gross language (see CENSORSHIP), but finally permitted. GW

Ahmanson Theatre see CENTER THEATRE GROUP

Aidoo, Ama Ata 1942– Ghanaian playwright. Aidoo graduated from the University of Legon in 1964. Her reputation as a playwright rests upon *The Dilemma of a Ghost* and *Anowa*. *The Dilemma of a Ghost* was first produced at the University of Legon in 1964, and published in London a year later. It explores the problems of a marriage between a Ghanaian who has achieved academic honours in the USA and a black American woman whom he brings home to Ghana. The play is concerned with their decision not to have children immediately, and the consequent relationship with the husband's proud Ghanaian family, who cannot reconcile the wife's slave ancestry with their prejudices. But there is eventually a reconciliation between the women of the family, and the husband is chided for his insensitivity towards mother, aunts and wife. *Anowa* (1970), too, is concerned with slavery's legacy and is written from a woman's point of view. This time the perspective is not of reconciliation and of the good sense of traditional society, but the social visionary, and the outcome is tragic. The play embodies a powerful poetic vision of social values in the context of slavery and the position of women.

Aidoo has written a collection of short stories, *No Sweetness Here* (1970), novels and poetry. She held the post of Secretary for Education in the Rawlings government. She now lives in Zimbabwe. ME

Aiken, George L. 1830–76 American playwright known for one play: *UNCLE TOM'S CABIN; or, Life Among the Lowly*, a dramatization of Mrs Stowe's novel, presented at Troy, New York, on 27 September 1852, with Aiken in the part of George Harris. In response to audience demand for more episodes from the novel, Aiken prepared a sequel, *The Death of Uncle Tom; or, the Religion of the Lowly*, and in mid-November combined the two plays into one drama of six acts, now the standard version. G. C. Howard (see HOWARD FAMILY), manager of the company and Aiken's

cousin, rewarded the 22-year-old actor-playwright with a bonus of $40 and a gold watch for the 'week of extra work' required to devise a role (Eva) for his four-year-old daughter Cordelia. RM

Aikenvald, Yuly (Isaevich) 1872–1928 Russian literary critic and theatre reviewer for *Russian Thought* and other journals, who became embroiled in the pre-revolutionary crisis-in-the-theatre debate over theatre's true nature and proper function. His article 'Rejecting the Theatre' (*Studio*, 1912) asserted that theatre had no value except as dramatic literature, no justifiable aesthetic as an independent art form, and possessed an innate concreteness which defied all contemporary attempts – by the symbolists (see SYMBOLISM), MEYERHOLD, EVREINOV and others – to poeticize, stylize, conventionalize or psychologize it. The author's intentions are better realized and his rights served (went his argument) by an intelligent reading of his play rather than by the meddling of interpretative artists such as actors and directors. Aikenvald's broadside galvanized the loyal opposition – among them, directors VLADIMIR NEMIROVICH-DANCHENKO and FYODOR KOMISSARZHEVSKY, critic D. N. Ovsyaniko-Kulikovsky and dramatist-actor A. I. Yuzhin-Sumbatov – who published a volume of their own, *Debating the Theatre* (1912), in which they defended their roles as artistic interpreters. SG

Akalaitis, JoAnne 1937– American actress, director, founding member of the avant-garde group MABOU MINES and former producer of the NEW YORK SHAKESPEARE FESTIVAL. Her experimental works have been performed at major art centres and festivals throughout the USA and Europe, including the New York PUBLIC THEATER, The Kitchen (New York City), the Walker Art Center (Minneapolis), the Mark Taper (Los Angeles), Théâtre St Denis (France), Teatro Goldoni (Italy) and the National Galerie (Berlin). During 1983–4 she directed a controversial production of BECKETT's *Endgame* with music by her former husband Philip Glass at the AMERICAN REPERTORY THEATRE. A champion of German writer FRANZ XAVER KROETZ, she has directed a number of his plays, including productions in 1984 and 1990 of *Through the Leaves*. Other recent productions include *Green Card* (at New York's Joyce Theatre, 1988), *The Screens* (GUTHRIE THEATRE, Minneapolis, 1989), and, at the Public Theater, *Cymbeline* (1989), *Henry IV, Parts 1 and 2* (1991), *'Tis Pity She's a Whore* (1992) and *Woyzeck* (1992). After being named artistic director of the New York Shakespeare Festival in 1991, she was released in spring 1993 in a controversial decision by the company's board. Three months later she received an OFF-BROADWAY Obie for sustained achievement and continues as an active freelance director. DBW

Akerman, Anthony 1949– South African playwright and director. His plays are written in English but incorporate South African slang and idiomatic expressions from Afrikaans and Zulu. His first, *Somewhere on the Border* (1983), was written while he was living in exile in Amsterdam. An indictment of the South African military and its participation in the Angolan War, the play was banned in South Africa before its first performance by exiled actors in Holland. Then followed *A Man out of the Country* (1985), an exploration of the existential problems faced by exiles, and *A World Elsewhere* (1987), a mini-epic about growing up in South Africa during the apartheid era. All these plays deal with individuals trying to come to terms with their South African identity, and examine the ethical choices they feel compelled to make – themes further explored in *Dark Outsider* (1991), set in the 1920s and 30s and dealing with a period in the life of the South African poet Roy Campbell. After 19 years in exile, Akerman returned permanently to South Africa in 1992. His recent play, *First Loves* (1993), deals with memory and a returned exile's confrontation with his past. IS

Akimoto Matsuyo 1911– Doyenne of modern Japanese playwrights. Influenced by Miyoshi Jūrō (1902–58), Akimoto's *Kaison the Priest of Hitachi* (*Hitachibō kaison*, 1965; trans. 1988) signalled the return of the gods in full force to the Japanese stage in the 1960s. In more recent years, her work with director NINAGAWA YUKIO and designer ASAKURA SETSU for the commercial Tōhō Company on such works as *The Love Suicides of Chikamatsu* (*Chikamatsu shinjūmonogatari*, 1979) has attracted attention. JRB

Akimov, Nikolai (Pavlovich) 1901–68 Soviet designer, director, graphic artist, portraitist and teacher, whose distinctive, graceful, whimsical and vibrantly colourful stage realizations, especially of EVGENY SHVARTS's political fables, defined the character of the Leningrad Theatre of Comedy, where he was the long-time artistic director (1935–49, 1955–68). Akimov studied under artists M. V. Dobuzhinsky, A. E. Yakovlev and V. I. Shukhaev (1915–19), and in 1922 began his design career at the Kharkov Children's Theatre. His Leningrad and Moscow design career, dating from 1923, includes work at the Free Comedy Theatre, the Leningrad Theatre of Satire, the Bolshoi Dramatic Theatre, the Leningrad Academic Theatre of Drama, the Moscow Theatre of the Revolution and the MOSCOW ART THEATRE, on Soviet dramas by VSEVOLOD IVANOV, FAIKO, OLESHA, AFINOGENOV and KRON. He began directing in 1929 and in 1932 staged a controversial formalist production of *Hamlet* for Moscow's Vakhtangov Theatre, set at a decadent court with a not mad but drunk Ophelia and a Ghost invented by Hamlet. His sharp and witty style, a kind of satiric HOFFMANNesque romanticism, was most clearly demonstrated in his Theatre of Comedy productions, particularly Shvarts's *The Shadow* (1940, 1960), *The Dragon* (1944, 1962) and *An Ordinary Miracle* (1956) and in SUKHOVO-KOBYLIN's *The Case* (1964) and *Krechinsky's Wedding* (1966). From 1951 to 55 he served as the Lensoviet Theatre's artistic director, where he staged SALTYKOV-SHCHEDRIN's *Shadows* (1953) and an earlier version of *The Case* (1955).

Akimov also designed for films, and his theatre posters are among the most famous in Soviet history. He was the author of many articles and two books – *About Theatre* (1962), and its revised and expanded successor *Not Only About Theatre* (1966) – in which he blended memoir material with discussion of theatre aesthetics and practice. In 1960 he was named a People's Artist of the USSR. SG

Akins, Zoë 1886–1958 Prolific American playwright, scenarist and adapter of French and Hungarian plays. Akins began her career with an experimental *vers libre* drama, *The Magical City* (1916). Her early sophisticated comedies and wistful tragedies about worldly and slightly jaded women were followed by a rash of typical popular comedies. Her first and best hit was *Déclassée* (1919). Others which had either critical or popular success were *Papa* (1919), *Greatness: A Comedy* (1921; also called *The Texas Nightingale*), *Daddy's Gone A-Hunting* (1921), and *The Greeks Had a Word for It* (1929; later filmed as *The Golddiggers*). In 1935, in a controversial decision, Akins received the Pulitzer Prize for her adaptation of EDNA FERBER's *The Old Maid*. Her successful screenplays include *Morning Glory* (1932) and *Camille* (1937). FB

Aksyonov, Vasily (Pavlovich) 1932– Soviet novelist and dramatist, who continues the intellectual tradition of literary PARODY, satiric fable and grotesque REALISM of GOGOL, SUKHOVO-KOBYLIN, SALTYKOV-SHCHEDRIN, BULGAKOV, ERDMAN, MAYAKOVSKY, OLESHA and SHVARTS. The son of Evgeniya Ginzburg, whose *Journey into the Whirlwind* (1967) is a harrowing account of her imprisonment during the Stalinist purges, Aksyonov abandoned medicine for a literary career. As part of the Young Prose movement centred around VALENTIN KATAEV's journal *Youth* (1955), he became a spokesman for the post-Second World War generation. His early novels – *Colleagues* (1960), *A Ticket to the Stars* (1961), *Oranges from Morocco* (1962), *It's Time, My Love, It's Time* (1963) – reflect the problems of youth and maturation in Soviet society and are characterized by a highly eclectic 1960s feel: racy dialogue; Western-style dress, music and colloquialisms; and shifting and confused objective and subjective perspectives on reality.

His later writing, of which his two major plays are a part, tends towards the experimental and fantastic and suggests a conscious throwback to the Russian avant-garde of the 1920s. *Always on Sale*, at once a realistic social SATIRE and a highly theatricalist pastiche of popular culture – MASKS, songs and dances, film and television – was a great success in OLEG EFREMOV's 1965 production at Moscow's Sovremennik Theatre. *Your Murderer* (published in English, 1977), subtitled 'An Anti-alcoholic Comedy in Eight Scenes with a Prologue and an Epilogue', is a grotesque, fanciful parable of an artist who sells out, opts out and is destroyed by his own creation, an Ubuesque monster-become-folk-hero named Pork Sausage. This play is an even greater mix of popular junk culture and literary allusions than his former. A third play, *The Heron* (unpublished), 'A Comedy with Intermissions and Rhymes', is a CHEKHOVian parody set at a health resort and containing familiar Aksyonovian erotic touches. It received a staged reading at the Theatre at St Clement's Church in New York City in spring 1985.

Aksyonov emigrated to the USA in 1980, owing to the publication of his COMEDY *The Four Temperaments* (1967) in the *Metropol* literary anthology, which had been banned the previous year in Moscow. He has become a ubiquitous literary presence in America, discoursing on Russian and Soviet writers past and present and on the problems of the transplanted artist. SG

Aktie Tomaat (Action Tomato, or the Tomato Campaign) Late in 1969, tomatoes were thrown at actors during a performance by the Nederlandse Comedie at the municipal theatre of Amsterdam: students from the Toneelschool (Amsterdam School of Drama) were launching a protest both against the rigid theatrical opinions held by established theatre producers, who were accused of limiting their repertory to middle-of-the-road performances lacking any form of social relevance, and against the authoritarian status of the director, who subordinated everybody else – notably the actors – to his views.

This protest linked up with the call for democracy by students and workers that had started in the late 1960s in the United States and had then crossed over to Europe, particularly Paris (May 1968). Aktie Tomaat made its contribution to the breaking down of old structures: new companies emerged, organized on democratic principles, and old ones disappeared. This development was accepted by the Ministry of Culture, which subsidized the new theatre groups. The director became a creative assistant or member of a collective. Actors could start to explore their creative potential. Productions evolved from improvisation; dramatic texts had to be modernized before they could be performed.

Much thought was given to the social function of drama and theatre: performances were geared to sections of the population that had previously had no contact with drama because neither form nor content had appealed to them. Aktie Tomaat created a climate in which new theatrical companies could come into existence: WERKTEATER; Sater (political educational theatre (1971–84), director Peter de Baan); Baal (musical theatre (1973–88), director Leonard Frank); De Appel (modern stagings of classics such as the *Oresteia* and *King Lear* (founded 1972), director Erik Vos); and Onafhankelijk Toneel (environmental theatre).   HS MG

Alarcón (y Mendoza), Juan Ruiz de see RUIZ DE ALARCÓN (Y MENDOZA), JUAN

Alawada Theatre see ADEJUMO, MOSES OLAIYA

Albania Albania, about the size of Wales and with a population of just under three million, lies on the western coast of the Balkan Peninsula, between Greece and the former Yugoslavia. The history of the theatre in Albania goes back to ancient times: archaeologists have uncovered the remains of theatres dating back to the 4th century BC – that at Bylis in the south of the country could have accommodated an audience of more than 7000.

For 500 years – from the 15th to the 20th century – Albania lay under the occupation of the Ottoman Empire, which discouraged drama. The modern Albanian theatre came into existence only during the national renaissance of the late 19th and early 20th centuries, when Albanians at home and abroad were engaged in a fierce struggle for independence. This national struggle was naturally reflected in the arts, and the plays performed by the amateur dramatic groups which sprang up in the main towns at this time, as well as those written by playwrights of the Albanian communities abroad, were for the most part imbued with patriotic sentiments and played a significant

role in the development of national consciousness.

The first known productions in the Albanian language include *The Wedding in Lunxhëria* by Koto Hoxhi (1824–95), performed in the southern town of Gjirokastra in 1874; a FARCE, *Makka*, performed in Shkodër in 1870; a LITURGICAL DRAMA, *Christmas Night*, by the Italian-Albanian writer Leonardo de Martino (1830–1923), performed in Shkodër in 1880; Shakespeare's *Othello*, staged in Korçë in 1889; and various didactic and patriotic sketches by Gjerasim Qiriazi and Petro Nini Luarasi during the same period.

In southern Italy the former priest Anton Santori (1809–94) wrote *Emira* (1887), a love story set among the Albanian community in the author's native Calabria. In Turkey Sami Frashëri (1850–1904), the youngest of the three distinguished Frashëri brothers, wrote the six-act play *The Vow* in Turkish, translated into Albanian in 1902. The Orthodox bishop Fan Noli (1882–1965) – poet, historian, playwright, translator, composer and statesman (he was briefly prime minister in 1924 before settling in the USA) – made brilliant translations of a number of SHAKESPEARE's tragedies, as well as of IBSEN's *An Enemy of the People*, and was the author of *Israelites and Philistines* (1902), ostensibly biblical in theme but in fact portraying problems of the contemporary Albanian national movement. In Egypt the lawyer-poet Andon Zako Çajupi (1866–1930) wrote several plays, including the one-act comedies *The Fourteen-Year-Old Bridegroom* (1902) and *Post Mortem* (1910), and the classical verse tragedy *Man of the Earth* (1907), based on Albania's 15th-century leader of the resistance against the Turkish invaders, Skanderbeg. Mihal Grameno (1872–1931), an émigré in Romania and America, was the author of the anticlerical COMEDY *The Curse of the Albanian Language* (1905) and the historical drama *The Death of Pirro* (1906). In predominantly Catholic northern Albania, the Franciscan priest and poet Gjergj Fishta (1871–1940) translated plays by EURIPIDES and MOLIÈRE and was himself the author of the verse plays *The Civilized Albanian* and *Judas Maccabaeus*.

Kristo Floqi (b.1875?) wrote a number of comedies and nationalistic dramas, among them *Religion and Nationality* and *Triumph of Liberty*. Vinçenë Prennushi (1885–1954), Catholic archbishop and lyric poet, adapted two plays by Ambrogio Rolando, *The Betrayed Girl* (1919) and *From Slavery to Freedom* (1931). Another priest, Ndré Zadeja (1890–1945), wrote MELODRAMAS about Albanian life, including *The Mountain Fairy of Albania*, *The Siege of Shkodër*, *Roadfa* (the name of the fortress of Shkodër) and *Oso Kuka* (about the 19th-century Albanian hero of that name). Foqion Postoli (1890–1927) wrote the drama *Mother Duty* (1919), and Haki Stërmilli (1895–1953) wrote patriotic dramas on the subject of Serbian aggression against the Albanian people, including *The Unfortunate Dibrane* (1923), *Love and Faithfulness* (1923) and *Happy Dawn* (1924). Etëhem Haxhiademi (b.1902) wrote tragedies based on mythological and historical characters – *Ulysses* (1921), *Achilles* (1921), *Alexander* (1921), *Pyrrhus* (1934), *Skënderbeg* (1935) and *Diomedes* (1939). Ilo Mitkë Qafëzezi (1889–1954) wrote a comedy of school life, *The Teacher Gjoka* (1936).

The proclamation of independence in November 1912 brought little development in the Albanian theatre, since it was quickly followed by foreign occupation during the First World War, by the autocratic rule of King Zog, and by the further occupation by Fascist Italy and Nazi Germany. During most of this period the arts were not encouraged – indeed, many amateur dramatic groups were victims of savage persecution and the dream of establishing a professional national theatre came to nothing. The Paris-trained director Sokral Mio (b.1902) attempted to create a professional theatre company, but worked mainly with amateurs, with the female roles usually played by men.

1944 to the present National liberation from German occupation was achieved in November 1944 under the leadership of the Communist Party of Albania (now the 'Party of Labour'), and the People's Republic of Albania (now the People's Socialist Republic of Albania) was established with a programme of building a socialist society on Marxist-Leninist principles. The new state adopted a policy of actively encouraging the arts and of making them available to a mass audience. Even during the War of National Liberation, partisan theatre groups presented plays aimed at stimulating national morale, and on 24 May 1944 the first professional theatre was established in the liberated town of Përmet; this company later moved to the capital to become the People's Theatre of Tirana. In fact the organizer of the theatre was a Yugoslav actor-director – Boža Nikolić – who was invited to Tirana by the new communist government in 1945, a fact not given official publicity. On 26 September 1945 the company performed *The Lover*, and an adaptation of a folkloric play with music, *Dido*, by the 19th-century Serbian playwrights Janko M. Veselinović and Dragomir Brazk.

Today almost every factory, cooperative farm, school and military detachment has its own amateur dramatic company, and frequent drama festivals and competitions are organized for these thousands of groups. There are 8 professional theatres (apart from 15 VARIETY theatres and 26 PUPPET theatres), the best-known of which are the People's Theatre in Tirana, the A. Z. Çajupi Theatre in Korça, the Migjeni Theatre in Shkodra, the Scampa Theatre in Elbasan and the A. Moisiu Theatre in Durrës – named after the famous Albanian actor ALEKSANDËR MOISIU (1879–1935), who was compelled to carry on his profession outside Albania.

In 1946 the first art school with a drama deparment, the Jordan Misja School, was opened; this was followed in 1959 by the inauguration of the Aleksandër Moisiu School of Drama, transformed in 1960 into a department of the Higher Institute of Art, training actors, directors and stage technicians.

Although each professional company has its own permanent theatre, it spends approximately half of each year playing to audiences in the countryside and helping to raise the artistic standards of amateur drama groups. Theatre artists who are considered the most outstanding may be awarded the title of Honoured Artist or People's Artist.

The Party of Labour, which is constitutionally the guiding force within society, maintains that good art must be realist in formand, in the case of contemporary art, must accord with the principles of socialist realism. Plays, whether Albanian or foreign, are selected for production on this basis. The most popular non-Albanian playwrights who figure in the repertoire of the contemporary theatre include BRECHT, CHEKHOV, Euripides, GOGOL, GOLDONI, Ibsen, MILLER, PRIESTLEY, SCHILLER and Shakespeare.

However, prime attention has been paid to the development of a national drama, and among the most successful plays in recent years have been *The Prefect* (1947) by Besim Levonja (b.1922); *Dom John* (1947), *Halili and Hajrija* (1949) and *Our Land* (1954) by Kolë Jakova (b.1916); *The Fisherman's Family* (1955) by Sulejman Pitarka; *The Carnivals of Korça* (1961) by Spiro Çomora (1918–73); *The Second Face* (1963) by Dritero Agolli (b.1931); *Koste Bardhi's Mill* (1971) by Naum Prifti; *The Girl from the Mountains* (1967) by Loni Papa; *Short Cloudiness* by Teodor Laço (b.1936); and *The Lady from the City* (1975) by Ruzhdi Pulaha. One of the best playwrights was Fadil Paçrami (b.1922), a high communist official. In 1973 he was criticized by party leader Hoxha for liberal comments in his work, and his plays were banned. In *The Event of the Factory* (1968), *The Case of the Engineer Samiri* (1971) and other plays, he treated the theme of the individual's relationship to collectivism. A whole galaxy of gifted actors – such as Naim Fashëri, Pjetër Gjoka, Zef Jubani, Loro Kovaçi, Marie Logoreci, Violeta Manushi, Mihal Popi and Sander Prosi- and directors – such as Andrea Malo, Pirro Mani, Esat Oktrova and Pandi Stillu – has emerged, many of them having graduated from the ranks of amateurs.

In 1965 there were eight professional theatres, 26 puppet theatres and many amateur theatres. After the fall of the communist regime in 1991 theatre creativity in Albania became democratized. In 1993 Beckett's *Waiting for Godot* was produced for the first time. WBB PI

See: K. Bihiku, *A History of Albanian Literature*, Tirana, 1980; *Fjalori enciklopedik shqiptar* (*Albanian Encyclopedia*), Tirana, 1985; K. Gurakuqi, *Shkrimtarët shqipturë* (*The Albanian Writers*), vol. 2, Tirana, 1941; S. E. Mann, *Albanian Literature*, London, 1955; S. Skendi (ed.), *Albania*, 2nd edn, New York, 1958; K. Velça and Gj. Zheji (eds), *Historia e teatrit shqiptar* (*History of Albanian Theatre*), Tirana, 1984, vols 1 and 3 (vol. 2 censored).

Albee, Edward 1928– American playwright, who made a spectacular debut with four one-act plays in an absurdist style (*The Zoo Story*, written 1958 (see THEATRE OF THE ABSURD); *The Death of Bessie Smith*, 1959; *The Sandbox*, 1959; and *The American Dream*, 1960) and capped his reputation with the BROADWAY productions of *Who's Afraid of Virginia Woolf?* (1962) and an audacious and belligerent metaphysical mystery, *Tiny Alice* (1964).

Albee was greeted as the leader of a new theatrical movement and his name was linked with those of TENNESSEE WILLIAMS, ARTHUR MILLER and WILLIAM INGE as a major American playwright. Refusing, however, to capitalize on the qualities that made *Virginia Woolf* so powerful – the lacerating wit and incendiary character conflict – he has pursued an increasingly rarefied style, one that is emotionally and sexually evasive and that often forsakes dramatic impact for mandarin elegance. Despite critical and commercial defeats, Albee has continued to write prolifically in three forms: adaptations (Carson McCullers's *Ballad of the Sad Café* (1963), James Purdy's

Malcolm (1965), Giles Cooper's *Everything in the Garden* (1967) and Nabokov's *Lolita* (1980)); short chamber plays that are musical in their repetitions and juxtapositions of image and motif (*Box* and *Quotations from Mao-Tse Tung*, 1968; *Listening*, 1975, and *Counting the Ways*, 1976); and full-length plays in which ordered lives are invaded and transformed. His settings may appear realistic (see REALISM), but Albee is at heart a fabulist; like the imaginary child in *Virginia Woolf*, surreal surprises hover over most of his work. In his wisest play, *A Delicate Balance* (awarded the Pulitzer Prize in 1966), Harry and Edna carry a mysterious psychic plague into their best friends' living room. The title character in *The Lady from Dubuque* (1979) is an angel of death. Talking sea creatures emerge from the water to confront sedate picnickers in *Seascape* (which won the Pulitzer Prize in 1975).

After a long dry spell, Albee's mainstream reputation is now on the rise. His last Broadway production (in 1983), *The Man Who Had Three Arms*, was decimated by the critics. His recent plays – such as *Marriage Play* (1987), which did not have a US premiere until 1992 in his own staging (co-produced by the ALLEY THEATRE and Princeton, New Jersey's McCarter Theatre), *Three Tall Women* (1991) which had its New York viewing in January 1994 (Pulitzer Prize), and *Fragments* (first seen in Cincinnati, 1993) – premiered outside New York, several at the English Theater in Vienna. Albee will surely reclaim his place as an important stylist, a writer of wit and sensibility, as recent events suggest. In 1993–4 he was playwright-in-residence at New York's Signature Theatre; in recent years, primarily at the University of Houston, he has taught and directed.   FH

Albee, Edward F(ranklin) 1857–1930 American VAUDEVILLE producer and executive. Born in Maine, the great-grandson of one of the original Colonial Minute Men, Albee left home in 1876 to join a CIRCUS, serving first as common roustabout and later as ticket seller. In 1885 he joined B. F. KEITH in Boston, where Keith had opened a dime museum in a vacant store in 1883. With business poor, Albee supposedly suggested the exploitation of light OPERA at variety-theatre prices, which led to a pirated, condensed version of GILBERT and Sullivan's *The Mikado*, presented five times a day with vaudeville acts between performances. With the slogan 'Cleanliness, Courtesy and Comfort', Keith and Albee quickly built a vaudeville empire, with Albee largely responsible for planning the theatre structures that formed the Keith circuit. In 1900 they founded the Vaudeville Managers' Protective Association, followed in 1906 by the United Booking Office, both designed virtually to monopolize first-class vaudeville. After Keith's death in 1914 and his son's in 1918, Albee controlled the Keith Circuit, asserting power over his performers with his own in-house union, the National Vaudeville Artists (1916). The Keith circuit, dominating Eastern vaudeville, merged with other circuits in 1927 to form the Keith–Albee Orpheum Corporation, controlling 700 theatres in the USA and Canada and booking some 15,000 performers. Less a showman than a builder, Albee continued the policy of clean, family fare after his partner's death, eschewing coarseness and enforcing his standards with fines and blacklisting. A year before his death, Albee's empire was subsumed by RKO (the Radio–Keith–Orpheum Corporation), led by Joseph P. Kennedy.   DBW

Albertazzi, Giorgio 1925– Italian actor and director. Albertazzi began his career as an actor in the early 1940s, acquiring wide range and experience in touring companies as well as in films. He became internationally known through the latter, notably in films like *L'Année dernière à Marienbad* and *Morte di un bandito*. He is a strong lead player with an impressive stage presence. Among his major roles in classic drama have been SHAKESPEARE's Hamlet, Macbeth and Richard III (the last in his own version and done most recently in 1988), PIRANDELLO's Enrico IV and IBSEN's Peer Gynt (1988). He has directed in theatre and film, and since 1985, with *Lucia di Lammermoor*, for the musical stage. He has supported the work of modern foreign dramatists on the Italian stage, most recently directing the Italian premiere of ARNOLD WESKER's *Letter to a Daughter* (1993). He has published an autobiography, *Un perdente di successo* (1988).   KR

Albery, James 1838–89 British playwright whose one outstanding success, *Two Roses* (1870), established HENRY IRVING as a star. Albery tried in vain to live up to the reputation *Two Roses* had gained for him as a true successor to T. W. ROBERTSON, and undervalued his ingenious adaptations from the French. CHARLES WYNDHAM, who recognized the sophistication of Albery's dialogue, set him the task of making palatable for Criterion audiences the saucy marital farce *Les Dominos Roses*. *The Pink Dominos* (1877), whilst raising a few hackles, was the effective outcome. *Where's the Cat?* (1880) was another vehicle for Wyndham and another disappointment for the critics, who ruined Albery's talent by expecting too much of it.   PT

Aldredge, Theoni 1932– Greek-born American COSTUME designer. Aldredge studied and then worked at the GOODMAN THEATRE in Chicago before going to New York in 1958. From 1962 onwards she was a principal designer for the NEW YORK SHAKESPEARE FESTIVAL. From the mid-1970s she was part of the collaborative team – MICHAEL BENNETT, ROBIN WAGNER and THARON MUSSER – that produced *A Chorus Line* and *Dreamgirls*, among others. Aldredge designed landmark productions such as *Who's Afraid of Virginia Woolf?* and *Hair* (prior to BROADWAY), and also designs for ballet, OPERA, television and film, including *Network* and *The Great Gatsby*. She is an excellent collaborative artist, and her designs are integrated with and supportive of the direction and overall visual statement of a production. Costumes for the elegant but troubled and short-lived musical *Nick and Nora* (1991) were designed by her, as were those for *Annie Warbucks*, the 1993 sequel to the MUSICAL *Annie*, which she also designed and for which she won one of her three Tonys.   AA

Aldridge, Ira 1807–67 African-American actor who, starting with the AFRICAN THEATRE in New York, moved to England at the age of 17 and was a touring provincial actor in Britain and Ireland for over 25 years. In 1833, to a mixed press, he replaced the mortally ill EDMUND KEAN as Othello at London's COVENT GARDEN Theatre, and in 1852 began a series of highly successful appearances in Europe and

Russia, receiving several decorations from heads of state. His return to London's WEST END in 1865 was widely praised. Aldridge played over 40 roles, black and white, many of them Shakespearian. Equally brilliant in TRAGEDY and COMEDY, he often performed Othello and Mungo (in BICKERSTAFFE's comic OPERETTA *The Padlock*) on the same bill. He introduced psychological REALISM in acting in the 1850s, well before his European counterparts. He died while on an engagement in Lódz, Poland, in 1867. EGH

Alegría, Alonso 1940– Peruvian playwright, director and professor. Born in Santiago de Chile, he studied architecture from 1958 to 60, and later organized the theatre group Alba (1960–2). Between 1964 and 69 he received BA and MFA degrees in theatre from Yale, studied with John Gassner, and worked in the NEW YORK SHAKESPEARE FESTIVAL with PAPP. He was director of the National Popular Theatre in Lima from 1971 to 75, and later professor in the USA (Texas Tech, Florida International and Kenyon College). Author of *Remigio, el huaquero* (*Remigio, the Huaco Collector*, 1965), his major play is *El cruce sobre el Niágara* (*Niagara Crossing*, 1969), a powerful rendition of existential values predicated on the 19th-century French tightrope walker BLONDIN and his assistant Carlo. Later plays include *El terno blanco* (*The White Suit*), rewritten as *El color de Chambalén, una novela fantaseosa para teatro* (*The Colour of Chambalén, a Vain Novel for Theatre*, 1981) and *Daniela Frank* (1982), the latter written in English. GW

Alekseev, K. S. see STANISLAVSKY, KONSTANTIN

Aleotti, Giovanni Battista 1546–1636 Italian architect, engineer and stage designer. Aleotti spent most of his working life in the service of the court of the Estensi at Ferrara, where he built the Teatro degli Intrepidi in 1605 (destroyed by fire in 1679). His finest surviving work is the Teatro Farnese in Parma, constructed in 1618 in the Pilotta and one of the largest and finest of baroque theatres. Its U-shaped auditorium has a seating capacity of 4500. Inauguration was delayed until 1628, when it opened with the tourney *Mercurio e Marte* with music by Monteverdi. To Aleotti is ascribed the introduction, possibly as early as 1606 but certainly by 1618, of sliding flat wings; these rapidly came to replace the traditional Serlian (see SERLIO) fixed angle wings and permitted frequent and rapid shifts of scene, particularly after TORELLI developed the system further by devising machinery for synchronizing wing changes. KR

Alexander, George [George Samson] 1858–1918 Anglo-Scottish actor and theatre manager. Intended by his parents for a respectable career in the city, Alexander turned actor in 1879 and was with IRVING at the London LYCEUM during 1881–9, most notably as Valentine in *Faust* (1885). After a brief spell as manager of the Royal Avenue Theatre, he bought the lease on the ST JAMES'S and retained it until his death. His declared policy was to encourage and support the writing of new plays by British authors. Alexander was the first English producer of OSCAR WILDE – *Lady Windermere's Fan* (1892) – and the creator of Jack Worthing in *The Importance of Being Earnest* (1895). His greatest (and boldest) success was PINERO's *The Second Mrs Tanqueray* (1893), which made a star of MRS PATRICK CAMPBELL and confirmed Alexander's own quality as a strong-jawed 'straight' man in the part of Aubrey Tanqueray. Later Pinero premieres included *The Princess and the Butterfly* (1897), *His House in Order* (1906), *The Thunderbolt* (1908) and *Mid-Channel* (1909). HENRY JAMES's *Guy Domville* (1895) did not long survive a disastrous first night, and it was the 1902 production of STEPHEN PHILLIPS's *Paolo and Francesca* which earned for Alexander an undeserved reputation as an upholder of literary standards. He was, in fact, a shrewd businessman and a punctilious and efficient theatre manager, who took risks only occasionally. He had a highly developed sense of fair play – he was prosecuted in 1895 for defending a prostitute from police harassment – and was loyal to his company. He was knighted in 1911. PT

Alexander [née Quigley], **Jane** 1939– American actress, who gained stardom as the white mistress of the black boxing champion in *The Great White Hope* (1968), a role she first created at the ARENA STAGE in Washington, DC. A New Englander dedicated to regional theatre, she was critically acclaimed as Lavinia in *Mourning Becomes Electra* at the AMERICAN SHAKESPEARE THEATRE in 1971 and at the Eisenhower in Washington, DC, and the Huntington Hartford in Los Angeles in 1972. Other New York theatre appearances include *Six Rms Riv Vu* (1972), *First Monday in October* (1978), WILLIAM GIBSON's *Monday after the Miracle* (1982), *Shadowlands* (1990), *The Visit* (1992) and *The Sisters Rosensweig* (1992) in an Obie-winning/Tony-nominated performance.

Selected in 1993 to head the controversial National Endowment for the Arts, Alexander became the first artist to hold the post. In the theatre community it was believed her appointment would make the agency less vulnerable to conservative attacks. DBW

Alfieri, Vittorio 1749–1803 Italian dramatist and poet. Born into a noble family, he was at first destined for an army career, but in 1766 abandoned military studies in Turin and spent the next few years travelling widely throughout Europe. It was after his return to Turin in 1772 that he began seriously to write in both French and Italian, his first TRAGEDY *Cleopatra* appearing in 1775. Over the next decade or so he produced the bulk of his dramatic work, including 19 tragedies, a substantial amount of non-dramatic verse, and many highly personal social and political writings in which he challenged the authoritarian institutions of his day and the mass servility and passivity they bred. The tragic form, in particular, permitted him to tap a vein of melancholy deep-rooted in his temperament, and at their best his plays reveal a distinctively personal blend of the classical and the romantic, his taste for the economy and austerity of classical models, and tight adherence to the Aristotelian rules (see ARISTOTLE) balanced by powerful emotion and a highly individual insistence on the exercise of heroic will. The prominence of the authorial voice limits the stageworthiness of his great poetic dramas, and although 19th-century actors like SALVINI performed some of them abroad, and several have survived on the modern Italian stage, none has entered the European repertoire. Of Alfieri's 21 tragedies perhaps the best are *Oreste* (1778), *Virginia* (1778), *Saul* (1782) and *Mirra* (1786); none of his six comedies now attracts interest. LR

Algarotti, Francesco 1712–64 Italian author of an influential *Essay on Opera* (1755), originally published in Italy, which appeared in English (1767), in German (1769) and in French (1773). It is still a striking account of the state of OPERA in the middle of the 18th century and makes reasoned proposals for its reform and development. One random illustration of its anticipation of the ideas of GLUCK, CALZABIGI and many others is its claim that it is almost impossible to convince the composer 'that he ought to be in a subordinate position, that music derives its greatest merit from being no more than an auxiliary, the handmaid to poetry'. Algarotti was a man of wide culture, friend of many European artists and intimate of Frederick the Great, who created him count. GH

Algeria see FRENCH-SPEAKING NORTH AFRICA; MIDDLE EAST

Alkazi, Ebrahim Indian director and educator. Arguably the most influential Indian theatre artist of the 20th century, Alkazi started his theatre career after basic college education in Bombay in the 1940s. He studied in London at RADA and the Royal Academy of Art. In 1951 he returned to Bombay where he and friends and relatives founded Theatre Group, an English-language theatre organization. Shortly thereafter he founded Theatre Unit, where he successfully produced plays in Hindi. His reputation for organization and his workshops in theatre education earned him the post of director of the National School of Drama in New Delhi in the early 1960s, which he brought to national and international prominence. Alkazi was responsible for forging a respected team of teachers who established the standard for theatre education for the contemporary generation of theatre artists, many of whom are now leaders in film, television and theatre. After resigning from the National School of Drama in the late 1970s he returned to his earlier love – collecting and selling modern art for Indian and foreign dealers. In 1991 he made a brief return to the New Delhi stage with several new productions, among them *The House of Bernarda Alba* and *Othello*. FaR

Allen, Gracie see BURNS, GEORGE

Allen, Viola 1869–1948 American actress, who made her stage debut in *Esmeralda* in New York in 1882. In 1884 JOHN MCCULLOUGH engaged her to play his daughter in *Virginius*, then made her his leading lady. In subsequent seasons she played opposite W. E. Sheridan, the Italian TOMMASO SALVINI and JOSEPH JEFFERSON III. For four years she was leading lady in CHARLES FROHMAN's Empire Stock Company. An intelligent and appealing actress, sometimes thought to be over-technical, she was, until her retirement in 1918, a popular touring star, highly regarded for such portrayals as Viola, the double roles of Hermione and Perdita, and Dolores (*In the Palace of the King*). FHL

Alley Theatre (Houston, Texas) Established as an amateur organization by Mr and Mrs Robert Altfeld and Nina Vance, who became artistic head, the theatre began production in November 1947 in a rented 87-seat dance studio, the name inspired by a narrow alley-way that led to the studio. Its second home, an attic-fan manufacturing plant converted to a 231-seat arena theatre, opened on 8 February 1949 with a production of *The Children's Hour* utilizing professional actors. In 1954 the theatre became fully professional. The current building, which opened in November 1968, was named after Nina Vance following her death in 1980. Pat Brown, an actress-director appointed artistic head in 1981, attempted to fill the two theatres in the complex (one seating 824 and another, arena-style, holding 296) with more adventurous and experimental fare than its previous conservative offerings. Under Brown, a landmark exchange in June 1983 with the Stephen Joseph Theatre in Scarborough, England, was initiated; in July 1985 they presented ALAN AYCKBOURN's *Season's Greetings* at New York's Joyce Theatre. After Brown's departure in 1988, Gregory Boyd became artistic director in 1989, adding to the theatre's mission 'the intent to create for leading theatre artists from around the world a home where they can develop their work'. DBW

Alleyn, Edward 1566–1626 English actor, known to have been with Worcester's Men in 1583 and with the ADMIRAL'S MEN at London's ROSE by, at the latest, 1592. It was above all as the creator, for the latter company, of MARLOWE's towering heroes that Alleyn was celebrated. He shared with RICHARD BURBAGE the acknowledged leadership of his profession. But unlike Burbage's, Alleyn's career as an actor was interrupted. A friendship with the Rose's manager, HENSLOWE, led to marriage to Henslowe's stepdaughter and a business partnership that eventually made Alleyn a rich man. He retired from the stage in 1597, presumably to join in some of Henslowe's enterprises. Together they ran the Bear Garden, possibly from as early as 1594, and built the FORTUNE as a new home for the Admiral's Men. When the Fortune opened in 1600, Alleyn returned to the stage. His highly rhetorical style may by then have seemed old-fashioned, but he was still with the Admiral's Men when the change of monarch saw the company renamed Prince Henry's Men. Alleyn's final retirement from acting probably came in 1604, when he and Henslowe received a joint-patent as Masters of the Royal Game of Bears, Bulls and Mastiff Dogs. By 1605, he was negotiating to buy the manor of Dulwich (then a few miles southeast of London), where, in 1613, he began the building of the College of God's Gift. The papers he deposited in the library there, including Henslowe's *Diary*, are a unique record of the business side of the Elizabethan and Jacobean theatre. Assured of his social status, Alleyn took as his second wife the daughter of the Dean of St Paul's, the poet John Donne. PT

Alonso de Santos, José Luis 1942– Spanish playwright, adapter, professor of acting at the Royal School of Dramatic Art, and frequent contributor to the theatre journal *Primer Acto*. He became associated with the independent, collective theatre movement during his student years. The premiere of his first original play coincided with Franco's death in November 1975; he is recognized as a major author of the new theatre of democratic Spain. Among important works are *La estanquera de Vallecas* (*Hostages in the Barrio*, 1981), *El álbum familiar* (*Family Album*, 1982) and *Bajarse al moro* (*Going Down to Marrakesh*). The latter was the smash hit of the 1985 and 1986 Madrid theatre seasons and was awarded the National Theatre Prize for 1985. *Bajarse al moro* has been translated into several languages and aired on Spanish television; both it and *La estanquera de Vallecas* have been made into films. Typically, Alonso de Santos's plays are bitter-sweet comedies. Their surface humour, creative use of contemporary slang and intertextual references to filmic codes make them particularly appealing to a younger generation of theatregoers. PZ

Alpers, Boris (Vladimirovich) 1894–1974 Soviet theatre critic and scholar who, following the 1917 Revolution, adopted a Bolshevik bias in his writing. A former member of MEYERHOLD's Dr Dapertutto Studio on Borodinsky Street (1914–15), Alpers, along with fellow Dapertutto alumni V. V. Dmitriev, K. K. Tverskoi (pseudonym of Kuzmin-Karavaev), K. N. Derzhavin, A. L. Gripich and V. N. Solovyov (artistic director), established the Ligovsky Dramatic Theatre in Petrograd (1921–4), whose 'industrial programme' called for a more democratic actor–audience relationship.

Renamed the Theatre of New Drama (1922–3), the company turned away from its original position and towards EXPRESSIONISM. Alpers and Gripich later helped to organize the Moscow Theatre of the Revolution, where Alpers headed the literary section (1924–7) and where many of the social themes originally proposed at the Ligovsky were realized. He began his literary career in 1921, which included reviews, theoretical articles and books such as *The Theatre of the Revolution* (1928), *M. S. Shchepkin* (1933), *The Actor's Art in Russia* (1945) and *The Path of the Soviet Theatre* (1947). Most important was his *The Theatre of the Social Mask* (1931), written in the late 1920s, which presented the first conceptual, developmental assessment of Meyerhold's work to that point. Alpers believed that Meyerhold's art was always the art of 'type masks', which 'embrace the entire living variety of types from the past', and especially 'the ossification of a social type', drained of individual traits, schematized, generalized and resistant to 'character'. Although opposed in its own time by the trend towards concrete, individuated character psychology, the term is still quoted in contemporary criticism. SG

alta comedia see COMEDIA

alternative theatre (USA) One of the terms developed to describe theatrical work growing out of the burgeoning cultural movement of the 1960s and 70s. As the name suggests, alternative theatre defined itself against dominant work – whether in commercial, political or aesthetic terms – and sought to challenge the status quo as it was represented by mainstream middle-class theatre. Early on, alternative theatres aligned themselves with particular social movements: for instance, the Free Southern Theatre in Louisiana, New Feminist Theater in New York and EL TEATRO CAMPESINO in California not only responded to but

were part of the civil rights, feminist and farmworkers' movements, respectively. As such, they sought out new audiences, hoping to reflect and represent the experiences of those whose voices were never heard on mainstream stages.

These theatres, and a spate of others like them (there were more than 100 FEMINIST THEATRES in the USA in the early 1970s), by definition rejected the values of commercial theatre. More interested in helping to forge political movements than in earning a profit by selling entertainment, they redefined the relationship between spectator and performer, developed new performance styles and, perhaps most important, attracted a new army of theatre workers – the term itself revealing new attitudes towards the process of theatrical production. Few of those drawn to work in these political theatres were theatre professionals; instead, the theatres were staffed by constituents of the political movements. Thus, alternative theatres often established programmes to train people as actors – and for virtually every other theatrical task. More often than not, plays presented by alternative theatres were developed through group improvisation or, at the very least, were written specifically for the group by company members. As part of its alternative impulse, the alternative theatre rejected the mainstream theatre's definition of a script as a commercial property, as well as its rigid divisions of labour. In the alternative theatre, scripts often were not even written down. Meanwhile, company members not only acted but painted scenery, hung lights, played musical instruments and helped round up an audience.

Although most of the specific issue-related theatres had died out by the 1980s, another strand of the alternative theatre movement persisted. While groups like the Free Southern Theatre or the LIVING THEATRE primarily looked outward, concentrating on theatre's role in changing society through its direct engagement with social issues, others looked inward, searching for ways of changing society by offering spectators new ways of seeing and of thinking about themselves and their place in the world. These theatres, often politically radical as well, concentrated more on new aesthetic forms, new styles of creating work, and new approaches to acting.

The OPEN THEATRE, for instance, which began in 1963 (and closed 10 years later), concentrated on developing what director JOSEPH CHAIKIN described as the actor's 'presence' – that is, the performer, rather than the character, was to be the central focus of his theatre. The REALISM of the conventional theatre was to be replaced by self-conscious attention to the unique qualities of live performance.

Over the past two decades, techniques pioneered by these early alternative theatres – such as the acting exercises of the Open Theatre or the collective structure (see COLLECTIVE THEATRE GROUPS) of feminist theatres – were adopted and adapted by new alternative theatres. While these theatres also defined themselves in opposition to the mainstream, that definition tended to become more and more aesthetic, if only because the social movements of the 1960s and 70s and the counterculture that had grown up with them had themselves faded away. In urban centres like New York, the countercultural life was less possible in the 1980s than in the turbulent decades before:

rents had skyrocketed, making it difficult for alternative theatre artists to support themselves at odd jobs while spending the bulk of their time making theatre; the avant-garde was getting commodified, bringing to alternative theatre mainstream media attention and audiences.

Thus, many of the alternative theatres that remained in the 1980s, and those that started up, were more interested in artistic exploration than in political commitment. The formalism of ROBERT WILSON, for instance, can be counted as part of the alternative theatre in this sense, as can the often autobiographical but still highly formal work of RICHARD FOREMAN, the WOOSTER GROUP and MABOU MINES.

Many of these theatres remain active in the 1990s, and a new generation of alternative theatre artists has grown up under their influence. In the absence of a vibrant counter-cultural movement, however, this new generation more often finds itself working in fragmented ways – experimental directors like Anne Bogart and PETER SELLARS, for example, do not work consistently with the same company. Also, nowadays the term 'alternative theatre' tends to describe a physical space – such as New York's Dance Theatre Workshop and Performance Space 122, or San Francisco's Life on the Water – where alternative works can be booked. AS

Altweibermuehle 'The mill for old women', a Tirolean FASTNACHTSPIEL. The idea of a mill or forge which rejuvenates old women, traceable to the 16th century in both dramatic and iconographic form, turns up in the work of the 18th-century showman Barzanti, and in Yugoslavian folk-paintings of the 18th and 19th centuries. In the Tirolean play, a series of local character types drag their ageing wives to the miraculous mill, run by a clownish apprentice. The apparent sexism is turned on its head when the women, once more young and desirable, refuse to return to their husbands until a change of attitude and behaviour is negotiated. AEG

Alvarez Lleras, Antonio 1892–1956 Colombian dentist, diplomat and playwright, author of 15 plays that earned him recognition as the father of the modern COLOMBIAN theatre. Without breaking from the 19th-century romantic tradition, he wrote both comedies and dramas that portrayed problems within society, such as hypocrisy in *Víboras sociales* (*Social Vipers*, 1911), parentally arranged marriages in *Los mercenarios* (*The Mercenaries*, 1924) and incest in *El zarpazo* (*The Blow*, 1927). His best play, *El Virrey Solís* (*The Viceroy Solís* 1948), recounts the adventures of the 18th-century historical figure José Solís, nobleman, viceroy and priest. Alvarez Lleras's works are often heavy-handed and moralistic, but his successful plays opened pathways for a new generation. GW

Alvarez Quintero, Serafín 1871–1938 and **Joaquín Alvarez Quintero** 1873–1944 Spanish playwright brothers who collaborated on 200 works. *El genio alegre* (*Happy Spirit*, 1906) and *Puebla de las mujeres* (*The Women Have Their Way*, 1912) are comedies of Andalusian manners, revealing charming wit and psychological subtlety. Also successful in its day, *Malvaloca*, 1912, is the serious drama of a woman who overcomes her past.

Their major plays were once widely performed internationally and are still revived in Spain. Short pieces, like *Mañana del sol* (*A Bright Morning*, 1905), which describes the chance encounter of former sweethearts in their old age, remain popular with independent and amateur groups. PZ

Amalrik, Andrei (Alekseevich) 1938–80 Independent, outspoken Soviet dissident historian, memoirist and absurdist dramatist (see THEATRE OF THE ABSURD), in the tradition of GOGOL, SUKHOVO-KOBYLIN and the OBERIU (the Association of Real Art) of the 1920s. Amalrik was expelled from Moscow University in 1963 for attempting to convey his controversial diploma dissertation on foreign influence in 9th-century Kievan Russia to a Danish professor. He was exiled to a collective farm in Tomsk, Siberia (1965), for two and a half years on charges of 'parasitism' (vagrancy) and disseminating pornography (i.e. his plays and the avant-garde art of others).

Following the commutation of his sentence and his release in 1966, he published *Involuntary Journey to Siberia*, which documented his experiences as a shepherd and cart driver. He was dismissed in 1968 from his job at the Novosty Press Agency for 'nonconformist dissident behaviour', and worked thereafter as everything from translator of technical literature and private tutor to construction worker, cartographer and timekeeper at sporting events. His long theoretical essay, 'Will the Soviet Union Survive until 1984?' (1969), was a pessimistic rejoinder to those who foresaw a growing liberalization of Soviet society, and predicted war between the USSR and China. His three-year labour camp sentence for spreading 'falsehoods derogatory to the Soviet state' (1970) was extended in 1973, and he emigrated in 1976. His *Notes of a Revolutionary* (1982), its title suggested by the memoirs of Prince Peter Kropotkin, is a personal biography and a cultural history of the USSR, 1966–76, focusing upon the individual's destruction by the governmental system.

Amalrik's five short plays reflect his childhood interest in the puppet theatre (see PUPPETS), as well as the influence, in addition to those already mentioned, of the Russian transrationalist, futurist poet-dramatist (see FUTURISM) Velimir Khlebnikov, BECKETT and, especially, IONESCO. *My Aunt Is Living in Volokolamsk* (1963, 1964, 1966), *East-West: A Dialogue in Suzdal* (1963), *The Fourteen Lovers of Ugly Mary-Ann* (1964), *The Story of the Little White Bull* (1964), *Is Uncle Jack a Conformist?* (1964) and *Nose! Nose? No-se!* (adapted from Gogol's short story, 'The Nose', 1964), all one-acts, are characterized by Freudian-based sex and violence; illogical character behaviour and plot structuring; role reversals and identity confusion; sudden appearances and disappearances of characters; language ranging from aphoristic to freely associative to nonsensical; ritualistic patterning; parodied stage conventions. Amalrik was killed in a car accident while travelling to Madrid to testify at a conference examining Soviet compliance with the Helsinki Accords on Human Rights. At the time of his death, he was working on a biography of Rasputin. SG

Ambigu(-Comique) see BOULEVARD

American Academy of Dramatic Arts The first and oldest conservatory of professional acting training in the USA. Located in New York City, the Academy was founded in 1884 as the Lyceum Theatre School of Acting by Franklin Haven Sargent. In 1974 it opened a campus in the Los Angeles area. The Academy's stated purpose is 'to provide a broad and practical education to those desiring to make acting their profession'. Distinguished alumni include JASON ROBARDS JR, LUCILLE LORTEL, RUTH GORDON, HUME CRONYN, COLLEEN DEWHURST, Anne Bancroft and GARSON KANIN. TLM

American Conservatory Theater (ACT) (previously Theatre) Non-commercial regional repertory company that combines performing with a training school. Founded in 1965 by the late William Ball, ACT has made its home in San Francisco since 1967. Ball attracted critical notice in 1958 with an OFF-BROADWAY staging of ANTON CHEKHOV's *Ivanov*. Subsequent productions throughout the USA and Canada made him one of the most promising young directors in America. In 1965 he established ACT at the Pittsburgh Playhouse as an experimental and educational company with a more 'dashing style' than he saw elsewhere. Arrangements quickly soured, and Ball took ACT on the road for much of 1966, settling permanently in San Francisco for a January 1967 opening. Playing in two theatres, the downtown Geary and the Marine Memorial, the 50-member company offered 15 plays during the 1967-8 season, including *A Flea in Her Ear*, *The Three Sisters*, *The Devil's Disciple*, *Little Murders*, *A Delicate Balance* and *Hamlet*. The late Allen Fletcher joined ACT in 1970 to head the Conservatory training programme, now with some 70 acting students annually. The company ran up deficits of $900,000 in 1973, which required reductions in the size of the company and its repertoire. Ball was succeeded in 1987 by Edward Hastings, who resigned in 1991, replaced in 1992 by Carey Perloff, formerly artistic director of New York's Classic Stage Company. As a result of earthquake damage to the Geary, during 1990-1 ACT resituated at the Palace of Fine Arts Theater. TLM

American Laboratory Theatre (ALT) Inspired by the first American visit of the MOSCOW ART THEATRE in January 1923, the ALT (originally termed the Theatre Arts Institute) was founded in New York six months later by a group of wealthy American patrons as a school for training young actors in the STANISLAVSKY system. Providing a well rounded three-year programme, the school was a significant first step in translating Stanislavsky's ideas about truth in acting into an American idiom. Although courses were offered in MIME, ballet, fencing, phonetics and corrective gymnastics, the school's focus was the classes taught by RICHARD BOLESLAVSKI and Maria Ouspenskaya, two impassioned émigrés from Stanislavsky's company. During 1925-30 the Lab sponsored a theatre, under Boleslavski, modelled on the MAT but billed as America's first native, creative theatre. Most of its productions were of new and revived European plays rather than the American originals its charter promised. The Lab (disbanded in 1933) and its theatre were an important link between the historic appearance of Stanislavsky's company and the establishment in 1931 of America's first truly theatrical collective, the GROUP THEATRE, co-founded by CLURMAN, STRASBERG and CRAWFORD, who had listened intently to Boleslavski's inspiring lectures. FH

American National Theatre and Academy (ANTA) (New York City) Chartered in 1935 as a tax-exempt, self-supporting 'people's' theatre, ANTA languished until after the Second World War, when a board of directors, infused with theatre personalities and entertainment industry leaders, raised money to help ANTA acquire New York's Guild Theater (1950), renamed the ANTA Playhouse. Non-commercial works such as *The Tower beyond Tragedy*, Robinson Jeffers's adaptation of AESCHYLUS' *Oresteia*, and revivals such as *Twentieth Century* (1932) by BEN HECHT and CHARLES MACARTHUR, were featured. In 1963 ANTA built the Washington Square Theatre, which temporarily housed the Repertory Theatre of Lincoln Center. WD

American Place Theatre (New York City) Established as a producing organization dedicated to the presentation of new American plays by living authors, the American Place Theatre was founded at St Clement's Church on West 46th Street by Wynn Handman and Reverend Sidney Lanier, the church's vicar. In 1971, an underground complex of theatres, offices and workrooms at the rear of the Stevens building on the Avenue of the Americas was presented to the group, through changes in the building and zoning laws that permitted the builder of an office skyscraper to add extra storeys if a theatre was also added within the structure. The company pays $5 per year (25-year lease) for this space. Handman continues as artistic director (he was assisted by Julia Miles, who ran the Women's Project (now WOMEN'S PROJECT AND PRODUCTIONS) there during 1978-87). The company mounts full-scale productions as well as numerous works-in-progress during its 10-month season. MCH

American Repertory Theatre (ART) The first company of this name, founded in 1946 by EVA LE GALLIENNE with MARGARET WEBSTER and CHERYL CRAWFORD, was located in an obsolete theatre on Columbus Circle, New York. Despite a notable company of actors and the objective to become the city's version of Britain's OLD VIC or the COMÉDIE-FRANÇAISE, it was defunct by 1948. The second company of this name (ART), under ROBERT BRUSTEIN, began an association in 1980 with Harvard University. Dedicated to neglected works from the past, new American plays and innovative classical productions, the theatre has staged controversial productions (such as *Endgame* (1984-5), disclaimed by BECKETT), innovative direction and experimental work, such as the 1985 production of portions of ROBERT WILSON's *the CIVIL WarS*, and Wilson's 1991 staging of IBSEN's *When We Dead Awaken*. It has also mounted inaugural productions, such as MARSHA NORMAN's *'night, Mother* (1982) and the 1985 Tony-winning MUSICAL *Big River*, later seen in New York. In 1986 ART received a special Tony and a National Endowment for the Arts Ongoing Ensemble Award. In 1987 ART began its Institute for Advanced Theatre Training. DBW

American Shakespeare Theatre Founded in Stratford,

Connecticut, in 1951 as the American Festival Theatre under the guidance of LAWRENCE LANGNER, its name was changed in 1972. Designed by Edwin Howard, the octagonal theatre suggests the exterior of the original Globe Theatre, with a thrust stage and an auditorium seating about 1500. It opened on 12 July 1955 with *Julius Caesar*, as part of an eight-week season. Under a series of artistic directors approximately 75 productions were staged, including non-Shakespearian works beginning with SHAW's *Caesar and Cleopatra* in 1963. In 1959 special spring performances for students were added. Among the better-known actors to have appeared here were MORRIS CARNOVSKY, JESSICA TANDY, Katharine Hepburn, KATE REID, JAMES EARL JONES, CHRISTOPHER PLUMMER and ALFRED DRAKE. In 1977 the Connecticut Center for the Performing Arts was established, to expand the season to include guest artists and touring companies. The last full summer season was 1979, followed by sporadic production and finally virtual inactivity since 1982. In January of that year the theatre filed for bankruptcy, with a debt of almost $2 million. A proposed solution to its financial woes has yet to lead to full-time operation, despite the inauguration in 1988 of the Stratford Institution by the University of Connecticut and a brief summer season (as the American Festival Theatre) in 1989 by a company from the AMERICAN CONSERVATORY THEATER. DBW

American Theatre (New Orleans) English-language theatre was successfully established in New Orleans with the American Theatre, lit with gas and boasting a 38-ft proscenium opening, which flourished during 1824–40. A substantial brick structure accommodating 1100 on upholstered seats, the house was built by JAMES H. CALDWELL, who served as its manager for eight years before leasing it to others. Caldwell and his successors assembled competent companies, provided novelties along with the standard repertory, and brought in whatever stars were available each season. After he had launched his larger and more opulent ST CHARLES, Caldwell disposed of the 'pretty little playhouse' on Camp Street, which was rebuilt as the Camp Street Exchange in 1840. MCH

Ames, Winthrop 1871–1937 American producer and director. Ames, a wealthy Bostonian, was a leader in the art movement: at Boston's Castle Square Theatre (1904–7), at New York's ill-fated NEW THEATRE (1909–11); and finally at the two theatres he built, the Little Theatre (1912, West 44th St) – 'a little Pullman car of a place', he called it – and the BOOTH (West 45th St). Ames was the first American to make a serious study of the European art theatres. In 1907 he visited 64 theatres, saw 53 productions in Paris, London, Berlin, Vienna and Munich, and kept a detailed notebook including 154 sketches of scenic innovations. In 1912 he introduced the 'new stagecraft' to New York by bringing over REINHARDT's production of *Sumurun*. He also encouraged NORMAN BEL GEDDES's experiments in STAGE LIGHTING at his two theatres.

Ames prepared minutely detailed prompt scripts ('mother copies', he called them) for his productions, the results reflecting his lively imagination and impeccable taste. Most notable were GALSWORTHY's *The Pigeon* (1912),

SCHNITZLER's *The Affairs of Anatol* (1912, starring John Barrymore (see DREW-BARRYMORE FAMILY), SHAW's *The Philanderer* (1913), *Snow White* (1913, his own adaptation), MAETERLINCK's *The Betrothal* (1918) and KAUFMAN and CONNELLY's *Beggar on Horseback* (1924). RM

Amsterdamse Schouwburg In 1637 the Dutch architect Jacob van Campen built the first municipal theatre of Amsterdam, the famous Schouwburg, by order of the trustees of the local orphanage and old people's home. It opened on 3 January 1638 with a performance of *Gijsbrecht van Aemstel*, written by JOOST VAN DEN VONDEL especially for the occasion. The event initiated a New Year's tradition that would continue for centuries. It was in this theatre that in 1655 the first Dutch actress, Ariana Roozemond, appeared on stage. In 1664 the trustees decided to have a new theatre built, in the Venetian mode. A system of side-wings and backdrops in the baroque style was introduced, which facilitated quick scene changes. In 1772 the theatre was destroyed by fire. Two years later a new theatre was built at the Leidseplein; this was a wooden building, destined to go up in flames – which indeed happened in 1890. The present theatre, made of stone, was built in 1894, also at the Leidseplein.

The resident company in the Schouwburg chooses its repertory from the best of world drama. This Amsterdam municipal theatre faces stiff competition from the Muziektheater, also known as the Stopera, built in 1986. MG WH

Anderson, J(ohn) H(enry) 1814–74 Scottish conjuror known as 'the Great Wizard of the North'. The son of an Aberdeen tenant farmer, he had a genius for publicity, broadcasting posters, staging parades and publishing newspapers to advertise his advent. After years of success in the provinces and London, he opened his 5000-seat City Theatre in Glasgow in 1845, producing MINSTREL SHOWS, OPERAS and VARIETY as a setting for his demonstrations of MAGIC and second sight. Anderson originated the pulling of rabbits from top hats and of a live goose from 'The Magic Scrapbook' (Queen Victoria's favourite trick). Five months after the opening, the theatre was consumed by fire, and all his conjuring apparatus destroyed, so he resumed touring, taking in Europe (1846–7), the USA (1851, 55–6, 59–61) and Australia (1858). Two more stage fires helped reduce him to bankruptcy, prompting an unsuccessful appearance as Prospero in a BURLESQUE, pro-Union *Tempest* (Winter Garden, New York, 1861). His final performances were assisted by a bevy of daughters, some adopted. LS

Anderson, John Murray 1886–1954 American producer, designer and director. After beginning his theatrical career as a producer of pageants and civic MASQUES, Anderson applied the New Stagecraft of GORDON CRAIG and his followers to the American REVUE when he presented the *Greenwich Village Follies* (1919). The show's success, due largely to its simple, imaginative and beautiful scenery and costumes, launched an annual series of revues that rivalled the ZIEGFELD *Follies* in the taste and artistry of its *mise-en-scène*. The *Greenwich Village Follies* were also noted for their 'ballet ballads', poems and stories set to music and dance. Anderson was soon in demand as a designer, director and producer. Over the next 30 years he was primarily known as a facile director of musicals, nightclub floor shows and CIRCUSES. Among his MUSICAL THEATRE productions were two editions of the revue *Murray Anderson's Almanac* (1929 and 1953). His autobiography was published in 1954.   MK

Anderson, Judith [Frances Margaret Anderson-Anderson] 1898–1992 First Australian-born actress appointed DBE (1960). She consistently excelled in powerful, tragic roles. Failing in her planned singing career, she turned to acting and made her debut in Sydney in 1915, followed by a two-year tour with an American STOCK COMPANY. Her first New York appearance was in 1918; her first substantial success was as Elise in *Cobra* (1924), followed by the Unknown One in *As You Desire Me* (1931) and Lavinia in *Mourning Becomes Electra* (1932). In 1936 she was Gertrude to JOHN GIELGUD's Hamlet in New York; in 1937 she made her London debut (OLD VIC) as Lady Macbeth opposite LAURENCE OLIVIER (repeated with MAURICE EVANS, New York, 1941). She played the title role in Robinson Jeffer's adaptation of EURIPIDES' *Medea* in 1947 (revived in 1974). At the Old Vic in 1960 she appeared as Irina Arkadina in *The Seagull*. In 1970, with minimal success, she toured as Hamlet. During 1984–7 she appeared regularly as a domineering matriarch on the US television daytime drama *Santa Barbara*. In 1984 a theatre on New York's THEATRE ROW (West 42nd St) was named after her.   DBW

Anderson, Laurie 1947– Chicago-born performance artist, composer and musician whose work addresses mass audiences and explores popular music idioms. As a child, she studied the violin; then studied art history at Barnard College and sculpture at Columbia University (MFA, 1972), and wrote for major art journals. Her work is influenced by Sol LeWitt, John Cage, Fluxus, Conceptual Art and popular culture. Supported by voice filters, loops and sequencers that manipulate the pitch and texture of her natural voice, Anderson's media image emphasizes androgyny and explores the ambiguities of language and sound. Her work ranges from *Automotive* (1972), scored for car horns; and a Fluxus-inspired street performance, *Duets on Ice* (1974), in which she played a prepared violin while standing in blocks of melting ice; to *Empty Places* (1988–90), a concert with media images, projections, songs, storytelling and stand-up comedy. Her multimedia event *United States* (1978–83) was recorded by Warner Bros, and a section of it, *O Superman* (1980), became a hit in the USA and in Britain.   AF

Anderson, Lindsay (Gordon) 1923–94 British director who began his career by making documentary films. He met GEORGE DEVINE through a mutual friend, Tony Richardson, at a time (1956) when Devine was establishing the English Stage Company at the ROYAL COURT THEATRE. He became a forceful member of Devine's team, directing Willis Hall's *The Long and the Short and the Tall* (1959) and JOHN ARDEN's *Serjeant Musgrave's Dance* (1959); but his qualities as a director were better revealed through his long association with the plays of DAVID STOREY, which began with *In Celebration* (1969) and continued through

several lovingly detailed studies of contemporary life: *The Contractor* (1969), *Home* (1970), *The Changing Room* (1971), *The Farm* (1973) and *Life Class* (1974). In 1969, he became part of a three-man management running the Royal Court with Anthony Page and WILLIAM GASKILL, but his talents did not lie towards administration. The success of his film, *If* (1968), about British public school life and aberrations led to a new career in films and television, to which he brought his left-leaning, half-satirical NATURALISM. In recent years he has worked less in the theatre, although his partnership with Storey continued at the Royal NATIONAL THEATRE with *Early Days* (1980), *The March on Russia* (1989) and *Stages* (1992). In 1987, he directed a revival of PHILIP BARRY's 1928 US comedy, *Holiday*, at the OLD VIC.   JE

Anderson, Mary 1859–1940 American actress. At 16 she made her debut as Juliet at Macaulay's Theatre in Louisville, and this quickly led to other engagements. Her major assets were her classical beauty and a rich, expressive voice. She made her New York debut in 1877. W. S. GILBERT wrote a short play, *Comedy and Tragedy*, for her. Americans proudly called her 'Our Mary'. During her 14-year career on both sides of the Atlantic, she played 18 leading roles, including such favourites as Rosalind and Galatea in *Pygmalion and Galatea*. She was also the first actress to double the roles of Hermione and Perdita. In 1890 at the height of her career, she retired from the stage, settled in England and married Antonio de Navarro. She returned to the stage during the First World War, appearing in various benefit performances. Her memoirs were published as *A Few Memories* (1896) and *A Few More Memories* (1930).   FHL DJW

Anderson, Maxwell 1888–1959 American playwright and dramatic theorist whose prolific career spanned three decades, although the bulk of his critically acclaimed work came in the 1930s. He won a Pulitzer Prize for *Both Your Houses* (1933), the Drama Critics' Circle Award for *Winterset* (1935, the first such award ever given), and another for *High Tor* (1937). He gained a reputation as an anti-war dramatist; and *What Price Glory* (1924), co-authored with Lawrence Stallings, pioneered by bringing onstage the realistic, salty language of men at war. Other Anderson plays with wartime settings or themes include *Valley Forge* (1934), *Key Largo* (1939), *Candle in the Wind* (1941) and *The Eve of St Mark* (1942).

Anderson turned frequently to the lives of monarchs and other political leaders for the subject-matter of his dramas. Important examples include *Elizabeth the Queen* (1930), *Mary of Scotland* (1933), *Knickerbocker Holiday* (1938, a MUSICAL written in collaboration with KURT WEILL), *Joan of Lorraine* (1947), *Anne of the Thousand Days* (1948) and *Barefoot in Athens* (1951). He also successfully adapted others' work for the stage, such as *Lost in the Stars* (1949, also in collaboration with Weill) and *The Bad Seed* (1954). Anderson never tired of attempting to justify the use of blank verse in modern drama, and with *The Essence of Tragedy* (1939) became the first American playwright to publish a detailed theory of TRAGEDY. An astute businessman, he was one of the founders of the Playwrights' Company (1938).   LDC

Anderson, Robert W(oodruff) 1917– New York-born and Harvard-educated playwright. Anderson first drew attention by winning the National Theatre Conference prize with *Come Marching Home* (1945). After an eight-year hiatus during which he taught playwriting and adapted 36 plays and several novels for the Theatre Guild of the Air, he burst upon BROADWAY with the long-running *Tea and Sympathy* (1953), starring Deborah Kerr. This sensitive study of a young man's growth from innocence into experience, originally staged by Elia Kazan at the Ethel Barrymore Theatre, is still considered his outstanding work. He was the only new playwright ever elected to membership (1953) of the Playwrights' Company, which produced three of his plays: *All Summer Long* (1953), *Tea and Sympathy* and *Silent Night, Lonely Night* (1959). His *The Days Between* (1965) helped inaugurate the American Playwrights' Theatre. He proved that an evening of one-act plays was still viable Broadway fare with *You Know I Can't Hear You When the Water's Running* (1967) and *Solitaire/Double Solitaire* (1970). Anderson adapted several of his plays to film, including the autobiographical *I Never Sang for My Father* (1968), the screenplay for which earned him a 1970 Academy Award nomination. LDC

Andersson, Bibi 1935– Swedish actress. While best known internationally for her films, Andersson's outstanding stage career dates from early work at DRAMATEN, after which she joined INGMAR BERGMAN'S MALMÖ STADSTEATER company in the late 1950s. Most of her recent stage successes have been at Dramaten, in classical and contemporary plays, including SCHILLER'S Maria Stuart, Mary in *Long Day's Journey into Night* (1988), and Åse in *Peer Gynt* (1991). Andersson has an enormous range, and her work is marked by unusual spontaneity and complete emotional and intellectual commitment to the moment. In the early 1990s she directed plays by SHEPARD and Suzanne Brøgger at Dramaten. HL

Andrade, Jorge 1922–84 Brazilian playwright, born to one of São Paulo's most traditional rural aristocratic families. He was educated in the capital city and returned to work on the family estate, but discovered his vocation on enrolling in the Drama School of São Paulo, where he finished in 1954. His plays divide into the 'rural' cycle and the 'urban'. In the rural cycle are *O Telescópio* (*The Telescope*, 1954), *A Moratória* (*The Moratorium*, 1955), *Pedreira das Almas* (*Stone Quarry of Souls*, 1956) and *Vereda da Salvação* (*Path to Salvation*, 1964). Of the several urban plays, the best-known is perhaps *Os Ossos do Barão* (*The Baron's Bones*, 1963). Andrade specialized in showing the decadence of the Paulista society in its various phases, with special emphasis on the coffee plantations that were a singular part of his heritage. The publication of *Marta, a Arvore e o Relógio* (*Martha, the Tree and the Clock*, 1970) climaxed his entire production, one of the most heterogeneous in Brazil. *Rasto Atrás* (*Step Backwards*), his last major play, dealt explosively with an undercurrent that had permeated his other plays – that is, the autobiographical projection of a father–son relationship with a public confession of personal issues in a context of class decadence. GW

Andreev, Leonid (Nikolaevich) 1871–1919 Prolific and controversial Russian prose writer, dramatist and journalist, who rivalled CHEKHOV and GORKY in popularity and importance during the pre-revolutionary period (c.1905–17). Andreev is an extreme example of the soul sickness, spiritual confusion and sense of isolation suffered by the Russian artistic intelligentsia of this era. In his work, one finds a growing pessimism bordering on nihilism and a concomitant hope for spiritual regeneration and a reprieve from mankind's dark fate. In his search for faith he assumed many roles: realist, pro- and anti-symbolist, pro- and anti-revolutionary, militarist and neo-romantic allegorist. Gorky's neo-realist Znanie (Knowledge) publishing house printed his early stories, but Andreev eventually rejected his sponsor's naive revolutionary politics. The symbolists (see SYMBOLISM), with the exception of BLOK and BELY, disowned him. The futurists (see Futurism), with whom he shared a primitivist tendency, parted with him after 1915, when he proclaimed them philistines and bourgeois entertainers. His real kinsmen were E. T. A. HOFFMANN, Poe, MAETERLINCK, GOGOL and Dostoevsky. His macabre short stories, like his metaphysical dramas, contemplate man's folly, vanity and brutality and life's horror and falsity, and feature madness, death and all manner of sexual and spiritual perversion.

On the basis of these stories and plays (he wrote some less interesting realistic and satirical dramas as well), Andreev has been lauded by some for his ambitious scope, his modernism and truthfulness, and attacked by others for his pretence, abstract moralizing and humourless contrivance of theme, plot and character, which makes his people and situations inaccessible and unbelievable. Both assessments are partly correct. Despite the audacity of his conceptions, their realization is too often melodramatic and in time redundant. His language tends to be stilted and his tone self-important. Nevertheless, he is an artistic phenomenon. His most representative 'cosmic' dramas include *The Life of Man* (1906), *Tsar Hunger* (1907), *Black Masks* (1908), *Anathema* (1909) and his international classic, *He Who Gets Slapped* (1915). *The Life of Man* utilizes puppet-like characters, stylized speech and action, *chiaroscuro* lighting effects (Andreev was a painter) and 'Someone in Grey', representing God-Fate-Death, to relate in schematic fashion the central episodes in the life cycle. MEYERHOLD and STANISLAVSKY gave the play impressionistic mountings on grey- and black-draped stages in St Petersburg and Moscow, respectively (1907).

Black Masks, a romantic *doppelgänger* tale, suggests the extreme subjectivism and externalization of psychic experience posited in EVREINOV's theory of 'monodrama', SOLOGUB's 'theatre of one will' and Andreev's own 'panpsychism'. *Anathema* depicts the struggle for man's soul between Satan's logic and God's irrational love. *He Who Gets Slapped* combines aspects of Russian folk puppet theatre, COMMEDIA DELL'ARTE, oriental theatrical conventionalism and romantic CIRCUS themes in a mythic-symbolic story of alienation, pain and humiliation. Andreev's sombreness was parodied in his time. His mysticism, eroticism, nihilism and eventual repudiation of the revolutionary cause conspired to deflate his reputation in the Soviet Union. SG

Andreini family Italian actors, originally from Tuscany. The family's founder **Francesco** Dal Gallo (1548–1624) took the name Andreini when he entered a COMMEDIA DELL'ARTE troupe. His best roles included a good Sicilian Dottore and a polyglot romancer, and as Capitano Spavento da Vall'Inferno he perfected the type of the braggart soldier. He headed the GELOSI company on its pioneering visit to Paris in 1603–4. His wife **Isabella** (born Canali, 1562–1604) played Innamorata with the Gelosi and was the most famous actress of her time. Much lauded for her grace, virtue and beauty, she lent her name to many commedia heroines. She was also celebrated as a writer of poetry and pastoral (Mirtilla, 1588). Their eldest son **Giovan Battista** or Giambattista (1576 or 1579–1654) played Innamorato under the name Lelio, and insisted on a form of stage NATURALISM and splendour. With TRISTANO MARTINELLI he founded the FEDELI troupe, which toured Italy (1613–14) and went to Paris, where he became a favourite of Louis XIII. He was a prolific playwright, his works comprising tragicomedies, comedies, mystery plays (L' Adamo, 1613, which was once thought to be Milton's inspiration for Paradise Lost) and PASTORALS (La Florinda, 1603). This last piece featured his wife **Virginia** (born Ramponi, 1583–1638), a frigid beauty who performed under the name Florinda. After her death, he married Virginia Rotari, known as Lidia. LS

Andrianoú, [Kyría] Kyvéli ?1887–1978 Greek actress. Together with the better-known Katína Paxinoú and the more versatile MARÍKA KOTOPOÚLI, Kyvéli Andrianoú or Kyría Kyvéli, as she was usually referred to ('Kyría' suggesting a respect similar to that evoked by 'Dame'), graced the modern Greek stage for decades. Her springboard was Constantíne Christomános's Néa Skiní (New Stage, 1901–5). She distinguished herself in ingénue roles and played in a great number of bourgeois dramas, captivating audiences with her melodious voice and sentimental gestures. Eventually she acted in mature roles: Mary Stuart (against Kotopoúli's Elizabeth) in SCHILLER's classical drama, Kontéssa Valéraina in Gregory Xenópoulos's best play The Secret of Kontéssa Valéraina, and the mother in BRECHT's Mother Courage. Several Greek playwrights wrote dramas especially for her to act in. Kyvéli's two daughters, Alíki and Miránda, became actresses. GT

Andronicus, Lucius Livius d.?204 BC Early Roman dramatist, said to have been a freed slave from the Greek colony of Tarentum. His chronology was disputed by Roman scholars, but it is now generally accepted that he produced the first of all literary dramas in Latin in 240 BC. He wrote tragedies and comedies, all adapted from Greek originals, as well as non-dramatic works, and must have established the main conventions of Roman drama, though his work seemed crude to later generations. ALB

Anglin, Margaret 1876–1958 American actress. Daughter of the Speaker of the Canadian parliament, she trained at CHARLES FROHMAN's EMPIRE THEATRE School, made her debut in 1893, and toured opposite JAMES O'NEILL and RICHARD MANSFIELD. She became leading lady of the Empire Company opposite HENRY MILLER (1899–1905), and under their own management (1905–8)

they produced The Great Divide by WILLIAM VAUGHN MOODY. She then devoted herself to classical plays in productions designed by Livingston Platt in the manner of GORDON CRAIG. Highlights were her summer productions of Antigone, Electra and Medea in the Hearst Amphitheatre at the University of California, Berkeley (1910, 13, and 15), and her tour in The Taming of the Shrew, Twelfth Night, As You Like It and Antony and Cleopatra (1913–14). Except for a few revivals of her Greek productions, she appeared in modern plays from 1915 to 43. In 1911 she married the actor Howard Hull. A large, commanding woman, she lacked warmth and charm but was unsurpassed at tears and dark interior emotions. DMCD

Angola see PORTUGUESE-SPEAKING AFRICA

angura Japanese theatre movement. A perversion of English 'underground [theatre]', angura refers to the theatrical activity in the 1960s and after, that challenged the hegemony of Western-style modern drama in Japan. In the 60s this revolt against SHINGEKI sought to recapture the pre-modern Japanese imagination as the source of Japanese theatrical creativity. Also referred to as the shōgekijō undō ('little theatre movement'), and the post-shingeki movement. JRB

Anicet-Bourgeois, Auguste 1805–71 French dramatist. A prolific author of pieces for the BOULEVARD theatres, Bourgeois nearly always worked with a collaborator. He wrote MELODRAMAS, vaudevilles and FÉERIES and was an active adapter of popular novels for the stage. An excellent dramatic craftsman, he had a hand in a number of the major theatrical successes of the 19th century, including Latude (with PIXÉRÉCOURT, 1834), La Nonne sanglante (The Bleeding Nun, 1835), Gaspard Hauser (with DENNERY, 1838), Marceau, ou les enfants de la République (Marceau, or The Children of the Republic, 1848), Les Orphelins du Pont Notre-Dame (The Orphans of the Pont Notre Dame, 1849), Les Pilules du diable (The Devil's Medicine, 1854), Les Pirates de la Savane (1858), La Fille des chiffonniers (The Rag-and-Bone Man's Daughter, 1861), La Bouquetière des Innocents (The Flower-girl of Les Innocents, 1862), Le Bossu (The Hunchback, 1862) and Rocambole (1864). JMCC

animal impersonation Possibly the earliest form of acting, as primitive tribesmen or their SHAMANS disguised themselves as animal divinities to ensure successful hunts, evoke fertility daimons or propitiate malign influences. The painting of the deer dancer in the Trois Frères cave in Ariège, France, probably shows such an impersonation, and the Indians of New Mexico preserved such a deer dance to the 20th century. Horns continued to appear on the Wild Men of Bavarian folk festivals and in the Abbots Bromley horn dance. The daimonic element can be traced in surviving folk customs, such as the whirling Padstow horse (Cornwall, England) and hobbyhorses of the mummers' plays, and particularly in the combats against dragons, usually portrayed by a collective. These range from the grotesque Balinese barong to the dragon marched in procession in Suffolk as late as 1903. In Beijing

The Italo-American pantomimist Joseph Marzetti (d.1864) as Jocko, the Brazilian ape.

opera (see JINGXI), the mischievous monkey god plays a leading role.

The folk plays of Attica (see GREECE, ANCIENT) were strong on animal impersonation, while the *maenads* in their ecstatic worship of Dionysus wore fox- and doeskins, and the satyr chorus from which TRAGEDY is traditionally claimed to have sprung was clad in goatskins, horsetails and fox ears. Vase paintings of c.500 BC show dancing men dressed as birds and horses. Vestiges of these practices recur in the fantastic choruses of ARISTOPHANES' comedies: birds, wasps and frogs. One of his legendary predecessors Magnes, a writer of beast-fable comedies, is said to have flapped wings and dyed himself green to amuse the Athenian audiences.

The portrayal of animals as individual characters by human actors became immensely popular after the French Revolution, as a byblow of ROUSSEAU's ideas; the noble savage was held to exist even under the skin of an ape. Thus, the sensitive anthropoid in Gabriel and Rochefort's pantomimic scenario *Jocko; or The Ape of Brazil* (1825) was one of the most successful tear-jerkers of all time. A number of skilled performers, including the Frenchman MAZURIER, the Englishman Gouffe and the Italo-American Marzetti, made careers of imitating the behaviour of simians in MIMES, ballets, and plays, part

MELODRAMA, part FARCE, composed to feature them. Edward Klischnigg (1813–77), an English contortionist, lent his name to the *emploi* in the German-speaking theatre, and NESTROY wrote his *Ape and Bridegroom* (1836) for him.

English PANTOMIME was another important setting for animal impersonation. Hogarth portrayed JOHN RICH in a dogskin from *Perseus and Andromeda* (1730), and GRIMALDI was almost killed at the age of three as he played a monkey swung round on a chain by his father. The 19-year-old HENRY IRVING practised villainy as a wolf in an Edinburgh panto. The leading artists in this field were GEORGE CONQUEST the elder, George Ali and Charles Lauri. Conquest triumphed in such outlandish parts as an octopus, a crab and a giant porcupine whose costume consisted of 2500 separate pieces; his son Fred is considered the greatest goose of all time, and his son Arthur ended his career with the act 'Daphne the Chimpanzee'. Lauri was an expert at reproducing the movement of a poodle, an ape, a bear, a wolf, an ostrich, a kangaroo, and especially a cat, in which role he introduced his famous walk round the dress circle balcony. The Brothers Griffiths kept MUSIC-HALL audiences in stitches with their wrestling lion and the famous BLONDIN donkey, which seemed lifelike but contorted its legs in cartoon fashion as soon as it was forced on to the tightrope.

Modern drama, fixated on REALISM, has been chary of this type of performance. In a playful mode, MAETERLINCK made a dog and cat major characters in *The Blue Bird* (1908) and SHAW provided his Androcles with a waltzing lion (1913); but despite such fine actors as Lucien Guitry and MAUDE ADAMS, ROSTAND's attempt in *Chantecleer* (1910) to turn barnyard fowl and forest creatures into alexandrine-spouting humanoids could not be taken seriously by adult audiences.

Nevertheless, realism was challenged by such experiments as the dinosaur and mammoth in THORNTON WILDER's *Skin of Our Teeth* (1942) and the scaly amphibians in EDWARD ALBEE's *Seascape* (1975). For the most part, modern animal impersonation has been relegated to pantomime and MUSICAL COMEDY: the cat in *Dick Whittington*, Nana the St Bernard in *Peter Pan* (1904), the beagle Snoopy in *You're a Good Man, Charlie Brown*, Caroline the cow in *Gypsy* (1959), the feline cast of *Cats* and the wolf in *Into the Woods*. Horses have been merged with their riders in ANOUILH's *Beckett* (1959) and KOPIT's *Indians* (1968) and stylized into elegant gymnasts in SHAFFER's *Equus* (1973). However, a more three-dimensional and moving equine hero appeared in Mark Rozovsky's dramatization of *Kholstomer*, TOLSTOI's story of a gelding (directed by GEORGY TOVSTONOGOV, Leningrad, 1975); it was recreated in English as *Strider*. Several recent adaptations of Kafka's *Metamorphosis* have provided the greatest stretch for an actor: when STEVE BERKOFF's version was played in New York, the cockroach was interpreted by the great ballet dancer Mikhail Baryshnikov. LS

animals as performers From the dawn of time, man has used animal totems and established animal cults to achieve a dominance over nature. The training of animals not to perform an agricultural or military function but simply to entertain, most specifically by imitating human behaviour, blatantly advertises man as Lord of Creation. The earliest recorded example is the lion Antam-Nekht under Pharaoh Rameses II (1292–1225 BC); trained tigers that would allow a man to put his head safely in their mouths were known in early China and India (12–9th centuries BC). The Romans were more expert at slaughtering beasts than at schooling them, but the name of at least one of the *bestiari* or animal-trainers survives, the Gallic gladiator Paulus Superbus. Wandering performers in both the ancient and medieval worlds showed off simple tricks with bears and apes.

The most famous trained animal of SHAKESPEARE's day was the bay horse Morocco, shown by John Banks; as exhibited in the yard of the Belle Sauvage, London, it returned gloves to their owners, told the number of coins, and danced (warranting a mention in *Love's Labour's Lost*). Sir Walter Raleigh praised it, and BEN JONSON, referring to the rumour that beast and master had been executed for sorcery in Europe, described Banks as 'our Pythagoras, / Grave tutor to the learned horse; both which / Being, beyond the sea, burned for one witch'.

The heyday of the performing animal came in the 'Age of Enlightenment', when *animaux savants* rivalled the noble savage as exemplars of natural perfectibility. The almanacs of Parisian fairs and boulevards (1773–87) report on the 'volatile troupe' of birds at the St Germain fair doing acrobatics and military exercises, rats that danced a saraband and NICOLET's ape Turco, a rope-dancer; during the Restoration the spaniel Munito was a celebrity. In England learned pigs were frequently on view solving mathematical puzzles. During the early romantic period of MELODRAMA and pantomime, animals starred: Coco the stag, a headliner at the CIRQUE OLYMPIQUE, was seriously compared to ballet dancers when he overleapt 16 horses in 1813. When Karsten of Vienna visited the Weimar Court Theatre in 1817 with *The Hound of Aubry*, featuring a poodle, GOETHE gave up the management in disgust.

COVENT GARDEN and DRURY LANE admitted horses, lions and elephants to their pantomimic spectacles, with Chunee, the first pachyderm on the English stage, seen in the Garden's *Harlequin and Padmanaba* in 1811. Gasparo Spontini added an elephant to his opera *Olympia* (Berlin, 1821) and Mlle Djeck took the title-role as *The King of Siam's Elephant* (Cirque Olympique, 1829). Dog drama retained its favour on the Bowery and transpontine London stages well into the century. In the 1850s, when CHARLES KEAN revived 'legitimate' drama at the PRINCESS'S THEATRE, he followed the example of William Cooke, who had equestrianized Shakespeare at ASTLEY's (see HIPPODRAMA), and put horses on stage. Contretemps were not infrequent: the horse starved to play Rosinante at the Cirque Olympique in 1843 died in rehearsal, and the OPERETTA *Barkouf* by SCRIBE and OFFENBACH (1860) which featured a dog and music that imitated howling was damned by the critics as *chiennerie*.

Meanwhile, the exhibition of wild animals at CIRCUSES was undergoing a change. Most trainers entered the cage and with more or less violence put the beasts through their paces. Isaac van Amburgh (1811–65) performed before Queen Victoria and was painted by Landseer, in his cage. Henri Martin was the first to break out of the cage into pantomime in *The Lions of Mysore* (Paris, 1831), and

was followed by Thomas Batty at the Zirkus Renz (Berlin, 1861).

New training methods stressed animal psychology and work therapy, based on Pavlov's experiments and those of the Swiss psychologist J. Gaule. The result could be seen in the work of Carl and Wilhelm Hagenbeck, who worked on the trust system and developed the round cage that filled the entire arena, allowing the animals more freedom (1888), Julius Seeth who let himself be 'eaten' by lions nightly in *Quo Vadis?*, and the Russian clown VLADIMIR DUROV whose rats and pigs made satirical political points. In the 20th century, although Clyde Beatty and Alfred Court continued to use the whip and chair as trademarks, the stress was now laid on glamour, culminating in the quasi-erotic displays of Günther Gebel-Williams.

Almost every kind of animal has been recruited into show business, from Fink's mules in American VAUDEVILLE to Floridian alligator-wrestling. Trained bees were shown by an Englishman at the St Germain fair in 1774, and the first recorded flea circus was opened by the Swiss Heinrich Degeller in Stuttgart in 1812. The VARIETY stage housed boxing kangaroos (first shown by Prof. Landermann at the London Aquarium in 1892), Harald Winston's sea-lions dancing with chorus-girls in 1924, hyenas acting villains in 'The Shepherdess in the Desert' (1927), and Peter Alupka's (1905–18) cats singing 'O Tannenbaum'. The chimpanzee Consul, Lockhart's Elephants and Capt. Woodward's seals were public favourites for many years, but snake-charming was segregated into dime museums and side-shows. Today live animals are still to be seen in GRAND OPERA and MUSICAL COMEDY: Billy Rose's *Jumbo* (1935) put down a spoor to be picked up by the dog Sandy in *Annie*. LS

Anisfeld, Boris (Izrailevich) 1879–1973 Bessarabian-born painter and designer. As a member of the World of Art group he worked with Diaghilev's Ballets Russes and the Pavlova Ballet before going to the USA in 1918. An exhibition of his paintings toured the country that year, and in 1919 he began an extended association with the Metropolitan Opera. Known for his brilliant use of colour, he helped introduce unit settings and folk motifs into the vocabulary of the new stagecraft in America. His production of the world premiere of Prokofiev's *The Love for Three Oranges* (1921) at the Chicago Opera is one of his best-known. In 1928 he joined the faculty of the School of the Art Institute of Chicago and taught there for more than 30 years. AA

ankiya nat Religious theatre form found in Assam, a beautiful state in remote northeastern INDIA. *Ankiya nat* was created by Sankaradeva (c.1449–1568), who was an ardent devotee of Lord Vishnu, an earthly manifestation of Krishna worshipped by many Assamese Hindus. *Ankiya* means 'act' and *nat* means 'drama'. Thus, *ankiya nat* means a one-act drama composed in a particular form. Sankaradeva created *ankiya nat* and wrote many plays as a means of maintaining and spreading the tenets of Vaisnavism among his people.

Performance of *ankiya nat* usually takes place within the confines of a prayer hall (*nam-ghar*), a roofed structure open at the side, located in the sacred confines of a monastery. The acting area is a narrow central corridor marked off by ropes running down the length of the building. Usually audiences sit on the ground or stand at the back facing each other while the players make their way up and down the narrow acting corridor. At times, scenes are played behind one side of the audience, literally enfolding spectators in the dramatic action.

At one end of the prayer hall is a shrine (*manikut*) where the sacred text (*Bhagavata Purana*) is kept, symbolizing the presence of the words, the teachings, of Krishna (Vishnu). Entrances are usually made at the end opposite the shrine and, to begin the performances, the players progress down the passageway in a slow RITUAL dance toward the text. The large orchestra of musicians provides a hypnotic musical background during the overture and throughout a show.

Usually companies consist of about 15 amateur actors, either made up of devotees who regard it as their sacred duty to portray the stories of their god, or village artists who take particular pride in playing the roles of the gods and goddesses of the plays. Men normally play all the parts in the monastery productions, but women may participate in performances in communities where taboos do not forbid it. The boys who take the role of Krishna and his brother Balarama are thought to be temporarily possessed by the spirit of god and are approached with great reverence, particularly by female spectators.

Shimmering white costumes are worn by the musicians, and leading characters wear colourful costumes and crowns to symbolize their stations in life. Perhaps the most striking characters are giant effigies made of bamboo covered with papier-mâché and painted to represent demons and animals. Some of these figures, which are at least 15ft high, must be manipulated by several actors. MASKS of birds, snakes, monkeys and bears are worn when actors portray such fanciful characters.

Typically, performances are organized to coincide with religious festivals, such as the birth of Krishna or the memorial-day celebration of Sankaradeva or some local preceptor, or held on a full-moon night. The holiday season coincides with harvest and planting (mid-January to mid-April). A performance event usually begins around 9 p.m. and continues until sunrise.

Performance begins with an elaborate ritual of drumming. Songs and dances commence at an archway of lights (*agni-gad*) constructed on the acting area, opposite the sacred shrine. Special songs are sung in praise of Krishna and distribution of sacred food (*prasada*) to the musicians follows. At last the stage manager (*sutradhara*) makes a spectacular entrance from behind a curtain at the archway. He is accompanied by fireworks and dancing. In a stately dance before the shrine, he offers his humble respects to Krishna. Then he recites a verse from the play to be enacted and concludes with a song. A red curtain is held up and Krishna makes his entrance, dancing majestically towards the shrine. Only now does the actual drama begin. Throughout the action which follows, the stage manager stands near the actors, referring to the text of the play in order to make certain that they perform all the dialogue correctly. He inserts the necessary directions to the musicians and interprets the action of the play for the audience when necessary. In this respect, the stage manager

reminds one of the medieval directors depicted in the famous painting of the martyrdom of Saint Apollonia.

Like other forms of traditional theatre, scenes of conflict between the forces of good and evil highlight an evening of *ankiya nat*. Brief songs and dances close the performance in the early hours of the morning.

The strength of *ankiya nat* lies in its close links to the religious beliefs of the Assamese people, particularly devotees (*bhaktas*) of Krishna. It has sustained itself for centuries because it is prominent among the religiously minded Hindus of the state. It seems to be relatively unchanged over time, even though Assam has undergone many dramatic changes in its economic and social organization in recent times. FAR

Annenkov, Yury (Pavlovich) 1889–1974 Russian designer, graphic artist, portraitist, art critic and memoirist, whose witty, sharp and eccentric style, suggestive of EXPRESSIONISM, CUBO-FUTURISM and constructivism, abetted noteworthy pre-revolutionary and early post-revolutionary theatrical experiments by NIKOLAI EVREINOV, FYODOR KOMISSARZHEVSKY and others. He designed at two of the most popular 'theatres of small forms' – NIKITA BALIEV's Moscow Bat (later, Chauve-Souris) and (from 1913) KUGEL's and Kholmskaya's St Petersburg Crooked Mirror Theatre, where Evreinov served as artistic director and resident playwright (1910–17). The Annenkov–Evreinov collaboration extended from Crooked Mirror parodies of classical and contemporary literature genres to a portrait, book covers and illustrations, and expressionist designs for Evreinov's Soviet mass spectacle *The Storming of the Winter Palace* (1920) and *The Chief Thing* premiere at the Theatre of Free Comedy (1921). Annenkov also contributed large-scale designs to *The Field of Mars May Day Celebration* (1918) and *The Hymn to Liberated Labour* (1920), staged in front of the old St Petersburg stock exchange. He helped introduce futurist theatre ideas into Russia via his 1919 design-*mise en scène* for LEV TOLSTOI's *The First Distiller* at the Petrograd Hermitage Theatre, his 1921 broadside 'Merry Sanitorium' and his 1921 manifesto 'The Theatre to the End' – these two literary pronouncements owing much to MARINETTI's 'Variety Manifesto' (1913).

Annenkov posited a 'theatre of pure method', based upon gymnastic and CIRCUS performance and a kinetic stage space which would be anti-psychological and heroic. This approach inspired the Factory of the Eccentric Actor (1922) of Kozintsev, Trauberg and Kryzhitsky and MEYERHOLD's 1922 staging of *Tarelkin's Death*. In 1924 Annenkov emigrated to Germany and France, where he published articles, prose tales and an illuminating memoir of his Russian years, *Diary of My Acquaintances* (2 vols., 1965–6). SG

Annensky, Innokenty (Fyodorovich) 1856–1909 Russian symbolist-based poet (see SYMBOLISM), impressionist critic (he dubbed GORKY a symbolist), translator of all of EURIPIDES' plays, neo-mythic dramatist, teacher, Hellenist and Slavist – and one of Russian modernism's forebears and unallied elder statesmen. A man of exceptional classical erudition, he attempted in his four dramas to contemporize the Greek myths while maintaining their universality. Euripides was his model and master in his questioning of religious belief (i.e. the classical myths) and his search for a way to believe; in his interest in human psychology and his journalistic approach to the personalities, themes and events of the day; in his hybridization of metre and style; in his penchant for introducing music, dance, spectacle and melodramatic devices; and in his unabashed virtuosity. All four of Annensky's plays – *Melanippe, the Philosopher* (1901), *King Ixion* (1902), *Laodamia* (1906), *Thamira, the Cither Player* (1906) – deal in some sense with the conflict between art and life, beauty and suffering, and display a well developed auditory and visual sense. Only *Thamira* was staged, by TAIROV in a cubist production at Moscow's Kamerny Theatre (1916). The story of Laodamia was retold by SOLOGUB in *The Gift of the Wise Bees* (1907) and by BRIUSOV in *Protesilaus Deceased* (1913). SG

Anouilh, Jean 1910–87 French playwright and script-writer. Probably the most successful modern French playwright in financial terms, Anouilh worked in theatre (and films) after his first job, as secretary to JOUVET. GIRAUDOUX and PIRANDELLO were important influences on his work, but his first plays were written in a naturalist vein (see NATURALISM) – e.g. *Le Voyageur sans bagage* (*Traveller without Luggage*; directed by GEORGES PITOËFF, 1937). However, he soon moved towards a more light-hearted style of bitter-sweet comedy, perfected in *Le Bal des voleurs* (*The Thieves' Carnival*; directed by BARSACQ, 1938). This started a fruitful collaboration with Barsacq, which included Anouilh's best-known play *Antigone* (1944). The play identifies role-play with fate: because she is called Antigone, the heroine must say 'no' to Creon; in this, the play is derivative of Pirandello and of revivals of Greek myth between the wars. Anouilh's *Antigone* lacks the political and religious elements of SOPHOCLES' play and contains anachronistic references to contemporary life. As a result, the 1944 production appealed both to Nazi sympathizers and to Resistance workers.

After the war, Anouilh established a place as a writer of high-quality plays which could bridge the gap between the classics and the BOULEVARD. His output in the 1950s and 60s was voluminous but his themes, notably the contrast between youthful purity and adult compromise, varied little. His characters are mostly reduced to the dimensions of a single role or mask, which lends a certain similarity to his plots whether they be set in the Middle Ages (*L'Alouette* (*The Lark*), 1953), the French Revolution (*Pauvre Bitos* (*Poor Bitos*), 1956) or modern times (*Cher Antoine* (*Dear Antoine*), 1969). The vapidity of his work has been partly concealed by his choice of familiar subjects (e.g. St Joan in *The Lark*, Thomas Becket and Henry II in *Becket*, 1959) and by his unquestionably brilliant theatrical craftsmanship. Some of the credit for this must go to the directors with whom he worked: Barsacq during the 1940s, Roland Piétri in the 1950s and 60s; but Anouilh showed his own acumen in directing revivals of MOLIÈRE and of VITRAC's *Victor*. DB

Anski, S. [Solomon Z. Rapoport] 1863–1920 Russian-born writer immortalized by his play *The Dybbuk*, which resulted from research into small mystical ethnic sects, in this case the Chassidim. Written in 1914 in Yiddish (see YIDDISH THEATRE), it was first produced with outstanding success by the VILNA TROUPE two weeks after Anski's death, and subsequently toured throughout the world. Translated into Hebrew by the poet Bialik, it became the outstanding success of HABIMAH. AB

anti-masque SEE MASQUE

Antigua SEE EASTERN CARIBBEAN STATES

Antoine, André 1858–1943 French actor and director who started life working for the Paris gas company. While a member of an amateur company, the Cercle Gaulois, he persuaded friends to perform some new plays and adopted the name Théâtre Libre (Free Theatre). In his first programme was an adaptation of *Jacques Damour*, a story by ZOLA, with whom Antoine was friendly. Surprised by the success of this and a subsequent programme of new plays, Antoine turned professional. Between 1887 and 1894 his Free Theatre operated as a small experimental theatre club that was to have a remarkable influence, since it laid the foundations of stage NATURALISM, a form that was to dominate Western theatre for the next century. His lead was followed by OTTO BRAHM who opened his Free Theatre in Berlin in 1889 and J.T. Grein who founded the Independent Theatre in London in 1891.

Antoine was not a programmatic director, though his memory has become imprisoned in a myth of total stage illusionism. His prime aim was to free theatre from the constricting conventions of the time: instead of frivolous bedroom farce or spectacular melodrama, he wanted to be able to perform new plays dealing with contemporary issues. He taught his audience to enjoy evenings of short new plays known as *quarts d'heure* (quarter-hours – though they lasted more than 15 minutes). He also introduced the work of major German, Scandinavian and Russian naturalists to the Paris stage, e.g. IBSEN's *Ghosts* (1890), *The Wild Duck* (1891) and STRINDBERG's *Miss Julie* (1893). In 1888 he saw performances by the MEININGEN COMPANY and was deeply impressed by the ensemble playing, especially in crowd scenes. He aimed for similar effects, notably in HAUPTMANN's *The Weavers* (1893).

In 1894 bankruptcy forced him to close down but in 1897 he was able to reopen as the Théâtre Antoine, and he received public recognition when in 1906 he was appointed director of the ODÉON. In this period he revived many early successes but also developed and refined the techniques of naturalist theatre. He was the first director in France to do away with footlights, to lower house lights completely during performances and to treat the set like a real environment rather than a decorative background. He anticipated modern trends by always attempting to build the set in time for rehearsals so that the actors would be thoroughly familiar with it. Some rehearsal sets were even constructed with a fourth wall, later removed for performances. Above all, Antoine revolutionized acting in France, doing away with grand postures and declamatory speech and encouraging an intimate acting style and realistic use of space (e.g. being prepared to turn one's back on the audience).

Antoine was also the first French director of modern

Adolphe Appia's design for The Magic Garden, *Parsifal*, 1922.

times to take SHAKESPEARE seriously, beginning another trend that was to dominate 20th-century French theatre. During his time at the Odéon he produced the first unbowdlerized French *King Lear* (1904) as well as other plays little known at the time, e.g. *Troilus and Cressida* (1912). For these he adapted his usual naturalistic settings to achieve a more fluid production style. After the First World War he worked in films for a while and continued to campaign for the ideals on which the Théâtre Libre had been founded. DB

Anzengruber, Ludwig 1839–89 Austrian playwright. After a disastrous career as an actor, Anzengruber turned to playwriting. He was happiest writing about the Austrian peasantry, whose dialect he was able to capture in a masterly way. Two of his greatest successes, *The Parson of Kirchfeld* (1870) and *The Cross-Makers* (1872), reflect the conflict between orthodox Catholicism and liberalism in contemporary Austria, while *The Perjured Peasant* (1871) is a grim study of family life among the peasantry. Anzengruber's major achievement in the genre of the Viennese VOLKSSTÜCK was *The Fourth Commandment* (1877), a play that advocated the maintenance of traditional family values and loyalties. Anzengruber's plays were first produced in the commercial theatres of Vienna, not at the BURGTHEATER. SW

Apollo Theatre (New York City) Historic showplace of black entertainers at 125th Street, Harlem. Originally a BURLESQUE theatre, this two-balconied, 1700-seat playhouse became the mecca of black show business when it was taken over in 1935 by Frank Schiffman and Leo Brecher. Now-famous big bands, instrumentalists, singers, dancers and stand-up comedians all graced the Apollo stage, some making their first public appearance at the regular Wednesday amateur night show. The theatre was closed in 1977 and later reopened as a television studio for the black cable market. The building was granted landmark status in 1983. Its future as a venue for live entertainment is currently in jeopardy. EGH

Appia, Adolphe 1862–1928 Swiss theorist and designer who regenerated theatrical and operatic scenography. During 1880–1, he pursued musical studies in Geneva; 1882 saw his first trip to BAYREUTH and musical studies in Leipzig. From 1882 to 90, he travelled extensively: Leipzig, Geneva, Paris, Bayreuth, Dresden, pursuing studies in music and drawing. He twice attempted suicide (1888 and 90).

In 1888, after a performance of WAGNER's *The Master Singers*, Appia resolved 'to reform the art of the theatre [*la mise en scène*]'. Cosima Wagner invited him to design the costumes for Bayreuth (1888), but he declined the offer as too premature. It was not repeated. In 1891–2 he wrote his notes towards the production of *The Ring* and *La Mise en scène du drame wagnérien* (published in Paris in 1895), and in 1892 he also wrote his most important work, *La Musique et la mise en scène* which was first published, with his own drawings, in German as *Die Musik und die Inszenierung* (Munich, 1899). In 1905 he saw the *Fête des vignerons* in Vevey (which awakened his interest in popular festivals) and in 1906 he met Émile Jaques-Dalcroze, the creator of the system of eurhythmics. In 1909 he began sketches for his 'rhythmic spaces'.

Appia and Dalcroze prepared plans for an ambitious school and festival in Hellerau (Germany), where singers, dancers, musicians and designers would work in creative harmony. The institute operated from 1911 to 1914 and staged two festivals (1912 and 1913). In 1914 he exhibited 53 drawings in Zurich and met GORDON CRAIG: they respected each other's work and recognized a kindred spirit. COPEAU became a personal friend in 1915 and the two men remained in close contact, although they never worked together. *L'Oeuvre d'art vivant* was published in 1921. Craig and Appia shared an exhibition in Amsterdam (1922). Eventually, on 20 December 1923, a full design by

Appia for an OPERA by Wagner was completed, when the Scala of Milan under Toscanini performed *Tristan and Isolde*, to a mixed reception. In 1924, the young director WÄLTERLIN asked him to design the whole of *The Ring* for his theatre in Basle. But after a few performances of *Rhinegold* and *The Valkyrie* the plan had to be abandoned, as Appia's work was deemed 'too revolutionary'.

Although Appia's output as a theatre designer was pitifully small (his shyness and the establishment's philistinism combining to keep him away from the stage), his influence on designers and lighting designers cannot be overstressed. He abolished *trompe-l'oeil* scenery, called for non-naturalistic and symbolic architectural sets (see NATURALISM; SYMBOLISM), used light creatively and insisted on the alliance of music and action, of body and spirit. (See also STAGE LIGHTING; THEATRE DESIGN.) CIS

Aquarium French theatre company which has successfully maintained the principle of *création collective* developed by many companies after 1968. Originally a student group, they turned professional in 1970 and moved to a permanent space in the Cartoucherie at Vincennes in 1972. Their work has been distinguished by a rigorous search for effective theatrical treatment of contemporary documentary material, e.g. *Marchands de ville* (*Town Merchants*, 1972) about housing problems or *Un Conseil de classe très ordinaire* (*A Very Ordinary Staff Meeting*, 1981) about education. DB

Arbuzov, Aleksei (Nikolaevich) 1908– Soviet actor, director and one of the most prolific and popular dramatists at home and in the West. His plays employ the theatricalist devices of late-1950s 'new lyricism' to punch up a cagey mix of irony, sentimentalism, melodrama, fantasy, romanticism and self-consciously evoked CHEKHOVIAN character eccentricities and themes – time's passage, life's disappointments, youth's coming of age and the old becoming young again. An 'orphan of the Revolution', raised by an aunt – his father left home and his mother was hospitalized (1919) – Arbuzov's sense of love and fantasy as twin salvations from the fragility and cruelty of life is reflected in his plays.

He began by writing AGIT-PROP skits for the Moscow Proletkult Theatre, having already performed in a MIME troupe and in an amateur travelling company of his own. His first full-length plays – *Class* (1930), *Six Favourites* and *The Distant Road* (1935) – were followed by the extremely popular *Tanya* (1939; revised 1946; operatic version by G. G. Kreitner, 1954). A chronicle play centring on a negative, dependent woman, who through losing her husband transforms herself into a self- and socially aware heroine, *Tanya* is typical of Arbuzov's work and of much Soviet playwriting. His next plays, written for the Second World War front-line theatre, the Moscow Theatrical Studio, which he co-founded with V. N. PLYUCHEK, include *Sunrise City* (co-written with the collective, 1940), *The Immortal One* (with A. K. Gladkov, 1942) and *The Little House in Cherkizovo* (revised as *The Little House on the Outskirts*, 1943). Following *A Meeting with Youth* (1947), a dramatization of TURGENEV's *On the Eve* (1948), and *European Chronicle* (1952), Arbuzov wrote the youth chronicle play, *The Years of Wandering* (1954); the strongly Chekhovian *The*

Twelfth Hour (1959); and his most popular drama, *Irkutsk Story* (1959), which became the model for much of his later work. This simple, naive tale of young love, personal hardship and growth is given a socially resonant setting – a Siberian hydro-electric plant – and a flashback structure through which the story is told in part by a chorus, direct audience address and mime.

In his international hit, *My Poor Marat* (English title: *The Promise*, 1965), Arbuzov compresses space (a claustrophobic Leningrad apartment) and expands time (1942–60), and offers us dreams deferred and love redeemed, with the individual assuming responsibility for his own life. His plays of the 1970s, published in the collection *Choice* (called after the least memorable among them), focus upon more mature adults, either saved from loneliness by love or punished for withholding it when it was needed. These include *Tales of the Old Arbat* (English title: *Once Upon a Time*), a 'COMEDY' featuring a puppeteer-Prospero battling with his son for the love of a Hilda Wangel (*The Master Builder*) type; *In This Pleasant Old House*, a 'vaudeville-MELODRAMA' with songs and dances, in which an estranged wife is fittingly denied readmission to a warm, eccentric musical family she has earlier rejected; *My Eye-Catcher*, an 'optimistic comedy' of super-animated flat characters and improbable situations *à la vaudeville*; *An Old-Fashioned Comedy* (English title: *Do You Turn Somersaults?*), a gentle 'presentation' for two ageing and lonely people, set to romantic musical themes; and *Evening Light*, a Chekhovian 'tale for the theatre', linking serious moral themes on personal and social levels. *Cruel Games* (1978), which takes its epigraph from EDWARD ALBEE's *Who's Afraid of Virginia Woolf?*, is a disturbing picture of disaffected youth passing through cruelty to kindness, which aroused considerable controversy when produced. His most recent plays, *Remembrances* (1981) and *The Victorious One*, return to the safe, familiar conflicts between extracurricular romance and family, professional and personal life. A long-time supporter of young talent, Arbuzov runs a theatre studio, from which have graduated playwrights LYUDMILA PETRUSHEVSKAYA, Olga Kuchkina-Pavlova and Anna Rodionova. SG

Arce, Manuel José 1935–85 Playwright and director, as well as one of GUATEMALA's best poets and the most read columnist of his generation. His best plays, *Delito, condena y ejecución de una gallina* (*Crime, Punishment and Execution of a Chicken*, 1968) and *Sebastián sale de compras* (*Sebastian Goes Shopping*, 1971), have been translated and performed in several countries. He wrote several one-act plays. GW

Arch Street Theatre (Philadelphia) Believing that Philadelphians would support a newer, more elegant playhouse than the CHESTNUT, a group of citizens pledged the money to build the Arch Street Theatre and leased it to WILLIAM B. WOOD, late of the rival theatre. It opened in 1828, but Wood did not last long as manager, and it passed to other hands. Starting in 1861, it enjoyed its most prosperous and famous period when Mrs John Drew (see DREW–BARRYMORE FAMILY) became manageress. For nearly a decade, she maintained a peerless company of actors in excellent productions. In 1879, Mrs Drew was forced to drop her stock company and accede to the 'combination system', in which each play is individually cast and presented for as long a run as it has the public's interest. After she retired from the theatre's management in 1892, it was often closed. Before it was demolished in 1936, the theatre had been used by German and YIDDISH companies. MCH

Archer, William 1856–1924 Scottish journalist and drama critic, whose alliance with GEORGE BERNARD SHAW in the promotion of IBSEN was influential in the move to raise the literary standards of British drama at the end of the 19th century. The first of Archer's own translations from Ibsen was performed in London in 1880 under the title *Quicksands: or The Pillars of Society*. A collected edition in 11 volumes was published in 1906–8. Archer was a fierce defender of the best of contemporary drama against what he considered a dangerous and indiscriminate preference for the 'classics'. *The Old Drama and the New* (1923) is a vigorously argued and unashamedly partisan statement of his critical view that the plays of T. W. ROBERTSON raised the English drama to a new level of excellence and that they, together with the work of Robertson's immediate successors, should command a dominant place on the stage. PT

Arden, John 1930– British dramatist, whose first plays were seen at the ROYAL COURT THEATRE during GEORGE DEVINE's pioneering seasons. *Serjeant Musgrave's Dance* (1959), about a band of deserting soldiers who try to recruit the inhabitants of a bleak Northern town into a dance of death, is now widely regarded as a modern classic. Other Arden plays from this period such as *Live Like Pigs* (1957) and *The Happy Haven* (1960) reveal a blend of social concern and technical experimentation. For *Armstrong's Last Goodnight*, which was presented at the NATIONAL THEATRE in 1965, he invented a medieval Scottish dialect with regional variations to express a theme originally inspired by political events in the Congo. His Arthurian epic, *The Island of the Mighty* (1972), written with his wife Margaretta D'Arcy, was produced by the ROYAL SHAKESPEARE COMPANY only after violent disagreements; and since 1970, Arden's Marxist convictions have increasingly distanced him from the mainstream of British theatre. He writes with Margaretta D'Arcy for nonprofessional groups and lives in Ireland, whose troubled history has provided them with the content of several plays, such as *The Ballygombeen Bequest* (1972) and *The Non-Stop Connolly Show* (1975).

The literary preoccupations of his early years, which lent him the reputation of being an English BRECHT with a summary song for every moral, have changed towards a populist directness of speech, often harsh and polemical, but at best stirring and powerful. His views on the theatre have been collected into a book of essays, *To Present the Pretence* (1978). Although he has largely kept to his promise, sworn after *The Island of the Mighty*, never to write for mainstream British theatres again, he has written with D'Arcy plays for smaller and touring groups, and programmes for BBC radio, including *Whose Is the Kingdom?* (1988), a nine-part series on early Christianity. JE

Arden of Feversham, The Tragedy of Mr An anonymous play, at one time attributed to SHAKESPEARE, published in 1592 and probably first performed in the same year. It is of great interest as an early example of domestic TRAGEDY and, insofar as it is based on an actual recent murder, as a forerunner of the popular criminal drama of the 18th and 19th centuries. GEORGE LILLO adapted and sentimentalized it for the audience of his day. PT

Arena Stage (Washington, DC) In 1950, a group of six people associated with George Washington University founded a theatrical company, Arena Stage, under the guidance of Professor Edward Mangum. They opened their first season in a cinema, presenting their plays 'in the round'. When most of the original group drifted away to other pursuits, ZELDA FICHANDLER, one of the founding members, took over the reins of leadership and remained its director until 1991. In 1956, the company moved into an old brewery and gradually built an audience. In 1961, sharing the management with her husband Thomas, Mrs Fichandler moved into a new modern theatre with the help of grants from the Ford Foundation and others. In phase two of its development (1970), a 500-seat, modified-thrust-stage playhouse (the Kreeger) joined the 800-seat mainstage; later, a CABARET theatre (the Old Vat Room) was added. In 1991 Douglas C. Wager, who had been associated with Arena in various capacities since 1974, succeeded Fichandler. The Arena Stage Company supports a full company of actors, directors and designers, and presents new American and European plays along with MUSICALS and classical revivals. MCH

Aretino, Pietro 1492–1556 Italian writer and dramatist noted for his vigorous SATIRES against papal and secular figures and his scurrilous dialogues, *I ragionamenti* (1534–6). His early work was written in Rome under the patronage of Leo X, but the hostility it attracted later prompted him to move to the more liberal atmosphere of Venice. Although he wrote one tragedy, *L'Orazia* (1545), his wide-ranging interests, eye for social detail and vigorous, colloquial language were better suited to COMEDY, in which genre he wrote some of the most lively and enduring of the period, among them *La cortigiana* (*The Courtesan*, 1525) and *Il marescalco* (*The Stablemaster*, 1527). For the production of his comedy *La Talanta* at Venice in 1541 VASARI prepared a theatre in the Casa di Cannaregio, one of the significant early developments in the evolution of indoor fitted stagings. KR LR

Argentina Buenos Aires, often referred to as the Paris of South America, was an insignificant city at the time of independence in 1816. Neither Argentina nor the River Plate, contrary to the connotations of the names, yielded up silver to the colonizers; neither did the explorers find gold, as they did in many other Spanish colonies. Buenos Aires was founded in 1580, but the interior cities were more important in early years. In Córdoba theatre activity was documented as early as 1610 as the Jesuit missions worked with the local Native American population. Comedies, dramas and religious plays were performed by such authors as Luis de Tejeda, Valentín de Céspedes and Cristóbal de Aguilar, all from Córdoba.

In Buenos Aires the first permanent construction for musical theatrical events dates from 1757. The Teatro de la Ranchería (Settlement Theatre) was built in 1783 on the site of the present Manzana de las Luces (Block of Lights). Before it burned in 1792, one play now considered part of the early heritage was presented there: *Siripo* (1789) by Manuel José de Lavardén (1754–1801), an early tragedy of which only a fragment survives. The anonymous *sainete* (see GÉNERO CHICO), *El amor de la estanciera* (*Love of the Ranch Lady*), recognized as the precursor of *gaucho* drama for its popular verse form, rustic speech and setting on the pampa, is probably later (c.1814). Existing records show that LOAS and other Spanish and French classics were also presented in several cities – such as Santiago del Estero, Buenos Aires, Catamarca, Santa Fe, Corrientes and Córdoba – throughout the 18th century.

After independence the Sociedad del Buen Gusto del Teatro (Society of Good Taste in Theatre, 1817) aspired to create an autonomous theatre, but internal dissensions over CENSORSHIP issues caused it to cease operations after only two years. The theatre still reflected the 18th-century French neoclassical styles in such plays as the tragedy *Dido* (1821), a work inspired by the *Aeneid* and written by Juan Cruz Varela (1794–1839), whose *A río revuelto ganancia de pescadores* (*Turbulent River, Fisherman's Delight*), written during his student years, is a fresh comedy still of interest today. Luis Ambrosio Morante (1775–1837) was a major director and actor of this period, and several plays are attributed to him, in addition to various translations and adaptations. He captured the new spirit of independence in such plays as 25 *de mayo* (25th of May, 1812) and *Tupac Amaru* (1817). A series of anonymous plays followed, written from a historical–political perspective and revivifying the revolutionary battles.

During the federal government (1829–53) of Juan Manuel de Rosas, theatre became a favourite entertainment with new buildings and good public support. Romantic theatre appeared in Buenos Aires following the satiric-costumbristic style (see COSTUMBRISMO) established by Bretón in Spain. The circus was popular. Ten plays, plus as many *sainetes* by local writers, were performed. In addition to such authors as Bartolomé Mitre (1821–1906) and José Mármol (1817–71), the principal exponent was Juan Bautista Alberdi (1810–84), whose *El gigante Amapolas* (*The Giant Amapolas*, 1841) is a one-act FARCE satirizing Rosas and the myths of power. The play was comic and entertaining, it sowed the seeds of the grotesque theatre that was to follow, and it has retained its popularity up to the present. A theatre in exile presented works critical of Rosas; after his fall Pedro Echagüe (1821–89) wrote his play *Rosas* (1860), a politically recriminatory caricature. Echagüe also marked the transition to a post-romantic period during the years of growth and expansion of Presidents Mitre and Sarmiento, but even so the theatre did not flourish. Instead, travelling shows and imported groups dominated. At least ten new theatres were built during the century, including the impressive Teatro Colón (1857–1944 in its first epoch), which regularly attracted world-class performers.

The year 1884 marked a turning point in the Argentine theatre. The distinguishing geographical feature of Argentina was the enormous pampa, originally an inland sea, a fertile agricultural area unbroken for miles that served as the heartland of the nation and produced myths and legends about the *gaucho*, the inimitable Argentine cowboy. The 19th-century literature included the play *Las bodas de Chivico y Pancha* (*The Wedding of Chivico and Pancha*, 1823); Mitre's poems (1840s); Sarmiento's historical-fictional account of civilization and barbarism in the life of Quiroga (1845); and especially the epic poem of José Hernández, *Martín Fierro* (1872–9). After the publication of Eduardo Gutiérrez's serialized novel, *Juan Moreira*, in 1884, the Carlo Brothers' Circus commissioned the author to prepare a pantomimic version, which was performed with José J. Podestá in the title role. This popular figure representing the fates and fortunes of the *gaucho*, the free spirit of the pampas in conflict with civil authority, captured the Argentine spirit. The CIRCUS tradition became an integral feature of Argentine theatre, and in the centennial revival of the play in 1984 the circus tent was still a dominant scenographic reminder of this heritage. Martiniano Leguizamón's (1858–1933) *Calandria* in 1896 continued the tradition, as did many others who wrote *sainetes gauchescos* about rural conflicts. On the other hand, the *sainete urbano* revealed conflicts of the city in a stage of development.

The 20th century Before the turn of the century, impoverished European emigrants began to deluge Argentina in search of opportunities and prosperity. The fusion of the new arrivals with the national atmosphere provided the raw materials for the modernized *sainete*, the principal mouthpiece of this social class. For all their faults, the plays had the merit of depicting a typically Argentine reality. The theatre in Argentina cannot easily be separated from that of URUGUAY, since the capital cities are only 100 miles apart and communication across the River Plate has been continuous. The realistic–naturalistic influence of the European theatre and the local *sainete criollo* tradition merged to produce the most renowned dramatist of South America: FLORENCIO SÁNCHEZ (1875–1910). Born in Uruguay, the self-taught Sánchez was a faithful observer of daily life, of the customs and people of his time. During the so-called Golden Decade (1900–10) he wrote plays that reflected values in an age when the predominance of urban life and the immigrant population signalled rapid change in lifestyles. *La gringa* (*The Foreign Girl*, 1904) and *Barranca abajo* (*Down the Gully*, 1905) are his two masterpieces that depict characters struggling against insurmountable obstacles; Don Zoilo of the latter play is a memorable tragic figure whose despair leads him to suicide.

Other dramatists also captured the life of the times. Gregorio Laferrère (1867–1913) wrote popular theatre with spontaneous characters such as those in *Las de Barranco* (*Those of Barranco*, 1908), and Roberto J. Payró (1867–1928) also dealt with social injustices. The *sainete* maintained box-office success for many years through such authors as Alberto Vacarezza (1888–1959), who showed the picturesqueness of popular types in caricature. Throughout the first 30 years of the century, the Argentine theatre was dominated by these *sainetes criollos*. This term actually includes such diverse forms as drama, comedy and political theatre. In a total production of possibly 5000 plays, the following writers stood out: Nemesio Trejo (1862–1916), Carlos M. Pacheco (1881–1914), Enrique García Velloso (1880–1938) and José González Castillo (1885–1937). Other writers in a similar vein included Pedro E. Pico (1882–1945), Camilo Darthés (1889–1974), Carlos S. Damel (1890–1930) and Francisco Defilippis Novoa (1890–1930). Armando Discépolo (1887–1952) developed the Creole grotesque, and served as the model for later generations.

SAMUEL EICHELBAUM was touted as a major force, but his plays are at times exaggerated and unrealistic. His *La mala sed* (*The Bad Thirst*, 1920) dealt with hereditary sexual impulses, and *Dos brasas* (*Two Live Coals*) is an exercise in greed and moral misery. Conrado Nalé Roxlo (1898–1971), on the other hand, achieved a lyrical, poetical quality in plays such as *La cola de la sirena* (*The Mermaid's Tail*, 1941), a farcical examination of reality and egotism. Juan Oscar Ponferrada (b.1907) played with folkloric material from the pagan *calchaquí* carnival in *El carnival del diablo* (*The Devil's Carnival*, 1943).

The rise of the independent theatre movement in 1930 gave new impulse to the Argentine theatre. The movement brought fresh life to techniques of stage performance. The first group was the Teatro del Pueblo (People's Theatre), formed by Leónidas Barletta, whose motivation was to develop a new public, to give new importance to the role of the director, and to impose vanguard techniques of production. In Argentina, this independent theatre also had a political commitment, inspired by Marxism, for addressing social concerns and vices. The Juan B. Justo group (1933) and La Máscara (the Mask, 1939) shared the problems, anxieties and successes of the Teatro del Pueblo, as did 50 other groups founded in Buenos Aires and the provinces as modern successors of the so-called *filodramáticos* (union groups, immigrant community groups, neighbourhood social clubs, and so on) that formed from 1890 to 1930. The usual foreign authors were presented – COCTEAU, LENORMAND, SYNGE, PIRANDELLO, O'NEILL – as well as new national dramatists including ROBERTO ARLT, César Tiempo, Juan Oscar Ponferrada, Carlos Carlino and Tulio Carella. Of these, Arlt was the author of the most consistent body of vanguard work. Better known by his contemporaries as a novelist, he mixed the possible with the impossible and the world of reality with the world of dreams. Of his eight plays, *Saverio el cruel* (*Saverio the Cruel*, 1936) has become a revisionist classic for its metatheatrical techniques and the experimentation with illusion and insanity.

The year 1949 was a turning point, when CARLOS GOROSTIZA first staged *El puente* (*The Bridge*) in La Máscara, an independent theatre. The play metaphorically bridged two separate social classes with a common denominator – the pathos of death. From 1950 onward, the theatre in Argentina entered a new phase of growth and development. The costumbristic theatre continued to exist, but a greater consciousness of national social and political issues impinged on the creative arts. Gorostiza continued to be a major realistic writer, with plays that reflected the changing milieu of Buenos Aires but that at the same time honoured traditional values. Gorostiza experimented with game theory form in *A qué jugamos?* (*What Shall We Play?*, 1968) and other plays, always faith-ful in language to the social stratum. AGUSTÍN CUZZANI wrote what he called *farsátiras* that pointed out the deficiencies in the standards of middle-class society, willing to sacrifice the most helpless fellow human beings. Another important author of the period was ANDRÉS LIZÁRRAGA, whose *Tres jueces para un largo silencio* (*Three Judges for a Long Silence*), *Santa Juana de América* (*St Joan of America*) and *Alto Perú* (*High Peru*) constituted a revisionist history of the 1810 Revolution under the common title *Trilogía sobre mayo* (*Trilogy about May*).

OSVALDO DRAGÚN captured international attention with his *Historias para ser contadas* (*Stories to Be Told*, 1957), expressionistic (see EXPRESSIONISM), BRECHTian-flavoured vignettes of dehumanization and exploitation that translated easily and were understandable around the world. Disillusioned with Peronism and more disillusioned with the political anarchy that followed, Dragún sought to translate the injustices of Argentine social and economic systems for the stage. *La peste viene de Melos* (*The Plague Comes from Melos*, 1956) and *Tupac Amarú* (1957) launched his career with the theatre group Fray Mocho, and marked his orientation as a committed realistic dramatist – a tendency he was to follow in many subsequent plays, some of which echoed the *Historias* model. Although his theatre has become more symbolic over the years, his insistence on portraying flaws in society has not waned.

In spite of, or ironically perhaps because of, the political turmoil in Argentina since the 1950s – the constant military intervention that interrupts civilian authority – the theatre has shown remarkable vitality. In addition to Gorostiza, Cuzzani and Dragún, other writers who dealt with the problems and issues of the Argentine middle class through a style of social REALISM that earned them the denomination of the 'new realist generation' were Julio Mauricio (b.1919), Sergio de Cecco (b.1931), CARLOS SOMIGLIANA, ROBERTO COSSA, RICARDO HALAC, RICARDO TALESNIK and GERMÁN ROZENMACHER. In their early plays, many of them focused on the frustrations and rebellion of a disillusioned generation of youth, such as Halac's *Soledad para cuatro* (*Solitude for Four*, 1961) and Cossa's *Nuestro fin de semana* (*Our Weekend*, 1964). By constantly searching out the value systems within society, they captured the realities of their generation, becoming more cynical with time and veering towards the traditions of the Argentine grotesque, as in Cossa's *La nona* (*The Grandmother*, 1977) or Halac's *El destete* (*The Weaning*, 1978).

In 1970 Cossa, Rozenmacher, Somigliana and Talesnik collaborated on a play, *El avión negro* (*The Black Airplane*), an episodic documentary in future time that foretells Perón's return from exile in a mythical black plane. Mauricio's plays looked at the human condition to find a means of happiness in spite of the stresses of everyday existence. Rozenmacher, a talented and active journalist and writer, focused on the problems of the Jewish middle class with its hopes, fears, and generational and religious conflicts. Talesnik began in television and film; of his several works in theatre, he was brought international fame by *La fiaca* (*The Doldrums*, 1967), a poignant play about a man who tries to assert his independence one abulic Monday morning by not going to work.

Almost simultaneously with the generation mentioned earlier, another group of writers began to make its mark by adhering more to the vein of absurdist theatre (see THEATRE OF THE ABSURD) and to Theatre of Cruelty. Principal among them were GRISELDA GAMBARO, EDUARDO PAVLOVSKY, Alberto Adellach (b.1933) and RICARDO MONTI. Gambaro's *Los siameses* (*The Siamese Twins*, 1967) and *El campo* (*The Camp*, 1968) are characteristic of the violence inherent in human nature and the dependency syndromes that penetrate love–hate relationships. Gambaro well deserves her reputation as one of the best women playwrights in all of Latin America. Pavlovsky, a psychiatrist trained in psychodrama, turned from his early experimentation with psychoanalytic situations towards the problems of the Argentine socio-political situation in *El señor Galíndez* (*Mr Galíndez*, 1973), a study of torture and physical/mental cruelty. His *Telarañas* (*Spiderwebs*, 1976) was banned during the height of the political repression. He used the brutality of Haiti and the Duvalier regime in similar fashion in *El señor Laforgue* (*Mr Laforgue*, 1982). Monti experimented with expressive and symbolic language in *Una noche con el señor Magnus e hijos* (*A Night with Mr Magnus and Sons*, 1970) as well as *Visita* (*Visit*, 1977) and *Marathón* (*Marathon*, 1980). All are restaged frequently and reveal his particular style of relating political and historical themes of Argentina. His *Una pasión sudamericana* (*A South American Passion*, 1989) and *Una historia tendenciosa* (*A Tendentious Story*, 1990) confirmed his reputation as one of Argentina's leading playwrights. Oscar Viale (b.1932), author of *El grito pelado* (*The Shriek*, 1967), *Chúmbale* (*Go get 'em!*, 1971) and *Convivencia* (*Living Together*, 1978), is an author of grotesque NATURALISM with black humour.

At a low point in Argentine political freedom, a group of authors and directors collaborated on a project known as TEATRO ABIERTO (Open Theatre). Designed to revitalize the stagnant stage and to encourage new experimentation, the first cycle (in 1981) resulted in 20 new one-act plays staged by different directors, three each night for a week on a repeating cycle. The theatre building, the Teatro Picadero, burned mysteriously at the end of the first week, but the project continued almost immediately in the Teatro Tabarís with determination and enthusiastic public support. Osvaldo Dragún was instrumental in organizing the movement, which disclaims any relationship to JOSEPH CHAIKIN's 1963 experiment. The 1982 cycle was less successful aesthetically and unfortunately coincided with the Argentine–British dispute over the Falklands. Activities were organized for subsequent years, but the election of Raúl Alfonsín in 1983 returned democracy to Argentina and diminished pressures for maintaining the project.

The few authors and directors mentioned do scant credit to the multiplicity of themes, styles and techniques that characterize Argentine theatre in the 20th century. Economic and political problems have taken their toll, disrupting attendance and clouding the artistic atmosphere, but during the present regime new theatres are being constructed and new personnel are being formed. The national theatre (Cervantes), the municipal theatre complex (San Martín), the Manzana de las Luces and a host of independent theatres promote a wide variety of national, Latin American and worldwide plays. New playwrights and directors have emerged, such as BEATRIZ SEIBEL, Eugenio Griffero (b.1936), Roma Mahieu (b.1937), Aída Bortnik (b.1938), Enrique Pinti (b.1940), Jorge Goldenberg (b.1941), Pacho O'Donnell (b.1941), Susana Torres Molina (b.1956), MAURICIO KARTÚN and EDUARDO ROVNER. In the years following the infamous Dirty War in Argentina, which saw unmitigated terror with many 'disappeared persons', the country has attempted, especially under President Menem, to stabilize its economy and its politics. The theatre is active and dynamic with wide-ranging themes and techniques. The work of Osvaldo Pellettieri and his group of critics has helped to stimulate interest both inside and outside Argentina.

Theatre in the provinces has followed much the same history as that of Buenos Aires, with *filodramáticos* groups and later independent theatres, although commercial and professional theatres are notably lacking. Important provincial dramatists include Miguel Iriarte in Córdoba, Oscar Quiroga in Tucumán and Hugo Laccoccia in Neuquén. With the coming of democracy a flurry of festivals and regional meetings has stimulated the theatre, especially in Córdoba.

A panoramic view of Argentine theatre could not be complete without mention, at least, of many other forms: RITUAL theatre in the Native American communities; Creole circuses; radio theatre companies; street theatre in the large cities; popular festivals and CARNIVALS; and the innumerable religious festivals such as the Fiesta of Santa Ana in Tilcara. Argentores, the playwrights' theatre organization, as well as the Argentine Association of Actors, the Association of Critics and Researchers and other private and state institutions, continue to promote the dramatic arts and to sustain the long theatrical tradition which inheres in Argentina. GW

See: A. Blanco Amores de Pagella, *Iniciadores del teatro argentino*, Buenos Aires, 1972, and *Motivaciones del teatro argentino en el siglo 20*, Buenos Aires, 1983; R. Castagnino, *El teatro en Buenos Aires durante la época de Rosas*, Buenos Aires, 1944; J. Marial, *El teatro independiente*, Buenos Aires, 1955; N. Mazziotti, *El auge de las revistas teatrales argentinas*, Madrid, 1985; L. Ordaz, *Breve historia del teatro argentino*, Buenos Aires, 1985, and *Los artistas trashumantes*, Buenos Aires, 1985; O. Pellettieri, *Teatro argentino contemporáneo (1980–1990): Crisis, transición y cambio*, Buenos Aires, 1994; J. L. Trenti Rocamora, *El teatro en la América colonial*, Buenos Aires, 1947; N. Tirri, *Realismo y teatro argentino*, Buenos Aires, 1973; P. Zayas de Lima, *Diccionario de autores teatrales argentinos (1940–90)*, Buenos Aires, 1991.

aria Feature of OPERA, absent at the beginning of the 17th century, that achieved its peak in the first half of the 18th and thereafter became increasingly modified. As distinct from RECITATIVE, an aria has a formal musical structure. It expresses feeling rather than presenting information, reflecting rather than forwarding the action. The most prevalent type of aria during the 18th century was the *da capo* (literally, 'from the beginning') aria in which there are three sections, the third being a repeat of the first. Musical rather than dramatic considerations prevailed in the *da capo* aria, although skilled composers were able to use such arias to dramatic effect. Arias were elaborately codified into a dozen or more types according to the feelings they expressed and the kind of music they involved. After the 18th century, arias became more flexible and recitative more musically fluent and their abrupt distinction disappeared. GH

Ariosto, Ludovico 1474–1533 Italian poet and dramatist. Ariosto was one of the first major Italian dramatists to write in the vernacular rather than in Latin. His first play *La cassaria* (*The Chest*, performed 1508), in addition to being important in its own right as perhaps the first *commedia erudita*, is significant in theatrical history for being presented with painted perspective settings. His second, *I suppositi* (1509, and mounted with settings by Raphael in 1519), was one of the first Italian prose comedies to be widely imitated and exerted considerable influence on the development of scripted COMEDY, not just in Italy but elsewhere – as in England through George Gascoigne's version, *The Supposes*. Both prose plays Ariosto later recast into verse. His *La Lena* and *Il negromante* (*Lena* and *The Magician*, 1528 and 1529 respectively) were both put on during CARNIVAL at Ferrara. Ariosto's plays carried additional authority by virtue of the reputation he won by his non-dramatic verse epic *Orlando furioso*, one of the major poetic works of the Renaissance. This has several times been adapted for stage performance, notably by LUCA RONCONI in 1968, the production later being transferred to film. LR

Aristophanes c.447–after 388 BC Greek comic playwright. Aristophanes was regarded as the greatest poet of the Athenian 'Old Comedy' (see GREECE, ANCIENT), and is the only such poet whose work survives. He spent most of his adult life during the Peloponnesian War (431–404), a bitter struggle between Athens and an alliance led by Sparta. His first play was performed in 427. Because of his youth he gave his first three plays (*Banqueters*, *Babylonians* and *Acharnians*) to another man to produce instead of doing so himself, and for some reason he did the same with some of his later plays. He seems to have been unsuccessfully prosecuted by the demagogue Cleon on a charge of slandering magistrates and citizens in his *Babylonians* (426), and again, perhaps after *Knights* (424), on a charge of falsely claiming to be an Athenian citizen. He wrote about 40 plays in all, some for the Great Dionysia and some for the Lenaea.

Eleven plays survive. In *Acharnians* (*Men of Acharnae*, a village near Athens; 425) an Athenian makes a private peace treaty with Sparta. *Knights* (424) is a savage attack on Cleon. *Clouds* (produced in 423, though the version we have was revised by its author c.418) ridicules the philosopher Socrates. *Wasps* (422) satirizes the Athenians' alleged passion for jury service. *Peace* (421) celebrates an imminent peace treaty with Sparta. In *Birds* (414) two Athenians found an ideal city among the birds. In *Lysistrata* (411) the women of Greece hold a 'sex strike' to force the men to end the war. *Thesmophoriazusae* (*Women Celebrating the Thesmophoria*, a women's festival; 411) travesties EURIPIDES. In *Frogs* (405) the god Dionysus visits the underworld to fetch Euripides back. In *Ecclesiazusae* (*Women*

Holding an Assembly; c.392) the women take control at Athens. In *Plutus* (*Wealth*, 388) the god Wealth is cured of his blindness.

The plots of these plays are exuberant fantasies set in a world in which anything is possible – in which an ordinary citizen can make a private peace treaty and enjoy the blessings of peace while the city remains at war, or can fly to heaven on a giant dung-beetle to rescue the goddess Peace, or can join the birds to found the city of Cloudcuckooland. Typically the play centres on a 'comic hero', elderly (unless female) but lusty, and a 'great idea' for setting the world, or at least the 'hero's' own problems, to rights. The 'great idea' encounters opposition, and the Chorus is called in either to assist the 'hero' or to oppose him. At least once in each of the 5th-century plays the Chorus steps forward in a *parabasis* to address the audience directly; and the main issues of the play are usually debated in a formal *agôn* or battle of words between two characters. The 'hero' usually triumphs (but in *Clouds*, *Wasps* and *Frogs*, where he has ideas that Aristophanes disapproves of, he is made to see the error of his ways); and the play often ends with a series of short, farcical scenes in which enemies or spongers are beaten off.

A bracing feature (or a deplorable one, according to taste) of all the plays except *Plutus* is their total lack of moral uplift. Honesty, decency and courage barely exist, and subjects for cheerful humour include torture, rape, blindness and starvation. The way to deal with enemies is sometimes to defeat them by argument (of a sort), but just as often to cudgel them from the stage. Even the 'hero' seldom rises above a certain shrewd peasant cunning (it takes some effort to apply the word 'hero' to the truly appalling Philocleon of *Wasps*, perhaps Aristophanes' funniest character). If we identify with him, it is because he contrives to enact with impunity our more disreputable fantasies. *Plutus*, however, which should perhaps be classed as Middle Comedy rather than Old, presents a rather sentimental idealization of honest poverty.

Aristophanes never allows considerations of relevance, dramatic illusion or consistency of character or motive to get in the way of a good joke; and his humour covers the widest possible range. There are passages (generally choral) of innocent and whimsical charm (notably in *Birds*); there is skilful PARODY of tragedy, implying close study of it (notably in *Acharnians*, *Thesmophoriazusae* and *Frogs*); but these can exist side by side with sheer slapstick and the crudest of schoolboy jokes.

Though Aristophanes is capable of satirizing sentimental traditionalism (the personification of Right Argument in *Clouds* turns out to be the archetypal scoutmaster), he generally assumes that his audience is highly conservative in its attitudes. While he would certainly have called himself a democrat, and while he would not have dreamed of suggesting that any living politician was *not* a thief, foreigner and sexual pervert, the main targets of his political attacks are the so-called demagogues – politicians (including his arch-enemy Cleon) who depended on the support of the poorer classes in Athens. More attractive, perhaps, is his constant devotion to the cause of peace, a devotion that is surely sincere and not merely a function of the hedonism expected in comedy (it seems not to have been shared by his rival EUPOLIS).

Similarly, among intellectuals, Aristophanes' favourite targets are the new-fangled sophists, whom he accuses of corrupting the morals of the young and among whom (in defiance of all our other evidence) he includes Socrates. With these he associates Euripides, who also upset traditional assumptions, and who is the favourite object of Aristophanic parody.

While much of his abuse of living figures is obviously unfair, it is unclear how seriously it was taken. The Athenians appointed Cleon to the post of general shortly after awarding first prize to *Knights*; but Cleon himself seems to have reacted sharply to Aristophanes' attacks on him, and indeed these can hardly be dismissed as good clean fun. Plato's *Apology* holds Aristophanes partly responsible for popular prejudice against Socrates, but his *Symposium* portrays him with affection, and shows him at ease in Socrates' company. There is no doubt that Aristophanes' *main* purpose was to entertain his audience and win their applause, not to alter their views.   ALB

Aristotle 384–322 BC Greek philosopher, pupil of Plato, and author of numerous works concerning logic, the natural world and human activities. Though he often alludes to drama in the *Rhetoric* and elsewhere, his importance for theatre lies mainly in his *Poetics*, which probably dates from the 330s or 320s. From this we have only one book, on TRAGEDY and epic poetry, a second book, on comedy, being lost. Moreover, what we have is (for whatever reason) preserved in such a compressed, disorganized and corrupt form that its meaning is often highly obscure.

Aristotle approaches poetry not as a literary critic but as an analytical philosopher. He regards it as a phenomenon among other phenomena, needing to be defined, accounted for and classified into its different varieties, each of which must itself be defined and analysed into its constituent parts (this, at least, is the plan, though it is very imperfectly realized in the work as we have it). Any phenomenon, however, is best exemplified by its highest forms, and Aristotle must therefore establish what is the highest form of poetry (in his opinion tragedy) and what is the best type of tragedy (exemplified for him by the *Oedipus Tyrannus* of SOPHOCLES). It is in this way that literary evaluation enters in; though, when Aristotle is defending the existence of poetry or of tragedy (*Poetics* 4, 9, 26 etc.), we may often detect the ulterior motive of replying to the charges brought against them by Plato.

The factual information which Aristotle gives, especially on the origins of tragedy and comedy (see GREECE, ANCIENT), can seem contradictory and implausible, and it is doubtful how far it is based on evidence and how far on mere theorizing. His definitions, such as the famous definition of tragedy in chapter 6, tend to reflect his philosophical preoccupations rather than ordinary usage. The analysis of the structure of a tragedy in chapter 12 is unsatisfactory, and may not be his work at all. His literary judgements are often based on *a priori* reasoning rather than a direct response to literature – or at least, they *claim* to be so based, though at times it may be that a direct response to literature is being rationalized. His emphasis on the preeminence of plot over character (chapter 6 etc.) may reflect the priorities of the Greek dramatists, and his guidance on effective plot construction (7–14) is of wide, though not

universal, application. For anyone seeking to understand Greek drama, however, his unargued assumptions may be of greater interest than his conclusions.

Nevertheless, the influence of the *Poetics* – or of doctrines purporting to be derived from it – has been immense ever since it became known to Renaissance Europe through a Latin translation by Giorgio Valla, published in 1498. One famous 'Aristotelian' doctrine is that of the three unities – of time, place and action – which were considered canonical by, in particular, the 17th-century dramatists of France and England. The *Poetics* does insist on 'unity of action' (chapters 7–8 etc.), but the idea of 'unity of time' derives merely from a remark in chapter 5 that tragedy 'tries as far as possible to limit itself to a single revolution of the sun, or a little more', and 'unity of place' is not mentioned at all.

In more recent times certain terms which do occur in the *Poetics* have become clichés of literary criticism, notably *katharsis* ('purgation' or 'purification'?) from chapter 6 and *hamartia* ('sin', 'error' or both?) from chapter 13. What Aristotle himself meant by these terms is still hotly disputed. We may be fairly certain, however, that his *katharsis* had little in common with the Freudian ideas now associated with it, and that his *hamartia* was not the 'fatal flaw' of the 'tragic hero'. (See also DRAMATIC THEORY.)   ALB

Arlecchino see COMMEDIA DELL'ARTE; HARLEQUIN; ZANNI

Arlequin see HARLEQUIN

Arliss, George [George Augustus Arlis-Andrews] 1868–1946 British-born character actor and playwright, whose greatest successes occurred in the USA after 1901. Arliss, immediately recognizable on account of his long, narrow face, pointed nose, habitual monocle and charming voice, spent 40 years perfecting the playing of villains, great historical leaders and wise old men with an apparent effortlessness that concealed his polished technique. Louis Parker, author of his best known vehicle, *Disraeli* (1911), said Arliss could 'express more with one finger than most actors can express with their entire bodies'. His most notable stage roles, in addition to Disraeli, were in *The Second Mrs Tanqueray* (1901) with MRS PATRICK CAMPBELL, *The Darling of the Gods* (1902) with BLANCHE BATES, *Hedda Gabler* (1904) and *Rosmersholm* (1907) with MINNIE MADDERN FISKE; in *Paganini* (1915), *The Green Goddess* (1921) and *Old English* (1924); and his last formal stage appearance as Shylock (1928). In 1923 he returned to London after a 22-year absence to appear in William Archer's *The Green Goddess*. His successful film career began in 1920, and during the 30s he made over 20 films, portraying among other characters such historical figures as Voltaire, Rothschild (Meyer and Nathan), Cardinal Richelieu and Wellington. He wrote or collaborated on six plays and wrote two important autobiographies: *Up the Years from Bloomsbury* (1927) and *My Ten Years in the Studio* (1940).   DBW

Arlt, Roberto 1900–42 Argentine playwright. Also journalist and novelist, Arlt is the link between the celebrated Golden Decade (1900–10) of Argentine theatre and the contemporary movement. His experimental style and technique were apparent in his first novel, *El juguete rabioso* (1926), but were greatly refined in his later novels, which he peopled with anguished, nonconformist characters who anticipated later existentialist trends. His dramatic career spans the ten years from 1932 until his death. The essential characteristic of his dramaturgy is the transformation of a conventional reality by means of illusions, dreams, fantasies and the grotesque in order to create a new world. He denied the influence of PIRANDELLO, although Pirandello's works were played in Buenos Aires during those years, and preferred to say that he had found his inspiration in the European master painters – Goya, Dürer and Brueghel. He wrote eight plays, most of which were premiered by Leónidas Barletta, the father of the Argentine independent theatre movement, in his Teatro del Pueblo. Major titles are *Saverio el cruel* (*Saverio the Cruel*), which shows strong influence of the *Quijote*, Arlt's favourite book; *La isla desierta* (*The Desert Island*, 1937); and *La fiesta del hierro* (*The Iron Fiesta*, 1940). GW

Armin, Robert c.1568–1615 Elizabethan actor, who may have attracted the attention of the great clown RICHARD TARLTON while serving an apprenticeship to a goldsmith. We do not know when Armin became an actor, though it was certainly some years before he succeeded WILL KEMPE as leading 'CLOWN' in the LORD CHAMBERLAIN'S MEN. We know from Armin's own *Quips upon Questions* (1600) that he inherited some of Tarlton's (and Kempe's) skills as an extemporizer, but also that he considered himself a 'foolosopher'. The recognizable transition in SHAKESPEARE's plays from broad clown to wise fool must owe something to the contrasting playing styles of Kempe and Armin. The passage from Dogberry (Kempe's creation) to Feste (Armin's) is a change from rustic clown to motley jester. If, as is sometimes supposed, Armin was also the original Lavache, Pandarus and Fool to King Lear, he was obviously an actor whom Shakespeare trusted, as well as a talented singer. Armin's collection of comic tales, *Foole upon Foole, or Sixe Sortes of Sottes* (1600), was successful enough to earn a second edition in 1605 and republication in enlarged form as *A Nest of Ninnies* (1608). His play, *The Two Maids of Moreclacke* (1609), was performed by the Children of the King's Revels. PT

Arneaux, J. A. 1855–? African-American actor. Born in Georgia of a white French father and a black mother, Arneaux received a good post-secondary education in northern cities and in Paris. A journalist by profession, he took to the stage first as a song-and-dance artist at TONY PASTOR's Metropolitan Theatre on BROADWAY, then as a legitimate actor and manager of the Astor Place Company of Colored Tragedians, the leading black dramatic troupe in America in the 1880s. Based in New York, the company also performed to great acclaim in both Philadelphia and Providence, Rhode Island. Arneaux's roles included Iago, Macbeth and Pythias, but his favourite part, in which he excelled, was Richard III – being ranked with MACREADY, EDWIN BOOTH and LAWRENCE BARRETT. EGH

Arniches, Carlos 1866–1943 Spanish playwright whose *sainetes* represent the culmination of the 19th-century

GÉNERO CHICO. In his short FARCES, comedies of manners, and ZARZUELAS, he creatively invented popular speech and character types drawn from Madrid reality. Although once brushed aside by critics, his works have endured. Director José Osuna was responsible for numerous revivals in the 1970s and 80s, including a series of summer productions of *sainetes* of old Madrid, in Lauro Olmo's modernized versions. Among Arniches's most frequently performed farces are *La venganza de la Petra* (*Petra's Revenge*, 1917). *Los caciques* (*The Political Bosses*, 1920), a riotous SATIRE of rural politics, received a major Madrid production in 1987, directed by José Luis Alonso. Arniches's greatest impact on Spanish and Spanish American theatre (see HISPANIC THEATRE (USA)) stems from his grotesque tragicomedies. *La señorita de Trevélez* (*Miss Trevelez*, 1916), his masterwork, caricatures a small-town spinster but aims its critical barbs at the cruelty of idle young men who make fun of her. PZ

Aronson, Boris 1898–1980 Russian-American painter, sculptor and set designer. Aronson is still for many the most respected American designer of the mid-20th century. He was born in Russia and studied with ALEKSANDRA EKSTER, a constructivist designer with the Kamerny Theatre. He left Russia for Berlin in 1922, and in 1923 emigrated to the USA, where his first assignments were for the Unser Theatre and the YIDDISH ART THEATRE. By the 1930s he was designing major shows on BROADWAY and working with the GROUP THEATRE. His early work reflected the influences not only of Ekster but of Marc Chagall and Nathan Altman, who designed for the Moscow Jewish Theatre. The cubist-fantastic style characteristic of Chagall's paintings can be seen in much of Aronson's early work and even in later works, such as the acclaimed 1959 set for *J.B.*

Despite his enormous output and critical success for plays by WILLIAM SAROYAN, TENNESSEE WILLIAMS, CLIFFORD ODETS, ARTHUR MILLER, WILLIAM INGE and others, he did not achieve widespread recognition until he teamed up with director HAROLD PRINCE on the 1964 musical *Fiddler on the Roof*. This was followed by six more musicals, including *Cabaret* and *A Little Night Music*. This collaboration seemed to bring out Aronson's creativity. His designs ranged from realistic detail for plays like *Awake and Sing!* to technological fantasies such as *Company* that used steel, plexiglass and projections. His constructivist influences could be seen throughout his work. His sets always had a strong sense of line and form and a generally subtle but evocative use of colour employed symbolically to support the mood of the play. For the 1940 production of Ballet Theatre's *The Great American Goof*, Aronson employed, for the first time, a technique he called 'projected scenery' – a method of projecting coloured slides on to neutral, abstract shapes in order to create and change the mood and space of a piece. This technique was displayed in the 1947 exhibition of his work at the Museum of Modern Art, aptly titled 'Painting with Light'. A major study of his work, co-authored by his wife, Lisa, and Frank Rich, was published in 1987. AA

Aronson, Rudolph 1856–1919 American impresario, theatre manager and composer. After studying music in

Berlin and Paris, Aronson presented a series of orchestral concerts in New York. In 1882 he opened the Casino Theatre, where for 12 seasons he mounted lavish productions of European and British comic OPERAS, most notably *Erminie*, which tallied some 1200 performances in the decade after its premiere in 1886. Among the many performers who attained stardom at the Casino were LILLIAN RUSSELL, FRANCIS WILSON, DE WOLF HOPPER and JEFFERSON DE ANGELIS. Aronson also introduced New Yorkers to the pleasures of the roof garden, as he brought his comic operas to the Casino's roof during the summer months. After leaving the Casino, he managed the Bijou Theatre for several years, and was the proprietor of the Metropole Hotel at his death. He also composed more than 150 musical works and left an autobiography, *Theatrical and Musical Memoirs* (1913). MK

Arrabal, Fernando 1932– Spanish/French playwright. Arrabal's work is dominated by the traumas of his Spanish childhood when his mother, a Catholic, betrayed his father, a Republican, to Franco's police. His early plays, written in French and published in 1958, are dream works in which naive characters behave according to basic Freudian drives. In the 1960s he achieved notoricty, especially with SAVARY's production of *Le Labyrinthe* (1967). The same year Garcia produced Arrabal's *Automobile Graveyard* and Lavelli *The Architect and Emperor of Assyria*. Since then his voluminous work has appeared under the title 'panic theatre'. Designed to provoke psychological shock waves in its audience, it often appears merely self-indulgent. DB

Arriví, Francisco 1915– Puerto Rican dramatist, director, critic, essayist and major figure in Puerto Rican theatre. Arriví studied pedagogy in Puerto Rico, and radio and theatre at Columbia University. His early plays – *Club de solteros* (*Bachelors' Club*, 1940) and *El diablo se humaniza* (*Humanizing the Devil*, 1941) – are fantastic and farcical. *María Soledad* (*Maria Solitude*, 1947) is a Jasperian search for absolute purity. The trilogy *Máscara puertorriqueña* (*Puerto Rican Mask*, 1956–9) deals with the complex racial and cultural heritage of the Puerto Ricans. Other major plays include *Cóctel de Don Nadie* (*Mr Nobody's Cocktail*, 1964) and the MUSICAL *Solteros 72* (*Bachelors 72*). Arriví founded the theatre group Tinglado Puertorriqueño in 1945 and was for years director of the theatre wing of the Puerto Rican Cultural Institute that sponsors the annual theatre festival. GW

Arrufat, Antón 1935– Cuban playwright and poet. Arrufat abandoned university studies to write; he initiated with two one-act absurdist plays (see THEATRE OF THE ABSURD) – *El caso se investiga* (*The Case Is Being Investigated*) and *El último tren* (*The Last Train*), both written in 1957 but without initial success. *El vivo al pollo* (*Chicken for the Living*, 1959) uses traditional BUFO theatre to PARODY a natural fear of death in the case of a woman who embalms her husband. With *La zona cero* (*Zero Zone*, 1959) the illogical patterns and comedy routines he developed earlier reached a climax in a BECKETT-style absurdism. After *La repetición* (*The Repetition*, 1963), a duplicative process that shows the influence of the

Revolution, and *Todos los domingos* (*Every Sunday*, 1965), he wrote *Los siete contra Tebas* (*Seven against Thebes*), which won the UNEAC prize for 1968, but he was censured along with Herberto Padilla for a work considered antithetical to revolutionary goals. He remains in Cuba and works as a journalist/writer. His later plays are unpublished and unstaged: *La tierra permanente* (*The Solid Earth*), *Retrato de Juan Criollo* (*Portrait of John Creole*) and *La divina Fanny* (*Divine Fanny*). His preoccupation with language and the search for language adequate to express new concepts are strong characteristics of his work. GW

Artaud, Antonin 1896–1948 French poet, actor, director and theoretician. Born in Marseille, Artaud moved to Paris in 1920 where he acted in DULLIN's company and in productions by GEORGES PITOËFF. He sent some poems to Jacques Rivière, director of the *Nouvelle Revue Française*, who rejected them but published the correspondence that followed, in which Artaud attempted to explain the difficulties he experienced in expressing himself. This analysis of the gap between the poet's vision and the expressive means at his disposal stands as a paradigmatic statement for all 20th-century artists. Artaud was a member of Breton's surrealist group (see SURREALISM) from 1924 until they expelled him two years later. He took acting roles in films, notably Abel Gance's *Napoléon* (Marat) and Dreyer's *Passion of Joan of Arc* (Brother Massieu).

But his extraordinary influence on subsequent theatre is based largely on his two short-lived attempts at directing and on his volume of essays, *The Theatre and Its Double*. The first directing venture was in 1926, when he founded the Théâtre Alfred Jarry together with Robert Aron and ROGER VITRAC. The manifestos for this theatre stressed the idea that theatre should no longer be mere entertainment but genuine action with real effects on the real world. A suggested model for theatre was a police raid on a red-light district, rounding up prostitutes on the streets and flushing them out of the brothels. The features of what he later called Theatre of Cruelty are all to be found here: violence, sexuality, social taboos, and the eruption of dramatic action outside the safe confines of the stage. The Théâtre Alfred Jarry never had its own premises and could only manage occasional productions, among which were STRINDBERG's *Dream Play* and Vitrac's *Victor* (both 1928).

In 1931 Artaud was dazzled by a performance of dances from Bali that he saw at the colonial exhibition. Under their influence, he published the essays collected and published in 1938 as *The Theatre and Its Double*. The double of theatre was life, the vital, metaphysical reality that shadows our everyday actions. Western society had lost contact with this life and so theatre had to be like the plague, a violent, overwhelming crisis, both socially and individually, from which people would emerge either dead or purged. In 1935 he founded his second theatre, the Théâtre de la Cruauté, which failed to outlive its first production, an adaptation of Shelley's *The Cenci*. Artaud's direction was precise, even balletic, but he was obliged to give the main part to an indifferent actress who put up the money for the production. The circumstances of the production were also to blame for its failure: primeval theatre did not harmonize with fashionable Parisian theatre-going. He travelled to Mexico and to Ireland but, with his health gradually deteriorating, he was committed to an asylum at Rodez. He remained in institutions throughout the war and only emerged two years before his death. His last two years produced a torrent of work including an essay in which he identified with Van Gogh, and a radio programme of his own work which was banned at the last minute.

Artaud's writings do not form a coherent body of DRAMATIC THEORY, but, rather, a visionary expression of the loss of the spiritual dimension in the life of Western civilization. His proposed remedy involves rediscovering the sense of danger and of total, physical commitment in both art and life. Artists, he says in the preface to *Theatre and Its Double*, should be 'condemned men at the stake, signalling through the flames'. He dismisses clever, witty writing and the cult of the masterpiece, moving the emphasis from the writer to the director and stressing the essentially physical, three-dimensional quality of theatre. The director becomes a new kind of author, writing in space by means of sound, colour, lights, objects and, above all, actors, who take on the force of moving hieroglyphs. Though he himself failed, his work has been enormously influential, especially since the 1960s; many directors, e.g. BROOK, GROTOWSKI, PLANCHON and BLIN, have acknowledged their debt to him.   DB

Artef YIDDISH acronym for Workers' Theater Group; begun in New York in 1925 as a dramatic studio/collective under the auspices of the communist daily, *Freiheit* (*Freedom*). Several more cohorts of actors entered in successive studios and studied together until assimilated into the performing nucleus. Like other Soviet-influenced groups of the period, Artef's members were committed to spreading radical politics through expressionist (see EXPRESSIONISM), even AGIT-PROP, productions that stressed stylized groupings and mass movement. The press outside the Yiddish community praised its colourful vitality, in repertory adapted from the Yiddish canon or translated into Yiddish from contemporaneous American and Soviet plays – some 80 productions in all. After a last major effort in 1939, Artef performed only sporadically until 1953. NS

Arts Council of Great Britain (ACGB) The agency through which funds from central government sources are distributed to the arts in Britain. The Arts Council was incorporated by Royal Charter on 9 August 1946. Like its wartime predecessor CEMA, the ACGB had links with the adult education movement and its aims were philanthropic – to improve artistic standards and to encourage the appreciation of the arts (originally the 'fine' arts) around the country. It was allowed to subsidize non-profit-distributing companies, registered under the Charities Act, and not commercial ones. The Council itself consisted of up to 16 members, appointed by the government which was afterwards expected not to interfere with its decisions but stay 'at arm's length'. The day-to-day running of its affairs was left in the hands of a secretary-general and his/her staff, assisted by unpaid boards of expert advisers.

Initially the ACGB's funds, received directly through the Treasury, were small, rising from £230,000 (1945/6) to £830,000 (1955/6), of which a third was allocated to the Royal Opera House, COVENT GARDEN. By 1965/6, described in its annual report as a 'key year', this total sum had risen to about £4 million. This was the year when the incoming Labour government published its White Paper on the Arts, which transformed the ACGB's role. It was now funded through the Department of Education and Science, whose under-secretary, Jennie Lee MP, was known as the Arts Minister. Its resources rose rapidly year by year under Labour and Conservative governments, although it was supported by a new department of Arts and Libraries under Margaret Thatcher's government. Its grant-funding from the government topped £100 million by 1984/5 and £200 million by 1992, when it became the responsibility of a newly created National Heritage Ministry.

During this evolutionary process, the ACGB's role greatly changed. For the first twenty years of its existence, it was a small but influential adjunct to a predominantly commercial arts world. It helped some ambitious new companies, such as the English Stage Company, encouraged the local authorities to lay the foundations for a new regional theatre movement and conducted an influential survey, 'Housing the Arts' (1961). It was a significant factor in the establishment of the national companies, the NATIONAL THEATRE and the ROYAL SHAKESPEARE COMPANY. Under Jennie Lee and her immediate successors, the ACGB took a more active role in transforming the British arts scene. The commercial companies fell into decline, while the subsidized ones thrived with a mixture of support from the ACGB, the regional and the local authorities. The Council became the main source of funding for the 12 Regional Arts Associations (RAAs), modelled after its example. It subsidized most forms of theatre, from the dissident wings to the establishment centre; and it could be argued that the ACGB, which claimed merely to respond to the arts initiatives emanating from elsewhere, was the shaping factor in determining the value system of modern British theatre. It was the ACGB of the 1970s which determined the financial priority given to the two national companies as 'centres of excellence'.

Margaret Thatcher's government was opposed in principle to such quangos (quasi-autonomous non-governmental organizations), but the system had become too well established to be easily changed. Many of the old commercial theatres had gone and been replaced by non-cost-effective civic arts centres, which could not survive without subsidies. In *The Glory of the Garden* (1984), a modestly reformist document largely written by the ACGB's new chairman, Sir William Rees-Mogg, it was envisaged that many of the ACGB's grant-giving powers should devolve to the RAAs, while new money should be sought from sponsorship. His secretary-general, Luke Rittner, helped to found ABSA (the Association for Business Sponsorship of the Arts); he came from a non-academic background, unlike his predecessor, Sir Roy Shaw. The ACGB was no longer a body which shunned market principles. Indeed, it embraced them.

British theatre and the arts in general had previously lived within a mixed economy, whose system disadvantaged the small company and the independent producer. Broadcasting, the main provider of popular drama for mass audiences, was strictly under the control of the government. Intellectual property rights (including COPY-RIGHT) were poorly monitored. The paradox of the 1980s was that state subsidies more than doubled within ten years under a government which did not believe in subsidy, but needed to compensate the arts for the weaknesses of its market system. In 1992, after winning a general election, Prime Minister John Major introduced the National Heritage Ministry, which embraced many arts fields (including broadcasting) previously scattered among several ministries. The ACGB's main role was now to fund the national companies, with the RAAs responsible for the regional ones. The beneficial effects of the growth of the ACGB's resources and the establishment of the new ministry do not yet seem to have percolated down to many arts companies, which tend to be as uncertain of their futures as they have always been. The wages of actors have not improved in real terms since the 1950s and unemployment rates are still high, facts noted in *Theatre for All* (1988), an ACGB report, and repeated in an ACGB discussion document, *Towards a National Arts and Media Strategy* (1992). JE

Arts Theatre (London) Opening in 1927, the theatre gave private performances of unlicensed experimental plays for members. Successful from the first, with a series of productions transferring to the commercial theatre, including JOHN VAN DRUTEN's first play *Young Woodly* in 1928, it continued this role until sold to the film producer NATHAN COHEN in 1962. It hosted tours by foreign artists such as YVETTE GUILBERT, and the COMPAGNIE DES QUINZE appeared there in 1931. Under the management of ALEC CLUNES from 1942 to 1950 it gained a national reputation, with premieres of work such as CHRISTOPHER FRY's *The Lady's Not for Burning* (1948). The intimacy of the small stage and 347-seat auditorium was particularly suited to the new wave of absurd drama (see THEATRE OF THE ABSURD) in the 1950s, and BECKETT's *Waiting for Godot*, PINTER's *The Caretaker* and ALBEE's *Zoo Story* were all given their first English performances there. The ROYAL SHAKESPEARE COMPANY leased it for a major season of new work and seldom-performed classics in 1962, and since then it has served as a WEST END transfer house for FRINGE THEATRE productions, with Robert Patrick's *Kennedy's Children* from the King's Head (Islington, London) in 1975, and STOPPARD's *Dirty Linen* and *New Found Land* in 1976. CI

Asakura Setsu 1922– Japan's best-known modern stage designer, a professor at Kuwasawa Institute of Design in Tokyo. Asakura was influenced by Itō Kisaku (1899–1967), who began his career in 1925 with a design for *Julius Caesar* at the Tsukiji Little Theatre. Asakura reached prominence after the Second World War designing complex sets for a range of commercial, avant-garde and *SHINGEKI* productions. She worked with NŌ actor KANZE HISAO and KYŌGEN actor Nomura Mansaku on SENECA's *Medea* (1975). She has designed for directors SUZUKI TADASHI, KARA JŪRŌ and NINAGAWA YUKIO. For Inoue Hisashi's play *The Great Doctor Yabuhara* (*Yabuhara kengyōgo*, 1974) she used lighting to sculpt and transform a single open space. Typifying her bold and dynamic design sense are the mammoth three- and four-storey sets for Ninagawa's production of BRECHT's *Threepenny Opera*

(1977), *The Love Suicides of Chikamatsu* (*Chikamatsu shinjū monogatari*, 1979) and Kara Jūrō's *A Tale of Tokyo* (*Shitaya mannenchō monogatari*, 1981). JRB

Asch, Sholom 1880–1957 Polish-born playwright and novelist who wrote in YIDDISH. His plays mainly concern the conflict between orthodox and emancipated Jew, and he achieved early fame and notoriety with *The God of Vengeance* (1907), closed down by the police for immorality when produced on BROADWAY in 1923. Other notable plays include *Downstream* (1904), *The Messiah Period* (1906), *Sabatai Zevi* (1908), *Wealthy Reb Shloime* (1913) and *Mottke the Thief* (1917). Several of his novels were dramatized and performed by MAURICE SCHWARTZ. AB

Asche, Oscar 1872–1936 British actor, who worked with F. R. BENSON and BEERBOHM TREE, from whom he took over the management of His [Her] MAJESTY'S THEATRE. He made his reputation in Shakespearian roles, though he also played opposite ELLEN TERRY in GORDON CRAIG's 1903 production of IBSEN's *The Vikings*, and gained his greatest success in his own MUSICAL fantasy *Chu Chin Chow* (based on *Ali Baba and the Forty Thieves*), which ran from 1916 to 1921. CI

Ashcroft, Peggy (Edith Margaret Emily) 1907–91 British actress, who first took the WEST END by storm as the innocent Naemi in *Jew Suss* (1929). Her special quality of radiant freshness caused some critics, including JAMES AGATE, to state that she was too simple and lightweight for major classical roles, but the 1932/3 OLD VIC season revealed her range as an actress in such parts as Juliet, Rosalind, Lady Teazle and SHAW's Cleopatra. Her subsequent career was remarkable for its versatility, command and, not least, her instinct for major challenges. Against all expectations, she was a brilliantly sluttish Cleopatra to MICHAEL REDGRAVE's Antony at the Shakespeare Memorial Theatre in 1953, an electric Beatrice to JOHN GIELGUD's Benedict in 1950 and 1955, a savage Hedda Gabler in 1954, and Shen Teh in BRECHT's *The Good Person of Setzuan*. Her roles in contemporary plays ranged from Hester in TERENCE RATTIGAN's *The Deep Blue Sea* (1952) to Beth in HAROLD PINTER's *Landscape* (1969) and Winnie in SAMUEL BECKETT's *Happy Days* (1975). Her last stage performance was as LILIAN BAYLIS in *Save the Wells* at the Royal Opera House in 1986, although she continued to act in films and TV dramas until shortly before her death, appearing in *Madame Soutsatzka*, a film directed by John Schlesinger in 1988. A committed socialist, Ashcroft energetically furthered the interests of her profession by serving on the council of Equity, on the ARTS COUNCIL and on the artistic committee of the English Stage Company. She became a director of the ROYAL SHAKESPEARE COMPANY in 1968 and, among her many honours, she received a DBE in 1956. In 1962 a new theatre in her place of birth, Croydon in south London, was named after her. JE

Asian and Pacific Island theatre Tens of thousands of theatre troupes perform traditional and modern plays in the enormous area of the Asian mainland and the adjoining islands of the Pacific Ocean. No one knows the full extent of the performing arts among the over two billion people who live in the 50 plus nation states within this region. What is certain, though, is that the theatrical arts in Asian and Pacific Island cultures have an ancient heritage, are highly developed, are rich almost beyond imagining in their diversity, and are still very much alive for large segments of the population.

From Turkey (see MIDDLE EAST) in the west to the Hawaiian Islands in the east, from Siberia in the north to AUSTRALIA in the south, the theatrical arts have evolved into perhaps a thousand distinct forms or genres, each reflecting the language, religious views, social structures and daily lives of the people who have created it, and each distinguished by its own constellation of music, movement, acting techniques and staging conventions, as well as by its dramatic content and form. Even to the relatively uninitiated observer, KYŌGEN comedies in JAPAN stand apart from KABUKI or from BUNRAKU, also from Japan; and they are artistic and cultural worlds away from ludruk in INDONESIA, BHAVAI in INDIA, or JINGXI (Beijing opera) in CHINA – forms which also stress comic elements. Still, shared features do link genres within and between countries, and it is possible – with considerable caution – to identify interregional and even Pan-Asian-Pacific traditions because of centuries – even millennia – of interactions that have led to similarities, as well as to differences, in ethnicity, religion, politics, language and literary traditions.

The major cultural regions Six major geographic and cultural regions may be identified within this vast sweep of land and ocean – though all of these regions blur at their borders, all have divergent tendencies within them, and all have been affected by and had an effect upon other regions.

South Asia encompasses the present nation states of the Indian subcontinent: BANGLADESH, Bhutan, India, Nepal, PAKISTAN and SRI LANKA. This region has been the birthplace of Hinduism and of Buddhism, and, hence, the source of the *Ramayana* and *Mahabharata* epics and *Jataka* tales which have provided narratives and themes for a multitude of theatrical forms, not only in the subcontinent but in Southeast Asia as well. The region is also the home of a pervasive, multifaceted and extremely influential classical dance, theatre and music tradition, described in BHARATA MUNI's treatise, the *Natyasastra* (written sometime between 400 BC and AD 200). Rooted in Hinduism, this tradition was itself enriched as well as challenged by contact with successive Islamic courts since the 8th century AD, while the performing arts of Nepal and Bhutan have maintained a great affinity with those of Buddhist Tibet (see TIBETAN DRAMA). An outpouring of fecund detail, a baroque love of brilliant theatrical display and the vibrant use of colour, emotion and rhythm in performance mark the profusion of South Asian forms.

Abutting this subcontinent is the area of Southwest Asia and, beyond this, Asia Minor, which are treated in this volume along with the Islamic states of North Africa as the MIDDLE EAST (but see also FRENCH-SPEAKING NORTH AFRICA). The rich storytelling and musical traditions developed and performed in this region have also had an enormous impact on the performing arts of South and Southeast Asia, as well as on the cultures of Mediterranean Europe

and sub-Saharan Africa. The satirical *karagöz* puppet theatre (see KARAGÖZ) has spread from Turkey to Greece and North Africa and the region has provided the models for numerous traditions of secular farce *(orta oyuni* in Turkey, *ru-howzi* in Iran, *bhand jashna* in Kashmir, *alkab* in Bengal), as well as traditions of intensely devotional Islamic performance (the whirling Sufi dance in Turkey, *ta'ziyeh* in Iran (see MIDDLE EAST), *qu'wali in* Pakistan). When encountering other traditions, the approaches honed here have often encouraged a more contemplative and abstract aesthetic in dance and theatre, as indicated by changes to *wayang kulit* (see SHADOW PUPPETS) in Indonesia (Java) and to *kathak* in India under Islamic patronage and rule.

China, HONG KONG, Japan, KOREA (North and South), Mongolia and TAIWAN comprise East Asia. These countries all have cultures that have been shaped, in large part, by Confucian civil ethics, systems of imperial rule and Buddhist philosophy, as well as by an ancient and enduring legacy of SHAMANism shared, particularly, with Siberia to the north. The Chinese writing system of calligraphic characters was widely adopted throughout this region and, in the process, Chinese literature and brush painting and Chinese approaches to music and dance were introduced. Traditions range from those featuring a love of clamorous noise and dazzling primary colours to those that stress an opposing spirit of decorum and restraint and a concern for structural simplicity and clarity, as theorized in ZEAMI's writings from the early 15th century.

The countries of Southeast Asia – BURMA (Myanmar), CAMBODIA (Kampuchea), Indonesia, LAOS, MALAYSIA, the PHILIPPINES, Brunei, SINGAPORE, THAILAND and VIETNAM – have welcomed religions, literature and dance from both South and East Asia, as well as from Asia Minor, and have fused these with rich, indigenous performance traditions, typically based on an animist world-view. Merging with previous populations, Malay peoples settled Indonesia, Malaysia, southern Thailand, Cambodia and the Philippines, and these countries share many traits in their approaches to theatrical arts. Related musical traditions, indicating a Chinese influence, are heard in theatrical traditions of northern Burma, Laos, Thailand, Cambodia and Vietnam, while dance traditions showing a close affinity with classical Indian models are found in Burma, Cambodia, Thailand, Indonesia and Malaysia. The small island nation of Singapore, settled by Malays and site of a more recent influx of peoples from China and India, presents a unique cornucopia of interacting traditions.

OCEANIA contains some 20 Pacific Island nations in the subregions of Melanesia, Micronesia and Polynesia, whose original settlement can often be traced back to common ancestors arriving in successive waves from the Asian mainland and then advancing from island to far-flung island. These Pacific voyagers brought with them their religious songs, genealogical chants, and dances, spreading them across the island groupings, eastward through Papua New Guinea, Fiji, Tahiti, Samoa and Hawaii, and southward towards NEW ZEALAND and Australia, which stand apart from most of the cultures in Asia and the Pacific because of their unique patterns of colonization and settlement (but see MAORI THEATRE, as well as the coverage of aboriginal performance in the entry on Australia).

The various Pacific cultures tend to be rich in dance, music, storytelling and RITUAL forms, with less traditional emphasis on formal theatre and drama.

Genres in relation to social milieu We can identify four quite different social milieux that have nourished theatre forms within the countries that lie in and are adjacent to the western Pacific and northern Indian Oceans. Elite forms of theatre were created with the support of the ruling classes, propounding the ideology of rulers and serving audiences drawn from those at or near the centre of political and economic power. In the past, these were court forms, performed by court functionaries – sometimes by courtesans, catamites or members of the royal family – for court occasions. In this context, performance constituted a civic political ritual, demonstrating and confirming royal prerogatives; it also reflected the culture's most esteemed literary and artistic values (a status attained, for example, by Sanskrit drama in India, BUGAKU and NŌ in Japan, bedaya and gambuh in Indonesia, zat in Burma, hat boi in Vietnam and the hula in Hawaii). In the course of time, and especially during the late 19th and early 20th centuries, the royal courts which had supported these arts diminished in power or were replaced, and performers were forced to turn to other patrons and audiences for support. Today, many former 'royal' theatre forms continue to be enacted as important 'cultural artefacts', preserved as 'state arts' with modest levels of government support.

'Folk theatre', created by local villagers-turned-performers and enacted by them at community festivals, on religious occasions and for the entertainment of their own neighbours, has existed throughout Asia for as far back as we can research – usually in an active give-and-take relationship with the more elite forms. It has often provided the artistic base from which the elite forms develop (sarugaku and dengaku nō in Japan), and sometimes has preserved the elite forms' artistic legacy (KUTIYATTAM Sanskrit theatre in India). In thousands of village communities, and in urban enclaves as well, folk performances continue to be organized as religio-civic rites, expressing and helping to form the cultural identities of local communities. Although the artistic quality may be high and a performer may enjoy social esteem, performing in such genres has traditionally been an occasional activity and rarely an occupation. Today, if the economic environment is encouraging, outstanding folk performers may gain favour and move towards professionalism – usually performing for national and foreign tourist audiences; but this is often done at the cost of being separated from the communities that have fostered the forms and given them meaning in the first place. Among the many forms of Asian folk theatre are mani-rimdu in Nepal, hat cheo in Vietnam, SANDAE-GŬK in Korea, kuda kepang in Indonesia, ruhozi in Iran, YAKSHAGANA and THERUKOOTHU in India, and KOLAM in Sri Lanka.

In urban environments, significant forms of commercial theatre have evolved for a public audience of commoners, workers, artisans and merchants. Typical commercial troupes perform regularly – some of them daily – in permanent enclosed theatre buildings, sensitive to the tastes of the general ticket-buying public. Most important urban commercial theatre genres began with ventures despised by the intelligentsia (ludruk and ketoprak in Indonesia, zarzuela (distantly related to the Spanish ZARZUELA) in the Philippines, bangsawan in Malaysia, likay in Thailand, mawlum moo in Laos, lakon bassak in Cambodia, TAMASHA, JATRA and NAUTANKI in India, ZAIJU in China). As is true of THIRD WORLD POPULAR THEATRE elsewhere, government suppression of these genres in the name of public order and morality has been common. Ironically, some of these forms have seen their official standing metamorphose with the passage of time and today they are considered reputable – even 'classical' – forms of intangible national treasures (kabuki in Japan, YUEJU from Shaoxing in China, wayang orang in Indonesia, cai luong in Vietnam).

A completely different elite theatre was created in the 20th century by and for a new Western-oriented, university-educated, professional, managerial and student class. The theatre of this elite was spoken drama, adapted from the West and representing modernism. It began as an amateur enterprise, idealistically motivated, in the manner of Europe's 'little theatres', and even today audiences are small and economic self-sufficiency elusive. In the 1910s–30s this was primarily a theatre of REALISM, devoted to the gospel of social reform. By the beginning of the Second World War, artists had divided sharply into two opposing groups: those committed to a humanistic, psychological drama of the individual (sometimes identified as 'non-political', 'psychological', or 'art' theatre), and those allied to 'progressive', socialist ideologies, who saw the theatre as a means of struggling to build and maintain a socialist/communist society.

This division continues today, with profound consequences: communist governments (China, North Korea and Vietnam) have often attempted to restrict or completely ban 'bourgeois' theatre as a corrupting and counter-revolutionary phenomenon, while capitalist governments with varying degrees of democracy have frequently censored or banned theatre from the 'revolutionary' left (South Korea, Taiwan, Indonesia, Malaysia, Thailand and Iran). Though modern theatre is generally valued as a part of the modernizing process, its independent-minded creators are often at odds with whatever government is in power, and there is widespread CENSORSHIP of new plays (often alternating with periods of relative artistic freedom). Current modern theatre in Asia and the Pacific region encompasses the older realism, Western classical drama (especially SHAKESPEARE's plays), variations of 'socialist realism', and avant-garde experiments with new forms – often in international and 'intercultural' settings – as well as unique local movements (see e.g. SHINGEKI (Japan); SHINGŬK (Korea); HUAJU (China)).

Religion and theatre Everywhere in Asia and Oceania, the earliest performances seem to have been associated with man's relationship to the gods. The reaffirmation of human bonds with spirits of the land ('dina) underlies many of the popular dances and chants in Polynesia and Micronesia (Oceania), and SHAMANISM was at the base of many theatrical forms of Asia. In the animist systems of belief and practice that typically form the substratum of Asian and Pacific cultures, performance may constitute an honouring of the gods, a request for good health, a successful hunt or a bounteous harvest, or may serve to invite the spirits of the sacred world into the ephemeral world of mankind: e.g. in Sri Lanka, *sanniya yakuma*; Thailand, *nora*; Indonesia, *sanghyang*; Japan, *kagura*; India, *teyyam*, *dandanata*, DASHAVATARA, and many RITUAL forms from Melanesia (Oceania). The belief that the human performer is a vessel for a god's appearance is widespread, and trance possession underlies such ritual performances as *barong* in Indonesia, PRAHLADA NATAKA in India, *duk-duk* in New Britain (Oceania) and *nat pwe* in Burma.

The prevalence of such ritual traditions has encouraged the use of MASKS in Asian theatre – allowing the performer to transcend the limits of everyday identity and represent gods, ancestors, demons, mythological figures and animals, as well as idealized or satirized human types (*nō* of Japan; HAHOE PYŎLSIN-GUT of Korea; *topeng* in Indonesia; KOLAM of Sri Lanka). It has also encouraged an extraordinarily rich heritage of puppetry: MARIONETTE, rod, glove and doll PUPPETS are all used, and forms include *kathputli* in India, *wayang golek* in Java, KKOKTU in Korea, *mua roi nuoc* in Vietnam, and *bunraku* in Japan. There are also dozens of varieties of SHADOW PUPPETS and shadow plays in Asia, from the satirical *karagöz* of Turkey (and Greece and much of North Africa; see KARAGÖZ) to the cardboard *carillo* of the Philippines, including at least seven varieties in China, five in India, the giant puppets of Cambodia *(nang sbek thom)* and Thailand *(nang yai)* and the many variations on Indonesian *wayang kulit* that are spread throughout Southeast Asia. Devoid of mortality, puppets – particularly shadow puppets with their seeming lack of material substance – have proved an ideal medium for representation of gods, heroes from the past, and their demon antagonists. Throughout Asia, such puppet forms have served as a model for (and have been affected by) later developments of human theatre and dance. While many puppet forms appeal to a broad-based audience, nowhere in Asia is this medium relegated to 'children's theatre': some of the most sophisticated dramatic constructions in the world have been created within the context of Asian puppet theatre.

Asia has been the birthplace of Zoroastrianism, Hinduism, Taoism, Judaism, Buddhism, Shintoism, Jainism, Christianity, Islam and Sikhism. Not surprisingly, religion and theatre are intimately intertwined throughout Asia and the Pacific Islands: religious myths, legends and stories, the characters of saints, gods, spirits and demons and underlying religious world-views all provide material for performing traditions that dramatize religious belief and devotion; as community events, temple-based ceremonies also provide occasions for more secular performances. Storytelling traditions – often focused on religious themes and frequently elaborated with music and dance – have proliferated throughout Asia and the Pacific (e.g. *awang* in Malaysia, *pala* and BURRAKATHA in India, *mawlum* in Laos, P'ANSORI in Korea). Buddhist *Jataka* stories – tales about Lord Buddha in a former life – are the source for scores of dramatic narratives in Thailand, Laos, Burma and Cambodia. Krishna and Rama, incarnations of the Brahmanic god Vishnu, are heroes not only in Indian regional theatre forms – KATHAKALI, KRISH-NATTAM, KUCHIPUDI, RAMLILA, RASLILA, ANKIYA NAT, *dhanu*

jatra and so forth – but are prominent in the repertoires of many Southeast Asian genres, such as the many forms of *wayang* in Indonesia and Malaysia and the masked *khon* and *lakon khol* dance-dramas of Thailand and Cambodia. The Confucian ethical code – entailing fidelity to ruler, husband and father – informs Japanese *bunraku*, Chinese *jingxi* and SHINPA of Korea. *Ta'ziyeh* of Iran (see MIDDLE EAST) is based on the martyrdom of the Shi'ite saint, Iman Hussein. Persian and Arabic stories also entered Pakistan, India and Bangladesh with the introduction of Islam: the Arabian hero, Amir Hamza, is featured in *bangsawan* of Malaysia and in *ketoprak* and *wayang golek* in Indonesia (home to more Muslims than any other nation on earth). Muslim and Christian influences contend in *komedya* of the Philippines, and Christian biblical stories, along with later medieval romances, are dramatized in the PASKU of Sri Lanka, Indian CAVITTU NATAKAM, and *sanakulo* of the Philippines.

It should not be imagined that this dramatic material has travelled intact and unaltered from one culture to another, or even from genre to genre within the same culture. Just as Japanese Buddhism is different from Chinese or Tibetan Buddhism (and even more different from Sri Lankan Buddhism), Chinese stories dramatized in Korea and Japan are greatly altered and acquire a local flavour. When Rama appears on Balinese or Javanese puppet screens in Indonesia, he is treated as a Balinese or Javanese king. In Buddhist Burma, Thailand and Cambodia, Rama is portrayed as the Buddha in a former life and Sita may be his sister, not his wife. In Malaysia, Rama eventually converts to Islam. The legend of the one-horned wizard who traps the rain gods and brings drought to the world – a legend also originating in India and brought to Japan by way of China – is dramatized in Japan as *nō kyōgen* and *kabuki*; it has a different tone and a different thematic emphasis in each of its dramatic reincarnations.

The historical intermixture of genres Over time, Asian and Pacific performance techniques, as well as philosophies and narratives, have been carried by performers to neighbouring countries, creating similar theatrical forms. Dancers, actors and musicians have either transported their performance skills to foreign countries or, conversely, learned performance skills while abroad and then brought them home. Thus, a millennium ago (by either or both of these procedures), Indian dance styles became known to performers far beyond that country's boundaries. These fused with local traditions, creating numerous related, yet distinct, dance forms: e.g. Balinese *legong* and Javanese *wayang orang* of Indonesia, *lakon kabach boran* of Cambodia, *lakon fai nai* of Thailand, and *mak yong* of Malaysia. Javanese shadow puppetry (*wayang kulit*) was carried to neighbouring Malaysia, Cambodia and Bali (as, perhaps, shadow players from India had earlier brought forms such as RAVANA CHHAYA to Java). Artists from Korea and Japan learned masked dances at the Chinese court in the early Tang dynasty (618–907), returned home, and adapted what they had learned to their own courts, establishing *kiak* in Korea and *gigaku* and *bugaku* in Japan. During national wars between Vietnam and China (11th–13th centuries) and between Cambodia, Thailand and Burma (15th–18th centuries), entire court troupes were captured as booty, resulting in a significant intermixture of theatre forms and performance techniques among these countries.

Finally, beginning in the 16th century, Western entrepreneurs and colonial administrations brought popular forms of Western music, dance and theatre into India, the Philippines and Japan, and into other countries somewhat later. From these and later European and American contacts stem such urban popular entertainments as *bodabil* (VAUDEVILLE) in the Philippines and the all-female operetta, *takarazuka*, in Japan, as well as the touring professional Parsi theatre troupes of 19th-century India. By the late 19th century, intellectuals and members of an emerging middle class in Calcutta under British rule had formed their own troupes to perform Western modern drama and plays of their own making. In the early decades to the 20th century, students from China and Korea studying in Japan discovered Western MELODRAMA (notably, *UNCLE TOM'S CABIN*) and modern theatre (especially IBSEN) through Japanese productions and translations and brought their new-found enthusiasms home. By the time of the Second World War, a considerable number of Asian playwrights, directors and actors had travelled to Europe and the United States, learning the 'realistic' techniques of Western 'spoken drama'. Modern Western plays were translated into Asian languages, and new plays were written in this style by major authors such as RABINDRANATH TAGORE, Yu Ch'i-jin and TIAN HAN, while English-language companies became strongly established in Singapore and the Philippines, and, to a lesser extent, in Hong Kong, Malaysia, India and Burma – all areas under long-lasting British or American colonization.

Concurrently, traditional Asian artists were performing on tour in the West for the first time. Artists of the European avant-garde were able to see MEI LANFANG perform Beijing opera, *kabuki* actors from Japan, and dance troupes from Cambodia, Bali and the Middle East. BRECHT, ARTAUD and MEYERHOLD were deeply influenced, and so were artists in other fields – including Eisenstein, Rodin, Loie Fuller and Isadora Duncan – responding to the vividly 'exotic other' of the epochal performances in the early decades of the 20th century.

In the nearly 50 years following the end of the Second World War, theatrical interchange between Asia–Oceania and Europe–America has become established as a continuous process of mutual interaction; recent developments in theatre anywhere in the world are quickly known to at least some theatre practitioners in most of the countries of Asia and the Pacific Islands. When political conditions and regional tastes allow it, happenings, absurdism (see THEATRE OF THE ABSURD), deconstructionism and multiculturalism echo in urban theatre practice in Asia and the Pacific, as well as in the West. At the same time, Western actors, dancers, musicians, directors and playwrights – and sometimes scholars – are seriously studying the performance techniques and aesthetic principles of Asia and Oceania, occasionally gaining considerable mastery of Asian forms. In its diversity of forms and practice, and in its imaginative exuberance and physical rigour, traditional Asian theatre has become a stimulus and a model for such contemporary theatre figures in the West as JERZY GROTOWSKI, EUGENIO BARBA, PETER BROOK, ARIANE MNOUCHKINE, David Henry Hwang, ROBERT WILSON, Peter Schumann, PETER SELLARS, Richard Schechner and LEE BREUER (see ASIAN INFLUENCES ON WESTERN THEATRE).

Speech, movement and aesthetic principles It is often said that all traditional Asian performance is dance. This is true in the sense that the actor follows well established and carefully controlled movement codes. Beyond this, there are many forms that incorporate sections of choreographed movement (or dance movement improvised from previously mastered strips of behaviour) in order to introduce characters, enact battle scenes or otherwise engage the audience as the play moves towards its dramatic conclusion. The degree to which dance *per se* predominates varies greatly: to take three forms from India as examples, in Seraikella *chhau*, dance carries the narrative; in *kathakali*, the dancer-actors are supported by singers and elaborate on the sung texts with their movements; in *prahlada nataka*, the dancer-actors also sing and speak the lines from a complex script; yet all three are commonly called 'dance dramas'. In other forms, sung lyrics are the major component of the dramatic structure and the actor is required to develop exceptional vocal skill. For convenience – and lack of a better term – these forms are often called operas in English (Korean *p'ansori*, Chinese KUNQU, Taiwanese *gozai xi*, Balinese *arja* (see INDONESIA), Indian *KHYAL*).

Highly choreographed and stylized movements may alternate with more natural movement patterns *(natya dharmi* and *lokadharmi* in the Indian classical tradition), while song, chant or formal recitation of poetry – sometimes in archaic languages – may alternate with colloquial speech. In many theatres, the bearer of the colloquial, present-day speech and movement is the omnipresent clown: Indonesian *wayang* and *topeng* take this approach, which has precedents in the Sanskrit theatre of India. In Iranian *ta'ziyeh* the martyred heroes sing and the villains orate. The nature and definition of each theatrical form are largely dependent upon the particular balance struck among its many components and constituent parts – which elements and means of performance are emphasized and which are neglected – as well as upon the specific performance codes that are mastered and employed.

These behavioural codes – ways of speaking, ways of moving – are, of course, generated and enacted in relation to larger aesthetic and philosophical systems. There is no single Asian-Oceanic aesthetic of theatre, nor is there an all-embracing structural pattern, but rather numerous divergent, and even opposing, aesthetic principles and structures. Just as there are important differences in social and religious values, there are vastly different approaches to time, space, narrative and audience–actor relationships. For example, ZEAMI of 15th-century Japan and, much earlier, BHARATA MUNI of India both wrote extremely important treatises on theatrical aesthetics that dealt in subtle and sophisticated ways with the impact of performance upon the audience. Bharata Muni's *bhava-rasa* theory stresses congruencies – though not identities – between the emotional states (*bhava*) projected by the actor through the use of an elaborately detailed system of behavioural codes and the audience's aesthetic savouring (*rasa*) of these performed emotions through empathetic response. Zeami, on the other hand, recommended that an *in-yo* (*yin-yang*) principle of contrasting opposites should regulate an actor's relationship to the audience, working against the grain to gain the advantage of surprise, pique the audience's interest and eventually to alter its mood. Bharata Muni's theatre is one of abundance and simultaneity, flooding the senses; Zeami's theatre, while also complex in its semiotic cues, is one of spareness. While the two authors share many aesthetic interests, their approaches here are quite different.

At a more immediate structural level, a day's (or night's) performance in Asia will almost always follow well known structural and temporal principles; but those principles vary greatly. In Indonesia, Javanese (but not Balinese) *wayang kulit*, for example, conforms to a three-part structure in which the musical pitch rises in stages through a nine-hour evening performance and certain kinds of characters confront each other at certain temporal and structural junctures: the plot must be juggled accordingly. Or, to take another well known example, a four-part structure is in effect in Japanese *kabuki* performances: scenes are arranged so that the audience will experience, in sequence over a four- to six-hour performance, strong, slow formality, languid essence, lively casualness, and colourful, rhythmic action. Within a given performance, refined concepts of timing, dynamics and temporal flow regulate the actor and supporting musicians and singers in their interactions. One of the most famous of these is *jo-ha-kyu*, literally, 'opening – breaking apart – speeding up', which is observable in the continual tempo changes that occur in dance, moment by moment, and in song, phrase by phrase, during a *nō* performance.

Training, transmission and performance codes Most Asian traditional theatre is centred on the actor, for the actor is the source and repository of performance information. While in many forms there are strong dramatic texts that have been written by superb writers (including Zeami and CHIKAMATSU MONZAEMON in Japan, and KALIDASA and Tulsidas in India), in others the centrality of the actor extends to script composition, often through improvised dialogue and song. Whether or not improvisation is expected or allowed, however, the first task of the actor-dancer-musician – before grappling with the issues of text – is to become proficient in the received codes of the theatrical form. Thus, the Indian *kathakali* actor spends his childhood forming his body into a pliable instrument for the leaps and whorls of dance, the eye, mouth and cheek movements that are expressive of emotion, and the 600 hand gestures (*hasta* and *mudra*) that he must execute when on stage enacting a role. Zeami, writing in 15th-century Japan, said the actor should spend from the age of seven to 17 mastering the arts of chanting and dance, before focusing on 'role playing'. The student of Chinese *jingxi* must master scores of movement techniques – 'water sleeve' (*shuixiu*) gestures, tumbling, and ACROBATICS in the fighting arts (*wushu*) – and, at least in the past, carried out demanding vocal exercises outdoors at 5 a.m., summer or winter. Only after a firm artistic base has been laid does the actor learn to enact roles in specific plays. Then, he or she acts in reference to generic role types that have been developed by earlier generations of performers.

It would be incorrect to assume that the performance codes mastered by the traditional Asian performer are merely matters of technique. Meaning adheres to them. They are lenses through which human life is refracted into patterns unique to each genre; this is no simple mirroring of nature, but an artistically elaborate and symbolically complex process of reflexion and recreation. The performance codes of Asian theatre traditions suggest a world larger than that of characters in a single play. The codes encompass all of the plays or scenarios for potential plays in the repertoire (or at least of subgroups within the repertoire); and they facilitate the embodiment of a coherent artistic and philosophical vision. In conjunction with more or less fixed character types, the codes allow for an enormous range of transformations across boundaries of age, gender, epistemology and metaphysics. Both MALE and FEMALE IMPERSONATION are common: some forms are enacted only by men, some (though fewer) only by women; old men play young lovers; young men play vamps and crones; young women play god-kings. The embodiment of the codes in performance – when the actor 'becomes' the character – is neither a mechanical act nor a formulaic exercise. Playing in reference to a known type and behaving by means of the received codes allows the actor the paradoxical freedom to be alive, present, focused and communicative: the water coursing through the river banks, the light burning within the lantern's glass. The body is 'dilated', the action 'decided'. His or her negotiation of dramatic action by means of the performance codes at hand becomes an exemplary human action.

A performance constitutes one momentary arrangement of pre-established elements; it is one in a series of performances which are like the changing patterns of the kaleidoscope. The play is *not* the thing: the performance is, and, beyond the performance, the genre, the art form, and a vision of life. An emphasis on training replaces the reliance on rehearsal common in the West. To put on a traditional performance does not usually require the special outside vision of a director. Well trained actors, dancers and musicians are themselves the source of knowledge of how to perform and they are capable of working as a self-directing ensemble, often without benefit of rehearsals at all, and frequently in forms that require intricate coordination as well as substantial improvisation.

In this performer-based theatre, then, proper transmission of performance codes becomes of vital importance. The most common method of training has traditionally been for a pupil to apprentice himself or herself to a master and to learn by assisting, watching and receiving informal instruction over an extended period of time, perhaps a lifetime. The art may be passed down from father to son (the present ICHIKAWA DANJŪRŌ is a 12th-generation *kabuki* actor) or within hereditary castes (as in Indian *bhavai* and *kutiyattam*). In some cases, a master may take a group of students and train them together in a school – in Hawaii called a *halau*, 'temple', indicating the sacred nature of transmission. Today, numerous formal academies also exist to teach young performers of Chinese *jingxi*, Indian classical dance, Indonesian, Thai and Cambodian dance-dramas, Korean *sandae-g'uk*, and many other forms. These have large classes, multiple teachers and formalized curricula over a fixed number of years. Knowing that if one generation of students fails to learn the necessary skills a theatre genre may be irrevocably lost, most governments in Asia now either run or subsidize training academies, sometimes supplemented (as in *kabuki)* by the more traditional master–disciple system. These same academies, paradoxically, are sometimes centres for theatrical experimentation.

The present situation A truly remarkable number of traditional theatre forms, some over 1000 years old, continue being skilfully performed for Asian and Pacific audiences today, while others have recently vanished or are in a serious state of decline. If the historical continuity in the region is impressive, it is also true that change occurs without cease; and the rate of change is also being profoundly quickened by the increasing interrelatedness of nations and peoples and the availability of electronic media.

Two opposing currents swirl and push against each other. While it is unlikely that there will ever be such a thing as a uniform global village, intercultural mixing of theatre traditions is happening at an unprecedented rate today. Asian and Oceanic theatre artists regularly tour abroad and attend international symposia and conferences, absorbing the latest happenings in world theatre. Pacific governments proudly host international and regional theatre festivals. And, everywhere, tourism is expanding exponentially. The walls that only a few decades ago separated culture from culture and genre from genre are falling rapidly, and the impact of international television, via satellite and video cassette, is increasingly apparent and important.

The current opposing this merging of cultures flows from an intense pride in one's self and one's culture, often with a concomitant aversion to the import of foreign culture and arts. Not very long ago, local intellectuals might have accepted Western theatre theories that held that Sanskrit drama was inferior because it did not achieve tragedy, and that *nō* was not even drama because it was not based on dramatic conflict. No longer. Many want to accept Western political and economic systems while simultaneously preserving local cultural values. In modern theatre, this originally meant taking the dramatic structure of realist drama and realistic (i.e. illusionistic) approaches (see REALISM) to acting and staging and filling that structure with the content of Asian and Pacific social and political situations. Now, though still used, that formula is suspect.

The sense of ambivalence felt towards Western models underlies both policies and strategies affecting the traditional theatre and the activities and projects of the avant-garde. Throughout Asia and Oceania, governments and broadly based social and artistic organizations seek to preserve and invigorate traditional, indigenous theatre forms that reflect their cultural legacy. At the same time, avant-garde playwrights and directors have sought since the 1960s and 70s to return to traditional performing roots in their search for new theatre forms that reflect national and cultural identities, rejecting the Western realist theatre imported and imitated over the past century and attempting to tap into the vital theatricality of traditional forms. This approach has its own problems: urban actors

and directors rarely have adequate training in the specific codes of traditional forms, and the performers of those forms are often uninterested in the enterprises of contemporary theatre. Moreover, many of the traditional forms came into being to support religious and social values and hierarchical structures that contemporary artists may well reject. Some directors and authors – SUZUKI TADASHI in Japan, K. N. Pannikar and B. V. KARANTH in India, Putu Wijaya and Rendra in Indonesia – have attempted with considerable success to deconstruct the old codes, abstracting principles and approaches and applying them to new ventures: sometimes productions of Western classics, sometimes projects focusing on regional narratives and events. It is not surprising that Asian theatre today should exhibit the *in yo* of opposites precariously balanced within the whole; the old and the new are inescapable aspects of contemporary Asian-Oceanic circumstances.   JRB JEM

See: G. L. Anderson (ed.), *The Genius of the Oriental Theatre*, New York, 1966, and (ed.), *Masterpieces of the Orient*, New York, 1961; E. Barba and N. Savarese, *A Dictionary of Theatre Anthropology*, tr. R. Fowler, London and New York, 1991; F. Bowers, *Theatre in the East: A Survey of Asian Dance and Drama*, New York, 1956; J. R. Brandon, *Theatre in Southeast Asia*, Cambridge, Mass., 1967, *Brandon's Guide to Theater in Asia*, Honolulu, 1976, and (ed.), *The Performing Arts in Asia*, Paris, 1971, *Traditional Asian Plays*, New York, 1972; E. van Erven, *The Playful Revolution*, New York, 1992; V. R. Irwin (ed.), *Four Classical Asian Plays in Modern Translation*, Harmondsworth, 1972; E. T. Kirby, *Ur-Drama: The Origins of Theatre*, New York, 1975; M. R. Malkin, *Traditional and Folk Puppets of the World*, Cranbury, N. J., 1978; J. O. Miettinen, *Classical Dance and Theatre in South-East Asia*, Singapore, 1992; M. T. Osman (ed.), *Traditional Drama and Music of Southeast Asia*, Kuala Lumpur, 1974; L. C. Pronko, *Theater East and West: Perspectives Toward a Total Theater*, Berkeley, Calif., 1974 (1967); A. C. Scott, *The Theatre in Asia*, New York, 1972; J. Tilakasiri, *The Puppet Theatre of Asia*, Colombo, 1968; Tokyo National Research Institute of Cultural Properties (ed.), *Masked Performances in Asia*, Tokyo, 1987; H. W. Wells, *The Classical Drama of the Orient*, New York, 1965.

Asian influences on Western theatre Since antiquity, performance traditions from Asia and North Africa have influenced theatre created in civilizations to the West. Though the extent of influence is debated, the culture of ancient Greece was clearly indebted to Egyptian, Canaanite and Phoenician precedents (see MIDDLE EAST). The Furies-turned-Eumenides of Aeschylus' *Oresteia* are variants of an apotropaic tradition long shared between Greece and INDIA (connected by Phoenician trade routes). Dionysus – the god honoured by the Athenian tragic festival – had himself arrived from the East (most likely from Phrygia, via Thrace); the ecstatic dancing of the new 'Asian' religion depicted in Euripides' *The Bacchae* gives evidence that, from ancient times, performative traditions, along with gods and goods, have moved between Asia and Europe.

These early encounters – like many of those that followed – were framed by war as well as by trade. The first extant play of classical Greek tragedy, AESCHYLUS' *The Persians* (472 BC), has arch-enemy Xerxes as its protagonist, while the centrality of the Trojan War in the Greek sense of history made Asia Minor a pivotal locus in EURIPIDES' anti-war plays of the late 5th century BC. The Asian peoples of Persia and Phrygia were thus depicted both as exotically 'other' – irrational, autocratic, opulent, excessive, and somehow more 'feminine' – even as they were embraced as sharing a common humanity through their capacity to suffer. This conception of Asia as both familiar and irreducibly strange – at once threatening and alluring – was enhanced by the conquest and occupation of lands in Southwest Asia and North Africa by Alexander the Great and the legions of Rome; and was hardened in the long struggle between Islam and Christianity that began soon after the fall of the Roman Empire and persisted throughout the Middle Ages and Renaissance.

The characterizations of MARLOWE's Tamburlaine and SHAKESPEARE's Othello exemplify the West's fascination with and distrust of the exotic East. So do the eccentric, black-faced moriscoes (morris dances) which swept through Europe as a popular fad in the 15th century, and the exotic Asian locales and costumes used in the court MASQUES of the 16th and early 17th centuries. Even when most aggressively opposed as opposites, however, the cultures of East and West were intricately intertwined. Arabic and Sephardic Jewish influences came into Europe through Moorish control of southern SPAIN from 711 to 1492, bringing the lute to Europe, as well as traditions of epic and lyric poetry and recitation. In the 11th century, Moorish *joglars* and troubadors and Jewish translators and scholars were prominent in the Christian courts of Northern Spain and Provence.

Influences from the Islamic world also came more directly from the Middle East, through trade and successive Crusades. Until its collapse in 1453, Byzantium's capital, Constantinople, on the Bosporus straits dividing Europe and Asia, provided grounds for a fertile exchange of popular theatrical traditions as Christian troubadors there interacted with Islamic counterparts. Egypt and Persia had been among the first medieval centres with court fools, and a lively tradition of popular satiric farce is evidenced by the 13th-century SHADOW PUPPET plays of Ibn Daniyal from present-day Iraq. Traditions brought from Central Asia by the Mongols in the 12th and 13th centuries may well have also influenced early Christian theatre; the chthonic image of hellmouth, for example, is thought to be derived from Central Asian models.

With the revitalization of sea trade in the late Middle Ages and early Renaissance, Venice emerged as the principal European port of contact with the expanding Ottoman Empire, and skilled masked players and street performers from Western Asia were most likely an important source of inspiration for the COMMEDIA DELL'ARTE (*maschera*, mask, is believed to derive from an Arabic word, *mascara*, comic actor). Improvised farcical forms strikingly similar to the *commedia* are still extant in Turkey, Iran and Kashmir (which may themselves have been influenced by remnants of the Greek and Roman MIME traditions). Popular European PUPPET traditions, such as the PUNCH and Judy theatre of England, are similarly linked to forms of shadow and glove puppetry developed in Egypt and Turkey and transported to Europe through Venice and Naples. Despite such an intricate interweaving of popular traditions, however, the Islamic East remained conceptualized as the exotic other. The West's continuing fascination with (and ambiguous feelings about) its neighbours to the south and east are evident, for example, in the contrast between Mozart's first opera, *The Abduction from the Seraglio* (1782), and VOLTAIRE's more jaundiced view of Islam in *Zaire* (1732) and *Mahomet, ou le Fanatisme* (1741). The sensuous and exotic Islamic Orient could be idealized or demonized; it was near enough to provide a sense of danger and far enough to ensure mystery and allow free scope to the imagination; it provided an ideal setting for MELODRAMA.

In the 14th century, travels of Marco Polo along the silk routes of Central Asia had rekindled interest in lands further East – an interest that eventually spawned numerous tragedies pitting love against honour in exotic locales (e.g. DRYDEN's *Indian Queen* (1664) and *Aureng-Zebe* (1675)) along with maritime trade, exploration and European colonialism. Still, direct influences from South and East Asian drama on European theatre are not evident until the middle of the 18th century. A French translation of a 14th-century drama from CHINA, *The Orphan of the House of Tschao*, was published in 1736 (without music or lyrics and adapted to neoclassic conventions), and in 1755 Voltaire further adapted this drama for performance by the COMÉDIE-FRANÇAISE. The 5th-century Sanskrit drama, *Shakuntala*, translated into German from William Jones's English translation of 1789, so impressed GOETHE that he not only extolled its virtues as a dramatic masterpiece but borrowed some of its conventions for *Faust* (1808, 1832).

Since then, KALIDASA's play has been adapted and produced by a number of Western directors, including THÉOPHILE GAUTIER (1858), LUGNÉ-POE (1895), TAIROV (1914), GROTOWSKI (1960) and BARBA (1993). Stanislas Julian's 1832 translation of the Chinese *Tale of the Chalk Circle* has had a similarly long-lasting impact on German theatre, through the adaptations of Klaubund (1925) and BRECHT (1945). CARLO GOZZI's *Turandot* (1762), a transposition of a tale from Persian history via the *Arabian Nights* into a China of his own invention, has been restaged by VAKHTANGOV (1922), set to music by PUCCINI (1926), and adapted by Brecht (1954). The variety of approaches represented by these productions – ranging from exotic fantasy creations of the Orient, to respectful evocations of Asian traditions, to a free adaptation of Asian techniques and principles, to jarring examinations of the contradictions and paradoxes of the role of the Orient in the Western imagination – give one indication of the complexity of the East's legacy to the Western stage.

By the end of the 19th century perhaps a dozen Chinese operas, classical Indian dramas and JAPANESE NŌ plays had been published in English, French and German translation, and accounts from travellers and missionaries (none of them theatre practitioners) had called attention to the riches of East Asian theatre. These translations and travelogues were aspects of the chinoiserie and japonaiserie that suffused European popular art after the Paris Exposition of 1867, and which became a significant source of inspiration for such major painters as Manet and

Monet, Van Gogh and Gaugin, and Degas and Whistler, as well as composers such as Saint-Saëns and Debussy. The initial impact on theatre was considerably less impressive. Following the general rage for things oriental, plays and musicals set in the exotic East became extremely popular on European stages in the late 19th century – e.g. GILBERT and Sullivan's *Mikado* (1885) and the ubiquitous *The Indian Widow* (performed in half a dozen languages). These dramas were not inspired by theatre forms of Asia: the authors and directors had no personal knowledge of Asian performance, and – like the moriscoes and masques that preceded them – the plays often presented gross parodies of Asian cultures. Similar exotic tales of the Orient were popular in the nascent American MUSICAL THEATRE: e.g. *The Pearl of Pekin* (1888), *Wizard of the Nile* (1895) and *Shogun* (1904). By century's end, however, a more sympathetic (though not necessarily better informed) use of Asian materials was deployed by the artists involved in the French symbolist movement (see SYMBOLISM): Lugné-Poe's commercially successful productions of *Shakuntala* in 1895 and the Chinese *La Fleur Palan Enlevée* in 1896 looked to Asia for a lyrical suggestiveness and a way to harness the emotive force of silence.

These same qualities appealed to the artists who were to create the modern dance movement of the early 20th century. While Isadora Duncan was more directly inspired by impressions of classical Greece, Émile Jaques-Dalcroze, who was developing eurythmics in Switzerland, combined this predilection with an interest in Indian philosophy and aesthetics obtained through his association with the philosopher and educator Rudolph Steiner. Loie Fuller, Ruth St Denis, Ted Shawn and Martha Graham created the vocabulary and direction of modern dance in large part from their impressions of the gestural forms and spiritual underpinnings of Indian and Japanese theatre and dance. Their interest in the work of Jaques-Dalcroze and Françoise Delsarte (whose codification of emotions through gesture mirrored classical Indian aesthetics) helped provide pathways linking Indian traditions with their modernist agendas.

Fuller was also directly involved in the first modern Western tours of performers from East Asia. Sada Yakko, a Japanese geisha trained in *nihon buyo* dance, and her husband, Kawakami Otojiro, had embarked on a study tour of Western theatre intent on founding a modern theatre in Japan. With Fuller's help, they organized a troupe of 30 and brought the first 'complete' Asian theatre performances to audiences in America and Europe. Touring America and then Europe from 1898 to 1902 and, again, in 1908, they performed adaptations from the KABUKI repertoire, as well as scenes from Shakespeare and *La Dame aux camélias*. Their performances at the Paris Exposition of 1900 were greatly praised – especially for the 'supernatural realism' of Sada Yakko's death scenes; ELLEN TERRY and HENRY IRVING counted themselves among her admirers. Though women were not allowed on the public stage in Japan, the geisha Hanako also performed 'kabuki' in major theatres of Europe and America for 20 years (1901–22), and her emotional, 'realistic' dying scenes were similarly praised by DUSE and BERNHARDT, and were sculpted by Rodin. In these and other early tours, Asian performers drastically tailored their performances to suit Western tastes, creating ersatz pieces such as Hanako's *The Samurai and the Geisha* (conceived and written by Fuller). Still, the taste for 'oriental' performances was established, and in 1906 the dancers of the Cambodian royal court were the sensation of the Colonial Exposition in Marseille (see CAMBODIA). By then, a more profound impact of Asian theatre practice on acting and scenography was emerging.

While the original enthusiasm for oriental theatre had been based on its 'realistic' depiction of extreme emotions and violent death (rendered intriguingly exotic by lavish COSTUMES), the next wave of theatre artists influenced by Eastern theatre forms were attracted by the frank use of artifice, incorporation of music and dance, alternations of narrative and dramatic modes, and unembarrassed access to supernatural and spiritual domains common to many Asian traditions – all qualities that contrasted sharply with the newly dominant naturalistic conventions of the Western stage. Though many of the Asian theatre forms that would become influential in the West had been stimulated by the same growth of urban culture and rise of a mercantile class in the late 16th and early 17th centuries that encouraged the burgeoning of Elizabethan, Spanish and French baroque and neoclassical forms – and though numerous parallels can be found in shifting patterns of patronage, in the growth of vernacular, actor-based theatres, and in struggles over the representation of gender and the regulation of pleasure – the theatrical forms developed in Asia had never taken the extreme turn towards a 'realistic' mode of representation presaged by Renaissance painting and reaching its apogee in Europe and America under the influence of positivism in the late 19th century. Their exuberant and acknowledged theatricality made them a useful counterweight in the avant-garde's struggles against the limitations of NATURALISM.

Thus, in 1905, GEORG FUCHS recommended *kabuki* as offering an exemplary stylization of movement; and MEYERHOLD, following this lead, was inspired by the theatrical, arrested poses of this Japanese tradition in his staging of *Hedda Gabler* a year later. In 1913 Meyerhold took on his own studio, in which he combined his enthusiasm for Indian, Chinese and Japanese theatre (known to him mainly through illustrations), a taste for the 'fairground' arts of the circus and *commedia*, a love of the grotesque and a fascination with the 'science' of the body, in order to evolve a new psycho-physical approach to training actors, as well as to production. Also in 1913, JACQUES COPEAU founded the VIEUX COLOMBIER in France – an experimental theatre cum studio that similarly took inspiration from Asian theatre forms, as well as from such diverse Western sources as the Italian *commedia*, Greek tragedy, Jaques-Dalcroze's eurythmics, and Diaghilev's Ballets Russes (which had toured Paris in 1909). Beginning in 1908, GORDON CRAIG devoted several issues of the journal *Mask* to Asian theatre, providing inspiration for such ventures. His own scene designs were influenced by Chinese landscape painting – abandoning environmental verisimilitude for a suggestive spareness; and the flat planes of colour and expressive shapes of Asian art came into European theatre through the scene designs of such painters as Vuillard and Toulouse-Lautrec. In 1918, however, as these experimental companies were re-establishing themselves after a hiatus caused by the First World War, Craig inveighed against learning directly from Asian forms, predicting that the resultant hybrids would be artificial and essentially lifeless.

Craig may have been reacting to such ludicrous orientalist enterprises as Paul Anthelme's *Japanese Honour* (1912), directed by – of all people – ANDRÉ ANTOINE. Then again, he may have been dubious about the attempts of W. B. YEATS to write plays inspired directly by Japanese *nō*. First interested in Sanskrit drama through his friendship with RABINDRANATH TAGORE, Yeats encountered *nō* plays in the then unpublished translations of Ernest Fenollosa and Ezra Pound in 1913–14 (published in 1916). Collaborating with Ito Michio (a Japanese dancer in London who had trained with Dalcroze), he created his *Plays for Dancers* using *nō* as the model for a theatre of poetry, myth and symbol. Yeats's *At the Hawk's Well*, first staged in 1917 and then restaged in 1918 with music by Kosaku Yamada, featured Ito in the leading role. Ito went on to introduce minimalist decor and choreography to BROADWAY musicals in the 1920s and 30s, while *At the Hawk's Well* – despite all the idiosyncrasies that distance it from its Japanese prototypes – was rewritten and performed as a *nō* play by the Kita school in Tokyo in 1949 and as a fusion piece in Kyoto under American Jonah Salz's direction in 1981.

Craig's warnings notwithstanding, during 1923–4 the company of the Vieux Colombier worked on an adaptation of Zeami's *nō* drama, *Kantan*, under Suzanne Bing's direction, seeking inspiration from Japanese aesthetic principles to achieve a compelling acting style marked by discipline, rigour and constraint. Though never presented to a public audience, the work was seen and applauded by STANISLAVSKY, GRANVILLE BARKER and APPIA during a dress rehearsal. While Yeats's experiments remained *sui generis,* the attempts at the Vieux Colombier to combine principles gleaned from Asian theatre practice with the techniques of *commedia* and other Western forms were continued by Copeau's students and colleagues: in addition to Bing, these included LOUIS JOUVET, JEAN DASTÉ, CHARLES DULLIN and MICHEL SAINT-DENIS. Dullin, who retained a particular interest in Japanese theatre, numbered among his students JEAN VILAR, ANTONIN ARTAUD, JEAN-LOUIS BARRAULT, ROGER BLIN and ÉTIENNE DECROUX; Dasté, Copeau's son-in-law, taught JACQUES LECOQ. Michel Saint-Denis, Copeau's nephew, became one of the most influential theatre educators of the 20th century. It would be difficult to over-emphasize the effect of Copeau's legacy on the French stage, or the importance of Asian theatre as an exemplary model within that legacy. Also influenced by Copeau's work were Russian émigrés GEORGES PITOËFF and MICHAEL CHEKHOV. Chekhov, already drawn to Asian forms by his associations with Meyerhold and Vakhtangov, as well as through his interest in Rudolph Steiner's anthroposophical writings, used yogic principles in devising a psycho-physical approach to character that has posed a significant alternative to the American Method.

PAUL CLAUDEL, who lived in China and Japan for nearly two decades, composed his late poetic dramas of the 1920s and 30s with an extensive knowledge of *nō, kabuki* and the Chinese theatre. The lessons of Asian theatre are particu-larly evident in *The Satin Slipper* (1923), with its extensive use of narration, song, dance and MIME. In 1927, FIRMIN GÉMIER produced *The Maskmaker,* a modern Japanese play by Okamato Kido, with direct guidance of visiting artists from Japan. These productions, based on extended cultural contact with Asian cultures and performers, were exceptions, however: for the most part, the next wave of influences from Asia came from the inspiration provided by brief visits of touring Asian performers.

At the frequent Colonial and World Expositions of Europe and North America, traditional Asian theatre forms were featured as exotic fruits of colonial enterprise – equivalent to the captives and goods paraded before the hometown populace by the Caesars of Rome and the oligarchies of Athens in order to demonstrate the power of the realm. None the less, in the 1920s and 1930s several outstanding classical dance and theatre troupes performed in the West and, for the first time, Western audiences and theatre artists could directly experience the artistry of some of the most accomplished performers of Asia. Though these performances were still shaped to Western tastes, the impact on the European avant-garde was overwhelming. Meyerhold and Eisenstein greeted the 1928 visit of Ichikawa Sadanji II's Grand Kabuki Troupe to Russia with rhapsodic responses. In 1930, the pre-eminent Beijing opera performer, MEI LANFANG, toured the United States, where he was befriended by an admiring Charlie Chaplin; in 1935, he made a triumphal appearance in Moscow at the head of his New Theatre of Ancient Forms. Stanislavsky and Meyerhold, Brecht and PISCATOR, Tairov and TRETYAKOV, and Craig and Eisenstein all attended. In the wake of Mei's performances, Beijing opera (*JINGXI*) became a pervasive theatrical model. Jean-Louis Barrault used its techniques in staging Shakespearian fight scenes in Paris. THORNTON WILDER and EUGENE O'NEILL were inspired to write plays for a bare stage in New York. Shioh I. Hsiung's translation of *Lady Precious Stream* (1934) enjoyed a great success in London. In Moscow, while Tretyakov – who had lived in Beijing and written *Roar China!* (1930) as a 'factographic' exposé of colonialism – denounced Mei's performance as decadent and dangerous, for the other Russians present the Chinese performer's ability to hold the audience's rapt attention without any of the trappings of naturalism was an argument against the aesthetic of Soviet socialist realism being murderously imposed by Stalin and his regime; even Stanislavsky defended Mei's 'truthfulness within the constraints of his art'.

While the Russian 'formalists' would fail in their last-ditch effort to stave off a repressive aesthetic, for Brecht the encounter with Mei – in conjunction with his concurrent discovery of Viktor Shklovsky's theory of estrangement – consolidated an aesthetic that was to guide him and others for decades to come. The combination of joyful athleticism with moral teaching, the prominence of music and mime, the use of 'pre-acting' to frame narrative sections of a play, the deployment of sudden freezes to arrest the action and focus attention, the refusal to blacken the auditorium, the maintenance of a 'minimum of illusion', the use of a turntable to indicate travel and fluidly change scenes *a vista* (a device first adapted by Piscator) and, perhaps most importantly, the privileging of the presence of actor over character – all fitted Brecht's needs as he sought to define an EPIC THEATRE that could resist Fascism. Chinese stories and theatrical principles remained important to Brecht, and he later also deployed narrative techniques drawn from *BUNRAKU* and sceno-graphic ideas taken from *nō* and *kabuki*. So pervasive was his indebtedness to Asian theatrical traditions that his plays and theoretical writings have, ironically, been used as levers to reclaim access to traditional modes of story-telling and theatrical presentation in the urban centres of India and other Asian sites once dominated by European colonial models.

Antonin Artaud's encounter with Balinese dance-drama (see INDONESIA) at the Paris Colonial Exposition of 1931 was similarly serendipitous. Artaud had already been impressed by Cambodian dance-drama viewed at Marseille in 1922, and he had been deeply involved in the surrealist movement (see SURREALISM) in Paris and with the Japanese-inspired experiments of Copeau and Dullin. Viewing a pot-pourri of Balinese dance and dance-drama forms stripped of their verbal play and narrative signifi-cance, Artaud consolidated his vision of a rigorous, 'cruel', essentially non-verbal theatre, capable of giving form to metaphysical forces through 'animated hieroglyphs'. Though skewed by the limitations of the Parisian exhibit and by his own romanticism, his vision of Balinese dance-drama as an exemplary, brave and bracing art led to the formulation of a Theatre of Cruelty that, in its inverse Platonism, strove to be in all ways antithetical to the 'the-atre of idiots, madmen, inverts, grammarians, grocers, anti-poets, and positivists, i.e. Occidentals'. His theories were to be enormously influential, both through the work of his colleagues and protégés Roger Blin and Jean-Louis Barrault, and through the later impact of his writings from 1931 to 37, collected as *The Theatre and Its Double* and translated into English in 1957. These writings were to have a profound effect on JEAN GENET, Julian Beck and Judith Malina (see LIVING THEATRE), JOSEPH CHAIKIN, PETER WEISS, PETER BROOK, CHARLES MAROWITZ, Jerzy Grotowski and Richard Schechner (see PERFORMANCE GROUP), among many others (and, indirectly, may have in turn influenced Japanese *BUTŌ* and Balinese dance-drama itself).

Meyerhold, Copeau, Yeats, Brecht, Artaud and Michael Chekhov were not part of any 'Asian theatre movement'. None of them ever travelled to Asia and none envisioned the staging of Asian drama by Westerners as a desirable end in itself. Their political utopias differed, and so did their visions of theatre; but they all found in the bits and shards of Asian theatre available to them – viewed through the multiple prisms and isms of the avant-garde of the early 20th century – an antidote to what they all regarded as a stultifying lack of imagination on and off the stage. Asian techniques and principles were freely inter-preted (and misinterpreted), combined with elements of Greek theatre, the *commedia dell'arte* and modern dance, and pressed into service as exemplary alternatives to the hegemony of REALISM: they were tools to restore theatri-cality to the theatre.

Contact between performers and traditions of Eastern and Western theatrical forms has become commonplace in the late 20th century. Wars and their aftermath took many Americans to the South Pacific, Korea, Japan and Southeast Asia, and the mixed legacy of these encounters has included an increased interest in Asian cultures. Conferences, festivals, research fellowships and joint ven-tures have frequently brought Asian and Western theatre workers together. Still, the orientalist impulse continues well into the post-colonial era. The construction of Asia as a set of exotic locales and of Asians as exotic peoples has continued in the commercial musical theatre pieces that reach New York, London and Paris: e.g. *Lute Song* (1946), *South Pacific* (1949), *The King and I* (1951), *Kismet* (1953), *Flower Drum Song* (1958), *Pacific Overtures* (1976) and *Miss Saigon* (1992).

Ironically, while these shows often reflect and project Asian stereotypes, the Western musical form itself has been deeply affected by Asian practices in ways that go far beyond surface exoticism. This has occurred through the influence of Indian, Chinese and Japanese (together with Latino and African) dance traditions on the work of influ-ential choreographers such as JACK COLE and JEROME ROBBINS, and through Chinese and Japanese influences evident in the set designs of JO MIELZINER, BORIS ARONSON and their student, the Chinese-born MING CHO LEE. HAROLD PRINCE has acknowledged that, since his work on *Pacific Overtures* (1976), shows such as *Evita* (1976), *Sweeney Todd* (1979) and *The Phantom of the Opera* (1992) have all been influenced by a sense of ceremony derived from his observations of *nō* and *kabuki*. In OPERA – ever a magnet for Asian influences – Benjamin Britten's *Curlew River* (1964) constitutes a rethinking of the *nō* play *Sumidagawa*, while, less obviously, ROBERT WILSON and Philip Glass's collaborations, *Einstein on the Beach* (1976) and *Satyagraha* (1981), are deeply indebted to Balinese and Javanese principles in their music and to Japanese and Sufi traditions in their use of space, time and movement.

One major change since the end of the Second World War has been the increased study of Asian theatre practice by Western theatre artists. While none of the early research on Asian theatre was conducted by theatre prac-titioners, a great deal of the scholarly work published since 1960 has been written by people who are themselves working directors, choreographers and designers, who have studied practical aspects of performance in the field, and who have combined the traditional concerns of the historian, anthropologist and performing artist in their research, scholarship and related production work. Today, scores of young actors, dancers, musicians and perfor-mance scholars are living in Asia, often for extended peri-ods, and studying under master performer-teachers.

Prominent performing troupes and individual artists from Asia have also visited Europe and America with increased frequency since the last war. Outstanding Beijing opera, *nō*, *kabuki*, *bunraku* and Balinese dance troupes have visited European and American theatres since the mid-1950s, influencing many Western theatre artists in the process. Jean Genet, for example, noted the effects of the Beijing Opera's visit to Paris in 1955 on his subsequent work.

In the 1960s IASTA (the International Association for the Study of Theatre Arts), under John D. Mitchell's direc-tion, brought in leading exponents of Asian theatrical forms, such as *kabuki* actor Onoe Baiko, Indian choreographer Mrnalini Sarabhai, *nō* performer Sadayo Kita and British scholar of Chinese theatre A.C. Scott, to direct American professional actors in classical Asian works. During the early 1970s, the summer institutes of the American Society for Eastern Arts under Robert Brown's direction brought outstanding dancers, musicians and puppeteers from Java, Bali, Japan and India to programmes that have had a long-lasting effect on participants who have gone on to adapt Asian techniques and principles in their own work; these include Julie Taymor (mask-maker, puppeteer, choreographer and director), Larry C. Reed (shadow master and director) and Judy Mitomo (choreographer and co-producer with PETER SELLARS of the Los Angeles International Arts Festival of 1990). Fred Curchak is another performer who has studied with Asian masters of numerous Asian forms in America and has creatively used their techniques and principles in staging his one-man confrontations with Shakespeare's texts.

Several American universities now provide an institutional basis for the serious study of Asian traditional performances. This trend started in 1954, with Earle Ernst's seminar in oriental theatre at the University of Hawaii, where the first comprehensive graduate programme in Asian theatre studies was established in the 1960s. Productions of traditional and modern Asian plays have become a regular part of the educational theatre programmes at Hawaii, Wisconsin, Pomona, Michigan State, Kansas, UCLA and SUNY Stony Brook, often with the participation of master actor-teachers from Asia. A.C. Scott's programme in Asian theatre at the University of Wisconsin took an early lead within American universities in encouraging the application of principles gleaned from careful study of Asian theatre to the production of plays such as SAMUEL BECKETT's *Mimes for One and Two Actors* and *Waiting for Godot*. More recently, contemporary Asian directors have begun to exert a strong influence through their practical training of Western actors in institutional settings. SUZUKI TADASHI has been teaching American and European actors his systematic disciplines of body and voice at Toga Village and the Mito Art Centre in Japan; his system of movement training is now taught in conservatory programmes in New York, Milwaukee, San Diego, Berkeley and Seattle. He has directed Western actors and bilingual casts in recent productions of *Lear, Hamlet* and *The Bacchae* and has teamed with director Anne Bogart to form a summer institute for theatre research and training in Saratoga Springs, NY. Suzuki is not alone among contemporary Asian directors who work in non-traditional ways with traditional Asian elements, and American universities have also provided homes for such contemporary directors as Indonesia's Putu Wijaya and India's N.K. Raina and K.N. Panikkar. Professional theatres, too, have hired Asian professionals. Shozo Sato has staged a number of *kabuki*-inspired productions in Chicago; ŌTA SHŌGO trained a joint German-Japanese cast in Berlin in 1992 for a revival of his silent play, *The Water Station*; and India's Girish Karnad has been commissioned to write a new work for the GUTHRIE THEATRE in Minneapolis following the success there of *Nagamandala* (1992).

While the benefits of learning a performance culture through study with master teachers and the application of the skills learned to texts in translation include an 'in-body' appreciation of an Asian theatrical form and the experience of focusing the actor's energy within a rigorous system of movement, other directors and performers have followed Craig's caution (echoed by LeCoq and Michel Saint-Denis in the 1940s and 50s) to look to the spirit of Asian theatre rather than imitate its forms. Jerzy Grotowski was inspired by *KATHAKALI* and *JINGXI* training methods in his influential Polish Laboratory Theatre productions of the late 1960s. Principles drawn from Japanese traditional theatre have been openly used by Carol Sorgenfrei in *Medea: A Nō Cycle* (1975) and *Cordelia Victorious* (1982), while ROMULUS LINNEY has subtly used the influence of *nō* drama in the construction of his play, *Childe Byron* (1978) and, more obviously, of *bunraku* in *The Love Suicide at Schofield Barracks* (1972). Meyerhold and Copeau's attempts to draw freely on Asian principles in creating an arresting, athletic and flexible style of performance has been continued by several groups, sometimes with the inclusion of Asian performers. ARIANE MNOUCHKINE's THÉÂTRE DU SOLEIL has drawn on *kabuki* for the fight scenes of *Henry IV Part I* (1984), on Javanese dance for the court etiquette of *Richard II* (1981), on Balinese *topeng* (see INDONESIA) for *The Terrible and Tragic History of Norodom Sihanouk, King of Cambodia* (1985), and on *kathakali* and *KUTIYATTAM* in her production of the *Oresteia, L'Indiade* (1992), freely mixing impulses and stylistic elements from these traditions with aspects of European folk arts and popular culture and African dance. The result is often an eclectic, original style of great energy and verve.

Peter Brook, whose connections with Asian philosophical and religious traditions date back several decades through his interest in Gurdjieff's teachings, has used lessons from Persian *ta'ziyeh* and *ru-howzi* (see MIDDLE EAST) as well as from Japanese and Chinese theatre in staging such productions as *The Tragedy of Carmen* (1983) and *A Midsummer Night's Dream* (1970). At the International Centre for Theatre Research in Paris, he has been working with a company including performers from Japan, India and Bali, most notably and controversially staging Carriere's adaptation of *The Mahabharata* in Paris and New York (1984–6). Along with Robert Wilson, LEE BREUER has been deeply influenced by Japanese theatre: the use of space, of narration, of chorus and of decor in his *Gospel at Colonus* (1983) – a project that more obviously brings together a Greek classic text with the African-American Gospel tradition – was suggested by the *nō* conventions, and he has used *bunraku* puppeteers (as well as Balinese and Caribbean performers) in his ongoing stagings of *The Warrior Ant*. Richard Schechner has used techniques from a wide variety of Asian and Pacific locales in his productions, most notably the dynamic interactions of audience and performers in the fluid space of popular Indian devotional forms such as *RAMLILA* in his 'environmental theatre' productions of the late 1960s and 70s with the Performance Group. Peter Schumann has interwoven Asian techniques and principles with Western medieval tropes and contemporary political concerns in the BREAD AND PUPPET THEATRE's many plays, pageants and 'domestic resurrection' circuses.

The most common criticism of intercultural productions – from those of Klabund and Yeats through to those of Brook, Breuer and Mnouchkine – is that the cultural 'property' of others is being appropriated without genuine understanding, creating performances that are mere pastiches of ill-fitting techniques and styles, through which the notion of the exotic Asian other is only reinforced. While intercultural endeavours have sometimes produced theatre that seems created in the mode of interior decoration, vital theatrical experiences have also been forged in which the whole has transcended the various parts (through synthesis or resonant juxtapositions), exciting audience–actor relationships have been established and rigorous physical forms for thoughts and feelings have been found – imbued with intense psychological energy and unbounded by the conventions of realism.

Of particular note in contemporary American theatre is the work of ASIAN-AMERICAN playwrights and directors such as David Henry Hwang and PHILIP KAN GOTANDA that employs elements of traditional Asian theatre. Ethnic Chinese theatres have existed in the United States since 1852 (in San Francisco) and Japanese theatres since the 1870s, only a decade after the forced opening of Japan's markets. In the 1960s and 70s, theatres dedicated to plays in English by Asian-American playwrights came into existence: first the East-West Players in Los Angeles, then the Asian American Theatre Workshop and Yuriko Doi's Theatre of Yugen in San Francisco, Tisa Chang's Pan Asian Repertory in New York, and other theatres from Seattle to Toronto. Some of the plays produced by these theatres and in independent productions have deployed techniques of Asian performing traditions. In a cruel irony of cultural history these usages of Asian techniques have been especially controversial. For example, Hwang's *M. Butterfly* (1988), in which Beijing opera collides with PUCCINI, and *The Dance and the Railroad* (1981), which uses Beijing opera as a means of communication as well as an emblem of identity, have been criticized by some within the Asian-American community as reinforcing exotic stereotypes.

Also of note are productions in North America drawing from NATIVE AMERICAN performing traditions. These first Asian-Americans – who arrived in waves out of Siberia starting over 30,000 years ago and, archaeological evidence suggests, have also had intermittent cultural influences from Asia by way of the Pacific – share certain iconography, myths and SHAMANIC practices with Asian cultures, past and present. *Yupik Antigone* at the Perseverance Theater in Alaska drew upon one of the many complex cultures that evolved, as well as on Sophocles' drama. One effect of such intercultural productions may be to reveal the complex, multi-layered construction of current cultural identities. In London, Jatinder Verma (who grew up in an Indian family in Kenya) has made imaginative use of Indian theatrical traditions to underline the complex and changing ethnic and cultural nature of contemporary England. His production of *Tartuffe* (1990) with his multiracial TARA ARTS Company set the performance of that play in the court of Aurangzeb, exposing and playing with cultural parallels and contrasts between Aurangzeb's court and those at Versailles; his production of the Sanskrit classic, *The Clay Cart* (1992), deployed a company of Indo-English and Irish actors to give the play a new resonance.

Amidst all of the current transcultural and intercultural projects, the question emerges as to what various performance cultures – of both East and West – may share in regard to their understanding of the theatrical. At Eugenio Barba's International School of Theatre Anthropology in Denmark (ISTA), visiting Asian artists Sanjukta Panigrahi (Odissi dance), Kanho Azuma *(kabuki)* and I Made Bandem (Balinese dance), among others, have collaborated to 'barter' theatrical expertise with Barba's Western acting company in over a decade of meetings in search of such common principles underlying different traditions. Grotowski has similarly been interested in exploring a Theatre of Sources with international artists, and Brook has sought to find a style of performance that 'transcends' culture through work with his International Centre in Paris. Such projects – though beset with traps of their own – have further de-stabilized the separation between 'East' and 'West'. The separations, fusions, secret marriages and unstable alliances that have marked the East-West theatrical interactions in Eurasia and beyond since the earliest recorded times continues, in both familiar and unforeseen ways. JEM JRB

See: M.M. Badawi, 'Medieval Arabic Drama: Ibn Daniyal', *Journal of Arabic Literature*, 13, 1982; G. Banu, 'Mei Lanfang, a Case against and a Model for the Occidental Stage', *Asian Theatre Journal*, 3, 2, 1986; E. Barba and N. Savarese (eds), *A Dictionary of Theatre Anthropology: The Secret Art of the Performer*, London and New York, 1991; M. Bernal, *Black Athena: The Afroasiatic Roots of Classical Civilization*, vol. 1, New Brunswick, NJ, 1987; R. Bethune, 'Describing Performance in the Theatre: Kabuki Training and the Western Acting Student', *TDR*, 33, 4, 1989; R. Bharucha, *Theatre and the World: Essays on Performance and Politics of Culture*, Columbia, Mo., 1990; E. Blumenthal, 'West Meets East Meets West', *American Theatre*, Jan. 1987, and 'The Unfinished Histories of Ariane Mnouchkine', *American Theatre*, April 1986; J.R. Brandon, 'A New World: Asian Theatre in the West Today', *TDR*, 3, 1, 1989, and 'On Little Hanako', *ATJ*, 5, 1, 1988; R. Briffault, *The Troubadors*, Bloomington, Ind., 1965; E. Ernst, 'The Influence of Japanese Theatrical Style on Western Theatre', *ETJ*, 21, 1969; J. Feral (ed.), 'Orient– Occident', in *Cahiers de théâtre jeu*, 49, 1988; K. Foley, 'Hanako and the European Imagination,' *ATJ*, 5, 1, 1988; E. Fulchignoni, 'Oriental Influences on the Commedia dell'Arte,' *ATJ*, 7, 1, 1990; T.H. Gaster, *Thespis: Ritual, Myth, and Drama in the Ancient Near East*, Garden City, NJ, 1950; B. Hunningher, *The Origin of the Theatre*, New York, 1961; C. Innes, *Avant Garde Theatre 1892–1992*, London and New York, 1993; L. Logie, 'Training the Actor's Body to Express: A Cross-Cultural Study', PhD diss., Murdoch University, 1993; B. Marranca and G. Dasgupta (eds.), *Interculturalism and Performance*, New York, 1991; A.D. Napier, *Masks, Transformation, and Paradox*, Berkeley, 1984; P. Pavis, *Theatre at the Crossroads of Culture*, London and New York, 1992; L.C. Pronko, *Theater East and West: Perspectives Toward a Total Theater*, Berkeley, 1967; E.W. Said, *Orientalism*, New York, 1978; N. Savarese, *Teatro e spettacolo fra oriente e occidente*, Rome and Bari, 1992, and 'A Portrait of

Hanako', *ATJ*, 5, 1, 1988; S. Snow, 'Intercultural Performance: The Balinese-American Model', *ATJ*, 3, 2, 1986; E. Welsford, *The Fool: His Social and Literary History*, New York, 1935.

Asian-American theatre This term could apply to the work of all American theatre artists of Asian ancestry – from the avant-garde spectacles of PING CHONG to the BROADWAY playmaking of David Henry Hwang. More often, however, it refers to a contemporary movement of ethnic-identified theatre that has yielded several regional companies and provided encouragement, training and professional exposure to scores of Asian-American actors, directors and, perhaps most significantly, playwrights. Whether it has also produced a unified aesthetic or political outlook is open to debate. Historically, artists of Asian extraction have been performing in the USA for over a century; but until recently an intricate nexus of social and cultural factors kept them marginalized or excluded from mainstream theatre, and impeded the development of Asian-American stage literature.

Traditional operas, puppet shows and acrobatic displays were imported into the USA from CHINA as early as the 1850s. Exotic and baffling to many Westerners, these vivid spectacles were welcomed by the masses of Chinese labourers who emigrated to California to mine gold, build the railway and start up Chinatowns. Tung Hook Tong was, in 1852, probably the first such opera company to tour nationally. Other Chinese performers played extended runs in San Francisco; some eventually toured in VARIETY and VAUDEVILLE. Anti-Chinese sentiment flared in the economically depressed 1870s, and in 1882 Congress passed the Asian Exclusion Act to stem immigration. Related racial violence drove many Chinese from California to other regions of the country. The new Chinatowns soon had their own amateur opera clubs, and by 1900 there were professional Chinese opera houses in New York, Portland (Oregon) and Boston as well as San Francisco.

Interest in traditional performance gradually diminished, and by the 1930s many Chinatown theatres had become Chinese-language cinemas. By then a large contingent of Japanese (and a smaller number of Filipinos) had also settled in the USA, mostly in the West. However, apart from the variety artists who imitated such Caucasian celebrities as FRED ASTAIRE, SALLY RAND and Bing Crosby in Chinatown nightclubs during the 1930s and 40s, few Asian Americans appeared in Western-style live entertainment. The American theatre continued periodically to produce shows with Asian themes – from *The First Born* (a 19th-century MELODRAMA set in San Francisco's Chinatown), to GILBERT and Sullivan's *Mikado*, to the post-Second World War Broadway hits *Teahouse of the August Moon* and *The King and I*. But Asiatic actors were usually relegated to playing stock character maids, cooks, vamps and spies, while Caucasians played the 'Oriental' leads. (The same was often true in Hollywood films.)

The differences between Western and Asian drama kept some Asian immigrants away from theatre, as did language barriers and moral qualms about show business. Moreover, Japanese Americans were virtually banished from all public life when the government interned them in relocation camps during the Second World War. But as third- and fourth-generation Asian Americans appeared, the stereotyping and casting practices remained. The 1958 RODGERS–HAMMERSTEIN MUSICAL *Flower Drum Song* was the first (and for many years the only) professional New York production set in a modern Asian-American milieu.

In 1965, finding little meaningful stage or screen work, Alberto Isaacs, Mako and other other Asian-American actors and directors created East West Players in Los Angeles. It was the thick of the civil rights era, and EWP was a self-help venture, talent showcase and declaration of ethnic pride. Unlike contemporary AFRICAN-AMERICAN ensembles, however, EWP had no repertoire of new plays or stable of writers to draw on; at first it staged classics and scripts set in Asia (*Rashomon*). In 1973 two sister ensembles were formed: the Asian Exclusion Act (now Northwest Asian American Theatre) in Seattle and the activist Asian American Theatre Workshop in San Francisco. AATW (later renamed the Asian American Theatre Company) caused the bigger splash, with new plays high on its agenda – plays exploding the old media images of Asians and aggressively revealing the frustrations and contradictions of Asian-American experience. In this vein, co-founder Frank Chin's hip, nervy scripts garnered immediate national attention: first *Chickencoop Chinaman* and later his *Year of the Dragon* and *Gee, Pop!*. Chin was the first Asian-American dramatist to have a 'legit' production in New York (*Chickencoop Chinaman*, 1972, AMERICAN PLACE THEATRE).

In 1977 actor-director Tisa Chang founded New York's Pan Asian Repertory Theatre, the fourth regional outlet for Asian-American drama. This loose network of subscription theatres boosted the careers of many fine Asian-American actors, including John Lone, Mako, Nobu McCarthy, Dennis Dun and Joan Chen, and introduced works by dozens of US writers with ancestral roots in Japan, China, Korea, the Philippines and other Asian countries. Repeated themes include the Japanese-American Second World War internment, generational clashes between Asian-bred immigrants and their Americanized children, the history and persistence of racism, the mythic reverberations from Asian cultures. REALISM laced with satiric SURREALISM is the predominant style, but much variety exists. Noteworthy texts include: Velina Hasu Houston's *Tea* (a Japanese war bride who kills her US husband); PHILIP KAN GOTANDA's memory play *Song for a Nisei Fisherman*; Wakako Yamauchi's *And the Soul Shall Dance* (set on a Depression-era farm); Laurence Yep's *Pay the Chinaman* (about Chinese con men in early California); Ric Shiomi's *Yellow Fever* (detective tale with an ethnic twist); Ernest Abuba's *An American Story* (about a mixed-raced family in San Diego); Han Ong's gritty *L.A. Stories* (about a Los Angeles street hustler); and Reggie Cheong-Leen's *The Nanjing Race*, a unique look at the Asian-American dilemma of cultures at odds.

A few Asian-American playwrights have 'crossed over' into mainstream venues. Most prominently, David Henry Hwang's early works (*F.O.B.*, *Dance and the Railroad*) debuted at New York's PUBLIC THEATER, and his *M. Butterfly* won a Tony on Broadway (his second Broadway effort failed). Berkeley Repertory Theatre, Eureka Theatre,

MANHATTAN THEATRE CLUB, Mark Taper Forum and Los Angeles Theatre Center have mounted scripts by Hwang, Gotanda, Houston and others.

Not all dramatists of Asian descent have worked within the Asian-American theatre axis; some prefer not to affix any ethnic labels to their work. The many linked with the movement have, however, kept involved in it long after finding success in other realms. In 1990 Hwang and actor B. D. Wong led a protest by Asian-American artists over the casting of a white actor (JONATHAN PRYCE) in a major Eurasian role in the Broadway musical *Miss Saigon,* igniting a vigorous public debate about the meaning of 'non-traditional' casting and multiculturalism.

As their ranks continue to swell, Asian Americans have repudiated the notion that they are a 'silent, invisible' minority by actively participating in all areas of popular culture; and while some critics now decry ethnic-specific cultural expression as a 'balkanization' of the arts, Asian-American drama leaders defend its ongoing importance. East West Players artistic director Nobu McCarthy commented in 1991: 'Our artists should graduate and perform shoulder-to-shoulder with white artists in the mainstream. But first we must discover who *we* are, before we become the mainstream.' MBer

Astaire [Austerlitz], **Fred** 1899–1987 and
Adele Astaire 1898–1981 American dancers, singers and actors. As children the Astaires spent 10 years in VAUDEVILLE, where they perfected their dancing and teamwork. In 1917 they made their New York MUSICAL THEATRE debut in *Over the Top.* Influenced by the ballroom dancing of Vernon and Irene Castle, the Astaires also studied with BROADWAY choreographer and director NED WAYBURN. Their dances were fluid, stylish and often witty, in keeping with the frothy musicals in which they appeared. After featured roles in several shows, the Astaires were the stars of *Lady, Be Good!*(1924), for which GEORGE AND IRA GERSHWIN wrote the score. The successful partnership with the Gershwins was repeated with *Funny Face* (1927). They starred with MARILYN MILLER in *Smiles* (1930), and made their last appearance as a team in the Howard Dietz–Arthur Schwartz REVUE, *The Band Wagon* (1931). After Adele's retirement, Fred appeared alone in *The Gay Divorcee*(1932) before leaving for Hollywood and a career in musical films. Critics generally considered Adele to be the stronger dancer and more vivid personality of the partnership. Equally popular in England, the Astaires brought several of their American successes to the London stage during the 1920s. MK

Astley, Philip 1742–1814 English equestrian and manager, who first distinguished himself as a horse-breaking sergeant-major during the Continental wars (1760). On leaving the cavalry, he opened a riding school outside London (1768), where he combined equestrianism with CLOWNS and tumblers to constitute the first true CIRCUS. After a stint in Dublin, he erected his Royal Amphitheatre (1788). When a rival, Charles Hughes, built the Royal Circus and began staging plays without a licence, Astley followed suit. Both managers were closed by the authorities, and Astley sought new pastures in Paris where he prospered with his *cirque*(1782–9). The French Revolution

forced him home, where he published his *System of Equestrian Education* (1801). His London amphitheatre burned to the ground in 1794, to be rebuilt the next year; it burned again in 1803 to rise phoenix-like as a splendid new house, seating 2500 spectators, in 1804. He left this business to his son and then built the Olympic Pavilion from the timber of an old frigate at a cost of £800. It lost £10,000 in its first season. His last enterprise was an amphitheatre restricted to equestrianism in the Faubourg du Temple in Paris (October 1814).

His son John Philip Conway (1767–1821), as a child equestrian, had been dubbed the English Rose by Marie Antoinette. Indolent and handsome, he excelled at devising fanciful equestrian PANTOMIMES but, a prodigal businessman, he spent more than the amphitheatre earned and died of high living. (See also HIPPODRAMA.) LS

Aston, Anthony [Matt Medley] c.1682–c.1753 English actor-manager. Born into a wealthy family, he abandoned law to become an actor. A strolling player with DOGGETT in the provinces and in Ireland in the late 1690s, he became a soldier and a lawyer in the West Indies and may also have acted in America. By 1709 he was acting again in Ireland, where his first play *Love in a Hurry* was performed. In 1710 he began performing the medleys for which he became famous. These were variety shows of short plays, scenes, songs and dances performed by Aston and members of his family, and their success earned him the nickname Matt Medley. Though he attempted a full-scale production in London in 1717 (closed down because of the monopoly of the Patent companies) and briefly joined the LINCOLN's INN FIELDS company in 1722, he spent most of his career touring the country with the medleys, adding extra features such as ANIMAL IMPERSONATIONS from time to time. In 1735 he campaigned successfully against the proposed Playhouse Bill, which would have strengthened the power of the Patent companies against shows like his. He gave his last known performances in 1744. His play *The Fool's Opera* contains an autobiographical sketch. As a contemporary said, 'he is a monopoliser ... he plays all characters, he fills none: he is the whole comedy in his single person'. PH

Astor Place Opera House (New York City) In their pursuit of operatic pleasure, well-to-do New Yorkers built the Astor Place close to an exclusive enclave on Lafayette Street settled by the Astors and their friends; but opera did not remain for long the house's principal fare, and the 1800-seat theatre was given over to other entertainments. In 1849, during an engagement by the English star W. C. MACREADY, a riot was triggered from a long-smouldering feud between Macready and the American star EDWIN FORREST, which was also fed by anti-English sentiment among the Irish denizens of the Bowery area. The militia was called in to quell the riot, and the order was given to fire at the crowd. When the smoke had cleared, at least 22 (possibly as many as 31) people had died and 150 were wounded. A 1990 play by RICHARD NELSON (*Two Shakespearean Actors*) deals with the Macready–Forrest rivalry. In 1852, the theatre was renamed the New York to rid it of its tainted past, but in 1854 it was sold at auction to the Mercantile Library Association; thereafter it was known as Clinton Hall, until it was torn down in 1891. MCH

Atelier, Théâtre de l' (Paris) A 19th-century melodrama theatre in Montmartre; then a cinema from 1914 till 1922 when DULLIN reopened it as L'Atelier. It became well known as one of the CARTEL theatres, producing a wide repertoire, including the classics, the Elizabethans and modern playwrights, notably PIRANDELLO and SALACROU. Alongside the producing company, Dullin ran a school in which many famous French actors and directors trained, e.g. ARTAUD, BARRAULT, BARSACQ, BLIN and VILAR. When Dullin moved to the Théâtre Sarah Bernhardt in 1940, Barsacq took over the theatre with his Compagnie des Quatre Saisons. He remained its director till his death, preserving a similar tradition to that of Dullin but with the addition of more light modern works. DB

Atkinson, (Justin) Brooks 1894–1984 American drama critic. Educated at Harvard University where he attended GEORGE PIERCE BAKER's Workshop 47, Atkinson taught English for a year (1917–18) at Dartmouth College and worked as a reporter on the Springfield (Mass.) *Daily News*. A year later, he began a four-year stint as assistant drama critic to H.T. Parker on the *Boston Daily Evening Transcript*. In 1922 he became book review editor for the *New York Times*, succeeding STARK YOUNG as the paper's theatre critic in 1926. When war broke out in 1941, he took an overseas assignment, later receiving a Pulitzer Prize (1947) for his reports on the Soviet Union. After the war (1946) he returned to reviewing the BROADWAY theatre. The most respected critic of his generation, Atkinson offered commonsense opinions in a graceful style, and was known for both his fairness and his candour. He thought that the theatre should reach out and relate to the world outside of the art; therefore he did not mingle with theatre people or attend rehearsals, believing that his reviews were for the 'average guy who goes to the theatre'. At his retirement in 1960, the Mansfield Theatre (built in 1926) was renamed in his honour. His many books include *Broadway Scrapbook* (1948), *Brief Chronicles* (1966), *Broadway* (1970) and *The Lively Years: 1920–1973*. TLM

Auden, W(ystan) H(ugh) 1907–73 British poet and dramatist. Auden was a founder member of the GROUP THEATRE in London, which was responsible for the production of his first performed play, *The Dance of Death* (1934). A didactic celebration of the destruction of the bourgeoisie using music and ballet, and influenced by the AGIT-PROP form of workers' theatre, its doggerel verse and Marxist themes point forward to his collaborations with CHRISTOPHER ISHERWOOD, *The Dog Beneath the Skin* (1935), *The Ascent of F6* (1936) and *On the Frontier* (1938). These political fables, mixing symbolic quests, epic techniques (see EPIC THEATRE) derived from BRECHT, and satiric pastiche are among the most powerful English plays of the 1930s. Auden was awarded the Pulitzer Prize for his modern MORALITY PLAY *The Age of Anxiety* (1947), which explores loneliness as the human condition through characters derived from Jungian psychology. As well as translations of ERNST TOLLER, Brecht and COCTEAU, he is known for his opera librettos – in particular, *Paul Bunyan* (1941)

for Benjamin Britten, *The Rake's Progress* (1951) for Igor Stravinsky, and *Moralities* for Hans Werner Henze (1969). CI

Audiberti, Jacques 1899–1965 Prolific southern French writer of poetic rather than dramatic bent. Audiberti's first play to be seen on the French stage, *Quoat-Quoat* (directed by Reybaz in 1946), was written without thought of performance. However, his poetic exuberance led him to be linked with writers of the post-war avant-garde such as Schéhadé and VAUTHIER. Many of his plays were directed by Georges Vitaly and then enjoyed a second life in productions by MARCEL MARÉCHAL in Lyon in the 1960s. His multi-layered texts (including 26 plays) deal with the eternal conflict between forces of good and evil in settings often borrowed from history or myth. DB

Auditorium Theatre (Chicago) Set within a multipurpose building encompassing a hotel, offices and stores, the Auditorium was intended to be supported by the commercial enterprises in the complex. Designed by the experimental firm of Dankmar and Adler, it introduced no stunningly new concepts architecturally but was provided with near-perfect acoustics and sightlines, a flexible auditorium and stage and striking interior decoration. It opened in 1889 and was in use as an opera house and theatre until 1942, when it was largely abandoned. Once threatened with destruction, it was restored and reopened in 1967 after a civic campaign was launched to save it. Today it is used for BROADWAY road shows, dance companies and pop concerts. MCH

Augier, Émile 1820–89 The most important French social dramatist and chronicler of society of the Second Empire and Third Republic. He exposes the bourgeoisie of the period, in play after play, for its hypocritical and false moral values. His plays helped move the French theatre in the direction of NATURALISM by offering serious examinations of a number of topical issues – for example, *Madame Caverlet* (1876) dealt with the question of divorce. The 19th-century bourgeois's obsession with money and his confusion of moral and monetary values provided a favourite theme of Augier's, most strongly expressed in his last play, *The House of Fourchambault* (1878), in which a character states that 'marriage is the lowest of human institutions when it is no more than the union of two fortunes'.

Augier's first play, *Hemlock* (1844), had a classical theme, but revealed a talent which he would soon turn to more contemporary issues. In *Le Mariage d'Olympe* (*The Marriage of Olympia*, 1855), which was booed by its first audiences, he attacked the romantic sentimentalizing of the courtesan. *Le Gendre de Monsieur Poirier* (*Monsieur Poirier's Son-in-Law*), written with Jules Sandeau for the Gymnase in 1854 (it joined the repertoire of the COMÉDIE-FRANÇAISE in 1864), explored the subject of the *nouveau riche* bourgeois and the impoverished nobleman in a 19th-century version of MOLIÈRE's *Le Bourgeois Gentilhomme*. *A False Step* (*The Poor Lionesses*, 1858) showed the lengths to which the wives of the bourgeoisie were prepared to go to satisfy their taste for ostentation and luxury and the risks which they might run.

By the 1860s Augier was dealing with more and more contentious subjects, constantly attacking the frenetic pursuit of material wealth. In *Les Effrontés* (*The Shameless Ones*, 1861) he exposed the link between manipulation of the stock exchange and the press. This play created the character of Giboyer (brilliantly interpreted by the actor GÔT), and its success led to a sequel, *Le Fils de Giboyer* (*Giboyer's Son*). The play contained a strong dose of anti-clericalism. His virulent attack on the political manoeuvring of the Jesuits was continued in *Lions et renards* (*Lions and Foxes*, 1869). *Maître Guérin* (1864), which had a long run, is a return to the comedy of manners, focusing on the character of a dubious lawyer who turns the law to his own advantage. The French critic Gustave Lanson felt that this was the most original and the most closely observed character to be put on the stage since Molière. Augier was elected to the French Academy in 1857. After *The House of Fourchambault* he virtually stopped writing because of a nervous complaint. JMCC

Auriol, Jean-Baptiste 1806–81 French acrobatic CLOWN, son of a ballet master. Auriol studied under the rope dancer Pierre Forioso and married the English performer Aurelia Belling, before taking his first job with DUCROW, performing his famous bottle dance. After appearances throughout Europe he made his Parisian debut with Franconi (1847), where his leaps had a phenomenal success: he performed a *salto mortale* over 24 soldiers and a double *salto* over 12 horses (see ACROBATICS). Auriol's non-use of make-up, his voice 'like a child's trumpet' and his jester's costume set the style for European clowns for two decades. He retired in 1862. LS

Australia

Aboriginal dance drama In the 40,000 years the Aborigines are believed to have inhabited Australia, many forms of dance drama or 'corroboree' evolved. These dance traditions, which Aborigines believe are passed on from the spirits of ancestors, have religious significance and are associated with initiation, tribal, totemic and magic ceremonies. A fusion of music, dance and drama, they have varied from the large formal patterns of the southeastern traditions to the looser formations and individual dancing of northern Australia. Sometimes only men dance; on other occasions both men and women dance, sometimes separately. Dance is usually accompanied by singing and clapsticks; in northern Australia a wooden trumpet (didjeridu) is also played. Dancers are painted with coloured ochres and decorated with feathers and plants, preparing themselves behind a screen of boughs and performing, often by firelight, in a specially prepared area. The dances often depict animal movements; among the distinctive steps are the leg-quivering movement and dancing on all fours. These dances combine religious rite and theatrical entertainment; those of the southeastern areas, now largely inhabited by white settlers, have for the most part disappeared, but Aboriginal dance remains a living tradition in other parts of Australia.

Early colonial theatre, 1789–1850 European settlement of Australia began in 1788 with the founding of a British penal colony at Sydney, and for a generation afterwards theatre was largely a convict activity. The first theatrical performance took place in 1789 – FARQUHAR's *The Recruiting Officer* staged in a decorated bark hut in honour of the king's birthday. In 1796 Robert Sidaway opened a theatre which convicts could attend for payment of meat, flour or spirits, but their rowdy behaviour spelt its closure two years later, and another theatre, for officers, in 1800 was also short-lived. But convict performances were permitted at Norfolk Island in 1793–4; in 1826 performances were held in the Debtors' Room at Sydney Gaol, and at Emu Plains a convict theatre group established in 1825 was patronized by free settlers until abruptly disbanded in 1830.

Professional theatre in New South Wales, however, emerged only after a struggle with officialdom and some community disapproval. In 1827 a stage-struck Sydney businessman named Barnett Levey advertised for shareholders in a theatre, and in 1829 began holding balls and entertainments in his mill and hotel complex known as the Colchester warehouse. After repeated applications and a change of governor he was finally granted a theatre licence, and professional theatre was born on Boxing Night 1832 with *Black Ey'd Susan* staged in the hotel saloon; his Theatre Royal opened on 5 October 1833 with *The Miller and his Men*. Many associated with Levey, including the actors Conrad Knowles, George Buckingham and John Meredith, and the managers Joseph Simmons and Joseph Wyatt, helped consolidate the profession in Sydney and the other colonies in the next decade, while the lively actress Eliza Winstanley went on to perform with CHARLES KEAN at the London PRINCESS's THEATRE in the 1850s. The Theatre Royal survived until 1838 when Sydney gained a second theatre, the Royal Victoria, seating almost 2000 and with a solid professional company under Joseph Wyatt. The 1840s saw short-lived competition from Signor Dalle Case's Olympic Theatre (1842) and Joseph Simmons's Royal City Theatre (1843), but the Royal Victoria remained a major Sydney theatre until 1880.

Theatre was also established in the other Australian colonies in the 1830s and 1840s, with Sydney performers and others newly arrived from England, including the Samson Camerons, Theodosia Yates, Francis Nesbitt, Francis Belfield, Gustavus Arabin and Anne Clarke, moving with surprising frequency between widely separated settlements. In Van Diemen's Land (Tasmania) John Phillip Deane held concerts in Hobart from 1826, and in 1833–4 the Samson Camerons at the Freemason's Tavern and Deane at the Argyle Rooms presented professional entertainments; by 1841 the provincial town of Launceston had regular performances.

Though Tasmania was also a penal colony, unlike New South Wales its Colonial Secretary was one of the sponsors of a theatre, and in 1837 Hobart's Theatre Royal was opened. Though much altered, it still stands as Australia's only working theatre from early colonial days. Adelaide, a free settlement, gained a professional theatre in 1838, and two more under the Camerons and Buckingham, before the Queen's Theatre opened near the Shakespeare Tavern (later the New Queen's) in 1841. The English actor-manager GEORGE COPPIN became Adelaide's most prominent theatrical figure in the late 1840s, managing the Royal

Victoria (the old Queen's) with John Lazar, and opening a theatre in Port Adelaide in 1850. Melbourne was founded later in 1835, and not until 1841 did its makeshift Pavilion Theatre open next to the Eagle Tavern – another example of the common link between early theatres and public houses. As the Royal Victoria it was managed by Knowles and Samson Cameron until 1845, when a New Queen's Theatre Royal opened under Francis Nesbitt. The nearby township of Geelong also had a thriving theatre from the 1840s. Perth had theatrical entertainments from 1839, and from 1842 Hodge's Hotel presented amateur performances; Brisbane was to wait till the 1850s for its earliest theatricals, and till 1865 for its first theatre.

The repertoire of such theatres was that of the British stage, from SHAKESPEARE to MELODRAMA, FARCE and BURLESQUE – indeed, Levey's original licence had specified 'such Plays and Entertainments only as have been performed at one of His Majesty's Licensed Theatres in London'. But the indigenous drama dates from 1828 when David Burn wrote his melodrama *The Bushrangers* (staged at Edinburgh in 1829), based on a Tasmanian convict, Matthew Brady. Burn's other dramas were performed in Sydney and Melbourne during the 1840s, while the Melbourne Queen's Theatre staged several plays by local authors, including the actor Francis Belfield's melodramas.

In Sydney, still cautious towards theatre because of its convict population, a system of licensing locally written plays on the pattern of the Lord Chamberlain's CENSORSHIP in Britain developed in the 1840s, though it favoured plays with little or no local content. The convict Edward Geoghegan became Sydney's most prolific playwright, writing or adapting ten pieces for the Royal Victoria, including a charming musical trifle with a Sydney setting, *The Currency Lass* (1844). Most of his plays, however, like those of Conrad Knowles and Joseph Simmons, are romantic melodramas with exotic settings, as was the first locally written OPERA staged in Australia, Isaac Nathan's *Don John of Austria* (1847). Apart from Burn's drama, the most specific depiction of colonial society is the anonymous comedy *Jemmy Green in Australia* (c.1845), attributed to the convict James Tucker, which transplants a naive cockney character from W. T. MONCRIEFF's *Tom and Jerry* to confront bumbling constables and bushrangers in New South Wales.

Years of expansion The early 1850s saw theatre's expansion into a fully fledged entertainment industry, with the discovery of gold in New South Wales and Victoria, and subsequently in Queensland. Melbourne, barely 15 years old, became almost overnight a cosmopolitan city, and with Bendigo, Ballarat and other goldmining centres provided a ready market for performers such as LOLA MONTEZ, who toured in 1855 with her notorious 'spider dance'. George Coppin quickly established himself as Australia's leading entrepreneur, with four theatres in Melbourne by the mid-1850s, and it was he who introduced the practice of importing noted artists to tour an established circuit of major cities and provincial towns, a policy which was to dominate the Australian theatre throughout the 19th century. Coppin's first overseas star was the Irish tragedian Gustavus Vaughan Brooke, his partner at the Melbourne

Queen's Theatre in the 1850s, and over the next 20 years many theatrical celebrities toured Australia, most under Coppin's management. From the British and European theatre came Charles Kean and Ellen Tree (1863), the Shakespearians Barry Sullivan (1862–6) and Walter Montgomery (1867–9), CHARLES JAMES MATHEWS (1870–1) and MADAME CÉLESTE (1867), while from America came JOSEPH JEFFERSON III for several years in the early 1860s, Adelaide and Joey Gougenheim (1856), EDWIN BOOTH in the 1850s and again in 1872, and Avonia Jones (1859–61), among many others. Such theatrical celebrities, and others sometimes less well known, while undoubtedly raising theatrical standards, inevitably fostered the attitude that 'the best' came from abroad and consolidated the emerging Australian theatre in the mould of British and American tradition.

A number of Australian-based managements became well established in the 1860s–70s, pre-eminent among whom was William Saurin Lyster's Grand Opera Company, which established opera as the popular form it was to remain until after the First World War. But not surprisingly, in the light of so many imported plays and players, the local drama was even less evident than in the 1840s. Farces and comic afterpieces with local settings were sometimes staged, but PANTOMIMES emerged as the form most readily adaptable to local colour and topicality. The prolific William Mower Akhurst, and later Marcus Clarke and Garnet Walch, wrote numerous pantomimes and extravaganzas which combined fairy tale and mythology with colonial characters to satirize the new pretensions to urbanity of Australian society, though in the most light-hearted and ephemeral way.

The golden years, 1870–1914 The period from 1870 to the First World War saw rapid growth in theatrical activity. Sydney, for example, which in the early 1870s had two or three regular venues, could boast six major theatres by the late 1880s, as well as several smaller venues for VARIETY theatre. By the 1890s Australians had access to the full spectrum of 19th-century theatrical fare, from Shakespeare, GRAND OPERA and OPERETTA to melodrama, farce and variety theatre. From the 1870s the Australian-born population outnumbered immigrants, producing homegrown stars such as the ravishing NELLIE STEWART, but the theatre remained largely dominated by performers and managers who had come from abroad. Australia was still a provincial outpost of British theatre, and increasingly part of an international touring circuit. Some performers came for brief, highly publicized tours – Julius Knight in 1891 and 1897, H. B. Irving (the son of HENRY IRVING) in 1911, EMILY SOLDENE and her showgirls in 1877, Mrs Brown Potter and Kyrle Bellew in 1891; JANET ACHURCH in the controversial *A Doll's House* in 1889, soon after its London staging; the expatriate OSCAR ASCHE with Lily Brayton in 1909; and, most celebrated of all, SARAH BERNHARDT in 1891.

Others returned so often or stayed so long that they became identified with the Australian stage: the actor-manager George Rignold, the Majeroni family who had arrived in 1875 with ADELAIDE RISTORI, the Italian tragedienne, the English actor George Titheradge and the American Grattan Riggs, among many others. The famous melodramatist DION BOUCICAULT arrived in 1885 with his son and daughter, and the younger Dion (Dot) remained to found in 1886, with Robert Brough, the Brough–Boucicault Company, based in Melbourne, which for a decade set the standard for stylish productions of sophisticated new plays.

Many such performers were initially brought to Australia by Coppin's successor as Australia's foremost entrepreneur, the American J. C. WILLIAMSON, who himself had first arrived as one of Coppin's imported stars in 1874. In 1882 Williamson formed a partnership with Arthur Garner and George Musgrove, known as the Triumvirate, which lasted until 1890 and led to the Williamson managerial 'Firm' which dominated Australian theatre for two generations. Williamson, a shrewd businessman with little interest in serious drama and even less in that of his adopted country, consolidated the policy of importing proven successes with overseas stars, justifying it with the dictum that 'Australians don't want Australian' – a view that was almost unquestioningly accepted as fact until the mid-20th century.

Williamson's middle-brow entertainment, leavened with spectacular seasons of 'high culture' such as the Melba Grand Opera tour in 1911, set the pattern for commercial theatre until the 1950s. Ironically, his denigration of the local playwright came just as Australian authors were finding enthusiastic audiences in the melodrama theatres, though the local drama was always heavily overshadowed by overseas successes. Walter Cooper, journalist, member of parliament and playwright, in the 1870s wrote comedies and sensation dramas depicting the 'new chum' immigrant's experience, sometimes with spectacle scenes of bushfires and floods; and George Darrell, an English-born actor-manager and author, consolidated the Anglo-Australian melodrama with pieces such as *The Forlorn Hope* (1879), showing a band of colonials coming to Britain's aid in a future European war, and *The Sunny South* (1883), in which an aristocratic English household 'strike it rich' on the goldfields and have various colonial adventures before returning triumphant to England.

In the 1890s and early 20th century Alfred Dampier, Bland Holt and William Anderson staged local melodramas with bush settings and stock figures such as the bushranger, squatter, bushman, gold-digger and spirited colonial heroine in adapted melodramatic plots; Dampier's bushranging play *Robbery under Arms* (1890) and the stage version of the chronicles of the hayseed Rudd family, *On Our Selection*, as dramatized by Bert Bailey and Edmund Duggan in 1912, remained popular favourites until well into the 1920s. There is no Australian genre equivalent to the 'society drama' of the British theatre, nor did there develop, despite the great popularity of musical theatre, a distinctively Australian strand of operetta or opera. Melodrama with a heavy weighting towards farce remained the predominant form of Australian popular drama until the advent of the 'talkies' virtually spelt its end.

The commercial theatre, 1920–60 The years after the First World War saw the transition from the last of the old actor-managements, providing a wide spectrum of entertainment, to a theatre run largely by entrepreneurs and presenting light entertainment with occasional seasons of culture from abroad. The J. C. Williamson management consolidated its dominance of Australian theatre by absorbing its major competitors, and in 1920 effected a merger with its most significant rival, J. & N. Tait. This virtually monopolistic 'Firm', in the tradition laid down by its founder, staged proven MUSICALS, thrillers and light comedies, usually with imported stars. A number of talented Australians, including GLADYS MONCRIEFF, ROBERT HELPMANN, Madge Elliott and Dorothy Brunton, had their first opportunity in the lavish Williamson musicals of the 1920s, but in later years local performers were relegated to supporting roles, and many notable performers were lost to the British theatre. The procession of visiting stars continued – Pavlova toured in 1926, Dion Boucicault Jr and his wife Irene Vanbrugh made several visits in the 1920s, and in 1932 SYBIL THORNDIKE and LEWIS CASSON toured in a memorable *St Joan*. Often the visiting stars were Australians who had made their names abroad: Melba made two farewell tours of her homeland in 1924–8, Oscar Asche returned in 1922–3, JUDITH ANDERSON returned from America for a season in 1927, and Cyril Ritchard and Madge Elliott toured in 1946, followed by Cicely Courtneidge two years later. In the 1930s two musicals presented by F. W. Thring, *Collit's Inn* (1933) and *The Cedar Tree* (1934), together with the Williamson production *Blue Mountain Melody* (1934), gave promise of an indigenous musical theatre which, apart from Williamson's much later success with *The Sentimental Bloke* (1957), was not fulfilled. By the 1950s the commercial theatre was even less grounded in Australian life than had been the popular theatre of the 19th century.

The VAUDEVILLE and variety theatre, however, developed its own indigenous quality. The variety and MINSTREL SHOW had been popular since the 1870s, but large-scale vaudeville dates from 1892 when Harry Rickards (Benjamin Harry Leete), a London-born comic singer, opened the Sydney Tivoli theatre, first of a circuit which was to last 75 years. By 1915 Rickards's successor Hugh D. McIntosh was rivalled by the New Zealand management Fuller's (two brothers, Ben and John), who established their own city theatres while also working with the suburban theatre circuits and the travelling TENT SHOWS, such as Sorlie's and Barton's Follies, which carried entertainment to the widely dispersed rural populations.

Where the Tivoli chain imported stars from the British and American MUSIC-HALL and variety theatre, including MARIE LLOYD, Little Tich, W. C. FIELDS and the Australian-born Florrie Forde, Fuller's cultivated local artists. In 1916 their Australian pantomime *The Bunyip* at the Sydney Grand Opera House brought together two comedians whose legendary partnership as 'Stiffy and Mo' lasted until 1928. 'Mo', or ROY RENE, Australia's first national comedian, with a grotesquely insinuating manner, and his 'straight man' Nat Phillips, together with Jim Gerald, a clown and outrageous pantomime dame, and George Wallace, a 'hayseed' type who specialized in comic falls, turned the vaudeville theatre between the wars into the vehicle for a characteristically Australian style of broad humour and irreverence.

The Depression was a major setback for the commercial theatre, with economic difficulties compounded by a crippling entertainment tax at both state and federal levels. Many larger theatres were forced to close, the Tivoli circuit was reduced to one theatre for a time, and Fuller's exchanged live theatre for film: but in the 1930s Rene led a Mike Connors–Queenie Paul company which merged briefly with the Tivoli management. A revival of local variety theatre during the Second World War created new stars such as Gloria Dawn, but in postwar years the Tivoli, under David N. Martin, reverted to imported artists, and many former vaude-villains ended their careers in radio.

The 'literary' drama, 1900–55

The serious drama was not entirely neglected, though it played to a small and fairly literate audience. The first repertory theatre was established in Adelaide in 1908 by Bryceson Treharne, followed in 1911 by GREGAN MCMAHON's Melbourne Repertory Theatre and later his Sydney semi-amateur groups; while Shakespeare was regularly performed from 1916 to the Depression by ALLAN WILKIE's touring company, and in the 1950s by the John Alden Company, at times with the backing of the Williamson management. But there was little if any place for the Australian playwright in the professional theatre. From 1904, when Leon Brodzky had attempted to organize an Australian Stage Society, there were moves to cultivate an indigenous drama of greater depth than the sensation melodramas. From 1909 to 1912 William Moore held annual Australian Drama Nights in Melbourne, at which the earliest work of Australia's first realistic playwright, LOUIS ESSON, was staged; and in 1922, influenced by Dublin's ABBEY THEATRE, Esson co-founded the Pioneer Players in Melbourne, to perform only Australian works. The group disbanded in 1926, and its attempt to create a folk theatre must be counted a failure, but it remained an inspiration to those committed to the indigenous drama.

From the early 1930s many small amateur and semi-amateur theatres were founded, many by talented women. Carrie Tennant opened her Community Playhouse in Sydney in 1930, and in 1932 the Independent Theatre, also in Sydney, was founded by Doris Fitton. May Hollingworth's Metropolitan Theatre in Sydney, the Little Theatre, Frank Thring Sr's Arrow Theatre and Gertrude Johnson's National Theatre Movement, all in Melbourne, and the various branches of the left-wing New Theatre in several cities, kept alive the serious drama until the 1950s, and in some cases for much longer. These 'little theatres' were virtually the only outlet for the work of Australian playwrights, and fostered a large number of writers, including Oriel Gray and Mona Brand (both associated with the New Theatres), Henrietta Drake-Brockman, Sydney Tomholt, George Landen Dann, George Farwell, and Frank Hardy. Their plays, for the most part in the prevailing realistic style, drew on historical themes, or depicted the cultural clash between country and city folk, or whites and Aborigines, in the harsh 'outback'. Among the best plays are Betty Roland's *The Touch of Silk* (1928), the touching story of a French war bride whose marriage is destroyed by the tensions of drought and small-town bigotry, and Katharine Susannah Prichard's *Brumby Innes*, a study in black–white relations and unromantic sexuality written in 1927 but not performed until 1972.

Many playwrights turned to radio, the major producer of Australian drama between the wars; of the radio playwrights the most important was Douglas Stewart, whose historical verse dramas, several of which were subsequently staged, extended the language of Australian drama beyond the REALISM of the vernacular. Most Australian plays were seen only by coterie audiences, but in 1948 the Independent Theatre's production of Sumner Locke-Elliott's *Rusty Bugles* caused a minor furore when the New South Wales police investigated its alleged 'profanity'. The vigour and humour of its depiction of a group of soldiers stationed at an isolated ordnance depot in Northern Territory, cut off from both family life and the action of the war, won the play a wide audience throughout Australia.

The little theatres struggled against great difficulties, apart from their financial precariousness. The spectacular high-budget commercial productions inevitably made the amateur groups seem merely 'worthy' by comparison, while the lack of opportunity outside the overseas-dominated commercial theatre led many actors and actresses who had gained their initial experience in the little theatres to pursue their careers abroad – Peter Finch, Coral Browne, Marie Ney, Frank Thring, Ray Barrett and later ZOË CALDWELL, among many others – so that the smaller theatres were constantly depleted of their finest talent. Until well into the 1950s the highlights of Australian theatre were still the highly publicized tours of overseas stars and companies. The acclaimed OLD VIC tour of 1948 with LAURENCE OLIVIER and VIVIEN LEIGH, the 1949 and 1952–3 tours of the Stratford Memorial Theatre, the latter including the expatriate actors LEO MCKERN and KEITH MICHELL, and the Old Vic tour of 1955 with Katharine Hepburn and Robert Helpmann, could only underline the deficiencies of a country unable to provide opportunities for its own talent.

The Australian Elizabethan Theatre Trust, 1954

From the 1940s, increasing dissatisfaction was voiced about the theatre's stratification into entertainment industry and amateur substitute for a profession. In 1943 an Australian Council for Music and the Arts was established to take the arts to schools and country areas, and in 1947 the Australian government invited the British director TYRONE GUTHRIE to Australia to report on the feasibility of establishing a national theatre. Guthrie's report, suggesting that such a move was premature, was resented in some quarters, but helped to fuel nationalistic feeling. In 1954 Dr H. C. Coombs, Governor of the Commonwealth Bank, announced a theatre trust to be set up by public subscription and government pro rata payments. Named the Australian Elizabethan Theatre Trust to commemorate the queen's recent Australian visit, it was formally inaugurated on 29 September 1954. Though initially the Trust came under some criticism for appointing an English director, HUGH HUNT, and presenting two English plays in conjunction with a commercial management, Garnet H. Carroll, as its opening season, the national aspirations for theatre and drama were acknowledged the following year with the return of Judith Anderson to play Medea, and the production in 1956 of Douglas Stewart's verse drama *Ned Kelly*, with Leo McKern in the title role of Australia's most famous bushranger.

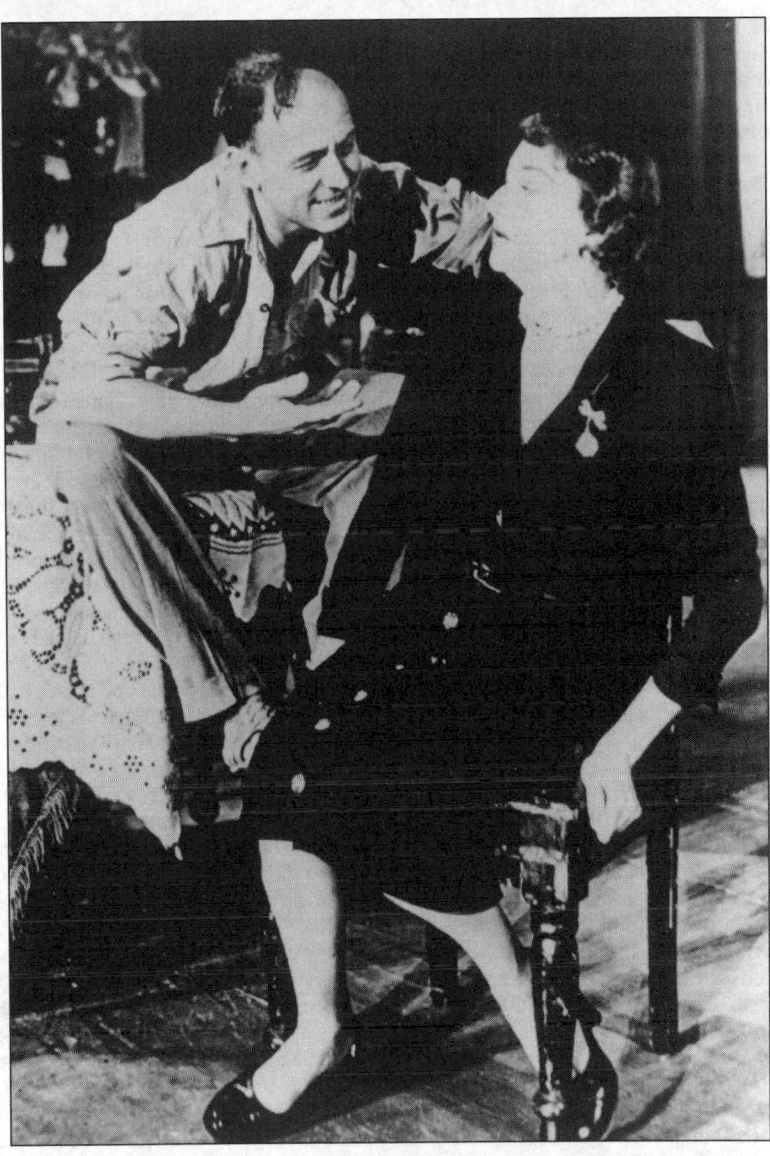

The first production of Ray Lawler's *Summer of the Seventeenth Doll*, Union Theatre Company, 1955.

Throughout the 1950s and 1960s the Trust set up theatrical structures through which, in time, an indigenous drama and theatre could mature. In 1956 the national Elizabethan Theatre Trust Opera Company was created, becoming the Australian Opera in 1969; and in 1962 the Australian Ballet under Peggy van Praagh was established after the demise of the Borovansky Ballet which had performed since the 1940s, often with the backing of the Williamson 'Firm'. When barely a year old the Trust was remarkably lucky to find what is still Australia's best-known and most loved play – *Summer of the Seventeenth Doll*, by a then unknown author, RAY LAWLER. *The Doll*, as it became known, co-winner in a competition run by the Playwrights Advisory Board (an organization for the encouragement of Australian drama set up by Leslie Rees in 1938), was an immediate success from its first production at the Union Theatre, Melbourne, in 1955, and after touring Australia under the Trust's auspices, went on to London and New York. The stimulus to Australian playwriting was immediate, and gave rise to a school of plays in *The Doll*'s mould of three-act realism, making vivid use of the vernacular and colourful working-class characters. Of these the most lasting have been Richard Beynon's drama of immigrant Italians, *The Shifting Heart* (1957), Peter Kenna's underworld drama *The Slaughter of St Teresa's Day* (1959), and Alan Seymour's play of the conflict between generations over war remembrance, *The One Day of the Year* (1960). Most of them were staged by the Trust Players, a core company of eight actors under the director Robin Lovejoy, which was established in 1959 and performed widely throughout Australia until the rigours of touring brought about its disbanding in 1961.

The effects of subsidy The 1960s saw radical changes in Australian theatre thanks to government subsidy of the performing arts, consolidated in 1968 with the formation of the Australian Council for the Arts (renamed the Australia Council in 1975). Fully professional subsidized companies were set up in each of the state capital cities, largely superseding the little theatres of the previous three decades. Two of these new 'state companies' grew directly out of links with universities; in 1968 the Union Theatre Repertory Company, initially at Melbourne University, became the Melbourne Theatre Company under John Sumner, while in Sydney the University of New South Wales Drama Foundation under Robert Quentin comprised Australia's first training school for theatre professionals, the National Institute of Dramatic Art (NIDA), founded in 1958, the first academic drama department, and the Old Tote Theatre Company. (The Old Tote was replaced as New South Wales's state company by the Sydney Theatre Company in 1980.) The creation of the South Australian Theatre Company (1965) in Adelaide, and Queensland Theatre Company (1969) in Brisbane, together with the National Theatre Company which had been formed from the Perth Repertory Club in 1956, and the Tasmanian Theatre Company (1973) in Hobart (the latter two superseded by the Western Australian Theatre Company and the Tasmanian Theatre Trust), meant that within two decades of the Trust's foundation Australia had a professional theatre network providing regular employment for performers, directors and designers who in an earlier generation would have made their careers abroad.

The change came about not only at the expense of the little theatres – the 1960s saw the closure of many of the large commercial theatres. The vaudeville and variety tradition dating back to the 1890s virtually came to an end in 1966 with the closure of the Tivoli circuit, though its spirit had seen a revival in the 1950s and 1960s in the wickedly satrical Phillip Street revues in Sydney. The J.C. Williamson management had become increasingly conservative in its musical entertainments, and the spiralling costs of its spectacular productions caused the almost century-old Firm to close in 1976, though the famous name continued to be used by a new management under Kenn Brodziak, Michael Edgley and several others.

The indigenous drama was slower to develop. The short-lived burst of realistic drama after *The Doll* had ended with several playwrights emigrating to Britain, but the early 1960s saw two significant developments – the rise to international stardom of BARRY HUMPHRIES, whose archetypal housewife character Edna Everage had had a cult following since the mid-1950s, and the emergence of the celebrated novelist PATRICK WHITE as playwright. In contrast to the prevailing realism of the drama since the First World War, both writers, Humphries in particular, opened up a rich vein of satirical caricature, anticipating the cartoon style of a 'new wave' of playwrights later in the decade. (The rejection of White's first play, *The Ham Funeral*, as 'unpleasant' by the Adelaide Festival Committee, before its staging at Adelaide University and subsequent production by the Trust, epitomized the CENSORSHIP battles of the 1960s, in which attempts to suppress such productions as the Sydney New Theatre's *America Hurrah!* in 1968 eventually led to the more liberal attitudes of the 1970s.)

From 1966, seasons of new Australian plays were held in a small church, the Jane Street Theatre, initially under the University of New South Wales Drama Foundation with assistance from the Gulbenkian Foundation, and from 1969 under the management of NIDA. The Jane Street seasons, intended primarily as workshop experience for the authors, staged the work of a number of new playwrights, including the novelist Thomas Keneally, DOROTHY HEWETT and Rodney Milgate; but the response to an adventurous season of plays at the Old Tote in 1968 seemed to confirm the long-standing managerial scepticism towards the Australian playwright. By the late 1960s the performance of Australian plays by the professional theatre was still minimal. The new state companies based their repertoires firmly on the classics and recent British or American successes, and though not yet a decade old, were increasingly seen as the reactionary 'establishment' by a new generation of potential actors and writers.

The alternative theatres, 1967–75 A new era in Australian theatre began in 1967 in Carlton, a working-class and immigrant suburb of Melbourne with a large student population, when Betty Burstall opened an intimate coffee-theatre on the model of the alternative venues in New York, and named La Mama after one of them (see LA MAMA). La Mama quickly became a focus for new poets, musicians and actors, and a group of playwrights including JACK HIBBERD, JOHN ROMERIL, DAVID WILLIAMSON and Barry Oakley. The La Mama Company of actors and writers also presented street theatre, often at the large anti-Vietnam War demonstrations, and toured factories in AGIT-PROP political pieces. In 1970 they moved to a large warehouse theatre, the Pram Factory, and renamed themselves the Australian Performing Group, reflecting their commitment to an indigenous drama and playing style; the Pram Factory quickly gained a reputation for robust and irreverent productions drawing on the old Australian vaudeville, variety and pantomime traditions. For ten years the APG remained a theatrical cooperative and umbrella organization for factory tours, innovative versions of the classics, Soapbox Circus (antecedent of the internationally known Circus Oz), film-making and a writers' agency. Though essentially an actors' company and committed to collective creation, which produced such successes as *The Hills Family Show* (1975), a hilarious backstage view of an old-time travelling theatre troupe, the APG also fostered a number of talented playwrights, some associated with the company since the La Mama days – Hibberd, Romeril, Oakley – and others, such as Barry Dickins and Tim Robertson, sharing the Pram Factory's radical political and theatrical commitment and often anarchic comic style.

Sydney's version of ALTERNATIVE THEATRE grew out of the blockbusting Jane Street success in 1970 of *The Legend of King O'Malley*, Michael Boddy's and Bob Ellis's REVUE-style portrait of a former political figure, which went on to an Australia-wide tour. Later the same year its director JOHN BELL, with Ken Horler, founded the small Nimrod Street Theatre in the inner-city suburb of Darlinghurst. Unlike the APG, which even as a subsidized company remained anti-establishment in philosophy and structure, Nimrod was a fully professional, if unconventional, theatre. Its early productions included irreverent musical treatments of Australian history, innovative productions of Shakespeare, and an outrageous transvestite pantomime, *Hamlet on Ice* (1972). It also attracted new Sydney playwrights such as Boddy and Ellis, Ron Blair, Jim McNeill, Dick Hall and ALEX BUZO, who, like their Melbourne counterparts, bypassed traditional forms to create works of an almost journalistic immediacy, and in demolishing the pretensions and hypocrisies of Australian society quickly found a responsive young audience. While the APG remained by choice an alternative group until its self-dissolution in 1981, Nimrod moved in 1974 to larger premises and established itself as a major mainstream company, often more adventurous than the state companies with which it stands comparison.

The acceptance of the new playwrights by the professional theatre came about largely through the work of David Williamson, whose *The Removalists* and *Don's Party*, initially staged at La Mama and the Pram Factory, had notable successes in Sydney – the former in 1971 at Nimrod followed by a commercial production by Harry M. Miller, and the latter at Jane Street in 1972 prior to an Australian tour and production in London. These, with *O'Malley* and the many long-running productions of Jack Hibberd's participatory wedding play, *Dimboola* (1969), removed any doubt that audiences would respond enthusiastically to Australian plays. By the mid-1970s, after a century and a half of theatrical activity, Australia had a theatre created by its own actors, directors and designers, and a drama that, at least in part, reflected its own society.

Contemporary Australian theatre Today the theatre has a range and diversity comparable to that of many older cultures. Public acceptance of the performing arts as an important part of Australian life is seen in the building of large performance complexes in several capitals, the most famous of which is the Sydney Opera House. Built to a modified design by the Danish architect Joern Utzon, it has some limitations as a performance space, but since its opening in 1973 its flamboyant white 'sails' on the edge of Sydney Harbour have become a symbol of renewed interest in the performing arts. Similar complexes, incorporating large auditoria and intimate studio theatres, have been opened in Adelaide, Melbourne and Brisbane. The marked increase in theatrical activity is largely due to the Australia Council, whose Performing Arts Board, composed of theatre and music practitioners, distributes annual grants to the major companies (the Australian Opera and Australian Ballet are funded by special grants) and to the many smaller companies, FRINGE and community groups, and individual artists through direct grants, special projects and travel grants. State governments and some local councils also offer assistance, and business sponsorship is increasingly important. The Elizabethan Theatre Trust, in provisional liquidation during 1991, was revived in 1992 as an entrepreneurial body, while branches of the federal Arts Council body promote touring and local enterprises in various states. Four major international arts festivals, the biennial Adelaide Festival and the annual Perth, Sydney and Melbourne festivals, as well as an annual gay theatre season in conjunction with Sydney's Gay and Lesbian Mardi Gras, provide first-class overseas theatre as well as promoting Australian work.

The six state theatre companies are the mainstay of traditional performance, though most state companies present a wide spectrum of classical and modern work, and have access to informal flexible venues for experimental productions. A number of smaller theatres in each capital (Sydney's Q Theatre in the outer suburbs, Ensemble Theatre, Belvoir Street Theatre and Griffin Theatre; La Boite in Brisbane; Playbox Theatre Company, the Malthouse and Gasworks (now home to Anthill Theatre) in Melbourne; Troupe, the Red Shed, and the Stage Company in Adelaide; and the Hole in the Wall in Perth) have been important outlets for recent overseas drama and new Australian writing. Australian material is now integral at all levels of activity; directors of European classics often commission Australian translations, while outstanding directors such as JIM SHARMAN, GEORGE OGILVIE, the late Rex Cramphorn, Richard Wherrett and Rodney Fisher have made their reputations as much through Australian plays as the classics and overseas works – Sharman has been associated with the work of Patrick White, and Fisher with that of David Williamson and DOROTHY HEWETT. Innovative new directors include Polish-born Bogdan Koca, Gale Edwards, who has directed both classical works and international productions of major musicals, and Barrie Kosky of the Jewish company Gilgul in Melbourne. Since 1975 the annual National Playwrights Conference (which now runs a permanent Australian National Playwrights Centre in Sydney) and the Playworks Women Writers Workshop have provided workshops and readings of new plays, many of which have subsequently received full professional production, and certain theatre companies, such as the Griffin Theatre in Sydney, are orientated towards staging Australian material.

For more than 20 years Currency Press has published Australian plays and dramatic criticism, and with smaller publishers such as Yackandandah has helped create a body of widely read and performed texts. Though David Williamson remains the most successful playwright, the energetic, topical and celebratory drama of the 1970s has to some extent been supplanted by a more urbane, cosmopolitan and even cerebral style in the work of LOUIS NOWRA and STEPHEN SEWELL; other established playwrights include Steve J. Spears (whose monodrama *The Elocution of Benjamin Franklin* won the New York Critics' OFF-BROADWAY Award for 1980), Ron Elisha, Doreen Clark, Jennifer Compton, Hannie Rayson, David Allen, George Hutchinson, ALMA DE GROEN, Kath Thomson, Jill Shearer, Barry Dickins, MICHAEL GOW, and director-writer Nick Enright, who has also created several musicals with Terence Clarke. The solo performers Reg Livermore, with his outrageous lampoons of reactionary social attitudes, and Max Gillies, a brilliant mimic of political and public figures, are the successors to Barry Humphries in satirizing Australian society.

Three important areas of growth are youth, women's and Aboriginal theatre. The Patch Theatre in Adelaide, and numerous children's theatre and THEATRE-IN-EDUCATION teams – including Arena in Melbourne and Jigsaw in Canberra; Toe Truck, Pipi Storm, Pact and the Theatre of the Deaf in Sydney; the Magpie team in Adelaide and Salamanca company in Hobart; and PUPPET companies such as Handspan in Melbourne, Spare Parts in Perth, and the Marionette Theatre of Australia in Sydney – have all presented schools shows or holiday entertainment. There are also participatory youth theatres such as the Carclew Youth Performing Arts Centre in Adelaide, and the Australian Theatre for Young People and Shopfront in Sydney; the latter has since 1977 conducted national Young Playwrights' Conferences, and in 1985 initiated the first international Young Playwrights' Conference in Sydney. Youth theatre festivals are held in most cities, with the annual 'Come Out' festival in Adelaide as the major national event.

Women's theatre largely began in the early 1970s when an offshoot of the Carlton alternative theatre, the Women's Theatre Group, provided opportunities for performers, directors and writers such as Val Kirwin, Jan Cornall, Jenny Kemp, Kerry Dwyer and Fay Mokotow, while in Sydney in 1981–2 a Women and Theatre Project for established professionals was funded by the Australia Council. Among the many groups featuring women's theatre have been the Canberra group Fool's Gallery, directed by Carol Woodrow, Women on a Shoestring, also in Canberra, Vitalstatistix in Adelaide, Women in Comfortable Shoes Theatre Company in Melbourne, and Home Cooking in Melbourne and later Darwin; while the singer-author Robyn Archer has brought a wider public to theatre with a feminist orientation through shows such as *The Pack of Women* (1983), a cabaret-style evening of songs, poems and sketches first performed in London, *Café Fledermaus* (1990), a satirical portrait of Viennese life in the first half of this century, and *See Ya Next Century* (1993), commenting on the present and future state of the world. Peta Murray's *Wallflowering* (1989), showing a middle-aged couple's adjustment to feminism, and Katherine Thomson's *Diving for Pearls* (1991) and *Barmaids* (1992) have been popular successes. Other new writers include Tobsha Learner, Sandra Shotlander, Hilary Bell, Karen Mainwaring, Rhondda Fleming, Tes Lyssiotis and Andrea Lemon, who works with the performer Sarah Cathcart.

In the early 1970s, following a revue titled *Basically Black* (1972) at Nimrod Theatre, a Black Theatre group was created under the direction of Betty Fisher in Redfern, a Sydney inner suburb with a large urban Aboriginal population. Its most notable production was Robert Merritt's *The Cake Man* (1975), a depiction of so-called 'benevolent' white influence on Aboriginal life which represented Australia at the World Theatre Festival in Denver, Colorado, in 1982. One of the most significant developments of the 1980s was the emergence of a vigorous, sophisticated and varied Aboriginal theatre and drama, widely staged throughout Australia and also seen overseas. Perth poet JACK DAVIS has become one of Australia's most notable playwrights; other writers include Richard Walley (*Coordah*, 1987; *Munjong*, 1990), Sally Morgan (*Sistergirl*, 1992), Eva Johnson (*Murras*, 1988), and the director Bob Maza (*The Keepers*, 1988). Aboriginal Playwrights Conferences in 1987 (when an Aboriginal National Theatre Trust was formed) and 1989 have encouraged new writers. Bob Maza, Justine Saunders, Jack Charles and Ernie Dingo are noted Aboriginal performers. The MUSICAL *Bran Nue Dae*, by Jimmy Chi and the Broome band Kuckles, which premiered at the 1990 Perth Festival, subsequently became a major success throughout

Australia; a new production by Black Swan Theatre in Perth, with a chorus enlarged through a training scheme for Aboriginal performers, began a return Australian tour in 1993. In performances using dance, song, traditional musical instruments, story-telling and dramatic interludes, groups throughout Australia now present Aboriginal culture, traditional and contemporary. These include the Aboriginal Islander Dance Theatre Company, a Sydney-based training school and company which has made a number of overseas tours; the Bangarra Dance Theatre in Sydney, formed in 1989 by graduates of the AIDTC; the Eora group in Sydney's inner suburb of Redfern; and Ilbjerri, an Aboriginal and Torres Strait Islander theatre company.

The 1980s and 1990s have seen a renewal of 'alternative' theatre, though less directly political and writer-orientated than that of the 1960s. Political and popular groups such as the Popular Theatre Troupe in Queensland and Death-Defying Theatre in Sydney have performed in shopping centres, factories and schools, but the fringe theatre of the 1980s seemed directed more to the exploration of theatrical styles, sometimes through evocative images, as in the All Out Ensemble's work and Kim Carpenter's Theatre of Image, and sometimes in combination with MIME and dance in companies such as Entr'acte and the One Extra Company in Sydney. The Sydney Dance Company, under its director Graeme Murphy, has also been particularly innovative in combining modern dance with theatrical and dramatic qualities. Contemporary dance groups such as Meryl Tankard's Australian Dance Theatre in Adelaide, the Chrissie Parrott Dance Company in Perth, Leigh Warren and Dancers from Adelaide, and Paul Mercurio's Sydney-based collective, the Australian Choreographic Ensemble, have proliferated; a more radical combination of mime, acrobatics and comedy is found in companies such as Legs on the Wall, Etcetera Inc., and the Popular Mechanicals. A feature of the 1990s has been actors' creation of their own material, singly or in small companies, and the direct exploration of the performers' own experience in groups such as Open City. Numerous theatre restaurants and CABARET-style venues, and the annual Melbourne Comedy Festival, have led to a resurgence of often anarchic comedy from comedians such as the Melbourne duo Los Trios Ringbarkus and the trio the Doug Anthony Allstars, the Sydney group Funny Stories, and a large number of stand-up comics, many of whom, like Maryanne Fahey, Jean Kittson and Sue Ingleton, deal specifically with women's issues.

If the 1970s impetus was towards nationalism, the more recent emphasis has been on decentralization and diversification. Australia has 17 million people on a continent almost the size of the United States, but the concentration of population in the capital cities (Sydney and Melbourne together have over one-third of the population) has inevitably led to theatre's focus on the urban areas, and recently to a drift towards the largest city, Sydney – compounded in the view of some by the Australia Council's headquarters being in that city. Extensive touring in country areas has not always proved feasible, and regionally based theatres such as the Riverina Theatre Company on the Victorian–New South Wales border, and the Hunter Valley Theatre Company in regional New South Wales, as well as companies in many larger towns throughout the country, have been established to counter the isolation of country communities from the performing arts.

The Australia Council's policy from 1986 has been to limit grants to the major companies to an indexed 'ceiling', in order to promote a wider range of smaller groups more closely related to specific audiences. In some rural areas theatre-in-education teams and community theatres have already developed a strong local identity, and regional growth of this kind is the present aim of funding. Community theatre groups, both urban and regional, are also encouraged, some fully professional companies focusing on local issues, and other participatory groups in which professional leaders work with local amateurs or disadvantaged groups such as the physically handicapped and unemployed. The Australia Council's art-in-working-life policy encourages performances staged in work-places such as factories and building sites, for audiences who would otherwise not have access to theatre. The Victorian College of the Arts, the second major training institution for theatre professionals (the third is the Western Australian Academy of the Performing Arts), and many of the training courses in the newer universities, place a strong emphasis on community theatre arts in addition to traditional theatre skills. Regional and grass-roots growth, it is hoped, will bring the performing arts to those formerly isolated, either geographically or socially, from mainstream theatre, though the development has not been without its critics among those who see theatre in more traditional terms.

Television drama Australia gained television in 1956; besides a government-funded national network run by the ABC (Australian Broadcasting Corporation), there are a number of commercial networks – the larger cities each have three commercial channels – and since 1980 there has been a government-sponsored multicultural channel in several cities. Initially local drama was submerged by British and American imports, though Crawford Productions' police series *Homicide*, beginning in 1964, and the ABC's serial of country life, *Bellbird* (1967–77), had popular followings. From 1967 a quota for locally produced drama was imposed on the commercial channels, initially 30 minutes per week, and currently 102 hours per year. This, with the founding in 1973 of a national Film and Television School in Sydney (there is a second training institution at the Swinburne Institute of Technology in Melbourne), has led to a marked increase in both the quantity and the quality of local drama.

Since the 1970s local serials and series, most created by the two major production companies, Crawfords and the Grundy Organization, have become a feature of commercial television. Among the longest-running have been *The Sullivans* (1976–83), showing a working-class family during war years; the hospital series *The Young Doctors* (1976–82); the domestic dramas *The Restless Years* (1977–82) and *Sons and Daughters* (1982–); *Prisoner* (1979–), set in a women's penitentiary; and *A Country Practice* (1981–), set in a country town. While similar to American soap operas, such serials are an important balance to the still dominant imported drama, and sometimes explore current social issues. The ABC has produced many high-quality shorter serials, including the goldmining story *Rush* (1973–4) in collaboration with France's Antenne 2 and Scottish Global Television; the bushranging drama *Ben Hall* (1974–5), a joint Australian–Canadian production; *I Can Jump Puddles* (1980–1), the story of a country youth between the wars; *Scales of Justice* (1983), an exposé of police corruption; and *Palace of Dreams* (1985), a story of Jewish immigrants in Sydney. It has also presented seasons of television plays and comedy series, though neither the self-contained play nor situation comedy has been as important in Australia as in some other countries.

The 1980s saw a number of mini-series, thanks to the federal government's generous tax concessions from 1981 for investment in Australian films, now replaced by the Film Finance Corporation. Produced by companies such as Kennedy Miller for the commercial channels, some, like the Pegasus production *Against the Wind* (1979), have been set in the colonial past; others, including *Waterfront* (1985) and *Bodyline* (1984), have been set in the more recent past. Among the more controversial have been *The Dismissal* (1983), a semi-documentary depicting the 1975 Labour government's dismissal from office; *The Last Bastion* (1984), exposing the Allies' tenuous commitment to Australia in the Second World War; *The Cowra Breakout* (1985), based on the escape attempt of Japanese prisoners-of-war in a country town; *Brides of Christ* (1991), set in a Catholic girls' school in the 1960s; and *The Leaving of Liverpool* (1992), the harrowing story of British children taken to Australia as orphans during the Second World War. These mini-series have been culturally significant in bringing local drama to a wide audience, and sometimes in provoking heated re-examination of Australian history. (See also TELEVISION DRAMA.)

Prospects Much diverse theatrical activity has developed in the 40 years since the founding of the Elizabethan Theatre Trust. That the increasing respectability and acceptance of theatre in the 1980s was gained at the expense of the nationalistic fervour and exuberance of the 1970s was perhaps inevitable after heady pioneering days, and perhaps also a reflection of grimmer economic times. In particular the more cosmopolitan drama of Nowra and Sewell, after the earlier 'folk' drama of the previous decade, has tended to polarize those who believe the theatre's function is to celebrate and explore Australian society, and those who see theatre in less localized terms. The vitality, irreverence and freshness of theatre in the 1990s, ranging from stylistic exploration to social comment, is evidence that the two aims need not be incompatible.

Australian theatre in the 1990s reflects Australia's position as one of the most culturally diverse societies in the world. Increasingly this diversity is the subject of plays, including Richard Barrett's *The Heartbreak Kid* (1987), a school romance between Greek teacher and student; Janis Balodis's two plays on Latvian immigrants, *Too Young for Ghosts* (1985) and *No Going Back* (1993), and Peta Murray's *One Woman's Song* (1993), a tribute to the Aboriginal poet and activist Ooodjeroo of the tribe Noonuccal (formerly known as Kath Walker).

Australia is closer to Asia than to anywhere except New Zealand, and immigration, business and travel contacts have greatly strengthened its ties with the Pacific region. Individual directors and groups such as Rex Cramphorn's Performance Syndicate in the 1970s have explored Asian styles, and cultural exchange with Asia has been frequent. In 1983–4 Chinese acrobats from Nanjing spent several months training the children of the Albury-based Flying Fruit Fly Circus, Japanese artists have worked with Australian puppetry companies, and the Western Australia Ballet is developing a relationship with the Singapore Dance Theatre. The One Extra Company's director until 1991 was Kai Tai Chan, a Malaysian Chinese who has since worked with the Chinese group, City Contemporary Dance Company. Sydney's Sidetrack Theatre, and the Australian People's Theatre attached to the Sydney Theatre Company, both have multicultural acting companies, and bilingual performances are not uncommon – such as those by Teresa Crea and the Adelaide-based Italian company Doppio Teatro, and the plays of Tes Lyssiotis, notably *The Forty Lounge Café* (1990), based on her Greek mother's life in an Australian country town.

Under the auspices of the Multicultural Theatre Alliance a number of groups are devising their own performances in languages other than English, and finding new audiences. The huge popular success of the Greek revue-style piece *Wogs out of Work* in 1988, satirizing stereotypical attitudes to immigrant Australians, led to a long-running television comedy series, *Acropolis Now*; and the 'Wogs' sequel in 1993, *Wog-a-Rama*, now incorporates Aboriginal and Vietnamese characters. With many new performers and directors also coming from non-English-speaking backgrounds, after almost two centuries of predominantly European orientation Australian theatre is becoming remarkably diverse and eclectic.   MW

See: J. Allen (ed.), *Entertainment Arts in Australia*, Sydney, 1968; M. Clunies Ross, 'North-Central Arnhem Land'; C. Ellis, 'Antatirinya Dance'; A. Grau, 'YOI: The Dance of the Tiwi'; M. Llinos Dail-Jones, 'Warlpiri Dance'; J. von Sturmer, 'Cape York Peninsula'; S. Wild, 'Australian Aboriginal Dance' – all in *International Encyclopaedia of Dance*, ed. S. J. Cohen, Univ. of California, Berkeley, 1991; P. Fitzpatrick, *After 'The Doll'*, Melbourne, 1979; P. Holloway (ed.), *Contemporary Australian Drama*, Sydney, 1987; E. Irvin, *Theatre Comes to Australia*, St Lucia, 1971, and *A Dictionary of the Australian Theatre*, Sydney, 1985; H. Love, *The Golden Age of Australian Opera*, Sydney, 1981, and (ed.), *The Australian Stage: A Documentary History*, Sydney, 1984; L. Rees, *A History of Australian Drama*, Sydney, 1978; J. West, *Theatre in Australia*, Sydney, 1978; M. Williams, *Australia on the Popular Stage, 1829–1929*, Melbourne, 1983.

Austria

To 1914 The cultural traditions of Austria are quite distinct from those of her larger neighbour, Germany. This is clearly apparent in the history of their respective theatres. While professional theatre in Germany was, for much of the 18th century, an alien hybrid, the Austrian theatre was an indigenous phenomenon, growing spontaneously as a popular institution. Furthermore, unlike Germany, whose theatrical tradition has grown around several provincial cities, in Austria most significant developments in the theatre have taken place in the capital city, Vienna.

During the Middle Ages, Vienna had been a major centre for the production of religious drama, PASSION PLAYS with massive casts being given in various locales of the city on Good Friday and CORPUS CHRISTI. The familiarity of the Viennese with theatre no doubt eased the way for the acceptance of secular, humanistic drama, based on Roman models, staged under the aegis of Konrad Celtis (1459–1508) at the University of Vienna early in the 16th century. But no continuous theatrical activity occurred at this time; indeed, it was not until the mid-17th century that the three modes of theatre that would have a potent formative influence on the subsequent development of Austrian theatre had fully evolved. The first of these was the Jesuit drama (see *JESUITENDRAMA*), which was to give the Austrian theatre one of its most characteristic themes, the conflict between supernatural and human planes of experience; it flourished in the schools. The second was the *COMMEDIA DELL'ARTE*, which engendered in audiences and actors alike a strong taste for improvisation, and could be seen in the work of several travelling Italian troupes and, occasionally, in the ENGLISCHE KOMÖDIANTEN. Thirdly, there was Italian OPERA, first produced solely at the Habsburg court, but it gained in popularity and created among the Viennese a widespread taste for musical expression and lavish spectacle on stage.

These three forms of theatre were gradually united on the Viennese stage in the course of the 18th century, forming one of the most attractive theatrical cultures of Europe. The founding of the popular theatre has traditionally been dated as 1711 when JOSEF STRANITZKY, an improvisational player who led his own wandering troupe, took over the Kärntnertortheater in Vienna from an Italian company. He instantly won the support of the populace for his racy plays on local life, which required considerable improvisation. Stranitzky was also famed for his creation of the generic figure of HANSWURST, a wily, coarse servant, initially of rustic origin, but after Stranitzky's translation to Vienna he was made into an urban figure who had much in common with his Italian counterpart HARLEQUIN. The irreverent spirit of Hanswurst was the dominant influence on the early years of the Viennese popular theatre, but in the hands of Stranitzky's successor GOTTFRIED PREHAUSER and, later, the comic actor Josef Felix Kurz (1717–83) the tone was softened, even sentimentalized, greater attention being paid on the one hand to realistic characterization, on the other to the relationship between the human and magic world – a concern which links the Viennese popular drama with its Jesuit predecessors. During the middle of the 18th century, improvisation gradually disappeared from the stage. Though this change might initially seem to indicate a decline in energy, towards the end of the century the Viennese theatre produced one of the greatest works of any popular theatrical tradition, *The Magic Flute* (1791) by Mozart and SCHIKANEDER.

The change in the popular theatre was caused in part by external pressure. JOSEF VON SONNENFELS, one of the Viennese literati, was a follower of the German professor JOHANN GOTTSCHED, and in his *Letters on the Viennese Stage* (1767) he advocated a decorous, unimprovised drama that could lead towards the education of the populace. These ideas were fundamental to the establishment by the Emperor Josef II of the Habsburg Court Theatre, the BURGTHEATER, as a national theatre. Despite early vicissitudes, this grew to be the pre-eminent theatre of the German-speaking world. During the 19th century, especially under the direction of JOSEF SCHREYVOGEL and HEINRICH LAUBE, the repertoire came to include all ages and styles of Western drama, while the elegant underplaying and ensemble of the Burgtheater's famous company became a byword in the German theatre. Although the Burgtheater has always regarded itself as an 'actor's theatre', it has also had some notable house playwrights, especially during the 19th century. By far the most important was FRANZ GRILLPARZER, whose adaptation of various foreign forms of drama, especially of the ancient Greek and Spanish baroque, was very characteristic of his country's international outlook. EDUARD VON BAUERNFELD, whose skilfully written, light comedies of Viennese life were immensely popular in his time, was another of the mainstays of the Burgtheater repertoire during the 19th century.

The great resilience of Viennese theatre is demonstrated by the refusal of the popular theatre to be overshadowed by the successful and prestigious Burgtheater. In fact, despite Sonnenfels's wish to extinguish the popular theatre, the last decades of the 18th century and the first half of the 19th represent the full flowering of this theatre. In addition to *The Magic Flute*, the 18th century saw other significant additions to the popular repertoire, most notably in the plays of Philipp Hafner, whose famous work *Megära the Terrible Witch* (1755) is possibly the first example of the Viennese VOLKSSTÜCK (folk play), in which magic and human characters are mingled.

The turn of the century saw countless additions to the repertoire, most significantly in the highly theatrical plays of the prolific ALOIS GLEICH, KARL MEISL and ADOLPHE BÄUERLE. While the literary level of their works is not especially high, a colleague of these playwrights, FERDINAND RAIMUND, made out of the magic *Volksstück*, or *Zauberstück*, plays that are among the few masterpieces of the romantic theatre, especially *The Alpine King and the Misanthrope* (1828) and *The Spendthrift* (1834). Raimund committed suicide, possibly in apprehension of the rise of a new playwright, whose work seemed to threaten the fundamental assumptions and integrated vision of the *Zauberstück*, JOHANN NESTROY. Over the middle of the 19th century, in Nestroy's plays the satirical vein of the popular theatre, which had never entirely disappeared, reached complete fulfilment. In fact, Nestroy's dramatic work, both parodies and social comedies, possibly represents the most consummate achievement in stage comedy in the German language. After Nestroy's retirement in 1860, the energy seemed to leave the popular theatre. In its years of decline, the most characteristic genre of the popular theatre was the attractive though comparatively devitalized OPERETTA.

During its heyday, the Viennese popular theatre, like the Burgtheater, maintained an unusually sophisticated level of acting. Several actors, like Stranitzky with Hanswurst, evolved generic comic figures; Kurz was responsible for introducing the figure of Bernadon, a young adventurer; Johann Laroche (1745–1806) introduced KASPER, a figure with some affinities to PUNCH; and Anton Hasenhut (1766–1841) created the pathetic Thaddädl. These characters recurred in several of the hundreds of plays that composed the popular repertoire, and the audiences' affection for them ensured well packed auditoriums. The particular enjoyment of the Viennese audiences for the discipline of acting suggests that improvisation did not disappear entirely from the stage; in fact Nestroy, as versatile and celebrated an actor as he was a playwright, was occasionally in trouble for passages of action, for speeches and ripostes, that had not passed the censor's approval (see CENSORSHIP), as they had been made up on the spur of the moment.

The widespread popularity of theatre in Vienna meant a consistent expansion in the number of theatres. In its most flourishing years, three of the most famous 'suburban' theatres – i.e. those theatres not in the city centre like the Burgtheater – opened their doors; of these, two, the Theater in der Josefstadt and the Theater an der Wien, are still in use today. The third, the Theater in der Leopoldstadt, was replaced by the Carltheater in the middle of the 19th century. The abundance of theatres in Vienna has led several historians to characterize it as quintessentially a 'theatre city'. Although this epithet has been used to describe the supposedly Viennese trait of treating life as a play, as if in ironic denial of its more serious aspects, it also identifies the unique role of theatre in the city's social life. In the early 19th century the suburban theatres and the Burgtheater dominated, but as the century progressed, several more theatres opened, such as the Stadttheater (1880) and the Deutsches Volkstheater (1889), which attempted a more serious repertoire than the declining popular theatre. In addition, the Court Opera, which opened a splendid new opera house on the Ringstrasse in 1869, was one of the centres of the city's closely aligned musical and theatre lives.

As the popular theatre declined during the latter half of the 19th century, the most successful works of Raimund and Nestroy passed into the Burgtheater repertoire. Meanwhile, a school of playwriting emerged which owed as much to European as it did to Viennese models. A deep concern with the injustices and deprivations of everyday life had been apparent in the rather grim, realistic plays of LUDWIG ANZENGRUBER, who wrote about the peasantry as well as about city life. However, both a more characteristically Viennese note and a European tone could be heard in the plays of ARTHUR SCHNITZLER, all of which are impressionistic or naturalistic dramatizations of Viennese life. In them the playwright's unceasing and stringent irony points towards, though never rigorously spells out, a moralistic judgement of the city's society, especially in matters of sexual morality.

Early in life Schnitzler belonged to an informal group of writers known as Jung Wien (Young Vienna), who were set upon modernizing the city's literature. Among the most prominent writers in this group were HERMANN BAHR, who achieved more as a contentious theatre critic and as an interpreter of contemporary literary theory than as a dramatist, and HUGO VON HOFMANNSTHAL. As a young man, Hofmannsthal wrote verse drama that showed clearly the influence of French SYMBOLISM. Later, having suffered a crisis of confidence in the ability of language to express his thoughts effectively, Hofmannsthal turned to writing librettos for the opera composer, Richard Strauss. Hofmannsthal did not, however, abandon the legitimate theatre, and his later plays are remarkable for their author's ability to combine a concern for the modern world with traditional dramatic material. In this respect his greatest and most Austrian play is *The Tower*. Not only does the play focus on the rise of totalitarianism, but thematically it expresses the tension between human and supernatural planes of experience. In this play, Hofmannsthal's rich, allusive technique reminds us of past ages of drama, of SHAKESPEARE, the Spanish baroque (it is based on CALDERÓN's *Life Is a Dream*), and the various indigenous forms of Austrian drama. This arouses in the audience a profound sense of what has been lost by the modern world. In doing so the play expresses in the most positive and humane way its country's characteristic, deep attachment to the past. SW

Since 1914 With the First World War and the destruction of the Austro-Hungarian Empire, Austrian theatre effectively lost its existence as an independent entity, becoming increasingly integrated with that of Germany. Sharing much of the same history of the dissolution of the monarchy and a weak republic, the Anschluss and Fascism – which drove almost all the leading writers into exile and shut down the stages completely in 1945 – plus foreign occupation and, more recently, a high standard of material prosperity, Austrian dramatists have been preoccupied with the same kind of themes as their German counterparts, and adopted comparable styles of representation. In addition there has been a continual interchange of actors and directors, with MAX PALLENBERG, FRITZ KORTNER and, in the younger generation, HANS HOLLMANN, who established themselves on the German stage; and BERTHOLD VIERTEL, who eventually returned to lead the rebuilt Vienna Burgtheater after making his reputation at the DEUTSCHES THEATER in Berlin and working with the BERLINER ENSEMBLE.

Despite the dominance of Berlin as a centre for theatrical experimentation during the 1920s, however, this influence has by no means been one-sided. It was an Austrian, MAX REINHARDT, who became perhaps the most significant single figure in German theatre during the first part of the century with his eclectic range of productions. His stagings of WEDEKIND and STRINDBERG (1912–13) set the style for early expressionist works, and it was under his aegis at the Deutsches Theater that the plays of the Young Germany movement were performed, while productions like Karl Vollmoeller's *Miracle* (1917) brought the traditional Austrian religious themes and spectacular pageant production to Germany. But he also founded the modern Salzburg Festival together with Hofmannsthal in 1918, which under Reinhardt's direction became the leading festival theatre in Europe, characterized by his open-air productions of Hofmannsthal's *Everyman*.

Even in movements specifically identified with Germany such as EXPRESSIONISM, Austrian dramatists made significant contributions. OSKAR KOKOSCHKA's work prefigured its violent sexual themes and psychological symbolism as early as 1910, ARNOLT BRONNEN and FRANZ WERFEL were among its leading exponents, while the drama of Anton Wildgans (1881–1932), who also directed the Burgtheater during the 1920s, transposed expressionist elements into a distinctively Austrian form. Alongside this avant-garde work, traditional Austrian theatre continued to flourish with the revival of the MIRACLE PLAY by Max Mell (1882–1971), the historical tragedies of Richard Beer-Hoffman and FERDINAND BRUCKNER, both of whom turned to themes of radical persecution in response to the Jewish Holocaust, and the drama of ideas developed by FRITZ HOCHWÄLDER.

Successful as they were, these traditional works seem dated from a modern perspective in contrast to the plays of ÖDÖN VON HORVÁTH. Following KARL KRAUS and Franz Csokor (1885–1969), he transformed the satiric popular theatre of Nestroy into highly political images of social hypocrisy and the corruption of cultural values. Rediscovered in the 1960s, his work inspired the modern *Volksstück*, one of the major forms of contemporary German drama, whose Austrian exponents are WOLFGANG BAUER, Harald Sommer (b.1935) and PETER TURRINI. Another influence has been the Vienna Group, active between 1954 and 1964. Its playwrights Konrad Bayer (1932–64) and H. C. Artmann (b.1921) adapted the traditional Kasper figure for dialect dramas that prefigure the linguistic themes of PETER HANDKE, whose experimental 'speaking plays' have achieved an international reputation, while his later surrealistic drama (see SURREALISM) – like the nihilistic symbolism of the other leading contemporary Austrian playwright, THOMAS BERNHARD – continues to be recognized as among the most significant work on the contemporary German-speaking stage. CI

See: C.E. Williams, *The Broken Eagle: The Politics of Austrian Literature from Empire to Anschluss*, London, 1974.

auto sacramental In medieval Spain, a one-act play, religious or secular. Early authors of religious *autos* included JUAN DEL ENCINA and GIL VICENTE. By the mid-16th century *auto sacramental* denoted an allegory of eucharistic theme performed at the feast of Corpus Christi. TIRSO DE MOLINA, LOPE DE VEGA and others contributed to the form, which culminated with CALDERÓN, sole author of Madrid's *autos* from 1648 to 1681. The highly visual spectacles were staged outdoors with scenery mounted on carts. In 1765, under the Bourbon Enlightenment, these symbolic works were suppressed. (See also MEDIEVAL DRAMA IN EUROPE.) PZ

Averchenko, Arkady (Timofeevich) 1881–1925 Russian writer of humorous stories, *feuilletons* and dramatic miniatures satirizing contemporary mores, vulgarity, pretence and artistic trends. He contributed to and was eventual editor of St Petersburg's leading satirical weekly, *Satyricon* (1908–14), whose staff included writers N. A. Teffi, B. F. Geier and MIKHAIL KUZMIN and artists ALEXANDRE BENOIS and M. V. Dobuzhinsky. Averchenko left in 1913 to edit *New Satyricon*, until it was closed for publishing anti-Bolshevik SATIRE. From 1912 to 16 he contributed short comic sketches and *vaudevilles* to the Liteiny, Crooked Mirror and Troitsky Theatres in St Petersburg. These included parodies of LEV TOLSTOI's *The*

Power of Darkness and of FUTURISM (Woe from Futurism). He published four volumes of one-act plays and miniatures, a highly popular collection of stories entitled Jolly Oysters (1910), the three-volume Stories (1910–11), and in 1920 the anti-Bolshevik collection Unclean Power, which led to his emigration that same year, eventually ending in Prague (1922). SG

Avignon Festival French theatre festival established by JEAN VILAR in 1947 in order to provide a context for theatre-going different from that of the Paris BOULEVARD theatres. The Festival was, and still is, held in July, when commercial and state theatres in France are closed. Vilar's work at Avignon successfully created an atmosphere of celebration and participation, and laid the foundations for his production style at the THÉÂTRE NATIONAL POPULAIRE in the 1950s; his choice of Avignon helped give impetus to the DECENTRALIZATION MOVEMENT. The Avignon Festival grew rapidly in the 1960s and 70s and is now one of the largest and most prestigious in the world. It has played a significant role in the development of French theatre at large, especially in the introduction of foreign influences – such as the LIVING THEATRE, who called the whole Festival into question in 1968, or, more recently, the Polish company of TADEUSZ KANTOR. DB

Avilés Blonda, Máximo 1931– Dominican Republic playwright and poet, with degrees in philosophy and law; founder and director of the University Theatre. Las manos vacías (Empty Hands, 1959) is a postwar study; La otra estrella en el cielo (The Other Star in the Sky, 1963) deals metaphorically with a 15th-century Italian struggle for power: Yo, Bertolt Brecht (I, Bertolt Brecht, 1966) is a vanguardist adaptation of epic scenes, and Pirámide 179 (Pyramid 179, 1969) applies BRECHTian techniques to national hatred over the Haitian boundary issue. GW

Ayalneh Mulat fl.1970s Ethiopian playwright. After being director of the University of Addis Ababa Cultural

Centre, Ayalneh was for some years responsible for culture at the Commission for the Party of the Working People of Ethiopia. In the early days of the Marxist state he was a popular writer of pro-revolutionary, AGIT-PROP theatre. His plays include Isat Sined (When the Fire Is Burning, 1975), Shater Beyeferiu (Sabotage in Different Colours), The Peasant Woman's Beacon (1977) and Pumpkin and Gourd (1979). He is now once more director of the University Cultural Centre. JPL

Ayckbourn, Alan 1939– British playwright, director and actor, who has written nearly 50 full-length plays, as well as directing and running his own company in Scarborough. He began his career as a stage manager and actor with DONALD WOLFIT's touring company, joined STEPHEN JOSEPH's theatre-in-the-round at Scarborough in 1959, became a drama producer with the BBC in Leeds and a founder of the VICTORIA THEATRE, Stoke-on-Trent, before returning to Scarborough as director of productions in 1970.

Ayckbourn has been the most successful writer of sharp comedies about middle-class manners and morals since the war, and his only rival internationally would be the American dramatist, NEIL SIMON. Although his first play to reach the WEST END, Mr Whatnot, was written in 1963, Ayckbourn's major commercial successes began with Relatively Speaking (London, 1967) and How the Other Half Loves (1970). Throughout the 1970s he was prolific – with a sequence of COMEDY hits which started with Time and Time Again (1971) and Absurd Person Singular (1973), rose to the complicated heights of The Norman Conquests (1974), a trilogy of plays set in different areas of one house over one weekend, and was rewarded by productions at the NATIONAL THEATRE of Bedroom Farce (1977), Sisterly Feelings (1980), Way Upstream (1982) and his own production of A Small Family Business (1987).

Ayckbourn's plays have received critical acclaim and popular approval, despite the predictable objection that they have concentrated on too narrow a class range in life.

Alan Ayckbourn's *Way Upstream*, National Theatre, London 1982.

His success is partly due to a rare professionalism in writing plays, revealed through his brilliantly terse dialogue and intricate situations, but it also comes from his clear observation of how people behave. His humour is tinged with sadness and sometimes bitterness, but his most remarkable quality is his evenness of tone. In *Henceforward* (1988), with its elements of science-fiction, in *Man of the Moment* (1989) about a bank clerk living in the south of Spain, in *Body Language* (1990) where a plump brainy girl and a skinny dumb model exchange bodies and in *The Revenger's Comedies* (1991), the same qualities of craftsmanship prevail. His children's plays, *This Is Where We Come In* (1990) and *Callisto 5* (1990), are intricate puzzle games. WILDEST DREAMS (1993) is a dark comedy with the appearance of a sit-com but the substance of a sci-fi psychodrama. Some friends eke out their lonely suburban lives by playing fantasy board games, but their wildest dreams are not as extreme as the different realities from which they are trying to escape. Ayckbourn directed ARTHUR MILLER's *A View from the Bridge* (1987) for the NT, where he became an associate director, and *Othello* (1990) for his Scarborough theatre, both with MICHAEL GAMBON, an actor with whom he has frequently worked.

Until 1992, Ayckbourn was thought to have a weakness with MUSICALS, demonstrated by one of his rare flops, *Jeeves* (1975); but *Dreams from a Summer House* (1992) was an effective musical play, whose songs parody a range of musicals and operettas without ceasing to be part of a good plot. With that last chink in his professional armour closed, he can lay a claim to being the most complete all-rounder in British theatre.   JE

Ayers, Lemuel 1915–55 American scenic and COSTUME designer. From the late 1930s until his death, Ayers designed some of BROADWAY's most memorable plays and MUSICALS including *Oklahoma!* (1943), *Kiss Me, Kate* (also co-produced; 1948), *Camino Real* (1953) and *Pajama Game* (1954). He developed a painterly, almost whimsical style, but was also capable of evocative REALISM as in *Angel Street* (1941), which had an unusually shallow set painted on black velour.   AA

Ayrer, Jacob 1543–1601 German playwright. Several of the plays of this popular and extremely prolific dramatist shared sources with the plays of SHAKESPEARE. However, the quality of Ayrer's drama, written as it is in *Knittelverse* (irregular popular verse), is far from Shakespearian.   SW

Azenberg, Emanuel 1934– American producer, called by the *New York Times* one of BROADWAY's 'most successful producers and one of its outspoken critics'. Although he has worked closely with the SHUBERT ORGANIZATION, in the mid-1980s he essentially left the Broadway establishment by walking out on the League of American Theatres and Producers. Although he has been producing in New York since 1961 (almost 40 Broadway plays in 30 years), his greatest successes have been since 1982. His single major client has been NEIL SIMON, all of whose plays since 1972 have been produced by Azenberg. Recent productions have included *Biloxi Blues*, a revival of *Joe Egg*, SONDHEIM's *Sunday in the Park with George* and Simon's *Lost in Yonkers* (1991). In 1990 he ventured into film by producing TOM STOPPARD's *Rosencrantz and Guildenstern Are Dead*.   DBW

Baba Sala see Adejumo, Moses Olaiya

Babanova, Mariya (Ivanovna) 1900–82 Russian-Soviet actress, former student of Fyodor Komissarzhevsky, and a mainstay of Meyerhold's acting company at the RSFSR (Russian Soviet Federated Socialist Republic) Theatre 1, the Moscow Theatre of the Revolution and the Meyerhold Theatre (1920–7). Babanova brought humanity, lyricism, psychological depth, a melodic voice, strong rhythmic sense and a child-like quality to her roles in Meyerhold's formalist productions, most notably Stella in Crommelynck's *The Magnanimous Cuckold* (1922), Polinka in Ostrovsky's *A Profitable Post* (1923), an erotic Maria Antonovna in Gogol's *The Inspector General* (1926) and the Chinese boy in Tretyakov's *Roar China!* (1926). Unhappy with Meyerhold's promotion of his wife Zinaida Raikh to the rank of the company's lead actress, Babanova left and appeared in a series of new Soviet plays, including Faiko's *The Man with a Briefcase* (1928), Pogodin's *Poem about an Axe* (1931) and *After the Ball* (1934) and Arbuzov's *Tanya* (1939), in which she created the new Soviet dramatic heroine. She appeared briefly as a too old Ophelia in Okhlopkov's 1954 production of *Hamlet* and played Ranevskaya in *The Cherry Orchard* (1956). Radzinsky's play *An Old Actress in the Role of Dostoevsky's Wife*, written for Babanova and partially based upon her memories of the 1920s and 30s, was completed after her death. SG

Babel, Isaak (Emmanuilovich) 1894–1941 Odessa-born Russian Jewish short story writer and dramatist, noted for his textured and polished language, careful attention to character and environmental detail and vivid sense of historical time and place. His two famous short story collections, *The Odessa Tales* (1921–3) and *Red Cavalry* (1926), are based upon personal experience. The former is a rich tapestry of the Jewish underworld in Odessa. The latter evokes the brutality of the Russian Civil War. The stories are characterized by exoticism, eroticism, moral and political ambiguity, paradox and grotesque – all qualities which impeded his full critical acceptance in the Soviet Union. His play *Sunset* (1928) borrows themes and characters from *The Odessa Tales* (which also appeared in his scenario for the film *Benya Krik*, 1926). It was successfully produced at the Moscow Art Theatre in 1928 and translated into Yiddish in 1929. His play *Mariya* (published 1935), set in Petrograd in 1920, dramatizes the disintegration of a family in the wake of the Bolshevik victory and evokes Chekhov's *The Cherry Orchard*. It was banned while in simultaneous rehearsal at the Vakhtangov Theatre and at the State Jewish Theatre, under the direction of Solomon Mikhoels. A third play, *The Chekist*, was seized and believed destroyed at Babel's arrest on undisclosed charges in 1939. The official Soviet account lists the date of his death in a prison camp as 17 March 1941. SG

Bacon, Frank 1864–1922 American actor and dramatist. A native of California, Bacon emphasized Yankee character parts in melodramas such as *Ten Nights in a Barroom* and in comedy sketches, mainly in the San Francisco area until the 1906 earthquake, when he departed for New York. There he performed in such plays as *Alabama*, *Pudd'nhead Wilson* and Winchell Smith's *The Fortune Hunter*. In *Lightnin'* (1918), written in collaboration with Smith, Bacon achieved his greatest acting success as Lightnin' Bill Jones, a charming rascal and ne'er-do-well who enjoys tall tales and strong drink. Dependent upon Bacon's acting, which he interrupted to participate in the 1919 actors' strike, the plays ran for three years, breaking the old record held by Hoyt's *A Trip to Chinatown* with 1291 performances. WJM

Bagnold, Enid [Lady Roderick Jones] 1889–1981 British playwright and novelist. Bagnold became well known in the interwar years through her novels, *Serena Blandish* (1925), which S. N. Behrman adapted for the stage (1929, New York), and *National Velvet* (1935), which was made into a film and dramatized by the author herself for the theatre. She also adapted another of her novels, *Lottie Dundas* (1943), and her later stage plays, including *The Chalk Garden* (1955, New York; 1956, London) and *The Chinese Prime Minister* (1964, New York; 1965, London), retain a literary flavour, as if written by someone who was not closely in touch with the shifts of theatrical fashion. Of her plays *The Chalk Garden* was the most successful, described by Kenneth Tynan as perhaps 'the finest artificial comedy to have flowed from an English (as opposed to Irish) pen since the death of Congreve'. *The Last Joke* (1960) and *Call Me Jacky* (1967) failed to find a public in either New York or London, although the latter was revived as *A Matter of Gravity* with Katharine Hepburn in 1976. JE

Bahr, Hermann 1863–1934 Austrian playwright and critic. After some years as a student in Germany, Bahr settled in Vienna, where he became a leading light of an informal group of writers known as Jung Wien (Young Vienna), whose intent was to introduce into Viennese literature themes and literary modes of the avant-garde writers in other European countries. Bahr, whose prime importance was as a dramatic critic (see criticism), first introduced naturalism, which he quickly repudiated in an essay in 1891; he then acted as the harbinger of other literary movements for his Viennese readers. He was also a prolific playwright, but only his comedy *The Concert* (1909) has proved to be durable. In 1918 he was briefly part of a directorial triumvirate at the Burgtheater. SW

Baierl, Helmut 1927– German dramatist. He was dramaturge at the Deutsches Theater, then at the Berliner Ensemble, which staged *Frau Flinz* (1961), a socialist-realist version of Brecht's *Mother Courage* set during the collectivization of agriculture in the GDR, with HELENE WEIGEL in the title role.   HR

baiju The form of music-drama – literally, 'Bai drama' – found among the Bai minority, a people numbering 1.6 million according to the 1990 census and living in Western Yunnan province with their heartland in Dali. The age of the Bai drama is unclear. There is no incontrovertible evidence that it goes back further than the 18th century, but because it is folk drama the lack of written records does not necessarily show non-existence. At least one Bai authority, Yang Ming, considers that it may have a history of as much as 500 years, which would make it the oldest form of surviving minority drama in China other than that of the Tibetans.

The Bai drama is derived from the Han drama, and specially from the *yiyang qiang* system. The categorization of performers follows the pattern familiar in Han drama: *sheng*, *dan*, *jing* and *chou*. Costuming and make-up also follow the patterns favoured in the Han regional styles. Most of the stories are based on Han legends or love stories, with a few even using Chinese language. However, the Bai drama has one major feature very characteristic of Bai literature since at least the 10th century – namely, that the stanzas of the libretti are usually of four lines with seven, seven, seven and five characters respectively.

Under the People's Republic, the Bai drama has done well, except during the Cultural Revolution decade. Indeed, Bai dramatists and composers have tried, with some success, to emphasize the Bai features of the drama more than was the case in the past. One example illustrating the point is the creation by Yang Ming of a drama called *The Husband-Gazing Cloud* (*Wangfu yun*). This is not only based on a Bai legend, about a princess who marries a hunter against her father's opposition, but incorporates melody and dance special to the Bai people, making its feel very definitely more Bai than Han.   CPM

baiting Obsolete popular entertainment, notable for its cruelty. In the Roman games, specialized gladiators, the *venationes* and *bestiarii*, were set to kill exotic beasts in epic numbers, though we are told that an audience at Pompey's show pitied the massacred elephants in their frantic confusion. In the Middle Ages, the baiting of bulls was required by law as a hygienic measure prior to their slaughter by butchers, and survived in English towns like Tutbury and Stamford as 'bull-running'.

Bear-baiting may have been introduced into England by Italians during the reign of King John; it began as an exclusively aristocratic pastime, a degenerate form of hunting, until the 15th century when nobles allowed their bear wards to institute a commercial exhibition of bears at lesser manors. Erasmus wrote (c.1500) of the 'many herds of bears kept in England for the purpose of baiting'. Under Henry VIII a certain John Cooper was licensed to put on public animal combats; prior to 1574, there were two baiting rings in London, but by SHAKESPEARE's day, they had merged into one, the Bear Garden, which was permitted to play on Sunday (when playhouses were closed) until 1603. This monopoly of Sunday amusement had led to a collapse of the building beneath an overflow crowd in 1583, and

the Bear Garden was immediately rebuilt as a three-storey amphitheatre, managed by HENSLOWE of the ROSE. In 1598, a German traveller, Hentzner, watched bulls and bears teased by dogs and a blind bear whipped there; its proximity to the playhouses may have enabled Shakespeare to use the genuine article when *The Winter's Tale* requires an 'Exit pursued by a bear'. Elizabeth I was a great enthusiast, and some bears enjoyed star status; in *The Merry Wives of Windsor*, Slender tells sweet Anne Page he has seen 'Sanderson' loose 20 times. The Queen's Treasury paid for the provisioning and replacement of the baiting animals, and the actor EDWARD ALLEYN was made Royal Keeper of Bulls and Mastiffs in 1604, a source of considerable profit. Three bear gardens existed in Restoration London (Evelyn thought it 'a rude and dirty pastime') and one persisted in Birmingham until 1773. Parliament finally forbade the practice in 1835, but it was carried on in private for at least another 50 years.

Bears, boars and deer were baited by dogs in Dresden in the early 17th century, and tigers and buffaloes in the later part of the century. A special amphitheatre was built to house the combats in the 18th century. Baiting was also carried on in Königsberg, Berlin, Moscow (till 1867) and Vienna, where a commercial baiting pit was opened in 1699. A new establishment was designed in 1735 by no less distinguished artists than ANTONIO GALLI DA BIBIENA and Antonio Caradini. As late as 1828, John Orlando Parry saw dogs in Paris gored and tossed to a height of 12 metres by savage bulls, bears placed on a pole with a fire above and below them, wild asses and bulldogs tearing each other to pieces, and a bull chained to a stake fighting an elkhound. Such diversions were offered for three hours every Sunday afternoon to a crowded attendance. Rats killed by terriers provided a popular sport for Victorian gamblers, as Henry Mayhew attests in his reportage. More recently, deer-baiting has been observed at Midwestern American county fairs.   LS

Baker, Benjamin (A.) 1818–90 American playwright. 'Uncle Ben Baker' deserted his prompter's post at William Mitchell's Olympic Theatre and, for Mitchell's benefit, wrote *A Glance at New York in 1848*, which opened on 15 February 1848 starring FRANK CHANFRAU as Mose. Encouraged by the 'shouts of delight from the Bowery B'hoys in the pit', and a run of 74 performances, Baker created more adventures for Mose: *New York as It Is* (1848), *Mose in California* (1849) and *Mose in China* (1850). Mose took on epic proportions as a folk hero, a man of the city who could simultaneously fight fires, sing songs, tell jokes and love women.   RAH RM

Baker, George Pierce 1866–1935 American educator, who a year after graduating from Harvard University in 1887 returned as an instructor in the English Department. In 1905, he began offering a course in playwriting entitled English 47. Three years later he founded the Harvard Dramatic Club and served as its sponsor. And in 1912 he established Workshop 47 as a laboratory theatre for plays written in English 47. The programme and Baker's growing reputation attracted to Harvard such promising talents as EUGENE O'NEILL, SIDNEY HOWARD, Thomas Wolfe, EDWARD SHELDON and PHILIP BARRY. He resigned and moved to Yale in 1925 as head of its first Department of Drama, retiring in 1933. Beginning in 1927 he worked to establish the National Theatre Conference, and served as its first president in 1932. He is remembered as a teacher and mentor to the generation of American playwrights who came to the front in the 1920s. His ideas about the craft of playwriting are set forth in *Dramatic Technique* (1919); his contributions to American theatre are explicated in W. Kinne's 1954 biography. TLM

Baker, Joséphine [*née* Josephine Freda McDonald] 1906–75 AFRICAN-AMERICAN entertainer, who left her indigent family in St Louis at the age of 16 to play in all-black REVUES in Philadelphia and New York. Her outrageous comic antics had a *succès de scandale* in Paris in *La Revue Nègre* (Théâtre des Champs-Élysées, 1925). Some celebrated her as a combination of 'boxing kangaroo, sen-sen gum and racing cyclist' (*Candide*), while moralists condemned her as the decline of the West made flesh. La Baker's rubber-limbed Charlestons and black-bottoms, and her cincture of phalliform bananas, became a fixture of Parisian night life. Her repertory of American classics ('Always'), French nostalgia ('La Petite Tonkinoise'), and the signature tune 'J'ai Deux Amours' was sung in a thin soprano. After the Second World War, when she had worked for the Resistance, she made many 'farewell tours' to raise money for the orphans she housed on her estate in Milandes. She returned to the USA in 1948 and 1951 and was active for civil rights, though as a performer she never equalled her success abroad. Needy and ailing, she died during the run of a revue at the Paris Bobino. LS

Bakst, Léon [Lev Rozenberg] 1866-1924 Russian painter and designer; emigrated to Paris in 1909. He began his stage career designing at the Hermitage, the Imperial private theatre. Bakst was a co-founder, with ALEXANDRE BENOIS, of the World of Art Group and was one of the primary designers – many believe the most significant – of the first period of the Ballets Russes, where he worked with Diaghilev until 1914. In Paris he also designed for Ida Rubinstein. Bakst's use of colour revolutionized all of Western design. Drawing on motifs, line, and palettes from ancient Greece, Egypt, central Asia and the orient, he simplified the shape and line of COSTUMES, designed costumes and sets that suggested free-flowing movement, and bathed decor in nearly overwhelming, deep, rich, sensual shades of blue, green, gold, orange and yellow (see THEATRE DESIGN). He believed that colour – and the fusion of colours – had significant emotional effects upon the spectators. This is most evident in *Scheherazade* (1910). Other significant designs include *Cléopâtre*, *L'Oiseau de feu* (*The Firebird*, 1910), *Le Dieu bleu* (1912), *Thamar* (1912), *L'Après-midi d'un faune* (1912), *Daphnis and Chloë* (1912), and *La Belle au bois dormant* (1921) with the Ballets Russes in London. AA

Balanchine, George [Georgi Balanchivadze] 1904–83 Russian-born ballet dancer-choreographer and theatre choreographer. Recognized as one of the leading figures in 20th-century dance, Balanchine is credited with establishing the American balletic style. In addition to his work in ballet, he also contributed to American MUSICAL theatrical

dance, choreographing such shows as *The ZIEGFELD Follies* (1935), *On Your Toes* (1936), *Babes in Arms* (1937) and *Song of Norway* (1937). Balanchine's theatrical choreography is considered to have been well integrated in the shows, and he never demanded the insertion of a ballet segment. His dances interpreted the essence and feeling of the musical score within the context of the script. LF

Baldwin, James (Arthur) 1924–87 African-American novelist, essayist and playwright. The most widely read of contemporary black authors, Baldwin wrote two plays. In *The Amen Corner* (produced at Howard University in 1954 and on BROADWAY in 1965) a fanatical woman pastor tries unsuccessfully to turn her son against the father whose love she has rejected. Despite a convincing performance by Beah Richards, the play was coolly received by leading critics. In *Blues for Mr Charlie* (1964) Baldwin examined racial attitudes in the murder of an angry black youth by a white bigot. The writing is often shrill, characters' motivations are questionable and the author's viewpoint remains ambivalent. EGH

Bale, John 1495-1563 English playwright. Trained as a Carmelite friar, he threw over the Roman Catholic religion and became an outspoken Protestant. His now best-known play *Kynge Johan* blends the allegorical figures of the MORALITY PLAYS with chronicle history, for a violent attack on the papacy and clerics. Of his other surviving pieces three are MYSTERY PLAYS transformed into Protestant polemic; and one, *The Three Laws*, an anti-Catholic morality. After exile in Germany he was made Bishop of Ossory in Ireland by Edward VI; he just escaped to Basle with his life and his wife under Mary, where he seems to have revised *Kynge Johan*; then returned to England and died a canon of Canterbury Cathedral in November 1563. His other great literary work was his biographical catalogue of English writers up to his time. PM

Bali see INDONESIA

Baliev, Nikita (Fyodorovich) ?1877–1936 Co-founder (with Nikolai Tarasov), director and jovial master of ceremonies of Moscow's Bat (1908–22), Russia's first real CABARET. The Bat grew out of the 'cabbage parties', the informal, in-house VARIETY evenings held at the Moscow ART THEATRE (MAT) in pre-revolutionary days during Lent when the theatres were officially closed. Baliev became part of the MAT company (1906–11) after meeting STANISLAVSKY in Berlin during the Theatre's European tour (1906). He appeared as Bread in MAETERLINCK's *The Blue Bird* and as the Guest in ANDREEV's *The Life of Man*.

The Bat began as a semi-independent, MAT-related enterprise, originally playing to an invited audience, but after 1910 and the first of two address changes, it opened its doors to the paying public. The Bat's main attraction was the rotund, moon-faced Baliev who, as Russia's first *conférencier*, was expert at improvising horseplay with the customers from the stage and cavorting in specially designed entr'acte numbers. The Bat did not imagine itself a serious artistic enterprise with an articulated aesthetic credo like the Crooked Mirror Theatre, for example. It catered to Moscow's *nouveaux riches*, not St Petersburg's intelligentsia. It offered light-hearted, slightly varied and occasionally uneven performances of sketches, MIME, COMEDY and musical acts; and, especially, short dramatizations and modestly conceived parodies of Russian classics by PUSHKIN, LERMONTOV and, above all, GOGOL. In 1920 Baliev emigrated to Paris with part of the company. As the Chauve-Souris they offered 273 performances in Paris, 175 in London and nearly 1000 in America (1920–4). After some success, its audience dried up, and the cabaret closed. SG

Ball, William 1931–91 Flamboyant, charismatic American actor-director, and founder in 1965 of the AMERICAN CONSERVATORY THEATRE in Pittsburgh. When he took the company to San Francisco in 1967 Ball almost single-handedly revived legitimate theatre in that city. In 1986 he resigned amid financial and artistic controversy, leaving behind a career record of over 300 productions, 87 of which he directed (including legendary productions of *The Taming of the Shrew* (1976) and *Cyrano de Bergerac* (1974) – both subsequently televised). Prior to ACT, Ball had acted with regional companies and SHAKESPEARE festivals, and in the late 1950s and early 60s directed several award-winning OFF-BROADWAY productions, in 1964 directing two plays for Lincoln Center (at the ANTA Theatre (see AMERICAN NATIONAL THEATRE AND ACADEMY), Washington Square). His book, *A Sense of Direction: Some Observations on the Art of Directing*, was published in 1984. DBW

ballad opera Although called a type of OPERA, ballad opera is more nearly a play interspersed with songs, the songs having new words set to already known tunes. The most famous example is *The Beggar's Opera*, which enjoyed phenomenal popularity in its own day and is now the only ballad opera to be regularly revived. Ballad opera, strictly defined, disappeared after the middle of the 18th century. It was succeeded by what is often called English opera, in which many of the tunes were written by the person named as composer and others were extracted by him from various sources, including foreign operas, and interpolated in the work. Sometimes English opera is for obvious reasons referred to as *pasticcio* opera, although the term is also used to indicate operas in which each act is by a different composer. GH

Ballard, Lucinda 1908–93 American COSTUME designer. An assistant to scenic designers NORMAN BEL GEDDES and Claude Bragdon early in her career, Ballard was an active designer (principally of costumes) for theatre, film and ballet. She received the first Tony for Costume Design for the plays *Happy Birthday*, *Another Part of the Forest*, *Street Scene*, *John Loves Mary* and *The Chocolate Soldier* in the 1947 BROADWAY season. She also won a Tony in 1961 for *The Gay Life* and the 1945 Donaldson Award for *I Remember Mama*. In recent years she supervised the costumes for revivals of productions she originally designed. BO

Bancroft, Squire 1841–1926 English actor-manager, who made his London debut in T. W. ROBERTSON's *Society* at the PRINCE OF WALES's in 1865. Two years later, having

created the role of Captain Hawtree in Robertson's *Caste*, he entered into management and matrimony with the theatre's lessee, MARIE WILSON. The Bancrofts' subsequent tenure of the Prince of Wales's was a fashionable triumph, and Bancroft himself, tall, distinguished, habitually sporting a monocle, was a social success. Impeccable manners and cultivated elegance were hallmarks of the Bancroft management at the Prince of Wales's (1867–79) and the HAYMARKET (1880–5). Despite their rigid sense of hierarchy, they had the good sense to play lesser roles in several productions, thereby providing an ensemble alternative to the star-centred regime of IRVING at the LYCEUM. Like Irving, they were enamoured of pictorial staging, but their feeling was less for the grand than for the exquisite. The aesthetic link between visual and theatrical art in Victorian England is embodied in Bancroft's decision, when renovating the Haymarket in 1880, to build in a proscenium 'in the form of a large gold frame, with all four sides complete'. This, after all, was the logical conclusion of the picture-frame stage, turning plays into moving pictures. The cinema was not far away. Bancroft retired from the theatre, already rich, at the age of 44. *Mr and Mrs Bancroft, on and off the Stage* (1888) was the first of a sequence of self-regarding professional reminiscences. In 1897, Bancroft became the second actor to receive a knighthood. Irving had beaten him by two years. PT

bandi nata A regional Indian theatre form of central and western Orissa, which takes its name from Bandi, the nickname of the sister of Chandrasena, Radha's husband in the mythological tales surrounding the life of Krishna. The stories concern Bandi's self-sacrifice for her husband Krishna so that he may sport with Radha. The form is acted by members of the untouchable community. The actors mix with the spectators and only join in the action when their turn comes. They are accompanied by the *dhol* drum. Performance lasts about three hours. Dances, songs, actions and humour are freely mixed to keep the spectators entertained. FaR

Bandō Tamasaburō 1950– Perhaps the most popular young Japanese KABUKI actor of female roles. The adopted son of Morita Kanya XIV (1907–75), he took the name Kinoji for his stage debut in 1957 and his present name in 1964. Tall and willowy with a beautiful face, his somewhat haughty persona draws adoring young fans. He is popular in seductive roles – Lady Taema in *The Thundergod*, Princess Sakura in *The Scarlet Princess of Edo* – and multiple quick-change roles – seven roles in TSURUYA NAMBOKU's *Osome and Hisamatsu*. He has successfully played in films, in Mishima's modern play *Madame de Sade*, and as Lady Macbeth. JRB

Bang-Hansen, Kjetil 1940– Norwegian director. Much of his work has been outside Oslo, beginning in 1967 in Trondheim, under the tutelage of Erik Pierstorff. With several associates (dubbed the 'Molde Group') Bang-Hansen established Teater Vårt in Molde in 1972, before moving to Rogaland Teater, Stavanger, and the NATIONALE SCENE, Bergen. He believes in theatre as an artistic end in itself, an encounter between performers and spectators, unrestricted by political ideology, and in the need to discover performance styles in free approaches to texts. Among many extraordinary productions, often with designer Helge Hoff Monsen, have been *Peer Gynt* (1978), *Raskolnikov* (1982) and *The Royal House of Thebes* (1985). After briefly heading NATIONALTHEATRET (1986–8), Bang-Hansen has freelanced, often at the Norske Teatret, where key productions have included *The Pretenders* (1989) and *The Tidings Brought to Mary* (1993).   HL

Bangladesh Bangladesh was created in 1971 as an independent state from former East Pakistan. The population is predominantly Muslim, sharing this heritage with Pakistanis, while being ethnically and linguistically Bengali, thus sharing a common culture with the Bengali people of northeastern INDIA. This linguistic and cultural tie has been a determining factor in the development of the theatre: Bangladesh theatre is intimately linked to the history of theatre in the whole Bengali-speaking region, including the state of West Bengal in India. Peasants form the majority of the Bengali population both in Bangladesh and West Bengal. Consequently, Bengali-language JATRA troupes have long enjoyed popularity among villagers throughout the region and have generally been able to cross from one country into the other while touring. *Jatra* is therefore an exceptional example in Asia of a theatre form that can be considered the 'joint' cultural property of two nations.

Urban theatre had modest beginnings during the 19th century in Dacca, the present capital of Bangladesh, expressing the concerns of the small but growing middle class of urban, intellectual Bengalis. Syed Abul Hasain wrote one prose and one musical play espousing the unity of Hindu and Muslim Bengalis. Until the partition of India and Pakistan in 1947, artists and writers in Dacca and Calcutta shared the ideas and common concerns of Bengali art and culture. After partition and the establishment of Muslim East Pakistan, amateur groups in Dacca broke the conventional prohibition against women on stage and began mounting 'co-acted' modern plays in 1950–1. In the 1950s and 60s the Drama Circle at Dacca University organized numerous amateur productions, and it hosted performances by the famous Bohorupee modern-drama troupe from Calcutta. Beginning in the 1960s the Bangla Academy established an annual Drama Season, which subsidized new productions, sponsored playwriting competitions and brought in troupes from England and the United States, thus opening their theatre to world influences. These influences are apparent in Syed Ali Ahsan's *Kalbela* and *Milepost*, inspired by the Japanese NŌform, and in London-trained Sayeed Ahmed's *Korbani*, *Julkaikha* and *Johra O Mushtari*, which echo SAMUEL BECKETT. STRINDBERG's *The Father* was staged in the style of local *jatra*, showing a maturing of theatre in this Muslim culture.

As the struggle for an independent Bangladesh grew stronger, many urban theatre people were motivated to work for liberation through their plays. Dramas were written on the theme of the repression of the Bengali people and their plight. In the late 1960s this struggle moved from the theatre halls to the streets and theatre people helped coalesce public support for the independence movement.

A new era was ushered in after independence, in which groups of young players have struggled to establish artistic roots in the community and survive economically. Among the groups founded in the 1970s are Aranyak, Bahubachan, Nagorik, Theatre, Dacca Drama, Padatik, Dacca Padatik, Samasthi and Kathak. In smaller urban centres other groups have sprung up in recent years. All the groups share common concerns through affiliation with the Bangladesh Centre of the International Theatre Institute. (See also ASIAN AND PACIFIC ISLAND THEATRE.)   FAR

Bankhead, Tallulah 1902–68 American stage and film actress noted for her vibrant energy, sultry voice, explosive speech and impetuous behaviour. The daughter of one of the most famous political families of Alabama, she debuted on Broadway in 1919 and achieved fame in 1923 in London in *The Dancers*. She returned to the USA in 1923 for film work, reappearing on BROADWAY in 1933. After a revival of *Rain*, she was widely acclaimed as Regina in *The Little Foxes* (1939) and won the New York Drama Critics' Circle Award for Best Actress as Sabina in *The Skin of Our Teeth*. She won the Best Actress Award from the New York Film Critics in 1944 for *Lifeboat*. She published her autobiography, *Tallulah*, in 1952. Her final stage appearance was in *The Milk Train Doesn't Stop Here Anymore* (1964, Brooks Atkinson Theatre, New York City).   SMA

Banks, John c.1652–1706 English playwright. Trained for the law, he turned to the theatre and wrote seven plays. After three heroic plays, of which the best is *The Destruction of Troy* (1678), Banks established an entirely new form of drama which was decisively influential. Using as his source British history, he centred his plays, dubbed 'she-tragedies', on the sufferings of the heroine, creating an overwhelming emphasis on pathos. *The Unhappy Favourite* (1681), on Queen Elizabeth and Essex, was markedly successful and Banks pursued the genre with plays on Anne Boleyn, Lady Jane Grey and Mary Queen of Scots. The latter two, *The Innocent Usurper* (1683) and *The Island Queens* (1684), dealing in threats of usurpation and the execution of monarchs, were far too politically sensitive and were banned from performance.   PH

Bannister, Jack [John] 1760–1836 English actor, son of the comedian Charles Bannister (1741–1804). Bannister was a student at the Royal Academy before making his acting debut at the HAYMARKET in 1778, and remained a close friend of his fellow student Thomas Rowlandson until Rowlandson's death in 1827. After moderate successes in tragedy at DRURY LANE, he began a new career as a comedian when he created the part of Don Ferolo Whiskerandos in SHERIDAN's *The Critic* (1779). A popular light comedian with a genial temperament and a fair singing voice, he was particularly associated with the summer seasons at the Haymarket. The manager was GEORGE COLMAN THE YOUNGER, who wrote a part for Bannister in almost all his plays and who helped him to compile one of the first authentic one-man shows under the title of *Bannister's Budget*. The success of these performances enabled Bannister to retire in 1815.   PT

Bannister, Nathaniel (Harrington) 1813–47 American actor and dramatist, who began his career in New York and Philadelphia before going to New Orleans in 1834, where he married the widow of JOHN AUGUSTUS STONE and established his reputation as a playwright. After 1837 the Bannisters performed regularly in New York. The author of at least 40 plays, ranging through ancient history (*Gaulantus the Gaul*, 1836), national incidents (*The Maine Question*, 1839), romantic COMEDY (*The Gentleman of Lyons*, 1838) and moral dilemmas (*The Destruction of Jerusalem*, 1837), Bannister wrote mainly to please the public. His popular spectacle, *Putnam, the Iron Son of '76* (1844), opened with 78 performances and exploited the considerable feats of Black Vulture, a horse. The most distinctive actor-dramatist of his time, with six published plays, Bannister was a thoughtful and well read man, an innovator who enriched theatre managers and died young and a pauper. WJM

Baraka, Amiri [(Everett) LeRoi Jones] 1934– African-American poet, essayist and playwright. Baraka assumed his new name and mission in the 1960s, when he became leader of the black arts revolutionary movement that viewed theatre as a weapon in the struggle for black liberation. He has produced some 20 plays, many of them one-acts, that powerfully dramatize social and racial problems in expressive forms and with unnerving frankness. Hailed for his 'fierce and blazing talent', condemned for his blatant anti-white posture, Baraka was notwithstanding the most prominent American dramatist of the 1960s with such plays as the Obie-winning *Dutchman* (1964), *The Slave* (1964), *A Black Mass* (1966) and *Slave Ship* (1969). He founded the Black Arts Repertory Theatre/School in Harlem (1965–6) and Spirit House in Newark, NJ (1966), where his plays were produced. Baraka's earlier writings and speeches had a profound influence on the younger generation of playwrights. He later rejected black nationalism for revolutionary socialism, as shown in his play *The Motion of History* (1975). His autobiography was published in 1984. EGH

Barba, Eugenio 1936– Italian theatre director and theorist whose major work has been done with the ODIN TEATRET, exploring the possibilities of what he has called 'the Third Theatre', a socially aware, exploratory, actor-oriented drama, distinct from that of commercial BOULEVARD theatre on the one hand and director-dominated, dramatist-oriented art theatre on the other. After university study in Italy and a period at the directors' school in Warsaw, he joined GROTOWSKI's Laboratory Theatre as an observer in 1961. The influence of the three years he spent there has remained fundamental in his later work, inspiring him to found the Odin Teatret, first in Oslo, then on a more firm and regular basis as a centre for theatre research at Holstebrö in Denmark. That research has been pursued in a variety of ways, including the mounting of international conferences at which like-minded groups can exchange information on aims and methods; working in communities traditionally deprived of drama other than that projected by the mass media; exploring the possibilities of 'bartering' entertainment and founding, as a focal point for collective research, the International School of Theatre Anthropology in 1979. He edited and contributed to Grotowski's seminal *Towards a Poor Theatre* (English translation 1968), and has published many articles on actor research and theatre anthropology, some of which have been gathered and further developed in *The Floating Islands* (1984), *Beyond the Floating Islands* (1986), *A Dictionary of Theatre Anthropology* (with Nicola Savarese, 1991) and *The Paper Canoe* (1994). KR

Barbados Most easterly of the Caribbean island chain, Barbados had been deserted by indigenous Carib Indians by the time it was settled by the English in 1625. The first African slaves were brought to the island in 1627, and by 1668 its population consisted of 40,000 blacks and 20,000 whites. Today the population is virtually homogeneous, with more than 90 per cent of African descent and the rest of European or non-African mixed ancestry.

Because, at 66 square miles, the island is relatively small and its open terrain allows access to all parts of the country, it has been assumed that the slaves, engulfed by the dominant European culture, lost all traces of their African past. While this conjecture may be partly true of the coloured middle class, there is little doubt that Barbadian working-class blacks, like those in other Caribbean islands, retained aspects of an African-Caribbean performance culture that was despised or, at best, tolerated during the colonial period. Since the achievement of political independence in 1966, these performance modes have been openly encouraged in events such as the annual Crop Over festival, the Kadooment CARNIVAL, the Talk Tent and the calypso contest; and in the Landship marching band and the Tuk music band.

As far as formal theatre is concerned, the 18th century witnessed spurts of dramatic activity: in 1729 by local 'gentlemen players', and in 1752–3 and again in 1783–4 most probably by travelling players from England or America. The plays shown were standard works for the period – for instance, GEORGE LILLO's *The London Merchant, or, The History of George Barnwell* and GEORGE FARQUHAR's *The Beaux' Stratagem*. Although press advertisements referred to the theatre venues as 'playhouses', they were most likely large rooms fitted up for the purpose, such as Marshall's Great Room in the city of Bridgetown used in 1752.

During the 19th century several theatres were opened, the most important being the Theatre Royal, built in Bridgetown in 1810 at a cost of £10,000. It was destroyed by a hurricane in 1831 and was succeeded two years later by a second Theatre Royal built of wood, which was demolished in 1844. The British garrison in 1818 set up its own theatre space at St Ann's for the entertainment of troops, their families and friends. Known as the Garrison Theatre and set up in one hall after another, it survived into the mid-20th century. Speightstown, the second town of importance, also boasted at least two theatres in the 19th century. Professional players, mainly from North America, visited the island quite regularly in the latter half of the century. These included the J. W. Lanergan Company, Brooks and Fyffe's Dramatic Combination, an Italian opera company, and the E. A. McDowell Vaudeville Company that came in 1881, 1882 and 1886 and performed GILBERT and Sullivan's *HMS Pinafore* for the first time in Barbados. Although these touring companies played for no more than two weeks at a time, their appearance usually stirred the local thespians into renewed activity, so that over a four-year period performances were given by no less than six different amateur groups.

The final decade of the 19th century brought Bridgetown yet another theatre – Wilhelmina Hall. Erected in 1894 by J. H. Inniss, with seating for 900, it became the principal venue for visiting companies such as the Russ-Whytal Dramatic Company from New York in 1900, and the F. R. BENSON Shakespeare Company (in 1905) and the Florence Glossop-Harris Dramatic Company (in 1920) from England. The hall was eventually converted into a cinema and renamed the Olympic Theatre. The urge to build a proper civic theatre had existed since the 1880s, when a group of Barbadian businessmen jointly offered shares to the public in order to raise capital of £8000. This and other similar schemes proved abortive, until 1918 when construction was begun on the Empire Theatre on Probyn Street. At a cost of £15,000 this handsome, spacious, limestone-brick playhouse opened its doors to the public in 1922, by which time it had been decided that the city could not support a theatre of stage productions only. The opening bill consisted of VAUDEVILLE items and screen snapshots, and it was inevitable that film shows would eventually overwhelm theatre productions.

Up to the 1930s, live theatre in Barbados was primarily a white concern, both participants and audiences comprising resident Europeans and the military, native-born whites or near-whites. Exceptions to this pattern were rare. As far back as 1805, when members of the free coloured population of Bridgetown staged JOHN HOME's tragedy, *Douglas*, one critic, while favourably impressed with the performance, felt constrained to point out that non-whites should not have been permitted to engage in this sort of cultural activity. His remarks had the effect of increasing the attendance of whites at subsequent performances. Then in 1830 the Lyceum Amateur Theatre on Reed Street was organized by Samuel Jackman Prescod and other leading coloured figures of the community, but the group was apparently active for only a few months.

At no time before the 1930s do the records disclose the production in Barbados of a locally written play or a play of local relevance. *The West Indian*, a sentimental comedy chosen for the opening of the newly built Theatre Royal in 1810, had been written by the English dramatist RICHARD CUMBERLAND, and though it was about a rich, hot-blooded, young Jamaican planter who becomes entangled in a love affair, it was set in London. This situation would change in the years ahead.

The first real departure came when the Guyana-born Joyce Stuart, a coloured woman who had studied dance in New York and London, staged her first *Revuedeville* at the Drill Hall in 1938, featuring students from her dancing academy. A second presentation took place the next year, and in 1950 the show was revived at the Empire Theatre as a MUSICAL COMEDY under the title *Passport to Heaven*. It introduced to the stage the inimitable comedian Joe Tudor. According to one critic, the show had 'broken virgin ground, filled with possibilities and promise for the future'. Stuart took her show to Trinidad, making it one of the first Caribbean productions to travel to a neighbouring country – an event that had become commonplace two decades later.

In the 1930s other popular REVUES were staged at the Empire Theatre, displaying the talents of local writers and performers, among them Frank Collymore who became one of the island's leading actors. Amateur groups such as the Bridgetown Players and the Barbados Dramatic Club (which merged into the Green Room Theatre Club in 1953) continued to function. As these observed a finely drawn colour line, it was left to the British Council, which set up regional offices in the Caribbean in the 1940s, to provide a pocket theatre at its own premises where fledgeling drama groups that could not afford the cost of hiring the Empire Theatre or other commercial halls could stage their plays. The Council also undertook to sponsor theatre arts workshops, conducted by drama officers of the Extramural Department of the University of the West Indies and others; the contribution of Daphne Joseph-Hackett, as organizer and producer of these sessions, was substantial. With the growth of indigenous theatre groups, the 250-seat theatre in Queen's Park House (now the Daphne Joseph-Hackett Theatre) was put into service, and it has proved an ideal home for intimate productions.

As racial barriers in the theatre began to come down, two major concerns were voiced. First was the issue of interracial casting, and second was the need for more Caribbean plays. These issues, raised in articles published in the *Advocate*, were soon overtaken by events. In 1955 the university's extramural drama office began publishing a series of Caribbean plays which were quickly disseminated throughout the area, encouraging new writers who wished to take advantage of a wider field. Meanwhile, graduates who had been members of the University Dramatic Society in JAMAICA returned home and mounted plays with mixed casting, as they were accustomed to do in their campus productions.

Strides in dramatic production were paralleled in music and dance. Beginning in 1966 and continuing for over a decade, the Barbados Festival Choir produced a series of original MUSICALS called *Bimshire*, loosely patterned on the annual Jamaica PANTOMIME. The originators of this experiment were Noel Vaz of Jamaica and Joseph-Hackett. The Barbados Dance Theatre Company, founded in 1968, has gone from strength to strength in its annual season of dance, much of it theatrical in form, which has attracted increasingly enthusiastic audiences. The company has presented original dances based on folklore or historical anecdote, such as the RITUAL dance *Shango* and *Yarico*, a legend about an Arawak girl (1973); the ingenious *Licks for Six*, based on Barbados cricket (1974); and *Dreams and Visions*, inspired by Caribbean poetry (1983).

With the attainment of independence in 1966, competitive festivals for schools and adult groups were introduced under the aegis first of the Barbados Arts Council and later of the National Cultural Foundation. These festivals spurred the writing and production of more Barbadian and other Caribbean plays. The leading playwright in Barbados is Anthony Hinkson, and others of note include Winston Farrell and the New York-based dancer-dramatist Glenville Lovell, whose play *When the Eagle Screams* deals with the 1983 American invasion of Grenada. Popular theatrical experiments include *Laff It*

Off, an earthy, vernacular romp set in a bar in a Barbadian village and directed by Thom Cross; the satiric *Pampalam*, a series of staged encounters in rhyme written by journalist Jeannette Layne-Clark; and the Talk Tent – initiated by director Earl Warner and based on the 19th-century fundraiser known as a tea meeting with its emphasis on speechifying and song. The popularity of these forms of theatre has pushed the homegrown effort towards professionalism.

Another type of production is epitomized by the Popular Theatre Movement, a group that encourages rural communities to participate in solving communal problems through research and play enactment, using a variety of expressive forms. The programme is part of the Eastern Caribbean Popular Theatre Organization, based in Dominica. Perhaps the most notable recent development in Barbadian theatre has been the establishment of professional organizations that aim to put the theatre on a sound financial footing while ensuring that the best talent is able to travel throughout the islands and abroad. Stage One, organized in 1978, has over 25 productions to its credit, and W.W.B. Productions (1987) has recruited Caribbean-wide performers and toured its productions to other territories and to London. EGH

See: W. Alleyne, 'A Tradition of Theatre', *The Bajan and South Caribbean*, 1981; K. Corsbie, *Theatre in the Caribbean*, London, 1984.

Barbeau, Jean 1945– Quebec playwright. Barbeau was one of the first to follow the lead of MICHEL TREMBLAY in the use of *joual*, the popular French of Quebec, in plays such as *Manon Lastcall* (1970) and *Joualez-moi d'amour* (*Speak to Me of Love*, forging a new verb, *joualer*, to replace *parler*, 1970). These plays deal humorously with the cultural schizophrenia of Quebec, joined by shared social heritage to France but divided by an uncommon tongue. *Le Chemin de Lacroix* (*The Way of Lacross*), *0–71* and *Ben-Ur*, all published in 1971, deal in more serious fashion with the social victims of his province's malaise. After the election of the Parti Québécois in 1976 Barbeau, like many another Quebec intellectual, turned to more universal concerns in plays such as *Le Jardin de la Maison Blanche* (*The White House Garden*, 1979) and *Les Gars* (*The Guys*, 1984), which attack the materialistic values of contemporary society and the problems of modern masculinity. LED

Barker, Harley Granville see GRANVILLE BARKER, HARLEY

Barker, Howard 1946– British dramatist, whose first plays were produced at the ROYAL COURT THEATRE and the Open Space in the early 1970s. His early works looked at British society from the stance of the underworld as well as the underdog – of twin gangsters in *Alpha Alpha* (1972), of pimps in *Claw* (1975) and of the criminal in *Stripwell* (1975), who invades the house of the judge who condemned him. Barker is adept at choosing telling dramatic situations in which many different incidents can take place, but he reverses what might be regarded as the moral expectations. The prison governor in *The Hang of the Gaol* (1978) becomes an arsonist, while the entrepreneur who capitalizes on graveyard mementoes in *The Love of a Good*

Man is the hero of a black comedy set in 1920, after the carnage of the First World War. In *No End of Blame* (1980) he debates the issue of the different censorships, East and West, favouring the former. He relishes, as WEDEKIND and BRECHT did before him, reversing the expected moral order of capitalist societies. In *The Possibilities* (1988) and *The Last Supper* (1988), he turns religious parables inside out: his Christ-like figure, Lvov, has to ask his disciples to eat him to gain posthumous fame. *Scenes from an Execution* (1990) concerns an artist, Galactia, commissioned by the state of Venice in the 16th century to paint a triumphant war picture commemorating the Battle of Lepanto, but she paints its horror instead, which paradoxically proves popular with its public.

Barker deliberately attempts to upset expectations, denying the value of reason, continuity and NATURALISM, but there is a certain predictability about his wildness. His characters seem to be at the emotional extremes, to speak in the same overwrought, rhetorical language. *A Hard Heart* (1992), concerning a female architect who tries to save a ruined city from the enemy nearly within, and *The Europeans* (1993), set in Vienna after the siege of 1683, rage with feverish despair, as if black spattered with blood were fashionable colours this year. Barker cuts a Byronic dash in British theatre – sardonic, detached, the insider's outsider. He has said that he tries to liberate his audiences 'from the nightmare of being entertained'. A theatre group, the Wrestling School, has been formed to realize his plays. JE

Barker, James Nelson 1784–1858 American playwright, poet and politician. Born into a politically and socially influential family, Barker combined his love of country with his love of theatre. Among his plays are *America* (1805); *Tears and Smiles* (1807), a patriotic COMEDY; *The Embargo* (1808), a defence of Jefferson's Embargo Act; *The Indian Princess* (1808), the first produced American play about Pocahontas; and *Marmion; or, The Battle of Flodden Field* (1812), in which England's treatment of 16th-century Scotland was translated to America. Barker's greatest achievements are his 11 essays on drama in the *Democratic Press* (18 December 1816–19 February 1817) and his remarkable TRAGEDY of New England intolerance, *Superstition; or, The Fanatic Father* (1824), in which the villain protagonist, a clergyman, mistakes his own passions for the word of God. Thereafter, Barker, an avid supporter of President Andrew Jackson, absorbed himself in politics, contributing to literature with poetry rather than plays. WJM

Barlach, Ernst 1370–1938 German sculptor, artist and dramatist who, like his symbolic plays (see SYMBOLISM), was deeply rooted in his native Mecklenburg. His work coincided with that of expressionists 20 years his junior (see EXPRESSIONISM), but JESSNER's expressionist stylization of Barlach's *Die echten Sedemunds* (*The Real Sedemunds*) in 1921 repelled the author, who viewed his strange characters as real. *Der tote Tag* (*The Dead Day*, 1917) treats the expressionist generation conflict in religious terms. The hero of *Der arme Vetter* (*The Poor Cousin*, 1919) sacrifices his life to save his cousin from materialism. *Die Sintflut* (*The Flood*, 1924), for which Barlach was awarded the Kleist Prize, projects his personal mysticism on the Noah story. In *Der blaue Boll* (*Boozer Boll*, 1926) the squire almost seduces an impoverished young mother – she needs the money for poison to put her children out of their misery – before spiritual regeneration sets in on both sides.

Barlach's central theme is salvation. His syntax is involved, his language thick with images and neologisms, and his characters lapse frequently into monologue, making his dialogue difficult in performance. These heavy North German comedies are nevertheless periodically revived, most successfully by Hans Lietzau.   HR

Barnabee, Henry Clay 1833–1917 American MUSICAL COMEDY actor. A passionate amateur singer, he worked as a retail clerk in Boston until 1865 when he became a Lyceum (see CHAUTAUQUA AND LYCEUM) entertainer. He made his professional stage debut in Boston the following year and later headed his own concert company. He was a founding member of the BOSTON IDEAL OPERA COMPANY (1879) and their successors, the Bostonians (1887). A tenor, he specialized in such GILBERT and Sullivan roles as Sir Joseph Porter and Bunthorne, but he was also noted for his Dr Dulcamera in Donizetti's *The Elixir of Love*. He created the role of the Sheriff of Nottingham in *Robin Hood* by HARRY B. SMITH and REGINALD DE KOVEN. In 1913 his autobiography, *My Wanderings*, appeared.   DMCD

Barnay, Ludwig 1842–1924 German actor. Before he joined the MEININGEN COMPANY as an actor of heroic roles, Barnay had acquired a considerable reputation as a guest in theatres in Pest, Graz, Mainz, Vienna, Leipzig and Frankfurt am Main. After his years with the Meininger, he made tours of England and America. In 1883 he was a co-founder with L'ARRONGE of the DEUTSCHES THEATER, though he soon left the company to start his own Berliner Theater in 1887. His last years were spent directing the BERLIN ROYAL THEATRE and the Court Theatre in Hannover. Barnay is also noted as the founder of a fledgling German actors' union, the Genossenschaft Deutscher Bühnenangehörigen, in 1871.   SW

Barnes, Clive (Alexander) 1927– London-born and Oxford-educated dance and drama critic, who first established his credentials as a dance critic for *Dance and Dancers* (1950–) and for *The Times* (1961–5). In 1965 he went to the USA as dance critic for the *New York Times*, adding the drama post in 1967. A decade later he was replaced as drama critic, and within the year (1977) resigned from the *Times* to become dance/drama critic for the *New York Post*. Noted for his clever style, Barnes wrote of *Agnes of God*: 'Some plays are so concerned with being theatrical that they forget to be dramatic.' He has been accused of being pro-British and of supporting the avant-garde more than the BROADWAY theatre.   TLM

P. T. Barnum kneeling before Mercy Lavinia Warren Bump (1841–1919), who became Mrs Tom Thumb.

Barnes, Peter 1931– British dramatist, whose plays combine trenchant SATIRE with a delight in shock effects. Although his first play, *Sclerosis*, an attack on British colonialism, was seen in Edinburgh and London in 1965, Barnes achieved success with his second play, *The Ruling Class* (1968), which contained many distinguishing features of his style – a fierce PARODY of the English upper classes; rapid changes of mood and atmosphere, from the farcical to the macabre; an unusual delight in rhetoric; and several *coups de théâtre*, not least in the play's final moments, where a grotesque House of Lords with skeletal figures swings on stage. In subsequent plays, he has chosen major moral and historical themes as subjects for black comedy – the Spanish Succession in *The Bewitched* (1974), the Holocaust in *Laughter!* (1978) and the Black Death in *Red Noses* (1985). Barnes consciously looks back to the Jacobeans and to the German dramatist FRANK WEDEKIND for his technical style, despising NATURALISM; and he has adapted plays by BEN JONSON (whom he admires more than SHAKESPEARE) and Wedekind's *Lulu* plays (1971). His taste for tackling large themes of Good and Evil within medieval settings was reflected in *Sunset and Glories* (1990), about the risks of electing a saintly pope, Celestine, given its premiere at the West Yorkshire Playhouse; and his adaptation of a Japanese play, *Tango at the End of Winter* (1991) by Kunio Shumizu, was seen in the WEST END in 1991. JE

Barnum, P(hineas) T(aylor) 1810–91 American entrepreneur and showman, a hard-headed businessman of personal integrity, yet whose *modus operandi* used deceit and innovative methods of publicity to promote both popular and high culture. Starting as a shopkeeper and editor of a weekly newspaper in Danbury, Conn., he moved to New York in 1834 and the next year commenced as a showman by exhibiting an ancient black woman he claimed was 160 years old and George Washington's nurse. In 1841 he purchased a museum (see BARNUM'S AMERICAN MUSEUM), where he mixed freak-shows with 'moral' drama and displayed the midget Tom Thumb (Charles Stratton), whose European appearances in 1844 made Barnum and the notion of 'humbug' notorious. In 1849 the Museum became a STOCK COMPANY and the next year he organized the American tour of the Swedish soprano Jenny Lind, who received 1000 dollars a night. Barnum retired in 1855, but soon resumed his business. He did not enter the CIRCUS trade until 1871, merging with James A. Bailey in 1881 to create 'The Greatest Show on Earth', a combination of circus, menagerie and side-show; the acquisition of the elephant Jumbo was his greatest feat there. Throughout his busy life, Barnum regularly issued versions of his life story and optimistic philosophy: these included his *Autobiography* (1854), *The Humbugs of the World* (1865) and *Struggles and Triumphs* (1869; the best edition is that edited by G.S. Bryan, 2 vols., 1927). A definitive biography by A. H. Saxon appeared in 1989. LS

Barnum's American Museum (New York City) In 1841 P. T. BARNUM, America's greatest showman, bought Scudder's Museum and quickly turned it into a city landmark. As part of the price of admission to see real and fake curiosities and an assortment of human freaks and oddi-ties, he provided concerts and light entertainment in a lecture room. In 1849, this was expanded into a full-scale theatre for dramatic performances. In 1850, the seating was increased to 3000 for the presentation of *The Drunkard*; or, *The Fallen Saved* by William H. Smith, a temperance drama. Thereafter, Barnum presented a series of moral plays in a moral manner with a STOCK COMPANY of actors of unimpeachable morality. In 1865, the museum and theatre burned to the ground. Although he moved to 559 Broadway, Barnum's second venture never achieved the success of the first, and was destroyed by fire after only a few years of operation. MCH

Baron [Michel Boyron] 1653–1729 French actor and protégé of MOLIÈRE. The son of theatrical parents, he was orphaned in childhood and at the age of 13, while acting in a children's troupe, he so impressed Molière that the latter offered him individual coaching and took him into his own company, where he developed into a successful *jeune premier*. On Molière's death he moved to the HÔTEL DE BOURGOGNE, creating some of RACINE's young heroes, and thence to the COMÉDIE-FRANÇAISE on its formation in 1680. In 1691, at the height of his powers, he inexplicably retired from the stage, not acting again, except for occasional private performances, until he made an equally unexpected comeback 29 years later, whereupon at the age of 67 he cheerfully resumed most of his former roles, including those of young lovers, and created a number of new ones. He continued to act until shortly before his death nine years later.

At his peak his outstanding ability, allied to good looks, intelligence and an air of distinction, enabled him to take leading roles in TRAGEDY and COMEDY alike and was apparently enough to ensure a sympathetic hearing for mediocre plays. Contemporary critics remarked upon his attention to detail and the relative simplicity of his playing – a quality he is supposed to have encouraged in the young ADRIENNE LECOUVREUR – though he could also be self-important and disagreeable to his colleagues. He was the author of several comedies, the most interesting of which are *L'Homme à bonnes fortunes* (*The Philanderer*, 1686) and the one-act *Le Rendez-vous des Tuileries* (1685), in which several actors of the Comédie-Française appeared as themselves. DR

Barr [Baer], **Richard (Alphonse)** 1917–89 American producer-director and president of the League of American Theaters and Producers for 21 years, best known for bringing early works by EDWARD ALBEE to the American public by co-producing (with CLINTON WILDER) *The Zoo Story*, *The American Dream* and *The Death of Bessie Smith*. These were followed by all of Albee's major plays, including *Who's Afraid of Virginia Woolf?*, Albee's first BROADWAY production, which thanks to Barr's initiative established preview performances in New York (1962). Barr also championed other young playwrights: alone and in partnership, he produced early works by LANFORD WILSON, William Hanley, TERRENCE MCNALLY, Jack Richardson, JOHN GUARE, A. R. GURNEY, AMIRI BARAKA (as LeRoi Jones), JEAN-CLAUDE VAN ITALLIE and Paul Zindel. He also presented American premieres of works by BECKETT and IONESCO. DBW

Barrault, Jean-Louis 1910–94 French actor and director, who made a significant contribution to five decades of theatre. His first performances were at the ATELIER in the 1930s; one of these was hailed by ARTAUD as achieving his own ideal. In 1940 Barrault joined the COMÉDIE-FRANÇAISE where he met Madeleine Renaud, an outstanding actress and later his wife and co-director. Here he began to direct as well as act: his production of CLAUDEL's *Le Soulier de satin* (*The Satin Slipper*) in 1943 was a particular success. In 1946 he and Renaud left to found their own company. At the Marigny Theatre as a private company and, after 1959, at the ODÉON with state subsidy, their policy was to produce a mixture of new plays and classics. Barrault's greatest achievement was to have seen that Claudel's apparently wordy plays could succeed in the theatre, given a sufficiently concrete and gestural production style: he produced six of his plays. He had learned much from the MIME artist ÉTIENNE DECROUX before the war (as he demonstrated in the role of DEBURAU in Carné's film *Les Enfants du paradis*), and his performances were outstanding for the detail and inventiveness of their physical action. He produced many new authors, including IONESCO, DURAS and VAUTHIER, and made a number of his own adaptations for the stage. The most famous was *Rabelais* (1968), performed in a Montmartre wrestling hall. This production, celebrating freedom from authority, was his reply to Malraux, who had dismissed him from his post at the Odéon for allowing students to use it as a debating forum during the near-revolution. In 1972 he converted the former Orsay station into a performance space, erecting a circus tent inside the building, and in 1981 he moved to the Théâtre du Rond-Point, a former skating rink on the Champs-Élysées.

Originally identified with total theatre, Barrault became, in old age, a star actor viewed with the same respect as LAURENCE OLIVIER in England. DB

Barrett, Lawrence 1838–91 American actor and manager. Lawrence made his debut as Murad in *The French Spy* in Detroit in 1853 and his first important New York appearances in 1857 as a member of WILLIAM E. BURTON's Metropolitan Theatre Company. He subsequently was a member of Boston's Howard Athenaeum Company (1858–61). Barrett was associated with EDWIN BOOTH throughout his career. In 1863 he acted with Booth at the WINTER GARDEN THEATRE, and in 1871–2 at BOOTH's THEATRE he was the leading supporting actor, appearing most notably as Adrian de Mauprat to Booth's celebrated Richelieu, but also alternating Othello and Iago with him. At Booth's Theatre, Barrett also starred as James Harebell in W. G. WILLS's *The Man o'Airlie* (one of his most acclaimed roles), as Leontes in a spectacular production of *The Winter's Tale*, and as Cassius with Booth's Brutus in a lavish revival of *Julius Caesar*. This last production was later toured by Barrett under the management of Henry C. Jarrett and A. M. PALMER. Although a professional disagreement estranged them for the next seven years, Booth and Barrett were reconciled in 1880, and their relationship continued to be close for the rest of their lives. Barrett managed Booth's last starring tours (1886–91), and for the last three seasons they made nationwide 'joint starring' tours. Barrett managed the CALIFORNIA THEATRE in San Francisco (1866–70, with JOHN McCULLOUGH) and the Variety Theatre in New Orleans (1871–3). In 1884–5 he leased HENRY IRVING's LYCEUM THEATRE (London) during the latter's first American tour. Generally, however, Barrett spent most of his career as a touring star, often with his own company. He was also keenly interested in encouraging American drama and dramatists, commissioning numerous original plays and adaptations during his career. He presented WILLIAM DEAN HOWELLS's first full-length play, *Counterfeit Presentment* (1877), and William Young's *Pendragon* (1881) and *Ganelon* (1888), and successfully revived GEORGE HENRY BOKER's *Francesca da Rimini* (1883).

Slender, with a sensitive face, deep-set expressive eyes and an unusual vocal range, Barrett was regarded as a studious, sometimes compelling, but also overly technical actor. His most successful roles after Harebell were Lanciotto in *Francesca da Rimini,* Hernani, Cassius and (late in his career) Othello. DJW

Barrett, Wilson 1846–1904 British actor-manager, who too often wasted his good looks and fervour for greatness on inferior material, much of it written by himself. The supreme example is *The Sign of the Cross* (1895), a MELODRAMA of frantic spirituality which requires a Roman patrician to face the lions for love of a Christian maiden. He opened the play in the USA, took it to the Grand Theatre in Leeds, of which he was the first lessee (1878–95), and only then to London, where, outrageously, it was a huge success. Barrett was, at various times, manager of theatres in Leeds and Hull as well as in London (the Court, the PRINCESS's, the GLOBE, the OLYMPIC, the LYCEUM). Among his Shakespearian roles, his Mercutio was better received than his Hamlet and his Benedick, but his real gift was in rampantly wholesome melodrama, preferably with religious overtones. He had major successes with George R. Sims's *The Lights o' London* (1881) and the HENRY ARTHUR JONES/Henry Herman collaboration *The Silver King* (1882), and with his own adaptations of *The Manxman* (1894) and *Quo Vadis?* (1900). PT

Barrie, J(ames) M(atthew) 1860–1937 Scottish playwright whose journalistic career took him to London in 1885. Barrie had already made a mark with a novel, *The Little Minister* (1891), when J. L. TOOLE staged his first successful play, *Walker, London* (1892). Ten years and several plays later, Barrie discovered, in *Quality Street* (1902) and *The Admirable Crichton* (1902), a profitable way of combining his own predilection for escapist romance with the contemporary dramatic interest in social problems. He was a craftsman who should not be too easily condemned as merely whimsical or classified as a permanent adolescent, unwilling or unable to join the adult world, like the leading character of his most famous play, *Peter Pan* (1904). If *Alice Sit-by-the-Fire* (1905) and *Mary Rose* (1920) are fatally flawed by mawkishness, *What Every Woman Knows* (1908) and *Dear Brutus* (1917) are strengthened by the quiet SATIRE that is present in everything that Barrie wrote. Certain of his one-act plays, *The Twelve-Pound Look* (1910), *The Will* (1913) and *The Old Lady Shows Her Medals* (1917) among them, remain effective examples of that difficult form. Best of all, perhaps, is the teasing *Shall We Join* the Ladies? (1921), the first act of an uncompleted murder-mystery, which is a masterpiece of trail-laying. Barrie was knighted in 1913.   PT

Barrison [Bareisen] **Sisters, Five** Swedish VARIETY performers, who first appeared in 1893 at the Chicago World's Fair in a children's ballet. Despite their ages (one was married), they dressed in pink pinafores, ruffled petticoats and babies' caps. The contrast between this innocent exterior and the *double entendre* of their songs and dances, as they held black pussy-cats below their midriffs, created a sensation in Europe, especially at the FOLIES-BERGÈRE and the Berlin Wintergarten, and founded a new genre of sisters act. Their best number was 'Linger Longer, Loo'. They retired in 1908, although the youngest, Gertrude, continued to dance in CABARETS.   LS

Barry, Elizabeth c.1658–1713 English actress. According to tradition, after a poor start in the theatre, she was trained by the Earl of Rochester and became his mistress. Her first known role was in OTWAY's *Alcibiades* (1675) for the Duke's Company, and she quickly established herself as the outstanding actress of her day. Her great success as Monimia in Otway's *The Orphan* (1680) showed her ability to move the audience: DOWNES, the prompter, recorded, 'she forced tears from the eyes of her auditory, especially those who have any sense of pity for the distressed'. By the late 1680s, she was effectively co-manager of the United Company with BETTERTON, and joined his group of actors who seceded in 1695 to form a company at LINCOLN'S INN FIELDS THEATRE. She retired in 1710. Her acting was marked by an unusual control and intensity. She was praised for her identification with the role ('she is the person she represents') and for what COLLEY CIBBER described as her ability to 'pour out the sentiment with an enchanting harmony'. At her best in TRAGEDY, she had many major parts written for her by Otway, CONGREVE and others. For nearly 30 years she proved her right to be regarded as the first great English actress.   PH

Barry, Philip (James Quinn) 1896–1949 Popular American dramatist of the 1920s and 30s. Barry got his start with two plays written in GEORGE PIERCE BAKER's Workshop 47 at Harvard: *A Punch for Judy* (1921) and *You and I* (1923), a BROADWAY success. Focusing on the problems of family relations, romance, sexual intrigue and professional vocation, he developed a modern comedy of manners: *In a Garden* (1925), *Paris Bound* (1927), *Holiday* (1928), *The Animal Kingdom* (1932) and *The Philadelphia Story* (1939), which starred Katharine Hepburn. These plays regularly feature the 'Barry girl', a well heeled if somewhat spoiled young woman who rejects the smug conventions associated with materialist culture and upper-class society. Barry's protagonists, male and female, struggle to serve the liberal ideals of personal integrity, tolerance, art and freedom. Less well received were his quasi-allegorical plays on metaphysical themes: *Hotel Universe* (1930), *The Joyous Season* (1934), *Here Come the Clowns* (1938, perhaps his best serious play) and *Liberty Jones* (1941). Productions in the 1940s were only moderately successful, even though Hepburn acted in *Without Love* (1942), and TALLULAH BANKHEAD starred in *Foolish*

Notion (1945). His last play, *Second Threshold* (1951), was finished posthumously by ROBERT E. SHERWOOD.   TP

Barry, Sebastian 1955– Irish playwright. Barry's first important play was *Boss Grady's Boys* (1988), a moody evocation of the lives of two old men on a hill farm. *Prayers of Sherkin* (1990), set in an isolated fundamentalist community, and the unworldly outlaw gang of *White Woman Street* (1991) underline Barry's penchant for odd and apparently remote subjects. His deployment of lyrical language within a restrained theatrical formalism makes him the most YEATSian of the neo-poetic Irish dramatists.   GF

Barry, Spranger ?1717–77 Irish actor-manager. Born in Dublin, he began acting at Smock Alley Theatre in 1744, playing Othello at his debut. In 1746 he moved to DRURY LANE, playing Othello and Macbeth in his first season. He quickly established a high reputation as an actor of sighing lovers, acting opposite GARRICK in plays by OTWAY and ROWE with great success. In 1750 he joined COVENT GARDEN and played Romeo in direct competition with Garrick's performances in Drury Lane for 12 successive nights, eventually giving way to Garrick, though praised for 'the amorous harmony of his features, his melting eyes and unequalled plaintiveness of voice'. In 1756 he played Lear with great majesty. The following year he took over a theatre in Dublin and built a new one, the Crow Street Theatre, but returned to London in 1767, nearly bankrupt. He remarried and often acted with his wife, but he rowed incessantly with Garrick who accused him of avoiding performing whenever possible. In the 1770s, frequently ill, he moved again to Covent Garden and continued acting till his death.   PH

Barrymore see DREW–BARRYMORE FAMILY

Barsacq, André 1909–73 French theatre director of Russian origins, who began as a designer for DULLIN. With JEAN DASTÉ and Maurice Jacquemont he founded the Compagnie des Quatre Saisons in 1937. In 1940 he took over from Dullin as director of the ATELIER, where he succeeded in continuing the work of the pre-war CARTEL directors, like them largely unsubsidized and relying on exquisite revivals of classics, especially the Russians, combined with popular modern playwrights such as ANOUILH, Marcel Aymé, Félicien Marceau, René de Obaldia and occasionally a media-hyped author such as Françoise Sagan. He made a fine adaptation of Dostoevsky's *The Idiot* (1966).   DB

Bartoli, Francesco 1745–1806 Italian actor and writer who worked his way up in the trade, first directing amateur improvising groups, then in minor professional companies, and finally joining the major troupe led by Pietro Rossi. In 1769 he married one of the lead actresses of the time, Teodora Ricci, and with her two years later joined one of the most important companies of the age, that led by ANTONIO SACCO. A competent, second-string actor at a time when most players were uneducated, in addition to his wide professional experience he brought intelligence and a cultivated mind to his most important writing on the theatre, *Notizie istoriche de'comici italiani che fiorirono intorno all'anno MDL fino a'giorni presenti* (*Historical Particulars of Italian Players who Flourished Around the Year 1550 to the Present Day*, 1782). Although full of errors, it is an indispensable early source book for information on Italian performers and companies, particularly those of the COMMEDIA DELL'ARTE. It was published in the year he left the profession. Abandoned by his wife, who in 1777 had left to pursue an independent career in Paris, he took up bookselling. He also wrote poetry and plays, and a study of Italian architects.   KR

Barton, John (Bernard Adie) 1928– British director, who directed Marlowe Society productions at Cambridge while he was a Fellow of King's College during the 1950s. His particular strength lay in his detailed understanding of Elizabethan and Jacobean verse, and under his guidance the Society's SHAKESPEARE productions were renowned for the vivid naturalness of the verse-speaking. In 1960 he joined the Shakespeare Memorial Company at Stratford (later, the ROYAL SHAKESPEARE COMPANY) under its new leadership from PETER HALL. Barton helped the company to present Shakespearian texts in ways that were immediately understood by modern audiences. Sometimes this involved a simplification or reduction of the original texts, as in *The Wars of the Roses* (1963), which condensed the *Henry VI* trilogy and *Richard III* into three evenings of power struggles. He devised recital performances for the RSC, such as *The Hollow Crown* (1961) and *The Art of Seduction* (1962), and helped to bring the RSC's touring Theatre-go-Round into existence. As a resident director with the company, he was responsible for many Shakespearian productions on the main stages and in the studio theatres. In 1980 he devised *The Greeks*, ten plays shown in a cycle which tell the story of the Trojan wars. In recent years, he has directed 19th- and 20th-century plays for the RSC by such writers as IBSEN, SCHNITZLER, GRANVILLE BARKER and JOHN WHITING.   JE

Bassermann, Albert 1862–1952 German actor. After acting in Mannheim and with the MEININGEN COMPANY, in 1899 Bassermann joined BRAHM'S DEUTSCHES THEATER in Berlin. Here he was specially noted for his interpretations of IBSEN. Later he acted for several years with REINHARDT. Upon Hitler's rise to power, he emigrated to America. In 1944, he appeared on BROADWAY, then returned to Europe at the end of the war.   SW

Bateman family Hezekiah Linthicum Bateman 1812– 75 American manager, first relied on his child-prodigy daughters before managing London's LYCEUM THEATRE, where he brought HENRY IRVING to prominence in *The Bells* (1871) and then in *Hamlet* (1874, for 200 performances).

His wife **Sidney** (1823–81) wrote *Self* (1856), assumed the Lyceum management at her husband's death, and later managed SADLER'S WELLS (1879).

Daughters **Kate** (1843–1917) and **Ellen** (1844–1936) began performing SHAKESPEARE in New York (1849) when they were six and five, then in London (1851). Kate played Portia, Richmond and Lady Macbeth; Ellen played Shylock, Richard III and Macbeth. Later, Kate played in *Leah, the*

Forsaken (1862, New York; 1863, London) and appeared with Irving. Daughters **Virginia** (1853–1940) and **Isabel** (1854–1934) made their London debuts in 1865, then joined Irving. Virginia married Edward Compton and was the mother of Fay Compton and Compton McKenzie. Isabel co-managed Sadler's Wells before becoming Reverend Mother General of the Community of St Mary the Virgin at Wantage (1898).   RM

Bates, Alan (Arthur) 1934– British actor, who played the passive Cliff to Kenneth Haigh's vitriolic Jimmy Porter in the ROYAL COURT production of *Look Back in Anger* (1956). Bates here revealed his capacity for a taut stillness, an eloquent calm, which has stayed with him in more demanding roles, such as Mick in HAROLD PINTER's *The Caretaker* (1960), the title role in SIMON GRAY's *Butley* (1971), Simon in Gray's *Otherwise Engaged* (1975) and the Inquisitor in Pinter's *One for the Road* (1984). He is also at home with flamboyance, and brought to two Gray plays, *Butley* (1971) and *Melon* (1987), a biting invective unmatched by any other modern British actor, with the possible exception of JOHN WOOD. His performance in PETER SHAFFER's *Yonadab* (1985) helped to redeem an ill-fated play at the NATIONAL THEATRE. He provided the WEST END with performances in classic plays, such as the title role in ANTON CHEKHOV's *Ivanov* and Benedick in SHAKESPEARE's *Much Ado About Nothing*, both in 1989; but his most memorable performances have been in contemporary plays, particularly perhaps in DAVID STOREY's *Stages* at the National Theatre in 1992, a thoughtful study of an artist in anguish.   JE

Bates, Blanche 1873–1941 American actress. Daughter of Frank Bates, manager of noted stock companies (see STOCK COMPANY) in Portland and San Francisco, she made her debut in the latter (1893) after an early marriage and a brief career as a schoolteacher. By 1895 she had become a leading lady there. A successful tour opposite JAMES O'NEILL (1899–1900) brought her to New York and to the attention of DAVID BELASCO, who starred her as Cho-Cho-San in *Madame Butterfly* (1900), Cigarette in *Under Two Flags* (1901), Yo-San in *The Darling of the Gods* (1902) and Minnie in *The Girl of the Golden West* (1905). She retired in 1926. Full of power and humour, she portrayed a liberated woman who was always energetic, resourceful and faithful.   DMCD

Baty, Gaston 1885–1952 French theatre director, the only member of the CARTEL who was not also an actor. Baty brought the stage techniques of EXPRESSIONISM to the Paris theatre. Like CRAIG, he admired PUPPETS and had an ambitious view of the director's art. Like ARTAUD he attacked the predominance of literary theatre in France between the wars. From 1930 to 1947 he ran the Théâtre Montparnasse, where he strove for complex staging methods with an emphasis on pictorial qualities.   DB

Bauer, Wolfgang 1941– Austrian dramatist who was, with HANDKE, a member of the Graz Group. *Party for Six* (1967), *Magic Afternoon* (1968), *Change* (1969) and *Gespenster* (*Ghosts*, 1974) captured the idiom of the Swinging Sixties in the Styrian capital with an authenticity reminiscent of HORVÁTH. These evocative, largely plotless situation pieces were part of the VOLKSSTÜCK revival. Bauer's characters inhabit an escapist, self-destructive world of drugs, dreams, pop music, promiscuity and role-playing into which violence occasionally intrudes. With *Magnetküsse* (*Magnet Kisses*, 1976) and *Memory Hotel* (1980) he abandons intuitive REALISM and loses his touch. HR

Bäuerle, Adolf 1786–1859 Austrian playwright. Although less prolific than his colleagues ALOIS GLEICH and KARL MEISL (he wrote only 78 plays), Bäuerle had as great an impact on the Viennese repertoire, primarily because of his greater sense of dramatic structure and his capacity to construct complex, comic plots. His first great comic success, *Die Bürger in Wien* (*The Bourgeois of Vienna*, 1813), introduced the character of Staberl the umbrella-maker to the Viennese stage. *Der Fiaker als Marquis* (*The Cabdriver as Marquis*, 1816) has some telling moments of social SATIRE, while *Die falsche Primadonna* (*The False Prima Donna*, 1818) at times almost touches comic greatness. From 1806 to 1860 Bäuerle edited the *Theaterzeitung*, in its time the only journal in Europe devoted solely to theatre. SW

Bauernfeld, Eduard von 1802–90 Austrian playwright. Prolific writer of comedies of manners on Viennese life, most of which were produced at the BURGTHEATER. These plays are considered to capture the essence of Viennese society during the Biedermeier period. Best-known among Bauernfeld's plays, several of which were effective SATIRES, are *Bourgeois and Romantic* (1833), *Of Age* (1846), *The Categorical Imperative* (1850) and *From Society* (1867). SW

Bax, Clifford 1886–1962 British playwright, poet and critic, heavily influenced by W. B. YEATS. Bax's major success was in historical tragedy. Besides his portrayal of Henry VIII in *The Rose without a Thorn* (1932) and *The House of Borgia* (1935), he also adapted KAREL ČAPEK's *The Insect Play* (1922–3) together with Nigel Playfair, and experimented with COMMEDIA DELL'ARTE and PARODY in *Midsummer Marriage* (1924). During the Second World War he turned to radio plays (see RADIO DRAMA) on mystical themes, and in 1945 published a work of theatrical theory that contained a strong plea for the establishment of a NATIONAL THEATRE. CI

Baxter, James K. 1926–72 New Zealand playwright. He was already established as a poet when his first radio play, *Jack Winter's Dream*, was produced in 1958, and other radio plays (see RADIO DRAMA) followed during a fellowship at the University of Otago (1966–7). His first stage plays were written for the director Richard Campion; *The Wide Open Cage* (1959) was the most successful of these. Patric Carey encouraged him to write other plays on religious, social and Greek themes, contained in *Collected Plays*, published in 1982. HDMCN

Bay, Howard 1912–86 American stage and film designer whose designs included *The Little Foxes*, *Show Boat*, *The Music Man*, *Finian's Rainbow* and *Man of La Mancha*.

Although he became associated with the sentimental MUSICALS of the 1940s and 50s, which were very painterly in style, he virtually began his career with a super-realistic tenement set for the FEDERAL THEATRE PROJECT's *One Third of a Nation*. Bay believed that a designer 'must not polish a single style', but rather must be adaptable to any situation; he was thus known as a pragmatist and for his ingenious solutions to design problems. During 1965–82 Bay taught at Brandeis University. He authored the well respected book *Stage Design* (1974). AA

Bayes, Nora [Eleanor or Leonora Goldberg] 1880–1928 American VAUDEVILLE singer-comedienne who, despite an undistinguished voice, was a major star in America and England, praised for her ability to dramatize or 'put over' a song. She introduced such standards as 'Shine on Harvest Moon', 'Has Anybody Here Seen Kelly?' and GEORGE M. COHAN's 'Over There' (1917), the most famous song of the First World War. Her second husband of five, Jack Norworth, was her stage partner during 1908–13 (the billing was 'Nora Bayes, Assisted and Admired by Jack Norworth'). Star of numerous REVUES and MUSICALS, she had a theatre named after her in 1918 (later the Forty-fourth Street Theatre). She was known for her egocentrism and temperament. Bayes nonetheless devoted much time and money to charities, especially those concerned with children (three of whom she adopted), and earned as much as $5000 a week touring. DBW

Baylis, Lilian (Mary) 1874–1937 British theatre manager. Trained as a musician, Baylis began her association with the Victoria Theatre (popularly known as the OLD VIC) when it was run as a temperance hall providing cheap family entertainment under her aunt, Emma Cons. Taking over in 1912, she mounted a complete cycle of SHAKESPEARE's First Folio plays from *The Taming of the Shrew* in 1914 to *Troilus and Cressida* in 1923, an undertaking that no theatre had attempted before. Directed by BEN GREET and with players of the stature of SYBIL THORNDIKE, these established a reputation for the theatre that continued after her death up to 1963, when it became the temporary stage of the new NATIONAL THEATRE company. Appointed a Companion of Honour for her services to the arts in 1929, she reopened SADLER'S WELLS THEATRE in 1931, founding the companies that eventually became the Royal Ballet and the English National Opera. CI

Bayreuth This Franconian city has two notable theatres. First there is the Margrave's Opera House, designed by members of the BIBIENA FAMILY, opened in 1748 and regarded nowadays as a perfect example of rococo theatre architecture. Then there is the Festival Theatre, opened by RICHARD WAGNER in 1876, built specifically for the performance of *The Ring of the Nibelung* and, as it transpired later, for his other mature music dramas. The auditorium of the Festival Theatre is one of the first examples of the arrangement known in America as the 'European style'. It has a wedge-shaped auditorium, a sunken orchestra pit and a proscenium arch, which is repeated on the side walls of the auditorium. These features, combined with the unusually long acoustic reverberation of the wooden auditorium, have created a theatre space where Wagner's spectacular, large-scale works can be seen and heard under conditions of remarkable concentration, even intimacy. Wagner's music dramas are still performed at annual music festivals at Bayreuth, under the direction of the Wagner family. (See also THEATRE DESIGN.) SW

bear-baiting see BAITING

Beaton, Cecil 1904–80 British theatrical set and COSTUME designer, photographer and writer. Beaton's career as a designer (see THEATRE DESIGN) began after he was permitted to photograph Edith Sitwell, who introduced him into theatrical circles. His neo-romantic style is illustrated in his well known designs for the stage which include costumes for the MUSICAL *My Fair Lady* (1956), and for *Lady Windermere's Fan* (1946). He also created exuberant designs for film – *Gigi* (1958), *My Fair Lady* (1964) and in 1970 *On a Clear Day You Can See Forever* (which he co-designed). Beaton's style, particularly suited to the ballet, is evident in his designs for Frederick Ashton's *Les Sirènes* (1946), *Swan Lake* (1952) and *Marguerite et Armand* (1963). TM

Beatty, John Lee 1948– American designer, educated at Brown and Yale Universities. Active since the early 1970s with the MANHATTAN THEATRE CLUB and CIRCLE REPERTORY COMPANY, among others, by the mid-1980s Beatty had become the most prolific designer in New York, having as many as six shows running simultaneously. A master of poetic or lyric REALISM, he designed the premieres of virtually all the plays of LANFORD WILSON and several by BETH HENLEY. His ability to create evocative settings through deceptive simplicity has worked well for many new plays at the NEW YORK SHAKESPEARE FESTIVAL and many regional theatres, as well as for McNALLY's *Lips Together, Teeth Apart* (1991) and *Ain't Misbehavin'* (1978) and several other small MUSICALS. He is also known for playful and theatrical settings, such as the caricature environment for *Song of Singapore* (1991) and the shows by magicians Penn and Teller. A 1993 Lucille Lortel Award recognized the 'body of his work'. AA

Beaumarchais, Pierre-Augustin Caron de 1732–99 French playwright, whose work for the stage occupied only a fraction of his energetic life as government agent, financial speculator, litigant and commercial entrepreneur. Son of a Paris watchmaker, he used this skill to gain an entrée to court, where he advanced himself with characteristic opportunism, giving music lessons to the king's daughters, acquiring a position and the title Beaumarchais by marriage to a rich widow and purchasing various royal charges. His dramatic career began with *parades*, short sketches modelled on those acted at the fair theatres and written for private performance; but with *Eugénie* (1767), a domestic drama, he produced his first serious work and published it with a supporting essay showing clearly the influence of DIDEROT's advocacy of this new genre (see DRAMATIC THEORY). The play was quite well received, but another in the same vein, *Les Deux Amis* (*The Two Friends*, 1770), proved a failure.

With a display of tongue-in-cheek contrition he turned to COMEDY, contriving an exquisite confection of all the genre's traditional devices. This was the first of his Figaro plays, *The Barber of Seville*, which despite some initial difficulties with the censor was a huge success at the COMÉDIE-FRANÇAISE in 1775, but the underlying note of seriousness in its sequel, *The Marriage of Figaro*, fell badly foul of CENSORSHIP. It was considered dangerously critical of authority, and permission to present it publicly was withheld for several years. The opening night at the Comédie-Française in 1784 was a keenly anticipated and historic occasion: ecstatic applause came from all parts of the house, not least from the aristocracy themselves, and a record run of performances ensued. Because of its proximity to the events of 1789 the play's political significance can too easily be overestimated, but as a comedy it is remarkable for having captured a sense of grievance and dissent in the air of its time.

Beaumarchais's next work was an opera, *Tarare* (1787), with music by Salieri, and in 1792 he returned to heavy-handed domestic sentiment with the last Figaro play, *La Mère coupable* (*The Guilty Mother*). Using the same central characters, the trilogy as a whole thus charts in miniature a progression from 'artificial' comedy to 'realistic' domestic drama. Meanwhile, he had founded the Société des Auteurs, introducing an author's royalty on all theatrical performances; established a printing press to publish the first complete edition of VOLTAIRE's works; and exported arms to the American colonies during the War of Independence. A protracted arms mission on behalf of the Revolution led to accusations of fraud, seizure of his property, temporary exile and disgrace for his entire family, but he still managed to avoid the guillotine and died peacefully in his bed. DR

Beaumont, (Hugh) Binkie [Hughes Griffiths Morgan] 1908–73 British theatre impresario, who became the managing director of H. M. Tennent Ltd and its non-profit subsidiary, Tennent Productions Ltd. For a quarter of a century, from the mid-1930s to the early 1960s, Beaumont was one of the most powerful impresarios in British theatre, concerning himself mainly with dramas and comedies. His tastes were restrained: he liked fine writing in plays and helped such dramatists as CHRISTOPHER FRY and TERENCE RATTIGAN. H. M. Tennent Ltd became associated in the 1950s with star-studded WEST END productions of small-cast, opulently dressed and staged plays, and, consequently, became a target for such 'angry young men' as KENNETH TYNAN. Beaumont became a governor of the Shakespeare Memorial Theatre in 1950 and was also a member of the NATIONAL THEATRE board from 1962 to 68. Modest and retiring, he was an astute businessman and clearly understood the middle- and upper-middle-class tastes for which his productions were mainly intended. JE

Beaumont, Francis 1584–1616 English playwright and poet, a member of the rural gentry, who left Oxford University without a degree in 1598 and was a casual law student at the Inner Temple in London after 1600. His first play, *The Woman Hater* (1605), is a COMEDY OF HUMOURS written for the BOYS OF ST PAUL'S. A second, the only other extant play of which he was sole author, was performed by the CHILDREN OF THE CHAPEL ROYAL. This is the witty and

John Kani as Vladimir and Winston Ntshona as Estragon in Beckett's *Waiting for Godot*, the Old Vic, London, 1981.

splendidly good-humoured *The Knight of the Burning Pestle* (1607), in which the bourgeois taste for chivalric romance is kindly mocked. The rest of Beaumont's dramatic work was written in a famous collaboration with JOHN FLETCHER. They succeeded SHAKESPEARE as leading playwrights for the King's Men in about 1609, providing the company with a sequence of popular successes including *Philaster* (c.1609), *The Maid's Tragedy* (c.1610) and *A King and No King* (1611). Perhaps because they shared a fashionably educated audience's fondness for mellifluous verse, spicy sexual encounters and neatly paralleled situations, Beaumont and Fletcher became leaders of refined theatrical taste. Their natural home was less the GLOBE than the King's Men's newly acquired indoor theatre in the BLACKFRIARS. Beaumont's active involvement did not long survive his marriage in 1613, and of the many plays sometimes ascribed to the two friends, only a handful can be confidently attributed, in any significant part, to him. These include, in addition to the three finer works already mentioned, *Cupid's Revenge* (c.1611), *The Coxcomb* (1612), *The Scornful Lady* (c.1613) and *The Captain* (1613).
PT

Beck, Julian see LIVING THEATRE

Beckett, Samuel 1906–89 Irish-French playwright and novelist. Like ADAMOV and IONESCO, Beckett only became known as a playwright relatively late in life when, in 1953, *En attendant Godot* was successfully produced by BLIN. The play was both so brilliant and so different from anything audiences were accustomed to that it became a great talking point in cultural circles. The British premiere of *Waiting for Godot* (directed by HALL, 1955) had a similarly explosive effect on English theatre. But when Beckett wrote *Godot* he had already completed the greater part of his prose *oeuvre*, including the trilogy *Molloy*, *Malone Dies* and *The Unnamable*.

He had grown up in Dublin in a Protestant family, and taken a job briefly teaching French at Trinity College. But he soon moved into self-imposed exile in London and then in Paris, where he lived almost continuously after 1937. Some of his plays were written in French, some in English; in each case Beckett did his own translations into the other language. In *Godot* and subsequent plays, especially *Endgame* (first performed as *Fin de partie* and directed by Blin in London, 1957), *Krapp's Last Tape* (1958) and *Happy Days* (1961), Beckett succeeded in creating rituals for celebrating nothing which are both philosophically uncompromising and theatrically inventive. He appears to have been influenced by the Dublin MUSIC-HALLS he visited in his youth and his characters' dialogue owes much to comic cross-talk acts. But his achievement was that through whittling away the traditional elements of plot, setting and character he created a dynamic image for the static experience of waiting, remembering and struggling with the characteristically modern sense of futility. His characters are often devoid of 'personality', possessing only the clown's self-conscious and anguished awareness that his sole function is to keep the game going. Their appeal on stage stems from Beckett's gift for creating literal images for degenerating life conditions, and some of these have become proverbial: Hamm's parents living in dustbins (*Endgame*) or Winnie, buried in a mound, first up to her waist, then up to her neck (*Happy Days*). By such means, Beckett creates compressed images of the whole human situation.

After the late 1960s he wrote only short dramatic fragments in which the clown figure has disappeared, to be replaced by ghostly shapes, only half seen, struggling to retain a feeble hold on their sense of themselves and of the space in which they move or speak. But Beckett also became more involved in the production of his own works, and records of his direction – e.g. of *Waiting for Godot* in Berlin, 1975 – have led to increased understanding of his dramaturgical originality.   DB

Becque, Henry 1837–99 French dramatist. Becque's significance for the development of NATURALISM in the theatre is out of proportion to his actual dramatic output. His early play, *Michel Pauper* (1870), was already a committedly socialist piece. *La Navette* (*The Shuttle*), about a lady with three lovers, a foretaste of *The Parisienne*, disgusted audiences at the Gymnase in 1878. Two years later his MUSSET-ish badinage *Les Honnêtes Femmes* (*Honest Women*) had a better reception. In 1882, five years after its writing, having been turned down by a number of theatres, *Les Corbeaux* (*The Crows*) received its premiere at the COMÉDIE-FRANÇAISE. This was a stormy event followed by long battles in the press, and signalled the arrival of naturalism in the national theatre. Becque had moved beyond the WELL MADE PLAY to the well observed play, an accurate depiction of the less pleasant side of late-19th-century society. The 'crows' are birds of prey who descend on the women of a family after the death of the father. One of the daughters finally 'saves' the family by marrying the man whom she knows to have been the cause of their poverty.

The Parisienne (1885) had even less plot, lacking exposition and denouement, and was the prototype of the 'slice of life' play. It presented a married woman with a complaisant husband, a jealous lover and another lover. In a short piece, *Veuve!* (*Widow!*), Becque explored the situation after the death of the husband. *The Parisienne* was first staged at the Renaissance with RÉJANE, and joined the repertoire of the Comédie-Française in 1890.

Becque wrote little in his later years apart from some one-act sketches and an unfinished work, *Les Polichinelles, ou Le Monde d'argent* (*Polichinelles, or The World of Money*), but in 1895 he published his *Memoirs of a Dramatist*. His two major plays heralded the bitter comedies, the *comédies rosses*, that would become a major fea-

ture of the Théâtre Libre repertoire, and his achievement is best measured by comparing him with such 'realist' dramatists as AUGIER and DUMAS *père*, still working within the framework of the well made play.   JMCC

Bedford, Brian 1935– British-born actor. Since his 1959 US acting debut in PETER SHAFFER's *Five Finger Exercise*, Bedford has devoted his career to US and Canadian stages, winning awards in *The Knack* (Obie, 1965) and *School for Wives* (Tony, 1971). His numerous appearances at the STRATFORD FESTIVAL (Ontario) over a dozen seasons have included Malvolio, Angelo (*Measure for Measure*), Leontes, Richard II, Tartuffe, Bottom, Richard III, and six roles opposite MAGGIE SMITH. His most recent New York roles were Alceste in CIRCLE IN THE SQUARE's production of *The Misanthrope* (1982–3) and the British actor W. C. MACREADY in RICHARD NELSON's *Two Shakespearean Actors* (1992) and Timon of Athens for the National Actors Theatre, New York (1993). In addition to periodic New York engagements he has been seen (primarily in SHAKESPEARE or MOLIÈRE) at the JOHN F. KENNEDY CENTER, the Old Globe Theatre (San Diego) and the Shakespeare Theatre at the Folger, Washington, DC. Since 1975 he has had starring roles in national tours of *Equus*, *Deathtrap*, *Whose Life is It Anyway?*, *The Real Thing* and his own one-man show based on Shakespeare's life and works, *The Lunatic, The Lover & The Poet*.   DBW

Beeston, Christopher c.1580–1639 English actor and theatre manager who may have been trained for the stage by AUGUSTINE PHILLIPS, and was briefly with the LORD CHAMBERLAIN'S MEN and then with Worcester's Men at the ROSE. Beeston made his reputation at the RED BULL during that theatre's boisterous occupation by Queen Anne's Men, for whom, during 1612–19, he was an autocratic business manager. In 1616, he acquired the lease of the COCKPIT in Drury Lane, converting and renaming it the PHOENIX in 1617. It was as manager and impresario at the Phoenix that Beeston exerted a major influence on the Jacobean and Caroline theatre. His dominance was acknowledged in the popular name of the last of the many companies he established there, Beeston's Boys (1637–40). PT

Beeston, William c.1606–82 English theatre manager, the son of CHRISTOPHER BEESTON, from whom he inherited control of Beeston's Boys at the PHOENIX in 1639. He was replaced by DAVENANT in 1640, after twice offending the authorities by his choice of plays. Certainly he maintained his theatrical ambitions during the Interregnum. His activities at the indoor theatre in SALISBURY COURT may have provoked its dismantling by soldiers in 1649. Beeston refurbished it for performance in 1660 and probably retained a managerial interest until the building's destruction in the Great Fire of 1666. In retirement, he was a noted theatrical raconteur.   PT

Behan, Brendan 1923–64 Irish playwright. A child of the tenements, Behan credited his education to his prison terms, though he owed much to his family – well read and of strong Republican sympathies. At 14 he joined the IRA, and spent two years in an English Borstal, convicted in

1939 of carrying explosives. Released and deported, in 1942 he got 14 years for shooting at a policeman during an IRA ceremony.

Amnestied in 1947, Behan continued the writing begun in prison, mainly short stories in an inventive stylization of Dublin vernacular. His plays brought him celebrity. In 1954 the Pike Theatre presented *The Quare Fellow*, a grimly comic drama of the hours preceding a prison hanging. Much more than propaganda against judicial execution, it captures, with remarkable economy of form and neutrality of tone, the condition of the outcast and the emotions excited by barbaric revenge. JOAN LITTLEWOOD's 1956 Theatre Workshop production in London made Behan famous.

Success was unmanageable. Behan's irresolute discipline collapsed into international drinking bouts. *The Hostage* (1958), his next play, derived from his one-act Gaelic play *An Giall*, was acclaimed in London, Paris and New York. Much influenced by Joan Littlewood's improvisational theatre, it travesties with song and danceand Behan's easy connivancethe tragic simplicity of its original. His last serious work, *Borstal Boy* (1958), is an imaginatively controlled account of his Borstal years, itself the testimony to a sophisticated creative power and great generosity of feeling.

A clamorous Dublin presence, belligerent or convivial, Behan illuminated the theatrical drabness of the 1950s. He subdued his vivid personality to an objective form, and his work, however brief, is continuous with a tradition, that of O'CASEY's urban drama. DM

Behn, Aphra 1640–89 The first English woman to be a professional playwright. She lived in Surinam from 1663 to 1664, an experience on which her novella *Oroonoko* was based. In 1666 she was employed as a spy by the English government in Antwerp but, arriving back in London in 1667 penniless, she was imprisoned for debt and had to appeal for her government pay. She wrote at least 17 plays, mostly comedies but including one FARCE OPERA, *The Emperor of the Moon* (1687), which made use of massive stage spectacle and a French COMMEDIA DELL'ARTE plot. Her comedies, well crafted and vigorous, return frequently to the miseries of mercenary, loveless marriages. She wrote political comedies of Tory propaganda, e.g. *The Roundheads* (1681), as well as SATIRES on contemporary behaviour, e.g. *The Lucky Chance* (1686) and *Sir Patient Fancy* (1678). Her best play, *The Rover* (1677), was based on THOMAS KILLIGREW's *Thomaso* and sets the rake's freedom against the independence and wit of Hellena. She produced a sequel in 1681. PH

Behrman, S(amuel) N(athaniel) 1893–1973 American playwright. Though Behrman came from a middle-class family, his plays are typically set in genteel upper-class drawing rooms. Dramatizing conflicts of conscience and values among wealthy, privileged characters, Behrman produced a steady series of urbane and curiously impersonal high comedies such as *The Second Man* (1927), *Biography* (1932), *End of Summer* (1936), *No Time for Comedy* (1939) and *But for Whom Charlie* (1964). Two recurrent character types haunt his salons: fashionable, tolerant matrons (often played, charmingly, by INA CLAIRE) and cynically detached self-made artists and sybarites. Not quite problem plays or plays of ideas in the Shavian mould, Behrman's discussion dramas (notably weak in story and structure) chart the progress of his well-spoken characters towards a position of worldly compromise, a sophisticated *via media*. The THEATRE GUILD presented most of Behrman's work, and his smart comedies have come to be identified as the Guild's prevailing house style. FH

Beijing opera see JINGXI

Béjart family French actors, whose careers were intimately linked with that of MOLIÈRE. **Joseph**, the eldest brother (c.1616–59), was a co-founder in 1643 of Molière's first theatrical venture, the Illustre-Théâtre, and subsequently shared his fortunes as a strolling player in the provinces but died prematurely without participating in the years of success in Paris. Afflicted with a stammer on which he doubtless capitalized in comic roles, he was a useful and well liked company member who also contrived to publish two books on heraldry. **Madeleine** (1618–72) was already an experienced actress when she helped to establish the Illustre-Théâtre, and became Molière's touring companion as well as his mistress before returning with him to the capital in 1658. Her devoted support as performer (and for a time as business manager) was of incalculable importance to him for almost 30 years, until she predeceased him by exactly a twelvemonth. She played tragic heroines (e.g. Jocaste in RACINE's first play, *La Thébaïde* (*The Thebaid*), and created several of Molière's outspoken soubrettes (e.g. Dorine in *Tartuffe*). Her sister **Geneviève** (1624–75), who adopted her mother's maiden name, Mlle Hervé, was another of the original members of the Illustre-Théâtre and thereafter a constant member of Molière's company – more noted for tragic roles, though she played Bélise in *Les Femmes savantes* (*The Learned Ladies*). **Louis** (1630–78), known as L'Éguisé on stage, joined the company later to play old men and supporting roles such as La Flèche in *L'Avare* (*The Miser*), where Molière made use of his limp and had Harpagon call him a 'lame devil'. When he retired in 1670 he was the first member of the company to be awarded a pension.

Armande **(-Grésinde-Claire-Élizabeth)** (1641–1700), Madeleine's youngest sister or possibly her illegitimate daughter, was brought up as a member of Molière's itinerant company and became his wife in 1662. Gossip, articulated by the playwright's lampooned enemy MONTFLEURY, suggested that Molière had thus married his own daughter by his mistress, though Louis XIV's willingness to stand as godfather to their first-born two years later effectively stifled the aspersion. Although the marriage itself was not happy (and the widowed Armande later remarried), the parallel stage partnership was probably a vital element in her husband's success. Benefiting no doubt from his advice, she proved a fine actress and after her debut in 1663 she played most of Molière's young heroines (e.g. Célimène in *The Misanthrope*, Elmire in *Tartuffe*, Henriette in *The Learned Ladies* and Angélique in *Le Malade imaginaire* (*The Imaginary Invalid*)), parts which he had fashioned for her. It was she too, with the help of LA GRANGE, who rallied the company after his death. DR

Bel Geddes, Norman 1893-1958 American set and industrial designer, who pioneered the use of lenses in STAGE LIGHTING equipment. Bel Geddes is probably better known for his industrial designs, ranging from cars to stoves; he is sometimes called 'the father of streamlining'. The number of his designs for the theatre was small in comparison with his contemporaries, but they were often visionary and influential. His most ambitious design was for an unrealized project based on *The Divine Comedy*. The set was to include 70-ft towers and a performance area some 100ft wide. His designs are suggestive, emblematic, and possessed of towering grandeur, thus creating a theatrical sense of space. Most of his scenic designs that were executed were detailed and naturalistic, such as *Dead End*, because of the demands of the theatre at the time. He is best known for transforming the Century Theatre (the renamed NEW THEATRE) into a cavernous gothic cathedral for MAX REINHARDT'S production of *The Miracle*. Bel Geddes also had projects for innovative theatre spaces that altered the traditional audience–performer relationship. His autobiography, *Miracle in the Evening*, was published in 1960. AA

Belasco, David 1853-1931 American director, playwright and manager. A San Francisco native, he made his acting debut there (1872) and toured the West as a supporting player, settling at San Francisco's Baldwin Theatre as stage manager and playwright (1878-82). There he collaborated with JAMES A. HERNE in writing and producing, and first worked with Gustave Frohman, who took him to New York as stage manager and resident dramatist for the new MADISON SQUARE THEATRE (1882). In 1884 he moved to DANIEL FROHMAN'S LYCEUM THEATRE, performing the same tasks until 1890, when he became an independent producer. His long apprenticeship involved the staging of scores of productions and the writing, alone or in collaboration, of more than three dozen plays. The first play of which he was sole author was *May Blossom* (1884), but his first successes were in collaboration with HENRY C. DeMILLE, beginning with *The Wife* (1887). Until 1902 Belasco produced plays for booking by the THEATRICAL SYNDICATE. His most notable productions in this period were *Madam Butterfly* (1900), *Under Two Flags* (1901), *The Auctioneer* (1901) and *Du Barry* (1901). He broke with the Theatrical Syndicate in a dispute over fees, leased a theatre from OSCAR HAMMERSTEIN, and entered into the richest phase of his career (1902-15). During this period he did 42 original productions and revivals in New York City and on tour. The most famous were *The Darling of the Gods* (1902), *The Girl of the Golden West* (1905), *The Rose of the Rancho* (1906),

Norman Bel Geddes's famous set for *Dead End* by Sidney Kingsley, Belasco Theatre, 1935.

The Easiest Way (1909) and *The Governor's Lady* (1912). He also built a new theatre (1907) and kept both houses active for the rest of the period. Though he was responsible for another 35 productions between 1915 and his retirement in 1930, his influence had waned, and his work was treated condescendingly.

Though prodigiously active as a playwright, affixing his name to some 70 works, none still holds the stage. Even in playwriting his greatest contribution was in creating and managing stage effects. In collaborating with DeMille, Belasco would pace the stage, describing scenes and effects while DeMille took notes. DeMille would then write out the dialogue, which Belasco would polish during rehearsals. As a producer Belasco did nothing that had not been done before, but he did it more elaborately and carefully. Desiring to be realistic without being unpleasant, he combined a scenic REALISM, which demanded solid, three-dimensional pieces and actual objects whenever possible, with MELODRAMATic action and sentimental idealization of character. Working with the designer Louis Hartmann and the technicians John H. and Anton Kliegl, he pioneered the use of electric lights to create mood. He selected talented but relatively unknown performers (BLANCHE BATES, MRS LESLIE CARTER, FRANCES STARR and DAVID WARFIELD) whom he cast to type in vehicles created for them. Each piece was rehearsed for 10 weeks (rather than the normal four), so that as nearly as possible the leading performers were playing carefully derived extensions of their own personalities on stage. Belasco's memoir, *The Theatre through Its Stage Door*, was published in 1919. DMCD

Belasco Theatre (New York City) Opened on 16 October 1907 with a production of *A Grand Army Man*, starring DAVID WARFIELD and directed by the new theatre's owner, producer DAVID BELASCO. (Until 1910 the theatre was called the Stuyvesant, to avoid confusion with another house bearing Belasco's name.) The theatre, which cost $750,000 to build, was elaborately decorated. The stage and backstage areas were unusually well equipped, and the lighting system – a special interest of Belasco's – was considered to be particularly innovative. In 1909 Belasco added a penthouse, which contained offices and a lavish apartment for himself. Belasco continued to produce at the theatre until his death in 1931: among his spectacularly conceived productions there were *The Return of Peter Grimm* (1911), with David Warfield; *The Governor's Lady* (1912), in which an accurate replica of a Child's Restaurant (a US chain) was built onstage; and a memorable 1922 presentation of *The Merchant of Venice*, with Warfield as Shylock. After Belasco's death the theatre was leased, at various times, to KATHARINE CORNELL, ELMER RICE, the GROUP THEATRE and the National Broadcasting Company, which used it as a radio playhouse in the early 1950s. It became a legitimate theatre again in 1953. The Belasco, which seats approximately 1000 spectators, is currently owned by the SHUBERT ORGANIZATION. Tony Randall's new classical repertory company, the National Players, was housed in the Belasco in 1991. BMCN

Belaval, Emilio (S.) 1903–72 Puerto Rican essayist, playwright, director and producer. Belaval studied law at the University of Puerto Rico; he was later president of the Puerto Rican Atheneum and a member of the Supreme Court. In 1939 he created Areyto, a popular but short-lived theatre group. He was a major contributor to the development of modern Puerto Rican theatre because of his books and essays, his work in promoting theatre, and his plays: *La presa de los vencedores* (*The Victors' Prey*, 1939), *Hay que decir la verdad* (*The Truth Must be Told*, 1940), *La muerte* (*Death*, 1950), *La vida* (*Life*, 1958) and *Cielo caído* (*Fallen Sky*, 1960). GW

Belgium (See also MEDIEVAL DRAMA IN EUROPE (The Low Countries).) The earliest history of Belgian theatre, particularly that of Flanders where Dutch was spoken, bears a close resemblance to that of the Netherlands. In fact, the two countries, then called the Low Countries, were one until 1830. A major difference lies in the fact that in the south (present-day Belgium) two languages are spoken – namely Dutch and, in the Walloon part, French).

The Mons PASSION PLAY, written in French and dating from 1501, is an important point of reference for LITURGICAL DRAMA, just as the *First* and *Seventh Joy of Mary*, composed in Flemish and dating from around 1440, are early witnesses of MIRACLE PLAYS. The miracle plays *Mariken van Nieumeghen* and *Elckerlijc* present two highlights of the genre. With the rise of the *Rederijkers* (Rhetoricians) in the 16th century, drama in the Low Countries became better organized, and came to the fore in Flanders. A tendency towards the didactic, and a preference for abstract characters by means of allegorical presentation, dominated poetic and dramatic works of art. Particularly noteworthy for their cultural importance were the spectacular *landjuwelen* ('country jewels'), in which the *Kamers van Rhetorike* (Chambers of Rhetoric) took part and which covered several days.

Pyramus and Thisbe by Matthijs de Castelein (1488–1555) would seem to offer a first, if somewhat cautious, pointer to the Renaissance. However, a large number of these allegories exercised an ever-increasing impetus to the spread of Protestantism. As a result, the *Rederijkers* fell into disgrace with the Roman Catholic authorities. Moreover, Spanish Catholic rule claimed many victims, particularly among the *Rederijkers*, who remained loyal to their faith and country. Consequently, after the fall of Antwerp in 1585 many artists fled to the north and to Amsterdam, which now became the new cultural centre of the Low Countries. Because of constant wars, the Renaissance never flourished in Belgium.

In the 17th and 18th centuries there was hardly any theatrical activity; drama relapsed into medieval allegory and *vaudevilles*, modelled on French lines. Michiel de Swaen (1654–1707), however, proved an exception. His *The Blessed Cobblers, or The Crowned Boot* (1688) showed force and originality.

In 1830 Belgium achieved independence and French became the official language. In reaction to this development, the Flemish started to become more self-assured. The Vlaamse Beweging (the Flemish Movement) gave a strong boost to Flemish drama. The first official Flemish theatre, the Koninklijke Nationale Schouwburg (KNS) (Royal National Theatre), was opened in 1853. In 1887 another theatre, the Koninklijke Vlaamse Schouwburg

(KVS) (Royal Flemish Theatre), followed in Brussels, a city mainly inhabited by French-speaking citizens. Cyriel Buysse (1859–1932), a well known novelist, was one of many who contributed to this gradual revival. In his play *The Paemel Family* (1903), the economic decline of the Flemish labourers is portrayed in a sombre style, following the realistic-naturalistic tradition (see REALISM).

The best-known playwright from around 1900 is MAURICE MAETERLINCK. This Fleming, who wrote in French and reached international fame through plays like *Les Aveugles* (1890), *La Princesse Maleine* (1889) and *Pelléas et Mélisande* (1892), represents the victory of SYMBOLISM over NATURALISM. Maeterlinck was fascinated by the dimensions that make life elusive, such as mysterious forces and blindness. Only through contemplation, absolute silence and inactivity could these be elucidated. His plays are characterized by their lack of action or conflict. This made him, in the eyes of some, a precursor of absurdism (see THEATRE OF THE ABSURD). In *Le Cocu magnifique* (1920) Fernand Crommelynck (1885–1970), in inimitable style, portrayed marital jealousy and the obsession with sin. MEYERHOLD's famous staging of the play in 1922, acted in bio-mechanical style, is still a highlight in the history of modern theatre.

Another Fleming who wrote in French, MICHEL DE GHELDERODE, became known after the Second World War. His comedies pictured a world in which madness and sanity, the tragic and the burlesque, meet and clash, and the power of death is everywhere – as in his *Pantagleize* (1929), *Magie rouge* (1931) and *Hop Signor* (1935). Herman Teirlinck (1879–1967) is important primarily as a theorist (he introduced APPIA and CRAIG), and as a founder of the Antwerp school of drama, which now bears his name. As a playwright, he is an exponent of EXPRESSIONISM (*De vertraagde film* (*The Slow-motion Film*, 1922)).

After the Second World War, Belgian theatre was dominated by repertory companies such as the KNS and the KVS. The Vlaamse Volkstoneel (Flemish People's Theatre) did not receive financial support, because in the eyes of the suppliers of subsidy it showed too much interest in social and political causes. From 1922 onwards this company became a household name, under the inspired leadership of Jan de Gruyter (1885–1929). He renewed the repertory and built up a solid company without employing the star system. However, after the war it proved difficult to continue. The most important author of this postwar generation is HUGO CLAUS.

In Belgium as in other European countries around 1968, a strong reaction took place against the established theatre and what were considered its rigid structures (see AKTIE TOMAAT; VORMINGSTONEEL). A group by the name of Kollektief INTERNATIONALE NIEUWE SCENE (New International Stage) was one of the companies to emerge from this dissatisfaction. They are a political theatre movement with a strong socialist tendency. In particular, their performance of DARIO FO's *Mistero buffo* gave them an international reputation. Developments in this period in Belgium run strikingly parallel to those in the Netherlands.

The main interest of Belgian theatre in the 1980s derived from a young generation of theatre artists who were experimenting with new forms of theatre, e.g. Jan Decorte. Jan Fabre (b.1958) has risen rapidly to international fame with two works, namely *Het is theater zoals te verwachten en te voorzien was* (*It Is the Kind of Theatre One Could Expect and Foresee*, 1982–3) and *De macht der theaterlijke dwaasheden* (*The Power of Theatrical Follies*, 1984), performed also outside Belgium. Originally a plastic artist, he produces strongly RITUAListic and visual theatre. During his frequently lengthy plays (five to eight hours), Fabre puts the theatrical conventions under constant discussion – e.g. traditional differences between actor and character become unclear, and traditional story-lines or themes disappear. He prefers to work with people who have not been to drama school, whom he pushes almost to the limits of their physical endurance; the repetition of act and movement seems to express a postmodern sense of life. Recent performances include *Das glas im kopf wird vom glas* (*The Glass in the Head Becomes Glass*, 1987) and *Sweet Temptations* (1991).

In the field of dance, especially where minimal dance is concerned, Anne Therese de Keersmaeker plays an important part. In cooperation with Steve Reich she put on *Phase, Four Movements on the Music of Steve Reich* (1982). Her performances are characterized by the linking of music with complicated dance constructions, which move in phases; the repeating movements stand alone and abstract, stripped of all traditional dramatic impact (*Bartok-Aantekeningen*, 1987; *Ottone Ottone*, 1988).

During the 1980s a powerful generation of young directors increasingly dominated the Flemish theatre landscape, with their own interpretations of the established drama repertory. Because of their influence on the Dutch theatre, this generation is known as the Flemish Wave. Working with little companies of motivated actors or with ad hoc groups, they present refreshing, ironic and non-emotional visions of the classics: Jan Decorte with his group the Trojaanse Paard – Trojan Horse (*King Lear*, 1983); Jan Lauwers with his Needcompany (*Antony and Cleopatra*, 1987; *Julius Caesar*, 1990); Guy Joosten and Luk Perceval with the Blauwe Maandag – Blue Monday (CHEKHOV's *Meeuw* (*The Seagull*), 1988, directed by Luk Perceval); Ivo van Hove with the Tijd – Time (SCHILLER's *Don Carlos* and SHAKESPEARE's *Macbeth*, both 1988).

HS MG WH

See: G. Cohen, *Le Théâtre français en Belgique au moyen âge*, Brussels, 1953; L. van den Dries, *Omtrent de opvoering: Een pragmasemiotische benadering van opvoeringsanalyse, getoetst aan enkele Heiner Müller-produkties in Vlaanderen*, Antwerp, 1991; *Humus: Vijftien jaar Kaaitheater*, Brussel-Brugge, 1993; A. van Impe, *Over toneel: Vlaamse kroniek van het komediantendom*, Amsterdam and Tielt, 1978; M. van Kerkhoven, *De vernieuwing van het Zuid-Nederlands Toneel tussen 1950 en 1960*, Brussels, 1968; S. Lilar, *The Belgian Theatre Since 1890*, New York, 1950; F. Peeters, *Het Vlaamse Volkstoneel 1920–1924*, Antwerp, 1986; Th. de Ronde, *Het Toneelleven in Vlaanderen door de Eeuwen heen*, Leuven, 1930; C. Tindemans, 'Theater en Drama 1920–1970' in *Een halve eeuw Kunst in België*, Brussels, 1973, and *Mens, Gemeenschap en Maatschappij in de Toneelletterkunde van Zuid-Nederland 1815–1914*, 1973.

See also: bibliography of the NETHERLANDS.

Bell, John 1940– Australian actor and director. After acting in student theatre and with the Old Tote Theatre Company in Sydney, a British Council scholarship took him to Britain in 1964, where he acted with the ROYAL SHAKESPEARE COMPANY from 1964 to 69, and acted and directed at Lincoln Repertory Theatre. A co-founder of Nimrod Theatre, Sydney, in 1970, he remained an artistic director there till 1985, directing several innovative Shakespearian productions. His major roles include Arturo Ui (1971, 1985), Hamlet (1973), Henry V (1964) and Cyrano de Bergerac (1980–1). He was awarded an OBE in 1978. He is director of the Bell Shakespeare Company (initially privately funded but now part-subsidized), a touring company dedicated to innovative Shakespearian productions of appeal to young audiences as well as to the general public. MW

Bellamy, George Anne ?1731–88 Irish actress. Named George because she was born on St George's Day, she appeared as a child actress at COVENT GARDEN in 1741, playing Prue in CONGREVE's *Love for Love* and appearing with GARRICK in private performances in Kingston. In 1744 she made her debut as an adult actress, playing Monimia in OTWAY's *The Orphan*. After a brief stay in Ireland she returned to London in 1748. Her lifestyle was already established: many lovers, extravagant spending, heavy gambling and furious rows with Garrick and others in the company. It did nothing for her acting: as a contemporary commented, 'were but her love to her profession, her application to its necessary studies and her patience ... equal to her abilities, she would have few equals'. In 1750 she played Juliet to Garrick's Romeo. Performing as Euridice in *Oedipus* she was so 'overcome by the horror of the piece that she was carried off in a state of insensibility'. She was severely ill in 1757 and by the 1760s, still only in her thirties, she looked old and wrinkled. She finally retired in 1770, returning to the stage for a single benefit performance in 1780. Her ghosted autobiography in six volumes was published in 1785. PH

Belleroche see POISSON, RAYMOND

Bellerose [Pierre le Messier] ?–1670 French actor-manager, one of the leading exponents of TRAGEDY in the first half of the 17th century. Apprenticed to VALLERAN LE CONTE in 1609, he presumably remained attached to his master's itinerant company for several years, but by 1620 he was leading his own company in Marseille. He joined the Comédiens du Roi under GROS-GUILLAUME at the HÔTEL DE BOURGOGNE in 1622 and succeeded the latter as director in 1635, before selling the position to FLORIDOR in 1647 while remaining a member of the company for many years. He had a fine speaking voice which he used to good effect as company 'orator' in formal addresses to the audience and in a whole range of leading parts in tragedy and COMEDY, though some contemporaries, perhaps preferring the greater aggression of his arch-rival MONTDORY at the MARAIS, regarded Bellerose as insipid and somewhat affected. He was one of the actors appearing *in propria persona* in Gougenot's *La Comédie des comédiens* (*The Actors' Comedy*, 1631/2). DR

Bellew, Kyrle 1855–1911 British-born actor. Son of a popular preacher and public reader, Bellew served in the British Navy and merchant marine. Emigrating to Australia (1870), he abandoned gold-mining for the stage (1874). His English debut was in Brighton (30 August 1875). Subsequently, he acted with the Bancrofts (see SQUIRE BANCROFT) and with HENRY IRVING. He was a fixture in New York at WALLACK'S THEATRE during 1885–7 and from 1902 until his death. Noted for his graceful bearing and beautiful voice, he excelled in polite comedy. DMCD

Bellotti-Bon, Luigi 1820–83 Italian actor and company manager. Born into the profession, Bellotti-Bon was acting from an early age. In his twenties he acquired a wide range of experience with a number of companies, the enduring influence perhaps being that of GUSTAVO MODENA's young company in 1845 (together with TOMMASO SALVINI). In the 1850s he was a member of the Reale Sarda with RISTORI and ROSSI, and went with them to Paris, Dresden and Berlin on what was one of the first 'international' tours undertaken by an Italian company since the decline of the *COMMEDIA DELL'ARTE*. In 1859 he formed a company of his own, distinguished for the range and quality of the talents it included and the manager's own concern for high standards. He particularly encouraged new drama, and most of the leading and emerging playwrights of the day wrote for his company. The troupe enjoyed great success, and in 1873 he expanded his single company into three. Unfortunately the bid was over-ambitious, stretching both his financial and his artistic resources. He turned increasingly to French adaptations, but failed to hold his audience. Too late, he attempted to cut back, reducing the companies first to two, then to one, but was unable to cover mounting debts. After delaying for several years the inevitable financial collapse, when a bank foreclosed on him he shot himself. Bellotti-Bon was one of the most accomplished and innovative actor-managers of the century, and his tragedy sent a shock wave through the Italian theatrical and cultural scene, prompting intense discussion of the problems confronting Italian drama and theatre. KR

below Sometimes used in Elizabethan stage directions simply to indicate the location of a character on the main stage in contrast to a character ABOVE, the 'below' was also the area underneath the trestle stage from which access was possible through a trap. Very occasionally it was put to use by actors and dramatists, as, for example, by the Ghost in *Hamlet*. On medieval stages, the below could represent Hell, the abode of the Devil and his minions. Christ's harrowing of Hell could release the righteous pre-Christians from the below on to the platform. PT

Bely, Andrei [Boris (Nikolaevich) Bugaev] 1880–1934 Russian symbolist poet (see SYMBOLISM), novelist, critic, theorist and dramatist, whose 'crisis of consciousness' mirrored that of his society and produced works of stylistic brilliance. Vladimir Solovyov's moral philosophy (1905–10) engendered in him a belief in imminent apocalypse to be precipitated by the 1905 Revolution and resulting in a reconciliation with God. He embraced Rudolf Steiner's anthroposophic philosophy (1912–23), which gave scientific coherence to Christian doctrine and Eastern mysticism. He believed with the symbolists that the creative act makes life meaningful, but wavered on the question of how conscious or intuitive creation should be. He found in poetry the desired synthesis between concrete space and abstract time, and in poetry conceived as music a transcendent force. His dramas – *He Who Has Come* (1903) and *The Jaws of Night* (1907) – are from the period (1900–6) in which he championed the MYSTERY PLAY as generator of religious experience.

His 'mysteries' describe a portentous moment in time in which the earth is poised between apocalypse and the Second Coming, a situation recreated in his 1910 novel, *The Silver Dove*. Their imitative MAETERLINCKian dialogue and settings are infused with Bely's intense, hallucinogenic orchestration of rhythms, sound, light and colour. His prescient (pro-MEYERHOLD, anti-STANISLAVSKY) critical essay on *The Cherry Orchard* (1904) already pointed in a new direction, towards a more IBSENite-CHEKHOVian symbolic REALISM in which the infinite is revealed in the instant, the eternal in the seemingly quotidian. His essay 'Theatre and Modern Drama' not only rejected the mystery play but announced that 'the theatre is no place for symbolist drama'.

Bely's final experiences with theatre involved adapting his two city novels for the stage. The right to produce his Joycean symphonic *Petersburg* (1913) was awarded to MICHAEL CHEKHOV over Meyerhold and TAIROV and resulted in a much cut and altered stage version entitled *The Death of a Senator* (1925). Although Chekhov won rave reviews in the title role, the production at the MOSCOW ART THEATRE's Second Studio received mixed reviews. Impressed by Meyerhold's musically constructed theatricalist stagings of classics, Bely gave him his Moscow adaptation, but it never reached the stage. SG

Bemba, Sylvain [Michel Belavin; Martial Malinda] 1934– Congolese dramatist and novelist. His literary career began in the late 1950s with pieces in *Liaison*, the organ of the French cultural centres of French Equatorial Africa. Before turning to playwriting he wrote sketches for radio (he was trained as a journalist in Strasbourg) under the pseudonym Belavin, and produced a short feature film and a pageant on the colonial experience of the Congo. His first play *L'Enfer c'est Orfeo* (*Hell Is Orfeo*, 1966), published under the pseudonym Malinda, is about an African doctor-intellectual, Orfeo, who finds salvation in revolutionary action from his hell of self-hatred and contempt for his pleasure-seeking social class. In its preoccupation with social and economic injustices, in its use of SATIRE, fantasy (in the scene where the wounded Orfeo hallucinates) and popular African French speech, this play is typical of the rest of Bemba's dramatic work – which consists of four other published plays: *L'Homme qui tua le crocodile* (*The Man Who Killed the Crocodile*, 1973), *Une Eau dormante* (*Sleepy Waters*, 1975), *Tarentelle noire et diable blanc* (*Black Tarantula and White Devil*, 1976) and *Un Foutu de monde pour un blanchisseur trop honnête* (*A Rotten World for an Over-honest Laundryman*, 1979). Bemba is also the author of four novels and a collection of short stories. JCM

Ben-Ami, Jacob 1890–1977 Russian-born actor and director, who achieved critical acclaim on both Yiddish- and English-speaking stages. Born in Minsk, he worked with the Hirshbein Troupe in Odessa, the VILNA TROUPE and, for a short period, the Fineman Art Theatre in London. Ben-Ami emigrated to New York in 1912 and joined MAURICE SCHWARTZ's Irving Place Theatre in 1918. Dissatisfied with the superficial quality of YIDDISH THEATRE, Ben-Ami sought to modernize the repertoire. Differences with Schwartz in 1919 led him to found his own JEWISH ART THEATRE, where he discarded the old starring system and offered works by SHOLOM ALEICHEM, TOLSTOI and HAUPTMANN. (Schwartz reorganized as the YIDDISH ART THEATRE.) Discovered by ARTHUR HOPKINS, in 1920 he was given his first English-speaking role as Peter Krumback in *Samson and Delilah*. His BROADWAY acting career extended to 1972 and included Michael Cape in O'NEILL's *Welded* (1924), Arthur Kober in *Evening Song* (1934) and Forman in *The Tenth Man* (1959). He was a member of EVA LE GALLIENNE's CIVIC REPERTORY THEATRE (1929–31), portraying a memorable Trigorin in *The Seagull*. He acted and directed for the THEATRE GUILD and toured his Yiddish productions to Africa and South America. TLM AB

Benavente, Jacinto 1866–1954 Spanish playwright who from 1894 to his death wrote and staged 172 plays. His early realistic works (see REALISM), requiring a natural acting style, rejected the MELODRAMAS of ECHEGARAY then in vogue. Ironically, his subsequent domination of the Spanish stage led to protests over his Nobel Prize in 1922, comparable to those against Echegaray's award two decades before. Because of his prolific output of formula works, Benavente's name is associated with bourgeois comedies characterized by mild social SATIRE, well constructed dialogue and final scenes of reconciliation.

Neither of two masterworks that have entered the international repertoire fits this mould. *Los intereses creados* (*Bonds of Interest*, 1907) is an elaborate metaplay that uses COMMEDIA DELL'ARTE characters and classic farcical devices to satirize materialism and hypocrisy, while simultaneously PARODYing romantic love. *La malquerida* (*The Passion Flower*, 1913) reworks Greek tragedy as rural drama. The suppressed desires of the title character and her stepfather lead to the killing of her suitor and her mother. Among other major plays are *La noche del sábado* (*The Witches' Sabbath*, 1903), a blend of satire and fantasy; *Los malhechores del bien* (*The Evil-doers of Good*, 1905), a criticism of hypocrisy underscoring upper-class charity; and the rural drama *Señora ama* (*The Lady of the House*, 1908). He also wrote children's theatre. PZ

Benchley, Robert 1889–1945 American humourist, actor, drama critic and professional celebrity. Educated at Harvard University, Benchley wrote for the *New York Tribune* and *Vanity Fair* before becoming dramatic editor of the old *Life* (1920–9) and of the *New Yorker* (1929–40). His short humorous sketches on minor problems of the middle class appeared in *Life*, *Liberty* and other popular magazines. Many of these were recycled into VAUDEVILLE sketches, and later into short films in which Benchley appeared. In the 1930s, he appeared in numerous feature films. A charter member of the Algonquin Round Table and of the New York Drama Critics' Circle, Benchley was noted for his sophisticated wit and urbanity. TLM

Bene, Carmelo 1937– Italian actor, director and dramatist who began his career as an actor playing traditional roles in established theatre, but quickly went his own way and developed his combined talents of actor, writer and director. His stage presentations, often radical reorchestrations of classic drama, like his versions of SHAKESPEARE – Amleto (1975), Romeo e Giulietta (1976) and Riccardo III (1977) – or compositions such as Nostra Signora dei Turchi (Our Lady of the Turks, 1973) and S. A. D. E. (1974), have been highly original, if often controversial attempts to evolve contemporary, post-ARTAUDian performance styles centred on the physical and vocal qualities of the actor but exploiting all the technical facilities available to the modern stage, particularly light, sound and costuming. The range of his skills and the idiosyncratic nature of his work have won him considerable succès d'estime and a wide following, but have also drawn charges of empty flamboyance, exhibitionism and decadence. He is an intelligent, ambitious and always innovative writer, director and actor whose performance skills were remarkably demonstrated in his tour de force oratorio version of MANZONI's Adelchi (1984), first presented on stage, then transferred to Italian television. His commitment to striking scenic adaptation has persisted in work like Hammelette for Hamlet, 'Operetta inqualificabile' (1987), adapted from Laforgue, and in revivals such as his versions of BENELLI's La cena delle beffe (1989) and of MARLOWE's Tamburlaine (1992). Bene is a prolific commentator on his own approaches to the art of the theatre, as in Otello o la deficienza della donna (Othello, or The Inadequacy of Woman, 1981). KR

Benedetti, Mario 1920– Uruguayan playwright, novelist, short story writer and critic. After three plays, including Ida y vuelta (Return Trip, 1958), a bitter Pirandellian SATIRE (see PIRANDELLO) on problems of moral decay in the national identity, Benedetti left the theatre because productions fell short of his expectations. He subsequently wrote Pedro y el capitán (Pedro and the Captain, 1979), a virulent play about torture written during the worst period of Uruguayan political repression. ICTUS, a major professional theatre in Chile, adapted his novel Primavera con una esquina rota (Spring with a Broken Corner, 1984) for the stage, in order to portray the issues of exile and escape from political upheaval. GW

Benedix, Roderich 1811–73 German playwright and director. Benedix managed theatres in Frankfurt, Cologne and Leipzig, and was a prolific writer of light COMEDY in the manner of SCRIBE. Highly popular in their day, his plays have now disappeared totally from the repertoire. SW

Benelli, Sem 1877–1949 Italian dramatist and poet. Benelli's best work was done in the decade or so before the First World War: costume drama in the manner of D'ANNUNZIO that exploited a fashionable taste for pseudo-Renaissance dash, colour and dastardly deeds. Most cele-brated of such pieces in Italy and abroad was La cena delle beffe (The Jest, 1909), an exotic blank-verse tragedy of Renaissance court revenge. A prolific dramatist in his day, he was too much of his age to be of more than historical interest, although some have seen his La maschera di Bruto (The Mask of Brutus, 1908) as anticipating later experimental drama, and his comedy Tignola (1908) retains a certain charm. LR

Benin A former French possession which until 1975 was known as Dahomey, Benin has, like its eastern neighbour NIGERIA, a strong heritage in the traditional performing arts. Examples of these theatrical displays are the gelede masquerade performers (see MASQUERADES IN AFRICA); the adjogbo dancers, who are believed to seek out evil spirits; and the watchmen, the zangbeto. A thriving PUPPET theatre also existed, up to the early 20th century, in the Ouwème region of Benin.

While these activities continue to inform the cultural life of traditional Benin, they have not provided, as in Nigeria, the framework for the emergence of a modern drama, either in the national languages or in French. In fact Benin's achievements in this area are negligible. And yet Dahomey students at the École William Ponty in SENEGAL were noted in the 1930s for significant collective productions such as La Dernière Entrevue de Béhanzin et de Bayol (Béhanzin and Bayol, the Last Meeting, 1933) and L'Élection d'un roi au Dahomey (The Election of a King in Dahomey, 1935). But this early promise has not been borne out. Only a handful of Beninois have published plays, among them Maurice Mêlé (Danhômé, 1965), André Pognon (Le Trône vacant, The Vacant Throne, 1975), Henri Héssou and Kossi Attiga-Tsogbe (L'Aventurier sans scrupules, The Unscrupulous Adventurer, 1982; Droits d'auteur en Afrique, Copyright Laws in Africa, 1982), and Camille Amouro (Goli, 1991). Fourteen Dahomean plays are summarized by Julian Alapini in his Les Acteurs noirs (Black Actors, 1965). But of Benin's dramatists, only Jean Pliya, with his historical drama Kondo le requin (Kondo the Shark, 1981) and social SATIRE La Secrétaire particulière (The Confidential Secretary, 1973), has a reputation beyond the national frontiers. This inactivity has been partly blamed on successive governments which have failed to create the necessary infrastructure – theatre buildings, drama departments, competitions – for the growth of theatre.

However, Benin does not lack performance troupes, which are mostly concerned with presenting cultural dances and folklore. The more important are the Troupe Théâtrale et Folklorique d'Ekpe, founded in 1956; the Troupe Théâtrale Towakonou, founded in 1976 by a former footballer turned professional storyteller, Déhumon Adjagnon; and the Zamahara ('Voice of the People'), which under the Marxist-Leninist government of former president Mathieu Kérékou was little more than a propaganda machine. JCM

See: R. Cornevin, Le Théâtre en Afrique noire et à Madagascar, Paris, 1970; B. Koudjo, 'La pratique théâtrale au Benin', Notre Librairie: La Littérature beninoise, 69, May/Jul. 1983.

Bennett, Alan 1934– British actor and dramatist, who

was part of the highly successful *Beyond the Fringe* revue team (1960). As a character actor, Bennett specialized in woolly-minded English eccentrics, whose nursery language revealed political realities. The satiric qualities of his acting are more fully developed in his writing, which started with a REVUE-like play, *Forty Years On* (1968), recalling the changes in a minor public school. The school's pageant described the decline of Britain and while, in subsequent plays, Bennett left behind the dependence on short satiric scenes, he retained his mournful obsession with the twilight of British imperialism. *Getting On* (1971) described the disillusionment of a Labour MP, and in *The Old Country* (1977) ALEC GUINNESS played a British traitor in exile in the Soviet Union. Bennett's small-town comedy, *Habeas Corpus* (1973), contained amusing jokes about British middle-class sexual inhibitions, while *Enjoy* (1980) offered the life-cycle of a working-class couple. In 1988 he adapted his short television play, *An Englishman Abroad*, about the British spy Guy Burgess's life in Moscow, to form part of a double bill with *A Question of Attribution*, about Sir Anthony Blunt, the Keeper of the Queen's Pictures, who was also a spy – played in the NATIONAL THEATRE's production by Bennett himself. These plays (presented under the title of *Single Spies*), successful in themselves, have led to further triumphs at the NT – his adaptation of *The Wind in the Willows* (1990) and *The Madness of George III* (1991), in which NIGEL HAWTHORNE gave a masterly performance as the king who was not as mad as he looked. Bennett's television plays, *Talking Heads*, were successfully staged in 1992. JE

Bennett, (Enoch) Arnold 1867–1931 British novelist and dramatist, resident in France after 1903. After early romantic comedies (*Cupid and Common Sense*, 1908; *The Honeymoon*, 1911) he made his reputation with *The Great Adventure* (1911), based on his novel *Buried Alive*. Dealing with an artist who fakes his own death to escape the pressure of fame, it was followed by his most successful play *Milestones* (in collaboration with Edward Knoblock, 1912), which covers the human and political machinations of an English industrial family over several generations. After the First World War, in which he served as director of propaganda for the Ministry of Information, he turned to more metaphysical themes in plays like *Sacred and Profane Love* (1919) and *Body and Soul* (1922), though these were less well received than his naturalistic comedies (see NATURALISM) *London Life* (1924) and *Mr Prohack* (1927, with CHARLES LAUGHTON in the title role), both of which again were written in collaboration with Knoblock. CI

Bennett [Di Figlia], **Michael** 1943–87 American choreographer and director who began his BROADWAY career as a dancer, creating his first choreography for *A Joyful Noise* (1966). Bennett served as both director and choreographer for *Promises, Promises* (1968) and *Coco* (1969). In the early 1970s he teamed with HAROLD PRINCE and STEPHEN SONDHEIM in the creation of two 'concept MUSICALS', *Company* (1970) and *Follies* (1971), for which he served as choreographer and co-director. He next directed and choreographed the more traditional *Seesaw* (1973), followed by the critically acclaimed *A Chorus Line* (1975). A concept musical about the lives of Broadway's chorus dancers, *A Chorus Line*'s brilliant dance sequences were the most vivid element of the production. Bennett went on to direct and choreograph *Ballroom* (1978) and *Dreamgirls* (1981). Illness forced him to withdraw as director of the London production of *Chess* (1986). As a choreographer, he most often employed a precise, rhythmic, but emotionally expressive style of jazz dance admirably suited to contemporary characters and situations. MK

Bennett, Richard 1873–1944 American actor, born in Deacon's Mills, Indiana, who first appeared on the stage at the Standard Theatre, Chicago, in 1891, and made his debut on BROADWAY at NIBLO's Garden in *The Limited Mail*. His first London appearance was as Jefferson Ryder in *The Lion and the Mouse* in 1906, and his film career began in 1913. Among his more successful roles were He in *He Who Gets Slapped*, Judge Gaunt in *Winterset*, Tony in *They Knew What They Wanted* and Robert Mayo in *Beyond the Horizon*. Bennett excited considerable controversy by berating audiences and critics, even stopping shows to lecture the audience. Three of his daughters, Constance, Barbara and Joan, had successful film careers. SMA

Benois, Alexandre 1870–1960 Russian painter, art historian and designer; born in St Petersburg and emigrated to Paris in 1926. Except for a few productions at the MOSCOW ART THEATRE and elsewhere, most of his design was for OPERA and ballet. Together with Serge Diaghilev he founded the journal *Mir Isskustva* (*The World of Art*) in 1898, which resurrected Russia's folk art and became a focal point for the World of Art Group – the emerging modern artists of Russia. Benois served as artistic director for the early years of Diaghilev's Ballets Russes, and together with LÉON BAKST shaped the visual aesthetic of that group and thus exerted a profound influence on the development of European design and ballet.

Benois's designs, which were often of 18th- and 19th-century scenes, exhibit deep, rich colours; an evocative, romantic – though non-sentimental – atmosphere; and an attention to detail and scale. He designed both sets and COSTUMES, since he considered them an inseparable scenographic unit (see THEATRE DESIGN). His crowning achievement with the Ballets Russes was *Petrushka* (1911). After the mid-1920s he designed throughout Europe, primarily with the Paris Opéra, the Ballets Russes de Monte Carlo, and especially at La Scala in Milan where his son Nicola (b.1901) was resident designer. AA

Benson, F(rank) R(obert) 1858–1939 British actor-manager, whose lifelong interest in sport and in theatre was established while he was an Oxford undergraduate. In 1881, for example, he produced the *Agamemnon* in Greek and won the three-mile race against Cambridge. He made his professional debut in London at IRVING's LYCEUM in 1882, joined a touring Shakespearian company whose manager absconded, bought the remaining assets and found himself, at the age of 25, manager of the F. R. Benson Company. Engaged by Charles Flower to initiate an annual SHAKESPEARE Festival at Stratford, Benson retained his association with the Festival during 1886–1919. When he was not at Stratford, he was touring the British Isles, providing for many provincial audiences their only experience of professional Shakespearian performance. Responses to Benson's acting were to remain mixed. HERBERT BEERBOHM TREE found his Henry V beyond praise 'as a branch of university cricket', but less impressive 'as a form of acting'. For other critics, he was at his best in the HISTORY PLAYS. To his credit, he played an uncut *Hamlet* (1899) and all but two of Shakespeare's plays, and many actors did their apprenticeship in his busy company. Benson was knighted in the Royal Box at DRURY LANE in 1916. PT

Bentley, Eric (Russell) 1916– British-born drama critic, translator, editor, playwright, educator and director. Educated at Oxford and Yale (PhD, 1941), Bentley gained recognition in the late 1940s for his translations of BRECHT's plays. He worked in both the US and the European theatre, co-directing the German-language premiere of *The Iceman Cometh* in Zurich (1950) and directing his translation of *The Good Person of Setzuan* in New York (1956). Drama critic of the *New Republic* during 1952–6, Bentley also held distinguished academic positions as BRANDER MATTHEWS Professor of Dramatic Literature at Columbia University (1952–69), KATHARINE CORNELL Professor of Theatre at State University of New York–Buffalo (1977–82) and professor of comparative literature, University of Maryland (1982–). He is a noted translator of Brecht, PIRANDELLO and SCHNITZLER, author of 10 original plays, and author or editor of numerous books, including *The Playwright as Thinker* (1946), *The Life of the Drama* (1964), *The Brecht Commentaries 1943–1980* (1981) and *Thinking about the Playwright* (1987). TLM

Beolco, Angelo see RUZZANTE

Berain, Jean 1637–1711 French engraver, architect and designer, whose style represents a transitional phase between baroque and rococo. He was appointed official designer to Louis XIV in 1674, his chief function being to devise the costumes and decorations for royal ceremonies such as marriages, baptisms and funerals and for all court entertainments. Given the king's taste, these consisted predominantly of ballets, OPERAS and the elaborate open-air *fêtes* arranged by LULLY and his various associates in the gardens of Versailles and other royal palaces. He also collaborated with Lully at the Paris Opéra, where he succeeded VIGARANI as designer-machinist in 1680. If Berain's approach to scenic spectacle was rather more restrained than that of his Italian predecessors, his COSTUME designs were sumptuous and idiosyncratic, without the least regard for period accuracy or local colour but showing an inspired conjunction of fantasy and contemporary dress which amounted to a truly personal style. It was inherited, along with his post, by his son Jean (1678–1726). (See also THEATRE DESIGN.) DR

Bérard, Christian(-Jacques)
1902–49 French theatrical and film designer, graphic artist, painter and fashion designer. Bérard combined his painting with a theatrical career, much like EUGENE BERMAN and PAVEL TCHELITCHEW, two neo-romantic artists with whom he exhibited works in Paris in 1926. His sketches of Paris fashions, which he submitted to such magazines as *Vogue* and *Harper's Bazaar*, were so well recognized that he was said to have inspired fashion designer Christian Dior to create the 'New Look' in the mid-1940s.

When he was 22 Bérard designed the ballet *Les Elves* (1924), for Michel Fokine. He subsequently worked for other famous choreographers and executed such works as GEORGE BALANCHINE's *Mozartiana* (1931), Roland Petit's *Les Forains* (1945) and Léonide Massine's *Symphonie Fantastique* (1936). Along with Petit and Boris Kochno, he founded and served as co-director of the Ballet des Champs-Élysées. His designs included highly stylized productions such as JEAN COCTEAU's *The Infernal Machine* (1934), the film *Beauty and the Beast* and LOUIS JOUVET's production of JEAN GIRAUDOUX's *Madwoman of Chaillot* (1945). Bérard, a ubiquitous personality in the theatre world, was a short, dishevelled man with an unruly beard whose appearance belied the stunning beauty of his stage designs. TM

Berber, Anita see NUDITY

Berghof, Herbert 1909–90 Austrian-born actor, director and teacher who studied with ALEKSANDËR MOISIU (Alexander Moissi), MAX REINHARDT, LEE STRASBERG and at the ACTORS STUDIO (charter member). His professional debut was in *Don Carlos* (Vienna, 1927), and he was introduced to the New York theatre world as director of *From Vienna* (1939). He first appeared on BROADWAY in 1940, co-directing and performing in *Reunion in New York*. He staged the first US production of *Waiting for Godot* (1956). Berghof taught acting at Columbia University, the New School for Social Research, the NEIGHBORHOOD PLAYHOUSE and the American Theatre Wing. In 1945 he founded the Herbert Berghof Studio, which he directed with his wife, UTA HAGEN. In 1946 he founded the HB Playwrights Foundation, where he gave his last performance in August 1990 in his production of STRINDBERG's *Easter*. SMA

Bergman, Hjalmar 1883–1931 Swedish playwright. Bergman's first significant plays were his one-act *Marionette Plays* (1917), including *Mr Sleeman Is Coming*, a blend of the realistic and symbolic (see REALISM; SYMBOLISM) reminiscent of MAETERLINCK. *An Experiment* (1919) is an uneasily playful social comedy echoing SHAW's *Pygmalion*, but with *The Gambling House* (1916–23) and *The Legend* (c.1920) he attempted ambitious symbolist fantasies on moral issues. Popular success in the theatre eluded Bergman until his final plays, which are still performed: *Swedenhielms* (1923), *The Rabble* (1928), *The Markurells of Wadköping* (1929) and *The Baron's Will* (1930), the last two being dramatizations of earlier novels. These are inventive comedies, with spirited dialogue, well prepared confrontations, sudden changes of mood, and eccentric characters that make splendid acting vehicles. They remain popular in Sweden. HL

Bergman, Ingmar 1918– Swedish director, one of the century's greatest film makers, but constantly active in theatre. He began at provincial city theatres: Helsingborg, including a stark anti-Nazi *Macbeth*; GÖTEBORGS STADSTEATER (1946–50), including an intensely physical

Caligula; and MALMÖ STADSTEATER (1952–8), where he is one of few to master the huge main stage, not only for large-scale works like *The Merry Widow*, but for MOLIÈRE, IBSEN and STRINDBERG. His stagings of *The Crown Bride*, *The Ghost Sonata* and *Erik XIV* established his special grasp of Strindberg.

For three years (1963–6) Bergman headed DRAMATEN, introducing open rehearsals, higher salaries and better programmes, and directing some extraordinary productions (including a provocative *Woyzeck* and an intimate, formalistic *Hedda Gabler*). He returned to Dramaten in the 1970s for major guest engagements, especially to direct Strindberg: an intimate *Dream Play* (1970), an extraordinary, grotesque *Ghost Sonata* (1973) and an adaptation of *To Damascus*, Parts 1 and 2 (1974). Suddenly, in 1976, erroneous tax-evasion charges made him leave Sweden for nine years; he joined the Munich Residenztheater, and staged Strindberg, Molière, Ibsen, CHEKHOV and GOMBROWICZ. Particularly ambitious was his 1981 'Bergman Project': *A Doll's House*, *Miss Julie* and his own *Scenes from a Marriage*, all opening on the same evening. He has occasionally directed in Sweden (including a lavish *King Lear* in 1984) and in 1985 rejoined Dramaten, where he usually directs two productions annually, including SHAKESPEARE, Strindberg, Ibsen, O'NEILL, Mishima and Tabori. While his productions are often hotly debated in Sweden, Dramaten has very successfully toured them internationally; Bergman himself is in demand to direct abroad, but has done so infrequently, apparently preferring the security of artists and working conditions that he knows.

Bergman's directing often involves a radical reformulation of the text, rather than 'mere word fidelity', to capture in contemporary terms his sense of its perceptions. Seeing theatre as a form of conjuration, in which actor and text interact with spectator, he avoids literal REALISM, preferring to re-theatricalize rather than reproduce a text's traditional terms of representation. His stage productions have much in common with his films: they are often formal and picturesque, and they mostly support acting that is emotionally courageous. HL

Bergner, Elisabeth 1900–86 Austrian actress, a sexy, boyish star in 1920s Berlin. She was a natural for classical BREECHES roles – SHAKESPEARE's Viola, Rosalind, Portia – and also played moderns, STRINDBERG's Miss Julie and SHAW's St Joan, the latter bringing her international acclaim in 1924. Exiled in England from 1933 – BARRIE wrote *Boy David* for her – she never returned to Germany except to tour. HR

Berkoff, Steve(n) 1937– British playwright, performer and director. He first became known with the formation of the London Theatre Group in 1968, whose tightly choreographed productions of well known texts (which he adapted) featured in the programmes of major alternative theatres, from the Roundhouse to the MICKERY in Amsterdam. These included works by Kafka (*The Penal Colony*, 1968; *Metamorphosis*, 1969; and *The Trial*, 1970), SHAKESPEARE, AESCHYLUS and Edgar Allan Poe, whose *Fall of the House of Usher* (1974) transferred to the NATIONAL THEATRE. He has often featured as his own star actor, once

playing Hamlet, and his intense face, savage MIME and grating voice are hard to forget. His own plays have similar characteristics. The writing is often a mannered PARODY of other styles: *East* (1975), about his East End (London) boyhood, in a blank verse which simultaneously echoed Shakespeare and the football terraces; *Greek* (1979); *Decadence* (1981), where he writhed like Laocoön in the coils of upper-class vowel sounds; *Kvetch* (1987) and *Acapulco* (1992). As a guest director, he staged *Coriolanus* (1989) at New York's PUBLIC THEATER and notably *Salome* (1989) with the GATE THEATRE in Dublin, a production which did much to rescue OSCAR WILDE's verse drama from nearly a century of neglect. JE

Berlin, Irving [Israel Baline] 1888–1989 American composer and lyricist. With his family he emigrated to the USA from Russia at age two. He received little formal education and held a variety of jobs before publishing his first song in 1907. Four years later his 'Alexander's Ragtime Band' became an international sensation, launching a vogue for popular songs written in a ragtime or pseudo-ragtime rhythm. Berlin wrote his first complete BROADWAY score for *Watch Your Step* (1914). After contributing songs to other musical comedies and REVUES, he created the score for an all-soldier show, *Yip, Yip Yaphank* (1918), and in the following year wrote several songs for *The ZIEGFELD Follies*. During 1921–4 he and producer SAM H. HARRIS offered a series of *Music Box Revues*, which introduced many of Berlin's standards, such as 'What'll I Do?' and 'All Alone'. His other shows of the 1920s were *The Cocoanuts* (1925) and *The Ziegfeld Follies* (1927).

In the 1930s Berlin responded to a trend towards treating social and political issues in MUSICALS by creating the score to *Face the Music* (1932), a SATIRE on police corruption. He also included in his score for the revue *As Thousands Cheer* (1933) the song 'Supper Time', a lament about the lynching of a Southern black.

After spending several years writing for Hollywood films, Berlin returned to Broadway with the score for *Louisiana Purchase* (1940) and an updated all-soldier show, *This Is the Army* (1942). Four years later he wrote the music for *Annie Get Your Gun*, proving that he, like RODGERS and HAMMERSTEIN, could write a score in which the song grew naturally out of the dramatic action. In 1950 he wrote the songs for *Call Me Madam*, and 12 years later Broadway heard his final score, written for *Mr President* (1962).

Berlin was one of America's most successful composers of popular music. His most memorable contributions to the musical stage were individual songs rather than complete scores. He was rarely interested in experimentation or innovation; his strength was his ability to adapt to changing musical styles and to reflect in his music the thoughts, feelings and aspirations of average Americans. An enormous collection of Berliniana is housed at the Library of Congress. MK

Berlin Royal Theatre In 1786, DÖBBELIN took over the Komödienhaus on the Gendarmenmarkt in Berlin, where he received a royal patent to perform plays. In 1796, AUGUST IFFLAND was appointed director of this court theatre. Under him it achieved the status of a national theatre. Iffland's attention to production values, especially in the performance of plays with historical settings, did much to raise theatrical standards in Germany. After Iffland's death in 1812, the direction was taken over by Count Karl von Brühl (1772–1837), who cultivated the WEIMAR STYLE of acting in the company, despite the presence in it of LUDWIG DEVRIENT. After Brühl's retirement and Devrient's death, the pre-eminence of the National Theatre began to decline, and, although actors such as KARL SEYDELMANN and ADALBERT MATKOWSKY occasionally energized its work, its influence over the development of the German theatre fell off rapidly. SW

Berliner Ensemble German theatre company founded by HELENE WEIGEL in 1949 in the Soviet sector of the city to promote BRECHT's EPIC THEATRE. Established in the Theater am Schiffbauerdamm from 1954, it was the most influential force in the German theatre of the 1950s and 60s. Here Brecht tried out his concepts of acting and directing – on his own plays (*Mother Courage*, *The Mother*, *The Caucasian Chalk Circle*) and on the classics (KLEIST's *Broken Jug*, *Drums and Trumpets* after FARQUHAR, and LENZ's *Tutor*), as well as promoting new writing. He developed an anti-illusionistic style in which a bare stage, a cyclorama, revealed lights and overall unatmospheric lighting were regular features.

In his uncluttered sets, often by Caspar Neher, a portal stood for a palace (*Chalk Circle*), and the materials employed looked not only appropriate, but real and worn. He rehearsed for months, used *Verfremdung* (alienation or estrangement) with discretion and aimed for a critical audience response. His productions were carefully documented in 'model-books' for the guidance of others.

The BE's *Courage* took prizes for best play and best production at the 1954 THÉÂTRE DES NATIONS in Paris, and its visit to London in 1956 profoundly influenced the ROYAL SHAKESPEARE COMPANY and the ROYAL COURT. Worldwide tours disseminated the BE style.

After Brecht's death the company flourished, and then gently ossified under Weigel until 1971. Ruth Berghaus attempted to revitalize it, but was replaced in 1977 by MANFRED WEKWERTH under whom the BE became a Brecht museum. Divorced from Brecht and his heirs after 1989, its future is uncertain. HR

Berman, Eugene 1899–1972 Set and COSTUME designer and painter. Born in St Petersburg, Russia, Berman lived in Paris during 1918–39, then in the USA. He first visited Italy in 1922, and his studies of Italian landscape and Renaissance and baroque theatrical design influenced him greatly. His wispy, almost surreal sketches (see SURREALISM) are filled with such architectural elements as arches and colonnades and have a strong sense of proportion, all reminiscent of Piranesi. In the 1920s he was classed with a group of artists known as neo-romantics. Most of his designs were for ballet and OPERA, and he worked frequently with GEORGE BALANCHINE. Berman's design for Anthony Tudor's *Romeo and Juliet* with American Ballet Theatre is considered one of his best. AA

Berman, Sabina 1953– Mexican playwright, one of the bright lights of the postmodern generation. Berman's plays are complex and provocative, and many exist under a second title. *Yankee* (originally named *Bill*, 1980) involves a Vietnam veteran with a Mexican novelist and his wife; *Rompecabezas* (*Puzzle*, 1982) interprets Trotsky's death in Mexico; *Aguila o sol* (*Eagle or Sun*, 1985) deals with conquest; *Muerte súbita* (*Sudden Death*, 1988) examines value systems in a young relationship; and *Entre Villa y una mujer desnuda* (*Between Villa and a Naked Woman*, 1990) uses the figure of Pancho Villa to dramatize politics and *machismo* in Mexico. GW

Bernal, Ligia 1930– Guatemalan playwright and director. Founder of the University Art Theatre (1950), Bernal studied theatre in Paris. Her most important works are *Una piedra en el pozo* (*Stone in the Well*, 1959) and *Tus alas, Ariel* (*Your Wings, Ariel*, 1970). She is presently director of AMARES, a student theatre institution. GW

Bernard, John 1756–1828 British actor-manager, who had an extensive career in the USA. Born in Portsmouth, he played provincial theatres before his debut at COVENT GARDEN in *The Beaux' Stratagem* in 1787. WIGNELL took him to Philadelphia's CHESTNUT STREET THEATRE, where he remained until 1803, then moving to Boston's FEDERAL STREET THEATRE, which he co-managed during 1806–10. He then toured the USA and Canada extensively, returning in 1819 to England, where he died in poverty. He describes his career as a leading low comedian in two books, *Retrospections of America, 1797–1811* (1887) and *Retrospections of the Stage* (1832). SMA

Bernhard, Thomas 1931–89 Austrian dramatist and novelist with musical training whose plays are relentless, skilfully orchestrated cascades of words, set as verse without punctuation. *Ein Fest für Boris* (*A Party for Boris*, 1970), in which the legless Kind Lady dragoons 13 other cripples into a party for her husband – who dies unnoticed during the proceedings – is typical of his grotesque comic bleakness. In *Der Ignorant und der Wahnsinnige* (*The Ignoramus and the Lunatic*, 1972) an international soprano laments that she has become a coloratura-machine. Artistic perfectionism, with its destructive effects, is also the theme of *Die Macht der Gewohnheit* (*The Force of Habit*, 1974) and of *Der Theatermacher* (*The Showman*, 1985), in which ALAN BATES appeared at the Almeida Theatre in 1993.

Bernhard's pessimism develops into cynical wit when he reflects on German history in *Vor dem Ruhestand* (*Before Retirement*, 1979), in which an ex-SS officer, now an MP, celebrates Himmler's birthday; and, in *Heldenplatz* (1988), on Austria's continuing antisemitism. Sickness and stupidity, desperation and death, are his constant themes. The plays often take the form of interrupted monologues by one dominant character; they were written for Bernhard's favourite actors – *Minetti* (1976) for BERNHARD MINETTI and *Ritter, Dene, Voss* (1986) for GERT VOSS and two actresses in PEYMANN's company, which premiered most of his plays. HR

Bernhardt, Sarah [Sarah Henriette Rosine Bernard] 1844–1923 French actress, incontestably the greatest star of the 19th-century French theatre. The 'divine' Sarah's reputation depended partly upon her very great talent as an actress (notably the purity of her diction), partly upon her personal charisma and particular brand of femininity, and partly upon her extravagant lifestyle and productions. Her tempestuous departure from the COMÉDIE-FRANÇAISE in 1880, her well publicized exhibitions of sculpture and painting, her liaisons and her 'scandalous' balloon ride in 1878, all kept the journalists busy. Her numerous tours abroad, especially to the USA but also to Russia and Australia, ensured that her reputation travelled well beyond the boundaries of France. Thanks to her mother's highly placed protectors, Sarah was able to go to the Conservatoire and to make her debut at the Comédie-Française in 1862 in the role of Iphigenia – an unremarkable performance, and she left under a cloud, having slapped a senior member of the troupe. In 1869 she appeared at the ODÉON in the BREECHES PART of Zanetto in François Coppée's *The Passer-by*, making both her own reputation and that of the young Coppée. By 1872 she was back at the Comédie-Française, making a triumphant appearance as the Queen in the major revival of HUGO's *Ruy Blas*, and by 1875 had risen to being a *sociétaire* of the company. She appeared in a number of roles including Phèdre (1877), which would become one of her greatest parts, Andromaque and Hernani (in which she was much admired by Hugo and had a strong partner in Mounet-Sully).

Sarah Bernhardt as Hamlet.

Bernhardt was at home in both the classical and the modern repertoire, notably in the plays of DUMAS *fils*, especially as Mistress Clarkson in *The Outsider* (*L'Étrangère*); later, Marguerite in *The Lady of the Camellias* would become one of her great parts. The Comédie-Française found her hard to contain on the occasion of their visit to London in 1878. After her departure from the troupe, she developed a pattern of long foreign tours. In 1882 she found one of her two major authors in VICTORIEN SARDOU, whose *Fédora* was written for her to perform at the Vaudeville. From now on she was virtually her own manager, and it is noticeable how many of the plays chosen became vehicles for her talent and opportunities for her artistic delight in sumptuous *mise-en-scène*. In 1883 she took over the Porte-Saint-Martin and showed her versatility by appearing in MEILHAC and Halévy's light COMEDY, *Froufrou*, followed by Jean Richepin's much darker drama *Nana Sahib*. She was also involved in the Ambigu Theatre through her son, Maurice.

However, these ventures led her to bankruptcy. In 1884 she gave one of the finest performances of her career in *The Lady of the Camellias*, with her husband, Jacques Damala, as Armand. That autumn she was ill (her health was often a problem), but by December was appearing at the Porte-Saint-Martin in Sardou's *Théodora*, another lavish spectacle, for which her cloak alone was reputed to have cost 8000 francs. In 1893 she took on the direction of the Renaissance, her intention being to have a theatre where she could prepare and launch productions which would then tour. It was here that she created the title role in Sardou's *Gismonda* (1894), in which she was joined by COQUELIN who had left the Comédie-Française, and in *La Princesse lointaine* (*The Distant Princess*) by ROSTAND (her other major author); and staged the first production of MUSSET's *Lorenzaccio*, adapted for her by Armand d'Artois and in which she played Lorenzo. In 1899 she moved to the former THÉÂTRE DES NATIONS on the Place du Châtelet, which now became the Théâtre-Sarah-Bernhardt (a title it would retain until the Occupation). She opened with one of her great roles in Sardou's *Tosca*, revived Rostand's *La Samaritaine* (*The Woman of Samaria*), and appeared in Marcel Schwob's adaptation of *Hamlet*. The most significant production of this period was Rostand's *L'Aiglon* (another breeches part for Bernhardt, as Napoleon's son). When she went on tour that autumn she allowed the Comédie-Française, which had just suffered a serious fire, to use her theatre. During the First World War she turned to fund-raising on a massive scale to help the war-wounded – she had much earlier, in 1870, turned the Odéon into a field hospital. She continued playing to the bitter end, even after the amputation of one of her legs, which often required her to be propped up on stage. After her death her son Maurice continued the management of the theatre for some years. JMCC

Bernini, Gian Lorenzo 1598–1680 Italian architect, sculptor, stage designer, dramatist, actor and stage manager. Perhaps the greatest artist of the Italian baroque, throughout his life he was fascinated by, and involved in, theatrical activity; some would argue that his architecture and sculptures are essentially theatrical in tone and organization. No visual material has survived to illustrate his scenographic work, which was undertaken in his main workplace, Rome, in venues like the Vatican Fonderia and the Teatro Barberini, as well as at his own house for private theatricals. Such baroque spectacles as *De'due teatri* (*The Two Theatres*, 1637) and *L'inondazione del Tevere* (*The Tiber in Flood*, 1638) he stage-managed himself. His output also included plays, a particularly interesting example of which was discovered only in the 1960s and given the title *La fontana di Trevi* (*Trevi Fountain*, 1966), a scripted treatment of subject-matter in the COMMEDIA DELL'ARTE tradition   KR

Bernstein, Aline 1880–1955 American set and COSTUME designer, who became involved in theatre as a founding member of the NEIGHBORHOOD PLAYHOUSE (1915). Her successful designs there, such as *The Little Clay Cart*, led to work with the THEATRE GUILD and on BROADWAY, and in 1926 actress EVA LE GALLIENNE asked her to design for a newly founded CIVIC REPERTORY THEATRE. Bernstein first worked with producer Herman Shumlin on *Grand Hotel*, then continued her association with him through the 1930s, most notably on the plays of LILLIAN HELLMAN, including *The Little Foxes*. Her early designs utilized adaptable unit sets, whereas some of her later work employed mechanical devices for a cinematic change of scenes. Bernstein founded the Costume Museum, which later was absorbed by the Metropolitan Museum of Art. Her autobiography, *An Actor's Daughter* (her father was Joseph Frankau), first appeared in 1941.   AA

Bernstein, Leonard 1918–90 American composer. Although his primary career was as a conductor of symphony orchestras, Bernstein wrote the scores for six MUSICALS. In 1944 he composed the music for JEROME ROBBINS's ballet 'Fancy Free'; when this was expanded into the full-length musical *On the Town* (1944), he wrote the entire score. Critics complimented him for the fresh, lively sound of his music. Nine years passed before Broadway heard another Bernstein score. *Wonderful Town* gave him the opportunity to write a nostalgic score full of pastiches of the 'swing' music popular in the 1930s. In 1956 he wrote the music for *Candide*, a musical adaptation of the VOLTAIRE novel. Although the show was not a commercial success, Bernstein's score, with its echoes of various classical composers and its dry, satiric sound, was recognized as one of the finest written for the BROADWAY stage. A 1974 revival of *Candide* proved to be more successful with audiences. His most famous score, that for *West Side Story*, premiered in 1957. Critics praised the music for its ability to embody the tensions and passions of the show's teenage characters. Although his contributions to the Broadway stage were relatively few, Bernstein's musically sophisticated and inventive scores earned him a reputation as one of the foremost Broadway composers   MK

Bertinazzi [Bertinassi], **Carlo Antonio** [Carlino; Carlin] 1710–83 Italian actor, the last great Arlecchino (see COMMEDIA DELL'ARTE; HARLEQUIN) in France. Already famous in Italy, he first appeared at the Théâtre Italien, Paris, as a replacement for the unpopular ANGELO COSTANTINI; unsure of his French, he chose LUIGI RICCOBONI's *Arlecchino Constrained to Be Mute* as his premier offer-

ing. His grace, elegance, precision of movement, and the wittiness of his MIME and vocal inflexions won him approbation; the rapport between himself and his audience was so great that he was always chosen to make the addresses to the public. He was admired by DAVID GARRICK and by GOLDONI, in whose *Arlecchino's Son Lost and Found* and *Paternal Love* he played, but his best vehicles were written by Jean-Pierre de Florian.   LS

Bertonov, Yehoshua 1879–1971 Hebrew actor. Born in Vilna to poor parents, Bertonov joined HABIMAH in 1922 and was at the time the only member with previous acting experience. He played Old Ekdal in IBSEN's *The Wild Duck* (1954), and the title role in SHOLOM ALEICHEM's *Tevye the Milkman* (1943). He was noted for his readings, especially from the Bible.   HAS

Besson, Benno 1922– Swiss director who, until 1982, was best known for his close collaboration with BRECHT and his work in East Germany. In 1942 he joined Geneviève and JEAN-MARIE SERREAU in Lyon, then studied English and French at Zurich University, where he met Brecht. In 1947–9, he toured the French occupation zone in Germany with Serreau (*The Exception and the Rule*); in 1949 Brecht invited him to East Berlin. His first *mise-en-scène* was MOLIÈRE's *Don Juan*, in Besson's own adaptation (BERLINER ENSEMBLE, Rostock, 1952). He remained in East Berlin until 1977: with the Berliner Ensemble, 1949–58; as director of the DEUTSCHES THEATER, 1960–9; and of the VOLKSBÜHNE, 1969–77. Besson also directed in Rostock, Vienna, Frankfurt, Stuttgart, Lausanne, Zurich, Munich, Sofia and Avignon, amongst other cities. In 1982 he was offered his first appointment in Switzerland, as artistic director of the Comédie de Genève. In 1985 he received the Reinhart-Ring, highest Swiss award for exceptional achievements in the theatre.

Besson has directed over 50 plays, bringing to his work a high degree of visual inventiveness, insisting on the playful quality of the art of theatre and on the need for true communication between actors and spectators. He has, like Brecht, modernized the classics and staged the work of young playwrights. His main productions are Brecht's *The Days of the Commune* (premiere, 1956), *The Good Person of Setzuan* (1956, 57, 70, 73), *Man Is Man* (1958: two different productions with the same cast), *Saint Joan of the Stockyards* (1961, 62, 73, 81), *The Caucasian Chalk Circle* (1978); SHAKESPEARE's *The Two Gentlemen of Verona* (1959, 63), *As You Like It* (1975, Berlin and Sofia; 1974, Paris), *Hamlet* (1977, Paris; 1983, Geneva and Zurich; 1985, Helsinki). He premiered PETER HACKS's *Moritz Tassow* (1965), Gerhard Winterlich's *Horizons* (1969), Flaubert's *Le Sexe Faible* (*The Weaker Sex*, 1984) and Élie Bourquin's *Lapin Lapin* (*Rabbit Rabbit*, 1986). Besson left Geneva in 1989 to resume his international work as a freelance director in OPERA as well as theatre.   CLS

Betsuyaku Minoru 1937– Japanese playwright. A prolific writer whose minimalist plays, profoundly influenced by the work of SAMUEL BECKETT and EUGENE IONESCO, have been a staple of the Japanese theatrical scene for three decades. *The Little Match Girl* (*Matchi-uri no shōjo*, 1966; trans. 1992), one of Betsuyaku's earliest works, treated the deprivation of the immediate postwar period. He subsequently rejected the style as too 'literary' and moved toward more abstract, absurdist works like *The Move* (*Idō*, 1973; trans. 1979). DGG

Betterton, Thomas 1635–1710 English actor, manager and playwright. Without doubt the greatest actor in England between RICHARD BURBAGE and GARRICK. He probably started acting with John Rhodes's company in 1659, and was immediately recognized as their leading man and a major talent. By 1661 he had joined DAVENANT's company as their star actor and also became a shareholder in the company. Pepys frequently praised his excellence. Davenant trained him as Hamlet: 'having seen Mr [JOSEPH] TAYLOR of the BLACKFRIARS company act it, who being instructed by the author Mr SHAKESPEARE, he taught Mr Betterton in every particle of it'. In 1662 he married Mary Saunderson, one of the first English actresses and a leading member of the company. In the same year he visited Paris to learn about French theatre machinery and stage design. He starred in virtually every play his company put on: playing, for instance, Bosola in WEBSTER's *The Duchess of Malfi*, Sir Toby Belch, Macbeth and Henry VIII.

On Davenant's death he became co-manager of the company with particular responsibility for rehearsals and for training young actors. He also began writing comedies and adapting earlier ones for the Restoration stage. He continued as manager when the two companies were amalgamated in 1682 into the United Company. The following year he visited France again, pursuing his interest in spectacular stage effects, and brought over Louis Grabu, a composer who collaborated with him on a series of OPERAS of great expense and technical brilliance. After a series of arguments with Christopher Rich, who was financial director of the company, Betterton led the senior actors in revolt against the management and by 1695, under licence from the king, they had established themselves in the LINCOLN'S INN FIELDS THEATRE under Betterton's control. But, after an initial success, the company was a failure, with Betterton failing to be sufficiently innovative and to preserve discipline. In 1704, when the company moved into VANBRUGH's HAYMARKET Theatre, he retired as manager, continuing to act. Not long after a famous benefit performance of CONGREVE's *Love for Love* for him in 1709, he retired as an actor as well.

Throughout his long career he played all the major parts available to him: over 120 roles can be specifically ascribed to him. He was known for his careful preparation of roles, always consulting the playwright, always ready to respond to criticism. His acting style in tragedy was majestic and restrained, with an impressive self-discipline, a long way from the excessive styles of his contemporaries. Some of his thoughts on acting may survive in a history of the stage, written largely by Gildon but published under Betterton's name (1710). PH

Betti, Ugo 1892–1953 Italian dramatist, poet and critic, and after PIRANDELLO regarded by many as the major Italian playwright of the 20th century. Although Betti's legal training and practice are strongly felt in his major plays of the 1940s, he began as a poet, and for a period in the late 1920s essayed a number of experimental drama

Thomas Betterton's Hamlet meeting his father's ghost in his mother's chamber.

forms, including dance-drama. He achieved his first major success with what many consider his finest play, *Frana allo scalo nord* (*Landslide*, 1936), cast in the form of a judicial inquiry following an accident, and concerned with the revelation and exploration of guilt, weakness and spiritual need. His standpoint is liberal and Christian, but he avoids moral and religious simplicities and dogmatic judgements, exploring, in his best work, the nature of social and individual responsibility. The austere tone of his work was for long little appreciated in Italy until he achieved international success with plays like *Corruzione al Palazzo di Giustizia* (*Corruption in the Palace of Justice*, 1944), *Delitto all'Isola delle Capre* (*Crime on Goat Island*, 1946) and *La regina e gli insorti* (*The Queen and the Rebels*, 1949). LR

Betty, William (Henry West) 1791–1874 Anglo-Irish actor, a child prodigy, who for two seasons (1804–6) threw the London theatre into an undignified flutter. Billed as the 'Young Roscius', he outshone JOHN PHILIP KEMBLE at COVENT GARDEN, threatening that theatre with bankruptcy when he was tempted over to DRURY LANE. During those heady years Betty played Hamlet, Romeo, Rolla in SHERIDAN's *Pizarro* and Young Norval in JOHN HOME's

Douglas – to the utter delight of indulgent audiences, until the craze dwindled. Beautiful and, within limits, talented, Betty was first ignored and then hissed into oblivion, despite the endeavours of his grasping father. After an abortive spell at Cambridge University, he attempted a comeback in 1812, but the magic was gone. Disheartened by the struggle, he attempted suicide in 1821 and retired into a tolerably prosperous obscurity in 1824. PT

bhagavata mela Folk dance drama of Melattur, a village in Tamil Nadu state in south India. The term *bhagavata* refers to the *Bhagavata Puranas*, collections of Indian epic stories about Lord Vishnu's incarnations. Those who perform these stories are known as *bhagavatar* or *bhagavatulu*. *Mela* refers to a troupe of dancers or singers.

The origin of *bhagavata mela* is traced to the state of Andhra Pradesh where it appears to have been inspired by KUCHIPUDI dance drama around 1502. After the fall of the Hindu Vijayanagar Empire, which included Andhra Pradesh, in 1565, cultural activities came to a virtual standstill. About 500 Brahmin families who performed *kuchipudi* in the Telugu language were left homeless. They travelled south to Tanjore, a Tamil-speaking region, and appealed to King Achyutappa Nayak (1561–1614) for support. The ruler granted them cultivable land and six villages near the city of Tanjore. Today, Melattur, one of the six villages, retains *bhagavata mela* as an annual performance. The other villages also present truncated versions of *bhagavata mela* during the annual festival season.

In Melattur, during the last few weeks of April or early May, two troupes of devotees present an annual performance before the Varadraja Perumala Temple and at the village tank in celebration of Narasimha Jayanti, a festival honouring Vishnu's terrifying man-lion incarnation which destroyed a demon king. Venkatarama Sastri (1759–1847) sparked new life in the form by creating appealing musical compositions to suit about a dozen dance dramas which he also wrote. The object of Sastri's compositions was to spread among the people of this region the devotional movement of Hinduism (*bhakti*), which began in the Middle Ages and continues unabated up to the present day.

The traditional site for the so-called 'temple performance' is on a narrow raised proscenium stage erected in the street between rows of houses of Brahmin families opposite the Varadraja Perumala Temple. A long protective roof of thatch is stretched from the top of the proscenium about 100ft down the street. Before performances begin around 9.30 or 10.00 p.m., the temple deity is carried in lavish procession through the streets of the town. Then he is installed on a special roofed structure opposite the stage, so that performances take place in the divine presence.

Performance begins with the entrance of the clown (*konangi*) who dances and jests with the spectators. Then musicians enter and sing invocations praising Vishnu and songs appropriate to introduce the particular play to be enacted. Next, the chief teachers of the art are honoured with sandal paste and flowers. This is followed by the appearance of a small boy wearing the mask of Ganapati, the elephant-headed god of good fortune. It is said that the child is chosen because his parents have made a vow to

present their son on the stage in this role. After brief dances and songs asking Ganapati's blessings, the drama begins.

All the actors who participate are men, the younger and more attractive of whom play female roles. Elaborate entrances of each character are made behind a curtain held by two attendants. The dance entrances incorporate stylized gesture and intricate patterns of movement characteristic of Indian classical dance. An entrance song (*patra pravesha daru*) introduces each character.

The scenes that follow depict episodes of the drama through dialogue, song and dance. Actors combine stylized and complicated patterns of gesture-language with naturalistic movement and gesture to convey the meaning of the text. The climax of performance occurs in the early hours of the morning when a dramatic crisis is reached.

One particular drama is noteworthy for its dramatic impact and RITUAL significance – that of *The Story of Prahlada* (*Prahlada Charitram*).

This story demonstrates the faith of Prahlada, a youthful prince who worships Lord Vishnu. Forsaking his father's love for that of his god, Prahlada's faith is tested in various ways. With each successive test his wicked father becomes more and more furious. Eventually Prahlada's father is tricked and loses his life when Lord Vishnu, in the form of a man-lion (Hiranyakashipu), rips open the tyrant king's guts and kills him. (See also PRAHLADA NATAKA.)

According to tradition, the actor who portrays the role of the man-lion fasts and prays before wearing a special MASK depicting the god. The mask is said to possess special powers endowed by the deity and the actor goes into a trance to become the violent man-lion. To protect actors playing the other roles, this actor is restrained by attendants. After the ritual killing all the actors climb down from the stage and walk to the temple where they circumambulate the deity. Ragas appropriate to the early hours of the morning are sung by the chief musician. Offerings of rice are then received at households along the street, and the ritual ends with a visit to another temple on the outskirts of the village where the actor playing the man-lion takes off his mask. Immediately he falls into another trance and lies motionless on the ground until revived by water sprinkled over him to restore him to consciousness and symbolically return him to his normal state. To conclude the ceremony, benedictory verses are chanted and the exhausted actors return to their homes.

Owing to family conflicts, two parties of performers now work in this tiny village. They share the performance space considered sacred for the festival and each presents a dramatic work as part of the celebrations.

The music of *bhagavata mela*, following the Karnataka style of classical music, has garnered much praise from music critics. Classical musical instruments are used in performance – the *mridangam* drum, traverse bamboo flute, a violin played in the Indian manner and bell-brass cymbals. The voice of the singer is a particularly important instrument completing the musical ensemble.

The dance techniques are a mixture of those inherited from *kuchipudi* and those adapted from the classical *bharata natyam* of Tamil Nadu. (See also FOLK THEATRE, ASIAN.) FaR

bhamakalapam Regional devotional dance-drama form of Andhra Pradesh state, India. The word is composed of two parts: *bhama*, an abbreviation of the name of Lord Krishna's beautiful and jealous wife Satyabhama, and *kalapam*, meaning 'dialogue' or 'argument'. *Bhamakalapam* is both a play and a theatre form. The play was written in the 17th century by Siddhendra Yogi for use as a devotional ritual by KUCHIPUDI performers. Several versions of the story have been created since that time, but none is better known or more popular than his. Although *bhamakalapam* is called *vithi natakam* by some scholars, in form and content it is markedly different from *veedhi natakam*, the well known street drama of south India.

Bhamakalapam is enacted by all-male troupes (*mela*) which function throughout Andhra Pradesh. Until recently it was patronized by local landowners (*zamindar*) and other wealthy patrons. Owing to the general deterioration of folk arts and traditions in modern India, the form is in serious danger of disappearing altogether.

Unlike the dance dramas KATHAKALI, YAKSHAGANA or THERUKOOTIIU, which emphasize masculine dance movements (*tandava*), *bhamakalapam* provides a superb example of graceful feminine dance movements (*lasya*). Today there is less scope for *bhamakalapam* than *kuchipudi* because it has gained little recognition among dance critics and scholars and, as tastes have changed, the support of wealthy patrons has disappeared. FaR

Bharata Muni Reputed author (INDIAn) of *A Treatise on Theatre* (*Natyasastra*), in which is formulated the ideas which have shaped centuries of dramatic literature and patterns of performance practice throughout much of South Asia. The work has served actors, dancers, playwrights and musicians over the centuries and is the earliest complete text of Indian dramaturgy and among the most important works of its kind in the world. Bharata is not only the author's name, but also the name of the first tribe of India and has come to mean 'actor' as an occupational group. 'Muni' is scholar or seer. Although many stories about the author speak of him as a Brahmin and the father of a hundred sons, the man remains a mystery. FaR

Bhasa 4th–5th centuries AD Major playwright (Indian) of ancient Sanskrit drama. Bhasa probably worked in the city of Ujjain in north central India. He composed plays based on dramatic incidents from the *Ramayana*, the *Mahabharata*, and the *Purana*, as well as semi-historical tales. He also created original stories. Bhasa's works follow many of the dramatic rules of the *Natyasastra*; when he violates them at times it is with outstanding results. Bhasa seems to have been a man of the theatre, as well as a capable poet. His works are as fresh today as they must have been when he first wrote them. Many modern Indian directors have been drawn to Bhasa's plays and have given them new, and often lively, modern interpretations.

The texts of 13 plays attributed to Bhasa were discovered in 1912. The most important and one of the most elegant in Sanskrit literature is *The Vision of Vasavadatta* (*Svapnavasavadatta*), a play fusing the pain of love in separation with a political intrigue. Among Bhasa's short plays are *The Broken Thighs* (*Urubhangam*) and *Karna's Task*

(*Karna-bharam*), dramatizations of episodes in the great battle which concludes the *Mahabharata*. FaR

bhavai Form of rural theatre – raucous, bawdy, obscene, satiric, poignant – performed over a broad area of north Gujarat and Saurashtra, Madhya Pradesh state and Rajasthan state in western India. Once extremely popular, the number of troupes has declined today. Local legend has it that *bhavai*'s origin may be attributed to Asaita Thakar, an outcast Brahmin who lived during the mid-14th century in what is now Gujarat state.

The story goes that Asaita Thakar was born a Brahmin and served as the family priest of Patel Hema, headman of Unza, a small village in north Gujarat. One day Hema's daughter Ganga was abducted by a Muslim captain who had an eye for a pretty face. Asaita felt obliged to save the girl and so he sought audience with the captain on the pretext of entertaining him with songs. After winning the captain's praise, Asaita begged that Ganga be released saying that she was his only daughter. The shrewd captain suspected that Asaita was lying, but he agreed to release Ganga if Asaita dined with her in his presence. The wily captain knew that Brahmins were strictly forbidden to dine with lower caste Hindus – indeed, it was an unpardonable act. To the captain's amazement Asaita readily agreed and did as he was bade, thus gaining Ganga's freedom. When Asaita returned to Unza with Ganga safely in tow he was promptly excommunicated by his Brahmin brethren. In ancient India excommunication meant that Asaita could no longer practise his hereditary profession and consequently could not earn a living. A lesser man would surely have been ruined by this sudden reversal of fortune, but Asaita accepted his fate and turned to singing and dancing for a living, which has historically been considered an appropriate profession for many of India's outcastes. With the help of his sons and other outcaste Brahmins he formed Gujarat's first company of strolling players (*bhavaiya* – literally, 'those who arouse sentiment' in the spectators through their performance). This community still preserves the hereditary right to perform *bhavai* in Gujarat.

In gratitude for the safe return of his daughter, Patel Hema bestowed a small plot of land and financial support on Asaita, thereby initiating a pattern of village patronage of *bhavaiya* which persists today.

Bhavai is traditionally performed in connection with religious festivals in praise of mother goddesses, such as Ambaji and Bahucharaji, the latter regarded as the patroness of *bhavai* actors. *Navaratri*, the nine-night festival in September–October honouring the goddess, is particularly auspicious. A performance is normally arranged in the sacred confines of a temple courtyard or a street in front of the temple. The performance space (*paudh*) is sanctified by the stage manager who draws a large circle of oil on the ground and lights a torch symbolizing the presence of the goddess. Songs in praise of the goddess are also sung prior to other ritual overtures and the actors and audience alike sometimes shout 'Long life to the Goddess!' during the show.

The contents of most performances centre on the vices and virtues of members of various communities in village society. The Brahmin, the tailor, the potter, the scavenger, the money-lender are all satirized. Some performances deal with Hindu mythology; others provide vignettes of famous historical personages of the area.

Humour is the dominant sentiment (*rasa*), although a variety of other emotions may be evoked. The predominance of humour makes *bhavai* unique in the catalogue of regional forms of traditional Indian theatre.

The language of performance is a generous mix of Gujarati, Hindi-Urdu and Marwadi, indicating the historical connection of many castes and communities throughout this wide geographic region. Songs in verse, set to a wide variety of metres, and prose dialogue characterize the structure of the stories.

Bhavai is linked to the past through performance rather than through written stories. Texts were collected and published in Gujarat for the first time in the 19th century. The stories are known as *vesa* (literally 'costume') and they bear the names of the chief characters around which they are composed. For example, *Ganapati-no-Vesa* is the ritual introduction and dance of the elephant-headed god Ganapati; *Juthana-no-Vesa* tells the story of the trials of a Muslim crown prince, Juthana; *Zhanda Zulan-no-Vesa* concerns the love affair between a Muslim policeman and a wife of a rich Hindu merchant; *Brahmana-no-Vesa* depicts the mad antics of a priest, and so the catalogue goes on and on. There are said to have been 360 *vesa*, one for every day of the year, but far fewer survive in the repertory today.

Commonly used musical instruments are *bhungal*, *pakhawaja*, *tabla* drums, small cymbals (*jhanjha*), harmonium and the classical north Indian stringed instrument, *sarangi*. *Bhungal* are unique to *bhavai*. They are 4-ft-long copper pipes which are blown to provide a forceful cadence during dance sequences and to announce the entrance of important characters. Normally, two *bhungal* are used, a male and a female instrument. On occasion, other instruments are introduced for special effects.

Performance begins around 10 p.m. after villagers have taken their evening meals. Music accompanies the action and initially serves to attract the spectators to the performance area. Hindustani, or north-Indian-style, music predominates but popular local tunes and rhythms are integrated throughout. When a sufficient number of spectators has been drawn to the playing area and important guests have been seated, prayers to Ambaji commence. These are followed by songs describing the love affair of a famous couple from Marwad. The songs serve as a cue to the stage manager (*nayaka*) to enter the arena and begin the RITUALS.

Asaita Thakar must have considered this phase of the preliminaries important because he formalized the pattern of the preliminaries in a separate *vesa*. On cue from the musicians, an actor dressed to represent Ganapati, the elephant-headed god of beginnings and successes, enters holding a brass plate before his face. As he dances, the musicians sing his praises. Like all of the dances of *bhavai*, the style is a simplified version of *kathak*, the classical dance of north India, combined with *garba*, a folk dance of the region. After Ganapati makes his exit, another actor enters impersonating the goddess Kali. The stage manager asks her name and business but gets nothing other than monosyllables as a reply. Kali dances in a frenzy to loud songs of praise. At the end of the dance the musicians implore her to remove all impediments that might hinder their performance, which she symbolically does by forming a circle over their heads and cracking her knuckles on her temples.

To conclude the preliminaries, an actor dressed as a Brahmin priest comes from the dressing room through the crowds of spectators which circle the arena. He provides the first bit of humour of the evening. When questioned by the stage manager as to his name and business he gives a ridiculous reply, using all kinds of obscenities to the delight of the spectators. His costume caricatures a Brahmin priest. Sometimes an actor portrays the role wearing small clay pots on his stomach and on his hips which are concealed under the folds of his costume. His grotesque appearance provokes roars of laughter. When he dances his movements are the very antithesis of grace. After his antics have been completed the Ganapati preliminaries are concluded by a song. At this point the regular story begins.

Although rural interest in *bhavai* has waned over the last several decades, urban theatre people have been attracted to it for a variety of reasons. First, in the wake of a national desire to preserve valuable and endangered folk traditions, urbanites have sought to support *bhavai* performances and prominent educational institutions have recruited some of the best actors to be part-time teachers at college level. In this way *bhavai*'s folk traditions are being preserved and passed down to future generations in this rapidly industrializing society. Second, the form of *bhavai*, its attention to COMEDY, SATIRE and political details, accompanied by music with stylized movements and dance, has been imitated by urban theatre groups.

Actors in modern drama troupes have taken *bhavai* and rendered their own versions of the form to the delight of city audiences. More faithful imitators have attempted to replicate *bhavai*'s rural flavour. *Mena Gujari* and *Jasma Odan*, produced by Deena Gandhi and Shanta Gandhi respectively, two well known theatre directors, have run successfully in Ahmedabad, Bombay and Delhi in recent years. With all the expressed interest, no major movement has occurred which has led the way toward a genuine revival of *bhavai*, and so the original actors and their community continue to struggle to survive. (See also FOLK THEATRE, ASIAN.) FAR

Biancolelli family Italian actors. **Isabella** Franchini (d. c.1650), the daughter of the famous Pantalone Francesco Franchini and a famous Colombina in her own right, took as her third husband the Bolognese **Francesco** Biancolelli (d. c.1640). Their son **Giuseppe Domenico** (c.1636–88) played with Locatelli's company in Paris from 1659, and from 1680 acted at the newly founded HÔTEL DE BOURGOGNE in the COMÉDIE-ITALIENNE, under the stage name Dominique. Short, svelte and supremely agile, he naturalized the Arlecchino (see COMMEDIA DELL'ARTE; HARLEQUIN) type to the French stage with an admixture of dance, wisecracks and acrobatics and a quantum of elegance. He was on bantering terms with Louis XIV, who permitted him to interject French dialogue in his harsh voice. He died of pneumonia, following a particularly strenuous exhibition. He had married (1663) Orsola Cortesi, called Eularia (c.1632–1718), who took the veil at his death. Their children included three actors: Francesca Maria Apolline, called **Isabella** (1664–1747), a witty, brilliant *amorosa*, who made her debut in 1683; Caterina, called **Colombina** (1665–1716), who excelled her grandmother in that role and was painted by Watteau before her retirement in 1697; and Pier Francesco, called **Dominique** *fils* (1680–1734). He made his debut with an Italian troupe in Toulouse, toured the French provinces, and had an extraordinary success as Arlecchino in Venice and Genoa. On his return to Paris, he took over the management of the foundering Opéra Comique. When LUIGI RICCOBONI reopened the newly organized Comédie-Italienne in 1716 under the protection of the Duc d'Orléans, he joined it, soon becoming one of its favourite players. Contemporaries unanimously hailed him as the best Arlequin of his time; he wrote a number of scenarios for the improvised comedy. LS

Bibiena, (Galli da) family Italian theatre architects and scenic designers, who took their name from the birthplace of Giovanni Maria (1625–65), known as Il Vecchio, a designer of modest talents who established the family connections with theatre and whose sons and grandsons acquired European celebrity. His eldest son, **Ferdinando** (1657–1743), is said to have begun his career with GIACOMO TORELLI, but quickly rose to prominence under the patronage of the Farnese at Parma, where he was chief court architect for many years. He went to Spain in 1708 to direct the festivities at Barcelona in celebration of the marriage of Charles III, and between 1712 and 1717 was in the service of the Emperor Charles VI in Vienna. His major contribution to scenic design, the scenes set at an acute angle (*scena per angolo*), revolutionized baroque staging: these were first used at Piacenza in mounting Lotti's *Didio Giuliano* (1687), and are described in his *L'architettura civile preparata nella geometria* (*Civic Architecture on Geometrical Principles*, 1711). His brother **Francesco** (1659–1739) likewise worked widely throughout Italy and elsewhere on the Continent, at first often with Ferdinando, developing the latter's angled scenes, then on his own account. In 1702 he was responsible for the celebrations mounted to mark the arrival of Philip V in Naples; between 1708 and 1709 he built the splendid theatre at Nancy in France and, later in his career, the Teatro Filarmonico at Verona.

Ferdinando's eldest son **Giuseppe** (1696–1757) long worked with his father at the Viennese court, and was noted for the quality of his OPERA sets there, as well as those he did for major theatrical centres like Dresden, Prague and Venice: in 1740 he published a rich collection of his stage designs. He appears to have been the first to use transparent scenery lit from behind. His younger brother **Antonio** (1700–74) followed him as first court architect at Vienna, and in Italy designed a number of theatres including the Teatro Comunale in Bologna (from 1755) and the Teatro dei Quattro Cavalieri in Pavia (1773). Giuseppe's son **Carlo** (1728–87) continued the family tradition, working with his father – for example, on the Opera House of the Palgrave at Bayreuth, then at various courts, including those of Vienna and Dresden. KR

Bickerstaffe, Isaac 1733–?1808 Irish playwright. Born in Dublin, he was a page to the Earl of Chesterfield before going to London in 1755. In 1760 his 'dramatic PASTORAL' or 'ballad farce' *Thomas and Sally*, with music by Arne, was performed. *Love in a Village* (1762) is probably the first English comic opera. Its success led Bickerstaffe to write many more, including *The Maid in the Mill* (1765). His collaborations with DIBDIN were particularly successful, influencing the whole development of MUSICAL COMEDY as a dramatic form. Their play *Love in the City* failed at its first performance but succeeded when abbreviated as *The Romp*. He adapted WYCHERLEY's *The Plain Dealer* for GARRICK in 1765, and his short FARCE *The Padlock* (1768) starred Dibdin as Mungo, the first blackface comic role seen in London. In 1772 he escaped to France to avoid prosecution after a homosexual affair and he lived abroad until his death. PH

bidesia Minor regional theatre form from the villages of Bihar, India – literally, 'one who emigrates from his homeland'. Apparently it was created in the early part of the century by Bhikhari Thakur, a barber who left the security of his home to form a company of itinerant actors. Plays depict the trials and tribulations of villagers, and some concern the confrontation between the traditional values of rural life and the modern values of city dwellers. FAR

Bill-Belotserkovsky, Vladimir (Naumovich) 1884–1970 Soviet dramatist, whose propagandistic tales of heroic communism and decadent capitalism introduced many of the theatrical themes, devices and character types which were consolidated under socialist realism (1934–53). Bill-Belotserkovsky's work reflects his proletarian beginnings, his years at sea, his sojourn as an unskilled worker in the USA (1911–17, hence his American nickname, 'Bill'), his active participation in the October Revolution and ensuing work on behalf of the Communist Party. As a member (in 1921) of the Proletkult (the Proletarian Culture Organization) and later of the Glavrepertkom (the Central Committee for the Control of Repertory, 1929), he helped to develop and to police the new Soviet drama. Derived from the *agitka*, or AGIT-PROP, presentations of the Civil War period, his plays are naive, crudely energetic, episodically structured and transparently diagrammatic in character and thematic development, ranging in style from primitive psychological REALISM to heroic monumentalism.

His first four plays – *Beefsteak, Rare* (1920), *Stages* (1921), *Echo* (1922) and *Steer to the Left!* (1926) – traverse the path to World Revolution through Europe and America, underscoring, sometimes in allegorical terms, the inevitability of the climactic struggle. *Storm* (1924) is the author's classic Civil War play. Melodramatically conceived and martially scored at a brisk tempo, its tale of an heroic Party chairman (the first 'positive hero' on the Soviet stage) battling to rid his quarter of class enemies and bring about a new order out of chaos gave birth to VISHNEVSKY's genre-defining *An Optimistic Tragedy* (1933) and a host of socialist-realist progeny. It was popular throughout Eastern Europe and was revised by the author for the 1952 YURY ZAVADSKY production at the Mossoviet Theatre. His second most influential work, *Life Is Calling* (1953), is an attempt to deal with the social problems of assimilation into and alienation from the new regime within the framework of a small-scale psychological realistic play. Its use of romantic subplots, pairings of ideological types and a climactic conversion speech – really a clarion call to the audience – became familiar elements in the theatrical language of the new Soviet drama. His other plays include *Calm* (1926), an attempt at NEP (New Economic Policy) SATIRE, *Moon on the Left* (1927), a weak comedy about the positive hero and love, and *The Voice of the Depths* (1928), a First Five-Year Plan reconstruction play, none of which were successful. SG

Birch-Pfeiffer, Charlotte 1800–68 German actress and playwright. Among the several plays she adapted from novels, *The Orphan of Lowood* (1856), based on *Jane Eyre*, was the most widely performed. Despite her considerable dramaturgical skill, Birch-Pfeiffer's plays disappeared soon after her death. SW

Bird, Robert Montgomery 1806–54 American playwright, whose major plays – *The Gladiator* (1831), *Oralloosa* (1832) and *The Broker of Bogota* (1834) – were prize-winners in EDWIN FORREST's playwriting contests and were performed by him. *Gladiator* and *Broker* were retained in Forrest's repertoire, with extraordinary profits for him and only $2000 for Bird; *Pelopidas* (1830), another winner, was never produced. Discouraged by his bitter financial quarrels with Forrest, Bird turned to novels: *Hawks of Hawk Hollow* (1836) and *Nick of the Woods* (1837) are the best-known.

Bird received a medical degree in 1827, practised for a year, wrote two plays in 1827 (*The Cowled Lover* and *Caridorf*), then taught at Pennsylvania Medical College (1841–3). At his death his notebook outlined plans for 11 tragedies, 12 comedies, 33 melodramas and 25 novels. RM

Birmingham Repertory Theatre This, the first purpose-built repertory theatre in Britain, was opened in February 1913. Seating 464, it was designed to be intimate, every seat in the steeply raked auditorium having an unrestricted view of the stage. Under BARRY JACKSON, theatre owner and artistic director, with JOHN DRINKWATER as its general manager, the resident company quickly gained a reputation for consistent, high-quality and often adventurous productions of the 'uncommercial' drama, and notable successes included Eden Phillpotts's *The Farmer's Wife* (1916), Drinkwater's *Abraham Lincoln* (1918), modern-dress productions of SHAKESPEARE (1923 onwards) and SHAW's *Back to Methuselah* (1923). From 1925 Jackson added a series of London seasons to the work of a rapidly expanding company. Recurring financial difficulties, however, led in 1935 to a board of trustees taking over ownership of the theatre. In 1971 a new theatre was opened to replace the old. A 900-seat auditorium facing a wide stage, spacious foyers and backstage facilities and a small studio theatre for experimental work contrast markedly with the old building, though there has been some loss of intimacy too. Jackson's policy of an all-embracing repertoire of new, old and popular works continues but there is no longer a resident acting company and the lower levels of subsidy now available have meant considerably fewer home-produced shows each season than in the new Rep's first ten years of life. Actors whose careers were launched at Birmingham include RALPH RICHARDSON, LAURENCE OLIVIER, Cedric Hardwicke, PAUL SCOFIELD and ALBERT FINNEY. AJ

Bjørnson, Bjørn 1859–1942 Norwegian director and actor. The son of BJØRNSTJERNE BJØRNSON, he studied in Vienna before acting with the MEININGEN COMPANY. Joining Christiania Theater in 1884, he introduced the principles of naturalistic acting and staging (see NATURALISM), in productions of SHAKESPEARE, MOLIÈRE and IBSEN, often in collaboration with the realistic acting of JOHANNE DYBWAD. In the 1890s his tremendous energies strengthened the campaign for the new NATIONALTHEATRET, which opened in 1899 with Bjørnson at its head. He threw himself into almost every aspect of production and created a remarkable ensemble, until ill-health forced his resignation in 1907. Apart from a brief return to Nationaltheatret in the 1920s, he spent the rest of his life in Germany and Italy, returning frequently to Norway to act and direct. Although he was sometimes attacked for poor artistic taste, Bjørnson was crucial in the modernization of Norwegian theatre HL

Bjørnson, Bjørnstjerne 1832–1910 Norwegian playwright, novelist and journalist, winner of the 1903 Nobel Prize for Literature. As a journalist, he actively supported the campaign for the Norwegianization of the Danish-speaking Christiania Theater, and succeeded IBSEN as stage director of the Norske Theater, Bergen (1857–9), before successfully directing at Christiania Theater (1865–7). His playwriting began in the 1850s with romantic history plays in the manner of Oehlenschläger; the most enduring is *Sigurd the Bad* (1862). From the mid-1860s, his plays dealt realistically with social problems: marital, as in *The Newlyweds* (1865), *Leonarda* (1879) and *A Gauntlet* (1883); financial, as in the internationally successful *A Bankruptcy* (1874); and political, as in *The King* (1877) and *Paul Lange and Tora Parsberg* (1898). Beginning with *Beyond Our Power, I* (1883), he explored more spiritual issues. Bjørnson's plays are limited by his obvious plot manipulations, and by their good-natured sentimentality, allowing the solution of problems by characters' superficial changes of heart. HL

Black, George 1891–1945 British impresario, noted for the rapid pacing of his shows. He originated the Royal Variety Performances and injected the sumptuousness of REVUE into MUSIC-HALL. As managing director of the General Theatre Corporation (1928) and Moss Empires Ltd (1933) he controlled 40 halls, including the London Palladium, where, by conflating three teams of comedians, he created the CRAZY GANG (*U-Kay for Sound*, 1936–7). His lavish revues at the HIPPODROME include *The Fleet's Lit Up* (1938), *Black Velvet* (1939) and *Black Varieties* (1941). LS

blackface minstrelsy see MINSTREL SHOW

Blackfriars Theatre (London) Of the two theatres built in rooms formerly part of the Blackfriars monastery, the earlier dates from 1576, the same year in which JAMES BURBAGE erected the THEATRE. The private and public theatres of Elizabethan London were, thus, virtually twin-born. The prime mover in the Blackfriars enterprise was Richard Farrant, Deputy Master of the CHILDREN OF THE CHAPEL ROYAL and already an experienced instigator of their occasional plays at court. Speculation on a basis of scant detail suggests that the room Farrant converted was the old refectory. The dimensions (46.5ft x 26ft) are those of an intimate theatre, with a presumed capacity not much in excess of 100. The convenient fiction was that the choristers were there 'rehearsing' plays for performance before the queen, but patrons were charged for admission and Farrant's boys were effective rivals to the BOYS OF ST PAUL'S. After Farrant's death in 1580, the two BOYS' COMPANIES were briefly united under the creative leadership of JOHN LYLY, but in 1584 the Blackfriars landlord, for reasons unknown, decided to recover possession of his property.

Speculation has again many gaps to fill in our knowledge of the second Blackfriars, but the outline of its story is discernible. When James Burbage was looking to replace the Theatre, whose lease was due to expire in 1597, he bought, from the same landlord who had evicted the Children of the Chapel Royal, several rooms in the Blackfriars, including the Parliament Chamber (66ft x 46ft). It was probably in this Chamber, rather than the lower paved hall beneath it, that Burbage set about his conversion work. That work was, however, halted late in 1596 when a petition from Blackfriars residents against the licensing of a public playhouse in their exclusive precinct was circulated. Burbage died in 1597, leaving the unusable Blackfriars to his equally practical son, the actor RICHARD BURBAGE, and it was he who in 1600 leased it to Henry Evans, operating on behalf of the Children of the Chapel Royal. The residents evidently found it easier to stomach a 'private' playhouse, occupied by a boys' company. The Parliament Chamber was high enough to accommodate galleries, and its capacity was also increased by onstage seating for privileged or showy spectators. The artificial lighting and scenic refinements of the indoor stage, together with a faddish interest in boy performers, made the Blackfriars a formidable rival to the outdoor houses of the adult companies, but Evans, notoriously unscrupulous in his treatment of the choristers and possessed of a tabloid temperament, pushed his players too far into controversy. The repertoire included many of the finest plays of the period, but Evans came increasingly to miscalculate the amount of licence permissible to boys, and his management ended in disorder in 1608. It was then that Richard Burbage brought the King's Men into occupation of the prized indoor theatre, although their first performances there may have been delayed until 1610. The playhouse remained in the company's possession until the CLOSURE OF THE THEATRES in 1642, after which it fell into disrepair.   PT

Blake, Eubie see SISSLE, NOBLE

Blake, William Rufus 1805–63 Canadian-born actor, playwright and manager, noted for his portrayal of old men on the American stage. With the possible exception of WILLIAM BURTON, he was without equal in this line.

Blake made his New York debut at the Chatham Garden Theatre in 1824 and subsequently appeared with great success in the USA and Britain. In the 1820s and 30s he managed successively the TREMONT THEATRE, Boston; the WALNUT STREET in Philadelphia; and, with H. E. Willard, the Olympic Theatre, New York. Later he was principal comedian in the New York stock companies (see STOCK COMPANY) of Burton, LAURA KEENE and LESTER WALLACK. His final appearance was as Sir Peter Teazle at the BOSTON THEATRE on 21 April 1863; he died suddenly the next day. DBW

Blakely, Colin (George Edward) 1930–87 British actor, who turned to the theatre at the age of 28 in Belfast and was invited to join GEORGE DEVINE's English Stage Company for a small part in SEAN O'CASEY's Cock-a-Doodle-Dandy. He joined the NATIONAL THEATRE company under LAURENCE OLIVIER in 1963, where he achieved immediate success as the rugged adventurer, Pizarro, in PETER SHAFFER's The Royal Hunt of the Sun (1964). The range of Blakely's work was impressive – equally successful as Titus Andronicus in a ROYAL SHAKESPEARE COMPANY production as in a play by HAROLD PINTER (Old Times, 1972) – and he starred in the WEST END, with the national companies, in films, TV and in FRINGE theatres. Blakely's particular asset was the feeling of authenticity which he brought to his various roles, a quality of being dramatically untheatrical, so that, as with his performance in AYCKBOURN's Just Between Ourselves (1977), the audience was drawn into what seemed an intimate eavesdropping on human life. JE

Blakemore, Michael (Howell) 1928– Australian-born actor and director, who studied at the Royal Academy of Dramatic Art in London. He started as an actor with several major regional repertory companies, including the BIRMINGHAM REP and the Shakespeare Memorial Company at Stratford-upon-Avon. In 1966 he was appointed co-director of the Glasgow CITIZENS' THEATRE, where his sensitive production of PETER NICHOLS's A Day in the Death of Joe Egg (1967) attracted much attention. His Arturo Ui production in 1969 first drew the attention of many other directors to the potentiality of this BRECHT play. His association with the work of Peter Nichols continued with successful productions of Forget-me-not Lane (1971), The National Health (1969) at the NATIONAL THEATRE and Privates on Parade with the ROYAL SHAKESPEARE COMPANY. LAURENCE OLIVIER invited him to become an associate artistic director of the National Theatre in 1971; and there he directed several major NT successes in quick succession, including Long Day's Journey into Night (with Olivier as Tyrone), The Front Page, The Cherry Orchard and Plunder. He stayed on under PETER HALL's regime at the National Theatre until the opening of the new theatre, but the relationship between them was never happy.

After a brief spell as resident director at the LYRIC THEATRE, HAMMERSMITH, in 1970, Blakemore returned to being a freelance director in Britain and Australia, directing MICHAEL FRAYN's hit FARCE, Noises Off (1982), in Britain and the USA. His film, A Personal History of the Australian Surf (1981), is a splendid evocation of his boyhood, while his novel, Next Season (1969), provides a telling account of his life as an actor with the Shakespeare Memorial Company. In 1987 he directed the WEST END premiere of PETER SHAFFER's *Lettice and Lovage*, and briefly returned as a guest director to the National Theatre with a revival of ARTHUR MILLER's *After the Fall* (1990). After staging the premiere of Miller's *The Ride Down Mount Morgan* (1991) in London, he directed his first major MUSICAL, LARRY GELBART's *City of Angels*, in the USA, which won six Tony awards on BROADWAY and triumphantly transferred to London in 1993. JE

Blau, Herbert 1926– American director and postmodern critic who, in *The Impossible Theater: A Manifesto* (1964), vowed 'to talk up a revolution', and has. Blau's later critical work – *Take up the Bodies: Theater at the Vanishing Point* and *Blooded Thought: Occasions of Theatre* (1982), *The Eye of Prey: Subversions of the Postmodern* (1987), *The Audience* (1990) and *To All Appearances* (1992) – propounds a Foucaultian *theatrum philosophicum* of the mind. His main themes are 'the self-abolishing [and self-observing] thought of theatre', the co-opting of theatrical performance by writing, and the de-centring of culture based in logocentric language via the complicating of thought's linguistic expression. Blau and Jules Irving pioneered stage work on BRECHT and BECKETT at San Francisco Actors Workshop, which they co-founded (1952), before becoming co-artistic directors of the Repertory Theatre of Lincoln Center, New York City (1965). Resigning his position in 1967, following his controversial production of *Danton's Death* (which opened the VIVIAN BEAUMONT THEATRE), Blau co-founded the California Institute of the Arts (1968), where he was in charge of actor training. His later work with KRAKEN (formerly the Oberlin Group) was rigorously physical and group-created. Blau continually promotes modes of seeing – authorship and spectatorship – that address and partially redress the new cultural subjects of division and pastiche SG

Bleasdale, Alan 1946– British dramatist, whose comedies, MUSICALS and dramas are often set in his home town, Liverpool. His early plays, *The Party's Over* (1975), *Down the Dock Road* (1976), *It's a Madhouse* (1976) and *No More Sitting on the Old School Bench* (1977), were produced in the North of England but failed to make an impact on London, where they were occasionally staged in the FRINGE theatres. Despite the popularity of *Having a Ball* (1981), about four men waiting for treatment in a vasectomy clinic, his national success came with two drama series on television – *Boys from the Blackstuff* (1983), about the unemployed on Merseyside, and *GBH* (1991), about the rise and fall of the leader of a far-left faction of the Liverpool Labour Party, supposedly satirizing Derek Hatton and the Militant Tendency. These illustrate his strengths as a writer. His comedy veers towards FARCE, his characterization is lively rather than subtle, and although he cannot be described as a writer who stirs the emotions Bleasdale is gifted with a feeling for pathos. This fellow feeling for people who are down on their luck emerged in his musical hagiography of the last days of Elvis Presley, *Are You Lonesome Tonight?* (1985).

Bleasdale is not a calculating writer, and the weaknesses of his plots derive from the fact that his themes have not been sufficiently considered. It strained credulity to believe that his Hatton-like character in *GBH* was an unwitting *agent provocateur* for the far right, while *The Boys from the Blackstuff* handled the politics of unemployment naively, although it captured a British mood under Mrs Thatcher. His stage play *On the Ledge* (1993), co-produced by the Nottingham Playhouse and the NATIONAL THEATRE, was a bleak parable set in Liverpool on Guy Fawkes night. An honest man is on the ledge of a tower block and threatening to jump, driven to despair by the state of the world and a riot in the streets below. The characters are drawn with a broad brush and the allegory leads towards the apocalypse, which is averted, as so often in Bleasdale's plays, by northern common sense and a sprinkle of one-line gags. JE

Blin, Roger 1907–84 French actor, director and designer. Drawn to stage acting as a way of overcoming a stammer, Blin acted with ARTAUD, DULLIN, BARRAULT and the OCTOBER GROUP in the 1930s, also studying MIME. After the war he began directing in avant-garde theatres, producing two of ADAMOV's plays as well as BECKETT's *En attendant Godot*, with which he made his name in 1953. He became the friend and trusted director of Beckett (*Fin de partie*, 1957; *La Dernière Bande*, 1960; *Oh les beaux jours*, 1963) and also of GENET (*Les Nègres* (*The Blacks*), 1959; *Les Paravents* (*The Screens*), 1966). Genet's published letters to him about his production of *The Screens* testify to an unusually close collaboration between author and director. For Blin, the functions of director and designer were inseparable: to direct a play was to reveal reality in a new light, making every element in the production speak its own particular language. DB

Blitzstein, Marc 1905–64 American composer, librettist and adapter, born in Philadelphia, who studied at the Curtis Institute of Music and later trained with Nadia Boulanger in Paris and Arnold Schönberg in Berlin. He is best known as the composer-librettist for *The Cradle Will Rock* (1937), a pro-labour OPERETTA developed within the FEDERAL THEATRE PROJECT. The controversial production, famously recounted in JOHN HOUSEMAN's *Run-through* (1972), was revived a few months later by ORSON WELLES and Houseman as part of the MERCURY THEATRE's first season. He later translated and adapted BRECHT's *The Threepenny Opera* (1952), an OFF-BROADWAY success (2611 performances). Other musical works include *Regina* (1949), based on LILLIAN HELLMAN's *The Little Foxes*, and *Juno* (1959), based on SEAN O'CASEY's *Juno and the Paycock*. At the time of his death, a murder victim in Martinique, he was developing an OPERA about the Sacco and Vanzetti case. TP

Bloch, William 1845–1926 Danish director, who introduced naturalistic staging (see NATURALISM) at the KONGELIGE TEATER in the 1880s. His richly textured IBSEN productions established him as Denmark's most perceptive interpreter of the new drama. Anticipating many of STANISLAVSKY's ideas, Bloch increased rehearsal time, planned and researched productions and, although he was working with actors trained in the romantic theatre, strove (sometimes unsuccessfully) for ensemble acting that captured individuality and inner truth. He typically coordinated a mass of carefully planned details to create the 'atmosphere' of a play's specific world, as in his productions of *An Enemy of the People* (1883) and *The Wild Duck* (1885). Opposition to his methods and repertoire led to his resignation in 1893, until he returned in 1899 for a ten-year engagement during which he revolutionized the theatre's approach to HOLBERG, by treating his plays as though they were new.   HL

Blok, Aleksandr (Aleksandrovich) 1880–1921 Russian poet and dramatist, considered 'the last romantic' and 'the greatest symbolist', who helped to define 20th-century self-conscious, conventional theatre. The latter half of his career is an ironic commentary on his earlier naive romance with SYMBOLISM and the mystical philosophy of Vladimir Solovyov. When the latter's 'Divine Sophia', 'God's ideal humanity', failed to materialize with the defeat of the 1905 Revolution, Blok underwent a spiritual crisis from which he never recovered. He rejected the 'decadent charlatanism' of symbolist mysticism, an impulse reinforced by the relationship that was forming between his wife (L. D. Mendeleeva) and symbolist colleague ANDREI BELY. *The Lyrical Dramas* (1908) which resulted – *The Puppet Show*, *The King on the Square* and *The Unknown Woman* (all 1906) – along with his later plays offer a mixture of autobiographical existentialist drama, artistic and sociopolitical SATIRE, and elegy for what was lost, never was and might never be found. His tragi-farce *The Puppet Show*, based on an earlier poem, casts Bely as HARLEQUIN, Mendeleevna as Columbine – symbolist image recast as sensual betrayer – and Blok as Pierrot; and mystical God-seekers and apocalyptic seers from the symbolist ranks – among them Gippius, Merezhkovsky, BRIUSOV – as the Mystics, whose philosophical drama here collides with COMMEDIA DELL'ARTE. Infused with doubleness of vision, self-conscious role-playing, grotesque juxtapositions, direct audience address and 'laying bare the device', the play unites the GOGOLian tradition with modern metatheatrical and absurdist perspectives (see THEATRE OF THE ABSURD). Blok's *liebestod* created an exceptional furore when staged by MEYERHOLD (Vera Komissarzhevskaya's Theatre, 1906), who appeared as Pierrot.

The King on the Square, which was denied production by the censor (see CENSORSHIP), and *The Unknown Woman*, staged by Meyerhold in 1914, find the poet alienated from the untransformed society of post-1905 Russia and from his Eternal Feminine, who has been transformed into a prostitute. The allegorical *The Song of Fate* (1908), dealing with similar themes, was rewritten by Blok in 1919 to make it more realistic, a change which STANISLAVSKY had thought necessary when he rejected it for production in 1908. Blok's verse drama *The Rose and the Cross* (1913) grew out of his libretto for a Glazunov OPERA and, more generally, from his affinity for and knowledge of medieval culture. Drawing upon materials gathered for his translation of *The Miracle of Théophile*, produced at the Ancient Theatre in 1908, he again brings together joy (the rose) and suffering (the cross), concluding that the former is transient, while the latter, if selfless,

yields true and lasting happiness. The play, planned for the MOSCOW ART THEATRE, was not produced. In 1919 Blok served as chairman of the production board of Leningrad's Bolshoi Dramatic Theatre and was appointed to the repertory section of the Theatre Division of the People's Commissariat for Education.   SG

Blondin, Charles [Jean-François-Émile Gravelet] 1824–97 French wire-walker. The son of nomadic performers, he studied with the RAVEL FAMILY, taking his name from his tutor Jean Ravel Blondin and cultivating the bayonet springboard. Fame came in 1859 when, on a US tour with the Ravels, he crossed Niagara Falls on a tightrope; he later repeated this feat blindfolded or pushing a man in a wheelbarrow, or stopping halfway across to cook an omelette. He was much imitated, especially by 'female Blondins'. His first London appearance at the Crystal Palace (1861) earned him £100 a performance, enabling him to buy an estate near Birmingham. He pursued his altitudinous profession till the age of 70.   LS

Bloolips See FEMALE IMPERSONATION; REVUE

Bloom, Claire 1931– British actress. Bloom made her debut at the Oxford Repertory Theatre in 1946 and has developed a distinguished career that encompasses the stage, film and television. She has played an extensive repertoire of Shakespearian roles, including Cordelia to JOHN GIELGUD's King Lear in the 1952–3 OLD VIC season, and acted major roles in both classic and modern plays, such as Hedda in *Hedda Gabler* (1971), Blanche du Bois in *A Streetcar Named Desire* (1974) and Mary Queen of Scots in *Vivat! Vivat Regina!* (1972). Her films have included Chaplin's *Limelight* (1952) and *Look Back in Anger* (1959), and for television more Shakespearian roles and *Brideshead Revisited*. Her acting has been consistently remarkable for her great sensitivity and intelligence, as well as for her personal beauty.   MB

Blue Blouses The first of these Soviet Russian workers' groups was founded by Boris Yuzhanin in 1923 at the Moscow Institute for Journalism; the name derived from factory workers' loose blue smocks. Essentially, it was a LIVING NEWSPAPER, presenting a montage of current events skewed to a proletarian ideology in a MUSIC-HALL format of songs and sketches. Because of its flexibility, a troupe could tour widely, performing AGIT-PROP in factories, clubs and the open air. In their heyday, there were more than 5000 of these groups, both professional and amateur collectives, with 100,000 members. SERGEI TRETYAKOV promoted them, though he warned of the dangers of too much didacticism and stylization. After a tour of Germany in 1927 by a professional troupe, the Blue Blouses were forcibly merged with the more orthodox TRAM movement.   LS

Boaden, James 1762–1839 English dramatist and biographer. Educated for a career in commerce, Boaden became a journalist and editor. In 1794 his adaptation of Ann Radcliffe's *Romance of the Forest*, *Fountainville Forest*, was performed, one of the first transformations of a Gothic novel into Gothic drama. He led the attack on the

Soviet Blue Blouse Troupe, Moscow, 1927.

SHAKESPEARE forgeries of WILLIAM HENRY IRELAND in 1796. The following year he adapted Mrs Radcliffe's *The Italian* as *The Italian Monk*. A great admirer of KEMBLE and MRS SIDDONS, he wrote important biographies of them in 1825 and 1827 as well as of DOROTHY JORDAN, ELIZABETH INCHBALD and GARRICK.   PH

Boal, Augusto 1931– Brazilian playwright, director and theoretician. Boal premiered as an author with *Mulher Magra, Marido Chato (Lean Wife, Mean Husband)* in 1957. His *Revolução na América do Sul (Revolution in South America)* in 1961 by Arena Theatre opened a new epoch of political protest theatre. Teatro Oficina in 1962 presented his third play, *José, do Parto a Sepultura (Joe, from the Womb to the Tomb)*. During the 1960s he worked closely with GIANFRANCESCO GUARNIERI on various classical plays about LOPE DE VEGA and GOGOL, and in 1965 they launched their famous *Arena conta ...* series (on Zumbi, Tirandentes, Bolívar, among others). An inveterate experimenter and Marxist ideologue, Boal encountered problems with the Brazilian political situation. After a period of imprisonment, he sought exile in Argentina and other countries, where he continued to develop new forms of radical theatre such as the *teatro jornal*, a documentary drama based on current events (newspaper events), and the *teatro invisible*, which consists of staged performances in public places before unsuspecting audiences. Boal has written theoretical works explaining his techniques of theatre: *Categorías de teatro popular (Categories of Popular Theatre*, Buenos Aires, 1972), and *Técnicas latinoamericanas de teatro popular (Latin American Techniques of Popular Theatre*, Buenos Aires, 1975). His *Teatro do Oprimido* (1975, translated as *Theatre of the Oppressed*, 1979) gained international recognition as a theoretical model of revolutionary theatre.   GW

Boar's Head Tavern (London) Situated in Whitechapel, just outside Aldgate, the Boar's Head was the first of London's inns to undergo radical transformation for the purpose of accommodating plays (1598–9). Details of the conversion are known from a complicated legal wrangle involving the innkeeper Richard Samwell, a city haberdasher Oliver Woodliffe, the owner of the SWAN Francis Langley and the actor ROBERT BROWNE. We know that a stage was erected on one of the long sides of a rectangular yard, that the galleries were extended to increase the capacity and that a TIRING HOUSE was provided behind the stage. The ambitious plan was to combine three companies, Worcester's, Derby's and Oxford's, as serious rivals to the dominance of the LORD CHAMBERLAIN'S MEN at the GLOBE and the ADMIRAL'S MEN, still at the ROSE in 1599. The combined company, renamed Queen Anne's Men under James I, soon moved to the RED BULL, and the subsequent history of the Boar's Head is unimpressive. By 1621 it was no longer in use as a theatre. It may be that PHILIP HENSLOWE's decision to bring the Admiral's Men north of the river to the FORTUNE in 1600, thereby challenging the geographical uniqueness of the Boar's Head, was too quick and too powerful a blow.   PT

Bobèche [Jean-Antoine-Aimé Mandelart] 1791–c.1841 and
Galimafré [Auguste Guérin] d. c.1870 These artisans' sons played together in *parades*, open-air performances given on trestle stages before the show-booths of the Parisian boulevards. In his yellow shorts, red coat, stringy wig and tricorne hat with its butterfly cockade, Bobèche represented the naïf whose half-closed eyes and caustic

smile concealed shrewdness. His salty comments, unbridled puns and *non sequiturs* were taken up by society; and whenever he played with Galimafré, a tall scrawny figure with a fringe of hair and a Norman costume, the Boulevard du Temple was jammed with carriages. They separated in 1814; Galimafré became a stage-hand at the ODÉON for almost 30 years; Bobèche failed in theatre management in Rouen and Bordeaux and was reduced to playing the violin in low MUSIC-HALLS. LS

Bocage 1797–1863 French actor and director. Bocage was a major figure in the establishment of the *drame romantique*, but for which he might never have made a serious career. He owed much to DUMAS *père*, who understood his talent and made use of it. His political views were strong and coloured his performance and, in the later 1840s, his management of the ODÉON theatre.

Bocage's career began with a travelling troupe. He was taken on at the Odéon in 1822, where the intensity of his acting was noticed. Attracted by the *drame*, he moved to the Gaîté in 1829, playing Sir Jack in *Alice, ou Les Fossoyeurs d'Écosse* (*Alice, or The Scottish Grave-diggers*), then on to the Porte-Saint-Martin (see BOULEVARD), where he played Shylock. Described as 'the boldest barnstormer of the capital', he reached the peak of his career in 1831–2 with the title role in Dumas's *Antony*, as Didier in *Marion Delorme* and as Buridan in *La Tour de Nesle*. Antony allowed him to display a sombre, melancholy and wildly passionate nature which established him as the romantic actor *par excellence*; but the COMÉDIE-FRANÇAISE, where it was staged, was not the theatre for him and he returned to the Porte-Saint-Martin. He moved from theatre to theatre, appearing at the Ambigu in PYAT and Luchet's *Ango* in 1835 (performances were stopped by the censors), at the Porte-Saint-Martin in 1836 in *Don Juan de Marana*, at the Ambigu in 1839 in *Christophe le suédois* and at the Théâtre du Gymnase in Souvestre's *L'Interdiction* (*Forbidden* – a sort of modern-day *Hamlet*). In 1843 he enjoyed a huge success as Brute in PONSARD's *Lucrèce*. During his brief and disastrous period as director of the Odéon, he staged George Sand's *François le champi*, which spurred her to write for the theatre.

Bocage was a great actor, a good director, but a mediocre theatre manager. In 1859 the last of his savings went into a brief management of the Saint Marcel Theatre, and in 1861 he was playing Buridan at Belleville. He was to know one more great triumph – with Paul Meurice and George Sand's play *Les Beaux Messieurs de Bois Doré* (Ambigu Theatre, 1862). JMCC

Bock, Jerry 1925– and
Sheldon Harnick 1924– American composer and lyricist, each of whom began writing for the BROADWAY musical stage in the 1950s; however, they did not work as collaborators until *The Body Beautiful* (1958). In the following year their show *Fiorello!* won the Pulitzer Prize for Drama. Among their other notable scores were *She Loves Me* (1963; revised with critical acclaim, 1993), *Fiddler on the Roof* (1964), *The Apple Tree* (1966) and *The Rothschilds* (1970), after which they ended their partnership. Writing in an era when most MUSICALS had an exotic or period setting, Bock and Harnick were adept at varying their style to match the time and place of each show, while at the same time working within the traditional forms of Broadway show music. MK

Boeuf sur le Toit ('Ox on the Roof') Parisian CABARET, founded by JEAN COCTEAU in 1921; the name derives from an orchestral suite by Darius Milhaud (1919), exploiting MUSIC-HALL tunes. The club served as a retreat for avant-garde artists like Tristan Tzara, who could hear Mozart or GERSHWIN played there by virtuoso pianists. The German émigrée Marianne Oswald introduced its audiences to the songs of BRECHT and Weill, as well as the lyrics of anarchist poet Jacques Prévert and the Hungarian Josef Kosma. The Nazis closed it in 1943, but after the war it reopened featuring Resistance songs, and took on an existentialist aura in 1949 when Juliette Gréco sang works by SARTRE and Mauriac. LS

Bogusław ski, Wojciech 1757–1829 Polish actor, director, manager and playwright, who abandoned a military career for the stage. He is the father of the Polish National Theatre in Warsaw, which he directed from 1783 to 1814. There he staged the first OPERA sung in Polish, Salieri's *Axur*, playing the title role in 1793. In 1798 in Lwów he presented the first Polish *Hamlet*, adapting it from German and French versions. In 1811 he founded the first theatre school, where he taught and wrote a textbook on acting. Among over 80 original plays and adaptations, best known are his musical *Cracovians and Mountaineers* (1794), and the historical drama *Henry IV at the Hunt* (1792). DG

Boileau(-Despréaux), Nicolas 1636–1711 French poet and critic, whose independent spirit, shrewd literary judgement and keen satirical style made him a powerful arbiter of contemporary taste and demolisher of individual reputations. In particular, his adroit exposition of neoclassical doctrine, *L'Art poétique* (1674), conveniently and elegantly summarizes his own critical thinking on the various literary forms, giving prominence to TRAGEDY and COMEDY. He was the friend and supporter of MOLIÈRE and RACINE and was elected to the Académie-Française in 1684. DR

Boker, George Henry 1823–90 American playwright and poet. His principal play, *Francesca da Rimini* (1855), first performed by E. L. DAVENPORT (Lanciotto), did not achieve major success until 1882 when LAWRENCE BARRETT appeared as Lanciotto and OTIS SKINNER as Paolo. It was retained in Barrett's repertoire and was revived by Skinner (Lanciotto) in 1901. Boker wrote 10 other plays. The best-known are *The World a Mask* (1851) and *The Bankrupt* (1855). He once confided to writer Bayard Taylor that he had no ambition to become 'a mere playwright' but wanted to be 'acknowledged as a poet'. He wrote several volumes of poetry: *The Lesson of Life* (1848), *Poems of the War* (1864) and *The Will of the People* (1864).

Boker served as Minister to Turkey (1871–5), as Minister Plenipotentiary to Russia (1875–8), and as president of Philadelphia's Union League (1878–84). RM

Boleslavski [Boleslavsky], **Richard** [Boleslaw Ryszard Srzednicki] 1887–1937 Original member of the Moscow

ART THEATRE's first Studio. Boleslavski left Russia in 1920, joined the Kachalov Group (a MAT offshoot) in Prague (1921) and settled in the USA in 1922. His Princess Theatre (New York City) lectures and his article 'First Lesson of Acting' (1923) introduced Americans to the Stanislavskian concept of 'concentration' in acting (see STANISLAVSKY) and were the basis of his book *Acting: The First Six Lessons* (1933). Boleslavski and former MAT actress Maria Ouspenskaya co-founded the AMERICAN LABORATORY THEATRE (1923–30), where a full theatre curriculum was taught. Boleslavski's development of the actor's expressive means and intellectual and cultural awareness linked the MAT tradition to the GROUP THEATRE, though he believed that one of the founders and a former student, LEE STRASBERG, erroneously stressed affective memory over dramatic action in his teaching. Boleslavski had a varied New York City stage directing career (including the ALT subscription series begun in 1925), directed 15 major Hollywood films in the 1930s, and wrote two autobiographical books, *Lances Down* and *The Way of the Lancer* (published 1932). SG

Bolger, Dermot 1959– Irish playwright. Bolger's trademark is his fusion of nightmarish urban settings, cinematic fluidity and a stylish use of language. *The Lament for Arthur Cleary* (1989) employs formal Gaelic lament to structure its treatment of urban decay, thuggery and drug dealing. The neo-nomadic exile figure of that play also appears in *In High Germany* (1990) – a monologue, later coupled with *The Holy Ground* (1990). His most recent work, *One Last White Horse* (1991), explores the outer and inner nightmares of a drug addict. GF

Bolger, Ray 1904–87 American dancer and singer. After making his debut with a musical STOCK COMPANY in Boston, Bolger spent a few years in VAUDEVILLE before appearing on BROADWAY in *The Merry World* (1926). His loose-limbed, comic dancing style was featured in several REVUES, including GEORGE WHITE's *Scandals of 1931*. He appeared in *Life Begins at 8:40* (1934) and created the part of Junior Dolan in RODGERS and HART's *On Your Toes* (1936), in which he performed GEORGE BALANCHINE's choreography for the 'Slaughter on Tenth Avenue' ballet. During the 1940s Bolger starred in such popular MUSICALS as *By Jupiter* (1942) and *Three to Make Ready* (1946). In *Where's Charley?* (for which he was awarded a Tony, 1948), a musical version of *Charley's Aunt*, he stopped the show with his rendition of 'Once in Love with Amy'. After a decade away from Broadway, he returned to the musical stage in the 1960s for *All American* (1962) and *Come Summer* (1969), neither of which was a hit. MK

Bolivia Since the time of the Spanish Conquest, and even before, there has been theatrical activity in this land-locked nation, although a sustained tradition is lacking. Possible causes include the imposing geography, relative isolation, a series of devastating wars that decimated Bolivia's spirit, and an unstable political climate that produced on average more than one head of state per year since independence. During the colonial period, plays focused on religious themes and important historical events before and during the Conquest. They were often trilingual in Spanish, Quechua and Aymará, but no individual plays of artistic merit can be cited. Upper Peru was part of the viceroyalty of La Plata, and for over 300 years supplied the Spanish with a steady supply of silver, tin and other riches. Bolívar and Sucre liberated this territory in 1825, relatively late in the independence movement in Latin America, and it was named Bolivia, but political independence did not sever Spanish cultural linkages. Traditional Spanish styles continued to dominate through the 19th century.

A major 19th-century play, *Plan de una representación* (*Plan of a Performance*, 1857) by Félix Reyes Ortiz, satirized military coups from university students' perspectives – an ominously prescient view of later Bolivian reality. Historical plays with bombastic verse and exaggerated situations were set vicariously in Argentina (about Juan Manuel de Rosas) and Mexico (about Iturbide). In the War of the Pacific (1879-83) with Peru and Chile, Bolivia lost valuable territory, including its access to the sea, but the theatre did not reflect major changes. An emphasis on verse monologue related to historical drama exalted such figures as Pedro Domingo Murillo, a La Paz revolutionary hero, and Simón Bolívar. Major playwrights of the period are José Palma y V. in the monologue, and Ricardo Jaimes Freyre (1868–1933) and Franz Tamayo (1880–1956) in poetic drama.

The 20th century Modern Bolivian theatre began with Fabián Vaca Chávez's *Carmen Rosa* (1912), a play that portrayed human characters rather than glorified heroes. In a new flurry of interest during the 1920s, the young intellectuals tried to renovate poetry and the arts with vanguard European techniques, but their theatre still resonated with 19th-century romanticism. The Ateneo de la Juventud (Youth Atheneum) and the Sociedad Boliviana de Autores Teatrales (Bolivian Society of Theatrical Authors) in 1922 and 1923 respectively promoted the dramatic arts. The major contribution of these years was to raise the consciousness level regarding the Native American, as well as other national sociopolitical issues. Wenceslao Monroy, better known as Tío Ubico, taught actors and directors for three decades – until 1954. The most prolific playwrights of the period are Mario Flores and Alberto Saavedro.

The War of the Chaco (1932-5) helped unify the country in the quest for a national identity. After the war, Antonio Díaz Villamil advanced the Bolivian theatre by incorporating the lively language of the lower classes, while Valentín Meriles and Joaquín Gantier experimented with the psychological play. A major transformation in government systems led to the National Revolution of 1952 that imposed agrarian reform, nationalized the mines, and introduced universal suffrage – traumatic events that failed nonetheless to stem the revolutions, political assassinations and disastrous economics that plague modern-day Bolivia. A new wave of theatrical activity was evident from 1967 forward that included the formation of new theatre groups such as the Experimental University Theatre, both of Santa Cruz and of Cochabamba. Since 1967 IBART (Bolivian Art Institute) has sponsored nine theatre festivals in Cochabamba.

Another generation of playwrights took a fresh look at

age-old problems. Raúl Salmón in the 1950s and 1960s wrote social plays with a didactic purpose. One of them, *Tres generales* (*Three Generals*, 1969), places three presidents of the 19th century into contemporary Bolivia to emphasize the ubiquitous problems of Bolivian politics and governance. In *La lanza capitana* (1967) Raúl Botelho Gosálvez used a historical framework to advocate Native American rights. Sergio Suárez Figueroa, born in Uruguay, wrote two major plays – *El hombre del sombrero de paja* (*Man in the Straw Hat*, 1967) and *La peste negra* (*Black Plague*, 1967) – the latter a medieval pestilence play with political overtones of modern-day Bolivian governments of terror. GUILLERMO FRANCOVICH pressed for educational reform by dramatizing Simón Rodríguez, the teacher of Simón Bolívar, in *Como los gansos* (*Like the Geese*, 1957). Other playwrights worthy of note are Guido H. Calabri Abaroa and Adolfo Costa du Rels (1895–1980), author of *Los estandartes del rey* (*The King's Standards*, 1956), the only Bolivian play to have won international recognition. In 1972 the play was selected over one by BUERO-VALLEJO for the Gulbenkian Award, given by the Academy of the Latin World.

More recently, without a proper infrastructure, the Bolivian theatre has continued to languish. Maritza Wilde acts and directs in La Paz, Bolivia's capital city, while Santa Cruz is now recognized as the theatrical capital because of René Hohenstein's efforts as director. The few playwrights currently active include Gastón Suárez, Adolfo Mier Rivas, Joaquín Aguirre Lavayén (*Guano maldito*; *Damned Guano*, 1986) and Oscar Barbery (*Laberinto*; *Labyrinth*, 1988).   GW

See: E. M. Dial, 'The Military in Government in Bolivia: A View from the Theatre of Raúl Salmón', *Latin American Theatre Review*, 9, 1, Fall 1975; O. Muñoz Cadima, *Teatro boliviano contemporáneo*, La Paz, 1981; J. Ortega and A. Cáseres Romero, *Diccionario de la literatura boliviana*, La Paz, 1977; M. T. Soria, *Teatro boliviano en el siglo 20*, La Paz, 1980; C. M. Suárez Radillo, 'El teatro boliviano: De lo histórico a lo humano contemporáno', *Cuadernos Hispanoamericanos*, vols. 263–4, May–June 1972.

Bolt, Robert (Oxton) 1924–95 British dramatist, whose first performed plays, *The Critic and the Heart* (1957), *Flowering Cherry* (1957) and *The Tiger and the Horse* (1960), kept closely to the requirements of the serious, WELL MADE PLAYS of the 1950s. RALPH RICHARDSON and Celia Johnson were notably successful in *Flowering Cherry*, which ran for 400 performances at the HAYMARKET. Bolt's training as a historian not only provided the material for later plays but also encouraged him to break away from the somewhat constricting formulae of his early work. In *A Man for All Seasons* (1960) about the life and death of Sir Thomas More, Bolt chose to link together short scenes by employing a narrator, the Common Man, in a style which was then dubbed BRECHTian. Subsequent historical plays included *Vivat! Vivat Regina!* (1970) and *State of Revolution* (1977), and Bolt also wrote the screenplays for such films as *Lawrence of Arabia* (1962), *Dr Zhivago* (1965) and *Ryan's Daughter* (1970). Other sides to his talents were revealed in his children's play, *The Thwarting of Baron Bolligrew* (1965), and *Gentle Jack* (1963), a pantheistic parable.   JE

Bolton, Guy 1883–1979 American librettist and playwright. He began writing plays in 1911, and soon after turned to writing librettos. In 1915 he joined composer JEROME KERN for the first of the Princess Theatre (New York City) musicals, *Nobody Home*. The success of this modest and ingratiating MUSICAL COMEDY was repeated with *Very Good Eddie* (1915), *Have a Heart* (1917), *Oh, Boy!* (1917) and others. Bolton's Princess Theatre librettos were praised for their unusually coherent plots and well developed characters. His career as a librettist spanned 40 years, encompassing such hits as *Sally* (1920), *Lady, Be Good* (1924), *Oh, Kay!* (1926) and *Anything Goes* (1934). With lyricist P. G. WODEHOUSE, he co-authored an autobiography, *Bring on the Girls* (1953).   MK

bommalattam [*gombeyata*] Doll-MARIONETTE theatre form of south-central India, similar in some respects to the better-known Rajasthani doll theatre (*kathputli*) of north India. The age and origin of *bommalattam* is as yet uncertain. Three parties of performers exist at the present time: Kumbhakonam, led by Mani Iyer, near Tanjore in Tamil Nadu state, and Haluvagalu and Padmanabhan Kamath in northern Karnataka.

Play themes are drawn from the *Puranas*, with local folk elements added. The Mysore troupes use YAKSHAGANA performing style as a base and the Tamil troupe imitates *bharata natyam* classical dance. Puppets are 1–3ft tall and are manipulated by strings attached to the head and back, and by rods or strings attached to the arms and legs. The puppet's head and hands are constructed of light wood and the costume is stuffed with paper to give the figure a soft, round appearance.

Manipulators stand above the puppets in an area about 4ft high and 11ft wide in order to move the puppets via overhead strings. The puppet area is created by black cloth stretched across benches or any improvised framework to form a proscenium opening. Light from two petromax lamps or small oil lamps made of coconut shells illuminates the acting area from the front. Like SHADOW PUPPETeers in India, *bommalattam* puppeteers wear bells on their ankles which sound the rhythm of their movements. The stories are told in song and dialogue with passages of dance added for colour. Usually, a cymbal player keeps time, the *mridangam* drum emphasizes movements, and the harmonium provides the base sound for the singers. In the Mysore form, a wind instrument (*ottu*) is used when songs are not sung.

Occasions for performance include temple festivals and religious celebrations. Puppets are also used to ward off evil, prevent epidemics and drought, or bring rain.   FAR

Bond, Edward 1934– British dramatist, whose second play, *Saved*, created a furore when it was first performed at the ROYAL COURT THEATRE in 1965. The most controversial scene involved the stoning to death of a baby in a pram, but Bond used this savage incident to illustrate the moral and cultural deprivation of contemporary life. The technical range and imaginative strength of Bond's plays are impressive. In *Early Morning* (1968) he offered a surrealistic FARCE (see SURREALISM) on Victorian values and mock-heroism, set in a cannibalistic heaven, while in *Narrow Road to the Deep North* (1968) the Japanese *haiku* poet,

String marionettes of the ten-headed Ravana, or Dasamuka, and the monkey Hanuman in *bommalattam*, Tamilnadu state.

Matsui Basho, is the central character in a myth about power lords, good and bad, the worst ones being British imperialists. Despite his sombre views, Bond can sometimes be a funny writer, as in *The Sea* (1973); a lyric poet capable of portraying convincingly other poets, such as John Clare in *The Fool* (1976) and SHAKESPEARE in *Bingo* (1974); and a persuasive naturalistic writer, as in his first play, *The Pope's Wedding* (1962), set in East Anglia. The intensity of his vision can verge on the apocalyptic, as in *Lear* (1972) and particularly in his *War Plays* (1985), about life after the nuclear holocaust.

Bond is the most celebrated and powerful dramatist to have emerged from a group of left-wing writers who were originally encouraged through the Royal Court in the 1960s and went on to write both for FRINGE THEATRE in the 1970s and for the national companies. In 1978 his version of the Greek myths, *The Woman*, was presented at the NATIONAL THEATRE. As with other left-wing dramatists, the collapse of the Soviet Union and international communism left him in ideological isolation. The 1980s were as notable for the absence of Bond's plays as the 1970s were remarkable for their presence. In 1990, *Jackets II* was produced by the Leicester Haymarket and briefly seen at the Bush Theatre in London.   JE

book-holder Combined the functions of prompter and stage-hand, in the Elizabethan theatre. There is insufficient evidence to provide a detailed job description.   PT

book-keeper In the Elizabethan theatre, the company member responsible for the copies of the plays owned by the company was generally called the book-keeper. His first task, on receipt of the author's manuscript ('foul papers'), was to commission a fair copy and to supervise the preparation of the rolls on which individual parts, with short cues, were written out. He was then entrusted with the safe-keeping of the playhouse copy and the parts. Any inefficiency he displayed would have simplified the theft of a popular success by another company or by an opportunist publisher. The continuing reputation of a company might, on the other hand, have been sustained by his effectiveness.   PT

Booth, Barton ?1679–1733 English actor and manager. At Westminster School with ROWE, he was praised for his performance in school productions of TERENCE. After performing in Dublin, he joined BETTERTON's company in 1700, Rowe giving him a part in *The Ambitious Stepmother*. He played secondary roles until he joined AARON HILL's company at DRURY LANE in 1710, taking over some of Betterton's old roles. Often arguing with Hill, he rioted against him with the other actors. He scored a great triumph as Cato in ADDISON's play (1713) and became a partner in the management of the company. In the 1720s his laziness interfered with his success, though he could be inspired on occasions and was expected to take on a heavy acting load, leading to wrangling with COLLEY

CIBBER and Wilks. He retired in 1728 because of ill-health. At his best in majestic roles in TRAGEDY from the start (e. g. the Ghost in *Hamlet*), he thought it 'depreciated the dignity of tragedy to raise a smile in any part of it' (Cibber). PH

Booth, Edwin (Thomas) 1833–93 American actor and manager, who made his debut in 1849 at the BOSTON MUSEUM as Tressel in support of his father's Richard III. Booth continued to act with his father, accompanying him to California in 1852. When the elder Booth left California, Edwin remained, playing in San Francisco and Sacramento and touring various small towns and mining camps. During 1854–5, he toured with LAURA KEENE to Melbourne and Sydney, with a brief engagement in Honolulu on the return voyage. In 1856 he returned to the East, making starring engagements in Baltimore, Richmond and Boston. He made his first major New York appearance at Burton's Chambers Street Theatre (see WILLIAM E. BURTON) in May 1857. From this point until his retirement in 1891, his acting career was generally a series of unbroken successes. For 10 years (1864–74), Booth was involved in the management of several theatres, most notably the WINTER GARDEN (1864–7) and his own BOOTH'S THEATRE (1869–74). His management was particularly distinguished by his carefully mounted, visually splendid productions of *Hamlet*, *Julius Caesar*, *The Merchant of Venice*, *Othello* and *Richelieu*. However, after he lost his theatre in 1873 through poor financial management, he abandoned management and spent the remainder of his career touring.

Early in his career (1861–2) Booth had starred in London (where his only child Edwina was born) and in Manchester and Liverpool. In 1881–2, at the height of his powers, he played at London's PRINCESS'S THEATRE and alternated Othello and Iago with HENRY IRVING at the LYCEUM THEATRE, London. He appeared in London again in 1883 and then toured the provincial circuit. In 1883 he also made a highly successful tour of several German cities. During 1886–91 he completed several extensive US tours in association with his close friend, LAWRENCE BARRETT. Booth's last performance was as Hamlet at the Brooklyn Academy of Music in 1891.

Darkly handsome and gifted with a slender, graceful figure, a clear, musical voice and luminous, expressive eyes, he was the finest American tragedian of his time. At his best portraying brooding, melancholy characters like Brutus or Hamlet – his greatest characterization – or capturing darkly sinister personalities like Iago or Bertuccio (*The Fool's Revenge*), Booth was also successful in the playfully comic roles of Benedick and Petruchio, and especially as the wily, histrionic Cardinal Richelieu. Late in his career, his King Lear and Shylock were widely admired.

The hallmark of his acting style was a certain vocal, physical and emotional restraint, or 'quietude'; this was the chief quality that distinguished his acting from the often violent excesses of the earlier romantic school to which his father JUNIUS BRUTUS belonged. An amateur Booth-watcher, Mary Isabella Stone, commented not only on the 'naturalness' of Booth's speaking, but also on the richly suggestive, complex 'tonalities' of 'exquisite sarcasm' or of 'sincere, friendly interest and sympathy', or of 'mingled grief, astonishment, and anger'. His gestures, facial expressions and movements were also regarded as 'natural'. He did not strain after effect. Perhaps because of his concentration on feeling, he reportedly lost his own personality in a role, creating vivid, completely different, believable characters.

Throughout his career, Booth diligently tried to better not only his art, but also the theatrical profession. He eagerly shared the stage with fellow stars, including not only Irving and Barrett, but also BOGUMIL DAWISON, TOMMASO SALVINI, HELENA MODJESKA, CHARLOTTE CUSHMAN and FANNY JANAUSCHEK. In 1888, he established the Players as a social and cultural club for actors and others interested in theatre. DJW

Booth, John Wilkes 1839–65 American actor, brother of EDWIN. He made his professional debut in 1855 at the Charles Street Theatre in Baltimore as Richmond in *Richard III*, and subsequently played supporting roles for several seasons, principally at the ARCH STREET THEATRE in Philadelphia and the Richmond Theatre. By the early 1860s he was an established popular touring star, playing mainly in the Midwestern and Southern theatrical circuits. He was undoubtedly a talented, sometimes compelling, but also erratic and undisciplined actor, who was probably at his best playing romantic characters and melodramatic heroes and villains. His first New York appearance was as Richard III at the old WALLACK'S THEATRE (1862); his last stage appearance was as Pescara in *The Apostate* at Ford's Theatre, Washington, DC, on 18 March 1865.

Almost a month later (14 April 1865) in the same theatre, Booth, a Southern sympathizer, assassinated Lincoln while the President was watching a performance of TOM TAYLOR's *Our American Cousin*. His motive may have been misguided patriotism or a desire for notoriety. DJW MB

Booth, Junius Brutus 1796–1852 Anglo-American actor who rose to stardom in London, but who spent the bulk of his career in America. Born in London, Booth tried various occupations before becoming an actor in 1813. After a continental tour in 1814–15, he performed at Brighton and Worthing before starring in 1817 at COVENT GARDEN. EDMUND KEAN, concerned with a possible new rival, invited Booth to DRURY LANE to play Iago to his Othello. After one performance, Booth retreated to Covent Garden, where he starred for a few months, then toured the provinces, playing London only occasionally. In 1821 he deserted his wife and child and emigrated to America with Mary Ann Holmes.

Booth bought a farm in Maryland and toured the USA until his death, except for visits to England in 1825–6 and 1836–7. He sired 10 children in Maryland, six of whom reached their majority. His London wife, Adelaide Dellanoy, learned of Booth's American family and in 1851 divorced him; he married Holmes a few weeks later.

As an actor, Booth was often compared to Kean, even accused of imitating him. Romantic, passionate, frequently seeming out of control, Booth gained such notoriety in the New World with his often aberrant behaviour as to be billed 'The Mad Tragedian'. Heavy drinking complicated his situation, but Walt Whitman said of him, 'The words fire, energy, *abandon*, found in him unprecedented meanings. I never heard a speaker or actor who could give such a string to hauteur or the taunt.'

About 1852 Booth began construction on his farm of Tudor Hall, based on an English design – a structure that still stands. He played San Francisco and Sacramento in 1852, appeared for the last time in New Orleans, and died on a Mississippi River steamboat near Louisville. He is buried in Green Mount Cemetery in Baltimore. SMA

Booth, Junius Brutus, Jr 1821–83 American actor and theatre manager who made his debut in 1834 at the Pittsburgh Theatre as Tressel to his father's Richard III. After over a decade of playing stock (see STOCK COMPANY) at various theatres, including New York's BOWERY and Boston's Howard Athenaeum, he migrated to California in 1851 where he acted and managed several theatres in San Francisco until he returned east in 1864. At various times he managed, for his brother EDWIN, the BOSTON THEATRE, the WALNUT STREET THEATRE, the WINTER GARDEN and, for one season, BOOTH'S THEATRE. He was a competent manager, but generally an undistinguished actor, although he was well regarded for his King John and Cassius. He married three women, all actresses: first Clementine DeBar, then Harriet Mace (d.1859) and finally Agnes Land Perry (d.1910), who was a successful leading actress for many years as Agnes Booth. Four of Junius's children pursued stage careers: Blanche DeBar, Marion, Junius Brutus III (d.1887) and Sydney Barton Booth (1873–1937). DJW

Booth, Shirley [Thelma Booth Ford] 1907–92 American actress, whose career began in 1919 with the Poli STOCK COMPANY. Her first New York appearance was in *Hell's Bells* (1925). She is best known for her haunting portrayal of the anguished and slovenly Lola in INGE's *Come Back, Little Sheba* (1950), for which she received a Tony and, for the film version, an Academy Award. In addition she appeared in such productions as *Goodbye, My Fancy* (1948), *A Tree Grows in Brooklyn* (1951), *The Time of the Cuckoo* (1952), *By the Beautiful Sea* (1954), *The Desk Set* (1955), *Juno* (1959), and *Look to the Lilies* and *Hay Fever* (1970). In 1972 she toured as Mrs Gibson in *Mourning in a Funny Hat*. During the 1960s she played the comic strip character Hazel on American television. DBW

booth stage To render themselves visible in a flat playing space, actors have to raise themselves if they cannot raise the audience. A booth stage provides a simple solution. Boards placed across barrels or trestles make a platform, and a curtain strung at the back conceals off-stage actors. It was on stages such as these that Europeans witnessed the gradual emergence of the professional actor – in venues such as streets, market-places and fairgrounds. PT

Booth Theatre (New York City) Built by the SHUBERT BROTHERS in partnership with producer WINTHROP AMES, the Booth opened in 1913 with its sister house, the Sam S. Shubert, the flagship of the Shubert enterprises then and now. Ames envisioned the Booth – a small house, seating about 800 – for his productions of intimate dramas and comedies, which have been its staple ever since. When Ames retired in 1932, the theatre reverted to the Shuberts,

in whose possession it still remains. It has housed four Pulitzer Prize-winning productions: *You Can't Take It with You* (1936), *The Time of Your Life* (1939), *That Championship Season* (1972) and the MUSICAL *Sunday in the Park with George* (1984). MCH

Booth's Theatre (New York City) Built for EDWIN BOOTH at the corner of 6th Avenue and 23rd Street, it opened on 3 February 1869 with a production of *Romeo and Juliet*. Constructed in granite, in an ornate Second Empire style, Booth's Theatre measured 150ft by 100ft deep and rose to a height of 125ft. Attached to the west end was a five-storey wing, the ground floor of which was for shops, with three floors above for artists' studios and apartments and the top floor reserved for Booth's private flat. The lavishly decorated and appointed auditorium followed the standard 19th-century horseshoe-shaped configuration, although it had a fairly narrow apron and a sunken orchestra pit similar to that designed for the BAYREUTH Festspielhaus some seven years later. There were a number of other mechanical innovations in the design of the theatre, including a forced-air heating and cooling system, a set of hydraulic ramps that raised vertically moving bridges or platforms for changing scenery, a sprinkler system for fire protection, and an electrical spark ignition device that for the first time in the USA permitted both the auditorium and the stage lights to be extinguished during performances.

Some of the finest Shakespearian productions of the era were mounted at the theatre during Booth's four-year tenure. After he lost control of it in 1873 – the result of poor financial management – Booth's Theatre was leased and managed by various individuals including JUNIUS BRUTUS BOOTH JR, Henry C. Jarrett and Henry David Palmer, AUGUSTIN DALY, George Rignold and DION BOUCICAULT. In 1883 the theatre was rebuilt as a department store, which in turn was razed in the 1960s. DJW

Borchers, David 1744–96 German actor. Borchers was a celebrated intuitive actor who began in the ACKERMANN troupe, then played with FRIEDRICH SCHRÖDER in the Hamburg Town Theatre. He was noted for the elemental power of his stage presence and for his wild good humour. He never learned his roles and often improvised. From 1782 to 1785 he was the director of the Linz Town Theatre. He was notorious for his irregular private life: he once gambled with his wife as the stake, and lost. SW

Borchert, Wolfgang 1921–47 German dramatist. His only play, *Draussen vor der Tür* (*The Man Outside*, 1947), deals with a soldier's return from the war. It was an emotive subject treated in emotional language, with many echoes of EXPRESSIONISM. First performed the day after Borchert died, it became the first postwar hit in Germany. HR

Borovsky, David 1934– Soviet-Russian stage designer, best known for his work with director YURY LYUBIMOV at the Taganka Theatre in Moscow. Some of Borovsky's more important productions include *Hamlet* (1972), *Comrade Believe*, GORKY's *Mother* (1978) and *Valentin and Valentina* (1978). His design is characterized by the creation of highly textured, three-dimensional, interactive playing environments using real objectsrelated metaphorically to the plays' themes, which can be transformed by the actors. A good example is the use of a wooden army truck in *The Dawns Are Quiet* (1972), which was transformed into trees, living quarters and coffins. In *Hamlet*, a movable woollen curtain transformed the space into 12 different configurations. AJN

Bosnia see YUGOSLAVIA; MEDIEVAL DRAMA IN EUROPE (Eastern Europe)

Boston Ideal Opera Company [the Bostonians] American comic OPERA company. Founded by Miss E. H. Ober in 1879 in order to present an 'ideal' production of *HMS Pinafore*, the company, made up primarily of church choir singers from the Boston area, was noted for its high standards in both the singing and the mounting of comic operas. Although based in Boston, the company toured extensively. Reorganized as the Bostonians in 1887, they announced their intention of encouraging the development of American comic opera. They launched the career of composer REGINALD DE KOVEN with their production of *Robin Hood* (1891), and performed the same service for VICTOR HERBERT with *Prince Ananias* (1894). After a defection by several members of the troupe in 1898, the company declined, ending its existence in the 1904–5 season. MK

Boston Museum (USA) In 1841, Moses Kimball opened the Boston Museum and Gallery of Fine Arts at the corner of Tremont and Bromfield Streets, Boston, Massachusetts, to offer a collection of curiosities to the public at a small admission charge. In combination with the museum was a

'concert saloon', which in 1843 was transformed into a regular theatre with a STOCK COMPANY. In 1844, after the phenomenal success of *The Drunkard*, which played for 100 performances, it provided a steady diet of moral plays, earning it the name of 'deacon's theatre'. In 1846 the entire enterprise was moved into its new building, and under a succession of astute managers, particularly R.M. Field, it housed the finest dramatic corps in America during the 1860s and 70s. Its most distinguished member, WILLIAM WARREN THE YOUNGER, spent almost his entire career (1847–82) with it. The company was disbanded in 1894, and the theatre fell into the THEATRICAL SYNDICATE's hands until it was razed in 1903. MCH

Boston Theatre (USA)Built on Washington Street, Boston, Massachusetts, in 1854 through public subscription in response to the closing of the FEDERAL STREET and TREMONT THEATRES; DION BOUCICAULT called it 'the finest theatre in the world'. A technical showplace, its seating capacity of 3140 made it the largest theatre in the USA. EDWIN BOOTH made his first starring appearance there (1857), and JOSEPH JEFFERSON III first played Rip Van Winkle there (1869). By 1885 the theatre's well regarded STOCK COMPANY operated independently and spent most of its time touring New England; it dissolved sometime in the late 1890s. B. F. KEITH turned the theatre into a VAUDEVILLE and motion picture house after 1909. Sixteen years later it was torn down to make way for the Keith Memorial Theatre. TC

Botswana, Lesotho and Swaziland Botswana and Lesotho became independent in 1966; Swaziland, in 1968. The population of the three states totals some 3 million,

A scene from *Kopana Ke Matla* (*Unity is Strength*), a play about the problems facing an agricultural co-operative, produced by the National University of Lesotho's Theatre in Community Development Project, 1984.

including many who live and work in South Africa. Sharing the southern African subcontinent with the Republic of SOUTH AFRICA, the three states have had much of their modern history determined by events taking place on that troubled stage. Established as discrete nations in the early 19th century, Lesotho (formerly Basutoland) and Swaziland developed quite differently. In Basutoland, Moshoeshoe I of the Basotho welcomed immigrants of many ethnic backgrounds, and encouraged his people to engage in the emerging industrialization and urbanization of South Africa. This policy, however, had unfortunate results, as labour migrancy over the past 150 years has led to catastrophic soil erosion and the fracturing of the family unit. Religious divisions have created additional tensions within Lesotho, further worsened by the oppressive South African experience of many Basotho men. In Swaziland, a conservative ethnic exclusivity and the centralized power of the monarchy have not encouraged experimentation in the arts. Botswana (formerly Bechuanaland) – with the most varied citizenry of the three, ranging from the Khoi-Khoi and San 'bushmen' of the Kalahari to the urbanites of the modern capital Gaborone – has had the most pacific history and the greatest measure of political democracy. But scattered settlement over a large but sparsely populated territory has not, until recently, stimulated a great deal of theatrical activity beyond traditional forms.

Sharing a regional experience, playwrights of the three nations tend also to share thematic preoccupations: history (often exploring intracommunal dissonance, rather than conflicts with colonial authorities or settlers); strain between generations and between Western-Christian and customary ways, including the enduring dilemmas of bride price, polygamy and traditional magic; the changing pattern of family relations; the life of the sojourner in South African cities; the corrosive effects of apartheid; and the social and psychological consequences of labour migrancy. Interestingly, while writers working in English have tended to be identified with their nations of citizenship, writers in African languages are often seen as members of a larger transnational ethnic community. Thus, South African Joseph M. Ntsime (b.1930) is considered a Setswana-language playwright, while Sesotho-speaking B. L. Leshoai (b.1920), who writes in English, is perceived as a South African.

Of the surviving traditional performance modes in the three countries, the one with the most prominent dramatic component is the mimetic game-enactment of the hunter-gatherer Khoi-Khoi and San of Botswana's desert region. In sung and danced sketches, involving rudimentary forms of plot and characterization and the use of costuming and make-up, both animals and humans are represented. Like the cave paintings for which these cultures are noted, such plays often deal with the processes and skills of hunting.

Written drama in Setswana, the language of the Batswana people, dates only from the 1930s, with SHAKESPEARE translations by South African Solomon T. Plaatje (1877–1932) and, later, by the Motswana Michael O. Seboni (1912–72). The first original play published in Setswana was the work of the Botswana playwright Leetile Disang Raditladi (1910–71). *Motsasele II* (1937) deals with a

critical moment in the history of Botswana's Bakwena people, and was eventually followed by the tragedy, *Dinshontsho tsa Lorato* (*The Many Deaths of Love*, 1956), and *Sekgoma I* (1967), which recounts the events of a disruptive chieftaincy dispute amongst the 19th-century Amangwato people.

Of the next generation, Ntsime's *Pelo e Ja Se Rati* (*A Loving Heart Knows No Bounds*, 1965) is a domestic comedy setting chiefly and paternal authority against decisions of the heart; his *Kobo e Ntsho* (*The Black Robe*, 1968) is a darker and partly autobiographical study of the effects of a father's pressure on his son to become a clergyman; and *Pelo e Ntsho* (*A Black Heart*, 1972) is an attack on witchcraft. But by far the most innovative theatrical initiative in Botswana in recent years has been the Laedza Batanani (The Sun Is Risen, Come Out and Work) scheme, begun by Jeppe Kelepile in 1974, using theatre to encourage both discussion of and action on community problems (health, illiteracy, crime, economic issues) at village level.

Largest of the countries and the first to have a printing operation, Lesotho has seen the greatest number of published plays, if disproportionately fewer stage productions. The first script published in the Sesotho language, Twentyman M. Mofokeng's *Sek'ona Sa Joala* (*A Calabash of Beer*, 1939), is concerned with the clash of cultures, traditional and modern. Later, numerous plays on moral and religious themes, many of them unproducible closet dramas, were circulated, often in cyclostyled form, by the Roman Catholic centre at Mazenod and the Evangelical Mission at Morija.

Lesotho's first major playwright emerged in 1947, with the publication of B. M. Khaketla's *Moshoeshoe le Baruti* (*Moshoeshoe and the Missionaries*). Khaketla (b.1913) – a teacher turned politician, and founder, in 1960, of the small Marematlon Freedom Party – is best-known as a novelist, poet and polemicist. His stage pieces include the historical *Tholoana tsa Sethepu* (*The Fruits of Polygamy*, 1954), about a succession to kingship, and its sequel, *Bulane* (1958), in which the disinherited son finally becomes king. Khaketla's wife, N. M. Khaketla, is probably the most widely read Sesotho author today. Amongst her plays, which deal with both domestic and broader social problems, are *Mosali Eo U 'Neileng Eena* (*The Woman Thou Gavest Me*, 1956), in which a shell-shocked former seminarian returns from the First World War, survives difficulties in love and becomes a cleric; the two short pieces collected as *Ka U Lotha* (*I'm Posing You a Riddle*, 1976); the unpublished *Mahlopha a Senya* (*Creating and Destroying*, early 1980s), which mixes Sesotho and the local English of the streets; and *Ho Isa Lefung* (*Unto Death*).

Lesotho's best-known playwright, and one of Africa's major theatrical voices, is ZAKES MDA. Son of a central figure in South Africa's banned Pan-Africanist Congress, Mda emigrated to Lesotho in 1963, and began writing for the stage while at secondary school. By the mid-1980s his plays had been performed both within and outside Africa, and translated into several languages. *We Shall Sing for the Fatherland* (1978), set in an unnamed African country, examines the disparity between the promises of nationalist politicians before independence and the reality of deprivation afterwards. In *Dark Voices Ring* (1978), Mda anatomizes the system of contracted prison labour in

South Africa and the psychological cost to the family of a black farm overseer of complicity with apartheid. *The Hill* (1979), his most finished piece, is a powerful TRAGICOMEDY on the social and ethical distortions created by labour migrancy. This theme is further developed in *The Road* (1982), a stark parable with resonances of BRECHT, BECKETT and GENET, in which a Lesotho migrant worker confronts an Afrikaner farmer in a bizarre melange of misperception, hostility and desperate territoriality.

In the mid-1980s Lesotho also saw the emergence of popular theatre, with the Theatre for Community Development Project of the National University, which combines the improvisational stage techniques of the Laedza Batanani scheme with radio, videotape and narrative comic-book production, and is directed at rural, urban and prison groups. From this has grown the Marotholi Travelling Theatre and the University of Lesotho Theatre Group – both working as theatre-for-development (see THIRD WORLD POPULAR THEATRE) companies into the early 1990s. Playwrights and theatre workers active from the late 1980s include Masitha Hoeane, Buti Moleko and Afelile Sekhamane.

Swaziland's theatre remains the least developed in the region, with its best-known published play by a writer who is neither a Swazi nor primarily a playwright – anthropologist Hilda Kuper's statement on the position of women in Swazi society, *A Witch in My Heart* (1970). However, from the 1980s a great deal of work has been done in participatory community theatre as part of public education campaigns. Swaziland also has a rich tradition of RITUAL and ceremonial performance, including the six-day sacred harvest and kingship rites of the *ncwala* and the annual secular *mhlanga* (reed dance) for young girls.   AH

See: C. M. Doke, 'Games, Plays and Dances of the Khomani Bushmen', *Bantu Studies*, 10, 1936; A Gerard, *African Language Literatures*, London, 1981; A. Horn, *The Plays of Zakes Mda*, Johannesburg, 1987; R. Kidd, M. Byram and P. Rohr-Rouendaal, *Laedza Batanani: Organizing Popular Theatre*, Gaborone, 1978; Z. Mda, *When People Play People: Development Communication through Theatre*, London, 1993; L. Nichols, *African Writers at the Microphone*, Washington, DC, 1984.

Bottomley, Gordon 1874–1948 British poet and dramatist, who wrote specifically for groups such as the Community Theatre and the Scottish National Theatre, though his early work also had some success on the London stage. Bottomley's poetic dramas, influenced by SYNGE'S REALISM, dealt with subjects from Norse history (*The Riding to Lithend*, 1907, first performed 1928) or from SHAKESPEARE (*King Lear's Wife*, 1915; *Gruach*, 1923). Discarding these as 'plays for the Theatre Outworn', he turned to experimental choral work based on Celtic legend – which he called pieces 'for a Theatre Unborn' – following NŌ drama in reducing scenery to a portable folding screen.   CI

Bouchard, Michel Marc 1958– Quebec playwright and actor. Bouchard began writing plays while in his teens but first attracted attention in 1983 with *La Contre-Nature de Chrysippe Tanguay, écologiste* (*The Counter Nature of Chrysippos Tanguay, Ecologist*), in which a male homosexual couple seeking to adopt a child discover the limits of social tolerance. It was followed by a score of plays in rapid succession, notably *La Poupée de Pélopia* (*Pelopia's Doll*, 1984) and especially *Les Feluettes, ou la Répétition d'un drame romantique* (1987), one of the major works of modern Canadian dramaturgy, both in French and in its English translation, *Lilies; or, The Revival of a Romantic Drama* (1988). The latter, like most of Bouchard's work, deals with homosexuality in conflict with evolving social values.   LED

Bouchardy, Joseph 1810–70 French dramatist and engraver. Beginning to write for the theatre in the mid-1830s, Bouchardy was often thought of as the direct descendant of PIXÉRÉCOURT, and his name became almost a byword for the rather naive, old-fashioned MELODRAMA. His main output was a score of dramas, of which the most popular were *Gaspardo le pêcheur* (*Gaspardo the Fisherman*, 1837), *Le Sonneur de Saint-Paul* (*The Bellringer of Saint Paul's*, 1838) and *Lazare le pâtre* (*Lazarus the Shepherd*, 1840). Most were written for the Ambigu or the Gaîté (see BOULEVARD), and their general tone is resolutely populist, with powerful villains who always meet their deserts. Bouchardy's plots are infinitely more complicated than those of Pixérécourt, and generally revolve around the avenging of a crime committed either in a prologue or 20 years before the beginning of the action proper. His avenging heroes are thus usually middle-aged men. Bouchardy's stagecraft helped ensure his popularity, which lasted until the 1850s. His last play, *The Armourer of Santiago*, was performed at the Châtelet in 1868. Bouchardy's work as an engraver includes theatrical scenes for the *Monde dramatique*.   JMCC

Boucicault, Dion(ysius Lardner) 1820–90 Irish-born playwright, actor and theatre manager whose energy and facility combined with a flair for self-advertisement to make him a leading figure in both the English and the American theatre. The success of *London Assurance* (1841) at COVENT GARDEN during the regime of MADAME VESTRIS and CHARLES JAMES MATHEWS brought Boucicault into youthful prominence. This artful five-act comedy, Regency rather than Victorian in tone and setting, held the stage throughout the 19th century and was effectively revived by the ROYAL SHAKESPEARE COMPANY in 1970. *Old Heads and Young Hearts* (1844) was a second and similar success. Like the cleverly contrasting two-act comedy *Used Up* (1844), it was staged at BENJAMIN WEBSTER'S HAYMARKET.

It was partly to provide Webster with plays 'from the French' that Boucicault went to Paris in 1845. Mostly on the strength of intelligent plagiarism, he continued to supply the London theatres for a further decade, most notably with *The Corsican Brothers* (1852) and *The Vampire* (1852) at CHARLES KEAN'S PRINCESS'S THEATRE. Not only as a playwright, but also as the actor of the sensational title role in *The Vampire*, Boucicault was London's rising star in 1852, but the scandal of his liaison with the actress Agnes Robertson ended his contract with Kean. It was as Agnes Robertson's manager that the resourceful Boucicault began his career in the American theatre in

1853. As man and wife they toured the USA, managed theatres in New Orleans (1855), Washington (1858) and New York (1859) and made Boucicault's name familiar in the New World. With *The Poor of New York* (1857), he established the vogue of the sensation scene in MELODRAMA, continuing it with *Jessie Brown* (1858), *The Octoroon* (1859) and *The Colleen Bawn* (1860). It was in the last of these that Boucicault and Agnes made a brilliant comeback in London in 1860, where they remained until 1872. Outstanding successes during this period included an adaptation of *Rip Van Winkle* (1865) for JOSEPH JEFFERSON III, a horse-racing melodrama *The Flying Scud* (1866) and a courtesan-play, *Formosa* (1869), which scandalized the audiences – which it also delighted at DRURY LANE. A second Irish melodrama, *Arrah-na-Pogue* (1864), was followed ten years later by a third, *The Shaughraun* (1874), which is among the best of the genre.

Of Boucicault's remaining plays (he is credited with nearly 200), only *The Jilt* (1885) did anything to sustain his reputation. Always controversial, he had contributed to the establishment of a new COPYRIGHT law in the USA, to the development of fire-proofed scenery, to a profit-sharing system for playwrights which led in time to their receiving royalties, and to the foundation of actor-training in the USA. His own style of acting was extravagant and idiosyncratic. Outstanding as the lovable Irish rogues he had written into his accomplished trio of melodramas, he also relished the oriental exoticism of the villainous Nana Sahib in *Jessie Brown* and the Indian chief Wahnotee in *The Octoroon*. Quite as roguish in his own life as his finest creation, Conn the Shaughraun, he made a bigamous marriage to an American actress 44 years his junior in 1885, defiantly claiming until his death that his common-law wedding to Agnes Robertson was not legally binding. PT

Bouffé 1800–88 French actor. A performer of considerable sensitivity and simplicity, Bouffé was known particularly for his attention to nuance and accurately observed detail and for a tendency to underplay in the genre in which he excelled, the *vaudeville*. His first roles were at the Panorama Dramatique, playing Mère Simonne in *La Fille mal gardée* and the Chinese emperor in *La Petite Lampe merveilleuse* (*The Wonderful Little Lamp*, 1822). With the closure of the Panorama he moved to the CIRQUE OLYMPIQUE, and then to the Gaîté (see BOULEVARD), where he showed a talent for cameo character parts. From 1827 to 31 he appeared in 52 plays at the Nouveautés, moving then to the Théâtre du Gymnase, where he was said to be the best comic actor in Paris. Bouffé's great triumph there was in *Le Gamin de Paris* (*The Urchin of Paris*), which he played 315 times between 1836 and 1844 (Vanderbuck, one of the authors, was able to buy a chateau with his share of the royalties).

In 1842 the Gymnase trapped him into a 15-year contract, which he managed to buy himself out of so as to move to the Variétés in 1843. His appointment there changed the deficit of that theatre into a handsome profit, and DÉJAZET was appointed to complement him. In 1848 his career was interrupted for five years by a nervous disease. He then began playing again in the provinces, appearing in Paris in 1854 at the Porte-Saint-Martin with *Michel Perrin*, and then in *La Fille de l'avare* (*The Miser's Daughter*), which gave him one of his greatest roles. In 1855 the Cogniards invited him back to the Variétés, but without a fixed contract, because of his health. His last appearance was in a special matinée given for him in 1878, and in 1880 he published his memoirs. JMCC

boulevard In the late 19th century the term applied broadly to the commercial theatre in Paris purveying meretricious entertainment to the more affluent bourgeoisie. Between 1750 and 1830, 'boulevard' had a more precise geographical reference – the Boulevard du Temple (sometimes called the Boulevard du Crime because of the violent MELODRAMAS shown there), and was associated with the popular theatres. Two fairground showmen, Nicolet, a harlequin (see HARLEQUIN), and Audinot, a puppet-showman (see PUPPETS), set up booths on the Boulevard which ultimately became the Théâtre de la Gaîté and the Ambigu-Comique, where the melodrama was born out of the 18th-century pantomime – a development greatly accelerated by the abolition of the monopoly of the COMÉDIE-FRANÇAISE in 1791.

The Gaîté, the theatre associated with PIXÉRÉCOURT in particular, was rebuilt after a disastrous fire in 1835, and then demolished in 1862, when the Boulevard du Temple made way for the present Place de la République. The new Gaîté moved to the Square des Arts et Métiers, becoming more an operetta theatre than one for melodrama. The Ambigu, after a fire in 1827, moved to the adjacent Boulevard Saint-Martin and continued into the 20th century as a theatre for popular melodrama. Napoleon's decree of 1807 limited the number of theatres in Paris to eight (plus the CIRQUE OLYMPIQUE, where much equestrian melodrama (see HIPPODRAMA) developed). The Gaîté, the Ambigu, the Variétés and the Vaudeville were 'secondary', or boulevard, theatres. The Variétés, going back to 1785, occupied MLLE MONTANSIER's theatre in the PALAIS-ROYAL, but in 1807 moved into a new theatre, Boulevard Montmartre (the oldest extant theatre building in Paris). Its licence permitted 'short plays in the *grivois*, *poissard* or *villageois* genres, sometimes also containing songs set to popular tunes'. By the 1850s the Variétés had abandoned its popular repertoire (drag parts such as Madame Angot, played by the popular comic actor Brunet) and under Hippolyte Cogniard introduced REVUES and OPERETTA, including Offenbach's *La Belle Hélène*, with Hortense Schneider (1864). The Vaudeville opened in 1792, as a result of the liberty of the theatres. Its repertoire, like that of the Variétés, consisted largely of the *vaudeville*, short comic pieces with sung couplets, a genre which would find its highest expression in the plays of LABICHE. In 1838 the Vaudeville was demolished but it reopened in a theatre opposite the Stock Exchange, the unsuccessful Nouveautés (1827–32), where it remained until 1869 and where, in 1852, Eugénie Doche and CHARLES FECHTER appeared in the first production of *La Dame aux camélias* (*The Lady of the Camellias*).

The largest of the boulevard theatres, the Porte-Saint-Martin, was originally built as a temporary opera house in 1781, opened as a melodrama theatre in 1802, closed for a time because of the 1807 decree, was burnt in the Commune of 1871, then rebuilt. In the early 1800s it was important for its *ballet-pantomimes*, forerunners of the romantic story-ballet. For the dramatists of the romantic school (HUGO, DUMAS *père* and even DELAVIGNE), the Porte-Saint-Martin became a sort of alternative Théâtre-Français. After the first Empire the number of theatres gradually increased, until 1864 when Napoleon III granted freedom to build and run a theatre to anyone wishing to do so. As a result, the latter part of the century saw a vast boom in theatre building, and the disappearance of the concept of theatres limited to a specific repertoire or genre.

In the 20th century these theatres changed their staple from melodrama to light COMEDY, though some managers have attempted to include more literary plays in a repertoire mostly composed of commercial productions. The boulevard's most flourishing period was the *belle époque* (1890–1914), before there was serious competition from the modern media. In this period the contemporary playwrights most favoured were GEORGES FEYDEAU, Tristan Bernard and Georges Courteline. These authors continued the tradition of the well made sex comedy, designed to entertain a well heeled after-dinner audience and providing a suitable vehicle for star actors such as SACHA GUITRY, who himself wrote boulevard comedies. Other writers whose plays partly fall into the boulevard category also had higher ambitions, such as Édouard Bourdet, Henri Bernstein, Henri Bataille and Georges de Porto-Riche. Between the wars a sub-genre of psychological portrait theatre set in rural France was provided by Marcel Pagnol and Jean-Jacques Bernard, and other comedy writers emerged, notably Marcel Achard. But the essential nature of boulevard theatre as an upper-middle-class club was maintained by the obligatory wearing of evening dress, the series of tips required from the *vestiaire* to the *ouvreuse*, and the fact that performances never started until at least half an hour after the advertised time of 9 pm. These were not favourable conditions for serious drama, as reformers such as COPEAU, ANTOINE and GÉMIER never ceased to point out.

After the Second World War boulevard theatre again flourished, benefiting from the habit of theatregoing acquired by Parisians during the German occupation. New successful playwrights emerged, notably André Roussin and Félicien Marceau. Plays by more literary dramatists, especially SALACROU, SARTRE and ANOUILH, were also performed on the boulevards in the 1950s, and many private managers prided themselves on their commercial flair, fighting hard against every encroachment of subsidized theatre (e.g. the THÉÂTRE NATIONAL POPULAIRE of VILAR). But since the 1960s, with escalating costs and the inexorable rise of the subsidized sector, the commercial theatres of the boulevards have gradually been reduced in number. Some have tried to broaden their appeal with imported successes from Britain and the USA; others have tried to develop a particular brand of whimsical, semi-cynical, semi-poetic humour through authors such as François Billetdoux, Romain Weingarten and René de Obaldia. Today the distinctive snob value of these theatres has largely disappeared, and some are even able to claim government subsidy. JMCC DB

Bowery Theatre (New York City) When a sprinkling of wealthy and fashionable New York families began to settle near the Bowery, they decided to build a playhouse more conveniently located for them than the PARK THEATRE. Pledging money and buying land on which Henry Astor's tavern had stood, they erected what came to be known as the Bowery Theatre, although it passed through a succession of other names. Superior to the Park in appearance, both inside and out, it presented several seasons of drama, OPERA and ballet before its audience left it to return to the older house. In 1830, Thomas S. Hamblin secured its lease and, for the next 20 years, dominated its policies. Hamblin's tenure included the highwater years for the playhouse, during which the greatest names of the American theatre (J. B. BOOTH, EDWIN FORREST, the WALLACKS, Mrs John Drew (see DREW–BARRYMORE FAMILY), FRANK CHANFRAU) appeared on its stage. Hamblin eventually bought the theatre, but bad times forced him to lose it. A succession of managers followed, who presented spectacle and MELODRAMA to please the neighbourhood.

The surrounding district became the haven for the newly arriving immigrant groups who poured into New York in the mid-19th century, and the theatre began increasingly to reflect the new populations of the area, becoming the temple of entertainment for New York's Lower East Side. Until 1879 the dramatic fare was in English; thereafter it was the turn of German acting troupes, who renamed the theatre the Thalia. Then came Yiddish performers in 1891; next, Italian vaudevillians; and finally came Chinese VAUDEVILLE, which was playing at the time of the theatre's fiery demise (1929). It had burned down and been rebuilt five times previously (1828, 30, 36, 38, 45), and each reconstruction had carried it further away from its original neoclassical façade into a strange mixture of architectural styles. MCH

Boyd, John 1912– Irish playwright. Boyd's major theme is the North of Ireland's divided heritage, mainly in urban settings and expressed in the local idiom paradoxically common to the antagonistic faiths. *The Assassin* (Gaiety, Dublin, 1969) explores the psychology of a clerical demagogue. *The Flats* (Lyric Theatre, Belfast, 1971; also produced in New York and Germany) places domestic tragedy in the collective violence of Belfast. These naturalistic plays (see NATURALISM) – along with *The Farm* (1972) and *The Street* (1977), *Summer School* (1987) and *Round the Big Clock* (1992), a Belfast chronicle play – are acutely discerning of the brutalities behind factional slogans. DM GF

Boyle, Roger, Earl of Orrery 1621–79 Irish playwright. He ended the Civil War as a favourite of Charles II and began writing plays after the king had suggested he try to write a TRAGEDY in heroic couplets. The result, *The General*, was first performed privately in Ireland in 1662 and in London in 1664. He continued writing whenever recurrent bouts of gout interrupted his political career as one of the Lord Justices of Ireland. *Henry V* (1664), *Mustapha* (1665) and *The Black Prince* (1667) established his reputation for the creation of a new mode of heroic drama, placing the hero between love and honour. His work was much admired by DRYDEN, though his later comedies, written when heroic drama ceased to be fashionable, were unsuccessful. PH

Boyle, William 1853–1923 Irish playwright. The ABBEY, to judge by the reviews, made uproarious comedies of Boyle's plays. Except for *The Eloquent Dempsey* (1906), a FARCE about dishonest politics, his plays are desolate enough. *The Building Fund* (1905) is a black study in avaricious competition for an inheritance, *The Mineral Workers* (1906) a kind of 'problem play' about the conflict between industrial development and rural values, their representatives equally unsavoury. Boyle broke with the Abbey in the row over SYNGE's *Playboy*, but gave it his last two plays, *Family Failing* (1912) and *Nic* (1916). DM

boys' companies There are records of performances at the English court of plays by choristers as early as the 14th century, but the significant history of the two major companies, the BOYS OF ST PAUL'S and the CHILDREN OF THE CHAPEL ROYAL, begins in the 16th century. The Paul's Boys were probably the first English company, adult or child, to have their own theatre (c.1575), though they were quickly followed by the Chapel Children at the BLACKFRIARS (1576). The early repertoire probably consisted of MORALITY PLAYS, but the engagement of JOHN LYLY as the major writer for both companies (1582–90) brought a new sophistication to their work. Lyly's allegorical plays could be deciphered by alert audiences more readily than by the choristers themselves, and the dangerous precedent of employing boys to speak lines that would have been considered censurable if spoken by adults was established. But Lyly misjudged the mood of the established Church when he used the Paul's Boys on its behalf in the Marprelate Controversy (1589–90), and the activities of the boys' companies were summarily curtailed.

After a ten-year silence, during which Elizabethan drama had grown by leaps and bounds, the boys began a decade of astonishing and controversial activity. Only SHAKESPEARE among the major dramatists of his day remained aloof. Others, like CHAPMAN and MARSTON, wrote their best plays for the boy actors, demanding of them rhetorical skill in delivering lines whose import they cannot always have grasped. We must assume that audiences took a mischievous delight in hearing pubescent boys mouth sexual innuendoes or satirical jibes. There was also the advantage of indoor performance and the sensible exploitation of the choristers' musical skills, which the adult companies could not match. Never far from controversy, the boys came under more vigilant scrutiny after the accession of James I. Diplomatic blunders mounted. Chapman, Marston and JONSON offended with *Eastward Ho* (1605), JOHN DAY with *The Isle of Gulls* (1606) and Chapman again with his *Biron* plays (1608).

The Paul's Boys declined after 1606 and the Chapel Children were forced to abandon the Blackfriars to the King's Men in 1608. This was not the end of the boys' companies, but it marked the climacteric. As the Children of the King's Revels (1608–9) and of the Queen's Revels (1609–13), groups continued to perform at the less attractive WHITEFRIARS, but without the special privileges of choristers they struggled to rival the adult troupes. The last of the major children's companies performed at the COCKPIT from 1637 to 42, where they were familiarly known as Beeston's Boys after their manager, CHRISTOPHER BEESTON. But this, though a youthful company, was probably not composed of boys as young as the choristers of the early-17th-century ascendancy, when SALATHIEL PAVY had been three years a star on his death at the age of 13. PT

Boys of St Paul's Although the choristers of St Paul's may have acted in plays as early as the 14th century, the significant history of what is arguably England's first home-based drama company begins with the mastership of Sebastian Westcott in 1553. Licensed to impress suitable children, Westcott seems to have been as interested in an aptitude for acting as an ability to sing. Recent scholarship has established the existence, but not the exact whereabouts or dimensions, of a playhouse within the precinct of St Paul's. The likeliest site is a corner of the Chapter House cloisters. We know that a portion, known as the shrouds, was roofed over to form a secure house in c.1575, and this may in effect mean that an open-air playing space was converted into a private theatre. The ten choristers of St Paul's were sporadically employed as actors before Westcott's mastership. They 'recited' TERENCE's *Phormio* for Cardinal Wolsey in 1528, and an earlier master, John Redford, probably wrote *Wit and Science* for them during his period of office (c.1534–c.1547). But Westcott, despite his defiant Catholicism, was favoured and protected by the queen during his 30 years (1553–82) as Master. There are records of over 30 court appearances by the Paul's Boys under his direction. We have, for example, the names though not the texts of seven plays they presented at court for the Christmas celebrations of 1567–8.

Westcott's successor, Thomas Gyles (1584–1600), was not discernibly interested in drama, and he entrusted their preparation to JOHN LYLY. For a while (1582–5) the Paul's Boys combined with the CHILDREN OF THE CHAPEL ROYAL to present Lyly's courtly plays, which simultaneously increased the prestige and reduced the audience of the BOYS' COMPANIES. Even more disastrously, Lyly enlisted the boy actors in the Marprelate Controversy, after which their right to perform was summarily removed. Only after a ten-year silence and under a new Master, Edward Pearce, did the Paul's Boys re-emerge as an acting company. The major influence now was JOHN MARSTON, who wrote his extraordinary *Antonio* plays (1599) for the choristers before plunging them into the adult Poetomachia (see WAR OF THE THEATRES), in which he was worsted by BEN JONSON. This time, though, the Paul's Boys benefited from the publicity of controversy. Major playwrights DEKKER, CHAPMAN, MIDDLETON, JOHN WEBSTER and BEAUMONT wrote for them, and they were popular enough to ruffle the adult companies. Around 1605, almost unaccountably, the tide began to turn against the boys' companies, and the St Paul's group was the first to crack. There are records of sporadic performances during 1606–8, but these were evidently no more than death throes. PT

Bracco, Roberto 1862–1943 Italian dramatist and critic whose prolific output spans a range of dramatic kinds: light, sophisticated comedies, naturalistic pieces, and explorations of social and domestic problems in the manner of IBSEN. It was for the last, with plays like *Tragedie dell'anima* (*Tragedies of the Soul*, 1899) and *Maternità* (*Maternity*, 1903), that he was particularly admired in his own day, although the play for which he is now best remembered, *Il piccolo santo* (*The Little Saint*, 1909), was more innovative than derivative in its Freudian-like treatment of the workings of the subconscious. In the 1920s his liberal views ran foul of Fascist opposition, which effectively put an end to his career in the theatre.   LR

Bracegirdle, Anne 1671–1748 English actress who first appeared on the stage in 1688. From the beginning she chose to play the pathetic heroine in tragedy and the witty, sophisticated woman in comedy, particularly if the role called for her to be disguised in BREECHES. She also gained a considerable reputation as a singer. She worked for the United Company until 1695 when she joined BETTERTON's group of seceding actors. CONGREVE wrote for her such roles as Angelica in *Love for Love* (1695) and Millamant in *The Way of the World* (1700). Her carefully made reputation for virtue and virginity was frequently challenged but never overthrown. She retired in 1707, probably recognizing that she could not compete with the talents of ANNE OLDFIELD, and enjoyed a long and dignified retirement.   PH

Brackenridge, Hugh H(enry) 1748–1815 American author and playwright. Writing for his students at Maryland Academy, he did not consider his plays – *The Battle of Bunker's-Hill* and *The Death of General Montgomery in Storming the City of Quebec* (1777) – finished dramas. Both plays, composed in blank verse, emphasize patriotic virtue and stress the strong emotional qualities that characterized much of Brackenridge's writing. As teacher, judge, legislator, and chaplain in Washington's army, he exhibited a belief in persuasive oratory in writing and a sense of mission.   WJM

Brady, Alice 1892–1939 American stage and film actress and singer, and daughter of WILLIAM A. BRADY. Making her New York debut as a chorus girl in *The Mikado* at 18, she appeared in major GILBERT and Sullivan roles for the next two years, then as Meg in *Little Women* (1912). In 1914 she entered silent pictures for Famous Players Company. By 1923 she had made 32 films, but continued working in the theatre. In 1928 she joined the THEATRE GUILD; her most memorable stage role was as Lavinia in O'NEILL's *Mourning Becomes Electra*. She returned to films as a singer-actress in 1933.   SMA

Brady, William A(loysius) 1863–1950 American manager and producer. Born in San Francisco, Brady made his first stage appearance in 1882, and his debut as a producer in 1888. He purchased the rights to *After Dark* from DION BOUCICAULT in 1899 and presented it at the BOWERY THEATRE. AUGUSTIN DALY sued him for plagiarizing the locomotive scene from *Under the Gaslight*; Brady eventually lost, but attained publicity by hiring prizefighter James J. Corbett to appear in the cast and later featuring him in several vehicles. In 1896 he leased the Manhattan Theatre, where he enjoyed several successes, including *Way Down East* in 1898. A year later he married actress Grace George and promoted her career. She opened his Playhouse in 1911 with *Sauce for the Goose*, and later appeared in *The School for Scandal* and SHAW's *Major*

Barbara. Brady managed the careers of numerous players including his wife's and his daughter, ALICE's. His more than 260 productions included *Street Scene* (1929), which ran for 600 performances and won a Pulitzer. Also a sports promoter and film pioneer, Brady was recognized as a 'born gambler' with an 'uncanny instinct for drama'. His memoir, *Showman*, was published in 1937.   TLM

Bragaglia, Anton Giulio 1890–1960 Italian theatre director and critic. Bragaglia was founder and director of the Teatro degli Indipendenti, an experimental avant-garde company working in Rome between 1923 and 1930, and conceived radically to reform the conservative and conventional Italian stage of his day. He pioneered new staging techniques and introduced the work of innovative young playwrights, including BRECHT. Connected early on with the futurist movement (see FUTURISM), he looked to technology to revolutionize a moribund theatre by emphasizing the spectacularity of the art. He was a theorist as well as a practitioner: many of his early ideas found expression in his controversial *Del teatro teatrale, ossia del teatro* (*About the Theatrical Theatre – that is, the Theatre*, 1927), a work which puts him among the major early-20th-century prophets of a new theatre to meet modern needs. His own experimentation as director, however, was handicapped, as were futurist experiments, by the technical backwardness of the Italian stage, as well as by his limited funds. During the Fascist period he directed the Teatro delle Arti in Rome, seeking where possible to advance new work and encourage young directing talent: in both respects his positive longer-term effects on the Italian stage were substantial, and he ranks as one of the few significant figures in the Italian theatre of the interwar years. Like other members of the futurist movement he was interested in photography and the cinema, making an early experimental film, *Perfido incanto* (*Perfidious Enchantment*, 1916). His last years were devoted to theatre criticism and to studies of popular theatre.   KR

Brahm, Otto 1856–1912 German director and critic. Brahm began his career as drama critic of somewhat conservative tastes on the Berlin newspapers *Vossische Zeitung* and *Die Nation*. However, he became enthused by the European naturalist movement (see NATURALISM) and, especially, by the plays of IBSEN. As a result, in 1889 he founded the FREIE BÜHNE (Free Theatre), an organization devoted to the production of naturalistic drama on an irregular basis but in established theatres and using well known Berlin actors. In these years Brahm was substantially responsible for bringing the plays of GERHART HAUPTMANN to public attention. In 1894 Brahm was appointed director of the DEUTSCHES THEATER. However, as a director, he was limited by his unremittingly naturalistic approach to production, so that he was unable to adapt to changing trends in theatre. In 1904 the more versatile MAX REINHARDT took over the Deutsches Theater, and Brahm's final years were spent as the director of the less prominent Lessingtheater.   SW

Branagh, Kenneth (Charles) 1960– British actor. Born in Belfast, Branagh won a scholarship to study at RADA at the age of 18 and joined the ROYAL SHAKESPEARE COMPANY at Stratford when he was 22. His stocky appearance and rugged good looks, coupled with his evident acting ability, brought him immediately into contention as a possible leading man; and he was chosen to play the title role in *Henry V* (1984), the youngest actor in the RSC's history to tackle this part. This led to other major but less rewarding roles with the RSC – in *Hamlet*, Louise Page's *Golden Girls* and *Love's Labour's Lost*. Wanting to escape from the limitations of the RSC's policies, he launched his own company, Renaissance, in 1987, which attracted other leading actors and became one of Britain's major touring companies. Renaissance concentrates on Shakespearian productions, directed by actors, rebelling against the directors' theatre of such companies as the RSC. Branagh himself directed *King Lear* (1990) and *Uncle Vanya* (1991) and played the title role in *Coriolanus* (1992). He has been successful on television, playing Guy Pringle in the BBC's series, *Fortunes of War*, where he met the actress Emma Thompson, whom he married. He was by now already being described as a new OLIVIER, a comparison underlined by his starring part in the film *Henry V*, which he also directed. This was the first of several successful movies, in which he played this dual role of actor-director, including a film noir, *Dead Again*, and a comedy, *Peter's Friends*. He returned to the RSC to play Hamlet in ADRIAN NOBLE's Edwardian production in 1992, his third version of this part. JE

Brandão, Raúl 1867–1930 Portuguese playwright. Before the vogue for literary existentialism caught on anywhere, Brandão wrote theatre which takes as its dominant theme the existential position of man, with the emotional accents on the pain, the deprivations and frustrations and the very brevity, pointless and tragic, of life. Two apprentice plays of the turn of the century were followed by *O Gebo e a Sombra* (*Hunchback and Shadow*, 1927), the only play performed professionally in his lifetime; two longish one-acters; two dramatic monologues; and a TRAGICOMEDY, *Jesus Cristo em Lisboa* (1927). In spite of the exiguous repertoire, Brandão's burning compassion and his dramatic single-mindedness and power have ensured the growth of his reputation and influence in latter years. LK

Brandes, Georg 1842–1927 Danish critic, the major promoter in 1870s Scandinavia of the 'modern breakthrough' of rational, progressive thinking and naturalistic (see NATURALISM) problem-oriented literature. As a theorist, Brandes was an assimilator rather than an originator, but his assertion in *Main Currents in Nineteenth-century Literature* that contemporary literature was alive insofar as it submitted problems to debate was enormously influential. Controversy over his questioning of accepted social views led to his spending the years 1877–83 in exile, where he had frequent contact with IBSEN, BJØRNSON and STRINDBERG, who were inspired by Brandes to write their naturalistic plays. Through his prolific writings, Brandes promoted their work, as well as that of Kierkegaard, J.P. Jacobsen and other Scandinavian writers. Equally importantly, he promoted within Scandinavia such diverse figures as John Stuart Mill (whose *Subjection of Women* he translated), Taine, Dostoevsky and, above all, NIETZSCHE. HL

Brandes, Johann Christian 1735–99 German actor and playwright. An actor of little distinction, Brandes made his mark by his facile pen. His plays, thoroughly forgotten now, were successful in their day. He is best known now for his autobiography (1800), one of the chief sources for the theatre history of the late 18th century. Brandes was briefly, and unsuccessfully, manager of the Hamburg Town Theatre while FRIEDRICH SCHRÖDER was away in Vienna. SW

Brando, Marlon 1924– American actor. Although his major reputation comes from his work as a film actor (*A Streetcar Named Desire*, *On the Waterfront*, *The Godfather*), it was as Stanley Kowalski in ELIA KAZAN's stage production of TENNESSEE WILLIAMS's *A Streetcar Named Desire* (1947), his final theatre role, that Brando first made his mark as an actor of moody intensity. Among his other limited stage appearances were *I Remember Mama* (1944), *Truckline* (1946) and *Candida* (1947). His style is often seen as the most famous product of the ACTORS STUDIO. Brando is currently completing his autobiography. MB

Brassens, Georges 1921–81 French poet and singer. The son of a mason, he went to Paris in 1939, worked in a factory and after the war joined the anarchist movement. Although he already had an underground reputation for performing his unconventional compositions in clubs, he was 'discovered' in 1952 by Jacques Grello and his recordings soon became best-sellers. Accompanying himself on the guitar, Brassens would sing of friendship, atheism, self-sacrifice, losers and nostalgia in a gruff and ursine manner, that smacked a bit of the blues. The Académie-Française awarded him its poetry prize in 1967; he made his last public appearances at the Bobino in 1972 and 1976. LS

Braun, Volker 1939– German dramatist, the third most important, after HACKS and MÜLLER, in the GDR. *Die Kipper* (*Tippers*, 1972) and *Tinka* (1974) exposed inadequacies in GDR working conditions and practices. *Guevara, oder der Sonnenstaat* (*Guevara or the Sun State*, 1977), which was banned, encapsulated Braun's own predicament – how to justify utopian Communism while embroiled in the real thing. *Der grosse Frieden* (*The Great Peace*, 1979) was a parable celebrating Communist utopia, while *Die Übergangsgesellschaft* (Temporary Society, 1989), which transposed CHEKHOV's *Three Sisters* to East Berlin, was a popular hit because of the criticism of existing socialism clearly visible between the lines. HR

Brayne, John c.1540–86 English theatrical entrepreneur, brother-in-law of the more famous JAMES BURBAGE. Brayne was a prosperous grocer, who ventured his wealth in at least three London theatrical projects – firstly at the RED LION in Stepney in 1567, secondly at the THEATRE in 1567, and thirdly at the George Inn in Whitechapel in 1579. It has been too readily assumed that Burbage was the main instigator of Elizabethan theatre-building. The true (and unsung) pioneer may equally have been Brayne. PT

Brazil In all of Latin America, Brazil is a unique phenom-

Grupo Pau Brasil's *Macunaíma*, at the Lyric Hammersmith, London, 1981.

enon. This gigantic territory, occupying as it does nearly half the land mass of South America, was settled by Portuguese explorers after discovery in 1500. Even though it shares a border with every country in South America except Chile, the linguistic and cultural differences in formation have created a vast chasm that impedes close contact with Spanish-speaking neighbours. Brazil is remarkably heterogeneous: in addition to the Portuguese and the Native Americans, Africans were brought to sustain slavery, which endured until 1888. Waves of Italian, Spanish and German immigrants, followed by the Japanese and various other nationalities, produced a melting-pot of traditions and heritages in a country enormously rich in natural and human resources and with a strong international presence.

The theatre in this great land has developed separately from that of its neighbours but is similar in many respects because of dominant external influences over an extended period of time. The early immigrants included the Jesuit missionaries who incorporated indigenous elements, extracted from the flora, fauna and ethnology, into their productions that were designed to help catechize the native populations. One early example is the *Auto de Pregação Universal* (*Auto of Universal Prayer*, 1570), written by Padre José Anchieta and considered a typical manifestation of the early religious plays. *Autos* (short plays), comedies and tragedies were all cultivated, written in combinations of Latin, Spanish or Portuguese with the native language, of which many existed in this vast territory.

The excitement of the Conquest and settlement produced some dramatic activity, but the ensuing 17th and 18th centuries have been described by Brazilian critic Sábato Magaldi as the 'vacuum of two centuries'. This period marks the decline of the activities of the Jesuit theatre; in general the dramatic representations were linked to religious festivals or to other popular feasts and public occasions. Manuel Botelho de Oliveira (1636–1711) was one of the first Brazilians to publish his works, but they are Spanish in spirit, technique, themes and even in language. The other significant figure of the period was Antonio José de Silva ('the Jew') (1705–39). During his short lifetime, punctuated by persecutions from the Inquisition, he dedicated himself to satiric theatre as a reaction against the decadence of the Portuguese theatre, which was dominated by a taste for Spanish COMEDY and Italian OPERA. His facility in caricaturing nobles and churchmen probably contributed greatly to his being beheaded and burned at the stake.

In 19th-century Brazil the political and social upheaval produced the same kind of theatrical anarchy that was evident in other countries. When King Dom João fled with his nobles to Brazil to escape Napoleon's invading armies, he ordered the construction of the Royal Theatre of St John in order to transplant to Rio the Italian opera he dearly loved. Through his protection and encouragement, governmental subsidies were granted to support dramatic enterprises. *Antonio José, ou o Poeta e a Inquisição* (*Antonio José, or The Poet and the Inquisition*, 1838) by Gonçalves de Magalhães (1811–82) merited attention as the first work on a national theme written by a Brazilian. The author wrote his play as a classical tragedy to represent his violent reaction against the 'horrors of the modern school' of romanticism, the outmoded literary movement still dominant at that time in Latin America.

The first period of monarchy under King John was followed by that of Pedro I (1822–31), who failed to find favour with the Brazilian populace and abdicated his throne in disgrace. He left a young son, Pedro II, who after a period of regency (1831–41) ruled Brazil for nearly 50 years (1841–89) and despite all odds managed to keep the country intact. This unique political situation did not produce the kind of political and propagandistic drama often found in the other Latin American countries. Instead, the comedy of manners flourished under the inspiration of Martins Pena. His one-act comedy, *O Juiz de Paz de Roça* (*The Frontier Justice of the Peace*, 1833), revealed his unusual ability to capture the essence of the people. His plays, in fact, represented a compendium of the life and times of the first half of the century, and are still produced because of the humour and the agility of his dramatic constructions.

Other writers of the period succumbed to the liberal excesses of romanticism. Their premature deaths reflected their ebullient spirits but cut short their production. Gonçalves Dias (1823–64) left one important work, *Leonor de Mendoça* (1847), a historical play based on jealousy and intrigue. In 1852 Alvares de Azevedo (1831–52) wrote *Macário*, a wickedly nightmarish dream. Castro Alves (1847–71) does not belong chronologically to the romanticists but his work reflected the aesthetics of the period. His masterpiece, *Gonzaga ou a Revolução de Minas* (*Gonzaga, or The Minas Revolution*, 1867), advocated his greatest aspiration, the abolition of slavery.

The second half of the 19th century has been divided into two stages: from 1855 to 1884, and 1884 to 1900. In 1855 Joaquim Heliodoro Gomes organized his new theatre, the Ginásio Dramático (Dramatic Gymnasium), modelled on the Gymnase in Paris, where the repertoire of French realism triumphed. The new works, thesis plays illustrating the important social questions of the time, were presented there and for a while were received enthusiastically by the public. The COMEDIA more accurately reflected the true interest of the public, however, rather than the theatre of social thesis and psychological analysis, and the initial step towards REALISM fell short because of the intervention of the OPERETTA and the musical REVUE.

Artur Azevedo (1855-1908), more than any other writer, was responsible for the trend of the Brazilian drama during the latter half of the century. He was a prolific writer, and his adaptations and translations were regularly performed in Rio de Janeiro. His most popular work, *A Capital Federal* (*The Federal Capital*, 1897), itself an adaptation of one of his earlier plays, turned on humorous contrasts between rural and urban lifestyles. The REVISTA (revue) form he cultivated gained quick popular acceptance. A satire of customs, primarily political issues, the *revista* ranged from a unified plot to independent sketches without continuity. In either event, the *revista* attracted a greater public during those years than the more serious theatre, and Azevedo responded to his critics by pointing out the public choices. When Azevedo and Moreira Sampaio presented *O Mandarim* (*The Mandarin*) in 1884, the *revista* was established as a literarydramatic genre that has survived to the present day to a minor extent, although it was essentially discredited by the early 1940s.

Although the quality was not exceptional, the operetta, the *revista* and PARODY were all popular forms at the end of the century.

The 20th century During the early years of the century, the greater degree of commercial success available to writers and impresarios of the *teatro ligeiro* (light theatre) inhibited the expansion of serious works. Revues, BURLESQUE, FARCES and operettas continued as the dominant forms, represented by Gomes Cardim, Coelho Neto, Cláudio de Sousa and João de Rio, who continued these traditions after Azevedo's death in 1908. In the next two decades, several attempts were made to establish new theatre companies, most of which produced only fleeting impressions on national drama. The popular Cláudio de Sousa (1876-1954) continued the romantic, sentimental traditions of the past century in *Flores na Sombra* (*Flowers in the Shadow*, 1916). The Semana de Arte Moderna (Week of Modern Art, 1922) brought to Brazil the postwar vanguard movement in literature and the arts, although the movement had little effect on drama. Alvaro Moreyra (1888-1964) and Oswald de Andrade (1890-1954), leading writers in 'modernism', failed to achieve public acceptance, although the latter's *O Rei da Vela* (*King of the Candle*), for example, revealed a technical virtuosity too early for its time.

The worldwide economic and social crisis of the 1930s produced an incipient revolution in the theatre. JORACY CAMARGO and Oduvaldo Vianna (1892–1972) wrote pompous, 19th-century-style thesis plays utilizing an anachronistic Camões language. The initiative to reform the theatre along the lines of the European vanguardists such as COPEAU, REINHARDT and STANISLAVSKY fell to several theatre groups knowledgeable about the new techniques, such as Colméia (1924), Alvaro Moreyra's Teatro de Brinquedo (Game Theatre, late 1920s), the Teatro Universitário (University Theatre, 1940s) and the Teatro do Estudante do Brasil (Brazilian Student Theatre, 1940s).

The new orientation took solid form in 1938 with the formation of Os Comediantes (the Comedians), an amateur group, later professional, that dared to disobey the traditional rules and customs by experimenting with new techniques of lighting, staging and acting. The arrival of the Polish refugee Zbigniew Ziembinski in 1941 provided substance to their efforts. Ziembinski was trained in German EXPRESSIONISM and brought with him experience in directing, acting and lighting as well as techniques for training new actors and a new theatre public. Their production of *Vestido de Noiva* (*Bridal Gown*) in Rio in 1943 marked the beginning of the modern Brazilian theatre. This play by NELSON RODRIGUES was ideally suited to the expressionistic techniques in lighting, rhythm and movement that enhanced the presentation of the psychic disassociations of a moribund woman in three levels of past and present time. Rodrigues's morbid attraction for shocking scenes and themes revealed an analogy with the THEATRE OF THE ABSURD. A prolific though not always popular dramatist, Rodrigues often lacked commercial success although he continued to write about the perversions, sexual and otherwise, he considered indicative of contemporary society. From that point forward, the Brazilian theatre began to reflect the aesthetic revolution that occurred in other genres during the modernist movement in 1922.

In the oft-repeated pattern of Latin American theatre, a number of amateur and experimental companies developed to accept the challenge of establishing a new theatre: Teatro de Amadores de Pernambuco (Amateur Theatre of Pernambuco, 1941), Teatro Experimental do Negro (Black Experimental Theatre, 1944, established in protest about the lack of blacks on the Brazilian stage), Grupo dos Quixotes (Quixote Group, 1951) and others. Without question the most significant group was the Teatro Brasileiro de Comédia (Brazilian Play Company), established in São Paulo in 1948, where it formed a permanent company of 15 to 20 actors with two Italian directors, Celi and Salce. By 1954 the TBC had acquired sufficient stability and a sound artistic and commercial base in order to open a parallel company in Rio de Janeiro, where it inspired rival groups along similar lines, such as the Teatro Maria Della Costa.

From the 1940s onward, the critics have commented on the dichotomies in the Brazilian theatre – between the public that favours light, frivolous comedies and those who support serious artistic fare. Originally, the distinction was geographic, with the light farce and comedy associated with Rio de Janeiro and the serious comedy with São Paulo, although these lines are not severely drawn. In Rio the tradition of Martins Pena and Artur Azevedo was continued by Silveira Sampaio (1914–65) and Henrique Pongetti (b.1898). Sampaio satirized the customs of marriage and middle-class society in three comedies filled with irony and comic talent known as the *Trilogia do Herói Grotesco* (*Trilogy of the Grotesque Hero*, 1948–9). Two political SATIRES followed; Pongetti also wrote farces disparaging politics and high-society morals. Other playwrights of the Rio tradition included Raimundo Magalhães Júnior (b.1907) and Pedro Bloch (b. 1914). Bloch was consistently popular with the public, if not with the drama critics. His two-act monologue, *As mãos de Eurídice* (*Euridice's Hands*, 1951), achieved international acclaim, more for its interesting techniques than for the convincing psychology. He also wrote psychodramas with didactic tendencies.

The theatre in São Paulo began to develop a serious, realistic tradition. One of the major playwrights affiliated with the TBC was JORGE ANDRADE, whose interest in the decadence of the rural Paulista society led to *A Moratória* (*The Moratorium*, 1955), *Pedreira das Almas* (*Stone-Quarry of Souls*, 1956), and a group of plays known as the 'coffee cycle'. Abílio Pereira de Almeida (1906–77) had already portrayed the decadence of the rural aristocracy in *Paiol Velho* (*Old Barn*, 1951), but as the unofficial dramatist of the TBC he lapsed briefly into sensationalism for commercial success before returning to criticism of venal public officials and the political, moral and economic corruption of the metropolis.

In the late 50s and early 60s various experimental theatre groups with the perspectives inspired by vanguard European and North American groups (such as the LIVING THEATRE) launched new directions. Three groups were particularly important. In São Paulo the Teatro Arena (Arena Theatre) made initial efforts with both foreign plays (TENNESSEE WILLIAMS and others) and domestic productions. The focus was on politically committed theatre

which would elaborate a unique and characteristically Brazilian dramatic 'language'. The founder and first director was José Renato; after the American-trained AUGUSTO BOAL joined the company in 1956, they staged a series of *Arena Conta ...* (*Arena Tells ...*) plays with an arena stage, actor/audience contact, NUDITY and daring language in an effort to Brazilianize BRECHT. Their production of *Eles não Usam Black-tie* (*They Don't Use Tuxedos*) by GIANFRANCESCO GUARNIERI (born in Italy in 1934) set new standards of realistic theatre by focusing on lower-class problems of life in the *favela* (the Brazilian slum). The Teatro Oficina (Workshop Theatre) under the direction of José Celso promoted street theatre, staged GORKY and Brecht, and the first production in 1967 of *O Rei da Vela* (*King of the Candle*), the long-ignored 1929 play by Osvaldo de Andrade. The most important production since *Bridal Gown* in 1943, it again revolutionized Brazilian stagecraft. The Teatro Opinião (Opinion Theatre) in Rio functioned along similar lines, staging *Liberdade, Liberdade* (*Freedom, Freedom*) by Flavio Rangel and Millor Fernandes in 1965.

The dominance of Rio and São Paulo as theatrical centres did not preclude the development of a religious and folkloric theatre (see FOLK DRAMA) in the Northeast, where unique combinations of cultural, social and religious elements produced moralizing and regionalistic farces. The principal playwrights were ARIANO SUASSUNA and ALFREDO DIAS GOMES. Suassuna's *Auto da Compadecida* (*The Rogue's Trial*, 1957) integrated the 17th-century-style AUTO SACRAMENTAL with modern comedy, folklore and colloquial language. An instant success in Brazil, the play was soon known around the world in various translations. Dias Gomes achieved international recognition with *O Pagador de Promessas* (*Payment as Pledged*, 1960), a moving drama staged by the TBC in 1960 that reflected the insensitivity of the modern world towards an ingenuous peasant victimized by the hypocrisy and syncretism of his native region. The film version of this play won at the Cannes Film Festival in 1962, and launched a long and productive career for Dias Gomes – whose other plays include *O Berço do Heroi* (*The Hero's Cradle*, 1965) and *O Santo Inquérito* (*The Holy Inquisition*, 1966).

Deteriorating political conditions in Brazil in the 1960s led to major changes in the theatre. The military regime of General Castello Branco at first dealt lightly with the theatre, but after the worldwide protests of 1968 brought strikes and student demonstrations to Brazil, restrictions and CENSORSHIP were imposed. PLÍNIO MARCOS was the most sensational new playwright, with *Dois Perdidos numa Noite Suja* (*Two Lost Souls in a Dirty Night*, 1966) and *Navalha na Carne* (*Knife in the Flesh*, 1967), plays that captured the marginal society of pimps, prostitutes and homosexuals with candour and scabrous language. In *O Assalto* (*The Assault*, 1969), José Vicente painted the fragility of the human condition in a two-character play with homosexual motifs that turns violent and destructive. Homosexual themes coupled with revolutionary motifs are still in evidence in 1984 in such plays as *As Três Moças do Sabonete* (*Three Girls on a Bar of Soap*) by Herbert Daniel.

During the radicalized period of the 1970s, the newspapers resorted to such absurd tactics as publishing recipes when articles were censored. In the theatre innovative groups such as Arena Theatre and Workshop Theatre disappeared. Plínio Marcos was unable to stage his plays. Augusto Boal after a period of torture and imprisonment went into exile, where he continued his vanguardist experiments with 'newspaper theatre' (*teatro jornal*, a kind of documentary drama) and the 'invisible theatre' (street theatre in which the public is unaware of a rehearsed performance). Within Brazil, social commentary was permissible only if cleverly disguised, such as in the brilliant *Apareceu a Margarida* (*Miss Margarida's Way*, 1973) by Roberto de Athayde (b. 1949), a monologue by a frustrated and foul-mouthed schoolteacher lecturing to her students. *Um Grito Parado no Ar* (*A Scream in the Air*, 1974) was a symbolic, nationalistic piece by Guarnieri (in collaboration with Boal). Chico Buarque de Holanda brought his musical genius to notable productions such as *Gota d'Agua* (*Drop of Water*, 1977), the tragic theme of Medea set in the Brazilian *favela*. His *Opera do Malandro* (*The Rogue's Opera*, 1980), an adaptation of *The Threepenny Opera*, is critical of commercial relationships between Third World countries and the USA. The most important Brazilian theatre company in the 1970s was Rio's Asdrubal Trouxe Seu Trombone (Hasdrubal Brought His Trombone).

The new regime of General João Figueiredo in 1979 restored greater freedoms to the Brazilian people and to the stage, which led to a resurgence of activity. The spectacular productions of recent years include *Macunaíma*, a staged version of the recondite novel by Mário de Andrade, written in 1927 and staged in 1979 by the Grupo Pau Brasil, a group that subsequently adopted the name of its own production. Based on a cyclical and mythical journey by an ingenuous Native American from the innocence of the jungle to the sophisticated and wicked metropolis and back again, the play recreates with freshness and ingenuity the true genius of Brazilian theatre. Grupo Macunaíma was Brazil's most successful company in the 1980s and achieved international acclaim. Its subsequent productions were *O Eterno Retorno* (*The Eternal Return*), 1981, based on plays by Nelson Rodrigues; *Romeo and Juliet* (1984); and *Augusto Matraga* (1986), based on a short story by Guimarães Rosa. Cacá Rosset has directed such notable productions as a Brazilian version of Brecht's *Mahagonny* and, more recently, a clever, fascinating version of *Père Ubu* with all the humour, sensuality and freedom of expression that typify the Brazilian theatre.

With the previous fierce censorship lifted, directors and plays took on previously taboo topics, including torture and other political themes. Older playwrights have continued to be active: Plínio Marcos returned with *Madame Blavatsky* (1985), a work that echoes Brazilian mysticism through the Ukrainian-born founder of the Theosophy Society (1875), while new names appear: Naum Alvez de Souza (b.1942), Júlio César Conte (b.1955) and Gerald Thomas (b.1954). Of these, Thomas is perhaps the most ingenious. Educated in London and apprenticed to LA MAMA in New York, he has developed a provocative style in *Eletra com Creta* (*Electra with Crete*, 1985), *Carmen com Filtro* (*Carmen with Filter*, 1986) and *Carmen com Filtro 2* (*Carmen with Filter 2*, 1990).

Important women writers in Brazil include Maria Clara Machado, Rachel de Queiroz, Luiza Barreto Leite, Leilah Assunção and Maria Adelaide Amaral. Denise Stoklos (b.1950) has captured international attention with her acting, and productions such as *Mary Stuart* (1987), *Hamlet* (1988) and *Casa* (*Home*, 1990).

In a country with a multiplicity of regional customs and traditions, the theatre is diversified and active. Although theatre companies in Brazil are notoriously unstable (the exceptions are Os Comediantes, TBC, Arena, Oficina and now Grupo Macunaíma), new companies, often with colourful names, are constantly being formed as only slightly older ones disappear. Such groups include Asdrúbal Trouxe Seu Trombone, Tá na Rua (It's in the Street) and Boi Voador (Flying Bull). The level of theatre activity in Brazil is high and the quality is often exceptional. Language differences continue to impede the transmission of recent Brazilian drama to the consciousness of the Western world – a serious loss.   GW

See: S. J. Albuquerque, *LATR*, 25, 2, Spring 1992; A. Boal, *Teatro do Oprimido*, Rio de Janeiro, 1975; H. Borba Filho, *Fisonomia e Espírito de Mamulengo* (*O Teatro Popular do Nordeste*), São Paulo, 1966; A. S. da Silva, *Oficina: do Teatro ao Te-ato*, São Paulo, 1981; M. Garcia Mendes, *A Personagem Negra no Teatro Brasileiro*, São Paulo, 1982; D. George, *Teatro e Antropofágia*, São Paulo, 1985, and *Grupo Macunaíma: Carnavalização e Mito*, São Paulo, 1990; A. Guzik (ed.), *Teatro Brasileiro do Comédia*, Rio de Janeiro, 1980; L. B. Leite, *A Mulher no Teatro Brasileiro*, Rio de Janeiro, 1965; S. Magaldi, *Panorama do Teatro Brasileiro*, Rio de Janeiro, 1979, and *Um Palco Brasileiro: Arena*, São Paulo, 1984; M. Silveira, *A Contribuição Italiana ao Teatro Brasileiro*, São Paulo, 1976, and *A Outra Crítica*, São Paulo, 1976; *Teatro e Realidade Brasileira* [*caderno especial*], *Revista Civilização Brasileira*, 2, 1968.

Bread and Puppet Theatre Founded in New York in 1961 by Peter Schumann, who had previously organized the New Dance Group in Germany, Bread and Puppet has never been an orthodox group in manning, finance or artistic policy. Not an ensemble but a loose association of performers under Schumann's firm direction, and supplemented as needed by amateurs, the company has so mistrusted the idea of purchasing entertainment that, whenever possible, it offers its services free. This principle is based on its founder's maxim – 'theatre is like bread, more like a necessity' – which is enacted literally in the course of each performance by the giving of bread to the audience. Deeply involved in the contemporary reaction against what is perceived as the over-intellectualization of Western culture, as epitomized in its powerful tradition of literary theatre, Schumann and his associates work with larger-than-life PUPPETS to create a non-narrative theatre that addresses contemporary issues – such as the Vietnam War – through disturbing visual images rather than words. In performances such as 'The Cry of the People for Meat' and 'The Domestic Resurrection Circus' (the latter first mounted in 1970 and subsequently most years since 1974), religious iconography and political message are combined in an attempt to offer a critique of contemporary society in terms of its own values.

After a four-year residence at Goddard College, in 1974 Schumann moved to a farm near Glover, Vermont, and the company nominally disbanded. In practice it has continued to regroup for summer festivals at Glover (in 1993 a new structure was erected for modest winter productions), and for specific tours and commissions such as the 1975 'Anti-Bicentennial' at the University of California – an angry and moving elegy to the last Indian survivor of white genocide in the state. More recently, Schumann and his associates have performed both scripted plays such as BÜCHNER's *Woyzeck* (New York, 1981) and large-scale devised pieces such as *Uprising of the Beast*, which toured Europe in 1990. AEG DBW

Brecht, Bertolt [Eugen Berthold Friedrich Brecht] 1898–1956 German dramatist, director and poet. Brecht is a seminal figure in the 20th-century exploration of drama as a medium, and of theatre as a forum for political ideas. In the Weimar Republic his cynical, anti-bourgeois plays were a riposte to both the soothing illusionism of MAX REINHARDT and the idealistic pathos of the expressionists (see EXPRESSIONISM). In *Drums in the Night* (1922) a returning soldier spurns the revolution in favour of bed with his fiancée. *Baal* (1923) is a small-town ballad of libertinism as self-fulfilment; *In the Jungle of Cities* (1923) shows a purposeless feud in Chicago; and *Man Equals Man* (1926) demonstrates how the army turns docile citizens into ruthless killers.

Brecht was already experimenting with 'alienation effects' such as whiteface for frightened soldiers in *Edward II* (1924, after MARLOWE). This anarchic phase culminated in *The Threepenny Opera* (1928) with its sexy jazz score by KURT WEILL, which transposed JOHN GAY's *Beggar's Opera* to a tough, modern underworld. Influenced by PISCATOR, Brecht now turned to Marxism to give his plays an ideological focus and began to experiment with short, schematic, communist *Lehrstücke* ('teaching-plays') designed to sharpen the class-consciousness of actors as much as audiences. These choral pieces for amateurs were set to music by Paul Hindemith (*Flight over the Ocean*, 1929), Kurt Weill (*He Who Said Yes* and *He Who Said No*, 1930), and Hanns Eisler (*The Measures Taken*, 1931). *The Mother* (1932, after GORKY), also an exercise in awakening class-consciousness, provided a famous part for HELENE WEIGEL.

To escape Nazi persecution Brecht settled in Denmark in 1933, where he completed *Round Heads and Pointed Heads* (1936), a version of *Measure for Measure*, and contributed two uncharacteristically naturalistic plays (see NATURALISM) – *Señora Carrar's Rifles* (1937) and *Fear and Misery of the Third Reich* (1938; in the USA, *The Private Life of the Master Race*) – to the struggle against Fascism. The 'ballet' *The Seven Deadly Sins* (1933) was written with Kurt Weill for performance by Lotte Lenya in Paris. Isolated from his native audience with its specific political problems – from 1933 to 1945 he could only be performed in the original in neutral Zurich – he began to write parable plays on historical or exotic subjects where the political message is oblique and the communist premises are embedded deep in the structure. These are his epic masterpieces: *Mother Courage and her Children* (1941), with its anti-war theme; *Life of Galileo* (1943), a perennially top-

ical critique of science in society; *The Good Person of Setzuan* (1943), on the conflict between business efficiency and private morality; and *The Caucasian Chalk Circle* (1948).

The term EPIC THEATRE was in the air in German political theatre in the 1920s before Brecht codified it in his *Notes on the Opera 'The Rise and Fall of the City of Mahagonny'*. He saw his plays as experiments designed to identify and improve the principles governing social behaviour; so epic theatre replaced the unbroken illusion of conventional 'dramatic' or 'Aristotelian' theatre (see ARISTOTLE) with a montage of separate scenes to expose the social dynamics of the action, which were highlighted by 'alienation' or estranging effects. This was to appeal to the intellect, limit empathy and invite critical appraisal of the narrative. These ideas were developed in the *Small Organum for the Theatre* (1948).

In 1941 Brecht moved to Finland, where he wrote his gangster FARCE *The Resistible Rise of Arturo Ui* (1958) which parodies the rise of Hitler, and the Finnish comedy *Mr Puntila and His Man Matti* (1948). He then went via the Soviet Union to California. His relationship with Hollywood was uneasy – though he did script *Hangmen Also Die* (1943) for Fritz Lang – and he failed to break into the American theatre despite his fruitful collaboration with CHARLES LAUGHTON, which reconstructed the title role in *Life of Galileo*. *The Visions of Simone Machard* (1957) and *Schweyk in the Second World War* (1957) were written in the USA.

Brecht returned to Europe after successfully defending himself against charges of un-American activities in 1947, and in 1948 he settled in East Berlin, where he directed a string of internationally acclaimed productions with the BERLINER ENSEMBLE. He was a pragmatist who saw rehearsals as a stage in the writing process, and performance as 'the proof of the pudding', his favourite English expression. He reworked his plays in an effort to get a politically correct audience response to characters like Mother Courage and Galileo, but the plays refused to be tamed. From the 1920s Brecht was a collaborative writer, trying out scenes on his friends and incorporating their suggestions – a practice that relied on female assistants like Elisabeth Hauptmann, Margarete Steffin and Ruth Berlau. With the collapse of communism Brecht is ripe for reinterpretation – as DAVID HARE's intimate version of *Life of Galileo* at the Almeida Theatre, Islington (London), in 1994 has shown. HR

Bredero, Gerbrand Adriaansz 1585–1618 Dutch poet and dramatist, famous primarily for his comedies and farces. The impact of his plays lies in the apt portrayal of the middle classes, the farmers and citizens, seen in plays like *The Farce of the Cow* (1612) and *The Miller's Farce* (1613). In his *Moortje* (1616), based on TERENCE's *Eunuchus*, and in *The Spanish Brabanter* (1617) his use of dialect and the way in which he depicts ordinary Amsterdam life is striking. Today, his plays are still regularly performed. *The Spanish Brabanter* has been translated into English, and has been staged in England. Bredero wrote tragedies too. He was, however, less familiar with the genre, and, as a result, these plays have remained relatively unknown. MG WH

breeches part Male role played by an actress. Peg Woffington's portrayal of Sir Harry Wildair in Farquhar's *The Constant Couple* (1699) established a tradition that extends, in the English theatre, through to the principal boy in pantomime. In the 19th century the breeches role often accommodated a roguish young man of good, if mischievous, nature – as, for instance, the part of Sam Willoughby in Tom Taylor's *The Ticket of Leave Man.* (See also male impersonation.) MB

Brel, Jacques 1929–78 Belgian song-writer and performer, who renounced his middle-class inheritance to sing in Paris. Originally, his songs were idealistic and tinged with Catholic pieties, but gradually grew more trenchant, misogynistic and obsessed with death. His performance technique used illustrative gesture to caricature his own lyrics, which he almost spat out at the adoring audience. Brel's fame spread to the English-speaking world with the musical *Jacques Brel Is Alive and Well and Living in Paris* by Mort Shuman and Eric Blau (1968). He retired from the stage in 1972 and died of cancer six years later. LS

Brenton, Howard 1942– British dramatist, whose first play, *Ladder of Fools*, was staged in 1965 in Cambridge where he was a student. After leaving university, he wrote for various fringe companies, winning Arts Council bursaries in 1969 and 1970, together with the John Whiting Award (1970) for his short play, *Christie in Love*. Brenton was influenced by a group of intellectuals in France, the 'situationists', who described Western liberal democracies as the societies 'of the Spectacle' in which politicians deceived the public with confidence tricks, aided by the mass media. Brenton saw his task as being to 'disrupt the Spectacle', and his full-length plays such as *Magnificence* (1973), *The Churchill Play* (1974) and *Brassneck* (with David Hare, 1973) have all attempted to shock the British public out of their bourgeois complacency. In *The Romans in Britain* (1980) Brenton drew a parallel between the presence of British troops in Northern Ireland and the conquest of Britain by Julius Caesar, stressing the analogy with a graphic scene of homosexual rape. The ensuing controversy led to a private prosecution being brought under the Sexual Offences Act of 1956, though it was eventually withdrawn.

Brenton's vivid dialogue, his narrative flow of powerful incidents and his polemical attacks brought him quickly to the fore in the state-subsidized sector of British theatre, with productions at the National Theatre, the Royal Court and major regional reps. As a translator/adapter, he has provided the National Theatre with English versions of Brecht's *Galileo* and Büchner's *Danton's Death*. During the 1980s, he wrote plays which considered the end of the Cold War and its consequences, such as *Moscow Gold* (1990, with Tariq Ali) about Mikhail Gorbachev's *glasnost*, and *Berlin Bertie* (1992); but his 'Three Plays for Utopia', *Bloody Poetry* (1984), *Sore Throats* (1979, revised in 1988) and *Greenland* (1988), tried to revive the vision of a Marxist utopia, while recognizing the failures of the past and present. *Hesse Is Dead* (1989), staged by the Royal Shakespeare Company at the Almeida in London, demonstrates how historical facts can be manipulated to suit present political purposes. JE

Breuer, Lee 1937– American actor, playwright, director, and founding member of the avant-garde theatre company Mabou Mines. Breuer, who calls himself a 'reluctant radical', began his career in the early 1960s with the San Francisco Actors' Workshop, moving to Europe in 1965 to study with the Berliner Ensemble and the Polish Theatre Lab. For Mabou Mines he served as director, author, adapter, producer and performer. His staging and adaptation of Beckett's work has earned him three Obies. His trilogy *Animations* (*The Red Horse* (1970), *The B. Beaver* (1974) and *The Shaggy Dog* (1978)) was published in 1979, and *Sister Suzie Cinema* (Public Theater, 1980) in 1986. In 1988 he wrote and directed a gender-reversed adaptation of *King Lear* with former wife Ruth Maleczech as Lear. Outside Mabou Mines his most notable effort has been *The Gospel at Colonus* (1983), which he conceived, adapted and directed for the Brooklyn Academy of Music's Next Wave Festival; it was performed later at Broadway's Lunt-Fontanne, Washington's Arena Stage, and in San Francisco, as was *The Warrior Ant* (1988), heard first in concert at New York's Lincoln Center in 1986. In the 1980s, while serving as director of the directing programme at the Yale School of Drama, his focus was on creating a new theatre that merges Asian and African arts with American performance techniques. A recent effort (*Ma Ha Bhar ANT a*, 1992), a satiric look at American cultural conflicts, owed its focus to the influence of Balinese shadow puppet theatre. DBW

Brewster, Yvonne 1938– Jamaican actress and producer, and artistic director of the Talawa Theatre Company, London. Brewster left Jamaica in 1956 for England, to study speech, drama and mime at the Rose Bruford College in Kent and at the Royal Academy of Music. She then worked as an actress in London before returning to Jamaica, where she became a radio announcer and television producer.

In 1971 she founded with Jamaican Trevor Rhone the Barn Theatre in Kingston, Jamaica, from a converted garage on her family's compound. Later that year in London she directed *Lippo, the New Noah* by Sally Durie, with an African-Caribbean cast at the Institute of Contemporary Arts and, to mark the tenth anniversary of Jamaica's independence, she staged Rhone's *Smile Orange*, which toured to black communities in London. Other productions at this time included Derek Walcott's *Pantomime* and a musical version of Jamaican playwright Barry Reckord's *Skyvers*. Brewster was also production manager or assistant director on the films *The Harder They Come*, *Smile Orange*, *The Marijuana Affair* and *The Fight against Slavery*.

In 1986 she founded the all-black Talawa Theatre Company, aimed at enriching British theatre and enlarging audiences in the black community. She directed seven productions – four by Caribbean authors (*The Black Jacobins* by C. L. R. James, *An Echo in the Bone* by Dennis Scott, *O Babylon* by Derek Walcott, and *The Dragon Can't Dance* by Earl Lovelace of Trinidad and Tobago), one Nigerian (*The Gods Are Not to Blame* by Ola Rotimi), one Irish (Wilde's *The Importance of Being Earnest*, co-produced with the Tyne Theatre Company in Newcastle) and one English (SHAKESPEARE's *Antony and Cleopatra*, co-produced with Merseyside Everyman Theatre in Liverpool) – all staged in venues around London, as well as Newcastle and Liverpool, respectively. In 1988 she directed Rhone's *Two Can Play* at the BRISTOL OLD VIC, and in 1991 GARCÍA LORCA's *Blood Wedding* at the NATIONAL THEATRE in London. In 1992 she took over the renovated Cochrane Theatre in Holborn, creating a new home for black theatre in central London. There she directed SOYINKA's *The Road* (1992).

Brewster was drama officer of the Arts Council of Great Britain from 1982 to 1984, and has served on the London Arts Board, the British Council's Drama and Dance Advisory Committee, and the Black Theatre Forum. She is a member of the National Theatre Trust and a Fellow of the Royal Society of Arts. In 1993 she was awarded an OBE. She has published two collections of plays: *Black Plays* (1987) and *Black Plays: Two* (1989). EGH

Brice, Fanny [Fannie; *née* Frances Borach] 1891–1951 American comedienne and singer whose gawky walk, repertoire of comic faces and ability to sing both satiric and serious songs with equal success made her a star of REVUES for over a quarter of a century. After serving an apprenticeship in amateur shows and BURLESQUE, Brice appeared in ZIEGFELD's *Follies of 1910*. She remained with the *Follies* for six more editions until 1923, then switched to IRVING BERLIN's *Music Box Revue* (1924). An attempt to star in a book musical, *Fioretta* (1929), was a failure. Brice appeared in four more revues: *Sweet and Low* (1930), *Billy Rose's Crazy Quilt* (1931) and two editions of *The Ziegfeld Follies* (1934, 1936) produced by the SHUBERTS after Ziegfeld's death. In most of her songs and sketches Brice affected a Yiddish accent that heightened her satirical treatment of such subjects as the ballet and silent film 'vamps'. The MUSICAL *Funny Girl* is loosely based on portions of her career, recently re-explored by Barbara Grossman (1991) and Herbert Goldman (1992). MK

Bridges-Adams, William 1889–1965 British director. Bridges-Adams toured the provinces as an actor and stage-managed for WILLIAM POEL before taking over the Bristol repertory theatre, where between 1914 and 1915 he introduced a programme of SHAW, MASEFIELD and STANLEY HOUGHTON. From 1919 to 1934 he directed the festival at Stratford-upon-Avon, where he founded the New Shakespearian Company, and toured Canada and America with them after the old theatre burned down in 1926. His last production was *Oedipus Rex* at COVENT GARDEN in 1936. CI

Bridie, James [Osborne Henry Mavor] 1888–1951 Scottish playwright. Bridie was a doctor, and he certainly did much to keep Scottish theatre healthy, not only through his playwriting (which included *Tobias and the Angel* (1930), *Jonah and the Whale* (1932), *Mr Bolfry* (1943), *Daphne Laureola* (1949) and *The Queen's Comedy* (1950)), but also through his association, as a founder, with the Glasgow CITIZENS' THEATRE and with the establishment of drama training in the Royal Scottish Academy of Music and Drama. His playwriting, though often on serious

themes, was distinguished by a very personal wit and charm, and he created roles relished by such performers as Alastair Sim and EDITH EVANS. MB

Brieux, Eugène 1858–1932 French dramatist. His naturalistic dramas (see NATURALISM) on social themes dealt frankly with matters ranging from syphilis to birth control. GEORGE BERNARD SHAW wrote a famous introduction to the English translation of three of the plays, *Les Avariés* (*Damaged Goods*, 1902), *The Three Daughters of M. Dupont* (1897) and *Maternity* (1903), in which he compared Brieux to IBSEN. In terms of Brieux as a campaigner, the comparison is valid. MB

Brighouse, Harold 1882–1958 British playwright, who wrote prolifically and mainly about the people and affairs of his home county of Lancashire. The GAIETY THEATRE in Manchester was the venue for much of his work, including his best-known play *Hobson's Choice* (1915). This play and *Zack* (1916) have established a firm place in the national repertory. His one-act plays, which are particularly well crafted, form an important part of his work. (See also STANLEY HOUGHTON.) MB

Bristol Old Vic Company Shortly after the end of the Second World War, the ARTS COUNCIL OF GREAT BRITAIN, in association with the OLD VIC in London, set up a permanent repertory company in Bristol, based at the recently reopened Theatre Royal (itself dating from 1766). Beginning in 1946, under the direction of HUGH HUNT, it soon became established as one of the country's leading theatre companies: a position it has continued to hold under its subsequent directors, with a record of many transfers of successful productions to London and worldwide tours. Notable productions have included *Salad Days*, *The Killing of Sister George*, *Conduct Unbecoming* and *A Severed Head*. Since 1972, when alterations to the Theatre Royal were completed, the company has also been able to present small-scale new and experimental work in a theatre studio, the New Vic. The Bristol Old Vic Theatre Trust, independent of the Arts Council since 1963 though still receiving substantial grant-aid, also runs the highly regarded Bristol Old Vic Theatre School. AJ

Bristow, James c.1585–? English actor, whose experience provides unique information on the trade in boy actors in the Elizabethan theatre. HENSLOWE's *Diary* records the purchase of Bristow from William Augusten, 'player', for £8. That purchase price is greater than Bristow's yearly wage as an employee of Henslowe's in 1600, when he received three shillings per week. Nothing is heard of him after 1603. PT

Briusov, Valery (Yakovlevich) 1873–1924 Russian poet, novelist, critic, translator, scholar and chief theoretician of the symbolist movement (see SYMBOLISM), whose call for a conventional theatre of essence greatly influenced MEYERHOLD and other anti-realistic directors of the early 20th century (see REALISM). His symbolist activities included the anthology *Russian Symbolists* (1894), which launched the movement; the editing of its journal the *Scales* (1904); numerous volumes of poetry and short fiction; theoretical and critical articles; the novel *The Fiery Angel* (1907–8); over 20 produced plays, and sketches of many more.

His comparison of STANISLAVSKY's realistic approach to poetic drama at the MOSCOW ART THEATRE (MAT) with the naive poeticism of the native folk theatre helped convince him that the latter's stylized conventionality better realized theatre's innately symbolic nature. In his seminal essay 'Unnecessary Truth' (*World of Art*, 1902) and later in 'The Theatre of the Future' (1907) and 'Realism and Convention on the Stage' (1908), he argued his preference for a conventional (*uslovny*) theatre which would give the actor the centrality he enjoyed in the ancient Greek and Elizabethan theatres. Stanislavsky attempted to adopt these ideas in his work on MAETERLINCK's, Hamsun's and ANDREEV's dramas at MAT (1903–7), then sponsored Meyerhold's more dramatic experiments at the Theatre Studio on Povarskaya Street (1905), of which Briusov was literary head. Briusov attacked Meyerhold's mechanization of the actor in his production of Maeterlinck's *Pelléas and Mélisande*, which Briusov translated, at Vera Komissarzhevskaya's Theatre (1907). However, he supported GORDON CRAIG's bid to stylize the acting in his *Hamlet* collaboration with Stanislavsky at MAT (1912).

Briusov's own dramas have been labelled 'cosmic' and offer spectacular scenic and lighting effects, philosophical themes and heightened language, symbols and imagery rather than credibility. *Earth* (1904) is the only published one of four science fiction plays which Briusov wrote, the others being *Piroent* (*Pyroesis*), *The Dictator* (1921) and *The World of Seven Generations* (1923). The lone symbolist play set in the future, it is an apocalyptic urban tale with echoes of Plato and of GOETHE's *Faust*. *The Wayfarer* (1910) is a one-act 'psychodrama' resembling EVREINOVian monodrama and featuring a Maeterlinckian 'silent stranger' (later used by PINTER) in a study of repressed female eroticism. *Protesilaus Deceased* (1911–12) is a version of the EURIPIDES-dramatized myth, which was also the subject of dramas by ANNENSKY and SOLOGUB. Briusov's plays have had no meaningful production history in Russia. Briusov, who sided with the 'clarists' against the 'mystics' in the 1904–5 symbolist split, later broke with the movement (1908–10) and, in 1917, embraced the October Revolution. SG

Broadhurst, George H(owells) 1866–1952 London-born playwright and theatre manager, who emigrated to America in 1886 and managed several regional theatres before gaining some success in New York with FARCE-comedies – *What Happened to Jones* (1897) and *Why Smith Left Home* (1899). Primarily concerned with commercial theatre, Broadhurst made his best contribution to American drama with *The Man of the Hour* (1906), a MELODRAMA about a young mayor who successfully resists organized political corruption; and *Bought and Paid For* (1911), which exploits the problems of a wealthy, self-made man who counts his wife among his possessions. One of the better writers of social melodrama before the First World War, Broadhurst produced a number of successful plays and eventually became known for his light musical comedies. In 1918 a new BROADWAY venue at West 44th Street was named the Broadhurst Theatre in his honour. WJM

Broadway Broadway is to New York as the WEST END is to London – the district that is thought of as the traditional theatrical heart of the city. Centred on and around the street of that name in New York City since the 1890s have been the major theatres that have represented the professional and commercial theatrical core of the nation, extending, from the 1950s, into OFF-BROADWAY locations (to accommodate generally smaller and somewhat more innovative theatres) as economic pressures restricted work in the big old theatres. OFF-OFF BROADWAY is distinguished from Broadway and Off-Broadway not only by a further diminution in scale and eclectic experimentation, but also by the radically different contractual relationship with actors, based on non-profit-making companies (see NEW YORK CITY THEATRES; RESIDENT NON-PROFIT PROFESSIONAL THEATRE (USA)). MCH

Broadway, Off- and Off-Off see OFF-BROADWAY and OFF-OFF BROADWAY

Brockmann, Johann 1745–1812 Austrian actor. Brockmann achieved prominence when, in 1776, he acted the title role in FRIEDRICH SCHRÖDER's famous production of *Hamlet* in Hamburg. The grace and naturalness of his expression were highly admired. After successful guest appearances in Berlin, Brockmann was called to the BURGTHEATER where he remained for the rest of his life. Here he helped form the characteristic style of the company. SW

Brome, Richard c.1590–1652 English playwright, certainly among the finest of the Caroline period. According to *Biographia Dramatica* (1764), 'his extraction was mean, he having originally been no better than a menial servant to the celebrated Ben Jonson', and a Jonsonian influence is detectable in much of his work. But Brome was uncommonly versatile – *The Queen and Concubine* (1636) is a courtly play, *The Wedding of Covent Garden* (c.1633) a socially alert CITIZEN COMEDY; but the finest of Brome's works, *The Damoiselle* (1637), *The Antipodes* (1638), *The Court Beggar* (1640) and *A Jovial Crew* (1641), display a sturdy faith in the popular tradition and an acutely critical political awareness. Brome's is the earliest surviving playwright's contract. It amounts to being a job description of his attachment to the company at the SALISBURY COURT playhouse. PT

Bronnen, Arnolt 1895–1959 Austrian dramatist; friend of BRECHT. The erotic, anti-bourgeois, black EXPRESSIONISM of *Vatermord* (*Parricide*, 1922) caused a sensation, which he followed up with *Geburt der Jugend* (*Birth of Youth*, 1922) and *Die Excesse* (1923). He later wrote reportage-plays and supported the Nazis. After 1945 he turned communist. HR

Brook, Peter (Stephen Paul) 1925– British director. Born in London of Russian descent, Brook first attracted attention as an Oxford undergraduate staging ambitious plays under the difficult conditions of London's little theatre clubs during the war. BARRY JACKSON invited him to direct *Man and Superman* and *King John* (1945) at the BIRMINGHAM REP, whose success led to an engagement at the Shakespeare Memorial Theatre, Stratford-upon-Avon, then struggling to revive its summer festival seasons. His enchanting *Love's Labour's Lost* (1946), designed after Watteau, began his long association with what became in 1961 the ROYAL SHAKESPEARE COMPANY.

The charm and visual style of Brook's early productions aroused the interest of WEST END and BROADWAY managements, for whom he directed plays by ANOUILH, Roussin and CHRISTOPHER FRY; but the true power of his imagination was felt through the Stratford Shakespearian productions, notably of *Measure for Measure* (1950) and of *Titus Andronicus* (1955), which starred LAURENCE OLIVIER as Titus and featured Brook's own set designs and *musique concrète*. Later Brook productions for the RSC included *King Lear* (1962) with PAUL SCOFIELD; PETER WEISS's *The Marat/Sade* (1964); *US* (1966), a documentary attack on the USA's involvement in Vietnam; and *A Midsummer Night's Dream* (1970), set in an adult adventure playground, with trapezes, stilts and spinning plates.

During the 1960s, Brook was influenced by the seemingly contradictory theories of ANTONIN ARTAUD and BERTOLT BRECHT, shock tactics and analytical calm, and his reconciliation of these extremes became a feature of the RSC style. His collection of four brief essays, *The Empty Space* (1968), influenced many directors in Britain and overseas as an acute analysis of the basic problems facing contemporary theatre. By 1970, however, Brook was moving towards a style of performance which would have been equally out of place in a major subsidized company as on the West End stage. With the help of JEAN-LOUIS BARRAULT and a Ford Foundation grant, he established an International Centre of Theatre Research (CIRT). Their first production was a play by Ted Hughes, *Orghast*, written in an ancient Persian ceremonial language, Avesta, and staged in the magnificent setting of Persepolis during the Shiraz Festival (1971). Brook and the co-founder of CIRT, Micheline Rozan, found a deserted music-hall near the Gare du Nord in Paris, where he assembled a team of actors, dancers, musicians, acrobats and mimes from many countries. Brook wanted to encourage a group approach which could transcend the boundaries of national cultures. His company took myths to remote villages in the Sahara, as in *The Conference of the Birds* (1976), and the experience of living on the verge of starvation they took back to Paris and London in *The Ik* (1975). Although the Centre has been acclaimed for its productions of *The Cherry Orchard* (1981) and *The Tragedy of Carmen* (1983), its most celebrated and daunting achievement has so far been to tell the entire story of the Indian religious epic, *The Mahabharata* (1985; see INDIA), in nine hours in a quarry outside Avignon. His productions since *The Mahabharata* have seemed more modest – *The Tempest* (1987) and *Pelléas and Mélisande* (1992) – but have been distinguished by a luminous clarity and simplicity. JE

Brougham, John 1810–80 Irish-American playwright and actor, whose reputation rests principally on his outlandish Indian BURLESQUES: *Po-ca-hon-tas; or, The Gentle Savage* (1855), 'An Original Aboriginal Erratic Operatic Semi-Civilized and Demi-Savage Extravaganza', and *Metamora; or, The Last of the Pollywogs* (1857). He poked

fun at the stage version of the 'noble savage', particularly that of EDWIN FORREST in *Metamora; or, The Last of the Wampanoags*. Brougham had a facile pen – too facile, he once admitted. He wrote 126 wide-ranging pieces – adaptations (*Dombey and Son*, 1848), gothic MELODRAMA (*The Gunmaker of Moscow*, 1857), tearful melodrama (*Night and Morning*, 1855), sensational melodrama (*The Lottery of Life*, 1868) and social SATIRE (*The Game of Love*, 1856) – but never with any 'gall in his ink', according to one critic. As principal actor in most of his pieces, he was praised for his joviality, versatility, topical interpolations and impromptu 'before-the-curtain' speeches.

Born in Dublin, Brougham performed in amateur theatricals at Trinity College, appeared at London's OLYMPIC THEATRE (1830, with MADAME VESTRIS) and at COVENT GARDEN; leased the London LYCEUM (1840); then went to America (1842), appearing at the PARK THEATRE and touring the country; became stage manager at WILLIAM E. BURTON's Chambers Street Theatre (1848); had two flings at management (at Brougham's Broadway Lyceum (1850–2) and the old BOWERY (1856–7)); and was employed as actor-playwright at WALLACK'S THEATRE for seven seasons – 'the brightest part of my artist's life,' he reported. He spent the Civil War years in London, returning to the USA in 1865 to continue as actor-playwright at the WINTER GARDEN and at AUGUSTIN DALY's FIFTH AVENUE THEATRE. RM

Brown, John Mason 1900–69 American drama critic. Educated at Harvard University, Brown began his journalistic career on the *Louisville Courier-Journal* in 1917. During 1923–4 he reported on the European theatre for Boston and Louisville newspapers before becoming associate editor and drama critic for *Theatre Arts Monthly* (1924–8). In 1929 he moved to the *New York Evening Post* and established his column 'Two on the Aisle', which remained popular throughout the 1930s. In 1941 he accepted a similar position on the *New York World-Telegram*, but the outbreak of the war prompted him to join the Navy in 1942. Two years later he became associate editor and drama critic of *Saturday Review*, where his column 'Seeing Things' remained a standard for 10 years. Brown wrote in an easy, informal style that JOHN SIMON characterized as 'chatty urbanity'. His many books include *The Modern Theatre in Revolt* (1929), *Two on the Aisle* (1938), *Seeing Things* (1946), *Dramatis Personae* (1963) and *The Worlds of ROBERT E. SHERWOOD* (1965). TLM

Brown, Lew see DESYLVA, (B. G.) BUDDY

Brown, William Henry fl.1820s African-American theatre manager and playwright. An ex-West Indian seaman, Brown became the father of AFRICAN-AMERICAN THEATRE when he established the AFRICAN THEATRE in New York in 1821 with a repertoire including condensed versions of plays such as *Richard III*, *Pizarro*, *Tom and Jerry* and *Obi; or, Three-Fingered Jack*, as well as pantomimes. He also wrote and produced the first African-American play, *The Drama of King Shotaway* (1823), based on personal experience of the 1795 Black Caribs' insurrection on St Vincent. From his African Theatre emerged James Hewlett, the first black Shakespearian actor, and IRA ALDRIDGE, black actor renowned in England and Europe in the 19th century. Brown may also have founded a theatre in Albany, New York, in 1823.   EGH

Brown, William Wells 1819–84 African-American playwright. An escaped slave, Brown joined the abolitionist movement from his Boston home and wrote two anti-slavery plays that he read from lecture platforms. The first, *Experience; or, How to Give a Northern Man a Backbone* (1856), satirizes a pro-slavery Northern preacher who recants after being sold into slavery and later released; the second, *The Escape; or, A Leap for Freedom* (1858), describes domestic life on a Southern plantation as slaves plot their escape.   EGH

Browne, E(lliot) Martin 1900–80 British director, instrumental in reviving poetic religious drama. Appointed director of religious drama for the diocese of Chichester in 1930, Browne founded the Religious Drama Society and encouraged T. S. ELIOT to write for the theatre, directing all his plays from *Murder in the Cathedral*, in which he also acted the Fourth Tempter (1935), to *The Elder Statesman* (1958). After directing the Pilgrim Players, who toured with works by Eliot and BRIDIE, he took over the MERCURY THEATRE in London in 1945, making it a centre for new poetic plays that included CHRISTOPHER FRY's first success, *A Phoenix Too Frequent* (1946). In 1948 he succeeded Geoffrey Whitworth as director of the British Drama League, and in 1951 produced the first revival of the York cycle of MYSTERY PLAYS since 1572. CI

Browne, Robert fl.1593–1603 English actor, about whose career contradictory records survive. It may be that there were two actors of this name, one of whom was the active leader of a group of English players on the Continent, particularly in Germany, from 1592 to 1620, and the other a leader of Derby's Men, prosperous enough to finance the innkeeper Richard Samwell's conversion of the BOAR'S HEAD in 1598–9 and then to buy Samwell's interest in the new theatre. This may be the 'Browne of the Boar's Head' referred to in 1603, in a letter to EDWARD ALLEYN from his wife, as 'dead and died very poor'   PT

Bruant, Aristide 1851–1925 The first outstanding author-composer-performer of the French CABARET. A former soldier and railway clerk, he sang in *CAFÉS CHANTANTS* before opening his own cabaret Le Mirliton in 1885, where middle-class audiences flocked to be insulted by him (one refrain ran 'All customers are swine!') and hear his 'realistic songs'. These ballads, couched in the authentic slang of the Parisian slums, hymn the desperate plight of the outcast and outlawed with sardonic impassivity. Bruant, a striking combination of *apache* and lion-tamer in his black sombrero, boots and red scarf, recorded by Toulouse-Lautrec, made a fortune and in 1900 retired to the bourgeois private life he had earlier attacked.   LS

Bruce, Lenny [Alfred Schneider] c.1924–66 American stand-up comic, who became a martyr to his cult image. After serving in the Navy in the Second World War, he studied acting under the GI bill and began as a nightclub comedian. Working out of small clubs in Greenwich Village, he first gained notoriety for his liberal use of four-letter words; gradually, he became noted for his savage attacks on establishment hypocrisy. As his act developed into intimate, improvisational harangues of the audience, he shocked the conventional and rejoiced the 'hip' with his freewheeling SATIRE on narcotics legislation, organized religion, sexual taboos and race relations. Frequently arrested for drug abuse and blasphemy (the Home Office refused to let him perform in England), he sank into paranoia and died of an overdose of narcotics. After his death, he became a totem – in KENNETH TYNAN's words, 'the man who went down on America's conscience' – and a play, *Lenny*, was devoted to him.   LS

Bruckner, Ferdinand [Theodor Tagger] 1891–1958 Austrian dramatist. After his early experiments with EXPRESSIONISM, his plays ranged from brutally realistic studies of suicide (*Malady of Youth*, 1926) or the persecution of Jewish students (*Races*, 1933) to historical dramas such as his best-known work *Elizabeth of England* (1930). In 1936 he emigrated to America, where he worked with PISCATOR, returning in 1951 to become dramaturg at the Schiller Theater in Berlin. Though technically innovative, his postwar attempts to revive verse tragedy in *Pyrrhus and Andromache* (1952) or *The Fight with the Angel* (1956) were unsuccessful.   CI

Bruno, Giordano 1548–1600 Italian philosopher and dramatist. A Dominican priest and one of the greatest philosophers of the Renaissance, he ran foul of the Inquisition, and after a peripatetic life was burnt at the stake in Rome. His only known play, the comedy *Il candelaio* (*The Candlemaker*, Paris, 1582), is a subtle, complex and verbally difficult piece. It is one of the few great Italian Renaissance comedies, but is rarely performed, although for all its verbal density it stages well and was given an impressively theatrical production by LUCA RONCONI in 1968   LR

Bruscambille [Jean Deslauriers or Du Laurier] French actor of the 17th century, who may have trained at fairgrounds and in Italy, where he claimed to have learned *la charlatannerie*. He was seen at Toulouse c.1598 and joined the company of the HÔTEL DE BOURGOGNE, Paris, in 1606; he was playing there still in 1632, but no trace of him survives after 1634. His prime function was as a master of ceremonies, delivering vivacious satirical prologues. Several collections of jokes attributed to him were published between 1610 and 1619, including the famous sally that his was 'une vie sans souci, et quelquefois sans six sous'. LS

Brustein, Robert 1927– American critic, actor, and director and founder of the YALE REPERTORY and AMERICAN REPERTORY THEATRES. He has served on the faculties of several universities, and was the Dean of the Yale Drama School during 1965–79, years recalled in his book *Making Scenes*. The author of nine other important books on theatre and society (most notably *The Theatre of Revolt* (1964), *The Third Theatre* (1968), *Revolution as Theatre* (1970), *Who Needs Theatre?* (1986) and *Reimagining American*

Theatre (1991)), Brustein has been one of the most respected and controversial critics, primarily as drama critic for the *New Republic* since 1959 (regularly until 1968; he was also sometime critic for the London *Observer*). He received the GEORGE JEAN NATHAN Award for Dramatic Criticism in 1962 and 87. In 1979 he was unexpectedly released as Dean at Yale and moved to Harvard, where ART was established. At Yale and Harvard, he has supervised over 170 professional productions.   DBW

Bruun Olsen, Ernst 1923– Danish playwright and director, who made a breakthrough at the KONGELIGE TEATER in 1962 with his MUSICAL *Teenage Love*, satirizing the exploitative nature of the entertainment industry. His work reflects his involvement in live theatre (often as resident dramatist and director) in its orchestration of simultaneous effects. For example, in *Prometheus Trapped* (1981), a split stage and two-level script interweave a broadcast political debate with private commentary by production staff. Political critique also dominates his musical *Ball at the Social Club* (1966) and *Where Did Nora Go When She Went Out?* (1968), a sequel to IBSEN's *A Doll's House* exploring social constructions of gender and class. His work on the classics also reflects his politics; in his 1979 production of MOLIÈRE's *Tartuffe*, Tartuffe's deceptiveness reportedly suggested modern political parallels; when asked to direct a HOLBERG play in 1985, he adapted one into a 'nightmare FARCE' about modern business.   HL

Bryant, Dan [Daniel Webster O'Brien] 1833–75 American minstrel and manager. After his debut (as dancer) at New York's Vauxhall Garden in 1843, Bryant graduated to blackface minstrelsy (1849) with the Sable Harmonists, and in 1850 joined Charley White at the Bowery's Melodeon Minstrel Hall. In 1857 Dan and his brothers Jerry and Neil founded Bryant's Minstrels – Jerry and Dan the 'end men' and Neil the interlocutor. Bryant's became New York's premiere MINSTREL SHOW company. 'Dixie', written by troupe member Dan Emmett, was introduced by them (1859), though Bryant was best known for his 'rude and untutored' black character dance, 'Essence of Old Virginny'. Also a good Irish-dialect actor, Bryant appeared in that guise first in *Handy Andy* (1863). His natural inclination towards blackface comedy brought him back to minstrelsy in 1868.   DBW

Bryden, Bill [William Campbell Rough] 1942– British dramatist and director, who began his career as a documentary writer for Scottish television. He was drawn towards the theatre and was appointed assistant director at the Belgrade Theatre, Coventry (1965–7), and at the ROYAL COURT THEATRE (1967–9). From 1971 to 1974, Bryden was an associate director at the Royal Lyceum Theatre in Edinburgh and helped to raise the company towards the status of being Scotland's unofficial national theatre. Notable among many Lyceum productions were those of Bryden's own two plays, *Willie Rough* (1972), about the Greenock shop steward who led a shipyard strike during the First World War, and *Benny Lynch* (1974). Both plays were distinguished by the naturalistic detail, the clear handling of complex historical material and the socialist fervour which never became blindly polemical.

PETER HALL invited him to join the NATIONAL THEATRE in London in 1975, where he became director of the Cottesloe Theatre in 1978. Bryden developed the flexibility of the space by exploring the possibilities of 'promenade' productions, as in *Lark Rise* (1978) and TONY HARRISON's *Mysteries*, derived from the York mystery cycle (see MYSTERY PLAY), which were developed over four years from 1979 and presented in three parts. His play *Old Movies* (1977) was also seen at the Cottesloe, as were his productions of 20th-century American plays, by O'NEILL, ODETS and DAVID MAMET. To celebrate Glasgow's year as the European City of Culture he staged *The Ship* (1990), in the Harland and Wolff shipyards in Govan, his nostalgic and sometimes angry documentary play on Glasgow's history as a major shipbuilding and industrial city.   JE

Buatler de Kolta [Joseph Buatier] 1847–1903 French illusionist, who gave up studying for the priesthood to become assistant to the Hungarian prestidigitator De Kolta. Buatier's claim was that he never bought a trick but invented all the illusions in his act: scarves passing through bottles, a seated woman disappearing from her chair, the apparition of a giant black glove, and many others. His last great invention was 'the Growing Die', which expanded at the conjuror's command until it was the size of a trunk, at which point a woman stepped out of it. (See also MAGIC.)   LS

Büchner, Georg 1813–37 German dramatist. During his brief life, Büchner achieved notoriety as the leader of an abortive conspiracy to revolution in Hesse, and distinction as a lecturer in comparative anatomy at the University of Zürich, a post to which he was appointed in 1836. His first play, *Danton's Death* (1835), reflects his disillusionment with revolutionary politics; Danton's humanity is the sole positive element in this nihilistic view of the French Revolution as being nothing but the power struggle of ambitious individuals and interests. *Leonce and Lena* (1836) is a lively satirical COMEDY, while *Woyzeck* (1837), a possibly incomplete drama, expresses his sympathy for the socially downtrodden. Because of his unorthodox dramaturgy, his plays were not performed for several decades after his death. *Leonce and Lena* was first produced in 1895, *Danton's Death* in 1903, and *Woyzeck* in 1913. It is possible that Büchner left another play in manuscript when he died, *Pietro Aretino*; this may have been destroyed by his fiancée, who objected to the obscenity in the play.   SW

Buckingham [George Villiers], 2nd Duke of 1628–87 English playwright. After service in the Civil War, exile with Charles II and imprisonment in the Tower, Buckingham became effectively chief minister of state from 1668 in spite of his notorious affair with the Countess of Shrewsbury whose husband he had killed in a duel. In 1668 his adaptation of FLETCHER's *The Chances* was very successful, with NELL GWYN in a minor role. In 1669 he collaborated with SIR ROBERT HOWARD on *The Country Gentleman*, contributing a scene which mocked Sir William Coventry so accurately that Coventry succeeded in having the play banned. His best play, *The Rehearsal*, was first written in 1665, in collaboration with Clifford,

Sprat and Butler, as a SATIRE on DAVENANT and Sir Robert Howard, but by the time the play was first performed in 1671 it had become a satire on DRYDEN who was portrayed as Bayes, a pompous writer of heroic plays. A brilliant BURLESQUE of the heroic drama then particularly popular, the play parodies plays and playwrights unmercifully. The form, a writer outlining his ideas to his friends during a rehearsal of one of his plays, was the model for burlesque drama thereafter and particularly influenced SHERIDAN in *The Critic*. Buckingham fell from power soon after his disastrous negotiations with France in 1674. He retired from politics after the accession of James II.   PH

Buckstone, J(ohn) B(aldwin) 1802–79 English actor, playwright and theatre manager. After three seasons in the provinces, he made his London debut at the Surrey Theatre in 1823–4, establishing himself in the 'low comedian' line which he sustained for over 50 years. Of the 160 or so dramatic pieces Buckstone wrote between 1825 and 1850, most were short FARCES, OPERETTAS or burlettas – the staple accompaniment of MELODRAMA at the minor theatres of London; but one of the earliest, *Luke the Labourer* (1826), helped set the fashion for domestic melodrama. *The Wreck Ashore* (1830) is a hyperactive adventure story, typically larded with low-life comic characters. Here, as in the lively COMEDY of *The Irish Lion* (1838) and *Single Life* (1839) and in the tear-jerking of *The Green Bushes* (1845), Buckstone upholds manly fortitude and decency, assuring his heroes and heroines the satisfaction of victory or of superior self-sacrifice in defeat. Most of his plays provided him with meaty comic roles during the years 1827–40, when he wintered at the ADELPHI and played at the HAYMARKET during the summer months. It was with the Haymarket that he came finally to be identified, initially as part of BENJAMIN WEBSTER'S company (1842–53) and from 1853 to 76 as manager. His announced policy was to make the Haymarket the home of comedy, and prospective playwrights were expected to provide suitable parts for the resident company. TOM TAYLOR, WESTLAND MARSTON and, after 1870, W. S. GILBERT were Buckstone's preferred playwrights.   PT

Buenaventura, Enrique 1928– Colombian playwright, director and theoretician. Born in Cali, Buenaventura studied architecture, painting and sculpture in Bogotá, all of which give to his work a plastic vision of dramatic art. In 1955 he helped establish the TEC (Theatre School of Cali, which was renamed the Experimental Theatre of Cali in 1970), one of the most respected and enduring theatre groups in Latin America. His style and dedication to principles of Third World theatre (the so-called 'new theatre') have brought him international recognition. The early *A la diestra de Dios Padre* (*On the Right Hand of God the Father*, 1958) is modelled on folkloric versions of the Devil and St Peter, as told by Colombian novelist Tomás Carrasquilla. Buenaventura's later plays have stronger messages of social and political protest. The vitriolic one-act segments of *Los papeles del infierno* (*Documents from Hell*, 1968) and *Historia de una bala de plata* (*Story of a Silver Bullet*, 1980) are representative of this change in his theatre.   GW

Buero-Vallejo, Antonio 1916– Spanish author of modern tragedies in which the destiny of the individual and of society are interwined.

Historia de una escalera (*Story of a Stairway*, 1949) marked the resurgence of serious theatre in postwar Spain. It presents the harsh realities of several families of a Madrid tenement. A school for the blind in *En la ardiente oscuridad* (*In the Burning Darkness*, 1950) instils an illusion of normality in its students, who come to prefer comfortable fiction to the truth of their condition. In *El tragaluz* (*The Basement Window*, 1967) victims of the Spanish Civil War inhabit a basement apartment which, like the school for the blind, is both an escape from reality and a prison. *La doble historia del doctor Valmy* (*The Double Case History of Doctor Valmy*, 1968) deals with police torture and those who prefer to deny its existence; prohibited by CENSORSHIP, it premiered in London.

Buero's history plays likewise search for truth and freedom. *Las Meninas*, 1961, presents Velázquez as the conscience of his time. In *El Concierto de San Ovidio* (*Concert at St Ovide Fair*, 1964), a group of blind beggars in pre-revolutionary France are exploited by an unscrupulous manager. In *El sueño de la razón* (*The Sleep of Reason*, 1970), Goya's solitude is underscored by his deafness and by the obsessions of a mind close to insanity. Slides of his *Black Paintings* provide social commentary on his times and, by extension, the Franco era.

To reveal his characters' inner nature and promote audience identification, Buero uses 'immersion effects'. He immerses spectators in his students' blindness by plunging the theatre into darkness, and makes them deaf with Goya by having other characters mouth words silently while he is present. *La Fundación* (*The Foundation*, 1974) exploits this technique to its limits. A political prisoner, responsible for his cellmates' death sentences, cannot accept his guilt. His mind creates an elegant room in a research foundation to replace the sordid prison cell. Since the set shows what he sees, the audience is immersed in his illusory world. As he gradually returns to reality, the set changes.

Buero's most recent plays are set in the 1980s: *Diálogo secreto* (*Secret Dialogue*, 1984), *Lázaro en el laberinto* (*Lazarus in the Labyrinth*, 1986) and *Música cercana* (*The Music Window*, 1989).

Buero's theory of TRAGEDY reflects his dialectical view of history and he always offers a degree of hope, at least for spectators if not for the characters. His plays have long been popular in Eastern Europe, Russia, Scandinavia and Japan. In the English-speaking world the best-known are *Concert at St Ovide Fair*, *The Foundation*, and *The Sleep of Reason*.   MH

bufo Caribbean, especially Cuban, equivalent of the *sainete* (see GÉNERO CHICO), a popular theatre form that incorporates the types, characters and language typical of the lower social classes. *Bufo* also implies a criticism of some aspect of life, and is normally presented with the intention of destroying false illusions. After a period of relative disuse, the form has been reincorporated into Cuba's new social theatre.   GW

Bugaev, Boris N. see BELY, ANDREI

bugaku Formal Japanese court dance, dating from the 7th century, that originated in CHINA. A rarefied art, *bugaku* is performed and taught primarily at the Music Department of the Imperial Household Agency and at large temples and shrines in Kyoto, Osaka and Nara. Public performances also are given annually at the National Theatre in Tokyo. *Bugaku* is performed on a square, raised dance floor. Unroofed, its space is demarcated visually by a red-lacquered railing on four sides and by a green silk cloth that covers its surface. The stage is often set outdoors, in a garden or over a pond, to enhance the beauty of performance. Performers, divided into 'left' and 'right' groups and performing different items of the repertory, enter between two enormous drums that stand at the rear of the stage. MASKS are worn for some roles. Costumes are court dress of the 7th century: elegant silk robes, black hats, white *tabi* covering the feet. No scenery is used. Musicians playing flute (*ryūteki, komabue* and *hichiriki*), mouth organ (*shō*), gong (*shōko*), drums (*taiko, sannoko* and *kakko*) accompany the dance while seated, often in small pavilions, offstage. There are no singers. The repertory of about 50 dances can be classified into pieces of Chinese or KOREAN origin; old or new; large, medium or small cast; or, most commonly, into military or civil pieces, a classification well known in China.

Although performance today has lost almost all dramatic function, reminders of *bugaku*'s previous dramatic content can be seen in the grotesque mask worn by the young king Ranryō who wished to frighten his enemy in battle, in Batō where the dancer is supposedly mounted on a white horse, and in some now extinct pieces that were comic parodies of *gigaku* dances. Associated with the Imperial court from its beginnings, the decorous, four-square movements and ethereal music of *bugaku* evoke, to a remarkable extent, the refined elegance of the Japanese court of 1000 years ago (the dances from which *bugaku* grew have long since died out in China). *Bugaku* performance was structured into an opening (*jo*), a breaking apart (*ha*), and a fast conclusion (*kyū*). This fundamental aesthetic construct of emotional progression was later adopted in NŌ and other forms of Japanese theatre.

See: M. Togi, *Gagaku: Court Music and Dance*, Tokyo, 1971; C. Wolz, *Bugaku: Japanese Court Dance*, Providence, R.I., 1971. JRB

Bugge, Stein 1896–1961 Norwegian director, theorist and dramatist, whose ideas and writings have influenced many leading Scandinavian directors. Inspired by Belgian and French modernists such as Jan de Gruyter and JACQUES COPEAU, whose work he had studied first hand, he published a manifesto in 1928, 'The Ideal Theatre', attacking NATURALISM and arguing for a theatricalization of the theatre. In Bergen he started the annual festival performances that eventually became the Bergen Festival, and he was briefly head of NATIONALE SCENE (1946–8). As a director he was admired for his productions of SHAKESPEARE, HOLBERG, GOGOL and IBSEN. HL

Bulgakov, Mikhail (Afanasievich) 1891–1940 Russian novelist, short story writer and dramatist who, perceiving post-revolutionary Russia as a spiritual vacuum for the artist-intellectual, attempted to maintain a continued relationship with a civilized past while defining an ethical response to the present. He was uniquely able to embroider mystical, allegorical and parallel historical threads into the fabric of his texts, successfully mixing all manner of literary allusions and styles. The medically trained son of a Kiev theologian, he soon embarked on careers in journalism and literature, the latter including such major narrative works as the story collection *Diaboliad*, the novelette *Heart of a Dog* and the epic and, some say, best Soviet Civil War novel *White Guard* (all 1925). His adaptation of this novel, *The Days of the Turbins* (1925), commissioned by the MOSCOW ART THEATRE (MAT) which premiered it in 1926, realistically depicts the rush of events (1918–19) leading to the destruction and exile of a White officer's family in the author's native Kiev. Its sympathetic portrayal of the White enemy and its downplaying of the constructive role the Red Army played in these events resulted in Bulgakov's being labelled an 'internal émigré'.

'Former people' again are featured in his first major comedy, *Zoika's Apartment* (1926), a 'satiric MELODRAMA' similar to those of the New Economic Policy period (e.g. by ERDMAN and FAIKO), dealing with Khlestakovian deception, financial speculation and petty demonism in a time of severe economic shortages. It played 100 times at the Vakhtangov Theatre and elsewhere in Moscow before being totally banned with Bulgakov's other plays in 1929. *The Crimson Island* (1927), a COMEDY-allegory written for TAIROV's Kamerny Theatre where it ran briefly in 1928, parodies CENSORSHIP and officially sanctioned drama. *Flight* (1927), his most ambitious play and the first to be banned before it premiered (at MAT), is a hallucinatory epilogue to *The Days of the Turbins*. Via a series of dreams and ever shifting time–space matrices the author creates the surreal experience of White émigrés in confused psychological and moral transit. The play received its Soviet premiere in 1957. Preceding his biography of MOLIÈRE (1933), Bulgakov wrote *The Cabal of Hypocrites* (*Molière*, written 1929; banned 1930), a cinematically structured, onstage–backstage retelling of the difficulties experienced by *Tartuffe*'s author in getting his play produced and in reconciling the tensions of his personal and professional lives. The obvious parallels with Bulgakov's own life and work, together with STANISLAVSKY's disapproval of the author's anti-heroic portrayal of this admired artist, contributed to the play's difficulties, and it ran for only seven performances. Bulgakov satirized his uneasy tenure at MAT as playwright and as an assistant director (1930–6) in his theatrical novel (*Black Snow*, 1936).

Of the remaining 30-odd plays written by Bulgakov that were not either burned by the author or confiscated by the government, some worth mentioning are *Last Days* (1935), in which an unseen PUSHKIN is discussed as a victim of the Tsarist police state; an apocalyptic science fiction play, *Adam and Eve* (1931); two fantasy-SATIRES on time travel, *Bliss* (1934) and *Ivan Vasilievich* (1935); his adaptations of *Dead Souls* (1932) and *Don Quixote* (1938); and *Batum* (1938), about the young Stalin. His brilliant novel *The Master and Margarita*, a veritable compendium of topical, literary (especially biblical) and personal themes and styles completed at his death, established him as a true heir to GOGOL, SUKHOVO-KOBYLIN and Dostoevsky. Long a

Soviet underground classic, it was finally brought to the stage by YURY LYUBIMOV at Moscow's Taganka Theatre (1977). SG

Bulgaria Despite a scant history that extends back only to the mid-19th century, Bulgarian theatre thrives today on a par with the rest of European theatre.

The beginning of Bulgarian theatre is usually identified with two performances in 1856: the 15 August performance of a Serbian COMEDY, *Mihal Mishkoed*, in Shumen where Sava Dobroplodni staged his farcical adaptation to a coffee-house audience; and the 12 December showing of a German MELODRAMA, *Longsuffering Genoveve*, in Lom, staged by Krastu Pishurka in his home before an audience of over 100. The first Bulgarian theatrical troupe was founded by Dobri Voinikov in 1865 in Braila, Romania. Its location outside the country reflects the long legacy of Bulgaria's political suppression under Turkish rule and the cultural hegemony of the Greek Church. From its beginning the theatre in Bulgaria was devoted to two themes: national independence and cultural revival. The oral folklore tradition (see FOLK DRAMA) and the art of recitation, widely used in the schools, were fertile ground for the emerging dramatic form.

Two works stand out from the original plays written prior to the national liberation in 1878: *Ivanko, Assassin of Asen I* (1872), a historical play by Basil Drumev (1840–1901), author of the first modern Bulgarian novel; and *Civilization Misunderstood* (1871) by D. Voinikov, a comedy satirizing the popular fashion for embracing all things French to the disdain of everything Bulgarian. Both plays retain a currency today that bears occasional performance.

From the arrival of national independence to the First World War the dominant influence in Bulgarian theatre was poet and novelist Ivan Vasov (1850–1921). Vasov's historical/patriotic plays *Khushove* (1894) and *Under the Yoke* (1910) were adapted from his novels. He also wrote several original plays, among them *Jobchasers* (1903), a colourful comedy ridiculing the widespread careerism of his day. Two theatre companies, Foundation, established in 1888 in Sofia, and Tears and Laughter, established in 1892, led to the founding of the Bulgarian National Theatre, which moved into a new building in the heart of Sofia in 1907 and became the centre for theatrical life in the country. A nucleus of talented performers and directors, mostly educated in Europe and Russia, formed under the direction of poet and drama critic P. Slavejkov.

Dramatic literature as an independent form dates from the first two decades of the 20th century. Its founders were Anton Strashimirov (1872–1937), a novelist, Petko Todorov (1879–1916) and poet Peio Yavorov (1878–1914). Strashimirov is best remembered for a drama, *Vampire* (1901), and *Mother-in-Law* (1907), a satiric comedy; Yavorov, artistic director of the National Theatre, foreshadowed his own suicide in *In the Foothills of Vitosha* (1911); Todorov invented a ballad-like genre combining mythic folk motifs with realistic characters in *The Masons* (1902), *The Woodsprite* (1904) and *The Dragon's Wedding* (1911). Influences of the period include IBSEN, CHEKHOV, STRINDBERG and HAUPTMANN.

A series of catastrophes struck in the mid-1920s. The National Theatre building was destroyed by fire in 1923; the same year an abortive uprising against the regime led to the black-listing of many theatre professionals. Then, in 1925, an assassination attempt against the Bulgarian Tsar cost the lives of hundreds of intellectuals in the purge that followed. Among those purged was Geo Milev (1895–1925), an avant-garde modernist poet who, as director of the National Theatre, stressed highly experimental directorial methods and introduced Bulgarian audiences to the work of German playwright ERNST TOLLER.

A vital resurrection was signalled in 1929 by the opening of a 1150-seat modern theatre building. This theatre, standing on the site of the old, offered the most advanced production technology; renovated in the 1970s, it now bears the name of Ivan Vasov.

The dozen-odd years before the Second World War saw a new emphasis on directorial techniques (H. Tzankov, B. Danovski, N. Fol). In 1948 Bulgaria was declared a People's Republic and the theatre reaped the benefit of full state support together with the bane of supervised repertoire. The High Institute for Theatrical Arts (VITIS) offered a diverse curriculum for training actors, directors and dramaturges; specialized theatre companies were created and a film industry was founded.

The torpor of the postwar period gave way to a new vital phase for the theatre in the 1960s. The energy released generated a rebirth of the spirit that had infused the first quarter of the century. G. Ostrovski's 1961–2 productions of *When the Roses Dance*, a MUSICAL by V. Petrov, and *Improvisation* by V. Petrov and R. Ralin, both staged in the Theatre of Satire, started a series of innovative productions there. *Sumatoha*, written by Y. Radichkov and directed by M. Andonov, was not only a new kind of dramaturgy but an example of superb ensemble and character acting. In Andonov's revival of *Mihal Mishkoed* the actors were encouraged to improvise freely. The close collaboration of directors and playwrights shaped the modern drama. Such teams produced *We Are Not Angels* by N. Yordanov (directed by A. Shopov) and *The Poet and the Mountain* by I. Teofilov (directed by L. Daniel), *The Prosecutor* by G. Gjagarov (directed by E. Halachev), *Romeo, Juliet and Petroleum* by I. Radoev (directed by A. Shopov) and *The Old Man and the Arrow* by N. Russev (directed by M. Andonov).

In the 1970s and 80s Bulgarian drama showed its appeal before Western audiences. Director Andonov screened his feature film *The Goat's Horn*, scripted by playwright N. Haytov, at the 1972 Chicago Film Festival where it won the Golden Hugo; in 1981 M. Kisselov, a student of Andonov's, staged a production of Radichkov's *An Attempt at Flying* at the Yale Repertory Theatre in New Haven, Connecticut, after staging it at the National Theatre in Sofia. *Official Status: Batman*, adapted from a short story by playwright G.P. Stamatov and directed by K. Kolarov, won the Golden Ear of Wheat at the 1980 Feature Film Festival in Valladolid, Spain.

Today Bulgaria has 56 repertory theatres spread around the country, against a pre-war maximum of 13. Bulgarian National Television has, from its beginning in 1958, featured a weekly TV drama series which has drawn from the best theatre professionals for its players, directors and playwrights. Bulgaria is a member of the INTERNATIONAL THEATRE INSTITUTE. BL

See: *Bulgarian Encyclopaedia*, 1936; G. Konstantinov, *New Bulgarian Literature*, 1943; *Modern Bulgaria*, Sofia Press, 1981; B. Penev, *History of Bulgarian Literature*, vols. 1–3, 1933; L. Tenev, 'Dramaturgy and Reality', *Literaturen Front*, 7 May 1981.

bull-baiting see BAITING

Bullins, Ed 1935– African-American playwright who began writing fiction but, seeing BARAKA's plays on stage, felt drama was more effective in reaching black audiences. Since 1965 Bullins has written several dozen plays and has been produced internationally. In 1967 he joined the New Lafayette Theatre as resident playwright, became its associate director, and edited its periodical *Black Theatre*. Among his best-known plays are *Goin' a Buffalo* (1966), *In the Wine Time* (1968), *The Duplex* (1970), *In New England Winter* (1971), *The Fabulous Miss Marie* (1971) and *The Taking of Miss Janie* (1975). His experiments in form combine rhythmic, racy dialogue, black RITUAL, and jazz and blues music as integral elements of his dramaturgy. His work has been recognized by an Obie and in 1975 the New York Drama Critics' Circle Award. In 1982 Bullins moved to San Francisco, where he has had several new plays produced. EGH

Buloff, Joseph 1899–1985 Gifted YIDDISH THEATRE actor and director – first with the VILNA TROUPE where he distinguished himself in the title role of OSSIP DIMOV's *Yoshke Musikant*, then in America where he acted with MAURICE SCHWARTZ's YIDDISH ART THEATRE and directed for the FOLKSBIENE, forming the New York Art Theatre in 1934/5. He eventually moved to English-speaking roles on BROADWAY and was active in Israel during the 50s and 60s. AB

Bulwer Lytton, Edward (George Earle) [1st Baron Lytton] 1803–73 English novelist, playwright and politician, who changed his name from Bulwer to Bulwer Lytton on inheriting Knebworth House from his mother Elizabeth Lytton and was created Baron Lytton of Knebworth in 1866. Richly talented and damagingly vain, Bulwer Lytton found himself suddenly needy when his parents opposed his disastrous marriage, and he wrote to earn money. Already famous as the author of *Eugene Aram* (1832), a fashionable 'Newgate novel', and *The Last Days of Pompeii* (1834) when he wrote his first plays, he was also a far-sighted agitator for theatrical reform. As a member of parliament, he had led a Select Committee of Inquiry into the state of the theatre in 1832. The Committee's three aims were impeccable – to protect playwrights by establishing an effective COPYRIGHT law, to investigate the propriety of the Patent theatres' monopoly over 'legitimate' drama, and to challenge the Lord Chamberlain's role as dramatic censor. (The first was a limited success, the second bore fruit 11 years later and the third faded into obscurity.)

Bulwer Lytton's perceptive analysis of contemporary theatre can be read in Book 4 of his acute social survey, *England and the English* (1833). The best of his plays were solicited and performed by MACREADY. They are *The Duchess de la Vallière* (1837), a Gothic drama in verse, *The Lady of Lyons* (1838), a drama of mixed verse and prose which remained a favourite of audiences throughout the 19th century, *Richelieu* (1839), a polished verse drama which provided IRVING as well as Macready with a major role, and the prose comedy, *Money* (1840), which offers a particularly sharp commentary on contemporary values. It was revived by the ROYAL SHAKESPEARE COMPANY in 1982. PT

Bunn, Alfred 1798–1860 English theatre manager whose scuffle with MACREADY (Macready punched him in the eye and Bunn bit Macready's finger) has earned him a partly merited notoriety. Bunn was appointed stage manager at DRURY LANE by ELLISTON, whose view that there was nothing so special about the proud Patent theatres he inherited. His simultaneous management of Drury Lane and COVENT GARDEN (1833–5) gave him a unique opportunity to test his views, but his singular tactlessness aroused such vigorous opposition that he was never able to pursue a consistent policy, and by 1840 he was bankrupt. *The Stage: Both Before and Behind the Curtain* (1840) is an argumentative and by no means negligible self-justification in three volumes. Bunn, who was mockingly nicknamed 'Poet' Bunn in response to his published verse, loved comic opera more than he loved plays. He wrote several librettos, including one for Balfe's popular *The Bohemian Girl* (1843). PT

bunraku Highly sophisticated, adult, commercial Japanese doll-puppet theatre. Since 1652, all professional performers have been male. The name *bunraku* derives from the 19th-century theatre manager, Uemura Bunrakuen (or Bunrakuken), who moved from Awaji Island to Osaka, where he staged puppet plays at shrines and professional theatres. His troupe was the only group of professionals to continue into the Meiji period (1868–1912), hence the association of his name with the current genre. A chanted puppet performance may also be called *jōruri*, after the generic style of narrative music, *ayatsuri* ('manipulation') *jōruri*, or *ningyō shibai* ('puppet play').

In the 1590s *jōruri* narrative chanting and accompanying *shamisen* music was joined to puppet manipulation to form this complex style of puppet theatre. For perhaps a thousand years before this, bards had chanted religious tales and military epics, especially, after the 12th century, *The Tale of the Heike* (*Heike monogatari*). Because of the respected tradition of oral narrative (*katari*), the chanter (*tayū*) took social and artistic precedence over puppeteers and musicians. Until the 20th century, only he was allowed to own property or live outside the confines of the licensed theatre districts. An indication of the status of chanting can be seen in the visit in 1614 of the emperor Go-Yozei to a puppet performance in Kyoto of the Buddhist miracle play, *The Chest-Splitting of Amida Buddha* (*Amida no munewari*). Numerous chanting styles competed in the early 17th century. In Edo (Tokyo), the chanter Satsuma Jōun (1593–1672) joined his highly bombastic chanting style with violent puppet manipulation to create *kimpira jōruri*. It is said that the bravura acting style of *KABUKI* was in part inspired by performances of the *kimpira* puppeteer Izumi Dayū who decapitated puppets with an iron bar in knockabout battle scenes.

In 1657 the Great Edo Fire destroyed the three professional puppet theatres operating in the capital (as well as four large and eight small *kabuki* theatres). When these puppet troupes fled to Osaka that city became the undisputed centre of puppet theatre. From 1686 audiences thrilled to TAKEMOTO GIDAYŪ's beautiful melodies and powerful interpretations at the Takemoto Theatre. His vocal style displaced all others and today the general term for *bunraku* music and chanting style is *gidayū* (or *takemoto* when played and sung in *kabuki*).

A day's programme traditionally consisted either of a history and domestic play in sequence, or selected scenes. More important than act divisions (*dan*), are the two or three scenes (*ba*) into which they are divided: opening (*kuchi*), middle (*naka*), and conclusion (*kiri*). In performance a different chanter is assigned to each scene: young chanters take early, less important scenes; star chanters take difficult scenes, especially each act conclusion. Occasionally 4 or 5 chanters perform a scene together, each providing the voice of one character as an actor might, an indication of *kabuki* influence.

Influenced by NŌ's *jo-ha-kyū* structure, most history plays are in five acts and last 8–10 hours in performance. Several subplots intersect, providing opportunity for display of a variety of emotions: love, pathos, the excitement and horror of battle, auspicious celebration. The dramatic high point is the 'final scene of the third act' (*san dan no kiri*), an agonizing scene in which a parent sacrifices a child (*migawari*) or a warrior commits ritual suicide out of feudal loyalty (*seppuku*). Most domestic plays are in three acts. They followed the history play and closed the programme (*kiri kyōgen*). Critics today regard the domestic play more highly than the history form, a reversal of 18th-century opinion. History and domestic plays alike portray an ethical conflict fundamental to feudal society: duty (*giri*) to a lord or master versus human feelings of love and generosity (*ninjō*). In CHIKAMATSU's *The Battles of Coxinga* (*Kokusenya kassen*) the mother and sister of Coxinga willingly kill themselves to protect the honour of the two male heroes.

A text is composed in alternating sections of prose (*kotoba*), which is usually spoken dialogue, and verse (*fushigoto*), which is usually sung narrative, that call upon various vocal techniques (*ji, naka, kami, suete*, and so on). A chanter must perform at a tremendous pitch of emotional fervour to match the dramatic intensity of the text. Chanter and *shamisen* player sit in audience view on a dais (*yuka*) stage left of the proscenium that revolves to change performers between scenes. The chanter 'reads' from the text (actually memorized) which rests prominently on a lacquered stand before him.

Bunraku is performed on a proscenium stage, somewhat smaller than a *kabuki* stage and without *hanamichi* or revolving stage. It is divided by low railings into two or three zones from front to back. Since a puppet's feet reach to around the knees of the puppeteers, the low front railings provide a ground level on which a puppet character can walk when moving outside. The innermost railing ('first railing', *honte*) is at about hip level, allowing a puppet to be seated on a mat of an inner room. Elaborately painted sets surround the PUPPETS with 'realistic' interior and exterior environments.

Some 50 types of puppet heads match a wide variety of character types; in a long play five heads may be used for one character to show changes in emotion. Heads are carved of paulownia wood, hollowed to hold the mechanisms for moving eyes, eyebrows and mouth, and painted in realistic detail. Fingers may be jointed so the hand can open wide or close in a fist. Puppets of vigorous male characters have the largest number of movable parts. Three puppeteers surround, hold and move a puppet. The chief puppeteer (*omo zukai*) controls a puppet's right arm (with his right hand) and head and body (with his left hand). The second puppeteer (*hidari zukai*, 'left puppeteer') controls the left arm. The third puppeteer (*ashi zukai*, 'foot puppeteer') moves the feet of the male puppet or kimono hem of the legless female puppet. Puppeteers may improvise movements in performance, using a wide repertory of accepted mimetic gestures (*furi*) and stylized movements (*kata*). The former include sewing, smoking, walking or weeping in highly realistic fashion. The latter include displays of technical virtuosity, such as the beautiful one-handed manipulation of a woman looking over her shoulder (*ushiro buri*). Although it is inanimate wood and cloth, the energy infused into a puppet by the manipulators, chanter and musician make it appear lifelike and real, while a *kabuki* character may seem quite unreal. Puppets, puppeteers, chanter and musician all have their own visual presence in *bunraku* and vie for attention. Puppeteers in the West are now borrowing from *bunraku* many of its performing techniques because of their theatrical effectiveness. JRB

See: B. Adachi, *The Voices and Hands of Bunraku*, Tokyo, 1978; T. Ando, *Bunraku: The Puppet Theatre*, New York, 1970; D. Keene, *Bunraku: The Art of the Japanese Puppet Theatre*, Tokyo, 1965, and (tr.), *Major Plays of Chikamatsu*, New York, 1961; C. J. Dunn, *The Early Japanese Puppet Drama*, London, 1966; C. A. Gerstle, *Circles of Fantasy: Convention in the Plays of Chikamatsu*, Cambridge, Mass., 1986; C. A. Gerstle, K. Inobe and W. Malm, *Theater as Music: The Bunraku Play 'Mt. Imo and Mt. Se: An Exemplary Tale of Womanly Virtue'*, Ann Arbor, Mich., 1990; T. Izumo, *Chūshingura: The Treasury of Loyal Retainers*, tr. D. Keene, New York, 1971; S. H. Jones Jr (tr.), *Sugawara and the Secrets of Calligraphy*, New York, 1984; S. Saito et al., *Masterpieces of Japanese Puppetry: Sculptured Heads of the Bunraku Theater*, Rutland, Vt., 1958.

Buontalenti, Bernardo 1536–1608 Italian architect and scenic designer. In 1547 Buontalenti began service to the Medici court assisting designer and architect GIORGIO VASARI. In addition to designing palaces, villas and fortresses, he organized firework displays and designed COSTUMES and machinery for transformation scenes in festivals directed by Vasari (1565) and Lanci (1569). By 1574 he had succeeded Vasari as architect and supervisor of Florentine court entertainments. In honour of the marriage between Virginia de'Medici and Cesare d'Este (1585) he designed the Teatro degli Uffizi, with a system of revolving *periaktoi* and elaborate stage machinery. His decors were used for Giovanni Bardi's *L'amico fido* (*The Faithful Friend*) and the accompanying six intermezzi written for the occasion. Another achievement was direction of the month-long festivities honouring the marriage of Ferdinand I of Tuscany to Catherine de'Medici (1589). In addition to the animal hunts, masquerades and NAU-MACHIA on the Arno which he supervised for the occasion, he designed the production of Girolami Bargagli's *La pellegrina* and its six intermezzi. Characteristic of his style, these elaborate and sumptuous productions were noted for the ingenious cloud machines, glories, traps, revolving *periaktoi* and moving side wings, which facilitated the almost magical scene changes taking place in full view of the spectators. AJN

Burbage, James c.1530–97 English actor and tradesman, better remembered as the entrepreneur responsible for the building of the THEATRE. Trained as a joiner, Burbage probably turned actor in middle life, and is known to have been a member of LEICESTER'S MEN by 1572. Anticipating the spread of interest in plays, he borrowed money from JOHN BRAYNE, his brother-in-law, to finance the erection of the Theatre on the estate of the dissolved Holywell Priory. After its opening in 1567, Burbage spent the rest of his life in theatre management. With the lease of the land approaching its expiry date, he took out a second lease on a large room (probably the Parliament Chamber) in the old Blackfriars monastery, and, in 1596, set about converting it for use as an indoor playhouse, but his plans were frustrated by the opposition of residents of the BLACKFRIARS precinct. He died with the situation unresolved, leaving the Theatre and its problems to his elder son, Cuthbert, and the Blackfriars and its problems to his younger son, RICHARD (see ENGLAND). PT

Burbage, Richard c.1568–1619 English actor, who, as the leading member of the LORD CHAMBERLAIN'S/King's MEN from 1594 until his death, created many of SHAKESPEARE's greatest roles. As the son of JAMES BURBAGE, he was involved in theatre management from an early age. His name is first encountered in a lawsuit of 1590, when, in defiance of a court order, he physically resisted the attempts of his father's business partners to collect a share of the takings at the THEATRE. The impression that Richard Burbage was strong and sturdily built is confirmed by a surviving portrait in the Dulwich Picture Gallery. Whether or not this is a self-portrait, Burbage is known to have been a talented painter as well as an actor. He was engaged for the important job of scene-painting at the Earl of Rutland's tilts in 1613 and 1616, and these are unlikely to be isolated occasions. In 1594, when STRANGE'S MEN, to which he belonged, either dissolved or moved out of London, Burbage remained in the capital as a founder-member of the new company, the Lord Chamberlain's Men, resident at the Theatre. Over the next two decades, he is known to have played Hamlet, Othello, Lear and Richard III, Ferdinand in WEBSTER's *The Duchess of Malfi*, Malevole in MARSTON's *The Malcontent* and 'Jeronimo', probably in a lost play opportunistically exploiting the success of KYD's *The Spanish Tragedy*. Contemporaries, comparing him perhaps with EDWARD ALLEYN, considered his acting true to life, though he was certainly faithful also to rhetorical conventions. With his brother Cuthbert he owned half the shares in the GLOBE and, later, the BLACKFRIARS, and he must be accounted, in the company's sharing system, *primus inter pares*. PT

bürgerliches Trauerspiel ('bourgeois tragedy') Genre that arose in the German theatre during the latter half of the 18th century, partially as a result of the introduction of English plays into the repertoire, partially due to the rise in economic power of the bourgeoisie. It is a TRAGEDY set neither in princely or noble courts nor in a heroic period of history, but in the home of the bourgeoisie, who are regarded as serious subject-matter for drama. The first significant examples of the genre are LESSING's *Miss Sara Sampson* (1755), written under the influence of the English writers GEORGE LILLO and Samuel Richardson, and *Emilia Galotti* (1772). SCHILLER described his *Love and Intrigue* (1783) as a *bürgerliches Trauerspiel*. The genre is universally recognized as foreshadowing the work of HENRIK IBSEN, GERHART HAUPTMANN and other late-19th-century naturalist dramatists (see NATURALISM). SW

Burgess, Neil 1846–1910 American actor, who made his debut with Spalding's Bell Ringers in 1865. Born in Boston, he gained attention in a dame role, Mrs Benjamin Bibbs, in *The Quiet Family*; he won stardom in 1879, touring extensively in a dramatization of Alice B. Neal's 1858 novel *The Widow Bedott Papers*, in which he played the garrulous, malapropistic 'widdy-woman' wooed by seedy Deacon Sniffles. He equalled but did not surpass this success as Betsy Puffy in *Vim* (1882) and Aunt Abigail Prue in his own production of Charles Bernard's *The County Fair* (1888). Burgess's comic cross-dressing (see FEMALE IMPERSONATION) made him one of the richest actors in America, but his fortune evaporated in ill-advised speculations and, as the stock system (see STOCK COMPANY) declined, he was reduced (from 1899) to playing tabloid versions of his best parts in VAUDEVILLE. LS

Burgtheater (Vienna) Founded in 1741 as the court theatre of the Habsburgs. In 1776, the Emperor Josef II declared it to be a national theatre; in so doing, Josef was influenced partially by the ideas of JOSEF VON SONNENFELS on the educative potential of the theatre. Under the aegis of actors such as Stephanie the elder (1773–98), J. H. F. Müller (1738–1815), BROCKMANN and FRIEDRICH SCHRÖDER, the Burgtheater developed a style of acting noted for its moderation and evenness of expression among the whole ensemble. In the 19th century, under the directorship first of JOSEF SCHREYVOGEL, then of HEINRICH LAUBE, this style became widely admired and imitated throughout the German-speaking world.

Among the greatest actors who perfected the Burgtheater style were Heinrich Anschütz (1785–1865), famous for his moving Lear; Bernhard Baumeister (1828–1917), a magnificently robust actor; Josef Lewinsky (1835–1907), a masterly player of villains; SOPHIE SCHRÖDER; Charlotte Wolter (1834–97), a great tragedienne; and Adolf von Sonnenthal (1834–1909), whose gracious bearing both on and off stage established him in the eyes of the public as the epitome of the Burgtheater. In 1888, the company moved from their intimate theatre in the Hofburg to a palatial construction on the Franzen-Ring. This threatened their traditional style of ensemble, but through the direction of Max Burckhard (1854–1912), then intendant of the Burgtheater, and the acting first of MITTERWURZER, then of KAINZ, this difficult period of transition passed without the company declining. The Burgtheater is still the pre-eminent theatre of the German-speaking world and continues to practise, in modified form, the ideals of acting developed during the 18th and 19th centuries. SW

Burian, E(mil) F(rantišek) 1904–59 Czech avant-garde theatre artist, who began his career in the 1920s as composer, musician and actor. Concurrently he developed 'voiceband', a synthesis of music and syncopated choral recitation. In 1933 Burian established his own theatre collective, D34 (the number changed annually to indicate the current season). There, his early work contained elements of PISCATOR-like AGIT-PROP, but his most successful productions combined his musical talents more artistically with his intense political concerns. Burian often created his own poetic scenarios, most strikingly in *War* (1935), a moving anti-military work of village life. An auteur of the stage, he tended to regard every text as a libretto, for which he would be editor, composer, orchestrator and conductor. Although he produced in very small spaces, he achieved sophisticated technical effects: e.g. *Theatergraph*, in 1935, a system that blended cinema projections with live action in poetic ways and thus anticipated the Czech LATERNA MAGIKA of the 1950s. JMB

Burk, John Daly c.1776–1808 American playwright. Burk was known for his patriotic spectacle *Bunker-Hill; or, The Death of General Warren* (Boston, February 1797; New York, September 1797) and for his detailed account of the primitive staging: 'Our twelve-minute battle ... Charlestown on fire and Warren animating the Americans amidst the smoak [*sic*] and confusion produce an effect scarce credible.' For 20 years *Bunker-Hill* was the American theatre's standard offering for the Fourth of July and for Evacuation Day (25 November).

Expelled from Dublin's Trinity College, Burk went to Boston in 1796, and in 1808 was killed in a duel. He edited two newspapers, practised law, and wrote six other plays – *Female Patriotism; or, The Death of Joan of Arc* (1798), the best-known – as well as a *History of Virginia* and *History of the Late-War in Ireland* (1799). RM

Burkina Faso Formerly Upper Volta, Burkina Faso gained its independence from France in August 1960. It is remembered by older French-speaking African theatre enthusiasts for the excellent performance of its Banfora Cultural Centre Troupe at the drama competitions of 1955 and 1957 organized among French West African states. But this promising beginning has not been followed up. Only two Burkina plays in French have been published to date: *Le Fou* (*The Madman*, 1986) by Jean-Pierre Guingané, playwright and Burkina theatre historian, and Pierre Dabiré's *Sansoa* (1969). The other six that exist in print were issued by the country's Ministry of Culture and are not widely available.

But theatrical activity certainly exists in Burkina Faso. The country boasts at least four notable companies that are engaged either in the creation of new plays or the stag-

ing of the many unpublished ones – estimated at five hundred by Guingané. These four are the Troupe du Théâtre Radiophonique, the Troupe de la Mutuelle Nouvelle Génération, the Atelier Théâtre Burkinabé and the Théâtre de la Fraternité, the last two being currently the most influential. The Atelier Théâtre, under the direction of Prosper Kampaoré, advocates a theatre of participation: one that breaks the barriers between actor and spectator and transforms the latter from passive consumer to creative agent. Although he is said to derive this idea from his traditional heritage, he also admits to being inspired by the forum-theatre techniques of the Brazilian playwright-director AUGUSTO BOAL. His productions are followed by debates between actors and spectators, during which the latter are encouraged to criticize the 'model' performances and propose alternative scenarios, which are then produced. Kampaoré's themes are mostly developmental. The Théâtre de la Fraternité, on the other hand, under its director Guingané, concentrates on sociopolitical topics. The performance style that he is trying to develop is based on that of the folk-tale, where the storyteller acts different characters, effecting costume changes in full view of the audience, and where the action is narrated, sung or dramatized. JCM

See: B. Benon, 'Deux expériences théâtrales. Jean-Pierre Guingané et le Théâtre de la Fraternité; Prosper Kampaoré et l'Atelier Burkinabé', *Notre Librairie: La Littérature du Burkina Faso*, 101, Apr./June 1990; Thérèse-Marie Deffontaines, 'Théâtre-Forum au Burkina Faso et au Mali', *Notre Librairie: Théâtres*, 102, Jul./Aug. 1990; J. B. Guingané, 'Du manuscrit à la scène', *Notre Librairie: La Littérature du Burkina Faso*, ibid.; J.-C. Ki, 'Dix ans de théâtre 1979–1989', *Notre Librairie: La Littérature du Burkina Faso*, ibid.; W. Zimmer, 'Jean-Pierre Guingané, un "fou" de théâtre au Burkina Faso', ibid.

burlesque Burlesque, PARODY and SATIRE are often treated as synonyms for ridicule through distortion, but it is useful to suggest distinctions between them. None of the three words refers exclusively to drama; yet all have been applied to drama. Burlesque as derisive imitation enters the English language in the 17th century, *after* such signal achievements as the Pyramus and Thisbe scene in SHAKESPEARE's *Midsummer Night's Dream* and the mockery of romance in BEAUMONT and FLETCHER's *Knight of the Burning Pestle*. In general, burlesque tends to be broader than parody, mocking a style, class, or genre. Seventeenth-century France and 18th-century England showed a marked taste for burlesque, and plays of that genre were standard fare in the 19th-century theatres of most European countries. Twentieth-century burlesque survives in skits and REVUES, but TOM STOPPARD's *Travesties* is a rare example of a full-length burlesque. RC

burlesque show, American Raucous and bawdy style of VARIETY performance, partly inspired by LYDIA THOMPSON and her British Blondes, partly by blackface MINSTREL SHOWS and 'leg shows' like *The Black Crook*. The manager Michael B. Leavitt is credited with its invention by creating Mme Rentz's Female Minstrels (Rentz from a popular CIRCUS), later the RentzSantley troupe (after

Mabel Santley, its star). One of its earliest personalities was May Howard, who ran her own company in the 1880s.

Burlesque rapidly developed a tripartite structure: in the first third, dance and song rendered by a female company, was intermingled with low comedy from male comedians; part two was an olio of specialities in which the women did not appear; and part three comprised a grand finale. 'Clean' versions of these preponderantly female productions were widely sponsored by the Miner family. Sam T. Jack, who opened the first exclusively burlesque theatre in Chicago, pioneered 'dirty' burlesque or 'turkey show', which was especially popular in the Western 'honky-tonks'. The Empire and Mutual Circuits or Wheels revelled in such maculose entertainment, while the Columbia Circuit booked only clean shows, until 1925, when it too was forced by dwindling receipts to go dirty.

Leading entrepreneurs were the MINSKY BROTHERS: Abe, who brought belly dancers (known as 'cootchers') and the illuminated runway from Paris; the publicists Billy and Morton; and Herbert, who introduced OPERA. From the early 1900s to 1935 they moulded the image of American burlesque, at the Republic Theatre and the National Winter Garden, New York. By present-day standards the offerings were tame, for the girls never disrobed completely. But the blatant *doubles entendres* in the dialogue between straight man and 'talking woman', and runway interplay between strippers and audience, enraged moralists. The strip-tease (see NUDITY), which achieved extraordinary invention and daring, entered burlesque in 1921 with 'Curls' Mason, and Carrie Finnell performed the first tassel dance, twirling the fringe from her nipples; the most memorable personalities among the strippers were Millie De Leon, the urbane GYPSY ROSE LEE (a protégée of the gangster Waxy Gordon) and the indestructible ANN CORIO. Among the comedians nurtured by the form were Sliding Billy Watson, Billy 'Beef Trust' Watson, Al Shean (see GALLAGHER AND SHEAN), WILLIE HOWARD, Phil Silvers, Abbott and Costello and Jackie Gleason, while routines like 'Floogle Street' became classics.

Changing times brought classic burlesque to an end. New York courts banned the runway in 1934 and all burlesque in 1942, and the Burlesque Artists Association had its charter revoked in 1957. Gogo dancing, the Las Vegas-style REVUE, and television siphoned off the remaining talents, and revivals, like Corio's widely toured *This Was Burlesque*, tend to be steeped in nostalgia. The form has inspired ARTHUR HOPKINS's play *Burlesque* (1927), Ralph Allen's MUSICAL *Sugar Babies* (1979), and feminist dramas that stress the exploitation of the stripper as commodity. LS

Burma [Myanmar] This Southeast Asian country borders on India, Bangladesh, China, Laos and Thailand; the country is 600 miles by 800 miles in its major land area

The refined female and male roles, the princess and the hero, performed by members of the Burmese National Theatre.

with a thin strip running another 500 miles down the Malay peninsula. The population of 41 million is composed of hill people and lowlanders. Though music and dance are important among the hill groups, drama is historically a development of the lowland areas where the Burmese predominate. The Burmese speak a Tibeto-Burman language and have adopted cultural patterns from the ethnically related Pyu and Mon who established themselves in the area prior to Burmese migration from Tibet. From the Pyu they learned Theraveda Buddhism, a belief system which, mixed with animist elements, has contributed to performance practice in terms of aesthetics, performance occasions and plot patterns. The recorded history of the Burmese begins with the founding of the kingdom of Pagan in the 11th century.

Though Indian, Chinese and Tibetan influences (see INDIA; CHINA; TIBETAN DRAMA) are evident in the music and repertoire, general Southeast Asian features underlie performance: the assertion that human performance is modelled on the PUPPET theatre, the function of the clown, set character types, such as the refined hero who clashes with an ogrely villain, and the dramatic structure that moves from court to the wilderness. Written records are rare and theatrical practice is passed orally from teacher to student in training and performance. Four categories can be distinguished: (1) animistic performance; (2) Buddhist theatre; (3) court dance drama; (4) popular performance.

Animistic performance Until the late 1700s, dance and music seem more significant for human performers than drama in the context of animist performance. Traditionally, the Burmese believe in spirits called *nat*, which, alongside place spirits, include the spirits of heroes, ancestors and even criminals. Throughout Burma, 37 major *nat* are honoured, and female and male transvestite spirit-mediums, *nat kadaw* ('spirit wives'), enter trance to manifest them during festivals or in private seances for divination. Set songs are used to summon specific spirits. The mediums dance till possessed, then speak in the voice of the possessing spirit. Male mediums are more common than female at present. SHAMANIC patterns of sickness accompanying the call to the medium role are the norm.

The jerky movements of the ecstatic *nat* dances have perhaps contributed to the percussive nature of Burmese theatrical dance. This aesthetic is ancient, as is attested by the poem of a Tang dynasty official who saw Pyu performers at the Chinese court in AD 802. The twirls and leaps, the costume crowns and the sound of gongs described by him would be appropriate to a contemporary performance. Trance performances may have established the aesthetic, and *nat pwe* ('spirit shows') may have provided the early format for drama activities, for legend claims that in the 1400s two outcast princes became the first secular performers by emulating seances of female mediums.

Nat pwe and *anyein pwe* are two major genres still performed today with roots in trance traditions. In *nat pwe* a group of mediums dress in theatrical garb: the chief medium in the costume of a prince, a junior medium in a princess's costume. *Anyein pwe* features a female singer-dancer and a pair of clowns who perform while she rests, or joke with her. The form may be a secularization of the female trance tradition. The performance structure relates to *nat* dancing: the opening piece of all traditional drama is a *nat* dance executed by a female performer. The low status traditionally accorded to actors may have been accentuated by the animistic association: *nat* mediums hold a devalued position in the Buddhist society.

Buddhist theatre Some Burmese scholars hold that the first dramas presented were of *Jataka* stories – that is, tales presenting prior lives of the Buddha. By being reconceived as stories of incarnations of the historical Buddha, plots and tales from older and indigenous sources were incorporated into this tradition as well. *Nibhatkhin* were religious plays on *Jataka* themes. Scenes were presented on cart stages which stopped in various parts of the town. Aside from *nat pwe*, these were probably the main dramatic presentations in the period prior to 1752. Stories were derived from *hawsa*, the storytelling tradition of Burma, in which a reciter told *Jataka* tales. When enacted as *nibhatkhin*, plays included a clown character (*lubyet*) who served the prince and added satirical comment. Like all Southeast Asian clowns, the *lubyet* of today is free to break the story frame as he improvises on any topic. Though he may have come to the *nibhatkhin* from earlier genres, he became ensconced in the Buddhist theatre and associated with the *Jataka* tradition. Because *Jataka* were important themes, classical drama as a whole was called *zat pwe* (literally, '*Jataka* show') and the name was retained even after the repertoire widened to include historical episodes and legends.

Tradition relates that the now rare puppet show, *yokthe pwe*, became the first non-devotional format for the presentation of *Jataka*, and that the repertoire and movements of the MARIONETTES were later emulated by human dancers. Puppet performances of *Jataka* stories were common in the reign of King Bowpaya (1782–1819) when a court minister assigned to oversee theatrical activities gave the form considerable support. Some scholars think puppetry may only have been developed in this era, under the influence of Siamese puppeteers. But the use of marionettes (the complex princess puppet could have 60 strings), rather than shadow figures like Thai *nang yai* puppet theatre, and distinctively Burmese pre-play scenes may be evidence to support the Burmese oral tradition of this form's indigenous origin.

Court dance drama The human dance drama emerged under Thai influence (see THAILAND). Scholars believe the major impetus was the capture of the Siamese capital of Ayutthya in 1767 by troops of the Burmese King Hsinbyushin. Siamese court dancers and musicians were taken into exile where they helped develop the indigenous Burmese theatre. Performers modified Siamese dance style, musical instrumentation and plot materials in creating the new art. The relatively high status of these captured performers as compared to *nat* dancers, and the sudden increase in court support of the arts helped raise the status of performance and performers as a whole.

The Thai female group dances probably became the basis for the *yein* Burmese group court dance. Thai MASK dance *khon* with its *Ramayana* repertoire became the model for the Burmese court mask dance, *zat gyi*. The

Burmese, in borrowing the Vishnavite religious epic, considered the hero Rama as a previous incarnation of the Buddha. As in Thai court performance, professional dancers and courtiers mingled in the cast, and ornate COSTUMES and crown-like headdresses adorned the performers who mimed the actions while narrators and chorus sang the text to musical accompaniment.

Soon new texts were introduced: a minister, Myawaddi, created a version of the Panji story called *Inaung* which, like its Thai model titled *Inao*, dwells on the amorous exploits of that Indonesian prince. In the 19th century, court dramas written by U Kyin U and U Pon Nya are the most notable achievements of court literary activity. Their plays abound in political intrigue, murder and betrayal. The Buddhist mistrust of worldly things, the murderous struggle for power that characterizes Burmese history and the malaise in the wake of the first Anglo-Burman war in 1823 combined to create a dark world-view in their writing.

Popular performance As court support waned due to British control in the 1800s, the new dance drama took to the villages. The *History of Thaton* (1877) was typical, reflecting the tensions between hill-tribe Shan and Burmese lowlanders: a *nat* spirit is the reincarnation of a murdered Shan girl who brings reconciliation between her Shan brother and Burmese husband. Saya Yaw's play was immensely successful on stage and page. U Ku, a musician and songwriter, wrote *Baboon Brother and Sister* in the same period, a tale of two children born of the mating of man and beast.

Performers worked as assiduously as writers to seize their audiences' imaginations. Major matinée idols at the turn of the century included Aungbala (d.1910), Sein Kadon and Po Sein. Sein Kadon danced with electric bulbs all over his costume. Po Sein hired two armed English mercenaries to guard the stage. Simultaneously he revolutionized stagecraft. He rejected the traditional, ground-level dancing circle of earlier drama for a raised stage modelled on the puppet platform. He incorporated new Western-influenced techniques in lighting, scenery and story. Such display combined with artistry attracted the masses.

Until recently, a classical *zat pwe* play remained the major offering on a typical theatre programme. The prince, princess, clown and ogre-villain were the staple character types of the performance. But modern troupes have increasingly found that their audiences hunger for *pya zat* plays that contain contemporary events and common characters for their theme. Such plays in recent years have been pushing out the older repertoire.

Troupes include 50–150 performers under the direction of a leading performer who plays the refined male lead. The writer, who generates scripts, and the chief musician, who writes the musical accompaniment, are other important contributors. Major troupes of the late 1970s and early 80s include the Golden Mandalay Troupe (*Shwe-Man-thabin*) led by Bo Win, noted for his romantic performances, Golden Mandalay (*Shwe-Man*) led by Kyaw Aung, and Capital (*Myo-daw*) directed by Thein-Aung, which specialize in modern plays. The Great Sein Troupe (*Sein-Maha-thabin*) carries on the tradition of excellence begun by Po Sein. Each town will have a troupe, and large cities two or three. Troupes tour to the surrounding countryside, and major groups tour nationally. Insurgency and political instability in the last 20 years, however, have impeded their free movement. Young performers traditionally were trained in the troupe, but since independence Burma's Government Department of Performing Arts has founded two training schools at Rangoon and Mandalay.

The show is presented in a thatched enclosure built for the occasion – only in major cities are there permanent structures or actual enclosed theatres to utilize. Audience members bring rugs to sit on and a pavilion may seat 700. In addition to watching, viewers eat or nap during the show.

Theatrical preliminaries begin at 9 p.m. and the programme continues until dawn. A typical programme begins with a solo *nat* dance, followed by an *opaya* ('opera') which is usually a *Jataka* tale using classical music sung in a modern mode. This is followed by a *pya zat*, written by the troupe playwright, which generally takes contemporary life as its theme. In recent years this part of the programme has enjoyed increased audience popularity. Next comes a *thay-tha-yot-hpaw*, which literally means 'the performance to display the song'. For about 30 minutes actors MIME the story of a song. The featured play, traditionally a *zat* in classical dance style, occupies the final major spot in the programme. *Jataka*, historical, or mythical materials are dealt with in this story, and the writer may take liberties to make the material significant to his audience. A plot, for example, may deal with the efforts of three Shan princes to win over the Mongols, a reference to the current need for unity against insurgents.

The major roles in a *zat* remain constant: heroes, princesses, clowns and ogres–villains. Long sequences of song and dance by the major characters, or comic improvisations by the clowns, punctuate the flow of dramatic events. According to anthropologist Ward Keeler, who did field work in 1988, the story may almost disappear and the presentation resemble *anyein pwe* with its short sequences of acts and songs. The pattern arises from the original theatrical impulse and continued theatrical taste of Burma: dance, song and clowning have more seniority than drama. (See also ASIAN AND PACIFIC ISLAND THEATRE.) KF

See: J. R. Brandon (ed.), *The Cambridge Guide to Asian Theatre*, Cambridge, 1993.

Burns, George [Nathan Birnbaum] 1896– and **Gracie Allen** [Grace Ethel Cecile Rosalie Allen] 1895–1964 Burns and Allen were the paradigm of American male–female double acts, his wry underplaying setting in relief her staccato dizziness. Burns had been a trick roller-skater, dance teacher and song-and-dance man in VAUDEVILLE; Allen entered show business as a child in an Irish sisters act. They teamed up in 1923 and married in 1926, Burns playing the quizzical straight man to her Dumb Dora. 'Lamb Chops', one version of their cross-talk act, was signed to a six-year contract in the KEITH theatres (1926–32). They had their own radio show (1932–49) and moved successfully to television. After Allen's retirement in 1958, Burns, wielding his omnipresent cigar, continued to perform, a high point being his Carnegie Hall recital in 1976. LS

burrakatha Popular form of Indian narrative entertainment, especially in the rural areas of the state of Andhra Pradesh. The form is thought to have been derived from bands of roving minstrels (*jangam*) who sang the praise of the god Shiva as they travelled the rural areas in ancient times. When listeners' social and religious affiliations shifted, the minstrels responded by absorbing secular materials into their shows.

Burrakatha's predecessor was known as *jangam katha*, literally, 'stories of the *jangam*'. In this theatrical form, a storyteller, accompanied by his wife, gave recitals of two or three days' duration. He sang, danced and recited before the people of a village under the patronage of a village elder. At some undetermined point in its history, perhaps in the early 20th century, *burrakatha* evolved from these beginnings.

The term *burra* refers to *tambura*, a stringed instrument worn across the right shoulder of the performer. *Katha* means a story and the main performer (*kathakudu*) plays the *tambura* with his right hand as he dances rhythmically forward and back on the stage while reciting a story. The performer also wears, over his right thumb, a hollow ring with metal balls inside and holds a similar metal ring in the palm of his hand. With the rings, he beats the basic tempo of the songs. At regular intervals during the narration, he addresses and responds to his co-performers, two drummers who play two-headed earthen drums (*dakki*). The drums produce a distinctly metallic sound to accentuate the songs and are regarded as an indispensable ingredient of *burrakatha* performance.

The drummer to the right of the performer is known as the *rajkiya*. He comments on contemporary political and social issues even if the story concerns historical or mythological events. The drummer to his left, the *hasyam*, cracks jokes and provides comic relief.

Performance begins in the evening with devotional songs in praise of various celestial beings. Then the performer introduces the main story by establishing the place, time and historical context of the action. During this section the *rajkiya* and *hasyam* repeat the refrain of the narrative. When the introduction is concluded, the main plot begins in which all three individuals take an active role assuming various characters in the incidents, as well as providing narrative bridges between incidents. Dance, recitation, song and enactment of scenes provide variation within a strong narrative line. Generally a story continues for two to three hours. A longer work may be serialized into several consecutive evenings.

Burrakatha stories fall into three categories – mythological, historical and sociopolitical. Although the form was originally improvised, today popular stories have been written down and committed to memory by performers.

In the 1940s, the Indian People's Theatre Association (IPTA), then closely associated with the Communist Party of India, used rural forms of theatre throughout INDIA as a vehicle to convey its political and social message. In the state of Andhra Pradesh, the Praja Natak Mandali revised *burrakatha* in order to reach vast numbers of voters. Soon other political parties followed suit. Today *burrakatha* troupes are used by a wide range of political organizations and also by the state and central government as a medium of traditional communication to attract members.

Although communist organizations maintain devoted *burrakatha* performers who believe in their political ideology, most artists are politically neutral and willing to work for anyone who wants them to convey social and political ideas through *burrakatha*, provided the price is right. Today more than 200 troupes of artists bring *burrakatha* to rural and urban audiences of Andhra Pradesh. Many derive their full livelihood from performance and a few have become celebrities.   FaR

Burrows, Abe [Abram S.] 1910–85 American playwright, librettist, 'play doctor' and director. Born in New York City, Burrows moved to Hollywood in 1939 and divided his time between these two entertainment centres for the rest of his life. Following a successful career in radio (he was the chief writer for 'Duffy's Tavern', for example), he first scored as a playwright in 1950 by co-authoring *Guys and Dolls* with Jo Swerling and FRANK LOESSER. This success (Tony, New York Drama Critics' Circle Award) propelled him during the next decade into several assignments as lyricist or librettist for MUSICALS, including *Three Wishes for Jamie* (1952), *Can-Can* (1953), *Silk Stockings* (1955), *Say, Darling* (1958), *First Impressions* (1959) and *How to Succeed in Business without Really Trying* (1961; Tony, Pulitzer Prize). He also adapted *Cactus Flower* from a French COMEDY by Barillet and Gredy for a successful 1965 BROADWAY production. He made his debut as a director with *Can-Can*, and soon became known for his ability to infuse stage comedies with the kind of wit and gentle humour that characterized his personality and allowed him to work harmoniously with testy writers when called upon as an unbilled 'doctor' for shows in trouble. In 1991 a theatre at New York University was named after him. LDC

Burstyn, Ellen [Edna Rae Gillooly] 1932– American actress, past president of the Actors' Equity Association (1982–5) and former artistic director of the ACTORS STUDIO. Once a showgirl on Jackie Gleason's television show and now a champion of women's status in American film and theatre, Burstyn, who has long striven to play roles that intrigued her irrespective of their size, has played significant parts in plays as disparate as *Same Time, Next Year* (1975, Tony), *84 Charing Cross Road* (1982), *Driving Miss Daisy* (1988), *Shirley Valentine* (1989) and *Shimada* (1992). She won an Academy Award for her sensitive portrayal in *Alice Doesn't Live Here Anymore* (1974).   DBW

Burton, Richard (Jenkins) 1925–84 Welsh actor. Burton's early work for the stage, in productions of FRY's *The Lady's Not for Burning* (1949) and *Hamlet* at the OLD VIC in 1953 amongst others, established him as one of the most brilliant actors of his generation. He abandoned the stage for a life of film stardom, which meant that his remarkable talent was never fully realized.   MB

Burton, William E(vans) 1804–60 British-born actor and manager who ran one of the best stock companies (see STOCK COMPANY) in the USA, earning at the same time the reputation, according to critic Laurence Hutton, as the 'funniest man who ever lived'. Burton's first professional appearance was in 1831 at London's Pavilion Theatre, followed the next year by an engagement opposite EDMUND KEAN at the Theatre Royal, HAYMARKET. In 1834 he made his American debut at the ARCH STREET THEATRE. In 1841 he entered management in New York at the National Theatre, a short-lived appointment because of the destruction by fire of the theatre seven weeks later. He also managed briefly the CHESTNUT and Arch Street Theatres in Philadelphia, the Washington Theatre and the Front Street Theatre in Baltimore. In 1848 he leased Palmo's Opera House (New York), renamed Burton's Chambers Street Theatre, and in 1856, with increasing competition from J. W. WALLACK, moved to the Metropolitan Theatre, BROADWAY, renamed Burton's New Theatre. He withdrew from management in 1858.

Burton's theatres operated successfully during 1848–56 largely without visiting stars, boasting such company members as HENRY PLACIDE, WILLIAM RUFUS BLAKE, GEORGE HOLLAND, Charles Fisher, LESTER WALLACK and JOHN BROUGHAM, who also wrote numerous new pieces for Burton. Audiences, however, came primarily to see Burton himself perform such roles as Bob Acres, Tony Lumpkin, Bottom, Falstaff, and especially Timothy Toodles in his own *The Toodles*; Aminidab Sleek in Morris Barnett's *The Serious Family*, and Captain Cuttle in Brougham's stage version of DICKENS's *Dombey and Son*. His last New York appearance was at NIBLO's Garden in 1859. Burton also wrote plays (non-extant). His biography, by William L. Keese, was published in 1885. DBW

Bury, John 1925– Senior British stage designer, with three major affiliations in his career. For more than ten years immediately after the Second World War he worked with JOAN LITTLEWOOD's Theatre Workshop. From 1963 to 1973 he was chief designer at the Royal Shakespeare Theatre, and from 1973 to 1985 he was head of design at the NATIONAL THEATRE, in addition to freelancing at other theatres in England and abroad. With no formal training in art or design, Bury developed a mode of selective, abstractly treated REALISM, eschewing the consciously decorative and theatrical in favour of stark, large-scale images, and relying on authentic materials rather than the artifices of the scene shop. *The Wars of the Roses* (1963) employed steel for most surfaces and shifted scenes by means of twin, mobile *periaktoi* towers. In later years a conscious sense of form and style has become more apparent: *Tristan und Isolde* (1971), *Amadeus* (1979), *Yonodab* (1985), *Salome* (1988), *Elektra* (1991). Throughout his career Bury has designed his own lighting in order to increase the expressiveness of his sets. JMB

Bush Theatre (London) A leading FRINGE theatre, with a remarkable record in the promotion of new plays and unknown dramatists. It was founded in 1970 by the actor Brian McDermott in the 'social functions' room of a public house. Originally self-financing, it quickly became the venue for many lively touring companies, including the PEOPLE SHOW and LINDSAY KEMP's company, whose hit show, *Flowers*, was premiered at the Bush. In the mid-1970s the Bush Theatre received its first substantial ARTS COUNCIL grants and, under the direction of (among others) the playwright DUSTY HUGHES and the director Simon

Stokes, it evolved into a 'new plays' theatre, specializing in an imaginative use of its black-box auditorium and excelling in its acting standards. Among the many dramatists whose early plays were promoted through the Bush are STEPHEN POLIAKOFF (*Hitting Town, City Sugar*) and TOM KEMPINSKI (*Duet for One*). With Dominic Dromgoole as its artistic director, the Bush has pioneered the work of BILLY ROCHE, producing the premieres of the award-winning Wexford Trilogy (*A Handful of Stars*, 1988; *Poor Beast in the Rain*, 1989; and *Belfry*, 1991). JE

butō Japanese theatre movement. Often referred to as *ankoku butō* or 'dance of darkness', and in Roman transcription *butoh*. Butō originated in the 1950s and 60s with the work of Ohno Kazuo and Hijikata Tatsumi. Maro Akaji brought together *butō* choreography and post-*SHINGEKI* dramaturgy when he founded the first *butō* troupe, Dairakudakan (the Great Camel Battleship), in 1972. Other current troupes are Sankai-juku (literally, Mountain-Ocean School, founded 1975), Byakkosha (literally, White Tiger Brigade, founded 1980) located in Kyoto, and Tanaka Min's Dance School (Mai-juku, founded 1981). The essence of the movement is its attempt to recapture the SHAMANIC basis of the Japanese performing arts and rearticulate it as modern art. DG

Buzo, Alex(ander John) 1944– Australian playwright. His first success was *Norm and Ahmed* (1968), a dialogue between an old Australian and a Pakistani student. His subsequent plays tend to focus on misfit idealists in contemporary suburbia or historical settings; his style, sometimes misconstrued as realism, is a brittle comic-ironic surface with complex subtext and evocative images. His plays include *The Front Room Boys* (1969), *Macquarie*, written while he was resident playwright with Melbourne Theatre Company in 1972–3, *Coralie Lansdowne Says No* (1974), *Martello Towers* (1976), *Makassar Reef* (1978) and *The Marginal Farm* (1984). MW

Byron (George Gordon), Lord 1788–1824 English poet and playwright, who scandalized and excited contemporary England to a degree rivalled only by Napoleon. Byron's interest in the theatre, and his admiration in particular for EDMUND KEAN, can be traced in his *Letters and Journals*. He was even appointed to the committee of London's DRURY LANE in 1815, shortly before the publicity surrounding his separation from his wife drove him out of the country. He wrote all his plays during his Italian exile. There is good reason to doubt his frequent claims that they were not intended for the stage, though his determination to write 'studiously Greek' tragedies was a conscious challenge to English theatrical tradition.

Only *Marino Faliero* was performed in his lifetime, not only at Drury Lane (1821), but also in New York and Paris. MACREADY, who revived it in 1842, had long maintained *Werner*, a gloomy Gothic MELODRAMA which Byron certainly wrote with performance in mind, in his repertoire. IRVING selected *Werner* for a charity matinée at the LYCEUM in 1887. It is Byron's worst play. His best is probably *Sardanapalus*. Macready was the first to stage it, in 1834, but the most famous revival was CHARLES KEAN's at the PRINCESS's in 1853, enriched by the pageantry of

Thomas Grieve's 'historical' sets, based on Layard's *Nineveh and its Remains* (1849). *Manfred*, unmistakably a dramatic poem rather than a play, was wrestled into shape by ALFRED BUNN for performance at COVENT GARDEN in 1834, in a shameless attempt to capitalize on the vogue for witch-drama inspired by Weber's *Der Freischutz*. More surprisingly, SAMUEL PHELPS chose to open his Drury Lane season of 1863 with his version of *Manfred*. *The Two Foscari*, tedious as a poem and clumsy as a play, was first staged by Macready in 1838. *Cain* was directed by STANISLAVSKY for the MOSCOW ART THEATRE in 1920 and transformed by GROTOWSKI in 1960. There is every chance that Byron's plays will be further revived. PT

Byron, H(enry) J(ames) 1834–84 British playwright, actor, theatre manager and journalist, who abandoned legal training when his BURLESQUE version of *Fra Diavolo* (1858) proved a popular success at the Strand Theatre. Over the next seven years, Byron had 40 pieces staged at the Strand and other London theatres, and he continued to write at much the same rate throughout his life. His prodigious punning and irreverent treatment of familiar stories made a distinctive contribution to the development of the British PANTOMIME. (To his burlesque versions of *Cinderella* (1860) and *Aladdin* (1861) we owe the invention of Buttons and Widow Twankey.) In 1865, together with the star of many of his Strand burlesques MARIE WILTON, Byron took on the management of the PRINCE OF WALES'S THEATRE and it was at his instigation that the first of T. W. ROBERTSON's plays was staged there; but he resigned in 1867, when it became clear that Marie Wilton had no further interest in burlesque.

He was, by then, manager of three Liverpool theatres, a venture that ended in bankruptcy in 1868. It was for Liverpool that he wrote *The Lancashire Lass* (1867), a melodrama full of the effects he delighted to burlesque. Other melodramas include *Blow for Blow* (1868) and, in collaboration with BOUCICAULT, *Lost at Sea* (1869). They were less successful than the comedies, *Cyril's Success* (1868) and the phenomenally popular *Our Boys* (1875), which ran for over four years at the Vaudeville Theatre. Byron, who was an indifferent actor, made his London debut in his own *Not Such a Fool as He Looks* (1869), and he continued to make irregular appearances thereafter. More successful was his return to burlesque at the GAIETY. His delightful *The Gaiety Gulliver* (1879), for example, set the pattern for the famous Quartette of NELLIE FARREN, EDWARD TERRY, KATE VAUGHAN and EDWARD ROYCE. PT

cabaret (from the Spanish *caba retta* or 'merry bowl', then the French *cabaret* or tavern) A small-scale entertainment, occasionally improvised, for the presentation of songs, sketches, SATIRES and speeches, usually commenting on social, political or artistic conditions. Strictly an urban form, it originated as an avant-garde amusement for a select audience but later became commercialized for a broader public.

In 1878 Émile Goudeau founded such a club for the Hydropathes (a polyglot pun on *goût d'eau*) at Le Sherry Cobbler in Paris, where poets read their own work. But it was the Chat Noir, a name taken from Poe's tale, that gave the generic term *cabaret artistique* to programmes put on in cafés and pubs. It was founded on 18 November 1881 by the painter Rudolphe Salis, who called it a cabaret because the songs and sketches were set forth like courses on a menu. His Montmartre premises, seating 60 and designed in an antiquarian Louis XIII style, housed not only Friday night poetry readings but elaborate shadow plays, scripted, designed and musically accompanied by leading artists. When it moved to elegant new premises in 1885, the old building was taken over by ARISTIDE BRUANT's Le Mirliton, one of the numerous Montmartre cabarets it inspired. The intimate milieu allowed performers like YVETTE GUILBERT to develop a subtle new manner of delivery and to treat 'naturalistic' subjects.

In Germany, the first true cabaret was the Bunte Bühne (the Motley Stage), a self-styled *Überbrettl* (supergaff) created by Baron Ernst von Wolzogen and Otto Julius Bierbaum in 1901 to offer a superior form of VARIETY show. Its self-conscious artiness led Alfred Kerr to criticize it for philistinism. The same year saw the founding of Berlin's Schall und Rauch (Noise and Smoke) by the young MAX REINHARDT and actors of the DEUTSCHES THEATER; and of Munich's Elf Scharfrichter (Eleven Executioners), where FRANK WEDEKIND sang his own macabre ditties to guitar accompaniment. The writers and artists connected with the satirical journal *Simplicissimus* performed at the homonymous cabaret of Kathi Kobus in Munich. These artistic cabarets mixed ballads, art songs, one-act plays, dance, puppet drama and instrumental music in a programme held together by a master of ceremonies. The primary aim was to amuse and to air new fashions in literature.

Similar goals were served in Barcelona at Els Quatre Gats (the Four Cats) and in Cracow at Zielony Balonik (the Green Balloon), evolved from painters' gatherings. In Russia, the associations were more theatrical. Letuchaya Mysh (the Bat) was developed by NIKITA BALIEV from the hilarious 'cabbage parties' held by the MOSCOW ART THEATRE, and rapidly turned into a miniature theatre presenting plays and tableaux based on classic Russian literature and folk art. As the Chauve-Souris it became world-famous after the Revolution. Krivoe Zerkalo (the Crooked Mirror), founded in St Petersburg in 1908, was, under the directorship of NIKOLAI EVREINOV, a house

excelling in PARODY and experimental forms such as monodrama. The most literary of these cabarets was Brodyachaya Sobaka (the Stray Dog, 1913–15), a haunt of futurists (see FUTURISM) and acmeists. It was succeeded by the Prival Komediantov (Comedians' Rest, 1916–19), an intimate theatre whose presiding genius was VSEVOLOD MEYERHOLD.

The most extreme of these artistic playgrounds was the Cabaret Voltaire in Zürich (1916–17), where Hans Arp and Tristan Tzara enunciated dadaism, soon to branch out as an independent art movement. After the First World War, German cabarets grew more political, breeding-grounds for dissent, particularly in Berlin. Kurt Tucholsky coined the term *Kabarett* to describe the newly engaged cabaret, with an ensemble company and a programme founded on a given theme (in German, *Cabaret* suggests a less structured series of solo numbers). They included Trude Hesterberg's Wilde Bühne (Wild Stage, 1921), the Kabarett der Komiker (Comedians' Cabaret, 1924), the anti-Fascist Katakombe (Catacombs, 1929) of WERNER FINCK, and Friedrich Hollaender's Tingel-Tangel (1930; see TINGELTANGEL). Although these did not always pack the political punch they promised, by 1935 the Nazis had banned cabaret. Some performers, like Finck, were sent to concentration camps; others emigrated to carry on exile cabarets, such as the Pfeffer-Mühle (Pepper-Mill) of Klaus and Erika Mann and Therese Giehse (1933).

Post-war cabaret in Germany, both East and West, tried hard to renew its political activity. There was a tendency towards carefully structured programmes and precise staging at Munich's Schaubude (Show-Booth), Düsseldorf's Kom(m)ödchen (the Commody) and Munich's Lach- und Schiessgesellschaft (Laugh and Shooting Society). But they, like West Berlin's Stachelschweine (Porcupine, founded 1949), found it hard to compete with television; and the East Berlin cabarets had to direct their satire exclusively at foreign targets. In times of political turmoil they proved to be less pungent than street theatre and AGIT-PROP groups.

In the English-speaking world, cabaret was equated with nightclubs until the 1960s, when Chicago's Second City emphasized improvisation and devised sketches before the audience's eyes. It spawned a shoal of imitations, such as San Francisco's the Premise and Boston's the Proposition, manned by university graduates. Following the highly successful run of the REVUE *Beyond the Fringe*, the Establishment (1961), an after-hours club in London, tried to maintain the atmosphere of irreverence.

Recent developments include comedy clubs where untried performers air their material before uncritical audiences at little cost to the management. (This phenomenon had been foreshadowed in Berlin in 1926 by the Cabaret of the Nameless, where amateurs made fools of themselves.) The haphazard nature of the enterprise is a far cry from the programmatic intentions of the artistic cabaret. More in line with the avant-garde tradition has been the short-lived New Wave Vaudeville, a lunatic musical assemblage deriving from punk rock. LS

See: L. Appignanesi, *The Cabaret*, London, 1975; K. Budzinski, *Pfeffer ins Getriebe*, Munich, 1984; R. Hösch, *Kabarett von gestern und heute*, Berlin, 1967; P. Jelavich, *Berlin Cabaret*, Cambridge, Mass., 1993; L. Richard, *Cabaret, cabarets: Origines et décadence*, Paris, 1991; L. Senelick, *Cabaret Performance: Europe 1890–1940*, 2 vols., New York, 1989, 1992.

Cabrujas, José Ignacio 1937– Venezuelan playwright and director. One-third of the Venezuelan 'Holy Trinity' (with CHALBAUD and CHOCRÓN), Cabrujas made his start with the theatre group of the Central University in 1956. Until he joined the NUEVO GRUPO (New Group) in 1967, he participated as an actor, director and writer with various groups and was a founding member of the Teatro Arte de Caracas (Art Theatre of Caracas) in 1961. A committed writer with multiple talents, he composed for the New Group (which closed in 1988) such plays as *Profundo* (*Deep*, 1970), *Acto cultural* (*Cultural Act*, 1976) and *El día que me quieras* (*The Day You Love Me*, 1979), the latter an enormously popular play that intermixes the Argentine tangos of Carlos Gardel with the Marxist movement of the 1930s. He has won many prizes for acting and directing, and since the early 60s has written and adapted for film as well. Other plays include *Los insurgentes* (*The Insurgents*, 1961), *El extraño viaje de Simón el malo* (*The Strange Voyage of Simon the Evil*, 1962) and *Fiésole* (1967). His *El americano ilustrado* (*The Illustrious American*, 1988), based on the 19th-century Venezuelan president Guzmán Blanco, brought mixed reviews. GW

Caecilius Statius d.168 BC? The leading Roman comic playwright in the period between PLAUTUS and TERENCE; considered by some critics the best of all writers of Roman COMEDY. One of the prologues to Terence's *Hecyra* says that his work was unpopular until championed by Turpio, later Terence's own patron. This should imply that Caecilius, like Terence, cultivated Greek refinement; but the surviving fragments display a thoroughly Plautine exuberance. ALB

café chantant, café concert The leading French VARIETY entertainment of the 19th century. The first musical taverns that sprang up along the Parisian boulevards in the 1770s were called *musicos*, from the Dutch; their growth was fostered during the Revolution by a decree of the National Assembly which gave theatres total licence, and they proliferated around the Palais-Royal and the Boulevard du Temple, becoming so popular that the singer Déduit of the Café Yon was dubbed the *chansonnier national*. When theatrical freedom was suppressed under the First Empire, these cafés were supplanted by summer theatres along the Champs Élysées; they spread rapidly and by 1850 there were some 200 in Paris alone. However, by law, their actors had the status of fairground performers, were not allowed to perform in stage costume (until 1867), and had to pass the hat personally once or twice a night.

These open-air *cafés chantants*, which popularized the *vaudeville* traditions of the French stage, multiplied under the Second Empire, but when the Boulevard du Temple and its cheap theatres were torn down they were replaced by *cafés concerts*, long rooms with a high stage, where popular performances combined with smoking and drinking were accessible to small budgets. The decline of the public dance-halls also contributed to their proliferation. The *caf' conc'*, as it was known, specialized in romantic ballads, erotic innuendo and *scies* or catchy, nonsensical choruses. Between 1870 and 1914 there were as many *caf' conc's* in Paris as there are now cinemas. The most important were the Eldorado and the Alcazar, which showcased the talents of THÉRÉSA, JUDIC, PAULUS, POLIN, Dranem and MAYOL, among others. The types of performers included the 'comic trooper', the 'dude' or *gommeux*, the 'naturalistic' singer of urban low life, and the sentimental balladeer.

A decree of 1864 allowed some of these houses to become *cafés spectacles*, blending songs with FARCES and OPERETTAS, and by the turn of the century the largest had taken on the English name of 'MUSIC-HALLS'. The first was Joseph Oller's Olympia (1893) which, under Jacques-Charles's management, launched MISTINGUETT and introduced American jazz. The music-hall, which dominated the scene by the end of the First World War, banned smoking and drinking from the auditorium; it still offered a central role to song, but this became increasingly the *tour de chant*, a recital by a single performer – e.g. Georgius, Fréhel and, later, PIAF. In 1949 the historian Romi founded a nostalgic, amateur *caf' conc'*, but it had scant success. LS

Caffe Cino (New York City) The USA's Ur theatre of the OFF-OFF BROADWAY movement. Joseph Cino, a former dancer, opened his coffee-house on Cornelia Street in Greenwich Village in December 1958. Soon local poets were doing readings and actors were performing scenes. While the first play presented was a condensed version of OSCAR WILDE's *The Importance of Being Earnest*, a new generation of dramatists whose sensibilities were at odds with the commercial mainstream soon made the Cino's 8 × 8-ft stage their home, paying the expenses of their brief runs by passing the hat. Robert Patrick, Paul Foster, Tom Eyen, LANFORD WILSON, Robert Heide, MARIA IRENE FORNÉS, William M. Hoffman, Megan Terry, Leonard Melfi, Jeff Weiss, JOHN GUARE and JEAN-CLAUDE VAN ITALLIE were among the regulars whose plays Joe Cino introduced with a whoosh of steam from the espresso machine as he swirled a black thrift-shop cape. While Cino imposed no artistic criteria, the quintessential Caffe Cino playwright was H.M. Koutoukas, whose plays had a tacky, high-camp glamour suited to an atmosphere that Patrick describes as 'a cross between Lourdes and Sodom'. The Cino burned down on Ash Wednesday, 1965. Although it did reopen, Joe Cino committed suicide under the influence of drugs in 1967. *Village Voice* critic Michael Smith tried to keep the coffee-house going for a while, but the spirit had died with Cino, the first Off-Off Broadway impresario. CLJ

Caigniez, L. C. 1762–1842 French dramatist. Born into a legal family which suffered at the Revolution, Caigniez went to Paris in 1798 and had his first play, *La Forêt enchantée* (*The Enchanted Forest*), a fairy extravaganza, performed at the Gaîté in 1799. The MELODRAMA was the new popular genre, and the one in which he would excel. In 1802 his *Jugement de Salomon* (*The Judgement of Solomon*) ran for over 300 performances at the Ambigu (see BOULEVARD). He followed it with *Le Triomphe de David* (*The Triumph of King David*, 1805) and then turned to the type of play favoured by PIXÉRÉCOURT, *La Forêt d'Hermanstadt, ou La Fausse Épouse* (*The Forest of Hermanstadt, or The False Wife*), set in a brigand-ridden Bulgaria and employing the souterrains and other devices of the early melodrama. *L'Illustre Aveugle* (*The Illustrious Blind Man*, 1806), exploiting the dramatic possibilities of a physical defect and the device of switched identity, showed him at the height of his powers. His name is linked most closely with *La Pie voleuse, ou La Servante de Palaiseau* (*The Thieving Magpie, or The Servant of Palaiseau*, 1815), a rewriting of a play submitted by an unknown author to the Porte-Saint-Martin, which made the fortune of the theatre director, Saint-Romain, and later provided the plot of Rossini's opera. Caigniez remained popular until about 1830, but died in poverty. JMCC

Calderón de la Barca, Pedro 1600–81 Spanish playwright whose plays, together with those of the older LOPE DE VEGA, dominated Spain's GOLDEN AGE. Born in Madrid, he attended a Jesuit school and the Universities of Alcalá and Salamanca and did military service in Italy and Flanders. In 1636 he was made a Knight of the Order of Santiago.

A skilled dramatic craftsman, Calderón refined and polished the style shaped by Lope de Vega and his followers. He became a priest in 1651 but continued his lifelong dedication to dramatic writing, which resulted in over 100 known *COMEDIAS* and nearly as many *AUTOS SACRAMENTALES*. He wrote comedies and serious plays for the public *CORRALES*, and spectacular productions with the Italian stage architect Cosme Lotti for the Coliseo Theatre of the Buen Retiro during the reigns of Philip IV and Charles II. Calderón continued the polymetric verse structure of the *comedia*, but his poetry reflects the complexities of baroque rhetoric. He favoured the repetition of suggestive images and motifs which engaged the listener both intellectually and emotionally while exploring deeper philosophical meanings.

His most famous play, *La vida es sueño* (*Life Is a Dream*), examines the conflict between free will and predestination, showing ultimately the importance of individual moral responsibility and self-control. A misguided and superstitious king of Poland incarcerates from birth his only son to protect his reign from the terrible predictions of astrologers. Woven into this tale is a secondary plot which tells the story of a dishonoured young woman who dresses as a man to recover her wayward lover and her honour. Among his plays on religious subjects are *El príncipe constante* (*The Constant Prince*), in which the Portuguese Prince Fernando dies rather than surrender Ceuta to the Moslems; *El mágico prodigioso* (*The Wonder-Working Magician*), which relates the legend of Saint Cyprian who sells his soul to Satan for love and is later redeemed through faith; and *Devoción a la cruz* (*Devotion to the Cross*), in which again faith alone ensures salvation.

El Alcalde de Zalamea (*The Mayor of Zalamea*), successfully revived by the Spanish National Classical Theatre Company in 1988, develops the theme of peasant honour in conflict with the abuse of power by social superiors popularized by Lope de Vega. Pedro Crespo, a wealthy farmer, must deal with the kidnapping and rape of his daughter by a visiting captain. The latter, confident of his impunity, refuses to marry the woman and is killed. Crespo is pardoned and the dishonoured daughter retires to a convent.

A trilogy of wife-murder plays has identified Calderón closely with Spanish concepts of honour and tragedy. *El médico de su honra* (*The Physician of his Honour*), *A secreto agravio secreta venganza* (*Secret Insult, Secret Vengeance*) and *El pintor de su deshonra* (*The Painter of his Own Dishonour*) all show the effects of real or assumed female adultery. In each case the wife is murdered directly or indirectly by the husband to restore honour lost by her infidelity. Although the husbands are pardoned by the king for their terrible personal vengeance, the subtle working-out of the plots shows the generalized destructive effect of such actions.

Several comedies of the cape-and-sword variety have enjoyed recent revivals. His *La dama duende* (*The Phantom Lady*) and *Antes que todo es mi dama* (*My Lady before Anything*) were performed by the Spanish National Classical Theatre Company in 1990 and 1987 respectively. Characterized by complicated and highly structured plots revolving around themes of love, honour and jealousy, they also feature clever female protagonists.

Re-evaluations of Calderón's court dramas reveal a brilliant synthesis of theatrical entertainment and serious political consciousness within the ceremonial context of their performance. Based mainly on classical mythology and performed with spectacular stage effects, these plays and their shorter companion pieces, *LOAS*, *entremeses* and songs, celebrated the glory of the attending Habsburg monarchs while also illustrating their moral and political flaws. *El mayor encanto, amor* (*Love, the Best Delight*, 1635) was based on the Ulysses and Circe story; *Hado y divisa de Leónido y Marfisa* (*Fate and Emblem of Leónido and Marfisa*, 1680) was his last court play.

Calderón enjoyed enormous success and patronage during his lifetime. His intellectual and philosophical depth and superb dramatic poetry and craftsmanship have singled him out as the most read and performed Golden Age author outside of Spain. Rediscovered by the German romantics, he remains popular in Spain and abroad. GROTOWSKI received international acclaim for his versions of *The Constant Prince* in the 1960s, and Calderón's works have entered the repertoire of national theatres in France, England and elsewhere. EJB

Caldwell, James H. 1793–1863 British-born actor-manager, who pioneered the theatre in the Mississippi valley. He made his debut in Manchester, and went to the USA in 1816 to perform in Charleston; but he soon began managing in Kentucky and assembled his own touring company. On New Year's Day, 1824, he opened the Camp Street or AMERICAN THEATRE, the first English-language house in New Orleans and the first US theatre illuminated by gas. Caldwell built theatres for his companies in such cities as Mobile, Nashville and Cincinnati, thus rising to dominate the Mississippi and Ohio river valleys. His success was such that in 1835 he opened the St Charles Theatre with a first-rate company and visiting stars of the highest magnitude. Intense competition with Noah Ludlow and Sol Smith fostered excellent theatre in the area; but in 1837 a financial panic ruined Caldwell, in 1842 the St Charles Theatre burned down, and by 1843 he could no longer successfully compete and so retired from the stage. He held several official positions in New Orleans, fled to New York at the beginning of the Civil War, and died there in 1863.   SMA

Caldwell, Zoë (Ada) 1934– Australian-born actress and director, whose professional debut was with the Union Theatre Company, Stratford-upon-Avon (1958–9); she made her London debut at the Royal Court in 1960. After seasons in Canada and Australia, her US debut occurred in 1963 at the Tyrone Guthrie Theatre in Minneapolis, followed by her New York debut in 1965 as the Prioress in John Whiting's *The Devils*. While remaining active in regional theatre, she is best remembered for the Tony-winning title roles in *Slapstick Tragedy* (1966), *The Prime of Miss Jean Brodie* (1968) and *Medea* (1982). Her directing credits include *An Almost Perfect Person* (1977), *Richard II* (1979), *The Taming of the Shrew* and *Hamlet* (1985), *Park Your Car in Harvard Yard* (1991) and *Vita and Virginia* (1994). In 1988 she assumed the direction of the Glenda Jackson–Christopher Plummer *Macbeth*. After a period teaching in Florida, she returned to the New York stage in Terrence McNally's *A Perfect Ganesh* (1993). A superb technician with great power on stage, she has avoided being typecast, while leaning toward work in the classics. The wife of producer Robert Whitehead, she was awarded the OBE in 1970.   DBW

California Theatre The most respected San Francisco playhouse of its day opened on Bush Street on 18 January 1869 with Bulwer Lytton's *Money* – an apt choice because Bank of California honcho William C. Ralston had bankrolled the luxurious 2400-seat, $250,000 theatre for actors John McCullough and Lawrence Barrett. Under McCullough's extended management, a first-rate stock company supported top guest stars (Modjeska, Edwin Booth, Boucicault) and introduced such innovations to San Francisco as the box set. The theatre's fortunes fell after Ralston's death and McCullough's 1877 departure; it was torn down in 1888. The New California, on the same site, stayed active until the 1906 earthquake, though never recapturing its predecessor's glory.   MBer

Callow, Simon 1949– British actor and director who has worked in a variety of theatrical situations, from the National Theatre (Mozart in Shaffer's *Amadeus*1979) to the innovative Joint Stock theatre company. His book *Being an Actor*, published in 1984, offers a lively and important debate on the relationship between the actor and the director in the contemporary British theatre. In his case, his actor's instincts merge into his directorial ones; and after playing the title role in Goethe's *Faust* in 1988, he directed Willy Russell's *Shirley Valentine* (1988) with Pauline Collins in the West End, and Alan Bennett's one-actor *A Question of Attribution* (1988) for the NT, both great successes. In 1991 he won a Laurence Olivier Award

as Best Director of a Musical, the revival of *Carmen Jones* at the Old Vic; while in 1992 his production of Sharman Macdonald's *Shades*, with Pauline Collins, just failed to repeat their triumph with *Shirley Valentine*.   JE

Calmo, Andrea 1509/10–71 Venetian actor and playwright, considered to be the leading literary influence on the *commedia dell'arte*. The son of a gondolier, he made his reputation playing fussy, amorous old men of the Pantalone type. His six comedies spice the intrigues of the *commedia erudita* with regional dialects, horseplay and comic invention. He is said to have retired in 1560 because pastoral and tragedy were dominating the stage.   LS

căluş Romanian Whitsuntide ritual dance of great semiotic complexity, performed by men who during the performance period abstain from sex and keep normal social contact to a minimum. It has a strong magical element, involving trance and the healing of people possessed by spirits. In one form, prevalent in Muntenia, the dances alternate with short comic plays, led by a paradoxical phallic clown, the 'mute' (he is not silent), on subjects such as money, sex and fighting.   AEG

Calzabigi, Raniero de 1714–95 Italian man of letters, and something of an adventurer, who is principally remembered as Gluck's collaborator. His early works were commended, with some reservation, by Metastasio. Calzabigi went to Paris and, along with Casanova, established a lottery. Arriving in Vienna in about 1761, he there made the acquaintance of Gluck, to whom he supplied three librettos, *Orpheus and Eurydice* (1762), *Alcestis* (1767) and *Paris and Helen* (1769), of which the first two were the basis of Gluck's earliest successful essentially dramatic operas. Calzabigi aimed at the natural expression of genuine feeling and was skilled at keeping his main theme free from excrescences. His aesthetic and Gluck's were identical, and there is much doubt as to how far Gluck's writings on opera are the composer's own work and how far they are unacknowledgedly Calzabigi's. A letter from Gluck to the *Mercure de France* in 1774, in which he comments on the success of his operas, is no doubt genuine. It contains the tribute, 'It is to Signor Calzabigi that the chief praise is due, and if my music has found approbation I think I must gratefully acknowledge that I am indebted to him, since it was he who gave me the opportunity to pour forth my art.'   GH

Camargo, Joracy 1898–1973 Brazilian playwright: a precursor of the reformation of the Brazilian theatre. His career began with the revue, and later shifted to the serious play. A major contribution was *Deus Lhe Pague* (*May God Pay You*, 1932), a play generally considered to mark the beginning of the social theatre in Brazil with its examination of bourgeois values under the microscope of Marx and leftist ideology during the heady years of the 1930s.   GW

Cambodia Cambodia (recently Kampuchea) is a Southeast Asian nation which boasts a refined heritage of performance dating back at least 1700 years. The country of eight million borders on Laos, Thailand and Vietnam.

Ethnic Khmer make up 93 per cent of the population and their performance traditions predominate, though arts of the minority Chinese, Vietnamese, Cham and the ethnically related but culturally distinct hill tribes (called Khmer Loeu) are also found. Since the 13th century Theraveda Buddhism has been the predominant religion, overlaying Hinduism and Mahayana Buddhism. Recently, socialist thought has had an impact on the performing arts.

The first reports of performance are Chinese court records which note that musicians from Funan, an early kingdom of the area, were part of an embassy sent to the Chinese emperor in AD 243. Performance under temple and royal patronage flourished during the Angkor period (9th–15th centuries) with INDIAN and Indonesian influences apparent in the repertoire and performance system. During this time the classical theatre forms of today were created. After 1431, with the sack of Angkor by the Thai, came a decline of Khmer power in the area.

In the 19th century Thai performers were brought in to help restructure Cambodian court performance, and this Thai–Khmer tradition was modified in the 20th century as palace performance developed, until 1970 when the Southeast Asian war and its aftermath disrupted the arts. Something of a renaissance came about in the 1980s.

Khmer arts can be conceptually divided into three categories: (1) traditional village performance; (2) classical court forms; (3) modern popular genres. The village and court forms are part of a single continuum, while the more recently developed popular genres have borrowed significantly from Thai, Malay and Vietnamese models of the last 100 years.

Traditional village performance Village performance corresponds to a general Southeast Asian pattern in which the arts are used for entertainment, social integration and spirit propitiation, sometimes serving more than one of these functions simultaneously. For example, *ayay*, a kind of folk chant inspired by legends, provides both entertainment and courting opportunities. Young men and women form two groups and sing dialogues to the tune of a two-stringed fiddle or zither. Improvisation and satirical comment are encouraged in the form, and simple dance movements are executed. The music quickens as the verbal jousting intensifies. LAOS's *mawlum* and INDONESIA's *ronggeng* traditions show certain affinities with this form.

The *trott* (stag dance) is a genre in the area around Siamreap (Angkor) and Battambang which has both entertainment and ritual functions. Dancers impersonating deer and hunters, accompanied by musicians, go from house to house dancing and collecting payment. The dance is said to end drought and brings luck at the beginning of the new year. The deer is conceived of as a demonic creature, related to the ogre who assumes the guise of a golden deer in the *Ramayana*.

Some performance specialists are found at village level. These include blind musicians and wandering singers, who reinterpret legends to the accompaniment of a *cha pei*, a long-necked lute. Female dancers also perform at village shrines as an invitation to spirits. Once a spirit arrives it will then possess the village spirit-medium. Though none of these village performances represent drama in which an actor impersonates a character in a sustained narrative, they contain mimetic elements and probably contributed elements that were elaborated in the court drama tradition.

Classical court forms Classical court forms include female dance drama (*lakon kabach boran*), shadow play (*nang sbek thom*), and mask dance drama (*lakon khol*). Indigenous, Indian and Indonesian influences were probably important in the creation of these arts a millennium ago, but the current forms are close to THAILAND's *lakon fai nai*, *nang yai* and *khon*, respectively. The term *lakon* (also spelled *lakhon*) means 'play' or 'drama' in both Khmer and Thai. Research has yet to clarify whether Thai shadow play and masked dance were, like the female dance form, first developed in Cambodia. The confusion on this question is exacerbated by the fact that the current Cambodian variants on the ancient arts are only about 150 years old, and were influenced by Thai models in the 19th century.

Indigenous elements probably contributed to the RITUAL importance of performance in Khmer courts. As early as the 7th century, dance was a feature of the funeral rites of kings – a court tradition continued into this century. A palace dance-ritual, a weekly ceremonial salutation to teachers and spirits, was thought to promote good luck. More elaborate ceremonies might be staged to promote rain and fertility; *buong suong* ('paying respect to heavenly spirits') performances were enacted to promote rain and for other ritual purposes. Such rites show the link between performance and communication with the supernatural common in Southeast Asia.

Indian influence shows in the popularity of the *Ramayana* in the repertoire and the primary importance of female dancers. The preference for *Ramayana* materials results from Vaishnavite influence which may have come via Indonesia or Bengal. The Indian temple dancers (*devadasi*), who were ritually married to temple idols and, in Vaishnavite practice, became associated with god-kings, probably formed a model for the Khmer court dancers. The references to female dancers in Cambodia begin as early as AD 611 when there are reports of female dancers being dedicated to Hindu temples. The practice of dedicating performers to temples was continued after Buddhism became the state religion, and the practice was most popular in the reign of Jayavarman VII (1181–?1219) when over 3000 dancers were in residence.

Indonesian practices are believed to have been introduced in 802 when Jayavarman II, the founder of the Khmer kingdom and of the *devaraja* ('god-king') cult, reportedly returned from Sriwijaya, a kingdom in the Malay archipelago. The fact that the major Khmer court arts all have clear counterparts in the Malay world bolsters the belief in this venerable connection. The Javanese (see INDONESIA) semiritual court dance (*bedaya*), puppet-derived forms (*wayang*), and the mask dance (*topeng*) are, like the Khmer court arts, modern versions of ancient forms that linked the ruler with the world of ancestors and spirits, ensuring him godlike power.

Similarly, the Cambodian *pinpeat* orchestra shares many structural features with the *gamelan* ensembles indigenous to the Malay world, probably as a result of borrowing in past ages. It is, however, difficult to prove when and how this interchange occurred, for trade contacts with the Malay Archipelago and MALAYSIAN mainland have persisted over many centuries.

The exact nature of ancient Khmer performance is obscure. Some scholars feel that non-dramatic dances by large groups of women were part of the repertoire. Couple dances by women impersonating a prince and a princess appear ancient as well. One 13th-century inscription, cited by Cravath, indicates that a *Jataka* (Buddhist birth-story) was played by female performers, but such reference to dance drama is rare in the Angkor period. Written evidence for shadow play and masked dance is completely lacking. This leads some scholars to feel that narrative drama was not highly developed during the Angkor period. Indeed, to the present, genres that are thought to be the oldest female dance forms of the Malay and Indonesian courts are largely non-dramatic. It is possible that the common dramatic repertoire of Khmer and Thai performance largely evolved in the more secular environment of the Thai courts after Angkor's decline beginning in 1431. Many of the tales currently in the repertoire may first have come from Thai sources.

Information concerning Khmer court arts is scant from the 15th century to the mid-19th century, when, according to the oral tradition, King Ang Duong directed a reformation of the arts. The practice of court performers prior to that time is said to have been close to village dance, as in *ayay*, described above. The King, who had spent time in the Thai court, directed that the movement, especially of male dancers, be made more rounded and less jerky. Elbows that were held stiffly at shoulder level were lowered. Meanwhile, COSTUMES were modelled on those of the Thai court. Whether these refinements were, as Cambodian oral tradition reports, a return to the past or the expropriation of Thai models can be debated. The innovations do, however, explain the close similarities between Khmer and Thai arts in the present era. Current performance of female dance drama, puppetry, and mask dance derives from this period.

The *lakon kabach boran*, the dance of the palace ladies, is the most important of the court arts. The performers were wives, concubines or relatives of the ruler. A new troupe would normally be organized at the beginning of each ruler's reign, under the direction of a matron appointed by the king. The women would be trained for a single role – male, female, monkey or ogre – according to their body type. Prior to the last generation, men would not be allowed to appear with the ladies. Exceptions to this rule were the man who played the hermit role and had certain ritual functions in training and graduating dancers, and the men who played clown roles (cf. Thailand's *lakon fai nai*, and Malaysia's *mak yong*). Floor patterns in the female dance tend toward circles and lines, and the hand gestures are, like most Southeast Asian systems, abstract or pantomimic rather than the gesture language of Indian *mudras*.

The repertoire of the female court dance, which came to be known in the West as the Royal Cambodian Ballet, is currently composed of about 60 *robam* ('pure dance pieces') and 40 *roeung* ('dance dramas'). In the dance dramas, actresses mime the action as an offstage chorus of female singers delivers the text to *pinpeat* musical accompaniment. The stories performed include episodes from the *Reamker*, the Cambodian version of the *Ramayana*, the Javanese *Panji* cycle, the tale of *Anrudh* (a grandson of Krishna), *Jataka* stories including the tale of the bird-woman, *Manora*, and the conch prince, *Preah Sang*, and local legends. The tales typically focus on the struggle of the noble hero with an ogrely villain for the love of a woman. An episode of great popularity is the story of *Sovann Macha*, a fish queen who is courted by Hanuman, the monkey general leading Rama's troops. The artists trained and performed in the palace, dancing when required by the king, and commoners would not normally be allowed to view presentations. But the traditional system has been modified considerably in the last generations.

The history of the dance in the last 100 years is an abstract of the struggle for royal autonomy during the colonial era. The kings strove to maintain the female dance during the French protectorate, inaugurated in 1863, but found the allowances accorded the monarch were not sufficient to support the 500-dancer entourage of former times. By 1904, 100 dancers remained and about half accompanied King Sisowath to Europe to perform at the Marseilles exhibition in 1906. European acclaim followed, but the decay in numbers continued as dancers left the palace to go to school or marry. Frenchmen like George Groslier, who as art director of the colony pleaded for support for the troupe, became significant in fostering the dance. In 1928 the Palace administration and French proponents agreed to place the troupe under the University of Fine Arts (École des Beaux Arts). During the 1930s the French authorities gave support to a non-court troupe organized by a former dancer, Say Sangvann, whose dancers, unlike the royal troupe, were willing to appear in French salons. It was a sign of the times that dance was taught and performed outside the palace. The magico-religious significance of the art as a symbol of the potent ruler was on the wane, and kings were forced to quibble about allowances for dance costumes with French civil servants.

Yet the politics of the period were, in a sense, reflective of the tradition of female dance in Cambodia – he who controlled the dance controlled the nation. When the ruler was no longer powerful enough to support his dancers and prevent performance outside the palace, his arts were expropriated by the new rulers, the French.

The former queen mother, Kossamak, was instrumental in a renaissance of the court troupe, which flourished during the reign of her son, Prince Norodom Sihanouk (1922–), who ascended the throne in 1941 and reigned until he was set aside by the Lon Nol government in 1970. She regained control of the dance and effectively revamped the programme, venues and costuming. The queen mother made the royal dancers a significant feature in the emerging culture politics of modern Cambodia.

In the 1960s Sihanouk's daughter Bopha Devi was the major dancer in the group, and, following Kossamak's innovations, the Royal Cambodian Ballet performed at capitals around the world on cultural missions and for visiting heads of state in Cambodia. The 254 members of the troupe (2 male dance teachers, 17 female dance teachers, 6 prime dancers, 25 corps de ballet, 160 pupils, 30 dressers, costumers, jewellery persons and make-up artists, 10 singers, and 4 male clowns) in 1962 show that in this era *lakon kabach boran* was again an important attribute of the Khmer king's power.

Of lesser significance to the Khmer court were the two male forms, the shadow play (see SHADOW PUPPETS) and the masked dance. *Nang sbek thom* shadow play involves 10 manipulators dancing with large leather panels portraying multi-person scenes of the *Ramayana* story in front of and behind a white screen, while a narrator tells the story to *pinpeat* musical accompaniment. In addition to providing entertainment and edification, some performances might be done to promote rain or cure epidemics. A single troupe was operating in Siam Reap in the early 1970s, and the form had considerable support during the late 1980s from Chheng Phon, Minister of Culture. The form can be compared to the Thai *nang yai*, and the curative powers of performance, the use of a percussive orchestra and the strategy of depicting heroic action in a theatre of character types make it analogous to the *wayang* tradition of Indonesia and Malaysia. The mask dance *lakon khol* is believed to have developed from the shadow play, as puppeteers exchanged their leather panels for MASKS and crown headdresses. The footwork of the dancers is derived from the dance of the puppet manipulators, and the dramatic and musical repertoire corresponds to the shadow theatre.

In the early 1970s Prince Sihanouk was deposed, and in the following 20 years the court arts were attenuated. After the advent of the Khmer Rouge government in 1975 many dancers fled the country or were killed. With the takeover of the country in 1979 by a Vietnamese-backed government, classical dance experienced some resurgence. Performers adapted lyrics to express themes relevant to the current socialist government. Outside of Cambodia training continued in refugee camps in Thailand, and what had been a palace prerogative began thus to reach a new part of the Khmer population. But as Khmer have moved overseas, the art has been difficult to maintain, since the expatriates' life in Western society makes it virtually impossible to maintain the kind of daily, intensive rehearsal needed for the dance to flourish. In Paris a group operates under Bopha Devi's direction and a Maryland-based group in the United States toured that nation in 1984.

Modern popular forms Cambodian popular forms borrow from foreign genres, adapting the performances to suit Khmer tastes. Arts like *yike*, *lakon bassac*, *ayang*, and spoken drama have this mixed heritage.

Yike developed in response to tours by Malay *bang-sawan* troupes in the late 19th century. The art also parallels *likay* of Thailand in its mixture of classical and modern features. The introduction of wing-and-drop scenery, the rough approximation of classical dance used for entrances and exits, the humorous burlesques of classical legends and the introduction of new plots coupled with witty improvisation by performers, helped *yike* gain wide popularity among the populace. Performances were even staged at court.

Lakon bassac combines elements borrowed from Vietnamese theatre with indigenous techniques. The form developed in the 19th century in the Bassac river region in VIETNAM, where Khmer peoples live, and spread to Cambodia. It mixes traditional Cambodian features and elements of the Chinese-influenced Vietnamese theatre. Brandon notes that *pinpeat* music may play in one scene and a Chinese two-stringed fiddle in the next; while one costume will seem fit for a classical Khmer dance, the next may resemble a Chinese opera outfit.

A third popular form is *ayang* (or *nang kalun*), a shadow-puppet theatre related to the *nang talung* of Thailand. Both the Khmer and Thai shadow genres derive from the Indonesian/Malay *wayang* tradition, but *ayang* is unusual in its use of multiple puppeteers. Stories from the *Reamker* and *Jataka* tradition can be presented, and the buffoonery of the clown endears the form to the peasant audience.

A final form that has developed in the 20th century is spoken Western drama, based on French models. Prince Sihanouk himself wrote and produced plays in this genre. The fate and the future of all Khmer performance art awaits the stabilization of the country.

The current situation: 1980s–1990s When performers returned to Phnom Penh to re-establish the performing arts after the fall of the Khmer Rouge regime in 1979, they discovered that nearly 90 per cent of their professional colleagues (dancers, musicians, actors and playwrights) had perished during the four years of murderous Khmer Rouge rule or had fled overseas. Virtually all documents on performance – libraries and photographs – had been destroyed. Current efforts, guided by former Minister of Culture Chheng Phon, are directed to rebuilding shattered professional troupes and to recruiting and training a new generation to replace the nation's appalling artistic loss. The National Department of Arts, Ministry of Culture, under the direction of Pich Tum Kravel, actor and playwright, and Hang Sot, musician, operates two theatres in Phnom Penh, the Bassac and Chatomuk. Ten professional theatrical troupes are supported by the Department, including troupes devoted to *lakon khol*, *lakon mahori*, *nang sbek thom*, *yike*, *lakon bassac*, modern drama, and *apee*, a newly revived genre that mixes *yike* and classical dance. The Department's *lakon kabach boran* troupe, to which many former members of the Royal Ballet now belong, performs its classical dance-drama repertory for state occasions, ceremonies and festivals as in the past, as well as for tourists and the general public. It has toured abroad, to England and Italy (1990) and Thailand and Hong Kong (1992). To stimulate professional and amateur groups, the Department sponsors yearly festivals in Phnom Penh. The Municipality of Phnom Penh supports three professional troupes: dance, modern drama, and *lakon bassac*.

Young performers are trained in classical performance (classical dance drama, *lakon bassac*, *yike* and shadow puppetry) at the University of Fine Arts as well as in Khmer folk dance and in modern drama. The dean of the Faculty of Choreographic Arts, Proeung Chhieng, and the chief instructor in the Department of Classical Dance, Mme Chea Samy, are former stars of the Royal Ballet, representing two of the last links with Cambodia's great prewar dance-drama traditions. Students perform in their own theatre and in a rehearsal hall (modelled on the Chan Chhaya Pavilion in the Royal Palace) on the university campus, and have toured with their teachers to India, Japan, eastern Europe and the United States.

Modern spoken drama (*lakon ciet*, 'national drama', or *lakon niyey*, 'spoken drama') began in 1949 with adaptations of short French plays. The National School of Theatre, directed by Peau Yuleng, and its modern drama troupe were established in the 1950s and through the 1960s was extremely active. Training focused on the STANISLAVSKY technique. The national troupe toured with great success through the country, eventually developing into three troupes. A major playwright of spoken drama was Hang Thun Hak, affectionately known as the 'second MOLIÈRE'. There was a conscious effort to educate society and build national culture through spoken drama. In 1964–5 the school and troupes became incorporated into the University of Fine Arts. In 1975 all modern theatre activity ceased when the Khmer Rouge evacuated the cities and made its violent attempt to radically alter Khmer culture and society.

Spoken drama is extremely popular with contemporary audiences. In 1992, in addition to the three Phnom Penh troupes affiliated with the government institutions mentioned above, professional troupes are found in Kandal, Takeo, Prey Veng and Svay Rieng provinces. The Voice of the People radio station has its own modern drama troupe that regularly broadcasts original spoken dramas. Contemporary dramas explore tensions in society – between rich and poor, between the powerful and the powerless – the consequences of these tensions, and ways in which people either overcome their material and moral dilemmas, or are defeated by them and learn to suffer with dignity. Pring Sakon, a famous actor teaching at the University of Fine Arts, combines Western and Khmer theatrical forms, following Chheng Phon's belief that 'modern isn't foreign'.

All provincial seats have a theatre, many with resident companies. In 1992 several hundred amateur troupes existed, both in the capital and throughout the country. Most specialize in popular *lakon bassac*, while those in Kampot and Takeo provinces are famous for *yike*. Recently, as video tapes have become the preferred form of entertainment at festivals and ceremonies, the number of amateur troupes has declined. (See also ASIAN AND PACIFIC ISLAND THEATRE.) KF

See: J. R. Brandon (ed.), *The Cambridge Guide to Asian Theatre*, Cambridge, 1993.

Cameroon Cameroon, like Togo, was under German rule between 1814 and 1916 before passing into Franco-British control as a League of Nations mandated territory. The French section became independent in January 1961 and was joined by the British Cameroons ten months later. There is a modern Cameroonian theatre in all three languages: insignificant in German – represented by one play, Alexandre Kuma N'Dumbé's *Kafra-Biatanga* (1973), which was first written in that language – but substantial in the other two.

The modern Cameroonian theatre goes back to the

1940s, but with the exception of GUILLAUME OYONO-MBIA and NICOLE WEREWERE-LIKING it has produced no dramatists of the stature of Ferdinand Oyono in the novel, let alone of Mongo Beti. It is basically a comic theatre: refreshingly undidactic and very playable in Oyono-Mbia's works, Ndedi-Penda's *Le Fusil* (*The Gun*, 1970), Protais Asseng's feminist *Trop c'est trop* (*Enough Is Enough*, 1981) and Stanislas Awona's *Le Chômeur* (*The Unemployed*, 1968), among others.

Although not comparable with the output of the Sahel countries, historical and political drama is also present, exemplified by Paul Tchakouté's *Les Dieux trancheront* (*The Gods Will Decide*, 1971, written under the pseudonym Franz Cayor) and his *Samba* (1980); by Kuma N'Dumbé's *Amilcar Cabral* (1976), Ndam Njoya's *Dairou IV* (1973) and Benjamin Matip's *Laisse-nous bâtir une Afrique debout* (*Allow Us to Build a Strong Africa*, 1979).

Cameroon also had in the 1940s the beginnings of a modern theatre in the local languages: its practitioners included Jean-Baptiste Obama with his *Mbarga Osono* (1943) and Adalbert Owona with *Fada Jean* (*Father Jean*, 1944); and in 1956 an erotic comedy, *Ebudundu*, was staged. But this promise of a popular theatre in the local languages did not materialize. What has emerged, however, since the 1970s is a popular, crowd-pulling theatre that uses colloquial French. It treats topics of concern to the mass of people, and depicts characters sometimes dressed in rags, singing, narrating or dancing out their many adventures. Slapstick and licentious jokes and songs figure prominently. Plays in this genre include *Le Moule cassé* (*The Broken Mould*, 1974) by Zomo Bel Abel, Daniel Ndo's *Le Mariage de Folinka* (*Folinka's Marriage*, 1976), and others, mostly unpublished, by writers such as Dieudonné Afana, Jean-Michel Kankan, Michel Ndi and Dave Moktoi.

Since the mid-1980s, under the influence of Jacqueline Leloup, the Frenchwoman who ran the University of Yaoundé theatre, there have been attempts to found a theatre based on RITUAL, such as Bamiléké funeral and enthronement ceremonies. Examples are Jean-Marie Tueche's *La Succession de Wabo Défo* (*The Succession of Wabo Défo*) and Leloup's *Guéido* (1984), performed at the first Limoges Festival of Francophone Theatre. Other recent plays include: D. Ndachi-Tagne's *Monsieur Handlock, ou le boulanger poétique* (*Mr Handlock, or The Poetic Baker*, 1985); R. Ekossono's *Ainsi s'achève la vie d'un homme* (*So Ends a Man's Life*, 1989); and M.-C. Mbarga's *Les Insatiables* (*The Insatiables*, 1989). The relative weakness of Cameroonian theatre, which has no national company or professional troupes, has been partly blamed on governments which prefer to sponsor activities like football rather than one that is largely devoted to criticizing their pompous and corrupt officials. JCM

See: R. Cornevin, *Le Théâtre en Afrique noire et à Madagascar*, 1970; G. Doho, 'Théâtre et représentation au Cameroun', *Notre Librairie: La Littérature Camérounaise*, 99, Oct./Dec. 1989; C. Mbom, 'Le Théâtre camerounais en pleine mutation', *Notre Librairie*, ibid.; C. Wake, 'Cameroon', in *The Cambridge Guide to World Theatre*, ed. M. Banham, Cambridge, 1988; C. Wake and M. Banham, *African Theatre Today*, London, 1976.

Camp Street Theatre   see AMERICAN THEATRE

Campagnol, Théâtre du French theatre company founded in 1975 by Jean-Claude Penchenat. Its most notable productions have been *David Copperfield* (1977) and *Le Bal* (*The Ball* or *Ballroom*, 1981). The latter relied entirely on gesture, MIME, movement and dance, containing no speech at all. It was filmed by Ettore Scola in 1983. Like the THÉÂTRE DU SOLEIL (which Penchenat had helped to found), it often works through *création collective* and relies on meticulous observation of physical realities. In 1983 it became an official Centre Dramatique, based in south Paris.   DB

Campbell, Bartley 1843–88 American playwright. Born in a Pittsburgh suburb and privately educated, Campbell turned to journalism and then to playwriting. The first of his 35 plays was *Through Fire* (1871). During 1872–6 he wrote and staged plays for R. M. Hooley in Chicago. From 1876 until his mental breakdown in 1885 he was America's most popular melodramatist. His greatest success was the mining camp MELODRAMA *My Partner* (1879), which became a starring vehicle for Louis Aldrich as Joe and Charles Parsloe as Wing Lee. Though Parsloe went on to other parts, Aldrich, having purchased the rights to the play for a paltry $10 a performance, played it for the rest of his career. Campbell's other outstanding plays were *The Galley Slave* (1879) and *The White Slave* (1881).   DMCD

Campbell, Ken 1941– British actor, director, clown and playwright. As the leader of the anarchic FRINGE touring group, Ken Campbell's Roadshow, which featured such unlikely acts as the World 'Ferret down Trousers' Competition, Campbell became a popular entertainer around the fringe circuit during the 1960s; but his talents drew him towards writing and directing, with a particular fascination for strange and wonderful tales, including science fiction. *The Great Caper* (1974) speculated about time warps, while in 1976 he adapted with Chris Langham the science fiction novel, *Illuminatus*, for the stage, which ran for seven hours. It was originally presented by the Science Fiction Theatre of Liverpool, but transferred to the NATIONAL THEATRE to open the Cottesloe auditorium in 1977. Its sequel, Neil Oram's *The Warp*, transferred to the Institute of Contemporary Arts in London in 1979. In 1980 Campbell became the artistic director of the Everyman Theatre, Liverpool, for which he adapted and directed KAREL ČAPEK's novel, *The War with the Newts*, later seen at RIVERSIDE STUDIOS in London. His partly improvised monologues, *Recollections of a Furtive Nudist* (1988), have found appreciative audiences in fringe theatres.   JE

Campbell, Mrs Patrick [Beatrice Stella Tanner] 1865–1940 British actress, whose formidable personality sometimes hid or overshadowed her artistry. No more than a minor name before 1893, she became a star when she created the title role in PINERO's *The Second Mrs Tanqueray* (1893) at London's ST JAMES's. Playwrights clamoured to provide her with opportunities to repeat herself as the superficially urbane but secretly passionate *demi-mondaine* – Haddon Chambers with *John-a-Dreams*

(1894), HENRY ARTHUR JONES with *The Masqueraders* (1894) and Pinero again with *The Notorious Mrs Ebbsmith* (1895) among them – but she had higher artistic aspirations than such parts allowed. With JOHNSTON FORBES-ROBERTSON, who loved and encouraged her, she played Juliet (1896), Lady Teazle (1896) and Ophelia (1897). Her performances were considered dangerously modern against the classical purity of Forbes-Robertson. As Macbeth and Lady Macbeth (1897), they were attacked in England and applauded on a German tour. Mrs Patrick Campbell had made it a condition of her agreement to tour that she would stage the first English production of MAETERLINCK's *Pelléas and Mélisande* on her return to London in 1897. Forbes-Robertson, who thought the play morbid, gave Pelléas to JOHN MARTIN-HARVEY. Mélisande became Mrs Campbell's favourite part. She even played Mélisande in French to SARAH BERNHARDT's Pelléas (1904).

It was a dangerous fondness for operatic roles that marred her career at its height and that spoiled her attempts at IBSEN (Rita in *Little Eyolf* (1896) and the title role in *Hedda Gabler* (1907)). SHAW, who recognized in her a supremacy in COMEDY, wrote *Caesar and Cleopatra* for her and Forbes-Robertson, but she never performed it. Instead, nearing 50, she created Eliza Doolittle in *Pygmalion* (1914), the last and greatest scandal of her London career.   PT

Campion, Thomas 1567–1620 English poet and musician, best remembered as a writer of songs, though his versatility is exemplified also by his studies of poetic theory, the law and medicine. Campion's theatrical importance rests on his composition of words and music for three Jacobean MASQUES, *Lord Hayes' Masque* (1607), the *Lords' Masque* and the *Squires' Masque* (both 1613).   PT

Campistron, Jean Galbert de 1656–1723 French dramatist whose work marks a decline in the power and rigour of 17th-century classical TRAGEDY. His tragic situations, best exemplified by *Tiridate* (1691), are too often vitiated by a treatment which is tame and insipid, though occasionally affecting in an elegantly melancholy vein, and seem but a pale imitation of RACINE and PIERRE CORNEILLE. He also wrote comedies and the text of two *tragédies en musique* for LULLY. He was sufficiently esteemed in his day to be admitted to the Académie-Française in 1701.   DR

Camus, Albert 1913–60 French novelist, essayist, playwright and director. Camus's plays, which were a significant part of the vigorous revival of French theatre following the Second World War, no longer seem as innovative as they did in the 1940s and 1950s. His reputation rested largely on *Le Malentendu* (*Cross-Purpose*, 1944) and *Caligula* (1945), in which GÉRARD PHILIPE played the title role. But *Les Justes* (*The Just*, 1949) confirmed Camus's tendency to write extended debates rather than true dramatic actions. He had run an amateur theatre company in Algiers before the war and he directed his own adaptations of works by Faulkner and Dostoevsky in Paris in the 1950s; these were successful with audiences and critics alike. He appreciated the team work involved in theatre production and once said that the only places he felt really happy were the football field and the theatre.   DB

Canada: 1 English
The colonial theatre to 1879 The first record of theatrical activity in what is now Canada is probably found in Richard Hakluyt's *Principal Navigations*, where Captain Edward Haies reports on his 1583 voyage with Sir Humphrey Gilbert's expedition to Newfoundland that 'we were provided of Musike in good variety: not omitting the least toyes, as Morris dancers, Hobby horsse, and Maylike conceits to delight the Savage people'.

Of course, Canada's native peoples had their own theatrical rites and ceremonies and had had them for many centuries before. These included secret initiation ceremonies and communal performances such as Micmac marriage and funeral RITUALS, the Ojibway war dance, the prairie sun dance, the Cree shaking-tent ceremony, Iroquois false-face curing rituals, Tlingit SHAMANIC displays, the Coast Salish spirit dance and Inuit ritual dramas.

By the time of the arrival of the first Europeans some of these ceremonials had become very elaborate. The most theatrical were those of the Nootka and Kwakiutl Indians of coastal British Columbia. Staged at night and indoors around a huge fire, their ceremonial cycles re-created incidents from clan mythology and visionary encounters between young initiates and supernatural beings. They

were performed by members of dance societies wearing costume and intricately carved wooden MASKS. During the performances, some masks opened to reveal other masks beneath, monsters flew through the air on strings, actors disappeared into tunnels and trap-doors, and voices were transmitted through hollow kelp stems. These were stage effects unsurpassed in the Americas.

The European theatrical tradition had to await the arrival of permanent European settlers. New France was settled early in the 17th century, but it was not until the mid-18th century that we find the first traces of theatrical production in English. In the constant state of war that reigned between England and France in the 18th century it is not surprising that among the first English-speaking residents of Canada were the military garrisons. As a natural consequence, the earliest English theatre was 'garrison theatre', staged by the officers and men for their own diversion and for that of settlers and traders in the vicinity. As the settlements grew larger the military men were often joined by local 'gentlemen amateurs'. The first recorded production of a play in English occurred on 6 January 1744, MOLIÈRE's *Le Misanthrope*, translated and staged by the lieutenant-governor of Nova Scotia, Paul Mascarene.

The first professional troupe to play in English Canada was advertised under the name of the American Company of Comedians led by a Mr Mills and Henry Giffard, who

The Theatre Royal and William's Creek Brigade Hall, Barkerville, British Columbia, 1869.

spent the late summer and early autumn of 1768 in Halifax. But the main source of theatrical entertainment in the colonies continued to be provided by the garrison amateurs, such as the production of *The Suspicious Husband* by 'the gentlemen of the Army and Navy' in 1773. Another garrison production, *Acadius; or, Love in a Calm*, performed in Halifax in 1774, was probably the first English-language play written in Canada. The first play in English by a Canadian-born author, WILLIAM RUFUS BLAKE'S MELODRAMA *Fitzallan*, was staged at the Halifax Theatre on 27 April 1833.

The fall of New France in 1760 brought British military installations and theatricals to Quebec and Montreal, though the population remained overwhelmingly French-speaking. The real development of English Canada did not begin until the American Revolution, especially after 1783 when thousands of United Empire Loyalists fled inhospitable surroundings and made new homes in British North America. The Atlantic colonies grew and prospered with this new wave of immigration, and the first settlements were established in what is now Ontario.

While the earliest performances were given in inns and assembly rooms, soon various associations of garrison amateurs and local theatrical societies fitted up special buildings as playhouses. The first such theatre, the 500-seat Grand Theatre, was constructed under the guidance of the 'Gentlemen of the Navy, Army and Town' in Halifax in 1789. Besides housing garrison performances, it was rented out to other amateurs and to occasional visiting professional companies. More than a hundred different pieces were presented in Halifax in the last 15 years of the 18th century.

As other centres grew, theatrical activity spread to them. The English actor William Moore performed in Nova Scotia in May 1785 and then toured to Quebec. In 1786-7, the company of Moore and Edward Allen provided the first performances in Montreal and Quebec City. Another company, led by a Mr Ormsby, 'from the Theatre Royal, Edinburgh', came from Albany, New York, and acted in Montreal in 1804. We find them again as the first professional company in Newfoundland, appearing in St John's in July 1806, presumably a stop-over on the way back to Britain.

Montreal and Quebec City attracted many visitors. EDMUND KEAN played in Quebec City and Montreal in 1826 and was made an honorary chief by admiring Huron Indians. CHARLES and FANNY KEMBLE appeared in 1833, and W. C. MACREADY in 1844. In Ontario the same pattern held true. In Kingston and Toronto, military and local amateurs performed in improvised settings until the population justified dedicating a building or part of a building to theatrical entertainments. This facility then attracted the strolling professional troupes. Throughout the first half of the 19th century this was the basis for theatre in all of British North America.

Garrison players were usually officers and, consequently, of a relatively elevated social class. The local amateurs were often also leading figures in local society - such as lawyers and merchants. They represented a small coterie in frequent contact with the home country, and imbued with the expected sense of decorum and respectability only slightly marred by unprofessional attempts at female impersonation. It was with such amateurs that CHARLES DICKENS acted during his visit to Montreal in 1842.

The professional companies were a very different story. They were usually small, led by a married couple, and often made up of other couples. Extensive travel in early Canada could only easily be undertaken by water in the summer or by sleigh in the winter. Performers came to Toronto in the spring by way of the Erie Canal, for example, and left in the autumn by way of the Ohio and Mississippi Rivers. When the size of the settlements warranted it, larger companies could come by water, and Saint John, New Brunswick, with the benefit of J.W. Lanergan's Dramatic Lyceum, became a summer home for actors from New York and Boston. E. A. SOTHERN managed a company in Halifax in 1856, 1857, 1858 and 1859.

But transportation difficulties meant that the growing demand for more and larger-scale entertainment could only be satisfied by resident repertory companies. Across the eastern part of the country substantial theatre buildings seating from 750 to 1000 were constructed (Theatre Royal, Quebec City, 1824; Theatre Royal, Montreal, 1825; Royal Lyceum, Toronto, 1849; Saint John Dramatic Lyceum, 1857), and these were owned or leased by managers who engaged good-quality companies for an entire season. J.W. Lanergan in Saint John, John and Kate Buckland in Montreal, and John Nickinson in Toronto established long and close relations with their respective communities. Variety was provided by a constant round of touring stars, who joined these resident companies for a few nights or a few weeks. In Canada the visiting stars were more often British than American, but the supporting company usually came from New York.

The presence of a resident company in the community offered the possibility of local plays being produced. Unfortunately, Canadian poets and writers had insufficient opportunity to become an integral part of the theatre production process, and the number of original pieces produced through this period is slight. Many writers did produce either closet verse dramas - such as Eliza Lanesford Cushing's *The Fatal Ring* (1840), Charles Heavysege's *Saul* (1857), Charles Mair's *Tecumseh* (1886) and Sarah Anne Curzon's *Laura Secord, the Heroine of 1812* (1887) - or journalistic social and political SATIRES, usually anonymous, such as *The Female Consistory of Brockville* (1856) or Nicholas Flood Davin's *The Fair Grit; or, The Advantages of Coalition* (1876), which were never intended for the stage.

The system of visiting stars impeded the development of original dramas and limited the repertoire to the standard London drama and SHAKESPEARE - plays familiar to both the star and the company. Early in the century the bills were filled with short FARCES and burlettas, which later gave way to SHERIDAN and GOLDSMITH; COLMAN THE YOUNGER'S *The Heir at Law*, KOTZEBUE'S *The Stranger*, HOME'S *Douglas* and the plays of BOUCICAULT were also great favourites. It is interesting, however, to note that the military men, with their frequent rotation, were often able to stage relatively recent London successes. EDWARD FITZBALL'S *The Inchcape Bell*, first presented in London in May 1828, was staged by the garrison amateurs in Kingston in July 1830.

As the population grew, so did the number and size of

the theatres. By the 1870s, playhouses seating from 1250 to over 2000 people appeared across the country (Grand Opera House, Toronto, 1874; Academy of Music, Montreal, 1875; Academy of Music, Halifax, 1877), and many cities had several theatres, each one appealing to a different audience segment: for example, in Toronto in 1875 the Grand Opera House presented the standard drama, the Royal Opera House tended towards the melodramatic and sensational, while the Queen's Theatre was what was known as a 'VARIETY dive'. All these theatres had their own companies, generally engaged in New York and filled out with local residents, but they were very much a part of the community.

As the Canadian population spread westward across the prairies, so did the theatre. Garrison amateurs were active in the Red River settlements from 1866, and so were the employees of the Hudson's Bay Company. The first visiting professionals arrived in Winnipeg soon after a rail link was established with Minneapolis in 1878. E.A. McDowell's company was a frequent visitor to most eastern Canadian cities, and one of the first to make the long trek to Winnipeg. His company spent a month there in the summer of 1879 and two months in 1880. By 1883 Winnipeg audiences could support the 1300-seat Princess Theatre.

On the west coast, the naval installations at Victoria saw the same kind of garrison theatre that had been performed in the east almost a century earlier. But Victoria and the west coast also saw another remarkable kind of colonial theatre arise with the discovery of gold in the Fraser River in 1858. Thousands of treasure hunters flocked to the tent cities that sprang up along the rivers and creeks of British Columbia. Many of them wintered in Victoria or mainland towns such as New Westminster. Among various kinds of diversions provided for them, the theatre played a surprisingly large role.

The first professional company to visit Victoria was George Chapman's Pioneer Dramatic Company in 1859, and in 1860 Chapman created the city's first theatre, the 360-seat Colonial Theatre, converted from a recently built concert hall. Even the tiny mining settlements created playhouses for visiting and local entertainers.

The Pioneer Theatre at Barkerville, for example, also served as headquarters for the local fire brigade. San Francisco was the main source for these visiting companies, who often made Victoria the terminus of their route up the coast. Further developments quickly followed the established pattern in the rest of the country, and by the end of the 1870s Canada could boast a chain of large theatres and established repertory companies from coast to coast.

The touring era, 1880–1945 The years from 1880 to the First World War were a golden age of popular theatre in Canada. At the end of the 1870s economic, artistic and technological forces combined to produce a major change in the way the theatre worked, not only in Canada but across North America. Almost overnight the system of resident companies and visiting stars was replaced by touring companies presenting a single or several plays, changing nightly. This new system brought with it higher standards of production and a new and more varied repertoire. However, it was a North American rather than a Canadian theatre, almost entirely focused on New York, where companies were formed, productions mounted, and tours booked by monopolies such as the THEATRICAL SYNDICATE and the SHUBERT ORGANIZATION. If there had been a chance of a Canadian drama emerging from the local repertory companies, it had now completely disappeared. The Canadian market was simply too small and undercapitalized for Canadian theatre producers to create special products for it that could be distributed Canada-wide, for the theatre had become a major industry dedicated to the production of mass entertainment.

There had been touring companies before, of course, particularly OPERA companies. After mid-century, OPERETTA, OPÉRA BOUFFE and other light musical concoctions were extremely popular in English Canada. The Holman English Opera Company, based in London, Ontario, and Toronto, regularly toured eastern Canada and the northern USA throughout the 1860s and 1870s with works by Balfe, Lecocq and OFFENBACH, as well as their own creations. It is no surprise, then, to find that the most successful original productions of the Canadian theatre in this period were musical entertainments. W.H. Fuller's satirical attack on the Canadian government, *HMS Parliament* (1880), an adaptation of *HMS Pinafore*, enjoyed a remarkable cross-Canada success in the hands of the McDowell company; another musical pastiche, *Bunthorne Abroad* (1883), assembled from GILBERT and Sullivan by Toronto caricaturist J.W. Bengough, enjoyed several revivals before disappearing.

Local booking circuits had already begun to spring up in the 1870s to allow for more efficient planning of tours by the stars and their entourages. These circuits gradually became larger and more exclusive. Local entrepreneurs such as Ambrose Small in Toronto, the Whitney family in southwestern Ontario and C.P. Walker in Winnipeg, with his Red River Theatre Circuit, either associated themselves with the larger American chains or simply sold out to them. The resulting syndicate control of virtually all North American playhouses effectively dealt the death blow to any hopes for a distinctive Canadian theatre.

Canadians, however, participated fully in this North American theatre industry, and many became very prominent parts of it. There was room for small local companies within the continental scheme, and essentially Canadian troupes such as the Marks Brothers or Ida Van Cortland and the Tavernier Dramatic Company played on both Canadian and nearby American circuits. Harold Nelson's Canadian Dramatic Company played the classics regularly on the Walker circuit in the west, while the Dumbells, a VAUDEVILLE company that had grown out of a First World War army show, enjoyed international fame in the 1920s.

Many individual Canadian-born performers and producers such as MARGARET ANGLIN, Julia Arthur, WALTER HUSTON, MARIE DRESSLER, BEATRICE LILLIE and Mary Pickford began their careers in local stock companies (see STOCK COMPANY). Among playwrights, W.A. Tremayne of Montreal was the most successful, writing several farces and melodramas, including *The Secret Warrant* (1897) and *The Dagger and the Cross* (1900) for ROBERT MANTELL, and *The Black Feather* (1916). Canada's more serious writers such as Wilfred Campbell still avoided the contemporary stage, though they continued to write in dramatic forms.

But even as this primarily foreign professional theatrical activity was at its peak, the Canadian public was not completely satisfied with the productions provided. The community, little theatre, and art theatre movements were a widespread reaction to the state of commercial theatre at the turn of the century. In Canada, the journalist and theosophist Roy Mitchell made Toronto's Arts and Letters Club an important centre of theatrical experimentation during 1908–14, but the plays produced were those of MAETERLINCK, YEATS, TAGORE and SYNGE. The visits of the Irish Players from the ABBEY THEATRE provided an important model to those who were crying out for a Canadian theatre. By the 1920s the art and little theatre movements in Canada displayed overt nationalistic aspirations.

In 1919 Roy Mitchell was appointed the first director of the University of Toronto's Hart House Theatre, and helped it become one of the centres of the little theatre and indigenous playwriting movement in Canada. Mitchell left in 1921 to teach and write in New York, but under succeeding directors more Canadian plays were produced at Hart House Theatre, though almost always one-act works. Merrill Denison, whose *Brothers in Arms* (1921) and *From Their Own Place* (1922) were produced at Hart House and the Arts and Letters Club respectively, emerged as the first serious Canadian playwright to write about Canadian themes and locales in his anthology *The Unheroic North* (1923). Disillusioned that a Canadian professional theatre did not emerge in the 1920s, Denison moved to the USA in 1932 to write radio dramas for CBS and NBC.

The attempt to create a Canadian national theatre and drama was continued in the 1930s by playwrights and directors such as Herman Voaden, whose Play Workshop produced not only his own multi-media experiments in symphonic EXPRESSIONISM but also the work of many local writers. Voaden's most important romantic and mystical dramas include *Rocks* (1932) and *Earth Song* (1932), *Hill-Land* (1934), *Murder Pattern* (1936) and *Ascend as the Sun* (1942). The women writers of the Playwrights Studio Group (Dora Smith Conover, Rica McLean Farquharson, Leonora McNeilly, Lois Reynolds Kerr, Marjorie Price, Virginia Coyne Knight and Winnifred Pilcher) also produced dozens of original scripts, mostly comedies, at Hart House Theatre between 1932 and 1940.

In Montreal, Martha Allan and Rupert Caplan were among the founders of the Community Players in 1921. W.A. Tremayne was their stage director. The Players disbanded after four years and Rupert Caplan joined the PROVINCETOWN PLAYERS before returning and becoming a major force in Canadian radio. Martha Allan went to the PASADENA PLAYHOUSE and returned to form the Montreal Repertory Theatre in 1930, which survived until 1961.

In the west Carroll Aikins, whose poetic tragedy on American Indian themes, *The God of Gods*, had been produced at the BIRMINGHAM REPERTORY THEATRE in 1919, constructed a well equipped little playhouse on his Okanagan valley farm at Naramata, British Columbia, where he tried to create a professional troupe in the early 1920s. He was director of Hart House Theatre from 1927 to 1929. Playwriting in Alberta was pioneered in the 1930s by Elsie Park Gowan, who also became an important radio dramatist, and by Gwen Pharis Ringwood whose most suc-

cessful prairie folk plays include *Still Stands the House* (1938) and *Dark Harvest* and *The Rainmaker* (1945).

One of the reasons for all this indigenous theatrical activity was the gradual disappearance of the imported product. Just as Canadian writers were beginning to find some success in the theatre, the professional stage was falling before the onslaught of vaudeville and the cinema. The movies took over not only the theatre audience but also its buildings, and the Depression did the rest.

A consequence of the death of the road was the limited return of local stock companies presenting weekly rep. They were not really local, of course, for even they were bound to New York and the booking circuits, but in their long-term residencies in the larger cities they provided opportunities for local participation.

From the beginning of the century occasional companies had tried to avoid the cost of touring by spending long periods in one city or region, particularly in those parts of the country not well served by the major touring circuits. Among the more long-lived examples were the Permanent Players, who were an institution in Winnipeg through the first two decades of the century. In Toronto the Vaughan Glaser Players played through the 1920s, for the first six years in the 3000-seat Uptown Theatre. The John Holden Players, who grew out of a summer actors' colony near Toronto in 1934, played for several winter seasons in both Toronto and Winnipeg. But by 1939 they were billing themselves as the only professional theatre in North America doing weekly stock on a year-round basis, and by 1942 the Second World War had put an end to such activity.

Outside the larger cities the professional theatre was virtually dead by the 1930s, but it was replaced to a degree by amateur theatre. The 1920s had seen the beginnings of a large number of little theatre groups across the country. Complementing the art theatres, they carried on the tradition begun in the military garrisons a century and a half before. In 1932 the Dominion Drama Festival was founded to provide a focus for this amateur activity, with an annual competitive festival. Adjudicators such as Robert Speaight, HARLEY GRANVILLE BARKER and particularly MICHEL SAINT-DENIS contributed a great deal to the high standards of amateur theatre in Canada. The Barry Jackson Trophy, awarded from 1934 for the best Canadian play, stimulated the creation and production of works by Mazo de la Roche, John Coulter, Robertson Davies and Gwen Pharis Ringwood.

The 1930s also saw the rise of the social theatre and AGIT-PROP presentations by theatre groups associated with the leftist Progressive Arts Clubs in major cities across the country. The high point of this movement, *Eight Men Speak* (1933) – a creation of Toronto's Workers' Theatre to protest against the arrest and attempted prison murder of a Communist Party leader – was performed to great public controversy and subsequent suppression (see CENSORSHIP). These groups also brought Canadian audiences the works of radical American writers such as CLIFFORD ODETS, Sinclair Lewis and Irwin Shaw.

Far more important for the future of the theatre in Canada was the establishment of the Canadian Broadcasting Corporation in 1936. Radio broadcasts of plays had begun as early as 1925 on the trans-Canada

CNRA network operated by Canadian National Railways. In 1931 TYRONE GUTHRIE produced 'The Romance of Canada', a series of historical plays written by Merrill Denison for the network. That network eventually became the CBC and, especially during the 1940s and 1950s under Andrew Allan, was a major producer of original drama (see RADIO DRAMA). Playwrights and performers now were able to work professionally and consistently, though not on the stage. The talent pool that the CBC supported led directly to the postwar theatrical explosion that finally created an indigenous, professional theatre and an important body of Canadian dramatic work.

The new Canadian theatre The Canadian nation, formed in 1867, became almost totally independent in 1931 when passage of the British Statute of Westminster gave autonomy to the British Empire's Dominions. Its new nationhood was confirmed in the Second World War. Following the war there was an unmatched explosion of creative activity in all the performing arts. Recognizing the need for a comprehensive cultural policy, the federal government in 1949 appointed a Royal Commission under Vincent Massey to study the role of the arts in Canadian life. The resulting Massey Report in 1951 was a major document in the evolution of Canadian culture. It recognized the importance of the arts and called for government subsidy to provide the necessary facilities for their growth. This recommendation led directly to the formation of the Canada Council in 1957 and, later, various provincial Arts Councils, which provided 'arms-length' support to artists and arts organizations.

But long before the Canada Council and even before the Massey Report, Canadian theatre experienced a postwar rebirth from coast to coast. Sydney Risk's Everyman Theatre mounted a truck-and-train tour from Vancouver to Winnipeg in 1946 and 1947 – with a repertoire that included Elsie Park Gowan's social comedy *The Last Caveman* (1938) – before settling into its own studio theatre in Vancouver.

In Toronto Dora Mavor Moore's New Play Society, founded in 1946, produced international classics and the annual satirical REVUE, *Spring Thaw* (1948–71), as well as successful original works such as Morley Callaghan's *To Tell the Truth* (1949) and John Coulter's epic drama about the leader of the 19th-century Métis rebellion in western Canada, *Riel* (1950). When the NPS turned towards education and musical theatre, the Jupiter Theatre, founded in 1951 by Lorne Greene, John Drainie and other CBC artists, took over its original role, producing the works of BRECHT, SARTRE, O'NEILL and PIRANDELLO, but also Canadian plays such as Lister Sinclair's *Socrates* (1952) and *The Blood Is Strong* (1953). Robertson Davies's plays of ideas exploring Canadian cultural life began to be widely produced and published in 1948 and 1949. His most important stage works include *Fortune, My Foe* (1949), *At My Heart's Core* (1950) and *Question Time* (1975).

In Montreal, the Montreal Repertory Theatre renewed its activities after the war and was joined by the Canadian Art Theatre, which presented ambitious productions at its Open Air Playhouse, including a 1950 *Cymbeline* directed by FYODOR KOMISSARZHEVSKY. In the same year the first productions were mounted at the indoor Mountain

Playhouse. Malcolm Morley went from Montreal to Ottawa in 1948 to join the Ottawa Stage Society and help turn it into the Canadian Repertory Theatre, which produced full 34-play seasons of professional weekly rep in a school auditorium. And in Newfoundland a group of players from the Birmingham Repertory Company played long seasons from 1947 to 1957, first as the Alexandra Players and then as the London Theatre Company. Most of those London players remained in Canada.

Summer theatre also flourished, from Quebec's Brae Manor Playhouse and Ontario's Red Barn and International Players to Winnipeg's Rainbow Stage and the Totem Theatre and Theatre Under the Stars in Vancouver. But undoubtedly the one event that catalysed and revolutionized theatre in Canada was the opening of the STRATFORD FESTIVAL in Stratford, Ontario, in 1953. Almost overnight a major theatrical force was born that was to set standards of production for the whole continent. The intense postwar activity had produced a Canadian theatre community more than ready for the challenge of a world-class classical theatre. All but four of the first Stratford company were Canadians who had already been working in the nascent professional theatre and who were determined to continue. Among them were Robert Christie, Richard Easton, Amelia Hall, William Hutt and Douglas Rain. Subsequent seasons included Frances Hyland, Lorne Greene and CHRISTOPHER PLUMMER.

In January 1954, four months after the close of the first Stratford season, Donald and Murray Davis opened the Crest Theatre in Toronto to produce full winter seasons of two-week repertory. Over the next 12 years it provided a strong continuing presence that balanced many other short-lived theatrical enterprises. Among the 16 original works produced at the Crest were plays by Robertson Davies, Mavor Moore, Ted Allan, Jack Gray and Bernard Slade. In 1959 George Luscombe's TORONTO WORKSHOP PRODUCTIONS began offering a more radical alternative in both style and content.

The founding of the Manitoba Theatre Centre in 1958, a merger of the long-established amateur Winnipeg Little Theatre and JOHN HIRSCH's newly formed professional Theatre 77, marked the beginning of the regional theatre movement. The next decade saw the establishment of a chain of relatively large, important theatre companies across the country. The Vancouver Playhouse and Neptune Theatre in Halifax presented their first seasons in 1962 and 1963; Edmonton's Citadel Theatre opened in 1965, followed by the Globe Theatre in Regina the next year, Fredericton's Theatre New Brunswick and Theatre Calgary in 1968, Centaur Theatre in Montreal in 1969, Toronto's CentreStage in 1970, Bastion Theatre in Victoria in 1971, and the Grand Theatre in London, Ontario, in 1978. In succeeding years professional theatres were established in almost every significant city in the country. Theatre critics such as NATHAN COHEN and HERBERT WHITTAKER made the whole country their 'beat', and marshalled public support for an indigenous Canadian theatre and drama.

The year 1969 also saw the opening of the National Arts Centre in Ottawa which, despite inadequate government financial support, attempted to showcase the best in English and French-language theatre from across the country. The Stratford Festival was joined in 1962 by the

SHAW FESTIVAL in Niagara-on-the-Lake, dedicated to the plays of GEORGE BERNARD SHAW and his contemporaries. The Charlottetown Festival, established in Prince Edward Island in 1965, quickly found a role as the major producer of original MUSICAL THEATRE, presenting over 40 shows in its first 20 years, including the perennially popular *Anne of Green Gables* (1965).

Many professionals were trained for these theatres at the National Theatre School, founded in Montreal in 1960. The School continues to offer intense training in acting, production, design and playwriting in both English and French. Other professional training programmes have been connected with theatres themselves, especially in Vancouver, Winnipeg and Stratford. A growing number of university theatre departments have been training students for the profession since the 1970s.

Funding came from a variety of sources. After 1957 the Canada Council and certain provincial bodies provided operating subsidies for established companies, but these had to be supplemented by significant private fund-raising. The centennial of Canadian confederation in 1967 provided an impetus to the building boom, and many a theatre building or arts centre was designated a centennial project and thus eligible for special capital grants. While perhaps too much money was poured into concrete and not enough into art, the result was a living, reasonably healthy theatre network covering the country, providing professional production standards and popular entertainments. Show business had returned to Canada.

The centennial celebrations also provided an impetus to Canadian playwriting. The 1967 Dominion Drama Festival allowed only Canadian plays, and the regional theatres made determined efforts to find and produce Canadian scripts. The 1967 Vancouver Playhouse production of GEORGE RYGA's *The Ecstasy of Rita Joe* was an important landmark in this new emerging Canadian drama. Also in 1967, the Stratford Festival staged JAMES REANEY's memory play, *Colours in the Dark*, and the Manitoba Theatre Centre produced Ann Henry's *Lulu Street*.

But these main-stage productions of new Canadian works were the exception, not the norm. The regional theatres were large, expensive and necessarily conservative institutions. Their subscription seasons were generally made up of a recent American or British success, a classic or two, and the occasional Canadian work. The most successful Canadian play of 1967, John Herbert's *Fortune and Men's Eyes*, had to look to the Actors Playhouse in New York for a full-scale production following its 1965 Stratford workshop because its homosexual content was deemed too disturbing.

The 1970s saw the arrival of the 'alternative theatre movement'. The energy and revolutionary idealism of the 1960s led to the growth of what were originally called 'underground' and later 'alternative' theatres. The term was widely used in Canada to suggest a movement diametrically opposed to the established regional theatres. On small and often improvised stages they explored new movements in radical theatre. Their arrival was marked by a large Festival of Underground Theatre in Toronto in 1970 in which Canadian, American and European companies presented their work all over the city. While their initial impulse was not particularly nationalistic it quickly became so, especially after the Gaspé Manifesto issued by a meeting of Canadian playwrights in 1971, which called for 50 per cent Canadian content at all publicly subsidized theatres. Toronto and, to a lesser extent, Vancouver were the centres of this movement. From the late 1960s to the early 1970s there was a rapid expansion in theatre production, and of new Canadian plays in particular.

In the west, the Savage God experiments of John Juliani had begun in Vancouver as early as 1966, but with the establishment of the all-Canadian play development, New Play Centre, in 1970, a new generation of playwrights began seeing their works on stage and in print. The collective and improvisational found its outlet with Tamahnous Theatre, founded in 1971. West Coast Actors and the Arts Club Theatre occupied the middle ground between the established Playhouse Theatre and the experimenters.

In Toronto, THEATRE PASSE MURAILLE emerged from the car park of the radical Rochdale College and, under the direction of Paul Thompson, became a leader in a style of collective documentary drama that has become an important Canadian tradition. Ken Gass founded the Factory Theatre Lab in 1970 with a firm commitment to produce only new Canadian plays, and in its first season introduced writers and plays as different as GEORGE WALKER's *Prince of Naples* (1971), Herschel Hardin's *Esker Mike and his Wife Agiluk* (1971) and David Freeman's *Creeps* (1971). Bill Glassco left the Factory Lab to found TARRAGON THEATRE, which quickly became the most established of the alternatives with successful productions of the works of David Freeman and DAVID FRENCH – especially French's *Leaving Home* (1972) – and English translations of Quebec playwright MICHEL TREMBLAY.

Much of the alternative theatrical activity was fuelled by special federal government employment programmes. Local Initiative Programs (LIPs) and Opportunities for Youth (OFY) projects often turned into theatrical companies that flowered briefly before disappearing as quickly as they had arisen. One important survivor was the Toronto Free Theatre, founded in 1972 as literally a 'free' theatre with no admission charge. Its merger in 1988 with Toronto's regional theatre, CentreStage, to form the Canadian Stage Company was initially heralded as a breakthrough legitimizing the indigenous creativity and cultural nationalism espoused by the alternative theatre movement. The ongoing economic recession and resulting artistic retrenchment have unfortunately blunted much of this artistic promise.

Alternative theatres were not confined to the larger cities. Almost everywhere a regional theatre existed an alternative company rose to challenge it, from Halifax's Pier One to Edmonton's Theatre Network and Calgary's Alberta Theatre Projects. In many cases the regionals themselves established second stages or workshops for the production of new and experimental works. Even smaller cities such as Thunder Bay, Ontario, developed a mainstream company, Magnus Theatre, and an alternative, Kam Theatre Lab.

The result of all this activity was the production of over 200 new Canadian plays between 1970 and 1972. Many of them were of uneven quality, but through their productions playwrights had a chance to learn. A whole new generation of writers found success, often continuing success, on the stage. Besides those mentioned already, Carol Bolt, Rick Salutin, SHARON POLLOCK, Rex Deverell, Michael Cook, Linda Griffiths, JOHN MURRELL, David Fennario, JUDITH THOMPSON, TOMSON HIGHWAY and Brad Fraser have established themselves as important and widely produced writers.

The trend towards collective creations, led by Theatre Passe Muraille's *Farm Show* (1972), found adherents in the east and west; Newfoundland's Mummers Troupe and Saskatoon's 25th Street Theatre toured the country with productions such as *They Club Seals, Don't They?* (1978) and *Paper Wheat* (1977), both obviously deeply rooted in populist politics and in their regional environment and culture. Another trend evident in the early 1970s was the popularity of small-scale naturalistic looks at Canadian life. Although often most closely connected with the Tarragon Theatre, this style was a pervasive influence and not unrelated to the achievements of the Canadian documentary film-makers.

After such an explosion of playmaking, it was inevitable that a certain retrenchment and consolidation would follow. The drying up of LIP and OFY funds after 1974 certainly helped, but there still remained a vigorous and active alternative theatre presenting a large proportion of new work. An 'edifice complex' took hold in the late 70s and early 80s, and the abandoned warehouses and factories that had housed these fledgling companies were bought, restored, and equipped as playing spaces that would be the envy of similar companies in many other parts of the Western world.

Most of this theatre was non-profit, subsidized theatre receiving up to 50 per cent of its budget from various government sources. With the active encouragement of the Canada Council the regional theatres almost universally adopted subscription systems in the 1970s. Many of the alternative theatres followed suit. Subscription guarantees an audience, but it also prohibits extended runs of popular shows. In the larger cities, the need for transfer houses where a successful production can have its run extended has become evident.

As the alternative theatres became more established, a new generation of alternatives arose, catering to special audiences (such as feminist, gay and lesbian, native peoples, multicultural, labour union) or special styles of performance. Popular FRINGE festivals, beginning in Edmonton in 1980 and now also including Victoria, Vancouver, Saskatoon, Winnipeg, Toronto, Montreal and Halifax, provide work opportunities for emerging playwrights and performers and continue the alternative theatres' experimentation and artistic renewal. Together with the over 300 producing companies active to various degrees in English Canada, the fringe festivals have raised the number of new Canadian plays produced annually to approximately 1000 since the mid-1980s.

A full spectrum of theatrical activity was available to Canadians by the end of the 1980s: a few remaining large touring houses for BROADWAY or WEST END successes, the established, traditional regional theatres, the more adventurous alternatives, and the radical fringe. Theatre once more has become a major industry in Canada, and companies are attempting to work more closely together through tours, exchanges, co-productions and organizations such as the Professional Association of Canadian Theatres.

The most serious artistic and economic challenge facing Canadian theatres in the early 1990s, particularly in Toronto, has been the rise of commercial theatre producers and the renewed dominance of large-scale British and American musicals. Toronto audiences have had a continuous connection with Broadway since the opening of the 1500-seat Royal Alexandra Theatre in 1907. The opening of the city-operated 3200-seat O'Keefe Centre in 1960 increased the number of touring Broadway musicals and Las Vegas type VARIETY shows. In 1985 the Ontario Heritage Foundation reopened the 2100-seat Elgin Theatre, a vaudeville house built in 1913. Its inaugural production, a locally mounted, two-year run of ANDREW LLOYD WEBBER's *Cats*, demonstrated the tremendous box-office potential of British and American musicals.

By 1989 producer Garth Drabinsky had renovated the 2200-seat Pantages Theatre, another Toronto vaudeville house, built in 1920, at a cost of $22 million. By the end of 1994, with audiences of 800,000 a year, his inaugural production of *The Phantom of the Opera* had grossed over $300 million. Ed and David Mirvish, the owners and producers of the Royal Alexandra Theatre, also had a major commercial hit with *Les Misérables*, and in 1993 built the $35 million 2000-seat Princess of Wales Theatre for an open-ended run of *Miss Saigon*. In 1993 Garth Drabinsky's Live Entertainment Corporation also opened the $48 million publicly owned 1850-seat Ford Centre for the Performing Arts with a revival of *Show Boat*, which subsequently transferred for a popular run on Broadway.

While Drabinsky was able to create an international hit with *Kiss of the Spider Woman*, neither he nor the Mirvishes have as yet been able to produce Canadian plays for the international market. Their commercial success with American and British mega-musicals, with their multi-million-dollar advertising budgets and box-office receipts, has marginalized the smaller subsidized companies and has also undermined public support for subsidized theatre at a time of economic recession and severe cutbacks in government support for the arts.   JA AW

See: J. Ball and R. Plant (eds), *Bibliography of Theatre History in Canada: The Beginnings through 1984*, Toronto, 1993; E. Benson and L.W. Conolly, *English Canadian Theatre*, Toronto, 1987, and (eds), *The Oxford Companion to Canadian Theatre*, Toronto, 1989; D. Bessai, *Playwrights of Collective Creation*, Toronto, 1992; *Canadian Theatre Review*; M. Edwards, *A Stage in our Past*, Toronto, 1968; A. Filewod, *Collective Encounters: Documentary Theatre in English Canada*, Toronto, 1991; D. Johnston, *Up the Mainstream: The Rise of Toronto's Alternative Theatres*, Toronto, 1991; R.P. Knowles (ed.), *Theatre in Atlantic Canada*, Sackville, 1988; E.R. Stuart, *The History of Prairie Theatre, 1833–1982*, Toronto, 1984; *Theatre Research in Canada*; *Theatrum*; R. Usmiani, *Second Stage: The Alternative Theatre Movement in Canada*, Vancouver, 1983; A. Wagner (ed.), *The Brock Bibliography of Published Canadian Plays in English, 1766–1978*, Toronto, 1980, and (ed.), *Contemporary Canadian Theatre*, Toronto, 1985; R. Wallace, *Producing Marginality*, Saskatoon, 1990.

Canada: 2 French

Theatre in French Canada to the Second World War

The first record of theatrical activity in French and the first dramatic text come from Port Royal in Acadia (today's Annapolis Royal, Nova Scotia), where MARC LESCARBOT's aquatic pageant, *The Theatre of Neptune in New France*, was written and performed in November 1606. The text was composed to celebrate the return of the colony's leaders from a prolonged and dangerous mission: this function identifies it as a *réception*, a dramatic sub-genre long popular in France, performed mainly by students in Jesuit colleges to welcome visiting dignitaries. But Lescarbot's short verse play has none of the stuffy formality associated with traditional *réceptions*: although relying heavily on neoclassical references, it is a good-natured frolic intended to amuse and entertain.

Only two other texts survive from the French regime, both belonging to this category: the *Réception for Governor D'Argenson*, written by the Jesuits and performed by their pupils in Quebec in 1658, to mark the arrival of the new governor; and another *réception* with many elements of a PASTORAL, composed again by a Jesuit and performed by children for Bishop Saint-Vallier in 1727. A surprising characteristic of all three texts is their strong political component: their authors intercalate precise messages for the reader/spectator, advising strategies for colonization, recommending war against the Iroquois, pleading for administrative support of church projects. This political element would be a lasting trait of French Canadian theatre.

Throughout its history, material conditions in New France were not conducive to the establishment of an enduring theatrical tradition. In Quebec fashionable plays (particularly those of CORNEILLE) were staged for the social elite as early as the 1640s; such performances were surprisingly frequent at times, especially in the 1650s and early 1690s. But primary social factors – a sparse, transient population in a huge colony, the indifference and later the hostility of the powerful Catholic Church – militated against sustained theatrical activity. These difficult conditions were exacerbated by a direct confrontation between civil and religious authority in 1693–4. Word had spread that Governor Frontenac intended to stage, along with plays by Corneille and RACINE, MOLIÈRE's controversial *Tartuffe*. Bishop Saint-Vallier was scandalized, and used all the power of his office to block the plan. Their conflict ended with bishop bribing governor handsomely for not staging *Tartuffe*. Theatre's cause was the loser, however: the bishop now forbade all public theatricals; and such was the authority of his office that there are only sporadic references to other performances after 1694. In fact, Bishop Saint-Vallier's prohibition would create problems for theatre in French Canada for the next 200 years.

Soon after the formal cession of New France in 1763 the British garrison in Quebec was actively performing classical French plays (mainly by Molière), in French. Garrison theatre of this sort appeared in Montreal in the following decade, and would continue well into the 19th century, with frequent participation of local amateurs. After 1763 drama returned to the curriculum of schools and colleges as well, attested to by newspaper reports of such performances and by surviving manuscripts of college plays

from the 1780s. Independent amateur troupes also appeared at this time, the most important being Montreal's Society Theatre which in the season 1789-90 staged eight separate plays, one of them written by a naturalized French immigrant, Joseph Quesnel, entitled *Colas et Colinette, ou Le Bailli dupé* (*Colas and Colinette: or The Bailiff Confounded*), published in 1812 (with an imprint of 1808).

At this point the Catholic Church decided to intervene, first from the pulpit and then more effectively through the confessional. Its discreet strategy proved effective, and would continue to be so for the next half-century, with the result that theatre in French, unlike its English Canadian counterpart, would long remain cyclical, endangered and amateur. In such conditions it is not surprising that the most successful dramatic form to evolve would be a literary-journalistic one: political theatre (or 'paratheatre', since it would not be performed until the 1860s). Intensely partisan, it began appearing in French Canada's newspapers in the 1760s and would continue well into the 20th century. It represents the most original indigenous genre, and for good reason: surviving texts from the 1790s show that some at least were intended to be read aloud at public meetings, thus 'performed' in a sense, in a period when less than 5 per cent of the francophone population could read. An apogee of this paradramatic form came in 1834, with the publication in rival newspapers of five amusing playlets, the *Status Quo Comedies*. Satirical, vituperative to the point of libel, they were an effective political weapon. Not being destined for performance, they could escape the Church's ire, as could the religious-pedagogic theatre performed for a restricted public in educational institutions.

In the 1830s, as in the late 1780s, the public stage received much-needed catalysis from abroad. France's political turmoil of the early 1830s brought an influx of dissident intellectuals, the most notable being Firmin Prud'homme, Napoléon Aubin and Hyacinthe Leblanc de Marconnay. The latter helped found an Amateur Canadian Dramatic Society and composed two plays, *Le Soldat* (*The Soldier*, 1835), perhaps written in conjunction with Aubin, and *Valentine, ou La Nina canadienne* (*Valentine: or, The Canadian Nina*, 1836), both performed and published in Montreal. In 1837 came the first published play by a native French Canadian (apart from the closet political playlets mentioned above): *Griphon, ou La Vengeance d'un valet* (*Griphon: or, A Valet's Revenge*), written by PIERRE PETITCLAIR. It was never performed, but was followed by two others that were: his MELODRAMA *La Donation* (*The Legal Donation*), first staged in 1842, making it the first play by a native Canadian to be published and performed; and *Une Partie de campagne* (*A Country Outing*, 1857), satirizing French Canadians who aped English speech and manners.

More solemn in intent, more formal in style, is *Le Jeune Latour* (*Young Latour*) by Antoine Gérin-Lajoie, performed by him and his fellow students at the Collège de Nicolet in 1844. A verse tragedy dealing with the short-lived conquest of New France by the English in 1629–30, it is the first in a long line of patriotic historical works that would characterize the 19th century. It also signals a renaissance of drama in the institutions of secondary education in

Quebec, from which would come the intellectual and social elite on which theatrical activity depended. Most of the college texts performed were, unlike *Young Latour*, either written by instructors (usually priests) or adapted by them from existing texts, the 'adaptation' consisting largely in the removal of all female roles, even for plays by Racine, Corneille and Molière.

By mid-century the Catholic clergy, recognizing the propagandistic potential of theatre, took active measures to harness it to the Church's ends: for combating heresy, in works such as the anonymous *Soirées du village, ou Entretiens sur le Protestantisme* (*Village Evenings: or, Conversations on Protestantism*, 1859–60); for alerting the faithful to the dangers of alcoholism, in *L'Hôte à Valiquet, ou Le Fricot sinistre* (*Valiquet's Guest: or, The Sinister Stew*) by Father Jean-Baptiste Proulx (1869); for attacking individual enemies, as in Father Alphonse Villeneuve's *Contre-Poison: Faussetés, erreurs, impostures, blasphèmes de l'apostat Chiniquy* (*Antidote: or, Falsehoods, Errors, Deceits and Blasphemies of the Apostate [Charles] Chiniquy*, 1875); for eloquent pleas on behalf of colonization and social action, as in Father Proulx's *Les Pionniers du Lac Nominingue, ou Les Avantages de la Colonisation* (*The Pioneers of Lake Nominingue: or, The Advantages of Colonization*, 1882) and Father Édouard Hamon's *Exil et Patrie* (*Exile and Fatherland*), performed in 1870.

Concomitant with the Church's increasing use of dramatic forms was its growing tolerance of public theatre. LOUIS-HONORÉ FRÉCHETTE's hyperpatriotic *Félix Poutré* (1862), dealing with the Rebellion of 1837–8, continued to be performed, even in institutions under church control, well into the 20th century; and college performances were opened to the general public, notably in the case of *Archibald Cameron of Locheill*, based on the most popular novel of the century, Philippe Aubert de Gaspé's *Les Anciens Canadiens* (*Canadians of Old*): its premiere in 1865 at the Collège de l'Assomption was a cultural highlight of the decade. But native dramaturgy was slow to respond, its most significant evolution in this period being in the realm of political theatre: the unplayable, often wooden journalistic dialogues of the 1830s and 40s are enlivened with satirical songs in the following decade. And in 1868 came Elzéar Labelle's witty *La Conversion d'un pêcheur de la Nouvelle-Écosse* (*The Conversion of a Nova Scotian Fisherman*), no longer anonymous, no longer unilaterally partisan but directed at both sides in the Confederation debate. This play would continue to attract sell-out audiences to the end of the century. It points the way towards one of the few genres that would prosper in French Canada until the 1940s: the satirical revue, replete with music, dance and monologue, brimming with contemporary political allusions.

Another important factor influencing theatrical activity and eventually dramatic composition was the more and more frequent visits by touring companies from France. From 1858 professional troupes crossing to the USA began to add Montreal and occasionally Quebec to their itinerary, as the continent's railway system developed sufficiently to allow this. Some visiting troupes remained in Canada, notably that of Alfred Maugard after 1871. The most celebrated of these tours were those of SARAH BERNHARDT, beginning in 1880. She would return six times by 1916, arousing on each occasion great interest among French- and English-speaking audiences and greater opposition from the Church, scandalized by her choice of plays. This overall injection of lighter, more modern repertory fostered a sharp revival of amateur activity in both cities, and led to the establishment of the first professional troupes in Montreal in the 1890s. Soon playwrights like Ernest Doin and J. George Walter McGown were 'adapting' successful Parisian fare to less worldly local tastes, thereby adding scores of ephemeral titles to Canadian repertory. Influenced also by imported tastes but much more original is the work of Félix-Gabriel Marchand, premier of Quebec, 1897–1900. His five plays, from *Fatenville* (1869) to *Le Lauréat* (*The Laureate*, 1899), brought welcome variety to a dramaturgy otherwise committed to solemn historical and patriotic themes.

Similar in inspiration is the work of Régis Roy in popular comedies such as *Consultations gratuites* (*Free Consultations*, 1896) and *Nous divorçons* (*We're Divorcing*, 1897). But the most frequent source for dramatists remained the history of French Canada: the heroic age of exploration, as in Joseph-Louis Archambault's *Jacques Cartier, ou Canada vengé* (*Jacques Cartier: or, Canada Avenged*, 1879); the Conquest of 1759–60, in Laurent-Olivier David's *Le Drapeau de Carillon* (*The Flag from [the Battle of] Carillon*, 1901); the Patriote Rebellion of 1837–8, in Fréchette's *Félix Poutré* (1862) and his *Papineau* (1880); and contemporary national concerns such as the suppression of the French-speaking Métis under Louis Riel in 1885, which inspired in the following year two plays entitled *Riel*, one written in collaboration by two recent French immigrants, the other by Quebec-born Elzéar Paquin. This sometimes turgid nationalistic-historical vein would continue to be the mainstay of dramatic composition until the Second World War.

The result of this modest dramaturgic and theatrical activity was the establishment of the first permanent French-language theatres in Montreal. The opening of the Monument National in 1894 and of the Théâtre des Nouveautés in 1898 marks an important progression, although it was mainly European French actors who continued to play there, with only minor roles given to locals. In 1898 the first lay company officially sanctioned by the Catholic Church was formed, appositely named Les Soirées de Famille (Family Evenings), dedicated to providing 'wholesome' theatre in more or less open opposition to the fare offered by touring troupes. The most important pioneer in the Canadianization of troupes and repertory at this time is Julien Daoust, founder in 1900 of the Théâtre National Français, actor, director, and author of some two dozen works, most of them played but never published. The period 1898–1914 is frequently referred to as the Golden Age of theatre in Montreal, an epithet that is only valid compared to the debased coinage that preceded it. And the glitter continued to be largely imported: of nearly 500 plays staged in French between 1890 and 1900, only 15 were composed by French Canadians; less than a third of the 85 known plays by native playwrights between 1890 and 1914 were ever performed. In this respect the college stage remained exceptional, most of the works it offered continuing to be of local composition while the public stage continued to prefer insubstantial comedies adapted for local tastes. By 1914 a noticeable change had occurred in the origin of source materials and models, however, and the Americanized genres, VAUDEVILLE, BURLESQUE and REVUES, crowd out Parisian 'BOULEVARD theatre'.

The First World War had a drastic effect, putting an end to international tours and sending most French professionals back to their homeland. After these barren years, attempts to revive traditional repertory theatre were not successful: after 1918 the American genres mentioned above were the only ones capable of offering competition for cinema, a sad symptom being the regular conversion of theatres to cinemas. This is when the dichotomy between dramaturgy and performance is most striking, as the favourite inspiration for local playwrights remained stubbornly patriotic and nationalistic. More than twice as many plays were published in French Canada in the 1920s as in any preceding decade, the majority of them belonging to this category. Yet most of the local texts performed were sketches and comic monologues. Drama remained primarily a literary form, with occasional exceptions such as Paul Gury's Le Mortel Baiser (Kiss of Death, 1923) and Léopold Houlé's Le Presbytère en fleurs (The Presbytery in Flower, 1929), both staged with success before and after their publication. Best example of the tenuous link between performance and printed text is the case of Aurore l'enfant martyre (Aurora, Child Martyr), based upon a sensational crime that took place in 1920 in a Quebec village. First staged in 1921, this melodrama relying heavily on sadistic voyeurism was performed no less than 5000 times by the late 1940s, yet remained unpublished until 1982.

Cinema had been a serious competitor with live theatre since its appearance in Montreal in 1902. When radio arrived in the 1920s its influence soon became pervasive, rapidly becoming the most important vehicle of cultural solidarity, since for the first time the basic problem of demographic dispersion could be overcome. Initially radio's influence was pernicious to theatrical activity, but in the early 1930s broadcasts of plays and serials became immensely popular, providing fertile nurseries for indigenous authors and performers. Many passed with surprising ease from one medium to the other, notably Henry Deyglun and Henri Letondal. And since they could now live by their craft, they had spare energies to invest in keeping alive the unprofitable, 'serious' stage, as did actor-managers Fred Barry and Albert Duquesne in 1930, buying out a small cinema and renaming it the Stella. During its five-year span this company provided the best theatrical fare Montreal had known for decades, staging some of the few home-grown plays of the period such as Yvette Mercier-Gouin's Cocktail in 1935. At the same time the Stella helped train future professionals on whom live theatre and radio would depend, through its subsidiary troupe, the Académie Canadienne d'Art Dramatique. This proved to be merely a holding action, however: the effect of the Depression, along with increased competition from vaudeville, burlesque, film and radio, made the Stella's demise inevitable.

Only the Americanized forms of popular theatre were secure, their principal practitioners (Olivier Guimond, Rose Ouellette, Juliette Petrie) becoming household names on whom any impresario could depend for a full house. On a non-competitive level, religious-pedagogical drama continued to thrive throughout the period in Quebec's educational institutions. In the 1930s it began to seek a broader public, primarily through the efforts of prolific writer-directors like Laurent Tremblay and GUSTAVE LAMARCHE. With hundreds of participants, their creations took on the panoramic dimensions of medieval PASSION PLAYS: Lamarche's La Défaite de l'enfer (Hell Defeated, 1938), Notre-Dame-des-Neiges (Our Lady of the Snows, 1942) and Notre-Dame-de-la-Couronne (Our Lady of the Crown, 1947) are reported to have attracted up to 100,000 spectators for a single performance. With energetic, imaginative priests like Georges-Henri d'Auteuil at Montreal's Collège Sainte-Marie and ÉMILE LEGAULT at the Collège Saint-Laurent, academic theatre came to the fore, rescuing the public stage from its own worst instincts. This is especially true in the case of Legault's Compagnons de Saint-Laurent: from their formation in 1937 to the time they disbanded in 1952 they would be a seminal group, providing most of the professional actors, directors and designers who would make possible a renaissance of stage arts after the Second World War. As that conflict approached, however, only what was peripheral to traditional theatre appeared to have any real chance of survival.

Theatre in Quebec since the Second World War Theatre historians have been almost unanimous in recognizing in the staging of GRATIEN GÉLINAS's 'Tit-Coq (1948) the beginning of contemporary theatre in Quebec. In this play's theme of a foundling's frustrated search for identity, French Canadian audiences perceived something of their own quest, formulated in familiar language. Its 500 performances over the next few years attest to this, and its undeniable success immediately stimulated renewed interest in traditional theatre. Yet 'Tit-Coq was not the spontaneous phenomenon it has often been made to appear: it is a mature outgrowth of processes observable over the preceding 60 years. Its premiere was at the Monument National, the opening of which in 1894 had marked a previous summit in Montreal's cultural history. Its cast included Fred Barry and Albert Duquesne, two of the founders of the Stella in 1930, as well as Juliette Béliveau, whose career had been launched at the turn of the century, during Montreal's so-called Golden Age. The author, who directed the play and played the title role, had received a solid grounding in college theatre before going on to write and perform sketches in the 1930s. In the years 1938–46 he wrote annual revues called Fridolinades from their title-character Fridolin, a sort of Québécois Everyman played by the author himself; and from this character much of the essence of 'Tit-Coq's titular hero is distilled. One man had pulled together all these disparate threads, and his play came at an auspicious moment in Quebec's history.

The war years had brought changes, some of them beneficial to theatrical activity – the economic recovery that ensued, first of all, with money disposable for arts and entertainment after basic needs had been met; the partial eclipse of cinema, especially that hitherto imported from

France; the arrival of European refugees with theatrical training such as LUDMILLA PITOËFF, who came to live for a time in Montreal; the visitors like JEAN-PAUL SARTRE, who witnessed for the first time a performance of his own *Huis Clos* (*No Exit*) in that city in 1946. New troupes appeared, especially L'equipe, founded in 1943 by Pierre Dagenais, a disaffected member of Legault's Compagnons, and Le Jeune Colombier, established by Jean Duceppe, whose contribution continues today in a theatre bearing his name. The most enduring of these companies is Montreal's Rideau Vert, established in the disused Stella in 1948 by Yvette Brind'Amour and Mercédès Palomino and still flourishing today. Soon after the war young Québécois began returning to Paris to study stage arts under the great masters, as Legault had done before them. Two such students in particular, JEAN GASCON and JEAN-LOUIS ROUX, would play a central role on their return, founding the THÉÂTRE DU NOUVEAU MONDE in 1951. This remains French Canada's most prestigious company: its influence has been pervasive, although it now represents an 'establishment' against which young troupes rebel.

But the most significant event of the 1950s came from offstage: the establishment in 1957 of the Canada Council and of Montreal's Regional Arts Council, followed four years later by that of Quebec's Ministry of Cultural Affairs. By the very nature of their decision to fund one group at the expense of another, these three agencies, deliberately or not, have wielded much influence, not all of it positive, upon the repertory chosen. A stridently anti-establishment troupe or play has had less of a chance for subsidy, with the result that playwrights and theatre managers have sometimes had to compromise their principles. But positive effects have been many, including the establishment in 1960 of the National Theatre School of Canada (its first executive director was Jean Gascon, with MICHEL SAINT-DENIS as artistic director); and the differing criteria employed by the three granting agencies have frequently led to healthy rivalry.

In dramaturgy, the example of Gélinas was not immediately emulated. He himself did not compose another stage play until 1959, preferring to write for television and to concentrate on his career as director and actor. Other playwrights appeared in the 1940s and early 50s without achieving his sort of recognition: singer-folklorist Félix Leclerc; the neoclassicist Paul Toupin; novelists André Langevin and Yves Thériault; Robert Élie, Éloi de Grandmont – for all of them dramaturgy was an avocation, as it had been for those before 1948. More innovative were JACQUES LANGUIRAND and JACQUES FERRON, the former a bursary student who returned from Paris indelibly stamped by the THEATRE OF THE ABSURD in vogue there in the early 1950s. In works such as *Les Insolites* (*The Unusual Ones*, 1956) and *Les Grands Départs* (*Great Departures*, 1958), Languirand captured the attention of a public athirst for novelty, before the Quiet Revolution of the 1960s that would again turn its gaze inward. Ferron, on the other hand, had begun with satirical works such as *Le Licou* (*The Halter*, 1947) and *L'Ogre* (*The Ogre*, 1949), but in the following decade had anticipated Quebec's radical awakening with *Les Grands Soleils* (*The Great Sunflowers*, 1958), which centres upon the Patriote Rebellion of 1837-8 and attacks the province's mythologized history.

The most important and most productive dramatist, however, was MARCEL DUBÉ, author of more than 40 plays, many of them written for television and most of them visibly influenced by it, the most important being *Zone* (1955) and *Un Simple Soldat* (*Private Soldier*, 1958).

The Quiet Revolution brought with it an unprecedented flourishing, in quality as in quantity, of theatre arts. With the encouragement of state funding agencies new troupes thrived, their number in Montreal alone trebling between 1959 and 68. Television provided a lucrative outlet for this exuberance, exercising in turn considerable influence on themes and structures of stage plays. Dubé continued to dominate both media in the 1960s, with plays such as *Florence* (1960), *Octobre* (1964), *Bilan* (*The Accounting*, 1968), and *Au Retour des oies blanches* (*The White Geese*, 1968), the latter often considered his finest play as well as a clear example of his steady progression away from the working-class characters and concerns of his early works.

Many of the salient texts from this decade spring from the politico-social context: Gélinas's *Hier les enfants dansaient* (*Yesterday the Children Were Dancing*, 1966) portrays within one family the political divisions then plaguing Canada; FRANÇOISE LORANGER's *Le Chemin du Roy* (*The King's Highway*, 1968) satirizes, in the guise of a penalty-filled hockey game between Ottawa and Quebec, the confrontation caused by President De Gaulle's visit during centennial year; ROBERT GURIK's *Hamlet, Prince du Québec* (*Hamlet, Prince of Quebec*, 1968) is a PARODY of the same federal-provincial antagonism, close in form and inspiration to French Canadian political theatre of the 19th century. Yet the most revolutionary play of the decade has no direct reference to the political situation: MICHEL TREMBLAY's *Les Belles-Soeurs* (*Sisters-in-Law*). Its setting is a drab flat in working-class Montreal, its characters all female, its theme that of cultural and economic dispossession. Most importantly, its language is unalloyed *joual*, the impoverished, eroded, heavily anglicized French of the urban proletariat, hitherto considered too ugly for public display except in VAUDEVILLE and BURLESQUE. In Tremblay's stylized text, language itself becomes the metaphor of collective frustration and individual solitude. Its remarkable success led to an immediate proliferation of plays composed in Quebec's homely vernacular, the most notable being those of JEAN-CLAUDE GERMAIN, JEAN BARBEAU, MICHEL GARNEAU and Victor-Lévy Beaulieu.

Les Belles-Soeurs had first been read and approved in 1965 by the Centre d'Essai des Auteurs Dramatiques, a loose organization of young theatre professionals established that year whose activities continue to prove catalytic today. The CEAD and, after 1972, the Association Québécoise du Jeune Théâtre assembled the discordant voices of those opposed to the directions established theatre had been taking – an opposition that expressed itself most noticeably in an attack upon the traditional supremacy of the dramaturgic text and of the iniquitous 'star system', which militated against young actors. The dynamic movement it generated is best exemplified in the offerings of troupes such as the iconoclastic Grand Cirque Ordinaire (1969–77), founded by a group of dissatisfied graduates of the National Theatre School, and by Jean-Claude Germain's short-lived Théâtre du Même Nom

(TMN), a parodic anagram of the Théâtre du Nouveau Monde, that most established of Canadian companies. Influenced by such groups as BREAD AND PUPPET, LIVING THEATRE and EL TEATRO CAMPESINO of California, some of these young experimental troupes adopted activist political ideology, as did the Marxist Théâtre Euh! (1970-8); others produced plays on demand for workers' unions, collectives and schools. Although economic conditions have since caused the demise of many of these companies there are still more than 50 of them, most clinging to a precarious existence. Their purgative influence has proved salutary for surviving groups and even for established theatre. The practitioners of 'young' theatre age ineluctably, however: if there is at present an 'establishment' in French Canadian dramaturgy, its most established author is the prolific Michel Tremblay, whose works have attracted national and international acclaim such as no Canadian before him has known.

After the election of the independentist Parti Québécois government in 1976, the agressive political stance frequently visible hitherto in text and performance was greatly mitigated. There has since been less preoccupation with Quebec's domestic problems and a return to more universal concerns. Jean-Pierre Ronfard's brilliantly innovative seven-play cycle, *Vie et mort du roi boiteux* (*Life and Death of the Lame King*, 1981-2) is a dramaturgic *tour de force*, inspired in part by SHAKESPEARE's royal tragedies and requiring some 15 hours of playing time. Some of the most successful plays have been apolitical comedies such as the bilingual *Broue/Brew* (1979), written in collaboration by seven authors and situated entirely in a Montreal tavern. Another interesting and largely apolitical phenomenon has been the Ligue Nationale d'Improvisation, spectacularly successful on stage and TV, its 'contests' spoofing National Hockey League games, with uniformed teams and referees, and an improvisational format that recalls both COMMEDIA DELL'ARTE and American burlesque's comic 'bits'.

A more universal revolution continues to produce far-reaching effects upon theatre in Canada: that of women. One of the earliest feminist playwrights was Françoise Loranger, in plays such as *Encore cinq minutes* (*Five Minutes More*, 1967), which portrays the identity crisis of a middle-aged, middle-class housewife. In the 1970s the first women's troupes appeared, staging collective works created by and for women, the most notable being Montreal's Théâtre des Cuisines (1973-81), the Théâtre Expérimental des Femmes (1979-), and Quebec City's Commune à Marie (1978-). Their anonymous and collectivist preferences underline these troupes' affinity with Jeune Théâtre, as does their iconoclasm. To date their most remarkable production has been *La Nef des sorcières* (1976; tr. as *A Clash of Symbols*, 1977), comprising six monologues by different authors. More recently, individual feminist playwrights have come to the fore: Denise Boucher, whose *Les Fées ont soif* (*The Fairies Are Thirsty*) led to a memorable confrontation between state funding agencies and the stage in 1978; Elizabeth Bourget; Jeanne-Mance Delisle; Luisette Dussault; Jovette Marchessault, whose *La Saga des poules mouillées* (*The Saga of the Wet Hens*, 1981) attracted much scandalized attention; Maryse Pelletier; Francine Ruel; France Vézina; and especially MARIE LABERGE, whose plays have received much recognition at home and abroad, particularly *L'Homme gris* (*The Man in Grey*), which brought her membership of France's prestigious Ordre des Arts et des Lettres after its successful run in Paris in 1986. Since 1980 women have also moved into more influential roles in Quebec theatre as designers, administrators and artistic directors with major theatrical companies, including the Théâtre du Nouveau Monde, the Nouvelle Compagnie Théâtrale and the Théâtre Populaire du Québec.

Although many current female authors voice, often eloquently, issues of deep concern to women, a label like 'feminist' is nonetheless misleading for many of them, particularly for a Marie Laberge, whose theatre transcends any such reductive categorization. Her best works, by any criteria, stand comparison with those of the foremost playwrights of French Canada in the last decade of the 20th century. Currently, the first rank of francophone dramatists would include, along with those mentioned in the preceding paragraph, MICHEL MARC BOUCHARD, Normand Canac-Marquis, Normand Chaurette, the Ontarian Jean Marc Dalpé, RENÉ-DANIEL DUBOIS, ROBERT LEPAGE, the Acadian ANTONINE MAILLET, Serge Marois, Marco Micone, Claude Poissant, André Ricard and Louis Saia.

The 1960s saw the serious gap between performed theatre and published texts diminish when the Montreal firm Leméac initiated an extensive collection of plays proven in performance. Partially as a result, in the 1970s interest in French-language theatre heightened in colleges and universities across the nation. From a position subservient to that of poetry and the novel, drama has since moved to a privileged rank in the curricula of post-secondary institutions, with the status of research and criticism enhanced accordingly.

The first serious attempt at tracing the history of theatre had been made in 1958 by the critic Jean Béraud, in his *350 ans de théâtre au Canada français*. Although incomplete, it remained almost the only source of information until the 1970s, when several important studies were published. In 1978 came the first volume of the *Dictionnaire des oeuvres littéraires du Québec*, the most ambitious literary-historical undertaking to date, now comprising six volumes and nearly 6500 pages. Specialized theatre journals also began to appear in the 1970s, notably *Jeu* and *Theatre History in Canada/Histoire du théâtre au Canada*. Particularly useful as well are *The Oxford Companion to Canadian Theatre* (1989), edited by E. Benson and L. W. Conolly, P. Lavoie's *Pour suivre le théâtre au Québec: Les Ressources documentaires* (1985) and the *Bibliography of Theatre History in Canada: The Beginnings through 1984* (1993), edited by J. Ball and R. Plant.

In the last decade of the 20th century the stage remains troubled but vibrantly alive in Quebec. Its problems are primarily financial, resulting from years of curtailed support from public granting agencies and a generally depressed urban economy. Its vigour emanates from the current generation of dynamic authors, directors and actors whose talents, conjoined with those of the preceding generation, will certainly ensure the survival of the theatre in Quebec.

Theatre in French outside Quebec Although French-language theatre in North America began in Acadia in 1606 it did not return there for another 260 years; and it took an additional century before a viable theatrical tradition arose. The area's francophone population was too widely scattered for cultural centres to develop, and this dispersion was accentuated by the Deportation of the 1750s. But as soon as the first French-language colleges were established in the last quarter of the 19th century, drama became an integral part of their curricula and an important interface with the local communities on which they depended.

At first the plays were imported, written mainly by clerics for college theatre in France and Quebec, with occasional use of adapted, expurgated classics, especially the works of MOLIÈRE. By the 1870s theatre had extended to the French-speaking parishes of the Maritime Provinces and New England, and the first Acadian texts, those of Pascal Poirier, were performed. Father Alexandre Braud's *Les Derniers Martyrs du Colisée* (*The Last Martyrs of the Coliseum*, 1898), and in particular his *Subercase* (1902), the latter commemorating the last French colonial governor of Acadia, attracted critical and popular acclaim. In the late 1920s Father James Branch composed the first of his five plays, remarkable for their provocative political stance, such as *Vivent nos écoles catholiques! ou La Résistance de Caraquet* (*Long Live Our Catholic Schools! or, Resistance at Caraquet*, 1932). These and other such plays were performed by amateur troupes, providing the only sustained theatrical activity until the late 1950s while serving as important vehicles of cultural cohesion. The first full-fledged theatrical company was founded by Laurie Henri in Moncton in 1956. It has survived two name changes and lives on as the Théâtre Laurie Henri since his death in 1981. Two of its most important productions were by Acadian playwrights Germaine Comeau (*Les Pêcheurs déportés*; *Deported Fishermen*) and Antonine Maillet (*Les Crasseux*; *The Unwashed*), both in 1976.

The 1960s saw the birth of half a dozen other troupes, operating generally in the vicinity of Acadian colleges and offering plays by local, by Québécois (especially Marcel Dubé, Françoise Loranger and Michel Tremblay) and foreign dramatists. The most prominent of these was Moncton's Les Feux-Chalins, 1969–76, celebrated for its production of Maillet's immensely popular *La Sagouine* in 1971 and of Lavel Goupil's first play, *Tête d'eau* (*Water Head*) in 1974. There has since been a succession of small companies, such as the touring educational troupe L'Escaouette, the Petit Théâtre de Memramcook, Le Théâtre Amateur d'Acadie and Théâtre Acadie. In dramaturgy Antonine Maillet has been the outstanding figure to date. Her first plays, *Entr'acte* (*Intermission*, 1957) and *Poireâcre* (1958), attracted local attention, but her *La Sagouine* (*The Slattern*), first performed on radio in 1970–1, fascinated national audiences in French and English and kindled an interest in her people. She has since composed a dozen more plays, not all Acadian in focus. Other contemporary playwrights of note are Laval Goupil, Jules Boudreau, Herménégilde Chiasson, Germaine Comeau, Roger Le Blanc, and Léonard Forest.

In Ontario French-language theatre began in the Ottawa Valley in the 1860s, with the fare offered much the same as in Montreal. Theatrical activity in the Hull–Ottawa area remained vigorous but amateur until after the Second World War, producing actor-directors like Guy Beaulne who have had to pursue professional careers elsewhere. In the 1970s focus shifted westwards to the Sudbury area, home of the Théâtre du Nouvel Ontario, which has staged the plays of the most important dramatists writing in French: André Paiement (whose three volumes of plays, most of them produced successfully, were published posthumously in 1978) and Jean-Marc Dalpé, whose *Le Chien* (*The Dog*, 1988) has been produced in Ottawa, Toronto, Montreal and elsewhere, in French and English. There are currently more than a dozen French-language troupes active in the province, mainly in the east and northwest. Ottawa's importance was enhanced by the opening of the National Arts Centre in 1969, and since 1967 Toronto's Théâtre du Petit Bonheur (renamed Le Théâtre Français de Toronto in 1987) has offered a rich succession of plays in French, mostly of Quebec origin.

In Western Canada theatre in French has also been surprisingly widespread, with virtually all the scattered francophone communities serving at one time or another as centres for local amateur activity. Theatre was introduced into the educational institutions of Manitoba in the 1870s, with many of the texts composed by members of the local clergy. After 1885 the Jesuit Collège de Saint-Boniface offered regular dramatic performances that attracted spectators from the tiny settlements along the Red River. Soon local amateur groups appeared in towns and villages, and continued to flourish until the Second World War. The most famous of these is the Cercle Molière in Saint-Boniface, founded in 1925 and still active in the 1990s. Its success led to the establishment of Edmonton's Théâtre Molière in the following decade, and of Vancouver's active Troupe Molière, which flourished between 1946 and 67. Belying their titles, these troupes' repertory has included everything from the French classics to MUSICALS and light, modern theatre from Paris and Montreal.

Despite this healthy dramatic activity, only in Manitoba has a tradition of native dramaturgy developed. Auguste-Henri de Trémaudan published five plays between 1925 and 30, while André Castelein de la Lande had 50 titles to his credit, most of them performed but only four published, all in the mid-1930s. They and other playwrights of the period dealt with general, non-controversial themes. More recently, the tribulations of Manitoba's embattled francophone community have been the focus of plays such as Roger Auger's *Je m'en vais à Régina* (*I'm Off to Regina*, 1976), Claude Dorge's *Le Roitelet* (*Kinglet*, 1976) and Rosemarie Bissonnette's *Une Bagarre très politique* (*A Very Political Quarrel*, 1981). LED

See: *Archives des lettres canadiennes*, vol. 5, *Le Théâtre canadien-français*, Montreal, 1976; J. Ball and R. Plant (eds.), *Bibliography of Theatre History in Canada: The Beginnings through 1984*, Toronto, 1993; E. Benson and L. W. Conolly (eds.), *The Oxford Companion to Canadian Theatre*, Toronto, 1989; J. Béraud, *350 ans de théâtre au Canada français*, Montreal, 1958; *Dictionnaire des oeuvres littéraires du Québec*, Montreal, 6 vols., 1978–94; L. E. Doucette, *Theatre in French Canada: Laying the Foundations, 1606–1867*, Toronto, 1984; J. C. Godin and L. Mailhot, *Théâtre* québécois I, Montreal, 1970, and *Théâtre québécois II*, Montreal, 1980; J. Laflamme and R. Tourangeau, *L'Église et le théâtre au Québec*, Montreal, 1979; P. Lavoi, *Pour suivre le théâtre au Québec: Les Ressources documentaires*, Montreal, 1985; E.-G. Rinfret (ed.), *Le Théâtre canadien d'expression française: Répertoire analytique des origines à nos jours*, 4 vols., Montreal, 1975-8.

Cañas, Alberto 1920– Costa Rican playwright, director, and Minister of Culture. Under Cañas's direction, the Costa Rican government launched a major new effort in the 1970s to promote theatre. Cañas is himself a major writer of at least ten plays, including such titles as *El luto robado* (*Stolen Mourning*, 1962); *En agosto hizo dos años* (*Two Years Ago in August*, 1966), about an individual returned from the dead; *La segua* (1971), an untranslatable mythical creature in a play that used the Pirandellian techniques (see PIRANDELLO) found in his earlier plays; and *Ni mi casa es ya mi casa* (*My House Is No Longer My Home*, 1982), in which he dealt with the socio-economic crises produced by world inflationary and recessionary spirals. GW

Cano, Joel 1966– Cuban playwright, who studied theatre at the Art Institute of Havana. Cano is the author of several texts, including *Fábula de insomnio* (*Insomniac Fable*) and *Beatlemania*, but his stunning play is *Timeball* (1992), a complex, non-linear postmodern experiment that combines music, time, poetry, history and imagery into a work that has become a marker in the development of Cuban dramaturgy. GW

Cantor, Eddie 1892–1964 American singer and comedian who, after spending his early years in VAUDEVILLE and English MUSIC-HALLS, made his legitimate theatre debut in a London REVUE. His first American appearance was in *Canary Cottage* (1917). FLORENZ ZIEGFELD hired Cantor for his cabaret show *The Midnight Frolic*, and then featured him in the *Ziegfeld Follies of 1917*. Cantor also appeared in the next two *Follies* (1918, 19). Like AL JOLSON he often appeared in blackface, a vestige of the American MINSTREL SHOW. During his musical numbers he would skip across the stage and clap his hands while smirking his way through some slightly suggestive lyrics. Cantor also appeared in several *Follies* sketches as a timid but potentially hot-tempered young man. He switched to the SHUBERT management for a few years, after which Ziegfeld presented him in a book musical, *Kid Boots* (1923). Cantor appeared in two more Ziegfeld shows, the *Follies of 1927* (for which he collaborated on the libretto as well as being the star performer), and *Whoopee* (1928), another book musical. His final BROADWAY appearance was in *Banjo Eyes* (1941). In addition to his work in the theatre, he appeared in numerous films and was a star of radio and television. He co-authored two autobiographies: *My Life Is in Your Hands* (1928) and *Take My Life* (1957). MK

Cao Yu [Wan Jiabao] 1910– Chinese dramatist. Born in Hubei, he graduated in Western literature from Qinghua University, Beijing, and at one time taught at the National Academy of Dramatic Art, Nanjing. In 1934 he published the four-act play *Thunderstorm* (*Leiyu*) which received instant acclaim. Its involved plot covers a single day's events set against the menace of a gathering storm. A tangled history of seduction revealed through the interrelationships of a wealthy industrialist's household ends in tragedy when incest is exposed as a consequence of a misalliance. Five other plays written within the next six years include *Sunrise* (*Richu*) and *Wilderness* (*Yuanye*), which, with *Thunderstorm*, form the trilogy that constitutes his major achievement. Their theme is the decadence of Chinese pre-war society. During the war Cao Yu taught at Fudan University and in 1946 observed theatre in the United States with the playwright–novelist LAO SHE.

In the 1950s he held a number of cultural and administrative posts in the new government and served on the presidium of a conference of writers, artists and theatre people called by the CCP. Soon he came under fire for bourgeois thinking and he remained creatively inactive until his propagandist play *Bright Skies* (*Minglang de tian*) was staged at the Beijing People's Art Theatre in 1956. Cao Yu became a CCP member in 1957 when there was a drive to recruit older intellectuals. In 1966 he was seized from his home at night and sent to a reform school in the country. He was rehabilitated like his fellow intellectuals after 1976 and recognized as a father figure of the modern theatre. Reverting to historical themes in 1961, *The Gall and the Sword* (*Dan jian pian*) takes as its theme the wars between the two ancient kingdoms of Wu and Yue in the 5th century BC. The play has an ideological implication in its eulogizing of the people. In 1979 his full trilogy was revived to an enthusiastic reception. From the late 1970s he was concerned with the experimental use of conventions from traditional theatre for historical themes. ACS

capa y espada, comedia de see COMEDIA

Cape Verde see PORTUGUESE-SPEAKING AFRICA

Čapek, Karel 1890–1938 Czech dramatist. Educated at Charles University, he was a philosophic, ironic humanist deeply committed to the democratic ideals of his nation. After writing a variety of prose works including a major trilogy of novels, he achieved world recognition for several plays, especially *RUR* (1921), *The Insect Comedy* (written with his brother Josef in 1922), and *The Makropolus Affair* (1922), which became the libretto for Leoš Janáček's opera. These theatrically effective works displaying a fanciful, witty yet compassionate vision of humanity coping with its own weaknesses amid the stresses of a high-technology age were followed by the equally powerful *The White Disease* (1937), a disturbing parable of the seemingly inevitable devastation triggered by power-hungry dictators, and *The Mother* (1938). More than any other Czech dramatist, he combined a talent for drama with acute insight into issues central to his time. JMB

Capon, William 1757–1827 British scene designer and architect. Capon's first major employment was as scene designer for JOHN PHILIP KEMBLE at DRURY LANE (1794–1809). He impressed the critics with his design of a Gothic-style chapel for Handel's *Oratorio*, performed for the opening of the reconstructed theatre (1794), and his

Karel and Josef Čapek's
The Insect Comedy,
Prague National Theatre,
1965. The designer was
Josef Svoboda.

six Gothic chamber wings designed for *Macbeth* that same year. During his tenure at Drury Lane his most impressive designs were for Kemble's MELODRAMAS: the Gothic library and ancient baronial hall for *The Iron Chest* (1796), a chapel with side aisles and choir for *De Montfort* (1800), and a Gothic castle for *Adelmorn, the Outlaw* (1801). When Kemble moved to COVENT GARDEN in 1809 Capon joined him and designed many scenes for Shakespearian revivals, including an Anglo-Norman hall for *Hamlet* (1812). The designs he contributed were intended not only to serve for a particular production, but also as part of the theatre's stock scenery. An antiquarian, he insisted upon accurate representations of the external construction materials and architectural features of the existing historical buildings upon which he modelled his designs. His Gothic and pre-Gothic street scenes and building interiors, for which he was famous, remained part of the stock scenery used in productions at Covent Garden long after his death.   AJN

Capuana, Luigi 1839–1915 Italian novelist, short story writer and dramatist. Capuana was a prolific writer who began as a poet, and throughout his life he produced a substantial body of journalistic writings and literary and theatrical criticism. The influences of many late-19th-century artistic movements can be felt in his work, particularly that of SYMBOLISM; he is above all identified as a practitioner and theorist of VERISMO. Among his many plays the most enduring are his drama of peasant life, *Malia (The Spell*, 1895), and his study of the Sicilian petty bourgeoisie, *Lu Cavalieri Pidagna* (1909).   LR

Caragiale, Ion Luca 1852–1912 Romanian dramatist whose comedies are masterpieces of meticulous craftsmanship. Associated with the conservative literary circle Junimea, he lashed out violently at the Romanian society of his time. His sarcastic wit found its most celebrated expression in *A Lost Letter* (1884), the zenith of Romanian playwriting, dealing with a corrupt provincial electoral

campaign won unexpectedly by a hilariously doltish blackmailer, the basest and most empty-headed of all the candidates. His other comedy, *A Stormy Night* (1879), portrays the moral hypocrisy of the middle class, while the FARCE *Carnival Scenes* (1885), whose action takes place in a barber's shop, draws a ludicrous picture of the lower strata of urban society. Caragiale's scant dramatic output also includes the one-act farce *Mr Leonida Facing Reaction* (1880), in which a senile blockhead takes street revellers for revolutionaries; and the less successful psychological drama, *The Bane* (1890). A highly sophisticated use of colourful and often nonsensical language provides much of the appeal of his comedies, which, consequently, lose much in translation. Romanian productions still invariably present these plays as period pieces, thereby reducing them to a critique of bourgeois society, and narrowing the universality of the playwright's vision. Caragiale also wrote many humorous short stories, a number of which were later performed as dramatic sketches.   BM

Carballido, Emilio 1925– Mexican playwright, director and professor, who has fomented theatre in Mexico since 1948. Carballido was born in Córdoba, Veracruz, and his ties to the province remain strong although his professional career belongs to the capital. Founder of the theatre journal *Tramoya* (1975), he has taught, promoted and anthologized an entire generation of young playwrights in Mexico. He is Mexico's premier playwright, both in quantity and quality: his plays are marked by an inexhaustible creative spirit. Drawing on both the realistic and the fantastic, he has written more than 100 plays, several novels and cinema scripts. *Rosalba y los Llaveros (Rosalba and the Llavero Family*, 1950) is a psychological play that contrasts the moral codes of metropolis and province; *La hebra de oro (The Golden Thread*, 1955) integrates the fantastic into a provincial setting with existential intentions. *Yo también hablo de la rosa (I Too Speak of the Rose*, 1965) dramatizes the complexities of human experience and the process of creativity through a metaphorical rose. Later titles include *Las cartas de Mozart* (*Mozart's Letters*, 1974), *Fotografía en la playa* (*Photo on the Beach*, 1977) and *Mimí y Fifí en el Río Orinoco* (*Mimí and Fifí on the Orinoco River*, 1982). *Tiempo de ladrones: La historia de Chucho el Roto* (*Time of Thieves: The Story of Chucho el Roto*, 1984) provided the interesting technique of two full-length plays with some interchangeable scenes, based on a Mexican Robin Hood story. With *Una rosa de dos aromas* (*A Rose with Two Scents*, 1986), he explored male–female relationships from the perspective of two women married to the same man. The distinctive notes in his theatre are the constant experimentation, authentic language and an irrepressible sense of humour.   GW

Carey, Henry [Benjamin Bounce] 1687–1743 English playwright. His early work was as a song-writer and librettist, including songs for GAY's *The Beggar's Opera* (1727) and COLLEY CIBBER's *The Provoked Husband* (1728). He wrote librettos for operas like *Amelia* (1731) and a farcical afterpiece, *The Contrivances* (1715). In 1734 his brilliant PARODY of the bombast of contemporary TRAGEDY, *Chrononhotonthologos*, was performed under the pseudonym Benjamin Bounce. In the wake of *The Beggar's Opera*, Carey joined the attack on the excesses of Italian opera in England with his OPERA *The Dragonfly of Wantley* (1737), performed 67 times in its first season at COVENT GARDEN. Its sequel, *The Dragoness* (1738), was less successful. Carey committed suicide five years later.   PH

Caribbean theatre see BARBADOS; CUBA; DOMINICAN REPUBLIC; EASTERN CARIBBEAN STATES; GUYANA; JAMAICA; PUERTO RICO; TRINIDAD AND TOBAGO

Cariou, Len 1939– Canadian-born actor, director and singer. A classically trained actor whose early career was most closely associated with the STRATFORD [Shakespeare] FESTIVAL (Ontario) and the Tyrone GUTHRIE THEATRE in Minneapolis, Cariou has received his greatest acclaim as a leading man in BROADWAY musicals. His first MUSICAL COMEDY appearance was in the role of Bill Sampson in *Applause* (1970). Critics praised his performance as Fredrik Egerman in *A Little Night Music* (1973), complimenting him for his acting ability and fine singing voice. He returned to the musical stage in 1979 to portray the monomaniacal 'Demon Barber of Fleet Street' in *Sweeney Todd*. His bravura performance in one of the musical theatre's most demanding roles earned him the Tony for Best Actor in a MUSICAL. A later musical role, that of Teddy Roosevelt in *Teddy and Alice* (1987), was less successful. In addition to performing, Cariou has directed several plays, and has served as artistic director of the Manitoba Theatre Centre. In 1991 he appeared on Broadway in Steve Tesich's *The Speed of Darkness*, the first play produced under the new Broadway Alliance.   MK

carnival (See also TRINIDAD CARNIVAL.) The pre-Lent festival of the Christian, and especially Roman Catholic, world. Features of the carnival occur in many seasonal festivities, varying according to both culture and climate, such as May Games, the Feast of St Bartholomew (25 August; JONSON's play gives a lively contemporary picture), the Jamaican Christmas masquerade of Jonkonnu, the Feast of Fools (28 December, Holy Innocents) or, outside Christianity, the Jewish PURIM PLAY. The word is known from the 11th century. Its Latin root signifies the 'removal' of flesh; Italian popular etymology gives us the literally equivalent but metaphorically more graphic 'farewell' to flesh – the meat about to be forsworn for the Lenten fast.

J. Caro Baroja has shown that the wild indulgence of carnival, though set immediately in opposition to the austerity of Lent, forms, in a larger context, the mediating term in a shift from the *alegría* of Christmas to the *tristeza* of Ash Wednesday to Easter Sunday, so that a secular celebration of carnality stands between the year's two key spiritual occasions, looking back to one and forward to the other. Nor is this a structuralist abstraction. Observers of the carnival in Trinidad, or the now heavily commercialized event in Rio de Janeiro, have noted their capacity to absorb, in planning and debriefing, more than their allotted span; and while, in principle, carnival is restricted to Shrove Tuesday, it has often tended to creep forward to *lundi gras*, *dimanche gras*, and sometimes further. In 1739, Thomas Gray wrote from Italy that it 'lasts only from Christmas to Lent; one half of the remaining part of the year is passed in remembering the last, the other in expecting the future Carnival'.

In its activities, its visual imagery and its verbal expressions, carnival is a bewildering set of variations on the theme of oppositions and their inversion or dissolution, which together create a COCKAIGNE-like universe. LIVING PICTURES are processed through the street, illustrating versions of the world turned upside down: the judge sentenced by the accused, the horseman riding backwards, the husband spinning while his wife ploughs. Distinctions between rich and poor, high status and low, are dissolved in the promiscuous mingling of the crowd in the public square, or disguised behind zoomorphic and demonic MASKS and costumes. Men and women cross-dress, and the normal rules of sexual deference are relaxed or abandoned. Informal abuse and obscenity are the order of the day, together with their formal counterpart, the bawdy or satirical song. People throw things – fireworks, water, eggs, dirt – putting physical safety at risk and marring the very clothes that they have donned for the occasion. Animals are subjected to BAITING, and so, sometimes, are minorities such as Jews. Competitive games may be organized, but even then they are virtually rule-free and extremely robust (like the Shrove Tuesday football at Ashbourne, Derbyshire, England), or tend to deny their own rules, by ensuring that the fattest and slowest man wins the foot race. Informal associations of young men process, mount shows, or simply roam the streets – the *SCHEMBARTLÄUFER* of Nuremberg, the Compagnie de la Mère Folle at Dijon, the Venetian Compagnia della Calza; and even, though not in inception a carnivalic organization, the 17th-century London apprentices who used their Shrove Tuesday holiday to express trade rivalries in gang fights and to make common cause against playhouses and brothels (not because they had anything against either, but because it caused a cheerful nuisance and offered the opportunity of stoning the constable and his men when they arrived to break it up).

Such internally democratic and loosely constituted

associations at once express the egalitarian ideal of carnival, and parody the guilds, societies and orders of the everyday, hierarchically organized world. Above all, people eat and drink as if there is no tomorrow – especially pork, hams, chitterlings and innumerable variants of the phallomorphic sausage – turning on its head the usual cautious husbandry of the pre-industrial world, with the glorious excuse that if it is not eaten today, tomorrow we may not eat it.

The organization of all these activities, while obviously requiring planning and preparation, is on the day as loose and anarchic as is consistent with their occurring at all, and they go on simultaneously: a carnival is not primarily a spectator sport, and has no need of the sequential patterning which audiences require. Its chronological frame of reference is external, not internal. Nevertheless, its activities cover a spectrum from wholly informal socializing and milling about, through the relatively formal processions of floats and perambulations of societies, to the wholly formal protodramatic or dramatic performance. Some of these derive directly from the parodic thesis of carnival – mock marriages, trials, burials (such as the burial of the sardine in Madrid depicted by Goya), jousts between Carnival and Lent (Brueghel's painting of 1559, though it should not be taken overall as a depiction of a Flemish carnival – it is a masterly synthesis of the festive calendar from winter to spring – shows in the foreground just such a combat between their gross and emaciated figures). Others extrapolate the ambiance of carnival into fully developed little FARCES, such as the FASTNACHTSPIELE of southern Germany, or the *sottie* 'Le Jeu du Prince des Sots', which Pierre Gringore and his Enfants sans Souci gave in Paris in 1511. From plays such as these derive stock comic characters such as the German HANSWURST, and possibly the English Pickleherring.

This is carnival at its most organized, crystallized into a conscious aesthetic. At its least, always rowdy and rough, it could degenerate into serious public disorder or be used by conflicting interest groups as a violent expression of political and personal rivalry, as happened at ROMANS in 1580.

No single analytical strategy will explain a phenomenon as historically complex, semiotically diffuse and intrinsically paradoxical as carnival. In a sense it is a ritual of revolt, and sometimes this has specific political connotations. But to equate its dialectic between official and popular culture with class struggle in a general sense is too simple, for patricians as well as plebeians are involved as organizers and participants, and share its symbolic vocabulary. Often it seems that a whole society is reacting against its own disciplinary framework, in order, as Victor Turner puts it, to break through the constraints of structure into the euphoria of *communitas*, to discard social norms in favour of human contact. Obviously some members of society have a greater interest than others in changing the norms more permanently, in establishing a free, equal and fraternal ideal of community as a basis for social life; whence the event's potential for political conflict. But for the most part, masters and servants alike seem willing to accept the collective hangover that follows the collective binge. Carnivals have led to riot and repression; they have never led directly to social revolution. Their indirect influence in posing questions of the relationship between the spiritual and the carnal, authority and equality, order and licence, and in offering an image of what the world might be like if it were turned upside down, remains a matter of speculation. AEG

Carnovsky, Morris 1897–1992 American actor who, beginning his long acting career with the THEATRE GUILD in the 1920s, departed in 1931 to join the GROUP THEATRE. Among his many distinguished performances with the Group were those in CLIFFORD ODETS's *Awake and Sing!* (1935), *Paradise Lost* (1935), *Golden Boy* (1937), *Rocket to the Moon* (1938) and *Night Music* (1940). With his mobile face, leonine profile and commanding voice, he played characters much older than himself. Like other Group members, Carnovsky developed his own version of the Method (see ACTORS STUDIO); he disagreed with LEE STRASBERG's emphasis on the actor's own emotions but believed that, used properly, the Method could help actors to create classic roles. Beginning in the mid-1950s, in a series of acclaimed Shakespearian interpretations, Carnovsky achieved a fusion of the Method's psychological REALISM with the demands of poetic style. For the AMERICAN SHAKESPEARE [Festival] THEATRE and various universities he performed Lear, Falstaff, Prospero and Shylock. Like all the Group alumni he was a lifelong student of the art of acting and continued to be active as both a performer and a teacher. In 1983, with lovely simplicity, he portrayed Firs in ANTON CHEKHOV's *The Cherry Orchard* at New Haven's LONG WHARF THEATRE, and in 1984 he published a book of reflections, *The Actor's Eye*. FH

Carrillo, Hugo 1928–94 Guatemalan playwright and director. Carrillo studied in Paris and the USA, and was one of the founders of University Art Theatre (1950). He directed the National Theatre Company until 1968, and from 1972 was artistic director of the independent Theatre Club. A committed writer, his major works include *El corazón del espantapájaros* (*The Scarecrow's Heart*, 1962); *La herencia de la Tula* (*Tula's Inheritance*, 1964); *Mortaja, sueño y autopsia para un teléfono* (*Shroud, Dream and Autopsy for a Telephone*), three one-act plays (1972); and *El señor Presidente* (*Mr President*, 1974) from the novel by Guatemala's Nobel Prize-winning novelist, Miguel Angel Asturias. Carrillo founded the Educational Theatre for school and college students for which he adapted classic Latin American novels to the stage. His plays are translated into many languages and presented widely. GW

Carroll, Earl 1892–1948 American producer, theatre manager and composer who began his theatrical career as a programme seller in Pittsburgh. He tried his hand at song-writing and, after serving as a pilot in the First World War, launched into theatrical producing with *The Lady of the Lamp* (1920). Three years later he inaugurated a REVUE series called the *Earl Carroll Vanities*, which continued annually until 1932, with sporadic editions thereafter. Although they featured established performers such as W. C. FIELDS, Jack Benny and Milton Berle, the *Vanities* were most noted for their daring use of NUDITY in 'living curtain' tableaux, and for Carroll's barrage of outrageous publicity stunts. He opened his own theatre in New York in 1923 but lost it in the Depression. In 1936 he left for Hollywood, where he was an associate producer at 20th Century-Fox. In 1938 he opened the Earl Carroll Theatre and Restaurant in Hollywood.   MK

Carroll, Paul Vincent 1900–68 Irish playwright, co-founder of Glasgow's CITIZENS' THEATRE. He emigrated when he was 21, then taught in Glasgow until 1937, when his plays gave him financial independence. Carroll's early plays satirize the clerical authoritarianism of his youthful experience.

In 1932 the ABBEY presented *Things That Are Caesar's*, in which a woman escapes from an odious marriage engineered with the approval of the local priest. *Shadow and Substance* (1937), acclaimed in Dublin and New York, is a study of Canon Skerritt, whose cold erudition disables his care of souls. In *The White Steed* (1939), Father Shaughnessy is a ruthless puritan vigilante, credibly sinister in the Europe of 1939.

Carroll's dialogue is robust and convincing, his SATIRE precisely directed against subservience to power abused. Yet his first is his only play not to sentimentalize its conclusion: in *The White Steed* an implausibly benign canon, previously implausibly inactive, defeats Shaughnessy's theocratic tyranny, displacing the antagonists who have really challenged it.

Apart from two lightly satiric comedies, *The Devil Came from Dublin* and *The Wayward Saint* (1955), Carroll's later work is heavily didactic. The acrid scenes from provincial life in his first three plays put him worthily in the line of COLUM and T. C. MURRAY.   DM

Cartel An association, formed in France in 1927 by DULLIN, JOUVET, GEORGES PITOËFF and BATY, originally to give mutual support in the face of hostile or frivolous drama critics; this grouping committed each director to publicizing the productions of the other three and to encouraging its audience to see theatre as an art rather than as mere entertainment.   DB

Carter, Mrs Leslie 1862–1937 American actress. Mrs Carter and DAVID BELASCO, her tutor and director, discovered that striking beauty, emotional pyrotechnics and a sensational divorce could make a star performer – first in *The Heart of Maryland* (1895, for a three-year run), in which she swung on the clapper of a bell to keep it from ringing, and then in such slightly lurid dramas as *Zaza* (1899), *Du Barry* (1901) and *Adrea* (1905). According to one critic, Mrs Carter would 'weep, vociferate, shriek, rant, become hoarse with passion, and finally flop and beat the floor'. Although after breaking with Belasco (1906) she continued to perform, on the road and sometimes under her own management, in *Camille*, *The Second Mrs Tanqueray* and *The Circle*, she never matched her successes with Belasco.   RM

Cartwright, Jim 1958– British dramatist, whose first play, *Road* (1986), was seen in a promenade production at London's Theatre Upstairs, but transferred quickly to the main ROYAL COURT THEATRE, where it won Cartwright the Most Promising Playwright Award from *Plays and Players*.

It was a study of the unemployed in Lancashire, as witnessed by its narrator Scully, in short, telling scenes with a lyrical commentary which reminded some observers of DYLAN THOMAS. It was considered to be a play for Mrs Thatcher's Britain. *Bed* (1989) could be described as a dormitory production, in that the stage consists of a giant bed in which seven elderly people are sleeping. Their thoughts and dreams at night provided the action, which had its moments of SURREALISM, its stream-of-consciousness and its lyricism, expressed in an unsophisticated manner which was also its strength. Cartwright, who claims to have read only four books in his life, is a naive writer, but an intuitively skilled one. While *To* (1990) was a less ambitious collection of sketches about working-class life, *The Rise and Fall of Little Voice* (1992) offered roles for two splendid comic actresses, Jane Horrocks, as the little voice of the title whose skills at impersonating the stars are exploited by her mother, played by Alison Steadman. It was staged at the NATIONAL THEATRE with the support of MICHAEL CODRON, the commercial impresario, to whose Aldwych Theatre in the WEST END it transferred.   JE

Cartwright, William 1611–43 English playwright, preacher and Royalist, claimed as a poetic 'son' by BEN JONSON. Of a handful of plays, the most notable is *The Royal Slave* (1636), in which a condemned slave, made king for his last three days, provides a model of virtuous and effective government. Charles I and, particularly, his queen were so impressed by its performance in Oxford that they commanded a repeat at Hampton Court.   PT

Casarès, Maria 1922– French actress of Spanish origins, who performed in *Cross-Purpose* and *The Just* by CAMUS and in COCTEAU's film *Orphée*, and was a permanent member of the THÉÂTRE NATIONAL POPULAIRE company during 1954–9. Since then she has established a reputation as the outstanding French tragic actress, although her style is somewhat too violent for traditional tastes. Major performances include the Mother in *The Screens* (directed by BLIN (1966), a role she repeated in CHÉREAU's production of 1983), Medea in Lavelli's 1967 production and SHAKESPEARE's Cleopatra in 1975.   DB

Casona, Alejandro [Alejandro Rodríguez Álvarez] 1903–65 Spanish playwright forced into exile in 1937 on account of Loyalist sympathies. He wrote his major plays in ARGENTINA, returning to Spain only in 1963. Reacting against REALISM, Casona brought poetry and fantasy to the stage. Through illusion his characters often escape cruel reality; however, they return to find happiness in love, sacrifice and suffering. His theatre evinces optimism and faith, without denying life's tragic side. *La dama del alba* (*Lady of the Dawn*, 1944), written for MARGARITA XIRGU, portrays death as a beautiful woman with human feelings who is victim of her own tragic destiny. *La barca sin pescador* (*The Boat without a Fisherman*, 1945) dramatizes the redemption through love of a ruined stockbroker who sells his soul to the devil. *Los árboles mueren de pie* (*Trees Die Standing*, 1949) depicts an heroic grandmother who pretends to believe pious lies of those attempting to bring her happiness. Among Spain's most frequently performed playwrights internationally, Casona is also well known for one-act plays recreating Spanish classics. MH

Cassidy, Claudia 1905– American drama critic. Born in Illinois, Cassidy spent her girlhood in Chicago and attended the University of Illinois in Urbana. She began her career as a drama and music critic with the *Chicago Journal of Commerce* in 1925, quickly gaining a reputation for being tough but fair. In 1941, she left the *Journal* to organize the music and drama departments of the new *Chicago Daily Sun* (now the *Sun-Times*). Within a year, she was hired by the *Tribune*. Until her retirement in 1965, she wrote a daily column, 'On the Aisle', plus contributing to the Sunday edition. She toured Europe during the summers, sending back to the *Tribune* her impressions of 'Europe on the Aisle'. Considered the most powerful Chicago critic, Cassidy was credited with stopping New York producers from putting weak companies on the road. Her major credo was that the 'only way to judge a play is to wait and see if the theatre brings it to life'. TLM

Casson, Lewis 1875–1969 British actor and director. From 1904 to 1907 he was a regular player at the ROYAL COURT THEATRE during the historic VEDRENNE–BARKER seasons, and Granville Barker's influence on his directing and commitment to the repertory movement (see REGIONAL THEATRE (BRITAIN)) was lifelong. In 1908 he joined ANNIE HORNIMAN's company in Manchester and was its director from 1911 to 1914. After the war he continued to mix acting (in plays ranging from SHAW to SHAKESPEARE and EURIPIDES) with directing, and with his wife SYBIL THORNDIKE frequently toured abroad in both plays and recitals. During the Second World War he became a leading force in CEMA (Council for the Encouragement of Music and the Arts), directing and playing in *Macbeth* for the first tour of the Welsh coalfields in 1940. Knighted in 1945, he is remembered for his clear and subtly expressive stage speech, his catholicity of taste and his concern to extend the reach of the theatre. AJ

Castelvetro, Lodovico 1505–71 Italian dramatist and writer; perhaps the most influential of the many Renaissance translators and interpreters of ARISTOTLE. Castelvetro's liberal understanding of the dramatic unities, decorum and characterization as expounded in his *Poetica di Aristotele vulgarizata et sposta* (*Aristotle's Poetics Translated into the Vernacular and Explicated*, Vienna, 1950) generated intense critical debate on the degree of freedom that might reasonably be enjoyed by modern writers in adapting classical rules to contemporary needs and practice. KR

castrato Mature male, castrated before his voice broke, singing in the soprano or contralto register. The original reasons for the occurrence of such singers have never been satisfactorily determined. They appeared in Italian OPERA from its beginning and achieved their greatest celebrity in the 18th century. It was claimed that their advantage over boys was that they were more amenable to discipline and, of course, their voices would not break after several years: also, they were said to have more powerful voices than women. They were noted for their brilliant execution rather than for their dramatic accomplishment, and they frequently ornamented their singing with the most elaborate embellishments, to the increasing anger of many serious composers. The castrati performed male roles, giving rise to such occasions as that on which a heroic character was sung by a castrato in a soprano voice and that of his wife by a woman contralto. The most famous of all operatic castrati was Carlo Broschi, known as Farinelli (1705–82). The comment attributed to Lady Rich, 'One God – one Farinelli', was well enough known for Hogarth to include it in plate 2 of his *Rake's Progress*. The last of these celebrated singers was Giovanni Battista Velutti (1781–1861), who created the last operatic role written for his kind of voice in Meyerbeer's *Il crociato in Egitto* (Venice, 1824). Castrati were sometimes referred to as sopranists (or contraltists), *musici* or *evirati*. GH

Castro y Bellvís, Guillem de 1569–1631 Spanish playwright who began writing in the flourishing theatrical tradition of his native Valencia and whose contact there with the older LOPE DE VEGA and the *COMEDIA nueva* is evident in his later work. He is best known for his two-part work inspired by ballads on the youth of Spain's national hero. The first, *Las mocedades del Cid* (*The Young El Cid*), is the source of PIERRE CORNEILLE's *Le Cid* (1636), but stresses the heroic dimensions of the protagonist rather than the love interest of the French version. Three plays in the comic cape-and-sword tradition, inspired by works of CERVANTES, are *Narciso en su opinión* (*Narcissus in His Own Eyes*) and *Los mal casados de Valencia* (*The Unhappily Married of Valencia*). ElB

Catalan theatre (See also MEDIEVAL DRAMA IN EUROPE (Spain).) Catalan is the language of northeastern Spain: Catalonia, Valencia and the Balearic Islands. After producing a flourishing medieval literature, it virtually disappeared until a mid- 19th-century renaissance. Among innovators in the revival were Santiago Rusiñol (1861–1931) and ANGEL GUIMERÀ, Catalonia's major end-of-the-century playwright.

The following decades witnessed a lively theatre movement at both amateur and professional levels. In 1913 the modernist playwright and director Adrià Gual (1872–1943) founded the Catalan School of Dramatic Art (since 1931, the Theatre Institute). Josep Maria de Sagarra (1894–1961) created original verse dramas and superlative SHAKESPEARE translations. Actress MARGARITA XIRGU gained international fame. The Gran Teatro del Liceo became a major European OPERA house, and popular theatres along the Paralelo were home to VAUDEVILLE and musical REVUES. In 1929 the outdoor Teatre Grec was inaugurated in conjunction with the city's second World Exposition.

Franco's victory in the Civil War (1936–9) forced many theatre people into exile and introduced a period of repression for Catalan culture. Although some provincial groups defied the prohibition, there were no authorized performances in Catalan until 1946. Subject to CENSORSHIP, the first postwar plays followed conventional formulas, but the establishment of the Agrupació Dramàtica de Barcelona in 1955 provided a viable alternative to this commercial stage. Along with classic Catalan and foreign theatre, the ADB premiered works by important postwar playwrights: Salvador Espriu (1913–85), known for his modernizations of Greek legends; Maria Aurèlia Capmany (1918–91); absurdist (see THEATRE OF THE ABSURD) Manuel de Pedrolo (1918–90); and Joan Brossa (b.1919). The group was disbanded by government order in 1963 for staging BRECHT's *The Threepenny Opera*.

Despite the prohibition, Brecht's theory underpinned the Adrià Gual School of Dramatic Art. Founded in 1960 and directed by Ricard Salvat (b.1934), the school is credited with professionalizing the Catalan stage. Among its collaborators was NÚRIA ESPERT, already a nationally acclaimed actress. While the training programme closed in 1978, the group continued to produce foreign and Catalan works.

In the early 1960s, an independent theatre movement replaced the aborted ADB. Associated with younger authors like Josep Benet i Jornet (b.1940) and Jordi Teixidor (b.1939), it also gave rise to troupes specializing in pantomime and collective creation. Notable among these are ELS JOGLARS (founded 1962) and Els Comediants (1972), that have successfully toured internationally and remain active.

Although Barcelona has never supported as many playhouses as Madrid, paradoxically it has produced some of Spain's most innovative theatre. The Lliure, founded in 1976 by LLUÍS PASQUAL and Fabià Puigserver, and the Poliorama, directed since 1985 by JOSEP MARIA FLOTATS, are among the country's most prestigious theatres. Also highly praised are the productions of Carles Santos, a multifaceted avant-garde composer, actor and writer from Valencia. Newer troupes, like La Fura dels Baus, La Cubana, Tricicle and Sèmola, tour widely and enjoy enormous popularity.

Among Catalan-language playwrights whose works are translated and staged abroad are Rodolf Sirera (b.1948) and Sergi Belbel (b.1963). Sirera's *El verí del teatre* (*The Audition*, 1978) was produced in London in 1988, and two of Belbel's texts were performed in Paris in 1992. PZ

cavittu natakam Form of theatre that emerged in the mid-16th century in south INDIA to satisfy the cravings of Latin Christian communities for an entertainment centred on Christian subject-matter. *Cavittu natakam* of Kerala state was inspired by the zeal of Roman Catholic priests who proselytized the area. They were protected by Portuguese military and political authorities who had recently consolidated their power along the eastern seacoast of the Indian subcontinent.

The plays contain quasi-historical and mythological characters of Christian history and figures of medieval romances, like Charlemagne, St George and St Sebastian, who are the equivalents of the great archetypal heroes of the Hindu myths and legends, such as Rama, Krishna and Arjuna. Among the plays, *The Play of Charlemagne* is famous and frequently performed. It requires 15 nights to complete and includes a cast of nearly 80 characters. The play is based on ARIOSTO's *Orlando Furioso* and deals with the heroic adventures of the 8th-century French emperor and his 12 valiant peers. Replete with battles and court scenes, it provides the quintessential *cavittu natakam* performance. Other works created for the *cavittu natakam* stage present Old and New Testament stories, lives of the

saints and contemporary plays with social and historical significance. The dominant sentiments (*rasa*) of this form of theatre are heroism (*vira*) and love (*srngara*).

Cavittu means 'step' or 'stamping' and *natakam* means a 'play' or 'drama'. A great deal of violent dance movement occurs in performance, in which the actors, who are all male, stamp their feet vigorously on the stage. In posture and walk, the actors exaggerate masculine movement patterns to the extreme. Battle scenes loosely incorporate martial art techniques of the region (*kalarippayatt*) which have been adapted to suit the demands of the plays, especially in conflicts with swords and shields. The style of movement contrasts markedly with that of Hindu theatre forms popular in the same region – KATHAKALI, KRISHNATTAM and KUTIYATTAM. Some hand gestures and facial expressions seem to have been borrowed from classically derived forms, but the traces are faint.

The master of the performance is the teacher (*asan*) who stage-manages and trains the players in martial arts, ACROBATICS, singing and dancing, not to mention the memorization of the parts. Most plays are written in Tamil, which is not the language of the players, who speak Malayalam. The teacher sets up a schedule of work at his household, and after ritual initiation into the art, provides regular lessons in the specific roles that are to be learned. General training is not given. Those who play kings come from special families of Christians. Each of the actors is assigned to a character of an appropriate play according to his family connections.

The *cavittu natakam* stage is unique. Located in open ground in a village or town near a church or cathedral, it may be 30ft wide and 100ft long. Flanking each end are tall wooden platforms that must be scaled from the stage by ladders. The kings hold court on the high platforms while the action scenes and battles take place centre stage. A door up right serves for all entrances and one up left serves for exits. A small opening up centre provides a clear view of the stage for the chorus and musicians who work backstage. A large bell-metal lamp fed by coconut oil and cloth wicks is located down centre, although it is used more for RITUAL purposes than for illumination. The main illumination is provided by electric lights such as floods, scoops and fluorescent tubes.

Costumes are local versions of historical Western dress, sumptuous in appearance and very colourful. Make-up is realistic, except for false beards, moustaches and wigs. Villainous characters often wear sunglasses and tennis shoes, which are thought to be appropriate for individuals of an evil nature. The clown character (*katiyakkaran*) keeps spectators amused with various antics, especially when he parodies the songs and dances of the other characters. He even makes cutting remarks about the teacher, who stands on stage throughout performance guiding the progress of the action. The clown interprets the action in Malayalam so that spectators are able to follow the meaning of the Tamil songs and they can appreciate his satiric comments.

Chief among the musical instruments are the barrel-shaped drum played by two sticks (*centa*) and the large bell-metal cymbals (*elattalam*). The teacher controls the tempo of performance with small hand cymbals and he may cue scene changes and entrances with a whistle. A wide variety of other musical instruments may also be used – harmonium, clarinet, *mridangam* drum and *tamboora*, a stringed instrument made from a gourd, among others. Even snare and trap drums make an appearance, adding to the general chaos of sound that typifies the *cavittu natakam* performance.

Cavittu natakam is best known in the Cochin and Quilon districts of central Kerala where Latin Christians make their home. The season lasts from December to March, coinciding with major church festivals. A group of performers can count on perhaps a dozen shows a season; therefore, they all have other occupations and even the teachers resort to outside income to survive. FAR

Céleste, Madame (Céline) [Céleste Keppler] 1810/11–82 French dancer, most of whose unusual career belongs to the English theatre. Most works of reference accept her own claim that she was born in 1814, but her marriage in Baltimore in 1828 and the birth of a child in 1829 make that improbable. She had visited the USA with a Parisian dance troupe, and had already divested herself of husband and child when she made her English debut in 1830. A graceful dancer and mime, she solicited from English playwrights pieces that would either allow her to remain speechless throughout or accommodate her unrepentant French accent. The first was PLANCHÉ's *The Child of the Wreck* (1837) at DRURY LANE. Céleste was by now a wealthy woman, after several lucrative and wildly popular American tours, and her move to the HAYMARKET in 1838 was partly managerial and partly romantic. It signalled the start of a long relationship with BENJAMIN WEBSTER, confirmed in 1844, when they became joint lessees of the ADELPHI, where Céleste was to be an acknowledged favourite. The part of the noble American Indian, Miami, in BUCKSTONE's *The Green Bushes* (1845) was to remain in her repertoire until her retirement. BOUCICAULT and TOM TAYLOR also tailored parts for her at the Adelphi. After quarrelling with Webster, she became lessee of the LYCEUM (1860–1), opening as Madame Defarge in Tom Taylor's version of *A Tale of Two Cities*. She returned to the Adelphi, after an extended foreign tour (1863–8), in 1870 to make her farewell appearance as Miami, a 'final' appearance which she repeated in 1872, 73 and 74. PT

CEMA (Council for the Encouragement of Music and the Arts) Formed in Britain in 1940 to provide entertainment for wartime factory and evacuation areas, CEMA was responsible for transferring the bombed-out OLD VIC Company to Burnley, Lancashire (1941), and sponsoring tours by the Pilgrim Players and ASHLEY DUKES's Mercury Players. It took over the Bristol Theatre Royal in 1943 and through JAMES BRIDIE founded the Glasgow CITIZENS' THEATRE. In 1946 it was transformed into the ARTS COUNCIL OF GREAT BRITAIN. CI

censorship Although sometimes pretending to other concerns, especially religious and moral, censorship of the theatre is fundamentally a political act. Endemic to most present-day hardline regimes, it attempts to sedate or suppress whatever elements in the drama the exercising authority considers contrary to its interests or values. Historically, too, censorship has been as useful to spiritual

as to temporal masters. Its agents tend to be shadowy Kafkaesque figures, whose decisions are rarely open to question or appeal. A well tamed theatre is the ally of the state machine; an unruly one, potentially its bitterest enemy and critic.

In contrast to censorship of the theatre, institutionalized pre-publication censorship, with roots going back to the invention of printing in the 15th century, has in most cases been long abandoned, especially in Western Europe, though legal recourse against published materials may still be permitted. Even in Britain, where the press has been nominally free since 1695, controls on blasphemy, sedition and obscenity have continued to be applied with varying degrees of rigour over the centuries, including the present – most notably in the case of Regina v. Penguin Books (1960) over the publication of the uncut text of LAWRENCE's *Lady Chatterley's Lover*. But the theatre has always been a special case, because of the immediacy of its impact on an audience and its potential propaganda value; and the widespread survival of dramatic censorship into the 20th century, even in Western liberal democracies, reflects belief in the power of the stage to move audiences and mould attitudes.

To be effective, censorship does not have to be institutionalized: it may be exercised in various less overt (often equally damaging) ways, including self-censorship by authors or editors, and managerial, proprietorial and publishers' censorship. In Britain SHAKESPEARE was heavily edited on moral and religious grounds for 19th-century readers (e.g. Thomas Bowdler's *Family Shakespeare*, 1808), while Restoration comedy was unavailable in print until late in the century and almost never produced on stage. An increasing recent trend has been censorship by withdrawal of sponsorship, or state or local funding, from theatre companies which perform plays regarded as challenging political, moral or religious orthodoxies. This discussion, however, is mainly concerned with the commonest version of dramatic censorship – institutionalized governmental censorship – which aims in one sense or another to constrain the intellectual and artistic freedom of the playwright. Extreme forms may involve an embargo on publication as well as performance.

Ancient Greece and Rome Evidence for the existence in antiquity of dramatic censorship in the modern sense is scarce and unreliable. Scattered references (e.g. in Cicero, *De Republica*) suggest that personal SATIRE in Attic comedy was occasionally bridled, though not in any systematic way and not necessarily prompted by the state. Free speech was in any case a deeply rooted Athenian concept, and ARISTOPHANES' comedies show that the limits, if any, were really very broad. Roman comedy was more restrained, especially at the level of personal allusion, after Naevius' imprisonment on orders of the powerful Metelli family whom he allegedly insulted in his plays. Laws on libel and slander were harsh and may have inhibited comic dramatists like PLAUTUS (who alludes to Naevius' fate in the *Miles Gloriosus*). Another form of censorship is implied by Donatus' claim that in the *fabula togata* (native comedy) it was forbidden to depict masters outwitted by their slaves; but how common this prohibition was is unclear. Popular though it was, the theatre was distrusted by the authorities, which at various times tried to discourage its spread; and it came to be regarded with contempt by commentators such as Livy. Towards the end of the Roman Empire Tertullian's *De Spectaculis* shows evidence of the early Christian Church's animosity to the whole spectrum of dramatic activity, culminating in Justinian's closure of the theatres in the 6th century AD.

Europe c.1400–1900 The roots of modern European censorship lie within the medieval theatre (see MEDIEVAL DRAMA IN EUROPE). In England the Church exercised considerable control over the content of MYSTERY PLAYS and was apparently responsible, before the Reformation, for elimination from the York and Chester cycles of pieces devoted to the life of the Virgin Mary. At Chester in 1531 the secular authorities removed references to papal power from the banns of the city's cycle; and similar measures were probably later taken elsewhere. In France as early as 1402 Charles VI asserted court authority over the presentation of religious drama by granting the CONFRÉRIE DE LA PASSION the right to stage *mystères* only on condition that his own officials kept a critical eye on performances. Such controls, limited in effect, foreshadowed more aggressive attempts to regulate the theatre in Western Europe as it became more secularized. In France the satirical exploits of troupes like Les Basochiens and Les Clercs prompted edicts against them in 1442 and 1448. By the early 16th century some local authorities became impatient with itinerant troupes and their disruptive potential: at Lille in 1514 they prohibited the practice of *farcer les princes*, attacked the insolence of actors in 1552, and in 1544 suppressed *des jeux scandaleux*.

Religious drama, disinherited by the Church and vexatious to the state, came under growing threat during the 16th century. The French *parlement* introduced a form of preventive censorship in 1538, leading to withdrawal of the privileges enjoyed by the Confrérie de la Passion in 1548 and a ban on the performance of mystery plays. During the upheavals of the Reformation in England, government regulation of the drama was a vital instrument of Tudor statecraft. One of the provisions of the Act 'for the advancement of true religion and for the abolition of the contrary' (1543) banned all plays likely to challenge the newly established Protestantism, while in 1548 the Feast of CORPUS CHRISTI (with all attendant dramatic activities) was suppressed. It was temporarily reinstated under Mary, but by 1581 Elizabeth I had achieved complete prohibition of the mystery cycles, followed by a ban (lasting for over 300 years) on all plays based on, or quoting from, the Bible.

The key to effective censorship was centralized control. In many parts of Western Europe (e.g. Germany and Italy) the fragmented political situation made that impossible; but France had some success via its *parlement* in Paris, and Spain had its native-bred Inquisition (though the drama never figured prominently in the proscription lists). Most adept at handling stage censorship was Elizabethan England. Although local authorities in 1559 were empowered to prohibit plays 'wherein either matters of religion or the gouvernance of the estate of the common weale shall be handled, or treated', Elizabeth always understood that proper control meant active supervision by the Court itself.

The powers of the MASTER OF THE REVELS as censor, nominally subject to the Lord Chamberlain (chief officer of the royal household), are first mentioned in the patent granted in 1574 to the Earl of Chesterfield's troupe to perform only those plays 'sene and allowed' by the Master. The advent of the first permanent theatres in London in 1576–7 obliged fuller definition of the powers of the Revels Office, and in 1581 a royal patent gave the incumbent, Edmund Tilney, sweeping powers over plays, players and playhouses 'to order and reforme aucthorise and put downe as shalbe thought meete or unmeete unto himselfe or his said deputie'. Those who 'obstinatelie refuse[d]' his commands became liable to imprisonment. By the time Shakespeare came to London a centralized and surprisingly effective system of censorship was operating. Further royal edicts of 1598, 1603 and 1622, and the 1606 Act prohibiting profane oaths, helped secure the Master of the Revels' control of the drama during the 17th century, interrupted only by the Puritans' CLOSURE OF THE THEATRES from 1642 to 1660.

Court supervision had both positive and negative effects. While it gave acting companies protection from interference by hostile local authorities, it also meant that plays were very carefully scrutinized. The MS of *Sir Thomas More* (c.1593) – of which it is likely Shakespeare was part-author – bears the instruction: 'leave out the insurrection wholy & the Cause ther off'. There is evidence of extensive political censorship in some other plays of the period – e.g. *The Second Maiden's Tragedy* (1611), MASSINGER and FLETCHER's *Sir John van Olden Barnavelt* (1619) and Massinger's *Believe As You List* (1631) and *The King and his Subject* (1638) – though it is not certain that the censor (as opposed to the playhouse) was responsible for all of the deletions. Some early printings of Shakespeare's plays also suffered: texts of *Richard II* up to Q4 (1608) lack the abdication scene and the Folio *Othello* omits the oaths present in the Quarto (but the same caution applies, especially in the latter case). The substitution of Falstaff for Sir John Oldcastle in *Henry IV Part 1* probably indicates the censor's attempt to protect a prominent personality.

There are more definite examples of the same practice later – e.g. MIDDLETON's *A Game at Chess* (1624) was licensed but then proscribed, supposedly for representing the king on stage, though its anti-Spanish political stance, supported by a caricature of the former Spanish ambassador, was just as important a reason. Middleton may have been imprisoned for his satire; others certainly were – e.g. BEN JONSON, CHAPMAN and MARSTON, whose unlicensed *Eastward Ho* (1605) aroused James I's wrath for irreverent portrayals of his Scottish courtiers.

The relative strength of censorship in 17th-century England under Masters of the Revels Sir George Buc and Sir Henry Herbert contrasts with its relative weakness elsewhere. In France, where pre-production censorship brought only limited returns, Louis XIII abolished censorship altogether in 1641. But actors could still be punished for indecency and playwrights were not completely free. MOLIÈRE's portrait of religious hypocrisy in *Tartuffe* (1664) aroused such a storm of abuse from *parlement* and the Archbishop of Paris that Louis XIV, though privately sympathetic to Molière, was forced to ban the play. A much revised version was allowed for public performance in 1669, in the presence of the king.

During the 18th century dramatic censorship became more firmly entrenched in Western Europe, particularly in Britain and France, where measures were introduced which (with periodic remissions in the latter case) persisted into the 20th century. On 31 March 1701 Louis XIV ordered that all new plays be officially examined before performance which, with a strengthening edict in November 1706, set up the formal mechanism of pre-Revolution control over the stage. Victims of censorship included La Harpe, Chénier and Lemierre; but pre-eminent was BEAUMARCHAIS, whose comedies *The Barber of Seville* (1775) and (in particular) *The Marriage of Figaro* (1784) were regarded as offensive to the *ancien régime*.

Britain's system of censorship was comprehensively revised and tightened in 1737. Sir Robert Walpole's Stage Licensing Act granted the authorities sweeping new powers, a direct result of damaging lampoons on the government by HENRY FIELDING and others. Drawing on the practice of the Revels Office, the new law centred on the Lord Chamberlain, who was empowered (in addition to certain licensing responsibilities for theatres) to forbid 'as often as he shall think fit' any dramatic piece acted 'for hire, gain, or reward' anywhere in Great Britain. Modified only in details by the Theatre Regulation Act, which replaced it in 1843, Walpole's legislation laid the foundations for government control of the theatre for well over 200 years. Though not normally applied retrospectively, the Lord Chamberlain's powers were occasionally used to prohibit performances of plays such as OTWAY's *Venice Preserv'd* on grounds of political sensitivity and, during the madness of George III, *King Lear*.

No formal system of censorship existed in Russia until the beginning of the 19th century, but the Tsars attempted to bring the drama into close alliance with the Court, just as in England. The motives were similar, though the methods were different and more confining, since Russia relied on generous state patronage – in effect government sponsorship of the theatre – to ensure that what was performed was tailored to meet the political needs of the day. While there could be no centralized censorship in the politically confused climate of Germany and Austria, controls did operate locally. SCHILLER's famous *STURM UND DRANG* drama *The Robbers* (1781; described by HAZLITT as the quintessence of all that was noble in the struggle for liberty) terrified the director of the 1782 Mannheim production so much that he decided to camouflage its revolutionary spirit by transplanting it into a 16th-century context, forestalling in the process action on the part of the authorities. Even so, the play was prohibited altogether in other parts of Germany–Austria (e.g. in Leipzig), and its Viennese premiere was delayed until 1808, when it was given at the Theater an der Wien rather than at the more illustrious BURGTHEATER (where it was eventually allowed in a cut version in 1850). Only in France was the play welcomed with unbridled enthusiasm as a salutary lesson for the times.

Censorship, inimical to the spirit of the French Revolution, was temporarily abolished by order of the Legislative Assembly, 13–19 January 1791. However, only three years later it was revived in an attempt to 'republi-canize' the drama. Theatres were ordered to delete all references to *duc*, *baron*, *marquis*, *conte* and *monsieur*. No playwright was immune – not even RACINE, whose *Andromaque* (1667), *Phèdre* (1667) and *Britannicus* (1668) suddenly became proscribed works. During the summer of 1794 at the height of the Terror, out of 151 scripts submitted over three months 33 were suppressed and another 25 severely cut. Fear of contamination by France's revolutionary spirit induced other countries to exercise sterner vigilance in political censorship than ever before. In Britain, under the scrutiny of the Lord Chamberlain's deputies – John Larpent (between 1778 and 1824) and GEORGE COLMAN THE YOUNGER (between 1824 and 1836) – plays bearing resemblances to events in France or to insurrection in general were prohibited. These included Joseph Holman's adaptation of Schiller's *The Robbers* (c.1799); Martin Archer Shee's *Alasco*, a drama of Polish patriotism (published in 1824 with all of Colman's cuts conspicuously marked); and Mary Russell Mitford's historical tragedy of regicide, *Charles the First* (1825).

A general antipathy to revolutionary topics also characterized the growing power of Habsburg censorship. The Vienna Order (1794) banned all dangerous political works and by 1819 Metternich, supported by a spy system which had ramifications well beyond the dramatic and literary, sought to impose a rigid censorship through all states of the Austrian Empire. During the 1830s and 1840s JOHANN NESTROY and FRANZ GRILLPARZER were frequently at odds with the censor in Vienna. The former's *Freedom Comes to Krahwinkel*, saturated with ad-libbed political allusion, was banned shortly after its first performance in 1848, and the latter's *King Ottakar, His Rise and Fall* (written 1819–23) was branded as seditious. When *Thou Shalt Not Lie* was vetoed in 1838, Grillparzer refused to permit any further performances of his works.

The theatre in Tsarist Russia was already virtually a department of the state when formal censorship was established in 1804. Over the next 50 years the regulations were progressively tightened. By 1828 censorship had been brought under the wing of the Third Department of His Majesty's Personal Office, which introduced new rules for censorship in Moscow, St Petersburg and the larger provincial cities, and from 1842 embraced all provincial troupes. When Nicholas I set up his secret committee for censorship (known officially as the Committee of April 2nd) in 1848, the Tsar took over personal control of the system, which prohibited representation of the Tsar and satire on the nobility, landowners and state or local officials. Victims included PUSHKIN (*Boris Godunov*, 1825; performed 1870 under the more flexible policies of Alexander II), LERMONTOV (*Masquerade*, 1836; full version performed 1862), OSTROVSKY (*The Bankrupt*, 1849), TURGENEV (*A Month in the Country*, 1850; performed 1872), SUKHOVO-KOBYLIN (*The Case*, 1862; performed as *Obsolete Time*, 1882; and *Tarelkin's Death*, 1869; performed 1900), and LEV TOLSTOI (*The Power of Darkness*, 1886; performed 1895). Surprisingly, GOGOL escaped a veto on *The Inspector General* (1836), as Tsar Nicholas apparently counted on its frightening corrupt provincial officials.

On the European continent political censorship was an important weapon against the increasing use of the drama as a vehicle for expression of national libertarian sentiment. In France VICTOR HUGO's *Le Roi s'amuse* (1832), which provoked disorder in the theatre for supposed reference to Louis-Philippe, was prohibited after two performances. It was instrumental in bringing about the reimposition of state censorship in 1835, after abolition in the 1830 Revolution.

The situation in Italy was confused. In some areas (e.g. Lombardy–Venetia) the Austrian censor was in control; in most other states and duchies there were localized systems. A royal committee was set up in Naples in 1807 to supervise all aspects of theatrical production, while at the Vatican Pius VII appointed a censorship board of six *cavalieri* and a prelate. ALFIERI's tragedies were prohibited in the 1820s in Lombardy–Venetia and in Piedmont: Victor Emmanuel, suspicious of their political allusiveness, ordered deletions of patriotic expressions from *Rosmunda* and *Oreste*. The need to anaesthetize nationalist emotions was confirmed by the fervent reception of the 'Va pensiero' chorus in Verdi's opera *Nabucco* (Milan, 1842). In consequence Verdi's works attracted special attention from Italian and other European censors. Among playwrights who suffered political censorship in the period before Unification were Ugo Fosco, Giovanni Battista Niccolini, Silvio Pellico and Vincenzo Monti (whose tragedy *Caio Gracco* was banned posthumously in Tuscany in 1847).

In Europe generally, after about 1850, the balance began to change in favour of a more persistent concern with moral issues. After 1852 (and another brief respite from censorship in the wake of the 1848 Revolution), the French censors turned their attention to the supposed immoralities of the plays of, among others, ALEXANDRE DUMAS *fils* (who fell victim to the system when he adapted his novel *La Dame aux camélias* for the stage in 1850), VICTORIEN SARDOU and ÉMILE AUGIER.

Much of Britain's theatrical life in the later 19th century was dependent on adaptations of the latest Parisian novelties, and because moral censorship was more restrictive than in France all plays of French origin were thoroughly deodorized before being rendered fit for British audiences. Some pieces (especially those which seemed to attack the sanctity of family life) proved too *risqué* in language and situation to pass muster with the censors (successively William Bodham Donne, Edward Pigott and George A. Redford) and were banned outright. A typical comment (on *Le Songe d'une matinée de printemps*, in which SARAH BERNHARDT was to star at the Lyric and was refused a licence in 1898) reads: 'a tissue of moral beastliness which could only disgust any healthy minded audience'. Most notorious of all – indeed, for many years a benchmark of immorality – was *La Dame aux camélias*, banned in Britain first in 1853 (a year after it was allowed in France) and several times thereafter in a variety of adaptations. Ironically Verdi's version as *La traviata* (Venice, 1853) was allowed in English translation in 1856 because OPERA as a matter of policy enjoyed more latitude than straight drama.

The arrival of the 'advanced drama' in the 1890s, heralded by IBSEN, accelerated the embryonic anti-censorship campaign led in Britain by WILLIAM ARCHER and BERNARD SHAW, a movement fuelled by the suppression on moral grounds of several plays of European stature: Ibsen's *Ghosts* (Pigott described its author as 'morally deranged' and the play was not approved for public performance until 1914), Tolstoi's *The Power of Darkness*, MAETERLINCK's *Monna Vanna* (in French, 1902), and some plays by EUGÈNE BRIEUX (including *Damaged Goods*, 1902; performed 1914, also prohibited for a time in France). On the native front Shaw's *Mrs Warren's Profession* (copyright performance 1898, but not licensed until 1925) and HARLEY GRANVILLE BARKER's *Waste* (refused 1907, approved 1920) – both plays were given private performances by the STAGE SOCIETY in 1902 and 1907 respectively – were victims of a censorship that was beginning to inflict severe damage on playwrights committed to the serious discussion of moral and sexual issues on the stage. Conditions were hardly more favourable in Germany, where censorship was strengthened after about 1889: FRANK WEDEKIND's *Spring Awakening* (1891) and *Earth Spirit* (1893) were both banned from public performance until 1906 and 1902 respectively. One solution to the restrictions was a theatre dedicated to private (i.e. club) performances only which would escape the attentions of the censor and be freed from the demands of commercial theatre. Of such the most prominent were the Théâtre Libre (see ANDRÉ ANTOINE), founded in Paris in 1887, Berlin's FREIE BÜHNE (1888) and London's INDEPENDENT THEATRE SOCIETY (1891).

Only in France was the anti-censorship lobby victorious, with the ending of formal, pre-production censorship for practical purposes in 1905, when funding by central government was withdrawn. In Britain a petition by 71 dramatists (including PINERO, HENRY ARTHUR JONES, W. S. GILBERT, GALSWORTHY, Granville Barker and Shaw), supported by leading novelists and poets, resulted in the setting up of a parliamentary committee specifically to consider the problem of stage censorship. Its report (1909), recommending a system of voluntary censorship, found little favour in parliament or the theatre – managers relied on the protection offered by the Lord Chamberlain's licence – and the idea lapsed, though a few years later a modified version was adopted by the new British Board of Film Censors under George Redford (who resigned from the Lord Chamberlain's Office in 1911 after 16 controversial years as Examiner of Plays).

20th-century Europe In Britain, as in the past, the Lord Chamberlain claimed to have majority feeling behind his decisions, and the practice of the censors in the 20th century – latterly a committee of advisers rather than one individual – was gradually to adjust to public acceptance of what had been formerly considered outrageous, indecent or taboo. The rule on the ineligibility of scriptural drama on the stage, which had induced the ban on WILDE's *Salomé* in 1893 (privately described by the censor as 'a miracle of impudence'), was slowly relaxed during the first decade of the century. Nonetheless, in 1958 BECKETT's *Endgame* was censored for references to the nonexistence of God (whereas the original 1957 version in French had emerged unscathed) and a translation of FERNANDO ARRABAL's *Car Cemetery* – which has the distinction of being the last play to be refused a licence by the Lord Chamberlain – was vetoed in June 1968 because of an allegedly blasphemous crucifixion scene. Political censorship prohibited Shaw's *Press Cuttings* and *The Shewing Up of Blanco Posnet* (to which there were also religious objections) in 1909, but the latter was staged in Ireland at Dublin's ABBEY THEATRE after YEATS and LADY GREGORY averted threatened use by the Lord Lieutenant of his power of *ex post facto* censorship. NOËL COWARD's *The Vortex* (1924) narrowly escaped a veto (even the king was consulted at one stage) for its cynical portrayal of the upper middle classes, bordering, in the opinion of one of the Lord Chamberlain's advisers, on 'socialist propaganda'.

Leftish political attitudes were always examined with care, even in reference to matters abroad (e.g. pro-Bolshevik sentiments were deleted from plays in the 1920s). The censor habitually intervened on behalf of public figures: the licence for *The Mikado* was suspended in 1907 in anticipation of offence to the crown prince of Japan, then on a state visit; and in the 1930s all references to Hitler and Mussolini were excised. (Ironically the MUSIC-HALLS, immune from the Lord Chamberlain's jurisdiction, delighted in exploiting just the kind of material that the censors insisted on deleting.) Members of the royal family (dead or alive) continued to be dutifully protected, even when sympathetically treated as in LAURENCE HOUSMAN's *Victoria Regina* (1934). But the rule prohibiting personal allusion was severely undermined by 1961, when a send-up of the prime minister, Harold Macmillan, was allowed to feature in the satirical REVUE *Beyond the Fringe*.

Concern for moral standards – in effect the upholding of what was conceived of as ordinary, decent, middle-class morality – was the mainstay of British censorship. Much of it was of a fairly minor, if annoying, nature to do with innuendo and 'bad' language (e.g. 'tickle your arse with a feather', which was cut from AUDEN's *Paid on Both Sides* for the Cambridge Festival Theatre in 1934). But among censorship's more important effects was the suppression on moral grounds, for varying periods, of important plays like STRINDBERG's *Miss Julie*, PIRANDELLO's *Six Characters in Search of an Author*, O'NEILL's *Desire under the Elms*, LILLIAN HELLMAN's *The Children's Hour* (not licensed until 1960), Wedekind's *Spring Awakening* and *Earth Spirit* (not licensed until 1964), and ARTHUR MILLER's *A View from the Bridge*. Most of these plays were first performed privately under club conditions, the only legitimate method of evading the censor's ban. Such members-only institutions as the Stage Society, the Pioneer Players (formed under EDITH CRAIG), London's GATE THEATRE (founded 1925 and especially active in the 1930s), the ARTS THEATRE Club, the English Stage Company (in the late 1950s and 1960s) at the ROYAL COURT THEATRE, and the Watergate Theatre Club staged at least some banned plays and helped bring closer the eventual abolition of censorship.

After 1956 the Lord Chamberlain was very much on the defensive. Dramatists such as JOHN ARDEN and JOHN OSBORNE had difficulties with the censor (especially the latter), yet steadily undermined the conservatism of the authorities and widened the perspective of British theatre. Though pressure to end censorship ultimately proved irresistible, the Lord Chamberlain's Office exercised its authority to the last.

Because it was too explicit in its handling of themes of homosexuality and transvestism, Osborne's *A Patriot for Me* (1964) was permitted only club performances at the Royal Court. A similar restriction applied to EDWARD BOND's *Saved* (1965), described by a censor as a 'revolting amateur play ... the writing is vile and the conception worse'. In January 1966, after visits from the police, the Royal Court was prosecuted for abusing the necessary conditions for private performance, and the play was not performed publicly in Britain until 1969. More controversy was generated with Bond's *Early Morning*, which, apart from unflattering portrayals of Queen Victoria, Florence Nightingale, Gladstone and Disraeli, directly challenged the Lord Chamberlain by including his Victorian counterpart in the cast. It was refused a licence on 8 November 1967. Subsequent club performances at the Royal Court ended abruptly after threats to withdraw the theatre's ARTS COUNCIL subsidy. In June 1968, only three months before the formal ending of censorship, Bond's *Narrow Road to the Deep North* was heavily cut for its premiere at Coventry's Belgrade Theatre. This the author refused to accept and, though a compromise was reached with St James's Palace, Bond maintained that in performance the required deletions were never observed.

With the formal abolition of the institution of censorship in France after the Second World War, municipalities continued to retain the powers of local veto first granted in 1701. These were used against JEAN GENET's *The Balcony* (1956), which was considered too offensive, sexually and politically, to be staged in Paris until 1960 – ironically the world premiere took place in London in 1957 – and the authorities in Nancy also banned a production in 1970. British theatre suffered no such restrictions after 26 September 1968, when the powers of the Lord Chamberlain as censor of plays ceased under the terms of the new Theatres Act.

Since then prosecution under the common law has been the only potential regulator of theatrical performances. Deliberately provocative productions such as the American MUSICALS *Hair* – refused a licence in the summer of 1968 – and *Oh! Calcutta!* (1969), both featuring full-frontal male and female NUDITY, quickly tested the new autonomy, but the deluge of immorality predicted by advocates of continued censorship never really arrived. The law has been called in to mediate only once since 1968, when a private prosecution was brought in 1982 against Michael Bogdanov's NATIONAL THEATRE production of HOWARD BRENTON's *The Romans in Britain* (1980), which showed a simulated male rape. It was unsuccessful because the prosecution, in some confusion, abandoned its case, and the courts have not been troubled since. Exceptionally, in 1993 another Brenton play *Christie in Love* (Royal Court, 1970) was banned in Jersey (where, as an offshore dependency, different laws apply) under a statute dating from 1778, when an amateur group applied for a licence from the island's Bailiff.

Outside Britain the pattern of European censorship was mainly political. In Germany during the 1930s and 40s (and in Austria after the *Anschluss*) it was exceptionally severe. The Nazis took measures which not only prohibited the entire works of authors of whom they disapproved but, as part of a sophisticated propaganda machine, sought directly to manipulate theatrical production and choice of repertoire. On the proscription lists were GEORG

KAISER (Germany's leading expressionist playwright (see EXPRESSIONISM) and ARTHUR SCHNITZLER (an Austrian Jew, whose work was banned posthumously). BERTOLT BRECHT suffered police harassment and fled abroad in 1933 to temporary refuge in the USA and elsewhere, returning to East Berlin in 1948 to Marxist censorship. Prohibitions of a similar nature operated in Nazi-occupied countries – French drama was censored by the German authorities in Paris and the puppet government at Vichy. In Fascist Italy, Alfieri's classic tragedy *Saul* was forbidden (because the hero was a Jew), as was GARCÍA LORCA's *Blood Wedding*, and a version of *Julius Caesar* because it reflected too critically on Mussolini. Under Mussolini Italian censorship became centralized for the first time. Official censorship ceased in West Germany and Italy after the Second World War.

Repressive and long-lasting censorships operated in the Iberian peninsula: in Portugal under the Salazar regime from 1928 to 74, and in Franco's Spain, where, after the Civil War, pre-existent Catholic censorship was overlaid with an extreme right-wing political element. When García Lorca was murdered by the Falangists in 1936 at the start of the Civil War, there was a mass exodus of intellectuals and artists, including Arrabal (who became a French citizen and thereafter wrote in French). Those who stayed included ALFONSO SASTRE – he published a severe indictment of the damage caused by censorship in 1961 – and ANTONIO BUERO-VALLEJO. Both playwrights endured terms of imprisonment under Franco. Buero-Vallejo's *Adventure in the Grey* was banned in 1949 but allowed in a version more critical of the state in 1963, when censorship eased slightly after the appointment of a new supervising committee. Though he achieved some successes in circumventing the censor, *The Double Story of Dr Valmy* was suppressed in 1964, followed in 1970 by *The Sleep of Reason* (in which Goya's refusal to submit to tyranny by Ferdinand VII bore intentional parallels with contemporary resistance to Franco). Most other Spanish drama of significance was produced abroad until the demise of Franco in 1975, when censorship was relaxed.

East European censorship in the 20th century was, until the late 1980s, dominated by the model of the former USSR. Although a short period of relative freedom for the theatre followed the Bolshevik Revolution, from the 1920s the USSR (taking inspiration from the excesses of Tsarist censorship) engineered a system whereby the state was in absolute control of literature and the theatre. As a consequence much of the history of 20th-century Soviet drama is of slow critical and intellectual emasculation in the name of socialist realism, a concept of uncertain definition which forced everything into the mould determined by the state machine. All writers were obliged to belong to the Union of Soviet Writers, an organ of the Communist Party, whose first president was the playwright MAKSIM GORKY (a victim of early-20th-century Tsarist censorship). Glavlit, the state censorship office, was established in 1922 and by about 1930 was virtually a branch of the security police. Its staff were empowered to read all plays at least ten days beforehand and to have representatives allocated two seats (no further back than the fourth row) at every performance. Along with its sister organization Glavrepertkom (responsible for determining theatre

repertoires), Glavlit effectively determined what was art, since by definition anything not approved could not be art.

Stalinist censorship was uncompromising and vindictive (e.g. in 1936-7 over half the plays earmarked for production at the main theatres were banned). Dramatists who suffered in the late 1920s and 30s included BULGAKOV (e.g. *Zoika's Apartment* (1926), and his SATIRE on Glavrepertkom in *The Crimson Island* (1928) – on appeal to Stalin he was made resident playwright at the Moscow ART THEATRE, but further suppressions followed, including *Bliss* (1934), *Ivan Vasilevich* (1936) and *The Cabal of Hypocrites*, an attack on cultural dictatorship (1936)); MAYAKOVSKY (whose imaginative satires on Soviet philistinism and bureaucracy, *The Bedbug* and *The Bathhouse*, were vetoed in 1929-30); and LEONOV (*The Snowstorm*, suppressed during rehearsals in 1939). Some dramatists managed to emigrate (e.g. EVGENY ZAMYATIN in 1932), but ISAAK BABEL, whose last play *The Checkist* disappeared after his arrest by the secret police, presumably shared a similar fate – death in a labour camp – to the director VSEVOLOD MEYERHOLD, a protégé of STANISLAVSKY's arrested during the same 1938-9 purge.

The period came to be dominated by the hardline orthodoxy of Andrei Zhdanov (Stalin's associate and ultimately Party spokesman on cultural affairs), who was responsible for the notorious 'Zhdanov Theses' (1946) and the drab, uniform mediocrity of approved Soviet drama until the early 1950s. Nearly all suppressed plays and their authors were subsequently rehabilitated during one or other of the periodic post-Stalin cultural thaws (e.g. Babel in the late 1950s; but some of Bulgakov's work was restricted until 1965). In the 1960s several new dissident dramatists emerged. Solzhenitsyn's play *The Love Girl and the Innocent* (based on first-hand experience in a Stalinist labour camp) was banned after the dress rehearsal in 1962. ANDREI AMALRIK's absurdist dramas (see THEATRE OF THE ABSURD) and Muza Pavlova's satirical pieces *Boxes* and *Wings* were eventually published in Frankfurt in 1970.

With Mikhail Gorbachev's rise to power, a new policy of *glasnost* (openness) swept over Soviet society. Strikingly, in the summer of 1986, official approval was given to *Sarcophagus* (by Vladimir Gubarev, a senior journalist with *Pravda*, based on personal observation of the aftermath of the Chernobyl nuclear disaster). Widely performed in the USSR, extracts from it even appeared in official journals, including *Sovietskaya Kultura*, the Communist Party newspaper. Glavlit was soon being stripped of its former power – a decline which accelerated after 1988 – and by August 1990 its 60-year stranglehold on Soviet theatre was over.

Most states in Eastern Europe (especially Romania and the Prussian-dominated areas of Poland) endured harsh political censorships in the 19th century. After the Second World War, exceptionally, the Yugoslavian theatre escaped the strictness of Stalinist controls despite, as elsewhere, being heavily subsidized by the state; but from 1948 onwards all other East European Communist states operated systems of state censorship based on the parent model of socialist realism. There were, however, important differences of emphasis. Generally speaking, East Germany, Bulgaria and Albania were among the more repressive, while Hungary (until 1956), Czechoslovakia (until 1968) and Poland (until the early 1980s) enjoyed degrees of relative freedom. Following the Soviet invasion of 1968, which ended the revival of the Czech theatre in the 1960s, harsh restraints were imposed: the plays of leading dramatists like Milan Kundera and Pavel Kohout were banned, as was the entire work of VÁCLAV HAVEL. His later plays *Audience*, *Private View* (both 1975) and *Protest* (1978), written in the knowledge that public performance was impossible and staged privately with friends, were later professionally presented in the West. Havel spent over four years in prison following his arrest for subversion in 1979; Kohout wrote in exile in Vienna.

Romanian theatre, after a period of relative tolerance by the authorities in the 1960s, was severely tested by censorship under Ceausescu and fell into a backwater from which it is still struggling to recover. In Poland, where the theatre has always had a distinctive nationalist dimension some interesting avant-garde drama was allowed to develop in the late 60s and 70s, though SŁAWOMIR MROŻEK's *Vatzlav* (written in the tense political climate of 1968) was denied its premiere until 1979, when the power of the popular movement known as Solidarity was strong. But after the imposition of military rule under General Jaruselski in late 1981, the theatres were closed altogether for a while. When they reopened under strict military censorship all plays were subject to scrutiny before rehearsals began and again at the dress rehearsal stage. Dissident drama went underground, and banned plays were read at gatherings in private houses or churches.

One prominent victim of official censorship was Kazimierz Braun's *Dżuma* (*The Plague*) – based on motifs from CAMUS and Defoe and drawing parallels with modern-day Poland – which was permitted a few, heavily cut, performances after a visit from the censors to the dress rehearsal in April 1983. Though later admitted into the repertoire of the Teatr Wspolczesny (of which Braun was director), it was allowed abroad only on a restricted basis and never made its planned visit to London. In late 1984 Braun was dismissed from his post and further performances were stopped. In 1985 an underground group (Theatre of the Eighth Day, which had attracted government sponsorship during Solidarity's heyday) performed in Scotland at the EDINBURGH FESTIVAL FRINGE and won a prize; but the Polish authorities denied the company's existence. In 1989–90, after the collapse of Soviet domination, censorship ceased throughout the former Communist bloc including Czechoslovakia, where, ironically, Václav Havel was elected state president from 1989 to 1992.

Outside Europe In the USA early Puritan settlers were hostile to the theatre, and in some areas like Boston the theatre was initially outlawed completely. While dramatic censorship has never existed on a formalized basis since 1776, as free speech is guaranteed under the Constitution, constraints may operate at community or state level, in closing down allegedly offensive productions which endanger public morals or are regarded as politically insulting. On the whole, however, theatre managers in the USA have been their own censors, as offences against public taste endanger their theatre licences.

The absence of institutionalized censorship allowed the world premiere of *Ghosts* to take place in Chicago in 1882 (no theatre in Scandinavia would touch the play); but when Shaw's *Mrs Warren's Profession* was staged by ARNOLD DALY in New York in 1905 – it was still banned in Britain – the actors were prosecuted; and in 1926 MAE WEST's theatrical debut as a waterfront whore in *Sex* earned her an eight-day prison sentence for offence against public decency. Left-wing drama came under attack in the 1930s, effectively through withdrawal of sponsorship (e.g. MARC BLITZSTEIN's *The Cradle Will Rock* was suppressed in 1939 and led to the collapse of the left-wing FEDERAL THEATRE). After the Second World War several playwrights (including Arthur Miller and Brecht) were called before the House Committee on Un-American Activities. Currently in the USA, as in most other countries free from formal censorship, the most potent weapon against what is regarded as politically or morally unacceptable in the arts is financial.

Censorship began in Australia soon after colonization. All theatrical performances by convict settlers were prohibited between 1800 and 1832; and in 1828, after the first permanent theatre was set up in Sydney, the Legislative Council was panicked into passing an Act to regulate all places of public entertainment, which drew heavily on Walpole's 1737 Stage Licensing Act and survived, as in Britain, into the late 1960s. By the 19th century the British authorities in India began to entertain suspicions about native theatre, especially in Bengal, where the drama was seemingly used as an instrument for anti-British propaganda. Deenabandhu Mitra's *The Mirror of the Indigo* (1860) – on British exploitation of Bengali labour in the tea plantations – was eventually banned when taken on tour to Lucknow and Delhi. In 1879 the colonialists introduced the Dramatic Performances Act, which lasted until well after independence and was used, among other things, to suppress plays on sensitive issues like Kashmir.

In the African dominions censorship during the 19th and early 20th centuries was generally very informal (though nonetheless damaging), with Christian missionaries, in the attempt to 'civilize', trying to modify or even suppress native theatre forms. The colonial authorities sometimes also intervened, and in western Nigeria some Yoruba-language operas by HUBERT OGUNDE – e.g. *Strike and Hunger* (1945), *Bread and Bullets* (1949) and his post-independence play *Yoruba Ronu!* (*Yoruba Awake!*, 1964) – were banned for fear of public disturbances. WOLE SOYINKA, Africa's leading playwright, suffered imprisonment during the Nigerian civil war and went into exile until 1976.

Censorship survived in post-independence Africa. This occurred particularly where Muslim influences prevail and hostility to the theatre carried over from colonial times. In some areas, including those formerly under British rule, censorship has also taken a remarkably extreme form. Under the Obote and Amin dictatorships in Uganda theatrical activity was virtually suppressed altogether until about 1986, while in Malawi the Censorship Control of Entertainment Act (1968) imposed strict regulations on religious, political and sexual matters. ADRIAN MITCHELL's *Man Friday* (1972) and Soyinka's *Giants* (1984) were victims, as was Garton Sandifolo, whose work has never been produced in Malawi. In Kenya the government frequently intervened to suppress unwelcome developments, notably in community theatre: at the Kamiriithu centre at Limuru the open-air theatre was destroyed by police action in 1982. All scripts – even school and college plays – are subject to censorship and require an official licence before performance. In March 1991 the government vetoed a production in Nairobi of DARIO FO's *Can't Pay, Won't Pay* (1974) on the grounds that it might stir up trouble about prices in the shops.

In the 19th century Turkish drama suffered censorship under the rule of Sultans Abdulaziz (1861–76) and Abdulhamit II (1876–1908): traditional SHADOW PUPPET theatre (KARAGÖZ), often satirical in content, was as much affected as the more westernized forms of theatre that were beginning to emerge (e.g. Namik Kemal's strongly nationalistic *The Fatherland: or, Silistria* (1873), which the sultan, afraid of its inciting a revolution, banned with its author). Though in the early 20th century drama started to flourish once more – ANTOINE helped establish a National Theatre in Istanbul in 1914 – Turkey's record in political censorship was punctuated by periods of quite severe restriction. Only after the 1960 Revolution was political drama allowed relative freedom of expression; but it is still a sensitive issue.

Until 1989, Israeli playwrights (whether writing in Arabic, Hebrew or English) were required to submit all scripts for prior approval by the Interior Ministry's Committee of Censorship of Plays and Films; and in the Occupied Territories (Gaza and the West Bank) Palestinian theatre was subject to strict military censorship into the mid-1990s. Any play judged to compromise Israeli state security could be closed without notice. Islamic fundamentalism is not sympathetic to the stage, and Middle Eastern states under such influence operate rigorous censorships. Among the more extreme is Iran, which, having formerly enforced rigorous censorship under the Shah, became even more repressive in the early 1980s. The theatre was viewed with extreme suspicion, and directors were required to seek approval of text and manner of performance before rehearsals were allowed to begin. All productions were subject to unannounced visits by officials from the Ministry of Islamic Guidance. Some Iranian playwrights suffered under both regimes (e.g. Gholam Hoseyn Sa'edi, who died in exile in Paris in 1985). In present-day Iran no play may be performed unless the text is published beforehand, which is a guarantee of its acceptability to the regime.

Japanese censorship has a history dating back to the mid-17th century, when the Shogunate, always distrustful of eruptions of popular feeling, imposed restrictions on *KABUKI* theatre, the irreverent alternative to classical *NŌ* drama. From 1629 women were prohibited from acting on the stage, and reappeared only in the present century. For centuries Japanese theatre developed in virtual isolation from the rest of the world, yet the activities of its censors – mainly of a political nature, occasionally disguised as moral concerns – were strikingly similar to those of their European counterparts. After the Meiji Restoration in 1868, when Japan's contacts with the West assumed importance, the theatre, considered crucial to the country's dignity and prestige, was encouraged to project wholesomeness and sobriety. At this time *kabuki* theatre came under renewed attack for alleged superficiality and licentiousness. After the First World War Japan intensified its grip on the theatre at home and in those countries subject to its rule, especially in Korea. Social criticism was severely restricted (e.g. Senzaburo Suzuki's *Burned Alive*, banned in 1921), and by the late 1930s political drama was outlawed completely, with the government's disbanding of left-wing theatre groups. It began to re-emerge only in the 1950s.

China has laboured under strict censorship since the People's Republic was established in 1949. But even in the 1930s the theatre was made to serve the interests of the Party in areas under Communist control, while the Nationalists similarly operated a censorship to ensure that the theatre reflected its best interests. China's most intense (and chaotic) period of censorship began in the mid-60s with the Cultural Revolution, which was to some extent precipitated by attacks in 1964 on the play *Hai Jui Dismissed* (by Wu Han, deputy mayor of Beijing) for its alleged veiled criticism of Chairman Mao. During the Revolution itself even Beijing and Shanghai classical opera suffered, and some of China's most distinguished playwrights (e.g. T'ien Han) fell from grace in a hysterical purge of modern drama. In the name of the theatre-as-education, Madame Mao (gaoled in 1976 on her husband's death) reduced the drama to a mechanical procession of Communist heroes triumphing over gutless class enemies, in praise of Chairman Mao and the Revolution. Although the injustices of the period have been largely corrected since 1977 – Western drama slowly began to reappear, notably with Arthur Miller's arrival in 1984 to direct a production of *Death of a Salesman* in Beijing – the Chinese theatre has remained in an uncertain state, marked by the repressive atmosphere following the Student Movement and the Tiananmen Square massacre. Art and politics are inseparable in China. How far the theatre may act as a subversive political vehicle was demonstrated at a revival in Beijing in 1991 of Madame Mao's revolutionary opera *The Red Lantern* (1964), when the first-night audience unexpectedly applied its message of vengeance to the existing political climate.

In many areas of Southeast Asia after the emergence from colonial rule, censorships proliferated: under the regulations of martial law in the Philippines after 1972; in Indonesia under Sukarno and in the 1970s, when the actor and director W. S. Rendra was imprisoned and, on release, prevented from undertaking any further public performances for seven years; and in Singapore where anti-establishment drama had a difficult time (e.g. the left-wing director and playwright Kuo Pao Kun was gaoled between 1976 and 1980). After the Japanese left Korea at the end of the Second World War, having imposed strict military censorship during their long occupation from 1910, and the country was divided, the theatre in the North became a direct instrument of the state, dedicated to praise of its leader Kim Li-song. A period of uncertainty followed his death in 1994.

The restless and unstable political climate of Central and South America makes dramatic censorship an almost continually self-renewing feature of cultural life. It is as common to right-wing dictatorships (e.g. Chile) as to left-wing regimes (e.g. Cuba). Although the subcontinent has produced some dramatists of international repute, the predominance of military-inspired censorships has restricted (and in some periods stifled) growth. In Brazil severe constraints were imposed after the 1964 *coup d'état*, which initiated years of very active and repressive censorship, particularly between 1968 and 1979 (a period marked by torture and imprisonment or exile for many left-wing playwrights and actors); similarly in Chile after the military coup of 1968 (when an attempt was made to make the theatre reflect the ideas of the revolution); in Uruguay between 1974 and 84; and also in Argentina during the Peronist regime and, in the early 1980s, the rule of the Generals.

Anti-totalitarian dramatists have tended to have little voice in modern Latin America for much of the century. Among those who chose self-exile were the Chilean dramatist ALEJANDRO SIEVEKING (who lived and worked in Costa Rica, 1974–84), AUGUSTO BOAL of Brazil, and the Argentinian playwrights EDUARDO PAVLOVSKY and GRISELDA GAMBARO (who wrote in exile in Spain for some time, though both later returned). Political changes after 1984 lightened the atmosphere generally: e.g. in Argentina Gambaro's plays found favour again (*El campo* received its first airing for ten years in Buenos Aires in 1984) and Pavlovsky's *Paso de dos*, a forthright play about torture and repression, was performed in 1990.

South Africa's censorship laws, which until recently possessed a rigour unmatched outside the former Soviet bloc, date back to the early years of Afrikaner rule. But the Entertainments (Censorship) Act (1931) and the Publications and Entertainment Act (1963) gave real force and substance to earlier, more haphazard arrangements. Several leading playwrights were forced into exile (e.g. Alfred Hutchinson, Lewis Nkosi), while others (e.g. ATHOL FUGARD, a white writer hostile to the regime) continued to produce under increasingly daunting conditions. Strict censorship also extended to the work of foreign dramatists (e.g. EDWARD ALBEE's *Who's Afraid of Virginia Woolf?*, banned in 1963). By 1975 theatre groups promoting black consciousness had been largely silenced. An appeals procedure operated through the Ministry of the Interior. Political changes towards ending apartheid in the late 1980s and early 1990s brought about more liberal attitudes to the theatre, which assumed a less dangerous aspect in the eyes of the authorities. The arrival of majority rule in 1994 brought formally to an end what was once one of the most repressive of all modern censorships. JRS

Center Theatre Group (Los Angeles)

Center Theatre Group (Los Angeles) Founded in 1966 to serve as the umbrella organization for activities at both the Ahmanson Theatre and the Mark Taper Forum, which, with the Dorothy Chandler Pavilion, form the principal venues of the Music Center of Los Angeles County. Both were completed in April 1967, and are owned and operated as public trusts. GORDON DAVIDSON serves as artistic director.

The 2100-seat Ahmanson is a commercial theatre that typically mounts productions with wide appeal (five of NEIL SIMON's plays have premiered here), and features well known film and stage actors. The non-profit company at the smaller (750-seat) Taper in its first 23 seasons (1967–90) presented 137 mainstage productions, 57 West Coast or American premieres and 38 world premieres, including works by ROMULUS LINNEY, A. R. GURNEY, LUIS VALDÉZ, Neil Simon, LANFORD WILSON and JEAN-CLAUDE VAN ITALLIE. In the 95-seat John Anson Ford Theatre in Hollywood, the company develops new plays through staged readings, workshops and fully mounted productions, including *Sundays at the Itchey Foot* (1980), a literary CABARET.

Taper productions have won 8 Obies and 11 Tonys, and in 1977 the company received the special Tony for regional theatre. Artists have included directors TYRONE GUTHRIE, HAROLD CLURMAN, MARSHALL W. MASON, ATHOL FUGARD, Ellis Rabb, JOSÉ QUINTERO, Robert Woodruff and KENNETH BRANAGH; designers MING CHO LEE, Peter Wexler, THARON MUSSER and Ralph Funicello; and many well known film and stage actors. JDM

Centlivre, Susannah 1669–1723 English playwright. Born in Lincolnshire, she was a strolling player from c.1685 and may have spent some time in Cambridge. In 1700 her first poems and letters were published and her first play produced. Her sharp attack on the contemporary addiction to gambling, *The Gamester* (1705), was her first significant success as a dramatist and its sequel, *The Basset-Table*, dealt with the same theme. She married in 1707. Of her 20 plays the most popular were *The Busy Body* (1709) and *The Wonder: A Woman Keeps a Secret* (1714), both of which lasted well into the 19th century. Her best work, *A Bold Stroke for a Wife* (1718), provides a virtuoso acting part for the hero in his multiple disguises. PH

Century Theatre (New York City) see NEW THEATRE

Cervantes, Miguel de 1547–1616 Spanish novelist and playwright. He claimed to have staged 30 plays in the 1580s, but this early neoclassical theatre was eclipsed by the new COMEDIA of his rival LOPE DE VEGA, and his works were no longer performed. His later theatre, published in 1615, includes eight full-length plays and eight *entremeses* (farcical interludes).

Although frustrated in his lifetime, Cervantes has been assured a place in world theatre through adaptations of *Don Quixote* and other novels, as well as through his original plays. His TRAGEDY based on the heroic defence of a city against Roman invaders, *El cerco de Numancia* (*The Siege of Numantia*), has sometimes been revived as a political statement. In Paris it was given an ARTAUDIAN staging in 1937 by BARRAULT to draw attention to the Spanish Civil War. In Spain NIEVA's spectacular free adaptation of *Los baños de Argel* (*The Baths of Algiers*) earned him the National Theatre Prize of 1979.

The most enduring of Cervantes's theatre works are the one-act *entremeses*, humorous pieces noted for their rapid pace, sparkling wit and REALISM. Foremost among them are *El retablo de las maravillas* (*The Miracle Show*) and *El viejo celoso* (*The Jealous Old Man*). The former uses a nonexistent play-within-the-play, visible only to the racially pure, to satirize antisemitism and the fear of illegitimacy. The latter is a bawdy treatment of the classic FARCE of the young wife deceiving the old husband. PZ

Césaire, Aimé 1913– Martiniquan poet, politician, essayist and playwright. Césaire has enjoyed a successful career as a politician and author, being one of the founders (with Léopold Senghor) of the negritude movement in the 1930s. He is better known as a poet than as a playwright, but his plays are among the most important new French-language work of the 1960s. They administered a shock to the French theatre world very similar to that produced by SOYINKA's work in England. An early play, *Et les chiens se taisaient* (*And the Dogs Were Silent*), celebrates the themes of revolt to be found in his major plays, but remains essentially a poetic work.

His three plays for the theatre were written in the 1960s, partly under the influence of JEAN-MARIE SERREAU, who directed them. In *La Tragédie du Roi Christophe* (*The Tragedy of King Christopher*, 1964) the historical figure of Christophe (King Henry of Haiti, 1811–20) is used to present the conflicting views of black African liberation current in the 1950s and 1960s. The play has a vigorous, BRECHTian epic structure, combined with a rich and powerful French poetic idiom, drawing on the language of Africa and the Caribbean as well as that of France. Through the very different dramatic style of the African hero play, *Une Saison au Congo* (*A Season in the Congo*, 1967) centres on Patrice Lumumba's attempts to establish an independent Congolese Republic. European critics misunderstood its intentions, but it is as powerful in its own way as *Christophe*, and very much more critical of the effects of white decolonization. This theme is taken up in *Une Tempête* (1969), a brilliant reworking of SHAKESPEARE's *Tempest*, in which Prospero represents a white settler and Caliban a black slave, follower of Shango. The play ends differently from Shakespeare's, with Prospero unable to leave the island, remaining locked in a power struggle with Caliban which he is doomed, in the end, to lose.

Césaire turned to the theatre to reach a broader audience than the readers of his poetry and to deal directly with African politics. His plays are revered more than they are performed in France, but his work has become a staple for young racially aware theatre companies in the USA. DB

Chaikin, Joseph 1935– American director, actor and producer. Born in Brooklyn and educated at Drake University, Chaikin made his New York debut in *Dark of the Moon* (1958). He joined the LIVING THEATRE the following year and appeared in *Many Loves* and *Tonight We Improvise* (1959); *The Connection* and BRECHT's *Jungle of Cities* (1961–2); and *Man Is Man* (1962). For the Writers' Stage (1964), he performed in IONESCO's *The New Tenant* and *Victims of Duty*. He founded the OPEN THEATRE in 1964 as an experimental company to build and perform new scripts. The success of *America Hurrah!* in 1966 (1967 in London) established his reputation. His workshop approach to composition also produced *Terminal* and *The Serpent* in 1970, the latter a series of episodes on the history of murder. Chaikin has directed for the NEW YORK SHAKESPEARE FESTIVAL, MANHATTAN THEATRE CLUB, Magic Theatre of San Francisco, and Mark Taper Forum of Los Angeles (see CENTER THEATRE GROUP). An articulate spokesman for the 1960s avant-garde movement, he has won numerous awards, including five Obies. After a stroke

in 1984 resulted in aphasia, he appeared in New York City for the first time in 1991 (AMERICAN PLACE) in plays he co-authored with SAM SHEPARD (*The War in Heaven*) and VAN ITALLIE (*Struck Dumb*) that reflected that experience. TLM

Chaillot Theatre (Paris) The first theatre on the Place du Trocadéro, opposite the Eiffel Tower in Paris, was a Second Empire monstrosity built for the exhibition of 1878. It was allotted to GÉMIER when he set up the first THÉÂTRE NATIONAL POPULAIRE in 1920. Situated at the heart of the most fashionable residential district, it could never be the centre for a popular community theatre. Gémier could only arrange reduced-price performances of productions by other companies. In 1935 it was demolished and the present complex of museums and theatres was built for the 1937 exhibition. The main theatre had a stage 75ft wide and its auditorium held 2800. It made a perfect debating chamber for the United Nations Organization, which met there from 1947 to 51. Heading a revived TNP, VILAR managed to make a going concern of this theatre between 1951 and 1963, but audiences declined after his departure and in 1972 the theatre was closed for renovations. The interior was completely remodelled to designs commissioned by ANTOINE VITEZ and Jack Lang, later Minister of Culture under Mitterrand. But the first director to be put in charge of the new auditorium, André-Louis Périnetti, claimed that it was too cumbersome to work with. It was left to Antoine Vitez, who took over in 1981, to regenerate something of Vilar and Gémier's vision with bold new productions of both new plays and world classics. Since 1988 it has been under the direction of JÉRÔME SAVARY. DB

Chalbaud, Román 1931– Venezuelan playwright and director. One-third of the Venezuelan 'Holy Trinity' (with CABRUJAS and CHOCRÓN), Chalbaud has written more than a dozen plays. A pioneer in film techniques, he has also been a leading figure in Venezuelan film since the mid-50s, with a grotesque Buñuelesque reliance on abnormal and deformed characters. As a director of the NUEVO GRUPO (New Group) from 1967 until its closure in 1988, he mounted both national and foreign plays, ranging from the classics to the absurd (see THEATRE OF THE ABSURD), in order to promote a national theatre movement. As a writer, he has been eclectic in both theme and style, but his plays often depict marginal characters within society and deal with poverty, social maladjustment, sexuality, and political and ontological problems. Often dealing with multiple issues at the same time, he characterizes the sociological concerns of Venezuelan society with a cinematic technique. *Caín adolescente* (*Adolescent Cain*, 1955) dealt with rural adaptation to an urban environment; later plays include *La quema de Judas* (*The Burning of Judas*, 1964), *Los ángeles terribles* (*The Terrible Angels*, 1967), *El pez que fuma* (*The Smoking Fish*, 1968) and *El viejo grupo* (*The Old Group*, 1984). GW

Champion, Gower 1921–80 American dancer, choreographer and director. Champion appeared as a dancer in *The Streets of Paris* (1939) and several other shows before turning to choreography with *Small Wonder* (1948). After dancing with his wife Marge in several Hollywood films, he returned to BROADWAY as the director and choreographer of *Bye, Bye, Birdie* (1960). The charm and energy of his staging led to further directing and choreography assignments – for *Carnival* (1961), *Hello, Dolly!* (1964), *I Do! I Do!* (1966), *Irene* (1973), *Mack and Mabel* (1974) and others. He died just as his last show, *42nd Street*, was about to open. His initial directorial work evinced a fresh and inventive approach to staging a musical. *Carnival*, in particular, was praised for its imaginative, stylized production. Champion, along with BOB FOSSE and MICHAEL BENNETT, made the choreographer-director the dominant figure in the MUSICAL THEATRE of the 1970s.   MK

Champmeslé, Mlle [Marie Desmares] 1642–98 French actress, noted for her performances in the tragedies of RACINE. First mentioned at Rouen in 1665, she went to Paris three years later and subsequently appeared at all the established theatres in turn – first the MARAIS from 1668, the HÔTEL DE BOURGOGNE from 1670, and after 1679 with MOLIÈRE's former company at the Hôtel Guénégaud, which became the first COMÉDIE-FRANÇAISE in the following year. Although not beautiful she was renowned for her touching voice, which could readily move an audience to tears and made her a potent attraction even in indifferent plays. Having deeply impressed Racine as Hermione in *Andromaque*, she became the playwright's mistress and created all his major heroines from Bérénice to Phèdre, which he wrote expressly for her. Illness forced her to retire in 1698 and she died a few months later. Her husband Charles Chevillet, whose stage name she had taken after their marriage in 1666, was an actor with the same companies, also predominantly in tragic parts. He was a friend of La Fontaine and the author of a number of satirical comedies, notably *Crispin Chevalier* (*Crispin Knight*, 1673) and *Le Florentin* (*The Florentine*, 1685).   DR

Chancerel, Léon 1886–1965 French actor, director, playwright and researcher. After training with COPEAU Chancerel founded the Comédiens Routiers in 1929, a semi-amateur touring company linked to the Scout movement. Like Copeau, he revived the style and spirit of the *COMMEDIA* for productions of MOLIÈRE and of adaptations of medieval tales. He promoted the revival of medieval religious drama, established a children's theatre (Le Théâtre de l'Oncle Sébastien) and, in 1939, was put in charge of the Centre Dramatique de Kellermann, a research institute in which he continued to work after the war.   DB

Chanfrau, Frank 1824–84 American actor. Born in New York, Chanfrau was inspired to become an actor by a performance of EDWIN FORREST; he gained recognition through his ability to imitate Forrest, starting on a tour of theatres and cities across America that eventually led him to the Olympic Theatre in New York in 1848. As Mose the fire b'hoy in *A Glance at New York*, written for him by BENJAMIN A. BAKER, Chanfrau became the 'lion' of the town. Dressed in the red shirt, plug hat, and turned-up trousers of the New York fireman, he was featured in several Mose plays, particularly *The Mysteries and Miseries of New York* by Henry W. Plunkett. Friends leased the Chatham Theatre for Chanfrau, who renamed it the

National and continued to perform the role of Mose for about three and a half years. After this popularity, he performed the title role 560 times in *Kit the Arkansas Traveller*, and played the lead character in Thomas de Walden's *Sam* 783 times.   WJM

Channing, Carol 1921– American singer and comedienne. Seattle-born and Bennington-educated, Channing made her BROADWAY debut in *No for an Answer* (1941). Critics praised her work in the REVUE *Lend an Ear* (1948), and in the following year she became a star with her larger-than-life performance as 1920s vamp Lorelei Lee in the musical version of *Gentlemen Prefer Blondes*. She succeeded Rosalind Russell in *Wonderful Town* (1954), appeared in the short-lived MUSICAL *The Vamp* (1955) and the revue *Show Girl* (1961), and toured with the SHAW play *The Millionairess* (1963) before starring in the long-running hit *Hello, Dolly!* in 1964. As matchmaker Dolly Gallagher Levi, Channing gave a warm, funny, and at times outrageous performance. In subsequent years, she was unable to find vehicles worthy of her unique talents. *Lorelei* (1974) lasted only a few months, and the play *Legends* (1986) closed before reaching Broadway.   MK

Channing, Stockard [Susan Williams Antonio Stockard] 1944– American actress. New York-born and Radcliffe-educated (BA, 1965), Channing began professional stage work in 1967 with the Theatre Company of Boston and, after a stint in California, made her BROADWAY debut in 1971. Despite some dozen major New York City appearances since, a failed TV series, and poorly received films (excepting *Grease*), it was not until her Tony-winning portrayal in *Joe Egg* (1985 Broadway revival) that her extraordinary stage talent began to be recognized. Other notable appearances include NEIL SIMON's *They're Playing Our Song* (1980), GUARE's *The House of Blue Leaves* (1986 revival, as Bunny), AYCKBOURN's *Woman in Mind* (1988, Drama Desk Award), GURNEY's *Love Letters* (1989) and especially Guare's *Six Degrees of Separation* (New York, 1990; London, 1992), in which she was critically acclaimed as Ouisa. Her most recent New York appearances were in PETER HALL's production of Guare's *Four Baboons Adoring the Sun* (1992) at the VIVIAN BEAUMONT THEATRE and the title role in STOPPARD's *Hapgood* (1994). Gurney has said that Channing has the ability 'to combine a sense of comedy with a sense of pathos to get at the ache underneath'.   DBW

Chapelain, Jean 1595–1674 French scholar, critic and man of letters, who played an influential part in the formulation of the neoclassical aesthetic in 17th-century France. As founder member of the Académie-Française in 1634 he guided its counsels for many years and was the principal, if not sole, author of the Academy's public censure of PIERRE CORNEILLE's *Le Cid* for its irregularities. In this and other critical writings he staunchly upheld the formal conventions derived by Renaissance scholarship from the ancients, stressing the importance for drama of credibility (as distinct from truth to the facts), decorum, and the three unities, of time, place and action. In so doing he postulated two crucial factors – the existence of absolute rules for judging the quality of contemporary plays, and the paternalistic role of the Académie-Française as the guardian of these standards – in effect, the genesis of the 'academy-spirit': 'we must not say with the crowd that a work is good merely because it pleases, unless the learned and the expert are also pleased'. DR

Chapman family see SHOWBOATS

Chapman, George c.1560–1634 English poet and playwright, as famous for his translations of Homer as for his idiosyncratic and often difficult plays. He was one of many writers associated with HENSLOWE and the ADMIRAL'S MEN during the final decade of the 16th century. Surviving plays from this period are *The Blind Beggar of Alexandria* (1596) and *An Humorous Day's Mirth* (1597), which influenced JONSON's more famous comedy of humours, *Every Man in His Humour* (1598). Francis Meres, in *Palladis Tamia* (1598), considered Chapman among the best poets for both TRAGEDY and COMEDY, which strongly suggests that several of his plays have been lost.

Those that survive date mostly from the first decade of the 17th century, when Chapman was writing for the sophisticated audiences of the BOYS' COMPANIES. They include *May Day* (c.1601), *The Gentleman Usher* (c.1602), *All Fools* (1604), *Monsieur D'Olive* (1604) and *The Widow's Tears* (c.1605). These comedies yield less to the reader than does the work of many of Chapman's contemporaries. They are sometimes morally as well as linguistically complex. In his tragedies, Chapman writes repeatedly of deeply flawed Titanic heroes, distanced by their author's classical stoicism from the recent French history in which they figured. It is these overreachers who give their names to *Bussy D'Ambois* (1604), *The Conspiracy and Tragedy of Charles, Duke of Byron* (1608), *The Revenge of Bussy D'Ambois* (c.1610) and *Chabot, Admiral of France* (c.1613). The second of these plays so offended the French ambassador that Chapman was threatened with imprisonment, something he had already suffered for his part in the writing of *Eastward Ho* (1605). It is this lively collaboration with Jonson and MARSTON that has had the longest theatrical life of all Chapman's plays. PT

Chappuzeau, Samuel 1625–1701 French man of letters, author of a number of comedies and farces but preeminently of *Le Théâtre français* (1674), the only contemporary account of its kind. Apart from presenting an apologia for the theatre in general and actors in particular, it contains a catalogue of dramatists and lives of many prominent performers, including a long section on MOLIÈRE. Despite inaccuracies, it is a valuable source of information on the 17th-century professional theatre. DR

Charabanc Theatre Company Established in Belfast in 1983 by Marie Jones, Eleanor Methven and Carol Scanlan. The company won immediate success with *Lay Up Your Ends,* a play about the Belfast linen mills, which exemplifies its most distinctive work: sparse staging of a script devised by company and playwright, based on women's experience of local working-class life and history. Charabanc also do feminist productions of classic European plays, but their best work is original: *The Girls in*

the *Big Picture* (1984), *Somewhere Over the Balcony* (1987) and *The Hamster Wheel* (1988). GF

charivari The *chalvaricum,* as 14th- and 15th-century church bans refer to it, was originally a 'tumult' directed against a marriage the community disapproved of; remarried widows and unequal matches would be treated to a barrage of catcalls (the German *Katzenmusik*). The term came to mean a procession of noisy maskers, dancers, drummers and singers who made the streets unsafe by night. Once the staid citizens realized the fun in singing and saying what one would under the anonymity of devil MASKS, the charivari became organized as a mass 'happening' for its own sake. Among the *buffones* or masks were depraved monks with bare behinds and lions' manes, demons rattling pots and pans (as in the modern FASTNACHTSPIELE) of Basle), and the wild man Hellequin or Herlequin whose name becomes transformed into HARLEQUIN. In England this 'rough music' came to be performed by concerts of butchers on marrow-bones and cleavers at the weddings of members of their craft and, later, of the *beau monde,* as Hogarth shows in his illustrations to *Hudibras.* LS

See: R. Johannsmeier, *Spielmann, Schalk und Scharlatan,* Reinbek bei Hamburg, 1984.

Chautauqua and **Lyceum** Prominent American cultural, educational and religious organizations of the late 19th–early 20th century, part of a movement initiated by evangelists travelling the 'sawdust trail' along the Western frontier in gospel tents, beginning in an organized fashion with the Millerites in 1842. Both Chautauqua and Lyceum ultimately offered theatrical or platform entertainment.

Chautauqua, founded by John Heyl Vincent and Lewis Miller, began in New York State during the summer of 1874 as a tent meeting on the shores of Lake Chautauqua. By 1884 Chautauqua had expanded beyond its original intent to offer only religious instruction, and had begun to include cultural edification of all sorts, including dramatic interpretation and stereoptican views. Experiments with summer Chautauqua circuits began in 1904, first organized by Keith Vawter and Roy J. Ellison; soon there were Chautauqua tents throughout the country, covering established circuits (by 1912 there were over 1000 independent Chautauquas) in the summer. Very soon, show business became part of the formula of the brown tents (see TENT SHOW) of Chautauqua – brown, in contrast to the white top of the CIRCUS, became a symbol of its quasi-cultural inspiration – and because of the extensive circuits, a good Chautauqua act could survive for years. Typically, a Chautauqua programme combined elements of VAUDEVILLE (especially as vaudeville became more 'refined') and dramatic sketches, in addition to the usual smattering of lectures and other 'cultural' programming. Since early Chautauqua was generally hostile to traditional theatre, preference was given to platform performances, in particular the one-person show; as Victorian intolerance for the stage weakened, more actual drama was offered in Chautauqua. As early as 1904 the New York Chautauqua offered BEN JONSON'S MASQUE *The Sad Shepherd,* and in 1910 plays of SHAKESPEARE were presented by the

Nicholson Sylvan Players. The ultimate cause (of many) of Chautauqua's abrupt demise in the 1920s was the radio, although there is still an active programme at the permanent home in New York.

The Lyceums, active as early as 1826, operated in the winter, in permanent venues and in urban settings, in contrast to tent Chautauqua in rural areas. Although different institutions, they often shared a common pool of talent; but there was less pure entertainment in Lyceum. Still, with skilled promoters – in particular James Redpath in the last half of the 19th century – Lyceum prospered, with a less perceptible collapse than Chautauqua, continuing into the 1940s and gradually having its function usurped by college and university lecture, writer, and performance series. During its heyday, some of the great celebrities of the time appeared as Lyceum presentations, including Daniel Webster, Edgar Allan Poe, FANNY KEMBLE, CHARLOTTE CUSHMAN, CHARLES DICKENS and Mark Twain. DBW

Cheek by Jowl Small-scale company touring classic plays, founded by its director, Declan Donnellan, and its designer, Nick Ormerod, in 1981. Its policy combines what might be considered 'safe' SHAKESPEARES (*The Tempest*, 1988; *As You Like It*, 1991; *Measure for Measure*, 1994) with unusual or little-known classics, such as CORNEILLE's *Le Cid* (1986), SOPHOCLES' *Philoctetes* (1988) or G. E. LESSING's *Miss Sara Sampson* (1990). Donnellan's directorial style allows the plays to unfold with little trickery, but when he pursues an idea (as with the all-male *As You Like It*) he does so consistently; and this may be the secret of his successful partnership with Ormerod, who is an economical designer, precise with effects. Having worked on small-scale productions, they were invited to stage LOPE DE VEGA's *Fuente Ovejuna* (1989) at the NATIONAL THEATRE's Cottesloe, where in 1992 they directed a new play by the US playwright TONY KUSHNER, *Angels in America*, where AIDS offers a symbol for the downfall of Western civilization as we know it. JE

Chekhov, Anton (Pavlovich) 1860–1904 The most notable and celebrated 19th-century Russian dramatist in the West. His plays helped establish psychological REALISM, although possessing symbolist, impressionist and even proto-absurdist traits (see SYMBOLISM; THEATRE OF THE ABSURD). By fragmenting the WELL MADE PLAY, scattering exposition throughout, compressing, internalizing and excising action, Chekhov created the 'theatre of mood', of misdirection, non-eventfulness and partially stated meaning. A physician by training, he was especially sensitive to the individual's predisposition towards wastefulness as opposed to the conservationist potential of life.

His short story writing career, begun at Moscow University Medical School (1879–84) and extending to his commissions for Suvorin's conservative newspaper *New Time* (1886–93) and beyond, taught him to select and delicately weave idiosyncratically revealing details, symbols, images and themes into a rhythmically constructed musical structure. His work reveals the influence of the great Russian realists – TOLSTOI, Dostoevsky, TURGENEV, the *bytovki* (those who wrote of everyday life) – as well as that of de Maupassant's and SALTYKOV-SHCHEDRIN's

atmospheric character studies, MAETERLINCK's symbolist-rendered inner worlds, GOGOL's grotesquely stylized illogicality and PISAREV's vaudevillian FARCES. Also, in such stories as 'The Steppe' (1888), 'A Dreary Story' (1889), 'The Duel' (1891), 'Ward No. 6' (1892), 'The Lady with the Dog' (1899) and 'In the Ravine' (1900), Chekhov learned to strike a balance between 'subjectively painful' and 'objectively comedic' perspectives on life, to link the catastrophic with the trivial, to create a sense of mystery, multiplicity, recurrence and non-occurrence.

His earliest plays are farces, vaudevilles and 'comedy-jokes' based upon his stories *On the Highroad* (1884), *The Harmfulness of Tobacco Smoking* (1886), *Swan Song* and *The Bear* (1888), *The Wedding* and *The Tragedian in Spite of Himself* (1889), *The Marriage Proposal* (1890) and *The Anniversary* (1891). In these succinct, dynamic and compassionate pieces, Chekhov began to erase the boundary between COMEDY and drama and to forge the tragi-farcical approach built upon 'seeming irrelevancy' which so confounded the audiences and critics of his full-length plays, with the notable exception of NEMIROVICH-DANCHENKO, MEYERHOLD and BELY.

Chekhov's ambivalence towards art as either 'sacred mystery' or 'debased entertainment', and his uncertainty *vis-à-vis* his own career as a dramatist, were reinforced by the failure of his early plays. *Platonov* (1878), *Ivanov* (1887) and *The Wood Demon* (1889) dealt with provincial Don Juans and Hamlets, 19th-century 'superfluous men' of the intelligentsia, sunk in the mire of false and disillusioned romance and realism. His major plays – *The Seagull* (following a dismal 1896 production at the Aleksandrinsky Theatre), *Uncle Vanya* (a revised *Wood Demon*, 1899), *The Three Sisters* (1901) and *The Cherry Orchard* (1904) – all staged by STANISLAVSKY at the MOSCOW ART THEATRE (MAT) in what were for Chekhov unsatisfactorily sentimental and naturalistic productions, developed the full array of his characteristic dramaturgical devices: contrapuntal dialogue, structure and theme; offstage and inner action; spatial iconography; and metatheatrical doubleness in settings, characters, time- and story-frames. Time moves relentlessly forward in his plays, while seeming simultaneously, via homecomings and departures, memories and fixations, to cycle endlessly back, and characters manage to waste what little time they have in the present. This describes both universal human folly and the situation of the pre-revolutionary Russian intelligentsia.

The grandson of a serf, Chekhov well understood the necessity for change and the burden of legacy. A long-time sufferer from what would prove to be fatal tuberculosis, he lived more consciously than most with the reality of transience. GORKY, later to become the voice of Soviet Russia, was befriended and supported by Chekhov, who would have found the new world which he helped imagine utterly foreign to his spirit and intentions. SG

Chekhov, Michael [Mikhail] **(Aleksandrovich)** 1891–1955 Russian stage and film actor, director, teacher and creator of an acting system which has become increasingly influential in the West. ANTON CHEKHOV's nephew, Michael (his professional name following emigration to the West in 1928) was a self-styled mystical philosopher, who used the language of acting to reveal inner truth. He was a member of the Moscow Art Theatre's First Studio from 1912 (later the second Moscow Art Theatre, of which he became artistic director, 1924). His mentors were Stanislavsky, from whom he received personal training in the 'system', Leopold Sulerzhitsky, the Studio's head and the system's best teacher, and Vakhtangov, with whom he often quarrelled but who was perhaps his most influential director-teacher.

A combined artistic-spiritual crisis led Chekhov to study Eastern philosophers and finally to embrace Rudolf Steiner's anthroposophy (1930), which pointed him in a more mystical symbolist direction (see Symbolism). His system of acting evolved into an alternative to Stanislavsky's, emphasizing more universal, imagistic and intuitively contacted and communicated spiritual resources of energy, rather than historical, emotional and psychological details of the actor's life. Organized around the 'psychological gesture', an iconographic physicalization of inner thought and emotion which transforms rather than repeats itself in outer expression, the Chekhov approach is designed to be highly spontaneous, plastic and dialogic between inner and outer tempo-rhythms. Chekhov the actor was noted for his ability to transform himself into a simultaneously symbolic-realistic character mask and to animate his body, largely improvisatorily, into a varied code of precise gestures and movements.

The major roles of his Russian career include Caleb Plummer in Dickens's *The Cricket on the Hearth* (1914), Malvolio in *Twelfth Night* (1917), the title role in Vakhtangov's production of Strindberg's *Erik XIV* (1921), Khlestakov in *The Inspector General* (1921), *Hamlet* (1924), and Senator Ableukov in *The Death of a Senator* (adapted from Bely's *Petersburg*, 1925). His émigré career included acting for Max Reinhardt (1928–30) and in Hollywood (Academy Award nominations for Hitchcock's *Spellbound*, 1945), directing the Habimah Theatre (1930) and several companies and studios of his own – the Chekhov–Bonner company (1931), the Moscow Art Players (1934) and the Chekhov Theatre Studio (1936–42) – through which he disseminated his ideas as actor-director-teacher. His books include *The Path of the Actor* (autobiography, 1928), *On the Actor's Technique* (in Russian, 1946), *To the Actor* (1953) and *To the Director and Playwright* (1963). SG

Cheney, Sheldon 1886–1980 American critic and author. Cheney championed the modernist movement in the American theatre of the 1910s through his books *The New Movement in Theater* (1914) and *The Art Theater* (1916), and through *Theatre Arts [Monthly]* magazine, of which he was founding editor (1916–21). A graduate of the University of California at Berkeley (1908), he studied with George Pierce Baker at Harvard (1913), and later spent five years in Europe, touring and studying theatres. Cheney called for a non-naturalistic aesthetic (see Naturalism) for the American stage, for a poetic and symbolic treatment (see Symbolism) of human experience that engaged rather than eliminated the imagination. His 13 books on art history, architecture and theatre include *The Theatre: 3000 Years of Drama, Acting and Stagecraft* (1929), considered the first comprehensive history of theatre written in the USA. TLM

Cheng Changgeng c.1812–80 Chinese actor of old male (*laosheng*) roles in JINGXI. Born in Anhui, he moved to Beijing in childhood and first studied acting under his maternal uncle. Cheng rose to become leader of the Three Celebrations, one of the four major acting companies in the capital. He was outstanding in male roles portraying great statesmen and warriors, and his style of acting was influential on later performers. A man of great personal integrity and dignity, he was well regarded at court. ACS

Cheng Yanqiu 1904–58 Chinese actor in JINGXI. Born in Beijing the son of an impoverished Manchu family, he studied both *jingxi* and KUNQU techniques under leading teachers. Specializing in women's roles (*dan*), he rose to professional recognition as one of the 'four great famous *dan*' (*sida mingdan*). MEI LANFANG, Shang Xiaoyun (1900–76) and Xun Huisheng (1900–68) were the other three. Cheng developed an individual style of vocalization and was noted for grace and skill in acting. An influential teacher, in the 1930s he directed the new Academy of Dramatic Art in Beijing and under the PRC spent his last years training a new generation of actors. He played in one film made expressly to record his technical expertise. ACS

Chéreau, Patrice 1944– French director, who made his name by winning the competition for young companies with Lenz's *The Soldiers* in 1967. He joined Planchon as director of the Théâtre National Populaire at Villeurbanne in 1972 and moved to the Théâtre des Amandiers at Nanterre in 1982. His productions are distinguished by great scenic brilliance together with an ability to create modern archetypes. His *Ring* cycle at Bayreuth in 1976–80 recast the Norse legends in images of the industrial revolution, and his revivals of Marivaux, Ibsen (*Peer Gynt*, 1981) and Genet (*Les Paravents*, 1983) have brought international recognition. Between 1983 and 88 he directed the first performances of the plays of Bernard-Marie Koltès. DB

Chestnut Street Theatre (Philadelphia) Prominent Philadelphians raised the capital to underwrite a theatre, to be located in the centre of the city and to replace the deteriorating Southwark. It was leased to Thomas Wignell and Alexander Reinagle, who set about assembling an acting company. Completed in 1793, its opening was delayed for a year because of an outbreak of yellow fever. Handsome and well appointed, by 1805 it was considered the finest playhouse with the best acting company in America. In 1816, gaslighting was introduced for the first time in a theatre, but in 1820 the playhouse burned down, to be rebuilt in a version that bore little resemblance to the original. Its most prosperous years occurred under the management of William Warren the elder and William B. Wood, which ended in 1828. Thereafter, it went steadily downhill, as new theatres were built and better acting companies arose to challenge it. In 1855, the theatre was demolished. A new one bearing the same name was built six blocks away; it, too, was razed in 1917. MCH

Chettle, Henry c.1560–c.1607 English playwright and pamphleteer, very few of whose plays survive. Forced into hackwork by financial need, Chettle had a hand in about 50 plays, including several for the ADMIRAL'S MEN. The REVENGE TRAGEDY, *Hoffman* (c.1603), was probably his alone. With ANTHONY MUNDAY he wrote *The Downfall* and *The Death of Robert, Earl of Huntingdon* (1598), with JOHN DAY *The Blind Beggar of Bethnal Green* (1600), and with DEKKER and William Haughton *Patient Grissel* (1600). Chettle is almost as well remembered as the printer of ROBERT GREENE's *Groatsworth of Wit* (1592), and for dissociating himself from Greene's attack on SHAKESPEARE in the preface to his own dream fable, *Kind Heart's Dream* (1593). PT

Chevalier, Albert [Albert Onésime Britannicus Gwathveoyd Louis Chevalier] 1862–1923 British actor and MUSIC-HALL singer, who made his professional debut under the BANCROFTS at the PRINCE OF WALES'S THEATRE in 1877. After a decade of work in the legitimate theatre, appearing with the KENDALS, JOHN HARE and GEORGE ALEXANDER, he reluctantly branched out in 1888 into recitals of comic songs and monologues, many written by his brother and manager Augustus (Charles Ingle). He first appeared 'on the halls' at the London Pavilion, 5 February 1891, as a coster comedian and made an immediate hit; although, or perhaps because, he lacked the cockney authenticity of Gus Elen and Alec Hurley, he was a favourite with royalty and the upper classes, often performing in drawing-rooms, and widely appreciated outside London as well. A master of make-up and stage business, he introduced the now traditional coster gestures in such songs as 'Knocked 'Em in the Old Kent Road' and the maudlin 'My Old Dutch', playing the latter as a full-scale *scena*. In 1906 he toured the USA and Canada with YVETTE GUILBERT, who admired his technique but found his material old-fashioned. After his death, his wife Florrie (daughter of GEORGE LEYBOURNE) wrote an account of her post-mortem conversations with him. LS

Chevalier, Maurice 1888–1972 French singer and actor, who began his career at the age of 11. In MUSIC-HALL, he imitated popular comedians before developing the character of a peasant aspiring to be a dandy. At the FOLIES-BERGÈRE by 1908, he was later sponsored by MISTINGUETT, who became his mistress and his partner, leading to a phenomenal rise in REVUE, OPERETTA and singing tours, with such numbers as 'Valentine' and 'Ma Pomme'. In the 1920s Chevalier's straw boater, dinner-jacket and casual soft shoe stood for a sporty new generation. A stint in Hollywood (1928–35) earned him international fame and he cultivated a somewhat artificial French accent, much imitated. Because of his collaboration with the Vichy government during the Occupation he temporarily fell out of favour, but he regained popularity with a series of one-man shows, begun in 1948. The chat gradually elbowed out the singing and he bade his final farewell to the stage at the Théâtre des Champs-Élysées in 1968. Chevalier's rapport with his audiences was a triumph of manner over matter: his trivial material, weak voice and bland personality were compensated for by abundant charm and a knowing use of *Sprechgesang*. LS

Chiarelli, Luigi 1880–1947 Italian dramatist. In his early years Chiarelli was primarily a journalist. His first tentative attempts to write short pieces for the theatre met with little success until in 1916 the company of VIRGILIO TALLI produced his three-act *La maschera e il volto* (*The Mask and the Face*) in Rome. This ironic comedy, about the conflict between the individual and social conventions, helped to launch the TEATRO DEL GROTTESCO. Although he wrote many other plays in the 1920s and 30s, these never enjoyed the same success, and indeed tended to expose the extent to which the thought underlying *La maschera e il volto* was essentially superficial. LR

Chiari, Pietro 1712–85 Italian dramatist who worked mainly for the Venetian theatres. A prolific writer of competent but unambitious stock pieces, Chiari is remembered primarily for his literary and theatrical disputes with GOLDONI. His work was enormously popular in its day, mingling as it did comic, tragic and satiric elements. Much of it turned on PARODY or ridicule of Goldoni's plays, notably *La scuola delle vedove* (*The School for Widows*, 1749), a parody of Goldoni's 'reform' play, *La vedova scaltra* (*The Cunning Widow*, 1748). A former Jesuit and known as the *abate*, Chiari also wrote romances and *novelle*, and his writing output as a whole is a useful index to the tastes of the Venetian middle classes at the time of that city's theatrical heyday. KR

Chicano theatre Chicano theatre belongs to the larger category of Spanish-speaking theatre in the USA. Its origins date from the arrival of the Spanish conquerors, including the priests interested in the spiritual conquest, in the 16th century. Dramatic performances were recorded in the Southwest as early as 1598, when Juan de Oñate's band of explorers performed an early religious play near El Paso, Texas. Throughout the period of settlement and growth of the following centuries, the dominant Hispanic culture and language in the area gave attention to the theatre. During the 19th century, both San Francisco and Los Angeles were major centres of HISPANIC THEATRE activity that sponsored visits by operatic companies even before the California gold rush. As the railway linked major cities throughout the Southwest, especially Laredo, San Antonio and El Paso, the ethnic communities with a strong sense of their heritage and traditions maintained local cultural activities and hosted travelling road companies en route to and from Mexico City.

By the 1920s Chicano theatre flourished from Los Angeles to Chicago. Productions of musical REVUES and ZARZUELAS coincided with serious plays that addressed issues particular to Chicano communities. The problems of adapting culturally and linguistically to a predominantly Anglo culture were standard themes. The level of activity subsided during the Depression and Second World War years, although it did not disappear entirely.

The more recent Chicano theatre movement coincided with activism in the US civil rights movement in the 1960s. In the summer of 1965, LUIS VALDÉZ joined César Chávez as he was organizing the farm workers' strike in the fields of Delano, California – using politically orientated improvisational theatre to underscore the migrant workers' cause – and became the acknowledged father of the new direction in Chicano theatre. His *actos*, as they came to be called, were short AGIT-PROP pieces that dramatized the essence and spirit of the Chicano reality. The new Chicano theatre was, suddenly, a revolutionary theatre committed to social change. From this initial experience, Valdéz established EL TEATRO CAMPESINO (Farm Workers' Theatre).

This group served as the model for a host of other Chicano theatre groups created throughout the West and Southwest, and extending across the country into Illinois, Indiana and Wisconsin. Adrian Vargas created Teatro de la Gente (People's Theatre) in 1967. In 1971 Jorge Huerta developed the Teatro de la Esperanza (Theatre of Hope) in Santa Barbara, a group whose stability is second only to that of El Teatro Campesino. In 1972 Joe Rosenberg established the Teatro Bilingüe (Bilingual Theatre) in Kingsville, Texas. At the peak of the movement, as many as 100 groups were functioning throughout the USA. Rubén Sierra, Roberto D. Pomo, Romulus Zamora and Manuel Pickett are but a few of the other major directors. A national network was established in 1971 to maintain linkages among the groups. Called TENAZ (El Teatro Nacional de Aztlán; National Aztlán Theatre), it has sponsored the annual festivals that bring together groups from all over the USA as well as from Latin America to learn about their common heritage and share their experiences. The road has not always been smooth: differences in function and orientation were particularly evident at the fifth festival celebrated in 1974 in Mexico City, where Valdéz was severely criticized. Nevertheless, the festivals provided a useful interchange and gave opportunity for fresh perspectives on techniques.

The farm-worker issue catapulted El Teatro Campesino into existence, but the themes captured in its BRECHTIAN-style *actos* were many and varied. *Soldado razo* decried the mistreatment of Mexican-Americans in the Vietnam War; *Vendidos* depicted the worst of Chicago stereotypes. Valdéz's *Zoot Suit*, based on a historical episode of racial violence in East Los Angeles in the summer of 1943, opened in Los Angeles in 1978 as a tremendous critical and popular success – a record that unfortunately did not hold true when it opened months later as the first Chicano show to arrive on BROADWAY. After a period of reorganization in San Luis Obispo, the company has in more recent years staged Valdéz's *I Don't Have to Show You No Stinking Badges* and *Simply Maria* (1986) by Josefina Lopéz, a young Mexican woman brought up in Los Angeles. The latter play builds on Valdéz's inherent sense of the comic while at the same time cutting into the pain and prejudice of cross-cultural living.

An entire generation of Chicano writers has picked up the cue, adding original notes derived from the rich traditions and folklore of the Chicano people. Most plays are identified by author; others are the product of a group effort, a kind of *creación colectiva*. Teatro de la Esperanza was particularly active in the latter vein. Growing out of a student movement at Santa Barbara into a professional theatre group, it staged its first full-scale production, *Guadalupe* – a play that chronicled the exploitation of Chicanos in a small California community – in 1974. That success led to *La victima* (1976), another documentary experiment based on the deportation of Mexican workers alleged to be injurious to the American economy. Later plays include *Hijos: Once a Family* (1979), *Lotería de pasiones* (*Lottery of Passions*, 1984) and Lalo Cervantes's *Teodolo's Final Spin* (1988).

Among the women playwrights Estela Portillo Trambley is notable for her *Puente negro*, *Autumn Gold*, *Blacklight* and *Sor Juana*, the last an impressive and stimulating work that captures both the intellect and the emotion of the 17th-century Mexican nun, herself a brilliant poet and playwright. Several writers who are not exactly Mexican-American are claimed by the movement. One is Milcha Sanchez-Scott, born to a Columbian father and an Indonesian-Chinese-Dutch mother, whose play *Roosters* (1987) deals with family conflicts and Chicano issues around a metaphor of cockfighting. Another is Arthur Giron, born of Guatemalan parents; his play *Money* chronicles the fast and vicious world of high finance and corporate foundations. Other important writers include Rubén Sierra and Carlos Morton.

The Chicano theatre is normally written and performed in the peculiar linguistic mixture typical of the Chicano population. Words and phrases in the two languages are constantly interchanged according to the context. Most groups perform in the 'Spanglish' dialect most comfortable to their situation; some prefer to maintain the separation and will alternate performances in Spanish and English. A new generation of Hispanic writers is losing the language entirely and now prefers to write almost exclusively in English, with only an occasional word or expression in Spanish. Economic difficulties have dimmed some opportunities for Chicano theatre at the same time as social issues have changed some of the needs. The effort to educate the majority population about Chicano issues while serving the interests of the Chicano population itself presents a major challenge, especially now that not as many groups are functioning as before. The publication of texts continues to be a high priority as an incentive to production. From its humble beginnings the Chicano theatre has achieved an impressive level of accomplishment. GW

See: J. W. Brokaw, *Educational Theatre Journal*, Dec. 1977; Y. Broyles-González, *El Teatro Campesino: Theater in the Chicano Movement*, Austin, 1994; D. Chávez and L. Feyder, *Shattering the Myth: Plays by Hispanic Women*, Houston, 1992; J. A. Huerta, *Chicano Theatre: Themes and Forms*, New York, 1982, and (ed.), *Necessary Theater: Six Plays about the Chicano Experience*, Houston, 1989; J. A. Huerta and N. Kanellos, *Nuevos Pasos: Chicano and Puerto Rican Drama*, Houston, 1979; M. E. Osborn, *On New Ground: Contemporary Hispanic-American Plays*, New York, 1987; E. C. Ramírez, *Footlights Across the Border: A History of Spanish-language Professional Theatre on the Texas Stage*, New York, 1990.

Chichester Festival Theatre The first large thrust-stage theatre in Britain. Seating nearly 1400 people around its stage, it opened on 3 July 1962. It was also one of the first theatres to be built in a park, outside a small country city in the south of England. It was built largely by local subscriptions, raised by Leslie Evershed-Martin, who had been inspired by the example of the STRATFORD (Ontario) FESTIVAL Theatre in Canada. These two theatres share the ideals for theatre construction first argued for by TYRONE GUTHRIE and derived from Elizabethan models, stressing close audience–actor contact, all-round visibility and the use of the whole auditorium as the stage set. Such ideas, radical in their day, were first put to the test at Chichester by LAURENCE OLIVIER, the first director, who was also appointed the director of the still embryonic NATIONAL THEATRE company at the OLD VIC. The productions, including *Uncle Vanya* (1962), *The Royal Hunt of the Sun* (1964) and *Armstrong's Last Goodnight* (1965), transferred from Chichester to the Old Vic. In 1965 Olivier was succeeded by another famous actor-director, John Clements. The tradition of actor-managers at Chichester continued until Peter Dews's appointment in 1978.

The theatre was unusual among postwar civic reps in that it received little grant income from the state but more from its box-office and supporters' club. This led to the charge that its programmes were over-commercial and orientated towards WEST END transfers with star names. It is certainly the most English-looking of reps (see REGIONAL THEATRE (BRITAIN)) and favours English repertoires, with SHAKESPEARE and the Edwardian writers predominating. MICHAEL RUDMAN, born in the USA, had problems with finding the right blend of styles, although under his leadership the studio theatre at Chichester, the Minerva, flourished. In 1991 he was replaced by a former artistic director, Patrick Garland, whose tastes were more traditional.   JE

Chifunyise, S. J. 1948– Zimbabwean playwright, educated in Zambia and the United States. A Chikwakwa Theatre product (see ZAMBIA), he taught at the University of Zambia and was National Director of Culture. He is now Director of Arts and Crafts at the Ministry of Youth, Sport and Culture in Zimbabwe. His short plays and dance-dramas are extremely popular in both Zambia and Zimbabwe. Some of these have been published in his collection, *Medicine for Love* (1984). Chifunyise is now Deputy Secretary, Culture, in the Ministry of Education and Culture, and active in many cultural and arts organizations.   RK

Chikamatsu Monzaemon 1653–1725 The most important Japanese playwright of *KABUKI* and *BUNRAKU* plays in Kyoto–Osaka during his lifetime. Born the second son of a minor provincial samurai and placed in service as a court page in his youth, his background and education are apparent in the literary quality of his texts. His first *kabuki* play, *Seventh Year Memorial for Yūgiri* (*Yūgiri nananenki*, 1684), was written for SAKATA TŌJŪRŌ and for a decade he was that actor's staff playwright in Kyoto. Abbreviated illustrated scripts (*eiri kyōgen bon*) of 31 of his *kabuki* plays are preserved, including *The Prostitute and the Whirlpool of Love* (*Keisei Awa no naruto*, 1695), *The Prostitute of Buddha Field* (*Keisei hotoke no hara*, 1699), and *The Prostitute and Prayers to Buddha* (*Keisei mibu dainenbutsu*, 1702). The juxtaposition of religion and eroticism is typical of early *kabuki*. In these plays Chikamatsu skilfully balanced bravura history scenes with gentle lovers' scenes.

During this period he also wrote PUPPET plays, such as *The Soga Heir* (*Yotsugi Soga*, 1683) for chanter Uji Kaga no Jō and *Kagekiyo Victorious* (*Shusse Kagekiyo*, 1685) for

chanter TAKEMOTO GIDAYŪ. At Gidayū's invitation he moved to Osaka in 1705 and over the next 20 years composed nearly 100 puppet plays for the Takemoto Theatre. The history play *The Battles of Coxinga* (1715), showing a Japanese hero restoring the Ming dynasty in China, was immensely successful and influential. In a dozen lovers' suicide plays (*shinjūmono*), Chikamatsu carried *kabuki*'s erotic prostitute-buying themes to tragic conclusions, creating a new independent domestic play in *The Love Suicides at Sonezaki* (*Sonezaki shinjū*, 1703), *The Courier to Hell* (*Meido no hikyaku*, 1711), *The Love Suicides at Amijima* (*Shinjū ten no Amijima*, 1721) and others.

Chikamatsu's narrative passages contain sections of great verbal beauty, especially lovers' travel scenes (*michiyuki*). He used verbal techniques of alliteration (*kakekotoba*, 'pivot words') – in which a word contributes one meaning to the phrase preceding and a different meaning to the phrase following – and related words (*engo*), as, for example, mist, rain, dew and wetness convey related images of eroticism. More than any other playwright he created significant dramatic literature for the puppet theatre.   JRB

Children of Blackfriars, Children of Whitefriars
see CHILDREN OF THE CHAPEL ROYAL

Children of the Chapel Royal Under the mastership of William Cornish, the choristers of the Chapels Royal in Windsor and London supplied the young Henry VIII's demand for entertainment in a number of lost plays. JOHN SKELTON's *Magnyfycence*, if not representative, at least underlines that most of them would have been in the MORALITY tradition, which also governed the elaborate disguisings in which Cornish and his king delighted. The mid-century Master, Richard Edwardes, putative author of the TRAGEDY *Damon and Pithias* (1565), extended the dramatic range of the Chapel Children. He may have been the first to admit spectators to the 'rehearsals' of court entertainments in the paved hall of the disused Blackfriars monastery, where the MASTER OF THE REVELS previewed royal command performances.

It was in the Blackfriars refectory that Richard Farrant, Deputy Master of the Chapel Children, established an indoor theatre in 1576. With a home of their own, Farrant's choristers became serious rivals to the BOYS OF ST PAUL'S, with whom they teamed up under the creative leadership of JOHN LYLY after Farrant's death in 1580 and that of Sebastian Westcott, Master of the Paul's Boys, in 1582. The Chapel Children shared the disgrace of the Paul's Boys after Lyly had drawn them into the Marprelate Controversy in 1589–90, and there is no evidence of further dramatic activity until 1600. It was then that Henry Evans leased the converted Parliament Chamber of the Blackfriars from RICHARD BURBAGE and led his choristers into eight years of intense and brilliant activity. The publicity provided by the WAR OF THE THEATRES, which lined JONSON and the Children of the Chapel against MARSTON and the Boys of St Paul's, turned Jonson's *Poetaster* (1600) into a *cause célèbre*.

The talented boys, including at various times EZEKIEL FENN, NATHAN FIELD and SALATHIEL PAVY, gave the first performances of major plays by Jonson, CHAPMAN,

MIDDLETON, BEAUMONT and even Marston. Their repertoire was no less distinguished than that of the King's Men. It may be that playwrights as well as audiences took a perverse delight in the boys' utterance of bawdy or scurrilous material, but the authorities were increasingly unamused. *Eastward Ho* (1605) angered James I, as did JOHN DAY's *The Isle of Gulls* (1606), and by 1608 the company was in crisis. Henry Evans surrendered his lease of the Blackfriars and fled to the Continent, and Richard Burbage led the King's Men into the BLACKFRIARS THEATRE. A remnant of the Children of the Chapel Royal survived ingloriously at the WHITEFRIARS, where they performed Jonson's *Epicoene* (1609) and other plays before being finally disbanded in 1615. PT

Childress, Alice 1920–94 African-American playwright. Born in Charleston, South Carolina, and brought up in Harlem, Childress opened the New York stage to black women writers when her play *Gold through the Trees* (1952) was professionally produced OFF-BROADWAY. She had for 12 years been an actress with the American Negro Theatre, and her most important play, *Trouble in Mind* (1955), voiced the protest of a veteran black actress against playing a stereotypical 'darkie' role in a BROADWAY-bound production. It won the Obie for best original Off-Broadway play. Other notable plays by Childress that feature strong black women of compassion and dignity are *Wedding Band* (1966) and *Wine in the Wilderness* (1969). More recent works include the screenplay *A Hero Ain't Nothin' but a Sandwich* (1977), on teenage drug addiction, and *Moms* (1987), a play recalling the life of comedienne Jackie 'Moms' Mabley. EGH

Chile Mexico, and later Peru, became the principal centres of commercial development and intellectual formation in the New World because the Spanish were able to build on well developed indigenous cultures. In Chile, on the other hand, the Native Americans had not achieved a high level of cultural development, and their fierce resistance made the conquest by the Spaniards extremely difficult. Much of the colonial literature in Chile dealt with aspects of heroic fighting on the part of the *araucanos*, and the names of the American Indian leaders – Colocolo, Caupolicán and Lautaro, for example – survived as well as those of the Spanish *conquistadores* such as Pedro de Valdivia.

The earliest theatre representations recorded in Chile took place around 1612 when the Spanish king ordered the celebration of the Mystery of the Conception in the American colonies. Especially on Corpus Christi, AUTOS SACRAMENTALES were commonly performed with elaborate processions, along with the 'mysteries' (see MYSTERY PLAY) and *pasos* (see GÉNERO CHICO). Performances took place in the churches, convents and cemeteries until the corruption in the *autos sacramentales* invoked a ban by King Carlos III in 1765. The so-called 'divine' comedies were allowed to continue, but the strong position of the Church impeded the development of secular drama. Women were not allowed to perform in the theatre, and strict regulations about seating arrangements were enforced. The essence of good drama present in epic poetry, nonetheless, was picked up in far-away Spain. Ercilla's

La araucana (1569, 78, 89), Pedro de Oña's *El arauco domado* (1596) and the chronicles of Don Cristóbal Suárez de Figueroa provided inspiration for at least three Spanish plays, one of which involved nine participating authors including Mira de Amescua, JUAN RUIZ DE ALARCÓN, Vélez de Guevara and GUILLÉM DE CASTRO Y BELLVÍS. Francisco González Bustos's play, *Los españoles en Chile* (*The Spanish in Chile*, 1665), which finally played in Chile after 1800, was a play of literary merit that showed the nobility of the *araucanos*. Towards the end of the 18th century Peruvian-born Juan de Egaña stimulated theatre in Santiago with translations of European plays, and it is significant that throughout the nearly 300 years of colonial rule no single play by a Chilean author captured critical attention as a major work.

In the period following independence in 1818, Camilo Henríquez (1769–1825) advocated governmental support of the theatre. One of his own plays, *La Camila, o la patriota de Sudamérica* (*Camila, or the South American Patriot*, 1817), is an early Chilean play but is poorly written and therefore did not gain much recognition. During much of this period Valparaíso, the port city, was a more important centre of theatre activity than Santiago, the capital, where the first permanent theatre building opened in 1820. In the new republic the major influences for promoting theatre came from Bernardo O'Higgins, the country's patriot and new leader, and Andrés Bello (1781–1865), a VENEZUELAN-born poet and philosopher who became rector of the university and reformed education throughout the country. During this period of transition between the aesthetics of neoclassicism and romanticism, Bello wrote plays, as did his son, Carlos Bello (1815–54). Other important foreign influences were Juan Casacuberta (1799–1849), an actor who arrived from ARGENTINA with a repertory of romantic plays. Also from Argentina were Luis Ambrosio Morante, actor, director and sometime playwright, and Domingo Faustino Sarmiento (1811–88), a writer and essayist fleeing the dictatorial Rosas regime. The latter's critical editorials in *El Mercurio* of Valparaíso deploring the lack of culture produced a sharp reaction.

If the rest of the century did not produce transcendental works, it did see the emergence of nationalism and several plays and authors that attempted through the romantic mode to capture a Chilean ambiance. Rafael Minvielle (1800–87), with a European background, achieved success with *Ernesto* in 1842. Alberto Blest Gana (1830–1920), better known as a novelist, attempted one play that in turn inspired the major playwright of the latter half of the century, Daniel Barros Grez (1834–1904). Barros Grez, in a sense the founder of the Chilean theatre and the first major *costumbrista* (see COSTUMBRISMO), wrote scores of plays and essays about the popular figures he wished to satirize with his moralizing, didactic tone. He is considered a successor of the Spanish MORATÍN and a precursor of PIRANDELLO; one of his best plays is *Como en Santiago* (*As in Santiago*, 1874), revived and made popular in the 20th century for its engaging view of rural life that tries to emulate urban mores with its satirical and humorous view. Other writers of the century include Daniel Caldera y de Villar (1852–91), author of *El tribunal del honor* (*Honour of the Court*, 1877), a historico-nationalistic play, and Mateo Martínez Quevedo (1848–1923), author of *Don*

Lucas Gómez (1885), an extremely popular play that highlighted rural/urban differences with great humour.

The 20th century The development of a Chilean middle class began to change the character of the theatre, which at the beginning of the century belonged, for the most part, either to an outdated and romantic melodramatic style or to the reality of the incipient social class. The War of the Pacific (1879–84) not only ended the domination of the upper class, but it led as well to a period of great immigration and the foreign domination of Chilean economic interests, especially mining. A new sense of nationalism emerged, in spite of the strong foreign influences (French, German and British), and a rising consciousness of social problems. Antonio Acevedo Hernández (1886–1962) left home at age ten and learned the world through personal experiences. His plays focused on all aspects of the marginal classes in urban, rural, mining and other settings; while he criticized the social order,he avoided the worst aspects of politically committed theatre. His major works are *Chañarcillo* (1936), *Los caminos de Dios* (*The Paths of God*), which premiered in Poland, and *El triángulo tiene cuatro lados* (*The Triangle Has Four Sides*).

The formation of the Compañía Dramática Nacional (National Drama Company) in 1913 fomented new interest in the theatre and barely preceded the opening of the Panama Canal (1914), which curiously had a negative impact on Chilean theatre. Foreign troupes that had traditionally visited Chile now could choose to bypass the country, given the flexibility offered by the Canal. In 1915 the Sociedad de Autores Teatrales de Chile (Society of Chilean Playwrights; SATCH) was formed, composed primarily of writers who followed the traditional lines of romantic MELODRAMAS as well as the satirical and costumbristic plays.

Santiago's first theatre company, formed in 1917, was headed by actors Enrique Baguena and Arturo Burhle; it still adhered to the old styles of theatre (such as prompter's box, candles and painted sets). The other major writers of the period were Armando Moock (1894–1942) and Germán Luco Cruchaga (1894–1936). Moock broke with the naturalist/determinist (see NATURALISM) school and anticipated the relevant themes of the 1950s in such plays as *Pueblecito* (*Little Town*), *Mocosita* (*Brat*, 1929) and *Rigoberto* (1935), which captured typical elements in the daily lives of urban dwellers concerned about education, family and especially the artistic existence. Luco Cruchaga is the author of the now classic play *La viuda de Apablaza* (*The Widow of Apablaza*, 1928) with its touching portrayal of loneliness, love and disappointment.

Throughout the 1920s and 30s the Chilean theatre continued along similar lines, unable to break with the strong traditions. A number of factors, including the world Depression, Chile's relative isolation and the rise of movies, contributed to the delay in creating an independent theatre in Chile – some 10 to 15 years after its development in Mexico or Argentina, for example. The visit by the famous Spanish company of MARGARITA XIRGÚ prepared the way for new concepts of staging, with plays by SHAW and LENORMAND.

With the creation of the Teatro Experimental de la Universidad de Chile (University of Chile Experimental Theatre) in 1941, renovation of the Chilean theatre began. Under the leadership of Pedro de la Barra, its first director (until 1958), the group (renamed the Instituto de Teatro de la Universidad de Chile (ITUCH) in 1959) undertook to bring to the Chilean theatre the new conceptions of acting and staging that were implemented in Europe by PISCATOR, ANTOINE, COPEAU and STANISLAVSKY. The famous French actor LOUIS JOUVET visited Chile with a French company in 1942 and provided additional impetus. The group's first major success was THORNTON WILDER's *Our Town* in 1945.

A similar thrust at the Catholic University led to the creation of the TEUC (Teatro Experimental de la Universidad Católica) in 1943, also with its own professional company and, since 1956, its own theatre. Both ITUCH and TEUC brought together the most important theatre practitioners in the country and provided theatre training for a new generation of directors, actors and technicians. In their formative years, both professional groups normally staged the best foreign plays. Plays by national authors were the exception, as a new group of playwrights was being formed. In addition to Enrique Bunster, Fernando Cuadra and Pedro de la Barra, the most notable are María Asunción Requena's (1915–86) *Fuerte Bulnes* (*Fort Bulnes*), a drama of heroic proportions in the colonization of southern Chile (Magallanes); Fernando Debesa's *Mama Rosa* (1957), an engaging costumbristic middle-class family story; and LUIS ALBERTO HEIREMANS's *Versos de ciego* (*The Blind Man's Verses*, 1961). Chile has produced exceptional women writers in addition to Requena, such as Isidora Aguirre (b.1919) and Gabriela Roepke (b.1920).

The solid quality of productions by ITUCH and TEUC brought about a new generation of Chilean playwrights who have dominated the Chilean scene since the mid-50s. The major theatrical mode has been REALISM that focuses on the socio-economic issues within Chilean society, drawing on representative psychological figures. EGON WOLFF and SERGIO VODANOVIĆ have written exceptional plays. Wolff, trained as a chemical engineer, is the author of more than 20, of which *Los invasores* (*The Invaders*, 1962) and *Flores de papel* (*Paper Flowers*, 1970) illustrate his technical control by combining pressing social concerns with artistic integrity. Vodanović was less experimental but achieved success with *Deja que los perros ladren* (*Let the Dogs Bark*, 1959) and *Nos tomamos la universidad* (*We Took the University*, 1970), in which he exposed corruption in the political sphere and hypocrisy in revolution. Another major realistic writer was Fernando Cuadra (b.1926), author of *La niña en la palomera* (*The Girl in the Dovecot*, 1966), and JUAN RADRIGÁN, author of *Hechos consumados* (*Accomplished Deeds*, 1981).

The realistic overtone in the recent theatre has not precluded, however, a more abstract and symbolic theatre. JÒRGE DÍAZ, Chile's best-known playwright internationally, began in an absurdist vein (see THEATRE OF THE ABSURD) with overtones of BECKETT, but even from the beginning demonstrated a concern about social issues which became more apparent in his later plays. His *El cepillo de dientes* (*The Toothbrush*, 1961) is a masterful two-character play of miscommunication within a circus atmosphere. Many of his later plays combine political and social topics with a constant experimentation for an adequate language of expression. His successor in this vein is MARCO ANTONIO DE LA PARRA, whose several plays to date have woven sociopolitical themes into an abstract technique. In a different vein, ALEJANDRO SIEVEKING has pursued vigorously and prolifically a popular theatre with social overtones that often depends on folkloric tendencies. A psychological, religious and eclectic writer, he works in collaboration with his actress wife, Bélgica Castro.

The fall of the Allende regime in 1973 coincided with the death of Chile's Nobel poet laureate, Pablo Neruda, who himself had experimented with theatre in a curious work entitled *Fulgor y muerte de Joaquín Murieta* (*Splendour and Death of Joaquín Murieta*, 1966). The ensuing dictatorship of General Pinochet brought on a climate of repression difficult for the artistic community (see CENSORSHIP). Light comedies were admissible, but certain groups gradually became more insistent, with socially committed themes. After 1976 the plays became more daring, with such examples as *Pedro, Juan y Diego* (1976) by ICTUS and David Benavente; *¿Cuántos años tiene un dia?* (*How Many Years in a Day?*, 1978) by ICTUS and Sergio Vodanović; *Los payasos de la esperanza* (*Clowns of Hope*, 1977) by Taller de Investigación Teatral; and *Tres Marías y una Rosa* (*Three Marys and a Rose*, 1979) by the same group in collaboration with David Benavente. De la Parra's *Lo crudo, lo cocido y lo podrido* (*The Raw, the Cooked and the Rotten*, 1978) created a sensation when it was banned at the Catholic University the day before its scheduled opening, ostensibly for its gross language. The collective work begun in 1967-8 with the so-called Teatro Taller (Theatre Workshop) was gradually transformed during these years into collaborative work that often incorporated a textual author into the process.

In 1984 a new political policy encouraged the return of the émigrés. The theatre has flourished, with many functioning groups and festivals. A pattern of self-censorship avoids massive confrontations, but generally the regime has not bothered the recent theatre, which it treats as an intellectual safety valve. The current theatre is dynamic in dealing with psychological realism, socio-economic matters and problems of the émigré.

Among the most important functioning groups is ICTUS, directed by Delfina Guzmán and Nissim Sharim, a group established in 1956 and at present the strongest professional company in Santiago outside the universities. Teatro Imagen, Teatro del Ángel and other smaller groups help maintain an active theatre fare. Two major novelists have entered the theatre in recent years: José Donoso (b.1924) with his *Sueños de mala muerte* (*Second-Class Dreams*, 1983), developed in collaboration with ICTUS, and ANTONIO SKÁRMETA with *Ardiente paciencia* (*Burning Patience*, 1982), a poetic version of Pablo Neruda's final days that exalts his human qualities over his roles as diplomat and poet.

In the last 25 years Chile has benefited from an abundance of talented and productive directors, such as Pedro Orthus, Agustín Siré, Pedro de la Barra, Fernando Colina, Eugenio Dittborn, Eugenio Guzmán, Fernando González, Raúl Osorio and Gustavo Meza. In addition to the young directors on the current scene, a new generation of writers is also emerging, including the original work of Ramón Griffero and Jaime Miranda. Griffero, with *Historia de un galpón abandonado* (*Story of an Abandoned Barn*, 1984) and *Cinema Utopia* (1986), opened up new visual spaces with scenes of terror and ambiguity. Marco Antonio de la Parra has gone on to fulfil his original promise and is now the hottest item of his generation. The 50th anniversaries of the theatre programmes at both the University of Chile (1991) and the Catholic University (1933) have brought revivals of interest.

Theatre of the marginal classes and an active programme of children's theatre complement the experiments of some of the more forward young playwrights and directors. It is still true that most of the solid theatre activity is concentrated in Santiago. Theatre in the provinces is limited to small amateur groups, although cities such as Valdivia, which sponsored its first theatre festival in 1985, and Concepción, also in the south, have a tradition of active support. GW

See: C.M. Boyle, *Chilean Theater, 1973-1985: Marginality, Power, Selfhood*, London and Toronto, 1992; E. Castedo-Ellerman, *El teatro chileno de mediados del siglo 20*, Santiago, 1982; J. Durán Cerda, *Repertorio del teatro chileno*, Santiago de Chile, 1962; A. M. Escudero, *Apuntes sobre el teatro en Chile*, Santiago, 1967; T. Fernández, *El teatro chileno contemporáneo (1941-1973)*, Madrid, 1982; E. Pereira Salas, *Historia del teatro en Chile desde sus orígenes hasta la muerte de Juan Casacuberta*, Santiago, 1974; G. Rojo, *Muerte y resurrección del teatro chileno (1973-1983)*, Madrid, 1985; O. Rodríguez and D. Piga, *Teatro chileno del siglo 20*, Santiago, 1964.

Chilly, Charles Marie de 1804-72 French actor and theatre manager, who first appeared in the smaller theatres, making his debut at the ODÉON in 1827. He then toured the provinces with a troupe run by Sabatier and BOCAGE, returning to the Odéon in 1829. He followed HAREL to the Porte-Saint-Martin, where he attracted attention as the Jew in HUGO's *Marie Tudor*. In 1837 he joined the Ambigu (see BOULEVARD) taking on the parts of the late FIRMIN, and began to find his vocation in 'third roles', the villains of MELODRAMA. His sharp features and clipped, measured diction created a new type of villain, and his greatest role was that of Rodin in *The Wandering Jew*. In 1858 he became manager of the ailing Ambigu, and brought back audiences. From 1866 to 72 he was director of the Odéon, and was responsible for the triumphal revival of *Ruy Blas*. JMCC

China Theatre has been and remains an omnipresent force in the social life of the Chinese. It is first described by a single ambiguous term, *xi*, which originally designated PLAY, games and ACROBATICS. The name is still current but retains a connotation of plurality as an umbrella word covering a host of theatrical entertainments. When the Chinese speak of theatre specifically they use the names of the musical and dialectal forms which animate their numerous regional dramatic styles. These constitute the corpus of theatre in a national sense. A varying length of tradition lies behind them. Some, like the rice-planting song of northern China, persist as simple forms of song and gestural expression with an uncomplicated musical

A county official as a *chou* character, showing the typical white patch on the face, headgear, whiskers and red garment.

accompaniment. Other styles, practised within the orbit of more sophisticated urban areas, developed as the transmitters of polished theatrical form. Three seminal events mark the long time-span such progress involved. The rise of ZAJU theatre in the 13th century set precedents for structured stage practices which endured. The flowering of the KUNQU in the 16th century ushered in a theatre of lyrical elegance and scholarly playwrights, while the domination of the Beijing theatre style in the 19th century proclaimed the triumph of an aesthetic for the man in the street.

Chinese traditional theatre is a presentational, secular style of performance essentially musical and choreographic in its basic structure. Synthesis of forms and variety of offering are operative factors. Categorized archetypal character roles predominate, each having its particular formalized speech and movement techniques together with a distinctive make-up and costume style.

The composition of a dramatic text and its interpretation by the actor are conditioned by an ordered arrangement of song, narrative and declamation. Their structural basis results from the dual relationship between musical sound and the spoken word arising from the homonymic nature of the Chinese language. Because of the pitch variations, or tones, which differentiate the meanings of otherwise identically sounding words in Chinese, the sound pattern accruing from the formal organization of rhythm has acquired a particular literary significance. The number of syllables and tonal patterns contained by a line of text became a first element of verse and song composition

for the traditional drama. Metrical pattern and rhyme schemes were given priority by the old Chinese dramatist in devising his text. Rhyme tables classifying words with the same tonal movement were the tools of his craft. The playwright did not set words to music; he sought appropriate words to match the auditory permutations of his lines and stanzas. Because of this, there has been handed down an extensive repertoire of tunes, that is to say metrical arrangements having their separate tonal patterns and rhyme schemes, which can be used over and over again in relation to specific emotional situations. Because of this also, the stage musician can command stereotyped styles embodying fixed metrical patterns which complement the tonal–rhythmic format of a play text as stipulated by the dramatist. Dialect naturally affects a compositional style so dependent on auditory effects. The melodic differences resulting from dialectal usage in regional dramatic forms were broadly classified as northern and southern styles by the Chinese in the past. A complex history of borrowing and cross-fusion between the two divisions brought about the musical genres which identify major theatrical styles such as those of Suzhou or Beijing.

Antecedents of theatre Performance goes back to the earliest times in China. SHAMANistic rituals from many centuries before the time of Christ probably involved a combination of song, dance, gesture and COSTUME. The performing arts functioned also as entertainment. An example is shown in a wall painting in a tomb excavated in the early 1960s in Mixian, central Henan Province, dating from about AD 200. It shows a large-scale banquet, probably hosted by the main tomb occupant when alive. A series of small-scale performances is taking place between two long rows of guests. There are dancers, JUGGLERS, plate-spinners and musicians.

The Tang dynasty (618–907) witnessed a climax in the political power and culture of medieval China, with many quite developed forerunners of theatre already in existence. An example is the 'adjutant plays' (canjun xi), which were comic skits. They included dialogue, string and wind and perhaps percussion instruments as musical accompaniment, and role categories. Both actors and actresses took part, and sometimes there were three roles or even more. Puppet shows were not new to the Tang, but certainly flourished then and were popular in the marketplaces of the cities. The Emperor Minghuang (r.713–56) loved to watch puppet shows in the inner palace. The 20th-century scholar Sun Kaidi has argued that drama in China imitates and derives from PUPPETS. The arts of the storytellers were also highly developed by that time. The late-Tang-period poet Li Shangyin records how storytellers would expound the deeds and wars of the heroes of the Three Kingdoms period (AD 220–65). These were later to be a major arm of the content of all popular Chinese theatre. It was already quite common for entertainers to mount high platforms or stages so that they could better be seen by their audiences. Religious impulses, from shamanism, Taoism and Buddhism, remain important in many regional 'minority' theatres in outlying areas today, including TIBETAN DRAMA.

Origins of theatre The Song dynasty ruled all China from 960 to 1127 and southern China until 1279. Meanwhile the Jin dynasty, ruled by the Jurchen people, ancestors of the Manchus, seized the Northern Song capital of Kaifeng in 1126, forcing the Song to relocate their centre of government to Hangzhou in the south.

The Song dynasty is notable for the rise of commerce, together with a class to organize it, and the growth of cities. In this more urbanized environment China's first fully developed theatres arose. Called goulan (literally, 'hook balustrades'), they were contained within amusement centres termed wazi ('tiles') or washe ('tile booths'). The largest amusement centre in early-12th-century Kaifeng held 50 theatres or even more, and the grandest theatre could accommodate several thousand people. They were covered, not open-air, structures and so not subject to the vagaries of the weather. All classes of people frequented them.

In the north such performances were termed zaju ('various plays') or, under the Jin dynasty, yuanben, and included dancing, acrobatics, the core play, comic patter and a musical conclusion. The terms zaju or yuanben refer also to the core playlet, which was short and funny and might concern a love affair or satirize officialdom. Apart from a musician, these plays needed actors for four or five characters. Role categories included clown (fujing) and jester (fumo). MASKS were probably used for supernatural roles, and make-up was common.

In the south a new style arose from early in the 12th century: 'southern drama' (nanxi). Its place of origin was Wenzhou in southern Zhejiang Province. Its music was based partly on folk songs and it may also have been influenced by Indian drama. The seven role categories of southern drama are the foundations on which most later Chinese theatre has built. Sheng and dan were respectively the principal male and female characters, mo and wai secondary male, and tie secondary female roles. Jing were strong male characters and chou, according to Xu Wei (1521–93), had a 'face daubed with black powder and was very ugly'. The jing and chou roles were frequently interchangeable. In contrast to the zaju, all characters sang.

The plays of southern drama were longer and had more complex story lines than earlier performances and in this sense they may be taken as the first stage of a fully developed Chinese drama. The great majority appear to have been love comedies. The two most famous, Chaste Woman Zhao (Zhao zhennü) and Wang Kui Renounces Guiying (Wang Kui fu Guiying), deal with unfaithful scholar-lovers who come to a bad end. Most scripts are anonymous, many having been written by 'writing societies'.

The first great age of Chinese theatre In 1234 the Mongols conquered the Jin and in 1279 the Southern Song armies, and established the Yuan dynasty (1279–1368). After the Mongol conquest of the south, southern drama lost popularity, although it did revive in the middle of the 14th century not long before the fall of the Mongol Yuan dynasty (1368). The form of theatre which replaced it over the intervening century was zaju, marking the first great age of Chinese theatre. The apex of Yuan zaju was probably reached in the reign of Kublai Khan (1260–94), the man who reunited north and south China.

The texts of just over 160 zaju dramas survive. They are contained in two collections, the more important of them entitled Selection of Yuan Songs (Yuanqu xuan, 1615), collected and edited by Zang Maoxun. They deal with romance, courtesans, friendships between men, tyrannical rulers or rebels, recluses or supernatural beings. Many focus on politics or war, including the heroes of the Three Kingdoms period. Others centre on law cases, the main judge being the famous historical figure Bao Zheng (999–1062), known for his harshness but canonized in Yuan theatre for his benevolence and fairness. Quite a few end sadly or with the death of the leading positive character.

Dramatists were mainly Han Chinese (but also included Uygurs, Mongols and others). They were minor officials, entertainers and traders, not in general men of high social status. It has been suggested, by Chung-wen Shih among others, that Mongol rule blocked off opportunities for educated Han Chinese to enter the bureaucracy, through such measures as the suspension of the civil-service examinations (not reinstated until 1315), and that playwriting was an outlet for their literary talents.

The four most famous zaju dramatists are GUAN HANQING, Bai Pu (1226–after 1306), Ma Zhiyuan (1250–c.1325), and Zheng Guangzu (died c.1320). Bai Pu came from an official family which had been torn apart by the Mongol invasion. A Jin loyalist, he refused an offer of service in the Mongol court. He wrote at least 16 dramas, of which three are still extant. His best known play is Rain on the Paulownia Tree (Wutong yu) about the doomed love of the Tang Emperor Minghuang for his favourite concubine Yang Guifei, among the most popular stories in Chinese literature.

No musical scores of Yuan dramas have survived. Possibly they were never used much, since the music could be transmitted from teacher to disciple. In any case Yuan drama music appears to have died out during the following Ming dynasty (1368–1644). Musical accompaniment was mainly by stringed instruments, especially the four-string plucked lute (*pipa*). The famous wall painting of a scene from a Yuan *zaju* performance, dated 1324 and found in a temple in Shanxi Province, shows no string players, but does include a player of the side-blown flute (*dizi*), and a clapper player, as well as a drum.

The main role categories of *zaju* are *mo* (male), *dan* (female), *jing* (villain) and *chou* (clown). A play has one male lead and one female character and a number of subsidiary characters. The categorization is similar but not identical to that of the earlier southern drama. The costuming shown in the 1324 mural is colourful and fairly complex. Two characters have heavy black make-up on their eyebrows and white around the eyes. Several male characters are bearded, one with highly stylized whiskers. The mural shows a tiled stage, heavy backdrop painted with two elaborate pictures, but no stage properties.

Performers of either sex acted male or female roles. The heading of the 1324 mural informs us that a certain famous actress 'Elegance of Zhongdu performed here', while the main character depicted, the one presumably played by the named female star, is male. Actresses may well have dominated Yuan theatre. Certainly we know much more about them than the actors because Xia Tingzhi (1316–after 1368) wrote a work called *Green Bower Collection* (*Qinglou ji*) which is a set of biographies of actresses of the 13th and first half of the 14th centuries. Prostitutes as well as performers, they were wooed, sometimes even married, by high-ranking ministers, generals and literary figures. Although Mongol rulers were initially favourably disposed to the acting profession, one of them later issued a ban on teaching or performing *zaju* and damned such entertainments as lewd. Probably few people took any notice of such an edict, but in general performers held a very low social status.

Why was it that this new theatrical tradition should blossom so suddenly into the magnificent body of art which Yuan *zaju* appears to have been? After all, Han Chinese scholars blocked from the bureaucracy might more easily have turned to other branches of art. James Crump suggests the Jurchen people of the Jin dynasty were accomplished singers and dancers. Other component parts of theatre – acrobatics, pantomime, music, farce – were already flourishing and there was no shortage of good stories in Chinese literature and history. Yuan *zaju* represents the synthesis of several strong existing traditions. The Mongols became acculturated and 'welcomed the dramas which were shaped by music probably already familiar to them and which incorporated the less sophisticated arts that had always delighted them'. It was such processes, he concludes, from which 'the golden age of Yuan drama began'.

The revival of southern drama: marvel dramas Under the last of the Mongol emperors Shundi (1333–68), the dormant southern drama revived. The term used to refer to the form was one which had been in use to describe stories or novellas during the Tang dynasty: *chuanqi*, literally 'transmitting the marvellous'.

The first of these 'marvel dramas' was *The Story of the Lute* (*Pipa ji*) by Gao Ming. It is based on the same story as *Chaste Woman Zhao*, namely the abandonment by the 2nd-century writer and scholar Cai Yong of his newly-wed wife Zhao Wuniang. However, Gao Ming has altered the characterization to portray Cai in a positive light. In place of his bad end, Gao has him reunited with Zhao, redeemed and rewarded. Zhu Yuanzhang (r.1368–99), founder of the Ming dynasty, was an admirer of Gao and his play. When Zhu had become the Hongwu Emperor, he urged all noble families to possess a copy and he ordered his actors to perform *The Story of the Lute* every day. Regretting the lack of stringed accompaniment, he commanded members of his Academy of Music to rectify the weakness, so Liu Gao rearranged the orchestra adding the 15-string zither (*zheng*) and 4-string lute (*pipa*).

In the late Yuan and early Ming periods, the 'four great marvel plays' appeared: *The Story of the Thorn Hairpin* (*Jingchai ji*), *The Moon Prayer Pavilion* (*Baiyue ting*), *The Story of the White Rabbit* (*Baitu ji*), and *The Story of Killing a Dog* (*Shagou ji*). The first two concern scholars who leave behind their faithful wives to sit for the examinations, do brilliantly in them and are reunited with their beloveds. The marvel dramas have romantic themes, with scholars and beauties in central roles, and lack the warlike content of *zaju* drama.

A prologue, sometimes found in earlier southern dramas, always introduces the action of marvel dramas. It explains the story and announces the title of the play. Sometimes, as in *The Story of the Lute*, it explains the moral as well. Marvel dramas, at least in Ming editions, are divided into scenes, whereas earlier southern dramas were apparently performed without breaks. Yet a basic continuity of style, form and performance connects southern and marvel drama.

The decline of *zaju* The rise of the marvel drama did not at first negatively affect *zaju*. On the contrary, the early Ming dynasty was a prolific period for *zaju* and quality was also good. Major authors of this period include Zhu Quan (1378–1448) and Zhu Youdun (1379–1439). Zhu Quan was the 17th son of the Hongwu Emperor Zhu Yuanzhang. He wrote twelve *zaju* dramas of which two survive. He also either wrote, or had written, a work entitled *Great Peace Table of Correct Sounds* (*Taihe zhengyin pu*), which not only lists the titles of 689 *zaju* plays written from the Yuan period to his own time, but also gives titles of 335 *zaju* melodies arranged into 12 modes, each with poems illustrating the appropriate tonal patterns. Zhu Youdun, a grandson of the Hongwu Emperor, wrote over 30 *zaju* plays, all extant, many dealing with religious subjects, and in which women, either prostitutes or saints, are given prominence.

Xu Wei was a somewhat later dramatist, an eccentric best known for *Four Howls of the Ape* (*Sisheng yuan*), which in fact consists of four *zaju* plays. Xu's plays were unconventional in two ways. Firstly, in several of them he departed from the rule that *zaju* should have four acts and a wedge. He was not the first to write a one-act *zaju* drama, but he also wrote two-act and five-act plays, signalling the collapse of the rigid *zaju* structure. Secondly, Xu Wei combined northern and southern music. Again, he was not the first to do this, but his experiment led on quite soon to an even more radical departure from *zaju* tradition when Wang Daokun (1525–93) used only southern music in writing *zaju*. The break was very important because it meant the abandonment of a type of music which had imposed a quite clear northern stamp on the drama.

Thereafter, *zaju* sharply declined in popularity. By the time the Ming dynasty fell in 1644, *zaju* was no longer performed at all and it survives only as a genre of literature.

The southern theatre of the educated At the time *zaju* was declining, various local dramas rose to prominence, their differences, region to region, revealed in dialect, and especially music. One southern city with a particularly rich musical tradition was Haiyan, a major trading port in Zhejiang Province. The 'music of Haiyan' (*haiyan qiang*) had long flourished as a local form of southern drama. Xu Wei claims that in his own day it was 'in use' in four parts of Zhejiang Province, and it appears to have spread even further afield, including Jiangsu Province and even Beijing, later in the 16th century. Dramas using Haiyan music were probably accompanied by percussion instruments only, but the singing was soft and melodious. Role categories followed the normal patterns of southern drama. The audience came mainly from the educated classes, rich families and officials. By the end of the 17th century, this earlier form of Haiyan music had died out as an independent style. However, Xu Wei lists it among those musical traditions absorbed into *kunqu*, that drama form which by the end of the Ming dynasty was monopolizing the affections of educated theatre-lovers.

Credit for the creation of *kunqu* is often given to WEI LIANGFU, a 16th-century musician and actor. Wei adapted various familiar musical styles, including not only *haiyan qiang* but also *zaju*, *yiyang qiang* and the local music of Kunshan, to a new form which was called the 'music of Kunshan' (*kunshan qiang*), now known as *kunqu*. It was Wei's achievement to impose those main musical features which to this day make *kunqu* instantly identifiable. These are a slow-moving melismatic rhythmic melody, and an orchestration dominated by the flute and including the four-string lute and wind organ (*sheng*). The language of the libretti was classical, with many unexplained literary allusions. Stage motions tended to be slow and action sparse. The overall effect was melodious, delicate, refined and even melancholy. *Kunqu* quickly came to be known as 'elegant drama'. Its language and style closed it off from the masses, whose theatre was known, by contrast, as 'flower drama', a term covering most styles other than *kunqu*.

Role categories in *kunqu* closely followed those of marvel dramas. Companies took over stories from preceding styles, especially marvel dramas and *zaju*. Many early pieces had 40 or 50 scenes, like the marvel dramas from which they had been adopted. Performance might require three days and nights. By the 17th century the practice of performing a single scene became the norm. The most

famous *kunqu* dramatists were Liang Chenyu, TANG XIANZU, HONG SHENG and KONG SHANGREN.

Kunqu eventually spread throughout most of China, in part transmitted by officials who loved the elevated style. They sponsored their own private companies and took the actors with them when posted to various cities around the country. Of many famous professional companies, the Jixiu of Suzhou is worth special mention. It was formed in 1784 to provide entertainment for the Manchu Qianlong Emperor (r.1736–96) during his visit to the south in that year. Its members were drawn from among all the best actors of the cities of the Lower Yangzi Valley. It stayed together after the emperor's departure and survived until 1827.

The Hongwu Emperor of the Ming dynasty had founded a eunuch agency in 1390 to provide court entertainment, including theatre. Initially the favoured form was *zaju* but the court was happy to follow the fashion of the upper classes and patronize *kunqu* from the 16th century on. Early in his reign the Qianlong Emperor set up an organization to control court theatre. An official, Zhang Zhao (1691–1745), wrote five lengthy and highly moralistic dramas for the imperial theatre, including *Golden Statutes for Encouraging Goodness* (*Quanshan jinke*) about Mulian's saving his mother from hell. The Manchu Prince Yinlu (1695–1767), an uncle of Qianlong's, adapted the stories of the Three Kingdoms to compile the play *Annals of the Tripod* (*Dingzhi chunqiu*). During their heyday in the 18th century the court companies contained well over 1000 actors, including eunuchs and well known artists, especially from the south.

Popular theatre: *yiyang qiang* Originally a mass form of theatre, *zaju* had been taken over by the educated elite by the 16th century. At about the same time, new forms of popular theatre began to emerge and prosper, numbering by the 20th century some 350 styles. The great majority were popular in one or more localities, some major ones in whole provinces. Many belong to the *yiyang qiang* system of musical theatre.

Yiyang is a place name in eastern Jiangxi Province. Southern drama and *zaju* were heard there about the 13th century and melodies from these combined with local folk music to form the 'music of Yiyang' (*yiyang qiang*). In the 16th century it spread to other places, including the capital at Beijing, and Jiangsu, Anhui, Hunan, Fujian, Guangxi and Guangdong Provinces, and by the middle of the 17th century as far as the south-western province of Sichuan. Its role categories and stories were similar to those of southern and marvel dramas. Since *yiyang qiang* was popular drama, normally scripts were not written down and only a few texts of the various forms survive from the 16th century. From them it is clear that the libretti were adapted from marvel dramas, and performed in single short scenes.

Several features of the *yiyang qiang* styles are noteworthy. Short sections in colloquial language were added to an original classical text. Thus, a literary allusion to a classical poem might be supplemented by a full recitation of the poem. An educated audience could be expected to recognize a literary allusion, but the ordinary masses who made up the audiences would need to have it pointed out.

These added passages, *gundiao* (literally, 'rolling tunes'), could be either sung or, despite their name, spoken. One very important corollary of the *gundiao* was that libretti were much longer than for a corresponding *kunqu* and performances were often of excerpted scenes, rather than whole dramas. Moreover, as the well known 17th-century drama theorist LI YU put it, 'characters are many but sounds are few'. What he meant was that, in strong contrast to the melismatic *kunqu*, the music of Yiyang was syllabic. It was also rather fast-moving on the whole.

A second feature, which applied to all popular theatre in China, was that these plays used local dialect. The ordinary people did not normally understand the 'official words' of the music of Haiyan or of the bureaucrats who had composed them.

A third feature was the 'helping' or offstage chorus (*bangqiang*). Apparently adopted from earlier southern drama, it is not found in Ming or Qing period drama systems other than the music of Yiyang. Li Yu writes that 'one person would start singing and then several would take up the tune'. The offstage chorus is still a strong feature in contemporary music-of-Yiyang styles, such as Sichuan opera (*CHUANJU*). The practice of a chorus accompanying solo singers in folksongs is extremely ancient in China. It probably arose because instrumental accompaniment was impossible for people at work in the fields and 'labour songs' have always been a normal category of folksong. *Yiyang qiang* styles, like southern drama before them, lacked the accompaniment of string or wind instruments and had only percussion.

The initial net effect of these features was to irritate the refined members of the educated classes, who used terms like 'bawl' to describe the singing of the music of Yiyang. Such contempt did not prevent the rapid and extensive spread of this mass drama, and in any case began to abate in the course of time. By the 18th century there were in Beijing six famous companies devoted to 'capital music drama' (*jing qiang*), which belonged to the music-of-Yiyang systems. Chief of these was the Great Company of the Princely Mansions, indicating that members of the aristocracy were patronizing this popular theatre.

Popular theatre: clapper opera Another important system of popular theatre styles is 'clapper opera' (*bangzi qiang*). A tune identified as belonging to clapper opera is noted in Shaanxi in the 16th century. The music of this system was initially prevalent only in northern China and today is known in almost all the provinces north of the Yangzi River. By the late 18th century there was a thriving clapper-opera tradition in Sichuan, and it was even popular in the lower Yangzi Valley in places like Suzhou and Yangzhou. Merchants and bankers from Shaanxi and Shanxi, who traded all over the country, may well have brought with them private actors who could perform it.

As its name implies, the chief characteristic linking the styles of the clapper-opera system is the use of the clapper, a datewood block struck with a stick, to beat out the rhythm. In contrast to *kunqu*, the clapper opera emphasizes rhythmic change. In most styles there are eight different rhythms, the main one termed 'one beat, three eyes' (*yiban sanyan*) which corresponds to quick, common time (4/4) in Western music. In sung sections, the dominant

poetic structure is seven- or ten-character couplets. Another characteristic of its music is the dominance of stringed instruments. The scholar Li Tiaoyuan (1734–1803) writes that the four-string plucked moon-guitar (*yueqin*) 'responds to the clapper in rhythm which is either hurried or slow', and all clapper styles feature a two-string bowed instrument.

A flourishing clapper opera attracted the attention of scholar-official Yan Changming (1731–87) who wrote that 36 famous companies were in operation in Xi'an, Shaanxi's capital, in the 1780s. The most distinguished was called Shuangsai. At the same time, a group of actors of female roles (*dan*) from Sichuan, led by Wei Changsheng (1744–1802), were captivating Beijing audiences with their clapper-opera performances. They probably arrived to take part in the Qianlong Emperor's 70th-birthday celebrations in 1780 and stayed until 1785 when the court prohibited their performances as obscene. In this short time they exercised a tremendous influence on the theatre of the capital and many elements of their art were later absorbed into Beijing opera. Among his innovations, Wei Changsheng wore a false foot beneath his foot and tied to the leg with cotton bandage, enabling him to imitate the gait of a woman with bound feet. Clapper actors were popular not only among the masses, but even among the educated elite.

Popular theatre: the *pihuang* system Ten years later, a new group of actors came to Beijing to take part in the celebrations for the Qianlong Emperor's 80th birthday in 1790. These actors were members of companies from Anhui Province and their style of performance belonged to the *pihuang* musical system. Since this was the first time *pihuang* had been heard in the capital, the event is usually regarded as the birth of 'Beijing opera' (see *JINGXI*; *PIHUANG XI*).

Pihuang is actually a combination of two styles, *xipi* and *erhuang*, each of which remains identifiable and separately designated. Both styles can be varied greatly in their rhythm, melody and feeling. A.C. Scott wrote in 1957 that in general *erhuang* 'is used for more serious occasions' in Beijing opera, while *xipi* 'is, on the whole, happy and spirited in feeling'. Each style includes 'counter' (*fan*) tunes which 'are used for sad and tragic occasions'.

Of several theories advanced to explain the origin of *erhuang*, the most likely is that the term is a derivative of *Yihuang*, the place in Jiangxi Province where the style began. The style was adopted in Anhui Province and became far more popular there than in its original home. *Xipi* was a southern offshoot of clapper opera which spread to Hubei and other provinces from its northern roots in Shaanxi and Shanxi. From the 18th century the two styles became inseparable, their association perhaps beginning in Anhui. Together they spread to all the southern provinces and to Beijing. They formed at least 20 important styles, including not only Beijing opera but also Anhui opera (*huiju*), Hubei opera (*hanju*), Guangdong opera (*YUEJU*), and Jiangxi opera (*ganju*). They also form part of such forms as Sichuan opera (*chuanju*), and Yunnan opera (*dianju*).

Although each regional opera form in *pihuang* style has its own special points, such as the use of the local dialect and the influence of local folk music, they share many characteristics in common. These include several probably inherited from clapper opera: the use of seven- or ten-character couplets in the libretti, emphasis on rhythmic change, and, with the exception of a very few styles, the domination of the accompanying orchestra by a two-string bowed fiddle.

The actor Gao Yueguan (c.1770–?1830) is mainly credited with introducing *pihuang* music to Beijing. He and his followers were *dan* performers and early Beijing opera flourished on a kind of slave trade in which parents in Jiangsu and Anhui provinces sold sons to entrepreneurs who took them to Beijing to be trained for the stage. Within a short time after 1790, the 'Four Great Anhui Companies' established themselves as pre-eminent: Spring Stage (Chuntai), Three Celebrations (Sanqing), Four Joys (Sixi) and Harmonious Spring (Hechun). The Spring Stage company continued in the capital for 110 years, and only disbanded in 1900 when the Boxer uprising resulted in the burning down of the theatres of Beijing.

In the 1830s yet another wave of actors, this time from Hubei Province, entered Beijing. From this time Beijing opera changes substantially from an art in which *dan* actors and civil items were dominant, to an art that emphasized *sheng* actors and military plays. The most famous actors of 19th-century Beijing were all *sheng*: CHENG CHANGGENG, Yu Sansheng (1802–66) and Zhang Erkui (1814–64).

In 1860, the court for the first time brought in Beijing-opera actors from the city to perform. The initial experiment was short-lived, but revived by the Empress Dowager Cixi in 1884 to celebrate her 50th birthday. She was an avid enthusiast of the Beijing opera and ensured a continuing flow of fine actors from the city to the imperial court.

The growth of regional theatre in the Ming and Qing periods was paralleled by a similar expansion in local storytelling forms. The music, instruments and dialect varied from place to place, but on the whole the stories were constant and like those of the dramas. *Pingtan*, popular in and near Suzhou, Jiangsu Province, was a particularly well known storytelling form.

Society, stage and stage arts during the Ming and Qing periods

Theatre in the Ming (1368–1644) and Qing (1644–1911) dynasties was very much a part of the people's lives. Performances accompanied popular festivals and marked prayers to the gods for good harvests in the spring or thanksgiving in autumn. Rich families held performances to accompany sacrifices to their ancestors or banquets for their guests. Theatre was also tightly related to commerce. Temple or other fairs included performances which crowds watched between or even during business transactions. The government treated such occasions with suspicion. Authorities believed that large gatherings of people provided opportunities for political sedition and the planning of rebellion, or for sexual immorality: 'men and women mix unrestrainedly' is a phrase found constantly in the sources describing large crowds of people gathered to watch drama. Many edicts restricted or banned certain plays or practices associated with the theatre.

There was great variety in sites of performance. The permanent, covered, commercial theatres (*goulan*) of earlier centuries tended to go out of fashion. Some temples and guild halls had permanent stages, but otherwise a temporary stage was constructed as required. The market-place also provided a convenient venue, even without a stage. Performances given during private banquets of the rich needed no stage, only an empty carpeted space near the banqueting tables. A very high-ranking or rich family might have a permanent stage constructed in its mansion. In Beijing a few of these were given over to the public as teahouse-theatres. The entry of Wei Changsheng and his clapper-opera actors led to the repair of these buildings and the construction of others. The period covering the end of the 18th and all of the 19th century was the high point of the traditional teahouse-theatre in Beijing. The best were concentrated in one part of town, just outside the main wall separating the residential areas of the masses from that part of the city where the officials and Imperial court lived.

The stage itself was very simple. There was a curtain at the back but none at the front. Several records of Ming-dynasty plays describe elaborate scenery and stage properties, but these are exceptional cases. The norm was a nearly bare stage with no scenery and very simple or no properties.

The simplicity of the stage was balanced by the complexity and symbolism of the actors' art. Manners of walking, differing from character to character, hand gestures and the use of the fingers were all highly stylized and told the audience the nature and behaviour of the character. Costuming and make-up were extremely elaborate and expressive. Even their minor aspects assumed great theatrical significance, an example being the delicate way characters manipulate the very long and loose 'water' sleeves. Although it is not possible to trace the origins of all aspects of the performance of Chinese theatre, it is likely that 'water'-sleeve dance techniques were an artistic skill before the time of Christ. There was undoubtedly change during the Ming and Qing periods, and it took the direction of refining performance techniques and the arts of the stage, making them more complicated and integrating them better into the totality of theatre.

Make-up is a very ancient feature of the Chinese performing arts. In theatre it appears originally to have been simple. Only one of the characters in the 1324 wall-painting has make-up over an area more extensive than that around the eyes. From early Ming times make-up became more complicated and the practice became established of painting the whole face of *jing* characters with a coloured design to show moral or other qualities. Pictures dating from the Ming dynasty show that both in early *kunqu* and *yiyang qiang* dramas the faces of the *jing* characters were fully painted. Red indicated loyalty and patriotism in generals, black honesty, and so on. The complex painted face became a major feature of Beijing opera, where some of the colours hold essentially the same significance as in Ming times.

For many centuries ACROBATICS have been a major form of entertainment in China. Tumbling, somersaults, and other gymnastics appear to have featured in military plays of Yuan *zaju*, and they became well integrated into the performance of *yiyang qiang* dramas and later popular theatre forms, especially Beijing opera. Military scenes climax in an acrobatics display, with rapid and numerous cartwheels, somersaults and finely timed throwing, kicking back and catching of spears and swords. It is notable that through the Ming period acrobatics were not incorporated into southern drama. Instead Ming-period *kunqu* emphasized the synthesis and synchronization of song and dance movements. In the clapper-opera system actors were allowed to sing while not dancing and vice versa, thus breaking this unity. This process probably emerged late in the 18th or early in the 19th century. The change, added to the earlier absorption of acrobatics, made for greater variety and liveliness in the stage movements of the popular theatre forms than in *kunqu*.

Performers in the Ming and Qing periods The troupes in the Ming and Qing dynasties were basically of two kinds: private and professional. Private troupes belonged to individual rich families and the members were drawn from among their servants or house-slaves. They could give private entertainment to the family or perform for invited guests. The majority of such troupes specialized in *kunqu* drama, but by the 18th century we find cases of private companies performing popular regional styles, an example being the Spring Stage company in Yangzhou, Jiangsu Province, which belonged to the rich salt merchant Jiang Chun (1725–93).

Professional troupes named in the sources were concentrated in particular cities and periods, especially Beijing in the 18th and 19th centuries. The normal pattern was for professional companies to go wandering throughout the countryside in certain seasons of the year, especially before sowing and after the harvest had been reaped. They would stay at a particular place a few days, present a festival and then move on. They financed their activities by sending representatives from door to door collecting, the records claim sometimes extorting, money. Only the best companies were semipermanent. The majority disbanded and reformed themselves from year to year, and the turnover of actors was substantial.

Acting companies of the time were usually either all-male, or all-female, mostly the former. Therefore many actors excelled in women's roles, many actresses in men's. Among professional women's *kunqu* companies, one type was composed of female prostitutes. Several patrons have left behind records of their admiration for the beauty and artistic skills of these women. Their bound feet made the gymnastic movements of military dramas impossible on the stage, as well as preventing them from moving away from their home base.

Training procedures were initially very rudimentary. Examples can be found from both the Ming and Qing periods of actors who in effect taught themselves the necessary skills by sheer determination. The normal procedure was for troupe managers to apprentice or buy small boys and have them taught the trade on a master–disciple basis. The practice reached a high point late in the 18th and in the first half of the 19th century and supplied Beijing opera companies with a virtually limitless number of actors. The main companies in Beijing ran special training schools (*keban*) that taught the slave-boys the necessary arts.

Performers held a very low status in society, one symbol of this being edicts forbidding them to sit for official examinations, the main gateway to the bureaucracy. Edicts of 1369 and 1652 were extended in 1770 to include actors' sons and grandsons. Actors were despised as vagabonds because they wandered about. Some members of the official classes were quite happy to take advantage of the sexual favours offered by performers, but still despised them as immoral. Not only were actresses prostitutes, among actors homosexuality was widespread. A 19th-century law forbade government officials to visit female prostitutes, and as a result the boy actors became effective substitutes. The excellence of mature stars after about 1780, especially in Beijing, raised actors' status slightly, but in general the social position of the acting profession remained extremely low well into the 20th century.

Traditional theatre in the 20th century Beijing-style theatre continued to dominate the traditional stage through the first half of the 20th century. It retained an unequalled appeal on a national scale and had an enormous following among the ordinary public. This successful transition in an age of cultural iconoclasm was possible because of a particularly talented body of actors. They bore the artistic integrity of the old theatrical tradition forward while adjusting to social change. A towering figure was Beijing-born MEI LANFANG. His artistry and breadth of perception helped the old theatre attain a new pinnacle of public esteem. Not the least of Mei's achievements was his success in international cultural relations resulting from his tours to America and Russia in the 1930s. He stirred Western thinking to new aesthetic insights on theatre. BERTOLT BRECHT and VSEVOLOD MEYERHOLD were among those who admired and were deeply influenced by seeing Mei's performances.

Two major reforms were accomplished in the professional world of Mei Lanfang and his peers during the 1920s and 30s. An improved system of training and education for theatre apprentices was introduced and actresses began to achieve professional emancipation. A first attempt at improved training conditions was the founding in 1903 of the Xiliancheng (later renamed the Fuliancheng) School in Beijing. Some of China's greatest Beijing actors graduated from this institution. Boys only were accepted; admitted at the age of seven, they were taken on contract for a seven-year period. They lived in, and tuition, board and lodging were free. In return, the school demanded complete professional control, including an obligation to perform in public to fill the school's coffers. It was a hard life demanding meticulous standards and intensive application but it represented a clear advance on older methods when boys could be victimized by unscrupulous individuals.

A revolutionary step came in 1930 when Li Yuying founded a co-educational conservatory for dramatic training in Beijing. The actor CHENG YANQIU was appointed principal. Cheng was highly regarded both for his stage talents and personal integrity. In 1932 Cheng was sent to Europe for a year on behalf of the school to study drama and OPERA. The first of its kind to admit both sexes on an equal basis, the school provided a general education simultaneously with professional training. An ambitious syllabus was taught by special tutors. Professionals were in charge of theatrical training. Although only one class graduated, it set the pattern that today's training methods follow. In 1934 a School for Experimental Drama was founded by Wang Bozheng at Jinan in Shandong. It aimed to develop a new national theatre form based on traditional methods while drawing scientifically on Western methods when required. A four-year course was set up with one year devoted to empirical experiment. In 1937 all of these schools were closed by the War of Resistance against Japan.

The professional rise of the actress in the 1920s and 30s overcame long-standing prejudices. Women were all but excluded from the theatre both as performers and spectators during the 19th century. In the early 1900s one or two all-women troupes were active in Beijing and Shanghai. They performed at private gatherings and were not allowed into theatres. By 1920 women were performing at several Beijing theatres but never alongside actors. During the 1920s Wang Yaoqing (1881–1954), a teacher of Mei Lanfang, and Mei himself ignored old prejudices and took female pupils, a hitherto unknown practice.

In 1928 the actresses Xue Yanqin (1906–86) and Xin Yanqiu (1911–) appeared on the stage of the Great Theatre (Da Xiyuan) in Shanghai with male actors. From the age of eight Xue had studied women's roles, combat techniques and *kunqu* in Beijing under Jin Guorui and later Zhang Cailin. From 1930 through a long acting career Xue appeared regularly with mixed casts, doing much to enhance the theatrical prestige of the actress. In 1960 she assumed a teaching post with the Beijing School of Dramatic Art. Xin Yanqiu studied with Mei Lanfang and Wang Yaoqing. When she began performing with Cheng Yanqiu, she took that famous actor's professional name. Xue and Xin were the vanguard of a galaxy of accomplished women artists who rose to prominence in the prewar years and brought new lustre to traditional theatre.

The rise of the modern theatre The 20th century began with a movement to create a new theatre inspired by Western example. The old theatre became a target for change. The Western impact on 19th-century China resulted in many young intellectuals being sent abroad to study. Thousands went to JAPAN where progressive modernization had followed the Meiji Restoration of 1868. Japan was geographically and culturally closer to China than the West. The synthesis of tradition with modernity they found there made cultural adjustment easier. Intellectuals who returned from Japan became a major influence on the early development of modern Chinese theatre.

In 1907 a Chinese group in Tokyo founded the Spring Willow Dramatic Society. Assisted by the Japanese actor Fujisawa Asajirō, who ran an acting school (see SHINPA), they staged a version of *Camille* (*Chahua nü*) by ALEXANDRE DUMAS *fils* in February 1907. The play appealed to the Chinese because the heroine's plight mirrored the rigidity of their own marital conventions and suitably echoed their own social protest.

A five-act adaptation of Uncle Tom's Cabin followed in June. Entitled *The Black Slave's Cry to Heaven* (*Heinu yut-ian lu*), it was staged at the Hongo Theatre in Tokyo where *shinpa*, an early westernized Japanese genre, was featured. The play's action was expanded with extraneous interludes to please Chinese tastes. A curtain and scenery added novelty of effect. Harriet Beecher Stowe's story was well received for it offered a melodramatic vehicle for protest against racial discrimination from which the Chinese too suffered.

Both productions used translations by Lin Shu, who first put SHAKESPEARE into Chinese, and were performed by all-male casts. Hybrids, they nevertheless offered a substitute for the old song-declamation form and the beginning of a new genre, eventually to be named *HUAJU*, spoken drama.

Shanghai became the centre for early experiments in the new Western form. The Spring Sun Society under Wang Zhongsheng (d.1911), who had studied in Japan, staged *The Black Slave's Cry to Heaven* in 1907. Lu Jingruo (1885–1915), also returned from Japan, organized the New Drama Association in 1912. In 1914 Lu revived the Spring Willow Dramatic Society which produced *Camille*, among other productions, in a commercial theatre. Stage expertise was slight in these years, and old theatre conventions remained, including female impersonation.

The years 1915–19 marked a turning point. A Western-educated generation was agitating for cultural change. New journals supporting the New Culture Movement proliferated. Drama ignored by the old literati became recognized as a mouthpiece for social reform. In May 1919 students protested in Beijing against the surrender of Chinese sovereignty that was proposed at the Paris Peace Conference, and when the Treaty of Versailles formalized the proposals to China's detriment, national outrage forced the Chinese government to refuse to sign. The new intelligentsia closed ranks in affirming an era of definitive cultural change called the May 4th Movement.

Succeeding events brought new impetus to change in the theatre. One of the early attempts to develop a new theatre consciously hostile to the weaknesses of the old was in Hu Shi's *The Greatest Event in Her Life* (*Zhongshen dashi*). Premiered and set in 1919, it deals with a progressive young woman who elopes with her chosen husband in defiance against her parents; agree about little else, they are nevertheless united in their opposition to him as a son-in-law. In 1921 Gu Jiachen founded the Shanghai Dramatic Association which became a forceful sponsor of new drama. Two of its outstanding members were OUYANG YUQIAN and Hong Shen (1892–1955), stage director, playwright, teacher and film director. The latter studied in America from 1916 to 1922 and aroused controversy on his return by refusing to countenance men playing women's roles. Endorsed by conservative public opinion, this convention remained a barrier to developing a naturalistic acting style. Hong Shen defied long-standing prejudice by recruiting actresses from the more open-minded women of the universities and the Shanghai film world.

In 1921 Ouyang and Hong joined forces with TIAN HAN to found the Creation Society in Shanghai. The first issue of its journal *Creation Quarterly* in 1922, contained Tian Han's play *A Night at a Coffeehouse* (*Jiafei dian zhi yiye*) which became an immediate theatrical *cause célèbre*. The Society toured productions throughout the country until, in 1923, it was dissolved by government order. Although it was short-lived, the Society was influential in introducing broad audiences to modern theatre.

In the 1930s, the Japanese military threat compounded by the Nationalist–Communist political feud overshadowed intellectual life. People in literature and the arts responded to a new political awareness. In 1931 the League of Left Wing Dramatists was formed. Tian Han and Hong Shen became active members. Plays written and produced to portray current political–social problems were vigorously promoted in schools and factories. The Japanese attack on Shanghai in 1932 intensified theatrical protest, to which the Nationalist government responded with a campaign of repression, forcing leftist theatre underground. Tian Han and other League members were arrested as a deterrent.

The Chinese Communist Party (CCP) began organizing theatre for political action soon after the party's establishment in 1921. In 1931 the Chinese Soviet Republic was declared with its capital at Ruijin. Performers were recruited locally and provided with dramatic training, political education, their food, clothing and a subsistence pittance. Troupes trained at the CCP school in Ruijin were then attached to army units for service in rural territory and the front line. This work culminated in the organization of a Workers and Peasants Dramatic Society. Song, dance and MIME were indispensable to appeal to audiences whose sole concept of theatre was provided by traditional opera. An extensive dramatic network functioned on this basis and contributed to establishing a permanent theatre-training school at the CCP wartime base in Yan'an.

Advocacy of drama as a factor in social education was also manifest on the National side. In 1932, Xiong Foxi (1900–65), a playwright-teacher-producer who had studied theatre in America, was invited by the National Association for Advancement of Mass Education to initiate a theatre project in the rural district of Dingxian, Hebei Province. Living among the peasant community provided him with authentic material for writing and producing plays with local people as actors. Within three years the troupe was staging self-supporting productions which attracted considerable notice. The Japanese invasion forced Xiong to lead his group to unoccupied west China. There, as the Farmers Resistance Dramatic Corps, they performed to mass audiences.

Political tensions notwithstanding, the 1930s witnessed the rise of a socially conscious theatre given credibility by the commitment of its practitioners. New dramatists were at work to capitalize on this advance, at times working in film with its emotive capacity for evoking human values and national sentiment. Tian Han, Ouyang Yuqian and Hong Shen all turned to film as advisers, directors and scenario writers. A complementary and continuing relationship was established between the modern stage movement and the film studios. Xia Yan (1900–95), Japan-returned dramatist and scenario writer, was representative of this trend. His two early stage plays *Under a Shanghai Roof* (*Shanghai wuyan xia*) and *Sai Jinhua* were considered major contributions to the modern repertoire. The first portrayed the alienation and suffering of tenement dwellers in a great city. The second concerned a celebrated Chinese courtesan, one of whose alliances was with Count Alfred von Waldersee, the German commander of the allied forces which occupied Beijing to relieve the Boxer siege in 1900.

Arguably the most important playwright of this period was CAO YU, a graduate in Western literature from a Beijing university. His first play, *Thunderstorm* (*Leiyu*), directed by Hong Shen and Ouyang Yuqian in 1935 for the Fudan University Dramatic Club, Shanghai, was an immediate success. Cao Yu had studied Greek drama and admired EUGENE O'NEILL and ANTON CHEKHOV, influences discernible in this play with its dark commentary on the Chinese family system and the social degradation it caused. Credibility of characterization and realistic dialogue, allied to an intuitive sense of theatre, stamped this play as a breakthrough for indigenous dialogue drama. Cao Yu's second play *Sunrise* (*Richu*) portrayed the corruptive power of materialism and won him a literary prize. *Wilderness* (*Yuanye*), *Metamorphosis* (*Shuibian*), *Peking Man* (*Beijing ren*) and *Family* (*Jia*) followed, establishing him as a dramatist of social conscience.

Thunderstorm was taken throughout the country by the China Travelling Dramatic Troupe, founded in Shanghai in 1934 by Tang Huaiqiu. His goal was a modern repertory theatre on a financially viable basis. A co-operative unit, they achieved a homogeneous quality in their acting. *Thunderstorm* broke all box-office records for modern theatre and this was followed by Hong Shen's equally successful *Lady Windermere's Fan*. The troupe's aim seemed close to realization when in 1937 war intervened. They moved their base to Hong Kong for a brief period, but that too fell to the Japanese at the end of 1941.

In December 1937 theatre leaders, including Tian Han, met in Hankou to organize the National Dramatic Association to Resist the Enemy, an umbrella for all wartime theatrical activities. In February 1938 Tian Han became director of the government's Cultural Work Committee and head of the Propaganda Section, and a zealous censorship was applied to all dramatic activity. Henceforward modern theatre was subordinated to national propaganda needs. A call for resistance united theatre people as never before. Itinerant by vocation, they responded with travelling troupes to take propagandist theatre to the rural masses. Nationalists and Communists shared a common concept if with divergent ideological intent.

The rapid advance of the invading forces drove the Nationalist government to set up their capital at Chongqing, Sichuan Province. Universities and major educational organizations followed them, together with those prominent in every field of the arts. The emotional climate was typified by the manifesto of Xiong Foxi for his theatre students in west China: 'Cultivate modern drama with an artist's passion and a soldier's discipline to aid China's spiritual regeneration.'

Students of the co-educational Nanjing National Academy of Dramatic Art, founded in 1935 and evacuated to Chongqing, made their professional debut staging street plays and LIVING NEWSPAPERS. A favoured technique entailed actors anonymously entering teahouses and drawing an audience by seemingly spontaneous dialogues on current affairs. Lack of permanent stages and technical equipment in wartime territory did not deter the hundreds of itinerant troupes. Academics and literary men frequently joined forces with professionals. Urban intellectuals and the rural population shared a new direct relationship as the result of dramatic activities.

Tian Han, official spokesman for theatre in wartime, encouraged these trends as a healthy portent for the future. He adapted such traditional Beijing-opera favourites as *The White Snake* (*Baishe zhuan*) for modern production. Criticized at the time, his version became standard after the war. Ouyang Yuqian worked closely with Tian Han during those years, leading a troupe that toured patriotic plays. Hong Shen ran a theatrical troupe and taught film and drama in the universities. It was a time of shared skills and commitments.

Xia Yan's plays successfully caught the public's mood. Typical was *City of Sorrows* (*Choucheng ji*) satirizing life in Japanese-occupied territory. *Put down Your Whip* (*Fangxia nide bianzi*) denounced Japanese aggression and was outstanding among the mass of propaganda pieces being produced. Cao Yu, in contrast, wrote nothing after his adaptation in 1941 of Ba Jin's novel *Family*. Xiong Foxi became disillusioned with government censorship policy after serving as head of the Sichuan Provincial College of Dramatic Arts. He left for Guilin in the southwest where he engaged in writing and editorial work until 1945.

Wartime Chongqing saw the germination of a national dance movement resulting from the work of Dai Ailian (1916–), a Trinidad-born Chinese danseuse. After studying ballet in England, patriotic motives led her to wartime China. While teaching in Chongqing she began studying local folk and minority nationality dances. With a team of pupil assistants she travelled to outlying areas researching and notating choreographic techniques, eventually forming her own company. Her pioneering work then prepared the way for organized dance education in China later.

The tangential ingredients of narrative, song and descriptive gesture in folk dance embodied primal elements of Chinese theatrical communication. They appealed directly to the uncomplicated emotive responses of peasant audiences. Both Nationalists and Communists sought to profit from this factor in their wartime sensitivity to folk tradition. The Communists were the more uncompromising. The artistic criteria of folk genres were subordinated to theories of proletarian drama created to eliminate the aesthetic 'elitism' of the old theatre.

Following the Long March of 1934–5 the Communists set up their base in the loessic caves at Yan'an in northern Shaanxi Province. There in May 1942 Mao Zedong gave his 'Talks at the Yan'an Forum on Literature and Art'. In them he expounded his Marxist manifesto destined to become the bible of all Chinese cultural endeavour. He spoke at the Lu Xun Art Institute which trained troupes to adapt old folk-performance methods to new content.

One such ancient form much utilized by the Communists was the *yangge* rice-planting song. Originally *yangge* referred to simple rhythmic steps danced to a chant and percussion while planting the rice fields. When Communist troops entered the big cities in 1949 they were preceded by files of dancers performing this simple work form as a victory theme. In time *yangge* was applied collectively to various other types of performances that were developed from it.

During the 19th century the style of *yangge* prevalent in Dingxian, Hebei Province, gradually became elaborated as village performance: 20 to 30 dancers performed with a leader, male and female characters confronted each other with a question–response narrative followed by singing and dance movements extended with representational gesture. Elemental themes from village life and ethics were introduced. A comic character frequently added the necessary touch of earthy humour. Drum, gong, flute and cymbals provided musical accompaniment.

Two scholars, Li Jinghuan and Zhang Shiwen, conducted a government-sponsored field project on the Dingxian style in 1932, afterwards publishing an anthology of plays. It was this genre of performance the Communists found so adaptable and were quick to develop for their needs. *Yangge* troupes proliferated. More than 30 of them staged performances at the 1944 Yan'an spring festival. Their repertoire included a play called *The White-Haired Girl* (*Baimao nü*).

Reputedly of ballad-recitative origin and based on some actual facts, the play had undergone collective revisions prior to the 1944 presentation. In 1945 a new five-act version was prepared with a script and lyrics by He Jingzhi (1924–) and Ding Yi (1921–). Music based on authentic folk sources was composed for it by Ma Ke (1918–76) and five colleagues. Being directed against abusive social practices long familiar to village tenant farmers, it became a theatrical symbol of the revolutionary cause and was constantly performed in the late 1940s and 1950s. The fusion of song, music, chorus work and ordinary speech allied to a contemporary setting set *The White-Haired Girl* apart from either traditional Chinese or modern Western stage practices, though both had clearly offered some inspiration. It appealed to an audience for whom theatre without song and music was inconceivable and dialogue drama in the Western vein meaningless in the context of their lifestyle. *The White-Haired Girl* was the first full-length representative of a new national genre named GEJU, song drama. Flexible in subject matter and musical form it was contemporary but adaptable to regional traditions. It was one solution to finding a middle way between past and present, a long-standing problem of Chinese theatre.

Re-establishment of the Nationalist capital at Nanjing in May 1946 followed Japan's defeat in 1945. In 1946 full-scale civil war broke out as the CCP began its drive for ultimate power. Crippling inflation led to economic chaos and social disintegration. The plight of the universities was desperate, the mood of intellectuals despair.

In 1946 Xiong Foxi became head of the Shanghai Municipal Experimental School of Dramatic Art, which shared the premises of a local museum and primary school. Xiong's faith in theatre was matched by that of his students and staff. Combining classroom study with working experience they sustained a continuing series of performances for the public in spite of neglible government support. Tian Han, Cao Yu and Hong Shen all taught there after the war. Xia Yen had given up playwriting for film work and Ouyang Yuqian was working for Hong Kong film studios. Dai Ailian, the dancer, another guest of the United States during this period, returned to set up her own school in Shanghai. In 1949 when the Nationalist government left for Taiwan these key artists stayed on to work under the new government. It was a decision which was shared by a large proportion of people prominent in both traditional and modern theatre circles.

The People's Republic: policy and theory On 1 October 1949 the Chinese Communist Party (CCP) established the People's Republic of China (PRC) under its Chairman Mao Zedong. In 1966 Mao launched his radical Cultural Revolution in an attempt to preserve revolutionary purity. With his death in September 1976 and the fall of the radical 'gang of four' the following month, economic modernization soon assumed top priority in China's policy, and in 1981 both the Cultural Revolution and Mao's leadership from 1958 on were largely discredited.

Attitudes towards theatre reflect overall CCP policy, which means that there have been substantial changes from period to period. However, at no time has the CCP believed it should relax its concern with theatre activities altogether. As a result, the fact of CENSORSHIP has been consistent, even though the extent has varied enormously.

Until 1981, the basic CCP policy and theory of theatre (and other arts) were those Mao advanced in his 'Talks at the Yan'an Forum on Literature and Art'. Mao declared there that theatre reflected society but also influenced it as a means of propaganda, whether it intended to or not. He held all theatre as representing the interests of one class or another and advocated that it should oppose the bourgeoisie and favour the masses of workers, peasants and soldiers. Elsewhere, Mao pushed for the critical assimilation of traditional and foreign theatres.

In July 1950 the new government's Ministry of Culture set up a Drama Reform Committee to determine precisely how practice in the theatre should be brought into line with theory. Among traditional music dramas it retained those which emphasized Chinese patriotism, peasant rebellion or heroism, equality between the sexes, or the political prominence of women. Newly arranged dramas on historical themes were expected to emphasize similar topics. On the other hand, many items considered 'feudal' and siding with the rich against the poor were banned. While the mannerisms, costumes and other aspects of the traditional actor's craft were retained, reform demanded the abolition of some 'unhealthy' usages. No people's hero should be shown in a position which humiliated him before a feudal person such as a monk. Kowtowing and the 'false foot' devised by Wei Changsheng were banned. The Great Leap Forward of 1958 gave strong emphasis to dramas of all forms on contemporary themes, but did not discourage traditional themes. Throughout the 1950s and early 1960s, although the theories of STANISLAVSKY were dominant in spoken-drama circles, those of BERTOLT BRECHT also had a following, led by Huang Zuoling of the Shanghai People's Art Theatre.

At a meeting of heads of CCP Cultural Bureaux held in April 1963, Mao's wife Jiang Qing had a circular distributed calling for 'the suspension of the performance of ghost plays', by which she meant any traditional music drama or newly arranged historical item. In mid-1964 a Festival of Beijing Opera on Contemporary Themes was held, signalling the near total disappearance of all such 'ghost plays' from the stage for 13 years. In February 1966

Jiang Qing held a forum on 'Literature and Art in the Armed Forces' which laid down the line on theatre demanded during the Cultural Revolution (1966–76). It followed Mao's ideas closely in its emphasis on class and class struggle and the mass line, but placed an extreme interpretation on them. Thus 'critical assimilation' of tradition meant retention of little more than the name Beijing opera. All content must praise the revolution and the CCP directly, almost all the traditional content, mannerisms and costumes were banned as espousing feudal ideas and class interests. The forum also pushed the notion of a 'model' drama, one which encapsulated perfectly all the Cultural Revolution's theory of theatre. Over the following years a small number of these 'models' was devised, and professional drama companies were allowed to perform more or less nothing else. One of the main features of the 'models' was their characterization, which portrayed the heroes as faultless, and the villains as without redeeming features.

Jiang Qing was the leader of the 'gang of four' and it was not long after their fall that the Cultural Revolution's theatre theory was discredited. In May 1977 several scenes of a newly arranged historical drama were restaged in Beijing. Early the following year the main power-holder of the new leadership, Deng Xiaoping, gave explicit approval for the revival of traditional music dramas and these began to trickle back, very quickly becoming a veritable torrent. Love-stories and patriotic dramas, as well as those about peasant rebels, again received encouragement and the theme of righted injustice set in the dynastic past became a useful propaganda weapon on behalf of legal reform. Humour again became a dominant part of the Chinese regional drama, and entertainment was accepted as a main purpose of theatre. The ancient RITUAL masked *nuo* theatre, assumed to have died out, was rediscovered and re-performed, the main focus being on Guizhou province.

The main linchpin in the CCP's theatre policy is the need for variety. The range of form and content continued to broaden until 1989, on the whole with CCP approval. Up till 1989 attempts to hold back this trend towards liberalization, such as the Campaign against Spiritual Pollution in 1983, proved short-lived. In 1982 Mao's 'Talks at the Yan'an Forum' were partly discredited. In theory, theatre should still serve the interests of the 'people' but the emphasis on its use as a propaganda weapon for socialism tended increasingly to weaken. As a result, modern dramas ignoring the role of the CCP in society, and those advocating no solution for its ills, became common. Psychological drama became popular among the urban intelligentsia. The theories of acting and theatre of Bertolt Brecht increased in influence especially among younger playwrights. Since 1979 various forms of foreign theatre have received CCP sponsorship, not only performed by foreign companies in the original language, but also by local troupes and translated into Chinese.

The crisis of 1989, which climaxed in the bloody Tiananmen Square incident in Beijing on 4 June, exercised a highly detrimental effect on modern forms of drama because it placed a clamp on new experiments and ideas in theatre which could be construed as non-supportive of the CCP. In the period following the crisis, the man with chief responsibility for literature and the arts was Li Ruihuan. In a major speech made on 10 January 1990 he emphasized the magnificence of Chinese tradition and called for the critical absorption of foreign cultures. He summarized the relationship between art and politics as follows: 'We do not require literature and art to be directly subordinate to temporary and specific political tasks. At the same time, this does not mean that literature and art can deviate from serving socialism.' Certainly there would be no return to the policies of the Cultural Revolution, when literature and art were indeed directly subservient to political tasks. At the same time, Li's position implied a strong tendency to glorify the Chinese 'nation' through theatre and other arts.

Early in 1992, the senior though retired leader Deng Xiaoping reinvigorated the reform policies through a visit to selected parts of southern China. The implication in the arts, and in theatre, was a greater liberalism, wider variety and a lightening of censorship. In a speech of August 1992, Li Ruihuan welcomed a 'healthy proliferation' of 'politically harmless, but artistically superior works welcome to the masses', and argued against banning any work unless it was directly against the constitution. Plays with messages distinctly critical of the government were allowed performance. Several mid-century European plays were put on in Chinese production and translation and with Chinese performers, which carried social or political overtones clearly out of line with current official thinking – among them, plays concerning homosexuality or extramarital relationships, even including a near-nude bedroom scene. One item with anti-government political ramifications was Li Zhaohua's production of Swiss playwright FRIEDRICH DÜRRENMATT's 1949 drama *Romulus the Great*. Set in AD 476, it deals with the last Roman emperor's use of his power to abandon the empire to barbarians storming the gates of Rome, despite outrage from patriots. Li Zhaohua denied that the play was more than a comedy about ancient history, but with Deng Xiaoping in his late eighties and the shape of the post-Deng era still very uncertain, it is hard to avoid seeing the piece also as a commentary on China's possible future.

Yet the CCP continued to push its emphasis on patriotism. In his address to the 14th Congress of the CCP, held in October 1992, CCP Secretary-General Jiang Zemin emphasized 'maintaining and enriching the fine traditions of the Chinese nation'. In the early 1990s government support for traditional music-drama and plays set in the distant past grew noticeably at the expense of those dramas or drama forms focused on modern history or contemporary society. In 1990, the 200th anniversary of the entry of the Anhui companies into Beijing in 1790, a major stage along the path of development of the Beijing opera (*jingxi*), was celebrated enthusiastically throughout China. By way of climax, a festival featuring traditional music-dramas was held in Beijing, attended by Li Ruihuan and Jiang Zemin. In 1992 *Top Graduate Zhang Xie*, the earliest Chinese drama with a surviving script, was restaged, again marking enthusiasm for China's ancient national heritage.

Form, performance The main forms of theatre in China since 1949 are traditional music drama, newly arranged historical drama (*XINBIAN LISHI JU*), spoken drama (*huaju*),

song drama (*geju*), dance drama (*wuju*) and ballet. There are about 350 regional styles of traditional music drama, as explained in the sections on imperial China. The content is always from the distant past. As in the past, stage properties are simple, there is no scenery, but COSTUMES and make-up are elaborate, mannerisms, posture and body movements stylized. An evening's entertainment will normally feature three or four short items. Reform and censorship have removed certain items and passages, but this is the form least affected by the modern age. 'Newly arranged historical dramas' are traditional in most aspects of style, but as the name suggests, are created by contemporary writers and performers. In addition, scores of amateur and professional puppetry troupes perpetuate various regional traditions of puppet play (*kuilei xi*), shadow play (*piying xi*), and rod-puppet play (*zhangtou kuilei*) performance (see PUPPETS; SHADOW PUPPETS).

Among Westernized forms, the most important is spoken drama (*huaju*). Only of this form can it be said, since the 1980s, that most items are set in the present or even since 1949. The best representative writer before the Cultural Revolution was LAO SHE. Spoken drama in the 1980s showed inventiveness and innovation and the most outside, mainly Western, influence. Social commentary remained strong, but among avant-garde playwrights, propaganda of the type favoured by the CCP became less and less direct, more and more subdued. Individualism and feminism are hallmarks of contemporary female playwrights such as Bai Fengxi (1934–). Directors have experimented with techniques new to China, for example, variation in the colour and intensity of STAGE LIGHTING to show emotional or psychological atmospheres or qualities. Spoken dramas of the PRC normally use elaborate scenery and stage properties and in urban theatres the act curtain is drawn to mark beginning, end or intermission. However, since 1982, a few plays have adopted extremely simple stage properties, and abandoned scenery and the curtain altogether. Body movements and postures are realistic, not stylized as in traditional music drama. But whereas the plays with heavy propaganda content tended to show ideal characters through rather stilted, even stereotypical, movements and postures, natural style became more popular in the 1980s to portray characters who themselves conform less to images laid down as good, mediocre or bad by the CCP.

The introduction of Western ballet is due principally to Soviet influence. Before 1966, ballet meant mainly items of classical European repertoire, especially *Swan Lake*. The 'model' dramas of Jiang Qing included two ballets: *The White-Haired Girl* and *The Red Detachment of Women* (*Hongse niangzi jun*). Since 1976, these items have disappeared as ballets and classical works have returned. At the same time, Chinese artists are making very tentative steps towards creating their own national ballet, including composing new works and training ballet dancers. However, no high priority is given to this form, and it is most unlikely ever to gain great popularity in China outside a small urban intellectual elite.

Illustrative pieces Of all newly arranged historical dramas, none is more famous than *The White Snake* (*Baishe zhuan*). Originally a folk story about a white snake that turns into a beautiful woman, it underwent numerous adaptations, including a *kunqu* version by an anonymous playwright in the 18th century. Tian Han, one of the PRC's most famous dramatists, adapted it as a Beijing opera, completing the work in 1953. A monk in the *kunqu* is a positive character who succeeds in curbing the power of the wicked snake, but Tian Han has changed the characterization to present him as evil, the snake turned woman as positive. Even though an element of magic is preserved, the item thus advocates a positive role for women.

The theme of patriotism supplements advocacy of equality for women in *Women Generals of the Yang Family* (*Yangmen nüjiang*), arranged as a Beijing opera in 1960 by Lü Ruiming on the basis of a late-Ming novel and a Yangzhou music drama entitled *Centenarian Takes Command* (*Baisui guashuai*). Like all others on traditional themes, this item was banned during the Cultural Revolution. However it was revived in 1978. It is set in the 11th century. A centenarian dowager surnamed Yang persuades the women of her family to resist an enemy aggressing from the north, and their forces win the final victory.

One regional drama on a modern theme is *The Story of the Red Lantern* (*Hongdeng ji*), which features three generations of Communist heroes and their struggle against a Japanese general during the War of Resistance against Japan. The representatives of the two elder generations are killed by the general, but the youngest lives to fight victoriously against him. The item was adapted into a Beijing opera by the playwright-director Ajia (1907–) and performed at the 1964 Festival of Beijing Opera on Contemporary Themes. It was taken over by Jiang Qing and recognized as one of her model dramas from 1970 on. The characterization was made starker to emphasize the class struggle; Western instruments were added to the accompanying orchestra and the music made more staccato to express the heroism of the Communists better. The item was revived in the festival of December 1990 and January 1991 to mark the 200th anniversary of the entry of the Anhui companies into Beijing. That this was not a sign of a Cultural Revolutionary revival was demonstrated by the fact that the form chosen was Ajia's, with Jiang Qing being accused of having seized the item through an act of robbery.

In the 1980s several spoken dramas and newly arranged historical music dramas appeared on the subject of Li Shimin, one of China's greatest emperors (r.626–49). He was the second ruler of the Tang dynasty and held the imperial title of Taizong, and so is known also as Tang Taizong. One of the music dramas is the Beijing opera *Tang Taizong*, arranged by Li Lun. It deals with Li Shimin's success in winning over a Turkish invader through mediation and popular support, not force, thus securing national unity. The incident which forms the core of the drama is historical, but the characterization and plot are adapted to advocate political lessons appropriate to the present. An item to be premiered after the 1989 crisis was *Painting Dragons and Filling in Eyes* (*Hualong dianjing*) by Sun Yuexia and others. Set in 627, it portrays Li Shimin as a kind of 'people's emperor' and an example for the Chinese nation and concerns his search for good officials and suppression of corruption. In the 1980s the best writer of

newly arranged historical music drama was probably WEI MINGLUN.

More modern national heroes portrayed on the stage since the late 1970s are revolutionaries such as Mao Zedong and Zhou Enlai. In 1981, the 70th anniversary of the overthrow of the last dynasty by Sun Yatsen and his followers was the occasion for several spoken dramas about him. His wife Song Qingling, who died in 1981, figures prominently in them. The first of the plays was *Sun Yatsen's London Encounter with Danger* (*Sun Zhongshan Lundun mengan ji*). Its focus was Sun's arrest by the Chinese legation in 1896 and later release through the efforts of his former teacher, the British doctor Sir James Cantlie. This enables the playwright, Li Peijian, to emphasize not only the courage and unselfishness of Sun, but also the power and wisdom of the British people, represented by Cantlie and others, and Sun's good relations with his 'foreign friends'. The play was unusual in China, even in the 1980s, in being set in a foreign country.

Sites of performance, audiences Theatre performances can take place in a variety of sites in China, including workers' or rural clubs, a market-place or any open space. Street theatre is common only on special occasions such as festivals. In the cities and towns, cinemas are readily used as theatres for live performances. A major theatre encyclopedia published in Beijing in 1983 stated that there were 891 theatres in China in 1949 and 2227 in 1957. It claimed that 'after 1958 [we] continued to build quite a few new theatres' but gave no figures. In the main cities there are a few large theatres, of special note being one opened in Beijing in 1984 which has a 600-square-metre stage able to hold 1000 performers.

Most theatres built since 1949 follow a somewhat stark Soviet architectural style, both internally and externally. In sharp contrast to the teahouse-theatres of the 19th century, the audience is expected to concentrate fully on the performance, and sits in rows facing one side of the stage. In the case of musical items, the text is projected beside the stage to facilitate comprehension. The seats are rarely padded. The large 1984 Beijing theatre has a stage with rising and revolving platforms, a stereo sound system, lamps, spotlights and curtains all controlled by computer, the first of its kind in China. But the most modern theatre in China is the Grand Theatre (*Da juyuan*) in Shenzhen, a 'special economic zone' very near Hong Kong. Apart from a large concert hall, it has a playhouse with a gigantic and computerized stage. It is similar to up-to-date theatres in the West, including its modern coffee shop. Tickets are considerably more expensive than in most Chinese theatres, but unfortunately it is rarely booked out.

Some companies own their own theatre. Those not so fortunate negotiate with a local government Bureau of Culture, which co-ordinates the timetables of the various troupes and theatres. Tours are planned through an annual meeting organized by the central Ministry of Culture. In a few parts of China there are special theatres for balladeers or storytellers. Here people sip tea and listen to stories sung out by one or several performers, accompanied by musical instruments. However, in most cases storytellers perform by themselves in parks or squares.

Performances are advertised partly through the local

press. Theatres announce forthcoming items and performances through bills in the foyer. Most important of all, advertisements are stuck on special billboards, poles or any free space along the streets or in the markets. This is especially necessary in small towns or villages which lack their own newspaper. Tickets for professional performances are cheap and entry to amateur ones often free. Simple printed programmes are very cheap. Full houses are quite common, especially for good and well performed pieces, but companies frequently complain of low attendances, and nearly empty theatres are distressingly common in provincial centres.

Those involved with the traditional and the newly arranged historical music drama have become very worried over the defection of young people from their audiences. Possibly the gap in performance of over a decade during the Cultural Revolution dealt a crippling blow to youth's interest in such theatre. It was excluded from their education and cultural life for so long that by the time of its revival they simply did not understand it and saw no reason why they should make the effort. In the 1980s audiences at urban performances of traditional music dramas were mainly over 40 years of age, with men outnumbering women two to one or more. Moreover, the situation appears to be getting even worse in the 1990s, with audiences continuing to dwindle and theatre workers more and more worried about the future. The same problem affects the countryside, but is not nearly so pronounced there.

Young theatregoers prefer the spoken drama because they can understand it and it has more to say of relevance to their own lives. However, since the mid-1980s even spoken-drama troupes have been finding it increasingly difficult to make ends meet and to attract large audiences. The form of entertainment which is more and more attracting the largest audience is not theatre, but television. The State Statistical Bureau's 1994 communiqué on the previous year's economy and society declared that there were 683 television stations and 1085 television transmitting and relay stations. Television is available not only in the cities but to very large and increasing areas of the countryside. Ironically the screen does support all drama forms in the sense that both traditional and modern music-dramas and spoken dramas are shown both on television and in the cinema, but the fact is of little comfort to the average performer.

Audiences at traditional music dramas tend to be noisy, possibly in part a reflection of their incomplete understanding of what is happening, but those at spoken drama are quiet. Applause is reserved mainly for notes held an unusual length of time or an excellent acrobatics display. Even very good troupes are lucky to elicit more than a patter at the conclusion of the performance.

The performer The number of fully professional art troupes in 1950 was 1676 and in 1965 3458, but fell to 2514 by 1971 as a result of the policies of the Cultural Revolution. The year with the highest figure was 1980, with 3533 troupes and 245,659 personnel, but the trend since then has been downwards. By 1993 there were only 2723 troupes and the average size was very much smaller than in 1980. The reason for this was that performers who did not pull their weight or for whom no work could be found were dismissed.

The nationalization of professional troupes began in the mid-1950s and was completed during the Cultural Revolution. After the fall of the 'gang of four' the process was reversed and in the early 1980s reform directed towards free enterprise began to be introduced even in state companies. Under the new system, state subsidies to troupes are reduced and the troupe keeps a larger portion of its box-office earnings. Box-office earnings thus assume far greater importance. This aims to 'break the iron rice bowl' and in theory improves quality because it intensifies competition among actors. Now the possibility of dismissal becomes quite real for lazy or incompetent members. Above all, inequalities increase greatly because performers with big roles in successful plays can earn substantial sums from box-office returns, in addition to their salary, and thus become rich by Chinese standards quite quickly. In a speech made just after his appointment as Minister of Culture in 1993, Liu Zhongde stated that only a few very special theatre troupes, such as 'those of historic worth and great impact in China and abroad', would remain under state sponsorship, with the remainder being forced to rely on market forces. Those which could not make money would simply go out of business.

Immediately after coming to power, the CCP abolished the training system of the past and instituted the principle that potential performers should receive a general as well as theatrical education in order to wipe out illiteracy. The training of almost all traditional music-drama students was suspended during the Cultural Revolution and then revived after 1976. Most professional companies run schools through which to recruit, train and educate new performers. For traditional music drama, especially Beijing opera, the main national school is the Chinese Music Drama Institute (Zhongguo Xiqu Xueyuan), set up in 1950. It now has five departments: Beijing-opera performance, music, directing, dramaturgy and stagecraft. Between 1956 and 1982 the institution produced some 1300 graduates.

Entry into training schools at all levels is through highly competitive examination: about 5 per cent of applicants gain admission. There is still a strong bias in favour of males, the rationale being that casts require more men.

CCP policy is to train women to sing female roles and men to sing male. In 1951 Premier Zhou Enlai told the famous *dan* actor Zhang Chunqiu: 'up to you the male *dan*, and that's the end'. If this policy is continued, in time women will perform all *dan* roles, but it appears that a handful of female impersonators (see FEMALE IMPERSONATION) are being trained, so the art may not die after all.

The social status of performers has risen greatly under CCP rule. Among the reasons for this are the elimination of the social discrimination which previously afflicted them, a highly organized recruitment and training system, an improved standard of living, and the government's high evaluation of 'art workers' as a profession. There are, however, still strong gradations in the status of performers: stars may be among the most influential and respected members of society, while ordinary performers live in serious poverty and social disregard.

Since the earliest days of its existence the CCP has

strongly encouraged amateur artists who, it considered, could assist its propaganda work among the masses to an extent even greater than professionals. The slogan pushed was 'small in scale, rich in variety' (*xiaoxing duoyang*), meaning that long or complicated pieces requiring extensive training or elaborate and expensive costumes should be avoided. The spoken drama, simple songs and dances, or balladry items, were greatly preferred to traditional music drama. The Cultural Revolution gave great priority to 'mass amateur propaganda troupes' and for several years in the late 1960s they were more or less the only source of China's theatrical life.

Since the late 1970s amateur troupes have declined markedly. To fill their place semi-professional troupes have arisen everywhere in China, especially in the countryside where fully professional theatre is less accessible than in the cities. Peasants form troupes on their own initiative and only the most talented and skilled local performers are chosen. They spend most of the year as peasants, and during the slack season they go around performing, mainly traditional regional music dramas. The reward is financial, for although the performers do not receive salaries, they are paid out of box-office returns according to their contribution to the particular drama. Even if they perform in the street and there is no box office, they are quite likely to be thrown tips from the audience. In 1992 the number of such troupes nationwide was 46,945.

Conclusion Clearly the period since 1978 has brought enormous changes to the Chinese theatre in all respects. A major feature of society in general and the theatre in particular is a dichotomous impulse towards modernization on the one hand and a traditionalist revival on the other. The major thrust is still socialist in that content tends to reflect socialist society and many fully professional troupes remain state-owned. The direction of change until mid-1989 was towards greater variety and liberalism in terms of form and content, and free enterprise in organization. Between then and early 1992 the trend towards liberalism was reversed in favour of a more rigid application of ideology – Marxism–Leninism and especially nationalism – but this proved temporary, with the liberal notions implied by economic reform reasserting themselves from that time. Experience in other countries suggests that economic modernization affects traditional arts adversely. Despite the current enthusiasm in China for traditional music drama as an example of its national arts, the same could easily happen there in the next few decades. (See also ASIAN AND PACIFIC ISLAND THEATRE.) CPM ACS

GENERAL

See: J. R. Brandon (ed.), *The Cambridge Guide to Asian Theatre*, Cambridge, 1993; W. Dolby (tr.), *Eight Chinese Plays from the Thirteenth Century to the Present*, New York, 1978, and *A History of Chinese Drama*, London, 1976; E. M. Gunn (ed.), *Twentieth-Century Chinese Drama: An Anthology*, Bloomington, Ind., 1983; Tao-Ching Hsü, *The Chinese Conception of the Theatre*, Seattle and London, 1985; C. Mackerras, *Chinese Drama, A Historical Survey*, Beijing, 1990, (ed.), *Chinese Theatre from its Origins to the Present Day*, Honolulu, 1983, 1988, *The Chinese Theatre in Modern Times from*

1840 to the Present Day, London, 1975, and *The Rise of the Peking Opera 1770–1870, Social Aspects of the Theatre in Manchu China*, Oxford, 1972; A. C. Scott (tr. and ed.), *Traditional Chinese Plays*, 3 vols., Madison, 1967, 1969, 1975; S. H. West, *Vaudeville and Narrative: Aspects of Chin Theatre*, Wiesbaden, 1977; E. Wichmann, *Listening to Theatre, The Aural Dimension of Beijing Opera*, Honolulu, 1991.

REGIONAL AND FOLK DRAMA

See: B. Yung, *Cantonese Opera: Performance as a Creative Process*, Cambridge, 1989.

THE PEOPLE'S REPUBLIC

See: B. S. McDougall (ed.), *Popular Chinese Literature and Performing Arts in the People's Republic of China 1949–1979*, Berkeley, Calif., 1984; C. Mackerras, *The Performing Arts in Contemporary China*, London, 1981; W. J. and R. I. Meserve (eds.), *Modern Drama from Communist China*, New York, 1970; Peking Opera Troupe of Shanghai, *Taking Tiger Mountain by Strategy: A Modern Revolutionary Peking Opera*, Peking, 1971; J. Riley and E. Unterrieder (eds.), *Haishi Zou Hao, Chinese Poetry, Drama and Literature of the 1980s*, Bonn, 1989; C. Tung and C. Mackerras (eds.), *Drama in the People's Republic of China*, Albany, 1987; R. G. Wagner, *The Contemporary Chinese Historical Drama, Four Studies*, Berkeley, Calif., 1990.

Chirgwin, G. H. 1854–1922 'The white-eyed kaffir': British blackface comedian, singer, multi-instrumentalist and eccentric dancer. London-born, he got his early experience busking with his brothers both in the metropolis and at small seaside resorts, and subsequently as a 'nigger MINSTREL' and cross-talk act at the minor halls. He seems to have made his London stage debut as early as 1861: he began to play solo at the Middlesex Music Hall, and became unfailingly successful after a booking at the Oxford in 1878. Tall and long-legged, he was a striking figure in black tights and leotard, floor-length frock-coat and enormous stove-pipe hat, with a contrasting white lozenge over his right eye. In a stage career of over 40 years, the only variation in his appearance was that he sometimes performed with the colours reversed. Though his act never changed, his instrumental versatility (and his ability to dance while playing the bagpipes) gave it variety, as did his habit of alternating baritone and falsetto delivery in both speech and song. He was also much given to topical rhymes and allusions, and liked to set up a relationship of impromptu banter with his audience. He is best remembered for his performance of the old Christy Minstrel tearjerker 'The Blind Boy' and the punning 'My Fiddle is my Sweetheart (and I'm her only Beau)'. AEG

Chocolat see FOOTTIT, GEORGE

Chocrón, Isaac 1932– Venezuelan playwright, director, critic and novelist. One-third of the Venezuelan 'Holy Trinity' (with CABRUJAS and CHALBAUD), Chocrón has written more than a dozen plays, plus several novels. He was a director of the NUEVO GRUPO (New Group) from 1967 until its closure in 1988. Winner of the National Theatre Prize in 1979, in 1984 he was chosen by the Venezuelan president to direct the newly formed National Theatre Company.

Trained as an economist, he studied in both the USA and England. His first play, *Mónica y el florentino* (*Monica and the Florentine*, 1959), used an international guest-house to manifest problems of isolation and difficulties of communication. Chocrón has experimented with a variety of styles: his popular *Asia y el lejano oriente* (*Asia and the Far East*, 1966), about the selling of a country, was restaged with music and dance added as the first offering of the National Theatre Company in 1985. *Okey* (1969) presented a *ménage à trois* addicted to consumerism, and *La revolución* (*The Revolution*, 1971) dealt frankly with homosexuality. Later plays include *La máxima felicidad* (*Maximum Happiness*, 1974), *El acompañante* (*The Accompanist*, 1978), *Mesopotamia* (1979) and *Simón* (1983), the latter a view of young Bolívar and his mentor. Along with his colleague Cabrujas, Chocrón has remained a dominant force in the Venezuelan theatre; *Clipper* (1987) is inspired by personal and emotional memories of family members. GW

Chong, Ping 1946– Toronto-born experimental theatre director, choreographer, performer and film-maker who also produces videotapes and site-specific installations. Chong was brought up in the Chinatown section of New York. During 1971–8 he was a member of MEREDITH MONK's company; he continues to collaborate with her on video productions and performances, such as their opera/music theatre, *The Games* (1984). He founded his own company, the Fiji Theater Company (1975; since 1988 known as the Ping Chong Company). Beginning with his first theatre piece, *Lazarus* (1972), Chong's multimedia hi-tech and science fiction works have explored, among other themes, the alienation of humanoid and android races (*Angels of Swedenborg* (1985), *Kind Ness* (1986), *Elephant Memories* (1990), *Deshima* (1990; revised 1993). His influences – Chinese opera, BRECHT, MEYERHOLD, Kafka and film producer Robert Bresson – represent postmodernist fragmentation. Chong uses futuristic (see FUTURISM), cinematic and theatrical stage effects to explore bureaucratic regimentation and the psychological states of the outsider. AF

Christie [*née* Miller], Dame Agatha (Mary Clarissa) 1891–1976 British detective novelist and dramatist, whose dramatizations of her own novels have been successful both on stage and in film, notably *Ten Little Niggers* (1943; produced in New York as *Ten Little Indians*, 1944) and *Murder on the Nile* (1946). *The Mousetrap*, which opened in 1952 at the Ambassadors Theatre and had already achieved the record for the longest continuous London run of any play before 1973 when it transferred to St Martin's Theatre, is still (1995) running. Although the most conventional of her plays, it was also seen in New York (1960), and has been running for the last twelve years in Toronto. Her work also established a record of another sort when *Spider's Web* was staged in 1954 while *Witness for the Prosecution* (1953) was still on, so that she had three plays running simultaneously in the WEST END. CI

chuanju (Sichuan opera) Form of music drama found in Sichuan, China's most populous province, and one of the most important of the country's regional styles. It grew out of five different musical and theatrical styles that originally were independent, four belonging to the main systems of Chinese theatre and introduced from outside the province. The earliest of these, *gaoqiang*, came into Sichuan around the 17th century. A variant of the 'music-of-Yiyang' drama, it featured an offstage chorus. Slightly later, clapper opera, known in Sichuan as *tanqiang* ('strum music'), was introduced from Shaanxi to the north. Next *huqin qiang* ('music of the *huqin*'), a variant of the PIHUANG system, introduced the two-string *huqin* instrument. Aristocratic KUNQU was popular with the officials of Sichuan. The one form native to Sichuan was *dengxi* ('lantern theatre'), a folk style based on local MASK dances of village SHAMANS.

Early in the 20th century, the theatre was reformed and the five styles began to be performed on the same stage and were regarded as a unity, though every item still retained its style of origin in its music. The first teahouse-theatres were introduced into Sichuan's cities. Probably the greatest of the reformers was Kang Zilin (1870–1931), a fine actor, teacher and leader of the famous Three Celebrations (Sanqing) Company (est. 1912). Apart from the decade of the Cultural Revolution, Sichuan opera has flourished under the Communists, especially since 1978. The Sichuan Province Chuanju Research Institute holds the texts of over 2000 plays, most of which follow stories familiar from the literature and theatre of China as a whole.

In performance, stagecraft, costuming and make-up, Sichuan opera is essentially similar to other Chinese regional styles, including Beijing opera (JINGXI), though some of its stage arts are distinctive. For instance, Kang Zilin devised a kick in which the foot, touching the middle of the lower forehead for a split second, leaves the image of a third eye there, a breathtaking technique still practised in Sichuan. Make-up styles are also somewhat different: the painted-face character (*jing*), is restricted to four colours – black, red, white and grey – rather than the many colours used in Beijing opera, and grey rather than green and gold identifies a supernatural being. CPM

Churchill, Caryl 1938– British dramatist, who started to write radio plays in the early 1960s about 'bourgeois middle-class life and [its] destruction'. A hatred of injustice characterized her early stage plays, notably *Owners* (1972). While not at first a playwright to be described as politically committed, she came to write for left-wing and feminist companies such as Joint Stock and Monstrous Regiment, for whom she wrote *Light Shining in Buckinghamshire* (1976) and *Vinegar Tom* (1976). She accepted the then standard connection between the class struggle and the role of women in an imperialist and capitalist society. This broad-brush approach to the problems of our time helps to explain the leaps in logic which occur in *Cloud Nine* (1979), a play about sexual role-playing, and *Top Girls* (1982), a dinner party in which famous women from various epochs describe the struggles that they faced to succeed in a male world. She was much praised by the left, for whom she became a shining example in herself, although her popularity with audiences amounted to a kind of political warning. Her SATIRE on the City financiers in *Serious Money* (1987) was observed to be more welcomed by 'yuppies' than by 'trendies', while her lack of didacticism was thought by some supporters to be more of a weakness.

At best, Churchill is a witty, literate writer whose wide-ranging references reveal the eclectic scope of her interests. Her play from Romania, *Mad Forest* (1990), developed on-site in the weeks after the downfall of the Ceaușescus, is a rare example of a British play that attempts to understand the havoc left by totalitarianism in Eastern Europe. *The Skriker* (1994) derives its title from a kind of northern goblin, brilliantly played at the NATIONAL THEATRE by Kathryn Hunter, whose powers shape the lives of two Lancastrian women visiting London. Churchill's text uses an associative dream logic, which some critics found nonsensical, but which the supernatural yearnings of its theme required dance, music (by the opera composer Judith Weir) and much MIME to realize.   JE

Cibber, Colley 1671–1757 English actor, manager and playwright. Son of Caius Gabriel Cibber, a sculptor, he joined the United Company as an actor in 1690. After the secession of the senior actors with BETTERTON in 1695, he stayed with Christopher Rich, recognizing the opportunity to take over major roles, and was successful as Fondlewife in CONGREVE's *The Old Bachelor*. His first play, *Love's Last Shift* (1696), including a superb role for himself as a fop, Sir Novelty Fashion, contains a last-act repentance for the rake-hero and is often labelled the first sentimental comedy. He played Lord Foppington, Sir Novelty elevated to the peerage, in VANBRUGH's rebuttal of the argument of *Love's Last Shift*, *The Relapse* (1698). In 1699 he produced his adaptation of SHAKESPEARE's *Richard III*, and though his own performance as Richard was much ridiculed the adaptation was performed for the next 120 years: it, not Shakespeare's play, contains the famous line 'Off with his head. So much for Buckingham.'

His best original COMEDY, *The Careless Husband*, with Lord Foppington again, was first performed in 1704. By this time Cibber was beginning to be involved in theatre management, and by 1708, together with DOGGETT and OLDFIELD, he was running the Queen's Theatre for its owner, Swiney, triumphing over Rich, the much hated previous manager. In 1710 a triumvirate of Wilks, Doggett and Cibber took over the management of DRURY LANE.

Cibber was a broadly successful manager, with occasional blunders such as the rejection of GAY's *The Beggar's Opera*; he was particularly good at teaching acting. His adaptation of MOLIÈRE's *Tartuffe* as *The Nonjuror* and his completion of Vanbrugh's *A Journey to London* as *The Provoked Husband* (1728) are his best plays of this period. Often mocked by satirists for his snobbishness and conceit, Cibber became an oddly obsessive butt, after his appointment as Poet Laureate in 1730, both for FIELDING and, especially, Pope, who made him King of the Dunces in *The New Dunciad* (1742). From 1733, when he retired as manager, he acted less frequently, though he was still acting in 1745 in his adaptation of Shakespeare's *King John*. His brilliant autobiography, *An Apology for the Life of Colley Cibber*, was published in 1740.   PH

Cibber, Susanna (Maria) 1714–66 English actress, who began her career as a singer at the HAYMARKET in 1732. Partly trained by COLLEY CIBBER, she made her debut as an

actress in AARON HILL's *Zara* with huge success. She had a small but carefully chosen repertoire of roles, including Desdemona, Cordelia and Monimia in OTWAY's *The Orphan*, and was particularly famed for her use of her handkerchief in performances of tragedies. Her pathetic style led Hill to comment: 'When Mrs Cibber weeps, who won't weep with her?'. She was off the stage during the scandal of her husband's (THEOPHILUS CIBBER) suing her lover for damages for adultery, but returned triumphantly in 1742 to Dublin and COVENT GARDEN. She worked with GARRICK and with RICH but recurrent illnesses frequently hindered her from acting, though she worked up to her death.   PH

Cibber, Theophilus 1703–58 English actor, manager and playwright, son of COLLEY CIBBER. He joined the DRURY LANE company in 1719 and was a precocious and appealing actor. From 1727 he assisted Wilks as manager. He gained particular success as Pistol in *Henry IV Part 1* and *Henry V*, in spite of his over-acting. Distrusted by his father, who refused to appoint him his successor as manager, he led a rebellion of actors against the management and in 1734 was granted a licence for the HAYMARKET Theatre. His appalling treatment of his wife, SUSANNA CIBBER, culminated in his attempt to sue his wife's lover for damages for adultery, though he condoned and encouraged the affair; he was awarded only £10 damages and was hissed off the stage. In spite of frequent attempts to take on other companies he never really succeeded. He drowned on his way to Ireland to act at Smock Alley Theatre.   PH

Ciceri, Pierre(-Luc-Charles) 1782–1862 French stage designer and scene painter. The most admired designer of the first half of the 19th century in Paris, Ciceri began studying drawing and painting with stage designer F. J. Belanger in 1802. In 1806 he became a staff painter to the Paris Opéra, specializing in landscapes. By 1818 he was promoted to chief painter and from 1822 to 1847 he was scenic director for the Paris Opéra. Imaginative landscapes and classical ruins painted on flats and backdrops using a central vanishing point were characteristic of his early designs. With the completion of the new opera house in 1822, the dimming and brightening of gas footlights were taken into account in his designs. In 1826, for the COMÉDIE-FRANÇAISE, he began designing detailed depictions of historical epochs. Some of his most important works were executed in his scenic studio established in 1822: designs for Liszt's *Don Sancho* (1825), *La Muette de Portici* (1828), *Guillaume Tell* (1829), *Robert le diable* (1831) and *Hernani* (1830). The romantic style developed at his studio dominated the scene designs of the next generation in France.   AJN

Cinquevalli, Paul [Paul Kestner] 1856–1918 Polish JUGGLER. His debut took place in Odessa (1873) as an aerialist; but after a fall from a 75-ft height and eight months in hospital, he switched to juggling. He was first seen in London in 1885 and was soon a headliner on MUSIC-HALL bills, as 'the Human Billiard Table'. He would often conclude his act by catching a cannon ball on the nape of his neck. Absolute tops in his field, some of his tricks never copied, he retired in 1915, depressed by anti-German sentiment inaccurately directed at him.   LS

Cinzio see GIRALDI, GIOVAN BATTISTA

Circle in the Square   New York's oldest company, founded in 1951 by JOSÉ QUINTERO, Theodore Mann, Emilie Stevens and Jason Wingreen. Starting as the Loft Players in 1949 (originally the Villetta Studio Players in Woodstock, NY) and producing in the round (originally on Sheridan Square, whence its name), the company is 'artistically committed to the art of acting'. Never avant-garde, the company 'hold[s] the classics up to our sunshine in the hope of making them glow'. Its 1952 revival of *Summer and Smoke* launched Circle's success, Quintero's and GERALDINE PAGE's careers, and OFF-BROADWAY's heyday. In 1961, Circle opened its school, briefly associated with New York University. In 1969–70, it produced six shows at Washington's Ford's Theatre, and in 1972, maintaining its Greenwich Village house, occupied its BROADWAY theatre. In 1992–3 a fiscal crisis threatened the closing of this venue although in 1994 Josephine R. Abady joined Mann as co-artistic director to resuscitate the operation.

Under previous artistic director Mann, Circle produced many O'NEILL works directed by Quintero, contemporary plays, and classics with such stars as GEORGE C. SCOTT, Cicely Tyson, JASON ROBARDS JR, JAMES EARL JONES, Joanne Woodward, Philip Bosco, VANESSA REDGRAVE and DUSTIN HOFFMAN. Its productions include Capote's *The Grass Harp* (1953), *The Iceman Cometh* with Robards (1956), DYLAN THOMAS's *Under Milk Wood* (1961), FUGARD's *Boesman and Lena* (1970), *Medea* with Irene Papas (1973), a contemporary adaptation of MOLIÈRE's *The Cheats of Scapino* (*Scapino!*) with Jim Dale (1974), *The Glass Menagerie* (1975), IBSEN's *The Lady from the Sea* with Redgrave (1976), *Macbeth* directed by NICOL WILLIAMSON (1982), *Heartbreak House* with REX HARRISON (1983), *Design for Living* directed by Scott (1984), *Arms and the Man* with KEVIN KLINE and RAUL JULIA (1986), Tina Howe's *Coastal Disturbances* (1987), *Sweeney Todd* (1989) and *The Miser* with Bosco (1990). Many later ran on Broadway or television. Circle in the Square's numerous awards include Tonys, Obies and Drama Desk Awards.   REK

Circle Repertory Company (New York City) OFF-BROADWAY theatre, founded in 1969 by MARSHALL W. MASON, Robert Thirkield, Tanya Berezin and LANFORD WILSON, dedicated to rediscovering 'lyric realism as the native voice of the American theatre'. Formed 'for the needs of the artists, based on the relation between the actors and the playwright', the group, at Café LA MAMA and CAFFE CINO since 1965, founded the American Theatre Project in 1968. Devoted to new American writers, CRC operates a playwrights' workshop, projects-in-progress series and script evaluation service, and launched the Young Playwrights Festival (now at the NEW YORK SHAKESPEARE FESTIVAL). CRC's informal alliance of over 200 artists is committed 'to making the action of the play become the experience of the audience'. In 1987, founding artistic director Mason turned the company over to Berezin, who left in early 1995.

Many of Wilson's plays moved to BROADWAY (*The Hot l Baltimore* (1972), *Talley's Folly* (1979), *5th of July* (1977), *Angels Fall* (1983), *Burn This* (1987)). Other productions include *When You Comin' Back, Red Ryder?* (1973), *Battle of Angles* (1974), Jules Feiffer's *Knock Knock* (1976), *Gemini* (1977), Marty Martin's *Gertrude Stein, Gertrude Stein, Gertrude Stein* (1979), *Buried Child* (1979), *Fool for Love* (1983), *As Is* (1985), *Prelude to a Kiss* (1990) and *Three Hotels* (1993). In 1985, CRC became the first American company to tour Japan, presenting *Who's Afraid of Virginia Woolf?* and *Fool for Love*. Its many awards include Wilson's Obie for *The Mound Builders* (1975) and a Pulitzer Prize for *Talley's Folly* (1980). CRC received the 1991 Lucille Lortel Award for 'outstanding body of work'. A study by Mary Ryzuk covering the first 15 years of the company's history was published in 1989.   REK

circus   From the Latin for 'ring', but specifically from the Circus Maximus in Rome; defined by Marcello Truzzi as 'a travelling and organized display of animals and skilled performance within one or more circular stages known as "rings" before an audience encircling these activities'.

The modern circus, which JEAN GENET has called 'an instance of the ultimate truth', incorporates the individual acts into one serial, often simultaneous, presentation. It developed from the riding school in European cities of the late 18th century, often under the guidance of former cavalry officers. Fairs were declining, owing to newer forms of consumerism and tighter municipal licensing laws, and their entertainments could more easily be controlled within the rings of the equestrian shows. Unemployed rope dancers, acrobats (see ACROBATICS) and JUGGLERS drifted to these arenas. Although Jacob Bates had set up such a show, the Cirque Équestre, in Paris in 1767, credit for the first true circus is usually bestowed on PHILIP ASTLEY in London (1768), for he supplemented the horsemanship with CLOWNS and trained animals and later added PANTOMIMES. (The Royal Circus, founded in 1782 by CHARLES DIBDIN, was the first theatre to use the term.) The circus of this period has been called 'one of the most abstract depictions of the ideals of the French Revolution' (Alexander Kluge), a picture which put man in an omnipotent position in regard to the world. The fairground, located in a natural setting, was less anthropocentric than the controlled space of the *manège*, which first resembled the theatres of its time with box, pit and gallery.

Once permanent buildings for the circus were created, its spontaneity diminished, but in recompense it provided an 'opera for the eyes' through its pantomime spectacles. The oval or race-track ring was characteristic, the round ring a later introduction by Americans. Astley's tradition of elegant riding was carried on in Paris by Antonio Franconi's *exercice de grâce*, in Vienna by de Bach, and in St Petersburg by Tournaire. This so-called romantic period of the circus enjoyed considerable cross-fertilization with the ballet and pantomimic MELODRAMA. But with an increasingly heterogeneous audience and larger buildings, elegant horsemanship gradually declined until the exclusively equestrian circus disappeared in 1897 with Berlin's Zirkus Renz. Meanwhile, new genres began to dominate, with an emphasis on sensation rather than grace: aerialism, wild-beast taming, and daredevil feats. Travelling circuses became a major concern only after the spread of railways, when it became easier to transport elaborate machinery, huge cages and a numerous troupe. With touring, which entailed an enormous staff of roustabouts and workers to set up and strike the tents, came the need for standardization, particularly so that the horses would not be upset by any deviation in environment. The standard European arena was invariably 13 metres in diameter, surrounded by a low barrier broken by two apertures on opposite sides, and strewn with sawdust or sand six to eight centimetres thick.

England Astley's Royal Amphitheatre (1798) burned down in 1803 but was rebuilt the following year. Under the management of ANDREW DUCROW (1830–41) and with a company of 150, it enjoyed a period of glory, especially with HIPPODRAMAS such as *The Battle of Waterloo* (1824), and survived as a building until 1893. These shows presented burlettas, pantomime, and *ballets d'action*, which used dramatic actors. Other managements include the Ginnetts, the Cookes, E. T. Smith who starred ADAH ISAACS MENKEN, and GEORGE SANGER who bought Astley's in 1871 to stage spectaculars. The circus empire of Charles Hengler, the son of a rope dancer, began in Liverpool when he converted the Argyll Street Theatre to an amphitheatre. At the turn of the century, competition from MUSIC-HALLS forced many circuses to convert to VARIETY stages, although a reversal of this trend can be seen in the London Hippodrome, which was built to amalgamate the two genres. C. B. COCHRAN planned a circus building that could hold 6000 spectators, but the war prevented its realization. Important modern managers include Bertram Mills, whose circus played at the London Olympia (1920–66) and on the road (1930–64); Billy Russell, Jimmy and Dick Chipperfield, Robert Brothers and Jerry Cottle. Circus at Christmas is as sure a tradition as the pantomime. Historically, the English influence in circus can be seen chiefly in the fields of equestrianism, gymnastics and clowning.

France The first true circus after Bates's was that of Astley in the rue des Vieilles-Tuileries, Paris (1772), later enlarged as the CIRQUE OLYMPIQUE (1782), where a medley of equestrian acts (including a horse minuet), rope dancing and pantomime was presented. Astley fled during the Revolution, to be replaced by his erstwhile partner Antonio Franconi (1737–1836), a bird trainer turned horse trainer, who rented the circus in 1793 and produced elaborate pantomimes dominated by riding (such as *The Death of Marlborough*). It was Franconi who first used the term *cirque* in 1807 because of a Napoleonic ban on *théâtre* to describe fairground entertainments. His sons Laurent (1776–1840) and Jean-Gérard-Henri (1778–1840), among the best equestrians of their time, opened the Cirque Olympique (1807–16), which featured stylish spectacles in Empire taste ('The Egyptian Pyramids', 'The Death of Bayard') and trained animals like Coco the stag and the elephant Baba. Their new building in the Boulevard du Temple was sold in 1835 to a banker, Louis Déjean, who called it the Cirque National and later opened the Cirque Napoléon (1852) and the Cirque de l'Impératrice, a summer circus in the Champs Élysées. These were veritable cultural centres that introduced the first English clowns

and the aerialist LÉOTARD to Paris; Déjean obtained a licence to stage plays there, provided that horses always took part. Victor Franconi carried on his family tradition with the Hippodrome (1846), a wooden oval some 108 metres long and 104 metres wide, which held an audience of 15,000; it excelled in military spectacles and Roman chariot races, arranged by Lucien Arnault. Victor Franconi also created the Cirque d'Hiver (1852) and the Cirque d'Été. The Nouveau Cirque under Joseph Oller used tanbark (brown coconut matting) rather than sand, and featured naumachic (sea-battle) shows (see NAUMACHIA).

The Cirque Pinder, founded in 1854 in England by the brothers Pinder, was taken over by Spessardy in 1928 and carried on in partnership with the radio station ORTF until it was bought in 1972 by Jean Richard. Richard, a film actor, who founded his own circus in 1968, now runs a small empire, including the modern travelling Cirque Medrano, and is affiliated with the Grüss family of performers, who have expanded into management on their own. The Cirque Rancy et F. Lalanne, founded in 1856 by Théodore Rancy and F. Lalanne, was maintained until 1932, and revived 10 years later by Henry Rancy. The Cirque Bouglione, founded by Sampion Bouglione, played at the Cirque d'Hiver in winter and the Cirque de Montmartre in summer. The Cirque Amar, founded by the Algerian Ahmed Ben Amar as a menagerie, was active in the 1930s and was bought in 1973 by Bouglione.

Central and Eastern Europe Most German circuses followed the French pattern. The leading managements were and are Renz (1851–97), founded in Berlin by Ernst Jacob Renz (1815–92); Busch (1884–1960, after 1963 billed as the Roland Circus), founded by Paul Busch; Sarrasani (1912–48, newly reopened 1956), founded by Hans Stosch (1874–1934); Krone (1905–49; as a tent circus, next a winter building in Munich, then a new building in 1962), founded by Carl Krone (1870–1943). The Circus Knie has become the unofficial Swiss national circus, and responsible for many innovations. The major Russian circus of Tsarist days was Salamonsky's, founded by the German Jew Albert Salamonsky (1839–1913); the building in Moscow which opened in 1880 is still in operation. Ciniselli's was its St Petersburg counterpart. In the Soviet bloc countries the circus was nationalized and heavily subsidized, organized and promoted as a tool of popular enlightenment (such as the Soviet State Circus, the Zentral-Zirkus of the German Democratic Republic).

USA The first American circus performance may be that given by rope dancers in Philadelphia in 1724. A Mr Pool clowned in the first equestrian show in New York, Philadelphia and Boston in 1785. The first true circus was opened in Philadelphia on 9 April 1793 by John Bill Ricketts as a combination of riding academy and show; George Washington was among its patrons. Foreign troupes toured extensively, as did the pioneer companies of James West, Spalding & Rogers, and Van Amburgh, as travelling menageries began to be absorbed into circuses and 'mud shows' by 1824. New York's first circus building, which held 4000 persons, opened in 1826. Native talent, such as the transvestite equestrian Ella Zoyara (Omar Kingsley) and the Shakespearian clown DAN RICE helped to naturalize the form, as did innovations like the circus parade and the SHOWBOAT. The first railway circus to make a transcontinental tour was Dan Costello's in 1868; the last was the Cooper Brothers, which closed in 1936.

P. T. BARNUM entered the circus business in 1871; two years later, W. C. Coup originated the two-ring arrangement in a Barnum show, and in 1881 James Bailey, who had combined with Barnum the previous year, instituted the three-ring circus, over his partner's protestations. The emphasis now fell on spectacle, and intimacy was lost; this gigantism, as well as new methods of publicity and railway transport, were the major American innovations. When Barnum and Bailey's 'Greatest Show on Earth' went abroad in 1898, Europeans were most impressed by the quasi-military organization, the advance troops of press agents, and the whole notion of a gargantuan tenting show. As circuses began to run into competition from WILD WEST EXHIBITIONS, the five German-born Ringling brothers who managed the Forepaugh-Sells show cleaned up the act by banishing midway con-games in an attempt to bring respectability to the sawdust arena. Their sensational pantomimes, performed in Madison Square Garden in imitation of the KIRALFYS, grew to hyperthyroid proportions; their *Cleopatra* required 1500 performers and their 1919 show allowed 12,000 spectators to see seven *manèges* simultaneously in the confines of two and a half acres. Such size naturally shifted the emphasis from clown patter, small-animal training and elegant equestrian pantomime, but made a strong impact on circus management throughout the world.

After a long period of competition, the Ringlings bought Barnum and Bailey's in 1907 and, later, other rivals such as John Robinson, Hagenbeck-Wallace and Sells-Floto, to become the biggest concern in the world. These massive operations with their huge deployment of performers, labourers and animals continued until the Depression. Ringling Brothers was reduced to only two tent circuses, with few baggage horses, parades or railway cars, and finally folded its tents in 1956, a year that also proved disastrous to Clyde Beatty and the King Brothers. Ringling now plays only indoors, with an infusion of show-business glitter, in an attempt to attract audiences weaned on television.

Historically, the appeal of the circus has derived in part from its variety, the romantic aura of its bohemianism, and the fact that it can be appreciated on many levels, from child-like wonder to the perception of a Laszlo Moholy-Nagy who envisaged acrobats as human machinery. It has had a powerful influence on the modern theatre, in reaction against the psychological drama of the late 19th century. The avant-garde was attracted to its physical skills and timing, clown routines, space–time continuum, the reduction of speech to merely one among many means of communication, and the arena itself. Although the circus is the setting for such plays as LEONID ANDREEV's *He Who Gets Slapped*, Marcel Achard's *Voulez-vous jouer avec moâ* [in imitation of an English accent], Pavel Kohout's *August, August, August* and THOMAS BERNHARD's *The Force of Habit*, more significant has been the use of the circus aesthetic in modern staging. OSKAR SCHLEMMER's *Triadic Ballet* (1912) was followed by his invention of the clown Mr Ey as an expression of physical

mechanics (1933–7). As early as 1919, YURY ANNENKOV in Russia staged TOLSTOI's *First Distiller* as a circus show, and GORKY provided a circus scenario in *The Hard-Worker Wordflow* (1920). The experiments of Eisenstein in his 'montage of attractions' and MEYERHOLD in biomechanics were grounded in circus gymnastics. JARRY, GORDON CRAIG, ARTAUD, the futurists (see FUTURISM), and later PETER BROOK with his ingenious *Midsummer Night's Dream*, found inspiration in the circus ring.

One of the liveliest trends in North America during the last generation has been the resurgence of the one-ring show: these include the Royal Liechtenstein Circus, founded in San José, California, in 1971, as a Jesuit ministry; the Pickle Family Circus, founded in San Francisco, 1974; the Big Apple Circus, founded by Paul Binder in New York, 1977, which unifies its acts around a theme or story; and the Cirque du Soleil, founded by the fire-breather Guy Laliberte in Montreal, 1984.   LS

See: D. Amiard-Chevrel (ed.), *Du Cirque au Théâtre*, Lausanne, 1983; G. Bose and E. Brinkmann, *Circus: Geschichte und Aesthetik einer niederen Kunst*, Berlin, 1978; J. Culhane, *The American Circus: An Illustrated History*, New York, 1990; A. Hippisley-Coxe, *A Seat at the Circus*, rev. edn, Hamden, Conn., 1980; M. J. Renevey, *Le Grand Livre du Cirque*, 2 vols., Paris, 1977; G. Speaight, *A History of the Circus*, London, 1980; H. Thétard, *La Merveilleuse Histoire du Cirque*, rev. edn, Paris, 1978; R. Toole-Stott, *Circus and Allied Arts: A World Bibliography*, 5 vols., Derby, 1958–71, Liverpool, 1992.

Cirque Olympique [Théâtre du Châtelet] In 1782 PHILIP ASTLEY established his equestrian amphitheatre in Paris (see HIPPODRAMA). He left France at the Revolution, renting the establishment to Antonio Franconi and his two sons. Dramatic elements crept increasingly into the programmes. In 1798 and 1799 the Franconi troupe was engaged by the Théâtre de la Cité to provide equestrian scenes for pantomimes by J. A. G. Cuvelier. This led to the Franconis adding pantomime material to their own performances, especially after they opened a new CIRCUS at the rue du Monthabor in 1807. They were not subject to the legislation restricting the number of theatres, as they counted as a circus. In fact they increasingly developed the old historical pantomime, now called a *mimodrame* (see MIME), in which they celebrated all the major Napoleonic victories. In 1816 they moved to the more popular Temple suburb and, after a fire in 1826, to the BOULEVARD itself, the new theatre being built largely by popular subscription (with a handsome contribution from the royal family).

The Cirque Olympique was a people's theatre, its dearest seats costing only 2 francs in 1835. It had a large and well equipped stage which communicated with the arena. After the equestrian part of the programme, more spectators came into the arena and an orchestra was pushed out from under the stage. In 1835 the name changed to the Théâtre National du Cirque. The repertoire had become increasingly the sumptuously mounted fairy extravaganza. In 1853 Napoleon III gave it the title of Théâtre Impérial du Cirque, and in 1862, with the demolition of the Boulevard du Temple, the whole establishment moved to a new theatre on the site of the old fortress of the

The Taking of Peking at the Théâtre Impérial du Cirque, 1862. The equestrian melodrama with combats was an important part of the repertoire of the Cirque.

Châtelet. This was the largest theatre of the time, with a stage 35 metres deep, and excellently equipped for spectacular productions. Some lean years followed and the theatre closed in 1869, reopening after the Commune of 1871, when a new management turned essentially to the dramas and MELODRAMAS of the Ambigu. In 1874 another attempt was made to create a popular opera theatre, but audiences were not interested. Finally, the theatre found an appeal with the sensation drama, notably adaptations of Jules Verne's *Around the World in Eighty Days* and *Michel Strogoff.* JMCC

citizen comedy The term used to describe a group of Elizabethan and Jacobean plays whose setting is London and whose characters are predominantly the day-by-day tradesmen of the city. The SATIRE of mercantile values and financial opportunism is, for the most part, good-humoured, but no quarter is given to social overreaching or the pursuit of commercial success by fraud. That is to say that citizen (or 'city') comedy is characteristically moral and determined to castigate whatever or whoever discredits the good name of London. Outstanding examples include DEKKER's *The Shoemaker's Holiday* (1599), *Eastward Ho* (1605) – on which CHAPMAN, JONSON and MARSTON collaborated and which outdoes the two joint works of Dekker and WEBSTER, *Westward Ho* (1604) and *Northward Ho* (1605) – and MIDDLETON's *A Chaste Maid in Cheapside* (1611). The combination of a romantic plot and plain characters was sufficiently familiar by 1607 to provoke the lively mockery of BEAUMONT's *The Knight of the Burning Pestle*, but citizen comedy was both durable and adaptable. It reflected the secure London base of many of the public stage's greatest dramatists. Jonson, too various and too original to be confined within a category, evoked the teeming life of the city in *Epicoene* (1609), *The Alchemist* (1610) and *Bartholomew Fair* (1614). The

increasing tensions of London under the Stuarts, which contributed to the hardening tone and eventual decline of citizen comedy, are well represented by the distance between *Eastward Ho* and MASSINGER's altogether darker version of the same plot in *The City Madam* (c.1632). PT

Citizens' Theatre (Glasgow) Founded in 1943 by JAMES BRIDIE, who aimed at the establishment of a Scottish National Theatre, the Citizens' began operation at the small Athenaeum Theatre but in 1945 transferred to the Royal Princess's Theatre in the Gorbals, where it has since remained. The policy continued to be the presentation of the best of British and European drama and the encouragement of new Scottish playwrights, until 1969 when Giles Havergal was appointed artistic director. Audience numbers had been dwindling and Havergal, together with (from 1970) his co-directors PHILIP PROWSE and Robert David MacDonald, embarked on a radical new policy. Their aim was to find production styles that would make every performance, of whatever type of play, a fresh, eye-opening experience. Design (under Prowse) was accorded a high priority; NATURALISM was shunned; plays as far removed as *Hamlet*, *The Balcony* and MacDonald's *Chinchilla* (about Diaghilev) were invested with an assertively, sometimes outrageously, theatrical style; within ten years the Citizens' became, and has remained, one of the most distinctive of the UK's theatre companies, with an international reputation. AJ

Ciulei, Liviu 1923– Romanian-born director, scene designer, actor, film-maker (with a background in architecture) and seminal figure of the Romanian stage. From 1948 until the 1970s he worked at the Lucia Sturza Bulandra Theatre in Bucharest, after which he took assignments as guest director in Germany, France, Canada, Australia and, finally, the USA. During 1980–6 he was artistic director at the GUTHRIE THEATRE, where his eclectic, idiosyncratic and cerebral productions included *The Tempest*, *Eve of Retirement*, *Peer Gynt*, *The Threepenny Opera*, *A Midsummer Night's Dream* and a stunning *The Bacchae* (1987). Other US credits include Wedekind's *Spring Awakening* and *Hamlet* (1986) at the NEW YORK SHAKESPEARE FESTIVAL (PUBLIC THEATER); *Leonce and Lena* (1974 debut), *Émigrés*, *Hamlet*, *Don Juan*, *The Lower Depths*, Viktor Slavkin's *Cerceau*, *The Time of Your Life*, PIRANDELLO's *It's the Truth (If You Think It Is)* and *Hedda Gabler* (1994) at ARENA STAGE; and *Inspector General* at CIRCLE IN THE SQUARE. In recent years he has directed OPERA throughout the world, and he is currently on New York University's graduate acting faculty. BM DBW

Civic Repertory Theatre (USA) Opened in 1926 by EVA LE GALLIENNE at New York City's 14th Street Theatre with BENAVENTE's *Saturday Night*. Management's progressive ideas for a non-commercial repertory theatre specializing in modern classics and charging low admission was inspired by European subsidized theatres and influenced such American theatres as the THEATRE GUILD and the GROUP THEATRE. CRT boasted an all-female professional staff, promoting, for example, the design talents of ALINE BERNSTEIN and IRENE SHARAFF. Other than modern classics, CRT staged three CHEKHOVS, five IBSENS and two ROSTANDS; premiered three American plays; and introduced GIRAUDOUX, GOLDONI and SUSAN GLASPELL's *Alison's House* to New York – for a largely neighbourhood audience. Throughout 10 seasons and a 37 play repertory CRT was beset by financial difficulties, which forced Le Gallienne to bend her repertory rule and in 1933 to move her adaptation of *Alice in Wonderland* uptown for a long run. Nevertheless CRT disbanded in 1935, as a result of these fiscal problems. EII

Cixous, Hélène 1937– Born into a Jewish family living in Oran, Algeria, Cixous grew up speaking fluent French and German and specialized in English at university. Her North African childhood and polyglot sense of 'otherness' placed her in a powerful position to question white male perspectives on the world.

Her main project has been to develop a specific *écriture féminine* and she now heads a Centre de Recherches et d'Études Féminines in Paris. In the early 1980s she became associated with the THÉÂTRE DU SOLEIL, then performing a cycle of four plays by SHAKESPEARE. The company commissioned her to write two plays inspired by Shakespearian models, one on the history of Cambodia and the other on that of India. The first, *Norodom Sihanouk* (1985), was in two parts, like *Henry IV*, and ran for more than eight hours. The second, *L'Indiade* (1987), was less monumental, but still dealt with a vast swathe of Indian history, from the beginnings of the independence movement to partition. She continues her association with the company, scripting a film for them (*La Nuit miraculeuse*) in 1989, and *La Ville parjure, ou le retour des Erinnyes* in 1994. Before this her one notable success in the theatre had been *Portrait de Dora* (*Portrait of Dora*, 1976) in which she had used the Dora case to question Freud's methods and motives. DB

Claire, Ina [Inez Fagan] ?1892–1985 American actress noted for her insouciant charm and high comedic sense and style. Claire specialized – from her first appearance in a straight play (1917) to her final one (*The Confidential Clerk*, 1954) – in what *Time Magazine* called 'highly varnished comedies of bad manners and good breeding in which the characters misbehave in venomous, perfectly timed epigrams'. HAROLD CLURMAN considered her 'the most brilliant comedienne of our stage' in vehicles such as S. N. BEHRMAN's *Biography* and *End of Summer*. She also had an active career in pre-First World War VAUDEVILLE, the ZIEGFELD *Follies*, silent films and later the talkies. DBW

Clairon, Mlle [Claire-Josèphe-Hippolyte Léris de la Tude] 1723–1803 French actress, considered the finest tragedienne of her age. After a brief engagement as a juvenile at the COMÉDIE-ITALIENNE and some years in provincial theatres, she entered the COMÉDIE-FRANÇAISE as an understudy and made a sensational debut as RACINE's Phèdre in 1743. This youthful success led to a whole series of major tragic roles for which her beautiful voice, graceful figure and range of feeling provided a natural endowment. Later she was persuaded by the critic Marmontel, whose mistress she had become, to moderate the solemn, declamatory style of the day in favour of a simpler, more conversationally direct form of diction, and again at his instance and that of DIDEROT she tempered the worst excesses of fashion and ornament in her stage dress to make room for some sense of propriety and historical period, as did her contemporary LEKAIN for male COSTUME. She was admired by GARRICK and particularly by VOLTAIRE, many of whose tragic heroines she created and in whose private theatre she gave performances during a visit to Ferney in 1765.

In the following year she took a premature retirement, ostensibly on grounds of ill health but also perhaps because of friction with fellow members of the company, thereafter opening a school for young actors and appearing occasionally in private theatricals. Towards the end of her long life she published an interesting autobiographical work, *Mémoires d'Hippolyte Clairon et réflexions sur l'art dramatique* (1799). She died in virtual penury, her theatrical pension having lapsed under the Revolution. DR

Clapp, Henry Austin 1841–1904 American drama critic. Educated at Harvard, Clapp practised law in Boston, pursuing drama criticism as an avocation. He was music and drama critic of the *Boston Daily Advertiser* from 1868 to 1902, and of the *Boston Herald* during 1902–4. An authority on SHAKESPEARE, he was viewed as an erudite, incorruptible and fair critic. His *Reminiscences of a Drama Critic* (1902) provides an overview of late-19th-century Boston theatrical life. TLM

claque Organized band of applauders. Such bands have been known since ancient Greek times; their members would be under the orders of some powerful figure, or were motivated by a common desire to further the interests of some writer, performer or cause. By the 18th century claques organized on a business footing had become established in European theatres, especially in France and Italy. The first three-quarters of the 19th century probably saw the claque at its peak.

Each claque had a leader, sometimes paid by the theatre but sometimes, as at the Paris Opéra, paying the theatre for acknowledging his office. He recruited applauders by distributing free tickets, adding from time to time a free drink and, very rarely, a small amount of cash. The leader was paid by, or extorted payment from, the artists and authors who desired guaranteed public approbation. Some leaders had a list of charges for different lengths and intensities of applause. The kind of reaction required at any given moment was signalled by the leader to his claqueurs. Leaders occupied a prominent position in theatrical circles and the most celebrated took their jobs very seriously, attending rehearsals and discussing both the appropriate moments for applause and the levels at which it should be given. Louis Castel's *Memoirs of a Claqueur* (1829) deals with 'the theory and practice of the art'. Even different ways of using the hands were a matter of concern – e.g. striking both open palms together, bringing the fingers of one hand against the palm of the other, or snapping the fingers.

Claques of unpaid enthusiasts continued to assemble from time to time, but it was the paid claque that persisted with regularity; however, even the paid claque began to disappear after the 19th century, leaving the playhouse before it left the opera house. Whether or not paid claques still operate on at least some occasions in some European theatres is unclear. Those on the outside have no direct evidence. Those on the inside are not forthcoming on the matter. By far the best, and most amusing, account of the modern claque is to be found in *Looking for a Bluebird* (1945) by Joseph Wechsberg. GH

Clark, Bobby 1888–1960 and
Paul McCullough 1883–1936 American comedy team that perfected their raucous, physical style in the CIRCUS and VAUDEVILLE, Clark and McCullough made the transition to musical theatre in a London REVUE, *Chuckles of 1922*. Their first BROADWAY show was *The Music Box Revue 1922–23*, and after other revue appearances they brought their acrobatic antics to a book MUSICAL, *Strike up the Band* (1930). Following McCullough's suicide in 1936, Bobby Clark continued alone, appearing in revues such as *The* ZIEGFELD *Follies of 1936,* musical comedies such as *Mexican Hayride* (1944), revivals of classical comedies such as *Love for Love* (1940) and revivals of OPERETTAS such as *Sweethearts* (1947). His last engagement was in the touring company of *Damn Yankees* (1956). The crouching, scampering Clark, with his painted-on eyeglasses, everpresent cigar and stubby cane, was perfectly matched with the tall, giggling McCullough, the straight man of the act. MK

Clark-Bekederemo, J(ohn) P(epper) [J. P. Clark] 1936– Nigerian playwright, poet, critic and academic. J. P. Clark-Bekederemo was born in Kaigbodo in Ijo country in the Niger Delta. In 1958, as an undergraduate at Ibadan University, he edited the poetry magazine *The Horn*, which created both context and outlet for a new literacy discourse in Nigeria amongst the young Nigerian 'Euromodernists' (as they were later called). After a spell in journalism, Clark-Bekederemo held research fellowships at Princeton and Ibadan. Three early plays in English were widely acclaimed, despite some reservations about their use of a stylized, metrically organized variety of English. The first, *Song of a Goat*, is a tragedy of two brothers, one of whom becomes impotent. His younger brother sleeps with his wife, which results in both men committing suicide. *Masquerade* is the tragedy of the child of that wife's coupling with the husband's brother. *The Raft*, the third play, is a quasi-existentialist work about four men adrift on the Niger on a lumber raft; like *Song of a Goat*, it has been widely produced (all published 1964).

Clark-Bekederemo has continued to publish poetry, with a collection on the Nigerian civil war arousing fierce controversy (*Casualties*, 1970). His reputation for outspoken social criticism was confirmed by his account of his visit to the USA in *America, Their America* (1964). His years as an academic were marked by his creative and scholarly work on the monumental Ijo saga of *Ozidi*, a substantial piece of sustained research into the traditional antecedents for Nigerian theatre. This resulted in his own English-language play, *Ozidi* (1966), and a transcribed version of the full saga (1977). In 1980 he resigned his Chair of English at Lagos University, and in 1982 he founded with Ebun Odutola Clark the Pec Repertory Theatre in Lagos. This is a commercial venture committed to the professional presentation of outstanding African plays in English before a subscription audience and, through this initiative, to the creation of a theatre industry in Nigeria. Since the early 1990s the repertory theatre has been leased to other performing companies, such as that run by Chuck Mike.

Amongst Clark-Bekederemo's more recent plays are *The Wives' Revolt* (1985) and *The Bikoroa Plays* (1981; published 1985). The action of the *Bikoroa* trilogy extends from the beginning to the close of the colonial period. Essentially a domestic chronicle, set in the Niger Delta, it offers oblique insights into Nigeria's social and political history. CD

Clarke, Austin (Augustine Joseph) 1896–1974 Irish playwright, educated at University College, Dublin. A major poet, realizing his full strengths in later life, Clarke was much under the shadow of YEATS, whose ideals for verse drama fascinated him. In 1940 Clarke founded the Dublin Verse-Speaking Society, giving readings on Radio Eireann and three drama seasons (1941–3) at the Peacock. His Lyric Theatre Company presented biannual evenings (1944–51) at the ABBEY, putting on nine of Clarke's plays, reviving FITZMAURICE, and giving the first performances of Yeats's *The Death of Cuchulain* and *The Herne's Egg*.

Clarke's plays, set mostly in the 6th–12th centuries, turn, sometimes comically, on the nature of faith, on medieval and modern Catholicism, to the latter's disadvantage: *The Flame* (1930), *Black Fast* (1941), *The Moment Next to Nothing* (1953). They constitute another brave but unavailing attempt to bring verse to the 20th-century stage. DM

Clarke, John Sleeper 1833–99 American actor and theatre manager, who made his professional stage debut in

1851 at Boston's Howard Athenaeum as Frank Hardy in *Paul Pry*. A friend of EDWIN BOOTH since childhood, Clarke married Booth's sister Asia in 1859. He was a popular, skilful comedian, highly regarded for his portrayal of eccentric characters like Major Wellington De Boots in Joseph S. Coyne's *A Widow Hunt*, Dr Pangloss and Zekiel Homespun in COLMAN THE YOUNGER'S *The Heir at Law*, and Bob Acres in SHERIDAN'S *The Rivals*. In the 1860s Clarke was associated with Booth in the management of several theatres, including Philadelphia's WALNUT STREET THEATRE, the BOSTON THEATRE and the WINTER GARDEN. In 1867 he emigrated to England, where he remained for the rest of his life, except for occasional starring tours to America. At various times he successfully managed several English theatres including the HAYMARKET, the Charing Cross (Toole's) and, for over a decade (From 1883), the Strand. His sons Creston Clarke (1865–1910) and Wilfred Booth Clarke (1867–1945) also had relatively successful careers in theatre.   DJW

Clarke, Martha 1944– Baltimore-born American experimental theatre director and choreographer. Clarke studied dance as a child and at Juilliard with Louis Horst and choreographers Anthony Tudor and Anna Sokolow, whose company she joined (1965–7). She co-founded Pilobolus (1972–8) and Crowsnest dance companies (1978). *Nocturne* (1978) and *Portraits* (1979) were early sketches that evolved into large-scale productions, *The Garden of Earthly Delights* (1984, inspired by Hieronymus Bosch's painting), *Vienna Lusthaus* (1986, inspired by Egon Schiele's watercolours of women) and *Endangered Species* (1990, based on Toulouse-Lautrec's circus pastels, the American Civil War and the Holocaust). Clarke explores the grotesque body, archetypical and psychological preoccupations with forbidden pleasures, and the loss of innocence. Influenced by Martha Graham's modern dance style and 1960s theatre of the body (GROTOWSKI, the LIVING THEATER), her work also shares an affinity with Pina Bausch's Tanztheater and ROBERT WILSON's Theatre of Images.   AF

Claudel, Paul 1868–1955 French poet, diplomat and playwright; the most important French dramatist of the last 100 years. A more unlikely figure for this stature is hard to imagine. Claudel was authoritarian, pious, secretive, and wanted to be a priest not a writer. When he was turned down by the Church he joined the diplomatic service, spending time in the Far East and experiencing an unhappy love affair that was to form the basis of *Partage de midi* (*Break of Noon*, written 1905). His experience of Eastern theatre and his interest in ancient Greek theatre (he made a fine translation of the *Oresteia*; see GREECE, ANCIENT) helped him to develop a dramatic style of great theatrical resourcefulness and flexibility.

At first influenced by SYMBOLISM, he wrote his plays in three creative bursts. The first, between about 1895 and 1905, includes *Tête d'or* (*Golden Head*, 1889), *La Ville* (*The Town*, 1890), *L'Échange* (*The Exchange*, 1893), *Partage de midi* and *La Jeune Fille Violaine* (*The Young Girl Violaine*, 1892), later to become *L'Annonce faite à Marie* (*The Tidings Brought to Mary*). This was the first of his plays to be staged (directed by LUGNÉ-POE, 1912). The second is a

trilogy – *L'Otage* (*The Hostage*, 1909), *Le Pain dur* (*Hard Bread*, 1914) and *Le Père humilié* (*The Humiliated Father*, 1916). And the third is *Le Soulier de satin* (*The Satin Slipper*, 1924). They all rely for their power partly on Claudel's peculiar verse style. This is quite unlike anything before it in the French tradition, being based on the breath group, not on the number of feet in a line. Written for declamation, his verse nevertheless has a variety and subtlety that can fairly be compared with Shakespearian blank verse.

Claudel admired the Spanish GOLDEN AGE and many of his plays deal with the discovery of the New World, but material confines can only restrict his ambitious characters, who constantly yearn for other, wider worlds of the spirit. By picking subjects and characters of the Renaissance period, Claudel managed the improbable task of welding together elements of medieval mysticism, Renaissance optimism and modernist anguish. His most ambitious, and perhaps his theatrically most successful play, *Le Soulier de satin*, includes a presenter figure whose linking commentary enables Claudel to achieve a striking alienation effect and also ties together the disparate elements of the play. These range from high TRAGEDY to low FARCE, from soul-searching monologue to animated dialogue, and include song, dance and MIME. The play was thought unproducible because written at inordinate length and divided into four 'days'. But in 1942 the young BARRAULT persuaded Claudel to cut and rewrite his text for stage presentation and this production (COMÉDIE-FRANÇAISE, 1943) was a triumph. Claudel's work became one of the mainstays of Barrault's career as a director. Works written at the beginning of the century gradually took on a new life as their theatrical power was released in Barrault's productions. These included *Partage de midi* (1948), *L'Échange* (1951), *Christophe Colomb* (1953), *Tête d'or* (1968). The new generation of directors have made their own reinterpretations e.g. – Jorge Lavelli, *L'Échange* (1967); VITEZ, *Partage de midi* (1976), *L'Échange* (1976), *Le Soulier de satin* (1987); and Gildas Bourdet, *Le Pain dur* (1984).   DB

Claus, Hugo 1929– Distinguished Flemish playwright, novelist, translator and director of the postwar generation. His plays, written in Dutch, focus on themes such as loneliness, the purity of childhood in a corrupt world, love between brother and sister, and the Oedipus complex. The action is frequently of a RITUAL nature. As a result, his plays rise above their Flemish settings. In particular, *Bruid in de morgen* (*Bride in the Morning*, 1953), *Suiker* (*Sugar*, 1958), depicting the tough life of seasonal labourers in France, and *Vrijdag* (*Friday*, 1969) have established Claus's reputation as a playwright. He directed the film version of *Vrijdag* himself. This story of the home coming of a prisoner who, having been released from gaol, hears his wife confess that she has given birth to a child after an affair with a neighbour, is presented soberly, almost as a factual account.

Claus has adapted several classical plays, e.g. SENECA's *Thyestes* (1966), Sophocles' *Oedipus at Colonus* (1986) and *Phaedra* (1980); JONSON's *Volpone*, as *De vossenjacht* (*The Fox Hunting*, 1972); and DE ROJAS's *La Celestina* as *De spaanse hoer* (*The Spanish Whore*, 1970). Many of his plays have been translated and are performed all over the world. HS MG

Cleveland Play House (Cleveland, Ohio, USA) In 1915 Raymond O'Neil, a Cleveland journalist, founded a small amateur theatre group for the production of native plays. Out of it grew the Cleveland Play House, now the oldest producing regional theatre in America. In 1921, Frederic McConnell took over the amateur company and transformed it into a professional organization. Six years later, the company moved into its complex of two theatres, the 500-seat Drury and the 160-seat Brooks, plus offices and workrooms. When McConnell retired in 1958, he was succeeded by K. Elmo Lowe; then Richard Oberlin; in 1988, Josephine Abady, until the 1993–4 season; and Peter Hackett in late 1994. In 1983 the 625-seat Bolton was added to the complex. The theatre maintains its policy of presenting classics, contemporary and new plays, and MUSICALS. MCH

Clive, Kitty 1711–85 English actress. Her debut in 1728 quickly led to success, particularly as a wry actress and singer in COMEDY, BURLESQUE and BALLAD OPERA. She was briefly married in 1732 to a lawyer. She performed at DRURY LANE until 1769, apart from a brief spell at COVENT GARDEN in the 1740s, enjoying a high reputation in spite of her long-running battles with GARRICK over her choice of parts. Her performance as Portia in *The Merchant of Venice* was often attacked for its high comedy and its mimicry of contemporary lawyers, but it was a popular success. Her long friendship with Horace Walpole led to her moving into a cottage near his home at Strawberry Hill in 1754; it became known as Cliveden (Clive's den). She retired there in 1769. PH

Close, Glenn 1947– American actress, who in only a decade established herself as one of the most respected of her generation. Though best known for films such as *The Big Chill, Fatal Attraction* and *Hamlet,* she is a versatile stage performer as well, noted for her 'charged stillness'. Her BROADWAY debut – Angelica in a revival of CONGREVE's *Love for Love* (1974) – was followed by a series of major roles in regional theatres, OFF-BROADWAY appearances (including WENDY WASSERSTEIN's *Uncommon Women and Others* and an Obie-winning performance in Simone Benmussa's *The Singular Life of Albert Nobbs* at the MANHATTAN THEATRE CLUB), and various Broadway appearances, including *The Crucifer of Blood* (1978), the MUSICAL *Barnum* (1980) and Annie in the American premiere of STOPPARD's *The Real Thing* (1984), for which she won a Tony – an honour repeated in the spring of 1992 in MIKE NICHOLS's production of *Death and the Maiden* by Ariel Dorfman. In 1993–4 she appeared as Norma Desmond in LLOYD WEBBER's *Sunset Boulevard* (Los Angeles, late 1993, and Broadway, autumn 1994). DBW

closure of the theatres In England in 1642, a parliamentary ordinance signalling the imminent triumph of Puritan forces commanded the closure of all theatres. Although occasional surreptitious performances continued during the Interregnum and although Cromwell licensed certain private entertainments and approved

school plays, the ordinance was surprisingly effective. It brought a great age of English drama to an end. PT

clown The distinction between a clown and a comedian, said 'the Perfect Fool' ED WYNN, is that the former does funny things, the latter does things funny. According to the social psychologist William McDougall, there are six primary components to clowning: the fall (slipping and sliding); the blow (slaps, custard pies); surprise (incongruity between what is expected and what happens); harmless and childish naughtiness; mimicry, usually with an element of PARODY; and stupidity which can turn out to be cleverness. This last trait may be the most basic, a false contrast: the clown's assumed clumsiness is revealed to be true virtuosity, his naïvety to be wisdom, his hilarity to be sorrow disguised. The mythic dimension of the clown may derive from this tension.

Some scholars have seen the clown's archetype in the arch-trickster of Native American cults, who possessed fertility and healing powers. Others have identified it with a wonder-working but diabolic opponent to the divine Establishment, like Lucifer. There are no clowns in the Hindu epic the *Mahabharata*, but its stage version features Vedusaka, a bald dwarf with fangs and drooping limbs who speaks Prakrit, the language of women and low castes; he is teamed with Vita, a parasitic slyboots. This yoking of the dim-witted fallguy and the scheming conniver is constant in clowning: in China the contrast is between Wu Ch'ou and Wen Ch'ou, in Renaissance Italy between the two ZANNI Arlecchino and Brighella. Clownish types also appear in the ithyphallic satyr choruses of classical Greek drama (see GREECE, ANCIENT) and in the phlyakes comedies of southern Italy in the 3rd century BC, and become discriminated in the Atellan farces into the pop-eyed boaster Bucco, the awkward Maccus and the hunchbacked Dossenus, and the Stupidus of the *ludi scenici*. In Roman comedy, the comic figure is usually the slave, for the clown is commonly in an underdog position, working within and hence against his social context.

This anti-social aspect was confirmed by medieval distrust of the itinerant entertainer (see MEDIEVAL THEATRE IN EUROPE). A Saxon law governing municipal outskirts declared that 'players and minstrels are not people like other men, for they have only the appearance of mankind and are almost akin to the dead'. Clowns became the symbol of a lack, an absent quality, which enabled them to perform as 'constructive anarchists', and through their garish make-up and outlandish costume to assert that they are of another world. Typically, the clown of the miracle and MYSTERY PLAYS was a devil, and in the MORALITY PLAYS, the eloquently named Vice, obtuse and buffeted, with his sword of lath. The first named German clown is Rubin, zany to the mountebank of the medieval PASSION PLAY; this function as stooge to a quack descends through the merry andrew and TABARIN to HARPO MARX and Lou Costello.

In the German *FASTNACHTSPIEL* the low comic is usually a peasant. Indeed, the English word 'clown' first meant a country clotpoll, and this booby begins to be polished by the professionals of SHAKESPEARE's day, THOMAS HEYWOOD, RICHARD TARLTON and WILL KEMPE. The Shakespearian comic is multiform: in *As You Like It* he runs the gamut from the thick ploughboy William to the professional jester Touchstone to the moody philosopher Jaques. (The jester or fool, native to courts, was distinctly not a clown in the modern sense; his comedy was more consciously verbal and ambiguous, and he has been seen by modern critics as the ancestor of the dandy and the art of high camp.)

The Elizabethan clown was conveyed to Europe by the English Comedians (see ENGLISCHE KOMÖDIANTEN). Robert Reynolds introduced Pickelhering (pickled herring) c.1618; his bizarre costume, grotesque MASK and movements were comic exaggerations of reality. Naturalized in Germany, he not only amused the audience and acted as a bridge between it and a play's action, but enlarged the scope of the pompous tragedies in which he appeared. Other clowns spawned by the English Comedians include John Posset (Jean Bouschet) invented by Sackville of the Brown troupe, who spoke a macaronic medley of broken German, witty English and Dutch; and Hans Stockfisch, created by Spencer at Dresden (1617).

The Italian COMMEDIA DELL'ARTE was immensely influential in disseminating its types – the zanni, the Dottore, Pantalone, the Spanish Captain – throughout Europe; but over time these types became submerged into complex dramatic characters with broader dimensions. MOLIÈRE, for example, transforms Mascarille, Sganarelle and Scapin from masked clichés to recognizable human beings with individuated psychologies. Only Arlecchino as Arlequin and HARLEQUIN managed to retain a being independent of the plot requirements; but even his diabolical vestiges began to be domesticated in the 18th century, in the fêtes galantes of MARIVAUX and Watteau and the more sophisticated figures of Figaro and Papageno. He was also gradually edged out by the melancholy PIERROT, created c.1682 by G. B. Giaratoni as a foil to the turbulent Arlequin. This pale-faced etiolation of Pedrolino evolved into the elegant white clown of the European circus.

As romantic and, later, realistic drama insisted on integrating the clown into a recognizable social entity (GOETHE's Mephistopheles may be seen as one surviving avatar of the Vice figure), he found a refuge in PANTOMIME and then CIRCUS. JOSEPH GRIMALDI established the type of the Joey, greedy, amoral, gloating over his triumphs and cringing at his defeats; henceforth the clown of the harlequinade would wear tufts and frills, brandish a red-hot poker, and butter slides for policemen. Successors to Grimaldi, like Tom Matthews and 'Whimsical Walker', embellished but did not substantially alter this outline, until MUSIC-HALL comedians like DAN LENO assumed their function in the spectacular pantos of the 1880s and 1890s; then the clown was relegated to the vestigial harlequinade, and the comedian, in dame or villain role, reigned supreme.

The circus clown has also gone through several stages. In England he resembled the Grimaldi type, trading crosstalk with the ringmaster. On the Continent, under AURIOL's influence, he dressed as a jester and specialized in ACROBATICS; this culminated in the 1870s in the knockabout pantos of the HANLON-LEES and the Byrne Brothers. The Shakespearian clown, exemplified in England by William Wallett and in America by DAN RICE, was possible only in a one-ring circus, exchanging puns and patter with the audience, and mangling hackneyed quotations from the Bard. Around 1869, according to tradition, Tom Belling (1834–1900) created the Dumme August at the Zirkus Renz in Berlin, by making an impromptu appearance in a ringmaster's outfit and fright-wig; this radical innovation expanded the usual clown–ringmaster duet to a trio. (The invention was also claimed by Chadwick (d.1889)). The term august, signifying a stupid, grotesque clown, first occurs at the Cirque Franconi in 1877; it never caught on in English (the American Bozo is analogous).

Clown teams dominated the latter half of the 19th century: the exchange of slaps between FOOTTIT AND CHOCOLAT, or the Price Brothers' 'Evening at Maxim's', with its demolition of a private room at a restaurant, injected social SATIRE into the ring. Dan Rice had dabbled in political commentary; this factor became dominant in pre-revolutionary Russia with the DUROV brothers and was carried on, in a carefully monitored form, under the Soviets (VITALY LAZARENKO, ARKADI RAIKIN). Harsh economic conditions, such as the American slump of the 1890s, spawned tramp clowns, like VAUDEVILLE's Nat Wills and the trick cyclist Joe Jackson; but they did not invade the circus until the Great Depression, when Otto Griebling with his rickety barrel organ and Emmett Kelly with his pathetic broom made their debut.

Although there was a recrudescence of genius in musichall clowning with GROCK, the FRATELLINI and CHARLIE RIVEL, many of the clown's prerogatives were usurped by the silent film comics; circuses became overrun with Chaplin imitators. Contemporary clowns perform very much in the shadow of their illustrious forebears. Barring such exceptions as JANGO EDWARDS who added a drug-culture anarchy to the tradition, and Coluche (Michel Colucci) who enlarged the clown's sphere of action by running for the French presidency in 1981, the clown today has become a hackneyed subject for Sunday painters, a huckster for hamburgers and cereal (not unlike the merry andrew who pitched for mountebanks), a filler between circus acts rather than a number in himself. In the USA, however, the so-called 'new vaudeville' has provided performance artists like BILL IRWIN and Avner the Eccentric with a chance to revive the clown as an eloquent mediator between age-old techniques and post-modern aesthetics. The resurgence of the one-ring circus in North America has also facilitated the merging of the clown with the performance artist: among others, Geoff Hoyle as Mr Sniff at the Pickle Family Circus in San Francisco, and Barry Lubin as Grandma at the Big Apple Circus in New York, have recovered the intimacy and detailed characterization of their forebears.

The modern theatre has drawn deeply on the clown tradition, transmuting him into characters like BRECHT's Arturo Ui, Schweyk and Puntila, or absorbing his techniques, as DARIO FO has done. Germany, in particular, has been fascinated by the clown as a political symbol, and he is used by such playwrights as WEDEKIND, HANDKE, PETER WEISS and HEINER MÜLLER; but the clown also informed the plays of MAYAKOVSKY, BECKETT and IONESCO, and the productions of the Brazilian AUGUSTO BOAL. LS

See: J. Fabbri and A. Sallée (eds), Clowns et Farceurs, Paris, 1982; P.-R. Levy, Les Clowns et la tradition clownesque, Sorvilier, 1991; T. Rémy, Les Clowns, Paris, 1945; J. Schechter, Durov's Pig: Clowns, Politics and Theatre,

New York, 1985; G. Speaight, *The Book of Clowns*, London, 1980; J. H. Towson, *Clowns*, New York, 1976; C. von Barloewen, *Clown*, Frankfurt, 1984.

Clun, Walter d.1664 English actor who began as a boy in women's parts and became a leading member of KILLIGREW's company after the Restoration of Charles II. Much admired by PEPYS, Clun played the lead in the opening production of the new playhouse in DRURY LANE in 1663. The following year he was attacked and robbed in Kentish Town, London, where he bled to death in a ditch.   PT

Clunes, Alec [Alexander S. de Moro] 1912–70 British actor, director and theatre manager, who ran London's ARTS THEATRE for eight influential seasons from 1942 to 1950. Clunes was born into a theatre family and became a professional actor when he joined BEN GREET's company in 1934. He was never a major star, but he played a variety of roles at the OLD VIC and at the Malvern Festival; in the 1950s he joined the Shakespeare Memorial Theatre at Stratford, where he was Claudius to PAUL SCOFIELD's Hamlet in 1955. His last acting appearance came in HOCHHUTH's *Soldiers* in 1968. His main achievement, however, began during the war years when he ran an ambitious and intellectually demanding repertory at the tiny Arts Theatre in the heart of London's WEST END. In addition to pioneering the work of such writers as CHRISTOPHER FRY, and creating the part of Thomas in *The Lady's Not for Burning* (1948), he unearthed forgotten English classics and searched for plays from abroad.   JE

Clurman, Harold 1901–80 American director, critic, author and teacher, who left his mark on the American theatre as founder of the GROUP THEATRE (1931–40). In 25 midnight sessions with New York actors and directors he 'talked the Group into existence', becoming its inspirational leader and one of its principal directors. He nurtured the talents of CLIFFORD ODETS and directed five of his plays: *Awake and Sing!* (1935), *Paradise Lost* (1935), *Golden Boy* (1937), *Rocket to the Moon* (1938) and *Night Music* (1940). He also directed Irwin Shaw's *The Gentle People* (1939) and wrote *The Fervent Years* (1945), a history of the Group. After the Group's demise Clurman continued directing: *The Member of the Wedding* (1950), *The Autumn Garden* (1951), *Bus Stop* (1955), *The Waltz of the Toreadors* (1957), *Incident at Vichy* (1965, in Tokyo), *Long Day's Journey into Night* (1965) and *The Iceman Cometh* (1968).

He was theatre critic for the *New Republic* (1949–52), the *Nation* (1953–80) and the London *Observer* (1955–63). He also assembled three volumes of essays: *Lies Like Truths* (1958), *The Naked Image* (1966) and *The Divine Pastime* (1974), and wrote *On Directing* (1968), *Ibsen* (1977) and *All People Are Famous* (1974), the last in lieu of an autobiography. In addition, he was a professor at Hunter College, City University of New York (1964–80).

Born in New York, he was 'reborn in Paris in the 20s' (his words), and became a playreader for the THEATRE GUILD (1929–31). Among his awards, which included the Donaldson, the GEORGE JEAN NATHAN and four honorary doctorates, he was proudest of La Croix du Chevalier de la Légion d'Honneur.   RM

Coburn, Charles Douville 1877–1961 American actor and manager, remembered for his films, who with his wife, Ivah Wills, founded the Coburn Shakespearean Players (1906), touring major Shakespearian plays and other classics. Additional stage appearances included *The Better 'Ole* (1918), *The Yellow Jacket* (1921, 1926), *So This Is London* (1922), *The Farmer's Wife* (1924), *Trelawny of the Wells* (1925, all-star revival), *Diplomacy* (1928) and *Three Wise Fools* (1936). The Coburns helped to found the Mohawk Drama Festival (1934) at Union College, Schenectady, New York, performing there in the summers. He retired from the stage in 1937 on his wife's death, returning to play Falstaff in *The Merry Wives of Windsor* for the THEATRE GUILD in 1946, his final appearance on the BROADWAY stage.   DBW

Cochran, C(harles) B(lake) 1872–1951 The leading English showman of his time, whose enterprises ranged from roller-skating competitions to ballet. He began in the USA as an actor and then secretary to RICHARD MANSFIELD; his first production was IBSEN's *John Gabriel Borkman* (New York, 1897). He returned to London in 1902. His taste was eclectic and not invariably tied to profit: he was capable of booking REINHARDT's *The Miracle* into the London Olympia in 1911, and then housing Hagenbeck's circus there. From 1914 he was distinguished as a producer of smart REVUES: *Odds and Ends* (1914), *Pell Mell* (1916), *As You Were* (1918), *London, Paris and New York* (1920), among others. More highbrow efforts, including the first London showing of an O'NEILL play (*Anna Christie*, 1925), led to bankruptcy, but he recouped his fortunes by collaborating with NOËL COWARD and producing *On with the Show* (1925), *This Year of Grace* (1928), *Bitter Sweet* (1929), *Private Lives* (1930), *Cavalcade* (1931), *Words and Music* (1932) and *Conversation Piece* (1934). After the war, he seemed incapable of tapping into the new public taste. He published volumes of memoirs in 1925, 32, 41 and 45, the best being the first, *The Secrets of a Showman*. In 1973 a MUSICAL COMEDY based on his career, *Cockie*, by Peter Saunders, opened at the Vaudeville Theatre, London.   LS

Cockaigne Land of idleness and luxury known in Europe under various names (Cocagne, Cuccagna, Schlarrafenland, Lubberland, the Land of Prester John) since the 14th century. This popular utopia, in which houses are thatched with pancakes, people are paid for sleeping, and pigs run around with forks stuck in them looking for diners, is an important theme of European folk drama and CARNIVAL.   AEG

Cockpit-in-Court (London) Built in the Palace of Whitehall for the entertainment of Henry VIII and his Court, the royal cockpit was, from time to time, adapted to accommodate plays. Few records survive, though it can be reasonably surmised that the King's Men staged *The Merry Devil of Edmonton* there in 1618, shortly after CHRISTOPHER BEESTON had successfully converted the public COCKPIT THEATRE in Drury Lane. Beeston's attractive little theatre may have encouraged Charles I to undertake a similar permanent conversion in his own artistic Court. As Surveyor-General of the King's Works, INIGO JONES undertook the work, which was completed in 1629–30. His drawings of a ground plan and an elevation, extant in Worcester College, Oxford, have recently been identified. They give us clearer information about this intimate theatre than we have about any other pre-Restoration theatre. An octagonal auditorium with tiers of seats and an upper gallery was set within a 58ft-square frame. The semicircular stage had five entrance doors and was 36ft wide at the front. Only from the royal box was there a central view across the stage to the large central arch of the *scaenae frons*. Even the placement of the candelabra (ten small and two large on stage) is known. What is not known is the repertoire nor the frequency of performances. Charles I would have wished to give pride of place to the King's Men in a theatre readily comparable to their own BLACKFRIARS, but it is unlikely that they were the only users. Unused during the Interregnum, the Cockpit-in-Court was never again more than sporadically a playhouse. PT

Cockpit Theatre (London) Built in Drury Lane in 1609 to house the popular 'game' of cockfighting, this small (c.50ft square) tiered house was permanently converted for the performance of plays by CHRISTOPHER BEESTON in 1616. He renamed it the Phoenix, intending it as the indoor theatre of Queen Anne's Men during their popular tenure of the outdoor RED BULL. Beeston retained the management until his death in 1639, employing and dispensing with several companies, the last of which, nicknamed Beeston's Boys, was inherited by his son William. When the younger Beeston's choice of plays offended the Court, DAVENANT replaced him as manager. The Cockpit's irregular use for surreptitious performance during the Interregnum led to a raid by Commonwealth soldiers in 1649. More important to the future of English theatre (and OPERA) was the licensed staging by Davenant of two musical spectacles, *The Cruelty of the Spaniards in Peru* (1658) and *Sir Francis Drake* (1659). After the Restoration, the Cockpit was quickly returned to regular use until the establishment of the Patent companies disenfranchised it. There is no record of performances there after 1665. PT

Cocteau, Jean 1889–1963 French poet, novelist, essayist, cineast and playwright. Cocteau was at his best when indulging his highly developed sense of playfulness, well exemplified in the visual puns and gentle SATIRE of *Parade* (1917), *Le Boeuf sur le toit* (*The Ox on the Roof*, 1920) and *Les Mariés de la Tour Eiffel* (*The Eiffel Tower Wedding Party*, 1921). These were ballets or MIME dramas written in collaboration with such luminaries as PICASSO, Satie and Milhaud and were successful, especially with fashionable high society. Plays based on ancient Greek models – *Antigone*, directed by DULLIN, 1922; *Orphée* (*Orpheus*), directed by GEORGES PITOËFF, 1926; *La Machine infernale* (*The Infernal Machine*), directed by JOUVET, 1934 – were very uneven, ostensibly seeking to develop a modern form of tragedy but in reality coming perilously close to PARODY. *Les Parents terribles* (*Intimate Relations*, 1938) was a more vigorous, realistic tragedy of modern family life. It had the distinction of being banned under the Occupation as prejudicial to morality and public order. His later plays were weak, wordy and unoriginal: *Chevaliers de la Table Ronde* (*Knights of the Round Table*, 1937), an Arthurian fantasy; *Les Monstres sacrés* (*The Sacred Monsters*, 1940), a techni-

cal MELODRAMA; *La Machine à Écrire* (*The Typewriter*, 1941), a thriller; *Renaud et Armide* (1943), a neoclassical fairy tale; *L'Aigle à deux têtes* (*The Eagle with Two Heads*, 1946), a neo-romantic love story; and *Bacchus* (1951), a sub-SARTREAN philosophical drama.

His real genius was for the cinema, where his gift for organizing brilliant visual images was able to develop its full potential. His first full-length feature was *La Belle et la bête* (*Beauty and the Beast*, 1945), followed by *Orphée* (1950) and *Le Testament d'Orphée* (1960). DB

Codron, Michael (Victor) 1930– British producer, whose adventurous promotion of new playwrights during the 1960s transformed the WEST END. His first London venture came in 1957, when he took a college REVUE, *Share My Lettuce*, from Cambridge to London, recasting it to include the then unknown actors, MAGGIE SMITH and Kenneth Williams. In 1958 he staged the first plays of JOHN MORTIMER (*The Dock Brief* and *Shall We Tell Caroline?*) and HAROLD PINTER's *The Birthday Party*, which ran for less than a week at the LYRIC THEATRE, HAMMERSMITH. Codron retained his faith in Pinter and in 1960 produced *The Caretaker* at the ARTS THEATRE Club, which transferred to the West End and was recognized as one of the finest plays of its time. Other dramatists whose careers began with Codron productions include HENRY LIVINGS, Charles Dyer, ALAN AYCKBOURN, JAMES SAUNDERS, CHARLES WOOD, FRANK MARCUS, JOE ORTON, DAVID HALLIWELL and SIMON GRAY, and he also enabled writers like DAVID MERCER and CHRISTOPHER HAMPTON to see their plays transferred from smaller subsidized theatres to the West End.

Codron rarely produced musicals, and for much of his career he had no particular theatre with which he was associated. By the end of the 1960s the West End contained a range of drama that could barely have been conceived when the decade began, and Codron had led the way among the younger impresarios. He sat on advisory and governing boards in the subsidized sector, forming long-standing associations with HAMPSTEAD THEATRE, the English Stage Company and other managements. In the 1980s he became co-owner of the Vaudeville Theatre in London, where he produced MICHAEL FRAYN's award-winning play, *Benefactors* (1984). He has since moved his offices to the Aldwych Theatre, where his policy of intelligent, non-musical and usually new plays in well staged productions continues. He produced STOPPARD's *Hapgood* (1988), Ayckbourn's *Henceforward* (1988), *The Revengers' Comedies* (1991) and Frayn's *Look, Look* (1990) – safe middle-brow productions, perhaps, but he also helped to produce MARTIN CRIMP's *Dealing with Clair* (1988) and JIM CARTWRIGHT's *Rise and Fall of Little Voice* (1992). JE

Cody, (William Frederick) Buffalo Bill 1846–1917 American (Iowa-born) Western scout, who parlayed his notoriety into success as actor and showman. Buffalo Bill Cody personified the excitement of the American FRONTIER in the second half of the 19th century. Publicity gilded his accomplishments, but the stories had some factual basis. His nickname came from a job supplying buffalo meat for railway workers. Cody gained attention after the Civil War as scout for Generals George Custer and Philip

Sheridan. Ned Buntline (E. Z. C. Judson) glamorized his exploits in a serial in December 1869, and in November 1872 John B. Studley enacted him in a play in New York. The immense popularity of plays about Buffalo Bill persuaded Cody to take the stage himself in Buntline's *The Scouts of the Prairie*, on 18 December 1872 in Chicago. Audiences tolerated the weak play and Cody's amateurish acting to glimpse the hero with the beard, moustache and flowing hair. For the next 10 years he cultivated a striking stage presence as he played himself in action-filled melodramas.

Between seasons Cody scouted for the Army and arranged hunting parties and entertainments for influential businessmen and European aristocrats. In 1883 he and sharpshooter William F. Carver presented an outdoor WILD WEST EXHIBITION. Problems undermined the partnership, and Nate Salsbury soon replaced Carver. The Wild West enjoyed phenomenal popularity in America and Europe, but financial setbacks rendered Cody a victim of his success. For 34 years, right up to his death, Buffalo Bill rode out to shoot glass balls and entertain audiences, playing successive farewell tours to pay his bills. Although a 20th-century perspective has altered the perception of Cody's border exploits, his stature as the man who brought the frontier to life for generations of Americans is undeniable. RAH

Coe, Richard (Livingston) 1916– American drama critic. Born in New York and educated at George Washington University, Coe served as assistant drama and film critic for the *Washington Post* during 1938–42. After military service in the Middle East, he returned to the *Post* in 1946 as its principal critic, a position he held until his semi-retirement in 1979. Coe has been regarded as one of the most perceptive, impartial and supportive critics of the American stage. He was named Critic of the Year in 1963 by the Directors' Guild of America. TLM

Coghlan, Charles 1842–99 British-born actor who, after several successes in London, was taken to New York in 1876 by AUGUSTIN DALY. At the FIFTH AVENUE THEATRE he became a favourite in leading roles such as Alfred Evelyn in BULWER LYTTON's *Money* and Orlando to FANNY DAVENPORT's Rosalind. Subsequent seasons found him at the Union Square Theatre, WALLACK's and in England again. In 1897 he created the part of Alex opposite MINNIE MADDERN FISKE's Tess. He joined his sister, ROSE, on several of her tours; together they were outstanding in SHERIDAN's comedies. Coghlan died in Galveston, Texas, on tour in his own play, *The Royal Box*. DBW

Coghlan, Rose ?1850/3–1932 British-born actress, whose debut as a child was as one of the witches in a Scottish production of *Macbeth*. Her first New York appearance was in 1872 at WALLACK's THEATRE, where she would reign as leading lady during the 1880s. Her Lady Teazle and Rosalind were declared 'unsurpassed' on the American stage. During the 1890s and 1900s she appeared principally in London, including starring in the first production of WILDE's *A Woman of No Importance* (1893); after a 1907 US tour in SHAW's *Mrs Warren's Profession*, she divided her time between New York and London. At her retirement in 1921 she had completed a stage career of more than 52 years. DBW

Cohan [Keohane]**, George M(ichael)** 1878–1942 American performer, playwright, director and producer who was born in Providence, Rhode Island, while his parents were touring in VAUDEVILLE. He first appeared on stage as a child with his family's vaudeville team, the 'Four Cohans', and by 15 was writing material for their act. His New York debut came in 1901 with his first full-length play, *The Governor's Son*. In 1904 he formed a producing partnership with SAM H. HARRIS, which lasted until 1920. In 1911 he opened his George M. Cohan Theatre on BROADWAY (razed in 1938). Outstanding among the 50-odd plays and MUSICALS credited to him are *Little Johnny Jones* (1904) – featuring the song that most identifies Cohan ('Yankee Doodle Dandy') – *Forty-five Minutes from Broadway* (1905), *The Talk of New York* (1907), *Get-Rich-Quick Wallingford* (1911), *Seven Keys to Baldpate* (1913), *The Tavern* (1921) and *The Song and Dance Man* (1923). His most famous song, 'Over There' (1917), won him a Congressional medal. His most notable performances in plays other than his own were as the father in O'NEILL's *Ah, Wilderness!* (1933) and as the President in GEORGE S. KAUFMAN and MOSS HART's *I'd Rather Be Right* (1937).

Although Cohan was always the archetype for the glories of turn-of-the-century show business and the representation of a simplistic patriotism to his audience, he was also a complex and lonely man, rarely popular with critics and something of an outcast to his fellow performers when in 1919 he refused to support the establishment of an actors' union. His life story was filmed by Warner Bros in 1942 (*Yankee Doodle Dandy*); a statue of Cohan was erected in 1959 in Duffy Square, New York City; and a musical based on his career, *George M!*, was produced on Broadway in 1968. DBW

Cohen, Alexander H. 1920– American producer. Born in New York, educated at New York and Columbia Universities, Cohen began producing on BROADWAY in 1941 with *Ghost for Sale* and *Angel Street*. In 1950 his casting of *King Lear* with blacklisted actors established him as a producer of meritorious if not always commercially successful works. In 1959 he began a series called 'Nine o'Clock Theatre' and presented *An Evening with Mike Nichols and Elaine May* (1960), *Beyond the Fringe* (1962) and a revival of JOHN GIELGUD in *The Ages of Man* (1963). He has presented foreign productions in New York, including the ROYAL SHAKESPEARE COMPANY's *The Homecoming* (1967), which won a Tony; DAVID STOREY's *Home*, starring Gielgud and RALPH RICHARDSON (1970); Ben Kingsley as EDMUND KEAN (1983); PETER BROOK's *La Tragédie de Carmen* (1983); and DARIO FO's *Accidental Death of an Anarchist* (1985). Other productions include *Anna Christie* (1977), *I Remember Mama* (1979), *A Day in Hollywood/A Night in the Ukraine* (1980) and *Brightlights* (1987). Cohen has produced in London and for television, including the Emmys and the ANTOINETTE PERRY (Tony) Awards. Married to producer Hildy Parks (1926–), he is a trustee of the Actors' Fund of America and since late 1992 the producer of the Stamford (Connecticut) Center for the Arts. His reminiscences, *Sold Out!*, were published in 1993. TLM

Cohen, Nathan 1923-71 Canadian theatre critic. Through his involvement in journals, radio and television, and as drama critic for the Toronto *Star* from 1959 to 1971, Cohen helped shape the aesthetic standards for the developing professional theatre in Canada. He was an ardent champion of indigenous Canadian theatre and dramatic literature, but his outspoken, provocative style and his belief in the critic's responsibility to maintain high standards often gained him the enmity of the Canadian theatrical community. Nonetheless, Cohen firmly established the idea in Canada of developing a Canadian theatrical tradition that would command international respect. In 1981, the Nathan Cohen Award for excellence in theatre CRITICISM was established, and *Tarragon Theatre* produced *Nathan Cohen: A Review*, by Rick Salutin. DAH

Cokayne, Aston 1608-84 English dramatist. Born in Derbyshire and educated at both Oxford and Cambridge Universities, he toured France and Italy in 1632. He wrote three plays, *The Obstinate Lady* (published 1657), a tragedy heavily influenced by FLETCHER, *Trappolin Suppos'd a Prince*, a farce later successful when adapted by NAHUM TATE as *A Duke and No Duke*, and *The Tragedy of Ovid*, an account of the poet's life in exile. It is not clear that any of the plays were ever performed. After the Restoration he wasted his wealth, had to sell off the family's estates, and died in poverty. His most important contribution to English drama may be the revelation in a poem that MASSINGER collaborated on many of the plays published under the authorship of BEAUMONT and Fletcher. PH

Cole, Bob 1869-1912 and
J. Rosamond Johnson 1873-1954 African-American lyricist and composer. Pioneers in bringing black MUSICALS to the New York stage, Cole and Johnson were prolific song-writers, librettists and performers. Cole, in conjunction with Billy Johnson, had written and starred in *A Trip to Coontown* (1898), the first musical entirely created and performed by African Americans. Cole teamed with the classically trained composer J. Rosamond Johnson in 1900. In an era when it was a common practice for songs by several composers to be interpolated into a single musical, Cole and Johnson were in constant demand, providing songs for such shows as *The Belle of Bridgeport* (1900), *Mother Goose* (1903) and *Humpty Dumpty* (1904). Their biggest hit, 'Under the Bamboo Tree', was interpolated into *Sally in Our Alley* (1902). Cole and Johnson wrote and appeared in two musicals, *The Shoo Fly Regiment* (1907) and *Mr Lode of Koal* (1909), but critics of the time were unwilling to accept black performers in musicals that had plots and sympathetic characters. After Cole's death, Johnson continued to write songs and sketches for musicals. Late in his career he appeared in the musicals *Porgy and Bess* (1935) and *Cabin in the Sky* (1940). MK

Cole, Jack 1914-74 American choreographer and dancer, who received his training in modern dance at the Humphrey-Weidman school and as a member of the Denishawn Company, after which he and his own company of dancers appeared in nightclubs. He danced in *Thumbs Up* (1934) and *Keep 'Em Laughing* (1942), and in

1943 was given his first choreographic assignment for *Something for the Boys*. Among the many other shows that he choreographed were *Alive and Kicking* (1950), in which he also appeared; *Kismet* (1953); *Jamaica* (1957); and *Man of La Mancha* (1965). Cole served as both director and choreographer for the short-lived *Donnybrook!* (1961). A student of the Chinese dancer MEI LANFANG, Cole frequently used oriental movements and gestures in his choreography. He is most noted for creating 'jazz dancing', a form characterized by small groupings and angular movements. It became the dominant choreographic style of the 1950s and 60s. MK

Coleman, Cy 1929- American composer. A child prodigy, he attended the New York College of Music before playing in nightclubs with a jazz trio. With lyricist Carolyn Leigh he contributed songs to the REVUE *John Murray Anderson's Almanac* (1953), and wrote the scores for the MUSICALS *Wildcat* (1960) and *Little Me* (1962). He then teamed with Dorothy Fields for the score of *Sweet Charity* (1966). Among his more successful scores with other lyricists were those for *I Love My Wife* (1977), *On the Twentieth Century* (1978), *Barnum* (1980), *City of Angels* (1989; 1990 Tony for Best Musical) and *The Will Rogers Follies* (1991). Coleman's early interest in modern jazz influenced the upbeat, rhythmic style of his compositions for the musical stage. MK

Coliseum London MUSIC-HALL and VARIETY theatre, seating 2358, and the first English stage to be equipped with a revolve. It opened under OSWALD STOLL in 1904; performances included actresses of the stature of ELLEN TERRY, EDITH EVANS, SARAH BERNHARDT and LILLIE LANGTRY, and companies such as Diaghilev's Ballets Russes (in three seasons between 1918 and 1925). GROCK, the most accomplished CLOWN of the period, presented his musical MIMES there from 1911 to 1924. After 1931 it alternated between MUSICAL COMEDY, the most successful of which were *White Horse Inn* (1931) and *The Vagabond King* (1937), and spectacular ice-shows or Christmas PANTOMIME. From 1945 to 1960 it housed a series of American MUSICALS, including *Annie Get Your Gun* (1947), *Kiss Me Kate!* (1951) and *Guys and Dolls* (1953). After some years as a cinema, it reopened in 1968 under the SADLER'S WELLS company as the permanent home of the English National Opera. CI

collective theatre groups (USA) During America's burgeoning theatre movement throughout the 1960s, various performance ensembles formed to create an alternative to the prevalent commercial methods of producing. These groups produced such a wide spectrum of work OFF-OFF BROADWAY that, aesthetically, it is difficult to generalize about the nature of their productions; what they have in common, however, is an organizational structure – or sometimes simply an organizational point of view – that values each participant in a production as a creative collaborator. Collectives tended – sometimes explicitly, sometimes implicitly – to reject both the commercial aims of BROADWAY and OFF-BROADWAY and their hierarchical and increasingly bureaucratic organization.

Actors, especially, gravitated to collectives, disenchanted by what they considered the exploitation of their talents in the service of commercial products in the mainstream theatre. Indeed, many collectives, among them the OPEN THEATRE and the Talking Band, developed plays out of actors' improvisational exercises.

In many cases 'collective' is a misnomer, since some groups have distinct directors whose own style stamps the groups' work and who make the final artistic decisions. This is true, for instance, of some of the theatres that emphasized formal experimentation: the PERFORMANCE GROUP, Manhattan Project (see ANDRE GREGORY), MABOU MINES and the WOOSTER GROUP. Nevertheless, these ensembles, too, involved actors and other company members in a collaborative process of developing plays that was not bound by the short rehearsal periods of Broadway.

Perhaps the prototype of the American collective was the LIVING THEATRE, founded in 1948 by Julian Beck and Judith Malina. In many groups that followed, the plan to work collectively reflected overt political aims, as in the BREAD AND PUPPET THEATRE, started by puppeteer Peter Schumann in the early 1960s; the SAN FRANCISCO MIME TROUPE founded in 1959 by R.G. Davis, which produced open-air political *commedia*-like plays (see *COMMEDIA DELL'ARTE*); EL TEATRO CAMPESINO, a group of Chicano farm workers, founded by LUIS VALDÉZ in response to the 1965 California grape strike; and, an outgrowth of the civil rights movement in the American South, the New Orleans-based Free Southern Theatre.

According to the same principle, in the 1970s the collective became the main organizational approach for feminist theatres, among them Minneapolis's At the Foot of the Mountain and New York's Spiderwoman Theatre, Women's Experimental Theatre and Split Britches. The collective ideal remains a potent precedent for theatres being formed to this day. (See also ALTERNATIVE THEATRE (USA).) AS

Collier, Jeremy 1650–1726 English moralist and divine. Educated at Caius College, Cambridge, Collier was ordained in 1677. In 1689 he refused to take the oath of allegiance to William and Mary and was briefly imprisoned. In 1697 he published the first volume of *Essays upon Several Moral Subjects* and in 1708 the first volume of *An Ecclesiastical History of Great Britain* (neither of which would earn him an entry in this *Guide*). In 1698, however, he published *A Short View of the Immorality and Profaneness of the English Stage*, a lengthy, violent and combative attack on blasphemy, abuse of the clergy, abuse of sacraments like marriage and other offences he cited as present in contemporary drama, particularly in the work of CONGREVE, DRYDEN, D'URFEY and VANBRUGH.

The resulting pamphlet war was intense, rapid and acrimonious. By the end of 1698 Vanbrugh had written his defence, *A Vindication of The Relapse and The Provoked Wife*, Congreve his *Amendments of Mr Collier's False and Imperfect Citations*, and had been attacked in turn by Collier's supporters. Among Collier's subsequent contributions to the debate were *A Defence of the Short View* (1698), *A Second Defence* (1700), *A Dissuasive from the Playhouse* (1703) and *A Farther Vindication of the Short View* (1707). In addition to the battle in print, actors and playwrights found themselves prosecuted, from evidence collected by informers in the audience, for blasphemy,

both in ad-libbed lines and in speeches previously licensed. Collier's attack also encouraged the establishment of Societies for the Reformation of Manners, which monitored plays. Collier's diatribe was well timed to catch the growing sense of middle-class morality and was undoubtedly a major contributory factor in the development towards unrealistic, sentimental forms. PH

Collins, Lottie [Charlotte Louise Collins] 1865–1910 British MUSIC-HALL performer, the daughter of a Jewish blackface MINSTREL. She began at the age of five as a skipping-rope dancer and joined her sisters Marie and Lizzie as a song-and-dance trio on the music-halls. In 1890 she leapt to fame with 'Ta-ra-ra-boom-de-ay', a laundered version of an American brothel song, which she introduced at the Tivoli Music-Hall, London. The infectious chorus and her high-kicking display of red petticoats for four years 'affected the country like an epidemic' (Holbrook Jackson) and has been interpreted as the revolutionary anthem of the Naughty 'Nineties. Collins toured America in 1892, and later became a sketch artist. Her eldest daughter Jose (1887–1958) was a popular MUSICAL COMEDY singer, best known for her Theresa in *The Maid of the Mountains*. LS

Collins, Sam [Samuel Vagg] 1824–65 'Irish' comic vocalist and step-dancer, turned entrepreneur. Despite his stage persona, he was born in London and worked as a chimney-sweep before gaining fame at the London tavern halls and concert rooms of the 1840s (such as Evan's Late Joys) with still-celebrated songs such as 'Limerick Races', 'No Irish Need Apply' and 'The Rocky Road to Dublin'. Having increased his status and prosperity by bookings at CHARLES MORTON's Canterbury Hall, he took over the Rose of Normandy in Edgware Road, turning it into the Marylebone Music Hall, and in 1861 initiated the venture which still bears his name (if only as a Greater London Council blue plaque) by converting the Lansdown Arms, Islington Green, into a thousand-seater hall which opened in 1863 as Sam Collins's Music Hall. AEG

Colman, George, the elder 1732–94 English playwright and theatre manager. Born in Florence where his father was an envoy, he was educated at Westminster School and Oxford University, becoming a barrister in 1757. Considering theatre at this stage an amateur amusement, he began a long friendship with GARRICK in 1760 when his first play, *Polly Honeycombe*, a SATIRE on the sentimental novel, was produced. His first full-length play, *The Jealous Wife* (from FIELDING's *Tom Jones*), appeared in 1761. Disappointed in expectations of the will of his uncle, the Earl of Bath, in 1764, he was still able to give up law and turned to the theatre full-time. While Garrick was on tour he took part in the management of DRURY LANE. His fine translation of TERENCE appeared in 1765 and the following year he collaborated with Garrick in writing *The Clandestine Marriage*, though arguing for years afterwards about the precise share each had in the play. The play, at times a serious consideration of social class and marriage, was a major success.

In 1767 he invested both time and money in COVENT GARDEN, becoming principal manager. In 1769 he beat Garrick in putting on a play about the SHAKESPEARE Jubilee celebrations organized by Garrick in Stratford. Though he continued to write plays, none of them are more than hack work or adaptations, including a number of burlettas. In 1773 he was persuaded by GOLDSMITH to accept SHERIDAN's *The School for Scandal*, which Garrick had turned down. He retired from Covent Garden in 1774 and negotiations for him to take over from Garrick at Drury Lane failed. In 1776 he bought the HAYMARKET Theatre from SAMUEL FOOTE and, in spite of heavy investment in scenery and costumes, made the theatre a financial and artistic success. From 1785 management began to pass to his son, particularly after a bad stroke in 1789, which led to his spending his last years in an asylum.   PH

Colman, George, the younger 1762–1836 English playwright and theatre manager, son of GEORGE COLMAN THE ELDER, from whom he inherited the Little Theatre in the Haymarket in 1794, having already assumed the responsibilities of management five years earlier. Gregarious, bibulous and personally improvident, Colman nevertheless defended and improved the status of the Little Theatre, with which he remained associated until 1817. His fourth play, *Inkle and Yarico* (1787), was a deserved success there. Described as an opera, it is a COMEDY with songs, humanely if uninsistently critical of the slave trade. Colman's undoubted facility as a writer of comic verse (the collection of 'tales in verse', *My Nightgown and Slippers* (1797), has genuine merit) enlivens, with some strain of plausibility, the historical romances *The Battle of Hexham* (1789) and *The Surrender of Calais* (1791), as well as colouring the otherwise sombre adaptation of Godwin's *Caleb Williams*, *The Iron Chest*

(1796). Such impure writing from a man with a reputation as a superior dramatist forms a natural prelude to the wildness of the 19th-century theatre. Colman's more traditional five-act comedies, *The Heir at Law* (1797), *The Poor Gentleman* (1801) and particularly *John Bull* (1803), are not without incidental merits, but he was at his best as a popular entertainer. It is ironic that his appointment as Examiner of Plays in 1824, and his conduct in the office between then and his death, should have left him with the reputation of a spoiler of other people's entertainment. PT

Colombia Indigenous groups in the Americas often ceremonialized their myths and legends in dramatic form. Before the arrival of the Spanish, the Muiscas reached a modest level of development in the area known in colonial times as New Granada. In the colony itself, theatre records indicate presentations as early as 1580, and the first known play is *Laurea crítica* (*Critical Laurel*, 1629), a satirical sketch by Fernando Fernández de Valenzuela (1616–?). Only sporadic activity is recorded through the next two centuries, with an occasional religious play or LOA for special occasions such as the canonization of St Thomas in 1660 and the crowning of Fernando VI in 1752. Nevertheless, the first theatre structure, the Coliseo Ramírez (Ramírez Coliseum), built in 1791 following Spanish models, attracted travelling companies presenting ZARZUELAS, dances and songs. In general the colonial period was, however, one of limited theatrical activity.

Independence in 1819 did not bring major changes. Luis Vargas Tejada (1802–29) and José Fernández Madrid (1789–1830) both wrote neoclassical historical tragedies

Bread and Puppet Theatre (USA) performing *The Crucifixion and Resurrection of Archbishop Oscar Romero of El Salvador*, Manizales International Theatre Festival, Colombia, 1984.

with exalted Native American themes. Local authors imitated the Spanish costumbristic (see COSTUMBRISMO) imports of MORATÍN and Bretón de los Herreros, followed later by the popular romantic movement. The prolific José María Samper (1828–88) exercised both styles, perhaps never more successfully than in the musical version of *Un alcalde a la antigua* (*An Old-Fashioned Mayor*, 1856) that encapsulates the tension between tradition and progress in a rapidly changing society, a typical *costumbrista* theme of the period. The most important national theatre company at mid-century was that of Romualdo Díaz. José Caicedo Rojas (1816–97) and Santiago Pérez (1830–1900) were major writers of the late 19th century, a period that included Constancio Franco (1842–1917), José María Vergara y Vergara (1831–72) and Adolfo León Gómez (1858–1927).

The 20th century The creation of the Society of Authors of Bogotá in 1911 touched off a brief period of theatrical activity. The father of the modern Colombian theatre is considered to be ANTONIO ALVAREZ LLERAS (1892–1956), the author of 15 plays. From his first effort in 1907 to his masterpiece, *El virrey Solís* (*The Viceroy Solís*) in 1948, he sought to internationalize Colombian themes with psychologically realistic plays that were didactic and often historical. Luis Enrique Osorio (1896–1966) promoted theatre with a quarterly journal, a national theatre company and his own plays that were openly critical of Colombian politics and manners. Other playwrights of this first half of the century included Ángel María Céspedes (1892–1956), Jorge Zalamea (b.1905) and Oswaldo Díaz Díaz (1910–67), and Gerardo Valencia Verjarano ('Chonta', b.1911). The most important theatre group was Arturo Acevedo Vallanino's Benavente Company, which toured the entire country.

The contemporary theatre movement in Colombia dates from the 1950s. The Experimental Theatre of the Institute of Fine Arts was created in 1950 in Medellín to promote acting and directing. In 1955 the Rojas Pinilla government invited the Japanese-born, STANISLAVSKY-trained and Mexico-based director, Seki Sano, to train actors and directors for the new television industry. Change came rapidly during his one-year stay (1955–6), before he was expelled in a governmental purge. The generation of writers and directors that emerged – ENRIQUE BUENAVENTURA, SANTIAGO GARCÍA and others – had new expectations about activist and committed theatre. Buenaventura aired BRECHT's *The Trial of Lucullus* on national radio, and El Buho (the Owl), one of the early experimental groups in Bogotá, staged a Brecht play in 1958. An incipient absurdist (see THEATRE OF THE ABSURD) and escapist theatre disappeared under a rising tide of Brecht productions: Fausto Cabrera's version of *Man Is Man*, Jorge Alí Triana's *The Guns of Mother Carrar* and Santiago García's *Galileo*.

During the 1960s the university theatre movement responded to the consolidated labour movement and the Cuban Revolution. In the National University, as well as the Universities del Valle, los Andes and Antioquia, theatre became the vehicle for a politicized student movement. In 1968 the first festival of university theatre was celebrated in the 1500-seat ultramodern theatre Los Fundadores (the Founders) in Manizales, with a blue-ribbon panel of judges (including Jack Lang of France and Pablo Neruda of Chile) and Guatemalan Miguel Angel Asturias as honorary president. Political disruptions closed this international festival after five years, but it was reinstated in 1984. The Festival of New Theatre, sponsored annually after 1975 by Colcultura (Colombian Culture), was equally important in promoting national theatre with a strong sociopolitical commitment.

The history of the recent theatre in Colombia is closely related to several active groups. The TEC, established in 1955 under the direction of the Spaniard Cayetano Luca de Tena but soon taken over by playwright and director Enrique Buenaventura, was reorganized in 1969 as the Teatro Experimental de Cali (Experimental Theatre of Cali). Buenaventura was instrumental in restructuring theatre throughout Latin America by adapting Brechtian techniques and Marxist ideology from collective theatre to traditional dramatic theory. As university theatre became more ideological and less artistic, repressive measures brought to bear within the university led to the formation of the CCT (Colombian Theatre Corporation) in 1969, a new theatre union that embraced the 100 or more theatre groups in the country. Mostly non-professional and experimental in nature, the groups derived strength from each other in the absence of governmental or corporate support. Many groups have subsequently disappeared, but the spirit of solidarity and community was sustained by, among others, several core groups: the TEC of Buenaventura; Santiago García's La Candelaria (originally the Casa de Cultura but renamed after its sector of the city); Ricardo Camacho's Teatro Libre de Bogotá (Free Theatre of Bogotá); Miguel Torres's El Local (the Place); La Mama of Bogotá, established by Ellen Stewart in 1968 and directed by Edy Armando; and Jorge Alí Triana's TPB (Popular Theatre of Bogotá), also established in 1968, which merged in 1984 with CARLOS JOSÉ REYES's El Alacrán (the Scorpion).

The technique of collective theatre (*creación colectiva*) that appeared in Latin America around 1968 was particularly strong in Colombia, and served to coalesce sociopolitical issues. The 'new theatre', as it was called, often dramatized historical issues. The TPB's *I Took Panamá* (1974) used an English title to document Teddy Roosevelt's imperialistic move to gain canal rights. La Candelaria's *Guadalupe, años sin cuenta* (*Guadalupe, Years without Number*, 1975) took advantage of a titular word play to focus on the years of 'the violence' that marked the endemic struggle between liberals and conservatives that had devastated life and politics in Colombia since the 19th century. The TEC's *Nosotros los comunes* (*We the Peasants*, 1972) was also representative of the ongoing class struggle.

Street theatre is popular in Bogotá and other major cities in Colombia (Manizales, Cali and Medellín, for example). Groups that are to some extent a product of the National Dramatic Arts School – with inspiration from the USA's BREAD AND PUPPET – create lively and spontaneous performances. La Máscara (the Mask), El Globo (the Balloon), Nuevo Teatro de Pantomima (New Pantomime Theatre), Teatro Taller de Colombia (Workshop Theatre of Colombia), La Fanfarria and Pequeño Teatro (Little

Theatre) (both of Medellín), Acto Latino (Latin Act), Súcubos, Tecal and others utilize PUPPETS, MASKS and pantomime in combinations of ARTAUDian and grotesque forms that relate to popular native forms such as those Buenaventura used in *A la diestra de Dios Padre* (*On the Right Hand of God the Father*, 1958). Performances of *Gukup* by Teatro Taller de Colombia and *Blacamán* by Acto Latino, the latter based on a short story by Gabriel García Márquez, Colombia's Nobel-laureate novelist, are noteworthy. The coastal area has enjoyed its own theatrical forms, derived from the myths and traditions of the syncretic culture (black, white and Native American). Manuel Zapata Olivella's thoroughly researched and documented *Rambao* (1975) is a good example.

Despite its problems, the Colombian theatre continues to be lively and dynamic. Younger authors include Fernando González Cajiao (b.1938), also an important theatre historian, whose *Huellas de un rebelde* (*A Rebel's Tracks*, 1970) placed him in the mainstream. In 1993 his *Popón* echoed his continuing interest in indigenous historical material. Jairo Aníbal Niño (b.1941) is known for his *El Monte Calvo* (*Bald Mountain*). Esteban Navajas Cortés won the Cuban Casa de las Américas prize in 1978 for *La agonía del difunto* (*The Agony of the Deceased*). Fernando Peñuela's metafictional *La trasescena* (*Behind the Scenes*, 1984), written for La Candelaria, followed on the success of Santiago García's *Diálogo del rebusque* (*Hermetic Dialogue*, 1982), based on texts by the Spanish baroque poet Francisco de Quevedo. The monumental Iberoamerican Theatre Festival, launched by Fanny Mickey and Ramiro Osorio and celebrated in alternate years (1990, 92, 94), has stimulated local theatre by bringing world-famous groups to Bogotá.

An active theatre movement in the regional city of Medellín includes Gilberto Martínez, playwright, director and theatre journal editor; Rodrigo Saldarriaga, director of El Pequeño Teatro; and dramatists José Manuel Friedel, author of the vanguard *Las desdichas de la Bella Otero* (*The Misfortunes of the Beautiful Otero*, 1985) and Henry Díaz, whose *El cumpleaños de Alicia* (*Alice's Birthday*) won first prize in a Medellín University contest in 1985.

The theatre in Colombia includes a number of *café concierto* establishments; perhaps the most significant feature of the recent theatre is that it is not limited to political or engagé aspects. GW

See: F. González Cajiao, *Historia del teatro en Colombia*, Bogotá, 1986; C. M. Suárez Radillo, 'Dos generaciones de la violencia en el teatro colombiano contemporaneo', *Anales de Literatura Hispanoamericana*, 2–3, Madrid, 1973–4; M. Watson Espener and C. José Reyes, *Materiales para una historia del teatro en Colombia*, Bogotá, 1978.

Colum, Padraic 1881–1972 Irish playwright. A founder member of the National Theatre Society, Colum, with other ABBEY notables, soon disputed YEATS's autocracy, and left to form the rival Theatre of Ireland (1906–12) under Edward Martyn. In 1914 he emigrated to America, where he spent most of his life, celebrated for his poetry, children's stories and travel books.

The National Theatre Society's first season included Colum's first major play, *Broken Soil* (1903). There followed *The Land* (1905), *The Fiddler's House* (Theatre of Ireland, 1907, a revision of *Broken Soil*), and *Thomas Muskerry* (1910). Although they are essentially plays about individuals at moments of decision which reflect an era of social flux, the subdued lyricism of Colum's prose amplifies their essential REALISM, making them more than documentaries of historical circumstances.

Colum wrote few plays subsequently, none matching his early work. It had an influence out of proportion to its quantity, establishing a ground between SYNGE's exuberant poetry and T. C. MURRAY's plainer speech. DM GF

combination company see STOCK COMPANY

Comden, Betty 1915– and
Adolph Green 1915– American librettists, lyricists and performers. After writing and appearing in a satirical nightclub act, Comden and Green made their BROADWAY debuts as librettists, lyricists and featured performers in *On the Town* (1944). Their wry wit appeared to best advantage in the librettos and/or lyrics they created for shows with a satirical tinge (see SATIRE), such as *Wonderful Town* (1953), *Bells Are Ringing* (1956) and *Say Darling* (1958). When their fast-paced, wisecracking style of MUSICAL COMEDY declined in popularity in the 1960s, their contributions to the Broadway stage became less frequent. As a taste for satirical books and lyrics returned in the late 1970s and 80s, the partners were again successful with their work for *On the Twentieth Century* (1978) and *Singin' in the Rain* (1985). They began the 1990s with Tony-winning lyrics for *The WILL ROGERS Follies*, music by CY COLEMAN. Comden and Green also wrote the screenplays for several popular musical films of the 1950s. In 1991 they were honoured at the Kennedy Center. MK

comedia Spanish term referring ambiguously, even in its own time, to any full-length play in verse whether serious or comic written during Spain's GOLDEN AGE of literature. Often called *comedia nueva* (new comedy), these plays are generally of mixed types; and attempts to classify them by themes (history, saints' lives, mythology and so on) or by dramatic action (*de costumbres* (manners), *de enredo* (intrigue), *de figurón* (character)) are often futile. (See also SPAIN.) ElB

Comédie-Française French theatre and theatre company. Formed in 1680 by a royal decree merging the troupes of MOLIÈRE (d.1673) and of the HÔTEL DE BOURGOGNE, the Comédie-Française is proud of its uninterrupted tradition as the oldest European theatre company. For most of its first 100 years it performed in a theatre constructed in 1688–9 on the site of a tennis court in the rue des Fossés-St-Germain-des-Prés, now rue de l'Ancienne-Comédie. This was designed by François d'Orbay with a large parterre, a U-shaped amphitheatre at the back and 3 rows of boxes, giving a total audience capacity of around 1500. Until the Revolution the company enjoyed a virtual monopoly on all new plays performed in the capital (shared for just some of the time with the COMÉDIE-ITALIENNE), and so the history of its repertoire is also the history of playwriting in France. The company has always retained a collective structure, with shares held by full members and decisions about repertoire and so on taken in common.

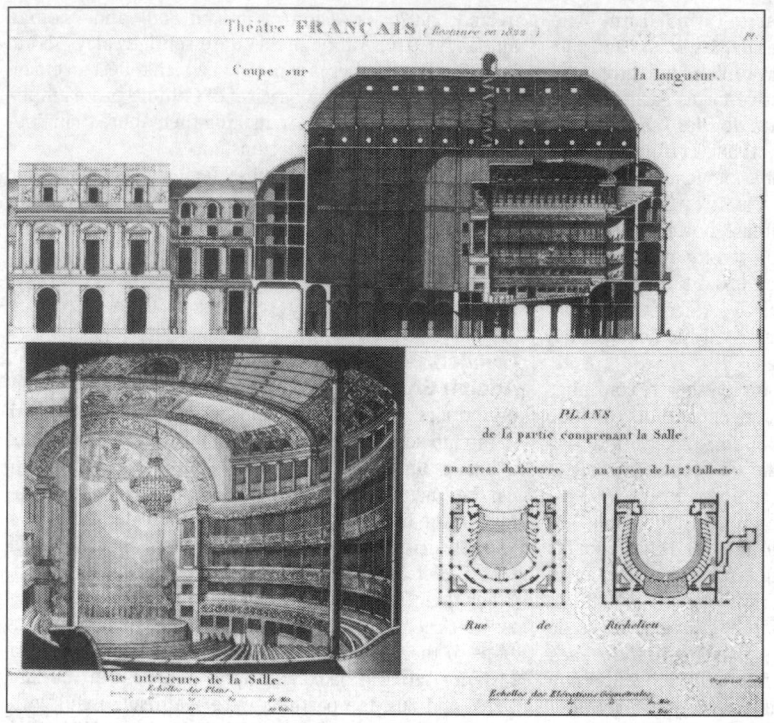

A plan of the Théâtre-Français in the 19th century. This is substantially Victor Louis's theatre. It is interesting to note how he placed a large theatre on a small site (vestibule under the auditorium, no large foyers or monumental staircase).

At first the main influence was wielded by LA GRANGE, one of Molière's main actors, together with ARMANDE BÉJART, Molière's widow. Other important players were BARON and Noël-Jacques Hauteroche, both of whom followed Molière's example by writing comedies for performance by the company. As Madame de Maintenon's influence grew at court, life became more difficult for the company, who frequently had to close for periods of official mourning or religious observance. The accession of Louis XV brought easier times and the company was able to recruit powerful performers both in TRAGEDY and in COMEDY, among whom were ADRIENNE LECOUVREUR, MLLE CLAIRON, LEKAIN and the POISSON family. They were received in society and their finances established on a sounder footing. For the repertoire, they continued to rely on the plays of RACINE, PIERRE CORNEILLE and Molière, but also enjoyed considerable success with the tragedies of VOLTAIRE and the *comédies larmoyantes* of LA CHAUSSÉE; their greatest success was *The Marriage of Figaro*, whose opening night in 1784 had been delayed for several years by the censor (see CENSORSHIP). Between 1770 and 1782 the company performed in the SALLE DES MACHINES at the Tuileries palace, before moving into a new building designed for them by Peyre and Wailly, the present ODÉON.

From the opening of the new theatre in 1782 to the burning of the Salle Richelieu in 1900, the Théâtre-Français had a chequered career. During the Revolution the title of the theatre was changed to Théâtre de la Nation (1789). In 1790 it went through a stormy period of internal dissension occasioned by Chénier's historico-political tragedy, *Charles IX*, which led to TALMA, Dugazon, MADAME VESTRIS and other revolutionary members of the troupe leaving to set up at the Théâtre de la République (Salle Richelieu, formerly the Variétés Amusantes). The sit-

uation of the Comédie was made more difficult by the law of the liberty of theatres of 1791, which abolished its monopoly, and, in 1793, by the arrest and near-execution of the more conservative members as a result of performances of LAYA's moderate play *L'Ami des lois* (*The Friend of the Law*) and François de Neufchâteau's *Paméla*. In 1798, the same François de Neufchâteau, now Minister for the Interior, arranged for the government to acquire both the old Comédie-Française (Odéon) and the Théâtre de la République, and to pay off the heavy debts incurred during the Revolution. A fire at the Odéon in 1799 brought the troupe together again. In 1800 the building of the Théâtre-Français became state property, and in 1802 a regular subsidy of 100,000 francs was established. An act of 1803 forbade the *sociétaires* to appear at any other theatre without special government permission.

Napoleon had a great interest in the theatre, seeing the Théâtre-Français (where he attended some 270 performances) as essential to national prestige. The decree of Moscow of 1812 set forth the new organization of the theatre and removed some of the administrative authority of the actors by installing an imperial commissar, whose job was to transmit to the actors the wishes of the *surintendant des spectacles*, even on such details as casting. After 1816 a not very happy attempt was made to revert to the organization of 1766. The theatre went through a difficult period – *Tartuffe* was banned and a series of rather dreary medieval tragedies was staged. Finally, in 1825, the new royal commissar, Baron Taylor, was appointed. Taylor had already been involved with the Panorama Dramatique, where he was co-author of the very successful adaptation of Maturin's *Bertram*. A widely travelled man and a keen archaeologist, he also produced a series of volumes, illustrated by well known artists, called *Voyages pittoresques de l'ancienne France.* Taylor opened wide the doors of the Comédie to the romantic movement, and also to a much more elaborate conception of *mise-en-scène* than had previously been contemplated at that theatre. In particular he was responsible for *Henri III et sa cour* (*Henry III and His Court*), *Le More de Venise* (*The Moor of Venice*) and *Hernani*. After the battle of *Hernani* (see HUGO), Taylor drifted off on long trips, leaving the company in a state of internal chaos which nearly led to its dissolution. In 1833 the Théâtre-Français abandoned its right to administer itself and a director was appointed, the first being Jouslin de la Salle, a former stage director, who saw himself as the saviour of the theatre and continued Taylor's policy, staging *Angelo* (Hugo), *Chatterton* (VIGNY), *Les Enfants d'Édouard* and *Marino Faliero* (DELAVIGNE), and introducing the repertoire of SCRIBE. He had to resign in 1837 over an illegal ticket racket.

In 1838 RACHEL was engaged and turned the classical repertoire into box-office. In 1840, Buloz (of the *Revue des Deux Mondes*) became director, introduced gas lighting, discovered the plays of AUGIER, and tried to interest the theatre in ancient and foreign repertoires. 1843 saw the disaster of *Les Burgraves*. In 1847 an attempt was made to create an administrator who would be an almost all-powerful civil servant independent of the company itself. Buloz lost his post with the 1848 revolution and was replaced by a protégé of Rachel's, the actor Lockroy. A decree of 1849 established a commissar-administrator – in fact, Arsène Houssaye, a man of letters – and in 1850 Louis Napoléon fixed the rights and duties of the administrator by decree. Houssaye met with hostility from the company, but when they offered to walk out, he simply told them he would employ BOULEVARD actors. The Théâtre-Français became very fashionable under the Second Empire, and Houssaye attached much importance to the presentation of new works. Under Empis (1856–9) there was a return to a more traditional repertoire. Édouard Thierry, appointed in 1859, introduced the repertoire of SARDOU and Pailleron. In 1870 the theatre was set up as a field hospital, and the fall of the Empire brought considerable financial difficulties. After the Commune, Thierry was replaced by Émile Perrin, a former director of the Opéra, who brought back financial stability, introducing Tuesday subscription nights and Sunday matinées. It was also decided that actors should no longer be responsible for their own costumes in modern-dress plays. The troupe was now strong, but Perrin was criticized for attaching more importance to *mise-en-scène* than to literary quality. Perrin was followed by Jules Clarétie, whose administration lasted for 28 years.

In 1900 a disastrous fire caused the death of an actor and the wholesale destruction of stage and scenery at the Salle Richelieu. A year later the company moved back into the renovated theatre, following the fashion of the times by performing mainly comedy of an undemanding kind. They continued to perform throughout the First World War, travelling to the Front to entertain the troops. After the war, as COPEAU and the CARTEL directors tried to raise standards of production, the Comédie-Française lagged behind. An attempted improvement was the appointment of Bourdet as administrator in 1936, with four associate directors: BATY, Copeau, DULLIN and JOUVET. During the German occupation the theatre's reputation rose again,

partly thanks to BARRAULT's production of CLAUDEL's *The Satin Slipper* (1943), but Barrault left with Madeleine Renaud in 1946 when they set up the independent Renaud-Barrault company. Since then the Comédie-Française, though strong in boulevard comedy, has continued to be a conservative force in the French theatre, claiming to preserve the traditions of 17th-century performance. In fact its styles have changed, both in acting and production, but always considerably *after* rather than *with* the times. There are now 40 full *sociétaires*, who elect new members as vacancies occur from the 30 *pensionnaires*, who are actors drawing a salary, not full shareholders. The current 350 technical and administrative staff account for the theatre's large subsidy, which is considerably higher than that of any other French theatre.

Despite many reconstructions, the theatre retains VICTOR LOUIS's basic lay-out with a horse-shoe-shaped auditorium and four shallow superimposed balconies. Originally designed to hold 2000 spectators, it now contains seating for a maximum of 892. The stage, too, has had the latest technology installed without altering the fundamental design of the original building. The main training ground for actors, the Conservatoire, until recently employed almost exclusively Comédie-Française actors as its teachers, which contributed to the company's conservative influence. After 1968 various reforms were introduced, notably in the Conservatoire, and a policy of performing more contemporary plays was initiated. In 1983 JEAN-PIERRE VINCENT was appointed director, the first to come to the post from a decentralized theatre (Strasbourg); however, he left three years later without having been able to accomplish the reforms he deemed necessary to make the Comédie-Française into a representative national theatre. In 1985 Vincent was succeeded by Jean Le Poulain, a senior member of the company, who died in 1988. Further reforms were attempted by ANTOINE VITEZ, who was appointed director in 1988, but his early death in 1990 came before he had achieved what he set out to do. JACQUES LASSALLE (director from 1990 to 1993) was equally unsuccessful in changing a company that remains self-consciously a 'national treasure', and which politicians, especially of the Gaullist persuasion, are determined to maintain as a monument to the national heritage. DB JMCC

Comédie-Italienne Italian theatre company resident in France. *COMMEDIA DELL'ARTE* troupes were familiar visitors to France from the mid-16th century and increasingly into the 17th. Summoned to appear at Court and entertaining the general public en route, companies led by GANASSA, FRANCESCO and ISABELLA ANDREINI, TRISTANO MARTINELLI, TIBERIO FIORILLI and others were so popular with Paris audiences that eventually Louis XIV resolved to establish the last-named under royal protection, first at the PETIT-BOURBON and then at the PALAIS-ROYAL. After a further spell in the rue Guénégaud they finally moved to the HÔTEL DE BOURGOGNE (made available by the formation of the COMÉDIE-FRANÇAISE in 1680), where they took the name of the Comédie-Italienne. The company, which still featured the veteran Fiorilli alongside DOMENICO BIANCOLELLI, his two daughters and the COSTANTINI brothers, now went beyond occasional French interpolations in their performances to the adoption of whole scripted plays by such dramatists as REGNARD, Dufresny and Palaprat, and slowly their traditional reliance on improvisation diminished as they turned their attention to contemporary SATIRE and COMEDY of manners.

Their success suffered a setback in 1697 with Lenoble's *La Fausse Prude* (*The False Prude*), which was seen as an attack on Mme de Maintenon, the king's second wife, and the Italians were promptly banished. In 1716, after Louis's death, a new company under LUIGI RICCOBONI and numbering some of the finest *commedia* actors of the day returned to the Hôtel de Bourgogne, but the initial warmth of their reception soon cooled and they too were forced to abandon Italian for French. They were granted a royal pension in 1723 and despite competition from the fair theatres, the *comédiens italiens ordinaires du roi* now enjoyed a period of great prosperity, thanks largely to their partnership with MARIVAUX, some 20 of whose plays they presented between 1720 and 1740, though their link with *commedia* became progressively more tenuous. Gradually the enormous popularity of *vaudevilles* and comic OPERAS at the fair theatres induced the Italians to follow suit and led ultimately to their amalgamation with the Opéra-Comique under FAVART in 1762. Most of the older actors had now retired and the traditional Comédie-Italienne had effectively ceased to exist by the time the joint company opened the new Salle Favart in 1783.   DR

comedy From classical Greek times, comedy has been viewed in contrast to TRAGEDY, but by the late 20th century a considerable corpus of criticism has broken free of tragedy to comment independently on comedy and its several subgenres. Although ARISTOTLE presents rival claims to the etymology of comedy, modern scholars agree that 'comedy' means 'revel-song', and a correspondingly festive spirit has been associated with many forms of comic drama. Aristotle's definition of comedy as 'the painlessly ugly' has proved less resonant than his famous definition of tragedy (which has more to do with his philosophy than with ordinary usage), and the centuries have brought scant agreement about the nature of dramatic comedy, its function, or its components. Critical consideration of comedy has often strayed into theories of laughter.

Played at the Dionysian Festival as well as the Lenaea in the 5th century BC (see GREECE, ANCIENT), Greek comedy by the next century was classified as Old, Middle or New. What the three forms shared were avatars of the laughable. Old Comedy, which is extant only in the plays of ARISTOPHANES, was a rich blend of satire and fantasy, physical farce and subtle word play; it featured an ingenious trickster and closed on a lavish choral song and dance. Whatever Middle Comedy may be (scholars disagree), burlesque of heroes and divinities dilutes the comic brew. New Comedy depicted ordinary citizens beset by ordinary problems; the playwright's concern was with the individual. The plot of New Comedy was often structured on the most durable formula of all drama: young lovers separated by an obstacle are united at the grand finale. New Comedy thrived on asides, eavesdropping, quid pro quo and mistaken indentity, and it evolved such comic types as the old grouch, the pedant, the braggart soldier– often the obstacle in the path of the young lovers. Although MENANDER may not have invented New Comedy, he was admired for his deft creations. Admiration took the form of imitation by PLAUTUS and TERENCE (see ROME), and, through them, by a host of neoclassical European playwrights in both Latin and the vulgar tongues. The scheming slave of New Comedy was the ancestor of Italian Arlecchino, German HANSWURST and the Spanish GRACIOSO.

Before that harvest, however, dramatic comedy was eclipsed by comic theory, with Cicero offering a widely quoted definition of comedy as 'an imitation of life, a mirror of customs, and an image of truth'. In the Middle Ages comedy was associated with the vulgar tongue (as opposed to Latin) and with a happy ending; thus Dante called his great epic a comedy. On the late-medieval stage – both amateur and professional – comedy displayed a spectrum of techniques from slapstick to puns, from topical SATIRE to tropical fantasy. Moreover, in religious plays devils and vice figures were simultaneously funny and evil, implicitly contradicting an Aristotle they did not know – for the medieval mind the comic was painfully ugly.

By the Renaissance, neoclassical playwrights imposed decorum on comedy as on tragedy – the proverbial unities and five acts – as well as a realistic and prosaic tone. In contrast, neoclassical playwrights like SHAKESPEARE rejected such constraints when they created what was later called romantic comedy. Both neoclassical and romantic comedies often ended in marriage, but different paths to wedlock might suggest different subgenres of comedy, even while comedy in the Romance languages gradually came to mean any play. Thus, Italian and Spanish drama introduced comedy of intrigue with elaborate plots. MACHIAVELLI's *Mandragola* may well be the pinnacle of this subgenre, but the anonymous *Ingannati* (*The Deceived*) became a fertile model. BEN JONSON in England created COMEDY OF HUMOURS (named after the particular humour, or body fluid, which was believed to determine character), but in Jacobean times the broader panoply of CITIZEN COMEDY replaced obsessive monsters. In France MOLIÈRE usually observed classical decorum, but ranged from a FARCE like *The Flying Doctor* to character comedy like *The Misanthrope*. French comedy of morals crossed the English Channel as comedy of manners, which ridiculed social foibles. Type characters from COMMEDIA DELL'ARTE sprang across national boundaries into the written comedies of several languages.

Despite such gifted practitioners of comedy as Shakespeare, Molière, LOPE DE VEGA and Jonson, critics and even practitioners tended to view comedy as a genre inferior to tragedy. In the 18th century, with the rise of the bourgeoisie, comedy tried to be serious in such subgenres as LA CHAUSSÉE's *comédie larmoyante* (tearful comedy) or STEELE's sentimental comedy (resurrected belatedly in today's sit-com (see TELEVISION DRAMA)). At approximately the same time, the stock type of the scheming servant towered above his master in BEAUMARCHAIS's Figaro trilogy. Romantic dramatists preferred tragedy to comedy, but MUSSET's bittersweet armchair comedies set the tone not only for BÜCHNER's *Leonce and Lena* but also for playwrights as different as CHEKHOV, GARCÍA LORCA, GIRAUDOUX and BARRIE. At the turn of the 20th century comedy gained staturelargely through BERNARD SHAW, with his comedy of ideas. Although stage humour abounds in many times and places, the 20th century commercial stage has been particularly hospitable to frivolous entertainment that goes by the name of comedy. In contrast, the zany humour of the dadaists and surrealists (see SURREALISM) was only rarely seen in the theatre before the absurd (see THEATRE OF THE ABSURD) exploded in the 1950s.

Is dramatic comedy still with us as a distinct genre? The reply will depend on how the viewer defines comedy: the new comedy formula holds in plays as different as Harvey Fierstein's *Torch Song Trilogy* and NEIL SIMON's *Barefoot in the Park*: wit scintillates in plays as bleak as SAMUEL BECKETT's *Endgame* and HAROLD PINTER's *Betrayal*. Various comic subgenres linger residually as devices – BURLESQUE, farce, PARODY, satire, even the grotesque in such a play as STOPPARD's *Travesties*, of undesignated genre. Comedy has been the obstreperously preferred genre of political radicals from BRECHT to FO. What is hard to find today is the festive spirit implied by the etymology of comedy, which has been periodically revived in times less threatening and threatened than our own.   RC

comedy of humours The distinctive style of English comedy of humours was popularized by the enormous success of JONSON's *Every Man in His Humour* (1598) in its performance by the LORD CHAMBERLAIN'S MEN. Jonson peopled his play with characters, each of whom was dominated by a single attitude or 'humour'. It was a comic technique familiar from ARISTOPHANES, and it was possibly the excellence of the acting that brought it into new prominence, denying what may have been a merited historical

precedence to CHAPMAN's *An Humorous Day's Mirth* (1597). Jonson followed it up with the less successful *Every Man out of His Humour* (1599), written in the 'old comedy' style of Aristophanes and including satirical portraits of MARSTON and DEKKER. The comedy of humours became a weapon in the WAR OF THE THEATRES, with Jonson countered by Dekker's *Satiromastix* and Marston's *What You Will*, and he himself then struck back with *Poetaster*. Almost all contemporary and subsequent writers of COMEDY have been in various degrees reliant on the comic potential of 'humours'. SHAKESPEARE, though exceptional, displays its influence in the creation of Jaques in *As You Like it* (1599) and in *Twelfth Night* (c.1600) as well as in the more slapdash *The Merry Wives of Windsor* (c.1600). JOHN DAY looked back over a rich decade in the title and conduct of his *Humour out of Breath* (c.1608), and the special tone of Restoration comedy is, in part, the result of a preservation of humours comedy alongside the sophisticated comedy of manners. Through the 18th and 19th centuries, with an often wearying predictability, professional dramatists deposited humours into FARCE, where the situation comedies of modern television have kept them.   PT

commedia dell'arte 'Comedy of the profession' – a term in general use since the 18th century to describe what until then had been known as *commedia degli zanni* or *all'improvviso*: i.e. the dramatic form associated with the new acting companies which sprang up in northern Italy towards the middle of the 16th century, as distinct from the *commedia erudita* of gentlemanly amateurs. An immediate problem arises. There was never in reality a

French and Italian players in the *commedia dell'arte* style, c.1670.

strict and fixed distinction between the *dell'arte* and the *erudita*: some *dell'arte* actors, such as GIOVAN BATTISTA ANDREINI and Brigida Fedele, were dramatists or translators in their own right; the celebrated GELOSI company were as comfortable with literary theatre as with improvised FARCE (they premiered TASSO's *Aminta* in 1573); some of DELLA PORTA's work exists in both composed and scenario forms; and throughout their history the major companies played repertories of great generic diversity, including OPERA and spectacular 'machine plays' as well as the improvised comedy of fixed social types for which they are better known.

It was, indeed, this strand in their work for which they were best known in their own time, and which has remained influential to the present day; and it is reasonable to distinguish between the *dell'arte* as an institution (professional touring companies, some of which sometimes took up permanent residence) and as an artistic form.

The original setting of that form was the simple trestle-or booth-stage – easily portable or organized on the spot by a company on tour, and adaptable to any context from the public piazza to the courtly hall. On this uncluttered platform the actors improvised their plays (usually farcical comedies of sex, greed and status) from skeletal scenarios, ringing the changes on a set of caricatures and a repertory of traditional situations and GAGS.

Two centuries saw numerous changes of detail and nomenclature in the dramatis personae of the *commedia dell'arte*, sometimes in response to the success of particular performers (ISABELLA ANDREINI probably gave her own name to the first *inamorata* of the Gelosi company, and SILVIO FIORILLO popularized Policinella (see PUNCH)), but its basic character format remained the same: two contrasted male clowns or ZANNI, of low social status, the crafty and unscrupulous Brighella and the dim-witted and famished Arlecchino (HARLEQUIN); two older male characters of high social status, bourgeois heads of household, the avaricious, lustful and suspicious merchant Pantalone and the pedantic and ineffectual Dottore; and at least one pair of lovers, the *inamorato* (under a variety of names) and *inamorata* (often Isabella), the latter frequently the overprotected daughter or younger wife of one of the senior male characters. To this basic list were added the *capitan*, a braggart soldier; the witty serving-wench Colombina; the obese and malicious Pulcinella; and numerous others – additional or alternative *zanni* such as Coviello, Pedrolino and Tartaglia, and further female characters such as the widow, to complicate the sexual intrigue.

Most of the roles had their own half-MASK and COSTUME, so that they were instantly recognizable and the actor was freed from the need to establish his character, to concentrate on improvising the action. Arlecchino, whose rise in theatrical status (partly attributable to DOMENICO BIANCOLELLI's innovative fusion of the two *zanni* into a single, paradoxical character) is itself a miniature history of popular stereotypes, wore an unembellished black or dark-brown mask and a patched and motley costume which subsequently became refined into the familiar overall pattern of lozenges, and carried a wooden slapstick. Brighella was identifiable by his green and white stripes

and dagger, and sometimes played a guitar. Pantalone's attributes were a beard and long nose, loose gown, red stockings, Turkish slippers and brimless hat. The female characters were not invariably masked – or, if so, not in character, but with the black velvet domino – but they were equally recognizable by clothes appropriate to their status, and could rely on a contemporary understanding of 'what colours signify love or hope or jealousy'. Such emblematic costuming, for both men and women, was reinforced in its visual impact by the actor's ability to relax into the characteristic posture and movement of a role which he or she might inhabit throughout a professional lifetime.

An improvised masked comedy of traditional situation, social caricature, emblematic costume and high visual impact, with no basis in a written script – all points to a form in which action takes precedence over character, where physical skills are at least as important as verbal skills, and verbal skills are of a very particular kind. The impression is reinforced when we consider that Italian actors were able to play in France or Bavaria as successfully as on their Cisalpine stamping-ground. Further, in its early days, *commedia* made great play with local frames of reference and vernaculars, and its improvised texts must have been a pot-pourri of Italian dialects in an age when there was no spoken standard. Arlecchino hailed from Bergamo and Pulcinella from Benevento, near Naples, both Gothamite communities; Pantalone was a Venetian grandee, the Doctor a university man from Bologna, the captain a Spaniard. Not that the actors necessarily came from these places, but they mimicked the dialects or broken Italian, and we cannot be sure that they were always wholly intelligible – for Arlecchino to speak virtual gibberish would be consistent with his role, and the parodied technical language of academicians and soldiers in itself approaches meaninglessness. Such clashes of discourse are a common source of Renaissance humour. But on stage, if their appeal is not to wane through repetition, or be confined to an intellectual coterie, they must be allied with unflagging physical energy and narrative drive.

The basis for this was the scenario, a chronological plot summary that was pinned up backstage. Though scenarios are referential – they were designed as an *aide-mémoire* for actors – they provide a schematic account of the intrigue (typically concerned with the ploys of tricksters in getting the girl, or the money, or both) and indicate the interpolation of the stock comic device known as a LAZZO. The *burla*, typically a practical joke, is a more developed form, though in practice the terms overlap. Either could be used as the action demanded or at the discretion of the players. The scenario was the framework which every improviser required to support a performance, providing, in essence, given circumstances, lines of action, and needs. The performer brought to bear on this a physical training in ACROBATICS and comic business, and a verbal training in mimicry. We may also reasonably infer a formulaic technique of the kind widely used by oral improvisers from poets to preachers – certainly the extant *bravure* of the hyperbolical *capitan* suggest it – and perhaps certain memorized set pieces such as the rhymed declarations of the lovers and the cross-talk acts of the *zanni*. Again, literary evidence exists for these, and combinations of memorization and improvisation are not unknown in other art forms.

The origin of the *commedia dell'arte* is unknown. Attempts have been made to trace it back to Roman comedy (see ROME): certainly Pulcinella resembles the CLOWN Maccus, Capitano Spavento da Vall'Inferno is *miles gloriosus* to the life, and PLAUTUS would have recognized immediately the outwitting of masters by their servants. There is, however, no historical evidence to cover the millennium and a half that separate Plautus, TERENCE and the Atellan farces from GANASSA and his comrades, nor to bridge the gap between literary scripts and improvised action. There is no single clear line of descent: in an age of syntheses, *commedia* is another. Plautus and Terence were known to the educated, and their conventions mediated into popular consciousness through the plays of CALMO and RUZZANTE, who added elements of local vernacular language and anarchic comic business. Further material was readily available in printed *novelle* and chapbooks, not to mention oral literature. Professional entertainment was nothing new, and it is likely that the patter, storytelling, clowning, acrobatics, dancing and music of the minstrel, the buffoon and the mountebank contributed their techniques. As for improvisation, in 16th-century Italy, where most of the population had to rely on it for verbal expression of any kind, the opportunity to acquire its disciplines may be taken for granted, and even the elite culture's training in rhetoric played its part. Finally, models for dialogue might be acquired from the FLYTINGS associated with CARNIVAL, and the same source could have provided the concept of masked performance.

Most innovations are a form of *bricolage* under a given economic and cultural stimulus. The Mantua-based ACCESI, the CONFIDENTI who toured in Spain, the DESIOSI whom Montaigne admired when visiting Pisa in 1581, and the FEDELI who played at the HÔTEL DE BOURGOGNE in 1613 and 1614, were constructing a new art form from classical and traditional sources, just as they combined the old financial model of aristocratic patronage with the new supply-and-demand model of performing to popular audiences in the growing cities of the early modern world. Certainly there is nothing unambiguously old-fashioned about their way of doing business. They may sometimes be known as 'families' – some actors were related, and some masks inherited; but the word should not be taken too literally. Performers such as FRANCESCO GABRIELLI, a musical Scapino, the great Arlecchino TRISTANO MARTINELLI, and the actor and scenarist Flaminio Scala (whose collection of 1611 is the earliest printed source of scenarios) moved freely from company to company in pursuit of their own ends, as actors do today.

As modern Europe's first fully fledged professional drama, the artistry of *commedia* rapidly created a demand outside its homeland. The first evidence of a professional touring company (its contracts) is from 1545 (though we know nothing about their repertoire): by 1568 Ganassa was working in Mantua and the Gelosi in Milan; and by 1577 DRUSIANO MARTINELLI was probably in London. Before 1600 the troupes had infiltrated every important European country. France, particularly Paris, was their second home, and the later history of the form is as much French as Italian. The touring of earlier decades was con-

solidated, by 1662, in the long-term use of the PALAIS-ROYAL (shared with MOLIÈRE's company) by TIBERIO FIORILLI and his colleagues, including Domenico Biancolelli and ANGELO COSTANTINI. In 1680 they moved to the Hôtel de Bourgogne under the name of the COMÉDIE-ITALIENNE, staying there until 1697 when they were expelled following a scandal. In 1716, after the accession of Louis XV, the company re-formed – 11 actors under LUIGI RICCOBONI. By 1720, when MARIVAUX wrote *Arlequin poli par l'amour* for them, they were *ipso facto* no longer a *commedia dell'arte* troupe in the old sense. This literalization of a performer's art was the inevitable conclusion of uprooting the *commedia* from its indigenous culture. Its potency of local and topical reference was inevitably lost, and replaced by the universalism of sentimental comedy; the performers began to work in a language that was not their own, and, unsurprisingly, relied increasingly on the memorization of macaronic texts; the permanent theatre building replaced the opportunistic venues of earlier days.

Nor was the process confined to France. In a world of growing literacy and literature, the *commedia* had its back to the wall. In its heartland, GOLDONI wrote *The Servant of Two Masters* (1745) for SACCO's Venetian company, although he disliked masked acting and improvisation. GOZZI liked them, and his self-defeating response was to write another script, *The Love of Three Oranges* (1761). Fine plays both, but a cultural world away from the *improvvisa*.

The influence of *commedia* is sometimes overestimated: all regions of early modern Europe had traditions of improvised performance, and their own local comic stereotypes such as HANSWURST, Gilles and Pickelhering; these are sometimes analogous to *commedia*'s *tipi fissi*, but analogy does not imply derivation. Nevertheless, the particular synthesis of demotic traditions of performance with the humanist learning of the Renaissance was original, and immensely influential, both in its own day and subsequently.

In Italy itself (not then a nation state) – though in its northern heartland the *improvvisa* was assimilated to the literary theatre – *commedia* continued to thrive in Naples where the local favourite Pulcinella entertained popular audiences until the late 19th century. Further afield, the energetic touring of the Italians contributed to the foundation and growth of art theatre in CZECHOSLOVAKIA, POLAND, DENMARK, SWEDEN and RUSSIA. Everywhere they influenced actors, writers and impresarios: great dramatists like Molière and JONSON; little-known puppet-masters (see PUPPETS) and fairground showmen such as those who made a hard living at Paris's *foires* of St Germain and St Laurent; the innovative actor-managers of 18th-century London who originated the English PANTOMIME.

In the 20th century's reaction against NATURALISM, *commedia* has found a vigorous second existence. In the cultural and political maelstrom of pre-revolutionary Russia and the Soviet Union, it had both technical and ideological attractions. EVREINOV and BLOK explored the equivocal relationship between mask and performer in vivid theatrical experiments, and MEYERHOLD assimilated the idea of a sharply defined, non-naturalistic physical style in his biomechanical system. Others, too, have recognized the usefulness of *commedia* techniques in actor training.

JACQUES COPEAU's school (founded 1921) was an early centre of mask work as part of a programme for liberating the actor's physicality. Later, inside Italy, *commedia dell'arte* has been an important inspiration in the work of the Piccolo Teatro in Milan (see GIORGIO STREHLER) and of DARIO FO; outside, its techniques have been applied very successfully to modern situations and issues, on both sides of the Atlantic, by the SAN FRANCISCO MIME TROUPE (founded 1959) and the Belgian company INTERNATIONALE NIEUWE SCENE. AEG

See: R. Andrews, *Scripts and Scenarios*, Cambridge, 1993; G. Attinger, *L'Esprit de la commedia dell'arte dans le théâtre français*, Paris, 1950; C. Cairns (ed.), *The Commedia dell'Arte from the Renaissance to Dario Fo*, Lampeter, 1988; P. L. Duchartre, *The Italian Comedy*, New York, 1966; T. Heck, *Commedia dell'Arte: A Guide to the Primary and Secondary Literature*, New York, 1988; K. M. Lea, *Italian Popular Comedy*, Oxford, 1934; C. Mic, *La Commedia dell'Arte*, Paris, 1927; A. Nicoll, *The World of Harlequin*, London, 1963; G. Oreglia, *The Commedia dell'Arte*, New York, 1968; D. Pietropaolo (ed.), *The Science of Buffoonery: Theory and History of the Commedia dell'Arte*, Ottawa, 1989; K. and L. Richards, *The Commedia dell'Arte: A Documentary History*, Oxford, 1990; V. Scott, *The Commedia dell'Arte in Paris 1644–1697*, Charlottesville, Va., 1990; R. Storey, *Pierrot: A Critical History of a Mask*, Princeton, 1978.

commedia erudita see COMMEDIA DELL'ARTE

Community Arts Service Theatre New Zealand theatre organization active from 1947 to 1962, touring productions extensively in the North Island. Organized from the Adult Education Centre of Auckland University, the company's professionalism was often in conflict with the amateur resources available on tour. Though only one New Zealand play was ever presented (Curnow's *Moon Section*), successive directors (Arnold Goodwin, Harold Baigent and Ronald Barker) did introduce rural audiences to SYNGE, CHEKHOV and BECKETT, and stimulated amateur drama considerably. HDMCN

community theatre (Britain) see REGIONAL THEATRE (BRITAIN)

community theatre/Little Theatre movement (USA) Thespian societies and parlour theatricals were common in America long before the advent of the Little Theatres. In 1901 Jane Addams and Mrs Laura Dainty Pelham organized the Hull-House Players in Chicago because they believed that good plays performed by amateurs could have 'a salutary influence on the community'. The big movement came a decade later with the Players (1909) in Providence, Rhode Island; Thomas H. Dickinson's Wisconsin Dramatic Society in Madison and Milwaukee (1911); Mrs Lyman Gale's Boston Toy Theatre (1912); Alfred Arvold's Little Country Theatre in Fargo, North Dakota (1912); and Maurice Browne's Chicago Little Theatre (1912). The sudden and simultaneous flowering of Little Theatres can be attributed to the following: the visit of Lady Gregory's Irish Players (1911); PERCY MACKAYE's call for 'constructive leisure' in his book *The Civic Theatre*

(1912); the founding of the DRAMA LEAGUE (1909); GEORGE PIERCE BAKER's Workshop 47 at Harvard (1912); the numerous articles about the European art theatres; dissatisfaction with the offerings of the commercial theatre; and a passionate belief, if sometimes ill-founded, that the arts and crafts of the theatre could be grasped by enthusiastic and ambitious amateurs eager for 'self-expression'.

The pioneers were quickly joined by Samuel Eliot's Little Theatre in Indianapolis (1915), SAM HUME's Arts and Crafts Theatre in Detroit (1916), Frederick McConnell's CLEVELAND PLAY HOUSE (1916), Gilmore Brown's PASADENA PLAYHOUSE (1918) and Oliver Hinsdell's Dallas Little Theatre (1920). By 1920 there were more than 50 groups scattered across the country, who found further support for their endeavours from Gordon Craig's *Toward a New Theatre* (1913); Hume's exhibition of the New Stagecraft (1914); New York's PROVINCETOWN PLAYERS (1914) and WASHINGTON SQUARE PLAYERS (1915); *Theatre Arts* (1916, later THEATRE ARTS MONTHLY); and from Constance D'Arcy Mackay's *The Little Theatre in the United States* (1917).

By the Second World War, the number of groups had grown to more than 100. They performed in improvised quarters (family mansions, livery stables, churches, community centres), on temporary platforms framed by proscenium openings of 15ft or less and with accommodation for fewer than a hundred spectators, most of whom were season subscribers. They specialized in bills of one-act plays, which required minimal scenery and few rehearsals and offered less demanding roles to more members. The more ambitious attempted the plays of SHAW, IBSEN and STRINDBERG, and at one time or another (in the 1920s) most took a turn at laughing at themselves with GEORGE E. KELLY's *The Torchbearers.* They also sponsored lectures, playreadings, and classes in theatre arts and crafts.

Community theatres (now numbering more than 5000) have become an integral part of the cultural life of their communities, and many have built their own theatre complexes. A 1984 survey by the American Community Theatre Association found nearly 100 that have been in continuous operation for 50 years or more, including the Footlight Club of Jamaica, Massachusetts (1877); the Players of Providence, RI (1909); Indianapolis Civic Theatre (1915); Le Petit Théâtre du Vieux Carré in New Orleans (1919); Theatre Memphis (1920); and the Omaha Community Playhouse (1925). Some have been transformed into regional professional theatres (e.g. Cleveland, Houston, Washington, Dallas), and even those that have maintained their amateur (or semi-amateur) status can hardly be called 'Little': they operate on budgets approaching a million dollars and present full seasons of major plays, both old and new.

Numerous attempts to organize such theatres into an association include the Little Theatre Conference at the Pasadena Playhouse (1924), the National Theatre Conference (1920s), and the American Educational Theatre Association (AETA, starting in 1936). In 1958 the National Association of Community Theatres joined members of AETA to form ACTA as a division of the American Theatre Association (formerly AETA). The demise of ATA resulted in a new group, the American Association of Community Theatres (1986), which meets annually and sponsors a play festival (ACT-FEST) every other year. RM

See: S. Cheney, *The Art Theatre*, New York, 1917; A. L. Crowley, *The Neighborhood Playhouse*, New York, 1959; N. Houghton, *Advance from Broadway: 19,000 Miles of American Theatre*, New York, 1941; A. McCleery and C. Glick, *Curtains Going Up*, Chicago, 1939; K. Macgowan, *Footlights Across America*, New York, 1929; P. MacKaye, *The Civic Theatre*, New York, 1912.

Compagnie des Quinze French theatre company directed by MICHEL SAINT-DENIS and drawn from former pupils of COPEAU. The company formed in 1929 when work with Copeau in Burgundy was no longer possible, and gave performances at the VIEUX-COLOMBIER THEATRE and the ATELIER as well as on foreign tours between 1931 and 1934. Their aim was to create a style of theatre at once poetic and acrobatic; their success was partly due to close collaboration with ANDRÉ OBEY, who wrote several plays for them. DB

Condell, Henry ?–1627 English actor, a long-serving member of SHAKESPEARE's company, the LORD CHAMBERLAIN'S MEN. Condell is known to have acted the Cardinal in WEBSTER's *The Duchess of Malfi* and was in the cast list of several other plays, all dating from before 1619, when he may have turned from acting to management. He shared with his colleague HEMINGES in the editing of the Shakespeare Folio of 1623 and in the churchwardenship of St Mary's, Aldermanbury, in London. He accumulated sufficient wealth to buy a country house in Fulham. PT

Confidenti Company of Italian COMMEDIA DELL'ARTE actors, 'confident of the public's indulgence', which travelled throughout Italy and to France and Spain between 1574 and 1620. In the early years it was headed by Vittoria Piisimi assisted by Giovanni Pellesini (Pedrolino), and for a brief time in 1584 merged with the UNITI. Its leading players were then DRUSIANO, and TRISTANO MARTINELLI as Arlecchino. From 1612 until its break-up, the troupe was managed by Flaminio Scala (Flavio), who was also its scenarist. LS

Confrérie de la Passion (Confraternity of the Passion) Medieval guild of Parisian artisans and merchants, formed in the latter part of the 14th century for the performance of religious drama and recognized by letters patent of Charles VI in 1402. Their privileges, which included a monopoly on dramatic activity in the capital, were confirmed by successive French kings and by the *parlement* in 1548. In the same year they built their own theatre, the HÔTEL DE BOURGOGNE, but were deprived of much of their repertoire by a *parlement* decree banning the performance of 'sacred mysteries'. Turning to moralities, farces, romances and other secular pieces, they continued to perform until almost the end of the century, whereafter their occasional practice of leasing their theatre to itinerant companies rapidly became the norm and their own performances ceased. The Hôtel de Bourgogne was soon a hub of professional theatre, though as landlords the Confrères proved strict, imposing rigorous conditions and a stiff rental on their tenants and resolutely pursuing defaulters or those who sought to evade their monopoly by performing elsewhere without paying them the requisite fee. In this way they hindered the development of theatrical activity in Paris, until the centralization of social and cultural life on the capital in the 1620s made change irresistible. With the establishment of the Comédiens du Roi in their theatre after 1629 and that of another company at the MARAIS in 1634, the Confrères' authority was slowly eroded and their monopoly was finally abolished in 1675. (See also MEDIEVAL DRAMA IN EUROPE.) DR

Congo, Republic of Formerly part of French Equatorial Africa, the Republic of Congo, renamed the People's Republic of Congo in 1969, gained its independence in 1960. Before the rapid development of the past 15 years, modern theatre was, of all the literary genres, the poor relation. Modern theatre in the Congo started only in 1950, and even then it consisted largely of school plays put on in mission institutions and performances at the French Cultural Centre by visiting French troupes. By the end of the 1960s, the country had three troupes of its own: the Théâtre Congolais founded by Guy Menga, Patrice Lhoni and others; the Troupe Municipale; and the Kamango Players of the country's second city Pointe-Noire. Their repertory was drawn from the few existing plays: Menga's *La Marmite de Koka Mbala* (*Koka Mbala's Pot*, 1969) and *L'Oracle* (*The Oracle*, 1969); Lhoni's *L'Annonce faite à Makoko* (*The Announcement to Makoko*, 1967); and Ferdinand Mouangassa's *Nganga Mayala* (1969).

The mid-1970s saw a quickening of the tempo, which had started with the publication some years earlier of SYLVAIN BEMBA's political classic *L'Enfer c'est Orfeo* (*Hell Is Orfeo*, 1968), and Letembet-Ambily's prize-winning *L'Europe inculpée* (*Europe Convicted*, 1969). In addition to Bemba, who also wrote *L'Homme qui tua le crocodile* (*The Man Who Killed the Crocodile*, 1972), a comedy of manners, and *Tarentelle noir et diable blanc* (*Black Tarantula and White Devil*, 1976), the other important dramatist of the 1970s was SONY LABOU TANSI. Poets like FELIX TCHICAYA U'TAMSI with his *Le Zulu* (*The Zulu*, 1977), and Maxime Ndébéka with *Le Président* (*The President*, 1970) – both plays against dictatorship – also turned dramatists about this time. There also emerged a theatre of socialist propaganda by Jacob Owei-Okanza.

Acclaimed recent plays include: U'Tamsi's *Le Bal de Ndinga* (*Ndinga's Ball*, 1987); Labou Tansi's *Moi veuve de l'empire* (*I, Widow of the Empire*, 1987); and Maxime Ndébéka's *Equatorium* (1987).

The 1980s saw the formation of troupes. Of the 15-odd that exploded on to the scene, only four are reported to be doing well: Labou Tansi's Rocado Zulu, Emmanuel Dongala's Théâtre de l'Éclair, both private and benefiting from financial and logistical support from the French Cultural Centre in Brazzaville; the Troupe Artistique Ngunga, and the state-run Théâtre National. What characterizes these troupes is the constant search for a new aesthetic. They all practise the technique of collective creation, and emphasize the actors' physical presence on stage and stylized body movements; they reduce the decor to the barest minimum, integrate dance, MIME and song into the activity, and make use of MASKS and symbolism. With the Ngunga and the Rocado now earning an international reputation with their regular participation in the

Limoges Festival of Francophone Theatre, Congolese theatre has come of age. JCM

> *See*: R. Chemain and A. Chemain-Dégrange, *Panorama critique de la littérature congolaise contemporaine*, Paris, 1979; R. Cornevin, *Le Théâtre en Afrique noire et à Madagascar*, Paris, 1970; J.-B. Tati-Loutard, 'Itinéraire', *Notre Librairie: La Littérature Congolaise*, 92–3, Mar./May 1988; M. Turé, 'Panorama du théâtre et quelques réflexions', *Notre Librairie*, ibid.

Congreve, William 1670-1729 English playwright; in its brilliant wit and taut control his comic style marks the greatest achievement of its age. Born in Yorkshire, he was brought up in Ireland and went to Trinity College, Dublin. In 1689 he wrote his first play *The Old Bachelor* before moving to London, ostensibly to study law. Through meeting THOMAS SOUTHERNE he became known to DRYDEN and his circle. His novel *Incognita* was published in 1692.

Southerne and Dryden helped Congreve revise *The Old Bachelor*, which was a brilliant success when it was performed in 1693. Using the materials of earlier Restoration comedies, the play is a witty examination of courtship and marriage with the rake seen as an odd anachronism. Congreve's next play, *The Double-Dealer* (1694), published with a prefatory poem of high praise by Dryden, was less successful. Its claustrophobic atmosphere and contrast of good with evil rather than wit with folly was too different from the norm to be understood. When BETTERTON's group split from the United Company, they opened their new theatre with Congreve's *Love for Love* (1695). Its blend of wit and generosity, with the rake in retreat for much of the play as his mistress seems about to marry his father, was immediately triumphant. Congreve's only tragedy, *The Mourning Bride*, much admired by DR JOHNSON, was performed in 1697; its rhetoric is restrained and its action less exotically improbable than most Restoration tragedies.

When JEREMY COLLIER launched his attack on the immorality of the stage Congreve was one of the dramatists singled out for especial attention: Congreve's reply, his *Amendments of Mr Collier's False and Imperfect Citations* (1698), does not show him at his wittiest for all its care in defending his practice. His last comedy, *The Way of the World* (1700), was not the success he had expected. It is the greatest of all Restoration comedies, exploring the battle for wealth and fortune as well as the search for security and constancy in courtship. Mirabell and Millamant are both witty and serious in facing the difficulty of proving their love. His libretto *The Judgement of Paris* was set in 1701, but apart from collaborating with VANBRUGH and William Walsh on a MOLIÈRE adaptation, *Squire Trelooby*, in 1704, Congreve did not write for the stage again. He briefly joined Vanbrugh in the management of the new Queen's Theatre in London's Haymarket in 1704, but gave it up when he gained the sinecure of commissioner for wines. Failing eyesight did not prevent his attending meetings of the Kit-Kat Club, and his *Works* were elegantly published in 1710. Financially secure when made Secretary for Jamaica in 1714, his long affair with the Duchess of Marlborough led to their daughter receiving his fortune in the form of a necklace after his death. PH

Conklin, John 1937– American set and COSTUME designer, whose career began in the late 1950s at Yale and the WILLIAMSTOWN THEATRE FESTIVAL (Massachusetts). In the 1960s he began an ongoing association with the HARTFORD STAGE COMPANY (Connecticut). Most of his work through the 1970s was at these and other regional theatres, but he also began to design for OPERA and teach at New York University (1980). By the 1990s he was designing regularly for the San Francisco, New York City, Metropolitan and Chicago Lyric Opera Companies as well as at opera houses throughout Europe. He worked extensively with directors ROBERT WILSON, Mark Lamos, JONATHAN MILLER and Robert Falls, among many others, and developed close relationships with such theatres as the AMERICAN REPERTORY THEATRE and the GOODMAN as well as Hartford, where he frequently collaborates with lighting designer Pat Collins. These associations and his teaching at NYU have made him one of the most influential designers in the USA. Working in a largely architectural style, Conklin fills his work with rich detail, texture and historical reference. His intelligent use of historical art and culture within his settings has been a strong influence on postmodernist tendencies in design. AA

Connelly, Marc [Marcus Cook Connelly] 1890–1980 American playwright, actor, producer and director who first became known on the BROADWAY scene as a collaborator with GEORGE S. KAUFMAN on such plays as *Dulcy* (1921) and *Beggar on Horseback* (1924), the latter being the most successful of their work together. His greatest contribution as a playwright came with *The Green Pastures* (1930), a Pulitzer Prize-winning adaptation of Roark Bradford's dialect stories. By holding the stage for 640 performances, this funny, touching and naturally truthful work showed America that a play with an all-black cast could be good box office. Connelly's Broadway acting credits include the Stage Manager in a 1944 production of *Our Town* and Professor Osman in *Tall Story* (1959), a role he repeated for the motion picture. As a producer-director, his greatest success was *Having Wonderful Time* (1937). His memoirs, *Voices Offstage*, appeared in 1968. LDC

Conquest [Oliver] **family** English theatrical family. **Benjamin** Oliver (Conquest; 1804–72), a low comedian famous for his rendition of 'Billy Barlow', married the dancer Clarissa Ann Bennett (1803–67). He managed the Garrick Theatre in London's Whitechapel from 1830 until 1846 when it burned down, and then took over the Grecian Theatre (1851–72), where he initiated a series of PANTOMIMES featuring his son **George** (**Augustus Oliver**) Conquest (1837–1901). George was the most spectacular acrobatic performer of his day, excelling in grotesque characters, strenuous leaps and aerial combats; his best parts were *Spitz-Spitze the Spider Crab* (1875) and the Monkey in *Grim Goblin* (1876). He managed the Grecian (1872–8) and then the Surrey Theatre (1881–1901), specializing in pantomime and full-blooded MELODRAMA, written in collaboration with Paul Merritt and Henry Pettitt. His biggest melodramatic successes were *Mankind* (1881) and *For Ever* (1882), in which he played the man-monkey Zacky Pastrana. His son **George Benjamin** (1858–1926) rose from ACROBATICS to roles as giants and carried on at the Surrey till 1904. His brothers were outstanding animal impersonators (see ANIMAL IMPERSONATION): **Fred** (1871–1941) excelled as the Goose in *Mother Goose*, while **Arthur** (1875–1945), after a successful career at DRURY LANE and COVENT GARDEN, appeared as Daphne the Chimpanzee on the MUSIC-HALLS in a double-act with his daughter Elizabeth. LS

Contat, Louise 1760–1813 French actress, who made her debut in 1776 and created the role of Suzanne in *The Marriage of Figaro* (1784). A particularly fine comic actress, she excelled in the plays of MARIVAUX, and was responsible for bringing *Les Fausses Confidences* into the COMÉDIE-FRANÇAISE repertoire. A tendency to stoutness made her gravitate towards roles of mothers and duennas. An ardent royalist (one of her lovers was the Comte d'Artois), she belonged to the anti-TALMA faction of the Comédie-Française, threatened to retire, and only reappeared (in *Les Victimes Cloîtrées* (*The Victims of the Cloister*) 1793) after he had departed. She was one of the members of the troupe condemned to death in 1793, but she reappeared with the reunited troupe in 1798. Bonaparte disliked her for her royalist association and *ancien régime* style, but this also accounted for her popularity. JMCC

Cook, Michael 1933–94 Canadian playwright. Born in London, England, Cook served in the British Army for twelve years before training as a teacher in Nottingham. He emigrated to Newfoundland, Canada, in 1965 where he later became a member of Memorial University's English department.

Cook was a prolific writer of RADIO DRAMA; representative samples of this genre are found in his *Tiln and Other Plays* (1976). The best of his stage plays are the historical dramas *Colour the Flesh the Colour of Dust* (1972), *The Gayden Chronicles* (1977) and *On the Rim of the Curve* (1977), and two plays dealing with contemporary Newfoundland life, *The Head, Guts and Sound Bone Dance* (1974) and *Jacob's Wake* (1975). *Colour the Flesh the Colour of Dust*, which shows the influence of BRECHT's EPIC THEATRE, dramatizes the 17th-century struggle between France and England to assert sovereignty over the North American seaboard; the play is an indictment of the colonialism represented by both European powers. *The Gayden Chronicles* and *On the Rim of the Curve* also interrogate Canada's colonial past, the latter documenting the extermination of the native people of Newfoundland, the Beothuks, by the British colonizers.

Cook characterized *The Head, Guts and Sound Bone Dance* as 'a controversial play that deals with Newfoundland's future', but the work is, rather, an elegy that contrasts an heroic and idealized past with a morally bankrupt present. *Jacob's Wake* is an even harsher condemnation of contemporary values, represented by a corrupt Newfoundland family embroiled in confrontations. The final apocalyptic scene in which a storm sweeps away the family home and its inhabitants has been compared with the conclusion to G. B. SHAW's *Heartbreak House*. But Cook's play is marred by an uneasy collocation of SURREALISM and NATURALISM, and its language again reveals how the genuinely poetic speech of his *oeuvre* is too often marred by an overheated rhetoric. EBEN

Cooke, George Frederick 1756–1812 Dublin-born English romantic actor; the first major foreign star on the American stage. Cooke was a travelling actor in the British provinces from at least 1773 until 1800, essaying some 300 roles. After a successful debut at COVENT GARDEN in 1800, where during 1800–3 he rivalled JOHN PHILIP KEMBLE, he restricted himself to a few roles – Shylock, Iago, Macbeth, Sir Giles Overreach, MACKLIN's Sir Pertinax MacSycophant and Sir Archy MacSarcasm, and especially Richard III – those seen most frequently during his American visit (1810–12), and those most admired for their satanic humour. Although there was a coarseness in his character and acting, Cooke was often noted for his stately carriage, as well as his broad torso and prominent nose. A chronic alcoholic, he was taken to the USA by THOMAS A. COOPER and STEPHEN PRICE to appear first at the PARK THEATRE on 11 November 1810. Although his reputation for drunkenness and debauchery preceded him, he was on his best behaviour (for the most part) during his 160 performances in New York, Boston, Baltimore, Philadelphia and Providence (where he gave his final performance, on 31 July 1812). He intended to take his US-met last wife (of a possible three to five) back to England, but died of cirrhosis of the liver in New York City that September. Buried in St Paul's churchyard in New York City, his remains were reinterred in 1821 by his admirer EDMUND KEAN, who erected a monument over them – still a notable theatre shrine refurbished six times (most recently in 1948). His earliest biography was penned by his contemporary WILLIAM DUNLAP (1813), though efforts by Arnold Hare and D. B. Wilmeth published in 1980 are generally more reliable. PT DBW

Cooke, T(homas) P(otter) 1786–1864 English actor, uniquely celebrated as a hero of nautical MELODRAMA, an illusion aided by the fact that he had served in the Royal Navy during his teens. His most famous roles were Long Tom Coffin in FITZBALL's *The Pilot* (1825), William in JERROLD's *Black-Eyed Susan* (1829) and Harry Hallyard in J. T. Haines's *My Poll and My Partner Joe* (1835). Cooke also provided the nautical interest in BUCKSTONE's domestic melodrama, *Luke the Labourer* (1826). His natural successor was WILLIAM TERRISS. PT

Cooper, Giles 1918–66 British playwright. Although best-known in his lifetime as a prolific adapter for television (see TELEVISION DRAMA), notably the *Maigret* series for which he won a Writer of the Year award in 1961, Cooper produced 70 original plays for radio, television and theatre. He had some critical success with the stage play *Everything in the Garden* (1962) and in 1964 created one of the most spectacular television plays of its time, *The Other Man*, an alternative history of Anglo-Nazi relations. His best work, however, was in radio, a medium whose extreme flexibility suited his acerbic mixture of the absurd and the naturalistic. Typically, the Cooper hero inhabits a world without meaning; he may be a small cog in an industrial machine of crushing pointlessness, or, often, a displaced soldier in a world with no room for his values. Cooper charted the decline of the British Empire in the postwar years with a sardonic verve tinged with compassion; it symbolized for him the inability of the human race to make sense of itself.

Despite their nihilism, his plays were charged with an economical wit. Pushing out radio's technical frontiers, he pioneered electronic sound effects to reinforce the cartoon-like nature of some of his stories (see SOUND IN THE THEATRE); he moved adroitly between his characters' inner and outer lives, between dream and reality. Six of his radio plays (see RADIO DRAMA) were published by the BBC in 1966, a rare tribute to a single radio author. He also received distinctions for his radio work from Czechoslovakia and West Germany. FG

Cooper, Thomas A(bthorpe) 1776–1849 British-born actor and manager, who became the first star of the American stage and initiated the practice of travelling from one company to another performing only prominent roles. While in his teens Cooper performed in Edinburgh and at various provincial theatres; his London debut was as Hamlet in 1795. In 1796, unhappy with his English acceptance, he went to the CHESTNUT STREET THEATRE in Philadelphia. After the settlement of an alleged breach of articles with the Philadelphia management, he joined WILLIAM DUNLAP at the PARK THEATRE in New York in 1801; during 1806–15 he was in management at the Park. With STEPHEN PRICE as his partner he played the Eastern circuit, excelling in heroic characters in poetic drama, such as Pierre in *Venice Preserv'd*. His popularity continued into the 1820s, but by 1830 it was waning and by 1835 'he had sadly become the seeker instead of the sought after'. DBW

Copeau, Jacques 1879–1949 French actor, director, critic, essayist and playwright. Generally considered to be the major influence on the development of French theatre since the First World War, Copeau was a tormented genius, never satisfied with what he achieved. He was a co-founder (with GIDE and Schlumberger) of the *Nouvelle Revue Française*, which published art and theatre CRITICISM, until in 1913 he founded his own theatre company in the VIEUX-COLOMBIER on the then unfashionable Paris left bank. From here he planned to launch a renewal of theatre art, rejecting both NATURALISM and spectacular decorativism in favour of a concentration on the actor and a bare stage.

His repertoire consisted mainly of SHAKESPEARE and the French classics, though he attempted to encourage new young playwrights. Associated with the theatre was a school in which an all-round training was given, not concentrating merely on theatre skills. Interrupted by the outbreak of war, Copeau was asked by Clémenceau to reconvene his company and perform in New York (GARRICK THEATRE, 1917–19). They returned to Paris in 1920 and performed on a stage remodelled by JOUVET to achieve something close to an Elizabethan playing space. In 1924 a religious crisis led to Copeau's conversion and withdrawal to the Burgundian village of Pernand-Vergelesses, accompanied by a few students. From 1925 to 29 he and the 'Copiaus' continued their quest, as much spiritual as theatrical, for artistic perfection. When Copeau again withdrew, some of his disciples formed the COMPAGNIE DES QUINZE.

His subsequent work consisted of isolated productions, especially of religious works in the open air, occasional productions at the COMÉDIE-FRANÇAISE, plus a brief spell as its director (1940–1); and the writing of plays and of an influential essay, *Le Théâtre populaire* (1941), which articulated the theoretical foundation for the post-war DECENTRALIZATION MOVEMENT. An extraordinary number of directors and actors (most notably DULLIN and Jouvet) trained or worked with him at some stage, and underwent the influence of his charismatic personality. His search for a new performance style, truthful and direct yet inventive and flexible, is still acknowledged as a source by contemporary groups such as the THÉÂTRE DU SOLEIL. DB

Coppin, George (Selth) 1819–1906 Australian actor-entrepreneur. A child performer and low comedian in England, Coppin arrived in Sydney with Maria Burroughs in 1843, and performed and managed theatres in several Australian colonies. By the mid-1850s he had four Melbourne theatres, including his famous Iron Pot, prefabricated in Manchester: based at the Melbourne Theatre Royal, he established a lucrative touring circuit for international performers. A member of the Victorian parliament and public figure for over 25 years, he retained his theatrical interests until the 1890s. MW

copyright: 1 Anglophone and European Copyright is ownership of, and right of control over, all possible ways of reproducing a work. In this context a work is an object which is the product of an original creative act (by one or more people), in a form which makes it subject to one or other means of copying. Copyright protection is given to literary, dramatic, musical and artistic works.

There are two qualifications for protection. First, that the work is capable of being 'in copyright' – that is, that it was not created or published at a time outside the period of protection offered by the law of the country in question. Second, that the work is 'original' – that is, the product of some skill and labour in composition other than the skill and labour involved in mere copying. The emphasis here is on expression rather than content. The copyright in an article expressing a new philosophical theory, for example, is in its unique sequence of words rather than in the theory as such. You do not infringe copyright in paraphrasing this theory and publishing your paraphrase (although you may be guilty of plagiarism). Indeed your paraphrase secures its own copyright protection as another sequence of words.

Ownership The creator of a work is normally the copyright owner, and no special act (e.g. registration) is required in order to establish ownership. The main exceptions are where the creator has already assigned copyright to another party via a contract entered into before the work was finished, or where the act of creation was a legitimate part of the creator's role under a contract of employment (broadly speaking, what United States copyright legislation refers to as a 'work made for hire').

Duration of copyright In the main, copyright is finite: there comes a time when a work goes out of copyright and falls into the public domain. The term of copyright varies widely from country to country – from 20 years after first publication at one extreme to 80 years after the death of the author at the other.

Transfer of rights 'Copyright' is really a bundle of rights, and the bundle grows as more means of reproduction and dissemination are invented. The copyright in an original play, for example, will contain the performing right, the right to publish in the original language, the right to translate and to perform and publish that translation, the right to quote, the right to turn into a film, and so on. The playwright is the original owner of all these rights by virtue of authorship; and in the normal run of events they are leased out on an exclusive basis, and possibly for a fixed period of time. An 'assignment of copyright', on the other hand, is the granting of the complete copyright to another: it is a transfer of ownership.

Dramatic copyright It is a surprising fact that the United Kingdom did not establish a performing right in a play (as distinct from a right to copy words on paper) until 1833. The moving force was BULWER LYTTON, whose eloquence in parliament led to a committee of inquiry into the laws affecting dramatic literature and the condition of the drama. Other countries have their different histories; enlightenment came very early to some and very late to others. Roman law appears to have identified a performance right, for example, and playwrights sold this right to the organizers of games, whilst in pre-revolutionary France the monopoly of the COMÉDIE-FRANÇAISE led to the poor author having neither rights nor payment.

Nowadays, the copyright laws of all countries contain specific protection for drama, and almost invariably a distinction is drawn between the right of publication and the right of performance. The differences and complexities arise when one starts to try to find out what each country means by 'performance', whether it takes some types of performance out of the realm of copyright, and what performance protection it gives to works other than straightforward plays (to dance or mime, for example).

Dramatization In all countries which recognize an author's rights, the right to dramatize (a novel, short story, or whatever) is held by the author as part of his copyright. The majority of countries assume that there is a point, however, where a dramatization is so remote from the original novel (for example) as to take it outside the dramatization right held by the novelist. The dramatist may be inspired by a dominant idea or theme in a novel, and produce a work which enshrines that idea but has its own set of characters and incidents. In any event, whether the work is a faithful dramatization of the novel or whether it is remote in everything but theme, the playwright will enjoy the copyright protection that is given to an 'original' play. CS

copyright: 2 Asian In traditional theatres in Asia, varied extra-legal systems evolved in the past to protect theatrical rights, with results similar to those of formal copyright laws. Rights to perform certain plays, roles and styles are understood by custom to belong to those artists who have created them. This does not mean that one actor cannot learn from an actor in another group, or that learning, borrowing and even stealing of specific techniques, bits of business or styles never occurs. However, in general, traditional performers stay within well defined language and cultural boundaries, if for no other reason than the fact that audiences, who belong to the same culture as the performers, are not attuned to non-indigenous styles or dramatic materials. Because play texts are inseparable from complex systems of singing, dancing and acting, it is almost impossible for a performer from outside a theatre tradition to profit much from stealing just the text; hence, formal copyright is rarely necessary to protect traditional texts.

However, it is common for performers within a given genre to jealously guard their individual styles of performance, and the texts associated with them, from rival performers working in the same genre. A powerful deterrent to improper appropriation is to deny access to training except to those in one's own family or group, or to one or two carefully selected pupils. In INDIA, performers of *KATHAKALI* and *KUCHIPUDI* must be male members of a particular caste. The puppeteer, *dalang*, of *wayang kulit* in INDONESIA and MALAYSIA passes on his art only to a few disciples who have spent years studying with him. In CHINA, only those pupils who received personal instruction from the great actor-singer MEI LANFANG may continue his style of performance.

In JAPAN, traditional rights of possession are primarily located within a theatre family. Between the 14th and 20th centuries, government edicts made the family legally responsible for acts of its members, thus setting a legal basis for theatrical 'family' rights over the plays and styles of performance created by past generations of that family. Exclusive authority over performance has contributed importantly to the fact that in Japan acting, dance and musical traditions have been transmitted unbroken for centuries. Thus, in *KABUKI* today the actor ICHIKAWA DANJŪRŌ XII is responsible for maintaining the integrity of the 'famous eighteen plays' of his family. As head of the family he must preserve the traditional form (*kata*) in his own performances of, for example, *Narukami the Thundergod*, which his ancestor, Danjūrō I, wrote and starred in three centuries ago. Further, he holds full authority to grant or deny another actor permission to perform the role of Narukami or similar role that 'belongs' to the Ichikawa family.

In *NŌ* theatre, each leading actor (*shite*) is a member of a 'school' or guild (Kanze, Hōshō, Kongō, Komparu or Kita). These five guilds operate as wholly independent and separate organizations. Each sponsors its own performances, and the actors in one guild would not dream of appearing in a play together with actors from another guild, or of mixing acting styles in a joint performance or of using the text of another school. (Supporting actors – *waki* and *kyōgen* – as well as musicians are also organized into guilds, but they may participate in performances of any of the five major guilds.) An acting family head, such as the great 15th-century playwright-actor ZEAMI MOTOKIYO, passed on to a single heir the written 'secrets' of his family's style, hidden from public knowledge.

The exclusivity typical of Japanese theatre guilds is

most clearly seen in the 'family head' (*iemoto*) system of *nō*, KYŌGEN, BUGAKU and classical dance (*nihon buyō*). The head has exclusive right to teach, to allow a disciple to learn a particular piece in the repertory, to grant approval to perform in public, and to supply texts and COSTUMES or MASKS necessary for performance. Further, portions of fees received by those lower in the system are channelled to the guild head, thus providing strong economic control over the entire guild. The performer who transgresses the internal rules can be expelled from the guild by the head, or by its senior members. While expulsion is not a legal matter today, it effectively denies the transgressor his occupation and is therefore a powerful deterrent to boundary transgression. Today, with few exceptions, exclusive ownership of theatrical materials by a theatre family or guild is universally accepted within traditional theatre in Japan. Today, modern drama texts are published under international copyright law, and performance rights to these texts are similarly protected by copyright law everywhere in Asia – with the notable exception of the People's Republic of China and the Republic of China (TAIWAN). JRB

Coquelin, Constant 1841–1909 French actor. Coquelin's name is associated with Cyrano de Bergerac (1897), which he played over 400 times at the Porte-Saint-Martin. Essentially a comic actor, he made his debut at the COMÉDIE-FRANÇAISE in MOLIÈRE's *Dépit amoureux* in 1860, but soon showed that his talents could be put to equally good use in the modern or the classical repertoire. One of his greatest successes was as Figaro. In 1886 he broke his career at the Comédie-Française to tour in Europe and America. He returned in 1889 for a brief period, which included the stormy reception of SARDOU's *Thermidor*, which had to be taken off after two nights in 1891 and replaced by a production of *The Taming of the Shrew*. The next year he joined SARAH BERNHARDT at the Théâtre de la Renaissance for Sardou's *Gismonda*. Their association was short, as the personalities of both were too strong to work together. The rest of his career was spent on the BOULEVARD. His last role was to have been ROSTAND's Chantecler, but he died while studying it. His great parts included Tartuffe and Don César de Bazan in *Ruy Blas* (1879).

An artist very aware of his profession, Coquelin wrote an important manual of acting in 1880, in which he emphasizes the need for authenticity in performance and stresses that the actor must always be in control of his means and leave nothing to chance. For him the voice was fundamental. In his last years he founded a retirement home for old actors at Pont-aux-Dames, and died there himself. His brother Ernest (1848–1909), generally known as Coquelin *cadet* (junior), was also an actor and tended to specialize in broader comic parts. JMCC

Corio, Ann [Anna Coria or Coreo] ?1907– With Georgia Sothern and GYPSY ROSE LEE, one of the premiere American strip-teasers of the 1930s, although Corio, 'probably the prettiest girl in burlesque', took off few clothes. From a member of the chorus in a BURLESQUE SHOW in her home town of Hartford, Connecticut, she rose to soubrette and then headline stripper. Her gimmick became 'innocence', dressing as a pretty little girl in a ruffled skirt. 'The

more innocent I was, the more wicked they [the audience] felt.' Under the tutelage of impresario Emmett R. Callahan (who married her), she became the star of *Girls in Blue* and other shows. Probably her most important contribution, however, was the revival of old-time burlesque in her *This Was Burlesque* (also the title of a book she co-wrote in 1968), which opened in 1962 and featured some of the great top bananas, including Steve Mills and Conny Ryan. DBW

Corneille, Pierre 1606–84 French dramatist and poet, one of the dominant figures in the evolution of 17th-century neoclassical drama. In the course of a long association with the Parisian theatres he produced over 30 plays, and proved equally successful in TRAGEDY and COMEDY. His first play *Mélite*, written while he was practising law in his native Rouen, was taken up by an itinerant company under Le Noir and MONTDORY and well received when they presented it in Paris in 1629. After an unfortunate foray into TRAGICOMEDY with *Clitandre* (1631), Corneille returned to favour with a string of four comedies set in contemporary Paris – *La Veuve* (*The Widow*, 1631/2), *La Galerie du Palais* (*The Palace Gallery*, 1632), *La Suivante* (*The Maidservant*, 1633) and *La Place Royale* (1633), all performed by Montdory's company. Their success brought him to Paris, where his first tragedy *Médée* (1635), possibly inspired by MAIRET's regular tragedy *Sophonisbe*, was produced at the MARAIS, as was his most original, 'theatrical' comedy, *L'Illusion comique* (*The Theatrical Illusion*, 1636). Corneille had also become one of the group of five authors employed by RICHELIEU to write plays under his direction, but after a disagreement with the Cardinal over some point of plotting the engagement was terminated and he returned to Rouen, where he wrote his most celebrated play *Le Cid*, derived from his reading of Spanish literature.

The triumph of this tragicomedy at the Marais early in 1637 signalled a resurgence in French drama, but it provoked the enmity of fellow writers, notably Mairet and SCUDÉRY, and a polemical exchange of pamphlets for and against the play, the *querelle du Cid*, ensued. In its wake Corneille wrote nothing for several years, but his series of 'Roman' plays, *Horace* (1640), *Cinna* (1641), *Polyeucte* (1642) and *La Mort de Pompée* (*The Death of Pompey*, 1643), followed by *Rodogune*, *Théodore* (both 1645) and *Héraclius* (1646), established him as the foremost tragedian of his day and led to his election to the Académie-Française in 1647. All were premiered at the Marais, where the leading roles were played by FLORIDOR, who also appeared alongside JODELET in Corneille's best comedy, *Le Menteur* (*The Liar*, 1643) and its sequel *La Suite du menteur* (1644).

The remainder of his career was attended by rather mixed fortunes. An inferior 'heroic comedy', *Don Sanche d'Aragon* (1649), and a 'machine-play', *Andromède* (1650), designed to exploit TORELLI's new mechanical installations at the PETIT-BOURBON, were followed by one of his finest tragedies, *Nicomède* (1651). But the failure of *Pertharite* in the following year induced him to abandon the stage and devote himself to verse, and later to the preparation of a complete edition of his plays containing commentaries on each and a considered exposition of his dramatic theory – the three *Discours sur l'art dramatique*

(1660). He resumed with further tragedies for the HÔTEL DE BOURGOGNE and the Marais – *Oedipe* (1659), *Sertorius* (1662), *Sophonisbe* (1663), *Othon* (1664), *Agésilas* (1666) – while another machine-play, *La Toison d'or* (*The Golden Fleece*), was produced in honour of the king's marriage in 1660 and later re-staged at the Marais. Having finally settled in Paris in 1663, the veteran dramatist was now in a good position to witness the rise of a formidable young rival in RACINE. He collaborated to good effect with MOLIÈRE and QUINAULT on *Psyché*, a *tragédie-ballet* presented at the Tuileries in 1671, but the two tragedies that Corneille entrusted to Molière's company at the PALAIS-ROYAL, *Attila* (1667) and *Tite et Bérénice* (1670), were both eclipsed by concurrent successes of Racine, and Corneille's last two plays, *Pulchérie* (1672) and *Suréna* (1674), fared little better.

Comparison with Racine is perhaps inevitable, if essentially unprofitable. As tragedians, the two evoke contrary responses in the spectator, Corneille's characters impressing us as emblems of nobility and heroic virtue and inspiring admiration above all else, Racine's as portraits of emotionally and psychologically divided individuals who arouse our appalled compassion. Not surprisingly, the latter's much smaller *oeuvre* is still largely familiar, whereas Corneille holds his place in the modern repertoire with only a handful of tragedies and even fewer comedies. DR

Corneille (de l'Isle), Thomas 1625–1709 French dramatist, younger brother of PIERRE CORNEILLE, with whom he remained on close terms throughout his life. His first comedies were produced when he was in his early 20s, and over the next 30 years he turned his hand with equal facility to a variety of genres, not least OPERA, with librettos for LULLY. Derivative but skilfully contrived, his plays followed the fashions of the day and proved consistently popular with audiences. In particular his TRAGEDY *Timocrate* was a triumph at the MARAIS in 1656, and he scored further successes with two other tragedies, *Ariane* (1672) and *Le Comte d'Essex* (*The Earl of Essex*, 1678); a COMEDY for JODELET entitled *Le Geôlier de soi-même, ou Jodelet prince* (*Jailer to Oneself, or Jodelet Prince*, 1655); and the 'machine-play' *La Devineresse* (*The Fortune-Teller*, 1679). In 1681 he became co-editor of the *Mercure Galant* and in 1684 was elected to the Académie-Française in succession to his brother. DR

Cornell, Katharine 1893–1974 American actress. Called 'the First Lady of the Theatre' by ALEXANDER WOOLLCOTT, Cornell, with HELEN HAYES and Lynn Fontanne (see LUNT, ALFRED), was the reigning actress on the BROADWAY stage during the second quarter of the 20th century. An accomplished interpreter of romantic and character roles, she brought to her characterizations a resonant voice and a remarkably expressive face that captivated audiences; she could create the illusion that a memorable play was being witnessed when in fact the vehicle was weak. Her New York debut was with the WASHINGTON SQUARE PLAYERS (1916); her London debut was as Jo in *Little Women* (1919). Prominence in the American theatre came with *A Bill of Divorcement* (1921). She is best remembered as Elizabeth Barrett in *The Barretts of Wimpole Street* (1931) and as SHAW's Candida (1924). Other notable appearances included *Romeo and Juliet* (1934), *The Doctor's Dilemma* (1941), *Antony and Cleopatra* (1947), *The Dark Is Light Enough* (1955) and *Dear Liar* (as MRS PATRICK CAMPBELL) in 1959. In 1921 she married GUTHRIE McCLINTIC, who was responsible for most of her productions. On his death in 1961 she retired. A lively biography was written in 1978 by the playwright Tad Mosel. DBW

Corpus Christi play Play performed on the feast of Corpus Christi, sometimes as part of the procession, which was an essential part of the celebration. The feast (instituted 1264) became generally celebrated in the west of Christian Europe in the early 14th century. Evidence for Corpus Christi plays comes primarily from England and Germany (*Fronleichnamsspiele*), though processions in Spain and Italy also show clear signs of dramatic activity as well as simple tableaux. The term is medieval, but its meaning in relation to the content of the play (and sometimes even day of performance) is not fixed. PM

corral de comedia A converted courtyard or patio, performance site of GOLDEN AGE popular theatre. In the mid-16th century charitable brotherhoods sponsored performances in hired yards, and by 1579 space had been purchased in Madrid for the first permanent *corral* on the Calle de la Cruz, followed in 1582 by another on the Calle del Príncipe. Eventually, the principal benefactor of the performances was the General Hospital.

The shape of the *corral* was determined by its position among existing blocks of buildings. The exposed stage was apron-shaped; against the back wall were narrow galleries supported by pillars and divided into sections, which could be curtained off allowing for dressing rooms or for use in performances as DISCOVERY SPACES or for balcony scenes, for instance. There might be two or three levels of balconies, with the highest one containing stage machinery. The stage itself could hold portable lateral graded bench seating. Trap doors were set into the stage, which was six or more feet above the floor. On each side of the *corral* were graded benches to the first-floor level. Above them the windows of the surrounding buildings, probably covered in iron grills, served as privately rented viewing spaces. Opposite the stage, the front or entrance area was set off by two enclosures where refreshments were sold; above this ground level was the women's section, probably protected by a grill and with boxes on either side. Above this level were more box spaces for dignitaries and, above them, more women's space and room for clerics. A projecting roof covered all sides but left the patio area open. This could be covered, however, by a canvas awning. Fees were charged at entrance and again for special seating; women were separated from men, except in the boxes. The patio area was for standing room, and the groundlings were infamous for their disruptions.

Performances were held all year except during Lent, and began at 2 p.m. in autumn and winter and 4 p.m. in spring and summer. Plays can be seen today in a reconstructed *corral* in the city of Almagro, but the *corral* was essentially replaced by the proscenium stage theatre in the 18th century. ELB

Corrie, Joe 1894–1968 Scottish dramatist. Corrie was a miner who wrote for the Scottish Community Drama Association and his own amateur group, the Bowhill Village Players, which toured the mining towns in Southern Scotland and (in 1929–30) Northern England. His first plays – *The Shillin'-a-Week Man* and *The Poacher* – were written for performance in the 1926 General Strike, but he rejected the more experimental techniques of AGIT-PROP theatre, calling for 'old technique' to be applied to working-class Marxist themes. The majority of his plays were short political pieces depicting everyday scenes of mining and rural life in Scottish dialect, some of which gained an international reputation, being translated into Russian, German and French; he also completed two full-length historical works – a drama on Robert Burns and *Master of Men* (1944). CI

Corvan, Ned 1830–65 British Tyneside comedian and song-writer. He joined BILLY PURVIS's company in his late teens, played fiddle in his band, took bit parts, and performed comic songs, including his own compositions, between the scenes. Finding himself increasingly successful in this line, notably with the genially antimilitaristic 'He Wad be a Noodle', he left Billy's employ in 1850 to join the Olympic concert-hall, Newcastle, as a singer-composer. A great hit with his songs and patter on local issues such as 'The Toon Improvement Bill' ('But still thor's folks 'boot here that smells/The cash buik wiv its flaw') and the price of coal ('They ken hoo to swindle poor folks'), he went freelance, playing the growing number of northeast MUSIC-HALLS. After a short-lived and costly attempt to set himself up in business as publican, impresario and leading artist at Corvan's Music Hall, South Shields, he went back to touring until his death from tuberculosis. A versatile performer, who incorporated impromptu cartooning into his act alongside self-accompanied song and character monologue, he stuck strictly to his northeastern base. His work has a concrete precision of reference that is unusual on the British VARIETY stage, as well as an anarchic imagination that looks forward to DAN LENO. AEG

Cossa, Roberto 1934– Argentine playwright and journalist, admirer of FLORENCIO SÁNCHEZ, ANTON CHEKHOV and ARTHUR MILLER. His first play, *Nuestro fin de semana* (*Our Weekend*, 1964), revealed him to be a major force in Argentine theatre, at the head of the so-called 'new realistic generation'. After several plays in the 1960s, in collaboration with GERMÁN ROZENMACHER, CARLOS SOMIGLIANA and RICARDO TALESNIK he wrote *El avión negro* (*The Black Airplane*, 1970), a collage of scenes dealing with the myth regarding Perón's possible return to Argentina. *La nona* (*The Grandmother*, 1977), the story of a voracious nonagenarian who metaphorically consumes and destroys, is perhaps the best-known play outside Argentina. *Los compadritos* (*The Bullies*) describes a particular style of urban strong-man, and is based on the sinking of a German U-boat off the coast of Uruguay at the beginning of the Second World War. In 1987 his *Yepeto* (of Pinocchio fame) explored the complex relationship of art, literature and life through two men enamoured of the same young woman. GW

Costa Rica Costa Rica is an anomaly within the Central American republics. With a high literacy rate, a record of stable democratic government and no military force, it has been a model imitated all too rarely. After the division of the United Provinces in 1838, this small country developed good working relationships between principal families and working-class citizens. The coffee and sugar industries flourished, and the growth of the banana industry in the latter part of the 19th century was consolidated into United Fruit, led by railroad tycoon Minor Keith. Petroleum shortages and inflationary trends in the 1970s and 1980s escalated the economic crises in Costa Rica, but the country remains decidedly stable in a geographic area characterized by political violence, socio-economic upheaval and class struggle.

The theatre before the 20th century has few national traits. Records exist regarding performances in the colonial capital of Cartago as early as 1722, but the few foreign troupes that presented plays did not provide sufficient impetus to create national theatre consciousness. Theatre houses were constructed by 1837 in San José, first in the Plaza Principal. Later constructions included the Teatro Mora, renamed the Teatro Municipal in 1861. The Costa Rican National Theatre, inaugurated in 1897 and renovated in 1974, bears testimony to cultural processes in this small democracy. Throughout the 19th century visiting theatre troupes, primarily from Spain, brought ZORRILLA's plays and other productions to enhance the scant activity being staged locally.

The 20th century In the 20th century the Costa Rican theatre began to assume national characteristics. The first national text is considered to be *Magdalena* by Ricardo Fernández Guardia (1867–1950), a costumbristic (see COSTUMBRISMO) play of the Costa Rican coffee families in which the central theme is a marriage of convenience that exacerbates class distinctions. A restaging of this play by the National Theatre Company in 1983 affirmed the importance of value systems at the turn of the century. Emilio Pacheco Cooper also wrote plays about local customs, such as *Venganza de un poeta* (*A Poet's Vengeance*, 1902), a lyrical work about intellectual pursuits which won the author a laurel wreath. Raúl Salazar Alvárez's *San José en camisa* (*San José in Night-shirt*) and *El hombre que buscaba el verdadero amor* (*The Man who Sought True Love*) were major successes; the latter pointed up the problem of local women who marry foreigners with different expectations. The visit of Díaz de Mendoza and his company in 1912 stimulated local actors and writers such as Eduardo Calsamiglia (?–1918), who wrote a dozen plays, all in verse. José Fabio Garnier (1884–1956) studied in Italy and wrote plays in an Italian Renaissance style, notably *Boccacesca* (1910) inspired by the *Decameron*. During the period between the two world wars, Costa Rica continued to be a regular stopping place for foreign theatre companies. Héctor Alfredo Castro Fernández (1889–1966), who used the pen name Marizancene, revealed a strong French influence and often wrote his plays in French for later translation.

Major outputs of recent years include the more traditional urban middle-class theatre of ALBERTO CAÑAS (b.1920) whose play, *Ni mi casa es ya mi casa* (*My House Is*

No Longer My Home, 1982), illustrates the devastating effects of inflation/recession in the modern world. Cañas is interested in folklore and popular myths. DANIEL GALLEGOS (b.1930), perhaps Costa Rica's most important playwright, has written cosmopolitan theatre with more universal tendencies, as seen in *La colina* (*The Hill*, 1968), a penetrating play that raised important religious and metaphysical questions about the death of God. SAMUEL ROVINSKI (b.1932), a more committed playwright in sociopolitical terms, has written several plays that demand greater accountability of those in positions of authority. Historical theatre became an important form for a younger generation of writers that included Fernando Cerdas and Miguel Rojas, and Víctor Valdelomar dealt with drugs and violence in a metropolitan setting in *Como semilla e' coyol* (*Like Seed and Fruit*, 1982).

The congenial climate of Costa Rica causes foreigners to assimilate easily, and the country has extrapolated to good advantage the experience and talent of outsiders while developing a national theatre. Plays from London, New York, Paris, Mexico and Buenos Aires are commonly staged, and a series of annual theatre festivals and showcases has helped to disseminate theatre in San José. A popular theatre movement has gained momentum; the Grupo Tierra Negra which opened in 1973 with a *creación colectiva* called *La invasión* (*The Invasion*) celebrated its tenth anniversary with Fabián Dobles's *El barrilete* (*The Cylinder*), a Revolutionary play about a man who wanted to fly. A PUPPET theatre, the Moderno Teatro de Muñecos, was established by Juan Enrique Acuña in 1968. Since 1979, *Escena*, a major theatre journal, has reported on theatrical activities and events in the country. About five groups or theatre houses are functioning regularly through impresarios who mount appealing and independent works; they interact with other forms of commercial theatre. After extensive damage in the earthquake of 1990, the National Theatre was closed for repairs and opened again only in 1994. For its size and population, Costa Rica has an active and vital theatre movement.   GW

> *See*: Cajiao Salas and A. Herzfeld, *El teatro de hoy en Costa Rica; perspectiva crítica y antología*, San José, 1973; G. Fernández, *Los caminos del teatro en Costa Rica*, San José, 1977; L. Garrido, *La imagen teatral*, San José, 1972.

Costantini [in France, Constantini] **family** Italian actors. The earliest noticed Costantino (c.1634–c.96) played first ZANNI under the name Gradellino and appeared in Paris from 1687. His son **Angelo** (c.1654–1729) alternated Arlecchino with DOMINIQUE BIANCOLELLI, but Dominique's death concentrated his powers on the role of Mezzetino, his red-and-white striped costume a contrast to the green and white livery of Brighella. He performed it in Paris (1683–97) and Dresden, where he was a successful rival in love to Duke August the Strong, who clapped him in prison for twenty years. Back in Paris, he was only sporadically successful. He wrote a life of TIBERIO FIORILLI. His brother **Giovan Battista** (d.1726) played second *amoroso* under the name Cintio, succeeding Marc Antonio Romagnesi in Paris in 1688.   LS

costumbrismo Spanish term (adjective: *costumbrista*) which refers to a type of theatre (or other genre) that captures the customs, style, characters and local colour of a particular region. Particularly strong in Spain in the early 19th century, it became characteristic of theatre in Spanish America in later periods.   GW

costume Actors often find costumes more important than scenery when making theatre. Many performance traditions throughout the world, and many 'golden ages' of theatrical history, have eschewed scenic display while lavishing resources on clothing, accessories, MASKS and disguises. Costumes have often been an actor's or a professional troupe's most valuable property. For companies constantly on the move, a greater reliance on dress than on scenery is understandable. The importance for the performer, however, is more intimate than this. The transformation of the human body, at rest and in motion, is central both to the craft of acting and to the craft of costuming.

Ancient Greece and Rome In 5th-century Athenian drama both actors and Chorus wore masks which were fully three-dimensional. They concealed the entire head of the wearer and were designed to be viewed from all directions. These helmet masks incorporated full heads of hair and often headgear or hair adornments which served to

Figures from the Pronomos Vase.

identify the characters impersonated. Facial characteristics on comic masks were exaggerated or caricatured, but on tragic masks were more lifelike and finely delineated (the distortions usually associated with the tragic mask belong to later Hellenistic and Roman practice).

Mask and costume formed a unified image. In COMEDY, lots of padding was worn on the abdomen and buttocks, to complement the exaggerated lineaments of the mask. On top of this padding a leotard and tights – to which, when appropriate, was affixed a ludicrously long leather phallus which could be coiled and uncoiled – represented stage NUDITY. Over this basic costume a character wore everyday clothing that was deliberately shortened or ill-fitted to reveal something of the 'stage body' underneath. In TRAGEDY, on the other hand, the flowing outlines of long tunics and elaborately draped cloaks complemented the finely delineated features of the masks, while subtle modifications to these everyday items of clothing served to create a sense of the familiarly unfamiliar.

The most distinctive of these modifications was the fitted sleeve, extending from shoulder to wrist, which was worn both by the piper (who accompanied the lyrics and dances) and by the tragic actors. Another was the *kothornos*, or calf-length boot, which became a definitive element of tragic costume. It was soft, with thin soles, and often with a pointed toe. It could be undecorated or decorated, loose or laced, but it always covered most of the leg. Outside the theatre *kothornoi* were worn by women: in tragedy they were worn by men, irrespective of the gender of the character being portrayed. In tragic costume, ceremonial and emblematic detail seems to have taken precedence over any literal naturalism. Colour and ornamentation were used to emphasize or symbolize aspects of the tragic action, as were contrasting costume changes, as the importance of clothing as an image throughout AESCHYLUS' *Persians* clearly shows.

Chorus members in tragedy wore *kothornoi* like the actors, although it is clear that they could also perform barefoot, but appear never to have worn the fitted sleeves which distinguished both piper and characters. Comic Choruses were usually dressed in padded costumes similar to those worn by the actors but, where appropriate, they also dressed in colourful and elaborate animal disguises. A comedy such as ARISTOPHANES' *Birds*, for example, would have given an ambitious *choregos* (producer) plenty of scope for a spectacular display of avian costumes and masks. Early evidence, on vases which pre-date the beginnings of organized comedy in Athens, indicates that Choruses costumed as animals, as well as Choruses costumed as fat revellers, formed part of the prehistory of Old Comedy.

In satyr plays the Chorus wore loin cloths, which sported an equine tail and a human phallus, and the distinctive mask of the satyr (clearly illustrated on the well known Pronomos vase) with snub nose and pointed ears. Actors in satyr plays wore the same costume as in the preceding tragedies, except for the performer playing the satyrs' father, Silenus, who donned a white-tufted, tightly fitting costume which covered the whole body, and a white-bearded mask.

From the 4th century BC onwards, with the spread of theatrical activity throughout the Hellenistic world – leading, over a period of time, to the formation of guilds of Dionysiac artists – there were significant changes in Greek attitudes to dramatic costumes and staging conventions which in turn influenced Roman theatre practice. The transition from Old to New Comedy saw more realistic comic masks and costumes, while the popularity of mythological burlesque (particularly in southern Italy) led to a blurring of some of the distinctions between comic and tragic genres. A 4th-century vase fragment from the theatrically active city of Taras (Taranto) shows a tragedian wearing a short fringed tunic, suggesting that a greater variety in theatrical costuming accompanied the rise of the professional actor. That costuming had a valued artistic status and played an important role in dramatic festivals throughout the Graeco-Roman world is testified by numerous inscriptions recording guild membership, or prizes and expenses, for costumiers (*himatiomisthai*).

Roman actors in the comedies of PLAUTUS and TERENCE wore masks and Greek costumes that were appropriate to the type of stock character portrayed. Some, like the Slave and Old Man, were grossly exaggerated, larger than life; others, like the Young Man and Young Woman, wore a more naturalistic disguise. A statue of a courtesan, found in Pompeii, shows how colourful costumes for the *palliata* (comedy in Greek dress) must have been. The mask has red hair and red lips, and a pale rose-violet mantle with fringes is draped over a light-blue short-sleeved robe. The influence of Italian FARCE can be detected in some of the grotesque stock disguises: the mask for the Old Man, for example, resembles that of the Attellan Pappus. Costumes in these native farces, as well as in the *togata* (comedy in Roman dress) which came to rival the *palliata* in popularity, reflected Roman and other local forms of dress. Three terracotta statuettes of masked actors, at present in the British Museum, show something of the variety that was possible: one is dressed in the Roman *sagula*, another in a Roman *toga* and the third in the Roman *paenula*.

A tendency, observable in late-Hellenistic tragic costume, towards vertical distortion was developed to an extreme degree on the Roman stage. The tragic actor wore boots with platform soles and heels or, eventually, stilts. The features of the tragic mask became distorted and stylized, and the forehead and hair were heightened in an increasingly two-dimensional dome. Lucian, writing in the 2nd century AD, gives an unsympathetic but graphic description of this artificial and conventional theatrical costume: 'How frightful and repellent a spectacle is a man tricked out to disproportionate size, mounted on high boots, wearing a mask that extends above his head with a mouth yawning wide as though to swallow the audience; not to mention the padding he wears on chest and paunch so that his own slender figure will not betray this excessive stature.' (See also GREECE, ANCIENT; ROME.)

Asia In ancient INDIA, costume was carefully regulated in the Sanskrit theatre to indicate such features as character type, profession and social status, and to evoke emotional states and sentiments. Dress, ornaments and make-up were viewed as essential elements in the transformation that was central to the art of the actor. As the *Natyasastra* puts it: 'Just as the soul after renouncing the nature proper to one body assumes another character related to the

Brick carvings showing costumed actors of the Yuan dynasty *zaju*, c.1279.

body of another, so a person having a different colour and make-up adopts the behaviour connected with the clothes he wears.' The use of colour was particularly emphasized. Abhira maidens wore dark-blue clothes; wandering ascetics, sages and Buddhist monks wore dark red; ministers, bankers and merchants wore white. Colouring of the face and limbs was an important part of the overall design. Different gods and demi-gods had their appropriate colour, while human characters were painted 'in conformity with their habitation, birth and age'.

Many of the traditional theatre forms found throughout India today continue something of this elaborate codification of make-up, dress and adornment. In KATHAKALI, for example, an audience can tell from the details and colours of a character's disguise not only what type of character is being presented but also what kind of behaviour they should be prepared for. Types range from the refined and heroic (*pacca*, or green roles) to the grotesque and primitive (*kari*, or black roles). A great deal of time and care can be taken in such codified costuming; for instance, the voluminous and complexly folded skirt worn by heroic characters in KUTIYATTAM takes three hours of patient preparation before it can be tied to the performer's waist. Visual spectacle, in traditional theatres as different as *chau*, *teyyam* and YAKSHAGANA, frequently depends entirely on the care and resources lavished on the actor's appearance.

From the evidence of early murals, brick reliefs and figurines, it is clear that a similar emphasis on costume and make-up was a distinguishing feature of theatrical performances in ancient CHINA. However, the symbolic system of painted-face roles encountered in modern Beijing opera is part of a tradition of stylization which appears only to have begun during the Ming dynasty. In *yuan* drama, make-up was used sparingly and the range of colours was restricted. Character types could be delineated by the use of false beards, but more particularly by specific and detailed items of clothing. In a players' edition of ZAJU dramas 46 types of hat and an even larger number of different jackets are listed for the male roles.

It was during the Ming and Qing periods that elaboration, synthesis and standardization of make-up and costume occurred as part of the conventional codes and symbolic modes of acting developed both in the private and the professional troupes. The close relationship between costume and acting conventions can be seen in the way such items as the extremely long and loose 'water' sleeves, which as early as the Han dynasties had been a feature of dancers' costumes, were incorporated into the symbolic systems developed for character portrayal by the acting companies. Costumes for KUNQU and PIHUANG XI became increasingly luxurious, often made of silk and richly embroidered, with headgear and adornments that extended the performer's referential and aesthetic powers. The four flags sewn to the back of the Great General's costume in Beijing opera, for example, allowed an actor to indicate the presence of his army at his back, and the long silver-pheasant tail feathers that adorned his headdress could be manipulated to punctuate thoughts, words, emotions and actions.

This interplay between symbolic and formal codes in acting and in costuming is particularly marked in JAPANESE NO and KABUKI traditions. In *kabuki* the exaggerated embellishments in form, texture and colour of the actor's bodily image both intensify and are intensified by the convention of freezing the action at moments of heightened emotion. In the Edo style of *aragoto* (the heroic mode of the ICHIKAWA DANJŪRŌ acting dynasty), the thick red and black lines of face-paint on a white base form an expressive background against which 'acting with the eyes' can stand out vividly, framed by the ferocious formalism of the *kurumabin* wig. At the same time the padding, the recurved toes and fingers, and the gigantic sword fuse with the extended outlines and brilliant colours of the costume to transfigure every motion or pose and imbue the actor's patterns with a sense of superhuman energy.

Whatever the style in *kabuki*, however, the colouring and ornamenting of a costume also convey specific symbolic information. In *The Actor's Analects*, for example, we learn that in the early pre-Genroku period of *kabuki* the white silk costume of a courtesan's client had 'an allover silver decoration of a wasp stinging a deer's antlers' which symbolized toughness and immunity from pain. Today, each of the lavish and aesthetically spectacular dresses worn by the courtesan Agemaki in the play *Sukeroku*, which were designed by Iwai Hanshiro V, are rich with such emblematic references. In the scene where Agemaki turns away her lover's mother, for instance, her sash is composed of a bush-like profusion of poems, a design which alludes to the custom of hanging scrolls from bamboo branches at the Star Festival in celebration of the love of the Herdsman star and the Weaving Maiden star who met briefly, once a year, across the divide of the Milky Way.

In contrast to the expressive exuberance of *kabuki* costume and acting styles, the symbolism and formalism in *nō* theatre is more restrained and subtle. The *waki* or Sideman is normally dressed in dark colours and mat fabrics to highlight the revelations encoded in the bright robes (*shozoku*) and elegant masks (*nohmen*) worn by the

Frontispiece to Shakespeare's *Henry VIII* in Rowe's edition (1709). Note that whereas the major characters are in historical costume, supporting actors wear contemporary dress.

shite, or Doer. Both mask and costume are crafted so that the slightest movement pattern can alter a character's appearance and liberate, through suggestion and context, a sense of universal flux. Masks are attached to the front of the head and are usually rather small, thus emphasizing rather than disguising the performer's body. It is the skill with which the Doer animates the polished surface of the mask in combination with the colours, textures and distinctive cut of the robes that is accentuated.

The aesthetic qualities of surface and detail represent differences of character and type: an under-robe with foil appliqué on white satin indicates a woman's skin – gold foil with red, a young woman; silver foil without red, an older woman. When portraying a female character, the way that outer robe and under-robe are worn in combination can indicate whether the character is a court lady or is mad or is half-dressed. The stress on the quality of material, colour, ornamentation and stylized beauty of the Doer's disguises is an essential element in *nō* theatre, guiding the audience's concentration towards the slow tempo and minimalism of the action.

Europe before 1900 In MEDIEVAL DRAMA, theatrical costumes ranged from the exotic to the stylized and ceremonial and to the realistic and everyday. Church vestments were worn in the early *Quem queritis* tropes (albs and copes are specified in the *Regularis Concordia* prepared at Winchester between 965 and 975), but as the variety of enactment increased so MIMEtic and representational details were added. Costume specifications in an *ordo prophetarum* of the 13th century from Laon in France record this development: a beard for Isaiah, dressed in a dalmatic with a red stole, and a beard and a hunchback for Habbakuk; while the clergy playing Daniel and Elizabeth are respectively said to be 'dressed as a young man in a gorgeous robe' and 'dressed as a woman pregnant'. A 14th-century *visitatio sepulchri* from Dublin distinguishes John from Peter by dressing one in white and the other in red, one carrying a palm, the other keys (their emblems as saints).

Outside the Church, theatrical costuming often showed a similar emphasis on indicative or symbolic detail: a money-bag for Judas, a crown for Mary, and a scarlet gown with a blue tabard and a mitre 'after the old law' for Annas in the English N. town PASSION PLAY. Such details were occasionally combined with recognizable items of contemporary clothing, although numerous costume inventories show that imaginary or quasi-historical disguises were also common. Materials and colours could be sumptuous and varied – Herod's queen in the Bourges (France) *Acts of the Apostles* (1536) wore a purple satin cloak, lined with silver, over a gown of violet velvet which had sleeves of cloth of gold – and wigs, masks and other elaborate bodily extensions were frequently employed.

Heads of yellow hair, suits of gold skins and pairs of iridescent wings for the angels contrasted with the distorted animality of the masks worn by the devils, who were covered all over with hair, feathers or serpent-like scales, or wore coats and trousers with bat-like flaps and ferocious faces painted on their bellies, knees and bottoms. Lucifer could descend to hell 'apparelled foul with fire about him' and then transform into 'a fine serpent made with a virgin face and yellow hair upon her head'. Adam and Eve regularly wore wigs and appeared 'nude' in special tights or in suits of white leather. Death, in Saragossa in 1414, was dressed in tight-fitting yellow leather so that his body and head looked like those of a skeleton – 'quite cadaverous, without substance, without eyes' – beckoning now to one, now to another of the onlookers to come with him. The range and often lavish nature of theatrical costuming in the Middle Ages are apparent from the many references in the records that survive.

This visual exuberance, its conventions and symbolism, were developed in the English MORALITY PLAYS and Tudor moral INTERLUDES in ways which significantly influenced later practice on the Elizabethan public stage. On the one hand, abstract characters – identified by an emblematic detail or prop – could be clothed in contemporary fashions indicative of specific social types, thus involving audiences both in current political and social concerns and in the human persona presented. On the other hand, abstractions could be dramatized wholly as abstractions, often in new and spectacular designs which, while part of a growing set of recognizable emblems, could provoke thought through brilliant and arresting images.

Money, for example, in Lupton's *All for Money*, 'cometh in having the one half of his gown yellow, and the other white, having the coin of silver and gold painted upon it'. Fame can appear in a coat and cap painted with 'eyes, tongues and ears', Report can be 'appareled in crimson satin full of tongues', while Catholic False-Report's outfit can have cross keys and scallop shells interwoven with the eyes, tongues and ears. SHAKESPEARE's Rumour 'painted full of tongues', in *Henry IV Part 2*, is heir to this tradition.

Elizabethan fashion, with its extravagant stiffening, padding and distorting of all natural lines (in male as well as female dress), reflects the age's intense interest in clothes. It is an interest which also dominates the theatre of the time. Dramatic texts are studded with observations on their characters' clothes, costume being seen both as an expression of power, status and wealth and as a mirror of inner qualities or transitory moods. On the largely bare platform, a hero or heroine's changing fortunes were visibly emphasized by changes of costume rather than changes of scenery. The wardrobe master, or TIREMAN, had an important task to fulfil, and, as we learn from HENSLOWE's diary, an actor could expect the fine for removing a costume from the playhouse to be some 40 times greater than the fine that might be imposed for missing a performance. No wonder, when the sum expended on taffeta to make two gowns for a single production in 1598 cost three times the average takings for a performance!

Contemporary styles and emblematic conventions clearly dominated theatrical costume on the Shakespearian stage, but some suggestion of historical or exotic dress, appropriate to the period or place depicted, may also have been employed for individual characters. Henry Peacham's drawing of characters in *Titus Andronicus* shows Titus, Aaron and two kneeling figures in fanciful versions of Roman attire, while Tamara and two soldiers are in English costumes. In the court MASQUE, particularly in the work of INIGO JONES from 1605 onwards, this mixture of character-specific styles began to be transformed by a more unified and pictorial sense of design. Jones introduced to England, alongside Italian perspective scenery, the scholarship and ideals of the Renaissance theatre designer.

Designers like BUONTALENTI and his successor PARIGI embodied the ideals of nobility and magnificence in theatrical costume articulated by YEHUDA LEONE DE' SOMMI in his dialogues on scenic representation. The fusion of the imaginary, the contemporary and the classical in their designs proved an influential model for aristocratic display, festivities and entertainment outside, as well as inside, Italy (a model that was developed and transformed at the court of Louis XIV in the work of the great JEAN BERAIN). In particular, the dissemination – throughout the courts of Europe – of the image of the stage hero dressed as an imperial Roman conqueror affected theatrical practice for more than two hundred years.

A Roman tunic and breastplate with overskirt, together with a helmet plumed with ostrich feathers, define the heroic or tragic actor throughout the baroque period. Changing notions on decorum and display continually modify details, but the exalted status of the Roman image remains a constant. Inigo Jones, when costuming Prince Henry in JONSON's *Oberon, The Fairy Prince*, eschewed an actual Roman skirt and created the illusion of its leather strips on more decorous trunk-hose; MOLIÈRE added a highly fashionable periwig when playing Julius Caesar in 1659; Boquet at Versailles, and Messelreuther at Bayreuth, used paniers to widen and stiffen the tonnelet or overskirt to form a surface for rococo design; SPRANGER BARRY and DAVID GARRICK added contemporary long, cuffed sleeves to their armour and wore knee-breeches under their tonnelets (though Barry's skirt remained hooped while Garrick's hung loose). Examples from the DROTTNINGHOLM SLOTTSTEATER of this baroque tragic attire are covered with sequins, crystals, spangles and copper threads that are designed to act as reflectors and enhance the illusion of heroic glory. In the soft candlelight of the indoor theatres the whole costume would shine and shimmer.

Plumes and classical overskirt also defined the baroque heroine, although the transformations due to changing tastes and fashions were even more pronounced. The overskirt might be reduced to tasselled lappets, or the hair piled higher and higher in place of the plumes. Whatever identified social superiority in high society, the theatre appropriated in order to emphasize the status of the tragic heroine. A train highlighted her nobility and grandeur; its length and degree of impracticability revealed her rank. The dialogue between off-stage and on-stage styles of dress was a complex one. Baroque theatre costumes did not simply ape current trends and values: they also refashioned them and even, at times, created them. The *fontange* or towering hairstyle, for example, was conceived on the stage.

For any actor or actress, respect for the geographical or historical context of a character vied with respect for the task of imaginative re-creation in terms of contemporary values and issues. It was not a matter of one or the other, but of balance. How different and individual a resolution any talented performer might come to on the baroque stage is revealed in the contrast between CHAMPMESLÉ's costume and Dumesnil's for RACINE's Phèdre.

Champmeslé wore a light, full-length, sleeveless gown, which was split on the left side so that her leg was revealed up to the knee, and a trailing cloak with gold-embroidered edges. On her head she wore a diadem with an embroidered veil, which fell to the level where her tunic parted to bare her knee. Dumesnil, in contrast, was robed in the latest contemporary style. Her wide-paniered white skirt – edged with gold – was decorated with a delicate flower-and-leaf design that contrasted with the billowing red and gold of her overskirt, bodice and puffed sleeves. Her train, white and patterned like her skirt, was bunched on her left hip as though it was in the process of slipping from the red billows of her overskirt. Her fashionable hair-do was red-ribboned and white-plumed and her veil trailed, bunched, behind her.

The quest for authenticity, REALISM or historical accuracy in theatrical costuming was a recurrent theme in stage theory and practice throughout the 19th century. With ever larger and less homogeneous audiences, the task of imaginative re-creation in terms of agreed and shared social values became more complex and volatile; and, as the fictional world on the stage became more pictorially and physically separate from the audience, so it became possible for a performer's concern for the 'truth' of a character's geography or history to predominate. Hence many of the costume 'reforms', initiated largely by actors and actresses, that electrified the latter half of the 18th century and prefigured the systematic, 'scientific' 19th-century achievements that culminated in NATURALISM.

These 'reforms', which at the time were lauded as authentic, realistic or historically accurate, now seem little more than tinkerings with the fashions of the day in defiance of outmoded stage conventions. Garrick and IFFLAND's concern for realism and truth in stage costume,

for example, entailed adapting 'modern dress' and selected historical features to suit the characteristic and individualized details of a role. LEKAIN's concern for 'costumes appropriate to the period and manners of the action represented' amounted to little more than exotic and magnificently fulsome adaptations of conventional heroic attire, as depictions of his oriental disguise for VOLTAIRE's *Orphelin de la Chine* clearly show.

Far more significant was TALMA's appearance, as a minor character in a 1789 revival of another of Voltaire's dramas, dressed in a toga faithfully copied from a Roman sculpture. Influenced by his friend, the painter David, Talma's innovations throughout his career were based on the conviction: 'Truth in the costume as well as in the scenery increases the illusion, takes the spectator right into the century and the country where the characters are living.'

A similar conviction sustained the unremitting researches of figures like Count Carl von Bruhl in Germany or J. R. PLANCHÉ and CHARLES KEAN in England – researches which informed every aspect of every costume in spectacular productions that sought to re-create, as it were, accurate pictures from the past. Under von Bruhl's direction, at the BERLIN ROYAL THEATRE from 1814 onwards even the cloth for a particular costume could be 'woven specially to reproduce the identical texture it would have had in the period concerned'. In Kean's production of *King John* (1852), the individual coat-of-arms for each noble in the play had been researched in the heraldic records and every detail was scrupulously reproduced.

This passion for exactitude was more consistently and influentially developed in the work of the MEININGEN COMPANY, who performed in most of the major cities in Europe from 1874 to 1890. Every detail of costume was intended not only to be historically correct, and actual rather than simulated in construction, but also to be harmonized with the scenery, the properties, the lighting, the sound, the movements on stage. Costume was considered as part of a total impression, of an authentic living picture. Such verisimilitude influenced ANTOINE in France, BRAHM in Germany, and STANISLAVSKY and NEMIROVICH-DANCHENKO in Moscow. For the first production of the MOSCOW ART THEATRE in 1898, the costumes of the Tsar, the boyars and the people were exact replicas of historical documents and were fashioned from genuine old materials gathered by the company from villages and markets. 'We wanted to depart from vulgar and theatrical gilding and cheap scenic luxury; we wanted to find another simpler, richer finish informed with some of the real spirit of the past.'

The 20th century Fidelity to period, place and psychology in theatrical dress, together with a desire for the authentic detail, 'the real spirit', is a legacy that has lingered throughout this century in spite of the numerous anti-naturalistic movements that have transformed so much of theatre practice. APPIA and CRAIG had far more influence on scenery and light than on costume. However, Craig's interest in masks, his symbolist designs for YEATS, and his fusion of costume and set in a single image (as, for instance, Claudius' enormous cloak, enveloping most of the stage, through which the courtiers of Elsinore

Edward Gordon Craig's design for the mask of the Blind Man in Yeats's *On Baile's Strand*, 1911.

appeared) adumbrated future developments. Many of Beckett's arresting stage images, for example, show a similar fusion of environment and dress.

The extension of the image of the human body outside the dictates of fashion – or the conventions established through performance traditions – is perhaps the single most innovative strand in 20th-century costume design. EXPRESSIONISM in Germany and constructivism in Russia both used distortion and abstraction to play on the 'normal' expectations concerning human appearance (although stage settings were often more adventurous in this respect). Far more radical was the work of OSKAR SCHLEMMER, whose transformations of the human body in motion through mask and costume influenced modern dance and foreshadowed developments in both performance art and experimental theatre in the second half of the century. The work of BREAD AND PUPPET THEATRE, WELFARE STATE INTERNATIONAL and ODIN TEATRET is indicative of this strand.

The other major shift in this century is the triumph of the designer. Although costumiers and costume designers have been important figures in the past, actors have also been actively involved in the issue of appearance (as the wardrobes of the great actors of the past amply illustrate). During the 20th century, such involvement has diminished. With the rise of the modern director, the notion of a unified vision shaped from outside the action has become a standard assumption, and the individual style of a designer has become a central feature of any production (see THEATRE DESIGN). LSR

See: M. D. Anderson, *Drama and Imagery in English Medieval Churches*, London, 1963; M. Baur-Heinhold, *Baroque Theatre*, London, 1967; M. Bieber, *The History of Greek and Roman Theatre*, London, 1951; T. Komisarjevsky, *The Costume of the Theatre*, New York, 1932; K. Komparu, *The Noh Theater*, New York, 1983; J. Laver, *Drama, Its Costume and Decor*, London, 1951, and *Costume in the Theatre*, London, 1964; D. de Marly, *Costume on the Stage 1600–1940*, London, 1982; P. Meredith and J. Tailby, *The Staging of Religious Drama in Europe in the Later Middle Ages*, Michigan, 1983; S. M. Newton, *Renaissance Theatre Costume*, London, 1975; S. Orgel and R. Strong, *Inigo Jones: Theatre of the Stuart Court*, London, 1973; A. Pickard-Cambridge, *The Dramatic Festivals of Athens*, 2nd edn, Oxford, 1968; F. P. Richmond, D. L. Swann and P. B. Zarrilli, *Indian Theatre: Traditions of Performance*, Honolulu, 1990.

Côte d'Ivoire Modern theatre in Côte d'Ivoire, which became independent in 1960, has enjoyed over the past 70 years a steady and richly varied development. It can be traced back to the late 1920s in Grand-Bassam, and its first signs seen in the secondary school pupils of the then Gold Coast, whose itinerant acting groups toured border regions of both countries during summer vacations, performing sketches in the common local languages. But it was in the 1930s at the École Primaire Supérieure de Bingerville that this new theatre was really to develop. The French headmaster Charles Béart, committed to nurturing his pupils' natural dramatic talent, encouraged them in their spontaneous improvisations. Beginning with extracts from French classical plays, soon the pupils were composing their own pieces and staging them to an outside audience.

This fledgeling theatrical activity was strengthened by the founding in 1938 of the Théâtre Indigène troupe by ex-Bingerville and École William Ponty (see SENEGAL) Ivorians – BERNARD DADIÉ, Koffi Gadeau and, especially, Amon d'Aby – whose period of study in the latter institution had further developed their taste for the theatre. The troupe's repertory was drawn from their historical, satirical and biblical dramas. Performances took place in the popular district of Abidjan, in a pidgin French (*français de moussa*) that is now widely used in popular dramas. Then in 1953 the Cercle Culturel et Folklorique was formed, and its members, including the three founder-members of the by then defunct Théâtre Indigène, wrote and produced new plays that reflected their growing nationalist consciousness.

In the immediate pre-independence years, France strengthened Ivorian theatre by creating cultural centres and founding the École Nationale d'Art Dramatique for training Ivorians in the theatre arts. The newly independent state built on this programme by instituting in 1963 a scholarship programme, which sent young students to France for advanced study of the theatre, and by founding in 1967 the Institut National des Arts. Short seminars by visiting French specialists were organized, and troupes sprang up: the Kourouma Moussa, the Guézaba and the Houphouët-Boigny.

If before 1960 Ivorian theatre was dominated, in terms of sheer production, by d'Aby (with 14 dramas by 1957) and Gadeau, the period after independence has been Dadié's. His plays, serious but also theatrical, are constantly being performed not just in his country but throughout French-speaking Africa. Other Ivorian playwrights include Charles Nokan, with his *Abraha Poku* (1971); the Martiniquan naturalized-Ivorian Eugène Dervain, with *La Reine scélérate* (*The Villainous Queen*, 1968) and Amadou Koné, with *Les Canaris sont vides* (*The Pots are Empty*, 1984).

In the late 1970s, several new currents revitalized Ivorian theatre by pulling it free from its European-inspired aesthetic. Thus Niangoran Porquet with his Théâtre Griotique evolved a style of acting derived from the 'theatre-ballets' of the Guinean Fodéba Keita and the performance of the traditional *griot*, which combines the spoken word with music, song, dance and MIME. Souleymane Koly, of Guinean origin, founded the Ensemble Kotéba which, like its Malian ancestor, explores social problems for a popular audience. His plays such as *Didi par-ci, Didi par-là* (*Didi Here, Didi There*, 1979) use a plurality of languages – French, pidgin French and Dioula – and mix spoken parts with stylized dance roles.

Sidiki Bakaba is experimenting with a theatre based on collective creation – usually a collection of loosely strung episodes – where scene and costume changes are all done in full view of the audience and where the director sometimes goes on stage to act a character. But perhaps the two most notable innovators of these years are BERNARD ZADI ZAOUROU with his Didiga Theatre of Symbolism, and NICOLE WEREWERE-LIKING, who has written plays which in content, form and function derive from RITUAL ceremonies. JCM

See: R. Bonneau, 'Panorama du théâtre ivoirien', *Afrique Littéraire et Artistique*, 23, 1972, and '*C'est quoi même*: *une improvisation collective de Sidiki Bakaba'*, *Afrique Littéraire et Artistique*, 27, 1973; R. Cornevin, *Le Théâtre en Afrique noire et à Madagascar*, Paris, 1970; F. J. d'Aby, 'Des origines du théâtre de Bingerville', *Notre Librairie: La Côte d'Ivoire*, 86, Jan./Mar. 1987, and *Le Théâtre en Côte d'Ivoire*, Abidjan, 1988; M.-J. Hourantier, *Du Rituel au théâtre rituel*, Paris, 1984, and 'La Parole poétique du Didiga de Zadi Zaourou', *Notre Librairie*, ibid.; A. Koné, 'La Griotique de Niangoran Porquet', *Notre Librairie*, ibid.; B. Kotchy, 'New Trends in the Theatre of the Ivory Coast 1972–1983', *Theatre Research International*, 9, 3, 1984; C. Wake, 'Ivory Coast', in *The Cambridge Guide to World Theatre*, ed. M. Banham, Cambridge, 1988.

court theatres (England) The various entertainments at the Tudor and Stuart courts were often elaborate enough to demand the temporary adaptation of indoor spaces. The Great Hall at Hampton Court, the Banqueting Houses as well as the Great Chamber at Whitehall and the Great Halls at Greenwich, Richmond and Windsor were all put to use, particularly during the Christmas festivities at which professional theatre companies were privileged to perform and well rewarded for doing so. Under Charles I, more permanent structures were adapted or built. INIGO JONES converted the COCKPIT-IN-COURT (1629–30) into an intimate theatre along the lines already tested at the COCKPIT THEATRE in Drury Lane, and the Stuart delight in MASQUES was gratified by the costly erection of the Masquing House (1637), close to Jones's magnificent Banqueting Hall (1619–22). Under Charles II and his successors, the custom of adaptation declined and the court theatres dwindled into insignificance. PT

Courtenay, Tom [Thomas] **(Daniel)** 1937– British actor, who helped to change the image of English acting in the early 1960s. Not conventionally handsome, with a northern accent, Courtenay played Konstantin in an OLD VIC production of CHEKHOV's *The Seagull*, stressing not just the doomed romanticism but also the provincialism of Arkadina's son. Courtenay took over from ALBERT FINNEY in the title role of *Billy Liar* (1961) and established himself quickly as a brilliant deadpan comic, starring in two ALAN AYCKBOURN comedies, *Time and Time Again* (1972) and *The Norman Conquests* (1974) in which he played Norman, the 'gigolo trapped in a haystack'. In Manchester, where he was part of the 69 Company at the ROYAL EXCHANGE THEATRE for several seasons, the range of his acting was more visible and better appreciated than in London, for he played Hamlet, Peer Gynt and the title role in RONALD HARWOOD's *The Dresser*.

Courtenay's style of acting adapts well to television and films, retaining its down-to-earth credibility. In 1964 he acted in the NATIONAL THEATRE's production of MAX FRISCH's *Andorra*, but his most memorable London role perhaps was as John Clare, the Northamptonshire poet-peasant, in EDWARD BOND's *The Fool* (1975) at the ROYAL COURT THEATRE. His stage appearances became less frequent in the 1980s, although he was a memorable Argan in MOLIÈRE's *The Imaginary Invalid*. In 1988 he played James, the innocent victim of an estate agent, in MARTIN CRIMP's *Dealing with Clair*. JE

Cousin, Gabriel 1908– French playwright, poet and sportsman. Cousin's career has been entirely outside Paris in the theatres of the DECENTRALIZATION MOVEMENT. His plays deal with major world problems of our time – hunger, racism, exploitation, the nuclear threat – but approached through the experience of communities of the working class, like himself, or the peasants. His first success, *Le Drame du Fukuryu Maru* (*The Drama of the Fukuryu Maru*; directed by DASTÉ, 1962), was a poetic evocation of the real experience of fishermen affected by a hydrogen bomb test in the Pacific in 1954. An original play about loneliness and exploitation used techniques reminiscent of the THEATRE OF THE ABSURD: *L'Aboyeuse et l'automate* (*The Barker and the Automaton*; directed by LECOQ, 1961). *L'Opéra noir* (*Black Opera*; directed by Garran, 1967) is a MUSICAL about racial violence and *Le Voyage de derrière la montagne* (*The Journey behind the Mountain*; directed by Lepeuve, 1966) is a powerful version of a Japanese tale about old age and poverty. His most accomplished play is *Le Cycle du crabe* (*The Crab Cycle*; directed by Cousin, 1975) about the inhabitants of a shanty-town in South America. His plays are filled with songs and movement; he believes that an essential element in *théâtre populaire* is festivity and celebration, however austere the subject. Since 1972 he has run a centre for encouraging creative activity, in Grenoble. DB

Covarrubias, Francisco see CUBA

Covent Garden, Theatre Royal (London) There have been three theatres on or near the Bow Street site, formerly part of a convent garden. The first was designed by James Shepherd for JOHN RICH, then proprietor of the theatre in LINCOLN's INN FIELDS and holder of one of the two Royal Patents. With a greater capacity (nearly 3000) than Lincoln's Inn Fields, it opened with a revival of CONGREVE's *The Way of the World* in 1732. Rich's company was led by JAMES QUIN, though Rich himself continued to feature in the annual PANTOMIME and his theatre's payroll had also to cater for followers of OPERA and ballet. Rivalry with DRURY LANE intensified when SPRANGER BARRY went to Covent Garden in 1750, though Barry rarely drew blood in his duels with DAVID GARRICK. For a few years after Rich's death in 1761, opera predominated at the theatre, but the stormy partnership of GEORGE COLMAN THE ELDER and Thomas Harris (1767–74) restored the balance. GOLDSMITH's *The Good-natured Man* (1768) and *She Stoops to Conquer* (1773) belong to this period, as does CHARLES MACKLIN's innovatory playing of Macbeth in Scottish costume (1773). Colman was eased out in 1774, but Harris remained active in the management of Covent Garden until 1809. His was the chief credit in spotting SHERIDAN's promise in *The Rivals* (1775) and in the decision to ask Henry Holland to oversee the massive structural alterations and enlargement of 1792. GEORGE FREDERICK COOKE made his London debut at Covent Garden in 1800, and the first self-proclaimed MELODRAMA, THOMAS HOLCROFT's *A Tale of Mystery*, was staged there in 1802. A major coup of Harris's was the theft of JOHN PHILIP KEMBLE from

The interior of Covent Garden Theatre at the time of the 'Fitzgiggio' Riot, 1763.

Sheridan's Drury Lane in 1803. Having bought a sixth share of the Patent, Kemble remained at Covent Garden until his retirement in 1817. It was he who engaged the prodigious Master BETTY in 1804, suffering in silence the indignity of unfavourable comparison.

When the first theatre was destroyed by fire in 1808, a second, designed by Richard Smirke after the Temple of Minerva on the Acropolis, was speedily built and opened in 1809 with an ill-fated production of *Macbeth*. Smirke's Covent Garden (capacity 3000) was slightly less capacious than Holland's remodelled auditorium, and Kemble had agreed to a compensating increase in prices. The fierce Old Price Riots forced the management into eventual submission. SARAH SIDDONS gave her farewell performance at Covent Garden in 1812, four years before MACREADY made his unwilling debut there. Having already installed gas to illuminate the entrance hall and grand staircase in 1815, the management of Covent Garden was quick to follow the LYCEUM and Drury Lane in the installation of gaslight for auditorium and stage (1817), an innovation which had an incalculable effect on the development of English acting. In 1821, John Kemble resigned his interest in Covent Garden to his brother Charles, who was to take responsibility for the staging of *King John* in historical costume (1823), according to the researches of J. R. PLANCHÉ. It was an idea that caught the imagination of audiences in the era of the Waverley novels. It was a rare success for CHARLES KEMBLE, who was one among many to be impoverished by his involvement with Covent Garden. Even the popularity of his daughter Fanny, a reluctant actress from 1829 to 32, was insufficient to save him, and his appointment as Examiner of Plays in 1832 came as a welcome relief. Subsequent managers – Laporte (1832–3), ALFRED BUNN (1833–5), Osbaldiston (1835–7), Macready (1837–9) and MADAME VESTRIS and CHARLES JAMES MATHEWS (1839–42) – were no luckier. The Patent houses could no longer afford their supremacy. After the Vestris management, Covent Garden remained closed until 1847, when it entered on a new life as the Royal Italian Opera House, with its capacity increased to over 4000. It was burnt to the ground in 1856.

The third theatre (capacity 2141), designed by Edward Barry, opened in 1858 with a performance of Meyerbeer's *Les Huguenots* and has been associated with opera ever since. It has been known as the Royal Opera House since 1939.   PT

Coward, Noël 1899–1973 British playwright and actor. Coward's most substantial work for the theatre was in the late 1920s to the early 1940s, with a series of rather precious but witty comedies (*Fallen Angels*, 1925; *Hay Fever*, 1925; *Private Lives*, 1930; *Design for Living*, 1933; *Blithe Spirit*, 1941; *Present Laughter*, 1942). The Second World War brought from him some patriotic pieces that were successful in their time but seem somewhat excessive in retrospect (*This Happy Breed*, 1942; *Peace in Our Time*, 1947), reworking a flag-waving enthusiasm first seen in *Cavalcade* (1931). As a composer and song-writer he produced work that the messenger-boy whistled then and whistles still, and in the theatrical orbit that he graced he was termed 'the Master'. He was knighted in 1970. MB

Cowell, Joe (Leathley) [Joseph Hawkins Witchett] 1792–1863 English-born actor, manager and scene painter who, after an abortive career in the Navy, became an itinerant actor, establishing a reputation as a low comedian. Emigrating to America in 1821, Cowell became a well known figure in the American theatre, both as an actor and as a manager of theatres and CIRCUSES. His vivid memoirs appeared in 1844. In 1863 he returned to England. Through marriages he was related to SARAH SIDDONS and the BATEMANS. His second son, SAM, became a MUSIC-HALL star. DBW

Cowell, Sam(uel Houghton) 1820–64 British actor-vocalist, born in the USA. Cowell, one of the earliest recognized MUSIC-HALL performers and an early star at the Canterbury Hall (see MORTON, CHARLES) in Lambeth, London, was the son of JOE COWELL and began his career in the legitimate theatre, touring the USA with his father in the 1830s in Shakespearian productions, billed as 'The Young American ROSCIUS'. Returning to England at the age of 20, he rapidly converted himself into a comic vocalist – he had already done 'coon' songs as entr'actes in America – and BURLESQUE performer. By 1850 he had abandoned the legitimate stage entirely in favour of the song and supper rooms of the WEST END, though his early career continued to serve him well in burlesques of SHAKESPEARE. An ugly little man with a lugubrious expression, he specialized in cockney song-and-patter acts, notably 'The Ratcatcher's Daughter' and 'Vilikins and his Dinah'. AEG DBW

Cowl, Jane 1884–1950 Boston-born American actress. Jane Cowl made her New York stage debut in 1903 in *Sweet Kitty Bellairs*. Her portrayal of the wronged woman, Mary Turner, in *Within the Law* (1912) established her as a star. Cowl appeared in plays that she wrote or co-wrote, including *Lilac Time* (1917); *Daybreak* and *Information Please* (1918); and *Smilin' Through* (1920). In 1923 she offered a 'breath-taking' Juliet in a production that ran for 174 consecutive performances. Her successful rendering of Larita in NOËL COWARD's *Easy Virtue* (1925) was followed by an 'appealing' Amytis in *The Road to Rome* (1927) and a 'brilliant' Lucy Chase Wayne in *First Lady* (1935). BROOKS ATKINSON praised her 'personal beauty, impeccability of manners, humorous vitality, and simple command of the art of acting'. The dark-haired, dark-eyed actress was regarded as a distinguished 'lady of the theatre' in London as well as New York. TLM

Cowley, Hannah 1743–1809 English playwright. Her first play, *The Runaway*, was produced by GARRICK in 1776 after he had 'embellished' it. Prolonged battles with SHERIDAN, Garrick's successor at DRURY LANE, and Harris at COVENT GARDEN delayed production of her next play, but her afterpiece *Who's the Dupe?* (1779) proved immensely successful in its vitality, using traditional figures of COMEDY such as the pedant. Her best play, *The Belle's Stratagem* (1780), and *A Bold Stroke for a Husband*

(1783) make extensive and unfashionable use of Restoration comedy as sources. In 1783 her husband moved to India (where he died in 1797) while she continued to pursue her writing career. PH

Crabtree, Lotta [Charlotte] 1847–1924 American actress. Born in New York, she and her mother followed her father to the gold mining town of Grass Valley, California, in 1853. She soon learned to dance and sing, and became a featured performer in mining camp VARIETY troupes. She conquered San Francisco in 1859 and headed east. She achieved widespread popularity when she made the transition to legitimate drama in the dual leading roles of *Little Nell and the Marchioness* (1867), dramatized for her from DICKENS's *The Old Curiosity Shop* by JOHN BROUGHAM. Though she later had other vehicles, they were only excuses for this tiny, red-haired, black-eyed elf to exhibit her skills at mimicry, banjo-picking and clog dancing. She never married, and retired with comfortable wealth in 1891. DMCD

Craig, Edith 1869–1947 British actress and director. Sister of GORDON CRAIG and daughter of ELLEN TERRY, she began her career performing with HENRY IRVING at the London LYCEUM in 1890. She constructed the costumes designed by her brother for his productions in 1900–1, and stage-managed her mother's 1907 American tour. She designed and directed for the Pioneer Players (between 1911 and 1921) and in London. CI

Craig, (Edward Henry) Gordon 1872–1966 British theorist, director and stage designer. Trained under HENRY IRVING, on whom he later wrote a definitive study (1930), Craig established a reputation as one of the leading young actors before leaving the London LYCEUM in 1897. Influenced by Hubert von Herkomer and the symbolists (see SYMBOLISM), he directed and designed a series of highly praised but financially unsuccessful productions, ranging from opera (*Dido and Aeneas*, 1900; *The Masque of Love*, 1901; *Acis and Galatea*, 1902) to LAURENCE HOUSMAN's nativity play *Bethlehem* (1902) and IBSEN's *The Vikings* (1903), before leaving for Germany where he designed productions for OTTO BRAHM and ELEONORA DUSE and influenced MAX REINHARDT, as well as beginning his association with Isadora Duncan.

In 1905 he published his first and most famous essay *The Art of the Theatre*, calling for the development of a non-naturalistic aesthetic (see NATURALISM) through which the theatre could become an art form equivalent to music or poetry, and establishing the dominant position of the modern director. This was followed by one of the first proposals for an English NATIONAL THEATRE and an attack on conventional acting, apparently demanding the elimination of the human performer, which was published in the first issue of the *Mask*. From 1908 until 1929 this quarterly journal, published and largely written by Craig himself using over 30 pseudonyms, ranged over the whole history of the stage, arguing for an abstract and ritualistic theatre that would have an equivalent spiritual significance to the tragedy of classical Greece or the Japanese Nô drama, and against the literary elements of drama as well as REALISM. The basis of his new drama –

Craig was comparable in some ways to his contemporary ADOLPHE APPIA – was to be light and rhythmic movement. In attempting to realize this, he pursued the notion of a flexible stage by means of which an endless variation of architectural shapes could be created during a performance (*Scene*, 1923). He founded a school of theatre in Florence in 1913 (closed by the First World War in 1915), and invented movable screens to substitute for scenery. These were used by W. B. YEATS at the ABBEY THEATRE, Dublin, in 1911, and by Craig himself in the famous 1912 *Hamlet*, which he directed for STANISLAVSKY's MOSCOW ART THEATRE.

Although, apart from this production, he directed only one other play – Ibsen's *The Pretenders* for the Poulsens at the Royal Theatre in Copenhagen (1926) – and only a single set of designs for live performance – GEORGE TYLER's 1928 production of *Macbeth* in New York – the originality of Craig's writings and the visionary nature of his designs have had a lasting impact on 20th-century theatre.　CI

Crane, William H(enry) 1845–1928 American actor who, after a long apprenticeship with a small touring OPERA company, achieved his first major success in *Evangeline* at NIBLO's Garden in 1873. During 1877–89, Crane and STUART ROBSON joined forces to produce a series of very popular American domestic comedies, such as *Our Boarding House*, *Our Bachelors* and *The Henrietta*. Crane was also noted for his Dromio, Falstaff and Sir Toby Belch. In 1890, he began a successful career as a producer-actor in his own-vehicle productions when he appeared as Senator Hannibal Rivers in *The Senator*, with which he was to be associated for the rest of his career. In 1896 he toured in JOSEPH JEFFERSON III's 'All Star' production of SHERIDAN's *The Rivals* as Anthony Absolute. A thoughtful artist who contributed a number of essays on acting and the theatre to popular journals of the day, he published his autobiography *Footprints and Echoes* in 1927.　MR DJW

Cratinus active c.450–c.423 BC The most prominent Greek poet of Old Comedy (see GREECE, ANCIENT) in the generation before ARISTOPHANES. He was noted for his invective, uninhibited even by Aristophanes' standards. Numerous brief fragments survive.　ALB

Craven, Frank ?1875–1945 American actor, playwright and director, best known for creating the Stage Manager in THORNTON WILDER's *Our Town* in 1938. Born in Boston of theatrical parents, Craven was a child actor. At 16 he played in repertory in Philadelphia; his first New York success was in 1910 as James Gilley in *Bought and Paid For*. He later wrote several successful scripts for the stage, such as *Too Many Cooks* and *This Way Out*. He played leading roles in several films, adapted some of his scripts to film, and wrote dialogue for Laurel and Hardy. He last appeared on BROADWAY in 1944. BROOKS ATKINSON called him 'the best pipe and pants-pocket actor in the business'.　SMA

Crawford, Cheryl 1902–86 American producer. As executive assistant to THERESA HELBURN at the THEATRE GUILD in the late 1920s, as co-founder with HAROLD CLURMAN and LEE STRASBERG of the GROUP THEATRE (1931), as creator of the AMERICAN REPERTORY THEATRE (1946) with EVA LE GALLIENNE and MARGARET WEBSTER, and as co-founder with ELIA KAZAN and ROBERT LEWIS of the ACTORS STUDIO (1947), Crawford was at the centre of the most vital and idealistic enterprises in the American theatre. A wry, poker-faced Midwesterner, she was a remarkably self-effacing impresario. Surrounded by highly strung, visionary colleagues, she always remained level-headed. She kept the peace between Clurman and Strasberg, whom she called Old Testament prophets; she raised money, trimmed budgets, found rehearsal space, arranged theatre rentals, and could always be counted on for a frank opinion of the artistic merit and commercial appeal of both plays and players. For all her commitment to serious theatre, she thought of plays as potential hits or flops, and withdrew from the organizations she helped to foster in order to pursue a career as an independent stage producer with a particular interest in MUSICALS. Her biggest commercial success was *Brigadoon* (1947); other notable Crawford productions include the 1942 revival of *Porgy and Bess*; *One Touch of Venus* (1943); *Paint Your Wagon* (1950); *Mother Courage* (1963); and four plays by TENNESSEE WILLIAMS – *The Rose Tattoo* (1951), *Camino Real* (1953), *Sweet Bird of Youth* (1959) and *Period of Adjustment* (1960). Her autobiography, *One Naked Individual*, was published in 1977.　FH

Crazy Gang Troupe of British comedians, who brought comedy techniques from VARIETY and CIRCUS to create a unique brand of knockabout satirical FARCE. (Bud) Flanagan (born Chaim Reuben Weinthrop) and (Chesney William) Allen, Jimmie Nervo (James Holloway) and Teddy Knox (Albert Edward Cromwell-Knox), Charlie Naughton and Jimmy Gold (James McConigal), with 'Monsewer' Eddie Gray, were brought together by GEORGE BLACK for 'crazy weeks' at the London Palladium in 1932. These improvisations developed into a popular series of REVUES from *Life Begins at Oxford Circus* (1935) to *These Foolish Things* (1938); and their success was repeated at the Victoria Palace from 1947 (*Together Again*) to 1960 (*Young in Heart*).　CI

Crébillon, Prosper Jolyot de 1674–1762 French dramatist, whose work offers an early hint of 18th-century sensibility and taste for the macabre. As if to galvanize audience response or to eclipse the memory of RACINE, he cultivated the most passionate and sensational of subject-matter. His most wildly successful tragedies, *Atrée et Thyeste* (1707), *Electre* (1708) and *Rhadamiste et Zénobie* (1711), are rhetorical tissues of pathos, horror and complicated plotting, which in retrospect offer at best a MELODRAMATIC *frisson*. He became a member of the Académie-Française in 1731.　DR

Crimp, Martin 1956– British dramatist, whose plays are particularly associated with the small suburban theatre the Orange Tree, Richmond, in Surrey. Crimp has been likened to HAROLD PINTER in that behind his studies of an apparently tranquil suburban life there are signs of menace, although a better comparison might be with the US postmodern TV soap opera, *Twin Peaks*. *Dealing with Clair* (1988) concerns the relationships between an estate agent (Clair), a yuppie couple and an innocent cash buyer. When

Clair disappears, it is assumed that she has been murdered. *Play with Repeats* (1989) concerns a man who, feeling himself to be inadequate, seeks advice from a guru – which he follows, only to find that he really is inadequate. *No One Sees the Videos* (1990) is a scrappy but sometimes brilliant attack on market research, while *Getting Attentions* (1991) starts like a sit-com but develops into a frightening study of child abuse. Crimp's dialogue is dry, witty and with interesting turns of phrase. His sense of construction can recall AYCKBOURN'S, but his characters seem currently to lack the depth required for full-length plays. JE

criticism: 1 European There is little theatre criticism in a modern sense before the 16th century in Europe, because of the lack of an established theatre or of pamphlets. What criticism there was confined itself to academic discussions of the merits of classical dramatists; and the classical bias accordingly entered into the first major critical discussions which emerged during the 17th century. In Britain, PHILIP SIDNEY (1554–86) entered into a debate with a minor playwright, STEPHEN GOSSON, who had become convinced of the sinfulness of all fiction; and the result, Sidney's *Apologie for Poetrie* (or *Defence of Poesie*), published in 1595 but written before 1583, became a model defence for the theatre (and all art) against the charge of lying. Nevertheless, the immorality or otherwise of the theatre has preoccupied much critical discussion until today, and has been well documented in Jonas Barish's *The Anti-theatrical Prejudice* (1981).

In France, theories of classical drama were discussed in Jacques Grevin's *Bref discours pour l'intelligence de ce théâtre* (1561) and Jacques de la Taille's *L'art de la tragédie* (1573); while in 1630, JEAN CHAPELAIN (1595–1674), a founder member of the French Academy and a friend of CARDINAL RICHELIEU, wrote a *Letter on the Twenty-four Hour Rule* to his fellow Academician, Abbot Godeau, which starts to apply classical rules to contemporary texts, emphasizing among other matters *bienséance* (decorum). This letter suggests that of the famous three unities (of time, place and action), only that of time had yet been formulated. Chapelain also took the dramatist PIERRE CORNEILLE (1606–84) to task over his triumphantly successful tragedy, *Le Cid* (1637), and the following *querelle du Cid* prepared the way for the formation of neoclassical opinion. This was still textual criticism and confined to a limited social circle; but by the 1650s, public pamphlets on stage performances began to appear. A collection of these loose sheets, started in 1650 by Jean Loret, was published in 1656 as *Muse Historique*; while Charles Robinet's *Lettres*, begun in 1654, contained some theatre criticism. The most important of these gazetteers was DONNEAU DE VISÉ, who from 1672 onwards started seriously to discuss criteria suitable for the public performance of plays in his *Mercure Galant*; and he, together with Charles de Saint-Denis de Saint-Évremond (1613–1703), were the real pioneers of neoclassical criticism in Europe, rather than the better-known NICOLAS BOILEAU (1636–1711).

Boileau's *L'Art poétique* (1674) was originally conceived in four cantos as a witty commentary on his fellow poets; and Mme de Sévigné has described the amusement caused by its early readings in 1672. In comparing his contemporaries, often unfairly, with classical writers, Boileau described the three unities, which specified that plays should concentrate on single situations which might (in real life) have occurred in one place in a time span not exceeding one day. These rules, which suited Boileau's friend, JEAN RACINE, better than anybody else, became incorporated (together with decorum in speech, manner and moral behaviour) into the general tenets of neoclassicism, which spread from the Court of the Sun King, Louis XIV of France (1638–1714), to other European monarchies, affecting the Enlightenment associated with the reign of Frederick II (the Great) of Prussia (1712–86) and the Age of Reason in Britain. Boileau himself became known throughout Europe as 'the lawgiver of Parnassus'.

Among British writers strongly influenced by Boileau was JOSEPH ADDISON (1672–1719), whose essays on theatre topics for the *Tatler* and the *Spectator*, a periodical which he edited with SIR RICHARD STEELE, mark the rapid transformation from Restoration pamphleteering with its polemical tone into the urbane journalism of the Augustan age. Addison's tragedy, *Cato* (1713), is modelled on Boileau's precepts. Addison was not, however, a theorist and, as the successor to the poet, dramatist and critic, JOHN DRYDEN (1631–1700), could not be regarded as a pioneer of criticism. The success of the *Spectator* led to many imitations; and aesthetic discussions, together with gossip, became a familiar feature of 18th-century literary life. Alexander Pope's *Essay on Criticism* (1711) and *The Dunciad* (1728) have in their satirical sketches and their conventional neoclassical wisdoms much in common with *L'Art poétique* which Pope greatly admired. While DR SAMUEL JOHNSON's *The Lives of the Poets* (1781) represents the pinnacle of Augustan criticism – sane, terse and moral without being sententious – the capacity to take part in critical discussion at a high level was shared by most men of letters of his time, despite the fact that in Britain the Theatres Act of 1737 had severely restricted the development of the theatre.

Among the German-speaking countries, Boileau's influence spread through the Enlightenment critic, JOHANN GOTTSCHED (1700–66), who became a professor at Leipzig University. He not only introduced neoclassical criticism into German dramaturgy through his *Versuch einer kritischer Dichtkunst* (1729) and compiled a bibliography of German drama from the 16th century onwards, but also translated (with his wife) plays from French and English sources, including Addison's *Cato*. He found the existing German repertoire lacking in seriousness, and he particularly disliked the touring bands of players with their slapstick comedies, in which the commentator CLOWN, HANSWURST, so frequently figured. In France, Britain and the German-speaking countries, neoclassicism was soon to come under attack for being rule-bound, snobbish and inhibiting to the creative spirit; but, at best, the critics were not dogmatic but sought to combat barbarism with the standards of the two highest civilizations of which they were aware, those of the Greek city-states and of Rome in the time of Augustus. They also pursued a reconciliation between Reason and Nature, for Reason was deemed mechanical and lifeless by itself, just as Nature was wild and anarchic without Reason. The critic sought a judicious balance, the harmony of opposites, which was also held to be the secret of behavioural and moral decorum.

The challenge to neoclassicism The first major challenge to neoclassical opinion came from G. E. LESSING (1729–81), who attacked Gottsched's reforms in *Briefe, die neuste Litteratur betreffend* (1759). He became the dramaturge to the National Theatre at Hamburg (1767–8), publishing a series of papers as *Hamburgische Dramaturgie*. The aesthetic principles described in *Laokoon* (1766), of which only the first part was finished, were developed through his own plays, which range in style from the early prose comedy, *Minna von Barnhelm* (1767), to his final tragedy, *Nathan the Wise*, not produced until two years after his death. Lessing, with the SCHLEGEL brothers, AUGUST WILHELM (1767–1845) and Karl Wilhelm Friedrich (1772–1829), first proposed the theories which became known as romanticism. Gottsched was criticized for importing artificial French rules into Germany, and Lessing cited the example of SHAKESPEARE as a dramatist who followed no sterile formula but achieved a directness of utterance unparalleled since the ancient Greeks. This enthusiasm for Shakespeare was shared by all the romantic critics and A. W. Schlegel's translations of Shakespeare's plays still hold pride of place on the German stage.

Naturalness and sincerity became key words in the critical vocabulary; and although Lessing anticipated the lawless aspirations of the *STURM UND DRANG* movement, he was too steeped in classical humanism to endorse them. Johann Georg Hamann (1730–88) and his one-time pupil, Johann Gottfried Herder (1744–1803), finally broke with classical doctrine and declared that only the unfettered creative imagination could contemplate God and His works. In *Kritische Wälder* (1769), Herder argued that plays have to be seen in relationship to the prevailing circumstances of their times, not judged by any absolute standards, although the *Kraft* (energy, power) of the poet could transcend social conditioning. Herder championed not just Shakespeare but folk poetry and those early German plays which Gottsched had despised; and he influenced the great romantic writer, JOHANN WOLFGANG VON GOETHE (1749–1832), who brought him to Weimar in 1776.

Herder was also an early admirer of JEAN-JACQUES ROUSSEAU (1712–78), who in a tormented life came to reject the debilitating effects, as he saw them, of urban civilization, calling for a return to simpler, more primitive human values. Through Rousseau's *Du contrat social* (1762), romanticism acquired a political stance (for populism, democracy and folk loyalties) which it never subsequently lost. Romanticism reversed the neoclassical doctrines, perhaps too neatly. It was anti-academic, anti-monarchical, individualistic, passionate rather than polite, stressing the aspirations of the human soul. The artist became a prophet and a seer, the 'unacknowledged legislator of mankind', while the critic was his apostle and interpreter.

In Britain, until the restrictions of the Theatres Act were partially lifted in 1843, the theatre was damned in the eyes of many romantic critics by its aristocratic leanings and state CENSORSHIP. Shakespeare, however, was exempt from these strictures, and Samuel Taylor Coleridge, among others, wrote eloquently about him. WILLIAM

HAZLITT (1778–1830), the finest theatrical essayist to have emerged in Britain, described Elizabethan drama and Shakespeare's characters in powerful articles, as well as providing vivid portraits of actors like JOHN PHILIP KEMBLE and EDMUND KEAN, for which he is best remembered. Hazlitt's collection of essays, *A View of the English Stage* (1818), remains a model for British critics; and he excelled in describing the social contexts of drama, which he dubbed (translating from German) the 'spirit of the age'. *Tales from Shakespeare* by CHARLES LAMB and his sister Mary introduced generations of schoolchildren to the basic plots. Among academics in Britain, Shakespearian interpretations owe a considerable debt to German romantic scholarship. Even A. C. Bradley's *Shakespearian Tragedy* (1905), a standard university textbook for 50 years, referred back to the pioneering work of Lessing and the Schlegels, and in particular adopted Lessing-like interpretations of the tragic hero and the importance of empathy and catharsis.

In France, what became bardolatry among lesser critics was slower to arrive and existed side by side with conventional neoclassical opinion, which received a new lease of life through the BOULEVARD drama of EUGÈNE SCRIBE (1791–1861) and the formulae of the WELL MADE PLAY. Nevertheless, Mme de Staël's *De l'Allemagne* (1813) and Stendhal's *Racine et Shakespeare* (1823, 1825) paved the way for the flowering of French romanticism in the works of Vicomte François-René de Chateaubriand (1768–1848) and particularly of VICTOR HUGO (1802–85), whose *Préface de Cromwell* (1827) went out of its way to reject two of the three unities, retaining only that of action in a modified form. He praised Shakespeare's alternative technique which organized a play through contrasts, tone colour and the juxtaposition of themes. Hugo's passion for Shakespeare is fully expressed in *William Shakespeare* (1864). By the 1840s, however, a reaction against romanticism had begun to be expressed through the writings of Charles Augustin Sainte-Beuve (1804–69), who came strongly to deplore the vaunting of egoism as inspiration. His *Chateaubriand et son groupe littéraire sous l'Empire* (1860) scathingly denigrated the romantic movement in France and proposed a new role for theatre critics, who should aim towards the sophisticated broadmindedness of Montaigne, the 16th-century essayist whom he particularly admired.

One consequence of the romantic movement was that aesthetics became detached from ethics or from any classical concept of civilization. Criticism necessarily became more subjective, the reflection of the likes and dislikes of the individual critic; and in the early 19th century, magazines and periodicals which appealed to the new middle classes developed, whose pages contained the work of critical essayists whose personalities defined their aesthetic standards and whose charm became a major selling point. JULES JANIN (1804–74) was one such, the critic of the *Journal des Débats* who could make and break theatrical reputations following no guide other than his own instinct. His main rival, Gustave Planche of the *Revue des Deux Mondes*, specialized in iconoclasm. Das Junge Deutschland (with Lüdwig Börne (1786–1837), the dramatist KARL GUTZKOW (1811–78), and briefly Heinrich Heine (1797–1856)) was a literary and political movement of the

1830s which sought to direct the idealism of the romantics towards specific political ends, anticipating social realism. Its main principles were expressed in Ludolf Wienbarg's *Aesthetische Feldzüge* (1834). Apart from such political movements, which were reflected to different degrees in other countries, the main feature of European criticism at this time lay in the growth of those elegant, personal descriptive essays which became known as *feuilletons*, a word still used to describe the review sections of newspapers in some parts of Europe; and the master of the *feuilleton*, who preached 'art for art's sake', was THÉOPHILE GAUTIER (1811–72), who wrote for the *Monde Dramatique* and *La Presse*.

Despite the popularity of the *feuilletonistes*, criticism aspired towards a greater precision of thought, something of that discipline which had been lost with the decline of neoclassicism. One of Sainte-Beuve's disciples, Hippolyte Taine (1823–93), turned to science as the method for the objective description of a work of art, which could 'tackle the human soul' as well as the surrounding social history. Such faith in science was criticized by even his supporters, such as Paul Bourget (1852–1935) and Ferdinand Brunetière (1849–1906), who came to theorize about tragedy from a neo-Darwinian point of view, in his lectures at the École Normale in 1889. Nevertheless, Brunetière eventually proclaimed the bankruptcy of science as an approach to art. Other French critics, such as Jules Lemaître (1853–1914) of the *Journal des Débats* and Anatole France, the pseudonym of Anatole-François Thibault (1844–1924) who wrote extensively for many papers but particularly for *Le Temps* from 1887 to 92, scrupulously avoided scientism, adopting an impressionistic style of considerable brilliance in which the first consideration was of an epicurean delight, and the second vaguely left-wing sentiments.

In the 43 years which separated the birth of the Third Republic in France in 1871 and the First World War, the growth of theatre criticism defies short, comprehensive analysis. In Paris, major poets and dramatists wrote regular columns, such as Alphonse Daudet (1840–97), Catulle Mendès (1841–1909), Jean-Jacques Weiss (1827–91) and even ÉMILE ZOLA (1840–1902), whose contributions to *Le Roman experimental* (1880) argued a fundamental, if extreme, case for NATURALISM. By 1911, there were no less than 150 theatre columns in Paris; and in 1907 a daily newspaper, *Comoedia*, was exclusively devoted to the theatre. Paul Léautard (1872–1956), Léon Blum in the *Écho de Paris* and the *Grande Revue*, Henri Bordeaux in the *Revue Hebdomadaire* and the *Revue des Deux Mondes*, Paul Souday in *Le Temps* and Anatole France – all had reading publics which spread beyond the borders of France.

In Germany, the proliferation of newspapers was one factor in the development of a split between ordinary theatre reviewing and academic criticism. Whereas the academics increasingly sought to apply scientific criteria, or at least sustainably objective ones, to the study of drama, the daily critics had neither the time nor the inclination to do so, although they tended to be more academic than the British critics. Before 1870, much German criticism was political in character, with Wolfgang Menzel (1798–1873) insisting that the critic should confront the nation with major moral questions and such writers as Theodor

Vischer (1807–87), Robert Prutz (1816–72) and HERMANN HETTNER seeking to combine historical and social analysis with politics and aesthetics. The establishment of the Kaiserreich in 1870 and the new commercialism of the press changed the context in which critical discussions took place. As the theatre itself, under censorship, lost its political bite, so such journalists as Karl Frenzel of the *Nationalzeitung*, Berlin, concentrated on drama as entertainment, ignoring its other dimensions. As in France, there were brilliant *feuilletonistes*, such as Theodor Fontane (1819–98) and PAUL LINDAU (1839–1919), whose stylistic excellence compensated for their unwillingness to take part in wider speculation. Their approach was challenged, however, by those critics who came to embrace naturalism, led by Julius Hart (1859–1930), and whose arguments, as expressed by OTTO BRAHM (1856–1912), Paul Schlenther (1854–1916) and Alfred Kerr (1867–1948), laid the foundations for contemporary German criticism. Through Brahm and Kerr criticism recovered its wider interests, notably in the avant-garde, without losing its journalistic panache – although their approaches could still be attacked as too subjective. A Marxist critic such as Franz Mehring (1846–1919) would turn any aesthetic discussion into a political seminar, while Herbert Ihering (1888–1977), an early supporter of BERTOLT BRECHT, stressed the importance of a factual examination of the performance. Between 1933 and 1945, all criticism under the Nazis in Germany had to be dedicated to the goals of nationalism.

British theatre criticism, like British theatre itself, was slower to develop than in France or Germany; and less space was devoted to it within its press. Matthew Arnold (1822–88) attacked what he dubbed the philistinism of Victorian smugness and its moral values and the coarse popularity of proletarian theatre. His essay, 'The French Play in London', for the August issue of *Nineteenth Century* (1879), based on a visit of the COMÉDIE-FRANÇAISE to London, called for the establishment of a British National Theatre and was continually cited by those who wanted to establish Continental-style repertory theatres in Britain. Clement Scott (1841–1904), the theatre critic for the *Daily Telegraph* for 30 years and a minor dramatist, became notorious for his attacks on IBSEN and the naturalistic writers, mainly on the grounds of preserving a moral decorum of language and subject-matter within the theatre. Scott also edited the *Theatre*, which he founded in 1877, but withdrew in 1890 after a dispute with WILLIAM ARCHER (1856–1924), the dramatist and critic of the *World*, who was Ibsen's champion and translator in Britain. Archer with HARLEY GRANVILLE BARKER (1877–1946) provided a blueprint for a British National Theatre (1907), which offered the model for fund-raisers and other enthusiasts for 50 years. The most brilliant and successful theatre critic, however, and the best since Hazlitt, was BERNARD SHAW, whose columns for the *Saturday Review* from 1895 to 1898 combined wit, seriousness of intent and a voluminous, if superficial, general knowledge. His successor was almost equally remarkable, Max Beerbohm (1872–1956, the half-brother of HERBERT BEERBOHM TREE the actor-manager), who wrote for the *Saturday Review* from 1895 to 1910, and was also an essayist and playwright.

Themes of 20th-century criticism From this welter of turn-of-the-century criticism, certain themes emerged which often transcended national boundaries and sometimes derived from ideas promulgated through romanticism. The great debating issue was that of the new naturalistic drama, pioneered by Zola and ANTOINE's Théâtre Libre in Paris but which came to be associated with Ibsen and the Scandinavians. Systematically attacked by conventional moralists and often censored in Britain, the new naturalists were stoutly defended by most left-of-centre critics, including Shaw, who used the evident seriousness of Ibsen, BRIEUX and Zola as a means to attack the superficiality of state censorship. CENSORSHIP itself was an issue which divided critics around Europe. But naturalism was only one manifestation of the avant-garde which preoccupied critics. In some countries, such as Ireland, still under British rule, nationalism and the rediscovery of national languages dominated critical discussion; and straight patriotism was incorporated into the aesthetic theories of Russia, Italy, Norway and the several nations which comprised the Austro-Hungarian Empire (1867–1918). In line with romantic theory, the folk origins of their national theatres were discussed, usually praised at the expense of those from other countries; and, for example, the Polishness of being Polish was debated, with the different imperialisms of France, Britain and Prussia coming under attack.

There was also a European growth of interest in SHAKESPEARE, with the first translations appearing in Hungary (1864), Spain (in the 1870s), Belgium (1884), Denmark, Sweden, Norway and Russia. Shakespeare Associations developed in many countries, while in Britain the interest in Shakespearian scholarship and production led to the foundation in 1894 of the Elizabethan Stage Society, under the actor-director WILLIAM POEL whose experiments with open stages and minimal settings profoundly influenced Shakespearian performances in the 20th century. British Shakespearian scholarship moved away from its German intellectual roots towards practical staging – exemplified in Granville Barker's *Prefaces to Shakespeare* (1927–47), in which his experience as a director and actor is of paramount importance – and towards sensitive research and the brilliantly imaginative work of G. Wilson Knight and Caroline Spurgeon, whose analysis of Shakespeare's poetic images provided the ROYAL SHAKESPEARE COMPANY in the 1960s with a supply of set designs. The Polish-born critic JAN KOTT (b.1914) bravely attempted to strip 19th-century moralizing away from the canon in his *Shakespeare, Our Contemporary* (1964), in which the absurdity of Shakespeare's world and its power struggles was stressed and related to modern preoccupations.

But theatre criticism was also indebted to romanticism in other, less direct ways, for the romantics had uncovered problems and ideas which continued to haunt all intellectuals until the 1950s, whether they considered themselves to be part of the romantic movement or not. One such major theme was that of individualism and the search for the self. While many turn-of-the-century critics derided the spectacle of the doomed tragic hero, as hammed by actor-managers in countless MELODRAMAS, nevertheless they continued to be confronted by the consequences of

individualism, such as the conflicting demands of the state, the private conscience and religious belief. NIETZSCHE's assertion that God was dead was capable of many interpretations, one consequence being that without God there could be no inherent order within the universe. Edmund Husserl (1859–1938), the mathematician-philosopher, in common with some British empiricists argued that the true study of philosophy lay in the accurate description of consciousness, which he christened 'phenomenology'. One of his pupils was the existentialist, Martin Heidegger (1889–1976), although Husserl's impact on criticism was more evident through the dominance in postwar Paris of JEAN-PAUL SARTRE (1905–80). Sartre's particular contribution lay in his attempt to reconcile the apparently irreconcilable – faith in existential individualism, an individualism which discovers its own 'essence' through the act of being, and Marxist collectivism.

While such philosophical speculation coloured European criticism particularly in the 1950s, there were other less abstract ways in which individualism affected aesthetic theory. One was the growth of EXPRESSIONISM, which began in Germany in 1910, a movement of social revolt and a reaction against NATURALISM in which the playwright or director is considered to speak directly to the audience, albeit in a variety of ways, including AGIT-PROP imagery. The Swedish critic PÄR LAGERKVIST (1891–1974), who received the Nobel Prize for Literature in 1951, cogently argued the case for the expressionism in AUGUST STRINDBERG (against the naturalism of Henrik Ibsen) in *Modern Teater* (1918); but the greater international impact came from the work of the German expressionists, TOLLER and WEDEKIND among them, who influenced a generation of writers and directors, of whom the most systematic in developing his ideas was the dramatist-critic, BERTOLT BRECHT (1898–1956). Brecht's theoretical writings were considerable and appeared in essays and dialogues throughout his life; but the ideas on 'epic' theatre, 'alienation' (*Verfremdungseffekte*) and the 'gest' were summarized in *Kleines Organon für das Theater* (1949). Brecht borrowed some techniques from expressionism to provide the basis for what was essentially an instructional theatre, devoted to furthering Marxism, although his own theatrical sense and poetic instincts prevented his plays from being narrowly propagandist. With customary thoroughness, however, he argued the case for his EPIC THEATRE from the roots of dramatic theory, attacking the Aristotelian concept of theatre, as he understood it.

Brecht's views were not initially well received in the Soviet Union, whose official views, after the outpouring of modernism in the early 1920s, remained wedded to social realism, in which naturalistic stagings were wedded to socialist analysis. The first Commissar for Education in Soviet Russia was ANATOLY LUNACHARSKY (1875–1933), a dramatist and comparatively liberal in his views, who furthered the cause of theatre under the intellectually restricted circumstances of Stalinism. The main purges of intellectuals, however, took place after his death and continued throughout the Eastern bloc until long after the death of Stalin. A particular target for Soviet attacks was, however, not Brecht, not even bourgeois theatre, for

OPERETTA houses still comprised a third of the theatres in the Soviet Union, but another and more fundamental off-shoot of expressionism, the THEATRE OF THE ABSURD.

Absurdist theatre has many roots, well described in Martin Esslin's *The Theatre of the Absurd* (1962), but what all its different manifestations had in common was a hatred of conventional bourgeois theatre, scientific logic and middle-class ethical restrictions. While ALFRED JARRY's *Ubu Roi*, conceived as a MARIONETTE play in 1888 but performed as a stage play in 1896, is generally regarded as the seminal work (leading to the mock-scientific theories of Jarry's pataphysics and to French SURREALISM), the leading theorist was STANISŁAW IGNACY WITKIEWICZ (1885–1919), 'Witkacy', a Polish dramatist and artist whose impact on postwar absurdist writers and directors, including SAMUEL BECKETT, EUGÈNE IONESCO and the director TADEUSZ KANTOR, was considerable. His use of visual imagery – for Witkacy had studied as an architect and painter – remains (despite the plays of PICASSO) the most effective dramatic extension of surrealism; and as a philosopher, he was able to connect his ideas with those of existentialism. The French theorist, poet and playwright, ANTONIN ARTAUD (1896–1948), was more violent in his rejection of bourgeois codes, both in the theatre and outside it, declaring in his collection of essays, *Le Théâtre et son double* (1938), that the theatre would 'never find itself again ... except by furnishing the spectator with the truthful precipitates of dreams', in which crime, erotic obsessions and savagery loomed large. Artaud in turn influenced JERZY GROTOWSKI (b.1933) whose book, *Towards a Poor Theatre* (1968), and whose example as a director working solely through those means supplied by the expressiveness of actors, made a great impact on the fringe theatres of the 1960s.

This often bewildering variety of theories and philosophies became absorbed into critical journalism, sometimes as little more than useful terms employed without questioning their background or meanings. In the interwar years in Britain, it was possible for critics such as JAMES AGATE (1877–1947), who wrote for the *Sunday Times* from 1923 until his death, or W. A. Darlington (1890–1979) who was with the *Daily Telegraph* for 48 years, to be resolutely anti-intellectual, relying on their flair for judging the theatrical moment and their good-humoured relationship with their readers. 'Touchstone' criticism was in fashion: for Agate, IRVING was the touchstone by which he judged great acting. Agate's successor at the *Sunday Times*, Harold Hobson (1904–92), was another touchstone critic, although in his case Edwige Feuillère represented a kind of acting excellence. KENNETH TYNAN (1927–80), the last flowering of the *feuilletoniste* tradition in Britain, employed touchstone criticism in his early essays, published in *He That Plays the King* (1950), which much impressed Agate.

The 1960s to the present day In the 1960s, theatre journalists were confronted not only with a bewildering variety of new genres, such as happenings, total theatre and environmental theatre, but also with a new critical vocabulary. Words such as 'alienation' and the 'V-effect', derived from Brecht, quickly became commonplace. Others came from Antonin Artaud's Theatre of Cruelty or from the street and FRINGE THEATRE movements. Method acting had

its own technical language and jargon. But the most pervasive new critical language stemmed from structuralism, which influenced even those critics who claimed to know nothing about it and took pride in their ignorance.

Structuralism derived from the teachings of Ferdinand de Saussure (1857–1913), a Swiss linguistics professor, whose lecture notes were published posthumously. *Cours de linquistique générale* (1915, Paris; 1959, New York) described language as a system of signs, in which every item both defines and is defined by its surrounding signs. The study of signs, which do not have to be verbal signs but can be other visual and aural signs – of music, painting and the theatre – became known as structuralism or semiology, the science of signs. The appeal of structuralism lay in its claim to be a 'science', provable and thus objective. Critics who were not structuralists merely responded to their likes and dislikes; but the initiated claimed to be analysing society from the standpoint of social scientists.

The background to most of their theories derived from Marxism. The French anthropologist, Claude Lévi-Strauss, applied the principles of Saussurean linguistics to the problems of communication in many cultures, from primitive to modern societies, and his *Les Structures élémentaires de la parenté* (1949) remains a classic study of social structures and their origins. Roland Barthes (1915–80) approached literature from a similar point of view. His first book, *Le Degré zéro de l'écriture* (1953), described the cultural conditioning inherent in all writing, and in his various essays, including *Sur Racine* (1963) and *Essais critiques* (1964), he attempted to analyse certain works following structuralist methods. In *Critique et vérité* (1966) he offered a phrase-by-phrase analysis of a Balzac story, describing the act of reading and the relationship of the reader's experience to the following of the text.

Barthes reflected a transition between structuralists and the post-structuralists, who followed Saussure's methods but denied that there could be any 'objective' study of language, in that the study had also to be conducted within language and shared the strengths and weaknesses of all sign systems. He was a forerunner of such linguistic philosophers as Jacques Derrida (b.1930) and Michel Foucault (1926–90), who specialized in 'deconstruction', the taking apart of the text to illustrate its component parts.

Structuralism, post-structuralism and deconstruction became the fashionable words, particularly among the postwar generation of academic critics around Europe; and different schools of structuralism emerged, notably in Paris, Prague and Antwerp. In terms of theatre criticism, one effect was to encourage a much broader approach to the analysis of drama within universities. It was considered unreliable simply to study the text of a play, but the staging, the performances, the financing, the audiences and their social surroundings, all had to be taken into account. These new preoccupations affected programme notes. Those of the ROYAL SHAKESPEARE COMPANY were often as much about Shakespeare's England as about his plays. This total approach was not well suited to journalists, who had to give overnight reactions to performances.

The gap which already existed between academic critics and journalists widened further. In France, there was a gulf between the structuralists and the journalist critics, such as Guy Dumur, André Camp and Georges Banu, even when the journalists had (like Banu) university appointments. Banu's books on PETER BROOK, on the art of acting and on JAPANESE theatre combined the observation of a journalist with the analysis of an academic. The German magazine, *Theater Heute*, which laid claim to being the best theatre magazine in Europe and featured such critics as Michael Merschmaier and Peter von Becker, contained detailed analyses of performances, play texts and short notices, in which the Olympian tone of traditional German criticism mingled uneasily with the casual language of cool deconstruction.

In Britain, the structuralists and post-structuralists (such as Terry Eagleton and Catherine Belsey) were mainly confined to the universities. The leading journalists, Michael Billington (the *Guardian*), Irving Wardle (*The Times* and the *Independent on Sunday*), Benedict Nightingale (*The Times*) and Paul Taylor (the *Independent*), were little influenced by semiology, even in their books. Billington's *Peggy Ashcroft* (1988) and Wardle's *The Theatres of George Devine* (1978) were straightforward biographies with little attempt at critical analysis, although Wardle's *Theatre Criticism* (1991) gave many insights into the work of the journalist critic. British critics often had practical experience in the theatre. Billington was once a director, Wardle a playwright. One British critic who bridged the gulf between journalism and academic life was John Elsom, once the theatre critic of the *Listener* (1972–82), who established a postgraduate course in criticism at London's City University. His books are primarily surveys, such as *Post-War British Theatre* (1976), *The History of the National Theatre* (1978) and *Cold War Theatre* (1992), but they contain an element of critical theory, concentrating on the way in which social myths are promoted through the theatre, reflecting and changing the climate of opinion within which politicians have to work.

The separation between journalism and academic criticism has tended to weaken both modes of describing the theatre. Too many academic critics who write about the theatre in structuralist terms see relatively few stage productions; while journalists see many productions but lack the critical theories which can best evaluate them. The critical debate thus becomes either rarefied or so pragmatic that it lacks serious reflection. Few modern European critics carry the broad popular appeal of their 19th-century predecessors or can launch a major debate about the theatre in the press or on television. Among the broadcast arts programmes, the presenters are nearly always better known and more powerful than the critics or commentators. JE

criticism: 2 American Critics experienced a difficult time establishing themselves as an important force in the American theatre. Since the theatre itself was considered a dangerous public institution in the late 18th century, the role of the critic was seen more in terms of CENSORSHIP, guarding against violations of social and moral laws. The earliest extant review of a play appeared anonymously in the *Maryland Gazette* (1760) at a time when papers usually 'noticed' a performance with little or no critical evalua-

tion. The subject prompted WILLIAM DUNLAP in his *History of the American Theatre* (1832) to devote a chapter to critics, explaining that in 1796 a group of six 'gentlemen' organized themselves into a 'band of scalpers and tomahawkers' to write anonymous reviews about New York productions. A few years later, Washington Irving wrote the charming and lightly satirical 'Letters of Jonathan Oldstyle, Gent.' (1802–3), to comment upon the New York stage. Irving also penned reviews for *The Salmagundi* (1807) and *Select Reviews*, later the *Analectic Magazine* (1815). He is regarded as the first American drama critic of importance.

Few daily newspapers published reviews regularly until the 1850s, and even fewer allowed bylines by their critics until the end of the century. Theatre notices and criticism became associated more with short-lived dramatic magazines such as *Theatrical Censor* (1806), *Rambler's Magazine* and *New York Theatrical Register* (1809), *Mirror of Taste* and *Dramatic Censor* (1810) and the *Broadway Journal* and *Stranger's Guide* (1847), as well as sporting weeklies such as *Spirit of the Times* (1831) and *New York Clipper* (1853). The first important theatrical weekly was the *New York Dramatic Mirror*, founded in 1879. Play reviewing, like the theatre itself, was held in low esteem. It was not uncommon for editors to send untrained reporters to 'write up' the opening night of a play; nor was it uncommon for critics to review only productions that advertised in their papers. In 1836, Edgar Allan Poe called professional reviewers 'illiterate mountebanks'. Walt Whitman, writing in 1847, blamed the vulgarity and coarseness of the theatre upon the 'paid puff' system.

The expansion of the newspaper business in the 1850s prompted separate 'amusement' departments and separate dramatic columns of news and reviews. Moralists and puffers tended to dominate the profession, although Henry Clapp Jr returned from France in 1855 or 56 to set up a coterie of critics at Pfaff's Restaurant to rail against tradition and convention. He advocated that the theatre be judged on aesthetic rather than moral grounds, and wrote bright and witty essays for the *Saturday Press* and other weeklies. The Civil War destroyed the movement, however, and what emerged afterwards was a highly moralistic and conservative school headed by WILLIAM WINTER, JOHN RANKEN TOWSE and HENRY AUSTIN CLAPP. Winter made his reputation on Horace Greeley's *New York Tribune* from 1865 to 1909. Towse headed the dramatic department of the elitist *New York Evening Post* during 1874–1927. Clapp wrote for the *Boston Daily Advertiser* from 1868 to 1902. These 'genteel' critics shared the values of the cultured elite and endured until these values changed.

The popular press, however, demanded bright and clever reviews, not moralistic essays, and the innovations introduced by Henry Clapp Jr were carried on in the aggressive and colourful writing of ANDREW C. WHEELER (alias Nym Crinkle) in the New York *Sun*, *World* and 'lesser' dramatic and sporting journals. Alfred J. Cohen (alias ALAN DALE) popularized his 'School of the Flippant Remark' from coast to coast for Hearst publications in the late 1890s and early 1900s. Other critics sought reform. Stephen Ryder Fiske of Wilkes's *Spirit of the Times* (1879–1902) ridiculed shoddy business practices and productions. He viewed the theatre as a worthwhile place of amusement that should be conducted in a professional manner. Epes W. Sargent served VAUDEVILLE in a similar way, writing for a number of trade papers including *Variety* in 1905. HARRISON GREY FISKE of the *New York Dramatic Mirror* (1880–1911) worked to improve business practices and sought to establish a charity (the Actors' Fund) to help the profession. He fought to protect the legal rights of playwrights and to bring an end to the blackmailing efforts of the *New York Dramatic News*. Still other critics worked to improve the American drama. WILLIAM DEAN HOWELLS in the 1880s sought a realistic native drama from his editor's desk at *Atlantic Monthly*, and encouraged JAMES A. HERNE and BRONSON HOWARD. EDWARD A. DITHMAR of the *New York Times* (1884–1902) encouraged American dramatists and broke with tradition by refusing to judge a play on moral grounds. Academicians such as Clayton Hamilton, Walter Prichard Eaton and BRANDER MATTHEWS wrote books about the history, practice and theory of the drama, thus educating the public. An important voice for change, JAMES G. HUNEKER, promoted the new European drama of IBSEN and SHAW, and insisted (as had Clapp) that art be judged on aesthetic rather than moral grounds. Huneker influenced a generation of writers, including GEORGE JEAN NATHAN.

As drama critic of *Smart Set* (1909–23), Nathan attacked the shop-worn dramatic devices of BELASCO, the pomposity of the cultured elite, and the ignorance of the masses. He used ridicule, sarcasm and SATIRE to rid the theatre of stultifying tradition and convention. Like Huneker, he championed Ibsen, Shaw, STRINDBERG, MAETERLINCK and HAUPTMANN, and unlike Huneker he found value in the new American drama. He discovered EUGENE O'NEILL and published his early work in *Smart Set*. Although he never wielded the power of his New York peers on the daily press, he commanded the respect of the young intellectuals in the 1910s and 20s. His unwillingness to find value in the political theatre of the 1930s eroded his influence as a vital force in the theatre.

The exuberant ALEXANDER WOOLLCOTT established the power of the *New York Times* in the 1910s with his enthusiastic prose and his battle with the SHUBERTS. PERCY HAMMOND moved from the *Chicago Tribune* (1908–21) to the *New York Tribune* (1921–36) and brought his urbane and satirical style to bear upon that theatre's pretensions. He could dismiss a Shakespearian actor with the flick of his pen by noting: 'he wore his tights competently'. BURNS MANTLE provided good journalistic prose and sound opinions for the *New York Evening Mail* (1911–22) and *Daily News* (1922–43). BROOKS ATKINSON served for 34 years as chief critic of the *New York Times* (1926–60), enhancing the paper's reputation and his own for fairness and accuracy. Unlike Nathan, he encouraged the more revolutionary theatre of the 1930s as did other critics, including John Anderson (*Post* and *Journal*), Gilbert Gabriel (*Sun* and *American*), JOHN MASON BROWN (*Post* and *Saturday Review*) and Richard Watts Jr (*Herald-Tribune* and *Post*). In 1950 WALTER KERR began reviewing for *Commonweal*, and a year later for the *Herald-Tribune*. A former drama professor, Kerr brought to his position a historical perspective lacked by most of his colleagues. Upon the retirement of Atkinson in 1960, Kerr was acknowledged as the foremost New York critic, a position he held until his retirement

from the *New York Times* in 1983.

Outside New York, the reputation of critics has usually remained local or regional, reflecting the institutions they review. Exceptions include Henry Taylor Parker of the *Boston Transcript* (1905–35), Claudia Cassidy of the *Chicago Tribune* (1942–65), ELLIOT NORTON of the *Boston Post* (1934–56) and other papers, and RICHARD COE of the *Washington Post* (1946–79). These critics gained widespread recognition because their writings had an impact upon the national theatre.

As the number of New York newspapers declined after 1920 (15 in 1920; seven in 1950; three in 1970), magazine critics gained in importance. STARK YOUNG appealed to educated tastes in the *New Republic* (1921–47), as did Joseph Wood Krutch in the *Nation* (1924–52), and KENNETH MACGOWAN, Rosamond Gilder and EDITH J. R. ISAACS in *Theatre Arts Monthly* (1916–64). Discriminating readers have also turned to HAROLD CLURMAN in the *Nation*; ERIC BENTLEY, Stanley Kauffmann and ROBERT BRUSTEIN in *New Republic*; Henry Hewes in *Saturday Review*; ROBERT BENCHLEY, Wolcott Gibbs, Brendan Gill, Edith Oliver and JOHN LAHR in *The New Yorker*; and JOHN SIMON in *New York Magazine*. The general public has depended more on Louis Kronenberger, T. E. Kalem and William Henry III in *Time* magazine and Jack Kroll in *Newsweek*; members of the theatrical profession have relied on *Billboard* and *Variety*. *Village Voice* critics Julius Novick, Alisa Solomon, Michael Feingold and others have kept its readers abreast of the avant-garde. Television critics have been part of the BROADWAY scene for over a decade but there is no agreement over their role and influence.

In the 1990s, the *New York Times* remains the most important and powerful newspaper to review the American theatre, and their daily critic, FRANK RICH (1980–94; replaced by David Richards), the most powerful individual. However, the nature of this power has changed over the past two decades. In the 1980s and 90s, with decentralization of the American theatre and the demise of major papers nationwide, critics for dominant papers in major markets have gained immense power over theatre in their areas. Dan Sullivan and Sylvie Drake in Los Angeles, Richard Christiansen in Chicago, Kevin Kelly in Boston and Bernard Weiner in San Francisco, for example, have had real power to make reputations and close shows. And with local productions originating with an eye to Broadway, these local critics, indirectly, have gained power over what is seen in New York. The *New York Times*'s critic has immense power in New York but less in the regions, and is no longer as important to theatre in Los Angeles, for example, as is Sylvie Drake. TLM

criticism: 3 Asian Theatrical genres in CHINA, JAPAN, KOREA, INDIA, INDONESIA, THAILAND, CAMBODIA, VIETNAM and neighbouring countries developed a rich palette of expressive means: acting (role-playing or mimesis), narrative, speech, chant, song, instrumental music, dance, codified gesture language, expressive make-up patterns, and often the iconography of PUPPETS and MASKS. Consequently, theories which describe, or prescribe, the theatre and drama in Asia are as much devoted to concerns of music, diction and spectacle – the three poor sisters of ARISTOTLE's 'six parts' of the theatre – as they are to plot, character or meaning. Written theory describes only a few Asian theatre genres, but comprehensive, coherent 'systems' of performance practice, play composition and audience expectation undergird all forms of traditional theatre. For example, the performance 'system' of KABUKI is extremely detailed and precise, but it must be extracted from observing and studying performance since much of it is not in written 'theory' form.

The most complete analysis of any theatre form in the world lies in the 1000-plus pages of *A Treatise on Theatre* (*Natyasastra*), attributed to one BHARATA MUNI and written perhaps 2000 years ago. Its 36 chapters describe an immensely detailed interlocking structure of performance, in which actors express basic and transitory human emotions (*bhava*) on stage, thereby inducing in the prepared spectator a state of 'aesthetic bliss' (*rasa*). The staged emotion of sadness, as an example, is transformed within the spectator into an 'appreciation', a 'savouring', of the general condition of sorrow. The process universalizes, or objectifies, the specific, individual emotions dramatized in the play. (The Western term 'aesthetic distance' similarly identifies this depersonalized or objective aspect of the experience, but while the Western concept says nothing about the spectator – it describes a 'neutral' situation – the spectator's contribution of 'appreciation' is basic to *rasa*.)

The *rasa-bhava* theory is based on correspondences: the playwright, director, actor, musician and dancer are enjoined to make those choices which are mutually reinforcing of the play's basic nature. Thus, if the hero's emotional state is love, appropriate scenes to be written by the playwright include assignations set in flowery gardens at night time and dialogue of endearing phrases; the actor expresses the durable and the transitory emotions of love through hundreds of identifiable hand gestures (*hasta*), eye, lip, brow, chin and chest expressions, bodily movements, vocal styles and physical attributes; the music and the decorative dances are elegant, romantic and in all ways 'appropriate'. Complementary *bhava* provide variety, but the focus is strongly on one dominant emotional state, richly elaborated upon.

Eighteen chapters name and list technical aspects of performance: several scores of hand gestures, 108 body stances, many hundreds of verse forms and thousands of rhythmic, verse and drum patterns, all of which are described as appropriate to one or more emotional conditions and hence dramatic situations. This minute cataloguing by name suggests that the work represents a description of actual performance practice. Only the dance system has been transmitted in part, and with many changes, to the present time (for example, in *bharata natyam* and KATHAKALI of India). Most other parts of the performance system are irretrievably lost, with the notable exception of the *rasa* aesthetic theory. *Rasa*, first propounded for theatrical performance in ancient times, gradually became a pan-Indian theory, employed to explain all other artistic forms in the culture. The theory has been expanded and elaborated upon in the process, with a ninth and transcendent *rasa* – peace, or *santi* – being added in the medieval period, for example.

Chinese traditional scholarship excelled in exegesis and classification but not in criticism or theory. Early works about theatre consisted mainly of lists of works, melodies or songs, or of classifications of items. Confucian scholars regarded the theatre and those who performed it with great distaste, according them a very low position in the social scale.

The first major work of criticism of theatre in China was *A Temporary Lodge for My Leisure Thoughts* (*Xianqing ouji*, 1671) by LI YU, which proposed a somewhat higher status for theatre than other writers and put forward a detailed set of criteria by which to judge a drama. In terms of content Li believed that dramas should advocate moral principles like loyalty, filial piety, purity and righteousness, but also wanted them to be entertaining. Because of the latter principle he proposed using new and imaginative topics rather than well known historical stories. For structure his principle was 'one character, one plot' (*yiren yishi*), meaning that there should be one central plot to which all subplots should be subject, and one main character around which all others should be grouped. He emphasized dialogue and stageability. Li's treatise, which he himself regarded as rather original, remained the only published work focused on drama criticism until the Republican period.

Drama criticism was one of the areas of contention in the intellectual revolution known as the New Culture Movement which began about 1915. One of the less radical leaders of the revolution was the American-educated Hu Shi (1891–1962), who held strong views on literature. As he was a dramatist – among his many other attributes – his ideas extended also to drama. He insisted that literary allusions should be avoided, and eschewed imitating the ancients. On the other hand, he advocated using colloquial language. Conservatives found such ideas anathema and tantamount to the destruction of traditional Chinese drama and culture.

During the period of the Republic (1912–49), criticism in the spoken drama tended to a large extent to follow Western canons. In 1918 *New Youth*, a radical monthly edited by Chen Duxiu (1879–1942), devoted an issue to HENRIK IBSEN whose work was discussed as an example to follow, while CHEKHOV and O'NEILL were regarded as positive models by several of the main dramatists of the 1930s and 1940s, in particular CAO YU. While he and many of the other leading dramatists were left-wing in their sympathies, only a few actually joined the Chinese Communist Party (CCP), led by Mao Zedong.

At a forum in his headquarters, Yan'an, in 1944, Mao put forward his Marxist theories on literature and art. He believed that the arts should be judged according to the interests of which class they served. Drama should derive from the masses, who should occupy centre stage, with content favouring the people against the ruling classes and the language colloquial or simple enough to be understood by ordinary people. Another criterion was patriotism. Mao was not only Marxist but nationalist, and at the time of the Yan'an Forum China was suffering invasion by the Japanese. When the CCP came to power in 1949 it implemented these ideas, with the result that the criteria used for criticism became dominantly political. This is not to say that nothing else mattered, but accessibility to ordinary people was always paramount. Selected dramas held to be either anti-people or unpatriotic were banned.

STANISLAVSKY's ideas on acting became the yardstick for performance in the spoken drama as long as China remained on good terms with the Soviet Union.

The Cultural Revolution period (1966–76) saw a much more rigid application of Mao's ideas, with Stanislavsky condemned and class interests and struggle being the almost exclusive criteria for judging theatre. Traditional drama was criticized as feudal and banned (see CENSORSHIP), while even drama on contemporary themes was condemned unless it put forward a very stereotypical characterization which showed the proletariat as heroic and the bourgeoisie as evil.

Drama criticism has remained to some extent political in the 1980s and 1990s. In official publications, dramas are sometimes criticized and occasionally even banned on ideological grounds. However, criteria for judging drama are incomparably broader now than during the Cultural Revolution. Criticism has become strongly influenced by Western notions of what constitutes a good drama, with playwrights such as GAO XINGJIAN consciously trying to follow models of composition and criticism imported from FRANCE. Many playwrights no longer care what the CCP thinks in terms of good and bad on the stage, and Marxist views on criticism tend towards the irrelevant. For traditional drama and items on historical themes, patriotism is more important than alliance with the people, and characters who 'contributed to the Chinese nation' are regarded as worthier than rebels or revolutionaries, even if they were emperors or other members of the feudal ruling classes.

In 16 treatises written over his lifetime, ZEAMI MOTOKIYO, the famous 15th-century Japanese NŌ playwright-actor, combines subtle elucidation of theory with practical advice on how to train child actors (don't force the child but let him learn naturally, according to his age and abilities), write a successful drama (choose a known subject and structure the dances and songs effectively), defeat a rival in competition (perform in an unexpected way), and please a patron (adjust your performance to suit the mood at the moment of his arrival). From medieval thought, and especially from Zen Buddhism, Zeami took two significant concepts: the absolute necessity of being fresh and spontaneous in performance, expressed in the image of the flower (hana) that blooms and soon fades; and a mysterious subdued beauty (yūgen) that represents the highest level of acting achievement. Because nō is a song-dance drama, the young actor should thoroughly master these two artistic techniques before attempting to act any specific role. Zeami's suggestions to actors make splendid sense for performers on any stage: nourish the beginner's spirit at all times (be open to improvement), 'feel ten, express seven' (hold something in reserve), 'see yourself from afar' (be objective), when 'playing a woman keep strength' and when 'playing a demon keep gentleness' (shallow characterization is not interesting, whereas complexity is).

He elaborates on two important East Asian principles of art: jo–ha–kyū, and yin and yang. The former means 'introduction–breaking–speeding' and identifies the three-stage rhythmic sequence that even the first-time spectator can immediately identify in nō dance movement and vocal patterns. The concept, Chinese in origin, was introduced to Korean and Japanese court dance of the 7th century and eventually absorbed into the very fabric of nō where it operates at every level, from acts and scenes down to a half-measure of music. The latter is the well known principle of balancing opposites (black–white, male–female, strong–weak) within a single entity. Much of nō's subtle complexity derives from the operation of yin-yang principles. Thus, throughout his writings, Zeami speaks of the need to evaluate time, place, season and mood of an audience, in order to perform in a contrasting manner: he notes that during the brightness of the day, you should perform a subdued play for the sake of contrast and to interest the spectator. In this respect, Zeami and Bharata work from contrary points of view: Zeami is interested in oppositions, contrasts, freshness and surprise; Bharata describes correspondences among likes within an all-encompassing and interlocking system. Zeami's writings acknowledge that it is difficult for an actor to hold to internal ideals of a 'good' performance, all the while being dependent on audience approval for a livelihood. In the end, the audience is the final judge in both of these Asian systems. Bharata hopes for the 'knowledgeable' spectator who can experience rasa; Zeami says the actor must please the country bumpkins as well as the ideal sophisticated aristocratic patron.

After Japan slavishly borrowed realistic theory from ZOLA and Stanislavsky in the early decades of the 20th century, playwright-critic KISHIDA KUNIO signalled the beginning of a revolt against REALISM in his critical writings. His trenchant 1920s remark that modern drama was insufferably dull because it is 'theatre that is not theatre', opened a passionate and still continuing search for a contemporary theatre rooted in Japanese traditions.

Two important contemporary author-directors who have written extensively about their theories of theatre are SUZUKI TADASHI and ŌTA SHŌGO. Suzuki's actor-training method, now widely studied by Western performers, emphasizes the expressive power of the physicalized body. In writings in the 1960s, Suzuki described the lowered torso and stamping feet found in nō and kabuki as important models in constructing a contemporary acting style that would be uniquely Japanese ('the grammar of the feet'). The function of character within a text is to stimulate an actor to express the actor's own self – the obverse of realistic acting. The actor 'narrates' a character, an idea utilizing Japan's long tradition of narrative theatre forms, such as BUNRAKU. Ōta, in a 1972 essay 'Silence and Theatre', argued that far from humankind's being the 'speaking animal', we spend 90 per cent of our lives in silence and the appropriate dramatic expression of this condition was a 'theatre of silence' (Ōta has written and directed 20 silent, or nearly silent, plays). Spoken language is learned, hence artificial and inevitably a lie. Because the daily conversation which forms the core of realist and naturalist theatre (see NATURALISM) masks the truth, only the body's physical actions, arising from deep and compelling emotions, are genuine. Ōta deprives his actors of voice speech so that they can physically express fundamental human nature with truth.

In Southeast Asia, criticism and theory were traditionally embedded in performance. In both indigenous dance/RITUALS and Indian-influenced arts (puppetry, masked and female dance), the meaning was encoded in iconography, choreography and ritual texts. Animistic village rites are relatively forthright presentations of communal meanings, with access to theory a matter of age/sex/community membership. As a villager became an elder or leader he or she would simultaneously become the arbitrator of performances, interpreting meanings to younger members.

The arts formulated under Hindu-Buddhist influence are more esoteric, on account of tantric influences. Wayang (see SHADOW PUPPETS) will serve as an example. While any viewer could gain a preliminary sense of the ideas through performances, in practice only the specialists, the performers or those they trained, would have full access to meanings. Explanations of ideas or texts of critical *mantra* were, and are, jealously guarded secrets in these large oral traditions. Secrecy was important since performances were considered powerful acts. Initiation and spiritual stamina were prerequisites, so the guru ideally should only teach those with the qualities to handle the power responsibly. A more pragmatic outcome of this restrictive approach was to maintain the power within the gurus' families, which benefited economically and socially from the arrangement. Thus what for the average audience member was entertainment cum magic was, for the initiated, theory and hermeneutics.

Consideration of Indian antecedents is helpful. Tantrism urges the practitioner to enlightenment by understanding the energy that infuses the universe, and posits that this macrocosmic power can be experientially encountered in one's own body (the microcosm). By spiritual practice (*sadhana*), *mantra*, the construction of cosmic symbols (*yantra*, *mandala*), powerful gestures (*mudra*), and imaginative reconfiguration of the body identifying the self with the deity (*nyasa*), the hidden dimensions and meaning of the macrocosm can be revealed. Tantric rituals and performances were the vehicles for this enlightenment. Tantric arts were important in Java in its Hindu-Buddhist period (2nd to 16th centuries) and had reached Cambodia by about the end of the 10th century. As a legacy of this influence, it is common for vocal, movement and ideological practices embedded in Southeast Asian traditional performance structure to point towards psycho-physical enlightenment.

For example, at the opening of each *wayang* play of Indonesia and Malaysia, performers contemplate the 'tree of life' (*kayon*) puppet, knowing that its imagery relates microcosmic human life and the analogous macrocosm – the universe. Next, in archaic language and with symbolic movement, the opening passage of the *wayang* plays out the birth of the world from chaos and sets up analogies to the story, which will inevitably explore the chaos that human desire introduces into this universe. The remainder of the story, through the ordering logic of the *dalang* who is compared to god in the opening *mantra*, allows for redress of this violation. Books of *wayang* lore like the *Dharma Pawayangan* (the Balinese book of the *dalang*) contain formulas that range from lofty meditative practice to simple sorcery. The obscure language of some of the material will bewilder the uninitiated, but it is rich with theoretical implications for the enlightened puppet-master. Enlightenment via performance is, in some sense, the method of the *wayang*.   JRB CPM KF

Croatia see YUGOSLAVIA; MEDIEVAL DRAMA IN EUROPE (Eastern Europe)

Cronyn, Hume 1911– Canadian actor, director and writer, born in London, Ontario. Cronyn studied acting at the New York School of the Theatre and the AMERICAN ACADEMY OF DRAMATIC ARTS, making his professional debut with Cochran's STOCK COMPANY in Washington, DC, in 1931. He also worked for the Barter Theatre, Abingdon, Virginia, during their second season. His BROADWAY debut was as the Janitor in *Hipper's Holiday* (1934).

Cronyn soon became a much sought-after character in Hollywood, where he married JESSICA TANDY in 1942. While in Los Angeles, he directed Tandy as Miss Collins in TENNESSEE WILLIAMS's *Portrait of a Madonna* (1946). This exposure led to Tandy's being cast as Blanche Dubois in 1947 on Broadway.

Cronyn and Tandy appeared together for the first time in 1951 in *The Fourposter*, in which they were 'compared to the LUNTS, in that the team had enough grace, skill, and wit to hold a stage and an audience by themselves'. They have since co-starred in *The Physicists* (1964), EDWARD ALBEE's *A Delicate Balance* (1966), *The Gin Game* (1977), *Noel Coward in Two Keys* (1974) and *Foxfire* (1982; co-authored by Cronyn). Between these projects, Cronyn and Tandy played several seasons at the GUTHRIE THEATRE and at the STRATFORD FESTIVAL in Ontario. In 1994 they received the first special Tony for Lifetime Achievement. In 1964 Cronyn played Polonius to RICHARD BURTON's Hamlet, winning a Tony. His memoir, *A Terrible Liar*, was published in 1991. Cronyn's and Tandy's daughter, Tandy Cronyn (1946–), is an accomplished actress.   SMA

Crossroads Theatre (USA) An active and innovative AFRICAN-AMERICAN theatre, founded in 1978 and located in New Brunswick, New Jersey. Under the resourceful artistic leadership of Ricardo Khan, the theatre has attained a distinguished record, presenting an average of six productions each season (including GEORGE C. WOLFE's first success, *The Colored Museum*), often to critical acclaim. It has supported new playwrights, encouraged new forms of staging, presented world premieres, and toured a production annually during Black History Month (February). In 1991 the theatre acquired a new home on Livingston Avenue as part of New Brunswick's Cultural Center complex and in 1993 it received the fifth annual Rosetta LeNoire Award, given by American Actors' Equity for 'outstanding artistic contributions to the universality of the human experience in American theatre'.   EGH

Crothers, Rachel c.1878–1958 American actress, playwright and director; the 'NEIL SIMON of her day'. Crothers's many commercially successful plays chronicled the tension in early-20th-century women between their new economic and sexual freedom and their old traditional values. Her first success, *The Three of Us* (1906), was followed by some 30 BROADWAY plays, most of which she directed and staged herself. Although she wrote some sentimental plays in the 1910s, her best works were her serio-comic, women-centred plays: *Myself Bettina* (1908), *A*

Man's World (1910), *Ourselves* (1913), *Young Wisdom* (1914), *He and She* (1920; first produced 1911), *Expressing Willie* (1924), *Let Us Be Gay* (1929), *As Husbands Go* (1931), *When Ladies Meet* (1932) and *Susan and God* (1937).

Besides her undisputed position as the leading commercial woman playwright and director of her time, Crothers was instrumental in the founding of Stage Women's War Relief Fund (1917), United Theatre Relief Committee (1932) and American Theatre Wing for War Relief (1940; best-known for the Stage Door Canteen). She received the Chi Omega National Achievement Award for 1938. FB

Crouse, Russel 1893–1966 American playwright, librettist and producer. Crouse began his stage writing career as librettist for *The Gang's All Here* (1931); but it was only after he teamed with HOWARD LINDSAY on *Anything Goes* (1934) that he achieved continued success. Crouse and Lindsay became prolific collaborators. Their first straight play was *Life with Father*, a nostalgic bit of Americana that captured the hearts of the BROADWAY audience for a contemporary long-run record that held until the 1970s. Working with Lindsay throughout the remainder of his career, Crouse helped write more than 15 plays and librettos, a highly successful example of the latter being *The Sound of Music* (1959). They also teamed to produce many plays in New York, including several of their own and the profitable *Arsenic and Old Lace* (1941). LDC

Crowne, John c.1640–1712 English playwright. Crowne emigrated to America in 1657, when his father was granted estates in Nova Scotia by Cromwell, was educated at Harvard, then returned to England in 1660 when the family lost the estates at the Restoration. He began writing in the 1660s and his first play was performed in 1671. In 1675 he wrote the last court MASQUE, *Calisto*. His heroic play *The Destruction of Jerusalem* was successful in 1677. His finest TRAGEDY, *The Ambitious Statesman* (1679), is a serious study of political power. A favourite of the king, Crowne was given the subject for his popular COMEDY, *Sir Courtly Nice* (1685), by Charles himself. His political comedy, *City Politiques* (1682), mocked leading lawyers and politicians. *The Married Beau* (1694), Crowne's last comedy, is a cynical SATIRE on the torture of marriage. He died poor and obscure. PH

Cruelty, Theatre of see ARTAUD, ANTONIN

Cuadra, Pablo Antonio 1912– Nicaraguan poet, historian, journalist and playwright. Cuadra has also been a lawyer, professor of history and literature, and founder of important cultural periodicals in Managua such as *Vanguardia* (*Vanguard*) and *Trinchera* (*Trench*). His dramatic work includes *El árbol seco* (*The Dry Tree*), *Satanás entra en escena* (*Satan Enters on Stage*, 1938), *Pastorela* (1939) and his masterpiece, *Por los caminos van los campesinos* (*Along the Roads Go the Peasants*, 1937). The latter is set during the intervention of the USA in Nicaragua during the 1920s and protests against the injustices committed against the poor in the name of politics. During the Sandinista government, Cuadra served as editor of the opposition newspaper, *La Prensa*. GW

Cuba Early manifestations of theatrical activity in Cuba parallel those of the other Caribbean islands. The *areytos* of the indigenous peoples were complex theatre–dance forms that incorporated music with full-dress costume to recount the historical, religious and cultural repertoire of the society. When the Spanish colonizers banned the *areytos* in 1512 on grounds of primitive hereticism, they extin-

Cabildo Teatral de Santiago in Raúl Pomares's *De cómo Santiago Apóstol puso los pies en le tierra* (*About how the Apostle James put his Feet on Earth*), Santiago, Cuba, 1975.

guished an important part of the indigenous culture and took another step in obliterating the native population itself. Later, when black slaves were imported to work the developing sugar plantations, other traditions of culture and art forms came to exert an influence.

Cuba's strategic location generated a long struggle for military and economic control. The British occupied Havana in 1762–3; French refugees from Haiti arrived in the late 18th century. For centuries, sugar has been the single most important product, and its fluctuating price determined the local prosperity. Theatrical activity existed only sporadically during the first two centuries (1500–1700). The first Cuban play is considered to be *El príncipe jardinero y fingido Cloridano* (*The Presumed Gardener Prince Cloridano*) by Santiago Pita. Published in Spain around 1730, this play treats chivalry in a mythical Grecian setting far removed from Cuba's reality. Beginning late in the century, a round of theatre construction facilitated local productions: the Coliseo (Coliseum) (1775), later restored as the Teatro El Principal (the Principal Theatre, 1803), the Diorama (1829), the Tacón (1838) and others. The acknowledged father of the Cuban national theatre is Francisco Covarrubias (1775–1850). Impresario, actor and author of more than 20 plays, he was famous for his representation of the *negrito* (the white actor in blackface), probably before the famous roles created by THOMAS RICE and Dan Emmett in the USA (see MINSTREL SHOW). Covarrubias integrated popular Cuban figures into forms of the Spanish *sainete* (see GÉNERO CHICO), without political implications or character development, but no play has survived.

During the 19th century Cuba continued to chafe under colonial domination, since the Spanish American struggle for independence (1810–25) excluded the island. In other countries the new freedom ushered in the unrestrained liberties of romanticism, and Cuba also was touched as early as 1836 with the production of *Don Pedro de Castilla* by Francisco Javier Foxá (1816–65). This Dominican exile's play drew a storm of protest and CENSORSHIP. José María Heredia (1803–39), Cuban poet and patriot who spent years of exile in the USA and Mexico, wrote romantic poetry, but his plays, translations and adaptations retained neoclassical styles and techniques. José Jacinto Milanés (1814–63) took the title figure of *El conde Alarcos* (*Count Alarcos*, 1838) as a dramatic symbol of tyranny and oppression; in his later plays he turned towards picturesque popular figures presented in natural language, such as *El mirón cubano* (*Cuban Busybody*, 1840), which consists of several scenes of a costumbristic nature (see COSTUMBRISMO) in which Milanés censures habits and customs of the age. The outstanding figure of the period was GERTRUDIS GÓMEZ DE AVELLANEDA, an extraordinary poet, novelist and playwright. With 20 plays, she was a major woman playwright of the Americas who dominated both tragic and comic form, and knew how to create solid characters while avoiding the excesses of romanticism.

At mid-century the theatre was replete with writers whose humour and comic intrigue reflected the foibles of a developing society, and the problems created by politics, social status and racial mixtures. José Agustín Millán wrote his *Una aventura, o El camino más corto* (*An Adventure, or The Shortest Route*) in 1842, a play considered to be the beginning of the national COMEDY, a form characterized by its humble, popular language and comic intrigue. Joaquín Lorenzo Luaces (1826–67) was Cuba's best playwright of the 19th century. His plays, *El becerro de oro* (*The Golden Calf*), *La escuela de los parientes* (*School for Relatives*), *Dos amigas* (*Two Friends*) and *El fantasmón de Aravaca* (*The Ghost of Aravaca*), are of good quality with Cuban characteristics. His plays captured the same comic style and anticipated the BUFO theatre that took Havana by storm in 1868. The US MINSTREL SHOWS that visited Havana shortly before (1860–5) left an influence on this musical dance theatre that specialized in PARODY, caricature and SATIRE. The linguistic salad of the *bufo* drew on a French, English and black cuisine, and though their popular format excited the Cuban public the colonial regime was not pleased. The havoc of the Ten Years' War (1868–78) suspended the Bufos Habaneros (Havana *bufos*), but they returned for a second cycle from 1879 to 1900.

Late in the century, the great Cuban poet and patriot José Martí (1853–95), who also wrote patriotic and moralistic plays, spearheaded an invasion by the government in exile. Martí was killed in battle. Spain was ready to concede defeat, but the episode of the battleship *Maine* provoked American intervention, and in 1898 Spain relinquished Cuba as well as Puerto Rico and the Philippines to US control.

The 20th century The USA ruled Cuba militarily for four years and withdrew as planned, leaving Cuba to self-rule under the Platt Amendment, although the USA reserved the right to intervene 'as necessary'. A series of inept and corrupt presidents led to the dictatorship of Fulgencio Batista from 1934 to 1959, when he himself was ousted by Fidel Castro and the Bearded Ones, an event that ushered in a period of Marxist domination. The century also ushered in the Alhambra Theatre, which served as the centre of popular theatre in Havana. The music and dance REVUES programmed by Regino López as principal actor and Federico Villoch as impresario championed the popular Cuban character types in lavish and colourful productions that entertained Cubans for 35 years.

Efforts to organize a serious theatre movement came in 1910 with the formation of the Sociedad de Fomento del Teatro (Society for the Promotion of Theatre), later redesignated the Sociedad del Teatro Cubano (Society of Cuban Theatre), but in spite of the efforts of such distinguished participants as José Antonio Ramos (1885–1946) and Max Henríquez Ureña (1885–1968), the effort failed. Ramos did write serious plays, and his *Tembladera* (*Trembler*, 1917) was a precursor of the theatre of protest against exploitative bourgeois policies.

Another impetus came in 1928 when Luis A. Baralt (1892–1969) launched the Teatro La Cueva (the Cave Theatre) that represented an early effort to bring vanguard European techniques to the Cuban theatre. The Academia de Artes Dramáticas (Academy of Dramatic Arts) was established in 1941, the Patronata del Teatro (Patrons of Theatre) in 1942, and the Teatro Experimental (Experimental Theatre) of the University of Havana in 1949, all fundamental to the development of an internationalized theatre capable of stimulating national playwrights and directors. Nevertheless, authors such as Carlos Felipe (1911–75), VIRGILIO PIÑERA and Rolando Ferrer (1925–76), the most established playwrights during the 1950s, wrote without benefit of an atmosphere conducive to serious theatre. The decadence of Havana during the later Batista years yielded to prostitution and commercialized, semi-pornographic shows catering primarily for the tourist trade. In the years immediately preceding the Castro Revolution, few theatre companies existed and few serious plays were presented.

The revolutionary years The Revolution brought a new perspective on theatre and the arts. Under the new regime, government support was available and theatre became, in fact, an arm of the revolutionary process. Salaries were provided for writers, directors, actors and technical crew. Buildings, some of them old movie houses, were converted or adapted for use as theatre space, but the theatre also took to the streets and parks. The Escuela de Instructores de Arte (School of Art Instructors) was established in 1961 and the Escuela Nacional de Arte (National School of Art) in 1962. By the mid-70s a wide network of sites offered instruction in theatre, music, plastic arts, ballet and dance to nearly 5000 students. An active publication programme accompanied the literacy campaign; plays were published in great numbers and the theatre journal *Conjunto* (1964) began publishing criticism, plays and information about theatre from countries throughout the Americas.

ABELARDO ESTORINO joined the Teatro Estudio (Studio Theatre) group in 1960 and became a professional writer in 1961. His *El robo del cochino* (*The Theft of the Pig*, 1961) signalled his ability to create true-to-life characters in the tense political situation that anticipated the Revolution. His subsequent plays such as *La casa vieja* (*The Old House*, 1964), *Los mangos de Caín* (*Cain's Mangoes*, 1967), *La dolorosa historia del amor secreto de don José Jacinto Milanés* (*The Tragic Story of the Secret Love of Don José Jacinto Milanés*, 1974), *Ni un sí ni un no* (*Neither a Yes nor a No*, 1981) and *Morir del cuento* (*To Die from the Story*, 1983) lived up to the original promise, as he became the only writer who continued over an extended period.

ANTÓN ARRUFAT performed an absurdist play (see THEATRE OF THE ABSURD), *El caso se investiga* (*The Case Is Being Investigated*), as early as 1957, which was followed by several more plays during the early revolutionary years. When his *Los siete contra Tebas* (*Seven against Thebes*) won the UNEAC prize in 1968, the play was censured for its alleged counter-revolutionary spirit, along with Herberto Padilla's poetry. Arrufat continued writing for the theatre but his later plays have not been staged.

JOSÉ TRIANA became Cuba's best-known writer internationally for his *La noche de los asesinos* (*Night of the Assassins*, 1965), an intriguing metatheatrical play of three adolescents playing various roles as they prepare for the ritual murder of their parents. Triana resumed writing for the theatre after 1980. Other writers of the early years of the Revolution included José Brene (b.1927), whose *Santa Camila de la Habana vieja* (*St Camille of Old Havana*, 1962) dramatized the ideological reorientation of a parasite in the society, and the precocious Nicolás Dorr (b. 1947), whose first work at age 14 was a remarkably mature picture of human relationships captured in a farcical and even absurdist style. In this vein are Dorr's *Las pericas* (*The Parrots*, 1961), *El palacio de los cartones* (*The Cardboard Palace*, 1961) and *La esquina de los concejales* (*The Councillors' Corner*, 1962), although later works are more realistic (see REALISM), such as *La chacota* (*The Racket*, 1974) and *Confesión en el barrio chino* (*Confession in the Chinese Quarter*). As director of Teatro Popular Latinoamericano (Popular Latin American Theatre), Dorr launched an ambitious programme for Cuban theatre and continued writing ideologically oriented plays about the new society. In 1967 the Cuban theatre was shaken by the appearance of *María Antonia*, a tragedy by Eugenio Hernández Espinosa (b.1936) rooted in the mythical Afro-Cuban universe that reflects the marginal society preceding the 1959 Revolution. Hernández is the Cuban playwright who represents with greatest authenticity the world of the blacks in such recent works as *Oba y Shangó* (*The King and Shango*) and *Odebí el cazador* (*Odebí the Hunter*).

By 1968 the theatre in Cuba was entering a second phase. The Teatro Escambray (Escambray Theatre), established that year by Sergio Corrieri in the province of Las Villas, was representative of the search for the methods and contacts that would lead to the so-called 'new theatre'. The term refers to the anti-bourgeois theatre that grew out of close interaction between theatre groups and the public they served. The Escambray group, for example, developed a model of interviewing regional people about their concerns, attitudes and values in order to develop meaningful dramatic experiences for them. The plays relied on local language and colour, almost always with music. Other groups with a similar orientation soon followed: La Yaya (1973–6), Cabildo Teatral de Santiago (1973), Teatrova de Santiago (1974), Cubana de Acero (Cuban Steel, 1977), Teatro Juvenil Pinos Nuevos (Pinos Nuevos Children's Theatre, 1974) and others. Cuban Steel operated directly out of the steel factory, and performances took place between shifts. Juglares y su Peña Literaria performed in Lenin Park in Havana. The very first revolutionary group, the Studio Theatre, was consolidated in 1959 after the Revolution and dedicated to Marxist–Leninist principles.

Even though the Cuban theatre has operated in a collective style, individual authors have played a prominent role. In addition to those cited, others of note are Flora Lauten, Herminia Sánchez, Albio Paz, Francisco Garzón Céspedes, Roberto Orihuela, Lázaro Rodríguez, Rafael González, Freddy Artiles, and Abraham Rodríguez. The immediacy of the revolutionary process called special attention to aspects of societal change, education, male/female roles and relationships, work ethics, and individual commitment to revolutionary goals in a rapidly changing economy and society. The theatre did not merely reflect the process, but because of its popular nature it became instrumental in helping to shape attitudes and opinions.

From the 1970s Cuban playwriting signalled a frequent recognition of current themes by means of a critical investigation of reality. Throughout the 1980s the government continued to invest heavily in theatre and the arts, and sponsored an international theatre festival on an alternate year basis. A new journal *Tablas* (1982), edited by Rosa

Ileana Boudet, complemented the long-standing publication of *Conjunto* (1964), the theatre arm of Casa de las Américas. Before the demise of the Soviet Union signs of change were already apparent, as creative artists sought to break the ideological hammer-lock of the Revolution. Alberto Pedro (b.1954) with *Pasión Malinche* (*Malinche Passion*) examines treason, opportunism and false morality through the historical figure of the Conquest. Carmen Duarte (b.1959) in *¿Cuánto me das marinero?* (*How Much Will You Give Me, Sailor?*, 1989) took a fresh look at generational conflicts and teen problems in Havana. The most promising of the new writers is JOEL CANO (b.1966): his *Timeball* (1992) is an innovative postmodern non-lineal performance text. Cuba in 1994 is economically destitute, with no paper or ink for publication, no lights for theatre. Nonetheless, an indomitable artistic spirit continues to produce good results.   GW

See: N. González Freire, *Teatro cubano* (1927–61), Havana, 1961; R. Leal, *Breve historia del teatro cubano*, Havana, 1980; M. Montes Huidobro, *Persona, vida y máscara en el teatro cubano*, Miami, 1973.

Cuban-American theatre The origins of Cuban theatre in the USA are to be found in the MELODRAMAS and Cuban blackface FARCES that were staged by the Cuban immigrant communities in New York City and Ybor City–Tampa during the final decade of the 19th century. In New York City these were produced by groups made up of professional and amateur players, such as the Club Lírico Dramático directed by Luis Baralt, a 30-year veteran of the Havana stage; these first productions raised funds to support the war for Cuban independence from Spain.

In the early 20th century, Cuban melodrama and lyric theatre became staples of the commercial stage in the Hispanic community, which supported its own theatre houses and repertory companies, as well as hosting companies on tour from Havana and Tampa. Before the Second World War, one of the most popular theatrical genres in the Hispanic community was the *obra bufa cubana*, or Cuban blackface farce, written and/or improvised by such local playwrights as Alberto O'Farrill and Juan C. Rivera, as well as by such masters from Cuba as Arquímides Pous and Armando Bronca.

Hispanic theatrical culture developed in Ybor City–Tampa during the late 19th and early 20th centuries on the stages of Cuban and Spanish mutualist societies; these were allied to the tobacco industry that had been transplanted there from Cuba. A mix of amateur and professional players, plus tours by professional companies from abroad, helped to nurture the creation of a full-fledged commercial stage by the 1920s, one that produced talent for the HISPANIC THEATRE in New York, Cuba and Spain. On the strength of this intense activity, Tampa became the site for the only Hispanic (often called Cuban) FEDERAL THEATRE PROJECT, which produced 14 shows during 1936–7, including a Spanish-language version of *It Can't Happen Here*.

The Cuban Revolution of 1959 is the most recent event resulting in large-scale theatrical activity in Cuban US communities, principally those in Miami and New York. At first, stages were founded in these two cities to accommodate a primarily political theatre of exile, as well as a

VAUDEVILLESque commodity theatre that still relies upon the humour, stereotypes and music of the *obras bufas cubanas* as entertainment. Among the most active and recognized of the serious exile playwrights are José Cid Pérez, Leopoldo Hernández, Matías Montes Huidobro, Fermín Borges, René Ariza and José Sánchez Boudy, all of whom primarily write their plays in Spanish and have depended on publication for reaching broader audiences than those attending their limited university-sponsored productions. Of primary concern to these writers has been criticism of Fidel Castro and the communist revolution, and a nostalgic longing for the land and culture left behind upon taking refuge in the USA.

Another generation of playwrights has appeared, primarily comprising writers who were educated or began their theatrical careers in the USA. These are more likely to write their works in English as well as Spanish and to deal with acculturation, bilingualism, culture conflict, the generation gap between immigrant parents and US-raised children, and other themes pertaining to life in the USA. Included among what can be properly called a generation of Cuban-American playwrights are Iván Acosta, Manuel Martín, Mario Peña, Dolores Prida and Omar Torres. This generation is characterized by extensive work on the stage as playwrights, actors and directors in primarily Hispanic non-profit theatres in New York and Miami, with Acosta and Torres also venturing off to work in the commercial cinema.   NK

See: J. A. Escarpanter, *Latin American Theatre Review* (Spring 1986); N. Kanellos, *A History of Hispanic Theatre in the United States, Origins to 1940*, Austin, Tex., 1990; M. Watson-Espener, in *Hispanic Theatre in the United States*, ed. N. Kanellos, Houston, Tex., 1984.

Cubitt, William fl. late 18th–early 19th century English actor. Described as a useful performer, this subordinate actor, singer and instrumentalist of DRURY LANE and, especially, COVENT GARDEN, was also a well known summer performer in small theatres, and it is for his playing of Hamlet during his summer engagements that he ought to be remembered. On one of these occasions, 'musicians being scarce, he actually descended into the orchestra, in the dress of the royal Dane, and played the fiddle between the acts'. So reported the principal oboist at Covent Garden, who also records an occasion when Cubitt, having one night given an indifferent performance of Hamlet, suddenly became ill the following night just as the play was about to begin. The manager 'was constrained to request the audience to suffer them to go through the play, omitting the character of Hamlet; which being complied with, it was afterwards considered by the bulk of the audience to be a great improvement'. An actor responsible for a performance of *Hamlet* without the Prince of Denmark surely deserves to escape oblivion.   GH

Cumberland, Richard 1732–1811 English playwright. Born in Trinity College, Cambridge, where his grandfather was Master, and educated there, he entered politics as secretary to Lord Halifax in 1751. After a successful career with Halifax, he began writing plays in 1761 and became a prolific dramatist. He is best remembered as the original of Sir Fretful Plagiary, SHERIDAN's caricature of him in *The*

Critic, but he was rapidly and deservedly successful, particularly after GARRICK's production of *The West Indian* (1771), a highly moral account of an essentially good rake making his way through London society, a domestic comedy with a strong dose of sentimentalism. Among his outpouring of dully conventional plays, Cumberland's best work is intriguingly original, particularly *The Mysterious Husband* (1783), a prose tragedy set in contemporary London among the fashionable aristocracy, and *The Jew* (1794), a reasoned argument against contemporary anti-semitism, a play which restored Cumberland's reputation after some years of only moderate success. Secretary to the Board of Trade from 1775 to 1780, he retired to Tunbridge Wells on its abolition, continuing to write plays until his death.   PH

Curtain Theatre (London) Erected not far from the THEATRE, possibly by the Henry Lanman who was its proprietor from 1582 to 92, the Curtain was London's second purpose-built playhouse. Almost certainly polygonal and constructed after the model of the Theatre, it had a surprisingly long and almost entirely undistinguished life. For a brief period, between the dismantling of the Theatre and the opening of the GLOBE, it was probably the home of the LORD CHAMBERLAIN'S MEN. If, as is often claimed, it was the theatre which first staged SHAKESPEARE's *Henry V*, the apologetic Chorus may be drawing attention to the short-comings of a theatre that was already old-fashioned in 1599. Even so, it was the home of Queen Anne's Men for a short period after 1603 and remained open and in occasional use by many other companies until the Restoration. PT

Cusack, Cyril 1910–93 Irish stage and film actor, director and playwright. Cusack performed with the ABBEY THEATRE in Dublin from 1932 to 1945, and again from 1968, when he started the revival of BOUCICAULT's plays in the Abbey production of *The Shaughraun* at the World Theatre Season in London. He directed the Gaelic Players in 1935–6, and in his own play *Tareis an Aifreann* (*After the Mass*) at the Dublin GATE THEATRE in 1942. After taking over the Gaiety Theatre, Dublin, in 1945, he formed his own company, with which he presented SYNGE's *Playboy of the Western World* at the first International Drama Festival in Paris in 1954, and in 1960 he won the International Critics' Award for his performance in BECKETT's monologue, *Krapp's Last Tape.*   CI

Cushman, Charlotte (Saunders) 1816–76 The first native-born American actress of the top rank. Cushman, described as commanding rather than handsome, was considered the most powerful actress on the 19th-century stage. Appearing somewhat masculine, with a tall, strong body, unusual voice and powerful personality, her stage characterizations emerged in heroic outline. Trained as an opera singer, she misused her voice and was forced to alter her career.

Her acting debut was as Lady Macbeth under JAMES H. CALDWELL in New Orleans (1836), repeated the same year in New York at the BOWERY. Her first sensational success was as Nancy Sykes in *Oliver Twist* (1839). A failed manager of Philadelphia's WALNUT STREET THEATRE, she appeared opposite W. C. MACREADY on his American tour in 1843–4 and then went to London, appearing first in 1845 at the PRINCESS'S THEATRE. After 1844 she performed about 35 roles, with only 10 repeated regularly. By her return to the USA in 1849, she was considered by many the greatest living English-speaking actress. During her long career she played over 200 roles, excelling as Meg Merrilies in *Guy Mannering*, Romeo opposite the Juliet of her sister Susan, Lady Macbeth and Queen Katharine in *Henry VIII*. During 1852–69 she gave a series of farewell appearances, returning permanently to the stage in 1869 to forget the pain she suffered from cancer.

Cushman's style was marked by sweep, power and majesty, sometimes overly expressive and extravagant. One critic described her movement as 'a galvanized distortion of nature', and said her constant activity conveyed the impression she was 'suffering under a violent attack of colic'. Her definitive biography, *Bright Particular Star* by Joseph Leach, was published in 1970.   DBW

Cuzzani, Agustín 1924–87 Argentine playwright, novelist and lawyer. Famous for his *farsátiras* in the 1950s, he wrote several major plays: *Una libra de carne* (*A Pound of Flesh*, 1954), based on the Shylock story, *El centroforward murió al amanecer* (*The Centre-Forward Died at Dawn*, 1955) and *Sempronio* (1958). The latter presents a man who has become radioactive from his Japanese stamp collection but is redeemed by the power of his family's love over the vindictive state bureaucracy. His plays depend on farcical situations to advocate positions of individual liberty for mankind within oppressive set-ups.   GW

Czechoslovakia [Czech Republic; Slovakia]
The beginnings to the 18th century The evolution of theatre in Czechoslovakia falls into several periods, most of which have been demarcated by religious, political or military events. Evidence of a flourishing medieval religious drama gradually incorporating secular and comic elements, as well as vernacular Czech by the 14th century, is found in many sources: e.g. two 'Mastičkář' texts from c.1350 that present a quack healer and his scolding wife with not only the three Marys but also Abraham and Isaac. The social comment and theatricality in such surviving fragments suggest a lively theatre culture, but its potential growth was aborted by the Hussite wars in the 15th century. Theatre revived with Renaissance humanism in the 16th century. TERENCE and PLAUTUS were performed in schools and occasionally in public by students, almost always in Latin, but biblical dramas based on the lives of saints were performed in Czech. Pavel Kyrmezer, a Slovak, but the first known playwright in Czech, composed several, with comic characterization and realistic detail, from the 1560s to the 1580s.

Several other forms of theatre emerged in the second half of the 16th century. Jesuit school drama (see JESUITEN DRAMA) developed rapidly after 1566 in Bohemia and was an important force in Czech theatre for two hundred years. Eventually incorporating Czech history and other secular themes, the Jesuits also expanded the use of scenery, costumes and other production elements, as well as the use of Czech in performance. Theatricality also marked Italianate spectacles that reached a peak in

Prague with the first movable scenery north of the Alps (*Phasma Dionysia*, 1617). Additional foreign influence came with touring Italian, German and English companies towards the end of the 16th century. Concurrently, the indigenous folk tradition in theatre revived in the form of Shrovetide processions, skits and plays in Czech that mixed moralizing and social SATIRE with peasant FARCE. *The Feast at Sedlec* (printed 1588) is the best-known. More formal and purely secular drama includes Jan Campanus Vodňanský's *Břetislav* (1603) and the first known Czech interlude, *The Apprehended Infidelity* (anon., 1608).

The vital theatre implicit in these examples ended with the Czechs' defeat at the Battle of White Mountain (1620). Not only Czech theatre but Czech culture and national identity were virtually erased for a century and a half as the Czechs languished under Habsburg authority.

Although no professional theatre in Czech was to exist until the National Revival in the late 18th century, other forms of theatre bridged the gap. Foreign theatre companies introduced Neapolitan opera, COMMEDIA DELL'ARTE and marionettes. Equally important, they brought technical advances in staging: e.g. for the coronation of Charles VI in Prague in 1723, GIUSEPPE BIBIENA designed the total outdoor, nocturnal theatre and scenery for *Costanza e Fortezza*. Drama and theatre of native origin took two forms. Jan Amos Komenský wrote Latin plays in the 1640s based on classical or biblical themes, to be performed by schoolboys as part of their education. Later in the 17th century Václav Kocmánek wrote a Christmas play and numerous interludes in Czech; Karel Kolčava composed several plays in Latin but based on Czech history. Of greater significance for Czech theatre, the folk theatre reappeared after 1650 in the form of amateur village productions in Czech of primarily religious material but also comprising pre-Christian elements as well as theatrical techniques indirectly derived from Jesuit and foreign productions. This fascinating blend of naive and sophisticated theatre was profoundly important in sustaining the faith, culture and language of the Czechs.

The national revival to 1900 Playing a leading role in the revival movement, which began in the 1780s, theatre became intimately linked with Czech national and cultural aspirations. One symptom of the increasing interest in theatre was the building of the Nostitz Theatre in Prague in 1783; later known as the Estates Theatre and the Tyl Theatre, it has been in use to the present. It embodied the latest technical equipment of its day and was the site of the original production of *Don Giovanni*, directed and conducted in 1786 by Mozart himself. The first performance in Czech at this theatre occurred in 1785.

Of greater consequence for Czech culture and theatre was the establishment by a group of Czech actors of the Bouda (Hut) Theatre in 1786 in order to be able to perform in Czech on a more regular basis, usually four times a week. That season included the performance of the first play in nearly two hundred years with Czech subject-matter written and performed in Czech: *Břetislav and Jitka*, by Václav Thá, the first of many indefatigable Czech actor-writer-translators dedicated to the cause of reviving theatre in their native tongue.

The Hut Theatre lasted two years, but sporadic Czech performances continued into the 19th century in similar temporary, bilingual theatres as well as in the Nostitz Theatre. Jan Nepomuk Štěpánek, playwright, translator, and theatre producer-administrator, was instrumental in increasing the number and regularity of Czech performances on the professional stage in Prague. Václav Kliment Klicpera was the first Czech playwright of undisputed talent. Whether in the genre of history, COMEDY or PARODY-farce, Klicpera had a sure theatrical sense and special gift for characterization and sharp social observation, as is evident in *Hadrian of Rimsy* (1821) and *Everyone Does His Bit for the Homeland* (1829). Widespread MARIONETTE theatre activity by touring professional groups also sustained the public use of Czech, most notably in the years 1820–50. Matěj Kopecký was a leading practitioner.

Surpassing the achievements of all others up to this time in the cause of theatre and emergent nationalism was Josef Kajetán Tyl; as actor, playwright, dramaturge, director, editor, publisher, and even representative to the Habsburg Assembly, he devoted himself entirely to his countrymen and his art. He was the first to formulate the concept of a Czech National Theatre, in the 1840s, when he was also a leading figure in Prague theatres and writer of some dozen major plays: e.g. *The Bagpiper of Strakonice* (1846), *The Miners of Kutná Mountain* (1848) and *Hardheaded Woman* (1849), works that blend patriotic romanticism with wry comedy and socially realistic detail.

In 1850 a committee for the establishment of a National Theatre became the focal point for the entire national revival movement. From then until the 1880s, when the dream was realized, most of the funds came from voluntary contributions by the Czech people. In the meantime, the Provisional Theatre was built in 1862, and thus became the first exclusively Czech professional theatre with a regular schedule. The National Theatre itself had two inaugurals: two months after the first one in 1881 the theatre burned down, but two years later it reopened with the premiere of Bedřich Smetana's opera *Libuše*. From then until now its motto, emblazoned above the proscenium arch, has been 'A Nation's Gift to Itself'.

Smetana was the most significant artistic force in the National Theatre movement, and his operas were the strongest productions during the years leading up to the opening of the theatre and even later. But playwrights and other theatre artists were also developing talents and experience necessary for so demanding a project. SHAKESPEARE and SCHILLER, idealized models for the Czech theatre of the 19th century, were especially influential in the career of Josef J. Kolár, a major actor, producer, playwright and translator of Shakespeare. French, Russian and German theatre also became influential; Emanuel Bozděch was known as the Czech SCRIBE. A cluster of other playwrights reflected the shift to critical social realism sweeping Europe in the second half of the century. Among the realist playwrights and their chief works were L. Stroupežnický, *Our Hotheads*, 1887; F. V. Jeřábek, *The Servant of His Master*, 1869; the Mrštík brothers, Alois and Vilem, *Maryša*, 1894; and G. Preissová, *The Housewife Slave*, 1889. A counter-movement towards deliberately poetic, imaginative drama was evident in the work of Jaroslav Vrchlický, whose prolific output included lyrical treatments of Czech history, *A Night at Karlštein* (1884), and classical myth, the *Hippodamia* trilogy (1890–1). Similar neo-romantic impulses were evident in the poetic dramas of Julius Zeyer, *An Old Story* (1882) and *Radúz and Mahulena* (1898), while Jaroslav Hilbert strove to combine an IBSEN-like ethical REALISM with symbolist overtones: *Guilt* (1896), *About God* (1898).

Theatre practice was also maturing and becoming more sophisticated. With the National Theatre serving as prime inspiration and showcase, and with opportunities to observe visiting luminaries like the MEININGEN players, Czech performers were able to build a promising foundation for a genuinely world-class Czech theatre in the 20th century. F. A. Šubert, playwright and director of the National Theatre until the turn of the century, led Czech theatre towards the mainstream of European theatre; 20th-century directors plunged it into that current and guided it to a leading position.

The 20th century Although other Czech theatres existed by 1900, the Prague National and Municipal Theatres (the latter built in 1907) dominated Czech theatre during the first two decades of the 20th century. Each of the two major Prague theatres was led by a director with a distinctive creative personality.

In his concern with the total integration and harmony of all components of production, Jaroslav Kvapil was the first modern Czech director. At the National Theatre from 1900 to 1918, he raised the level of performance to European standards. A gifted lyric poet, he brought his sensitivity to language, form and nuance to the stage, where he was particularly drawn to Ibsen and CHEKHOV. His most notable productions, however, were of Shakespeare, especially his cycle of Shakespeare's plays in 1916. He mounted a similar cycle of Czech historical dramas in 1918 to support the hope for an independent state, which in fact materialized in October 1918 with the overthrow of the Habsburg regime. Kvapil worked with a number of great actors, above all the legendary Eduard Vojan, whose Hamlet (1905) is regarded as the highwater mark of Czech acting, Hana Kvapilová, his peer in Shakespearian and modern psychological roles, and Marie Hübnerová, whose forte was earthier genre types.

Kvapil's successor at the National Theatre was KAREL HUGO HILAR, who had established a reputation for bold staging at the Municipal Theatre. More flamboyant and forceful than Kvapil, Hilar repeatedly attracted international attention to the National Theatre in the 1920s and early 1930s. Hilar had a notable collaborator in his chief designer, Vlastislav Hofman, whose stage settings based on both painting and architectural techniques matched the expressiveness of Hilar's vision.

Several Czech playwrights in the early 1900s reflected the growing maturity of Czech dramaturgy. Although primarily a novelist, Alois Jirásek brought skill and imagination to the writing of historical drama, particularly his plays known as the *Hussite Trilogy* (1903–14), and a lighter, fanciful touch to a play of Czech folk life, *The Lantern* (1905). Less social in its orientation was the work of the poet Fráňa Šrámek, who dealt sensitively with themes of youthful eroticism and other subjective states: *Summer* (1915), *Moon above the River* (1922). Irony and

disenchantment characterized the plays of Viktor Dyk: *The Coming to Wisdom of Don Quixote* (1913) and *Revolutionary Trilogy* (1917), on the French Revolution. Overlapping the work of Hilar and Kvapil in the 1920s and 1930s was the work of another group of important theatre artists primarily associated with smaller, avant-garde Prague stages. At the crossroads of Europe, these artists were sensitized not only to theatre in Germany, France and Soviet Russia but also to the political forces that threatened their new state.

Jindřich Honzl was a major theoretician and critic of theatre as well as an active director whose work encompassed communist proletarian mass spectacles and small-scale experimental staging of surrealistic and other unorthodox texts: e.g. JARRY's *Ubu Roi* and COCTEAU's *Orphée* in the 1920s. For a brief period in 1926, Jiří Frejka joined with Honzl in the leadership of the most active of the avant-garde groups, the Liberated Theatre. Frejka was a more lyrical, intuitive director; inspired by the *commedia dell'arte*, he was less intellectual or politically committed than Honzl. He leaned towards a more fanciful theatre and worked more intimately with actors. In the 1930s Frejka moved to the National Theatre, where he began to work on a larger scale and eventually directed productions that clearly took a stand against the growing threat of Fascism in Europe: e.g. ARISTOPHANES' *The Birds* (1933) and *Julius Caesar* (1936). Collaborating with Frejka on *Caesar* and many other major productions at the National Theatre was František Tröster, a stage designer with an architectonic approach to the handling of stage space. Other highly creative stage designers of the 1920s and 1930s included Bedřich Feuerstein, Antonín Heythum and František Muzika.

A distinctive new form of theatre was created by JIŘÍ VOSKOVEC and Jan Werich. In 1927 their semi-improvised entertainment, *Vestpocket Review*, became an overnight sensation in Prague. Authors, librettists and chief actors of their REVUES, they eventually took over the Liberated Theatre and renamed it the Liberated Theatre of V+W, where they continued to mount provocative socio-political combinations of music, dance and Aristophanic farce. Particularly in the 1930s their productions became a rallying point against the Fascist threat to the brief independence of Czechoslovakia. Among their successes were *Executioner and Fool* (1934), *Heavy Barbora* (1937) and *A Fist in the Eye* (1938).

Probably the most important avant-garde theatre artist of the interwar period was EMIL FRANTIŠEK BURIAN. In the 1930s he combined his talents for music and theatre with his political activism and established D34, a theatre that gained international recognition for its stage artistry and social relevance. Other directors of the 1920s and 1930s included Jan Bor and Karel Dostal, who did important work at the Municipal and National Theatres, respectively; Viktor Šulc, noted for his expressionistic productions in Bratislava and his interest in BRECHT; and Oldřich Stibor, an eclectic, politically engaged director most of whose work was done in Olomouc. The single best-known theatre figure in Czechoslovakia in the interwar years was KAREL ČAPEK, whose highly imaginative, provocative plays (e.g. *RUR*) achieved worldwide production in the 1920s and 30s. František Langer, who explored questions of ethical choice and social implications in more conventional ways, also achieved international recognition: e.g. *Camel through the Needle's Eye* (1923), *The Periphery* (1925), *Grandhotel Nevada* (1927).

From the Munich capitulation in October 1938 to the liberation in May 1945, a censored theatre subsisted at the discretion of the German forces of occupation. Several of the leading theatre artists survived this period to extend their creativity for varying lengths of time, but none surpassed Čapek's pre-war achievements. One reason may be found in still another radical sociopolitical dislocation, in 1948: the fall of the postwar Republic, the ascension to power of the Communist Party, and the establishment of the Czechoslovakian Socialist Republic. Private enterprise in theatre was abolished and all theatre activity brought under state control. In the arts, a dogmatically imposed policy of socialist realism stifled for some ten years virtually all creativity not in accord with ideological guidelines. Then Czech theatre gradually began still another revival, which in several respects surpassed even the accomplishments of the interwar era before being reined back again after the military and political suppression of Czechoslovakia by the Moscow Pact nations in 1968.

The 1960s and their aftermath As in the interwar period, the blooming of Czech theatre in the 1960s was largely evident in the work of directors and designers who mounted a stream of highly imaginative, powerfully executed productions in both large institutional theatres and small studio environments. But playwrights, too, made their mark.

Two directors stood out for their large-scale work. OTOMAR KREJČA became chief director and head of drama at the National Theatre in the late 1950s. In 1965, he became head of his own producing organization at the Gate Theatre. In both places his most frequent collaborator was the designer JOSEF SVOBODA, with whom he formed a creative team that was reminiscent of Hilar and Hofman. Some of Krejča's memorable productions included CHEKHOV's *Seagull* (1960) and *Three Sisters* (1966), *Romeo and Juliet* (1963), Topol's *Their Day* (1959) and *End of Carnival* (1964), and his own conflation *Oedipus–Antigone* (1971). After directing abroad exclusively between 1976 and 89 because of political pressures, Krejča returned to Prague and revived his Gate Theatre in 1990.

ALFRED RADOK's work at the National and the Municipal Theatres of Prague in the 1950s and 1960s was distinguished by subjective, highly metaphoric production concepts. An outgrowth of Radok's creativity in the late 1950s was a unique fusion of live action and projected film called *LATERNA MAGIKA*, which he evolved with Josef Svoboda. Radok's single most outstanding production, however, was his adaptation of ROLLAND's *The Game of Love and Death* (1964), designed by Czechoslovakia's other leading scenographer, LADISLAV VYCHODIL. Radok worked abroad after the 1968 crushing of the Prague Spring. Other important directors of the 1960s and beyond were Jaromír Pleskot and Miroslav Macháček.

Josef Svoboda, who has designed over 500 productions of drama, opera and ballet since the late 1940s, was for nearly thirty years chief designer at the National Theatre while also working extensively in other world theatre centres. In the early 1980s he became head of the Laterna Magika operation as well. Outstanding among his Prague productions have been *Hamlet* (1959), *Romeo and Juliet* (1963), *Insect Comedy* (1965), *Mother Courage* (1970), and the OPERAS *Fidelio* (1976) and *Rusalka* (1990).

Other vital theatre in the 1960s occurred on smaller stages that provided an outlet for creative energies dormant during the previous decade. One of the earliest examples was the Balustrade Theatre; established in the late 1950s, it reached its peak of creative production under the leadership of JAN GROSSMAN in the last half of the 1960s with productions of Kafka's *Trial*, Jarry's *Ubu Roi*, BECKETT's *Godot* and the plays of VÁCLAV HAVEL. Sharing the theatre was the internationally known MIME troupe of LADISLAV FIALKA. The Drama Club, founded in 1965, is more an actors' theatre than is the text-oriented Balustrade Theatre. The Semafor Theatre, under Jiří Suchý, has since the late 1950s specialized in satiric REVUES with heavy emphasis on music, echoing the prototypal V+W revues of the 1930s. Krejča's Gate Theatre (1965–72) was the other outstanding small theatre operation in Prague.

As Čapek's plays brought world attention to Czech theatre in the pre-war years, so too did the plays of Václav Havel in the 1960s, while he was dramaturg and resident playwright at the Balustrade, for which he wrote all his plays until 1968. Echoing the implications of Čapek's works, Havel's themes centre on the plight of civilized values in a dehumanized world. Josef Topol is essentially a poet whose work is highly suggestive, intuitive, at times cryptic in its explorations of complex sensibilities. His chief works (all directed by Krejča) include *Their Day* (1959), *End of Carnival* (1964), *Cat on the Rails* (1965) and *Hour of Love* (1968). His work was banned between 1969 and 1990, after which time newer works such as *Goodbye, Socrates* and *Voices of the Birds* were staged. František Hrubín, like Topol a poet and Krejča collaborator, presented more traditionally drawn characters and incidents with Chekhovian overtones: for example, *Sunday in August* (1958) and *Starry Night* (1961). Other interesting authors in the 1960s included František Pavlíček (*The Heavenly Ascension of Saska Christ*, 1967); Pavel Kohout (*August, August, August*, 1967); Milan Kundera (*Owners of the Keys*, 1962); Ivan Klíma (*The Castle*, 1964; and Ladislav Smoček (*Cosmic Spring*, 1970).

The radical military and political events of August 1968 did not dramatically truncate theatre activity in Czechoslovakia; challenging, creative work occasionally surfaced for the next season or two. But the main flow was turned off, and although some of the principal writers and artists continued to work, theatre in Czechoslovakia once again marked time. Important playwrights of the 1970s and 1980s were Oldřich Daněk (*The Duchess of Waldstein's Armies*, 1980, and *You Are Jan*, 1987); Karel Steigerwald (*Period Dances*, 1980); Arnošt Goldflam (*Sand*, 1988); and Daniela Fischerová (*Princess T.*, 1987). Jan Kačer, Ewald Schorm, Petr Scherhaufer and Ivan Rajmont were noteworthy directors in the 1970s and 80s. During that same era, scenographers Jaroslav Malina, Jan Dušek, Ivo Žídek and Marta Rozkopfová did significant work. The studio theatre tradition of the 1960s was enriched in the 1970s and 80s, though in somewhat muted form, by the

Ypsilon Theatre in Prague, and the Theatre on a String and the Hadivadlo theatre in Brno.

Slovak theatre Retarded in its development by its people's centuries-long vassalhood to Hungary and Austria, Slovak professional theatre began in 1918 with the formation of the Czechoslovak Republic. Prior to that time, theatre activity was limited to amateur performances, which dated back to 1830 and echoed the nationalistic aspirations of the Czech theatre. Early playwrights included Ján Chalupka and Ján Palárik, authors of satiric comedies; the major poet P. O. Hviezdoslav; the prolific, extremely popular Ferko Urbánek, and the naturalistic social critic J. G. Tajovský.

The Slovak National Theatre was established in 1920, but for years it performed not only in Slovak but also in Czech and relied on experienced Czech actors and directors. Two men were especially significant in building the foundations of a truly Slovak professional theatre: Andrej Bagar and Ján Borodáč, both of whom were central to National Theatre activity from the 1920s to the 1960s as actors, directors and administrators. Ján Jamnický was a strong, more overtly theatrical director in the early 1940s.

The most notable playwright of the interwar years was Ivan Stodola, whose sharp sense of social SATIRE combined with a firm grasp of theatre values; his work ranged from contemporary satire, *The Career of Jožka Púčik* (1931), to Slovak history, *King Svätopluk* (1931). Július Barč-Ivan, a religiously oriented playwright, attempted to blend EXPRESSIONISM with neo-realism: *3000 People* (1934), *Mother* (1943).

The dominant figure in Slovak playwriting after the Second World War was Peter Karvaš, whose plays were especially effective in dealing with the problematics of wartime morality in Slovakia (*Midnight Mass*, 1959; *Antigone and the Others*, 1962) and the follies of the 1950s (*The Big Wig*, 1964). Two directors dominated the postwar era. Jozef Budský developed into Slovakia's most expressive director, employing great imagination and theatrical metaphor in his bold stagings. Beginning his directing career in the 1940s, he endured the limitations of the socialist realism era and was the first to reintroduce conscious art into production. Karol Zachar, more traditionally realistic and actor-centred in his work, had a special talent for fantasy and lyricism.

Slovakia's pre-eminent scenographer, Ladislav Vychodil, was chief designer and technical chief of the Slovak National Theatre in Bratislava from the end of the Second World War until the 1980s. Less prolific than Svoboda, Vychodil also differed in being more emotive and lyrical in his designs and in not using complex technical methods as extensively. Vychodil also established the stage design training programme at the School of Fine Arts in Bratislava. Of subsequent scenographers, Jozef Ciller, who succeeded Vychodil at the Bratislava school, has been the most important. Noteworthy younger playwrights have included Osvald Zahradník, Štanislav Štepka and Karol Horák, while directors Vladimír Strnisko, Miloš Pietor, Lubomír Vajdička and Jozef Bednárik, as well as designers Jan Zavarský and Milan Ferenčík, have done stimulating work. The Korzo Theatre of Bratislava carried on its significant avant-garde studio work of the 1960s into the 70s and 80s.

The present The relatively unfruitful era of the 1970s lasted until the late 1980s, when the principles of *glasnost* and *perestroika* led to liberalization in the arts and culminated in fundamental changes of government after the Velvet Revolution of 1989. Although Czechoslovakia was transformed in 1993 into the Czech and Slovak Republics, respectively, the long-standing, largely subsidized repertory theatre system still prevails in both sovereign states, with virtually no private, commercial theatres. Nevertheless, the reorganization or revival of some theatres, the folding of others, and the creation of new ones indicate that the theatre world of what was Czechoslovakia is in the process of substantial transformation. JMB

See: J. M. Burian, *The Scenography of Josef Svoboda*, Middletown, Conn., 1971; F. Černý (ed.), *Dějiny Českého Divadla* (*The History of Czech Theatre*), 4 vols., Prague, 1968–83 (the most recent and most definitive study, but available only in Czech), and *Divadlo Nové Doby 1945–1948* (*Theatre of the New Age*), Prague, 1989 (an objective and thorough coverage of the revival of Prague theatre in the critical three years after the war; only in Czech); M. Goetz-Stankiewicz, *The Silenced Theatre*, Toronto, 1979; J. Honzl (ed.), *The Czechoslovak Theatre*, Prague, 1948; M. Rutte and F. Bartoš, *The Modern Czech Scene*, tr. A. R. Weir, Prague, 1938; J. Svoboda, *The Secret of Theatrical Space*, New York, 1992; P. Trensky, *Czech Drama Since World War II*, White Plains, NY, 1978; O. Vočadlo, 'The Theatre and Drama of Czechoslovakia', in *The Theater in a Changing Europe*, ed. T. H. Dickinson, New York, 1937. See also the journal , *Theatre*, Theatre Institute, Prague.

Dadié, Bernard (Binlin) 1916– Ivorian novelist, poet, dramatist and politician; generally recognized as one of the founding fathers of French-language Ivorian drama. Dadié was educated in the Ivory Coast at the École Primaire Supérieure at Bingerville, and at the École William Ponty in SENEGAL, where he was involved in the school's nascent but already dynamic dramatic activities. On graduation, he worked in Dakar at the French Research Institute for African Studies (IFAN), from 1936 to 1947. Also in Dakar, under various pseudonyms he was involved in nationalist journalism, an activity he pursued on his return to Abidjan in 1948 for the Ivorian section of the Rassemblement Démocratique Africain mass political movement. Dadié has had a distinguished career in his country as a top civil servant in the Ministry of Culture and Information, then as Minister of Culture. His first play, *Les Villes* (*The Towns*, 1933), now missing, was written while he was still at Bingerville. It was followed in 1934 at Ponty by a historical chronicle, *Assémien Déhylé*. Between 1955 and 1960 he wrote five sketches for the Cercle Culturel Folklorique de Côte d'Ivoire, which he had helped found: *Serment d'amour* (*Love Vow*, 1955), *Situation difficile* (*A Difficult Situation*, 1955), *Les Enfants* (*The Children*, 1956), *Min Ajao* (*My Inheritance*, 1956) and *Sidi, maître escroc* (*Sidi, Master Crook*, 1960).

But it is for the plays of his mature period that he is best known: *Béatrice du Congo* and *Îles de tempête* (*Beatrice of Congo*, 1970; *Islands of Storm*, 1973) and *Les Voix dans le vent*, *Monsieur Thogo-Ghini*, *Mhoi-Ceul* and *Papassidi maître escroc* (*Voices in the Wind*, 1970; *Mister Thogo-Ghini*, 1970; *I Alone*, 1979; *Papassidi Master Crook*, 1975). In their preoccupation with political power and social criticism, all reflect the major concerns of the French-language African dramatist.

The success of Dadié's plays lies in the fact that they are both humanly engaging and theatrically lively. He has also written four prose narratives, volumes of poetry, folk-tales and short stories. JCM

Daldry, Stephen 1947– British director, whose LIVERPOOL PLAYHOUSE production of *The Ragged Trousered Philanthropists* in 1988 won him instant comparisons with JOAN LITTLEWOOD for his liveliness of staging and economy of means. He started to direct on London's FRINGE and staged ÖDÖN VON HORVÁTH's *Judgement Day* at the Old Red Lion in 1989, praised by the *Guardian* critic Michael Billington as 'a remarkable event'. In 1990 he became the director of the tiny Gate Theatre in Notting Hill, and at once started to explore the repertoire of neglected European plays, including Horváth's *Figaro Gets Divorced* (1990), MARIELUISE FLEISSER's *Pioneers in Ingolstadt* and *Purgatory in Ingolstadt* (1991, with co-director Annie Castledine) and TIRSO DE MOLINA's *Damned for Despair* (1991). His ingenuity at finding, casting and staging major plays which other directors had overlooked drew the Gate Theatre from the fringe to the centre of London's theatrical life. There was relatively little surprise when it was announced in 1991 that Daldry would join the ROYAL COURT THEATRE as a co-director with Max Stafford-Clark with a view to succeeding him, but before he had directed one production there the NATIONAL THEATRE had claimed him for London's South Bank, inviting him to direct a revival of J. B. PRIESTLEY's *An Inspector Calls* (1992), where the magnificent set, designed by Ian MacNeil, rather overwhelmed the acting and the thoughtful text. In 1994 Daldry triumphantly revived WESKER's *The Kitchen* at the Royal Court, where he is now established as sole artistic director JE

Dale, Alan [Alfred J. Cohen] 1861–1928 British-born critic, who went to New York in the early 1880s to write for the *Dramatic Times*. In 1887 Joseph Pulitzer employed him as drama critic for the *World*. Dale switched to Hearst's *Morning Journal* in 1897 and *Cosmopolitan* magazine in 1904. Except for the period 1914–17, he remained a Hearst regular until his death. Dale popularized an aggressive and 'smart' style of reviewing. *Who's Who in the Theatre* (1914) concluded that his opinions 'probably carry more weight than any others in New York'. TLM

Dale, Charlie see SMITH, JOE

Dallas Theater Center (Texas, USA) Founded in 1959 by Baylor University (Texas) professor Paul Baker and a group of Dallas citizens, the Dallas Theater Center sprang into being in the only theatre designed by Frank Lloyd Wright that he ever lived to see built. A gift of Dallas businessmen and named after a Texas actress who was killed in a plane crash, the Kalita Humphreys Theatre consists of a geometric poured-concrete structure set into a hilly, wooded area a few miles from the centre of the city. Its original stage was set at one end of the auditorium and was equipped with a revolve and two side stages. Professor Baker's plan to assemble a permanent acting company to present classics and contemporary plays and to introduce new works in conjunction with a graduate programme at Baylor (later at Trinity University, where he transferred his activities) was largely fulfilled but has been discontinued. To the original 516-seat theatre have been added an experimental and flexible stage, In the Basement, seating 50–100, and the Arts District Theatre in downtown Dallas (up to 750 seats). Under the leadership of Adrian Hall (1983–9), DTC became an Equity (actors' union) company. Hall was replaced by 35-year-old Ken Bryant, who died suddenly in October 1990 following a car accident. In December 1991 Richard Hamburger, formerly with Maine's Portland Stage, was appointed artistic director. MCH

Daly, (Peter Christopher) Arnold 1875–1927 American producer and actor. Daly should be remembered as SHAW's first truly effective champion in the USA. Even as he was establishing himself as a player of supporting roles in England and America, he pursued his interest in Shaw by directing and acting in a trial matinée of *Candida*, which opened for a regular run in New York in 1903 and then went on tour with *The Man of Destiny*. After visiting Shaw, he returned for the 1904–5 season to produce *How She Lied to Her Husband* (written for Daly), *You Never Can Tell*, *John Bull's Other Island* and *Mrs Warren's Profession*. The first New York performance of this last play was cause for Daly's arrest on moral charges, although he was acquitted. In 1906, he added *Arms and the Man* to his repertory and, under the management of the SHUBERTS, conducted a successful national tour. Somewhat dismayed by the vitriolic response of conservative critics, Daly abandoned Shaw for a time to pursue more conventional roles. MR

Daly, (John) Augustin 1838–99 American dramatist, managing director and critic, who dominated the theatrical scene in the USA during the last half of the 19th century. His plays and especially his productions set a new standard for American theatre and exerted a strong influence in England, beginning with a first European tour in 1884 and culminating with the opening of Daly's own theatre in London in 1893. He began his theatre career as a critic, writing for five newspapers during 1859–67. During this period he also wrote or adapted his first plays, most notably *Leah, the Forsaken* (1862) and the melodrama *Under the Gaslight* (1867). From the inception of his writing career he was assisted at every turn by his brother Joseph, though this collaboration was kept secret. Ultimately, the Dalys had over 90 of their plays or adaptations performed. Of this large number few are significant literary accomplishments, though many show Daly to have been an exceptional contriver of effects and theatri-cal moments and, during the 1870s and 80s, a writer of MELODRAMAS and sentimental comedies superior to most of his contemporaries. Among his more successful productions were *A Flash of Lightning* (1868), *Frou-Frou* (1870), *Horizon* (1871), *Divorce* (1871), *Article 47* (1872), *Needles and Pins* (1880), *Dollars and Sense* (1883), *Love on Crutches* (1884) and *The Lottery of Love* (1888). He also produced adaptations of English classics and SHAKESPEARE, one of the most successful of which, *The Taming of the Shrew*, was presented at Stratford-upon-Avon in 1888, supposedly the first performance of the play given there.

Many of his more notable productions featured ADA REHAN, John Drew (see DREW–BARRYMORE FAMILY), Mrs G.H. Gilbert (1821–1904) and James Lewis (?1837–96), known as the 'Big Four'. Daly was usually adept at discerning and developing talent: over 75 prominent actors owed their success to his training. He also managed and built several important theatres, beginning with the rental in 1869 of the FIFTH AVENUE THEATRE, and took over briefly the Grand Opera House. In 1879, with these theatres behind him, he took over the old Wood's Museum (built in 1867), which he opened as Daly's on BROADWAY, remaining there until his death (after which it was run by a succession of managers, including DANIEL FROHMAN and the SHUBERT BROTHERS). Constantly striving for an ensemble effect in his productions, Daly was one of the first directors in the modern sense and the first American *régisseur*. DBW

Dalrymple, Jean 1910– American producer, director and publicist. Dalrymple began her career as an actress in VAUDEVILLE, then became personal representative with JOHN GOLDEN, and in 1940 formed her own publicity organization. Her initial venture as producer was in 1945 when she presented *Hope for the Best* by William McCleery.

A poster advertising the sensation scene from Augustin Daly's *Under the Gaslight*, 1867.

Associated with the New York City Center Light Opera Company and the City Center Drama Company from its inception in 1943, in 1953 she became its general director, a position she held for the next 15 years. This experience was recorded in her book *From the Last Row* (1975). During 1968–70 she was executive director of the American National Theatre and Academy, and in 1958 she was coordinator of the performing arts for the USA at the Brussels World's Fair. DBW

dame role see PANTOMIME, ENGLISH; FEMALE IMPERSONATION

Dancourt [Florent Carton] 1661–1725 French actor and playwright who, after several years with provincial companies, joined the COMÉDIE-FRANÇAISE in 1685. Between then and his retirement in 1718 he pursued a dual career and wrote over 80 plays, including many in one act. Most are comedies of manners in prose, closely based on the contemporary scene and depicting an unscrupulous and pleasure-seeking society, as in *Le Chevalier à la mode* (*The Fashionable Knight*, 1687) and *Les Bourgeoises à la mode* (1692), which was imitated by VANBRUGH in *The Confederacy* (1705). Amongst the characteristic types surveyed – social-climbing bourgeois, financiers, magistrates, aristocratic gamesters and adventurers – there are few sympathetic figures, and the perspective offered looks forward to LESAGE, if in a less sardonic and more light-hearted mood. DR

Dane, Clemence [*née* Winifred Ashton; Diana Cortis] 1888–1965 British dramatist and novelist, once hailed (by the critic ST JOHN ERVINE) as 'the most distinguished woman dramatist'. Trained as a portraitist, Dane began her theatrical career as an actress (under the stage name of Cortis) before turning to writing MELODRAMATIC 'problem plays' focusing on sexual issues from a female perspective. *A Bill of Divorcement* (1921) was followed by *The Way Things Happen* (1924), and a morality play on adultery, *Granite* (1926). She also used biblical subjects (*Naboth's Vineyard*, 1925; *Herod and Marianne*, 1938) or historical settings (a dramatization of the lives of the Brontë sisters, *Wild Decembers*, 1932; *The Golden Age of Queen Elizabeth*, 1941) to illustrate her themes. She wrote a seven-play religious cycle for radio (see RADIO DRAMA), *The Saviours*, part of which was adapted for the stage (1942, with JOHN MILLS and SYBIL THORNDIKE). Her last work, *Eighty in the Shade* (1959), was specially written for Sybil Thorndike and LEWIS CASSON, who had played the leading roles in the premiere of *Granite*. CI

Daniel, Samuel 1562–1619 English poet and occasional playwright, who enjoyed the patronage of many noble benefactors and was thus spared the rough and tumble of the public theatres. Daniel wrote two SENECAN tragedies, *Cleopatra* (1594) and *Philotas* (1604), supervising the production of the second by the CHILDREN OF THE CHAPEL ROYAL. James I was among those troubled by supposedly covert references in the play to the fate of the Earl of Essex, and Daniel fell into further disfavour when the Children of the Chapel Royal, over which he exercised formal control, presented *Eastward Ho* (1605), the joint work of JONSON, MARSTON and CHAPMAN, offensive to the king for its anti-Scottish jibes. But Daniel knew the virtues of timely sycophancy. The composition of a number of court entertainments, including the PASTORAL *The Queen's Arcadia* in the dangerous year of 1605, re-established him at court. We do not know why, nor precisely when, he retired from public life to a farm in Somerset. PT

D'Annunzio, Gabriele 1863–1938 Italian poet, dramatist and novelist. D'Annunzio was a prolific writer, whose literary and theatrical activities and adventurous life had a powerful, if not always positive, influence on his contemporaries.

The flamboyant writing and lifestyle of this poet and novelist of *fin-de-siècle* decadence rapidly made him a prominent figure in the 1880s, particularly after the publication of *Canto novo* and *Terra vergine*, volumes of verse marked as much by stylistic experimentation as by exotic language and subject-matter. His theatrical activity began comparatively late, in 1896, after the start of his seven-year relationship with the actress ELEONORA DUSE, with whom he projected a revitalization of theatre that turned its face boldly against the constraints of bourgeois NATURALISM. The ideals of this new theatre he passionately described in his novel, *Il fuoco* (*The Flame of Life*, 1900), and he wrote the one-act *Sogno di un mattino di primavera* (*Dream of a Spring Morning*) and *Sogno di un tramonto d'autunno* (*Dream of an Autumn Sunset*) for Duse in 1898. Audiences remained indifferent, and he won no substantially greater success with the full-length pieces which immediately followed: *La città morta* (*The Dead City*), first produced in Paris by SARAH BERNHARDT in 1898, and *La Gioconda* and *La gloria* (*The Glory*), both mounted by Duse and ERMETE ZACCONI in 1899.

D'Annunzio's search for a poetic drama led him to abandon prose, and with his next play, *Francesca da Rimini* (1901), he attempted a verse tragedy in the historical vein. It proved enormously successful and was widely imitated. Even more popular was his next piece, *La figlia di Iorio* (*Iorio's Daughter*, 1904), a modern peasant drama set in his native Abruzzo and considered today to be by far his best stage work. Later plays, enjoying variable success, included *La nave* (*The Ship*, 1908) and *Le Martyr de Saint Sébastien* (*The Martyrdom of St Sebastian*), produced with music by Debussy in Paris in 1911, where D'Annunzio had gone into self-imposed exile to escape critical hostility and debts.

During the First World War he became increasingly a man of action, involved in Italian political and military affairs. He remained as colourful a figure as ever, never more so than during the Fiume adventure: with a group of volunteers he occupied the disputed city and held it for a year, defying the European powers and embarrassing the Italian government. In the 1920s he retired to his exotically decorated and furnished villa, Il Vittoriale, on Lake Garda. Of his last works perhaps the most effective was the libretto he wrote for Mascagni's *Parisina*. Increasingly from 1913 he wrote more for the cinema than for the theatre, collaborating on the scenario for *Cabiria* (1913) and writing others independently. Many films have been made from his novels, stories and plays. These last, like *La città morta* and *La gloria*, turned from the concerns of contemporary naturalistic drama to treat of the struggles of exceptional NIETZSCHEan individuals in a language verbally rich but too often flamboyant, precious and replete with neologisms and antique terms and turns of phrase.

The best of D'Annunzio's plays are not wholly lacking in dramatic power, but they are often marred by contrived conflict and vapid grandiloquence. He was invariably active in the preparation of his own plays for performance: his emphasis on detail and accuracy in the reconstruction of historical settings was obsessive to the point of pedantry, and his attempts to wed stage upholstery to the quasi-mystical and symbolic suggest that his rejection of naturalism was partial rather than complete, as too perhaps does his dependence on familiar love triangle conflicts in *La città morta*, *La gloria*, *La Gioconda*, *Francesca da Rimini* and *La figlia di Iorio*. Some of his work is occasionally revived in the Italian theatre today.   LR

dashavatara Popular form of rural theatre in Konkan and Goa on India's west coast: literally, 'ten' (*dash*) 'incarnations' (*avatara*) of Lord Vishnu, two of whom, Rama and Krishna, are widely worshipped in India.

Dashavatara is thought to have been introduced to the area by a Brahmin 400 years ago. Some claim that it is derived from *KUCHIPUDI*; others maintain that it owes its origin to *YAKSHAGANA*. The actors who preserve *dashavatara* worship a small image of a deity which is said to have been brought from Kerala. Most of the actors come from the lower strata of society, although a few Brahmins also perform. The all-male troupes are itinerant, moving from village to village half the year, carrying simple baskets and trunks and sleeping out in the open most of the time. Their earnings are generally meagre.

Performances usually begin around 11 p.m. with songs in praise of Ganapati, the elephant-headed god, sung by the stage manager (*sutradhara*). A Brahmin enters and comic dialogue ensues. Two men dance dressed as women. An elementary dance is then performed by an actor who impersonates Saraswati, goddess of learning. After the dance, two women enter symbolizing rivers. With them is Madhavi, a comic Brahmin. Next the frightening figure of Shankhasura bursts on to the playing area dressed from head to foot in black and sporting a red cloth representing a tongue. Shankhasura is thought to be capable of exposing the scandals and private lives of the villagers. He carries on a lively improvisational conversation with the stage manager. Then an actor playing the god Brahma, the creator, enters and a story about the theft of the sacred *Veda* is related, in which Shankhasura and the stage manager participate. The events in the elaborate overture described above continue for approximately two hours.

Finally the drama (*akhyana*) begins, lasting until sunrise. The drama includes well known episodes from epic literature and introduces mythological and historical characters with whom village audiences are familiar. The decision as to which episodes should be performed is negotiated between the village patron and the stage manager, sometimes less than an hour before the show.

A small boy dressed in the costume of a woman moves among the spectators during the performance soliciting contributions from the villagers. The job is said to help cure the boy of stage fright and his costume gives him access to the women, who usually huddle together apart from the village men.

A harmonium and drum (*mridangam*) assist the actors with their songs and set a lively tempo for the simple dances. Tunes from popular film music are also liberally used as accompaniment to song lyrics.

The stage area is simple – an open space in a temple hall or a temporary raised platform set up in the village, surrounded on three sides and roofed by thatch and leaves. A rough wooden bench from the local town-council hall or school serves as the only piece of furniture. Special properties, such as swords, spears and clubs, are introduced by the actors when the need arises. A company's belongings include an elaborately carved ten-headed wooden mask depicting Ravana, the demon king of Lanka, and one representing Ganapati's elephant head. Costumes and ornaments are rather elaborate, considering the simple means the actors have of transporting them. Various cloth pieces, saris, jewellery and headdresses are worn to symbolize nobles, gods and goddesses; red and white make-up distinguishes the characters from their village patrons.

Very little has been written about this form and scholars have only recently begun to reveal the extent and nature of its impact on village life in this area of India.   FaR

Dasté, Jean 1904–94 French actor and director. One of COPEAU's original band of disciples (he married Copeau's daughter, Marie-Hélène), Dasté was a pioneer in the DECENTRALIZATION MOVEMENT. After working with the Compagnie des Quatre Saisons (he was a co-founder with BARSACQ and Jacquemont in 1936) and a touring offshoot of this group under the Occupation, Dasté established a touring company of his own in Grenoble after the Liberation. Local opposition led to his departure for St Étienne in 1947, where he remained until 1971. His repertoire followed Copeau's lead but included new dramatists (COUSIN, GATTI) and BRECHT (his *Caucasian Chalk Circle*, 1956, was that play's French premiere). His policy involved vigorous prospection of a working-class audience. St Étienne's Maison de la Culture, built in consultation with Dasté, was denied him because of a disagreement with the local board of management. He played many character roles in French films, notably Truffaut's *L'Enfant sauvage* (*The Wild Child*, 1970), in which he played the role of Professor Pinel.   DB

Daubeny, Peter (Lauderdale) 1921–75 British impresario, best known as the artistic director of the World Theatre Seasons in London from 1964 to 1973. He began his career as an actor, studying with MICHEL SAINT-DENIS's London Theatre Studio and joining the LIVERPOOL PLAYHOUSE under William Armstrong. During the war, he served as a lieutenant in the Coldstream Guards and lost a left arm during the Salerno invasion in 1943. This injury caused him to abandon his acting career and concentrate on management. He staged his first production, of William Lipscombe's *The Gay Pavilion*, at the Piccadilly Theatre in London in 1945, but his first major successes as an impresario came in the early 1950s, when he brought over to London a dazzling array of dance companies from Spain, India, France, Yugoslavia and Soviet Russia. He concentrated at first on those forms of theatre where language was no barrier, but following the triumphant success of the Compagnie Edwige Feuillère in *La Dame aux camélias* (1955) he looked to major drama companies as well.

The BERLINER ENSEMBLE was brought to London's Palace Theatre in 1956, providing British audiences with their first opportunity to see BRECHT's company, which was then little known. Other major visiting companies included the COMÉDIE-FRANÇAISE, the MOSCOW ART THEATRE, the MÄLMO STADSTEATER Company in INGMAR BERGMAN's production of *Urfast*, Zizi Jeanmaire and her company and VITTORIO GASSMAN's Teatro Popolare Italiano. Daubeny introduced London audiences to the new wave of American theatre with Jack Gelber's *The Connection* (1961). As a result, he managed to build up an audience prepared to look at forms of theatre as various as the Classical Theatre of China and Dublin's ABBEY THEATRE in a SEAN O'CASEY play. This public provided the financial basis – Daubeny received no government grants – for the World Theatre Seasons, which ran usually at the Aldwych Theatre for two to three months in the spring. These became an established feature of London's theatrical year, a major reason for the new-found cosmopolitanism in British drama.

Daubeny travelled tirelessly, and the success of the World Theatre Seasons was due to the width and perceptions of his tastes, his energy and his outstanding diplomatic skills. He was knighted in 1973. After his death, there was nobody who could adequately succeed him in running the World Theatre Seasons. He was the author of *Stage by Stage* (1952) and *My World of Theatre* (1971). JE

d'Aubignac, François Hédelin, abbé 1604–76 French critic and dramatist. As a member of RICHELIEU's household he came to share the Cardinal's passion for the drama and evolved an authoritarian view of its nature and current practice, to the extent of advancing a proposal for the radical reform of the theatre under state control. His principal work, *La Pratique du théâtre*, published in 1657 but begun much earlier, is a manual of dramatic writing and stage presentation in which he elaborates the neoclassical rules of composition into a systematic code of practice for the playwright. He insists on a strict division of the genres, the consequential decorum of character and incident to each, and above all the importance of *vraisemblance* (credibility) which inclines him to a severe interpretation of the unities of place, time and action, the presumed length of the latter being ideally comparable to the actual duration of the performance. For him, such rules are founded not on the authority of the ancients but on that of reason and will be conducive to the production of a satisfying artefact, capable of pleasing an audience in performance. Sadly, they did not serve to enhance his own three tragedies, intended as models but indifferently received. The *Pratique* itself, however, had a profound influence on dramatists, extended by its translation into English as *The Whole Art of the Stage* in 1684. DR

Davenant, William 1606–68 English playwright and manager, who claimed to be the illegitimate son of SHAKESPEARE. He joined the household of Fulke Greville and was soon a member of the circle of writers including SHIRLEY and Suckling. His first play, *The Cruel Brother*, was performed in 1627, and in the 1630s he produced a steady stream of plays including the comedies *The Platonic Lovers* (1635) and *News from Plymouth* (1635) and court MASQUES, (especially *Britannia Triumphans* (1638) and the last Caroline masque *Salmacida Spolia* (1640)). After a bout of syphilis his nose collapsed. In 1638 he succeeded JONSON as Laureate. In 1639 he secured a patent from the king to open a theatre, and the following year on WILLIAM BEESTON's imprisonment he ran the Phoenix Theatre (see COCKPIT THEATRE) in Drury Lane.

After active service during the Civil War and imprisonment when captured attempting to sail to Maryland, he joined the king's circle in Paris. In 1656 he avoided the government's prohibition on plays by performing operas at Rutland House, including his own heroic play *The Siege of Rhodes*, which marked a major advance in the development of English OPERA and was produced with changeable scenery by JOHN WEBB. He followed these performances with one at the Cockpit in Drury Lane in 1658. In 1660 he leased Lisle's Tennis Court in Lincoln's Inn Fields and converted it into a theatre. With KILLIGREW he persuaded the king to grant them a patent giving them a monopoly on theatre performances in London. Davenant's troupe, the Duke's Company, after eliminating the rival companies apart from Killigrew's, began acting at LINCOLN'S INN FIELDS in 1661, the first professional company in England to act in a theatre equipped with changeable scenery. In his agreement with the company Davenant controlled the rent and production costs and maintained the actresses in return for two-thirds of the company profits.

Shorn of rights to almost all pre-Restoration drama, Davenant began adapting plays: *Hamlet* in 1661, *The Law against Lovers* from *Measure for Measure* and *Much Ado about Nothing* in 1662, and operatic versions of *Macbeth* (1663) and *The Tempest* (with DRYDEN, 1667). He also carefully encouraged new work by ETHEREGE, BOYLE and others. Shrewdly identifying the tastes of his middle-class audience, he gave them spectacular dramas and good FARCES, establishing the success of his company, which continued under his widow's management. PH

Davenport, E(dward) L(oomis) 1815–77 American actor, known for his versatility, grace, good taste, musical voice and gentlemanly manners. ANNA CORA MOWATT said that he simply looked like a leading man. He began his career in Providence (1835), became Mowatt's leading man (1846), went with her to London, remained there for seven years (often playing in support of W. C. MACREADY), and returned to acclaim for his 'intelligent and impressive' conception of Lanciotto in BOKER's *Francesca da Rimini* (1885). From then until his final season (1875–6, playing Brutus to LAWRENCE BARRETT's Cassius), he became known for his extraordinary versatility. He was equally effective as Bill Sykes, Hamlet, Sir Lucius O'Trigger or Othello.

He was the father of the actress FANNY DAVENPORT, and three of his descendants have been active in recent years: Anne and WILLIAM SEYMOUR as actors, and the late May Davenport Seymour as theatre curator at the Museum of the City of New York. RM

Davenport, Fanny 1850–98 British-born actress and

daughter of actor E. L. DAVENPORT. 'Miss Fanny' was a popular child actress before her New York debut in 1862 at NIBLO's Garden Theatre. In 1869 she joined AUGUSTIN DALY's FIFTH AVENUE THEATRE company and demonstrated remarkable versatility in light comedies, SHAKESPEARE, and finally serious dramatic works like Daly's *Pique* (1876), in which she created Mabel Renfew, one of her most popular roles, along with Nancy Sykes in *Oliver Twist*. A beautiful, 'spirited' actress, she formed her own company and gave the American English-language premieres of four BERNHARDT vehicles by SARDOU: *Fedora* (1883), *La Tosca* (1888), *Cleopatra* (1890) and *Gismonda* (1894).   FHL

Davenport brothers Ira Erastus (1839–1911) and **William Henry Harrison** (1841–77), credited as the first successful stage mediums. Beginning in their home town of Buffalo, New York, they first toured the USA successfully in the 1860s, producing 'inexplicable manifestations' from their mysterious wooden cabinet in which they were securely tied. Denounced as fakes by such prominent British conjurors as J. H. ANDERSON and J. N. MASKELYNE, they nevertheless toured until William's death, and influenced all subsequent producers of 'spirit music'. DBW

Davidson, Gordon 1933– American director. Educated at Cornell University (1956) and at Case Western Reserve (1957), Davidson has directed at the Paper Mill Playhouse (New Jersey), the Barter Theatre and other venues, and stage-managed for Martha Graham. At the AMERICAN SHAKESPEARE [THEATRE] Festival he assisted JOHN HOUSEMAN, who chose him to co-direct *King Lear* with the Theatre Group and serve as managing director (1964–6). He is producing director of the Ahmanson (CENTER THEATRE GROUP, Los Angeles) and artistic director/producer of that city's Mark Taper Forum, where he directs nearly 20 per cent of the mainstage productions.   JDM

Davies, Hubert Henry 1876–1917 British dramatist. By profession a journalist, Davies wrote a series of social comedies between 1899 and 1914. These included a depiction of female domination, *The Mollusc* (1907), and *Outcast*, his last and most successful play, about sexual double standards.   CI

Davis, Henrietta Vinton 1860–1941 African-American actress. For 35 years a pre-eminent actress and solo elocutionist, Baltimore-born Davis was 'a singularly beautiful woman ... with illustriously expressive eyes [and a] rich, flexible and effective voice'. She was universally hailed by audiences across America for her powerful and moving interpretations of a range of dramatic heroines that included Juliet, Portia, Ophelia, Rosalind, Lady Anne, Desdemona, Lady Macbeth and Cleopatra. Excluded by racial prejudice from the established professional stage, Davis gave concert readings and performed dramatic scenes with other black actors. She produced and played leading roles in three plays by African-American dramatists: *Dessalines* (1893) and *Christophe* (1912), both by William Edgar Easton, and *Our Old Kentucky Home* (1898), written for her by the journalist John E. Bruce. During 1919–31 Davis held a major office in the Marcus

Garvey movement, working for racial equality and the establishment of a black nation-state in Africa.   EGH

Davis, Jack 1917– Australian playwright. Davis is the most distinguished and prolific of a number of Aboriginal dramatists who came to prominence during the 1980s. *Kullark* (1979) chronicles the conflict between European settlement and Aboriginal tribal life; *The Dreamers* (1982), *No Sugar* (1985), *Barungin: Smell the Wind* (1988) and *Wahngin Country* (1992) chart the history of Aboriginal dispossession in mission settlements earlier this century, juxtaposed with contemporary Aboriginal town life, drawn with great warmth and humour. Like many Aboriginal dramas, his plays fuse the realistic depiction of everyday life with traditional dance, music and poetry, linking the characters with their tribal heritage. He has been widely performed throughout Australia and overseas, and has a special association with Black Swan Theatre in Perth and its director Andrew Ross.   MW

Davis, Ossie 1917– African-American actor and playwright. Davis began acting with the Harlem-based ROSE McCLENDON Players and made his BROADWAY debut in the title role of *Jeb* (1946). He joined the national tour of *Anna Lucasta* (1947) and played in various New York productions, including *Stevedore* (1949), *The Green Pastures* (1951) and *No Time for Sergeants* (1955), before succeeding Sidney Poitier in *A Raisin in the Sun* (1959). In 1961 Davis assumed the lead role opposite his wife RUBY DEE in his hilarious COMEDY *Purlie Victorious*, which pungently ridiculed racial stereotyping. The film version, *Gone Are the Days* (1963), was unimpressive, but success was renewed with the MUSICAL *Purlie* (1970). Davis also wrote *Curtain Call, Mr Aldridge, Sir* (1963), and has appeared in numerous films and television shows (in the early 90s as a regular on 'Evening Shade'), some of which he scripted and directed. Louis D. Mitchell has called him 'one of the most gifted men in the modern American theatre'.   EGH

Davis, Owen 1874–1956 The most successful American writing MELODRAMA at the turn of the 20th century. From *Through the Breakers* (1899) to *The Family Cupboard* (1913), Davis wrote 129 melodramas, such as *Nellie, the Beautiful Cloak Model*. Then he stopped, and in 'Why I Quit Writing Melodrama' (*American Magazine*, September 1914) explained his art – for example, the importance of the play title and of the stage carpenter in the third act, on which he later elaborated in *I'd Like to Do It Again* (1931). Abandoning his Harvard-trained writing style, he began to write realistic plays (see REALISM), such as *Detour* (1921), in which he depicted a spiritual barrenness. *Icebound* (1923), concerned with the lost illusions of a New England family, won a Pulitzer Prize. Among later plays, only his adaptation of Edith Wharton's *Ethan Frome* (1936), with his son Donald Davis, was successful. He could not keep pace with the new rank of American dramatists during the 1930s. His autobiography, *My First Fifty Years in the Theatre*, appeared in 1950.   WJM

Davydov, Vladimir (Nikolaevich) [Ivan Gorelov] 1849–1925 Russian actor, born of impoverished gentry. After work in the provinces, he became a luminary of the

Imperial Alexandra Theatre in St Petersburg (1880–1924). Best in GOGOL (eight roles in *The Government Inspector* over the course of his career) and OSTROVSKY, noted for subtlety and versatility, Davydov was one of the first interpreters of CHEKHOV (title role in *Ivanov*, 1887; Firs in *The Cherry Orchard*, 1905; Chebutykin in *Three Sisters*, 1910). Perhaps he was greatest as the rogue Raspluev in *Krechinsky's Wedding*. Unfortunately, his talent was squandered on trivial vehicles and, despite his inspiring teaching, he failed to transmit a distinct tradition.   LS

Dawison, Bogumil 1818–72 Celebrated Polish virtuoso actor, whose career was spent mainly in the German theatre. He was a member of the Vienna BURGTHEATER from 1849 to 1852 and of the DRESDEN COURT THEATRE from 1852 to 1864. Dawison was noted for his aggressive, often unpolished interpretations of Shakespearian and other classic roles. As he was a bitter rival of EMIL DEVRIENT, his acting was widely regarded as the antithesis of the WEIMAR STYLE. He was one of the first German actors to tour America.   SW

Day, John 1574–1640 English playwright and poet whose recorded theatrical activity is confined to the period 1598–1608. He was, for a time, one of HENSLOWE's circle of writers, part-author with CHETTLE of one of the ADMIRAL'S MEN's major successes, *The Blind Beggar of Bethnal Green* (1600). Two satirical comedies for BOYS' COMPANIES, *Law Tricks* (1604) and *The Isle of Gulls* (1606), were followed by another collaboration, with WILLIAM ROWLEY and George Wilkins, on the ramblingly peculiar romance *The Travels of the Three English Brothers* (1607), based on the adventures of the extraordinary Shirley family and including an interesting scene in which the Shakespearian CLOWN WILL KEMPE displays his extempore skills. Day's known dramatic work is completed by an attractive COMEDY, *Humour out of Breath* (c.1608), and the strange collection of semi-dramatic monologues in *The Parliament of Bees* (published 1641), boldly critical of Charles I's personal rule. Day's is a minor talent, but a pleasing one.   PT

De Angelis, Jefferson 1859–1933 American comedian-singer and one of the most beloved stars of comic OPERA. De Angelis performed in VAUDEVILLE as a child, and later on tried his hand at dramatic acting. In 1887 he joined the McCaull Opera Company, appearing as a featured performer in comic operas such as *The Lady or the Tiger?* (1888). For several years he was a regular member of the Casino Theatre company, along with LILLIAN RUSSELL and FRANCIS WILSON. His first solo starring part was in *The Caliph* (1896). De Angelis brought to his comic opera roles both an ability to create consistent and individualized characters and the physical skills of an acrobat. His greatest successes were in *The Jolly Musketeer* (1898), *The Emerald Isle* (1902), *Fantana* (1905) and *The Girl and the Governor* (1907). From 1910 until his death, he performed in revivals of comic operas and in straight plays such as *The Royal Family* (1927). His autobiography (*A Vagabond Trouper*) was published in 1931.   MK

De Filippo family Italian actors, directors and playwrights. **Eduardo** (1900–85), like his sister **Titina** (1898–1963) and brother **Peppino** (1903–80), was born into the profession and at an early age acted in the SCARPETTA troupe. In 1932 the three formed their own company which lasted until 1945 when Peppino left to work independently, and Eduardo and Titina set up Il Teatro di Eduardo.

A brilliant comic actor with an economic, realistic style of playing, Eduardo had an engaging stage presence and a wide range of technical skills honed to perfection by his apprenticeship in the Neapolitan theatre. From the late 1920s until his death he was also a prolific dramatist, acting in and directing much of his own work; indeed, many of his plays have been most effective on the stage when he performed them with his own troupe. The best of them rank as the most vital in the modern Italian theatre, and attest to the enduring invention of the Neapolitan dialect stage.

Eduardo wrote some 40 plays, several of the finest of which – like *Filumena Maturano* (*Filumena*, 1946), *Sabato, domenica, e lunedì* (*Saturday, Sunday, Monday*, 1959) and, at least in its film version, *Napoli milionaria!* (*Affluent Naples!* 1945) – have enjoyed not only great popularity in Italy but considerable success abroad. They draw on a wide range of popular forms and on the Italian and dialect 'prose' theatre traditions. Detailed stage directions show the hand of the professional practitioner, and for all that there are strong literary-dramatic influences, notably that of PIRANDELLO, the plays are very much of the theatre. But they are firmly placed too in the language, life and attitudes of the Neapolitan petty-bourgeois and working classes, and character and situation are handled in basically naturalistic ways (see NATURALISM). Eduardo's view of the world was essentially tragicomic: in many of his plays the action turns on the attempts of a good-natured, even naive, individual to change a society that is rapacious and materialistic.

A darker, more melancholy tone tends to emerge in his later work. At the centre of nearly all of it, however, is the family, and familiar ties and obligations remain the one certainty in an otherwise unstable world. At times this can prove treacherous subject-matter, and some of the plays are marred by sentimentality and a simplistic moral didacticism. One play, *L'Arte della commedia* (*The Art of Comedy*, 1964), stands rather apart, its subject being the condition of the modern Italian theatre. Eduardo demonstrated his concern for the stage too in practical ways, notably in his renovation of the Teatro San Ferdinando in Naples, which he undertook at his own expense. He both acted in and directed a number of films.

Eduardo's brother Peppino, after forming his own company, came increasingly to specialize in Italian light comedy and farce and excelled in much foreign comic drama, from MOLIÈRE to PINTER. He too wrote plays and was a well known film actor, often appearing with the comedian TOTÒ. His son **Luigi** has continued in the family's actor-management tradition. Titina de Filippo worked mainly with Eduardo, interpreting many of the female lead roles in his plays, notably Filumena Maturano.   LR

de Graft, Joe [J. C.] 1924–78 Ghanaian playwright and critic. Joe de Graft taught drama at the University of

GHANA (and later in East Africa) and was active as a performer as well as a writer. In 1962 he appeared in the first performance of EFUA T. SUTHERLAND's *Edufa* at the Ghana Drama Studio in Accra, and in 1964 his play *Sons and Daughters* was published. This was followed in 1970 with *Through a Film Darkly*. Both plays are of their time in setting and concern, dealing with the tensions and dissensions that he suggested plagued the apparently sophisticated lives of modern educated Ghanaians. They present the 'clash of cultures' theme popular in much African theatre in the years leading up to and following independence, with young people in revolt against their parents and students abroad experiencing the humiliation of racism. ME

De Groen, Alma 1941– Australian playwright. Her early play *The Joss Adams Show* (1973) portrayed a teenage mother who kills her child; subsequent plays focused on social misfits and lone figures – *The Secret Life of Arthur Cravan* (1973) and *Chidley* (1977). Her more recent work is imbued with a feminist perspective: *Going Home* (1976) depicts a group of Australian art-world expatriates in Canada, *Vocations* (1982) wittily explores the conflicts in women pursuing independent careers and relationships with men; and her most ambitious work, *The Rivers of China* (1987), juxtaposes the New Zealand writer Katherine Mansfield's last weeks at Gurdjieff's Institute near Paris in 1923 with the story of a hospitalized man in a future female-governed world. MW

De Koven, Reginald 1859–1920 American composer. After an extensive musical education in Europe, De Koven, in partnership with librettist HARRY B. SMITH, set out to prove that Americans could write a comic OPERA in the European style. Their first show, *The Begum* (1887), while not an unqualified success in New York, drew large audiences in Chicago, De Koven's home town. In 1891 De Koven composed the score of *Robin Hood*, the most popular American comic opera of the era. Carefully mounted by the Bostonians (see BOSTON IDEAL OPERA COMPANY), *Robin Hood* was an immediate hit, and the song 'O Promise Me' became an enduring American standard. Although he continued to compose comic operas until 1913, De Koven never had another success of the stature of *Robin Hood*. Although his music was largely imitative of European modes, he is remembered for his courage in challenging the supremacy of European comic opera composers on the American stage. MK

de la Parra, Marco Antonio 1952– Chilean playwright and diplomat, with an MD in psychiatry and an extraordinary talent for interweaving sociopolitical situations and abstract techniques. Cast into the limelight when *Lo crudo, lo cocido y lo podrido* (*The Raw, the Cooked and the*

Scenic pieces by De Loutherbourg for the creation of a boat/cliff scene. In place, they create a realistic perspective.

Rotten) was suddenly banned (see CENSORSHIP) in 1978 hours before its scheduled opening in the Catholic University theatre, de la Parra settled into a rhythm of regular productions. *Matatangos* (*Kill Tangos*, 1979) examines the process of myth-making regarding Carlos Gardel, famous Argentine *tanguista*; *La secreta obscenidad de cada día* (*The Everyday Secret Obscenity*, 1984) disguised Karl Marx and Sigmund Freud as would-be exhibitionists instead of political assassins; *Infieles* (*Beds*, 1987) deals with life for the yuppies of the Pinochet years in Chile; *El deseo de toda ciudadana* (*The Desire of Every Citizen*, 1989) is a thriller based on loneliness, invasion and an eventual homicide; *King Kong Palace, o el exilio de Tarzán* (*King Kong Palace, or The Exile of Tarzan*, 1990) is a postmodern intertextual experience about power and corruption. GW

De Liagre, Alfred, Jr 1904–87 Yale-educated American producer and director. De Liagre began his professional career in 1930 as stage manager at the Woodstock Playhouse. In 1933 he began producing professionally and worked in both New York and London. He produced or co-produced more than 30 plays, a number of which he also directed. His more noteworthy credits included *The Voice of the Turtle* (1943), *The Madwoman of Chaillot* (1948), *Second Threshold* (1950), *The Golden Apple* (1954), *The Girls in 509* (1958), *J.B.* (1959, Pulitzer Prize), *Photo Finish* (1963), *Bubbling Brown Sugar* (1976), *Deathtrap* (1978) and *On Your Toes* (revival, 1983). TLM

De Loutherbourg, Philip (James) 1740–1812 Alsatian scene designer. Born in Strasbourg, he studied painting in Paris, becoming particularly interested in the use of colour. In 1771 he moved to London to work with GARRICK and proposed improvements in the lighting and scene systems at DRURY LANE, particularly in the quantity of theatre lighting available. In 1773 he began designing extravagant theatre spectacles, like a naval review for Arne's *Alfred*. His new techniques concentrated on transformation scenes and on light effects (e.g. sunlight, castles in moonlight) as well as on developing a landscape and perspective style of exotic romantic views of England for, e.g., SHERIDAN's *The Wonders of Derbyshire* (1779). In 1781 he left the theatre to set up the Eidophusikon, a display of scenes as panoramic pictures, scenery for its own sake, using rear-lit transparencies and experimenting with coloured plates. His later years were obsessed with faith-healing. His brilliant developments of STAGE LIGHTING and of naturalistic romantic landscapes enabled the actor to step back into the scenic spaces and prepared the ground for the development of pictorial modes of theatre. (See also THEATRE DESIGN.) PH

de Mille, Agnes 1905–93 American choreographer, director and author, daughter of playwright/film director William C. de Mille (1878–1955). Trained in the techniques of classical ballet, de Mille appeared as a dancer in the *Greenwich Village Follies* (1928). After choreographing two shows in London, she returned to New York to create the dances for *Hooray for What* (1937) and *Swingin' the Dream* (1939). In 1943 RODGERS and HAMMERSTEIN hired her to choreograph *Oklahoma!*, and her use of modern bal-

let techniques revolutionized MUSICAL COMEDY dance. In particular, the success of *Oklahoma!*'s dream ballet made such sequences a common feature of 1940s MUSICALS. She went on to choreograph *One Touch of Venus* (1943), *Bloomer Girl* (1944), *Carousel* (1945) and *Brigadoon* (1947). Her choreography for *Brigadoon* was acclaimed for its dramatic intensity and its use of traditional Scottish dances. Agnes de Mille served as both choreographer and director for *Allegro* (1947) and *Out of This World* (1950). In the 1950s she created the dances for such shows as *Paint Your Wagon* (1951), *The Girl in Pink Tights* (1954) and *Goldilocks* (1958). Less active in the 1960s, she choreographed *Kwamina* (1961), *110 in the Shade* (1963) and *Come Summer* (1969). Best remembered for her pioneering work in musicals of the 1940s, de Mille is credited with demonstrating dance's potential for furthering a musical's dramatic action. Her dozen books include *Dance to the Piper* (1952), *Speak to Me, Dance With Me* (1973), *Reprieve: A Memoir* (1981), *Portrait Gallery* (1990) and *Martha* [Graham] (1991). MK

de Rojas, Fernando ?–1541 Reputed author of the classic Spanish work, *La Celestina*. Written c.1492 and first published in 1499 as *La comedia de Calisto y Melibea*, this novel in dialogue was long considered unstageable because of its length; the definitive version of 1526, labelled a TRAGICOMEDY, has 21 acts. *La Celestina* juxtaposes the romanticized passion of courtly lovers and the seamy underworld of the bawd with whose name it is now identified. Major Spanish revivals have featured adaptations by CASONA (directed by José Osuna, 1965), by Nobel Prize-winner Camilo José Cela (directed by José Tamayo, 1978) and by Gonzalo Torrente Ballester (directed by Adolfo Marsillach, 1988). Since CAMUS's first French-language version in Algiers in 1936, it has also been staged frequently in France. MARÉCHAL's 1975 COMÉDIE-FRANÇAISE production proved highly controversial. Less scandalous was VITEZ's 1989 staging, which premiered at AVIGNON before moving to the ODÉON in Paris. PZ

de' Sommi (de Portaleone), Yehuda Leone [Leone di Somi (or Sommo)] 1527–92 Jewish-Italian author of the first Hebrew play (see HEBREW THEATRE), *A Comedy of Betrothal* (c.1550, English translation 1988), a typical Renaissance comedy with a racy Hebrew flavour. The main plot, based on the Midrash, tells the story of a young man, Shalom, whose father died far away bequeathing all his possessions save one to his slave. Shalom may claim any one of them as his. On the advice of the wise rabbi, the young man chooses the slave, thus obtaining the full inheritance. This tale is intertwined with a conventional romantic plot. The play was rediscovered by modern scholarship and produced first by a university group and in 1968 by the Haifa Municipal Theatre.

De' Sommi was a prolific writer of poetry and plays in both Italian and Hebrew, but most of his work was destroyed by a fire in 1904. Apparently he produced plays for the Duke of Gonzaga at Mantua. He wrote an important theoretical treatise, *Four Dialogues on Scenic Representation* (English translation by Allardyce Nicoll, 1937). HAS

De Wahl, Anders 1869–1956 Swedish actor, popular until the late 1920s, when his pre-eminence was challenged by the more natural style of LARS HANSON. A personality actor whose lyricism and physical grace precisely reflected the ideals of *fin-de-siècle* romanticism, De Wahl excelled in emotionally troubled roles, including STRINDBERG's Erik XIV (1899) and King Magnus (1901), and in plays on religious themes such as *Everyman* (1916) or ELIOT's *Murder in the Cathedral* (1939). Firmly rooted in 19th-century tradition, he was outspokenly opposed to modernism in theatre, although the early popularity of PIRANDELLO in Sweden probably resulted from De Wahl's performances in *Six Characters in Search of an Author* (1925), *Henry IV* (1926) and *The Pleasure of Honesty* (1930). HL

Dean, Basil (Herbert) 1888–1978 British actor, director and producer. Dean joined ANNIE HORNIMAN's company in Manchester in 1907 as an actor, where he stayed until in 1910 he was invited to help start a new repertory theatre in Liverpool. Appointed director of productions in 1911, he had established the theatre as a major force in the repertory movement before leaving in 1913 (see REGIONAL THEATRE (BRITAIN)). From 1919 to 1926 he was in partnership with Alec Rea and, as the 'ReandeaN' management, they were responsible for a series of major productions on the London stage, including *The Skin Game, R.U.R.* and *Hassan*. Dean continued both to produce and to direct, staging, among others, the premieres of several plays by PRIESTLEY. In 1939, he started and became director of ENSA (Entertainments National Service Association); and in 1948 organized the first British Repertory Theatre Festival in London. He directed a number of films, including *Lorna Doone* and the films of GRACIE FIELDS. The two volumes of his autobiography are *Seven Ages* (1888–1927) and *The Mind's Eye* (1927–72); and his *Theatre at War* is the official history of ENSA. AJ

Dean, Julia 1830–68 American actress. Her mother, Julia Drake, was the daughter of pioneer Kentucky manager, SAMUEL DRAKE; her father, Edwin Dean, was a pioneer manager in Buffalo. Making her debut at the age of 11, she was the leading American tragic actress by 1846. Marriage to Samuel Hayne in 1855 was disastrous, so she went west in 1856 and established herself as a star in California and Utah for the rest of her life. She specialized in suffering heroines, such as SHAKESPEARE's Juliet and BULWER LYTTON's Pauline, in which her height, blonde good looks and deep voice were assets. DMCD

Dear, Nick 1955– British playwright whose first works were produced in the early 1980s (*The Perfect Alibi*, 1980) but who first received national attention with *The Art of Success* (1986), directed by ADRIAN NOBLE at the ROYAL SHAKESPEARE COMPANY's the Pit. This won him an Olivier Award as the Most Promising Newcomer, but when the play was revived in 1989 its message already seemed dated. *The Art of Success* was set in the early 18th century, but there were echoes of Thatcherism in the tussles between its central character, William Hogarth, and the prime minister, Robert Walpole. It was another RSC attack on get-rich-quick societies, but Dear's robust language, vivid and scatological, made a powerful impact. He adapted OSTROVSKY's *A Family Affair* (1988) for CHEEK BY JOWL and TIRSO DE MOLINA's *The Last Days of Don Juan* (1990) for the RSC. A few of his own plays have been recently produced: a short monologue, *Food for Love* (1988), and a staged radio play, *In the Ruins* (1990), a near-monologue from a mad King George III, played by Patrick Malahide at the New Vic, Bristol. JE

Dearly, Max [Lucien-Max Rolland] 1874–1943 French actor and VARIETY artist, trained in an English circus at Marseilles. At his Paris debut at the Concert Parisien, his ingratiating manners, lantern-jawed face and 'British' elegance made him a favourite. In his heyday, 1905–10, he launched the *valse chaloupée*, or 'apache dance', with MISTINGUETT and mimed an entire horse race in his 'Jockey américain'. As his vocal powers diminished, he abandoned OPERETTA and REVUE for the plays of De Flers and Caillavet, and the screen, where he was seen as Homais in Jean Renoir's *Madame Bovary* (1934). LS

DeBar, Ben 1812–77 British-born actor-manager who went to America as an equestrian performer (see HIPPODRAMA) in 1837, but soon specialized in low COMEDY. He was also stage manager for NOAH LUDLOW and SOL SMITH at the ST CHARLES THEATRE, New Orleans; when they retired (1843), he assumed management of their New Orleans and St Louis theatres. At the outbreak of the Civil War he moved to St Louis, retaining ownership of the St Charles until 1876. In St Louis he moved from the St Louis Theatre to DeBar's Grand Opera House in 1873. He remained active as a performer, touring the Mississippi River valley as a star every season, and was the most influential manager in the region. DMCD

Deburau, Jean-Gaspard [Jan Kaspar Dvorak] 1796–1846 French mime artist, born in Bohemia. In 1812 he went to Paris with his family, long active as acrobats and fairground performers. From 1816 he appeared at the THÉÂTRE DES FUNAMBULES, rapidly becoming a favourite of the working-class audiences in such pantomimes as *Harlequin Doctor*, *The Raging Bull* (1827), *The Golden Sleep* (1828), *The Whale* (1832), *Pierrot in Africa* and *The Old Clo' Man* (1842). He developed the secondary character PIERROT into a versatile protagonist, hapless, ingenious, often macabre and aggressive; puffed by the literati, including Nodier, GAUTIER, Baudelaire and Heine, his pale-faced, elongated hero took on mythic proportions. Personally taciturn and touchy (he once killed a youth who molested his wife), on stage Deburau extended the physical vocabulary of MIME into broadly lyrical directions; most modern mimes, MARCEAU especially, acknowledge their debt to him. Deburau was the subject of a play by SACHA GUITRY (1918), and Marcel Carné's film *Les Enfants du Paradis* (1945) incarnated Baptiste, the Deburau figure, in JEAN-LOUIS BARRAULT. His son, Jean-Charles (1829–73), succeeded him at the Funambules and sublimated Pierrot into an elegant moonstruck romantic. LS

decentralization movement Theatre in France has always been more centred on the metropolis than theatre in other European countries, but it was the conversion of provincial theatres into cinemas in the early years of the 20th century that led to a situation where almost no producing company existed outside Paris. GÉMIER formed a Théâtre National Ambulant (National Touring Theatre) in 1911 to try to fill this provincial vacuum. He was followed by COPEAU, CHANCEREL and others between the two world wars, who began to feel that a move away from Paris was a necessary prerequisite for theatrical renewal. In 1937 DULLIN was commissioned by the Popular Front government to produce a plan for decentralizing the theatre. His plan was for provincial centres of dramatic excellence, each with the responsibility for touring their region. The project was interrupted by the war years, but formed the basis of the policy vigorously pursued by Jeanne Laurent, who worked for the Department of 'Arts et Spectacles' during 1939–54. Under her guidance the first provincial Centres Dramatiques were established in Alsace at Colmar (later moving to Strasbourg and becoming a Théâtre National in 1968), at St Étienne, at Rennes, at Toulouse and at Aix-en-Provence. VILAR, who had founded the successful AVIGNON FESTIVAL in 1947, was installed as director of the THÉÂTRE NATIONAL POPULAIRE at the CHAILLOT THEATRE. No more official centres were established until De Gaulle came to power in 1959 and appointed Malraux his minister of culture. Malraux dreamed of creating a modern equivalent of the medieval cathedrals: Maisons de la Culture devoted to interdisciplinary practice of the arts. In reality, many of the first Maisons were constructed around an existing theatre company (e.g. Gabriel Monnet's at Bourges, Jo Tréhard's at Caen), although subsequent differences of opinion sometimes led to these directors being deprived of the building. The dual funding of the Maisons, half by the ministry, half by the municipality, often led to the Maison becoming a political football.

The near-revolution of 1968 brought these differences into the open, and the 70s were a period of stagnation from which the 15 Maisons were rescued by the socialist government's injections of cash and enthusiasm after 1981. Malraux also promoted the network of Centres Dramatiques, entirely funded by the ministry, and introduced the status of Troupes Permanentes de la Décentralisation for young provincial companies serving a particular area. Among important companies to emerge in the 60s, following the Théâtre de la Cité at Villeurbanne, were companies based in Angers, Beaune, Besançon, Caen, Carcassonne, Grenoble, Lille, Limoges, Lyon, Marseille, Nice, Reims and Tourcoing. A number of new theatre companies were also established in the 'red belt' of workers' suburbs around Paris, notably the Théâtre des Amandiers directed by Pierre Debauche at Nanterre; the Théâtre de la Commune directed by Gabriel Garran at Aubervilliers; the Théâtre Gérard Philipe directed by José Valverde at Saint-Denis, and the Théâtre de Sartrouville where PATRICE CHÉREAU was beginning to make his name. The title of Théâtre de l'Est Parisien was conferred on the company of Guy Rétoré, working in the East End of Paris.

In the 1970s, PLANCHON's company became the TNP while remaining in Villeurbanne, and a new generation of directors and actors began to make their names in the decentralized theatres, notably JEAN-PIERRE VINCENT at Strasbourg; Michel Dubois at Caen; Georges Lavaudant at Grenoble; MARCEL MARÉCHAL at Lyon, then at Marseille; Gildas Bourdet at Tourcoing; and, in the Parisian red belt, Bernard Sobel at Gennevilliers and ANTOINE VITEZ at Ivry. In the mid-80s there were 29 Centres Dramatiques in the provinces or Paris suburbs which had benefited from the Mitterrand government's determination to breathe new life into the decentralization movement.

Basing itself on the ideas articulated in Copeau's Le Théâtre populaire (1941) and on Vilar's vision of theatre as a public service, the decentralization movement has had an important influence on the development of directing, acting and playwriting in France and has encouraged a greater level of social and political awareness among theatre artists. The theatre school attached to the Strasbourg centre by MICHEL SAINT-DENIS has trained a whole generation of actors and directors who have gone out to work in the decentralized theatres. New playwrights have been slower to emerge: while the new THEATRE OF THE ABSURD was the glory of the Parisian stage, the decentralized theatres were digesting the lessons of BRECHT. But in the 1960s new work by French playwrights began to be performed. Some of these have acquired national reputations, e.g. ADAMOV, COUSIN, GATTI; others have had a more local following, identified with a particular community, e.g. Pierre Halet at Bourges. In the 1970s the decentralized theatres were in the avant-garde of new playwriting, promoting the work of the théâtre du QUOTIDIEN. DB

Decroux, Étienne-Marcel 1898–1991 French actor, who, according to GORDON CRAIG, 'rediscovered mime'. A student of CHARLES DULLIN (1926–34), he developed a systematic grammar of physical expression he called *mime corporel* or *pantomime de style*, a method of corporal extension geared to make abstract statements. He had a strong influence on JEAN-LOUIS BARRAULT, playing DEBURAU *père* to the latter's Baptiste Deburau in the film *Les Enfants du Paradis* (1945). In 1941 he opened a school, performing for tiny audiences of two or three persons, and through his students Éliane Guyon, Cathérine Toth and MARCEL MARCEAU his ideas were diffused throughout modern MIME. He toured the Western world and Israel (1949–58) and ran a studio theatre in Paris. His son Maximilien was also a mime. LS

Dee, Ruby [*née* Ruby Ann Wallace] 1923– African-American actress and playwright. Born in Cleveland, Ohio, Dee first acted with the American Negro Theatre, and took over the title role for the tour of *Anna Lucasta* (1944). She appeared in various New York productions, attracting attention as Ruth Younger in *A Raisin in the Sun* (1959), after which her reputation advanced. She was acclaimed as Lutiebelle, the innocent pawn in *Purlie Victorious* (1961), and as the long-suffering Lena in *Boesman and Lena* (1970), for which she won an Obie and a Drama Desk Award. Her performance in ALICE CHILDRESS's *Wedding Band* (1973) also earned a Drama Desk Award. In SHAKESPEARE, Dee has played Katharina in *The Taming of the Shrew* (1965), Cordelia to MORRIS CARNOVSKY's King Lear (1965), and Gertrude in *Hamlet* (1975). She coauthored the screenplay *Uptight* (1968), in which she starred, and has written plays including *Twin Bit Gardens* (1976), the MUSICAL *Take It from the Top* (1979), the biographical *Zora Is My Name* (1983), about Harlem Renaissance writer and folklorist Zora Neale Hurston, and *The Disappearance* (1993), adapted from a Rosa Guy 1979 suspense novel. In 1988 she was elected to the Theatre Hall of Fame. Dee possesses an irresistibly enchanting stage personality and is infectiously funny in comedy.   EGH

Déjazet, (Pauline) Virginie 1798–1875 French actress. After a debut at the Variétés (see BOULEVARD) in 1817, she appeared in Lyon and Bordeaux, and in 1821 was taken on at the Gymnase, where her roles included a number of BREECHES PARTS. In 1828 she joined the Nouveautés, playing the youthful Napoleon in *Bonaparte à Brienne, ou Le Petit Caporal* (*Bonaparte at Brienne, or The Little Corporal*, 1830). In 1831, now a 'star', she was at the Montansier (PALAIS-ROYAL) playing a series of *grisette* roles with a strong element of sexual suggestiveness. By 1844 she was earning 20,000 francs a year, with a fee of 20 francs for every act performed, four months' holiday and three benefit performances. In 1843, Béranger's *Lisette* provided her with a monologue she would use for the next 30 years. From 1844 to 1850 she was at the Variétés, then moved on to the Vaudeville, still playing breeches parts; but she had herself freed from her contract because of the long run of *La Dame aux camélias*, and became freelance. In 1857 she took over the Folies Nouvelles, which was managed by her son. She intended to produce the young SARDOU's *Candide*, but this was banned by the censor (see CENSORSHIP), so she fell back on her old repertoire. In 1866 she had to give up her theatre and resume touring, playing the 15-year-old Richelieu at the age of 70. Her frenetic touring was largely forced on her by her exploitative son and daughter. In 1874 a huge benefit performance was given to create a pension for her, and her funeral, the following year, attracted some 30,000 people.   JMCC

Dekker, Thomas c.1570–1632 English playwright and pamphleteer, whose vivid accounts of London life support the view that he was a Londoner by birth and upbringing. There are frequent references to Dekker's plays (and to his debts) in HENSLOWE's *Diary* for 1598–1602. He was prodigiously busy – Henslowe lists 16 plays in which he had a hand in 1598 – but even such industry could not keep pace with his expenditure. Dekker was briefly in prison for debt in 1599 and again from 1613 to 19. Of the 50 or so plays on which he is known to have worked, some 20 have survived. The earliest, *Old Fortunatus* (1599), is a rambling moral COMEDY. The second, *The Shoemaker's Holiday* (1599), is his masterpiece. Its exuberant plotting and vivid portraits of London tradesmen established the distinctive form of CITIZEN COMEDY.

The other plays of which Dekker was sole author are, by comparison, disappointing. *Satiromastix* (1601) is a broken-backed rejoinder to JONSON's abuse of Dekker (in *Poetaster* as well as in the earlier caricature of Orange in *Every Man out of His Humour*), notable only for its contribution to the WAR OF THE THEATRES. It was probably with an eye to the profitability of controversy that the King's Men chose to stage it. Careless construction (the outcome of too much haste?) also mars *The Whore of Babylon* (1606), *If It*

Be Not Good the Devil Is in It (c.1610) and *Match Me in London* (c.1611). Needing to accept all commissions, Dekker was involved in numerous collaborations: with CHETTLE and William Haughton on *Patient Grissel* (1600), with WEBSTER on *Westward Ho* (1604) and *Northward Ho* (1605), with MIDDLETON on *The Honest Whore* (1604) and *The Roaring Girl* (c.1610), with MASSINGER on *The Virgin Martyr* (1620) and with WILLIAM ROWLEY and FORD on *The Witch of Edmonton* (1621). His lively satirical pamphlet, *The Gull's Hornbook* (1609), contains some telling observations of audience behaviour in the London theatres.   PT

Delaney, Shelagh 1939– British dramatist. Her first and most successful play, *A Taste of Honey*, about a girl who, abandoned by her lover, rears her child with the help of a maternally minded gay, was written when she was only 17 and staged in 1958 by JOAN LITTLEWOOD at the Theatre Workshop, Stratford, East London. The freshness of the writing and Littlewood's dynamic production took *A Taste of Honey* to the WEST END and afterwards to BROADWAY, where it won the New York Drama Critics Award. Delaney's second play, *The Lion in Love* (1960), was less successful, and she turned away from the theatre to writing screenplays, *The White Bus* (1966) and *Charley Bubbles* (1968); and for television, *Did Your Nanny Come from Bergen?* (1970).   JE

Delavigne, (Jean François) Casimir 1793–1843 French dramatist. Delavigne, who aligned himself with the liberal, anticlerical bourgeoisie of the Restauration, began his career with a volume of patriotic poems, *Les Messéniennes*. His play *Sicilian Vespers* was turned down at the COMÉDIE-FRANÇAISE in 1818, but ran for some 300 performances when staged at the ODÉON in 1819. Delavigne followed timidly in the wake of the romantics in his choice of medieval themes, but remained a second-rate (if much more frequently performed) dramatist, giving the audience what they wanted and avoiding shocking. His uninspired style continued the poetic diction of the 18th century with its inversions and periphrases. In *Le Paria* (1821) he introduced an important element of local colour with the Indian setting, and used Brahmin fanaticism as a way of attacking Catholic fanaticism, a theme he would pick up again with *Une Famille au temps de Luther* (*A Family in the Time of Luther*, 1836).

The liberalism of Delavigne's sentiments lost him his job, but gained him the good opinion of the Duke of Orleans, who offered him a post as librarian. At the 1830 revolution Delavigne's popular patriotic song, *La Parisienne*, was sung in all the theatres. *Marino Faliero* (1829) converted LORD BYRON's model heroine into an adulterous wife (played by MARIE DORVAL). It was meant to be a TRAGEDY, but drew heavily on the effects of MELODRAMA, and even had to be described as such for its first performances at the Porte-Saint-Martin (see BOULEVARD) with music by Rossini. *Louis XI*, seen sometimes as his greatest play, moved towards the romantic mixture of genres. In England, in BOUCICAULT's adaptation, it offered a splendid role to CHARLES KEAN and later HENRY IRVING. One critic saw the play as a modern tragedy and a response to the excesses of the romantics. With *Les Enfants d'Édouard* (1833), the romantic mixture of genres was taken further in a play that reduced *Richard III* to three acts, concentrated on the element of pathos and played down anything that might shock. His other main plays are *Don Juan d'Autriche*, *La Fille du Cid* (*The Daughter of the Cid*) and an opera, *Charles VI*, with music by Halévy. Delavigne was elected to the French Academy in 1825. His brother Germain was also quite well known as a dramatist.   JMCC

Della Porta, Giambattista 1535–1615 Italian dramatist, scientist and philosopher. Della Porta was a prolific writer on a wide range of subjects: his output included three tragedies, a tragicomedy and 29 comedies (of which 14 have survived). The best-known of his plays are *Olimpia* (1589) and *Il moro* (*The Moor*, 1607) which, like most of his dramatic work, show the influence both of the classical tradition and of the later *novelle* and romances, uniting the example of the ancients in structure and characterization with elements more reflective of Renaissance life and assumptions. Particularly interesting are his *L'astrologo* (*The Astrologer*, 1606) and *La Trappolaria* (*The Comedy of Trappoia*, 1596), of which both scripted and scenario versions exist, indicating some of the ways in which the Italian *commedia erudita* and COMMEDIA DELL'ARTE interconnected.   LR

Delpini, Carlo (Antonio) 1740–1828 Italian dancer, CLOWN and scenarist. He was first seen at COVENT GARDEN in 1776 as PIERROT in *Harlequin's Frolicks*, and for the rest of the century was involved in performing and creating pantomime there and at the HAYMARKET. Willson Disher credits him with having invented the Regency PANTOMIME by stressing character and scenic transformation, as in the DUMB SHOW of *Robinson Crusoe* (DRURY LANE, 1781). He also worked at Hughes's Royal Circus where, in the panto *What You Please*, he contrived a spectacular exhibition of 'The Four Quarters of the World' (1788).   LS

Demidova, Alla (Sergeevna) 1936– Russian actress. Trained as a chemist and thereafter at the Shchukin Theatre Institute, Demidova graduated to the role of lead actress in her teacher LYUBIMOV's new Taganka Theatre company. She was Elmire in *Tartuffe* (1968), a passionate Gertrude in *Hamlet* (1971), the old peasant woman Vasilisa Melentevna in Abramov's *Wooden Horses* (1974), and played major roles in *Rush Hour* (1969), *The Exchange* (1976), *Crime and Punishment* (1979), *Vladimir Vysotsky* (1981) and *Boris Godunov* (1982). Other Taganka credits include an intensely neuresthenic Ranevskaya in EFROS's 1975 production of *The Cherry Orchard* and the title role in Marina Tsvetaeva's verse TRAGEDY *Phaedra*, staged by VIKTIUK, which also ran at the American Repertory Theatre in Cambridge, Massachusetts, in 1990. Demidova performed Tsvetaeva's and Anna Akhmatova's poetry with CLAIRE BLOOM in Europe and the USA in 1993. Her film roles include Arkadina in *The Seagull*, and she has written two books, *Vladimir Vysotsky As I Knew and Loved Him* (1989) and her autobiography, *The Second Reality*.   SG

DeMille, Henry C(hurchill) 1850–93 American playwright. A native of North Carolina, DeMille prepared for his career by securing a position as a playreader at the MADISON SQUARE THEATRE in 1882. His first play, *John Delmer's Daughter* (1883), dealing with family problems resulting from social climbing, failed. His next, a FRONTIER MELODRAMA, *The Main Line* (1886), written with Charles Bernard, succeeded not only in New York but on tour, in later productions, and even as revised with Rosabel Morrison as *The Danger Signal* (1891). DeMille made his reputation, however, collaborating with DAVID BELASCO. *The Wife* (1887), which dramatized a husband's resolve to win the love of his wife who had married him out of pique, received 239 performances. They wrote *Lord Chumley* (1888) for E.H. SOTHERN, who made the young English nobleman a memorable theatre experience. *The Charity Ball* (1889) contrasts a strong clergyman with his weak brother in a plot revealing seduction and greed resolved by love. Their last collaboration, *Men and Women* (1890), builds upon banking, speculation, love and family. Together they produced four of the most popular plays of that period in America.   WJM

Dench, Judi [Judith] **(Olivia)** 1934 British actress, who first attracted critical acclaim as Ophelia to JOHN NEVILLE's Hamlet at the OLD VIC in 1957. She was invited to join the ROYAL SHAKESPEARE COMPANY in the exciting first season, 1961, after its transformation from the Shakespeare Memorial Company, and became an established leading actress in PETER HALL's team, playing Anya in *The Cherry Orchard*, Isabella in *Measure for Measure* and Dorcas in JOHN WHITING's *A Penny for a Song*. Her association with the RSC has continued for more than 30 years, during which time she has played a wide variety of great classical roles, from the Duchess in *The Duchess of Malfi* to Beatrice in *Much Ado* and Lady Macbeth, as well as Mother Courage in BRECHT's play. She has also appeared in the WEST END, as Sally Bowles in *Cabaret* (1968), her first MUSICAL. Among the actresses of her generation, Judi Dench is technically the best equipped, with a naturally soft and expressive voice, an appearance versatile enough to match an imposing beauty for one play and dowdiness the next, and a keen intelligence which provides fresh insights into the most familiar texts. She played Cleopatra in Peter Hall's production of *Antony and Cleopatra* (1987) and Gertrude in RICHARD EYRE's *Hamlet*, both at the NATIONAL THEATRE; and directed *As You Like It* (1988) and *Look Back in Anger* (1989) for the Renaissance Theatre Group.   JE

Denison, Michael 1915– British actor. In the time before and just after the Second World War which produced so many fine British actors, including OLIVIER and GIELGUD, Denison's career was somewhat overshadowed; but for 50 years, often partnered by his wife, the actress Dulcie Gray, he has been one of the most popular and skilled artists in Britain. He rarely attempts to stray beyond his apparently narrow range of gentlemanly roles, but within these limits he excels. He first appeared in a London theatre as Paris in *Troilus and Cressida* (1938); but he was taken up by BINKIE BEAUMONT for H.M. Tennent Players for whom he toured. After serving in the army from 1940 to 1946, he became a star of stage and screen in the later 1940s and 50s; and joined the Shakespeare Memorial Company in 1955, playing Andrew Aguecheek, Bertram (in *All's Well That Ends Well*) and Lucius in BROOK's *Titus Andronicus*, in which Olivier played the title role. He was much in demand for Edwardian revivals, of plays by WILDE and SHAW in particular, and was a notable Ekdal in IBSEN's *The Wild Duck* (1970). He is perhaps best known for his screen performances in *My Brother Jonathan* and *The Importance of Being Earnest* from the 1939 stage production. His many television roles include the title role in the long-running 1960s series, *Boyd QC*. His recent stage roles include a brief appearance in COWARD's last play, *Star Quality* (1989), and the Earl of Caversham in PETER HALL's revival of Wilde's *An Ideal Husband* (1992). JE

Denmark Danish theatre probably began in medieval churches, with tropes introduced into Easter and Epiphany masses. Physical evidence, such as sepulchres for the RITUAL burial of crosses or effigies of Christ, dates from the 15th century, but an earlier tradition is commonly assumed. Outdoor MIRACLE PLAYS began in the 15th century, as did visits by German players, performing popular FARCES. Although LITURGICAL DRAMA was stopped by the Reformation, school and university performances were encouraged as morally improving; Latin comedies were acted, as well as modern derivations, such as the biblical *Susanna* (1576) and the satirical *Niding the Niggard* (1606). Meanwhile, 16th- and 17th-century monarchs mounted lavish festivals with Italianate scenery, allegorical processions and *ballets de cour*. Both Christian IV (reigned 1596–1648) and Frederik III (1648–70) were especially supportive; a royal marriage in 1634 occasioned 13 days of festivities, including a huge production of *The Tragedy of Virtues and Vices* in Copenhagen's Castle Square.

Influence from abroad continued in 1662, when a Dutch merchant obtained a patent to build Copenhagen's first, short-lived, public theatre (1663–6). Denmark's first opera house opened in 1703, and at court there was a succession of French troupes, among whom was René Magnon de Montaigu, whose father knew MOLIÈRE. In 1722, Montaigu's company occupied a new theatre in Lille Grønnegade street and after a few months obtained permission for Danish-language performances, beginning with Molière's *The Miser*, and *The Political Tinker*, one of 32 comedies written for the company by the Norwegian-born LUDVIG HOLBERG. This company survived (with interruptions) until 1728, when the great Copenhagen fire (followed in 1730 by the accession of the pietistic Christian VI) put a stop to theatrical activity. However, his successor Frederik V (1746–66) vigorously supported its revival, with a court opera company, and French and German troupes in the city, and the Danish company, with Holberg as advisor, performing from 1748 in the new KONGELIGE TEATER (the Royal Theatre) on Kongens Nytorv.

Its repertoire consisted primarily of comedies, including Molière and Holberg, acted by gifted comedians such as Gert Londemann. Attempts in the 1770s to introduce TRAGEDY in the French style produced Denmark's most brilliant literary PARODY, Johann Wessel's *Love without Stockings* (1772). By 1800, tragedies, sentimental dramas and Johannes Ewald's serious SINGSPIELE were popular, helped by the heroic acting of Michael Rosing. In 1790, the Kongelige Teater first presented KOTZEBUE, beginning a flood of 1000 performances over three decades. The first

Danish SHAKESPEARE performance was of *Hamlet*, in Odense (1792); the Kongelige Teater staged it in 1813.

The last decades of the 18th century witnessed a wave of amateur dramatic clubs that opened theatres for their productions. Copenhagen had several, and most significant provincial towns had at least one. In the early 1800s, these small provincial theatres were gradually improved or replaced for professional touring companies to use, and the amateur activity diminished. Odense's theatre was first (1795), followed by Århus (1816) and Helsingør (1817).

In some ways, the Kongelige Teater achieved a high point in the mid-19th century, under the aegis of JOHAN LUDVIG HEIBERG and his celebrated actress-wife JOHANNE LUISE HEIBERG. The Heibergs promoted GOETHE's concept of classical beauty, and the urbanity of French BOULEVARD comedy. They discarded Kotzebue's plays, replacing them with SCRIBE, Heiberg's own *vaudevilles*, and the sentimental dramas of Henrik Hertz. A new, lighter acting style was in vogue, exemplified by the work of Fru Heiberg and her partner MICHAEL WIEHE. But by the 1850s the Heibergs were being challenged by demands for a more progressive repertoire. In 1874, the Kongelige moved to its present building, where the struggle to introduce naturalistic (see NATURALISM) staging methods would be fought in WILLIAM BLOCH's Ibsen productions in the 1880s, with actors like BETTY HENNINGS.

The Kongelige's first competitor in Copenhagen was the privately owned Casino (1848), where some major dramatists began their careers. Ibsen's first Copenhagen production was at the Casino, and it gave the world premiere of STRINDBERG's *The Father* in 1887. Folketeatret (1857) specialized in comedies and OPERETTAS, but from the 1880s presented plays rejected by the Kongelige, including Ibsen's *Ghosts*. Private theatres were greatly aided in 1889, with the end of the Kongelige's monopoly on every play it had ever performed.

New theatre buildings opened in several provincial cities: Aalborg (1882), Århus (1900), Odense (1914). Copenhagen acquired the Ny Teater (1908) and the Betty Nansen Teatret (1917), which pioneered new plays until NANSEN's death in 1943. Dagmarteatret was particularly successful in the 1920s, with Bodil Ipsen and POUL REUMERT acting there. At the Kongelige there were experiments with spectacular, non-realistic staging, such as Johannes Poulsen's two-evening production of Oehlenschläger's *Aladdin* (1919), and in 1928 Ibsen's *The Pretenders*, designed by GORDON CRAIG. However, the theatricalized theatre really advanced in the 1930s, with directors like Per Knutzon, theatres such as the experimental Riddersalen, and a new generation of actors including Bodil Kjer, Mogens Wieth, John Price and Ebbe Rode. After the war, the Ny Teater, under Peer Gregaard, seriously challenged the Kongelige, with outstanding productions of new plays and classics.

In the 1960s came rapid expansion and diversification. Fiolteatret (1962) staged PINTER, ALBEE, BECKETT and Danish modernists like Klaus Rifbjerg. There was a proliferation of satirical (and increasingly political) REVUES, such as Erik Knudsen's *Freedom – The Best Gold* (1961); the Kongelige echoed this trend with BRUUN OLSEN's *Teenage Love* (1962). Danish theatre's growing political consciousness emerged most clearly in the many 'group' theatres

Hotel Pro Forma,
Copenhagen, in *The
Enigma of the Late
Afternoon*, 1992.

that started: Svalegangen (1964) and Teatervaerkstedet den Blå Hest (1976) in Århus, Boldhusteatret in Copenhagen (1965), Jomfru Ane Teatret in Aalborg (1967). Fiolteatret became increasingly political, as did Banden (1969), in Odense. Political theatre flourished in the anarchist 'action theatre' of Solvognen (1969–80); their *Santa Claus Army* (1974) exposed the capitalist Christmas by having Santas distribute 'gifts' from department-store shelves.

The contemporary situation In the 1980s, the Kongelige Teater still dominated Danish theatre in terms of prestige and resources, although it was challenged, in repertoire and production standards, by Folketeatret and the provincial theatres in Odense, Aalborg and Århus. Århus led in promoting new Danish plays, with its resident playwright programme. From 1975 most of the former private Copenhagen theatres had combined in the 'greater Copenhagen regional theatre', receiving government subsidies and using the national ticket agency Arte to sell two-thirds of Copenhagen's tickets; Arte sells 80 per cent of provincial tickets. The resulting security freed some of them, such as the Gladsaxe, Betty Nansen and Aveny Theatres, to be courageous in their programming, as are some of the alternative companies such as Café Teatret, Bådteatret (both 1972) and Mammutteatret (1983).

An important new company was the Nyt Skandinavisk Forsøgsteater (1989–92), directed by the Swedish director Staffan Valdemar Holm. Several renovated rental facilities, such as Husets Teater and Kanonhallen, have aided the work of alternative companies. Meanwhile, Aveny

Teater has been taken over by the sometimes iconoclastic company, Dr Dante. Avant-garde companies produce some of Denmark's most provocative work. ODIN TEATRET, part of the Nordisk Teaterlaboratorium, in Holstebro since 1986, remains Denmark's most internationally regarded company. Led by EUGENIO BARBA, it has done remarkable productions as part of research into the nature of performance. In nearby Fjaltring, TUKAK TEATRET (1975) continues as the major training ground for Greenlanders and other indigenous peoples. In Greenland, Silamiut has been active for a number of years, and on the Faeroe Islands is Teater Gríma. HOTEL PRO FORMA (1985) is Denmark's most ambitious visual performance company; others include Exment (1984) in Århus, and Cantabile 2 (1992) in Vordingborg.

Danish theatres have been governed by a theatre law since 1963 (revised 1970 and 1991), establishing the formula by which various categories of theatre can receive public funding. The range of theatres has increased over the years, to include smaller companies. A significant provision until 1990 was the so-called 'guarantee against loss', by which theatres were not only provided with grants but could also be reimbursed with extra funding when a production took in less box-office than expected. Theatres began each season without a deficit, but could not accumulate capital. The new law provides for fixed grants, but removes the guarantee against loss, and some fear that this will discourage theatres from risk, including production of new plays.

Nevertheless, in the late 1980s and early 1990s, Danish theatres seemed to be producing more new Danish plays than before. Among important dramatists are Ernst Bruun Olsen, Stig Dalager, Sven Holm, Sten Kaalø, FINN METHLING, Svend Åge Madsen, Ulla Ryum, Astrid Saalbach, Pia Tafdrup and Jens Ørnsbo. Denmark's outstanding directors include Eugenio Barba, Sam Besekow (still working in his eighties), Kaspar Rostrup, Emil Hansen, Klaus Hoffmeyer, Søren Iversen, PETER LANGDAL, Jan Maagaard, Henrik Sartou and Ib Thorup (1941–90). Significant scenographers are Karin Betz, Nina Flagstad, Bente Lykke-Møller, Birgitte Mellentin, Nina Schiøttz, Kim Witzel and Steffen Aarfing. Among the hosts of excellent actors are Birgitte Federspiel, Frits Helmuth, Henning Jensen, Bodil Kjer, Ghita Nørby, Kirsten Olesen, Ulla Henningsen, Henning Moritzen, Søren Pilmark, Jørgen Reenberg, Ebbe Rode, Ove Sprogøe, and Susse Wold.   HL

See: K.O. Arntzen, T.O. Svendsen and M. Moi (eds.), *Kunnskapsforlagets Teater- og Filmleksikon*, Oslo, 1991; P. Brask (ed.), *Drama Contemporary: Scandinavia*, New York, 1989; H. Fenger and F.J. Marker, *The Heibergs*, New York, 1971; A. Henriques, *The Royal Theatre Past and Present*, Copenhagen, 1967; S.J. Jensen, K. Kvam and U. Strømberg (eds.), *Dansk Teater i 60erne og 70erne*, Copenhagen, 1983; K. Kvam, J. Risum and J. Wiingaard (eds.), *Dansk Teaterhistorie*, 2 vols., Copenhagen, 1992; F.J. and L.-L. Marker, *The Scandinavian Theatre*, Oxford, 1975; *Nordic Theatre Studies*, Copenhagen, 1988– ; L. Senelick (ed.), *National Theatre in Northern and Eastern Europe, 1746–1900*, Cambridge, 1991; *Teater Et* (journal), Copenhagen, 1989– ; *Teater i Danmark* (annual), Copenhagen, 1965–87, 1992– .

Dennery [D'Ennery], **Adolphe** 1811–99 French dramatist. Dennery was author or co-author of some of the best-known MELODRAMAS of the 19th century. *Émile, ou Le Fils d'un pair de France* (*Émile, or The Son of a Peer of France*, 1831), written with Charles Desnoyer, was the first of some 200 plays. Dennery had an excellent sense of theatre and of dramatic situations, and many of the plays had a strong populist appeal which ensured them hundreds of performances on the BOULEVARD. His first major success, *Gaspard Hauser* (1838), based on recent real-life events, showed the inhumanity of social convention in respect of illegitimacy. *La Grâce de Dieu* (*The Grace of God*, 1841), perhaps the greatest tear-jerker of the century, depended heavily on the opposition of the social classes. *Marie-Jeanne, ou La Femme du peuple* (*Marie Jeanne, or The Woman of the People*, 1843) provided MARIE DORVAL with her most pathetic role and looked at the social problems of a drunken husband who will not work. *Les Deux Orphelines* (*The Two Orphans*, 1874), written in collaboration with Eugène Cormon, with its persecuted heroines, is his best-known play. Its popularity continued into the 20th century, ultimately becoming the D. W. Griffith film, *Orphans of the Storm*.

In the latter part of his career Dennery moved heavily into the spectacular sensation drama with his adaptations of Jules Verne's novels – *Around the World in Eighty Days* (1874), *Captain Grant's Children* (1878), and *Michel Strogoff* (1880), with its thrilling theme, impossible hero and astounding pyrotechnic effects. Other popular Dennery plays were *Les Bohémiens de Paris* (*The Bohemians of Paris*, 1843), *Don César de Bazan* (1844), *La*

Prière des naufragés (*The Prayer of the Castaways*, 1853), *Uncle Tom's Cabin* (1853), *Cartouche* (1858), *Le Lac de Glenaston* (*The Lake of Glenaston*, 1861) – an adaptation of *The Colleen Bawn* – *The Taking of Peking*, with much equestrian excitement (1861), and *Les Mystères du vieux Paris* (*The Mysteries of Old Paris*, 1865). In addition, Dennery was the author of some of the most celebrated FÉERIES, or extravaganzas, of the century: *Les Sept Châteaux du Diable* (*The Seven Castles of the Devil*, 1844), *La Poule aux oeufs d'or* (*The Hen with the Golden Eggs*, 1848), *Rothomago* (1862) and *Aladin, or The Magic Lamp* (1863); and he wrote librettos for Adam's opera *Si j'étais roi* (*If I Were King*, 1852) and Massenet's *Le Cid* (1885). He also provided the first stage version of Balzac's *Mercadet, le Faiseur* (*Mercadet, or The Financier*), reducing it from five acts to three for the Gymnase in 1851.   JMCC

Dennis, John 1657–1734 English critic and playwright. After studying in Cambridge he settled in London in 1680. His early CRITICISM, e.g. *The Impartial Critic* (1693), established his reputation as an intelligent and tolerant neoclassicist. He began writing plays in 1696 with a comedy *A Plot and No Plot*, and wrote a spectacular opera *Rinaldo and Armida* (1698). He defended the stage in the COLLIER controversy in his pamphlet *The Usefulness of the Stage* (1698). He put his principles to the test in the classical TRAGEDY *Iphigenia* (1699) and in the restrained version of *Appius and Virginia* (1709). Of his other plays, he wrote two poor SHAKESPEARE adaptations, *The Comical Gallant* (1702, from *The Merry Wives of Windsor*) and *The Invader of His Country* (1719, from *Coriolanus*), and a heroic drama set among Canadian Indians, *Liberty Asserted* (1704). His later critical writings, e.g. *Remarks upon 'The Conscious Lovers'* (1723) and *The Causes of the Decay of Dramatic Poetry* (1725), are remarkable for their nostalgic admiration for the drama of the Restoration against the anaemic contemporary specimens.   PH

Denver Center Theatre (USA) The $13 million Helen G. Bonfils Theatre Complex opened on New Year's Eve, 1979, as part of the Denver (Colorado) Center for the Performing Arts. The Bonfils complex consists of three separate theatres: the 550-seat thrust; the 450-seat environmental; and a 150-seat theatre laboratory/rehearsal hall for new American works. Maintaining a professional resident company, the Denver Theatre in its inaugural season (December–April) performed five plays: *The Caucasian Chalk Circle*, ORSON WELLES's *Moby Dick – Rehearsed*, *The Learned Ladies*, *A Midsummer Night's Dream* and Steve Tesich's *Passing Game*. It now stages 10–12 productions annually plus a new play festival (US West) each spring.   TLM

Derain, André 1880–1954 French theatre designer and artist. Derain's entry into the theatre came about in 1919 when Serge Diaghilev recruited him and other Paris-based painters to design for the Ballets Russes. He successfully designed *La Boutique fantastique* (1919) for Léonide Massine, and *Jack-in-the-Box* (1926) for GEORGE BALANCHINE. Derain's theatrical design career, which lasted into the 1950s, was distinguished by a painterly style which simplified reality into a highly decorative stage picture. This style is evident in such productions as *Mam'zelle Angot* (1947) and *Les Femmes de bonne humeur* (1949). As an artist, his fauvist style was said to have influenced early modern painting, and he was also known as an accomplished illustrator and sculptor. TM

D'Errico, Ezio 1892–1972 Italian writer, painter, graphic artist, photographer and dramatist. Remarkably versatile, and variously described – negatively as 'a genial dilettante' and positively as 'an eclectic artist' – D'Errico was keenly responsive to early-20th-century avant-garde movements, particularly FUTURISM, EXPRESSIONISM and SURREALISM. He began to write for the theatre only in 1948, producing some 40 plays. The early work included light COMEDY, MELODRAMA and traditional pieces in the manner of the WELL MADE PLAY, which were in the main more successful than his later, more serious work. This last was for the most part ignored in his lifetime by critics and practitioners alike, although it has come to attract increasing interest; the best of the plays, including *Tempo di cavallette* (*Time of Locusts*, 1956), *La foresta* (*The Forest*, 1956), *Il formicaio* (*The Ants' Nest*, 1957) and *L'assedio* (*The Siege*, 1959), are dark, pessimistic pieces treating of abstract existential issues, reflecting the influence of PIRANDELLO, IONESCO and BECKETT, and place him quite firmly in the 'absurdist' category (see THEATRE OF THE ABSURD). Largely ignored in Italy, they were more successful abroad, particularly in Germany. D'Errico was for long associated with the influential Italian theatre journal, *Ridotto*. LR

Derwent, Clarence 1884–1959 British-born actor-director who fled his London home to become a provincial bit player. By 1910 he appeared back in London; in 1915 he went to the USA to appear with Grace George in SHAW's *Major Barbara*. He went on to appear in some 500 plays and several films, and occasionally directed. In 1945 he founded the Clarence Derwent Awards in London and New York for the best performers in supporting roles. Among his many professional offices were two terms as president of American Actors' Equity and the presidency in 1952 of the AMERICAN NATIONAL THEATRE AND ACADEMY. He also chaired the National Center of the International Theatre Institute and was president of the Dramatic Workshop. His autobiography, *The Derwent Story*, appeared in 1954. SMA

design see theatre design

Desiosi, Compagnia dei (meaning 'those desirous', i.e. of pleasing the public) A *COMMEDIA DELL'ARTE* troupe first noted in 1581, when Montaigne saw them in Pisa and admired their comic Fargnoccola. The company also included the celebrated Arlecchino, TRISTANO MARTINELLI, and Flaminio Scala served in it both as comedian and manager; but its star from 1585 was Diana Ponti, who acted under the name Lavinia. When she joined the ACCESI in 1600, the Desiosi dispersed. LS

Deslys, Gaby [Gabrielle Caïre] 1881–1920 French REVUE artiste of scant talent but blonde good looks and elegant manner, who made her debut at the Parisiana in 1898. From the start, her alleged romance with the ex-king

of Portugal and her regularly imperilled pearls were the stuff of press agents' fables. Her importance lies in her introducing Europe to American jazz styles in the revue *Laissez-les tomber* (1910): dancing with her American partner Harry Pilcer to such exotic instruments as xylophones, saxophones and banjos, she opened up a New World to Paris. She was also the first to make a grand entrance descending a staircase in ostrich plumes and pearls, setting the style for MISTINGUETT, who was her stand-in when her health failed. LS

Dessoir, Ludwig 1810–74 German actor; a virtuoso noted for the contrast in his acting between restraint and carefully judged outbursts of passion. From 1849, Dessoir was a member of the BERLIN ROYAL THEATRE. In 1853, he appeared with EMIL DEVRIENT at the ST JAMES'S THEATRE, London. SW

Destouches [Philippe Néricault] 1680–1754 French dramatist, whose early career was divided between writing for the stage and diplomatic service for the regent, Philip of Orleans, whose protection probably ensured his admission to the Académie-Française in 1723. Thereafter he devoted himself exclusively to playwriting, producing about 30 plays in all, in which he gradually threw off a MOLIÈRESQUE manner and discovered a more individual and more obviously moralizing voice. The most characteristic, and certainly the most successful, were *Le Philosophe marié* (*The Married Philosopher*, 1727) and *Le Glorieux* (*The Conceited Count*, 1732). DR

DeSylva, (B.G.) Buddy [George Gard], 1869–1950, lyricist, librettist;
Lew Brown [Louis Brownstein], 1893–1958, librettist, lyricist, director, producer; and
Ray Henderson [Raymond Brost], 1896–1970, composer. Although they each worked with others, DeSylva, Brown and Henderson are best known for the American MUSICALS they created together in the 1920s. DeSylva studied at the University of Southern California before writing songs for AL JOLSON's shows *Sinbad* (1918) and *Bombo* (1921). With GEORGE GERSHWIN he wrote the score of *La, La, Lucille* (1919) and the 1922–4 *GEORGE WHITE's Scandals*. Born in Russia, Brown wrote popular songs for the publisher Albert von Tilzer and had some of his songs interpolated into BROADWAY shows. Henderson received musical training at the Chicago Conservatory of Music before becoming a VAUDEVILLE accompanist, music arranger and song plugger. Together, the three wrote the score for the 1926 and 1928 editions of the REVUE series *George White's Scandals*. In 1927 they created the book and score of *Good News*, a frothy musical with a college setting that ran for 557 performances. Their subsequent shows included *Hold Everything* (1928), *Follow Thru* (1929) and *Flying High* (1930).

DeSylva went to Hollywood to become a film producer in the early 1930s, eventually becoming head of Paramount Studios. He continued to write lyrics and librettos, some in partnership with Brown and Henderson, for such shows as *Take a Chance* (1932), *Strike Me Pink* (1933), *Du Barry Was a Lady* (1939), *Louisiana Purchase* (1940) and *Panama Hattie* (1940). Brown continued to work on Broadway as a librettist, director and producer, with shows such as *Calling All Stars* (1934) and *Yokel Boy* (1939); he also produced films in Hollywood. Henderson continued to write music for both Broadway shows such as *Say When* (1934) and the *ZIEGFELD Follies* (1943), as well as for Hollywood films. DeSylva, Brown and Henderson perfectly captured the light-hearted spirit of the 1920s in songs such as 'The Best Things in Life are Free' and 'You're the Cream in My Coffee'. MK

Deutsches Theater Theatre company in Berlin, founded by ADOLF L'ARRONGE in 1883 to provide the city with a repertory company that had standards of ensemble similar to those of the MEININGEN COMPANY. Thanks to the contribution of actors such as JOSEF KAINZ and others, L'Arronge succeeded in his efforts. In 1894 the direction was taken over by OTTO BRAHM, who developed a naturalistic approach to the performance of the classics and established the plays of the naturalists firmly in the repertoire (see NATURALISM). In 1904 MAX REINHARDT, who had been a member of Brahm's ensemble, assumed the direction. In the following year he established a theatre school and built a chamber theatre. The Deutsches Theater remained the centre of Reinhardt's Berlin operations until his withdrawal from Nazi Germany in 1933. It is still one of the most prominent theatre companies in Berlin. SW

Devant, David (Wighton) 1868–1941 'The greatest [British] magician of all times', as *The Times* called him. Devant was presenting his first original illusion, 'Vice-Versa', a man-into-woman transformation, on the London MUSIC-HALLS when he was discovered by J. N. MASKELYNE, who took him on as assistant and, in 1905, as partner. Devant discarded the hitherto indispensable MAGIC wand and other suspect apparatus, appeared in the first Royal Command Variety Performance of 1912, and withdrew from co-managing London's St George's Hall in 1915 to offer a series of matinées at the Ambassador Theatre. His illusions, always eschewing the gruesome, included 'The Giant's Breakfast', in which a girl dressed as a chicken materialized from a huge egg; 'The Magic Mirror', wherein the figures of Devant, a volunteer from the audience, and Satan changed position around a mirrored frame; and 'Bif', in which a rattling motorcycle and its rider were pulled into the air and made to vanish. He retired in 1919 after the onset of a nervous palsy that reduced his sleight of hand to nil. LS

Devine, George (Alexander Cassady) 1910–65 British actor and director, who established the English Stage Company at the ROYAL COURT as a 'writers' theatre'. As president of the Oxford University Dramatic Society, he invited JOHN GIELGUD to direct *Romeo and Juliet* in 1932, in which he played Mercutio. This led to an early professional engagement with the OLD VIC, before joining Gielgud's company at the New Theatre in 1934 to act the Player King in what was recognized to be the most celebrated *Hamlet* of the time. He met MICHEL SAINT-DENIS, the innovative French director, who had founded the London Theatre Studio.

The partnership between them, at the Studio from 1936 to 1939 and at the Old Vic School with Glen Byam Shaw after the war, was fruitful both in the testing of new theatrical ideas and in the training of the next generation of actors. The Old Vic Centre, with its school and YOUNG VIC theatre company, was intended to become the experimental heart of the proposed new NATIONAL THEATRE, but was axed in 1951. Devine returned to being a freelance actor and director, playing Tesman in a memorable *Hedda Gabler* with PEGGY ASHCROFT in 1954 and directing at SADLER'S WELLS and Stratford-upon-Avon with the Shakespeare Memorial Company.

But he became convinced that the conditions within British theatre had to change before good new work could be achieved, and in 1954 he joined forces with the playwright Ronald Duncan and the businessman Neville Blond who, together with the director Tony Richardson, founded the English Stage Company for the purpose of staging contemporary plays. In April 1956, the English Stage Company began its first season at the Royal Court Theatre in London's Sloane Square, an event which had an immediate impact upon the course of British theatre. The success of the first season was the premiere of JOHN OSBORNE's *Look Back in Anger*, an unknown play by a then unknown writer, which lent the tone of crusading radicalism, often bitter and angry but never lazy or complacent, to the Royal Court's programmes.

The subsequent years provided new plays by SAMUEL BECKETT, N. F. SIMPSON, ARNOLD WESKER, JOHN ARDEN and ANN JELLICOE; and Devine provided as artistic director a stabilizing influence in what were often stormy times, supporting his young protégés while helping them with sound common sense. He bore the main burden (with Tony Richardson) of directing the early seasons, staging plays by BRECHT, ARTHUR MILLER and JEAN-PAUL SARTRE, and also acting with the company – notably in IONESCO's *The Chairs* (1957) and in Osborne's *A Patriot for Me* (1965), his final role. The George Devine Award was instituted in his memory in 1966 to encourage young professional workers in the theatre, and has been awarded primarily to playwrights. JE

Devrient family The most famous family of German actors in the 19th century. **Ludwig** (1784–1832) is almost universally regarded as the quintessentially romantic actor, thanks mainly to his celebrated interpretations of roles such as Franz Moor in SCHILLER's *The Robbers*, Shylock, and Lear. His ability to bring the unconscious of the characters he played to the fore fascinated and often disturbed his audiences. He was also celebrated for his comic roles, among which was a matchless Falstaff. His early career was spent in the Dessau Court Theatre and the Breslau Town Theatre. In 1815 he joined the BERLIN ROYAL THEATRE, but soon his powers began to wane on account of his chronic alcoholism. Nevertheless, he continued to act both in Berlin and on numerous tours, acquiring for himself a legendary reputation until his early death.

His three nephews were the most distinguished perpetuators of the family name. **Carl** (1797–1872) was a solid, heroic actor. **Eduard** (1801–77) was a distinguished director of the Karlsruhe Court Theatre, where he raised standards of ensemble and production; he was also author of the great *History of German Acting* (1848–74). **Emil** (1803–72) was an idolized virtuoso, his acting being considered the finest expression of the WEIMAR STYLE in the middle years of the century. Later family members continued the tradition into the 20th century. SW

Dewhurst, Colleen 1926–91 Canadian-born American actress. Dewhurst's robustness qualified her ideally for certain EUGENE O'NEILL heroines, most notably Josie in *A Moon for the Misbegotten*, for which she received a Tony in a 1973 revival directed by JOSÉ QUINTERO. 'I love the O'Neill women,' she said. 'They move from the groin rather than the brain. To play O'Neill ... you can't sit and play little moments of sadness or sweetness.' Ironically, her professional New York career began as one of the Neighbours in *Desire Under the Elms* in 1952 (in 1963 she played Abbie Putnam at CIRCLE IN THE SQUARE). Other O'Neill productions of note included *More Stately Mansions* (1967), a 1972 revival of *Mourning Becomes Electra*, and 1988 revivals of *Long Day's Journey into Night* and *Ah, Wilderness!*. She also appeared in three EDWARD ALBEE plays, including a 1976 revival of *Who's Afraid of Virginia Woolf?*. In 1960 she received her first Tony for Mary Follet in *All the Way Home*. Dewhurst was also praised for her work in the classics, especially SHAKESPEARE, most notably for JOSEPH PAPP's NEW YORK SHAKESPEARE FESTIVAL in the 1950s. In recent years she appeared at Papp's PUBLIC THEATER in several productions, including *O'Neill and Carlotta* (1979). In 1985 she was elected president of US Actors' Equity, a position she held until shortly before her death. Her final New York stage appearance was in GURNEY's *Love Letters* (1989); her final film was 1991's *Dying Young* with her son Campbell Scott. DBW

Dexter, John 1925–90 British director, who joined the English Stage Company at the ROYAL COURT in 1957 primarily as an actor but quickly became their most innovative director. He established his reputation with productions of new plays by ARNOLD WESKER, including the *Roots* trilogy (1958, 1959, 1960), *Chips with Everything* (1962) and, in 1959, *The Kitchen*, where Dexter brilliantly choreographed the preparation of restaurant meals. His skill at MIME and movement drew him towards a WEST END MUSICAL, *Half a Sixpence* (1963), and he was one of two Royal Court directors to be invited to join LAURENCE OLIVIER in the formation of the NATIONAL THEATRE company.

From 1963 to 1966, Dexter was an associate director at the National Theatre, responsible for such revivals as *St Joan*, *Hobson's Choice* and *Othello* (with Olivier in the title role). But his most striking NT achievement was his production of PETER SHAFFER's *The Royal Hunt of the Sun* (1964), which had been rejected as unplayable by most London managements. He directed the NT company into such feats as miming the ascent of the Andes, the invention of an Inca language, musical as well as spoken, and the convincing desecration of an empire. This triumph led to other Dexter/Shaffer collaborations, particularly on *Equus* (1973).

After leaving the National Theatre, Dexter directed on BROADWAY and in the West End, returning sometimes to the National Theatre on a freelance basis, for TREVOR GRIFFITHS's play *The Party* (1973), *Phaedra Britannica*

(1975; adapted by TONY HARRISON from RACINE's play) and BRECHT's *Galileo* (1980). From 1974 to 1981, Dexter was director of productions at the Metropolitan Opera House in New York. His last success before his premature death was with the London production of David Henry Hwang's *M. Butterfly* (1989). JE

Dhlomo, H(erbert) I. E. 1903–56 South African playwright, poet and essayist. Known in SOUTH AFRICA as 'the father of black drama', H. I. E. Dhlomo was the first black man to have a play published there in English. He wrote heroic historical dramas such as *Dingane* (1937), *Cetshwayo* (1936) and *Moshoeshoe* (1937), as well as plays that explored the social and political relations of his time such as *The Girl Who Killed to Save: Nongqause the Liberator* (1936) and *The Workers* (1940). Frequently misrepresented as a middle-class intellectual appropriated by European liberal discourse, Dhlomo was in fact one of the most important progressive thinkers of his time. He grappled with the crucial themes for black South Africans of modernization and urbanization, rejecting tribalism at a time when political figures in South Africa were embarking on retrogressive 'native' policies which sought to entrench tribal identities in order to retard black development. He exerted an important influence on the development of black writing in English which matured in the 1950s before it was effectively truncated by political repression in the 60s. An essayist of considerable stature, he wrote about art and politics in South Africa. His *Collected Works*, edited by N. Visser and T. Couzens (1985), reveal him as the most prolific black writer of the mid-century in South Africa. IS

Dias Gomes, Alfredo 1922– Brazilian playwright from Bahia. Dia Gomes began writing in the 40s, and by the 50s had published several novels and written ten plays. Problems with Brazilian CENSORSHIP turned him towards radio and television, but did not dampen his interest in the theatre. In 1960 he catapulted to national prominence with his play *O pagador de promessas* (*Payment as Pledged*), the story of a simple peasant whose efforts to repay a religious promise bring down upon him the entire religious and civic authority of his town. In 1962 the film version of the play won him the coveted Gold Palm at the Cannes Film Festival. A series of successful plays followed. *A Invasão* (*The Invasion*, 1962) depicted problems of the urban poor, *A Revolução dos Beatos* (*The Revolution of the Devout*, 1962) dealt with political and religious fanaticism and intrigue; *O Berço do Herói* (*The Hero's Cradle*, 1965) emphasized the humour, SATIRE and expressionistic vein (see EXPRESSIONISM) of early plays; and *O Santo Inquérito* (*The Holy Inquisition*, 1966) dealt with a historical figure burned at the stake in the 18th century who served as a metaphor of the political repression in Brazil at that time. Dias Gomes continued with *Dr Getulio, Sua Vida e Sua Glória* (*Dr Getulio, His Life and His Glory*), written in collaboration with Ferreira Gullar; *O Rei de Ramos* (*The King of Boughs*, 1979), a MUSICAL collective; and *Campeões do Mundo* (*World Champions*, 1980); all have a political current strongly based in contemporary Brazilian military repression, censorship, political intrigue and hypocrisy. *Amor em Campo Minado* (*Love in a Mine Field*, 1984), first published as *Vamos Soltar os Demonios*, chronicles the last hours of an intellectual accused of subversive activities and consists primarily of a verbal battle between the protagonist and his wife over levels of commitment. Erotic elements turn obscene as political issues are interrelated with sexuality. GW

Díaz, Grégor 1933– Peruvian playwright, actor and director. Born in Cajamarca, Díaz received his theatre training first in Lima in the National Institute of Dramatic Art, later in Chile in the University Experimental Theatre. Affiliated with the Theatre Club, he has won national prizes for many of his plays. His major works are *La huelga* (*Strike*, 1966), *Los del 4* (*The Ones in* 4, 1969), *Sitio al sitio* (*Siege of the Site*, 1978), *El mudo de la ventana* (*The Mute at the Window*, 1984) and *Harina mundo* (*Flour World*, 1993). Committed to redressing political and socio-economic injustices, his theatre presents the evils of oppression with artistic sensitivity. GW

Díaz, Jorge 1930– Chilean playwright. Born in Argentina of Spanish parents, Díaz became a naturalized Chilean citizen. After studying architecture at the University of Chile, he began his theatre career as a set designer with the group ICTUS in Santiago in 1959. In 1965 he moved to Spain, and currently holds dual Chilean–Spanish citizenship. His early plays fell into the following categories: those written with ICTUS, which showed the strong influence of European absurdism (see THEATRE OF THE ABSURD), such as *El cepillo de dientes* (*The Toothbrush*, 1961); and those from the first years in Spain, which still carried a strong Latin American influence, such as *Topografía de un desnudo* (*Topography of a Nude*, 1966). After 1970 he wrote plays of strong political protest such as *Americaliente* (1971), a bombastic collage about US intervention in Latin America, and commentaries about contemporary life in Spain, such as *Mata a tu prójimo como a ti mismo* (*Kill Thy Neighbour as Thyself*, 1975). More recent plays include *Piel contra piel* (*Skin against Skin*, 1982), an anniversary interpretation of his earlier *Toothbrush*, and a series of plays that depict contemporary life in Spain as well as in Chile, reflective of his dual allegiances and cultures. In 1992 *El jáguar azul* (*The Blue Jaguar*) won the Premio Born for a novel interpretation of the Spanish Conquest.

A prolific writer of more than 40 major plays, he also wrote children's theatre (more than 20 works) and television scripts. Díaz is an inveterate experimenter with language, who loves to challenge societal conventions regarding basic aspects of human existence. His major themes are love, sex, violence and death. GW

Dibdin, Charles 1745–1814 English actor, dramatist and composer. After early success as a chorister in Winchester and as a singer and song-writer in London (by his death he had written 1400 songs), he began to collaborate with ISAAC BICKERSTAFFE on comic operas – for example, for GARRICK'S SHAKESPEARE Jubilee in 1769, an event which was part of his endless feuding with Garrick. In 1768 he starred as Mungo, a black-faced servant, in his own play *The Padlock* with such success that he gave his son Charles the name Mungo. In 1776 he left DRURY LANE,

sacked for his neglect of rehearsals or because of Garrick's dislike of his mistress, and settled in France for two years, in debt. Apart from numerous works for COVENT GARDEN he also flirted with popular entertainments, creating a riot at a puppet play in 1780 when the audience had expected live actors, and becoming a partner in 1782 in an equestrian theatre (see HIPPODRAMA), the Royal Circus, later the Surrey Theatre, another financial failure that landed him in a debtors' prison. From 1789 he began to perform one-man shows of songs, playlets and monologues. From 1796 he wrote plays and entertainments for the Sans Souci Theatre, which he managed. He was granted a civil list pension in 1803 for his songs celebrating the British sailor. PH

Dickens, Charles (John Huffam) 1812–70 British novelist, whose dependence on the theatre can be sensed even where it cannot be documented. His famous gift for eccentric characterization owed much to his youthful observation of actors, and he repaid the debt by providing actors with unrivalled opportunities in the countless adaptations of his novels. Outstanding examples include IRVING's Jingle, JOSEPH JEFFERSON III's Caleb Plummer (also in the repertoire of J. L. TOOLE), BEERBOHM TREE's Fagin and JOHN MARTIN-HARVEY's Sydney Carton. Among the playwrights to have dramatized Dickens are W. T. MONCRIEFF, TOM TAYLOR, T. W. ROBERTSON, BOUCICAULT, JAMES ALBERY, W. S. GILBERT and, most recently, DAVID EDGAR (*Nicholas Nickleby*, 1980). The famous public readings, with which Dickens boosted his income in his declining years, served only to confirm that it was partly as an armchair actor that he created characters and dramatic episodes. No novelist of stature has so fed off the world of MELODRAMA. Dickens's own plays – he had two burlettas and a FARCE performed in his lifetime – are lightweight, but he was immensely serious about his amateur theatricals in the small private theatre in his London home, Tavistock House, where he relished the opportunity to act on a real stage instead of only in his imagination. PT

Diderot, Denis 1713–84 French philosopher, novelist, playwright and critic, whose DRAMATIC THEORY represents an attempt to liberate the 18th-century stage from the artificial constraints of neoclassical dramaturgy and to provide it with a moral rationale. Between the mutually exclusive poles of classical TRAGEDY and traditional comedy of intrigue there is, he argued, a vast neglected territory ripe for dramatic exploration: the 'conditions' of men, their professions and trades, their conjugal and family lives, their social virtues, are susceptible to treatment either in the form of 'serious' COMEDY or domestic tragedy. Both are related aspects of what he calls the *genre sérieux*, in which tears and laughter should mingle as they do in the real world. With its recognizable situations and characters such drama will correspond to the audience's own experience of life, will touch them to the heart and thereby make them better people. His thinking exerted a widespread influence on European drama and proved, in fact, more compelling than the plays that he wrote to illustrate it: *Le Fils naturel* (*The Natural Son*, published 1757 and performed 1771) and *Le Père de famille* (*The Father of the Family*, 1758 and 1761), which are implausibly elevated in style and moralizingly over-sentimental in tone. Most memorable of all his theoretical work, perhaps, is his dialogue on the nature of acting, *Paradoxe sur le comédien* (published posthumously in 1830), which assesses the relative importance to the performer of genuine feeling and conscious control by the intellect. DR

Digges, Dudley 1879–1947 Dublin-born actor and director, and a member of the original Abbey Players. He made his New York debut in 1904 with MINNIE MADDERN FISKE. In 1919 he appeared in *Bonds of Interest* for the THEATRE GUILD, for whom he eventually played more than 3500 times (including the role of James Caesar in *John Ferguson*) and staged four plays. Reviewing his final appearance as Harry Hope in O'NEILL's *The Iceman Cometh*, BROOKS ATKINSON remarked that Digges's 'command of the actor's art of expressing character and theme is brilliantly alive; it overflows with comic and philosophical expression'. Digges also appeared in over 50 films and served as vice-president of US Actors' Equity Association. SMA

Dimov, Ossip 1878–1959 Russian-language writer of over 30 Jewish plays, at first for the MOSCOW ART THEATRE, later in America. Devoted to improving the literary quality of YIDDISH THEATRE as both writer and producer, his best-known plays are *The Eternal Wanderer*, *Hear O Israel, Yoshke Musikant* and *Bronx Express*. AB

Dingelstedt, Franz von 1814–81 German director. After several years as a journalist with ideas akin to those of the liberal writers of the Junges Deutschland (Young Germany) movement, Dingelstedt underwent a conversion to royalist beliefs. For some years, he was a librarian at the royal court in Stuttgart, then in 1851 he was appointed director of the Munich Court Theatre. Here he staged productions of unusual splendour, which were so expensive that in 1857 he was dismissed for running the theatre deeply into debt. He was immediately appointed director of the Weimar Court Theatre, where his most significant achievement was the production in 1864 of all of SHAKESPEARE'S HISTORY PLAYS. This created such a name for him that, in 1867, he was appointed director of the Vienna Opera and, in 1870, of the BURGTHEATER. Here he repeated his success with Shakespeare's histories and staged numerous other classical plays in a notably spectacular manner. Dingelstedt is regarded by many historians as a forerunner of both the Duke of Saxe-MEININGEN and MAX REINHARDT. SW

directing Directing is part of that complex of seeing and doing that makes theatre. At all levels, the need to intervene to shape the theatrical event can be felt but, because of the processual nature of PLAY, the best of directing comes from within the activity. However, throughout the history of theatre a need can be discerned for unification, direction and encouragement from without – for leadership.

The authority to intervene on behalf of others has been, in the past, mainly the prerogative of playwright or actor (sometimes the same person, as with ZEAMI and MOLIÈRE). Social and economic power, though often influential, has rarely been directly responsible for the crafting of play. For example, in 472 BC at Athens, the politics and wealth of the young Pericles as *choregos* (the citizen entrusted with financing certain aspects of a production) must have affected the ideology and spectacle of *The Persians*, but the teaching of the songs and dances, the vision and government of the overall event, was in the hands of AESCHYLUS, who was both playwright and leading actor. By Hellenistic times there is evidence to suggest that training was a separate professional business, but by then directorial authority had been abrogated by the 'star' performer. Likewise in Rome, the *dominus gregis*, as chief actor of the troupe, was responsible for production. In the Middle Ages the *maître de jeu* or BOOK-KEEPER worked both on the preparation and on the smooth-running of the show, although often it is unclear how separate such figures were from poet or player. Many must have been similar to the 'property players' of early-16th-century England – actors engaged from the metropolis to supervise and furnish material for provincial productions; but some were, without doubt, separate managers and machinists like the two *conducteurs des sccrets* of the Mons PASSION PLAY. With the growth of scenic illusion in the West, such stage-management increased, but it is not until late in the 19th century that the figure of the director can be discerned.

In Asia, given the historical importance of the transmission of performance genres (see ACTING), masters often took control of the preparation for a production. The *sutradhara* in classical Indian theatre, for example, was often responsible for selecting, organizing and training the cast, for overseeing the building of a theatre, conducting offerings to the gods and appearing on stage in the preliminaries to the play. Production manuals (*kramadipika*), alongside acting manuals (*attaprakara*), have been passed on through generations of actors of KUTIYATTAM. However, as James Brandon has observed: 'To put together a traditional performance does not require the special outside vision of a director, as we in Western theatre expect.'

The modern concept of the director grew from the work of the Duke of Saxe-MEININGEN and his stage-manager Chronegk. It was nurtured by pioneers like ANTOINE, STANISLAVSKY and REINHARDT. The latter gave up acting completely in 1903 to devote all his time to directing. The new authority, fundamental to the thoughts of APPIA and CRAIG on the coherence of theatre as art, is exemplified in the careers of MEYERHOLD, VAKHTANGOV, and TAIROV, COPEAU and PISCATOR. The work of such masters heads a rich and varied tradition, of which more recent exponents include BROOK, GROTOWSKI and PETER STEIN (all of whom began as directors). This tradition shares with film a parallel development and a common notion of the director as *auteur*. While this notion may be valid in film, where a final intervention is made in the cutting room, in theatre the live performance mocks its grandeur. In many ways the hegemony of the director – the director seen as an authority separate and separable from either actor or dramatist – is problematic. Reliance on this authority can too often sap the creativity, intelligence and initiative of the player; while for the playwright, production more and more usurps the power once held by the play. Interpretation is all! The idea of the director is the most dominant feature of Western theatre in the 20th century. LSR

discovery space It is clear from numerous stage directions that Elizabethan theatres, both public and private, had the capacity to conceal and reveal actors and scenes. The assumption that the platform had a large alcove or 'inner stage' at the back was undermined by the publication in 1888 of De Witt's drawing of the SWAN, which shows a blank wall between two large stage-doors in the TIRING HOUSE façade. It would have been possible to create a small discovery space by hanging a curtain between the inward-opening doors of the Swan, an easy solution which would have had the advantage of increasing visibility for observers above or beside the thrust stage. For some scenes, as is suggested by the 1633 title-page drawing in KYD's *The Spanish Tragedy*, a separate free-standing structure would have been more appropriate. What is certain is that, once the concealed scene or character had been revealed, the action was brought out on to the platform proper. Having served the story, the discovery space was not allowed to contain or constrain it.   PT

Dithmar, Edward A. 1854–1917 American drama critic. Born in New York, Dithmar began his career in 1871 with the *New York Evening Post*. He moved to the *New York Times* in 1877 where he became night editor in 1882 and drama critic in 1884, replacing George Edgar Montgomery. After giving way to John Corbin in 1901, he served as the *Times*'s London correspondent (1901–2), editor of its *Saturday Review of Books* (1902–7) and editorial writer (1907–17). He authored *John Drew* (1900) and *Memoirs of Daly's Theatre* (1897), and coedited with AUGUSTIN DALY *A Portfolio of Players*. His business relationship with Daly may have compromised his reputation. Dithmar is best remembered as an outspoken advocate of American drama.   TLM

Dmitrevsky [Dmitrevskoi]**, Ivan (Afanasievich)** 1734–1821 The first Russian actor of real artistic distinction and social prominence. Dmitrevsky began his career with FYODOR VOLKOV's acting troupe in Yaroslavl (1750) and continued with the Moscow company co-founded by Volkov and playwright ALEKSEI SUMAROKOV in 1756. Known as 'the Russian GARRICK', whose acting he studied along with LEKAIN's and CLAIRON's while abroad (1765–8), Dmitrevsky is credited with having introduced into Russia the loud, artificial declamatory acting style which MIKHAIL SHCHEPKIN's simple, natural approach replaced in the 1830s.

Dmitrevsky's intelligent but unemotional approach to acting contributed to the success of his second career as teacher-director-administrator, beginning in 1780 with one of Russia's first private acting companies, the Free Knipper Theatre in Moscow, and extending through various enterprises over the next 38 years. Among his most distinguished pupils were such leaders of the next generation of actors as PYOTR PLAVILSHCHIKOV, A. S. YAKOVLEV, E. S. SEMYONOVA and I. I. SOSNITSKY. Dmitrevsky wrote more than 40 dramas, comedies and operas, and regularly advised his more influential contemporary playwrights Sumarokov, YAKOV KNYAZHNIN and especially DENIS FONVIZIN, in whose comedy *The Minor* he scored a notable acting success as Starodum. His co-translations of Tacitus, play analyses, contributions to joint scholarly projects and individual research efforts, including an unpublished history of the Russian theatre (1792), earned Dmitrevsky election to the Russian Academy on 3 May 1802.   SG

Döbbelin, Carl Theophil 1727–93 German actor. After some years in SCHÖNEMANN's troupe, where he practised the LEIPZIG STYLE, in 1756 Döbbelin founded his own troupe; it gave the first performance of LESSING's *Götz von Berlichingen* in 1774. From 1775 on, the troupe formed a permanent company in Berlin; in 1786 it was established, still under Döbbelin's leadership, as the Berlin National and Court Theatre, later to become the important BERLIN ROYAL THEATRE.   SW

Dockstader, Lew [George Alfred Clapp] 1856–1925 American comedian, who preserved the MINSTREL SHOW's vitality while injecting it with political SATIRE. He had begun in blackface as a teenager and formed his own company with Charles Dockstader in 1876, retaining the name after his partner retired in 1883. His new partnership with George Primrose created the most popular turn-of-the-century minstrel troupe in the USA (1898–1913). Dockstader performed in two-foot-long shoes and a coat with a 30-in tail; his best song was 'Everybody Works but Father'. Before he became a solo monologuist on the KEITH circuit, he had given a start to AL JOLSON.   LS

Dodin, Lev (Abramovich) 1944– Russian director who has made his career in St Petersburg as Boris Zon's student at the Theatre Institute; as a member of Zinovy Korogotsky's children's theatre workshop; and since 1983 as artistic director of the Maly Dramatic Theatre. In 1976–9, using Institute students, Dodin developed a stage adaptation of 'village prose' novelist Fyodor Abramov's *Brothers and Sisters*, which along with *Home* (Dodin's first major success at the MDT, 1980–1) dealt with the falsely propagandistic ideal of collective farm life and the spiritual bankruptcy of contemporary Soviet society. Dodin's later two-evening-long production of *Brothers and Sisters* at MDT combined ethnographic costumes, music and action, newsreel footage and an evocative set by EDVARD KOCHERGIN. It toured widely abroad, along with Dodin's 1987 production of GALIN's *Stars in the Morning Sky*, which featured NUDITY as an example of the new openness in the Russian theatre. Dodin's other productions include TENNESSEE WILLIAMS's *The Rose Tattoo* and staged adaptations of William Golding's *Lord of the Flies* (1987) set among plane wreckage, Nikolai Kaledin's black novella *Construction Battalion* and Dostoevsky's *The Brothers Karamazov* and *The Devils*.   SG

Dodsley, Robert 1703–64 English playwright and publisher. He ran away from his apprenticeship to a stocking weaver and became a footman in London where, encouraged by Alexander Pope, he became a writer and bookseller. His first play, *The Toyshop* (1735), was a light FARCE. He had his greatest success with *The King and the Miller of Mansfield* (1737), a folk-tale COMEDY, and with *Cleone* (1758), an emotionally violent TRAGEDY with GEORGE ANNE BELLAMY in the title role. But Dodsley's most important contribution to drama was as editor and publisher of *A Select Collection of Old Plays* (12 vols., 1744), a major attempt to rescue the work of many Renaissance dramatists from obscurity – the work was re-edited by Hazlitt in 1874. He also turned DAY and CHETTLE's *The Blind Beggar of Bethnal Green* into a BALLAD OPERA in 1741.   PH

dog drama see ANIMALS AS PERFORMERS

Doggett, Thomas c.1670–1721 English actor, manager and playwright. He performed in Ireland in the 1680s but joined the DRURY LANE company by 1691, scoring a great success as Solon in D'URFEY's *The Marriage-Hater Matched* (1692) and being nicknamed Solon thereafter. He was praised by DRYDEN for his intelligence as an actor and by ASTON as 'the best face-player and gesticulator'. He was careful in his costuming and in his observation of life. Though he joined the secessionists in 1695, he could not settle with them and oscillated between the companies and touring outside London. In 1709 he joined Wilks and COLLEY CIBBER in running the Queen's Theatre and later Drury Lane. He left the triumvirate in 1714 in an argument over BARTON BOOTH's joining them. In 1716 he established a race for Thames watermen from London Bridge to Chelsea for a cap and silver badge: it is still rowed annually.   PH

Domínguez, Franklin 1931– Dominican Republic playwright, director and actor. A graduate of the National School of Dramatic Art in 1949, Domínguez was instrumental in creating the experimental theatre movement in the DOMINICAN REPUBLIC. With degrees in philosophy (1953) and law (1955), he occupied important positions in national theatre and culture. He has served as director of the Fine Arts Theatre and has his own theatre group, Franklin Domínguez Presents. He is an eclectic writer; his works have been translated and staged in French, German, English, Portuguese, Flemish and Chinese. Among his more than 30 plays are *El último instante* (*The Last Moment*, 1957), the anguished monologue of a suicidal prostitute; *Se busca un hombre honesto* (*The Search for an Honest Man*, 1963); and *Lisístrata odia la política* (*Lysistrata Hates Politics*, 1965), a socially committed play based on ARISTOPHANES. His plays have won prizes in many countries.   GW

Dominica see EASTERN CARIBBEAN STATES

Dominican Republic On this Caribbean island, one of Columbus's first settlements, the native *taínos* practised both the *areyto*, a historical music-dance drama that transmitted the cultural heritage orally, and the *cohaba*, a priestly ceremonial dance induced by hallucinogenic drugs. The early extinction of the indigenous population through the imposition of a Spanish hierarchical system and the importation of European diseases reduced the demand for catechetical theatre. In the colonial years, theatre tended to reflect religious concerns in the form of *LOAS*, *entremeses* (see GÉNERO CHICO) and COMEDIAS, although a secular theatre, realistic and comic, sometimes in open opposition to Catholic dogma, was performed and naturally censured by the Church (see CENSORSHIP).

Cristóbal de Llerena is the first playwright of record born in the New World. Author of several works, only his *entremés* performed in 1588 survives. The work reflected social conflicts and corruption within the Dominican society during a period of external and internal pirating. Sir Francis Drake had sacked the city shortly before this date, and Llerena's brief two-scene play resulted in his immediate but temporary deportation. In 1616–18 TIRSO DE MOLINA, the famous Spanish playwright of the GOLDEN AGE, lived on the island, but there is no record that his plays were performed there or that his idealistic conception of the world left any lasting impact on Dominican theatre.

New governors, slave rebellions and political instability produced by invasions and the wars between Spain, France and England characterized life on the island during the 17th and 18th centuries. Theatrical events took place in the churches, plazas and viceregal houses and palaces, but no plays are preserved. The 19th-century foreign occupation by the Haitians (1822–44) and the Spanish (1861–5) perpetuated the turbulence, but such theatre groups as the Trinitarians, the Philanthropics and the Dramatic Society attempted to maintain a semblance of activity, generally with foreign plays by such authors as ALFIERI and Francisco Martínez de la Rosa.

Don Felix María del Monte is considered to be the first national playwright, with a work that criticizes the first president of the nation for the assassination of the patriot of the title – *Antonio Duvergé, o Las víctimas del 11 de abril* (*Antonio Duvergé, or The Victims of 11 April*, 1856). Indigenous and heroic tendencies, embedded in a romantic framework, were typical of the other major authors of the period such as Javier Foxá (1816–65) and Javier Angulo Guridi (1816–84), the latter the author of *Iguaniona* (1867). Groups such as La Juventud (Youth) (1868) and Amigos del País (Friends of the Nation) (1871) contributed to the theatre movement.

The 20th century After 1911 the cultural societies began to produce comedy sketches, and the North American occupation of the island (1916–24) inspired some political plays. Rafael Damirón's (1882–1946) *Alma criolla* (*Creole Soul*, 1916) continued the romantic tradition with elements of the ZARZUELA, however. For the most part, the early years of the century saw little new development.

In the 1940s the arrival of Spanish immigrants, refugees of the Civil War, gave new impulse to the theatre and promoted local authors such as MANUEL RUEDA and HÉCTOR INCHÁUSTEGUI CABRAL. The contemporary theatre movement dates from 1946, the year that Generalissimo Trujillo's wife urged the creation of the Fine Arts Theatre. The theatre occupies a handsome building; the government provides regular, though minimal, salaries. The experimental theatre movement in Santo Domingo dates from 1952; MÁXIMO AVILÉS BLONDA and FRANKLIN DOMÍNGUEZ were instrumental in using the latest production techniques to stage translations of foreign plays, along with their own works. Both are major authors with a commitment to serious theatre; Domínguez, the island's best-known playwright internationally, has for years directed the Fine Arts Theatre. Other writers of importance include Marcio Veloz Maggiolo, Carlos Esteban Deive (b.1935), IVÁN GARCÍA GUERRA (b.1938), Carlos Acevedo, Rafael Añez Bergés, Juan Carlos Mieses (b.1947) and Efraím Castillo. The latter has published two plays: *Viaje de regreso* (*Return Trip*) and *La cosecha* (*The Crop*).

The experimental movement spawned such groups as the Jockey Club Group, the Popular Experimental Theatre (1976), Intec Projection (1978) and Chispa (Spark). Domínguez created his own independent group; and the Gratey Theatre, directed by Danilo Ginebra and others, has been responsible for a wide range of publications and activities, including the first national popular theatre festival in 1983. Rafael Villalona, Delta Sota and María Castillo have done important work with the Nuevo Teatro (New Theatre). In 1985 Reynaldo Disla won the coveted Casa de las Americas prize in Cuba for the best new play, *Bolo Francisco*.

Theatre activity continues to be sporadic, centred mostly in the capital city of Santo Domingo which embraces the non-professional, independent and university theatre activity – that of the Autonomous University of Santo Domingo, Pedro Henríquez Ureña National University and the Technical Institute of Santo Domingo. Isolated movement in the provinces includes the work of Rubén Echavarría and Lincoln López in the theatre programme of the Catholic University Madre y Maestra. Robinson Aybar, a young director, actor and writer from Santiago de los Caballeros, counts more than 20 groups on the island, but the theatre still suffers from a lack of infrastructure, with the result that the numbers encourage false expectations about the availability of staged performances.   GW

> *See*: D. Ginebra (ed.), *Teatro dominicano*, vol. 1, Santo Domingo, 1984; P. Henríquez Ureña, *Obras completas: El teatro de la América española*, vol. 7, Santo Domingo, 1978; J. Lockward, *Teatro dominicano: Pasado y presente*, Santo Domingo, 1959.

Donnellan, Declan   see CHEEK BY JOWL.

Döring, Theodor   1803–78 German actor. A natural and versatile imitator, Döring was known for the REALISM and completeness of his characterizations. He had a refreshing vital energy, though at times he became so absorbed in a role that it was difficult to hear him. Before joining the BERLIN ROYAL THEATRE in 1845, he acted in companies in Mannheim, Hamburg, Stuttgart and Hannover.   SW

Dorset Garden Theatre (London) Begun in 1669 by Wren on a frontage facing the river with a site measuring 140 by 57ft, the Dorset Garden Theatre had seven boxes on each of the lower and middle galleries and an undivided upper gallery above. It opened in November 1671 for use by the Duke's Company with a production of DRYDEN's *Sir Martin Mar-All*. It was soon apparent that the theatre's acoustics were poor and it was increasingly used only for spectacular productions of operatic extravagances. It was demolished in 1709.   PH

Dorst, Tankred   1925– German dramatist of notable versatility and range. *Die Kurve* (*The Curve*, 1960) was an absurdist piece (see THEATRE OF THE ABSURD); *Grosse Schmährede an der Mauer* (*Tirade at the Wall*, 1961) was an inverted *Lehrstück* affirming the primacy of private over public life. *Toller* (1968), a researched reconstruction of ERNST TOLLER's role in the Munich Soviet built around

scenes from his play *Masses and Man*, explores the theme of the writer and politics. *Eiszeit* (*Ice Age*, 1973) examines the same theme in a conversation between Knut Hamsun in old age and a young German probing the Norwegian novelist's collaboration with the Nazis.

In 1972 Dorst turned Hans Fallada's novel *Little Man, What Now?* into a 1920s REVUE for PETER ZADEK, with whom he works regularly. His major project, *German History*, a family saga in various media ranging from the 1920s to the present, to date comprises *Auf dem Chimborazo* (*On Chimborazo*, 1970), *Die Villa* (1980), *Heinrich, oder Die Schmerzen der Phantasie* (*Heinrich, or the Pains of Imagination*, 1984), a novel *Dorothea Merz*, and a TV film *Klara's Mutter*. The grand poetic sweep of his eight-hour *Merlin* (1985), an anachronistic, kaleidoscopic dramatization of the decline of Christian chivalry, stands as an Arthurian metaphor for the collapse of utopia today. *Fernando Krapp hat diesen Brief geschrieben* (*Fernando Krapp Wrote This Letter*, 1992) is a critical comedy based on Miguel de Unamuno.   HR

Dorval, Marie   1798–1849 French actress who best represented the romantic movement in the French theatre. Her passionate temperament and instinctive playing, defying the 'rules' of good acting, set her in opposition to the great classical actress MLLE MARS, with whom she shared the stage in HUGO's *Angelo* (1835). Dorval was the offspring of travelling players, and made her first appearances at the age of eight in such popular MELODRAMAS as *Les deux petits savoyards* (*The Two Little Savoyards*). At 15 she married a poor ballet master, Allan Dorval, and, having been noticed in Strasbourg by the actor POTIER, was taken on at the Porte-Saint-Martin in 1818. Her greatest triumph there came in 1827 with VICTOR DUCANGE's *The Hut on the Red Mountain; or, Thirty Years of a Gamester's Life*, in which she played opposite FRÉDÉRICK LEMAÎTRE. This gave her the sort of strong dramatic role that suited her talent.

CASIMIR DELAVIGNE's *Marino Faliero* (1829) established her as the first actress of the BOULEVARD. She moved briefly to the Ambigu, then back to the Porte-Saint-Martin to play Adèle d'Hervey with BOCAGE in DUMAS *père*'s *Antony* (1831). Her role was that of a passionate woman forced by society into a loveless marriage and trapped into an adulterous affair. In Hugo's *Marion de Lorme* she incarnated the golden-hearted courtesan. Her style of play, with a tremor in her voice, could send a wave of emotion through audiences. From 1833 to 1835 she had a liaison with VIGNY, who wrote *Quitte pour la peur* (*Getting Off with a Fright*) and *Chatterton* (1835) for her. She made her debut at the COMÉDIE-FRANÇAISE in 1834, taking on some of Mlle Mars's parts, but she was not really a Comédie-Française actress, and left again in 1835. In *Chatterton*, as the silent and pathetic Kitty Bell, she introduced an unforgettable final stage effect, fainting at the top of a flight of stairs and allowing her inanimate body to slide the entire length of the banisters.

After the Comédie-Française she had a brief period at the ODÉON and then moved to the Gymnase in 1837. It was mutually agreed that her talents were not suited to Gymnase comedy and the contract was cancelled in 1840. She returned for a time to the Comédie-Française, appearing at the request of George Sand, who admired her, in the latter's *Cosima*, then moved back to the Odéon to appear in the title role of PONSARD's *Lucrèce* (1842). In 1845 she was back on the boulevard in her final huge triumph, the melodrama *Marie-Jeanne*. By this stage her health was undermined and, after some further appearances at the Odéon and a revival of *Marie-Jeanne* in 1848, she died in poverty. JMCC

Dotrice, Roy 1923– British actor. Dotrice made his reputation after joining the ROYAL SHAKESPEARE COMPANY in 1958, where he demonstrated his versatility with memorable performances in the contrasting roles of Gaunt, Hotspur and Justice Shallow, all presented on a single day in the first half of PETER HALL's history cycle, *The Wars of the Roses* (1963). He made an international reputation with his solo adaptation of John Aubrey's *Brief Lives* (1966), which set a record for the longest-running solo performance, and has been followed by other one-man shows. His range remains eclectic, though concentrating on SHAKESPEARE and modern classics from IBSEN to PINTER. CI

Douglas, James 1929– Irish playwright. Douglas made an impressive debut with *North City Traffic Straight Ahead* (Gaiety, Dublin, 1961), an ironic and spare drama of wasted urban lives. His television drama includes some long-running series, and a number of plays – *The Bomb* (1962), *Babby Joe* (1966), *The Hollow Field* (1965), *Too Short a Summer* (1973). Douglas's other stage plays – such as the successful *Carrie* (1963), *The Ice Goddess* (1964), *The Savages* (1968) – did not quite recapture the force of his debut, but did bring a hard-edged urban REALISM to Irish theatre in the 60s. DM GF

Douglass, David ?–1786 British-born actor-manager. Douglass became the central figure in the history of the American theatre from his marriage in 1758 to the widow of LEWIS HALLAM SR, in JAMAICA, to the American Revolution. He returned to New York from London in 1758 as head of Hallam's Company of Comedians (renamed in 1763 the American Company of Comedians). For 17 years Douglass's company played up and down the East Coast, erecting temporary theatres in most towns. In 1766 he built the first permanent theatre in the USA, the SOUTHWARK in Philadelphia, followed in 1767 by the JOHN STREET THEATRE in New York. In April 1767 he announced the first professional production of a play by an American-born writer, a comic OPERA called *The Disappointment*; this was replaced at the last minute by Thomas Godfrey's *The Prince of Parthia*, the first native TRAGEDY to be presented professionally . Before the outbreak of hostilities, Douglass and his company returned to the West Indies in 1775, where he became a justice, an officer in the militia, and a member of the Council. He was America's first Falstaff and King John; though a poor actor, he was a superb manager. DBW

Dowling, Eddie [Joseph Nelson Goucher] 1889–1976 Pulitzer Prize-winning American producer, playwright, song-writer, director and actor. Dowling began his career doing a song-and-dance act in his native state of Rhode Island. His BROADWAY debut was in VICTOR HERBERT's *The Velvet Lady* in 1919; he appeared in the ZIEGFELD Follies of 1919, 20 and 21. In 1945, after rejecting a sure-fire commercial project, he co-produced and co-directed (with MARGO JONES) TENNESSEE WILLIAMS's *The Glass Menagerie*, in which he also played Tom. The production made theatrical history and brought Williams out of obscurity. Dowling produced *Richard II* in 1937 with MAURICE EVANS, and during his long career worked with such playwrights as WILLIAM SAROYAN, PAUL VINCENT CARROLL, SEAN O'CASEY and PHILIP BARRY. DBW

Downes, John fl.1661–1719 English prompter. He began as an actor but failed because of severe stage fright in a performance of DAVENANT's *The Siege of Rhodes* in 1661. He became prompter for the Duke's Company and worked for the United Company and BETTERTON's Company until 1706, being responsible for writing out actors' parts, attending all rehearsals and all performances. In 1708 he published *Roscius Anglicanus*, a brief history of the stage from the Restoration. PH

drag shows See FEMALE IMPERSONATION

Dragún, Osvaldo 1929– Argentine playwright and director. Born in Entre Ríos, San Salvador, Dragún is committed to denouncing social injustices and has consistently censured the materialism and hypocrisy of our times. His *Historias para ser contadas* (*Stories to Be Told*, 1957) were written with a COMMEDIA DELL'ARTE flavour, to be performed by his theatre group Teatro Popular Fray Mocho. Internationally known, these vignettes with long titles condemn the sacrifices of human dignity on the altar of economic survival. Other titles, *La peste viene de Melos* (*The Plague comes from Melos*, 1956) and *Tupac Amarú* (1957), show perverted economic and moral values in classical settings. Later plays include *Y nos dijeron que éramos inmortales* (*And They Told Us We Were Immortal*, 1963), *El milagro en el mercado viejo* (*Miracle in the Old Market*, 1964), *El amasijo* (*The Hodgepodge*, 1968) and sequels to the *Historias* (*Stories*). Dragún played a major role in the creation of the TEATRO ABIERTO (Open Theatre), an experiment organized in 1981 to produce viable theatre during the most repressive years of the military government. Recent works include *Al violador* (*To the Rapist*, 1981), *Hoy comen al flaco* (*Today They Eat the Thin Man*, 1981), *Mi obelisco y yo* (*My Obelisk and Me*, 1981), *Al perdedor* (*To the Loser*, 1982), *Al vendedor* (*To the Seller*, 1982) and *Arriba corazón!* (*Upward Heart!*, 1987). For the last several years Dragún has directed the Institute for Latin American Theatre in Havana, Cuba. GW

Drake, Alfred 1914–92 American singer and actor. One of the most versatile leading men of the American musical stage, Drake began his musical career in GILBERT and Sullivan revivals and made his BROADWAY debut in the chorus of *White Horse Inn* (1936). After featured roles in such shows as *Babes in Arms* (1937) and *The Straw Hat Revue* (1939), he created the role of Curley in RODGERS and HAMMERSTEIN's *Oklahoma!* (1943). Five years later, he played Fred Graham in *Kiss Me, Kate*. He was praised by critics for his romantic, swaggering portrayal of a

Shakespearian actor, and his comic abilities received a large share of the acclaim. Among his subsequent MUSICAL THEATRE appearances, only his performance as Hajj in *Kismet* (1953) was notable. Drake's career as an actor included performances as Othello and Benedick at the AMERICAN SHAKESPEARE [Festival] THEATRE, and Claudius opposite RICHARD BURTON in *Hamlet* (1964). His last major role was in a 1975 revival of *The Skin of Our Teeth*. MK

Drake, Samuel 1769–1854 American actor-manager. After managing in the English provinces, Drake took his family to America in 1810. They spent a few years in Boston, then joined JOHN BERNARD's company in Albany, New York (1813), and in 1815, at the invitation of Luke Usher, Drake took his three sons, two daughters and five assistants as a company to Frankfort, Kentucky. He extended his influence to Louisville, Lexington and Cincinnati, a circuit he controlled for many years. While not the leading company in the West at the time, Drake's group improved performance levels in the area and firmly established the FRONTIER THEATRE. Drake was the grandfather of JULIA DEAN. SMA

Drama League (USA) Founded in 1909 by an Evanston, Illlinois, ladies' literary society, the Riley Circle. Their first national gathering was held at a church in Evanston (1910), and at their constitutional convention (1910) at the Chicago Art Institute, attended by some 200 delegates representing 63 local centres, Mrs A. Starr Bast was elected president and proclaimed their goals: 'to stimulate interest in the best drama'; 'to awaken the public to the importance of the theatre as a social force'. The organization expanded rapidly from 12,000 members in 25 states in 1911 to 23,000 members, 100,000 affiliated members, and 114 centres throughout the country by the early 20s. They published a quarterly, *The Drama* (1911), 'to cultivate a deeper understanding and appreciation for American drama and theatre'; issued 250 bulletins (1910–16) endorsing current productions; sponsored tours of the HULL-HOUSE Players, the Irish Players, MINNIE MADDERN FISKE, GEORGE ARLISS and others; published 20 volumes of 'good' plays; conducted summer instructional institutes; and held annual conventions in Chicago, New York, St Louis, Pittsburgh and Detroit. After the national organization was disbanded (1931), local centres continued to function, in particular the New York Drama League which celebrated its 75th anniversary in 1992. In addition to offering a number of major awards, this remnant of the League assists young playwrights and oversees the Directors Fellows Program, which provides young directors with intensive entry-level professional experience. RM

Dramaten The Royal Dramatic Theatre, Stockholm, was founded in 1788 by Gustav III to develop Swedish as a literary language, and to establish a national repertoire. It occupied various premises (a tennis court, the royal arsenal) before acquiring a new theatre in 1863. Until 1842 it enjoyed a 50-year monopoly of spoken drama in the capital. Royal and parliamentary subsidies supported it until 1888, when it was denationalized and run by an association of actors, in strong competition with Albert Ranft's Svenska and Vasa Theatres. Dramaten moved to its present building and regained its subsidies in 1907 and has become one of the world's most celebrated companies, especially under the leadership of PER LINDBERG, OLOF MOLANDER, ALF SJÖBERG and INGMAR BERGMAN. STRINDBERG has been important in the modern repertory, along with IBSEN, BRECHT and O'NEILL, who awarded it several world premieres. In the late 1980s contemporary Swedish writers, such as LARS NORÉN, were encouraged to write for Dramaten. The neighbouring Small Stage opened in 1945, joined in the 1970s and 80s by ancillary performance spaces in the main theatre and in nearby buildings. HL

Dramatic Authors' Society (Britain) The first professional association of British playwrights. Though it may have had an informal existence as early as 1830–1, the Society was properly established in 1833, in parallel with the reform in dramatic COPYRIGHT. Its purpose was to provide the machinery whereby authors' performance fees could be centrally collected for redistribution and to guard against unauthorized performances of members' plays, especially in the provinces, where copyright abuse was common. Among its founders were J. R. PLANCHÉ, DOUGLAS JERROLD and T. J. Serle, the two latter becoming chairman and secretary respectively.

The Society quickly secured the loyalty of many of the most active dramatists of the period and, in its early years, the bookseller-publisher John Miller (described as 'Agent to the Dramatic Authors' Society') of Henrietta Street, Covent Garden, London, acted as publisher for members' plays. Its agency function was gradually refined, and scales of performance fees relative to the popularity and length of plays were issued for the convenience of theatre managers. The Society was perhaps at its strongest in the 1850s and 60s, when it fulfilled the function of professional club as well as commercial organization, with nearly every playwright of note as a member. In 1865 more than 2000 plays were under its protection. By then it had agents all over the country to report on copyright infringements of members' plays. But it failed to move with the times, lacking sufficient commercial dynamism on behalf of its membership in the resurgent theatre of the 1870s. A number of high-flying playwrights like DION BOUCICAULT and W. S. GILBERT, who were making substantial sums in performance fees quite independently of the Society's system and tariff, quit in frustration.

Decline was relatively swift. In January 1883 the Dramatic Authors' Society ceased to exist as an agency for fee collection, and it faded away entirely in 1884, when it was said to have merged with the newly established Society of Authors. In fact this much more powerful body effectively consumed it. Dramatic authors had no separate voice in the literary establishment until HENRY ARTHUR JONES took up the chairmanship of the dramatic sub-committee in 1897, and it was 1908 before dramatists had a fully fledged dramatic section set up within the Society of Authors, embracing most British playwrights of any standing. JRS

dramatic theory Most theorists of drama agree that one of their tasks is to define dramatic theory itself. In many instances, the agreement stops there because individual theorists often hold divergent views of both theory and drama. This is not to say that dramatic theory ought to be, or even could be, done without. Anyone arguing against dramatic theory would have to make some general statements about theory, drama, and their proper relationship (if any). He or she would thus add arguments to the growing body of dramatic theory which, for the purpose of these comments, may be defined as follows: systematically generalizing discourse about the nature and function of plays, about their genres, modes and styles, and about their production by performers and reception by readers or spectators including theorists and other critics.

Such a broad definition is needed if we are to account for both guises in which drama can appear to its audience. Some theorists view the text, others the performance, as a play's ultimate reality. In both camps, however, there tends to be sufficient willingness to heed both the literary and the theatrical dimension of drama. Even the most devout believers in drama as literature hardly ever deny that the potential for being performed sets plays apart from other kinds of literary works. Conversely, even the most fervent proponents of the view that the 'playscript' is a mere recipe for a more or less delicious production stop short of suggesting that the assignment of readings in a drama course is like the serving up of loose leaves from a cookbook at the dinner table. On the evidence of 2500 years of dramatic theory and practice in the West it is reasonable to conclude that plays need not be considered as *either* performable texts *or* scriptable performances. They can be, and usually are, both.

Whether designed for the page or the stage, many plays themselves contain theoretical observations about drama and performance. Since the Roman times of PLAUTUS and TERENCE, prologues and epilogues have proved to be the most convenient dramatic sites for such self-reflective theorizing. But SHAKESPEARE was by no means the only playwright to put elements of dramatic theory into the mouth of a major character, as when Hamlet tells the Players that the theatre's purpose has always been 'to hold, as 'twere, the mirror up to nature'. Hamlet's memorable phrase merely echoes the opinion, often expressed since Plato and ARISTOTLE, that art in general and drama in particular 'imitates' or 'reflects' reality. Yet playwrights have also been known to initiate debates about important theoretical issues, and not only in prefaces, postscripts, or other writings designed to vindicate their own dramatic practice. For example, the contest in Hades between AESCHYLUS and EURIPIDES at the thematic climax of *The Frogs* by ARISTOPHANES foreshadows one of the fundamental dilemmas of later theory: is the playwright's first commitment to morality or reality, is he mainly to improve or to inform his audience?

As subsequent theorists pondered drama's impact on its audience, they often described or prescribed several distinct but combinable goals for the endeavours of playwrights and performers. On the whole, they tended either to share HORACE's view that plays like other poetic constructs may 'benefit' or 'delight' us, or else to agree with Cicero's Renaissance disciple, Bishop Minturno, that plays like other rhetorical constructs should 'instruct, delight, and move' us. CASTELVETRO was a rare exception, and not only among 16th-century theorists, in that he rejected the didactic function of drama altogether, insisting that 'poetry was invented solely to delight and to recreate'.

Disparate rankings of the two or three widely endorsed objectives of drama did, however, occur. In the preface to his edition of Shakespeare's plays, for example, SAMUEL JOHNSON subordinated delight to instruction as a means to an end ('the end of poetry is to instruct by pleasing') without explicit mention of the all-too-human need for motivation. The latter had, however, been stressed two centuries before in PHILIP SIDNEY's *Defense of Poesy*. According to Sidney, the potential achievement of poetry (including drama) is 'of higher degree' than that of philosophy because imaginative works are more adept at the crucial task of 'moving' their audience, yet for any moral teaching to occur and be effective, it is necessary for us 'to be moved with desire to know' and 'to be moved to do that which we know'. Recent proponents of a politically activist theatre (e.g. AUGUSTO BOAL, DARIO FO, ARIANE MNOUCHKINE) hold comparable views even if, following BRECHT, they pay more attention than Sidney to the especially strong motivating power of the theatre to trigger the desired audience response during or after a live performance. The theory and practice of ANTONIN ARTAUD and some of his American followers (e.g. Julian Beck and Judith Malina of the LIVING THEATRE, JOSEPH CHAIKIN and Viola Spolin of the OPEN THEATRE, Richard Schechner of the PERFORMANCE GROUP) in turn demand of the stage an almost hypnotic ability to 'move' performers and spectators alike – not towards specific intellectual, moral or political commitments but, through participatory search for personal liberation, ultimately beyond them.

Plato's rejection of the theatre in the *Republic* and elsewhere was tangential to his summary censure of poets and other artists for imitating transient objects (rather than contemplating eternal ideas) and for exciting the passions (rather than promoting truth, patriotic courage, and the love of justice). By contrast, Aristotle's *Poetics* defended the arts against such charges with frequent and specific reference to tragic drama. He argued that tragedy's skilful representation of events, linked together into a unified action by probability or necessity rather than mere chance, makes it 'more philosophical than history'; and he appears to have held the paradoxically profound view that the tragic poet's artistic arousal of pity and fear serves to purge us – perhaps by clarifying their causes – of the potentially harmful intensity of such emotions. Later theorists have made countless attempts to elucidate Aristotle's key concepts, including the two just mentioned: representation (*mimesis*) and purging (*catharsis*). But untutored theatregoers, too, are in the Greek philosopher's debt for a good deal of their pertinent vocabulary. In most languages spoken today in Europe and the Americas, even informal conversations about plays and productions heavily rely on words whose ancient Greek prototypes prominently figure in the *Poetics*: theatre and drama, tragedy and comedy, poet and critic, scene and rhythm, to name a few. Aristotle did not coin any of those terms, but his usage contributed greatly to establishing their future currency.

The extant text of the *Poetics* is terse, fragmentary, and enigmatic in several respects. Yet no single work has had a comparable commanding influence on almost all subsequent theorizing about plays the vast majority of which was, of course, unknown to its author. Needless to say, the critical tradition has been appropriating Aristotle according to its historically changing needs and circumstances. Following Robortello, some neoclassical theorists of the 16th and 17th centuries were to derive, for instance, ironclad rules of the 'unity of time' from Aristotle's empirical observation that 'tragedy attempts, as far as possible, to remain within one circuit of the sun or, at least, not to depart from this by much'. Some pre-romantic and romantic critics of the 18th and early 19th centuries (e.g. La Motte, A. W. SCHLEGEL, Coleridge) were in turn so dissatisfied with their predecessors' 'mechanical' application of supposedly Aristotelian rules that they even replaced Aristotle's explicit demand for the unity of dramatic action by what they felt was a more flexible and more natural organizing principle: the unity (or totality) of 'interest'.

The major spokesmen for the various 'isms' of the late 19th and early 20th centuries (the naturalist ZOLA, the symbolist MAETERLINCK, the futurist MARINETTI, the surrealist Apollinaire, the expressionist Pinthus, and the dadaist Tzara, for example (see NATURALISM; SYMBOLISM; FUTURISM; SURREALISM; EXPRESSIONISM)) neither used nor abused the *Poetics* as a frequent point of reference in their respective manifestos. Yet few theorists today doubt that Aristotle's overview of the principles of Greek drama has considerable relevance to the analysis and evaluation of most later plays as well. His preference for heroes that are neither completely virtuous nor completely evil is one good example. His insistence on the desirability of connecting the tragic figure's conduct and his or her fate through some grave 'error', 'transgression' or 'flaw' (*hamartia*) is another. Still more impressive is the degree to which some of the most basic conceptual tools of all later theorizing about drama have been anticipated by Aristotle's magisterially simple delineation of the 'six parts' of tragedy: plot (*mythos*), character (*ethos*), thought (*dianoia*), diction (*lexis*), music (*melos*) and spectacle (*opsis*).

Five of the six Greek terms on the list are clearly recognizable ancestors of modern English and foreign words (myth, ethics, lexicon, melody, and optics, for example). All six Aristotelian concepts, however, relate to what still appear to be the most essential components of a performed play. The first three concepts encompass three aspects of the fictive world represented by a dramatic text or performance: what is done ('plot'), by and to whom ('character'), and why ('thought' as the characters' reasonings or as the playwright's and director's thematic message). The last three in turn apply to three aspects of theatrical world-making whose chief vehicles are, indeed, either verbal ('diction') or nonverbal and either acoustic (sometimes even 'musical') or visual (sometimes even 'spectacular').

Of the six categories, the first two have received privileged attention from both Aristotle – he called plot 'the soul of tragedy' – and the majority of later theorists. As a rule, 'plot' has prompted structural explorations in quasi-Aristotelian terms such as exposition, complication, denouement; deserved or undeserved suffering; rising or falling action; conflict, suspense, change of fortune; crisis,

climax, reversal and catastrophe. 'Character' has in turn been approached most frequently from the vantage point of the theorist's own system of psychology and morality. Theories of 'thought' (or theme) usually address the spiritual or ideological implications of drama and the sociopolitical relationship between a play's world and the worldview of its author or audience. Primary concern with 'diction' prompts theorists to stress the literary aspects of drama, while close study of 'music' and 'spectacle' (in the extended sense of the words as the acoustic and visual features of an actual or imagined production) points them towards every play's theatrical dimension. The last two 'parts' were relatively neglected by Aristotle but take centre stage among theorists of the OPERA, ballet, the PANTOMIME, the cinema, and various forms of unscripted theatre (including 'happenings' and other types of partially improvised performance in both literate and oral cultures).

Theories of staging – whether articulated or merely implied – likewise vary in orientation. They may be principally geared towards a unified plot of human interaction (STANISLAVSKY's atmospheric ensemble style); towards a few highlighted characters (the almost exclusive attention paid to 'leading men' and 'leading ladies' in some periods and many histories of acting); towards the direct communication of thought to the audience (Brechtian *Verfremdung*, or estrangement); towards the unimpeded enactment of diction (JACQUES COPEAU's almost 'bare boards' on which highly literate actors declaim the precious lines of dramatic masterpieces); towards the lavish forthpouring of nonverbal or partly verbal sound (the practice, if not the theory, of most operatic performances); or else towards the markedly non-literary creation of an imaginative visual design (GORDON CRAIG's artistic sets and light effects and his proposed reduction of each performer to a masked *Über-Marionette*). In pure theory it seems possible and desirable to achieve a 'total work of art' through the mutual enhancement of all relevant components (RICHARD WAGNER's operatic *Gesamtkunstwerk*) or through their mutual subordination (JERZY GROTOWSKI's 'poor theatre'). In actual practice, however, the attention of most spectators (and of most theorists) is likely to remain riveted to just one of the six 'parts' as the dominant factor in a particular performance (or in a certain type of drama or production). The acknowledgment of such dominance need not lead to theoretical claims for absolute supremacy, of course. In most plays and performances, each 'part' significantly contributes to drama's representation of a world and its communication of a worldview.

Theorists seeing drama chiefly as communication aspire to varying degrees of precision as they explore just who does the communicating. Many assume that author and director – the ultimate senders of the dramatic 'message' – are absent from each part of the play while present in its total design by way of implication. For most purposes, the view expressed by Stephen Dedalus in Joyce's *Portrait of the Artist as a Young Man* is accurate enough: the playwright, 'like the God of the creation, remains within or behind or beyond or above his handiwork, invisible, refined out of existence, paring his fingernails'. On closer inspection, however, the image of an absent deity appears to do better justice to the director's role in individual performances than to the actual or implied author's concrete ubiquity in the text of his or her play. In their search for the concealed author, various modern theorists have been concentrating on a number of different components and aspects of drama in and through which that elusive spirit may have assumed material existence after all: stage directions and poetic diction (Roman Ingarden), Greek chorus and Elizabethan soliloquy (Una Ellis-Fermor), prologues, epilogues, narrator figures, and other devices of an EPIC THEATRE (Peter Szondi). Somewhat more impressionistically, T. S. ELIOT in *The Three Voices of Poetry* even wondered whether Macbeth's speech beginning 'Tomorrow and to-morrow and to-morrow' especially moves us because 'Shakespeare and Macbeth are uttering the words in unison'.

A similar interplay of presence and absence has long been discerned in the representation of characters: each human participant in the action evoked by a performed play is, at the same time, magically present in and tantalizingly absent from the performer of the role. To give a particular example, the man we see on the stage is *neither* Hamlet *nor* LAURENCE OLIVIER but Olivier *as* Hamlet, which means that both character and performer simultaneously are and are not what they seem to be. To be sure, actors and actresses are merely implied when a play is being read rather than performed. Yet readers of a dramatic text imaginatively substitute their minds and bodies for the 'missing' performers whose assigned roles they enact on the mental stage of their reading experience. Theories of acting thus have considerable bearing on our understanding of the reception of printed drama as well. When, for disparate reasons of their own, Horace and Stanislavsky recommend – while DIDEROT and Brecht reject – the performer's emotional identification with his or her role, they thereby propose or presuppose very different methods of properly playing the implied reader's role. As a result, they also offer quite different views of drama as the textual basis of various kinds, degrees or mixtures of empathy and distance.

Distinguishing among different kinds of plays tends to be an important part of theorizing about them. Often enough, the contrast outlined by Aristole between TRAGEDY and COMEDY has served as the principal model for drawing generic distinctions. Since the extant portions of the *Poetics* say far too little about comedy, some aspects of the contrast had to be reconstructed or constructed by other theorists in the light of Greek and later examples of comic drama. In any event, tragedy and comedy have remained the conceptual poles between which many sparks of genre criticism have been generated even beyond the confines of dramatic literature. For example, elementary observations about plot structure – happy *versus* unhappy ending – sufficed for Dante and Chaucer to subsume narrative texts under their respective concepts of comedy and tragedy. The majority of more recent, and usually more complex, attempts at defining the 'essence' or 'spirit' of tragedy and comedy likewise point beyond drama and the theatre in their theoretical implications. Even in middle-brow conversations, it is not uncommon to characterize the mood of poems and novelsor paintings and symphoniesas either 'tragic' or 'comic' (sometimes

called 'comedic' to avoid the connotation of being unintentionally laughable).

The experience of tragic and comic drama has prompted numerous profound thinkers to evolve elaborate explanations as to why we find the contemplation both of grave suffering and risible levity both pleasurable and edifying. To name just a few, Plato, Augustine, Descartes, Hobbes, Hume, Kant, Schopenhauer, NIETZSCHE, Bergson and Freud all have addressed at least one side of the puzzling fact that humans are rather proud of being able to indulge themselves in certain kinds of tears and laughter. It is, however, in Hegel's posthumously published lectures on aesthetics that tragedy and comedy have received their most ambitiously systematic treatment. In brief, Hegel sees drama as the art form best suited to make visible the dialectical truth that the universal World Spirit or Ethical Substance exists dispersed in a multiplicity of particular beings and conflicting values. Tragedy (especially the kind of Greek tragedy exemplified in SOPHOCLES' *Antigone*) shows the ultimate victory of the undivided Substance over the human representatives of particular and thus one-sided moralities. When both Creon, who embodies the principle of the state, and Antigone, who stands for the principle of family, are crushed we pity each doomed hero and fear the ethical principle he or she has violated by embracing an equally divine yet momentarily opposed principle. Comedy in turn asserts the subjective right of what *is* by declining to relate it too closely to what *should* be, that is, to the objective goals of the Ethical Substance. In particular, the comedies of Aristophanes and Shakespeare show the victory of the 'serene subjectivity' of individuals who are able to laugh at themselves as their more substantive aspirations (should they have any at all) remain unfulfilled.

Hegel's views of tragedy and comedy have been received with much admiration, as well as irritation, by later critics who have not stopped offering their own new perspectives on that old, and somewhat odd, couple. Susanne K. Langer's *Feeling and Form* may well contain the best-known 20th-century attempt by a philosopher to interrelate tragedy and comedy. Langer considers the two 'great dramatic forms' not only in the more conventional terms of a 'tragic theme' (guilt leading to expiation) and a 'comic theme' (vanity leading to exposure). Rather, she argues that tragic and comic works bear the marks of one of two fundamental 'rhythms' of life; they contrast the human awareness of individuation and death to the survival of species. While comedy exhibits the vital rhythm of nature's self-preservation, tragedy imprints on the dramatized events the rhythm of self-consummation – the 'death-ward advance' of multicellular life through the irreversible phases of growth, maturity and decline.

Throughout the centuries, quite a few playwrights have reacted to the constraining tragic–comic dichotomy by turning into theorists of various alternatives. In the prologue to his *Amphitruo*, Plautus made the god Mercury (disguised as a slave) call the play a 'tragicomedy' because such traditionally tragic figures as gods and kings and such comic figures as slaves would appear in it. With different arguments (and under different historical circumstances) GUARINI, FLETCHER and HUGO also spoke out in favour of their respective versions of a 'mixed' genre.

DRYDEN, Diderot, BEAUMARCHAIS and GOETHE were in turn among the many playwrights who wished to fill what may be called the dramatic gap between tragedy and comedy by contributing to the theory and practice of such 'middle' categories as the heroic play, *le genre sérieux, le drame*, or *das Schauspiel*. More recently, DÜRRENMATT, IONESCO and PINTER were among the numerous modern authors claiming that there isn't, or need not be, any essential difference between tragedy and comedy. By contrast, ARTHUR MILLER insisted on his *Death of a Salesman* being a tragedy even though the play had not met some critics' expectations as to the social status and intellectual stature of its central character. In 'Tragedy and the Common Man' Miller argues that for tragic feeling to be aroused in us it is sufficient that a character be 'ready to lay down his life to secure his sense of personal dignity'. Recalling that Miller gave the first name 'Willy' and the last name 'Loman' to his tragic antihero, one might sum up his position as follows: *man*, however *low*, can rise to tragic height if he has the *will* to do so. Among earlier defenders of bourgeois or even working-class tragedy, FRIEDRICH HEBBEL may have anticipated Miller's argument most closely when he suggested that all tragedy, whether 'high' or 'low', exemplifies some universal human conflict through a significant clash of individual wills.

Major modern attempts to account for and then transcend the tragic–comic polarity include Northrop Frye's *Anatomy of Criticism* and ERIC BENTLEY's *The Life of the Drama*. According to Frye's view of tragedy, similar acts of 'narrowing a comparatively free life into a process of causation' are performed by Macbeth when he accepts the logic of usurpation, by Hamlet when he accepts the logic of abdication. The typical plot structure of comedy reverses the process and leads the hero out of bondage into a 'stable and harmonious order' which, at the end of most comic works, turns out to have been only temporarily 'disrupted by folly, obsession, forgetfulness, "pride and prejudice" '. Frye's theory goes well beyond drama in its range of cross-disciplinary reference and textual illustrations; he uses the terms tragedy and comedy (as well as romance and SATIRE) to designate narrative categories 'broader than, or logically prior to, literary genres'. Modelled on mythic narratives rather than their 'displaced' literary or dramatic versions, the four 'pre-generic' story patterns represent archetypal movements within a highly desirable world (romance), within a painfully defective world (satire), downward from innocence through hamartia to catastrophe (tragedy), or upward from the threatening complications of the fallen world of experience to 'a general assumption of post-dated innocence in which everyone lives happily ever after' (comedy).

Bentley favours a more theatrical fivesome of generic types: MELODRAMA, FARCE, tragedy, comedy and TRAGICOMEDY. While melodrama derives its basic formula – innocence surrounded by malevolence – from 'more or less paranoid phantasies', farce reveals the fierce pleasure of aggression with which 'innocence' retaliates. Tragedy thwarts our impulse to identify with innocence and exacts identification with the hero's guilt, thereby promoting self-knowledge instead of melodrama's wishful gratification of the ego. Comedy also promotes self-knowledge when, unlike farce, it makes us face the misery of the human condition before it allows us 'to look the other way'. As for tragicomedy, Bentley distinguishes two kinds. The first is, really, 'tragedy with a comic sequel' (e.g. Shakespeare's *Measure for Measure* and Goethe's *Faust*); it celebrates forgiveness instead of tragic justice, which is a higher form of melodramatic revenge. In the second and more harrowing strain of this complex genre, dark and bitter comedy either refuses 'to look the other way' (e.g. IBSEN's *The Wild Duck*) or else permeates the entire play with the grotesquely zestful despair of 'gallows humour' (e.g. BECKETT's *Waiting for Godot*).

Most 20th-century critics addressing the question of dramatic kinds subscribe to Frye's view that 'the purpose of criticism by genres is not so much to classify as to clarify traditions and affinities, thereby bringing out a large number of literary relationships that would not be noticed as long as there were no context established for them'. For better or worse, however, the majority of playwrights, directors and theorists today show relatively little explicit interest in problems of genre. Perhaps because nature abhores a vacuum, two other concerns have begun to hold sway in the dramatic theory of the last decades. The first prompts structuralist-semiological scrutinies of how everything in the theatre – the text, the performer, the decor, the music, and so forth – functions as a constructed sign of something else. The second leads to hermeneutic-phenomenological studies of how all those things, while functioning as decodable signs, manage to retain their phenomenal thingness or existentially interpretable humanity.

Readers wishing to explore both approaches and to become acquainted with the views of some influential and current proponents of each should consult the books by Keir Elam, Bert O. States, and Bruce Wilshire listed below. Some vital issues raised in those books are not restricted to 'dramatic theory' as defined at the beginning of this discussion. But this is precisely what we should expect. Theatrical enactment shares its reliance on semiotic codes and hermeneutic horizons not only with ceremonies, rituals, sporting events and the like. Our ordinary acts of self-presentation in the socially assigned roles of daily life must likewise be decoded and interpreted. Recognizing their mutual affinities, philosophy, psychology, sociology, anthropology and other human sciences have in recent years been interacting with dramatic theory very forcefully indeed. As a result, each alert participant in the ongoing cross-disciplinary dialogue has become increasingly aware of the many ways in which every stage is a world and in which, as Shakespeare's Jaques has put it, 'all the world's stage' (*As You Like It*).

In addition to the approaches cited above there is now a developing body of thought which is considering the implications for dramatic theory arising out of the work of French post-structuralist thinkers such as Michel Foucault, Jean-François Lyotard, Julia Kristeva, HÉLÈNE CIXOUS and Jacques Derrida. This work reviews the key dramatic classifications of plot, character and narrative structure, offered by Aristotle as the organizing principles of dramatic material, and critiques these categories as forms of closure held in place by the concept of a 'knowing' but elusive author. The post-structuralist approach turns on its head the notion that art reflects life and follows

Nietzsche's famous dictum that man 'has himself become a work of art'. To follow the implications of this about-turn is to ask the reader or spectator to renounce his search for the hidden profundity of authorial intent in dramatic literature, and to focus rather upon the play of textured surfaces which offers a proliferation of meaning in place of Aristotelian containment. Thus, the denial of the fixed and knowing subject in dramatic literature opens up the possibility of the creative spectator who participates in the theatrical urge to create and re-create identity by willing a relationship to the text which is premised upon doubt and an awareness of the wholly provisional category of the 'I' which speaks and acts upon the world.

For those interested in exploring this complex, and often perilous, area of dramatic theory, the work of Blau, Phelan and Barker (see below) will be useful as an introduction. PHE AP

See: Aristotle's Poetics, trans. L. Golden, commentary O. B. Hardison Jr, Englewood Cliffs, NJ, 1968; H. Barker, Arguments for a Theatre, Manchester, 1993; E. Bentley, The Life of the Drama, New York, 1967; H. Blau, To All Appearances: Ideology and Performance, London, 1992; M. Carlson, Theories of the Theatre: A Historical and Critical Survey, from the Greeks to the Present, Ithaca, NY, 1984; K. Elam, The Semiotics of Theatre and Drama, London, 1980; N. Frye, Anatomy of Criticism, Princeton, NJ, 1957; S. Greenblatt, Renaissance Self-Fashioning from More to Shakespeare, Chicago, 1980; G. W. F. Hegel, Philosophy of Fine Art, trans. F. P. B. Osmaston, London, 1920; P. Hernadi, Beyond Genre: New Directions in Literary Classification, Ithaca, NY, 1972; S. K. Langer, Feeling and Form, New York, 1953; P. Phelan, Unmarked: The Politics of Performance, London, 1993; B. O. States, Great Reckonings in Little Rooms: On the Phenomenology of Theatre, Berkeley, Calif., 1985; J. Willett (ed.), Brecht on Theatre, New York, 1964; B. Wilshire, Role Playing and Identity: The Limits of Theatre as Metaphor, Bloomington, Indiana, 1982.

Draper, Ruth 1884–1956 American actress and monologuist. Draper created and performed a repertoire of 54 different characters in some 35 sketches. The range of personalities that she assumed was broad, as was the scope of her travels and reputation. In addition to accolades for her finely wrought characterizations of women of all ages, types and cultures she received plaudits for her ability to evoke throngs of other 'unseen' characters. Before her professional debut in 1920, at the Aeolian Hall, London, she had been perfecting her craft before family, friends and charity audiences. In the three and a half decades that followed, she performed almost non-stop, on every continent, and often at the command of royalty. Her letters, edited by Neilla Warren, were published in 1979. DBW

Dresden Court Theatre The first record of performances in Dresden dates from 1585, when the ENGLISCHE KOMÖDIANTEN visited the court. In the late 17th century, JOHANNES VELTEN was employed with some regularity at the Dresden court. Operatic and dramatic performances continued regularly throughout the 18th century, but the high point in the Court Theatre's history was the long intendancy of August von Lüttichau (1785–1863), which

lasted from 1824 to 1862. During these years Dresden became known as the theatre where the WEIMAR STYLE was most assiduously cultivated. From 1831 until his death in 1872, EMIL DEVRIENT was an idolized member of the company, though his pre-eminence was challenged between 1853 and 1864, when BOGUMIL DAWISON was also in the company. In 1841, the Dresden Court Theatre was housed in a splendid new theatre designed by Gottfried Semper, which was in use until its destruction in the Second World War. The restored theatre was reopened in 1985. SW

Dressler, Marie [Leila Koerber] 1869–1934 Canadian comedienne, daughter of an itinerant musician. At 14 she joined the Nevada STOCK COMPANY playing ingénues, but her mastiff-like features and stocky build soon relegated her to farcical roles. She entered New York VAUDEVILLE with coon songs and impersonations, and had a real success as the MUSIC-HALL singer Flo Honeydew in the comic opera The Lady Slavey (1896). JOSEPH WEBER invited her to join his company in Higgledy-Piggledy (1904). Her most memorable role was the day-dreaming boarding-house drudge Tillie Blobbs, in Tillie's Nightmare (Herald Square Theatre, 1910), singing 'Heaven Will Protect the Working Girl'. This led to a film contract with Mack Sennett for Tillie's Punctured Romance (1914), in which she was wooed by Charlie Chaplin; but she never flourished in

An advertising card for Marie Dressler in Tillie's Nightmare, on tour 1910.

silent pictures. She was prominent in the Liberty Loan drives of 1917–18 and the actors' strike of 1919, but reached such a low ebb in her career by 1927 that she contemplated opening an hotel in Paris. Fortuitously she returned to Hollywood and won a new public with *Anna Christie* (1930), *Dinner at Eight* and *Tugboat Annie* (both 1933). Her autobiography appeared in 1934.   LS

Drew–Barrymore family The name Barrymore, with Lionel, Ethel and John its foremost exponents, stands as a synonym for acting. Franklin Delano Roosevelt was called 'a newsreel Barrymore'; Mahatma Gandhi was 'the Barrymore of the talking newspapers'. *Time* magazine coined 'Barrymorishly' to describe how Ethel held the stage. Thirty years after she, the last of the triumvirate, died in 1959, the Barrymores remain the undisputed royal family of a kingdom called BROADWAY.

Their theatrical pedigree is genuine, traceable to 1752 and, according to family tradition, to strolling players in Shakespeare's time. Their maternal grandmother, **Mrs John Drew** (1820–97), was born Louisa Lane in London to Thomas Frederick Lane, an actor of some provincial fame, and Eliza Trenter, a sweet singer of ballads. After her father's early death, the child toured provincial theatres, playing such roles as Prince Agib in *Timour, the Tartar*, before sailing for America with her mother. After playing such roles as the Duke of York to JUNIUS BRUTUS BOOTH's Richard III and Albert to EDWIN FORREST's William Tell (10 years later, she would graduate to Lady Macbeth opposite Forrest's Thane), she made her debut as a child star in 1828, playing Little Pickle in *The Spoiled Child* and five characters in *Twelve Precisely*.

In 1850, after a distinguished adolescent and adult career, she married her third husband, **John Drew** (1827–62), whose father managed NIBLO's Garden in New York. Famous for such popular Irish characters as Dr O'Toole (*The Irish Tenor*) and Tim O'Brian (*The Irish Immigrant*) and SHAKESPEARE's Andrew Aguecheek and Dromio, Drew briefly managed Philadelphia's National and ARCH STREET Theatres. Mrs Drew undertook the management of the Arch in 1861, one year before her husband's untimely death. During 30 subsequent years at the helm, she essentially contributed to the achievement and acceptance of theatre in America, while continuing to act, by popular demand, in such roles as Mrs Malaprop and Mistress Quickly.

Two of her children by Drew began illustrious careers at the Arch. **John Drew** (1853–1927) trained under his mother's stern supervision before joining AUGUSTIN DALY's FIFTH AVENUE THEATRE company in New York (1875). Among his most popular old and new COMEDY parts were Orlando, Petruchio and Charles Surface. By the mid-1800s, he and his fellow Fifth Avenue players, ADA REHAN, James Lewis and Mrs G.H. Gilbert, were called 'the Big Four'. In 1892, Drew agreed to star for manager CHARLES FROHMAN at the unheard-of salary of $500 per week. Following his sensational debut in *The Masked Ball*, his naturalistic acting (see NATURALISM), elegant bearing and sartorial correctness won him the uncontested title 'First Gentleman of the American Stage' and kept him a reigning star for 35 years.

Georgiana Drew (1856–93), after a strict Arch Street

apprenticeship, followed her older brother to the Fifth Avenue in 1876. She made an immediate hit with her breezy manner and unique way of tossing lines like nosegays to an audience – a technique that established her as a popular comedienne in such subsequent hits as *The Senator* (1889) with WILLIAM H. CRANE and *Settled Out of Court* (1892) with Frohman's Comedians. Her Fifth Avenue debut, in Daly's popular *Pique*, cast her opposite a young newcomer from England, **Maurice Barrymore** (1847–1905), whom she married in 1876.

The son of a British district commissioner in India, Barrymore left Oxford, became amateur middle-weight boxing champion of England, changed his name from Herbert Blyth to spare his proper family, and tried acting. After his 1872 debut at the Theatre Royal, Windsor, he toured the provincial theatres for three years before sailing for America. His early years there were distinguished by successive inclusion in the companies of America's foremost managers: Augustin Daly, LESTER WALLACK and A. M. PALMER. His striking beauty, sharp wit and carefree manner made him a popular matinée idol and a sought-after leading man. His most successful characterizations included Orlando (particularly opposite HELENA MODJESKA), and the title roles in *A Man of the World* and *Captain Swift* (1888), which reviewers considered his 'Monte Cristo' – a role in which he, like JAMES O'NEILL as the count, might have toured profitably for years. But Barrymore's volatile temperament and profligate ways precluded such security. Although three of the eight plays he wrote – *Reckless Temple*, *Roaring Dick & Co* and *Nadjezda* – also were potentially durable vehicles, the author never exploited them. He died of paresis at the age of 58, deranged and unfulfilled, leaving a legacy of three children by Georgie Drew.

Ethel Barrymore (1879–1959) became the first of the three siblings to achieve stardom. At the age of 21, after six years of apprenticeship with her grandmother, her uncle John Drew, and SIR HENRY IRVING in England, her name went above the title during the Broadway run of *Captain Jinks of the Horse Marines* in 1901. Under the astute management of Charles Frohman, she became a darling of *fin-de-siècle* society on two continents. The term 'glamour girl' was coined for her, and sons of American millionaires and English peers courted her. Declining Winston Churchill's proposal of marriage, she explained, 'I didn't think I could live up to his world. My world was the theatre.' Her world remained the theatre, as 'Ethel Barrymore vehicles' such as *Alice-Sit-by-the-Fire*, *Cousin Kate*, *Lady Frederick* and *Déclassé* alternated with the stronger stuff of *A Doll's House*, *The Second Mrs Tanqueray*, *The Constant Wife*, Lady Teazle, Camille, Portia and Juliet. By birth she was queen of the royal family; by achievement, with regal bearing and fluid style, she became the First Lady of the American Theatre – a fact underscored in 1928 when the SHUBERTS opened on West 47th Street the intimate (1100 seats) Ethel Barrymore Theatre, with Ethel interpreting three ages of woman in *The Kingdom of God*. After the climax of her stage career in *The Corn Is Green* (1940), she opted for lucrative, less taxing film work until her death in Hollywood two months before her 80th birthday.

Her older brother, **Lionel Barrymore** (1878–1954), began

acting at 15 under the tutelage of his grandmother and his uncle **Sidney Drew** (1868-1919); Sidney was Mrs Drew's illegitimate son – probably by Robert Craig, an actor in her Arch Street company. Sidney became a noted stage and VAUDEVILLE comedian, usually opposite his first wife, Gladys Rankin, daughter of actor-manager ARTHUR MCKEE RANKIN, and his actress wife Kitty Blanchard. Lionel, in support of his uncle John Drew in *The Mummy and the Humming Bird* (1903), excelled in the small role of an Italian organ grinder without speaking a word of English. His inspired gift for characterization flourished in several subsequent productions – notably as boxer Kid Garvey in *The Other Girl* (1904), written for him by his father's friend AUGUSTUS THOMAS. But in 1906, Lionel retreated to France with his first wife, Doris Rankin (Gladys's sister), to indulge his first love – painting. Three years later they returned to America and what Lionel called 'the family curse' – acting. Interspersed with his pioneer acting in the 'flickers' from 1912, his foremost stage vehicles – *The Copperhead* (1917), *The Claw* (1921) and *Laugh, Clown, Laugh* (1923) – were eclipsed by two co-starring ventures with his brother: *Peter Ibbetson* (1917) and *The Jest* (1919). 'To the future of such actors,' predicted the *New York Times*, 'it is impossible to set any limits.' But after the failure of his *Macbeth* in 1921 and a series of mediocre plays, Lionel turned irrevocably to Hollywood. The elder Barrymore became acting's unchallenged Grand Old Man after nearly 200 film roles – the last 40 played in excruciating rheumatic pain, but with no less power, on crutches or in a wheelchair until his death at the age of 76.

His younger brother, **John Barrymore** (1882-1942), was more resistant to acting. After a brief stint as a newspaper illustrator, he half-heartedly pursued, with the help of family and friends, a career as a stage comedian, while whole-heartedly pursuing debutantes and chorus girls. (Among his conquests in the former category: Katherine Harris, who became his first wife in 1913; in the latter, Evelyn Nesbit and Irene Fenwick, who later became Lionel's second wife.) Then, after a run of light comedy roles like *The Fortune Hunter* (1909), John stunned critics and theatregoers with his expert delineations of tragic roles in *Justice* (1916) and *Redemption* (1918). He followed them with two of the theatre's towering achievements: the ARTHUR HOPKINS–ROBERT EDMOND JONES productions of *Richard III* (1920) and *Hamlet* (1922), illuminated by his poetic beauty, vocal grandeur and subtle strength. 'The new prince was entering his kingdom,' observed Hopkins. But at the height of his powers, touted as America's greatest actor, the crown prince of the royal family abdicated. He left the stage for films, returning only once after alcohol and self-indulgence had diminished his talents, playing a parody of himself in a travesty of a play (*My Dear Children*, 1939) three years before his death at 60.

Artistry and industry, combined with the colour and glamour of their private lives, earned the Barrymores a unique niche in the annals of American theatre. Subsequent Drew–Barrymore generations have pursued theatrical careers with considerably less distinction. Ethel's three children from her marriage to socialite Russell Colt made attempts: two sons, half-heartedly; a daughter, **Ethel Barrymore Colt** (1912-77), with some success, particularly as an OPERA singer and acting teacher.

John's daughter **Diana** (1921-60), by his second wife, socialite-poetess Michael Strange, had a brief, promising acting career curtailed by excesses similar to those of her father. John's only son (by his third wife, actress Dolores Costello), known as John Barrymore Jr or **John Drew Barrymore** (1932-), also sacrificed a promising screen and stage career to alcohol, drugs and self-indulgence. But his daughter, named appropriately **Drew Barrymore** (1975-), gained stardom, as her great-great-grandmother Mrs Drew had, at the age of seven in the film *E.T.* (1982) and, despite a teenage bout with alcohol and drugs, continues in the 1990s to appear in films.   JK-D

Drinkwater, John [John Darnley] 1882-1937 British dramatist, director, poet and biographer. Drinkwater is best-known for his part in the revival of poetic drama, although he made a more lasting contribution to the theatre as a founder member of BARRY JACKSON's Pilgrim Players and as the first general manager of the BIRMINGHAM REPERTORY THEATRE. There he directed over 60 productions as well as acting under the stage name of Darnley. He experimented with MASQUES before writing his first full-length play, *Rebellion* (1914), an allegorical attack on Victorian morality. This was followed by *The Storm* (1915), inspired by SYNGE's *Riders to the Sea*, but after his bitter lament against war, *X=O: A Night of the Trojan War* (1917), he abandoned verse. His most successful work was in historical drama, in particular *Abraham Lincoln* (1918), though he also wrote a popular comedy, *Bird in Hand* (1927), the first play in which PEGGY ASHCROFT and LAURENCE OLIVIER played major roles.   CI

Drottningholm Slottsteater As a summer palace of the Swedish kings, Drottningholm had temporary theatres from at least the 1740s, and from 1753 a permanent playhouse for Italian OPERA and French drama. After fire destroyed this in 1762, Carl Fredrik Adelcrantz designed the present building, which opened in 1766. Its stage is extremely deep, with elaborate Italianate machinery by Donato Stopani: wing-chariots, a glory, movable traps and cloud and wave machines. The auditorium, adjustable in size, is itself a painted setting, matching the illusory world on stage.

The theatre's most brilliant era was the reign of Gustav III (1771-92), when the royal opera and acting companies spent the summers there. After his assassination, it fell into disuse (which paradoxically ensured its survival), until rediscovered in 1921, miraculously preserved, with about 30 complete 18th-century settings by such artists as CARLO BIBIENA and Louis Jean Desprez. Since 1922 it has staged summer seasons of 18th-century opera and dance, and its present director, Elisabeth Söderström, is working to recover its original repertoire and performance styles.   HL

Drury Lane, Theatre Royal (London) For nearly two centuries, any of the four buildings erected along the network of narrow streets including Drury Lane, Bridges Street and Catharine Street could reasonably have claimed to be London's leading theatre. The first, generally known as the Theatre Royal, Bridges Street, opened in 1663 with a performance of JOHN FLETCHER's

The Humorous Lieutenant. It was a small theatre (capacity c.700), built at the behest of THOMAS KILLIGREW to house the King's Men, one of the two companies licensed by Royal Patent to perform the legitimate drama in the city of Westminster. A strong company included Charles Hart, Michael Mohun and, for a while after 1665, NELL GWYN. It was destroyed by fire early in 1672.

A second theatre, probably designed by Sir Christopher Wren, opened in 1674. Its foundations are still visible under the present stage. The building was rectangular, 114 feet in length. Nine rows of backless pit benches were ringed by boxes on three sides and the stage (c.66 feet from the probably curved front of the apron to the rear wall) in front. There were two galleries, the upper probably open as a 'footman's gallery'. The prominence of the stage doors, two on either side, emphasizes the fact that the action would have been confined to the apron, where it could be illuminated by chandeliers more concentrated than those in the auditorium. The middle section of the stage accommodated the grooves and shutters of the new scene-craft and the rear section was available for 'vistas'. Despite the compact elegance of its design, DRYDEN was not alone in considering this important theatre 'plain built – a bare convenience only'. Restoration audiences preferred the Duke's Men at the rival DORSET GARDEN THEATRE, and Drury Lane experienced three decades of struggle, exacerbated by the unpopularity among actors of the new patentee, Christopher Rich. Its fortunes were restored in 1711, when three actors – Robert Wilks, THOMAS DOGGETT (replaced by BARTON BOOTH in 1713) and COLLEY CIBBER – assumed the active management and ANNE OLDFIELD was in her prime.

But the costs of satisfying public demand for OPERA, ballet, PANTOMIME and scenic spectacle as well as constant novelty in drama were cripplingly high for the Patent theatres, and Drury Lane experienced a series of crises from 1733 to 47, only temporarily alleviated by such outstanding events as CHARLES MACKLIN's startlingly original playing of Shylock (1741) and the debut of DAVID GARRICK in OTWAY's *The Orphan* (1742). It was Garrick himself, in association with JAMES LACY, who inaugurated the greatest years in the whole history of Drury Lane. His long management (1747–76) was a model of combined caution and daring. Although he failed in his attempts to abolish the custom of half-price admission – always an invitation to drink first and make trouble at the theatre afterwards – he succeeded in much else, not least in removing audience members from the stage. But it was in the practices of the stage that Garrick's regime most notably advanced the cause of the British theatre. He took rehearsals seriously, challenged assumptions about individual actors' 'possession' of their roles, treated the texts of the classical repertoire with a new respect and, particularly in association with PHILIP DE LOUTHERBOURG, raised the status of scenic design (see THEATRE DESIGN) and explored the field of STAGE LIGHTING. He surrounded himself with a strong company, including at various times SPRANGER BARRY, Charles Macklin, KITTY CLIVE, PEG WOFFINGTON, SUSANNA CIBBER, HANNAH PRITCHARD and such comedians as Harry Woodward, Ned Shuter and Richard Yates. He was also responsible for the alterations to the interior of the theatre, undertaken by Robert Adam in 1775.

Garrick's unlikely successor was the playwright SHERIDAN, a man temperamentally unsuited to the chores of management. He began well with the production of his own *The School for Scandal* (1777), the most successful opening in the theatre's history. The following year, he engaged John Henderson in an attempt to replace Garrick as well as writing *The Camp*, and in 1779 he produced his last major work, *The Critic*. It was after the damage caused to Drury Lane during the Gordon Riots of 1780 that a detachment of Guards was posted nightly at the theatre, a custom not discontinued until 1896, though insufficient to prevent the attempt on George III's life in 1800. Sheridan's financial problems were eased by the success of SARAH SIDDONS in 1782 and of her brother JOHN PHILIP KEMBLE in 1783. It was to Kemble that Sheridan entrusted the effective management in 1788, but the theatre had so deteriorated that Sheridan decided to demolish it in 1791.

The third Drury Lane, designed by Henry Holland and opened in 1794, was a massive building with a capacity of 3611. Better suited to spectacle than to drama, it marked a low point in theatrical taste. To judge from his last play, *Pizarro* (1799), Sheridan was aware of its limitations. No less aware of Sheridan's limitations, Kemble defected to COVENT GARDEN in 1803, taking Sarah Siddons with him. Increasingly occupied with parliamentary affairs, Sheridan presided over a declining theatre, whose destruction by fire in 1809, notwithstanding the iron safety-curtain proudly exhibited at its opening, threatened him with utter ruin. Whilst a committee of management, ably chaired by the brewer Samuel Whitbread, set about raising funds for rebuilding, the Drury Lane company performed at the LYCEUM from 1809 to 12.

The fourth theatre (original capacity 3060), designed by Benjamin Wyatt, opened in 1812 with a prologue by LORD BYRON and with a performance of *Hamlet* with ROBERT ELLISTON in the title role. The manager was Samuel Arnold, hampered by a committee of well connected amateurs. It was the sensational debut of EDMUND KEAN in 1814 that delayed inevitable financial disaster, the joint fate of both Patent companies in the last decades of their monopoly. For nearly five seasons, Kean reigned supreme, but high living and scandal increasingly damaged him after 1819, the year in which the equally boisterous Elliston became manager of Drury Lane. By 1826, Kean was past his best and Elliston bankrupt. The improvident manager, CHARLES LAMB's 'Great Lessee', had arranged for the addition of the portico in 1820 (John Nash's colonnade would be moved to Drury Lane from Regent Street in 1831) and Samuel Beazley's extensive remodelling of the interior in 1822. Equipped with gas lighting since 1817, the Drury Lane which ruined successive managers until the abolition of the Patent monopoly in 1843 was a superb but costly toy. Even MACREADY's admired attempt to restore it to its place at the head of English drama (1841–3) resulted in a loss to him of about £20,000.

It was as a house of spectacle that Drury Lane survived the vicissitudes of the mid-century, a trend fully endorsed by the famous managements of Sir Augustus Harris (1879–96) and Arthur Collins (1896–1923). Their prosperity was based on sensation drama and the annual pantomime, though both men were hospitable to incursions of high art provided they were profitable. Under

Alfred Butt (1924–31) Drury Lane became the home of the English musical, as it did of the American MUSICAL in the years following the Second World War, with Ivor Novello dominating the years between. A 1980 guide to London theatres described the policy of London's greatest theatre as 'to present top musicals with wide appeal and likely to enjoy long runs'. PT

Dryden, John 1631–1700 English playwright. In the range of his work over 30 years he dominated English drama of the Restoration. Educated at Westminster School and Trinity College, Cambridge, he settled in London in 1657 and worked as a professional writer. Though he wrote, adapted and collaborated on at least 30 plays during this time, they do not represent his greatest achievements as poet nor the best drama of the period. But they are marked by a consistently incisive intelligence and a seriousness that is invigorating. His first play, the comedy *The Wild Gallant*, was a failure at its first performances in 1663 – he revised it in 1668. He collaborated with SIR ROBERT HOWARD on *The Indian Queen* (1664), an attempt to create the new genre of heroic tragedy, depending on the hero's choice between love and honour in an exotic setting. His sequel, *The Indian Emperor* (1665), is a better and fully formed example of the genre, teetering on the edge of bombastic self-PARODY. In 1667 he experimented with mixing heroic TRAGEDY and contemporary COMEDY in *Secret Love*, a form he returned to frequently.

Sir Martin Mar-All, a bright comedy, possibly written with William Cavendish, Duke of Newcastle, marked a shift of allegiance from KILLIGREW's DRURY LANE to DAVENANT's LINCOLN'S INN FIELDS, and he followed it with an adaptation of SHAKESPEARE's *The Tempest*, written with Davenant, playing up the spectacular and creating erotic frissons with new characters to balance Shakespeare's so that Miranda and Caliban each acquire sisters. In 1668 he was appointed Poet Laureate and published his major critical study, *An Essay of Dramatic Poesy*, constructed as a debate on the merits of French and English plays and establishing new principles of neoclassical judgement as applied to English drama. *Tyrannic Love*, on the martyrdom of St Catherine, was performed in 1669 but his largest-scale heroic drama, *The Conquest of Granada*, appeared in two parts in 1670 and 1671. Of his later tragedies, *Aureng-Zebe* (1675) is noticeably more restrained and points towards *All for Love*, a version of Shakespeare's *Antony and Cleopatra*, fully embodying neoclassical unities and morality, to tearful effect. He adapted Milton's *Paradise Lost* into an unperformed and unperformable OPERA, *The State of Innocence* (1677), and produced a blood-filled *Oedipus* with NATHANIEL LEE (1679). Of his comedies, *Marriage à-la-Mode* (1672) is as witty and perceptive as *The Kind Keeper* (1678) is coarse.

In 1685 Dryden became Roman Catholic, and while this earned him prestige under James II he lost the laureateship in 1689 on the accession of William and Mary. His best two plays date from this late period of his work: *Amphitryon* (1690) is a virtuoso retelling of the myth with an energy and lightness of wit that is continually surprising; *Don Sebastian* (1689), for all its comic sub-plot, is a dark and depressing tragedy of a king defeating rebellion but abdicating on discovering himself guilty of incest.

Dryden also wrote operas at this time, notably *King Arthur* (1691) with music by Purcell. He contributed numerous prologues and epilogues to others' plays and frequently engaged in literary pamphleteering on theatrical matters, particularly over SETTLE's *The Empress of Morocco* and Rymer's attack on Shakespeare. PH

Držić, Marin 1508–67 Croatian playwright from Dubrovnik. Educated in Siena, Držić held minor offices in his Adriatic city state, and travelled to Italy and Austria. He plotted the overthrow of patrician rule in Dubrovnik, and solicited Florentine help for the purpose. He died in Venice as an exile, perhaps liquidated by a killing squad sent by Dubrovnik. But between 1548 and 59 Držić was the main animator of amateur theatricals in Dubrovnik, and creator of a small repertoire of PASTORALS and comedies. Some are lost, others are preserved only in incomplete form. Most famous and probably the best of these is *Uncle Maroje*, rediscovered and restaged for the first time by Marko Fotez in Zagreb just before the Second World War. *Uncle Maroje* became a regular feature in the Croat and Yugoslav repertoire, and the national play most frequently produced abroad – in Scandinavia, Eastern Europe, Belgium, Holland, Turkey and America. In *Uncle Maroje*, *Tirena*, *The Farce of Stanac* and *The Miser* Držić fuses the motifs and style of Italian Renaissance drama with local traditions, circumstances and temperament, but instances of melancholy and bitterness occasionally break through the spirit of merriment. DK

Du Maurier, Gerald (Hubert Edward) 1873–1934 British actor-manager, who began his career under FORBES-ROBERTSON and made his reputation with BEERBOHM TREE. Du Maurier specialized in popular drama of the clubland heroes variety (Raffles, Arsène Lupin, Bulldog Drummond), though his most important roles were in the premieres of BARRIE's *The Admirable Crichton* (1902), *Peter Pan* (1904) and *Dear Brutus* (1917). In 1910 he took over the management of Wyndham's Theatre in London, and was knighted in 1922. CI

Du Ryer, Pierre c.1600–58 French dramatist, one of a group of young writers who emerged in the late 1620s in response to the establishment of permanent theatre companies in Paris. His workmanlike output, which evolved from romance-like TRAGICOMEDY, PASTORAL and one interesting COMEDY of manners, *Les Vendanges de Suresnes* (*The Grape Harvest at Suresnes*, 1633), to a more regular, heroic TRAGEDY, as in *Alcionée* (1637) and *Scévole* (1644), which compares well with PIERRE CORNEILLE's Roman plays, is a convenient barometer to trends in dramatic taste at the time. He was elected to the Académie-Française in 1646. DR

Dubé, Marcel 1930– Quebec playwright, poet and novelist. The most prolific and most popular dramatist of the 1950s and 60s, Dubé began writing for Radio-Canada in 1950 and for national television two years later. His first stage play, *Le Bal triste* (*The Sad Ball*), was produced by a troupe he helped found, La Jeune Scène, in 1950, but he first attracted critical acclaim with *Zone*, winning first prize at the Dominion Drama Festival in 1953. This play, highly successful in its televised adaptation the same year, is typical of the first 'hungry' period of Dubé's work, portraying economically and culturally dispossessed urban youth in their defiance of social norms. A second important play from this period is the even more popular *Un Simple Soldat* (*Private Soldier*, 1957), first produced on television, then revised for stage performance in 1958. His mastery of cinematic technique is evident in all his published work: no other Quebec dramatist passes as easily from one medium to the other. His themes and plots are realistic, yet his dialogue is infused with a poetic quality that heightens its symbolic strength, particularly in plays such as *Le Temps des lilas* (*Lilac Time*, 1958), depicting love and disillusion in a decaying urban lodging-house.

Having attained financial success, Dubé's attention turned more to middle-class characters and concerns. In the 1960s his vision remained tragic, in works such as *Bilan* (*The Accounting*, 1960), *Florence* (1960), *Les Beaux Dimanches* (*Fine Sundays*, 1965) and, especially, in *Au Retour des oies blanches* (*The White Geese*, 1966), generally considered his finest play. In the 1970s, despite frequent illness, he turned his hand to comedy, in *L'Été s'appelle Julie* (*The Summer Named Julie*, 1975) and *Dites-le avec des fleurs* (*Say it with Flowers*, 1976), the latter written in collaboration with JEAN BARBEAU. Author of some 50 plays to date, plus a score of radio and television scripts, Dubé dominated his age as no previous Quebec dramatist had done. LED

Dublin Drama League Irish company, founded in 1919 by LENNOX ROBINSON with YEATS's support. Managed by subscribing members, the League was allowed to use the ABBEY stage on Sundays and Mondays, when the Abbey did not play. As a complement to the Abbey's almost wholly Irish repertoire the League presented PIRANDELLO, TOLLER, STRINDBERG, CHEKHOV and ANDREEV. Abbey actors participated with amateurs, including DENIS JOHNSTON. The League was an enthusiastic venture, successfully bringing world drama to a Dublin audience, SEAN O'CASEY among them. The League dissolved itself in 1929, recognizing the legitimate succession of the Edwards–MacLiammóir GATE THEATRE. DM

Dublin International Theatre Festival (Ireland) Begun in 1957 as part of a national annual festival called An Tostal, its purpose was to have plays by Irish and foreign dramatists staged by outstanding local and imported companies. The early years were rocky: clerical objection to O'CASEY and Joyce meant its second year was cancelled. The Festival survived, and, despite modest funding and intermittent financial crises, has managed to become truly international in style and cultural range. It occurs every October and its 40-odd productions have, in recent years, included OPERA, dance, MIME, puppetry and CIRCUS as well as conventional theatre; companies have come from Australia, China, Brazil, Japan, Africa, America and all parts of Europe.

In 1991 the Festival and the GATE THEATRE pulled off a particular coup in staging all of SAMUEL BECKETT's theatre works, several for the first time, over a three-week period. Under Tony O'Dalaigh's leadership, the Festival has also extended into children's and young people's theatre, while continuing to act as a showcase of indigenous theatre work and to host many notable Irish premieres. DM GF

Du Bois, Raoul Pène 1914–85 Staten Island-born American scenic and costume designer. Starting with a single costume design for *The Garrick Gaieties* in 1930, Du Bois went on to pursue a 50-year career designing creative and colourful COSTUMES, imaginative sets and occasional lighting designs. In addition to notable BROADWAY credits, including *Du Barry Was a Lady* (1939), *Sugar Babies* (1979) and *No, No, Nanette* (1971), his costumes and scenery were seen in London and Paris and graced films, ice shows, ballets, nightclubs, aquacades and commercial illustrations. He received Tonys for costumes (*No, No, Nanette*, 1971) and scenery (*Wonderful Town*, 1953). BO

Dubois, René-Daniel 1955– Quebec playwright and actor. Dubois's first play, *Panique à Longueuil* (*Panic in Longueuil*, 1980), fascinated Montreal audiences with its oneiric and Freudian overtones. *Ne blâmez jamais les Bédouins* (*Never Blame the Bedouins*, 1984) was an even greater success, its startling fantasy combining with REALISM of language and action to produce a disturbing, intensely theatrical experience. One of the finest actors of his generation, Dubois himself played all the roles in this work, and the main role in most of his others. *Being at Home with Claude* (1985), dealing with a homosexual's confession to the murder of his lover, is another powerful text, consecrating his status in the front rank of contemporary Quebec dramatists. LED

Ducange, Victor 1783–1833 French novelist and dramatist. Ducange is historically important for his hostility to the restored monarchy and his activity as a political journalist. He began to write for the stage in 1812 and his first real success was *Calas* (1819), a MELODRAMA on the theme of religious fanaticism. Ducange's hallmark was his emphasis on strong emotional effect provoked by horror and pathos, well exemplified by the persecuted heroine of *Thérésa, ou L'Orpheline de Genève* (*Theresa, or The Orphan of Geneva*). His most lasting success was *Thirty Years of a Gamester's Life* (1827), a piece on the evils of gambling. His anticlericalism resurfaced in *Le Jésuite* (*The Jesuit*, 1820), and his final play *Il y a seize ans* (*Sixteen Years Ago*, 1831) was another famous tear-jerker. His own novels provided sources to some of the plays, and he also drew on Sir Walter Scott. JMCC

Duchesnois, Mlle [Catherine Joséphine Rafuin] 1777–1835 French actress. Born in Valenciennes, she first appeared in an amateur production there in 1797. After a debut in Versailles in 1802 she joined the COMÉDIE-FRANÇAISE, where she made up for lack of physical advantages by warmth, verve, instinct, and a strong and flexible voice. TALMA found her an ideal partner, and audiences loved her, even calling her back on stage (which was not the custom at the time). There was a celebrated rivalry between Mlle Duchesnois and MLLE GEORGE, which was fed by the press. Both became *sociétaires* the same day, but Duchesnois really came into her own in 1808 when George ran off to Russia. From 1804 to 1829 she created 36 roles, including Andromaque in *Hector* (1809), Marie Stuart (1820) and Clytemnestra (1822).   JMCC

Ducis, Jean-François 1733–1816 French dramatist and man of letters. Ducis is best known for his adaptations of SHAKESPEARE's plays according to the rules of the three unities and French neoclassical taste. His *Hamlet* (1769) was very successful and, despite the indignation of VOLTAIRE, who felt that Shakespeare was a desecration of the French stage, remained popular into the 19th century. Ophelia is the daughter of Claudius; Hamlet shames his mother by presenting her with the urn containing his father's ashes; and at the end of the play he decides that the best thing he can do is to live and reign. Ducis also adapted *King Lear* (1792), *Macbeth* (1783), and *Othello* with two possible denouements (1792), as well as *Romeo and Juliet* and *King John*. Ducis's own most popular play was *Abufar, ou La Famille arabe* (1795), which provided TALMA with one of his greatest roles. In 1778 Ducis succeeded Voltaire at the Académie-Française.   JMCC

Ducrow, Andrew 1793–1848 This uneducated son of a Belgian strongman was, in his way, a genius: an exquisite MIME artist, an outstanding acrobat, a superb equestrian and an absolutely peerless contriver of spectacular shows. He won his fame in London at ASTLEY's in 1814 as Eloi the dumb boy in *The Forest of Bondy*, in Paris at Franconi's CIRCUS, where he was noted for his quick changes on horseback as in *The Peasant's Frolic* and *The Flying Wardrobe*, and his *poses plastiques équestriennes*, in which he impersonated Greek statuary on horseback. He managed Astley's with great success from 1830 to 1841, introducing brief dramas played entirely on horseback and such spectacles as his leading attraction, *The Battle of Waterloo* (1824), based on field research. Despite his theatrical acumen, he was scorned as a surly illiterate by many, who quoted his rehearsal directive, 'Cut the dialect and come to the 'osses.' His brother John (1796–1834) played at Astley's as Mr Merryman the CLOWN from 1826, serving tea for his ponies Darby and Joan; and his second wife Louisa Woolford (1814–1900) was a distinguished equestrienne. (See also HIPPODROMA.)   LS

Duff, Mary Ann (Dyke) 1794–1857 London-born actress, known as 'the American SARAH SIDDONS'. She seems to have made her debut in Dublin, but went to America with her husband, John Duff, in 1810 and made her first appearance as Juliet on New Year's Eve that year. Until 1817 she went relatively unnoticed, then suddenly changed her style, showing the 'true fire of genius', and emerged as a star. She won fame in Philadelphia and Boston rather than New York as a tragic actress, noted by critics for her 'uniformity of excellence'. The death of her husband in 1831 left her with seven children; she then married the actor Charles Young, but the marriage was soon annulled. She married again in 1835 and retired in 1838, but returned to the stage sporadically, appearing as late as 1850 in Toronto. Many of the leading actors of the time considered her the greatest actress in America. A biography by J. Ireland appeared in 1882.   SMA

Dukes, Ashley 1885–1959 British theatre manager, drama critic and dramatist. Dukes founded the MERCURY THEATRE in London in 1933 as a permanent base for the ballet company run by his wife, Marie Rambert. In his critical writing he consistently championed new dramatists, becoming English editor of the American journal *Theatre Arts Monthly* in 1926. He adapted plays by Anatole France (1914), GEORG KAISER and ERNST TOLLER (1920–3 – thus introducing German EXPRESSIONISM to the British stage), LION FEUCHTWANGER, FERDINAND BRUCKNER and CARL STERNHEIM, as well as NICCOLÒ MACHIAVELLI's *Mandragola* (1939). His most successful original play was *The Man with a Load of Mischief* (1924). In 1935 he organized a Poets' Theatre Season at the Mercury in cooperation with the GROUP THEATRE, at which T. S. ELIOT's *Murder in the Cathedral* was given its successful London premiere. Plays by W. H. AUDEN and CHRISTOPHER ISHERWOOD followed, and the theatre continued its reputation for poetic drama in 1945–6 with work by Norman Nicholson, Ronald Duncan and CHRISTOPHER FRY, produced by E. MARTIN BROWNE. In 1941 Dukes joined CEMA, and later became a member of the building committee for the NATIONAL THEATRE.   CI

Dullin, Charles 1885–1949 French actor and director. After performing in MELODRAMA and at the Théâtre Antoine, Dullin was part of COPEAU's first company at the VIEUX-COLOMBIER. He went to America with Copeau but on his return he left to join GÉMIER, being interested in *théâtre populaire*. He took on responsibility for Gémier's theatre school and when, in 1922, he assumed direction of the ATELIER, he retained the school, in which many notable actors and directors including ARTAUD, BARRAULT, BLIN and VILAR received training. At the Atelier he emphasized acrobatic training, employing techniques from MUSIC-HALL, COMMEDIA DELL'ARTE and Japanese theatre. His repertoire followed Copeau's, attempting to combine vigorous versions of the classics with modern plays. He directed plays by SALACROU and ROMAINS and was one of the first to perform PIRANDELLO in France. He helped found the CARTEL in 1927. His most famous performances, often revived, were in the central roles of MOLIÈRE's *The Miser* (1922), JONSON's *Volpone* (adapted by Romains, 1928) and SHAKESPEARE's *Richard III* (adapted by OBEY, 1933). In 1937 he compiled a report which became the basis for the postwar DECENTRALIZATION MOVEMENT. In 1941 he moved to the large Théâtre Sarah Bernhardt (renamed Théâtre de la Cité under the German Occupation), hoping to reach a broader, more popular audience than was possible in the tiny Atelier. He produced a demanding repertoire there, including SARTRE's first play *The Flies* (1943), but did not achieve the popular success he had hoped for.   DB

Dumas, Alexandre, *fils* 1824–95 French novelist and dramatist, son of ALEXANDRE DUMAS *père*. The younger Dumas's main area of interest was the wealthy society of the Second Empire and Third Republic, which he examined with the eye of a severe moralist whilst dealing with themes considered risqué at the time. In 1844 he met Alphonsine Duplessis, a high-class courtesan, who became his mistress and was the model for his novel *La Dame aux camélias* (1848), which he adapted for the stage. This was accepted at the Vaudeville (see BOULEVARD) in 1850, but rejected three times by the censors before a change of Minister of the Interior made performance possible in 1852 (see CENSORSHIP). The play subsequently became the basis for the libretto of Verdi's *La Traviata* (1853). The title of his COMEDY, *Le Demi-monde* (Théâtre du Gymnase, 1855) virtually created a new term for the French language, as well as a new role, the woman with a past who will appear so frequently in the drama of the late 19th century. In 1865 the Théâtre-Français (see COMÉDIE-FRANÇAISE) opened its doors to Dumas (and his collaborator Émile de Girardin) for his drama *Le Supplice d'une femme* (*A Woman's Torture*). His other most important play for this theatre was *L'Étrangère* (1876), which explored the theme of marital infidelity. The same year, under the pseudonym Pierre Newsky, his rewriting of a play by an amateur author, *Les Danicheff*, became one of the greatest and least expected successes of the 19th century at the ODÉON (the cast included SARAH BERNHARDT's dog). JMCC

Dumas, Alexandre, *père* 1802–70 French dramatist and novelist. Son of a Napoleonic general who had fallen from favour with the emperor, he was first attracted to the theatre by a provincial production of DUCIS's adaptation of *Hamlet*. By the early 1820s he had written some *vaudevilles*, and a meeting with TALMA finally decided him on his career. His first major historical drama, *Christine, ou, Paris, Fontainebleau, Rome*, was accepted by the Théâtre-Français (see COMÉDIE-FRANÇAISE) in 1828, but was not performed until 1830, in a revised version, at the ODÉON. *Henri III et sa cour* (*Henry III and His Court*, 1829) was the first great romantic drama to be staged at the Théâtre-Français. The play, which contains many elements of the MELODRAMA, opened the way at the first French theatre to a staging which attempted in COSTUMES and scenery to recreate a given historical period, and thus to an overall concept of *mise-en-scène*. The 1830 revolution led to a wave of new plays about Napoleon (no longer a forbidden subject). Dumas's contribution was *Napoléon Bonaparte; ou, Trente Ans de l'histoire de France* (*Napoleon Bonaparte; or, Thirty Years of French History*), a six-act drama in 23 scenes, with FRÉDÉRICK LEMAÎTRE in the title role.

His first real triumph was a modern-dress play, *Antony*, with BOCAGE and MARIE DORVAL, at the Porte-Saint-Martin (see BOULEVARD) in 1831. This powerful play with its theme of the outsider is an exciting melodrama, but the villain is society with its prejudices against illegitimacy. It is the first great 'problem play' of the 19th century. In 1834 it was banned at the Théâtre-Français. In 1831 the Odéon staged another major historical drama by Dumas, *Charles VII chez ses grands vassaux* (*Charles VII with His Great Vassals*). In 1832, he rewrote Gaillardet's play submitted to HAREL at the Porte-Saint-Martin, *La Tour de Nesle*, a cloak-and-dagger piece in which crime from the past catches up on its perpetrators in the most horrible manner possible. This piece, which afforded Bocage, as the avenger/villain/hero Buridan, one of the most flamboyant roles of the 19th century, remained immensely popular and continued to be revived well into the 20th century. Further dramas include *Angèle* (1833), *Cathérine Howard* (1834) and *Kean; or, Disorder and Genius* (1836), another actor's vehi-

cle, about the English actor EDMUND KEAN, in which the most striking scene is a defiant insult hurled from the 'stage' at the Prince of Wales.

Dumas had long wanted a theatre of his own for the 'new drama', and in 1837 he and VICTOR HUGO rented the Ventadour and renamed it Théâtre de la Renaissance, opening it with Hugo's *Ruy Blas*. The popularity of the *drame romantique* was on the wane and this venture lasted less than three years. In 1839 Dumas's talents as a writer of historical COMEDY were shown in the successful *Mademoiselle de Belle-Isle* at the Théâtre-Français. The 1830s saw the rise of the serial story in newspapers. In 1838, Dumas adapted Fenimore Cooper's *The Pirate* as *Le Capitaine Paul* for the *Siècle*, increasing the number of subscribers by 5000 in three weeks, and in 1844 his two most famous novels appeared in serial form: *The Three Musketeers* and *The Count of Monte Cristo*. In 1846 there was *The Chevalier de Maison Rouge* and *The Lady of Monsoreau*, in 1848 *The Viscount of Bragelonne*, in 1849 *The Queen's Necklace* and in 1850 *The Black Tulip*. His second venture into theatre management came with the creation of the Théâtre Historique (1847) on the Boulevard du Temple, built according to his specifications, which opened with his *Reine Margot* and presented a series of adaptations of his own novels, often written in collaboration with Auguste Maguet. The theatre closed in 1851, becoming an opera house until its demolition in 1863.

Dumas's later years were largely devoted to the 20 volumes of his *Mémoires* (1852–4), to eight volumes of *Souvenirs de 1830 à 1842* (1855) and his *Souvenirs dramatiques* (1868) – interesting, if inaccurate, sources of theatre history. He also launched his own newspapers, the *Mousquetaire* (1853–7 and 1865–6) and the *Monte Cristo* (1857–62). Dumas's own life was as colourful and extravagant as his fiction, and in total contrast to that of his rather puritanical illegitimate son, ALEXANDRE DUMAS *fils*, author of *The Lady of the Camellias*. JMCC

dumb show Dumb shows as a feature of serious drama flourished in Tudor England. In the actionless tragedies that followed in the wake of *Gorboduc* (1562), they were a spectacular element. Early dumb shows were characteristically allegorical, employing symbolic figures rather than actual characters from the play, but the professional playwrights of Elizabethan England perceived the theatrical advantages to be gained by exploiting dumb shows to focus the attention of the audience on significant deeds outside the strict sequence of the play's narrative. There are famous examples in KYD's *The Spanish Tragedy* (c.1589), PEELE's *The Old Wives Tale* (published 1595) and the anonymous *A Warning for Fair Women* (1599). MUNDAY, like many other writers of plays on legendary heroes, found the dumb show particularly useful in the control of an awkwardly spreading plot. SHAKESPEARE was less addicted than many of his contemporaries, though the dumb show that introduces the play-within-the-play in *Hamlet* is the most familiar of all. It is deployed in a consciously archaic way, since the vogue for introductory dumb shows had long passed. Still more unusual is its description of the whole play rather than of a single episode. WEBSTER and MIDDLETON continued to exploit dumb shows to sensational effect after they had been incorporated in the more spectacular MASQUE, but they ceased to be a feature of TRAGEDY during the reign of James I. PT

Dunlap, William 1766–1839 American playwright and manager, often termed 'the father of American drama'. He wrote or translated and adapted more than 50 plays. Half of them were originals; the other half adaptations from the French and German, principally from KOTZEBUE. He managed the PARK THEATRE (1798–1805), an undertaking that ended disastrously, as he was apparently too good-natured to be hard-headed about financial matters. Still he persisted, managing the Park again (1806–11) for the actor THOMAS A. COOPER. Even if poor at business, he was the first manager to write and present his own plays, the first to champion native subject-matter and dramatists, and the first to record his experiences and those of others in his *History of the American Theatre* (1832).

Born in Perth Amboy, New Jersey, Dunlap began his artistic life as a painter, studied with Benjamin West in England (1784–7), became fascinated with the theatre when he saw R.B. SHERIDAN's *The School for Scandal* and *The Critic* with their original casts, and on his return to New York where he saw ROYALL TYLER's *The Contrast*.

Most notable among his original plays are *Darby's Return* (1789); *The Father* (1799); *André* (1798), which he later transformed into a patriotic spectacle for holiday performance as *The Glory of Columbia* (1803), with backdrops and transparencies by PIERRE CICERI; *Leicester* 1806); and *A Trip to Niagara; or, Travellers in America* (1828), with a diorama of 18 scenes along the Hudson as a steamboat moves up the river from New York to Catskill landing. His most popular adaptations include (from Kotzebue) *The Stranger* (1798), *False Shame* (1799) and *Pizarro in Peru* (1800), as well as (from the French) *The Wife of Two Husbands* (1804, PIXÉRÉCOURT) and *Thirty Years; or, the Life of a Gamester* (1828, Goubaux and DUCANGE).

Besides his work in the theatre, he painted a host of miniatures (one of George Washington), and monumental religious canvases such as *Christ Rejected* (12 × 18ft). He was director of the American Academy of Fine Arts (1817), a founder of the National Academy of Design (1826), and a professor of historical painting at the National Academy (1830–9). He wrote biographies of the actor GEORGE FREDERICK COOKE (1813) and the novelist Charles Brockden Brown (1815), a *History of the Arts of Design* (1834), *Thirty Years Ago; or, Memoirs of a Water Drinker* (1836), and a *History of New York for Schools* (1837). His revealing diary was published in 1930. RM

Dunlop, Frank 1927– British director, who trained at the OLD VIC School and started his own theatre company, Piccolo Theatre, in 1954. After being appointed resident director at the BRISTOL OLD VIC and directing *Les Frères Jacques* in the WEST END, he was appointed artistic director of the Nottingham Playhouse from 1961 to 64, inaugurating its new theatre. In 1967 he joined OLIVIER's NATIONAL THEATRE as an associate director, and founded the YOUNG VIC in 1970 as a small stage adjunct to the Old Vic, which was then the NT's home. The Young Vic quickly acquired a reputation for lively, popular productions of classic plays, notably *Scapino* (from MOLIÈRE's *The Tricks of Scapino*, 1970) and *The Taming of the Shrew* (1970), both of which he directed, but he also spotted the talents of the young TIM RICE and ANDREW LLOYD WEBBER, staging *Joseph and the Amazing Technicolour Dreamcoat* (1968). He was appointed director of the EDINBURGH FESTIVAL in 1983, to which he contributed what might be considered a prototype Dunlop production, *Treasure Island* (1990), at the Assembly Rooms – imaginative, energetic and buoyantly cheerful. But after staging a post-*glasnost* festival in 1991, with many companies from Eastern and Central Europe, he resigned, in protest at the low funding and inadequate support of the Festival from the Edinburgh and Lothian authorities. JE

Dunnock, Mildred 1901–91 American actress and director, remembered by ARTHUR MILLER as 'a fiercely dedicated artist'. She first appeared in New York in 1932, then played several seasons of stock (see STOCK COMPANY). After a number of BROADWAY appearances, she achieved stardom with such roles as Linda Loman in *Death of a Salesman* (1949) and Big Mama in *Cat on a Hot Tin Roof* (1955). She played a number of seasons with the AMERICAN SHAKESPEARE [Festival] THEATRE in both classic and modern roles, and in 1965 directed *Graduation* on Broadway. She usually appeared in major supporting roles (mothers, spinsters and eccentric ladies), relying on a bird-like fragile stature and tremendous voice to project an ineffectual gentility. She made her film debut in *The Corn Is Green* (1945), and later appeared in such successful films as *Death of a Salesman* (1951), *Viva Zapata!* (1952), *The Jazz Singer* (1953), *Baby Doll* (1956) and *Sweet Bird of Youth* (1962). She also appeared in many television series and specials. Her daughter Linda McGuire is an actress, as is her granddaughter Patricia McGuire Dunnock. SMA

Dunsany [Edward John Moreton Drax Plunkett], Lord 1878–1957 Anglo-Irish dramatist, novelist and critic, whose ironic fantasies in exotic settings were connected with the Irish literary revival. After *The Glittering Gates* (1909) and *King Argimenes* (1911) at the ABBEY THEATRE in Dublin, his work was mainly produced at the HAYMARKET and EVERYMAN Theatres in London and in the USA, the most successful being *If* (1921), in which time is reversed and telescoped. CI

Durang, Christopher 1949– American playwright and actor, born in Montclair, New Jersey, and educated at Harvard and Yale. Durang had his first play produced in 1971, emerging as a new breed of American dramatist in the late 1970s and early 80s. His best-known scripts include *A History of the American Film* (1976), *Sister Mary Ignatius Explains It All for You* (1979; Obie, 1980), *The Actor's Nightmare* (1981), *Beyond Therapy* (1981), *Baby with the Bath Water* (1983), *The Marriage of Bette and Boo* (1973, revised 1985) and *Laughing Wild* (1988). Durang's style, according to *New York Times* critic Mel Gussow, 'has the wiggishness of four Marxes and the malice of a Jonathan Swift'. His satirical bent, especially when he attacks religion, has provoked considerable controversy and attempted CENSORSHIP. In recent years he has devoted much time to CABARET and REVUE performance. SMA

Durante, Jimmy 1893–1980 American comedian, actor and singer, known affectionately as 'Schnozzola' for his prominent nose, butt of many of his jokes. One of America's most beloved entertainers, Durante began as a saloon pianist on Coney Island and opened his own night-club in 1923 with Eddie Jackson and Lou Clayton. He debuted on BROADWAY in *Show Girl* in 1929. He later toured England, then appeared on Broadway in such shows as *Jumbo* (1935), *Red, Hot, and Blue!* (1936) and *Stars in Your Eyes* (1939). He made his film debut in *Roadhouse* (1930); among his other films were *Palooka* (1934), *The Man Who Came to Dinner* (1941) and *Two Girls and a Sailor* (1944). He starred in American radio's 'Rexall Show' (1944–50) and later in his own TV show, being voted best television performer in 1951. More a clown than comic, Durante's style eluded analysis, yet his sayings ('Stop the music', 'I got a million of 'em' and 'Goodnight Mrs Calabash, wherever you are') were assimilated into the language, and the presentation of his songs, including his signature tune 'Inka Dinka Doo', prompted Fred Allen to characterize his singing as 'a dull rasp calling its mate'. SMA DBW

Duras, Marguerite 1914– French novelist, script-writer and playwright. Duras's contribution is to have blurred the distinctions between the genres: her disembodied voices speak hauntingly through novels and films as much as through the theatre. Her plays, sometimes adapted from her stories like her first, *Le Square* (*The Square*, 1956), present a stream of discourse, through which characters seek to make contact with one another but seldom succeed. Her plays have been successful on radio, where their lack of dramatic action is less of a disadvantage. Madeleine Renaud has performed in many of her plays, including *Des Journées entières dans lès arbres* (1956; *Days in the Trees*, starring PEGGY ASHCROFT at the Aldwych in 1968) and *L'Éden-cinéma* (1977). DB

D'Urfey, Thomas 1653–1723 English playwright. Born in Devon and probably trained for the law, he settled in London, becoming a close friend of the king, Charles II, and of all his successors, in itself an achievement. Constantly mocked for his stutter and his ugliness, he became best known for his songs, collected as *Pills to Purge Melancholy* (six vols., 1719). Making his living as a professional writer, he wrote 33 plays, including five poor sensationalist tragedies and four equally weak operas. But his comedies, beginning with *Madam Fickle* in 1676, have an energy far beyond their frequently imitative plots. D'Urfey often adapted earlier plays by FLETCHER and others, including a version of SHAKESPEARE's *Cymbeline* as *The Injured Princess* (1682), but his best work is sharp contemporary SATIRE, particularly on the connection between financial intrigue and marriage in *Love for Money* (1691) and *The Richmond Heiress* (1693), both plays combining a nascent sentimentalism with a harsh cynicism. His most ambitious work was a three-part adaptation of CERVANTES as *The Comical History of Don Quixote* (1694–5), partly faithful recreation of his source and partly delightfully coarse invention – like Sancho Panza's daughter, Mary the Buxom. The plays' bawdiness made them a particular target for the attacks of JEREMY COLLIER. PH

Durov family Russian CLOWNS and animal trainers. The brothers **Vladimir (Leonidovich)** (1863–1934) and **Anatoly (Leonidovich)** (1864–1916), scions of the gentry, left school and played in show-booths and menageries in several capacities before discovering their proper role as satiric clowns. Vladimir was renowned as a trainer, using new principles based on Pavlov's experiments; with his pigs, rats and dogs in such sketches as 'The Pied Piper of Hamelin' and 'The Russo-Japanese War' he attacked bureaucratic corruption and administrative malpractice. Both brothers frequently got into trouble with the police and authorities, but it was Anatoly, the more sardonic and poetic satirist, who was gaoled in Berlin for *lèse-majesté* to Wilhelm II. Wearing almost no make-up, Anatoly always began his act with a monologue in verse; he toured Europe from 1890, and enunciated a theory of COMEDY.

After the Revolution, Vladimir, who had founded his own menagerie in 1912, retired to experiment in animal behaviour. Of his progeny, four children and two grand-children went into the CIRCUS, as did two children and two grandchildren of Anatoly. These successors, the most important being **Yury (Vladimirovich)** (1910–71), **Anatoly (Anatol'evich)** (1894–1928) and **Vladimir (Grigor'evich)** (1909–72), concentrated on animal tricks rather than SATIRE under the Soviets. LS

Dürrenmatt, Friedrich 1921–90 Swiss playwright, novelist and essayist, arguably the best-known 'German' dramatist of the 20th century beside BRECHT. Born in Konolfingen, son of a Calvinist pastor, Dürrenmatt studied classics, German literature and philosophy at the Universities of Berne and Zurich (1941–5), leaving without taking his exams. He was interested in drawing and, especially, caricatures.

His first play *It is Written* was presented at the Zurich Schauspielhaus in 1947, and caused a scandal because of the satirical nature of the work. Scandal and controversy attended many of Dürrenmatt's best plays, as he cynically asked uncomfortable questions about the complacency of post-Second World War Switzerland. Success came with *Romulus the Great* (1949), 'an unhistorical historical comedy', compound of JARRY's *Ubu Roi* and PIRANDELLO's *Henry IV*, containing already the quintessential mixture of sour comedy and unfulfilled tragedy which is Dürrenmatt's hallmark. *The Marriage of Mr Mississippi* (1952) plays freely with theatrical conventions and turns a string of murders into so many comic events. In *The Visit* (1955), which triumphed the world over, and *The Physicists* (1962), Dürrenmatt cast a desperate look over mankind and concluded that hope is not reasonable. The bleakness of the parables is redeemed, as often in his plays, by a dazzling theatrical inventiveness.

The Visit concerns millionaire Claire Zachanassian's return to her small home town where, in her youth, she was seduced and abandoned by Ill. She seeks revenge and, to get it, bribes the entire population: every man, woman and child will be rich for the rest of their lives if they agree to put Ill to death. After a feeble moral struggle and a travesty of a trial, the people of Güllen condemn and execute the erstwhile lover. In so doing they condemn themselves, and Dürrenmatt condemns society as a whole. In *The Physicists* a Pirandellian device cleverly blurs the edges separating reality from fiction, sanity from reason: the confusion between the sane world and the asylum presented on stage, and between the responsible scientists and the mad atomic physicists, is never 'happily' resolved. *Frank V* (1959), 'opera for a private bank', is an indictment of the modern totalitarian state and mocks the derisory situation of the individual. For the Basle Stadttheater, Dürrenmatt adapted SHAKESPEARE's *King John* (1968–9), directed by Werner Düggelin, and STRINDBERG's *The Dance of Death* which became *Play Strindberg* (1969), an even sparer and harsher drama than the original, now Dürrenmatt's most performed play. *Woyzeck* followed in 1972. *The Partaker* (1973), a bleak descent into a putrid, post-Dachau netherworld where injustice rules supreme, had little success.

In his last years, Dürrenmatt concentrated on prose writing. His essays on playwriting and theatre theory (see DRAMATIC THEORY) are an important contribution to the field. Like IONESCO, he was convinced that the profound tragedy of our time can only be expressed through FARCE, and that is why his iconoclastic theatre is full of scenic pyrotechnics relying on SATIRE, PARODY, CABARET and the exploitation of the grotesque. CIS

Duse, Eleonora 1858–1924 Italian actress. Born into the profession, as a child she acquired considerable stage experience touring throughout Italy with her parents, who were poor players of modest rank. Her apprenticeship was long and hard, and more than once she came close to abandoning the profession. In 1879 she joined the company of GIOVANNI EMANUEL: her parts opposite him included Desdemona and Ophelia. Later she achieved notable success in ZOLA's *Thérèse Raquin* (1879), which gave her status in the profession but did not deliver her of the need, standard in the Italian theatre of the day, to tour constantly from one city to another. Such touring was particularly demanding on Duse, for her health was poor and she suffered frequent illness. Again she was tempted to leave the stage, but persevered when she saw performances by SARAH BERNHARDT, during one of that actress's Italian visits. In Turin in 1884 she achieved a major triumph, in VERGA's *Cavalleria rusticana* (*Rustic Chivalry*). Following this she toured for the first time abroad, to South America, and in 1887 formed with the lead actor, Flavio Andò, the Compagnia Città di Roma, playing in 19th-century stock pieces – particularly adaptations from French dramatists like SARDOU and DUMAS *fils*, as well as in GOLDONI and GIACOSA.

Duse had a long and intimate relationship with the composer and librettist Arrigo Boito, who questioned the worth of her stock repertoire and encouraged her to undertake artistically more ambitious work. He translated SHAKESPEARE's *Antony and Cleopatra* for her, first performed at the Teatro Manzoni in Milan in 1888 and transferred to London in 1893, though not to the satisfaction of English critics. Her first significant triumph abroad was in 1891, when she opened in St Petersburg with *La signora dalle camelie* (*The Lady of the Camellias*); it was the start of a long international career that took her to most parts of Europe and to the United States and won her wide acclaim.

If it was in the 1890s that Duse established her international career, it was in the late 90s too that she entered into one of the most influential and painful relationships of her life: that with the Italian poet and dramatist, GABRIELE D'ANNUNZIO. For several years from 1896 she devoted much of her time, art and money to seeking to realize D'Annunzio's dream of a new, revolutionary, poetic drama that would achieve in modern times a theatre comparable to that of classical Greece. Notwithstanding her disappointment that D'Annunzio gave his first play, *La città morta* (*The Dead City*), to Bernhardt for performance in Paris in 1898, in the same year she acted in his short pieces, *Sogno di un mattino di primavera* (*Dream of a Spring Morning*) and *Sogno di un tramonto d'autunno* (*Dream of an Autumn Sunset*), and went on to produce his *La Gioconda* (1899), *La gloria* (1899) and *Francesca da Rimini* (1901), playing these abroad as well as in Italy. Her later repertoire expanded to embrace other serious modern drama, notably the work of IBSEN, including *A Doll's House*, *Hedda Gabler*, *Rosmersholm* (for which GORDON CRAIG did the scenery) and *The Lady from the Sea*, the part of Ellida being one of her last major roles. After the break-up of her relationship with D'Annunzio, she continued to tour both in Italy and abroad into the 1920s.

In Italy, at least, Duse was considered by many to be more than just a 'star' performer: her very individual talent, her high seriousness of purpose, and her working associations with many of the leading cultural figures of the age in Italy and abroad seemed to bring an intellectual prestige to the Italian theatre which it had long lacked. Certainly her acting style was felt by many to embody something new. Commenting on Duse in an interview ADELAIDE RISTORI perceptively, if rather waspishly, characterized the stage persona of her younger colleague as that of the archetypal *fin-de-siècle* woman: 'Duse has created for herself her own mannerisms, she has created a kind of convention peculiar to herself: according to this she is the modern woman with all her maladies of hysteria, anaemia and neurosis, and with all their consequences.' A keen admirer, BERNARD SHAW defined her 'modernist' style more generously, seeing it as the application of the grand tradition of theatrical romantic realism – the disciplined, restrained force of a Ristori or a SALVINI – to interpretations appropriate to the new age: Duse was, claimed Shaw, 'the first actress whom we have seen applying the method of the great school to characteristically modern parts, or to characteristically modern conceptions of old parts'. KR LR

Dutt, Utpal 1929– Indian director: perhaps India's best-known exponent of theatre for political and social purposes. He began his career in the 1940s with the Shakespeareana International Theater Company. Later he produced many of SHAKESPEARE's plays in English for the Little Theatre Group of Calcutta. Attracted to political causes, he joined the Indian People's Theatre Association in 1950 but remained for less than a year, needing more independence and flexibility. As director, playwright, stage and film actor, Dutt has been acknowledged for his dynamic personality, energy and determination. Among his memorable productions are *Coal* (*Angar*), *Invincible Vietnam* (*Ajeya Vietnam*), *Arrow* (*Teer*), and *Barracade*. For a time he wrote performance pieces for JATRA, the popular folk-theatre form of Bengal.　FaR

Duym, Jacob 1547?–1612/20 Flemish playwright. In the career of Jacob Duym the history of the Low Countries (see BELGIUM; NETHERLANDS) in the second half of the 16th century is reflected. Duym, of a noble Brabant family, was invalided out of the army of William of Orange after having been in Spanish captivity and moved to Leyden in 1588, where he became poetic leader (*keizer*) of the Flemish Chamber of Rhetoric in exile, the Orange Lily (founded 1590). In that capacity he wrote 12 plays, using classical and national historical material. He created a new type of play which combined the allegorical character and the didactic moralizations of the *spel van sinnen* (see MORALITY PLAY) with the narrative epic character of secular and religious 16th-century drama. The plays are no longer merely dramatized disputes, the characters more than allegorical abstractions or collectives. The traditional *sinnekens* develop into characters of flesh and blood, who keep to some extent their usual role of scandalmongers and entertainers, but are portrayed as servants of the main characters and take on the role of reporters for and informers of the audience. New, too, is Duym's frequent use of comic intermezzi, similar to the comic INTERLUDES in Elizabethan drama and employing lower-class characters. The *rondeau*, often used in *sinneken* scenes, is here employed for the comic interlude.

Each of Duym's plays is accompanied by elaborate stage directions. Costumes, decor and special effects are carefully described and often fairly complex. He uses three different types of staging according to the kind of play performed. Allegorical abstract plays, less abstract plays or siege plays are, respectively, performed on a stage with neutral entrances and *mansions*; a stage with more and specific entrances and *mansions*; or a larger stage with specific and realistically rendered locations.　ES

Dybwad, Johanne 1867–1950 The greatest Norwegian actress of her generation. Dybwad trained at the NATIONALE SCENE, Bergen, before moving to Christiania Theater and NATIONALTHEATRET, where she acted for some 50 years, often opposite Egil Eide and August Oddvar. Her best work was under the direction of BJØRN BJØRNSON, who nurtured her realistic style. Later in her career, she was sometimes accused of over-exploiting her virtuosity to create sensational effects. Among her 20 IBSEN roles were a complex, serious Nora, Hedvig, a very natural Hilde Wangel, Mrs Alving and Aase. Other celebrated roles included the title parts in GUNNAR HEIBERG's *Aunt Ulrikke* and BJØRNSTJERNE BJØRNSON's *Paul Lange and Tora Parsberg*. From 1906 she frequently directed, sometimes with herself in the lead. Intense and demanding, she took liberties with texts to support her individualistic readings. HL

Eastern Caribbean States When the West Indies Federation collapsed in 1962 with the withdrawal of JAMAICA and TRINIDAD AND TOBAGO, the smaller English-speaking islands of the eastern Caribbean sought to establish a loose association from which they might benefit economically as trading partners. At present they use the same currency, although politically they range from crown colony to fully independent states. With a total population of about 600,000, these islands – referred to as the Windward and Leeward Islands, according to whether they are in the path of the trade winds and thus subject to rain, or on the lee side and therefore drier – form the eastern rim of the Caribbean basin. The Windwards comprise Grenada, Martinique, St Vincent and the Grenadines, St Lucia and Dominica. The Leewards are Montserrat, Antigua and Barbuda, St Kitts and Nevis, and Anguilla. Only the three states where theatrical activity is of particular interest are dealt with here.

The islands were first inhabited by Arawak Indians who were driven out by the fiercer Carib Indians from South America. These in turn were crushed by the Spanish adventurers who followed Columbus to the area. In the 1500s and 1600s Great Britain and France fought over these Eastern Caribbean States, which had become British colonies by the early 1800s. Little is known of early theatrical activity in the islands, but English companies no doubt put on performances in the area from the late 18th century. A Leeward Islands company of comedians is reported to have performed *King Lear*, *Richard II* and other popular plays of the day at Christiansted, Danish West Indies, in 1771.

Antigua A party of amateurs opened Antigua's first theatre in 1788 with OTWAY's *Venice Preserv'd*, after which visiting companies came for a few weeks' run, their performances reinforced by local actors. The West India Sketch Book (1835) mentions a theatre in Antigua with amateurs performing GOLDSMITH's *She Stoops to Conquer* along with a PANTOMIME called *Harlequin Planter, or The Land of Promise*. This latter – containing 'aboriginal savages', their evil spirit Maboya, white settlers, black slaves, Astraea the goddess of justice, members of the Anti-Slavery Society, HARLEQUIN and Columbine – might count as one of the earliest pieces of native Caribbean theatre, dealing as it does with the local scene. The audience of white, coloured and black, freemen and slaves, were said to be delighted by the performance.

Antiguans recall, from the 1930s, the OPERETTAS and MUSICALS presented by one Nellie Robinson of the TOR Memorial High School. In 1952 the Community Players were formed, causing a stir in local circles when, led by the drama tutor of the University of the West Indies, they created the village play *Priscilla's Wedding* using local dialect, thought at the time to undermine the teaching of 'proper' English. The Players have since performed their folksongs and operettas internationally. In 1956 the UWI extramural tutor based in St Kitts organized the first Leeward Islands drama festival, and in 1967 the Antigua University Centre was established, with a 400-seat open-air theatre. Several short-lived theatre groups sprang up at this time. The Little Theatre, led by Bobby Margetson, presented Caribbean plays including two from Antigua by Oliver Flax: *The Legend of Prince Klaas*, entered in the Carifesta (Caribbean festival of creative arts) in GUYANA in 1972, and *A Better Way* (1976), directed by Edgar Davis. The Grammarians took their *Obeah Slave* (1969), by Lester Simon, to Montserrat and BARBADOS, and the Open-Air Theatre travelled to St Kitts and Barbados in 1971 with Lonne Elder's *Ceremonies in Dark Old Men*.

These last two groups merged in 1972, under Antiguan playwright and director Dorbrene O'Marde, to become the Harambee Open-Air Theatre, considered the most important group of recent times. The Third World Theatre led by Leon Symester, also known as Chaka Wacca, presented two protest plays, *Voices of Protest* (1976) and *Time Bomb* (1977), dealing with the political situation in Antigua. *Time Bomb* was considered libellous and not allowed to be entered in the local festival, but drew crowds when it played at the University Centre. Chaka Wacca left Antigua in 1980 for New Jersey, where he practises law. Eliston Adams, known also as Nambulumba, in 1979 started the Rio Revealers Theatre for staging what have been described as his 'slapstick plays', which the company took to Montserrat, St Martin (Dutch) and St Thomas (American). In 1988 the Popular Theatre Movement was started in village communities, where role-playing, discussion and creative play-making help to identify issues and suggest solutions. The group toured their self-made play, *Rising from the Ashes*, to Dominica. In 1990 Rick James began his fully professional Theatre Ensemble, playing short plays with small casts at beach hotels.

As in Antigua, groups in other island states have taken productions to neighbouring islands in order to extend their run, improve working skills and advance careers. But this constant movement has posed survival difficulties, because such groups tend to be disparate and short-lived instead of becoming consolidated under strong, lasting leadership.

Dominica The only Eastern Caribbean island with a history of significant Carib and free African populations, Dominica was captured from the French by the British navy in 1761. Its mountainous terrain was not suitable for large plantations, and thus peasant farming controlled by French mulattos from neighbouring Guadeloupe and Martinique remained the dominant mode in coastal villages. From this mélange of Carib, African, and French mulatto, plus a small English administrative community, emerged a rich heritage of folk-songs, dances, music-making, storytelling and masquerades, cultural manifestations in which the Creole language predominates.

According to the historian Lennox Honychurch 'there is no tradition of theatre or creative interpretative dance in

Dominica'. Only in this century have productions of GILBERT and Sullivan's operettas been organized, and in 1945 an adaptation of Jane Austen's novel *Pride and Prejudice* was memorably staged. In 1964 a SHAKESPEARE festival brought to the fore Amah Harris and Alwin Bully. Harris formed the Little Theatre, which she led during 1965–70 before leaving for Toronto. Bully took a BA at the Cave Hill, Barbados, campus of the University of the West Indies during 1967–71. On his return to Dominica he directed Daniel Caudeiron's *Speak, Brother, Speak*, a social commentary with music and dance which was produced for the Little Theatre in 1972. He then formed his own group, the People's Action Theatre (PAT), whose intention was to be socially active, taking productions to village audiences. In 1975 Bully's play *Streak* confirmed this approach.

The work of the PAT inspired the formation of other groups such as, in 1976, the Aquarian Xpression group; in 1977, the Karifouna Cultural Group, dedicated to the preservation and promotion of Carib culture; in 1982, the Movement for Cultural Awareness which, as part of the Eastern Caribbean Popular Theatre Organization, focused on popular theatre in the villages; and in 1984, the New Dimensions Theatre led by playwright-director Steve Hyacinth, principal of the Mahaut Government School. This group has produced six of Hyacinth's plays, all taken on tour to village audiences. In 1990, combining the talents of the People's Action and New Dimensions Theatres, the Popular Theatre Movement produced *The Swine and the Pearl*, written by Hyacinth, Philbert Aaron and Delmance Moses and directed by Nigel Francis. Dealing with issues pertinent to the Year of Environment and Shelter, to which it was a contribution, the play was presented in the capital, Roseau, and to ten communities around the island. Creole translations of plays such as DEREK WALCOTT's *Ti-Jean and His Brothers* and Trinidadian Errol John's *Moon on a Rainbow Shawl* have proved popular in a country where the first, and sometimes only, language of the people is Kweyol (Creole). Demonstrating the theatre's consciousness of the needs of its public, both plays have been staged in Dominica, the latter having also been taken to the Martinique Theatre Festival in 1989.

The most serious and successful dance-drama group is the Waitukubuli Dance Theatre Company led by Raymond Lawrence. ('Waitukubuli' is the Carib name for Dominica, to be interpreted as 'tall is her body' or 'land of many battles'.) Founded in 1971, the company has produced four dance-dramas: *Kabouki* (1977), *Papa Toussaint* (1978), and two biblical pieces, *The Resurrection* (1986) and *The Power and the Glory* (1987). It has also presented works set to the poetry of Dominican writers.

The major problem facing theatre and dance companies in Dominica is the lack of a proper performing space. For years theatre groups have endured inadequate school halls, and even today, troupes in Roseau are obliged to perform in an old, hurricane-damaged cinema.

St Lucia A Theatre Royal was first established in the capital, Castries, in 1832. The theatre was used by English and French amateurs, aided by a company of artists from Martinique under the direction of one M. Charvet. They performed two or three times a week for six months. The historian Henry Breen has commented: 'it was a spectacle at once novel and pleasing to behold the same audience successively applauding the representations, on the same stage and in different languages, of *Othello* and the *Médicin malgré lui*'. Charvet brought his company for a second visit in 1834, when they were joined by amateurs from the Royal Regiment stationed on St Lucia. The phenomenon of French and English performers sharing the same stage reflects the duality of the colonial powers that, for over 160 years, contended for the island. Eventually, in 1804, the English prevailed, but, as with Dominica, the French left their mark on the language and customs of the island, with its population of basically African or part-African, as well as bequeathing them what is still their principal religion – Roman Catholicism.

Any theatre performed up to the mid-20th century might be expected still to be European in content, if not always in personnel. In 1950, however, a new era was ushered in with the founding of the Arts Guild of St Lucia by Maurice Mason and Derek Walcott. Within months Walcott left St Lucia to take up a scholarship at the University of the West Indies, and the leadership of the Guild was taken over by his twin brother Roddy Walcott. With members recruited primarily from pupils and ex-pupils of Castries's secondary schools, the Guild started with an ambitious programme to promote the arts in general, but soon found itself drawn primarily to the theatre. For over 20 years it was the principal play-producing organization in the country, with a growing emphasis on Caribbean drama. In 1966 the Creative and Performing Arts Society – primarily a training operation supported by the university extramural tutor, Patricia Charles – came into being. Tutors were drawn from among the British residents on the island who were trained in theatre, and from JAMAICA and TRINIDAD in the case of workshops in dance. As well as indigenous works, the society produced plays such as SHAW's *Dark Lady of the Sonnets*, Henri Ghéon's *Christmas in the Market-Place*, Errol Hill's *Square Peg* and Eric Roach's *Letter from Leonora*.

The Society ceased to exist in 1974, but it was in that year that the Folk Research Centre was established. George Alphonse, one of its foundation members, was sent for two years (1983–5) by the St Lucia government to the Cultural Training Centre in Jamaica, and on his return he organized popular theatre groups in villages around the country, as well as conducting an annual festival for them. His work is closely associated with the Eastern Caribbean Popular Theatre Organization. Allan Weeks, a former Arts Guild member now teaching at the Community College, formed the St Lucia Creole Theatre Workshop, for which he has translated into Creole several St Lucian and other Caribbean plays and performed them in Castries, in Vieux Fort and on tour to Martinique.

In 1989 the government of St Lucia opened a cultural centre with funds provided by the French government, but since the fees charged for both rehearsal and performance are reportedly too high to encourage its frequent use by individual theatre groups, Kendal Hippolyte, another past member of the Arts Guild, has opened the Lighthouse Theatre in Castries, seating up to 120. Plays recently performed there include his own *The Drum*

Maker, Trinidadian Lennox Brown's *The Trinity of Four*, Derek Walcott's *Pantomime*, and FERNANDO ARRABAL's *Picnic on the Battlefield*. Apart from the Walcott brothers and Hippolyte, the most important St Lucian playwright is Stanley French, a University of London graduate in civil engineering who now lives in Barbados. His plays include *The Rape of Fair Helen* (1962), *Ballad of a Man and Dog* (1967), *No Rain No Play* (1967), *The Light and the Dark* (1968), and *Under a Sky of Incense* (1977).   EGH

See: H. Breen, *St Lucia: Historical, Statistical and Descriptive*, London, 1834, repr. 1970; D. J. Crowley, 'Festivals of the Calendar in St Lucia', *Caribbean Quarterly*, 4, 2, 1955; E. Hill, 'The Emergence of a National Drama in the West Indies', *Caribbean Quarterly*, 18, 4, 1972; K. Omotoso, *The Theatrical into Theatre: A Study of the Drama and Theatre of the English-speaking Caribbean*, London, 1982.

Ebb, Fred see KANDER, JOHN

Echegaray, José 1832–1916 Spanish mathematician, government official and playwright, who wrote 100 plays and dominated the Spanish stage for several decades, starting in 1874. Author of neo-romantic works in verse, paradoxically he was influenced by realists IBSEN and STRINDBERG. The resulting MELODRAMAS are no longer staged. His receipt of the Nobel Prize in 1904 was greeted by protests from younger Spanish intellectuals. His most famous work, *El gran Galeoto* (*The Great Galeoto*, 1881), is a criticism of contemporary society dealing with the disastrous results of idle gossip. Among several English translations, the most popular was titled *The World and His Wife*. PZ

Ecuador The territory of the Incas extended into what is present-day Ecuador, but because the centre of power was located in Peru, that rich cultural heritage is affiliated more with Ecuador's neighbour to the south. Rich in natural resources but poor in development, Ecuador sits astride the Equator, after which it is named, with four major divisions in its geographical configuration, ranging from the tropical coastlands to the remote and exotic jungle regions. Progressively diminished in size over the years by avaricious neighbours, Ecuador has been overshadowed by a combination of foreign exploitation, overt admiration of France, and internal politics that have systematically, since the time of independence, wreaked havoc with the socio-economic structure of the country. Of all the South American countries, Ecuador may be among the poorest in early cultural development, although both Quito, the capital, and Guayaquil, the coastal city, are important metropolitan centres. Ricardo Descalzi, an indefatigable researcher and playwright as well, has documented the history of the Ecuadorian theatre in six volumes, even though an independent theatre activity from the early period is notably lean.

As with other colonial sites, however, visiting troupes brought theatre to the area. They performed primarily in the grand rooms of manorial houses or in churches and plazas. There is evidence of some original local production, but many texts have been lost. The earliest pieces preserved were an *entremés* (see *GÉNERO CHICO*) and some

LOAS by the priest Diego Molina, performed around 1732. After independence in the early 19th century, the internationally known poet José Joaquín de Olmedo (1780–1847) wrote plays that were performed in Lima where he was studying, but all have been lost with the exception of one small *loa*. Throughout the 19th century a broad array of dramatists was active, including Juan Montalvo (1832–89) who wrote five plays in *The Book of the Passions*. Much of the work of the period, however, now appears to have had little transcendental value.

The 20th century The first decades of the 20th century continued the hyperbolic romantic tendencies of the previous century. In 1925 the National Dramatic Company was created in Quito and produced plays of JACINTO BENAVENTE and FLORENCIO SÁNCHEZ, Spaniard and Uruguayan, respectively. After a 1926 contest for dramatic companies, however, in which the National won first place, it soon ceased to exist. Jorge Icaza (b.1906), who later achieved international fame for his Native American novel *Huasipungo* (1934), wrote six plays between 1928 and 1932 that combined psychoanalytical techniques and class consciousness.

The so-called Generation of 1930 and the Guayaquil Group had a major impact on arts and letters in Ecuador. The five creative individuals who comprise the Group were dedicated to leftist, social reforms. The important theatrical figure to emerge from the Group was DEMETRIO AGUILERA MALTA, also novelist and diplomat, whose earliest play is from 1938, *España leal* (*Loyal Spain*). His plays revealed his dedication both to social justice and to artistic integrity, as he experimented with techniques of EXPRESSIONISM and magical REALISM, seen especially in *El tigre* (*The Tiger*, 1955) and *Dientes blancos* (*White Teeth*, 1955). Another novelist, Pedro Jorge Vera (b.1914), followed with *El Dios de la selva* (*God of the Jungle*) in 1941 and *Luto eterno* (*Eternal Mourning*, 1954), an adaptation of a homonymous novel in which he satirized the family rituals that accompany death.

The creation of the Teatro Experimental Universitario (University Experimental Theatre) in 1955 brought some coherence to the Quito theatre movement, when Sixto Salguero with his ties to the Generation of 1930 provided new impetus to the popular theatre movement. Francisco Tobar García had organized the Teatro Independiente in 1954, and the group functioned until 1970. In Guayaquil the Teatro Experimental Universitario Agora was founded in 1958 by Francisco Villar, and later directed by Ramón Arias. In this formative period many other groups were also created, and gave rise to what Gerardo Luzuriaga has described as the Generation of 1960, when the Ecuadorian theatre for the first time achieved a sense of national identity.

In 1962 the Casa de la Cultura (House of Culture) requested through UNESCO a technical director who could infuse fresh life into the Ecuadorian theatre. In October 1963 the Italian director Fabio Pacchioni arrived under the auspices of the Ministry of Education to organize theatre seminars and to begin the process of building a new artistic expression. When the first seminar was concluded in 1964, the Teatro Ensayo (Rehearsal Theatre) was formed to train actors and other theatre personnel. The

Teatro Ensayo staged several plays in each of the succeeding seasons, drawing on classical works by LOPE DE RUEDA and CERVANTES, while at the same time mounting both old and new works by Ecuadorian writers such as Aguilera Malta and JOSÉ MARTÍNEZ QUEIROLO. The latter's *Requiem por la lluvia* (*Requiem for the Rain*, 1960) is a socially committed monologue with international appeal. The group went on tour within the country in an effort to raise the consciousness of theatre on a wider national scale. Antonio Ordóñez was a member of the original group and became the functional director in 1968.

Other groups that have influenced the direction of Ecuadorian theatre include the Teatro Experimental Ecuatoriano, established in 1971 and directed by Eduardo Almeida. A popular theatre group with a strong sociopolitical commitment, it has participated in many national and international festivals, including those of Rennes, Oporto, Amsterdam and Stockholm. Carlos Villalba has worked tirelessly with the Colegio Luciano Andrada Marín (CLAM) to form groups of actors who have at times splintered off to form other groups. Mojiganga was formed by a Belgian, Carlos Theus, in 1977. Other groups include the Ollantay (directed by Carlos Villarreal), El Juglar (directed by Ernesto Suárez) and the Taller de Teatro Popular (Popular Theatre Workshop), directed by the talented Ilonka Vargas, an actress and professor at the Central University. For the most part, these groups share in a commitment to develop a serious popular theatre that can respond to the needs and aesthetic sensibilities of the Ecuadorian public.

The functioning groups have not only promoted national theatre, but, as a part of the consciousness-raising process, have presented a range of Latin American works by such authors as AGUSTÍN CUZZANI, OSVALDO DRAGÚN and ANDRÉS LIZÁRRAGA of Argentina, JORGE DÍAZ of Chile, and Millor Fernandes and João Cabral de Melo Neto of Brazil. ENRIQUE BUENAVENTURA of Colombia and AUGUSTO BOAL of Brazil have worked with groups to develop techniques of collective or group theatre, common throughout Latin America in the 1970s. As the Ecuadorian groups have become more disciplined, and more exposed to regular participation in international theatre festivals in Manizales, Caracas and Europe, for example, the impetus for the growth and development of a national theatre has been even greater. After José Martínez Queirolo, whose later works include *Los unos vs. los otros* (*Some against Others*, 1968), a story of rich versus poor set in a boxing context, younger authors worthy of mention are Jorge Dávila Vásquez with *Con gusto a muerte* (*With a Taste of Death*, 1977), Hugo Salazar Tamariz's *En tiempos de la colonia* (*In Colonial Times*, 1979) and Eliécer Cárdenas's *Polvo y ceniza* (*Dust and Ashes*, 1980).

The Ecuadorian theatre is still struggling in its process of self-identification and self-realization, but the efforts of talented individuals in the two major cities of Quito and Guayaquil, not to mention smaller cities in the interior, spur new levels of excitement and activity. While many groups continue to mount foreign plays, a competition sponsored by the Ecuadorian House of Culture in 1990 resulted in three prize-winning plays: Jorge Dávila's *El espejo roto* (*The Broken Mirror*), Luis Miguel Campos's *San Sebastián*, and Iván Toledo's and Raúl Arias's *Luces y espe-*

jos de la vida en el rincón más oscuro de la tierra (*Lights and Mirrors of Life in the Darkest Corner of the World*). The repressive political climate has taken its toll over the years, but the theatre movement, while still not healthy, appears to be growing.   GW

> *See*: R. Descalzi, *Historia crítica del teatro ecuatoriano*, Quito, 1968; G. Luzuriaga, *Del realismo al expresionismo: El teatro de Aguilera Malta*, Madrid, 1971, and 'La generación del 60 y el teatro', *Caravelle*, 30, 1980.

Edgar, David 1948– British dramatist, born in Birmingham, one of a group of left-wing writers who were politicized by the events of 1968. After a spell as a reporter on the *Bradford Telegraph and Argus*, he turned to writing AGIT-PROP plays for the General Will, a touring political theatre company whose targets then included Edward Heath's Conservative government, the Rent Act and a strike on the Upper Clyde. These illustrated Edgar's gift for quick research, lively writing and the telling image. In two years, from 1971 to 1973, he wrote ten plays and collaborated on two others, *England's Ireland* (1972) and a *Fart for Europe* with HOWARD BRENTON (1973).

In the best of these plays, he found popular forms to match his political arguments. The PANTOMIME *Tedderella* (about Edward Heath, 1971, touring; in London, 1973) and the MELODRAMA *Dick Deterred* (1974), about President Richard Nixon and the Watergate scandal, were enjoyable polemical romps. He started to write for the ROYAL SHAKESPEARE COMPANY which, in the early 1970s, described itself as orientated towards socialism and not at all elitist, despite its privileged position in the British theatre system. With the greater resources of a national company, he began to tackle more ambitious subjects. *Destiny* (1976) concerned the rise of a fictitious political party, Nation Forward, a neo-Fascist group akin to the National Front, a real though marginal British political party. In *Maydays* (1983), Edgar described the growing disillusion of British socialists since the Second World War, but his greatest RSC success was his adaptation of *Nicholas Nickleby* (1980), a mammoth project which spread over two evenings and recreated Dickensian London in a manner which suggested that the evils of capitalism have changed little since then. In 1991 he adapted another Victorian novel for the Royal NATIONAL THEATRE – Robert Louis Stevenson's *The Strange Tale of Dr Jekyll and Mr Hyde* (1979) – which was presented at the ROYAL COURT, revealing another side to his work. Its story about a disturbed child was based on an R.D. Laing case study, and stressed the social causes behind mental illness.

During the 1980s, the confident if simplistic left-wing assumptions of his early plays became harder to sustain. As well as the growing doubts expressed in *Maydays*, he described how the collapse of the 1984 miners' strike affected the left-wing (in *That Summer*, 1987) and how the political maps of Eastern Europe were redrawn after Gorbachev's *perestroika* (in *The Shape of the Table*, 1990). Edgar is the most prolific and skilled of the socialist dramatists in Britain; but, as might be expected, his plays have dated, as some practical side effects of socialist rhetoric have come under greater scrutiny. It now seems odd that in *Destiny* he should have concentrated on the threat of Fascism in Britain, at a time when the Militant

Tendency was taking over the Labour Party in Liverpool. JE

Edinburgh Festival The Edinburgh International Festival of Music and Drama (1947 to the present day) presents a programme of first-class international music and drama, as well as art exhibitions, opera and dance, in August and September each year. It is primarily an international occasion, but it has also provided a focus for Scottish theatrical achievement. Here, its most notable success was TYRONE GUTHRIE's production of Sir David Lindsay's medieval MORALITY PLAY, *An Satyre of the Thrie Estaites* (first performed at the Assembly Halls on the Mound in 1948). From the very beginning, the official festival attracted a large number of smaller events. Their presence was ultimately recognized by the formation of the Edinburgh Fringe Festival Society (see FRINGE THEATRE). The Fringe offers a wide range of theatrical activities in halls and on the streets throughout the city. It has long been seen as a spawning ground for new talent and, on occasion, outshines its official counterpart. LM

Edwall, Allan 1924– Swedish actor, director and playwright. Edwall is known internationally for his work in film, but has worked on stage since the 1950s. He acted mostly at DRAMATEN, frequently with ALF SJÖBERG, at first in colourful secondary roles but later in leading roles in MOLIÈRE, STRINDBERG, FRISCH, BRECHT and BECKETT. In 1986 he opened his own cellar theatre in Stockholm, called Brunnsgatan 4 (after the theatre's address). It contains two small stages, on which Edwall has performed much admired one-man versions of SOPHOCLES' *Oedipus*, EURIPIDES' *Alcestis* and his own adaptations of Hjalmar Söderberg and Kafka. HL

Edwardes, George 1852–1915 Irish-born theatre manager whose first important job was that of managing London's newly opened Savoy in 1881. Under direction from Richard D'Oyly Carte, he there supervised the staging of three GILBERT and Sullivan OPERAS. In 1885, Edwardes entered partnership with JOHN HOLLINGSHEAD at the GAIETY, becoming sole manager the following year. His flair was immediately apparent in his employment of FRED LESLIE as his leading comedian. Almost from the start, Edwardes was known as the 'Guv'nor'. He trained and made famous the chorus of Gaiety Girls and was the supreme impresario of the new style of MUSICAL COMEDY, which he introduced not only at the Gaiety, but also at the other London theatres he came to manage – Daly's, the ADELPHI, the PRINCE OF WALES's and the Apollo. Among the many stars who first made their name under Edwardes's management were Gertie Millar, Ellaline Terriss, SEYMOUR HICKS, Marie Tempest, Constance Collier and Gladys Cooper, and among the many musicals he promoted were *The Merry Widow* (1907), *Our Miss Gibbs* (1909) and *The Quaker Girl* (1910). PT

Edwards, Jango [Stanley Ted Edwards] 1950– American CLOWN. After phases as a student and a hippy, he studied clowning in London in 1971, when he founded his first theatre group; this developed into the Friends' Roadshow, which toured Europe regularly. Obscene, anarchic and using rock-concert techniques, Edwards revolutionized the European concept of clown shows and in 1975 organized a mass international gathering of clowns, musicians and FRINGE THEATRES at his Amsterdam headquarters – a Feast of Fools, which became an annual event. LS

Efremov, Oleg (Nikolaevich) 1927– Soviet-Russian stage and film actor, director in the STANISLAVSKY tradition of inner-directed emotional experiencing (*perezhivaniye*). Upon graduating from the studio school of the Moscow Art Theatre (1949), he joined Moscow's Central Children's Theatre as an actor, making his directing debut in 1955. In 1957 he founded and directed the Studio of Young Actors, composed of actors from various theatres as well as students from the MAT studio school. In 1958 this became the Sovremennik (Contemporary) Theatre, so named because it sought to become the voice of the post-Thaw generation of the later 1950s. In intimate, psychologically based realistic plays through which the actors engaged in lyrical self-expression, they paid homage to the Stanislavskian collective ideal while opposing the moribund 'REALISM' which then characterized MAT productions. The company, performing at first in the ballroom of the Moskva (Moscow) Hotel, opened with VIKTOR ROZOV's family war drama *Alive Forever*, which became the theatre's signature piece. Rozov and ALEKSANDR VOLODIN, whose *Two Flowers* (1959), *The Elder Sister* (1962) and *The Appointment* (1963) they also produced, became house playwrights.

Other notable Sovremennik productions included EVGENY SHVARTS's *The Naked King* (1962) and *The Dragon*, which was removed from the repertoire after only four performances; Rozov's *On the Wedding Day* (1964), *The Reunion* (1967) and *From Night to Noon* (1969); VASILY AKSYONOV's social SATIRE *Always on Sale* (1965); contemporary Western plays such as WILLIAM GIBSON's *Two for the Seesaw* (1963), JOHN OSBORNE's *Look Back in Anger* (1966) and EDWARD ALBEE's adaptation of Carson McCullers's *Ballad of the Sad Café* (1967); an adaptation of Ivan Goncharov's classic novel *An Ordinary Story* (1967); and a trilogy on Russia's revolutionary history, consisting of LEONID ZORIN's *The Decembrists*, A. Svobodin's *The Populists* and Mikhail Shatrov's *The Bolsheviks* (1967), commemorating the 50th anniversary of the October Revolution.

The brilliant young company, once thought to be the best in Moscow if not Russia – including Efremov, Igor Kvasha, Evgeny Evstigneev, Oleg Tabakov, L. Tolmachova, Mikhail Kazakov – divided in 1971, some following Efremov to MAT, where he became artistic director (succeeding Boris Livanov), some staying on under actors Oleg Tabakov and Galina Volchyok, and some joining other companies. Appropriately, Efremov's final productions at the Sovremennik included MAT perennials – *The Lower Depths* (1969) and a purposely crowded staging of *The Seagull* (1970), in which a stuffed seagull, thrown at the stage curtain by the actor playing Treplev, hung ingloriously in mockery of MAT's emblem and the spiritual and artistic ideals that theatre no longer served. In the hope of reviving MAT but with some trepidation arising from the institution's prescribed social role, and under some official pressure, Efremov accepted his new position and produced such plays as Volodin's *Dulcinea of El Toboso* (1973), about Don Quixote's legacy; BUERO-VALLEJO's *The Sleep of Reason*, about Goya's last days; MIKHAIL ROSHCHIN's *Old New Year* (produced 1973) and *Troop Train* (1975); and G. Bokrev's *Steel Workers* (1974), an industrial ethics play whose claim to fame was its realistic-looking open-hearth furnaces, shower room with running water and functional elevator.

In 1973 MAT moved into its new 1370-seat theatre on Tverskoi Boulevard, which increased audience expectations of Efremov's directorship, although his play selections and stagings were fast disappointing the *cognoscenti*. Although he failed to unify the MAT collective in spirit and acting style and relied heavily on guest directors, the innovative Little Stage which he opened in 1980–1 as an adjunct to MAT helped develop young actors and directors and new and seldom seen Russian plays. Following his unsuccessful staging of CHEKHOV's *The Seagull* (1980), Efremov mounted provocative productions in the 1980s of Roshchin's satirical comedy *Mother-of-Pearl Zinaida*, ALEKSANDR GELMAN's social-conscience play *Alone among Many*, SHATROV's controversial Lenin play *Blue Horses on Red Grass* and BULGAKOV's *Molière*, in which he played the title role. In 1990, he directed Chekhov's *Ivanov* at the Yale Repertory Theatre. In 1992, he staged GRIBOEDOV's *Woe from Wit* at Moscow's first Anton Chekhov International Theatre Festival. SG

Efros, Anatoly (Vasilievich) 1925–87 Soviet Moscow-based director of distinctive productions in which the kinetic enactment of actor temperament through character spoke to contemporary Soviet man's problem with expressing his personality and maintaining his humanity. Trained by N. V. Petrov and M. O. KNEBEL at the Moscow State Institute of Theatrical Art (GITIS), Efros began his directing career in Ryazan and was the artistic director of several Moscow theatres: the Central Children's Theatre (1954–63); the Lenin Komsomol Theatre (1963–7), where he lost his position on account of 'ideological deficiencies' (i.e. placing individualistic innovation above collective ideology) in his productions; and the Taganka Theatre (1985), as the exiled YURY LYUBIMOV's replacement. From 1967 to 85 he served in a reduced official capacity as staff director at the Theatre on Malaya Bronnaya, where he mounted some of his most celebrated productions.

With an ensemble of like-minded performers assembled over the course of the past 25 years, Efros forged a uniquely athletic style of play in which characters seemed always to be running or otherwise violently physicalizing, and where 'machines for acting', most successfully designed by David Borovsky and Valery Levintal, made strongly tactile, mobile, sculpted, non-decorative statements, somewhat reminiscent of 1920s constructivism. The stage itself was conceived as a boxing ring where the actors-characters' anxieties escalated via absurd repetition into weird rituals of alternating and simultaneous acceptance and denial. Efros sensitively staged contemporary Soviet plays dealing with confused and disaffected youth and spiritual crisis, including his most frequent collaborator VIKTOR ROZOV's *On the Wedding Day* (1964) and *Brother Alyosha* (adapted from Dostoevsky's *The Brothers Karamazov*, 1972); EDVARD RADZINSKY's *104 Pages about*

Love (1964) and *Making a Movie* (1965); and ALEKSEI ARBUZOV's *My Poor Marat* (1965). His staging of BULGAKOV's *The Cabal of Hypocrites* (*Molière*, 1967), a Soviet classic on the talent-as-crown-of-thorns theme, was repeated for television with embattled Taganka director Lyubimov in the title role, and re-created at the invitation of Minneapolis's GUTHRIE THEATRE in 1979.

His highly controversial production of CHEKHOV's *The Three Sisters* (1967) emphasized enervation and repressed sexuality, dealt ironically with dreams of the future (i.e. the communist utopia) and transformed characters into convulsively moving puppets. His *Romeo and Juliet* (1970), which pitted violently expressive youth against their indolent, banal and spiritually corrupt parents beneath the scenically rendered wings of death, was called a distortion of SHAKESPEARE's intentions. Efros interpreted MOLIÈRE's *Don Juan* (1973) as the last rites of a self-destructive, anti-heroic man, victimized by his own myths. His best production, GOGOL's *Marriage* (1974; restaged at the Guthrie Theatre, 1978), was a hyperbolic and alternately frenzied and dream-like evocation of fear and loneliness engaged in a violent tug of war, and featured overpopulated tracking stages and revolving scenic panels reminiscent of MEYERHOLD's 1926 production of *The Inspector General*. Efros's rendering of Chekhov's *The Cherry Orchard*, as guest director at the Taganka (1975), was a study of heightened neurasthenia mounted in a white island-graveyard (perhaps the Moscow Art Theatre tradition's burial ground) in an empty white sea. His 1981 staging of *The Road*, B. Baliasny's adaptation of GOGOL's *Dead Souls*, combined the novel with the author's letters and other writings and made Gogol a character in the play. His version of Molière's *Tartuffe* (1983), at the revitalized Moscow Art Theatre, viewed Orgon's household as a madhouse and featured such MARX BROS-inspired antics as Elvire hiding from Tartuffe in the theatre's prompter's box and Orgon disappearing from underneath the table (which splits in half) where he had been seen to be hiding.

In 1984, facing expulsion from the Malaya Bronnaya theatre staff and seeking to save the Taganka Theatre from Party bureaucrats, Efros replaced the fired Lyubimov as that company's chief director. Amidst severe criticism from the Taganka company and staff and from the Russian émigré press, Efros staged a series of productions, including GORKY's *The Lower Depths* (1984) and Molière's *The Misanthrope* (1986), that were not up to his previous standards. He died suddenly from a heart attack brought on by administrative interrogation. His books include *Rehearsals Are My Passion* (1975), *Profession: Director* (1979), *Sequel to a Theatre Story* (1985) and *The Fourth Book* (1987). SG

Egypt see MIDDLE EAST

Eichelbaum, Samuel 1894–1967 Argentine dramatist who dominated the Buenos Aires stage for nearly 50 years with more than 30 productions. *Un guapo del novecientos* (*A 1900s Dandy*, 1940) marks the beginning of a second period in his writing when he departs from the earlier introspective, often abstract, plays in order to concentrate on more localized themes. Major titles include *Divorcio nupcial* (*Nuptial Divorce*, 1941), *Rostro perdido* (*Lost Face*,

1952), *Dos brasas* (*Two Live Coals*, 1952) and *Subsuelo* (*Underground*, 1966). GW

Ekhof, Konrad 1720–78 German actor. Ekhof acted mainly with the travelling troupes of JOHANN SCHÖNEMANN (from 1740 to 1764), KONRAD ACKERMANN (from 1764 to 1771) and Abel Seyler (from 1771 to 1774). He was the leading actor of the short-lived Hamburg National Theatre project, where his performances led LESSING towards many of the insights into acting recorded in the *Hamburg Dramaturgy*. From 1774 to his death, Ekhof was director of the first troupe of actors to become permanently resident in a German court theatre, at Gotha. Deeply concerned about raising the social status of the acting profession and exploring the fundamental principles of performance, while he was in the Schönemann troupe, Ekhof attempted without much success to found an 'academy' among the actors to study these matters. In Gotha he was able to train young actors systematically. On stage he always gave performances that were realistic, in contrast to the still, rhetorical LEIPZIG STYLE then in vogue. He was often profoundly moving. He had a major influence over the development of German acting at a crucial point in its development. SW

Ekman, Gösta 1890–1938 Swedish actor. Ekman's erratic career alternated between periods of relatively superficial personality acting, which exploited his charm and charisma, and periods in which he achieved great depth, especially in collaboration with PER LINDBERG, under whose direction he gave many important performances: Kurano in MASEFIELD's *The Faithful* (1931), Hamlet, Peer Gynt and the title role in LAGERKVIST's *The Hangman* (all 1934); Shylock, Hjalmar Ekdal and Fedja in LEV TOLSTOI's *The Living Corpse* (all 1935). HL

Ekster, Aleksandra (Aleksandrovna) 1884–1949 Soviet painter and theatrical designer (see THEATRE DESIGN), who helped to introduce cubist and futurist ideas (see FUTURISM) into Russia and lyrically to adapt the constructivist concrete aesthetic in her work with TAIROV. Ekster's outlook was highly cosmopolitan, a result of training and studio work in Paris (following the Kiev Art School), where she met PICASSO, Braque, Apollinaire and MARINETTI. Her sense of solid forms bursting out of three-dimensional space led her to Tairov's Kamerny Theatre, where she designed sets and COSTUMES for ANNENSKY's *Thamira, the Cither Player* (1916), WILDE's *Salome* (1917) and SHAKESPEARE's *Romeo and Juliet* (1921). Her cubist-influenced designs contributed to Tairov's concept of a 'synthetic theatre' in which all visual elements were extensions of the actor's will. This was expressed via a carefully orchestrated three-dimensional score of saturated and symbolic colours, rhythmic shapes, levels and spatial planes. The attempt to avoid both decorative illusionism and two-dimensional stylization coincided with Ekster's interest in exploring the 'dynamic use of immobile form' and the architectural potential of the stage. She designed constructivist costumes from industrial materials (in collaboration with Vera Mukhina) for the film of A. N. TOLSTOI's science fiction novel, *Aelita* (1923), as well as the costumes for MICHAEL CHEKHOV's 1924 MAT Second Studio

production of CALDERÓN DE LA BARCA's *The Phantom Lady*. She emigrated to France in 1924 and pursued an international career as a theatre, ballet and fashion designer and book illustrator. Her legacy to Russian design includes the 'Kiev school' of artists she trained – Pavel Chelishchev, Aleksandr Tyshler, Nisson Shifrin and Anatoly Petritsky – who had distinguished careers of their own. SG

El Salvador If theatre existed in Salvadoran territory during the three centuries (16th–18th) of colonial rule, no records documenting it have survived. The first play of record is titled *La tragedia de Morazán* (*The Tragedy of Morazán*). Written by Francisco Díaz (1812–45) and staged posthumously, it dramatizes the life of the Honduran Francisco Morazán, the general who served briefly as president of the United Provinces of Central America. During the 19th century the principal force in the Salvadoran theatre was Francisco Gavidia (1863–1955). A contemporary and friend of the Nicaraguan modernist poet Rubén Darío, he established the National Theatre with the help of Francisco Antonio Galindo, and over a 60-year period wrote a dozen plays about conflicts from the national past using romantic and symbolist (see SYMBOLISM) styles. One of his best efforts was *Júpiter esclavo o Blanca Celis* (*Jupiter Enslaved or Blanca Celis*, 1895), on the issue of education as a means of personal freedom. Another playwright of the period was José Emilio Aragón (1887–1938).

The 20th century Visiting Spanish and Mexican troupes began to bring modern European influences to El Salvador during the 1920s. In 1927, the Guatemalan-born José Llerena (1895–1943), long-term resident of El Salvador, established the Escuela de Prácticas Escénicas (School of Dramatic Practice) along with the actor Gerardo Neva. He also wrote plays protesting against the encroaching North American influence, but the REALISM of his SATIRE was tempered by weak constructions and excessive moralizing.

In 1952 the government established a department of theatre within the programme of Fine Arts. The impetus brought new playwrights to the fore. Walter Béneke (b.1928) served as his country's ambassador to Germany and Japan, and wrote two prize-winning plays. *El paraíso de los imprudentes* (*Paradise of the Imprudent*, 1956), with its disconcerting look at the 'lost' postwar generation in Paris, was the first play published in the series Colección Teatro (Theatre Collection) of El Salvador. The English title of *Funeral Home* (1958) reflects its setting in the USA, where an anguished young widow faces an existential choice between happiness or adherence to a meaningless standard of values.

A contemporary of Béneke's was Roberto Arturo Menéndez (b.1931), who shared with him first prize in the national culture contest of 1958 for *La ira del cordero* (*The Ire of the Lamb*), a modernized version of the Cain and Abel story rooted in the jealousy and envy produced by parental favouritism. His later plays, *Prometeo II* (*Prometheus II*, 1965) and *Nuevamente Edipo* (*Oedipus Once Again*, 1968), showed his affinity for classical motifs in modern guise. Alvaro Menéndez Leal (b.1943), author of the surrealistic (see SURREALISM) *Luz negra* (*Black Light*, 1966), represented El Salvador in the Olympic Theatre Festival in Mexico in 1968. In the play the two 'severed' heads that compare death with life show clear ties to BECKETT's theatre, but with more humour. Roberto Armijo (b.1937) won first prize in the Central American Theatre contest of 1969 for his *Jugando a la gallina ciega* (*Playing Blind Chicken*), a chilling story about entrapment in the modern world. A group formed in 1982, Teatro del Alba (Theatre of Dawn), presented an ambitious work by a new author, José Roberto Cea (b.1939), in 1983. His *Escenas cumbres* (*High Points*) dramatizes the anguish, solitude and rebellion of man, searching for his authenticity, in contemporary society.

Drama in El Salvador in the 80s was found in the streets, as the vicious civil war brought death and destruction to many and exile to a fortunate few. At the end of the decade J. Luis Ayala García wrote *Crónica de una traición* (*Chronicle of a Treason*); the young Edgar Roberto Gustave also captured the violence of the times in his short plays. Peace has been formally restored to the country, but the theatre has not yet received much attention, even though some exiles have returned. GW

El Teatro Campesino (Farmworkers' Theatre) Founded by LUIS VALDÉZ in 1965 to support Filipino and Mexican-American strikers against the grape farmers of the San Joaquin Valley in Calfornia. Initially an AGIT-PROP group tailoring its *actos* (short plays) to the issues and needs of the moment, in a style at once cartoon-like, comic and realistic, the company took on a wider political involvement – though still focusing on CHICANO concerns – during the period of maximum opposition to the Vietnam War. In the 1970s, disillusion with the growing violence of Chicano politics, together with a need to develop artistically, prompted a change of direction. El Centro Campesino Cultural was created on 40 acres of farmland at San Juan Bautista, south of San Francisco, for Valdéz and his people to research Indian myth and RITUAL as a basis for life and theatre. In performance, the early *actos* were replaced by *mitos* ('myths') such as *El baile de los gigantes* (*The Dance of the Giants*, 1974), though the basic principle of a bilingual theatre using a vivid physical style remained the same. Valdéz's MUSICAL *Corridos*, based on Mexican ballad traditions, opened in 1983; and each year sees a performance of *La Pastorela*, the company's adaptation of a traditional shepherds' play. The interest in Spanish-American (and autochthonous) culture has not, however, replaced the earlier polemical thrust, so much as provided a wider context for it. Valdéz's drama of racial violence, *Zoot Suit* (1978), played to critical and popular acclaim in Los Angeles (though not on BROADWAY), and more recently the company has had success with Valdéz's *I Don't Have to Show You No Stinking Badges* and Josefina López's *Simply Maria* (1986). During the 1990s three to six productions have been mounted annually, and the company has toured extensively. AEG

Elder, Eldon 1924– American designer, who studied with DONALD OENSLAGER at Yale. Though he designed over 200 productions for BROADWAY, OFF-BROADWAY, OPERA and regional theatre, his lasting legacy is as designer of the Delacorte Theater, the Central Park home of the NEW YORK SHAKESPEARE FESTIVAL, where he was resident designer during 1958–61. He also designed or consulted on several other theatres, including many regional ones, with over 30 productions at the St Louis Municipal Opera. Elder taught for many years at Brooklyn College, City University of New York. AA

Elder, Lonne, III 1931– African-American playwright and film/TV scriptwriter. After the critical acclaim accorded to his play *Ceremonies in Dark Old Men* (1969), Elder joined the NEGRO ENSEMBLE COMPANY as director of its Playwrights' Unit. He then moved to Hollywood to write scripts for film and television. Among the best-known of his screenplays are the award-winning *Sounder* (1972), which shows the effect of the Depression on a black sharecropping family; its sequel *Sounder, Part II* (1976); and *Melinda* (1972), about a black disk jockey's entanglement with a crime syndicate. In 1988 Elder's one-person play *Splendid Mummer* opened in New York City: based on the career of the 19th-century black actor IRA ALDRIDGE and featuring Charles Dutton, it failed, however, to win critical approval. EGH

Eldridge [*née* McKechnie], **Florence** 1901–88 American actress, whose BROADWAY debut in 1918 was in the chorus of *Rock-a-Bye Baby*. After several appearances on Broadway, she toured with her husband, FREDRIC MARCH, in THEATRE GUILD's productions such as *Arms and the Man*, *The Silver Cord* and *The Guardsman* in 1927–8. She made her film debut in 1929 in *Studio Murder Mystery* with her husband. She frequently appeared with March, as in *The Skin of Our Teeth* (1942) and again in RUTH GORDON's *Years Ago* (1946). One of her greatest successes, again with March, was as Mary Tyrone in *Long Day's Journey into Night* (1956), for which she won the *Variety* New York Drama Critics' Poll. SMA

Eliot, T(homas) S(tearns) 1888–1965 American-born British poet and dramatist. From St Louis in Missouri, Eliot was educated at Harvard, the Sorbonne and Oxford, then settled in London after 1915. His plays mark the high point in the modern revival of English poetic drama. He was a founder member of London's GROUP THEATRE, his first short stage pieces portraying the spiritual wasteland of 20th-century social values and political movements: the fragmentary 'Aristophanic melodrama' *Sweeney Agonistes* (1928) and the choral BURLESQUE *The Rock* were produced by Rupert Doone and E. MARTIN BROWNE in 1934. They reflected Eliot's suggestion that poetry might be restored to the theatre by adapting popular forms or MUSIC-HALL techniques, as did his first major play, *Murder in the Cathedral*, with its incorporation of jazz rhythms and direct address as well as liturgical structures. Commissioned for the 1935 Canterbury Festival and performed in the chapter house of the cathedral, it is the clearest expression of the integral connection between verse and religious experience that characterizes Eliot's work. Despite its medieval subject and static form, it transferred successfully to the commercial theatre and has been more frequently revived than any of Eliot's other plays.

However, Eliot came to see it as a dead end in his attempt to create a contemporary poetic language for the stage, and from *The Family Reunion* (1939) he increasingly disguised the verse, spiritual themes and archetypal paradigms of his drama. Based on the *Oresteia*, this play retained visionary choral passages and the supernatural machinery of the Eumenides in the context of a modern country house detective drama. But in *The Cocktail Party* (1949), *The Confidential Clerk* (1953) and *The Elder Statesman* (1958), all of which were first performed at the EDINBURGH FESTIVAL, the rhythms of the dialogue become progressively closer to prose. The incongruity of overtly ritual elements in a realistic setting is avoided. There are no direct references to alert the audience to the mythical basis of the plots – drawn respectively from the *Alcestis* and *Ion* of EURIPIDES and SOPHOCLES' *Oedipus at Colonus*, and designed to work on a subconscious level. Instead, the surface situation is that of a conventional comedy of manners or modern problem play, and the plays suffer by comparison with more normal examples of these genres since the underlying religious significance tends to flatten the characters and remove dramatic tension. Even so, with Eliot's prestige as a Nobel Prizewinner for his poetry (1948) and the intrinsic interest of his continuing theatrical experimentation, these plays ran successfully in London and New York as well as attracting considerable critical attention.

At the beginning of his career Eliot also edited a literary quarterly, the *Criterion*, becoming a director of the publishing house Faber and Faber in 1925, and the difficulties of his first marriage have recently formed the subject of a successful play, *Tom and Viv*, by Michael Hastings. A revival of *The Cocktail Party* (London 1986) and the production of the MUSICAL *Cats*, based on Eliot's 1939 poems *Old Possum's Book of Practical Cats*, suggest a renewed interest in Eliot in the 1980s and 90s. CI DBW MB

Elizabethan theatre companies The richer households of 14th- and 15th-century England customarily included minstrels and other entertainers among their numerous servants. The playing of INTERLUDES at feasts in great halls encouraged the development of small troupes (four men and a boy) like Henry VII's Lusores Regis. Protected by the livery of a noble patron, these players avoided the stringent penalties inflicted on rogues and vagabonds in Tudor England. There was prestige to be gained for the lord of an impressive acting troupe. LEICESTER'S MEN (1559–88) proclaimed the munificence of their patron as well as their own special skills. Other companies– Sussex's, Oxford's, STRANGE'S, Worcester's – operated along similar lines. They performed before visiting dignitaries in the great halls of their patrons' homes, toured the provinces in his livery and aspired to the honour of playing at the queen's court.

Performance in London was more likely to catch the eye of the Lord Chamberlain, and so it was to London that the companies gravitated, playing in inn-yards like the Saracen's Head and the BOAR'S HEAD. It was a former member of Leicester's Men, JAMES BURBAGE, who first tested the potential profitability of a purpose-built playhouse. His erection of the THEATRE in 1576 began a change in the priorities of the household companies. The command of London audiences proffered a new financial independence to any company that could seize it. As more theatres were built, leading companies became associated with

particular homes – the LORD CHAMBERLAIN'S MEN with the Theatre, the ADMIRAL'S MEN with the ROSE, Pembroke's Men (disastrously) with the SWAN, Worcester's and Oxford's Men with the Boar's Head. The theatre owner would claim his share of the takings but the companies were artistically independent. The custom was for senior members to become sharers (in the risks as well as the profits). Buying and dealing in such shares was hazardous, since London's theatres were threatened by competition, by hostile authorities and by the recurrent plague epidemics, but prudence and good fortune brought riches to some sharers. A loyal and successful company like the Lord Chamberlain's Men probably included six actor-sharers, four hired men and two boys apprenticed to a sharer. But the Chamberlain's Men stole a march on all their rivals when they moved to the GLOBE in 1599. For the first, and probably the only, time the actors owned their own theatre.

Although briefly (1583–94) the nominal patron of her own company, QUEEN ELIZABETH'S MEN, Elizabeth I endorsed the household groups of the Tudor aristocracy. James I was anxious to centralize and assert the cultural ascendancy of the court. He adopted the Chamberlain's Men as his own King's Men and the Admiral's Men became Prince Henry's Men. London's third company, playing at the Boar's Head, became Queen Anne's Men and moved to the RED BULL, where they gratified a boisterous audience with violence and spectacle. Other companies formed and disbanded and other theatres, both public and private, opened and closed in London. The challenge of the BOYS' COMPANIES faded after 1608, and the adult companies, once the principle of higher admission charges for small indoor theatres had been established, vied for the privilege of performing under cover. The King's Men maintained their outdoor supremacy at the Globe and added indoor success at the BLACKFRIARS after 1609. CHRISTOPHER BEESTON caused dissension when he tried to provide Queen Anne's Men with an indoor home at the COCKPIT THEATRE, and became instead an autocratic theatre manager, who hired the Cockpit to any high-bidding company before establishing there his own troupe, nicknamed Beeston's Boys.

The last theatres to be built before the Civil War, the SALISBURY COURT and the COCKPIT-IN-COURT, were both small indoor houses, which suited a Caroline taste for decorous display. The Salisbury Court was successively the home of Prince Charles's Men (1631–35) and Queen Henrietta's Men (1636–42). The Cockpit-in-Court was used primarily but not exclusively by the King's Men during their regular royal command performances. With the CLOSURE OF THE THEATRES, the great theatre companies were perforce disbanded. The great majority of the actors, conscious of the hand that buttered their bread, took and fought on the Royalist side. A few remained in London to seek out opportunities for surreptitious performance at the abandoned theatres. PT

Elliot, Michael 1931–84 British director. In 1959 Elliot formed the 59 Theatre Company at the LYRIC THEATRE, HAMMERSMITH, for which he directed his highly acclaimed production of IBSEN's *Brand*. He directed at Stratford-upon-Avon in 1961–2, was appointed artistic director of the OLD VIC for its final season in 1962–3, and directed for the NATIONAL THEATRE in 1965. In 1968, together with several members of the original 59 Company, he founded the 69 Theatre Company in Manchester which in 1976 metamorphosed into the ROYAL EXCHANGE THEATRE Company. He aimed from the start to make the new theatre of front-rank quality, independent of current London trends. His own productions of (for example) *Uncle Vanya*, *The Lady from the Sea* and *The Dresser* all helped to guarantee the success of the enterprise. He won a deserved reputation as England's foremost interpreter of Ibsen and STRINDBERG, and also directed many successful productions for television (see TELEVISION DRAMA). AJ

Elliott, Gertrude [*née* May Dermot] 1874–1950 American actress; sister to MAXINE ELLIOTT. After making her New York debut in 1894, she acted with Marie Wainwright (1895) and NAT GOODWIN (1897–9), playing Emily in *In Mizzoura*, Lucy in *The Rivals*, and Angelica Knowlton in *Nathan Hale*. She made her London debut in 1899 as Midge in *The Cowboy and the Lady*, and remained in England to play Ophelia to FORBES-ROBERTSON's Hamlet. After the two were married in 1900, she returned to America several times, playing Maisie in *The Light That Failed* (1903), a character in the mould of Hedda Gabler, and creating the role of Cleopatra in SHAW's *Caesar and Cleopatra* (1906). Critics praised her girlish spirit, playful humour, eloquent speech and dusky beauty. After her husband retired, she managed London's ST JAMES'S THEATRE (1918). TLM

Elliott, Maxine [*née* Jessie Dermot] 1871–1940 American actress and stage beauty; older sister to GERTRUDE ELLIOTT. After making her New York stage debut at PALMER's Theatre in 1890, Maxine Elliott rose rapidly in the theatre, spending a season each with ROSE COGHLAN's and AUGUSTIN DALY's companies (1894, 95) before her London debut as Sylvia in *Two Gentlemen of Verona* (1895). After an Australian tour with NAT GOODWIN (1896), she became his leading lady (1897) and his wife (1898). They co-starred in numerous successes, including her first big hit as Alice Adams in *Nathan Hale* (1899). They separated in 1902, after which she established herself as a star with Georgiana Carley in *Her Own Way* (1903) written for her by CLYDE FITCH. Two years later, her Georgiana attracted the attentions of Edward VII in London. She built the Maxine Elliott Theatre in New York (1908) with help from the SHUBERTS, and appeared there in numerous comedies, including *Myself*, *Settina* and *The Chaperon*. In 1911 she retired to England, making only occasional stage appearances thereafter. She was praised as a 'rare comedienne of the drawing room' during her 1918–19 American tour of *Lord and Lady Algy*. Although she appeared stiff and mechanical to some critics, all praised her dark and lustrous beauty and her statuesque stage presence. She retired to the Riviera after 1920 to live out her life as a 'lady of society'. TLM

Elliston, Robert (William) 1774–1831 English actor and theatre manager, who disappointed his respectable uncles by running off to make a stage debut at Bath. Known for his versatility, since he was at home in TRAGEDY as well as COMEDY, Elliston is remembered as 'the Great Lessee', lauded for his good spirits by CHARLES LAMB and a redoubtable opponent of the Patent theatres' monopoly over the legitimate drama during his years in management of such minor theatres as the Royal Circus (1809–14), which he converted and renamed the Surrey, and of the OLYMPIC (1813–19), where he was the first manager to install gas in a theatre auditorium (1815). Having failed to beat the powerful Patent houses, he did the next-best thing by assuming management of DRURY LANE (1819–26). The company was led by EDMUND KEAN, whom Elliston had been the first London manager to recognize, and was in full-scale rivalry with COVENT GARDEN. Elliston relished the competition and set about securing the best actors by raising salaries. For the first few years the policy paid off, but the end was bankruptcy.

The failure owed as much to Elliston's private life – he had followed his watchmaker-father into alcoholism and was required to maintain at least three bastards as well as a wife and their nine children. His policy, which he bequeathed to the notorious ALFRED BUNN, was to run Drury Lane as he had run the Surrey (and would run it again from 1827 until his death), as a home for spectacle and PANTOMIME as well as the classical drama. The secret of his acting was the bond he established with his audience (as Charles Surface or Falstaff, in particular), and he managed his theatres in the same way. Almost alone among Regency managers, Elliston had the common touch. PT

Ellsler, John 1822–1903 American manager. Originally an actor, he assumed management of his own company at Cleveland's Academy of Music in 1855. He opened his lavish Euclid Avenue Opera House in 1875, but the Academy of Music remained his centre of operation until 1885. His company toured extensively to surrounding towns in the summers, and between 1871 and 87 he managed at least one theatre a year in Pittsburgh. His theatre was noted as a nursery of talent: CLARA MORRIS, JAMES O'NEILL, James Lewis and Mrs G.H. Gilbert apprenticed there. His daughter, Effie Ellsler (1854–1942), became a leading lady of the next generation, remembered primarily for her Hazel Kirke, a role written for her by STEELE MACKAYE. John Ellsler's memoirs were not published until 1950. DMCD

Eltinge, Julian [William Dalton] 1883–1941 American female impersonator (see FEMALE IMPERSONATION), first seen professionally in *Mr Wix of Wixham*, a MUSICAL COMEDY (1904). His biggest hit was *The Fascinating Widow* (1911 and tours), in which he outshone fashion-plate Valeska Surratt. Its success led grateful producer Al Woods to build the Eltinge Theatre on 42nd St, New York. 'The ambi-sextrous comedian', as PERCY HAMMOND called him, chose vehicles that enabled him to shift gender by quick change (one act required 11 separate changes). With his company, the Julian Eltinge Players, he played VAUDEVILLE (1918–27) and starred in silent films. A large man with a passable baritone voice, he was a favourite primarily with female audiences, not least for the chic of his wardrobe. His last VARIETY appearance – at the White Horse, Los Angeles (1940) – was a fiasco, owing to a police ban on public transvestism. LS

Emanuel, Giovanni 1848–1902 Italian actor-manager. Emanuel early became a lead player opposite the principal actresses of his day, formed his own company and, in the way of Italian players of the age, toured widely abroad, as far as Latin America and Russia. He was noted for his strongly naturalistic style (see NATURALISM) in interpreting the classics, including SHAKESPEARE, being particularly strong as Othello and Lear. The care with which he prepared productions, and the scrupulous attention he gave to detail in the roles he played, are well evidenced in his extant prompt books. KR

Emery, John 1777–1822 English comic actor, the son, father and grandfather of notable actors. Emery completed his apprenticeship under TATE WILKINSON in the York circuit, and was, from 1798 until his death, a leading low comedian at COVENT GARDEN. He is the first actor known to have been encored for his playing of a scene, that of Fixture's jealousy in THOMAS MORTON's *A Roland for an Oliver* (1819). Emery had spent much of his childhood in Yorkshire, and his pre-eminence in rustic roles established the Yorkshire dialect as an acceptable alternative to 'Mummerset' for comic country bumpkins. His Tyke in Morton's *The School of Reform* (1805) was famous in his time, and the play died with him. His melancholy end is tersely recorded in James Winston's diary: 'Emery is given over. Emery became latterly incapable of fulfilling his duty. He drank excessively, was in a public house great part of his time.' PT

Emmet, Alfred see QUESTORS THEATRE

Emmett, Dan see MINSTREL SHOW

Empire Theatre (New York City) In 1893, when CHARLES FROHMAN built the gem-like Empire on BROADWAY some 25 blocks north of the theatre district at Union Square, the spark was ignited to create a new theatre district uptown. This theatre remained the headquarters of Frohman's activities until he died on the *Lusitania* in 1915. During his lifetime, Frohman was Broadway's principal starmaker, a member of the THEATRICAL SYNDICATE, and the Napoleon of the American theatre. The roster of the stars who appeared at the Empire is etched into a plaque affixed to the wall of the characterless office building that replaced the theatre after it was torn down in 1953. The theatre was managed by Alf Hayman for the Frohman estate on a run-of-the-play basis, and was later leased to producer GILBERT MILLER until 1931. With just over 1000 seats, it was a compact, well designed playhouse and a favourite among actors and audiences alike. It enjoyed a latter-day reputation as a house of hits, crowned by the arrival of *Life with Father* in 1939, which did not leave its stage for six years. The theatre changed ownership several times before its demise. At the time it closed, it was presenting *The Time of the Cuckoo* with SHIRLEY BOOTH. MCH

Encina, Juan del c.1468–c.1530 Spanish poet, musician and playwright, sometimes called the Father of Spanish Drama. Born and educated in Salamanca, he served the Duke of Alba in several capacities, then lived in Rome from 1498 until 1509. In 1496 he published eight of his 14 dramatic *églogas* (eclogues), along with poetry and songs. The early plays are PASTORAL sketches featuring comic shepherds, topical allusions, songs and dances. They were performed on high feastdays by Encina and other courtiers. Later eclogues are longer, more complex, and influenced by secular Italian Renaissance forms. CL PZ

Engel, Johann Jakob 1741–1802 German playwright and aesthetician. A minor figure at best, Engel's most important contribution to theatre was his book *Ideas on Mimesis* (1786), which catalogued in detail gestures and poses of characteristic emotions. From 1787 to 1794, he was director of the BERLIN ROYAL THEATRE. SW

England (See also MEDIEVAL DRAMA IN EUROPE (England, Scotland and Ireland; Cornwall and Wales).

The Tudor period The English theatre owes more than can be accurately determined to the fondness for display of the Tudor family. Henry VII had his own company of players. Grandiloquently called the Lusores Regis, the group probably comprised four men and a boy, all adept at quick costume changes and the doubling or trebling of parts. But it was not only, nor even primarily, through the patronage of plays that the Tudors announced their theatricality. The elaborate disguisings that greeted the arrival of distinguished guests, the royal progresses and tournaments often placed the monarch at the centre of the spectacle. Although such events were 'amateur', they were planned and managed with professional thoroughness and observed, or participated in, by the men who would later plan and manage the Elizabethan companies of professional players. The taste for display and spectacular expenditure (or the appearance of spectacular expenditure) should be recognized by any student of English drama under the Tudors and Stuarts.

The irregular but persistent increase of professional actors is a feature of the 16th century. Their attachment to noble families protected them from the worst effects of religious and political turbulence, which threatened and finally silenced the amateur performers of medieval MYSTERY PLAYS. The suppression of the Feast of Corpus Christi in 1548 was a sign of the new times. In the midlands and the North, remote from the centres of power, the mystery cycles continued for three decades, but by 1581 they had been effectively destroyed. The English theatre's secular history was decisively launched, and the fraternity of professional actors was ready for it.

Their readiness was owed in part to the slender growth of secular drama during the first half of the 16th century. The influence of Roman comedy (see ROME) persisted, despite the sudden disfavour with which everything Italian was viewed after the Reformation, but the audience for such plays was restricted. *Ralph Roister Doister* (written 1534–52, printed c.1566), the first English COMEDY to capture successfully the comic vitality of PLAUTUS and TERENCE, was probably intended by its schoolmaster-author, NICHOLAS UDALL, for performance by the boys of Eton or Westminster. The more homespun *Gammer Gurton's Needle* (written 1552–63, printed 1575, the year in which its putative author, William Stevenson, died) was probably first performed by schoolboys, too. Like comedy,

Ralph Richardson and Laurence Olivier in Sheridan's *The Critic*, Old Vic Theatre, 1945.

English TRAGEDY was nurtured by a privileged audience. THOMAS NORTON and THOMAS SACKVILLE, men of substance whose involvement lent lustre to the craft of the playwright, wrote *Gorboduc* (1562), under the conscious influence of the Roman SENECA, for performance at London's Inner Temple before the queen. It was the scholarly study of classical form, supremely exemplified in the drama by Seneca and Terence, that established the formal, five-act discipline of tragedy and comedy in England. Since they were much studied at the grammar schools, it is reasonable to assume that Seneca and Terence were included in SHAKESPEARE's 'little Latin'.

If the outstanding plays of the mid-century were written for private performance, there were competent writers to cater for the immediate needs of professional players. In 1574, while the death-knell of religious drama tolled, regular weekday performances of plays were legitimized in London. One man who took particular notice was JAMES BURBAGE, a master-carpenter eager to raise himself, and a member (or former member) of the most prominent of early-Elizabethan household companies, Lord LEICESTER's MEN. Burbage calculated that there was sufficient interest in and around London to justify the erection of a building specially designed for the performance of plays. He was guided less by Continental precedent than by simple commercial considerations. Whilst professional players could expect *ex gratia* payments for entertaining the nobility, the collecting of money from casual audiences, particularly at open-air performances, was unreliable. We can reasonably assume that Burbage's main interest was the box-office, not the stage. Like many Elizabethans – explorers, alchemists, quack-doctors – he was a speculator, bold enough to risk all in a project. What he had not got, he borrowed, and his new playhouse, known simply as the THEATRE, was completed in 1576.

There is no more significant date in the history of English drama. Had Burbage's project failed, it is difficult to see how the great plays of the next 50 years could have been written. The circumstances of his success merit attention. There is, firstly, the question of location. The city of London was governed by men much less sympathetic to games and plays than was the Tudor nobility. Prudence dictated that the Theatre be built outside the city walls, beyond the immediate jurisdiction of the city fathers. Burbage took a lease on a site north of Bishopsgate, in Shoreditch, on land vacated by the dissolution of Holywell Priory. Since no records survive, the nature of the building must be inferred, partly from our knowledge of Burbage's likely models and partly from information on subsequent theatre-building. Plays had been performed in public places for long enough to provide the first theatre architect with certain guidelines. A raised stage, for instance, was of proven value. Simply mounted on barrels or trestles, it could be quickly removed to clear space for such popular entertainments as animal-baiting. Although he built the Theatre to house plays, Burbage was too good a businessman to neglect the advantages of adaptability. The new drama had still to capture public attention. Meanwhile, the medieval confusion of 'games' and 'plays' held good. Tiered seating, like that in contemporary cockpits, suited spectators of both. The Theatre was on a grander scale than the cockpits and more serviceable than the yards of coaching inns, whose open plan and first-floor walkways were familiar to Tudor actors, but it incorporated features of both. Arguing from later evidence, scholars propose that the first English playhouse had three galleries circling an open yard, about half of which was occupied by a removable scaffold stage. The TIRING HOUSE (dressing rooms) lay behind the stage, and entrances were made through either of two doors in the tiring house façade. This would have brought the actors into close proximity with the standing audience, who had paid one penny for admission to the yard, and also with the spectators seated in the lowest gallery, who had probably paid a further penny for the privilege of resting their legs.

This proximity was something with which audience and actors were familiar. There is disagreement among students of Elizabethan acting about the comparative formality or realism of performing styles. Either way, the actors had to confront a boisterous audience in an atmosphere closer to that of a public meeting than a decorously hushed modern theatre. On a wide stage (the later GLOBE and FORTUNE had platforms at least 43ft wide x 23ft deep), timid acting had no place. The Elizabethan player needed to dominate both platform and audience. The Theatre, like later Elizabethan playhouses, was no setting for inward acting. Passion had to be shown, not contained, and stories had to be told with emphasis and clarity. It was all too easy for a dissatisfied audience to make its feelings plain. The best Elizabethan actors were supreme showmen, many of them skilled swordsmen, athletes or musicians. Some learned their trade as apprentices, and the likelihood is that bodily prowess was as prominent in the training programme as rhetoric. No Elizabethan company could afford to neglect the drawing power of spectacle, and, since scene design and mechanical aids were in their infancy, that spectacle had to be provided by the actors themselves. Their chief support, in an age extravagantly interested in clothes, was COSTUME. The actor had no scenery to shelter in, no atmospheric lighting and no proscenium arch to protect him from the rude encounter with his audience. Sharing a confined space under the open sky with paying customers, he needed a good costume and a good voice. The great playwrights of the age could afford to write as they did because actors spoke well and audiences were used to listening. It is hard for us, in a period so dependent on visual stimulus, to recapture the priorities of an aural culture, when vital information was still conveyed by proclamation and the town-crier not yet a colourful archaism, when street ballads attracted crowds and, even in sophisticated court circles, it was the custom for poets to read their work aloud.

It is easy, with hindsight, to see that London was ready for a theatre in 1576, but Burbage's boldness should not be underrated. The repertoire of plays, now that religious drama was frowned on, was pitiably small. The rapid creation of a national repertoire is the most astonishing achievement of the period, but the innovatory work of CHRISTOPHER MARLOWE was still a decade away – *Tamburlaine* dates from c.1587 – and we have no record of the plays presented at the Theatre in its early years. Burbage probably leased it, at a fixed rent, to his old company, Leicester's Men, and, on demand, to other groups. Like-minded promoters soon followed his lead. The CURTAIN was built nearby in 1577, and an obscure theatre in the south-bank village of Newington was active by, at the latest, 1580. In addition, several inns remained in irregular use – the Bell and Cross Keys in Gracious (now Gracechurch) Street, the BOAR'S HEAD in Whitechapel, the Saracen's Head in Islington, the Bull in Bishopsgate, and the Bel Savage in Ludgate Hill among them. By 1587, the enterprising PHILIP HENSLOWE was running the newly built ROSE on the south bank of the Thames, where, like all Elizabethan public theatres, it was outside the jurisdiction of the city fathers. By 1595 Francis Langley, probably the most grasping of all Elizabethan theatrical entrepreneurs, had opened the SWAN in nearby Paris Garden. It is from the chance preservation of a drawing of the Swan's interior by a visiting Dutchman, Johannes De Witt, that we derive our only concrete evidence of the physical outlines of the stage during the early years of the public theatres.

The year 1576 is notable for another theatrical enterprise, one which introduces an important Elizabethan distinction. 'Public' theatres of the kind pioneered by Burbage were, initially at least, polygonal buildings enclosing covered galleries and a yard open to the sky. The partial covering of the stage, observable in De Witt's drawing, was a later refinement, copied at the first and second Globe (1599 and 1614), the square Fortune (1600), the adapted inn known as the RED BULL (1605) and Henslowe's last great enterprise, the HOPE (1614). But there was to be competition, after 1576, from a rival tradition of indoor 'private' theatres. In that extraordinary year, Richard Farrant, Master of the CHILDREN OF THE CHAPEL ROYAL, supervised the conversion of rooms in the dissolved BLACKFRIARS monastery for use as an indoor playhouse. His actors were choirboys, whose regular involvement in the performance of plays at Court had been affirmed by such earlier 16th-century Masters as William Cornish and Richard Edwardes. Not to be outdone, the BOYS OF ST PAUL'S, under the active mastership (1557–82) of Sebastian Westcott, had formed an effective rival company. The fondness for boy actors, sometimes in preference to adults, is mysteriously related to aristocratic cult interest in pubescence, and Farrant's Blackfriars plans were opportunistic. Although within the city walls, the Blackfriars precinct was constitutionally outside the jurisdiction of the civic authorities, and it had the extra advantage of being within easy reach of the Inns of Court, whose wealthy and pleasure-seeking residents became a staple audience of the private, as well as of the public, theatres.

The first innovative Elizabethan playwright, JOHN LYLY, whose earliest plays were staged at the Blackfriars in 1584, can be claimed by the BOYS' COMPANIES. Lyly was prominent among the group of UNIVERSITY WITS (others include PEELE, NASHE, GREENE, Lodge and Marlowe), whose alert response to theatrical expansion soon plumped out the meagre repertoire of plays. Proud of their sophistication, they poured scorn on the rising generation of professional playwrights, who eagerly peddled their work to boys and adults alike. Lyly went so far as to involve himself at managerial level, burning his own fingers as well as those of the boys' companies by involving them on the anti-Puritan side in the Marprelate Controversy of 1588–9. Under the Tudors, as under the Stuarts, it was a perilous thing for actors to involve themselves in politics. The boys' companies lay low for a decade, and when, under a new Master, Nathaniel Giles, the Children of the Chapel Royal returned to the Blackfriars, it was to new premises. The second Blackfriars theatre had been leased and converted by James Burbage in 1596, for adult use, but the precinct's residents petitioned against the unruly intrusion and the enterprise foundered. That Giles should have been allowed to present plays there after 1600 is evidence of the social status attached to boys' companies. For a while, as the famous references in *Hamlet* show, the children were a threat even to the best of the adult players, but more political indiscretions, together with a shift in taste, led to their disintegration. By 1608, the heyday of boy acting was over and the adult companies could take their pick from the choristers willing to play female roles in a single-sex profession.

Over one thousand professional players are known by name in the period 1590–1642, and there were probably at least as many again. Of the several companies under noble patronage (such as Pembroke's Men, Oxford's Men, Worcester's Men), two had established a clear supremacy by the end of the 16th century. Of these, the ADMIRAL'S MEN had been so called since 1585 and the CHAMBERLAIN'S MEN since 1594. The former became associated with Henslowe's theatres (the Rose and the Fortune) and the latter with Burbage's (the Theatre and the Globe). It was during the 1590s that the English theatre came of age, but the status of the playwright remained anomalous. 'Haply some plays may be worth the keeping: but hardly one in forty,' wrote the book-loving Sir Thomas Bodley in 1612, and his point can be supported by reference to careless publication or, more often, by the lack of publication. Even so, we can estimate that well over 2000 new plays were written between 1590 and 1642, each one a commodity for which a company would pay £6. Playwrights were employed by actors, and since speed of composition was vital, with several theatres competing for a limited audience and new pieces guaranteed a larger following at their first performance than ever again, the task of turning an agreed plot into a complete script was customarily shared by two or more writers.

Unlike the University Wits, the new generation of playwrights came often from within the profession. Shakespeare and JONSON, the two greatest, were both actors, and Shakespeare would never have achieved such prosperity if he had confined himself to writing. His name was sufficiently familiar by 1592 to inspire Greene's jealous abuse, but it was his purchase of a share in the newly formed Chamberlain's Men in 1594 that gave him a secure hold on an insecure profession. Until his retirement in c.1608, he remained an active member of London's leading company, adding outstandingly successful plays to a repertoire that also included work by Jonson, MARSTON, DEKKER, WEBSTER, MIDDLETON, TOURNEUR, FLETCHER and

BEAUMONT. It was a repertoire that the Admiral's Men could not match, except with the often revived plays of Marlowe. Evidently averse to collaborative composition, Shakespeare was adept at snapping up and improving popular styles. When Senecan tragedy (*Titus Andronicus*) was modified by the success of KYD's *The Spanish Tragedy*, he could lift REVENGE TRAGEDY to new heights in *Hamlet*. When the rough chronicle plays were challenged by Marlowe's *Edward II*, he produced *Richard II* and the finest of HISTORY PLAYS, *Henry IV* in two parts and *Henry V*. *Julius Caesar* was a response to a revived interest in Roman history. The late comedies, from *Pericles* to *The Tempest*, were written in full awareness of the popular romances of Beaumont and Fletcher. Even the uniquely Jonsonian COMEDY OF HUMOURS is alluded to in *Twelfth Night*, and CITIZEN COMEDY, of which Dekker's *The Shoemaker's Holiday* is the outstanding example, is embraced by *The Merry Wives of Windsor*. Shakespeare's greatest comedies and tragedies belong to no school, and the countless attempts through history to imitate them only serve to demonstrate their inimitability. But it should be stressed that they were written for performance by his known fellow actors. RICHARD BURBAGE and others enhanced the greatness of Shakespeare's plays, establishing their claims on contemporary audiences as surely as EDWARD ALLEYN's playing established Marlowe's pre-eminence a few years earlier. By any reckoning, the Chamberlain's Men were, during Shakespeare's years as a member, one of the finest companies of players the English theatre has known.

The Stuart period Within two months of his accession, James I had taken the Chamberlain's Men into his personal patronage, renaming them the King's Men. The Admiral's Men were assigned to his heir, Prince Henry. Unlike the Tudors, the Stuarts were anxious to centralize and specify cultural supremacy. Royal interest would prove a mixed blessing for the London theatre, but initially it was a lovely light in a dark world. The year 1603 would otherwise have been a financial disaster. Closed in March as a token of respect to the dying queen, the theatres had scarcely opened after the period of national mourning when London was struck by plague. While 30,000 citizens died between May 1603 and April 1604, the theatres remained closed, as they always were when plague deaths reached 40 in any week. James, who had prudently delayed his arrival in the capital, summoned the King's Men to Wilton House, rewarding them for their December performances with a generous £30. But his displeasure could be equally decisive, as the authors of the anti-Scottish tags in *Eastward Ho* discovered in 1604. Two of them, CHAPMAN and Jonson, were briefly imprisoned, and the third, Marston, took refuge abroad.

Some critics have perceived a darkening tone in Jacobean drama, a pervading cynicism about the preponderance of time-servers in corrupt courts and an unhappy recognition, shared with John Donne, that 'new philosophy' has 'put all in doubt'. The view is attractive but oversimple. The first Stuart decade encompasses the bitter work of Webster and Tourneur, the great tragedies of Shakespeare, Jonson's most biting comedies and the emergence of the distinctively caustic Middleton, but also the happy vogue for tragicomic romance, spearheaded by the gentleman-playwrights, Beaumont and Fletcher, who, together or singly, wrote with an easy grace that demonstrates the astonishingly rapid maturity of a national drama that was scarcely 30 years old.

The same decade saw important developments in staging techniques. In 1608, James Burbage's dream was posthumously realized when the King's Men took possession of the indoor theatre in the Blackfriars. Given the climate, indoor performance was certain, sooner or later, to become the norm in England, and it is appropriate that the King's Men should have led a move towards it. But the Globe, their home since 1599, was not abandoned. On the contrary, it was rebuilt after its gutting by fire in 1613, and the King's Men continued to conduct outdoor and indoor performances in tandem. This was nothing new. Actors were accustomed to presenting plays in a variety of spaces. The palace of Whitehall had several – the Great Hall (c.40ft wide), the splendid Banquet House (50ft wide x 110 long) and the compact COCKPIT-IN-COURT were all familiar to the King's Men, whose adaptability to the Royal Command was certainly enhanced by their possession of the Blackfriars. But the greatest transformation was not strictly in the field of drama.

James I and his Danish wife, though interested in drama, took particular delight in the elaborate courtliness of the MASQUE. Through the genius of one man, that royal preference came to exercise a decisive influence on the future of the English theatre. INIGO JONES brought firsthand experience of Italian theatres to his appointment in the household of Prince Henry (1604). For *The Masque of Blackness* (1605) he provided the first English example of perspective scenery (see THEATRE DESIGN) behind an artificial proscenium arch. In tune with the Stuart preparedness to spend lavishly on court entertainment, scenery came increasingly to dominate text in the masques that preceded the Civil War. Ben Jonson, who as court poet wrote at least eight of them, was predictably resentful, and his quarrels with Jones culminated in his angry withdrawal in 1634. But Jones's experiments with changeable scenery, involving the use of decorated shutters run in grooves parallel to the line of the proscenium arch, had already created the conditions that would govern the pictorial stage for well over two centuries.

Some spin-off effect on the drama was inevitable. It is observable in the visual and musical techniques of *The Tempest* as well as in the more riotous spectacle associated with the performances of Queen Anne's Men at the Red Bull (1605–17). Even so, the new generation of playwrights, of whom MASSINGER, FORD and SHIRLEY are the best known, were recognizably the inheritors of a sturdier Elizabethan tradition, embodied in Jonson's combative person. Typical of a group of minor dramatists, mocked in their time as 'Sons of Ben', is RICHARD BROME, whose contract as resident (or 'attached') playwright to Queen Henrietta's Men at the SALISBURY COURT THEATRE (1635) provides valuable insights into the writer's world. The contract stipulates that Brome shall write three plays per year and publish none of them, that he will provide epilogues, prologues, inductions, songs and new or rewritten scenes for old plays, and that he will receive 15 shillings per week so long as he does no writing for other companies. We can reasonably assume that other attached playwrights, like Shakespeare, worked under comparable conditions. It was only gradually that they achieved independence from actors or acting companies, and not until the end of the 17th century did their names figure on playbills. Jonson's publication of his own plays in the splendour of a Folio edition (1616) was unprecedented assertiveness, and the King's Men's decision to celebrate their late colleague, Shakespeare, in the same rich format (1623) must, in context, be seen as a vividly generous acknowledgement.

Concentration on theatrical activity in London gives a misleadingly narrow view, which recent scholarship is adjusting. It is, however, probably true that the centralizing disposition of the first two Stuart kings postponed the full development of provincial theatre, forcing would-be actors into the capital. The traveller Fynes Moryson recorded in 1626: 'The City of London alone hath four or five companies of players with their peculiar theatres capable of many thousands, wherein they all play every day in the week but Sunday, with most strange concourse of people ... as there be, in my opinion, more plays in London than in all parts of the world I have seen, so do these players or comedians excel all others in the world.' English actors were admired on the Continent, particularly in Germany and the Low Countries. A visitor to the 1592 Frankfurt Autumn Fair wrote to his wife: 'Here are some English actors whose plays I have seen. They have such splendid good music, and are perfect in their dancing and jumping, whose equal I have never seen. There are ten or twelve of them, all richly and magnificently clothed.' It was probably ROBERT BROWNE's company that he saw – specialists in JIGS, the popular and often bawdy afterpieces in which RICHARD TARLTON and, after him, WILL KEMPE featured in England. The Swiss visitor, Thomas Platter, was more struck by the jig that followed the Globe performance of *Julius Caesar* (1599) than by the play itself, although he thought that 'very well acted'. The theatre of Elizabethan and Jacobean London was popular, not purist, and a farcical jig had as rightful a place on the programme as a tragedy or one of the sour, satirical comedies written by, or in imitation of, Jonson that displaced Shakespearian lyricism during the troubled early years of the 17th century. It was the court entertainment that displayed an alternative elitist approach to theatrical art, adumbrating the distinction between a boisterous public form and a sophisticated private one that has bedevilled English drama ever since. The division is implicit in the architecture of the last two Caroline theatres. Invited to remodel the Cockpit-in-Court in about 1630, Inigo Jones incorporated Palladian features after the refined Italian model, and the Salisbury Court theatre, though public, was a neoclassically severe brick structure, which might well have intimidated a popular audience.

Puritan opposition to the theatre gathered force under the Stuarts. WILLIAM PRYNNE's *Histriomastix* (1632) is the best known of many attempts to expose in print the moral dangers of the lascivious stage. The city fathers, resentful of royal privilege, were in general alliance with the Puritans, though paradoxically prepared to employ playwrights and actors in the elaborate annual pageants at the inauguration of the Lord Mayor. Dekker, Jonson, THOMAS HEYWOOD, Middleton and Webster all wrote for Lord Mayor's shows, and these civic spectacles can be seen, in part, as the city's emulation of the masques at court. But if the evidence is contradictory, the outcome of Puritan hostility is clear. Soon after the outbreak of the Civil War, the London theatres, public and private, were closed (1642–3; see CLOSURE OF THE THEATRES).

This rupture of historical process is significant above all for its effect on audiences. Under Charles I, there had been a discernible drift among writers and entrepreneurs away from public theatres towards the more exclusive, though not formally or officially exclusive, private theatres. The enforced closure of the open-air houses broke the habit of popular playgoing in England. That remains true despite the fact that the closure was intermittently defied. Surreptitious performances of the kind that certainly occurred at the Red Bull, the COCKPIT THEATRE and Salisbury Court are likely to increase an audience's sense of its own exclusiveness. With few exceptions, actors took the Royalist side in the Civil War, and the king's defeat cost some their lives and all their livelihoods. The Puritans, Cromwell included, permitted the performance of plays in schools and, on occasions, in private houses, before discriminating audiences. It was the mixed crowds of the public theatres that they feared, their objection to plays being quite as much political as moral. By 1656, attitudes had sufficiently softened to allow WILLIAM DAVENANT, knighted by Charles I in 1643 for services to the Royalist cause, to resume an adventurous theatrical career. *The Siege of Rhodes* (1656) at Rutland House was followed, at the 'public' Cockpit, by *The Cruelty of the Spaniards in Peru* (1658) and *Sir Francis Drake* (1659). It is sometimes argued that *The Siege of Rhodes* was the first English OPERA, but its greater importance lay in its theatrical innovations. Assisted by Inigo Jones's pupil, JOHN WEBB, Davenant imported the changeable scenery of the masques into the public theatre. Wings, grooves and painted backcloths, augmented by machinery on demand, would become the stock-in-trade of the English stage before the 17th century ended.

The Restoration period The theatre during the period 1660–1700 was so markedly different from its pre-Cromwellian self that it has been habitually distinguished as 'Restoration theatre' and its drama as 'Restoration drama'. There was, of course, some continuity, provided not least by the two men who led the reform of the stage under Charles II, Davenant and THOMAS KILLIGREW. Davenant had written masques for Charles I and managed the Cockpit in the years immediately preceding the Civil War. Killigrew had written modish tragicomedies and acted at the Red Bull during the same period. Advised of the dangers of an unlimited theatre, Charles II rewarded the loyalty of these middle-aged men by granting them a monopoly over the performance of plays in the city of Westminster. He could not have predicted the effect that the Letters Patent, issued to Davenant and Killigrew in 1662, would have on the English theatre from then until the Theatres Act of 1843. His intention, quite simply, was to control the excited professionals who had greeted his Restoration by reoccupying abandoned theatres and staging plays from the old repertoire. Such unrestricted growth threatened the precarious balance of the monarchy, and the Letters Patent were a decisive reaction.

Killigrew led his King's Men to a newly constructed theatre in DRURY LANE and Davenant the Duke's Men to a converted tennis court in LINCOLN'S INN FIELDS, where he had installed the public theatre's first proscenium arch.

The greatest single difference between the Restoration stage and all that had preceded it lay in the debut of the professional actress. The first outstanding names are those of ELIZABETH BARRY, creator of THOMAS OTWAY's tragic heroines, and ANNE BRACEGIRDLE, creator of WILLIAM CONGREVE's liveliest ladies. From the outset, actresses occupied an ambiguous place in society. In the Green Room, the highest in the land would talk and flirt with them. It was probably the rakish Earl of Rochester's child that Elizabeth Barry bore. Anne Bracegirdle was the mistress of the gentlemanly Congreve. NELL GWYN's liaison with Charles II was the most notorious of several rags-to-riches progresses, nor was she the only actress to nestle in the royal bed. It was not until late in the 19th century that actresses were given patriarchal leave to pursue their new profession in acknowledged contradistinction from the oldest profession. Their presence on the Restoration stage made overt the latent sexuality of performance, and it elicited from the fashionable audience a seedy voyeurism that is an unattractive feature of the new theatre. The displacing of male actors from female roles was not completed overnight – NED KYNASTON, for example, was considered by Samuel Pepys 'the loveliest lady that ever I saw' in a revival of Fletcher's *The Loyal Subject* – but it was rapid, and it brought with it a measurable shift in the tone of English drama.

The best-known of the 'old' playwrights in the post-Interregnum theatre were BEAUMONT and FLETCHER. A large Folio edition of their work had been published in 1647. It was, in fact, an anthology of plays, few of them jointly written by the named authors and some by neither, and it provided a treasury of Jacobean plays to energize the Restoration theatre. Its influence is apparent in the escapades of APHRA BEHN's intrigue comedies, in Samuel Tuke's *The Adventures of Five Hours* (1663) and in the forgotten work of THOMAS D'URFEY, in which Spanish plots are grafted on to English manners. More solidly 'English' were THOMAS SHADWELL's attempts to revitalize the Jonsonian COMEDY OF HUMOURS, though Shadwell was also one of the many Restoration writers to plunder MOLIÈRE without remembering to steal the clarity of his moral vision. Released from Puritan restraints, the fashion-conscious intellectuals of Restoration England tested the scope of human liberty. The great poets and thinkers of the mid-century, men like Milton and Hobbes, had dared to inquire into the sources of human behaviour and to question the legitimate power of governments, and the Restoration quest for knowledge is exemplified at its best by the cool intelligence of John Locke. But, as in all permissive societies, the honest quest can be easily diverted, and it is such a diversion that is recorded in the Restoration's most original contribution, the comedy of manners.

Adultery, either plotted or achieved, and acquisitive sexuality are common themes of what has come to be known as Restoration comedy. Even where the tone is satirical, the cumulative tendency of these plays is to condone quick-witted conquests and easy virtue. The losers are usually less intelligent than the winners, and the dialogue sparkles most in contests of wit. Many of the female characters, like the actresses who played them, are willing sinners, plagued only by the fear of being found out, and the lords, knights and gentlemen stake their reputations on their effectiveness as seducers. The milieu is courtly and the *dramatis personae* predominantly aristocratic, though clever servants are often on hand to aid or thwart their betters' schemes. True to the spirit of comedy, the plays usually end with the imminent marriage of at least one couple, but the institution of marriage has taken such a battering by then that this represents the shape rather than the substance of a happy ending. There is something feverish about the anxiety of the characters to maintain their place in a society which threatens to corrupt all whom it has not already corrupted. To be forced out of town, away from fashionable assemblies, is a dread prospect. (To a dog that bit him, the Earl of Rochester said, 'I wish you were married and living in the country.') The status of Restoration comedy is still a matter of debate, but the artfulness, wit and ingenuity of its best writers, ETHEREGE, WYCHERLEY, VANBRUGH and Congreve, is undeniable.

The style and subject-matter of these comedies was controversial. The actor-playwright COLLEY CIBBER, a gifted sycophant, provided an antidote in *Love's Last Shift* (1696), whose rakish hero ultimately resolves to reform and to honour his marriage vows. Cibber lost face in the short term, when Vanbrugh's hurriedly written but brilliant *The Relapse* showed Cibber's repentant hero's speedy fall from grace, but he won in the long term. In retrospect, *Love's Last Shift* can be seen as a harbinger of the imminent triumph of sentimental comedy over the Restoration comedy of manners. A crucial blow was struck by JEREMY COLLIER, whose *Short View of the Immorality and Profaneness of the English Stage* (1698) focused hostility on Vanbrugh and Congreve. Congreve was stung into action, and a pamphlet war ensued, with points scored on either side, but Congreve withdrew from the theatre after writing *The Way of the World* (1700), and it was left to the more genial GEORGE FARQUHAR to preserve the spirit of Restoration comedy. When Farquhar died in poverty in 1707, a dramatic style died with him.

The change in taste was dictated by a changed audience. The early Restoration theatres were small and fashionable, but when the first Drury Lane was destroyed by fire (1672) it was replaced by a grander building, probably designed by Sir Christopher Wren, with a capacity increased from 700 to 2000. The Duke's Men, led by the actor THOMAS BETTERTON, had already moved from Lincoln's Inn Fields to a more capacious theatre in DORSET GARDEN (1671). The city's prosperous bourgeoisie could now exert its claims on the theatre. Less easy to particularize is the influence of Betterton, widely acknowledged as the age's greatest actor and accepted by colleagues as their leader. Respected and respectable in the loose world of the theatre, Betterton's image is solidly middle-class. When the Duke's and King's Men united at Drury Lane in 1682, it was Betterton who smoothed the rough passage, and it was he who, in protest against the malpractice of Drury Lane's Patent-holder Christopher Rich, led a breakaway group of actors to Lincoln's Inn Fields in 1695. Cibber's

finest service to the English theatre is his generous record of Betterton's acting in his *Apology for the Life of Mr Colley Cibber, Comedian* (1740). The long dominance of the school of Betterton, formal, rhetorically measured in its delineation of the passions, given to heightened verse-speaking not far from chanting, was about to face the decisive challenge of DAVID GARRICK when Cibber's book was published. But, in his own time, Betterton was admired as Hamlet and Falstaff and for his mastery of the awkward language of heroic tragedy.

The tragic drama of Restoration England is not, for the most part, impressive. Over-affected by the niceties of neo-classical theory, the courtly poets of the period tried to import into English heroic couplets the crisp language and high sentiments of CORNEILLE and RACINE. The outcome, even from a writer as fine as JOHN DRYDEN, was bombastic in a way that would have horrified Racine. Written at the height of the fashion for heroic tragedy, the two parts of Dryden's *The Conquest of Granada* (1670–1) exemplify the best and worst of the style. A notable theatrical consequence was the brilliant SATIRE of the DUKE OF BUCKINGHAM'S *The Rehearsal* (1671), which pilloried Dryden and accelerated the decline of heroic tragedy, though Dryden had still to write one of his best, *Aureng-Zebe* (1675). More admired today is his *All for Love*, a blank verse reworking of Shakespeare's *Antony and Cleopatra* according to the more 'correct' taste of the Restoration. Otway, whose early ventures into heroic tragedy were moderately successful, turned to blank verse for *The Orphan* (1680) and *Venice Preserv'd* (1682), in which he revealed a rhetorical gift that recalls the riches of Elizabethan dramatic poetry. Otway, melancholy victim of an unrequited passion for Elizabeth Barry, died young. NATHANIEL LEE, of whose ranting and death-strewn tragedies *The Rival Queens* (1677) proved most durable, was not much older when he died, confined in Bedlam, London, as a lunatic. Having held their place in the theatrical repertoire into the 19th century, Lee's plays dropped into obscurity when the melodramatic taste for spectacle and triumphant virtue challenged his commitment to vaulting verse and death throes. Unlike Otway's, they have not been successfully revived in the 20th century.

No survey of Restoration theatre can ignore the impact of dramatic theory. Dryden's *Essay of Dramatick Poesie* (1668) and Thomas Rymer's *Short View of Tragedy* (1693) provide a convenient frame. Both men, Rymer myopically, were partisans of French neoclassicism and of the rationalizing tendency of the 'new' philosophy. It was a movement on which Bishop Hurd would look back from the next century with a mixture of pride and ruefulness: 'What we have gotten by this revolution is a great deal of good sense. What we have lost is a world of fine fabling.' What were such 'ruly' critics to make of the unruly Shakespeare? Dryden's preparedness to admire him was characteristically generous, but characteristic also was his pragmatic decision to carry reproof of Shakespeare's barbarities to the point of improvement. It was during the Restoration period that the long tradition of rewriting Shakespeare began. Dryden contributed not only *All for Love* but also a corrected *Troilus and Cressida* (1679) with an influential critical preface. A version of *The Tempest*, on which he collaborated with Davenant, was further modified by Shadwell as an opera, *The Enchanted Island* (1674), in which scope was offered to the new excitement of changeable scenery. NAHUM TATE's *King Lear* (1681), which displaced Shakespeare's for 150 years, cut the Fool, preserved Lear and Gloucester and married Cordelia to Edgar. Cibber's *Richard III* (1700), which held the stage for even longer, imported passages from several other plays by Shakespeare, clearing all obstructions to Richard's absolute domination of the piece. Such alterations are of immense importance in the history of English acting. The testing of an actor's greatness by reference to Shakespearian roles, already emergent in 1700 and soon to become mandatory, was carried out under the controlled conditions supplied by rewritten texts.

The 18th century In 1700, the Patent theatres were in familiar disarray. At Drury Lane, Christopher Rich's unpopular regime continued, whilst the best actors remained with Betterton at Lincoln's Inn Fields. It was already difficult to trace with precision the legal status of the Patents since the custom of purchasing shares in them was established. The issue would haunt the London stage until 1843, when the power of the Patents was abolished by Act of Parliament. The opening of non-Patent theatres, irregular throughout the 18th century, would become a regular occurrence in the early decades of the 19th century. Despite the efforts of the Patent-holders, it was soon clear that the monopoly over the acted drama did not carry with it a monopoly over those forms of dramatic entertainment that could not be strictly categorized as 'drama', and as the popular taste turned more and more towards these 'illegitimate' forms, the holding of the Royal Patent for the presentation of legitimate drama teetered towards the condition of empty splendour.

But that condition was still many years away when, in 1705, Betterton led his company into a lavish new theatre, designed by the architect-playwright Vanbrugh for erection in the Haymarket. Within a few years, this unwieldy Queen's Theatre had become the home of opera, and the Patents had reverted to Drury Lane and Lincoln's Inn Fields. Drury Lane entered a controversial but comparatively prosperous period (1710–33) under a triumvirate of actor-managers, Cibber, Robert Wilks and THOMAS DOGGETT (later replaced by BARTON BOOTH). Ousted from Drury Lane, Christopher Rich took his share in the Patent to Lincoln's Inn Fields in 1714. He died before the renovations he initiated were complete and was succeeded by his son, whose regime proved more innovative than his father's could ever have been. JOHN RICH had taken part in Drury Lane DUMB SHOWS, imported from *COMMEDIA DELL'ARTE* by the dancing-master, John Weaver. Under the stage name of John Lun, he became a famous HARLEQUIN, figuring in the annual PANTOMIMES which he inaugurated at Lincoln's Inn Fields in 1717. They were soon to be emulated at Drury Lane and elsewhere. Rich made sufficient money from his pantomimes and from the popular success of JOHN GAY's *The Beggar's Opera* (1728) to undertake the construction of a new theatre, close to Drury Lane. The running rivalry of the Theatres Royal in COVENT GARDEN and Drury Lane is a leitmotif in the subsequent history of the Patent houses.

The legitimate drama over which the patentees squabbled is now largely confined to the bookshelves of collectors of the voluminous anthologies of British plays – Cumberland's, Bell's, Inchbald's, Lacy's, Dick's and eventually French's. The moralizing comedies of RICHARD STEELE, from *The Funeral* (1701) to *The Conscious Lovers* (1722), are competently crafted but over-earnest. There is more life and less substance in the work of his contemporary, SUSANNAH CENTLIVRE. Like most of the finest writers for the next 250 years, Steele was an uncertain dramatist. It is as an essayist and as the founder of the first English theatrical periodical, the *Theatre* (1719), that his reputation is most secure. The mid-century intellectual vogue for sentimentality found Steele's successors in comedy well equipped to exploit it. GOLDSMITH's *The Good-Natured Man* (1768) has a sentimental hero, but Goldsmith subjects his behaviour to a scrutiny beyond the range of opportunistic playwrights like HUGH KELLY, whose *False Delicacy* (1768) eclipsed Goldsmith's play in London, and RICHARD CUMBERLAND, whose hero in *The West Indian* (1771) is an 18th-century man of feeling bereft of any purpose beyond benevolence. This play was one of the great successes during Garrick's management of Drury Lane, bestowing on Cumberland a leadership of taste that stung SHERIDAN into caricaturing him as Sir Fretful Plagiary in *The Critic* (1779). Sheridan's own career as a playwright began auspiciously with *The Rivals* (1775), reached its peak with *The School for Scandal* (1777) and the glorious theatrical BURLESQUE *The Critic*, dwindling after his election to parliament in 1780 to culminate sadly in *Pizarro* (1799). Literary historians have tended to present Sheridan as an isolated phenomenon, supported in his struggle against sentimental comedy only by the excellence of Goldsmith's *She Stoops to Conquer* (1773). The truth is less bleak. The comedy of manners had other exponents – ARTHUR MURPHY, GEORGE COLMAN THE ELDER, JOHN O'KEEFFE and the actor-playwrights Garrick and CHARLES MACKLIN among them.

It was in tragedy that the 18th century was worst served. Essays at poetic tragedy were frequent, but few attracted audiences. NICHOLAS ROWE, better remembered for his regularizing edition of Shakespeare (1709), provided strong roles for women, particularly in *The Fair Penitent* (1703) and *Jane Shore* (1714). They were still in SARAH SIDDONS's repertoire as the century neared its end. As much for topical as for dramatic reasons, JOSEPH ADDISON's neoclassical tragedy *Cato* (1713) had a celebrated run at Drury Lane, but Addison's essays are a securer monument. The best-known, though not necessarily the best, of later poetic tragedies include DR SAMUEL JOHNSON's *Irene* (1749), JOHN HOME's *Douglas* (1756) and Murphy's *The Grecian Daughter* (1772), but none is great. The perennial problem for writers of tragedy has been the example of Shakespeare and his contemporaries. Throughout the 18th and 19th centuries, the writers' search for a voice of their own in poetic tragedy had drifted too soon into an attempt to sound like Shakespeare. The exceptional case is that of domestic tragedy, pioneered by GEORGE LILLO. That Lillo was conscious of Elizabethan precedent is evident from his adaptation of *Arden of Feversham*, but his plays belong firmly to their own age. The best, *The London Merchant* (1731), is a Hogarthian warning to idle apprentices. Its bourgeois author, speaking confidently to a bourgeois audience, commends industry, thrift and satisfaction with a middle station in life. Lillo's plays belong to an age that, in poetry, produced Pomfret's *The Choice* (1700) and Henry Baker's prayer: 'Grant me, ye gods, before I die/An happy mediocrity', and whose representative novel is Richardson's *Pamela* (1740). He had few followers in England – EDWARD MOORE's dreary play *The Gamester* (1753) is usually cited – though sentimental comedy shares his priorities, differing only in outcome. It was on the Continent, particularly in the German states, that his influence was felt. Lillo had, after all, dared to challenge the Aristotelian conviction that tragedy requires noble protagonists. Dull himself, he nevertheless initiated a movement that would provide the 19th century with IBSEN's plays.

It was outside the established modes of comedy and tragedy that the 18th century produced its liveliest drama. BALLAD OPERA, boosted by *The Beggar's Opera*, retained its theatrical hold throughout the century. Gay had intended to mock the fashionable cult of Italian opera by providing popular songs with comically inappropriate orchestral and harmonic frills. Instead, he fashioned a genre which, on the one hand, profoundly strengthened the world of 'illegitimate' drama and, on the other, offered to home-grown English opera a new, non-Italianate direction. That the political gibes of *The Beggar's Opera* had struck home was proved by the banning of its sequel, *Polly*, and ballad opera remained a convenient container for social and political satire even as the censors grew more vigilant. The best, and most irritating, exponent was HENRY FIELDING, in militant occupation of a small unlicensed theatre in the HAYMARKET, where he staged a series of his own ballad operas and burlesques, as well as work by his friends and political allies. The main target was Robert Walpole, financial wizard of the Whig administration, but even the royal family felt Fielding's lash, hilariously plied in *The Welsh Opera* (1731). Without the advantages of the Patent houses, the Haymarket was also free of their constraints. Not since Middleton's *A Game at Chess* (1624) had contemporary political leaders been so openly attacked in the theatre as they were in Fielding's *Pasquin* (1736) and *The Historical Register for the Year 1736* (1737). Walpole took offence (or fright) and engineered a counter-attack, choosing as his weapon a scurrilous play called *The Golden Rump*. The provenance of this piece, or even whether it ever existed outside the fertile brains of Walpole and his fellow schemers, is not known. It had, purportedly, been submitted to Henry Giffard, manager of another unlicensed theatre in GOODMAN'S FIELDS, who thought it his patriotic duty to show it to Walpole. It is to be hoped that Giffard was well rewarded, for it was by means of judicious 'quotation' from *The Golden Rump* that Walpole persuaded parliament of the need to curb the freedom of the turbulent theatre.

One result was Lord Chesterfield's exemplary speech on the dangers of CENSORSHIP, but a more repressive one was the Theatre Licensing Act of 1737. The Act aimed to consolidate the monopoly of the Patent theatres and to define for ever the terms of the Lord Chamberlain's control over the contents of performed plays. It was immediately effective on both fronts. Fielding's Haymarket operations were brought to an end and even Giffard had to close his theatre. In the longer term, though, it was only the processes of censorship that were adhered to. Once the heat was off, Giffard reopened his theatre – it was there that Garrick made his sensational debut in 1741. Deprived of an outlet for his plays, Fielding contributed his genius to the developing English novel, and it was the maverick SAMUEL FOOTE who reopened the Haymarket in 1747, charging patrons for tea and offering theatrical entertainment 'free'. The laws governing dramatic censorship were not so easily subverted. The Chamberlain's office retained legal authority over English drama until 1968, varying its rigidity according to the views of successive Chamberlains and Examiners of Plays. (The Examiner of Plays was appointed by the Crown to do or supervise the actual reading under the Lord Chamberlain's imprimatur. None distinguished himself.) However liberal the individual Examiner, the effect on English drama was unfortunate. To be confident of uncensored performance, playwrights had to avoid religious or political controversy. That is to say that they had to disengage themselves from the vital questions of their age. It is no surprise that the greatest writers of the next 200 years chose the freedom of the novel and of poetry.

Perversely, perhaps, the theatre did not shrivel under the Lord Chamberlain's scrutiny. There was always the refuge of innuendo or the risky exhilaration of altering the written text in performance. Working playwrights tailored their plays to suit the public. It was common practice for the author of a comedy to abbreviate it as an afterpiece when it had served its turn in full-length form. Afterpieces, knowingly contrived by professionals like Garrick, Foote, Murphy and Colman, were often deployed to sustain the run of a faltering tragedy. It was an opportunistic, pragmatic theatre, in which the actor shone more brightly than the dramatist. The early years of the 18th century saw the rise of ANNE OLDFIELD, supreme in Drury Lane comedy opposite Robert Wilks and Barton Booth. JAMES QUIN, Betterton's successor in Shakespearian roles, made his London debut in 1714. The year 1741 was a watershed. At Drury Lane in February, the fiery Macklin defied the pundits by playing Shylock as a serious, even dignified, figure. For Alexander Pope, 'This was the Jew that Shakespeare drew.' In October, a charismatic midlander drew fashionable audiences to see his (and Cibber's) Richard III at Giffard's theatre in Goodman's Fields. David Garrick was launched in London.

Garrick's impact on the English theatre was greater than any single person's before or since. There was nothing that he did not touch. Versatile enough to play tragedy and comedy, he also wrote prolifically, adapted Shakespeare, inaugurated the glorification of Stratford-upon-Avon as birthplace of the bard (though the English climate turned his 1769 jubilee into a fiasco), and established by his own conversational brilliance the actor's right of entry to intellectual society. But it was above all as manager of Drury Lane (1747–76) that Garrick raised the theatre. His supervision of stage business, though by no means that of a modern director, was unprecedentedly disciplined, and his clearing of the audience from the stage together with his ill-fated attempt to abolish the custom of half-price admission after the third act of the main piece – a custom which virtually invited roisterers to come drunk to the theatre – show the professionalism of his approach. Even on vacation, Garrick was at work. After a Continental holiday, he invited the Alsatian painter DE LOUTHERBOURG to Drury Lane. As scenic director, De Loutherbourg began the transformation from the old system of flats and wings to the new one of exquisitely painted backdrops and the breaking of the stage surface by load-bearing levels. His lighting innovations enhanced the illusion of reality in, for example, storms, fires and moonlit scenes. Garrick, although unashamedly conscious of himself as a star, built up a strong company at Drury Lane. Among many actresses who shared his glory were PEG WOFFINGTON, a trendsetter in BREECHES PARTS, the pert KITTY CLIVE, HANNAH PRITCHARD, SUSANNA CIBBER, GEORGE ANNE BELLAMY and FRANCES ABINGTON. More chary of male competition, Garrick released SPRANGER BARRY to Covent Garden in 1750. This fine-voiced and handsome Irishman was openly ambitious to usurp Garrick's crown, and their rivalry briefly brought competition between the Patent houses to a head.

A more serious problem was the alacrity with which financial backers greeted the increasing size of audiences by increasing the size of the theatres: Henry Holland's designs for the reconstruction of Drury Lane (1791) and Covent Garden (1792) raised both to a capacity in excess of 3000, thus capping a steady growth over several decades. A parallel broadening of acting styles was unavoidable, and many discriminating actors and spectators came to prefer the reduced scale of the Haymarket. This theatre had undergone a significant change in status since its reopening by Samuel Foote. Foote's legendary improvidence had already lost him two fortunes when, in 1776, he also lost a leg. In remorse, or perhaps to buy Foote's silence, the Duke of York, who had been party to the prank that resulted in the amputation, procured for Foote a 'limited licence' to stage the legitimate drama during the summer months, when the Patent theatres were closed. By the end of the century, the 'little theatre in the Haymarket' was able to mount a formidable challenge to its overgrown rivals. It was then being managed, in succession to his father, by the clever but indolent COLMAN THE YOUNGER. After wintering in the vastnesses of Drury Lane, many actors found the summer intimacy of the Haymarket a blessed relief, and dramatists were easily persuaded that their plays had a better chance to be heard there. The new generation, whose writing would span the centuries – THOMAS MORTON, ELIZABETH INCHBALD, Frederick Reynolds, the younger Colman himself – accustomed themselves to writing scenic spectacles for the Patent theatres and plays for the Haymarket; and the new generation of actors, particularly those in the comic line – Joseph Munden, DOROTHY JORDAN, JOHN LISTON, CHARLES MATHEWS – had to make a virtue of inconsistency, or risk penury. The all-purpose actors, like Colman's favourite, JACK BANNISTER, were natural products of this confused period in English theatre history. The established genres of tragedy and comedy split into numerous subdivisions, not least because unlicensed theatres sought to evade the law by mingling music and songs with the spoken text. Anything with music was 'illegitimate' and could, therefore, be performed anywhere. The range was wide, covering ISAAC BICKERSTAFFE's *Love in a Village* (1762), which, given original music by Thomas Arne, links ballad opera and English OPERETTA; Colman's *Inkle and Yarico* (1787), which is closer to modern MUSICAL COMEDY; and countless 'straight' plays interrupted without rhyme or reason by sudden solos or glees. The curious word 'burletta' was often applied to such pieces. Asked to define 'burletta' during his undistinguished tenure of the office of Examiner of Plays, the younger Colman could suggest only that it was a play with at least five songs in each act.

It was a difficult task to maintain the Patent theatres amid such confusion. At Covent Garden (1774–1820), Thomas Harris displayed for 50 years a greater interest in business than in art, whilst Sheridan, who had succeeded Garrick at Drury Lane, showed small concern with either, deputing effective control to JOHN PHILIP KEMBLE in 1788. Kemble and his sister, Sarah Siddons, were dominant figures in the London theatre, to which they brought an Augustan dignity. Kemble excelled as Shakespeare's Roman heroes, in each of whom he found and embodied a ruling passion. Mrs Siddons, the most Racinian of English actresses, chilled audiences as Lady Macbeth and made them sob as Constance in *King John*. Their combined social prestige was still a rarity in an unstable profession. As a manager, Kemble found his belief in high art troubled by the demands of accountancy. Exasperated by Sheridan's interference, he moved to Covent Garden in 1805, and his last active years were scarred by the Old Price Riots (1809), the ridiculous craze for the 'young Roscius' WILLIAM BETTY (1804–5) and the sudden rivalry, after 1814, of EDMUND KEAN.

The Kembles' careers began, as was by now almost invariably the case, in the provinces. It was during the 18th century that the English provincial theatre became established. The practice was for a STOCK COMPANY to occupy a theatre in one town or city and use it as a base from which to tour a circuit of theatres. Thus, the Lincoln circuit embraced Grantham, Boston, Peterborough, Wisbech, Huntingdon, Spalding and Newark. From Nottingham, the stock company visited Worcester, Wolverhampton, Derby, Retford and Stamford. The Norwich circuit included Ipswich, Colchester, Bury St Edmunds and Yarmouth. Particularly famous, both in their own right and as launching-pads for London fame, were the companies based in Bath and in York. TATE WILKINSON, who managed the York circuit (Hull, Leeds, Doncaster, Wakefield, Pontefract) for about 30 years, is one of the 18th-century theatre's most colourful figures. It became customary for London stars to appear in favourite roles in provincial theatres, where they were supported by the local stock company. On one such occasion, the majestic Mrs Siddons needlessly commiserated with the diminutive Edmund Kean: 'You have done well, sir, very well. It is a pity there is too little of you to go far.'

The 19th century With English acting reaching new heights and English drama in a trough, there was a vacuum to be filled. The leading name as the 19th century began was that of the German playwright, KOTZEBUE. His *Menschenhass und Reue*, decently disguised to satisfy English modesty, had appeared in Benjamin Thompson's adaptation as *The Stranger* (1798), and in the same year Mrs Inchbald had turned *Das Kind der Liebe* into *Lovers'*

Vows. Even watered-down Kotzebue was shocking enough to flutter domestic peace, as the younger generation discover in Jane Austen's *Mansfield Park* (1814), when their rehearsal of *Lovers' Vows* is interrupted by Sir Thomas Bertram's return. For the splendidly bad-tempered critic Thomas Dutton, this foreign domination of the English stage was deplorable, and in 1800 he filled successive numbers of his journal, the *Dramatic Censor*, with a celebration of the English renaissance as exemplified by Thomas Morton's new play, *Speed the Plough*. It is worth asking why Dutton should have so overrated a play which is now noted only for its invention of MRS GRUNDY. *Speed the Plough* has five acts – the length is significant because a five-act structure implied an attempt to write within one of the major genres, tragedy or comedy – and at least three plots, forced together rather than linked. Its main plot is a gallimaufry of castles, lost heirs, secret guilt, locked chambers and remorse. Its obvious reference is to the contemporary novels of such as Ann Radcliffe and Matthew 'Monk' Lewis, the latter of whom had recently succeeded with a Gothic play, *The Castle Spectre* (1797). The secondary plot centres on the domestic life of a salt-of-the-earth farmer, whose good-hearted wife, a little too anxious to keep up appearances, is plagued by fears about what Mrs Grundy (who never appears) will say if she fails. The sentimental view that simplicity is synonymous with goodness had already a long history in the theatre, and would have a long future. A third plot, involving the mismatched and uxorious Sir Abel Handy, is a grotesque comedy of manners. There are no songs, but the play is otherwise characteristic of the mixed drama familiar to contemporary audiences. It is not great literature, but it fairly represents the best that can be expected – though better work might sometimes have been achieved – from a national drama whose hands were tied by a predominantly philistine CENSORSHIP. Its virtues are those of good storytelling, its limitation a reliance on the existing stock of theatrical characters and situations.

Morton called *Speed the Plough* a 'comedy', but it belongs to the world of melodrama, into which Kotzebue had already guided the English theatre. The first self-styled melodrama on the London stage was THOMAS HOLCROFT's *A Tale of Mystery* (1802), adapted from a French play by PIXÉRÉCOURT. Melodrama in its many guises is a distinctively 19th-century genre. It gratified the greed for spectacle, which was met also by the HIPPODRAMAS at ASTLEY's Amphitheatre, the dioramas and panoramas, *tableaux vivants* (see LIVING PICTURE), waxworks, magic lanterns, freaks and machines that added to the proliferating shows of London. But melodrama also responded to the emotional needs of an increasingly humdrum industrialized society. Playing on the nerves rather than the feelings, it replaces tragic catastrophe with peril. Its threatened heroines, resisting 'a fate worse than death', wrapped eroticism in an acceptable disguise. Its thrills and spills aroused the excitability of the superficially placid 19th-century middle classes, that same erethism that fed on Newgate novels and the supremely 'theatrical' work of CHARLES DICKENS. Melodrama is a broad category, and there is little similarity between the rough justice of Isaac Pocock's *The Miller and his Men* (1813) or DOUGLAS JERROLD's *Black-Eyed Susan* (1829) and

the crafted composition of DION BOUCICAULT's *The Shaughraun* (1874) or HENRY ARTHUR JONES and Henry Herman's *The Silver King* (1882), but the audience for such plays remained broadly the same. Every journeyman-dramatist of the century needed to know how to turn a melodrama. There was ready employment for facile journeymen at London's now numerous theatres. SADLER's WELLS had been active since 1765 and Astley's Amphitheatre since 1784. After 1806, the OLYMPIC, the ADELPHI and the rebuilt Surrey led the illegitimate charge, to be joined in 1809 by the more stately LYCEUM, in 1818 by the Coburg (better known by its later nickname, the OLD VIC) and in 1832 by the Strand. For these and other rivals to the Patent theatres, melodrama was the staple fare.

The quest for great tragedies continued alongside the spread of melodrama, and the claims of Joanna Baillie, Thomas Beddoes, Henry Milman, Richard Sheil, Henry Taylor, Thomas Talfourd and W. G. WILLS were, at various times, vaunted. Most of the century's poets, from Wordsworth to Hardy, tried their hand at drama, with no one working harder on their behalf than the actor-manager, W. C. MACREADY. But even Macready could make nothing of Browning's plays, and the only one of BYRON's that he found marketable was the Gothic melodrama, *Werner*. Of Byron's 'studiously Greek' tragedies, *Marino Faliero* flopped at Drury Lane in 1823 and the 1853 revival of *Sardanapalus* at the PRINCESS's owed its cult success to the lavish pedantry of CHARLES KEAN's archaeological research. Even TENNYSON, despite his hold on the popular imagination, faltered in the theatre. His *Becket*, doctored and superbly performed by HENRY IRVING, was one of the glories of the century's last decade, but Irving died performing it and the play died with him. The only 19th-century tragedies to share literary and theatrical acclaim in their own time were those of SHERIDAN KNOWLES, which now read poorly and have not been revived.

The condition of comedy was only a little healthier. One of the best, Colman the younger's *John Bull* (1803), is typically dependent on the creation of eccentric 'characters', culled from past plays and loosely regrouped round an extravagant plot. The basic theme of comedy, as of melodrama, was money, a fact which EDWARD BULWER LYTTON frankly acknowledged in the title of his proficient *Money* (1840). Knowles's comedies, much better than his tragedies, were neglected even in his own time. Like Boucicault's *London Assurance* (1841) and *Old Heads and Young Hearts* (1844), and like TOM TAYLOR's *The Overland Route* (1860), they derive from the comedy of manners, maintaining a tradition that would culminate in the 19th century's single dramatic masterpiece, OSCAR WILDE's *The Importance of Being Earnest* (1895). A significant, even revolutionary, step was taken when, at the previously unfashionable PRINCE OF WALES's, under the bold management of MARIE WILTON, a succession of plays by T. W. ROBERTSON was staged. *Society* (1865), *Ours* (1866), *Caste* (1867), *Play* (1868) and *School* (1869) are exceptional only in manner. For the first time, English comedy was allowed to settle snugly into prose. Knowing his limitations, Robertson let his characters talk like real people and diverted the sensation scenes of melodrama into domestic routines: the pouring of tea, the carrying of milk-cans, the preparation of a roly-poly pudding. The recent innovation of the box set permitted the use of doors with real handles, and encouraged the fundamentally middle-class Robertson to depict the fundamentally middle-class. In his charming homage to the mid-Victorian theatre, *Trelawny of the Wells* (1898), PINERO portrays, through Tom Wrench, Robertson's delight in the mundane detail of stage business. Pinero was a beneficiary of the Robertsonian reformation, an inheritance which he used to guide comedy into the new territory of the social-problem play. *The Second Mrs Tanqueray* (1893), described as a 'drama' and certainly not a comedy, is the most famous example of the *fin-de-siècle* genre. Pinero wrote several more, as did Henry Arthur Jones, among others.

More dependent on MELODRAMA than on tragedy, the 19th-century stage was also more dependent on FARCE than on comedy. The long theatrical bills would conventionally end with a one-act farce, work for facile writers from Theodore Hook to W. S. GILBERT, and full-length farces 'from the French' were a frequent feature during the latter half of the century. The delight in childlike 'fun', which is so enigmatic an aspect of Victorian escapism, was expressed also in travesty, BURLESQUE, extravaganza and PANTOMIME, expertly composed by J. R. PLANCHÉ, H. J. BYRON, F. C. Burnand and others. The growth of the MUSIC-HALL and the continuing development of comic OPERA, OPERETTA and ballet are further evidence of the urban hunger for entertainment. The Patent theatres, forced to retain vast companies to cater for the variety of public taste, lost their distinctiveness and eventually, in 1843, their privilege. By 1900, Drury Lane was known as the home of pantomime and Covent Garden as the headquarters of opera.

The Patent theatres had narrowly survived the first four decades of the 19th century through the drawing power of actors and the opportunism of managers. For six seasons (1814–19), Drury Lane had the best of Edmund Kean, but after that, he and his equally profligate manager, ROBERT ELLISTON (CHARLES LAMB's 'Great Lessee'), slid together towards disaster. Macready, Kean's immediate successor, did his best to repair the damage done to the reputation of actors, with a dogged and thoroughly Victorian determination to improve the theatres he grudgingly adorned. Although Macready was a conscientious manager, he had too little respect for his fellow actors to be a great one. The story of the 19th-century theatre is elsewhere strung together by a succession of impressive actor-managers. Daniel Terry and Frederick Yates established melodrama at the Adelphi (1825–9). MADAME VESTRIS brilliantly staged Planché's extravaganzas at the Olympic (1831–9), where stylish COSTUME and scenic invention were part of the routine (see THEATRE DESIGN). Vestris engaged CHARLES JAMES MATHEWS in 1835, and it was at the Olympic that his relaxed comic style first challenged the gagging and caricatured oddness of his predecessors in comedy.

The installation of gas lighting in London's theatres (the Lyceum and Drury Lane led the way in 1817) allowed actors to perform within rather than in front of the scenery, inviting the evolution towards a greater NATURALISM, which Mathews accelerated. Charles Kean, the roguish Edmund's ultra-respectable son, made the Princess's a museum of pictorial staging (1850–9). Lavish productions and souvenir programmes that were illustrated records of

research helped disguise the limitations of Kean's own acting. BENJAMIN WEBSTER at the Haymarket (1837–53) and his successor, J. B. BUCKSTONE (1853–79), built up a comic ensemble that lasted long enough to become old-fashioned. Marie Wilton and SQUIRE BANCROFT at the Prince of Wales's (1865–80) not only staged Robertson's comedies, but also changed the style of theatregoing. Their replacing of the old pit benches with individual stalls was an influential innovation that, by quietening the audience closest to the actors, aided the development of unforced acting. The standards of Shakespearian production were raised by SAMUEL PHELPS during his astonishing years at Sadler's Wells (1844–62). Taking immediate advantage of the abolition of the Patent monopoly, Phelps staged all but four of Shakespeare's plays in an avowedly low-brow theatre. Henry Irving's long tenure of the Lyceum (1878–1902) exceeded even such outstanding precedents. The theatre was his temple, and he laboured to perfect each part of it, from dim-lit foyer to dressing-rooms. His decision to lower the auditorium lights during performance produced another major shift in theatregoing. Although Irving acted in several of Shakespeare's plays and brought their pictorial staging to its height, the Lyceum, particularly during the great years of his partnership with ELLEN TERRY, was dedicated to the actor's art. Irving's Hamlet was fine, but so was his Mathias in LEOPOLD LEWIS's melodrama of secret guilt, *The Bells* (1871). It was not the quality of a play but the quality of a role that determined his repertoire. For nearly 30 years, in all but name, the Lyceum was a national theatre, and Irving's knighthood (1895) acknowledged as much. The century ended with two notable actor-managers still in office, GEORGE ALEXANDER at the ST JAMES's (1891–1917) and BEERBOHM TREE at HER MAJESTY's (1897–1915).

Actor-managers worked closely with designers, inheriting from such as WILLIAM CAPON a concern for settings that were both grand and appropriate. William Beverley's was a major contribution to the success of Madame Vestris's Olympic seasons. The painter CLARKSON STANFIELD worked for Macready and others. JOHN HENDERSON GRIEVE's family brought flair and industry to the Patent theatres. Hawes Craven realized Irving's visions as William Telbin had realized Charles Kean's. Scenery and machinery were vital parts of the Victorian spectacular theatre, in which elaborate scene-changes prolonged intervals and drew attention to the importance of refreshment facilities and hospitable foyers.

It was not easy to accommodate the rapid scenes and multiple locations of Shakespeare's plays in such a theatre, and the rearrangement of scenes was a normal practice. But a growing reverence for the bard was variously expressed through the 19th century. CHARLES KEMBLE staged *King John* at Covent Garden (1823) in costumes researched and designed by the ubiquitous J. R. Planché, inaugurating a new concern for historical accuracy. Macready restored the Fool to *King Lear* (1838), albeit played by a woman. (Edmund Kean had played Shakespeare's ending in 1826.) Samuel Phelps was more faithful to the received text than any of his predecessors and most of his immediate successors. Irving, for example, surrendered to public pressure by cutting the final act of *The Merchant of Venice*, a play which, in the 19th century, rarely survived the departure of Shylock. The publication in 1888 of the newly discovered De Witt drawing of the Swan invited antiquarian interest in simpler Shakespearian staging, but WILLIAM POEL's was the only significant response. His 1895 *Twelfth Night* for the Elizabethan Stage Society was the first of several bare-stage productions by this singular prophet, whose influence on HARLEY GRANVILLE BARKER had a greater impact on Shakespearian production than anything he did himself. Meanwhile, it was individual actors rather than great playwrights who continued to draw the public to the theatres.

It is an anomaly of which historians have to take account that, during a period whose drama has generally been derided, the theatre was more popular than ever before or since. Great acting and ingenious stage design are the real theme of the age, and our understanding of this is enhanced by the unique brilliance of 19th-century theatre CRITICISM. The record of Shakespearian performances, from GEORGE FREDERICK COOKE's Richard III in 1800 to FORBES-ROBERTSON's Hamlet in 1897, was kept by the descriptive genius of WILLIAM HAZLITT, LEIGH HUNT, G. H. LEWES, WESTLAND MARSTON and GEORGE BERNARD SHAW. Given generous space in the journals for which they wrote, these men thought it the business of criticism to say what was seen and heard before encapsulating their own opinions. Even Shaw, for whom opinion was daily bread, is scrupulous to describe as well as to discriminate.

The 20th century Locked in its own past, the English theatre traditionally stole from abroad only those goods which could be confidently marketed at home. Against the strident advocacy of WILLIAM ARCHER and Shaw, actor-managers carried into the 20th century a 'native' dislike of Continental naturalism in general and of the 'wretched, deplorable, loathsome' (Clement Scott in the *Daily Telegraph*) IBSEN in particular. The dominance of the 'long runs', supported by elaborate staging and the new suppleness of electric light, downgraded experiment, and it was left to small semi-professional groups, like J. T. Grein's Independent Theatre (founded in 1891) and the STAGE SOCIETY (1899–1939), to pioneer the 'theatre of ideas'. It was the Stage Society's 1902 production of Shaw's prostitution play, *Mrs Warren's Profession*, that established the right of 'private' clubs to perform works banned by the Lord Chamberlain. Earlier examples, like the Shelley Society's 1886 production of *The Cenci*, had been more discreet, but even such discretion has its admixture of valour. Much of the initiative in the 'modern' English theatre belongs to individuals operating in isolation from the mainstream. JANET ACHURCH's tours of Ibsen and Shaw took her all over England and as far afield as Cairo. EDITH CRAIG, the elder of Ellen Terry's two children, took a lead in the women's theatre movement as director of the Pioneer Players (1911–21). The younger, GORDON CRAIG, was one of the rare English theatrical visionaries. Always a maverick, he had done little work in the English theatre, which he found stodgy, when he began his long residence in Italy, but his journal the *Mask* (1908–29) was a source of inspiration to many people. Craig's aesthetic interest in the actor as one element in the kinetic sculpture of theatre led him to the concept of the *Über-Marionette*, a creature wholly subservient to the totality of the work of art, and he found his unlikely model in the disciplined regime of Irving's Lyceum productions. Irving's example, very differently perceived, also inspired the Shakespearian tours of F. R. BENSON, whose annual visits to Stratford (1886–1916) established the provincial eminence of Shakespeare's birthplace.

More immediately significant than any of these was the sequence of seasons at the ROYAL COURT (1904–7) under the joint management of J. E. VEDRENNE and Granville Barker. Committed to repertory rather than to long runs, Vedrenne and Barker not only introduced to London several Continental dramatists (HAUPTMANN, MAETERLINCK, SCHNITZLER), but also affirmed the centrality of Ibsen, provided a platform for English NATURALISM in the plays of GALSWORTHY, ST JOHN HANKIN and Barker himself, and established Shaw as the chief playwright of the new English theatre.

Shaw's plays, though touched by many 'schools', belong to none. Passionate to argue, he would contradict himself in the absence of intelligent contradiction from others. His childlike exuberance and his conviction that ideas important outside the theatre have a proper place inside it go some way towards explaining the tone of English drama, part-boyish and part-knowing, during the first half of the 20th century. The best, like the most successful, plays of this period are not really Shavian, but they occupy the adult playground that he helped to build. It was a playground for the fantasies of J. M. BARRIE and the time plays of J. B. PRIESTLEY, for SOMERSET MAUGHAM, FREDERICK LONSDALE, BEN TRAVERS, R. C. SHERRIFF, John Van Druten and NOËL COWARD. Maugham pleased Edwardian audiences – he had four plays running in London in 1908 – with social comedies, brittly brilliant like Lonsdale's *On Approval* (1927) and Coward's *Private Lives* (1930), but in *For Services Rendered* (1932) he provided a harsh view of the effects of war that neatly balances Sherriff's depiction of war's conduct in *Journey's End* (1928). Travers carried into the 1930s the frivolity of the 20s with the sequence of farces (1925–33) he wrote for the talented Aldwych company. Controversial subjects, although they had to be charily handled to avoid censorship, were not avoided. Youthful sexuality, for instance, was displayed with some frankness in Coward's early plays, *The Young Idea* (1923) and *The Vortex* (1924), and in Van Druten's *Young Woodley* (1925), which the Chamberlain's office inanely banned. (It was given its first English performance 'privately' in 1928.) These plays have in common a comfortable acceptance of the conventions of stage reality. Shaw, by contrast, was constantly exploring the same conventions in order to draw attention to realities outside the theatre. When BARRY JACKSON founded the Malvern Festival in 1929, he gave Shaw a regular provincial base from which to launch on London *The Apple Cart* (1929) and its successors. Jackson had already taken the extraordinary *Back to Methuselah* (1922) from Birmingham to London.

The development of provincial theatre is a striking feature of the 20th century. The old stock companies (see STOCK COMPANY) had been thrown into disorder by the rail-based mobility of the 19th-century touring companies. A pre- or post-London tour extended the life of a play by many weeks, which suited managements whilst jostling provincial centres into theatrical parasitism. It was against this background that the repertory movement began (see REGIONAL THEATRE (BRITAIN)). Its champions aimed to hold several plays in repertoire instead of retaining one play for as long as its audience held. In the event, this Continental repertory system proved too much for English theatres, hit by inflation after the First World War, and it was quickly adapted to accommodate a sequence of short runs. Such a system had already been tested in London, by Florence Farr at the Avenue (1894) as well as Vedrenne and Barker at the Royal Court. The provincial initiative was taken by the tea heiress, ANNIE HORNIMAN, who had supported Florence Farr at the Avenue and financed the conversion of Dublin's ABBEY THEATRE (1904). Horniman bought the old GAIETY THEATRE in Manchester and presided over its repertory company from 1908 to 17. The company, which included SYBIL THORNDIKE and LEWIS CASSON, staged several plays by Manchester-based writers, including STANLEY HOUGHTON, HAROLD BRIGHOUSE and Allan Monkhouse. Other cities followed suit – Liverpool (1911), Birmingham under Barry Jackson (1913), Sheffield (1923), Oxford under J. B. Fagan (1923) and Cambridge (1926), where the idiosyncratic TERENCE GRAY made the Festival Theatre an influential, though sadly short-lived, centre for experimental staging. A postwar lull in new theatre-building ended with the opening of the Belgrade Theatre in Coventry (1958). A modest revival of theatre-in-the-round, strenuously advocated by STEPHEN JOSEPH, was represented by the VICTORIA THEATRE, Stoke-on-Trent (1962, and in new premises from 1986), the Stephen Joseph Theatre in Scarborough (1970) and the remarkable ROYAL EXCHANGE THEATRE in Manchester (1976), a glass module suspended from four pillars in the vast hall of the city's former cotton exchange. All these theatres are notable for the production of new plays in a period when few repertory theatres dare to risk the unknown. Other theatres of architectural interest include the Mermaid in London (1959), which has an end-stage unprotected by a proscenium, the cylindrical Nottingham Playhouse (1963), and the thrust-stage CHICHESTER FESTIVAL THEATRE (1962) and Sheffield Crucible (1971).

The heyday of the repertory and civic theatres of England, which followed hard on the foundation of the ARTS COUNCIL in 1946 and began to falter under challenge from the radical FRINGE after 1968, is over. Most companies, feeling the pinch of monetarist strategies in the 80s, have taken refuge in 'safe' plays, preferably with small casts. The Arts Council, underfunded itself, has passed along the underfunding to the regions, with the ironic result that its policy of regional growth, portentously outlined in The Glory of the Garden (1984), has proved to be a prelude to regional attenuation. It is not easy to see how the Arts Council can preserve, let alone strengthen, the best of live theatre in England. Without subsidy, few theatres outside London's WEST END can survive. High rents, spiralling production costs and the wage increases negotiated by Actors' Equity (founded in 1929) have seen to that. For a while, subsidy kept pace with inflation, but the signs are that this tendency will be reversed. Selected regional theatres may be allowed to die (pour encourager les autres?) and the two major companies, the NATIONAL and the ROYAL SHAKESPEARE, whose development is a

feature of the postwar theatre, preserved just below the level of significant growth.

When the Gothic Memorial Theatre that had housed Benson's Stratford performances was destroyed by fire (1926), it was replaced by the building which, with significant modifications, still stands. Under successive artistic directors – WILLIAM BRIDGES-ADAMS (1920–34), BEN IDEN PAYNE (1935–43), Barry Jackson (1945–8), ANTHONY QUAYLE (1948–56) and Glen Byam Shaw (1956–61) – the prestige of Stratford grew. Quayle was particularly successful in attracting major actors, like PEGGY ASHCROFT, JOHN GIELGUD and MICHAEL REDGRAVE, away from London. But the real leap came with the appointment of the young and ambitious PETER HALL in 1961. Hall negotiated a change of name to the Royal Shakespeare Theatre and rented a London base at the Aldwych. Now, whilst Shakespeare remained the staple diet at Stratford, the Royal Shakespeare Company could display its skills, in plays old and new, in London. Notable revivals have included Boucicault's London Assurance (1970), O'KEEFFE's Wild Oats (1976) and several plays by GORKY. TREVOR NUNN, who succeeded Hall in 1969, continued to blend revivals and premieres, signalling his interest in experiment by adding studio theatres in London – the Place (1971–4) and the Warehouse (1977–82); and at Stratford – the Other Place (opened 1974). With its occupation of the spacious Barbican Centre in London (1982), the Company stated its claims for parity with the National Theatre. The conversion of the old museum at Stratford into the open-stage Swan Theatre (1986), designed to stage post-Shakespearian classics, gives the RSC an important new venue.

The long-delayed establishment of a National Theatre Company finally came about in 1962, with a production of Hamlet at the Old Vic. The appointment of LAURENCE OLIVIER as artistic director was a tribute to the man himself and to the acting profession as a whole. In collaboration with his literary manager, KENNETH TYNAN, Olivier determined on an eclectic repertoire, with English and foreign classics balancing new work by TOM STOPPARD, PETER SHAFFER and TREVOR GRIFFITHS. In 1973, with work on the south-bank site well advanced, Olivier was replaced by Peter Hall, under whose supervision the three separate theatres – the Lyttelton, the Olivier and the small Cottesloe – were opened in 1976–7. The situation of the huge complex designed by Denys Lasdun to house the National Theatre is splendid, but size brings its own burdens. In unpredicted ways, the pains of the old Patent theatres have come back. Nunn and Hall, like earlier managers of Drury Lane and Covent Garden, have to reconcile artistic aims with the constant drain of an ever-lengthening permanent pay-roll.

The single most distinctive invention of the 20th century theatre is the non-acting director. Not that the actor-manager disappeared overnight. Beerbohm Tree, CHARLES WYNDHAM, JOHN MARTIN-HARVEY, OSCAR ASCHE and others imported to the new century the customs of the old, which perished splendidly with DONALD WOLFIT and Anew McMaster. We cannot name the first English 'director'. Actor-managers from Betterton onwards attended to the stage picture. T. W. Robertson's concern for detailed business influenced actors as well as playwrights. Irving took to heart the example of the visiting MEININGEN COMPANY

(1881), and his subsequent mastery of crowd scenes was an admired feature of Lyceum productions. But *quis custodiet ipsos custodies*? Modern purism would question the ability of an actor to direct himself. For Poel, and above all for Craig, the unifying vision had to be that of the artist-director. Granville Barker was the finest early master, above all in his Shakespeare productions at the Savoy (1912–14). Together with his designers, Charles Ricketts and Norman Wilkinson, Barker cut away the clutter of 'pictorial' Shakespeare to release the poetry of Shakespearian comedy. The escape from scenic realism was carried further by Claude Lovat Fraser during Nigel Playfair's 1920 season at the LYRIC, HAMMERSMITH. Fraser died, young and full of promise, in 1921, but Playfair, who had played Bottom in Barker's Savoy production of *A Midsummer Night's Dream*, continued at the Lyric until 1931, sharing with Norman MacDermott at the Hampstead Everyman (1920–6) an infectious optimism.

More influential than either of these notable ventures was the long regime (1912–37) of the extraordinary LILIAN BAYLIS at the Old Vic. From 1915 to 23, the Old Vic staged all the plays in the Shakespeare Folio, many of them starring Sybil Thorndike, but it was during the 30s that it became England's leading theatre. The Old Vic was, above all, an actors' house. Ashcroft, Wolfit, Olivier, Redgrave, Gielgud, CHARLES LAUGHTON, RALPH RICHARDSON, EDITH EVANS, FLORA ROBSON and EMLYN WILLIAMS all played there. It was a directors' theatre, too. TYRONE GUTHRIE's bold *Measure for Measure* (1933) and uncut *Hamlet* (1937), which, with Olivier in the title role, toured to Elsinore, were important productions. MICHEL SAINT-DENIS was brought from France to revive *The Witch of Edmonton* (1936), and remained to provide a vital focus for the reappraisal of theatrical values in England. Among the teachers at the London Theatre Studio, which he founded in 1936, was GEORGE DEVINE, who would later rejoin him at the influential Old Vic School. Other émigrés to bring flair and seriousness to the English theatre were MICHAEL CHEKHOV and Theodore Komisarjevsky (FYODOR KOMISSARZHEVSKY), whose Stratford productions (1933–9) were controversial enough to turn heads that way. Komisarjevsky liked to design his own productions, and his interest in the material as well as the appearance of his scenery anticipated by many years the original work of designers like Sean Kenny, JOHN BURY and RALPH KOLTAI (see also THEATRE DESIGN).

Since the Second World War, the primacy of the director has been increasingly taken for granted. The one undoubted genius, PETER BROOK, began young, with Barry Jackson's companies at Birmingham and Stratford (1945–6), where he established the rapport with PAUL SCOFIELD that culminated in a wonderful *King Lear* (1964). Two of his productions for the Royal Shakespeare Company, PETER WEISS's *Marat/Sade* (1964) and *A Midsummer Night's Dream* (1970), are already part of international theatre history, and Brook's explorations continue from the Parisian base to which he moved in 1970. The difficulty for lesser directors is the constant demand that they should inspire. Those without genius have too often to cultivate the appearance of having it.

For a while, after the Second World War, English drama retained its air of genteel irrelevance. AGATHA CHRISTIE's

The Mousetrap began its unprecedented run at the Ambassador's in 1952, when BRIAN RIX's seasons of FARCE at the Whitehall were in their third year. Christie and Rix provided material to bring bus tours to London theatres after the vogue for Ivor Novello's moonlit romanticism had passed. The initiative in MUSICAL COMEDY was briefly wrested from America by Sandy Wilson's *The Boy Friend* (1953) and Julian Slade's *Salad Days* (1954), as it would be again by Lionel Bart's *Oliver!* (1960). But it was the craftsmanlike realism of TERENCE RATTIGAN that best represented English drama during a period of nervous stasis. No one doubted that a change had to come. Poetic drama, briefly prosperous at the beginning of the century in the largely forgotten work of STEPHEN PHILLIPS, GORDON BOTTOMLEY and JOHN MASEFIELD, was made suddenly newsworthy by T. S. ELIOT's later plays and the verbal fireworks of CHRISTOPHER FRY's *The Lady's Not for Burning* (1948), but a growing impatience with plays written on the retreat from social confrontation, brilliantly spearheaded by Kenneth Tynan in the *Observer* (1954–8), swept the poetic revival aside. Three names previously unfamiliar to English theatregoers were being increasingly heard – BECKETT, IONESCO and BRECHT. *Waiting for Godot* opened at the capital's ARTS THEATRE in 1955 to mingled bewilderment and fascination, and in 1956, *The Bald Prima Donna* introduced the comic despair of Ionesco's absurdism (see THEATRE OF THE ABSURD) to London at much the same time as the BERLINER ENSEMBLE was bringing Brecht to the Royal Court. The triviality of English theatre was suddenly highlighted.

It has become almost axiomatic to date the revival of English drama from the performance of JOHN OSBORNE's *Look Back in Anger* at the Royal Court in 1956, and although this overrates the play, it allots proper credit to the vision of George Devine and the English Stage Company. Within a few years, the Royal Court had staged early work by JOHN ARDEN, ARNOLD WESKER, ANN JELLICOE and EDWARD BOND, and its writers' workshops generated an intense commitment to new plays and a preparedness to give offence when necessary. That the theatre might contribute to political debate, even under the eye of the Lord Chamberlain, had been proved by the socialist UNITY THEATRE in the 30s and by the Manchester Theatre Union, run by JOAN LITTLEWOOD and Ewan McColl (1935–9). Regrouped after the war as the Theatre Workshop, this company moved from Manchester to the Theatre Royal, Stratford East, in 1953. The high-spirited brashness of Joan Littlewood's productions caught the interest of West End managers and, largely to her disgust, her working-class community theatre was swept into the mainstream. Littlewood's methods were her own, but she shared Brecht's ripe delight in provoking the complacent into thinking and having fun while doing it. A more solemn commitment to Brechtian dramaturgy guided ROBERT BOLT's *A Man for All Seasons* (1960), in which the versatile Paul Scofield excelled, and Brecht has also exerted a strong influence on Arden and Bond, as well as on the generation of political dramatists who came into prominence after the abolition of the Lord Chamberlain's powers of CENSORSHIP (1968). More mannered playwrights – HAROLD PINTER, JAMES SAUNDERS, N. F. SIMPSON, Tom Stoppard – tend towards the philosophical buffoonery of Beckett or

Ionesco, reflecting the incongruities of human behaviour rather than the political structure which may, but may not, affect it, whilst Wesker, the most Shavian of recent playwrights, continues, in the face of critical disapproval, to try almost anything.

During the radical 1960s, the theatrical establishment spread to the repertory theatres, where it was shored up by the 'closed shop' strategies of Actors' Equity. Articulate minorities looking for a hearing rented outlying buildings on the fringe of the annual EDINBURGH FESTIVAL. By 1968, fringe theatre groups had completed their apprenticeship and were ready to launch an adult challenge against politicians in and outside the theatre. At their best, they brought a new vitality and originality to a still timid profession. Portable Theatre staged plays by the young HOWARD BRENTON and DAVID HARE. JOHN MCGRATH founded and wrote for 7:84 Theatre Company, which also revived Trevor Griffiths's *Occupations* and premiered DAVID EDGAR's *Wreckers* (1976). The Pip Simmons group interwove theatrical imagery and familiar stories. Monstrous Regiment was one of the many groups alert to the values of feminism. Belt and Braces, Red Ladder and North West Spanner strove to raise the political consciousness of the exploited workforce. Many groups worked collectively on a presentational style, Shared Experience specializing in storytelling techniques, Hull Truck developing plays through improvisation (as does MIKE LEIGH), Moving Being combining dance and drama in an associational theatre of their own devising. WELFARE STATE INTERNATIONAL masterminded large-scale environmental events, calling themselves 'Civic Magicians and Engineers of the Imagination'. They were pioneers of the community theatre movement, which spread to all the English regions during the 1970s. Many once-flourishing groups have ceased to exist. The Arts Council, having surprised them with subsidy, found it necessary to kill some in order to conserve its thinning funds. The 1980s witnessed a weakening of alternative theatre which has continued into the 90s. Three tendencies are discernible – an interest in a music theatre that is responsive to popular culture, the development of a distinctive performance art classically exemplified by the work of Impact Theatre, and a preparedness among larger, play-centred groups to operate almost as touring repertory theatre rather than as permanent ensembles.

The theatre of the late 20th century is not in easy command of audiences. Competition from the cinema has dwindled, to be replaced by the stay-at-home temptations of television. Few theatres have succeeded in holding down the price of tickets. Rising petrol costs and the decline of public transport are further discouragements. It is, however, to the credit of British television that it has continued to provide opportunities for original playwrights. John Hopkins, DAVID MERCER, Trevor Griffiths and DENNIS POTTER are among those who have generally preferred the wide and more popular audience of television (see TELEVISION DRAMA) to the diminishing and predominantly middle-class audience of the theatre. The modern actor has to learn to cope with television. Admired abroad and underrated in its own country, the English theatre treads uncertainly towards the 21st century. PT

See: E. L. Avery et al., *The London Stage, 1660–1800*, 11 vols., London, 1960–8; P. Barnes, *A Companion to Post-War British Theatre*, London and Sydney, 1986; G. E. Bentley, *The Jacobean and Caroline Stage*, 7 vols., Oxford, 1941–8; E. K. Chambers, *The Medieval Stage*, 2 vols., Oxford, 1903, and *The Elizabethan Stage*, 4 vols., Oxford, 1923; C. Leech and T.W. Craik (eds.), *The Revels History of Drama in English*, 8 vols., London, 1975–83; A. Nicoll, *History of English Drama, 1600–1900*, 6 vols., Cambridge, 1952–9, and *English Drama 1900–1930*, Cambridge, 1973; G. Rowell, *The Victorian Theatre 1792–1914*, 2nd edn, Cambridge, 1978; E. B. Watson, *Sheridan to Robertson*, Cambridge, Mass., 1926; G. Wickham, *Early English Stages 1300–1660: A History of the Development of Dramatic Spectacle and Stage Convention in England*, 3 vols., London, 1959–81.

English-speaking Caribbean see BARBADOS; EASTERN CARIBBEAN STATES; GUYANA; JAMAICA; TRINIDAD AND TOBAGO

English Stage Company see GEORGE DEVINE; ROYAL COURT THEATRE

Englische Komödianten Troupes of actors from the London theatres who toured Germany from the 1580s on, initially only when the London theatres were closed because of plague. By the start of the 17th century, however, their presence was more permanent and they enjoyed some aristocratic patronage. They performed plays of the Elizabethan and Jacobean dramatists in English, but soon German came to be substituted and the troupes took on German actors. By the end of the 17th century, all identification of the troupes with England had vanished, though the persistence of the HAUPT- UND STAATSAKTIONEN in the repertoire until the mid-18th century represents a continuation of English influence in the German theatre. SW

Ennius, Quintus 239–169 BC One of the most important of early Latin authors, active in various genres. His comedies seem to have been insignificant, but his tragedies, mostly adapted from EURIPIDES, were admired and influential. They are represented by 20 titles and over 400 surviving lines. ALB

Enquist, Per Olov 1934– Swedish playwright, novelist and journalist. After several important novels, he turned to playwriting with *The Night of the Tribades* (1975), which has since had some 400 productions. It initiated several projects about AUGUST STRINDBERG: Enquist later wrote *Strindberg: A Life*, which became a TV series, and directed *Miss Julie* in Denmark, where his work has been especially popular. Other plays include *To Phaedra* (1980), *From the Life of the Earthworms* (1981, about H.C. Andersen and the HEIBERGS), and *In the Hour of the Lynx* (1988). Enquist's plays metatheatrically explore the violence inherent in the ways in which his characters negotiate their identities in relationships. A new play, *Tupilak*, opened at DRAMATEN in 1993. HL

ENSA (Entertainments National Service Association)

British arts organization, formed in 1938 to enable performing artists to contribute to the war effort by sustaining the morale of troops and support staff, wherever they were stationed, in the British Isles or abroad. ENSA was the Services counterpart of CEMA, working through the NAAFI (Navy, Army and Air Force Institute). Its first performance took place immediately following the outbreak of hostilities in 1939. Under the directorship of BASIL DEAN and from its headquarters in London's DRURY LANE Theatre, it provided a touring programme that ranged from symphony orchestras, ballet companies and Shakespearian acting troupes to VARIETY shows, comedians, popular singers and mobile cinemas. CI

Enters, Angna ?1900–89 American dancer-MIME, writer and artist. Enters's international 40 year solo career began in New York in 1924 with her performance of 'stage poems without words'. She created the costumes, sets and often the music for 100 dance episodes, ranging from TRAGEDY to PARODY and portraying mainly women of many periods and countries. At MGM in Hollywood during the 1940s, she contributed a *COMMEDIA DELL'ARTE* sequence for *Scaramouche* and the story-line for *Lost Angel*. After her New York art show in 1933, she exhibited annually and also published three books of memoirs, a play, a novel and *On Mime* (1965); she also taught at Baylor (Texas) and Wesleyan (Connecticut). DMA

entremés see *GÉNERO CHICO*

Enzensberger, Hans Magnus 1929– German dramatist and poet of the 1960s protest movement, who demanded the replacement of conventional theatre by a radically political form – for which he devised *Der Verhör von Habana* (*The Havana Inquiry*, 1969), an unadorned collage of legal documents and news clippings to be delivered from a bare stage. The subject was the Cuban Bay of Pigs trial. In *The Sinking of the Titanic* (1980), an apocalyptic scenic poem, the liner's fate symbolizes the shipwreck of Enzensberger's earlier ideals. He wrote the libretto for H.W. Henze's MUSICAL *Rahel, la Cubana* (1975). HR

epic theatre The very juxtaposition of these two words would have horrified ARISTOTLE, and it was against Aristotle that ERWIN PISCATOR and BERTOLT BRECHT rebelled in their respective uses of the term. The Greek critic declared TRAGEDY a higher form of art than epic partly because of its economy and concentration. Reacting against EXPRESSIONISM's focus on emotion, Piscator and then Brecht separately wished theatre to embrace the larger social context of the epic. Towards this end, Piscator made varied and innovative use of film.

As early as 1924, in his adaptation of *Edward II*, Brecht introduced such epic elements as scene-by-scene summaries of the action and common soldiers in whiteface. In 1928 he and others collaborated with Piscator in dramatizing the Hasek novel *Adventures of the Good Soldier Schweik*; another collaborator, Gasbarra, refers to the novel's 'epic breadth', 'epic movement' and 'epic development' – which Piscator translated to the stage with the help of film, treadmills and moving cartoons by Georg Grosz. But Brecht in a 1927 newspaper article had already

announced epic theatre as the contemporary theatrical style: 'The essential point of epic theatre is perhaps that it appeals less to the feelings than to the spectator's reason.' By 1930, in connection with a production of his opera *Mahagonny* Brecht published an essay on epic theatre, in which he tabulated the contrasts between dramatic and epic theatre. In his 1931 production of his (revised) *Man Is Man* he first introduced the devices that were thereafter associated with epic theatre – half-curtain, half-MASKS, summary projections, few props, visible stage machinery, songs that punctuate the action, and 'cool' or estranged acting. Brecht demanded that the spectator use reason to reflect upon the performance.

Although the term rarely refers to theatre other than Brecht's, or adaptations of novels, the concept and devices of epic theatre have influenced playwrights as different as JOHN ARDEN, THORNTON WILDER, ROBERT BOLT, PETER WEISS, ARTHUR ADAMOV, ROGER PLANCHON and MICHEL VINAVER. It can be argued that every postwar director of stature is aware of the staging techniques of epic theatre. RC

Epicharmus 6th–5th centuries BC Sicilian comic dramatist, active at Syracuse in the reign of Hieron I (478–467 BC) and probably earlier. Surviving fragments of his plays, written in Doric Greek, show that they included burlesque treatments of myths as well as scenes from contemporary life; but many features are obscure (see GREECE, ANCIENT). ALB

equestrian drama see HIPPODRAMA

Erdman, Nikolai (Robertovich) 1900–70 Soviet dramatist who, in the tradition of GOGOL and SUKHOVO-KOBYLIN, brought grotesque SATIRE, intellectual irony and knowledgeable theatricalism to bear on the sociopolitical theme of the little man alienated from his technocratic society. Erdman began his theatrical career as a writer of REVUE sketches and speciality numbers for CABARET and MUSIC-HALL performers. The topical revue *Moscow from a Point of View* (1924), co-written with Vladimir Mass, Viktor Tipot and David Gutman, helped found the Moscow Theatre of Satire. Erdman's adaptation of Lensky's 1839 *vaudeville Lev Gurych Sinichkin* ran for nearly 10 years at the Vakhtangov Theatre in the 1930s.

Erdman wrote two major plays: *The Mandate* (1924), MEYERHOLD's most successful production at the Meyerhold Theatre and an influence on the work of MAYAKOVSKY; and *The Suicide* (1928), planned by the MOSCOW ART THEATRE and brought to dress rehearsal by the Meyerhold Theatre (1929) before it was closed. *The Laughter Conference*, an unfinished work, is rumoured to exist. His two major works cast ineffectual, anachronistic pre-revolutionary types – romantics, narcissists, prostitutes, intellectuals, artists, financial speculators and petty bourgeois (i.e. individualists and malcontents) – adrift in the so-called workers' utopia in search of what was promised them. They find that although society has progressed, man has been left behind without material means, and without his faith – which has been usurped by science – or even the right to protest. Erdman spent 1933–40 in Siberian exile and devoted the remainder of his career to stage adaptations of Russian classics and to writing OPERETTA, CIRCUS and cabaret libretti, and children's, animated and other film scripts, for which he received two Stalin Prizes. *The Mandate* was again produced in Russia in 1956 during the Thaw period. *The Suicide*, premiered in Sweden in 1969, ran for six performances at the Moscow Theatre of Satire in 1982 and, with *The Mandate*, was published in the Soviet Union in 1987. In 1990 LYUBIMOV, with whom Erdman had co-adapted LERMONTOV's *A Hero of our Time* at the Taganka (1965) and for whom he wrote the interludes to the staged adaptation of Sergei Esenin's dramatic poem *Pugachyov* (1967), staged *The Suicide* as a Chaplinesque tragi-FARCE in what was the most notable recent Soviet production of the play. SG

Ermolova, Mariya (Nikolaevna) 1853–1928 Daughter of a prompter at Moscow's Maly Theatre, who became its leading tragedienne and, with GLIKERIYA FEDOTOVA, one of the two most prominent Russian actresses of her day. STANISLAVSKY called her 'the heroic symphony of the Russian stage' and the equal of SALVINI and DUSE. She belonged to the realistic acting tradition (see REALISM) in the Russian theatre which includes SHCHEPKIN, whom she revered, Savina, Fedotova, Stanislavsky and KOMISSARZHEVSKAYA. She brought feminine strength, a mixture of inspiration and self-control, romantic idealism and a love of freedom to some 300 roles, excelling in those which emphasized heroic suffering: LESSING's Emilia Galotti (her earliest success, 1870); Judith in GUTZKOW's *Uriel Acosta* (1879); Schiller's Joan of Arc (*The Maid of Orleans*, her greatest success, 1884) and Maria Stuart (1886); RACINE's Phaedra (1890); and SHAKESPEARE's Ophelia (1878, 1891), Lady Anne (1878), Hermione (1887), Lady Macbeth (1896) and Volumnia (1902), among others.

In 1876 her incandescent, politicized portrayal of Laurentia in LOPE DE VEGA's tale of popular rebellion, *Fuenteovejuna*, made her famous, endeared her to progressive youth and resulted in the play's banning from the Russian stage for many years to come. She interpreted her favourite native writers, many of whom were radical – PUSHKIN, Nekrasov, Belinsky, Chernyshevsky, Dobrolyubov and PISAREV – as well as GOGOL and OSTROVSKY on the stage and concert platform and in progressive literary circles. The Maly Theatre administration sought to dismiss her in later years, but her career revived following the 1917 Revolution via a series of anti-bourgeois roles. She was the first actress to be given the honorary title of People's Artist of the Soviet Republics (1920) as well as Hero of Labour (1924). In 1930 one of the Maly Theatre's studios was named after her. In 1937 it became the Ermolova Theatre. SG

Ervine, St John [John Greer Ervine] 1883–1971 Irish playwright. On the basis of his plays, Ervine was appointed manager of the ABBEY THEATRE (1915–16) but, gifted and cantankerous, he eventually sacked the entire company, and resigned.

A prolific and quarrelsome drama critic, Ervine became a consequential figure in English theatre, author of many successful drawing-room comedies, faded now, such as *The First Mrs Frazer* (1929). His imagination finds a grip in the Northern Irish plays he gave to the Abbey: *Mixed*

Marriage (1911); *The Magnanimous Lover* (1912); *John Ferguson* (1915); *Boyd's Shop* (1936); *William John Mawhinney* (1940); *Friends and Relations* (1941).

Occasionally contrived and melodramatic, Ervine's Northern Irish plays display authentic though not profound characterization. His people fairly exhibit not only the intolerance and acquisitiveness of Northern Protestantism, but a conviviality, and, in some of his women especially, a charity beyond dogma. *Mixed Marriage* anticipates O'CASEY's urban REALISM, in a vigorous, less flamboyant vernacular, a Northern equivalent of T. C. MURRAY's. DM GF

esperpento see VALLE-INCLÁN, RAMÓN DEL

Espert, Núria 1938– Spanish actress and director. Born in Barcelona, she began her acting career at 11, in CATALAN THEATRE, achieving recognition in 1954 for her portrayal of Medea. In 1959 she and her husband, Armando Moreno, formed their own company. After establishing her reputation on the Madrid stage in classical works, she risked producing modern authors previously prohibited by CENSORSHIP; notable roles included BRECHT's *The Good Person of Setzuan* (1967, directed by Richard Salvat), SARTRE's *The Respectable Prostitute* and *In Camera* (1968, directed by Adolfo Marsillach) and GENET's *The Maids* (1969, directed by Víctor García).

The Maids brought international fame and was followed by other daring joint efforts: GARCÍA LORCA's *Yerma* (1971), performed on a trampoline, and VALLE-INCLÁN's *Divine Words* (1975), featuring NUDITY and erotically suggestive organ pipes. The García-Espert productions toured for years, as did her ventures with another Argentine-French director, Jorge Lavelli: García Lorca's *Doña Rosita the Spinster* (1980) and SHAKESPEARE's *The Tempest* (1983). Espert began directing in 1986, with a compelling London production of Lorca's *The House of Bernarda Alba*, starring GLENDA JACKSON. Other directing credits include several OPERAS, staged in London and Glasgow. For the 1992 Cultural Olympics she returned to Barcelona to direct EURIPIDES' *Medea*, with Irene Papas in the role that had first brought Espert fame. PZ

Esslair, Ferdinand 1772–1840 German actor. Of the romantic school, Esslair was second in popularity only to LUDWIG DEVRIENT. His grand stature, his good looks and his expressive, powerful voice made him an ideal interpreter of heroic roles. Reminiscent of FLECK, he was actually more reliable and methodical. Before settling at the Munich Court Theatre in 1820, Esslair acted in several companies throughout Germany. SW

Esson, (Thomas) Louis (Buvelot) 1879–1943 Australia's first realistic playwright. His early plays include *The Woman Tamer* (1910), *Dead Timber* (1911), and a Shavian political SATIRE, *The Time Is Not Yet Ripe* (1912). Between 1922 and 1926 his own company the Pioneer Players, co-founded with Vance Palmer and Steward Macky, staged his *The Battler*, *Mother and Son*, *The Drovers* (written in London in 1919) and *The Bride of Gospel Place* – all sensitive studies of outback or underworld life, written under the strong influence of YEATS, SYNGE and the ABBEY

THEATRE. Disillusioned artistically and politically, Esson eventually abandoned playwriting. MW

Estorino, Abelardo 1925– Cuban playwright and director. Estorino was born in Matanzas, studied at the University of Havana, and practised dental surgery for three years. In 1960 he joined the Studio Theatre, Cuba's first revolutionary theatre group, and in 1961 was contracted by the government as a professional writer. He often directs and occasionally acts and designs sets. Estorino interprets contemporary situations and immediate problems of Cuban reality into transcendent theatrical pieces. The constants in his work are the focus on family units and marital issues, and the need for openness, fairness and equality in human relationships. Essentially a realistic writer, he has remained loyal to the revolutionary ideals while experimenting with metatheatrical techniques in later plays. His best-known works are *El robo del cochino* (*The Theft of the Pig*, 1961), *La casa vieja* (*The Old House*, 1964), *Los mangos de Caín* (*Cain's Mangoes*, 1967), *La dolorosa historia del amor secreto de Don José Jacinto Milanés* (*The Tragic Story of the Secret Love of Don José Jacinto Milanés*, 1974), *Ni un sí ni un no* (*Neither a Yes nor a No*, 1981) and *Morir del cuento* (*To Die from the Story*, 1983). GW

Etherege, George 1636–92 English dramatist. Apprenticed to a lawyer, he went on to study at the Inns of Court in London. He may have been in France before appearing in London in 1663, already a friend of aristocrats. He quickly became an important member of the group of courtier-wits centred on Rochester and Sedley. His first play, *The Comical Revenge, or Love in a Tub* (1663), is a brilliant mixture of four separate plots, ranging from a serious action of high honour to a broad FARCE about a syphilitic servant. In 1668 *She Would If She Could* demonstrated Etherege's brilliance in a witty and thoughtful investigation of the problems of love and courtship; it was highly influential on the development of Restoration COMEDY. Immediately after its success Etherege was sent to Constantinople as a diplomat, returning in 1671. His last play, *The Man of Mode* (1676), is a complex exploration of the conflict between sexual appetite and genuine love in the rake-hero Dorimant, combined with a depiction of one of the great stage fops, Sir Fopling Flutter. In 1685 he became ambassador to Ratisbon and stayed abroad after the 1688 revolution. PH

Ethiopia Ethiopia is home to one of the most prolific theatre establishments in Africa. The capital, Addis Ababa, has five state theatre companies. There are state-supported *kinet* (performance arts) groups in all the regions, a Theatre Arts Department at the University of Addis Ababa, and a rapidly growing number of amateur groups in many urban centres. Some three hundred original works have been staged in Ethiopian theatres this century.

Ethiopian theatre is relatively unknown outside its homeland, primarily because almost all work has been written and produced in the dominant local language, Amharic. However, the history, geography and politics of the country have also encouraged insular attitudes. Pre-20th-century Ethiopia centred on a group of highland peoples living under the feudal overlordship of emperors who traced their descent back to a liaison between the Queen of Sheba and King Solomon. These highlanders were divided geographically from their neighbours on the surrounding plains and deserts. They were also religiously different. Ethiopians strongly identified with their Orthodox Christian Church, and from the 7th century AD, as Islam swept through much of the Horn of Africa, they were increasingly culturally isolated. Traditionally, Church and state reinforced each other's authority and encouraged conservative values. Control extended to CENSORSHIP of the arts. As early as the 6th century AD one Bishop Grigentius published a decree stating that public singers, harp-players, actors and dancers were all to be suppressed, and that anyone found practising these arts was to be punished by whipping and a year's hard labour.

Under Emperor Menelik in the late 19th century, Ethiopia was greatly expanded through conquest. Many new ethnic groups were brought into the Empire, so that today Ethiopia incorporates people of some 70 nationalities. The traditional performance cultures of many of these people have been little researched, although performance forms with dramatic elements such as music, dance, storytelling and RITUAL enactments are widespread. Within the dominant Amhara culture the Church promoted certain exclusive performance arts, such as priestly dance, *shibsheba*; religious music, *aquaquam*; and oral poetry, *qene*. For the ordinary people, traditional dance accompanied by improvised songs was the most common performance outlet, although rhetorical skills were and are widely revered. Ethiopian society also developed a caste grouping of professional singers and dancers, the *azmariwoch*, or azmaris, who were commonly attached to noble households as praise-singers.

Modern drama was first brought to Ethiopia by a nobleman, Tekle Hawariat, who had lived for many years in Europe. His SATIRE *The Comedy of Animals*, based on the work of La Fontaine, was performed to the Ethiopian court c.1916. The play was highly critical of the Ethiopian establishment, and as a result drama was banned at court by the then Empress, Zauditu. On his accession to the throne in 1930, Haile Selassie reversed Zauditu's ban and commissioned plays from two schoolmasters, Yoftahe Negussie and Malaku Baggosaw, who produced a succession of plays glorifying the Emperor, the Church and Ethiopian history. They had learnt the basics of modern drama by teaching in the elite European-style schools of Addis Ababa.

With the looming threat of the Italian invasion in 1935, the first national cultural group, the AGER FIKIR (Patriotic Theatre Association), was formed with a group of azmaris who were brought together to perform propaganda music, dance and theatre. The Italian occupation was a traumatic episode in Ethiopian history, and indigenous cultural production came to a temporary halt. However, after the restoration of the monarchy in 1941 there was a surge of artistic activity. The Ager Fikir was re-formed in 1942, and a second professional company was established in 1947 at the Addis Ababa City Hall. Both companies performed predominantly VARIETY-style shows comprising short plays followed by popular music and dance. At this time, too, drama was first toured through the regions.

Populist playwrights such as Mattewos Bekele and the

prolific Iyoel Yohannes, who wrote some 70 plays, produced largely slapstick comedies for popular urban consumption, but during the late 1940s and 50s it became fashionable for elite intellectuals to write serious drama for aristocratic consumption. Most of these playwrights had little idea of dramatic form, and they were primarily concerned with moralistic preaching. Makonnen Endalkachew was the prime exponent of the sermon play, with such works as *David and Orion*, *King David III* and *The Voice of Blood*. Patriotic and historical themes were also popular, and although some writers such as Kebede Michael with his *Hannibal* and the woman playwright Romana Worq Kasahun in her *The Light of Science* voiced mildly reformist ideals, most plays of this period reflect traditional values.

Many of the conventions for Ethiopian theatre were set during this early period. Action in serious drama is often minimal, long speeches abound, and many of the plays are written in verse form: rhetoric is the most important part of all Ethiopian plays. Characterization is generally sparse. Actors serve as symbols, and staging and lighting effects reinforce this iconographic style, which shows the strong influence of church culture. Playwrights as creators of rhetoric are honoured, and have usually come from the upper class. In contrast, actors until recently were either schoolboys or azmaris, and were regarded as mere servants of the play. Until the 1960s serious drama was still seen as an upper-class entertainment, while actors and the general populace tended to prefer traditional dance and music. A gulf has grown up between these two forms of performance art: theatre companies now have separate sections for the traditional performance arts, for modern music, and for drama. Actors now have the greatest prestige of all performers, and there is almost no interaction between the different forms of cultural representation.

Ethiopian plays may be up to four hours long and generally have no interval. Uniquely in Africa, Ethiopian theatre developed with minimal European influence. Unlike the drama of the colonized nations, Ethiopia's was always performed in the local language, dealt with matters of national concern, and was produced in ways which built on the country's cultural heritage and reflected the hierarchical, metaphysical world view of Amhara society as dominated by the Ethiopian Orthodox Church.

Haile Selassie's influence on the development of Ethiopian drama can hardly be overestimated. An autocrat who oversaw the running of Ethiopia in quite extraordinary detail, he frequently attended new productions, and no play could be published or performed without his approval. The value that the Emperor placed on drama is demonstrated perhaps most clearly in his commissioning of the 1400-seat Haile Selassie Theatre in 1955 for the Imperial Silver Jubilee. No expense was spared: the most modern technical equipment was bought from Europe, and a group of Austrians were employed to run the centre with enormous budgets for new productions.

From 1960, however, Haile Selassie's control over drama began to be challenged by a small group of young Ethiopians who had spent time abroad and who on their return started to use theatre to subtly challenge the established order. TSEGAYE GEBRE-MEDHIN, the most prominent of this group, returned home from Europe in 1960 and was

given artistic control of the Haile Selassie Theatre, ousting the foreigners. In partnership with TESFAYE GESSESSE, who had studied in America and now worked primarily as a director, Tsegaye started to stage a series of plays (mostly his own), which brought new ideas of social criticism into Ethiopian drama. Works such as *Mumps*, *The Crown of Thorns* and *A Man of the Future* examined the lives of ordinary Ethiopians, looking at issues such as the oppression of the poor, the degradation of much of city life and the loss of direction suffered by urban youth. Even in plays such as *Tewodros*, which took more traditional themes, he used history to question the role of rulers and to make strongly anticlerical statements.

Tsegaye was soon joined by other new playwrights. MENGISTU LEMMA in his *Marriage of Unequals* took a comic but critical look at aristocratic arrogance, ignorance and superstition. Abe Gubegna also criticized decadent aristocracy in *The Fall of Rome*, while Tesfaye's *Yeshi* studied the massive Ethiopian problem of urban prostitution.

The new style of theatre was increasingly popular with urban audiences, who for the first time could see their own lives mirrored on stage. However, the plays continually ran into trouble with the censors. Even though criticism was generally oblique – in the tradition of Ethiopian oral literature, which is famed for its use of *doubles entendres* – the plays of the 1960s and early 70s were increasingly either cut or ordered off stage after a few performances.

The revolution of 1974, which put in power a military council, the Dergue, led to a massive expansion of drama. Although the revolutionaries quickly became committed to socialism, for some time it was not clear what sort of left-wing ideology would be espoused or how the new state would organize itself. During this time of open debate, Ethiopian dramaturges seized the opportunity to express their views with a clarity which had previously been impossible. New plays discussing possible ways forward were now put on, and thousands flocked to this new drama of debate, so that runs lasted not for a few performances but for up to six months.

The military government quickly set up a new Ministry of Culture and Sport, and for the first time drama was used as a tool of widespread politicization. From the mass organizations that had been set up throughout the country, cultural groups were formed which started to put on short pieces of AGIT-PROP theatre. These propaganda plays, with titles like *The Red Sickle* and *Struggle for Victory*, were crude – but popular with audiences crying out for information about the revolution. And as the Dergue tightened its hold on power and created a Marxist-Leninist state, the theatres of the capital began to put on more committed plays. Two new theatres were opened in Addis Ababa in the late 1970s, and a new generation of playwrights, writing popular agit-prop plays, came to the fore: in particular, Getachew Abdi, Tekle Desta and AYALNEH MULAT. During the early years of Dergue control the previously despised actors won considerably improved working conditions, and a Theatre Arts Department was set up at Addis Ababa University which would from now on provide the most innovative voices in Ethiopian theatre.

By 1980 the military government, now run by President Mengistu Haile Mariam, had assumed total control of Ethiopia. In the theatres this meant a crackdown on freedom of expression, which came to a head in 1983 when the Ministry of Culture assumed the right to choose all plays to be put on in the professional theatres. At the same time there was increasing disillusion with Marxist rule, and as a result many of the plays of the 1980s were non-political and chosen primarily to make money. With many of the more prominent Ethiopian playwrights having been silenced by the censors, there was a rise in the incidence of foreign translations and comic drama. However, some new voices did emerge during this time, most notably those of Astelkachew Yihun and FISSEHA BELEY. Fisseha's work is particularly significant: in plays like *Simen Sintayehu* and *Hoda Yifejew* we see for the first time Ethiopian theatre based on an understanding of rural life and traditional customs.

The greatest area of theatre expansion at this time was in the regions where an amateur arts programme was set up in 1983 to help train interested groups in music, theatre, fine art and literature skills. The programme was of limited success, as it was under-resourced and subject to strict party control. The capital's fifth theatre opened in 1990, to put on plays for children.

The overthrow of the Dergue in 1991 has already led to some liberalization of the theatres. All the old senior management have been removed and replaced by much younger graduates. The Ministry of Culture is beginning to decentralize, and control over choice of plays may be handed back to the theatres, although it is unclear at present how far this process will go. Many dramaturges have been wary of the wish to democratize expressed by the transitional government, and in mid-1992 politics were only just starting to reappear on the Ethiopian stage. The most notable development has been the largely spontaneous emergence of many new urban theatre groups, seeking to earn an income by putting on a wide variety of improvised productions. JPl

See: A. Gerard, *Four African Literatures: Xhosa, Sotho, Zulu, Amharic*, Berkeley, 1971; T. L. Kane, *Ethiopian Literature in Amharic*, Wiesbaden, 1975; D. N. Levine, *Wax and Gold: Tradition and Innovation in Ethiopian Culture*, Chicago, 1965; R. K. Molvaer, *Tradition and Change in Ethiopia: Social and Cultural Life as Reflected in Amharic Fictional Literature 1930–1974*, Leiden, 1980; E. S. Pankhurst, *Ethiopia: A Cultural History*, London, 1955; L. Ricci, *Litterature dell' Ethiopia*, Como, 1969.

ethnic theatre (USA) Theatre by and for minority communities, whose cultural heritages distinguish them from the Anglo-American mainstream. A pluralistic nation with an indigenous population and immigrants from every corner of the earth, the USA has been host to a rich variety of ethnic theatres. Ethnic theatres have helped to meet the intellectual and emotional needs of people separated from the mainstream by language, culture, poverty and discrimination. They have reinforced indigenous or 'old world' languages and traditions, helped immigrants adjust to their new country, provided an arena for talented ethnic actors, directors and playwrights, and introduced new personalities and techniques to the Anglo-American stage.

Ethnic theatres sprang from a variety of historical conditions. Native American theatre (see NATIVE AMERICAN RITUAL/THEATRE) is rooted in communal celebrations and ancient rituals reflecting the religious outlook and shared values of the indigenous nations that created it. Conquest by whites destroyed entire 'Indian' nations, including, of course, their drama. Moreover, the confinement of Native Americans to reservations and the increasing dominance of Western culture often had a negative influence on the drama of nations that did survive.

White Americans were introduced to black performance as early as 1664 when captive Africans were forced to dance and sing for the crew of the English slaveship *Hannibal*. Autonomous AFRICAN-AMERICAN THEATRE began in 1821 in lower Manhattan, New York, where the AFRICAN THEATRE, founded by WILLIAM HENRY BROWN, performed Shakespearian drama for audiences of whites and blacks. In the 19th century whites in 'blackface' gave MINSTREL SHOWS, racist parodies of black entertainment; however, independent black theatre persisted, and by the early 20th century, MUSICALS written and performed by blacks were appearing on BROADWAY and in Harlem.

French theatre entered the country in 1803 when the USA purchased Louisiana from France, and Mexican-American (or CHICANO) theatre entered with the conquest of the Southwest from Mexico in 1848. Immigrants from Europe and Asia established theatres soon after their arrival. German theatres appeared in the rural Midwest in the early 1840s and in New York and New Orleans even earlier. Chinese theatre opened in San Francisco in 1852, and Japanese troupes entertained in Seattle several decades later. Polish, Yiddish, Italian and other Southern/Eastern European theatres were active in urban centres by the turn of the century.

Immigrant theatres faced significant problems, including lack of money, quarrels among the actors, directors and playwrights, and opposition from inside and outside the community. Scandinavian theatre was opposed by the conservative Lutheran clergy, who associated it with drinking; civil authorities closed Chinese theatres for performing on Sunday (when working-class audiences were free to attend); and German theatre was devastated by boycotts during the First World War.

Nevertheless, as the number of immigrants rose to a million a year in the decade before the First World War, immigrant theatres flourished. Actors trained in their homelands pursued careers in the USA, joined by enthusiastic amateurs who spent long days in the workplace and then rehearsed far into the night. Audiences with sparse resources saved their pennies for tickets. Large communities supported commercial theatres, and virtually every group enjoyed amateur theatre sponsored by lodges, athletic groups and schools, and cultural, nationalist and socialist societies. Road companies brought theatre to isolated farm and mining communities.

Moved by the same desire for economic opportunity and personal freedom that brought immigrants from foreign countries to the USA, native-born blacks migrated from the rural South to the industrial and commercial cities of the North in the opening decades of the 20th century. A burst of African-American theatrical creativity was part of the cultural and intellectual flowering of the 1920s known as the Harlem Renaissance. While black theatre flourished in many cities, its centre was Harlem, where race-conscious plays by, for and about black America were produced in the 1920s and 30s by companies such as the Krigwa Players (founded by W.E.B. Du Bois), the Harlem Experimental Theatre, the New Negro Theatre and the Harlem Suitcase Theatre (founded by LANGSTON HUGHES).

An integral part of the life of the immigrant 'ghettos' of the early 20th century, ethnic theatres supported the educational, charitable and political causes important to their communities. Theatre benefits financed Italian parochial schools in St Louis, social services for Danes and Japanese in Seattle, and orphanages and hospitals in the Ukraine. Their actors having unionized, YIDDISH THEATRES supported the 'uprising of the 20,000', the historic general strike of the largely Jewish shirt makers in New York City in 1909. Thaddeus Dolega-Eminowicz, star and founder of Polish theatres in many American cities, produced and acted in an original play, *With Whom to Side?*, in Detroit in 1917 to raise funds for the Polish Legion's participation in the First World War.

Immigrant theatres provided a place where the young and old, the educated and the uneducated, the newcomer and the old-timer, and the poor and the upwardly mobile could gather and share a common experience. To the inhabitants of cramped, dreary tenements, theatres were attractive places to court, gossip, quarrel, eat, joke and nurture friendships. To actors, directors and playwrights, the theatre was a self-sufficient social world in which marriages took place and children were reared, sometimes appearing on stage as soon as they could walk and talk. This world was especially important to intellectuals, whose lack of English cut them off from the professions they had pursued in the homeland. It was also important to women, who found in it an alternative to traditional domestic roles and a chance to win money and recognition and adopt unconventional life-styles with relative impunity. African-born Clara Lemberg made her reputation on the Finnish-American stage, Theofilia Samolinska on the Polish, Antonietta Pisanelli Alessandro on the Italian, and Sara Adler on the Yiddish. During the Harlem Renaissance (1918–30) eleven black women published 21 plays.

Ethnic theatre made the history and folklore of the homelands accessible to immigrants, many of whom had been deprived of education in the homelands, and introduced American-born children to the heritage of their parents. Based on the complex novel *Romance of the Three Kingdoms*, Chinese opera transmitted traditional Cantonese values of loyalty, self-reliance and personal integrity. Yiddish plays depicted episodes from centuries of Jewish history. German theatre dramatized the exploits of Frederick the Great. Polish theatres presented so many plays on historical and national themes that a Polish journalist called them 'schools of patriotism'.

Immigrant theatres introduced dialect-speaking audiences to the 'standard' pronunciation and vocabulary of their native languages and, through use of English expressions and performance of American plays, to the language and culture of the USA. Many also introduced the classics of world theatre. SHAKESPEARE was performed in Yiddish, German, Swedish and Italian. Yiddish theatres performed the works of MOLIÈRE, SCHILLER, GOETHE, TOLSTOI, GORKY,

SUDERMANN, HAUPTMANN, IBSEN, STRINDBERG, MOLNÁR and SHAW, as well as those of Jewish playwrights such as JACOB GORDIN, Leon Kobrin and SHOLOM ASCH.

Theatre groups of politically progressive Germans, Jews, Swedes, Finns, Hungarians, Latvians, Lithuanians and others used the works of Shaw, Ibsen and Strindberg as well as original plays to explore temperance, pacifism and the problems of workers, women and the aged. Latvian socialist theatres in New York, Chicago, Cleveland, Detroit, San Francisco and Boston produced dozens of AGIT-PROP-type plays, including original political dramas such as S\o(ı,¯)manis Ber\o(g,¯)is's *They Will Overcome* and D\o(a,¯)vids Bund\o(z,¯)a's *Celebrating May*. Theatres were prominent features in Finnish 'Labor Temples' (socialist community centres) across the nation, where plays, both original and imported from Finland, were used for the political education of children and adults. The first Polish play in Chicago was *The Emancipation of Women* (1873), by feminist actress, writer and community activist Theofilia Samolinska. Translated or adapted versions of Ibsen's controversial drama *A Doll's House* explored the 'woman question' in many immigrant theatres.

Despite the importance of educational and ideological plays, most immigrants attended the theatre for entertainment, glamour, diversion and emotional release. Folk dramas depicting the regional music, dance and customs of the homeland were popular in German, Swedish, Danish, Hungarian and Ukrainian theatres, appealing to nostalgia and the desire to escape urban life. A musical folk play, *The People of Varmland* (text by Fredrik August Dahlgren), was the most popular Swedish play, performed at least 62 times in Chicago alone between 1884 and 1921; 90 per cent of all Danish productions were folk plays or OPERETTAS.

'Formula' plays in which wily peasants outwitted landlords, true love triumphed, and villains were punished and heroes rewarded were popular among audiences for whom the problems of life were not so easily resolved. Also popular were VAUDEVILLE, COMEDY and SATIRE. Comic characters such as Olle i Skratthult (Olle from Laughtersville), created by Hjalmar Peterson, and Farfariello, created by Eduardo Migliaccio, satirized the immigrant community itself, especially 'green ones' (new immigrants), using wit and irony to help audiences understand, laugh at, and thus transcend their own often painful adjustment to the USA.

Plays filled with violence, revenge, suicide and murder were well received, whether classical tragedies or original MELODRAMAS. These plays moved audiences because they dealt with familiar problems, though in exaggerated form; Jacob Gordin's *The Jewish King Lear*, for example, about a pious father abused by heartless daughters, brought tears to the eyes of immigrants less than satisfied with the behaviour of American-born children. TRAGEDY, like comedy, provided emotional release, allowing immigrants to express their grief at the absence of loved ones and the frustrations of American life.

European and Asian immigrant theatres active in the early 20th century declined after 1930, undermined by the immigration restriction laws of 1924, the Americanization and geographic dispersion of audiences, and the rise of cinema, radio and television. Federal assistance through the Works Project Administration helped some immigrant and black theatre to survive during the Great Depression of the 1930s; and a few companies with an interest in artistic experimentation, such as the FOLKSBIENE (Yiddish) theatre in New York City and the Swedish Folk Theatre in Chicago, continued into mid-century. Meanwhile many actors, directors and writers from ethnic theatres passed into mainstream American entertainment, bringing elements of their traditions with them.

Ethnic theatre revived after the Second World War, stimulated by heavy migration of Puerto Ricans to the mainland, and, with liberalized quotas, new immigration from Europe, Latin America and Asia. The black civil rights movement touched off increased political activism and ethnic awareness not only among African-Americans but also among Hispanics, Native Americans and Asian Americans, stimulating new 'Third World' theatre activity across the nation. Many older European theatres were rejuvenated in the 1960s and 70s, not only by newcomers, but also by the nostalgia of ageing immigrants, the desire of acculturated children and grandchildren to explore their roots, and the 'new ethnicity', a heightened appreciation of cultural pluralism as an antidote for the anomie and homogenization of modern society.

In the 1960s hundreds of AFRICAN-AMERICAN theatres performed throughout the nation. In the late 1960s Miriam Colón's Puerto Rican Traveling Theatre brought bilingual productions to the Spanish-speaking neighbourhoods of New York City (see also NUYORICAN THEATRE), and by the early 1970s provided a laboratory theatre and an actors' training programme as well. Original plays about life in contemporary European-American ethnic communities as well as productions of Armenian, Latvian, Lithuanian, Polish and Yiddish classics (often in English) were mounted by ethnic churches and community centres, universities and professional companies.

By 1980 almost nine out of 10 new immigrants were from Asia or Latin America rather than Europe, a shift reflected in increased theatre activity in Asian and Latino communities. In the 1980s at least four ASIAN-AMERICAN THEATRE companies performed in New York City. The multi-ethnic East West Players of Los Angeles presented original Asian-American plays and trained actors of Chinese, Japanese, Filipino, Korean and Pacific Island backgrounds. Korean, Thai and other recent Pacific-rim immigrants introduced traditional forms of cultural expression that integrated theatre, dance and music. New Central and South American communities, some of which included foreign-trained actors, playwrights and directors, produced new Spanish-language theatre in New York, Los Angeles and other urban centres. CUBAN-AMERICAN THEATRE emerged in southern Florida.

Overshadowed by the mass media (now often available in ethnic languages), theatre in the post-Second World War decades was not as central to ethnic community life as it had been half a century earlier; nevertheless, it continued to educate as well as to entertain. In the 1970s Hanay Geiogamah's Native American Theatre Ensemble used 'Western'-style drama to transmit Native American traditions, values and aesthetics. Byelorussians, Hungarians, Latvians, Ukrainians, Slovaks and others used theatre in schools, summer camps and youth groups to teach ethnic language and history to a new generation.

Postwar ethnic theatres informed their communities about social and political issues and were more active than their predecessors in reaching out to inform the mainstream community as well. Dramas from the Baltic nations dealt with political oppression and resistance to tyranny in Eastern Europe and, by implication, everywhere. Similar themes were prominent in the theatres of the new Central and South American communities, including NYC's Teatro Cuarto, which followed the BRECHTian tradition of political theatre. The Theatre for Asian American Performing Artists in New York City gave a series of skits about anti-Asian discrimination for the United States Commission on Civil Rights, and produced a satirical review based on those skits at Lincoln Center during the 1976 Bicentennial. LUIS VALDÉZ's EL TEATRO CAMPESINO (Farm Workers' Theatre) developed original *actos* (short plays) to unionize migrant workers in California, and elaborated them into full-length plays that won national and international acclaim. Adopted by cannery workers in San José, tomato pickers in South Jersey, hospital workers in Chicago, and dozens of other groups, Valdez's 'Theatre of the People' became a vehicle for labour protest among Hispanics nationwide.

Ethnic theatre allowed Asian-, African-, Mexican- and Native-American actors, as well as those of other minorities, to move beyond the stereotypical roles usually assigned them in mainstream entertainment. It gave a new generation of playwrights an opportunity to use the language of the ethnic ghetto and to express sensibilities rooted in the unique historic experience of their own communities. 'America is illiterate ... deadset against the Chinese American sensibility,' wrote the militant Frank Chin, a seventh-generation Chinese American whose award-winning play *The Chickencoop Chinaman* was produced in New York in 1972; 'nothing but racist polemics have been written about us ... I don't like that ... All my writing is Chinaman backtalk.'

Ethnic theatre offered ethnic and mainstream audiences insights into minority experiences that, despite an increase of ethnic material in mainstream theatre, remained unavailable elsewhere. RENÉ MARQUÉS's celebrated play *The Oxcart*, which describes a family's disintegration as it moves from rural Puerto Rico to San Juan to New York City, helped Puerto Rican migrants evaluate their gains and losses. The problems of the black family, the impact of the Vietnam War on the Asian-American soldier, the destruction of ethnic neighbourhoods through 'urban renewal', Turkish genocide against Armenians in 1915, the impact of the Holocaust on Jewish survivors, the realities of growing up, getting old or being a woman in ethnic America, discrimination, assimilation and the survival of ethnic identities – these and similar themes were explored in post-Second World War ethnic theatre.

After the revival and expansion of the post-Second World War years, ethnic theatres have faced serious problems in the later decades of the century. In the 1980s political and social support for pluralism eroded. Funding provided in the 1960s and 70s by public and private foundations such as the Rockefeller Foundation, the National Endowment for the Arts, and stage and local cultural agencies was curtailed because of budget deficits and changing priorities. Many university and neighbourhood programmes that had trained ethnic playwrights and actors could no longer afford to do so.

Ethnic theatre had internal as well as external problems. New immigrant populations were sometimes so diverse and transient that neighbourhood theatres found it difficult to develop a stable base of support. An unprecedented array of foreign language entertainment – radio, TV, cinema and videos – competed for the immigrant's attention. Well educated, middle-class immigrants, now a sizeable proportion of newcomers, often preferred American theatre or imported classics to the ethnic genres popular with their largely working-class predecessors. The social class and cultural diversity of the new ethnic America was reflected in conflicts about the nature and purpose of ethnic theatre. Should its focus be local or international? Should its methods be traditional or experimental? Should its goal be artistic excellence or social relevance?

Despite the problems, there were reasons for optimism about the future. During the 1980s ethnic theatre gained increased recognition in academic theatre programmes, national theatre associations and scholarly journals, as well as among ethnic and mainstream audiences. Collections of ethnic plays and scholarly works about ethnic theatre were published. Actors, playwrights and directors experimented with new forms and materials, developed strategies to identify and train new talent, and responded with ingenuity to continuing economic scarcity. In New York City, for example, Italian-American playwrights organized the 'Forum' for mutual support, and Spanish-language theatres increased audiences and revenues by offering new ethnic plays in English to 'general' audiences. In Los Angeles ethnic theatres formed a consortium with other arts groups for more effective fundraising and marketing. The Black Repertory Company of Winston-Salem, North Carolina, drew financial and moral support from an active, dues-paying auxiliary, the North Carolina Black Theater Guild. Politics reinforced artistic and financial creativity: in 1989 a new law increased legal immigration, ensuring the continued growth of the nation's ethnic populations. These developments suggested that ethnic theatre would continue to survive in the USA, not as a curiosity or exercise in nostalgia, but as a living force in American culture. MS

See: Y. Broyles-Gonzalez, *El Teatro Campesino: Theater in the Chicano Movement*, Austin, Texas, 1994; E. Czerwinski, 'Emigrés, Skiers, and Messiahs: Polish Theater in the United States', *Journal of Popular Culture*, Winter 1985; H. Geiogamah, *New Native American Drama: Three Plays*, Norman, Okla., 1980; J. Huerta, *Chicano Theater: Themes and Forms*, Ypsilanti, Mich., 1982; N. Kanellos, *Mexican American Theatre*, Pittsburgh, 1987; F.A.H. Leuchs, *The Early German Theater in New York 1840–1870*, New York, 1928; D. Lifson, *The Yiddish Theatre in America*, New York, 1965; W. Mattila (ed.), *The Theater Finns*, Portland, 1972; H.C. Koren Naeseth, *The Swedish Theater of Chicago 1868–1950*, Rock Island, Ill., 1951; M. Schwartz Seller, *Ethnic Theatre in the United States*, Westport, Conn., 1983; A. Straumanis (ed.), *Baltic Drama: A Handbook and Bibliography*, Prospect Heights, Ill., 1981; L. Valdéz, *Actos*, San Juan Bautista, Calif., 1971.

Eugene O'Neill Memorial Theatre Center (Connecticut) In 1964, George C. White, then a 29-year-old TV executive, leased eight and a half acres of the former Hammon Estate – relevant to several plays by EUGENE O'NEILL – from Waterford, Connecticut, White's home town. Among other goals, White hoped to create a sheltered laboratory for a new generation of American playwrights. Then as now, his vision incorporated three basic elements of professional theatre: playwright, audience and critics. In 1965, he inaugurated the O'Neill's core programme, the National Playwrights Conference, with a five-day retreat. After three volatile shake-down seasons, LLOYD RICHARDS was appointed the NPC's artistic director; together with White, Richards established structures and methods of play development that would spread throughout the country and guided the O'Neill to international acclaim – as multiple awards, including a 1979 Tony, attest.

Other programmes followed, including the National Theatre of the Deaf (1966); the National Critics Institute (1967); the National Theatre Institute (1970), an academic programme; New Drama for Television (1976); and the National Opera/Music Theatre Conference (1978). The O'Neill also sponsors Creative Arts in Education, which integrates art into the community, trains teachers and runs a summer arts camp for teenagers. Media Arts explores the impact of technology on the performing arts, and various international programmes encourage cultural exchange and subsidize translations. Monte Cristo Cottage – the O'Neill summer house in adjacent New London, featured in *Ah, Wilderness!* and *Long Day's Journey into Night* – houses archives, resident artists and scholars, and hosts special events. CLJ

Eupolis Greek comic dramatist from Athens; contemporary with ARISTOPHANES, and his principal rival. As far as we can tell from the fragments of Eupolis, the work of the two seems to have been very similar. Aristophanes' *Frogs*, for instance, was evidently influenced both by Eupolis' *Taxiarchoi* (*Officers*), in which Dionysus was given a rowing lesson, and by his *Demoi* (*Villages*), in which great men of the past returned from the underworld to help Athens. ALB

Euripides ?485/4–407/6 BC Greek tragedian, from Phyla in Attica. Euripides was certainly of respectable birth; no attention need be paid to the allegation of comic poets that his mother was a greengrocer. Most of the anecdotes concerning his life are equally unreliable; it is doubtful, for instance, whether he became embittered at his lack of success at Athens, and whether he was prosecuted for impiety by the demagogue Cleon. Unlike his rival SOPHOCLES he seems to have taken little part in public life. In 408 or 407 he left Athens for the court of Archelaus, King of Macedon, and it was there that he died.

He produced his first plays in 455 but did not win a victory in the competition (see GREECE, ANCIENT) until 441. He is said to have produced 92 plays (we know the titles of about 80), but won first prize only four times in his life (and once after his death with plays that he had left unperformed). He did not usually write connected tetralogies, but there was a loose connection between the plays he produced in 415 (*Alexander, Palamedes,* the surviving *Trojan Women* and *Sisyphus*).

Nineteen plays survive under his name. One of these, the melodramatic *Rhesus,* is generally reckoned to be spurious, the only extant example of 4th-century TRAGEDY. Another, *Cyclops,* is not a tragedy but a satyr play (the only one that survives in full), probably one of his later works. Several of the remaining plays are securely dated, and progressive changes in Euripides' metrical practice enable scholars to fix the relative chronology of the rest within quite narrow limits, giving the following list: *Alcestis,* 438 (a tragedy performed in the position normally occupied by a satyr play); *Medea,* 431; *Heraclidae (Children of Heracles),* 430–428; *Hippolytus,* 428 (a revision of an earlier version); *Andromache,* c.425; *Hecabe,* c.424; *Suppliant Women,* c.423 (concerning the burial of the 'Seven against Thebes'); *Electra,* c.422–416; *Heracles,* c.415; *Trojan Women,* 415; *Iphigenia in Tauris (Among the Taurians),* c.414; *Ion,* c.413; *Helen,* c.412; *Phoenician Women,* c.409; *Orestes,* 408; *Bacchae* and *Iphigenia at Aulis,* both posthumously produced (the latter probably left unfinished and completed by a later hand). In addition we are well informed about many of the lost plays through numerous fragments and plot summaries.

The tragedies tend to contain certain stereotyped structural units, each developed for its own sake. A formal 'prologue speech' at the beginning, delivered by a god or a mortal character and placed outside the action, serves to set the scene and sometimes to foreshadow what will happen. A rhetorical *agōn,* or debate, occurs in every play, and is more self-consciously marked out than it would be in Sophocles; the same is true of the formal messenger-speech. At the end a god generally appears, not so much to tidy up loose ends in the drama as to remove the misapprehensions of the characters and to predict future mythical events. The Chorus tends not to be closely involved in the action, and in the later plays, especially, its songs are often evocations of a world remote from the characters' sufferings (though this need not be seen as mere light relief, as those sufferings may seem all the more poignant by contrast).

Euripides was not always greatly interested in organic plot construction (as ARISTOTLE complains). While the plot of *Medea* shows 'Sophoclean' concentration and that of *Iphigenia in Tauris* is a neatly worked out adventure story, *Trojan Women* hardly has a plot at all (being held together rather by unity of theme and mood), and some of the late plays, such as *Phoenician Women,* are highly episodic (though this is not true of *Bacchae,* which in many ways shows a reversion to earlier techniques).

Despite the uniformity of structure and style, the plays present a wide, even bewildering variety of tone. From the grim exploration of the mentality of child murder in *Medea,* or the bleak evocation of the sufferings of a captured city in *Trojan Women,* the plays range all the way to such light-hearted romances as *Iphigenia in Tauris* and *Helen,* with their daring rescues and happy endings. Between these extremes come various types of melodrama, such as *Hecabe* and *Orestes,* where the characters'

emotions and misfortunes are serious enough, but where the reader senses a certain detachment and lack of moral commitment in Euripides' portrayal of them. Some of these plays must simply be accounted failures (it takes a determined apologist to do anything for *Andromache*). There are also 'problem plays' of which the tone is variously assessed; should *Alcestis* and *Ion,* for instance, be read as cheerfully romantic or as bitterly ironic?

The plays leave a general impression, however, of men and women adrift in a world over which they have no control, at the mercy of passion, illusion and chance. Religion does not help, for, whatever the characters might wish (*Hippolytus* 120, *Bacchae* 1348), the action of the plays reveals the gods as behaving no better than mortals. Nor is the world redeemed by the possibility of noble self-sacrifice, like that of Alcestis or Iphigenia (*at Aulis*), owing to the lack of worthy causes in which this can be displayed.

In characterization Euripides is particularly fond of paradox and moral ambivalence, creating conflicts of sympathy in the audience. In some cases this involves abrupt shifts in behaviour, with little continuity of character (e.g. Alcmene in *Heraclidae,* Hecabe in *Hecabe*); in others it involves real psychological complexity (e.g. Medea, Phaedra in *Hippolytus,* Pentheus in *Bacchae,* all these being studies in the power of passion over reason).

The rhetoric of Euripidean speeches tends to broad generalization and theorizing, and characters can express highly unconventional views (e.g. questioning the subordinate position of women at *Medea* 230–51, or the nature of Zeus at *Trojan Women* 884–8) which show the influence of the sceptical 5th century thinkers called sophists. Such passages cannot be assumed to represent Euripides' personal opinions (no one wishing to promote feminist ideas would be likely to place them in the mouth of Medea), and it is hard to extract simple morals, whether modern or conventional, from the plays seen as wholes. The mere expression of sophistic ideas in tragedy, however, could evidently be regarded as subversive. ARISTOPHANES, who picked Euripides as one of his favourite targets (presenting him in person in *Acharnians, Themophoriazusae* and *Frogs*), portrays him as a pretentious, atheistic intellectual, who degrades tragedy by depicting trivial and vulgar subjects. After his death, however, he became by far the most popular and influential of the tragedians. ALB

Evans, Edith 1888–1976 British actress, awarded the DBE in 1946. After working with WILLIAM POEL and ELLEN TERRY, she established a leading reputation in Restoration and Shakespearian comedy with Millamant (1924) and Lady Wishfort (1948) in *The Way of the World,* and Rosalind in *As You Like It* (1926, at the OLD VIC, a role she returned to in 1959 with the ROYAL SHAKESPEARE COMPANY). Her most famous performance, using her superb voice to best advantage, was as Lady Bracknell in WILDE's *The Importance of Being Earnest* (first played in 1939, filmed in 1951); but she also gave definitive interpretations of SHAW and CHEKHOV and toured widely with ENSA between 1942 and 1944. Her last stage appearance was in *Edith Evans ... and Friends* in 1974. CI

Evans, Maurice (Herbert) 1901–89 British-born actor-director-producer. Evans became an American citizen in

1941, following a 15-year acting career in England, most notably as Raleigh in *Journey's End* (1929) and with the OLD VIC–SADLER'S WELLS company in 1934 (including a full-length *Hamlet*). In the USA he appeared with KATHARINE CORNELL as Romeo (1935) and in 1936 as the Dauphin opposite her Saint Joan. A series of notable Shakespearian performances followed, most directed by MARGARET WEBSTER, including Richard II (1937), gaining him the reputation as the foremost Shakespearian purveyor on the American stage. During the Second World War he entertained the troops with his so-called *GI Hamlet*. After the war (1947–59) Evans played major roles in four Shavian comedies (see SHAW), most notably John Tanner in *Man and Superman*. In 1952 he acted the uncharacteristic role of Tony Wendice in *Dial M for Murder*, in 1960 Rev. Brock in the MUSICAL *Tenderloin*, and in 1962 he appeared in *The Aspern Papers*. In the 1950s he presented SHAKESPEARE on television and produced several Broadway shows. In the 1970s and 80s he appeared mostly in films and TV, although at the age of 80 he played Norman in *On Golden Pond* in Florida. Shortly before his death he completed his autobiography, *All This ... and Evans Too!* (1987). DBW

Eveling, Stanley [Harry Stanley Eveling] 1925– British dramatist, who teaches philosophy at Edinburgh University. His plays first began to appear in the programmes of the adventurous TRAVERSE THEATRE in Edinburgh during the late 1960s, sometimes transferring to London's smaller theatres, such as the Open Space and HAMPSTEAD THEATRE. *The Lunatic, the Secret Sportsman and the Woman Next Door* (1968) and *Dear Janet Rosenberg, Dear Mr Kooning* (1969) were two such examples, whose intelligent dialogue and striking imagery made them popular particularly with young and student audiences. While not necessarily a dramatist of the absurd, for Eveling writes in many styles, he has expressed that sense of meaninglessness which leads to despair, although he often handles such moods in a light and comic vein. In the 1970s he wrote several plays concerning suicide in some form – mainly failed – such as *Caravaggio, Buddy* (1972), *Shivvers* (1974) and *The Dead of Night* (1975); but his funniest play, which transferred to London, was *Union Jack (and Bonzo)* (1973), a black FARCE about a Boy Scout camp and a serial killer. JE

Everyman Theatre (London) Founded by Norman Macdermott in 1920 as a non-commercial experimental playhouse, the Everyman became a showcase for SHAW's plays and mounted NOËL COWARD's first successful work, *The Vortex* (1924). Macdermott was also responsible for introducing many foreign dramatists to the English stage, including the first London performances of O'NEILL's early work, CHIARELLI's *The Mask and the Face* (1924) and PIRANDELLO's *Henry IV* (1925), as well as important productions of IBSEN's naturalistic dramas (see NATURALISM). This role was continued when RAYMOND MASSEY took over the management in 1926 and under Malcolm Morley, who directed the first English production of OSTROVSKY's *The Storm* in 1929. After that the building was used by various small companies such as the GROUP THEATRE (1932 and 1934), and even when converted into a cinema in 1947 it retained the line set by Macdermott, specializing in non-commercial and foreign films. CI

Evreinov, Nikolai (Nikolaevich) 1879–1953 A prolific and versatile anti-realist (see REALISM), mainly pre-revolutionary Russian man of the theatre. The central premiss of his work as director-dramatist-theorist-historian was 'theatricality', which consisted of the need to revitalize theatre (and not solely to stylize it as he believed MEYERHOLD had) by rediscovering its origin as pre-aesthetic, imaginative play; and the theatricalization of life (as opposed to the re-experiencing of life onstage as STANISLAVSKY proposed) in order to cure man's and society's ills, which largely derive from a fear of death.

Evreinov evolved this concept from several influences: Schopenhauer's 'the world as presentation'; NIETZSCHE's 'superman'; Bergson's 'creative evolution' or self-perfection; the symbolists' extreme subjectivism (see SYMBOLISM), which posited the artist-individual as the hero of his own life; the quasi-religious doctrine of transcendence via transformation; and COMMEDIA DELL'ARTE's spontaneity and creation of the theatrical MASK as real-life persona. He developed these themes in his interlocking theoretical treatises *An Introduction to Monodrama* (1909), *The Theatre as Such* (1912), *The Theatre for Oneself* (3 vols., 1915–17) and *Pro Scena Sua* (1915). Monodrama seeks to re-establish the audience as co-creator of the theatrical event as a first step in erasing the border between theatre and life. The expressionistic (see EXPRESSIONISM) transformation of characters and scenic effects to externalize the protagonist's consciousness in order to make him more accessible had little immediate impact, but foreshadowed cinematic and absurdist theatrical techniques (see THEATRE OF THE ABSURD). *The Presentation of Love* (1910) and *In the Stage-Wings of the Soul* (1911) are his earliest and best monodramas, respectively. His most significant commedia-based plays are *A Merry Death* (1908) and *The Chief Thing* (1921). The former, a tragi-farce after BLOK's *The Puppet Show*, and the latter, a 'dramatic paradox' and compendium of Evreinovian aesthetics and devices (and his one international success) based on GORKY's *The Lower Depths*, feature the author's alter-ego HARLEQUIN as death-defier and life-transformer.

In all, Evreinov wrote over 30 plays. Like his playwriting, his early directing as Meyerhold's successor at Vera Komissarzhevskaya's Theatre (1908–9) was an embryonic combination of symbolist and monodramatic tendencies. His interest in 'cultural retrospectivism', in contemporary vogue, led to his co-founding the Ancient Theatre (1907–8, 1911–12) with theatre administrator-censor-editor Baron Nikolai Drizen. The theatre's basic philosophy, 'artistic reconstruction' as opposed to antiquarianism, was manifested in its medieval and Spanish GOLDEN AGE cycles of productions.

Evreinov's penchant for pedantry was balanced by a highly parodistic nature, which he displayed at the Merry Theatre for Grown-up Children, co-founded with FYODOR KOMISSARZHEVSKY (1908–9), and especially at the Crooked Mirror Theatre, co-founded by editor-critic A. R. KUGEL and his wife, Maly Theatre comedienne Z. V. Kholmskaya, where Evreinov served as artistic director (1910–17). Here he directed, wrote, adapted, translated and composed

Oskar Kokoschka's *Murderer, the Hope of Women*, 1907, an early example of expressionism in the theatre; poster by playwright.

scores for some 100 plays – satirical monodramas, harlequinades, pantomimes and theatrical and literary parodies – which helped transform a late-night CABARET into one of Russia's leading 'theatres of small forms'. Of these compositions, *The Inspector General* (1912), PARODYING various directors' conceptual approaches to GOGOL's play, and *The Fourth Wall* (1915), which reveals the ludicrousness of applying Stanislavskian aesthetics and devices to the staging of opera, are of particular note. The summary achievement of Evreinov's Russian theatrical career was his scripting and staging of the Soviet mass spectacle *The Storming of the Winter Palace* (1920) with a cast of 10,000 on Uritsky Square in Petrograd, which realized his dream of merging theatre and life via heroic man. In 1925 he emigrated to Paris, where he continued his multi-faceted theatrical career, but with less impact and originality.   SG

expressionism In 1901, fittingly ushering in the new century, the French painter Julien-Auguste Hervé wanted to distinguish his painting from impressionism and coined the word 'expressionism', which soon found its way into several European languages. Not until the *Supplement to the Oxford English Dictionary*, however, do we find a formal definition in English: 'a style of painting in which the artist seeks to express emotional experience rather than impressions of the physical world; hence, a similar style or movement in literature, drama, music, etc.'. Despite the confusion of 'drama' with 'theatre', that definition points to one widespread use of 'expressionism' as NON-REALISM; sometimes, 'expressionism' is loosely used as a synonym of SURREALISM. The other, more rigorous, use of 'expressionism' in the context of theatre describes Central European, especially German, productions between 1907 (date of KOKOSCHKA's *Murderer, the Hope of Women*) and the mid-1920s, with productions of plays by SORGE, HASENCLEVER, KAISER, GOERING, TOLLER, Koffka, Unruh, BRONNEN, BARLACH and KORNFELD, directed by REINHARDT, JESSNER, FALCKENBERG, Barnowsky, MARTIN, Fehling and Hartung.

Although a few expressionist dramas pre-date the First World War, most of them bear the scars of that war. Aesthetically, the plays are marked by anti-mimetic predecessors, like Munch and Van Gogh in painting, and WEDEKIND, and especially STRINDBERG, in drama. Expressionists aimed at no less than the spiritual regeneration of mankind. Young men rebelling against the proprieties of the Hohenzollern Empire, they wrote of conflicts between generations, sexes and classes. They boldly treated taboo subjects, such as incest and patricide. In their plays, which verbalize emotions rather than dramatize conflicts, an autobiographical protagonist is involved not in a plot but in an apocalyptic quest – often for his essential identity. The protagonist sometimes meets avatars of himself (expressionist protagonists are unregenerately male), and other characters are schematically designed as nameless types. Short, often static, scenes are not causally linked, and the dialogue, varying from short phrases (telegraphese) to long rhapsodies, lacks interpersonal communication.

Originating in the visual arts, expressionism in the theatre was also highly visual (see THEATRE DESIGN). A strong directorial hand would employ light for atmosphere, stage crowd scenes; block his actors in jagged patterns, rather than the expected diagonals; colour garishly, and distort the architecture. Staircases, revolves, treadmills, traps and bridges extended the domain of the stage. And on that stage a new generation of actors rejected verisimilitude on the one hand, and declamation on the other, in order to express passion for its own sake; a strident voice and cadaverous face became hallmarks of the expressionist actor.

It was mainly through the theatre that expressionism travelled from Germany; its most triumphant playwright was the American EUGENE O'NEILL. The critic John Willett believes that O'Neill was the one great expressionist dramatist in any country; but expressionism is the creditor of all frankly theatrical exploitation of the modern stage. RC

Eyre, Richard 1943– British director. While at the Royal Lyceum Theatre, Edinburgh (1967–72), and later as a freelance director, Eyre gained widespread notice for his staging of contemporary drama. In 1973 he was appointed director of Nottingham Playhouse, where he remained for five years. His policy was to commission many new plays and, with premieres of such works as *Brassneck* (BRENTON and HARE) and *Comedians* (GRIFFITHS), the Playhouse quickly acquired a reputation as one of the major centres

in the UK for adventurous and often radical new drama. In 1978 he became producer of BBC TV's 'Play for Today', and in 1982 associate director at the NATIONAL THEATRE. Here, he demonstrated a mastery of the stage MUSICAL, with productions of *The Beggar's Opera* and the long-running *Guys and Dolls*, other recent successful productions including *The Inspector General* and, for the ROYAL COURT, *Hamlet*. His several full-length feature films include *The Ploughman's Lunch* and *Loose Connections*.

In 1986 he was appointed to succeed SIR PETER HALL as artistic director of the National Theatre, from whom he took over in September 1988. His classical productions, such as *The Changeling* (1988) and *Hamlet* (1989), seemed tentative after the self-assurance of Hall, although there was a refreshing search for new readings; but gradually his style of running the NT made itself felt. He issued few statements, but relied on his popularity within the profession to develop small teams of actors and directors, encouraging the younger ones in particular, such as Declan Donnellan (see CHEEK BY JOWL), NICHOLAS HYTNER, STEPHEN DALDRY, the Canadian ROBERT LEPAGE and THÉÂTRE DE COMPLICITÉ. Under Eyre, the NT lost any pretence of being primarily a classical repertoire theatre with some modern or avant-garde plays on the off-centre stages. He directed CHRISTOPHER HAMPTON's *The White Chameleon* (1991) and David Hare's *Murmuring Judges* and *Racing Demon* (both 1991); but his regime will be remembered more for the chances which he has given to others, such as Lepage's muddy *A Midsummer Night's Dream* (1992) and the promotion of ALAN BENNETT's work. The old balance between leftish and rightish new plays, characteristic of Hall's time, was replaced by a bias towards US plays and musicals, of which TONY KUSHNER's *Angels in America* (1992) and the revival of RODGERS and HAMMERSTEIN's *Carousel* (1992) are examples.

Eyre is an intuitive director and manager. He seems to be guided more by what he thinks will work than by a philosophy, which may prove to have been both the asset and the weakness of his running of the NT. He is due to retire from the NT at the end of 1995, after nine successful years. JE

Eytinge, Rose 1835–1911 American actress, author and teacher. Her professional debut was in 1852 as Melanie in BOUCICAULT's *The Old Guard* in Syracuse, New York. Considered temperamental and often unmanageable, she acted in England and the USA, specializing in high COMEDY and TRAGEDY. She worked under LESTER WALLACK, AUGUSTIN DALY and A. M. PALMER. Although she excelled in roles such as Cleopatra (1877), she was best known for her Nancy in *Oliver Twist* (1867) opposite E. L. DAVENPORT's Bill Sykes and the younger J. W. WALLACK JR's Fagin. She dramatized several novels, wrote a play and a novel, and recorded her colourful life in *The Memoirs of Rose Eytinge* (1905). DBW

Fabbri, Diego 1911–80 Italian dramatist notable particularly for his plays of Catholic emphasis written mainly in the 1950s, like *Inquisizione* (*Inquisition*, 1950), *Processo di famiglia* (*Family Trial*, 1953) and *Processo a Gesù* (*The Trial of Jesus*, 1955). The very titles of these indicate something of their concern with the serious, probing analysis of spiritual and religious issues, somewhat in the manner of the 'problem play' but under strong Pirandellian influence (see PIRANDELLO). Their tone and subject-matter, however, have limited their appeal outside Italy. Although the relationship between drama and religion, and the ways in which the theatre can be used to explore religious issues, were major preoccupations – as indicated too by his collection of essays, *Ambiguità cristiana* (*Christian Ambiguity*, 1954) – not all his work was in so serious a vein: more in the mainstream of BOULEVARD theatre are his light comedies of manners and matrimony, *Il seduttore* (*The Seducer*, 1951) and *La bugiarda* (*The Liar*, 1954). Of his later work, *Al dio ignoto* (*To the Unknown God*, 1980) and the posthumously published *Incontro al Parco Terme* (*Meeting in Terme Park*, 1982) are noteworthy. He was also an impressive stage adapter of novels, particularly those of Dostoevsky, and worked on scripts for film and television. The Italian dramatist with whom he is most frequently compared, and who shared many of his concerns, is UGO BETTI. LR

Fagan, J(ames) B(ernard) 1873–1933 British director and playwright, born in Northern Ireland. Beginning as an actor with F. R. BENSON's company and with BEERBOHM TREE, he took over the management of the ROYAL COURT THEATRE in 1918, where he mounted the British premiere of SHAW's *Heartbreak House* (1921) and a pioneering series of SHAKESPEARE productions. As well as a *Shakespeare vs Shaw* REVUE (1905) he also wrote over 15 plays, some specifically for GEORGE ALEXANDER and MRS PATRICK CAMPBELL, and his adaptation of *Treasure Island* became a regular Christmas show from 1922 until 1931. But his main contribution was in founding the Oxford Playhouse, where between 1923 and 1929 he directed a repertoire that included IBSEN, STRINDBERG, SYNGE and Shaw, and a 1925 production of *The Cherry Orchard* that was responsible for CHEKHOV's acceptance on the English stage. Here he developed a 'presentational' non-naturalistic style, and trained such young actors as JOHN GIELGUD, TYRONE GUTHRIE, RAYMOND MASSEY and FLORA ROBSON. After directing the Irish Players he abandoned the theatre for the American film industry. CI

Faiko, Aleksei (Mikhailovich) 1893–1978 Soviet author of quasi-expressionist plays (see EXPRESSIONISM) that were meant to counter the poster-sloganism and schematization of AGIT-PROP scenarios of the 1920s with clear, complex, emotionally saturated plots and characters. Following a brief career as teacher, actor and director, and some minor dramatic efforts – *Dilemma* (1921), *The Career of Pierpont Black* (1922), *Evgraf, Seeker of Adventures* (1926) – he wrote three plays which are remembered more for the artistic and social contexts in which they were produced than for the skill with which they were created.

Lake Lyul, a detective MELODRAMA staged by MEYERHOLD at the Theatre of the Revolution (1923), interwove 'pictures of capitalist bacchanalia', representing decadent individualism, with the then pervasive sense of 'NEP intoxication' – the Soviet audience's consciousness that the monetary liberal respite engendered by the New Economic Policy must be seized and lived to the fullest. Viktor Shestakov's three-tiered, caged, laddered and platformed set, featuring fully operative vertically and horizontally running elevators (a first on the Soviet stage), combined with slide projections and rapidly shifting action to create the effect of cinematic montage and anxious urbanism which, along with 'social mask' characterization (see BORIS ALPERS), fulfilled the director's if not the author's intentions. Meyerhold again strove for a 'theatre of social masks' in his 1924 staging of Faiko's *Bubus the Teacher*, which transformed that work from a naive *vaudeville*-OPERETTA into a pretentious social melodrama with a brilliantly visual and aural *mise en scène*. I. Schlepyanov's set, a semi-circle of bamboo hangings topped by intermittently flashing neon advertisements and a piano in a gilded half-shell on which a pianist performed live 46 'decadent' musical interpretations (Chopin, Liszt and jazz), combined with Meyerhold's experimental 'pre-acting' (pantomime preludes to and commentary upon dialogue) to produce an overall impression of alienation in the audience, akin to that experienced by the contemporary Soviet intelligentsia.

The Man with a Briefcase (1928), a melodramatic treatment of the rise and fall of a ruthless careerist doomed by a pre-revolutionary Tsarist military upbringing, was considered by the Soviets to be his best play and was popular during the Purges of the late 1930s. Faiko wrote six additional plays, two operetta librettos and several screenplays, including *Aelita* (with F. Ostep, from A. N. TOLSTOI's novel, 1924). SG

Falckenberg, Otto 1873–1947 German director and dramatist, whose work bridged SYMBOLISM and EXPRESSIONISM. After visionary plays like *Deliverance* (1899) and satirical CABARET, he became the artistic director of the Munich Kammerspiele from 1917 to 1947, establishing its reputation as one of the leading theatres for contemporary drama with productions of BRECHT's *Drums in the Night* (1922) and BARLACH's *The Dead Day* (1924). CI

Falkland, Samuel see HEIJERMANS, HERMAN

fantoccini SEE MARIONETTE

farce Farce as a technique is common to many forms of theatre, but it has been since the Middle Ages a popular genre which was neglected or scorned in criticism.

Although the word 'farce' is of medieval origin, the performance of raucous COMEDY is as old and as widespread as theatre. European farce has its provenance in elements of Greek and Roman theatre (see GREECE, ANCIENT; ROME) – for instance, the satyr plays of Greece and the comedies of PLAUTUS, with their inventive manipulation of incident and character. The English word 'farce' derives from a culinary word in French, and ultimately from Latin *farsa*, which means 'stuffing'. (The cook was evidently a staple of classical farce.) The genre may therefore have its origin in the medieval theatre custom of 'stuffing' the programme with several plays of various kinds, or of stuffing the liturgy with comic scenes.

French scholars have affixed the label of *farce* to some 200 short plays, mainly dating from the second half of the 15th century, but a minority of these carried genre tags in their own time. Consisting of scenes from daily life, these medieval farces in octosyllabic couplets (300 to 500 lines, on average) were simple in setting, sparse in properties, but inventive in acting – even though they lack scenic directions. Scholars debate whether the purpose was entertainment or edification (portrait of a fallen world), but the short plays are amazingly durable in evoking laughter. The two main subjects of medieval farce were the cuckolded husband and the deceiver deceived. The earliest extant farce – *The Boy and the Blind Man* – is a brutal but funny example of the latter. Over 50 medieval farces focus on conjugal conflict, of which *The Washbasin* is a fine example, typically reflecting medieval misogyny. *Master Pathelin*, the anonymous 15th-century masterpiece, is so nuanced in its character depiction, and so brilliant in its linguistic strategies, that it has led to the critical paradox that the best French farce is not a farce.

French farce influenced 15th-century German and English playwrights like JOHN HEYWOOD. After the Middle Ages, farce was perpetuated in a performing rather than a literary tradition, to which both SHAKESPEARE and MOLIÈRE in their different countries are indebted. In a celebrated essay (of 1901) the scholar Gustave Lanson traced Molière's greatness not only to Italian *COMMEDIA lazzi* (see *LAZZO*) of Scapino, Scaramouche and Brighella, but more importantly to the great French farceurs GROS-GUILLAUME, TABARIN, GAULTIER-GARGUILLE and TURLUPIN (see *TURLUPINADE*). Lanson inaugurated critical appreciation of farce – after a half-century of its popularity in the theatre – in the form called *vaudeville*, whose circumstantial plots hinged on preserving the fragile sexual proprieties. Characters were rudimentary, but sets and props were elaborate in the frenzied chase that might circle back to its point of origin. In France, LABICHE must have worn out a series of collaborators to produce his 175 plays (mainly farces), some of which were preposterous, but many were grounded in the daily life of the rising bourgeoisie in its pursuit of brides, pleasure and money. By the turn of the 20th century, FEYDEAU's farces had grown increasingly sour and cynical in his variations on bedmanship.

To succeed in Britain, farces had to emerge from bedrooms and terminate in weddings, and HENRY ARTHUR JONES and PINERO were able to accomplish this feat. By the 1920s the surrealists (see SURREALISM) sang the praises of farce – e.g. ARTAUD's delight at the MARX BROS. Across the Channel in London the Aldwych farces (mainly by BEN

TRAVERS) thrived on deception and manipulation. In the 1950s and 1960s farce was triumphant at the Whitehall Theatre, London, under the actor-manager BRIAN RIX. Silent films gave an international impetus to farce, through the brilliance of Buster Keaton, Laurel and Hardy, Harold Lloyd, and especially Charlie Chaplin. Farce is still the favourite genre on the BOULEVARDS – Achard and Roussin; on London's Shaftesbury Avenue – AYCKBOURN, FRAYN; and on BROADWAY – NEIL SIMON. Since the end of the Second World War, however, playwrights have deftly assimilated the devices of farce to expose a serious view: e.g. BECKETT's music-hall tramps in *Waiting for Godot*, IONESCO's proliferation of chairs in *The Chairs*, GENET's clown-show in *The Blacks*, PINTER's games in *The Collection*, STOPPARD's acrobats in *Jumpers* and travesties in *Travesties*, GRIFFITHS's comic turns in *Comedians*, and MAMET's BURLESQUE in *A Life in the Theatre*. Farce has acquired its ablest critic in ERIC BENTLEY in several essays, as well as in *The Life of the Drama* (1964).   RC

Farnie, H(enry) B(rougham) 1836–89 A prolific theatrical wordsmith who, sometimes in collaboration but often on his own, loosed a torrent of plays, BURLESQUES, librettos and, above all, adaptations of French *OPÉRA BOUFFE* on to the Victorian stage. He was reputed to go and see a work in Paris and then take no longer than the return Channel crossing to produce an English version. In 1880 five new English adaptations by Farnie appeared at different London theatres in a little over seven months. His pieces held the stage at the Strand Theatre continuously from 1879 until its closure for rebuilding in 1882. When it reopened later that year it was with another piece by him. Farnie was also a director of performances and an assiduous womanizer. This highly significant Victorian man of the theatre is now forgotten. BERNARD SHAW commented, 'The late H.B. Farnie was for an age, but not for all time.' GH

Farquhar, George 1677–1707 Irish playwright. Born in Londonderry and educated at Trinity College, Dublin, he tried a career as an actor at Smock Alley Theatre in Dublin, abandoning the stage when he wounded a fellow actor during a performance of DRYDEN's *The Indian Emperor* in 1697 by forgetting to use a blunted sword. Moving to London that year, his first play, a conventional comedy, *Love and a Bottle*, was produced in 1698. The following year, *The Constant Couple* was a phenomenal success, the greatest of the Restoration, mainly through the performance as Sir Harry Wildair of Robert Wilks, with whom Farquhar had acted in Dublin. Farquhar followed its success with a weaker sequel, *Sir Harry Wildair* (1701), an adaptation of FLETCHER's *The Wild Goose Chase* as *The Inconstant* (1702), a savage comedy in *The Twin Rivals* (1702) and a farce from a French source, *The Stage Coach* (1704). But none of these repeated his earlier success and a disastrous marriage to a penniless widow under the illusion that she was wealthy led to severe financial crisis, though the marriage surprisingly became an affectionate relationship.

As a way out of his money troubles he became a lieutenant in the Earl of Orrery's regiment in 1704 where, though he did not make money, his experiences in recruiting soldiers in Shropshire became the source of his next play, *The Recruiting Officer* (1706). In spite of its success, Farquhar, poor and ill, was soon to write his last comedy, *The Beaux' Stratagem*, in 1707, dying soon after the first performance. A lasting success, *The Beaux' Stratagem*, set in a country community of innkeepers and highwaymen, explores the problems of a loveless marriage, recommending the solution of divorce by mutual consent derived from the apparently unlikely source of Milton's divorce pamphlets. PH

Farrah, Abdelkader 1926– A native Algerian, most of whose work as a British freelance stage designer has been with the ROYAL SHAKESPEARE COMPANY. Self-trained as a painter, he became a protégé and collaborator of MICHEL SAINT-DENIS in France and later in England. Farrah's scenography is marked by an architectonic and theatrically expressive shaping of stage space (especially evident in *The Balcony*, 1971, *Henry V*, 1975, and *Coriolanus*, 1977), and a painter's talent for bold design and colour in COSTUMES and props (*Doctor Faustus*, 1968, *As You Like It*, 1980, *Poppy*, 1982, and *The Balcony*, 1987). Notable instances of his interest in stylized MASKS occurred in *The Tempest* (1963) and *Richard III* (1970), as well as in the 1968 *Doctor Faustus*. JMB

Farren, Elizabeth 1762–1829 English actress. She worked on the midlands theatre circuit with her mother and sisters in the 1770s and then joined Younger's company at Liverpool. By 1777 she was in London where she had little success in BREECHES PARTS, lacking the figure for them. From 1780 she acted at DRURY LANE, becoming very successful in the fine-lady roles previously played by FRANCES ABINGTON, and praised for her charm, beauty and art. Very successful and highly paid, she began an affair with the Earl of Derby in 1785 and started to move in high society. On the death of his first wife in 1797 she retired from the stage and married him. PH

Farren, Nellie [Ellen] 1848–1904 British actress, born into a famous theatrical family, who made her London debut in 1864. Known above all as a queen of BURLESQUE, she was a star of London's GAIETY from 1868 until her retirement in 1891 and a member of the famous Gaiety Quartette, with EDWARD TERRY, KATE VAUGHAN and EDWARD ROYCE. 'She was,' wrote H. J. BYRON in a poetic tribute, 'a peal of laughter, ringing its way through life.' PT

Fassbinder, R(ainer) W(erner) 1945–82 German dramatist, actor, director and film-maker. Fassbinder was an actor and founder member in 1968 of the Munich theatre commune Antitheater, for which he miniaturized BRUCKNER, FLEISSER, JARRY, GAY's *Beggar's Opera* and GOETHE's *Iphigenia*, turning them into montages of discordant scenes, without sets, costumes or psychological development. His later productions turned the amateurishness of his beginnings into a highly artistic, often luxurious, camp style.

He left the theatre for film-making in 1975, when charges of anti-Semitism halted rehearsals of his Frankfurt play *Der Müll, die Stadt und der Tod* (*The Refuse, the City and Death*). *Katzelmacher* (*Cock Artist*, 1968), a

look at suburban boredom, sex and racism, and *The Bitter Tears of Petra von Kant* (1971), a study of Lesbian masochism, later became films.

An artistic phenomenon in his own right, Fassbinder is connected with the VOLKSSTÜCK revival. He rediscovered Fleisser and filmed KROETZ and SPERR. He is best known as a prolific film director who could combine the texture of German life and the Hollywood panache of Douglas Sirk with a critical and personal view of German history, in films like *The Marriage of Maria Braun*, *Lola*, *Lili Marlene* and *Fear Eats the Soul*. His fascinating 14-part TV adaptation of Alfred Doblin's novel *Berlin Alexanderplatz* was shown on BBC2. HR

Fastnachtspiel The CARNIVAL or Shrovetide play of German-speaking Europe, known from the 15th century, popular in origin and content, though incorporating some learned elements. *Fastnachtspiele* are usually farcical comedies, as the term *Schwänke* ('jests'), sometimes applied to them, indicates, or allegorical debates. They are generally supposed to have been performed by students and artisans. The guild of mastersingers was also connected with them – Hans Folz, a member of the Nuremberg guild, is one of the few known 15th-century authors, and the 16th-century shoemaker and mastersinger Hans Sachs wrote a large number. AEG

Fatunde, Tunde 1951– Nigerian playwright, critic and journalist. Fatunde was born at Makurdi, Benue state. He studied at the Universities of Ibadan and Bordeaux, and later taught at the University of Benin. Among Nigerian playwrights he is the most notable exponent of AGIT-PROP theatre. His plays challenge economic exploitation in an authoritarian state that he sees as divided along class lines. Critical opinion is sharply split as to whether he has achieved an effective revolutionary theatre, raising his audience's consciousness, or whether his drama is 'ultimately reductionist ... [ignoring] the complexities with which [his] audience is daily contending', as the critic David Richards has said. His earliest plays, *Blood and Sweat* and *No More Oil Boom* (both 1985), deal, respectively, with the exploitation of labour in apartheid South Africa and with corruption and exploitation in the Nigeria of the oil-boom years. *No Food, No Country* (1985) dramatizes the massacre of peasants at Bakolori, northern Nigeria, as the government attempted to sequester land for a large-scale irrigation project. This play is significant as the first Fatunde wrote in pidgin, in an attempt to widen his potential audience and to bring his theatre's contents closer to the experience of working people. His later plays, *Oga Na Tief Man* (*The Big Man Is a Thief*, 1986) and *Water No Enemy Get* (1989), also written in pidgin, deal again with the themes of economic deprivation and attempts by workers to organize opposition to exploitation. Fatunde lectures at the Lagos State University. Since the early 1990s he has been an activist in Nigeria's Civil Liberties Organization. CD

Faucit, Helen Saville 1817–98 British actress, remembered primarily for her performance as MACREADY's leading lady. She made her debut at COVENT GARDEN in 1836, as Julia in SHERIDAN KNOWLES's *The Hunchback*, and was the creator, with Macready, of leading roles in the best-known plays of EDWARD BULWER LYTTON, *The Duchess de la Vallière* (1837), *The Lady of Lyons* (1838), *Richelieu* (1839) and *Money* (1840). Her refined portrayal of romantic passion attracted fashionable theatregoers, and she was an admired Juliet, Desdemona and Cordelia. After her marriage to the writer (and friend of the royal family) Theodore Martin, in 1851, she made only occasional appearances on the stage. Her husband was knighted in 1880, and it was as Lady Martin that she published her book *On Some of Shakespeare's Female Characters* (1892), an arch example of the 19th-century tendency to speculate on the unwritten biographies of dramatis personae.   PT

Favart, Charles-Simon 1710–92 French playwright and librettist, who wrote principally for the COMÉDIE-ITALIENNE and the Paris fair theatres of St Germain and St Laurent. In a long career stretching from the 1720s to the 1770s he produced some 150 pieces, mostly in the form of comic OPERAS, *ballet-pantomimes* or similar *divertissements* and frequently PARODYing other dramatic or operatic works. Many were devised in collaboration with such writers as Panard and the abbé de Voisenon and some, apparently, with his wife, a vivacious actress and singer who under the name of Mlle Chantilly (1727–72) appeared in most of his plays at the Comédie-Italienne and is reputed to have anticipated MLLE CLAIRON in incorporating touches of realism into her stage costume. Amongst the greatest of Favart's successes were *La Chercheuse d'esprit* (*The Adventuress*, 1741), *Les Amours de Bastien et Bastienne* (*The Loves of Bastien and Bastienne*, 1753), a parody of ROUSSEAU's *Le Devin du village* (*The Village Soothsayer*), *La Fée Urgèle* (*The Fairy Urgèle*, 1753) and *Annette et Lubin* (1762). In 1757 he replaced Monnet as director of the Opéra-Comique, a position he retained when it amalgamated with the Comédie-Italienne five years later. His lengthy correspondence in the 1760s with the intendant of court theatres in Vienna is a mine of information about Parisian theatrical life at the time.   DR

Faversham, William 1868–1940 London-born actor, who appeared briefly on the stage there before migrating to America in 1887. He was in the companies of both DANIEL FROHMAN and CHARLES FROHMAN, and played opposite MINNIE MADDERN FISKE and MAUDE ADAMS before becoming a leading man. His physical attractiveness and buoyant personality earned him the label of a 'matinée girl's idol'. Among his successful Shakespearian roles were Mark Antony in *Julius Caesar* and the title roles in *Romeo and Juliet* and *Othello*. He won his popularity, however, playing vigorous and masculine heroes in such plays as *Lord and Lady Algy*, *The Squaw Man* and *The Prince and the Pauper*. His last role came in 1933 when he played Jeeter Lester in the long-running *Tobacco Road*.   RAS

Fechter, Charles (Albert) 1824–79 Actor, born in London to a German father and an English mother, educated in France and speaking French as his first language. He made his debut in Paris in 1840 and became a leading melodramatic actor, particularly at the Porte-Saint-Martin. Restless and erratic, Fechter moved to London in 1860 and opened at the PRINCESS's in a version of HUGO's *Ruy Blas*. Despite (or because of) his French accent, the performance was a sensational success. He followed it with an equally melodramatic version of *Don Caesar de Bazan* (1861) and then floored the English public with a Hamlet that had all the ease and elegance of Ruy Blas. G. H. LEWES spoke for Fechter's female adorers in calling him 'lymphatic, delicate, handsome', and the ecstatic reception owed much to the innovatory blonde curls and the contrasting black suit, carefully tailored.

The innovations of his 'logical' Othello (1861) were more controversial, and Fechter returned to French melodrama for *The Duke's Motto* (1863). But his iconoclasm was something more than mere display. As manager of London's LYCEUM (1863–7) he initiated a mechanical revolution, substituting for wings and grooves the solid walls of an enclosing set and installing a system of lifts which allowed the sinking and lifting of complete scenes (see THEATRE DESIGN). His Lyceum repertoire mixed gentlemanly MELODRAMA with *Hamlet* and *Othello*, but his vogue passed. In 1870 he sailed to the USA, where he remained, with the exception of a short season in London in 1872, for the rest of his life. He toured for some time, then opened the Globe Theatre in Boston as Fechter's Theatre, again with many innovations. His managerial ventures in America, however, failed, owing to his personal vanity and what his fan and friend CHARLES DICKENS called 'a perfect genius for quarrelling'. Excessive drinking and a bigamous marriage forced him into retirement. He died in Quakertown, where he had tried to set up a farm.   PT SMA

Fedeli (meaning 'the faithful') A troupe of COMMEDIA DELL'ARTE actors founded (c.1603) and led by GIOVAN BATTISTA ANDREINI (Lelio, the male love interest), under the protection of the Duke of Mantua. Once allied to and often competing with the ACCESI, the Fedeli specialized in sumptuous court spectacles and featured Florinda (VIRGINIA ANDREINI) as its languishing prima donna in her husband's plays. It turned down Marie de Medici's invitation to give performances at the French Court in 1611, but three years later played publicly in Paris at the HÔTEL DE BOURGOGNE, when the company included TRISTANO MARTINELLI (Arlecchino), Barbieri (Beltrame) and FRANCESCO GABRIELLI (Scapino). Other French appearances occurred in 1623–4 and sometime between 1643 and 1647. The last notice of it mentions a performance of Andreini's *Magdalen Lustful and Repentant* (1652) in which a new young actress, Eularia Coris, enjoyed great personal success.   LS

Feder, Abe 1909– American designer who was a pioneer in the field of STAGE LIGHTING design. One of his earliest projects was *Four Saints in Three Acts* (1934) for director JOHN HOUSEMAN. He went on to do numerous productions with the FEDERAL THEATRE PROJECT, including many of the LIVING NEWSPAPERS and *The Cradle Will Rock* (1938). He designed the first season of Ballet Theatre (1941) and in the following decades designed extensively for the stage, notably lights for *The Skin of Our Teeth* (1942), *My Fair Lady* (1956) and *Camelot* (1960). As an architectural lighting designer, he designed or consulted on lighting for the 1964 New York World's Fair, exterior lighting for many buildings (including Rockefeller Center and the Pan Am Building), and lighting systems and interior lighting for several theatres, including the JOHN F. KENNEDY CENTER. AA

Federal Street Theatre (Boston, USA) When the 1750 law prohibiting play-acting was overturned, prominent Bostonians pledged money by shares to erect the city's first theatre. In 1794, a handsome brick building by Charles Bulfinch, one of America's first architects, opened under the management of Charles Stuart Powell. The theatre burned down in 1798 and was rebuilt by Bulfinch the following year. After a succession of managers, the theatre, known as 'Old Boston', was supplanted by newer theatres and was not used consistently. It closed in 1852. MCH

Federal Theatre Project (USA) Established under the Works Progress Administration (WPA) in 1935 by an Act of the United States Congress, this was the first American example of officially sponsored and financed theatre – and therefore the subject of much political controversy. Under the national direction of the indefatigable and intrepid HALLIE FLANAGAN, head of the experimental theatre at Vassar College, the FTP's objectives were to give meaningful employment to theatrical professionals out of work during the Depression and to provide 'free, adult, uncensored theatre' to audiences throughout the country. Indeed, 10,000 people were employed at its peak, with theatres in 40 states. During its almost four years of existence, the FTP launched or established the careers of such notable theatre artists as ORSON WELLES, JOHN HOUSEMAN, Joseph Cotten, Arlene Francis, Will Geer, John Huston, ARTHUR MILLER, Virgil Thomson, HOWARD BAY, PAUL GREEN, Mary Chase, MARC BLITZSTEIN, CANADA LEE and ELMER RICE. At low ticket prices, audiences were provided with a large variety of fare, ranging from classics to new plays, children's theatre, foreign-language productions, puppetry, religious plays, a Negro theatre, MUSICAL THEATRE, a circus, and a controversial innovation called the LIVING NEWSPAPER, designed to deal with issues of the day by utilizing documentary sources. In January 1936, with the urging of HELEN TAMIRIS, a separate Federal Dance Project was established, although congressional cut-backs forced a merger with the FTP in October 1937.

The FTP played to millions of people throughout the country; it is estimated that over 12 million attended performances in New York alone. Of the hundreds of productions presented by the FTP, those by its Negro theatre were among the most innovative and included the 'voodoo' *Macbeth* (1936), *Haiti* (1938) and *The Swing Mikado* (1939). In 1936 Sinclair Lewis's *It Can't Happen Here*, written for the FTP, was produced simultaneously in 22 cities. The US premiere of *Murder in the Cathedral*, which had been rejected by the THEATRE GUILD, was successful in 1936 at popular prices. The 1937 premiere of Paul Green's outdoor historical pageant *The Lost Colony* was in a WPA-built outdoor theatre on Roanoke Island, North Carolina, where it has been seen every summer since. The FTP was endlessly willing to take chances in its selection of plays and was, in HAROLD CLURMAN's words, 'the most truly experimental effort ever undertaken in the American theatre'.

CENSORSHIP was a problem frequently faced by various units of the FTP; its outspoken criticism, interpreted especially by Congressional conservatives as left-wing, ultimately led to a heated debate and the disbanding of the project on 30 June 1939. The epic and convoluted history of the FTP was first recounted by Flanagan in *Arena* (1940). In 1974 the Federal Theatre Project Research Center was established at George Mason University, though original material in the archive was moved to the Library of Congress in late 1994. DBW

Fedotova, Glikeriya (Nikolaevna) 1846–1925 The leading Russian actress of her day, protégée of SHCHEPKIN, the father of Russian realistic acting; and with her husband, actor-director A. F. Fedotov, STANISLAVSKY's teacher at the Moscow Society of Art and Literature. Her range was broader than that of the tragedienne ERMOLOVA, the other great Maly Theatre actress, extending to COMEDY and drama, both domestic and historical. She excelled in a series of 29 character roles from the OSTROVSKY canon, requiring emotional depth and truth to life. She was also memorable as many of SHAKESPEARE's strong women – Beatrice (1865), Isabella (1868), Katherina (1871), Portia (1877), Lady Macbeth and Mistress Page (1890), Volumnia (1902) – and as Queen Elizabeth opposite Ermolova's Maria Stuart in Schiller's play. SG

féerie Type of French spectacular show, whose action derives from magical, fantastic or supernatural elements; heavy on production values and stage machinery. Its forebears are the *pièces à machines* produced at the Théâtre du MARAIS in the mid-17th century, with classical mythology supplying the plots. Abbé Boyer's *Ulysse dans l'Île de Circe* (1648) was a grandiose example, while MOLIÈRE and CORNEILLE's *Psyché* (1670) represents a pocket version. In the late 18th century, the fantastic infiltrated fairground pantomimes, as in *Arlequin dans un oeuf* at the Théâtre des Jeunes-Artistes, to produce in the 19th century the synthetic *féerie*. The first true success was *Le Pied du mouton* (Théâtre de la Gaîté, 1806), a much revived extravaganza in which a magic sheep's trotter unleashes a host of miracles. It was superseded by *Les Pilules du diable* (CIRQUE OLYMPIQUE, 1839) and a succession of invariably successful shows, such as *La Biche au bois* (known in the English-speaking world as *The White Fawn*), *La Chatte Blanche* and *Peau d'Âne*, based on fairy tales and romances. Since the transformations, tricks and apotheoses required a large stage, the Châtelet and then the Porte-Saint-Martin (see BOULEVARD) under Marc Fournier became its favourite haunts. Romantic authors appreciated the dream-like qualities of the *féerie* (even Flaubert turned his hand to writing one, which went unproduced); it exercised an important influence on the development of BURLESQUE, MUSICAL COMEDY and early cinema. LS

female impersonation Among certain American-Indian, African and South Sea Island tribes, the androgynous SHAMAN or *bardache* serves an important function as intermediary with the supernatural which some scholars consider is, in civilized societies, sublimated in the actor. The origins of theatre in religious cults meant that women were barred from performance, a prohibition sustained by social sanctions against their public exhibition in general.

El Niño Farini, the English
trapeze and highwire artist,
in his transvestite costume
as Mlle Lulu.

Therefore, in Europe before the 17th century and in Asia before the 20th, female impersonation was the standard way to portray women on stage, and was considered far more normal than females playing females. The Greek and Roman theatre accepted the convention, and scandal arose only when an emperor lost caste by becoming a performer. Suetonius tells us that Nero enacted the incestuous sister in the MIME-drama *Macaris and Canace*, giving birth on stage to a baby that was then flung to the hounds; according to Aelius Lampridius, Heliogabalus played Venus in *The Judgement of Paris* with his naked body depilated.

In the Oriental theatre, the female impersonator constitutes a distinct line of business. The *dan* of Chinese opera, instituted for moral reasons in the reign of Chi'en Lung (1735–96), must be an exceptionally graceful dancer. It was the *emploi* of the great MEI LANFANG, voted the most popular actor in China in 1924, for whom Ts'i Zhou-chan wrote a special repertory. The *onnagata* role of Japanese *KABUKI* drama came about when women and boys were banished from the stage, lest they promote wantonness; mature men with shaven foreheads had to take over the female roles. Many specialists in *onnagata* parts possess an extensive range and are capable of dozens of distinct characters; in the past they were expected to behave offstage in as womanly a fashion as they did on.

Men dressing as women was a tradition of saturnalia, Feasts of Fools and medieval New Year's celebrations, still to be seen in rag weeks and end-of-term revels. Cross-dressing is a usual accompaniment to CARNIVAL time, when norms are turned upside-down; men giving birth was enacted at some Hindu festivals, and even Arlecchino in the late *COMMEDIA DELL'ARTE* was shown in childbed and then breastfeeding his infant. Just as the Catholic Church attacked unruly carnivals, Protestant clerics and Puritans censured the 'sodomitical' custom of the boy player on the Elizabethan and Jacobean stage. BOYS' COMPANIES dominated the English theatre until 1580, and NATHAN FIELD as Ophelia, Alexander Cooke as Lady Macbeth, and Robert Goffe as Juliet and Cleopatra shaped the image of these characters in the minds of SHAKESPEARE's contemporaries. NED KYNASTON was the last of the line, playing well into the Restoration when PEPYS saw him in skirts.

Women were members of *commedia dell'arte* troupes

from the 16th century but the male comics occasionally donned petticoats – to the delight of audiences – and this travesty aspect (already present in ARISTOPHANES) grew more important as actresses gained popularity. If beauty and sex appeal were to be projected from stage by a real, nubile woman, the post-menopausal woman could as easily be played by a comic actor; parts like Mme Pernelle in MOLIÈRE's *Tartuffe* and the nanny Yeremeevna in FONVIZIN's *The Minor* were conceived as male roles, and NESTROY's mid-19th-century FARCES contain several of these 'dame' parts. The comic dame had become a fixture of the English PANTOMIME by the Regency period, and would be a showcase for such comedians as DAN LENO, GEORGE ROBEY and George Graves; some performers like George Lacy and Rex Jamieson ('Mrs Shufflewick') played nothing but dames. The tradition was maintained on the American popular stage by Neil Burgess as Widow Bedotte and Gilbert Sarony (d.1910) as the Giddy Gusher; in France, OFFENBACH's OPERETTA *Mesdames de la Halle* (1858) created three roles of market-women to be sung by men.

Nor was it unusual in the CIRCUS for boy athletes to be disguised as girls to make their stunts seem more phenomenal: the American equestrian Ella Zoyara (Omar Kingsley) and the trapezist Lulu (El Niño Farini) were celebrated examples in the 19th century, the aerialist Barbette in the 20th. Such transvestite performers were said to be 'in drag', a term from thieves' cant that compared the train of a gown to the drag or brake on a coach, and entered theatrical parlance from homosexual slang around 1870. 'Dragging up' provides the central plot device in BRANDON THOMAS's *Charley's Aunt*, WILLIAM DOUGLAS HOME's sex-change play *Aunt Edwina* (1959) and SIMON GRAY's *Wise Child* (1968).

A new development arose in 19th-century VARIETY with the glamorous impersonator, who might be a comedian but dressed and made up to resemble a woman of taste, beauty and chic. In America they were stars. The baritone JULIAN ELTINGE usually selected vehicles that allowed him to vary sexes, accomplished by quick-change (one act required 11 separate changes); this 'ambi-sextrous comedian', as PERCY HAMMOND called him, wore costumes that rivalled those of the fashion-plate Valeska Surratt, whom he parodied in *The Fascinating Widow* (1911). Bert Savoy (Everett Mackenzie, 1888–1923), of Savoy and Brennan, introduced an outrageous caricature, garish and brassy, gossiping about her absent girlfriend Margie and launching such catch-phrases as 'You musssssst come over' and 'You don't know the half of it, dearie'; his arch camping influenced MAE WEST. Francis Renault (Anthony Oriema, d.1956), billed as 'the Slave of Fashion' and 'Camofleur', sang in a clear soprano, and Karyl Norman (George Podezzi, 1897–1947), 'the Creole Fashion-Plate', starred in MUSICAL COMEDY.

During the Second World War, all-male drag revues were popular in the British armed services, and persisted as postwar shows like *Soldiers in Skirts* and *Forces Showboats*. By the mid-1950s this activity had transferred to after-hours clubs, while London's East End pubs with their drag amateur nights were frequently subject to raids. In the USA, annual extravaganzas like *The Jewel Box Revue* arose. Drag ensembles sprang up in West Berlin (Chez Nous, 1958; Chez Romy Haag, 1972) and in Paris

(Alcazar, 1972; L'Ange Bleu, 1975; Chez Madame Arthur and Le Carrousel), often featuring transvestites such as the Bardot clone Coccinelle, who had taken hormone treatments to improve the likeness.

The mid-1960s to 1970s saw a resurgence of female impersonation as a virtual article of theatrical faith. DANNY LA RUE's club in Hanover Square, London (1964–70), was a resort of fashion; and drag MIMES, lip-synching to tapes, were ubiquitous. This style reached an apotheosis in Paris's La Grande Eugène, seen in London in 1976. The drag ball in OSBORNE's *A Patriot for Me* (ROYAL COURT, 1965) hastened the demise of dramatic CENSORSHIP in England, thus enabling such impressive impersonations as Tim Curry's Dr Frank'n'furter in *The Rocky Horror Show* (1972). Androgyny had infiltrated the rock-music scene with Alice Cooper and David Bowie, and reached a logical terminus in the asexual Boy George. More anarchic uses of 'gender-fuck' came from the American group the Cycle Sluts, hairy bruisers in net stockings, and the 'radical drag queens' Bloolips (founded 1970), while the LINDSAY KEMP company and the Glasgow CITIZENS' THEATRE adapted female impersonation to the interpretation of classical texts. Comedy persisted in the cod ballet of the all-male Ballets Trockadero de Monte Carlo (founded 1974) and the Trockadero Gloxinia Ballet; in impersonators like Charles Pierce and Craig Russell, and dames, such as BARRY HUMPHRIES as Edna Everage and the piano-entertainers Hinge & Brackett (George Logan and Patrick Fyffe).

Contemporary American performance art has latched on to the conventions of drag to explore gender identity and confusion, as in the work of Los Angeles comedian John Fleck (b.1953). A mixture of avant-garde innovation and the traditions of popular culture is clear in the work of John Epperson (Lypsinka) and Ethyl (Roy) Eichelberger (1945–91). 'Alternative drag' in the UK was a short-lived phenomenon, as such FRINGE performers as the Joan Collins Fan Club (Julian Clary) became show business personalities. The success of the MUSICAL *La Cage aux Folles* and David Henry Hwang's play *M. Butterfly* also testify to the co-opting of drag by the commercial theatre. The Afrikaner comedian Pieter-Dirk Uys (b.1946), who had evolved his female impersonations to attack South African society, found that his satiric creation Mrs Evita Bezuidenhout had become as beloved to Boers as to anti-apartheid activists. However, the rise of 'voguing', a transvestitic dance and beauty competition among American urban blacks and Hispanics, revealed a new strain of populism. As the politically correct gay community turned its back on drag, a radical edge was attributed to such outrageous clowns as Vaginal Creme Davis, Brenda Sexual and Glennda Orgasm of *The Brenda and Glennda Show*, and Hapi Phace, some of whom came out of the Pyramid Club in New York. (See also MALE IMPERSONATION.) LS

See: R. Baker, *Drag: A History of Female Impersonation*, London, 1968; K. Kirk and E. Heath, *Men in Frocks*, London, 1984; L. Senelick (ed.), *Gender in Performance*, Hanover, NH, 1992; C. Shaw and A. Oates, *A Pictorial History of the Art of Female Impersonation*, London, 1966.

feminist theatre (Britain) Feminist theatre evolved in the 1970s as part of the alternative/political theatre movement. The first feminist companies were set up by women involved with the women's movement (the Women's Theatre Group, 1973) or by women active in, or critical of, Left theatre (Monstrous Regiment, 1975).

Feminist theatre developed rapidly in the 1970s and 1980s. Many theatre companies emerged. Some addressed feminist politics in 'issue-based' theatre – the Women's Theatre Group, Monstrous Regiment, Clean Break, Mother Hen, Siren, Spare Tyre and Theatre of Black Women. Others focused on feminist comedy and physical theatre – Beryl and the Perils, Bloomers, Clapperclaw, Cunning Stunts and Les Oeufs Malades; or concerned themselves primarily with the aesthetics of feminist performance – Burnt Bridges, Hesitate and Demonstrate and the international Magdalena Project. One company, Sadista Sisters, was a band as well as a theatre group; another, Mrs Worthington's Daughters, specialized in recovering feminist plays from the early 20th century. The companies were usually workers' collectives; most were women-only and most began by group-devising their shows. All were touring companies – the aim of the Women's Playhouse Trust to establish a permanent theatre for women has never been achieved – playing to audiences composed predominantly of women. In London two venues, Oval House and Action Space/the Drill Hall, became particularly associated with women's theatre. Funding agencies began to recognize the importance of the genre, giving grants to companies and venues.

Nurtured by feminist theatre groups and pro-feminist policies in other theatres – notably the ROYAL COURT THEATRE in London – feminist playwrights became more numerous. Their plays explored the family, gender roles and sexuality from different political (socialist feminist, radical feminist, black feminist) and national, class and ethnic perspectives. Representative writers of this period include CARYL CHURCHILL, Sarah Daniels, Andrea Dunbar, Marcella Evaristi, PAM GEMS, Bryony Lavery, Deborah Levy, Jackie Kay, Liz Lockhead, Clare McIntyre, Rona Munro, Louise Page, Winsome Pinnock, Christina Reid, Sue Townsend, Michelene Wandor and TIMBERLAKE WERTENBAKER. The wider influence of feminism in the theatre was to be seen in the protests of actresses working in major theatre companies against the male 'directocracy', and in the gradual appointment of women artistic directors to major repertory houses.

In the l990s that vibrancy seems to have faded. Challenges have come from within feminism itself to the idea of an inclusive politics of 'female identity'. Protest theatre is out of favour. Public funding for the theatre has been reduced. Few feminist theatre companies have survived into the l990s and few new ones have emerged. In women's writing for the theatre there has been a perceptible shift in tone – Wertenbaker's most recent play *Three Birds Alighting on A Field*, for example, is markedly less critical of patriarchy/masculinity than her earlier plays – and, significantly, Britain's oldest feminist theatre company changed its name from the explicit Women's Theatre Group to the feminine mystery of the Sphinx.

The emphasis of women's work in the theatre has moved away from companies and collectives to individuals, and from political issues to personal/body exploration (perhaps influenced by the interest of feminist perfor-

mance theorists in HÉLÈNE CIXOUS's ideas of *écriture féminine*). Performance artists Annie Griffin, Rose English and Bobby Baker, whose work explores 'the feminine', have a large following, but there are no British performance artists as radically experimental with or on the female body as, for example, the American KAREN FINLAY. Claire Dowie's one-woman attacks on the constraints of the sexed body are rare moments of challenge, but radical deconstruction of gender and role is now the province of GAY and LESBIAN 'Queer theatre'.

Women's work in the theatre continues, but there are signs that feminist theatre may be suffering the fate of popular feminism: it has become unfashionable and, fearful of the taunt of 'political correctness', it is mutating into a more fashionable post-feminist humanism. Perhaps it is also of significance that the Royal Court's hit of 1993 was DAVID MAMET's backlash piece, *Oleanna*. JD

See: A. Castledine (ed.), *Plays by Women*, vols. 9 and 10, London, 1991, 1994; T. R. Griffiths and M. Llewellyn-Jones (eds.), *British and Irish Women Dramatists since 1958*, Milton Keynes, 1993; G. Hanna (ed.), *Monstrous Regiment: A Collective Celebration*, London, 1991; M. Remnant (ed.), *Plays by Women*, vols. 5–8, London, 1986, 1987, 1988, 1990; M. Wandor (ed.), *Plays by Women*, vols. 1–4, London, 1982, 1983, 1984, 1985.

feminist theatre (USA) This ALTERNATIVE THEATRE movement began and proliferated in the early 1970s. In tandem with the political movement from which they sprang, activist women's theatres with radical techniques and manifestos organized in major urban centres around the country. The groups were innumerable and local, since the theatre they produced spoke directly to its constituents about women's subordinate position in dominant culture and about possibilities for change.

The theatrical and political radicalism of feminist theatre grew from the second wave of US feminism, which followed the civil rights movement and the formation of a vocal, active New Left. From within the political upheaval of the late 1960s, activists tried to revise interpersonal relationships and cultural value systems according to more egalitarian ideology. However, within the Left's rhetoric of racial and economic liberation, gender politics remained conservative. The contemporary US women's movement rekindled itself partly out of profound disaffection with the misogyny of the male Left. Through a network of ad hoc consciousness-raising groups, white middle-class women with some background in radical politics spoke to each other for what seemed like the first time, without mediation. These groups allowed women to exchange previously unheard details of their personal lives. The apparent commonality of their shared experience provoked a political analysis based on the private sphere their lives seemed to inhabit, and the slogan 'the personal is the political' gained currency.

What began in the late 1960s as a grass-roots political movement became, through the 1970s, a political and ideological movement with organized impact and increasingly divergent strains. Networks such as the National Organization for Women (NOW), for example, developed strategies for influencing existing social and political systems around women's issues. The liberal feminist movement that was generated works to reform US systems towards women's equality.

Radical feminism, in contrast to the reformism of liberal feminism, theorized women's oppression as systemic and began to analyse how patriarchal domination relegated women to the private sphere and alienated them from the power that men wielded in public life. Radical feminism in the late 1960s and early 70s proposed that gender roles were socially constructed and could be changed only after a revolutionary restructuring of cultural power. This position was claimed in the late 80s by materialist feminist ideology.

Early feminist theatre began as a voice of radical feminism and the first manifestations of what eventually came to be celebrated in women's culture. New York's It's Alright to Be a Woman Theatre, for example, one of the earliest groups, transposed the political movement's consciousness-raising format to performance and used the new public forum to help validate women's personal lives. The troupe used AGIT-PROP techniques with a long tradition in political theatre, as well as street theatre and guerrilla tactics that they borrowed from the leftist experimental theatres that had multiplied in the USA in the late 1960s and early 70s.

Although these experimental theatres addressed in vital ways civil rights issues and the protests against the Vietnam War, they did no more for women than the Left in general. Women such as Megan Terry and Roberta Sklar, who had both worked in the shadow of JOSEPH CHAIKIN's fame at the OPEN THEATRE, left to form specifically women's or feminist theatre groups. At the Omaha Magic Theatre (OMT) and the Women's Experimental Theatre (WET), respectively, they brought along many of the experimental theatres' innovations with theatre form, including RITUAL-based theory and borrowings from BRECHT, ARTAUD and GROTOWSKI.

The LIVING THEATRE, the Open Theatre and the PERFORMANCE GROUP, for example, had broken with the psychological REALISM that dominated professional US stages. They had formed collectives that disrupted the politically constricting hierarchy of the playwright-actor-director triumvirate and the separation of spectators and performers formalized by the proscenium arch. The text was no longer sacred; 'happenings' and rituals became the primary base of theatre work; and social issues and politics explicitly informed every performance choice. Feminist theatre, however, set these theatrical techniques in a political arena where the spectators and performers moved along a revised gender axis.

WET, for example, produced a trilogy of plays called *The Daughters' Cycle*, which recuperated the House of Atreus myth from a female perspective, discussing relationships between mothers and daughters that had been elided in male versions of the story. Their later trilogy focused on women's relationship to food. The OMT, administered by Terry and Jo Ann Schmidman, continues its work in Nebraska; WET's Sklar and her collaborator Sondra Segal took time off from production.

While such examples of separatist-inclined women's culture thrived through the 1970s, in the 80s liberal feminism continued to gain viability. Although dogged attempts to pass the Equal Rights Amendment failed, consistent lobbying around women's issues instituted a focus on the 'gender gap' in US politics. The situation of urban black women and other minorities received little attention on the liberal feminist agenda, but the movement's focus on political and economic equity for white middle-class women became a force with which the dominant culture had to contend.

Mainstream theatre in the 1980s – no doubt as a result of liberal feminism – began to dole out its major awards to women. The visibility of women playwrights, in particular, led to three Pulitzer Prizes for women in that decade: BETH HENLEY for *Crimes of the Heart* (1981), MARSHA NORMAN for *'night, Mother* (1983) and WENDY WASSERSTEIN for *The Heidi Chronicles* (1989). Lily Tomlin and Jane Wagner's *Search for Signs of Intelligent Life in the Universe* (1985) proved a major BROADWAY success. Women's caucuses in professional theatre organizations and the vitality of Julia Miles's WOMEN'S PROJECT at the AMERICAN PLACE THEATRE helped women playwrights, directors, producers, designers and actors seem suddenly to appear where they had never been before in the ranks of Broadway and regional US theatres.

Mainstream plays by women, however, conformed to more traditional forms and styles, such as psychological realism and social comedy. Feminist theatre troupes in the 1970s and 80s continued to search for a 'feminine' or 'feminist' aesthetic that would give voice to new contents by developing new theatre forms and modes of production. Because of increasing economic burdens and the fractionalization of radical feminism as a concerted political movement, however, the tradition of flourishing, alternative feminist theatres failed to sustain itself.

Of the numerous radical feminist theatre groups that began in the 1970s, only Spiderwoman Theatre, a collective of Native-American women operating in New York, and At the Foot of the Mountain Theatre in Minneapolis continued to produce and tour by the early 90s. The multicultural or ethnic focus of these groups indicates the growing awareness in US feminism in the 1990s of differences between and among women. Split Britches, a popular feminist and lesbian troupe that began in the 1980s in the East Village lesbian community in New York City, appropriates popular cultural forms once anathema to feminist theatre to investigate sexuality as well as gender (see GAY THEATRE; LESBIAN THEATRE).

While alternative feminist theatre practice declined in the 1980s, the decade witnessed the beginning of committed feminist criticism and theory that has become a vital site for activist and intellectual work in the theatre profession and in academia. Such critical feminist writing – sponsored by such organizations as the Women and Theatre Program of the Association for Theatre in Higher Education – holds the potential to revitalize the radical practice of feminist theatre.   JDO

See: G. Austin, *Feminist Theories for Drama criticism*, Ann Arbor, 1990; E. Brater, *Feminine Focus: The New Women Playwrights*, New York, 1989; S. E. Case, *Feminism and Theatre*, New York, 1988, and (ed.), *Performing Feminisms*, Baltimore, Md., 1990; H. K. Chinoy and L. W. Jenkins (eds.), *Women in American Theatre*, New York, 1981 (rev. edn, 1987); J. Dolan, *The Feminist as Critic*, Ann Arbor, Mich., 1988, 1991, and

Presence and Desire, Ann Arbor, 1993; L. Goodman, *Contemporary Feminist Theatre*, New York, 1993; L. Hart (ed.), *Making a Spectacle*, Ann Arbor, 1989; L. Hart and P. Phelan (eds.), *Acting Out:Feminist Performances*, Ann Arbor, 1993; H. Keyssar, *Feminist Theatre*, New York, 1985; E. Natalle, *Feminist Theatre: A Study in Persuasion*, Metuchen, NJ, 1985.

Fenn, Ezekiel 1620–? English actor who, in 1635, played two demanding female roles for Queen Henrietta's Men at London's COCKPIT THEATRE, that of Sophonisba in Nabbes's *Hannibal and Scipio* and that of Winifred in a revival of *The Witch of Edmonton*, by DEKKER, FORD and WILLIAM ROWLEY. He remained at the Cockpit as one of BEESTON's Boys, and is the subject of an interesting poem by Henry Glapthorne (1639), 'For Ezekiel Fenn at his first Acting a Man's Part'. Glapthorne makes clear the magnitude of the transition from female to male roles. Since nothing further is known of Fenn, we cannot be sure that he accomplished it successfully.   PT

Fennell, James 1766–1816 London-born actor, who had a substantial career in America. Fennell first studied law, but made his debut in Edinburgh in 1787 as Othello, which became his most successful role; he soon appeared at COVENT GARDEN, with minimal success. WIGNELL took him to Philadelphia in 1792, where he soon became a star. Well over six feet tall with an expressive, handsome face, Fennell brought considerable dignity to such roles as Othello, Lear, and Jaffier in *Venice Preserv'd*; he was also much admired as Hamlet, Glenalvon in *Douglas* and Iago. However, he invested his theatrical income in various unsuccessful money-making schemes (including salt manufacture), was arrested for debt, and spent a time in prison. He retired from the stage in 1810, and in 1814 published his memoirs. In 1815 he attempted Lear, but his memory was gone and the exhibition was one of 'pitiable imbecility'.   SMA

Ferber, Edna 1885–1968 Celebrated American author of fiction, who began her theatrical career in 1915 with *Our Mrs McChesney*, a collaboration with George V. Hobart that starred Ethel Barrymore (see DREW–BARRYMORE FAMILY). In 1920 she wrote the unsuccessful *$1200 a Year* with Newman Levy and *The Eldest*, her only solo venture in playwriting, which was composed for the PROVINCETOWN PLAYERS. *Minick* (1924) began a lucrative partnership with GEORGE S. KAUFMAN, which also yielded *The Royal Family* (1927), depicting chaotic life in a theatrical dynasty; *Dinner at Eight* (1932), which examined the lives of guests at a fashionable dinner party; and *Stage Door* (1936), which focused on young actresses in a theatrical boarding-house. Less successful for Ferber and Kaufman were *The Land Is Bright* (1941) and *Bravo!* (1948). Two of Ferber's novels were adapted into the MUSICALS *Show Boat* (1927) and *Saratoga* (1959). Her autobiographies, *A Peculiar Treasure* (1939) and *A Kind of Magic* (1963), contain valuable impressions of the theatrical writing process.   KF

Ferrari, Paolo 1822–89 Italian dramatist whose long career and substantial output provide an index to many of the tastes, characteristics and deficiencies of the mid-19th-century Italian stage. The range of his work was wide, and included dialect pieces, comedies of manners, historical dramas and plays concerned with contemporary social and moral issues. French influence, particularly of the bourgeois *drame* of AUGIER and DUMAS *père*, is pronounced in much of his later writing, little of which has continued to hold the stage, although in their time plays like *Goldoni e le sue sedici commedie nuove* (*Goldoni and His Sixteen New Comedies*, 1853), *La satira e Parini* (*Parini and Satire*, 1856), *Il duello* (*The Duel*, 1868), *Cause ed effetti* (*Cause and Effect*, 1871) and *Il suicidio* (*The Suicide*, 1875) enjoyed considerable success and esteem. At its best his drama, notwithstanding a tendency to prolixity and artificiality, is marked by wit and lively characterization.   LR

Ferreira, António 1528–69 Portuguese playwright. He is known mainly for his *Tragédia de D. Inês de Castro* (*The Tragedy of Lady Inês de Castro*), usually known simply as *A Castro* (*The Castro*) to underline its great affinity with the plays and heroines of classical Greek tragedy. It was performed in Ferreira's lifetime at Coimbra, but published only in 1587.

The Castro, based on a real-life episode of Portuguese history, portrays the illicit love of the heir to the throne, D. Pedro (Prince Peter), for the Lady Inês – a liaison which, as in RACINE's *Bérénice*, is perceived as being completely at odds with reasons of state. The two lovers have their own dilemmas but they are not so cruel as that faced by the king, whose choice is between kingly prudence and compassion. The king, spurred on by counsellors, first condemns Inês to death, then rescinds his sentence and finally (Pilate-like) washes his hands of the responsibility while the counsellors, like chief priests, take the guilt upon themselves. Inês is dispatched, and the prince in the last short act threatens vengeance and that serious social disjunction that high tragedy characteristically entails. The fine management of tensions, the poetic atmosphere of foreboding, the Chorus's highly dramatic evocation of pity and terror make this one of the most theatrically effective and enduring of neoclassical tragedies – it played to packed houses in 1982 at the Lisbon Comuna theatre.

Ferreira also wrote two comedies, *O Cioso* (*The Jealous Man*) and *O Bristo* (protagonist's surname) – both pleasant, actable plays.   LK

Ferrer, José [José Vicente Ferrer Otero y Cintron] 1912–92 Puerto Rican-born actor, director and producer. His professional debut was in a SHOWBOAT MELODRAMA on Long Island Sound in 1934. He made his BROADWAY debut in 1935, but his first substantial role came in *Brother Rat* (1936), and he achieved stardom in *Charley's Aunt* (1940). Ferrer employed his rich and powerful voice in two subsequent revivals, as Iago to PAUL ROBESON's Othello (1943) and in the title role of *Cyrano de Bergerac* (1946; Tony, 1947). In the latter role, critics praised his 'throbbing, vigorous performance'. He directed the New York Theatre Company at the City Center for a time, appearing in several classical revivals.

Two other acting successes were *The Silver Whistle* (1948) and *The Shrike* (1952; Tony). Among his directing assignments were *Stalag 17* (1951), *The Fourposter* (1951), *My Three Angels* (1953) and *The Andersonville Trial* (1959). Ferrer appeared often in films, and won an Oscar for his filmed Cyrano; he also appeared in OPERA and on television. His last stage appearance was in a 1990 musical version of IONESCO's *Rhinoceros* in England. Ferrer, ninth president of the Players Club, was the first actor to receive the National Medal of Arts (1985).   SMA

Ferron, Jacques 1921–85 Quebec playwright, novelist and essayist. A physician by profession, Ferron early began to write satirical plays such as *Le Licou* (*The Halter*, 1947) and *L'Ogre* (*The Ogre*, 1949), pointing towards the nationalistic political commitment of his later works. Chief among these are *Les Grands Soleils* (*The Great Sunflowers*, 1958), which re-examines the Patriote Rebellion of 1837–8 and the myths that had distorted its perception, and the even more political *La Tête du roi* (*The King's Head*, 1963), dealing on intersecting historical planes with the 19th-century Métis Revolt and contemporary revolutionary violence in Quebec, crystallized in the decapitation of the statue of Edward VII, symbol of Empire. A major novelist and essayist, Ferron played an important role in the formation and victory of the separatist Parti Québécois in 1976. He was also the founder of the parodic Rhinoceros Party, an iconoclastic grouping which perished with him.   LED

FESTAC The first 'World Festival of Negro Arts' was held in Dakar in 1966. This was followed in January 1977 by the second 'Black and African Festival of Arts and Culture' held in Lagos, for which the acronym FESTAC was coined. The festivals were planned as Pan-African celebrations; and the ingredients ranged from performance to debate, dominated primarily by dance and theatre. Further FESTACs remain an ambition; past ones evoke fond nostalgia.   MB

Feuchtwanger, Lion 1884–1958 German dramatist and novelist; and a valued collaborator of BRECHT's, especially on *Life of Edward II* and *The Visions of Simone Machard*. Brecht for his part helped him to turn his play *Warren Hastings* (1924) into *Calcutta, May 4th*. Feuchtwanger rewrote his play *Jew Süss* (1917) as a novel, which was twice filmed.   HR

Feydeau, Georges 1862–1921 French dramatist. Often thought of as the father of French FARCE, Feydeau took over the 19th-century *vaudeville*, as perfected by LABICHE and others. His subject and audience was the wealthy bourgeoisie of the Third Republic, whose sexual and matrimonial activities he examines with great accuracy. Feydeau understood the mechanics of farce supremely well, moving his plot with enormous speed, invariably bringing the wrong people together at the wrong

Act II of Feydeau's *A Flea in her Ear*, showing the complex hotel set with split-stage and bedroom with revolving bed. The set is an integral part of the mechanism of the farce.

moment, and usually leaving a character caught, literally, with his trousers down. The world of Feydeau presents man helplessly out of control of his destiny, caught in situations for which he ultimately is responsible, in settings with multiple doors, any of which may open at any moment to reveal disaster, and surrounded by objects which seem to take on a perverse life of their own.

Feydeau's dramatic output was relatively limited. His first full-length play to be staged was *Tailleur pour dames* (*A Gown for His Mistress*) at the Théâtre de la Renaissance in 1886. The formula of matrimonial infidelity prepared in act 1, of all the characters coming together at the same place of assignation in act 2, and of sorting out the situation to everybody's 'satisfaction' in act 3, was firmly established. Feydeau's subsequent plays were unsuccessful, until 1892 when *Monsieur Chasse* (*Monsieur Is Hunting*) was accepted by the PALAIS-ROYAL, and *Champignol malgré lui* (*A Close Shave*) was staged at the Nouveautés, which would become the main theatre associated with his work. *Cat among the Pigeons* (*Un Fil à la patte*, 1894) shows the attempt of a young man to dispose of his *cocotte* mistress (a forerunner of the later 'Mome Crevette' of *The Lady from Maxim's* or of Amelia of *Look After Amelia* (1908)), in order to marry a young lady of large fortune. Feydeau wrote this on his own, unlike *Hotel Paradiso* (*L'Hôtel du Libre Échange*, 1894), on which he collaborated with Maurice Desvallières, who had also collaborated on some of his earlier plays. *Hotel Paradiso*, like *A Flea in Her Ear* (1907), his other most popular play, brings all the characters to an extremely dubious hotel in the second act, much of the comedy being derived from the respectability of the characters and the hypocrisy of their attitudes. With *Sauce for the Goose* (*Le Dindon*, 1896) Feydeau was moving towards a more serious portraiture of the mores of the bourgeoisie or the *belle époque*. Increasingly his focus is on marriage itself as an institution. *The Lady from Maxim's* (1899), one of the most popular plays running during the 1900 Exhibition (so popular that he wrote a 'sequel', *The Duchess of the Folies-Bergère*), exposes social snobberies by setting up a situation in which a group of respectable provincial ladies emulate the speech of a Parisian *cocotte*.

In his later years Feydeau's view of marriage (perhaps as a result of the failure of his own) became darker, with wives seen as invariably nagging and trivial. He wrote several shorter plays, including *Feu la mère de Madame* (*Madame's Late Mother*, 1908) and *On purge bébé* (*We're Giving Baby a Laxative*, 1910), in which the emphasis is no longer on complexity of plot, but on conjugal relationships. In these and *Mais n'te promène donc pas toute nue!* (*Don't Walk Round with Nothing On!*, 1911) and *Hortense dit 'Je m'en fous'* (*Hortense Says, I Don't Give a Damn!*, 1916), Feydeau was far closer to the naturalist theatre than to the fashionable BOULEVARD.   JMCC

Fialka, Ladislav 1931–91 Czech MIME artist. Trained as a ballet dancer, he was one of the founders of the Prague Balustrade Theatre (1958), where he directed and starred in pantomimes wearing the traditional whiteface of PIERROT. Working with a regular ensemble, he based his mimodramas mainly on traditional material: *Les Amants de la Lune* (1959) from DEBURAU; *The Castaways* (1959), in the style of silent films; *The Fools* (1965), which traced the type from the Bible to Kafka. He also worked in *Hamlet* (1959) and *Ubu* (1964), and toured Europe and America.   LS

Fichandler, Zelda 1924– American co-founder, and from 1951 sole producing director, of Washington DC's ARENA STAGE, the longest artistic tenure in regional theatre annals. From the beginning she was committed to having a resident acting company present the classics, American drama, and recent plays that had failed on BROADWAY – an artistic mission that continues to this day. Fichandler spent much of the 1950s articulating the promise of the regional theatre movement, and in 1961 built a permanent home for her company; there she continued to nurture her resident ensemble and began to produce new plays, such as *The Great White Hope* (1967), *Indians* (1969) and *Moonchildren* (1971). A tour to the Soviet Union in 1973, the first for an American theatre, fed her interest in Soviet and Eastern European drama and led to productions in the 1970s of works by FRISCH, MROŻEK, ÖRKÉNY and others, many of which she directed. In 1976 the theatre's successes culminated in a Tony for Arena – a first outside of New York City. Continuing her dedication to the development of young actors, Fichandler became chair of the graduate acting programme at New York University's Tisch School of the Arts in 1984, and, in 1990, concluded her visionary tenure at Arena to become artistic director of New York's ACTING COMPANY (1991–May 1994). In 1993 she was elected president of the Theatre Communications Group.   LM

Field, Nathan 1587–c.1620 English actor and playwright, whose father was a Puritan clergyman of vehemently anti-theatrical views. Field was probably impressed into the CHILDREN OF THE CHAPEL ROYAL in 1600 and quickly made a reputation as an outstanding boy actor. By 1613 he was the leader of the adult Lady Elizabeth's Men, from which he transferred to the King's Men in about 1615. Praised by BEN JONSON, the flamboyant Field was well suited to the role of CHAPMAN's Bussy d'Ambois, in which he excelled. That he was himself something of an overreacher is implied by his relationship with the Countess of Argyll, who bore his child in 1619. Field's two surviving comedies, *A Woman Is a Weather-Cock* (c.1609) and *Amends for Ladies* (c.1610), are competent exercises in the style of Jonson and he is known to have collaborated with MASSINGER, in *The Fatal Dowry* (c.1618) and other plays, as well as with FLETCHER.   PT

Field Day Theatre Company Inaugurated in Londonderry by actor Stephen Rea and playwright BRIAN FRIEL with the premiere of Friel's enormously forceful *Translations* (1980). The company's productions and publications have been designed to stimulate debate on current political and cultural controversies. Plays have included *Communication Cord* (Friel, 1982), *Pentecost* (STEWART PARKER, 1987), *Double Cross* (TOM KILROY, 1986), *Saint Oscar* (Terry Eagleton, 1989) and *The Madam Macadam Travelling Theatre* (Kilroy, 1991), as well as new versions of CHEKHOV, SOPHOCLES and MOLIÈRE by Brian Friel, Tom Paulin, Seamus Heaney and Derek Mahon.

Publishing *The Field Day Anthology of Irish Writing* appears to have exhausted the energies of the company for the moment. GF

Fielding, Henry 1707–54 English playwright. His first play was produced before he went to study in Leyden but his reputation as the finest satirical dramatist of his age effectively began with the production of *The Author's Farce* in 1730, a BALLAD OPERA which in its experimentation with dramatic form and the brilliance of its SATIRE established the model for his later work. His mockery of contemporary tragedy, *Tom Thumb* (1730), was later revised under the grandiose title *The Tragedy of Tragedies* (1731). After trying full-length FARCE, Fielding turned to political satire on both parties and the royal family in *The Welsh Opera* (performed 1731), revised as *The Grub Street Opera*, again using the ballad opera form as a vehicle for satire. His only attempt at a serious play on sexual intrigue and marriage, *The Modern Husband* (1732), analyses marriage as prostitution and adultery by consent.

Of the 15 plays before 1734, only *The Welsh Opera* was openly political satire but, with Walpole's Excise Bill threatening, Fielding moved openly into the Opposition, and into political drama again, attacking Walpole in *Don Quixote in England* (1734). For the next three years he made his attacks on the government clearer and clearer in plays like *Pasquin* (1736) and *The Historical Register for the Year 1736* (1737). He used the Little Haymarket Theatre, which he managed, as a platform for his and others' attacks on the government. Walpole was provoked to limit the freedom of the theatres and using a particularly vicious attack, *The Golden Rump* (a play scheduled for production at GOODMAN'S FIELDS THEATRE), as a convenient pretext for action, his government rushed through the Licensing Act which created CENSORSHIP over plays through the Lord Chamberlain's office, which lasted until 1968. Fielding, censored and with his theatre closed because unlicensed, turned to the law and to writing novels, with a few infrequent plays. PH

Fields [Stansfield]**, Gracie** 1898–1979 British singer and comedienne. 'Our Gracie' was born over a fish-and-chip shop in Rochdale, Lancashire, and worked part-time as a mill girl and shop clerk, while she sang in working men's clubs. Her professional debut at a local cinema, as a member of a juvenile troupe, came in 1908. In 1915 she joined the REVUE *Yes, I Think So* at the Hulme Theatre, Manchester; three months later she made her London debut as Sally Perkins in *Mr Tower of London*, which enjoyed a phenomenal run (1918–25) at the Alhambra, Leicester Square. She was a headliner in VARIETY by 1928, played the New York PALACE in 1930 and in 1931 first sang her signature tune, 'Sally'. Audiences adored her for her clogs-and-shawl manner and her ability to move smoothly from the vocal clowning of 'The Biggest Aspidistra in the World' to the mawkishness of 'Ave Maria'. She received a CBE in 1937.

When Britain went to war, her second husband, an Italo-American, was deported as an enemy alien, and she attracted much opprobrium by moving to Hollywood. Even though she raised £1,500,000 in the USA for the war effort in 1941, adverse comment also attached to her leav-ing her ENSA tours to honour American contracts. She played ten Royal Variety Performances, before retiring to Capri in 1959; by the time she was made Dame of the British Empire in 1979, all was forgiven and she was appreciated for her wartime efforts, with their theme song 'Wish Me Luck As You Wave Me Goodbye'. ERIC MORECAMBE opined that she and George Formby were the only show business persons 'really loved by the public'. LS

Fields, Lew see WEBER, JOSEPH

Fields, W. C. [William Claude Dukenfield] 1880–1946 American comedian, who ran away from home at the age of 14 and taught himself to juggle. As an eccentric tramp juggler he was the first American headliner at the FOLIES-BERGÈRE (1902) and a great hit at the London HIPPODROME (1904) for his trick pool game and frustrating golf lesson. Taking his cue from HARRY TATE's MUSIC-HALL persona, the bibulous, bottlenosed Fields developed the character of a grandiloquent but seedy curmudgeon, muttering indignant asides. He starred in the ZIEGFELD *Follies* (1915–18, 1920, 21, 25), and in 1923 in *Poppy* created the type of the moth-eaten but brazen showman he would later repeat on film. His earliest film appearance had been in a short of 1915, and after 1925 he settled in Los Angeles, filming a series of comic masterpieces. LS

Fifth Avenue Theatre (New York City) Amos Eno, the owner of the Fifth Avenue Hotel on West 24th Street, erected a small structure adjoining it for surreptitious and illegal stock-exchange activities, which he was forced to abandon. In 1865, he decided to convert it into a theatre, and for several years it functioned as a minstrel hall (see MINSTREL SHOW). The railway magnate James Fisk took it over, gutted the interior, and transformed it into a handsome little theatre, which eventually fell into the hands of AUGUSTIN DALY for his introduction into theatrical management. During 1869–73, Daly assembled an attractive company, staged comedies and dramas in perfectly tuned productions, and made this theatre the most fashionable and popular playhouse in New York. When it went up in flames in 1873, he transferred his company to the New Fifth Avenue Theatre on Broadway. In 1879, STEELE MACKAYE rebuilt the old house, renaming it the MADISON SQUARE. MCH

Finck, Werner 1902–78 German CABARET performer, co-founder of Berlin's Die Katakombe, where he was a cheeky and courageous compère and actor from 1929 to 1935. His puns and word-games constituted a veritable critique of his times, for which he was interned in a concentration camp in 1935. But he survived to make numerous postwar appearances as a solo cabaretist, particularly at Die Mausefalle, Stuttgart (1948–51). LS

Finland There exist no records of the very beginnings of theatrical activity in Finland. The main emphasis in the rich heritage of folklore is epic in nature, and no investigations have been made into the possible dramaturgy of the narrative event. The SHAMAN was a locally sanctioned performer in primitive Finnish society. The bear-hunting and wedding ceremonies certainly included role-playing. From the late 18th century onwards, one finds descriptions of games and ring dances with an elementary plot structure.

Although the Church in the Middle Ages first allowed and even organized religious performances and processions, a ban was imposed on all theatrical activities in the 17th century. The Finnish theatre thus lacks entirely the courtly traditions that have characterized the development of the theatre in other European countries.

At the end of the 18th century, when Finland was still part of Sweden, the first Swedish theatre companies started to extend their tours to include Finnish cities. At the same time amateur acting became popular in upper-middle-class families. The plays were all Swedish and later also in German, when German touring companies entered the country via St Petersburg. Interest in plays and spectacles was also considerable among the lower classes, but the popular performances in market-places and public gardens were not generally considered to have any artistic value.

After Finland had become a grand duchy of Russia in 1809, the interest shown in drama as an art form was one manifestation of the rising ambition to create a national literature, both in Finnish and in Swedish. A vigorous, and successful, effort was made to develop Finnish – which had not earlier been used at all by upper-class people – in such a way that it could compete with Swedish as a cultural language. Russian was never used as an artistically creative language in Finland.

For all these reasons, literary and verbal elements have always been strong in the Finnish theatre, and REALISM its main performing style. The first important themes were found simultaneously in Finno-Ugric mythology and in regional history. Aleksis Kivi wrote the first tragedy in Finnish (*Kullervo*, 1864), the protagonist being one of the heroes of the 'Kalevala', and the Swedish poet J. J. Wecksell dramatized a complicated sequence of 16th-century Finnish–Swedish relations in *Daniel Hjort*. Both acknowledged their debt to SHAKESPEARE. The first comedies, notably Kivi's *Cobblers on the Heath*, were influenced by the moderate rationalism of HOLBERG. In the 1860s, theatre enthusiasts accepted the idea of founding a bilingual theatre, but their plans turned literally to ashes, when the new theatre house in Helsinki burned down. Soon after that, the time seemed ripe for strengthening the position of the Finnish language in the performance of drama. The first professional theatre was founded by Dr Kaarlo Bergbom, a playwright and scholar, in 1872.

The Finnish Theatre, which in 1902 became the National Theatre, had an extensive and ambitious programme for building a theatrical culture based in both 'straight' drama and opera. Its primary objective was the promotion of drama in Finnish. Almost equally important was the task of making the great classical works available to Finnish audiences. This led, among other things, to the translation of the entire SHAKESPEARE canon by the poet Cajander.

The next outstanding Finnish dramatist after Aleksis Kivi was Minna Canth (1844–97), who wrote most of her plays in collaboration with Bergbom. Canth protested against the injustices of woman's position in society and created a series of remarkable studies in social conscience – for example, *The Worker's Wife* and *The Parson's Family*. The rebellious gipsy girl in *The Worker's Wife* was played by Ida Aalberg, who became the first great actress of the Finnish Theatre. She came of a humble family, her father being a railway employee, but soon she was playing all the great tragic parts. Later she toured with her own company and became known in Scandinavia, Russia and Germany. Greatly loved and greatly envied, Ida Aalberg was in the tradition of ELEONORA DUSE and SARAH BERNHARDT.

The Finnish Theatre toured the country extensively until it finally settled down in its present house in Helsinki in 1902. Meanwhile, professional and semi-professional theatres were founded in its wake. The newly urbanized workers were especially interested in theatre. They wanted to produce plays for their own amusement as well as for the social enlightenment of their fellows. Out of this interest sprang up a number of Workers' Theatres, simultaneously with the 'bourgeois' houses. By 1920, after the deadlock of the Civil War, almost every city had two theatre companies, with professional status and a measure of support from both the central government and the local authorities. The economic burden involved in all this soon became very heavy, and because of the generally right-wing policies that prevailed, the theatres were progressively amalgamated. Only the biggest industrial city, Tampere, has succeeded in maintaining an independent Workers' Theatre, now having almost the status of a National Theatre.

Living drama in the Swedish language was for long dependent on visits by touring companies from Sweden. There was uncertainty as to whether the Swedish spoken in Finland was sufficiently refined for the stage. The first 'national' Swedish theatre was founded in Turku in 1894, but it was not until 1915 that it became fully established in its own house in Helsinki.

When Finland became an independent state in 1917 and the Civil War was over, the theatre was needed both to consolidate the strong new cultural base and to open the windows to current cultural ideas elsewhere in Europe. The principal influences came largely from Germany and France and were mixed with the STANISLAVSKY-influenced 'national' realism.

The Workers' Theatres were particularly eager to embrace EXPRESSIONISM. This brought about a remarkable change in the style of acting. Expressionism gained a foothold through the success of various German plays, but it was soon also to receive Finnish and Swedish voices in plays by Lauri Haarla, Arvi Kivimaa and Hagar Olsson. Stage decor was relieved of the burden of stock realism and soon became an important element in dramaturgy itself, attracting both artists and architects (e. g. Wäinö Aaltonen, Alvar Aalto).

There existed simultaneously a quite different tradition, based on old Finnish folk characters. Scepticism and irony were characteristic of the comedies of Maria Jotuni and Maiju Lassila. These two dramatists created vivid social types – Jotuni, a woman herself, mostly women, and Lassila mostly men – and their plays were often built on a triangle of love, money and death. Lassila, a socialist journalist and novelist, was killed during the Civil War, but his comedies have shown enduring qualities. Jotuni continued writing right up to the 1940s, towards the end composing sombre and powerful tragic plays.

The most important directors in the period between the two world wars were Eino Kalima and Eino Salmelainen. Kalima was familiar with the style of acting of the Moscow ARTS THEATRE, and it was he who introduced Stanislavsky principles to Finland. He was also influenced by the ideas of COPEAU, and in the 1960s he presented a series of CHEKHOV productions which have become legendary in Finnish theatre history. The special atmosphere of these performances was the result of a thorough study of Russian life and the nostalgia of the upper classes combined with an implied criticism of the futility of their way of life. Eino Salmelainen was active in the People's Theatre of Helsinki and as director of the Tampere Workers' Theatre. He was largely responsible for bringing to the stage the life of Finnish peasants and workers in plays depicting their social conflicts especially through the works of Hella Wuolijoki (1886–1954). Wuolijoki's series of 'Niskavuori' plays, a family story centred on the heritage of agrarian culture, has become an apotheosis of the strength of Finnish womanhood.

The Second World War put a brake on the development in the theatre, which sent its troupes to tour the fronts with lightweight comedies, but soon after the war the Finnish theatre saw a remarkable renaissance. Directors like Arvi Kivimaa, who had succeeded Kalima as the director of the National Theatre, Wilho Ilmari and Sakari Puurunen all displayed an interest in moral and psychological problems. It was difficult to produce such plays because the theatres were usually too large and the audience too remote from the actors. The demand for a more intimate type of drama led to the building of studio and workshop stages. The first to be constructed was the small stage of the National Theatre, which, by presenting a repertory of plays by authors like SARTRE, BECKETT, OSBORNE and PINTER, paved the way to similar developments elsewhere, and also served as an inspiration for young Finnish directors and playwrights. The new interest in man's inner life became visible – e.g. in the plays of Eeva-Liisa Manner (b.1921), Paavo Haavikko (b.1931) and Veijo Meri (b.1928).

Arvi Kivimaa was active in building up international relationships, which led to membership of the INTERNATIONAL THEATRE INSTITUTE in 1959, foreign tours by Finnish companies and also visits to Finland by famous troupes from abroad. The native avant-garde was represented by the Intimiteatteri, which saw a period of splendid acting and fearless and original direction during its first decades (1950–70). In the Finnish Theatre School, directed by Wilho Ilmari, training was in the 1950s largely based on an adaptation of the methods of Stanislavsky. The School has produced generations of talented actors and actresses, well acquainted with the demands of psychological character study. Eeva-Kaarina Volanen (b.1926) is a fine actress who, during the course of a long career, has moved on from her earlier portraits of soulful youth (ANOUILH) to interpretations of the experienced and careworn women in modern American and Scandinavian drama. Lasse Pöysti (b.1927), who began his career as a greatly admired child actor, went on to become a skilful interpreter of the psychological problems of 20th-century

man. Later he worked for a period as director of the Tampere Workers' Theatre and finally as director of the Royal Dramatic Theatre, Stockholm.

The situation today In the 1960s a new emphasis on the theatre's social utility and its importance as a political tool became as evident in Finland as elsewhere. The new viewpoint was encouraged by a number of different factors. Democratization of culture was seen as one of the tasks of society, and public funds were allocated for the support of art and artistic institutions. It was recognized that although the audience that the theatre attracted was eager, it was predominantly middle-class, and whole sectors of society had become almost totally alienated from the theatre. At the same time, young people, influenced by the ideas of BERTOLT BRECHT, began to apprehend the theatre's potential for influencing the thinking of audiences.

The style and use of music also underwent a change; where homely folk melodies had been associated with comedy, and music had been used to point up the nuances of psychological relations, it now became possible to use music directly in CABARETS and in plays in AGIT-PROP style. The theatre first became a place for political debate in 1966, in Arvo Salo's Lapua Opera, which, despite the name, was not really profoundly Brechtian in character. Here was a clearly pacifist proclamation, inspired by memories of Finland's history in the 1930s and by American peace songs. This production, directed by Kalle Holmberg, with the Helsinki Students' Theatre and music by Kaj Chydenius, represented a final breakthrough in theatrical thinking.

The radical theatre of the young people was not easily accepted by the institutions, which had a more conservative bent. The result was the formation of new, independent theatre groups which emerged in the 1960s and 70s. The most vigorous of them still survive, such as KOM, which started as a subgroup of the Swedish Theatre in Helsinki but soon became independent and has since toured extensively both in Finland and abroad, and Unga Teatern (earlier, Skolteatern), a Swedish-language theatre performing mainly for children. The Ryhmäteatteri has, under the direction of Arto af Hällström and Ralla Leppäkoski, become an important avant-garde group with acclaimed new interpretations of both Finnish and foreign classics. A younger generation of actors and directors in the Q Theatre in Helsinki usually create their plays themselves, often based on the experience of lonely urban childhood.

There are also many dance theatre groups, the oldest being Raatikko; and, more or less in its footsteps, Aurinkobaletti, Dance Theatre ERI, Zodiac and Hurja-Ruuth. Dance theatre is a rapidly expanding sector of theatre life, and the groups strive to find an appropriate modern mode of expression, involving mythological stories and postmodern music as well as visual arts.

Meanwhile, many of the institutional theatres have tried to balance their activities between artistic ambition and popular appeal. The Turku City Theatre reached remarkable heights of achievement during the years 1973–7, when RALF LÅNGBACKA and Kalle Holmberg were directors there. Later they worked together at the Helsinki City Theatre. Långbacka is a BRECHT specialist and has directed many Brecht plays with a firm sense of their message. He has used his critical insights to create a new way of producing CHEKHOV, and recently also Shakespeare, together with a youthful Swedish-language company, Vilrus. Holmberg has directed a series of analytical plays on the social and moral conflicts in Finland. His 'rag' adaptation of the classic novel *The Seven Brothers* by Aleksis Kivi was immensely popular on the Turku stage. Holmberg has more lately deepened his human portraiture in works by STRINDBERG and Dostoevsky.

A striking picture of the Finns' idea of themselves has been given by Jouko Turkka, both at the Helsinki City Theatre and the Theatre Academy. Turkka uses the stage as a musician uses his instrument, exploiting to the full its physical and emotional possibilities. One of his most remarkable pupils and colleagues is Jussi Parviainen, a playwright, director and theatre manager who fills the stage with cruelty, morality and passion. Kurt Nuotio, also a one-time head of the Theatre Academy, has directed with great success chamber plays analysing the self-deception of modern man. Otso Kautto has established himself as a young director with an exceptional sense of irony and of postmodern lifestyles.

During its short history, the Finnish theatre has had a number of important female directors. The tradition established by Mia Backman and Glory Leppänen has been continued by Vivica Bandler (a long-time director of Stockholm City Theatre, now the artistic director of Tampere Theatre Festival), Ritva Arvelo, Kaisa Korhonen, Kristin Olsoni, Eija-Elina Bergholm, Ritva Siikala and Katarina Lahti. Their work has included new interpretations of the Finnish classics, notably the plays of Jotuni and Wuolijoki. Ritva Siikala has created a women's theatre group, Raivoisat Ruusut, which has performed both Shakespeare and AESCHYLUS with all-female casts.

During the period of economic growth in the 1970s and 80s, many new venues were built, e.g. in Rovaniemi and Jyväskylä (both designed by Alvar Aalto), in Helsinki for the City Theatre and in Tampere for the Tampere Workers' Theatre. The latest testimony to the strong position of the theatre arts in Finland's cultural life is the new Opera House in Helsinki (1993), a magnificent facility for productions on a Wagnerian scale. Less prestigious productions have been staged with good results in disused factories and warehouses (for instance KAAPELI in Helsinki).

A special feature of the Finnish theatre is the open-air stages on which plays are produced in the summer, notwithstanding the vicissitudes of the Finnish weather. These productions are becoming more and more popular because of their high artistic level and the experience of participation they can offer to their audiences. In Savonlinna there is a special summer festival for opera at which both Finnish and classical works are mounted.

Music has always had a prominent place in the Finnish theatrical tradition. Several works by Sibelius were originally composed for the stage (the music for *The Tempest* probably being the best-known). Finnish OPERA has recently been enriched by the prestigious works of Joonas Kokkonen (*The Last Temptations*), Aulis Sallinen (*The Horseman, The Red Line, The King Goes Forth to France*, *Kullervo* – the last as the opening production of the Opera

House, with Kalle Holmberg directing), Erik Bergman (*The Singing Tree*) and Iikka Kusisto (*The Moomin Opera*, *Jäger Ståhl*).

Theatre policy in Finland is largely directed by the wish to ensure that there will still be audiences in the 21st century in spite of the all-pervasive influence of television and video. The government supports annually approximately 50 theatres and theatre groups with 10–70 per cent of their total budget. The municipalities still have the main responsibility for the financing of theatre. Some good work is also done by the drama section of Finnish television (see TELEVISION DRAMA). RADIO DRAMA, which has a long and honourable tradition of attracting talented actors and promising new playwrights, also has a nation-wide audience. Numerous educational organizations exist to foster an interest in the theatre and to guide amateur groups, which arrange annual festivals at which their work is presented. IN

See: *Finnish Cultural Policies: A National Report to the Council of Europe*, Helsinki, 1994; *Finnish Theatre Today*, Helsinki, 1974; M. Savutie, *Finnish Theatre*, Helsinki, 1980.

Finlay, Frank 1926– British actor, who first attracted national attention as a versatile member of the English Stage Company at the ROYAL COURT in the late 1950s. He was a memorable Harry Khan in ARNOLD WESKER's *Chicken Soup with Barley* (1958), Attercliffe in JOHN ARDEN's *Sergeant Musgrave's Dance* (1959) and Hill in Wesker's *Chips with Everything* (1962). LAURENCE OLIVIER invited him to join the NATIONAL THEATRE Company, where he played such major roles as Willie Mossop in *Hobson's Choice*, Iago in *Othello* and Joxer Daly in *Juno and the Paycock*.'

Finlay acquired a certain identity as an actor, playing mainly middle-aged characters, often quiet and passive but with a controlled power which rose to emotional climaxes. As Bernard Link in DAVID MERCER's *After Haggerty* (1970) and the paterfamilias in DE FILIPPO's *Saturday, Sunday, Monday* (1973), Finlay retained the audience's attention with what seemed to be minimal effort until he reached the explosion of despair and anger towards the end of the play. This gift for pacing a performance proved especially useful to the director in such discursive plays as JOHN OSBORNE's *Watch It Come Down* (1976) and HOWARD BRENTON's *Weapons of Happiness* (1976) at the National Theatre. After taking over from COLIN BLAKELY in De Filippo's *Filumena* and from PAUL SCOFIELD as Salieri in *Amadeus* (1981), Finlay turned to a WEST END MUSICAL, *Mutiny!*, in which he played Captain Bligh (1985). In 1987 he appeared as Sir David Metcalfe QC, the barrister charged with the murder of his wife in Jeffrey Archer's courtroom drama, *Beyond Reasonable Doubt*. JE

Finley, Karen 1956– Chicago-born American visual and performance artist, and writer. Though her material is somewhat cliché-ridden and obvious, Finley represents the ever-increasing visibility of performance artists, especially since she became the centrepiece in the controversy over the refusal of funds for the National Endowment for the Arts in 1991 (as one of the 'NEA four'). She studied performance art and painting at the Chicago Art Institute

(1975–7) and the San Francisco Art Institute (MFA, 1981). She collaborated (1981–4) with Brian Rout (aka Harry Kipper, one of Britain's performance art duo, the Kipper Kids), to whom she was briefly married. In her theatre piece *The Theory of Total Blame* (1988) and her solo performances, such as *The Constant State of Desire* (1987), *We Keep Our Victims Ready* (1989) and *A Certain Level of Denial* (1992), her subject is the dysfunctional nuclear family and victimizing social conditions. Her strategy of over-exposing the body is to de-eroticize it.   AF DBW

Finney, Albert 1936– British actor, who led the postwar generation of actors towards a less upper-class, less cerebral and more physical style of playing. He had an early opportunity to take major roles with the BIRMINGHAM REPERTORY THEATRE, where he was one of BARRY JACKSON's protégés from 1956 to 1958; he then moved to the Shakespeare Memorial Theatre at Stratford-upon-Avon to play Edgar to CHARLES LAUGHTON's King Lear, and to take over as Coriolanus from LAURENCE OLIVIER. He became nationally known in 1960 when he created the title role in *Billy Liar*, the north-country comedy by KEITH WATERHOUSE and Willis Hall, and in 1961 played Luther in JOHN OSBORNE's historical epic at the ROYAL COURT THEATRE. He starred in major British films such as *Saturday Night and Sunday Morning* (1960) and *Tom Jones* (1963); and his rugged physique, stocky, determined manner and rich voice attracted the hero-worship of teenagers.

He joined the NATIONAL THEATRE Company in 1965 to play a variety of parts, ranging from the rebellious border baron, Armstrong, in JOHN ARDEN's *Armstrong's Last Goodnight* (1965) to the limp-wristed antiques collector in PETER SHAFFER's *Black Comedy* (1966). He started to direct both plays and films, notably *Charlie Bubbles* (1967), and was considered to be one of several possible successors to Olivier as director of the National Theatre. He co-presented PETER NICHOLS's *A Day in the Death of Joe Egg* (1967) in London and New York, and became an Associate Director at the Royal Court Theatre from 1972 to 1975. When PETER HALL took over from Olivier at the National Theatre, he invited Finney to star in the first NT seasons in their new home on London's South Bank, as Hamlet, Tamburlaine and Macbeth. Finney's many-sided talents have never, however, been matched by a single creative challenge which could absorb his full energy and concentration. He has appeared in many films and often on television, but his most recent stage appearances have been in two RONALD HARWOOD dramas, *Another Time* (1989) and *Reflected Glory* (1992).   JE

Fiorilli, Tiberio [Scaramuccia; Scaramouche] c.1600–94 Italian comedian, putative son of SILVIO FIORILLO. He popularized the character Scaramouche, an amalgam of the *ZANNI* and the Capitano, in a sober black costume, with no MASK and a guitar in lieu of a sword. Despite his squint, deafness and withered arm, his French and Italian contemporaries were charmed by his naturalness and comic power; one mute scene of fear in *Colombine Lawyer Pro and Con* (1685) kept a Parisian audience dying of laughter for 15 minutes. In 1658 he alternated performances at the PETIT-BOURBON with MOLIÈRE, who suggested a repeat of this experiment at the PALAIS-ROYAL

in 1661. Fiorilli enjoyed success in London in 1673 and 1675. A picaresque but untrustworthy biography, *La Vie de Scaramouche*, was written by ANGELO COSTANTINI in 1695.   LS

Fiorillo [Fiorilli] **family** Italian actors. **Silvio** Fiorillo (d.1633) began in the COMMEDIA DELL'ARTE playing Captain Matamoros, then c.1609 appeared in Naples as the first Policinella, brandishing a cuckold's horn; his success led to this episodic servant becoming a lead comedian. He also published some scenarios. His son **Giovan Battista** (fl.1614–51) played second *ZANNI* under the name Trappolino; his wife Beatrice Vitelli (fl.1638–54) played first *amorosa*.   LS

fireworks As a dramatic auxiliary, fireworks were used in 14th-century religious plays, particularly for hell mouth, and became a standard requisite of the medieval and baroque theatres. Vanuzzi Biringuccio and Bishop Abram of Suzdal testify to wooden figures and metal cylinders shooting off fireworks in plays produced in Siena and Florence on the Feast of St John and the Assumption, in the 16th century. In England, the 'wild men' of the Lord Mayor's show were associated with pyrotechnics; in George Whetstone's *Historie of Promos and Cassandra* (1578), green men enter with their clubs spouting fire. By the 18th century, fireworks displays, now with coloured lights, had been transferred to pleasure gardens, and only the COMÉDIE-ITALIENNE in Paris still employed them indoors. That they had become old-fashioned claptrap is clear in *Nicholas Nickleby* when Crummles proposes that a fireworks display, 'awful from the front', could be bought for 18 pence. A brief resurgence in their use came in the late 19th century in the spectaculars of the KIRALFY brothers and their competitors.   LS

Firmin 1784–1859 French actor. Firmin first appeared with the Théâtre des Jeunes Élèves c.1800. His talents suited him to COMEDY rather than TRAGEDY, and he joined PICARD's troupe at the Louvois in 1806, having an immediate success in *Le Jeune Homme à l'épreuve* (*The True Young Man*) and *L'Amour et la raison* (*Love and Reason*). He moved to the ODÉON, where Napoleon noticed him in *Les Querelles des deux frères* (*The Quarrels of the Two Brothers*) in 1810 and had him transferred to the COMÉDIE-FRANÇAISE. He was a lively, intelligent and sensitive actor, playing MARIVAUX's lovers remarkably well. He ventured into the *drame* in 1829 as Saint Mégrin in *Henri III et sa cour*, and was the original Hernani the following year. In 1831 he left the Comédie to play in the provinces and abroad, but returned in 1833. Between 1813 and 1843 he created at least 100 parts at the Comédie, including Torquato in *Tasse* (1826), Frédéric in SCRIBE's *Bertrand et Raton* (1833) and Richelieu in *Mlle de Belle-Isle* (1839). In 1845 he retired as his memory was failing, and died in rather mysterious circumstances at his country property.   JMCC

Fisher, Clara 1811–98 London-born actress who debuted at DRURY LANE at age six, toured England for a decade, and then went to the USA in 1827 for a triumphant debut at the PARK THEATRE. LUDLOW called her 'the finest comedy actress in the United States'. Among her more noted roles were Viola, Lady Teazle, Lady Gay Spanker, Pauline and the Fool in *King Lear*. She was first Singing Witch in MACREADY's *Macbeth* on the night of the ASTOR PLACE OPERA HOUSE riot. Although she retired in 1884, Fisher would occasionally appear in 'old-lady parts' and in 1897 completed her autobiography. SMA

Fiske, Harrison Grey 1861–1942 American drama editor, critic, producer, manager and playwright. Born of wealthy parents, Fiske served an early apprenticeship on the *Jersey City Argus*, *New York Star* and *New York Dramatic Mirror*. He left New York University after his sophomore year (1880) to edit the *Dramatic Mirror* when his father bought him one-third interest in it. He made the paper an important theatrical journal by attacking corruption in the profession and working to raise the tone of the American stage. He led a crusade in 1880 to establish the Actors' Fund. In 1890, he married the actress Marie Augusta Davey (MINNIE MADDERN FISKE) and managed her career as well as that of a number of leading actors. For her he wrote or adapted numerous plays, including *Hester Crewe* (1893) and *Marie Deloche* (1895). He leased the Manhattan Theatre in 1901 for Mrs Fiske, and formed the Manhattan Theatre Company to support her. His producing successes included *Kismet* (1911), starring OTIS SKINNER. Financial problems forced him to sell the *Dramatic Mirror* in 1911, and he declared bankruptcy in 1914, although he was discharged the following year. The death of Mrs Fiske in 1932 effectively ended his career. Fiske fought commercialism in the theatre, and did much to establish IBSEN on the American stage. TLM

Fiske, Minnie Maddern [*née* Marie Augusta Davey] 1864–1932 American actress and director. From a theatrical family, she began her career at age three, remaining in steady demand as a child actress. Her adult New York debut was in Charles Callahan's *Fogg's Ferry* (1882). After a brief first marriage, she wed her second husband, HARRISON GREY FISKE, editor of the *New York Dramatic Mirror*, in 1890, retiring for four years after her marriage. During this interlude she wrote several one-act plays and became interested in the realist movement (see REALISM). After 1893 she focused her energies, despite opposition, on plays of this ilk, and worked towards what she called 'natural, true acting' in her productions, especially with her Manhattan Theatre Company (1904–8). At the turn of the century she fought the THEATRICAL SYNDICATE, almost alone, and became a noted humanitarian, fighting against cruelty and abuse to animals. Some of her notable stage appearances were in *Hester Crewe* (1893), *A Doll's House* (1894), Lorimer Stoddard's dramatization of *Tess of the d'Urbervilles* (1897), LANGDON MITCHELL's adaptation of *Vanity Fair* (1899), *Becky Sharp* (1899), *Hedda Gabler* (1903), *Leah Kleschna* (1906), *The New York Idea* (1906), *Rosmersholm* (1907), *Salvation Nell* (1908), *The Pillars of Society* (1910) and *Ghosts* (1927). She is considered today one of the most distinguished actresses ever to have performed on the American stage and its chief promoter of IBSEN. A contemporary critic noted, 'She had a peculiar gift of emotion, uniting tears and smiles in the same breath, which was more pathetic than undiluted grief and

more diverting than undiluted laughter.' Her views on acting were edited by ALEXANDER WOOLLCOTT in 1917. DBW

Fisseha Beley fl.1980s–90s ETHIOPIAN playwright, the most popular of the generation to have emerged from the Theatre Arts Department of Addis Ababa University. Unusually for an Ethiopian playwright, Fisseha comes from a rural background and has drawn heavily on his understanding of rural culture and custom to create plays which have widespread appeal in both the cities and the regions. His work deals with serious social problems such as marriage rights and wife-beating, but takes the form of comedies. His plays in Amharic include *Simen Sintayehu* (1984), *Hoda Yifejew* (1985) and *Alkash Na Zefegn* (*The Mourner and the Singer*, 1988). JPL

Fitch, Clyde 1865–1909 American playwright. Born in Elmira, New York, he graduated from Amherst College, Massachusetts (1886), where he had been a leader in the dramatic club and frequently played female roles. Fitch was extraordinarily successful and prolific, writing 60 plays from *Beau Brummell* (1890, starring RICHARD MANSFIELD) to *The City* (1909). In 1901 four of his plays were running simultaneously in New York: *Lover's Lane*, *Captain Jinks of the Horse Marines* (with Ethel Barrymore (see DREW–BARRYMORE FAMILY)), *The Climbers* and *Barbara Frietchie*. Best known among his others are *The Moth and the Flame* (1898), *Nathan Hale* (1898), *The Cowboy and the Lady* (1899), *The Girl with the Green Eyes* (1902), *Her Great Match* (1905) and *The Truth* (1907). Fitch was a master of sprightly dialogue and documentary-like scenes from contemporary life, and as a director he meticulously controlled every detail of the staging. One critic said that his plays gave a better idea of American life than did newspapers and historical records. He died at Châlons-sur-Marne in France. His letters were published in 1924. RM

Fitzball, Edward 1793–1873 English playwright, the author of at least 150 plays as well as four novels, six volumes of bouncy verse and an informative autobiography, *Thirty-Five Years of a Dramatic Author's Life* (1859). Most famous for his spectacular MELODRAMAS, some of which advanced the patriotic taste for nautical heroism, Fitzball wrote nothing better than *Jonathan Bradford* (1833), based on a recent murder and provided with special music by Jolly, musical director of the Surrey Theatre. Particularly striking was the scenic innovation of showing four separate rooms in an inn simultaneously. Fitzball's quest for gallery-gripping effects can be read in his titles, *The Burning Bridge* (1824), *The Earthquake* (1828), *The Negro of Wapping* (1838), *The Wreck and the Reef* (1847). It was the bursts of red and blue fire rather than the skeletal text that brought *The Flying Dutchman* (1827) its phenomenal popularity. But managers thought highly enough of his feeling for what would 'go' on the contemporary stage to make him reader of plays for COVENT GARDEN (1835–8) and DRURY LANE (1838–51). His output, in both quantity and quality, is typical of the journeyman dramatist's work in the busy London theatres. Adaptations of popular novels (Fenimore Cooper, BULWER LYTTON, VICTOR HUGO), thefts from the French stage, comic OPERAS, BURLESQUES – whatever was wanted he provided, at the rate of six a year. From the fact that he added the pre-fix Fitz- to the plain Ball he was born, some *amour propre* is discernible, but his autobiography disarmingly records an occasion on which the manager and actors neglected to invite him to a first-night celebration of one of his own plays. It was not a writer's theatre during Fitzball's heyday. PT

Fitzgerald, Geraldine 1914– Dublin-born actress and director. Educated at the Dublin Art School, Fitzgerald made her stage debut at the GATE THEATRE in Dublin (1932) and her first appearance in New York as Ellie Dunn in SHAW's *Heartbreak House* (1938). While working in both films and the theatre, she has played onstage in the USA an impressive array of classical and modern characters: Jennifer Dubedat, *The Doctor's Dilemma* (1955); Goneril, *King Lear* (1956); Gertrude, *Hamlet* (1958); Queen, *The Cave Dwellers* (1961); Mary Tyrone, *Long Day's Journey into Night* (1971); Jenny, *The Threepenny Opera* (1972); Juno, *Juno and the Paycock* (1973); Essie Miller, *Ah, Wilderness!* (1975); Amanda Wingfield, *The Glass Menagerie* (1975); Felicity, *The Shadow Box* (1977); and Nora Melody, *A Touch of the Poet* (1978). She has also per-formed in a one-person show, *Songs of the Streets: O'Neill and Carlotta* (1979). One of America's most distinguished character actresses, Fitzgerald has been widely acclaimed for her 1973 portrayal of Juno, of which the *New York Time*'s Mel Gussow wrote: 'Geraldine Fitzgerald is exactly the actress to play her, managing to be resilient without sacrificing her vulnerability. Informed of her son's death, she marshals her resources, calms her hysterical daughter and then with a spasm of anguish reveals her own per-sonal loss.'

Fitzgerald has made over 30 films including *Wuthering Heights* (1939), *The Pawnbroker* (1965), *Arthur* (1981) and *Pope of Greenwich Village* (1984). She is as active today directing as she is acting, and in 1993 debuted as a lyricist and book writer with *Sharon*, a MUSICAL based on JOHN B. KEANE's *Sharon's Grave*, which she also directed. TLM

Fitzmaurice, George 1877–1963 Irish playwright. Fitzmaurice's first play, *The Country Dressmaker* (1907), a SATIRE of peasant chicanery, was a success. The two one-acters that follow – *The Pie-Dish* (1908) and *The Magic Glasses* – establish his fantastic 'folk world' of the human and the supernatural, the domestic and the magical. The latter concerns witchcraft, quack, sinister and diabolic possession, and the killing of the fey Jaymony by his enchanting, murderous magic glasses.

In *The Dandy Dolls*, discourteously rejected by YEATS in 1913, Roger Carmody and his dolls are the prize in an occult feud (or alliance) between the Gray Men and the Hag. Its 'rhythmic, gibing speech' (AUSTIN CLARKE's phrase) materializes its fabulous world, realized again in the extravagant comedy of *The Enchanted Land* (pub-lished 1957), where match-making goes astray in the Land-under-Wave.

Disparaged by Yeats, Fitzmaurice withdrew into silence, a loss to the poetic impulse Yeats desired to foster. His later, solitary work includes *One Evening Gleam* (1949) – a sombre and moving tale with an uncharacteristically realistic, urban setting.

Fitzmaurice's was an imagination of the most unusual temper, uniting the macabre and the exuberant. Austin Clarke's Lyric Theatre Co. restored it to the stage in the mid- and late 1940s; and more recently, in belated tribute, the ABBEY has put on productions. DM GF

Flanagan (Davis) [*née* Ferguson], **Hallie** 1890–1969 American playwright, educator and administrator. Franklin D. Roosevelt called Flanagan the third most pow-erful woman in America – 'after my wife and Frances Perkins' – when she supervised the FEDERAL THEATRE PROJECT. Born in South Dakota, she graduated from Grinnell College in Iowa, studied with GEORGE PIERCE BAKER at Workshop 47, and in 1927 received a Guggenheim Award to study theatre in Europe. On her return she ran a highly successful experimental pro-gramme at Vassar College. In 1935 Harry Hopkins invited her to administer the new theatre programme that had been established under WPA supervision to put qualified people back to work. For the next four years she managed the huge national theatre as it struggled with its double charge of art and relief. In spite of government harass-ment, crippling bureaucratic regulations and opposition from the professional theatre, the FTP achieved a remark-able record of accomplishments including LIVING NEWSPA-PERS, Negro companies, children's theatres and distinguished alumni. With the demise of the project in 1939 (after a skirmish with HUAC), Flanagan returned to Vassar. There she wrote a memoir (*Arena*, 1940), then moved to Smith College, where she continued to write and direct. She died leaving behind several books and a vision of the theatre as a vibrant social institution that must dare to be dangerous. A definitive biography by Joanne Bentley was published in 1988. BBW

Flanders, Michael 1922–75 British VARIETY performer, who contributed lyrics for such London REVUES as *Air on a Shoestring* and translated Stravinsky's *A Soldier's Tale* for the EDINBURGH FESTIVAL (1954), but is best remembered for *The Drop of a Hat* (1956) and other entertainments created and performed with Donald Swann. CI

Fleck, Ferdinand 1757–1801 German actor. After a few years in Hamburg, from 1786 to his death Fleck acted with the BERLIN ROYAL THEATRE. He was adulated for his power-ful, spontaneous interpretations of roles in both the clas-sics and contemporary romantic drama. LUDWIG TIECK's ideas on acting were profoundly influenced by his experi-ence of Fleck's acting. Fleck's performance as SCHILLER's Wallenstein provided a standard for most 19th-century actors. SW

Flecker, James Elroy 1884–1915 British poet and dramatist. The sensuous lyricism of his two plays, *Don Juan* (1911, which was not publicly performed until 1950) and *Hassan* (1914), owes more to the decadent movement at the end of the 19th century than to the modern revival of poetic drama. However, the colourful exoticism of the second play that lends itself to spectacle, together with incidental music by Delius and ballets by Fokine, gave it considerable popularity when it was first produced (in Germany, then in London by BASIL DEAN) in 1923, and it has since been revived in 1931 with PEGGY ASHCROFT and, less successfully, as part of the Festival of Britain in 1951. CI

Fleisser, Marieluise 1901–74 German dramatist; protégée of BRECHT, who had a hand in *Purgatory in Ingolstadt* (1926) which deals with small-town religion and sexual repression. *Pioneers in Ingolstadt* (1928), also set in her home town, sketches a brief encounter between a sentimental housemaid and a passing soldier with an authenticity that later influenced MARTIN SPERR, R. W. FASSBINDER and especially FRANZ XAVER KROETZ. *Tiefseefisch* (*Deep Sea Fish*, 1980; written 1930–72) documents her struggle to find space of her own, first with Brecht, then back home with her tobacconist husband. HR

Fletcher, John 1579–1625 English playwright, son of a bishop, who wrote elegantly and prolifically for London's theatres for at least 20 years. Probably after writing for BOYS' COMPANIES, he became associated with the King's Men and may have collaborated with SHAKESPEARE on *Henry VIII*, *The Two Noble Kinsmen* and the lost *Cardenio* (all c.1613). By then, Fletcher's famous collaboration with BEAUMONT had provided the King's Men with such outstanding successes as *Philaster* (c.1609), *The Maid's Tragedy* (c.1610) and *A King and No King* (1611). Themselves 'gentlemen', Beaumont and Fletcher easily gratified the gentlemanly taste for undemanding poetry, sexual intrigue and patterned composition. Their success tempted contemporary publicists and later publishers to ascribe to the partnership far more work than properly belongs to it. Thus, a 1647 edition includes 34 plays and a MASQUE, and a 1679 revision adds a further 18. Fletcher's hand is present in most of these, but Beaumont's in only about ten. It was MASSINGER who became Fletcher's most frequent collaborator in plays for the King's Men. Among the best of their joint work are *Sir John van Olden Barnavelt* (1619), *The Custom of the Country* (c.1619), *The Beggars' Bush* (1622) and *The Spanish Curate* (c.1622).

A happy combination of industry and facility allowed Fletcher to write, singly or in collaboration, at least four plays per year, and his single-minded commitment to drama makes him a rarity among contemporary poets. His was the major influence on the post-Restoration development of intrigue comedy. An immensely flexible writer, he eased into the Jacobean theatre a taste for romantic TRAGICOMEDY which perfectly suited the sophisticated audiences of the private theatres. Among the best of the plays for which he may have been singly responsible are *The Chances* (c.1617), *The Humorous Lieutenant* (c.1619), *The Wild-Goose Chase* (c.1621) and *Rule a Wife and Have a Wife* (1624). PT

Fletcher, Laurence d.1608 Scottish actor, a leader of the English players in Edinburgh at the end of the 16th century, and a favourite of the Scottish king. On inheriting the English throne, James I seems to have brought Fletcher south and enrolled him as one of the King's Men. We do not know what SHAKESPEARE and his colleagues thought of this arrangement, but there is no record of Fletcher's performing with the company. PT

Florence, Billy [William] **(Jermyn** or **James)** [Bernard Conlin] 1831–91 American actor. Florence's professional stage debut occurred in 1849 at the Marshall Theatre in Richmond, Virginia, as Peter in *The Stranger*. In 1853 he married Malvina Pray, the sister of Maria Pray Mestayer Williams, wife of actor BARNEY WILLIAMS. For almost 40 years, the Florences were a successful starring team in both England and America, often in Irish-American roles such as *The Irish Boy and the Yankee Girl*. Florence was a skilful comedian noted for his striking, convincingly human characterizations. After his Irish roles, his outstanding performances were as Bob Brierly in TOM TAYLOR's *The Ticket-of-Leave Man*, Bardwell Slote in Benjamin Woolf's *The Mighty Dollar*, Sir Lucius O'Trigger in *The Rivals*, and Zekiel Homespun in COLMAN THE YOUNGER's *The Heir at Law*. He also presented the first American production of T. W. ROBERTSON's *Caste* in 1867, only four months after its London premiere. DJW

Floridor [Josias de Soulas, sieur de Primefosse] c.1608–71 French actor-manager, scion of the minor aristocracy who opted for the life of a strolling player. First mentioned in 1635 as leader of a company of French actors in London where they played before the Court and at the COCKPIT THEATRE in Drury Lane, he made his debut at the MARAIS in 1638. Having prospered there, notably in the plays of PIERRE CORNEILLE, he purchased BELLEROSE's position as director of the rival Parisian company, as well as his wardrobe, and moved to the HÔTEL DE BOURGOGNE in 1647, which may well have persuaded Corneille, with whom he was on friendly terms, to entrust his later plays to that theatre. His career continued to flourish until the very year of his death and he was much admired by Louis XIV, who granted him some remunerative commercial concessions. Of noble bearing, with a sonorous voice and an unforced delivery, he was most successful in roles calling for dignity and authority; some critics found him too cold, though he created the role of Nero in RACINE's *Britannicus* (1669). Significantly, he was the one leading actor of the Hôtel de Bourgogne whom MOLIÈRE forbore to ridicule in his *Impromptu de Versailles* (1663). In fact, he seems to have been universally esteemed in his profession and to have led a blameless private life. DR

Flotats, Josep Maria 1939 Spanish actor and director, educated at a French institute in his native Barcelona. He went to Strasbourg in 1960 to study theatre, then launched an acting career that led to numerous roles in Paris at the THÉÂTRE NATIONAL POPULAIRE, the Théâtre de la Ville and the COMÉDIE-FRANÇAISE. Since 1985, when he assumed direction of the government-subsidized Poliorama, he has been a major figure in CATALAN THEATRE. Serving as a bridge between Catalonia and France, he has brought to Barcelona both French theatre people and important texts, including ones in which he has recreated roles he previously performed in France. Among notable productions, directed by and starring Flotats, are ROSTAND's *Cyrano de Bergerac* (1985), Natalie Sarraute's *Per un sí o per un no* (*For the Least Little Thing*, 1986), Brian Clark's *Whose Life Is It Anyway?* (1987), MUSSET's *Lorenzaccio* (1988) and MOLIÈRE's *The Misanthrope* (1989). In 1991 he produced his first Catalan text: *Ara que els* *ametllers ja estan batuts* (*Now That the Almonds Have Been Harvested*). This dramatic monologue, based on Josep Pla's narrative, was written, acted and directed by Flotats. PZ

flyting Stylized exchange of insults, or formalized debate, often in verse or formulaic prose. At its simplest it appears as 'kidding' among friends. It is more obviously rule-bound among young American and West Indian blacks ('playing the dozens' or 'sounding'), and calls for considerable poetic skill among the Inuit, whose impromptu obscene verses are a favourite form of entertainment, and in Italy where contests in the satirical stanzas known as *contrasto a braccio* are sometimes organized enough to have a panel of judges. The pattern of the *contrasto*, in which each contestant takes on one role in an oppositional theme (wine versus water, atheist versus priest, and so on), is common in CARNIVAL plays, and influenced the dramatic work of JOHN HEYWOOD and Hans Sachs. AEG

Fo, Dario 1926– Italian actor, director and dramatist. A versatile MIME artist, improviser and satirist, he began his career as a writer and performer in comic sketches and political CABARET. In 1957 he and his wife FRANCA RAME, herself from a family of popular entertainers, formed a company that worked a comic repertoire that included materials drawn from 19th-century FARCE and the techniques and strategies of popular street, fair and club theatre. Although this repertoire incorporated political SATIRE, it was crafted principally for bourgeois audiences: it was mocking, irreverent and anarchic, but essentially amiable, and included pieces like *Aveva due pistole dagli occhi bianchi e neri* (*Had Two Pistols with White and Black Eyes*, 1960) and *Settimo: Ruba un po'meno* (*Seventh: Steal a Bit Less*, 1964).

In the mid- and later 60s, Fo established a national reputation as a writer and performer of satirical pieces, the barbs of which became increasingly sharp in their cuts at capitalism, imperialism and the scandals and abuses of Italian government. The political disturbances of 1968, however, brought an important shift in the direction of Fo's work: abandoning mainstream theatre, he and his wife formed a new company, Nuova Scena (New Stage), and under the auspices of the Communist Party toured factories, clubs and halls in search of working-class audiences. His search for a genuinely political theatre issued in some quasi-BRECHTian didactic pieces like *L'Operaio conosce 300 parole, il padrone 1000; per questo lui é il padrone* (*The worker Knows 300 Words, the Boss 1000; That's Why He's the Boss*, 1969); *Grande pantomima con bandiere e pupazzi piccoli e medi* (*Great Pantomime with Flags and Medium-sized Puppets*, 1968), a satirical presentation of Italian politics since the fall of Fascism; and the highly original *Mistero buffo* (1969), a unique one-man spectacle performed with great success in Italy and abroad.

But tensions between him and the Party led Fo to break with the orthodox left, and in 1970 he and Franca Rame formed the theatre collective La Comune and turned their skills to the service of the New Left. The work of this group was more aggressively revolutionary, dramatizing topical political issues and seeking to expose the corruption, oppression and incompetence of bourgeois capitalist governments. Products of this new direction of Fo's work came in the later 70s and 80s to attract attention throughout Europe: notably, plays like *Morte accidentale di un anarchico* (*Accidental Death of an Anarchist*, 1970), *Non si paga! Non si paga!* (*Can't Pay, Won't Pay*, 1974) and *Female Parts* (1981) written jointly with Franca Rame. More recent work has included *Il Papa e la strega* (*The Pope and the Witch*, 1989) and *Johan Padan a la descoverta de la Americhe* (*Johan Padan and the Discovery of America*, 1992). Increasingly he has worked as a guest director abroad, notable work including brilliant stagings of two MOLIÈRE farces, *Le Médecin malgré lui* and *Le Médecin volant*, at the COMÉDIE-FRANÇAISE in Paris (1992). His theoretical and polemical writing includes *Manuale minimo dell'attore* (*The Tricks of the Trade*, 1987) and *Fabulazzo* (1992).

Fo is perhaps foremost a brilliant actor and exploiter of theatrical means for politico-satiric purposes: most notably in *Mistero buffo*, in which his consummate skill at drawing on a wide range of popular materials and traditions of improvised performance was put to the service of an ideological engagement that transcended merely national political concerns. In the view of some critics his deep political commitment at times co-exists uneasily with theatrical needs, creating a gap between ideological content and dramatic form: a criticism levelled at, for example, the ending of *Clacson, trombette e pernacchi* (*Trumpets and Raspberries*, 1981). But no one in the contemporary theatre has more effectively wedded comedy and savage political comment than Fo in pieces like *Mistero buffo* and *Morte accidentale*. LR

Fokin, Valery (Vladimirovich) Russian director who established his career at Moscow's Sovremennik Theatre with productions of ROSHCHIN's *Valentin and Valentina* (1971), Dostoevsky's *Notes from Underground* and *Dream of a Ridiculous Man* (1976) and Enn Vetemaa's *Monument* (1978), which dealt with the issue of suppressed freedom in Soviet society. As artistic director (since 1986) of Moscow's Ermolova Theatre, he has staged Aleksandr Buransky's *Speak*, a critical depiction of village life under Stalin (adapted from Valentin Ovechkin), which contrasts propagandistic newsreel footage with a chorus of dissatisfied peasants; Vladlen Dozortsev's psychological suspense drama *The Last Visitor* and RADZINSKY's *Jogging* (*Sporting Scenes*), both of which criticized the Soviet ruling elite or *nomenklatura* in the time of *glasnost*. Fokin also directed the Russian premiere of EDWARD ALBEE's *Who's Afraid of Virginia Woolf?* (1985) at the Sovremennik, VAMPILOV's *The Elder Son* at the Actors' Theatre of St Paul (Minnesota, 1989) and the Soviet television series *TASS Is Authorized to Announce*, on the KGB's foreign operations. SG

Folies-Bergère A Parisian MUSIC-HALL that opened in 1869, offering pantoMIME and OPERETTA. Léon Sari, who managed it until 1885, indulged the prostitutes who haunted its promenade so that it became a fashionable resort of young men-about-town. Under various managements, during 1885–1918, it alternated singers like MAURICE CHEVALIER and YVETTE GUILBERT with speciality acts like LITTLE TICH and Loïe Fuller. Paul Derval, who took it over in 1918, endowed it with the style that made it world-famous: lavish *revues à grand spectacle* with cohorts of naked women, exotic tableaux, monumental staircases, and acres of sequins and ostrich plumes. The titles, always of 13 letters, had to include the word *folie*. This 'hypertrophy of sumptuousness', as Roland Barthes called it, became the tourist trap *par excellence*, a must-see for French provincials and foreigners alike. Since 1974, it has been managed by Hélène Martini.   LS

folk drama, European and European-based

'Folklore' was not identified as an autonomous area of cultural activity until 1846, under the stimulus of romanticism, nationalism and rapid social change. The ensuing burst of collecting soon found its theoretical underpinning in cultural evolution, a bastard offspring of Darwin, which held that all societies pass through savagery and barbarism on their way to civilization. In the process, much is discarded in favour of more adaptive ways of living and thinking; but some relics of earlier patterns live on into the modern world, particularly among the more conservative members of society, notably the peasantry (rightly or wrongly so called).

The interest of these 'survivals in culture', to the 19th-century intellectual, lay in the light they shed on the prehistory of a people; that they might have a meaning in the present, for the 'peasants' who cherished them, rarely occurred to anybody. Meaning was consigned to the past, usually so remote that no documentary source could be used to test the scholar's analysis. Thus it came about, especially in the English-speaking world, that folk drama, rather than being treated as an artistic genre with its own development and conventions, was regarded as a corrupt and misunderstood RITUAL corpus. Where it could be shown that other phenomena – such as the chapbook press – had influenced it, these influences were rejected as late accretions. This idea of folk drama is still with us, not least among theatre historians, for all that professional folklorists have abandoned it, along with the general theory of culture from which it derived.

Not that folk drama contains no ancient elements; but, for the most part, we neither know nor are ever likely to know. Sometimes we do know, or may reasonably infer. The occasional association of ritual healing with folk drama (notably in the Romanian CĂLUŞ) may be of considerable antiquity. For certain, the zoomorphic trend in folk drama takes us back a long way.

There is graphic evidence of ANIMAL IMPERSONATION from prehistory; written sources show it in the classical period; and by the early Christian epoch we find churchmen embarking on a litany of complaints against animal guisers which they will waste their breath on for the next millennium and more. There even exists a clay MASK of a calf, clearly designed to be worn, and thought to date from about AD 400. It was found in Liechtenstein, and would not be out of place in an Alpine CARNIVAL in the 20th century. As the graphic and documentary sources of medieval art, scholarship and administration pile up, so does the evidence for zoomorphic masquerades. Of course, we never know exactly what the maskers were doing, though we sometimes know it was seasonal (New Year being a

favourite time, just as it was in pre-Christian ROME, and still is for the youngsters in Derbyshire and Nottinghamshire in England, who take their OLD TUP play around the pubs). But seasonality does not, in itself, imply religious observance, whether Christian or pagan (which is what the ritual survival thesis is about); ritual can be secular as well as sacred, and that St Augustine denounced a masquerade as ungodly in the 5th century no more makes it so than when Erasmus did the same in the 16th. What we have is a satisfying combination of archaeological, iconographic and written sources which support a continuous history of a particular kind of dramatic manifestation from the earliest times to the present day.

It does not therefore follow that all folk drama is ancient, and we merely lack the evidence to show it. Lying above this ancient cultural stratum are others demonstrably more recent. An important group of plays in Europe, and in Catholic Central America, celebrates major Christian feasts by the enactment of Bible stories; self-evidently, there is nothing pre-Christian about these. Though their age is unknown, they are analogous to and in some cases possibly derived from the scriptural drama of the late Middle Ages and Renaissance (see MEDIEVAL DRAMA IN EUROPE). They are not, however, cyclic, but concentrate rather on a specific event such as the arrival of the Magi (recorded in Germany from the 16th century and in Norway from the 17th); or the adoration of the Shepherds, known in Italy, Germany and Spain from the 16th century, in Czechoslovakia, Hungary and Poland from the 17th, and France from the 18th, as well as passing from Spain to Mexico, where *Los Pastores* is still performed. The overwhelming popularity of the Nativity and Epiphany as subjects is no doubt attributable to the growing importance of Christmas, as against Easter, in the modern world. Old Testament plays are less common, though folk redactions of Hans Sachs's *Tragedy of the Creation, the Fall and Expulsion of Adam from Paradise* have survived into the 20th century in Germany and Austria.

Cognate with these scripturally based plays in the secular domain are the numerous performances which are related to popular or, more rarely, elite literature. The English HERO-COMBAT PLAY (often called the mummers' play) owes something textually to Richard Johnson's *The Seven Champions of Christendom*, which went through at least 26 editions between 1596 and 1770; the Swiss *Tellspiel* (William Tell play) derives from ballad and literary sources of the 15th and 16th centuries; the Wandering Jew Ahasuerus wanders off the pages of the *bibliothèque bleue* into a Liège PASSION PLAY for puppets; and the so-called *pastorales* of the Basque country draw on a variety of hagiographical and romance sources for their content. Boccaccio's tale of patient Griselda, probably mediated through chapbooks, gives rise to Austrian folk plays. The northern Greek *Panaratos* (a sensational tale of forbidden love, judicial murder and revenge, framed by a prologue and epilogue from Charos, the personification of death) is a heavily cut and reworked version of the five-act tragedy *Erophila*, written in c.1600 by the Italianate Cretan Georgios Kostatzes. Even CONGREVE's *Love for Love* lends a few lines to the admittedly unusual text of the Ampleforth sword dance: the contribution is important neither quantitatively nor dramatically, but it is a useful indication of folk drama's tolerant exploitation of the most unlikely-looking material.

Each tradition, or group of related traditions, needs to be carefully scrutinized for its autochthonous elements, its debt to official traditions of religious expression (including the PARODY of them), and its borrowings from the great tradition of literacy, at high social and aesthetic levels as well as low, without granting theoretical precedence, *a priori*, to any one of these.

If the 'folk' element in folk drama is problematic, the 'drama' element is no less so. Everyone would agree, in principle, that it cannot be conceptualized according to an Aristotelian thesis of plot construction (see ARISTOTLE), or to the literary theatre's preoccupation with character and motive. Even in the elite theatre, the presence or absence of a text is not easy to use as a criterion of 'drama', and in folk theatre we are faced with the question of what a text is. Some folk actors (for that they unquestionably are, and if drama is what actors do, the problem is solved) may not use language at all, or speech may be optional: processional characters in CARNIVAL, the New Year *Dziady* (vagabonds) of Poland, the Slovenian *Kurenti* with their animal-skin coats, long-nosed masks, and feathered headdresses. But they may vocalize: grunts, snorts, roars, gibberish. Is this a 'text', and, if not, what is it? In any case, their behaviour, though apparently idiosyncratic to the point of anarchy, is neither unplanned nor incoherent. It has its own set of performance conventions, founded on the principle of reversing everyday behaviour.

Other maskers, though they do not offer a 'play' in the sense that the literary theatre uses that term, engage in an improvised dialogue with their audience. This may be a guessing game, in which the 'audience' (now effectively performers) have to identify the actors (TOLSTOI incorporated it in *War and Peace*, since when it has been reported in Ecuador, Trinidad, Ireland and maritime Canada – in Newfoundland the mummers frustrate their efforts by speaking ingressively); or an interrogation of the audience by their disguised visitors (Norwegian *Julegeita* – Christmas goats – and in Labrador the Inuit NALUYUKS – literally, 'heathens' – question children about their behaviour). Again, these dialogues, though improvised, follow entirely predictable lines, and occur within a recognized pattern of symbolic behaviour. We can, if we wish, deny these activities the status of 'drama', for pragmatic or ideological reasons; but then we are confronted by the strawboys of County Fermanagh, who would follow their performance of a hero-combat play with the guessing game – not to mention singing and dancing at their hosts' request, and eating and drinking at their expense.

Unless we are to risk overlooking vital conceptual links in a performance tradition (the strawboys, masked, enter as 'strangers' and, in role, perform their play; through the guessing game they become 'not-strangers'; only then can they be invited to sit and eat), it is essential that we be prepared to take events as a whole, rather than force them into the procrustean bed of an alien classification. Because folk traditions are so protean, not only among themselves (variation in space) but within themselves (variation in time), it makes sense to think in terms of a continuum of performance behaviour, rather than of clear demarcations.

Structurally, folk drama lies between two poles. One is the silent or non-verbal performance by masked actors, often constantly on the move, acting the goat (interesting phrase), frightening the children, grabbing girls, making mischief. The other is the virtually Aristotelian narrative of the subliterary *Panaratos*, or the *Tellspiel*, which covers the fundamental elements of the legend – Gessler's imposition of the apple-shot, Tell's success and disclosure of the second arrow's destination, his arrest as a subversive and subsequent escape, his assassination of the tyrannical landgrave. Between them lie a multitude of forms, with more or less emphasis on text or narrative development. The Italian *I Mesi* (Play of the Months) is a cavalcade of the 12 months personified, each with a laudatory verse and an emblematic property (a posy of flowers for May, figs for September, a pot of soup for December), introduced by New Year and the COMMEDIA DELL'ARTE figure of Pulcinella. The whole text is addressed directly to the audience. This highly formal succession of speeches of equal length is also used in FLYTINGS, such as the Swiss *Sommer-und-Winterspiel* (Play of Summer and Winter); here, however, two allegorical characters are set in dialogue against one another, each praising himself and denouncing the other, until Winter concedes. Greater narrative development is seen in the hero-combat play, but the Aristotelian expectations of its first phase (quarrel – conflict – killing – cure) are frustrated by its second phase, a pageant of apparently unconnected characters using only direct address. Traditional FARCES, such as the Tirolean carnival-play ALTWEIBERMUHLE (*The Mill for Old Women*) or the Russian PAKHOMUSHKA, by definition develop character relationships within a plot, though often as much through the playing of variants on the same theme as through a steady and integrated forward movement.

At any point in this continuum the dramatic action may be interrupted by or culminate in music and dance. The Basque *Pastorales* are interspersed with dances, selected from an independent repertory, regardless of whether the play is of St Eustace or Roland. The Papa Stour (Shetland) Sword Dance uses its text, a presentational pageant of characters, simply as a prologue to the dance. The important tradition of the MORESCA, a spectacular and bellicose Mediterranean-based dance-drama, also uses its text as a prologue, but one in which, through dialogue and character interaction, the conflict is established which will culminate in a choreographic battle.

Various as its sources and dramatic structures may be, the other formal properties of folk theatre are remarkably consistent. It is an open-space form: fitted-up stages are occasionally used, as is simple stage furniture. But the normal performance environment is a street, square, public house or domestic interior, unaltered but for the presence of costumed actors. The relationship between performer and audience follows from this. Dramatic performance is in itself abnormal; but for its abnormality to be acceptable within an environment created, in the first instance, for other reasons, the performers incorporate in their performance certain fundamental elements which belong to that environment. When we go into somebody's house, we do not ignore the occupants; in the street or the public house, if we merely talk amongst ourselves, politeness dictates that others present ignore us. Folk actors have the same way of dealing with both constraints – namely, direct address: even those performances which rely exclusively on dialogue, as many flytings do, are so formal in their construction and language as to invite a declamatory style which expressly includes the audience.

Intimacy between characters is foreign to folk drama; interestingly, in the 20th century, when some traditions have been influenced in their content by film and television, the fourth wall seems to have had no effect. This must indicate, within folk drama, a powerful artistic principle in favour of constructing a relationship of mutual acknowledgement between actor and audience. Characterization also militates in favour of this. It is without exception stereotypical: culture heroes and villains (including scriptural and hagiographical ones), allegorical figures, foolish old men and ugly old women, quack doctors, soldiers, schoolmasters, vagabonds. COSTUME and hand props either immediately represent these stereotypes, or are totally abstract. Finally, language and movement rarely pretend to realism. Rhymed verse, or a mixture of verse and prose, is typical, often interspersed with or framed by song. Movement is stylized, even ideographic (a fight may take the form of a metrical clashing of swords, a character decapitated may simply bow his or her head), and may become heightened into dance. Much of this also applies to performances by PUPPETS, such as PUNCH or the Turkish KARAGÖZ, which points to a high degree of stylization. Even the convention and implications of direct address, though they cannot literally apply to puppet-theatre, can be approximated by a skilful puppeteer.

If the style of folk drama is strikingly consistent, its content is not, and the analysis of it requires, strictly speaking, close attention to particular traditions. No more than a few introductory generalizations can be advanced here.

The first, and possibly the most fundamental, is that folk drama is frequently seasonal in its performance: that is, it is one item in a festive calendar. Since there is intrinsically no reason why folk plays should not be performed on demand, their calendric context must be significant. This may be marked in any of three ways: by reference to the official calendar whether liturgical (Christmas) or secular (New Year), or by reference to the pastoral or agricultural year (Anatolian shepherds perform their plays during the pregnancy of their ewes). Seasonality is sometimes a play's whole content; more frequently it is referred to in a prologue or epilogue.

The idea of continuity through change is central – obviously so in the religious plays which, through the re-enactment of, say, the Nativity, make concrete the community's commitment to a particular version of human history and its meaning. Small wonder that the shepherds have been so popular. The opportunities they offer for a certain level of realism in dialect speech and local costume, together with their representation of the poor and lowly, underscore the relationship – unmediated by a priest – between God and ordinary people.

In plays on secular themes may be seen a similar use of the past to validate the present, or particular values in relation to the present which are not necessarily those of the ruling class. The Russian plays which deal with the 17th-century peasant leader Sten'ka Razin embody an idea of justice which takes on a metaphysical dimension in the superhuman qualities attributed to him. Likewise the many plays about outlaws – ROBIN HOOD, the Catalan Joán de Serrallonga, the Mexican Agustín Lorenzo – all of them likely to be regarded as historical figures by actors and audience, invariably show the hero as just, magnanimous and brave, thereby implying a critique of a law that makes such men criminals; and, through the setting of the action in the past, the persistence of an alternative set of values through thick and thin. As for the widespread dramatic traditions based on death and resurrection (the hero-combat, the Thracian *Kalogheroi*, some versions of *Căluş*), their metaphorical correspondence to the clash and synthesis of past and future is self-evident.

The definition of a community in time is complemented by the representation of desirable and undesirable social types, and of insiders and outsiders. At its simplest, the behaviour of culture heroes and saints expresses positive social values, and that of villains and fools negative values. But not all norms are so obviously stated, and a lot of plays seem preoccupied with defining the normal by reference to its opposite. In the *moresca* both terms of the proposition are present in the defeat of blacks by whites. The Anatolian *Play of the Old Man* complicates the issue by making equally undesirable two suitors for a young woman's hand – the dangerous Arab, from an alien race and culture, and the foolish old man who demonstrates his unsuitability to claim the bride by his inability to fight for her. It is worth remembering that this violent comedy of sexual mismatch is set in the vital seasonal context of the reproduction of the flocks. The British hero-combat deals with two problematic social types, the untrustworthy stranger (soldiers, the itinerant mountebank, the light-fingered tramp) and the neighbour who is not fully integrated (the village idiot, the sexually ambiguous old woman).

The zoomorphic figure, where it occurs, is a central metaphor. It invariably has both human and animal attributes, an ambiguity which gives it special potency in a play of taxonomy. In the Anatolian plays the speaking characters are accompanied by non-speaking animal maskers. They represent both domestic animals such as the camel, and wild animals such as the hare and fox, echoing at an ecological level of imagery the outsider–insider dialectic which the text represents at a social and racial level. The hobby-horse who closes the Antrobus (Cheshire) hero-combat play is at once living and dead, domestic and wild, animal and human. Folk plays celebrate their community through a ludic representation of its definitions, including the PARODY of the dominant culture's institutions. Usually this remains at a fictional level, but there are examples in which play and real life merge. The Labrador *naluyuks* reward good children, and harass social undesirables. The Basque *Tobera Mustrak* is a highly developed CHARIVARI – based on the common carnivalic genre of the mock trial in which a play is constructed specifically to hold up to public ridicule particular persons and their offences against society.

This extreme example illustrates the close relationship between folk drama and its community. It is there in the seasonal context, in the value-laden texts, in the informal socializing that invariably accompanies them, in their strong sense of reciprocity among friends and neighbours. Fermanagh mummers use the proceeds of their collection to throw a party for everybody; a Polish Herod speaks of 'the good times we share together'. An Antrobus 'soulcaker' puts it succinctly: 'We're all one.' Theirs is an art in which text and context merge. AEG

See: V. Alford, *The Hobby Horse and Other Animal Masks*, London, 1978; G. Cocciara, *The History of Folklore in Europe*, Philadelphia, 1981; *Drama Review*, 18, 1974 (indigenous theatre issue); H. Glassie, *All Silver and No Brass*, Bloomington, 1975; A. E. Green, 'Popular Drama and the Mummer's Play', in D. Bradby, C. James and B. Sharratt (eds), *Performance and Politics in Popular Drama*, Cambridge, 1980; H. Halpert and G. M. Storey, *Christmas Mumming in Newfoundland*, Toronto, 1969; *Journal of American Folklore*, 94, 1981; G. Kligman, *Căluş*, Chicago, 1981; L. Schmidt, *Das Deutsche Volksschauspiel*, Berlin, 1962, and *Le Théâtre populaire européen*, Paris, 1965; P. Toschi, *Invito al folklore italiano: le regioni e le feste*, Rome, 1963; Arnold Van Gennep, *Manuel de folklore français contemporain*, Paris, 1939–58; E. Warner, *The Russian Folk Theatre*, The Hague, 1977.

folk theatre, Asian Uncounted tens of thousands of folk theatre groups perform in rural and urban settings in almost all areas of Asia. Folk theatre performances are closely linked to religious, social and communal celebrations. Performances occur at fixed intervals during the year, in conjunction with calendrical holidays, feasts, rituals, or significant social occasions such as marriage or birth (see RITES OF PASSAGE). Performers and spectators are residents of the same village or district within an urban area, or may be near-neighbours. Performers are farmers, shopkeepers, clerks or workers who act, sing and dance as participants in a social and often religious event on behalf of the community. They do not consider themselves professional. Entertainment of one's own community is a major motive, and the excellent performer often gains great prestige within his or her community. Expenses for a folk performance are borne by the community at large or by a local sponsor. Rarely are folk performers paid personally; funds paid to the performing group go to buy better costumes or musical instruments, or for performers' food and travel expenses. Folk theatre is usually performed on the bare earth, before a temple or shrine, or occasionally on a simple, often movable, platform stage.

In INDIA, JAPAN, INDONESIA, THAILAND, CAMBODIA, Samoa, Hawaii, Tahiti and elsewhere, folk dance, music and theatre forms are carefully learned and preserved. Although the value of performance may not be judged on aesthetic principles as much as on efficacy – if the performance is also a RITUAL – and social function, many folk performances are in fact sophisticated in conception and boast high artistic standards. With few exceptions, it is a myth that 'everyone' in a village can act or sing or dance; skill in performance is often so prized within the community that young pupils will seek out good teachers to assure their advancement. Specialization in performance may be linked to being an adept in religious practices as well – SHAMANism in particular. It is not possible to describe all the forms that are practised today. But a few examples will illustrate the range of dramatic material, performance techniques, and entertainment, social and religious function.

In Japan, villagers perform masked and unmasked Shinto plays and dances *(kagura)* in thousands of rural and urbanized areas at the five annual calendrical festivals, especially at New Year and the mid-summer ceremonies honouring the spirits of the dead. Performance follows the standard festival format: invocation of the god, entertainment of/by the god (the actual *kagura* performance) and the return of the god. The folk dance or play honours the deity, providing the mechanism for his or her presence in the community. Such a performance encompasses the explicit ritual function of assuring prosperity and freedom from disease for the community during the ensuing year or until the next performance. Performers are local villagers, people who normally perform the same roles year after year.

In India, such regional forms as KATHAKALI, KUCHIPUDI, CAVITTU NATAKAM, chaau and vithi natakam are folk theatre, performed in local regions, limited by language and custom, by local groups for communal occasions. The dramatic materials are drawn from vernacular versions of 'high' culture and literature: the epic *Ramayana* and *Mahabharata*, tales of the god Krishna and Hindu myth and, in the case of *cavittu natakam*, medieval European legends brought by Portuguese Catholic immigrants. In the PHILIPPINES, *komedya* (or *moro-moro*) represents the majority Catholic religion as practised in the countryside. It is performed as a social activity and a religious obligation by the young people of a rural *barrio* on the annual saint's day fiesta of the village church. Originally borrowed from Spain via Mexico, the plays dramatize the reconciliation of Christian and Islamic belief, reflecting the vying for converts of the two religions that has been a basic fact of life in Philippine culture for four centuries.

In SRI LANKA, folk theatre is intimately bound up with religious ritual. *SOKARI* is performed after the New Year as a devotion to the goddess Pattini, a pre-Buddhist deity, by devotees of a village, who have been trained by a master specifically for the performance. The play dramatizes the life and abilities of the goddess. Performers use MASKS, elaborate MIME and song. *Kolam is* a comic form of masked folk theatre that dramatizes Buddhist morality stories. As with many folk forms, ribaldry and sexual, reproductive humour are prominent, leading to speculation that both *sokari* and *kolam* derived from ancient fertility rites. The Sri Lankan performances are typical in that they take place at night (when farmers are not working), on the bare earth and without a theatre structure. In Indonesia, today's urban-based *ketoprak* in central Java and *ludruk* in East Java originated as informal village folk performances some 70 years ago. Primarily under the influence of professional *bangsawan* troupes who toured Indonesia in the early decades of the 20th century from home bases in MALAYSIA, professional Indonesian performers took up the styles, formed commercial troupes, and established touring or permanent theatres in major cities in Java.

'Folk theatre' is not a static concept, but rather it exists on a continuum with popular and elite theatre traditions, with the possibility always existing that folk performers may draw large audiences, become financially successful and thereby move into the popular, urban tradition of commercial performance; or that their art may become aestheticized, as has happened to many Balinese folk dances and plays, and thereby cross over into the elite tradition. JRB

Folksbiene (People's Stage) The longest continuously performing Yiddish theatre in the world. Beginning in New York City as one of hundreds of YIDDISH amateur theatres, it has presented at least one production every winter since 1915. Early on it hired professional directors, such as Joseph Buloff and JACOB BEN-AMI, and eventually began hiring some professional actors as well. Associated with the Workman's Circle, the group is generally committed to presenting Yiddish plays of literary worth, often classics; but in recent years it has also presented lighter entertainments, such as Yiddish translations of popular Israeli comedies. It is currently housed in the Central Synagogue, East 56th Street. NS

Folkteatern i Göteborg The Göteborg People's Theatre (founded 1954) is a corporation whose members are organizations and individuals associated with the Labour movement. This is reflected in its repertoire of new Swedish plays, many by working-class writers or about local labour concerns and history. Among the many artists who have frequently written, acted and directed for it are Kent Andersson, Bengt Bratt, STAFFAN GÖTHE, Lennart Hjulström, Roland Janson, Agneta Pleijel, Thomas van Bromssen and Staffan Westerberg. Its activities include a vigorous children's theatre, 'One Flight Down', and an extensive outreach programme. Local amateurs have sometimes participated, as in *A Shipyard Dream* (1981), a huge production about Göteborg's shipyards. HL

Fonda [Jaynes], Henry 1905–82 American actor. Born in Nebraska, Fonda made his first stage appearance in 1925 at the Omaha Community Playhouse, and his BROADWAY debut in 1929. He established himself as a leading actor in *The Farmer Takes a Wife* (1934) before turning almost exclusively to making films. After service in the Second World War, he played the title role in *Mister Roberts* (1948), which won him a Tony. Working in both Hollywood and New York, he won critical acclaim on Broadway in 1954 with his portrayal of Barney Greenwald in *The Caine Mutiny Court Martial*. He starred with Anne Bancroft in *Two for the Seesaw* (1958), and with Barbara Bel Geddes in *Silent Night, Lonely Night* (1959). Other important stage appearances include the COMEDY hit, *Generation*, in 1965, and the one-man show, *Clarence Darrow*, in 1974. Fonda's screen image as the quiet, unassuming man of integrity and strength dominated his appearances on stage. TLM

Fontanne, Lynn see LUNT, ALFRED

Fonvizin, Denis (Ivanovich) 1745–92 The creator of Russian national COMEDY, linking SUMAROKOV's neo-classicism and the satirical, social REALISM of GOGOL, OSTROVSKY, SALTYKOV-SHCHEDRIN and CHEKHOV. Fonvizin's social libertarianism and fierce moralism, influenced by the French Enlightenment philosophers Montesquieu, VOLTAIRE, ROUSSEAU and DIDEROT, foreshadowed the social philoso-

phy of art espoused by the critic Belinsky and the playwright-ideologue GORKY. He was an outspoken and periodically censored critic of Catherine the Great's regime: his favourite targets were the egoism and Gallomania of the provincial gentry, the institution of serfdom, and especially the harmfulness and abuses of foreign education (the 'tutors' in his plays are French coachmen and manicurists) – a snobbish attitude and dehumanizing behaviour directed at one's own culture and its people.

Fonvizin's satirical sensibility was sharpened by his reading of the Dane Holberg's fables, 183 of which he adapted and translated while a student at Moscow University (c.1760–2). He had joined the gymnasium of the university as a student in 1755, moving later into the main institution. In the early 1760s he served as a translator of Latin, French and German in the Ministry of Foreign Affairs, where he was involved with the circle of writers and translators headed by the writer and cabinet minister I. P. Elagin, whose secretary he became. Fonvizin's verse comedy *Korion* (1764), an adaptation of *Sidney* (1745), Gresset's *comédie larmoyante*, set the pattern for his later work, blending to an unprecedented degree Russian character and linguistic traits, scenic and quotidian details with such themes and conventions of European sentimental comedy as characters operating under the influence of vices, romantic entanglements and parental interference. In his major neo-classical comedies, *The Brigadier* (written 1769, produced 1780) and *The Minor* (1782), he individuated such familiar character types as the servant and the foolish old woman, and created such staples of the Russian actor's repertoire as Starodum ('Old Sense'), Mitrofan, Mrs Prostakova ('Mrs Simple'), the brigadier (whose rank has been laughable ever since) and his wife.

Fonvizin continued the practice of comedic portraiture (*na litso*, or drawn from life) while developing character and exposition via dialogue and action, a technique which would be perfected by GRIBOEDOV. His remaining plays include *Alzire, or the Americans* (1762, adapted from Voltaire's verse TRAGEDY), *A Friend of Honest People, or Starodum* (1788) and *The Choice of a Tutor* (1790). In 1782, Fonvizin followed his protector, the liberal ministry head Nikita Panin, into what was essentially for him a forced retirement from public life, and devoted himself to satirical essays, correspondence, an autobiography and an abortive journal project. SG

Foote, Samuel 1721–77 English actor, playwright and manager. After an extravagant youth ended with his being imprisoned for debt, he studied briefly with MACKLIN in 1743 and began acting with some success at the HAYMARKET and at Smock Alley in Dublin. In 1747 he published two interesting pamphlets on acting and DRAMATIC THEORY, *A Treatise on the Passions* and *The Roman and English Comedy Considered*, and began writing plays. He evaded the conditions of the Licensing Act with *The Diversions of the Morning*, a satirical REVUE, by inviting the audience to tea and staging the performance as a noon matinée. His next dodge, *The Auction of Pictures*, was similarly briefly legal and successful. While in Paris between 1749 and 1751, the basis for his play *The Englishman in Paris* (1753), he was incensed by GARRICK's permitting Woodward to mimic him in a performance of *Friendship* *in Fashion*, though most of Foote's own plays include similar pieces of personal caricature. His revue, renamed *Taste* (1752), was not a success and Foote tried fortune-telling, puppet plays and acting as well as theatre management in Dublin.

In 1760, with his SATIRE on Methodists, *The Minor*, he was at last a success in London and became the summer manager at the Haymarket. Thrown by a horse in 1766, he lost a leg but continued to act. In 1767 he bought and remodelled the Haymarket. His satire on doctors, *The Devil upon Two Sticks* (1768), exploited his own amputation. *The Nabob* (1722) attacked the East India Company. Apart from continued experiments with puppet shows, Foote's career as manager of the Haymarket was a success. His drama, with its recurrent concern with personal satire, led to his being nicknamed the English ARISTOPHANES. PH

Foottit, George [Tudor Hall] 1864–1921 and **Chocolat** [Raphaël Padilla] 1868–1917 French CLOWN act. Foottit, an Englishman trained in PANTOMIME and travelling shows, had already made a name for himself in Paris as a combination of the GRIMALDI clown and the pattering French Jocrisse when, in 1886, he teamed up with the black Cuban Chocolat at the Cirque Médrano. For 15 years, they delighted audiences with routines displaying Chocolat as 'he who gets slapped' and Foottit as his arrogant oppressor. They played the Nouveau Cirque and the Hippodrome, and in the REVUE *En selle pour la revue* (1888). After they retired, their sons carried on the tradition. LS

Forbes-Robertson, Johnston 1853–1937 British actor, who rejected the preferred but uncertain career of an artist when SAMUEL PHELPS offered him six guineas a week to act with him. Forbes-Robertson became Phelps's pupil (his portrait of Phelps as Wolsey hangs in the Garrick Club) and credited the old actor with the training of the voice that, with Henry Ainley's and JOHN GIELGUD's, has been the most praised in the English theatre. After working for BUCKSTONE at the HAYMARKET, Henry Neville at the OLYMPIC and the BANCROFTS at the PRINCE OF WALES'S, he was invited by IRVING to join the LYCEUM company. Irving may have seen in the ascetically gaunt features of Forbes-Robertson an image of his own youth, but his new recruit was a classical actor, not, like Irving, an idiosyncratic romantic. Irving had made a virtue of his physical awkwardness. Forbes-Robertson was graceful in movement and elegant in repose. In the event, it was during Irving's absence that he found his best opportunities, as Romeo to MRS PATRICK CAMPBELL's Juliet (1895) and above all as Hamlet (1897).

Forbes-Robertson was unquestionably the Hamlet of his generation, and the surviving silent film shows why. Grave and decorous, he displayed a feeling intelligence throughout the play. The part remained in his repertoire for the remaining 16 years of his theatrical career, and he made his farewell appearance in it at DRURY LANE in 1913. He was less suited to the emotional violence of other Shakespearian roles – Shylock, Leontes, Othello – though his admirers found no fault with him in them. It was the impish SHAW who perceived the classical Caesar in him and cajoled him into opening *Caesar and Cleopatra* dur-

ing an American tour (1906) with his American wife, GERTRUDE ELLIOTT (1874–1950), as Cleopatra. Forbes-Robertson's last famous creation was the Stranger in JEROME K. JEROME's *The Passing of the Third Floor Back* (1908). He was knighted in 1913, the year of his retirement from the stage. In his autobiography, *A Player under Three Reigns* (1925), he confesses that he never really enjoyed acting. PT

Ford, John c.1586–1640 English playwright of whose life very little is known. The order and precise dating of his work is the subject of scholarly debate, but it is generally believed that he wrote the subplot of *The Witch of Edmonton* (1621) and that he again collaborated with DEKKER on *The Welsh Ambassador* (1623) and *The Sun's Darling* (1624). This may mean that, by about 1620, he had abandoned a legal career and attached himself to an acting company. If so, the known products of his pen are surprisingly few. His subsequent fame rests on three plays. *Perkin Warbeck* (published 1634) may have revived in its original audiences memories of the old-fashioned chronicle play, but the characterization of the feckless hero is Ford's particular achievement. A startling interest in morbid psychology and emotional excess distinguishes his two major tragedies, *The Broken Heart* (c.1629) and *'Tis Pity She's a Whore* (c.1631). The second is the Caroline theatre's masterpiece. Its emotional centre is incestuous love, which Ford dares to treat with compassion and with a rhetorical delight in ethical paradox. His other surviving plays include three comedies, of which *The Lover's Melancholy* (1628) is the most interesting, and a tragedy, *Love's Sacrifice* (c.1632), most notable for its creation of the villainous D'Avalos, almost the last in a dramatic line of machiavellians. PT

Ford, John T. 1829–94 American theatre manager. A bookstore owner in Richmond, Virginia, Ford became the agent for a VARIETY troupe, and in 1855–6 leased theatres in Richmond, Baltimore and Washington, DC. The Richmond theatre closed at the beginning of the Civil War. In Washington he converted the First Baptist Church (1834) into Ford's Atheneum in 1861, and after it burned down in December 1862 he reopened it in August 1863 as Ford's Theatre; as a result of Lincoln's assassination, it was closed by the Army and purchased for offices and storage by the government (in 1893 during EDWIN BOOTH's funeral in New York the structure collapsed; in 1968 after government reconstruction it reopened). Ford continued to manage one or two theatres in Baltimore, and during 1873–86 he also managed the Grand Opera House in Washington, DC. In the 1880s he became the major producer of combination companies for the entire South. SMA DMCD

Foreman, Richard 1937– American director-designer-playwright. Foreman began the Ontological-Hysteric Theatre company in New York in 1968 as a means to present his own avant-garde works; since 1979 they have been co-produced by the NEW YORK SHAKESPEARE FESTIVAL, the Music Theatre Group/Lenox Art Center and the WOOSTER GROUP.

Until c.1975, Foreman was concerned with 'putting [an object] on stage and finding different ways of looking at it'.

In plays like *Total Recall* (1970), he used untrained performers directed not to show emotion; dialogue was disjointed, often recorded, and spoken without inflection. Furniture and props, which were suspended from the ceiling, were accorded as much focus and expressiveness as actors. Foreman ran the show like a conductor. Perched above the stage, he periodically sounded a loud buzzer that separated phrases of the attenuated action. More recently he has created pieces based directly on the ideas and sketches he collects in notebooks, often featuring a recurring character called Rhoda, played by Kate Manheim. With the stop-and-go action, accelerated parade of images, and his recorded comments on the performance in plays like *Pandering to the Masses* (1975), *Le Livre de Splendeurs* (Paris, 1976), *Penguin Touquet* (1981), *Egyptology* (1983) and *Film Is Evil: Radio Is Good* (1987), Foreman seeks to disrupt the audience's logical and teleological thought processes and 'force people to another level of consciousness'.

He has also directed plays by BÜCHNER, VÁCLAV HAVEL, Gertrude Stein and MOLIÈRE for such theatres as the HARTFORD STAGE COMPANY, the New York Shakespeare Festival and the AMERICAN REPERTORY THEATRE. In late 1991 he assumed control of the upstairs theatre at St Mark's Church in New York City ('Ontological at Saint Marks') to showcase his work and that of other companies, including *Samuel's Major Problems* (25th-anniversary production), an attenuated piece highlighted by a long meditation on death. Scripts and essays covering his first decade are collected in *Plays and Manifestos*, edited by Kate Davy (1976), and in *Reverberation Machines: The Later Plays and Essays* (1985); more recent work appears in *Love & Science* (1991) and *Unbalancing Acts* (1992). AS

Fornés, Maria Irene 1930– Cuban-born playwright and director who so exemplifies the concerns and style of OFF-BROADWAY theatre that she has won seven Obies since 1965, including one for sustained achievement (1982). Although her plays and MUSICALS deal with serious individual, national and global problems – *Tango Palace* (1964), *Promenade* (1965), *The Successful Life of Three* (1965), *Dr Kheal* (1968), *The Danube* (1984), *The Conduct of Life* (1985) and *Abingdon Square* (1987) – they are most acclaimed for their zany, whimsical humour and the use of innovative, cinematic techniques. Fornés's greatest critical success, *Fefu and Her Friends* (1977), is a feminist perspective on female friendship and women's roles in patriarchal society. In recent years her directorial interests have extended beyond her own plays to include standard works (*Hedda Gabler*, *Uncle Vanya*) and Latin American plays; other recent work includes *Lovers and Keepers* (1986) and *And What of the Night* (1989). FB

Forrest, Edwin 1806–72 The first American-born star. Forest dominated the American stage throughout the mid-19th century as Othello, Lear, Richard III, Coriolanus, Hamlet, Macbeth, Shylock and Richelieu; and in his repertoire of American plays: STONE's *Metamora*, BIRD's *The Gladiator* and *The Broker of Bogota* and Robert T. Conrad's *Jack Cade*, all of which had been winners in his playwriting contests (1829–47). Lear and Metamora were regarded as his best. Forrest's power derived from his commanding physique, penetrating voice, magnetic presence and strenuous REALISM in characters whose driving passions paralleled his own. Although only 5ft 10in in height, on stage his muscular frame seemed to tower like a giant. He was steady and predictable, in top form at every performance.

Born in Philadelphia, Forrest was stage-struck as a youngster, and at 15 studied the playing of THOMAS A. COOPER, EDMUND KEAN and JUNIUS BRUTUS BOOTH. Six years later, after appearing in Lexington, Louisville, Cincinnati and New Orleans, he performed with Kean and Cooper, and the next year alternated with Booth as Iago and Othello. He was quickly recognized as a star in the East and South, along the inland waterways, and later in the far West. He appeared in London in 1836 and again in 1845, when he challenged his British rival (W. C. MACREADY) – a rivalry that precipitated the disastrous ASTOR PLACE OPERA HOUSE riot (1849).

A superpatriot, Forrest was a colourful figure offstage and on. The lurid details of his divorce trial (1850) – *Forrest v. Catherine Sinclair* (she became a theatre manager in San Francisco) – filled the newspapers. He made a fortune, built Fonthill Castle on the Hudson, and had a spacious home in New York and another in Philadelphia (which was to become the Edwin Forrest Home for 'decayed' actors, in existence until the late 1980s). He closed his career with Shakespearian readings in Philadelphia, New York and Boston in 1872. RM

Forssell, Lars 1929– Prolific Swedish playwright, songwriter, poet, and a member of the Swedish Academy. He eschews REALISM in favour of a metatheatrical style employing songs and elements from CABARET, CIRCUS and popular entertainment. His plays mostly present a darkly pessimistic view of the world, frequently presenting the existential dilemma of characters who avoid the risk of love in an untrustworthy world, but thereby create solitudes of self-loathing from which they cannot escape. Examples are the Ventriloquist in *Charlie McDeath* (1961), Justus in *The Sunday Promenade* (1963), Gustav IV Adolf in *The Madcap* (1964), the Goat in *Show* (1970) and Fredman in *The Hare and the Buzzard* (1978). HL

Forte, Dieter 1935– Swiss dramatist, who writes in German and is known for *Martin Luther und Thomas Münzer oder die Einführung der Buchhaltung* (*Luther and Münzer, or the Introduction of Accountancy*, 1970), which applies the techniques of documentary theatre and polemical FARCE to the links between revolution, religion and finance during the Reformation. *Jean-Henri Dunant oder die Einführung der Zivilisation* (*Jean-Henri Dunant or the Introduction of Civilization*, 1975) is a similarly iconoclastic treatment of the founding of the Red Cross. HR

Fortune Theatre (London) Built in 1600, just outside Cripplegate in the Liberty of Finsbury, the Fortune was intended by HENSLOWE and ALLEYN to replace the ROSE as the home of the ADMIRAL'S MEN and rival to the GLOBE. The surviving building contract makes it abundantly clear that Henslowe had the Globe very much in mind and wished to copy many of its dimensions. In view of the fact that the Fortune was a square building, not a polygonal one, this emulation of the Globe posed (and poses) certain architectural problems. We know that the frame was to be 80ft square and the inner frame 55ft square. There were three tiers for spectators, and the covered stage was to be 43ft wide and 22-3ft deep, 'in all other proportions contrived and fashioned like unto the Stage of the said Play house called the Globe'. The venture was comparatively successful, and the Fortune was sufficiently prosperous to justify its rebuilding after destruction by fire in 1621. The second Fortune was probably polygonal. An important innovation was the use of brick in its building. It seems to have been an unlucky house whose reputation had declined some years before the CLOSURE OF THE THEATRES in 1642. Partially dismantled in 1649, it was demolished in 1661.

London's third Fortune was opened near Covent Garden in 1924. Successive managements have had to struggle to make it profitable largely because its capacity (424) is small for a commercial theatre.   PT

Fosse, Bob 1927-87 American choreographer and director. After beginning in VAUDEVILLE and BURLESQUE as a teenager, Fosse appeared as a dancer in touring companies of *Call Me Mister* and *Make Mine Manhattan*. He made his BROADWAY debut in *Dance Me a Song* (1950). His first choreography, created for *The Pajama Game* (1954), was influenced by JACK COLE's style of jazz dancing. His success with *The Pajama Game* was followed by choreography for *Damn Yankees* (1955) and *New Girl in Town* (1957). With *Redhead* (1959) Fosse began to direct as well as choreograph. In the 1960s he staged a number of successful MUSICALS, including *Sweet Charity* (1966). During the 1970s he created three unusual shows, closer in spirit to the SONDHEIM-PRINCE concept musicals: *Pippin* (1972), *Chicago* (1975) and *Dancin'* (1978). Fosse's frequent use of small groups, jerky, rhythmic steps, and sinuous, slow-motion movement, often coupled with bowler hats and white gloves, became his choreographic trademark. He also directed a number of films, including *Cabaret* and the autobiographical *All That Jazz*.   MK

Foster, Gloria 1936- African-American actress, noted for playing strong non-black characters. In her OFF-BROADWAY debut in the documentary collage *In White America* (1963), Foster won Obie and Vernon Rice awards. Playing the title role in Robinson Jeffers's *Medea* at the Martinique Theatre (1965-6), she gained the *Theatre World* Award for her outstanding performance. She was Yerma at the VIVIAN BEAUMONT THEATRE in 1966, and has appeared regularly at the PUBLIC THEATER in such roles as Volumnia (*Coriolanus*, 1979), *Mother Courage* (1980), and the mother in *Blood Wedding* (1992). She has also appeared in significant film roles and on television.   EGH

Fox, George W(ashington) L(afayette) 1825-77 American comedian who, after years of touring with the Fox-Howard clan (see HOWARD FAMILY), came into his own during his tenure at New York's National Theatre (1850-8), where his uproarious caricatures made him a favourite. He became influential in management by introducing his family's production of *UNCLE TOM'S CABIN*, himself in the role of Phineas Fletcher. He temporarily managed the Old

BOWERY, the New Bowery and the FIFTH AVENUE, losing as lessee what he earned as a comic star. Between 1862 and 67 he staged pantomimes at the Old Bowery, with himself as Clown and his brother Charles Kemble Fox as Pantaloon. More an expressive MIME artist than an acrobat, Fox tempered the stage trickery of the RAVEL FAMILY with his own antic drollery to create a purely American brand of PANTOMIME. This culminated in the immensely successful *Humpty Dumpty* (Olympic Theatre, 1868), which ran for more than 1200 performances. He also made a hit in BURLESQUES of *Faust*, *Macbeth*, *Richelieu* and EDWIN BOOTH's *Hamlet*. After recurring fits of insanity, he was forcibly removed from a performance in 1875 for committal to an asylum. Fox was reputed to be the funniest performer of his time; he contrived to raise American pantomime to a level of popularity it has never regained. A definitive biography by L. Senelick was published in 1988.   LS

Foy, Eddie 1856-1928 American comedian and singer. Beginning as a child performer in VAUDEVILLE, Foy brought his acrobatic style of comedy and his amusing delivery of comic songs to MUSICALS produced at the Chicago Opera House in 1889-90. His performance in *Bluebeard, Jr* (1890) received praise in both Chicago and New York. After appearing as a featured performer in several other comic OPERAS, he was hired as the principal comedian for *The Strollers* (1901). He starred in a number of musicals in the first decade of the 20th century, including *The Wild Rose* (1902), *Mr. Bluebeard* (1903), *Piff! Paff!! Pouf!!!* (1904), *The Earl and the Girl* (1905), *The Orchid* (1907), *Mr Hamlet of Broadway* (1908) and *Up and Down Broadway* (1910). Always a popular favourite in vaudeville, Foy spent most of his time on the VARIETY stage after 1910, when he began to include his children, billed as 'The Seven Little Foys', in his act. He published his autobiography, *Clowning through Life*, in 1928.   MK

Fragson [Fragmann], **Harry** [Leon Vince Philip Pott] 1866-1913 Anglo-French MUSIC-HALL performer, the son of a Belgian brewer. His career in England meeting with scant success, he tried his luck in Paris in 1891 and became an instant hit. His English accent, chic wardrobe, eloquent gestures and self-accompaniment on the piano (a novelty at the time) won him great popularity. Returning to London in 1905, he assumed a French accent and mannerisms. In the PANTOMIME *Cinderella* (DRURY LANE, 1906), the character Dandini was dubbed Dandigny in his honour. In France, his repertory had been comic and sentimental; in England it was dominated by such patter songs as 'The Other Department, If You Please'. The singer of the *entente cordiale*, as he was billed, was shot by his deranged father, who coveted one of his female admirers.   LS

France (See also MEDIEVAL DRAMA IN EUROPE (France).)
The 16th century The edict of the Paris parlement which in 1548 banned the performance of 'sacred mysteries' amounted to more than just the end of religious drama in France. It terminated a period in which theatre performance had given expression to the common beliefs held by all classes in the feudal order. The Roman Catholic Church, until then the biggest patron of the drama, became its most implacable enemy: for more than a

century French actors were not even allowed a church burial unless they made a deathbed renunciation of their profession. FARCES and MORALITY PLAYS continued to be performed, but they too were much restricted, especially in the capital, where the CONFRÉRIE DE LA PASSION was given a monopoly on all dramatic activity. Any company not performing in their new theatre, the HÔTEL DE BOURGOGNE, or with a licence obtained from them, was liable to a heavy fine.

One consequence of this was to silence the theatre as a voice of popular political protest: Pierre Gringore (d.1538) was the last performer of the century to be able to comment freely on affairs of state, though Brioché's puppet theatre on the Pont-Neuf indulged in mild SATIRE of Henri IV. Theatrical activity that survived in France through the 30-year period of civil war and religious persecution was precisely shaped to meet the needs of particular sectional interests. The Swiss Protestant Théodore de Bèze used biblical material, as the mysteries had done, for his *Abraham Sacrificing* (1550), and he had a certain following among Protestants, e.g. the *Tragédies saintes* (*Holy Tragedies*) of Louis de Masures (1563). Later Roman Catholic humanist writers were to turn to biblical subjects, but treated in a more classical manner, e.g. LA TAILLE's *Saul Enraged* (1572) and GARNIER's *The Jewish Women* (1583). The rapidly expanding Jesuit colleges also put on annual performances of religious plays, though the texts were, at first, in Latin. In academic and court circles a more important influence was the group of humanist poets known as the Pléiade. For the humanists the only suitable models of good dramaturgical practice were the authors of classical Greece and Rome, although their plays show them to have been at least as much influenced by the Italian *commedia erudita*. The first French tragedy of this kind was ÉTIENNE JODELLE's *Cleopatra Captive*, performed before the king in 1552 with the 20-year-old author in the role of Cleopatra, but the first to be written in Alexandrines (the 12-syllable line advocated by the Pléiade) was *The Death of Caesar* by Jacques Grévin in 1560. The main inspiration for these tragedies was SENECA; they were short on dramatic action and long on monologue. Moreover, their slavish imitation of the ancient world meant that reference to 16th-century France was almost entirely absent. The one author who managed to inject some contemporary urgency into his tragedies was Robert Garnier, whose *Antigone* (1580) was thus the first in a long line of French plays of that title using the downfall of the house of Oedipus as an oblique reference to contemporary events. Garnier's *The Jewish Women* also makes a powerful comment on cruelty at times of religious strife.

Many of the humanist authors also published theoretical statements of their dramaturgical aims: La Taille's treatise on the art of TRAGEDY (1562) echoes ARISTOTLE and HORACE; the same author's prologue to *The Rivals* (1574) heaps scorn on the native farce tradition, advocating a return to the methods of classical 'new comedy'. Jodelle's *Eugene* (1552) was the first such comedy, but although written in five acts and respecting the unity of time, the play's subject, cuckoldry, and its octosyllabic verse form were indistinguishable from those of French farce. PIERRE DE LARIVEY's comedies (the first six published in 1579) were close copies of the Italian *commedia*, but transposed into

a vigorous French idiom: Odet de Turnèbe's *The Happy Ones* (1584) managed a more original plot and characters while respecting the new humanist rules. The French humanists derived from their study of the classics and of the Italians the idea of theatre as an autonomous, stylized world, not as a simple transposition or symbolic representation of real life. The key factor was the change in the playing space. The medieval simultaneous staging, with actors visible throughout, had made no radical distinction between the world and the stage. By copying the Roman stage (see THEATRE DESIGN (Roman theatre)) and by building sets representing a public square or cross-roads set in perspective, the Italians had introduced a new kind of space: one which did not represent a particular location but which functioned as an empty space to be transformed by the presence of an actor.

In France, however, although authors were trying to apply new methods, the precarious state of the professional theatre made real progress difficult until the 1630s. In staging, especially, it was a long time before the medieval system of simultaneous staging gave way before Italian influence, as is shown by the manuscript *Mémoire* of MAHELOT. Henri IV attempted to improve the state of the theatre, even authorizing the performance of MYSTERY PLAYS, but the parlement confirmed its earlier veto. There is evidence of the existence of several itinerant companies working in the provinces at this time. In 1595 performances by such companies were permitted at the Paris fairs of St Germain in the spring and St Laurent in the autumn, and in 1598 the Confrérie allowed Pierre Venier's company to move from the St Germain fair into a hall at the Hôtel d'Argent on payment of a tax for each performance given. A year later VALLERAN LE CONTE took his company from the provinces to Paris, signing a three-month lease at the Hôtel de Bourgogne.

Valleran's company dramatist was ALEXANDRE HARDY, an immensely prolific playwright and the first to make this a professional career. He was more interested in lively dramatic action than in theoretical rules. In addition to the *commedia erudita*, he had been influenced by the COMMEDIA DELL'ARTE (the first of these Italian companies visited France in the 1570s, after which they were frequent visitors) and by the Italian vogue for PASTORALS. Hardy wrote many pastorals which, with their idealized worlds and analysis of emotional states, have been seen as the major source for French classical COMEDY. Hardy also borrowed from Spanish models and began another influential vogue for tragicomedies, often drawn from Spanish romance, filled with sensational action and quite unconcerned to observe the unities.

The 17th century For the first quarter of the 17th century, the theatrical profession continued precarious, theatres being associated with low life and crude performance. The favoured court entertainment was the ballet: Henri IV and Marie de Medici commissioned large numbers of allegorical ballets and passed their love of dancing on to Louis XIII and Louis XIV. But in the 1630s and 1640s RICHELIEU showed what could be achieved by determined patronage. Under a famous farce player, GROS-GUILLAUME, a company had established itself as the Comédiens du Roi at the Hôtel de Bourgogne. Richelieu put an end to their monopoly in 1634 by encouraging MONTDORY to bring his itinerant company to Paris and settle at the MARAIS theatre. This building was a former tennis court, previously hired out for occasional performances, which Montdory now rebuilt. Richelieu encouraged a spirit of rivalry between this new company and the Comédiens du Roi. He gave practical assistance to both by commissioning a group of five authors including MAIRET, ROTROU and PIERRE CORNEILLE to write tragedies, and he promoted a decree which, in 1641, recognized the legal status of the acting profession. Other important factors in making the theatre more socially acceptable were the salons, devoted to raising standards in literature, and the Académie-Française, which received its royal charter in 1635.

Encouraged by improved conditions, a group of new playwrights emerged; the definitions of tragedy formulated by La Taille's generation were taken up and refined, for example in Mairet's *Sylvanire*, whose preface formulated the three unities and advocated 'the study of a sudden psychological crisis'. Mairet's *Sophonisbe* (1634) and TRISTAN L'HERMITE's *Marianne* (1636), tragedies of high-flown verse and sentiment, were considered successful exemplars by contemporaries, which explains why the prodigious success of Pierre Corneille's TRAGICOMEDY of love and revenge, *Le Cid* (1637), sparked off the flurry of pamphlets and discussion known as the *querelle du Cid*. Corneille was mortified by the doubt cast on his work's classical credentials, and in the early 1640s followed it with four tragedies drawn from Roman history . These were perfectly regular, exalted duty and concern for honour, but also justice and clemency, and were written in sonorous Alexandrines of great rhetorical power, well exploited by FLORIDOR and other members of the Marais company who performed them.

Corneille had at first attracted attention with his comedies at the Marais in the 1630s. Characterized by elegant style and elevated tone, but also by a new realism, both in setting and in depiction of character, they were quickly perceived as models of classical comedy, owing little to farce and much to TERENCE and the *commedia*. SCUDÉRY's *The Actors' Comedy* (1635) and Corneille's *The Theatrical Illusion* (1636) demonstrate theatre's growing self-awareness concerning its own artistic and aesthetic means. These comedies at the Marais eclipsed the performances at the Hôtel de Bourgogne by the celebrated trio of farce players Gros-Guillaume, GAULTIER-GARGUILLE and Turlupin, which were a mixture of lewd jokes, expressive MIME and verbal comedy, the latter being the main inheritance from the old French farce tradition. While Gros-Guillaume retained the traditional floured face, Turlupin exhibited the influence of the Italian comedians with a costume similar to that of Brighella. Two other traditional stand-up comics, also known to act in plays, were TABARIN and BRUSCAMBILLE, both of whose comic monologues were sufficiently popular to be published during their lifetimes. The last of the old-style comic actors was JODELET, for whom SCARRON wrote a vehicle-play, *Jodelet, or The Master-servant*, in 1645, and for whom MOLIÈRE later wrote a leading role in *Les Précieuses Ridicules* (1659).

After the death of Gros-Guillaume in 1634 BELLEROSE took over management of the Hôtel de Bourgogne, but he and his resident dramatist Rotrou were no match for the Marais with Corneille as dramatist and actors such as Montdory and Floridor. The Marais theatre was extensively rebuilt after a fire in 1644. In 1647 the Hôtel de Bourgogne followed suit, also inducing both Floridor and Corneille to move there, after which the Marais lost its preeminence, turning more to 'machine plays'. The first building to be constructed specifically for theatre performance this century was the Palais Cardinal, built by Lemercier for Richelieu and inaugurated in 1641. After the cardinal's death in 1642 it reverted to the crown, becoming known as the PALAIS-ROYAL. Paris thus had three modern theatres by the 1640s and to these was added the auditorium in the PETIT-BOURBON palace, equipped by TORELLI, whom Cardinal Mazarin summoned from Italy in 1645 to install the latest machinery for spectacular scene changes, flying effects, and so on. This was at first used for Italian OPERA, but later also for machine plays. It was demolished in 1660 to be replaced by an even grander SALLE DES MACHINES at the Tuileries palace, equipped by Torelli's great rival VIGARANI.

During this period provincial companies continued to prosper: after the financial collapse of the Illustre-Théâtre founded by the BÉJARTS with the young Molière in 1645, they had earned their living touring the provinces for 13 years before returning to Paris in 1658. The centralizing tendencies of Louis XIV were to redress the balance in favour of the Paris region in the second half of the century, though Versailles did not acquire a permanent theatre building until just before the Revolution (1770). Under Louis XIV the lavish court festivities were given on large improvised stages. These provided the extensive acting areas required for the ballets in which Louis himself liked to dance. Many of Molière's plays and *comédies-ballets* were first performed as part of such festivities. In the town theatres the stages were more confined: long and narrow, with the acting area further reduced by the young nobles who would pay a high price for a seat on the stage. The practice of selling seats on the stage seems to have started at the Marais during the immensely popular run of *Le Cid* (1637). At first limited to about 30, the seating on the sides of the stage later expanded to more than 200. This crowd of spectators on the stage was a constant annoyance to actors, designers and playwrights. Not until 1759 was the practice abolished, after a campaign led by LEKAIN.

In the 1650s and 1660s the range of Parisian theatrical entertainment developed rapidly. As well as BURLESQUE comedy, whose major exponent was Scarron, and comedies of intrigue based on Italian or Spanish models by such writers as Rotrou, QUINAULT and THOMAS CORNEILLE, the Italian company of TIBERIO FIORILLI took up permanent residence, sharing a theatre with Molière. There was also a vogue for romanesque tragedy, with plots borrowed from contemporary novels, notably the influential and interminable pastoral *L'Astrée* by Honoré d'Urfé, but also the writings of Madeleine de Scudéry and La Calprenède. But the genre with most prestige (and the one in which Molière wanted to excel) was tragedy.

This period saw Corneille's late tragedies of political power in the ancient world and his eclipse by his younger rival RACINE who, in the ten-year period 1667–77, wrote the seven plays now considered to be the crowning glory of French classical tragedy. In these, he largely avoided the romanesque, borrowing most of his plots from classical antiquity and effortlessly observing the rules. Even when depicting the most extreme characters or situations, he strove to maintain *vraisemblance* – the quality of verisimilitude, without which, he held, it was impossible to touch the spectators' emotions. His own tragic formula was expressed in the preface to *Bérénice* (1670) as 'a simple action sustained by the violence of the passions, the beauty of the sentiments and the elegance of the language'. Unlike Molière, whose prose plays are as effective as those written in verse, much of Racine's power in the theatre stems from his supreme mastery of the Alexandrine verse form. Racine's first two plays were staged by Molière, but he transferred to the Hôtel de Bourgogne because of its pre-eminence in tragedy. He took with him, as his mistress, Molière's best tragic actress, Mlle du Parc, but again transferred his affections to MLLE CHAMPMESLÉ, another Marais actress, for whom he wrote his major female roles from Bérénice to Phèdre. After *Phèdre* (1667) he withdrew from the theatre, was reconciled with the Church, and only wrote two further tragedies, both on biblical subjects at Mme de Maintenon's request for performance by the girls at the Saint-Cyr school.

The works which have survived best from this period are the comedies of Molière, first written and produced in 14 years of intense activity from 1659 till his death in 1673. Their rich use of situation and dialogue, often exploiting traditional farce schemas to develop sophisticated comedy of character and ideas, has led to constant revivals in subsequent centuries. Part of their success at the time was doubtless due to the excellence of Molière's company, which included LA GRANGE, whose register of daily takings is one of the main sources of information about the company. Molière received a stream of royal commissions for court entertainments; because of his powerful protector he was also able to tackle dangerous subjects such as religious hypocrisy in *Tartuffe*. But Molière had to contend with intense professional jealousy, both from rival companies and from the composer LULLY, who also enjoyed the unstinting support of Louis XIV. Although Lully collaborated with Molière on many *comédies-ballets*, his ambition was to create a French opera in which pride of place would go to the music, reducing the role of the dramatist. He achieved this on Molière's death when he took possession of his theatre, the Palais-Royal. Vigarani converted the stage, which remained the home of Paris opera until 1763. Some of Molière's company went to the Hôtel de Bourgogne, the rest were merged with the Marais company which moved, with the Italians, into a theatre in the rue Guénégaud.

In 1680, on the death of La Thorillière, manager of the Hotel de Bourgogne, the king merged the two companies so as to create 'la seule troupe des comédiens du roi'. The new troupe contained 15 actors and 12 actresses who were none too pleased, at first, to be merged. But Louis rewarded them with a regular subsidy and monopoly of French-language performances in the capital; they quickly became known as the COMÉDIE-FRANÇAISE to distinguish them from the COMÉDIE-ITALIENNE, which moved to the Hôtel de Bourgogne. The Italians continued to be popular and began introducing more French material, but as Louis came under the influence of the devout Mme de Maintenon the Italians' brand of comedy became less acceptable. They were finally banished in 1697, to return in 1716 with the accession of Louis XV. The Comédie-Française also suffered from prevailing attitudes, when in 1687 the king ordered them to leave the rue Guénégaud because a new college was to be opened nearby and there were fears for the students' morals. They were allowed to buy an old tennis court in what is now the rue de l'Ancienne Comédie, St Germain des Prés, where they had a new theatre built. Their repertoire during the remaining years of the century consisted largely of plays by Molière, Corneille and Racine, to which were added Molièresque comedies written by members of the company, including the leading actor, BARON, whose most successful comedy was *The Philanderer* (1686); and Charles Champmeslé and Noël-Jacques Hauteroche, both of whom exploited the figure of the comic valet Crispin, originally developed by the actor RAYMOND POISSON. Molière's example was to dominate comic playwriting for a long time to come; without entirely escaping from his shadow, a group of playwrights including Dufresny, REGNARD, DANCOURT and LESAGE established a brilliant if cynical comedy of manners giving an uncomfortably realistic portrait of contemporary French society. Among the most effective are Lesage's *Crispin Rival of his Master* (1707) and *Turcaret* (1709), the latter exposing a society motivated entirely by greed through its central character, a tax-farmer.

The 18th century If Molière's example dominated the comic dramatists, writers of tragedy were completely overshadowed by Racine and Corneille. Their influence was reinforced by the work of critics, notably BOILEAU and D'AUBIGNAC, whose *Practice of Theatre* (1657) developed the neoclassical rules into a systematic code of practice for the playwright. Corneille himself published three *Discourses on Dramatic Art* in 1660, and the result of so much critical and theoretical analysis was that all subsequent writers of tragedy found themselves obliged to follow a formula. Nevertheless, new tragedies written in this way were a successful part of the Comédie-Française's repertoire throughout the 18th century, the most prolific author being VOLTAIRE, whose worthy but dull plays combined respect for the rules with crusades against bigotry. Voltaire helped to promote greater respect for the acting profession, protesting at the Church's refusal to bury ADRIENNE LECOUVREUR and assisting Clairon and Lekain in their campaign to clear the audience off the stage (this was partly to make room for the crowd scenes which he introduced under the influence of SHAKESPEARE). CRÉBILLON, while also respecting the rules, introduced more sensational subject-matter, pointing the way towards melodrama. But despite undistinguished tragic writing, the century marked a high point in the influence of French theatre throughout Europe. In aristocratic cultural circles the aesthetic purity and elevated tone of French tragedy in particular was widely admired. Comedy was marked by more innovation, partly because of the outstanding qualities of two playwrights, MARIVAUX and BEAUMARCHAIS, but mostly because of the growing importance of fairground theatres and other forms of entertainment.

Soon after the Comédie-Italienne returned under LUIGI RICCOBONI they were permitted to perform plays in French, and it was for them that Marivaux wrote most of his comedies. These at first exploited stock types such as HARLEQUIN in *Harlequin Refined by Love* (1720), but rapidly developed an original vein of psychological dialogue concentrating exclusively on the process of self-discovery occasioned by young love. Although not overwhelmingly successful in his own time, Marivaux has always remained in the repertoire and has enjoyed a great vogue among recent directors including PLANCHON and CHÉREAU. More successful in Marivaux's day were the *comédies larmoyantes*, or sentimental comedies, of DESTOUCHES and LA CHAUSSÉE. This new genre constituted the main French contribution to the development of comedy in the 18th century, although the plays have not weathered well. Their demonstrations of uncomplaining virtue rewarded after long trials soon palled, although they were the mainstay of the Comédie-Française repertoire in their time. Their generally improving tone paved the way for DIDEROT's demand, in his treatise published with his play *The Natural Son* (1757), for a new genre mid-way between comedy and tragedy named *le drame* — serious domestic drama investigating the real conditions in which people live. ROUSSEAU's celebrated condemnation of theatre for its frivolous and corrupting influence only led playwrights to make more emphatic claims for their moral seriousness; one of the few to match these claims with a good play was SEDAINE, whose *A Philosopher without Knowing It* was first performed at the Comédie-Française in 1765.

The bulk of Sedaine's output was written for the more theatrically vital Comédie-Italienne and the fairground theatres, home of the more vigorous forms of popular entertainment. In the course of the century, companies playing at the fairs became progressively cleverer at evading the monopoly, using MIME, dance, songs and placards to get round the ban on spoken dialogue. The *comédie-vaudeville* style that they evolved became so popular that it led the Italians to copy them, developing their own form of comic opera. In 1762 the Italians amalgamated with the Opéra-Comique, which had been playing at the fairs for many years and had experienced particular success under FAVART since 1757. In 1783 the combined troupe moved from the Hôtel de Bourgogne into a new theatre on the Boulevard des Italiens, so named in their honour. During this period the theatre booths of the Boulevard du Temple were also becoming more successful. The first person to establish a regular theatre here (despite opposition from the Comédie-Française) was NICOLET, with a troupe of acrobats and performing monkeys. He built a new theatre, named the Gaîté, and was followed to the Boulevard du Temple by Audinot, who in 1769 moved his MARIONETTES to the Ambigu-Comique, and by Fleury de l'Écluze, who opened the Variétés-Amusantes in 1779 (see BOULEVARD).

By the early 1770s both Nicolet and Audinot were flouting the monopoly laws by broadening their repertoires, but both were successful with all classes of theatregoers and were even invited to perform before Louis XV at Versailles. After the Revolution, restrictions on these theatres were lifted: article 1 of a law passed in January 1791 stated that 'any citizen will be able to open a public the-

atre and to have performed there plays in all genres'. Equally important was the lifting of a heavy tax that these theatres had been obliged to pay to the Opéra since 1784. French opera, like French tragedy, was widely admired in the 18th century as first Rameau and then GLUCK transformed it into a dramatic form in its own right. A similar development occurred in dance under the influence of Noverre. Together with the brilliant displays of the designer SERVANDONI, these developments help to explain the number of new theatres erected throughout France in the second half of the century. These included Gabriel's opera house at Versailles (1770), Ledoux's theatre at Besançon (1784) and VICTOR LOUIS's theatre at Bordeaux (1780).

The last major comic dramatist of the century was Beaumarchais. Influenced, like Sedaine, by Diderot, he wrote several serious domestic dramas but is remembered for his comedies *The Barber of Seville* and *The Marriage of Figaro*. Their combination of traditional comic devices with an underlying note of serious social and psychological comments makes them models of comic drama and suitable for setting to music, as Rossini and Mozart have shown. An astute businessman, Beaumarchais tried to institute a system of royalty payments to playwrights, something that became legally established early in the following century. *The Marriage of Figaro* was considered dangerously anti-authoritarian, and permission for performance at the Comédie-Française was withheld for 9 years. This only served to magnify the play's success when it was performed in 1784. More than any other play of its time, *The Marriage of Figaro* heralded a period when theatre was once again to become a focus for challenging political ideas.

The 19th century As well as liberating the theatres, the French Revolution set up open-air festivities organized by the painter David, at which the crowd were not merely spectators but participants as in the medieval mysteries. Rapidly a new theatre audience emerged, made up of citizens eager for powerful emotions and strong dramatic situations. These needs were met by MELODRAMA. Early French melodrama brought together the movement and energy of popular entertainment with the social concern of the late-18th-century domestic drama and the love of the picturesque characteristic of romanticism. The companies who performed the early melodramas were those who, before the Revolution, had relied on acrobatic turns or comic dance acts. When they doubled as actors, their performances were characterized by large, precise gestures tending to flow into grand spectacular tableaux. This was obviously appropriate for the popular comic *vaudevilles*, but also helped to shape the more tragic melodramas.

The outstanding writer of melodramas was PIXÉRÉCOURT, who claimed he wrote for 'those who cannot read' and often directed his own plays, attaching great importance to the visual aspects of production. Pixérécourt's protagonists are caught up in a cosmic battle between the forces of good and evil, often building up to a spectacular climax such as the eruption of Vesuvius on stage at the end of *Death's Head, or The Ruins of Pompeii* (1827). Another dramatic genre which found favour with new audiences was equestrian drama (see HIPPODRAMA) performed in a circus ring with a stage behind. The first such permanent CIRCUS was erected by ASTLEY in 1780. After the Revolution he abandoned it to the Franconi brothers, whose success led them to build the CIRQUE OLYMPIQUE in 1807. Here they put on mass spectacles celebrating the Napoleonic Empire, incorporating both equestrian acts and dramatic tableaux. In 1815 the Restoration put a stop to Napoleonic myth-making, but after 1830 such shows became even more popular and others followed, celebrating colonial conquest, e.g. *L'Empire* (1845), which concluded with an apotheosis of Napoleon. In the second half of the century circuses reverted to ACROBATICS, CLOWNing and animal acts (at one time there were 5 permanent circuses in Paris), while large Hippodromes were constructed for the performance of mass spectacle.

During the late 18th and early 19th centuries fruitful links grew up between the pictorial and dramatic arts, boosted by Diderot's concept of domestic drama as a succession of truthful pictures and by the popularity of the spectacular. In 1800, for example, a staging of Salieri's *Les Horaces* brought to life David's painting *The Oath of the Horatii*, a scene which had already been enacted at the Festival of the Supreme Being in 1794. This was also the period of the panorama and the diorama, in which audiences viewed tableaux displaying the skill of such scene-painters as Daguerre, inventor of photography. Further evidence of the renewed importance of visual aspects in theatre performance can be seen in the success of DEBURAU, whose MIME plays at the THÉÂTRE DES FUNAMBULES were continuously successful in the 1820s and 30s. The Revolution also sparked an enormous increase in the number of French theatres: in 1791 alone more than 20 new theatres were opened in Paris. But Napoleon soon limited this new-found freedom, reintroducing CENSORSHIP in 1804 and restricting the number of Paris theatres to eight (plus the circus) in 1807. Napoleon took a keen interest in the theatre and was a friend of TALMA, the actor who had led the pro-revolutionary faction of the Comédie-Française. By appearing in Voltaire's *Brutus* (1789) dressed in Roman garb, Talma had started a fashion for authentic costume which spread rapidly; delight in historical detail marks another point of contact between the visual and performing arts at this time.

Despite the vitality of theatre life after the Revolution, it was not until the 1830s that a major challenge to the literary tradition of classical tragedy appeared in the form of the romantic verse dramas of HUGO and DUMAS père. The riots in the theatre at the first performance of *Hernani* in 1830 were occasioned not merely by Hugo's open scorn for the classical rules. They were also a response to the introduction into the Comédie-Française of elements associated with popular drama: Pixérécourt's use of local colour had clearly influenced Dumas and Hugo. Other more respectable influences like SCHILLER and Shakespeare were still deemed barbarous by French aesthetic criteria, and also had demonstrable connections with melodrama – Schiller's *The Robbers* was the model for one of the earliest melodramas, Lamartellière's *Robert the Robber King* (1793). The first complete edition of Shakespeare's works in French had appeared in 1776–82 and he was to be a pervasive influence on dramatic writing, reinforced by visits of English theatre companies to Paris. A third important

element in the controversy surrounding *Hernani* was Hugo's standing as a political writer: his earlier historical drama *Marion de Lorme* had been banned by the censor, and many of his plays, especially *Ruy Blas* (1838), contain a meditation on the nature of political power clearly applicable to the contemporary French situation.

The theoretical basis for romantic drama had been set out three years earlier by Hugo in the preface to his play *Cromwell* (1827). It involved mixing the genres which had been so carefully separated by the French classical theatre, combining elements of the sublime and the grotesque in the same play. It also advocated a Shakespearian flexibility in the use of time and space, and looked to European rather than to Roman history for its subjects. For ten years, both at the Comédie-Française and at the Porte-Saint-Martin theatre, the plays of Hugo and Dumas drew enthusiastic audiences. Together with VIGNY, whose *Chatterton* (1835) gave MARIE DORVAL one of her greatest roles, they were responsible for establishing a new dramatic genre. But it was surprisingly short-lived – Hugo's *Les Burgraves*, a failure at the Comédie-Française in 1843, was the last of its kind, although EDMOND ROSTAND's verse plays, written some 50 years later, rely on many of the same qualities. Allied to the romantic dramatists through his historical epic *Lorenzaccio* (written in 1834), MUSSET did not at first imagine that this play could be staged, and he aimed many of his distinctive short comedies at the reader rather than at the spectator. He was, however, a skilful dramatist, successfully achieving a fluid, Shakespearian style and his works have enjoyed frequent revival; SARAH BERNHARDT played the title role of *Lorenzaccio* in 1896, and this play was important in the early success of VILAR at AVIGNON and the THÉÂTRE NATIONAL POPULAIRE, with GÉRARD PHILIPE in the title role in 1952.

The most prolific comic dramatist of the early 19th century was SCRIBE, who strengthened the somewhat unstructured *vaudeville* form, turning it into the comedy situation, subsequently dubbed WELL MADE PLAY by the critic SARCEY. Scribe was a master of complicated intrigue and *coups de théâtre*, and his methods were copied by the equally successful SARDOU. LABICHE took this form and used it for a biting SATIRE of the mid-19th-century bourgeoisie in plays whose visual qualities provoke comparison with Daumier. Labiche's combination of accurate social analysis and sense of the grotesque has led to recent revivals presenting him as a forerunner both of the THEATRE OF THE ABSURD and of political theatre. Other successful comic dramatists were the MEILHAC AND HALÉVY duo, who wrote witty librettos for OFFENBACH's OPERETTAS, and FEYDEAU, who developed the form known as French farce – a comic satire of the sexual mores of the bourgeoisie.

Melodrama continued popular throughout the century, with BOUCHARDY and DENNERY taking over from Pixérécourt. For a prolific author, this genre could provide rich earnings, but the people who profited most were the new breed of star actors or *monstres sacrés*, the most famous of whom was FRÉDÉRICK LEMAÎTRE. Frédérick, as he was known, achieved fame in 1824 by PARODYing a feeble melodrama and, in the process, creating the figure of Robert Macaire, who took on a life of his own. Like other successful actors and actresses of the period (e.g. BOCAGE, COQUELIN, DÉJAZET, Dorval, MÉLINGUE, POTIER, RÉJANE) his services were disputed by the different theatres. He performed in all types of play, from high romantic drama to popular melodrama, sometimes running into trouble with the censor for introducing political satire into his performances. Frédérick never performed at the Comédie-Française, which for many performers constituted the summit of their art. RACHEL, for example, had her greatest successes playing Racine and Corneille there, and Sarah Bernhardt rose to become a *sociétaire* before her reputation became so great that she was able to branch out on her own, becoming both star, director and theatre manager.

In 1864 Napoleon III removed the last restrictions on the exploitation of theatres and the result was an enormous boom in theatre building, especially along the new *grands boulevards* being constructed under Baron Haussmann. The most elaborate new theatre to be erected was the Paris Opéra, designed by Charles Garnier with the encouragement of Napoleon III. OPERA played an important role in the theatrical life of 19th-century France, an importance reflected in the four Parisian theatres – the Opéra, the Opéra-Comique, the Théâtre Lyrique, the Bouffes Parisiens – which gave regular performances in the second half of the century. Most successful were the light operas of composers Meyerbeer and Jacques Halévy, for both of whom Scribe wrote librettos. Georges Bizet had less success, initially, in his attempts to promote a taste for REALISM, e.g. with his music for Alphonse Daudet's *L'Arlésienne* (1872) and his opera *Carmen* (1875).

The realist movement in the other arts found a faint dramatic echo in the plays of AUGIER and DUMAS *fils*, but it was left to NATURALISM to bring about a real change in acting, production and playwriting. The force of naturalism as a cultural movement stemmed from its assertion that it was based on scientific principles. ZOLA, its main spokesman, borrowed ideas from contemporary medical and social theory as well as from Darwin. In addition to his novels and other writings, he mounted a campaign for the theatre to be treated seriously as a kind of laboratory of social relations. But, like Diderot in the previous century, though a powerful novelist and thinker, Zola was not a good dramatist. The French contribution to naturalism was largely the work of the pioneering director ANTOINE, who aimed to present new plays dealing with contemporary issues. He encouraged writers to attempt short one-act plays representing social conditions, and promoted a generation of minor dramatists including Ancey, BECQUE, BRIEUX, Bernstein, Courteline, ROMAINS and Mirbeau. Lacking major new French plays, he introduced the work of the German, Scandinavian and Russian naturalists to the French stage and also produced several of Shakespeare's plays for the first time. Antoine was a sensitive director of actors, encouraging an intimate, truthful performance style, and was also the first director to treat the stage setting as a realistic environment rather than a decorative or spectacular background. As a reaction against naturalism, Paul Fort set up the Théâtre d'Art in 1890 to promote poetic and symbolist work (see SYMBOLISM), an aim that was continued by LUGNÉ-POE at the Théâtre de l'Oeuvre from 1893. Lugné-Poe staged the work of several important new dramatists, including CLAUDEL, Crommelynck and MAETERLINCK. He also put on the first

performance of JARRY's *Ubu Roi* (1896), a play which was to be an inspiration to the 20th-century theatrical avant-garde.

The 20th century Although the innovations of both naturalism and symbolism were to prove influential, little seemed changed during the period of the *belle époque* (1890–1914). The majority of French theatres were devoted to light comic entertainment that could do nothing to shock the sensibilities of their newly prosperous bourgeois patrons. JACQUES COPEAU explicitly condemned this state of affairs as corrupt, and set up his VIEUX-COLOMBIER theatre in 1913 to restore the dignity of an art form that had once been the central expression of society's religious and social beliefs. Like Antoine, he failed to call forth any major new dramatists and his repertoire was based on the classics, especially Shakespeare and Molière. Under his guidance, JOUVET rebuilt the stage of the theatre to resemble the Elizabethan playing space; on this bare stage, almost devoid of scenery, he encouraged his actors to develop a performance style that was physically inventive (based on researches into the *commedia dell'arte*) but also truthful and direct. He also set up an influential theatre school, where many outstanding actors and directors of the century were trained.

Two of Copeau's original group, DULLIN and Jouvet, set up their own companies soon after the end of the First World War; in 1927 they joined together with GEORGES PITOËFF, a Russian émigré, and BATY to form the CARTEL. This group of actors and directors was responsible for introducing new standards of production and for creating an identifiable form of art theatre in the interwar years. Internationalist in outlook, their productions included work from Russia, Germany, Britain and America. They also brought a major new influence to bear on French playwriting with their productions of plays by PIRANDELLO, whose shadow hovers over the work of most successful dramatists of the 1930s and 1940s, notably SALACROU and ANOUILH. A long-lasting partnership between Jouvet and GIRAUDOUX helped the latter to develop into the outstanding dramatist of the interwar period. Urbane and witty, many of his plays return to the classical sources of 17th- and 18th-century settings, achieving their effects from unexpected juxtaposition.

Despite their considerable achievements, the Cartel did not affect the majority of French theatre output between the wars; this continued to consist of boulevard plays by such writers as Bataille, Bernstein, Bourdet and GUITRY. The success of the boulevard play continued well into the 1950s and 1960s, sustaining a large number of commercial theatres in Paris, including some of considerable artistic merit like the ATELIER which, under BARSACQ, produced an impressive number of new plays including the work of Anouilh, Marcel Aymé, Félicien Marceau and René de Obaldia. Other successful authors of the boulevard, such as André Roussin and Marcel Achard, were able to build up a personal following, but with the growing importance of the French cinema and television industry, star actors have been tempted away from the stage. This, combined with the growth of subsidized theatre, has contributed to the demise of French boulevard theatres. Those which survive do so mostly on sex comedies

Daguerre's setting for Act II of Ducange's *Elodie*, showing how he carried over the basic principles of the panorama and diorama into his stage design by dividing the stage into two main areas and varying lighting intensity to give a sense of considerable depth. Ambigu-Comique, 1822.

imported from the English-speaking theatre.

By the end of the 1930s the reforms of Copeau and the Cartel had helped to create conditions in which theatre was seen once more as a significant element in French cultural life; there was a revival of interest in Catholic theatre, and the Popular Front government promoted mass performances of socialist inspiration. Authors began once again to turn to the stage as a forum for serious political and philosophical ideas. Begun by Giraudoux in the 1930s, this continued in the 1940s and 1950s when SARTRE, CAMUS and Anouilh helped to promote the theatre to the forefront of French intellectual life. Sartre adopted old-fashioned dramaturgical models, revivifying the 19th-century melodramatic structures by an emphasis on existentialist choice. His first director was Dullin, who was permitted to put on *The Flies* in 1943 despite its clear call to resistance. In the following decade Sartre wrote a number of commercially successful plays dramatizing the problems of personal identity in the light of both moral and political choices. Similar concerns found expression in the plays of Camus and Anouilh, whose *Antigone* (1944) was interpreted by some as justifying collaboration, by others as encouraging resistance.

The four years of German occupation (1940–4) were an important period for the subsequent development of both commercial and subsidized theatre in France. The commercial theatre experienced a boom whose momentum carried it beyond the years of postwar austerity. In addition, the foundations were laid for the post-war DECENTRALIZATION MOVEMENT by men such as Vilar, DASTÉ and COUSIN, who shared a vision of theatre as a cultural force for freedom extended to all Frenchmen, not just the cognoscenti of the capital. They looked back to the pioneering work of GÉMIER, who had founded the Théâtre National Populaire in 1920, and to the work of LÉON CHANCEREL and the COMPAGNIE DES QUINZE in the 1930s. The immediate postwar years saw a flowering of new theatre work both in Paris and the provinces based on an affirmation of traditional French cultural values. In Paris, JEAN-LOUIS BARRAULT, with Madeleine Renaud, set up a company whose high reputation was built partly on brilliant productions of the classical French repertoire, partly on more recent playwrights, especially Claudel. With MARCEL MARCEAU and Jacques Lecoq, he also helped to revive the tradition of mime. The Grenier-Hussenot company breathed new life into the traditional French farce with inventive, acrobatic productions, half-way between theatre and CABARET. In the provinces five new centres of dramatic creation were established, supported by local and central government funding; strongly influenced by the example and writings of Copeau, these at first concentrated on the classical repertoire.

It was not until the 1950s that a major new dramaturgical form appeared, giving expression to the modern sense of anguish and despair by means of stage images both stark and concrete. The THEATRE OF THE ABSURD (or 'new theatre', by analogy with the *nouveau roman*) was the work of playwrights who were all outside the mainstream of French tradition – BECKETT, IONESCO, ADAMOV, GENET – and of actors and directors with roots in the surrealist avant-garde: Nicolas Bataille, BLIN and SERREAU. The surrealist movement between the wars had taken little active interest in theatre, but it had revived the work of Jarry and influenced ARTAUD and VITRAC who founded their Théâtre Alfred Jarry in 1926. Here they performed Vitrac's *Victor* (1928), a surreal satire of boulevard theatre and the bourgeois world it mirrors. Artaud went on to found the short-lived Theatre of Cruelty (1935) and to publish *The Theatre and its Double* (1938), in which he drew an analogy between theatre and plague, suggesting that theatre's effect should be that of a great collective nightmare from which few would emerge unscathed but which would leave society purged; theatre should be able to break through the encrusted shell of cultural tradition and fine discourse to discover a new language, essentially physical, concrete, spatial.

Although Artaud did not specifically influence the dramatists of the absurd, he helped to form the practitioners who, like Blin, were able to recognize the originality of these plays whose complex theatrical images combined tragedy and farce of the most extreme kind, thus decisively burying the great French tradition of separating the genres. At first misunderstood by the critics, plays such as Ionesco's *The Bald Prima Donna* staged by Bataille in 1950 and Beckett's *Waiting for Godot* staged by Blin in 1953 achieved rapid fame and have been constantly revived. Their influence also spread quickly in the English-speaking theatre world, thanks to fine translations of Beckett's work by himself and of Ionesco's by Donald Watson. In the course of the 1950s and 1960s both authors continued to write plays, but while Beckett's became shorter and starker, Ionesco's grew progressively longer and more verbose. Genet wrote only three full-length plays, *The Balcony*, *The Blacks* and *The Screens*; all were associated with scandal and protest, the first directed by BROOK and the other two by Blin. Adamov's work acquired a more political slant without abandoning the techniques of the new theatre. FERNANDO ARRABAL, Robert Pinget and MARGUERITE DURAS (better known for her *nouveaux romans*) also wrote plays which have been seen as part of the new theatre.

The triumph of the new theatre playwrights was almost exclusively confined to Paris. With a few exceptions, such as PLANCHON who produced Adamov and Ionesco at Lyon in the early 1950s, those working in the decentralized theatres at first shunned the absurd. Their aim was rather to rediscover theatre with a universal, popular appeal and to face up to issues of urgent political importance. The man who best represented this aim was Vilar, who had founded the Avignon theatre festival in 1947 and who, in 1951, became director of the Théâtre National Populaire at the CHAILLOT THEATRE. His choice of plays, drawn from the international classic repertoire, was made in order to comment on the current political situation, and he was among the first to produce BRECHT's work in France. Both Brecht's plays and his company, the BERLINER ENSEMBLE, exerted a

powerful influence over the decentralized theatres of the 1950s and 1960s. This was evident in a new playing style, more down-to-earth and less declamatory than traditional French acting, and in the renewed urgency with which theatre companies tried to identify and serve the cultural needs of the working class.

A new school of political dramatists emerged, including Adamov, CÉSAIRE, Cousin, GATTI, Planchon and YACINE. Although these playwrights were left-wing in their sympathies, the theatres at which they were performed were funded by a Gaullist government. Under de Gaulle's minister for culture, André Malraux, large sums of money were made available to subsidize theatre, especially outside Paris. By the end of the 1960s there were more than 30 permanent subsidized theatre companies working in provincial centres. Most were dedicated to an ideal of *théâtre populaire* inherited from Copeau, but becoming increasingly politicized. The near-revolution of 1968 persuaded many of these that they had lost touch with the people whom they were trying to serve. The result was a ferment of experimentation into new performance spaces, from the circus to the street, and new forms of actor–audience relationship. Cafés provided an ideal location for occasional small-scale performance; this fashion caught on and café-theatres of a more permanent kind were established. Many theatre companies now abandoned the traditional repertoire in favour of *création collective* – collaboratively devised shows, the outstanding example being the THÉÂTRE DU SOLEIL's *1789*, performed to packed audiences in a disused Vincennes warehouse from 1971 to 1973. This play, about the first year of the French Revolution, was acted on five separate stages placed around the audience, and marked the start of a decade of experiment into different actor–audience relationships: each new show by the Théâtre du Soleil involved a new arrangement of the spaces for performers and spectators. Similar experiments, emphasizing personal rather than political liberation, produced the Grand Magic Circus of SAVARY and the 'panic theatre' movement of Arrabal, whose work was produced by the South American directors Victor García and Jorge Lavelli.

Theatre was not favoured by governments from 1968 to 1981. Many provincial directors were dismissed for their part in the events of 1968, and even the apolitical Barrault was removed from the ODÉON. Spending on theatre was stagnant, although it continued to sustain a large body of work. In the French system the subsidy is paid straight to the director, who thus has complete control of artistic policy. Influenced by the work of Italian designers, particularly those who had worked for STREHLER, many directors have developed styles of great visual complexity. At its best, as in Chéreau's production of *La Dispute* by Marivaux, or in Planchon's productions of Racine and Molière, this produces work that is both compelling and profound, although it can also lead to productions that are scenically brilliant but intellectually vapid. The plays produced are frequently drawn from the classic repertoire. Today the major names in French theatre are no longer those of the new dramatists, nor of the star actors, but those of directors: Barrault, Planchon, MNOUCHKINE, VITEZ, Chéreau, VINCENT, LASSALLE, Lavaudant. The one major institutional change of the 1970s was the transfer of the title Théâtre National Populaire to the company of Planchon and Chéreau at Villeurbanne. Some of the decentralized theatres continued to produce new work. Those at Caen and Strasbourg, for example, were among the first to promote the school of playwright influenced by recent German-language drama, known as *théâtre du QUOTIDIEN* and including Michel Deutsch and MICHEL VINAVER.

Under Jack Lang, minister for culture in the Mitterrand government during 1981-6 and 1988-92, large sums of money were once again injected into the arts. In particular, a variety of financial incentives to playwrights were introduced, and the pendulum began to swing back from the director to the writer as the central creative force in the theatre. However, all sectors of theatrical activity benefited from increased government spending, and the number of new companies, both in Paris and outside, more than doubled in the course of the decade. The massive growth of decentralized theatre in France since the Second World War has transformed the pattern of theatrical activity, so that exciting new work is no longer available to Parisians only, but to audiences throughout the country. DB

See: D. Bradby, *Modern French Drama, 1940-1990*, rev. edn, Cambridge, 1991; M. Carlson, *The French Stage in the Nineteenth Century*, New Jersey, 1972; L. Champagne, *French Theatre Experiment since 1968*, Michigan, 1984; W. Deierkauf-Holsboer, *Histoire de la mise en scène dans le théâtre français de 1600 à 1673*, Paris, 1960; J. Guicharnaud, *Modern French Theatre from Giraudoux to Genet*, rev. edn, New Haven, 1975; W. D. Howarth, *Sublime and Grotesque*, London, 1975; D. Knowles, *French Drama of the Inter-war Years 1918-1939*, London, 1967; H. C. Lancaster, *A History of French Dramatic Literature in the Seventeenth Century*, 9 vols., Baltimore, 1924-42; T. E. Lawrenson, *The French Stage in the Seventeenth Century*, Manchester, 1957; M. Lioure, *Le Drame*, Paris, 1973; M. Meisel, *Realizations*, Princeton, 1983; J. Morel, *La Tragédie*, Paris, 1964; L. Moussinac, *Le Théâtre des origines à nos jours*, Paris, 1966; P. Peyronnet, *La Mise en scène au 18e siècle*, Paris, 1974; M. Root-Bernstein, *Boulevard Theatre and Revolution in Eighteenth-century Paris*, Michigan, 1984; J. Scherer, *La Dramaturgie classique en France*, Paris, 1959; A. Simon, *Dictionnaire du théâtre français contemporain*, Paris, 1970; R. Temkine, *Le Théâtre en l'état*, Paris, 1992; P. Voltz, *La Comédie*, Paris, 1964.

Franconi family see circus

Francovich, Guillermo 1901-90 Bolivian playwright, lawyer, university president and diplomat. In addition to numerous philosophical essays he has written more than a dozen plays, including *Como los gansos* (*Like the Geese*, 1957), *Un puñal en la noche* (*A Dagger in the Night*, 1953) and *El monje de Potosí* (*The Monk from Potosí*, 1954). In 1983 he published a volume of seven plays written after 1975, all of which have historical ramifications. GW

Fratellini family Italian CIRCUS performers, best known for the Three Fratellini, a CLOWN act composed of brothers, sons of the acrobat **Gustavo** Fratellini (1842-1905). **Paul** (Paolo, 1877-1940) was the subtle comedian, dressed as a parody of bourgeois respectability. **François** (Francesco, 1879-1951) was the elegant white clown in his spangled costume, strumming the guitar and mandolin. **Albert** (Alberto, 1886-1961) played the patsy with his huge nose, fright wigs, and musical instruments that were prone to squirt water or burst into flames. The trio first formed in 1905 and settled in Paris at the Cirque Médrano and then the Cirque d'Hiver, periodically touring Europe and America. They were so successful that in 1922 they were invited to join the COMÉDIE-FRANÇAISE as affiliates. Their descendants carry on the tradition. LS

Frayn, Michael 1933- British dramatist, who began by writing amusing columns for the (then) *Manchester Guardian* and the *Observer*, before turning his attention to the stage. While at Cambridge University, he contributed sketches to such REVUES as *Share My Lettuce* (1956), which transferred to London, and wrote *Zounds!* with John Edwards and the composer Keith Statham. But journalism and novel-writing took precedence over his theatrical enthusiasms, until in 1970 he wrote four short plays which were presented together as *The Two of Us*. His next play, *The Sandboy* (1971), was less successful, although both comedies demonstrated his knack for funny dialogue. *Alphabetical Order* (1975) about mayhem in a newspaper cuttings library, *Donkeys' Years* (1976) about university lives and loves, and *Clouds* (1976) based on a journalists' group visit to Cuba, all established him as a writer of intelligent comedies, although his first major success came with *Noises Off* (1982), a backstage comedy about an appalling touring theatre company. *Balmoral* (1978), retitled *Liberty Hall* (1979), can be considered as a comedy which signalled a change of mood in Britain, a new scepticism with political clichés. As in *Clouds*, Frayn contrasted in *Liberty Hall* the various perspectives offered by alternative assumptions. He has adapted foreign plays for Britain, notably from Russia with CHEKHOV's *Uncle Vanya* and *The Cherry Orchard*, LEV TOLSTOI's *The Fruits of Enlightenment* and Uri Trifomov's *Exchange*; and he wrote the filmscript for *Clockwise*. His most recent stage play, *Look, Look* (1990), attempted to balance *Noises Off* with an equally jaundiced impression of audiences, but its public failed to appreciate the joke. JE

Fréchette, Louis-Honoré 1839-1908 French Canadian poet, essayist and playwright, author of the most popular 19th-century Canadian play, *Félix Poutré* (1862), performed hundreds of times by amateur troupes well into the 20th century. The work draws heavily upon published memoirs of its titular hero, a participant in the 1837-8 Patriote Rebellion, who feigns madness to escape the gallows - exacting delicious vengeance onstage against stereotyped representatives of British rule. When research by historians proved Poutré to have been a double agent and liar, Fréchette shunned association with the work.

Two of his other three surviving plays have been shown to be suspect in origin: *Le Retour de l'exilé* (*The Exile's Return*, 1880), whose plot comes from a popular French novel, and *Véronica* (1903), written for a fee by French author Maurice de Pradel. Even Fréchette's only original drama, dealing with the leader of the Patriotes, *Papineau*

(1880), relies too heavily on the latter's published speeches. Only *Félix Poutré* has attracted critical and popular acclaim. LED

Fredro, Aleksander 1793–1876 Polish dramatist, who between 1815 and 1835 wrote over 20 comedies in octosyllabic rhymed couplets that have become a central part of the national repertory. Often set in pre-partition Poland, they depict the life of the landed gentry and feature lively plots and colourful, eccentric characters. Major works are *Ladies and Hussars* (1825), *Maiden Vows* (1833) and *Vengeance* (1834). DG

Fregoli, Leopoldo 1867–1936 Italian quick-change artist, who began by singing both male and female parts as an amateur actor. In 1896 he created the Fin-de-Siècle Company to present his one-man shows; it travelled round the world with a staff of 23, 370 trunks and 800 costumes until his retirement in 1925. In the course of a three-hour performance Fregoli would perform a one-act play, taking all the roles, then present imitations of 60 well known MUSIC-HALL performers, singing, dancing, performing magic tricks, ventriloquy and hypnotism; and end by screening 10 films he had directed and starred in – the 'Fregoligraph'. Using stand-ins and dummies to effect illusions of his presence, he became synonymous with proteanism, and NIKOLAI EVREINOV used his name to baptize the mercurial hero of his play *The Chief Thing* (1921). LS

Freie Bühne (Free Stage) A society in Berlin that was stimulated in part by the foundation of the Théâtre Libre in Paris (see ANDRÉ ANTOINE). Its purpose was to stage new plays that could not be seen, for a variety of reasons, in the repertoires of the commercial and state-subsidized theatres. Under the direction of OTTO BRAHM and with professional actors, the Freie Bühne staged IBSEN's *Ghosts* in September 1889 and the first performance of HAUPTMANN's *Before Dawn* in October 1889. Later productions included more plays by Hauptmann and works by, among others, TOLSTOI, STRINDBERG and ZOLA. The Freie Bühne was dissolved in 1894 when Otto Brahm was appointed director of the DEUTSCHES THEATER. Here he continued to pursue his mission of producing naturalist drama, though on a more permanent basis. SW

French, David 1939– Canadian playwright. Born in Newfoundland, French was raised in Toronto. The clash between the old, idealized values of life in Newfoundland (the rural, outport world of his parents) and the mores of contemporary life in the environment of a large metropolis is central to the tetralogy for which he is best known – *Leaving Home* (1972), *Of the Fields, Lately* (1973), *Salt-Water Moon* (1985) and *1949* (1989). Full-length plays, these established French as Canada's leading playwright in English, measured in terms of critical and commercial success. His other works include *One Crack Out* (1976), *Jitters* (1980) and *The Riddle of the World* (1981); French terms the latter play 'my one "flop"'.

Leaving Home and *Of the Fields, Lately*, both set in the late 1950s, focus on the Mercer family, who have left Newfoundland to settle in Toronto, and on the conflict between the father, Jacob, and his son, Ben. While both

plays may be termed naturalistic (see NATURALISM), they employ a heightened poetic speech (Irish in derivation) that invests the plays' domestic events with a surprising symbolic resonance. *Salt-Water Moon*, which takes place in 1926, is concerned with Jacob Mercer's courtship of his future wife, Mary. The development of their love is counterpointed with events that reveal the economic exploitation of the working class in Newfoundland and that cause Jacob and Mary to relocate in Toronto. *1949* concerns the entry of Newfoundland, a British colony, into Canada in 1949. The tetralogy may thus be viewed not only as the saga of a family spanning three generations but as an historical epic about the growth of nationhood and the shedding of a colonial past.

This viewpoint is reinforced by the openly ideological thrust of French's *Jitters*, the finest Canadian full-length COMEDY. In this play-within-a-play, a group of Canadian actors rehearse a Canadian play, revealing as they do so their ambivalence about American culture and the 'colonial cringe' that so often accompanies colonial literatures. EBEN

French-speaking Africa south of the Sahara 'Francophone' sub-Saharan Africa is the term used with increasing frequency since the 1960s, in both English and French, to describe a group of 16 African countries where, as a result of French and Belgian colonial rule (roughly between 1885 and 1960), French is the language of government, business and administration. While these countries, from SENEGAL in the west through ZAIRE in the centre to Chad in the east, each have a unique cultural identity, they have also evolved, by virtue of their similar colonial experience (especially those under a centralizing power like France), a distinctive modern African culture.

This francophone African culture, a synthesis of local African and imported French and Belgian traditions, has found expression in many forms: in the popular music of a Franco or Tabu Ley (Zaire), in the cinema of a Sembène Ousmane (Senegal) or a Souleymane Cissé (MALI), and in the philosophical writings of a Paulin Hountondji (BENIN) or Yves-Valentin Mudimbé (Zaire). But it is in literature that it has found its most powerful voice. The earliest practised genre was poetry in the 1930s, with Léopold Senghor; then came fiction in the early 50s with Camara Laye, Mongo Beti and Abdoulaye Sadji, and almost a decade later, in terms of significant published works, theatre dominated.

In spite of its relative youth, the theatre is now a vital aspect of the literature of sub-Saharan Africa in French, accounting for an important corpus of some 300 published plays. Many of these, by playwrights like CHEIK NDAO, BERNARD DADIÉ, SONY LABOU TANSI, FELIX TCHICAYA U'TAMSI, and GUILLAUME OYONO-MBIA, are of the highest standard and are regularly produced in francophone Africa. Some have been performed in France – at the AVIGNON FESTIVAL, and in Limoges, at the Festival International des Francophonies, launched in 1985 to promote world theatre in the French language. The Théâtre International de Langue Française, a troupe founded in 1985 by the French director Gabriel Garran, has been producing plays by U'Tamsi and Labou Tansi in theatres in Paris and its districts, while Françoise Kourilsky's Ubu

Repertory Theatre has been promoting francophone African theatre in New York since 1987, by organizing staged readings and performances of plays by BERNARD ZADI ZAOUROU, SENOUVO ZINSOU and Maxime Ndébéka (b.1944).

Over the years, francophone Africa has also produced actors of talent like the Paris-based Senegalese Bachir Touré and Douta Seck, Cameroonian Lydia Ewandé and, more recently, Malian Bakary Sangaré. The first three played roles in the 1960s in productions, mostly by JEAN-MARIE SERREAU but also by ROGER BLIN, of plays by JEAN GENET, AIMÉ CÉSAIRE and KATEB YACINE; while over the past five years Sangaré has appeared in plays by Abdou Anta Ka, U'Tamsi and Césaire, and in a production by PETER BROOK of *Woza Albert*.

That the theatre should prove an attraction to francophone Africans and become a crucial cultural nexus in their region is hardly surprising. Such a potential had always existed in this area of millennial cultures, where the performance of ancient oral narratives such as the Sunjata and Mwindo epics of old Mali and Zaire respectively by traditional bards, commonly known in francophone Africa as *griots*, as well as the enactment of RITUALS, takes on the quality of drama and theatre by the very circumstances of their performance. But beyond such 'framed' activities, a sense of theatre is perceptible in these cultures at an even more basic and unreflexive level: that of performed or expressive social conduct; conduct resulting from the conformity, demanded of members of these often hierarchical cultures, to a 'social script', that is, to immemorially prescribed and codified rules of saying and behaving. It is the sensitivity of early French educators like Charles Béart to these various dimensions of theatricality in Africa, and their decision to encourage and develop them into totally reflexive and modern artistic activities in their African students, first at the École Supérieure Primaire de Bingerville in the CÔTE D'IVOIRE and then at the École William Ponty in Senegal, that gave rise to the first dramatic compositions in French by sub-Saharan Africans. The best of these – Dadié's *Assémien Déhylé*(1936), for instance – were taken on tour to Paris for the Colonial Exhibition of 1937 and published in *Traits d'Union*, the cultural organ of French West African countries.

The subsequent development of francophone theatre was the result of concrete measures taken by the colonial authorities and later by the governments of some of the independent states. These include the building of theatres like the Daniel Sorano in Dakar; the founding of theatre arts institutes in Abidjan and Bamako, and other cities; the organizing of drama competitions by Radio France Internationale; and, in the immediate pre- and post-independence periods, the sponsoring of tours to Africa by French theatre directors and critics, including Raymond Hermantier, Henri Cordreaux and Jacques Schérer, to spot talent and train theatre specialists, and by theatre companies like the Greniers de Toulouse and the Théâtre des Amandiers. While, since the 1970s, the attitude of many francophone governments to the theatre has been at best lukewarm and at worst hostile, partly because of the increasingly oppositional role which this art has come to assume, French support for it has remained unwavering.

Of course, France no longer builds theatres in Africa, but it continues to second its specialists to work with francophone troupes, to make its local cultural centres and their material facilities available to these troupes and to sponsor their participation at international French theatre festivals.

Francophone African drama falls, in terms of themes, into three broad categories: historical, social and political. The first accounts for most of the plays produced so far. In exalting language, Ndao's *L'Exil d'Albouri* (*Albouri's Exile*, 1967), Jean Pliya's *Kondo le requin* (*Kondo the Shark*, first published 1966) and Séydou Badian's *La Mort de Chaka* (*The Death of Chaka*, 1962), for example, depict the careers of various 19th-century warrior-kings. In their heroic struggles to defend their territories, often against France, is conveyed a living sense of pre-colonial societies at their most glorious. This predilection for history is as much a legacy of the history-conscious oral traditions of the dramatists as it is a felt, nationalist need to present a dramatic corrective to the colonial view of the African past, or an instrument of legitimation of post-colonial régimes and rulers, by establishing parallels between the latter and heroic figures of the past.

The dislocating effects of modern culture on traditional beliefs and customs, and the retrograde nature of some of the latter, constitute the second, social, category of mostly comic plays: such as Oyono-Mbia's *Trois prétendants ... un mari* (*Three Suitors, One Husband*, 1964), Guy Menga's *La Marmite de Koka Mbala* (*Koka Mbala's Pot*, 1969) and Protais Asseng's *Trop c'est trop* (*Enough Is Enough*, 1981). The third group of plays by, among others, U'Tamsi (*Le Destin glorieux du Maréchal Nnikon Nniku*, *The Glorious Destiny of Marshal Nnikon Nniku*, 1979), Maxime Ndébéka (*Equatorium*, 1989) and Sony Labou Tansi explore the political corruption and ugly tyrannies that have sprung up in post-colonial African societies.

Over the past decade or so, francophone African theatre has moved in new directions. In the plays of dramatists like NICOLE WEREWERE-LIKING or Zaourou (*La Termitière*, *The Anthill*, 1981), ritual ceremonies – especially healing, initiation and purification rites – have provided the bases, in content and structure, for a new type of drama.

In terms of form, francophone theatre is heavily influenced by oral performance modes and the conventions of traditional genres. Elements of this influence include the episodic and undramatic nature of the action in many (especially historical) plays; the tendency to give epic grandeur to the most factual of events; the display of a vivid sense of spectacle through recourse to colourful ceremonies and to the visual and rhetorical presentation of the heroic deeds of the main characters, as in Pliya's *Kondo le requin*; the use of the cultural figure of the *griot* either as a character integrated into the action as in Eugène Dervain's *La Reine scélérate* (*The Villainous Queen*, 1968) or as presenter of and commentator on the dramatized events, such as the ghost-provocateur in Ndébéka's *Equatorium* or the public entertainer in SYLVAIN BEMBA's *L'Homme qui tua le crocodile* (*The Man who Killed the Crocodile*, 1972). The *griot*'s technique of acting several characters in the course of the same performance is also widely used: in Zinsou's *On joue la comédie* (*We Are Acting*, 1972), for instance, in which the presenter

Xuma acts the hero Chaka in a playlet within the play.

The use, as in traditional performances, of music, song and dance is also widespread. These elements signify and can contribute to dramatic action, as does the *lagyah* tune, for example, in Thiérno Ba's *Bilbassy* (1980). Sometimes they are used to entertain or to involve the audience in the action. Often, however, they degenerate into folklorism. A final legacy of oral performance to the modern theatre is to be found in the conception of scenic space as consisting of both stage and auditorium. Thus in Oyono-Mbia's *Trois prétendants ... un mari* it is the entire village community that is the stage.

Francophone theatre does not, though, merely borrow elements of form from tradition. It dramatizes actual *texts* of that tradition: that is, 'autonomous and isolated works ... highly organized as full and independent imaginative statements' irrespective of their orality, as the critic Abiola Irele has noted. An example is Dervain's *La Reine scélérate*, which is a staged version of the Da Monzon epic, an oral chronicle of the 19th-century exploits of the Diarra dynasty of the Bambara people of Mali. Nor is the degree of borrowing the same in all plays. A distinct trend is noticeable between the predominantly text-based plays of an earlier generation of playwrights (Ndao, Badian, Amadou Cissé Dia), for example, and the performance-centred works that emerged in the mid-70s – such as Zinsou's *On joue la comédie* – that now appear to dominate francophone theatrical production.

While the earlier drama used elements of traditional performances but within an essentially mainstream Western format, the more recent drama has proceeded to deprivilege text and author, in favour of actors and non-linguistic elements of communication. Examples are Werewere-Liking's *Singué Mura* (1990) and *Les Cloches* (*The Bells*, 1988), Souleymane Koly's *Commandant Jupiter et ses Black Nouchis* (*Commander Jupiter and His Black Nouchis*, 1988) and U'Tamsi's *Le Bal de Ndinga* (*Ndinga's Ball*, 1987). While such decentring of speech – the use of it as just another element of a theatrical language that now includes music, dance or puppetry – reflects political and cultural attempts to reach the larger (non-literate) audiences of the francophone area and to rescue from the margins African traditions of performance, it also runs the risk of transforming recent francophone theatre into mere spectacle. The need to satisfy the exotic expectations of the French audiences of Limoges, Avignon, Bordeaux – audiences that have become, over the past 14 years (through the international French-festival circuits), major patrons of francophone drama – might also account for this slide towards spectacle.

However, it should be mentioned that theatrical activity in francophone Africa is not limited to 'art' theatre. Neither has such 'art' or literary theatre always and uniformly been in French. There was also a *literary* drama in African languages (see TOGO, CAMEROON and ZAIRE). This was, though, later marginalized, especially in the first two countries, with the official promotion of a new, literary drama in the French language, when the adminis-

The stage of the Hotel Tonyeviadji in Lomé, Togo, photographed in the 1970s. This is typical of the simple performance spaces that still serve much African popular theatre.

tration of these territories passed over to France from Germany after the First World War. But like elite cultural forms the world over, French-language African drama's high visibility on local, and sometimes French, radio and television, at festivals, local and international, and on school syllabuses is more a reflection of the sociological and political importance of its language, its largely Western-educated producers and readers/spectators, than of its generalized impact on the wider society. For such an impact, one would need to turn to other types of theatre in the area, such as the dynamic, popular theatre of urban agglomerations. This is expressed, for example, in the concert parties and *kantatas* of Togo; in the performances of the Groupe Mufwankolo in the Shaba province of Zaire; and in the plays of Souleymane Koly of the CÔTE D'IVOIRE, and of Zomo Bel Abel, Daniel Ndo and Jean-Michel Kankan of Cameroon.

A common thread runs through this activity: there are no scripts; the plots are improvised; the themes treated are topical and of concern to the mass of the urban poor or unemployed who mostly constitute its audience; the language is a pot-pourri of pidgin French and local languages; and the action is conducted mostly through song and dance, though through dialogue too.

Another type of theatre in francophone Africa is the community development theatre, or theatre of social intervention. Its aim is to use the medium of the theatre to enable various target communities to better understand and participate in the development projects conceived for them. The plays are in the local languages, the actors are mostly drawn from members of the communities concerned, and the forms adopted are taken from their cultures. Mali, NIGER and BURKINA FASO are the great practitioners in francophone Africa of this type of theatre.

A final, and rather special, form of theatre worth mentioning because of its pervasiveness in two countries of the area – Zaire, where it started, and Togo, which quickly appropriated it – is the *théâtre d'animation politique et culturelle*, as it is known in these countries. Roughly translated as a theatre of political cheerleading, it is usually performed in airports, sports stadia or *les maisons du parti*, on the occasion of state visits by foreign dignitaries or the assizes of the ruling and only party. A mixture of praise-singing to the leader, recitals of party slogans and folkloric dances, this performance, put on by representatives of various regional and social groups, costumed in traditional dress or party colours, usually ends with an allegorical pageant on the near-supernatural nature and achievements of the leader. What one has in such performances, created and produced by the ruling parties in those countries, is an interesting case of the theatricalization of politics.

While all of this activity is, in one way or another, part of the new drama and theatre, francophone Africa is still home to a variety of traditional theatrical performances. The best-known is the Kotéba satirical theatre of the Bambara people of Mali, whose aesthetic is at the heart of current researches by the Groupe Dramatique of Mali to establish a new way of acting and writing. A less well known, but living, tradition of theatre in the francophone region is that of animated puppets. Examples include the *xouss-maniap* of the Wolof of Senegal, and more spectacu-

larly, the *konnou doukili* of the Bambara of Mali – the only documented example of theatre performed on water in Africa. The PUPPETS and their manipulators are on two rowing boats, while the spectators are on land. Like other forms of traditional theatre, puppetry is increasingly becoming an important component of modern francophone theatre, especially in the recent work of Werewere-Liking. JCM

See: D. Blair, *African Literature in French*, Cambridge, 1976; J. Conteh-Morgan, 'French-language African Drama and the Oral Tradition: Trends and Issues', *African Literature Today*, 18, 1992, and *Theatre and Drama in Francophone Africa*, Cambridge, 1994; R. Cornevin, 'Le Théâtre de langue française en Afrique Noire', *Culture Française*, 31–2, 1982/3; O. Darkowska-Nidzgorska, *Théâtre populaire de marionnettes*, Zaire, 1980; U. Edebiri, 'French Contributions to African Drama', *Research in African Literatures*, 6, 1975; A. Irele, 'Orality, Literacy and African Literature', in *Semper Aliquid Novi: Mélanges offerts à Albert Gérard*, ed. J. Riesz and A. Ricard, Tübingen, 1990; P. Manning, *Francophone sub-Saharan Africa 1880–1985*, Cambridge, 1988; J. Povey, 'The Mufwankolo Theater', *African Arts*, 8, 1975; F. Sahlien, *Panorama du théâtre africain d'expression française*, Zaire, 1983; J. Schérer, 'Le Théâtre en Afrique noire francophone', in *Le Théâtre moderne II*, ed. J. Jacquot, Paris, 1973; M. Schipper, 'Traditional Themes and Techniques in African Theatre and "Francophonie" ', *Theatre Research International*, 9, 3, 1984; B. Traoré, *Le Théâtre Négro-Africain et ses fonctions sociales*, Paris, 1958; C. Wake, 'French-speaking Africa South of the Sahara', in *The Cambridge Guide to World Theatre*, ed. M. Banham, Cambridge, 1988; H. Waters, *Théâtre noir: Encyclopédie des pièces écrites en français par des auteurs noirs*, Washington, DC, 1988.

French-speaking North Africa Algeria, Morocco and Tunisia are all Muslim countries and, in spite of the complex vicissitudes of Mediterranean history, have been so since the Arab conquest of North Africa in the 7th and 8th centuries. The dominant European influencemost profoundly effective in Algeriais that of FRANCE which, starting with the annexation of Algeria in 1830, eventually brought Tunisia (1883) and most of Morocco (1912), as well as protectorates, under its control. The resistance to the French occupation was as unrelenting as it had been to the conquest, and led to independence for Morocco and Tunisia in 1956 and, after a violent eight-year war of independence, for Algeria in 1962.

It has not been easy for theatre to flourish in these three countries. The Muslim tradition gave it little encouragement. French CENSORSHIP was always ready to suppress criticism of the colonial authority. Theatre tended to come, therefore, largely from outside the region. In the 19th century, shadow theatre from Turkey (see SHADOW PUPPETS; KARAGÖZ) was popular. Theatre companies from Egypt visited from time to time and after the First World War gave a significant impetus to the development of modern Moroccan literature, albeit mainly in genres other than drama. Visiting French theatre companies, although often of a high quality, provided entertainment chiefly for French expatriates (or citizens, in the case of

Algeria) and the French-speaking Arab elite; their offerings were almost by definition drawn from the Parisian BOULEVARD theatres. Since independence, there has been more indigenous activity, especially in Algeria. National Theatres have been established in Algeria and Tunisia, though not without difficulty. All three countries were well represented in the drama section of the 1969 Pan-African Festival, which was held in Algiers. The Moroccan entry won third prize with a play by Ahmed Taïeb El Alj entitled *Les Moutons répètent* (*The Sheep Rehearse*), which dealt with the theme of oppression through the medium of a fable. The Algerian entry, *Rouge l'aube* (*Red the Dawn*) by Assia Djebar and Walid Garn, was directed by Mustapha Kateb, who has had an important influence on the development of post-independence theatre in North Africa.

In addition to the difficulties created in pre-independence North Africa by religious and political restrictions, the development of the theatre has also been hampered, even into the present, by the firm hold of classical Arabic on literary production and the barrier to communication with the ordinary people that this causes. This is particularly harmful to the spread of theatre. Algeria did, however, have the major advantage of the work of Rachid Ksentini who, beween the wars, wrote and directed plays in spoken Arabic with considerable success. Directors and writers committed to the nationalist movement before independence realized the importance of Ksentini's work for the development of a people's theatre after independence. His ideas were adopted by Bachtarzi Mahiedine and Mustapha Kateb in particular; as directors of the Conservatoire Municipal d'Alger and the Théâtre National Algérien respectively, they were both in a good position to exercise influence. Mahiedine has also written plays which have been performed before enthusiastic audiences of workers, traders and women. They include *El Keddaïnes* (*The Traitors*), *Beni-oui-oui* (*The Yes-man*) and *Faqo* (*They Have Awoken*), as well as adaptations of MOLIÈRE, which are always popular: *El Mech-hak* (*The Miser*), *Sliman Ellouk* (*The Hypochondriac*).

The French-speaking Algerian playwright and novelist KATEB YACINE is well known in France, where he has more than once fallen foul of the authorities and French public opinion for his realistic and frank attacks on French colonialism in North Africa. His first play, *Le Cadavre encerclé* (*The Encircled Corpse*, 1958), was directed by JEAN-MARIE SERREAU and performed in Brussels after it provoked a near-riot in Paris. Serreau directed another of his plays, *Les Ancêtres redoublent de férocité* (*The Ancestors Redouble Their Ferocity*), published under the title *La Femme sauvage* (*The Savage Woman*); it was produced at the THÉÂTRE NATIONAL POPULAIRE in Lyon, where once again there was a strong reaction from the French. Along with a third play, *La Poudre d'intelligence* (*The Powder of Intelligence*), these plays have been published together in a volume entitled *Le Cercle des représailles* (*The Circle of Reprisals*). *L'Homme aux sandales de caoutchouc* (*The Man in Rubber Sandals*) appeared in 1971, and also in the early 1970s an Algerian company presented Yacine's bilingual comedy about immigrant life in France, *Mohamed, prends ta valise* (*Mohamed, Take Your Suitcase*), to immigrant audiences in Paris. His often violent language and style is as much that of the poet as the dramatist, and his theatre, like his novels, offers a vision of human behaviour that is far more nuanced than the simple portraits of political theatre (See also MIDDLE EAST.) CW

Freytag, Gustav 1816–95 German playwright, novelist and theorist. A writer of liberal sympathies, in his day Freytag was very widely read. His play *The Journalists* (1854), a genial comedy about the interrelationship of journalism and politics, was immensely popular and is still occasionally revived today. In his influential essay *The Technique of Drama* (1865), Freytag constructed a famous model by which each play was described as being structured like a pyramid; in essence, this was a refinement of the theory of the WELL MADE PLAY. SW

Friel, Brian 1929– Irish playwright. Teaching in Londonderry (1950–60), Friel began writing short stories and radio plays. *Philadelphia, Here I Come!* brought his first wide recognition, with a long BROADWAY run following its GATE premiere during the 1964 DUBLIN INTERNATIONAL THEATRE FESTIVAL. Thereafter his plays generally premiered at the ABBEY, apart from those staged in the 1980s by the FIELD DAY THEATRE COMPANY which Friel had co-founded.

The territory of Friel's short stories stretches from Co. Tyrone to West Donegal. Though they satirize Irish cant, their dominant tone is elegiac, commemorating the solace of illusions that do not wholly deceive. Friel's plays inhabit the same region. The variety of his work, taking on new strengths from the 70s, is exemplified in *Lovers* (1967), *The Gentle Island* (1968), *The Freedom of the City* (1973), *Aristocrats* (1979), *Faith Healer* (1979), *Translations* (1980) and *The Communication Cord* (1982). His more recent work includes *Making History* (1988), *Dancing at Lughnasa* (1990) and *Wonderful Tennessee* (1993), as well as versions of CHEKHOV and TURGENEV and a one-acter, *The London Vertigo* (1991), derived from CHARLES MACKLIN. While they occupy a common ground, each play secures a different perspective.

The figments of memory have always absorbed Friel's imagination. In *Philadelphia*, Gar on the eve of exile interrogates his past for corroborated 'truth'. *The Gentle Island* brutally revokes urban myths of idyllic pastoral on an island off Donegal. In *Aristocrats*, Casimir's fables of the Catholic Big House of his childhood collapse in the ruin of its decline. *Making History* explores the counterfeits of history through the ambiguities of Hugh O'Neill's noble Anglo-Irish rearing and European exile.

'But that's another story,' says Frank Harvey in *Faith Healer*, whose risky form – four monologues – delivers a riddling account of Frank's career and suicidal death; and a parable of the artist's capricious powers. A wider loss informs *Translations*, the dissolution of the old Gaelic culture, reinforced by the anglicizing of the Irish place names and mirrored in the love between an Irish girl and an English soldier. It is a lament, with farcical, questioning countertones, tones later developed in the apery of *The Communication Cord*'s 'restored' peasant cottage. These are in a sense political plays, but like *The Freedom of the City*, set in the present-day violence, they compose metaphors of individuals caught in a disintegrating society.

Lughnasa articulates afresh the questions ambient throughout the plays. In a small house outside Ballybeg, Friel's fictional Donegal village, five sisters barely sustain a home. The old Adam/Eve, which Catholic sanctimony can neither repress nor entertain, finally fragments it. Yet the household's remembered songs and dances defiantly temper, without evading, the tragic outcome. In *Wonderful Tennessee* a picnic party's all-night vigil of reminiscence, storytelling, song – an accordionist the animateur – partly exorcizes the illusion of the characters' sustaining fictions.

Though his latest plays more fully deploy effects of music and dance, and even gesture towards regions of experience beyond language, words remain Friel's necessary medium. His drama's conflict is between 'the lie of authority' – familial, communal, religious – the autocratic vocabulary of power, and the fictions of the antic, imaginative self, the victim, outsider, dispossessed. Their voices, having their eloquent say, seek a dignity, some accommodation with their place through stories, lies, fictions, histories. Success is at best partial. Within the tragedy and farce that his wide-ranging dramatic language encompasses, the characters' shifts, stratagems and inventions are more ends in themselves than a reforming force, a solace not a solution.   DM GF

Friml, Rudolf 1879–1972 Prague-born composer, who studied music under Antonin Dvořák before going to the USA in 1903. His first score for the MUSICAL stage was *The Firefly* (1912), which starred opera singer Emma Trentini. Over the next 20 years he composed the scores of numerous OPERETTAS and musical comedies (see MUSICAL COMEDY), notably *Rose-Marie* (1924), *The Vagabond King* (1925) and *The Three Musketeers* (1928). Although several of his shows were written in collaboration with lyricist OTTO HARBACH, Friml worked with many other lyricists, including P. G. WODEHOUSE, OSCAR HAMMERSTEIN II and Brian Hooker. Throughout his long career as a composer for the American musical stage, Friml never abandoned his musical roots; his scores were heavily indebted to the traditions of European operetta.   MK

fringe theatre (Britain) A movement which began in the 1960s in Britain and corresponds to the OFF-OFF BROADWAY theatres in New York and to the 'free theatre' groups in Europe. Although London has a long tradition of adventurous little theatres, fringe theatre developed from the many small companies which gathered around the main festival offerings at the EDINBURGH FESTIVAL. The term came into use in the late 1950s, and the REVUE *Beyond the Fringe* was first seen in 1960 in Edinburgh before transferring to London and New York. In 1963 Jim Haynes, an American bookseller, started the TRAVERSE THEATRE Club in Edinburgh which became the unlikely centre for many small groups from America and Europe, including such companies as the LA MAMA troupe, GROTOWSKI's 13 Rows from Opole and, later, SZAJNA's Studio Theatre from Warsaw.

The Traverse Theatre received state support and a new theatre in 1969, but Haynes was less successful in establishing his Arts Laboratory in London. Another American, CHARLES MAROWITZ, who with PETER BROOK ran the

Theatre of Cruelty season at LAMDA's little theatre in 1964, opened his Open Space Theatre in London's Tottenham Court Road in 1968. By then, the fringe theatre movement had become a major force in British theatre, developing not just in Edinburgh and London but in studios around the country, sometimes attached to repertory theatres but often just in back rooms of pubs or even converted garages.

Much fringe theatre has its origins in political protest movements, notably against the war in Vietnam. In the 1960s, the 'hippy' and 'flower power' movements, led by Julian Beck's LIVING THEATRE, were primarily American in origin, although they had many imitators in Britain. After 1968 and the May events in Paris, many young British writers, including DAVID HARE, HOWARD BRENTON and DAVID EDGAR, turned to fringe theatre companies to present left-wing AGIT-PROP plays. Not all fringe theatre, however, was political. In small theatre clubs such as the Ambiance and the Almost Free, various kinds of experimentalism could be attempted which might otherwise have fallen foul of the censor, theatrical CENSORSHIP being abolished only in 1968. Improvisatory drama, environmental theatre, plays with strong sexual impact or sometimes violent spectacles were staged in clubs to avoid the restrictions of the law. Companies like the PEOPLE SHOW, which started in 1966, developed a powerful imagistic language of their own.

At first fringe theatres were unsubsidized, although by the early 1970s many had started to receive small subsidies. The financial crisis in 1973–4 caused many companies to close, while the better-established fringe theatres survived. Of these, the BUSH THEATRE and the King's Head, Islington, London, became 'new plays' theatres, encouraging unknown writers. The touring fringe companies which survived included the left-wing 7:84 and Red Ladder Companies, while Shared Experience, under its director Mike Alfreds, turned the limitations of non-theatrical halls to their advantage, establishing a remarkable rapport with their audiences. The daring adventurousness of fringe theatres, the secret of their attraction in the 1960s, became less wild in the late 1970s, although the standards of production undoubtedly rose. It ceased to be polite to describe them as 'fringe', for most companies preferred the word 'alternative'. They regarded themselves as being different from mainstream theatre, but not on its edges.

This status was a sociopolitical distinction at first, claiming for the fringe its place among the avant-garde and politically radical movements, the cutting edge of modernism; but during the 1980s, shifts of political mood and outlook affected all fringe theatres. The ARTS COUNCIL became more selective in its choice of companies to support, leading to inevitable accusations of censorship by subsidy. The fringe theatres became more specialized, some concentrating on performance art, some on new plays, some (like the Gate Theatre in London's Notting Hill) on plays from Europe, some on Asian or West Indian drama and some on alternative comedy. During the 1981 season at the Boulevard Theatre in Soho, many of the comics who became household names through British television could be seen – Rik Mayall, French and Saunders, Alexei Sayle and Adrian Edmondson. The Comedy Store in Leicester Square was another metropolitan shop window for comics and would-be comics. The

Alternative Comedy circuit was not without its political aims. Ben Elton, who also wrote such plays as *Gasping* (1990), was a staunch supporter of the British Labour Party, while there were many feminists who chose comedy as their main vehicle.

Alternative comedy was one area where the fringe changed the course of mainstream British drama, as *Beyond the Fringe* had done for the previous generation. Another lay in the field of low-cost classical touring companies, such as CHEEK BY JOWL, THÉÂTRE DE COMPLICITÉ and Shared Experience (founded by the director Mike Alfreds in 1975), which were supported almost as much by the British Council for their overseas visits as by the Arts Council. Their leading directors, such as Declan Donnellan, and actors, such as Kathryn Hunter, were drawn into the national companies in the early 1990s, and became (as it were) the official 'alternative'. The Gate's theatre director, STEPHEN DALDRY, was similarly elevated as a guest director at the NATIONAL THEATRE.

Among the many companies established to reflect particular cultural groups or interests, several were perhaps outstanding. TARA ARTS, founded in 1977, became the first professional Asian company in Britain and under its director, Jatinder Verma, managed to blend Asian and Western theatrical traditions in such productions as *A Little Clay Cart* (based on an Indian classic) and *Tartuffe* (1990), which was produced by the National Theatre with members of the Tara Arts company, directed by Verma. The Black Theatre Co-operative (founded in 1982) emerged through the several Afro-Caribbean companies of the 1970s, among them Temba and the Dark and Light Theatre Club. Its pioneers were the dramatist MUSTAPHA MATURA and the director Charlie Hanson; and it was responsible during the 1980s for the promotion of plays by Jacqueline Rudet, Edgar White and Farrukh Dhondy.

Among the feminist groups, Monstrous Regiment and the Women's Theatre Group stand out; but the move towards establishing a theatre devoted to women's drama and performance was led by the Woman's Playhouse Trust. The most remarkable alternative theatre company must be Graeae, a professional group formed from disabled performers in 1980 by Nabil Shaban and Richard Tomlinson, which has staged plays (by such writers as Noel Greig) that stressed the problems of isolation rather than physical handicap.

Unlike the earlier fringe theatres such as the Bush, which have their own theatres, these companies were designed to tour the arts centres and similar venues which sprang up during the 1980s, such as London's Battersea Arts Centre and Watermans and the Almeida Theatre in Islington. Some were subsidized by the local authorities, others received project grants from the Arts Council or (usually) the regional arts association, but most of the new companies operated on a shoe-string – although by now some fringe theatres, including the Bush and HAMPSTEAD THEATRE, were subsidized towards the outer fringes of generosity. JE

Frisch, Max 1911–91 Swiss playwright, novelist and essayist. Born in Zurich, the son of an architect, he studied German, briefly, at Zurich University in 1931, but abandoned the course to travel extensively across Europe. He returned to read architecture (1936–41), and after graduation opened his architect's office, where he worked until 1954. His major project was a large municipal swimming pool (Zurich, 1948). He started writing seriously (novels, diaries) in his early 20s, but his first play dates from 1945: *Santa Cruz* (staged in 1946). His second play, *Now They Are Singing Again* (1945), was the first to be seen: it deals with the problem of individual guilt in war, the dichotomy of spirit and power. *The Great Wall of China* (1946) is a 'farce of the incommensurable', a structurally complex 'PARODY of consciousness' in which the contemporary (Swiss) intellectual comes face to face with totalitarianism in the wake of Hiroshima and Nagasaki. *When the War Was Over* (1949) and *Count Oderland* (1951) are two transitional plays. *Don Juan, or The Love of Geometry* (1953) is an ironic comment on the mythical character treated as an anti-hero and a playful study of the relationship between fiction and reality. His Don Juan, yet another intellectual, refuses at first to wear the mask, thus unmasking the hypocrisy of bourgeois society, until the mask is forced upon him and he willingly accepts it: Don Juan renouncing his individuality sinks into the comfort of conformity.

Frisch's two most important and successful plays are harsh and uncompromising indictments of the Swiss mentality and Swiss blindness to the world outside. *The Fire Raisers* (*Biedermann und die Brandstifter*, 1958), a BRECHTian parable or, according to Frisch, 'a morality without a moral', brought him international recognition. Biedermann, a complacent owner-occupier, worried about his property because of a recent series of arsons in the neighbourhood, not only invites two 'tramps' to settle in his attic, but also stocks them with petrol and finally gives them the matches to set his house alight. Beyond the deliberately grotesque situation, the most powerful theatrical ingredient is language: the disaster stems from 'the continual discrepancy between phraseology and reality'. *Andorra* (1961) proved to be Frisch's most contentious play, critically and politically, as it concerns the growth and explosion of antisemitism in a small, peaceful and peace-loving country. *Philipp Hotz's Fury* (1958), *Biography* (1968) and *Triptych* (1979) continue, in their various styles, the charting of the clash between the individual and society and the questioning of the position of man in the world. In 1989 Frisch took an active part in the campaign for the referendum to abolish the army, and wrote *Switzerland without Army? A Waffle*, a polemical dialogue staged in Zurich and in Lausanne by BENNO BESSON. Frisch received many literary prizes and academic awards in Switzerland, Germany, Israel and the USA. CLS

Frohman, Charles 1860–1915 American producer and theatrical manager. After a decade in theatrical business in various capacities, Frohman achieved his first major success as a producer with BRONSON HOWARD's *Shenandoah* (1889). In 1893 he formed the EMPIRE THEATRE Stock Company (see STOCK COMPANY), with John Drew as his leading actor. Frohman now began to develop and exploit the 'star and combination' system: members of his company would be made 'stars' as quickly as possible and sent, with a supporting cast, on national tours after opening in a Frohman theatre in New York. He successfully employed similar methods in London, principally at the

Duke of York Theatre after 1898. Stars who benefited from Frohman's patronage included, among many others, MAUDE ADAMS, WILLIAM GILLETTE, ARNOLD DALY, ANNIE RUSSELL, MARGARET ANGLIN, JULIA MARLOWE, WILLIAM H. CRANE, OTIS SKINNER, and John Drew and Ethel Barrymore (see DREW–BARRYMORE FAMILY).

In 1896, in association with Al Hayman, he joined Mark Klaw and Abe Erlanger, Fred Zimmerman and Fred Nixon to organize a monopoly known as the THEATRICAL SYNDICATE. With the security and efficiency afforded by such control, Frohman produced many contemporary playwrights and helped many aspiring actors to achieve stardom, giving him significant influence in matters of taste and method in the commercial theatre. After 1896 he regularly produced over a dozen shows a year, including WILDE's *The Importance of Being Earnest* (1895), Gillette's *Secret Service* (1896, New York; 1897, London; 1900, Paris), BARRIE's *The Little Minister* (1896, New York, with Maude Adams), FITCH's *Barbara Frietchie* (1899, with Julia Marlowe) and Barrie's *Peter Pan* (1899, New York, with Maude Adams; 1904, London). Frohman died with the sinking of the *Lusitania* in 1915. His brother DANIEL FROHMAN co-authored a 1916 biography. MR DJW

Frohman, Daniel 1851–1940 American theatre manager. With his brothers, CHARLES and Gustave, Frohman first came to prominence as business manager in 1880 with STEELE MACKAYE's organization at the MADISON SQUARE THEATRE, where he developed the system of 'auxiliary road companies' that toured the country while the original production was playing in New York. Frohman should be noted for his tenure as the producer-manager of New York's old LYCEUM THEATRE at 4th Avenue and its STOCK COMPANY from 1887 to 1902, and of the new Lyceum on 45th Street from 1902 until his retirement in 1909. Enlisting the talents of a fine acting company, from which E. H. SOTHERN's career was launched and that over the years included HENRY MILLER, WILLIAM FAVERSHAM, Effie Shannon, RICHARD MANSFIELD, MAUDE ADAMS and J. H. HACKETT, Frohman presented a fashionable repertory from contemporary authors including CLYDE FITCH, J. M. BARRIE, A. W. PINERO, HENRY ARTHUR JONES, WILDE and SARDOU. Notable productions that featured Sothern included *Lord Chumley* (1888), *The Charity Ball* (1889) and *The Prisoner of Zenda* (1895). The elaborate new Lyceum opened with Barrie's *The Admirable Crichton*. In 1899, Frohman began a four-year term as manager and lessee of Daly's Theatre, where he imported many musical comedies from London. He served as president of the Actors' Fund from 1903 until his death. Through his association with the Famous Players–Lasky Film Company after 1912, he brought many theatre stars to the infant film industry. Frohman authored three autobiographies (1911, 1935, 1937). MR

frontier theatre (USA) Just as the frontier has been described as the single most distinguished feature of American history in general, so it also left a distinguishing mark on American theatre history. Theatre in America began in the early settlements on the eastern seaboard, the frontier of the New World; and after Philadelphia, New York and Boston became theatrical centres, troupes of actors advanced into the western regions quick on the heels of the pioneers.

The following pattern was repeated several times: a principal city developed as the transportation, supply and finance centre for a series of outlying communities in which the region's raw materials were exploited. If these outlying communities were sufficiently remote, intermediate supply towns developed as well. Theatre responded to this pattern: permanent companies resided in large city theatres, and a dominant manager sent them on tour to the outlying communities. Intermediate towns were served in the same way, but on a more frequent basis. The first theatre opened in Williamsburg, Virginia, in 1718; the second, the Dock Street in Charleston, South Carolina, in 1736. When the Lewis Hallam company arrived from London in 1752, they performed in a new Williamsburg theatre. The HALLAMS and other troupes took to the road, found makeshift halls in such settlements as Annapolis, Norfolk, Newport and Providence, and set the pattern for the western trek that was soon to follow.

Thespian societies were a part of the cultural life of Lexington (1799), Cincinnati (1801) and St Louis (1815), even before professional troupes arrived. These troupes began their journey from Albany or Philadelphia to Pittsburgh, thence by flatboat down the Ohio River to Cincinnati and Louisville, and, as the frontier expanded, down the Mississippi to St Louis, Memphis, Nashville, Montgomery, Mobile and New Orleans. The James Douglass troupe arrived in Lexington, Louisville and Frankfort in 1810, and the SAMUEL DRAKE company in 1815. Typical of the accommodation they found was Luke Usher's Lexington theatre, a large room (30 × 60ft) on the second floor of his brewery. Two actors in Drake's company, NOAH LUDLOW and SOL SMITH, became the leading managers on the frontier, first as competitors and then as partners. Both wrote detailed first-hand accounts of their adventures.

Cramped and improvised quarters were common: a stage 10ft wide and 8ft deep, a Memphis theatre where only the women could be seated, and another that had formerly been a livery stable. Even proper theatres like the Columbia Street in Cincinnati (1821), boasting a 'spacious gallery', 'commodious lobbies' and 'two tiers of boxes', squeezed the stage and 800 spectators into a small area (40 × 100ft). JAMES H. CALDWELL was the first to provide adequate facilities with his three New Orleans theatres: the 1100-seat AMERICAN or Camp Street (1824), the St Charles (1835), and a second St Charles (1843). The first ST CHARLES, with 4000 seats, was said to be equalled in size and grandeur only by the opera houses in Naples, Milan and St Petersburg. When the theatre burned down (1842, a common occurrence), Caldwell built the second St Charles, less ornate and seating 1500, and turned the management over to Ludlow and Smith.

Frontier theatres were not all land-based. Showboating on the Ohio and Mississippi began early and continued into the 20th century, first with Ludlow's *Noah's Ark* (1817), then with William Chapman's *Floating Palace* (1831). SHOWBOATS lured audiences with their calliopes and their picturesque names: *French's New Sensation*, *Snow Queen*, *Wonderland*, *Goldenrod*, *Cotton Blossom* and *Majestic*.

Theatres appeared almost immediately after a community was settled; for example, Chicago (chartered 1837) was the location for John B. Rice's first theatre (1847), his second (1851) and McVICKER's (1857). Development of the trans-Mississippi West was similar to that of the East, but more extreme: distance was greater, population shift more volatile, and wealth more instantaneous and abundant. While playing conditions were conventional in the cities and towns, they were primitive in the small settlements: actors arrived by wagon and pack animal, often slept in the open, and performed in stores, houses and tents. However crude the conditions, though, western audiences were noted for the prodigality of their response.

California was the first region to develop. Its pioneer period began in 1849 and had passed its peak by 1857. The principal city was San Francisco, and the outlying communities were the gold mining camps in the Sierra Nevada. In between were the towns of Marysville, Sacramento and Stockton. During 1850–84 the Napoleon of California managers was Tom Maguire, an illiterate cab driver and saloon keeper. With few exceptions, he managed one or more theatres in the cities, and at least one in each intermediate town, thereby ensuring a smooth flow of attractions to the gold mines during the summer and early autumn. During 1859–67 the silver mines of Nevada's Washoe Valley became an extension of the California region, and Maguire used Virginia City as an intermediate town for them.

The West's second mining frontier began in 1857 along the eastern slopes of the Rocky Mountains near the South Platte River, and spread north and east with the gold strikes in Montana during the 1860s and in the Dakotas in the 70s. Denver was the region's city, and it was there that its most important manager, John Langrishe, first struck it rich. An actor seasoned by 15 years of barnstorming in the Mississippi Valley, Langrishe moved with his company in pursuit of bonanza: Denver (1859–67), Helena and Cheyenne (1867–71) and Deadwood (1876–9). The coming of the railways divided this frontier into separate regions. Denver became the centre of the Silver Circuit, which included the mining and resort towns of Colorado and the Mormon communities of Utah; it peaked under the management of Peter McCoart (1885–95). Montana and Wyoming were controlled by John Maguire (no relation to Tom), with its centre in Helena (1884–1900), whereas the Dakotas developed their own identity under the management of C.P. 'Con' Walker in Fargo after 1892.

Both the Northwest and Southwest waited for eastern rail links in the 1880s. Theatre followed population along the route of the Santa Fe Railroad in the Southwest. Los Angeles, where Henry T. Wyatt was the principal manager, became a theatrical centre servicing adjacent regions: southern California, the central coast, the central valley and Arizona–New Mexico. In the Northwest development followed the line of the Northern Pacific, which terminated in Seattle, where Calvin Heilig and John Cort were the leading managers. A second centre was Portland, which was on the way to San Francisco; John Howe was the principal manager there until the coming of the THEATRICAL SYNDICATE.

Western theatricals had two extensions beyond the continental USA: players had passed through San Francisco to and from the British colonies since 1855, but the management of an American, James Cassius Williamson, in Sydney after 1879 developed the route from Honolulu to Cape Town. The West's final frontier was the Klondike region of Alaska, where there was a gold stampede from 1896 to 1910. Vancouver was the city for this region, and Dawson, Fairbanks and Nome each had its turn as a principal town.

However unconventional playing conditions and audience behaviour in the frontier theatres may have been, productions were otherwise conventional. Each frontier saw the major actors of its day: JUNIUS BRUTUS BOOTH, EDWIN FORREST, W. C. MACREADY, EDWIN BOOTH, ANNA CORA MOWATT, JOSEPH JEFFERSON III, LAURA KEENE, TYRONE POWER, LOTTA CRABTREE, ADAH ISAACS MENKEN, JAMES MURDOCH, GEORGE HANDEL HILL, DANFORTH MARBLE, JOHN McCULLOUGH and others. These stars played their standard repertory of SHAKESPEARE, old COMEDY, contemporary FARCE, and domestic and sensational MELODRAMA in various permutations to suit the ability of the individual performer and the taste of the audience.   RM DMCD

See: M. Berson, *The San Francisco Stage: From Gold Rush to Golden Spike, 1849–1869*, San Francisco, 1989; W.G.B. Carson, *The Theatre on the Frontier*, Chicago, 1932; P. Graham, *Showboats*, Austin, Texas, 1951; M. Henderson, *History of the Theatre in Salt Lake City*, Salt Lake City, 1941; H. Hoyt, *Town Hall Tonight*, New York, 1955; H. W. Koon, *How Shakespeare Won the West*, Jefferson, NC, 1989; P.C. Lewis, *Trouping*, New York, 1973; D. McDermott, *Theatre Survey* (May 1978); D. McDermott and R. Sarlós (eds.), *Theatre West: Image and Impact*, Atlanta, Ga., 1990; R. Moody, *America Takes the Stage*, Bloomington, Ind., 1955; M. Watson, *Silver Theatre: Amusements of the Mining Frontier in Early Nevada, 1850–1864*, Glendale, Calif., 1964.

Fry, Christopher 1907– British playwright. His charming and witty verse plays of the 1940s and 1950s – *A Phoenix Too Frequent* (1946), *The Lady's Not for Burning* (1948), *Venus Observed* (1950) and *The Dark Is Light Enough* (1954) – were gentle successes that touched upon real concerns via unreal situations. Fry's view of mankind is marked by a tolerant Christianity that has sometimes made his plays unfashionable, especially as the poetic form is of rather specialized appeal. His translation of ANOUILH's *L'Invitation au château* (*Ring Round the Moon*, 1950) and *L'Alouette* (*The Lark*, 1955) and of plays by GIRAUDOUX, IBSEN and ROSTAND supplied more substantial plots for his skill with words .   MB

Fuchs, Georg 1868–1949 German director. Influenced by JOCZA SAVITS's experiments with the SHAKESPEARE stage in the Munich Court Theatre, in 1908 Fuchs founded the Munich Artists' Theatre. This had a relief stage, on which no attempt was made to create a realistic illusion. Fuchs's ambitions for the theatre are to be found in his most frequently read book, *Revolution in the Theatre*.   SW

Fuentes, Carlos 1928– One of Mexico's most celebrated novelists. Totally bilingual and bicultural in English, Fuentes has rarely ventured into theatre, but did so successfully with *Todos los gatos son pardos* (*All Cats Are*

Gray, 1970) and *El tuerto es rey* (*The One-Eyed King*, 1970). In 1982 he wrote *Orquídeas a la luz de la luna* in Spanish and the American version, *Orchids in the Moonlight*, to chronicle the myths and disintegrating values surrounding Dolores del Río and María Félix, two ageing Mexican American film stars.   GW

Fugard, Athol 1932– South African playwright; educated at the University of Cape Town, where he studied philosophy. Fugard's plays are written in English but incorporate many regional dialects and slang derived from vernaculars. His first plays and a novel (*Tsotsi*) were written from 1958 while he associated with black writers and intellectuals in the freehold suburb of Sophiatown outside Johannesburg. In the 1960s he wrote what are often referred to as 'the family plays' – including *The Blood Knot* (1961), *Hello and Goodbye* (1965) and *Boesman and Lena* (1969) – about the loneliness and isolation of working-class people of different races. In the early 1960s he worked through improvisation with actors to create what are referred to as 'the workshop plays', like *Sizwe Bansi Is Dead* (1972) and *Statements after an Arrest*

under the Immorality Act (1972), plays which dealt more directly with the oppression brought about by apartheid. In the second half of the decade he began writing alone again, and this period produced plays like *Master Harold ... and the Boys* (1982) and *The Road to Mecca* (1984), focusing on relationships and with a backdrop of politics. Indeed his plays are permeated by South African politics, but Fugard maintains that he is simply a 'regional' writer, and that his concern is with individual loneliness and pain in specific situations: politics, he suggests, provides only the context.

With the radical changes occurring in South Africa during the first half of the 1990s, however, his work has become more actively engaged with the political situation. His play *My Children, My Africa!* (1989) depicts characters actively confronting the violence of the streets which characterizes SOUTH AFRICA in the 90s: a society caught in civil war brought about by apartheid. And *Playland* (1992) depicts characters trying to find some way of communicating with each other and with themselves in the light of a history that has bruised every South African. Castigated by some for being a white liberal out of touch

Winston Ntshona in *Sizwe Bansi is Dead* by Athol Fugard, John Kani and Ntshona.

with the realities of black suffering and resistance, Fugard nevertheless succeeds in articulating an image of South Africa's peoples trying to live out their lives in a society deformed by race prejudice and all the insecurities spawned by such prejudice. IS

Fukuda Tsuneari 1912–94 Japanese playwright, critic and director. Fukuda graduated with a degree in English literature from Tokyo University in 1936 and later published a complete translation of SHAKESPEARE's works. He carried on the literary legacy of KISHIDA KUNIO in the post-war period, but, unlike Kishida, idealized Shakespeare and held the Bard up as the model Japanese theatre should emulate. During the 1950s Fukuda was active as a conservative social critic and as a playwright. In 1963 he founded the Contemporary Theatre Association (Gendai Engeki Kyōkai) and its affiliated Cloud (Kumo) troupe, which later became known as Subaru.

A proponent of conservative values in the theatre as in politics, Fukuda's major plays frequently parody Western works and are generally less stimulating than his theories. *Typhoon Kitty* (*Kitii taifū*, 1949), for example, may be read as a parody of CHEKHOV's *Cherry Orchard*; and *The Man Who Stroked the Dragon* (*Ryū o nadeta otoko*), often cited as Fukuda's best work, is based on ELIOT's *The Cocktail Party*. DGG

Fukuda Yoshiyuki 1931– Japanese playwright. Influenced by dramatist KINOSHITA JUNJI, Fukuda began his career as an orthodox left-wing playwright but contributed to the creation of the post-SHINGEKI movement with plays like *Find Hakamadare!* (*Hakamadare wa doko da*, 1964; trans. 1988), which introduced the dramaturgy of metamorphosis that characterized Japanese playwriting in the 1960s. As a founder of the Youth Art Theatre (Seinen Geijutsu Gekijō or Seigei) he influenced numerous younger playwrights, including BETSUYAKU MINORU, SATOH MAKOTO and KARA JŪRŌ, all of whom worked with the troupe. DGG

Fulda, Ludwig 1862–1939 German playwright. As a young man, Fulda was closely associated with the naturalist movement (see NATURALISM). His later plays were in verse. SW

Fuller, Charles 1939– African-American playwright. When *A Soldier's Play* (1981), dealing with the murder of an unpopular black army sergeant, received the Pulitzer Prize, Fuller was only the second black playwright to be so honoured. Philadelphia-born Fuller had several plays produced OFF-BROADWAY, notably by the NEGRO ENSEMBLE COMPANY, which nurtured his talent with productions of *In the Deepest Part of Sleep* (1974), *The Brownsville Raid* (1976) and the Obie-winning *Zooman and the Sign* (1980), as well as *A Soldier's Play*, which was turned into an absorbing film (*A Soldier's Story*, 1984). Since then, Negro Ensemble has produced other Fuller plays, including *Sally* and *Prince* (1988–9). Recently he has been working on a series of six plays about the post-Civil War quest for black self-determination; four have been produced at the NEC's Theatre Four to date, but have attracted little serious critical attention. EGH

Fuller, Isaac 1606–72 English scene-painter. A successful painter of portraits in the 1650s and 1660s, Fuller contracted with the King's Company in 1669 to paint 'a new scene of Elysium' for their production of DRYDEN's *Tyrannic Love*, agreeing to complete it in two weeks. It took much longer and the company sued him for £500 for the delay. He claimed he worked non-stop on it for three weeks and was awarded £325 10s as payment for the work. The case demonstrates the colossal expenditure on sets for the Restoration stage. PH

Furttenbach, Josef 1591–1667 German architect and scene designer. Having studied architecture and theatre design in Italy, Furttenbach absorbed the ideas utilized by GIULIO PARIGI and took them back to Germany. In 1631 he became municipal architect at Ulm and ten years later he designed and completed the city's Theater am Benderhof, which was used primarily for school performances. His designs are noted for their reliance upon a central vanishing point, *periaktoi*, a rear pit for the housing of special effects, and pictorial bow-shaped framing devices. He published several works on Italian architecture: *Civil Architecture* (1628), which only touches on theatre architecture and design; *Recreational Architecture* (1640), which illustrates *periaktoi*, cloud borders, flying machines and the chariot-and-pole mechanism for shifting scenery; and *The Noble Mirror of Art* (1663). The importance of these works is that they preserve and illustrate in great detail both the function and construction of scene-changing devices and stage machinery used in the Italian baroque theatre. (See also THEATRE BUILDINGS; THEATRE DESIGN.) AJN

futurism An artistic movement primarily of the second and third decades of the 20th century; founded by F. T. MARINETTI in 1909. The ideas and strategies of the futurists were rapidly diffused through manifestos, journals, exhibitions and the so-called 'futurist evenings'. The movement falls roughly into two phases, the first and most vigorous dating from Marinetti's 'The Founding and Manifesto of Futurism', published in the Paris *Figaro* of 20 February 1909, through to the early 1920s; the second during the period of Fascism, when it was little more than nominally avant-garde. Asserting an aesthetic of the 'new' and calling for an art attuned to the century of science and technology, futurism exalted what it claimed to be the essential characteristics of 'modernism': speed, movement, dynamism and spontaneity. It rejoiced in the machine – particularly motor car, aeroplane, speed boat and motor-cycle – and demanded a machine-age art. To achieve this it ruthlessly jettisoned the past, stridently denouncing most received artistic traditions, along with the conformism and academicism of museums, art galleries, concert halls and the regular 'prose' and 'musical' theatre.

Theatricality was of its essence, and the movement quickly developed a futurist theatre: the highly contentious 'futurist evenings' included readings, displays of painting and sculptures, and presentations of futurist performance 'works'. The presentations were deliberately calculated to provoke the verbal and physical wrath of audiences. Although they rejected most traditional forms of theatre, futurist practitioners recognized that their techniques had much in common with popular café and VARIETY entertainment, as Marinetti acknowledged in his important manifesto *Teatro di varietà* (*The Variety Theatre*, 1913).

A distinct advance came with the synthesis proposed in *Il teatro sintetico futurista* (*The Synthetic Theatre*, 1915). Syntheses were highly compressed dramatic pieces, intended to be demonstrations of that dynamic, autonomous, alogical, anti-psychological, abstract theatre that the futurists advocated as an ideal. The movement produced about 500 such syntheses, the best of which are more than mere musical GAGS and pat CABARET sketches, and anticipate certain themes and motives developed later by surrealist and absurdist theatre (see SURREALISM; THEATRE OF THE ABSURD) and by dramatists like PIRANDELLO and BECKETT. It inspired, too, some notable scenic design work, major figures in this field including the sculptor Giacomo Balla, the designer Fortunato Depero and the painter, and one of the leading theorists of the movement, ENRICO PRAMPOLINI. Futurist staging sought a dynamic use of chromatic effects in which the role of the human was either absent altogether or relegated to a robot-like function. An impressive example of futurist scenic design is that of Balla for Stravinsky's *Feu d'artifice* (1917), but most futurist scenic projects were never realized on the stage.

Marinetti early proposed the use of revolves to achieve that synthesis of activities and effects that should characterize futurist presentations. But as Prampolini later admitted, the movement lacked mechanical means, just as it lacked performers of skill, and an air of the amateurish invariably enveloped the theatre work it actually succeeded in mounting.   KR LR

Fuzelier, Louis 1672–1752 French playwright and librettist, a prolific author of comedies, comic OPERAS, *vaudevilles*, *ballet-pantomimes* and other *divertissements*, many of them parodies of existing works and totalling almost 200 in all. Apart from certain more formal works performed at the COMÉDIE-FRANÇAISE or the Opéra, the vast majority were written for the COMÉDIE-ITALIENNE or for the Paris fair theatres, where they were subject to an injunction outlawing spoken dialogue, imposed by the parlement at the instance of jealous actors of the legitimate stage. Accordingly the text was either set to music and sung or delivered in successive monologues or, again, in the so-called *pièces à écriteaux*, written in hand-held scrolls and on placards suspended from the flies, to which the actors mimed and the orchestra supplied a musical accompaniment of familiar airs, enabling the audience to join in. Fuzelier frequently collaborated with other playwrights (notably Panard, d'Orneval and LESAGE) or composers (Gilliers, J. B. Quinault, Rameau and Campra) and wrote on theatrical topics in the weekly *Mercure de France*, which he co-edited for several years in the 1720s and 1740s.   DR

Gabon and the Central African Republic The modern theatre of these two Central African countries, which with Chad and Congo constituted the former French Equatorial African Federation, remains the least developed in all French-speaking Africa. Gabon, which became independent in 1960, has only one playwright of note – the former Minister of Education Paul Nyonda, with 12 plays. The two most important of these are a dramatized legend, *La Mort de Guykafi* (*Guykafi's Death*, published 1981), performed at the 1966 Dakar Festival of Negro Arts, and *Le Soûlard* (*The Drunkard*, 1981), on the problems of alcoholism. The two other Gabonese writing for the stage are Laurent Owondo with *Les Impurs* (*The Impure Ones*), and one of francophone Africa's few female playwrights, Josephine Kama Bongo, whose play *Obali* (1974) deals with problems of forced marriages.

The Central African Republic, known in colonial times as Oubangui Chari, is better known, even today, for the literature on it by the French novelist André Gide in *Voyages au Congo* (*Travels in the Congo*, 1927) and by the French West Indian René Maran in *Batouala* (1921) than for its own literary productions. It has published no dramatic works, though four plays were shortlisted in various Radio France Internationale drama competitions: *A Molengue ti independence* (*The Children of Independence*, 1960) by Abbot Benoît-Basile Siango, *La Veuve Kiringuiza* (*Widow Kiringuiza*, 1968) by A. Franck, *Le Téléphone* (*The Telephone*, 1976) by Faustin-Albert Ipeko-Etomaner, and *La Petite Leçon* (*The Small Lesson*, 1976) by Étienne Goyémidé. JCM

> *See*: R. Cornevin, *Le Théâtre en Afrique noire et à Madagascar*, Paris, 1970, and 'Gabonese Writers and Dramatists', *The Courier: European Community–African Caribbean Pacific*, 50, Jul./Aug. 1978; E. Goyémidé, 'Le Théâtre existe!', *Notre Librairie: La Littérature Centrafricaine*, 97, Apr./May 1989.

Gabrielli family Italian actors. **Giovanni** (d. between 1603 and 1611), under the name Sivello, excelled at solo PANTOMIMES in which he presented a whole troupe of characters. His son **Francesco** (?1588–?1636), who amplified the ZANNI Scapino, toured Italy and France from 1612, mostly with the ACCESI and CONFIDENTI, though he was with the FEDELI under GIOVAN BATTISTA ANDREINI in Paris during1624–5. Accomplished at a dozen instruments, he was noted for virtuoso musical numbers. His daughter **Giulia** was seen in Paris under the name Diana in 1645. Girolamo Gabrielli, a famous Pantalone, and Ippolita Gabrielli, who was managing a troupe in 1663, may or may not be his children. LS

gag Originally, words interpolated by an actor into his part. The term derived from 'gag' as something forced into the mouth and was current theatrical slang in the 1840s. DICKENS uses it in *Bleak House* (1852). It came to mean a comic improvisation, and then, in silent film, a surprising or unmotivated wrinkle in the plot, often an elaborately structured piece of physical comedy. Now used to designate any joke or creative inspiration ('What's the gag?'). LS

Gaiety Theatre (London) Opened in 1868 on the site of the Strand Music-Hall by JOHN HOLLINGSHEAD. The Gaiety established a reputation for BURLESQUE, comic opera with the first collaboration of GILBERT and Sullivan, *Thespis* (1871), and then MUSICAL COMEDY after *In Town* (1892: generally considered the first of this genre), which survived the move to a new building in 1903 and continued until the theatre closed in 1939. Its initial popularity was partly due to a famous quartette of comedians – NELLIE FARREN, EDWARD ROYCE, EDWARD TERRY and KATE VAUGHAN – then during the 1890s to the 'Gaiety Girls'. These were initially introduced in a PARODY form as part of *Ruy Blas; or, The Blasé Roué* (1889), a burlesque which featured C. Danby, FRED LESLIE, Ben Nathan and Fred Story as ballerinas made up to resemble the actor-managers HENRY IRVING, J. L. TOOLE, WILSON BARRETT and Edward Terry. But the name came to refer to the musical chorus line of the 1890s, who were selected as much for their legs and looks as their singing and dancing ability. Among the later stars who made their name at the Gaiety the best-known were Gertie Millar and Leslie Henson. After standing empty for almost 20 years, the theatre was demolished in 1957. CI

Gaiety Theatre (Manchester, England) Built in 1884, the theatre achieved fame with the establishment there in 1908 of ANNIE HORNIMAN's repertory company, marking the beginning of the British repertory movement (see REGIONAL THEATRE (BRITAIN)). Miss Horniman rebuilt and refurbished the theatre interior and reduced its seating from 2500 to a more comfortable 1250. The first full season set the pattern for the next six years, offering plays by (among others) EURIPIDES, SHAW and GALSWORTHY and some one-act plays by Lancashire writers Allan Monkhouse, STANLEY HOUGHTON and HAROLD BRIGHOUSE – the core of what was later to be known as the 'Manchester school'. The Gaiety, under the artistic direction of BEN IDEN PAYNE and then LEWIS CASSON, soon built a reputation for its ensemble playing and its fostering of new writing, boosted further by a series of London seasons and tours to Canada and the USA. Success, however, brought its own penalties: the company over-extended itself and standards became inconsistent. During wartime the theatre's quality of output and its audiences declined, until in 1917 the company was disbanded. The Gaiety became a minor touring house until Miss Horniman sold it in 1920. Thereafter it served as a cinema, until finally demolished in 1952. AJ

Gaîté, Théâtre de la see BOULEVARD

Gala, Antonio 1936– Spanish playwright, novelist and poet who enjoys celebrity status for his television series and newspaper columns. His reputation as a major dramatist dates from the triumphant premiere of his first play, *Los verdes campos del Edén* (*The Green Fields of Eden*, 1963). *Los buenos días perdidos* (*The Bells of Orleans*, 1972), a SATIRE of contemporary materialism, and *Anillos para una dama* (*Rings for a Lady*, 1973), a feminist debunking of the Cid myth from the perspective of his widow Jimena, introduced a series of critical and box-office successes.

Gala's theatre blends sparkling surface humour with an underlying tragic reality. His protagonists typically seek a paradise of political and personal freedom where they may love the person of their choice. They champion the cause of the disempowered: women, Jews, homosexuals. With occasional exceptions like *Petra regalada* (1980), an allegory of the end of the Franco era, and *La truhana* (*The Comedienne*, 1992), their battle against repression meets with failure. Recent works include the long-running MUSICAL *Carmen Carmen* (1988) and the OPERA libretto *Cristóbal Colón* (*Christopher Columbus*, 1989; music by Leonardo Balada). The latter production, starring José Carreras, toured internationally in conjunction with the 1992 Quincentennial. PZ

Galich [Ginzburg]**, Aleksandr (Arkadievich)** 1918–77 Soviet Russian poet and playwright, popular in the 1940s and 50s for such romantic plays as *Moscow Does Not Believe in Tears* (1949). In the 1960s he became a prominent chansonnier, accompanying his own songs on guitar. As 'unofficial bard' he presented a satiric picture of everyday Soviet life dominated by the Party. He was expelled from the Writers' Union in 1972, and two years later emigrated to Paris, where he died of electrocution while repairing a tape recorder. His novel *Dress Rehearsal* (1974) is a fascinating account of backstage politics in Brezhnev's Russia. Galich was rehabilitated in 1987, when his banned play *Sailor's Rest* (1957), about three generations of a Russian-Jewish family, was staged at the MOSCOW ART THEATRE Studio by OLEG TABAKOV under the title *Big Land*. LS

Galich, Manuel 1913–84 Guatemalan playwright. Born to a theatrical family, Galich studied law at the University of Guatemala, directed an experimental theatre group (1938–42), and participated as a young revolutionary against Jorge Ubico (Guatemalan president, 1931–44). He was subsequently Minister of Education under Arévalo, Minister of Foreign Affairs under Arbenz, and Guatemala's ambassador to Argentina. His early plays were both historical and costumbristic (see COSTUMBRISMO), but his principal thrust was anti-imperialistic, political theatre. Major titles are *El tren amarillo* (*The Yellow Train*, 1954), *El pescado indigesto* (*The Undigested Fish*, 1960) and *Míster John Tenor y yo* (*Mr John Tenor and I*, 1975). Attracted by the Castro Revolution, he played a major role in the development of revolutionary theatre in Cuba, and served from 1964 to 1984 as the general editor of the theatre journal *Conjunto*. GW

Galimafré see BOBÈCHE

Galin, Aleksandr (Mikhailovich) 1947– Extremely popular Russian (St Petersburg) Jewish playwright, who

began his career in the puppet theatre after being refused admission to the Theatre Institute. Galin's breakthrough contemporary comedy of manners, *Retro* (1980), staged by Leonid Khaifits at Moscow's Maly Dramatic Theatre (1982), parodied GOGOL's *Marriage* and offered palatable social criticism of housing shortages and inadequate care of the elderly. DODIN's production of Galin's *Stars in the Morning Sky*, concerning the temporary deportation of prostitutes from Moscow during the 1980 Olympics, played in Los Angeles in 1988. Of his other produced plays (including *The Migratory Birds Are Flying*, *Delusion*, *The Last Meeting* and *Eastern Grandstand*), *The Group* (1990) is interesting for its treatment of the theme of contemporary Russian female identity, and *The Roof* for its semi-autobiographical treatment of Soviet college life in the early 1970s. Suppressed for nine years in Russia, the latter was produced at Florida State University, where Galin was in residence, in spring 1990. SG

Gallagher and Shean American vaudeville team. Straight man **Ed(ward) Gallagher** (?1873–1929) and comic **Al(bert) Shean** [Schoenberg] (1868–1949) formed a team in 1910 after years with other partners. For four years they appeared in VAUDEVILLE, BURLESQUE and REVUES; they then parted, reunited in 1920, and subsequently gained tremendous success, highlighted by 67 weeks in the ZIEGFELD Follies. An entire routine and career were built around one theme song ('Absolutely, Mr Gallagher?' 'Positively, Mr Shean'). The team dissolved in 1925, though Shean continued as a character actor on stage and in films. Shean's nephews, the MARX BROS, were given much support by their uncle early in their careers. DBW

Gallegos, Daniel 1930– Costa Rican playwright, director, professor and actor. Educated at home and abroad (USA and Europe), Gallegos was a major influence in the development of the Costa Rican theatre, as director of the Teatro Universitario and professor at the University of Costa Rica. His major plays are *Ese algo de Dávalos* (*Davalos's Certain Something*, 1964), *La colina* (*The Hill*, 1968), a metaphysical play about the death of God, and *En el séptimo círculo* (*In the Seventh Circle*, 1982), about violence in the current world situation. GW

Galsworthy, John 1867–1933 British novelist and dramatist; awarded the Nobel Prize for Literature in 1932 and best known for his novel sequence *The Forsyte Saga* that received international acclaim in a television dramatization (see TELEVISION DRAMA). His first plays, *The Silver Box* (1906), *Strife* (1909) and *Justice* (1910), were all produced by GRANVILLE BARKER. Dealing with the inequalities of justice in a class system, the causes of industrial unrest and the psychological effects of the prison system, their objective depiction of topical moral issues and social conscience made Galsworthy's plays a popular staple of the provincial repertory movement (see REGIONAL THEATRE (BRITAIN)) as well as WEST END successes. These themes were extended in *The Fugitive* (1913), dealing with the social victimization of women, and *The Mob* (1914), denouncing war hysteria, and repeated in a series of plays during the 1920s: *The Skin Game*, *Loyalties*, *Escape* and *Exiled*. His call for social reform was most effective in

Justice, which had a significant impact on the campaign for prison reform, and *Strife* was successfully revived at the NATIONAL THEATRE in 1978. But in general, like most 'problem drama', his plays have dated badly because the issues are defined too specifically in terms of a particular social context and the well made plots, several of which end with the protagonist's suicide, are overtly conventional. CI

Gambaro, Griselda 1928– Argentine novelist and short-story writer, and perhaps the foremost woman playwright in Latin America. Gambaro's hard-hitting psychological plays strike at the violence and oppression which have not only characterized Argentine politics and daily life in recent years but are inherent in the human condition. *Los siameses* (*The Siamese Twins*, 1967) contrasts aggression and passivity in two mutually dependent individuals, and *El campo* (*The Camp*, 1968) bears the stigma of a concentration camp whose leader is named Franco. Both earlier and later plays decry the trivialization and show the absurdity of contemporary lifestyles. During virulent periods of repression (see CENSORSHIP), she sought refuge in Spain; some of her plays have still not been performed in Argentina. Recent titles include *Decir sí* (*To Say Yes*, 1981) and *La malasangre* (*Bad Blood*, 1982), *Antígona furiosa* (*Furious Antigone*, 1986), *Efectos personales* (*Personal Effects*, 1988), *Morgan* (1989) and *Penas sin importancia* (*Unimportant Sorrows*, 1990). GW

Gambon, Michael 1940– Irish-born British actor. Gambon has become one of the most respected actors on the British stage, especially through his work at the NATIONAL THEATRE which he first joined in 1963 (at the OLD VIC) and to which he returned in 1978, and for the ROYAL SHAKESPEARE COMPANY. He played King Lear for the RSC in 1982–3, and as a comparable pinnacle in television took the title role in DENIS POTTER's play *The Singing Detective* (BBC, 1986). His is a quiet and unassuming talent, and a major one. His association with ALAN AYCKBOURN, which began with *The Norman Conquests* in which he played Tom the vet, has continued in productions which Ayckbourn has directed, not written, such as ARTHUR MILLER's *A View from the Bridge* (1987) and *Othello* (1990). He played Vanya in MICHAEL BLAKEMORE's production of *Uncle Vanya*, and the Sergeant in HAROLD PINTER's chilling *Mountain Language* (1988). He seems to work better with those directors who respect the stillness and economy of his acting rather than those who demand a more demonstrative style. MB JE

Ganassa [Zan Ganassa; Alberto Naseli or Naselli] ?1540–?1584 One of the first Italian COMMEDIA DELL'ARTE actors to perform beyond the borders of Italy. A specialist in ZANNI roles, he first crops up in 1568 as head of a troupe in Mantua. After giving private performances in France (1571, 1572), the latter occasion at the invitation of Charles IX, he spent nearly a decade in Spain (1574–84). There his success was so extraordinary that the municipal authorities of Seville revoked his company's licence because workers were slacking off to attend the shows. He is often mentioned by LOPE DE VEGA, who may have based his comic GRACIOSO on *commedia* figures. Fifty years after

Ganassa's departure, he was still cited in Spanish folk-sayings. LS

Gao Xingjian 1940– Chinese writer of HUAJU, and drama theorist. Influenced by Western, especially French, ideas he was the most innovative and challenging of the younger playwrights during the 1980s in terms of concept, performance and style. Graduating from the Beijing Foreign Languages Institute in 1962, he visited France in 1979 and after several further visits took up residence there. A highly prolific writer, he is best known for three spoken dramas from the first half of the 1980s: *Warning Signal* (*Juedui xinhao*), *Bus Stop* (*Chezhan*) and *Wild Man* (*Yeren*). *Warning Signal* is about unemployed youth. The main character, Blackie, intends to take part in a train robbery to get the money he needs to marry, but in the end turns against his accomplice and kills him. Like most other spoken dramas of the time, it is really about serious social problems in Chinese society – unemployment and juvenile delinquency. What is unusual is the play's symbolism and that it offers no solutions. Blackie's murder of his intended accomplice is shown as a redemptive not a criminal act. He is an anti-hero of a kind virtually unique in China in 1982. *Bus Stop* concerns characters waiting in vain at a bus stop and expressing their memories, disappointments and aspirations, inviting comparison with BECKETT's *Waiting for Godot*. It is a didactic play with a clear message in favour of forward movement. In *Wild Man*, Gao not only adopts contemporary notions of total theatre, but returns to the traditional style of drama in which singing, recitation, dance/movement and acting are combined in a total performance. The item has many messages, among which preservation of the environment is foremost. CPM

García Guerra, Iván 1938– Dominican Republic playwright, director, short-story writer and professor. García Guerra has been active in all phases of Dominican theatre. His first play was *Más allá de la búsqueda* (*Beyond the Search*, 1963), a Promethean existentialist exercise. Other major plays include *Don Quijote de todo el mundo* (*Don Quixote of the World*, 1964), a modernized revolutionary version of the idealistic dreamer, and *Fábula de los cinco caminantes* (*Fable of the Five Travellers*, 1965), a symbolic work representing major forces of contemporary society. GW

García Lorca, Federico 1898–1936 Spanish poet and playwright, executed in Granada at the outbreak of the Spanish Civil War. He reacted against the bourgeois realistic drama of his time, bringing to the stage his knowledge of plastic art, music and ballet.

Lorca's two popular FARCES, *La zapatera prodigiosa* (*The Shoemaker's Prodigious Wife*, 1930) and *El amor de don Perlimplín con Belisa en su jardín* (*The Love of Don Perlimplín with Belisa in her Garden*, 1933), like his MARIONETTE plays, integrate the lyric and the grotesque within a farcical framework. *Mariana Pineda* (1929) is an historical romance in verse about Granada's 19th-century martyr to the cause of freedom; it was premiered by MARGARITA XIRGU with decor by Salvador Dalí. *Doña Rosita la soltera* (*Doña Rosita the Spinster*, 1935) is the TRAGEDY of a woman betrayed who for 20 years awaits her fiancé's return; among notable revivals was the 1980 Lavelli production, staring Núria Espert, that evoked the text's Chekhovian undercurrents.

Lorca's most famous work is his tragic trilogy, where a profound fatalism renders the female characters powerless to struggle against blind passions at odds with society's traditional expectations. *Bodas de sangre* (*Blood Wedding*, 1933), based on a newspaper account of a bride who fled with a former lover on her wedding night, presents the woman's conflict together with a bloody clash between the two rivals – all framed by ancient clan rivalries. Symbolic figures of the Moon and Death, who participate in the pursuit through the forest, underscore the sense of fate.

Yerma (1934) is the tragedy of a barren woman obsessed with maternal needs and married to a man unable to fulfil them. Incapable of yielding to pagan erotic impulses by finding satisfaction with another man, she finally kills her husband. The action is heightened by the Washerwomen's lyrical paean poeticizing the joys of conception and the song of the barren wife during the archetypal fertility dance. Víctor García's polemical staging with Espert toured the USA and Europe in the 1970s. *La casa de Bernarda Alba* (*The House of Bernarda Alba*, 1945) is the tragedy of five daughters whose need for love clashes with the strict code of behaviour of their tyrannical mother. The youngest daughter, who rebels, hangs herself when she believes Bernarda has killed her lover. The tyrant's final words, protesting that her daughter has died a virgin, underscore the conflict between individual freedom and social convention.

Así que pasen cinco años (*When Five Years Pass*, 1945) and *El Público* (*The Audience*, 1986) are experiments in surrealism. The second, written in 1930, defends the right to love in its various dimensions, including the homosexual. Long considered unstageable, its production in Spanish by Pasqual was followed in 1988 by Lavelli's French version.   MH

García, Santiago 1928– Colombian playwright and director. García studied in Czechoslovakia, France and the USA. He is the founder of various theatre groups: El Búho (the Owl), Teatro Estudio (Studio Theatre, of the National University) and the Casa de la Cultura (1966–72), later renamed La Candelaria (1972). He was also the prime force behind the Colombian Theatre Corporation, which organized the 100 or more theatre groups in Colombia into a new union. The first Colombian director to stage Brecht and Peter Weiss, he promoted sociopolitical theatre with Marxist themes and structures. A major director, critic and theoretician, he has close ties with other experimental theatre groups throughout Latin America. Major productions include *La ciudad dorada* (*The Golden City*, 1974) and *Guadalupe, años sin cuenta* (*Guadalupe, Years without End*, 1975) – both dealing with war and violence in Colombia. *Morte y vida Severina* (*Life and Death Severina*) and *Los diez días que estremecieron el mundo* (*Ten days that Shook the World*) are adaptations of the Brazilian play by João Cabral de Melo Neto and the John Reed documentary on Russia, respectively. *Diálogo del rebusque* (*Hermetic Dialogue*, 1983) adapts the Spanish baroque

poet Francisco de Quevedo. García's group La Candelaria celebrated its 25th anniversary in 1991.   GW

Gardner, Herb 1934– Brooklyn-born American playwright and author of a successful syndicated cartoon (*The Nebbishes*). In 1962 *A Thousand Clowns* ran for 428 performances at the Eugene O'Neill Theatre in New York City and was adapted into a successful film, for which Gardner earned an Academy Award nomination. As a New Yorker he considers Broadway his 'neighborhood', and his plays are firmly rooted in urban life. *The Goodbye People* (1968) takes place on Coney Island and *I'm Not Rappaport* (1985) in Central Park. The latter, a poignant and comic study of ageing in America, was a success on Broadway and in London, winning the 1986 Tony. Gardner's most recent work, *Conversations with My Father* (1991), an autobiographical study exploring ethnic identity in America, premiered at the Seattle Repertory Theatre before moving to New York in 1992. Both *Rappaport* and *Conversations* were directed by Daniel Sullivan and starred Judd Hirsch.   BBW

Garin, Erast (Pavlovich) 1902–80 Russian-Soviet actor and director, who performed at the First Amateur Theatre of the Red Army (1921–3) and most notably at the Meyerhold Theatre in a physically expressive, theatrically eccentric mode – as Vanechka in Sukhovo-Kobylin's *Tarelkin's Death* (1922); seven characters in Podgayetsky's *D. E.* (1924); the tragicomic bourgeois Gulyachin in Erdman's *The Mandate* (1925); a sinister Khlestakov in Gogol's *The Inspector General* (1926); a romantic Chatsky in Griboedov's *Woe to Wit* (1928); and new Soviet heroes in Selvinsky's *Commandant 2* (1929) and Vishnevsky's *The Last Command* (1931). Garin directed at the Leningrad Theatre of Comedy (1936–50) and reconstructed Meyerhold's *Mandate mise en scène* in 1956 in Moscow. He performed on radio in the 1930s–50s and appeared in some 25 films, two of which, Gogol's *Marriage* (1937) and Sukhovo-Kobylin's *Rasplyuyev's Happy Days*, he co-wrote and directed.   SG

Garneau, Michel 1939– Quebec dramatist, poet, director and actor. Garneau's work is characterized by inspired irreverence for all that conservative Québécois consider sacred in politics, religion and language. His best-known play, *Quatre à quatre* (*Four to Four*, 1973), performed frequently at home and abroad, explores the constrictive effects of cultural heredity on four generations of Quebec women, while *Strauss et Pesant (et Rosa)* (1974) deals with the unsavoury collaboration between Church and state. *Émilie ne sera plus jamais cueillie par l'anémone* (1981), translated into English (*Émilie*, 1987), German and Spanish, is a sensitive, imaginative portrayal of the American poet Emily Dickinson. Garneau's dramatic texts, some 50 to date, include ten very liberal adaptations (he calls them 'tradaptations') of foreign classics, including Shakespeare and García Lorca.   LED

Garnier, Robert c.1545–90 French dramatist and poet, who divided his time between writing and the legal profession. His seven tragedies, though largely based on Greek mythology or Roman history, betray his own moral and religious concerns and may owe some of their power to his dismay at the doctrinal strife and civil wars then ravaging his native country. Despite their SENECAN manner, relying heavily on monologue and exaggerated pathos, they contain impressive choruses and other passages of lyrical and imaginative eloquence, particularly in the later works such as *Antigone* (1580) and *Les Juives* (*The Jewish Women*, 1583), which deals with Nebuchadnezzar's cruelty to Zedekiah and his family after the siege of Jerusalem. In *Bradamante* (1582), a TRAGICOMEDY derived from ARIOSTO's *Orlando Furioso*, he anticipated the genre that was to dominate the early part of the next century, and the play continued to be acted for many years. At its best Garnier's writing looks forward to PIERRE CORNEILLE and ROTROU, and two of his Roman plays were even translated into English in his own time.   DR

Garrett, João Baptista de Almeida 1799–1854 Portuguese playwright and theatrical motivator. After writing a neoclassical piece, *Catão* (*Cato*), in 1821 and putting on a play about the putting on of one of VICENTE's MASQUES, *Um Auto de Gil Vicente*, which pointed the way to a renewal of Portuguese theatre, Garrett tried his hand with a couple of moderately successful historical plays. He was chosen in 1836 to implement, as Inspector-General of Theatres (a post he held from 1836 to 1841), a plan that included renewing the national stage, setting up acting schools and building a National Theatre (eventually the TEATRO NACIONAL D. MARIA II). He set to work with great energy, built the theatre and provided its first repertoire – the aforementioned plays and five additional comedies, as well as the century's finest drama.

This, *Frei Luís de Sousa*, first performed in 1850, is classical tragedy with careful attention to detail of setting, correctness of costume – spelled out in long stage directions – and to historical events and atmosphere that would have been more typical of contemporary romantic theatre. Based on the true story of a nobleman, presumed killed in battle, who returns to the Portugal of the Spanish captivity under the Philips (to the consternation of his daughter, his remarried wife and her noble-minded husband), the play is strongly patriotic and instinct with a psychological truth which increases the impact of its denouement. With 239 performances in the first hundred years of the Teatro Nacional D. Maria II, it was the most often revived of all plays. Translated as *The Pilgrim* (for the husband returning from the dead), it was the New Vic theatre touring company's first venture into European drama, playing in their 1990–1 season both on tour and in the Lilian Baylis Theatre, SADLER'S WELLS, to considerable acclaim.   LK

Garrick, David 1717–79 English actor, manager and playwright. Born in Hereford, he was educated at Lichfield, enrolling in DR JOHNSON's school at one stage. In 1737 he and Johnson moved to London, where he opened a wholesale wine business with his brother. His first play, *Lethe*, a SATIRE, was performed at DRURY LANE in 1740. He began acting as an amateur but his family disapproved and he acted under a pseudonym in Ipswich. In 1741 at GOODMAN'S FIELDS THEATRE his performance as Richard III won him immediate success, and he followed it with Bayes

in BUCKINGHAM's *The Rehearsal* and King Lear (coached by MACKLIN). The triumph continued when he transferred to Drury Lane in 1742 and in Dublin, where he played Hamlet opposite PEG WOFFINGTON with whom he lived in London. He also began to perform one of his greatest roles as Abel Drugger in JONSON's *The Alchemist*, a realistic study of a low-comedy role.

Drury Lane was in deep financial trouble and Garrick joined the actors rebelling against the management. His willingness to capitulate infuriated Macklin. In 1744 Garrick prepared the way for his performance of Macbeth by publishing a pamphlet, *An Essay on Acting*, a satire on his own intentions. If he was always far from acting a true Shakespearian version of the text, Garrick was a careful restorer of many parts of SHAKESPEARE's plays that had traditionally been cut or adapted. Even his notorious version of *Hamlet* in 1772, which cut Ophelia's madness and the gravediggers in giving the play a remarkably rapid ending, put back numerous lines elsewhere. The *Macbeth* was advertised: 'revived as Shakespeare wrote it'.

During a season at COVENT GARDEN, Garrick produced the best of his 20 plays, the afterpiece FARCE *Miss in Her Teens*. In April 1747 Garrick and LACY signed an agreement of partnership in the Drury Lane Theatre and its patent, inaugurating Garrick's 29 years as the theatre's manager. Opening with a prologue by Dr Johnson assuring the audience that 'The drama's laws the drama's patrons give,/For we that live to please must please to live', Garrick, with a strong company, established Drury Lane as a standard of excellence in production and acting. In 1748 he added Benedick in *Much Ado about Nothing* and Romeo to his repertory, giving *Romeo and Juliet* its first production in London for 80 years and allowing the lovers a brief reunion in the tomb. Never at his best as young lovers, he still won the battle of the Romeos in 1750 when SPRANGER BARRY played the same role at Covent Garden. His production of Malet's *Alfred* (1751) inaugurated the spectacular Drury Lane PANTOMIMES. In 1754 Garrick bought an estate at Hampton with gardens laid out by Capability Brown and a new riverside temple dedicated to Shakespeare. His status was already far beyond any previous English actor's, a friend of the highest in London society, acclaimed as an intelligent critic as much as a performer. In 1755 Garrick coped with riots at the theatre over the employment of a French dance troupe as war broke out. Most of his own Shakespeare adaptations date from this period, with versions of *The Taming of the Shrew*, *The Winter's Tale*, *The Tempest*, *King Lear* and *Antony and Cleopatra* (its first performance since the Restoration).

Always ready to reform theatrical abuses, Garrick abolished the right of half-price admission after the third act, but the consequent riots forced him to give way. Frustrated, he left the stage for two years, travelling to France with his wife and lionized by French writers, players and society. His effect on the DIDEROT circle transformed the attitude to acting in France. For his part Garrick learned about scenic innovations – for instance, wing lights which he introduced at Drury Lane on his return. He collaborated with GEORGE COLMAN THE ELDER on *The Clandestine Marriage* in 1766, but refused to play Lord Ogleby and argued with Colman about their shares in the work.

In 1769 he was invited by the town council at Stratford to organize the Shakespeare Jubilee. Garrick, flattered and seizing the chance to display his idolatry of Shakespeare, arranged a massive series of processions, orations and entertainments at his own expense, nearly all of which were ruined by torrential rain. Undaunted, he mounted the pageants at Drury Lane as *The Jubilee* and recouped his losses. Suffering increasingly from gout and migraines, he began to withdraw from management, eventually selling the patent and his shares to SHERIDAN and retiring from acting with a series of farewell performances ending with SUSANNAH CENTLIVRE's *The Wonder* in 1776. On his death he was accorded a grand funeral at Westminster Abbey. Among other bequests he left his remarkable collection of English plays to the British Museum. An assiduous collector of drama, he was generous in making his library available to scholars like Dr Johnson and Steevens to help their study of Shakespeare and his contemporaries; the bequest extended his generosity.

Garrick's career as manager often seemed marked by disputes with other actors and playwrights but, if some showed him intransigent, he was firm in his policy of refusing bad plays even from friends and refusing actors parts which they could not successfully perform. If he was willing to satisfy public demands for spectacle he also inaugurated new forms of scenery and design, for example in his encouragement of DE LOUTHERBOURG. His cautious balance of commercial acquiescence and artistic responsibility carefully shaped public taste to his own standards, and the result was a rare combination of profit and artistic integrity. As a sustained success his management of Drury Lane is unparalleled.

As writer, his original work was usually no more than pragmatic and he aspired no higher. But his adaptations of earlier drama kept a broad range of major plays in the repertory in forms that the audience would accept. The adaptations show the consistent intelligence of the actor, crafting scenes to maximum effect, giving the cast (and himself) the best opportunities. They also show the producer recognizing in a new way on the English stage how to create a consistent interpretation of a play through cutting, rewriting and the use of scenery and COSTUME, a prototype for a much later concept of the director.

As actor, Garrick was incomparable, his range in classic and new plays unequalled, his virtuosity and daring brilliant and his effect on the audience profound. His terror as Hamlet meeting his father's ghost terrified the audience; his easy charm as Archer in FARQUHAR's *The Beaux' Stratagem* was infectious; his portrayal of Drugger as gentle simpleton was endearing.

Garrick's dominance of the English stage for over 30 years was absolute. His influence was as much social as theatrical; as Dr Johnson said, 'his profession made him rich and he made his profession respectable'.   PH

Garro, Elena 1922– Mexican playwright and novelist, an imaginative writer who finds abstract means of expressing external realities. *Un hogar sólido* (*A Solid Home*, 1956) is the title play of a collection dealing with characters and situations beyond the grave. *La señora en su balcón* (*The Lady on the Balcony*, 1963) is the dramatic encounter of an older woman with haunting illusions of her past. Garro stands as one of the best women writers of Mexico. The ex-wife of Octavio Paz, she recently returned to Mexico after years of self-imposed exile in Paris.   GW

Gascon, Jean 1921–88 French Canadian actor and director. Gascon acted with ÉMILE LEGAULT's Compagnons de Saint-Laurent in the 1940s before studying professional theatre in Paris, 1948–51. One of the founders of the THÉÂTRE DU NOUVEAU MONDE on his return, he was its artistic director until 1966, during the period when the TNM drew international acclaim for its interpretation of French classics, particularly the works of MOLIÈRE, many of them directed by Gascon and staged with the assistance of JEAN-LOUIS ROUX. Named first director-general (1960–3) of the National Theatre School of Canada, he was also active in English Canadian theatre and television, acting and directing at the STRATFORD FESTIVAL (Ontario), of which he was artistic director, 1969–74.   LED

Gaskill, William 1930– British director, who joined the ROYAL COURT THEATRE in 1957. Gaskill, whose experience had previously been as an actor and stage manager in rep, was confronted by N. F. SIMPSON's absurdist farce, *A Resounding Tinkle*, together with *The Hole* as his first assignment, whose unlikely success led to an engagement as assistant to the artistic director, GEORGE DEVINE. He directed plays by Simpson, Donald Howarth, JOHN OSBORNE and ARNOLD WESKER at the Royal Court, as well as *Richard III* (1961) and *Cymbeline* (1962) for the ROYAL SHAKESPEARE COMPANY and, in London, BRECHT's *The Caucasian Chalk Circle* and *Baal* (1963).

LAURENCE OLIVIER invited him to join the newly formed NATIONAL THEATRE Company in 1963 as associate director, and he provided a memorable production of their first season, FARQUHAR's *The Recruiting Officer*. His particular skill lay in encouraging the group acting of the new company through such methods as improvisation and discussion. After directing such National Theatre successes as Brecht's *Mother Courage* and JOHN ARDEN's *Armstrong's Last Goodnight*, he returned to the Royal Court, succeeding George Devine as artistic director. From 1965 to 1972 he led the company through some adventurous seasons, distinguished by the production of EDWARD BOND's first plays, *Saved* (1965), *Early Morning* (1968), *Lear* (1971) and *The Sea* (1973), which he also directed. After leaving the Royal Court he helped to found a theatre cooperative, the Joint Stock Company, which brought actors and writers together in the production of radical plays for what became the leading alternative theatre company in Britain. New plays by DAVID HARE, HOWARD BRENTON and Stephen Lowe were premiered by Joint Stock. Gaskill returned to the National Theatre as a guest director for GRANVILLE BARKER's *The Madras House* (1977). For RICHARD EYRE's NT he has directed LUIGI PIRANDELLO's *Man, Beast and Virtue* (1989) and particularly MIKHAIL BULGAKOV's *Black Snow* (1991), written in 1936, in which Bulgakov avenged himself on the great KONSTANTIN STANISLAVSKY, a situation developed with great panache in Gaskill's production.   JE

Gassman, Vittorio 1922– Italian actor and director. After studying at the National Academy of Dramatic Art in

Rome, he made his debut in 1943 and rapidly emerged on the postwar scene as a major stage actor. His handsome presence and strong, expressive voice made him particularly suited to classic parts like the titles roles in ALFIERI's *Oreste* (1950, directed by VISCONTI), and SHAKESPEARE's *Hamlet* (1952, jointly directed by Gassman and SQUARZINA) and *Othello* (1956). He later formed and directed the Teatro Popolare Italiano, for which he played a range of lead roles. Not only classic, but modern Italian and European drama has been prominent in his repertory, including the DUMAS *père*–SARTRE *Kean*, and plays by Zardi, Pasolini and others. His film career flourished after the international success of *I soliti ignoti* (*Unidentified People*, 1958, directed by Monicelli), in which he revealed a hitherto unsuspected talent for comic character roles. Perhaps his most notable achievements in Shakespeare have been his Richard III, King Lear and Prospero. The range and power of his talent were well illustrated in *Ulisse e la balena bianca* (*Ulysses and the White Whale*, 1972), adapted from Melville's *Moby Dick* and other sources, a production in which he not only performed but which he devised and directed. He has delivered on television a striking 40-part serial reading of Dante's *Divina Commedia* (1993–4), has written a play, *Camper* (1994), has established and runs a theatre school, Bottega Teatrale dell'Arte, and has published several books, including reminiscences and reflections on the theatre – among them *Un grande avvenire dietro le spalle* (*A Great Future behind Me*, 1981), *Memorie del sottoscala* (*Memoirs from under the Stairs*, 1990) and *Mal di parola* (1992). KR

Gate Theatre (Dublin) Created in 1928 by two Englishmen, Micheál MacLiammóir and Hilton Edwards, to diversify and Europeanize Irish theatre. MacLiammóir became a nationally known figure as an actor, but was also designer, director and playwright. His lifelong partner, Edwards, was principally known as a director. In 1930 the Gate moved from the Peacock to its own theatre, becoming noted for its brilliant productions of world classics, experimental plays, WEST END successes and FARCES. Without substantial subsidy, the theatre survived from 1936 to the 60s largely through the patronage of the theatrically inclined Lord Longford.

In the 1980s, with no permanent acting company but operating as an innovative producing house run by Michael Colgan, the Gate re-emerged as a theatrical force. It challenged the ABBEY THEATRE's role as a major producer of O'CASEY with Joe Dowling's highly acclaimed *Juno and the Paycock*, and visiting directors like JONATHAN MILLER, STEVE BERKOFF, Patrick Mason and Karel Reisz, combined with stylish design and distinguished casts, enlivened its staging of European classics and occasional new works. In 1991, with the DUBLIN INTERNATIONAL THEATRE FESTIVAL, the Gate staged the first complete festival of all SAMUEL BECKETT's plays. Although never a writers' theatre, it did much to encourage early work by JOHNSTON and FRIEL; in recent years it has premiered work by LEONARD, Friel, FRANK MCGUINNESS and DERMOT BOLGER. DM GF

Gatti, Armand 1924– French playwright, poet, journalist, script-writer and film-maker. Having experienced a

German concentration camp, Gatti struggled, in much of his early work, to come to terms with the survivor complex. He has tried to write plays that could intervene as incisively in world events as political journalism does. His autobiographical *Vie imaginaire de l'éboueur Auguste Geai* (*Imaginary Life of Auguste Geai*; directed by Rosner, 1962) was his first big success, after which his plays were hotly disputed by the decentralized theatres (see DECENTRALIZATION MOVEMENT). These plays explode the normal conventions of time and space, creating a revolutionary dramaturgy for revolutionary subjects. Since the 1970s, he has moved away from straight plays towards involvement of whole communities and the use of many different media at once, especially video. A series of hard-hitting documentary films was broadcast by French television, and in 1983 he became head of an audio-visual Atelier de Création Populaire at Toulouse, which he left five years later. DB

Gaultier-Garguille [Hugues Guéru; Fléchelles] 1572/3–1633 French actor, one of the most famous FARCE-players of his generation. A member of VALLERAN LE CONTE's troupe at the HÔTEL DE BOURGOGNE in 1606, he returned there in 1612 to join the company led by another of Valleran's ex-associates, GROS-GUILLAUME, thus cementing an acting partnership which was to endure until his death. In farce he was always masked and wore a tight-fitting black doublet with bright-red sleeves, narrow black breeches and stockings. A skull-cap, a cane and a belt holding a pouch and a wooden dagger completed the costume, which clearly owed something to the Pantalone of COMMEDIA and in which he played the old men of farce. In serious plays he adopted the name of Fléchelles, but he appeared under his farcical alias in Gougenot's *La Comédie des comédiens* (*The Actors' Comedy*, 1631/2). Just as popular as his comic acting were the engagingly crude and licentious songs that he contributed to the performance, a collection of which was published and went through several editions. DR

Gautier, Théophile 1811–72 French poet, novelist and critic. Gautier's main importance to the theatre is as a critic of drama and ballet. His first important review appeared in *Le Monde Dramatique* in 1835. From 1837 to 55 he had a regular column in *La Presse* and from 1855 to 71 in *Le Moniteur Universel*. He published a major collection of his theatre CRITICISM in his *Histoire de l'Art dramatique en France depuis vingt-cinq ans* (1858). He originally trained to be a painter. In 1830 he became actively involved with the romantic 'cohort', supporting HUGO's *Hernani* and sporting his celebrated red waistcoat. He soon distanced himself from the excesses of the romantic movement, and his criticism is marked by its common sense and honesty. He contributed to a number of minor dramatic works and librettos, but is best known for providing the scenarios for two major romantic ballets, *Giselle* (1841) and *La Péri* (1843). As a poet he is known for association with the Parnassian movement and for his volume *Émaux et Camées* (1852). JMCC

Gay, John 1685–1732 English dramatist. A schoolfriend of AARON HILL, Gay was apprenticed to a silk mercer in

London before finding employment with the Duchess of Monmouth and becoming a writer. His topical farce *The Mohocks* (1712) was unacted and his Chaucer adaptation *The Wife of Bath* (1713) was performed but proved a failure. A member of the Scriblerus Club with Swift and Pope from 1714, he aligned himself with the Tory party and sought court patronage fruitlessly. In 1715 his BURLESQUE of contemporary tragedy *The What D'Ye Call It* (1715), written with help from Pope, was successful, as was the SATIRE on other writers he wrote with Pope and Arbuthnot, *Three Hours after Marriage* (1717). After writing the libretto for Handel's *Acis and Galatea* (1719) and a PASTORAL tragedy *Dione* (1720), Gay produced the first volume of *The Fables* (1727). In 1728 JOHN RICH, manager of LINCOLN'S INN FIELDS THEATRE, produced Gay's BALLAD OPERA *The Beggar's Opera* with music by Pepusch, a success that made 'Gay rich and Rich gay'. Gay invented a new form with the work, using ballads to create a music theatre and setting his love story in the criminal world, through which he could attack sentimental drama and contemporary politics with immense verve. The work was later adapted by BRECHT as *The Threepenny Opera*. Walpole, stung by the portrayal of himself in *The Beggar's Opera*, banned performances of Gay's sequel *Polly* (1729) which moved Macheath to the West Indies; it was not performed until 1777 in a version by GEORGE COLMAN THE ELDER. None of Gay's later satiric plays matches the brilliance of *The Beggar's Opera*.   PH

gay theatre A term that describes theatre work by male homosexuals (see also LESBIAN THEATRE). 'Gay theatre' usually refers to performances and plays of the 1960s onwards which feature overtly gay characters and situations and/or gay political protest, but it can be extended to cover work before and since (particularly camp and drag) which exhibits a gay sensibility or aesthetic, even in the absence of a specific homosexual narrative. The key example is the work of OSCAR WILDE. Recent gay theorists have claimed Wilde as the originating point for a theatre of gay camp, and the 'bunburying' of *The Importance of Being Earnest* (1895) can be read as an image of covert homosexual practice.

The earliest play to feature a character whom the audience is invited to identify as homosexual is the British playwright HARLEY GRANVILLE BARKER's *The Madras House* (1910). The couturier, Mr Windlesham, is the first in a long history of stage representations of homosexuality as effeminacy. Interestingly, however, most early plays with discernible gay characters and/or narratives (J.R. Ackerley's *The Prisoners of War*, produced in London in 1925; MAE WEST's *The Drag*, 1927, and *The Pleasure Man*, 1928; and Mordaunt Shairp's *The Green Bay Tree*, produced in London and New York in 1933) were written by gay men or, in Mae West's case, a bisexual woman. This contrasts with the representation of lesbians in the same period, which is more overt but produced by heterosexual playwrights.

In the case of the British theatre in the period 1920–50, it can be argued that a gay sensibility, far from being excluded to the margins of theatre, came to dominate it. Many of the major playwrights of the period (SOMERSET MAUGHAM, NOËL COWARD, TERENCE RATTIGAN, for example)

were gay, as were powerful impresarios (BINKIE BEAUMONT of H.M. Tennant). While none of the plays of this theatre were overtly gay, some (Coward's *The Vortex*, 1924, and *Design for Living*, 1932; and Rattigan's *French without Tears*, 1936, to take just a few examples) were clearly, to gay audiences, gay plays. Much of the camp performance aesthetic of the theatre of this period also signals its gay origins.

The gradual liberalization of sexual attitudes in the postwar period – one sign of which, in Britain, was the 1967 decriminalization of sex between consenting adult males – meant that sex and sexuality began to feature as issues in drama. The abolition of the Lord Chamberlain as the British censor in 1968 (see CENSORSHIP) allowed for even greater freedom. It was heterosexual writers who were first to include homosexual characters or plots in their plays, inevitably from a heterosexual and somewhat negative perspective: in the USA, for example, ARTHUR MILLER's *A View from the Bridge* (1955); in Britain, BRENDAN BEHAN's *The Hostage* (1958), SHELAGH DELANEY's *A Taste of Honey* (1958) and JOHN OSBORNE's *A Patriot for Me* (1966). Interestingly, the three great gay playwrights of the period 1940–70 – TENNESSEE WILLIAMS, JEAN GENET and JOE ORTON – included few gay characters in their plays, although their style and narratives are unmistakably gay.

Gay theatre, in the sense of upfront plays about gay subjects for gay audiences, developed in the USA in the 1960s and in Britain in the 1970s. In both places the growth of an alternative circuit of small theatre venues where non-commercial theatre could be cheaply staged was an important factor. In the USA this was provided by the OFF-BROADWAY and OFF-OFF-BROADWAY movements. One such, the CAFFE CINO in New York's Greenwich Village, produced the work of gay playwrights Doric Wilson, Robert Patrick, Claris Nelson and William Hoffman. Off-Broadway also produced Mart Crowley's *The Boys in the Band* (1968), a huge success on both sides of the Atlantic. The 1970s in the USA saw further development of gay theatre with the founding of specifically gay companies and venues across America: for example, TOSOS Theatre Company, the Glines gay arts centre and the Meridian Gay Theatre in New York, the San Francisco Gay Men's Theatre Collective and Theatre Rhinoceros in San Francisco, and other companies in Phoenix, Houston, Minneapolis and Boston.

The growth of gay theatre testifies to the growth of gay communities in large cities. In the Stonewall Riots in Greenwich Village in 1969 the New York gay community took its first direct political action – fighting back against police harassment of gays and drag queens. This was to be a politicizing moment for gays around the world. Much of the gay theatre created post-Stonewall in both the USA and Britain was explicitly a radical, oppositional theatre. This radicalism took a variety of forms: disruptive 'situationist' spectacles (Notting Hill Street Theatre Group's drag/gender-bending performances on gay marches in London in the early 1970s, in which Betty Bourne, founder of the drag company Bloolips (see FEMALE IMPERSONATION; REVUE) took part; or transgressive/Queer performance (Hot Peaches in the USA and the LINDSAY KEMP Company in Britain); or political propagandist theatre. The latter was the ethos of Gay Sweatshop, Britain's first gay theatre company, founded in 1975.

In Britain gay theatre developed in the context of the alternative political movement of the 1960s and 1970s. Gay Sweatshop was as much influenced by the political agendas of socialism, feminism and anti-racism as by the Gay Liberation Front, and its plays reflect this. Noel Greig, whose plays were a mainstay of GS in its early years, came from a socialist-theatre background: his 1979 play *The Dear Love of Comrades* is about the turn-of-the-century Utopian socialist and homosexual propagandist Edward Carpenter, and his 1983 play *Poppies* deals with pacifism. Throughout its history Gay Sweatshop has been a mixed gay and lesbian company, with the agenda of feminism unavoidably part of its consciousness. Furthermore, Gay Sweatshop has had the role of political campaigner thrust upon it – it has had to fight battles with all kinds of state agencies (particularly local authorities and education authorities) to stop its productions from being summarily banned. Although the company has had difficult periods, when Arts Council funding has been withdrawn or when fatigue has threatened creativity, it has always been reinvigorated by new company members or new political campaigns – concerning Section 28 and AIDS, for example – or new turns in gay culture, as its recent Queer School events indicate.

Although in other areas of political theatre there was by the mid-1980s a feeling of weariness with overtly political/propagandist theatre, it was now, because of AIDS, that gay theatre entered its most strenuous campaigning phase. Gay theatre companies produced works to educate gay communities about AIDS and safe sex, to protest against state inertia in the face of the epidemic, and to challenge 'gay plague' hysteria. In the USA, *As Is* (William Hoffman, 1985) and *The Normal Heart* (Larry Kramer, 1985) both transferred to BROADWAY, the latter also playing to full houses in London. Gay Sweatshop produced *Compromised Immunity* (Andy Kirby, 1986/7), which toured Britain, often playing in mainstream venues which did not normally book gay shows.

In the 1990s AIDS remains an inescapable fact of gay life, and all gay art is made in its shadow – not, as was the case in the 80s, in the form of mourning and anger, but as an explosion of positive energy and creativity. Gay theatrical response has included TONY KUSHNER's huge, multidimensional epic of gay sex and politics, *Angels in America*, produced in Britain and across the USA. Gay theatre has reembraced the older traditions (often marginalized by gay politics) of drag and gay celebration: in Britain the collaboration of drag duo Bloolips and American lesbian company Split Britches on *Belle Reprieve*, a queer version of Tennessee Williams's *A Streetcar Named Desire*, was one of the gay theatre events of 1991. Gay bodies and sexuality have been publicly anatomized in the public health discourses around AIDS. Gay performers have responded with their own celebratory discourse of the body: in his show *My Queer Body* US gay performance artist Tim Miller performs a gay history – of a life in the time of AIDS – through his body, as map, as utterance. In Britain, audiences gay and straight flock to the work of the dancer/gay performer Michael Clark and dance/performance company DV8.

While plays about gays have enjoyed occasional popular success before – *Torch Song Trilogy* and *La Cage aux Folles*

were great hits on Broadway and in the WEST END in the 1980s, as were Martin Sherman's *Bent* and *The Normal Heart* – what is most interesting in the mid-1990s is that a gay theatre aesthetic seems, in Britain at least, to be at the very centre of the avant-garde of theatre. *Angels in America* has been one of the NATIONAL THEATRE's great critical successes; London's premier avant-garde art venue, the Institute of Contemporary Arts, is showing a great interest in gay (and lesbian) work, and Neil Bartlett, gay writer, director and performer with the theatre company Gloria (as well as novelist), has become artistic director of one of London's major repertory theatres, the LYRIC THEATRE, HAMMERSMITH.   JD WG

See: N. Bartlett, *Night after Night*, London, 1993; M. Meyer (ed.), *The Politics and Poetics of Camp*, London, 1994; P. Osment (ed.), *Gay Sweatshop: Four Plays and a Company*, London, 1989; essays on Queer Theatre, *Theater* (Yale School of Drama), 2, 1993; M. Wilcox (ed.), *Gay Plays* (3 vols.), London, 1984, 1985, 1988.

geju Chinese song drama. In broad usage *geju* can include Western OPERAS. Usually it refers to modern opera, created under CCP influence, that combines Chinese and Western techniques. The orchestra contains mainly Western instruments, with an admixture of Chinese traditional instruments. Melodies are Chinese in flavour, but strongly influenced by Western musical structure and harmonic principles. Complex scenery is used, and costumes and stage mannerisms, postures and gestures tend to be realistic, although retaining the influence of traditional theatre. A single item usually occupies a full evening, but the practice of combining key scenes from several pieces into a programme is not unknown.

The first important song drama was *The White-Haired Girl* (*Baimao nü*). A peasant girl raped by a tyrannical landlord flees to a mountain cave where her hair turns white from her privations. After a rumour of a white-haired spirit haunting the countryside spreads, Communist troops discover the truth. She is reunited with her former suitor and the landlord is publicly sentenced. *The White-Haired Girl* was premiered in April 1945 in Yan'an in conjunction with the Seventh Congress of the CCP and became exceptionally popular. Another example is *Red Guards on Hong Lake* (*Honghu chiwei dui*), about the CCP's revolutionary struggle against the Guomindang in 1930.

Creating new song dramas was encouraged in the 1950s and early 1960s, but they were totally suppressed in the decade of the Cultural Revolution that followed. *The White-Haired Girl* was adapted as a ballet, emphasizing the class struggle, and then revived in Beijing in the original song drama form in 1977. *Red Guards on Hong Lake* was also revived shortly after the fall of the 'gang of four'. Although new song dramas have continued to be written, they have not been large in number, and the song drama tends as a form to lack inventiveness and innovation.

One rather exceptional example, however, is *Wilderness* (*Yuanye*), the music of which was written by Jin Xiang based on the spoken drama by CAO YU (1937). Premiered in 1987, it differs from other song dramas in that the music is in the idiom of modern Western music, while the theme and language are Chinese. The singers fall into the categories standard for Western music – soprano, baritone and so on – while the orchestral instruments are nearly all Western. Although non-Chinese in style, the music captures the harrowing and gloomy oppression inherent in Cao Yu's original. CPM ACS

Gelbart, Larry 1923– Chicago-born American playwright, who has also written for radio, television (see RADIO DRAMA; TELEVISION DRAMA) and film. He began with comic sketches while still in his teens, and in 1958 won a television Emmy for an 'Art Carney Special'. In 1963 he and Burt Shevelove were awarded a Tony for *A Funny Thing Happened on the Way to the Forum*, and in 1975 he won the distinguished Peabody Award for the television series "M*A*S*H". Gelbart is one of America's most respected comic writers; his theatre credits include *Sly Fox* (1976), *Mastergate* (1989), *Power Failure* (1990), *Feats of Clay* (1991) and the book (Tony) for the highly praised MUSICAL *City of Angels* (1989). Among his film credits are *Oh, God* (1977) and *Tootsie* (1982), both of which earned him Oscar nominations. BBW

Gélinas, Gratien 1909– French Canadian playwright, actor and director. Gélinas began to write and perform radio scripts in the 1930s, creating in 1937 the comic character Fridolin, a satiric but sympathetic observer of contemporary Canadian foibles. The creation proved durable: from 1938 to 46 he wrote annual stage REVUES entitled *Fridolinons!* (published collectively as *Fridolinades* in 1980–1), interpreting the major role himself. Their immense popularity led to his first stage play, '*Tit-Coq* (1948), from which historians generally date the birth of modern Quebec theatre.

Much of Fridolin's character carries over into that of '*Tit-Coq*'s titular hero – played by the author, who also directed the production. A foundling seeking his identity through military service overseas, '*Tit-Coq* is defeated by an intransigent Catholic Church on his return. '*Tit-Coq* incarnated, for many Québécois, their own frustrated aspirations at the end of the Second World War. The play had more than 500 performances, in French and English. *Bousille et les justes* (*Bousille and the Just*, 1959), painting the bankruptcy of middle-class morality, was also an outstanding success, as was *Hier les enfants dansaient* (*Yesterday the Children Were Dancing*, 1966), which depicts a Quebec family riven by the same political forces then threatening to sunder Canada. Less topical is *La Passion de Narcisse Mondoux* (*Narcisse Mondoux's Passion*, 1986), a COMEDY written for himself and his wife, actress Huguette Oligny. Founder of the Comédie Canadienne in 1958, chairman of the Canadian Film Development Corporation in 1969, Gélinas continues to make a major contribution to the performing arts. LED

Gellert, Christian Fürchtegott 1715–69 German playwright. Gellert is best known for his *Fables*, but his effective sentimental comedies are among the more significant achievements of the early German theatre. Of these, *The Affectionate Sisters* (1747) and *The Sick Woman* (1747) are probably the best. SW

Gelman, Aleksandr (Isaakovich) 1933– Soviet Russian playwright who made his name as an exponent of 'workplace drama', an approved Soviet genre which pitted honest workers and Party members against corrupt management. A former Party official, construction worker and soldier, Gelman sophisticated the genre to explore the tensions between career and family, ethics and success. In the 1970s, he was discovered by OLEG EFREMOV, artistic director of the MOSCOW ART THEATRE, where most of his plays were to receive their premieres. The best-known are *Minutes of the Meeting* (1976), based on a film script, *The Bonus*, in which a work gang refuses to do shoddy work in order to meet a quota; *Feedback Circuit* (1978), for which JOSEF SVOBODA designed a pyramid of desks to suggest the impervious monumentality of the bureaucracy; and *We the Undersigned* (1979), which more openly defended the individual from the system. *Alone among Many* (1981), which abandoned Aesopian language for startling candour, is a two-character TRAGEDY about a foreman who neglects safety rules to meet a completion date and thus causes his son to lose his hands. It was banned, but under the title *A Man with Connections* was Gelman's first play to be produced abroad (EDINBURGH FESTIVAL, 1988; No Curtain Theatre, Washington, DC, 1991), partly because of its small cast but also because its questions of guilt and responsibility, reminiscent of ARTHUR MILLER's *All My Sons*, are more universally applicable. During the era of *glasnost*, Gelman abandoned playwriting for politics as a more effective means of changing the system. LS

Gelosi (meaning 'the jealous', i.e. of praise) Troupe of Italian actors, headed by FRANCESCO and ISABELLA ANDREINI, which collaborated with TASSO on *Aminta* in 1573 and undertook numerous tours from 1576. The Gelosi were the first professional Italian company to visit Paris, at the invitation of Henri III; seen there in 1576–7, 1588, 1600 and 1602, it demonstrated the superiority of professional playing and had a great influence on the development of the French stage. Its repertory included both COMMEDIA DELL'ARTE and *commedia erudita*. The troupe had long been troubled by internal dissension – the Arlecchino (TRISTANO MARTINELLI) was thought to have planned the murder of the Fritellino (Piermaria Cecchini) – and after Isabella died in 1604, her husband disbanded it. LS

Gémier, (Tonnerre) Firmin 1869–1933 French actor and director. At first a noted actor, Gémier was the first King Ubu in 1896. But the literary avant-garde interested him less than his vision of a mass theatre for the masses. In 1911 he bought a circus tent and built a mobile touring theatre with an audience capacity of 1650. In 1919 at the Paris Cirque d'Hiver he directed large-cast spectaculars and in 1920 was put in charge of the first THÉÂTRE NATIONAL POPULAIRE, but he was never given the means to run a permanent producing company. From 1921 to 30 he was director of the ODÉON, where he distinguished himself with his productions of SHAKESPEARE. He founded a Société Universelle du Théâtre, a forerunner of today's International Theatre Institute. DB

Gems, (Iris) Pam(ela) 1925– British dramatist, who turned to writing plays comparatively late in life after bringing up four children. She was involved in a women's theatre season at London's Almost Free in 1975, which included her full-length play, *The Amiable Courtship of Ms Venus and Wild Bill*. Two other lunchtime plays had been staged at the same theatre, *My Warren* and *After Birthday* (both 1973). Her first great success, however, came with the production in 1977 of *Dusa, Fish, Stas and Vi*, a study of four girls rooming together in a London flat, which transferred to the WEST END from the HAMPSTEAD THEATRE CLUB. The accuracy, good humour and specific awareness of feminist (as well as feminine) issues brought her recognition as a leading woman playwright, although her appeal was never confined to female audiences. The ROYAL SHAKESPEARE COMPANY produced *Queen Christina* at the Other Place in Stratford-upon-Avon in 1977; but it was her MUSICAL biography, *Piaf* which provided a splendid part for Jane Lapotaire – that moved, in the RSC's production, to the West End and New York (1980/81). Further productions with the RSC included *Camille* (1984) and *The Danton Affair* (1986). In 1991 she adapted *Uncle Vanya* for the Renaissance Theatre Company. JE

género chico Genre of one-act plays, introduced in 19th-century Spain with specific reference to popular, lyric theatre in Madrid. The modern theatre movement, which remained in vogue well into the 20th century, is related to a long tradition of short comic works, originating in the medieval Church and including the *paso*, *entremés*, *sainete* and shorter forms of the ZARZUELA.

In the 16th century, LOPE DE RUEDA created the name *paso* for comic pieces that depicted low-life characters in urban settings and featured lively, colloquial dialogue. In the GOLDEN AGE, the *entremés* was performed between acts of the COMEDIA to serve as a farcical counterpoint to the main play. Greatest exponent of the *entremés* was Luis Quiñones de Benavente (?1589–1651), to whom are attributed some 150 plays, ranging from realistic spoken texts to more imaginative interludes which incorporate song and dance. Among contributors to the popular genre was CERVANTES, whose texts are still frequently staged. While *sainetes* first appeared in the 17th century, the term became associated with Ramón de la Cruz (1731–94), who wrote 400 satires of Madrid society and customs. His short plays are the most enduring theatrical works of 18th-century Spain. By the late 19th century, some Madrid playhouses were devoted exclusively to the *género chico*. The minor genre's enormous popularity derived from its everyday characters and customs, its SATIRE of contemporary events and its blending of musical numbers and spoken text. Principal authors include Ricardo de la Vega (1838–1910), Carlos (1865–1911) and Guillermo (1893–1965) Fernández Shaw, ARNICHES, and the ALVAREZ QUINTERO brothers.

Both the *sainete* and the *zarzuela* served to inspire the popular theatre forms that began to develop in the River Plate (Argentina and Uruguay) area at the end of the 19th century. The *sainete criollo* depended on popular themes of the lower and middle class through an authentic language and presentation of customs, typical figures and, frequently, political satire. The *sainete gauchesco* was attuned to specific issues of the regional cowboy of the pampa, while the *sainete urbano* focused on popular types

and themes within the rapidly changing urban environment. CL GW PZ

Genet, Jean 1910–86 French poet, novelist and playwright. An orphan, Genet grew up to a life of crime and made his reputation with novels of homosexual eroticism written in prison. He published five plays: *Les Bonnes* (*The Maids*), produced by JOUVET in 1947; *Haute surveillance* (*Deathwatch*; directed by Genet and Marchat, 1949); *Le Balcon* (*The Balcony*, 1956; directed by BROOK, 1960); *Les Nègres* (*The Blacks*; directed by BLIN, 1959) and *Les Paravents* (*The Screens*) written in 1961 but considered too subversive to be produced until 1966, when Blin was invited to direct it at the ODÉON by BARRAULT. Two more have been published since his death: *Elle* (1989) and *Splendid's* (1993).

His plays embody a brilliant interplay of different levels of illusion which suggest both the interdependence and the potential treachery of all social roles, stressing the links between power and theatricality. But although considered subversive by right-wing forces in France, which made it difficult for many of them to be staged, his plays do not advocate revolutionary political solutions. The Algerians of *The Screens*, the blacks of *The Blacks* and the revolutionaries of *The Balcony* are all caught in a similar self-destructive circle, and the transformations which occur in these plays are mystic rather than material. Genet's work has been very influential, partly because it comes close to realizing some of ARTAUD's ideals: it does not rely on traditional plot or psychology, it is based in ritualized movements, dances, parades, interchanges of identity and a carefully worked contrast between the sumptuousness of poetic dialogue and the sordidness of dramatic situation.

Genet was contemptuous of theatre as mere entertainment; he professed admiration for children's games and the Catholic Mass. Among the many significant productions of his plays was *The Maids* produced by the LIVING THEATRE in 1965, *The Balcony* by Victor Garcia at São Paulo in 1969, *The Screens* revived by CHÉREAU in 1983, and *The Blacks* by STEIN the same year. DB

Gentleman, Francis 1728–84 Irish actor, playwright and critic. After a brief career in the army and an acting debut in Smock Alley Theatre, Dublin, he left for London on receiving a legacy and tried to ingratiate himself with GARRICK. A notorious self-publicist, he acted in the provinces in the 1750s, returning to London as a journalist in the 1760s. Most of his plays of this period were adaptations – e.g., of JONSON's *Sejanus* (1750) and *The Alchemist* (as *The Tobacconist*, 1760) and SOUTHERNE's *Oroonoko* (as *The Royal Slave*, 1760). His dramatic CRITICISM for the journal the *Dramatic Censor*, which he edited, was collected in 1771. Often pretentious and affected and with a concern for piety, his criticism provides remarkable descriptions of contemporary actors. In 1771 his SATIRE on the theatre attacked Garrick for plagiarism. In 1772 he prepared an edition of SHAKESPEARE for Bell's British Theatre, incorporating much material about stage business from the prompt books in use at the Patent theatres. PH

George, Mlle [Marguerite-Joséphine Weymer]

1787–1867 French actress. The daughter of travelling players, she appeared on the stage at Amiens at the age of five and was noticed by Mlle Raucourt, who took her to Paris to train her for the COMÉDIE-FRANÇAISE, where she made her debut in 1802 in the unusual role of Clytemnestra. She had a celebrated liaison with Napoleon, for whom she retained a deep affection. Like TALMA, she was the incarnation of the great classical roles to which her statuesque figure and sculptural beauty suited her. In 1808 she abandoned the Comédie-Française to go to Russia, where she was immensely popular. Back in Paris in 1813 she had to suffer the jealousy of her rival, MLLE DUCHESNOIS. In the late 1820s a new career opened up with the romantic drama: DUMAS *père*'s *Christine* (1829) and VIGNY's *La Maréchale d'Ancre* (1830). Under the director HAREL at the Porte-Saint-Martin (see BOULEVARD), her greatest roles were Marguerite de Bourgogne in *La Tour de Nesle* (1832) and Lucrèce Borgia and Marie Tudor (1833) in HUGO's plays. After 1842 her voice deteriorated, her majestic manner was out of fashion, and her weight problem had become chronic. She fell back on her old roles and in 1849 gave her farewell performance (a further one was given in 1853 at the Comédie-Française, when she played Rodogune).
JMCC

Germain, Jean-Claude [Claude-Jean Magnier] 1939– Quebec playwright, critic and director. Germain became involved with stage arts while still a student and worked on the periphery of theatre before founding in 1969 the Théâtre du Même Nom (TMN), a parodic anagram of the THÉÂTRE DU NOUVEAU MONDE, the most established of French Canada's troupes. Relying heavily on *joual*, Quebec's popular idiom, and laden with ingenious puns, his works are often virtually untranslatable. Most remarkable are *Diguidi, Diguidi, Ha! Ha! Ha!* (1969); *Le Roi des mises à bas prix* (*King of Discount Sales*, 1971); an adaptation into *joual* of 19th-century Quebec author F.-G. Marchand's *Les Faux-Brillants* (*False Diamonds*, 1977), and *A Canadian Play/Une plaie canadienne* (1979). LED

Germanova, Mariya (Nikolaevna) 1884–1940 Russian actress, protégée of NEMIROVICH-DANCHENKO at the MOSCOW ART THEATRE, making her debut as Calpurnia in *Julius Caesar* (1904). Her beauty and intelligence illuminated Agnes in *Brand* (1906), Grushenka in *The Brothers Karamazov* (1910) and Olga in *Three Sisters*. LEONID ANDREEV wrote *Katerina Ivanovna* for her (1912). In 1919 Germanova joined a number of colleagues abroad, who, as the Prague Group of the MAT, toured Europe and England until 1929. With them, Germanova created a new role, EURIPIDES' Medea, and staged most of the plays in imitation of the original Moscow productions. She died in Paris, leaving interesting unpublished memoirs of the life of an émigré actor. LS

Germany (See also MEDIEVAL DRAMA IN EUROPE (Germany, Switzerland and Scandinavia))
Up to 1914 Even though there was a vigorous religious and popular theatrical tradition in German-speaking countries during the Middle Ages, in contrast to England, France and Spain, the professional theatre in Germany was late in its development. Some historians have attrib-

uted this delay to the Thirty Years War and to the disastrous effect the war had on the German economy. However, it can also be argued, perhaps with more justification, that the absence of a regular professional theatre was primarily because there were no large cities that could nurture a permanent theatre in the way that London, Madrid and Paris did.

In several respects, in its early years the modern professional theatre was a phenomenon alien to Germany. Its origins can be traced first to the ENGLISCHE KOMÖDIANTEN, who, from the late 16th through to the mid-17th century, could be seen periodically on tours through the small towns and courts of Germany. Their repertoire consisted mainly of contemporary English plays, though from the very beginning of their tours comic scenes in Low German were inserted. Soon whole plays came to be given in German, especially as the companies were composed more and more of German actors. Italy also had a formative influence on German theatre, for the COMMEDIA DELL'ARTE troupes were frequent visitors. As these two national traditions of theatre were unified in the troupes of wandering German players towards the end of the 17th century, a unique dramatic hybrid emerged to form the basis of their repertoire, the HAUPT- UND STAATSAKTIONEN, plays that combined the episodic structure of the English chronicle play with the improvisational flexibility of the *commedia dell'arte*. Popular comic prototypical figures – like, for example, 'Pickelhering' – were evolved in this drama. Performances were normally given under rather primitive conditions, generally in spaces in the open air where it was possible to erect a stage structure. This may have borne some resemblance to the stage structure of the Elizabethan theatre.

Given the very lowly nature of the theatrical profession, it is not surprising that there were few German dramatists willing or capable of producing works of quality for the stage. JACOB AYRER, a late-16th-century playwright whose work has not endured, was the only significant contributor. In the 17th century, when Germany seemed ready to produce drama of some quality, primarily in the work of the classically influenced dramatist ANDREAS GRYPHIUS and the comparatively skilled baroque playwright CASPAR VON LOHENSTEIN, there were no adequate professional companies to perform their plays. Gryphius's plays were occasionally staged by schoolboys. Indeed, it is in the performance of the Jesuit drama (see JESUITENDRAMA) in the schools of Bavaria that the most continuous tradition of theatre exists for much of the 17th century.

If England and Italy were the major formative influences on whatever popular theatrical tradition there was in 17th-century Germany, France exercised the dominant influence on the development of theatre as a high art. Early in the 17th century, MARTIN OPITZ, a somewhat dry theoretician and translator, advocated that the German theatre model itself on the French and that dramatists respect the unities and classical decorum. His writings had little immediate effect but, by the end of the century, the actor-manager JOHANNES VELTEN, who received some patronage from the Duke of Saxony, began to introduce adaptations of French TRAGEDY and COMEDY. He also attempted, without much success, to control the frequently unpredictable and unruly improvisational actors in his company. By this time, the adoption of French dramatic form and actorial mannerisms carried with it potential social prestige, as the richer courts of German-speaking Europe were hiring companies of French actors in an attempt to impose a civilized culture on a society that was widely regarded by the courtly aristocrats as backward in matters pertaining to art and social customs.

However, it was not until well into the 18th century that the court theatre began to influence the public theatre – and then in a way that not all practitioners welcomed. This came about primarily through the efforts of JOHANN GOTTSCHED, who, with the aid of CAROLINE NEUBER, the most prominent actress of the time and the leader of Velten's old troupe, attempted to 'regularize' the public stage by introducing French classical tragedy in German adaptations, by abolishing improvisation (HARLEQUIN was 'banished' from the stage in a formal ceremony in Leipzig in 1737), and by adopting a stiff, rhetorical manner of acting, known as the LEIPZIG STYLE.

The endeavours of Neuber and Gottsched were thwarted by internal dissension and by an eventual lack of interest on the part of the public, who preferred the old *Haupt- und Staatsaktionen* and appreciated the freedom of the improvisational actors. Furthermore, actors in the public theatre failed at this time to attract the patronage of the aristocratic courts, who continued to prefer French actors and to enjoy the spectacle of Italian OPERA. In fact, despite the prestige earned by the troupe of KONRAD ACKERMANN, it was not until well into the second half of the century that German actors began to enjoy regular aristocratic patronage. Through the middle of the 18th century the number of touring troupes increased, but no permanent home was offered any troupe until 1776, when the Duke of Saxe-Gotha invited the actor KONRAD EKHOF to settle in his capital with his band of travelling players and to form the first regular court theatre staffed by German actors.

Although the Gotha Court Theatre lasted only three years, as it was disbanded on Ekhof's death, its foundation was a highly significant event as it was the first step in the 50-year creation of a network of permanent standing theatres that was eventually unequalled in Europe and gave the German theatre unique social prominence and prestige. In the late 1770s other important standing theatres devoted to the production of German drama and foreign drama in German translation were founded. The most notable of these were the Hamburg Town Theatre, formed in 1776 on a commercial basis by FRIEDRICH SCHRÖDER out of the Ackermann troupe, which had already attempted to form a National Theatre in Hamburg in the 1760s, and the MANNHEIM COURT and National Theatre founded by the king of Bavaria in 1778 under the directorship of Baron Dalberg (1750–1806). In its early days this latter theatre had one of the greatest actors of the time, AUGUST IFFLAND, as the leading member of its company. During the next two decades, national, court and municipal theatres came to be founded in most of the major German provinces and cities, so that by the early 19th century Germany possessed well over 65 permanent theatres, each of which was staffed with a company of actors. This network formed the basis for the present-day system of regional theatres in Germany.

As a result of these momentous changes, acting became a socially acceptable and, for those who were successful in it, a financially reliable profession. Partially as a consequence of the burgeoning prestige of theatre, the period from the late 1760s through to the late 1820s saw an increase in the volume and quality of playwriting, which ensured that Germany had a native popular and classic repertoire upon which to build. During the 1760s and 1770s LESSING's *bürgerliche Trauerspiele* (see BÜRGERLICHES TRAUERSPIEL), written under the influence of the comparatively realistic English drama, allowed the theatre to become a forum for the dramatization of issues close to the interests of the rising bourgeoisie. Lessing's plays, along with the *bürgerliche Trauerspiele* of other dramatists, encouraged a subdued style of realistic acting that was an alternative to the rather strident rhetoric of the Leipzig style. The 1770s saw the sudden eruption of the young STURM UND DRANG playwrights, whose works, though infrequently performed, both introduced themes of social protest into the drama and demonstrated the potent influence SHAKESPEARE was to have on the imagination of the German playwright. Among the most significant works of this movement were GOETHE's widely admired *Götz von Berlichingen*, first produced in Berlin and Hamburg in 1774, LENZ's *The Tutor*, produced in Hamburg in 1778, and SCHILLER's *The Robbers*, which received its immensely successful premiere in Mannheim in 1782.

But the most significant achievement in playwriting occurred at the end of the century, at the Weimar Court Theatre, which was directed by Goethe between 1719 and 1817. Here the great tragedies of Schiller's maturity and several of Goethe's generically various plays were first performed. Although neither Goethe nor Schiller rejected the influence of Shakespeare (though Goethe became increasingly sceptical about the viability of Shakespeare's plays on stage), their plays from this period also show other foreign influences, primarily ancient Greek and French neoclassical drama. However, Schiller's tragedy of idealism and Goethe's humanistic theatre had its own brand of uniqueness. Indeed, the first national drama of Germany was created in Weimar over the turn of the century. The plays of one of Germany's greatest dramatists, HEINRICH VON KLEIST, also date from this period, though because of the unpalatability of Kleist's outlook they went almost entirely unperformed in his lifetime and were only 'discovered' some decades after his death by LUDWIG TIECK. During this same period an extensive popular repertoire was also being created, primarily in the plays of the actor Iffland, who specialized in writing *Rührstücke*, sentimental domestic MELODRAMAS, and of KOTZEBUE, whose melodramas were performed not only in Germany but widely in England and the USA. The works of these two dramatists were to hold the stage for much of the 19th century.

The 50 years that span the end of the 18th and the beginning of the 19th centuries represent a major flowering of theatre, not only in the area of playwriting but also in that of performance. Standards of acting and production underwent radical improvement. Iffland was perhaps the most popular actor of the time, touring Germany ceaselessly, giving model performances of roles from his own plays and from classics. FERDINAND FLECK and LUDWIG DEVRIENT, though radically different from Iffland as they seemed to act from seemingly intuitive bases, served to focus public interest on the actor as a performing artist: in particular, they managed to bring to the surface the unconscious motivation of the characters they played. All three of these actors tended to encourage solo virtuosity at the expense of ensemble work. In contrast, Goethe at Weimar trained his actors both to respect the ensemble and to conduct themselves with great dignity on stage. The WEIMAR STYLE of acting that he evolved, which demanded that when the actor was performing tragedy he observe a formal aloofness from his audience, was to have a major influence on German actors for the next 100 years.

Indeed, in the course of the 19th century, German acting developed in the tension between the formality of the Weimar school and the realism of the so-called Hamburg school (see HAMBURG STYLE), first practised by Friedrich Schröder in the late 18th century. Standards of physical production also improved significantly. When Iffland was appointed director of the BERLIN ROYAL THEATRE, in 1796, he received a substantial subsidy from the Prussian court. He used this money to stage productions of Shakespeare, Schiller and other dramatists who used historical settings, under conditions of lavish splendour, achieving a level of spectacle previously unequalled in the German theatre. Although not all theatres could afford such luxury, Iffland's productions set the standard for the 19th century. In the German theatre as elsewhere in Europe, there was an increasing focus on spectacle, often at the expense of the impact that could be created by the individual actor and of the dramatic text itself.

As German cities grew in the course of the 19th century, so too did the theatres that serviced them. Although – in contrast to the theatre of Austria, France and England – German theatre remained provincially oriented, Berlin, as the capital of Prussia and after 1870 of a united Germany, saw the greatest growth and the most vigorous theatre. Early in the century, the Royal Theatre, under the direction first of Iffland and then of Goethe's disciple Count Carl von Brühl (1772–1837), had a monopoly on the performance of drama, similar in some ways to the royal patents possessed by DRURY LANE and COVENT GARDEN in London. However, this was soon abolished. The Königstadttheater was established by royal patent in 1824, with the specific purpose of providing competition for the Royal Theatre, and soon several other theatrical establishments sprang up in the city. Such expansion was common to other major German cities, in particular Hamburg and Munich. The growth of the German theatre did not, however, go unhampered. Until 1870, when Germany was united under Bismarck's rule, theatres could be opened only with governmental and police permission, which was not always forthcoming; after 1870, while freedom in building theatres was allowed, fairly stringent CENSORSHIP of the plays that were staged in them remained the rule.

After the achievements of Weimar classicism, the development of German playwriting during the 19th century might be regarded as disappointing. The romantic movement made little contribution to the lasting dramatic repertoire. There was no lack of effective light comedies, melodramas, and sentimental family pieces, written by such excellent dramatic craftsmen as RODERICH BENEDIX

and CHARLOTTE BIRCH-PFEIFFER. The plays of the Junges Deutschland (Young Germany) movement of the 1830s and 40s included themes of social protest but, because of the stringent censorship and the attachment of its major playwrights, HEINRICH LAUBE and KARL GUTZKOW, to the form of the WELL MADE PLAY, the work of Junges Deutschland lacked the urgency and exciting theatricality of the earlier *Sturm und Drang*. The most original playwrights of the age, and the only ones whose works have endured, were not widely performed. GEORG BÜCHNER, whose plays are generically similar to those of *Sturm und Drang*, never had one of his plays performed in his lifetime or for several decades after, while CHRISTIAN DIETRICH GRABBE, an eccentric but brilliant dramatist, also went unrecognized. Only FRIEDRICH HEBBEL, whose historical plays have complex characters drawn with remarkable psychological accuracy and whose *Maria Magdalena* is normally regarded as a forerunner of REALISM, achieved some degree of success and esteem in German theatres. GUSTAV FREYTAG's comedy *The Journalists* and OTTO LUDWIG's grim melodrama *The Hereditary Forester* are among the better plays of the mid-century.

Trends in performance in Germany during the 19th century demonstrate the same tension as in other countries. On the one hand, the rise of the virtuoso encouraged an approach to production that served mainly to highlight the principal star; on the other, an increasingly sophisticated technology seemed to militate against the predominance of the single actor in the interests of spectacle. Not many theatres could afford to stage magnificent spectacles, and most of the medium-sized and smaller theatres had relatively mediocre actors in their companies. Therefore they often had to rely on travelling stars to attract audiences. Thus, as the theatre expanded in the course of the century, increasing opportunities for skilled solo actors to make considerable fortunes opened up. Iffland and Ludwig Devrient were the important solo actors in the early decades, but the great age for the travelling virtuosi was in the middle years of the century. Although actors such as KARL SEYDELMANN, EMIL DEVRIENT – the greatest solo perpetuator of the Weimar style – BOGUMIL DAWISON, THEODOR DÖRING and Friedrich Haase were all members of major theatre companies, they would spend well over half the year touring both the provincial theatres and the major court and national theatres. As the century progressed and the American theatre developed, several of them crossed the Atlantic to make their name and sometimes a considerable sum of money by guest performances in the USA, often, like Dawison, acting in German to the English of colleagues on stage.

Even though the solo actor was frequently the centre of audience attention, evidence suggests that most theatre managers and directors would, whenever they had the resources, devote their energies to spectacle. In this regard, the most characteristic mid-century director was FRANZ VON DINGELSTEDT, who ran the Munich Court Theatre into debt because of his prodigiously extravagant productions. He then went on to Weimar and the Vienna BURGTHEATER. In both theatres he was especially noted for his magnificent production of the two Shakespeare history tetralogies (see HISTORY PLAY). The main attraction of these productions for contemporaries was the sense that the whole physical apparatus of the stage operated like a machine, while the actors were little more than well functioning cogs within it. Spectacle was also one of the ultimate goals of GRAND OPERA and, even though he claimed to be a theatrical revolutionary, RICHARD WAGNER's idea of the *Gesamtkunstwerk* existed in theory only when it came to staging. While the *Ring* cycle was of quite remarkable novelty in matters relating to the music drama and to the characterization, when it was presented in 1876 in BAYREUTH, the staging bore all the traditional trappings of the 19th-century spectacle theatre. Georg II, Duke of Saxe-MEININGEN, has often been acclaimed as the first stage director in the modern theatre. While this may be true in respect of the relationship adopted in his theatre between the actor and the director, the actor being allowed less freedom than was normally given him, one might well argue that aesthetically the Duke's work was no more advanced than that of his predecessors, a fact pointed out by several contemporary theatre critics. Even MAX REINHARDT, for all the technological innovations he achieved on stage, can be regarded as the heir to the traditional 19th-century stage director, in that his final ambition was to achieve on stage the impression of a physically dazzling performance that struck his audiences as a seamless whole.

Although theatre managers and *régisseurs* generally catered to the public appetite for spectacle, there were some who attempted to keep alive the ideal of ensemble, as had been practised either by Goethe at Weimar or by Schröder in Hamburg. Brühl, Iffland's successor at the Berlin Royal Theatre, perpetuated the Weimar style, though his productions were considerably more elaborate than Goethe's ever could have been at Weimar. August von Lüttichau (1785–1863), intendant at the DRESDEN COURT THEATRE, was also another notable perpetuator of Weimar acting; in fact, his theatre was nationally celebrated as a result. However, the spirit of Goethe's work was possibly better preserved in the work of ERNST KLINGEMANN at the Brunswick Court Theatre and, above all, of KARL IMMERMANN at the Düsseldorf Town Theatre. Immermann, in trying to focus attention on the actor, simplified the stage setting and encouraged an intimate ensemble among his actors that was more natural than that achieved by Goethe in Weimar. Towards the end of his life, Immermann also tried to revive the technique of open staging associated with theatres in England and Italy during the Renaissance. Immermann's private production of *Twelfth Night* in 1840, while it was seen by only a handful of people, was important as in it he rejected illusionistic scenery and multiple scene changes in order to achieve a simple, continuous production in which the ensemble was pre-eminent. Consequently the dramatic text was unfolded with remarkable simplicity.

Immermann was influenced by the ideas of Ludwig Tieck, who had been interested in the plays of the Elizabethan theatre since the late 18th century and, after a trip to England in 1817, also in the physical arrangement of that theatre. During his long career as playwright, critic and dramaturge – at the Dresden Court Theatre and, late in life, at the Berlin Royal Theatre – Tieck laboured without too much success to introduce simplified staging and natural ensemble. He did this in reaction both to the star

system and to the emphasis on spectacle. His efforts reached their peak in 1843 when he staged, at the Berlin Royal Theatre, an epoch-making production of *A Midsummer Night's Dream* with a staging that owed much to the Elizabethan theatre, even though it was far from being historically accurate. Although the challenge that arose from this, of greater simplicity in production and a denial of the prevalent illusionism of the stage, was not taken up again until close to the end of the century by JOCZA SAVITS in Munich, the idea of a non-spectacular theatre remained an ideal for some directors, most prominent among whom was Heinrich Laube. Laube's achievement as a stage director in Vienna and Leipzig was, arguably, of greater significance than his playwriting, for he developed to a higher degree of perfection than his predecessors or contemporaries the art of conversational ensemble on stage among settings that were severe in contrast to those normally seen in the conventional theatre. EDUARD DEVRIENT, the nephew of Ludwig, also created a highly admired ensemble theatre in Karlsruhe. No doubt it was the work of such theatre men that led G. H. LEWES to comment, after a visit to Germany, that the quality of ensemble even in the smallest theatres was far in advance of that of theatres in England.

If many historians have seen in the work of the Duke of Saxe-Meiningen the start of modern theatre, it is possibly because he asserted the pre-eminence of the director in the rehearsal process. In perceiving the rigorous discipline of the company, audiences became aware of this. The example of his well drilled ensemble inspired ADOLF L'ARRONGE and a few likeminded actors to found the DEUTSCHES THEATER in Berlin in 1883, in order to provide the capital city with a regular ensemble theatre of the quality of the Meininger. This project succeeded mainly on account of the quality of the company, which included actors such as JOSEF KAINZ and AGNES SORMA. In 1889 the drama critic OTTO BRAHM, an enthusiastic advocate of the plays of IBSEN and the naturalists (see NATURALISM) and stimulated by the example of the Théâtre Libre in Paris (see ANDRÉ ANTOINE), founded the FREIE BÜHNE, an informal company of professional actors who performed the works of the naturalist dramatists in the ensemble style that suited them. Their performances took place in regular theatres at times when these theatres were not being used for conventional, commercial productions. Brahm's productions appealed not to the broad audiences of the commercial theatre but to specific interest groups, especially the intelligentsia and the fledgling Social Democratic Party. Political rivalries quickly led to a split in the Freie Bühne movement, so that the more left-wing of Brahm's associates started the Freie Volksbühne, to be followed by yet a further splinter group, the Neue Freie Volksbühne. These organizations formed the basis of the present-day VOLKSBÜHNE movement, which, closely associated with trade unions, provides subsidized seats at performances in regional theatres for union members. Brahm was unsympathetic to the political aspirations of his colleagues so, in 1894, he gladly accepted the appointment of director of the Deutsches Theater, where he produced both modern and classical plays in the naturalistic style.

While Brahm was initially inspired by Ibsen, his innovations would not have been possible without the work of the German naturalist dramatists, of whom GERHART HAUPTMANN was undoubtedly the most important. Not only did Hauptmann successfully introduce on to the German stage both the subject-matter and style advocated by ZOLA in his two volumes of essays, *Naturalism in the Theatre*, but he also conducted a social polemic that was as capable of exciting and infuriating his contemporaries as were the plays of Ibsen. No other contemporary German playwright was as prolific as Hauptmann, not did any master such a variety of styles, for Hauptmann wrote successfully in the symbolist (see SYMBOLISM) and neo-romantic vein as well.

But all contemporary playwrights were influenced by him to the extent that subsequent German drama exhibited greater attention to individual psychology and, in most cases, a heightened awareness of the inequalities that vitiated German society. By far the most controversial playwright of this turn-of-the-century period was FRANK WEDEKIND, whose play *Spring Awakening*, which is about the effects of society's ignorance of the nature of puberty on adolescents, was written in 1892, but could not be performed – and then only in a severely modified version – until 1906. Wedekind, who found Hauptmann's relentless REALISM pedestrian, constructed his plot in disjointed episodes, in a manner reminiscent of *Sturm und Drang* and, as it transpired, anticipatory of the later expressionist movement in theatre. Wedekind never lost his position as an outsider in German theatre and society, as he unceasingly dramatized the sensational though socially tabooed topic of sex. This made him the most celebrated writer of the German theatrical avant-garde in the early 20th century. In the final year of his life, he sang in the company of the young BERTOLT BRECHT at a CABARET in Munich.

The years before the First World War were dominated by the work of the director Max Reinhardt. Reinhardt began his career as an actor in Brahm's ensemble at the Deutsches Theater. In 1903, ambition drove him to direct independently; in 1904 he took over the direction of the Deutsches Theater from Brahm, and for the following decade made it into the most celebrated theatre in Germany. Here, utilizing the work of designers influenced by the seminal theory and renditions of ADOLPHE APPIA and GORDON CRAIG, Reinhardt staged productions that were noted for their extraordinary polish and for an illusionistic spectacle that was perfect to the last detail. While Reinhardt claimed to enjoy working in chamber theatre conditions, he made his name staging vast spectacles, first in Berlin, then Vienna, then in London and other European capitals. By the outbreak of the war, his name was the byword for all that was respected internationally in German theatre – superlative ensemble, seamless spectacle, and a company repertoire that embraced a breadth of classics and modern work in a way unequalled elsewhere in Europe. SW

Since 1914 After 1914 Reinhardt continued to dominate the German stage, but was now challenged by innovations in the provinces. The first expressionist productions were of plays by KOKOSCHKA and HASENCLEVER in Dresden. From 1917 Hasenclever, KORNFELD, BRONNEN, Fritz von Unruh and director Richard Wiechert together developed

Frankfurt EXPRESSIONISM, while from 1920 Gustav Hartung cultivated his passionately pacifist strain in Darmstadt. Otto Falckenberg staged KAISER, SORGE, GOERING and early Brecht at the Munich Kammerspiele, and in Hamburg Erich Ziegel promoted Kaiser, Hanns Henny Jahn and BARLACH with a company including KORTNER and GRÜNDGENS.

Idealistic expressionism, with its generation conflicts and its themes of anti-materialism, pacifism and the renewal of mankind, reached its peak in the messianic socialist pathos of TOLLER and the cerebral ironies of Kaiser. It was a reaction against the First World War and the society that had started it, but hopes for a new dawn were dashed by the crushing of the Spartacist rising and the Munich Soviet in 1919, and the subsequent hyperinflation. By 1923 idealism had given way to pessimism, and the grotesque, violent black expressionism of Bronnen and Jahnn predominated. Reinhardt promoted many expressionists between 1917 and 1920 in an occasional series of productions called 'The Young Germany', but the extremism of the style was alien to him and he directed few plays himself. KARLHEINZ MARTIN's 1919 production of Toller's *Transfiguration*, at the Tribüne, gave Berlin its first taste of full-blooded expressionism, while JESSNER applied the style to the classics at the Prussian State Theatre. Few expressionist plays have stood the test of time, and the movement's lasting contribution was the introduction of non-naturalistic stage techniques, design and lighting (see THEATRE DESIGN; STAGE LIGHTING).

Reinhardt's middle-class audiences had been hard-hit by inflation, and he tried to adjust to the changing economics of theatre by converting the Circus Schuhmann into the 3500-seat Grosses Schauspielhaus – the so-called 'Theatre of the Five Thousand' – where he staged AESCHYLUS' *Oresteia*, *Hamlet* and ROMAIN ROLLAND's *Danton* before handing over to Karlheinz Martin. Now out of fashion, Reinhardt from 1922 concentrated on his Austrian productions.

ERWIN PISCATOR's Proletarian Theatre in 1919–20 toured simple communist AGIT-PROP productions round the meeting-halls and beer-gardens of Berlin's East End with a hand cart. He expanded this approach into the *Red Revue* (1924) and *In Spite of Everything* (1925), a polemical montage of film and documentation from the years 1914 to 1919 which filled the Grosses Schauspielhaus for a fortnight. At the VOLKSBÜHNE Piscator was also developing techniques for revealing the politico-economic context and implications of suitable conventional plays, using projections, film-clips and documentary inserts. In 1927 he founded the Piscatorbühne in the specially modernized Theater am Nollendorfplatz. Here he mounted a series of productions that, with their complex, multifaceted treatment of large contemporary political subjects, stretched the mechanical resources of the day to the limit. WALTER GROPIUS designed a highly flexible *Totaltheater* for Piscator's requirements, but it was never built. Piscator's stress on factual material and his constructivist sets were characteristic of the *neue Sachlichkeit* ('new sobriety') that had succeeded expressionism, and the seeds sown here flowered in the documentary drama of the 1960s. He used many of the outstanding actors of the period, including Ernst Deutsch, Tilla Durieux, Alexander

The figures on stilts in Brecht's production of *Man is Man*, 1931.

Granach and MAX PALLENBERG. Some of his younger actors like Ernst Busch later joined the Berliner Ensemble. After the collapse of the Piscatorbühne the political impulse survived in the naturalistic *Zeitstücke*, or topical-issue plays, of Carl Credé and FRIEDRICH WOLF, and in a more oblique form in the *Volksstücke* of FLEISSER, HORVÁTH and ZUCKMAYER. Horváth defined the genre as 'plays about the people, for the people, in the language of the people'.

Brecht was an occasional collaborator at the Piscatorbühne, and it was here that he came to believe in political theatre. His pre-ideological plays up to *The Threepenny Opera* had been cynical and anti-bourgeois, and he had been developing anti-illusionistic techniques from the moment he hung placards telling the audience at *Drums in the Night* in 1922: 'Don't gawp so romantically.' He had, however, always worked in state theatres – with the exception of *The Threepenny Opera*, which was the commercial hit of 1928.

From 1930, as his contribution to the communist fight against Nazism, he developed the *Lehrstück*, a concise 'teaching play' for performance by proletarian amateur groups. It was designed to raise the political consciousness of performers and audience alike. Brecht had codified the features of his EPIC THEATRE in his *Notes on The Rise and Fall of the City of Mahagonny* in 1930. His production of *Die Mutter* with HELENE WEIGEL in Berlin in 1932, with its bare stage, sparse props, banners and slogans, revealed lights and demonstrative acting, put those features into practice and marked the end of the revolutionary experiments that had given the Weimar theatre its vitality.

For the Nazis who came to power in 1933 modernism in all its manifestations was degenerate, its exponents to be hounded and silenced. Brecht, most of the other dramatists, and many of the key directors and actors of the Weimar period went into exile. Until 1945 the only place where exiled writers could be performed in German was at the Zurich Schauspielhaus, where a distinguished company of German exiles had been formed.

During the Third Reich Gründgens and Heinz Hilpert, directors of the Prussian State Theatre and the DEUTSCHES THEATER respectively, sustained those theatres' artistic standards, the former notably with productions by Jürgen Fehling. MINETTI, who was in Gründgens's company, claims that the theatre was relatively impervious to the directives of the propaganda ministry, though it avoided confrontation by concentrating on the classics – a controversial view still, but not to be dismissed out of hand. What is true is that the theatre in the Federal Republic of Germany after 1945 broadly remained in the hands of non-exiles like Gründgens and Hilpert, and that returning exiles like Piscator and Kortner felt less than welcome. The theatres were closed in 1944, and many of them were destroyed. It is testimony to the status of theatre in Germany that rebuilding them was an immediate priority in the shattered country.

In the immediate postwar years the first hits were BORCHERT's *The Man Outside* and Zuckmayer's *The Devil's General*, and audiences avid for new plays were offered ANOUILH, CLAUDEL, GIRAUDOUX, WILDER, TENNESSEE WILLIAMS, SHAW and T. S. ELIOT – plays from a world that had been cut off. The production style was apolitical and tended to formalism and SYMBOLISM. The probing REALISM of Kortner's productions, which was to influence PETER STEIN, was an exception; Kortner was never given a theatre of his own. New drama in German came first from Switzerland, with the plays of FRISCH and DÜRRENMATT in the 1950s. The Gruppe 47 (Group 47) provided a forum for progressive writers, and HILDESHEIMER, GRASS and WALSER read their early plays there. Discussion of the function of theatre in the wake of the Eichmann trial and the Frankfurt War Crimes Tribunal (1961–4) led to a re-politicization of the theatre with PETER WEISS's *Marat/Sade* and *The Investigation*, followed by ENZENSBERGER and the documentary theatre of HOCHHUTH and KIPPHARDT which Piscator staged at the newly opened Freie Volksbühne, of which he was made director after an exhausting decade of freelancing.

The late 1960s saw a revival of interest in the *Volksstück*, with the rediscovery of Fleisser and Horváth, and the stark and brutal new plays of KROETZ, SPERR and FASSBINDER. The appearance of HANDKE's first plays signalled a 'new sensibility', moving away from politics towards an examination of language and the nature of theatrical communication, and to the mythical realism of BOTHO STRAUSS. In Austria TURRINI exposes the crasser iniquities of the consumer society, while ELFRIEDE JELINEK and latterly Marleen Streeruwitz submit it to feminist scrutiny. In Germany the leading women dramatists are GERLIND REINSHAGEN and Friederike Roth.

The postwar theatre had been conservative – it was the Adenauer era. By 1968 the Vietnam protest campaign and the student movement were demanding general democratization, and the rigid command structure which allowed the actors little input came under scrutiny. A new generation of directors emerged. At the Schaubühne am Halleschen Ufer in Berlin Peter Stein established a company on egalitarian principles. The meticulous atmospheric realism of his carefully researched productions of the classics and of Botho Strauss made the company the West German flagship theatre of the 1970s. The equally anti-authoritarian PEYMANN at Stuttgart, Bochum and Vienna modernized the classics with a light, whimsical touch and commissioned much new work, notably from BERNHARD, Handke and HEINER MÜLLER, while the maverick ZADEK at Bochum and Hamburg de-gentrified SHAKESPEARE in provocatively unkempt style, and worked closely with DORST.

From 1945 the German Democratic Republic looked east. Approved Soviet bloc plays bulked large in the repertoire. Theatres cultivated links with state industry, offering talks and small-scale productions in canteens, while industry and the unions took block bookings and handed out tickets – which many threw away, leaving 'sold out' theatres half-empty. On the other hand, because audiences could read between the lines, the theatre was the one place where 'real existing socialism' could be criticized aloud, as in Ulrich Plenzdorf's *The New Sorrows of Young W.*, which voiced the jeans generation's disgruntlement, or in Heiner Müller's production of *The Scab*. Such events were real sell-outs.

Brecht returned to East Berlin in 1948 to found the BERLINER ENSEMBLE, which quickly achieved international acclaim. The regime funded him because of his eminence, though he never really conformed to their ideas any more

than they did to his. His epic treatment of *Mother Courage* in 1949 offered a contrast to both the histrionics of Nazi theatre and the Stanislavskian realism of socialist realism, the Stalinist style to which the GDR officially subscribed. West Germany was slow to accept Brecht, especially after the Berlin Wall of 1962, though PALITZSCH eventually introduced his style when he left the GDR in the 1960s.

The three main dramatists in the GDR after Brecht were VOLKER BRAUN, PETER HACKS and Heiner Müller. Braun's critical, realistic plays exposed sore points in the socialist system; Hacks developed from Brechtian historical parables into rarefied, 'post-revolutionary' verse comedy; while Müller, successful in both Germanies, moved from socialist realism to obscure, allusive avantgardism. Hacks and Müller were promoted by the Deutsches Theater and BENNO BESSON's Volksbühne respectively, both of which by the 1970s had outstripped the BE. There was also innovative work going on in Rostock under Anselm Perthen and in Schwerin under Christoph Schroth.

Since reunification, the German theatre has been exposed to cash restraints for the first time since the war. The Freie Volksbühne is now the Berlin Musical Theater, the Schillertheater with its three stages has been closed, and cuts are the order of the day. On the positive side, radical young ex-GDR directors have been appointed to two important theatres – the iconoclastic Frank Castorf to the Volksbühne in Berlin's East End, and the whimsical, inventive Leander Haussman to Bochum. HR

See: R. Hayman, *The German Theatre: A Symposium*, London, 1975; G. H. Huettich, *Theatre in the Planned Society: Contemporary Drama in the German Democratic Republic in Its Historical, Political and Cultural Context*, Chapel Hill, 1978; C. Innes, *Modern German Drama: A Study in Form*, Cambridge, 1979; R. Pascal, *From Naturalism to Expressionism: German Literature and Society, 1880–1918*, London, 1973; M. Patterson, *The Revolution in German Theatre 1900–1933*, London, 1981; L. R. Shaw, *The Playwright and Historical Change: Dramatic Strategies in Brecht, Hauptmann, Kaiser, Wedekind*, Wisconsin, 1970.

Gershwin, George 1898–1937 and
Ira Gershwin 1896–1983 American composer and lyricist. George's first connections with the musical stage were as a song-plugger and rehearsal pianist. In 1918 he teamed up with his brother Ira, who had written prose and verse for various periodicals, to write their first song, 'The Real American Folk Song'. A year later, George collaborated with lyricist Irving Caesar on one of the most popular songs of the day, 'Swanee'. For their first ventures in MUSICAL THEATRE, the brothers worked with other collaborators, George contributing songs to *La, La Lucille* (1919), *MORRIS GEST's Midnight Whirl* (1919), and the 1920–4 editions of *GEORGE WHITE's Scandals*, while Ira wrote lyrics for *Two Little Girls in Blue* (1921). George's early show music was steeped in the idioms of jazz, a form he had learned from listening to black musicians. In 1924 the brothers collaborated on *Lady, Be Good!*, a musical starring FRED AND ADELE ASTAIRE. Encouraged by the show's success, the Gershwins turned out a number of other popular 1920s musicals, including *Oh, Kay!* (1926), *Funny Face* (1927) and *Rosalie* (1928). Their songs of the 1920s were

characterized by George's infectious, driving music and Ira's clever, slangy lyrics.

In the early 1930s, the Gershwins created three satirical musicals, *Strike Up the Band* (1930), *Of Thee I Sing* (1931) and *Let 'Em Eat Cake* (1933). Acclaimed for its trenchant political satire and good-humoured score, *Of Thee I Sing* was the first musical to be awarded the Pulitzer Prize for Drama. The brothers did not totally abandon more light-hearted forms of MUSICAL COMEDY, however. *Girl Crazy* (1930) had a frivolous book, but contained some of the Gershwins' best songs, such as 'I Got Rhythm' and 'Embraceable You'. In 1992 it served as the inspiration for the Tony-winning musical *Crazy for You*, with book by Ken Ludwig but Gershwin songs. In 1935 the THEATRE GUILD produced the Gershwins' 'American folk opera' *Porgy and Bess*. Receiving mixed reviews from both drama and music critics, the original production of *Porgy and Bess* was not a success. Nevertheless, its magnificent score has proved to be the Gershwins' most enduring work.

After George's untimely death in 1937, Ira collaborated with other composers. *Lady in the Dark* (1941), which had a score by KURT WEILL, was innovative in confining its musical numbers to a few elaborate dream sequences. *The Firebrand of Florence* (1945), which Weill also composed, and *Park Avenue* (1946), with a score by Arthur Schwartz, were failures. In addition to composing for the musical stage, the Gershwins wrote a number of motion picture scores, and George also composed for the concert hall.

As a composer, George Gershwin helped to popularize jazz on the musical stage in the 1920s. His more serious compositions for the concert hall prepared him to write *Porgy and Bess*, one of the most ambitious scores ever created for the American musical theatre. Ira's abilities as a lyricist also grew from the facile rhyming of his 1920s songs to the deeper, more eloquent style of his later work. Together, the Gershwins were major forces in raising the level of musical theatre composition. Of the numerous books on the Gershwins, the most recent is J. Peyser's *A Memory of All That* (1993). MK

Gershwin Theatre (New York City) Originating as the Uris Theatre, this was the first large BROADWAY playhouse to be built under relaxed zoning constraints in the building code that permitted theatres to be incorporated within commercial structures. Erected by the Uris Corporation, the 1900-seat theatre is under long-term lease to the Nederlander Organization and Eugene Ostreicher. It opened in 1972 with a spectacular but unsuccessful rock musical; since then, its policy has fluctuated between MUSICAL productions and a series of concert appearances of well known popular performers, dance presentations and OPERA productions. In 1979, it received its first critical success with *Sweeney Todd*, the STEPHEN SONDHEIM musical. In 1983, it was renamed the Gershwin Theatre in honour of GEORGE AND IRA GERSHWIN. The theatre also encompasses the Theatre Hall of Fame within its spacious public areas. MCH

Gerstein [*neé* Gersten], **Bertha** fl. c.1900–20 Leading MUSICAL COMEDY and straight actress of the American YIDDISH THEATRE, notably with BORIS THOMASHEFSKY'S National Theatre and later with MAURICE SCHWARTZ'S company. Married to the actor JACOB BEN-AMI, she frequently played leads opposite him. AB

Gert, Valeska [Gertrud Valesca Samosch] 1892–1978 German CABARET dancer, an exponent of grotesque pantomime. After study with ALEKSANDËR MOISIU, she made her Berlin debut in 1916 and appeared at the Schall und Rauch from 1920. Her pugdog features and whirling movements were seen to advantage in macabre numbers like 'The Girl from the Mummy's Cellar'. Kurt Tucholsky called her harlot's dance, 'La Canaille', 'the boldest thing I ever saw on a stage'. She collaborated with BRECHT on a Red Revue and emigrated to New York (1938), where she founded the Beggar Bar. Back in West Berlin, she ran two more clubs, the Hexenküche (Witch's Kitchen, 1950) and the Ziegenstall (Goat Pen, 1978), adding parodic recitations to her dance repertory. LS

Gest, Morris 1881–1942 Russian-born American producer, who specialized in promoting foreign talent and in producing opulent spectacles at the Manhattan Opera House (1914–20) and Century Theatre (1917–19; see NEW THEATRE). Gest and his partner, F. Ray Comstock (1880–1949), imported the Ballets Russes from Paris, and the *Chauve-Souris* REVUE, featuring Nikita Balieff (Baliev). They produced the 1923–4 tour of the MOSCOW ART THEATRE, the 1924 presentation of MAX REINHARDT's *The Miracle*, and the 1925 tour of the Moscow Art Theatre Musical Theatre Studio, under the direction of VLADIMIR NEMIROVICH-DANCHENKO. After ending his partnership with Comstock in 1928, Gest sponsored the US visit of ALEKSANDËR MOISIU (Alexander Moissi), Reinhardt's leading actor, and he brought the Freiburg Passion Play to the USA. WD

Ghana Ghana achieved independence under Kwame Nkrumah in 1957, the first of Britain's African colonies to do so. Nkrumah's Convention People's Party was effectively organized at the grass roots and in the first years of independence proposed radical reform at the base of society. Nkrumah himself was a committed Pan-Africanist, eager to promote the liberation of the whole continent. His speeches and actions inspired millions in many parts of Africa. However, Ghana seems to frame new discourses that are fulfilled elsewhere. Nkrumah was overthrown by the military in 1966 and died in exile in 1972.

Political and economic factors have a direct effect on modern Ghanaian drama, for in Ghana playwrights have, from time to time, played an active role in central government, rather than finding themselves consistently in opposition to it. From 1957, one of the key Ghanaians involved in the development of theatre, EFUA T. SUTHERLAND, was associated with Nkrumah. She tried to translate some of the early ideals of the state into a socially based programme for the development of drama and performance out of traditional forms combined with professionalism. She founded the Ghana Drama Studio in Accra in 1957, and was involved, with J. K. Nketia, in the establishment of the School of Music and Drama under the aegis of the Institute of African Studies at the University of Ghana in Legon. Later, playwrights AMA ATA AIDOO and Asiedu Yirenkyi, who had worked at the Ghana

Drama Studio and with the university's Studio Players, held ministerial appointments in the military administration of Jerry Rawlings.

The deteriorating economy has meant that state funding for the performing arts has continually diminished. Just as new ideas have been promoted that make a virtue out of stringent economies, the funding has been further reduced. The result is that dramatic talent has been nurtured and then forced into exile – sometimes for economic reasons only, but always with a great deal of creative frustration. This has happened to Aidoo herself, as well as to another leading Ghanaian playwright and director, JOE DE GRAFT. Forced to work as expatriates in other African countries, away from the vigorous drama discourse within Ghana in which they were participating, their creative output has dwindled.

The influence of Ghanaian dramatists extends beyond their own artistic products, and to many African countries. However, the Ghanaian playwright in another African country is still classed as an expatriate and therefore caught in a contradiction: he or she is of the African culture, and yet politically separated from it. This can be particularly difficult for Ghanaian playwrights whose creative work has explored the political fusion of the traditional and the modern.

The traditional roots of drama in the oral culture are seen in Ghana as being highly significant for the forms, themes and tone of the new drama. The Ghanaian sources of theatre may be said to be dance-drama, ceremonies and storytelling. There are different traditions among ethnic groups, but research suggests that their dramatic elements all tend to emphasize the community as the basis for domestic well-being. The community can bring to light what the family may be tempted – to its cost – to hide. This can be seen in *aboakyer*, the deer-hunt festival in Winneba, which is a lord-of-misrule festival (an occasion for licensed mischief). The captured or killed deer is ceremonially sequestered while the entire community participates in an immense procession comprising bands and dancers, skits, SATIRE and transvestism. Another feature of the oral tradition is the participation of the audience, especially in the storytelling performances. The traditions of *anansesem* (spider stories) have been extended into a modern form of performance by Efua Sutherland. She describes the conventions of *anansegoro* in the foreword to her play *The Marriage of Anansewa*. Others, like Yirenkyi, have also been involved in developing *anansegoro*. Sutherland's use of this and other interesting forms of storytelling theatre and musical performance has led her also to evolve the architecture of performance space, like the *kodzidan*, the 'story house' in the village of Atwia.

The critic Charles Angmor divides modern dramatic expression in Ghana into operatic drama and literary drama. Under the former he lists folk-opera, cantatas (of various Christian congregations) and concert parties. Folk-opera may have developed out of the staging of GILBERT and Sullivan OPERETTAS in schools, although in colonial times the Ghanaian intelligentsia also acquired a taste for European GRAND OPERA. Saka Acquaye, in particular, wanting to indigenize the operatic form, composed operas in Ghanaian languages. In a similar way, perhaps, the can-tatas reflected a theatrical indigenizing of Christianity in the particular circumstances of fund-raising. However, it is in the concert parties that we find the most exciting development of theatre and dramatic form.

The concert parties of coastal Ghana and the neighbouring republic of Togo are the only professional theatre in the region, with the members of the many companies earning their livelihoods from their travelling shows. The concert parties are also called 'trios', their performers 'comedians', and their improvised performances 'comic plays'. The content of the plays is contemporary, depicting the actuality of the lives of their rapt audiences. Concert parties are reputed to have started in 1918 with a headmaster who performed solo, one Master Yalley; but the most famous company was that of 'Bob' Johnson in the 1930s. They were first known as the 'Two Bobs and their Carolina Girl' and then as the 'Axim Trio'. Sutherland states that they did not compose *anansegoro*, but that Johnson 'took ordinary life stories and then composed plays by the method of *kasa-ndwon* [speech and song]'. The trios flourished in the 1960s and 70s. Each company travels extensively with a large repertory of plays, which although improvised are actually maintained in a fairly stable performance 'text'. They have been researched by K. N. Bame in Ghana, and in Togo by Alain Ricard, who has published a performance on sound-tape of *Mister Tameklor* by the Happy Star Concert Band of Lomé. The great popularity of the concert parties has inspired writers like Patience Addo and Derlene Clems whose plays, *Company Pot* and *Scholarship Woman*, respectively, were broadcast by the BBC (1972).

The literary form that developed in the 1960s reflected in both content and form some Western models, but also showed a strong movement away from these, especially as theatre practice attempted to link the depiction of Ghanaian attitudes to the sensibilities of the audiences. This literary drama, says Angmor, 'does not operate as a rule on conflict and its resolution, but generally on consensus and consummation'. It continues to advance the discourse of traditional performance. These literary plays were prefigured by Kobina Sekyi's *The Blinkards* (1915; published 1974), which attacked European cultural influences; and, in the 1940s, by the literary and philosophical plays of J. B. Danquah and F. K. Fiawoo.

But the real flowering came only after independence. Although the corpus of published texts is small (about 30 plays, by fewer than 15 playwrights), the drama discourse has developed with depth and consistency, despite the divergent experiences and personalities of the playwrights. The plays deal with themes and ideas which are often far-reaching in their moral and political implications. *Foriwa* (1962), by Efua Sutherland, explores the transition from the old to the new, and the social mechanism for the transformation of the community at the grass roots. *The Mightier Sword* (1973) by Martin Owusu explores history for the sake of the present, as does de Graft's *Through a Film Darkly* (1966), offering a painful analysis of black racism. *Anowa* (1970), by Ama Ata Aidoo, considered by many critics to be one of the finest modern African plays, historicizes the present by investigating the implications of slavery for people's psyche. De Graft's *Muntu* (1975) mythologizes the present. The ordinary yet important domestic problems resulting from social transformations are expressed in Aidoo's *Dilemma of a Ghost* (1964), in *Sons and Daughters* (1964) by de Graft, in *Laughter and Hubbub in the House* (1972) by Kwesi Kay and in Yirenkyi's *Blood and Tears* (1973). On the other hand, the extraordinary domestic crises that result from secret and dubious short cuts to material prosperity are variously explored in *Kivuli* (1972) by Yirenkyi, *Amari* (1975) by Jacob Hevi, Owusu's *The Sudden Return* (1973), *Edufa* (1967) by Sutherland, and in a humorous vein in Sutherland's *anansegoro, The Marriage of Anansewa* (1975).

These plays are concerned with relationships and responsibilities within the household, which is almost always contextualized by a particularized community perspective – usually created off stage by the drama on stage. Though often not seen, the community is forever pressing in on the compound walls; and because of its absence it can also symbolize the nation-state, the well-being of which cannot be guaranteed until the family adjustments are properly made. In addition, the status of the women in the plays is often presented effectively as a problem, by both male and female playwrights. Efo Kodjo Mawugbe and other young playwrights give evidence of a new resurgence in Ghanaian theatre in the 1990s. ME

See: N. Akam and A. Ricard, *Mister Tameklor, suivi de Français-le-Parisien, par le Happy Star Concert Band de Lomé (Togo)*, Paris, 1981; C. Angmor, 'Drama in Ghana' in *Theatre in Africa*, ed. O. Agunba and I. Irele, Ibadan, 1978; K. N. Bame, *Come to Laugh: A Study of African Traditional Theatre in Ghana*, Legon, n.d.; M. Etherton, *The Development of African Drama*, London, 1982; S. Lokko, 'Theatre Space: A History Overview of the Theatre Movement in Ghana', *Modern Drama*, 23, 1980; A. Yirenkyi, 'Bill Marshall and the Ghanaian Theatre of the Early Seventies', *Journal of the Performing Arts*, 1, 1, 1980.

Ghelderode, Michel de [Ad(h)émar-Adolphe-Louis Martens] 1898-1962 The most powerful and significant Belgian dramatist of the interwar years. Ghelderode wrote some 60 plays as well as many stories and essays. His originals are in French but a number of his plays were first performed in Flemish or Dutch translations. They are the work of a national dramatist – they are not nationalistic, but essentially the product of a Belgian, heir to a mixed Flemish and French culture, with a powerful sense of his country's long and violent history.

Ghelderode's plays (several not performed until years after they were written, several still unperformed) can be divided very inexactly into three groups: those set in the past, e.g. *Escorial* (Théâtre Communal, Brussels, 1929), *Chronicles of Hell* (Théâtre de l'ATELIER, Paris, 1949), *The School for Fools* (Théâtre de l'Oeuvre, Paris, 1953); those with biblical origins – although these are far from being 'religious dramas' – e.g. *Barabbas* (Vlaamsche Volkstooneel, Ostend, 1929), *Miss Jairus* (Atelier, 1949), *The Women at the Tomb* (Théâtre Universitaire, Paris, 1953); and those with their roots in BURLESQUE and the MUSIC-HALL, e.g. *The Death of Doctor Faust* (Théâtre Art et Action, Paris, 1928), *Christopher Columbus* (Art et Action, 1929) and *Pantagleize* (Vlaamsche Volkstooneel, Saint-

Trond, 1930). All vividly display a theatre of sights and sounds as well as of words, a theatre of the senses – ARTAUD's theatre – and very much a theatre of cruelty wrought from the irresistible demands of the flesh, the agony of the spirit and the massacre of the innocent, frequently provoking laughter, but a very uneasy laughter.

It has been well noted that much of the avant-garde theatre of the postwar years had already appeared in Ghelderode's plays, which had nevertheless to wait many years before they escaped from print and from the obscurity of small cult theatres. His work has found appreciative audiences in both Eastern and Western Europe and in the USA, but he is still largely unknown in England. It is noteworthy that one of his most successful fictions was his account of his life and works. The true facts have been painstakingly established by Roland Beyen in *Michel de Ghelderode, ou la hantise du masque* (Brussels, 1971). Ghelderode, of whom JEAN COCTEAU said, 'His genius in the theatre is unsurpassed', has not yet received the honour that is his due. He was robbed even by death of his nomination for a Nobel Prize. GH

Gherardi family Italian actors. **Giovanni** (c.1645-83), a COMMEDIA DELL'ARTE player, who won his sobriquet Flautino from his virtuosity on the flute and guitar, went to Paris in 1674 or 1675. His son **Evaristo** (1663-1700) entered the COMÉDIE-ITALIENNE there as Arlequin in REGNARD's *Le Divorce* in 1689 and soon rose to manage it, often running foul of the police for his outspokenness. He wrote numerous scenarios for the HÔTEL DE BOURGOGNE, and when the Italian actors were turned out of Paris in 1697 he published 56 of them as *Le Théâtre italien*, the fullest edition being that of 1700. They comprise one of the most important sources for the history of the *commedia dell'arte* in France. LS

Giacometti, Paolo 1816-82 Italian dramatist, prolific in a range of play types but most important for his social dramas. The finest, *La morte civile* (*Civil Death*, 1861), is one of the more considerable Italian plays of the 19th century and was a main piece in the repertoire of many leading actors, including SALVINI, who after first producing it at the Teatro dei Fiorentini at Naples played it successfully in both Britain and the USA. LR

Giacosa, Giuseppe 1847-1906 Italian dramatist. Giacosa began as a poet and published 'a theatrical legend', *Una partita a scacchi* (*A Game of Chess*), in the journal *Nuova Antologia* in 1872. In the course of the 1870s he wrote a number of historical plays with mainly medieval and Renaissance settings, like *Il trionfo dell'amore* (*The Triumph of Love*, 1875), and comedies in a light GOLDONIAN manner like *Il marito amante della moglie* (*The Husband Lover of His Wife*, 1877). But his best work was written under the influence of NATURALISM in the 1890s: middle-class psychological dramas, the best-known of which are *Tristi amori* (*Sad Loves*, 1887) and *Come le foglie* (*Like the Leaves*, 1900), both of which were later made into films and still hold the Italian stage today. His best work is tightly constructed and is characterized by a mood of subtle melancholy. He was a distinguished librettist, collaborating with Luigi Illica on several pieces set by Puccini, including *La Bohème* (1896), *Tosca* (1899) and *Madame Butterfly* (1904). LR

Gide, André 1869–1951 French novelist, essayist and playwright. Gide was one of a group of writers concerned to reintroduce classical myth on the modern stage, as shown by his *Oedipus* (1931). He was a friend of Copeau and interested in the Vieux-Colombier, but his talents were essentially those of an introspective *moraliste* and novelist, not a dramatist. DB

Gielgud, John 1904– British actor and director, knighted in 1953. In his first roles under Granville Barker in 1921 and with J. B. Fagan's Oxford Repertory Company between 1924 and 1925 – when he had his first London success as Trofimov in *The Cherry Orchard* – Gielgud developed the elegant style and expressive clarity of voice that won him immediate acclamation as the leading interpreter of Shakespearian tragedy on his appearance with the Old Vic in 1929. His most famous role was Hamlet, which he returned to in his own production in 1933 and performed more than 500 times during his career. Another key role was John Worthing in Wilde's *The Importance of Being Earnest*, which he first played in 1930, while Gordon Daviot's *Richard of Bordeaux* (1932, under his own direction) established him as a popular star in the West End commercial theatre. His brilliant performances in *The Seagull* (1936), *The Three Sisters* (1937), *The Cherry Orchard* (1961) and *Ivanov* (1965), all of which he also directed, made a major contribution to Chekhov's acceptance on the English-speaking stage.

During the 1950s he promoted the work of such modern playwrights as Terence Rattigan, Graham Greene and Enid Bagnold, as both actor and director, in addition to extending his Shakespearian repertoire with the Royal Shakespeare Company (Lear, Angelo, Leontes: 1950–1) and at the Old Vic, and presenting his internationally acclaimed Shakespeare recital *Ages of Man* (1958). Since 1974 he has appeared frequently at the National Theatre, his most striking performances being in *The Tempest* (Prospero, 1974 – a role magnificently extended in the film *Prospero's Books* in 1988) and in Pinter's *No Man's Land* (1975). His six books of theatrical reminiscences offer a wealth of material on the development of the English theatre in the modern period. The Globe Theatre in London was renamed the Gielgud in 1994 to honour his 90th birthday. CI

Gilbert, John (Gibbs) 1810–89 American actor, famous for comic roles in classic English comedy. Gilbert, born in Boston, made his debut there at the Tremont Theatre as Jaffier in *Venice Preserv'd* in 1828. He played the frontier theatres until 1834 and made his New York debut in 1839. Although he started as a leading tragedian, his greater successes came in comedy, especially as old men. For a time he managed the Chestnut Street Theatre. For 26 years he was with Wallack's company. A very traditional actor, he resisted almost any theatrical change. He died on the road. William Winter published his biography and letters in 1890. SMA

Gilbert, Sir W(illiam) S(chwenck) [Bab] 1836–1911

British playwright, famous above all for his collaboration with Sir Arthur Sullivan in the series of Savoy Operas that made them both (and Richard D'Oyly Carte, their sponsor) rich. Gilbert was already well known as a writer some years before *Thespis* (1871) brought the two men together for the first time. He trained as a lawyer and was called to the Bar in 1863. Two years earlier he had begun contributing comic verse to the magazine *Fun*, under the pseudonym 'Bab'. The 1869 collection of *Bab Ballads* (other collections followed in 1873 and 1877) was illustrated by the author. It earns him an honoured place among Victorian 'nonsense' poets, but Gilbert's nonsense has often a satirical edge. He wrote his first play in 1863 and was consistently active in the theatre from 1866 to 97, during which time he wrote well over 60 plays, burlesques, operas and extravaganzas.

Although he wrote plays in many different styles, Gilbert's pessimistic assumption that manners and politeness are a mask for fundamental human selfishness is rarely absent from his work. This, certainly, is the basis of most of the successful 'fairy' plays, from *The Palace of Truth* (1870) through *Pygmalion and Galatea* (1871) to *The Wicked World* (1873), all written in blank verse that welcomes bathos. The vein of mockery that enlivens Gilbert's best work was happily exploited in the collaborations with Sullivan: *The Sorcerer* (1877), *HMS Pinafore* (1878), *The Pirates of Penzance* (1879), *Patience* (1881), *Iolanthe* (1882), *Princess Ida* (1884), *The Mikado* (1885), *Ruddigore* (1887), *The Yeomen of the Guard* (1888), *The Gondoliers* (1889), *Utopia Limited* (1893) and *The Grand Duke* (1896). The fame of the Savoy Operas has eclipsed that of even his best plays: notably *Sweethearts* (1874), *Engaged* (1877), which certainly influenced Shaw and Wilde, and *Rosencrantz and Guildenstern* (1891), a witty swansong of Victorian burlesque. When Gilbert was knighted in 1907, he was proud to claim that he was the first to be so honoured 'for dramatic authorship alone'. PT

Gilford, Jack 1907–90 American actor who began his career as a comedian, appearing in nightclubs, revues and vaudeville. His most successful appearances on Broadway included the roles of Bontche Schweig in *The World of Sholom Aleichem* (1953), Mr Dussell in *The Diary of Anne Frank* (1955), King Sextimus in *Once upon a Mattress* (1959), Hysterium in *A Funny Thing Happened on the Way to the Forum* (1962) and Herr Schultz in *Cabaret* (1966). His films included *A Funny Thing Happened*, *Catch 22* and *Cocoon*. He also starred in televised versions of *Sholom Aleichem* and *Anne Frank*. His last live appearance was in a stand-up comic routine (1988) at New York's Ballroom, a cabaret. SMA

Gill, Peter 1939– British director and dramatist, who joined the Royal Court company as an actor in 1959 but became best known there as the director of three hitherto underrated plays by D. H. Lawrence, presented as a group in 1968. In 1969 the Royal Court produced two of his first plays, *The Sleepers' Den* and *Over Gardens Out*, which revealed that Gill could evoke with economy of means but with lyrical skill the circumstances of his Cardiff boyhood. In 1977 he was appointed director of Riverside Studios, which he transformed into a major arts centre. On its rudimentary stages he directed classical productions of CHEKHOV's *The Cherry Orchard* (1978), MIDDLETON and ROWLEY's *The Changeling* (1978) and *Measure for Measure* (1979), as well as encouraging new dramatists and new forms of theatre. In 1980, he joined the NATIONAL THEATRE under PETER HALL, where in addition to directing such productions as TURGENEV's *A Month in the Country* (1981) and BÜCHNER's *Danton's Death* (1983) he pioneered new writing at the Cottesloe Theatre, running a season of premieres there in 1985. His best play, *Small Change* (1976), received its premiere at the Royal Court under his own directing. For the NT, he directed Nicholas Wright's *Mrs Klein* (1988), which afterwards transferred to the WEST END, and a revival of O'CASEY's *Juno and the Paycock* (1989). In 1992, he staged an elegant revival of Congreve's *The Way of the World* at the LYRIC THEATRE, HAMMERSMITH. JE

Gillette, William (Hooker) 1853–1937 American actor and playwright. Born into a prominent family in Hartford, Connecticut, Gillette left home in 1873 to seek a career on the stage. As an actor he is remembered for his performance in his own *Sherlock Holmes* (1899), which he played over 1300 times; his most significant achievement as a playwright was his Civil War spy MELODRAMA, *Secret Service* (1895), with its fast-moving action, suspense, and the tension between the demands of love and duty. Gillette was the author of numerous adaptations and dramatizations and several original plays in which he frequently appeared himself, in both the USA and England. In addition to Holmes, he played Blane in *Held by the Enemy* (1886), Billings in *Too Much Johnson* (1894) and Thorne/Dumont in *Secret Service*. His other notable appearances were in BARRIE's *The Admirable Crichton* (1903) and *Dear Brutus* (1918). Other Gillette plays include *The Private Secretary* (1884), *All the Comforts of Home* (1890), *Clarice* (1905) and *Electricity* (1910). In 1913 Gillette delivered his influential and subsequently published lecture 'The Illusion of the First Time in Acting', which explains his cool, understated approach to acting – a contrast to the florid and romantic style that dominated the theatre up to his time. DBW

Gilpin, Charles (Sidney) 1878–1930 African-American actor. Introduced at school to amateur theatricals, Gilpin left school at age 14 to become a vagabond vaudevillian (see VAUDEVILLE), his meagre earnings supplemented by sporadic jobs as printer, porter, barber and elevator boy. In 1907 he joined the all-black Pekin Stock Company of Chicago, and later acted at the Lincoln and Lafayette Theatres in Harlem. His impressive BROADWAY performance as the slave Custis in DRINKWATER's *Abraham Lincoln* (1919) led to the title role in *The Emperor Jones* (1920), in which he scored a resounding triumph. A victim of sudden fame and racial prejudice, Gilpin took to drink, which cut short his career. The black critic Theophilus Lewis lamented: 'He rose from obscurity to the peaks, lived his hour of triumph, and returned again to the shadows.' EGH

Giraldi, Giovan Battista [Cinzio] 1504–73 Italian dramatist, short story writer and literary theorist. Giraldi

was a prolific and influential writer. His nine plays in the tragic or tragicomic modes, exploiting SENECAn motifs of violence and the supernatural, were much admired in Italy and abroad, particularly *L'Orbecche* (1541), and his short stories provided plot lines or suggestions to many dramatists, among them SHAKESPEARE, who drew on his *Ecatommiti* (1565) for *Othello* and *Measure for Measure*. His theoretical writings on the unities of time, place and action, and the morality proper to dramatic subject-matter and treatment, were no less influential, particularly in France. KR

Giraudoux, Jean 1882–1944 French diplomat and writer. Giraudoux's success as a dramatist was largely due to his partnership with JOUVET, who directed and acted in almost all of his plays from the first, *Siegfried* (1928), to the last, *La Folle de Chaillot* (*The Madwoman of Chaillot*, 1945). At the time this pairing seemed the realization of COPEAU's dream of bringing poetry back to the modern stage, and each new production was eagerly awaited by Jouvet's audience. In fact much of Giraudoux's work is ill suited to the stage, verbose and lacking action, though it has great wit and charm. Largely unsuccessful in his attempt at tragedy, he seems at his best in light-hearted entertainments such as *Intermezzo* (1933) or *L'Apollon de Bellac* (*The Apollo of Bellac*, 1942), which combine brilliant humour with subtlety and occasional depth. Only perhaps in *La Guerre de Troie n'aura pas lieu* (*Tiger at the Gates*, 1935) did he succeed in tailoring his style to a subject of contemporary importance. Hitler's power was increasing and this story of civilized Trojans and Greeks dragged unwillingly into war struck a prophetic chord. Giraudoux's frequent use of classical mythology encouraged a vogue for myth on the French stage in the 1930s and 1940s. DB

Gish, Lillian 1893–1993 and
Dorothy Gish 1898–1968 American actresses and sisters who, although they worked together in several films, never considered themselves a team. Dorothy made her stage debut in 1907 in *East Lynne*. In 1912 she made her first film with D.W. Griffith, continuing with and without her sister until 1928. Among her films were *Orphans of the Storm*, *Nell Gwyn* and *Madame Pompadour*. She then returned to the stage, eventually succeeding Dorothy Stickney in *Life with Father* in 1941. She appeared the next year in *The Great Big Doorstep*, followed by *Magnificent Yankee*.

Lillian debuted in *In Convict's Stripes* (1902) and first appeared in New York as Marganie in *A Good Little Devil* (1913). She entered films and appeared in such early works as *The Birth of a Nation*, *Intolerance*, *Way Down East* and *The Orphans of the Storm*. She returned to the stage in 1930, starring in such productions as *Camille* (1932), JOHN GIELGUD's *Hamlet* (as Ophelia, 1937), *Life with Father* (1940–2) and *The Curious Savage* (1950). During 1969–70 she toured worldwide with a one-person concert programme. SMA

Glaspell, Susan 1876–1948 American theatre founder and playwright. Perhaps best known as one of the founders of the PROVINCETOWN PLAYERS (along with her husband, George Cram Cook), as a playwright (contributing 11 plays to the Players) Glaspell was second only to EUGENE O'NEILL in the founding of a modern American drama that combined contemporary American ideas with European expressionistic techniques (see EXPRESSIONISM). Glaspell's early one-act plays satirized contemporary attitudes and interests, such as pop psychology (*Suppressed Desires*, 1915) and ultra-idealism (*Tickless Time*, 1918), both written in collaboration with Cook. However, her *Trifles* (1916), one of the most frequently anthologized one-act plays, skilfully portrayed hidden, psychological motivation by using realistic settings and dialogue to reveal women's inner conflicts. This play was also her first to use the device of keeping the central female character offstage, a technique she repeated in *Bernice* (1919). In her most controversial play, *The Verge* (1921), she experimented with SYMBOLISM and expressionistic settings to reveal the state of mind of a 'new' woman who goes mad striving for both abstract idealism and individual fulfilment.

Throughout her career Glaspell never feared to tackle the new and the immediate. In *The Inheritors* (1921) she contrasted narrow post-First World War Americanism with earlier ideals of individual freedom and tolerance, again creating a female character who sacrifices ease and comfort to remain true to her ideals. In a controversial decision, she won the 1931 Pulitzer Prize for *Alison's House*, loosely based on the life of Emily Dickinson.

Glaspell's contribution to American drama includes her role in the founding of the Little Theatre movement (see COMMUNITY THEATRE/LITTLE THEATRE MOVEMENT), as well as her creation of modern female characters in search of autonomy, portrayed through new and experimental dramatic techniques. During 1936–8 she headed the Midwest Bureau of the FEDERAL THEATRE PROJECT, in Chicago.   FB

Gleich, (Josef) Alois 1772–1841 Austrian dramatist; one of the most prolific in the popular Viennese theatre (he wrote over 200 plays). Gleich's work is generally without character and generically various; however, in works such as *Die Musikanten vom hohen Markt* (*The Musicians from the Upper Market*, 1815) he movingly dramatized the miseries of contemporary Viennese life and provided FERDINAND RAIMUND with his first great role, the violinist Adam Kratzerl. Gleich also became an adept at the 'magic play' that was so characteristic of the Viennese repertoire: *Der Berggeist* (*The Mountain Spirit*, 1820) and *Ydor, der Wanderer aus dem Wasserreiche* (*Ydor, the Wanderer from the Water Kingdom*, 1820) still have some life in them. For 40 years, Gleich was also a civil servant.   SW

Globe Theatre (London) When the lease ran out on JAMES BURBAGE'S THEATRE in 1598, members of the LORD CHAMBERLAIN'S MEN had the building dismantled and most of its timbers carried across the Thames to a south-bank site close to HENSLOWE'S ROSE, where they were thriftily deployed in the construction of a new theatre. The Globe was a polygonal structure with a three-tiered gallery surrounding an open yard. Attempts to 'reconstruct' it are based on De Witt's drawing of the SWAN, which it probably resembled, and on references to it in the FORTUNE contract. Restricted excavations, begun on the site in 1989, are too inconclusive to settle disputes about its dimensions

and capacity (3350 according to John Orrell's 1983 argument), but it was certainly larger than the ROSE, its chief south-bank competitor. Of more general interest is the system of sharing costs and profits devised by the company at the Globe. SHAKESPEARE was among the six responsible 'housekeepers', and it was at the Globe from 1599 to 1608 that most of his finest plays were first publicly performed. The Globe continued in use after its resident company took possession of the indoor BLACKFRIARS THEATRE in 1608–9. That it was a profitable asset is emphasized by the speed with which it was rebuilt after destruction by fire in 1613. The second Globe remained active until the CLOSURE OF THE THEATRES in 1642. It was demolished in 1644.

Two later London theatres have shared the famous name. The first opened in 1868 with a production of H. J. BYRON's *Cyril's Success*, but was demolished in 1902 as part of the scheme for widening the Strand. The second, originally called the SEYMOUR HICKS after its first star, was opened in 1906 and still stands on Shaftesbury Avenue, though renamed in 1994 the GIELGUD THEATRE.   PT

Gluck, Christoph Willibald 1714–87 German composer of many OPERAS, the finest of which exhibit great dramatic power. In his later works Gluck dealt forceful blows at the decorative entertainment that opera had become in the 18th century. He was steeped in the aesthetic of the second half of the 18th century but created works that strongly foreshadow romanticism. In an age in which opera had become a mere succession of elaborate musical ornaments, he was preoccupied with opera as drama and sought to assign the libretto to its rightful position. He claimed that when composing he forgot that he was a musician. In fact he was an outstanding musician. His claim must be understood to mean that he did not aim to write music that proceeded in complete freedom, but music that bore a reciprocally supportive relationship with the libretto. His most successful operas were on classical themes, as had been the earliest of all operas and as were most serious operas in the 18th century. They are *Orpheus and Eurydice* (Vienna, 1762; revised, Paris, 1774), *Alcestis* (Vienna, 1767; revised, Paris, 1776), *Paris and Helen* (Vienna, 1769), *Iphigenia in Aulis* (Paris, 1774), *Armida* (Paris, 1777) and *Iphigenia in Tauris* (Paris, 1779). The librettos of the first three are by CALZABIGI, whose influence on Gluck was profound, and probably decisive.

In the prefaces to the scores of *Alcestis* and *Paris and Helen* and in letters to the *Mercure de France* Gluck stated his aims in operatic composition. Insisting on the necessity of a meaningful libretto and, in true 18th-century fashion, on the imitation of Nature, he declared that the overture should not be a free-standing musical item but a suitable introduction to the subsequent drama; that dramatically unnecessary vocal ornamentation and instrumental interpolation should have no place; and that the sharpness of distinction between RECITATIVE and ARIA should be reduced – a matter that was to be pursued by opera composers until it eventuated in WAGNER's 'continuous melody'. Gluck's grasp of the nature of theatre music as against concert or salon music is well illustrated by his comment that if someone up in the dome of the Invalides closely examining the paintings were to ask, 'What is intended here – a nose, an arm?' the proper reply from the painter at ground level would be, 'Come down here and judge for yourself.' GH

Godber, John 1956– British dramatist and stage director, who began his career at the age of 16 by writing for his local radio station, Radio Sheffield. He turned to television, contributing to such series as *Crown Court* and *Brookside*, before adapting *Blood Sweat and Tears* (1986) from his stage play, and *The Ritz* (1987), both of which were commissioned by the BBC. Since 1984 he has been the artistic director of Hull Truck, for whom he has staged his best-known comedies: *Up 'n' Under* (1984), which won the LAURENCE OLIVIER Comedy of the Year Award (a sequel, *Up 'n' Under 2*, was staged in 1993), *Bouncers* (1985), *Teechers* (1987), *Salt of the Earth* (1988) and *On the Piste* (1990), transferring to London's WEST END in 1993). Godber, like WILLY RUSSELL and ALAN BLEASDALE, is closely in touch with his Northern audiences, but has yet to make his full impact in the South. His plays are often set in leisure centres or rugby clubs, where it may be freely assumed that London's chattering classes are afraid to tread. He delights in physical and athletic GAGS, and jibes against the Establishment, which turned his Hull Truck production of *Twelfth Night* (1989) into something of a bunfight. His *Happy Families* (1991) had the privilege of being chosen for a group performance by 50 amateur companies throughout Britain, a record duly mentioned in the *Guinness Book of Records*, while *April in Paris* (1992) described the gloomy impression of foreign parts of one xenophobic couple. In 1992 Godber was listed as the fourth most performed British dramatist, after SHAKESPEARE, AYCKBOURN and Willy Russell. On *the Piste*, his first West End success, demonstrates why. Its title may suggest a crude farce, but the script is sharp and funny, and excels in its sketches of class warfare on the ski slopes. JE

Goerlng, Reinhard 1887–1936 German dramatist, whose *Seeschlacht* (*Sea Battle*, 1918) is a key expressionist text (see EXPRESSIONISM) and the first to put action from the First World War on to the stage. Set inside a gun turret, it uses unnamed types and condensed dialogue in the same way as KAISER and HASENCLEVER. *Die Südpolexpedition des Kapitäns Scott* (1930) was also shaped round an inescapable predicament with an aura of antique tragedy. HR

Goethe, Johann Wolfgang von 1749–1832 German playwright, director, novelist and essayist. Goethe's achievement in the theatre was as varied and as significant as his accomplishment in other fields of the arts, humanities and sciences. From his childhood in Frankfurt, where he eagerly attended both French TRAGEDY and PUNCH and Judy shows, he demonstrated an active interest in all things theatrical. He was a prolific playwright, but he is difficult to categorize as his work both typified and developed most genres current in his time. Hence while his early play *Götz von Berlichingen* (1773) reflects contemporary enthusiasm for the works of SHAKESPEARE and provided the young *STURM UND DRANG* writers with a model for their own dramas, after his

removal to Weimar Goethe's drama gradually came to express a more classical outlook. *Egmont* (completed in 1788) is still Shakespearian in structure, but Goethe's view of his hero, whose 'daimonic' personality and trust in the goodness of those around him leads to his death, shows a distrust of the values that had enthused him in his *Sturm und Drang* period.

Perhaps Goethe's most effective works for the theatre are the classical verse plays *Iphigenia in Tauris* (1787) and *Torquato Tasso* (1790), the former reflecting his belief in the superiority of moral strength and humanitarian impulse above barbarism; and the latter, which may well indicate his dissatisfaction with his position in the Weimar court, showing a profound scepticism as well as appreciation of the romantic spirit of the artist. Goethe's masterpiece, *Faust, Part 1* (1808) and *Part 2* (1832), while cast in dramatic form and exhibiting command of a vast range of dramatic styles, was not written with performance in mind. *Part 1* has, however, often been produced successfully; it focuses mainly on the private experience of Faust and on his erotic misadventures with Gretchen. *Part 2*, a far more formidable theatrical undertaking, has a wider scope, leading to meditations on such lofty and weighty subjects as the future of the human race.

From 1791 to 1817 Goethe executed, along with several other official duties in Weimar, the post of director of the Court Theatre, a position he shared for some years with SCHILLER. Apart from developing an admirable balanced approach to repertoire that was to be imitated by other court and municipal theatres, Goethe evolved the so-called WEIMAR school of acting, embodied in his 'Rules for Actors', that was to have a fundamental influence on the performance of tragedy in the German theatre until the end of the 19th century. His attempt to make the actor into a model of deportment and elegant speech might be regarded as a denial of the distrustful attitude he often expressed towards the acting profession, an attitude to which he gave vivid realization in *Wilhelm Meister's Apprenticeship* (1795–6), the great *Bildungsroman*. Despite Goethe's obvious suspicion of the artistic integrity of the actor, the novel is still one of the liveliest accounts of theatre life yet written.

Goethe's attitude towards Shakespeare underwent much modification during his lifetime. Initially, under the influence of J. G. Herder, he was in the forefront of the German Shakespeare revival. Latterly, most notably in his essay 'Shakespeare und kein Ende' ('No End to Shakespeare', 1815), he argued that Shakespeare's plays were best read and not performed. His notorious adaptation of *Romeo and Juliet* shows a lack of sympathy with Shakespeare's dramatic strategy and a distinct preference for French dramaturgy. SW

Gogol, Nikolai (Vasilievich) 1809–52 Nineteenth-century Russia's greatest comic writer and dramatist, whose special brand of grotesque REALISM and stated belief in the moral and social obligation of art influenced two centuries of artists, including TOLSTOI, Dostoevsky, SUKHOVO-KOBYLIN, TURGENEV, CHEKHOV, BELY and Nabokov. His early exposure to the puppet plays and folk tales of his native Ukraine with their mystery, superstition and coarse humour, and his psychological pleasures and embarrassments – spiritual health versus physical uncleanliness, food and sexuality, anonymity and exposure, the perfidy of woman and the hegemony of the Devil – mingled to produce his tormented art.

His St Petersburg career (1828–36) as lowly civil servant, bumbling history professor and developing writer broadened and deepened his fears for humanity and for the Russian people in particular. This period produced three volumes of short stories and miscellany – *Evenings on a Farm Near Dikanka* (1831–2), *Arabesques* and *Mirgorod* (1835), the last two containing his so-called 'Petersburg Tales'. He also composed three short comedies which feature his inimitable linguistic verve and fluidity, his farceur's sense of pace and plot and his relentless dissection of opportunism, eccentricity, self-delusion and social and moral hypocrisy. These include *Marriage* (1835), *The Gamblers* (1836) and *Decoration of Vladimir of the Third Class* (1832), this last concerning an upwardly mobile bureaucrat which Gogol left unfinished for fear of CENSORSHIP.

The Inspector General (1836) is his dramatic masterpiece. In it he creates a satirical, allegorical phantasmagoria of Tsarist Russia in the form of a woebegone provincial town whose greed, fear, pride, incomprehension and need for confession are awakened by the arrival of a nonentity mistaken for the titular government official. Variously regarded in Russia as the best early specimen of social realism and as a precursor of late-19th-/early-20th-century SYMBOLISM and formalist experiments, the play is pure Gogolian hyperbole. It amused the Tsar but confused and alienated many of the critics, upsetting the author – who fled to Rome, where he remained for 13 years. His paranoia, political conservatism and messianism intensified in his final years, as is reflected in his *Selected Passages from Correspondence with Friends* (1847) and in the picaresque epic *Dead Souls* (1842–52). The latter, a projected trilogy in the tradition of Dante's *The Divine Comedy* calling for the spiritual regeneration of Russia, was incomplete and partially burned prior to his death. The 20th century has seen several celebrated productions of his work: MEYERHOLD's and TOVSTONOGOV's *The Inspector General* (1926 and 1972, respectively), EFROS's *The Marriage* (1974) and LYUBIMOV's *The Inspector's Recounting* (1978). SG

Golden, John 1874–1955 American producer, who championed middle-class values through the production of wholesome family plays. He went from Ohio to New York at age 14 to be an actor, but abandoned this effort at age 21 for a profitable 13-year stint selling chemical products. While in this business he continued to write VAUDEVILLE sketches, short plays, and lyrics for show songs. Golden turned his full attention to writing and producing in 1918. His production of *Turn to the Right*, by Winchell Smith and John Hazzard – financed by royalties from 'Poor Butterfly', written for *The Big Show* (1916) – launched his career as a producer. He produced over 150 plays, more than a dozen of which achieved great popularity. His production of *Lightnin'* (1918), by FRANK BACON and Winchell Smith, ran for 1291 performances, a record that stood for most of the 1920s. He had enduring and productive professional relationships with Smith, actor-author FRANK CRAVEN and RACHEL CROTHERS. A founder of the American

Society of Composers, Authors and Publishers (ASCAP), he was noted for his gifts of money, personal time and organizational skill to many civic and cultural groups, including the Stage Relief Fund and the Stage Door Canteen. WD

Golden Age (Spain) Known as the *Siglo de Oro* in Spanish literature and the arts. In theatre it corresponds to the flourishing of the COMEDIA nueva (new comedy) or, approximately, 1580–1680. It coincides with Spain's political hegemony in Europe and its incipient decline. (See also SPAIN.) ElB

Goldfadn [Goldfaden], **Avrom** [Avraham Goldenfudim] 1840–1908 Playwright and producer, popularly called the 'father of YIDDISH THEATRE'. A Russian intellectual who could not make a living, in 1876 he tried writing sketches to be performed in a wine garden in Jassi, Romania, thereby becoming the first professional Yiddish playwright and producer. Typically, he wrote OPERETTAS whose form was European but whose substance was Yiddish folk material and life. Many plays were instant successes – for example, *Koldunye; or, The Witch* (1877); *The Fanatic; or, The Two Kuni-Lemls* (1880?); *Bar-Kokhba; or, The Last Days of Jerusalem* (1883); and *Shulamis; or, The Daughter of Jerusalem* (1883?). Some were also performed in other languages. However, Goldfadn spent much of his life wandering between Europe and America, rarely made a living, and fell from fashion entirely in old age. Nevertheless, about 30,000 mourners followed his funeral procession to Washington Cemetery in Brooklyn, New York, or much of his work had already taken on the status of folk culture: for example, the lullaby 'Raisins and Almonds', composed for *Shulamis*, and the clownish character types that he named Kuni-Leml and Shmendrik. His plays, in original form or adaptations, have often been revived. NS

Goldin, Horace [Hyman Goldstein] 1873–1939 Polish-born magician who emigrated to the USA at the age of 16. He started with a comic MAGIC act, but because of his heavy accent and stammer, converted it to a rapid-fire silent routine, '45 tricks in 17 minutes', baffling audiences with a quick succession of illusions. He appeared in the MUSICAL COMEDY *The Merry Magician* (Theatre Royal, Brighton, 1911) and was the first conjuror to play the PALACE THEATRE, New York (1913). His most famous illusion was an improvement on P. T. Selbit's 1879 trick, 'Sawing a Lady in Half': Goldin eliminated the box and used a buzz-saw, as Harry Blackstone (1885–1965) did as well. LS

Goldoni, Carlo 1707–93 Italian dramatist and librettist. Goldoni's career is primarily associated with the theatres of his birthplace, Venice. Although he qualified at the Venetian bar and intermittently practised law, he early had literary and theatrical ambitions: his tragedy for music, *Amalasunta*, he destroyed when it was rejected by the Milan opera; but he had better fortune with a tragicomedy, *Belisario*, produced in Venice by the company of Giuseppe Imer in 1734. Goldoni became the company's house dramatist at the San Samuele Theatre, writing mainly comic INTERLUDES and scenarios for improvising actors who worked in the tradition of the COMMEDIA DELL'ARTE. His literary aspirations led him to write tragedies, tragicomedies and librettos for OPERA SERIA, and in 1737 he became for a time literary director of the most distinguished Venetian opera house, the San Giovanni Grisostomo. Financial problems caused him to flee Venice in 1743 and for several years he practised law in Pisa, only occasionally writing dramatic pieces on demand. One such was *Arlecchino, servitore di due padroni* (*Arlecchino, the Servant of Two Masters*), reworked in 1745 from an old scenario at the request of the improvising actor ANTONIO SACCO: consisting part of scripted dialogue and part left for improvisation, in 1753 it was fully scripted by Goldoni into the form in which it now survives.

It was another improvising actor, the Pantalone Cesare d'Arbes, who brought Goldoni back to the theatre in 1748 by introducing him to the actor-manager GIROLAMO MEDEBACH. Goldoni joined Medebach's company (disparagingly called a troupe of rope dancers) as house dramatist at the little Sant' Angelo Theatre in Venice. There, between 1748 and 1752, he effectively began his reform of Italian COMEDY by gradually banishing the crudities and excesses of the old improvised comedy, subordinating on the one hand the traditional improvisation of masked types, and on the other the overly ornate language of baroque drama, to the needs of a scripted comedy more firmly located in a recognizable social milieu. He sometimes eliminated MASKS and improvisation altogether in order to focus, in a quasi-naturalistic way, on local morals and manners. The plays of this period include *La vedova scaltra* (*The Cunning Widow*), *La famiglia dell'antiquario* (*The Antiquarian's Family*), *I due gemelli veneziani* (*The Venetian Twins*), *La putta onorata* (*The Respectable Girl*) and *La locandiera* (*The Mistress of the Inn*). In the celebrated season of 1750–1, in a successful attempt to revive flagging attendance at his theatre, he produced 16 comedies: among them *Pamela nubile*, a version of Richardson's novel, and *Il teatro comico* (*The Comic Theatre*), a dramatized discussion between performers and company manager in which Goldoni outlined the nature and principles of his reform. In these years after 1748 he also contributed significantly to the comparatively new musical form, OPERA BUFFA, most notably in collaboration with the composer Baldassare Galuppi, who set more than 20 of Goldoni's librettos.

After quarrelling with Medebach over royalties and publication rights, in 1753 Goldoni moved to the larger San Luca Theatre run by the Vendramin family, achieving notable success there with a run of plays in the novel, if ephemeral, vein of exotic, Oriental TRAGICOMEDY; beginning with *La sposa persiana* (*The Persian Bride*, 1753), these capitalized on the size and facilities of the San Luca, and an audience taste for the strange mysteries of the East fostered by romances and travel writings. His comic drama became increasingly refined, subtle and ambitious in the ways in which it reflected mid-18th-century Venetian social mores, particularly those of the middle, and even lower, classes, both in comedies scripted in Venetian dialect and in plays which, while they rejected the external manifestations of the received tradition of improvised comedy like masks and impromptu perfor-

mance, yet absorbed its comic strategies, type figures and intricate balletic organization.

Among the most important comedies Goldoni wrote between 1753 and 1762 are *Il campiello*, *La casa nova* (*The New House*), *Gli innamorati* (*The Lovers*), *I rusteghi* (*The Boors*), *La villeggiatura* and *Le baruffe chiozzotte* (*The Chioggian Squabbles*). His librettos for *opera buffa* show a similar accommodation of inherited *commedia dell'arte* elements to a comic action rooted in a recognizable middle-class society and engaged with more local and immediate concerns. Goldoni helped give a new direction to such librettos by deftly translating mere stock types into engaging characters, investing ARIAS with ironic undertones, and building out ensembles and grand finales. His librettos became sought after and included two pieces which were among the century's most successful musical comedies throughout Europe: *Il filosofo di campagna* (*The Country Philosopher*, 1752) set by Galuppi, and *La buona figliuola* (*The Good Girl*), in the Piccinni setting of 1760. Goldoni's was a substantial contribution to the establishment of *opera buffa*, by the 1770s and 1780s, as a form of musical theatre as acceptable as *opera seria*. His reform of prose comedy similarly transformed the status of the genre in the Venetian theatres, elevating the 'prose theatre' to a level equal to that of the musical stage, and helping to create an audience taste for the simpler and the more verisimilar that was strongly felt in stage scenography and performance.

From the beginning Goldoni's success, and even more his attempts to reform comedy, provoked envy and hostility. In the late 1740s and 1750s his chief rival was the dramatist PIETRO CHIARI. The bitter hostility between the two (expressed in savage dramatic parodies, verse lampoons and offensive manifestos) led, in 1749, to the introduction of CENSORSHIP to the Venetian theatre. In the late 1750s another, and more dangerous, enemy appeared in the figure of the aristocratic writer and dramatist, CARLO GOZZI, defender of social, literary and linguistic tradition and champion of that masked and improvised comedy supposedly undermined by the Goldonian reform. Gozzi's *fiabe*, fantasy spectacles which exploited the talents of the improvising comedians, won considerable immediate success, and at the end of the 1761–2 season Goldoni left Venice to join the COMÉDIE-ITALIENNE in Paris. It is unlikely, however, that Gozzi's success alone led to his departure: Goldoni was now in his mid-fifties, he had exhausted much of his inspiration and he had a wife to support; the Venetian theatre offered a professional dramatist little long-term financial security, and Venetian patronage gave even less in the way of place or preferment. The Parisian theatre and French royalty had a reputation for generosity to foreign, particularly Italian, artists; he knew many Italian players in Paris, those close to Louis XV had invited him, his work was known there, and Italian *opera buffa* was becoming fashionable.

But whatever hopes he may have entertained, they were only partially realized. He remained in France to the end of his life, but his work never really adjusted to the cultural change: significantly, the best play he wrote there, *Il ventaglio* (*The Fan*, 1766), was done for a Venetian company, although plays he wrote in French, once he had mastered the language, have distinct quality, and *Le Bourru bienfaisant* (*The Beneficent Bear*) was highly successful at the Comédie when performed there in 1771. He accepted a post as Italian tutor to Louis XV's eldest daughter, and in 1769 was given a small court pension and joined the entourage at Versailles. There, and in Paris, in the 1780s he wrote his entertaining but not wholly reliable *Mémoires* (1787). He died destitute after the Revolution when his pension was abolished, a decision later reversed to the benefit of his widow.   KR

Goldsmith, Oliver 1728–74 Irish playwright. After studying at Trinity College, Dublin, he trained as a doctor at Edinburgh. He toured Europe in 1755 and settled in London, attempting to work as a physician. He began earning a living as a writer in 1757. His first play *The Good Natured Man*, first performed in 1768, was a serious attack on sentimentalism; the play's hero, Honeywood, suffers from an excess of good nature, though money always resolves the play's problems. *She Stoops to Conquer* (1773) mocks the snobbery of London through the manipulations of the country, embodied in Tony Lumpkin. The play's geniality mocks Marlow's inability to woo a woman unless he thinks she is a servant, celebrating the virtues of 'laughing comedy', which Goldsmith advocated in an important essay, over the prevalent sentimental forms.   PH

gollakalapam Indian theatre form, and also the name of a play. *Golla* means a 'female cowherd' (or *gopi*) and *kalapam* is a 'dialogue' or an 'argument'. Also known as *vithi bhagavata*, 'religious street stories', *gollakalapam* was created in Andhra Pradesh in the late 19th century by Bhagavatulu Ramayya, who developed the form out of KUCHIPUDI dance drama. Unlike *kuchipudi*, which is now the exclusive province of Brahmin men and boys, *gollakalapam* is performed by both women and men and has its own teachers knowledgeable in Sanskrit and the *Natyasastra*.

A typical performance proceeds as follows. A Brahmin acting as stage manager (*sutradhara*) performs the preliminaries and makes announcements. Then the main dancer (*golla*) enters and dances behind a curtain held by two attendants. Eventually the curtain is pulled aside and the dancer performs stylized dance patterns (*jati*) which are essentially the same as *daru* used in other dance-drama forms of the area. The dance includes intricate footwork and visual interpretation of songs through elaborate gestures. Following this, the Brahmin returns in the role of the clown (*vidushaka*) and converses with the dancer. They talk of the futility of religious rites, the superiority of the soul over the mind, the ideal family and so forth. The object of their conversation is to satirize the foibles of society and its conventions. A secondary female usually accompanies the chief dancer and performs less elaborate dances throughout the performance.

Songs are set to classical Karnatic melodies (*raga*) and the hand drum (*mridangam*) produces lively rhythmic accompaniment. Verbal recitations of the rhythmic patterns repeated in the dance (*jati*) make for very exciting moments and enrich the variety of an evening's performance.

Originally, *gollakalapam* was an all-night event which continued over three consecutive evenings. At its incep-

tion, it was a popular part of temple festivals and rich families invited parties to their homes to celebrate marriages or other happy family occasions. Today the form is rarely performed, owing to the absence of sympathetic patrons. It is somewhat less complicated to perform than *kuchipudi*, its parent form, and there are fewer restrictions regarding the time, place and process of performance.   FaR

gombeyatta Shadow-puppet theatre form of Karnataka, a state in southwest India. Puppets are made of goatskin and the largest are 30–40in tall. When constructing puppets of Ganapati, the elephant-headed god, and the epic hero-gods Krishna and Rama, the puppeteer performs RITUAL sacrifices and takes care in preparing and cutting the hides.

Performance requires at least 50 puppets from a set of more than a hundred figures. Puppet size generally indicates social rank and puppets fall into the following categories: divinities, demons, humans, monkey generals, clowns, animals of various kinds and natural objects, such as plants and trees. For some stories, a group of characters are clustered together to form a single puppet. As in other forms of shadow theatre, several puppets may be needed to represent the various moods of a single character.

A company of shadow players consists of the puppeteer, several male members of his family, his wife, who plays the harmonium, sings and speaks the female roles and a *tabla* drummer who also speaks the voices of some male characters. Three or four manipulators are needed to produce a shadow-puppet show and the number of instrumentalists may vary, depending on the wealth of the company. The construction of the stage, its size, shape and location, follow the pattern of *TOLLU BOMMALU*.

It is thought that about 300 families of shadow puppeteers make their living in Karnataka state. The Karnataka Chitrakala Parishath of Bangalore has pioneered collection and preservation of puppets and supports artists in maintaining their art.

Shadow performances in Karnataka are closely connected to religious holidays. Companies affiliated with particular temples must perform on demand, since temple authorities support them financially during the year. The main seasons for religious festivals are February–April and September–October. Plays are adapted from stories in the *Ramayana* and *Mahabharata* epics. (See also SHADOW PUPPETS.)   FaR

Gombrowicz, Witold 1902–69 Polish playwright, novelist and memoirist, who from 1939 lived in Argentina and France. His plays are grotesque theatricalist fables that oppose conflicting images of reality in a struggle between socially imposed, restrictive forms and creative immaturity. Since the mid-1970s, *Ivona, Princess of Burgundia* (1938), *The Marriage* (1947) and *Operetta* (1966) have been central to the national repertory.   DG

Gómez de Avellaneda, Gertrudis [Tula] 1814–73 Extraordinary poet, novelist and playwright, whose work reflected little of Cuban reality. Twice widowed, beset with major personal problems and mostly unappreciated in her native Cuba, Gómez de Avellaneda spent most of her life in Spain where she aspired to courtly grandeur. Her theatre belongs primarily to Spain, although she is considered one of the major women playwrights of the Americas. With 20 plays, she is a major figure who dominated both tragic and comic form. Her principal tragic works are *Munio Alfonso* (1844) and *Baltasar* (1858), the latter relating the Spanish crown to its biblical antecedents. On the lighter side, *La hija de las flores* (*Daughter of the Flowers*, 1852) and *El millonario y la maleta* (*The Millionaire and his Suitcase*, 1870) are entertaining comedies with good humour. For the most part, Tula, as she was called, managed to avoid the excesses of romanticism and create developed characters with good psychological basis. GW

Goncharova, Natalya (Sergeevna) 1881–1962 A talented and prolific Russian painter-designer (see THEATRE DESIGN) of the pre-revolutionary period who, with her companion the artist Mikhail Larionov, helped establish neo-primitivism (1910–14) as a trend in Russian art. Neo-primitivism returned to native-painted, handicraft art (such as the woodcut, primitive icons, toys) and Russian folkloric motifs to counter realist-naturalist illusionism, traditional perspective and proportion, the World of Art's *style moderne* with its decorative eclecticism, and the symbolists' (see SYMBOLISM) refined mysticism – all of which reflected the influence of the West. Goncharova embraced old Eastern forms – the Russian *skomorokhi* (mummers) and *balagany* (puppet shows; see PUPPETS) – with their frank and vital theatricality and spirit of buffoonery at a time when such features were becoming attractive to Russia's most innovative directors – MEYERHOLD, EVREINOV and TAIROV. Her movement towards rayonism (light rays as analogue for spatial linear dynamic), c.1912–16, led to the incorporation into her work of a forced perspective of subjective contemporaneity – what the Russian cubo-futurists called 'shift' and the Russian formalists dubbed 'making it strange'. She designed sets and COSTUMES for Diaghilev's production of the OPERA-ballet *The Golden Cockerel* (Paris, 1914) and the ballet *The Firebird* (London, 1926), for Tairov's Kamerny Theatre production of GOLDONI's *The Fan* (Moscow, 1915) and for BALIEV's *Chauve-Souris* (New York, 1931). Her work also included book and fashion design. She and Larionov emigrated to Paris in 1917. SG

González Dávila, Jesús 1942– Mexican playwright, born in the capital. González Dávila has succeeded with several prize-winning plays. *La fábrica de juguetes* (*The Toy Factory*, 1970) and *Muchacha del alma* (*A Girl with Soul*, 1983) are representative of his efforts to penetrate the contemporary Mexican psyche with realistic, often brutal, plays. GW

Goodman Theatre (USA) Chicago's Goodman is America's second-oldest regional theatre, founded in 1925. Originally funded as a memorial by the parents of playwright Kenneth Sawyer Goodman, the 683-seat theatre, built alongside the Chicago Art Institute, was to house both a resident professional company and a school of drama; however, the Depression forced the company to disband, whereas the school continued.

In 1969–70 a professional company returned to the Goodman to varying critical and popular reception. In 1978 its leadership was assumed by Gregory Mosher, who emphasized new works and classic revivals. Mosher frequently commissioned scripts from leading American playwrights, and in 1985 became co-director of the theatre wing at Lincoln Center in New York City. He was replaced at the Goodman in 1986 by Robert Falls, under whose leadership classical works have been staged with bold imagination and freshness and new works lavished with unusual care. World and American premieres have included MAMET's *Glengarry Glen Ross*, RABE's *Hurlyburly* and SOYINKA's *Death and the King's Horseman*.

In 1977 the Goodman Theatre ceased its affiliation with the Chicago Art Institute to become a self-sustaining operation, and in 1978 the School of Drama affiliated with De Paul University, Chicago. SMA

Goodman's Fields Theatre (London) Built in 1729 by Odell in Ayliffe Street, Goodman's Fields, the opposite end of London from the usual location for theatres. It was licensed, but after protests George II withdrew approval in 1730. Henry Giffard took over as manager and built a new theatre which opened in 1732, with a spectacular ceiling depicting the king surrounded by SHAKESPEARE, DRYDEN, CONGREVE and BETTERTON. It was used until 1736, when it was offered for sale, and again in 1740 to 1742 when it was the scene of DAVID GARRICK's spectacular London debut. PH

Goodwin, Nat(haniel Carl) 1857–1919 American actor and manager. Born and educated in Boston, Goodwin began his career as a mimic for drawing-room theatricals. In 1874 he made his professional stage debut at Boston's Howard Athenaeum, and in 1875 his first New York appearance at TONY PASTOR's Opera House. He enjoyed a major success in 1876 at the New York LYCEUM in *Off the Stage* by giving imitations of popular actors. While Goodwin excelled as a mimic and eccentric comedian, he was also effective in serious parts, such as Jim Rayburn in *In Mizzoura* (1893) and the title role in *Nathan Hale* (1899). Married five times, he gained notoriety for his offstage antics. With his third wife, MAXINE ELLIOTT, he starred in numerous plays including *Nathan Hale* and *When We Were Twenty-One* (1900). He was not, however, successful in Shakespearian roles, including Shylock (1901) and Bottom (1903). In his autobiography, *Nat Goodwin's Book* (1914), he took revenge upon his many enemies. TLM

gopalila [*kundhei nata*] Simple form of itinerant glove-puppet theatre of Orissa state, India. *Gopa* refers to the cowherd boys in the life of Lord Krishna and *lila* means 'play'. PUPPETS are made of wood and paper and their bodies are padded with cloth, the lower half being covered with a long skirt.

Puppeteers usually travel in pairs from village to village carrying their basket of puppets and a small box-like stage, large enough to mask the performer while he manipulates the puppets above his head. The second member of the party sits nearby, playing the drum (*pakhavaj*), singing and narrating incidents from the life of Lord Krishna. Religious occasions, especially those related to Krishna, provide puppeteers with the opportunity to entertain local villagers and to earn a living. Few performers are active today.   FAR

Gordin, Jacob 1853–1909 Yiddish playwright, driven because of socialist convictions from Russia to New York's Lower East Side, where he became a journalist of enormous personal authority and influence. Although the intelligentsia scorned YIDDISH THEATRE as parochial and vulgar, in 1891, trying to feed his nine children, Gordin wrote *Siberia*, and thus initiated the close identification of secular Yiddish literary culture with Yiddish theatre. Characteristic of his many plays was concern for verisimilitude, despite high-flown language and aphoristic tags. His work was most often dark and intense, achieving comic relief through colourful minor characters. Gordin wrote to teach: his plays' themes and subjects included socialism, women's rights, and the broader education of the Yiddish masses. He championed pure and literary Yiddish. He attracted the best Yiddish actors of his time – JACOB ADLER, Keni Liptzin, David Kessler, BERTHA KALISH, IDA KAMIŃSKA – and created juicy roles as vehicles for them. His best-known dramas include *God, Man and Devil* (1900), based on *Faust; The Jewish King Lear* (1892; see ETHNIC THEATRE (USA)); *Mirele Efros* (1898), sometimes called *The Jewish Queen Lear*, and *The Kreutzer Sonata* (1905). The first three were made into films; all remained staples of finer Yiddish intellectual repertory worldwide and are still considered classics.   NS

Gordon, Max [Mechel Salpeter] 1892–1978 American BROADWAY producer, remembered as 'a man of wide-ranging tastes, and the possessor of a capacity to gamble'. His production of *Born Yesterday* (1945) ran for 1642 performances. *The Women* (1936), *My Sister Eileen* (1940), *Junior Miss* (1941) and *The Solid Gold Cadillac* (1953) all achieved over 500 performances. His productions of *Roberta, Her Master's Voice, The Shining Hour* and *Dodsworth* all ran simultaneously in 1934. Gordon came to theatre as a VAUDEVILLE advance agent. Notable productions presented early in his career in association with SAM H. HARRIS include *Six-cylinder Love* (1921) and *The Jazz Singer* (1925). While continuing through the years to work with Harris, he also collaborated on *Missouri Legend* with GUTHRIE McCLINTIC and *Sing Out the News* with GEORGE S. KAUFMAN and MOSS HART (both 1938). Gordon also produced the film versions of *Abe Lincoln in Illinois* (1940) and *Years Ago* (retitled *The Actress*, 1953). He published an autobiography, *Max Gordon Presents*, in 1963.   MR

Gordon [*née* Jones]**, Ruth** 1896–1985 American actress and playwright. Gordon's New York debut in *Peter Pan* (1915) was followed by a succession of relatively insignificant roles. It was a revival in 1936 of WYCHERLEY's *The Country Wife*, in which she was the first American cast in an OLD VIC (London) production, that changed the direction of her career: her Mrs Pinchwife led to roles that exploited her individualistic technique, whirlwind vivacity and split-second timing. In 1937 (New York) she played Nora in *A Doll's House*, adapted for her by THORNTON WILDER; in 1942 she was Natasha in *The Three Sisters*. Her most memorable stage creation was Dolly Levi in *The*

Matchmaker (1954, London; 1955, New York), a role written for her by Wilder. Her last stage role was Zina in *Dreyfus in Rehearsal* (1974). Gordon was also a successful screen actress, playwright (*Over 21, Years Ago*) and, especially, screenwriter in collaboration with her second husband, GARSON KANIN. She was also the author of three lively autobiographies (1971, 1976, 1980).   DBW

Gorelik, Mordecai 1899–1990 Russian-born American director, stage and film designer. Gorelik studied with ROBERT EDMOND JONES, NORMAN BEL GEDDES and Serge Soudeikine and began his career with the PROVINCETOWN PLAYERS in 1920. His 1925 design for *Processional* was a rare example of successful EXPRESSIONISM on the American stage. During the 1930s he was the primary designer for the GROUP THEATRE, including *Men in White* and *Golden Boy*. He was an organizer of a short-lived leftist group, the Theatre Collective. Gorelik also designed *All My Sons* and *A Hatful of Rain*, among others on BROADWAY. He was a strong advocate of BRECHT's EPIC THEATRE, which he emphasizes in his book, *New Theatres for Old* (1940). Much of his design (some 40 productions) can be classified as suggestive REALISM.   AA

Gorky, Maksim [Aleksei (Maksimovich) Peshkov] 1868–1936 Soviet novelist, memoirist, short story writer, dramatist and critic, the 'stormy petrel' of the Revolution and the official hero of Soviet art. Born seven years after serfdom's abolition but within its memory into an extremely ignorant, cruel and impoverished milieu, Gorky learned about life on the road and soon became a self-educated rebel artist. His early romanticized peasant tales, leading to his first St Petersburg success, the short story 'Chelkash' (1895), transformed the author into a tramp-poet folk hero for the urban artistic intelligentsia, who sought to emulate his primitivism in their work. Always self-critical, even embarrassed by the clumsiness of his art and ambivalent towards the illiterate peasant life from which literature provided him with an escape, Gorky devoted his career to reconciling the classes into an enlightened society built upon education and communication.

His humanist philosophy – basically, to speak of what man can become by being made to believe in his goodness or potential for good – extended into the realistic literature which formed the basis of his developing art and of his growing role of mediator between art and society. His publishing house Znanie (Knowledge; 1900), although specializing in neo-REALISM, encouraged such writers as ANDREEV, BLOK and Bunin, whose aesthetics did not always agree with Gorky's own. Gorky was in turn befriended and championed (and also sharply criticized) by CHEKHOV, whose plays he sought unsuccessfully to emulate. Gorky's involvement in the 1905 and 1917 Revolutions, which led to arrest and an inevitable movement towards Bolshevism, focused and delimited the remainder of his career. He wrote 12 plays between 1901 and 1913, having already established himself as a short story writer (*Sketches and Stories*, 2 vols., 1898), novelist (*Foma Gordeev*, 1899), revolutionary poet (*Song of the Stormy Petrel*, 1901) and social force. His dramas are all sociopolitically slanted, lacking in psychological and stylistic subtlety, at times philosophically murky and morally ambivalent, mixing naive idealism with neo-puritanism, faith and cynicism. They offer stereotypically 'good' – i.e. strong-willed and productive – peasants and workers juxtaposed with 'bad' – i.e. ineffectual, self-serving, unenlightened, morally dishonest and effete – intellectuals, clerics and petty bourgeois. Plots are dialectically constructed so as to economize and maximize these conflicts and the theme of alienation between the classes. Language is often rhetorical, building towards and often interrupted by ideological tirades that are meant to educate the audience.

While Gorky garners raw power from his group portraits and folkloric elements, he is less effective with individuals, unless they inspire his rage or enthusiasm. His first play, *The Petty Bourgeoisie* (1902), beginning his long association with the MOSCOW ART THEATRE (MAT) which originally bore his name, presents the traditional Russian generational conflict theme, here emblematic of revolutionary societal change, resulting in the birth of the proletarian hero. *The Lower Depths* (1902) was celebrated in its time for the novelty of its tramp characters in an exotically downtrodden boarding-house as well as for the ensemble opportunities it afforded the MAT company, but it suffers from all of Gorky's ideological and dramaturgical faults. *Summer Folk* (1904), *Barbarians* (1905) and *Enemies* (1906) deal in various ways with philistinism and alienation among the classes, with blame invariably falling upon the intelligentsia and the merchants. These and other plays such as *Children of the Sun* (1905) and *Queer People* (1910) introduce romantic subplots and an overall spiritual malaise suggestive of TURGENEV and Chekhov, while Gorky's *Vassa Zheleznova* (1910), *The Zykovs* and *Counterfeit Money* (both 1913), the critically respected *Yegor Bulychov and Others* (1932) and its sequel *Dostigayev and Others* (1933) more directly suggest OSTROVSKY's dramatic portraits of merchant characters.

Gorky's most fully realized human drama may well have been his own life, recorded in his autobiographical trilogy – *My Childhood* (1914), *In the World* (1916) and *My Universities* (1924). The dramatic final chapter saw the humanitarian idealist returning from self-imposed exile (1921–8) to become first president of the newly formed Union of Soviet Writers and the somewhat unwitting artistic point man for the government's policy of 'socialist realism' in literature. His death has been variously ascribed to tuberculosis and, more dubiously, to Stalin-instigated assassination. SG

Gorostiza, Carlos 1920– Argentine playwright, actor and director. Gorostiza made theatre history when his play *El puente* (*The Bridge*, 1949) spanned the gap between the independent theatre and the commercial theatre in Buenos Aires, and opened a new epoch in REALISM on the Argentine stage. Other major works include *El pan de la locura* (*Bread of Madness*, 1958) and *Los prójimos* (*The Neighbours*, 1966), the latter based on the famous Kitty Genovese incident in New York in which unconcerned witnesses to an assault failed to intervene. *¿A qué jugamos?* (*What Shall We Play?*, 1968) uses a metatheatrical structure to investigate contemporary problems, especially those of the younger generation. Gorostiza has written

novels, worked in television, and in the Alfonsín government was named Secretary of Culture with broad responsibility for governmental support of the arts. Recent theatre titles are *Los hermanos queridos* (*Beloved Brothers*, 1978), *El acompañante* (*The Accompanist*, 1981), *Hay que apagar el fuego* (*We Have to Put Out the Fire*, 1982) and *Papi* (1984). GW

Gorostiza, Celestino 1904–67 Mexican playwright and director. A major figure in the independent movement of the 1930s, Gorostiza interpreted expressionist tendencies (see EXPRESSIONISM) in vogue in the European theatre in such plays as *Ser o no ser* (*To Be or Not to Be*, 1934). In a later wave, he dealt with the taboos of racism in Mexican society in *El color de nuestra piel* (*The Colour of Our Skin*, 1952) and took a new look at the story of Cortés and Malinche in *La Malinche*, later retitled *La leña está verde* (*The Firewood is Green*, 1958). GW

Gosson, Stephen 1554–1624 English anti-theatrical pamphleteer, who renounced his youthful interest in drama– he is known to have written some pastoral plays – under Puritan persuasion. His *The School of Abuse* (1579), attacking poets and actors, was dedicated, without permission, to PHILIP SIDNEY, whose *The Apology for Poetry* (written c.1580) was written partly to confute Gosson. The controversy was still at its height when Gosson wrote *Plays Confuted in Five Actions*. PT

Got, Edmond 1822–1901 French actor. Got's entire career of over 50 years was at the COMÉDIE-FRANÇAISE, where he made his debut in 1844, having received a first prize at the Conservatoire. In 1848 he played the Abbé in MUSSET's *Il ne faut jurer de rien* (*Nothing Is Certain*). This part (which he retained for 50 years) gave full rein to his specific vein of whimsical COMEDY. He created some 200 parts, being equally at home in the modern and the classical repertoires. An unforgettable Tibia in *Les Caprices de Marianne* (1851), his greatest successes were in *Le Duc Job* (1859), AUGIER's *Les Effrontés* (*The Shameless Ones*, 1861), PONSARD's *L'Honneur et l'argent* and *Le Fils de Giboyer* (1862) and the splendid 1868 revival of Balzac's *Mercadet*. In 1870, he steered the Comédie through a difficult period by organizing a tour to London. In 1873 he became *doyen*, and in 1877 was appointed to teach at the Conservatoire. He played Bernard in *Les Fourchambault* in 1878, created an interesting Harpagon in 1879, was made chevalier of the Légion d'Honneur in 1881, played Triboulet in *Le Roi s'amuse* (*The King's Fool*, which had been banned since its first performance 50 years earlier) in 1882, and gave his last performance in 1895. JMCC

Gotanda, Philip Kan 1950– Leading Asian-American (third-generation Japanese-American) playwright (and director), native of Stockton, California. First produced by small Asian-American companies, his work has crossed over to such theatres as Los Angeles's Mark Taper Forum and the MANHATTAN THEATRE CLUB. Though stylistically diverse, all his plays examine the psychosocial dynamics of the Asian-American experience. *The Wash* (1987), about an elderly Japanese-American couple in the throes of a wrenching divorce, and *Song for a Nisei Fisherman* (1980), the story of an immigrant doctor, are lyrical, naturalistic in texture. More satiric, *Yankee Dawg You Die* (1987) is a look at Hollywood stereotyping and the generation gap between two Asian-American actors, while *Fish Head Soup* (1991) is a surreal family drama and *Day Standing on Its Head* (1993) concerns an Asian-American professor grappling with middle age. His best work conveys the Asian-American milieu with a deftness and compassion that render it universal. MBER

Göteborgs Stadsteater Göteborg, Sweden, has a long theatrical history, with permanent playhouses throughout the 19th century and from 1916 the technically sophisticated Lorensbergsteatern. The Stadsteater, founded in 1917, performed there until it moved to its present building in 1934. The theatre's artistic reputation has fluctuated: PER LINDBERG's modernistic productions (1918–23) made it the theatrical focus of Scandinavia; Torsten Hammaren (1926–50) emphasized new writing, especially anti-Fascist plays; Mats Johansson (1962–82) developed its sociopolitical profile through productions by Lennart Hjulström, RALF LÅNGBACKA and PETER OSKARSON, and the early work of its suburban Angereds Ensemble. In the early 1980s, political and artistic conflict about the theatre's identity and mission caused chronic problems for the main company. However, Eva Bergman has led the Backa young people's company to extraordinary success, particularly with splendidly playful productions of SHAKESPEARE and IBSEN. HL

Göthe, Staffan 1944– Popular Swedish playwright, actor and director, who in 1972 began writing children's plays for the Växjöensemble company, in which he was an actor. Plays like *A Night in February* (1972) and *The Horrible Bang* (1978) are not only *for* young audiences, but incorporate their concerns and point of view, especially their attempts to survive, sometimes tragically, in a treacherous adult world. His plays for adults include a trilogy about the Cervieng family, exploring through a mix of REALISM and fantasy the breakdown of social–democratic Sweden as a 'people's home': *La Strada del Amore* (1985), *A Stuffed Dog* (1986) and *The Perfect Kiss* (1990). His plays focus, with both comedy and despair, on the vulnerability and loneliness prevalent in modern Swedish society, but allow spectators to discover their own sense of outrage. HL

Gottsched, Johann (Christoph) 1700–66 German playwright, critic and essayist. One of Germany's first significant men of letters, Gottsched wished to elevate German culture by modelling its literature and drama on the French. In his theatrical endeavours he was aided by CAROLINE NEUBER, whose troupe attempted to put into practice his tenets of acting, which were essentially abstracted from the acting of French companies in the German courts and developed from Gottsched's own conception of classical, rhetorical gesture. It became known as the LEIPZIG STYLE. His play *The Dying Cato* (1732), despite its woodenness, had some success when performed by the Neuber troupe. Gottsched was a man of little humour and had a limited idea of what could be achieved in the theatre. Hence, after his rupture with the Neubers in

1741, even though he had some communication with SCHÖNEMANN, his effective connections with the theatre were severed. SW

Goulue, La [Louise Weber] 1860–1919 French cancan dancer at the MOULIN-ROUGE, Paris, 1889–95. A former washerwoman, she was notorious in her day for her hot temper, vast appetite, lesbian attachments and huge salary. Her high kicks performed with her partner Valentin le Désossé (Jacques Renaudin) and red topknot remain familiar through the art of Toulouse-Lautrec. She later descended to belly-dancing, ran a show-booth as a lion-tamer and died alcoholic, obese and all but forgotten. LS

Gow, Michael 1955– Australian playwright. His first play *The Kid* (1983), a tragedy of dispossessed adolescents contextualized by WAGNER's *Ring* cycle, shows the juxtaposing of contemporary life with cultural myth characteristic of his work. His most popular play, *Away* (1986), links adults' gaining wisdom through a schoolboy's imminent death with fragments from *A Midsummer-Night's Dream* and *King Lear*; *Europe* (1987) explores an affair between a European actress and an Australian youth as a metaphor for Australia's relation to its cultural heritage. His other works include *1841*, a parable of Australia's lost libertarian ideals written for the Bicentennial in 1988, *Furious* (1991), and the television screenplay *Edens Lost* (1988). He is director of the Sydney Theatre Company's New Stages programme for innovative performances of classic texts. MW

Gozzi, Carlo 1720–1806 Italian writer and dramatist, who wrote plays primarily for the theatres of his birthplace, Venice. Although brought up in modest circumstances and largely self-taught, Gozzi was a younger son of an aristocratic family, and patrician attitudes strongly conditioned his views of society and the theatre. With his brother, the journalist Gasparo, he was a founder member of one of the most conservative Venetian academies, the Accademia dei Granelleschi, concerned to preserve the purity of traditional language, thought and artistic activity against the threatening incursions of the Enlightenment.

In the late 1750s, hostile to the bourgeois realistic and reformist tendencies of contemporary dramatists like CARLO GOLDONI and PIETRO CHIARI, he engaged first in vigorous literary polemics, then in the deliberate creation of an opposition drama. In this he sought initially to restore to the stage the MASKS and improvisation of the traditional COMMEDIA DELL'ARTE, supposedly undermined by the Goldonian reform of COMEDY, and later, drawing inspiration from Spanish drama, to reassert the courtly values of the aristocratic past. In neither was he successful for long, for all that much of his work was a product of his 25-year association with one of the finest Venetian acting companies of the 18th century, the troupe of ANTONIO SACCO. For them he wrote the most enduring of his work, the *fiabe*, which included *L'amore delle tre melarance* (*The Love of Three Oranges*, 1761), *Il corvo* (*The Raven*), *Il re cervo* (*The King Stag*, 1762), *Turandot* (1762), *La donna serpente* (*The Snake Woman*, 1762) and

L'augellino belverde (*The Green Bird*, 1765). These fantastic and scenically spectacular romances often wedded the comic strategies and masked figures of the improvised drama to the fairy-tale materials of exotic Oriental stories. Goldoni had capitalized in the mid-1750s on the Venetian taste for tales of the mysterious East, and Gozzi's highly theatrical concoctions proved equally successful in the 1750s – so much so, it is said, that they helped to drive his rival from Venice.

Underpinning Gozzi's work was his hostility to the local REALISM, scenographic simplicity and idiomatic language of Goldoni's new comedy, which in his eyes breached artistic decorum by mingling characters of high and low place, extolling the virtues and values of the Venetian bourgeoisie, and banishing imagination and invention from the stage. Significantly, his *fiabe*, although they have long provided plot lines for OPERA and ballet, only began again to attract the attention of the non-musical stage with the rediscovery of a primarily non-verbal, theatrical theatre in the stagings of MEYERHOLD and VAKHTANGOV in the early years of this century, and in the avant-garde visual theatre of the 1970s and 80s. Gozzi's witty and waspish memoirs, *Memorie inutili*, are a mine of information on the 18th-century Venetian theatre and provide an invaluable, if one-sided, account of his dispute with Goldoni and his association with the actors and actresses of Sacco's company. KR

Grabbe, Christian Dietrich 1801–36 German playwright. Grabbe had ambitions first to be an actor, then a professional playwright, but was forced to earn his living as an army lawyer in his native town of Detmold. Despite this, he was a prolific writer. However, as his plays were written in a manner that anticipated both the EPIC THEATRE of the 20th century and absurdism (see THEATRE OF THE ABSURD), it is not surprising they were not produced. His most significant works are large-scale dramas on great men of history, most notable among which are two plays from a projected cycle on the Hohenstaufen family, *The Emperor Friedrich Barbarossa* (1829) and *The Emperor Henry VI* (1830); *Napoleon, or The Hundred Days* (1831) and *Hannibal* (1835). The only one of his plays to be produced in his lifetime was *Don Juan and Faust* (1829), a study of the difference between the idealistic and realistic personalities. Grabbe is probably best known today for his grotesque comedy, *Joke, Satire, Irony, and Deeper Significance* (1827), though several of his plays have been revived with quite considerable success in the modern German theatre. SW

gracioso A comic servant, one of the chief sources of humour in the Spanish *COMEDIA*. (See also SPAIN.) CL

Graetz, Paul 1890–1937 German CABARET artist, who made a name for himself in SCHNITZLER roles before appearing at the Schall und Rauch and Kabarett der Komiker in Berlin. With his deep, raw voice and slow movements, he excelled at Berlin loudmouths and chatterboxes, his performances spiked with mother-wit. He collaborated with ARNOLT BRONNEN on the play *Katalaunische Schlacht* and worked for PISCATOR, before emigrating to the USA in 1935, where he died. LS

Gramsci, Antonio 1891–1937 Italian politician, political theorist and critic. As well as being an active politician and co-founder of the Italian Communist Party in 1921, he was a seminal commentator on a broad range of social and cultural matters, including the theatre. Between 1915 and 1920 he was theatre critic for *Avanti!*, and his penetrating articles, treating of drama and the stage from a firm and sophisticated ideological position hostile to the bourgeois and BOULEVARD values of the day, have since exercised considerable influence on thinking about the functions of theatre both in Italy and abroad. LR

Grand Duke's Opera House see PENNY THEATRES

Grand-Guignol Founded in 1895 as a *théâtre salon* by Oscar Méténier, the Théâtre de Grand-Guignol moved to its premises in the rue Chaptal, Paris, four years later, under the leadership of Max Maurey. At first merely a naturalistic theatre alternating one-acts of brutality and FARCE, it eventually specialized in horror, drawing on the works of E. A. Poe in particular. Its chief playwright was André de Lorde, nicknamed 'the Prince of Terror', who preferred psychological suspense to gore, though he was not averse to the eye-gougings and acid baths that were popular features of the genre. This skilled sensationalism pleased the Parisian public, but attempts to acclimatize it to England and America were not successful. By the Second World War, it was drawing heavily on detective fiction and finally closed its doors in 1962. LS

grand opera The term commonly used in England during the late 19th and early 20th centuries to describe any serious OPERA that contained no spoken dialogue. Properly it indicates opera of the kind presented at the Paris Opéra from about 1830 to 1865. This had no spoken dialogue, was on historical themes, and included extensive choral writing, ballets and elaborate stage spectacle. The most assiduous composer of grand opera for Paris was Giacomo Meyerbeer, whose librettist was EUGÈNE SCRIBE. GH

Granovsky [Azarkh]**, Aleksei (Mikhailovich)** 1890–1937 Russian-Soviet Jewish director, trained (by A. A. Sanin) at the St Petersburg School of Scenic Art (1910–11) and the Munich Theatrical Academy, and influenced by WAGNER, APPIA, CRAIG and Scriabin to create rituals for a theatrical congregation. His spectacular stagings of *Oedipus Rex* and *Macbeth* for Yury Yuriev's Theatre of Tragedy at Petrograd's Chinizelli Circus (1918) and of MAYAKOVSKY's *Mystery-Bouffe* (designed by Nathan Altman, 1921) at the former Salermonsky Circus recalled REINHARDT (with whom he worked in Berlin in 1913), MEYERHOLD, PISCATOR and BRECHT, and antedated the early Soviet mass spectacles. As a leader of the Petrograd Jewish Theatre Studio (1919) and its successor the Moscow State Jewish Theatre (GOSET, 1920–8), Granovsky selected and staged in YIDDISH (with designs by Chagall, Altman, Falk and Rabinovich) an international repertory of classic and contemporary plays that balanced Jewish assimilationist tendencies with pressures to preserve Jewish culture and create the new Soviet theatre. He also directed film and OPERA. He defected to the West on GOSET's 1928 European tour. SG

A scene from Granville Barker's *The Voysey Inheritance* showing the detailed realistic setting typical of his work.

Granville Barker, Harley 1877–1946 British actor, playwright, director and critic, who exerted a major influence on British drama and theatre both during and after his lifetime. As an actor he toured with various stock companies (see STOCK COMPANY) but became increasingly discontented with the low standards of commercial touring. Contact with WILLIAM POEL, WILLIAM ARCHER and BERNARD SHAW, however, at the turn of the century, together with membership of the STAGE SOCIETY, opened up new possibilities. He began acting in a new range of challenging roles (notably Marchbanks in *Candida*), and in 1900 directed his own first major play, written the year before, *The Marrying of Ann Leete*. In 1904, with J. E. VEDRENNE as his business manager, Barker took a lease on the ROYAL COURT THEATRE, London, and initiated three historic seasons of the new 'uncommercial' drama, presenting 11 plays by Shaw together with new plays by Continental and British authors and new translations of three plays by EURIPIDES. The enterprise proved the viability of such a programme on the public stage and gave a major boost to the repertory movement (see REGIONAL THEATRE (BRITAIN)).

During this period Barker wrote his second main play, *The Voysey Inheritance* (1903–5; produced at the Royal Court, 1905), and the publication during the next few years of *Waste* (1906–7) and *The Madras House* (1909) established him as an important dramatist of the new, realistic English drama (see REALISM). By 1907 he had practically abandoned acting, although his restrained, subtle and natural method of performance had made him an ideal player for the contemporary drama. His attention now focused upon directing and upon the promotion of the repertory movement in England. In 1910 he directed the experimental repertory season at the Duke of York's

Theatre, London, which proved an artistic success but a financial failure, underlining for Barker the case for subsidy of repertory. In 1912 the pinnacle of his directing career was reached with productions at the Savoy Theatre of *The Winter's Tale* and *Twelfth Night*, followed in 1914 by *A Midsummer Night's Dream*. He abandoned the elaborate, conventional methods of staging SHAKESPEARE, including the domination of 'star' actors, and produced instead ensemble performances of the highest quality. An apron stage was used, scenery and costumes were simple, colourful and impressionistic, and emphasis was given to the continuity of action, the full text being spoken with swiftness and intelligence. The freshness of interpretation and the vitality of the performances surprised and excited audiences and critics alike, and stimulated a new approach to Shakespeare in the theatre.

From 1918, Barker devoted himself almost totally to writing, lecturing and scholarship. In 1919 he joined the newly formed British Drama League and was its chairman for 13 years. He wrote several more plays and published many works on the role of theatre in society (e.g. *The Exemplary Theatre*, 1922; *A National Theatre*, 1930) and the nature and function of dramatic art (e.g. *On Dramatic Method*, 1931; *The Use of Drama*, 1944). But his most important and pioneering work of scholarship was his *Prefaces to Shakespeare* (in six volumes, 1927–46), in which he bridged the gap between the academic and theatrical approaches to the plays. AJ

Grass, Günter 1927– German dramatist and novelist; a prominent member of Group 47. His novel *The Tin Drum* is a modern classic. His short early plays *Hochwasser* (*Flood*, 1957) and *Die bösen Köche* (*The Wicked Cooks*, 1961) derive from the THEATRE OF THE ABSURD. The

Plebeians Rehearse the Uprising (1966) dramatized BRECHT's ambivalent behaviour during the workers' rising against the Communist regime in East Berlin in 1953. HR

Grasso, Giovanni 1873–1930 Italian actor-manager. Born into a Sicilian family of marionette specialists, Grasso turned to acting and after a long apprenticeship formed his own company with an emphasis on the performance of Sicilian plays and the work of contemporary Italian dramatists in dialect versions. He was one of the last Italian stage actors to tour extensively abroad, where the REALISM of his productions of dialect plays was particularly admired. He won notable success too, at home and abroad, as Othello, his version of the Moor outdoing SALVINI's for emotionalism and sensationalism, qualities little approved by English critics when he took the play to London in 1911. KR

Gray, Simon (James Holliday) 1936– British dramatist, whose first stage play in the WEST END, *Wise Child* (1967), featured ALEC GUINNESS as a transvestite. Gray's comedies often depict lonely, alienated men, rejected by society because of either their sexual inclinations or their shyness. His first major success came with *Butley* (1971), in which ALAN BATES played a university lecturer torn between his disintegrating marriage and love for a male student. Bates has starred in other Gray plays, for stage and television, including *Otherwise Engaged*, where he played a publisher who retreats into music to escape from people whom he dislikes and distrusts, and *Melon* (1987), in which he again played a publisher undergoing a nervous breakdown.

Publishing and university life provide the settings for several of his plays, leading to the criticism that his sympathies are with the articulate, if chattering, classes; but Gray's strengths lie in the way in which he can sustain a flow of comedy while exploring the nature of suffering. Among modern British dramatists, only RATTIGAN and AYCKBOURN have a similar skill; and Gray bears comparison well with them both. In *Close of Play* (1978), a distinguished academic stays silent during his last hours while his family bickers around him; in *Quartermain's Terms* (1981), a harmless, good-natured bachelor, teaching in a language school, is left defenceless against the loss of his job and the friendships which apparently went with it. *The Common Pursuit* (1984) is an intricate study of how a group of Cambridge arts graduates leave university and develop towards middle age, losing, retaining or forgetting their ideals as they do so; and Gray's book about the production, *An Unnatural Pursuit* (1985), described why it is so easy to lose faith in the theatre. The laughter in *Hidden Laughter* (1990), which he directed in the West End, is very hidden – it describes a family whose affluent lifestyle conceals the utmost loneliness, redeemed only by the quiet support of a well intentioned but dithering local vicar, memorably played by Peter Barkworth.

Gray's reputation has been overshadowed perhaps by his more prolific contemporary, Alan Ayckbourn, with whom he is often compared; but at best he has a strong sense of character, a flexible instinct for plot and a probing wit, so subtly dry that it is sometimes hard to tell which of the many nuances were primarily intended. JE

Gray, Spalding 1941– American actor-playwright; product of the avant-garde theatre movement of the 1960s. Gray spent five years as a traditional actor before joining Richard Schechner and the PERFORMANCE GROUP in 1970. With the disbanding of that group in 1980, he joined his collaborator and director ELIZABETH LeCOMPTE, James Clayburgh, Willem Dafoe, Libby Howes and Ron Vawter to form the WOOSTER GROUP. Gray's reputation, however, has transcended the Group, primarily because of two bodies of work: *Three Places in Rhode Island* (*Sakonnet Point*, 1975; *Rumstick Road*, 1977; *Nayatt School*, 1978), a trilogy devised by Gray (who says he is extremely 'narcissistic and reflective') and LeCompte from Gray's biography; and a series (1979–91) of 14 monologues ('without peer') drawn from his past, including *Terrors of Pleasure*, *Sex and Death to the Age of 14*, *Booze, Cars and College Girls*, *A Personal History of the American Theatre*, *India and After*, *Interviewing the Audience*, *Swimming to Cambodia*, *Monster in a Box* and in spring 1992 *Gray's Anatomy*. Theodore Shank calls Gray's pieces 'the most literally autobiographical work that has been presented in the theatre'. In 1988 he scored critical success as the stage manager in Lincoln Center's (see VIVIAN BEAUMONT AND MITZI E. NEWHOUSE THEATRES) *Our Town*. DBW

Gray, Terence 1895–?1987 British director and stage designer, heavily influenced by GORDON CRAIG. In 1926 Gray founded the Cambridge Festival Theatre, where he worked with NORMAN MARSHALL and the lighting expert Harold Ridge, mounting productions of classical Greek drama (see GREECE, ANCIENT) and German EXPRESSIONISM, ELMER RICE, early O'NEILL, PIRANDELLO and W. B. YEATS. His non-naturalistic style, which disregarded dramatic texts (*Twelfth Night* on roller-skates – an idea recently appropriated in one of ANDREW LLOYD WEBBER's musical spectaculars – and a 'flamenco' treatment of *Romeo and Juliet*), was accompanied by 'isometric scenic design', using pale-grey or luminous screens and columns as neutral architectural shapes for the play of light, together with arrangements of steps and multi-level rostra reminiscent of LEOPOLD JESSNER. TYRONE GUTHRIE took over the theatre for a season in 1929–30; and after Gray's final production, the first English performance of AESCHYLUS' *The Suppliants* in 1933, it finally closed in 1939. CI

Greece, ancient Greek drama as we know it was a relatively late development, arising when Greece already had a long and rich tradition of epic, lyric and other non-dramatic poetry. It was essentially the creation of classical Athens: all the dramatists who were later regarded as classics were active at Athens in the 5th and 4th centuries BC (the time of Athenian democracy), and all the surviving plays date from this period. It is convenient to consider first the religious festivals at which Athenian drama was performed, then the history of the different forms (see also TRAGEDY, COMEDY, MIME) and then some features of performance (see also GREEK THEATRES).

1 Dramatic festivals All dramatic performances at Athens took place at festivals of the god Dionysus. The main festival was the Great or City Dionysia, held in March or early April and centred on the temple and theatre of Dionysus beneath the Acropolis. The principal features were probably established in the late 6th century under the patronage of the tyrant Pisistratus. Every year three tragedians competed for a prize, each producing four plays on one day; and five comic poets (in wartime perhaps only three) competed for another prize, each producing one play. The four plays by a tragedian usually comprised three tragedies followed by a satyr play (but there were exceptions; see EURIPIDES). The four plays might be connected in theme to form a tetralogy in the proper sense (see AESCHYLUS), or might be wholly separate. The set of three tragedies from a tetralogy is called a trilogy.

The Great Dionysia also incorporated religious ceremonies and performances of dithyrambs (a form of non-dramatic choral song). The plays, however, were not religious rituals; they had no RITUAL function and their content had no necessary connection with Dionysus. At the beginning of the festival the competing dramatists paraded with their actors and choruses at a *proagōn*, a preliminary ceremony at which they probably announced the themes of their plays. The plays were mass entertainment, performed before an audience of several thousand (perhaps as many as 15,000) drawn from all social classes. In the 4th century at least, and perhaps earlier, the democratic state paid a small allowance to enable poor citizens to attend. Whether women attended is uncertain.

The festival was presided over by the principal *archōn* or magistrate. It was he who selected the competing dramatists and assigned to each a *choregus* – a wealthy citizen who volunteered, or was co-opted, to pay for the Chorus and for most other features of the production. Actors, however, were professionals paid by the state. The prize-giving was taken very seriously, ten judges being nominated by an elaborate process from the ten 'tribes' into which the citizen body was divided. From 449 there was a prize for the best tragic protagonist (leading actor) as well as one for the best tragedian. Official records (*didaskaliai*) were kept of the plays performed each year and the prizes awarded. These records date from c.501 for tragedy (though we hear, perhaps unreliably, of a victory by THESPIS as early as c.534), from c.486 for comedy.

The dramatists normally produced their own plays (though ARISTOPHANES did not always do so). Indeed the Greeks generally spoke not of a 'writer' but of a 'teacher' of tragedy or comedy, since his essential task was not simply to compose a text but to instruct the Chorus and actors in the performance through which his play was to be realized. Revivals of plays already performed did not become usual at the Great Dionysia until the 4th century, though Aeschylus is said to have received the unique distinction of a decree allowing his plays to be revived after his death.

All actors and Chorus members were male, and wore masks. The music to accompany songs was provided by the only unmasked figure, the player of the *aulos*, which was a double pipe with reeds. The Chorus normally sang in unison (though its leader could take part in spoken dialogue with actors), and danced in formation as it sang. Occasionally a second, subsidiary Chorus was used, and occasionally (but much less than in most modern productions) a song was divided between semi-choruses or individual Chorus members.

Another festival of Dionysus, the Lenaea, was held around the beginning of February. From c.442 it too was the occasion for dramatic competitions in the Theatre of Dionysus, with two tragic poets producing two plays each and five comic poets producing one play each. It was more important for comedy than for tragedy.

In the villages of Attica (the territory of Athens) plays were performed at the Rural Dionysia, usually held in December. In the 4th century and later we hear of touring companies who would go the rounds of theatres in Attica and beyond.

2 Tragedy: origins, development, form The origin of tragedy has been the subject of endless discussion. The tendency among recent scholars has been to abandon the elaborate theoretical constructions which had earlier been built around enigmatic remarks in ARISTOTLE, and to concentrate instead on the links between tragedy and various known types of non-dramatic poetry.

Tragedy contains two principal types of verse: spoken dialogue in iambic and trochaic metres, usually delivered by actors, and songs in lyric metres, usually delivered by the Chorus. There were non-dramatic precedents for both types. Iambic and trochaic poetry was composed for delivery by the poets themselves, for such purposes as attacking their enemies and giving moral and political advice to their fellow citizens. Choral songs, sometimes long and elaborate and incorporating mythical narratives, were performed on various religious and ceremonial occasions. Tragedy as we know it was born when these two traditions were combined together, verse spoken by the poet (who was at first the sole actor) being interspersed with songs sung by the Chorus. Even if Aristotle is right in deriving tragedy from 'the leaders of the dithyramb' (*Poetics* 4), the transformation of Chorus leader into actor, taking a mythical role and delivering spoken verse, was a monumental innovation. This innovation probably occurred at Athens in the second half of the 6th century, and may have been the achievement of the first recorded tragedian, Thespis.

Our sources do provide faint hints that before Thespis' time something called 'tragedy' may have existed outside Athens, in the northern Peloponnese. 'Tragedy' is attributed to the poet Arion, who was active at Corinth c.600, and we hear of 'tragic choruses' in the 6th-century Sicyon. But this Peloponnesian 'tragedy', if it existed at all, was presumably a purely choral and non-dramatic form. Certainly the Chorus is more prominent in the work of Aeschylus than in later tragedy, and it may well have been more prominent still in the work of Thespis; and the language and verse forms of tragic songs (as well as the assumption that every tragedy must *have* a chorus) clearly derive from earlier lyric traditions. But it is difficult to see how non-dramatic songs could have evolved into drama by any gradual process.

One feature which Thespis could not have borrowed from existing poetic traditions was the use of MASKS, enabling actor and Chorus to take on roles from the mythical past. Indeed, ancient sources claim that masks were his own invention. In other cultures, however, they are commonly employed in religious rituals, and there is some evidence for this in early Greece also. But any such ritual should be seen as at most another influence on the development of tragedy, not as its sole origin. There is no evidence that masks were ever used in the dithyramb.

The word 'tragedy' itself (*tragōidia*) remains most mysterious. It should mean something like 'goat-singing', but the Greeks themselves seem to have had no idea how tragedy was ever connected with goats. The sacrifice of a goat on the occasion of a tragic performance is a more likely explanation than any connection between tragedy and goat-like satyrs.

As long as the poet himself was the only actor, the dramatic possibilities must have been restricted. The important step of introducing a second actor is said to have been taken by Aeschylus, who also, according to Aristotle, 'reduced the choral element and gave dialogue the leading role', and who is often regarded as the true father of tragedy. The introduction of the third actor was ascribed to SOPHOCLES by most authorities but to Aeschylus by some, and evidently occurred around 460, in the period when both poets were competing. The three actors – protagonist, deuteragonist and tritagonist – shared the parts in any play between them. A fourth actor may have been employed on occasion, but seems never to have come into general use. In addition there were mute extras, generally functioning as attendants but sometimes portraying named characters; and Euripides sometimes has short singing parts for boys. The Chorus is usually thought to have numbered 12 in the extant plays of Aeschylus, 15 in those of Sophocles and Euripides.

The great majority of tragedies dramatized events from the Greek myths. These traditional tales were believed to be historically true in essence, but were also felt to provide paradigms of human fortunes, against which men could measure their own experience. The mythical material was usually taken from existing poetry, whether epic, lyric or tragic, but non-poetic traditions may have been used on occasion. The use of this familiar material meant that the outline of the story was always known to the audience in advance, and this knowledge could be exploited for purposes of dramatic irony. Nevertheless, the tragedian had great freedom in shaping his plot, and very different plays could be based on the same myth, as can be seen by comparing the *Choephori* of Aeschylus and the *Electra*s of Sophocles and Euripides. A few plays portrayed events in recent history (Aeschylus' *Persians* is the only surviving example, but see also PHRYNICHUS). These, however, were events that had already attained 'mythic' status, and the plays were set in exotic locations; no living Greek is mentioned by name in any tragedy.

The style of tragedy can be supple, lively and, up to a point, colloquial, but always retains a certain dignity; it avoids the jokes and indecencies associated with comedy and is enriched by poetic words and expressions unknown in ordinary usage. In theme and plot not all tragedies have the concentrated seriousness of Sophocles' *Oedipus Tyrannus* or Euripides' *Medea*; for those of Euripides also include sensational melodramas and plays of romance and intrigue, even of gentle humour. And there are happy endings, not only in these romantic tragedies but in such serious ones as Aeschylus' *Eumenides* or Sophocles' *Philoctetes*. The fact that a Greek tragedy *can* end unhappily, however, and can contemplate death and acute suffering without escapism or false consolation, is a

remarkable feature of the genre, distinguishing it from most independent dramatic traditions in other cultures, and doubtless owing much to the example of Homer's *Iliad*.

The scene of most tragedies is set in the open air in front of a palace or other building (exceptions include Aeschylus' *Persians*, apparently set *inside* a council chamber, and Sophocles' *Oedipus at Colonus*, set in a rustic grove). Occasionally (as in Aeschylus' *Eumenides* and Sophocles' *Ajax*) there is a change of scene, marked by the departure and re-entry of the Chorus. In Aeschylus there can also be a certain vagueness about the imagined location, allowing it to 'refocus' while the Chorus remains visible.

Events on the tragic stage never include acts of violence, and seldom include deaths. Violence and death, however, were central to most of the myths portrayed, and the tragedians dealt with this by means of messengers, who come to report what has happened inside the palace or elsewhere. Every play of Sophocles and Euripides contains at least one formal messenger speech, and the dramatists make the most of the opportunities which these provide for vivid and exciting narrative. Aeschylus uses messengers in rather different and more varied ways.

In structure a tragedy consists of several acts or 'episodes', normally separated by the major choral songs, which are preceded by exits of actors (though it is not uncommon for an actor to remain on stage) and followed by entrances. Most of the spoken dialogue takes the form either of extended speeches (often highly rhetorical) or of line-by-line exchanges (stichomythia), though more irregular patterns also occur. Besides spoken dialogue, an act may contain a sung (or partly sung) exchange between actor and Chorus (*amoibaion* or *kommos*) or a solo song by an actor (monody). *Amoibaia* become rarer and monodies more common in the course of the 5th century.

The rhetorical style of tragic speeches becomes most marked in the set-piece debate (known to scholars as an *agōn* or contest) between two characters. There is at least one such debate in almost every play of Sophocles or Euripides.

A choral song can have various functions. It can influence the audience's feelings by means of moralizing comments on what the Chorus has witnessed (though such comments are usually made from the viewpoint of the man in the street, not from one of exceptional wisdom). It can broaden the scope of the play by exploring the connections between present and past events (especially in Aeschylus). It can work ironically, evoking a mood of hope and joy before disaster strikes, or one of despair before salvation comes (especially in Sophocles). It can wistfully describe a remote and idyllic world which contrasts painfully with present realities (especially in Euripides). In Aeschylus the Chorus is always closely involved in what is happening on stage, and many of the actors' speeches are addressed to it (though it seldom intervenes decisively in the plot, outside the special cases of *Suppliant Women* and *Eumenides*). In Euripides (especially his later work) its role becomes less integral; its presence is ignored for long stretches (and can even be an embarrassment), and some of its songs are little more than interludes.

In the 4th century the tendencies seen in late Euripides

(and AGATHON) – melodramatic plot, episodic structure, a decline in the role of the Chorus – were apparently carried further. The period is usually seen as one of decline; but the genre continued to be popular and vigorously pursued, and some plays of the period, such as the *Hector* of Astydamas, attained classic status. Fourth-century vase paintings from the Greek colonies of southern Italy are often more closely inspired by tragic performance than was usual at Athens, and attest to the continuing popularity of both 5th- and 4th-century plays. Aristotle treats contemporary tragedians with respect, though he already sees the plays of Sophocles and Euripides (which were regularly revived) as classics.

In the Hellenistic period (from 323 BC) tragic performances, though widespread in the Greek world, were probably no longer attended by a wide public. While comedy remained popular and continued to develop, tragedy became fossilized. The stylized COSTUME and narrow stage must have made performances very static and statuesque. A five-act structure seems to have been usual, and the Chorus, when employed at all, was wholly detached from the action. We hear of a 'Pleiad' of seven admired tragedians in 3rd-century Alexandria, but the only Hellenistic tragedy of which we can form any impression is an oddity, the *Exagoge* (a play about Moses and the Exodus) of the Hellenized Jew Ezechiel.

3 Comedy: origins, development, form The word *kōmōidia* means singing connected with, or suitable for, a *kōmos* or drunken revel. The comedy of 5th-century Athens – 'Old Comedy' – combines the same principal types of verse as tragedy, namely iambic or trochaic dialogue and choral song. The combination of these elements can hardly be independent of the example of early tragedy. The earliest known comic dramatists were Chionides and Magnes, who seem to have competed in the earliest recorded contest, at the Great Dionysia c.486. Before this, according to Aristotle, there was informal comedy performed by 'volunteers' and derived from 'phallic songs'. The poet Susarion, who was claimed by some as the inventor of comedy, probably did not write comedies at all.

Matters are complicated, however, by the undoubted existence of a type of comedy in the Greek colony of Syracuse in Sicily. The chief exponent of this 'Doric Comedy' was EPICHARMUS, whom Aristotle places 'much earlier' than Chionides and Magnes, but who seems in fact to have been their contemporary. It is not clear whether his plays had a chorus and whether they influenced, or were influenced by, the comedy of Athens. Equally imponderable is the evidence of archaic vases showing dancers disguised as animals of one kind or another, which seem to provide a precedent for the animal choruses found in many comedies.

At Athens, though Aristotle assigns a formative role to one Crates (mid-5th century), the most admired poets of Old Comedy were CRATINUS, EUPOLIS and Aristophanes; and only the work of Aristophanes survives. All his extant plays have fantasy plots set at the time of their production, but burlesque treatments of mythical themes were also common.

Comedy evidently saw itself from the first as the anti-type of tragedy, which it constantly parodies; and we may suspect that neither the sustained dignity of tragedy nor the sustained buffoonery of comedy would have been possible if each form of drama had not been able to react against the other. Comic poets are much less concerned than tragedians with coherence and consistency of plot, and several of Aristophanes' plays degenerate by the end into a series of slapstick routines. An actor is always allowed to come out of character for the sake of a joke or a topical reference, and the 'dramatic illusion' may be deliberately broken for the sake of insulting the audience or playing with theatrical convention. There is no attempt at unity of place, a few lines of dialogue being sufficient to transform the imagined setting completely.

Actors are used less economically than in tragedy, some plays requiring at least four. The language of comedy (when it is not PARODYING tragedy or other literature, or foreign dialects) is an entirely colloquial Attic Greek.

A startling feature is the scurrilous and often quite unfair abuse which the comic poets heaped on contemporary individuals, from defenceless private citizens to powerful politicians (even gods are treated with scant respect). Some ancient scholars claim that attempts were made to place legal restrictions on the traditional freedom of comedy in this regard, but the evidence is confused, and it is clear that no such attempt had any lasting effect. There was certainly no restriction on the explicitness of the sexual and excremental jokes.

A play is usually called after the character assumed by its Chorus (24 in number), which may be human (e.g. *Men of Acharnae*), animal (e.g. *Frogs*) or even inanimate (e.g. *Clouds*). In the middle of most of Aristophanes' plays there is a long section (sometimes two sections) called the *parabasis*, in which the plot simply stops and the Chorus addresses the audience directly. In part of each *parabasis* it comes out of character altogether in order to act as the mouthpiece of the poet. The earliest examples have a strict and complex form, but this is progressively simplified in the course of Aristophanes' career, until finally the *parabasis* disappears completely. Formal complexity can be found elsewhere in the earlier plays, notably in the conventional *agōn* or battle of words, the structure of which is marked out by a pattern of interspersed stanzas from the Chorus.

The last two extant plays of Aristophanes, *Ecclesiazusae* and *Plutus*, dating from the early 4th century, exhibit the transition to Middle Comedy, which prevailed at Athens until about the 320s. We have only fragments, however, from such prolific 4th-century poets as Antiphanes, Anaxandrides and Eubulus. The importance of the Chorus declines rapidly; in *Plutus* only one of its songs is written out, others being marked by a mere stage direction. Obscenity and satirical abuse also decline to some extent, and the pervasive cynicism of Aristophanes' earlier work is replaced by homely moralizing. Fantasy plots and burlesque treatments of myths remain popular, but familiar figures from daily life, such as cooks, parasites and courtesans, start to appear in stereotyped roles.

Comic scenes are depicted in a vivid and lively series of 4th-century vase paintings from southern Italy. The vases have traditionally been known as Phlyax vases and taken to depict Phlyax plays, which were supposedly a local subliterary genre. Recent studies, however, in the light of newly discovered examples, have shown that the plays depicted are actually Athenian comedies (one vase clearly shows a scene from Aristophanes' *Thesmophoriazusae*). The vases thus provide good evidence for comic costumes and staging, and show that the plays were widely popular by an early date, despite their often parochial Athenian concerns. Little is known, then, about the genuine Phlyax plays, but they seem to have been burlesque treatments of myths, the speciality of one Rhinthon of Syracuse, who was active at Tarentum around 300 BC.

New Comedy, which prevailed from the late 4th century to the 2nd, is a gentle, whimsical comedy of manners, very different indeed from the anarchic fantasy of Aristophanes, and showing the influence of the romantic tragedies of Euripides. The great name here is MENANDER; other popular poets included Alexis (whose very long career spanned the transition from Middle to New), Philemon and Diphilus.

The only sign of the Chorus is now a stage direction between acts (which always number five) and a conventional warning that revellers are approaching, which signals its first entry. The scene is always set in front of two bourgeois houses in contemporary Greece, and the romantic plot, while it may be highly improbable, contains no actual impossibilities. Love, an almost unheard-of phenomenon in Old Comedy, is normally the mainspring of the action, and this proceeds through intrigues and misunderstandings to a happy ending, in which the sympathetic characters receive their reward. The situation is made clear to the audience by a formal prologue speech (not always situated at the very beginning), and most of the humour (and pathos) derives from the mistakes which the characters make and the human plausibility of their reactions. Somewhat broader humour is provided by slaves, cooks and the like, but indecency and topical allusions are very rare. While not all the sententious moralizing is to be taken at face value, an atmosphere of conventional decency and tolerance prevails.

The plays of New Comedy remained very popular throughout antiquity, but were lost in the Middle Ages. Our knowledge of them derives from imitations by PLAUTUS and TERENCE (through which they influenced the comic traditions of the Renaissance and later periods) and from more or less fragmentary texts (almost exclusively of Menander) excavated in Egypt in recent times.

4 The satyr play Satyrs are mythical subhuman creatures of the Greek countryside, drunken and lustful and often portrayed in the retinue of Dionysus or in pursuit of nymphs. On 5th-century vases they are depicted as men with bald heads, pointed ears, snub noses and horses' tails.

It is difficult to make anything of Aristotle's claim (*Poetics* 4) that tragedy developed from some 'satyric' form (a claim which seems to contradict much else that he himself says). More plausible is the tradition that the satyr plays were introduced at Athens by Aeschylus' contemporary PRATINAS, who perhaps knew them in some form at his native town of Phlius in the Peloponnese.

The 5th-century satyr play was always composed by a

A scene from a so-called Phlyax Vase showing Chiron and slaves.

tragedian, and normally formed a humorous tailpiece to a set of three tragedies. It consisted of a burlesque treatment of a mythical theme, which often concerned a popular figure such as Heracles, Dionysus or Odysseus, and always had a happy ending. Into this myth the satyrs (together with their father Silenus, who was regularly a character) had to be more or less artificially introduced. In metre and construction the plays were similar to tragedies, but less strict. The plot and 'dramatic illusion' were more carefully sustained than in Old Comedy, and the humour was less broad; indecencies did occur, but contemporary allusions did not.

The only example to survive complete is Euripides' *Cyclops*, but we also have about half of Sophocles' *Ichneutae* (*Trackers*) and some interesting scraps by Aeschylus, who was regarded as the greatest exponent of the form. In the 4th century the satyr play became separated from tragedy and assimilated to comedy, so as to include mockery of named individuals.

5 Mime The Greek colonies of Sicily and southern Italy evidently had a long and rich tradition of subliterary humorous drama, of which we can catch only glimpses. The Doric Comedy of Epicharmus (see section 3 above) may be an early offshoot of this tradition.

A mime (*mimos*) was a short monologue or (later) dialogue on a low-life theme, normally in prose and delivered by a single unmasked performer, himself called a mime. We possess brief fragments of the work of the most admired mimographer, the 5th-century Sophron of Syracuse, and some portions of anonymous mimes from later periods, when the form became widespread in the Greek world.

In the 3rd century a literary form of mime was composed in verse and in archaic dialect by Herodas (or Herondas). It is uncertain whether this was intended for performance. The eight surviving examples mostly portray women, engaged in such unladylike activities as flogging slaves or shopping for dildoes. Some of the poems of his more refined contemporary Theocritus are also, in effect, mimes, or strongly influenced by the mime form. The comedy of early ROME must also have been influenced by popular dramas of this type.

6 Actors and acting It is uncertain whether *hypokritēs*, the Greek for 'actor', originally meant 'answerer' (of the Chorus?) or 'interpreter, expounder'. Aeschylus may have taken the leading role in all his own plays (we are told the names of certain actors he employed, but not necessarily as protagonist). Sophocles, however, is said to have given up acting because of a weak voice, and the institution of a prize for actors shows that tragic poets did not act after the middle of the 5th century.

Tragic acting must have required considerable stamina and flexibility, since the same actors were used for all four plays which a tragedian presented on one day, and the roles assigned to a single actor might differ widely. The indications are that, as far as possible, the most important parts were given to the protagonist and the least important to the tritagonist, with little or no type-casting. It is uncertain whether a single part was ever divided between two or more actors (this would be necessary in Sophocles'

Oedipus at Colonus unless a fourth actor was employed).

Strength and clarity of voice were naturally considered important. Tragic texts sometimes call for quite vigorous movements (running, collapsing in agony, grasping another's knees in supplication), but we cannot know how realistically these were performed; there was doubtless some stylization, in keeping with the size of the theatre. Various anecdotes indicate that a certain NATURALISM was prized, but such things are relative, and we cannot assume that Greek acting would have appeared at all naturalistic to a modern audience. Old Comedy is full of such lively activities as dancing for joy, beating opponents, and chasing them off the stage. It is not likely that tragedy contained any significant actions not signalled by the words of the texts, but there are some passages of comedy that are hard for us to understand without the accompanying gestures.

7 Music and dance These were integral parts of a Greek dramatic performance, but are impossible for us to reconstruct (though we know something of the scales and rhythms employed, and have a scrap of musical notation for Euripides' *Orestes*). The metre shows that songs were often rhythmically complex but usually had a simple overall structure of paired stanzas (AABBCC...), the rhythms of the first stanza in each pair (the strophe) being recapitulated in the second (antistrophe). Where a song does not serve to separate two acts (often in comedy, more rarely in tragedy), the stanzas may be separated by dialogue passages. A freer form of song, without recapitulation, is also found, and becomes common in late Euripides.

Besides true song and spoken dialogue, there was an intermediate type of verse (often referred to as 'recitative'), accompanied, like the songs, on the *aulos*. This is often assigned to the Chorus leader, but sometimes to actors and sometimes perhaps to the whole Chorus.

Late sources tell us that a rectangular formation was employed for the entrance and the dances of the dramatic Chorus, but it is hard to believe that it was always as regimented as this. Sometimes the Chorus's movements can be imagined from its words (beating of the breast and head at Aeschylus *Choephori* 423–8, kicking out at Aristophanes *Peace* 331–4), but many songs do not obviously call for imitative gestures.

8 Masks, costumes and properties The Greek mask covered the whole head, with holes for the eyes and mouth. It was probably made of linen on a wooden frame. Vase paintings of the 5th century show that tragic masks of this period were realistic and undistorted. There must have been a range of types to show differences of age and sex, together with some special masks for such figures as the blinded Oedipus or the Phrygian in Euripides' *Orestes*. The mask of Old and Middle Comedy seems typically to have been ugly, with goggling eyes, wide nose and gaping mouth, but here again there must have been a wide variety according to the needs of the play; and there is evidence that portrait masks were used by actors playing real people.

Some 5th-century paintings of tragic actors show them wearing ordinary tunics and cloaks; but it seems that the *syrma*, a long, richly embroidered robe with sleeves, which had been worn by the *aulos*-player from the first, was progressively adopted by the actors also, becoming the standard tragic costume by the end of the century. Aristophanes repeatedly taunts Euripides with presenting his heroes in rags, and there are plays by the other tragedians in which ragged costumes seem to be called for (e.g. Aeschylus' *Persians*, Sophocles' *Philoctetes*), but we cannot tell how realistically ragged these were. The standard footwear was a calf-length boot, not normally worn by men in daily life.

Actors of Old and Middle Comedy wore the tunics and cloaks of everyday life, often with padding of the stomach and buttocks. It is disputed whether all comic actors wore a leather phallus (except when playing women or effeminates); it is likely that they did, but that this could be concealed beneath clothing on occasion. It is unclear whether the Chorus (when human) wore phalluses also.

In satyr plays the human characters wore tragic costume, while the satyrs wore drawers, usually of fur, equipped with phallus and horse's tail, and Silenus had a full-length costume covered with tufts of wool. A cast preparing to perform a satyr play is depicted on the Pronomos Vase, painted c.400 BC (see illustration, COSTUME).

From the latter part of the 4th century the appearance of tragic actors became more stylized. The mouth of the mask opened wider; the forehead was unnaturally raised, to make the actor appear taller; and, for the same reason, the sole of the boot was thickened, until the actor was walking on stilts which raised him several inches from the ground. Since most surviving representations of tragic masks and costumes date from a late period, it must be emphasized that they are very different from those worn in the first performances of the surviving plays.

At the same period comic masks and costumes became more lifelike, in keeping with the greater realism and decorum of New Comedy. The phallus ceased to be worn. The late writer Pollux describes an extensive repertory of comic masks for the various stock characters, and scholars have attempted to relate these both to the masks shown on terracottas and other monuments and to the characters in the plays themselves.

For stage properties (as distinct from sets and stage machinery – see GREEK THEATRES) we are dependent on the evidence of the plays. It is hardly likely (though possible in theory) that properties not mentioned in the text were used simply to create a realistic ambience. Those few which the tragic texts mention, however, are always dramatically significant and often memorably used (e.g. the carpet and the robe in Aeschylus' *Agamemnon* and *Choephori*, the urn and the bow in Sophocles' *Electra* and *Philoctetes*, the letter and the head of Pentheus in Euripides' *Iphigenia in Tauris* and *Bacchae*). The properties used by Aristophanes are more numerous, and include the scientific instruments of *Clouds* 200–17 and the arms-dealer's wares at *Peace* 1210–64.   ALB

GENERAL

See: P. E. Easterling and B. M. W. Knox (eds.), *The Cambridge History of Classical Literature*, vol. 1, Cambridge, 1985; *Greece and Rome: New Surveys in the Classics* – 13 (*Aristophanes*, 1979), 14 (*Euripides*, 1981), 16 (*Sophocles*, 1984), 18 (*Aeschylus*, 1986); A. Pickard-Cambridge, *Dithyramb Tragedy and Comedy*, 2nd edn rev. T. B. L. Webster, Oxford, 1962; E. Simon, *The Ancient Theatre*, tr. C.E. Vafopoulou-Richardson, London, 1982.

FESTIVALS

See: A. Pickard-Cambridge, *The Dramatic Festivals of Athens*, 2nd edn rev. J. Gould and D. M. Lewis, Oxford, 1968.

TRAGEDY

See: A. Brown, *A New Companion to Greek Tragedy*, London, 1983; C. J. Herington, *Poetry into Drama*, Chapel Hill, 1985; A. Lesky, *Greek Tragic Poetry*, tr. M. Dillon, New Haven, Conn., 1983; R. Rehm, *Greek Tragic Theatre*, London, 1992; O. Taplin, *Greek Tragedy in Action*, London, 1978.

COMEDY

See: K. J. Dover, *Aristophanic Comedy*, London, 1972; R. L. Hunter, *The New Comedy of Greece and Rome*, Cambridge, 1985; F.H. Sandbach, *The Comic Theatre of Greece and Rome*, London, 1977.

SATYR PLAY

See: R. A. S. Seaford, *Euripides: Cyclops*, Oxford, 1984; D. F. Sutton, *The Greek Satyr Play*, Meisenheim am Glan, 1980.

Greece, modern   Crete, still under Venetian rule, experienced its literary and artistic renaissance in the 16th to 17th centuries, and this is where modern Greek theatre began. Little is known about how plays were produced, but there exist a number of remarkable pieces of theatre in verse from that period: three tragedies, the best of which is *Erophili* (from the name of the heroine) by George Hortátjis, three comedies, a PASTORAL comedy and a religious drama. Although derivative, these works in Cretan dialect are often superior to their Western, mostly Italian, models.

The Ionian islands (an area which never fell under the Turks) seem to have known in the 18th century a flowering of theatre, with open-air performances of *omilíes* (literally, 'speeches'), skits in the vernacular Greek, often improvised, or of parts of the Cretan plays. The comedy *Hássis* (*The Loser*, 1795) by D. Gousélis, in 15-syllable lines, excels all other works of the period, which also produced classicizing dramas in purist Greek by Phanariot writers (educated Greeks associated with the Phanari, the Greek district of Constantinople).

The two traditions, the popular and the *loyía* (learned one), continued through the 19th century, with the former eventually gaining the upper hand. *The Basil Plant* (1830) by the Zanteot A. Mátesis is a social drama in prose and dialect. *Vavilonía* (*The Din of Babel*, 1836) by D. Vyzántios, in purist Greek but with heavily idiomatic dialogue (since the theme of the comedy is the very multiplicity of Greek dialects which supposedly makes communication among speakers impossible), has something of the spirit of *karaghiózis* (see KARAGÖZ), the shadow theatre which, with its set characters and farcical predilections, became popular towards the end of the century. The influence of SHAKESPEARE is evident in the scholar D. Vernardákis's archaicizing tragedies, such as *Merópi* (1866), and *Fáusta* (1893) which was performed simultaneously at two different theatres in Athens. Closer to reality is a type of popular theatre, in prose with inset songs, the so-called *komidílion* (1888–c.1900) that treats down-to-earth themes with everyday characters. This is often coupled with the *pimenikón idílion* (pastoral idyll), a more romantic type of play, also popular at the time. An outgrowth of both is the Greek *epitheórisis* (REVUE), skits with songs satirizing the social and political mores of the day.

Bourgeois theatre, which is represented by few plays in the 19th century (like *The Grocer's Daughter* by A. Vláhos and *The Late Evening Visit* by Il. Kapetanákis), made great advances in the first half of the 20th, thanks to a number of talented writers who creatively adapted to modern Greek realities the techniques and spirit that they found in STRINDBERG, IBSEN, CHEKHOV, MAETERLINCK, HAUPTMANN and other European playwrights. WAGNER influenced *The Ring of the Mother* (1898) by J. Kambísis– a play which was turned into an opera by M. Kalomiris – and NIETZSCHE and D'ANNUNZIO inspired the early plays of NIKOS KAZANTZÁKIS. *The Three Kisses* (1908) by C. Hristomános, subtitled 'A tragic sonata', is rather sentimental, but its author played a key role in the promotion of the performing aspects of modern Greek theatre and by launching actors who eventually dominated the Greek stage. The great actress KYVÉLI ANDRIANOÚ started at Christomános's Nea Skiní (New Stage, 1901–5), while MARÍKA KOTOPOÚLI and other fine actors first appeared at the Greek Royal Theatre (1901–8), whose founding also helped to encourage young writers and the translation of classical dramas, as well as contemporary European comedies and tragedies, into modern Greek.

It was a new era for Greek theatre. Special schools trained professional actors and more attention was given to the direction and staging of plays. It was in this climate that the leading poet of the day, Palamás, wrote his poetic drama *Thrice Noble* (1903), and Grégory Xenópoulos *The Secret of Kontéssa Valéraina* (1904). Xenópoulos, together with Spíros Melás, Pantelís Horn and others, enriched Greek theatre, in the decades following, with many new plays which proved rewarding both artistically and commercially.

The dominant trends were REALISM and NATURALISM. Xenópoulos wrote about 40 plays – tragedies and comedies – establishing himself as a great technician of the theatre (a NOËL COWARD of the Greek stage): *The Soul Father* (1895), *Fotiní Sándri* (1908), *Stélla Violándi* (1909), *The Temptation* (1910), *The Flower of the Levant* (1914) and many others. Melás's works were heavier but equally well crafted. The early pieces – *The Son of the Spectre*, *The Red Shirt* and *The Ruined Home* – have a poetic flavour and echo Ibsenic and Nietzschean ideas. More realistic are *The White and the Black* (1916) and *One Night, One Life* (1924). *Papafléssas* (1937), *The Kind and the Dog* (on Alexander the Great and Diogenes, 1953) and *Rígas Velestinlís* (1962) deal with themes from Greek history. Melás also wrote a successful comedy, *Dad Gets an Education* (1935), and for several years in the 1920s and 30s he was also active as a theatre director. Horn's most memorable play is *To Findanáki* (*The Young Plant*, an allusion to a pretty young woman, 1921), a drama of social conflict set in a poor neighbourhood of Athens.

The writer and critic Fótos Politis, who had a serious, idealistic view of theatre, became the first director of the Greek National Theatre (1932). This event, plus Károlos Koun's establishment of the Popular Stage and later (1942) of the Art Theatre, Sokrátis Karandinós's founding of his New Dramatic Stage (1933), and the operation of good private companies, helped advance the cause of the Greek theatre considerably. It held its own during the Second World War and the Greek civil war, to blossom again in the 1950s and 60s. There has also been another development – the revival of ancient Greek drama (see GREECE, ANCIENT), as, for instance, in the Delphic festivals of 1927 and 1930 sponsored by the poet Ángelos Sikelianós and his wife Eva Palmer. Formerly sporadic and amateurish, this is now practised on a regular basis and with elaborate productions in the ancient theatres of Epidaurus and Herodes Atticus (by the Acropolis), and in other extant theatres in Greece. Directors like Aléxis Minotís (d.1990), Dimítris Rondíris, Aléxis Solomós and Károlos Koun, and performers like Katirína Paxinoú, Anna Sinodinoú, Thános Kotsópoulos, Mános Katrákis and many others have distinguished themselves in this field.

At the same time, many successful plays from the theatres of London, Paris, and New York have been translated and presented in Greece, while writers of the generation of the 1930s, like Ángelos Terzákis and PANTELÍS PREVELÁKIS, and many younger writers have continued established traditions and also adapted fresh influences from abroad. The most popular types of theatre are still the *epitheórisis* (revue) and the so-called *farsokomodía*, a light comedy. But dramas of ideas as well as poetic plays are also presented frequently by various companies, often with the financial assistance of the state. Composers like Míkis Theodorákis and Mános Hadjidákis have contributed MUSICAL scores for the production of particular plays, and painters like Yánnis Tsaroúhis have specialized in stage and COSTUME designing.

Opera and operetta have not fared as well as other types of theatre in Greece, and the cinema and television have reduced the appeal of live theatre in general and of the Greek shadow theatre, *karaghiózis*, in particular. This is the era of the popular music concerts and of the big spectacular productions of drama and ballet by foreign companies visiting Greece, mostly in the summer. But modern Greek theatre has come a long way from its start in 16th- and 17th-century Crete.   GT

See: N. J. Laskaris, *Le Théâtre néo-grec*, Athens, 1930; F. M. Pontani, *Teatro Neoellenico*, Milan, 1962; Y. Sidéris et al., *The Modern Greek Theatre: A Concise History*, trans. L. Vassardaki, Athens, 1957; M. Valsa, *Le Théâtre grec moderne, de 1453 à 1900*, Berlin, 1960.

Greek theatres According to tradition the first tragedian, THESPIS, performed his plays on wagons with which he travelled, and seats were set up for performances in the *agora* (market-place) of Athens. By the end of the 6th century BC, however, a permanent *theatron*, 'watching-place', was set up in the precinct of Dionysus on the south slope of the Athenian Acropolis.

Since at first any construction above ground level was of wood, and since the theatre was later rebuilt many times, the surviving remains of this earliest Theatre of Dionysus are extremely scanty. (The remains to be seen on the site today are largely of the Roman period.) It has therefore to be reconstructed on the analogy of other Greek theatres and on the evidence of the plays performed there. The only features which *necessarily* existed in the early 5th century are wooden seats for spectators on the hillside, and a level, earth-floored *orchēstra*, 'dancing-area', in the centre. The *orchēstra* is usually believed to have been circular, like a threshing floor and like the *orchēstra* at Epidaurus (see below), with a diameter of perhaps 65 feet; but some have argued that it was rectangular, like that at Thoricus.

Most of the surviving plays also make use of a building, the *skēnē* or scene building, behind the *orchēstra*. This was used as a changing-room for actors and as a sounding board, but also served to represent the palace or house in front of which most plays are set. There seems to be no reference to it in the three earliest surviving plays, AESCHYLUS' *Persians*, *Seven against Thebes* and *Suppliants*, but it certainly existed by 458, the date of his *Oresteia*, in which it is very prominently used. It may at first have been a temporary building re-erected each year (*skēnē* means merely 'tent' or 'hut'). The number of doors in its façade is disputed; most tragedies require only one, but some of ARISTOPHANES' plays could more easily be performed with more, and it is likely that there were in fact three. Actors and choruses could also enter by paths, called *parodoi* or *eisodoi*, to right and left of the *skēnē*. Occasionally they did so on horse-drawn chariots, chiefly in Aeschylus (*Persae* 155, *Agamemnon* 783). The roof of the building could be used as an acting area; a Watchman is seen there at the beginning of *Agamemnon*, and it was probably there that gods entered when they appeared to mortal characters. It is possible that there was some sort of underground passage, allowing ghosts to appear from below, but this is uncertain.

There has been much dispute as to the existence of a stage (*logeion*) in front of the *skēnē*, raising the actors above the floor of the *orchēstra* where the Chorus per-formed. The evidence is sparse, but it is probable that this stage existed, although it will not have been so high as to prevent easy interaction between actors and Chorus. Other features of the *orchēstra* were a central altar and several images of gods, which could be noticed in the plays when required.

A sentence in ARISTOTLE connects painting of the *skēnē* with SOPHOCLES, while VITRUVIUS attributes it to the painter Agatharchus working for Aeschylus. If these traditions are of any value, they must refer to permanent painting, perhaps with *trompe-l'oeil* architectural effects, and not to sets for individual plays, which seem not to have existed even at later periods.

Various items of stage machinery are mentioned by late authors, but the only devices for which there is 5th-century evidence are the *ekkyklema* and the *mēchanē*. The former was a low platform on wheels, which could be pushed into view to reveal, in the form of a tableau, the consequences of events (normally killings) within the palace. It is a quite artificial device, but it seems to be an accepted convention as early as the *Oresteia*, which contains striking tableaux of Clytemnestra with the bodies of Agamemnon and Cassandra (*Agamemnon* 1372ff.) and of Orestes with the bodies of Clytemnestra and Aegisthus (*Choephori* 973ff.). Thereafter it is used in many tragedies and in comic parodies of tragedy.

The *mēchanē* was a kind of crane which could transport an actor through the air to give an effect of flying. It seems to be little used in surviving tragedy, though there are probable instances in the anonymous *Prometheus Bound* (284ff.) and *Rhesus* (885ff.), as well as in Aristophanes (e.g. Trygaeus' beetle at *Peace* 1ff.). Fifth-century tragedians probably did not use it for epiphanies of gods, though the 'god from the machine' (*deus ex machina*) became proverbial at an early date.

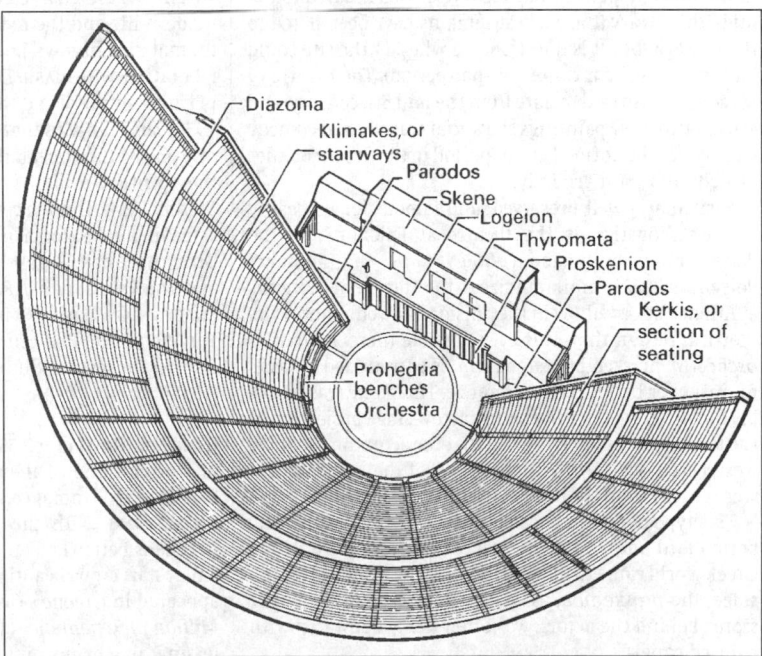

Diazoma
Klimakes, or stairways
Parodos
Skene
Logeion
Thyromata
Proskenion
Parodos
Kerkis, or section of seating
Prohedria benches
Orchestra

The theatre of Epidaurus, c.300 BC.

There are places in tragedy where more elaborate mechanical devices might seem to be needed – for instance, to represent the cataclysm at the end of *Prometheus Bound*, or the burning of Troy at the end of EURIPIDES' *Trojan Women*, or the collapse of the palace at Euripides' *Bacchae* 585ff. But it is far more likely that all these effects were left to the audience's imagination.

The only lighting was that provided by the sun. This cannot have been particularly good, as the theatre was oriented so that the central part of the audience faced south, and for much of the time the performers must have been lit from the back or overshadowed by the *skēnē*.

In the mid-5th century, at the instigation of the statesman Pericles, the Odeum, a square, roofed building for musical recitals, was built beside the theatre. Rather later (perhaps not until the 4th century) a long stone portico was built along the south side of the theatre, and the wooden *skēnē*, now at least 100 feet in length, backed directly on to this. Italian vase paintings of the 4th century show dramatic scenes played in and around porches or booths, consisting of a roof on narrow columns; such structures may or may not have existed in Athens. Around 330 the theatre was largely rebuilt in stone by the statesman Lycurgus; thrones were provided for priests and officials in the front row of the audience, and the ends of the stone *skēnē* were now equipped with forward-projecting wings, *paraskēnia*.

The lower rows of seats surrounded the *orchēstra* in approximately a semicircle, and further rows extended up the slope of the Acropolis behind. The capacity of the theatre has been calculated at a theoretical maximum of some 17,000, but this figure may not have been reached in practice.

Meanwhile drama spread rapidly outside Athens. The oldest theatre to survive in approximately its original form is a small one at Thoricus in Attica, with an *orchēstra* in the form of an irregular rectangle. This is dated to the mid-5th century (the earliest remains have been dated to the late 6th, but it is questionable whether the site could have been used for drama at that period). The theatre of Syracuse is also said to date from the mid-5th century, and 4th-century vase paintings show that tragedy and comedy were widely performed at this period in the Greek colonies of Sicily and southern Italy.

Particularly well preserved, and famous for its beauty and its acoustics, is the theatre at Epidaurus in the Peloponnese, built about 300 BC by the architect Polyclitus. This is similar in size to the Theatre of Dionysus at Athens, but a hollow in the hillside allowed a more symmetrical design than was ever possible there. A circular *orchēstra*, marked by a stone rim, is surrounded by seats for just over half its circumference. The *skēnē* was probably of two storeys, with a long, narrow stage projecting at the level of the upper storey, so that the actors on the stage were better seen by the upper rows of the audience but were cut off from the Chorus in the *orchēstra*.

This type of design became standard in the Hellenistic period (3rd and 2nd centuries), when every town in the Greek world came to have its theatre. The front wall of the stage, the *proskēnion*, as well as the façade of the upper storey behind the actors, was often richly decorated with painted panels. ALB

See: M. Bieber, *The History of the Greek and Roman Theater*, 2nd edn, Princeton, 1961; A. W. Pickard-Cambridge, *The Theatre of Dionysus in Athens*, Oxford, 1946; E. Simon, *The Ancient Theatre*, tr. C. E. Vafopoulou-Richardson, London, 1982.

Green, Adolph see COMDEN, BETTY

Green, Paul 1894–1981 American playwright. A student of Frederick Koch at the University of North Carolina, Green was taught that he should write about the life he knew – the South, its people and its religion. In *The Last of the Lowries* (1920) he re-created the rhythmic language of the Black and simple Southern folk characteristics. His best play, *In Abraham's Bosom* (1926), portrays the tragedy of a Black idealist, defeated by his own limitations and by the people he wants to help. In both *The Field God* (1927), showing the spiritual disintegration of a man condemned by the religiosity he rejected, and *Shroud My Body Down* (1934), he dramatized the fascination and violence of religious mania. A liberal and intelligent man of strong opinions, Green broadened his involvement with human protests in *Hymn to the Rising Sun* (1936), a condemnation of the chain-gang system, and *Johnny Johnson* (1936), in which he satirized warmongers through a hero who is confined by society for having 'peace monomania'. With *The Lost Colony* (1937), a symphonic drama about Sir Walter Raleigh's colony, Green found a new expression. After the Second World War, he continued to celebrate American history through such pageants as *The Common Glory* (1947), on the efforts of Jefferson during the Revolution; *The Founders* (1957), the story of the Jamestown colony; and *Cross and Sword* (1965). His letters were published in 1994. WJM

Greene, Graham 1904–91 British novelist and playwright, whose characteristic theme is the emptiness of modern life and the rediscovery of religious belief. After dramatizing his own novel *The Heart of the Matter* in collaboration with BASIL DEAN (1950), he wrote a series of plays on adultery and the loss of faith (*The Living Room*, 1953; *The Complaisant Lover*, 1959), on the effect of a miracle on an atheistic family (*The Potting Shed*, 1957) and on the spiritual pride of an untalented artist (*Carving a Statue*, 1964). Though conventional in form, these offered satisfying roles for a number of leading performers – DOROTHY TUTIN, RALPH RICHARDSON and JOHN GIELGUD – and *The Return of A. J. Raffles* was produced by the ROYAL SHAKESPEARE COMPANY in 1975. His plays *Yes and No* and *For Whom the Bell Chimes* were staged in 1980, and he also wrote several film scripts, notably *The Third Man* (1948). CI

Greene, Robert c.1558–92 English pamphleteer and playwright, one of the most voluble of the UNIVERSITY WITS. His romance, *Pandosto* (1588), provided SHAKESPEARE with the plot of *The Winter's Tale*, but Greene is better known for his attack on Shakespeare as 'an upstart crow, beautified with our feathers'. The attack appeared in *Greene's Groatsworth of Wit, Bought with a Million of Repentance* (1592), a death-bed pamphlet confessing and bemoaning his dissipated life. Of the five extant plays ascribed to him, the best is the COMEDY *Friar Bacon and Friar Bungay* (c.1589), a light-hearted treatment of the experiments with magic conducted by two 13th-century Oxford Franciscans. *James IV* (c.1591) combines Scottish history and fairy romance. *A Looking-Glass for London and England* (c.1590), written with Thomas Lodge, is a satirical dramatic treatment of material handled with more confidence in Greene's pamphlets. PT

Greenland Theatre is deeply rooted in the Inuit culture. Drama has always been an important vehicle of entertainment, celebration and communication. During folk festivities songs were used partly as community singing, partly performed solo, and created by the singers themselves. The songs were accompanied by movement, dancing, highly developed gestures and MIME. In various RITUALS and other activities performance skills were called upon. The SHAMAN – Angakoq – maintained his confidence by spiritual songs, expressed in the special language which urges and conjures the helping spirits of the shaman. Grave disagreements and disputes were settled by a unique kind of dueldrum-dancing and singing created by the disputants themselves for their defence, expressing their opinion of the conflict and at the same time trying to ridicule their opponents. The contestant who most convinced the audience won the case.

The wonders of life were praised by singing: a child's birth, and special events in the child's life, would be marked by a song composed by his or her 'special protector' – perhaps the grandmother. Likewise, the death of a loved one would be mourned in elegies of sorrow.

In these various ways drama was used in the culture of the Inuit people. Christian missionaries found such habits of spontaneity heathen and not suited for their congregation; they fought them to such a degree that the last representatives of these cultures had to perform their arts secretly.

During the 1930s a new kind of drama was introduced into Greenland. Some younger poets began writing plays in accordance with the European tradition – plays which became extremely popular with audiences, performed by amateur actors. Authors such as Pavia Petersen, Hans Lynge and Karl Heilmann are especially remembered for their works. During the following 20 to 30 years theatrical performances were strongly re-established, with successful plays such as Jorgen Pjettursson's *Itersamit qaqivoq* (*Out from the Deep*). Today professional theatre is established in Greenland. The first professional actors were trained in Denmark with the TUKAK (or Tuukkaq) TEATRET, which worked on ancient Inuit legends and myths and developed a strongly non-verbal approach. Many of the actors from that theatre have returned to Greenland. In the main town, Nuuk, they have formed the company Silamuit, which enjoys great success. JP

Greet, Ben [Philip Barling] 1857–1936 British actor-manager. Greet founded his own touring company in 1886 after playing in the provinces with Sarah Thorne and in London at the LYCEUM under LAWRENCE BARRETT. Best known for his open-air performances of SHAKESPEARE, particularly of *A Midsummer Night's Dream*, he followed WILLIAM POEL – with whom he had co-produced the 1902

revival of *Everyman* – in returning to the simplified staging techniques of the Elizabethan theatre. He toured widely in America and mounted a season at the New York Garden Theatre in 1910, before returning to London to become one of the leading directors at the OLD VIC, where he directed 24 Shakespeare plays between 1915 and 1918. Knighted in 1929, in 1930 he re-opened the Oxford Repertory Company (which had closed after the departure of J. B. FAGAN). CI

Gregory, Andre ?1934– American director, actor and producer, identified with the 1960s avant-garde. From producing OFF-BROADWAY (1959), Gregory directed at the Writer's Stage (1962), then founded the Manhattan Project, an environmental theatre group that adapted performance spaces to suit each script. He became famous overnight with the success of the company's *Alice in Wonderland* (1970) and *Endgame* (1973). JOSEPH PAPP presented the company at the PUBLIC THEATER in [The] *Seagull* (1975) and *Jinx Bridge* (1976). Always controversial, the Manhattan Project's six actors performed in an eccentric style with words articulated in a strange and often comic manner, and gestures exaggerated as they played the subtext more often than the text. CLIVE BARNES praised Gregory's work, but WALTER KERR dismissed the company as 'self-indulgent, slovenly in speech, and childish in antics'. Gregory's acting has included *Rumors* on BROADWAY (1988) and Prospero in *The Tempest* (1989–90) for Shakespeare & Company (Berkshires and Boston). He starred in the film *My Dinner with Andre* (1982) with Wallace Shawn, and has appeared subsequently in such offbeat films as *Protocol* (1984), *The Mosquito Coast* (1986) and *Street Smart* (1987). His staging of *Uncle Vanya* was recently filmed as in rehearsal by Louis Malle (1994). TLM

Gregory, Lady **Augusta (Isabella)** 1852–1932 Irish playwright and director. A staunch nationalist, Lady Gregory made three major contributions to the Irish dramatic movement: her organizational capacity, her personality and her writing.

From the founding of the Irish Literary, later the ABBEY, Theatre, she secured financial and political support from influential friends, gave the ideals of YEATS and Edward Martyn a local habitation and a name, and provided administrative stability. Her own writings – translations of Irish heroic literature, collections of folk tales, as well as comedies, tragedies and folk plays – were mostly rendered in Kiltartan Hiberno-English dialect and provided material and inspiration for many fellow writers. Yeats's Cuchulain plays drew on her *Cuchulain of Murtheimne* and she co-wrote, even ghosted, several of his early plays; SYNGE's use of dialect and LENNOX ROBINSON's interest in local, rural life were strongly influenced by her work. Along with the incalculable encouragement and support she gave to writers like Synge and O'CASEY, she gave the Abbey several of its most successful pot-boilers, some of which, like *The Workhouse Ward, Spreading the News* and *The Rising of the Moon*, continue to be revived regularly. DM GF

Gregory, Johann (Gottfried) 1631–75 Lutheran minister, born in Germany and practising in Moscow from

1662, who, at the behest of Tsar Aleksei Mikhailovich, founded and directed the first official court theatre in Russia (4 June 1672). A special wooden theatre was erected, an acting company of 64 (mostly the sons of German merchants) was trained, and a selection of plays on biblical themes (Esther, Judith) and adapted from English sources (MARLOWE) was drawn from the German dramatic repertory. Scenic, costume and musical effects were elaborate for their day, including perspective painting by the Dutch designer Engels (see THEATRE DESIGN). Attempts to educate the sons of Russian merchants as actors proved less successful, as did the theatre's general operation following Gregory's death, under former assistant George Huebner and later Latin teacher Stefan Chizhinsky. The Tsar's death in 1676 ended this theatre's brief career. SG

Grenfell, Joyce [Joyce Irene Phipps] 1910–79 British actress, who first made her name in intimate REVUE. She had entertained her friends privately with gently satiric sketches and monologues, which revealed her gifts for sharp observation and telling mimicry. Her first professional stage appearance, in *The Little Revue* (1939), was successful; and throughout the war she broadcast and toured, becoming one of Britain's best-loved comediennes. She appeared in NOËL COWARD's revue, *Sigh No More* (1945), in *Tuppence Coloured* (1947), in *Penny Plain* (1951) and in her one-woman show, *Joyce Grenfell Requests the Pleasure*, which went to New York in 1955. Her one-woman sketches were similar to those of the American actress RUTH DRAPER, and if Draper possessed a greater dramatic range, then Grenfell undoubtedly enjoyed the sharper comic instinct and, unlike Draper, was successful within a team. She was a memorable Gossage, the gawky games mistress, in the film version of John Dighton's *The Happiest Days of Your Life*. She could sing in a wistful, appealing soprano songs of her own devising, and was the author of three books: *Nanny Says* (with Sir Hugh Casson; 1972); an autobiography, *Joyce Grenfell Requests the Pleasure* (1976); and *George, Don't Do That* (1977). In 1988, a compilation of her songs and sketches was presented with great success by the actress MAUREEN LIPMAN, under the title *Re-Joyce*. JE

Griboedov, Aleksandr (Sergeevich) 1794–1829 Dramatist, diplomat and founding father of Russian stage REALISM. Interested in the theatre from his youth, Griboedov wrote and collaborated on a series of largely undistinguished adaptations of and variants on French comedies, while advancing from doctoral studies at Moscow University to a career in the Foreign Service. His early plays include *The Young Marrieds* (1815), an adaptation of Creuzé de Lesser's *Le Secret du Ménage* (*All in the Family; or, The Married Fiancée*; 1818), his best play of the group; *Feigned Infidelity* (1818), a translation of Nicolas Berthe's *Les Fausses Infidélités* (*The Student*; written 1817, produced 1904); and *Who's the Brother, Who's the Sister?, or, Deception for Deception*, the libretto of a *vaudeville* OPERA, co-written with Prince Peter Viazemsky (1823), among others.

Griboedov's reputation as a dramatist is based upon the verse COMEDY *Woe to Wit* (1824), the first truly classic Russian play. An indictment of Tsarist society etched in irony and melancholia, it is at once a romantic comedy of manners, psychological *comédie de caractère à la* MOLIÈRE, 'spiritual drama' of disaffected, revolutionary youth, progressive and grotesque sociopolitical SATIRE and *drame à clef*. Chatsky, the Byronic-Hamlet-Alceste-type protagonist, is both a positive variant of the generally parodistic neo-*philosophe* character type and the ambivalent thematic core of the play. His relationship with Sofiya, daughter of the ridiculous conservative government official Famusov (a starring vehicle for SHCHEPKIN and STANISLAVSKY), forms one half of the play's double intrigue. The second is Chatsky's disenchantment with and eventual fierce rejection of contemporary Russia's conservatism and Gallomania. Despite the play's pointed-

The Dining Room scene, from Griboedov's *Woe to Wit*, 1928.

ness of theme and characterization, Griboedov largely eschewed the didacticism and moralizing of contemporaries like PRINCE SHAKHOVSKOI, with whom and under whose influence he wrote some of his early works.

Technically, he improved upon the French models of *haute comédie* as well as on the Russian models of FONVIZIN, employing dialogue and action to advance character and Russian phraseology to texture witty verse form. The play's evocation of anti-government secret societies, especially the Decembrists with whom Griboedov was associated, earned its banning and underground celebrity prior to 1831. In the years following the 1917 Revolution Lenin and LUNACHARSKY characterized the enemies of the proletariat with images drawn from this play, and declared it to be one of the earliest 'people's creations'. MEYERHOLD staged a memorable production at his theatre in 1928. GEORGY TOVSTONOGOV mounted a famous production of the play at Leningrad's Gorky Theatre (1962), with Sergei Yursky as Chatsky.

Dispatched to Teheran as Russian ambassador in 1829, Griboedov was literally torn apart by a mob incensed by the harsh terms of a treaty which he had negotiated in order to end recent Russo-Persian hostilities. SG

Grieg, Nordahl 1902–43 Norwegian poet and playwright, instrumental in the introduction of modernism in Norwegian theatre. Educated partly at Oxford, Grieg was a journalist in China before turning to playwriting with *A Young Man's Love* (1927). His mature (and extremely controversial) plays – *Our Power and Our Glory* (1935), *But Tomorrow!* (1936) and *The Defeat* (1937) – reveal his admiration for Soviet theatre techniques (studied during a visit in 1932–4), his anti-Fascism and his belief that theatre must activate the spectator. During the German occupation, Grieg was close to the Free Norwegian government in London and died as an observer on a bombing raid over Berlin. HL

Grieve, John Henderson 1770–1845 The first of a notable English family of scene-painters, long associated with COVENT GARDEN. He was one of the major contributors to the vogue for picturesque SHAKESPEARE productions, encouraged under the management of JOHN PHILIP KEMBLE. Grieve was joined at Covent Garden by his sons Thomas (1799–1882) and William (1800–44). They were superior artisans, adept at adding to their moody landscapes slight antiquarian touches to gratify scholarly members of the audience. Like CLARKSON STANFIELD, they were quick to exploit the theatrical potential of the moving diorama, making them a feature of the annual Covent Garden PANTOMIME after the sensational success of their 1820 'seacrossing from Wales to Ireland'. Only William Grieve and Thomas's son, Thomas Walford Grieve (1841–82), showed any evidence of an individual talent to rival Stanfield's. Particularly admired for his command of moonlight, William was called for by the audience after the first performance of Meyerbeer's *Robert le Diable* at Covent Garden in 1832. In the last years of his life, he deserted the family to work at DRURY LANE. Over 700 designs by members of the Grieve family have survived, but so few are identified that it is difficult to distinguish the work of the individual members. PT

Griffiths, Trevor 1935– British dramatist, whose debate plays for stage and television reveal his training in Marxist dialectic. His first major play, *Occupations* (1970), was tried out at a Manchester FRINGE club, before the ROYAL SHAKESPEARE COMPANY brought it to London. It concerned the 1920 Fiat motor strike in Italy and the contrasting ideologies of the Marxist theorist ANTONIO GRAMSCI and the Soviet agent Kabak. *Sam, Sam* (1972) describes the careers of two brothers, one who stays happily loyal to his roots and the other who becomes a member of the new bourgeoisie. *Comedians* (1975) is a study of the social and class implications of popular comedy, set in a night school for would-be stand-up comics run by an ageing professional, Eddie Waters. In 1973 the NATIONAL THEATRE produced *The Party*, an analysis of why the events of May 1968 found so little response in Britain, which featured LAURENCE OLIVIER as Tagg, a Glaswegian Trotskyite. Griffiths has written for films and television, including the TV series *Bill Brand* (1976) and *Fatherland* (1986); and he has turned his hand to stage directing (*Saint Oscar*, 1990). He adapted a film script based on a CHEKHOV short story, *Piano* (1990), for the National Theatre; and in 1992 his most ambitious stage play for some years, *The Gulf between Us*, was produced at the West Yorkshire Playhouse in Leeds – a study of the Gulf War, in which he attempts to present it from the Arab point of view. IRVING WARDLE once described Griffiths as '[Britain's] most politically literate playwright since SHAW', but like Shaw, he is more literate at reading the left side of the argument than the right. The 1980s were cruel to the politically committed writers of the 1970s. *Thatcher's Children* (1993) brought together the life stories of seven members of sample ethnic groups in which they all express a similar frustration at their futures. The somewhat predictable message was that Mrs Thatcher had removed Hope from Britain, and the play ends with one actor attempting to foresee the next century through a virtual-reality machine. JE

Grillparzer, Franz 1791–1872 Austrian dramatist. The eclecticism of Grillparzer's work is typical of the variety of his country's dramatic tradition. His first success was a grim SCHICKSALTRAGÖDIE, *The Ancestress* (1817), but it is a measure of his talent that he did not repeat himself. His next play, *Sappho* (1819), was a classical tragedy on the irreconcilability of art and life, a work that earned him the position of house dramatist at the BURGTHEATER. Until 1838, Grillparzer wrote plays of a diverse nature. *The Golden Fleece* (1821), a mighty trilogy about Medea and Jason, contains a study of male–female relationships that, it might be argued, foreshadows the work of IBSEN. The last play of the trilogy, *Medea*, equals in power the Euripidean original (see EURIPIDES). *Waves of the Sea and Love* (1829) has a classical setting, as it is a dramatization of the story of Hero and Leander. Grillparzer was also noted for his historical tragedy *King Ottokar's Rise and Fall* (1823), while his play *A True Servant to His Master* (1826) owes much to the work of LOPE DE VEGA. Calderonian drama (see CALDERÓN DE LA BARCA) in an unlikely combination with the Viennese VOLKSSTÜCK inspired the most popular of his work with his contemporaries, *A Dream of Life* (1832). As a result of the failure of

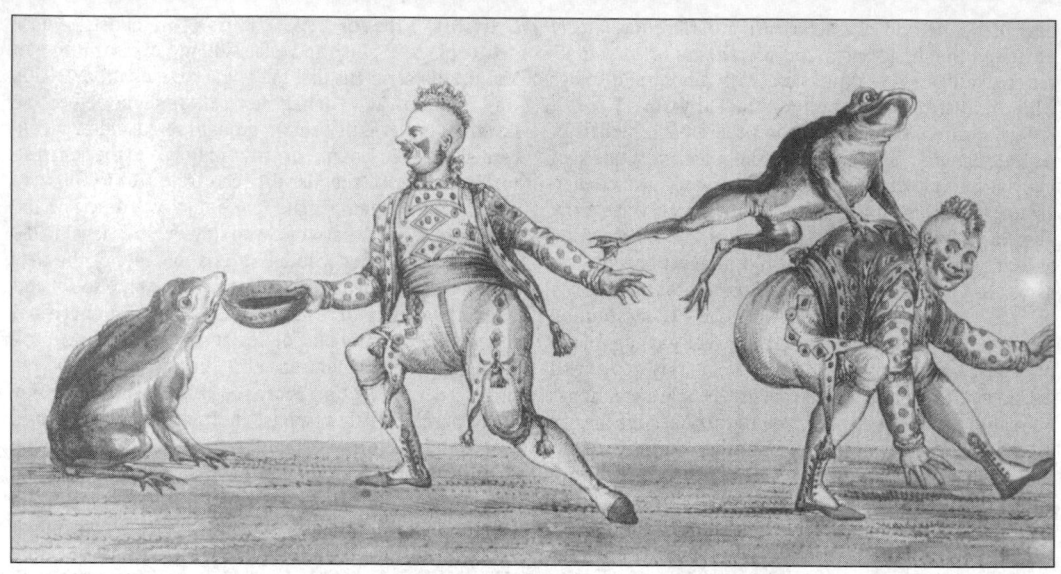

Grimaldi as Clown in *Harlequin and the Golden Fish*, feeding and playing leapfrog with a giant frog.

his comedy *Woe to Him Who Lies!*(1838), Grillparzer withdrew from writing for the public stage. His later works, *Family Strife among the Habsburgs*, *The Jewess of Toledo* and *Libussa*, were only performed after his death.

Although Grillparzer's plays incorporate wide-ranging political and social themes and, in *Libussa*, deal with the whole development of human civilization, their strength derives from their author's acute knowledge of human relations, especially in the sphere of sexuality. This was partially the result of his tormented private life: he could never find the fulfilment in love he was constantly searching for. His personal unhappiness was aggravated by the necessity for him to spend most of his life working in the Austrian civil service. Nevertheless, on his death he was publicly recognized as the pre-eminent dramatist of his country, and is still regarded as such today.   SW

Grimaldi, Joseph 1778–1837 'King of CLOWNS', grandson of the Italian dancer John Baptist 'Iron Legs' Grimaldi, known as Nicolini (fl.1740–2), and illegitimate London-born son of Giuseppe (?1710–88), a dancer and Pantaloon, noted for his agility and bad manners. He made his debut at SADLER'S WELLS or DRURY LANE at the age of four, and played sprites and fairies throughout childhood. Awkward in drama, he gravitated to PANTOMIME and first won acclaim as Clown in DIBDIN's *Peter Wilkins, or Harlequin in the Flying World* (Sadler's Wells, 1800), when he wore a costume more extravagant and particoloured than usual and changed the standard ruddy complexion for a white face with two red half-moons on the cheeks. His great success came in *Harlequin Mother Goose, or The Golden Egg* (COVENT GARDEN, 1806; much revived).

Grimaldi's clown was a greedy, amoral schoolboy, out to satisfy his appetites; his exuberant optimism was that of the survivor, and the fun derived from the overthrow of everyday inhibitions. His entering cry of 'Here we are again!', his songs 'Hot Codlins' and 'Tippitiwitchet' shared

with the audience, his tricks of construction, assembling 'living' creatures from assorted props, and, especially, his thieving, gluttony and violence, stealing sausages and attacking watchmen and police with a red-hot poker, became hallmarks of the panto clown or Joey. Lord High Chancellor Eldon himself exclaimed, 'Never, never did I see a leg of mutton stolen with such superhumanly sublime impudence as by that man.' Over-exertion rendered Grimaldi virtually crippled by 1823, and he gave two farewell performances, at Sadler's Wells and Drury Lane, in 1828. His son Joseph (1802–32) in whom he invested much hope of succession died of alcoholism, and the clown's last days were, as he described them, 'grim-all-day'. His *Memoirs* were edited, somewhat half-heartedly, by CHARLES DICKENS in 1838; his grave in Pentonville, London, is annually commemorated by a conventicle of clowns.   LS

Grock [Charles Adrien Wettach] 1880–1959 Swiss clown. He began as his father's partner in CABARET, and after 14 years as an acrobat took the name Grock when part of a musical-CLOWN tour of Europe and South America in 1903. Originally he played the dumb August to such white clowns as Antonet (Umberto Guillaume), but seldom got on with his partners, so he developed a solo act which gradually stretched to a half-hour. A virtuoso on 13 instruments, Grock in his routine demonstrated his inability to play properly on anything: concertinas, miniature fiddles, grand pianos – all turned into instruments of mental anguish in his hands. Combining the elegance of the white clown with the crude childishness of the August, he made his sketches parables of the malice of inanimate objects and human fecklessness. Personally pedantic and financially astute, on stage he tinged the hilarity with melancholy. His trademarks were an oversized coat, an egg-bald pate, a simian countenance, and frequent cries of (in France) 'Sans blague!', (in Germany) 'Nit mööööglich!'

and (in England) simply 'Oooh!'. He founded his own circus in 1951, retiring three years later. His acts have been preserved on film (1931, 48, 49). LS

Gropius, Walter 1883-1969 German artist and architect. In the 1920s, Gropius founded the Staatliches Bauhaus in Weimar, Germany, a School of Fine Arts and Arts and Crafts which focused on architecture, painting, sculpture, industrial design and theatre (see THEATRE DESIGN). Working with OSKAR SCHLEMMER who was in charge of the theatre workshop, Gropius hoped to fuse art with everyday life. In 1926, he conceived a new type of theatre building which he called the *Totaltheater*. This facility was intended through its design to change the actor–audience relationship, and was going to be used by director ERWIN PISCATOR. Gropius believed that there were only three types of theatrical stage: the thrust, the arena and the proscenium. In his new theatre design all three existed. Elliptically shaped, the 2000-seat arena featured a proscenium stage that was fronted by a circular thrust performing area, which could be rotated to the centre of the auditorium to create a theatre-in-the-round. In addition, the *Totaltheater* was designed to have a domed ceiling on which projections could be shown. This ceiling was supported by 12 pillars between which were additional projection screens. There was also a transluscent cyclorama for projections at the rear of the proscenium stage. When the Nazis came to power, the controversial Bauhaus was disbanded and thus the *Totaltheater* was never built. Nevertheless, its influence can be seen in many subsequent theatres. TM

Gros-Guillaume [Robert Guérin; La Fleur] ?-1634 French actor-manager, particularly celebrated under this guise in FARCE but who played in the remainder of the repertoire as La Fleur. First heard of at the HÔTEL DE BOURGOGNE in 1598, he joined VALLERAN LE CONTE's company there in 1610 and formed his own two years later. After some time in the provinces he returned to Paris as director of the Comédiens du Roi, who from 1622 took out successive leases of the Hôtel de Bourgogne before settling there permanently in 1629. A short, fat man, he accentuated his shape for comic effect by strapping two belts tightly round the midriff to give himself the appearance of a walking barrel; on his head he wore a flat cap askew and a sheepskin chin-strap, while his face, in the French theatrical tradition, was covered with flour, which by moving his agile features he would sprinkle over any actor who accosted him. Thus attired he was a perfect foil to the other popular farce-players with whom he regularly acted in the 1620s and 30s, GAULTIER-GARGUILLE and TURLUPIN, and like them he appeared under his stage name as a character in Gougenot's comedy about a company of actors, *La Comédie des comédiens* (*The Actors' Comedy*, 1631/2). DR

Grosbard, Ulu 1929- Belgian-born director, who emigrated to the USA in 1948 and attended the University of Chicago, Yale School of Drama and ACTORS STUDIO. He began his directing career in 1957, making his New York debut in 1962 with *The Days and Nights of Beebee Fenstermaker* at the Sheridan Square Playhouse. His notable productions since include *The Subject Was Roses* (1964); *A View from the Bridge* (1965); *The Investigation* (1966); *The Price* (1968); *American Buffalo* (1977); *The Wake of Jamie Foster* (1982); *Weekends Like Other People* (1982); and Paddy Chayefsky's *The Tenth Man* (1989 revival at Lincoln Center). Since 1961 he has worked also in films and television. TLM

Grossman, Jan 1925-93 Czech critic, dramaturge and director whose path led from literature to theatre. An assistant to E. F. BURIAN in the early 1950s, he became primarily associated with Prague's Balustrades Theatre in the 1960s as VÁCLAV HAVEL's intimate collaborator (*The Memorandum*, 1965). After 1968, political factors forced Grossman to become an itinerant director, occasionally abroad but chiefly in peripheral Czech theatres where his work developed conceptual and theatrical sophistication. In the late 1980s he was able to return triumphantly to the Balustrades Theatre with outstanding productions of MOLIÈRE's *Don Juan* (1989) and, after the Velvet Revolution, Havel's *Largo Desolato* (1990) and *Temptation* (1992), by which time he had become artistic head of the theatre. Never an overt social critic, Grossman nevertheless imbued his work with implicit questions of contemporary social values and practices, especially in his productions of Havel and works such as JARRY's *Ubu Roi* 1964 and Kafka's *The Trial* 1966. JMB

Grossmith, George [junior] 1874-1935 British actor and co-author of REVUES for London's Empire and GAIETY THEATRES. The son of George Grossmith, who was a regular performer in the Savoy Operas, he introduced the stock figure of the 'dude' to MUSICAL COMEDY, in which he starred between 1893 and 1912. CI

Grotowski, Jerzy 1933- Polish director, teacher and theoretician of the theatre, who since his departure from Poland in 1982 has become permanently located at the University of California in Irvine and at the Centro per la Sperimentazione e la Ricerca Teatrale in Pontedera, Italy. After studying at the State Drama School in Cracow and in Moscow, and directing in Cracow, he established the Theatre of 13 Rows in Opole, where from 1959 to 1964 he staged poetic works played against the texts as arguments with past cultural monuments and designed to transform traditional actor–audience relationships: BYRON's *Cain*, GOETHE's *Faust*, MAYAKOVSKY's *Mystery-Bouffe* and KALIDASA's *Shakuntula* in 1960; MICKIEWICZ's *Forefathers' Eve* in 1961; SŁOWACKI's *Kordian* and WYSPIAŃSKI's *Acropolis* (co-created with JÓZEF SZAJNA) in two versions in 1962; MARLOWE's *Faustus* in 1963; a third variant of *Acropolis* in 1964.

In 1965 he moved the group to Wrocław, adopting the name Laboratory Theatre. There he created a fourth and fifth variant of *Acropolis*, three versions of CALDERÓN's *The Constant Prince* (in Słowacki's translation), and three variants of *Apocalypsis cum figuris*, his final production, which brought to an end the first phase of his work, the Theatre of Performance (1959-69). In this phase Grotowski eliminated from theatre everything but the essential relationship of actor to spectator and developed training techniques stressing gymnastics, ACROBATICS, yoga and

Grotowski's production of *Faust*, Poznan, Poland, 1960.

pantoMIME. In the second phase, the Theatre of Participation (1969–75), Grotowski organized paratheatrical events that broke down barriers between actors and spectators, as both engaged in structured and spontaneous activities in natural surroundings. The third phase, the Theatre of Sources (1976–82), saw Grotowski and members of his circle explore the roots of theatrical experience. Travel to diverse cultures and invitations to native practitioners furthered study of RITUAL performance techniques. The fourth and final phase of Grotowski's work, first Objective Drama in California and then Ritual Arts in Italy (1983 to present), marks a return to the ancient mysteries in which there is no spectator, actor or theatre performance, but only the performer.

Grotowski's productions and theories, his concept of a 'poor theatre' and work on the training of actors have had a profound effect on world theatre. *Towards a Poor Theatre* (1968) is a collection of his seminal theoretical writings. DG

Group Theatre, The (USA) Founded in 1931 by HAROLD CLURMAN, LEE STRASBERG and CHERYL CRAWFORD, the Group was a pioneering attempt to create an American theatre COLLECTIVE, a company of players trained in a unified style and dedicated to presenting new American plays of social significance. With STANISLAVSKY's Moscow ART THEATRE as their model, Group members began a systematic study of an art that had few guidelines and virtually no written record. Prodded by their exacting teacher, Lee Strasberg, and fired by Clurman's messianic fervour, the actors experimented with improvisation, emotional and sensory memories, private moments, and exercises in relaxation and concentration. The inner technique they worked on – which became the basis of the American

Method and which Strasberg continued to develop during his 35 years at the ACTORS STUDIO – resulted in acting that was more natural and earthy, more private, more intense and more psychologically charged than previous styles. Debates over method erupted in the summer of 1934 when Group member STELLA ADLER returned from her studies with Stanislavsky in Paris to announce that the Master had abandoned his earlier emphasis on inner work in favour of a new external technique, the method of physical actions. Adler and Strasberg squared off in a craft war whose wounds have never healed, even after their deaths, Strasberg and his followers continuing to focus on the actor's own emotional resources while Adler and her colleagues have concentrated on the play as opposed to the player.

Among the superb realistic actors the Group helped to develop were John Garfield and Franchot Tone (both of whom defected to films), Margaret Barker, Ruth Nelson, MORRIS CARNOVSKY, Phoebe Brand, Art Smith and SANFORD MEISNER. Decades after the Group disbanded in 1941, Strasberg, Adler, Meisner and Carnovsky continued to be influential teachers, offering their own individual variations of the Method.

Although less successful than its actor-training programme, the Group's literary achievement was also substantial. The Group was not a political theatre and, in fact, was strongly criticized by more militant companies; but over a 10-year period it produced 22 new American plays on subjects of contemporary relevance. If only a few of these – JOHN HOWARD LAWSON's *Success Story* (1932) and CLIFFORD ODETS's *Awake and Sing!* (1935) and *Paradise Lost* (1935) – have enduring literary value, all of the Group's plays rose above the level of propaganda, and in Odets the company yielded an American original. A history appeared in 1990 by Wendy Smith (*Real Life: The Group Theatre and America, 1931–1940*), with another forthcoming by Helen Chinoy.   FH

Group Theatre (London) Founded by Rupert Doone (a choreographer who had danced with Diaghilev's Ballets Russes), together with Ormerod Greenwood and TYRONE GUTHRIE, as an ensemble company dedicated both to the performance of poetic drama and to socialist ideals comparable with those of the Workers' Theatre Movement. Its first successful production was the first revival in over 400 years of the recently discovered INTERLUDE *Fulgens and Lucrece* by HENRY MEDWALL. It provided a stage for *Sweeney Agonistes* (1935) by T. S. ELIOT, who also wrote a choral piece, *The Rock*, in collaboration with its members; and the verse plays of W. H. AUDEN and CHRISTOPHER ISHERWOOD – *The Dog beneath the Skin* (1936), *The Ascent of F6* (1937; re-staged at the Arts Theatre, Cambridge, in 1938 and at the OLD VIC in 1939) and *On the Frontier* (1938) – were written specifically for the Group. Louis MacNeice also provided texts, as did Stephen Spender (*The Trial of a Judge*, 1938), while Benjamin Britten contributed musical scores for many of the productions. It also functioned briefly between 1950 and 1954, presenting the first English production of a SARTRE play, *The Flies* (1951).   CI

Grumberg, Jean-Claude 1939– French actor, director and playwright; outstanding example of a playwright who successfully combined the styles of absurdist theatre and the social concern of the decentralized theatre in the 1970s (see THEATRE OF THE ABSURD; DECENTRALIZATION MOVEMENT). His use of theatre within the theatre (*Dreyfus* directed by Rosner, 1973) and of autobiographical material (*L'Atelier (The Workshop)* directed by Bénichou, Rosner and Grumberg, 1979) shows a craftsmanship similar to that displayed by the young ANOUILH.   DB

Gründgens, Gustaf 1899–1963 German actor and director, whose work epitomized the classical tradition in opposition to the REALISM of STANISLAVSKY. After working with REINHARDT in 1928, Gründgens established his reputation as the leading German actor with his performance of Mephisto in GOETHE's *Faust* in 1932, a role he had played as early as 1922 and which he repeated in his famous 1957 production. Appointed director of the Berlin Staatstheater under the Nazis from 1934 to 1944, he was attacked as a Fascist collaborator in the novel *Mephisto* by Klaus Mann (in whose 1925 play *Anja and Esther* he performed). But his wartime productions of SCHILLER and LESSING had drawn contemporary parallels as an oblique form of political protest – an approach continued when he was artistic director at Düsseldorf in 1947 and Hamburg from 1955, that has had a significant influence – and at BRECHT's request he directed the premiere of *St Joan of the Stockyards* in 1959.   CI

Grundy, Mrs The invention of the playwright THOMAS MORTON, Mrs Grundy is a character who never appears in his popular success *Speed the Plough* (1800), but whose approval is constantly sought and disapproval dreaded by Farmer Ashfield's worthy wife. The original Mrs Grundy is more like the Joneses, with whom the middle classes are constantly trying to keep up, than the ogre of prudish repression she has subsequently become.   PT

Grundy, Sydney 1848–1914 British playwright, born and educated in Manchester, where he was working as a barrister when his first play, *A Little Change* (1872), was staged at London's HAYMARKET. Grundy's normal practice was to adapt, and if necessary clean up, French plays. The bowdlerized and reshaped versions of ALEXANDRE DUMAS *père* – *A Marriage of Convenience* (1897), *The Silver Key* (1897), *The Musketeers* (1898), *The Black Tulip* (1899) – are typical, as is his best-known work, *A Pair of Spectacles* (1890), an adaptation from *Les Petits Oiseaux* by LABICHE and Delacour, which provided JOHN HARE with a popular success as Benjamin Goldfinch. An outspoken opponent of the 'demoralizing' IBSEN, Grundy nevertheless provided LILLIE LANGTRY with a *succès de scandale* in *The Degenerates* (1899), and enjoyed playing with fire in *A Fool's Paradise* (1889), a response to the Maybrick trial, and *Slaves of the Ring* (1894), in which he brushed with the adulterous passion of Tristan and Isolde. In the year of his death, he published an outrageously reactionary booklet, *The Play of the Future: by a Playwright of the Past*.   PT

Gryphius, Andreas 1616–64 German playwright. Although Gryphius's plays were not performed during his lifetime, they are now generally considered to be among the most significant achievements in German drama during the baroque period. His tragedies, classical in style and structure, deal with the sufferings of high-born nobility and royalty, though *Cardenio and Celinde* (1647) is closer to middle-class drama. *Murdered Majesty, or Charles Stuart* (1649) dramatizes, not very effectively, the execution of the English king. Of Gryphius's comedies, *Horribilicribrifax* (1663) and *The Beloved Rose with a Thorn* (1661) are the most refreshing and lively.   SW

Guan Hanqing fl. 13th century Chinese dramatist, regarded as the foremost Yuan dynasty ZAJU playwright. During celebrations of his 700th anniversary in 1958, tribute was paid to his affinity with the everyday life of his times. Of his presumed 63 plays, 18 are extant. *Injustice to Dou E (Dou E yuan)* is frequently performed in China and known in the West in translation. Its theme concerns the tragic fate of a young woman wrongly executed as the victim of false witness and a corrupt official. Her innocence is established by cosmic intervention. The emotional vigour of the characterization and an expressive lyrical style exemplify the formative contribution Guan made to early drama.   ACS

Guare, John 1938– American playwright. Guare's work is characterized by frank theatricality, lyrical quality, autobiographical base and satiric vivacity. Some critics have found his plays too cerebral or abstract, lacking focus, but few have failed to praise his use of language. Recognized first for his one-act play *Muzeeka* (1968), he received wide acclaim for his first full-length play, *The House of Blue Leaves* (1970; revived with critical acclaim in 1986). Since then his major works have included the adaptation and lyrics for *Two Gentlemen of Verona* (1971), *Rich and Famous* (1974), *The Landscape of the Body* (1977) and

Bosoms and Neglect (1979). A notable screenplay, *Atlantic City*, written for Louis Malle's 1981 film, was followed by *Lydie Breeze* and *Gardenia* (1982), two parts of a projected tetralogy set in 19th-century New England. *Women and Water*, chronologically first in this series, was seen in various drafts during 1984-5 in Los Angeles, Chicago and Washington, DC. *Moon over Miami*, originally meant as screenplay for John Belushi, was staged by Yale Rep in 1988. His most successful play to date is *Six Degrees of Separation* (1990), winner of the 1990 Dramatists Guild Hull-Warriner Award (also presented for *Landscape*) and the 1992 Laurence Olivier Award for best play in London, which delves into the vulnerability under New York's brittle surface. *Four Baboons Adoring the Sun* was given a 1992 production directed by PETER HALL at Lincoln Center's VIVIAN BEAUMONT THEATRE. DBW

Guarini, Giovan Battista 1538-1612 Italian poet, critic and dramatist. He obtained a Europeanwide reputation with his most important work, *Il pastor fido* (*The Faithful Shepherd*), written in the early 1580s in imitation of TASSO's PASTORAL play *Aminta*, but seeking to ring changes on that work by exploring the new vein of TRAGI-COMEDY. Guarini's play caught the taste of European courts, and his Preface, in which he set out a defensive theory of the genre against his critics, became widely influential: in England, JOHN FLETCHER's *The Faithful Shepherdess* was a version of the new tragicomic pastoral kind, and Fletcher's Preface, in which he defined tragicomedy as a form that 'wants deaths, but brings some near it', was indebted to Guarini's theory. LR

Guarnieri, Gianfrancesco 1934- Brazilian playwright. Born in Milan, Italy, Guarnieri arrived in Brazil as an infant. From a family of musicians, he became a major influence in the development of Brazilian realistic theatre (see REALISM) during the 1950s. Affiliated with the Arena Theatre in São Paulo as actor and director, he participated in the development of the *Arena Tells...* series (on Zumbi, Bolívar and Tiradentes, amongst others), which depended on concepts of open stage, simple sets, realistic dialogue and close interaction between actor and public. His *Eles não Usam Black-tie* (*They Don't Use Tuxedos*, 1958) became a Brazilian classic for its portrayal of the social problems of the slum areas. His other plays include *Gimba, Presidente dos Valentes* (*Gimba, President of the Brave*, 1959), *Um Grito Parado no Ar* (*A Scream Silenced in Air*, 1973), *Botequim* (*Tavern*, 1973) and *Ponto de Partida* (*Point of Departure*, 1976). Guarnieri has emphasized BRECHTian techniques in portraying the reality of Brazilian political and socio-economic situations with protest against military censorship and economic repression. GW

Guatemala Home of the only authentic pre-Colombian theatre piece, the *RABINAL ACHÍ*. Guatemala is a land rich in Native American tradition and folklore, a land where only about 50 per cent of the present-day population are native speakers of Spanish. As a major capital during the colonial period, Guatemala enjoyed religious presentations on special occasions. One form, the *LOAS del diablo* (*loas* of the devil), with fireworks and devils, is unique to the region. In 1793 the first theatre constructed in the present capital (Antigua was largely destroyed by the 1772 earthquake) was named Camato after its impresario, and designed for comedies. Through the 19th century a moderate level of theatrical activity was recorded. Although no plays of true dramatic value are known, several playwrights were active, especially Tiburcio Estrada (alias Tata Bucho), a talented actor, director, set designer and even ticket seller. The Carrera Theatre, originally built in 1859, became the National Theatre in 1871 and was renamed the Colon Theatre in 1892, on the 400th anniversary of discovery. Various travelling companies brought OPERAS, OPERETTAS and ZARZUELAS to Guatemala.

The 20th century The visiting troupes of the early part of the century (María Guerrero and her husband Fernando Díaz de Mendoza from Spain; Virginia Fábregas of Mexico, and others) helped inspire the formation of local groups: the National Artistic group (1912, renamed Renaissance in 1918), and Salomé Gill (1930). During these years the theatre provided light comedy or classical plays. Social and political criticism was inadmissible (see CENSORSHIP), especially during the Ubico dictatorship (1931-44). Rafael Arévalo Martínez (1884-1970) and Adolfo Drago Bracco (1894-1965) formed Tepeus in 1930 and wrote vanguardist Italian-style mechanistic plays, but the dominant pattern was costumbristic (see *COSTUMBRISMO*) with social criticism, and generally isolated from the main currents of North American and European theatre.

After the Ubico regime the Guatemalan theatre gained new strength in the October Revolution of 1944, responding to international theatre styles while often conserving elements of its rich folklore. New groups were created (Guatemalan Art Theatre and University Art Theatre, to name only two), and the Guatemalan theatre festivals sponsored by the Popular University annually since 1962 have promoted new authors. Two of Guatemala's major playwrights, CARLOS SOLÓRZANO and MANUEL GALICH, made their reputation in exile. A new generation of directors, actors and designers – some formed by Chilean director and actor Domingo Tessier, who established the National Theatre School in the university's Department of Fine Arts in 1957 – have struggled against repression and political and economic upheavals to keep the theatre alive. Principal playwrights are HUGO CARRILLO, MANUEL JOSÉ ARCE and LIGIA BERNAL, who in 1959 opened the first Young Playwrights Season with their plays *Green Sex Street*, *Stone in the Well* and *Orestes and the Apostle*, respectively, and defined the new profile of contemporary Guatemalan theatre.

When the government of President Vinicio Cerezo Arévalo opened the Ministry of Culture in 1985, it encouraged growth in the theatre. A few permanent groups now work year round in Guatemala City with performances at weekends. Some later present their works in the interior. Some, such as the Teatro Club and Grupo Diez, are independent. The annual theatre festivals do not attract the most representative works of the mainline authors nor the most transcendental works of the younger authors, according to Hugo Carrillo. GW

See: M. A. Carrera, *Ideas políticas en el teatro de Manuel Galich*, Guatemala, 1982.

Guignol MARIONETTE of the Lyons puppet theatre, presumably invented by the puppeteer Laurent Mourguet (1745–1844). Distinguished by a sharply satirical tongue and an earthy use of the vernacular, Guignol, costumed as a Lyons silk-weaver, was forbidden to improvise by the police of the Second Empire, became a parodist of opera, and eventually supplanted Polichinelle. The term *guignol* is now generic for any French PUNCH and Judy show. LS

Guilbert, Yvette [Emma Laure Esther Guilbert] 1865–1944 French song-stylist and *diseuse*, whose mordant attitude and clipped pronunciation revolutionized CABARET singing. She first appeared at the Théâtre des Variétés, Paris, 1889, and after various MUSIC-HALL engagements became a star in 1892 at the Divan Japonais and the MOULIN-ROUGE, singing verses by ARISTIDE BRUANT and Léon Xanrof. Her gaunt figure, long nose and neck, mop of red hair and invariable black gloves contrasted with the voluptuousness of her competition and were celebrated by Toulouse-Lautrec. According to Moeller van den Broeck, she had three styles: the lyrical, gruesome and coquettish. After 1901 she developed a fresh repertory of old French and English songs, religious and secular; made frequent appearances in REVUE and theatre (Mrs Peachum in the French *Threepenny Opera*, 1937); and in 1920 founded a school in New York. Her *How to Sing a Song* (1918) was the first textbook on the subject. LS

Guimerà, Angel 1845–1924 Spanish playwright and poet responsible for the development of modern CATALAN THEATRE. Influenced by SHAKESPEARE and HUGO, he began writing historical plays in verse before shifting to realistic theatre. He achieved international fame for his rural dramas of love and revenge. *María Rosa* (1894) was adapted to film by Cecil B. de Mille. His masterpiece, *Terra baixa* (*Marta of the Lowlands*, 1897), was translated into Castilian Spanish by ECHEGARAY, performed throughout the world, made into OPERAS in Germany and Belgium and into films in five different countries. He experimented with SYMBOLISM and ultimately turned again to historical drama. PZ

Guinea Of all the French-speaking countries in Africa, Guinea had the most tumultuous relations with France. It became a French colony in 1890 and remained so until 2 October 1958, when independence was thrust upon it after it voted 'no', in a historic referendum, to a French proposal to remain part of a wider French community of African states.

Modern theatrical activity was introduced to Guinea with the advent of colonial rule, but remained modest up to independence. It consisted mostly of performances of French plays from the classical repertory and of historical pieces by former Guinean students of the École William Ponty in SENEGAL, notably *La Rencontre du Capitaine Péroz et de Samory* (*The Encounter between Captain Péroz and Samory*, 1937). A typically Guinean theatrical activity of the period, which emerged in 1948 and was later to flourish, is what its founder Fodéba Keita called the 'theatre-ballet'. His play in this genre, *L'Aube africaine* (*The African Dawn*, 1965), on the shooting by French troops in Thiaroye, Senegal, of protesting, uncompensated Africans who had served in the French army during the Second World War, relates the action in the theatre-ballet tradition of mainly song and dance but also dialogue.

Since independence, theatre in Guinea has progressed. Recognizing its importance as an instrument of mass mobilization and propaganda, the socialist government of Sekou Touré (1958–84) encouraged and directed its growth. Arts festivals and competitions in which theatre played a large part were organized at district, regional and national levels. The local committees of the ruling Parti Démocratique de Guinée were charged with promoting it in their areas: the result was scores of collective productions of a fiercely anti-colonial stance on historical, political and social themes. The best of these, such as *Et la nuit s'illumine* (*And the Night Is Illuminated*, 1967) or *Thiaroye* (1973) from the Labé and Dabola regions, respectively, were performed to wide acclaim, the first at the Pan-African Arts Festival in Algiers in 1969, and the second in the 1977 Lagos Arts Festival.

But Guinean theatrical activity is not limited to plays. It also includes the other performing arts, such as traditional instrumental and choral music and African ballet, which national ballet troupes like the Ballets Africains de la République de Guinée and the highly acclaimed and award-winning Ballet Djoliba were created to promote.

Although almost all Guinean drama consists of unpublished collective productions, a few plays by individual artists have been published: the historical dramas *Continent-Afrique suivi de Amazoulous* (*Continent-Africa, Followed by Amazulus*, 1970) by a former Minister for Scientific Research, Condétto Nénékhaly-Camara, and Djibril Tamsir Niane's *Sikasso ou la dernière citadelle suivi de Chaka* (*Sikasso, or The Last Citadel Followed by Chaka*, 1976). Recent works include two by A.-T. Cissé: *Maudit soit Cham* (*May Cham Be Cursed*, 1982) and *Au nom du peuple* (*In the Name of the People*, 1990). JCM

> *See*: R. Cornevin, *Le Théâtre en Afrique noire et à Madagascar*, Paris, 1970; J. M. Touré, 'Mobiliser, informer, éduquer; un instrument efficace: le théâtre', *Notre Librairie: La Littérature Guinéenne*, 88–9, Jul./Sept. 1987.

Guinea-Bissau See PORTUGUESE-SPEAKING AFRICA

Guinness, Alec 1914– British actor. Guinness's first stage appearance was in 1934, and in 1936 he joined the OLD VIC theatre, playing various classic roles including Aguecheek in *Twelfth Night*. In 1938 he played Hamlet in the Old Vic's innovative modern-dress production, a performance which firmly established his reputation. After war service in the Royal Navy he returned to the theatre, rejoining the Old Vic company and playing a wide variety of modern and classic roles, ranging from Lear's Fool to Klestakov in GOGOL's *The Inspector General*. He also began to direct, with a production of *Twelfth Night* in 1948 and *Hamlet* in 1951, in which he also played the lead. A constantly busy actor, he displayed his range and ingenuity in parts ranging from Macbeth in GASKILL's experimental production for the ROYAL COURT THEATRE (1966) to Dr Wickersteed in *Habeas Corpus* by ALAN BENNETT (1973).

Guinness's film and television career developed alongside his work for the stage. His quizzical features became familiar in films such as *Kind Hearts and Coronets* (1949), *The Lavender Hill Mob* (1951) – the famous postwar Pinewood Studios comedies – and with *The Bridge on the River Kwai* (1957) his international stardom was established. For television (see TELEVISION DRAMA) his roles as a spy-catcher in John Le Carré's *Tinker, Tailor, Soldier, Spy* (1979) and *Smiley's People* (1982) were tailored for his enigmatic presence. He was knighted in 1959.   MB

Guitry, Sacha 1885–1957 French actor and playwright. Son of Lucien-Germain (1860–1925), sometime manager of the Renaissance and himself an actor and playwright, Sacha was a prolific writer predominantly of rather flimsy plays, many of them on vaguely historical themes.   MB

Gunter, Archibald Clavering 1847–1907 British-born playwright and novelist. Educated as a mining engineer in San Francisco, where he wrote his first play, *Found the True Vein* (1872), he moved to New York in 1879. During the next decade he wrote a number of moderately successful plays showing a broad Western influence upon his creativity: *Courage* (1883), with Effie Ellsler; *Prince Karl* (1886), RICHARD MANSFIELD's first starring role; *Two Nights in Rome* (1886); *The Deacon's Daughter* (1887); and *One against Many* (1887). In 1888 he dramatized his successful novel, *Mr Barnes of New York* (1887), the adventures of a rich, imprudent American, and thereafter mainly wrote fiction.   WJM

Gunter, John 1938– British stage designer, who worked for years on the Continent and in English REGIONAL THE-ATRE before establishing himself as a successful realistic designer at London's ROYAL COURT THEATRE in the late 1960s. Since then his work has been seen at both the Royal Shakespeare Theatre and, especially in recent years, at the NATIONAL THEATRE, in addition to productions in the WEST END and abroad. From 1974 to 1982 Gunter served as head of the THEATRE DESIGN programme at London's Central School, his own *alma mater*, and in 1988–90 he was head of design at the National Theatre. Based on painstakingly selective detail, his work has lately exhibited more conscious theatricality and metaphoric imagery. Outstanding productions have included *Guys and Dolls* (1982), *The Government Inspector* (1985), *Hamlet* (1989), *School for Scandal* (1990) and *Gift of the Gorgon* (1992).   JMB

Guo Moruo 1892–1978 Chinese dramatist, poet and historian from Sichuan province. In 1921 he was among the leaders of the Creation Society, spawned by the May 4th Movement of 1919. He lived in Japan as a student 1923–6 and again 1928–37. He played a prominent role in the resistance in Shanghai during the Second World War. Under the PRC he was given numerous government and cultural posts and was one of the very few artists and intellectuals to remain in favour during the decade of the Cultural Revolution.

A strong fighter for women's rights, this issue dominates much of his prodigious literary output. Among his early spoken dramas (written in 1923), *Wang Zhaojun* and *Zhuo Wenjun*, named after their respective heroines, present intelligent and defiant historical women of the distant past, whom Guo intended as positive models for his own times. In his last play, produced in 1962, *Wu Zetian*, the title role is the only woman in Chinese history ever to become emperor (r.684–705). The play praises both her and the concept that women should occupy high political positions. One of Guo's most productive periods was during the war against Japan. A representative play from those years is *Qu Yuan* (1942), which is about the famous poet of that name of the 3rd and 4th centuries BC and his struggle against tyrannical rulers of his time.   CPM

Gurik, Robert 1932– Quebec playwright and novelist. Born in France, Gurik went to Canada in 1950 and was soon active in amateur theatricals. His first play, *Le Chant du poète* (*Poet's Song*, 1964), attracted only local attention, but *Le Pendu* (*The Hanged Man*, 1967) won the Dominion Drama Festival prize for Best Play, along with general critical acclaim. With *Hamlet, Prince du Québec* (*Hamlet, Prince of Quebec*, 1968), a savage PARODY of the political rivalry between Quebec and Ottawa, Gurik moved towards social issues, a commitment continued in subsequent works, such as *Le Procès de Jean-Baptiste M.* (*The Trial of Jean-Baptiste M.*, 1972) and *La Baie des Jacques* (*Jacques's Bay*, 1976), the latter consciously emulating BERTOLT BRECHT's *Mahagonny* (1927) and depicting the dehumanizing effects of modern industrial development upon the individual.   LED

Gurney, A(lbert) R(amsdell) [Pete], **Jr** 1930– American playwright. The American theatre's John Cheever, Gurney writes feelingly about what he fears is an endangered species: well-to-do, or at least well bred, white Anglo-Saxon Protestants. His wry comedies unfold in a nostalgic haze. Typically, his plays are set in a time and place of poignant transition: at the end of summer, of adolescence, of an era. While his characters reluctantly confront the need for making changes, they also lament the passing of an enclosed and carefully regulated way of life. In one of his best plays, *The Dining Room* (1981), place is more important than any of the rotating cast of characters who pass through it; his dining room is a cultural artifact threatened with extinction, a metaphor for genteel traditions. In *The Middle Ages* (1983), the library of an exclusive club serves a similar thematic purpose. Other deft Gurney works include *Children* (1976), suggested by a Cheever short story, in which a matron chooses duty over pleasure; *What I Did Last Summer* (1982), about a teenager torn between propriety and bohemianism; *The Perfect Party* (1986); *The Cocktail Hour* (1990); *The Snow Ball* (1991); *The Old Boy* (1991); arguably his most successful, *Love Letters* (1989), a two-character play that relates a romance from primary school to middle age and has toured worldwide (1990–3); *The Fourth Wall* (1992); *Later Life* (1993); and a *Cheever Evening* (1994).   FH

Guthrie, Tyrone 1900–71 Anglo-Irish director. From the 1930s onward Guthrie was an innovative and popular international director, working extensively in Britain, the USA and Canada. His Shakespearian work included LAURENCE OLIVIER's *Hamlet* and *Henry V* (1937), and a modern-dress version of the former in 1938 with ALEC

GUINNESS. He was to repeat this experiment at the theatre named after him, the GUTHRIE THEATRE at Minneapolis, in 1963. His other productions included a notable *Peer Gynt* (1944) in which RALPH RICHARDSON starred, LINDSAY's *The Three Estates* (EDINBURGH FESTIVAL, 1948) and, with DONALD WOLFIT, *Tamburlaine the Great* (OLD VIC, 1951). He was director of the STRATFORD (Ontario) FESTIVAL theatre in Canada from 1953 to 1957, and it was here that he developed (together with TANYA MOISEIWITSCH) his thrust stage theatre form that was later permanently enshrined both there and in Minneapolis, and which was widely copied in new theatre building in Britain (Sheffield Crucible Theatre, Leeds (and its successor, the West Yorkshire) Playhouse). Guthrie was impressive in both stature and manner and (in Ronald Bryden's words) 'made his mark not only with adventurous productions, but also by gaining public acceptance for alternatives to the proscenium arch'. The architecture of his theatres indicated his devotion to the Elizabethan relation between actors and audience. He was knighted in 1961. MB

Guthrie Theatre (Minneapolis) Conceiving the idea of founding a theatre away from New York, Oliver Rea and Peter Zeisler searched the country for a hospitable city that would support such an enterprise. Enlisting the aid of the director TYRONE GUTHRIE, they eventually chose Minneapolis as their site and brought forth the Tyrone Guthrie Theatre after much effort in 1963. Part of the Walker Art Center, the 1315-seat Guthrie features a thrust stage, favoured by the late director, and in its early seasons presented mainly well cast productions of classics and significant modern plays. After Guthrie's departure, his place was taken by his assistant Douglas Campbell until

1967, and a few years later by MICHAEL LANGHAM (1971–5). In 1981, after years of declining audiences, the direction of the theatre fell to LIVIU CIULEI, the Romanian-born director, who materially changed its policy: the stage was enlarged, the exterior of the theatre altered, and the production of new American and European plays in addition to the classics in a different mode contributed to a new spirit within the enterprise. In 1986 Ciulei was succeeded by Garland Wright (who leaves the helm at the end of the 1995–6 season), whose work has included an innovative 1993 version of the Clytemnestra saga, a triptych based loosely on works by the three great classical writers of tragedy and starring African-American actress Isabelle Monk. MCH

Gutzkow, Karl 1811–78 German playwright, novelist and journalist. As a young man, Gutzkow was associated with the group of liberal writers Junges Deutschland (Young Germany), and was briefly imprisoned for his views in 1836. After his imprisonment, he turned from journalism to writing plays, many of which have a historical setting but refer to contemporary politics. Among his most widely performed works were *Richard Savage* (1839), the comedies *Pigtail and Sword* (1844) and *A Model For Tartuffe* (1845), and the powerful verse tragedy *Uriel Acosta* (1846), which has racial and religious intolerance as its theme. Gutzkow was briefly dramaturge at the DRESDEN COURT THEATRE (from 1846 to 1848), but after the 1848 revolution he seemed to lose interest in the drama and turned to novel writing. SW

Guyana Situated on the northeast coast of South America, of which it is the only English-speaking nation,

Tyrone Guthrie's 1963 production of *The Three Sisters* at the Guthrie Theatre, Minneapolis.

Guyana anchors the eastern chain of Caribbean islands. The Dutch were the first to found a settlement there, pushing the native Amerindians back into the rainforest. Later, both France and Great Britain claimed the area, and it changed hands repeatedly between the warring European powers before the British occupation was confirmed in 1808. In 1831 the three adjacent provinces of Demerara, Berbice and Essequibo, set up by the Dutch, were united into the colony of British Guiana, which in 1966 became the independent nation of Guyana, and in 1970 a republic.

The early settlers had brought in African slaves to work on the sugar plantations. The British outlawed the slave trade in 1807, and when they abolished slavery itself in 1834 the planters sought new sources of labour for this country of mountains and forest, rivers, grasslands and mudflats. It was a search that would produce one of the most racially diverse populations in the Caribbean. Planters came from the tired plantations of islands like BARBADOS, bringing their slaves with them to work the new lands, while liberated Africans captured from slaving vessels were deposited on Guyana's shores. Between 1838 and 1917 some 238,000 East Indians from the Indian subcontinent were introduced into Guyana, as indentured workers. Thirty-two thousand Portuguese came from Madeira under bounty, but abandoned field labour for commerce as soon as their work contracts permitted it. The Chinese came in smaller numbers – some 13,000 by the mid-19th century. The Amerindian word 'Guyana' means 'land of many rivers', but because of its varied populations the country has also come to be known as the land of six peoples – namely, Indian, African, European, Madeiran Portuguese, Chinese and Amerindian.

Records of theatre in Guyana before the late 19th century are incomplete. Providing the first evidence of theatre productions are strolling players from North America, who came in 1800 via Barbados and Grenada, charged $2 a head for each performance, and stayed three months. Where they performed is not known; it was not until 1805 that one M. Campbell constructed in Georgetown a new Union Coffee House, with a second-floor hall to be used for concerts, amateur theatricals, balls and meetings. Reconstructed by a Mr Goepel in 1810, the hall now combined a pit and stage with elegant transparencies on three sides, and bore the grandiose title of Theatre Royal. It was to accommodate both gentlemen amateurs in the tragedy *George Barnwell*, and another professional troupe that played for three months offering comedies and farces, ending its tour with SHAKESPEARE's *Richard III*.

Another company of players visited Guyana in 1817, and in 1826 the Dutch Amateur Dramatic Society were using the theatre. In 1828 this local group built its own theatre by public subscription. However, they soon disbanded, and in 1845 the theatre was sold to the Church of England for use as a chapel. Three other buildings functioned as theatres in the second half of the century: the Athenaeum, built in 1851; the Assembly Rooms (1857), with the ground floor occupied by the Georgetown Club, and a commodious ballroom and theatre upstairs – the flat auditorium could seat 700, while the gallery held another 100; and the Philharmonic Hall, built by one Charles Cahuac for staging concerts, but also available for plays and light operas. Without raked seating or an ade-

quately equipped stage, none of these buildings could be considered a proper playhouse. In 1893, when amateur theatre groups were unusually active, a resolution was put to the Georgetown council for the erection of a two-storey building, the upper part to be fitted up as a theatre, at a cost not exceeding $30,000. The council voted against, contending that a theatre would merely increase the burgesses' taxes and that sanitation and water supply were more important priorities.

In 1854 some Portuguese amateur players gave a performance in Georgetown in aid of the girls' orphanage. This was the first dramatic effort by the Portuguese in their adopted country, and its success both on stage and at the box office no doubt inspired subsequent performances by the group at the Philharmonic Hall – even though, since they were given in their native language, the audience must have been limited. In 1897, to mark the anniversary of the restoration of Portuguese independence from Spain, *29, or Honour and Glory*, with a cast of over 50, was staged in Georgetown, followed the next year by 'a rash of concerts and plays' to mark the fourth centenary of the discovery of the Cape route to India by Vasco da Gama. It was not until the last decade of the century, in a burst of patriotism transcending language, that presentations were made in English.

Apart from Portuguese amateurs, by 1870 the two major drama groups were the whites-only Amateur Dramatic Club and the Histrionic Club for coloureds. Two decades later the same racial distinctions obtained, but the groups were called the Demerara Dramatic Club (for whites) and the Georgetown Dramatic Club (for coloureds). The exclusiveness of the Demerara Club was resisted by some, who in 1898 formed the Demerara Dramatic Company, with membership open to all racial groups on payment of an entrance fee of 48 cents and a small monthly subscription. Women who appeared on stage were exempted from paying fees – an indication of the difficulty of getting respectable middle-class females to perform publicly.

On 1 November 1877 Chinese theatricals of an unspecified kind were recorded for the first and only time in Guyana. And for the next several years the Chinese celebrated their New Year's festival, which no doubt comprised a costumed street parade with music, singing and dancing, including the dragon dance to the beating of the big drum. (Such a parade was seen in TRINIDAD as late as the 1930s.)

The most important professional companies to visit Guyana in the late 19th century were W. M. Holland's Dramatic Company and E. A. McDowell's English Vaudeville Company. Holland's band of twelve, from New York, opened at the Assembly Rooms in Georgetown on 19 March 1872. It played three times weekly until the leading actor, Wallace Britton, died suddenly of a heart attack and the tour was cancelled. Holland's repertoire had relied on light comedies, and sentimental dramas or MELODRAMAS with farcical afterpieces. Schuler's Fanchon, the Cricket, based on a tale by George Sand, was his main piece, starring Effie Johns. Othello was the only Shakespeare drama to be performed by the company. McDowell's was a more solid outfit. With 19 members, it performed at the Philharmonic Hall five nights a week for six weeks. Its repertoire included plays by contemporaries such as

BOUCICAULT, BULWER LYTTON, W. S. GILBERT and T. W. ROBERTSON, along with short FARCES as afterpieces. Performances were of a high order, the actors being led by McDowell's wife, the esteemed Fanny Reeves. The company returned to Guyana in 1886 and again in 1891.

Early this century companies from England began once again to make the long journey to the Caribbean. In 1905 the F. R. BENSON Shakespeare Company gave performances at the Assembly Rooms that included at least two of Shakespeare's comedies and Hamlet. They were followed by the more ambitious Florence Glossop-Harris Company which made its first visit to the Caribbean in 1914, playing mostly Shakespeare. Audiences in Guyana would have been prepared for a season of Shakespeare by the regular lectures on his plays given by J. Veecock, a master at Queen's College, Georgetown, and director-manager of the Georgetown Dramatic Club. This club's halcyon days had been the 20-odd years up to about 1910 when, with the death of Veecock, it began to fall apart. The Glossop-Harris Company returned for seven more visits between 1920 and 1931, offering lighter dramas and musical comedies.

Curiously, it was the advent of film that generated the first flush of indigenous professional theatre in Guyana. As the crowds flocked to the cinemas, local vaudevillians seized the opportunity to present their dialect playlets before this ready-made audience, using the narrow strip in front of the screen as their stage, a bare minimum of properties and no special lighting or costumes, and relying on audience familiarity with the issues of the moment to sustain interest in the plot. Three leading entertainers appeared at this period: the Portuguese comedian Sidney Martin, who in 1916 published a collection of his sketches and witticisms; the shanty singer Bill Rogers; and Sam Chase. With remarkable ingenuity, Chase was able to involve his audience in the outcome of his plays. He flourished in the 1940s and 50s.

While the popular entertainers were laying the foundations of a folk-drama, two events conspired to uplift Guyana's two racial majorities, the Africans and the Indians. Beginning in 1931, Cambridge-educated Guyanese schoolmaster Norman Cameron began to write a series of historical plays, to be performed in high schools in Georgetown, that would give the African-Guyanese a sense of their glorious past in Africa and the Middle East, at times using biblical stories to win audience recognition of his principal characters. In the same decade the British Guiana Dramatic Society was formed in the city by a group of young Indians under the guidance of J. B. Singh, a prominent Hindu doctor, and his wife Alice. Active from 1937 to 1948, this group presented ten annual productions of works by Indian playwrights like TAGORE and KALIDASA, along with concerts and REVUES designed to bring to a wider audience images of Indian culture and achievement. In 1945 the group staged Asra, probably written by the Guyanese Basil Balgobin. Though set in India, its focus on nationalism and the conflict between traditional and Western values was pertinent to the situation in Guyana.

What was needed was to bring together not only the different races in Guyana but also the urban and rural classes; to create not a melting-pot of cultures but rather an understanding and appreciation of what each group had to offer to the whole. A move in this direction came in 1943 when Harold Stannard, cultural adviser to the British Council in the region, promoted the formation of the Union of Cultural Clubs, which, although presenting at its annual convention mostly British arts, influenced the government to sponsor in 1958 a History and Culture Week with the emphasis on creations of Guyanese origin.

The Sugar Estates Drama Festival, launched in 1956, encouraged plantation workers to combine their skills in the production of one-act plays. Soon drama workshops were being offered to the estate groups. In the same year, Cecile Nobrega broke new ground with her book Stabroek Fantasy, from which was devised a MUSICAL set in the colourful Stabroek market of Georgetown and among the 'pork-knockers' (gold-diggers) of the hinterland. In 1957 the Theatre Guild of Guyana was established, and two years later secured its own playhouse. It launched its first playwriting competition in 1958 and the first National Drama Festival in 1959. Among those responsible for founding the Guild was Bertie Martin.

The Guild proved to be a driving force in the development of Guyanese theatre. Its modest playhouse was open to all groups and its technical staff were on hand to help in mounting productions. Playwriting workshops and competitions stimulated the writing of local plays, and the Guyana Broadcasting Service added incentive by regularly broadcasting scripts. By 1973 the tally was 175 plays, most of which had been produced on either stage or radio. In one of its most productive decades, beginning in the mid-1960s under the leadership of people like Frank Thomasson and Ken Corsbie, the playhouse hosted six to eight major productions a year, running some of them for two to three weeks.

The Guild's policy was not to limit itself to Caribbean plays but to include international works of the highest standard, so that indigenous plays could be judged against the best work from anywhere. Among the Guild's established writers are Harold Bascom, Bertram Charles and Francis Farrier. Home-produced plays that have been staged overseas include Miriamy by Frank Pilgrim, The Tramping Man by Ian McDonald and Masquerade by Ian Valz. Among playwrights who have shown promise is Paloma Mohamed.

In summer 1972 Guyana held the first Carifesta (Caribbean festival of creative arts). Twenty-five countries participated, all except Brazil belonging to the Caribbean basin. For its drama contribution the host country presented Couvade: A Dream of Guyana by Michael Gilkes. In 1976 a new theatre and cultural centre opened. With an auditorium seating 2000 it is considered too large for the average production, yet popular local writers like Bascom succeed in filling it for plays that deal with contemporary issues in a realistic and stageworthy, if predictable, manner. Use of the local argot also enhances the popular appeal. In 1981 Ron Robinson formed the first registered professional company in Guyana – the Theatre Company. In its first ten years it produced nearly 60 plays, musicals and revues, one-third of which are original Caribbean works. The company has also gone on tours to Caribbean islands and to the USA.

The half-yearly literary magazine Kyk-over-al – edited by the late Guyanese poet and essayist Arthur Seymour from

1945 to 1961 and after 1984 revived and co-edited by him and Ian McDonald – has played a significant role in discussing issues of concern to writers and theatre people. It has reviewed local plays, raised questions regarding standards of criticism, published historical articles on Guyanese theatre and reports of festivals and other activities. It was the first serious literary journal, in June 1959, to publish the texts of two prize-winning one-act plays written in the vernacular: *It's Brickdam* by Sheila Van Sertima and *Porkknockers* by Sheik Sadeek.

Despite Guyana's potential mineral and agricultural wealth, its economy suffered a serious downturn under its late president L. F. S. Burnham, kept in power only because of the threat of a communist regime being installed by his closest rival, the Indian Cheddie Jagan, who was finally elected president in 1992. The depressed state of affairs sent many talented people off to more congenial shores. Among Guyanese theatre people who live and work abroad are playwrights Michael Abbensetts, Jan Carew and Ian Valz; actor-director Ken Corsbie and director-manager Henry Muttoo. The highly reputed actor, the late Wilbert Holder, worked professionally from Trinidad, and Clairmonte Taitt from Barbados. Writer-director Michael Gilkes and critic Gordon Rohlehr are with the University of the West Indies in Barbados and Trinidad, respectively. EGH

See: K. Corsbie, *Theatre in the Caribbean*, London, 1984; E. Hill, 'The Emergence of a National Drama in the West Indies', *Caribbean Quarterly*, 18, 4, 1972; *Kyk-over-al* (theatre issues), 25 (June 1959), 37 (Dec. 1987), 40 (Dec. 1989); K. Omotoso, *The Theatrical into Theatre: A Study of the Drama and Theatre of the English-speaking Caribbean*, London, 1982.

Gwyn, Nell [Eleanor] ?1642–87 English actress. After an early career as a herring-seller and, famously, an orange-seller in the theatre, she was taken up by Charles Hart and taught dancing by LACY, probably beginning to act in 1664. Her success as Florimel in DRYDEN's *Secret Love* led PEPYS to praise her 'both as a mad girl, then most and best of all when she comes in like a young gallant and hath the motions and carriage of a spark the most that ever I saw any man have'. She left the stage briefly in 1667 during her affair with Charles Sackville, Lord Buckhurst. She often attempted but was rarely successful in tragedy. In 1669 she played in Dryden's *Tyrannic Love*, speaking the epilogue with its mock epitaph on herself: 'Here Nelly lies who, though she lived a slattern, /Yet died a princess, acting in St Cathar'n.' Shortly after then she became mistress to Charles II, though she continued to act even after the birth of her first child, finally leaving the stage in the 1670s. PH

Habimah (Hebrew for 'the Stage') The national theatre of Israel, in Tel-Aviv. Originally founded by NAHUM ZEMACH as the Habimah Studio in 1918, in Moscow, it was the first Hebrew-speaking professional theatre (see HEBREW THEATRE). It soon won international acclaim with the production of S. ANSKI's *The Dybbuk* in 1922. Zemach recruited many gifted actors, among them Menahem Gnessin, HANNA ROVINA, YEHOSHUA BERTONOV and AARON MESKIN. They formed a collective singularly devoted to their art, which the great Russian directors STANISLAVSKY and VAKHTANGOV found exciting enough to bestow their energies upon. MAKSIM GORKY wrote that 'they have the element of ecstasy; theatre for them is a rite, a worship'.

The problem of repertoire haunted Habimah from the very beginning, because of the scarcity of original Hebrew plays. The debate over the company's future was formulated by the poet H. N. Bialik and the philosopher Martin Buber. While Bialik maintained that Habimah should turn its back on the Diaspora and forge a new culture for the nation in the making, looking to the Bible as a source, Buber contended that culture cannot be artificially created but can only grow through interaction with the foreign arts, and therefore advocated the translation of the best of world drama.

Habimah travelled extensively and became essentially a homeless wandering troupe until they finally settled in Palestine in 1931, where they found at last their natural audience. In 1958 the company became Israel's national theatre. Habimah's visit to the USSR in 1990, one of the consequences of *perestroika*, closed a circle in its history. HAS

Hackett, J(ames) H(enry) 1800–71 American actor, master dialectician and manager, and the first American to appear in London as a star. He first succeeded in New York as Sylvester Daggerwood in *New Hay at the Old Market*. In 1827 he appeared at London's COVENT GARDEN, but failed to win public esteem. Returning to the USA, he repeated his triumphant Dromio of Ephesus, but audiences preferred his FRONTIER and YANKEE roles, especially Nimrod Wildfire in *The Lion of the West* and Rip Van Winkle. He secured his reputation as the finest Falstaff of his time, first playing the role in 1828. Hackett periodically essayed management, and was manager of the ASTOR PLACE OPERA HOUSE at the time of the FORREST–MACREADY riot. His *Notes & Commentaries upon Certain Plays & Actors of Shakespeare, with Criticism & Correspondence* was published in 1863.

His son **James K(eteltas) Hackett** (1869–1926) was a member of DANIEL FROHMAN's LYCEUM company, starring in such vehicles as *The Prisoner of Zenda*. He married actress Mary Mannering in 1897 and co-starred with her in *The Walls of Jericho* (1905). In 1906 he managed Wallack's Theatre in New York (opened 1904 and not to be confused with the theatre associated with the WALLACK FAMILY). In 1914 he and JOSEPH URBAN collaborated on a scenically historic production of *Othello*. SMA

Hacks, Peter 1928– German dramatist, librettist and poet who was invited to East Berlin in 1955 by BRECHT, from whose EPIC THEATRE his early historical plays *Das Volksbuch von Herzog Ernst* (*The Chapbook of Duke Ernest*, 1967) and *Die Schlacht bei Lobkowitz* (*The Battle of Lobkowitz*, 1956) derive. *Die Sorgen und die Macht* (*Anxieties and Power*, 1962) offered a picture of working life and workers' aspirations according to the precepts of socialist realism, and *Moritz Tassow* (1965) explored the relationship between utopian and practical Communism. Both met with official disapproval.

Deciding in the late 1960s that COMEDY was the appropriate form for a post-revolutionary society, Hacks developed a light, ironic style, adapting ARISTOPHANES, SHAKESPEARE, GOETHE, SYNGE and JOHN GAY. Like HEINER MÜLLER, he writes masterly blank verse. His witty, elegant, occasionally bawdy treatments of historical or mythological themes – *Margarete in Aix* (1966), *Amphitryon* (1967), *Omphale* (1970), *Rosie träumt* (*Rosie Dreams*, 1975) – are always anchored in the contemporary world. *Ein Gespräch im Hause Stein über den abwesenden Herrn von Goethe* (*A Conversation in the Stein Household Concerning the Absent Herr von Goethe*, 1976) is a sparkling one-hander about a famous literary liaison. His popularity in the GDR waned after the 1970s, when he turned with *Prexaspes* (1976) and *Senecas Tod* (*Seneca's Death*, 1980) to arcane subjects and unusual verse forms. He is a successful writer of children's plays. HR

Hagen, Uta 1919– American actress and teacher. Hagen made her debut in 1938 in the LUNTS' production of *The Seagull* and has acted only sporadically since then, though almost always in circumstances as notable: in MAXWELL ANDERSON's *Key Largo* (1939); with PAUL ROBESON and JOSÉ FERRER in *Othello* (1945); opposite Anthony Quinn in *A Streetcar Named Desire* (1950); as the lead in ODETS's *Country Girl* (1950); and, most memorably, as tortured, caustic, vulnerable Martha in EDWARD ALBEE's *Who's Afraid of Virginia Woolf?* (1962). Known as an actor's actor, Hagen performs in a clean, masterly style; she has an earthy, assertive presence and a deep voice that suggests enormous power in reserve. Although her understatement is ideally suited to film, she has chosen to appear on screen only rarely (notably in *The Other* and *The Boys from Brazil*). Since 1947 she has taught at the HB Studio in New York, begun by her late husband HERBERT BERGHOF. Famous for the brevity and incisiveness of her comments, she speaks in technical code words – an actor's shorthand – that her students learn to interpret. Like most American teachers she derives her method from STANISLAVSKY; unlike LEE STRASBERG, another Stanislavsky disciple, she is strongly opposed to the use of emotional memory, which she considers both self-indulgent and self-destructive. She has written on acting in *Respect for Acting* (1973; a standard reference for both students and professionals) and *A Challenge for the Actor* (1991). Her memoir, *Sources*, appeared in 1983. FH

Hahoe pyölsin-gut (literally, 'SHAMANIC ritual of Hahoe') Well known folk masked play, formerly performed once every ten years as part of *pyölsin* RITUAL activities by farmers in Hahoe village, Kyongsang-pukdo Province, South Korea. Its MASKS are refined in their carving and old for, unlike other forms of Korean masked dance drama, it was not required that the masks be burned at the end of each performance. OKC

Haiti Few events in modern history have engendered the writing of as many plays as the Haitian war of independence (1791–1804). The idea of a successful slave revolt against the imperial forces of France and Britain accompanied by the tragic deaths of the revolutionary leaders seized the imagination of playwrights in the Western world. Vèvè Clark has estimated that from 1796 to 1975 no less than 63 dramas were published or performed about the event. Whilst most of these plays originated in Haiti, about one-third came from writers in England, France, Germany, Côte d'Ivoire, Martinique, St Lucia, Sweden and the United States.

During the period of the American marine occupation of Haiti (1915–34) several patriotic plays were written, some of which were censored by the authorities (see CENSORSHIP), such as Dominique Hippolyte's *Le Forçat* (*The Prisoner*, 1929). In 1953 playwright Felix Morriseau-Leroy produced his *Antigone in Creole* in response to Haitian intellectuals who felt that serious drama could not be written in Creole, the language of the ordinary Haitian. The play was successful in performances on Haiti as well as in Paris, New York and Montreal. Morriseau-Leroy also wrote a Haitian version of *King Creon* in which Creon was clearly meant to represent the Haitian dictator François Duvalier.

More recent playwrights have experimented in other ways. Franck Fouché, who died in 1978, not only had five of his plays performed in Creole but, according to Clark, he employed EPIC THEATRE techniques combined with Catholic and Vodoun RITUAL in his major work *Général Baron-la-Croix ou le silence masqué* (*General Baron of the Cross, or Masked Silence*, 1971). Yet another play in Creole, *Kaselezo* (*Womb Waters Breaking*, 1985), represents the collective creation of playwright, director and three actresses who play a blind Vodoum priestess and her two daughters. EGH

See: V. A. Clark, 'Haiti's Tragic Overture: (Mis) Representation of the Haitian Revolution in World Drama (1796–1975)', in *Representing the French Revolution*, ed. J. A. W. Heffernan, Hanover, NH, 1992; V. A. Clark, 'When Womb Waters Break: The Emergence of Haitian New Theatre (1953–1987)', *Callaloo*, 15, 3, 1992.

Halac, Ricardo 1935– Argentine playwright. A member of the realistic (see REALISM) generation of the 1960s. Halac studied in West Germany under the auspices of a Goethe Institute fellowship. His first play, *Soledad para cuatro* (*Solitude for Four*, 1961), dealt with the anxieties and frustrations of a younger generation in confronting an incomprehensible and valueless society, themes echoed in *Estela de madrugada* (*Morning Wake*, 1965) and *Fin de diciembre* (*End of December*, 1965). He moved away from the realistic tradition and towards the grotesque with *El destete* (*The Weaning*, 1978), recovering some of the BRECHTian tendencies he observed in his youth. After *Lejana tierra prometida* (*Distant Promised Land*, 1981) and *Ruido de rotas cadenas* (*The Noise of Broken Chains*, 1983), Halac continued to write committed plays, including *¡Viva la anarquía!* (*Long Live Anarchy*, 1992) and *Mil años, un día* (*A Thousand Years, One Day*, 1992), the latter focusing on the expulsion of the Jews from Spain in 1492. GW

Halbe, Max 1865–1944 German playwright and novelist. A prolific writer, Halbe was associated with the naturalist movement. His sole enduring success was the tragedy *Youth* (1893), one of the major works of German NATURALISM. SW

Halévy, Ludovic see MEILHAC, HENRI

Hall, Owen [James Davis] 1853–1907 The most celebrated provider (British) of books for turn-of-the-century MUSICAL COMEDY. As both a solicitor and a libellous journalist, Davis was familiar with both sides of the law. He was also an expert bridge player, the owner of racehorses, a lavish entertainer and, on two occasions, a parliamentary candidate. His financial insouciance gave rise to his sister's suggestion of the punning pseudonym that he adopted. Although he had never written for the theatre he boasted to GEORGE EDWARDES that he could write a better piece than the currently popular musical FARCE *In Town*. Edwardes called his bluff. Hall responded with *A Gaiety Girl* (PRINCE OF WALES'S THEATRE, London, 14 October 1893), and this first theatrical effort ran for an amazing 413 performances as well as touring the USA, Australia and New Zealand with great success. During the next dozen or so years of his relatively short life Hall wrote the books of a further ten musical comedies, all achieving long runs and all making their mark (not always under their London titles) in the USA. Of these his greatest successes were *The Geisha* (Daly's Theatre, 25 April 1896; 760 performances), *Florodora* (Lyric, 11 November 1899; 455 performances) and *The Girl from Kay's* (Apollo Theatre, 15 November 1902; 432 performances). GH

Hall, Peter (Reginald Frederick) 1930– British director and theatre manager, who was largely responsible for the creation of two British national theatres, the ROYAL SHAKESPEARE COMPANY and the NATIONAL THEATRE. At Cambridge University Hall was an energetic amateur director, who in 1953 received a professional production at the Theatre Royal, Windsor. He inherited the mantle of ALEC CLUNES at the Arts Theatre Club in 1954, where, like Clunes, he directed many British premieres of new plays from overseas, including SAMUEL BECKETT's *Waiting for Godot* (1956). He went as guest director to the Shakespeare Memorial Theatre in Stratford-upon-Avon where, after a successful *Love's Labour's Lost* (1956) and *Cymbeline* (1957), he was invited to become the new artistic director, taking up this post in 1960.

His plans for the Shakespeare Memorial Theatre were radical, ambitious and pursued with a dramatic speed. He wanted to transform what was then a prestigious regional festival theatre into a national company modelled on Continental lines. The company would be semi-permanent, a substantial nucleus of actors would be offered two- or three-year contracts, and in order to offer them a metropolitan shop-window Hall negotiated to take over the Aldwych Theatre in London. This enabled him to present a programme of new plays, as well as the SHAKESPEARE-based repertoire at Stratford-upon-Avon. He calculated that such a company would require subsidy on a level previously unknown in Britain; and accordingly, with the approval of the governors, he drew upon the accumulated reserves of the Shakespeare Memorial Theatre Company to launch the company's residency at the Aldwych Theatre. The name was changed to the Royal Shakespeare Company in 1961.

This managerial gamble was supported by an artistic vision which transformed the verse-speaking at Stratford, encouraged contemporary interpretations of Shakespeare's plays along the lines of JAN KOTT, and backed proposals from innovative directors such as PETER BROOK. Although the RSC never received the state support which Hall thought the company required, it became the second-largest recipient of subsidy to non-operatic theatre, and throughout the 1960s the RSC was the major 'directors' theatre' in Britain, although the National Theatre could be regarded as the 'actors' theatre'. Hall himself was responsible for several key RSC productions, including *The Wars of the Roses* (1963), adapted from the *Henry VI* trilogy and *Richard III*, and *Hamlet* (1965) with David Warner. He also directed HAROLD PINTER's plays, *The Homecoming* (1965), *Landscape* and *Silence* (1969) and *Old Times* (1971).

In 1968 he resigned as managing director of the RSC, becoming a freelance director in both the commercial and the subsidized sectors, and extending his range of interests to OPERA. In 1970 he was appointed director of productions at the Royal Opera House, COVENT GARDEN, but he left after a year, claiming that too much money was being spent on an elitist art form. He was immediately (if privately) invited to succeed OLIVIER at the National Theatre, although it was several months before this news became known even to Olivier. Hall took over from Olivier at the National Theatre under acrimonious circumstances, and his task there was not helped by the delays to the opening of the new building on London's South Bank. The climate of opinion, too, had changed by the mid-1970s. Demands for more state money, which had seemed swashbuckling when the RSC was founded, began to look selfish when almost every regional theatre was struggling to stay open.

As the National Theatre's director, Hall was responsible for the programmes in three contrasting theatres – the Olivier, the Lyttelton with its proscenium arch stage and the Cottesloe, the smaller studio theatre. One of his early policy decisions was to place individual directors, or teams of directors, in charge of the separate theatres, instead of retaining one large company structure. He himself directed such NT successes as MARLOWE's *Tamburlaine* (1976) which opened the Olivier Theatre, AYCKBOURN's *Bedroom Farce* (1977) and PETER SHAFFER's *Amadeus* (1979), which he also directed on BROADWAY. In 1983 he became artistic director of the Glyndebourne Festival, a post held jointly with his post at the National Theatre. In 1988 he directed Shakespeare's last elegiac tragicomedies, *The Winter's Tale*, *Cymbeline* and *The Tempest*, before handing over

the NT's directorship to RICHARD EYRE. With his own Peter Hall Company, he took his star-studded productions of mainly classic plays on tour before taking them to the Playhouse or HAYMARKET theatres – *Orpheus Descending* (1988, with VANESSA REDGRAVE), *The Merchant of Venice* (1989, with DUSTIN HOFFMAN), *The Wild Duck* (1990) and *An Ideal Husband* (1992). He also returned to direct at the RSC, with *All's Well That Ends Well* (1992) and Peter Shaffer's *The Gift of the Gorgons* (1992). In 1977, he was knighted for his services to the theatre.   JE

Hall, Willis see WATERHOUSE, KEITH

Hallam family English actors, and the first substantially documented company of professional players to appear on the North American continent. Hallams had apparently been in the English theatre from 1707, one being killed by CHARLES MACKLIN in a Green Room brawl at DRURY LANE in 1735. By 1750 **William** Hallam (d.1758) had suffered serious financial reverses while managing GOODMAN'S FIELDS, but creditors allowed him to try to raise his shortages. He therefore sent an advance agent, Robert Upton, across the Atlantic with considerable money to investigate theatrical conditions and potentials. Hallam never heard again from Upton, who joined the Murray–Kean company, took charge of it, headed an engagement in New York in 1751, and then returned to England. The Murray–Kean company soon afterwards disappeared.

In the meantime, William Hallam sent his brother, **Lewis** Hallam Sr (1714–55), Lewis's wife, their three children and an undistinguished company of 10 to America. (One daughter remained in England, later becoming British actress Mrs George Mattocks.) After a six-week voyage, the Hallam Company opened in Williamsburg, Virginia, on 15 September 1752 with *The Merchant of Venice* and *The Anatomist*. They remained in Williamsburg for about 11 months, presenting a repertory consisting of SHAKESPEARE, ROWE, LILLO, MOORE, FARQUHAR, ADDISON, CIBBER, VANBRUGH, STEELE and GAY. They next played New York, opening on 17 September 1753 with *The Conscious Lovers*. Although they faced considerable hostility from local Quakers, the company opened a Philadelphia engagement on 15 April 1754 with *The Fair Penitent* and *Miss in Her Teens*, but played only two months. After a three-month engagement in Charleston, the Hallams arrived in Jamaica about January 1755, where they joined forces with a company managed by DAVID DOUGLASS. After the elder Hallam's death, Douglass married **Mrs Hallam** (?–1773) in 1758, also securing **Lewis** Hallam Jr (1740–1808) as a leading man.

Mrs Hallam starred in the American Company, as Douglass called his group, being the first actress in New York to play such roles as Juliet, Cordelia and Jane Shore. Lewis Hallam Jr remained on the stage for some 50 years, playing almost every significant role in the repertoire of the time. He appeared in Thomas Godfrey's *The Prince of Parthia* (1767), the first script by an American to be given a professional production. After Douglass's death in 1786, the younger Hallam assumed leadership of the American Company with various partners. He retired from management in 1797, but continued to act until his death. His second wife, Miss Tuke, joined the company, but her quarrelsome and intemperate habits caused much friction.

Adam Hallam, the younger brother of Lewis Jr, left Jamaica with the company, but his name soon disappeared from the bills. Helen and Nancy Hallam eventually joined the company, as well.   SMA

Halliwell, David (William) 1936– British dramatist and actor, whose first (and most successful) play was a comic study of a student Hitler, *Little Malcolm and his Struggle against the Eunuchs* (1965), which was produced in New York as *Hail Scrawdyke!* (1966). In 1966 he started the adventurous FRINGE company, Quipu, which produced (as well as his own plays) new works by other young writers, including STEPHEN POLIAKOFF. Halliwell turned towards what he called 'multi-viewpoint' drama in which, as in *K. D. Dufford ...* (1969), different versions of the same incident, the rape and murder of a child, were played side by side. The technical problems of multi-viewpoint drama preoccupied Halliwell as a director and writer for many years, and although he wrote such plays as *Muck from Three Angles* (1970), *A Last Belch for the Great Auk* (1971) and *A Process of Elimination* (1975), he has never again reached the wider audiences of *Little Malcolm.*   JE

Halm, Friedrich [Baron von Münch-Bellinghausen] 1806–71 Austrian playwright. Halm wrote several romantic verse tragedies, which were produced at the BURGTHEATER. Of these, *The Gladiator of Ravenna* (1854) was the sole undisputed success of his career. Between 1867 and 1870 he was unhappily intendant of the Burgtheater.   SW

Hamburg style A realistic approach to acting, initially associated with FRIEDRICH SCHRÖDER and generally posited as the opposite to the WEIMAR STYLE. Although few German actors in the 19th century can have completely realized the unvarnished REALISM normally suggested by the term, it was a valuable conception as it provided a point of reference for the discussion of various actors' styles.   SW

Hammerstein, Oscar, I 1847–1919 American impresario, theatre owner and producer. After emigrating to America from Prussia, Hammerstein worked in a cigar factory. Money from his many patents for improvements in cigar manufacturing enabled him to indulge his passion for OPERA and theatre. He built a number of playhouses, including the Manhattan Opera House, where his operatic productions were so successful that he was bought out by the Metropolitan Opera, and the OLYMPIA theatre, whose location north of the established theatre district earned him the nickname 'the father of Times Square'. In 1899 Hammerstein opened the Victoria Theatre as a legitimate playhouse, but had to switch to VAUDEVILLE when the THEATRICAL SYNDICATE lured away legitimate attractions. During 1904–15 Hammerstein's Victoria, under the management of his son Willie, was the top vaudeville house in the country. His son Arthur (1872–1955) was also a producer, theatre owner and lyricist. An informative biography of Oscar by Vincent Sheean was published in 1956.   MK

Hammerstein, Oscar, II 1895–1960 American lyricist and librettist. Born into a theatrical family, Oscar Hammerstein II began his career as a lyricist while a student at Columbia University. In the early 1920s he wrote lyrics for four shows with music by Herbert Stothart and two shows composed by VINCENT YOUMANS. His first big success came with the lyrics for *Rose-Marie* (1924), an OPERETTA with music by RUDOLF FRIML. Among other shows of the 1920s for which Hammerstein provided lyrics were *Sunny* (1925) and *The Desert Song* (1926). In 1927 he wrote both the lyrics and the libretto for the era's most ambitious MUSICAL, *Show Boat*, which had a score by JEROME KERN. After writing several other musicals with Kern, Hammerstein teamed up with composer RICHARD RODGERS in 1943 to create one of the most influential of all American musicals, *Oklahoma!*. This collaboration continued through the 1940s and 50s, resulting in *Carousel* (1945), *South Pacific* (1949), *The King and I* (1951), *Flower Drum Song* (1958) and *The Sound of Music* (1959).

Although Hammerstein's lyrics have sometimes been criticized for their sentimentality, he is generally credited with making major innovations in the form and subjectmatter of the American musical through his contributions to *Show Boat* and his later musicals with Richard Rodgers. Of the numerous books on Rodgers and Hammerstein, Ethan Mordden's extensively illustrated study (1992) is the most recent.   MK

Hammond, (Hunter) Percy 1873–1936 American drama critic. Born in Cadiz, Ohio, and educated at Franklin College, Ohio (1892–6), Hammond began as a reporter, then drama critic, for the *Chicago Evening Post* (1898–1908), later serving as theatre critic for the *Chicago Tribune* (1908–21). In 1921 he began a 15-year career as critic for the *New York Tribune*, establishing his reputation as a master of irony and urbane humour. He wrote of the producer Al Woods: 'The anguish which Mr Woods experiences when he does a thing like *Gertie's Garter* ... is assuaged by the knowledge that with its stupendous profits he may speculate in the precarious investments of the worthier drama' (1921). A collection of essays on Hammond by Franklin P. Adams and others appeared in 1936.   TLM

Hampden (Dougherty), Walter 1879–1955 American-born actor, who began his career learning the classical repertory and the grand-manner acting style in the British company of F. R. BENSON during 1901–4. After playing leading and supporting roles in London and the provinces, he went to the USA in 1907 in support of ALLA NAZIMOVA in her repertory of IBSEN and other modern plays. Always more successful in poetic and romantic roles, his desire to act in *Hamlet* and similar plays was not realized until he was able to assume the financial risks for their presentation in 1918. In the 1920s and 30s he took SHAKESPEARE's plays to appreciative audiences in many American cities. In 1923, he added ROSTAND's *Cyrano de Bergerac* to his repertory and played the dauntless hero more than 1000 times in 15 years. From 1925 to 30 he leased his own theatre, adding the title character from BULWER LYTTON's *Richelieu* to his repertory in 1929. An active performer for most of his life, Hampden played

Cardinal Wolsey in the AMERICAN REPERTORY THEATRE production of *Henry VIII* in 1946 and Danforth in ARTHUR MILLER's *Crucible* in 1953. MR

Hampstead Theatre Club (London) The theatre opened at Moreland Hall in 1959 but moved in 1962 to a prefabricated shed by Swiss Cottage Underground station. It provides a historical link between the little theatres of pre-war London and the FRINGE THEATRE clubs of the 1960s. Its premises offered a plain end stage in a small auditorium, seating about 150, although its most recent theatre, which opened in 1970, is marginally more spacious with a more sharply raked seating. Within this simple setting, successive directors, who have included James Roose-Evans, MICHAEL RUDMAN and Michael Attenborough, have been able to pursue an adventurous policy of new plays, often tried out before WEST END runs, and visiting small companies. The Hampstead locale provides the club with loyal supporters; and its list of achievements, which include West End transfers of plays by MICHAEL FRAYN, PAM GEMS, BRIAN FRIEL and JAMES SAUNDERS, has resulted in the club's high reputation. JE

Hampton, Christopher (James) 1946– British dramatist. His first play, *When Did You Last See My Mother?* (1966), was produced in London and New York while he was still an undergraduate at Oxford. From 1968 to 1970 he was resident dramatist at the ROYAL COURT THEATRE, where his finely balanced study of the relationship between Rimbaud and Verlaine, *Total Eclipse* (1968), was staged, together with his comedy of linguistic misunderstanding, *The Philanthropist* (1970). Hampton was not a typical Royal Court playwright in that he disliked and resisted left-wing polemics. His plays were cool, poised, witty and cosmopolitan in outlook. An excellent linguist and, as a modern languages scholar, aware of the problems of translation, he sought to provide modern, actable versions of European classics, abused in many familiar English texts.

He adapted *Uncle Vanya* (1970), *Hedda Gabler* (1970) and *A Doll's House* (1971) and later, for the NATIONAL THEATRE, MOLIÈRE's *Don Juan* (1972), IBSEN's *The Wild Duck* (1979) and two plays by an Austrian dramatist, ÖDÖN VON HORVÁTH, then little known in Britain – *Tales from the Vienna Woods* (1977) and *Don Juan Comes Back from the War* (1978). Horváth's memory also inspired him to write *Tales from Hollywood* (1983), set in the émigré community in California during the war, in which Horváth, Thomas and Heinrich Mann and BERTOLT BRECHT appear as characters. Hampton can be a technically inventive writer, as his play *Savages* (1973) revealed, in which a British diplomat is captured by guerrillas in South America who, despite their populist ideology, despise and maltreat the native population.

Apart from his semi-autobiographical play *White Chameleon* (1991), about his boyhood in Egypt, Hampton has concentrated on adapting and translating plays in recent years. His adaptation of Laclos's *Les Liaisons Dangereuses* (1986) was a triumphant study for the ROYAL SHAKESPEARE COMPANY of malevolent sexual intrigue, while for the NT he translated and adapted Ibsen's *Hedda Gabler* (1989) and Horváth's *Faith, Hope and Charity* (1989). He also collaborated with Don Black to provide the book and lyrics for the ANDREW LLOYD WEBBER MUSICAL, *Sunset Boulevard* (1993), from the Billy Wilder film of the same name. Hampton has become a supreme script technician, an exponent of the craft of the 'play doctor', but his own distinctive voice comes through in the wit and craftsmanship of his comedies, of which *Treats* (1976) is a good but underrated example. JE

Handke, Peter 1942– Austrian dramatist and novelist who won instant recognition at the 1966 Experimental Festival in Frankfurt with his 'speaking plays' *Offending the Audience* and *Self-Accusation*, which rejected all the conventional elements of theatre and explored the manipulative potential of language. *Kaspar* (1968) develops this theme, using a naive clown who is bombarded from loudspeakers with clichés and slogans, to demonstrate that the acquisition of language is a process of ideological indoctrination. *The Ride across Constance* (1970) presents social interaction as a set of stereotyped gestures and conventional behaviour patterns.

These experimental plays derive partly from Ludwig Wittgenstein's linguistic philosophy. *They're Dying Out* (1973), an eccentric account of capitalism, is Handke's only play to use plot and characterization. An international trendy in the 1960s, he is now withdrawn, conservative and mystical. *Über die Dörfer* (*The Long Way Round*, 1982) is a dramatic meditation on rural roots, modernity and self-knowledge. *Das Spiel vom Fragen* (*The Play of Questioning*, 1990) is a dramatic essay on God and the world, and *Die Stunde da wir voneinander nichts wussten* (*The Hour When We Knew Nothing of One Another*, 1992) represents all human life, recorded without dialogue in the form of an extended stage direction, as it passed by Handke's café table one sunny day. HR

Hands, Terry [Terence] **(David)** 1941– British director, who helped to found the lively Everyman Theatre in Liverpool in 1964. Two years later he joined the ROYAL SHAKESPEARE COMPANY, initially to direct its travelling offshoot, Theatre-go-round, which took Shakespearian productions and anthologies to schools. His first production at the Shakespeare Memorial Theatre at Stratford-upon-Avon came in 1968 with *The Merry Wives of Windsor*, which transferred to the Aldwych in London and returned to Stratford for the following season – proof of its popularity. In subsequent seasons he directed *Pericles* and *Women Beware Women* (1969), *Richard III* (1970) and *The Merchant of Venice* (1971) at Stratford, and *Bartholomew Fair* (1969) and *The Man of Mode* (1971) at the Aldwych.

Hands was by then an established RSC director, but his Stratford Centenary productions of *Henry IV* and *Henry V* (1975) and his *Henry VI* cycle in 1977 indicated his love of major challenges. In 1978, he was appointed joint artistic director with TREVOR NUNN of the RSC. Hands, unlike other RSC directors, was not noted for his interpretations of Shakespearian texts, but he had a fine command of spectacle, particularly when he worked with the designer Farrah, and a panache in staging crowd scenes; and he developed a close working relationship with the actor ALAN HOWARD, who played Henry VI, Henry V, Coriolanus, Richard II and Richard III.

From 1975 to 1977 Hands was consultant director at the COMÉDIE-FRANÇAISE, where he had staged a triumphant *Richard III* in 1972. His flamboyant directing, however, has sometimes led to excess, as in his staging of PETER NICHOLS's satirical PANTOMIME, *Poppy* (1983), intended as a tatty Victorian show parading jingoism, but which in Hands's version became a glamorous WEST END MUSICAL. In 1987, Hands became the sole director of the RSC and remained in charge until 1990, before handing over to ADRIAN NOBLE. He suffered from having received what had become a large theatrical empire, with outposts in the regions and the West End, without being sure of enough subsidies or sponsorship to sustain it. Of his later RSC productions, those at the Swan Theatre seemed the most successful: *The Seagull* (1990) and *Tamburlaine* (1992), in which ANTHONY SHER played in the title role.   JE

Hankin, (Edward Charles) St John 1869–1909 British dramatist and critic. Hankin wrote social SATIRE and, influenced by BRIEUX and SHAW, *The Return of the Prodigal* (1905, revived by JOHN GIELGUD in 1948).   CI

Hanlon-Lees brothers Six English aerialists and knockabout comedians, who introduced a new style of stage FARCE. The sons of Tom Hanlon, manager of the Theatre Royal, Manchester, **Thomas** (1836–68), **George** (1840–1926), **William** (1842–1923), **Alfred** (1844–86), **Edward** (1846–1931), and **Frederick** (adopted; 1848–86) took the name Lees in honour of their trainer, the carpet acrobat John Lees (d.1856). After touring Europe as children, they created a sensation at NIBLO's Garden, New York (1860), with their daring trapeze stunts, including 'Zampillaerostation', and visited both Americas and Europe during 1862–6. Thereafter the troupe split up, and using lads they had trained, George, William and Alfred founded the Hanlon-Zanfretta company, while Frederick and Edward teamed with the French juggling clown Henri Agoust and performed in a series of slapstick PANTOMIMES, seen in Paris in 1867. Reconsolidated in 1868, they made a smash in St Petersburg and Berlin, and at the FOLIES-BERGÈRE in 1878, where their original mixture of spring-heeled acrobatics, sadistic sight-GAGS and poker-faced slapstick were hailed by Edmond de Goncourt and ÉMILE ZOLA as a new era in theatrical fantasy. This phase culminated in *Le Voyage en Suisse* (1879), a farce comedy enlivened with mechanical stunts which played for 400 nights in Paris before moving to the GAIETY, London, in 1880, and the PARK THEATRE, New York, in 1881. William and Edward settled in Massachusetts, and, working from their superbly equipped studio, developed and promoted the comic extravaganzas *Fantasma* (1884) and *Superba* (1890), which briefly revived the American taste for spectacular pantomime. George Jr, teamed in VAUDEVILLE with Ferry Corwey in a CLOWN act, the Hanlons, was a gagman much in demand (ED WYNN's *Hurray for What*, 1937).   LS

Hansberry, Lorraine 1930–65 African-American playwright. Born into a comfortable middle-class home but surrounded by poverty in Chicago's South Side, Hansberry early confronted the plight of black families living in ghetto conditions that formed the background for her landmark drama, *A Raisin in the Sun* (1959). This first play

on BROADWAY by a black woman had a black director, LLOYD RICHARDS, and predominant black financing. It ran for 530 performances and won the New York Drama Critics' Circle Award. Hansberry's next play, *The Sign in Sidney Brustein's Window* (1964), about uncommitted white intellectuals in Greenwich Village, was not successful. After her early death from cancer, her former husband completed and produced two plays from her unfinished manuscripts, *To Be Young, Gifted and Black* (1969) and *Les Blancs* (1970).   EGH

Hanson, Lars 1886–1965 Swedish stage and film actor, a leading exponent of the complex psychological REALISM which made DRAMATEN famous from the 1930s to the 1960s. Hanson's technical virtuosity was prodigious, enabling him to play Lear at 35 and Romeo at 49. His acting was chiefly distinguished by its inner subtlety, especially in his many STRINDBERG roles – from his early Gustav III (1916) to a series of Dramaten performances including Master Olof (1933), the Officer in *A Dream Play* (1935), the Unknown in *To Damascus* (1937 and 1944), Hummel in *The Ghost Sonata* (1942) and the Captain in *The Father* (1953). He excelled in SHAKESPEARE, above all as Richard III, and his work in O'NEILL included James Tyrone in the 1956 world premiere of *Long Day's Journey into Night*.   HL

Hanswurst (German, meaning Jack Sausage) The most indigenous of German CLOWN figures. The name first appears in literature as Hans Worst in a Dutch translation of Sebastian Brant's *Ship of Fools* (1519), and was used abusively by Martin Luther in disputations of 1530 and 1541. The earliest use of the name for a stage clown was in a FASTNACHTSPIEL of 1553 and in scholastic German in 1573. He became a permanent type under the influence of the ENGLISCHE KOMÖDIANTEN's Pickelhering and the Italian Arlecchino during the 17th and 18th centuries.

Hanswurst received a distinctive format from JOSEF STRANITZKY in Vienna, who turned him into a phlegmatic Salzburg peasant of coarse instincts, low cunning and mother-wit, clad in yellow trousers trimmed in blue, a bright-red jacket with wide sleeves, a blue bib with an arsenic-green leather heart monogrammed HW, a white ruff and a green pointed hat; he wore a short black beard, his hair in a topknot, and wielded the wooden sword or *pistolese*. In competition with the touring Italian COMMEDIA, the scurrilous, improvising (one stage direction reads, 'Here Hanswurst can perform his lazzi and fopperies') Hanswurst was interpolated into the pompous doings of the HAUPT- UND STAATSAKTIONEN, to the delight of audiences and the outrage of academics, scandalized by his sexual and scatological ad libs. With the aid of CAROLINE NEUBER, GOTTSCHED in Leipzig tried to expel him from the stage with their *Play of Hanswurst's Banishment* (1737) and JOSEF VON SONNENFELS in Vienna followed suit, but to no avail. He soon returned under other names, such as Hänschen, Kasperl or Claus Clump, usually in servant roles.

Stranitzky's chosen successor was the 26-year-old GOTTFRIED PREHAUSER, who made Hanswurst more Viennese: 'gallant, charming, agreeable'. Other outstanding Hanswursts were Phillip Hafner (1735–64) and Johann Josef Felix von Kurz (1715–84), who, under the name

Bernardon, sang improvised verses in rapid patter. Gradually, Hanswurst was effaced by the figure of KASPER, introduced by Johann Laroche in 1769, and his qualities were diffused among various Viennese comic figures – Larifari, Staberl, Thaddädl – until he wholly lost his improvisational clownishness in the comedies of RAIMUND and NESTROY and dwindled into a dramatically integrated character, usually a small comic tradesman. LS

Harbach [Hauerbach], **Otto** 1873–1963 American lyricist-librettist. Educated at Knox College, Illinois, Harbach taught English and worked as a reporter and copywriter before beginning his BROADWAY career with the lyrics for *Three Twins* (1908). Over the next 30 years he was one of the most prolific writers for the musical stage, producing books and/or lyrics to over 40 MUSICALS. He provided lyrics for several shows with composer RUDOLF FRIML, beginning with *The Firefly* (1912); collaborated with OSCAR HAMMERSTEIN II on lyrics and librettos for 10 shows, notably *Rose-Marie* (1924) and *Sunny* (1925); and contributed to shows ranging from the OPERETTA *Madame Sherry* (1910) to the bouncy 1920s musicals *Mary* (1920) and *No, No, Nanette* (1925), to the more innovative JEROME KERN musicals *The Cat and the Fiddle* (1931) and *Roberta* (1932). MK

Hardy, Alexandre c.1575–c.1632 French playwright, almost certainly the first to pursue a full-time career within the professional theatre. He probably began writing in the 1590s and by 1611 was attached as stock author to the itinerant company of VALLERAN LE CONTE, a position he still held with the Comédiens du Roi under BELLEROSE in 1625. Two years later he undertook to supply plays regularly to another troupe in return for one share as a company member. In all he reputedly wrote or adapted over 600 plays, though only 34 survive, predominantly tragedies and tragicomedies, which were published between 1623 and 1628. A further ten were still in the repertoire of the HÔTEL DE BOURGOGNE in the 1630s, and their staging is described in the *Mémoire* of MAHELOT.

Drawing his subject-matter eclectically from mythology and history and disdaining the neoclassical unities, he showed a true dramatist's instinct for propelling the action forward, promoting conflict or confrontation between protagonists and exploiting the possibilities of spectacle and violent incident, but as a writer of verse he was facile and was doubtless ill-served by contractual pressures and the easy popular success he achieved. In retrospect his real importance is to have animated the largely static, SENECAN dramaturgy of the French Renaissance and thus prepared the way for the generation of young playwrights emerging in the 1620s and 1630s in response to the establishment of permanent theatre companies in Paris, who disparaged but profited from his example. DR

Hare, David 1947– British dramatist and director, a co-founder with Tony Bicat of the influential FRINGE company, Portable Theatre (1968–72). After three apprentice plays, of which the best was *Inside Out*, adapted (with Bicat) from Kafka's diaries, Hare began his assault on male-dominated, capitalistic society with *Slag* (1970), about three teachers in a girls' school who abstain from sex as a protest. *The Great Exhibition* (1972) concerns a middle-class Labour MP who tries to opt out of parliamentary life but finds that the world's corruption pursues him; while *Knuckle* (1974), a neat Raymond Chandler pastiche set in England's Home Counties, describes how the hard-bitten Curly tries to discover who killed his sister, concluding that capitalism itself is the real villain. With HOWARD BRENTON he wrote *Brassneck* (1973), about corruption in local government; and, as a good team man, he contributed to several group plays, including *Lay By* (1971), about the origins of pornography in capitalism, and *England's Ireland* (1972), about British imperialism across the water.

Hare was a leader of the younger generation of dramatists politicized by the events of 1968, and was quickly absorbed into the subsidized theatre establishment. From 1970 to 71 he was resident dramatist at the ROYAL COURT, while in 1973 he became resident dramatist at the Nottingham Playhouse. He was a founder member of Joint Stock, for whom he adapted William Hinton's book about the Chinese Revolution, *Fanshen* (1975). After the success of *Teeth 'n' Smiles* (1975), in which HELEN MIRREN played a drunken lead singer performing at a Cambridge May Ball to an audience she despises, Hare started to write for the NATIONAL THEATRE, which produced *Plenty* (1978), *A Map of the World* (1983) and *Pravda* (1985), with Howard Brenton, about the subservience of journalists towards the power-mad tycoons dominating London's Fleet Street.

Hare was appointed an associate director of the National Theatre in 1984 and has directed several productions there, including Brenton's *Weapons of Happiness* and *King Lear* (1986), with Anthony Hopkins in the title role. *The Secret Rapture* (1988) was like an Edwardian society drama, with family crises, updated to suit Mrs Thatcher's Britain. His planned trilogy about the three estates of Britain was completed in 1993. The first two plays, *Racing Demon* (1990) about the Anglican Church, and *Murmuring Judges* (1991) about British law, were well received; the third, *The Absence of War* (1993), offered a sardonic assessment of why the Labour Party lost the 1992 General Election and its sense of purpose as well. But Hare's satirical edge can wear blunt with over-use. His too easy condemnations of anything British can verge on the supercilious. JE

Hare, John 1844–1921 British actor and theatre manager, who was part of the famous BANCROFT company at the PRINCE OF WALES'S (1865–75), where he created parts in all the T. W. ROBERTSON comedies (Sam Gerridge in *Caste* being the most famous). He was what would now be known as a 'character actor', with a meticulous eye for stage detail that made him *avant la lettre* an admired director. He was successively manager of the ROYAL COURT (1875–9), the ST JAMES'S with the KENDALS (1879–88) and the GARRICK (1889–95), where he created his best-known role as Benjamin Goldfinch in GRUNDY's *A Pair of Spectacles* (1890). He was one of the first to recognize PINERO's talents as a playwright, and was rewarded, late in his career, by the chance to create the title part in *The Gay Lord Quex* (1899). Hare was knighted in 1907 and retired in 1911. PT

Harel, Jean Charles 1790–1846 French theatre manager. Harel began his career as secretary to Cambacerès and was nominated sub-prefect at Soissons in 1814. With the return of the Bourbons, he left France, meeting MLLE GEORGE, with whom he would have a lifelong liaison. In 1820 he returned to France and founded a paper, the *Miroir (Mirror)*, in which he attacked the restored monarchy. During the 1820s he managed various provincial theatres, and in 1829 was appointed to the ODÉON. He remained there until 1832.

Harel was an extravagant manager who enjoyed scenic effects: DUMAS *père*'s *Napoleon Bonaparte, or Thirty Years of French History* (1831), starring LEMAÎTRE as the emperor, cost 80,000 francs and, after a few performances, had to be shortened from 23 scenes to 14. Harel was heading for bankruptcy when he became manager of the Porte-Saint-Martin (see BOULEVARD) in 1831 and promptly moved part of his troupe to that theatre. One of his most successful productions there was Dumas's *Richard Darlington*, which he then transferred back to the Odéon, keeping that theatre going for nearly a year with boulevard MELODRAMAS. His great period was the 1830s at the Porte-Saint-Martin, which he tried to make into an alternative COMÉDIE-FRANÇAISE. Unfortunately, although their plays were being staged by the talented Harel, the great romantic dramatists felt the lure of the Comédie-Française, and some of his actors were also drawn there.

Harel had to give up the Porte-Saint-Martin in 1840 and leave Paris to escape his creditors. In his last years he became insane and died in poverty. As a dramatist, he contributed to Théaulon and Alboize's popular play, *The War of the Servants* (1837). He also wrote a curious *Theatrical Dictionary, or, 1258 Truths about Various Managers, Actors and Actresses*. He was an excellent conversationalist and publicist. Good at extracting money from people, he was less precise about paying his actors or creditors. He had a reputation for uncleanliness and kept a pig in his apartment. JMCC

Harlequin The English name of a comic character who has persisted throughout the modern theatre. The names Herlekin and Hellequin occur in French folk literature as early as 1100 to denominate diabolic ragamuffins, and Adam de la Halle uses them in 1262 for spirits of the air. The Italian Arlecchino may, however, derive from *al lecchino*, the glutton. The character first appears as a doltish rustic from Lower Bergamo, teamed as a ZANNI with the shrewder Brighella; an early portrait, in TRISTANO MARTINELLI's *Les Compositions de rhétorique de M. Don Arlequin* (1601), shows him in a loose white blouse and trousers covered with patches, a flat cap and a black moustachioed half-mask; his dagger of lath was clearly descended from the ancient comic phalloi. By nature greedy, cowardly, slow-witted but inventive under compulsion, he retained the earthiness of his origins. GANASSA is one of the first actors reputed to have played the role, which soon became a leading feature of any *COMMEDIA DELL'ARTE* company, usually entrusted to one of the more skilful players.

Arlecchino's further metamorphoses took place in France, where he was first played by Tristano Martinelli, GIOVAN BATTISTA ANDREINI and ANGELO COSTANTINI. It was DOMINIQUE BIANCOLELLI who naturalized him as Arlequin and fused the two *zanni* by making his Arlecchino witty, neat and fluent in a croaking voice, which became as traditional as the squawk of PUNCH. His Arlequin was endowed with a motto by the poet Santeuil: *Castigat ridendo mores*. Biancolelli's successors carried on the polishing process: EVARISTO GHERARDI bestowed the power of macaronic speech, a *patois* of French and Italian, and Vicentini-Thomassin added the element of pathos, the ability to evoke tears as well as laughter.

With the dissolution of the COMÉDIE-ITALIENNE in 1697 Arlequin moved to the fairground theatre, where he appeared in plays by MARIVAUX, Boissy, Delisle, LESAGE and others; by this time, he was the leading character in these pieces, but with the return of the Italian players, was relegated to subservient status in the high comedies of Marivaux and Lesage. This prettified Arlequin is preserved in the porcelain figurines of Kändler. In Italy, GOLDONI penned vehicles for the popular Arlecchini SACCO and BERTINAZZI, but tried to confine them to the written text; his opponent GOZZI, in his attempts to revive the improvised comedy of the *commedia*, made Arlecchino merely one of a team of comics, no more important than Tartaglia or Truffaldino. In post-revolutionary Paris, Arlequin settled into the popular BOULEVARD theatres: at the Variétés-Amusantes he was played by Lazzari, at the Vaudeville by Laporte who enacted him in 500 plays. The last important French Arlequin was Bergamasque at the THÉÂTRE DES FUNAMBULES, but the character was already effaced by the PIERROT of JEAN-GASPARD DEBURAU.

Harlequin in England first appears in JOHN DAY's *The Travailes of the Three English Brothers* (1607) and Ravenscroft's *Scaramouch* (1644). APHRA BEHN adapted a French scenario into *The Emperor of the Moon* (1686) for the comedian Tom Jevon, who played the famous LAZZI of suicide in it; but Harlequin did not catch on in England until the introduction of the PANTOMIME by John Weaver and JOHN RICH. Rich, under the name Lun, presented an acrobatic Harlequin stripped of his complex French background, an antic mute most remarkable for his pantomimic tricks; this version was carried on by Henry Woodward, James Byrne who devised the close-fitting costume bespangled with glittering lozenges, John Bologna Jr, and Tom Ellar. By the time of the latter two, Harlequin had been elbowed aside by the popular Clown of JOSEPH GRIMALDI, and his chief functions were dancing with Columbine and effecting transformations with a touch of his magic bat. Despite his powers of invisibility, he performed chiefly as straightman to Clown and Pantaloon.

In modern times, Harlequin has become emblematic of a bygone theatre, despite attempts to revive him at the VIEUX-COLOMBIER and the Piccolo Teatro di Milano with Marcello Moretti in the part. Jacques Fabbri had a limited success in Santelli's *La Famille Arlequin* (1955). Fokine's use of Harlequin in his ballets *Arlequinade* (1900) and *Carnaval* (1910) is typical of the svelte, dandified character conjured up by many artists. The SAN FRANCISCO MIME TROUPE is one of the few groups to adapt Harlequin to the needs of contemporary SATIRE, while DARIO FO has managed to absorb the *commedia* in a comic persona all his own. LS

harlequinade see PANTOMIME, ENGLISH

Harnick, Sheldon see BOCK, JERRY

Harrigan, Edward 1844–1911 and
Tony Hart [Anthony J. Cannon] 1855–91 American playwright-actor and actor, Harrigan and Hart became the most popular comedy team on the American stage (1871–85). They sang, danced and played the principal roles (usually Harrigan as the amiable, fun-loving Irish adventurer Dan Mulligan and Hart, in blackface, as the Black wench Rebecca Allup) in Harrigan's high-spirited 'mêlées': *The Mulligan Guard Picnic* (1878), *The Mulligan Guard Ball* (1879), *The Mulligan Guard Chowder* (1879), *The Mulligan Guard Christmas* (1879), *The Mulligan Guard Nominee* (1880), *The Mulligan Guard Surprise* (1880), *The Mulligan Guard Silver Wedding* (1881), *Old Lavender* (1877), *The Major* (1881), *Squatter Sovereignty* (1882), *Cordelia's Aspirations* (1883), *Dan's Tribulations* (1884) and *Investigation* (1884). Harrigan's FARCES were not all 'knockdown and slambang'; his documentary explorations of New York's Lower East Side and his striking portraits of the Germans, Italians, Blacks and particularly the Irish in his 40 plays led WILLIAM DEAN HOWELLS to write, 'Here is the spring of a true American comedy, the joyous art of the dramatist who loves the life he observes.' Another critic called his plays the 'Pickwick Papers of a Bowery DICKENS'.

Harrigan was born on New York's Lower East Side and appeared first as an Irish comic singer in San Francisco (1867). In 1871 he met Hart, a falsetto-voiced singer from Worcester, Massachusetts, and wrote 'The Little Fraud', which alerted Boston to their extraordinary talents. They turned out 60 more sketches, most notable of which was 'The Mulligan Guard', a SATIRE on New York's pseudomilitary companies (with music by David Braham, Harrigan's future father-in-law and thereafter his musical collaborator). Their antics drew boisterous crowds to the Theatre Comique and then to Harrigan's Theatre Comique, both on Broadway.

When the second Comique burned down (1884), the partners separated. Hart stumbled in and out of three plays, was committed to an asylum, and died at the age of 35. Harrigan continued writing and acting – *The Leather Patch* (1886), *McNooney's Visit* (1887) and others – and opened a new Harrigan Theatre on Herald Square with *Reilly and the Four Hundred* (1890).

Three of his children – 'Eddie', William and Nedda (MRS JOSHUA LOGAN) – became actors. Harrigan, and Hart, have been studied extensively by E. J. Kahn (1955) and Richard Moody (1980). RM

Harris, Jed 1900–79 American producer and director. At the height of the 1920s, Harris presented four plays celebrated for their crisp, modern style: *Broadway* (1926), a raucous backstage MELODRAMA overrun with wisecracking gangsters and gum-chewing chorus girls; *Coquette* (1927), a tear-jerker about the risks of Flaming Youth; *The Royal Family* (1927), a SATIRE about a flamboyant theatrical dynasty modelled on the Barrymores (see DREW–BARRYMORE FAMILY); and *The Front Page* (1928), a whirlwind COMEDY-melodrama set in a newspaper office. Growing quickly bored with his success, Harris was content to rest on his laurels; he worked only sporadically thereafter, most notably on *Uncle Vanya* (1930), a response to critics who complained that he wasted his talents on light entertainment; *The Green Bay Tree* (1933), with LAURENCE OLIVIER as a kept homosexual; *Our Town* (1938); and *The Heiress* (1947), based on HENRY JAMES's *Washington Square*. After retiring to San Francisco, he broke silence with two books: *Watchman, What of the Night?* (1963), a crusty and self-justifying account of the backstage warfare on *The Heiress*, and *A Dance on the High Wire* (1979), a curiously muted memoir.

There are two enduring legends about Harris: one, obviously untrue, that he had a golden touch that turned every play he handled into a hit; and the other, which has much greater validity, that he was a monster. He directed only a few of his plays (including *Uncle Vanya* and *Our Town*), but all of his productions had superb taste and showmanship, achieved at great cost to his collaborators. GEORGE ABBOTT called him 'the Little Napoleon of Broadway', and stories of Harris's wild mood swings, withering sarcasm and cruelty are part of theatrical folklore. Martin Gottfried published an objective biography in 1984. FH

Harris, Julie 1925– American actress, whose BROADWAY debut was as Atlanta in *It's a Gift* (1945). She rose to stardom with such roles as Frankie Adams in *The Member of the Wedding* (1950); Sally Bowles in *I Am a Camera* (1951), for which in 1952 she won the first of her five Best Actress Tonys (a record); and Joan in *The Lark* (1955, 1956 Tony), performances she later filmed. In 1976 she successfully staged a one-person show, *The Belle of Amherst*, subsequently touring the show and playing a season at the PHOENIX THEATRE, London. Critics have been won over by her air of vulnerability and fragility, coupled with remarkable stage techniques. Her Emily Dickinson in *Belle* – one of numerous women she has portrayed culled from history – was called 'astonishing in its sagacity and passion ... shining'. She received a Tony in 1969 for *Forty Carats* and in 1972 for *The Last of Mrs Lincoln*. In 1980 she played the lead in *On Golden Pond* on the West Coast, and in 1989 toured in *Driving Miss Daisy* and in *Lettice & Lovage* in 1992–3. She appeared as Isak Dinesen in a one-woman play, *Lucifer's Child* (1991), in Timothy Mason's *The Fiery Furnace* for the Circle Repertory Company, OFF-BROADWAY (autumn 1993), and in a fiftieth anniversary production of *The Glass Menagerie* at New York's Roundabout Theatre. Harris has also won many awards during her illustrious career in film and television, including the 1993 Common Wealth Award for the Arts (a prize of $25,000). She is the author of an acclaimed and partially autobiographical text for beginning performers, *Julie Harris Talks to Young Actors* (1972). SMA

Harris, Rosemary 1930– British-born actress. Harris has appeared in over 140 roles in more than 30 years on the English and American stage, including affiliations with some of the great theatre companies (in England the BRISTOL OLD VIC, OLD VIC, the NATIONAL THEATRE, CHICHESTER FESTIVAL; in the USA the Association of Producing Artists, Lincoln Center, Brooklyn Academy of Music, AMERICAN SHAKESPEARE THEATRE and WILLIAMSTOWN THEATRE FESTIVAL). A versatile actress, who once described herself as 'a chameleon on a tartan' and was described in the *New York Times* as 'pure presence', she has appeared prominently in *Troilus and Cressida* (GUTHRIE's 1956 production), *Man and Superman*, *Much Ado about Nothing*, *The School for Scandal*, *The Seagull*, *Twelfth Night*, *The Broken Heart* (first Chichester season, 1952), *Hamlet* (Ophelia in National Theatre's inaugural season), *The Lion in Winter* (1966, Tony), *Old Times*, *Major Barbara*, *A Streetcar Named Desire* (1973 revival, VIVIAN BEAUMONT THEATRE), *The Royal Family*, *All My Sons* (1981 London revival), *Pack of Lies*, the BROADWAY revival of *Hay Fever* (1985–6 season), *The Best of Friends* (with JOHN GIELGUD), as the grandmother in *Lost in Yonkers* (Broadway replacement, 1991; and London, 1992–3), and in the acclaimed revival of *An Inspector Calls* (Broadway, 1994). DBW

Harris, Sam H(enry) 1872–1941 American producer, who began his theatrical career in 1899 as a stagehand. The following year he became a partner in the firm of Sullivan, Harris & Woods (1900–4), which produced eight MELODRAMAS and BURLESQUES including a hit, *The Fatal Wedding*. He began a 16-year partnership with GEORGE M. COHAN in 1904, producing more than 50 plays including Cohan's own *Little Johnny Jones*, *Forty-five Minutes from Broadway* and *Seven Keys to Baldpate*. After the partnership was dissolved in 1920, Harris independently produced *Rain* (1922), *The Jazz Singer* (1925), *Animal Crackers* (1928), *Dinner at Eight* (1932), *The Man Who Came to Dinner* (1939) and *Lady in the Dark* (1941). His productions of *Icebound* (1923), *Of Thee I Sing* (1932) and *You Can't Take It with You* (1937) won Pulitzer Prizes; and *Of Mice and Men* won the 1938 New York Critics' Circle Award. He preferred comedies and musical comedies to serious drama, and was noted for paying attention to the smallest details of a production. TLM

Harrison, Rex [Reginald Carey] 1908–90 British actor, knighted in 1989, active on both sides of the Atlantic. Underrated, despite considerable interpretative skills, he was described by Richard Coe as 'smooth as a pearl, prickly as a porcupine'. He began his professional career in London in 1930, where during a long career he appeared not only in the comedies of COWARD, RATTIGAN and VAN DRUTEN, but also in less obvious parts for an actor of his type-casting: the Uninvited Guest in ELIOT's *The Cocktail Party* (1950), Henry IV in PIRANDELLO's play (1973 and 1974), among others. This debonair star – the quintessential Henry Higgins in the MUSICAL version of SHAW's *Pygmalion*, *My Fair Lady*, his Tony-winning role of 1956 (revived in 1981) – appeared frequently in New York during his 66 years on the stage. From his BROADWAY debut in 1936 to his final role, Lord Porteous in *The Circle* (1989), Harrison appeared most notably as Henry VIII in *Anne of the Thousand Days* (Tony, 1948), Shepherd Henderson in *Bell, Book and Candle* (1950), The Man in *The Love of Four Colonels* (1953), Caesar in Shaw's *Caesar and Cleopatra* (1977) and Shotover in *Heartbreak House* (1983). He wrote two autobiographies: *Rex* (1974) and *A Damned Serious Business: My Life in Comedy* (1991). MB DBW

Harrison, Tony 1937– British playwright, translator and poet, whose brilliant adaptation of MOLIÈRE's *The Misanthrope* (1973), set in the time of General de Gaulle, was one of the delights of OLIVIER's NATIONAL THEATRE. He was known as a poet and classical scholar before he turned his attention to the theatre in the mid-1970s, and his version of the *Oresteia* with music by Harrison Birtwistle was staged at the NT, directed by PETER HALL, in 1981. Harrison modernized and strengthened the verse of the medieval MYSTERY PLAYS, *The Nativity*, *The Passion*, and *Doomsday* (1985), another NT hit. From a fragment of a Sophoclean satyr play he constructed a parable, *The Trackers of Oxyrhynchus* (1990), about two dons whose love for Greek culture helps them to overlook the disasters on their travels, which SOPHOCLES would have recognized too well. *Square Rounds* (1992) was described as a 'theatre piece' rather than a play, a meditation on armaments manufacturers which he directed himself and illustrated by MIME, juggling, conjuring and rhymed couplets, which seemed to fall below his normal standards – partly because they had to compete with everything else. JE

Hart brothers Heinrich 1855–1906 and Julius 1859–1930 German critics and playwrights, who did much to prepare the critical ground for naturalist theatre (see NATURALISM) in Berlin in the late 1880s. Their most important essays are collected in *Critical Conflicts* (1894). SW

Hart, Lorenz 1895–1943 American lyricist and librettist. Hart's first theatrical assignment was as a play translator for the SHUBERTS. In collaboration with RICHARD RODGERS, who was to be his partner for the rest of his career, he contributed four songs to the BROADWAY MUSICAL COMEDY *Poor Little Ritz Girl* (1920). The first complete scores by Rodgers and Hart were for *The Garrick Gaieties* (1925) and *Dearest Enemy* (1925). In the next 18 years they created an almost uninterrupted string of successful shows, including *The Girl Friend* (1926), *A Connecticut Yankee* (1927; revival 1943), *America's Sweetheart* (1931), *On Your Toes* (1936), *Babes in Arms* (1937), *The Boys from Syracuse* (1938), *I Married an Angel* (1938), *Pal Joey* (1940) and *By Jupiter* (1941). Hart's clever, sometimes sardonic lyrics, often employing complicated internal rhyme schemes, are considered among the finest ever written for the musical stage. MK

Hart, Moss 1904–61 American playwright, librettist and director. Although he had written several unsuccessful plays on his own, it was Hart's teaming up with GEORGE S. KAUFMAN during the 1930s that established his career. These two wits delighted American audiences with such hits as *Once in a Lifetime* (1930), *You Can't Take It with You* (1936, Pulitzer Prize) and *The Man Who Came to Dinner* (1939). On his own in the 40s, Hart wrote, among other offerings, the book for the landmark MUSICAL about psychoanalysis, *Lady in the Dark* (1941), and the funny theatre in-joke about a play in rehearsal, *Light up the Sky* (1948). Hart devoted much of the last decade of his career to directing, winning a Tony for his work on *My Fair Lady* (1956). His autobiography, *Act One* (1959), is a classic theatrical memoir. LDC

Hart, Tony see HARRIGAN, EDWARD

Harte, Bret [Francis Brett Harte] 1836–1902 American writer. Brought up in Brooklyn, New York City, Harte moved to California in 1853 and became famous for stories and poems in the *Overland Monthly* (1868–71). His popularity declined as rapidly as it rose, and after 1878 he lived abroad. His best work combines sentiment and low humour in the manner of CHARLES DICKENS. He wrote *Two Men of Sandy Bar* (1875) for STUART ROBSON, and collaborated with Mark Twain on *Ah Sin* (1877), a vehicle for actor Charles Parsloe. Though both failed, they established a genre that BARTLEY CAMPBELL perfected in *My Partner*. DMCD

Hartford Stage Company (USA) Since founding director Jacques Cartier opened this not-for-profit company (see RESIDENT NON-PROFIT PROFESSIONAL THEATRE) in an abandoned supermarket in 1964, the Hartford Stage, located in the capital of Connecticut, has developed into a first-rate regional theatre with a playhouse designed by postmodernist architect Robert Venturi. Cartier was succeeded as artistic director first by Paul Weidner in 1968, then by Mark Lamos in 1980. Initially a traditional company mounting old and modern standards, the Hartford now devotes about half of its season to new or recent American plays and dramatizations of non-theatrical works. Lamos, a prominent US director with a strong belief in regional theatre who consciously shuns New York, has revealed a special gift for large-scale productions of epics, such as SHAKESPEARE'S HISTORY PLAYS. His co-staging with Mary B. Robinson of *The Greeks* (1982), Kenneth Cavender's seven-hour cycle of Greek tragedies, earned the theatre wide acclaim. CLJ

Hartleben, Otto 1864–1905 German playwright, poet and short story writer. His plays, of which by far the most successful was *Rosenmontag* (*The Monday before Lent*, 1900), focus primarily upon the incompatibility of sexual attraction and social class. SW

Harwood, John Edmund 1771–1809 British-born comic actor, who was taken to the CHESTNUT STREET THEATRE by THOMAS WIGNELL in 1793, remaining in Philadelphia until engaged by WILLIAM DUNLAP for the PARK THEATRE in New York in 1803, where he acted until his death. Among his better roles was Falstaff, which he played first in 1806 opposite the Hotspur of THOMAS A. COOPER. Dunlap, who called him a man of wit and refinement and highly endowed as an actor, but indolent and careless of study, compared him to the British actor JOHN BANNISTER. He married a granddaughter of Benjamin Franklin and fathered Admiral Andrew Allen Harwood. DBW

Harwood, Ronald 1934– British dramatist, born in South Africa, who came to Britain where he joined DONALD WOLFIT's touring Shakespearian company as an actor. He turned his attention to writing novels and to writing for television in the early 1960s, but his first stage success came with *The Dresser* (1980), in which TOM COURTENAY played the dresser to a Wolfit-like star, whose life was reflected in a crumbling touring production of *King Lear*. Harwood's mixture of affection and despair at this downfall is reflected in somewhat similar studies of a loss in religious faith, in *J. J. Farr* (1987), in which ALBERT FINNEY and JANET SUZMAN played a Jewish Cape Town couple. He excels at collapses in confidence, whether of imperial, religious or aesthetic pretensions, and derives humour from the grubby other side of glamour; but his technique is wedded to the WELL MADE PLAY tradition. He can fall below the potential emotional intensity of his themes. It has been pointed out that *Another Time* has an O'NEILL plot and a NEIL SIMON impact. *Reflected Glory* (1992) describes the rivalry between a restaurant-owner and his younger and more successful playwright brother. It is written with professional skill and good humour, but leaves behind more questions (and more interesting ones) than it attempts to answer. JE

Hasenclever, Walter 1890–1940 German dramatist, novelist and poet whose first play, *The Son* (1916), was the first expressionist play (see EXPRESSIONISM) ever staged. It was a paradigmatic expressionist text – episodic, lyrical, and with a generation conflict between an idealistic son and a conservative martinet of a father which ends in parricide. His pacifist version of *Antigone* (1919) was directed by KARLHEINZ MARTIN at the 3500-seat Grosses Schauspielhaus in 1920. In 1927 Hasenclever turned successfully to comedy with *Ein besserer Herr* (*A Man of Distinction*), a piece about a confidence trickster, followed by *Die Ehen werden im Himmel gemacht* (*Marriages Are Made in Heaven*, 1928). In exile after 1933, he wrote *Scandal in Assyria*, which was performed in London in 1939. Hasenclever committed suicide in internment in Vichy France. HR

Haupt- und Staatsaktionen Plays performed by travelling troupes of actors in Germany during the 17th and early 18th centuries. They were derived from the Shakespearian drama that had been performed by the ENGLISCHE KOMÖDIANTEN, from the German literary drama, and from the improvised drama of the *commedia dell'arte* troupes that toured Germany then. By all accounts, this was a debased form of theatre that encouraged bombastic acting, sensational and gory manifestations on the stage, and frequent gross obscenity. As the German theatre became 'regularized' under the influence of GOTTSCHED and the quality of drama improved as a result of the efforts of such writers as J. E. SCHLEGEL and LESSING, both the style and the genre of representation began to decline. Although *Haupt- und Staatsaktionen* continued to be performed sporadically into the 1760s by the troupes of KOCH and DÖBBELIN, by the end of that decade they had disappeared entirely from the repertoire. SW

Hauptmann, Gerhart 1862–1946 German playwright and novelist. From the production of his first play *Before Dawn* (1889) at the FREIE BÜHNE, Hauptmann was celebrated as the leader of NATURALISM in the German theatre. The play shows the unmistakable influence of the theories of ZOLA and the dramaturgy of IBSEN, a legacy from which Hauptmann found it difficult to escape. *Lonely Lives* (1891) was clearly inspired by *Rosmersholm*, though with *The Weavers* (1892), a play of epic structure dramatizing

A scene from Gerhart Hauptmann's *Die Weber* (*The Weavers*), first produced in 1892. This is a classic example of naturalistic playwriting and staging.

the plight of Silesian workers during the riots of 1844, Hauptmann found a more individual tone. Although he continued to write naturalistic plays into the 20th century – *The Beaver Coat* (1893), *Carter Henschel* (1899) and *Rose Bernd* (1903) are notable examples – he also experimented with other genres and modes. *The Sunken Bell* (1896) was a widely performed, neo-romantic allegory that gave actors such as KAINZ an ideal opportunity to display their vocal skills. Hauptmann, who was awarded the Nobel Prize in 1912, continued to expand his range, producing historical dramas, fantasy plays, and tragedies written in both the Greek and Shakespearian forms. Up until his death after the Second World War, he remained one of the most respected German men of letters. However, his work never fulfilled the promise of the 1890s, when he was recognized, both in Germany and abroad, as a dramatist of primary significance. SW

Havel, Václav 1936– Czech playwright. A native of Prague, he studied at the Prague Theatre Academy and eventually became dramaturge and resident playwright at the Balustrades Theatre, for which he wrote all his plays until 1968. In his best-known plays, Havel focused on deformations in patterns of thinking (ideological and bureaucratic power stratagems run amok or become sclerotic). His stage world is essentially abstract, schematic and cerebral, characterized more by wit and farce than by humour, as is seen in *Garden Party* (1963), *Memorandum* (1965) and *The Increased Difficulty of Concentration* (1968), which form a triptych of variations on a theme. A frequently confined dissident, he continued to live and write in his homeland, although his only outlet for productions between 1969 and 90 was abroad: e.g. *A Private View* (New York, 1983), *Largo Desolato* (Vienna, 1985), *Temptation* (ROYAL SHAKESPEARE COMPANY, Stratford-

upon-Avon, 1987). The later plays, *Temptation* and *Urban Rehabilitation* (1989), reveal more interest in psychological characterization. His presidency of Czechoslovakia during 1990–2 and of the Czech Republic since 1993 has temporarily suspended his playwriting career. JMB

Hawthorne, Nigel 1927– British actor, educated in South Africa, who moved to London in the early 1950s. After some appearances in REVUES and in the touring production of *Oh, What a Lovely War!* (1967), he appeared in the WEST END as OSWALD STOLL in the Theatre Royal, Stratford East's production of *The Marie Lloyd Story* (1968). Having worked with JOAN LITTLEWOOD's company, he achieved his ironic touch by playing establishment figures in a gently tongue-in-cheek manner. This served him well as 'Roy Jenkins' in *Mrs Wilson's Diary* (1967) and in the long-running BBC TV series, *Yes, Minister* and *Yes, Prime Minister*, where he played the smoothly obstructive civil servant, Sir Humphrey. His acting range, however, extends from his appearance as Prince Albert in EDWARD BOND's *Early Morning* (1969) to his tender study of the writer C.S. Lewis in love in *Shadowlands* (1989) and his brilliant portrait of a not-mad king in ALAN BENNETT's *The Madness of George III* (1991). A subtle and easily underrated actor, Hawthorne is set to become the natural successor to ALEC GUINNESS. JE

Hayes [Brown], **Helen** 1900–93 American actress. With KATHARINE CORNELL and Lynn Fontanne (see LUNT, ALFRED), Hayes was often called 'the First Lady of the American theatre'. Diminutive and homespun, she was distinctly less glamorous than the other Great Ladies; and the qualities of modesty and common sense that she projected helped account for her enduring appeal. A stage star for over 50 years (she retired in 1971), she continued to

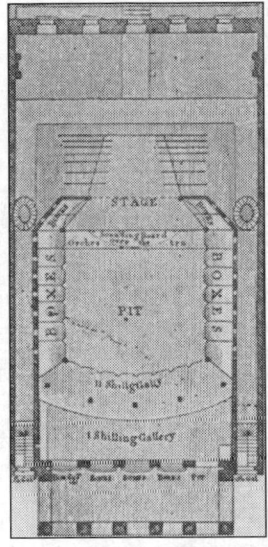

The Theatre Royal,
Haymarket, 1821.

act occasionally in films and on television, and for a time hosted a radio programme addressed to senior citizens.

As a youngster she appeared with John Drew (see DREW–BARRYMORE FAMILY) and WILLIAM GILLETTE, and worked for such fabled producers as CHARLES FROHMAN and GEORGE TYLER. Opposite Alfred Lunt in BOOTH TARKINGTON's *Clarence* (1919), she played a saucy flapper, as she did again in the THEATRE GUILD's *Caesar and Cleopatra*(1925) and *Coquette*(1927). In the 1930s, she had her greatest critical success as the gallant monarchs in *Mary of Scotland* (1933) and *Victoria Regina* (1935). In the 1940s and 50s she starred in showy vehicles like *Harriet* (1943), an episodic biography of Harriet Beecher Stowe; *Happy Birthday*(1946), in which she was a librarian turned siren; and *Mrs McThing* (1952), in which she was a society matron transformed into a charwoman. Her WEST END debut came in 1948 (Amanda in *The Glass Menagerie*). In her most memorable later work, the PHOENIX THEATRE 1967 revival of *The Show-Off*, she played GEORGE E. KELLY's no-nonsense mother-in-law with bracing tartness.

Often criticized for her choice of material and for being cloyingly demure, Hayes was more resourceful, modern and witty than her reputation generally allowed. She had a remarkably clear, low-pitched, resonant voice, and none of the hamminess that flawed the star acting of the tradition she grew up in. She was the author of several memoirs, most notably *My Life in Three Acts* (1990) with

Katherine Hatch. Two New York City playhouses were named the Helen Hayes Theatre, the first built in 1911 on West 46th Street and named in her honour in 1955 (torn down in 1982) and the second on West 44th Street, formerly the Little (built in 1912) and renamed the Helen Hayes in 1983. The major theatre awards given in Washington, DC, her birthplace, are named after her.   FH

Haymarket, Theatre Royal (London) Chief rival of the Patent houses for almost a century, the Haymarket opened inauspiciously in late 1720, scarcely justifying the speculative ambitions of its carpenter-builder, John Potter. It gathered notoriety in the 1730s, when HENRY FIELDING leased it to stage a series of anti-Walpole SATIRES. Walpole was sufficiently stung to engineer the passage of the Licensing Act in 1737, and the Haymarket was the most prominent of the illegitimate victims of this repressive legislation. After a fallow period, it was leased by SAMUEL FOOTE in 1747. Having ingeniously circumvented the law for several years, Foote was awarded a limited licence for the Haymarket in 1766, probably in compensation for the accident that cost him his leg. By the terms of the licence, the Haymarket was permitted to stage the legitimate drama during the summer months, when the Patent theatres were closed. Under the successive managements of GEORGE COLMAN THE ELDER (1776–94) and his son (1794–1817), the Haymarket provided a summer home for almost all the greatest actors and most popular plays of the period. The present theatre, with John Nash's famous portico, was built in 1820, though its interior has been refashioned many times since then. Among its best-known managers have been BENJAMIN WEBSTER (1837–53), BUCKSTONE (1853–79), the BANCROFTS (1880–5), BEERBOHM TREE (1887–96) and Cyril Maude (1896–1905).   PT

Hayward, Leland 1902–71 American producer. Hayward was responsible for two dozen plays and MUSICALS on BROADWAY between 1941 and his death, two-thirds of which were unqualified successes both critically and financially. Two of his productions (*State of the Union*, 1945; *South Pacific*, 1949) won Pulitzer Prizes. Before becoming a producer in 1944 with *A Bell for Adano*, Hayward had established a successful talent agency in Hollywood and New York. Other significant plays produced included *Mister Roberts* (1948), *Anne of the Thousand Days* (1948), *Call Me Madam* (1950), *Gypsy* (1959), *The Sound of Music* (1959) and *The Trial of the Catonsville Nine* (1971). He was also a film and television producer, a pilot and airline executive and a photographer. In 1936 he married the actress Margaret Sullavan, divorcing in 1948. OLIVER SMITH said that Hayward represented everything that was best in the theatre, being 'tenacious and at the same time elegant'.   DBW

Hazlewood, Colin Henry 1823–75 British playwright. Originally a low comedian in circuit theatres and a scribbler for cheap publications, Hazlewood became one of the most prolific and successful of 19th-century resident dramatists, spending most of his time in the employ of the Britannia, Hoxton, London. Although he could readily supply a PANTOMIME or a BURLESQUE, his most numerous pieces were MELODRAMAS. He and his assistants plundered popular periodicals and sensational magazines for gripping incidents, moral precepts and patriotic sentiments, sometimes copying them out, sometimes scissoring them out. The material accumulated and was then classified and stored in envelopes, which Hazlewood consulted when writing a play – or, as his contemporaries said, nailing down or sticking a play together. Some claim that he was paid 50 shillings per act; others, three pounds per week. It is not clear whether he or the management paid his assistants. Several of his pieces were based on popular novels. His *Lady Audley's Secret* was derived from Miss Braddon's tale, and his vividly entitled *The Headless Horseman, or The Ride of Death, A Strange Tale of Texas* from the novel by Mayne Reid. His dramatization of *The Heart of Midlothian* proved to be a most successful touring piece.   GH

Hazlitt, William 1778–1830 English essayist and critic whose unpredictable temperament, alternating from extremes of morbidity to extremes of enthusiasm, disqualified him from a potential role as the Boswell of the English romantics. Stirred almost equally in childhood by the promise of the French Revolution, the acting of SARAH SIDDONS and a reading of SCHILLER's *Die Räuber*, Hazlitt retained a fondness for the theatre, despite his clear perception of its faults and his literary refinement. 'We occasionally see something on the stage that reminds us a little of SHAKESPEARE,' he wrote in his *Champion* review of ELIZA O'NEILL's Juliet (1814), and yet, from so sceptical a stance, he could praise the grandeur of Mrs Siddons, the intensity of JOHN PHILIP KEMBLE, the gusto of EDMUND KEAN and the extravagance of LISTON. Hazlitt was most active as a dramatic critic for the *Examiner*, the *Champion*, the *Morning Chronicle* and *The Times* from 1813 to 18. It was in 1818 that he published a selection of his reviews under the title, *A View of the English Stage*. But his theatrical writing is by no means confined to that volume. He filled out and largely wrote the unfinished *Memoirs of the Late Thomas Holcroft* (1816), his famous *Characters of Shakespeare's Plays* (1817) is dotted with theatrical references, the metaphor of public life as a stage binds together the disparate essays of his most original work, *The Spirit of the Age* (1825); and he pursued with fascination the dangerous disparity between the actor, lofty in performance, and the actor, diminished in private, most notably in two essays, 'On Actors and Acting' (*The Round Table*, 1817) and 'Whether Actors Ought to Sit in the Boxes?' (*Table Talk*, 1824).   PT

Heath, Thomas see MCINTYRE, JAMES

heavens From the symbolic association of the 'heavens' above the stage and the 'hell' beneath it, the Elizabethans derived the custom of calling the canopy over the stage of the public theatres, supported as in De Witt's drawing of the SWAN by two pillars, the 'heavens'. It is probable that they decorated it with sun, moon and stars.   PT

Hebbel, Friedrich 1813–63 German playwright. After a childhood of abject poverty and an early manhood of dependency on various patrons, Hebbel settled in Vienna and, in 1846, married the BURGTHEATER actress, Christine Enghaus (1817–1910). The marriage gave him much-desired stability, both financial and emotional. Though most of Hebbel's plays have mythical or historical settings, his characters are recognizably figures of his time, struggling, not always with success, to come to terms with disturbing impulses that frequently border on the psychotic. The early prose drama *Judith* (1841) is an unorthodox treatment of the biblical myth, while *Maria Magdalena* (1844), a play with a contemporary setting, has been seen by many as anticipating IBSEN. *Herodes and Mariamne* (1849) treats the themes of trust and jealousy in marriage; *Agnes Bernauer* (1852), a powerful historical drama, has as its theme the guilt inherent in perfect beauty, while *Gyges and His Ring* (1856), a striking play about sexual tensions, also involves much discussion of political and moral issues. Hebbel's final work was a trilogy, *The Nibelungs* (1862). Though LAUBE at the Burgtheater was unwilling to stage Hebbel's work, he had little difficulty in finding theatres elsewhere in German-speaking Europe to accept his plays.   SW

Hebrew theatre Hebrew theatre is a relatively young theatre. Its history is intimately related to the national rebirth of the Jewish people and of the Hebrew language in the modern era. Although Hebrew, the language of the Bible, was continuously used by the Jews in the Diaspora for prayer, religious study and literature, it practically died out as a spoken language. Until the revival of Hebrew as an everyday language, since the turn of the century, Hebrew drama was handicapped by the lack of natural-sounding dialogue. This was not the case with drama written in Yiddish, the spoken language of the Jews of Eastern Europe (see YIDDISH THEATRE).

The growth of Hebrew theatre is also a concomitant of the gradual secularization of Jewish culture, for the Jewish religion was traditionally inimical to the theatre. The sages of the Talmud disapproved of it for a number of reasons, primarily because of the sacrifices offered in the theatre to idols. In their eyes it was also a scurrilous and bawdy place where the actors trespassed the Deuteronomy injunction against men wearing female dress. During the Hellenistic and Roman periods many theatres were built in Palestine, but they were regarded as gentile institutions, symbols of Hellenistic culture. Only in periods in which the Jewish community opened up towards its surroundings could it find interest in this essentially alien form of art.

The modern Hebrew theatre, closely tied as it is to the revival of the Hebrew language, has no theatrical tradition of its own. It consciously dissociated itself from the immediate heritage of the Yiddish theatre, which represented the culture of the Diaspora. Instead, the founders of the modern Hebrew theatre looked towards the European theatre for inspiration. But this relationship with foreign theatrical traditions on which it depends is often problematic. Where it finds the aesthetic form pleasing, it may yet find the ideology or religious values unpalatable and even offensive. This painful dialectic is especially poignant when the contemporary Israeli theatre grapples with antisemitic drama, such as SHAKESPEARE's *Merchant of Venice*.

Western dramatic art has often rejuvenated itself by reinterpreting classical drama. But Judaism saw Hellenism as a threatening alien and pagan culture to be opposed and rejected. Hence the Jews could not share in neoclassical movements. Instead, they could resort to a parallel stratagem and use the Bible as their artistic and moral paradigm and source of tales and themes. But for all its literary merit, the Bible could not teach dramatic structure and theatrical technique. For these, the Hebrew playwright had to turn to the works of other nations and languages.

The Purimspiel (Yiddish for PURIM PLAY) Most scholars see the folk origins of Jewish theatre in the Purim festival, the commemoration of the delivery of the Jews as recorded in the Book of Esther. It was traditionally celebrated with drink and revelry, dressing up and fooling, song and dance. The earliest recorded Jewish plays, dating from the 16th and 17th centuries, were meant for performance during the festival. Besides plays that retold the story of Esther, there were others on various biblical heroes, such as Joseph or Samson. These were written in Hebrew, Italian, Spanish, Portuguese, Provençal and Yiddish. Although not many of these plays have survived, we know about them from occasional catalogues of private libraries.

The beginnings in Italy, Holland and Eastern Europe It

was his wish to show that it was possible to write drama in Hebrew that brought YEHUDA LEONE DE' SOMMI to write the first original play in Hebrew, *A Comedy of Betrothal* (c.1550). In this comedy he successfully combined elements from both the *commedia erudita* and the *COMMEDIA DELL'ARTE* with a traditional Jewish story from the Midrash. Proud of his Judaism, de' Sommi attempted to prove in his *Four Dialogues on Scenic Representation* that it was the children of Israel rather than the Greeks who invented the tragic form, ingeniously arguing that the Book of Job is a tragedy in five acts. De' Sommi's singular enterprise does not seem to have influenced other Italian Jews and his work was forgotten until it was rediscovered by modern scholarship.

But at the beginning of the 17th century, because of the persecution of the Spanish Inquisition, a large number of Marranos left Spain and settled in Amsterdam. Here they revived their faith as well as the Hebrew language, in which they wrote not only religious treatises but also literary works and translations. Some of them, influenced perhaps by the Spanish *COMEDIA*, attempted to write plays in Hebrew.

The famous kabbalist Mosè Zaccuto, born in Amsterdam of Spanish descent and later a rabbi in Venice and Mantua, also wrote some Hebrew poetry and two dramatic works: *The Foundation of the Universe* (c.1650), ostensibly based on the Genesis story of Abraham and on the Midrash, but whose real theme is the martyrdom of the Spanish Jews; and *The Inferno Set Out* (date unknown), a poetic masterpiece but only questionably a play, exposing the tribulations of a recently deceased criminal who finds himself in the nether world faced with damnation.

His younger contemporary, Josseph Felix Penso de la Vega, emigrated with his family from Spain to Amsterdam, where he returned to the Jewish faith. He wrote in both Spanish and Hebrew and is reputed to have been the first to publish a book on the workings of the stock exchange, *Confusión de confusiones* (1688), a witty series of four conversations between a clever philosopher, a wary merchant and a knowledgeable stock-holder. As a 17-year-old student at a religious school, Penso de la Vega produced a play called *Prisoners of Hope* (1667), an allegory about a king who must choose between good and evil, somewhat like a MORALITY PLAY. Another renowned kabbalist who was also an occasional playwright was Moshe Hayim Luzzatto, from Padua. In his three plays he wrote about love's joys and pains: *The Tale of Samson* (1720), an adolescent biblical play intended perhaps as a Purim play, and two wedding plays, *The Tower of Strength* (c.1727), a PASTORAL play based on GUARINI's *Il Pastor Fido* (1596), and the highly allegorical *Praised be the Just* (1743).

Playwrights like Zaccuto and Luzzatto wrote against a background of a developing culture of plays performed at festivals and weddings. But at the end of the 18th century the Hebrew language lost favour with the Italian Jewish community as a literary medium, and the theatrical impulse died out.

The 19th century was a period of Jewish cultural renaissance in Eastern Europe. The *Haskalah* (Hebrew for 'Enlightenment') was a basically humanist and liberal movement, which aimed at introducing the Jews to the modern culture and science of other nations while at the same time effecting a revival of their own national culture. These new ideas, emanating from Germany, many of them put forth by the philosopher Moses Mendelssohn, swept through Eastern Europe in the second half of the 19th century. While the YIDDISH THEATRE blossomed during this period, the Hebrew drama, heavily influenced by Luzzatto, remained didactic and moralistic and devoid of theatricality.

The growth of the modern Hebrew theatre in Russia

The growth of the modern Hebrew theatre from the turn of the century onwards is closely associated with Zionism and its insistence on the return to Hebrew as an everyday spoken language. Unlike earlier cultural revivals, the Zionist movement was a national movement which succeeded in achieving its political goals with the founding of the state of Israel in 1948.

The first professional Hebrew theatre, HABIMAH ('the Stage'), was established in Moscow in 1918 by NAHUM ZEMACH. The founding of a Hebrew theatre was a truly visionary undertaking at a time when even in Palestine the language was spoken only by a few, and certainly in Russia, where only small groups of intellectuals understood it. While the Yiddish theatre enjoyed large popular audiences, there was no broad Hebrew-speaking audience. But Hebrew had become inextricable from the Zionist dream, and more and more literature was being written in it. Despite the ambivalent attitude of the Soviet authorities towards the use of Hebrew, Zemach obtained both recognition and financial support, and the Habimah became one of the three studios affiliated to the Moscow ART THEATRE, under the direction of KONSTANTIN STANISLAVSKY, and later grew into the Hebrew State Theatre Habimah.

Stanislavsky shaped the troupe's realistic acting technique, but it was EVGENY VAKHTANGOV's production of ANSKI's *The Dybbuk* (1922) that brought Habimah international recognition. Other notable early productions were *The Eternal Jew* by DAVID PINSKI, a play based on an ancient Talmudic legend, and *The Golem* by H. Leivik. In 1931 Habimah settled in Palestine.

Theatre in Palestine and Israel

The successive waves of Zionist immigration brought with them also the impetus to found a Hebrew theatre in Palestine. The first local group was the Lovers of the Hebrew Stage, who performed from 1904 to 1914. Various groups were formed in the early 20s: the Hebrew Theatre, the Dramatic Theatre, and the TAI (acronym for the Theatre of Eretz Israel). The Ohel ('Tent') was founded by Moshe Halevi, a Habimah veteran, in 1925. It was organized as a cooperative, much like a cultural kibbutz, and aimed at presenting plays on socialist themes. But it soon abandoned the idea of proletarian art in favour of national art, with a repertoire similar to that of Habimah. It remained the official theatre of the Histadrut (the General Labour Federation) until 1958, and closed down in 1969. The Ohel's most memorable production was Jaroslav Hašek's *The Good Soldier Schweik* (1935), starring the outstanding comedian MEIR MARGALIT.

While Habimah remained revered for its great past, a certain conservatism that had set in, a refusal to admit young actors into the collective and to face changes in Israeli society and in the spoken language, brought about the creation of the Cameri ('Chamber') Theatre, in 1944, by a group of young actors with a West European orientation, headed by Yosef Millo. Two of his recruits, HANNA MARRON and Yosef Yadin, were destined to become leading Israeli actors.

The Cameri's most important contribution to the theatrical scene was the performance of the first play by a *sabra*, a native Israeli, about a *sabra*. *He Walked the Fields*, by Moshe Shamir, was a topical play about the personal conflicts of the young heroes of the Israeli struggle for independence. The premiere took place in 1948, just two weeks after the proclamation of the state of Israel and in the midst of the war. The acting was devoid of the pathos that had come to be associated with Habimah. Millo staged the play in a non-illusionistic BRECHTian manner, with sets changed by the actors in front of the audience. Habimah followed suit with another play about the War of Independence, Yigal Mossinson's *The Wastes of the Negev* (1949), a thinly veiled stage reportage of a recent war episode.

Besides the three 'legitimate' public theatres there were also smaller ventures, such as the satirical theatres the Kumkum ('Kettle', 1927–8) and the Matateh ('Broom', 1928–54), which lampooned the British mandatory authorities.

The latest trends in avant-garde and experimental theatre were introduced in 1949 by Michael Almaz and his Zirah ('Arena') Theatre. In 1955, only three years after the Paris world premiere, the Zirah staged BECKETT's *Waiting for Godot*, and in 1957 it produced IONESCO's *The Bald Prima Donna* and *The Lesson*. But the theatre closed down after seven years, Almaz himself settling in England. In 1961 the Hammam Theatre opened in a disused Turkish bath in Jaffa. The Onot ('Seasons') Theatre was established in 1962, Bamat Hasahkanim ('the Actor's Stage') and Tzavta ('Together') in 1966.

All theatrical activity continued to be centred in Tel-Aviv until the opening of the Haifa Municipal Theatre in 1961, with Yosef Millo as artistic director. In its first years it hardly performed any original plays, but mounted a number of memorable productions, among them Brecht's *Caucasian Chalk Circle* (1962) with Zaharira Harifai as Grusha and HAIM TOPOL as Azdak, and *Richard III* (1966) with Millo himself in the title role.

Jerusalem, although the fast-expanding capital of Israel, has remained a theatrical backwater. In 1967 the municipality decided to convert an old *khan* into a theatre and to develop a local troupe. The Jerusalem Sherover Theatre is a striking modern edifice which has no troupe of its own but serves as the main auditorium for guest performances. Theatrical life in Israel also takes less conventional forms. For many years army troupes provided initial training for young actors and developed a distinctive style of acting and special brand of humour. The kibbutzim maintain their own semi-professional theatre, Bimat Hakibbutz ('Kibbutz Stage'). But perhaps its most striking feature is the government-sponsored tours of the established theatres, bringing performances to the remotest settlements.

Drama in the early years of the state

The War of

Independence and the establishment of the state of Israel (1948) made an enormous impact on the development of the theatre. A vogue of reportage-like drama followed the war plays of Moshe Shamir and Yigal Mossinson. Ben-Zion Tomer wrote in *The Children of the Shadow* about the encounter between refugees from Europe and the *sabras*. The failings of the new state were satirized by EPHRAIM KISHON and, in a lighter vein, by Aaron Megged (*Hedva and I*, 1954; *I Like Mike*, 1956).

From her broad European cultural perspective the poet Leah Goldberg dramatized the struggle between the old European culture and the new one being forged in Israel in *The Lady of the Manor* (1955). Nathan Alterman wrote a number of poetic plays, among them *The Inn of Ghosts* (1963), about the place of the artist in the world, and *Kinneret, Kinneret* (1962), on the early pioneers. Plays in the manner of the THEATRE OF THE ABSURD were written in the 50s and 60s by Nissim Alloni (*Most Cruel Is the King*, *The American Princess*, *Eddie King*, *The Bride and the Butterfly-Hunter* and several others) and by Amos Keenan (*That's the Man!*).

The contemporary scene While many successes from abroad continue to be imported for cultural as well as commercial reasons, the by now firm roots of the Israeli theatre have fostered the growth of new talent. The Haifa Municipal Theatre has been the most adventurous in soliciting new works – with remarkable returns, such as Ya'acov Shabtai's *Spotted Tiger* (1974) about the idealism of the early builders of Tel-Aviv, and A. B. Yehoshua's *A Night in May* (1968) about the effects of the pre-Six-Day War tension on a Jerusalem family. Especially fruitful has been the association between this theatre and Yehoshua Sobol (*Soul of a Jew*, 1982; *Ghetto*, 1984). Sobol has excelled in his imaginative use of historical and documentary material, and his plays have been well received abroad. Another outstanding Israeli playwright is HANOCH LEVIN.

The international vogue of adapting stories for the stage has not passed Israel by, where a number of plays based on stories by the two Nobel Prize-winners S. I. Agnon and Isaac Bashevis-Singer have coloured the local stage with nostalgia for the extinct Jewish culture of the Diaspora. The religious revival movement has also been reflected in a number of pieces, notably in Yossi Yizraeli's production of *The Seven Beggars* (1979), based on the Hassidic tales of Rabbi Nahman of Breslau.

The Israel Festival in Jerusalem has familiarized the Israeli public with the latest experimental work from abroad, while the young Acre Festival serves as a greenhouse for local alternative theatre. Since the beginning of the large wave of immigration from Russia in the late 1980s, some immigrant actors have found their way into the Hebrew-speaking theatres, especially the Be'er-Sheva Theatre, while others have founded Russian-speaking troupes. Notable among these is the Gesher ('Bridge') Theatre, headed by the director Evgeni Arieh, which performs in both Russian and Hebrew. They have won national recognition with performances of STOPPARD's *Rosenkrantz and Guildenstern are Dead*, BULGAKOV's *Molière*, and a stage adaptation of Dostoevsky's *The Idiot*.

Different aspects of the Arab-Israeli conflict, and especially the Palestinian question, have been widely addressed both in original plays and in provocative interpretations of traditional repertoire, as, e.g., Beckett's *Waiting for Godot* (Haifa Municipal Theatre, 1985), and *Romeo and Juliet* (co-production of the Israeli Khan Theatre and the Palestinian al-Casaba Theatre, 1994). HAS

See: G. Abramson, *Modern Hebrew Drama*, London, 1979; M. Kohansky, *The Hebrew Theatre: Its First Fifty Years*, Jerusalem, 1969; E. Levy, *The Habima – Israel's National Theatre 1917-1977*, New York, 1979; J. Schirman, *Studies in the History of Hebrew Poetry and Drama* (in Hebrew), Jerusalem, 1979.

Hecht, Ben 1894–1964 American playwright and librettist. Although a significant figure in American cinema, Hecht is important theatrically for two popular and frequently revived American plays, both collaborations with CHARLES MACARTHUR. Together the playwrights were viewed as bad boys of BROADWAY. *The Front Page*, a frenetic, funny, satirical MELODRAMA on the newspaper business (1928), is based on their experiences as reporters in Chicago. *Twentieth Century* (1932), an eccentric COMEDY depicting a desperate producer trying to make a comeback, inspired a John Barrymore (see DREW-BARRYMORE FAMILY) film and the MUSICAL *On the Twentieth Century*. Hecht wrote other plays and musical librettos as early as 1922 and as late as 1953. His autobiography, *A Child of the Century*, appeared in 1954. RHW

Heeley, Desmond 1931- British stage and COSTUME designer. Heeley began his career at the BIRMINGHAM REPERTORY THEATRE Company and then at the Shakespeare Memorial (now ROYAL SHAKESPEARE) Theatre, where he became designer in 1955. His first shows were *Toad of Toad Hall*, notable for its MASKS and headdresses and depiction of animals' hands and feet, and *Titus Andronicus* under the direction of PETER BROOK. He subsequently became an internationally known designer, working at the OLD VIC, the Shakespearian theatre of the STRATFORD FESTIVAL, Ontario, the GUTHRIE THEATRE in Minneapolis, and COVENT GARDEN. He was hired to design *Norma* at the New York Metropolitan Opera (1970) after Rudolph Bing saw his sets and costumes for the BROADWAY production of *Rosencrantz and Guildenstern Are Dead* (1968). He has subsequently designed many operas there. Heeley's lush, textured, layered and subtle but provocative use of colour in costumes has influenced a whole generation of designers (see THEATRE DESIGN). His style has been described as impressionistic SYMBOLISM combined with the texture of collage and junk art. His designs are most successful in the theatrical, larger-than-life world of SHAKESPEARE and opera. AA

Heiberg, Gunnar 1857–1929 Norwegian director, critic and playwright. Heiberg argued for a more modern repertoire and realistic acting style at Christiania Theater, and from 1884 attempted to realize them as director of the NATIONALE SCENE, Bergen, in his detailed world premiere productions of IBSEN's *The Wild Duck* and *Rosmersholm*. In 1888 he began a new career as a dramatist and essayist, only occasionally returning to directing. His 14 plays are influenced by IBSEN's in their handling of ideas, but are experimental in their tendencies towards theatricalism, SATIRE and formalized characterization. *Aunt Ulrikke* (1894) and *The Tragedy of Love* (1904) have been the most enduring.　HL

Heiberg, Johan Ludvig 1791–1860 Danish poet, playwright, critic and manager, husband of the actress JOHANNE LUISE HEIBERG. His extraordinary influence on Denmark's cultural life depended primarily on his promotion of the thought and literature of France and Germany, which he hoped would Europeanize Denmark. He praised 18th-century French classicism and GOETHE's WEIMAR classicism, and was at best ambivalent about SHAKESPEARE. He popularized Hegelian philosophy and admired CALDERÓN DE LA BARCA and the Jena romantics for their embodiment of speculative philosophy in drama. He considered REALISM tasteless, and sought to bring sophistication to Danish theatre by promoting and writing *vaudevilles*, in which his wife frequently performed; more enduring have been his comedies *Elves' Hill* (1828) and *A Soul after Death* (1841). In his management of the KONGELIGE TEATER (1849–56) his aristocratic values and conservative taste in repertoire were bitterly opposed by progressive-thinking actors like Frederik Høedt and MICHAEL WIEHE.　HL

Heiberg, Johanne Luise 1812–90 Celebrated Danish actress, who acted exclusively at the KONGELIGE TEATER. Heiberg's career was linked to that of her husband, JOHAN LUDVIG HEIBERG, who wrote a large number of *vaudevilles* specifically to suit her personality, while she shared his conviction that theatre should embody idealized beauty rather than reality. Her ironic, graceful style suited the *vaudevilles* and SCRIBEan comedies that dominated the Kongelige's repertoire in the 1830s, increasingly supplemented by the sentimental plays of Henrik Hertz in which she frequently partnered MICHAEL WIEHE. After her husband's death in 1860 she began her 'second career', playing more demanding roles such as Lady Macbeth and SCHILLER's Mary Stuart. In 1867 she began directing, and while her productions were tasteful rather than realistic, she staged several early plays by BJØRNSTJERNE BJØRNSON and IBSEN, whose writing clearly fascinated her.　HL

Heijermans, Herman [Samuel Falkland] 1864–1924 Dutch playwright and theatre director, who reached international fame through his socio-realistic plays. A convinced socialist, he wrote in order to protest against bad social conditions, under which the lower classes, particularly, suffered. Although he was a Jew, he had a strong dislike of orthodox Judaism (*Ghetto*, 1898): in general he opposed social and religious conventions and prejudices that forced man into a straitjacket.

In the 1900s Heijermans was a man of controversial opinions, but his plays, because of their social involvement, were very popular with audiences. Today, they are still regularly performed. The most popular ones are *Schakels* (*Links*, 1903), *Uitkomst* (*Relief*, 1907), *De opgaande zon* (*The Rising Sun*, 1908) and *De wijze kater* (*The Wise Cat*, 1917). *Ahasverus* (1893) was staged in Paris by ANTOINE. *Op Hoop van Zegen* (*The Good Hope*, 1900) and *In de Jonge Jan* (1903) were performed in England, the United States and Russia. *Op Hoop van Zegen*, his best-known play, deals with the oppression of poor fishermen by powerful ship-owners. The character of Kniertje, the old mother, has become a household name. His work has been compared with IBSEN, HAUPTMANN and CHEKHOV.　MG HS

Heiremans, Luis Alberto 1928–64 Chilean playwright, born to an illustrious and wealthy Santiago family with French ancestry. A talented and industrious student, he had early training in literature and languages (French and English), and discovered theatre at an early age. He received a medical degree, but preferred to devote his time and talents to literature and the arts. In addition to some 15 plays, Heiremans also published novels and short stories as well as translating and adapting French and English plays for the Chilean stage. He was a professor at the Teatro de Ensayo of the Catholic University, where he promoted Chilean theatre. The Heiremans Foundation, created after his premature death from cancer, continues to provide benefits for theatre students and the arts. Interested in vanguard theatrical techniques, Heiremans dealt with existentialist themes of anguish, frustration, solitude and alienation in his early plays. His *Esta señorita Trini* (*This Miss Trini*, 1958) was the first Chilean MUSICAL COMEDY, a play that enjoyed tremendous commercial success. His most mature plays are his final trilogy, *Versos de ciego* (*The Blind Man's Verses*, 1961), *El abanderado* (*The Standard Bearer*, 1962) and *El tony chico* (*The Little Clown*, 1964), representing a combination of religious-mythic, poetic and folkloric elements that point towards a higher Christian ideal.　GW

Helburn, Theresa 1887–1959 American director and producer. Born in New York, Helburn received her BA from Bryn Mawr College, Pennsylvania, in 1908, attended GEORGE PIERCE BAKER's playwriting course, English 47, at Radcliffe College and studied in Paris for a year at the Sorbonne. After a brief career as an actress, she pursued a writing career, becoming drama critic of the *Nation* (1918). Two years later she took over the administration of the struggling THEATRE GUILD with the title of executive director. In 1933 she left for a year in Hollywood but returned as administrative director with LAWRENCE LANGNER. She was responsible for bringing ALFRED LUNT AND LYNN FONTANNE together for *The Guardsman* in 1924, establishing them as the leading dual acting team in America. With Langner she brought *Oklahoma!* to the stage in 1943, and in the same year *Othello* with PAUL ROBESON. A woman of outstanding executive ability, she was described by Langner as possessing nerves 'like whipcord' and willpower 'like steel'. Her autobiography, *A Wayward Quest*, was published in 1960.　TLM

Hellman, Lillian 1906–84 One of America's leading playwrights. Since 1963, when she ceased writing for the theatre, revivals of her plays have been performed regularly throughout the USA. She is also known for her controversial books of memoirs: *An Unfinished Woman* (1969), *Pentimento* (1973) and *Scoundrel Time* (1976). In 1993 a play based on her relationship with Peter Feibleman (*Cakewalk*), starring Elaine Stritch, was staged at the AMERICAN REPERTORY THEATRE.

The Children's Hour (1934), based on an episode from William Roughead's *Bad Companions*, shocked and fascinated BROADWAY with the evil machinations of a child who destroys her teachers by whispering about their 'unnatural' relationship. Hellman was labelled a 'second IBSEN', 'the American STRINDBERG', and the play ran for 691 performances. Vigorous, unyielding confrontations became her dramaturgical trademark, both in *Children's Hour* and in *The Little Foxes* (1939), and in *Watch on the Rhine* (1941), *The Searching Wind* (1944), *Another Part of the Forest* (1946), *The Autumn Garden* (1951), *The Lark* (1955, adapted from ANOUILH's *L'Alouette*), *Candide* (1956, from Voltaire, with music by LEONARD BERNSTEIN) and *Toys in the Attic* (1960). Her plays were always given high-quality productions, first by Herman Shumlin and then by Kermit Bloomgarden. Only three plays failed at the box office: *Days to Come* (1936), *Montserrat* (1949, adapted from Emmanuel Roblés's play) and *My Mother, My Father and Me* (1963, adapted from Burt Blechman's novel, *How Much?*).

Born in New Orleans, she became an editorial assistant to Horace Liveright in New York, a theatre press agent, a playreader, and (in 1931) a script-reader in Hollywood, where she met detective-story writer Dashiell Hammett, who was to become her constant companion until his death in 1961. She wrote scripts for such films as *Dark Angel* (1935), *These Three* (1936, based on *The Children's Hour*), *Dead End* (1937) and *The North Star* (1943). In 1952 she was called before the House Un-American Activities Committee, and her name was automatically added to Hollywood's blacklist. RM

Helpmann, Robert (Murray) 1908–86 Australian dancer, actor, director and choreographer. As a youth he toured Australia with Pavlova in 1926, and became principal dancer in J. C. WILLIAMSON MUSICALS. Joining the Vic Wells/Sadler's Wells Ballet in 1933, he remained principal dancer until 1950, also working as dancer, choreographer and director at COVENT GARDEN from 1946. After appearing as Oberon at the OLD VIC in 1937 he played many Shakespearian roles at the Old Vic and Stratford-upon-Avon, and directed and acted in many modern plays. He was co-artistic director from 1965 to 76 of the Australian Ballet, which staged his ballets *The Display* (1964), *Yugen* (1965) and *Sun Music* (1968); he also directed the 1970 Adelaide Festival of Arts. He was awarded a CBE in 1964 and created a Knight of the British Empire in 1968. MW

Heminges, John d.1630 English actor and company manager whose claim to have been the original Falstaff is based on nothing more than the memory of a rumour. He was a sharer in the LORD CHAMBERLAIN'S/King's MEN from the company's foundation in 1594 until his death. He was an unexceptional actor, but his immortality is assured by his initiative in the publication of the SHAKESPEARE Folio of 1623. The task may have fallen to him in his role as business manager of the King's Men. After 1611, Heminges acted rarely, if at all. An ambiguous contemporary reference afflicts him with a stutter. There is no doubt that he was a reliable and widely respected administrator. He accumulated wealth and property, despite costly problems with at least two of his 14 children, and was for many years churchwarden of St Mary's, Aldermanbury. There

was nothing of the 'rogue and vagabond' about Heminges. PT

Henderson, Ray see DESYLVA, BUDDY

Henley, Beth 1952– American playwright (and actress) in the Southern Gothic tradition, whose comedies create empathy for bizarre characters who survive their disastrous experiences in outlandish ways. Her first professionally produced play, *Crimes of the Heart*, won the Pulitzer Prize in 1981, the first play to win it before a BROADWAY opening. A family drama gone awry, *Crimes* portrays with absurdist wit (see THEATRE OF THE ABSURD) and compassion the rallying of three eccentric Mississippi sisters because one of them has shot her husband. Henley's other plays include *The Wake of Jamey Foster* (1982); *Am I Blue?* (1982); *The Miss Firecracker Contest* (1984), another black COMEDY, about a Mississippi woman's effort to redeem her calamitous life by winning a beauty contest; *The Debutante Ball* (1985); *The Lucky Spot* (1986); and *Abundance* (1990), the exploration of a 25-year friendship of mail-order brides in the Old West. Henley also wrote screenplays for *Crimes* and *Miss Firecracker*. FB

Hennings, Betty 1850–1939 Danish actress, noted for her IBSEN performances at the KONGELIGE TEATER. Hennings specialized in ingénue roles, playing Agnes in *The School for Wives* and Selma in *The League of Youth*, before creating Nora in the world premiere of *A Doll's House* (1879). Her revelation of Nora's growing inner tension was a turning point in her career, leading to her casting as other, more complex, Ibsen characters: Hedda Gabler, Hilde Wangel, Hedvig Ekdal and Mrs Alving. Although her strength was in naturalistic modern drama (see NATURALISM), by the turn of the century her style was perceived as too mannered for modern taste. HL

Henry, John 1738–94 Early American actor, born in Ireland, who worked in London and the West Indies before joining DOUGLASS's American Company. Henry made his first American appearance in Philadelphia on 6 October 1767. The matinée idol of his time, he was the first actor in America whose lamentable morals were seized on by opponents of the theatre. A chronic sufferer from gout, Henry was also the first American actor to keep a carriage. He first married a Miss Storer; after her death he lived with her sister, Ann, and finally married a third Storer sister, Maria.

After the Revolutionary War, he co-managed the American Company with LEWIS HALLAM JR and in 1792 imported JOHN HODGKINSON, who shortly forced Henry into retirement. A tall, handsome Irishman, Henry was most successful in comedy, especially Irish characters. WILLIAM DUNLAP considered him 'one of the best performers in the colonies', but his arrogant manner made him many enemies. SMA

Henslowe, Philip c.1550–1616 English businessman whose many enterprises included theatre management. Henslowe was apprenticed to a dyer, whose widow he married and whose daughter married the actor EDWARD ALLEYN in 1592. By then, Henslowe already held the lease of the ROSE THEATRE, and may also have been in control of the theatre in London's Newington Butts. He and his son-in-law formed the most consistently successful partnership in the field of Elizabethan entertainment. When the Rose began to suffer under competition from the newly built GLOBE, they built the FORTUNE on the other side of the Thames (1600). In 1604, they purchased the Mastership of the Royal Game of Bears, Bulls and Mastiff Dogs, and ten years later they sought to combine their interests in drama and animal-BAITING by erecting the adaptable HOPE THEATRE on Bankside, London. Henslowe became involved in drama because he believed in its profitability. He was an energetic and not over-scrupulous businessman. Apart from maintaining some share in his brother's mines in Ashdown Forest, he was also engaged in the manufacture of starch, in real estate, in pawnbroking and in money-lending. It was partly by usury that he controlled his contracted actors and playwrights. Evidence of his dealings has survived in the uniquely valuable *Diary*, the gatherings of papers deposited by Alleyn in the Dulwich Picture Gallery in Southeast London.   PT

Her/His Majesty's Theatre (London) There have been four theatres on the Haymarket site and their names have varied with the sex of the reigning monarch. The first, designed by SIR JOHN VANBRUGH and named the Queen's Theatre, was intended as a home for the dissenting DRURY LANE players under the leadership of THOMAS BETTERTON. It opened in 1705, with Vanbrugh and CONGREVE in joint management, and soon proved more hospitable to OPERA than to drama. Handel wrote 29 of his 35 operas for performance there, and in its Georgian heyday the King's Theatre was a Mecca for the fashionable adherents of the Italian opera. It was destroyed by fire in 1789.

The second King's Theatre (capacity 2500), designed by Michael Novosielski, opened in 1791 and was recognized as a rival to La Scala in Milan (built 1788). After two seasons of drama (as host to the homeless Drury Lane company), it reverted to opera in 1793, remaining the undisputed centre of (predominantly Italian) opera until 1847, when COVENT GARDEN proclaimed itself the Royal Italian Opera House. Renamed Her Majesty's Theatre on the accession of Queen Victoria in 1837, the second theatre was destroyed by fire in 1867.

The third theatre, known throughout as Her Majesty's, had an undistinguished history. Designed by Charles Lee to house an audience of nearly 2000, it was completed in 1869, remained unused until 1874 when it was sold by auction, was occupied from 1875 to 77 by the American evangelists Moodey and Sankey, was first used for opera in 1877 and was demolished in 1891.

The present theatre (capacity 1263), designed by C. J. Phipps for HERBERT BEERBOHM TREE, opened in 1897 and remained under Tree's adventurous control until his death in 1917. It was there, in 1904, that he opened the drama school that would evolve into the Royal Academy of Dramatic Art, and there that he presented his spectacular SHAKESPEARE productions. The more typical future of Her Majesty's (His Majesty's between the death of Queen Victoria and the accession of Queen Elizabeth II) was foreshadowed by the phenomenal success of OSCAR ASCHE's *Chu Chin Chow* (1916). Later spectacular successes have included FLECKER's *Hassan* (1923), COWARD's *Bitter Sweet*

(1929) and such American MUSICALS as *Brigadoon* (1949), *Paint Your Wagon* (1953), *West Side Story* (1958) and *Fiddler on the Roof* (1967).   PT

Herbert, Jocelyn 1917– British stage designer in the austere, poetic tradition of COPEAU and SAINT-DENIS, by whom she became influenced while an art student in France and, later, as a theatre student in Saint-Denis's London Theatre Studio. Not until her 40th year did Herbert begin a theatre career, as stage designer at the ROYAL COURT THEATRE in London during its most creative years, under the leadership of GEORGE DEVINE, a former associate of Saint-Denis. Her work also came to reflect the spare functionality of BRECHTian theatre. In later years her scenography in England and abroad became more complex but has never lost its essential purity and fine sense of spatial proportion. Distinctive productions include *Saint Joan of the Stockyards* (1964), *The Abduction from the Seraglio* (1979), *Galileo* (1980), *The Oresteia* (1981), *The Mask of Orpheus* (1986) and *Square Rounds* (1992).   JMB

Herbert, Victor 1859–1924 Irish-born and German-educated composer, who went to America at the age of 27 to perform as a cellist with the Metropolitan Opera Orchestra. He became interested in composing for the theatre, and in 1894 his first score, *Prince Ananias*, was heard. The following year, his show *The Wizard of the Nile* had a long run in New York and on tour. After composing the music for several shows for comedian Frank Daniels, Herbert created the score for *The Serenade* (1897), which benefited from an excellent production by the Bostonians (BOSTON IDEAL OPERA COMPANY). In the last years of the 19th century, Herbert served as musical director of the Pittsburgh Symphony Orchestra. Some of his most enduringly popular songs were written for *Babes in Toyland* (1903) and *Mlle Modiste* (1905), the latter created as a vehicle for opera star Fritzi Scheff. Herbert's biggest commercial success came with *The Red Mill* (1906), which was also a big hit when revived on BROADWAY in 1945. Among his other popular MUSICALS were *Naughty Marietta* (1910), *Sweethearts* (1913) and *Eileen* (1917). He also contributed songs to the 1921 and 1923 ZIEGFELD *Follies*. He was one of the founding members of the American Society of Composers, Authors and Publishers.

Trained in the conventions and traditions of European operetta, Herbert was adept at composing music that appealed to American audiences. Equally at home writing for comic OPERAS, OPERETTAS and musical comedies, he raised the level of American theatre music through the richness and variety of his scores.   MK

Herman, David 1876–1930 One of the first and most influential of JEWISH ART THEATRE directors. Herman started with HIRSHBEIN's Troupe in Odessa in 1908, followed by the Arts Corner in Warsaw in 1910, and then the celebrated Vilna Troupe from 1917, where his most memorable of many productions was a stylistic production of *The Dybbuk*. After periods in Warsaw and Vienna, he emigrated to America, exerting a profound influence on the YIDDISH THEATRE scene with his inspired direction of the FOLKSBIENE.   AB

Hernández, Luisa Josefina 1928– Mexican playwright and novelist. Hernández occupied the theatre chair at the National University vacated by her professor and mentor, RUDOLFO USIGLI, when he accepted a diplomatic position. A prolific contemporary writer, she achieved early success with both *Los frutos-caídos* (*The Fallen Fruit*, 1957) and *Los huépedes reales* (*The Royal Guests*, 1957), the latter a brilliant study of incest. Always concerned with problems of history, she adapted several major works to the stage, such as *Clemencia* (the Altamirano novel, 1963), and *Popol-Vuh* (1967), based on the Mayan myths and legends, and *Quetzalcoatl* (1968). Hernández has integrated BRECHTian techniques into many works and has been an early and steady advocate of women's rights and social justice. Retired from the university, she continues to write plays that show great sensibility for the underprivileged classes. GW

Herne, James A. 1839–1901 American actor, manager and playwright. Responding to the forces of science and democracy that challenged contemporary society, Herne developed realistic themes and characters in his plays and created a realist creed for drama. Beginning his acting career in 1854, he became a stage manager in San Francisco, where he wrote MELODRAMAS with DAVID BELASCO (*Within an Inch of His Life*, 1879; *Hearts of Oak*, 1879). Among his own plays, *The Minute Men of 1774–75* (1886) suggested the New England local colour later developed in the temperance play *Drifting Apart* (1888) and *Shore Acres* (1892), in which Uncle Nat Berry, with his language and action, personified the down-easter (rustic New Englander) and made Herne a millionaire.

With the help of WILLIAM DEAN HOWELLS and others who rented Chickering Hall in Boston, Herne staged *Margaret Fleming* (1890–1), his best known-work. This insightful play, about a philandering husband whose illegitimate child is accepted by his morally superior and sensitive wife, revealed Herne's interest in REALISM and social determinism, as well as his playwriting skills; although revised before its New York production, it was still unsuccessful. *The Reverend Griffith Davenport* (1899), based on a novel by Helen Gardner, dramatized the struggle of a slave owner who opposed slavery during the Civil War.

Relating drama to contemporary literature, Herne wrote 'Art for Truth's Sake in the Drama' (*Arena*, February 1897) to emphasize the 'humanity' and 'large truth' in the drama that has a 'higher purpose' than to amuse. This was a new concept for commercially minded theatre entrepreneurs of this period. Praised by Howells for his 'epoch marking' play *Margaret Fleming*, Herne wrote plays that delineated the beginning of modern drama in America. WJM

hero-combat play The most widespread of the several British and Irish mumming plays. A comic drama of armed conflict, death and resurrection, performed seasonally, it is frequently described as medieval, or even pre-Christian, though there is no hard evidence of it until 1737. Its text appears to be based on one of the many editions of Richard Johnson's *Seven Champions of Christendom*, and on 17th-century broadside lampoons against mountebanks. It is probably a 17th- or 18th-century syn-thesis of popular literature with elements of indigenous traditions of mumming. The hero-combat play has been extensively revived in the present century under the aegis of the folk song and dance movements traditional gangs still perform at Antrobus, Bampton, Chipping Campden, Marshfield, Ripon and Uttoxeter in England. AEG

Heron, Matilda 1830–77 American actress, who made a life's work of *Camille*. Fascinated by Mlle Doche's playing of Marguerite Gautier in Paris (1854), she made her own adaptation of the play, opening it in New Orleans (1855) and then at WALLACK's (1857). New Yorkers were captivated by Heron's 'elemental power', her 'animal vivacity', her uninhibited exploitation of a woman's sexual life, and her lifelike naturalness (even turning her back to the audience); and when Camille coughed her way to the grave, tears flowed throughout the house. After an initial run of 100 performances, she toured the play for the next 20 years.

Born in Ireland, Heron played Juliet to CHARLOTTE CUSHMAN's Romeo (1852), made her New York debut as Lady Macbeth (1852), and appeared at London's DRURY LANE (1854) before she discovered Camille. RM

Herrmann, Alexander 1844–96 German-born MAGICIAN. His elder brother by 27 years, Carl, was the first Herrmann to achieve international acclaim, including initial appearances as a magician in the USA in the 1860s. Alexander, who succeeded Carl, was first seen in New York in 1869 and ultimately settled in the USA, though he continued touring internationally. Although Alexander was HARRY KELLAR's major competition in the 1880s – with illusions such as 'Cremation', in which a woman was set on fire and then spectral forms were made to rise from her coffin – Herrmann's widow Adelaide and his nephew Leon were unsuccessful in sustaining the popularity of the Herrmann show after his death, and for a time Kellar had little competition. Still, Adelaide performed until 1928, 31 years with her own show, longer than any other Herrmann. DBW

Herzegovina see YUGOSLAVIA; MEDIEVAL DRAMA IN EUROPE (Eastern Europe)

Hettner, Hermann 1821–82 German professor of literature. Hettner's most significant contribution to the theatre was his brief book *The Modern Drama* (1852), which, in validating the advances made by the bourgeois tragedy, prepared the way for the drama of IBSEN and the naturalists (see NATURALISM). SW

Hewett, Dorothy 1923– Australian playwright; initially a poet and novelist. Hewett's first work was the working-class drama *This Old Man Comes Rolling Home* (1967). Her plays, mainly expressionistic epics (see EXPRESSIONISM) featuring music and poetry, depict complex women characters trapped in ageing, domesticity, and the stereotyped images of women, or evoke an idyllic pastoral world. They include *The Chapel Perilous* (1971), *Bon Bons and Roses for Dolly* (1972), *The Tatty Hollow Story* (1974), *Pandora's Cross* (1978), *The Man from Mukinupin* (1979) and *The Fields of Heaven* (1982). She was made a Member of the Order of Australia in 1986. The much praised first volume of her autobiography, *Wild Card*, appeared in 1990. In 1992 she received one of the prestigious three-year Australian Artists' Creative Fellowships for established artists of excellence. MW

Heyward, Dorothy 1890–1961 and
(Edwin) DuBose Heyward 1885–1940 American husband and wife playwriting team, in which he primarily supplied stories from his novels, and she dramatic craftsmanship. Although DuBose wrote one other play and Dorothy had five others produced, their reputation rests on their folk dramas of Negro life – *Porgy* (1927) and *Mamba's Daughters* (1939) – both praised for their realistic depiction of the lives of Southern blacks. *Porgy*, the love story of a crippled black man and an erring woman, became an American legend, particularly after its conversion into a folk opera, *Porgy and Bess* (1935), by DuBose and the GERSHWINS (a 1977 revival won a Tony). The Heywards are credited with providing dramatic opportunities for AFRICAN-AMERICAN actors: ETHEL WATERS, in *Mamba's Daughters*, was the first black woman to star in a BROADWAY drama. FB

Heywood, John 1497–1580 English playwright. As a writer of INTERLUDES, Heywood is of importance in charting the development of the English theatre between the medieval period and the full fruition of the Elizabethan age. His plays *The Play of the Weather* (1533) and *The play called the foure P. P.* (*The Four Ps*, c.1543) are seen as his best. They, like the rest of his work, are jolly and simple. He was the son-in-law of JOHN RASTELL, and thus the nephew-in-law of Sir Thomas More – which probably helped. MB

Heywood, Thomas 1573–1641 English playwright, actor, poet and pamphleteer, who was, at various times, actor and attached dramatist with the ADMIRAL'S MEN, Worcester's Men and Queen Anne's Men. Heywood wrote industriously for money. Much of his work has been lost, and much that remains is ephemeral. Interest in his numerous mayoral pageants, for example, is likely to be confined to scholars. An early work, *The Four Prentices of London* (?1592), is a far-fetched chivalric romance. It was presumably a revival of this uncommonly popular work which inspired the jolly PARODY of BEAUMONT's *The Knight of the Burning Pestle* (1607). Heywood wrote plays of many kinds. His masterpiece is certainly the domestic tragedy, *A Woman Killed with Kindness* (1603), which rises to emotional heights without seeming to strive for them. Heywood's zest for the detail and range of Elizabethan life enriches the two-part chronicle of Elizabeth I's early years on the throne, *If You Know Not Me, You Know Nobody* (1605), and the eventful adventure play, *The Fair Maid of the West* (Part 1, c.1610; Part 2, c.1630). The dramatizations of Greek mythology in *The Golden Age, The Silver Age, The Brazen Age* and *The Iron Age* (1611–13) are, by contrast, oddly perfunctory. Heywood wrote them for Queen Anne's Men at the rough-and-tumble RED BULL THEATRE, and they are tuned to an audience that liked its poetry interrupted by spectacular action. By his own count he wrote, singly or in part, 220 plays, of which some 30 have survived. That he remained alert to topical issues is shown by a late play, written with RICHARD BROME, *The Late Lancashire Witches* (1634). He was well qualified by temperament and experience to write a defence of his profession, which he did in *An Apology for Actors* (1612). *The Fair Maid of the West* was the play chosen by the ROYAL SHAKESPEARE COMPANY to perform before Queen Elizabeth II when she officially opened the new Swan Theatre in Stratford-upon-Avon in 1986. PT

Hibberd, Jack [John] **(Charles)** 1940– Australian playwright. He studied medicine at Melbourne University where his first play, *White with Wire Wheels*, was staged in 1967; he later wrote for the Melbourne alternative theatres La Mama and the Pram Factory. His plays are characterized by caricature, black humour and flamboyant language: they include *Dimboola* (1969), *The Les Darcy Show* (1974) and *A Toast to Melba* (1976), both celebrations of famous Australians, the monodramas *A Stretch of the Imagination* (1972) and *Odyssey of a Prostitute* (1984), and a satirical OPERA, *Sin* (1978). He has abandoned the theatre for the present and returned to medicine. MW

Hicks, (Edward) Seymour 1871–1941 British actor-manager and dramatist, who toured America with the KENDALS before producing *Under the Clock* in 1893, the first REVUE staged in London. A versatile performer starring in everything from MUSIC-HALL to BARRIE's *Quality Street* (1904), Hicks was also a prolific author of light COMEDY such as *Sleeping Partners* (1917) and Christmas plays, one of which (*Bluebell in Fairyland*, 1901) was given regular performances until 1937; and he collaborated with the novelist Ian Hay on satiric FARCE (*Good Luck*, 1923). In 1905 he built the Aldwych Theatre, then the Globe in 1907, both in London, which he opened with performances in his own plays. Awarded the Legion of Honour in 1931 for his promotion of French drama on the English stage, he took over London's Daly's Theatre in 1934 and was knighted in 1935. CI

Highway, Tomson 1951– Canadian playwright of Native Cree heritage. Highway's plays mix a realistic portrayal of the lives of Canadian Natives with a plea for the revalidation of Native culture and spiritual mythology. His earliest performance pieces, *New Song ... New Dance* (1981) and *The Sage, the Dancer and the Fool* (1982), allowed him to combine his classical music training with his poetry in both English and Cree.

His first full-length play, *The Rez Sisters* (1986), about the lives of a group of women on an Indian reservation, won him international attention for its 'combination of the magical and kitchen-sink REALISM'. It won the 1986 Dora Mavor Moore Award for Best New Play of the Year, was a runner-up for the Floyd S. Chalmers Award for Best Canadian Play, and represented Canada at the EDINBURGH FESTIVAL, where it was enthusiastically received. His second contribution to the '*Rez* cycle', *Dry Lips Oughta Move to Kapuskasing* (1989), about the lives of the men on the same reservation, won several Dora Awards, including Best New Play, Best Production, Best Leading Male Actor and Best Female Supporting Actor. In 1991 it was performed at one of Canada's largest commercial stages, the Royal Alexandra Theatre in Toronto.

Hilar's production of *Hamlet* at the Prague National Theatre, 1926; set by V. Hofman.

The central figure in both *Rez* plays is Nanabush, or the Trickster – the sometimes male, sometimes female, sometimes tragic, sometimes comic central figure of Native spiritual mythology. Through his use of the Trickster figure, Highway tries to convey to non-native audiences a sense of the joyousness of Native spirituality, while at the same time providing a source of connection and pride for the Native cultural community. He is a founding member and former artistic director of Native Earth Performing Arts, a theatre company dedicated to developing and producing new works by Native artists.   DAH

Hijikata Yoshi   1898–1959 Japanese director. Born into the aristocracy, Hijikata soon became disillusioned with the nobility and took a lifelong interest in the theatre. After graduating from Tokyo University, he departed for a planned ten-year European tour in November 1922 but returned to Japan in December 1923 to help found the Tsukiji Little Theatre (Tsukiji Shōgekijō), which he financed almost single-handedly until 1929. As a director, Hijikata was influenced by MEYERHOLD and other avant-garde directors. In 1933 he left Japan for the Soviet Union. An avowed Marxist, the Japanese government stripped him of his title in 1934. During Stalin's purges Hijikata left the Soviet Union for France, but returned to Japan in 1941 and was immediately imprisoned, spending the duration of the war in gaol. After his release Hijikata resumed his theatrical activities, directing and serving as administrator for a number of influential theatrical enterprises. DGG

Hilar, Karel Hugo   1885–1935 Czech director. After early work as poet, critic and literary editor, he began his directing career in 1910 at Prague's Municipal Theatre, where he soon established himself as a director of great force attracted to the expressionistic mode (see EXPRESSIONISM). By his dynamic personality and artistic vision, he eventually surpassed the achievements of Jaroslav Kvapil, the first modern Czech director, as head of drama at the National Theatre (1921–35). After the mid-1920s his work became less extravagant and more reflective. Among his principal achievements were *Hamlet* (1926), *Oedipus* (1932) and *Mourning Becomes Electra* (1934).   JMB

Hildesheimer, Wolfgang   1916– German dramatist, novelist and painter. After a comedy based on *Turandot*, *The Dragon Throne* (produced by GRÜNDGENS in 1955), Hildesheimer became the leading German exponent of THEATRE OF THE ABSURD with plays such as *Behind Schedule* (1961) and *Nightpiece* (1963), before turning to historical subjects like *Mary Stuart* (1970).   CI

Hill, Aaron   1685–1750 English playwright, manager and critic. A schoolfriend of BARTON BOOTH and JOHN GAY, he toured Europe and the Middle East from 1700 to 1702. In 1709, as a complete novice, he was appointed manager of DRURY LANE and wrote his first plays, *Elfrid* and *The Walking Statue* (a good FARCE). He closed the theatre in 1710, after disputes with the actors, and moved to manage the HAYMARKET Theatre. His libretto for *Rinaldo* (1711), Handel's first London opera, and the spectacular machinery in the production ensured Handel's success.

After only one season Hill was forced to give up management. Of his next plays, *Fatal Vision* (1716) is significant for its use of FERDINANDO BIBIENA's angular perspective for the first time in England and *Fatal Extravagance* (1721) for its attempt at domestic bourgeois tragedy, though neither are good plays. Occasionally involved in theatre management in the 1720s, Hill continued to make interesting, if failed, experiments in playwriting and production. *Athelwold* (1731), a revision of *Elfrid*, was an early attempt at historical authenticity in design, with Hill producing drawings of 'old Saxon dress'; *Zara* (1735) is a translation of VOLTAIRE's *Zaïre*, the first of Hill's four translations from Voltaire. Apart from his numerous inventions and speculations, Hill also founded one of the most important periodicals to be concerned with theatre, the *Prompter* (1734–6), and wrote a poem

The Art of Acting (1746), encouraging the actor to develop the imagination to experience the emotions of the part and then reproduce the emotions in the physical appearance. PH

Hill, George Handel ['Yankee'] 1809–49 American actor. In the 1830s and 40s Hill was the leading exponent of the YANKEE roles in WILLIAM DUNLAP's *Trip to Niagara*, SAMUEL WOODWORTH's *The Forest Rose* and JOSEPH S. JONES's *The Green Mountain Boy*. Audiences delighted in his plausible cunning, his great industry and his pliant honesty. One critic said he was 'the funniest actor, and cleverest fellow in the Yankee signification of the word – in Christendom'. He appeared in London in 1836 and 38. He first undertook Yankee impersonations with solo recitations of 'Jonathan's Visit to Buffalo' and 'The Yankee in Trouble; or, Zephaniah in the Pantry'. His autobiography appeared in 1853. RM

Hill, Jenny 1851–96 British serio-comedienne ('the Vital Spark'), and the first female artist to achieve recognition as a MUSIC-HALL star. She and her contemporary Bessie Bellwood broke with the gentility of the lady duettist to create racy and original solo character acts, which paved the way for MARIE LLOYD, VESTA TILLEY and NELLIE WALLACE. Though details of her early life and career are sparse, it is clear that she had a hard time. The daughter of a cab-minder at a rank in London's Marylebone High Street, she began work at an artificial flower factory until transferred, under articles which bound her for five years, to the Bradford Tavern, one of the early 'sing songs', where, not yet in her teens, she 'had to be up with the lark to clean the bars' and 'by noon ... dressed and in the singing-room to provide harmony for the early-afternoon drinkers'. The long hours of virtual slavery while she was still a child may have contributed to the decline in her health and her early death, but evidently did not break her indomitable spirit; and it is likely that the experience of the tough performance conditions of the tavern halls contributed to her vibrant stage personality and gave depth to her later comic and MELODRAMATic realizations of suffering and oppression.

Following a disastrous early marriage to an acrobat, who abandoned her on the birth of their daughter, she talked her way into an engagement at the London Pavilion (c.1869) and from then on her brief career was made. She played all the big London halls, performed in New York, was a popular principal boy in PANTOMIME, did BURLESQUE, and even tried her hand at the legitimate theatre. Though not a success in the latter, even her failure moved the theatre manager JOHN HOLLINGSHEAD to describe her as 'one of the greatest female geniuses who ever appeared on the music hall platform'; specifically, he paid tribute to her 'sense of character – low life, of course – and her dramatic power of conjuring up solid pictures of men and women who never appear bodily on the stage'. The last remark probably refers to her emotive performance of narrative songs incorporating dialogue, but may also allude to the classic solo technique of inviting the audience to imagine the presence of other characters on stage.

Tiny in stature, with a generous smile, she had a powerful and flexible singing voice, danced well, and excelled in character songs both male and female, concentrating on representations of the poor and downtrodden: factory girls, domestic drudges, coster boys and street vendors. Among many fine performances perhaps the most popular was the eponymous hero of 'The Little Stowaway', a melodramatic song-sketch in which she played a small boy placed on board ship for Halifax, Nova Scotia, by his father who was unable to keep him. It is telling that no classic music-hall song is associated with her name; her fame came not from her material but from the power and generosity of her performance. AEG

hippodrama In A. H. Saxon's words, 'a play in which trained horses are considered as actors, with business, often leading actions of their own, to perform'. Horses had occasionally been brought on stage before the 19th century – PEPYS had seen some at the King's Playhouse in 1668 in a revival of SHIRLEY's *Hyde Park*, and a live Pegasus was flown in PIERRE CORNEILLE's *Andromède* in 1683. But the hippodrama first caught on at the turn of the 18th century, possibly because of cavalrymen, riding masters and stable grooms being made redundant after the Continental Wars, and the gradual closing of fairs. The innovation found a home in London at ASTLEY's Amphitheatre in 1803, at the Royal Circus and the Olympic Pavilion, and in Paris at the CIRQUE OLYMPIQUE. In Vienna, Christoph de Bach (1768–1834) presented equestrian pantoMIMES, such as *The Triumph of Diana* and *Marlborough's Heroic Death*, which constituted a synthesis of theatre and CIRCUS, and introduced a broader public to mythology and history.

Astley's *The Blood Red Knight* (1810) made £18,000, prompting COVENT GARDEN to follow suit with COLMAN THE YOUNGER's *Blue Beard* and 'Monk' Lewis's *Timour the Tartar* (1811), and DRURY LANE, reluctantly, with *The Cataract of the Ganges*. The outstanding performer was ANDREW DUCROW, but women took the title role in the frequently revived *Mazeppa, or The Wild Horse of Tartary*, in which the young prince, stripped to his fleshings, is strapped to a horse set loose on a treadmill and attacked by stuffed vultures and similar impedimenta. ADAH ISAACS MENKEN made her notorious name in the part.

The hippodrama, fallen into disuse by the mid-century, enjoyed a revival of sorts at the Châtelet, Paris, with military spectaculars like *Marengo* (1863) and the immensely popular *Michel Strogoff* (1880). The invention of a graduated treadmill that could simulate races inspired one final burst of horse-play in America with *The Country Fair* by Charles Bernard (Union Square Theatre, New York, 1889) and Lew Wallace's *Ben Hur* (Broadway Theatre, New York, 1899). Thereafter, equine stardom passed to the movies, where Trigger and Rex the Wonder Horse had fan clubs of their own. LS

Hippodrome (London) Built as a circus in 1900, with a large water-tank for aquatic spectacles, the Hippodrome was reconstructed as a MUSIC-HALL in 1909, where Tchaikovsky's *Swan Lake* was first danced in England by the Russian Ballet (1910). Its reputation was for REVUE and MUSICAL COMEDY, among them *Mr Cinders* (1929) and Ivor Novello's *Perchance to Dream* (1938); and from 1949 to 1951 it became the London equivalent of the FOLIES-BERGÈRE. In 1958 it was reconstructed again, becoming a dinner-CABARET – the Talk of the Town – until it closed in 1982. CI

Hippodrome Theatre (New York City) Conceived and built in 1905 by Frederic W. Thompson and Elmer S. Dundy, who had created the extravagant Coney Island amusement centre, Luna Park. Advertised as the world's largest theatre, its auditorium seated 5000 and its stage was equipped with every device known to create magnificent spectacles. The costs of production and the maintenance of the house overwhelmed even the canniest of producers, including the SHUBERTS and Charles Dillingham. In 1923, it was taken over by the KEITH–ALBEE VAUDEVILLE chain, then leased for popular-priced opera, then as a sports arena. In 1935, BILLY ROSE presented his production of *Jumbo* at the theatre, the last notable event in its history. It was torn down in 1939. MCH

Hirsch, John 1930–89 Canadian director. Hirsch fled the Holocaust in his native Hungary, arriving in 1947 in Winnipeg, where he was co-founder of the Manitoba Theatre Centre and its first artistic director (1958–66). He earned international attention for several of his productions there, including the first Canadian production of BRECHT's *Mother Courage* (1964), with ZOË CALDWELL in the title role. That same year he mounted his critically acclaimed French adaptation of *Mother Courage* (*Mère Courage*) for Montreal's THÉÂTRE DU NOUVEAU MONDE.

In 1965 Hirsch began his long and sometimes uneasy association with the STRATFORD FESTIVAL when he directed his brilliant adaptation of CHEKHOV's *The Cherry Orchard*; his production of JAMES REANEY's *Colours in the Dark* was the undisputed artistic success of the 1967 season. He was a master of theatrical effect: his productions were frequently provocative and controversial, but always marked by his distinctive style and focus. He became associate artistic director (with JEAN GASCON) at Stratford in 1968, a post he left in 1969 after confrontations with the Festival's board. He subsequently ran several major American theatres and taught at Yale. His production of Chekhov's *The Seagull* opened Israel's HABIMAH National Theatre in 1970.

After several years as head of CBC English-language Drama (1974–8; see RADIO DRAMA), Hirsch returned to the theatre, in 1981 becoming artistic director at Stratford, where he inherited a company reeling financially and emotionally from the abrupt departure of ROBIN PHILLIPS. His programme for renewal included profiling the successful Young Company, a reflection of his commitment to the development and training of actors. Artistically, however, his seasons were plagued by overspending and a general artistic blandness. Despite several noteworthy productions, he left Stratford in 1985, having seen audiences decline while the theatre's deficit tripled. He spent his remaining years teaching and directing, mainly in the USA. DAH

Hirsch, Judd 1935– American actor. Over 20 years Hirsch established a major reputation as a versatile actor in film and television and on stage, beginning with his BROADWAY debut in 1966, replacing Herb Edelman as the Telephone Repairman in *Barefoot in the Park*. Unlike many of his successful contemporaries in film or televi-

sion, he returns frequently to the New York stage, as the following partial list of credits illustrates: *The Hot l Baltimore* (1973) as Bill, the night manager; Feiffer's *Knock, Knock* (1976); NEIL SIMON's *Chapter Two* (1977); LANFORD WILSON's *Tally's Folly* (1979) as Matt Friedman, an immigrant Jewish accountant; CIRCLE REPERTORY COMPANY's *The Seagull* (1983) as Trigorin; and HERB GARDNER's *I'm Not Rappaport* (1985) at the AMERICAN PLACE THEATRE, later transferred to Broadway, and *Conversations with My Father* (1992), winning Tonys in both. According to one interviewer, Hirsch has a rugged 'street face, a face of interchangeable ethnicities and professions'. His career to date supports such a description. DBW

Hirschfeld, Al(bert) 1903– The doyen of American theatrical caricaturists, and well known internationally. Hirschfeld, a native of St Louis, studied fine arts in New York and Paris, intending to become a painter or sculptor. Instead, he became fascinated with the manipulation of the thin black line into shapes and attitudes, and hence was drawn into the art of the caricature. His early drawings were submitted to several New York newspapers, but since 1925 he has worked almost exclusively for the *New York Times*, flavouring its theatre journalism with drawings of current BROADWAY personalities and happenings. For many years, Hirschfeld has woven the name of his daughter Nina into the tapestry of his drawings, slipping a small numeral next to his signature to indicate the exact number of times it appears. He is the first American artist to be allowed to sign his name on postage stamp artwork (1991). Among his books are *The American Theatre as Seen by Hirschfeld* (1961), *Hirschfeld by Hirschfeld* (1979) and *Hirschfeld: Art and Recollections from Eight Decades* (1991). MCH

Hirschfeld, Kurt 1902–64 German director, whose major influence was in Switzerland where he staged the premiere of BRECHT's *Puntila* and helped to shape the drama of both DÜRRENMATT and FRISCH. CI

Hirshbein, Peretz 1880–1948 Yiddish playwright, who began writing in Hebrew in Russia but in 1906 started writing Yiddish plays, harshly realistic or subtly symbolist (see REALISM; SYMBOLISM). In Odessa he founded the Hirshbein Troupe (1908–10), an acting ensemble dedicated to intellectually ambitious YIDDISH THEATRE. After several years of travelling and writing he settled in New York, where his plays *Green Fields*, *A Secluded Nook*, *The Blacksmith's Daughters* and *The Idle Inn* (1912–18), all evocative romances of Russian Jewish rural life, won praise. The film version of *Green Fields* is still screened. NS

His Majesty's Theatre see HER/HIS MAJESTY'S THEATRE

Hispanic Caribbean see CUBA; DOMINICAN REPUBLIC; PUERTO RICO

Hispanic theatre (USA) From its earliest beginnings to the present time, Hispanic theatre has had a chequered and often interrupted history. In many cases documentation is scarce because of its depreciated value in traditional circles. Current scholarship divides the movement into three fairly discrete parts: CHICANO THEATRE, primarily in the West and Southwest; CUBAN-AMERICAN THEATRE, mostly in New York and Florida; and the New York theatre, sometimes called NUYORICAN, which has a heavily Puerto Rican component. None of these classifications is absolute or unilateral. Manifestations of Chicano theatre can be found across the land, from the Northwest to the East, and as the Spanish-speaking population has become more mixed and more integrated, categorization has become more difficult. The theatre is linguistically structured as well: Chicano theatre still tends to rely heavily on a mixture of both languages, combined into 'Spanglish'. Cuban-American theatre was earlier almost exclusively in Spanish, whereas the younger generation often writes and performs in English. The Nuyorican theatre depends heavily on English, in contrast with the island. (See also ETHNIC THEATRE (USA).)   GW

history play Because critics sensed a distinction between the plays SHAKESPEARE wrote on subjects drawn from English history and, for example, those he wrote on subjects drawn from Roman history, they came gradually to accept the invented term, 'history play'. Despite its specious appropriateness, the description is not particularly useful except as a convenient way of dividing Shakespeare's plays into sub-groups, as has also been tried with 'problem plays', 'Roman plays', 'last plays' and so on. The difference between the style of the Roman plays and that of the history plays owes more to the distinctive styles of Shakespeare's sources, Thomas North's translation of Plutarch for the Roman stories and Holinshed's *Chronicles* for the English, than to decisive authorial strategy. Nor could it be reputably maintained that the *Henry VI* trilogy has much in common with the great tetralogy comprising *Richard II*, the two parts of *Henry IV* and *Henry V*, whilst the untidy *King John* and the brilliantly melodramatic *Richard III* demand independent assessment. The Elizabethans would not have understood the modern distinction between history and legend, seeing both in terms of story. There is, however, some justice in the view that Shakespeare's history plays have, as a counterpoint to the story of English kings, the story of the country over which they ruled, and that they are further strengthened by the conviction, shared by playwright and original audience, that the story is still in progress. Even so refined, a term that may exclude TENNYSON's *Queen Mary* (1875), *Harold* (1876) and *Becket* (1884) but not plays as various as JOHN BALE's *Kynge Johan* (1538), MARLOWE's *Edward II* (c.1592) and JOHN ARDEN's *Left-Handed Liberty* (1965) is of limited use.   PT

Hjörtsberg, Lars 1772–1843 Popular Swedish comic actor. Hjörtsberg trained with Monvel's French troupe, brought to Sweden by Gustav III, and from 1788 to 1834 became a leading member of DRAMATEN. Admired for his powers of mimicry, improvisation and attention to detail, he specialized in playing eccentrics, such as the pedantic chatterbox Captain Puff, the daydreaming tailor in *The Imagined Prince* and Orgon in MOLIÈRE's *Tartuffe*. Short and somewhat plump, Hjörtsberg was unsuited to

tragedy, but succeeded in serious and sentimental drama such as the title role in RICHARD CUMBERLAND's *The Jew*.   HL

Hochhuth, Rolf 1931– German dramatist. His first play, *The Representative* (1963), is a closely printed 226-page indictment of Pope Pius XII for complicity in the Holocaust. Though part of the documentary movement, it is really a polemical piece shot through with SCHILLERian idealism and packed with documentary evidence. After PISCATOR's heavily cut and skilfully mounted Berlin production proved the play could work, its sensational subject brought Hochhuth 73 productions in 27 countries. Its US title was *The Deputy*. *Soldiers* (1970) takes issue with Dresden and the tactic of bombing civilians. It puts historical figures on the stage and accuses Churchill of murdering Sikorsky, wartime head of the Polish government in exile. Hochhuth has always had an eye for topical issues but has never learnt to cut them to dramatic size. At the BERLINER ENSEMBLE in 1992 Einar Schleef's striking production of *Wessies in Weimar*, an exposure of the West German colonialization of the former GDR, used one in ten of Hochhuth's lines.   HR

Hochwälder, Fritz 1911–86 Austrian dramatist, whose play *The Strong Are Lonely* (*Das heilige Experiment*, 1943) was performed world-wide. It explored the relationship between power politics and social utopia in the context of a 19th-century Jesuit colony in Paraguay. *Esther* (1940) used a biblical episode as a metaphor for the Nazi persecution of the Jews. Like the above, *Der öffentliche Ankläger* (*The Public Prosecutor*, 1947), dealing with justice during the French Revolution, is a conventional problem play.   HR

Hodgkinson (Meadowcroft), John 1767–1805 British-born actor and manager who, after some provincial experience, accepted an offer in 1792 from JOHN HENRY to join the American Company and spent the rest of his career in the USA. Although his personal reputation has been much maligned, his private life after his arrival in America seems to have been without blemish. He never became a star, but was a tall, handsome man with an exceptional voice and memory who excelled in high and low COMEDY, playing at least 379 roles during his 24-year career. During 1794–8 he was joint manager of the JOHN STREET THEATRE. Later he acted in all the principal cities of the Atlantic seaboard until his death from yellow fever.   DBW

Hoffman, Dustin 1937– American film and stage actor. Hoffman worked at the Theatre Company of Boston with David Wheeler before his 1965 New York debut as Immanuel in *Harry, Noon, and Night*. The next year he played Zoditch in *The Journey of the Fifth Horse*. Also in 1966 he appeared in *Eh?*, winning several awards, as he did in 1968 in the title role of *Jimmy Shine*. After an extraordinarily successful stint in films, he starred in a BROADWAY revival of *Death of a Salesman* (1984), acclaimed as a performance of genius and demonic intensity, and in 1989 (after a successful London engagement) appeared on Broadway as Shylock in PETER HALL's production of *The Merchant of Venice*.   SMA

Hoffmann, E(rnst) T(heodor) A(madeus) 1776–1822 German poet, novelist, composer and stage director. Known primarily as a writer of romantic short stories and novels, Hoffmann nevertheless had important theatre experience. From 1808 to 1813 he directed the theatre at Bamberg where, in cooperation with Franz von Holbein (1779–1855), he attempted to create a theatre in which all elements – the actors, the design and the lighting – contributed towards a vision of life beyond the appearance of everyday reality. While at Bamberg, he was among the first German directors to introduce the works of CALDERÓN to the stage. After his return to Berlin in 1814, where he joined the Prussian Civil Service, he became a close drinking companion of LUDWIG DEVRIENT. His poetic dialogue, *Strange Sorrows of a Theatre Director* (1818), apart from being an invaluable source for the acting of Devrient, also contains some of the liveliest accounts of the theatre of the time. Hoffmann was also a talented OPERA composer, his most famous work in this regard being the fairy opera, *Undine* (1814). SW

Hofmannsthal, Hugo von 1874–1929 Austrian poet, playwright and essayist. In the 1890s he was the youngest member of the Jung Wien (Young Vienna) circle, and his writings typified *fin-de-siècle* neo-romanticism and decadence. Among several plays he wrote at this time, *Death and the Fool* (1893) is notable for its elaborate verse and poetic atmosphere. As he matured, Hofmannsthal developed a profound awareness of the importance of traditional European culture and, throughout his career, worked to preserve its values in a period of radical, often violent, change. Hence he looked to the theatre of the past to provide him with both the structure and the substance of his work.

Elektra (1906) and his two Oedipus plays (1906 and 1907), while reflecting modern interest in psyche, clearly derive from classical sources. In plays that he wrote for the Salzburg Festival, *Everyman* (1911) and *The Salzburg Great Theatre of the World* (1922), he borrowed from medieval and Spanish baroque theatre. In *The Tower* (1925), his great festival play, the central situation is taken from CALDERÓN's *Life Is a Dream*, though thematically it relates to the destruction caused in Europe by the First World War. Hofmannsthal also adapted OTWAY's *Venice Preserv'd* (1905), and in his late comedy *The Difficult Man* (1921) he showed the influence of CONGREVE. He is possibly best remembered today for his librettos for OPERAS by Richard Strauss. In addition to *Elektra*, these included *Der Rosenkavalier* (1911), *Ariadne auf Naxos* (1912), *The Woman without a Shadow* (1919), *The Egyptian Helen* (1928) and *Arabella* (1931). SW

Holberg, Ludvig 1684–1754 Norwegian-born playwright, satirist, historian and philosopher. Holberg spent most of his life in Copenhagen, writing in Danish, and holding several university positions. Although his major impact on Danish letters has been in the theatre, playwriting occupied only short periods of his life. When Copenhagen acquired its first professional Danish-speaking theatre, on Grønnegade (1722–8), he wrote 27 comedies for it, and then six further plays for the new Danske Skueplads (Danish Playhouse) that opened in 1748.

Often dubbed 'the MOLIÈRE of the North', Holberg certainly echoes Molière, but also PLAUTUS, JONSON and *COMMEDIA DELL'ARTE*. His plays are still frequently performed in Scandinavia, and respond well to modern directorial approaches. His most enduring are those, such as *Jeppe of the Hill* (1722), *The Political Tinker* (1722), *The Busybody* (1726) and *Erasmus Montanus* (1731) which explore the irrationality of human behaviour. In Denmark the many plays that are built around *commedia*-like intrigues are almost as popular, while his specifically contemporary SATIRES have had a limited theatrical life. One view of Holberg's comedies is that they embody, at least by implication, an affirmative view of human rationality typical of the Enlightenment. This has been challenged by arguments that he is a complex ironist, presenting a chaotic, amoral world in which reason is threatened by irrational and antisocial forces. HL

Holbrook, Hal [Harold Rowe Holbrook] 1925– American actor and writer, who made his debut with a Cleveland STOCK COMPANY in 1942 and spent four seasons in stock. With his first wife he toured for six seasons, presenting famous scenes from the classics, from which developed his immensely successful one-person show, *Mark Twain Tonight!*. He first appeared as Twain in New York in 1955, and has revived the show periodically to immense critical and popular acclaim.

Holbrook spent the 1964 season with the Lincoln Center Repertory, alternating Quentin with JASON ROBARDS JR and playing Marco Polo in *Marco Millions*. Recently he has turned to classic roles, appearing at Cleveland's Great Lakes Theatre Festival in 1990 as King Lear (later seen at New York's Roundabout Theatre), as Uncle Vanya the following year and as Willy Loman in 1994, as well as Shylock at San Diego's Old Globe Theatre (summer 1991). SMA

Holcroft, Thomas 1745–1809 English playwright, the self-taught son of a shoemaker. Holcroft's life was a catalogue of disasters, sufficient to destroy a lesser man. After working successively as a pedlar, stable-boy, shoemaker and schoolteacher, he entered the theatrical profession in 1770 and was, for ten years, a strolling player. During this period of poverty, his first wife left him and his second died in childbirth; his first work, a comic opera called *The Crisis* (1778), was produced at DRURY LANE; and he published a novel based on his own theatrical experience, *Alwyn* (1780). The success of his COMEDY *Duplicity* (1781) at COVENT GARDEN encouraged Holcroft to commit himself to writing. Having taught himself French, as well as German and Italian, he went to Paris in search of plots and was lucky enough to witness an early performance of BEAUMARCHAIS's *The Marriage of Figaro*. Within two months, Holcroft's version, *The Follies of a Day* (1784), was staged at Covent Garden. It was followed by further adaptations: *Seduction* (1787) from Laclos's notorious novel *Les Liaisons Dangereuses*, *The German Hotel* (1790) from the German of JOHANN CHRISTIAN BRANDES, and *The School for Arrogance* (1791) from *Le Glorieux* by DESTOUCHES.

The source of Holcroft's best-known play, *The Road to Ruin* (1792), is not known. A moral comedy with excellent character roles, it held the stage for a century and was revived in London in 1937. Still dogged by tragedy,

Holcroft witnessed the suicide of his only son in 1789 and the death of his third wife in 1790, and was himself partially paralysed by a stroke in 1792. As a friend of William Godwin and defender of Thomas Paine (*The Rights of Man* was published in 1791-2), Holcroft was one of the 12 indicted for high treason in 1794, and although all were acquitted, Holcroft found his access to the theatre restricted for the rest of his life. Forced to avoid contentious topics, he mixed insipid comedies with the Gothic MELODRAMAS then in vogue in Paris. His first in this kind was *Deaf and Dumb* (1801), but the first to be advertised as a melodrama, thereby importing the word into the English theatre, was *A Tale of Mystery* (1802), hurriedly adapted from PIXÉRÉCOURT's *Coelina*. It is a shoddy monument to an extraordinarily vigorous man. Holcroft's *Memoirs* (1816), posthumously and grudgingly completed by WILLIAM HAZLITT, offer better evidence of his worth. PT

Holland Festival The first Holland Festival was held in June 1947 in Amsterdam, as a result of plans made during the German occupation in the Second World War to organize an annual celebration of the arts. The Festival belongs to the European Association of Music Festivals, but it has grown into an occasion for the presentation of other artistic forms as well, such as dance, the plastic arts and the atre. The aim is to investigate new artistic values. Hence, the Festival has featured experimental and controversial performances (particularly in recent years). Companies that specialize in drama, theatrical arts in general, music and dance, as well as individual artists from both the Netherlands and abroad, are invited according to the philosophy that the Netherlands, being a small country, should direct its attention to international developments. Regarded as a cultural highlight, the Festival is always held in June, a point at which the previous season has just ended and the new one has not yet begun. And most of it takes place in Amsterdam.

Significant performances have been BOTHO STRAUSS's *Gross und Klein* by Schaubühne am Hallischen Ufer, Berlin (1980); MacDonald's *Chinchilla* by the Glasgow CITIZENS' THEATRE (1981); a SHAKESPEARE trilogy by La Compagnia del Collettivo/Teatro Due, Parma (1982); *Rosas danst Rosas* by Anne Terese de Keersmaeker (1983); *De macht der theaterlijke dwaasheden* (*The Power of Theatrical Follies*) by Jan Fabre (1984); *Fairground '84* by MICKERY-THEATER (1984); *King Lear* by DRAMATEN, Stockholm (1985); and *Sihanouk* (1986) and *Les Atrides* (1991) by THÉÂTRE DU SOLEIL, Paris.

The Holland Festival is subsidized by both the government and local authorities, and further financial support is supplied by sponsorship. Now that television and radio show a growing interest in the event there is nationwide distribution of both live and pre-recorded broadcasts. MG HS

Holland, George 1791-1870 British-born actor, called a 'comedian of peculiar and irrepressible drollery'. After seven years on the London stage, he went to the USA in 1827, making his debut at the BOWERY THEATRE in *A Day after the Fair*. For 16 years he toured, gaining immense popularity, especially in the South, where he also entered

for a time into management with NOAH LUDLOW and also SOL SMITH. In New Orleans, where he remained from 1835 until 1843, he worked with JAMES H. CALDWELL. For the next six years he played in comedies and burlesques at WILLIAM MITCHELL's Olympic. Beginning in 1855, and for a total of 14 years, he was low comedian with WALLACK's company, leaving in 1869 to join AUGUSTIN DALY. Of Holland's six children, four became actors, most notably Edmund Milton and Joseph Jefferson. DBW

Holliday Street Theatre (Baltimore, USA) Built by THOMAS WIGNELL and Alexander Reinagle, the theatre was opened on 25 September 1794, intended as a satellite of their Philadelphia theatrical operations. Later in its history, it was managed prosperously by JOHN T. FORD. It was pulled down in 1813 and a new theatre built on its site; this the city of Baltimore razed in 1917, to construct War Memorial Plaza. MCH

Hollingshead, John 1827-1904 British theatre manager and journalist who was, for a while, a leading contributor to DICKENS's *Household Words* and dramatic critic of the *Daily News*. Fascinated by the theatre, Hollingshead was also a radical thinker, committed to improving the life of London's workers. As stage manager of the Alhambra, he sought to broaden its audience and to entertain it. If girls were the answer, girls he would employ. He was instrumental in introducing the cancan to England, and it was in the same spirit of daring that he opened his own London theatre, the GAIETY, in 1868. Almost accidentally, the Gaiety became the home of a new style of BURLESQUE, revolving round the talents of the famous Quartette of NELLIE FARREN, EDWARD TERRY, KATE VAUGHAN and EDWARD ROYCE. But it was also the first theatre in London to stage a play by the shocking IBSEN – WILLIAM ARCHER's translation of *Quicksands: or The Pillars of Society* (1880). Illness and financial troubles forced Hollingshead to sell out to GEORGE EDWARDES in 1886, but his love for his old theatre is vividly recorded in the books he wrote in his retirement, *Gaiety Chronicles* (1898) and *Good Old Gaiety* (1903). PT

Hollmann, Hans 1933- Austrian director, whose productions have tended towards sensationalism. Hollman has made a reputation for adapting the classics to reflect contemporary political issues, particularly SHAKESPEARE, and his influential productions of HORVÁTH between 1967 and 1971 helped to inspire the contemporary Volksstück (folk play). CI

Holm, Celeste 1919- American film, stage and television actress. Holm's professional debut was in *The Night of January 16* in a Deer Lake, Pennsylvania, summer theatre in 1936. Her first New York appearance was as Lady Mary in *Gloriana* in 1938. She created Ado Annie in *Oklahoma!* in 1943. Her first film was *Three Little Girls in Blue* (1946). Most recently (1991) she appeared with Nicol Williamson in Paul Rudnick's *I Hate Hamlet*. Her awards include an Oscar for *Gentlemen's Agreement* (1947) and the SARAH SIDDONS Award for her performance in the national touring company of *Mame* (1969). In 1979 she was knighted by King Olav of Norway. SMA

Holm, Hanya [Johanna Eckert] c.1898–1992 German-born modern dancer-choreographer and theatre choreographer, who began her training and performance career in her native country before arriving in the USA to direct the Wigman School in New York (1931). She opened her own school and embarked on a choreographic career that established her as a leading pioneer in American modern dance. Although primarily abstract in form, Holm's choreography was powerful, and critics wrote that she incorporated German constructivism in her work. Not limited to abstract invention, she also choreographed using more traditional dance movements for MUSICAL THEATRE productions. Among her most notable musical theatre credits are *Kiss Me Kate* (1948), *My Fair Lady* (1956) and *Camelot* (1960). LF

Holman, Robert 1952– British dramatist, born in Yorkshire, whose subtle studies of domestic and working lives express his gift for seeing wide-ranging issues in small examples. His early plays, *Coal* (1973), *Outside the Whale* (1976), *German Skerries* (1977) and *Mucking Out* (1978), are primarily naturalistic, well observed, atmospheric works, distinguished by their economy of means and compassion towards their characters. He is a reluctant moralist, who rarely diminishes his portraits by turning them into examples of some deplorable trait. Instead, as in *Today* (1984, about how a gifted young man develops during the interwar years), *The Overgrown Path* (1985) and *Making Noises Quietly* (1986), three short plays about encounters between people affected by war, Holman concentrates on the apparently trivial but pivotal incidents by which the lives of his characters are transformed. From 1977 to 79 he was the resident dramatist at the Royal NATIONAL THEATRE, but his plays seem better suited to the more intimate surroundings of London's BUSH THEATRE (which pioneered his early work) than to the larger studios of the national companies. *Across Oka* (1988), which was staged by the ROYAL SHAKESPEARE COMPANY at the Other Place in Stratford-upon-Avon and transferred to the Pit in London, is about two families, English and Russian, whose contrasting values emerge during a visit to a Soviet conservation reserve. Unlike his other plays, it seemed over-symbolic and polemical. *Rafts and Dreams* (1990) is an oddly poetic play about a young woman's obsession with cleanliness which spreads into a vision of the world as a vast lake. Holman is unquestionably a highly talented writer, but he has been talented for too long to take his ultimate success for granted. JE

Holtei, Karl von 1798–1880 German actor and dramatist. Holtei's comedies were extremely popular, especially *The Viennese in Berlin* (1824) and *The Berliners in Vienna* (1825). He had less success as an actor, but he held several important administrative positions in various German theatres. His autobiography, *Forty Years* (1843–50), provides an especially lively account of the theatre of his time. SW

Holz, Arno 1863–1929 German poet and playwright. Holz is best known for his collaboration with Johannes Schlaf (1862–1941) on the naturalistic play *The Selicke Family* (1892). Though he was initially identified with NATURALISM, his later plays were poetic. SW

Home, John 1722–1808 Scottish playwright. Born near Edinburgh, Home was educated at Edinburgh University and was ordained a minister in the Church of Scotland in 1745. In 1746 he took up a living and began a friendship with David Hume, the philosopher. His first play, *Agis*, was rejected by GARRICK in 1749 as was his second, *Douglas*. But his friends mounted the latter at the Canongate Theatre in Edinburgh in 1756. It was an extraordinary and lasting success, making Home the first major Scots playwright: as someone in the audience said, 'Whaur's yer Wullie Shakespeare noo?'. *Douglas* is perhaps the first romantic tragedy, a non-didactic exploration of the love of mother for long-lost son. The Church was outraged at a minister writing plays and had it denounced from pulpits. There was a prolonged pamphlet war for and against the play. Brought to COVENT GARDEN by RICH, it was equally successful. As a result Home gave up the ministry and became secretary to the Prime Minister, Lord Bute. *Agis* was mounted at DRURY LANE by Garrick in 1758, but neither it nor Home's four subsequent plays were successful. They all aim at a romantic pathos usually intensified by remote British settings. In 1778 Home fell from a horse with consequent brain damage. He moved to Edinburgh till his death. PH

Home, William Douglas 1912–92 British dramatist, whose upper-middle-class comedies and dramas made him a natural successor to FREDERICK LONSDALE in the postwar WEST END theatre. He began his career as an actor, which helps to explain why his plays contain not only amusing dialogue but star parts. He was an actor's playwright. His first political comedy successes, *The Chiltern Hundreds* (1947) and *The Manor of Northstead* (1954), were vehicles for the eccentric talents of A. E. Matthews. SYBIL THORNDIKE starred in *The Reluctant Peer* (1964), Alastair Sim in *The Jockey Club Stakes* (1970), RALPH RICHARDSON and PEGGY ASHCROFT in *Lloyd George Knew My Father* (1972), Celia Johnson in *The Dame of Sark* (1974) and REX HARRISON in the New York version of *The Kingfisher*, a part played by Ralph Richardson in London. Home's skill came in calculating exactly what the stars of his generation could achieve, but it was supported by a sound playwriting technique whose main weakness lay in a facile sentimentality. *Now Barabbas ...* (1947), however, showed his ability with a serious theme about prison life, while *The Secretary Bird* (1968) remains a thoughtful *ménage-à-trois* comedy. His last play, *Portraits* (1977), was a sympathetic study of the portrait painter Augustus John in his later years, as seen through the eyes of three who sat for him, General Montgomery, Matthew Smith and Cecil Beaton. JE

Honduras During the early years only the most sporadic evidence indicates some *pastorelas* written and performed by Fray José Trinidad Reyes (1797–1855), who arrived from Nicaragua and founded the University of Honduras. During the stormy years between independence from Spain and the creation of the five separate Central American republics, the young Francisco Morazán governed from 1829 to 1838 over the united provinces in the classic struggle between conservatives and liberals, between Church and state. Morazán was the subject of a successful 1852 play by the Salvadoran Francisco Díaz, as well as two patriotic plays by the Honduran Jorge Fidel Durón (b.1902), one-time rector of the National University. J. M. Tobías Rosas wrote children's theatre during these years. The Casa de la Cultura (Cultural Institute) was inaugurated in 1916 with another play on the Morazán period, *Los conspiradores* (*The Conspirators*), but no theatrical tradition was yet established.

After 1950, theatre activity belonged primarily to some active experimental groups that tried to establish a new consciousness of theatre in Honduras. Many, such as Teatro Ensayo (Rehearsal Theatre), Talía and Arlequín, soon ceased functioning; others had a longer life. The Grupo Dramático Tegucigalpa (Tegucigalpa Drama Group) was established in 1956. The émigré Andrés Morris created TESP (Teatro de la Escuela Superior del Profesorado/ Faculty High School Theatre), which merged with the newly formed Teatro Nacional de Honduras (National Honduran Theatre) in 1965. Francisco Salvador, who studied acting in Mexico, became director, and created an active programme for the National Theatre, by offering classes in acting, diction and history and by mounting four plays each year. Various groups brought for the first time to the Honduran state productions of SHAKESPEARE, GARCÍA LORCA, SARTRE, CAMUS and other theatre classics.

Honduras has not yet produced internationally known playwrights. Medardo Mejía's *Cinchonero* and Francisco Salvador's *El sueño de Matías Carpio* (*The Dream of Matías Carpio*) have limited merit. Andrés Morris (born in Spain in 1928, arrived in Honduras in 1961) is the author of a so-called 'tetralogy of underdevelopment': *La ascensión del busito* (*The Raising of the Little Bus*), *El Guarizama* (1966), *Oficio de hombres* (*Men's Job*, 1967) and *La miel del abejorro* (*Bumblebee Honey*, 1968) – all point out too clearly the violence, corruption and single-industry operations characteristic of an underdeveloped nation. Morris recently left Honduras, but he was recognized as an outstanding playwright for *Oficio de hombres* (*Men's Job*) and *La tormenta* (*The Storm*); the latter won the National Prize for Literature in 1955.

Recent activity includes a theatre movement with popular appeal. The Comunidad Hondureña de Teatristas (Honduran Theatrical Community) sponsored its first national congress in 1982 for the purpose of creating solidarity among the various groups with specific revolutionary objectives. The Teatro Taller Tegucigalpa (Tegucigalpa Workshop Theatre) and Teatro La Fragua (Forge Theatre), founded in Progreso in 1979, work closely with their public to develop folkloric and popular theatre. At the national theatre congress in July 1982, a dialogue between five active Honduran theatre participants (Saúl Toro, Rafael Murillo Selva, Emmanuel Jaen, Hermes Zelaya and Francisco Salvador) attested to the deplorable lack of organization and cohesion. The national theatre festival in November 1982, the first in 14 years, stimulated new levels of activity, and was followed in November 1983 by the third such festival. Awards were given in 1983 by the Camino Real Theatre Foundation to, among others, dramatist Salvador and critic Conrado Enríquez for their efforts to promote theatre. At the end of the 80s about seven groups could be considered permanent; the only one close to professional quality is Rascaniguas from Tegucigalpa. Few national authors or plays have emerged, although *Loubavagu*, a Mayan creation, caught international attention in Bogotá at the 1993 festival. By any measure, the theatre in Honduras continues to operate on a precarious level, with little or no institutional or governmental support. GW

See: A. Caballero and F. Salvador, *Teatro en Honduras*, 2 vols., Tegucigalpa, 1977; M. Fernández, *El Teatro en Honduras*, Nicaragua, 1976.

Hong Kong Hong Kong is a British colony on the south coast of China with a population of 5.6 million people, 98 per cent of whom are Chinese. Most come from neighbouring Guangdong Province in CHINA and speak the Cantonese dialect. After the Communist takeover of mainland China in 1949, many refugees came to Hong Kong. These mainlanders plus British, Americans, Europeans, Australians, Indians, Japanese and Portuguese have made Hong Kong a true melting pot of Eastern and Western cultures. Drama and theatre in Hong Kong also reflect this mixture.

The traditional theatre form in Hong Kong is *yueju*, or Cantonese opera, a regional drama of South China whose basic style of stage presentation is related to the more renowned and refined Beijing opera (*JINGXI*). The great difference is the use of the Cantonese dialect, which affects the style of singing and rhythmic emphasis. Just as Cantonese is a regional dialect, so the theatre there is related to, but different from, its parent form. Cantonese opera in China's Guangdong region (see *YUEJU* (Guangdong opera)) is usually considered inferior to Beijing opera in artistic quality and technical sophistication. The Hong Kong version of Cantonese opera reflects the influence of novelties introduced in performance before the 1960s, which removed the art considerably from its original, characteristically Chinese atmosphere. Its music is often called 'yellow music', meaning that it is mock classical and bears the same relationship to the art that the 'yellow press' has to respectable journalism. Arias, regardless of their classical base, came to contain a note of sentimentality and softness, and tunes were even danceable in a westernized ballroom way. Western instruments became part of the traditional theatre orchestra. COSTUMES were vulgarized, with sparkling sequins to keep the show glittering. Realistic settings, alien to classical Chinese theatre, showed everything from castle walls to gardens, temples, and palaces. Stylized gestures and movement patterns were still employed, though often sloppily rendered. Such debasement of the traditional art gave the Cantonese theatre of Hong Kong a bad reputation until very recently. At the present time, forward-looking theatre artists are returning Cantonese opera to higher standards, so it will be the equal of other major regional Chinese theatres.

Living side-by-side with the Cantonese opera is Western-style modern Chinese drama, *HUAJU* or 'spoken drama'. English is an accepted and popular language in Hong Kong; hence one strand of Western-style theatre consists of productions in the English language, almost always mounted by British and American actors for the foreign expatriate audience. The other and more important strand consists of Chinese-language productions staged by local theatre groups and by visiting mainland companies whose audience is the vast majority of the Hong Kong populace. The first known Western-style drama performance was staged in 1844 by British soldiers and their families stationed in Hong Kong. In 1911 two local amateur theatre groups were formed, staging Chinese plays such as *Zhuang Zi Testing His Wife's Virtue* (*Zhang Zi shiqi*) and *Flesh for the Debt of Gold* (*Jinchai roushang*, possibly an adaptation of *The Merchant of Venice*). It is notable that these productions of spoken dramas were mounted only four years after the first Chinese production of Western plays, *La Dame aux camélias* and UNCLE TOM'S CABIN, by students of the Spring Willow Society in Tokyo.

During the period of the Sino-Japanese War prior to Japanese occupation (1937–42), patriotic Hong Kong youths popularized spoken drama. Over 200 amateur groups staged some 300 productions for patriotic causes. A great number of these plays were original one-acts with anti-Japanese themes. Performances were given in school gyms or classrooms, and sometimes at street corners, or at sports fields following a sporting event. The most popular play of that period was *Lay Down Your Whip* (*Fangxia nide bienzi*), an AGIT-PROP piece about the suffering of Chinese people caused by the Japanese invasions of their homeland. To avoid persecution, many theatre workers burnt their mimeographed scripts just prior to Japanese military occupation in 1942. Thus most of the original plays written in this period were lost.

After the war Hong Kong modern drama came to life again. Many standard works of Chinese dramatists were staged, such as *Thunderstorm* (*Lei yu*), *Family* (*Jia*), and *Sunrise* (*Ri chu*), by CAO YU. Three professional theatre companies from the mainland also took residence in Hong Kong after the war and staged large-scale productions. *Sorrows of the Noble Family* (*Jumen yuan*), *The Story of Ah-Q* (*Ah-Q jengjuan*), *The Wedding March* (*Jiehun jinxinqu*), *Girls' Apartment* (*Nuzi gongyu*), *Hell on Earth* (*Renjian diyu*, adapted from GORKY'S *The Lower Depths*), and *The Imperial Inspector* (*Qinchai daqeng*, adapted from GOGOL'S *The Inspector General*) were their most frequently staged plays.

In the 1950s and 60s local dramatists wrote works of considerable maturity and sophistication. Three playwrights deserve mention. Perhaps the most respected theatre worker in Hong Kong was Hu Chun-bin, who wrote *Li Bo the Poet* (*Li Bo*) and *Dream of the Red Chamber* (*Honglou meng*, adapted from the famous Chinese novel of the same title). S. I. Hsiung (1903–91) was noted for his adaptation of classical Chinese plays into spoken dramas, such as *Lady Precious Stream* and *The West Chamber*. The English version of the former had been a London and BROADWAY hit in the 1930s, which made Hsiung a celebrity in the English-speaking world. Yao Hsin-nung, trained at Yale Drama School, was the youngest of the three. Besides being a playwright and stage director, he was a film producer and a scriptwriter in Shanghai and Hong Kong in the 1940s and 50s. His realistic social drama, *The Poor Man's Alley* (*Quongjen xiang*), became a hit on the mainland and in Hong Kong during the postwar era.

The contemporary situation The most important development on the contemporary Hong Kong theatre scene was the establishment in 1977 of the professional Hong Kong Repertory Theatre devoted to spoken drama. Founded and strongly subsidized by the Urban Council, its performances in Cantonese dialect and occasionally in Mandarin are seen in the two new theatres of the Hong Kong Cultural Centre and in various venues in the territory. In 1991, under the artistic directorship of Daniel S. P. Yang (1936–), former director of the Colorado SHAKESPEARE Festival, it staged eight productions totalling 120 performances, its repertory representing a unique balance of Chinese, Western, and Hong-Kong-written plays. As part of its services to the community, it offers educational theatre programmes and sponsors an annual Drama Festival.

Other leading theatre companies in contemporary Hong Kong are the Chung Ying Theatre Company, the Exploration Theatre, and the Carlsberg Wanchai Theatre Company. Chung Ying is a bilingual professional theatre company formed in 1979 with funding first from the British Council then from the Hong Kong government. Its charter was to do English-language THEATRE-IN-EDUCATION in schools and community centres, and occasionally in larger theatre venues as well. Its original company was British, but now consists of Hong Kong Chinese. Before 1985, Chung Ying actors performed mostly in Cantonese, and occasionally joined guest British actors in English-language productions. Now their productions are almost entirely in Cantonese. The Exploration Theatre (Hak Heng Fong) is a semi-professional company composed of theatre graduates of the Hong Kong Academy for the Performing Arts, with support since 1990 from the Hong Kong Council for the Performing Arts under its 'Green Sprouts Plan'. The Carlsberg Wanchai Theatre Company is the most active community theatre group in Hong Kong. Under the aggressive management of its artistic and managing director, Ho Wai-lung (1956–), this modest theatre company in the Wanchai district puts on four to six productions a year with partial funding from the Carlsberg beer company.

Among nearly 100 registered community, college and school theatre groups, the Seals Theatre Company, the Zuni Icosahedron, and the American Community Theatre are the most active. The Seals Theatre Company, established in 1979, produced four to five Chinese and translated works yearly until the retirement of its artistic director Vicki Oi in 1990. The Zuni Icosahedron's daring and controversial productions have featured NUDITY and homosexual themes. Under artistic director Danny Yung (1943–), the troupe has attracted considerable attention in other Asian countries due to its touring activities. The American Community Theatre is the most active English-language amateur theatre company. It stages eight productions a year including MUSICALS, with casts of resident expatriates and occasional professional English and American guest actors.

Young audiences show increasing interest in traditional Cantonese opera and new troupes have formed to accommodate budding young talent. With few professional troupes in residence, the Urban Council promotes amateur productions of Cantonese opera by providing funds and venues for performance. In 1980 a Cantonese-opera training school was formed by the Pak Wo Association, an umbrella organization for traditional theatre in Hong Kong. Graduates of this school later formed the Sun Moon Star Operatic Troupe (Yat Yuet Sing). Today, Hong Kong's most celebrated Cantonese-opera companies are the Chung Sun Sing Troupe, formed in 1965 by Lam Kar-sing, and the Cry of the Young Phoenix Troupe (Chor Fung Ming). The latter is an offshoot of the Cry of the Immortal Phoenix Troupe (Sin Fung Ming), which, under the leadership of Yum Kim-fai (d.1990) and Pak Suet-sin, had been extremely popular in the 1950s and 60s. Chor Fung Ming was established in 1973 by seven disciples of Yum and Pak, among whom Lung Kim-sang and Mui Suet-see are star actors. The Company is noted for ensemble acting, emphasis on creating new scripts and adaptation of modern theatre technology in its productions. It gives over 100 local productions annually and has toured Southeast Asia, Canada and the United States.

Hong Kong's first school for vocational training of actors, directors, designers, technicians and playwrights was established in 1985 when the Hong Kong Academy for Performing Arts was officially opened. The Academy has Schools of Music, Dance, Drama, and Technical Services. The 1200-seat Lyric Theatre in the Academy complex is one of the best performance venues in Hong Kong. Since Hong Kong is at the crossroad between East and West, the Academy designs its curricula to take advantage of the performing traditions of both Asian and Western countries. The School of Drama, headed by Chung King-fai, includes the study of the traditional theatre of China, with courses in T'ai Chi, Beijing-opera acting and acrobatic training, and traditional Chinese dance and music, as well as Western theatre.

Another impressive addition to the contemporary Hong Kong theatre scene is the Hong Kong Cultural Centre opened in 1989. Its Auditoria Building houses a 2100-seat Concert Hall, a 1750-seat Grand Theatre, and a 350- to 500-seat experimental Studio Theatre. In the 1980s and early 90s the urban council constructed some ten district theatres to accommodate cultural events in various areas of the territory and more are planned. It is estimated that by the year 2000 there will be a five-fold increase of theatre-seating capacity in Hong Kong, promising a considerable growth of theatre activities. (See also CHINA; TAIWAN; ASIAN AND PACIFIC ISLAND THEATRE.) DSPY

See: J. R. Brandon (ed.), *The Cambridge Guide to Asian Theatre*, Cambridge, 1993.

Hong Sheng 1645–1704 Chinese KUNQU dramatist. In Beijing, where he was appointed to the Imperial Academy, he made a reputation as a poet and playwright. His masterpiece *The Palace of Eternal Youth* (*Changsheng dian*, 1688) came to the notice of the Kangxi Emperor (r.1662–1723) and thereafter was performed frequently before court society. The plot concerns the love affair of the Tang Emperor Minghuang (r.713–56) and his favourite concubine Yang Guifei. The theme has been a constant inspiration to poets and dramatists and Hong's play is still regarded as one of China's greatest lyric dramas. In 1689 Hong was dismissed from the Academy for a breach of court etiquette. He spent his remaining days in poverty. ACS

Hooft, P(ieter) C(ornelisz) 1581–1647 Dutch dramatist. Together with VONDEL, P. C. Hooft was amongst the most distinguished men of letters of the Golden Age in the Netherlands. The themes of his tragedies refer to the classics, notably SENECA, and even more to Dutch history. *Geraert van Velsen* (1613) and *Baeto* (1616), although composed in conformity with Renaissance stylistic conventions, bear witness to a strong sense of individuality. His *Warenar* (1617), a comedy after PLAUTUS' *The Pot of Gold*, was very popular in Amsterdam during the 17th and 18th centuries. He was the central figure of the so-called *Muider-kring*, a group of talented artists who had regular meetings at his official residence, the Muiderslot. MG WH

Hope Theatre (London) Built in 1613–14 to replace the demolished Bear Garden, the Hope was intended by PHILIP HENSLOWE as a multi-purpose arena, with a removable stage and a cantilevered roof (or HEAVENS). JONSON's *Bartholomew Fair* was staged there in 1614, but it appears that professional actors preferred playhouses that were free of competition from animal-baiting, and the Hope attracted no regular acting company after 1617. There are licences, dating from 1623 to 38, for the exhibition of a camel, an elephant, a beaver, an opossum and two dromedaries, as well as the bears, lions and apes that were regularly baited. The Hope was demolished in 1656. PT

Hopkins, Arthur (Melancthon) 1878–1950 American producer and director who began his career as a newspaper reporter, then worked as a VAUDEVILLE press agent, and finally booked attractions himself. His first BROADWAY production was *Poor Little Rich Girl* (1913), which ran for 160 performances. Other early successes include *On Trial* (1914), *Good Gracious Annabelle* (1916), *A Successful Calamity* (1917), *Redemption* (1918) with John Barrymore and *The Jest* (1919) with John and Lionel Barrymore (see DREW–BARRYMORE FAMILY). He featured ALLA NAZIMOVA in revivals of IBSEN's *Wild Duck*, *Hedda Gabler* and *A Doll's House*. In the 1920s, Hopkins directed O'NEILL's *Anna Christie* (1921) and *The Hairy Ape* (1922); Stallings and MAXWELL ANDERSON's *What Price Glory* (1924); and PHILIP BARRY's *Paris Bound* (1927) and *Holiday* (1928). His output decreased after 1930, but he staged a successful *The Petrified Forest* in 1935 with Leslie Howard and Humphrey Bogart, and *The Magnificent Yankee* in 1946. His notable productions of SHAKESPEARE include John Barrymore in *Richard III* (1920) and in *Hamlet* (1922), and Lionel Barrymore in *Macbeth* (1921). Hopkins discovered Pauline Lord and Katharine Hepburn, and contributed to the success of ROBERT EDMOND JONES. He studied theatrical production in Europe and returned home to develop the revolving stage in America. He placed artistic above commercial merit. While many of his directing methods were modern, his reliance upon pictorial effect made his later productions seem old-fashioned. Hopkins's books include *To a Lonely Boy* (1937) and *Reference Point* (1948), both somewhat autobiographical. TLM

Hopper, De Wolf 1858–1935 American comedian and singer. His abnormally long legs, loose-jointed movements and strong singing voice made Hopper one of the most beloved performers in comic OPERA. His debut was in *Our*

Daughters (1879), after which he appeared in a number of shows under the aegis of the McCaull Opera Company. Hopper left the McCaull company in 1890 and under a new management was given his first starring role in *Castles in the Air* (1890). His two greatest successes, *Wang* (1891) and *Panjandrum* (1893), followed. After forming the De Wolf Hopper Opera Company, he appeared in *Dr Syntax* (1894), *El Capitan* (1896) and *The Mystical Miss* (1899). Hopper joined the WEBER AND FIELDS company for two shows, then starred in *Mr Pickwick* (1903), *Happyland* (1905), *The Pied Piper* (1908) and *A Matinée Idol* (1910). In 1911 he made the first of a number of successful forays into the GILBERT and Sullivan repertoire with a revival of *HMS Pinafore*. As the vogue for comic opera waned, Hopper's work was confined to REVUES, such as *The Passing Show of 1917*, and, on occasion, OPERETTAS. His last New York appearance was in *White Lilacs* (1928). Beginning his career at a time when comic opera was at its height, Hopper found ample opportunity to exercise his comic gifts and his forceful singing voice. He was especially noted for his ability to handle long comic speeches and involved patter songs, and for his amusing use of props. He published his autobiography, *Once a Clown*, in 1927. MK

Hopper, Edna Wallace 1874–1959 American actress and singer, who began her stage career at the BOSTON MUSEUM in 1891. As Edna Wallace, she appeared in a number of straight plays produced by CHARLES FROHMAN before making her comic OPERA debut as a replacement for Della Fox in *Panjandrum*. Soon after, she married DE WOLF HOPPER, and as Edna Wallace Hopper starred in *Dr Syntax* (1894), *El Capitan* (1896), *Yankee Doodle Dandy* (1898) and *Chris and the Wonderful Lamp* (1900). She played Lady Holyrood in the American production of *Florodora* (1900). Subsequently, she made the transition from comic opera to MUSICAL COMEDY in such shows as *About Town* (1906), *Fifty Miles from Boston* (1908) and *Jumping Jupiter* (1911). Hopper's popularity in comic opera was generally attributed to her sparkling and vivacious personality rather than to her singing voice, which was too small and delicate. Audiences especially enjoyed her appearances in trousers roles (see FEMALE IMPERSONATION; MALE IMPERSONATION). MK

Hopwood, Avery 1882–1928 Remarkably successful American playwright. With 18 hits in 15 years – four of them running simultaneously in New York theatres in 1920 – Hopwood understood both popular commercial theatre and the slight and ephemeral nature of his artistry. Most of his best works were written in collaboration with others: *Clothes* (1906), his first play, with Channing Pollock; four plays, including *The Bat* (1920), with Mary Roberts Rinehart; *Getting Gertie's Garter* (1921) with Wilson Collison; and *The Best People* with David Gray. Other play titles suggest the clever, *risqué* character of his work – *The Gold Diggers* (1919), *Little Miss Bluebeard* (1923), *Naughty Cinderella* (1925) – that almost guaranteed success. WJM

Horace [Quintus Horatius Flaccus] 65–8 BC Augustan poet. Though he wrote no drama himself, his verse epistle *Ars Poetica* (*The Art of Poetry*) includes advice on the writing of tragedies, comedies and satyr plays in the Greek manner (see GREECE, ANCIENT). There is no evidence that this advice had any effect in his own day, but it influenced neoclassical drama from the Renaissance onward. ALB

Hordern, Michael (Murray) 1911–95 British actor, who made his professional debut in 1937. Having been a popular actor in comparatively minor roles for 20 years, he first became a major London star with his portrait of the incompetent barrister in JOHN MORTIMER's *The Dock Brief*. This performance provided a general identity for the characters which Hordern came to play, of absent-minded, good-hearted English eccentrics. He played Riley in TOM STOPPARD's *Enter a Free Man* (1968) and George Moore, the traditional moral philosopher trying hard to defend his position in a world of materialists, in Stoppard's *Jumpers* (1972). He was the hippy vicar in DAVID MERCER's *Flint* (1970) and Pinfold in an adaptation of Evelyn Waugh's book, *The Ordeal of Gilbert Pinfold* (1977), which transferred from Manchester to London's Round House. He also appeared with major repertory companies such as the ROYAL SHAKESPEARE COMPANY and Nottingham Playhouse in a variety of classic roles – notably Malvolio at the OLD VIC in 1954, King Lear in JONATHAN MILLER's production of SHAKESPEARE's tragedy (1969), seen later on British television, and Prospero in *The Tempest* in the 1978 Stratford-upon-Avon version. He was knighted in 1983. In 1987 he appeared as the wise Walter in BERNARD SHAW's *You Never Can Tell*, in a Toby Robertson production from Mold in Wales which transferred to the HAYMARKET. JE

Hornblow, Arthur 1865–1942 English-born editor and author, who studied in Paris and worked as a correspondent for English and American newspapers before going to the USA in 1889. Hornblow pursued a career as a journalist, working first for the *Kansas City Globe* and then the *New York Dramatic Mirror*. He was foreign editor for the *New York Herald* during 1894–9, and copy-editor for the *New York Times* in 1899. During 1910–26 he served as editor of *Theatre Magazine*, frequently reviewing opening nights. Afterwards, for two years, he served as Dean of the JOHN MURRAY ANDERSON–Robert Milton School of Theatre and Dance in New York. Hornblow's greatest financial success came from novelizing popular plays, including *The Lion and the Mouse*, *The Easiest Way* and *Bought and Paid For*. His two-volume *A History of the Theatre in America* (1919) remains a flawed but standard reference work. TLM

Horniman, Annie (E. F.) 1860–1937 British theatre manager and patron. Born of a prosperous tea merchant's family, she inherited a large legacy in 1893 which she began, discreetly, to invest in theatrical enterprises that excited her. The first was a season at the Avenue Theatre, London, in 1894, which included W. B. YEATS's *Land of Heart's Desire*. She became Yeats's private secretary for five years and in 1904 financed the opening of the ABBEY THEATRE, Dublin, for the Irish National Theatre Society. She continued to subsidize the theatre until disagreement with the organizers led her to transfer her capital to Manchester, where in 1907 she founded a new repertory company (the first in England; see REGIONAL THEATRE

Hotel Pro Forma's production of *Why Does Night Come, Mother*, 1989 (scenography by Tomas Lahoda).

(BRITAIN)), opening its first season at the Midland Hotel Theatre. She purchased the nearby GAIETY THEATRE and made it, from 1908, her company's permanent home. Under her watchful eye the theatre became a major force in the repertory movement until the outbreak of war, when its fortunes fell and never recovered: she sold the building in 1920. In 1921 she donated her extensive library of plays to the British Drama League. AJ

Horovitz, Israel (Arthur) 1939– Harvard-educated American playwright. Horovitz spent two years at the Royal Academy of Dramatic Art (1961–3), London, and a year as resident playwright with the ROYAL SHAKESPEARE COMPANY (1965). He attracted critical attention in 1968 with the New York production of two one-acts: *It's Called the Sugar Plum* and *The Indian Wants the Bronx*, plays about urban violence in America. Also in 1968, his one-act *Morning* appeared on BROADWAY together with short pieces by TERRENCE MCNALLY and Leonard Melfi. Other Horovitz plays include *The Good Parts* (1982); *The Wakefield Plays* (1974–9), which include *The Alfred Trilogy* and *The Quannatowitt Quartet*; *Park Your Car in Harvard Yard* (1991); and *Unexpected Tenderness* (1994). In 1979 he founded the Gloucester Stage Company in Massachusetts, where most of his plays have since premiered (e.g. *Henry Lumper*, 1985; *A Rosen by Any Other Name*, 1987; *The Chopin Playoffs*, 1988). Horovitz deals in a realistic way with the angst of American life. TLM

Horváth, Ödön von 1901–38 Austro-Hungarian dramatist and novelist. Starting with realistic pieces like *Sladek der schwarze Reichswehrmann* (*Sladek the Blackshirt*, 1929), an exposure of the activities of Fascist paramilitaries, Horváth went on to develop the Austrian VOLKSSTÜCK to unmask the heartlessness and stupidity of the postwar common man, most famously in *Tales from the Vienna Woods* (1931), which subverts the OPERETTA image of golden-hearted Vienna with the tale of an ingénue exploited by her father, seduced by a small-time gigolo, and married off to a sadistic butcher. *Kasimir and Karoline* (1932) is a similarly ironic treatment of the genre, set at the Munich Oktoberfest. *Italienische Nacht* (*Italian Night*, 1931) is a subtle evocation of grass-roots politics – Social Democrats versus Nazis. Horváth's dialogue is not so much dialect as the cliché-ridden argot of the modern city, which, German not being his first language, is more effective for being a shade out of true. *Glaube, Liebe, Hoffnung* (*Faith, Charity and Hope*, 1936) is a fable of a woman caught in the poverty trap.

After his emigration a religious, metaphysical note enters his plays. *Himmelwärts* (*Heavenward*, 1937) is a mystery play with leanings towards CABARET; *Don Juan kommt aus dem Krieg* (*Don Juan Returns from the War*, 1952; written 1935) transposes Don Juan to the German hyperinflation of 1923, and *Figaro lässt sich scheiden* (*Figaro Gets Divorced*, 1937) picks up BEAUMARCHAIS's characters after six years of marriage and revolution. Banned during the Second World War and disregarded after it, Horváth's plays enjoyed a revival in the 1970s. HANDKE praised their openness and subtlety to the detriment of BRECHT's fixity and directness. *Tales from the Vienna Woods*, translated by HAMPTON, was performed at the NATIONAL THEATRE in London in 1977. Horváth was killed on the Champs Élysées when lightning struck the tree he was standing under. HR

Hôtel de Bourgogne (Paris) Theatre in the rue Mauconseil, built by the CONFRÉRIE DE LA PASSION in 1548 on the site of a former residence of the Dukes of Burgundy. Used for their own performances until the end of the century, it then became the principal focus in the capital for the rapidly developing professional stage and was leased to a variety of itinerant French and foreign companies, amongst them that of VALLERAN LE CONTE and many from Italy. After 1629 it became the permanent home of the Comédiens du Roi, who occupied it continuously, under the successive leaderships of BELLEROSE, FLORIDOR and Hauteroche, until their incorporation into the COMÉDIE-FRANÇAISE in 1680, and who performed there much of the most important dramatic writing of the 17th century, including many of PIERRE CORNEILLE's later plays and most of RACINE's work. As originally constructed, it was a long, rather narrow building, more than 108ft long by a little under 45ft wide, with a raked stage measuring some 35ft from the back wall and occupying the entire width of the building (minus wing space), and a smaller upper stage which, as the *Mémoire* of MAHELOT makes clear, was also used during the action, notably for mechanical effects. A large pit for standing spectators dominated the auditorium, which also contained boxes along the side walls, tiered benches facing the stage and galleries, giving a probable capacity well in excess of 1000. In 1647 the stage was extended forward by ten feet, raised slightly and fitted with a front curtain, and modifications were made to the auditorium modelled on seating arrangements at the MARAIS. In 1680 the vacated building was taken over by the COMÉDIE-ITALIENNE, who remained associated with it until 1783. DR

Hotel Pro Forma Danish performance group, founded in Copenhagen in 1986 by Kirsten Dehlholm, following her work with Billedstofteater (1977–85). The company's projects are close to visual performance, but combine visual imagery and architecture with spoken and sung text, music and action, using professional performers. The work is typically staged in formal locations such as museums and public buildings, and often incorporates an implicit dialogue between past and present. Important projects have included *Why Does Night Come, Mother*, about perspective and the law of gravity (1989), *The Enigma of the Late Afternoon*, a computerized performance inspired by the work of Giorgio de Chirico (1992), and *Opera: Orfeo* (1993). HL

Hou Baolin 1917– Veteran Chinese exponent of *xiangsheng*, a storytelling genre involving comic dialogue, wisecracks and mimicry. Hou was born in Beijing, was apprenticed to a street singer, joined a troupe of street entertainers skilled in reciting complete plays from the Beijing repertoire and eventually was accepted as an apprentice by the *xiangsheng* guild. He performed in Beijing and Tianjin and rose to fame partnered by Guo Qiru as his stage foil. He was denounced during the Cultural Revolution but survived to become a national celebrity. He is a master of improvisation and has a keen sense of characterization through dialect. Hou remains unsurpassed in the art of taking the audience by surprise, the essence of comic genius on the stage. ACS

Houdar de la Motte, Antoine 1672–1731 French dramatist, poet and critic. In his theoretical writings on drama he adopted an openly modernist stance, proclaiming the virtues of prose, even in TRAGEDY, rejecting slavish conformity to rules and conventions derived from the ancients, and identifying the pleasure given to an audience as the ultimate dramaturgic criterion. His own dramatic work, comprising six comedies, four tragedies, of which the most interesting and successful was *Inès de*

Castro (1723), and numerous librettos, was far more conservative in character and he was elected to the Académie-Française in 1710. DR

Houdini, Harry [Erik Weisz] 1874–1926 American MAGICIAN and escape artist, born in Budapest the son of a rabbi; his stage name was a homage to the 19th-century French conjuror ROBERT-HOUDIN. Starting in dime museums and CIRCUSES as the self-styled 'King of Cards', he gained prominence in 1895 with his escapes from handcuffs and straitjackets. A genius at self-promotion, he was soon challenging police forces throughout the world to keep him pent up, and once escaped from a chained packing crate at the bottom of a river; these escapes were often engineered by concealed keys, one passed in a kiss from his wife. Other tricks involved making an elephant vanish, and swallowing 70 needles and 20 yards of thread and bringing them up threaded. Houdini was also the first to fly an aeroplane in Australia (1910), enjoyed a career as a silent-film star and, after his mother's death in 1913, exposed fraudulent mediums. G. B. SHAW called him one of the three most famous persons in the world (the other two being Jesus Christ and Sherlock Holmes). *Houdini*, a 'circus-opera' by ADRIAN MITCHELL and Peter Schat, was performed in Amsterdam in 1977. A new biography is being written by Pulitzer Prize-winning author Kenneth Silverman. LS

Houghton, (Charles) Norris 1909– Indiana-born American producer, educator, designer and writer. A 1931 Princeton graduate, Houghton designed eight BROADWAY productions and directed four between 1932 and 57. As founder and co-managing director of the OFF-BROADWAY Phoenix Theatre, he helped mount almost 75 productions (1953–64). He has taught at numerous institutions; his last full-time position was at the State University of New York, Purchase (1967–80). A frequent writer and editor, Houghton is the author of six books, including the influential *Moscow Rehearsals* (1936), *Advance from Broadway* (1941) and *Return Engagement* (1962). His superb autobiography, *Entrances and Exits*, was published in 1991. Twice a Guggenheim Fellow, in 1962 he became a Fellow of the American Academy of Arts and Sciences. DBW

Houghton, Stanley 1881–1913 British playwright, one of the Manchester writers associated with the GAIETY THEATRE. *Hindle Wakes* (1912) is typical of the genre, a good Lancashire tale told with wit and care. *The Younger Generation* (1910) shows the radical social concern that is also evident in the clearly argued woman's point of view in *Hindle Wakes*. (See also HAROLD BRIGHOUSE.) MB

Houseman, John [Jacques Haussman] 1902–88 Bucharest-born director, producer and actor. Educated in England, Houseman began producing in New York in 1934 and was affiliated for a time with the FEDERAL THEATRE PROJECT. Some of his finest work was with ORSON WELLES and the MERCURY THEATRE, which he co-founded in 1937 – notably his production of *Julius Caesar* in modern dress. He served as artistic director for such producing agencies as the AMERICAN SHAKESPEARE [THEATRE] Festival (1956–9), the professional Theatre Group of the University of

California at Los Angeles (1959–64), and the Drama Division of the Juilliard School of the Performing Arts (1968–76). In 1972 he founded the ACTING COMPANY, originally known as the City Center Acting Company, directing several productions for them.

Houseman won great popular acclaim by playing an acerbic law professor in the television series 'Paper Chase'. He published three detailed and valuable accounts of his life in the theatre: *Run-Through* (1972), *Front and Center* (1981) and *Final Dress* (1983). The three were conflated into *Unfinished Business* (1989). SMA

Housman, Laurence 1865–1959 British dramatist and novelist. Most of Housman's work was banned from the public theatre because it presented the Holy Family or the royal family on the stage (see CENSORSHIP). His early play *Bethlehem* formed the basis of a brilliant production by GORDON CRAIG in 1902, and *Prunella*, written in collaboration with GRANVILLE BARKER, was one of the successes in his 1910 repertory season at London's Duke of York's Theatre. Three series of one-act dramas with the general title of *The Little Plays of St Francis* (1922, 1931, 1935) have retained their popularity on the amateur stage, but his best-known work was *Victoria Regina: A Dramatic Biography*. A loosely connected sequence of ten vignettes from before Queen Victoria's accession to her Diamond Jubilee, this was first presented privately by NORMAN MARSHALL at the London Gate Theatre and in a much acclaimed New York production with HELEN HAYES in 1935. CI

Howard, Alan (Mackenzie) 1937– British actor, who became a star leading man in the ROYAL SHAKESPEARE COMPANY (which normally prefers to emphasize its ensemble playing). He came from a theatrical family and his uncle was the film actor, Leslie Howard. He joined Bryan Bailey's company at the Belgrade Theatre, Coventry, going to the ROYAL COURT with the transfer of ARNOLD WESKER's *Roots* (1959). He stayed at the Royal Court for the Wesker trilogy (1960) and for *The Changeling* (1961), but his aristocratic good looks, diction and stage presence were not ideally suited to the Royal Court's programme of angry, working-class plays.

After playing Simon in *A Heritage and Its History* (1965), adapted by JULIAN MITCHELL from the Ivy Compton-Burnett novel, he joined the RSC, where his first major role was as Lussurioso, the voluptuary, in TOURNEUR's *The Revenger's Tragedy* (1966), an early TREVOR NUNN production. In 1968 he played Benedick in *Much Ado About Nothing*, then in 1970 Hamlet, before touring Europe as Theseus/Oberon in PETER BROOK's revolutionary *A Midsummer Night's Dream*, where his natural athleticism was turned into circus skills on the trapeze (1970). In 1975, he played Prince Hal and Henry V in the Stratford Centenary productions of *Henry IV* and *Henry V*, which led to a remarkable association with the director TERRY HANDS, who wanted to direct him in what almost amounted to the full span of kingly roles in SHAKESPEARE's HISTORY PLAYS, including Richard II, Richard III and, in 1977, Henry VI in Shakespeare's early trilogy, which Howard invested with a saintly innocence and dignity. In contemporary plays with the RSC, he took the leading role of the

liberal German professor who cooperates with the Nazis in C. P. TAYLOR's *Good* (1981), and appeared in revivals of plays by GORKY and OSTROVSKY. Howard has recently appeared frequently in films and on TV, but less often on the stage, one exception being as Higgins in the NT's revival of *Pygmalion*. JE

Howard, Bronson (Crocker) 1842–1908 The first professional American playwright; the first to distinguish the American businessman in his plays and one of the first to define his principles of drama in an essay, 'The Laws of Dramatic Composition'. Among his businessman plays are *Young Mrs Winthrop* (1882), a sympathetic treatment of the neglected wife; *The Henrietta* (1887), a SATIRE of life on the stock exchange; and *Aristocracy* (1892), which ridiculed new and old American wealth. Howard's awareness of social class stretched from *Saratoga* (1870), adapted to English circumstance as *Brighton* (1874), to *One of Our Girls* (1885), comparing American and French women. *The Banker's Daughter* (1878), given notoriety by Howard's lecture, 'Autobiography of a Play' (1886), and his Civil War MELODRAMA *Shenandoah* (1888) epitomized his popular success. Aided by his association with the THEATRICAL SYNDICATE, Howard raised the status of the American playwright with his plays and as a founder of the American Dramatists' Club in 1891. WJM

Howard, Sir Robert 1626–98 English playwright. Knighted for bravery at the Battle of Newbury in 1644, he was imprisoned during the Interregnum at Windsor Castle. At the Restoration he began a successful political career, becoming Auditor of the Exchequer in 1677, and a Privy Councillor in 1688. In the 1660s he wrote six plays and indulged in a prolonged argument with his brother-in-law, JOHN DRYDEN, about the relative merits of rhyming couplets and blank verse for tragedy and the desirability of writing tragicomedies, an early controversy in British DRAMATIC THEORY. *The Committee* (1662), a bitter play on the work of the Sequestration Committee during the Civil War, introduced the comic Irish servant Teague to the English stage. He collaborated with Dryden on *The Indian Queen* (1664), one of the most important plays in the creation of the genre of heroic play in England, an exotically set struggle between love and honour. *The Country Gentleman* was banned in 1669 because of a scene by BUCKINGHAM satirizing Sir William Coventry. Howard's brothers Edward and James were also successful dramatists. PH

Howard, Sidney (Coe) 1891–1939 American playwright who, in the 1920s, was a crucial figure in lifting American drama from provincial entertainment to an authentic native literature. In a group of provocative plays – *They Knew What They Wanted* (which won the Pulitzer Prize in 1924), *Lucky Sam McCarver* (1925), *The Silver Cord* (1926), *Ned McCobb's Daughter* (1927) and *Half Gods* (1929) – he looked at such subjects as sex, mother love, psychiatry and prohibition with a fresh point of view. Like EUGENE O'NEILL, Howard helped to popularize Freudian ideas about family and sexual relationships; but his focus, unlike O'Neill's, was intimate and his tone essentially comic. His best play, *They Knew What They Wanted*, advocates moral and sexual compromise, and in *Ned McCobb's Daughter* he created one of the era's most appealing New Women, a heroine with more sense than any of the men in her life. Because Howard thought of himself as a skilled craftsman rather than as an artist with a distinctive voice, he was a jack of all trades who wrote in a number of genres: spectacle, romance, the war story, and both urban and rural comedy. He frequently collaborated, and he translated and adapted the work of other writers (*The Late Christopher Bean* (1932) and *Dodsworth* (1934) were both acclaimed). He was also an active screenwriter, winning Academy Awards for *Arrowsmith* (1931) and *Gone with the Wind* (1939). His remarkably productive career – 27 plays and 13 screenplays – ended suddenly in 1939 when he had a fatal tractor accident on his Massachusetts farm. FH

Howard, Willie 1886–1949 and
Eugene Howard 1880–1965 American comedians. Like many performers of their day, the Howard brothers developed their comic personae in VAUDEVILLE. Their first joint appearance on the legitimate MUSICAL stage was in *The Passing Show of 1912*. Eugene served as the straight man for the act, while the sad-faced Willie got most of the laughs. Their talents were best displayed in REVUES: in addition to appearing in six of the *Passing Shows*, they starred in six editions of GEORGE WHITE'S *Scandals*. Willie's abilities as a mimic made him especially valuable in revues that emphasized travesties of the latest performers and shows. In addition to their comic talents, both brothers had fine singing voices, which they often displayed in parodies of GRAND OPERA. After Eugene's retirement in 1940, Willie continued as a solo performer, but never again had the success that the brothers had achieved as a team. MK

Howard family American performers. **G(eorge) C(unnabel)** Howard (1820–87), a Canadian-born actor, was engaged at the BOSTON MUSEUM, where he met and married (1844) the actress **Caroline** Emily Fox (1829–1908). With a STOCK COMPANY that included Caroline's mother and three brothers (see GEORGE W. L. FOX), they toured New England in abbreviated versions of *The Drunkard* and *The Factory Girl* intermingled with an olio of songs and dances. As a respectable family unit they acclimatized theatre in towns that had hitherto condemned all play-acting as damnable. The Howards achieved their most durable success with an adaptation of UNCLE TOM'S CABIN (1852), carpentered by their cousin GEORGE L. AIKEN and featuring George Howard as St Clare, Caroline as Topsy and their daughter **Cordelia** as Eva; when played in an expanded text at the National Theatre (New York, 1853), it captured the imagination of the times. Cordelia became the star of the family, also creating the title role in *Katy the Hot Corn Girl* and Little Gerty in *The Lamplighter*. LS

Howe, Tina 1937– American playwright whose plays, characterized by a strong central metaphor and contrapuntal, parallel speeches, present the contrast between polished public behaviour and quirky private characters. Heavily influenced by the MARX BROS, Howe's early works – *The Nest* (1969), *Birth and After Birth* (1973; unpro-

duced), *Museum* (1976) and *The Art of Dining* (1979) – are farcical criticisms of pretentiousness. Her later plays, all initially directed by Carole Rothman, are realistic works filled with fantasy. Her first big success was *Painting Churches* (1983, Outer Critics' Circle Award), an autobiographical play about a painter making peace with her ageing parents. *Coastal Disturbances* (1986), *Approaching Zanzibar* (1989) and *One Shoe Off* (1993) deal with more painful subjects, often in bizarre contexts but still in Howe's unique comedic style with themes concerning love, loss and denial of reality. In 1983, she won a collective Obie for Distinguished Playwriting. TH-S

Howells, William Dean 1837–1920 American novelist, critic and playwright. 'The father of realism' in America, Howells not only praised the work of EDWARD HARRIGAN, JAMES A. HERNE and HENRIK IBSEN, but contributed himself to the rise of REALISM in drama and the development of social COMEDY. Both *A Counterfeit Presentment* (1877) and *Yorick's Love* (1878) were acted successfully by LAWRENCE BARRETT. The author of some 36 plays, Howells wrote 12 one-act FARCES featuring social events in the lives of two couples (the Robertses and the Campbells), including *The Garroters* (1885), in which Roberts mistakenly garrottes a friend; *Five o'Clock Tea* (1887), when Campbell becomes engaged; and *The Unexpected Guest* (1893), when Mr and Mrs Campbell entertain. A writer of charming dialogue but incapable of producing the melodramatic confrontations demanded by 19th-century audiences, Howells pictured instead such man–woman struggles as broken engagements (*An Indian Giver*, 1897; *Parting Friends*, 1910). He was a gentle satirist of Boston manners who became bitter in later plays (*The Impossible*, 1910; *The Night before Christmas*, 1910), and his work appealed more to amateur than professional performers. WJM

Hoyt, Charles (Hale) 1860–1900 Major American writer of FARCE and SATIRE that, in his best plays, showed social themes and realistic characters. Hoyt wrote some 20 plays, drawing his material from his own interests and experiences: small-town life (*A Rag Baby*, 1884), his father's early occupation of hotel management (*A Bunch of Keys*, 1882), superstitions (*The Brass Monkey*, 1888), corrupt politics (*A Texas Steer*, 1890), prohibition (*A Temperance Town*, 1893), the hypocrisy of home guard companies (*A Milk White Flag*, 1893) and baseball (*A Runaway Colt*, 1895). *A Trip to Chinatown* (1891) had the longest run of any play produced in America to that date (650 performances). Theatre was strictly a business with Hoyt, who revised his work with extreme care and made £100,000 (roughly $485,000) in a good year. He suffered from stress, and was committed to the Retreat for the Insane at Hartford, Connecticut (in his native New England), in 1900. WJM

Hrotsvitha of Gandersheim c.935–73 German noblewoman living voluntarily within an order, but not a 'nun'. Hrotsvitha was the author of six plays, *Abraham*, *Callimachus*, *Dulcitius*, *Gallicanus*, *Pafuntius* and *Sapientia*, concerned with martyrdom for the Christian faith and the triumph of virginity over the temptations of the flesh. She wished to provide a Christian counterbalance to the plays of TERENCE, but despite successful modern productions both in the original Latin and in translation it remains unlikely that she had any idea of theatrical performance. JET

huaju Generic term for Chinese dialogue plays in Western style. Literally 'spoken drama', or 'speech drama'. *Huaju* had its tentative debut in the first decade of this century. Early inhibiting factors were public prejudice against women on the stage and an inability to dispense with old acting conventions. Since it appealed primarily to Western-educated intellectuals at first it offered no vital challenge to the mass appeal of the old theatre in the countryside. Even today, spoken drama is largely a theatre of the great cities.

The period 1915–19 was one of intellectual revolt against the old Chinese social–cultural order. Sweeping language reforms were introduced. Western literature, including drama, was being read and translated. IBSEN made a powerful impression and taught the intellectuals to use theatre as an art of social protest. In the 1930s actresses were accepted on stage and talented writers and directors returned to China with Western experience. The powerful realism of CAO YU's plays, beginning with *Thunderstorm* (*Leiyu*) in 1935, suggested a strong new direction. The Japanese invasion of China forced artists in new directions.

The war years were marked by the subservience of theatre to patriotic and party propaganda on both the Guomindang and CCP sides. In the event *huaju* remained the poor relation of theatre after the war, the prerogative of school and university drama clubs until the foundation of the PRC in 1949.

The Central Drama Institute, set up in Beijing in 1950, trained actors, directors and set designers for *huaju*. Sino-Soviet relations were then at their zenith and Russian advisers and teachers presided over the modern theatre scene, so that STANISLAVSKY's theories inform the work of many Chinese actors and directors today. During the Cultural Revolution (1966–76) Jiang Qing denounced Stanislavsky as bourgeois, along with virtually all spoken dramas performed in China since 1949. Companies were disbanded, their members dispersed and training institutions closed.

Following Jiang's downfall in 1976, Stanislavsky has been rehabilitated, training facilities re-organized and companies reformed. A younger generation of playwrights, of whom the most significant is probably GAO XINGJIAN, has increasingly broken away from stereotypes in terms of content, performance and style.

In 1979 a spate of spoken dramas attacked official corruption in contemporary society. *If I Were Real* (*Ruguo wo shi zhende*) by Sha Yexin and others, about a young man who gains great privileges by pretending to be the son of a high army officer, gained considerable attention in the West. *Power versus Law* (*Quan yu fa*) by Xing Yixun (c.1940–) denounced the widespread seizure of privileges by CCP officials for themselves and their families. The central theme shows the law, supported by the good CCP leader and the people, victorious over corrupt officials, thus attacking individuals, not the party itself.

The necessity of law is a strong theme also in *Fifteen Cases of Divorce* (*Shiwu lihun an*, 1983) by Liu Shugang (c.1941–), which probes the causes of divorce in contemporary China. The same two performers play the 15 couples suing for divorce. It introduced non-realistic staging techniques considered unusual in a Stanislavskian theatre: no curtain, changing costumes on stage, the use of MIME, and symbolic use of properties.

A Friend Comes in a Time of Stress (*Fengyu guren lai*, 1983) by feminist playwright Bai Fengxi (1934–) concerns a brilliant young mathematician who wins a scholarship to go to West Germany, but is pressured by her mother-in-law to withdraw in favour of her husband who has applied for the same scholarship. In refusing to yield to sexist blandishments the heroine appeals for a strong role for women in the professions, calling attention to the fact that professional competition between married couples is frequent in China.

Gouerye's Nirvana (*Gouerye niepan*), about an old peasant whose lifelong ambition is to own his own land, shows his misery and frustration under the rule both of the Guomindang and the CCP. The hero's 'nirvana' is a state between death and life in which he can reflect upon his life. Offering no solutions, the play is characteristic of plays prior to the mid-1989 political crisis: billed as a 'tragi-comedy', its overall impact is pessimistic and gloomy.

The 1989 crisis resulted in a campaign in the spoken drama called 'main melody' (*zhu xuanlü*), the aim of which was to stress the goals and achievements of the CCP and socialism. Many of the items produced focused on current attempts to fight corruption, and although the propaganda content was direct by comparison with the 1980s plays, there was still room for SATIRE and humour. This campaign was ended by the more liberal atmosphere resulting from Deng Xiaoping's visit to the south early in 1992.

Much attention has been given to Western drama in recent decades. ARTHUR MILLER's *Death of a Salesman* was directed by Miller and the forward-looking actor-director Ying Ruocheng (1929–) in 1983 at the Beijing People's Art Theatre. In 1986 Ying Ruocheng was co-director of PETER SHAFFER's *Amadeus* under the title *The Favoured Son of God* (*Shangdi de chonger*). The year 1986 also saw a major SHAKESPEARE festival in Beijing and in several other cities. CPM

Huerta, Jorge 1942– Chicano director and critic. Born in east Los Angeles, Huerta worked as a child actor in television. In 1971 he founded the Teatro de la Esperanza (Theatre of Hope) in Santa Barbara, California, and served as its artistic director until 1975. He was a founding member in 1971 of TENAZ (Teatro Nacional de Aztlán), the national CHICANO THEATRE network. He is the editor of various anthologies and newsletters (*TENAZ Talks Teatro*), author of books including *Chicano Theatre, Themes and Forms*, co-artistic director of the Old Globe's Teatro Meta and professor at the University of California, San Diego. GW

Hughes, Barnard 1915– American actor, born in Bedford Hills, New York, and educated at Manhattan College. Hughes made his New York debut in 1934 as the haberdasher in *The Taming of the Shrew*. After minor roles and military service, he developed his range and diversity in major supporting roles: *The Teahouse of the August Moon* (1956), *Enrico IV* (1958), *Advise and Consent* (1960), *A Doll's House* (1963), *Nobody Loves an Albatross* (1963), JOHN GIELGUD's *Hamlet* (1964), *Hogan's Goat* (1965), *How Now, Dow Jones* (1967) and *Sheep on the Runway* (1970). Since 1970, Hughes has become one of America's most distinguished character actors, acclaimed for his Dogberry in *Much Ado* (1972), Alexander Serebryakov in *Uncle Vanya* (1973), Falstaff in *The Merry Wives of Windsor* (1974), the title role in *Da* (1978), Father William Doherty in *Angels Fall* (1983), Philip Stone in *End of the World* (1984), Harry Hope in *The Iceman Cometh* (1985) and the father in *Prelude to a Kiss* (1990) by CRAIG LUCAS. Critic Mel Gussow regarded his award-winning Da as the high point of his career: 'he takes a most ordinary man ... and makes him lovable to his sardonic son and to the audience'. T. E. Kalem viewed his Da as 'an expansive field marshall of lifelong defeat who acts with the authority of an uncaged lion'. TLM

Hughes, Dusty 1947– British dramatist, who was a critic for the listings magazine *Time Out*, and joined London's BUSH THEATRE in 1974 as a co-director with Simon Stokes and Jenny Topper. He proved himself to be a capable stage director, but his interests lay in writing plays. After seeing his early plays, *Commitments* (1980) and *Heaven and Hell* (1981), on the small stage, he adapted two Russian works for the ROYAL SHAKESPEARE COMPANY, BULGAKOV's *Molière* (1982) and GORKY's *Philistines*. His interest in Russia at the time of the Revolution is reflected in *Futurists* (1986), directed by RICHARD EYRE at the NATIONAL THEATRE. It is set in a St Petersburg café in 1921, amid the excitement of an aesthetic movement which believed itself to be in tune with the politics of the time. *Metropolis* (1989) was a MUSICAL which went wrong and *A Slip of the Tongue* (1992) offered a part for JOHN MALKOVICH as a dissident in Eastern Europe, in hiding from all but the girls sent to wheedle out his secrets in bed. JE

Hughes, Holly 1951– Michigan-born American poet, playwright and performance artist. Hughes went to New York as a painter and entered the East Village scene of Piezo Electric, Club 57 and the WOW Café. As manager at the WOW Café until 1983, she organized regular 'talking slide shows', where artists showed slides and talked about their work. Hughes's first performances were *Shrimp in a Basket* and *The Well of Horniness*. She developed *Dress Suits to Hire* (1987) with Lois Weaver and Peggy Shaw. Her solo performances *World Without End* (1988) and *Dead Meat* (1990) explored the contradictions of multiple pleasures. In late 1993 she was developing *Snatches*, a potpourri of narratives dealing with relationships, gender and sexual orientation, among other subjects. Hughes's autobiographical style is inspired by 1970s feminist insistence on political and sexual autonomy, yet she performs in the stand-up comedic tradition of blasphemy and audience harangues made popular by LENNY BRUCE in the 1950s. AF

Hughes, (James Mercer) Langston 1902–67 African-

American poet, story-writer and playwright. Brought up by his grandmother, whose first husband died in John Brown's raid at Harper's Ferry, he acquired her racial consciousness and a love of literature. He published his first play, *The Gold Piece*, in 1921, and gained his first BROADWAY success with *Mulatto* (1935), a MELODRAMA on race relations in a Southern town. Hughes achieved substantial New York runs with his folk MUSICAL *Simply Heavenly* (1957) and with *Tambourines to Glory* (1963). He received several premieres at the interracial KARAMU Theatre in Cleveland, where he had attended school. Among these plays are *Little Ham* (1936), *Troubled Island* (1936), *Joy to My Soul* (1937) and *Front Porch* (1938). In addition, he wrote librettos for four produced OPERAS, and the book and lyrics for KURT WEILL's musical version of *Street Scene* (1947). Hughes founded three short-lived theatres: the Harlem Suitcase Theatre, where his polemical *Don't You Want to Be Free?* (1938) ran at weekends for 135 performances; the New Negro Theatre in Los Angeles (1939); and the Skyloft Players in Chicago (1949). In 1991 his previously unproduced play, *Mule Bone* (written with Zora Neale Hurston in 1930), was staged by Lincoln Center at the Ethel Barrymore Theatre. Hughes's plays are most appealing when his righteous anger is tempered by gentle satire, humour and lyricism. A Pulitzer Prize-winning biography in two volumes (1986, 1988) was written by Arnold Rampersad. EGH

Hugo, Victor 1802–85 French poet, dramatist and novelist. Hugo was the literary colossus of 19th-century France. Son of a Napoleonic officer, he developed an early interest in theatre and particularly in the historical MELODRAMA. His *Inez de Castro* was scheduled for production at the Panorama Dramatique in 1822, but forbidden by the censors. In the 1830s a number of Hugo's plays would have problems with CENSORSHIP, as he used historical themes to comment on the government and society of France at the time, expressed uncomfortable populist ideas, and harked back to Napoleon as an idealized ruler.

His first play to be performed was *Amy Robsart* (under the name of his brother-in-law, Paul Foucher) at the ODÉON in 1828, with COSTUMES by Delacroix. One of a number of adaptations of Scott's *Kenilworth*, it was not a great success and was Hugo's last attempt to adapt a novel for the stage. As Napoleon could not be represented on the stage in the 1820s, Hugo's great analysis of the legitimacy of power received its first expression in his unperformed play *Cromwell* (1827), originally intended for TALMA (d.1826), which developed his idea of a historical drama creating an understanding of its period and not simply concentrating on great historical protagonists. *Cromwell* was eclipsed by its preface, often seen as the manifesto of romantic drama. Many of the ideas of the preface were not new, but common practice in the popular melodrama theatres of the boulevards. However, Hugo was trying to find a new dramatic idiom to replace the played-out neoclassical TRAGEDY which was still favoured at the Théâtre-Français (see COMÉDIE-FRANÇAISE). His master was clearly SHAKESPEARE (though his plays are not particularly Shakespearian). He advocated a verse rather than a prose drama, but his practice was to free the Alexandrine rhythmically, to do away with 18th-century poetic diction and to introduce banal and unpoetic vocabulary. The most famous aesthetic thesis of the preface – significant in that the Théâtre-Français believed in keeping the genres separate – was the idea of the mixture of genres, the idea that the same play could contain elements of the 'sublime' and the 'grotesque'. Hugo also attacked the constrictions of the unities of time, place and action (the boulevard melodrama simply ignored them). His plays, with their slower speed and political purpose, though full of melodramatic scenes, situations and devices, differ from melodrama in their emphasis.

Hugo's first play to be accepted by the Théâtre-Français was *Marion de Lorme*, but its courtesan heroine and its attack on the power of the Church caused it to be banned. Finally, in 1831, after the 1830 revolution, it was performed at the Porte-Saint-Martin (see BOULEVARD), slightly upstaged by DUMAS *père's Antony* which has some resemblances to it. Meanwhile, *Hernani*, written at about the same time, was given an elaborate production at the Théâtre-Français in 1830, once the censors of Charles X had been satisfied by the excision of a number of lines expressing populist sentiment or harking back to the 'great' emperor, Charlemagne. The battle of *Hernani* was one of the famous theatre riots of history, representing the irruption into the temple of conservatism and classicism of the 'angry young men' of the romantic school. Ultimately the 'battle' was more symbolic than real. *Le Roi s'amuse*, source of the libretto of Verdi's *Rigoletto*, received a single performance at the Théâtre-Français in 1832, and was then banned because of the unfavourable light in which it showed King François I. Hugo took court proceedings, which he lost, and the play was not revived until 1882. His next three dramas were in prose. *Lucrèce Borgia*, a triumph at the Porte-Saint-Martin for MLLE GEORGE and FRÉDÉRICK LEMAÎTRE in 1833, resembled *La Tour de Nesle* with a sinful mother accidentally murdering her son. His *Marie Tudor*, at the same theatre the same year, was a flop. In 1835 he returned to the Théâtre-Français with *Angelo, Tyran de Padoue*, which offered two very strong female roles played by MARS and DORVAL. *Ruy Blas* opened Dumas and Hugo's Théâtre de la Renaissance in 1838. Despite a melodramatic framework, with clearly defined good and bad characters, the play continued a serious meditation on the nature of political power. A moderate success at the time, when revived with SARAH BERNHARDT in 1872 it ran for 300 performances. Hugo's last major romantic drama, *Les Burgraves* (Théâtre-Français, 1843), was of epic proportions, but audiences failed to take its 100-year-old lovers seriously, and this type of play was now clearly out of fashion.

In 1845 Hugo was elected a peer of France and in 1852 he had to go into exile for his opposition to Napoleon III. His later years were devoted to more novels (*Les Misérables*, 1862; *Les Travailleurs de la mer*, 1866; and *Quatre-vingt-treize*, 1874) and to some of his major poetic works, including *La Légende des siècles*. He also wrote a study of Shakespeare in 1864. During the years of exile he turned to armchair theatre, the plays of the *Théâtre en Liberté* – a freedom from censorship as much as from stage conventions. The most important of these was a modern play, *Mille Francs de récompense* (*1000 Francs Reward*), a melodrama in the style of *Le Chiffonnier de Paris*, which proved very playable when first performed in 1961. Hugo received a state funeral. JMCC

Hull-House Theatre (USA) Throughout most of its 90-year history, Chicago's Hull-House offered theatre along with, or as part of, its social work activity. Founders Jane Addams and Ellen Gates Starr felt from the start (1889) that theatre was an apt tool for social rehabilitation, and the efforts that ensued often exceeded that aim to achieve artistic excellence as well. The Hull-House Players (1897–1941) were leaders in the Little Theatre movement (see COMMUNITY THEATRE/LITTLE THEATRE MOVEMENT). Edith de Nancrede had long-term (1902–46) success with her children's theatre, and Robert Sickinger's revival of the Hull-House theatre programme (1963–9) is often credited with having a seminal effect on the re-emergence of theatre in Chicago.

Two theatre structures outlived the social work: the Jane Addams Theater on BROADWAY once housed the STEPPENWOLF THEATRE COMPANY (among others), and the Parkway Theater on the South Side housed X-BAG (Experimental Black Actors Guild) during the 1970s and the Chicago Theatre Company (and others) thereafter. SF

Hume, Sam(uel J.) 1885–1962 American set designer and founder of the Detroit Arts and Crafts Theatre. Hume was one of the pioneers of the New Stagecraft and the Little Theatre movement (see COMMUNITY THEATRE/LITTLE THEATRE MOVEMENT). He studied with GORDON CRAIG in Florence and subsequently applied Craig's idea of movable screens into 'adaptable settings' – unit sets utilizing flats, platforms, draperies, arches and pylons that could be rearranged or altered by lighting to fit individual scenes. It was thus a move away from NATURALISM towards simplification and suggestion, as well as being economical. AA

Humphries, (John) Barry 1934– Australian actor and author. He created his archetypal Australian housewife Edna Everage while working as an actor in the 1950s; his other characters include the ageing suburbanite Sandy Stone and the gross member of parliament Sir Les Patterson (Australia's 'Minister of Culture'). His satirical one-man shows, characterized by banter with the audience and a gladioli-waving finale, include *A Nice Night's Entertainment* (1962), *Excuse I* (1965), *At Least You Can Say You've Seen It* (1974), *Isn't It Pathetic at His Age* (1977), *An Evening's Intercourse with Barry Humphries* (1981), *Tears before Bedtime* (1985), *The Life and Death of Sandy Stone* (1990) and *Look at Me When I'm Talking to You* (1993). Early in his career he created the comic strip and film character Barry McKenzie; recently 'Dame Edna' has been the provocative hostess of satirical 'chat shows' on British television. His autobiography, *More Please*, was published in 1992. MW

Huneker, James G. 1857–1921 American critic, who brought serious public attention to European dramatists in the 1890s and early 1900s. Huneker made his debut as a music critic in 1875 for the *Philadelphia Evening Bulletin*. In 1886, after studying the piano in Paris, he moved to New York and a position as music critic for the *Musical Courier*.

He began writing drama criticism during his tenure with the *New York Recorder* (1891–5). In 1895 he became music and drama critic for the *Morning Advertiser*, and during 1902–4 held the drama post for the *New York Sun*. He also wrote for *Metropolitan Magazine*, *Puck*, *Smart Set* and *New York Times*. His 22 books include *Iconoclasts: A Book of Dramatists* (1905) and his autobiography, *Steeplejack* (1920). Huneker opposed the Genteel Tradition and championed the plays of IBSEN, STRINDBERG, SHAW, MAETERLINCK and SCHNITZLER. He brought a lively and impressionistic style to American criticism, and influenced a generation of writers including GEORGE JEAN NATHAN and H. L. Mencken. TLM

Hungary An offspring of the late-18th-century struggle to assert a national culture in the native language, modern Hungarian theatre was born with a sense of mission that, despite or because of the country's turbulent history, endures to this day. The earliest theatrical precedents can be found in medieval Hungary's participation in the European tradition of MYSTERY PLAYS and biblical PASSIONS.

The Renaissance in the 16th century yielded two noteworthy plays: *Electra* by Péter Bornemisza, a reworking of SOPHOCLES, and *A Fine Hungarian Comedy* by Bálint Balassi. Reformation-inspired college dramas became the main source of theatre in 17th-century Hungary, a strife-torn country fighting both Turks and Austrians, with no urban centres in which a theatrical culture could develop. The colleges kept theatre alive until the emergence of professional Hungarian theatre companies in the late 18th century. Though at first in Latin, Jesuit college drama created the pantheon of heroes that enabled the nation to identify with its past. Protestant college plays were mostly in Hungarian, as were Jesuit dramas by the mid-18th century. From that time on college performances attracted a wide audience, including peasants.

During the 18th century the ideas of the French Enlightenment flourished in Vienna, and influenced members of Empress Maria Theresa's Hungarian Guards, one of whom, György Bessenyei, initiated a national programme of cultural resurgence. This was followed by the language reform, a movement led by Ferenc Kazinczy, which reinvigorated native Hungarian culture, eliminating Latin as Hungary's official language and countering German influence. As part of his programme Bessenyei wrote plays such as *The Tragedy of Agis* (1772), which marks the traditional beginning of modern Hungarian literature, and the comedy, *The Philosopher* (1777), which delighted audiences when performed more than a decade after its publication. Mihály Csokonai, leading poet of his time, also contributed to early developments with plays like *The Dreamy Tempefői* (1793), a critique of class distinctions which abounds in social SATIRE. Both Bessenyei and Csokonai used drama as a means of social criticism.

The German-speaking middle class of Pest and Buda of the 18th century had two theatres: Pest (1774) and Buda (1784). Political, social and economic conditions impeded the emergence of a Hungarian urban middle class. Nevertheless, from 1780 to 1830 Pest became the Hungarian cultural centre of the country with its university, National Museum, Academy of Sciences and several publishing firms. Periodicals also flourished. Increasing numbers of impoverished noblemen moved to Pest as professionals, and the German-speaking middle class was gradually assimilated. Establishing Hungarian theatrical hegemony over Austrian colonial theatre became a national cause, especially after the building in 1812 of a large, German-language theatre in Pest.

In 1790, under the management of László Kelemen, a Hungarian acting troupe began performing in various locations in Pest, the repertoire consisting largely of translated German plays. The company received some local official support, which was withdrawn during the period of terror following the uncovering of the Martinovics conspiracy of 1794, an anti-monarchist plot. The company ceased functioning in 1796; a second attempt lasted from 1807 to 1815.

On the initiative of the leading Transylvanian Enlightenment intellectual, György Aranka, a Hungarian theatre company began performing in 1792 in Kolozsvár. This company survived through support from the aristocracy and the largely Hungarian-speaking Transylvanian urban middle class. Also, as an autonomous province of the Empire, Transylvania was less affected by the aftermath of the Martinovics conspiracy. In 1821 the company acquired in Kolozsvár the first permanent home of any Hungarian theatre.

Hungarian theatrical activity in Pest from 1815 to 1833 consisted of ten guest appearances by travelling troupes from other parts of Hungary. By the late 1820s about 15 such companies were touring the country, and several noteworthy troupes, based in Kassa, Miskolc and Székesfehérvár, emerged. The premiere in Pest of Károly Kisfaludy's *The Tartars in Hungary* (1819) by the Székesfehérvár troupe marked the beginning of a new era in Hungarian theatre. Kisfaludy's historical dramas satisfied the intense interest, characteristic of Hungarian romanticism, in the early history of the nation. Kisfaludy also popularized comedy (e.g. *The Suitors*, 1817) whose characters were recognizable Hungarian types. The plots, though standard, presented the clash of the social and cultural backgrounds of the characters, and made for social commentary.

The Academy of Sciences, founded in 1825, endeavoured to popularize the newly codified literary language by promoting the construction in Pest of a permanent home for Hungarian theatre, commissioning the translation of plays of international excellence and holding competitions for original Hungarian plays. Mihály Vörösmarty, the leading romantic poet, turned to writing plays in the 1830s. His one masterpiece is *Csongor and Tünde*, written in 1831 but not performed until 1879. This verse play describes Csongor's search for Fairyland, where he hopes to be reunited with his love, Tünde. Csongor is symbolic of the idealist who meets disillusionment and attains wisdom. At this time the greatest Hungarian play of the century, JÓZSEF KATONA's *Bánk Bán*, was not accorded its deserved recognition. Written in 1815, this TRAGEDY of an honourable palatine undone by conflicting loyalties was premiered in Kassa in 1833, but its merits were not recognized until 1845 at the National Theatre.

In 1833 the newly revived Hungarian Theatre Company of Pest took control of the former German theatre in Buda, and in 1837 moved into its new home in Pest, built with donations by citizens. At the Academy, Vörösmarty became head of the drama supervisory committee, and steered the repertoire towards SHAKESPEARE, SCHILLER and original Hungarian works. In 1840 the Theatre of Pest became the National Theatre under the management of József Bajza, renowned critic; he was succeeded in 1843 by Endre Bartay, a proponent of French romanticism. In 1847 the German theatre building in Pest burned down, an event signalling the rapid decline of German-language theatre in the capital, while in provincial cities assimilation led to the transfer of theatres to Hungarian companies. Between 1854 and 1867 six new theatres were built in provincial cities.

Hungary's Age of Reform (1825–48) was characterized by liberal political ideas and economic growth. By the 1840s there was widespread demand for the emancipation of the peasantry, and the National Theatre became a platform for these strivings. Hungarian political COMEDY was created by Ignác Nagy, whose *The County Election* (1843) satirizes social stereotypes and ridicules local political corruption. Comedies commenting on contemporary society became the vogue as interest in historical subjects waned. Károly Obernyik received an Academy award for his *Aristocrat and Serf* (1843), an open attack against class privilege. Zsigmond Czakó, influenced by French romanticism, depicted in *The Will* (1845) a hero who loses his social standing and sanity when it turns out he is not, as he thought, of noble descent.

In 1843 Ede Szigligeti emerged as the creator of a new type of play whose influence was apparent for half a century. *The Deserter* was the first *népszínmű* (roughly: folk play). This genre portrays peasant life with the aim of arousing sympathy for the peasantry; major ingredients are dialects, folk costumes, folk song and dance. Before the 1849 defeat in the War of Independence, the *népszínmű* was serious. Later the trappings and comic effects began to dominate, as the genre lost its reforming mission. Eventually the *népszínmű*, among whose practitioners was József Szigeti, degenerated into pseudo-OPERETTA. During the National Theatre's first four decades one-third of its repertoire consisted of plays by Ede Szigligeti. *Liliomfi* (1849) remains his most highly regarded comedy. He was the National's manager from 1873 to his death in 1878. Directorship was then assumed by Ede Paulay, who premiered Vörösmarty's *Csongor and Tünde* in 1879 and IMRE MADÁCH's *The Tragedy of Man* in 1883.

The reign of terror following defeat in the War of Independence (1848–9) crushed Hungarian intellectual life, and the gradual literary resurgence of the 1850s was much influenced by disillusionment over the present and future of the nation. This pessimism influenced Imre Madách's dramatic poem, *The Tragedy of Man* (1860), which nevertheless transcends national concerns and gives expression to man's inherent metaphysical insecurity. The work has proved to be one of the most enduring successes of the Hungarian theatre.

Political tensions eased following the compromise of 1867, which established the Austro-Hungarian dual monarchy. In the final decades of the century the middle class grew rapidly as Budapest became a major European city, and the demand for theatre grew. Between 1896 and 1907 five theatres were built in the capital, all in private

hands except for the National. Regional theatre was also experiencing an upsurge; by 1911, 38 theatres were operating throughout the country. But little of value was performed. The most popular domestic playwright of the period, Gergely Csiky, a keen observer of Hungarian society, has been called the SARDOU of the Hungarian stage.

At the beginning of the 20th century, drama was the weakest branch of Hungarian literature. In 1904 a group of intellectuals founded the Thalia Company, which championed the works of such writers as IBSEN, STRINDBERG, HAUPTMANN and SHAW. Its director, Sándor Hevesi, brought NATURALISM to the Hungarian stage. Though disbanded in 1909, the influence of the Thalia helped usher in a new breed of Hungarian playwrights, some of whom acquired international reputations. Their work, often called 'commercial drama', is based on a mastery of stagecraft and, often, a cosmopolitanism to which urban audiences in Europe and America could respond. These qualities are evident in the work of FERENC MOLNÁR, whose dramatic situations betray the influence of Freud, his sparkling dialogue that of WILDE, and whose treatment of reality versus illusion is reminiscent of PIRANDELLO. But Molnár's technical brilliance is not matched by depth of philosophical insight. The best-known of his nearly 30 plays are *The Devil* (1907), *Liliom* (1909), *The Guardsman* (1910) and *The Play's the Thing* (1926).

Another popular playwright of the period was Ferenc Herczeg. Whereas Molnár dealt mainly with the bourgeoisie, Herczeg in his historical dramas was an apologist for feudalism and the court of Vienna; in other plays he glorified the nationalist, conservative gentry. He is best-known for *The Blue Fox* (1917). Menyhért Lengyel achieved international acclaim with *Typhoon* (1909), a play about the clash of Eastern and Western world outlooks. Lengyel's attraction to oriental themes is demonstrated by his 1917 scenario for Béla Bartók's ballet, *The Miraculous Mandarin*. It was thanks to Bartók that Béla Balázs (later known as a film theorist) attained world fame with his symbolist play (see SYMBOLISM), *Bluebeard's Castle* (1910), which Bartók set to music. Lajos Bíró was also a popular, prolific, commercial playwright, best-known for *Yellow Lily* (1909). After the collapse of the short-lived Hungarian Republic of Councils in 1919, he settled in London and became a successful screenwriter. Dezső Szomory's historical dramas, many about Habsburg monarchs, are known for their use of lofty, ceremonious language. Jenő Heltai recorded his characters' foibles, social games and moral compromises with indulgence and cynicism. He is best-known for *The Tündérlaki Girls* (1914) and *The Silent Knight* (1936). Zsigmond Móricz, primarily a prose chronicler of peasant and small-town life, in his play *Judge Sári* (1910) gave one of the most true-to-life portrayals of peasant life ever to reach the Hungarian stage. Zoltán Thury and Sándor Bródy tried to bring genuine psychological conflict and social criticism to the stage, but could not compete with commercial drama. Thury was concerned in plays like *Soldiers* (1889) with revealing the passions behind false façades of social stability. Bródy's targets were middle-class families who corrupted and exploited their peasant maids. His best-known plays are *The Nanny* (1902) and *The Schoolmistress* (1908).

The First World War and its aftermath, the 133-day Republic of Councils followed by the White Terror, and the loss of two-thirds of the country's territory along with over three million ethnic Hungarians to the successor states, help explain why the legitimate theatre became the bourgeoisie's outlet for escapist entertainment and nostalgia. The most significant play of the period, Tibor Déry's Dadaist masterpiece, *The Giant Baby* (1926), was written in exile and remained unproduced for decades. It was left to the CABARET, the most vital Hungarian theatrical forum of the interwar years, to provide room for experimentation, political SATIRE and at times resistance. The cabaret was a phenomenon of Budapest, but had roots in folk traditions. Endre Nagy ran a cabaret from 1907 to 1929 in which some of the country's best performers, composers and writers including Móricz, Heltai and Molnár experimented. Between 1916 and 1936, 18 cabarets opened in Budapest. The cabaret pieces of Frigyes Karinthy, e.g. *The Magic Chair* (1917), foreshadowed absurdist drama. Cabaret continued to flourish under the new social order imposed after the Second World War.

Following the Second World War, playwrights who had left the country, or were silenced by the White Terror, the rise of Fascism or intolerance towards experimentation, returned or re-emerged. The most significant were Tibor Déry, Gyula Háy, Lajos Kassák, Áron Tamási and Béla Balázs. Their work was officially discredited, however, because the theatre was proclaimed a school for educating the masses in the new social order. In 1949 all of Hungary's theatres were nationalized. In the next five seasons 66 new Soviet plays, 13 Russian classics and only six Western plays were mounted, in addition to examples of domestic socialist realism conforming to the Party's aims. The pattern was broken by Tibor Déry's *The Sycophant* (1954), which ridiculed the over-eager Party functionary, and by Imre Sarkadi's *September* (1955), which in its realism broke with the Party's formula for the peasant-play.

The revolution of 1956, though crushed by Soviet tanks and followed by a period of severe repression, marked a turning point with far-reaching consequences. In response to the Party's requirement for plays justifying the suppression of the revolution, writers in official favour supplied plays in 1958–9 in which the hero is presented with a moral dilemma brought on by the uprising, and makes the 'correct' choice. Drama thus returned from schematic statements to the depiction of individuals in the throes of moral conflict. At the same time, many plays of BRECHT, previously banned as 'decadent', were produced, and EPIC THEATRE began to make its delayed inroads into Hungary.

In the early 1960s, the government began seeking legitimacy by increasingly respecting individual rights. Accordingly, compulsory artistic norms were abandoned in favour of growing tolerance in the areas of culture and art. From 1963, the Thalia Theatre, under the artistic directorship of Károly Kazimir, provided a much needed venue for new directions, beginning with Endre Fejes's *Scrap Yard*, a chronicle of a working-class family leading a meaningless life in the thick of the system's promises. Other important plays of this time also questioned Hungary's socialist system. Károly Szakonyi's *Sofie, My Life* (1963) and Imre Sarkadi's *Simeon Stylites* (1967) examine the post-

1956 intellectual's dilemma of becoming an unwilling member of the ruling class. The moral price of such reluctant compromise is examined by István Csurka in such plays as *Loser Takes All* (1969).

Though Miklós Mészöly was creating Hungarian absurdist drama in the late 1950s, as was Géza Páskándi in the early 1960s, their work remained unproduced for years. THEATRE OF THE ABSURD became visible in Hungary only in 1965, with productions of works by BECKETT, HAVEL and MROŻEK. Domestic absurdism first reached the stage in 1967, when the Thalia presented ISTVÁN ÖRKÉNY's *The Tóth Family*, a satiric play about a family actively undermining its own equanimity in order to curry favour with an authority figure, whom the Tóths ultimately murder. This production was followed in 1968 by Gábor Görgey's *Who's Got the Gun?* and István Eörsi's *Tombstone and Cocoa*. Hungarian absurdist drama, frequently called 'grotesque', tends to deal with the use of power and its effect on the individual. Thus absurdity arises not from existence *per se*, but from social and political conditions. Tibor Gyurkovics has also made significant contributions to the genre.

In the late 1960s, under László Gyurkó's directorship, the Twenty-Fifth Theater was established in Budapest specifically to air political and social issues. It was here in the early 1970s that the renowned film-maker Miklós Jancsó and his frequent scenarist, Gyula Hernádi, began their theatrical collaboration as director and playwright respectively. Other significant developments around this time include *Sojourn* (1970), GÉZA PÁSKÁNDI's first stage success, which introduced an absurdist approach to the historical drama, and *Please Stand By* (1970), Károly Szakonyi's SATIRE of middle-class mores, in which not even a 'second coming' can compete with the focus of family life: television.

While self-destruction, disillusionment and loss of moral equilibrium have been central themes in the Hungarian theatre since the 1970s, a more traditional school of drama has also been flourishing. Its main representatives are Gyula Illyés, László Németh, János Székely and ANDRÁS SÜTŐ. Their plays, mostly polemical historical dramas, recognize a stable moral order that gives meaning to action and choice, and reflect a concern with the nation's history and destiny. In Sütő's *Star at the Stake* (1975), the clash of the Reformation figures Calvin and Servetus illuminates the debate between political orthodoxy and the spirit of free inquiry. Illyés wrote that his play about the Albigensian Crusade, *Cathars* (1969), 'is about a nation that has perished, written for peoples and communities still alive'. National concerns naturally inform other genres as well. Even *Catsplay* (1971), Örkény's popular comedy about a sexagenarian love triangle, treats the issue of choosing the discomforts and insecurities of the homeland rather than emigrating to the West.

A remarkable generation of playwrights emerged in the late 1970s, bringing to Hungarian theatre a fundamentally new outlook based on the very absence of a moral order, of a meaningful past, of ideals, of the possibility of rational action or even a coherent personality. The most original among these playwrights is Péter Nádas, whose trilogy *House Cleaning* (1977), *Encounter* (1979) and *Burial* (1980) depicts rituals of purification and initiation. In *Halmi* (1979), Géza Bereményi reworks *Hamlet* into a play about a modern anti-hero. György Spiró's *Chickenhead* (1987) is a hypernaturalistic look into the consciousness of characters at the squalid margins of present-day Hungarian society. Mihály Kornis's *Kozma* (1986), a Dionysian orgy of confession set against the ravings of a chorus that recognizes nothing, examines a nation morally impoverished by recent history. Gábor Czakó and György Schwajda are also significant playwrights of this generation.

Two-thirds of Hungary's 30-odd theatres are in the capital. In the new political era, many of these have lost government subsidies and must rely on ticket sales and commercial sponsorships. Repertoire and the cohesiveness of acting companies, therefore, have suffered. Nevertheless, theatre remains an important repository and forum of national culture – a role upheld by such institutions as the National Theatre, the József Katona Theatre (presently a celebrated venue of new work) and theatres in the provinces, as well as by theatre companies of the Hungarian-minority populations in those parts of the surrounding states that were detached from Hungary after the First World War. There are six such companies in Transylvania (Romania), one in Slovakia, and a recently established one in Subcarpathia (Ukraine). The fate of Hungarian theatre in Vojvodina (Serbia) is uncertain at this time of strife. In recent seasons, these outlying theatres have been receiving guest performances of the National Theatre of Hungary, thus strengthening cultural bonds.

Hungarian theatre, its history rife with missed and crushed opportunities, now appears poised for a fruitful future. EB

See: L. Czigány, *The Oxford History of Hungarian Literature*, Oxford, 1984; I. Goldstein, 'A History of Hungarian Drama between 1945 and 1970', Ph.D. dissertation, City University of New York, 1974; F. Hont (ed.), *Magyar szihnáztörténet*, Budapest, 1962; T. Klaniczayt (ed.), *A History of Hungarian Literature*, Budapest, 1983; A. Szerb, *Magyar irodalomtörténet*, Budapest, 6th edn, 1978.

hunger artist Sideshow performer who fasts publicly for extended periods. Starvation had been used as a tragic theme in H. W. Gerstenberg's *Ugolino* (1768), and public fasting exploited by female charlatans passing themselves off as saints. Showmen took to it after 1880, when Dr Henry Tanner (d.1893) of New York fasted for 40 days to win a bet. Most hunger artists did drink during their ordeals, among them the leading performer of the turn of the century, Giacomo Succi of Milan. The phenomenon caught on in Germany during the Inflation period, when the populace was starving anyway; Succi's record was broken in 1926 by Ventego (47 days). As late as 1950 fasting could still be seen at European fairs, though it has now become a property of political protest in prisons.

TADEUSZ RÓZEWICZ's play *The Hunger Artist Departs* (1976), based on Franz Kafka, converts the starveling into a metaphor for the visionary artist in an uncomprehending world. LS

Hunt, Hugh (Sidney) 1911–93 British director, dramatist and critic. After directing a wide variety of plays in repertory (see REGIONAL THEATRE (BRITAIN)), Hunt became a director at the ABBEY THEATRE, Dublin, from 1935 to 1938, where his first play, written in collaboration with Frank O'Connor, *The Invincibles* (1937), was performed. In 1946 he was appointed the first director of the BRISTOL OLD VIC COMPANY, moving to the London OLD VIC in 1949, where he directed a series of SHAKESPEARE and SHAW productions. From 1955 to 1960 he played a significant role in the development of the Australian theatre as director of the Elizabethan Theatre Trust in Sydney, where he founded the Trust Players, the Young Elizabethan Players and the Elizabethan Opera Company. Returning to England in 1960, he directed a tour of PETER SHAFFER's *Five Finger Exercise* for the ARTS COUNCIL, and was instrumental in creating the Contact Company in Manchester, now the ROYAL EXCHANGE THEATRE Company. He was professor of drama at Manchester University during 1961–73, and between 1969 and 1971 was also artistic director of the Abbey Theatre. CI MB

Hunt, (James Henry) Leigh 1784–1859 English dramatic critic, essayist and poet. Hunt's father emigrated from the newly independent USA, where his vehement loyalty to the English Crown had made him too many enemies. His sons, John and Leigh, inherited his defiance. Leigh Hunt's first dramatic criticism was written for the *News*, of which John was editor. The volume of *Critical Essays on the Performers of the London Theatre* (1808) is a selection of these early reviews, the product of independent observation, seriousness and verbal facility. The absence of evident bias and the willingness to admire the art and chastise the artfulness of actors combined to enhance the status of dramatic CRITICISM in England. When his brother founded the *Examiner*, Hunt became its editor (1808), continuing his systematic visits to London theatres. The paper was prosecuted three times. On the first two occasions (they had exposed abuses in the British Army) the Hunts were acquitted, but in 1813 they were imprisoned for two years following what was adjudged a libel on the Prince Regent. As a result, Hunt missed the London debut of EDMUND KEAN. Released in early 1815, he saw Kean as Richard III and wrote one of his finest pieces of measured criticism to express his disappointment. Almost equally fine is his speedy recantation after watching Kean as Othello – 'the masterpiece of the living stage' was his conclusion.

Hunt was the father of a large and often hapless family, and he undertook far too much work in order to support it. He was probably mortified that so many of his friends – they included, at various times, Keats, Shelley, BYRON, LAMB, Carlyle, Browning, TENNYSON and DICKENS – were better writers than he. Of the ten or so plays he wrote, or started, two were staged in his lifetime, the verse tragedy *A Legend of Florence* (1840) at COVENT GARDEN, and a verse comedy, *Lovers' Amazements* (1858), at the LYCEUM.

To the end, Hunt aspired to be more than he actually was, a superior journalist. His *Dramatic Criticism, 1808–31* can be read in an excellent collection by L. H. and C. W. Houtchens (1949). PT

Hunter, N(orman) C(harles) 1908–71 British dramatist, whose two dramas of middle-class households in decline, *Waters of the Moon* (1951) and *A Day by the Sea* (1953), gave him the reputation of being an English CHEKHOV. He began by writing amusing comedies of which *All Rights Reserved* (1935) and *A Party for Christmas* (1938) reached the WEST END, but the plotting and dialogue seemed slick, without being particularly original or effective. After the war, however, his style became more leisurely, intricate and concerned with shifts in mood. The casting of *A Day by the Sea*, with JOHN GIELGUD, RALPH RICHARDSON, SYBIL THORNDIKE and IRENE WORTH, illustrates the esteem in which this autumnal play was held, and its command of atmosphere rewards the outstanding actor. Its dialogue now seems pedestrian, not like Chekhov but closer to minor RATTIGAN, but interest is retained through the interweaving of emotional themes. *A Touch of the Sun* (1958) and *The Tulip Tree* (1962) were less successful; and the fashion for N. C. Hunter's plays was one casualty of the new ROYAL COURT-led wave of angry young writers. JE

Hurt, William 1950– American actor of 'distilled and concentrated intensity'. Hurt's OFF-BROADWAY debut was *Henry V* (NEW YORK SHAKESPEARE FESTIVAL, 1977) and his BROADWAY debut was *Hurlyburly* (1984). He has been active with the CIRCLE REPERTORY COMPANY (1977–82); his most recent work includes Pintauro's *Beside Herself* (CRC, 1989) and *Ivanov* (YALE REPERTORY THEATRE, 1990), as well as the films *Body Heat* (1981), *The Big Chill* (1983), *Kiss of the Spider Woman* (Academy Award, 1984), *Children of a Lesser God* (1986), *The Accidental Tourist* (1988) and *The Doctor* (1991). Hurt won an Obie and *Theatre World* Award for his role in Corinne Jacker's *My Life* (CRC, 1977) and the 1988 Spencer Tracy Award. REK

Hurwitz, Moishe 1844–1910 and
Jacob Lateiner 1853–1935 The two main writers of *shund* theatre, characterizing the lowest quality of popular American YIDDISH THEATRE (sentimental and melodramatic) during the 1890s. Deliberately writing down to the tastes of the most uneducated and unsophisticated of the 'green' immigrants, 'Professor' Hurwitz (as he called himself) wrote about 90 plays, and Jacob Lateiner turned out over 150. AB

Hussein, Ebrahim 1943– Tanzanian playwright. Published plays include *Kinjeketile* (1970) originally in Swahili and translated into English, *Wakati Ukata* (*Time Is a Wall*, 1970), *Alikaona* (*The One Who Got What She Deserved*, 1970), *Mashetani* (*Devils*, 1971), *Arusi* (*Wedding*, 1980), *Jogoo Kijijini* (*The Dock in the Village*, 1976), *Ngao ya Jadi* (*The Traditional Shield*, 1976). Hussein's themes are closely related to the struggle for a just society in Tanzania, from the depiction of the Maji Maji uprising against the Germans in *Kinjeketile* to his portrayal of the unfulfilled dream for a better society in *Arusi*. Not only are his themes relevant to the Tanzanian situation but in many cases so are his forms, particularly his use of the traditional storytelling structure. Hussein was formerly Associate Professor in Theatre Arts at the University of Dar es Salaam. PMM

Huston, Walter 1884–1950 Canadian-born stage and film actor, noted for his artistic integrity, lack of affectation and economic style. Huston began acting in 1902, returned to school, then re-entered the theatre in 1909. For almost 18 years he toured the USA and Canada. His New York debut was in 1924 in the title role of *Mr Pitt*, and in the same year he achieved stardom as Ephraim Cabot in *Desire under the Elms*. STARK YOUNG called Huston's Ephraim 'trenchant, gaunt, fervid, harsh', lauding his 'ability to convey the harsh, inarticulate life' of the role. Later BROOKS ATKINSON called Huston 'the most honest of actors – plain, simple, lucid, magnetic'. He was also acclaimed for his title role in Sinclair Lewis's *Dodsworth* and for his work in *Knickerbocker Holiday*, in which he introduced 'September Song'. In 1948 he won an Academy Award for Best Supporting Actor in *The Treasure of the Sierra Madre*, a film directed by his son, John. His other films included *Dodsworth* and *Duel in the Sun*. SMA

Hyman, Earle 1926– African-American actor, renowned in classical and contemporary roles. Hyman began with the American Negro Theatre and at 17 appeared in *Anna Lucasta* (1944) on BROADWAY and in London's WEST END. His earliest Shakespearian role was Hamlet (1951) at Howard University, followed by the first of six Othellos played over a 25-year period in Antioch (Ohio), New York, Connecticut, Norway and Sweden. Hyman performed 10 other roles with the AMERICAN SHAKESPEARE THEATRE (1955–60), received rave notices for his Broadway performance in *Mr Johnson* (1956), and the State Award in Oslo for his portrayal of the title role in *The Emperor Jones* (1965). In 1989 he replaced Morgan Freeman as the Chauffeur in *Driving Miss Daisy*, performing the play in Norway and Denmark (in Norwegian and Danish). In 1991 he essayed the role of Pickering in New York's Roundabout Theatre's non-traditionally cast *Pygmalion*, and starred in 1994 in the PUBLIC THEATER's *East Texas Hot Links* by Eugene Lee. Despite his notable credits Hyman is best known by the public as comic Bill Cosby's father on Cosby's long-running television series (see TELEVISION DRAMA). EGH

Hytner, Nicholas 1956– British director, whose ROYAL SHAKESPEARE COMPANY debut with a clear and visually brilliant production of *Measure for Measure* (1987) marked him out as an exceptional young talent, the leader of a new generation of British directors. As if to prove that this was no accident, he provided a poetic *Tempest* (1988) with JOHN WOOD as Prospero. His NATIONAL THEATRE debut was equally impressive. His staging of Joshua Sobol's *Ghetto* (1989), about the sufferings of the Lithuanian Jews, showed his capacity to handle a large cast on the Olivier stage without losing his accurate sense of detail. He was picked by CAMERON MACKINTOSH to direct the MUSICAL *Miss Saigon* (1989) at DRURY LANE, which became an instant hit. Not even PETER BROOK made a more auspicious start to his career. His much shortened *Volpone* (1990) with Ian McDiarmid at London's Almeida and his *King Lear* with John Wood at Stratford-upon-Avon with the RSC were somewhat less convincing; but his productions of *The Wind in the Willows* (1991), *The Madness of George III*

(1991), *The Recruiting Officer* (1992) and the revival of *Carousel* (1992), all at the NT, were memorable. In his short career, Hytner has demonstrated that he has a remarkable range as a director: he is capable of staging big musicals, operas, classical tragedy and the intimate text-based nuances of an ALAN BENNETT play. It may seem ungenerous to add that he has still to prove that he can be a profound director, as well as versatile, and that his ideas do not always match the brilliance with which he expresses them. JE

Ibargüengoitia, Jorge 1928–85 Mexican playwright, author of a dozen plays. From an early tendency towards light comedies he found his niche in satiric comedies with black humour. His master work was *El atentado* (*The Assault*, 1966), with its sardonic view of the assassination of Mexican President Alvaro Obregón.   GW

Ibsen, Henrik 1828–1906 Norwegian playwright and poet. Ibsen's playwriting owed much to his early theatrical experience: having written only *Catiline* and *The Warrior's Barrow* (the latter staged at Christiania Theater), he was appointed resident dramatist and then stage director at the new Norske Theater in Bergen, Norway's first theatre to use Norwegian actors and attempt Norwegian (rather than Danish) speech. His next plays were written to meet his contract for a new play annually. In 1852, the theatre sent him to Dresden and Copenhagen, where he learned much from the methods and principles enforced by JOHAN LUDVIG HEIBERG at the KONGELIGE TEATER and from its acting ensemble, including JOHANNE LUISE HEIBERG and MICHAEL WIEHE. He also discovered HERMANN HETTNER's book *The Modern Drama*, which emphasized psychological conflict as the basis of drama; from Heiberg he may have learned the dramaturgical mechanics of SCRIBE.

In 1857 Ibsen moved to Christiania (now Oslo) to manage the new Kristiania Norske Theater, where resources were severely limited. When it closed in 1862, he was briefly engaged at Christiania Theater to direct his own *The Pretenders*, his final practical involvement with theatre before moving to Rome in 1864, beginning a 27-year voluntary exile.

Apart from the contemporary *St John's Night* (1852) and *Love's Comedy* (1862), Ibsen's early plays (including *The Pretenders*) owe much to the national romantic movement's fascination with Norway's past. His major transformation as a playwright occurred abroad, first in *Brand* (1865) and *Peer Gynt* (1867), both dealing with the dilemmas created by the claims of the absolute and the temptations of compromise. The immediate impetus was Ibsen's dismay at Norway's failure to assist Denmark in its struggle with Bismarck over Schleswig-Holstein. However, the plays' concerns reach back to the early *Catiline*, and resonate, with increasing complexity, in his later works. His characters are typically caught in a tension between the possible and the unattainable, driven to strive for the latter and tormented by guilt when they give in to the former. Despite his disclaimers, his mature plays are imbued with the ideas of Kierkegaard, particularly his differentiation between the aesthetic, ethical and religious ways of life and his use of Abraham as a representative 'Knight of Faith'. The motif of vocation, imperfectly understood by Brand and evaded by Peer, is also drawn from Kierkegaard and was to hold together the sprawling two-part *Emperor and Galilean* completed in 1873. Ibsen uses Julian the Apostate to explore the ironies of a man confusedly searching for vocation, while the world-will progresses regardless.

Despite his protests that he was a poet rather than a social reformer, his next plays were widely understood to be blows struck in support of social and political reform. For example, *A Doll's House* (1879) was critiqued as a feminist tract (shocking to many) rather than a study of self-realization and vocation; *Ghosts* (1881) was taken to be about venereal disease, rather than the dangerous social diseases it exposes; *An Enemy of the People* (1882) provoked more discussion of its supposed political targets than of its theme of the vocation to truth. However, with *The Wild Duck* (1884), the critics were bewildered. Ibsen had entered a new phase, in which his normally ambivalent perception of life became mysterious, raising more questions (both of fact and of principle) than he answered. In the character Gregers, the motif of vocation was perceived in a satirical and sinister light, an effect to be echoed in *Rosmersholm* (1886) and *Hedda Gabler* (1890), in which the female protagonists pursue missions that lead to disaster.

Ibsen's plays were now concerned more with individual destinies than with general moral or social principles, and his focus narrowed (and intensified) even more in *The Lady from the Sea* (1888) and the plays that followed: *The Master Builder* (1892), with its complex interweaving of guilt, ambition and fantasy; *Little Eyolf* (1894), in which Alfred and Rita seem possessed by a confused blend of guilt and frustrated personal ambition; and *John Gabriel Borkman* (1896), which exposes the frustrating failure of a family to live through others. Finally, in 1899, came what Ibsen called the 'dramatic epilogue' of the sequence of plays beginning with *A Doll's House* and later suggested was the conclusion of his entire dramatic output: *When We Dead Awaken* (1899). It does indeed seem to reach back through his 50 years of playwriting, drawing together many of the images and themes employed in earlier plays. However, he does not achieve a resolution of his characters' spiritual conflicts, but rather a final statement of their dilemma, caught between the temptations of the possible and the demands of the ideal.   HL

Iceland Under Norwegian and Danish rule respectively for seven centuries, Iceland regained independence, becoming a republic in 1944. Christianity was adopted in 1000, although heathen worship was tolerated. Roman Catholic until 1550, Iceland is now Lutheran Protestant. It has 265,000 inhabitants, more than half of whom live in the Reykjavík area.

Unlike the rich tradition of storytelling, evidence for early performance is scant. A definitive history of theatre goes back to the early 18th century, when students at the Cathedral School at Skálholt began performing the *Herranótt*, an annual RITUAL resembling the Boy Bishop tradition in England. This gave birth to Icelandic drama, for by 1790 the festivities included the performance of a play, the first significant dramatist being Sigurdur Pétursson, whose satirical comedies resemble HOLBERG's plays. The authorities eventually found these activities offensive, and banned them from 1799 until 1820. Plays were annually performed at the school after it moved to Reykjavík in 1846, and soon there were fairly regular amateur performances of plays and *vaudevilles* both in Danish and Icelandic, in Reykjavík and in villages around the country.

During the latter half of the 19th century, theatre became the most popular form of entertainment, a status it still retains. The chief exponent at the time was painter Sigurdur Gudmundsson. While studying in Copenhagen, Gudmundsson developed a keen interest in theatre, realizing its potential against foreign oppression, which led him to express the need for a national stage from which the people could be enlightened and made aware of their national identity. He became the first stage designer and may also have been the first stage director, as he frequently used to place the actors in such a way as to create tableaux.

Gudmundsson prompted poets to create a national drama from Icelandic folklore, suggesting the craft could be learned by translating great works of world theatre. Under his influence two students wrote plays from folklore. Matthías Jochumsson wrote *The Outlaws* (1862), and Indridi Einarsson wrote *New Year's Eve* (1871) inspired by HEIBERG's *Elverhöj* and SHAKESPEARE's *Midsummer Night's Dream. The Outlaws*, a popular COMEDY, remains the most frequently produced Icelandic play, but its initial success owed much to Gudmundsson's pioneering stage design depicting the Icelandic landscape. Jochumsson and Einarsson made several translations of Shakespeare – which were not superseded until Helgi Hálfdanarson's translations of the complete plays began appearing after 1950 – as well as writing historical plays in his fashion. These include Jochumsson's *Jón Arason* (1900) and Einarsson's *Sword and Crosier* (1899). Einarsson, a lesser writer than Jochumsson, was the first to concentrate on playwriting, and his folklore plays include *The Cave Dwellers* (1897) and the Faustian *The Dance at Hruni* (1921). Einarsson's major contribution is his dedication to Gudmundsson's national theatre ideal. Through his tireless efforts money was secured to begin construction of a National Theatre around 1930.

By the 1890s there were three main amateur companies in Reykjavík, two of which joined forces in 1897 to establish the Reykjavík Theatre Company (RTC), aiming to secure the growth of Icelandic drama and raise the standard of productions. The company, officially supported, found a permanent home with an intimate stage, and Einarsson became its first stage director. In 1903 the RTC produced their first Icelandic play, Einarsson's realistic *The Ship Is Sinking*, while the 1904–5 season featured IBSEN's *Ghosts* and *A Doll's House*, with MOLIÈRE, SCHILLER and SHAW crowning subsequent seasons. From 1908 to 1920 there were productions of 11 new plays, all but one directed by actor Jens B. Waage. In this period JÓHANN SIGURJÓNSSON, GUDMUNDUR KAMBAN and Einar H. Kvaran, three outstanding playwrights, were established, the first two gaining international reputations. The RTC, strong and ambitious although amateur, was joined by the first professional actors arriving from training abroad, mostly from Copenhagen, during the 1920s and early 1930s. These were Haraldur Björnsson, Anna Borg Reumert, Lárus Pálsson, Indridi Waage and Thorsteinn Ö. Stephensen. Björnsson, Pálsson and Waage became leading directors, while Stephensen also headed RADIO DRAMA for almost 30 years. Anna Borg Reumert soon returned to Copenhagen to become a leading actress there. In 1926 Waage directed *Twelfth Night,* the first Shakespeare production in Iceland.

The existence of the RTC was threatened in 1950 when the National Theatre opened, as nearly all the actors were recruited for the new theatre. A few idealists, including leading actors Stephensen and Brynjólfur Jóhannesson, decided to persevere, with Danish-born Gunnar R. Hansen as director. The RTC became fully professional in 1963 under artistic director Sveinn Einarsson and has since proved a vital alternative to the National Theatre. Vigdís Finnbogadóttir, now president of the republic, was artistic director from 1972 to 1980; the present incumbent is Sigurdur Hróarsson. The RTC moved into the new City Theatre in 1989.

The National Theatre opened with three productions on consecutive nights. Einarsson's *New Year's Eve* was followed by Jóhann Sigurjónsson's *Eyvind of the Mountains* (1911) and Lárus Pálsson's adaptation of Halldór Laxness's epic *The Bell of Iceland* (1943–6). New works and classics, both Icelandic and foreign, were staged, and it was not until the 1970s that new Icelandic drama became the backbone of the repertoire. Although the RTC had fine achievements to their credit, fully professional theatre begins only with the National Theatre. The NT Drama School (1950–70) offered the opportunity of professional training within the country, and the NT Ballet School made it possible to establish the Icelandic Dance Company in 1973, making ballet part of the repertoire, while OPERA has been included since 1951, the theatre being the only opera house until the Icelandic Opera was formed in 1982. The National Theatre building went through major renovations in 1990–1, and now has three playing stages with a total seating capacity of 700–800. The ensemble consists of 40 versatile actors. Björnsson, Pálsson and Waage were leading directors in the 1950s, and since 1960 the main directors have been Baldvin Halldórsson, Benedikt Árnason, Brynja Benediktsdóttir, Sveinn Einarsson, Stefán Baldursson, Bríet Hédinsdóttir, Thórhildur Thorleifsdóttir and Thórhallur Sigurdsson. Artistic directors have been Gudlaugur Rósinkranz, Sveinn Einarsson, Gísli Alfredsson and Stefán Baldursson.

The 1960s saw a renaissance of playwriting, and ever since Jökull Jakobsson's successful *Hard-a-Port* (1962) Icelandic plays have been predominant. This period produced a variety of playwrights, including Jakobsson with his impressionistic studies, absurdist satirist Oddur Björnsson, popular comedy writer Jónas Árnason, the versatile Kjartan Ragnarsson, the lyrical Nína Björk Árnadóttir, Birgir Sigurdsson with his psychological dramas, and GUDMUNDUR STEINSSON with his allegories and tragicomedies. Laxness also wrote a few absurdist satires in the 1960s, and dramatizations of his novels have proved popular.

The THEATRE OF THE ABSURD was influential in the 1960s,

and traces of it are detectable in nearly all the playwrights, but Icelandic absurdism is satirical rather than metaphysical, closer to early ALBEE and IONESCO than to BECKETT, while Jakobsson's plays echo PINTER. Now most writers have found different departures from the absurd – some towards REALISM, others towards social SATIRE and EXPRESSIONISM.

FRINGE theatre has made an impression since the 1960s, beginning with the Gríma Theatre, which, active throughout that decade, proved the need for an adventurous alternative theatre through productions of new avant-garde drama; whereas the short-lived Leiksmidjan (Theatre Workshop) made its mark, under director Eyvindur Erlendsson, with a return to folklore motifs. Fringe theatre gained a stronger foothold in the 1970s and 1980s, especially after the Icelandic Drama School was founded in 1973, training many promising young actors who were unable to find work with existing theatres. In 1973 the amateur theatre in Akureyri became the only professional theatre outside Reykjavík, and in 1975 the People's Theatre was established which, though initially a touring company, now performs in Reykjavík.

The fringe and avant-garde scene of the early 1980s was dominated by the People's Theatre, Vidar Eggertsson's Egg Theatre and the street theatre Svart og Sykurlaust, as well as the short-lived semi-professional University Theatre, while the Frú Emilía Theatre, based on the creative partnership of director Gudjón P. Pedersen and dramaturg Haflidi Arngrímsson, became a stronghold during the latter half of the decade and was virtually the only fringe theatre to survive unscathed the economic recession of the early 1990s. AI

See: A. Boucher, *Modern Nordic Plays*, Oslo, 1973; S. Einarsson, *A History of Icelandic Literature*, Baltimore, 1957; E. Haugen, *Fire and Ice: Three Icelandic Plays*, London, 1967; S. A. Magnússon, *Iceland Crucible*, Reykjavík, 1985.

Ichikawa Danjūrō Twelve generations of actors in the Ichikawa family of Japanese KABUKI actors have attained the illustrious name Danjūrō. Because of the importance of this acting family and its long history, Danjūrō is sometimes called the 'emperor' of *kabuki*. A brief description of the genealogy of this one acting name tells us much about *kabuki*'s hereditary acting system in general. Danjūrō, as family head (*soke*), is responsible for preserving the Ichikawa family's famous *aragoto* acting style and passing it to the next generation. The Danjūrō name was rather often given to child actors in the past, but more typically the expectant heir was awarded successively higher-ranking names during his early career (making identification of actors in historical sources a puzzle to unravel): the present Danjūrō XII was given the name Ichikawa Natsuo for his stage debut when he was three, Ichikawa Shinnosuke when he was 12, and Ichikawa Ebizo X when he showed his mature acting stature by playing the lead in *Sukeroku: Flower of Edo* at 23. He took the Danjūrō name at a three-month-long ceremony in the summer of 1985. Several Danjūrōs were adopted to continue the family acting line when there was no son.

Danjūrō I (1660–1704) Son of a country samurai, he was 13 when he played the boy-hero Sakata Kintoki in the play *The Four Guardian Gods* at the Nakamura Theatre in Edo (Tokyo) in bravura style, marking the beginning of *aragoto* acting. He wrote heroic roles for himself in a dozen plays under the pen name Mimasuya Hyōgo: an infatuated priest turned thundergod in *Thundergod* (1684), the superhero Kamakura Gongorō in *Wait a Moment* (1697), and the fierce protective god Fudōin *Immovable* (1697)', the powerful priest Benkei in *The Subscription List* (1702). He was murdered on stage by a jealous actor when he was 44.

Danjūrō II (1688–1758) The eldest son of Danjūrō I, he became Danjūrō II when he was 17. Over his long lifetime, he originated more than half the plays in the Eighteen Favourite Plays (*jūhachiban*) collection –*Sukeroku: Flower of Edo* (1713), *Medicine Seller* (1718), *Arrow Maker* (1725) and *Whisker Tweezers* (1742) among them. He introduced grace and gentleness into *aragoto* acting, especially in the dashing title role of Sukeroku, borrowing from the Kyoto-Osaka soft style of acting (*wagoto*). Having no son, he passed the Danjūrō name to a pupil and acted for the last 23 years of his life as Ichikawa Ebizō II.

Danjūrō III (1721–42) An adored child actor at six, he became Danjūrō III when he was 14. He had a beautiful voice and an elegant acting style. He died at the age of 21, after becoming ill while performing in Osaka with his adoptive father.

Danjūrō IV (1711–78) After Danjūrō III died, no successor was named for 12 years. The elderly Ebizō II (Danjūrō II) adopted 43-year-old Matsumoto Koshirō II, a specialist in villain roles, as his heir. A progressive, intelligent actor, Danjūrō IV added a dark tinge to *aragoto* acting in his role of the malicious warrior Kagekiyo, which he played 16 times in his life.

Danjūrō V (1741–1807) The son of Danjūrō IV, when he was 29 he changed his name from Matsumoto Koshirō III to Ichikawa Danjūrō V. He was the first actor to announce his new name in a formal name-taking ceremony (*shūmei hirō*). His boast that his name was known 'in all the corners of the world' (*sumi kara sumi made*) is now repeated by every Danjūrō. He addressed the audience, 'I will now cross one eye over the other', thus beginning the custom of demonstrating the Ichikawa family pose (*mie*) and eye-crossing glare (*nirami*), trademarks of each Danjūrō name succession. When he was 49 and at the height of his powers he gave the Danjūrō name to his son and retired as Ichikawa Hakuen, to a life of leisure and writing.

Danjūrō VI (1778–99) The son of Danjūrō V. Four magnificent prints by the woodblock artist Sharaku show a sensuously attractive teenage Danjūrō VI. He took his famous name when he was 13 and at 20 he was actor-manager (*zagashira*) of the Nakamura Theatre, a remarkable honour. Audiences loved his 'modern' acting as Heiemon in *The Forty-Seven Loyal Retainers* (1748), in which he expanded the range of the Ichikawa family acting style (*ie no gei*). His brilliant career ended the following year when he died on stage at the age of 21.

Danjūrō VII (1791–1859) Probably the child of Danjūrō V's daughter Sumi and the actor Maruya Shichibei. Precocious, he was three when he first acted in *kabuki*, became Ebizo at five, starred as Gongorō in *Wait a Moment* at the Kawarazaki Theatre at seven, and at the ripe age of nine became Danjūrō VII, only months after Danjūrō VI's sudden death. The greatest actors of the time – Matsumoto

KoshirōV, Iwai HanshirōV, Onoe KikugorōIII – spoke at his name-taking ceremony. He was highly original. He created gangster (*kizewamono*) roles, like the scoundrel Yoemon in TSURUYA NAMBOKU's *Kasane* (1823). He was a master at playing several roles in a play, accomplished by quick costume changes: he played four leading roles in Tsuruya Namboku's *The Scarlet Princess of Edo* (1817). He premiered new dance-dramas based on *NŌ*, such as *The Subscription List* (1840). Proud and ostentatious in his manner of living, the government banished him from Edo for seven years (1842–9). In all, he spent 15 years playing in the provinces.

Danjūrō VIII (1823–54) The eldest son of DanjūrōVII, he took his father's name when he was nine years old. He was idolized in such romantic roles as Sukeroku, but his father's banishment and the consequent burden he carried as head of the Ichikawa family led him into deep depression. He committed suicide when he was 31.

Danjūrō IX (1838–1903) The fifth son of DanjūrōVII had no reason to believe he would inherit his father's name. For 30 years he was an adopted actor in the Kawarazaki acting family, where he attained that family's highest name, Gonnosuke VII. Twenty years after the death of Danjūrō VIII and when he was 36 years old, he returned to carry on the Ichikawa family line as Danjūrō IX. He supported the Society for Theatre Reform that strove to modernize *kabuki* in the late 1880s. Danjūrō played Benkei in *The Subscription List* in the presence of the Emperor Meiji, the first time *kabuki* had been honoured by the imperial presence. He was a star of the Kabuki-za, a new theatre in the Ginza, which attracted a fashionable audience and helped make *kabuki* 'respectable' in society. DanjūrōIX possessed energy, courage and artistic vision; unquestionably, he was the greatest *kabuki* actor of the modern era.

Danjūrō X (1882–1956) Danjūrō IX had no son and no adoptive heir when he died. His eldest daughter was a talented performer but being a woman she could not act in *kabuki*, so responsibility for continuing the Ichikawa Danjūrō family line fell on her husband, a banker. Untrained in theatre, nonetheless he courageously revived long-forgotten plays in the Ichikawa repertory – *Immovable*, *Seven Masks*, *Pushing and Pulling*, and others – thus perpetuating the family acting style through a difficult period of Japanese history. He was awarded the name DanjūrōX posthumously.

Danjūrō XI (1909–65) DanjūrōX, too, had no son. For 60 years there was no Danjūrō on the *kabuki* stage. Danjūrō XI was the eldest son of Matsumoto KoshirōVII, a former pupil of DanjūrōIX, so it was considered appropriate that Koshirō's son should be adopted by the Ichikawa family. By nature he was reserved and modest, but on stage he excelled in dashing, romantic roles like Sukeroku or the Shining Prince Genji. He died, after a short illness, after holding the Danjūrō name for three years.

Danjūrō XII (b.1946) Twenty years after Danjūrō XI died, his eldest son became Danjūrō XII in a name-taking ceremony (*shūmei hirō*) that continued for three months in summer 1985. A modern person, he has combined a college education with a career as a classical *kabuki* actor. He had already attracted a youthful following as a teenager performing with Onoe Tatsunosuke and Onoe Kikunosuke (the present Kikugorō VII). When he took the name Ebizō,

at the age of 23, he was a veteran of 100 major roles. He is a genuine star, admired for restrained acting in modern plays as well as bravura performances of *aragoto* classics in the family line.   JRB

Ichikawa Ennosuke III 1939– Japanese *KABUKI* actor and director. The first son of Ichikawa DanshirōIII, he succeeded to his stage name in 1963. Ennosuke challenges the repertoire and the conventional system of *kabuki*, and revitalizes *kabuki* theatre. *Yoshitsune Thousand Cherry Trees* (*Yoshitsune Senbon Zakura*), for example, is a play with a plot about a fox appearing in the form of a human and following the drum made of his mother's skin. In this play in 1968 Ennosuke revived an old technique, *chūnori* (a flying trick). In his productions he emphasizes one of the characteristics of *kabuki*, *keren* (showing off, playing to the audience), with acrobatic movements and instant costume changes, and he has restored the spectacle and the liveliness to the genre. He has also formed a new *kabuki* theatre company, the Twenty-first-Century Kabuki Gumi, and promotes young actors who are not necessarily from *kabuki* families but who have been trained at the National Kabuki Drama School. With his company Ennosuke produces 'super *kabuki*', in the more elaborate and modern style. *Oguri* (1982) and *Yamato Takeru* (1987) are plays in 'super *kabuki*' style. He first toured abroad in 1977, and since then has regularly visited Europe and the USA. He has directed an opera in Germany and given acting workshops in other European countries.   MY

Iffland, August (Wilhelm) 1759–1814 German actor, *régisseur* and playwright. After being trained by EKHOF at Gotha, in 1779 Iffland joined the new MANNHEIM COURT THEATRE. He left in 1796 to become the director of the BERLIN ROYAL THEATRE, where he remained until his death. Iffland was honoured throughout Germany for the extraordinary versatility of his acting. Although not a performer of exceptional power, he was noted for the completeness of his characterization, his subtlety and his finely judged transitions. GOETHE was among his greatest admirers, though SCHILLER, who had approved of his Franz Moor at the first performance of *The Robbers* in 1782, later found him to be cold and artificial. Iffland was also a prolific playwright, specializing in *Rührstücke*, sentimental, MELODRAMATic pieces, generally with a domestic setting. Of these, *The Huntsmen* (1785) may be seen occasionally in Germany today. As director of the Berlin Royal Theatre, Iffland presented the plays of SHAKESPEARE, Schiller and contemporary historical dramatists in extremely spectacular productions, which foreshadowed the work of later directors such as DINGELSTEDT and the Duke of Saxe-MEININGEN. Iffland was decorated by the Prussian king. The eminence he achieved did much to elevate the professional status of the theatre in the eyes of the public.   SW

Ilinsky, Igor (Vladimirovich) 1901–87 Greatest Soviet Russian comic actor of his time. After proving himself in several Moscow theatres, he became one of MEYERHOLD's favourites, working with him from 1920 to 1935. A superb CLOWN, expert at biomechanics and eccentric physical expression, he was superb as Bruno in Crommelynck's *The Magnanimous Cuckold* (1922), as Arkashka in OSTROVSKY's

The Forest (1924) and as Prisypkin in MAYAKOVSKY's *The Bedbug* (1929). When Meyerhold fell into disfavour with the government Ilinsky was absorbed into the Maly Theatre troupe (1935), where his vitality was chastened by the stuffy house style. In the 1950s he had a resurgence of creativity, playing Akim in TOLSTOI's *The Power of Darkness* (1956) with tragic force, and directing his own adaptation of Thackeray's *Vanity Fair* (1958) and Sofronov's *Honesty* (1962). LS

'illegitimate' theatre see THEATRICAL MONOPOLY

Imbuga, Francis fl.1970s Kenyan playwright, author of a number of works including *The Fourth Trial* and *Kisses of Faho* (1972), *The Married Bachelor* (1973), *Betrayal in the City* (1976), *Games of Silence* (1977) and *The Successor* (1979). *Betrayal in the City* was KENYA's entry to FESTAC in Lagos in 1977. The play satirizes problems of independence and freedom in post-colonial African states. The same themes are seen in Imbuga's other plays, where the clashes between individuals or classes in society are used to comment on political and social tensions. The settings of the plays are usually contemporary, an exception being *The Successor*, a tale of ambition and political intrigue involved in finding a successor to a fictional emperor, set in 'semi-modern' time. KG NWAM

Immermann, Karl 1796–1840 German director, playwright and novelist. Immermann's most important contribution to the German theatre occurred during his directorship of the Düsseldorf Town Theatre between 1835 and 1837. Here, despite modest resources, he developed a company that achieved national renown for the standards of its ensemble playing. At this time most German theatres were subject to the pre-eminence of the virtuoso actor. In February 1840, Immermann staged *Twelfth Night* on a specially constructed stage that incorporated features of the Elizabethan and Italian Renaissance stages – a highly unusual enterprise in those days. His plays tended to be too reliant upon SHAKESPEARE, and only his TRAGEDY *Andreas Hofer* (1834) has any individual distinction. Immermann is remembered today primarily for his novel *Münchhausen*. SW

Incháustegui Cabral, Héctor 1912–79 Poet, critic, fiction writer and playwright. Born in Baní, Dominican Republic, Incháustegui Cabral practised journalism in his youth. He belonged to the so-called group of independent poets who produced important social poetry during the 30s to the 50s. His *Miedo en un puñado de polvo* (*Fear in a Handful of Dust*, 1968) is a collection of three plays based on Greek classics that express universal constants of the human spirit, but his theatre is more theatre of ideas than of action. GW

Inchbald, Elizabeth 1753–1821 English playwright and novelist, whose determination to become an actress, despite a speech impediment, led her to run away from home in 1772. Little is known of her marriage to Joseph Inchbald (d.1779), a minor actor. That she loved the much greater actor, JOHN PHILIP KEMBLE, is well known, not least from the reasonable inference that he served as the model for Dorriforth in her novel, *A Simple Story* (1791). Inchbald's acting career continued until 1789, after which time she devoted herself to writing. Her first play, *A Mogul Tale* (1784), cleverly exploited the current craze for hot-air balloons. It was followed by a number of comedies, of which the most successful include *I'll Tell You What* (1785), *Everyone Has His Fault* (1793), *Wives as They Were, and Maids as They Are* (1797) and *To Marry, or Not to Marry* (1805). *The Child of Nature* (1788) is a more ambitious piece, derived from ROUSSEAU by way of Madame de Genlis. A more famous adaptation is that of KOTZEBUE's *Das Kind der Liebe* as *Lovers' Vows* (1798), the play whose rehearsal in the Bertram household causes such consternation in Jane Austen's *Mansfield Park* (1814). Inchbald defied male prejudice by editing three collections of plays, *The British Theatre* (25 vols., 1808), *Farces* (7 vols., 1809) and *The Modern Theatre* (10 vols., 1809). PT

Independent Theatre Society Private theatre club, modelled on ANDRÉ ANTOINE's Théâtre Libre, founded in London in 1891 by J. T. Grein. His mission was to provide a platform for 'special performances of plays which have a literary and artistic, rather than a commercial value', including those which had fallen victim to the Lord Chamberlain's CENSORSHIP. The Society opened on 13 March 1891, spectacularly and to much hostile comment in the newspapers, with the British premiere of IBSEN's *Ghosts*, which did not receive a licence for public performance until 1914. But its controversial character was not sustained, though there was some intention to do so. SHAW, aware that *Mrs Warren's Profession* (1893) would be refused by the censor, hoped the Society might take it up, but in fact no further banned plays were staged because London managers proved unwilling to risk their theatres by upsetting the Lord Chamberlain, who sanctioned their annual licences.

A second Ibsen premiere, that of *The Wild Duck*, which was considered too heavy in its symbolism for commercial exposure, took place in 1894. The Society was a little slow at encouraging native talent – Grein was criticized for producing too many foreign dramas – but in retrospect this is clearly unfair. Between 1891 and its closure in December 1898, just over half the 28 pieces produced were of British origin, including the premieres of Shaw's *Widowers' Houses* (1892) and George Moore's only play *The Strike at Arlingford* (1893). As a matter of policy, most plays were restricted to a single performance, and Grein never had a permanent venue for his programme. A branch theatre was opened in Manchester in 1893, taking the London productions; and there was also a brief excursion into publishing Independent Theatre plays between 1893 and 1895.

The Society closed partly because of financial problems and partly because Grein felt he had fulfilled his aim in offering an alternative to commercial theatre. A number of similar, though smaller, club ventures appeared over the next decade, including the New Stage Club, the Afternoon Society and the Pioneer Players (under EDITH CRAIG), to which Grein gave his support; but the Independent Theatre's main successor was the STAGE SOCIETY (founded 1899), which performed under club conditions on Sunday evenings. JRS

India India is among the world's most populous nations, with nearly 850 million people inhabiting a vast and contrasting land bordered on the north and east by the Himalayan mountain range, on the west by the Great Thar Desert and with the southern half of the country a peninsula surrounded by the Arabian Sea on one side and the Bay of Bengal on the other. Because of its strategic location, Indian civilization has been shaped over time by a multitude of social, political and religious forces which, in turn, have had a direct bearing on the shape of its theatre.

The Indus Valley Civilization dating from 2300 BC was the first great culture to inhabit areas of the north, along the Indus River basin. But the advanced city-states that were formed there came to an abrupt and inexplicable halt by 1750 BC, and eventually India was populated by Indo-Aryans who migrated from Persia. Over the centuries, the Aryans developed a body of rituals and religious customs which came to be known as Hinduism. The Sanskrit language was the medium of communication among the priests and kings who dominated the social life. Myths developed which reinforced their ideas and the resulting society prospered and grew to take its place among the world's great ancient civilizations. Sanskrit drama and theatre came into being and flourished during this relatively peaceful period between the 1st and 10th

Manohar, actor-producer of Madras's National Theatre productions, performing the role of the gluttonous epic character Kumbakarna.

centuries AD, reinforcing the beliefs of the civilization.

India also served as the cradle of other great religions – Buddhism, Jainism, Sikhism and, though it did not originate there, Zoroastrianism. Even the Christian faith took root and flourished in parts of India.

Among the social and political influences that have had a major bearing on the development of Indian theatre was the introduction of Islam to the Indian subcontinent. After an initial period of conquest around the 10th and 11th centuries, the Middle Eastern people who introduced Islam integrated with the Indo-Aryans and produced powerful empires centred in Delhi, such as that of the Emperor Akbar. Owing to their religious convictions, the followers of Islam discouraged, or forbade entirely, the performance of theatre. Under the threat of mass conversion to Islam, the decline of Buddhism as a popular religion and the loss of social and political power, a new movement of Hinduism was born known as Vaisnavism. As a result of renewed faith in the values and ideas which were essentially indigenous to India, Vaisnavism nurtured the growth of theatre in village settings throughout the subcontinent. Theatre grew to service the needs of millions of people in a multitude of regional languages (by some counts today, there are 16 major regional languages in India). The period of development and growth of rural theatre forms began about the 15th century and continued through to the 19th century.

The British came to India in the 17th century, although they did not dominate the country until 150 years later. They established a presence at strategic locations on the subcontinent. Through their effort modern urban society was born. The colonial period extended from the mid-19th to the mid-20th century, bringing with it the centralization of power, industrialization, the development of mass systems of transportation and communication, as well as staggering growth in the population. During the colonial period modern theatre developed. It continues to develop in all the major regional languages as a reflection of the ideas and concerns of urban Indian audiences.

In order to understand Indian theatre, it is necessary to investigate each stage of its growth separately, beginning with the Sanskrit theatre, continuing through the rural theatre forms and concluding with modern theatre.

Fragments of the earliest known Sanskrit plays have been traced to the 1st century AD. The sophistication of the form of the fragments suggests that a living theatre tradition must have existed in India at a somewhat earlier date. The earliest traces of civilization in India date from between 2300 and 1750 BC and yet the enormous wealth of archaeological evidence provides no hint of the existence of a living theatre tradition. Dance and music seem to have been enjoyed by the people of those times, perhaps as part of religious celebrations, but theatre is not in evidence. A search of the *Vedas* – sacred hymns, among the world's earliest literary outpourings, dating from approximately 1500 to 1000 BC – yields no trace of theatre, even though a few of the hymns are composed in a short, elementary dialogue. Some of the ritual practices of the Vedic age have the potential of developing into drama but do not seem to have sparked a theatre tradition.

The period between 1000 and 100 BC saw the rise of the great Hindu epic literature, particularly the *Mahabharata*, the longest and arguably the most comprehensive document of ancient Indian life, the *Ramayana*, a somewhat shorter but no less important epic work which, like the *Mahabharata*, still provides rural and urban dramatists with source material, and the *Puranas*, a major collection of stories dealing with the life and exploits of Krishna, incarnation of the god Vishnu, all of whose incarnations have provided inspiration for dramatic compositions. There are references to a class of performers (*nata*) who may have been actors, which are to be found in major epic stories.

The earliest reference to events which may have been the seeds of Sanskrit drama is in 140 BC by Patanjali in his *Mahabhasya*. The work itself is a text of grammar. In order to make a point, Patanjali indicates that action may be determined in several ways: through (1) pantomime; (2) recitation; (3) song; (4) dance. Reference is made to individuals who recite and sing (*nata*). Given the existence of dramatic RITUALS, of ample epic stories which were later interpreted in dramatic form and of traditions of song, dance and recitation firmly established in Indian tradition, it is feasible that Sanskrit drama came into being about this point in time.

Sanskrit theatre has left no physical evidence of its early history. Only in the plays and dramaturgical texts which survive in palm leaf manuscript, and in descriptions from other sources, may one glean the outlines of the Sanskrit theatre.

The most important single source for establishing the character of the Sanskrit theatre tradition in ancient India is the vast compendium *A Treatise on Theatre* (*Natyasastra*) attributed to BHARATA MUNI and variously dated between 200 BC and AD 200. *Natya* means 'drama' or 'theatre'. *Sastra* is a generic term referring to any authoritative text.

The mythological origin of theatre is related in the *Natyasastra*. Theatre is said to have been the inspiration of Brahma, the god of creation, and Bharata figures prominently in its origin. In chapter one, Bharata tells a charming story of how theatre came into being.

When the world was given over to sensual pleasure, Indra, king of the gods (one of India's earliest major deities), approached Brahma and asked that he create a form of diversion that could be seen as well as heard and that would be accessible to the four occupational groups (*varna*) – priests, warriors, tradesmen and peasants. Out of his state of meditation, Brahma created drama (*natya*), which he referred to as a fifth *Veda* or sacred text.

Brahma requested that Indra compose plays and have the gods enact them. Not considering it appropriate for gods to act, Indra asked that the priests (*brahmana*) be recruited to take on this task. Bharata and his sons were summoned by Brahma and persuaded to serve as the first actors, which they willingly agreed to do. And Brahma, knowing what he had in mind when he created theatre, taught them the art himself.

To fulfil additional personnel needs, Brahma created heavenly nymphs to act and dance, and musicians were recruited to play and sing to accompany the show. The occasion of the first performance was established to depict and coincide with the defeat of the demons by the gods, celebrating Indra's victorious leadership.

All seemed well until malevolent spirits disturbed the dramatic action. Eventually Brahma summoned Visvakarma, his architect, to devise a space which would be sanctified and prevent spirits from bringing harm to the actors and the action to a complete halt. The architect did as he was bid and produced a facility all the parts of which were consecrated with rituals, from the very ground-breaking to the inauguration ceremony.

The show resumed in the newly sanctified theatre structure but the evil spirits continued to plague the actors. At last Brahma summoned the demons and in a mood of reconciliation explained the purpose of drama and the objective for which it was intended. In short, he indicated that no class of individuals is excluded from seeing it, including the demons, and that it is meant to educate and entertain, and thus no subject may be excluded from consideration, even the defeat of the demons in battle. As a final step to silence the objections of the malevolent spirits, Brahma proclaimed that those who correctly observe the ritual sacrifices connected with performance will be protected from evil and will enjoy success in their undertakings.

Bharata's simple story reveals many important facts about Sanskrit theatre: (1) it is composed of sacred material; (2) a specialist should witness it; (3) it should be performed by members of the priestly caste, the top rank in the hierarchy of the caste system; (4) its execution requires special knowledge and skill; (5) training is a hereditary process coming from father to son and descending directly from God; (6) special skills are necessary to execute theatre, such as dance, music, recitation and ritual knowledge; (7) it should be performed on consecrated ground; (8) its purpose is to entertain as well as to educate.

It is difficult to measure the influence of the *Natyasastra* in its historical context and virtually impossible to compare the multitude of dicta in it with actual stage practices. Perhaps a measure of its importance to scholarly concerns today is that it sheds light, sometimes the only light available, on many subjects of importance to a comprehensive understanding of the theatre in ancient India. Perhaps we cannot hope for more.

The work consists of 36 chapters and is the most complete book of ancient dramaturgy in the world. The *Natyasastra* covers acting, theatre architecture, costuming, make-up, properties, dance, music, play construction, as well as the organization of theatre companies, audiences, dramatic competitions, the community of actors and ritual practices, to name only a few of the more important subjects of the book. Coupled with the extant texts of plays, it is possible to develop a picture, incomplete though it may be, of the classical Indian theatre.

At the heart of the theatre companies was the stage manager (*sutradhara*) who may have also been a leading actor. It was his job to direct the players; perhaps he also served as their teacher. Like Bharata in the mythological story of the origin of theatre, he literally held the strings of the performance within his grasp (*sutradhara*, literally, means 'holder of the threads or strings', that is, a puppeteer, an architect or a manipulator). He also seems to have been assisted in his duties, perhaps by an apprentice who may have been one of his sons.

The actors studied under the guidance of a drama

teacher (*natyacharya*), probably the stage manager, who was usually an older and respected individual, perhaps, like Bharata, the father of the actors. Under his guidance, it was their job to keep physically and vocally fit for performance by undergoing rigorous periods of training. Also, through observation, they gained much insight from their elders in performance practices.

Men and women both seem to have been permitted to act together or in separate troupes of their own sex. They either played characters their own age or they played those of a contrasting age range. Younger actors might play the roles of older people and older actors might portray the young. Actresses were regarded as better suited to enact certain sentiments, not considered appropriate for men to perform. Given the plays, it may be assumed that the actors and actresses needed to be highly skilled in speech and singing, as well as adept at bodily movement, both realistic and abstract. The ability to dance may also have been required.

The Sanskrit plays that survive confirm the use of stock character types. Thus actors may have specialized in a particular role category, such as hero (*nayaka*), heroine (*nayika*), clown (*vidusaka*) and so forth.

The Indian system of acting is laid out in considerable detail in the *Natyasastra*. Many chapters are devoted to its discussion, more than for any other subject covered by the book. Two styles of acting appear to have been common – the realistic (*lokadharmi*) and the conventional (*natyadharmi*), the latter of which receives almost exclusive attention in the text.

Acting (*abhinaya*; literally, 'to carry towards') is defined as having four elements – bodily movement (*angika*), voice (*vacika*), spectacle (*aharya*) and sentiment or emotion (*sattvika*). Of these, bodily movement receives lavish attention in four chapters of the *Natyasastra*.

The body is divided into major and minor parts which are discussed in relation to the way they convey emotions to the spectators. A wide variety of hand gestures is described, indicating that a sophisticated language of communication had to be studied and perfected in order to act in the conventional style. Specific glances, movements of the eyebrows, cheeks, lips, chin and neck are all discussed according to their ability to communicate meaning. Broad categories of movement involving the whole body are also described, such as poses (*cari*) and gaits (*gati*) thought suitable in various situations depending on the age, sex, rank and temperament of a character. These discussions apply, in varying degree, to the actor and the dancer.

Another five chapters of the *Natyasastra* are devoted to voice, focusing on grammar, language and metres. Forms of address appropriate for characters of various ranks are discussed and regional dialects, thought appropriate to various characters according to their rank and station in life, are mentioned.

Costumes, ornaments and make-up of the actor are discussed as a vital part of character and of acting. Stage properties, too, are seen as an extension of acting and receive treatment in several chapters. Elaborate decorations (*alamkara*) of the body are described in detail – garlands, ornaments and costumes. From the top of the head to the tip of the toe, hardly any part of the human anatomy was not decorated according to the caste, station in life and occupation of the character. Real ornaments were considered inappropriate for stage use since their weight might tire the actor. Instead, ornaments were crafted of light wood and painted to resemble the actual object. It is not clear if the costumes were reproductions of historically accurate apparel, if they were the actual dress of the times or whether they were fanciful in shape, size and colour. A curtain (*yavanika*), held by two attendants, was used to mark entrances of characters and became a theatrical device for first introducing the character to the public.

The well rounded actor of Sanskrit plays was expected to go beyond external representation of character through correct execution of movement, speech and ornamentation. The *Natyasastra* states that there is something invisible (*sattva*) about performance, an intangible quality that transcends externals and reaches the hearts and minds of the spectators. This process has to do with conveying sentiments and emotions (*sattvika*) of the play through the content of the work. It is this intangible something, difficult to describe, which completes the Sanskrit actor's circle of obligations.

Although acting is obviously a very important part of theatre, the social status of the actors does not seem to have been particularly high in ancient India. Bharata may have been a Brahmin priest, but Sanskrit actors were classed with bandits and prostitutes according to most ancient authorities. In the final chapter of the *Natyasastra*, Bharata and his sons were cursed by respected sages who took offence at the caricatures of themselves by the actors. On the verge of suicide, the outcast actors were patronized by kings in order to preserve the art from extinction; thus began the historic practice of royal patronage which seems to have survived through ancient times.

Dancers and musicians were fundamental for performances and may have been commissioned to participate in a particular performance or as regular members of ancient companies of players. Among the musicians were male and female vocalists, flautists, who performed on bamboo instruments, players of stringed instruments, like the *vina*, a classical south Indian instrument, drummers and cymbal players. Ankle bells worn by dancers helped to accentuate the rhythmic patterns of the music and further contributed to the sophistication of the sound.

When reading a Sanskrit play it is difficult to determine how dance and music might have been integrated into the fabric of performance. Indeed, at first glance, the plays appear to be dialogue dramas. The stage directions do not indicate where music is to be inserted nor do they reveal when a dance should occur or whether a particular poetic passage is to be danced or sung. The *Natyasastra* does mention that songs (*dhruva*) were to be composed in the Prakrit language and inserted for specific purposes. Apparently these songs were composed for introducing characters, to mark a character's exit, to establish the middle or end of an act, to reinforce a dramatic mood, to establish the change of dramatic moods and to fill the gap when a temporary halt occurred in the action, for instance, when a costume had to be adjusted and the actor was forced to leave the stage.

None of the *dhruva* have survived the passage of time and it appears that the music in which they were composed may have differed considerably from that which we now know as Indian classical music, owing to the influence of Middle Eastern music after the Muslim invasions beginning in the 10th century AD.

Sanskrit theatre was performed to celebrate important religious occasions, in connection with temple festivals. The *Natyasastra* calls dramatic performance a visual sacrifice (*yajna*) to the gods and thus clearly identifies it as a sacred event. And yet we also know that performances were organized to celebrate secular events: a coronation, marriage, birth of a child, the return of a traveller or the defeat of an enemy.

The audience for theatrical events was known as 'those who see' (*preksaka*), clearly implying that seeing a performance was as important as hearing it. Owing to the sophistication demanded of the actors, it is not surprising that the *Natyasastra* identifies spectators in terms of certain ideal characteristics. Those of good character and high birth, who were quiet and learned – partial, advanced in age, alert, honest, virtuous, knowledgeable in drama, acting, music, dance and the arts and crafts which figure in their execution – were considered to have the attributes of an ideal spectator. Perhaps because few measured up to that ideal, God is the ultimate witness to the dramatic event, possessing all the attributes demanded.

Performance competitions, in which critics judged the merits of the acting and awarded prizes to those who excelled, are known during the classical period. Ultimately, those whose occupation was depicted were thought the best judge of the actors. Kings were thought fit to judge actors who portrayed kings, courtesans might judge those who played courtesans and so forth.

The *Natyasastra* laid down rules for the composition of plays and for rituals connected with their presentation. Published editions of the plays normally include a short benedictory verse (*nandi*) and a prologue (*prastavana*) along with the text of the work, if the original text contains a benediction and a prologue; however, the *Natyasastra* lists 18 separate preliminaries (*purvaranga*) among the steps that may have taken place prior to the first lines of a text, including the benediction and prologue. These preliminaries provide a gradual bridging between the world of the audience and that of the play. It begins with musical performances followed by dances and ritual observances. Eventually, events like those of the prologue occur in which the audience is addressed directly by the characters and their conversation leads to the introduction of the first character of the play. This special method of introduction to a play accomplishes the goal of warming the performers and the audience to the events at hand, sanctifying the performance area, blessing the proceedings, introducing the story in a novel way and focusing attention on the dramatic action.

Sanskrit playwrights had ten types of drama in which they could choose to compose their work. The best-known and most significant was the *nataka* which was required to have a well known story concerning a hero who might be a king or a royal sage. The theme of the *nataka* should exploit the sentiments of love and heroism. This type of drama was restricted to between five and seven acts.

Sakuntala and the Ring of Recognition (*Abhijnana-sakuntala*), *The Vision of Vasavadatta* (*Svapnavasavadatta*), and *The Latter History of Rama* (*Uttara-ramacarita*) are three of the better-known examples of this dramatic type.

The *prakarana* was the second major type. Of the two examples of this form which survive, *The Little Clay Cart* (*Mrcchakatika*) is the better known. According to the *Natyasastra*, it was to have an invented story; a Brahmin, merchant or minister was to serve as the hero; a courtesan was to serve as the heroine; and love was to be the dominant sentiment. It was restricted to between five and ten acts. The other types of plays listed in the *Natyasastra* were less complex forms, often in one or two acts, with small casts – one form was a monologue – and lacking some of the possible dramatic or theatrical elements of the longer, major play forms. Examples are best seen in the works of BHASA.

The smallest possible unit of a play was an act (*anka*) in which the hero's basic dramatic situation might be portrayed. Acts were to be made up of a series of incidents surrounding the main characters; the concerns of minor figures were not permitted to dominate an act. Curses, marriages, battles, loss of a kingdom or death were strictly prohibited from being depicted on the stage. Events such as these might be reported, but they could not be shown.

The plot (*vastu*) was considered the body of the play. Each stage in its development was carefully identified and thought to follow a prescribed pattern. Normally, the seed (*bija*) of the plot concerned the desire of the hero to achieve a specific end. The plot moved the dramatic action toward that goal with a reversal of fortune as an inevitable stumbling block to its achievement. Finally, the goal which was reached was to relate to one of the three ends of Hindu life – duty (*dharma*), pleasure (*kama*) or wealth (*artha*).

Sanskrit drama served as a model of ideal human behaviour. The idealization of the characters, their values and actions, all point to this lofty ultimate aim. Sanskrit drama is not a drama of protest or of reaction but a theatre of elevated ideals. Guided by the *Natyasastra*'s rules, the writers cooperated with and lived within their society rather than breaking down barriers or exhibiting individualistic points of view.

Among the unique contributions of Sanskrit drama to world literature is its aesthetic theory. The theory of sentiment (*rasa*) relates to the audience's perception of the theatre event, as well as the contribution of theatre artists to the process. According to the *Natyasastra*, which first articulated the theory of *rasa*, human experiences are divided into eight basic sentiments – the erotic (*srngara*), the comic (*hasya*), pathos (*karuna*), rage (*raudra*), heroism (*vira*), terror (*bhayanaka*), odiousness (*bibhatsa*) and the marvellous (*adbhuta*). These sentiments are aroused in the audience by corresponding emotions or feelings (*bhava*) represented by the actors. These emotions are achieved with the aid of 32 transitory feelings (*vyabhicaribhava*) and eight states of emotion or feeling (*sattvika*).

Every play has a dominant emotion (*sthayibhava*) which produces a corresponding sentiment (*rasa*) in the audience. And yet the play of the other *bhava* and resulting *rasa* are permissible in a work, as long as balance is maintained and one sentiment dominates the others.

The theory of *rasa* is much like the experience of savouring a good meal, excellently cooked and served, with contrasting complementary tastes abounding. The playwright provides the basic menu which the performers translate into an appropriate presentation. Given the refinement of the system, it is little wonder that spectators were expected to be cultivated and well educated in the arts, as well as in other aspects of life.

The place of performance of these refined works of art is still something of an enigma. No sketches remain, no drawings, floor plans, paintings or models, no ruins to contemplate. The *Natyasastra* is our only guide for a description of the physical facilities of the Sanskrit theatre building. And it speaks of the structures it describes as though they were ideal models rather than actual edifices.

Because the medium-sized rectangular building (*vikrstamadhya*) is spoken of in great detail, it may have been the favoured model. Bharata regards it as the most suitable space to see and hear a performance. The structure is comparatively small, perhaps holding between 200 and 500 people, certainly no more than 500. Although ideal for achieving intimacy between spectators and players, it seems to have been an exclusive space in contrast with the theatre structures of ancient GREECE and ROME, or those of Elizabethan ENGLAND.

The *Natyasastra* sets out specific steps in the selection and preparation of a site for a theatre structure. Rituals accompanied its construction and sanctification, following the plan described for the first theatre structure created by Visvakarma, the heavenly architect. A roof with high windows protected it from the elements and the walls and pillars were decorated with paintings.

Half of the 48 x 96ft structure was assigned to the spectators. It may be that they sat on risers. Different castes were assigned different seating locations according to their rank. The stage and dressing room made up the other half of the building. The stage space was 48 x 24ft and further subdivided in half. A space 48 x 12ft was raised above the floor of the building by perhaps a foot. The 48 x 12ft space near the dressing room was elevated still further. Two doors separated the dressing room from the acting area. The space between the doors was reserved for the musicians and one of the doors may have been used for entrances and the other assigned for exits. Curtains could have covered the doors.

Little is known about the dressing room and about the acting area. It appears from the plays that the acting area was regarded as a neutral space endowed with symbolic meaning depending on the dramatic action. By walking around (*parikramana*) the actors symbolically changed the locale of the action. The stage was also thought to be divided into separate zones (*kaksya*), although just how this was achieved is not clear from the text. There is no evidence that furniture was used to identify place. Perhaps a stool was the only item of furniture needed to symbolize various objects, such as thrones, benches and so on.

The *Natyasastra* also describes square and triangular theatre structures and indicates that there were small, medium and large varieties of all these shapes.

Although the *Natyasastra* categorizes playwrights (*natyakara*) among the members of theatre companies, historical evidence suggests that they were more likely to have been members of the courts of kings, if not kings themselves. Literally hundreds of plays were written from the 1st to the 10th century AD, the high point of the Sanskrit dramatic outpouring. Of these, several dozen have survived. The earliest are those of Asvaghosa, whose fragmentary works of the 1st century AD came to the attention of scholars in the early part of our own century. His plays concern Buddhist teachings and follow the rules pertaining to dramatic composition laid down in the *Natyasastra*.

The author for whom we have the greatest abundance of works is Bhasa, whose 13 surviving plays cover a wide range of subject-matter and at least one of which, *The Vision of Vasavadatta*, is among the best and most important works of Sanskrit dramatic literature.

Among the major dramatic works of classical India, the most monumental and perhaps one of the most popular is *The Little Clay Cart* attributed to SUDRAKA. No other works have been traced to Sudraka and yet it is hard to believe that a writer could have produced only one brilliant work and remained silent the rest of his life.

The Little Clay Cart is similar to Bhasa's unfinished work *Charudatta* (*Charudattam*). Scholars speculate whether Sudraka and Bhasa were one and the same individual, or whether Sudraka borrowed Bhasa's play and added his own poetic style to it, as well as embroidering the political plot into the fabric of the story.

The Little Clay Cart is a superb example of *prakarana*. It involves Charudatta, a hapless Brahmin merchant who is generous to a fault, brave and virtuous and who is in love with Vasantasena, a rich, beautiful and faithful courtesan. Their deep affection for each other is nearly spoiled by Samstanaka, a jealous ne'er-do-well brother-in-law of a corrupt king who is the very antithesis of Charudatta. He attempts to murder Vasantasena and blame the crime on Charudatta, only to find his plot is spoiled by fate. Despite its serious moments, the play basically centres on love and humour and historically has been one of the few popularly staged pieces of the classical Indian repertory.

Arguably India's greatest playwright is KALIDASA. His acknowledged masterpiece is *Sakuntala and the Ring of Recognition*, which, like *The Little Clay Cart*, has been produced frequently in modern times. The play is a delicate exploration of human love. The source of the story may be found in the *Mahabharata*. Kalidasa took liberties with the epic sources to suit his own particular needs. The plot surrounds King Dusyanta, his infatuation, love, marriage, separation and reunion with Sakuntala, daughter of a heavenly nymph and a sage. When the play opens, Sakuntala is a young girl on the verge of womanhood. Her unspoiled beauty attracts Dusyanta, who is sporting in a forest near Sakuntala's hermitage home. The first three acts explore the delicate relationship between the dashing king and the modest young maiden. After agreeing to a marriage by mutual consent, Sakuntala prepares to follow her husband to the city to take up residence in his palace as his chief queen. Her departure from the sacred grove provides ample food for some of the most beautiful lyrics in all of Sanskrit literature. They also parallel the anguish that parents experience when their children leave home for good.

Due to a seemingly minor offence to a saintly guest, on her arrival at court Sakuntala is punished when the king forgets her. Stricken with anguish, she is whisked away by a heavenly nymph and, up to the final act, the story revolves around the torments of the king, whose memory is restored too late and who learns that Sakuntala has disappeared. Ultimately fate intervenes and the king finds Sakuntala in the hermitage of the mother and father of the gods. She has given birth to a handsome son, his only child, who bears the marks of royalty. Dusyanta identifies the child, finds Sakuntala and experiences a tearful but happy reunion.

Among the major playwrights of a later period of Sanskrit drama, Bhavabhuti stands out above the others. He appears to have lived around AD 700 and was a member of the court of a north Indian king. His *The Latter History of Rama* is among the best plays of Sanskrit drama. The work adapts incidents from the epic *Ramayana* and develops unique and creative twists to the plot. Like other later writers, Bhavabhuti succumbs to the temptation to embellish his writing with lengthy poetic expressions.

Although there are other distinguished playwrights worth mentioning, none of them achieved the reputation of Bhasa, Sudraka, Kalidasa and Bhavabhuti. For all practical purposes, Sanskrit plays which deserve critical attention were not written after the 10th century AD.

The 10th century marks the end of the Sanskrit theatre as an active force in Indian art. Internal and external forces were at work several centuries prior to that time which brought about its demise. The successive invasions of Mohammed of Gazzni weakened the kingdoms of north India and eventually the temples and kingdoms could no longer patronize theatre troupes. Also the exclusivity of Sanskrit theatre must have weakened its ability to survive. The language of the courts and temples was Sanskrit, but various regional languages and literary traditions were on the verge of emerging in the rural areas. Then too, the rules laid down by the *Natyasastra* exerted a stranglehold on the creative imagination of some later writers. Few were able to make use of them without stifling their creativity. The flexibility that existed in the earlier period disappeared later, and the possibility of new ideas was suppressed.

In the great Mogul empires of the 15th century where Islam became the state religion, theatre no longer thrived because the religion did not condone it. Only at the southern tip of the subcontinent did a form of Sanskrit theatre manage to survive, KUTIYATTAM of Kerala. Little is known about other theatres of this period. For example, it is not known if the actors, once securely patronized at the court of Hindu kings, took to the road, abandoned Sanskrit and performed plays in vernacular languages of the rural areas, catering to the less sophisticated tastes of village spectators. To have done so would have been inconsistent and uncharacteristic but possible, given the will to survive. There is evidence of the existence of jugglers, acrobats, storytellers and singers, who are mentioned in various texts of the period. Certainly entertainment did not totally disappear.

Beginning around the 15th century, theatre emerged again in India through a dazzling array of village theatre forms, each with its own unique manner of presentation and, more importantly, in the vernacular language of a particular region to meet the needs of the people of that region. Sanskrit theatre had exhibited a national character because of the widespread use of Sanskrit at the court and in the temple: rural theatre forms did not travel beyond the boundaries of the communities in which they were originally created. The village troupes which sprang into being might be either amateur or professional. Many were itinerant groups that worked a particular area, sometimes operating within one community or religious group. From the 15th to the 19th century, forms of theatre developed in virtually every pocket of the subcontinent. Some of the earlier forms have disappeared today, but a large number of them still survive and continue to serve as a testament to the richness and variety of the creative minds of the people who invented them and invested them with a unique life.

A major catalyst for the re-emergence of theatre was Vaisnavism, a religious movement which centres on devotion of man for god in the person of Krishna, the incarnation of Vishnu. Unlike orthodox Hindus, followers of Vaisnavism believe that man may approach god directly, rather than with the aid of rituals. The simple act of repeating god's name is regarded as an act of faith. Thus, theatre became an excellent vehicle for communicating the faith by depicting the acts of god. Those who witnessed it, as well as those who performed it, were engaging in a religious act. Many theatre forms arose at different times and in different places to address the needs of Vaisnavism: ANKIYA NAT, BANDI NATA, BHAGAVATA MELA, BHAMAKALAPAM, DASHAVATARA, *dhanu jatra*, GOLLAKALAPAM, KRISHNATTAM, KUCHIPUDI, *nondi natakam*, PRAHLADA NATAKA and RAMLILA and RASLILA.

Most rural theatre forms in India begin with preliminaries and conclude with rituals. Some of these forms arose as an expression of religious zeal and have since made the transition to more secular concerns. Dozens of other regional theatre forms were originally secular in inspiration and are today played in commercial environs by professional troupes. Among these are: *bharatlila*, *BHAVAI*, *BIDESIA*, *BURRAKATHA*, *chaita ghoda gata*, *dandanata*, *daskathia*, *ghudiki nabaranga nata*, JATRA, KARIYALA, KATHAKALI, KHYAL, KURAVANJI, MAACH, *naqal*, NAUTANKI, *pala*, *rasdhari*, SVANGA, TAMASHA, THERUKOOTHU, *veedhi natakam* and YAKSHAGANA.

Most of India's rural theatre forms were created by Hindus primarily for Hindus and their content is derived from Hindu mythology. However, *bhagat* of Agra, and the *bhand jashna* of Kashmir were created for Muslim consumption, and CAVITTU NATAKAM of Kerala focuses on Christian concerns.

All of the above have their own unique form. In execution, organization, costume, make-up, staging and acting style they differ one from the other; yet there are some broad similarities that may be noted here. The south Indian forms lay stress on dance; indeed, some of them qualify as dance dramas, such as *kathakali* and *krishnattam* of Kerala. The north Indian forms emphasize song, among them *khyal* of Rajasthan, *maach* of Madhya Pradesh, *nautanki* of Uttar Pradesh and *svanga* of the Punjab. Those that lay stress on dialogue are *jatra* of Bengal, *tamasha* of Maharashtra and *bhavai* of Gujarat.

The last two mentioned forms are among the few which emphasize comedy and satire.

An amazing array of puppet-theatre forms is also part of the heritage of Indian village life. SHADOW, glove, doll and string PUPPETS have a place in various regions of the country. The shadow forms include GOMBEYATTA, PAVAIKUTHU, RAVANA CHHAYA and TOLLU BOMMALU. The glove forms include GOPALILA, PAVAI KATHAKALI and PAVAI KOOTHU. The doll forms are BOMMALATTAM and PUTUL NAUTCH. The string forms are kathputli and SAKHI KUNDHEI.

The proliferation of forms of the performing arts does not end here. Dramatic content may be found in the various solo forms of Indian classical dance – bharata natyam of south India, north Indian kathak, odissi from the east and mohiniyattam from Kerala – and in folk forms, such as gambhira of Bengal, seraikella chhau of Bihar, mayurbhanj chhau of Orissa and purulia chhau of Bengal. Also, dramatic content is richly woven in the ritual ceremonies of some areas, particularly those of Kerala state with its mudiyettu and teyyam. Storytelling too is part of the dramatic heritage of India. The acting in cakyar koothu and nangyar koothu of Kerala, the dance, acting and singing of solo performers of tullal, also of Kerala, and the songs and simple dances of the Khavads of Rajasthan, provide hints of the enormously rich variety of India's rural areas.

Modern theatre The seeds of the modern Indian theatre were sown in the late 18th century with the consolidation of British power in three distinct areas of the subcontinent – Bengal, Maharashtra and Tamil Nadu. More particularly, the British developed fortifications and centralized authority in villages which were later developed into the thriving metropolises of these three areas, Calcutta, Bombay and Madras, respectively. There they introduced their own brand of theatre, based on London models. In those days the playhouses tripled as performance spaces, meeting houses and storage rooms. Initially theatre was meant to provide entertainment for British soldiers and citizens who were serving out their days in an alien land and climate.

Before long it became evident that elaborate machinery was needed to govern a country much of which was already under British control. India, at that time, was a nation of a multitude of princely states most of which were weak and governed by ineffectual leadership in Delhi. To achieve their ends, the British introduced the English system of higher education as a means of developing a class of Indians educated in British ideas, tastes, morals and values. The theatre became an extension of that aim – a tool for conveying the British way of life.

At the same time, educated Indians were not content to merely watch the performance of British works: in the mid-19th century, rich young Bengalis in Calcutta established private theatres in their homes, which had space large enough for temporary acting areas and auditoria. There they produced plays for the consumption of their friends and family. Eventually they began to write plays following British models which wove in Indian music and songs. The work of RABINDRANATH TAGORE, the Nobel Prize-winning poet, was the product of this initial effort. He showed great empathy for the lives of poor villagers and his plays take such ordinary people as his subjects.

Among his dramatic achievements were Red Oleanders (Raktakurabi) and The King of the Dark Chamber (Raja).

These experiments stimulated the establishment of commercial public theatres during the last quarter of the 19th century, managed by Indian artists and designed to appeal to Indian urban taste. Thus, the modern Indian theatre was born.

The pattern of development of modern theatre differs from region to region, but it ultimately led to the same thing – construction of theatres with proscenium-arch stages, lighting with equipment suited to the needs of the space, audience control through sale of tickets, a sophisticated system of theatre management, an acting style suited to the demands of an enclosed building, separation of the audience from the actors by a raised stage and a front curtain, scenery designed to establish the place and time of the dramatic action, costumes, ornaments and make-up geared to the particular lighting effects, organization of the text into units which provided intermissions, and content which addressed issues pertinent to audience concerns. And, perhaps more importantly, the works were composed in the local regional languages. In Calcutta, Bengali was the language of the new and thriving theatre, in Madras it was Tamil and in Bombay, which was more cosmopolitan than the other cities, plays were composed in Marathi, Gujurati, Hindusthani, Urdu and sometimes in a blend of all these languages, plus English.

Dissatisfaction with British rule led some early patriots to produce works critical of the unfair and harsh treatment of Indian labourers. An itinerant band of Calcutta actors produced The Mirror of the Indigo Planters (Nildapana) in Lucknow in 1875, which criticized white planters for their cruel treatment of Indian peasants. The attempt led British audiences to send the actors packing. Sensitive to the potential of theatre to foment resentment and protest, the government passed the Dramatic Performances Act of 1879 which began a practice of CENSORSHIP that persisted until recently. Nevertheless, many Indians resorted to masking their protests under the guise of history and mythology. This practice continued, more or less unabated, until independence was achieved in 1947. The period of the late 19th and early 20th centuries saw the proliferation of theatre buildings, touring companies and an entrepreneurial spirit. Theatre was a popular art in urban areas and in small towns influenced by city commerce and trade, although not all companies were successful.

Sweeping changes in taste occurred in the early 20th century. The enormous popularity of cinema with the middle classes and its easy access led to the closing of live theatres virtually everywhere in the country. Artists abandoned the stage in large numbers to seek more lucrative careers in films. India quickly developed into one of the world's largest producers and consumers of films. Great studios thrived in Bombay, primarily creating films in Hindi, the language which constituted the largest potential market. Tamil-language films followed a close second. Today there are film studios in almost every major city and films are made in every major language of the country. While theatre retains some of its vigour, particularly in Calcutta and Bombay, the number of theatre troupes has declined from a peak in the early part of the century.

Goa Hindu Association in
Raigadala Jevha Jug Yele,
Bombay, 1962.

Commercial theatre companies performing modern drama exist in large cities today. The largest number of companies is in Calcutta, in the heart of the Bengali-speaking section of the city. The Star Theatre is among the oldest and best known, working out of a building constructed in 1888, renowned for famous theatre personalities that once performed there. Commercial companies also stage plays in the Circarena, Rangmahal, Biswaroopa, Minerva, Rangana and Bijon theatre buildings. In Kerala, the Kerala People's Arts Company (KPAC) and Kalidasa Kalakendra, both communist organizations, operate itinerant groups. The National Theatre of Madras still clings to 19th-century staging techniques, producing slick shows at various theatres and halls in the city, the state and even abroad. Trivandrum's Kalanilaya Vistavision Dramascope Company follows along the path of the National with melodramatic 19th-century fare still popular with a segment of Kerala's population.

The heart of the modern theatre in India today consists of amateur companies. Among the better known are Bohorupee, Little Theatre Group and Nandikar in Calcutta, and Goa Hindu Association's Theatre wing, Abhishek, Indian National Theatre, Theatre Unit and Theatre Group in Bombay. Many of the players who work with these organizations are theatre professionals who eke out a living performing a wide variety of jobs in films, television and advertising, as well as working on the stage. The groups retain their amateur status in order to benefit from tax concessions and because they cannot make enough money at the box office to support the players on a consistent basis.

Calcutta is said to have some three thousand registered amateur groups; Bombay may have as many as 500; Madras boasts at least 50 and Delhi several dozen.

Characteristically, each amateur organization has a director, or core of directors, at its head to choose plays, organize productions and provide momentum for its activities. Without a director these groups would collapse for lack of continuity and leadership. Distinguished directors with national reputations in the amateur theatre are Sombhu Mitra, UTPAL DUTT and Rudraprasad Sen Gupta of Calcutta; Kamalkar Sarang, Mansukh Joshi, Satyadev

Dubey, Alyque Padamsee, Pearl Padamsee, Vijaya Mehta of Bombay; EBRAHIM ALKAZI, HABIB TANVIR, Bansi Kaul and M. K. Raina of New Delhi; Manohar and Cho of Madras; and Kavalam Narayan Pannikar of Kerala.

Productions are normally organized on a show-by-show basis. Subscription seasons are virtually unknown. If a show is successful, it is repeated as many times as audiences will come to see it in sufficient numbers to warrant a showing. Often shows are kept in a group's repertory for years.

The bane of amateur theatre is the fact that virtually all the groups must rent theatre facilities which are owned by cooperatives, governments and private individuals. Only one theatre group, Theatre Centre of Calcutta, owns its own building, a tiny space seating less than a hundred people. This means that groups in all the cities vie with each other for theatre space. In Bombay, the situation has led amateur theatre producers to consolidate their efforts and to agree to a booking schedule that gives the busiest and most popular groups access to prime booking dates in the better houses.

Among the most popular amateur theatre houses are the Academy of Fine Arts in Calcutta; the Tata Theatre of the National Centre for the Performing Arts, Shivaji Mandir, Ravindra Natya Mandir, Gadkari Nangayatan, Baidas, Bhirla, Tejpal, Prithvi and Patkar in Bombay; and Kamani Auditorium, Gandhi Memorial Theatre, Sri Ram Centre and Sapru House in New Delhi.

Production expenses are relatively high for amateur theatre. Few of the groups have access to space to build scenery and props. Costume storage is virtually unheard of. Lighting equipment, such as it is, must be rented for each performance. Production costs in Bombay and Calcutta range from two or three thousand dollars for a single-set show to ten thousand dollars for a historical play or musical. In cities with a lower cost of living, such as Madras, Bangalore, Ahmedabad and Hyderabad, production costs are somewhat lower.

One of the greatest expenses is advertising. Newspaper advertisements are virtually prohibitive. Each one may run into hundreds of rupees for a small space on a single day. Negotiations for concessions are almost always going on between editors and heads of amateur groups. Word of mouth is considered the best, and certainly the cheapest, means of advertising a production.

If a performance fails at the box office, it may mean the demise of an amateur theatre organization. In recent years, organizers have realized that once a production has met with some degree of success in a large and prominent urban theatre, then it can profitably be marketed to organizations in smaller towns and cities. These so-called 'call' bookings have become a lucrative source of income for many groups and may make the difference between financial success and failure. Yet they are hard on organizers and performers, many of whom hold down jobs or have other commitments. By its very nature, amateur theatre in India is itinerant.

Plays that provide grist for the commercial and amateur theatre mill vary greatly from group to group, depending on the demands imposed by the organization. In the 19th century, plays were a blend of music, song and dialogue. During the 20th century music and song were dropped in favour of dialogue, as in modern Western drama. Today the trend, especially in major cities, is towards the incorporation of music and song into performance either as a primary or a secondary ingredient. The playwrights who create this work are as varied as the works themselves. Hack writers whose names do not appear on any marquee or in any programme are often engaged to develop an idea for the commercial theatres of Calcutta and Madras, much as hack writers do for films and television in the West. Socially committed playwrights like Thopil Basi are often commissioned by communist groups in Kerala. They frequently serve as playwright-directors, negotiating script changes directly with the actors. Utpal Dutt is also known for his contributions to the socially committed theatre of Calcutta. Dutt usually works as a playwright, director and actor. BADAL SIRCAR, Girish Karnad, Vijay Tendulkar, G. Sankara Pillai and K. Narayan Pannikar join Utpal Dutt among a small band of playwrights who have achieved national prominence and whose works have been produced beyond the confines of their own language and area of the country. These artists are concerned with social and political issues and their work is primarily serious in tone.

Examples of playwrights who deliver safer, more predictable works designed to appeal to the taste of the vast majority of urban audiences in their respective languages are N. N. Pillai of Kerala and Jaywant Dalve of Bombay. These writers focus on family life and the plight of the individual in a modern mechanized country. COMEDY and MELODRAMA are freely mixed in their work, leaving audiences satisfied at the conclusion of the show rather than disturbed or moved to take radical action.

Experimental work with limited public appeal has been presented in various areas of the country. Badal Sircar launched experimentation in Calcutta with his Satabdi group by producing work in 'found' spaces rather than in rented theatre halls, forgoing expensive lighting equipment, scenery and elaborate costuming. The work is presented every Friday evening on a regular basis with little or no advance advertising. A mere pittance is charged for admission. The Living Theatre of Khardah, a theatre group in a suburb outside Calcutta, attempts the same thing – a theatre of ideas, accessible to the public but free of commercial constraints. Experimental work has also been attempted in Bombay by Avishkar in a rented school hall and at the moderately expensive Prithvi Theatre in north Bombay. Work that is expected to attract limited audiences is also found in New Delhi and Madras. And in Kerala the work of Kavalam Narayan Pannikar has achieved critical acclaim for its integration of folk and classical theatre traditions.

For several decades the National School of Drama of New Delhi has been a leader in educational theatre by training young actors, directors and designers in modern theatre techniques. Under the guidance of Ebrahim Alkazi, it gained a national and international reputation during the 1960s and 70s. Theatre is taught at university level at the M. S. University of Baroda in Gujurat state, Rabindra Bharati University in Calcutta, Calicut University in Trichur, Kerala, and Chandigar University in the Punjab.

Short training programmes, workshops and retreats are

among the various methods used by teachers and leaders of amateur theatre organizations to promote theatre among the young. Regional and state competitions are also conducted to encourage interest in theatre. State and national governments help in a limited way to support the study of traditional and modern Indian theatre through grants to teachers, students and organizations. They also award annual prizes to distinguished individuals for their accomplishments. The government has helped to focus national attention on theatre. (See also ASIAN AND PACIFIC ISLAND THEATRE.) FaR

Children's theatre For the past decade the most active theatre for children in India has been Theatre Academy in Pune, directed by Mohan Agashe. Performed more than 800 times in Marathi, *No Daddy, We Are Masters of the House* and *The Day Is Yours* have brought images of contemporary Indian life to children in a huge region around Bombay. The new concern for reality is marked by the aim of the Sutrapat troupe in Calcutta, 'to teach children that wonderland does not exist'. In many productions the children select and present their own experiences on the stage, making their own characters and dialogue. More than 500 children created and performed *The Prism* under Barry John's direction in Calcutta in 1993. The famous traditional story *Lakshman's Deadly Arrow* from the epic *Ramayana* is reinterpreted for young audiences raised on TV commercial jingles so as to help them integrate their rich past with the rapidly changing present. JRB

Postscript The relationship between urban theatre activity and parallel developments in other genres is complex and of significance in representing the history of modern Indian theatre.

Until the 19th century, the performing artist was held in low esteem, except in the case of forms which had a RITUAL function or were part of temple celebrations. Secular performing arts were looked upon as degrading and morally corrupting. It was thanks to the influence of the British colonial rulers, who treated theatre as an acceptable – in fact, as a snobbish and exclusive – social indulgence, that theatre gained respectability in the metropolitan cities of Bombay, Calcutta and Madras. The system of selling tickets (in place of feudal or temple patronage) gave it a new economic base, further hastening the process of secularization.

In Bombay, for instance, the Parsis – Zoroastrian immigrants of several centuries ago from Persia – perfected the art of presenting even religious myths and legends as secular, commercially viable entertainment, decked out with music and spectacle, aimed at the predominantly Hindu audience but often written (since the most commonly understood language was Hindi/Urdu) by Muslim writers like Agha Hashr Kashmiri. Outside Bombay the new urban commercial theatre in Marathi was started, and monopolized by the emerging Maharashtran Brahmin middle class. The Marathi star, Bal Gandharva, who virtually invented stage 'glamour' with his female roles and was an exceptionally gifted singer, actor and businessman, is undoubtedly the most spectacular theatre personality of the 20th century.

In Calcutta, among the Bhadralok ('the direct product and the indirect beneficiaries of the colonial culture', according to sociologist Ashis Nandy) theatre started as a preserve of the gentry but was turned into a middle-class commercial enterprise by the playwright-actor-manager, Girish Chandra Ghose. Bengali theatre then reached dizzying heights under Sisir Kumar Bhaduri in the first half of this century.

Built on the twin selling points of music and spectacle, this theatre produced almost no drama of consequence, and hence collapsed without much resistance once Indian movies began to talk (or rather, sing). But by then the educated urban middle class had accepted theatre as the medium through which 'Indian culture' and 'Indian national identity' could be expressed and explored. Soon this notion spread to dance. (For reasons explained by James Brandon, developments in dance cannot be dissociated from those in theatre.) Indophile Westerners like Ruth St Denis, Ted Shawn and Anna Pavlova rekindled interest in 'classical' Indian dance. In 1931 the predominantly Brahminic Madras Music Academy adopted *dasiyattam* (the dance of the temple dancers) to save it from extinction, rechristened it *bharatanatyam* (dance of the Bharatans, or Brahmin gurus) and was persuaded by E. Krishna Iyer to present under its aegis temple dancers (such as the now legendary T. Balasaraswathi) as artists in their own right. Dance moved out of the temple on to the public stage. It also acquired social prestige.

It is no coincidence that within the next four years RABINDRANATH TAGORE had started a *manipuri* section in Shanthiniketan, Vallathol Narayana Menon had established the Kerala Kalamandalam to revitalize *kathakali*, and Rukmini Devi Arundale had founded the International Academy of Arts in Madras to propagate *bharatanatyam*. Academic scholars like Dr V. Raghavan and folklore activists like Kamaladevi Chattopadhyay travelled widely, identifying the 'Indian' classical or folk characteristics of regional forms. By the 1940s, we have Shivarama Karanth in Karnataka thinking of rejuvenating the ailing *yakshagana*.

With independence, the notion that traditional performance genres embody the true national identity of Indian culture received official backing. The Sangeet Natak Akademi (National Academy of the Performing Arts) in the 1960s and 1970s rediscovered, publicized and funded many genres – the medieval *dhrupad* singing, the folk *pandavani* and the ritualistic *therukoothu*. It ran institutions to teach *kathak*, *manipuri* and modern theatre (both Western and Indian). More recently it has begun to finance the teaching of *kutiyattam* and is at present planning a *chhau* centre. The *chhau* forms from Mayurbhanj (Orissa) and the neighbouring *seraikella* (Bihar), which were tribal ritual dances a hundred years ago, were remoulded to fit into Hindu religious festivals by local princes in the early part of this century, and continued to survive on princely support. But in 1961 a narrative dance-drama form was discovered in Purulia (Bengal), which still retained its tribal character and was staged by itinerant troupes. Within a decade *chhau* (in all its variety) was vying with *kathakali* in attracting world attention for its training techniques. If the immediate post-independence response was to stress the 'Indianness' of all these forms, recent scholarship has begun to focus on the regional and linguistic uniqueness of each form, with its roots in specific local beliefs and rites.

The phrase 'modern theatre' has to be understood in the context of this interconnected resurgence of activity in the various genres during the last hundred years. It is no accident that the first two important plays of post-independence India, Dharam Vir Bharati's *Andha Yug* (1955) and Mohan Rakesh's *A Day in Ashadh* (1958), went to myths and legends for their plots. The exploration of traditional forms in Girish Karnad's *Hayavadana* (1970), Chandrashekar Kambar's *Jokumaraswamy* (1972) and Vijay Tendulkar's *Ghashiram Kotwal* (1973), and the experiments of HABIB TANVIR, B. V. KARANTH, Ratan Thiyam, Kavalam Narayana Panikkar or Vijaya Mehta, make sense only against this background.   GK

GENERAL

See: S. Awasthi, *Drama: The Gift of Gods: Culture, Performance and Communication in India*, Tokyo, 1983; J. R. Brandon (ed.), *The Cambridge Guide to Asian Theatre*, Cambridge, 1993; C. Choondal, *Christian Theatre in India*, Trichur, 1984, and *Classical and Folk Dances of India*, Bombay, 1963; B. Gargi, *Theatre in India*, New York, 1962; M. Khokar, *Traditions of Indian Classical Dance*, Delhi, 1979; K. Kunjunni Raja, *Kutiyattam: An Introduction*, New Delhi, 1964; K. D. Kurtkoti (ed.), *The Tradition of Kannada Theatre*, Bangalore, 1986; G. Panchal, *Kuttampalam and Kutiyattam*, New Delhi, 1984; A. Rangacharya, *The Indian Theatre*, New Delhi, 1971; F. P. Richmond, D. L. Swann, and P. B. Zarrilli (eds.), *Indian Theatre: Traditions of Performance*, Honolulu, 1990; M. L. Varadapande, *Religion and Theatre*, New Delhi, 1983; K. Vatsyayan, *Classical Indian Dance in Literature and the Arts*, New Delhi, 1968, *Indian Classical Dance*, New Delhi, 1974, and *Traditional Indian Theatre: Multiple Streams*, New Delhi, 1980.

CLASSICAL SANSKRIT THEATRE

See: R. Van M. Baumer and J. R. Brandon (eds.), *Sanskrit Drama in Performance*, Honolulu, 1981; Bharata Muni, *Natyasastra*, ed. and tr., M. Ghosh, Calcutta, 1961; G. K. Bhat, *The Vidusaka*, Ahmedabad, 1959; C. M. Byrski, *Concept of Ancient Indian Theatre*, New Delhi, 1974; A. B. Keith, *The Sanskrit Drama in its Origin, Development, Theory and Practice*, London, 1964; E. W. Marasinghe, *The Sanskrit Theatre and Stagecraft*, Delhi, 1989; B. S. Miller (ed.), *Theatre of Memory, the Plays of Kalidasa*, New York, 1984; S. P. Pandya, *A Study of the Technique of Abhinaya in Relation to Sanskrit Drama*, Bombay, 1990; I. Shekhar, *Sanskrit Drama: Its Origin and Decline*, Leiden, 1960; H. W. Wells, *The Classical Drama of India*, New York, 1963, and *Six Sanskrit Plays*, Bombay, 1964.

REGIONAL AND FOLK THEATRE

See: M. Ashton and B. Christie, *Yakshagana*, New Delhi, 1977; S. R. Desai, *Bhavai*, Ahmedabad, 1972; R. A. Frasca, *The Theater of the Mahabharata*, Honolulu, 1990; B. Gargi, *Folk Theatre of India*, Seattle, Wash., 1966; J. S. Hawley, *At Play with Krishna*, Princeton, N. J., 1981; N. Hein, *The Miracle Plays of Mathura*, New Haven, Conn., 1972; C. R. Jones and B. T. Jones, *Kathakali: An Introduction to the Dance-Drama of Kerala*, San Francisco, 1970; K. S. Karanth, *Yakshagana*, Mysore,

1974; D. R. Kinsley, *The Divine Player: A Study of Krsna Lila*, Delhi, 1979; J. C. Mathur, *Drama in Rural India*, Bombay, 1964; M. Neog, *Sankaradeva and His Times*, Gauhati, 1965; G. Panchal, *Bhavai and its Typical Aharya*, Ahmedabad, 1983; R. Schechner, *Performance Circumstances from the Avant Garde to Ramlila*, Calcutta, 1983; M. L. Varadapande, *Krishna Theatre in India*, New Delhi, 1982; P. B. Zarrilli, *The Kathakali Complex: Actor, Performance, Structure*, New Delhi, 1984.

MODERN THEATRE

See: R. Bharucha, *Rehearsals of Revolution*, Honolulu, 1983; C. Choondal, *Contemporary Indian Theatre: Interviews with Playwrights and Directors*, New Delhi, 1989; S. D. Desai, *Happenings: Theatre in Gujarat in the Eighties*, Gandhinagar, 1990; U. Dutt, *Towards a Revolutionary Theatre*, Calcutta, 1982; C. H. Kullman and W. C. Young (eds.), 'India', in *Theatre Companies of the World*, vol. 1, Westport, Conn., 1986; S. K. Mukherjee, *The Story of the Calcutta Theatres, 1753–1980*, Calcutta, 1982; B. Narayana, *Hindi Drama and Stage*, Delhi, 1981; M. Aslam Qureshi, *Wajid Ali Shah's Theatrical Genius*, Lahore, 1987.

Indonesia This performance-rich Southeast Asian nation has a population of about 180 million located on over 3000 islands which extend from Sumatra to Irian Jaya (West New Guinea). Although most of the some 300 ethnic groups which speak over 250 languages have distinctive performance traditions, research in Western languages is just beginning to clarify their nature. The better-documented theatres of Java, Bali and Sunda (West Java) are fusions of drama, dance and music. Information on the arts of these areas has often been passed on by oral tradition, and taken with archaeological and performance evidence, reconstruction of the probable evolution is possible.

To understand the major theatres of Indonesia, it is important to comprehend four concepts: *wayang*, type, *gamelan*, and structured improvisation.

Wayang (see SHADOW PUPPETS) is the puppet tradition of the islands. The most venerable types of *wayang* are the recitation of stories from painted scrolls (*wayang beber*) and *wayang kulit purwa* (leather puppetry telling *Ramayana* and *Mahabharata* stories). *Wayang* uses a *dalang* ('storyteller', 'puppeteer') to direct the story. This individual manipulates the PUPPETS or, in human theatre modelled on the puppet tradition, forges the narrative link between characters' dialogue and episodes. *Wayang* is generally performed to a gong-chime orchestra, called a *gamelan*. Over its long history, its repertory changes from Hindu epics to indigenous legends (*babad*) to Muslim-influenced stories about King Amir Hamzah. And its medium changes from leather puppets (*kulit*) to round wooden puppets (*golek*) to masked dancers (*topeng*) to unmasked dancers (*orang*). Throughout, general rules of narration, music, structure and characterization identify the forms as variants of *wayang*.

Second is the concept of type. Actors strive to present the essence of a character type rather than a realistic portrait. Five character types – refined noble, proud refined aristocrat, strong male warrior, ogre king, and clown –

Balinese *baris*, the dance of a strong warrior, has been elaborated into a dance drama, *baris melamphan*.

appear in both puppetry and what is considered the oldest form of dance-acting, *topeng* masked dance. Later genres developed from these forms and, despite refinements, these five basic character types still form the substructure of theatre throughout Indonesia. The range from *alus* ('refined') to *kasar*, *gagah* ('rough', 'strong') characters underlies everything. Stylized gestures for mimetic action – walking, adjusting costume, gesturing – and pure dance movements are set for each type. Since all classical dance portrays one of these basic character types, all dance is dramatic. The refined hero, be he Rama from the *Ramayana*, Panji the prince of East Java, Amir Hamzah the uncle of Mohammed, or Arjuna (from the *Mahabharata*), will be identical in terms of movement, vocal usage, and demeanour. Only the COSTUME, the dialogue and story line will betray the individual identity.

Thirdly, music is a necessary component of all traditional performance. A tune, a tempo, a particular percussive pattern will alert a blind audience member that a character like Rama is on stage and making a specific gesture. In former times particular scales were probably linked with certain story materials: the five-tone *slendro* scale is widely found with the Hindu-derived tales, and the seven-tone *pelog* scale is more consistently used for local legends and Muslim tales (*Amir Hamzah*). In current Central Javanese practice, however, larger ensembles that can play either tuning have developed, blurring the earlier division. Most theatre forms are accompanied by some variant of *gamelan*, an orchestra in which instruments are a set tuned to each other rather than any absolute pitch. Hanging and horizontal gongs on racks generally sound on specific beats of the cyclical musical patterns. Smaller metallophones and xylophones play melodic patterns in interconnected parts. Drums provide the rhythmic lead – signalling starts, stops, and changes of tune – and may make sound effects or accent the moves of the dance. Singers, flute or a bowed lute (*rebab*) provide an elaborate melody within the structural frame the other instruments supply. The *dalang* cues the musicians with a wood mallet and/or metal plates. Specific tunes are associated with set scenes, character types or dramatic action (that is, battle). The *dalang* sings mood songs which have similar dramatic specificity. The *gamelan*'s singer, if present, will try to choose lyrics that reinforce the atmosphere of the scene. Voices of character types may be pegged to specific notes of the scale and defined by set vocal patterns.

Finally, one must consider the role of structured improvisation: traditional performances have no written text, nor are the songs to be played during a show preplanned by the troupe. The genre's set dramatic structure in conjunction with the scenario and rules of type allow performers to generate the text and song sequence in performance. A traditional epic episode or even a newly devised story can be presented by a good troupe at a moment's notice. Of the many theatre genres currently performed, only the recently developed Western-influenced genres like *sandiwara* and modern drama use a written script. Performances traditionally take place outdoors or in the pavilion of an aristocrat's house, and food stalls and other entertainments sprout just outside the performing area. Children wake up for clowning and battles, others turn their attention to the stage for love scenes or philosophical discussions. Audience members come and go, eat, gamble, sleep or visit neighbours throughout the night. The drama is only a part of a larger event in which audience and performers improvise within their set constraints.

These organizing principles provide a basis for considering theatre history. Four major categories of performance exist: (1) prototheatrical practices; (2) traditional court or folk performance; (3) popular urban drama of the last 100 years; and (4) modern spoken drama. By considering each of these strata as representing stages of development, a sense of the history of theatre may be deduced, though the interplay of strata is more complex than this evolutionary model implies.

Prototheatrical practices Throughout the archipelago features that characterize performance in most Malay cultures can be seen, notably: (1) epic recitation; (2) poetic dialogue games; and (3) use of performance for spirit communication. Singing of verse epics is found in many Indonesian cultures, and this custom seems to have continued with new content and metres as new cultural influences became accepted. For example, among the Sundanese of West Java, a *pantun* storyteller composes, in performance, his tale based on indigenous legends. Accompanying himself on a zither (*kecapi*), he sings octosyllabic, metred lines in nightlong presentations. Similar entertainments may have been a base from which puppet theatre developed after the advent of Hindu culture about the first century AD.

Javanese written epics of the 9th–14th centuries were probably presented in oral performance by reciters who are mentioned in early court records. These epics, based on Indian sources and written in Sanskrit-derived metres and language and known as *kakawin*, are still sung in Bali and may form the literary base for *wayang*. Tales include the *Ramayana*, which chronicles Sita's rescue by her god-incarnate husband, Rama, when she is kidnapped by the demonic Rawana. Other *kakawin* are based on the *Mahabharata*, telling of the exploits of five heroes, the Pandawa brothers, who fight their hundred Kurawa cousins in the *bharata yudha*, a great war that leaves the heroes heartbroken in their hour of victory. Middle-Javanese-language *kidung* were stories written in indigenous verse forms, dealing with the story of the heroic Panji and other indigenous tales. Although these texts, by virtue of being written, are more set than traditional theatre genres of today, they correspond to the story materials of most theatre. Such texts, presumably growing from and intended for oral performance, may have had interplay with theatrical enactment from an early period. Indeed, a few mood songs of the shadow-theatre repertoire correspond to passages from such texts.

A Cirebonese woman *dalang* lighting her oil lamp in a *wayang kulit purwa* performance.

Poetry games using indigenous verse forms are a root of some folk-theatre forms. The Sundanese four-line riddle poetry, *sisinderan*, is an example. These verses could be improvised courting games in which a male singer vied with a female, or sung in other contexts. A number of Sundanese folk-theatre forms, such as *godang*, *dog-dog*, *calung* (each of which uses a different kind of musical instrument to accompany singing), expand on such games by adding humorous improvised skits about village life.

Also significant are performances that communicate with spirits. Trance performance is common throughout the islands, since such dances allow spirits to enter the world in a controlled mode. In Balinese *sanghyang dedari*, a trance performance done in times of epidemic or difficulty, two small girls are put into trance by the chant of a male chorus and allowed to speak for the spirits. In West Java *sintren* or *lais*, the trance dance of a child medium, is probably a related form. In Central Java entranced dancers may rock a doll figure, *nini towong*, to make rain. In other islands of Indonesia, too, MASKS and puppets are used in rites for the dead, and a preference for puppet and mask in this culture may relate to such forms (cf. MALAYSIA's *ulek* and BURMA's *nat pwe*).

In Sunda, entranced dancers doing martial arts dance (*pencak silat*) may be entered by the spirit of a tiger (*pamacan*) or monkey (*pamonyet*). Horse trance dances are found in Bali (*sanghang jaran*), Java (*kuda kepang*, *jatilan*) and Sunda (*kuda lumping*) as well as in Malaysia. Dancers entered by horse spirits are able to eat glass or walk on hot coals. An important animal figure associated with trance performance is the lion-like being, Barong, perhaps derived from a Buddhist protective figure and related to the Chinese lion. In Bali the image has become linked to a magico-religious dance drama in which the protective *barong* pits its power against the malevolent witch, Rangda ('widow'). She prompts entranced dancers to turn their weapons against themselves; however, their trance prevents wounds.

In most trance performances a *dukun* (RITUAL specialist in dealing with spirits and curing) or a priest will be the significant figure who, by mantras and incense, calls the appropriate spirit into the performer. Often an assistant makes sure the trancers remain within acceptable bounds and adds comic quips to the possession rite at the same time. These two roles have some features in common with, respectively, a *dalang* who controls and narrates for a performance but does not 'act' himself, and a clown character who is part of every genre.

Content is also significant for placating the spirit world. *Wayang*'s exorcistic story, *The Origin of Kala* (*Murawakala*), is a case in point. In Java, Sunda and Bali certain individuals are believed to be threatened by the demon Kala, whose name means 'time'. The potential victim lives in danger of misfortune until a *dalang* plays the story of how the first *wayang* exorcism (*ruwatan*) calmed Kala's wrath. Another story, *Mikukuhan*, about King Mikukuhan was used in Java and Sunda to prevent diseases threatening rice crops, while *Watugunung*, named after its hero who married his own mother, was used in East Java to make rain. The Balinese *Calonarang*, named after the witch-widow of the title, tells how a king of East Java foiled her machinations. It may be presented in Bali as a shadow play or in conjunction with *rangda-barong* dance drama.

Performances are traditionally part of RITE OF PASSAGE ceremonies for the group or individual, and this tradition seems to have persisted through times of spirit worship, of Hinduism and of Islam. In areas like Cirebon, wooden-rod-puppet shows telling local chronicles (*wayang golek cepak*) take place annually at the cemetery to honour the dead. Indeed some scholars believe pre-Hindu performances told of ancestral exploits as a means of gaining the forebears' aid in promoting fertility. In Bali much performance takes place in the context of temple festivals when Hindu and local spirits are thought to be visiting earth. Throughout Muslim Java and Sunda weddings, circumcisions, a ceremony for an unborn or newly born child or a ritual cleansing of the village from bad spirits are important occasions for a performance that often lasts all night, since that is when spirits are nigh. Performances include food offerings for the spirits, and open with mantras and music meant for spirit propitiation. Although today most performances are primarily intended for the amusement of the audience who attend for free (the family celebrating the rite of passage pays the troupe), such evidence hints that old relationships of dancer and spirit medium, and of *dalang* and SHAMAN, give the performer an aura of power.

Traditional court and folk performance The elaboration of early performance practices into strong theatrical traditions seems largely to have come after Hindu–Buddhist religion was adopted by the ruling elite. In the kingdom of Sriwijaya (7th–13th centuries), centred in Sumatra but having influence in Java and the Malay peninsula, the ruler used ceremony as a mode of dramatizing his magico-religious power. In Java various dynasties perpetuated syncretic animistic-Hindu–Buddhist practices. By the 9th century Javanese inscriptions indicate that female dancers, clowns, mask performers and shadow players were resident in courts and temples. Indian influence may have been stronger in this early period: dancers in temple reliefs assume strong stances similar to current Indian dance and unlike contemporary Javanese style. The sign-MIME gestures of India (*mudra* or *hasta*) are not, however, apparent. Local aesthetics must soon have remoulded any strong outside stimuli: by the 13th century temple reliefs in East Java show scenes in which the costume, space usage and character typology bear a striking resemblance to current Balinese *wayang*.

In the 9th–15th centuries distinctive Javanese versions of the *Ramayana* and *Mahabharata* were developed. These epics probably reached Indonesia from Bengal and eastern INDIA, but soon events of the epics were believed to have occurred at specific sites in Java and the heroes were considered ancestors of the Javanese. Masked dance, female dance and shadow theatre became integral parts of ritual to enhance the aura of the king in magico-religious, as well as aesthetic dimensions. The importance of performance to such systems has led anthropologist Geertz to characterize such cultures as 'theatre states': court performance and ceremony became the way rulers acted out their power and, thereby, were empowered. The concept that *gamelan*, dances, puppets, MASKS and performers focused spiritual power and hence were necessary regalia for kings seems to have crystallized in this era. Tantric Hindu–Buddhist thought seems to have promoted such thinking. Kings in CAMBODIA, THAILAND and Malaysia eventually adopted similar strategies for articulating their glory, influenced, in part, by Sriwijayan and Javanese models.

Scholars currently debate the impact of Indian and Chinese culture in developing the arts. For example, female dance, shadow puppetry and mask theatre are all found in India. Though these are the oldest performance modes in Indonesia, each of these arts manifests itself in quite a different way than in Indian models. It seems likely that Indonesians largely borrowed forms which reinforced indigenous performance tendencies, upgrading them with Indian stories and the aura of a higher culture. The fact that theatre only developed strongly in areas of Indonesia where Hindu culture was firmly implanted implies that the impact of India was, indeed, important. Trade with CHINA was a significant feature in developing the economic base of the major kingdoms in Indonesia, and it is possible that puppetry techniques and typology of character were influenced by Chinese practice. Martial-arts dance and wooden-rod-puppet techniques, for example, are often associated with Chinese communities. Though less scholarship has focused on the connection between performance in Indonesia and OCEANIA, common threads might usefully be pursued. The importance of female dancers and child performers is a common link.

Muslim conversions began in the 13th century, and gradually all Java accepted Islam. The aristocrats of the last Hindu–Buddhist court, Majapahit, retreated to the neighbouring island of Bali around 1520. Balinese performance has developed greatly since these culture bringers slipped across those two miles of ocean, yet it seems likely that the aesthetic of Bali today may give some insight into Hindu Javanese arts. The Balinese hold that their theatre is the legacy of Majapahit, citing two forms in particular, *gambuh* dance drama and *wayang parwa*.

Bali *Gambuh* is said to have been developed in Majapahit Java and have changed little since the 16th century. The plays, presented in the inner temple courtyard during temple festivals, last all day or all night, and tell stories drawn from Javanese legends, notably the *Panji* cycle. The heroic characters speak Kawi (old Javanese), which the audience cannot understand, while the clowns use colloquial Balinese, and the narrator mixes Kawi and Balinese. This linguistic difference between epic characters and clowns is a significant part of traditional Balinese performance. Other Balinese dramatic forms, including *legong*, *topeng*, *wayang wong*, *arja* and *baris melamphan*, are said to derive from this ur-genre, which is preserved at Batuan, Gianyar and a few other places.

The other form considered as a direct legacy of Majapahit is *wayang parwa*, the hide-shadow-puppet theatre of Bali telling *Mahabharata* tales. The figures, the music ensemble and performance technique are more vigorous than current Javanese style, perhaps indicating an older practice. Less stylized puppet images, a simpler orchestra composed of four metallophones called *gender*, a smaller screen, a shorter performance duration and a more elaborate opening ritual are some of the characteristics differentiating it from Javanese practice. This vibrant puppet tradition is the most popular theatre form in Bali and performances are required for many life-cycle ceremonies.

The Balinese *legong* dancer, with darting eyes, high elbow placement, and dynamic changes of position, offers a more energized vision of the female than Muslim Java cultivates. The vibrancy may hint at an aesthetic more aligned with the Hindu–Buddhist heritage of Majapahit. In *legong* the most abstract of dramas is hidden in the movements of three prepubescent girls. The form as currently practised developed around 1800 when prince I Dewa Agung Made Karna, after dreaming he saw heavenly maidens dancing in a style similar to the sacred trance, *sanghang dedari*, ordered girls to be trained accordingly. As other rulers elaborated on this first attempt, *legong* was established. In times past, *legong* dancers often became wives of the ruler when they reached puberty.

Topeng is the mask dance of Bali: the stories are taken from Javanese and local legends. Major characters wear full masks, while clowns, who translate, wear half-masks. Some masks are said to be magically charged, and the oldest masks in the island are said to have been brought back from East Java in the Majapahit era by an aristocrat of the Jelantik clan. His descendants eventually used these masks and added new ones that tied at the back rather than being held by the teeth as in Java. The oldest Balinese *topeng* is the solo *topeng pajegan*, performed in the sacred inner courtyard of the temple. Four introductory mask dances begin the performance, then the dancer acts out a story alternating noble and clown masks. Finally, he puts on the mask of an old man, Sidha Karya ('Accomplishing the Task'), and enacts a dance ritual to bring a desired blessing. Ritually potent *topeng* dancers today include: I Made Jimat, I Made Sidja, Anak Agung Cebang and I Ketut Kantor. I Nyoman Kakul's death in the early 1980s was a major loss.

In the last hundred years two new *topeng* forms have become popular as entertainment. *Topeng panca* ('five'-person *topeng*) uses a larger group to present the traditional repertoire with more interaction and clown scenes. The Sidha Karya mask ritual is not presented in this version nor in the eclectic *topeng prembon* ('combination' *topeng*) created around 1940. The latter melds the *topeng* repertoire and clowning with females dancing and singing in *arja* (dance opera) style.

Gambuh, *wayang parwa*, and, to a lesser extent, *legong* and *topeng* may hint at Majapahit theatre practice and aesthetics. More recent Balinese genres continue to draw on these older forms. *Wayang wong* was created in the late 1700s when the ruler of Klungkung asked performers to use ancient masks in his collection. In the resulting form masked humans tell tales derived from the *Ramayana*. A parallel form is *wayang* (*orang*) *parwa* in which unmasked dancers and masked clowns enact *Mahabharata* stories. Sukawati was a centre for this genre, but the currently active group is in Bonkasa, Badung. Both these forms use a *dalang* and follow shadow-theatre performance practices. Masked *jauk* originated in the 18th century as dance dramas of *Ramayana* and *Mahabharata* stories.

More modern genres, created as secular entertainments, include: *jangger*, *arja*, *kecak*, *baris melamphan* and *sendratari. Jangger*, a group dance for young men and women, was considered daringly modern between 1920 and 1950, and it continues to be popular today. *Arja* is a romantic dance opera that began in the 1900s and features female performers. It is perhaps the most popular genre on the island today. *Kecak* is a modern creation devised for tourist audiences. The expatriot painter Walter Spies commissioned the first performance in Bedulu village for a German film *Island of Demons* in the 1930s. Thereafter it became a popular tourist genre. In its standard form, a 150-strong male chorus makes interlocking 'cak-cak' calls, playing a chorus of monkeys, as the stirring background for a danced episode of the kidnapping of Sita from the *Ramayana*. The abstract warrior dance drama *baris melamphan* uses *Ramayana* and *Mahabharata* stories. The all-male cast speaks in ancient Kawi language. The dancers are not distinguished from each other by costume or characterization, but by action and the talk of the translator-clowns.

Sendratari (literally, art-drama-dance) is a form of pantomimic dance drama developed at the High School of Traditional Music (KOKAR, now SMKI) in 1962. This genre was created simultaneously in Java and Sunda in government art schools. The narrative of the traditional *dalang* and dialogue were cut to eliminate the language barrier that kept members of other ethnic groups from understanding regional performance. In Bali *sendratari*'s appeal was heightened by the use of the most popular *gamelan* style of the last 25 years, *kebyar*, 'lightning' style, which has brilliant tone and quick transitions. The expert performance of the young dance students who often come from the best families of traditional dance, the proscenium stage, theatre lighting and costumes adapted from traditional dance apparel, all make the form popular. *Sendratari* as choreographed by I Wayan Beratha, I Wayan Dibia and I Made Bandem show much continuity with the past, but the imposition of a set choreography and the absence of the Kawi language and of a *dalang* show movement from the older theatre pattern.

Currently the Balinese maintain a vibrant theatrical life. Performers and cultural conservators, aware of potential contradictions between religious aims and modern commercial strains, have attempted to provide guidelines for usage of the different genres so that commercial and religious values need not clash. In the late 1970s the categories of sacred (*wali*), ceremonial (*bebali*) and entertainment (*bali-balihan*) were established, and different genres divided into these categories in an attempt to prevent commercial cannibalization of the *wali* genres. On any day dozens of tourist performances can be seen around the island and the glut of tourists has created a surplus of capital in many villages which is reinvested in performances for temple festivals, cremations and the annual Bali Arts Festival. At this point these attempts to distinguish tourist from religious performance appear successful.

Java With the energized Balinese drama as a perspective, the transitions made in 15th- to 17th-century Java toward a more subdued, inwardly focused and stylized theatre style become clear. A generation of Muslim teacher-rulers rose in cities along the north coast. Rather than abandon-

ing the arts, these leaders promoted them. Johns has suggested that Sufi mystical orders introduced Islam, and this would explain the performative orientation of Islam in Java. Further research is required to test the hypothesis: for example, a close comparison of *wayang kulit purwa* with the dervish-related KARAGÖZ shadow-puppet theatre of the Arab world, supposedly created in 1366 by a Sufi mystic, Mehmend Kushteri, might establish firmer links.

Documentation from earlier periods proves that shadow, mask and dance performance actually developed in the Hindu–Buddhist period. Still traditional Javanese artists invariably trace the origin of their theatre practice to the *Wali Sangga*, the 'Nine Saints' who converted the island to Islam. Wali Sunan Kalijaga is credited with devising *wayang kulit purwa*, performing it in mosques and requiring the Muslim confession of faith as the price of viewing.

Though not necessarily historical facts, these statements reveal inner truth – the local tradition was redefined, and new features characterized Muslim–Javanese as opposed to Hindu–Balinese arts. A greater stylization of puppet and mask was introduced, supposedly to circumvent the Islamic prohibition on representing the human form. A more inward-turning focus and flowing dance style were adopted, especially for refined character types. The Kawi language was abandoned for Javanese, though traces of the older tongue haunt mood songs and narration. The *Mahabharata* cycle, on which 95 per cent of current stories are based, was revised to suit a Muslim ethos: Indian religious figures were devalued and the polygamy of the five Pandawa and their wife, Drupadi, edited out. New content was introduced, including the Amir Hamzah stories glorifying that Muslim hero and tales of the nine *wali* themselves were soon developed. Pan-Islamic forms like Sufi *dikir* group chanting and the Muslim trance dance *dabus*, in which performers stab and cut themselves with impunity, also began in this era.

Many changes were made in Java's *wayang* tradition, leading toward the well known *wayang kulit purwa* of today. On an expansive screen a *dalang* presents the monodrama, manipulating about 50 leather shadow-puppet figures through a complex plot lasting from 8.30 p.m. till morning. The puppet-master controls the entire performance, cuing the *gamelan* which also accompanies the female singer. His story will ordinarily be based on Javanese-invented tales concerning the Hindu heros of the *Ramayana* and *Mahabharata* and will follow a strict performance structure: opening court scene, battle episode, hermitage and clown scene (*gara-gara*), second battle against ogre characters called the 'flower battle' (*perang kembang*), and closing battle. Individual scenes required for a story are added as necessary. The performance is divided into three parts, marked by change in musical pitch. The set character types of hero, strong warrior, clown and ogre, and known epic materials form the base for each improvised performance.

The meanings of these plays are multiple. For example, the three parts of the night correspond to youth, adolescence and adulthood. The child's precarious first steps become firm in the testing of youth, the 'flower battle'. There we overcome 'ogres' of greed and sensuality if we are to succeed in life. Another mode of looking at plays is to understand that the classes of characters correspond to different categories of Javanese society: the heroes are the Javanese elite; the clowns are the common people; the ogres, the demonic and non-Javanese powers or peoples. The myths of the Pandawas fighting their own cousins remind Javanese of the colonial experience. The Dutch used royal-family rivalries, splitting the royal house in 1755 into Surakarta and Yogyakarta and later subdividing these to form four competing royal houses. The inter-family quarrels helped make the rulers weak, and have given these stories deep resonance. Other scholars see old tribal patterns, spirit communication, royal propaganda or philosophical tolerance as important features of the form.

Other forms of Javanese *wayang* tend today to follow the structural-musical model of the *wayang kulit purwa*. The now infrequently played *wayang beber*, which tells various cycles using picture scrolls, may actually be older than the *wayang kulit purwa*. The oral tradition holds that this was the genre used to tell the exorcistic Kala tale until the early 1600s. Since *dalang* still fear changing this magically powerful story, earlier practices of it might have been maintained longer. Another genre that follows the *wayang kulit purwa* style is *wayang gedog* which uses *pelog gamelan* and leather puppets to tell *Panji* and other Javanese tales. It was supposedly created in 1553 by the wali, Sunan Giri. *Wayang golek cepak*, which has wooden doll-like rod puppets and tells Javanese chronicles and Amir Hamzah tales, was credited to Sunan Kudus's innovation in 1584. This form continues to thrive along the north coast, where Aliwijaya of Cirebon claims to be the 27th generation of his family to present the art. In East Java *wayang klitik* adopts flat wooden puppets to tell Javanese tales. One feature that distinguishes some of these genres from *wayang kulit purwa* is that there is no concept of 'branch' stories, and therefore *dalang*, in general, need to be better versed in all the particulars of the epic than the young *purwa dalang*, who may invent many of their tales. Another distinction is that puppet headdresses and costumes vary from *purwa* style and are reminiscent of Javanese court dress of the 17th century.

Some newer shadow forms are found only in the palaces or government offices, since they validate and glorify particular rulers: *wayang madya* uses leather puppets to tell tales of historical Central Javanese kings, while *wayang suluh* was created in 1947 and tells of figures like Sukarno who forged the new Republic of Indonesia. There are many other *wayang* forms, but none rival *wayang kulit purwa*, which remains a favoured entertainment for weddings and circumcisions. Cassettes of performances by superstars like narto Sabdho or Anom Suroto are found in every record shop. At institutions like Habiranda, a puppetry school founded by the Bureau of Performing Arts of the Yogyakarta palace in 1950, one can find many students studying formally what *dalang* of past generations learned by apprenticing themselves for a number of years.

The mask dance of the north coast, *topeng babakan*, is also attributed to Sunan Kalijaga. Over eight hours a solo dancer (who is also a *dalang*) presents a sequence of four or five masks. Today most *dalang* specialize only in dance; in times past performers, who might be male or female, often performed shadow plays as well. *Topeng* performances would be given during the day and *wayang kulit* *purwa* would be presented in the evening. The white-faced refined Panji, conceptually an innocent infant, yet spiritually perfected, opens the presentation. Then comes Pamindo ('two'), often a blue mask – a refined but proud and flighty adolescent; the third figure is a strong, mature male, Tummenggung ('minister'), whose mask has a reddish cast; and the final figure is Klana, a red-faced figure with bulging eyes and fangs', furiously grasping for life, even in the moment of death. A fifth mask, Rumiang, may sometimes be added. A second dancer plays the clown, and his half-masks let him engage in verbal as well as physical humour. The abstract story is less significant than the types which represent the different aspects of the personality that lie behind and within each person. The symbolism of the masks is complex: they are correlated with the four directions, the elements and emotions, and may be derived from rice-harvest ritual. Today Sujana Ardja of Salangit, Cirebon, is a major performer of this genre.

The second major mask theatre of Java is said to have evolved from this solo tradition. Multiple masked dancers enact stories in *wayang topeng* as a *dalang* delivers all the dialogue or just the narration, mood songs and cues. This form persists in rural areas especially along the north coast and on the island of Madura, while the courts and commercial theatre have largely abandoned it for unmasked dance drama.

The final legacy of this early Muslim period is the female dance of Java. Even more abstract than *legong*, it remains a potent symbol of past court glory. In *bedaya* nine refined female dancers move through intricate floor patterns via slow, stylized gesture. Somewhere within the piece a highly stylized struggle may be enacted, representing both an actual combat in the story and the extinction of worldly desire in the soul of the true aesthetic. The interplay of eroticism and enlightenment colours the form. Some practices of tantrism may have affected the genre, and the choreography creates a mandala-like floor pattern that works on a magico-religious level to simulate enlightenment in the ideal spectator – the ruler. The dancers would often become the wives or ladies-in-waiting of the ruler, and he might take them into battle to unleash the spiritual forces they represented against his enemy.

The oldest *bedaya* choreography still performed dates from the 16th century, but the genre is believed to be related to older Hindu–Buddhist forms. The *Bedaya Ketawang* is the inheritance of the Surakarta court of Central Java. It is said that Sultan Agung of Mataram (1616–45) was meditating on the shores of the southern ocean when the goddess of the seas tried to seduce him with this dance. Thereafter, it has been ritually performed once a year on the anniversary of the coronation day of his kingly descendants, perpetuating the spiritual compact between goddess and ruler. The goddess herself is believed sometimes to appear among the dancers.

Bedaya Semang, the similar ritual performance of the Yogyakarta court, lapsed around 1920. *Bedaya Madiun* presents the suppression of a rebellion by the Mataram monarch, and *Bedaya Arjuna Wiwaha* re-enacts the ritual union of the *Mahabharata* hero, Arjuna, with a heavenly nymph. In recent years *bedaya* has become a popular choreographic genre for new dances. *Srimpi*, a related form for four female dancers, dates from the 17th century.

Performers were traditionally daughters of rulers who, again, presented a stylized battle. *Srimpi Renggawati*, for five female dancers, shows the battle between two princesses in love with Amir Hamzah.

Solo female court dances do not have the same aura of the sacred as these group dances. It seems likely that they rise from the popular *ronggeng* (female singer-dancer) tradition which is found in many manifestations throughout Indonesia. *Tayuban* is a dance party in which a female dancer opens the performance by dancing classical character types but which ends up with the lady (or, in some instances, a female impersonator (see FEMALE IMPERSONATION)) doing partner dances with various male spectators. *Ronggeng* has always had an aura of prostitution attached, but the role has a significance that Western society does not accord the courtesan. Some scholars attribute these forms to archaic links between female dancers and rice fertility rituals, which are still found in some villages and require the presence of such a performer.

Beksan lawung ('lance dances') are 17th-century male court dances depicting military prowess performed at both the Surakarta and Yogyakarta courts. Perhaps because of the military expertise of its founder, Hamengku Buwana I, the Yogyakarta sultanate is especially noted for these dances, which recreate the pageantry and battles of the court. The Surakarta court, with its legacy of *bedaya*, is felt to excel in female-style dance.

Unmasked dance drama, *wayang orang* in Indonesian or *wayang wong* in Javanese, is also a speciality of Yogyakarta since it was supposedly created there after the split in the royal line. The first court dance drama, *Gondowerdoyo* (*Scent of the Heart*), was presented under the personal direction of Hamengku Buwana I in the 18th century. Then, as today, the performance used *wayang kulit purwa* and *wayang topeng* as models. The function of the *dalang* and the dramatic structure came from puppet theatre. Dancers took the puppet roles, and the flat plane of the blocking and the flowing quality of movement probably derived from the shadow play aesthetic. Female impersonators were the theatrical norm for *wayang wong* in Yogyakarta until the 1920s. Dance, in this era, was considered a necessary study for royalty, since it refined the spirit. Hence, princes were often fine dancers and apt to play major roles in these dance dramas. Performers were cast according to body type and personality, and would play the same role type for life. Though the conceptualization of role types was expanded from four to twelve in the court, the increased types can be considered a refinement, rather than a rejection, of the old four-character system.

The resources of the court promoted precision and elegance inconceivable in village performance. Performances ran three to four days with hundreds of dancers rehearsing up to a year in preparation. Twelve such epics were staged in the Yogyakarta court in the 1920s–30s, with the repertoire primarily drawn from *Mahabharata* material. The distinctive older headdress of the masked dancer, constructed of matted hair, was abandoned in favour of headpieces like those of *wayang kulit purwa* figures. Exquisitely dyed batik fabrics with set designs designated for specific characters wrapped the bejewelled dancers. Dance scarves, tossed and held as part of the dance technique, were prescribed for each role. The 'green-room' area where dancers waited to make their entrance to the dance area of the palace was called by the same name as the puppet chest of *wayang*. Still, behind the splendour of these costly court extravaganzas the *dalang* role of the ruler was already in decline.

In the first quarter of this century two major alterations in court support of theatre occurred. Firstly, Krida Beksa Wikrama was founded in Yogyakarta by Prince Surjodiningrat and Prince Tedjokusumo in 1918 to train dancers for performances outside the palace. Secondly, palace performers began producing *wayang orang* for a ticket-buying public in Sriwidari, a park in Surakarta opened in 1899. Originally commercial, travelling *wayang orang* companies played there, but by 1920 palace dancers took over the venue. The box office went into the palace treasury, and performers got a set salary. This early democratization and commercialization of palace arts accelerated after 1949, when, with independence, court resources diminished. Sriwidari itself came under city administration at that time.

Current commercial *wayang orang* troupes perform on a proscenium stage equipped with wing-and-drop scenery. Women often play refined male roles, a practice first introduced in the 1930s in Surakarta. Troupes have in recent years shortened performances to three hours and introduced new repertoire – Javanese legends, in addition to *purwa* tales – to attract audiences. Actors find these new materials difficult and must undertake unaccustomed rehearsals: *purwa* materials are easily improvised from the scenario, since actors generally play the same set character from performance to performance. Though the 1980s have brought declining audiences, major troupes like Ngesti Pandawa in Semarang and Surakarta's Sriwidari continue.

Other court dramas have largely disappeared. Surakarta's *langendriya* is rarely seen. This dance drama contained sung dialogue presented by a female troupe. It tells the story of Damar Wulan, a 14th-century Majapahit ruler. The form was created in 1876 by Raden Tummenggung Purwadiningrat and Prince Mankubumi. Also rare, *langen mandro wanara* was created by Danureja VII in the same era to present the *Ramayana* story. Related forms told stories of King Amir Hamzah (*langen asmara*) and Prince Panji (*langen pranasmara*).

As in Bali, a textless *sendratari* has grown popular in Java since the 1960s for both tourist and local audiences. Major tourist performances can be seen in the dry season at Prambanan and Pandaan temple complexes, where *Ramayana* and East Javanese tales, respectively, are presented. Noted *sendratari* choreographers, including Wisnu Wardhana, Bagong Kussudiardjo, Sudharso Pringgobroto, Sardono S. Kusumo, and Sudarsono, create works for urban Javanese and overseas tours. They sometimes incorporate techniques from Sundanese, Balinese, or even Western experimental dance in innovative productions. Story materials, music, and costume may also diverge from traditional sources. Still, the strong continuity with the classical tradition is apparent in most performances, which can also be seen at government academies of dance in Yogyakarta and Surakarta.

Sunda Since the 18th century the Sundanese, a distinct

ethnic group living in western Java, have developed a rich artistic tradition. As in Bali, genres show their relation to Javanese models while the aesthetic, movement style, music and language are Sunda's own. Sundanese performance strikes the viewer as occupying the middle ground between the almost frenetic dynamism of Bali and the mesmerizing, flowing aesthetic of Java. The drummer accents the dancers' steps with drum patterns appropriate for the movement, rather like the drum-dance syllables of Indian performance. This makes the movement and sound system seem more transparent than Java's. In conjunction with the lively musical style, the constant calls and quips that musicians are free to add to the performance, it also makes Sunda's arts seem earthy and spontaneous. This aesthetic probably results from the fact that palaces have had little part in forming the Sundanese arts – these are village arts.

Storytelling, harvest rituals, and poetry traditions involving skits were part of Sunda's indigenous culture. In the early 19th century Javanese officials assigned to govern parts of this area began importing *dalang* from the Cirebon area where north-coast Javanese had their own distinctive variants of Javanese arts. About the same time itinerant troupes from the north coast availed themselves of the road the Dutch colonial administration had opened into the Sundanese highlands. *Topeng* dancers and *ronggeng* singers might be found as part of market-day entertainments. As these artists settled in Sunda and intermarried with Sundanese, a new hybrid of *wayang ronggeng* and *topeng* performances developed. Meanwhile, *wayang golek purwa*, a rod-puppet theatre, was created about 150 years ago in the city of Sumedang when performers of Javanese *wayang kulit purwa* began to tell their Hindu-based *purwa* stories in the Sundanese language using wooden rod puppets. Until that time only leather puppets had been used to tell the *purwa* story, but the local preference for the comparative realism of the three-dimensional figures (used to tell Javanese and Muslim stories along the north coast) prompted the local regent to commission a set of wooden puppets with the distinctive *purwa* headdresses. From this start *wayang golek purwa* became a lively village entertainment. The most popular genre in Sunda, it is performed at life-cycle ceremonies and broadcast on radio and television. The story structure roughly follows the Javanese model, but much more freedom is allowed to the puppeteer in shaping his story, especially when the clown and ogre characters appear. At present some performers also do Sundanese chronicle tales and Amir Hamzah stories using the same set of *purwa* style puppets. These tales are the speciality of Bogor-city *dalang* who find Islamic fundamentalist audiences favour such material.

Today the Sunarya family of the Bandung area is probably the most popular *dalang* family: five major performers from two generations of the family are active. The eldest *dalang* in such a family can make holy water, used to cure and bring luck, or perform spiritually dangerous exorcisms. However, since major *dalang* are culture idols and command high fees, many boys who do not come from families of *dalang* aspire to the role, creating a current pool of about 2000 who have trained via the apprentice system. The female singer (*pasinden*), who was incorporated

into the form around 1900, is given more prominence than her Javanese counterpart, and the audience requests songs during interludes in the story. The first *pasinden* was, reportedly, a *ronggeng* dancer-singer who married a *dalang*. The popularity of these dynamic women rivals that of the *dalang* themselves.

Sundanese folk theatres like *topeng banyet* and *ronggeng gunung* are linked to the *ronggeng* tradition. They often open with solo character dances by a female, short sketches on village life, and culminate with performers dancing *ketuk tilu* partner dances with male audience members. Songs by the performers may come between sketches. Featured roles are the female actress-singer-dancer and clown. In recent years this *ronggeng* style has been reinterpreted for urban audiences in a performance called *jaipongan*. Begun in the late 1970s by Gugum Gumbira, *dalang* Nadang Barmaya and actress-singer Tatih Saleh, this dance-song-comedy genre became a pan-Indonesian craze.

Topeng mask dances came to Sunda from the north-coast area. The aggressive Klana character with his red face and demon energy has long been the favoured dance. Currently many Sundanese study with masters from the north coast and are reintroducing many mask dances into the highlands.

Wayang orang developed in Sunda, as in Java, by substituting people for puppets, and corresponds in most particulars to the *wayang golek purwa*. The dance of the performers has the grounded, three-dimensional feel of the wooden rod puppet that the dancer tries to emulate. *Sendratari* has emerged in the last 25 years, with Enoch Atmadibarata, Abay Subarja, Irawati Durban Arjo and Endo Suwanda as important choreographers. Though *purwa* stories are sometimes presented, Sundanese legends and history prevail. Tales of Pajajaran, the Sundanese kingdom that retreated to the spirit plane rather than accept the domination of the Javanese, may be presented with haunting Sundanese songs derived from the old *pantun* (storytelling) tradition. Where Javanese and Balinese may look for new materials from other areas, Sundanese tend to look to their own past.

Popular urban drama In the last hundred years popular drama forms which emphasize dialogue over dance, performed in permanent theatres for a ticket-buying audience, have arisen in the cities. Many of these forms developed in the early part of this century in response to touring *bangsawan* troupes from MALAYSIA. The Malaysian troupes presented a model of a commercial theatre where entertainment was the prime aim and presenting new plot materials was standard practice. Actors played set character types and generated the script from a scenario. A *dalang* was not needed, and the archaisms of language, rituals for spirits and formulaic phrases that characterize *wayang* were dropped. Plots could be set in modern times. Plot and language were emphasized and movement and the whole performance tended toward greater realism. The prominence given clown characters and tendency of plots to turn on problems of lovers and their parents make the forms reminiscent of COMMEDIA DELL'ARTE. Usually performances would be given in structures boasting a proscenium stage, painted scenery and a darkened auditorium. Though some forms, like *ketoprak*, show considerable continuity with *wayang*'s epic world, others, like *ludruk*, look more to the present.

Ketoprak is a Central-Javanese form created in the early 20th century based on musical rhythms elaborated from rice-pounding music. The music became a craze in court and villages around Surakarta, and dialogue-oriented, improvised dramas based on Javanese chronicle tales became associated with it in the 1920s. By 1927 *gamelan* replaced the original musical instruments. Current troupes like Ketoprak Mataram and Sapta Mandala in Yogyakarta perform nightly, and the backstage visitor will see actors checking the posted scenario before going on stage. Plot structure and character types correspond in many ways to *wayang orang* minus its dance and archaic language.

Ludruk is the urban popular theatre of Surabaya in East Java. It developed from folk entertainments into a drama-oriented genre under the influence of *bangsawan*. Performances begin with a dance, followed by a clown sequence and singing by the female impersonator. Then comes the story, usually a domestic melodrama with comic interludes, though some traditional stories are still presented. Though the female impersonator dances in a style rudely recalling the traditional female court dancer, the core of the show is the realistic spoken drama that probes problems of the modern urban audience.

Sandiwara, Sunda's response to *bangsawan*, has two major forms. The first is comparable to *ketoprak* and combines indigenous *gamelan*, Sundanese history tales, and *wayang*-like dramatic structure. The second variant is now more common and focuses on domestic melodramas climaxing in martial-arts scenes. A village girl may be kidnapped by a bandit, but rescued by her sweetheart, or the attempts of parents to marry a daughter for money will be foiled by her true love and the good offices of her clownish servant.

Other examples of similar 20th-century improvised forms aimed at popular audiences are found in Sumatra (*randai* of the Minangkabau), around Jakarta (the circle dance *lenong*), in Cirebon (*tarling*, accompanied by flute and guitar), and in Kalimantan (*mamanda*). Many troupes, however, have folded in recent years under the competition from rock bands, film and television. Sri Mulat, a company which has branches in Jakarta and East Java, is an exception, and its fine comedians perform often on television.

The traditional theatre comments on this world through the multifaceted clown, while music, dance, types and formulaic patterns communicate its deep message. It asks the audience to look at epic and archetypical worlds beyond and within, assuming the performance, crafted by forebears, will make viewers see a reality that the daily world obscures. Modern spoken drama, the youngest genre of theatre in Indonesia, on the other hand, demands that the audience look at the real world around them and take action on pressing social problems confronting the modernizing nation. Spoken drama is presented in contemporary Indonesian language, rather than the regional languages that characterize traditional dramatic forms. In hopes of reaching a wide audience with their message, playwrights and directors of modern the-

atre have increasingly in the last two decades moved toward television drama and film. For this reason, the history and development of modern theatre have had a profound influence on these two mass media and, conversely, some playwrights and directors work on the stage in a filmic manner. Arifin C. Noer's work appears in film, television and on the stage. Putu Wijaya's ironic sense of humour translates well into filmic scripts. Director Teguh Karya whose company excels in STANISLAVSKY-based realist theatre (see REALISM), has generated strong films like *Mother* (*Ibunda*). Within the limits of often strict government CENSORSHIP, modern drama, film and television speak tellingly of the faultlines and foibles in current Indonesian society. Producers who dictate what gets funded exert even stronger control, based on what they believe will draw audiences. These media play for a living, consumer audience.

Modern spoken drama The 1926 verse drama written by Rustam Effendi, *Bebasari*, opened the curtain on modern Indonesian theatre. Rustam's allegorical tale recalls the famous episode about the kidnapping of Sita in the Hindu epic, the *Ramayana*. Princess Bebasari (Indonesia) is abducted by Rawana (Holland) but she is subsequently rescued by Bujangga (Indonesian Youth). Performance of the play was obstructed by the Dutch colonial government and when Rustam published the play himself, it was proscribed.

Young literary dramatists such as Rustam and Mohammed Yamin, and those who belonged to the influential 1930s literary group, New Literati (Pujangga Baru), were pioneer writers in the newly proclaimed (1928) national language, Bahasa Indonesia. Collectively, they saw themselves as a beacon leading the nation towards the formation of a new culture. Their Western education had instilled in them progressive ideals, yet they were pulled towards fables of 'legendary and historical warriors' (*dongeng ksyatria*), gleaned from Indonesia's aristocratic classical literature. A leading figure of New Literati, Sanusi Pane, wove stories about imperious figures of the past in plays such as *Kertadjaja* (1932) and *Twilight of Majapahit* (*Sandhyakala Ning Majapahit*, 1933). But unlike Rustam's traditional hero, Sanusi's champions are flawed men, and vaguely tragic, surrendering either to fate or passion. Sanusi's ideal modern man, a synthesis of East and West, was raised in his only play with a contemporary setting (India), *New Man* (*Manusia Baru*, 1940). The most thoughtful play of the era was never performed.

Performance, however, was a main objective of the theatre company, Maya, formed by Usmar Ismail in 1944 at the close of the Japanese occupation. A literary intellectual and playwright cut in the same mould as the New Literati writers, Usmar was also a director and theatre professional. But this short tradition of professional modern theatre disappeared when Usmar turned to films in the 1950s, and was not revived again until the contemporary period.

In the 1950s, following Indonesia's independence in 1949, a proliferation of one-act plays pointed to two realities: firstly, the modest capacities of the playwrights; and secondly, the primary aim of writing plays was publication, preferably in literary magazines. Regarded as the father of Indonesian realistic drama, Utuy Tatang Sontani gained prominence because of his fecundity, deftness in creating verisimilitude, and his vision of the times. He wrote numerous one-act plays – one of the best-known, both in Indonesia and Malaysia, is *Awal and Mira* (*Awal dan Mira*, 1952) – and a few full-length dramas, that often alluded to that singular modern condition, alienation.

The inchoate in Indonesian realism was infused with a formal sensibility by the Indonesian National Academy of Theatre (Akademi Teater Nasional Indonesia, ATNI), instituted in 1955. The first modern theatre academy in Southeast Asia, ATNI taught Stanislavskian performance methods. Between 1955 and 1963, ATNI principally staged Western dramas, including MOLIÈRE, GOGOL, CHEKHOV and SARTRE. ATNI's choices reflected and reinforced theatre people's lack of confidence in indigenous modern plays. Nevertheless, ATNI raised the status of theatre in the national consciousness, and acted as a catalyst of increased theatre activity in major Indonesian towns and cities.

In the meantime, a doctrinaire 'socialist realism' in the arts was beginning to be preached in the late 1950s, following the ascendancy of the Indonesian Communist Party during President Sukarno's 'Guided Democracy' government. The aggressive promotion of the Marxist-Leninist line in the arts compelled neutrals and anti-communists to protect themselves against communist onslaughts, some surreptitiously supported by the army, the other major player in the Byzantine power game plaguing the late Sukarno era. The consequences were an intense politicization of and sectarianism in the arts, including modern theatre. Sukarno was discredited and the communists swept away in a holocaust of mass killings and arrests which followed an abortive coup against the generals on 30 September 1965. Soon after Suharto's New Order military government emerged in 1966, theatre too began to reveal a new visage.

In the growing mythology of contemporary Indonesian theatre, two persons are credited with its origins: W. S. Rendra and Arifin C. Noer. The watershed event was Rendra's staging of *Bip-Bop* in 1968. Nothing could have been more defiant of the literary, realistic theatre than this improvised and starkly non-verbal theatre exercise. Its principal resources – an ensemble of performers and a leader – collectively assembled a succession of non-linear images made up of movement and sound (natural and human and, occasionally, song). The overall impact of the piece was poetic, suggestive of a conflict between the mass and the individual – a theme that reverberated with political connotations in 1960s Indonesian society. Generously featured in the national press and on television, Rendra, also a considerable poet, soon rose in national perception to be a modern cultural hero. In subsequent years his communitarian-based company, Bengkel Teater Jogjakarta, staged Rendra's original plays, and various 'confrontations' with Western classics. Rendra, for example, transplanted the ambience of the Javanese folk theatre clowns into BECKETT's *Waiting for Godot* (*Menanti Godot*, 1969). SOPHOCLES' *Oedipus Rex* (1969) was mediated with a Balinese style of theatre, complete with Balinese MASKS and costumes.

Rendra's theatre became increasingly and explicitly political in the mid-1970s, as shown by the performances of *The Struggle of the Naga Tribe* (*Kisah Perjuangan Suku Naga*, 1974) and *District Secretary* (*Sekda*, 1977). Framed within Javanese *wayang kulit* shadow-theatre performance, the former warned that foreign exploitation, abetted by high-placed indigenous corruption, was jeopardizing the natural and harmonious order. From May to October 1978, Rendra was detained by the Indonesian authorities, and subsequently prohibited from public performance for seven years. In 1986 he returned to the stage with *Honourable Reso* (*Panembahan Reso*), a seven-hour event just two hours short of the traditional all-night *wayang kulit* performance. Staged in Jakarta's Senayan Stadium, the performance emphasized that Rendra, a charismatic actor with a unique Indonesian epic manner, is the only Asian avant-garde theatre personality who can command a mass audience cutting across age and class barriers.

Folk and popular theatre have also been Arifin Noer's resources in his explorations of a genuinely Indonesian theatre. His use of traditional sources is, however, informal, born of instinct and cunning, rather than of an *a priori* schema. He began his task with *Clouds* (*Mega-Mega*, 1964), and reached a momentary epiphany with *Moths* (*Kapai-Kapai*, 1970), which has become the best-known of all modern Southeast Asian plays. *Moths*' written text is as austere as a poem, but in its Jakarta premiere it was a multidimensional performance, profuse with non-linear events, crystallized by folk songs, children's games, irreverent popular-theatre comedy, topical commercial jingles and stylized movement. By so doing, Arifin wrested freedom from the thrall of the literary text. The relentless images revolved around the worker, Abu, whose plight was raised to spiritual and metaphysical heights by the performance strategy. (All of Arifin's contemporary plays focus on the spiritual vitiation of the underdog.) Mercurial juxtapositions of events and images were the means that opened up entry points to a reflexivity: juxtapositions between illusion and reality, sense and nonsense, TRAGEDY and COMEDY, horror and FARCE. In *Moths*, Arifin was the quintessential middleman, negotiating an autonomous status between Western and Asian theatre. The actor and playwright-director, Ikranagara, calls this stance 'postmodern'.

Throughout the 1970s, Arifin and his theatre group, Teater Kecil, forged ahead with a widely emulated style of play and performance. In 1985, after six years spent almost exclusively in film, Arifin staged *Interrogation or In the Shadow of God* (*Interogasi Atau Dalam Bayangan Tuhan*). His sense of play, provoking contrasts in tone and sensibility, was still intact. But he showed a renewed faith in story and verbal theatre. He explained that words, after all, are the last refuge of human contact in a world gone excessively rational and materialistic.

Once Putu Wijaya formed his theatre group, Teater Mandiri, in 1974, it was possible to talk of a 'Yogyakarta School of Contemporary Theatre'. (At separate times in the 1960s, both Arifin and Putu worked in Rendra's Yogyakarta theatre company.) Prominent also as an innovative and prolific novelist, Putu brought a posture of severe detachment to Indonesian contemporary theatre. Conventional characters were entirely absent on Putu's stage: his people appeared as dislocated beings in *Ouch* (*Aduh*, 1974) and *Insane* (*Edan*, 1973), dependent on the content of their dialogue to acquire 'character'. His evocation of the 'tragedy of language' made a mockery of human communication in plays titled *Dag-Dig-Dug* (1972) and *So and So* (*Anu*, 1974). Most of his plays present assemblies of contentious people caught in a state of shock or 'terror' over the power that mysterious individuals and happenings have on their lives, as in *Shit* (*Tai*, 1983). The sense of the mass on stage, initiated by Rendra, is amplified into a mortifying experience of paranoia. In contrast to his arid written texts, his performances, executed by a singularly stable and athletic ensemble, were as sensual, irrepressibly playful and grotesque as the Balinese folk theatre he imbibed as a high-born Balinese child. His last performance, *Front* (1985), however, also hinted at Putu's return to a narrative theatre.

In contrast, Teguh Karya, theatre director, film-maker and master of formal REALISM, has expanded his vocabulary of non-realistic gestures in recent performances staged by his group, Teater Popular. *Randai* Sumatran folk theatre was the informing style of his revival of GARCÍA LORCA's *Blood Wedding* (*Pernikahan Darah*, 1987). The Indonesian perception of Teguh as a prime mover of contemporary theatre is paradigmatic of the culture's plural and remarkably tolerant aesthetics. An ATNI product, Teguh, since his repertory days in the Bali Room of Hotel Indonesia (1968–72), gained fame and following mainly for his formalistic and finely wrought performances of Western dramas.

Direct contact with a 'concrete' audience is the root cause accounting for the ubiquitous 'rough and rude' (*kurang ajar*) humour characterizing much of contemporary Indonesian theatre. A specific audience, mostly young and numerically and geographically confined, was created in the 1970s, particularly in Jakarta's Ismail Marzuki Park (Taman Ismail Marzuki, TIM). TIM has been called 'the most successfully conceived arts centre in Asia'. Although financially supported by the Jakarta municipality, it is run by the artists themselves represented by their peers sitting on the Jakarta Arts Council (Dewan Kesenian Jakarta, DKD). Since 1968, TIM has housed a stable, diverse, innovative repertory of folk and popular theatre performances. TIM is also the mecca of regional contemporary theatres, notably those led by Wisran Hadi (Padang, Sumatra), and Suyatna Anirun (Bandung, Java). Conceived as a sanctuary of artistic freedom, TIM, however, has not been entirely immune from political interference. In the 1980s, TIM began to show signs of a creeping bureaucratization. Actually, TIM never fully recovered its glory days since the banning of Rendra and the prolonged absence of Arifin and Teguh due to film work.

In the 1990s the delicate equipoise between politics and the arts nurtured at TIM is threatened by the rise of liberal political parties. They represent a swelling middle class caused by the spread of education and economic stability under the New Order. Progressive cultural thinkers call for a socially 'contextual' literature and art. While TIM's leading lights, Arifin and Putu, have not demurred from contending with the social problems of poverty and oppression, their stance, shaped by the trauma of exces-sive politicization of the arts in the 1960s, is 'sly' and allusive while being responsible.

Teater Koma in Jakarta and Teater Gandrik in Yogyakarta exemplify the new shapes of theatre that emerged in the 1980s. Founded in 1977 by Nano Riantiarno, the former already has amassed new audiences from Jakarta's upper and middle classes. Teater Koma's 'operas', notably *The Cockroach Opera* (*Opera Kecoa*, 1985), reflect an accessible blend of Western rock and indigenous folk and popular performance applied to contemporary themes of poverty, slums, homosexuality and transvestism and to characters who live in the subterranean world of the dispossessed. Riantiarno's latest play, *Succession* (*Suksesi*, 1990), deals candidly with Indonesia's most controversial political issue – the succession to Suharto. Under the guise of folk *ketoprak* figures, he introduces extravagantly corrupt characters reminiscent of the president's family. The play was banned by the authorities in the midst of a hugely successful run in the Gedung Kesenian, Jakarta's newly renovated 'colonial' theatre.

Dwelling at the crossroads of town and country, Teater Gandrik leads a growing movement, centred in Java, that strives to inject contemporary theatre with the rural values of community through the malleable comic folk form of *dagalan mataram*. From its first performances in 1987, its style has been 'coarse', some of which seems to be erased in its most recent production, *Tree Spirit* (*Demit*, 1990). Gandrik's productions unveil the personal and political greed that lurks under the cover of commercial and intellectual pretence. (See also ASIAN AND PACIFIC ISLAND THEATRE.) KF

See: J. R. Brandon (ed.), *The Cambridge Guide to Asian Theatre*, Cambridge, 1993.

Inge, William (Motter) 1913–73 American playwright. Born in Independence, Kansas, and educated at the University of Kansas, he taught at Stephens College in Columbia, Missouri, and at Washington University in St Louis, and he toured for a season under canvas with a TOBY show; he was thus a product of mid-America, and his works reflected this background. On the strength of his first play, *Come Back Little Sheba* (1950), the critics touted Inge as having the promise to join ARTHUR MILLER and TENNESSEE WILLIAMS in a triumvirate of outstanding American dramatists. Although he never fulfilled that promise, he made considerable impact on American theatre with *Picnic* (1953), *Bus Stop* (1955) and *The Dark at the Top of the Stairs* (1957). Inge seemed to cherish his lonely characters: even as he laid bare their weaknesses, he surrounded them with love and understanding. He also recorded their speech with an accurate, appreciative ear. His later works, such as *A Loss of Roses* (1959), *Natural Affection* (1963) and *Where's Daddy?* (1966), drew neither critical acclaim nor much of an audience. He suffered from depression and alcoholism, and his death was by suicide. LDC

inner stage see DISCOVERY SPACE

inns as playhouses The yards of coaching inns were often used by touring players in 16th-century England. A simple trestle stage was set up along one side of a square or rectangular yard, and spectators accommodated in the first-floor walkways as well as in the yard itself. Innkeepers benefited from the extra custom, but the players probably had to rely on 'bottling' (taking a collection) for their remuneration. London inns known to have served as temporary playhouses include the Saracen's Head in Islington (first mentioned in 1557), the Bull in Bishopsgate and the Bell in Gracechurch Street, which were both used by QUEEN ELIZABETH'S MEN, and the Bel Savage in Ludgate (first mentioned in 1579). The Cross Keys in Gracechurch Street may have undergone some conversion for use by STRANGE'S MEN. It was no longer satisfactory for the increasingly professional companies to settle for bottling, once JAMES BURBAGE had demonstrated a safer way at the THEATRE. The public theatres of Elizabethan London had many features in common with inn yards, as the enterprising speculators who converted the BOAR'S HEAD near Aldgate (1597–9) and the RED BULL in Clerkenwell (1605) clearly knew. If Burbage used his experience of inns in planning the Theatre, they used their knowledge of theatres in planning the radical transformation of inns.   PT

Inter-Action Charitable trust founded in London by the American director, Ed Berman, in 1968, designed to be an umbrella organization for a variety of community activities, particularly concerned with theatre and play projects. Berman began with a little lunchtime theatre, the Ambiance in Queensway, West London, which put on new plays by mainly British and American authors, including TOM STOPPARD and ED BULLINS. When the lease ran out, the Ambiance moved to another short-term property and became the Almost Free in Piccadilly. At the main Inter-Action base in Kentish Town, North London, a bewildering range of little companies grew up around Berman – a Fun Art Bus, the Community Media Van, City Farm I (which created a farm in a city area), BARC (the British American Repertory Company), Professor Dogg's Troupe, Infilms (a professional film production company), Imprint (a small publishing house) and the International Institute for Social Enterprise. At one time, Inter-Action was considered to provide a model for inner-city community arts centres, an adventure playground primarily for adults but not excluding children.   JE

interlude The first recorded use of the term, at the beginning of the 14th century, is a theatrical one: in the title of the fragmentary English play of *The Clerk and the Girl* (*Interludium de Clerice et Puella*). It seems not to have been used elsewhere in Europe. During the 14th and 15th centuries it is applied to a variety of entertainments, some solo (e.g. the 1494 account of King Alfred disguised as a minstrel performing 'enterludes and songs' to the Danes). It is often associated with singing, but there are references which clearly indicate that it was also used of plays proper. The first-known named 'interlude' is MEDWALL's *Fulgens and Lucrece* (late 15th century), and during the 16th century it is used for any type of play: COMEDY, TRAGEDY, biblical play, MORALITY. It goes out of use in the later 17th century and was revived, as a critical term, by J. P. Collier to refer specifically to JOHN HEYWOOD's plays. It has since become a term for the miscellaneous, short, often comic, English plays of the first half of the 16th century.   PM

International Centre of Theatre Research see BROOK, PETER

International Popular Theatre Alliance see THIRD WORLD POPULAR THEATRE

International Theatre Institute UNESCO-based organization dedicated to furthering the cause of theatre world-wide. The ITI was founded in 1948 and is based in various national centres. Like many such organizations, it is a good idea in principle but has difficulties being as effective as it should be.   MB

Internationale Nieuwe Scene (New International Stage) Antwerp-based bilingual political theatre company founded in 1973. Its main theoretical influence is BRECHT; its main practical influence comes through personal and professional contact with DARIO FO and Arturo Corso. The company's first production was a reworking of Fo's *Mistero Buffo*, with the writer-actor's disquisitions on popular culture replaced by Flemish workers' songs. For preference the INS performs in a CIRCUS tent, whose connotations of popular entertainment and informal pleasure suit it better than a purpose-built theatre. The techniques of *COMMEDIA DELL'ARTE* are central to the company's work, in that they enable the actor to fulfil Brecht's criterion of showing rather than identifying with the character. However, their plays are in no sense archaeological exercises. The style (in itself impressively precise and imaginative) is one element in a thoroughly considered socialist aesthetic, seen at its most mature in *De Herkuls* (*Hercules*, 1980), a group-created piece about the life and work of dockers on the River Scheldt.   AEG

Ion of Chios d. c.422 BC Versatile Greek poet and prose author, noted for his tragedies, of which only meagre fragments survive. The author of the treatise *On the Sublime* ('Longinus') considered them faultless but lacking in the inspired boldness of SOPHOCLES. Ion knew Sophocles and AESCHYLUS and included anecdotes about them in his *Epidemiae*, a book of reminiscences.   ALB

Ionesco, Eugène 1909–94 French playwright. Ionesco was the child of separated parents, Romanian father and French mother; his youth was divided between France and Romania, but Paris was his home from before the Second World War until his death. His first play, *La Cantatrice chauve* (*The Bald Prima Donna*), was inspired by an English phrasebook, but when performed (directed by Nicolas Bataille, 1950) astonished its author by its comic force: he imagined he had written 'the tragedy of language'. A stream of one-act plays followed, e.g. *La Leçon* (*The Lesson*; directed by Cuvelier, 1951), *Les Chaises* (*The Chairs*; directed by Dhomme, 1952), which merit the author's epithet 'tragic farce'. In them language becomes reified and both physical and metaphysical elements fuse to generate strong concrete images of anguished mental states. Story-line, character and discussion are abandoned: events of a hallucinatory, surrealist quality take their place. With *Tueur sans gages* (*The Killer*, 1959) Ionesco wrote his first three-act play and his subsequent work, e.g. *Rhinoceros* (directed by BARRAULT, 1960) and *Le Roi se*

Ionesco's *The Chairs*,
Studio des Champs Elysées,
1956.

meurt (*Exit the King*; directed by Mauclair, 1962), was more conventional in form, returning to some of the dramatic traditions that his earlier work had castigated. Into a number of plays written during this period Ionesco introduced a character named Bérenger; naive, imaginative, alternately ecstatic and depressed for reasons he cannot identify, Bérenger is a transparently autobiographical figure and one with whom audiences could identify more easily than with the earlier, puppet-like figures.

In the 1960s Ionesco's plays were performed by companies all over the world, including the COMÉDIE-FRANÇAISE – *La Soif et la faim* (*Hunger and Thirst*, 1966). He was elected to the Académie-Française in 1970. Thereafter he was less prolific, writing memoirs and a novel. In 1981 a new play, *Voyages chez les morts* (*Journeys to the Homes of the Dead*), recaptured the hallucinatory quality of the early work using autobiographical material. It formed the basis of PLANCHON's massive biographical production *Ionesco*, starring Jean Carmet as the author, in 1982.   DB

Iran see MIDDLE EAST

Iraq see MIDDLE EAST

Ireland Literature in Irish – epic, saga and lyric – goes back some 1500 years, but in Gaelic culture there exists no equivalent to the European development of drama from the church to the secular stage. By the beginning of the 17th century the Gaelic social system, its aristocracy and culture had succumbed to increasingly efficient repres-

sion by the Tudor colonizers. In its place, 'the English born in Ireland', descendants of the original invaders, supplied the ruling class: an Anglo-Irish, Protestant ascendancy in a largely Catholic country.

The development of Irish theatre reflects these divisions. Theatres were built in Dublin, the first in 1637, and the more celebrated Smock Alley in 1662; and eventually in provincial towns. It was a colonial theatre: touring English companies gave English plays. In time, Irish players emerged – THOMAS DOGGETT (1660–1721), PEG WOFFINGTON (1714–60), CHARLES MACKLIN (1697–1797) – whose profession inevitably took them to London. This path was also followed by the Irish-born playwrights: FARQUHAR, GOLDSMITH, SHERIDAN, Murphy, O'Keeffe, BOUCICAULT, WILDE, SHAW. Their work is part of the English tradition, albeit constituting a separable thread within it.

A truly distinctive Irish drama began in 1897 with the conception of the Irish Literary Theatre by the poet W. B. YEATS, AUGUSTA LADY GREGORY and Edward Martyn. Though the enterprise allied itself with, in Douglas Hyde's phrase, 'the necessity for de-Anglicizing Ireland', it proposed a drama written mainly in Hibernicized English, versions of which had virtually replaced Gaelic as an authentic national speech; this medium would help create what the theatre's prospectus called 'a Celtic and Irish school of dramatic literature'. Lacking native models and contemptuous of English commercial theatre, the founders had quite divergent approaches to this end.

Lady Gregory's translations of Irish heroic legend and

peasant tales provided material for her own plays and many of Yeats's: images of Irish life to displace the caricatured 'stage Irishman' of the popular theatre. Yeats hoped to restore verse, and a poetic, non-realistic theatre to their bygone primacy: 'the theatre of SHAKESPEARE or rather perhaps of SOPHOCLES'. Martyn espoused the example of IBSEN. These divergent aesthetic purposes mattered less, perhaps, than the prospective audience's theatrically unsophisticated nationalism which, as a corrective to English disparagement, required of an Irish theatre flattering and idealized portrayals of Irish life and legend. The ILT's opening seasons (1899–1901) were a balance of its theories: heroic and pseudo-folk work from Yeats; Ibsenite socio-psychological drama such as Martyn's *The Heather Field* (1899); and peasant comedies like Douglas Hyde's one-acter, *The Twisting of the Rope* (1901). The possibilities had been shown; circumstances would direct their elaboration.

After Martyn's disgruntled withdrawal, Yeats, to solve the problem of having no native company to perform new Irish works, formed alliances with the brothers Frank and Willie Fay, enthusiastic amateurs with a strong commitment to the primacy of speech on stage, and with Maud Gonne's propagandist group the Daughters of Erin. The next year the Fays, Yeats, Lady Gregory and the newly recruited J. M. SYNGE formed the Irish National Theatre Society. When ANNIE HORNIMAN presented them with a permanent home in Abbey Street in 1904, it became the Irish National Theatre Society Ltd, commonly known as the ABBEY.

Among the first INTS presentations, most significant were PADRAIC COLUM's *Broken Soil* and J. M. Synge's *In the Shadow of the Glen* (1903). Though verse drama was still holding its own, Colum and Synge used prose as their medium to explore peasant life. They were both basically realist in staging, but Synge's prose was a dramatic rhetoric which stylized and elevated peasant speech, and Yeats recognized its enriching, poetic power. Colum's prose is less elaborately figured, and Yeats, deaf to its subdued poetry, saw it as colourless and common, incapable of any comprehensive range of expression. Colum, however, represented the future.

Irish drama had accepted the shape prescribed by the theatre available to it – the 19th-century proscenium stage – and Colum's successors established the dominance of the realist manner (see REALISM), a development that Yeats found 'a discouragement and a defeat'. Writers like WILLIAM BOYLE (*The Building Fund*, 1905), LENNOX ROBINSON (*The Clancy Name*, 1908) and T. C. MURRAY (*Birthright*, 1910) inaugurated a line of playwrights who wrote largely of rural and small-town life, took their subjects from contemporary social issues and employed a prose close to the common speech of their characters' real-life counterparts. With a couple of interesting exceptions – the strange fantasy plays of GEORGE FITZMAURICE (*The Pie-Dish*, 1908) and the verse plays of AUSTIN CLARKE (*The Son of Learning*, 1927) – the general run of Irish drama from the 1920s to the 50s was of that kind. This is not surprising. The granting of a state subsidy in 1925 had given the Abbey a pivotal role in Irish theatre. At the same time, the infamous *Silver Tassie* row in 1928 which led to O'Casey's self-imposed exile had arguably robbed the Irish

tradition of an individual genius who was to become a forceful exponent of European anti-naturalist forms. Abbey NATURALISM became the dominant mode of Irish theatre for almost 40 years.

Within that dominance, some dramatists' exploration of realist convention questioned its apparent solidity – as the early plays of SEAN O'CASEY (*The Shadow of a Gunman*, 1923) and DENIS JOHNSTON (*The Old Lady Says 'No'*, 1929) testify. In the work of these dramatists, language challenges the simply coded signals of a realist theatre, words assert their own primacy and create a rival world which may displace the world of facts, or alter it. This 'sovereignty of words' – Yeats's phrase – is pervasive in Irish drama as an assertion not only by the dramatists of an aesthetic principle but by their characters as a fact of life, a posture perfectly reflected in Denis Johnston's *The Old Lady*, when the Republican youth declares, 'We can make this country whatever we want it to be by saying so.'

That the dominant language used is English is itself a political consequence: displacing the mother tongue, it finds a sanction in its Gaelicized nature. In Irish drama, a language which is politicized turns to political matter. O'Casey's subjects are overtly so, as is much of Yeats, Johnston, and most recently BRIAN FRIEL. The realist work of GEORGE SHIELS (*Paul Twyning*, 1922) and PAUL VINCENT CARROLL (*Shadow and Substance*, 1937) centres on the social usages of post-independence Ireland and is implicitly political, and even SAMUEL BECKETT's desolate, unlocalized landscapes open fleetingly on an inheritance of ruined Irish hinterlands. These political reverberations are often muted, however – no equivalent to the public, post-BRECHTian politicization of British theatre, for instance.

The Abbey's role as the major nursery of new Irish writing was challenged though never superseded. Rivals, like the ULSTER LITERARY THEATRE (1904–34) or the Theatre of Ireland, were established and fell by the wayside, though the ULT did develop a Belfast variant on the Abbey style, imaginatively staging kitchen comedy and kitchen tragedy and developing the work of RUTHERFORD MAYNE. In Dublin only the GATE THEATRE (1928–) stayed the pace, but largely as a 'directors'' theatre, committed to a repertoire and a stagecraft more diversified and international than the Abbey's. Less ambitiously, Austin Clarke inaugurated his Lyric Theatre Company in Dublin in 1944 for occasional presentation of verse drama. Belfast acquired three companies: the Group Theatre, formed in 1940 through the amalgamation of three local companies, had a regional emphasis while also presenting classics of world theatre; the Arts Theatre, founded in 1950, presented studio productions of international drama; and Mary O'Malley's Lyric Theatre, founded in Belfast in 1951, shared some of the aims of the Arts in presenting world classics but gave a special place to verse drama, Yeats's specifically.

The contemporary scene The 1940s and early 50s were a dull period, enlivened by the work of M. J. MOLLOY and Louis D'Alton and by Alan Simpson's tiny Pike Theatre which staged BRENDAN BEHAN's *The Quare Fellow* (1954) and in 1955 shared the London premiere of Beckett's *Waiting for Godot*. Around the same time the recurrent attempts to create a Gaelic dramatic movement led to the opening in Dublin in 1956 of the Damer Theatre, where innovative and interesting work by writers like Sean O Tuama, Eoghan O Tuarisc and Cristoir O Floinn created a vision and generated a momentum which lasted for 10 or 15 years. (Brendan Behan's *The Hostage* was originally performed there as an Irish-language play, *An Giall*, in 1958.) But, despite individual talents, the revival did not reach critical mass and Gaelic drama is still only fitfully seen on the Irish stage.

These events did not redirect the mainstream of Irish drama but they were perhaps harbingers of the revival that would soon occur, when several elements conspired to broaden and intensify the scope of indigenous theatre considerably. The internationalization of Irish economic and cultural life in the early 1960s broke the isolationism of the previous 30 years and, on the heels of Behan, a generation of playwrights appeared – Brian Friel, TOM MURPHY, HUGH LEONARD and TOM KILROY – all individual in vision and international in theatrical awareness. Politics, and especially the pressures for change in the North, also had their impact: repeatedly the work of the newer dramatists shows, in domestic settings and individual lives, the instabilities of social and political inheritances no longer sure of themselves. Such patterns are directly evident in the work of SAM THOMPSON (*Over the Bridge*, 1960) and JOHN BOYD (*The Assassin*, 1969), and more obliquely so in Murphy (*A Whistle in the Dark*, 1961), EUGENE McCABE (*King of the Castle*, 1964), Friel (*Philadelphia, Here I Come!*, 1964), Kilroy (*The Death and Resurrection of Mr Roche*, 1968), where spiritual stresses reflect political futilities. The resurgent amateur theatre movement and the phenomenal strength and popular appeal of the work of JOHN B. KEANE – the latest in the line of pseudo-folk dramatists – added their own flavour to the stew. Finally, with the expanded role of the Arts Council from the 60s on, wider state subsidy encouraged the development of experimental, alternative theatre companies and forms, and of regional professional theatre.

Over the 20 years that followed, in Dublin alone, the Stanislavskian Focus Theatre grew in strength, the Project Arts Centre became a haven for experimental work, Rough Magic Theatre Company was established, the Gate Theatre underwent a transformation, and a group of young actors and writers established Passion Machine – a Northside company devoted to working-class plays by such as Roddy Doyle and Paul Mercier. A policy of regionalization in the late 1970s and early 80s helped establish professional companies in Galway (Druid Theatre), Cork (Cork Theatre Company), Derry (FIELD DAY THEATRE COMPANY), Limerick (Island Theatre Company) and Waterford (Red Kettle Theatre Company). Belfast saw the establishment of the highly innovative CHARABANC THEATRE COMPANY and, more recently, of Tinderbox Theatre Company. THEATRE-IN-EDUCATION and community arts were also fostered with the establishment of TEAM and Wet Paint Arts in Dublin, Graffiti in Cork, Replay in Belfast, and Macnas – a street theatre company – in Galway. All this, along with a host of experimental young companies, led to the hectic (and occasionally feverishly unhealthy) energy of Irish theatre in the 80s.

Encouraging and encouraged by that resurgence, a wave of new writing appeared. Major new works by established writers like Friel (*Translations*, 1980, and *Dancing at Lughnasa*, 1990) and Murphy (*The Gigli Concert*, 1983, and *Bailegangaire*, 1985) were one manifestation. But equally, the number, strength and diversity of the succeeding generation of playwrights – STEWART PARKER, TOM MACINTYRE, Bernard Farrell, FRANK McGUINNESS, SEBASTIAN BARRY, DERMOT BOLGER, Paul Mercier, BILLY ROCHE, Roddy Doyle, GRAHAM REID, CHRISTINA REID, BILL MORRISON, Marina Carr – have combined to make the last 15 years the most fruitful time in Irish theatre since the start of the century. It remains to be seen whether the companies, and the writers whose work they present, will survive the chill recessionary times of the early 1990s.

Irish drama has been a long experiment with the boundaries of realist theatre. Within those boundaries it seeks to introduce poetic transformations, beyond mere documentary paraphrase; it develops manners of presentation which are not discursive or sequential, which move away from literal portrayal towards modernist attitudes and methods. Although individual Irish dramatists have borrowed from other traditions and styles – Yeats from Japanese *NŌ* plays, Johnston and O'Casey from German EXPRESSIONISM, Friel from Russian NATURALISM, MacIntyre and Barry from American avant-garde – these are cavalier alliances within a self-sufficiency which continues to the present, informed by the sense of language as both reflecting and supplanting reality.

See: U. Ellis-Fermor, *The Irish Dramatic Movement*, rev. edn, London, 1954; D. E. S. Maxwell, *A Critical History of Modern Irish Drama 1891–1980*, Cambridge, 1984; K. Worth, *The Irish Drama of Europe from Yeats to Beckett*, Atlantic Highlands, 1978. DM GF

Ireland, William Henry 1775–1835 English forger. In 1794, desperate to please his father, Samuel Ireland, an obsessive idolizer of SHAKESPEARE, he began to forge legal documents with Shakespeare's signature. The papers early convinced a number of experts and other writers including BOADEN and Boswell, who knelt before them. Encouraged, Ireland went on to produce manuscripts of *King Lear*, part of *Hamlet* and a new play, *Vortigern*, which was accepted for production at DRURY LANE by SHERIDAN. Samuel Ireland published the documents as *Miscellaneous Papers* in 1795 but credulity had begun to wane, with Boaden now leading the attack. Two days before the first performance of *Vortigern* Edmond Malone, the most noted Shakespeare scholar of his day, published *An Inquiry into the Authenticity of Certain Miscellaneous Papers* which convincingly proved the forgery. *Vortigern* was performed on 2 April 1796, a day later than JOHN PHILIP KEMBLE had wickedly intended, and was a disaster – with Kemble delivering Ireland's line 'And when this solemn mockery is o'er' with calculated irony. Ireland's *Henry II*, another supposed Shakespeare play, was never performed. He admitted the fraud in his pamphlet *An Authentic Account*, but his father believed in the authenticity of the papers until his death. Ireland continued to write voluminously, but only one further play, *Mutius Scaevola* (1801), his best though unperformed. His full *Confessions* were published in 1805. PH

Henry Irving as Mathias in Leopold Lewis's *The Bells*:
'Take the rope from my neck…'

Irish Literary Theatre see Abbey Theatre

Irving, Henry [John Henry Brodribb] 1838–1905
English actor. Risking (and receiving) the disapproval of
his sternly Methodist Cornish relations, Irving escaped
from a London counting-house on to the professional
stage in 1856. For most of the next ten years he was a busy
provincial actor, notably in Edinburgh and Manchester,
distinguished from his colleagues only by the intensity of
his ambition. In 1866, he played in HANNAH COWLEY's *The
Belle's Stratagem* and BOUCICAULT's *Hunted Down* at the
St JAMES's with sufficient success to encourage him to stay
in London. He acted with ELLEN TERRY for the first time in
an 1867 revival of GARRICK's *Katharine and Petruchio*, but
it was his playing of Digby Grant in JAMES ALBERY's *Two
Roses* (1870) that gave the first sure indication of his idiosyncratic genius.

The American manager of the London LYCEUM, H. L.
BATEMAN, engaged Irving at a critical point in his theatre's
fortunes. As Jingle in Albery's *Pickwick* (1871), he was
asked to do little more than repeat Digby Grant, and the
public response was luke-warm. It was when Bateman
yielded to Irving's suggestion that they stage LEOPOLD
LEWIS's version of *Le Juif Polonais* that the fortunes of the
Lyceum changed decisively. *The Bells*, as Lewis agreed to
call it, gave Irving his first great part, that of the guilt-rid-
den burgomaster Mathias. It held a central place in
Irving's repertoire for the rest of his life. Secret guilt was
again the basis of his next major success, as Eugene Aram
in W. G. WILLS's indifferent play of that name (1873). In a

revival of EDWARD BULWER LYTTON's *Richelieu* (1873) it was
his embodiment of will-power that mesmerized audiences. His tender, sensitive Hamlet (1874) was an unexpected contrast, and the public had to be weaned before
accepting it as the generation's classic portrayal. It was in
the sinister and the aloof that they most readily recognized Irving – as Philip of Spain in TENNYSON's *Queen Mary*
(1876), as Richard III (1877), as the villainous Dubosc rather
than his virtuous double Lesurques in CHARLES READE's
version of *The Lyons Mail* (1877), as a coweringly senile
Louis XI in Boucicault's play and as Vanderdecken in the
Wills/Fitzgerald dilution of WAGNER's *The Flying
Dutchman* (1878).

At the end of 1878, Irving bought Bateman's widow out
of management of the Lyceum. For over 20 years he consecrated it as a temple to the actor's art, himself the high
priest. His first decision was to open with a revival of
Hamlet; his second, vastly more significant for the future,
was to invite Ellen Terry to play Ophelia. She, all grace,
charm and flowing lines, was aptly complementary to his
angular eccentricity. All their Shakespearian triumphs
were shared – Shylock and Portia (1879), Iago and
Desdemona (1881), Benedick and Beatrice (1882), Malvolio
and Viola (1884), Wolsey and Katherine of Aragon (1892),
Lear and Cordelia (1892), Iachimo and Imogen (1896). So
were their failures – Romeo and Juliet (1882), perhaps
Macbeth and Lady Macbeth (1888), certainly Coriolanus
and Volumnia (1901). Irving's SHAKESPEARE productions
were pictorially splendid and always embellished with
commissioned music. Sir Arthur Sullivan composed incidental music for *Macbeth*, Edward German for *Henry VIII*,
and the Lyceum musical directors (Hamilton Clarke,
1878–81, and Meredith Ball, 1881–99) provided overtures
as well as musical effects. Impressed by the staging techniques of the MEININGEN players at DRURY LANE in 1881,
Irving became a master of crowd scenes. In addition to his
resident designers, Hawes Craven and Joseph Harker, he
employed such luminaries as Alma-Tadema, Edwin Abbey
and Burne-Jones. There was a regular orchestra of 30 at the
Lyceum (35 for the lavish production of Wills's *Faust* (1885)
together with a chorus of 43 in the Brocken scene) and the
payroll for *Robespierre* (1899) amounted to a staggering
639, comprising 355 performers and musicians, 236 technical staff and 48 administrators and their assistants.

Despite his reputation as an interpreter of Shakespeare
and the intellectual leader of his profession, Irving was
primarily a showman, quite as likely to stage a tired MELO-
DRAMA like Watts Phillips's *The Dead Heart* (1889) as a classic revival, provided only that it contained a part in which
he could startle audiences. It was for this reason that he
selected Mephistopheles in Wills's shoddy *Faust*, the dual
role of Fabien and Louis dei Franchi in Boucicault's *The
Corsican Brothers* (1880) and the title role in Tennyson's
Becket (1893). GEORGE BERNARD SHAW's repeated complaints that Irving did nothing to advance the English
drama are just, not least because no other man was better
placed to do so. It was acting that interested Irving, not
writing. To that extent, he earned the knighthood
bestowed on him in 1895, the first actor to be so honoured.

Irving's two sons (his marriage to Florence O'Callaghan,
though maintained in name, formally ended in 1871) were
both active in the theatre. The elder, Henry, known as H. B.

Irving (1870–1919), made his debut in 1891, eventually forming his own company in 1906 and touring in many of his father's famous parts. His wife, Dorothea Baird (1875–1933), who had shot to fame as the creator of George Du Maurier's Trilby in 1895, was a member of the company until her retirement in 1913. Irving's younger son, Laurence (1871–1914), had aspirations as a playwright as well as an actor. There was some parental indulgence in the staging at the Lyceum of his unwieldy epic, *Peter the Great* (1898), and his adaptation of SARDOU's *Robespierre* (1899), but much was left unrealized when he was drowned in a shipwreck on the way to Canada. H. B. Irving's son, Laurence (1897–1983), was a regular designer for stage and films (he designed the first London production of T. S. ELIOT's *Murder in the Cathedral* (1935)), and the author of an excellent biography of his grandfather (1951) and an account of the family's subsequent history, *The Successors* (1967). PT

Irwin, Bill 1950– American actor, entertainer and playwright, the best known among disparate practitioners of the so-called NEW VAUDEVILLE. These performers focus on the creation, often in collaboration, of theatre works that draw upon American popular entertainment traditions, from the CIRCUS to VAUDEVILLE and experimental theatre techniques. Like others in this group, Irwin attempts to make innovative use of his CLOWN skills to create exciting visual metaphors for the broader actions and emotions of a play. He moved from conventional theatre training at the University of California at Los Angeles to experimental theatre training with HERBERT BLAU at Oberlin College, to the Ringling Brothers Clown College, the Pickle Family Circus and the avant-garde Oberlin Dance Collective before evolving what Ron Jenkins, a former circus clown, calls Irwin's 'metaphysical slapstick'. Irwin's first major New York vehicle was *The Regard of Flight*, played elsewhere before and after its 1982 performance at the AMERICAN PLACE THEATRE. This production effectively and comedically satirized the so-called new, postmodern theatre. It also established his stage persona of the beleaguered but resilient all-American, a character that he uses often.

Other appearances include *The Courtroom*; *Waiting for Godot* (a memorable Lucky at Lincoln Center in 1988); *Accidental Death of an Anarchist*; his Tony-nominated performance as 'Post-Modern Hoofer' in his nonverbal *Largely New York* (1989), which he also directed and choreographed, and for which he received a special citation from the New York Drama Critics' Circle; BECKETT's *Texts for Nothing* (1992; 1993 *Village Voice* Obie); and the clown show *Fool Moon* (special 1993 Outer Critics' Circle Award) with David Shiner, former star of Cirque du Soleil. In 1984 he became the first American performing artist to receive the prestigious MacArthur Foundation Fellowship. DBW

Irwin, May [Georgia or Ada Campbell] 1862–1938 Canadian-born actress. Dubbed 'secretary of laughter' in the 1910s by Woodrow Wilson, she began her career singing duets with her sister Flo at the Adelphi Theatre, Buffalo, New York (1875). By January 1877 they were stock members of TONY PASTOR's Music Hall company, remaining six years. In 1883 May joined AUGUSTIN DALY as a legiti-

mate actress, leaving in 1887 and returning to the legitimate stage only briefly in 1893 under CHARLES FROHMAN. The balance of her career was devoted to FARCE comedies with music. She reached star status in *The Widow Jones* (1895), and offered a series of comedies under her own management in the 1910s. A plump, jolly blonde, known for her rollicking exuberance, she introduced such popular songs as 'A Hot Time in the Old Town' and 'I'm Looking for de Bully' (in the style later known as Negro ragtime). She retired in 1922. DBW

Isaacs, Edith J(uliet) R(ich) 1878–1956 American editor and critic. Born and educated in Milwaukee, Wisconsin, Isaacs began her writing career as a reporter and later literary editor for the Milwaukee *Sentinel* before moving to New York in 1904 to marry and begin a family. She was a drama critic for *Ainslee's Magazine* and a freelance writer before joining the editorial board of *Theatre Arts [Monthly]* 1918. During 1922–46 she served as editor (and majority stockholder), moving the magazine from quarterly to monthly (1924) and featuring prominent new artists each month, such as EUGENE O'NEILL and ROBERT EDMOND JONES. She was actively involved in establishing the National Theatre Conference (1925), the AMERICAN NATIONAL THEATRE AND ACADEMY (1935), and the FEDERAL THEATRE PROJECT (1935–9) because she believed in a national theatre. TLM

Isherwood, Christopher 1904–86 British novelist and dramatist. Isherwood collaborated with W. H. AUDEN between 1935 and 1938 on the series of expressionistic verse plays (see EXPRESSIONISM) that established the reputation of the London GROUP THEATRE – *The Dog Beneath the Skin*, *The Ascent of F6* and *On the Frontier*. His novel *Goodbye to Berlin* (1939) won the New York Drama Critics Circle Award in the dramatization by JOHN VAN DRUTEN, *I Am a Camera*, and formed the basis for the film *Cabaret* (1966). Moving to Hollywood in 1940, he became an American citizen in 1946. CI

Isola brothers French impresarios **Émile** (1860–1945) and **Vincent** (1862–1947), who began as conjurors in their native Algeria and made a Parisian debut at the FOLIES-BERGÈRE in 1892 in a thought-transference act. That same year they founded the Théâtre Isola and were hailed for such illusions as 'The Muscovite Trunk'. Succumbing to competition, they gave up magic to become the managers of, in succession, Parisiana, the Olympia, the Folies-Bergère, the Gaieté-Lyrique, the Opéra-Comique (for 12 years), the Mogador and the Théâtre Sarah-Bernhardt, which they ran with taste and acumen. Failing to create a MUSIC-HALL monopoly after the British model and losing their money in the Depression, they returned to MAGIC. Vincent, with his aristocratic profile and monocle, presented grand illusions, while Émile specialized in shows of dexterity with cards and scarves. LS

Israel see HEBREW THEATRE

Italy (See also MEDIEVAL DRAMA IN EUROPE (Italy).) One of the difficulties in writing about Italian theatre is that until the middle of the 19th century Italy existed as a geographical, but not as a social or political, entity. Administrative divisions were reinforced by cultural and linguistic divisions: regional associations were strong; local customs, habits and assumptions informed most modes of artistic expression; and in the absence of an established national language, dialects like Neapolitan and Venetian enjoyed the status of quasi-independent languages with their own distinctive popular literatures. Conditions, then, for theatre differed quite considerably from region to region in terms of the pace of development, shaping influences, and even the organizational structures and kinds of innovation. No city in Italy enjoyed a status comparable to London or Paris as the administrative and cultural centre, and although Rome was made the national capital in 1870, the extent to which it is the *cultural* capital would even today be much disputed.

This political and cultural fragmentation in large measure accounts for one of the enduring features of much theatre in Italy since the formation of the professional acting companies, the COMMEDIA DELL'ARTE, in the mid-16th century: itinerancy. For all that many of the major troupes of the 17th and early 18th centuries turned regional differences and enforced travelling somewhat to their advantage, cultural divisions and the nomadic life endured by most theatre professionals were for long, and increasingly in the 19th and early 20th centuries, seen as artistically and economically debilitating, frustrating the development of a national drama and an effective organizational structure. Foreign political presences in the peninsula, too, helped to make the drama unduly dependent upon, or the more readily influenced by, foreign literary and dramatic norms – French cultural hegemony, in particular, being strong from the mid-17th century to at least the mid-19th.

Yet if the Italian theatre produced no significant body of dramatic literature, save for brief efflorescences at the early cinquecento courts, in settecento Venice and in the early 20th century, it was for long technically the most original in Europe. Renaissance Italy may not unreasonably be called the seeding-ground of the modern European theatre, breeding the genres of TRAGICOMEDY and PASTORAL, *OPERA SERIA* and *OPERA BUFFA*, and effecting a radical revolution in staging conventions, scenic design and theatre building. In the improvised drama, too, it produced an altogether unique actor-based theatre. Italian predominance in most of these fields remained supreme for more than two centuries and was widely influential throughout Europe, all the more so perhaps as the rapid economic decline of the peninsula during the 17th century helped to drive much of its most original talent abroad. Modest as has been Italy's contribution to European dramatic literature, in the arts and crafts of stage show perhaps no theatre in Europe since the Renaissance has been so consistently innovative for so long.

The Renaissance

The humanist theatre Post-quattrocento drama and theatre were in large measure shaped by the Renaissance rediscovery of ancient Greek and Roman achievement (see GREECE, ANCIENT; ROME). Medieval literary example and stage materials were not wholly ignored, but the work of humanist scholars and enthusiasts in the 15th century, aided by the invention of the printing press and the growth of aristocratic patronage, proved decisive. A new and keen interest in classical models and ancient authority was generated as work unknown to the Middle Ages increasingly came to light: the first edition of TERENCE's plays was printed in 1470, the first collected edition of PLAUTUS in 1472. Printing permitted the wide dissemination of texts, and this in turn encouraged stage production and translation.

Production inevitably generated curiosity about classical theatre structures and staging practices, a curiosity all the more excited by the publication of Vitruvius' study of ancient theatres, *De Architectura* (particularly in the Barbaro translation of 1567), while the ready availability of printed editions of HORACE's *Ars Poetica* and ARISTOTLE's *Poetics* raised questions about dramatic structure and composition. Rediscovery of the ancients was not just locally seminal, but of European-wide significance, and it came gradually to permeate all fields of drama and theatre – although in some countries, notably England, the Reformation prevented the new classicism from gaining a secure hold. In Italy it tended to license academicism.

The vernacular drama Nowhere was the dead hand of classical imitation more icily felt than on drama of tragic emphasis. Numerous tragedies were written in the vernacular during the period, and some were performed, but none has survived for other than historical reasons. The first regular Italian tragedy was TRISSINO's *Sofonisba* (1515), tightly organized on Greek lines in its observance of the three unities and use of chorus, song and spectacle, but artificially rhetorical and inert. So too is GIRALDI's *Orbecche*, first performed in 1541. It established the motives of SENECAN tragedy as fit for the cinquecento stage, initiating a vogue for revenge plots widely influential beyond Italy. One of the best of the 15th-century Italian tragedies, ARETINO's *Orazia* (1546), points up the limitations of TRAGEDY in this period: even though it jettisons some of the classical trappings, like the chorus, and is effectively plotted to achieve an unusual happy ending, it is stilted, remote and unfelt.

With COMEDY the case was somewhat different. Its structures, dramatic strategies, and some of its materials were likewise drawn from classical precedent, particularly Plautus and Terence. But classical precedent gave comic dramatists more freedom in their choice and use of language and subject-matter, and although nearly all the comedies of the period are of historical interest only – like, for example, two of the first Italian vernacular comedies, ARIOSTO's *La cassaria* (*The Chest*, 1508) and *I suppositi* (*The Supposes*, 1509) – several, like Bibbiena's (Bernardo Dovizi's) *La Calandria* (*The Follies of Calendro*, 1521) and MACHIAVELLI's *La mandragola* (*The Mandragola*, c.1518), had their roots in contemporary Italian life. The pool of stock classical characters was enriched by figures more particular to the age, like the devious priest, the hypocritical pedant and the sham doctor.

Machiavelli's play well illustrates this fruitful mingling of classical and more indigenous materials: its plot turns on a folk motif, and the stock Latin types, like the young people, the *senex* and the *servus*, are augmented by more distinctively Renaissance figures such as an accommodating friar. In its language, mocking wit, local reference and amoral tone *La Mandragola* is very much a comedy of its age, as too are the best comedies of Aretino, such as *La cortigiana* (*The Courtesan*, 1525) and *Il marescalco* (*The Stablemaster*, 1527), plays both picaresque and vibrant of local street life. Occasionally revived too on the modern Italian stage is the anonymous *La Venexiana*, a cutting and earthy low-life comedy written about 1550 mainly in the Venetian dialect. In the second half of the 16th century the quality of scripted comedy markedly declined. Only one play is occasionally revived today: *Il candelaio* (*The Candle Maker*, 1582), a tough, bitter comedy not performed in Italy in its own day, and the sole play by the greatest Italian philosopher of the age, GIORDANO BRUNO.

The drama so far mentioned was for the most part literary, was played in socially exclusive cultural centres and was often acted by amateurs. Since the 18th century many scholars have for convenience classified this drama as the *commedia erudita*, to distinguish it from the *commedia dell'arte*, acted by professional players in a wide range of performance venues, from the streets and squares of towns, to halls and the formal theatres of royalty and nobility. And here must be mentioned a drama that does not fall easily into either the *erudita* or the *dell'arte* category: the work of dramatists who wrote dialect comedies distinctive for their use of peasant characters or familiar local types. The 'popular' nature of their materials has encouraged some to see in their plays anticipations of the *commedia dell'arte*. Among these dramatists ANDREA CALMO acted as well as wrote, employed a wide range of dialect-speaking characters and developed a Venetian stage *vecchio* somewhat akin to the later Pantalone of the improvised comedy. But by far the most impressive writer of rustic comedy was Angelo Beolco, again an actor as well as a dramatist, who was known by the name of one of his stage characters, the boisterous peasant RUZZANTE. Beolco's plays have a vitality wanting in much cinquecento literary comedy, and express, though without any self-conscious didacticism, a sympathy and concern for the habits, pleasures and hardships of poor country people.

Virtually at the opposite pole to this rustic comedy, in content, organization, characterization and verbal tone, was the PASTORAL drama that enjoyed a remarkable vogue in Italy, and indeed throughout Europe, for at least a century and a half after its first tentative appearance with the *Orfeo* of Angelo Poliziano (1454–94) in 1480. Although many pastoral plays were written and produced in Italy in the 16th and 17th centuries, only two now merit serious consideration: TORQUATO TASSO's rich and complex masterpiece, the *Aminta*, first performed in 1573, and GIOVAN BATTISTA GUARINI's *Il pastor fido* (*The Faithful Shepherd*, 1590), a tragicomic pastoral highly influential throughout Europe for its subject-matter, its emotional and verbal extravagance, and the critical justification Guarini gave for his use of the tragicomic form. Aside from the influence that Tasso and Guarini exercised on the development of pastoral drama proper, their refinements of the form contributed significantly to the later development of other dramatic kinds, including MELODRAMA, tragicomedy, the French *ballet de cour* and, however indirectly, the English court MASQUE.

Sixteenth- and early-17th-century festivals, staging and theatres Italian Renaissance festivals had their roots deep in medieval religious drama, pageant and display, but came increasingly in the second half of the 15th century to be organized under the aegis of the courts, concerned symbolically to affirm their status and authority in public and private entertainments. Such festivals, whether devised to celebrate CARNIVAL, or visits by foreign dignitaries, or the baptisms or nuptials of members of the nobility, provided the occasion for the staging of plays, both scripted and improvised. Prodigious sums were spent on these entertainments, which might spread over days or weeks and were expressly designed to serve social and political purposes: whether public or private they demonstrated the wealth, generosity and influence of a patron, or of a ruler; they were used to assert political authority, underscore independence, affirm allegiances, or orchestrate possible new alliances.

The late-16th-century master of Florentine spectacle was BERNARDO BUONTALENTI: the six *intermezzo* designs he did in 1589 for a play, *La pellegrina*, indicate something of the high quality of his work. His successor at the Medici court was GIULIO PARIGI, responsible for such major shows as that of 1608, which included striking *intermezzo* designs for Buonarroti's *Il giudizio di Paride* (*The Judgement of Paris*) and for the elegant equestrian ballet, *La guerra d'amore* (*The War of Love*, 1615). Parigi's designs, not least through the wide dissemination of festival books, which included engravings of the shows and descriptive accounts pointing up the symbolic content of the elaborate decorations, exercised wide influence beyond Florence, notably on the work of INIGO JONES in England. Many were engraved by the Frenchman Jacques Callot who worked at the Medici court until 1621, and designed too for plays like Bonarelli's *Il Solimano* (1619).

Surviving illustrative material is most rich for the *feste* in Florence, but sumptuous shows were also mounted in many other major Italian cities during the period, most frequently and strikingly perhaps in Venice and Rome. It is records of these aristocratic festivals and processions which for the most part have survived; but the richness and abundance of these, and the fact that they often appealed to and addressed all social levels, should not conceal the continuing importance of more expressly popular festivals, like weddings and May Day revels, a distinctive and socially significant feature not just of the major cities, but of towns and villages.

The theatre of the festivals came in due course to contribute to a fundamental shift in staging conventions, from the multiple fixed or perambulatory stagings of the medieval drama, to the presentation of a play in a purpose-built theatre with end-stage and picture-framed perspective changeable settings. Recourse to perspective for stage settings had its roots in the work of quattrocento painters, and was furthered by the theoretical inquiries of the humanist academies. The first description we have of a perspective setting is of Pellegrino da Udine's set for Ariosto's *La cassaria* done at Ferrara in 1508. Other plays known to have been performed with painted settings in the early cinquecento include Bibbiena's *La Calandria* (1513 in Urbino, and 1514 in Rome), Ariosto's *I suppositi* (1519 in Rome) and Machiavelli's *La mandragola* and

Clizia (1521 and 1526 respectively in Florence). Early designers included Raphael, Andrea del Sarto, BASTIANO DA SANGALLO, BALDASSARE PERUZZI and SEBASTIANO SERLIO, the second book of whose *Dell'architettura* (Paris, 1545) treated of theatres, stage effects and settings – notably, the comic, the tragic and the pastoral (strictly, the satyric).

Perspective settings gave an illusion of depth and enhanced the three-dimensionality of the stage picture. Serlio's settings were achieved by spacing pairs of fixed angled wings at regular intervals on a raked stage, their painted fronts and the diminishing size of the wings at the rear of the scenic area, together with a painted back cloth, simulating distance. Later in the 16th century, such wings were set in continuous perspective. Perspective effects were also achieved by use of *periaktoi*: prisms with painted surfaces which could be rotated from face to face. Perspective settings were the response to a need generated by the new drama to establish unity of place for the stage action. That response, by focusing spectator attention on the action within and before a stage picture, made particular demands of the spectator, and turned the play in performance into a special event, while the special nature of the event came to require in its turn particular conditions of presentation.

Early stages were temporary wooden structures set up in courtyards or halls. Performance places in the courts, like those of say Florence, Mantua and Parma, were often decorated with tapestries and hangings, and were enhanced by diverse lighting effects. Elsewhere, however, as in the semi-private play performances given by Ruzzante, Calmo and others in the early decades of the 16th century around Padua and Venice, the venues were undoubtedly more modest in ambience and decoration. Permanent theatre buildings, the first known of which was that devised by Ariosto in 1531 at the Ferrarese court, were mainly a development of the second half of the century. Theatres were built at Mantua and Sienna, and in 1585–6 Buontalenti erected a permanent theatre in the Uffizi at Florence. By then the most famous of the Italian Renaissance theatres had been completed: the Teatro Olimpico at Vicenza, begun by PALLADIO in 1579 and finished according to his design by his pupil VINCENZO SCAMOZZI; with its permanent *scaenae frons* it stands rather apart from the main thrust of later Italian development, which was to favour the end-stage, housing changeable perspective scenery boxed behind a picture-frame proscenium. That direction was partly foreshadowed in 1588 when Scamozzi undertook the building of a small court theatre at Sabbioneta for the Duke of Mantua, moving the fixed architectural perspective behind a single arch that took in the entire stage opening.

The 17th century

Melodramma The last decade of the 16th century saw the beginnings of theatrical baroque and its most characteristic dramatic form, *melodramma*, or drama with music. The origins of *melodramma*, first called *opera* by the composer Pietro Francesco Cavalli (1602–76), are much disputed, but the form *sui generis* evolved gradually and in complex ways from a variety of theatrical kinds: from the musical spectacle that was an element of the *sacre rappre-*

sentazioni, from the *intermezzi* of music, dance and scenic display which punctuated the acts of plays given at courts, and which gradually became semi-independent entertainments; from the pastoral drama, in which music, dance, decoration and verbal lyricism were distinctive features; and from attempts by scholars and musicians to revive the musical dimension of classical staging.

Important beginnings were in Florence, but OPERA developed apace at Mantua where Monteverdi, *maestro di cappella* to the Gonzagas, composed *Orfeo* in 1607 and *Arianna* in 1608. The success of opera rapidly spread to other Italian courts; nor was its appeal confined to the social and cultural elites: the first public performances of opera were given in 1637 at the Teatro di San Cassiano in Venice; Monteverdi's *L'incoronazione di Poppea* inaugurated the opera house in Naples in 1651; houses were soon opened in other major cities throughout the peninsula. The rapid advance of opera offered stiff competition to the improvised drama and, indeed, with the exception of brief periods when the regular theatre temporarily flourished, was to constitute perhaps the most signal Italian contribution to European theatrical life until well into the 20th century.

Scenic design and theatre buildings The baroque theatre was pre-eminently one of expensive show and scenic marvels. In the early 17th century angle wing sets were displaced by sliding flat wings and back shutters, again spaced and painted for perspective effect, but now slotted through the stage floor and fixed to wheeled carriages which ran on rails under the stage. These movable 'flats' gave opportunity for increasingly sophisticated scenic changes. Increasingly elaborate ways of varying the settings were complemented by the rapid development of stage machinery, notably cloud machines and flying devices which could raise, lower or transport across the stage whole groups of performers or choirs of celestial beings. Ever more refined, too, were the mechanical contrivances for moving dragons, birds, chariots and ships, and for simulating storms at sea, cities on fire and disturbances in the heavens.

The early development of sliding flat wings is usually ascribed to GIOVANNI BATTISTA ALEOTTI. They were further developed by practitioners like Alfonso Parigi at Florence and, notably, GIACOMO TORELLI who in Venice and elsewhere developed an integrated wheel and roller system that allowed a single stage machinist to effect the synchronized movement of whole sets of wings and shutters. In 1645 Torelli translated his skills to the French court; he was but one of many Italian architects, designers and machinists who dominated baroque theatre throughout Europe, nowhere more so perhaps than in Vienna where particularly outstanding work was done by the Burnacini. Italian staging techniques, already disseminated by these native artists abroad, were further spread by technical treatises and handbooks, the most celebrated of the latter being NICOLA SABBATTINI's *Practica di fabricar scene e machine ne'teatri* (1638).

Aleotti is said to have first employed flat wings in 1618 at the magnificent theatre he built in Parma, the Teatro Farnese. This playhouse combined elements of the old and the new: its architectural *scaenae frons* formed an elaborate, decorated proscenium frame for the deep, square single stage opening within which eight or more sets of wings and shutters could be housed. It prefigures what was to become the basic shape of later baroque and 18th-century playhouses. As in the previous century, the construction of theatres, temporary or permanent, continued to be in the charge of distinguished engineers, designers and architects, among them the greatest artist of the age, BERNINI, and by 1650 many Italian courts could boast permanent theatres. But theatres were not built exclusively for courts and the elite. The public presentation of opera at the San Cassiano in Venice generated the development there of many public theatres. Both in Venice and elsewhere the design of public theatres posed architects special problems, not least in the need to increase seating and to provide social segregation. Traditional performance places, too, were refashioned into fully fledged permanent theatres, as was an erstwhile inn, the Teatro Falcone in Genoa (1653).

The drama If Italian *melodramma*, scenography and stage mechanics could scarcely be rivalled elsewhere in Europe during the 17th century, as much cannot be said for Italian scripted drama. The only dramatist of any real note was GIOVAN BATTISTA ANDREINI, and he is perhaps significant more as a resourceful *homme du théâtre* than as a playwright proper. A capable actor and leader of the FEDELI troupe, in addition to his religious verse pieces, the *Adamo* (1613) and *Maddalena* (1617), he wrote tragedies and comedies which exploited ingenious stagecraft, striking *coups de théâtre* and fresh reworkings of stock materials. Although his comedy-tragedy-pastoral novelty *La centaura* (1622) and the dramaturgically interesting if facilely bawdy comic play-within-a-play, *Le due commedie in commedia* (*Two Plays within a Play*, 1623), have been revived in the modern theatre, like his other plays, which included *Lo schiavetto* (*The Little Slave*, 1612) and *L'Amor nello specchio* (*Love in the Mirror*, 1622), they survive essentially as historical curiosities. Much the same must be said of the work of Michelangelo Buonarroti (1568–1646), whose plays reflect his concern less with the theatrically viable than with the variety of Italian dialects – nowhere more so than in the monstrously lengthy *La fiera* (*The Fair*) performed in 1618, a comedy in five parts, each part of five acts, that treats of the multitude of types and social groups who swarm in the play's fairground setting.

The extent to which Buonarroti's academician interests conditioned his dramatic writing is a fair measure of the extent to which virtually all 17th-century Italian scripted drama was governed by extra-theatrical considerations, to the detriment of authentic dramatic life. Vitality in drama lay elsewhere, at least during the early decades of the century, with the work of the improvising players. Increasingly in the course of the century, however, the major companies travelled abroad, as if in search of markets no longer so readily available at home. The increasing popularity of opera may have contributed to that decline. Whatever the causes, by mid-century no further records are found in Italy of the great troupes of the early decades – the UNITI, the ACCESI, the CONFIDENTI and the Fedeli.

The 18th century
Early-18th-century developments Well before the end of the 17th century the Italian theatre had become debilitatingly a prisoner of French influences: Paris drew off much of its best acting and scenographic talent, and French literary example and theatrical precepts strongly conditioned scripted drama. In the early 1700s the actor-manager LUIGI RICCOBONI made earnest but largely abortive attempts to reform the theatrical climate by touring a quality repertoire including the best serious Italian play of the early and mid-18th century, MAFFEI's *Merope* (1713). But although the Riccoboni troupe achieved a certain *succès d'estime*, it made little perceptible impact on the generally moribund Italian regular stage.

The lyric stage, however, remained very much alive, and produced a new theatrical form: *opera buffa*, or comic opera. Although the roots of *buffa* are hard to trace, a convenient *terminus a quo* is the decision in 1709 of the ailing Teatro dei Fiorentini in Naples to mount a season of comic musical entertainments in dialect. Gradually other cities took up the idea, if without the same emphasis on dialect and broad popular appeal, and with greater refinement of means in performance and presentation. Comic opera came quickly to appeal at all social levels. *Opera seria*, meanwhile, had been reformed by Zeno and others at the end of the 17th century according to French-inspired neoclassical notions of artistic decorum. The greatest serious librettist of the 18th century, METASTASIO (Pietro Trapassi), took advantage of this reform to secure an international reputation as a poet and dramatist. Classical in spirit and subject-matter, the best of his work is fluent, mellifluous and skilfully crafted for theatrical effect.

In another regard opera was particularly important. The 18th century in Italy saw the emergence of the fully fledged professional dramatist who worked for the most part independent of patronage. The market for opera librettos was considerable and paid better than did writing for the regular theatre. It is no accident that CARLO GOLDONI, the first major Italian professional dramatist, wrote for *opera seria* and *buffa* throughout his working life. Opera had become an important part of the entertainment business, most obviously in a tourist city like Venice.

The Venetian theatre By the early 18th century Venice had about 14 active theatres, of which some 7 were in regular commercial competition. Musical drama of course predominated, at theatres like the San Giovanni Grisostomo and the San Benedetto, but in the middle decades of the century several dramatists revitalized the Venetian regular theatre. One was PIETRO CHIARI, a tough and combative polemicist with a sharp eye for the immediately effective. Another was the aristocrat CARLO GOZZI, who sought to revivify the debilitated professional improvised comedy, the *commedia dell'arte*, in his *fiabe* – or fable plays – part-scripted, part-improvised. These enjoyed great success in the 1760s and some survive on European stages today, like *Il re cervo* (*The King Stag*) and *La donna serpente* (*The Snake Woman*). A third was their slightly older and decidedly greater contemporary, Carlo Goldoni.

Goldoni is important for his decisive reform of comedy: a reformation that entailed disciplining the crude and self-indulgent licence of the *commedia dell'arte* improvising players and reasserting the role of the dramatist in the Italian theatre. In the course of his career Goldoni essayed many kinds of comic play: 'low' comedy, comedy of middle- and upper-class life, comedy with a bias towards intrigue or towards character delineation, and tragicomedy that exploited the romantic, remote and mysterious settings of the Orient or the Americas. In many of his finest plays he gradually evolved a drama of character and manners with a certain emphasis on naturalistic depiction of persons and place, particularly in the Venetian dialect plays such as *Il Campiello* (*The Little Square*, 1756), *Le baruffe chiozzotte* (*The Chioggian Squabbles*, 1760) and *I rusteghi* (*The Boors*, 1760). But although his best drama is rooted in a recognizably Venetian social milieu, the determining influence remained the theatrical dimension. He was always a dramatist, never a mere documentarist. Much of his liveliest comedy, including *Arlecchino, servitore di due padroni* (*The Servant of Two Masters*), *Due gemelli veneziani* (*The Venetian Twins*) and *Il ventaglio* (*The Fan*), is distinguished by a highly developed sense of theatrical craftsmanship, learnt in his apprentice years in the theatre when he provided scenarios for masked improvisers.

The century saw a proliferation of acting troupes, most of them probably of mediocre quality, although their history has never been adequately investigated. Among them were companies led by Giuseppe Imer, Giuseppe Lapy, Pietro Rossi, Carlo and Maddalena Battaglia and, pre-eminently, by two actor-managers who were for long based in Venice – GIROLAMO MEDEBACH and ANTONIO SACCO. The former is primarily remembered today as the manager who brought Goldoni back to the theatre in 1747, but his career as a whole merits more attention than it has received. Active as a manager for more than 30 years, and employing at various times most of the lead players of the period, Medebach was an astute impresario with a professional buoyancy that enabled him to survive in what was an increasingly competitive market. Sacco, whose stage name was Truffaldino, was probably the leading Italian player of the century. Long associated with Carlo Gozzi, most of whose plays were first staged by his company, Sacco was noted for his histrionic agility, invention and improvising skill; and his death, while sailing from Genoa to Marseilles in 1786, is often taken as marking the demise both of the *commedia dell'arte* and of the great age of the Venetian theatre.

Theatres and scenic design

Theatres and scenic design The 18th century saw too the final efflorescence of Italian achievement in theatre architecture, mechanics and scenic design. In all areas, opera set the pace. By the end of the century few major Italian cities were without a theatre. The traditional conjunction of architecture and design was maintained in the work of many members of the great artistic families, like the BIBIENAS, the Mauri and the Galliari. The design and construction of theatres was very much the preserve of such professionals, but on one occasion at least the guiding spirit was an amateur: a lawyer, Benedetto Alfieri, carried through, on the initial plans of FILIPPO JUVARRA, the design and construction of the Teatro Regio in Turin (1738–40), an eclectic but harmonious conflation of baroque ideas

that set a standard for many theatres elsewhere in Europe.

Theatre architecture throughout the century was preoccupied with the accommodation of classical inspiration to social needs, and to achieving a balance between the decorative and the functional in auditorium size, shape and organization. Experiment produced a variety of theatres, from Luigi Vanvitelli's elegant Neapolitan court venue at Caserta (completed 1768) to Cosimo Morelli's modest little theatre at Imola (1779). By the late 18th century civic pride was invested in theatre buildings, and great emphasis was placed on internal comfort, notably in the great opera houses of La Scala in Milan (1778), La Fenice in Venice (1792) and the San Carlo in Naples (1810).

By the early 1700s recognition had been accorded to scenic design as a distinctive art form: some of the great designers published examples of their work, and others produced descriptive manuals of theatre architecture and design. Revolutionary in staging was the introduction in the 1690s of the *scena per angolo*, which broke with the traditional single perspective treatment of setting. These angled scenes helped to free the stage for more imaginative uses of space and were soon exploited by designers like Juvarra and the Bibienas, forming the base for a great deal of later scenic innovation. Although opera design remained sumptuous, elements of delicacy and refinement began to displace the ostentatious extravagances of the mythologically peopled stages of the 17th century. In addition, new influences came to be felt: more naturalistic rustic landscapes, and the novel, exotic tones of *chinoiserie*. Restraint was probably more characteristic of design in the later-18th-century regular theatre, if the illustrations to the Zatta edition of Goldoni's plays can be taken to reflect at least something of stage practice. But with the exception of special and court occasions, financial exigencies had always obliged the regular professional stage to be modest of decorative and mechanical means.

Alfieri

Alfieri If Goldoni was the greatest Italian dramatist of the 18th century, the most highly esteemed serious dramatist in Italy by the beginning of the next was VITTORIO ALFIERI: his independent political and patriotic stance caught the mood of the times, and helped to fuel that search for a national as opposed to a local or regional identity that lay at the heart of the Risorgimento. He sought to fashion a language and a structure for serious drama, and to bring to it intellectual and literary dignity. But despite its pre-romantic notes, his work looks back rather than forward: taking initial inspiration from French tragedy, absorbing elements from SENECA, and paring structure by the elimination of sub-plot and chorus, he sought more to refine the received literary tradition than to make any radical theatrical innovations. Certainly, Alfieri did what he could to encourage a reform of acting, emphasizing the need for discipline and restraint, but he met with little support either within the profession or from audiences apparently content with flamboyance and excess. Significantly, although his first tragedy, *Cleopatra* (1775), was staged by the Medebach Company, all his other plays were performed privately before socially exclusive audiences. Even the best, like *Saul* and *Mirra*, for all their grandeur of theme and economy of statement, tend to the formal and static and survive more as literary works than as stage pieces. They heralded no Italian dramatic renaissance.

The 19th and early 20th centuries

The drama Like so much else in the arts, the early-19th-century Italian theatre was dominated by the struggle for national independence and unification, all the more fuelled by the sentiments of the romantic movement which in Italy was a revolt not only against French-oriented classicism, but against foreign domination, political fragmentation, economic retardation and intellectual obscurantism. More perhaps than elsewhere, romanticism too had strong nationalist and popular emphases. Yet it cannot be said that cultural ferment generated any strikingly original or vital new drama, and for much of the century the theatre was dominated by translations, adaptations or imitations of French melodrama or the WELL MADE PLAY.

Perhaps the most distinctive of the comic dramatists was Giovanni Giraud, whose best plays have perceptible roots in the Italian social world in their criticism of clerical influence and bourgeois hypocrisy. In serious drama Alfierian influences were strong, and the Italian discovery of SHAKESPEARE was increasingly felt as the century progressed, particularly in the treatment of historical and biblical subject-matter. Prominent among those dramatists whose work bore Alfierian classical tones were Vincenzo Monti (1754–1827), notably in *Galeotto Manfredi* (1788) and *Caio Gracco* (1802), and the lyric poet Ugo Foscolo (1788–1827), who ran foul of CENSORSHIP and police intervention with his *Aiace*, performed at La Scala in 1811. Greater and more consistent stage success was enjoyed by the plays of the writer and critic Giovanni Battista Niccolini (1782–1861) and Silvio Pellico, whose *Francesca da Rimini* (1815) remained a stock piece in the repertoires of touring companies throughout the century. But perhaps the only dramatist before c.1850 to rise above literary mediocrity in drama was the poet and novelist ALESSANDRO MANZONI, who wrote two plays, *Il Conte di Carmagnola* (*The Count of Carmagnola*, 1816–19) and *Adelchi* (1820–2), neither of which, however, can be said to have succeeded in performance in its own time or since, notwithstanding evident Shakespearian influences.

The achievement of political independence and unification from 1861 led to intermittent attempts by central government to stimulate the growth of a national drama in the Italian language by the offer of official competitions and monetary prizes, but no dramatic revival followed. Dialect theatre occasionally threw up interesting and distinctive work, including in Piedmontese *Le miserie d' Monssu Travet* (*The Troubles of M. Travet*, 1863) of Vittorio Bersezio (1828–1900), in Venetian the strongly Goldonian-influenced light dramas of Giacinto Gallina (1852–97) and, most notably, the plays devised in or reworked from French farces into Neapolitan by the actor-dramatist EDUARDO SCARPETTA. For a time hopes for drama in the national language were pinned on Achille Torelli (1841–1922), whose *I mariti* (*The Husbands*, 1867) won considerable success, but the promise was little realized. Among other distinctive Italian plays of the middle decades may be mentioned PAOLO GIACOMETTI's *Elisabetta regina d'Inghilterra* (*Elizabeth, Queen of England*, 1853)

and *La morte civile* (*Civil Death*, 1861), both stock vehicles in the repertoires of leading players throughout the century, and the neatly crafted work of the versatile PAOLO FERRARI in comedy, historical drama and plays of Goldonian-inspired social observation. In virtually all this work, however, the influence of French BOULEVARD drama was strongly felt in plotting, characterization and theatrical emphases.

From France too came at least the initial inspiration for Italian theatrical VERISMO, triggered by the first Italian production of ZOLA's *Thérèse Raquin* in 1879. But *verismo* was distinctively Italian in its use of regional materials and subject-matter and its particular focus on the social psychology of bourgeois life. Foremost of the verist dramatists was the Sicilian GIOVANNI VERGA, in whose *Cavalleria rusticana* (*Rustic Chivalry*) ELEONORA DUSE secured a triumphant reception in 1884. Among other dramatists who worked in this line perhaps the most interesting was the Milanese, Carlo Bertolazzi, who in plays like *El nost Milan* (*Our Milan*, 1893) and *La Gibigianna* (1898) treated of communal and lower-class life. Other serious and competent work was produced by dramatists like MARCO PRAGA and Gerolamo Rovetta (1851–1910), but perhaps the finest dramatist of the movement was GIUSEPPE GIACOSA, whose *Tristi amori* (*Sad Loves*, 1887) and *Come le foglie* (*Like the Leaves*, 1900) remain the most durable plays of the 19th-century theatre. Limited as was the achievement of the *veristi*, they at least brought to the late-19th-century Italian theatre an attempt to treat serious themes, depict a recognizable social life, and eschew contrived and formulaic staginess. Not even the best of their plays, however, can compare with what was the greatest strength of the 19th-century Italian theatre: the musical drama from Donizetti and Bellini, through Verdi, to Mascagni and Puccini.

The practitioners If dramatic talent was in short supply, working conditions in the Italian theatre did little to encourage it. Throughout the century most acting companies remained, as they had been in the past, itinerant, touring the major cities, renting theatres for short seasons, and transporting props and scenery with them as they moved from place to place. The theatre never lacked either champions or enthusiastic new recruits, even if mainly *figli d'arte* (children of the profession), but its public was casual in attendance, conservative in attitude and all too prone to support modish foreign imports. A few companies enjoyed subsidy in permanent theatre buildings – as did the Compagnia Reale Italiana, first in Milan from 1806 to 1815, then in Naples until 1827, and the Turin-based Reale Sarda, perhaps the most celebrated company of the century, which from 1821 produced nearly 600 plays by Italian dramatists – until the Piedmontese state withdrew its subsidy on the ground that theatre was essentially entertainment and not an educative art. Ironically, the greatest Italian actor of the early decades of the century, GUSTAVO MODENA, a tireless supporter of reform in acting, staging and dramatic content, urged just such an educative purpose in his utopian *Teatro educatore* (1836).

This was the great age of 'star' performers, as much on the regular as on the operatic stage, and few acquired such wide international celebrity as did the major Italian players of the middle and later decades of the century: ADELAIDE RISTORI, ERNESTO ROSSI, TOMMASO SALVINI and Eleonora Duse. They were followed in the early 1900s by GIOVANNI GRASSO. By the time of the latter, however, taste for the novel REALISM and powerful emotionalism characteristic of much Italian playing was beginning to wane, as too was the domination exercised over international stages by the great star performers. None of these stars travelled as far and as frequently as did the Italians – north to Moscow and London, south to Egypt, and even more widely abroad to North and South America. Some, like Rossi and Salvini, came to spend as much if not more time playing abroad than in touring through Italy itself. Not least among their motives for travelling so much was the continuing instability and insecurity of acting company life in the peninsula itself, although by the final decades of the century the voices of players and managers were noticeably more concerted in their call for reform, and they were aided by the emergence of a new figure, the professional theatre critic.

Theatres and scenic design Nowhere is the decline of Italian theatrical influence beyond the peninsula more evident than in the very limited contribution it made to 19th-century developments in theatre architecture, mechanics and scenic design, areas in which hitherto the work of Italians had been prominent and seminal. Throughout the century many new opera houses were built and other major musical theatres were renovated, but for the most part Italian activity on these was either traditional or imitative of French and German models. The only really substantial new opera house built in the century was the Teatro Massimo at Palermo, which the Basile completed over a 20-year period in 1897. Little was done to increase the number or quality of theatres catering primarily for acting companies. Radically new ideas for theatres, lyric or regular, were for the most part confined to visionary writings like Benevello's *Azioni coreographiche* (1841) with its interesting anticipations of some of WAGNER's ideas for BAYREUTH.

Furthermore, what was distinctive in Italian scenic design, like the work of Antonio Basoli (1774–1843), Gaspare Galliari and Carlo Ferrario (1833–1907), was done for the musical stage. In the regular theatre production values were for the most part shoddy, their utilitarian nature dictated by limited funds and the requirements of constant touring: scenes consisted mainly of practicable and easily transportable flats and backdrops – often showing, as the dramatist Marco Praga complained in 1912, all the signs of excessive wear and tear – while the advanced technology found in many theatres elsewhere in Europe was unavailable in Italy. Reviewing an exhibition at La Scala in 1894 mounted as part of *Le Esposizioni Riunite di Milano*, the theatre critic of *Corriere della Sera*, Giovanni Pozza, delivered a broadside against the all-pervasive architectural and staging inadequacies of the Italian theatre.

Turn-of-the-century developments Although the Italian theatre's traditional strengths had lain in acting and stage decoration rather than in scripted drama, it was the work

of playwrights in the final years of the 19th century and the first decades of the 20th that offered promise of something new. Audaciously constructive were the dreams of the foremost Italian writer of the period, GABRIELE D'ANNUNZIO. Primarily a poet and novelist, D'Annunzio's interest in the theatre was sparked by his meeting in 1896 with the actress Eleonora Duse; for some years she was his artistic partner in an ambitious project to provide Italy with a great tragic drama. D'Annunzio took as his models the Greek classical theatre, the experiments of the Renaissance Florentine *camerata* with musical drama, the theory and practice of Wagner and the ideas of NIETZSCHE. With Duse he sketched plans for this new theatre and its future home – an open-air amphitheatre on the shore of Lake Albano where classical tragedy and his own plays would be produced. But although he wrote a number of highly individual plays, like *La città morta* (*The Dead City*, 1898) and *La nave* (*The Ship*, 1908), his ideal of a total theatre that would fuse words, movement, spectacle, music and dance was never adequately realized. The artistic and economic demands of D'Annunzio's programme were characteristically inflated, and were too remote from what could actually be achieved in the Italian theatre of his day. His ambitions, however, helped open up the Italian theatre to new staging ideas.

So too did the ostentatiously destructive experiments undertaken by the theatre practitioners of FUTURISM. Where D'Annunzio had sought to fashion a new theatre by drawing creatively on the ideas and practices of the past, the futurists very deliberately rejected the past and called for an art appropriate to the new age of technology. In theatre that art would reject not just bourgeois NATURALISM, but traditional genres, subject-matter, structures and verbal means, in favour of syntheses, or highly concentrated dramatic sketches. Much less aggressive and iconoclastic than the work of the futurists, but nonetheless charting distinctly new and promising territory, were the plays written by the dramatists of the TEATRO DEL GROTTESCO, whose cultivation of bizarre or absurd elements (see THEATRE OF THE ABSURD) within the apparently traditional love-triangle situations of boulevard drama challenged the validity of naturalism. All these activities can be seen as attempts to revitalize a theatre widely acknowledged to be hide-bound and unimaginative. Unfortunately, what new ideas and artistic movements could not contribute was what the Italian theatre needed, economic support. Unfortunately too, when that economic support did in some measure materialize there were political strings attached.

The later 20th century: Fascism to the present
Theatre under Fascism With the exception of PIRANDELLO's work, drama in Italy between the two world wars was undistinguished: the new directions taken by D'Annunzian, futurist and grotesque theatre led nowhere. Bourgeois naturalism and undemanding boulevard diversion prevailed. If any stage activity can be said to have been vital it was that of the popular CABARET entertainers like PETROLINI and TOTÒ. Also, dialect theatre remained strong, particularly in the Neapolitan plays of VIVIANI and the young EDUARDO DE FILIPPO. What changed quite significantly after the Mussolini government took

power in 1922 was the manner in which some theatre was organized: the *laissez-faire* structure and economy of the actor-manager system was partially modified by state intervention. Pirandello's acting company, the Teatro d'Arte, was established with a small grant from the state, and some encouragement was given to BRAGAGLIA's experimental Teatro degli Indipendenti.

From 1929 through to the early 1940s direct state encouragement of theatre was most evident in the activity of the so-called *carri di Tespi* (literally, Thespian carts, i.e. mobile theatres), which toured theatrical entertainment through the provinces. Although the support of this theatre shows that drama was now recognized as fulfilling an educative role in society, few of these itinerant shows were notable for their intellectual or artistic qualities; and although some may be seen as politically propagandist, particularly after censorship became centralized in the early 1930s, most were merely conformist, escapist and innocuous. A decidedly significant development of these years, however, was the founding in 1935 of the Accademia d'Arte Drammatica in Rome, a commitment to the idea of organized training for the stage that not only acknowledged the national importance of the profession, but implicitly challenged the more casual and arbitrary preparation provided by the *figli d'arte* system. Some of the groundwork was thus done in the 1930s for that reorganization of the structures and the economy of the Italian stage that for a century or more so many of its champions and practitioners had been demanding.

The postwar stage and the stabili In the years immediately following the Second World War, important new initiatives began significantly to modify the traditional system of private management far beyond anything that had occurred in the 1930s. The attractions of the *teatro stabile*, the permanently established company, had long been advocated by theatre reformers, and several *stabili* had been set up for short periods – as in 1898 were the Stabile Romana and the Teatro d'Arte in Turin – but subsidy had never been generous or regular. From 1947 onwards a more substantial attempt was made to pursue the idea. The first company funded was the Piccolo Teatro in Milan, under the joint direction of Paolo Grassi and GIORGIO STREHLER: the emphasis they placed on exploring the European classic repertory in studied but imaginative productions gradually won for the Piccolo an international as well as a national reputation, and the Milan *stabile* remains today one of the great theatres of Italy. Other early established *stabili* have similarly survived with distinction, like the Teatro d'Arte of Genoa (1951) and the Teatro Stabile of Turin (1955). Although most major Italian cities pioneered *stabili* in the late 1940s and 1950s, not all survived – for reasons artistic, economic and political.

While the development of *stabili* was of major importance, much significant work continued to be done by the independent actor-managed companies, one of the finest in the immediate postwar years being the Compagnia Morelli-Stoppa for which VISCONTI directed important new and classic drama. In the provinces too the centuries-old tradition of touring was maintained by stock companies (see STOCK COMPANY), often of very variable quality.

Such advances as theatre made in the decade or so immediately after the war were achieved in the face of severe competition – first from cinema and then, in the later 1950s, from television.

Actors, directors and dramatists The Italian regular theatre has traditionally been dominated by performers, and although the postwar stage has seen the emergence of the director the influence of lead actors and actresses has remained strong. This has been to the advantage of theatre when the ability and charisma of the star performer have been allied to intelligent and imaginative reinterpretation of classic roles, or been put to the service of new drama or radical reorchestrations of the received repertoire: such is the case with the contributions of actors as very different as VITTORIO GASSMAN and CARMELO BENE. On the other hand, the persistence of the star system has elsewhere, and not only in boulevard theatre, hampered the development of ensemble acting – as too, some would argue, has the increasing domination of the stage by 'star' directors. Aside from the work of between-the-wars pioneers like Bragaglia and TALLI, the director in the Italian theatre is very much a product of the post-1945 stage: figures like Visconti, Strehler and SQUARZINA are not only the most distinguished, but in effect the first Italian directors, and many of the most significant events in the modern Italian theatre are associated with them: Visconti's work on Goldonian comedy, Squarzina's treatments of Shakespeare, Strehler's productions of BRECHT.

Much in modern Italian theatre has been shaped by foreign influences: the drama of ARTHUR MILLER, TENNESSEE WILLIAMS and SARTRE in the late 1940s and early 50s, the impact of Brecht in the late 50s, a decade or so of radical experimentalism prompted from the mid-1960s onwards by the work of the LIVING THEATRE and the inspiration offered by GROTOWSKI. Much emphasis in Italian avant-garde theatre has been put on the non-literary: Bene's stage reworkings of classics, RONCONI's explorations of performance space, the experiments with light and sound characteristic of much Italian alternative theatre staging. Significantly, the contemporary Italian dramatist best known internationally, DARIO FO, is considered by many to be less a playwright than a performer or an *homme du théâtre*, and although the modern stage has seen interesting work by dramatists like BETTI and FABBRI, and one-off pieces by artists best known for their work in other fields, like Moravia and Pasolini, Italian drama has in the main been undistinguished, the strength of Italian theatre continuing to lie in the work of its actors, directors and designers. KR LR

See: M. Apollonio, *Storia del teatro italiano*, 2 vols., Florence, 1981; M. Carlson, *The Italian Stage, from Goldoni to D'Annunzio*, North Carolina, 1981; A. D'Ancona, *Origini del teatro italiano*, 2 vols., Turin, 1891; *Enciclopedia dello spettacolo*, 9 vols., Rome, 1954–62; *Enciclopedia dello spettacolo: cinema, teatro, balletto, TV*, Milan, 1976; V. Mariani, *Storia della scenografia italiana*, Florence, 1930; L. Rasi, *I comici italiani*, 3 vols., Florence, 1897–1905; G. Ricci, *Il teatro d'Italia*, Milan, 1971; V. Vivani, *Storia del teatro napoletano*, Naples, 1969.

Ivanov, Vsevolod (Vyacheslavovich) 1895–1963
Soviet prose writer and author of 15 plays, mostly relating
to the Russian Civil War, in which he fought on the Red
side, and to his native Siberia and Asiatic Russia. He led an
itinerant early life as circus fakir, day labourer and so on –
much like GORKY, who encouraged him in his early naturalistic short story writing (1915) and introduced him to
Petrograd's Serpion Brotherhood (1920). Reflecting
Gorky's and ZAMYATIN's influence, his personal experience
and his knowledge of Russian folklore, his early work
included the novelistic Civil War trilogy *The Partisans*
(1921), *Coloured Winds* (1922) and *Armoured Train 14–69*
(1922), the last of which he adapted for the stage in
1927 and which became his most important play.
Commissioned by the MOSCOW ART THEATRE for the 10th
anniversary of the Revolution, directed by STANISLAVSKY
(along with Sudakov and Litovsev) and starring KACHALOV,
it was the first Soviet play to be successfully produced by
MAT. In it a group of partisans, led by a peasant only
recently converted to the Bolshevik cause, seize a train of
White refugees in Siberia during the Civil War. The play
contains heroism and noble sacrifice, idealized Bolsheviks
and nefarious Japanese interventionists, ideological
themes – the people must win the battles of the Revolution
– virile action and earthy humour, and inflammatory
iconography (a martyred comrade's body borne upon the
train in inspirational evocation of Lenin).

Ivanov's other plays include: on Civil War themes –
Blockade (1929), *The Compromise of Naib-Khan* (1931), *The
Doves See the Departing Cruisers* (1937) and *Uncle Kostya*
(1944); on Russian historical themes – *Twelve Youths from
a Snuffbox* (1936), on Tsar Paul I's assassination in 1801;
Inspiration (1940), set in the 17th century in the time of
the false Dmitry; and *Lomonosov* (1953), on the 18th-cen-
tury Russian scientist and man of letters. Ivanov's plays
and narrative fiction after 1930 bear the unmistakable
imprint of socialist realism. SG

Ivanov, Vyacheslav (Ivanovich) 1866–1949 Russian
poet, dramatist, theorist and Hellenic scholar, and the
leader of the St Petersburg symbolists (see SYMBOLISM). His
major area of inquiry was the Dionysian cult, which he
linked to later Christian mysteries in an effort to establish
a philosophical foundation for a modern liturgical theatre. He here differed from NIETZSCHE – one of his ideological mentors, along with GOETHE, WAGNER and Vladimir
Solovyov – who had stressed their differences. In Ivanov's
theatre of myth-creation and communal action the actor-
priest and audience-congregants would co-create the
sacred rite of performance. He criticized those Russian
symbolist mystery plays that were conceived according to
purely aesthetic principles. He contributed two plays of
his own – *Tantalus* (1905) and *Prometheus* (1919) – which
imitated AESCHYLUS in structure, mythological subject-
matter and obscure, archaic language. The most scholarly
and profound of the symbolists, his ideas greatly influenced MEYERHOLD's thinking about conventional
(*uslovny*) theatre. Meyerhold mounted a reconstruction of
CALDERÓN DE LA BARCA's *The Adoration of the Cross* at the
Tower literary salon-theatre in the apartments of Ivanov

and his poet wife, Lidiya D. Zinovyeva-Annibal (1910),
where the leading lights of St Petersburg artistic society
gathered. BLOK dramatized his poem 'The Puppet Show' to
launch another Ivanov-conceived symbolist theatrical
(and journalistic) venture, 'The Torches', but this never
materialized.

As well as contributing to the major symbolist journals
of the day – the *Scales* and the *Golden Fleece* – and publishing several volumes of poetry, Ivanov collected his
major aesthetic essays in the volumes *Along the Stars*
(1909) and *Furrows and Landmarks* (1916). He emigated to
Italy in 1924. SG

Iwamatsu Ryō 1952– Japanese playwright, director and
actor. In the mid-1970s, performances of improvised
comic pieces were becoming dominant on the Tokyo
FRINGE, after the turbulent *angura* (underground) theatre
movement of the 1960s. It was the time when the Tokyo
Kandenchi (Electric Battery) Theatre Company was formed
(1976), which was to become extremely popular. Initially
Iwamatsu was invited to join the company to create situations and characters for improvisations and to write the
programmes for the performances. However, when the
company decided to change their direction in the mid-
1980s and to stage a written play rather than improvising,
Iwamatsu's role became that of company author, director
and actor.

Some elements of slapstick comedy (see FARCE) and
intriguing absurdity (see THEATRE OF THE ABSURD), which
developed through the experience of the previous ten
years, still remain in his plays. It has been said that his
naturalistic style (see NATURALISM), in its subtle detailing
of human emotions, is reminiscent of that of Kishida
Kunio (1891–1954), one of the leading playwrights in
early SHINGEKI. Iwamatsu unpretentiously discloses the
problems of Japanese society in his plays, giving the
impression to international audiences that his theatre
is akin to that of PINTER. His best-known works are
Tea and a Lecture (*O-cha to Sekkyo*, 1986), *Futon and
Daruma* (*Futon to Daruma*, 1988; translation 1992) and
The Man Next Door (*Tonari no Otoko*, 1990; translation
1994). MY

Izenour, George 1912– American theatre designer,
engineering consultant, and inventor of the electronic
console for STAGE LIGHTING control, the synchronous
winch system and the steel acoustical shell. He has been a
design and engineering consultant for over 100 theatres
around the world since the 1950s, and as such is a dominant force in theatre design and technology. Because economics dictates that a single theatre must be employed for
many uses (spoken drama, opera, concerts and so forth),
he is an advocate of the multi-use and multiform theatre,
in which the size and shape of the auditorium can be
altered for different needs and acoustical requirements.
Recipient of the Distinguished Service Award from the
American Theater Association, Izenour is the author of
three acclaimed books: *Theater Design* (1977), *Theater
Technology* (1988) and *Roofed Theaters of Classical
Antiquity* (1992). AA

Jackson, Anne see WALLACH, ELI

Jackson, Barry (Vincent) 1879–1961 British theatre director, manager and patron. Born in Birmingham of a prosperous merchant grocer's family, he founded the amateur Pilgrim Players in 1907 and the professional BIRMINGHAM REPERTORY THEATRE in 1913, for which he financed the building of a purpose-designed theatre. As owner and artistic director, and with extraordinary dedication, he established the theatre as the country's leading repertory venture (see REGIONAL THEATRE (BRITAIN)), committed to both new and classic plays. He occasionally designed and directed productions himself. Disappointed by lack of consistent public support, however, he threatened closure twice and in 1935 handed ownership of the theatre to a public trust. He was founder and director of the Malvern Theatre Festival from 1929 to 1937 and director of the Stratford Memorial Theatre during 1945–8. He also wrote, co-wrote and adapted a number of plays for adults and children, and was knighted in 1925. AJ

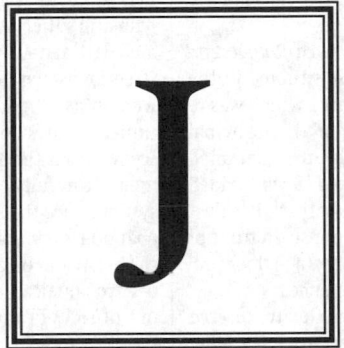

Jackson, Glenda 1936– British actress, who took part in a seminal Theatre of Cruelty season, organized by PETER BROOK and CHARLES MAROWITZ with the ROYAL SHAKESPEARE COMPANY at LAMDA (the London Academy of Music and Dramatic Art) in 1964. This prepared the way for her performance as Charlotte Corday in Peter Brook's production of PETER WEISS's *The Marat/Sade* (1965), celebrated on both sides of the Atlantic for its intensity and eroticism. In 1967, she was a notable Masha in CHEKHOV's *The Three Sisters* at the ROYAL COURT THEATRE, became known to wider audiences through her film appearances, such as in *Women in Love* (1970), and in 1975 she played Hedda Gabler in the RSC's production of IBSEN's play, which toured Britain, the USA and Australia.

Not conventionally pretty, Jackson nonetheless could radiate an emotional directness and intellectual honesty which transformed her *gamine* attractiveness into outright beauty. Her independence of mind, however, prevented her from working consistently within the structure of a permanent company such as the RSC. She returned to Stratford-upon-Avon in 1978 to play Cleopatra in Peter Brook's production of *Antony and Cleopatra* – with less than her usual success: but she has complained about the lack of good roles for actresses over 40. Of her several starring WEST END performances in recent years, in *Stevie* (1977), *Rose* (1980), *Summit Conference* (1982) and BOTHO STRAUSS's *Great and Small* (1983), she achieved a notable personal triumph in O'NEILL's *Strange Interlude* (1984). She appeared in GARCÍA LORCA's *The House of Bernarda Alba* (1987), in the title role of the Glasgow CITIZENS' *Mother Courage* (1990), and memorably in HOWARD BARKER's *Scenes from an Execution* (1990). A lifelong supporter of the Labour Party, she was elected to parliament as the MP for Hampstead, London, in 1992. JE

Jacobi, Derek (George) 1938– British actor. His debut was at BIRMINGHAM REPERTORY THEATRE in 1960, and in 1963 he joined the NATIONAL THEATRE at the OLD VIC, playing Laertes in *Hamlet*, Cassio in *Othello* and Lodovico in *The White Devils*, among various other major roles. He joined the Prospect Theatre Company in 1972, working with them for six years. He played Hamlet in 1978, memorably, and Peer Gynt and Prospero for the ROYAL SHAKESPEARE COMPANY in the 1982–3 season. He made a major popular impact as Claudius in the television drama serial, *I, Claudius*. He played the two title roles in *Richard II* (1988) and *Richard III* (1989) produced by a commercial company, Triumph Productions, in association with the JOHN F. KENNEDY CENTER in Washington, DC; and appeared as the actor Kean in *Kean* (1990) at the Old Vic, as Becket in *Becket* (1991) and as Byron, in *Mad, Bad and Dangerous to Know* (1992), roles indicating his ability to take centre stage and impose his strong but thoughtful personality on productions. MB JE

Jahnn, Hans Henny 1894–1959 German dramatist and novelist. His *Pastor Ephraim Magnus*, a prime specimen of nihilistic EXPRESSIONISM written in 1917 and stuffed with perversities and sado-masochistic motifs, was produced by BRONNEN in 1923 in a heavily cut version by himself and BRECHT. Jahnn's *Krönung Richards III* (*Coronation of Richard III*, 1922) was equally lurid. He re-emerged occasionally after the Second World War, when GRÜNDGENS produced *Thomas Chatterton* (1956) and PISCATOR *Der staubige Regenbogen* (*The Dusty Rainbow*, 1961). HR

Jamaica Theatre in Jamaica began with the English conquest of the island from Spain in 1655. By 1682 a theatre was in existence, probably situated in the then administrative capital of San Jago de la Vega, or Spanish Town, but whether the players were touring professionals from England or resident amateurs is unknown.

In 1733 an English company was successfully performing JOHN GAY's *The Beggar's Opera*, and 'a set of extraordinary good actors' is recorded at the Spanish Town playhouse in 1740–1. In 1776 a new theatre was opened in Spanish Town, at a cost of about £2500; it probably had a level-floor auditorium for dances and assemblies, since from 1792 to 1799 it was taken over by the government to house soldiers.

With the arrival in 1745 of the Irish actor John Moody, the centre of theatrical activity moved to Kingston, the present capital. Supported by local amateurs, Moody mounted a number of Shakespearian productions, then returned to England to recruit a professional company that included DAVID DOUGLASS; once back in Kingston, he set up a theatre in Harbour Street. There he remained until 1749, when he embarked again for England, leaving Douglass in charge of the company. Some years later Douglass abandoned the theatre Moody had set up and established his own in warehouses nearby. In 1755 an English company of comedians led by one LEWIS HALLAM arrived from America and joined the Douglass troupe. LEWIS HALLAM JR was a member of the company. When the older Hallam died within the year, Douglass married his widow, became company manager, and after three years took the troupe back to America with, as his principal actor, the 18-year-old Lewis. With the outbreak of the American War of Independence imminent, Douglass brought his company, now called the American Comedians, back to Jamaica, where they remained from 1775 to 1785. Eventually Douglass became a printer, leaving Lewis Hallam Jr and John Henry as co-managers of the troupe.

The players opened their first season with *Romeo and Juliet* on 1 July 1775, in a new playhouse situated in the parade ground (now St William Grant Park), which was to remain up to the present day the site of the principal Kingston theatres. Seating 600, this theatre contained a pit at floor level, and a second, stepped, level divided into boxes behind which rose an open gallery. Backless benches were provided throughout the house. In front of the curtain (raised in festoon fashion), the stage floor projected to accommodate entr'acte performances.

This was a slave-holding society, and the theatre catered primarily to the elite. Ticket prices were high, ranging from 6s8d to 13s4d when the average pay for skilled labour was 15s to 20s a week. The players offered a different programme each week, consisting of a major play followed by a FARCE or burletta, with solo entertainments between scene shifts. Along with SHAKESPEARE, the playwrights most often presented were CUMBERLAND, SUSANNAH CENTLIVRE, DRYDEN, GARRICK, GOLDSMITH and SHERIDAN. BICKERSTAFFE's *The Padlock* was the most popular farce. The company performed occasionally in Spanish Town and on the north side of the island in Montego Bay, where several long rooms had been converted into theatres to accommodate travelling players.

After the American Comedians left the island in 1785, theatrical activity declined. Natural disasters, the successful slave revolt in neighbouring San Domingue and slave uprisings at home preoccupied Jamaica in the ensuing decades. In 1812 a company arrived from Barbados, led by Charles Manning, Jesse Read and Mrs Elizabeth Shaw. They occupied the Kingston Theatre, but did not prosper until joined by William Adamson, also from Barbados. When the Jamaican fever claimed Adamson, his infant son, Read and other players, French-speaking refugees from France and San Domingue took to the stage with comic OPERETTAS and *vaudevilles*. Kingston amateurs also produced *Macbeth*, *Venice Preserv'd* and *She Stoops to Conquer*. It was a period of uncertainty, for the slaves were about to be freed and few could predict the future.

On 1 August 1838 a quarter of a million black slaves were set free: they joined a population of 15,000 whites and 40,000 already free blacks and coloureds. An increase in rowdiness in the theatre – which was to continue until the end of the century – was a problem that had begun before emancipation, when an attempt had been made to segregate the races by building a separate stairway into the theatre for people of colour. Overt segregation was now discontinued, but individuals were disposed to noisily assert their rights as free citizens and, moreover, the theatre continued to address itself to a small section of the

population, ignoring the vast majority whose behaviour was patterned on visits to the circus and other popular indigenous entertainments.

The slaves had developed their own modes of performance consisting of music-making, singing, dancing and storytelling; and Christmas masquerades (see MASQUERADES IN AFRICA) called jonkonnu, and the Set Girls. Their instruments comprised a variety of home-made drums, rattles, horns, flutes and fiddles; the songs were melancholy and satiric; and the dances often involved role-playing, while the stories suggested survival strategies to ease pain and suffering. Some of these exhibitions were associated with RITUALS that reached back to an African past. The street masquerades, often sponsored by freemen and women as a holiday pastime, presented elaborately costumed figures including the Actor Boy, who imitated scenes from the theatre. While these various entertainments, carefully controlled, were allowed under the slave system, once the slaves were freed they were expected to abandon such 'barbaric', 'heathen' practices and adopt the behaviour of 'civilized' Christians. But the suppression of Afro-Jamaican expression simply sent it underground, out of sight of the authorities, to emerge years later, in more favourable times, as the native culture.

Meanwhile the theatre on the parade ground, left behind by the American Comedians, had fallen into disrepair. Three more theatres were to be constructed on this site: the first Theatre Royal (1840); the second Theatre Royal (1897), which was destroyed in the great earthquake of 1907; and the Ward Theatre (1912), which is still in use today. All were built for the people of Kingston, and placed under the control of the city council. During the 19th century, members of the Jewish community – owners of the city's major newspaper and of other business interests – played a major role in ensuring the survival of Kingston's public theatre.

The opening of the first Theatre Royal brought a return of professional troupers from overseas, among them the Philadelphian John H. Oxley and his company. Oxley had been a supporting actor to EDWIN FORREST, and his Hamlet was viewed as 'the best ever presented to a Kingston audience'. Although his *Macbeth*, containing singing witches and a three-minute sword fight, and a visually spectacular *King Lear*, could fill the theatre, public support was generally disappointing. Nor did Signor Gastaldi's opera company that followed Oxley fare much better. When Oxley later teamed up with Mrs Monier and her daughter Virginia in an attempt to recoup his losses, only his *Othello* in 1842, the first ever production of the play in Jamaica, succeeded in filling the house.

It was time for the Kingston amateurs to take to the boards. Beginning in 1847, no fewer than eight groups competed for honours at the Theatre Royal, the most prestigious being the Kingston Amateur Theatre Association, which offered a major play once a month. There were a French troupe and two black groups, the Ethiopian Amateur Society and the Numidian Amateur Society. Spanish Town also had two amateur groups of its own. This activity terminated abruptly when a cholera epidemic struck the island in October 1850. By one estimate, between 25,000 and 30,000 of the working class perished.

Economic conditions deteriorated in the second half of

the century. The planters, now having to pay their labourers, were forced to compete against slave-grown sugar from Cuba and Brazil. In the theatre amateurs held the stage, their most important productions being two original plays in 1853 by the Jamaican Charles Shanahan, a newspaper reporter and president of the amateur Roscian Association. *The Mysteries of Vegetarianism*, a satiric farce on a current dietary practice, and his historical drama *The Spanish Warrior*, based on the career of the New World explorer Balboa, mark the first recorded instance of works written and performed by Jamaicans. The scripts have not survived, nor have any other scripts of local plays produced during this century. Some dramas, farces and skits were published in the press, but no productions of them are recorded.

In 1865 the English actor CHARLES KEAN and his wife, the actress Ellen Tree, visited Jamaica and gave Shakespearian readings and ballad recitations, to great acclaim. Seven years earlier the Jamaican Raphael de Cordova had embarked in the USA on an illustrious career as a humorous reader. Among other Jamaican professionals who worked abroad at this time was the esteemed actor Morton Tavares. Also in 1865, the first quartet of blackface minstrels (see MINSTREL SHOW) led by Frank Hussey arrived from New York, followed by other minstrel groups in 1869, 1872 and 1884. They established the tradition of blacking up to portray comic stereotypes that Jamaican comedians of the populist theatre adopted and maintained into the 1950s and 60s.

October 1865 witnessed the Morant Bay rebellion, started by landless peasants. The uprising was cruelly suppressed by the military, supported by British gunboats under the orders of a sadistic governor. Nineteen of the people's leaders were hanged without trial from the yardarm of one of the gunboats. In an attempt to redress the injury, gunboat officers and crews began a series of seven theatrical productions at the Theatre Royal to raise money for the victims' families. In 1866 Charles Selby's *Robert Macaire* was staged at the temporary barracks in Morant Bay, to which all classes were offered free admission after the first act. Military and naval amateurs continued to perform intermittently until 1869, when a calmer political atmosphere was restored. In that year Henry G. Murray, a black, began to deliver to audiences throughout the country his recitals of humorous stories based on Jamaican manners and customs. His appeal was immediate, and people flocked to hear him. After his death in 1877 his sons Andrew C. Murray and William C. Murray carried on the storytelling profession.

Touring troupers from abroad once again began to visit Jamaica, but few found it profitable, partly because the Kingston playhouse was unkempt and companies were forced to restore it, as well as provide their own scenery, before they could safely perform. Among the most reputable troupes at this time were J. W. Lanergan's, which paid three visits – in 1859, 1860 and 1861–2; E. A. McDowell's company, which played in 1880–1, 1885–6 and 1891; and William F. Burrough's New York Ideal Combination Company, in 1882. There was a distinct trend away from the old-fashioned romantic MELODRAMAS and towards contemporary realistic (see REALISM) plays by writers such as T. W. ROBERTSON and AUGUSTIN DALY. These pieces required a more naturalistic approach (see NATURALISM) to acting than hitherto, with greater emphasis on scenic decoration to achieve verisimilitude. Thus companies travelled with their own scene-painter and machinist.

In 1891 Jamaica held a three-month International Exhibition to stimulate trade. A temporary stage was built on the exhibition grounds, and the London Dramatic Company led by Warren F. Hill was installed. Meanwhile, McDowell's company, with the enormously popular Fanny Reeves, occupied the hastily refurbished Theatre Royal. Playing an average of five times a week, these two companies presented some 70 plays – light-hearted comedies, melodramas and historical romances by such authors as W. S. GILBERT, PINERO and BOUCICAULT – in a total of 128 performances.

The challenge of the 20th century was to develop an indigenous drama and theatre that could be identified as belonging to Jamaica and to the Caribbean region. The Murrays had shown that there was a popular audience for local material, and the last decades of the 19th century had witnessed the publication at home and abroad of Jamaican proverbs and Anansi stories. In 1907 Walter Jekyll published for the Folklore Society his collection of Jamaican stories and songs, and in 1913 the Jamaican Astley Clerk published his lecture on the music and musical instruments of Jamaica. The country did not shut out travelling professionals, as G. B. SHAW had urged on his visit in 1911, but gradually the homegrown product began to assert itself as the legitimate theatre of Jamaica. Touring English companies that used the newly built Ward Theatre into the 1930s included the Florence Glossop-Harris Company playing Shakespeare and modern drama, its successor the Empire Players, the W. S. Harkins Dramatic Company and the Klark-Urban Dramatic Company. These continued to provide a model for the schools and for those amateurs for whom theatre was simply an art form devoted to public entertainment of a high order. The native theatre, on the other hand, drew its energy from two sources: the populist theatre, including the comedians for whom theatre was principally a business catering to the largest audiences; and the art theatre, devoted to the establishment of a national culture.

Christmas morning concerts, most favoured of the VARIETY shows held on public holidays, were seen as opportunities for the seasoned professional as well as for the young and talented tyro to exhibit his speciality before a widely diverse audience. Another instrument for establishing a populist theatre, directed towards the social and political advancement of the Jamaican masses, was the Universal Negro Improvement Association (UNIA), founded in Kingston in 1914 by the Jamaican patriot and world-renowned figure Marcus Garvey. From the UNIA stage at Edelweiss Park issued the well known comedians Ernest Cupidon and Ranny Williams. Cupidon is credited with having dramatized two plays and a short story by the popular Jamaican writer H. G. de Lisser, and Garvey himself wrote several plays in 1930–2 aimed at uplifting his working-class audiences; but the most significant playwright of the 1930s was Una Marson, whose three plays dealt boldly and realistically with problems faced by the middle class of her time.

Following the workers' riots of 1937–8 that swept the

English-speaking Caribbean, Jamaican playwrights supported the nationalist cause with plays such as Frank Hill's *Upheaval* (1939), Roger Mais's *Hurricane* (1943) and W. G. Ogilvie's *One Sojer Man* (1945). The most successful playwright of the period was Archie Lindo, who treated topical issues such as colour prejudice and quasi-historical figures like the infamous White Witch of Rosehall. Two organizations that have had a profound impact on the Jamaican theatre are the Little Theatre Movement of Jamaica (LTM), formed in 1941, and the Caribbean Thespians (1946). The LTM generates the annual Jamaica PANTOMIME, while the Thespians have produced a number of outstanding theatre people including the actors Mona Chin Hammond and Charles Hyatt, the actor-playwrights Easton Lee and Mitzi Townshend, and the actor-director Ronald Harrison.

In 1950, under the aegis of the British Council, Nugent Monck of the Maddermarket Theatre in Norwich, England, visited Jamaica to work with drama students at secondary schools. From this resulted the first island-wide secondary schools drama festival, which has continued to the present day. In 1952 the Dramatic Society of the newly established University College of the West Indies (UWI) at Mona, Jamaica, gave its first production. The College, which became a full-fledged university in 1963, is significant because its students have spread the work of the Society throughout the West Indies.

In 1953 Errol Hill of TRINIDAD AND TOBAGO was appointed drama tutor in the UWI Extramural Department, dealing with the anglophone Caribbean as well as the Dramatic Society on campus. He started a collection of Caribbean plays, and by 1955 had begun to publish them. Also in 1955, a drama festival fostered by Wycliffe Bennett was held as part of the tercentary celebration of British rule. Under the Jamaica Drama League, this festival became an annual event, extending the work done in schools. In 1956 Louise Bennett was named drama officer for the Jamaica Social Welfare Commission. She travelled throughout the island, using the creative group play-making method to help villagers identify their needs and discover ways of satisfying them. In 1958, to herald the opening of the West Indies Federation, the St Lucian playwright DEREK WALCOTT was commissioned to write an epic drama called *Drums and Colours*, directed by the Jamaican Noel Vaz, who later became the second drama tutor in the UWI Extramural Department. Important playwrights to emerge in this decade were Cicely Waite-Smith (Jamaican by marriage) whose plays such as *Africa Slingshot* and *Uncle Robert* were greatly admired for their penetrating look at Jamaican society, and Barry Reckord, who first offered *Della* to Kingston audiences in 1954, then staged it at the ROYAL COURT THEATRE, London, as *Flesh to a Tiger*.

The next phase was the creating of more theatre spaces in Kingston to accommodate the increasing number of drama groups. In 1961, at a cost of £40,000, the LTM built the Little Theatre and rehearsal room. In 1967 Jamaican playwright Trevor Rhone and director YVONNE BREWSTER converted a garage into the intimate Barn Theatre. Several small theatres followed suit. Instead of playing for two or three times in the the 1200-seat Ward Theatre, companies could now offer several dozen performances in their much smaller houses, improve their scripts and acting skills and attract bigger audiences over the longer run – all of which helped to professionalize the local theatre. In 1968 the Creative Arts Centre was opened on the university campus, offering yet another theatre space in upper Kingston. The establishment of the Jamaica School of Drama (part of the Cultural Training Centre) in 1973 provided two additional performance areas, one an open-air arena.

Several producing companies emerged over the years, to take advantage of the upsurge in live theatre. Few have survived. Among those that have done significant work are the National Theatre Trust formed by Lloyd Reckord in 1968, and Sistren, a Jamaican women's empowerment group of the 1970s–80s, led by Honor Ford-Smith. New playwrights whose work merited attention in the 1960s included Samuel Hillary, Dennis Scott and Sylvia Wynter. The next two decades witnessed a flow of Caribbean productions to and from Jamaica, inspired in part by the university's Dramatic Society but also by the work of the Trinidad Theatre Workshop, as well as by productions originating in other Caribbean countries. The staging of Caribbean plays in London and in the USA has also opened up new opportunities for professional work to outstanding Jamaican and other Caribbean actors.

By the mid-1990s one can distinguish three types of live theatre in Jamaica. The Jamaica pantomime, a traditional form of seasonal entertainment, remains the most all-embracing theatrical experience for the widest audience. Its subject, real or fantasy, always has a contemporary flavour. It combines music and song with dance and speech in vigorous and innovative ways, and can fill the Ward Theatre for several months. Next in popularity is the 'Roots' (Grassroots) Theatre, exemplified by the work of producer Ralph Holness, who offers original plays with an emphasis on sexual behaviour that cater to a mass public. These are the successors to the Bim and Bam shows of an earlier time, translated to an age of sexual revolution. With small casts and limited scenery, they travel around the country playing in cinemas and public halls. Writer-directors Ginger Knight and Balfour Anderson also produce shows of this kind, but of a somewhat higher calibre. The third type of theatre consists of original Jamaican and Caribbean plays, plus those from the world repertoire that have a broader appeal than the Roots plays. The leading theatre critic on the island for 40 years was the late Irish-born, Yorkshire-raised and Jamaican-wed Harry Milner. His encyclopaedic knowledge of the arts generated reviews that were always informative and often controversial.

There has been a significant development in dance theatre since 1947, when the Jamaican Berto Pasuka formed in London a company called Les Ballets Nègres. His dances, mostly narrative in form, were accompanied by percussive instruments and piano. Pasuka's company toured Europe with great success, demonstrating the wide appeal of dance-drama. In Jamaica the form was adopted by the Ivy Baxter Dance Group, which took four original pieces to the Caribbean Festival in PUERTO RICO in 1951. The National Dance Theatre Company of Jamaica, formed in 1962, has continued the tradition, and has won considerable acclaim at home as in tours the world over. EGH

See: I. Baxter, *The Arts of an Island*, Metuchen, NJ, 1970;

K. Corsbie, *Theatre in the Caribbean*, London, 1984; E. Hill, *The Jamaican Stage, 1655–1900: Profile of a Colonial Theatre*, Amherst, Mass., 1992; R. Nettleford, *Mirror Mirror: Identity, Race and Protest in Jamaica*, Jamaica, 1970, *Caribbean Cultural Identity*, California, 1978, and *Dance Jamaica*, New York, 1985; J. W. Nunley and J. Bettelheim, *Caribbean Festival Arts: Each and Every Bit of Difference*, Seattle, Wash., 1988; K. Omotoso, *The Theatrical into Theatre*, London, 1982; R. Wright, *Revels in Jamaica*, rev. edn, Jamaica, 1986.

James, Henry 1843–1916 Expatriate American novelist and critic who found US culture provincial, and its theatre melodramatic and bombastic, lacking subtle character delineation and refinement of style. While spending much of his career in England, he wrote about the theatre in the *Nation*, the *Atlantic*, the *Century* and the *Galaxy* (1875–87), republished in *The Scenic Art* (1948). A failed playwright, James was too dependent on the well made dramas of SCRIBE and SARDOU. Dramatizations of his novels by others have been more successful, including *Berkeley Square* (1928), from *The Sense of the Past*; *The Heiress* (1947), from *Washington Square*; *The Innocents* (1950) from *The Turn of the Screw*; *The Spoils* (1968), from *The Spoils of Poynton*; and *A Boston Story* (1968), from *Watch and Ward*. TLM

Janauschek, Fanny [Francesca] 1830–1904 Czech-born actress, who made her debut at 16 at the Royal Theatre of Prague and two years later was engaged as leading actress of the State Theatre, Frankfurt, where she remained for ten years. Janauschek was an internationally renowned tragedienne before making her 1867 New York debut, performing Medea in German while the rest of the cast acted in English, as did EDWIN BOOTH opposite her German Lady Macbeth in 1868. After a year devoted to learning English, she launched her English-speaking career in 1870. With her statuesque figure, emotional power and vibrant but controlled voice, she excelled in heroic roles like Brunhilde, Deborah, Mary Stuart and later Meg Merrilies. She was also popular in the dual roles of the coquettish French maid and the haughty Lady Dedlock in *Chesney Wold* (based on DICKENS's *Bleak House*). She was one of the last great actresses in the 'grand style', but ended her career (after 1898) playing MELODRAMAS. FHL

Janin, Jules 1804–74 French critic. Known as the 'prince of critics', Janin commanded enormous influence and respect. He began his career as a journalist in 1825 with the *Figaro* (a small satirical paper) and then moved to the *Journal des Débats* as political correspondent. He temporarily took over the theatre column from Duviquet, and became so popular that he remained in this position for 41 years. He was particularly important for his championship of RACHEL and actively supported PONSARD (largely because he disapproved of HUGO). His disapproval of the COMÉDIE-FRANÇAISE was expressed indirectly in a curious volume devoted to the pantomime artist DEBURAU (1832), an invaluable source of information on the THÉÂTRE DES FUNAMBULES. His theatre CRITICISM appeared in two collections, *Histoire de la littérature dramatique* (1853–8) and *La Critique dramatique* (1877). He also published volumes on MLLE MARS (1843), on MLLE GEORGE (1862) and on ALEXANDRE DUMAS (1871). JMCC

Janis [*née* Bierbower], **Elsie** 1889–1956 American VAUDEVILLE entertainer, one of its greatest stars, and considered by many the queen of the form. The product of one of the archetypical stage mothers, from her debut in 1897 to the end of her career in 1932, Elsie appeared as a headliner in vaudeville, MUSICAL COMEDY and REVUE. During the First World War she frequently entertained the troops. The society darling of two continents, the attractive, slender Janis specialized in impersonations and comic songs, introducing such popular songs as 'Fo' de Lawd's Sake, Play a Waltz' and 'Florrie Was a Flapper'. On her death, lifelong friend Mary Pickford remarked, 'This ends the vaudeville era.' Her autobiography, *So Far, So Good!*, was published in 1932. DBW

Japan

Ancient and traditional Theatre permeates Japanese culture. Today, in spite of a surfeit of television and film, live theatre continues to draw huge audiences in major cities – Tokyo, Osaka and Kyoto – and in villages through folk festivals. There are arguably more theatre buildings in Tokyo than any other city in the world; 40 high-tech theatres and performance spaces were constructed in the 1980s alone. Perhaps because Japanese proscribe strong emotional display in daily life, they value sophisticated expression of emotion in the theatre. For whatever reasons, theatregoing is a normal facet of life for millions of modern Japanese.

Japanese share with most Asians the attitude that theatre is an open-ended form, with room for dialogue, song, music, dance and expressive elocution. The mode of expression may be first-person enactment, third-person narrative voice, a chorus substituting for the actor or a combination of modes. MASKS and PUPPETS are important expressive media. With few exceptions, traditional theatrical performance is exceptionally dynamic and based almost equally on textual and performance elements. The traditional word for theatre in Japanese is *geinō*, 'artistic skill', a linguistic indication that theatre arose primarily from the body and the voice of the performer. The Japanese conception of theatre as a complete performing art thus stands in marked contrast to Western critical analysis in which, historically, precedence has been given to drama (ARISTOTLE's plot, character, thought) while performance (Aristotle's spectacle, song, diction) has been felt to be unworthy of philosophic concern. With the exception of European OPERA and American MUSICAL COMEDY, the main line of Western performance development has been toward specialized arts: concert music, ballet, spoken drama. The NATURALISM of ZOLA and STANISLAVSKY, which took life, not art, as both subject matter and medium, was a movement consistent with the Western emphasis on dramatic content and its corollary, disdain for performance as an expressive art. Western visionaries such as ARTAUD, MEYERHOLD, Eisenstein and BRECHT responded to the wholeness of Asian and Japanese theatre, a wholeness that embraced all possible expressive means. Even today Japanese rarely treat play scripts as literature (*bungaku*). Text and performance together make up a single art which is understood to be quite distinct from written literature.

Significant theatre genres include Shintō-based celebratory dances and sketches (*kagura*), Buddhist dances and sketches (*gigaku*), semidramatic dances of the imperial court (*BUGAKU*), serious masked dance dramas of the samurai class (*NŌ*) and their companion comic plays (*KYŌGEN*), flamboyant commercial urban theatre (*KABUKI*), commercial puppet theatre (*BUNRAKU*), and, in this century, modern spoken drama inspired by Western models (*SHINPA* and *SHINGEKI*). Each genre reflects the historical period in which it was first created and the interests and the tastes of the social class which patronized it. Theatre's 2000-year history in Japan has not been 'cannibalistic', as has been the Western experience: succeeding genres did not devour existing genres, but rather coexisted in different societal niches. Performing traditions mentioned above (with the exception of *gigaku*) continue unbroken down to the present day. To see traditional theatre in Japan today is akin to entering a theatrical time capsule that transports the spectator to every period from the present to the ancient past.

Early religious performance: *kagura* Written history began in Japan in the 6th century, so we can only speculate about the origins of Japanese theatre. At excavations of Yayoi period settlements (350 BC to AD 250), clay miniatures of flutes, stringed instruments (*koto*), drums and masks have been found. Clay *haniwa* figures of the same era represent men and women singing, dancing and playing musical instruments. A great variety of folk dances and skits (*kagura*) celebrate Shintō festivals of the new year, rice planting and harvest in thousands of villages, leaving no doubt that performing arts trace their ancestry back to ancient times. The earliest written records of theatre are found in the *Records of Ancient Matters* (*Kojiki*, 712) and *Chronicles of Japan* (*Nihon shoki*, 720). They describe the origin of performance in Japan in a proto-shamanic myth. The Sun Goddess, Amaterasu, angered, has withdrawn from the community of deities into a rock cave, thus plunging the islands of Japan into darkness. Another goddess, Ame-no-Uzume, tries to lure her from the cave by showing her breasts, lowering her skirt, and dancing with a joyful beat of her feet. Hearing the laughter of the assembled gods and goddesses, Amaterasu leaves the cave to see what is causing their merriment and thus light is restored to the world. This is not only a mythological description of the 'first *kagura* performance'. It tells us theatre came into existence as a joyful welcome to a deity to enter a community, thus assuring the continuing life and prosperity of that community. This continues to be the function of *kagura* performances and Shintō festivals (*matsuri*).

Kagura came to be written with the Chinese characters meaning god-entertainment, but its original meaning was a deity's residence. *Kagura* performances occur at the site where the deity resides. The centrality of *kagura* to Shintō worship is clear from the fixed three-part structure of Japanese festivals: summoning the deity, entertaining the deity, and bidding the deity farewell. *Kagura* is that performance which entertains a deity during the mid-section of a Shintō festival and it may take many forms. In the lion

dance (*shishi kagura*), the deity is present in the large lion mask and it brings protection to those who invite it on to their premises. In folk *kagura* (*sato kagura*) a villager wears the mask of a deity and enters the village compound. Possession, role playing, and the enactment of a story, the fundamentals of drama and theatre, exist in prototypical form in village *kagura*. Female shamanic dance (*miko kagura*) by shrine priestesses uses music and dance to induce trance and to evoke a deity who speaks prophetically through the mouth of the priestess-dancer. *Mikagura*, court *kagura*, are performed by court musicians and dancers (courtiers in the past) as part of major Shintō rites sponsored by the imperial court to assure the prosperity of the land and the continuity of imperial rule.

A number of significant characteristics of Japanese theatre are first found in *kagura*. The journey of the deity along a sacred path, from the spiritual to the mundane world where the performance occurred, was marked out as a passageway of the gods. Open passageways to the stage – the bridgeway in *nō* and the flower path in *kabuki* – have their origins in this deeply ingrained conception of god–man relationships. In subsequent theatre forms, scenes of travel, journeys and impressive entrances became normal, indeed essential, parts of dramatic structure. *Kagura*'s square, raised wooden stage, permanent or temporary, is Japan's earliest theatre structure. In the form that influenced the development of *nō* and early *kabuki* theatres, it was covered with a roof and was a freestanding dance pavilion (*kagura den*), usually located at the entrance to the inner shrine compound. *Kagura*'s celebratory and joyous humour continues in *kyōgen* and in *kabuki*. Social or psychological humour that takes the form of SATIRE or FARCE in Western theatre is not a part of traditional theatre. Nor is there a clown or buffoon role, as there is in Indian, Southeast Asian, Chinese and Western theatre. The buffoon is a social outcast and the butt of humour, often cruel, that is based on ineptitude and failure, characteristics that do not fit the communal, egalitarian, felicitous nature of *kagura*. The easy acceptance of theatrical performance as part of both community and religious RITUAL carries forward into Japanese attitudes toward theatre today. We do not know whether the masking found in some *kagura* derives from ancient indigenous sources or is a later adoption influenced by Chinese or Korean theatre.

Early popular theatre: *dengaku, sangaku, sarugaku* Other early, popular entertainments are variously described, in personal diaries and official records of the 10th–12th centuries, as field entertainment (*dengaku*), miscellaneous entertainment (*sangaku*) and monkey music (*sarugaku*). It is difficult to know what kind of performances the terms refer to because sacred and secular, urban and country arts are mentioned first under one term and then under another. In part they referred to itinerant artists – acrobats, tight-rope walkers, JUGGLERS, and magicians – who worked the streets of Nara and Kyoto. *Sangaku*, a term borrowed from China, suggests arts introduced from CHINA (and KOREA). Until the 15th century, *dengaku* dramas were as popular as *nō* plays. Sacred *dengaku* rice-planting songs and dances have celebrated spring festivals as far back as records go; they are still performed as imperial rituals today. Professional *sarugaku* troupes gave variety shows in this early period. They set up in shrine or temple compounds at festival times or performed by invitation at the homes of court nobles. In the 14th century, *sarugaku* actors developed the serious dramas that came to be called *nō*.

Chinese and Korean influence: *gigaku, bugaku*

Between the 7th and 10th centuries, Chinese and Korean culture, including theatre, was widely admired and imitated in Japan. Chinese ideographs were adopted for writing and Chinese poetic forms and styles were learned at court. In 612, a Korean performer Mimaji (Mimashi in Japanese) introduced a Chinese-origin Buddhist dance play at the Japanese imperial court. Scattered masks, musical instruments and costumes of this form may have been brought from China as early as 550. This court-supported form, known as *kiak* in Korea, became *gigaku*, 'elegant entertainment', in Japan. The Japanese regent, Prince Shōtoku (r.593–621), ordered Mimaji to establish a school of music and dance at the court and he assigned boys to be his pupils. Other Korean musicians and dancers followed Mimaji to Japan.

Gigaku propagated Buddhism, a religion new to Japan which Shōtoku avidly proselytized during his reign. A 13th-century account describes a *gigaku* performance: first, ritual Buddhist music (*netori*) is played on flute, drums, gong and cymbals; then chanting monks masked as Buddha figures pass in procession (*gyōdō*) followed by a second procession of ten actors wearing masks of a Chinese woman, a king, Baromon (an Indian Brahman), Karora (Garuda, the King of Birds in Indian myth), lion tamer, wrestler and others. Finally, the masked figures mount a temporary outdoor stage and perform comic skits cautioning against Buddhist sins. By the 12th century, *gigaku* had lost imperial support and performances gradually ceased – an unusual case in Japan of a significant theatre form dying out. Some 250 *gigaku* masks are preserved in temple collections; the oldest date from the 7th century, the time when *gigaku* was first introduced, and may be of Chinese make. They are beautifully carved and painted, and are rare works of art.

A rival form of dance entertainment, *BUGAKU*, was introduced to the court from China via Korea in the 8th century. In 701 an Imperial Music Bureau was established at the court for instruction in *bugaku* and its music (*kangen*). (The composite dance-music art is called *gagaku*, 'musical entertainment'.) From the beginning, *bugaku* was an eclectic art. The Bureau had divisions for Chinese music and dance (*tōgaku*) and for Korean (*komagaku*) and apportioned its 255 performers to various specialities within the two divisions. In 736 performers were assigned to learn and perform new dances introduced from southern India and from Vietnam. The Emperor Ninmyō (r.833–49) was so devoted to *bugaku* he journeyed to the Tang court of China to study the original music and dance. He also composed many new dances. From the 13th to the 16th century *bugaku* entered a period of serious decline. An impoverished imperial court could not afford to support hundreds of performers after it lost political power to the rising samurai class. Many pieces in the repertory were lost and the early dramatic vitality of the genre was largely forgotten. The oldest dance pieces, such as 'Bunomai', a martial dance, suggest the present style of performing is considerably less dynamic than in the past. The dance 'Genjōraku' presents an intensely dramatic situation: a hero of Indian myth fights a poisonous snake, is victorious and returns triumphant to his castle. A number of the *bugaku* dances were borrowed and then absorbed into provincial performance genres, such as Buddhist longevity dances (*ennen*), because of their dramatic qualities. Today, however, *bugaku* is danced to instrumental music only and there is virtually no role-playing or dramatic interaction. Unison or mirror-image dancing in geometric patterns by two or four dancers is typical. Thus the earlier storytelling elements, song lyrics (and possibly dialogue), have not survived. *Bukagu*'s serene, stately qualities reflect the art's patronage by the imperial court and later by large shrines and temples closely associated with the throne, an association that is maintained at the present time.

Theatre of the samurai: *nō, kyōgen*

In Japan's medieval period (1185–1600), samurai generals wrested power from the imperial court and assuming for themselves the title of Shōgun, or General, ruled from lavish courts first in Kamakura and then in Kyoto. The chief theatre forms patronized by the samurai class were *sarugaku*, also called at that time *sarugaku nō*, and then later simply *NŌ* ('skill'), and its companion comic form *KYŌGEN*. In the middle of the 14th century, dozens of professional *sarugaku nō* troupes were attached to important shrines and temples. Four large troupes were based in Nara, the ancient capital city, where they performed for festival occasions and in public (*kanjin nō*). The head of one of these troupes, Kan'ami Kiyotsugu (1333–84), is credited with transforming *sarugaku* into *nō*. A skilled actor and troupe head, he conceived of combining a popular narrative song of the time (*kuse*) with rhythmic dance (*mai*) and used the resulting narrative song-dance (*kuse mai*) as the climactic scene of a performance. He structured his plays as virtual monodramas (in contrast to multirole plays of competing *dengaku nō* troupes), in which the crucial event in the life of the chief character (the *shite*, or Doer, role), often the grieving spirit of a dead person, was remembered and reenacted in a *kuse mai* scene. Kan'ami's son, ZEAMI MOTOKIYO, was an actor of singular genius whose superb acting focused even more attention on the Doer role. Kan'ami stressed convincing physical and vocal characterization (*monomane*) through observation of real people; hence he is considered the father of acting, as distinct from dancing and singing, in Japanese theatre.

Kan'ami's troupe, competing with other *sarugaku nō* and with *dengaku nō* troupes, had the good fortune to act before the Shōgun Ashikaga Yoshimitsu in 1374. The 14-year-old Shōgun was attracted by the playing of Zeami, who was 11 at the time, and invited him to be his companion in the palace. During the ensuing 50 years, Zeami performed at court and received shogunal patronage. Zen Buddhism was the official religion of the Ashikaga court, and under Zeami's guidance Zen artistic principles of restraint, austerity and economy of expression were incorporated into *nō* performance and plays. The unadorned stage, the deliberate pace of performance, masks for major characters and the significant gesture reflect Zen ideals. Zeami's advice to the actor to 'move seven if the heart feels ten' is a succinct expression of Zen precepts. Suggestive beauty (*yūgen*) was the quality most sought by Zeami in performance. Zeami became troupe leader when his father died and in his later years wrote important treatises on *nō* acting. He was succeeded by his eldest son Kanze Motomasa (?1394–1432), author of the play *The Sumida River* (*Sumidagawa*), and, following his early death, by his scholarly son-in-law KOMPARU ZENCHIKU. The last of the great actor-playwrights was Kanze Nobumitsu (1435–1516). He composed highly dramatic plays – *Benkei in the Boat* (*Funa Benkei*), *The Ataka Barrier* (*Ataka*), *The Maple Viewing* (*Momijigari*) – that used large casts and pitted Doer (*shite*) against Sideman (*waki*) in a dramatic conflict (originally he was a *waki* actor).

Shogunal patronage drastically declined during the civil wars of the 16th century. When Kyoto was burned, troupes fled to the provinces. To support themselves, actors instructed provincial samurai lords, priests and wealthy commoners in singing and dance. Texts for chanting (*utaibon*) were first printed and sold to the public in 1512. Hundreds of *nō* plays became available in print, as well as descriptions of staging, costumes, masks and music. *Nō* spread among the lower classes giving rise to amateur performances. Many surviving provincial *nō* styles trace their origins to this time. *Nō* troupes returned to the centre of political power when the country was unified at the end of the 16th century. The ruler Toyotomi Hideyoshi (1537–98) studied *nō*, ordered *nō* plays to be written about his battlefield victories, and played himself in them. The first Tokugawa Shōgun, Ieyasu (1543–1616), patronized the Kanze troupe even before he assumed rule in 1603. His successors ruled from the new capital of Edo (Tokyo), where they designated *nō* a 'ceremonial art' (*shikigaku*) to be performed on formal occasions through the long Tokugawa era (1600–1868). The third Tokugawa Shōgun, Iemitsu (1604–51), codified every aspect of *nō* and forbade deviation. *Nō* actors were given samurai rank and only the sons of actors were allowed to become performers. The troupe head (*iemoto*) was given absolute authority, and was held responsible for the actions of all members of the troupe. The freshness of performance (*hana*) that Zeami had prized was smothered by tradition and regulation. Popular audiences were forbidden to see or study *nō*. Actors devoted themselves to ever greater refinement and subtlety in their acting until, by the close of the 19th century, a play took two or three times as long to perform as during Zeami's time.

Nō evolved eclectically, its plays based on borrowed stories and its poetic forms mirroring earlier literature. Zeami advised playwrights to dramatize events from history and legend for these would be familiar and easily grasped: Chinese legend, and Japanese mythology and history, especially the 12th-century civil war between the Heike and Genji clans, are the source of most plays. *Nō*'s sonorous singing style grew out of Buddhist chant (*shōmyō*) and early popular songs (*imayō*); its restrained movement style shows the influence of professional female dance (*shirabyōshi*) as well as popular and religious performances (*jushi hashiri, ennen, dengaku, kōwaka*). The refined masks that mark *nō* as a uniquely suggestive art have antecedents in *gigaku* and *bugaku* masks of the court tradition and in village *kagura* masks as well. Masks for women's roles are especially beautiful. Often said to be 'neutral', in fact they express, usually in subtle fashion, a wide range of human emotions – happiness, pride, innocence, melancholy, elegance, grief. Except for the lavish costumes of the Doer role, dress is restrained in keeping with Zen precepts. Few properties are used and these tend to be symbolic – a fan as a drinking cup, a cloth-wrapped frame for a boat, for example.

Kyōgen, 'inspired or "mad" speech', is a performance genre that is both related to and separate from *nō*. *Kyōgen* actors perform in *nō* plays and they enact independent celebratory, often comic, plays that alternate in performance with them. (The term *nōgaku* encompasses the art of *nō* and *kyōgen* together.) *Kyōgen* plays and acting style are at least as old as *nō*. Some accounts trace *kyōgen*'s origins to comic dances – such as Ame-no-Uzume's – from the prehistoric Age of the Gods. The ritual play *Okina*, performed as an auspicious prayer for longevity at the beginning of a *nō-kyōgen* programme, is in both the *nō* and the *kyōgen* repertories and there is some evidence that the latter version is older. The humorous titles of 11th-century *sarugaku* plays (*A Nun Seeks Baby Napkins*, *Pranks by a City Boy*) show that *kyōgen* plays were a vital part of the *sarugaku* repertory. During Zeami's time specialist performers of *nō*, of *kyōgen*, of drums and of flute were combined into a comprehensive *sarugaku nō* troupe. When *kyōgen* actors of the Ōkura, Sagi, and Izumi families received direct patronage from the Tokugawa rulers toward the end of the 16th century, they became semi-independent of *nō* troupes. As with *nō*, all performers are men and acting is generally a hereditary profession passed down from father to son.

Within a *nō* play, the role of a commoner, servant or labourer is played by a *kyōgen* actor. Rarely is more than one *kyōgen* actor called for in a *nō* play, but in dramatic plays, such as *Benkei in the Boat*, the role is major and essential to the play's plot. The *kyōgen* role is also important in the interlude (*ai* or *ai kyōgen*) between parts one and two of the typical two-part *nō* play. When the Doer retires from the stage to change costume, the *kyōgen* actor recapitulates the story, in a monologue or in dialogue with the Sideman. Published *nō* texts do not contain the interludes, for these sections are the sole prerogative of *kyōgen* performers. Finally, *kyōgen* actors perform all roles in the independent comic plays that make up the separate *kyōgen* repertory. Most plays have two to four characters, a major role (*shite*), a second role (*ado*), and subsidiary roles (*koado*, 'small *ado*'). In all roles the *kyōgen* style of acting, in contrast to *nō* acting, calls for a clear and lively voice and movements that are active and precise. Actors improvised *kyōgen* in performance until at least the 17th century. Scenarios of 165 texts were written in manuscript form in 1578 and a collection of 203 texts of plays as they were performed were transcribed by Ōkura Toraakira, head of the Ōkura acting family, between 1638 and 1642. These were secret texts, shown outside the acting family only under exceptional circumstances. Some 200 *kyōgen* plays were published for the general public in 1660.

A *nō-kyōgen* programme is made up of thematically

unrelated plays chosen from the *nō* repertory of 240 plays and the *kyōgen* repertory of 260 plays. Each programme is given a single performance. Plays are chosen to match the season, the occasion and the aesthetic principle of ever-increasing emotional tension and tempo (*jo-ha-kyū*) that regulates performance. The *nō* repertory is divided into five groups based on the nature of the Doer role and the order in which the plays appear on a programme. A typical programme contains, in order, a play with a Shintō deity (*kami*), a male warrior (*asura*), a court lady (*katsura*), a deranged woman (*kyōran*) and a demon (*kichiku*) in the major role. The *kyōgen* plays that follow each *nō* play have as main roles a deity (*kami*), a wealthy land owner (*daimyō*), a small landholder (*shōmyō*), a bridegroom or son-in-law (*muko*), a Buddhist priest or mountain ascetic (*shukke* or *yamabushi*) or a demon (*oni*). A day-long programme in Zeami's time consisted of eight to ten *nō* plays and five or six *kyōgen* plays. Even a complete but shorter programme of five *nō* and four *kyōgen* is too long for modern audiences; shorter programmes, of as few as two or three *nō* and one or two *kyōgen*, fit the busy schedules of contemporary urban audiences. All-*kyōgen* programmes have gained acceptance in recent decades as the social status of *kyōgen* actors has grown.

Popular theatre of the Edo (Tokugawa) period: *kabuki, bunraku*

Professional, commercial KABUKI and BUNRAKU are products of a restless, assertive, mercantile society that flourished in the great cities of Kyoto, Osaka and Edo (Tokyo) under the xenophobic rule of successive Tokugawa Shōguns (1603–1868). Troupes of the two genres competed for the same audiences. They performed in theatres side by side and over the decades they borrowed each other's successful plays. Alike in certain ways, nonetheless they evolved out of different antecedents and they attempt mutually distinct artistic aims.

Kabuki grew out of popular, urban dances and sketches of contemporary life. In the 16th century, vagabond troupes congregated in Kyoto, then the capital, where they performed secularized forms of religious dances (*ennen*) and folk dances (*yayako odori* and *kaka odori*). Around 1600 one of these dancers, a woman named Okuni and advertised as a priestess of the Grand Shrine in Izumo, made a great success in a new dance called *kabuki*. She performed on a temporary stage set up first in the grounds of Kitano Shrine and later along the dry bed of the Kamo River (hence the disparaging term for *kabuki* actors, 'beggars of the riverbed'). *Kabuki* was unorthodox. It was the rock entertainment of the 17th century. Okuni performed the first Japanese plays of contemporary urban life: numerous painted screens and scrolls show her outrageously garbed as a handsome young warrior, exotic Christian rosary draped on her bosom, conducting an assignation with a prostitute. The Portuguese were newly arrived and licensed quarters for prostitution had only recently been established in Kyoto. Okuni's chief imitators were professional prostitutes who performed *kabuki* dances and songs on public stages as a come-on for their evening profession. Paintings of the early 17th century show prostitutes seated sensuously on tiger skins playing the *shamisen*, a lute recently introduced from China via Okinawa, as bevies of girls circle the stage.

The shogunate banned women from public stages in 1629 as part of its general policy of restricting each person to a single occupation; prostitutes could not also be actresses. Early *kabuki* was also performed by troupes of young boys (*wakashū*), doubling as catamites, and they were banned in 1652. After these events *kabuki* began to develop as a serious art. *Kabuki*'s major characteristics became established by the early 18th century: all-day multi-act plays, adult male casts (and therefore the evolution of the art of the *onnagata* or actor of female roles), a yearly season of five or six productions, and unique musical, dance and acting styles appropriate to various styles of play. Standard scene types are identifiable in the 1680s and 90s: the brothel assignation (*keiseigai*), the swaggering parade of a hero (*tanzen roppō*), the flight of lovers (*michiyuki*), the choreographed fight between a hero and a group of opponents (*tachimawari*). Government officials restricted the number and location of *kabuki* theatres and forced actors to live apart from others. Plays about current samurai were forbidden, leading playwrights to disguise contemporary events as history. In spite of government suppression of *kabuki*, samurai lords and their ladies, rich merchants, priests, workers and servants all attended the theatre and the despised art flourished as a major attraction of Japanese urban life.

Uniquely different plays and acting styles developed in *kabuki*'s two centres, Kyoto–Osaka and Edo. SAKATA TŌJŪRŌ performed in Kyoto for relatively cultivated audiences. In 1678 he portrayed Izaemon, the pampered scion of a wealthy merchant in *New Year's Remembrance of the Courtesan Yugiri* (*Yūgiri nagori no shōgatsu*). In the scene set in Osaka's current licensed quarter, Tōjūrō continued Okuni's original prostitute-buying plays. He developed a 'soft' acting style (*wagoto*) for romantic domestic scenes (*sewamono*).

In contrast, Ichikawa Danjūrō I wrote and acted in bravura history plays (*jidaimono*) for an audience of rough samurai and adventurers in the new city of Edo. He created a 'rough' acting style (*aragoto*) and specialized in playing heroes of superhuman strength. The bold red and black make-up (*kumadori*) and exaggerated COSTUMES that mark *aragoto* acting date from Danjūrō's first stage appearance as a boy of 14. Danjūrō's powerful poses (*mie*) and gestures are said to have been suggested by Buddhist guardian statues (the present Danjūrō XII worships at the same temple Danjūrō I did, dedicated to the Guardian Deity Fudō Myōō). Titles of plays in which he and his son Danjūrō II (1689–1758) starred are amply descriptive – *Indestructible* (*Fuwa*, 1680), *The Thundergod* (*Narukami*, 1684; trans. 1975), *Immovable* (*Fudō*, 1697), *Wait a Moment!* (*Shibaraku*, 1697), *Pulling the Elephant* (*Zōhiki*, 1701), *Repel!* (*Oshimodoshi*, 1714), *The Arrow Maker* (*Yanone*, 1725). Danjūrō II blended rough and soft styles when he created the role of the dandy hero in *Sukeroku: Flower of Edo* (*Sukeroku yukari Edo no zakura*, 1713; trans. 1975), written by Tsuuchi Jihei II (1679–1760). The wonderfully dramatic confrontations, erotic byplay, impromptu comedy verging on farce and brilliant settings of the licensed quarter justly make this *kabuki*'s most popular play. These and plays added by later generations comprise the Eighteen Favourite Plays (*jūhachiban*) of the ICHIKAWA DANJŪRŌ family.

Professional puppet theatre, today popularly called *bunraku*, began in the late 16th century from wholly different sources than *kabuki*. Doll figures manipulated by SHAMANS served as scapegoats, carrying away impurities and evil, in religious rites in ancient times and popular puppetry was influenced by travelling troupes of Chinese and Korean performers, as part of *sangaku*. Sophisticated mechanical dolls (*karakuri*) decorated festival floats and attracted audiences to commercial theatres as late as the 19th century. Narrative skills, long admired in Japan, found expression in dozens of religious and secular forms. Today, we can hear raconteurs of comic stories (*rakugo*) and reciters of historical epics (*kōdan*) carrying on their narrative traditions in variety halls. In the 1590s performers of the previously separate arts of puppet manipulation and of narrative storytelling joined forces with musicians who played the plucked three-stringed lute, the *shamisen*, forming commercial puppet-theatre troupes. One name for this tripartite theatre was *jōruri*, after the musical style used to chant a popular epic, *Twelve Tales of Princess Jōruri* (*Jōruri jūni dan*). The early-17th-century styles of commercial performance (*sekkyō bushi*, *ko jōruri*) were built around a narrative, sung, chanted and spoken by a single narrator (*tayū*), accompanied by a single *shamisen* player and illustrated by puppets. This remains the basic style of performance today. At first puppeteers, chanter and *shamisen* musician were concealed, but techniques of performance were of great interest to audiences, and by the early 18th century, when CHIKAMATSU MONZAEMON wrote the first psychologically persuasive 'modern' puppet plays, all performers were visible to the audience.

The first significant commercial puppet theatre was the Takemoto Theatre on the west bank of Dotombori Canal in Osaka. Its leading chanter TAKEMOTO GIDAYŪ specialized in serious, emotional delivery. The Toyotake Theatre (est. 1703) on the canal's east bank was set up by rival chanter Toyotake Wakatayū, whose style was light and flowery, hence a west style (*nishi fū*) and an east style (*higashi fū*) of chanting. The PUPPETS executed simple movements, each manipulated by one puppeteer. Audiences enjoyed the chanting, but early puppet theatre presented no challenge to *kabuki*. Between 1720 and 1740 performers revolutionized *bunraku* art and world puppetry. They adopted characteristics of a first-person theatre, thereby bringing it closer to *kabuki*. Yoshida Bunzaburō (?–1760) invented a three-man manipulation system in 1724. A nearly life-size doll with movable eyes, eyebrows, mouth, hands and fingers moved realistically within elaborately constructed scenery. Puppet-theatre producers and *kabuki* managers perfected the revolving stage (a century before Europe), multiple trap doors and lifts with which to move performers and entire scenes magically into and out of view.

Exciting new plays were written to capitalize on the expressive power of the three-man puppets. At the Takemoto Theatre the playwriting team of Takeda Izumo II (1691–1756), Namiki Senryū (1695–1751), and Miyoshi Shōraku (1696–1775) jointly composed the Three Great Masterpieces of puppet drama: *The House of Sugawara* (*Sugawara denju tenarai kagami*, 1746), a drama of feudal loyalty; *Yoshitsune and the Thousand Cherry Trees* (*Yoshitsune senbon zakura*, 1747), a war tragedy that pits brother against brother; and *The Treasury of Loyal Retainers* (*Kanadehon chūshingura*, 1748; trans. 1971), Japan's famous revenge play. The convoluted plots of these multi-act history plays are driven by Confucian conflicts between duty (*giri*) and human compassion (*ninjō*). In *The Treasury of Loyal Retainers* the stalwart hero Yuranosuke abandons his wife and debauches himself out of loyalty to his slain lord. The plays contain spectacular puppet effects – a flying fox, a statue coming to life – and horrifying scenes of sacrifice – ritual disembowelment (*seppuku*), verifying the severed head of your child (*kubi jikken*), killing a beloved relative to save one's lord (*migawari*) – draw powerful emotions from the chanters. In *Chronicle of the Battle of Ichinotani* (*Ichinotani futaba gunki*, 1751; trans. 1975), composed by Namiki Sōsuke and others for the Toyotake Theatre, the Genji general Kumagai slays his teenage son in order to save the life of the emperor's son, Atsumori. Then he is forced to show his son's head to his wife. Unable to bear the horror of his act, Kumagai abandons his rank and becomes a mendicant Buddhist monk. Basic to puppet narrative is the pathos of early death, symbolized by the quickly fading cherry blossoms.

Plays were now enacted with remarkable verisimilitude – real water and mud were used in staging the domestic play *The Summer Festival* (*Natsu matsuri*, 1745). Perhaps the *yin–yang* concept of balance through opposites explains why human *kabuki* is stylized while puppet *bunraku* is realistic. If the plays were lacking in dramatic coherence (scenes were parcelled out to the different writers), they provided wonderfully effective theatre. The popularity of the productions – *Chronicle of the Battle of Ichinotani* ran 12 months – was such that within a month or two *kabuki* troupes would mount pirated versions to keep their audiences. In the process of borrowing from each other, *kabuki* and *bunraku* became more alike, sharing a humanistic world view, a common audience and a flamboyant aesthetic.

Kabuki borrowed puppet movement techniques, *gidayū* music and third-person narration. Adaptations of puppet plays came to make up a third of the *kabuki* repertory. Conversely, puppeteers studied *kabuki* productions like *The Vendetta at Iga* (*Igagoe norikake kappa*, 1777) and *Dispute in the House of Sendai* (*Meiboku Sendai hagi*, 1777), and imitated the actors in later puppet performances. After Chikamatsu Hanji's popular *Moritsune's Battle Camp* (*Moritsune jinya*, 1769) and *Mount Imo and Mount Se* (*Imoseyama onna teikin*, 1771; trans. 1990), *bunraku*'s popularity rapidly declined. The Takemoto and Toyotake theatres closed by 1772 and by the beginning of the 20th century the Bunraku-za in Osaka was the only remaining puppet theatre.

Kabuki attracted fresh audiences with ever-changing performance styles. Playwright Namiki Shōzō I (1730–76) introduced traps, lifts and the revolving stage to enhance *kabuki*'s spectacle. *Onnagata* stars Segawa Kikunojō I (1693–1749) and Nakamura Tomijūrō I (1719–86) were adored for dancing in new versions of *The Lion Dance* (*Shakkyō*) and *Dōjō Temple* (*Dōjōji*). In 1784, the playwright Takarada Jurai created a new dramatic dance form (*buyō geki*) featuring male roles in *Love's Snowy Barrier* (*Seki no to*) and a new style of music, *tokiwazu*. The form was developed by playwrights Horikoshi Nisōji (1721–?81) and pupil Sakurada Jisuke I (1734–1806), who was also famous for his witty writing style. In Namiki Gōhei III's new dance drama *The Subscription List* (*Kanjinchō*, 1840; trans. 1966, 1972) all the roles were male. Danjūrō VII (1791–1859) created the leading part of Benkei, now considered the most difficult dance role in the repertory. *The Subscription List* is based on the *nō* play *The Ataka Barrier*. It was the first of a score of *kabuki* dance dramas, serious and comic, based on *nō* and *kyōgen* plays, that borrowed music and acting techniques from these forms.

In spite of the government's Tempo Reforms of 1830–42, which aimed at nothing less than the destruction of *kabuki* by forcing theatres to move to Saruwaka-cho outside of Edo city, *kabuki* flourished. Playwrights Tsuruya Namboku IV, Segawa Jokō III (1806–81), and Kawatake Mokuami in succession wrote 'raw' domestic plays (*kizewamono*) about thieves and gangsters, reflecting the riots, famines and peasant uprisings of the late feudal period, for actors Onoe Kikugorō V (1844–1903) and Ichikawa Kodanji IV (1812–66). Their scenes of murder (*koroshiba*), eroticism (*nureba*), torture (*semeba*) and extortion (*yusuriba*) illustrate a corrupt and decaying society. Namboku's masterpiece, *The Scarlet Princess of Edo* (*Sakura hime azuma bunsho*, 1817; trans. 1975), weaves together historical and outcast worlds (*sekai*), humour and soaring passages of poetic dialogue, and bloody, arresting visual effects. His imperial princess becomes a prostitute, his gangster becomes an official, and a samurai lord is murdered by a criminal.

The Western room: traditional theatre in the modern world Western warships forced Japan to open its society to foreign trade and culture in the mid-19th century. The last Tokugawa Shōgun was defeated in a brief civil war by citizen soldiers loyal to the new Emperor Meiji. Cultural, political and economic changes during the Meiji period (1868–1912) profoundly altered the social and economic basis of all existing theatre forms. Paradoxically, Japan's economic miracle since defeat in the Second World War has increased competition for theatre. Increasingly, traditional genres – *bugaku*, *nō*, *kyōgen*, *kabuki* and *bunraku* – must hold an audience in competition with film, television, rock concerts, travel and other amenities of modern life.

Nō and *kyōgen* actors suffered greatly when the Meiji emperor abolished feudalism in 1869. Overnight, *nō* actors lost their samurai status; without work or income, they were forced to sell heirloom masks and costumes to stay alive (hence the fine *nō* collections in Western museums). Within a year, however, actor Umewaka Minoru (1828–1909) began the process of bringing *nō* to the public by charging admission to performances in his home. Later he persuaded the reigning *nō* star Hōshō Kurō to return from retirement on his farm and to join him in performing in public. In Kyoto monthly public performances were started by actors of the Kongō school in 1877. New *nō* theatres were built in Tokyo's Aoyama Palace in 1878 and Shiba Park in 1881, encouraged by statesman Iwakura Tomomi who, returning from a study trip to Europe, realized that *nō* could be Japan's equivalent of Western OPERA. Former President Ulysses S. Grant, visiting Japan, praised *nō* and urged that it be preserved. Gradually *nō* occupied an elite position in the new society. After a short period of

government support, including imperial command performances, public support solidified.

Today the thousand or so professional actors that belong to the five *nō* and two *kyōgen* schools support themselves primarily by teaching many thousands of devoted amateurs, while only a portion of their income derives from performance (theatres seat 400–500 and each programme is performed a single time). Each *nō* school owns one or more theatres and the hereditary masteractor (*iemoto*) of each school exercises total artistic and financial control. On the surface, the repertory and style of performance appear unaffected by the modern world. With rare exceptions, new plays are not performed (Kanze Hideo was banished from *nō* in the 1960s for acting in modern plays).

The livelihood of *kabuki* and *bunraku* performers was not directly threatened by Meiji-period reform because their popular audiences did not immediately change. But through the 20th century both theatres gradually lost their 'popular' audiences and became classical arts favoured by a higher, better educated social class. In 1872 officials informed *kabuki* playwrights and actors of the emperor's 'command' that they must present only material suitable for family groups or foreign spectators. Throughout its 300-year history, *kabuki* had been 'contemporary theatre' and, like film and television today, everything new in society was eagerly placed on the stage. In the late Meiji period, Mokuami wrote plays featuring telegraph messages, locomotives and balloon ascents. In 1879, actor-manager Morita Kanya XII (1846–97) hired a British troupe from Hong Kong to act alongside *kabuki* actors in *A Foreign Kabuki* set in London. Modern 'cropped-hair plays' (*zangirimono*), acted by Onoe Kikugorō V (1844–1903), put current life on the *kabuki* stage. Ichikawa Danjūrō IX played in living-history plays (*katsureki geki*) that aimed at historical truth. Danjūrō joined the calls of the Society for Theatre Reform, formed in 1886, to modernize and sanitize *kabuki* in line with Western theatre practice. Leading literary scholars advocated abolishing traditional music, the wooden-clapper sound effects, the *hanamichi*, stage assistants and the female impersonator, so as to 'modernize' *kabuki*. These extreme reforms never came to pass, but the raucous nature of *kabuki* was irretrievably destroyed.

Literary men from outside the theatre replaced staff playwrights as the authors of new *kabuki* dramas (*shin kabuki*). Plays such as Tsubouchi Shōyō's *A Paulownia Leaf* (1904), Okamoto Kidō's *The Love Suicides at Mount Toribe* (1915), and more recently *kabuki* scripts by novelist-playwright Mishima Yukio are notable for having achieved *de facto* the aims of the discredited reform movement. Traditional *kabuki* dramaturgy is abandoned. Modern authors do not know seven-five dialogue, poetic name-saying speeches or traditional act and scene structure. They rarely incorporate *mie* poses, *shamisen* music or stylized battles. New *kabuki* plays continue to be written and staged at the Kabuki-za in Tokyo, but rarely do audiences like them, rarely are they revived, and rarely do they in any way deserve the name *kabuki*.

A handful of superb *bunraku* performers sparked renewed interest in the puppet theatre during the Meiji era, working primarily at two new theatres in Osaka, the

Bunraku-za (est. 1872) and its competitor the Hikoroku Theatre (est. 1884). The chanter Takemoto Harudayū V (1808–77) was greatly admired for his powerful and expressive voice. One of the few *shamisen* players to achieve personal fame, Toyozawa Danpei (1827–98) revolutionized the art of *bunraku* music. He composed complex scores that closely supported the emotional nuances of scenes rather than merely serving as accompaniment to the chanter. It was said a listener could understand the emotions of a character just by hearing Danpei play the *shamisen*. With his wife he wrote the touching Buddhist miracle play, *Miracle at Tsubosaka Temple* (*Tsubosaka reigenki*, 1879), the last important text to enter the traditional repertory. Chanter Takemoto Settsu-Daijō (1836–1917) performed for members of the imperial family and in 1902 was honoured with an imperial title. A decade before this, Settsu-Daijō began the fad of chanting puppet texts without puppets. Amateurs studied chanting under the instruction of professional *shamisen* teachers; in 1889 perhaps a thousand amateurs were chanting in theatres and recital halls in Osaka. Mass performances by 400–500 chanters were not uncommon. Women chanters (*onna jōruri*) gained enormous success in commercial variety theatres (*yose*) in the early decades of the 20th century. Settsu-Daijō attempted to restore 'historical truth' to classical plays, parallel to the efforts of Danjūrō IX in *kabuki*. He placed the old plays in their proper historical period and called characters by their real names. Lovers of *bunraku*, however, did not want their plays tampered with and by 1891 Settsu-Daijō had abandoned his reforms. *Bunraku*'s Meiji-period revival did not last when its charismatic performers passed from the scene. The one remaining puppet theatre, the Bunraku-za of Osaka, was purchased in 1909 by the Shōchiku Theatrical Corporation. Performers split into two competing groups following the Second World War, but in 1963 they rejoined to form the present single troupe under the auspices of the Bunraku Association and with generous financial support from the Ministry of Education. The troupe draws a stable, moderate-sized audience at its home theatre in Osaka and on yearly national tours.

Early in the Meiji period, when the government ceased regulating the number and location of theatres, *kabuki*-theatre owners moved to elite locations in the centre of Tokyo. In 1872 Kanya XII moved the Morita Theatre, which had opened in old Edo in 1660, into the heart of Tokyo and three years later rebuilt it as the New Tomi Theatre equipped with Western seats and gas lighting where he staged *kabuki*'s first nighttime performances. Foreign dignitaries, including former President Grant, attended this 'modern' theatre. The Kabuki-za, now the premiere *kabuki* theatre in the country, opened in the fashionable Ginza district in 1889. *Kabuki* managers were successful in drawing the new upper-middle class, but in doing so they abandoned their traditional supporters, the merchants, artisans and workers.

During the Second World War audiences for both *kabuki* and *bunraku* declined drastically. Performers were drafted into the army or sent on war-related entertainment tours. Theatres were gutted by bombing. After Japan's surrender in 1945 American-occupation censors banned 'feudal' *kabuki* and *bunraku* plays and it appeared that the survival of both forms was in doubt. The appeal of *kabuki* to a broad segment of the public remained strong, however, and as soon as CENSORSHIP was lifted audiences again filled the Kabuki-za, the Shinbashi Dance Theatre, and, from 1966, the new National Theatre. The Minami Theatre in Kyoto (remodelled in 1991) and the Naka Theatre in Osaka are located in traditional entertainment districts and retain the flavour of old *kabuki*.

Kabuki family acting traditions have been carried into the second half of the 20th century by a group of charismatic and talented actors: Ichikawa Danjūrō XI (1909–65); Living National Treasure Onoe Shōroku II (1913–89); Matsumoto Koshirō VII (1910–75); Living National Treasure Nakamura Kanzaburō XVII (1909–88); former President of the Kabuki Actors' Association Ichikawa Sadanji III (1898–1964); Morita Kanya XIV (1907–75); and two great *onnagata*, Living National Treasure NAKAMURA UTAEMON VI; and Living National Treasure Onoe Baikō VI (1915–). Today's young actors BANDŌ TAMASABURŌ, Kataoka Takao I (1944–), Onoe Kikugorō VII (1942–), Ichikawa Danjūrō XII (1946–) and even younger stars are idolized by fans. They have done much to attract a younger audience in the 1970s and 80s.

The imaginative staging by actor-director ICHIKAWA ENNOSUKE III, who insists upon reinterpreting each classic to make it interesting to a modern audience, is unusual. Today *kabuki* is a classical, orthodox theatre in which little change occurs. Spectators are mostly middle-class, block-booking by corporations fills 75 per cent of the house and a first-class ticket costs US $80–100 (£50–60). Once a despised theatre, it calls itself Grand Kabuki on foreign tours. Actors work exceptionally long hours: matinée and evening bills, usually different, begin at 11 in the morning and end at 10 at night. The programme changes monthly, performances are daily for 25 days, and four or five days at the end of the month are spent in intensive rehearsals on the next month's plays. Theatre owners and producers run *kabuki* today and the 500 or so professional actors are rotated among theatres each month as needed. There no longer is a functioning troupe system. Actors often perform in mixed-genre productions today.

Government support of theatre in the modern period has been negligible. *Bugaku* is the chief exception: the main troupe continues as part of the Imperial Household Agency. *Bunraku*, as noted, began receiving government subsidies in 1963. A distinguished artist who is named an Intangible Cultural Asset or Living National Treasure receives a small government annuity. Most significantly, in recent decades the government has built four modern and beautifully equipped theatres containing stages, research facilities and performer-training programmes: the National Theatre for *kabuki* and *bunraku* (1966), the National Variety Theatre (1966), and the National Noh Theatre (1983), all in Tokyo, and the National Bunraku Theatre (1985) in Osaka. Theatre staffs, but not the actors or musicians, are on government salaries.

Traditional performances have been televised regularly throughout Japan since the 1960s (*kabuki* most often), thereby reaching audiences that normally would never have the chance to attend the theatre. *Kabuki, bunraku, nō*, and *kyōgen* troupes are regularly sent on international tours, so that traditional theatre is no longer isolated.

Transition to modern theatre: *shinpa*

SHINPA, 'new school', developed as the theatre of the half-Westernized, half-traditional urban middle class that rose to prominence during the Meiji era. It was a transitional theatre whose rationale for existence was the rejection of 'old' values. The first *shinpa* plays were staged by the failed politician Kawakami Otojirō (1864–1911) who used patriotic events, such as the Russo-Japanese war, as subjects for MELODRAMA. He and his wife, Sada Yakko (1871–1946), a trained geisha, toured the United States and Europe in 1899–1901 where their troupe's emotional performances received astounded acclaim. Sada was compared to SARAH BERNHARDT for the 'realism' of her death scenes. Due to Sada, the 1629 law banning women from the public stage was repealed.

Kawakami successfully adapted Western plays such as *Othello*, *Hamlet* and *The Count of Monte Cristo* to Japanese settings. He introduced MAETERLINCK and SARDOU, and he produced Japan's first children's drama in 1903 at the Hongō Theatre. Between 1900 and 1915, Kawakami appeared in major theatres in Tokyo and Osaka in competition with rival *shinpa* troupes in topical plays that had great popular appeal. Titles of plays produced in 1904, the year that the Russo-Japanese war began, suggest their intense nationalist flavour: *The Fall of Port Arthur*, *The Imperial Army That Vanquishes Russia*, *The Great Russo-Japanese War, Battle Report*, and *Submarine*.

Shinpa producers inaugurated shortened performance hours, they brought actresses back to the stage, and they abolished the theatre teahouses that controlled ticket sales. Seeing that huge country audiences flocked to the cinema (introduced commercially in 1903), they placed live performances in front of film backgrounds in 1910. Most important, they gave new Japanese playwrights an opportunity to see their plays produced. TSUBOUCHI SHŌYŌ's modern drama *The Cuckoo* (1904) received its first performance at the hand of *shinpa* actors. Tsubouchi (1859–1935) was a seminal figure in early modern Japanese theatre – translator of SHAKESPEARE's canon, playwright, acting teacher, director, and founder of the influential Literary Arts Society. Satō Kōroku (1874–1949) wrote five plays in the space of two years (1907–08) for *shinpa* actors and Mayama Seika (1878–1948) dramatized contemporary novels for *shinpa* performance. By the 1920s *shingeki* had laid claim to Western drama and *shinpa* declined to routine domestic tragicomedies (see TRAGICOMEDY) marked by sentimental nostalgia for a past era. The superlative actress Mizutani Yaeko (1905–79) assured the popularity of the one remaining *shinpa* troupe through the postwar years, and her daughter, Mizutani Yoshie, continues with that troupe in the 1990s. Often *kabuki* and *shinpa* actors give joint performances, indicating the affinity of the two genres.

Modern Japanese theatre: *shingeki*

The history of modern Japanese theatre, known as SHINGEKI (literally, 'new theatre'), has been characterized by a break with traditional theatre forms in the early 20th century and attempts since the Second World War to recapture some of the resources lost in that rupture. In essence, the plethora of gods and demons who had populated classical *nō* and *kabuki* were exiled from the modern stage in the early period, only to return in force since the war. Five periods may be distinguished in this process: 1887–1928, the establishment of a modern theatre; 1928–45, the politicization of modern theatre; 1945–60, the establishment of an orthodox modernism; 1960–73, the rejection of modernism; and 1973 to the present, diversification.

Exile of the gods, 1887–1945: the classical legacy

In 1887, the government of Meiji Japan formed a blue-ribbon Committee for the Reform of the Theatre (Engeki Kairyō Kai) to clean up *kabuki* and make it acceptable to a Western audience. The Japanese oligarchy was self-conscious about *kabuki* because it was a highly erotic and frequently violent form of popular theatre that had provided a relatively harmless release for plebeian libido in the repressive Tokugawa period (1600–1868). The government's goal was to recast *kabuki* in the mould of 19th-century European REALISM. A number of attempts were made to achieve this end, including the *katsureki*, or 'living-history', plays performed by Ichikawa Danjūrō IX (1838–1903) in the 1890s and *shinpa* (literally 'new wave' drama), originated by Kawakami Otojirō, his wife Sada Yakko, and the actor Ii Yōhō (1871–1932). The experiments of Ichikawa Sadanji II (1880–1940) and OSANAI KAORU in the first decades of the 20th century are also worth noting. Most of these experiments failed, but some, like *shinpa*, survived and continue to be performed.

Nō and *kabuki*, Japan's premier traditional theatre forms, evolved in a pre-modern milieu where little distinction existed between art and religion. While very different from each other, *nō* and *kabuki* are nevertheless both religio-aesthetic forms. *Nō* is a sacred theatre where, typically, a god will appear and catharsis will be achieved through contact with the divine. By contrast, *kabuki* originated as a profane theatre, where catharsis was achieved through exposure to evil. What the Committee for the Reform of the Theatre and other would-be reformers tried to do was deny the religious function of *nō* and *kabuki* and re-establish them as purely aesthetic forms.

Exiled from the classical stage, the gods found little refuge in the emerging modern theatre. Troupes dedicated to producing Western plays and their Japanese equivalents appeared in the first decade of the 20th century. The Literary Arts Society (Bungei Kyōkai) was founded in 1906 by Tsubouchi Shōyō; the Free Theatre (Jiyū Gekijō), named after ANTOINE's Théâtre Libre, was founded in 1909 by Osanai Kaoru and Ichikawa Sadanji.

While the two troupes differed in their approach to modern theatre, there was little room in either of them for the displaced spirits of the Japanese pantheon. Tsubouchi, one of the Meiji period's outstanding men of letters, was professor of English literature at Waseda University and a translator of Shakespeare. As its name implied, his troupe took an academic and literary approach to the theatre and concentrated on performing Tsubouchi's translations of Shakespeare, including *The Merchant of Venice* (1906), *Hamlet* (1907, 1911) and *Julius Caesar* (1913). In contrast, the Free Theatre concentrated on the works of contemporary European writers, staging IBSEN's *John Gabriel Borkman* in 1909 and GORKY's *Lower Depths* in 1910.

The two troupes agreed that a new style of acting would be necessary to successfully perform Western drama (including the training of actresses, who had been banned from the Japanese stage more than 250 years earlier), but they differed on how this goal was to be achieved. The Literary Arts Society hoped to develop a new breed of actor by exposing amateurs to great works of dramatic literature; the Free Theatre sought to re-educate professional actors, like its cofounder Ichikawa Sadanji, to perform European works.

Neither approach was successful. *Kabuki* actors never successfully adapted to the realistic style of acting required by the modern European works staged by the Free Theatre; and the actors Tsubouchi helped to train were unwilling to remain dedicated to his stoic literary philosophy. The Free Theatre continued to perform sporadically until 1919. The Literary Arts Society collapsed in 1913, when the troupe's leading actress, MATSUI SUMAKO, left the troupe with Tsubouchi's erstwhile disciple, Shimamura Hōgetsu (1871–1918), to found their own Art Theatre (Geijutsuza), a more commercially oriented company that capitalized on Matsui's popularity as Japan's first modern actress.

The 1910s and early 20s were an era of much literary but little theatrical activity. Many plays were written but few performed with distinction. Among those writing plays during these years were Kikuchi Kan (1888–1948), Kume Masao (1891–1952), Yamamoto Yūzō (1887–1974), and Tanizaki Junichirō (1886–1965), all of whom are as well or better known as novelists.

It was at the end of this period of literary activity that the Tsukiji Little Theatre (Tsukiji Shōgekikjō) was founded. Ordinances had prevented the construction of new theatres in Tokyo, but after the Great Kanto Earthquake destroyed much of the city on 1 September 1923, the municipal administration eased restrictions in the interest of rebuilding the capital. Osanai organized and HIJIKATA YOSHI financed the project. A wealthy young nobleman and theatre devotee who had just left for an intended ten-year tour of Europe, Hijikata hastened home when he heard that a theatre could be built, and he placed the funds earmarked for his sojourn abroad at Osanai's disposal.

The Tsukiji Little Theatre opened on 13 June 1924. It had a seating capacity of just under 500 and was constructed along the most modern lines. The most renowned feature of its stage was a *Kuppelhorizont* that made sophisticated lighting design possible (see STAGE LIGHTING).

Construction of the Tsukiji Little Theatre was greeted with enthusiasm by Japanese playwrights. They had been publishing their works, first in *New Trends in Thought* (*Shinshichō*), a journal founded in 1907 by Osanai himself, and later in *New Trends in Drama* (*Engeki shinchō*), and had every reason to believe that the Tsukiji would stage them. They were thunderstruck, therefore, when Osanai announced at Keio University on 20 May 1924 that for a period of two years the Tsukiji would produce only works by Western playwrights.

Osanai's action precipitated a deep split in the *shingeki* movement. After his frustrating experience with the Free Theatre, his travels in Europe and his contact with STANISLAVSKY'S MOSCOW ART THEATRE, however, Osanai was determined to create a viable production system for modern plays in Japan, and he was convinced that this required a clean break with traditional methods and sensibilities. Even the remnants of Japaneseness found in the ostensibly 'modern' works of Japanese playwrights could subvert this project, he feared. Only by actually producing European plays in the European manner for an extended period could the goal of a modern theatre for Japan be achieved.

Politicization of modern theatre, 1928–45 By the time of Osanai's untimely death on 25 December 1928, the Tsukiji Little Theatre had established a modern system of theatre production in Japan. It had produced a diverse repertory of representative European works by playwrights including Ibsen, CHEKHOV, TURGENEV, STRINDBERG, ČAPEK, PIRANDELLO and GEORG KAISER; and it had trained an entire generation of theatre practitioners. With Osanai's passing, however, the tensions inherent in a troupe so diversely conceived immediately came to a head, and the company collapsed in less than three months.

The Tsukiji Little Theatre split into factions that continued to define the *shingeki* movement into the postwar period. Hijikata Yoshi led the New Tsukiji Troupe (Shin Tsukiji Gekidan), the 'political' faction, which incorporated the activist members of the original company, including such actors as Maruyama Sadao (1901–45) (who died from radiation poisoning he received in the atomic bombing of Hiroshima), Yamamoto Yasue (1905–) (later to become KINOSHITA JUNJI's favourite actress and to create the role of Tsū in his *Twilight Crane*), Susukida Kenji (1898–1972) (a founder of the People's Art Theatre company after the war) and others. Aoyama Sugisaku (1889–1956) represented the Tsukiji Little Theatre Company (Gekidan Tsukiji Shōgekijō), the 'artistic' faction, which included such notable actors as Higashiyama Chieko (1890–1980) (later of the Actors' Theatre), Tomoda Kyōsuke (1899–1937) and Tamura Akiko (1905–83) (husband and wife, who later joined the Literary Theatre), and Sugimura Haruko (1909–) (also of the Literary Theatre and one of the postwar period's finest actresses). Takizawa Osamu (1906–), one of Japan's most accomplished actors, originally belonged to the Tsukiji Little Theatre Company, but later shifted his allegiance to the politically engaged group.

Playwrights also helped to define the *shingeki* movement in the 1930s. Murayama Tomoyoshi (1901–77) (who was also a talented stage designer and director), Miyoshi Jūrō (1902–58), and KUBO SAKAE were left-wing writers associated with the political mainstream of the movement; Kubota Mantarō (1889–1963), Iwata Toyō (1893–1969), and KISHIDA KUNIO were representative writers for the artistic group. Kubota, Iwata and Kishida jointly founded the Literary Theatre (Bungakuza) in 1937; and it was the only pre-war *shingeki* troupe allowed to perform continuously through the war.

In August 1940, the government ordered the New Tsukiji and the New Co-operative (Shinkyō) troupes, the two remaining left-wing companies, to disband and imprisoned their leaders, including Kubo. Kishida, by contrast, became head of the cultural section of the Imperial Rule Assistance Association in 1940, the year it supplanted all political parties, and after the war he was purged by the Occupation as a collaborator in the war effort.

Modernism becomes orthodoxy, 1945–60: the postwar situation For a brief period after the war, it seemed that *shingeki* would become the centre, not only of Japanese theatre, but of Japanese culture as a whole. Of all the arts, its ardent devotion to REALISM had kept it relatively immune to the ultranationalist contagion. It was this same commitment to realism, however, that hobbled modern theatre's attempts to answer the profound questions raised by the war and defeat.

Influential playwrights in the 1950s included Kinoshita Junji (1914–), who represents the politically engaged group, and FUKUDA TSUNEARI, who was a leader of the literary faction. Both of these men were, incidentally, scholars and translators of Shakespeare. Mishima Yukio (1925–1970), whose *Five Modern Nō Plays* (*Kindai nōgaku shū*, 1956; trans. 1957) offers eerily effective one-act adaptations of the *nō* classics, was also an important innovator. Also significant were Hotta Kiyomi (1922–), whose play *The Island* (*Shima*, 1955; trans. 1986) was the first play of national importance to deal with the bombing of Hiroshima; and Tanaka Chikao (1905–), whose *Head of Mary* (*Maria no kubi*, 1959; trans. 1986) treated the tragedy of Nagasaki from a Roman Catholic point of view.

Institutionally, the postwar scene was dominated by three *shingeki* troupes that reflected the alliances that had existed in the Tsukiji Little Theatre. Mingei (the People's Art Theatre) represented the left wing; the Actors' Theatre (Haiyūza), led by SENDA KOREYA, an actor, director, and translator of BRECHT, most closely approximated the catholic, academic approach of Osanai; and the Literary Theatre continued to represent the literary faction.

With the easing of political tensions and the recovery of the postwar economy, the differences between these troupes became more apparent than real, however; and the postwar period was marked by a growing consensus on what modern theatre should be. Modernism, in short, became an orthodoxy. Among the tenets of this orthodoxy were a commitment to proscenium-arch realism, a belief in the primacy of the text and the actor's subservience to it, a commitment to a tragic and humanistic dramaturgy and a conviction that the principal function of theatre is didactic.

When the war ended, modern Japanese theatre faced a severe crisis. Most theatres had been destroyed, and troupes lacked the wherewithal to mount productions. By the 1960s, however, *shingeki* had achieved unprecedented success.

Two factors were responsible for the success of the postwar *shingeki* system. The first was the *gekidan* or company system. In the company system, actors work outside the theatre, especially in films and television, and pay a 'company tax' (*gekidanzei*) of up to 50 per cent of their earnings to support the activities of the troupe. A famous example of the efficacy of this system is the construction of the Actors' Theatre in 1954 with the earnings of actors like Senda Koreya, who performed in 29 films in two years and contributed 65 per cent of his income to the theatre. Actors like Senda, ununionized and unpaid or poorly paid for their stage work, are the altruistic foundation of all modern theatre in Japan. Another example of the success of the company system is the People's Art Theatre company. Founded in 1950 with eleven actors and one director, it had grown by 1970 to 250 members, producing ten plays for 600 performances a year.

The second factor was Rōen. Modelled after the German VOLKSBÜHNE, Rōen (Workers' Theatre Councils) provided troupes like the Actors' Theatre and the People's Art Theatre with a national audience by selling discounted tickets to members of trade unions. By 1969 the organization was sponsoring as many as a thousand performances each year for its 133,000 members.

In a sense, however, the postwar *shingeki* movement fell victim to its own success. Originality was frequently sacrificed in the interest of fiscal conservatism. Once the most innovative and adventurous form of theatre in Japan, by the 1960s *shingeki* had become a tradition in its own right, ripe for challenge by a new generation of theatre artists.

Return of the gods, 1960–73: emergence of the post-*shingeki* movement When the United States–Japan Mutual Security Treaty came up for renewal in 1960, the limitations of orthodox *shingeki* became painfully apparent to the emerging younger generation. Massive nationwide demonstrations had been organized to oppose renewal of the treaty, which permits the stationing of American military forces on Japanese soil and places Japan under the United States 'nuclear umbrella', and *shingeki* groups had taken an active part in them. When the demonstrations failed to prevent the renewal of the treaty, however, younger members of the movement began to feel that *shingeki* orthodoxy could no more effectively explain what had happened to them than it had been able to explain the war, and this led to a thoroughgoing re-assessment of theatrical priorities and goals that precipitated a countermovement in modern Japanese theatre called the ANGURA or post-*shingeki* movement.

The Youth Art Theatre (Seinen Geijutsu Gekijō or Seigei) company provided the transition from orthodox *shingeki* to the post-*shingeki* movement. It had been organized by youthful members of the People's Art Theatre troupe in November 1959. The Youth Art Theatre's leading playwright was FUKUDA YOSHIYUKI, whose early works, including *A Long Row of Tombstones* (*Nagai bohyō no retsu*, 1957), were written under the strong influence of Kubo Sakae and Kinoshita Junji. The experience of the 1960 demonstrations, street theatre in a real sense, changed the perspective of Fukuda and other members of the troupe, however, and the Youth Art Theatre began to develop an independent style that rejected proscenium-arch realism and the other major tenets of *shingeki* orthodoxy.

The Youth Art Theatre became a spawning ground for many of the writers and actors in the post-*shingeki* movement. Among the playwrights who were in some way connected with the troupe were BETSUYAKU MINORU, KARA JŪRŌ and SATOH MAKOTO.

In 1965, the Youth Art Theatre restaged Betsuyaku's *The Elephant* (*Zō*, 1962; trans. 1986), which eloquently articulated the new generation's frustration with the passivity of the orthodox movement and their desire to create a newly empowering rationale for action. The play deals with survivors of Hiroshima, but it was understood as a protest against a world in which any kind of action was impossible.

There was a widespread feeling after 1960 that if the past was to be successfully explained and a rationale for future action formulated, the dramatic conventions of a half-century would have to be discarded and some means found to make the gods once again appear on stage. In play after play, the writers of the post-*shingeki* movement engineered epiphanies, moments when gods once again came to populate the Japanese stage. This was their means of escaping the debilitating sense of enforced passivity and stasis they had been experiencing.

The mechanism was apotheosis: ordinary men and women were metamorphosed into gods before the audience's eyes. In 1964 the Youth Art Theatre produced Fukuda Yoshiyuki's *Find Hakamadare!* (*Hakamadare wa doko da*, 1964; trans. 1988), one of the first plays to clearly employ the dramaturgy of metamorphosis as an empowering theory of action. Based on a 12th-century legend, the play describes how a band of oppressed peasants take their fate into their own hands and become Hakamadare, their long-awaited saviour, when Hakamadare himself turns out to be a rapacious villain.

Kaison the Priest of Hitachi (*Hitachibō Kaison*, 1965; trans. 1988) by AKIMOTO MATSUYO describes the metamorphosis of a young man in the early 1960s into the immortal Kaison, a warrior from the 12th century who is still reputed to wander through northeast Japan doing penance for sins committed centuries ago. Through his metamorphosis the young man escapes from history into mythic time and is saved from the excruciating burden of guilt he carries from his experience as a child during the war. Kara Jūrō's *The Beggar of Love* (*Ai no kojiki*, 1970; trans. 1988) describes the metamorphosis of oppressed urbanites into their redeemer, an avenging peg-legged sailor named Silver. And Satoh Makoto's *Nezumi Kozō: The Rat* (*Nezumi Kozō Jirokichi*, 1970; trans. 1986) describes the transformation of a rag-tag band of lumpen proletarians into their awaited messiah, a Robin-Hood-like figure from the early 19th century named Nezumi Kozō.

A special feature of the post-*shingeki* dramaturgy of metamorphosis is that 'salvation' in each of these plays is virtually indistinguishable from damnation. Apotheosis into Kaison or Silver or Nezumi Kozō means abandoning historical time and responsibility and being sucked back into the maelstrom of eternal redundancy. This restatement of the existential situation of the Japanese, torn between the cruel reality of history and the ambivalent promise of salvation through assimilation to mythic time, has challenged the tragic–humanistic formula of orthodox *shingeki* and has been the major contribution of post-*shingeki* dramaturgy.

This contribution has been accompanied by innovations in stagecraft that break decisively with orthodox *shingeki* practice. Gone is the hegemony of the proscenium stage: two of the post-*shingeki* movement's major troupes, Kara Jūrō's Situation Theatre (Jōkyō Gekijō) and Satoh Makoto's Black Tent Theatre 68/71 (presently known simply as Kuro Tento or the Black Tent) perform in tents. SUZUKI TADASHI's SCOT (Suzuki Company of Toga), formerly the Waseda Little Theatre (Waseda Shōgekijō), abandoned Tokyo in 1976 for Toga village, a mountain retreat eight hours from the city, where the company lives and works together in a manner similar to JERZY GROTOWSKI's earlier Laboratory Theatre in Wroclaw, Poland, or EUGENIO BARBA's ODIN TEATRET in Holstebro, Denmark. The primacy of the text has been replaced by a renewed emphasis on the creative role of the actor, and Suzuki in particular has made a lasting contribution to actor training by creating a system of exercises suggested by *nō* and *kabuki*.

These three companies continue to perform today. An additional troupe from a slightly different lineage that played a seminal role in the revolt against *shingeki* orthodoxy was TERAYAMA SHŪJI's Tenjō Sajiki (literally, the Upper Gallery). Terayama, who was born in 1935 in Aomori prefecture in northeastern Japan, was deeply influenced by the French avant-garde, particularly ANTONIN ARTAUD and Lautréamont; and his first dramatic work, *Blood Sleeps Standing Up* (*Chi wa tatta mama nemutte iru*, 1960), was produced by the Four Seasons (Shiki) company headed by Asari Keita, which gained fame in the 1950s for its productions of the French playwrights GIRAUDOUX and ANOUILH. (Shiki is today a multimillion-dollar enterprise specializing in the production of MUSICALS like *Jesus Christ Superstar* and *Cats*.) The multi-talented Terayama, who was also a renowned poet, essayist and director, was a true scion of the European avant-garde. His principal aim was to shock the bourgeoisie, and he succeeded in this with happenings, street theatre, multimedia events and themes ranging from incest to transvestism.

Continuity and discontinuity: 1973 to the present By 1973 the dialectic of divine exile and return that had governed the evolution of modern Japanese drama for nearly a hundred years had been fulfilled. Orthodox *shingeki* was embattled. In 1971 30 members of the People's Art Theatre resigned, and 11 members of the Actors' Theatre quit in protest over the troupe's conservative repertory. Mishima Yukio's troupe, the Romantic Theatre (Roman Gekijō), folded in 1972, following the author's suicide two years earlier; and in 1973, writer Abe Kōbō (1924–93) ended his affiliation with the Actors' Theatre to found his own company, the Abe Kōbō Studio.

At the same time, the return of the gods to the Japanese stage reached its apex with the emergence of *BUTŌ* as a full-fledged dance form. The word *butō* is simply a variant of the Japanese word for dance. The style had originated in the 1950s and 60s with the pioneering work of dancer-choreographers Ohno Kazuo (1906–) and Hijikata Tatsumi (1928–86). In 1972 *butō* dovetailed with the post-*shingeki* movement. In that year, Maro Akaji (1943–), formerly a leading actor in Kara Jūrō's Situation Theatre, founded the first *butō* troupe, Dairakudakan (the Great Camel Battleship). Maro had lived and studied with Hijikata, and he effected a marriage of Hijikata's unique choreography with post-*shingeki* dramaturgy and organizational style.

The dancers in *butō* are ghosts and gods. Naked, heads shaven, covered in dead-white body make-up, arms raised, eyes rolled back, they are unmistakably apparitions from another world. Hijikata acknowledged this explicitly in a speech delivered in 1985: 'To make gestures of the dead, to die again, to make the dead re-enact once more their deaths in their entirety – these are what I want to experience within me.' The metamorphosis into transhistorical

Satoh Makoto's *Nezumi Kozō* (The Rat).

ghosts and gods that is the heart of post-*shingeki* dramaturgy appears in its most overt form in *butō*.

Having successfully challenged orthodox modernism, the consensus that had united various post-*shingeki* troupes in an informal movement began to collapse in the mid-1970s. A number of factors exacerbated this phenomenon. The first was political. The United Red Army Incident of 1972, the murder for 'ideological deviation' of student radicals by members of their own political sect, made theatre artists less sanguine about 'revolutionary' activity and signalled the end of the period of political radicalism that had begun in 1960. Productions like *When We Travel Down the Great River of Callousness* (*Bokura ga hijō no taiga o kudaru toki*, 1972), written by Shimizu Kunio (1936–) and directed by NINAGAWA YUKIO, reflected the impact. The second factor was economic. Following the OPEC oil embargo of 1973, 1974 was the first year since the Second World War that the Japanese economy experienced a recession. The concomitant inflation inevitably affected the theatre world.

More important than either of these factors, however, were the long-range changes in society brought about by the rapid economic growth of the 1960s. In particular, prosperity made it possible to construct numerous new theatres after 1973. The scarcity of theatrical space had always been the basic reality of modern Japanese theatre; now the construction of many new theatres accelerated the trend toward dramatic diversification. Similarly, the appearance in 1972 of *Pia*, a biweekly listing of theatre and other performances in the Tokyo area, brought accurate and timely information about the productions of new as well as established troupes to a mass audience. With the advent of easily accessed computerized ticketing in the

1980s, theatre attendance became simpler than ever, precipitating a boom in theatre that continues to this day.

Theatrical diversification began in the 1970s with the emergence of new, younger troupes: the Theatre Group (Engekidan) led by Ryūzanji Shō (1947–), the Gallery Troupe (Tsunbosajiki) led by Yamazaki Tetsu (1946–), and Space Acting (Kūkan Engi) led by Okabe Kōdai (1945–). It was the work of Tsuka Kōhei (1948–), however, that marked a real departure in style. Tsuka was the first playwright born after the war to receive the Kishida Prize for Playwriting, which he received for *The Atami Murder Incident* (*Atami satsujin jiken*) in 1974. Tsuka's apolitical, insightful human dramas were intensely funny and signalled an end to the underlying intellectuality that had continued to characterize post-*shingeki* productions.

The lure of commercialism was also felt. In 1974 Ninagawa Yukio defected from the avant-garde to direct *Romeo and Juliet* for the commercial Tōhō firm. Known for his highly theatrical effects, Ninagawa has gone on to direct many successful commercial productions. Avant-garde artists also began to work together on an *ad hoc* basis in what has come to be known as the 'producer system', but affiliation with quasi-familial companies remains the rule in Japan and a true system of independent artists and producers is yet to emerge.

Female playwright-directors also began to appear in the mid-1970s. Kishida Rio (1950–) had worked closely with Terayama Shūji, beginning in 1974. After his death in 1983, she established her own troupe, the Kishida Office & the Optimists (Kishida Jimusho + Rakutendan), and won the 1984 Kishida Prize for her feminist play *Woven Hell* (*Ito jigoku*). Kisaragi Koharu (1956–) and Watanabe Eriko (1955–) have also been influential. They and their troupes, respectively NOISE and 300 (Sanjūmaru), have frequently focused on family dynamics and have added a female perspective to contemporary Japanese theatre.

The 1980s have been called the decade of 'metatheatre'. The Dream Wanderers (Yume no Yū-minsha, founded 1976) led by NODA HIDEKI and the Third Stage (Daisan Butai, founded 1981) led by Kōkami Shōji (1958–) are representative. A fascination with play and nonsense, a fixation on childhood, and maze-like, anti-linear dramatic structure have earned these playwright-directors the title 'postmodern'. More traditional but no less innovative have been troupes like the Shinjuku Ryōzanpaku (literally, the Shinjuku Hideout, founded 1987), a unique ensemble organized by Japanese of Korean extraction who carry on the traditions of the Situation Theatre and the Black Tent, where many of them did their apprenticeship. In a similar vein, Tokyo Group One (Tokyo Ichikumi, founded 1988) has developed a uniquely satisfying combination of post-*shingeki* dramaturgy and the commercial comedy style of the immensely popular actor Fujiyama Kanbi (1929–90).

The 1980s were also a decade of acceptance. Prefectural and local governments began to actively support the theatre. Suzuki Tadashi's theatre at Toga and the Art Tower Mito with its resident theatre company, also directed by Suzuki, are examples of theatres built and supported with public funds. ŌTA SHŌGO, whose innovative Theatre of Transformation (Tenkei Gekijō) disbanded in 1988, became artistic director of the Shōnandai Cultural Centre Municipal Theatre in Fujisawa City in 1989. And the municipally funded Tokyo Art Theatre (Tōkyō Geijutsu Gekijō) opened in October 1990.

Corporations have also sought to improve their cultural image by building theatres and supporting theatrical activity. The Parco Theatre built in the Shibuya section of Tokyo by the Seibu department store chain in May 1973 was one of the first examples of corporate support for theatre. The Spiral Theatre in the Aoyama section of Tokyo was constructed by the Wacoal lingerie company in 1985. More recently, in 1989, the Tōkyū Corporation built the Culture Village (Bunkamura) complex adjacent to its flagship department store, also in Shibuya. The complex contains restaurants, a museum, an opera-concert hall, and the Theatre Cocoon presided over by Kushida Kazumi (1942–) and his Free Theatre troupe ('On Theatre' Jiyū Gekijō).

New theatres have provided expanded opportunities for stage designers. Japanese stage design began with the work of Itō Kisaku (1899–1967), who made his debut at the Tsukiji Little Theatre in 1925 with a modernistic set for *Julius Caesar*. Strongly influenced by GORDON CRAIG and ADOLPHE APPIA, Itō went on to influence the next generation of designers, most prominent among whom are Kanamori Kaoru (1933–80), Takada Ichirō (1929–) and ASAKURA SETSU. Hirano Kōga (1938–), who designed numerous sets for the Black Tent Theatre, and architect Isozaki Arata (1931–), who has designed several theatre spaces for Suzuki Tadashi, have also made original contributions to the conception and use of theatrical space.

Acceptance has also been international. In the 1970s and early 80s, Terayama Shūji made almost annual pilgrimages to perform at theatre festivals in Europe and the United States. Ninagawa Yukio's *Medea*, produced in Rome (1983) and Athens (1984), and *Macbeth*, staged in Amsterdam (1985) and London (1987), established his reputation internationally. Suzuki Tadashi, who has taught and directed in the United States, Europe and Australia, has also established a firm international reputation. In addition, since 1982, Suzuki has sponsored an annual international theatre festival in Toga, one of a growing number of international festivals being held in Japan.

Mainstream *shingeki* companies have remained active and have achieved a rapprochement with post-*shingeki* troupes. Chijinkai, literally, the Terrestrial Troupe, founded 1982, and the Komatsu Troupe (Komatsu-za, founded 1984) are two new *shingeki* troupes descended from the Literary Theatre. Both remain firmly literary in orientation and feature the work of director Kimura Kōichi (1931–) and writer Inoue Hisashi (1934–).

Youth theatre

The Shimpa actress Sada Yakko established Japan's first children's theatre company in 1903. For nearly a century since that time a dynamic youth theatre movement has been established, working primarily within the educational system. Especially since the end of the Second World War, large, highly successful commercial troupes have performed in major theatres and have also toured to school locations. Separate nationwide organizations support theatre activities at the primary school level, at the junior high school level, at the senior high school level, among parents and teachers, and in Japan's numerous private schools. The Japanese Educational Drama Association publishes the monthly journal *Drama in Education*. Some 70 professional troupes form the Japan Union of Theatre Companies for Children and Young People, and numerous unaffiliated troupes exist as well.

The artists and supporters of youth theatre strongly believe their productions have the major purpose of moulding socially desirable behaviour among the children for whom they perform. Children's theatre is expected to provide positive experiences in a child's formative years (Western children's stories about evil witches and ogres are rarely considered appropriate). The beauty of a peaceful society and the rewards of working cooperatively for the common good have been overriding themes for nearly 40 years. Foreign stories were popular in the 1950s – a non-threatening version of *Hansel and Gretel*, using Humperdinck's music, and the Russian *Stone Flower*, were extremely successful. Japanese local folk tales continue to provide fertile story materials.

Worldwide acclaim has greeted the innovative performances of several major troupes during the past 40 years. PUK has its own theatre, manages several troupes, and has regularly toured outside of Japan. Its large, rounded, friendly body puppets and distinctive vocal styles create large-scale visual effects. In contrast, Kaze-no-ko (Children of the Wind) performs with just a few trunks of properties – sticks, balls, paper and rope – which are manipulated by black-robed performers, *à la bunraku*, into various objects, a technique they call 'animated MIME', animime. Their work is highly physical, and their actors undergo rigorous training. Kaze-no-ko's five troupes continuously tour throughout Japan and are often invited to perform at children's theatre festivals in Europe, the United States and

Asia. The Nakama Theatre produces lavish spectacles for large audiences of parents and children on commercial stages. The Takeda Marionette Theatre continues a tradition of popular puppetry (which originally used mechanical dolls) that is three centuries old. The Elm Theatre bases many of its performances on the comic acting techniques of traditional *kyōgen*, in some cases adapting plays from the *kyōgen* repertory. A number of children's theatre directors, such as Sekiya Yukio of Kaze-no-ko, are important directors in the commercial theatre as well, often being invited to stage BROADWAY MUSICALS. (See also ASIAN AND PACIFIC ISLAND THEATRE.)   JRB DGG

GENERAL

See: J. T. Araki, *The Ballad-Drama of Medieval Japan*, Berkeley, Calif. 1964; P. D. Arnott, *The Theatres of Japan*, New York, 1969; F. Bowers, *The Japanese Theatre*, Rutland, Vt., 1974 (1952); E. Ernst (ed.), *Three Japanese Plays from the Traditional Theatre*, Westport, Conn., 1976 (1959); F. T. Immoos, *Japanese Theatre*, London, 1974; Y. Inoura and T. Kawatake, *The Traditional Theater of Japan*, New York, 1981; T. Komiya, *Japanese Music and Drama in the Meiji Era*, Tokyo, 1956; C. H. Kullman and W. C. Young (eds.), 'Japan', in *Theatre Companies of the World*, vol. 1, Westport, Conn., 1986; B. Ortolani, *The Japanese Theatre from Shamanistic Ritual to Contemporary Pluralism*, Leiden, 1990.

MODERN THEATRE

See: K. Abe, *Friends*, tr. Donald Keene, New York, 1969; D. G. Goodman (ed. and tr.), *After Apocalypse: Four Japanese Plays of Hiroshima and Nagasaki*, New York, 1986, and *Japanese Drama and Culture in the 1960s: The Return of the Gods*, Armonk, N.Y., 1988; T. R. H. Havens, *Artist and Patron in Postwar Japan: Dance, Music, Theater, and the Visual Arts, 1955–1980*, Princeton, N.J., 1982; E. Hoffman and M. Holborn, *Butō: Dance of the Dark Soul*, New York, 1987; A. Horie-Webber, 'Modernisation of the Japanese Theatre: The Shingeki Movement', in *Modern Japan: Aspects of History, Literature, and Society*, ed. W. G. Beasley, Berkeley, Calif., 1977; J. Kinoshita, *Between God and Man: A Judgement on War Crimes; A Play in Two Parts*, tr. Eric J. Gangloff, Seattle, Wash., 1979; K. Kishida, *Five Plays by Kishida Kunio*, ed. D. G. Goodman, Ithaca, N.Y., 1989; S. Kubo, *Land of Volcanic Ash*, tr. D. G. Goodman, Ithaca, N.Y., 1986; Y. Mishima, *Five Modern Nō Plays*, tr. Donald Keene, New York, 1957; Y. Mishima, *Madame de Sade*, tr. Donald Keene, New York, 1967; J. T. Rimer, *Toward a Modern Japanese Theatre*, Princeton, N.Y., 1974; R. T. Rolf and J. K. Gillespie (eds.), *Alternative Japanese Drama: Ten Plays*, Honolulu, 1992; T. Suzuki, *The Way of Acting: The Theatre Writings of Tadashi Suzuki*, tr. J. T. Rimer, New York, 1986; T. T. Takaya, *Modern Japanese Drama: An Anthology*, New York, 1979; J. Viala and N. Masson-Sekine, *Butoh: Shades of Darkness*, Tokyo, 1988; M. Yamazaki, *Mask and Sword: Two Plays for the Contemporary Japanese Theatre*, tr. J. T. Rimer, New York, 1980.

Jaques-Dalcroze, Émile see APPIA, ADOLPHE

Jardiel Poncela, Enrique 1901–52 Spanish playwright and novelist known for his near-absurdist dialogue (see THEATRE OF THE ABSURD), capricious humour and eccentric plots. He first achieved recognition with *Una noche de primavera sin sueño* (*A Sleepless Spring Night*, 1927). Between 1932 and 35 he worked intermittently as a film scenarist in Hollywood. Spain's most innovative playwright in the first decade of the Franco dictatorship, he became increasingly embittered by critical attacks. In his plays conventional dramatic forms are parodied or cleverly acknowledged, at times with extravagant metatheatrical turns. The popular successes *Eloísa está debajo de un almendro* (*Eloise Is under an Almond Tree*, 1940) and *Un marido de ida y vuelta* (*A Round-Trip Husband*, 1939) were followed by his scathing five-act SATIRE on Hollywood, *El amor sólo dura 2000 metros* (*Love Only Lasts 2000 Metres*, 1941), which was met with noisy disapproval. In the post-Franco years Jardiel's plays have been frequently revived, with favourable critical re-evaluation.   MPH

Jarry, Alfred 1873–1907 French author and dramatist, the creator of King Ubu, a grotesque, puppet-like figure who embodies every mean, destructive and ignoble quality. Ubu started life as a schoolboy send-up of Jarry's physics teacher at his school in Rennes; but he rapidly became a character in his own right, first in PUPPET performances given by Jarry and his friends, then in 1896 in a performance by FIRMIN GÉMIER, directed by LUGNÉ-POE, with COSTUMES, MASKS and scenery by Jarry, Bonnard, Vuillard and Toulouse-Lautrec. The play's two performances caused a legendary stir in literary circles. Jarry wrote three other Ubu plays, as well as an *Almanach du Père Ubu* and associated writings, but none of them matched the brutal simplicity of *Ubu Roi*. This Shakespearian PARODY, in which a lazy 'little man' is goaded by his wife into terrible acts of violence, had a prophetic quality. Ubu is quite without scruples because he thinks only of his own satisfaction. But he is also devoid of imagination: *merdre* (shite), the scandalously famous first word of the play, sums up Ubu's philosophy.

Jarry's stagecraft was simple and inventive, challenging the sacred cows of both naturalists and symbolists. He drank himself to death at the age of 34 but his work was championed by the surrealists and finally achieved 'classic' status in the 1950s, when the THEATRE OF THE ABSURD adopted similar techniques and characters.   DB

jatra The most popular regional theatre form in the rural areas of Bengal, INDIA, and among Bengali-speaking people of neighbouring Bihar, Orissa, Assam and Tripura. It also holds sway over village audiences in BANGLADESH (formerly East Bengal, and later East Pakistan), where Bengali is spoken. Versions of the form have been created in the Oriyan language as well.

Jatra means 'procession'. The form may have come into existence in the 16th century as a part of the Vaishnava devotional movement, introduced by Chaitanya, which swept the population into its fold through songs, dances and plays designed to propagate the faith. The earliest extant *jatra* scripts (*pala*) date from the late 18th century. Prior to that plays were preserved as a part of the oral tradition of the region.

Up to the early 19th century, *jatra* plays focused on religious themes and were instructive and moralistic in tone.

Companies of actors were owned and managed by the chief singer or actor. In the 19th century, amateurs, mostly the sons of the bourgeois of Calcutta, developed their own *jatra* groups and chose secular themes for their subject-matter rather than traditional religious fare. This led the older companies to adapt the secular stories as well. With the advent of the modern theatre movement in the mid-19th century, *jatra* borrowed the scenic displays of the proscenium-arch stage and imitated the Western style of acting and writing that was beginning to be popular among the middle and upper class of Calcutta. From the late 19th to the mid-20th century, *jatra* maintained its rural audiences, but urban audiences viewed its music, tone and style as old-fashioned and corrupt. It did not return to favour in urban areas until 1947, when the Communist Party employed it to win sympathetic support for its cause.

Jatra companies are generally professional and itinerant, booking throughout the Bengali-speaking regions of India. Today some 20 major troupes operate from their central headquarters in Calcutta. There, an agent books shows over the telephone, confirming engagements in the tea estates of Assam, in the steel towns and coal-mining centres of the northeast, or anywhere along the way that a group can afford to pay for the services of a *jatra* company. Troupes are dispatched to a locale for a flat fee, including food and shelter. Actors are hired by the company manager for the season, written contracts protect the interests of both parties and wages are paid according to a scale. Star performers' wages are handsome by Indian standards. Comedians and vocalists are paid somewhat less.

In the early history of *jatra*, actor-managers ran companies and exercised artistic control. Today, the owner-manager is normally not an artist but an entrepreneur who seeks a profit on his business and who has little motive other than to please the public, no matter what the artistic consequences.

Generally, actors come from the lower strata of society, joining companies at an early age because they fall in love with the romance of fame, fortune and travel. Boys aged 11 and 12 who join *jatra* companies are rigorously trained to sing, dance and act in *jatra* style. Frailer youths eventually train to play the female characters and those with powerful voices and strong bodies act the heroes and villains. Actors with a natural sense of humour become the comedians.

The *jatra* season begins in earnest in September, at the end of the monsoon, and extends to May or early June when the heavy rains return. A lucrative time for *jatra* in Bengali villages coincides with the major religious festivals, *Durga Puja* in late September and early October, *Kali Puja* three weeks later, and *Ratha Jatra* and *Manasa Puja* later in the year. The marriage of a daughter, the birth of a son or the winning of a lawsuit serve as an occasion of rejoicing and reason for a family, wealthy village merchant or headman to sponsor a *jatra* performance.

Jatra is highly melodramatic in character, with a liberal dose of songs and dramatic scenes. Actors are adept at vocal projection and can play before thousands of patrons out of doors without the aid of microphones. Among the more interesting of the old *jatra* characters is the Conscience (*bibek*) who is an allegorical figure who moves in and out of the action, commenting on its meaning and foretelling the consequences of evil deeds. The character of Fate (*niyati*), like that of the Conscience, comments on the action and warns characters of potential dangers. Traditionally this character is played by an actress.

The acting area (*asar*) is usually on ground level, covered with cloth mats (*durries*) or carpets and bounded by short bamboo poles linked together by string. Or a low, square wooden platform is used. The platform is connected to the dressing room by a rampway marked by bamboo posts or a wooden construction in the shape of a ramp. The ramp serves as an extension of the acting area and is used for dramatic effects, similar to those of the *hanamichi* in KABUKI theatres in Japan.

The audience enfolds the whole acting area, creating a sense of intimacy in the playing even when thousands of spectators gather on the ground, sit on chairs, stand on the verandas of nearby houses, or hang from the boughs of trees to watch. Women usually sit separately from the men.

Scenes flow rapidly one into the other, punctuated by songs which mark act intervals. The acting area is regarded as a neutral space, even when performing on a proscenium stage, to which meaning is assigned depending on the play's action. Scenery is not necessary and, indeed, would intrude. Experiments with scenery were undertaken in the 19th century in imitation of Western theatre practices; ultimately they failed.

Jatra music is provided by a drum (*pakhwaj*), harmonium, violin, clarinet or flute and bell-metal cymbals. Musicians normally sit at one side of the acting area so that they have a full view of the stage, the ramp and the dressing room. Normally a prompter sits with them, following the action in the script.

The performance begins with a musical concert which continues for an hour or two before the dramatic action starts. The concert is divided into two parts. In part one, evening melodies (*raga*) are played. Part two emphasizes fast-pace rhythms and virtuoso drumming. The concert attracts spectators to the playing area and entertains those who have already gathered. Mood music is inserted throughout a performance to accentuate a bit of dramatic business, to heighten the melodramatic sentiments of a scene or to underscore a character's emotional state.

The performance space is lit by a variety of means, ranging from simple oil torches in remote villages, to petromax pressure lamps, electric bulbs and even fluorescent lights in areas where there is access to better equipment. No attempt is made to vary the intensity of illumination or to control colour.

A chair is the only furniture found on stage. Like the stage itself, it is regarded as a neutral object until it is endowed with meaning. It may serve as a throne, a bed, the steps of a temple, the shrine itself, whatever is demanded by the action.

In the early 1960s, *jatra* underwent something of a revival among the middle classes of Calcutta. Before that time, it had been regarded as 'folksy' and not worth the attention of serious theatre patrons. In 1961, a *jatra* festival was held in the palace courtyard of the Shabhabazar Rajas in north Calcutta. It was a great success and has been repeated yearly with renewed acclaim.

Periodicals and newspapers devote space to *jatra*. *Jatra* scripts may be found in paperback editions in stalls and shops along the streets of Calcutta. And in 1968 Phanibhusan Bidyabinod became the first *jatra* artist honoured by the Sangeet Natak Akademi in New Delhi for his services to the art.

The Communist Party made use of *jatra*, as of other popular forms of rural theatre elsewhere in India, to propagate its political messages. In the 1930s and 40s, plays were written in *jatra* style and artists were recruited to the communist cause. Since that time, artists have taken a neutral political position so they may please the widest possible audience. In their headquarters it is not uncommon to find pictures of Communist Party leaders at home and abroad alongside those of popular Western politicians and Indian and Western religious leaders and prophets. In recent years the form has served as the model for various contemporary stage directors, actors and playwrights who have experimented with the application of contemporary social issues through the adaptation of the form.

The *jatra* of Bengal was introduced to the neighbouring state of Orissa in the 19th century. Local Orissi troupes soon took up the form and became popular in rural areas. *Jatra* of Orissa is similar to the Bengali version in most respects. However, the parties of actors prefer to use the words 'opera' and *natya* to describe their work rather than the term *jatra*.

In the Orissi form, the entrance and exit passageway, literally the 'flower way' (*puspa patha*), connects the low temporary wooden stage to the dressing room (*vesha ghara*). Plays are written in the Oriyan language following the structure and style of Bengali *jatra*. During the independence movement from the early 20th century up to 1947, Orissa *jatra* companies launched veiled attacks on their British rulers. Like Bengali *jatra*, Oriyan works emphasize virtuous upright characters pitted against villains and blackguards. Comic scenes add variety and spice to an all-night performance and sustain the interest of the audience.   FaR

Java see INDONESIA

Jefferson family Famous Anglo-American actors who can be traced back to **Thomas** Jefferson (1732–1807), an actor with GARRICK and occasional manager of provincial English theatres. One of his children, **Joseph** Jefferson I (1774–1832), went to America in 1795 and remained there. He became a favourite at the JOHN STREET and PARK THEATRES in New York, although somewhat overshadowed by JOHN HODGKINSON. In 1803 he moved to the CHESTNUT STREET THEATRE in Philadelphia, remaining until 1830. Most of his children worked in the theatre, including **Joseph** Jefferson II (1804–42), a better scene painter than actor. His marriage to the actress Cornelia Thomas in 1826 made him the stepfather of actor Charles Burke.

The greatest of the Jeffersons, however, was **Joseph** Jefferson III (1829–1905), who first appeared on stage at age four, in support of THOMAS D. RICE. Jefferson toured with his family, having garnered some fame by the mid-century and visiting Europe in 1856. He then joined LAURA KEENE's company, winning approval with such roles as Dr Pangloss in COLMAN THE YOUNGER's *The Heir at Law*. He

spent some time at the WINTER GARDEN THEATRE in New York, toured Australia for four years, and in London in 1865 first performed the role for which he was most noted, Rip Van Winkle, dramatized for him by DION BOUCICAULT. In this role, Jefferson's dignity and sympathetic personality soon won him popular and critical acclaim. Of him, the critic WILLIAM WINTER said: 'The magical charm of his acting was the deep human sympathy and the liveliness and individuality by which it was irradiated – an exquisite blending of humor, pathos, grace and beauty.'

Jefferson also triumphed as Bob Acres in SHERIDAN's *The Rivals*, Caleb Plummer in *Dot* and Salem Scudder in *The Octoroon; or, Life in Louisiana*. In 1893 he succeeded EDWIN BOOTH as president of the Players Club. His autobiography, a classic theatrical memoir published in 1890, indicates much of Jefferson's warmth and humanity.

Of his children, four went on the stage, the most distinguished being **Charles Burke** Jefferson (1851–1908), who served for a time as his father's manager.   SMA

Jelinek, Elfriede 1946– Austrian dramatist and novelist. Her experimental sequel to IBSEN's *Doll's House, Was geschah nachdem Nora ihren Mann verlassen hatte* (*What Happened after Nora Had Left Her Husband*, 1979), shows Nora unsuccessfully trying to make a living for herself in the early 1930s. Her 'musical tragedy' *Clara S* (1982) juxtaposes pianist Clara Schumann and her composer husband with the Fascist poet GABRIELE D'ANNUNZIO to examine the historical predicament of women artists. *Burgtheater* (1985) explores the behaviour of a popular acting dynasty at the Vienna BURGTHEATER during Nazi rule. *Krankheit oder moderne Frauen* (*Sickness or Modern Women*, 1987) is a female vampire fantasy involving Emily Brontë and Heathcliff in a drama of lust and female emancipation. *Totenauberg* (1992) reunites German racist, existentialist philosopher Heidegger in the Alps with his ex-pupil, the Jewish émigrée philosopher Hannah Arendt, for a wide-ranging discourse on post-Communist Europe. Jelinek's complex texts, with their radical Marxist and feminist arguments, are among the most challenging in German today.   HR

Jellicoe, Ann 1927– British dramatist and director, whose first full-length play, *The Sport of My Mad Mother* (1956), came joint third in a playwriting competition organized by the *Observer* newspaper and was subsequently staged at the ROYAL COURT THEATRE. Its speech rhythms, defiantly non-literary, were based on listening to young teenagers at play, and the 'mad mother' of the title was Kali, the Hindu goddess. Jellicoe, who trained at London's Central School of Speech and Drama, was a pioneer of community theatre in Britain and sought to release in her casts impulses towards drama which might be otherwise confined by formal texts. Her first successful plays, however, were conventionally written, notably *The Knack* (1961), contrasting two young men, one who has the knack of attracting women, the other who has not. *Shelley* (1965) was a clear, almost documentary account of the poet's life. In contrast, *The Rising Generation* (1967), originally written for but not performed by the Girl Guides' Association, was conceived in a spirit of orgiastic feminism. She was a founder-director of the Cockpit Theatre Club in 1950 and the literary manager of the Royal Court from 1973 to 1975. She founded the Colway Theatre Trust in Dorset in 1979 to stage community plays in village areas and West Country towns, but resigned as its director in 1985 as a protest against grant cuts.   JE

Jerome, Jerome K(lapka) 1859–1927 British playwright, novelist and journalist, remembered for the comic idyll *Three Men in a Boat* (1889). He was the author of several comedies and FARCES – two of the best, *The Prude's Progress* (1895) and *The MacHaggis* (1897), written in collaboration with Eden Phillpotts – in which pleasingly credible characters are asked to cope with pleasantly incredible situations. Of his social dramas, none has survived, though *The Passing of the Third Floor Back* (1908) gave JOHNSTON FORBES-ROBERTSON a famous part as the Christ-like stranger whose presence in a Bloomsbury boarding-house transforms the lives of his fellow lodgers. Jerome's early experience as an actor is amusingly embroidered in *On the Stage and Off* (1885), and the stock characters of 19th-century MELODRAMA are wittily anatomized in *Stage-Land* (1890).   PT

Jerrold, Douglas (William) 1803–57 British playwright and journalist, who was the leading contributor to *Punch* from its foundation in 1841 until his death. Jerrold was the son of an actor and the author of some 70 plays, many of them betraying his humane concern for the poor and oppressed in an uncaring society. He took more care over his comic and satiric sketches for *Punch*, of which the serial *Mrs Caudle's Curtain Lectures* is an outstanding example, than over his plays, but several are worthy of revival. A representative collection, published in 1854, contains one embarrassingly sentimental piece, *The Painter of Ghent* (1836); five charming comedies, *Nell Gwynne; or, The Prologue* (1833), *The Housekeeper* (1833), *The Wedding Gown* (1834), *The Schoolfellows* (1835) and *Doves in a Cage* (1835); a domestic drama which approaches its grim subject with unfamiliar glimpses of REALISM, *The Rent Day* (1832); and the incomparably ebullient nautical MELODRAMA, *Black-Eyed Susan* (1829). The addition of another domestic drama, *The Factory Girl* (1832), would provide a fair basis for assessment of Jerrold's dramatic output.   PT

Jessner, Leopold 1878–1945 German director. One of the early exponents of NATURALISM, Jessner later made his name by replacing representational scenery with multiple acting levels arranged in ascending steps on a bare stage (*Jessnertreppe*). These facilitated symbolic rhythms that reinforced the dramatic action. He transformed SCHILLER's *Wilhelm Tell* and SHAKESPEARE's *Richard III* into key examples of EXPRESSIONISM in 1919 and 1920, using a selection of single colours and lighting to represent different moods, and developing a rhetorical acting style, in which exaggerated gesture and facial masking were designed to project inner vision.   CI

Jesuitendrama Drama performed at Jesuit colleges throughout Europe, but associated generally with colleges in Bavaria and Austria. It was performed from approximately the mid-16th to the mid-18th century. The purpose of these dramas was to educate the student performers in the art of speaking and rhetoric and to instill in both audiences and actors a belief in the values of the Catholic Church, as propagated by the Society of Jesus after the Counter-Reformation. Initially the plays were in Latin, but in the course of the 17th century performance in the German vernacular became increasingly common. Jesuit drama demonstrated an increasing tendency towards spectacular and musical embellishment; in this regard, it has been considered a forerunner to the tradition of spectacular OPERA, which became established in several Austrian and southern German cities in the late 17th century. The most notable writers of Jesuit drama were Nikolaus Avancini (1611–86), an Austrian Jesuit of noble birth, and Jakob Bidermann (1578–1639), whose *Cenodoxus* (1609), written initially in Latin, might stand revival today. (See also UNIVERSITY AND SCHOOL DRAMA (16TH–18TH CENTURIES).)   SW

Jewish Art Theatre (USA) A company closely modelled on STANISLAVSKY's MOSCOW ART THEATRE, set up by JACOB BEN-AMI in 1919 at New York City's Garden Theatre, with Emanuel Reicher, associate of REINHARDT and a founder of the German FREIE BÜHNE, as play director. Rave reviews greeted PERETZ HIRSHBEIN's *The Haunted Inn* and *Green Fields*, with Ben-Ami scoring a personal triumph in both. In spite of further successes, including DAVID PINSKI's *The Dumb Messiah*, Ossip Dimov's *Bronx Express* and TOLSTOI's *The Power of Darkness*, internal dissension brought the venture – which had reached probably the high point of YIDDISH THEATRE – to a close after two seasons and 14 productions.   AB

Jewish Repertory Theatre (New York City) Founded in 1974 by artistic director Ran Avni. Located on 92nd Street, with production facilities at nearby Playhouse 91, the JRT presents plays in English relating to the Jewish experience. In addition to revivals such as *Awake and Sing!* and *Incident at Vichy*, JRT has rediscovered plays such as *Me and Molly*, *Success Story* and *Café Crown*; has produced such MUSICALS as *Vagabond Stars* and *Kuni-Leml* (1984), the latter winning four Outer Critics' Circle Awards; and has developed new works in its JRT Writers' Lab. The theatre also stages Jewish-oriented work by such established American writers as ARTHUR MILLER, Ira Levin and Jerry Herman, and reinterprets the work of non-American playwrights (such as PINTER, SARTRE, CHEKHOV) in the light of Judaism. In 1989 JRT won an Outer Critics' Circle Award for Continued Outstanding Productions. The first ten seasons of the JRT were chronicled by Irene Backalenick in 1988.   DBW

Jewish theatre   see YIDDISH THEATRE; HEBREW THEATRE

jig The Elizabethan jig, which was a popular item in the public theatres of London, developed from the song-and-dance acts of an older folk tradition and gained its name from the type of dance best known to its audiences. It was an inclusive term, used to describe a broadside ballad (danced as well as sung), a short satirical scene with music and rhyme and, most frequently, a broad and often bawdy FARCE in which doggerel and dance played a prominent part and in which a CLOWN was the central figure. The first great exponent of the theatrical jig was RICHARD TARLTON, and it was his example that provided the model for later clowns, of whom WILL KEMPE is the most notable. As an afterpiece, the jig was, for a while, the necessary conclusion to an afternoon performance. Kempe's unexplained resignation from the LORD CHAMBERLAIN'S MEN in c.1599 has led to speculation that SHAKESPEARE and his colleagues downgraded the jig, but Richard Knolles noted the continuing demand for a jig at the end of a tragedy in 1606, and the disorderly crowds that attended the FORTUNE for the jig only led, in 1612, to an Order 'for the suppressing of jigs at the end of plays'. The subsequent history of the theatrical jig is obscure, but it retained its popularity in fairgrounds and among strolling players until well into the 18th century.   PT

jingxi [*jingju*] Drama (*xi*) of the Chinese capital (*jing*) – that is, Beijing; therefore commonly 'Beijing opera' in English (earlier, 'Peking opera'). In Chinese theatre circles it is more specifically known as '*pihuang* drama' (PIHUANG XI), after the name of the musical system used in performance. In 1790 Anhui troupes visiting Beijing for the Qianlong Emperor's birthday celebrations staged innovatory performances incorporating the *pihuang* musical modes. They made a great impact and a new style of performance was born.

By the early 19th century *jingxi* dominated the Beijing stage and eventually usurped the national popularity of KUNQU. Brought to maturity in the venue of the stage connoisseurs and enthusiastically patronized by the court, it flourished along an axis defined by the traditional bastion of Beijing and the westernized sophistication of Shanghai. *Jingxi* achieved international recognition when MEI LANFANG toured America and Russia in the 1930s. For most of its history it has remained an adored national entertainment.

The great success of *jingxi* is due in part to a style which is neither too complicated nor precious. Plays, derived from historical epics and romantic novels of China's past, are familiar to everybody. Play texts are largely anonymous, being revisions made by actors from earlier *kunqu* and *zaju* to suit their performance skills. The repertory divides into civil (*wen*) or military (*wu*) plays, and into serious plays (*daxi*, 'great play') or comic plays (*xiaoxi*, 'small play') on the basis of character type and story content. An actor specializes in one of four role types: male (*sheng*), female (*dan*), painted-face (*jing*), or clown (*chou*), and more specifically in a subtype, for example old male (*laosheng*), old woman (*laodan*) or scholar lover (*xiaosheng*). Specific skills in speaking (*nianbai*), song (*chang*), and acrobatics characterize each role type.

In traditional performance the stage was essentially bare. Elaborate COSTUMES and make-up identify role types and major characters. The orchestra was seated onstage and was aurally and visually integrated with the actors. Written music was not used. The music's two principal styles, *erhuang* and *xipi*, contain a number of metrical arrangements defined in terms of accented and unaccented beats within a measure. The leader of the orchestra uses a pair of wooden clappers manipulated rather like castanets and a hardwood drum with a skin head to beat out

the measures. Singing is accompanied by a bowed two-string instrument, *huqin*, which has a florid, rippling line characterized by vibrato and glissando effects. Brass gongs and cymbals mark entrances, exits and emotional climaxes, and are particularly evident in the brilliant acrobatic and dance passages which highlight *jingxi* performance.

Singing is used to express human emotions and psychological reactions accentuated by musical rhythms conveying mood. Role types are vocally identified by pitch, volume and enunciation. Rhyme patterns are created from a system of 13-character groupings which provide a compositional key for the dramatist. The rhyme sounds themselves contain elements from the dialects of Anhui, Sichuan and Hubei. Stanzas of four lines rhyming alternately are standard for monologues and dialogue. Rhyme and melismatic effects serve a vital euphonic function in the actor's vocalization.   ACS

See: A. C. Scott, *Actors are Madmen, Notebook of a Theatregoer in China*, Madison, 1982, *The Classical Theatre of China*, London, 1957, and *Mei Lanfang, Leader of the Pear Garden*, Hong Kong, 1959; Wu Zuguang, Huang Zuolin and Mei Shaowu, *Peking Opera and Mei Lanfang, A Guide to China's Traditional Theatre and the Art of its Great Master*, Beijing, 1981; C. S. L. Zung, *Secrets of the Chinese Drama: A Complete Explanatory Guide to Actions and Symbols as Seen in the Performance of Chinese Drama*, New York, 1964.

Jodelet [Julien Bedeau] c.1590–1660 Celebrated French comedian, who adopted the floured face traditionally associated with FARCE. First heard of with a provincial touring company in 1603, he had graduated to the MARAIS by 1634, before being transferred with other members of MONTDORY's company to the HÔTEL DE BOURGOGNE at the king's behest towards the end of that year. Later, he spent a further period of approximately 16 years at the Marais, playing Cliton in PIERRE CORNEILLE's *Le Menteur* (*The Liar*, 1643) and the eponymous lead in several farces written especially for him, notably *Jodelet, ou Le Maître-Valet* (*Jodelet, or The Master-Servant*, 1645) by SCARRON and *Jodelet Prince* (1655) by THOMAS CORNEILLE. Capitalizing on his naturally comic appearance, with a large mouth, long snout-like nose and bushy eyebrows, he had only to walk on stage to provoke gales of laughter, which his nasal speaking voice then served to redouble. MOLIÈRE, doubtless intent on securing the collaboration or neutralizing the competition of a rival comedian who was already the favourite of Paris audiences, persuaded Jodelet to join his company soon after their arrival in the capital in 1658 and wrote for him the part of the Vicomte de Jodelet opposite his own Marquis de Mascarille in *Les Précieuses ridicules* (*The Affected Ladies*, 1659). Similarly, the title role in *Sganarelle, ou Le Cocu imaginaire* (*Sganarelle, or The Imaginary Cuckold*, 1660) might well have been played by Jodelet, had it not been for his death. His brother François (?–1663), also an actor, under the name of L'Espy, remained a close companion throughout his career.   DR

Jodelle, Étienne 1532–73 French dramatist and poet of the Pléiade group, who is of greater interest as pioneer of an indigenous literary drama of classical inspiration than for the indifferent quality of his achievement. Only three plays of his are extant, two of them – the TRAGEDY *Cléopâtre captive* and the COMEDY *Eugène* – dating from 1552, when they were performed before Henri II by the young Jodelle and his friends, and a further tragedy entitled *Didon se sacrifiant* (*Dido Sacrificing Herself*) from 1558. Both tragedies are excessively literary in the SENECAN manner, with no development of character, little action and lengthy soliloquizing and narration of events, and are more acceptable as lyric verse than as writing for the stage. A prologue to *Eugène* vaunts it as an original work which has turned its back on medieval forms and accommodated the classical dramatic tradition to present-day taste and expectations. In fact its subject – adultery and the complaisant cuckoldry of a stupid husband – owes much to medieval FARCE, and the play is at its best when commenting with satirical verve on aspects of contemporary life.   DR

Joffré, Sara 1935– Peruvian playwright and director. After travel and study abroad, she returned to Lima to found Homero, Teatro de Grillos (Homer, Cricket Theatre) in 1963. Author and director of six published one-act plays for adults, Joffré is primarily known for her work with children's theatre and festivals in Peru.   GW

Joglars, Els Collective, sometimes controversial, Barcelona theatre company (literally, the Minstrels) founded in 1962 by Albert Boadella (b.1943). The longest-lived avant-garde troupe to emerge in opposition to Franco's Spain, it is noted for its apocalyptic, ironic and humorous vision of contemporary society and Catalan bourgeoisie. Emphasizing visual rather than verbal texts, performances have been well received internationally. Major productions include *Olympic Man Movement* (1981), *Teledeum* (1983), *Virtuosos de Fontainebleau* (1985), *Bye, bye, Beethoven* (1987), and their irreverent contribution to the 1992 Quincentennial activities, *Yo tengo un tío en América* (*I Have an Uncle in America*). (See also CATALAN THEATRE.)   PZ

John F. Kennedy Center for the Performing Arts (Washington, DC) A national cultural centre had been created by law in 1958 under the presidency of Dwight D. Eisenhower, but did not get started until it was deemed a fitting monument to the assassinated president, John F. Kennedy. It opened in 1971 on the banks of the Potomac and encompassed three theatres: the Eisenhower with 1140 seats for dramatic presentations, the Concert Hall with 2670 seats, and the Opera House with 2200 seats. The Center was guided by ROGER STEVENS, its president during 1961–88; he was succeeded upon his retirement by Ralph Davidson (1989–90) and James Wolfensohn (1990–). In 1978 a fourth theatre was added on the roof terrace level: the Terrace Theatre, which seats 500 for films, dance concerts, experimental productions and children's theatre. Some productions originate at the Center, but many others are booked in.   MCH

John Street Theatre (New York City) The third and most substantial theatre to be built in New York by DAVID DOUGLASS, the playhouse in John Street served the city until 1798, when it was replaced by a new theatre after-

wards known as the PARK. There were three periods in the John Street's history. The first, before the Revolution, consisted of two long seasons beginning in 1767; the second commenced in 1777, when the British troops took it over, renamed it the Theatre Royal, and presented plays as an antidote to tedium in their long occupation; and the last and most important period began in the summer of 1785 with the return of LEWIS HALLAM JR, who started with 'entertainments' which blossomed into full-scale productions. Hallam established a permanent resident company and was joined by actor JOHN HENRY in its management, but both were replaced by JOHN HODGKINSON and WILLIAM DUNLAP in its final years.

No iconography exists of the John Street. William Dunlap described it as 'principally of wood, an unsightly object, painted red'. It contained two tiers of boxes, a pit and a gallery, with dressing rooms and a greenroom located in a shed nearby. A description of the interior was included in ROYALL TYLER's *The Contrast* (1787), which premiered at the theatre. When it closed, it was annexed to a feed-and-grain store next door.   MCH

Johnson, J. Rosamond see COLE, BOB

Johnson, Dr **Samuel** 1709–84 English critic, scholar, lexicographer, poet and man of letters. Having known GARRICK in Lichfield, he walked with him to London in 1737. In 1746 he began work on the *Dictionary*. He was invited by Garrick to write the prologue for the opening of his management of DRURY LANE in 1747 and formulated Garrick's managerial policy in the couplet 'The Drama's laws the Drama's patrons give,/ For we that live to please must please to live.' His only play, *Irene*, was produced by Garrick in 1749. Much of it had been written before he went to London; a sterile TRAGEDY, it survived for nine nights through Garrick's advocacy. In 1756 Johnson published his proposals for an edition of SHAKESPEARE. The edition, published in 1765, contains his remarkable preface as well as notes of acute critical perception, if vulnerable scholarship. Many of his *Lives of the Poets* (1779–81) are studies of dramatists, written with great sensitivity.   PH

Johnston, (William) Denis 1901–84 Irish playwright. Johnston had a remarkably varied career: barrister, actor, war correspondent, producer for BBC radio and television, critic, teacher. His prose work includes impressionistic journalism (*Nine Rivers from Jordan*, 1953), literary-historical surmise (*In Search of Swift*, 1959) and mystical speculation (*The Brazen Horn*, 1977).

Johnston's first play, rejected by the ABBEY (hence its title, *The Old Lady Says 'No!'*, 1929), is a sparkling expressionist SATIRE of Ireland after independence, superbly produced by the GATE at the Peacock. He followed it with *The Moon in the Yellow River* (1931), a wryly tragic, realist version of the same theme. Of his subsequent plays, only two use expressionist techniques, *A Bride for the Unicorn* (1933), a modernized MORALITY PLAY, and *The Dreaming Dust* (1940), in which seven actors from a Masque of the Seven Deadly Sins explore the enigmas of Swift's life. His other plays include two intelligent *pièces à thèse*, *The Golden Cuckoo* (1939) and *Strange Occurrence on Ireland's Eye* (1956). Johnston's last play, *The Scythe and the Sunset* (1958), is a treatment of the Easter Rising blending farce and tragedy, and, as its title suggests, a counterpart to O'Casey. It illustrates again Johnston's ability to push realist theatre beyond its normal boundaries.

Until recently, Johnston's work was undervalued, resisting categorization by its combinations of traditional and independently experimental forms, prose and verse, human scepticism and visionary consciousness. Though a relatively small body of work, his theatre is now rightly judged in the company of SYNGE and O'Casey.   DM GF

Jolly, George fl.?1630–73 English actor-manager. He started acting before the Civil War but from 1648 he continued the old tradition of touring Germany with a troupe of English actors, performing in English and German. In 1651 the company contained actresses and used changeable scenery, long before such innovations had been adopted on the professional stage in London, using SALISBURY COURT and the RED BULL THEATRE. In 1662 he temporarily signed the licence over to DAVENANT and KILLIGREW and took a group of actors on tour in East Anglia. Davenant and Killigrew convinced King Charles that the licence had been sold to them outright and Jolly was prevented from performing in London. As a scant recompense, they allowed him to run the NURSERIES in Hatton Garden in 1668 and subsequently at Vere Street, Bun Hill and the Barbican.   PH

Jolson, Al 1886–1950 American singer and comedian. After spending his early years in CIRCUSES, MINSTREL SHOWS and VAUDEVILLE, Jolson made his stage debut in *La Belle Paree* (1911). In *The Whirl of Society* (1912), he first played the blackfaced servant Gus, a character he was to impersonate in a series of loosely plotted MUSICALS, including *Robinson Crusoe, Jr* (1916), *Bombo* (1921) and *Big Boy* (1925). The use of blackface, a common practice in the minstrel shows where Jolson had received his early training, gave racist overtones to much of the humour in his productions. Most spectators came to Jolson's shows to hear him sing his repertoire of hit songs, and on many occasions he obliged them by stopping the performance, dismissing the other actors, and spending the rest of the evening singing directly to the audience. After his motion picture debut in *The Jazz Singer* (1927), Jolson moved to Hollywood. His only other BROADWAY appearances were in the REVUE *The Wonder Bar* (1931) and in the MUSICAL COMEDY *Hold on to Your Hats* (1940). Possessed of a good baritone voice, Jolson was a charismatic performer whose energy, good humour and emotional singing style made him the most popular American musical comedy performer of his day.   MK

Jones, David (Hugh) 1934– British director, who started as a television producer on the pioneering BBC arts programme, *Monitor*. He had acted at Cambridge University in some PETER HALL productions, and in 1962 Hall invited him to direct Boris Vian's *The Empire Builders* in an experimental season at the Arts Theatre Club. This was his first professional stage production, but it was not until 1964 that he joined the ROYAL SHAKESPEARE COMPANY, primarily in an administrative capacity. In 1968 he became a co-director of the RSC's operations at the Aldwych, and from 1975 to 1977 he was the director of the Aldwych Theatre, responsible for the London wing of the RSC's programmes. Although he has directed a wide variety of plays for the RSC by such writers as BRECHT, GÜNTER GRASS, DAVID MERCER and SEAN O'CASEY, he is best known for having introduced the plays of MAKSIM GORKY to British audiences. From 1979 to 81 he was the artistic director of the Brooklyn Academy of Music Theatre Co. in New York.

Jones's strengths as a director lie in the clear dramatic expositions, the encouragement of sensitive performances from his casts and his awareness of European theatrical traditions. In 1982, his first full-length feature film appeared, of HAROLD PINTER's *Betrayal*. After teaching and directing in the USA, he returned to the RSC in 1993 to direct a new play, *Misha's Party*, by the American-Russian writing team of Richard Nelson and ALEKSANDER GELMAN, first staged at the Pit.   JE

Jones, Henry Arthur 1851–1929 English playwright who was put to work in a draper's shop at the age of 12. He 'improved' himself by reading Herbert Spencer, Ruskin and, above all, Matthew Arnold, whose moralized view of culture Jones loosely translated into earnestness. He had his first play staged in 1878 and his first success when WILSON BARRETT staged a sensationally effective MELODRAMA, *The Silver King* (1882), written in collaboration with Henry Herman. *Breaking a Butterfly* (1884), another collaboration with Herman, was a version of IBSEN's *A Doll's House*, which solemnly distorted the point of the original by having Flossie (Nora) decide to stay with her husband. In the plays of his mid-career, Jones found a place for Ibsenite idealists, battered and sometimes broken by narrow-minded religiosity. *Saints and Sinners* (1884), *The Middleman* (1889), *Judah* (1890), *The Dancing Girl* (1891), *The Crusaders* (1891) (for which Jones leased the Avenue Theatre and commissioned William Morris to design the sets, and on which he lost £4000) and *Michael and His Lost Angel* (1896) belong to this period. They dramatize the war of flesh and spirit with some vigour, but without much subtlety, and are a marked improvement on the melodramas Jones had continued to write for Wilson Barrett until 1886.

He was, however, an opponent of the Shavian 'theatre of ideas', and his dialogue, though often urbane, exposes moral polarities without challenging them. It was his urbanity that attracted CHARLES WYNDHAM, whose interest launched Jones into producing his finest work, *The Case of Rebellious Susan* (1894), *The Liars* (1897) and *Mrs Dane's Defence* (1900). He had still 20 plays to write, none of them outstandingly successful, though his standing in the USA was higher than in England. His health began to fail in 1912, and his last years were marred by several rancorous outbursts against GEORGE BERNARD SHAW. Having flirted with socialism in his youth, Jones ended up a diehard Tory.   PT

Jones, Inigo 1573–1652 English architect and scene-designer who introduced to the English court the artistry and sophistication of Renaissance staging practices from the Continent, above all from Italy. Having been appointed to the household of Prince Henry in 1604, Jones supervised the design and construction of almost all the notable

Stuart MASQUES from then until the dissolution of the court at the outbreak of the Civil War. He introduced perspective scenery for JONSON's *The Masque of Blackness* (1605), having already followed the example of SERLIO by building a raked stage. Because perspective scenery demanded masking, he developed decorated sides for the proscenium – golden statues for *Hymenaei* (1606), pilasters for *Hue and Cry after Cupid* (1608) and giant figures of Neptune and Nereus linked by a frieze for *Tethys' Festival* (1610). The proscenium arch framing the stage picture owed its dominance over the English stage to the triumphant practice of Inigo Jones.

Visits to Paris in 1609 and to Italy in 1613–14 extended the range of his ideas. To the classical *periaktoi* he added the neoclassical devices of the *scena versatilis* (a front piece which swivelled to reveal a different scene on the reverse side) and the *scena ductilis* (a scene painted on shutters, which could be pulled apart to reveal another scene behind). *The Masque of Queens* (1609) achieved the effects of coloured lighting by placing candles behind bottles filled with tinted liquids. For THOMAS CAMPION's *Lords' Masque* (1613), Jones provided the first of his many relief scenes, further elaborated by a two-tiered design. The Banqueting House at Whitehall, which he designed (1619–22), was equipped with unprecedented mechanical facilities, enabling the raising and lowering of whole scenes. It was scarcely surprising that Jonson grumbled about the displacing of poetry by spectacle. Their collaboration ended in 1631, shortly after Jones had completed his clever conversion of the COCKPIT-IN-COURT. Later masques, designed to illuminate WILLIAM DAVENANT's text, showed no diminution of inventiveness, and Jones's enthusiasm for the form was expressed in his last great architectural project, the Masquing House at Whitehall (1637). Always dependent on court favour, Jones died in poverty during the Interregnum. A collection of his drawings and designs survives in Chatsworth House, Derbyshire, underlining his place as England's first scene-designer. (See also THEATRE DESIGN.)   PT

Jones, James Earl 1931– African-American actor. Son of the actor Robert Earl Jones, James Earl trained at the University of Michigan, the American Theatre Wing and with LEE STRASBERG before making his 1958 BROADWAY debut in *Sunrise at Campobello*. He soon attracted attention, winning several acting awards for performances in NEW YORK SHAKESPEARE FESTIVAL productions (1960–6) as well as in *Moon on a Rainbow Shawl* (1962) and *Baal* (1965) OFF-BROADWAY. Jones was unforgettable as the despised prizefighter Jack Jefferson in *The Great White Hope* (1968), a role that earned him a Tony. An actor of magnetic physical presence and vocal power, he has frequently been cast non-traditionally: he has played King Lear, Macbeth, Coriolanus, Lopahin in *The Cherry Orchard* (1973), Hickey in *The Iceman Cometh* (1973) and Lenny in *Of Mice and Men* (1974). He gave a memorable performance in the monodrama *Paul Robeson* (1978), despite controversy surrounding the production, and he won further acclaim for his Othello to CHRISTOPHER PLUMMER's Iago on Broadway in 1982. He has appeared in several of ATHOL FUGARD's South African plays under the direction of LLOYD RICHARDS. In 1987 he won a Tony in AUGUST WILSON's

Fences. In the early 1990s he devoted himself primarily to television. His autobiography was published (with Penelope Niven) in 1993.   EGH

Jones, John Gwilym 1904–88 Welsh playwright. After graduating from the University College of North Wales, Bangor, Jones developed an interest in the theatre while teaching in London. On his return to Wales in 1930 he continued teaching until appointed producer of radio plays with the BBC in Bangor (1949–53), thereafter returning to lecture at his old college and earning a high reputation as a teacher and literary critic. After SAUNDERS LEWIS he was the most distinguished Welsh dramatist of modern times. Like Lewis, he was alive to European influences, and the move away from NATURALISM in his later plays was inspired partly by the work of BERTOLD BRECHT; but he differs sharply from Lewis in his portrayal, with an almost IBSENesque intensity, of the destructive power of emotion and feeling, usually within family relationships. *Tad a'r Mab* (*Father and Son*, 1963) and *Ac Eto Nid Myfi* (*And Yet Not Me*, 1976) are generally considered his finest works.   MA

Jones, Joseph S(tevens) 1809–77 American actor, manager and playwright. Beginning with *The Liberty Tree* (1832), he may have written as many as 150 plays (he could never remember). In all, nonetheless, he infused his heroes with the qualities of individuality, personal conviction and freedom of spirit that identified Jacksonian America. For his good friend the YANKEE actor GEORGE HANDEL HILL he wrote *The Green Mountain Boy* (1833) and *The People's Lawyer* (1839), a favourite with several Yankee actors. MELODRAMAS such as *The Surgeon of Paris* (1838) and *The Carpenter of Rouen* (1840) provided the spectacles audiences demanded, but his most lasting play was *The Silver Spoon* (1852), in which WILLIAM WARREN THE YOUNGER acted until 1883. *Zafari the Bohemian* (1856) suggests Jones's greater ambitions as a playwright. Generally associated with Boston, where he managed the TREMONT and National Theatres, he was a thoroughly professional man of the theatre who supported COPYRIGHT protection and adequate recompense for playwrights. A medical doctor (Harvard, 1843), he was advertised in theatres as 'the celebrated Dr Jones'.   WJM

Jones, Margo [Margaret] **(Virginia)** 1913–55 American director, producer and pioneer in the regional theatre movement whose major contributions were made in her home state of Texas, where she managed a theatre in Dallas dedicated to the production of new plays. Her New York credits included the co-direction, with EDDIE DOWLING, of *The Glass Menagerie* (1945), Maxine Wood's *On Whitman Avenue* (1946), MAXWELL ANDERSON's *Joan of Lorraine* (1946), *Summer and Smoke* (1948) and Owen Crump's *Southern Exposure* (1950), the latter two first presented in Dallas. The Dallas theatre opened as Theatre 47 (with yearly name changes until Jones's accidental death, when it became the Margo Jones Theatre). During its 12 seasons, 133 plays were presented, 86 of which were new, including INGE's *The Dark at the Top of the Stairs*, TENNESSEE WILLIAMS's *Summer and Smoke* and LAWRENCE AND LEE's *Inherit the Wind*. Jones's theatre became the most celebrated home of arena staging in the USA and a pioneer in the decentralization of the American theatre; others emulated her example in part as a result of her book, *Theatre-in-the-Round* (1951). A biography by Helen Sheehy was published in 1989.   DBW

Jones, Robert Edmond 1887–1954 American set and COSTUME designer whose 1915 design for *The Man Who Married a Dumb Wife*, directed by HARLEY GRANVILLE BARKER, is generally considered the beginning of the New Stagecraft in America. Rebelling against the romantic REALISM of DAVID BELASCO and other producers of the late 19th century, Jones evolved a style of simplified sets that were suggestive, rather than a reproduction of the real world. Having travelled in Europe and observed MAX REINHARDT for a year at the DEUTSCHES THEATER, Jones returned to the USA with an appreciation for the power of symbolic or emblematic elements. Paraphrasing from *Hamlet*, he wrote, 'Stage designing should be addressed to [the] eye of the mind.' He advocated a style of design that elicited an underlying feeling for the play, not one that eliminated the imagination. For director ARTHUR HOPKINS, Jones designed the sets for several SHAKESPEARE plays in the early 1920s. The designs employed unit sets – then, virtually unknown – and a strong use of light and shadow in the style of ADOLPHE APPIA. For *Macbeth*, the three witches were portrayed by three large masks hanging over the stage.

Jones was also an early member of the PROVINCETOWN PLAYERS and designed most of EUGENE O'NEILL's plays, including *Anna Christie*, *The Great God Brown* and *Mourning Becomes Electra*. From 1923 to 29 he served as a producer, with KENNETH MACGOWAN and O'Neill, of the Experimental Theatre Inc. – the successor to the Provincetown. Perhaps as important as his revolutionary design was his writing – most notably *The Dramatic Imagination* (1941) – in which he expressed the visionary ideas that made him an inspiration to theatre artists in the next generation. His designs were published in 1958 and 70, and a previously unpublished collection of lectures appeared in 1992.   AA

jongleur see JUGGLER

Jonson, Ben(jamin) 1572–1637 English playwright, poet and actor, probably born as well as educated in Westminster, where his schooling, under the remarkable William Camden, was thorough. Jonson may have gone on to work with his stepfather, a master bricklayer, before serving as a mercenary in Flanders. We do not know how, nor precisely when, he entered the acting profession. Entries in HENSLOWE's *Diary* confirm that he was employed as both actor and writer by 1597, the year in which the *Isle of Dogs* furore threatened the whole future of London's theatres. The already controversial Jonson was probably co-author (with THOMAS NASHE) of this lost play, whose vigorous SATIRE provoked action against the public theatres and probably led to the imprisonment of Jonson and several of his fellow actors. Never a man to tread warily, Jonson was again in trouble in 1598, when he was arrested for killing another actor, GABRIEL SPENCER, in a duel. He escaped execution by pleading benefit of clergy.

The combative independence that was a leading characteristic was already unmistakable.

Jonson thought little enough of his earliest surviving play, *The Case Is Altered* (c.1597), to omit it from his own collected works in 1616, but its immediate successor, *Every Man in His Humour* (1598), turned him into a celebrity at the same time as it established the brief vogue for the COMEDY OF HUMOURS. He followed it, less successfully, with *Every Man out of His Humour* (1599) and *Cynthia's Revels* (1600), satirical comedies which displayed his classical scholarship and his delight in formal experiment. Jonson's quickness to give and take offence made him a leading participant in the WAR OF THE THEATRES, in which MARSTON and DEKKER were his chief adversaries and to which *The Poetaster* (1601) was his unattractive major contribution. His decision to portray himself there as HORACE indicates his admiration for the Latin poet, whose *Art of Poetry* he translated. It was to Roman history that he turned for his next play, the TRAGEDY *Sejanus, His Fall* (1603). That he laboured hard on the composition of this classically disciplined play is overevident in the text, though Jonson tells us that the published version differs from the one performed by the King's Men. He was probably surprised to find himself in trouble again, brought before the Privy Council to answer charges of 'popery and treason', but he had made no secret of his prison conversion to Roman Catholicism, and it was at least tactless for a Catholic to risk writing about conspiracy and assassination at court during the tense first months of James I's reign. Undeterred, the truculent Jonson was briefly imprisoned in 1604, when the anti-Scottish jokes of *Eastward Ho*, which he wrote in collaboration with CHAPMAN and his erstwhile enemy Marston, offended the king. It is all the more surprising that, in 1605, he should have begun a long association with the Stuart court by collaborating with the designer, INIGO JONES, on *The Masque of Blackness*. Jonson's MASQUES are far more numerous than his plays, and they contain some of his loveliest poetry. For *The Masque of Queens* (1609) he introduced the discordant anti-masque, which remained an exuberantly grotesque feature of his subsequent work in the genre. Increasingly disenchanted by the displacement of his poetry by the ingeniously spectacular scenery of Jones, Jonson complained and quarrelled and finally abandoned masque-writing in 1634.

The plays on which Jonson's enduring reputation is based are all comedies and all written in the ten years from 1605 to 14. They are *Volpone* (1605), *Epicoene: or, The Silent Woman* (1609), *The Alchemist* (1610) and *Bartholomew Fair* (1614). It is here that Jonson's stagecraft is at its most brilliant. The incidents and episodes are artfully controlled and yet preserve an air of improvisatory spontaneity. The characters, though strictly defined by their names, seem able to command the freedom of the stage. The cutting edge of Jonson's comedies is sharp. They are peopled with deceivers and dupes, and the virtuous intelligent have an unusually small part to play. The 'image of the times', promised in the Prologue to the revised *Every Man in His Humour* (1616), is an uncomfortable one. It is an age of usury, in which human folly gives living room to moral outrage. In such an ethos, it is not surprising that the junior devil Pug, permitted a day of earthly malpractice in *The Devil Is an Ass* (1616), finds himself outmanoeuvred by humans more devious than he.

The comparative failure of *The Devil Is an Ass* may have discouraged him. It was nine years before his next comedy, *The Staple of News* (1625), was staged, and his effective dramatic output is completed by *The New Inn* (1629) and *A Tale of a Tub* (1633). But Jonson was never inactive. His stubborn belief in his own superior talent is represented by the unprecedented publication, in folio, of his dramatic and poetic *Works* (1616) and by his continuing provision of masques for the Stuart court. He was rewarded with a royal pension and appointment as Poet Laureate. The songs and poems in the masques, together with the collected verse of *Epigrams* and *The Forrest* (both 1616) and *Underwoods* (1640), explain his hold over younger contemporaries, the self-styled 'tribe' or 'sons' of Ben. His prose style, founded like his poems on classical precedent, is memorably recalled in the published notes of William Drummond of Hawthornden (1632), based on conversations held during Jonson's visit to Scotland in 1618–19. Jonson's profound knowledge of London life was rewarded by his appointment as City Chronologer in 1628, the year in which he suffered a severe stroke. Many of the friends who remained loyal to him during his difficult last years attended his funeral in Westminster Abbey and contributed to the collection of memorial elegies, *Jonsonus Virbius* (1638). One of them, the forgotten Jack Young, inscribed the words 'O rare Ben Jonson' on his gravestone. PT

Jordan [*née* Bland], **Dorothy** 1761–1816 English actress. She made her debut in 1779 in Dublin and acted with JOHN PHILIP KEMBLE at Smock Alley Theatre in 1781–2. After an affair with the manager, Richard Daly, she fled to England, pregnant. She auditioned for TATE WILKINSON successfully and he recommended a change of name ('You have crossed the water so I'll call you Jordan'). She reached the London theatres by 1785 and, after a slow start, became a huge success in BREECHES and hoyden roles like Peggy in GARRICK's *The Country Girl* and Priscilla Tomboy in *The Romp*. She had three children by Richard Ford, a barrister, and in 1790 became mistress of the Duke of Clarence, by whom she had ten children. She continued to star successfully, even though no longer able to play the same roles: as HAZLITT commented, 'her person was large, soft and generous like her soul'. She was highly praised as Viola and Ophelia, particularly for her delivery of verse so that, as LAMB said, 'it was no set speech'. A devoted mother and an extravagant spender, she worked extremely hard as an actress both on stage and in her negotiations with managers: her daughters had dowries of £10,000 each. In 1811 she separated from the duke. In 1815, swindled out of a large sum of money, she fled to Paris fearing arrest and died there in poverty. PH

Joris, Charles 1935– Swiss director and actor. Joris studied French literature at Neuchâtel University and trained as an actor in Strasbourg (Centre Dramatique de l'Est, 1958–61) under Hubert Gignoux. In 1961 he founded the Théâtre Populaire Romand, the first professional French-speaking theatre ensemble in Switzerland. The TPR tours all linguistic regions of the country, and neighbouring France. In its 30 years the TPR has produced over 60 plays, mostly Swiss or world premieres. The style of presentation is scenographically highly inventive and relies on sophisticated acting skills (acrobatics, free improvisation). The TPR pursues a conscious community policy (youth theatre, courses for amateur companies, open workshops, summer festivals in Neuchâtel and La Chaux-de-Fonds) and performs in towns and villages which have never seen professional theatre before. In 1975 Joris was awarded the Reinhart-Ring, the highest Swiss distinction for work in the theatre. The TPR's most notable *mises en scène* include: Bernard Liègme's *Les Murs de la ville* (*The City Walls*, 1961) and *Le Soleil et la mort* (*Sun and Death*, 1966), Henri Deblüe's *Le Procès de la truie* (*The Sow's Trial*, 1962), BRECHT's *Man is Man* (1968), SHAKESPEARE's *Lear*, ARDEN's *The Workhouse Donkey* (1978), HANDKE's *Through Towns and Villages* (1984) and BECKETT's *Godot* (1985). In 1993, to mark the bicentenary of GOLDONI's death, the TPR collaborated with the Piccolo Teatro (see GIORGIO STREHLER) of Milan to great public and critical acclaim. CLS

Joseph, Stephen 1927–67 British director, lecturer and pioneer of theatre-in-the-round in England. Son of actress Hermione Gingold and publisher Michael Joseph, in 1955 he founded the Studio Theatre Company in Scarborough with which he toured theatreless towns in the North of England for several years, exploring at the same time the potential of performances 'in the round'. This venture, together with experience of theatres-in-the-round in the USA, convinced him of the potential of this staging form and he began to advocate its practice with increasing passion. With minimal financial support he set up the country's first permanent such theatre in Stoke-on-Trent in 1962 as a home for his company: the VICTORIA THEATRE. In 1961 he was appointed Fellow in Drama at the newly created drama department of Manchester University. His books include *New Theatre Forms* and *Theatre in the Round*. The Stephen Joseph Theatre in the Round at Scarborough was opened in 1976 as a memorial to his work. AJ

Jouvet, Louis 1887–1951 French actor and director. Like DULLIN, Jouvet joined COPEAU's first company at the VIEUX-COLOMBIER, but left in 1922 to found his own company. At first he was Copeau's technical and lighting director, only gradually revealing his qualities as a star actor. In 1923, at the Comédie des Champs Élysées, he scored a hit with a new play *Dr Knock, or The Triumph of Medicine* by JULES ROMAINS. In 1927 he was a co-founder of the CARTEL, and in 1928 he produced the first play by GIRAUDOUX.

His productions of Giraudoux's plays over the next 17 years involved a large measure of collaboration and rewriting in rehearsal. When the Popular Front government offered him the directorship of the COMÉDIE-FRANÇAISE he suggested instead a group of directors. He spent the war years on tour with his company in Latin America and returned to produce Giraudoux's last play, *The Madwoman of Chaillot* (1945), and GENET's first, *The Maids* (1947). He died while working on SARTRE's *The Devil and the Good Lord* in 1951. After 1934, when he took over the Athénée Theatre, he often worked with the designer CHRISTIAN BÉRARD, whose self-consciously picturesque style fitted Jouvet's theatrical performances. In the cinema, Jouvet was able to tone down his performance style admirably to suit the camera. He wrote several books about the art of actor and director. DB

Judic [Anne-Marie-Louise Damiens] 1850–1911 French actress and singer, who began playing COMEDY as soon as she graduated from the Conservatoire. She was an immediate hit at her music-hall debut (see *CAFÉ CHANTANT*) at the Paris Eldorado in 1869, because of her superb diction and talent for innuendo, which won her the nickname 'the School for Mimes'. Later she made a brilliant career in comic OPERA, especially in OFFENBACH, touring the USA. Her last appearance as a singer was at the FOLIES-BERGÈRE in 1900. LS

juggler The art of balancing objects, tossing and catching them in different rhythms, may be the oldest performance skill, known in ancient Egypt, Assyria, China, Greece and Rome. Roman jugglers were usually denominated by their specialities, as *ventilatores* (knife throwers) and *pilarii* (ball players), whereas the medieval Latin term *joculator* referred more broadly to the lower level of strolling entertainer. Hence its derivatives, 'juggler' in English, *jongleur* in French, *giullare* in Italian and *Gugelleute* in German, bore pejorative connotations, suggesting deception for criminal purposes. The Spanish *malabarista* came to mean an illusionist who also juggles. The first named juggler was Pierre Gringore (b.1475).

On the 19th- and 20th-century VARIETY stage a distinction is made between strength jugglers and salon jugglers. The former juggle heavy objects, including human beings, occasionally work on horseback or unicycle, and catch cannon balls on the backs of their necks; the most celebrated have been Karl Rappo (1800–54), Paul Conchas (Huett, d.1916) and John Holtum (b.1845). The latter juggle billiard balls, cigar boxes, diabolos and similar paraphernalia, sometimes with their mouths; among the most adroit have been PAUL CINQUEVALLI, ENRICO RASTELLI, Kara (Michael Steiner, 1867–1939) and W. C. FIELDS.

A MUSIC-HALL speciality was the restaurant scene, originated by Agoust and perfected by the Charles Perzoff Troupe (1890–1910), in which waiters and customers juggle a complete five-course meal; a variation was the plate-breaking number of Carl Baggessen (?1868–1931). Once a staple in the repertory of every itinerant performer, juggling is now a common item in the curriculum of drama schools, used to train agility and coordination. The Flying Karamazar Brothers have introduced comic juggling into stagings of classic works, such as *The Comedy of Errors*. LS

Julia, Raul 1940–94 Puerto Rican-born film and stage actor, whose New York debut was as Astolfo in *Life Is a Dream* in Spanish. Principal stage appearances included classical roles at the Delacorte (see NEW YORK SHAKESPEARE FESTIVAL) and the VIVIAN BEAUMONT THEATRE in New York. In 1982 he starred in *Nine* as Guido Contini, in which critics referred to him as 'a standout' and 'childishly wise, boyishly insincere, and totally right'. For *Nine* he was nominated for a Tony, as he was for *The Threepenny Opera* (1976), *Where's Charley?* (1974) and *Two Gentlemen of*

Verona (1971). In 1990 he was largely unsuccessful as Macbeth at the NYSF, where he essayed Othello for the second time the following year (the first was in 1979) opposite the Iago of Christopher Walken. He was seen as Don Quixote in a national tour of *Man of La Mancha* in 1991 (on BROADWAY in 1992). SMA

Junction Avenue Theatre Company Experimental SOUTH AFRICAN theatre company, based in Johannesburg. It has created a number of plays which have challenged ideas of content and form in the development of South African theatre. Since its foundation in 1976 with the production of their play *The Fantastical History of a Useless Man*, the company's policy has been to workshop plays which 'critically reflect South African society, reclaim hidden history and restore a voice to the voiceless'. Committed to non-racialism in a society where racial definitions have been the norm for most of the century, the company works collectively, sometimes spending up to six months researching, workshopping and improvising a text, then editing and rehearsing it for production. Using principles of MUSIC-HALL and popular theatre, African music and dance, and ideas derived from Workshop 71, BRECHT and GROTOWSKI, plus later elements of social realism, Junction Avenue has consistently engaged creatively with the relationship between theatre and political action.

Many of its plays, influenced by revisionist historiography emanating from, for example, the University of the Witwatersrand, attempt to reveal the history of repression in South Africa. Under the direction of Malcolm Purkey, plays such as *Randlords and Rotgut* (1978), *Marabi* (1982) and *Sophiatown* (1986) reveal aspects of the history of apartheid and its brutal influence over people's lives. In the late 1970s, inspired by the emergent trade union movement, members of the company, determined to push out in new directions, began working on short plays and sketches to take to union meetings and workers' halls. In 1980 *Security* and *Dikitsheneng* (*The Kitchen*), examples of this work, were presented in a double bill under the title *People's Plays*. Company members were subsequently invited by activists in the trade union movement to help devise plays with trade union members. The result was *Ilanga Lizophumela Abasebenzi* (*The Sun Will Rise for the Workers*, 1979), a seminal trade union theatre production.

The company has produced popular children's theatre and experimental works such as *Will of a Rebel* (1979), based on the life of poet Breyten Breytenbach, and an African version of *The Bacchae* (1983). It has also written and produced an award-winning television film, *Howl at the Moon* (1981). *Tooth and Nail* (1989) represents a departure in style: constructed as a series of flashes of South African life, the play suggests some issues to be confronted in a post-apartheid society. IS

Juvarra, Filippo 1676–1736 Italian architect and scene designer. Having studied architecture under Carlo Fontana in Rome, Juvarra won the Concorso Clementino prize and became a member of the Academia di San Luca in 1705. In 1706 he became assistant to designer Giuseppe Capelli at the San Bartolomeo Opera House in Naples. At this time he adopted the use of angled perspective, or *scena per angolo*. Under the patronage of Cardinal Ottoboni from 1708 to 1714, he designed and built the theatre at the Palazzo della Cancelleria and created the scenic effects for its productions. In 1713, he was also designing elaborate opera sets for the private theatres of both Prince Capricanica and the queen of Poland. By 1714 he became chief architect at the Savoy court in Turin. His style is characterized by the use of curvilinear settings which draw the observer's eye in a circle and then to the foreground. The effect is accomplished with the use of free-standing units and a permanent foreground with changing vistas. Draperies, tropical foliage and Near Eastern architecture are his hallmarks.

AJN

juvenile drama SEE TOY THEATRE

kabuki The major Japanese urban commercial theatre genre from its beginnings c.1600 into the 20th century. *Kabuki*, the noun form of the adjective *kabuku*, tilted or off-centre, meant the unorthodox, the strange, the new. The scandalous nature of early performance is clear from the fact that *kabuki* was written with the ideographs song (*ka*), dance (*bu*), and prostitute (*ki*). In response to the tuts of Victorian moralists, in the late 19th century the ideograph meaning 'skill' was substituted for the ideograph meaning 'prostitute'.

Kabuki performers depended on a popular audience, always creating new plays and acting styles to meet the temper of the times. They borrowed from *NŌ, KYŌGEN* and *BUNRAKU*. As a consequence, *kabuki* acting encompasses half a dozen substyles, leading the Meiji period scholar Tsubouchi Shōyō to call *kabuki* a multiheaded monster. It is notable that even a wildly successful play was rewritten as a matter of course when revived, which explains the scores of variant texts for an often-performed play like *Wait a Moment! (Shibaraku)*.

An actor masters forms or patterns (*kata*) of acting perfected over generations in his family. *Kata* are understood to encompass both outer form and inner content, so that varying interpretations are possible within one *kata*. Good actors create new, unique *kata*. The history of the ICHIKAWA DANJŪRŌ acting line illustrates the balance between tradition and creation over twelve generations. Today few actors go much beyond transmitted forms.

Actors in *kabuki* dance and speak. Song is the province of specialist singers who accompany the action from offstage or, in dance scenes, onstage. Actors of female roles (*onnagata*) display their charm and skill through solo dances (*shosagoto* or *keigoto*) that are worked into plays of all types. Actors characteristically freeze in tableaux (*mie*) at emotional climaxes, thus intensifying and prolonging moments of dramatic tension. A high level of energy in the actor sustains these silent, motionless moments. Actors command a repertory of vocal techniques, including versions of *nō* speech and *bunraku* chanting. Sukeroku's name-saying speech (*nanori*) requires a machine-gun-like tempo (*ippon chōshi*). Passages of antiphonal dialogue composed in lines of 7 and 5 syllables (*shichigochō*) are delivered in a melodious style (*yakuharai*) based on Buddhist chanting.

Nō and *bunraku* each have a single style of music; *kabuki* has many musical styles to match its many styles of drama and performance. Three basic types of instruments combine in *kabuki*. The *nō* ensemble of drums and flute (*hayashi*) can be seen in paintings of OKUNI's performances in Kyoto, c.1600–10. Later these combined with large drums, gongs, bells and other sound-effects instruments, to make up *kabuki*'s percussion ensemble (*narimono*). The plucked lute (*shamisen*) is seen in paintings of *kabuki* performance of the period 1610–20. Today percussion, *shamisen* and singers make up *kabuki*'s basic musical grouping, called *geza* ('lower seat') from its position offstage right. *Geza* musicians perform *nagauta* ('long

song') style music and provide sound effects. Their music is ubiquitous throughout a performance: instrumental *shamisen* melodies (*aikata*) set an appropriate mood for a scene; patterns beaten on the large barrel drum (*ōdaiko*) indicate rain, snow, wind, ocean waves or the time of day; *shamisen* and song accompany exits and entrances of characters along the rampway through the audience. More than 500 melodies and rhythms, as well as special gong and bell sounds, are part of the offstage musical repertory. Wooden blocks (*tsuke*) struck on the stage floor provide sound effects for running, walking, striking and other actions, while hard wood clappers (*ki* or *hyōshigi*) provide an aural frame for the opening and closing of the act curtain, for scenery changes, and to alert actors and audience that a scene will soon begin.

In dance plays, the musical ensemble – *nagauta*, *tokiwazu*, *tomimoto*, *kiyomoto* or other style – is seated onstage. The last three musical styles were created in the 18th century specifically for *kabuki* dance plays; they do not use percussion or flute and hence are softer and more romantic than *nagauta* music. *Takemoto* music accompanies borrowed puppet plays (*maruhonmono*) and some dance plays. The formally dressed musical ensembles contribute to the spectacular stage picture. Several ensembles can be used to provide variety of mood – *nagauta* and *tokiwazu* in *The Zen Substitute* (*Migawari zazen*; trans. 1966, 1972), or *nagauta*, *takemoto*, *tokiwazu* in *The Maple Viewing* (*Momijigari*), for example.

The bravura acting style of heroic figures (*aragoto*), developed by the Ichikawa Danjūrō acting family, is expressed through exaggerated COSTUMES and properties, and bold red and black face make-up (*kumadori*). It is familiar through actor portraits in wood-block prints. The comic-erotic acting (*wagoto*) for feckless heroes in domestic plays was developed in Kyoto–Osaka. When an actor acts a 'puppet' role, he may perform in exaggerated PUPPET style (*ningyō buri*). Styles are mixed within a play or scene. *Kabuki* dance incorporates lively rural and urban dances (*odori*) of the common people, as well as *nō*'s characteristic turning or pivoting technique (*mai*).

A *kabuki* performance is structured to provide changing moods and emotional states over time. The productions in the 1st, 3rd, 5th, 7th and 9th lunar months matched the Five Annual Festivals of the lunar calendar; the 11th-month production was the season opening, or *kaomise* ('face showing'). The nature of the play matched the season: love in spring, martial vigour on Boy's Day (5th month), lament for the spirits of the dead in the summer. A day's programme, 10–12 hours in length, began with casual 'practice' plays (*jobiraki* and *futatateme*) before dawn. The main play (*hon kyōgen*), consisting of formal history and legendary acts (*jidai*), domestic acts (*sewa*) and felicitous dance finale (*ōgiri*), ended at dusk.

Detailed information about performance was published in yearly rankings of actors (*hyōban ki*), production chronologies (*nendai ki*) and actors' commentaries (*gei-*

dan). *My Advice to Onnagata* (*Ayame gusa*) by the actor YOSHIZAWA AYAME I, *A Record of Theatrical Matters* (*Kezairoku*) by playwright Namiki Shōzō II (?–1807), *The Playwright's Seasonal Calendar* (*Sakusha nenjū gyōji*) by playwright Mimasuya Nisanji (1784–1856), and *Notes of a Kabuki Playwright* (*Kyōgen sakusha kokoroesho*) by KAWATAKE MOKUAMI provide fascinating inside views of *kabuki*'s vibrant place in society.

The Tokugawa government licensed 9 large *kabuki* theatres through most of the Edo period: 3 each in Edo, Kyoto and Osaka. A drum tower over the theatre entrance signified the owner was licensed to use *kabuki*'s unique three-coloured draw curtain, the revolving stage, *hanamichi*, and other *kabuki* symbols. Small, unlicensed *kabuki* houses, numbering up to a dozen in each city, could not. Spectators sat in side balconies, ground-floor boxes and a centre pit, and occasionally on the side of the stage and even behind scenes. Performance was restricted by law to daylight hours; lighting was by candle or indirect sunlight (shutters over the audience could be opened or closed).

In the autumn the theatre owner signed a one-year contract with a troupe actor-manager (*zagashira* or *zamoto*), a leading female impersonator (*tate onnagata* or *tate oyama*), a staff playwright (*tate sakusha*) and a company of 50 to 70 supporting writers, actors, musicians, singers, costumers, wigmakers and technicians. In addition, a staff of 150 barkers, ticket sellers, doormen, ushers, food vendors, cushion vendors and bouncers kept a large theatre running. Theatres were restricted by government decree to a single district of 2 or 3 blocks in each city.

A special theatre structure evolved for playing *kabuki*, an oblong box in which audience and stage are physically part of the same space. A rampway or *hanamichi* carried the stage space through the left portion of the audience nearly to the back of the house. *Hanamichi*, 'flower path', probably meant 'gift path' in the late 17th century, flower being a euphemism for a gift. It allowed an actor to walk through the audience when entering and exiting, or deliver a major speech standing in its midst. A second *hanamichi* ran through the right portion of most *kabuki* houses. In some scenes, two separated characters, one on each *hanamichi*, spoke alternate speeches over the heads of the audience, a technique not dissimilar to cinema montage. By the mid-18th century, theatres were equipped with floor-level revolving stages (often one within another) for moving elaborately painted scenery and actors, traps, hanging wires, pipes for water, and other staging devices. Stage assistants in black (*kōken* or *kurogo*) moved properties and scenery in audience view or lighted a star's face with a candle held out on a flexible pole.

Major changes occurred in staging *kabuki* during the 20th century. Cavernous new theatres were constructed, modelled on European OPERA houses. Auditoriums and stages expanded to three times the size of the traditional theatre – the present Kabuki-za in Tokyo has a 93-ft-wide stage and seats 2600. The actor used to stand out on the traditional small stage; he is now dwarfed by the theatre's dimensions. Acres of painted scenery fill the stage, competing with the actor for attention. Spectators in the overhanging balconies can no longer see actors on much of the *hanamichi*. The transformation of *kabuki* from a despised plebeian entertainment into a classic art of the middle class has been accompanied by the phenomenon of giganticism in theatre architecture and staging.

Kabuki's theatricalism has had a major impact on Western directors in the 20th century: Sergei Eisenstein, MAX REINHARDT, ERWIN PISCATOR, JOSHUA LOGAN and HAROLD PRINCE, among others. *Kabuki* is performed in English at the University of Hawaii and Pomono College, and its performing techniques are increasingly applied to various 'fusion' productions (for example a *Kabuki Macbeth*). JRB

See: J. R. Brandon (ed.), *Chūshingura: Studies in Kabuki and the Puppet Theatre*, Honolulu, 1982, and (tr.), *Kabuki: Five Classic Plays*, Cambridge, Mass., 1975; J. R. Brandon, W. Malm, and D. Shively, *Studies in Kabuki: Its Acting, Music, and Historical Context*, Honolulu, 1978; J. R. Brandon and Tamako Niwa (tr.), *Two Kabuki Plays: 'The Subscription List' and 'The Zen Substitute'*, New York, 1966; E. Ernst, *The Kabuki Theatre*, Honolulu, 1974 (1956); M. Gunji, *Buyo: The Classical Dance*, New York, 1971, and *Kabuki*, Palo Alto, Calif., 1970; Z. Kincaid, *Kabuki, the Popular Stage of Japan*, New York, 1977 (1925); S. L. Leiter (tr.), *The Art of Kabuki: Famous Plays in Performance*, Berkeley, Calif., 1979 and *Kabuki Encyclopedia*, Westport, Conn., 1979; A. C. Scott, *The Kabuki Theatre of Japan*, New York, 1966 (1955); R. Shaver, *Kabuki Costumes*, Rutland, Vt., 1966; Y. Toita, *Kabuki: The Popular Theatre*, New York, 1970;

Kachalov [Shverubovich]**, Vasily (Ivanovich)** 1875–1948 Russian-Soviet actor, who began his professional career in A. S. Suvorin's Theatre of the Literary Artistic Society in St Petersburg (1896–7), then in 1900 joined the MOSCOW ART THEATRE (MAT), where until 1948 he played 55 roles. An intelligent actor, he excelled at impersonating idealists, humanists and leading-man types, including the original Tuzenbach and Trofimov in *The Three Sisters* (1902) and *The Cherry Orchard* (1904), respectively, as well as the title role in CHEKHOV's *Ivanov* (1904); the Baron in the premiere of GORKY's *The Lower Depths* (1902) and Protasov in the same author's *Children of the Sun* (1905); Julius Caesar in SHAKESPEARE's tragedy (1903); Chatsky in GRIBOEDOV's *Woe from Wit* (1906 and 1914); Don Juan in PUSHKIN's *The Stone Guest* (1915); IBSEN's *Brand* (1906); and Hamlet in the famous GORDON CRAIG–STANISLAVSKY collaboration (1912). He also appeared as the definitive thinking man, Ivan Karamazov, in NEMIROVICH-DANCHENKO's famous 1910 production of Dostoevsky's *The Brothers Karamazov*. Kachalov's career continued unabated after the October Revolution – on the concert stage, in theatre, radio and film and in a full complement of roles from the classical repertory, including that of Chatsky in the 1938 *Woe from Wit* revival. He also appeared in the new Soviet drama: e.g. as Vershinin in VSEVOLOD IVANOV's *Armoured Train 14–69* (1927). In 1936 he was named a People's Artist of the USSR. SG

Kaduma, Godwin 1938– Tanzanian playwright. He has written two plays, both in Swahili, one published, the other not: *Dhamana* (*Pledge*, 1980), on the proper use of education, and *Mabatini* on the frustrations of the poor peasantry. Kaduma is Director of Culture in the Ministry of Culture, Youth and Sports. PMM

Kahn, Michael 1937– American director and educator, who during his career has staged plays ranging from avant-garde SATIRES to musical comedies (see MUSICAL COMEDY). He is known principally, however, as a talented Shakespearian director and as the artistic director of the AMERICAN SHAKESPEARE THEATRE (1969–74), the McCarter Theatre Company (1974–9), the ACTING COMPANY (1978–88) and, since 1986, the Shakespeare Theatre (Washington, DC). Drawing eclectically on both traditional and postmodernist directorial approaches, Kahn's Shakespearian stagings are noted for their vigour, clarity and originality and have contributed significantly to a revival of public interest in SHAKESPEARE on the American stage in the 1980s and 90s. In the training of actors, he also has been influential as the chair of the Acting Department of the Juilliard Drama Division (where he was appointed division head in 1992). DJW

Kahn, Otto H(ermann) 1867–1934 German-born banker, who emigrated to New York in 1893 and became the greatest individual patron of the arts the USA has yet known. The close personal friend and financial adviser of railway titan Edward H. Harriman, Kahn was regarded in his time as the most liberal and democratic multimillionaire in the country. He was the chief benefactor of the Metropolitan Opera Company and a founder and backer of the NEW THEATRE. His international contacts and his personal wealth facilitated the US tour (1916–17) of Serge Diaghilev's Ballets Russes, a visit that deflected American ballet from an Italian towards a Russian model. He backed the visits of COPEAU's VIEUX-COLOMBIER THEATRE (1917–19), the MOSCOW ART THEATRE (1922–3) and the Théâtre de l'Odéon (1924–5). He underwrote MAX REINHARDT's 1924 production of *The Miracle* to the amount of $600,000. He provided critical support for influential art theatres such as the WASHINGTON SQUARE PLAYERS, the PROVINCETOWN PLAYERS, the New Playwright's Theater, the CIVIC REPERTORY THEATRE and the Hedgerow Theatre (Moylan-Rose Valley, Pennsylvania), as well as for numerous individual writers, actors and artists. WD

Kainz, Josef 1858–1910 Austrian actor. As a young man Kainz acted with the MEININGEN COMPANY (from 1877 to 1880) and with the Munich Court Theatre (from 1880 to 1883). He was hired in 1883 by ADOLF L'ARRONGE to become a founding member of the company of the DEUTSCHES THEATER, Berlin. Here his emotional interpretation of the title role in *Don Carlos* brought him national fame. Kainz remained the leading actor of the Deutsches Theater until 1899, when he joined the Vienna BURGTHEATER. Here he remained until his death. He was undoubtedly the most popular actor of his day, on account of his aristocratic appearance, his phenomenally flexible and accurate voice and his unusual physical dexterity. His technique has been described as 'impressionist', and in his day his acting was compared to that of SARAH BERNHARDT, COQUELIN and ELEONORA DUSE. A common feature in his interpretation of the tragic roles of SHAKESPEARE, GOETHE, SCHILLER and GRILLPARZER was his representation of them as victories of the human spirit over adversity, rather than defeats. During the last decade of his life, these interpretations became darker and his acting revealed reserves of violent passion in the characters. Most famous among his celebrated roles were Romeo, Hamlet, Mark Antony and Torquato Tasso, not to mention his masterpieces of comic characterization in the plays of MOLIÈRE and NESTROY. SW

Kaiser, Georg 1878–1945 German dramatist, who with *Die Bürger von Calais* (*The Burghers of Calais*), *From Morn to Midnight* (1917), *Die Koralle* (*Coral*, 1917), *Gas I* (1918) and *II* (1920), and *Nebeneinander* (*Side by Side*, 1923) was the most successful expressionist dramatist (see EXPRESSIONISM). He wrote more than 60 plays, and with GERHART HAUPTMANN was the most frequently performed dramatist of the Weimar Republic.

The Burghers of Calais, his first success, heralded the arrival of the expressionist 'new man'. Written in 1913, it was only performed in 1917 when its themes of altruism and spiritual regeneration chimed with the war-weary public's aspirations. Another 'new man' tries in vain to coax the gas-workers in the *Gas* plays to abandon industry for life in a green-field settlement, then blows up the gasworks when it turns out to be making poison gas. In *From Morn to Midnight* (1917) a bank clerk seeks fulfilment in communal frenzy, commercial sex and salvationist religion, but finds materialism everywhere and commits suicide. Its episodic structure, compressed dialogue, typed characters (the Bank Manager, the Wife, and so on) and idealism, albeit frustrated, make it a characteristic expressionist piece. *Nebeneinander* uses the same structure to satirize the get-rich-quick postwar years, using rounder characters and the more realistic language of *Neue Sachlichkeit* (the new sobriety).

Kaiser's characters are not so much personalities as ideas in action, and his plays themselves were called *Denkspiele*, or games of ideas, by the critic Julius Bab. Kaiser wrote a MUSICAL COMEDY, *Zwei Krawatten* (*Two Ties*, music by Mischa Spoliansky, 1929), and the libretto for *Der Zar lässt sich photographieren* (*The Tsar Has His Photo Taken*, 1928) by KURT WEILL, who also set Kaiser's *Silbersee* (*Silverlake*, 1933) to music. Kaiser went into exile in Switzerland in 1938. He continued to write, latterly verse plays on Greek subjects. *Das Floss der Medusa* (*The Raft from the Medusa*, 1945) is a pessimistic reversal of the ethos of *The Burghers of Calais*, in which 13 children on a life raft drown the youngest to avoid bad luck. HR

Kalidasa mid-5th century AD Most revered playwright (INDIAN), of the classical Sanskrit theatre. Kalidasa may have been court poet for King Chandragupta II of Ujjain in north central India. He is known to have written the plays *Malavika and Agnimitra* (*Malavikagnimitra*) and *Urvasi Won by Valour* (*Vikramorvasiya*) and the dramatic poem *The Cloud Messenger* (*Meghaduta*). His most important work is the play *Sakuntala and the Ring of Recognition* (*Abhijnanasakuntala*), which has served as the ideal example of the *nataka* type of classical Sanskrit drama. Kalidasa adheres to the classical rules without sacrificing his own artistic integrity and his works are recognized as representing some of the finest examples of Sanskrit poetry. FaR

Kalish [Kalich], Bertha ?1872–1939 Polish (Lemberg)-born actress, who first performed in Polish OPERA but shifted to YIDDISH THEATRE. In 1896, already successful, she went to America with her husband and children. Her beauty, grace and dignity won her praise as the star of such plays as GOLDFADN's *Shulamis* and GORDIN's *Sappho* and *The Kreutzer Sonata* (which he supposedly wrote to show off her thrilling voice and beautiful thick hair). In 1905 she contracted with the American producer HARRISON GREY FISKE to star in productions such as *Fedora* and *Monna Vanna*, as well as English translations of her Yiddish successes, and for the next 20 years she performed at least as much in English as in Yiddish. However, near the end of her life, completely blind, she returned exclusively to the Yiddish stage. NS

Kamban, Gudmundur 1888-1945 Icelandic playwright and director. Like SIGURJÓNSSON he wanted to break the isolation of Icelandic literature, writing mostly in Danish, although his best plays, *Marble* (1918) and *We Murderers* (1920), are set in New York. His neo-romantic *Hadda-Padda* (1914) made his name in Iceland and Denmark. Mainly treating modern urban society, Kamban frequently deals with moral dilemma. Thus in *Marble* he questions the basis of the Western legislation regarding crime and punishment, while the debate in *We Murderers* is whether crime is the victim's responsibility. Another important play is the historical tragedy *Skálholt* (1934). An active director in Copenhagen and Germany during the 1920s, Kamban staged his own work as well as plays by BJÖRNSTJERNE BJÖRNSON, Knut Hamsun and others. He was the first Icelandic film director. His plays were seen in Scandinavia and Germany in the 1920s and 1930s and are still performed in Iceland. AI

Kamińska, Esther (Rachel) 1862-1930 and **Ida Kamińska** 1899-1980 Polish actress; and actress, director, producer, translator and teacher, respectively. Variously known as 'the Jewish DUSE' and 'mother of the Yiddish theatre', Esther Kamińska began as an actress in 1892 and achieved fame particularly in the fine series of female roles in JACOB GORDIN's plays, her most notable being the title role in *Mirele Efros*, with her young daughter Ida playing her stage daughter. In 1921 the Warsaw Yiddish Art Theatre (VYKT) was formed by the Kamińska family, all of whom were actors, performing in the highest traditions of European realistic theatre (see REALISM). In 1950 the Polish Jewish State Theatre was formed, housed in the specially built E. R. Kamińska Theatre in Warsaw, and Ida, who had inherited her father's administrative ability and her mother's acting talent, became its artistic director, a role she filled with distinction right up until her death. AB

Kampuchea see CAMBODIA

Kander, John 1927- and
Fred Ebb 1932- American composer, and lyricist. After receiving a Master's degree from Columbia University, Kander worked as a rehearsal pianist, conductor and arranger. His first BROADWAY score was for *A Family Affair* (1961). Ebb also received a Master's from Columbia; he wrote plays and song lyrics before joining with Kander to write scores for Broadway, notably *Flora, the Red Menace* (1964), *Cabaret* (1966), *Zorba* (1968), *Chicago* (1975),

Woman of the Year (1981) and *Kiss of the Spider Woman* (1992, Toronto and London; 1993, Broadway, winner of Tony). They wrote the songs for two of Liza Minnelli's one-person shows, and she appeared in their MUSICALS *Chicago* (as a replacement for GWEN VERDON), *The Act* (1977) and *The Rink* (1984). In several of their musicals they proved skilful at duplicating the sounds and idioms of foreign cultures and bygone eras. MK

Kanin, Garson 1912- New York-born (Rochester) actor, director and author of short stories, novels, documentaries, and stage, screen and television plays (often with his late wife RUTH GORDON; see TELEVISION DRAMA). Beginning in VAUDEVILLE, he debuted as Tommy Deal in *Little Ol' Boy* (1933), and appeared in *Spring Song* (1934) and *Ladies' Money* (1934) among others. He directed *Hitch Your Wagon* (1937) and *Too Many Heroes* (1937), and was assistant director to GEORGE ABBOTT (1935-7) before moving to Hollywood to direct feature films. With Carol Reed he received an Oscar for Eisenhower's army documentary, *The True Glory* (1945); alone he directed his best-known BROADWAY work, *Born Yesterday* (1946; directed film version in 1956), and his own libretto of *Die Fledermaus* (Metropolitan Opera, 1950). He also directed (among other films) *The Diary of Anne Frank* (1955); wrote the book for and directed *Do Re Mi* (1960); and directed *Funny Girl* (New York, 1964) and a revival of *Idiot's Delight* (Los Angeles, 1970). Known as a playwright of strong liberal sentiments, he received the American Academy of Dramatic Arts Award of Achievement (1958). GSA

Kantor, Tadeusz 1915-90 Polish scene designer, director and visual artist, who graduated from the Cracow Academy of Fine Arts in 1939. During the Nazi occupation he founded the underground Independent Theatre, staging SŁOWACKI's *Balladyna* (1943) and WYSPIAŃSKI's *Return of Odysseus* (1944). After the war he created avant-garde stage designs for the Teatr Stary in Cracow, including *Saint Joan* (1956), and for the Teatr Ludowy in Nowa Huta, notably *Measure for Measure* (1956). Dissatisfied with institutionalized avant-garde, he organized his own theatre in 1956 with a group of visual artists, calling it Cricot II, to mark continuity with the painters' theatre Cricot of the 1930s. In the 1960s Kantor produced happenings, exhibited widely, and travelled with his company, creating an autonomous theatre in which actors are used as props and manikins, and the text (usually by WITKIEWICZ) exists as an object on a par with other components of the production. In the 1970s he developed 'the Theatre of Death', where time, memory and the interpenetration of life and death hold sway, and Kantor himself appeared as master of ceremonies at a seance in the 'poor room of imagination'. Major productions include *The Cuttlefish* (1956), *In a Small Country House* (1961), *The Madman and the Nun* (1963), *The Water Hen* (1968), *The Green Pill* (1973), *The Dead Class* (1975), *Wielopole, Wielopole* (1980, created in Florence), *Where Are the Snows of Yesteryear?* (1982), *Let the Artists Die* (1985, created in Nuremberg), *I Shall Never Return* (1988) and *Today Is My Birthday* (1990). DG

Kanze Hisao 1924-78 The finest Japanese *nō* actor of

A scene from Tadeusz Kantor's *The Dead Class*, 1975. Kantor is designer, creator, director and performer.

the post-Second World War era, named an Important Intangible Cultural Asset; eldest of three sons (with Hideo and Shizuo) born into *nō* and trained by their grandfather, Kanze Kasetsu. He studied with JEAN-LOUIS BARRAULT in Paris and performed to acclaim on foreign tours. He brought new vitality to his performances of traditional plays, *The Fulling Block* (*Kinuta*), *The Feather Robe* (*Hagoromo*) and *Komachi on the Stupa* (*Sotoba Komachi*). He also acted in significant experimental productions: SUZUKI TADASHI's *The Trojan Women* (*Toroia no onna*, 1974), PIERROT in Takechi Tetsuji's fusion production *Moonstruck Pierrot* (*Tsuki ni tsukareta Piero*, 1955), leading roles in four productions of Yokomichi Mario's adaptation of YEATS's *At the Hawk's Well* (1967–71), and Oedipus in a 1971 production of the Dark Group (Mei no Kai) of which he was co-founder, with KYŌGEN actors Nomura Mannojō and Nomura Mansaku.　JRB

Kapnist, Vasily (Vasilievich) 1757–1823 Ukrainian dramatist and lyric poet whose satirical play *Chicanery* (1793) was the only 18th-century Russian COMEDY to approach FONVIZIN's work in skill and ferocity. Its tone is suggestive of GRIBOEDOV's later *Woe from Wit* and its subject, judicial corruption in a provincial town, foreshadows GOGOL's *The Inspector General*. Although the author's preface stresses the pastness of these abuses, Kapnist's play was refused permission for production and publica-

tion until after the death of Catherine the Great (1798), when it was performed for a brief time before being removed from the repertoire. It was revived in 1808 and again in 1812. Kapnist also translated MOLIÈRE's *Sganarelle* (1780, revised 1806), reflecting the penchant of Russia's most talented dramatists for the works of their French counterpart.　SG

Kara Jūrō 1940– Japanese playwright, director, actor and novelist. A graduate of Meiji University, Kara founded the Situation Theatre (Jōkyō Gekijō) in 1963. Influenced by J.-P. SARTRE's idea of a 'theatre of situations', Kara's work is characterized by the conviction that reality is nothing more than a social construction that can be altered by art. Ambivalent about the West, Kara and his troupe performed in Korea, Bangladesh and Lebanon in the early 1970s, but he found in the Middle East a reality that he could not easily countervail, and he subsequently devoted himself to less political themes and endeavours closer to home. In 1983 he won the Akutagawa Prize for a novel about a Japanese student in Paris who murders and cannibalizes his French girlfriend. Plays like *The Virgin's Mask* (*Shōjo kamen*, 1969; trans. 1992) and *John Silver: The Beggar of Love* (*Jon Shirubaa: ai no kojiki*, 1972; trans. 1988) are representative.　DGG

Karagöz [Karaghioz, Karagheuz, Kara-Goze] (Turkish,

meaning Dark Eyes) The comic character in Oriental SHADow plays of Turkish origin, said to have been invented by a Sheikh Kishteri. An entertainer named Karagöz may have lived in the 13th century, but from the mid-17th century the characterization was heavily influenced by Persian and Chinese PUPPET plays. Karagöz is the quick-witted, impudent young roisterer, endowed with a huge phallus, who is constantly misconstruing Hacivat (Hadj'Iwâz), the older, more pretentious show-off, and his wife Lachampiyya, in a series of bawdy, scatological dialogues. Secondary characters, usually racial stereotypes, were added later. The Karagöz plays were first performed only at nightfall during Ramadan in coffee-houses. They greatly influenced puppet drama throughout the Islamic world: in North Africa he pops up as Karagush or Karogheuz, a kind of priapic picaroon with a flexible leather member. The Greek version, Karaghiózis, emerged from the 1821 revolution as an exemplary spokesman for freedom and morality, who travelled the countryside accompanied by musicians. LS

Karamu House (Cleveland, Ohio) A private metropolitan centre for the arts, founded in 1915 by Oberlin College graduates Rowena and Russell Jelliffe. The original centre burned down in 1939, but a new and expanded facility opened 10 years later, after the Second World War. The adult theatre group, launched in 1921, was initially called the Gilpin Players, after actor CHARLES GILPIN. It was from the start multiracial, but a demographic change has given it a core constituency of inner-city blacks. The centre contains a proscenium and an arena theatre, both non-profit (see RESIDENT NON-PROFIT PROFESSIONAL THEATRE), in which some 11 productions are mounted each season, including MUSICALS and, in the past, OPERAS. Karamu enjoyed a special relationship with playwright LANGSTON HUGHES and premiered six of his plays. In 1981 an attempt was made to establish a black Equity unit, but traditional operating procedures thwarted the move and Equity personnel returned to New York. Karamu (Swahili for 'a place of enjoyment for all') considers its theatre to be the oldest continually active AFRICAN-AMERICAN THEATRE in America. EGH

Karanth, B. V. 1928– One of South INDIA's most important contemporary directors. B. V. Karanth began his career producing experimental works in Bangalore, where he attended college. He attended the National School of Drama and eventually became its director. Apart from many controversial stage productions he has also directed experimental films. He has headed Bhopal's Bharat Bhavan theatre school, where he forged numerous successful MUSICAL productions. Currently he heads the Karnataka Repertory in Mysore. FaR

Karatygin, Vasily (Andreevich) 1802–53 Famous Russian tragedian, born of an acting family, considered along with I. I. SOSNITSKY to be one of the best St Petersburg performers of his time. He was a former student of PRINCE SHAKHOVSKOI, with whose instruction he became disaffected, and later of Katenin, who compared his acting to TALMA's. He took a premeditated and declamatory approach to acting which created a coldly technical and

unsurprising, if often heroic, impression. In this he was abetted by a good education, native intelligence, a handsome figure and basso voice. These virtues proved more than sufficient for the neo-classical, MELODRAMATIC and historical-patriotic roles he was mostly called upon to play in the works of OZEROV, KUKOLNIK and POLEVOI. Although he was a court favourite, experts and literati such as SHCHEPKIN, PUSHKIN and Belinsky preferred the more impassioned, albeit inconsistent, performances of his Moscow counterpart, MOCHALOV. Karatygin was the original Chatsky in GRIBOEDOV's Woe from Wit (1831), Don Juan and the Baron in Pushkin's 'little tragedies', The Stone Guest (1847) and The Covetous Knight (1852), respectively; and Arbenin in LERMONTOV's Masquerade (1852). His wife, A. M. Kolosova, was a noted actress. SG

kariyala [kariala] Rural theatre form of Hindu villages in Himachal Pradesh state in northern INDIA.

The performance space or arena (akhara) is located between hillocks, permitting spectators to see the action easily. Musicians sit at one side of the playing area and the actors make a slow procession through the spectators from the dressing room to the playing area. As is typical in many rural settings, the men sit together on mats (durries) on one side and women huddle on the other. Children crowd close to the playing area to get a good view of the action and are carried home or join their parents in the early hours of the morning, when the all-night performance is over. Costumes are usually contemporary local dress to which brightly coloured headdresses and cloth pieces are added. Like bhand jashna, kariyala can be performed during the day as well as at night.

Performances begin when a clown and a female character dance and pantomime as the chorus sings songs of praise to the deities. Plays are loosely structured, simple stories built around character types and their acts (swang). SATIRE and the reinforcement of well known moral lessons characterize kariyala. Stories about money-lenders, village policemen, shepherds, religious medicants (sadhu) and old men who marry young wives are popular fare. FaR

Kartún Mauricio 1946– Argentine playwright with some notable successes in recent years. After Gente muy así (People Like That, 1976), El hambre da para todo (Hunger for Everything, 1978) and Chau Misterix (1980), he wrote Pericones (Dances, 1987), which presents a political intertext from the 19th century. El partener (The Partner, 1989) depends upon the tragicomic Argentine tradition of the sainete criollo (Creole FARCE) (see GÉNERO CHICO) to consider the loss of family values in contemporary society. GW

Kasoma, Kabwe fl.1970s Zambian playwright, whose published work includes The Black Mamba trilogy of plays on Kenneth Kaunda and the struggle for independence (1975). Kasoma is director of the University of ZAMBIA dance troupe and of the Centre for the Arts. RK

Kasper [Kasperl, Kasperle] Clown in the old Viennese folk comedy, who became the PUNCH of the Austro-German PUPPET play. He was originally created by stout

Johann Laroche (1745–1806), leading player at the Leopoldstadt Theatre, Vienna, from 1781; for 40 years, audiences rejoiced to hear his beery voice call, 'Auwedl' ('Deary me') from the wings. When Metternich forbade the good-natured dunce to speak, he cultivated his pantomime, giving rise to the Viennese expression, 'To laugh as if you were watching Kasperl'. The name was adopted by a hand-puppet, descending from the Meister Hämmerlein of the 16th century, who wielded a wooden bat; his partners were Gretel, Grandmother, Policeman, Death, the Devil and the Crocodile. In Munich Count Franz von Pocci (1807–76) and the puppeteer Josef Leonhard Schmid (1821–1912) tried to refine the dialect-speaking figure into the more literary Kasper Larifari, and early-20th-century educators used Kasperl as a spokesman for programmes of enlightenment. In the late 1920s, Max Jacob (1888–1967) developed a sardonic Kasperl, a displaced person given to officious preachments. The most popular puppet in the German-speaking world, Kasper has become a standard term for any puppet. LS

Kataev, Valentin (Petrovich) 1897–1986 Respected Soviet prose writer and dramatist, who survived Stalinism and is best known for his upbeat romantic social COMEDY of the New Economic Policy period, *Squaring the Circle* (1928), a tale of mismatched newly wed couples – one staunchly communist, the other quasi-bourgeois – thrown together in a Soviet housing shortage, who eventually swap mates. It premiered at the MOSCOW ART THEATRE under NEMIROVICH-DANCHENKO's direction and played successfully in New York and London. Most of his plays are comedies, *vaudevilles* and adaptations of his own novels, and are characterized by a generosity of spirit combined with acute SATIRE. *The Embezzlers* (1928), from his best-known novel, is an NEP adventure story with satirical overtones. *The Vanguard* (1930) is one of the first plays about collectivization. *A Lonely White Sail* (1937), describing the picaresque adventures of two young boys during the 1905 Revolution, was adapted from his novel (1936) for stage and screen. Along with the war-time dramas *The Soldier at the Front* (1937), *The Blue Scarf* (1943) and *Son of the Regiment* (1945), it reflects the author's sensitivity to young adults, children and sentimental themes. The drama *Time Forward!* (1932), a socialist-realist First Five-Year Plan drama inspired by MAYAKOVSKY's poem 'March of the Shock-Brigades', optimistically posits its theme of social progress through industrialization. Among his many produced comedies and *vaudevilles* are *The Road of Flowers* (1934), *Day of Rest* (1946) and *The Case of a Genius* (1955). Kataev was one of the few Soviet writers who successfully and acceptably coaxed comedy and even FARCE from sobering reality. SG

kathakali Major dance drama of Kerala state, south INDIA. It has gained a considerable international reputation in recent years for its vigorous masculine style of physical movement, bold superhuman characterizations and vivid emotionalism. Dance, music and acting blend in dramatizations of stories adapted from the *Ramayana* and *Mahabharata* epics and the *Purana*.

Kathakali emerged in the 17th century, borrowing heavily from various theatre and dance forms of a region rich in cultural traditions. RITUAL elements and emphasis on elaborate facial and eye expressions and hand gestures were perhaps adapted from earlier KUTIYATTAM. Its devotional character, style of dance, movement and music may have been borrowed from KRISHNATTAM. *Kathakali*'s direct predecessor was *ramanattam*, a form of theatre in which plays were composed from events adapted from the *Ramayana*. It is a popular belief that *ramanattam* was created because the Maharaja of Kottayam was jealous of the popularity of *krishnattam* and developed his own form of theatre as a form of self-aggrandizement.

When it became apparent that the fledgeling form of theatre needed a broader base for stories than the *Ramayana* provided, enthusiastic playwrights and patrons came forward to create dramas which included a wide range of popular epic material. *Ramanattam* then became known as *kathakali*, which literally means 'story play'. *Kathakali*'s patrons included rulers and rich landowners. The actors were Nairs, a caste trained in martial-art techniques which were long used in Kerala to develop soldiers to engage in ritual battle. Today actors hail from many different castes and communities, although prominent *kathakali* actors are Nairs.

Actor training is a long and arduous process, often taking from six to ten years to complete. As in many of the world's great art forms, it takes a lifetime to achieve greatness. Training usually begins between the ages of 10 and 14. Traditionally the sons of actors were trained in the art by their fathers, near relatives or trusted teachers.

Today the selection of potential candidates is a difficult task because so much time and energy is invested in the student once he is selected to participate in a programme, that the teachers must have a keen eye for spotting potential talent in the very young. Once selected, the student undergoes extensive body training to develop flexibility and the stamina needed to endure long hours of performance. Stress is placed on eye and facial exercises, and on mastery of an elaborate code of about 600 hand gestures.

The training day begins before dawn and extends until just before midnight. During a typical day, dance sequences suited to specific plays are taught. The rhythm and tempo of the action must be drilled into the physical being. And choreographic sections, including gestures, facial expressions and foot work, are committed to memory. Play texts (*attakatha*) are also learned by heart.

Actors do not speak, so the ideas of a play are conveyed through the lyrics of the song, sung by two singers, and by the actor's hand gestures, facial expressions, and body movements. Therefore precision and size of visual expression are crucial. The lead singer (*ponnani*) holds a heavy brass gong, striking it with a curved stick made of banana root. The second singer plays large bell-brass cymbals. The singers interweave their voices throughout the performance moving systematically through individual verses and dialogue portions of the text in a style of singing known as *sopana*. Three chief drums accompany the dramatic action. The large horizontal drum (*maddalam*) is carried across the waist of the drummer. It provides flexibility of pace and intonation. The vertical drum (*centa*) is used for battle scenes and scenes which require special sound effects and high drama. The small hourglass drum (*itekka*) has a delicate sound and is especially effective when female characters take stage. A harmonium keeps the singers on pitch and the conch shell (*sanka*) is used when gods or important ritual events are at hand. A close bond must be established between the musicians and the actors in order to create a unified dramatic effect.

Performance begins around nine or ten at night following an elaborate percussion overture and preliminaries danced by young apprentices. These take about two to three hours to complete.

Any spot is considered appropriate for a *kathakali* performance – temple compound, family home, large hall or proscenium-arch stage. Although a performance seems designed to be played on a rectangular space, 20 to 30ft square and demarcated by four poles, audiences prefer to gather at the front, near the brass lamp, opposite the musicians. No matter how audiences organize themselves, actors still play to the front.

The atmosphere at *kathakali* is charged with excitement, with children and women relegated to the front and to one side of the house and men arranged on the other.

Troupes of actors, musicians and backstage technicians and costumers, who are commissioned to perform, are able to choose a play at short notice from a limited repertory. The exact play may not be decided until a few hours before the performance begins, just in time for the actors to get into appropriate costumes and make-up.

A programme may include several favourite scenes from various *kathakali* plays or a single play performed from beginning to end. In village performances, shows conclude around 6 a.m. A band of enthusiastic devotees, awake to the very end, trudges wearily home with the sound of drums still ringing in their ears. FAR

Katona, József 1791–1830 Hungarian playwright. Born in Kecskemét, he became attracted to the theatre while studying law in Pest. He wrote *Bánk Bán* (*The Viceroy*) in 1815 for a competition held by the theatre in Kolozsvár, which never acknowledged the play. Discouraged, Katona had it published in 1821, and wrote no more for the stage. He died without realizing that *Bánk Bán* would eventually be considered the greatest Hungarian play of the century. Set in 13th-century HUNGARY, this TRAGEDY details the psychological undoing of Bánk, an honourable palatine, who is placed in a situation where his loyalties to his country, his king and his wife become irreconcilable. The 1845 production of *Bánk Bán* at the National Theatre made clear not only its dramatic merits, but also its political implications: the play treats the issue of foreign exploitation of the nation. EB

Katumba, Jimmy fl.1970s–80s UGANDAN musician and entrepreneur. In the late 1970s Katumba formed a musical ensemble which became very popular – the Ebonies. The group developed a large business enterprise, owning sound studios which produce Jimmy Katumba records. In 1988, extending their activities to drama, they formed the Ebonies, a group of actors who perform at the Theatre Excelsior, a converted school hall in Kampala. John W. Katunde's *The Dollar* (1988) and *The Inspector* (1990) are detective plays which are developed in performance by improvisation. *The Dollar* attacks materialism and corruption through a search for a murdered woman. In *The Inspector*, the main object of attack is hospital mismanagement and the medical profession. Both plays use the music for which this group is well known. Katumba now lives in the USA, and the group has become less active. MMAC

Kaufman, George S(imon) 1889–1961 American playwright and director. A founding father of the American popular theatre, Kaufman enjoyed a long and extraordinarily productive BROADWAY career. On his own he wrote only one full-length play, a SATIRE of the theatre called *The Butter and Egg Man* (1925); in collaboration he wrote 40 plays, more than half of them certified hits. His partners included MARC CONNELLY (*Dulcy* (1921), *Beggar on Horseback* (1924)); EDNA FERBER (*The Royal Family* (1927), *Dinner at Eight* (1932), *Stage Door* (1936)); Morrie Ryskind (*The Cocoanuts* (1925), *Animal Crackers* (1928) – two MARX BROS vehicles – and *Of Thee I Sing* (1931, Pulitzer Prize)); and MOSS HART (*Once in a Lifetime* (1930), *You Can't Take It with You* (1936, Pulitzer Prize), *The Man Who Came to Dinner* (1939)). While his partners were stronger on plot contrivance, Kaufman's speciality was dialogue, which he enlivened with witty, sarcastic rejoinders: the fabled Kaufman wisecrack. He was a born satirist whose targets included not only his own beat, the New York theatre world, but also Hollywood, big business, politics and provincialism (although Kaufman himself was accused of being parochial in his subject-matter). His subjects were drawn from life, but his artificial, WELL MADE plots were manufactured for the theatre. His dry wit earned him a seat at the Algonquin Round Table, and his instinctive abhorrence of romance, sentiment and melodrama provided a counterbalance to his less cynical collaborators. Though his tone was captious and ironic, Kaufman was never so abrasive as to offend the large popular audience that his bread and butter depended on; at the finale he tempered his sting with forgiveness.

Kaufman began his directing career in 1928 with a jumpy, frenetic production of *The Front Page*. Like a terse Kaufman script, a Kaufman-directed show had remarkable precision. Swift timing was his trademark; he had no patience for analysis or introspection, and when a solemn actor once made the mistake of asking about motivation, Kaufman snapped: 'Your job'. FH

Kawadwa, Byron c.1940–77 Ugandan playwright, producer and director. Kawadwa was educated at Aggrey Memorial School, Kampala, and founded the UGANDA Schools Drama Festival while still a student. On leaving school he worked at Radio Uganda but was arrested and imprisoned after the 1964 disturbances. On his release he worked with KIYINGI-KAGWE and his group. By 1965 the Kampala City Players had been formed with Kawadwa as writer and director and members drawn largely from young men and women in the Kampala business, commercial and government world. He was admitted to the Makerere University drama course in 1968. He was appointed artistic director of the Uganda National Theatre in 1973 and held a concurrent Creative Writing Fellowship at Makerere for one year. A staunch royalist, he used palace themes in his two most important works, written in collaboration with musician Wassanyi Serukenya.

Makula ga Kulabako (1970) tells the love story of Kulabako, a princess, and a commoner. It was immediately popular and has been made into a film. *Oluimba lwa Wankoko* (*The Song of Mr Cock*, 1971) tells of the attempt to oust the rightful heir to the throne by an ambitious politician. A covert SATIRE on the political situation in Buganda after the ousting of the Kabaka in 1966, it was later Uganda's entry to FESTAC in Lagos and is said to have been the cause of Kawadwa's murder. In both plays the music matches the words and the theme is both original and Ugandan. MMAC

Kawatake Mokuami 1816–93 The last great traditional Japanese KABUKI playwright, his work spanned the end of the feudal order and the early years of modern Japan. He apprenticed as a beginning playwright (*minarai sakusha*) at 20 and at 28 became staff playwright of the Kawarazaki Theatre in Edo. He wrote gangster plays (*kizewamono*) of grotesque humour for actor Ichikawa Kodanji IV (1812–66). Invited to the Ichimura Theatre and then the Nakamura Theatre, he developed the genre through mordant portrayals of thieves (*shiranamimono*) – *Three Thieves Named Kichisa* (*Sannin Kichisa kuruwa no hatsugai*, 1860) and *Benten the Thief* (*Aotozōshi hana no nishikie*, 1862; trans. 1976) – for Onoe KikugorōV. He wrote original 'puppet' scenes, using BUNRAKU-style music. He was the first writer to adapt Western literature to the *kabuki* stage in the 1870s. His impressive skill at composing dance plays, such as *The Ground Spider* (*Tsuchigumo*, 1881) which was witnessed by Emperor Meiji, helped socially elevate *kabuki*. In 120 history, domestic, modern and dance plays, he demonstrated an unrivalled ability to utilize acting technique, music, dance, costuming and staging for dramatic purposes. JRB

Kazan, Elia 1909– American director and actor, GROUP THEATRE member, and co-founder of the ACTORS STUDIO. Kazan was long considered America's leading director of actors for both stage and film. His stage productions of *A Streetcar Named Desire* (1947), *Death of a Salesman* (1949), *Cat on a Hot Tin Roof* (1955) and *Sweet Bird of Youth* (1959), and his films *Streetcar* (1951), *On the Waterfront* (1954) and *East of Eden* (1955) have earned him the reputation of pre-eminent Method director whose overheated, naturalistic style is synonymous with the work of the Actors Studio. A Kazan-directed performance is excitingly highly strung, notable for its depth and intensity of feeling, its verbal stammers and backtracking, its emotional ambivalences and its sexual vibrancy. Kazan's method, influenced by the ideas of STANISLAVSKY and LEE STRASBERG, depends on personal contact with his actors. A shrewd judge of character, he takes actors off to the side, his arm draped casually over their shoulders, to whisper some private confidence or observation. Although he has rarely directed, in films or theatre, since he resigned in 1964 as co-director of the VIVIAN BEAUMONT THEATRE, he remains a revered figure among New York actors. His controversial autobiography was published in 1988. FH

Kazantzákis, Nikos 1884–1957 Greek playwright and novelist. Better known for his novels and the long epic *Odyssey* (a sequel to Homer; see GREECE, ANCIENT), Kazantzákis was also a prolific author of plays, some of them in verse and most of them on subjects derived from Greek myth and history. *It Is Dawning* (1906) was praised at a drama contest but was refused the prize because of its passionate, anti-conformist character. The one-act tragedy *Comedy* (1908) has been likened to SARTRE's *Huis Clos* and BECKETT's *Waiting for Godot*. *The Master Builder* (1910) and all subsequent dramas show a NIETZSCHEan influence, with the Buddhist credo as a counterpoint: *Christ* (1921), *Odysseus* (1922), *Nikiphóros Phokás* (1927), *Mélissa* (1937), *Julian the Apostate* (1939), *Prometheus* (1943), *Capodistria* (1944), *Sodom and Gomorrha* (1948), *Koúros* (1949), *Christopher Columbus* (1949), *Constantine Paleológhos* (1951) and *Buddha* (1922–56). Disappointed by the reaction of critics and of the public, Kazantzákis wrote dramas with little attention to the practicalities of the stage, stressing the poetic and philosophic elements in them, tackling important existential issues. Several of his dramas were staged in Greece and other countries after his death. GT

Keach, Stacy 1941– American stage, film and television actor, who gained critical attention in the title role of *MacBird!* OFF-BROADWAY in 1967, as BUFFALO BILL CODY in KOPIT's *Indians* at the ARENA STAGE and on BROADWAY in 1969, and as Jamie in *Long Day's Journey into Night* (Off-Broadway 1971 revival). He has thrice played Hamlet, most recently at Los Angeles's Mark Taper Forum (1974). In 1990 he appeared as the title character in MICHAEL KAHN's production of *Richard III* at the Shakespeare Theatre in Washington, DC; Broadway appearances in *Solitary Confinement* (1992) and *Kentucky Cycle* (1993), both short-lived productions, followed. DBW

Kean, Charles 1811–68 British actor and theatre manager, the son of EDMUND KEAN, beside whom Charles looks even more of a prig than he actually was. He had been sent to Eton, and the lingering effect was to make him a gentlemanly actor and a pedagogic manager. He made his debut at DRURY LANE in 1827, playing young Norval in HOME's *Douglas* to mixed notices, and it was his name as much as his acting prowess that sustained him in leading roles in Britain and on American tours in 1830, 1840 and 1845–7 before his significant move into management at the PRINCESS's THEATRE in 1850. With a judicious mixture of SHAKESPEARE, BYRON and BOUCICAULT, Kean made the Princess's a centre of fashion. The admiration of Queen Victoria, who appointed him director of her private theatricals at Windsor in 1848, was a particular feather in his cap.

Kean's productions of classical plays were researched with a meticulous eye for historical accuracy. For *Macbeth* (1852) he sought advice on pre-Norman building from the architectural historian, George Godwin. For the revival of Byron's *Sardanapalus* (1852) he instructed his scene-painters to consult Layard's recent account of his excavations, *Nineveh and its Remains* (1849). Each production was accompanied by a nearly book-length documentation of historical sources, a labour of love for which Kean was rewarded by election as a Fellow of the Society of Antiquaries in 1857. He was concerned also to light his sets appropriately and was the first person to deploy focused

Charles Kean as Leontes with Ellen Terry as Mamillius in *The Winter's Tale*, 1856.

limelight effectively. The stubborn fact remains that he was a rather wooden actor. It is for the care he lavished on the look of his stage that Kean deserves to be remembered. Together with his wife, the actress Ellen Tree (1806–80), he exercised the Victorian virtue of thrift, and so could retire with a secure fortune in 1859. PT

Kean, Edmund 1789–1833 English actor who embodied the spirit of the romantic movement at its most turbulent. He was the illegitimate son of a minor actress who exploited his precocious talent. Probably resentful of the role of 'infant prodigy', Kean broke away from his mother in c.1804 and spent ten years as a struggling provincial actor, during which time he married and had two sons, the elder of whom died in infancy. Small, wiry and swarthy as a gypsy (which he was sometimes believed to be), Kean was also a skilful acrobat and mime, capable of playing the dumb HARLEQUIN as well as speaking roles in the STOCK companies of Irish and English towns and cities. He had already gathered a reputation for riotous living when he was culled from Exeter to London by ROBERT ELLISTON. Confusion over contracts, together with some sharp practice, led to his making his debut at DRURY LANE instead of at Elliston's OLYMPIC.

Drury Lane was at a point of crisis, and it was the miracle of Kean's triumph that saved its shareholders. He opened as Shylock, defying tradition by wearing a black beard in place of the established red and playing the Jew as a monster of energetic evil. The date was 26 January 1814 and it marked a turning point in the fortunes of Drury Lane as well as of Kean. Before the end of that first season, he added to Shylock his finest role, Richard III, as well as Hamlet, Othello, Iago and Luke Frugal in MASSINGER's *The City Madam*. It was already evident that demonic passions would be his forte. It was in the frenzy of Othello, as it would be in the final throes of Sir Giles Overreach in Massinger's *A New Way to Pay Old Debts* (1816), that he found his focus. Coleridge's famous observation that 'To see him act is like reading SHAKESPEARE by flashes of lightning' contains an important pointer to Kean's method. It was not on the sustained character study of a JOHN PHILIP KEMBLE that he relied, but on the making of startlingly indicative 'points'. His admired transitions, those sudden shifts from 'high' to 'low', were inspirational in the days of his greatness and became mechanical only in the long years of his decline.

That decline began all too soon. After the years of struggle, Kean succumbed quickly to the headiness of adulation. HAZLITT perceived a loss of concentration as early as his second season at Drury Lane (1814–15), when he added a controversial Macbeth and an often inert Romeo to his Shakespearian roles as well as restoring the neglected *Richard II* to the stage. Timon (1816), King John (1818), Coriolanus (1819), Lear (1820), Cardinal Wolsey (1822), Posthumus in *Cymbeline* (1823) – IRVING would later have the wisdom to prefer Iachimo – and a dismal fiasco as Henry V (1830) complete the catalogue of Kean's Drury Lane Shakespeare, but there was as much drama behind the scenes as on the stage. Frequently stupefied by drink, often in the company of Elliston with whom he had become dangerously reconciled, Kean lost all sexual restraint. Matters came to a head in 1824, when his affair with Charlotte Cox, wife of a member of the Drury Lane committee, was discovered. Kean was taken to court in January 1825 and booed throughout the playing of *Richard III* on 24 January. Bowing to public opinion, he paid a second visit to the USA (the first was in 1820), and, although accepted on his return, he was only intermittently fit to perform. He made his last appearance in March 1833, as Othello to the Iago of his son, CHARLES KEAN, but collapsed on stage and died a few weeks later. The supreme example of the charismatic actor, he had burned himself out by 1821, but there can be no doubt that for seven years he gave a lovely light. PT

Keane, John (Brendan) 1928– Irish playwright. For years Keane's many plays were known only through local amateur and semi-professional productions. Mostly in contemporary rural settings, they revive traditional themes of land hunger, made marriages and emigration, employing characters who often border on the grotesque. Most notable are *Sive* (1959), *The Year of the Hiker* (1963), *The Field* (1966) and *Big Maggie* (1970). In the 1970s Keane turned to humorous writing, novels and journalism, but his plays' enduring popularity finally led to critical re-evaluation, and the ABBEY – which originally rejected all but the uncharacteristically urban, English-set *Hut 42* (1962) – belatedly staged major revivals. *The Field*, in which land hunger and profiteering wound each other mortally, became a very successful film. Keane's plays are now understood not just as the last flourishing of the peasant play tradition, but as telling works about cultural change, occasionally reaching out towards myth. DM GF

Keeley [*née* Goward], **Mary Ann** 1806–99 British actress, extremely popular in FARCE and low COMEDY. She made her debut as a singer in 1825, but her fame was based on her playing of below-stairs characters. She was the ideal pert maid in MELODRAMA as well as farce, not least because of her ability to transform herself from soubrette to waif when the occasion arose. Two of her most successful parts required MALE IMPERSONATION. They were the title roles in BUCKSTONE's *Jack Sheppard* (1839) and Edward Stirling's *The Fortunes of Smike* (1840). She married Robert Keeley (1793–1869) in 1829, and from then on they always acted together. He was a chubby, round-faced comedian, who specialized in FEMALE IMPERSONATION – a famous Sarah Gamp in Stirling's *Martin Chuzzlewit* (1844) and the first actor to carry DOUGLAS JERROLD's Mrs Caudle (1844) from *Punch* on to the stage. The Keeleys retired in 1859, though

they continued to make occasional appearances thereafter. Managers considered them the safest 'draw' in the London theatre. PT

Keene, Laura [*née* Mary Frances Moss] ?1826–1873 British-born actress and manager. While facts about her origins, training and name are disputed, Laura Keene apparently made her London debut in 1851, a year before J. W. WALLACK hired her as leading lady for his company in New York. Her grace and charm as well as her comic ability endeared her to New York audiences in her favourite roles of Lady Teazle, Lady Gay Spanker and Beatrice in *Much Ado*. After a year with Wallack's company, she spent the next two seasons in Baltimore and San Francisco before touring Australia with young EDWIN BOOTH. In 1855 she returned to New York and opened her own Laura Keene Varieties Theatre. During 1856–63 she managed and acted in her Laura Keene's New Theatre, which became known for its lavishly mounted comedies. She encouraged the production of new American plays and closely supervised an excellent company that included E. A. SOTHERN, JOSEPH JEFFERSON III, Kate Reignolds, BILLY FLORENCE, Agnes Robertson, John T. Raymond and Charles W. Couldock. She returned to touring in 1863, and was performing in *Our American Cousin* at Ford's Theatre in Washington, DC, when President Lincoln was assassinated. During her career, she became closely identified with the emotional drama (e.g. *Camille*). TLM

Keith, B(enjamin) F(ranklin) 1846–1914 American VAUDEVILLE entrepreneur and theatre proprietor who, with EDWARD F. ALBEE, created the most extensive vaudeville theatre chain in the USA. New Hampshire-born Keith grew up on a farm, worked as a mess boy on a coastal freighter, and spent the 1870s working and travelling with CIRCUSES, where he most likely first met Albee. In 1880 he made and sold brooms in Providence, Rhode Island, but by 1883 had moved into the dime museum business with the rental of a vacant store in Boston. After Albee joined him in 1885 and continuous performances had been initiated, he became part-owner of the Gaiety Musée; in 1886 he added the adjoining Bijou Theatre. Keith is often credited with the first use of the word 'vaudeville' in order to circumvent the stigma attached to 'VARIETY' and the earlier concert saloon's sleazy reputation. With the formula of continuous, completely respectable vaudeville, the Keith–Albee circuit (nicknamed 'the Sunday School Circuit') grew quickly, aided by the construction or acquisition of vaudeville theatres in many cities, including Boston's Colonial Theatre (1894), New York's PALACE THEATRE (built by Martin Beck in 1913 but virtually controlled by Keith–Albee) and the Orpheum (built in 1899 by Percy Williams but bought by Keith in 1912). Despised by many vaudevillians, Keith–Albee sought to monopolize first-class vaudeville through the Vaudeville Managers' Protective Association (1900) and the United Booking Office (1906), headed by Keith and his major competitor, F. F. PROCTOR. After Keith's death, Albee ultimately gained control of the operation. DBW

Kellar, Harry [Heinrich Keller] 1849–1922 American MAGICIAN, who acted as assistant to the Fakir of Ava (I.

Harris Hughes) and the DAVENPORT BROTHERS before striking out on his own. Kellar tended to appropriate and refashion tricks conceived by others. A master of publicity, he won fame with BUATIER DE KOLTA's 'Vanishing Birdcage'; from MASKELYNE he derived the disappearing act 'The Witch, the Sailor and the Monkey' and his supreme illusion 'The Levitation of the Princess Karnac' (1904). After touring the world in 1880, he resettled in the USA, where he set a record of 323 consecutive performances at Philadelphia's Egyptian Hall (1884) and 179 at the Comedy Theatre, New York (1886–7). He retired on a well invested fortune in 1908, naming HOWARD THURSTON as his successor. His memoirs were published in 1886.   LS

Kelly, Fanny [Frances] **(Maria)** 1790–1882 Anglo-Irish actress and singer, niece of the musician and singing star, Michael Kelly (1762–1826). It was possibly he who took her into the DRURY LANE chorus for the production of GEORGE COLMAN THE YOUNGER's *Blue Beard* (1798), for which he was composer and musical director, and it was at Drury Lane that her adult career later took shape. She was a regular member of the company from 1810 to 33, playing leads in the ephemeral musical pieces that were a required part of the long evenings' entertainment.

Fanny Kelly owes her immortality to CHARLES LAMB rather than to her own skills. He adored her 'divine plain face', wrote a famous essay about her under the deceiving title 'Barbara SM', and proposed marriage to her in 1819. Her delicate refusal of the proposal is evidence of an interesting independence. Kelly was unprepared to dwindle into a wife. The madman who took a shot at her during a performance of O'KEEFFE's *Modern Antiques* in 1816 was another rejected suitor, and she further asserted the rights of women by promoting the all-female *Belles without Beaux* (1819), an anonymous piece which she may have helped to write. In 1833, she established a Theatre and Dramatic School at the Strand Theatre, boosting the income derived from pupils by performing a one-woman show of *Dramatic Recollections*, and transferring it in 1840 to a 200-seat theatre, built at the back of her house in Soho. She took her teaching seriously, and was proud of such famous pupils as BOUCICAULT and MRS KEELEY, but the venture had nearly bankrupted her by 1849, and she spent her last years in modest retirement in what was then the village of Feltham.   PT

Kelly, George E. 1887–1974 American playwright. One of the famed Philadelphia Kellys and uncle of Princess Grace, Kelly had three major BROADWAY successes in the 1920s: *The Torchbearers* (1922), a satire of Little Theatre (see COMMUNITY THEATRE/LITTLE THEATRE MOVEMENT) enthusiasts; *The Show Off* (1924), a COMEDY of provincial manners about the battle between a commonsensical mother and braggart son-in-law; and *Craig's Wife* (1925, Pulitzer Prize), an exposure of an American ice maiden whose immaculate home is more important to her than her husband. Although he was a practical man of the theatre – he began his career in 1912 as an actor on the VAUDEVILLE circuit – Kelly did not want to be labelled as a popular entertainer, and he insisted on directing each of his plays to preserve their distinctive rhythms. In later work such as *The Deep Mrs Sykes* (1945) and *The Fatal Weakness* (1946),

he deliberately muted comic elements. Kelly thought of himself as a moralist whose SATIRES were designed to instruct and improve as well as to amuse. His work gains its idiosyncratic stamp from the targets he chose: bossy, smug suburban matrons, untalented would-be actors and playwrights, and freeloaders. Although he worked within a conventional range of modest domestic settings, seemingly dictaphonic dialogue, and characters and situations drawn from middle-class American life, his writing achieves a unique voice: tart, scolding, droll and delightfully eccentric.   FH

Kelly, Hugh 1739–77 Irish playwright. He moved to London in 1760 and began writing, including essays on theatre for the *Babbler* and a SATIRE on actors, *Thespis* (1766). *False Delicacy* (1768) was produced to capitalize on the success of GOLDSMITH's *The Good Natured Man* at COVENT GARDEN and proved more immediately popular than its rival. *A Word to the Wise* (1769) closed after riots against Kelly for being a government apologist. Though he was often damned as a writer of sentimental comedy, Kelly's plays, particularly *The School for Wives* (1773), mock the absurd excesses of sentimentalism while appealing to feeling in pursuit of a moral argument.   PH

Kemble, Charles 1775–1854 English actor, the youngest brother of SARAH SIDDONS and JOHN PHILIP KEMBLE, who were playing the leads in *Macbeth* when he made his London debut as Malcolm in 1794. His finest Shakespearian roles were Mercutio and Faulconbridge in *King John*, though, unlike his better known siblings, he was effective also in COMEDY as Benedick, Orlando and Charles Surface in *The School for Scandal*. Intelligent, like most of the Kembles, Charles was a student of acting, but one who rarely excited audiences when he put his studies into practice. His reign as manager of COVENT GARDEN (1822–32) was uneasy. From the start, he was outmanoeuvred by ELLISTON at DRURY LANE, losing his best actors to the higher salaries of the rival house. The production of *King John* in 1823, with its pioneering devotion to historically accurate costumes (the research was done by J. R. PLANCHÉ), was an isolated triumph until the record-breaking production of Weber's *Der Freischütz* (1824).

By 1829 the position was critical and Kemble, reluctantly, cajoled his daughter into a profession from which he had hoped to spare her. FANNY KEMBLE's appearance as Juliet (1829) began a slow recovery, completed by a highly profitable tour of Philadelphia and New York (1832–3). Father and daughter played their favourite parts to more acclaim than they received in England. On his return home, Kemble was appointed Examiner of Plays (1836–40), a post which he resigned to his son. Despite increasing deafness, he played a final season at Covent Garden in 1842.   PT

Kemble, Fanny [Frances] **(Anne)** 1809–93 British actress, daughter of CHARLES KEMBLE. More ambitious to write than to act, she made her debut as Juliet in 1829 in a bid to rescue her father from financial disaster at COVENT GARDEN. Welcomed by a public that was curious to see the latest of the Kembles, she continued at Covent Garden until the end of the 1831–2 season, performing many of the parts from the repertoire of her aunt, SARAH SIDDONS, in addition to Portia, Beatrice and Lady Teazle. She also acted in her own tragedy, *Francis I* (1832), which required the audience's indulgence as well as her father's, and created the part of Julia in SHERIDAN KNOWLES's popular success, *The Hunchback* (1832). The restoration of Charles Kemble's fortunes was completed by a tour of theatres in New York and Philadelphia (1832–3) in which he shared star-billing with Fanny. When the tour was over she remained in Philadelphia to marry Pierce Butler (1834). The marriage turned out to be a battle of wills, finally foundering on the issue of slavery. Fanny was a vehement abolitionist, her husband a slave-owner. She left him in 1845 (he divorced her in 1849) and, after a year of rest with her sister in Rome, she reluctantly returned to the English stage.

Grown stout and already looking middle-aged, she was reduced to touring the provinces in *The Hunchback* for most of 1847, and her Lady Macbeth to MACREADY's Macbeth in London (1848) was not a success. But she was never easily deterred. For 26 years (1848–74) she financed herself by public readings from SHAKESPEARE, which became famous on both sides of the Atlantic. In retirement, she wrote three volumes of autobiography (1878, 1882 and 1890) and a novel, *Far Away and Long Ago* (1889). PT

Kemble, John Philip 1757–1823 English actor-manager; the greatest English classical actor. Born in Lancashire, the son of Roger Kemble, a theatre manager, he travelled with his father's company acting as a child. Intended for the priesthood, he trained at Douai, leaving there in 1775 to become an actor. After some successes in Liverpool he wrote to TATE WILKINSON for work, listing 126 roles in his repertory. At this stage in his career he also wrote a number of poor plays. He slowly built a substantial reputation and his acting was marked by careful preparation, which involved studying other actors' work. He made his London debut at DRURY LANE in 1783 as Hamlet and was highly praised for his gentleness and aristocratic grace, though there were already signs of the stiff and artificial technique and idiosyncratic pronunciation that marked his later work.

His performance as Jaffier in OTWAY's *Venice Preserv'd* was too cold: his sister MRS SIDDONS complained that 'his sensibilities are not so acute as they ought to be for the part of a lover'. In 1786 he published *Macbeth Reconsidered*, an erudite literary study focusing on Macbeth's courage and defining his later approach to the role. In 1787 his performance as Lear was praised for its tremendous grandeur, while his Othello was too studied and insufficiently passionate. In 1788 he took over the management of Drury Lane, inaugurating a series of spectacular productions like *Henry VIII* and *Coriolanus*, with an original interest in antiquarian realism and a disciplined classicism. His noble acting style reached its peak with Roman roles such as Coriolanus. The limitations of his approach were glaringly apparent as Charles Surface in SHERIDAN's *The School for Scandal* which, played as a serious role, was 'as merry as a funeral and as lively as an elephant'. Drury Lane, declared unsafe in 1790, was demolished, and Kemble opened the new theatre with its

huge stage and vastly increased capacity in 1794. By the following year he was suffering severely from gout and asthma. In 1796, he left Drury Lane after wrangles with Sheridan and moved to COVENT GARDEN with a repertory of classical and Shakespearian revivals. He allowed the Master BETTY hysteria to take its course but was nearly bankrupted when Covent Garden was destroyed by fire in 1808 and was under-insured. The new theatre opened in 1809 but arguments about prices led to the Old Price Riots, which lasted 67 nights and left Kemble disillusioned.

Mrs Siddons retired in 1812 and Kemble was seen as old-fashioned when EDMUND KEAN made his triumphant debut in 1814. He retired from the stage in 1817 to Lausanne. He accumulated a massive library of plays and playbills. His own many adaptations of earlier plays were published as *British Theatre* in 1815. His acting style of cultivated classicism was the result of sustained intellectual effort rather than genius, creating a performance that both was and appeared studied and lacking in spontaneity. Part of the deliberateness was the result of the asthma. His rare successes in new roles were in romantic MELODRAMAS like Penruddock in CUMBERLAND's *The Wheel of Fortune* (1795). Often regarded as progenitor of the director, his productions had aesthetic unity as well as atmospheric scenery and massive processional tableaux.   PH

Kemp, Lindsay 1939– British mime artist, choreographer, actor and director, who studied with Ballet Rambert and, in Paris, with MARCEL MARCEAU. During the 1960s he formed his own company, but earned an income by staging outlandish 'happenings' and Soho strip shows. He staged the Ziggy Stardust gigs for David Bowie, a former company member, and in 1974 appeared in a MIME show with the Great Orlando as well as staging his mime ballet, *Flowers*, based on JEAN GENET's *Notre Dame des Fleurs* at London's BUSH. *Flowers*, which went to the WEST END and toured widely, established his stage presence as a slow-moving, vulnerable coquette, surrounded by athletic male dancers – an image exaggerated in his version of OSCAR WILDE's *Salomé* (1977). He staged two ballets for the Ballet Rambert, *The Parade's Gone By* (1975) and *Cruel Garden* (1977), based on the life of FEDERICO GARCÍA LORCA. Resenting his lack of official support in Britain, he moved his company to Italy and then to Spain; but he has returned to stage productions at SADLER's WELLS, including *Alice* (1989), *A Midsummer Night's Dream* (1989) and *Onnagata, the Song of Orpheus* (1991). Kemp can outrage his critics with his blend of campness and kitsch, but beneath his deliberate bad taste there lies a profound instinct for beauty.   JE

Kempe [Kemp], Will(iam) d. c.1603 English CLOWN, the popular successor to RICHARD TARLTON, whom he may have replaced in the company of LEICESTER's MEN as early as 1583. Kempe is known to have acted in France, the Netherlands and Denmark at around this time, and his popularity there suggests that his routines had a strong visual element. This is further confirmed by a speech in the anonymous *The Pilgrimage to Parnassus* (1597): 'Clowns have been thrust into plays by head and shoulders ever since Kempe could make a scurvy face ... Why, if thou canst but draw thy mouth awry, lay thy leg over thy staff, saw a piece of cheese asunder with a dagger, lap up drink on the earth, I warrant thee they'll laugh mightily.' The stage business which made Kempe's appearance in a post-play JIG so popular is easily inferred.

After a period with STRANGE'S MEN, Kempe was a sharer in the newly formed LORD CHAMBERLAIN'S MEN (1594–9). He played Peter in *Romeo and Juliet* (presumably on the promise of a chance for something better in the jig) and Dogberry in *Much Ado About Nothing*. It is a reasonable guess that he also featured as Lancelot Gobbo and Bottom in *The Merchant of Venice* and *A Midsummer Night's Dream*, though we have no evidence of that. It may be that SHAKESPEARE had Kempe in mind when he had Hamlet complain of clowns who speak 'more than is set down for them'. Whatever the reason, Kempe left the Chamberlain's Men either just before or just after they had moved from the THEATRE to the GLOBE in 1599, taking his gift as a self-publicist into his fantastic morris dance from London to Norwich. His pamphlet account of this trip, *Kempe's Nine Days Wonder* (1600), is almost the last we hear of him, though it is thought that he went on a short visit to the Continent before joining Worcester's Men in 1601. PT

Kempinski, Tom 1938– British dramatist. Born in London of Jewish parents and once an actor, Kempinksi had a success with his first major production, *Duet for One* (1980), premiered at the BUSH THEATRE, in which his then wife, the actress Frances de la Tour, played a concert violinist stricken with multiple sclerosis, attempting to cope with her illness through psychotherapy. Psychoanalysis features in his other plays, notably in *When the Past Is Still to Come* (1992), an account of his own ten years in analysis, where he describes his 'struggle against the fear which kills', including in his case family memories of the Holocaust. He excels in intimate conversations between stricken individuals, as in *Self-Inflicted Wounds* (1985) and *Separation* (1987), where a reclusive writer in London conducts a long-distance relationship by phone with a sick, perhaps dying actress in New York. No other British dramatist handles Freudian theory with such insight, but his plays can seem sentimental to those not sharing his beliefs. In this, Kempinski has much in common with TENNESSEE WILLIAMS. When he has tried to broaden his range, as in *Sex Please, We're Italian* (1991), the results have been far from convincing. JE

Kendal, Madge [Margaret Sholto Robertson] 1848–1935 British actress, the youngest of 22 children, of whom the playwright T. W. ROBERTSON was the eldest. (This, at least, is what is always said, although there were only 19 years between them. The confusion is not lessened by Madge Kendal's autobiography (1933), in which she says not only that she was 30 years younger than Robertson, but also that there was a gap of several years between the birth of the 21st child and her own.)

Having acted as a child, most significantly in the Bristol circuit of James Henry Chute, she made her London debut in 1865, as Ophelia at the HAYMARKET. It was at this 'home of comedy' under BUCKSTONE that she established her reputation, above all in society COMEDY. Her partnership with W. H. Kendal (1843–1917), whom she married in 1869, was

broken only by his death. It was as 'the Kendals' that they continued to star at the Haymarket in *The Rivals* (1870), *As You Like It* (1875) and *She Stoops to Conquer* (1875) in a notable sequence of W. S. GILBERT premieres, *The Palace of Truth* (1870), *Pygmalion and Galatea* (1871), *The Wicked World* (1873) and *Charity* (1874), and at JOHN HARE's ROYAL COURT (1875–9). They were joint managers with Hare of the ST JAMES's from 1879 to 88, where they were adventurous and prosperous. They remained much in demand, at home and abroad, until their retirement in 1908. But Kendal, even during her management, was less notable as an actress than as a theatrical *grande dame*, the sort who inaugurates charity benefits, unveils plaques and opens fêtes. She was widely admired for taking up the case of John Merrick, the Elephant Man, in 1888 and lived to a ripe old age as the acme of respectability. She was appointed DBE in 1926. PT

Kennedy, Adrienne 1931– African-American playwright who blends symbols, historical figures, racial images and myths to create surreal, highly personalized one-act plays, all of which she claims are autobiographical. *Funnyhouse of a Negro*, which won an Obie in 1964, depicts the final moments before the suicide of Sarah, a mulatto psychically torn by an inability to reconcile herself to her mixed racial heritage. *The Owl Answers* (1969) portrays another mulatto woman caught in a hallucinatory nightmare of confused racial identity in which biographical and historical characters emerge, dissolve and metamorphose. Kennedy's other plays include *A Rat's Mass* (1966), a fantasy of war and prejudice; *The Lennon Play: In His Own Write* (1967), an adaptation of musician John Lennon's autobiographical writings; *A Movie Star Has to Star in Black and White* (1976); and *A Lancashire Lad* (1980), a children's theatre piece based on the early life of Charlie Chaplin. She has published two books on her work and life (1987 and 1990). FB

Kente, Gibson 1932– South African playwright and director. In 1967 Kente became SOUTH AFRICA's first black independent producer of theatre, and for the next quarter of a century remained virtually unrivalled as a theatrical entrepreneur, producing and directing on average more than one new play a year, all of them box-office hits. Even by the 1980s Kente's name remained virtually unknown in the established white theatres of the cities, but amongst black audiences he was the leading exponent of the 'township MUSICAL' and the unrivalled leader of the entertainment world. As writer, choreographer, composer and director of all his productions, Kente is a strict disciplinarian, and each of his productions has been likened to a course of study in a theatre school, in which new generations of performers have obtained their first rigorous training in the craft of theatre. Ranging from plays with a political message, such as *How Long?* (1971), *I Believe* (1972) and *Too Late* (1973), to simple township musical MELODRAMAS like *Hard Road* (1978), *Lobola* (1980) and *Mama and the Load* (1981), all of Kente's work draws upon popular cultural expression, refined and performed with extraordinary energy and professionalism, and his brand of musical melodrama has opened a window on the lives of black people in the townships. Many of his actors have gone on to establish careers as playwrights, directors and actors with an international reputation, but Kente has chosen to address his plays to the people of the townships. 15

Kenya The population of Kenya is estimated at about 20 million people, inhabiting 225,000 square miles, two-thirds of which is scarcely suitable for habitation. Formerly a British colony, Kenya achieved its independence in 1963 after many years of struggle and open war waged by the Mau Mau Land Freedom Army between 1952 and 1960. Since independence Kenya has developed a form of free enterprise capitalism which has divided the society into two worlds – that of a small class of Kenyans together with their foreign business partners and the broad masses of the people – a state of affairs depicted in the 1979 play *Thi Ni Igiri* (*There Are Two Worlds*).

As is to be expected in a colony with a significant settler population, theatre before independence was dominated by a tradition of 'Little Theatre', whose function was to provide its audiences with an opportunity to escape from reality and from the increasing challenge of the anti-colonial forces, who themselves were using theatre as a means of mobilizing opposition to the colonial regime. In 1952, at the height of the struggle for independence, the colonial government opened a cultural centre which also housed the National Theatre. Many of the productions performed there served to entertain and inspire the British soldiers who went to Kenya at that time, the settler community, white colonial administrators and industrial top management, as well as the educated Kenyan African petty bourgeoisie which had accepted colonial culture.

Apart from the traditional drama forms of the pre-colonial society, indigenous Kenyan drama first developed within the colonial education system and ultimately gave rise to the Kenya Schools Drama Festival, at which the set pieces, the adjudicators and the criteria were all foreign. In the late 1940s the Nairobi African Dramatic Society was formed, a group which was to initiate the idea of taking theatre to the people by performing in Machakos, Kiambu, Thika and Nakulu, all towns not far from Nairobi. In 1955 the Nairobi African Dramatic Society entered the white-dominated National Drama Festival with the play *Not Guilty* by Graham Hyslop, and won awards. Subsequently the development of indigenous theatre in Kenya was characterized either by an acceptance of the 'junior partner' tag or the struggle to find its own voice and direction. At first, most activity was very much an extension of the Little Theatre movement and the 'civilizing mission' of the mission schools. Comedians such as Athmani Suleiman (Mzee Tamaa) and Kipanga, who were trailblazers in the art of popular comedy, graced the stage of the National Theatre and were much enjoyed by settler audiences for their slapstick and *kisetla* (settler) *kiswahili*. They were to continue amusing people in live shows and radio and television broadcasts after independence, setting a tradition that has found worthy successors in such modern television programmes as *Vitimbi*.

At independence, the Kenya National Theatre, like the economic and other spheres and institutions of national life, was not democratized. It continued to serve foreign interests, now widened to include the tastes of those from European countries other than Britain. Plays and musicals of no relevance to the cultural life of the majority of Kenyans were performed.

In the years that followed more and more black schools entered the National Drama Festival, at first performing European set books, but later, as African plays began to be published, their entries changed in character. At the University of Nairobi, too, African plays such as WOLE SOYINKA's *Kongi's Harvest* (1966) and Lewis Nkosi's *The Rhythm of Violence* were produced and acted by Arthur Kemoli, Ben Chahilu, David Mulwa and others. A National Drama School was set up by the National Theatre, which produced artists such as KENNETH WATENE, Titus Gathwe, Sese Njugu and Frank Kimotho. In the meantime NGUGI WA THIONG'O, who had been active at Makerere writing and publishing his early plays, had joined the then Department of English at the university (a name which he and others fought to change to 'Department of Literature'). In addition John Ruganda, FRANCIS IMBUGA and later Waigwa Wachira were developing drama there, in particular the Free Travelling Theatre, which annually toured the country performing in schools and market-places.

It was in the 1970s that the social contradictions created by neo-colonialism became clearly visible. The increasing political and social polarization expressed itself in the arts, nowhere more clearly than in the novels and plays of Ngugi, in particular his collaborative drama with MICERE MUGO, *The Trial of Dedan Kimathi* (1976), which along with Imbuga's *Betrayal in the City* – Kenya's entries for FESTAC in 1977 – was performed at the National Theatre before a predominantly working-class audience. Both form and content were inspiring and created an atmosphere of communal song, dance and solidarity which served to highlight the role that a truly national theatre could play, thereby exposing the exclusiveness of the so-called National Theatre. The question of who controlled the art facilities in the country raised the more fundamental question of who controlled the economy. However, participants in this new and dynamic theatre were not ideologically united.

It is within the context of this quest for a national theatre that the performance of *I'll Marry When I Want* by Ngugi wa Thiong'o and Ngugi wa Mirii in 1977 should be seen – in its use of the Gikuyu language, the participation of workers, peasants and intellectuals of different nationalities bringing together town and rural areas – together with the move away from the National Theatre building into a more organically national context, the Kamiriithu Community Educational and Cultural Centre at Limuru. The potential of the Kamiriithu phenomenon to usher in a new, independent community-based theatre is best illustrated by the interest aroused by the performance of *I'll Marry When I Want* and its being able to tap and release an inexhaustible flow of creativity from ordinary people. The Kenyan government, however, moved to suppress the play (see CENSORSHIP). Its licence was withdrawn and subsequently Ngugi wa Thiong'o was detained without trial and Ngugi wa Mirii lost his job at the university. The Centre again, in 1982, was denied a licence to perform a play by Ngugi wa Thiong'o entitled *Mother Sing to Me*. The government publicly announced the deregistration of the

Centre on 11 March 1982, thus banning all its educational and cultural activities, and sent the police to raze the open-air theatre built by peasants and workers and the unemployed youth of Kamiriithu village.

By the 1980s Kenyan theatre was characterized by three trends: the colonial theatre, the 'African theatre' patronized by Western cultural missions, and the political national theatre symbolized by Kamiriithu. There was, though, a growing tendency towards more populist activity, sometimes of a militant nature, exemplified by Tamaduni Players' collectively evolved sketches on the life of the 'parking boys' in Nairobi, and their Swahili performance of *The Trial of Dedan Kimathi* before working-class and student audiences. Independent drama groups proliferated in most town-ships and working-class suburbs, laying the foundations for community-based theatre movements such as Capricorn Theatre Group and Wanamtaa. And an itinerant street theatre group with preachers, jokers and charlatans came into existence, performing at the Jeevanjee Gardens in Nairobi. In 1986 these groups gathered together to organize a four-day festival at the City Hall. All this signals an increased co-option, by the working classes, of theatre as an art form that can serve their interests.

In the face of the efforts of Kenyan artists to develop an independent and relevant theatre, the Kenyan government has repeatedly acted to suppress and thwart it. In 1979 Riara Mission School outside Nairobi entered the Schools Drama Festival with the play *There Are Two Worlds*. The school was raided soon afterwards by the Special Branch and the teacher in charge interrogated. In March 1982, officials tried to nullify the decision of the Schools Drama Festival judges to award a prize to the play, and it was only after a fierce struggle and because of the firm stand taken by the audience that they were forced to recognize the judges' decision. That April the government banned one school play, and in the October another. During the Teacher Training Colleges Drama Festival the Ministry of Education banned one of the entries, harassed the actors and the authors and confiscated the manuscript. The chief adjudicator at the festival commented that this intimidation was preventing young Kenyans from thinking about national issues that affected the majority, and that it suppressed not only creativity but also free democratic thinking in their everyday life.

More recently, there has been a move towards the establishment of a local repertory theatre company run along the same professional lines as the expatriate theatre companies. The first of these, Sarakasi Ltd, was established in 1990 and has recently staged two important plays, an adaptation of the Kikuyu legend *Wangu wa Makeri* and a translation in Kikuyu of the Cameroonian play *Enough Is Enough* (*Ciagana ni Ciagana*). In 1992 Phoenix Players started a new professional repertory company called Miujiza Players, to put on African plays. Mbalamwezi Players and Friends' Theatre are amateur groups, but average six to eight productions a year. These companies have found it hard to survive, and the increasing need for sponsorship has sometimes meant compromising the political content of their work with the result that they have taken to reviving relatively innocuous comedies such as OLA ROTIMI's *Our Husband Has Gone Mad Again* (published

1977). The expatriate companies, Phoenix Players and Nairobi City Players, faced with a dwindling pool of European actors, find themselves recruiting more and more Africans, who are frustrated by the roles available to them in European plays.

Touring continues to be important, and Sarakasi have toured successfully with their productions, as have other companies. Interest in areas outside Nairobi has been noticeably higher when the plays have been Kenyan, such as J. Nderitu's *Wangu wa Maeri*, which in 1991 Sarakasi toured in both its English and Gikuyu versions. The idea of festivals has also caught on well and in 1990 Theatre Workshop, a group of actors drawn from both within the University of Nairobi and outside it, attempted to host one at that university which was to include Soyinka's *Kongi's Harvest*, but they were refused permission to do so. In the last three years new published writing has included adaptations of oral narrative, *Lwanda Magere* (1991) by Okoiti Omtatah and *Nyamgondho* (1990) by Alakie Mboya. These have both been performed at the French Cultural Centre, which in 1992 hosted a festival of plays performed by various local groups.

In December 1992 *Can't Pay Won't Pay* by DARIO FO was performed after the High Court granted an injunction restraining the government from banning the play for the third time. The National Theatre has also seen a revival of interest in local theatre companies, and a grand scheme to modernize the Kenyan theatre is being funded by the Japanese government. By staging the annual winners of the Schools Drama Festival in 1991 the National Theatre tried to reassert its role as a national institution, but government interference and a lack of political will have thwarted these aims and ensured the continued domination of the National Theatre by foreign and expatriate companies. Every theatre group must register with the government, and performance licences are granted only after rigorous security checks and after each script has been read and approved by the administration. Theatre in Kenya now struggles to develop in a situation of growing confrontation between two worlds, and intensifying state repression and harassment.   KG NWAM

See: E. Gachuka and K. Akivaga (eds), *The Teaching of Literature in Kenya Secondary Schools*, Nairobi, 1979 (includes a section on drama in Kenya); R. Kidd, 'Popular Theatre and Popular Struggle in Kenya', *Theatrework*, 2, 6, 1982; C. D. Killam, *An Introduction to the Writing of Ngugi*, London, 1980; L. Mbughuni, 'Old and New Drama from East Africa', *African Literature Today*, 9, 1976; M. Mugo and G. Wasambu-were, *A New Approach to the Teaching of Literature in Kenyan High Schools*, Nairobi, forthcoming; Ngugi wa Thiongo, *Detained*, London, 1981; C. B. Robson, *Ngugi wa Thiongo*, New York, 1979.

Kern, Jerome 1885–1945 American composer. After studying musical composition, Kern began his theatrical career as a house composer for producer CHARLES FROHMAN in London. Returning to America, he worked as a song-plugger and rehearsal pianist. Individual songs by Kern were interpolated into several BROADWAY musicals before he was given his first opportunity to compose a complete score, *The Red Petticoat* (1912). In 1915 he was asked by producers F. Ray Comstock and Elisabeth Marbury to write the score for a modest musical that would be appropriate to New York's tiny, 299-seat Princess Theatre. The result, *Nobody Home*, enchanted critics and audiences with its personable cast, contemporary setting and lively score. An even greater success was the second Princess Theatre musical, *Very Good Eddie* (1915). With librettist GUY BOLTON and lyricist P. G. WODEHOUSE Kern created *Have a Heart* (1917), *Oh, Boy* (1917), *Leave It to Jane* (1917) and *Oh, Lady! Lady!* (1918). By replacing the mythical kingdoms and stilted language of European OPERETTA with recognizable characters, believable dramatic situations and American musical idioms, these shows strongly influenced the direction in which American MUSICAL COMEDY was to evolve in the 1920s.

After writing a number of successful, if conventional, musicals in the first half of the 1920s, Kern again pioneered a new style of musical theatre with his score for *Show Boat* (1927). Conceived as a musical drama, *Show Boat*, with book and lyrics by OSCAR HAMMERSTEIN II, proved that shows with serious librettos and songs that grew naturally out of the dramatic action could be successful. Kern's shows of the 1930s, although containing many fine songs, were more traditional operettas and musical comedies. His last complete score for Broadway was *Very Warm for May* (1939). He is remembered as an innovator whose scores for the Princess Theatre musicals and *Show Boat* were landmarks in the evolution of modern MUSICAL THEATRE. MK

Kerr, Walter 1913 American drama critic, playwright, lecturer, teacher and director. Kerr was educated at Northwestern University before beginning in 1938 an 11-year career as teacher of drama at Catholic University, Washington, DC. There he wrote or co-wrote and directed a number of new scripts, four of which reached BROADWAY. With his wife Jean he collaborated on several shows, including the MUSICAL COMEDY *Goldilocks* (1958). In 1950, Kerr began reviewing for *Commonweal*. The following year, he replaced Howard Barnes as drama critic for the *New York Herald Tribune*, a post he held until that paper's demise in 1966. The *New York Times* then hired Kerr as chief critic for the Sunday edition, a position he held until his retirement in 1983. Regarded as the most perceptive critic reviewing the Broadway theatre during the 1960s and 70s, Kerr brought intelligence, insight, knowledge and a graceful style to his work. He believed that a play's truths must be perceived by an audience intuitively rather than intellectually, and that a play must touch a group consciousness so that there is a 'single unified response'. His views are expressed in *The Decline of Pleasure* (1962), *The Theatre in Spite of Itself* (1963), *Tragedy and Comedy* (1967) and *Journey to the Center of the Theatre* (1979). He won a Pulitzer Prize for Dramatic Criticism in 1978. The restored Ritz Theatre in New York City, built in 1921 and renovated in 1983, was renamed the Walter Kerr Theatre in his honour (1990). TLM

Kerz, Leo 1912–76 Berlin-born theatre and film set designer. Kerz studied with BERTOLT BRECHT and Laszlo Moholy-Nagy, and from 1927 worked as an assistant designer to ERWIN PISCATOR. These influences remained with him throughout his career, and his sets tended towards sweeping proportions and emblematic scenic elements. Like Piscator, he also incorporated film and projections into many of his designs. He left Berlin soon after Hitler assumed power, and worked in London, Amsterdam and Prague before founding the Pioneer Theatre in Johannesburg. Kerz went to the USA in 1942, assisted Jo MIELZINER, Watson Barrett and Stewart Chaney, and resumed his work with Piscator. He made his BROADWAY debut in 1947 with the KATHARINE CORNELL production of *Antony and Cleopatra*. He is best known for his OPERA designs for the Metropolitan and New York City Opera companies, among others, and for his work at the *Arena Stage* during 1969–71. He also designed for television and film, including the controversial *Ecstasy* with Hedy Lamarr (1934). AA

Kessler, David 1860–1920 Moldavian (Kishenev)-born actor, who was 17 when the new invention, YIDDISH THEATRE, came to town. Fascinated, he first joined as a stagehand and, by 1886, when he arrived in New York, he had progressed to leading man. Kessler, an emotional actor, was capable both of melodramatic sensationalism, which excited the masses, and sensitive characterizations, which delighted the intelligentsia. His most famous roles were in GORDIN's *God, Man, and Devil* (1900) and *Shlomke Charlatan* and PINSKI's *Yankl the Blacksmith* (1906). For much of his career he functioned not only as actor but as star-manager of his own company. NS

Khmelnitsky, Nikolai (Ivanovich) 1789–1845 Russian dramatist. An early skilled practitioner of *vaudeville* and *haute comédie*, adapted from French salon comedy as a reaction against the moralizing tendency of Russian drama. Wit took precedence over didacticism in Khmelnitsky's plays, which were above all noteworthy for the simplicity, pliancy and native vitality of their dialogue; they advanced Russian COMEDY in the manner perfected by GRIBOEDOV, with whom he was friendly and whose *Woe from Wit* (along with PUSHKIN's and GOGOL's work) he probably influenced. His works include *The Chatterbox* (1871), adapted from the comedy *Le Babillard* by Louis de Boissy, and perhaps his best play; *Castles in the Air* (1818), his longest-running play; a dozen or more additional *vaudevilles*; two historical dramas from the 1840s, a tragedy based on the life of a famous ancestor who led a Cossack rebellion against Polish rule in 1648, and a treatment of Peter the Great's reign; and translations of MOLIÈRE's *School for Wives* (1821) and *Tartuffe* (1828) that were said to be superior to those of his predecessors. SG

khyal **[*khyala*]** Popular village theatre form in Uttar Pradesh and Rajasthan states in northwest INDIA. Some evidence suggests that *khyal* existed as early as the 18th century and that the city of Agra was its home.

Various styles of *khyal* exist and are named after a city: for example, *Jaipuri khyal*; a community: for example, *Gadhaspa khyal*; an acting style: for example, *abhinaya khyal*; or the author of the work: for example, *Alibaksh khyal*. Subtle differences in the music and language of performance, as well as staging techniques, distinguish the various styles.

Khyal stages are unusually elaborate. A main stage 3 to 4ft high is built as well as an adjacent acting area, either a lower-level stage (*laghu* or 'little stage') or an area demarcated by white sheets spread on the ground. At the four corners of the main stage platform, trunks of banana trees are placed in the ground and decorative flags are strung between the pillars to provide a festive appearance. Behind the main platform stage a balcony-like structure 12 to 20ft tall is erected on poles or supported by the roof of a nearby house. The balcony is wide enough to hold a few actors and is curtained at the sides and back. The high platform stage is connected to the main stage by a wooden ladder. Thus, *khyal* performances use three distinct acting areas to achieve a dramatic effect. Petromax lanterns, strategically placed at the corners of the main stage and at the front of the balcony, give off a harsh undirected white light which illuminates both acting areas and audience (originally oil lamps cast a flickering yellow light over the acting area). Today electric and fluorescent lights are fast replacing the petromax lamps as sources of illumination. The audience sits on three sides.

Prior to the building of the stage, there is a ceremony in which a pole is installed at the performance site, perhaps an ancient reminder of RITUAL practices found in the Sanskrit drama.

A performance begins with prayers to Ganapati, the elephant-headed god, and includes invocations to other gods and goddesses. This is followed by comic antics by clowns. The main play which follows is mythological, semihistorical or fanciful.

An accent on MELODRAMA and evocation of moods of romance, valour and pathos are typical. Like other rural theatre forms, music accompanies performance, played on *nagara* or *dholak* drums, bell-metal cymbals and harmonium. The human voice provides a strong melodic line and drums set various tempos for the action.

Male actors play all roles. The costumes of wealthy companies are elaborate and derived from long-vanished historical periods and styles. The action is carefully controlled by the director-producer (*ustad*), who sits in a chair on the main stage where he carefully follows the sequence of events in his prompt script.   FAR

Kidd, Michael [Milton Gruenwald] 1917– American ballet dancer and choreographer for theatre and film. Kidd performed with BALANCHINE's American Ballet, Ballet Caravan and Ballet Theatre before making his impact in American MUSICAL THEATRE. From his choreographic debut in *Finian's Rainbow* (1947) to the ever-popular barn-raising dance in the film *Seven Brides for Seven Brothers* (MGM, 1954), Kidd has been lauded for his energetic and spirited successes. He had a series of successes – *Guys and Dolls* (1950), *Can-Can* (1953), *Li'l Abner* (1956) and *Destry Rides Again* (1959) – for which he won four successive Tonys, becoming the first person ever so honoured. After a long absence from direction, he replaced GENE SAKS as director of *The Goodbye Girl* in 1993, for which he was nominated for a Tony.   LF

Kiesler, Frederick 1890–1965 Austrian-born architect and designer. Very little of Kiesler's visionary theatre was ever fully realized, yet his plans and projects exerted a strong influence on the development of mid-20th-century theatre architecture and on the emergence of environmental theatre. Most of his projects were variations on the so-called Endless Theatre – a futuristic theatre of ramps and spirals within an ellipsoidal shell. His more practical projects included flexible theatres capable of changing size and configuration, and 'space stages', which were essentially non-scenic architectural stages. He went to the USA in 1926 with the International Theatre Exhibit – the first look many Americans had at new European design – and stayed, but he never achieved the prominence he had known in Europe. Despite many projects, his only significant theatre fully realized in the USA was the Eighth Street Cinema in New York (1930).   AA

Killigrew, Thomas 1612–83 English playwright and theatre manager. He began acting as a child, playing devils at the RED BULL THEATRE in order to see the plays free. Though lacking a formal education, he had established himself as a courtier by 1633. His first plays were produced at the Phoenix (see COCKPIT THEATRE) and were tragicomic romances based on French models. His best play, *The Parson's Wedding* (c.1640), is an energetic and bawdy comedy. During the Interregnum he went into exile with the king, travelling throughout Europe and gaining further preferment from Charles. Some of his experiences were transmuted into his long romanticized dramatic semi-autobiography, *Thomaso the Wanderer* (written c.1654). He wrote a number of closet dramas during his period of exile, all extremely long and virtually unperformable.

In 1660, with DAVENANT, he secured a monopoly patent to set up a theatre company and established the King's Company, using the patent to close down all other companies except Davenant's. Killigrew's company was built around actors who had been players before the Civil War, particularly Hart, Mohun and LACY. He took over Gibbon's Tennis Court in Vere Street and converted it into a theatre much like pre-war private theatres without scenery. Claiming descent for his company from the earlier King's Men, Killigrew took for it the rights to the major part of the earlier drama, but he lacked the foresight to encourage new writers. In May 1663 the company moved to the Theatre Royal in Bridges Street. He established a nursery theatre (see NURSERIES) for the training of young actors in 1667. Though Killigrew boasted to PEPYS of his achievements as manager (wax candles, an orchestra of ten violinists, civil behaviour among the audience, visits from royalty and the provision of a prostitute for the company's younger actors), his lack of experience or good business sense prevented him from being financially successful or efficient. By the early 1670s he had pawned most of his interests in the company, having handed over management to his son Charles in 1671, and by 1676 was no longer directly involved in it. He was MASTER OF THE REVELS from 1673 to 1677.   PH

Kilroy, Tom [Thomas] 1934– Irish playwright. His novel *The Big Chapel* (1971) won a number of awards, but Kilroy is primarily a dramatist: *The Death and Resurrection of Mr Roche*, a success at the 1968 DUBLIN INTERNATIONAL THEATRE FESTIVAL; *The O'Neill* (1969); *Tea and Sex and Shakespeare* (1976); *Talbot's Box* (1977); *Double Cross*

(1986) and *The Madam Macadam Travelling Theatre* (1991), as well as versions of CHEKHOV's *The Seagull* (1981) and IBSEN's *Ghosts* (1989).

Mr Roche involves an all-male drinking party in a seedy Dublin flat, and (bogus or miraculous) otherworldly intimations when Mr Roche, a middle-aged, homosexual Jew, is immured, dies and revives. The action exposes and undermines the revellers' desperate self-deception. In *Talbot's Box*, kaleidoscopic, stylized scenes enact the life and agonized death of Matt Talbot, Dublin's 'workers' saint', searching the mystery of his frenzied devotion and its exploitation by lay and clerical power-seekers. *Double Cross* uses two linked plays to explore questions of nationality and identity through the lives of contemporaries Brendan Bracken and William Joyce.

These plays show real theatrical accomplishment, exploring the struggle for the individual between spirit and circumstances. DM GF

King, Woodie, Jr 1937– African-American producer and director. King was co-founder and artistic director of Concept East Theatre in Detroit during 1960–3 before moving to New York City. There in 1970 he co-founded and still serves as artistic director of the New Federal Theatre at the Henry Street Settlement, where he has produced and directed many plays by budding and significant black playwrights, including AMIRI BARAKA, ED BULLINS and NTOZAKE SHANGE. He founded and heads the National Black Touring Circuit. EGH

King's Men see LORD CHAMBERLAIN'S MEN

Kingsley, Sidney 1906–95 American playwright, who made his reputation with realistic social MELODRAMAS. *Dead End* (1935), concerned with the effect on a group of kids of slum life near New York's East River, is his most memorable success, but *Men in White* (1933), about a young doctor's experiences in a hospital, stabilized the financially troubled GROUP THEATRE and won Kingsley a Pulitzer Prize. His anti-war play, *Ten Million Ghosts* (1936), failed, and *The Patriots* (1943), contrasting the political theories of Thomas Jefferson and Alexander Hamilton, was a weak effort. Forsaking propaganda for realistic and vivid melodrama, Kingsley wrote *Detective Story* (1949), featuring a conscientious police detective whose emotional involvement drives him to sadism, and a dramatization of Arthur Koestler's novel *Darkness at Noon* (1951). Later plays include a FARCE entitled *Lunatics and Lovers* (1954) and *Night Life* (1962), a murder melodrama with overtones of labour relations and politics. A playwright whose career spanned more than half a century, Kingsley remained active in the Dramatists Guild in his last years. WJM

Kinoshita Junji 1914– Arguably the most influential JAPANESE playwright of the postwar period, 1945 to c.1965. Kinoshita graduated with a master's degree in English literature from Tokyo University in 1941. He specialized in Elizabethan literature and went on to produce an 8-volume translation of SHAKESPEARE's works. An ambivalent Christian, he was deeply influenced by both Hegelian theology and Hegel's theory of history. His work is compara-

ble to that of ARTHUR MILLER in the sense that he re-invented TRAGEDY in a modern idiom. Kinoshita identifies the historical dialectic with tragic dramaturgy, and in works from *Turbulent Times* (*Furō*, 1939, rewritten 1947) to *A Japanese Named Otto* (*Otto to yobareru Nihonjin*, 1963) an individual confronts history only to be simultaneously crushed and redeemed by it. Kinoshita has also been fascinated by Japanese folklore, and he has written numerous 'folktale plays', the most famous of which is *Twilight Crane* (*Yūzuru*, 1949; trans. 1956). The tension between his Christianity and his fascination with Japanese SHAMANism on the one hand and his Hegelian universalism and his sense of Japanese uniqueness on the other informs virtually all of his plays. A good example is *Between God and Man* (*Kami to hito to no aida*, 1970; trans. 1979), a two-part work that approaches the problem of Japanese war crimes through the Tokyo War Crimes Tribunal in the first part and through the eyes of a shaman in the second. DGG

Kiønig, Carl Jørgen 1949– Norwegian director. One of the first graduates of the Norwegian State Theatre School's directing programme in 1982, Kiønig quickly established himself as a leading director, on television and in both institutional and alternative theatres. His impact has been primarily with contemporary playwrights (ENQUIST, NORÉN, NORMAN, SHEPARD), but he staged a successful IBSEN's *Brand* at NATIONALTHEATRET in 1990. His work with the experimental group Lilith has included directing CECILIE LØVEID's *Time between Times* (1990) and his own play *In the Shadow of Electra* (1993). HL

Kipphardt, Heinar 1922–82 German dramatist who pioneered documentary drama with *In the Matter of J. Robert Oppenheimer* (1964), which is directly derived from transcripts of the hearings at which the physicist who developed the US atomic bomb was charged with treason. Originally a TV script, it was developed for the stage at the Freie VOLKSBÜHNE by PISCATOR, who claimed this was the material he had sought in vain in the 1920s. Piscator used film, tape recordings, news clips and headlines to give the impression of reportage. The piece attracted international attention and was produced in London (1965) and New York (1969). *Joel Brand, the Story of a Deal* (1965) exposes an aborted Nazi Jews-for-trucks deal. *Brother Eichmann* (1983) showed the Eichmann mentality as commonplace and used it to criticize NATO's nuclear strategy. HR

Kiralfy family Hungarian dancers and impresarios. After a distinguished career in German theatre, the three brothers **Imre** (1845–1919), **Arnold** (d.1908) and **Bolossy** (1848–1932) went to New York with their sister **Haniola** (d.1889) as dancers in GEORGE W. L. FOX's *Hiccory Diccory Dock* (1869). They soon branched out on their own, staging lavish spectacles. Arnold and Bolossy claimed the USA as their territory, building the Alhambra Palace in Philadelphia (1876). Imre, who had organized his first exhibition in Brussels in 1868, produced *Around the World in 80 Days*, *The Fall of Babylon*, an open-air spectacular with 1000 performers, and, with BARNUM, *Columbus* (1890) in the USA. He then settled in London, where his projects included *Venice in London* (1892), a refurbishment of the Earl's Court exhibition hall (1893), *India* (1896), the Victorian Era Exhibition (1897), the Military Exhibition (1901), *Paris in London* (1902) and the Coronation Exhibition (1912). The Kiralfys were distinguished by their magnificent deployment of extras, their innovative use of electricity, and their inability to get on with one another. LS

Kirshon, Vladimir (Mikhailovich) 1902–38 Soviet playwright, regarded by later Soviets as one of the founders of their modern dramaturgy. Kirshon's staunch advocacy (along with AFINOGENOV) of social and psychological REALISM (as opposed to romantic monumentalism) as the basis for the new drama encountered strong opposition from playwrights VISHNEVSKY and POGODIN, and in official circles. His plays attempt to balance clearly individuated characters against MELODRAMAtic situations and ideological themes without severely tipping the balance towards the latter. His first major play, *Konstantin Terekhin* (co-written with Andrei Uspensky; 1926), which deals with the problems of post-revolutionary Soviet youth, was produced under the title *Red Rust* by New York's THEATRE GUILD (1929), with LEE STRASBERG, Luther Adler and Franchot Tone in the cast. His most important play, *Bread* (1930), deals with the suppression of the *kulaks* – the prosperous peasant class – during the years of the First Five-Year Plan. The play has an episodic structure, with interpolated songs and musical themes, and calls for a revolving stage; in it Kirshon warns against oversimplification and idealization in confronting social problems, much as he did in relation to art. His other plays include *The Rails Are Humming* (1927), one of the first Soviet dramas to portray heroic labour; *City of the Winds* (1929), a revolutionary drama from which Kirshon created the libretto for Lev Knipper's OPERA *Northern Wind* (1930); *The Court* (1932), concerning the Social Democrats in Germany; *The Miraculous Alloy* (1934), an extremely popular social COMEDY about youth; and *A Great Day* (1936), about life in the Soviet army. Kirshon was arrested and executed on the charge of Trotskyism during the Stalinist purge trials. SG

Kishida Kunio 1890–1954 Japanese playwright. His devotion to drama as a form of literature helped establish an insightful form of psychological REALISM in Japan. Kishida spent several years in France in the early 1920s and was deeply influenced by JACQUES COPEAU and the VIEUX-COLOMBIER. In 1932 he founded *Playwriting* (*Gekisaku*) magazine as a literary showplace for younger playwrights ignored by the left-wing troupes that dominated the theatre at the time; and in 1937, he was instrumental in founding the Literary Theatre (Bungakuza) troupe as an alternative to the politically engaged theatre. The troupe continues to perform today. Kishida's best plays are the one-act sketches he wrote in the 1920s. Examples include *Paper Balloon* (*Kami fūsen*, 1925; trans. 1989) and *Cloudburst* (*Shūu*, 1926; trans. 1989). Multi-act works like *The Two Daughters of Mr Sawa* (*Sawa-shi no futari musume*, 1935; trans. 1989), regarded as Kishida's finest play, generally expand on the themes of his earlier work: family relationships and the inability of people to communicate with one another. In the postwar period, Kishida

returned to writing short works like *Adoration* (*Nyonin katsugō*, 1949; trans. 1989). DGG

Kishon, Ephraim 1924– Israeli satirist and playwright. Born in Budapest, he survived the Holocaust and emigrated to Israel in 1949. He arrived in Israel without a word of Hebrew, but three years later he produced his first Hebrew play, *His Name Goes before Him* (1952). He brought to the Hebrew stage a background of Central European culture and humour. For many years he wrote a daily satirical column. Kishon's plays and books have been widely translated and some have become international best-sellers, although he is less appreciated at home. Among his plays are: *Black on White* (1955), on racism amongst mice; *The Marriage Contract* (1961); *Plug It Out, the Water's Boiling* (1966), an attack on modern art and its upholders; *Oh, Julia* (1973), about Romeo and Julia in their 40s. HAS

Kiyingi-Kagwe, Wycliffe 1934– Ugandan playwright and producer, regarded as the doyen of Ugandan theatre. Educated at Kings College, Budo, and Makerere University, he founded the African Artists' Association, the first all-Ugandan dramatic society, in 1954. He writes well constructed topical SATIRE and FARCE, and was first successful with his radio series *Wokulira*, which began in 1961 and was then suppressed under Amin, but a new series is running in the 1990s. With the introduction of television in 1962, he began a very popular series, *Buli Enkya, Buli Ekiro* (*Day In, Day Out*), and with radio and TV reputation already made he produced *Gwosussa Emwanyi* (*The One You Despise*, 1963), the first full-length play performed in Luganda language in the UGANDA National Theatre. (It was published in 1967 and is a school set book.) In 1965 he spent a year studying theatre in Bristol. Another of his satirical farces, *Lozio ba Cecilia* (*Lozio, Cecilia's Husband*, published in 1972), is also a set book. Kiyingi-Kagwe acknowledges his debt to G. B. SHAW and SEAN O'CASEY, and is still writing and producing plays for stage, TV and radio. *Muduuma kwe Kwaffe* (1977) contrasts the exploiting Asian shopkeeper with the equally exploiting but less obliging Ugandan businessman in a witty three-act satire that gave rise to a TV series (see TELEVISION DRAMA), which is a vehicle for much social comment. MMAC

kkoktu kaksi Traditional KOREAN PUPPET theatre which is largely humorous, dealing with the corruption of Buddhist monks, domestic problems and immoral officials. During the performance, a puppeteer manipulates a single puppet at a time as he delivers lines and sings songs to the music. The puppet, called *kkoktu*, is easy to construct. Into the carved wooden or papier-mâché head, the main stick of the puppet, a 1 x 2in piece of light wood, is wedged. A rectangular main body frame of light wood is attached a few inches below the neck of the puppet. The upper horizontal bar of the frame forms the shoulders to which arm sticks are loosely fastened, enabling them to be manipulated from below by strings attached to the upper portion of the arms. Appropriate costumes are then fitted to the puppet. Traditionally, a puppet theatre company was made up of six or seven artists: three or four puppeteers and three musicians who played the small gong, an hourglass-shaped drum and a Korean oboe. Three melodies are associated with the puppet play: 'Kutkori', 'T'aryong', and 'Yombul'. OKC

Kleist, Heinrich von 1777-1811 German playwright. During his brief life, which was terminated by suicide, Kleist found neither acceptance in the military or civil service nor recognition as a writer. Today, however, his plays are regarded as being among the greatest achievements of a time when German culture was being enriched by both classicism and romanticism in art and literature. They do not fit easily into either category. Although it failed when first staged by GOETHE at Weimar in 1808, *The Broken Jug* has since been accepted as one of the greatest comedies in the language, especially because of the Falstaffian central figure, the corrupt judge Adam. *Amphitryon* (1807) offers in the development of its central situation a striking example of romantic irony. Among the later plays, *Penthesilea* (1808) is a remarkable portrayal of sexual frenzy, while *Das Käthchen von Heilbronn* (1810) is a deeply moving tale of love and devotion in a knightly, medieval environment. Kleist's final play, *The Prince of Homburg* (1811), is his masterpiece; in it, he reveals his profound attachment to and yet strong antipathy for Prussian militarism. Virtually unknown during his lifetime, a fact that no doubt contributed to his suicide, Kleist's plays were later produced through the agency of, among others, LUDWIG TIECK. SW

Kline, Kevin 1947- Missouri-born (St Louis) American actor, educated at Indiana University and trained at the Juilliard School, graduating in 1972. As a founding member of the ACTING COMPANY, he played numerous roles with that organization. On his own Kline won recognition as Bruce Granit in *On the Twentieth Century* (1978) and Paul in *Loose Ends* (1979), followed by critical acclaim as the Pirate King in *The Pirates of Penzance* (1980), which established him as a star, and as Bluntschli in a 1985 revival of *Arms and the Man*. In 1986 he first played Hamlet at the NEW YORK SHAKESPEARE FESTIVAL, a role he repeated for that organization in his own production in 1990 (and later televised). Kline's film appearances include *Sophie's Choice* (1982), *The Big Chill* (1983), *A Fish Called Wanda* (1988), *Grand Canyon* (1991) and *Dave* (1993). In 1989 he received the second William Shakespeare Award for Classical Theatre from the Shakespeare Theatre at the Folger, Washington, DC, and in June 1993 as a newly appointed artistic associate of the NYSF he appeared as the Duke in *Measure for Measure* at the Delacorte Theatre in Central Park. TLM

Klingemann, Ernst 1777-1831 German director and playwright. Klingemann directed two theatres in Brunswick, including the Court Theatre. Here he staged the first performance of GOETHE's *Faust, Part 1* in January 1829. He was moderately successful as a playwright, writing his own stageworthy version of the Faust legend. His travel volumes *Art and Nature* (1819-29) are an invaluable source for the theatre historian. SW

Klischnigg, Edward SEE ANIMAL IMPERSONATION

Klotz, Florence c.1920- American COSTUME designer who, by her own admission, became involved in design almost by accident. Through the 1960s she designed several light contemporary comedies. In 1971 she teamed up with director HAROLD PRINCE to design *Follies*, which had 140 costumes ranging from rags to lavish show costumes spanning half a century. She subsequently designed several Prince-STEPHEN SONDHEIM MUSICALS, each with a distinctly different style and period. Designs for *Kiss of the Spider Woman* won her a 1993 Tony. Her costumes manage to combine contemporary sensibilities with period style. AA

Knebel, Mariya (Osipovna) 1898-1985 Russian-Soviet actress, director and teacher, trained in the STANISLAVSKY system at MICHAEL CHEKHOV's studio (1918), the school of the MOSCOW ART THEATRE's Second Studio (1921) and as a member of the MAT acting company, where she mostly played character roles until her departure in 1950. She began directing in 1935, serving as artistic director of Moscow's Central Children's Theatre, 1955-60. She taught from 1932, most notably at the Shchepkin Theatre School (1940-8) and the Moscow State Institute of Theatre Arts (GITIS; from 1948), where her directing students included EFROS and VASILIEV. She was named a People's Artist of the Russian Soviet Federated Socialist Republic (1958) and wrote the book *A Whole Life*. SG

Knipper(-Chekhova), Olga (Leonardovna) 1868-1959 Russian-Soviet actress, who upon completing NEMIROVICH-DANCHENKO's course at the Music and Drama School of the Moscow Philharmonia (1896-8) joined the original company at the newly formed MOSCOW ART THEATRE (MAT, 1898). In the premiere season she played Tsaritsa Irina in A. K. TOLSTOI's historical tragedy *Tsar Fyodor Ioannovich*, and the actress Arkadina in CHEKHOV's *The Seagull*. The latter led to a personal and professional association with Chekhov. She married him in 1901 and played leading roles in all his major plays staged at the MAT: Elena Andreevna, in *Uncle Vanya* (1899); Masha, in *The Three Sisters* (1901); Anna Petrovna, in *Ivanov* (1904); and Ranevskaya, in *The Cherry Orchard* (1904), a role she laid claim to well into her old age. She was Nastya in the original MAT production of GORKY's *The Lower Depths* (1902), as well as the theatre's Anna Andreevna in *The Inspector General* and Natalya Petrovna in TURGENEV's *A Month in the Country* (1909). She was named a People's Artist of the USSR in 1937 and awarded a State Prize in 1943. SG

Knowles, (James) Sheridan 1784-1862 Anglo-Irish playwright. Knowles was born in Cork, the son of a lexicographer, but moved with his family to London in 1793 and studied medicine at the University of Aberdeen. After early practice as a doctor, he became an actor in 1808, a schoolmaster in 1811, an actor again from 1832 to 43 and an evangelical preacher after 1844. His decidedly sanctimonious *Lectures on Dramatic Literature* (2 vols., 1873) are pulpit pieces, written with the brief authority of a former playwright, considered in his time a rival to SHAKESPEARE. Almost forgotten today, Knowles is a victim of his own inflated reputation. Much of that reputation was owed to the actor, W. C. MACREADY, whose moving portrayal of suffering fatherhood in Knowles's *Virginius* (1820) brought the playwright into prominence. Later paternal tragedies included *William Tell* (1825) and *John of Procida* (1840). Written, like all his 23 plays, in over-regular blank verse, they are too mawkish to survive 20th-century appraisal. The romances, modelled on FLETCHER rather than Shakespeare, are more successful. They include *The Beggar's Daughter of Bethnal Green* (1828), revised as *The Beggar of Bethnal Green* (1834), and the understandably popular *The Hunchback* (1832). Best of all, though entirely neglected because of Knowles's claims as a writer of tragedies, are the comedies, *The Love-Chase* (1837) and *Old Maids* (1841).   PT

Knyazhnin, Yakov (Borisovich) 1742–91 Russian playwright; son-in-law of the influential Russian man of letters ALEKSEI SUMAROKOV, whom he succeeded as a writer of TRAGEDY after the French neo-classical models of RACINE and VOLTAIRE. His chief literary rival, IVAN KRYLOV, satirized Knyazhnin's tendency to plagiarize the French via the character Rifmokradov (Rhyme Thief) in his play *The Bombastics* (1787). The latter also contains a reference to Knyazhnin's conviction for embezzling government funds. While his career in public service faltered, however, his literary accomplishments earned him election in 1783 as one of the 30 charter members of the Russian Academy. His seven tragedies, beginning with *Dido* (1769) and extending through to his best-known and most controversial plays, *Rosslav* (1784) and especially *Vadim of Novgorod* (1789), are characterized by intricate plotting and dramatic stage effects but are short on originality, genuine historical detail and richly imagined characters. His heroes and villains are designed to argue for what Knyazhnin and Sumarokov believed to be the theatre's role – to propagate liberalism and civic responsibility. *Vadim*, which contrasted the virtues of republicanism and monarchism, so threatened Catherine the Great in the wake of the French Revolution that she ordered it burned. Although its complete text was not published until 1914, the play influenced Decembrist dramaturgy in the 1810s and resulted in a version by PUSHKIN.

Knyazhnin was a far better comic writer. His talented verse comedies (earlier Russian comedies were largely written in prose) satirize the abuses of serfdom and the corrupt nobility's pursuit of title and rank, Gallomania, reliance on foolish and fraudulent foreign tutors and 'valet-*philosophes*'. His comic OPERAS feature highly actable characters, richly aphoristic language and ample local colour. The comedies include *The Unsuccessful Mediator* (1785); *The Braggart* (1786), based on du Brieux's *L'Important* (1723) and featuring a prototype for GOGOL's Khlestakov; and *The Odd Fellows* (1790), based on DESTOUCHES's *L'Homme Singulier* (1764). His comic operas are highly successful: *The Mead-Seller* (1784), music by Byulant; and his best single work, *Misfortune from a Carriage* (written 1772, produced 1779), music by V. A. Pashkevich, which offered SHCHEPKIN one of his earliest roles. Knyazhnin's, like Sumarokov's, popularity was eclipsed by the Russian romantic writers of the early 1880s. SG

Koch, Heinrich Gottfried 1703–75 Major German actor of the 18th century, who worked with CAROLINE NEUBER and JOHANN SCHÖNEMANN. He took over the leadership of the Schönemann troupe when EKHOF was still a member, but the two had differences, especially over Koch's tendency to improvise, so Ekhof left to join the ACKERMANN troupe. Koch's troupe continued to travel in the Leipzig area until his death.   SW

Kochergin, Edvard (Stepanovich) 1937– Russian stage designer (see THEATRE DESIGN). Schooled under Soviet artists Bruni and Akimov, Kochergin became head of design at the Leningrad Theatre of Drama and Comedy in 1963. In 1966, he was appointed head designer of the Komissarzhevskaya Dramatic Theatre. He was later promoted to chief artist of the Gorky Theatre in Leningrad. Kochergin has refined a style which has been compared to GROTOWSKI's 'poor theatre' productions. His sparse, textured yet simple settings have been integral to such Gorky Theatre productions as *Hamlet* (1972), *Boris Godunov* (1973) and NIKOLAI GOGOL's *Notes of a Madman* (1978).

Among the many other productions which he designed for the Gorky Theatre are Shukshin's *Energetic People*, ROSHCHIN's *Valentin and Valentina*, VAMPILOV's *Last Summer in Chulimsk*, BULGAKOV's *Molière* and GORKY's *Summer Folk*. His design for LEV DODIN's production of *The House* (from Fyodor Abramov's family chronicle) at Leningrad's Maly Dramatic Theatre consisted of five wooden horses (used metaphorically) of the sort which traditionally decorate rural Russian houses. In 1975 Kochergin designed the striking set for the highly popular dramatization (by Mark Rozovsky) of LEV TOLSTOI's *The Story of a Horse* (*Kholstomer*) at the Gorky. Here the audience is seated inside the horse, looking into its worn flesh, which tears open to reveal paisley-lined flaps for actors' entrances and exits. Kochergin's design for LYUBIMOV's *The Inspector's Recounting* (based upon Gogol's works) at the Taganka made similar use of a textured background, a huge piece of felt representing the famous overcoat of Gogol's Akaky Akakyevich, which is being stitched together on numerous machines operated by *chinovniki* (clerks). The felt contained openings through which performers could make sudden appearances and cast various parts of their bodies (including nude knees representing noses). A series of small elevator platforms used for spectral ascents and descents completed the set. For Rozovsky's *High* (about MAYAKOVSKY) at the Mayakovsky Theatre, Kochergin designed a suprematist environment after Kazimir Malevich. Kochergin is generally considered to be one of Russia's greatest living scene designers.   SG TM

Kokoschka, Oskar 1886–1980 Austrian painter and dramatist, whose works were the earliest examples of EXPRESSIONISM, with their direct externalization of subconscious states. *Sphinx and Strawman* (1907) became one of the influences for dadaist theatre, while *Murderer, the Hope of Women* (1907), staged in 1918 and 1919 and as an opera with music by Hindemith in 1922, was a forerunner of ARTAUD's Theatre of Cruelty.   CI

kolam Sri Lankan masked folk theatre, once extremely popular along the southern coastal region. A dozen plays exist in this form. The word *kolam* in Sinhalese means appearance, impersonation or assumed guise, usually comic or exaggerated so as to provoke laughter. Full-face MASKS are used to identify at least 50 stock character types. Many are introduced through a ritual prologue and some assume importance in the dramatic action which follows. Among the characters that appear in the dramas are the king, the queen, the king's herald, his wife, a policeman, a washerman, the washerman's wife, a paramour, a village dignitary, celestial beings, demons and animals.

After RITUAL dances and chants in honour of the presiding deities, there is a colourful and elaborate ritual entrance of each character which is accompanied by the chanting of the verses of the musicians who outline the history of each character. The entrance of the characters is highlighted by dances appropriate to his or her station in life. The dramatic action of the play follows. The masks do not seem to have been designed for singing or speaking; therefore, in the dialogue portions of the play, masks are rarely worn.

Performances usually take place in any open space in a village, begin around nine in the evening and conclude about sunrise.

The origin of *kolam*, according to one of the dramas, is told in the story of a certain queen who, big with child, craved dances and amusements. The king ultimately satisfied her by ordering performances of *kolam*. This tale, along with other stories dealing with fertility, suggests that *kolam* may well have arisen as an ancient pregnancy rite. FAR

Koltai, Ralph 1924– German-born British stage designer, noted for his bold imagery and conscious sense of style in the service of a production concept. Suggesting the art of sculpture and architecture, his designs usually centre on highly expressive forms and constructions that often employ untraditional scenic materials such as plexiglass, styrofoam, steel and fibreglass. Primarily a freelance designer, almost half of whose work has been in OPERA, Koltai has also had extensive association with both the ROYAL SHAKESPEARE COMPANY and the NATIONAL THEATRE. The artistry of his work has frequently led to prizes and exhibitions. From 1965 to 1973 he was head of the THEATRE DESIGN programme at London's Central School. Notable productions have included *Doctor Faustus* (1964), *Back to Methuselah* (1968), the opera *Taverner* (1972), WAGNER's *Ring* (1970–3), *Brand* (1978), *Much Ado About Nothing* (1982), *Othello* (1985) and *Metropolis* (1989). With a production of *The Flying Dutchman* in 1987, he began to direct as well as design. JMB

Koltès, Bernard-Marie 1948–89 French playwright who developed a close relationship with PATRICE CHÉREAU, who produced all of Koltès's major plays at his Théâtre des Amandiers in the 1980s: *Combat de nègre et de chiens* (*Struggle of the Dogs and the Black*, 1983); *Quai ouest* (*Western Dock*, 1986); *Dans la solitude des champs de coton* (*In the Solitude of the Cotton Fields*, 1987); *Le Retour au désert* (*Return to the Desert*, 1988 – this last at the Théâtre du Rond Point). His posthumous *Roberto Zucco* was given its first production by PETER STEIN at the Berlin Schaubühne in 1990. Koltès wrote a number of shorter pieces and translated *The Winter's Tale* for Luc Bondy in

1988. Observing the classical unities, and written in a sumptuous prose style that carries echoes of JEAN GENET, Koltès's plays are widely regarded as the most important body of new work to emerge in the 1980s in France. The power of his writing lies in the multiple levels of meaning at work in the dialogue – dialogue that can convince an audience of the authenticity of particular characters, while at the same time carrying echoes of the larger ideological conflicts of our time. DB

Komissarzhevskaya, Vera (Fyodorovna) 1864–1910 A mystical, poetic actress of spiritual essences, who captured the restiveness and yearning of pre-revolutionary Russia's artistic elite. With her extreme nervosity and sensitivity, her virginal tenderness and sincerity, her luminous, other-worldly presence and an inner angst which seemed to play itself out via her roles, she became the perfect icon for the Russian symbolists (see SYMBOLISM) – BLOK, BELY, BRIUSOV, KUZMIN, SOLOGUB, Georgy Chulkov – a useful conduit for MEYERHOLD's directorial ideas and a possible model for characters in EVREINOV's plays. The daughter of a noted opera tenor, Komissarzhevskaya possessed a hypnotic, deeply resonant, 'inwardly musical' voice, which her contemporaries likened to a Stradivarius violin. She began her amateur acting career in St Petersburg in 1891 and shortly thereafter joined the amateur Moscow Society of Art and Literature run by her father, STANISLAVSKY and A. F. Fedotov. By the time she joined St Petersburg's Aleksandrinsky Theatre company, she had appeared in well over 60 roles in two separate professional theatres, mostly as ingénues and in musical *vaudevilles*. At the Aleksandrinsky she originated the role of Nina in the disastrous first production of *The Seagull*. She was the only company member who appreciated the play, and remained CHEKHOV's favourite interpreter of the role.

She left this theatre in 1902, and after two years touring founded the Dramatic Theatre of V. F. Komissarzhevskaya in St Petersburg. It immediately became a haven for symbolist artists and progressive students, who saw in her the social commitment of a latter-day ERMOLOVA. Her attraction to new ideas and to authoritarian figures led her to appoint Meyerhold as the theatre's artistic director and to become close to Briusov, who translated MAETERLINCK's *Pelléas and Mélisande* for their production, in which she played the title role (1907). To her admirers' chagrin, she subordinated her talent to Meyerhold's master plan, which at this time called for extreme stylization, scenic flatness, immobility, and puppet-like actors intoning in strangely rhythmic cadences. Excellent at playing victims, sufferers and visionaries – all touched by unreality – she here appeared as Maeterlinck's Sister Beatrice (1906) and as a bizarrely vampirish Hedda Gabler in the director's notorious, colour-coded production of IBSEN's play. This was a great act of faith for an actress who saw Ibsen as her special calling and who had given a memorable performance as Nora in *A Doll's House* and as Hilda Wangel in *The Master Builder*. It also reflected her theatre's commitment to innovative stage design by symbolist painters such as Nikolai Sapunov and Serge Soudeikine (Sergei Sudeikin).

In 1908 Komissarzhevskaya replaced Meyerhold with

Evreinov and her half-brother, FYODOR KOMISSARZHEVSKY, in an effort to reclaim authority for the actor, but she continued to perform Meyerhold's symbolist play choices. She even approved Evreinov's frankly erotic production of WILDE's *Salomé*, with Kalmakov's set design resembling huge female genitalia, which the Holy Synod banned in 1908. A falling-off in attendance and a personal psychological crisis led to her closing the theatre in 1908 and planning a school for the human development of actors with Andrei Bely. However, while on a fund-raising tour of Tashkent, she contracted smallpox and died.   SG

Komissarzhevsky, Fyodor (Fyodorovich) [Theodore Komisarjevsky] 1882–1954 Russian director, teacher, theorist; and half-brother of noted actress VERA KOMISSARZHEVSKAYA, whose theatre he headed with EVREINOV after MEYERHOLD's dismissal (1908). Here he staged ANDREEV's *Black Masks* and IBSEN's *The Master Builder* (1907–9), and during a company hiatus (1909) co-produced with Evreinov a programme of light fare, re-dubbing the playhouse the Merry Theatre for Grown-up Children. From 1910 he worked in Moscow, staging productions at the Maly (1913) and at Nezlobin's Theatre of OSTROVSKY's *Not a Kopek and Suddenly a Rouble* (1910), MOLIÈRE's *The Bourgeois Gentleman* (with exotic set and COSTUME designs by Sapunov, 1911), GOETHE's *Faust* (1912) and Dostoevsky's *The Idiot* (1913). Between 1910 and 1918 he directed productions at his own studio, including OZEROV's *Dmitry Donskoi* (1914), *Lysistrata* and plays by SOLOGUB, Andreev and KUZMIN.

In his many OPERA productions at the Bolshoi Theatre and elsewhere – such as *The Golden Cockerel* (1917), *Lohengrin* (1918) and *Boris Godunov* (1918) – Komissarzhevsky tried to realize his concept of a cultured, synthetic theatre, philosophically romantic in tone, created around a universal actor-singer-dancer. Following a year of directing a new studio theatre, he emigrated (1919), continuing in London, Stratford-upon-Avon, Rome, Paris, New York and Vienna to design and direct 'synthetic' productions of SHAKESPEARE, PIRANDELLO, Crommelynck and, especially, Russian classical dramas – by GOGOL and TURGENEV – and operas – by Mussorgsky and Borodin. He also directed films in England, and wrote *The Actor's Creative Work and Stanislavsky Theory* (1916), *Theatrical Preludes* (1916), *Myself and the Theatre* (1929), *Costume of the Theatre* (1931) and *The Theatre and a Changing Civilization* (1935).   SG

Komparu Zenchiku 1405–?68 Japanese playwright; second of ZEAMI's successors and head of the Kanze NŌ troupe from 1443 until his death. He composed the richly poetic plays *Yang Kuei-fei* (*Yōkihi*), *The Plantain Tree* (*Bashō*), and *Rain and Moon* (*Ugetsu*), which are admired for a profound, delicate and nostalgic sense of *yūgen*. In 23 treatises he developed a metaphysical philosophy of *nō* aesthetics based on doctrines of Kegon and Zen Buddhism. The actor who achieves unconscious performance enters the 'circle of emptiness', which is the highest level of artistic and religious accomplishment.   JRB

Kong Shangren 1648–1718 Chinese *KUNQU* playwright. A descendant of Confucius in the 64th generation and an authority on ancient rites and music, his *The Peach Blossom Fan* (*Taohua shan*, 1699), a 40-scene play written in southern style, is considered a masterpiece of poetic composition. It records the treachery and intrigue which facilitated the Manchu overthrow of the Ming dynasty in 1644. Characters are based on historical personages and its love story is one of the greatest in Chinese literature. The play won immediate popularity but resulted in the playwright's dismissal from office by the Manchu authorities. Kong was considered one of the two great playwrights of his day, the second being HONG SHENG.   ACS

Kongelige Teater (Copenhagen) Denmark's national theatre, located on Kongens Nytorv since 1748, comprises four organizations, performing on several stages: the theatre company, the Royal Opera, the Royal Danish Ballet and the Royal Orchestra. Its present building dates from 1874; the recently restored Old Stage is used almost exclusively for opera and ballet, with spoken drama relegated to the shabby and unsatisfactory New Stage and to studio theatres elsewhere in the city. The theatre company rightly claims its origins in the first Danish-speaking theatre founded in Lille Grønnegade Street in 1722. Traditionally, a peak in its history was the mid-19th century, when a company of fine actors were assembled around the HEIBERGS. In the 20th century, it has nurtured actors of undisputed genius such as Bodil Ipsen, POUL REUMERT, Bodil Kjer, Mogens Wieth, Jørgen Reenberg and Kirsten Olesen.   HL

Koonen, Alisa (Georgievna) 1889–1974 Russian-Soviet actress. One of STANISLAVSKY's favourite pupils at the MOSCOW ART THEATRE school, Koonen made her acting debut at MAT in 1906 and performed with the company until 1913, when she left to join MARDZHANOV's Free Theatre. After playing the title role in SCHNITZLER and Donanyi's *The Veil of Pierrette*, she and the production's director, her future husband TAIROV, co-founded the Kamerny (Chamber) Theatre (1914), where they sought to synthesize emotion and plastique. At the Kamerny, Koonen played a series of spiritually strong women searching for love, freedom and self-realization, either at odds with social conventions and demands or in service to a new social ideal. These roles included Sakuntala (1914); Salome (1917); Adrienne Lecouvreur (1919 and 1949); Juliet (1921); Phèdre (1922); St Joan; HASENCLEVER's Antigone (1927); EUGENE O'NEILL's Abbie and Ella in *Desire under the Elms* (1926) and *All God's Chillun' Got Wings* (1929); the heroic commissar in VISHNEVSKY's *An Optimistic Tragedy*; Cleopatra in the SHAKESPEARE-PUSHKIN-SHAW compilation *Egyptian Nights* (1934); Madame Bovary in her own adaptation (1940); and Nina Zarechnaya in CHEKHOV's *The Seagull* (1944). Koonen was named a People's Artist of the Russian Soviet Federated Socialist Republic in 1935 and in 1975 her memoir, *Pages of Life*, was published.   SG

Kopit, Arthur (Lee) 1937– New York-born and Harvard-educated American playwright, who has had a distinguished place in the US theatre as a serious and inventive writer for more than 30 years, though he has rarely gained popular acceptance. He first received international atten-

Yangju *pyolsandae*, Korean masked dance drama.

tion with *Oh Dad, Poor Dad, Mama's Hung You in the Closet and I'm Feelin' So Sad* (1960), a brilliant PARODY of the Oedipus complex. Since *Oh Dad* he has written a number of plays that experiment with dramatic form, most notably *The Day the Whores Came Out to Play Tennis* (1964), a comic portrayal of social-climbing country-clubbers; *Indians* (1968), a study of genocide of the Indians by white Americans; *Wings* (1978), a portrait of a stroke victim (the basis of a 1992 MUSICAL); *The End of the World* (1984), a dark COMEDY about nuclear proliferation; and *The Road to Nirvana* (1990), a scatological comedy about the business of Hollywood. Kopit also wrote the book for the musical *Nine* (1982) and a version of *Phantom of the Opera* (1991). DBW

Korea The peninsula of Korea, situated west of Japan and bordering on China and Russia on the north, is home to 60 million people speaking a single language and sharing one culture. Since 1948, the Korean people have been divided into two political states: the Republic of Korea with Seoul as its capital and the Democratic People's Republic of Korea with P'yongyang as its capital. For centuries folk theatre has existed in various geographical regions both in the North and in the South. During the successive rule of the three major kingdoms of Silla, Koryo and Choson (or Yi), court forms of dance and masked play were patronized and encouraged. In the first part of this century, modern Western drama and theatrical REALISM

were introduced. Before the Second World War, modern Korean theatre influenced by the West was limited in large part to Seoul, then capital of the whole country. Since 1948 modern theatre has been concentrated in the two capital cities, Seoul in the South and P'yongyang in the North. Regional theatre companies began to emerge in the South in the 1980s.

Folk theatre The precise origin of Korean theatre is unknown. The beginning of Korean theatre may be traced back to ancient ceremonies, folk observances and SHAMANistic rites, some more than 2000 years old. Among civic observances that are believed to have included incidental theatrical elements are *ch'ŏngun*, *much'ŏn* and *yŏngo*. They were mainly performed for the purpose of worshipping heaven and appeasing ancestral spirits. Presumably these RITUALS required the performers to sing and dance as well as wear MASKS. During the 7th century, *kiak*, originally consisting of music and dance, was probably imported from CHINA. This was performed at a Buddhist temple as a kind of simple didactic masked dance drama for a general audience. One theory suggests that *kiak* became the genesis of today's folk masked dance drama, SANDAE-GŬK ('mountain performance', probably indicating a performance on a raised stage). *Kiak* was also taken to JAPAN, where it was called *gigaku*.

During the long reign of the Silla Kingdom (57 BC–AD 935) *kŏmmu*, *muaemu* and *ch'ŏyongmu* were important dance forms containing theatrical elements. *Kŏmmu* was a masked sword dance, originating in the story of the death of a legendary young warrior who killed an enemy king. *Muaemu* was a dance performed without masks which promulgated Buddhism. Of these three, *ch'ŏyong-mu*, based on the story of legendary Ch'ŏyong, a son of the Dragon King of the East Sea, was the most grotesque and pungent early type of masked dance of Korea.

During the strongly Buddhist Koryo period (918–1392) there were no important amusements other than religious festivals such as *p'algwanhoe* and *yŏndŭnghoe*. The former was primarily a midwinter festival offered in honour of the earthly deity, while the latter, held in the first lunar month, was a Buddhist mass. Although the purpose of the two events differed, preparations for the festivities were strikingly similar: numerous lanterns of different sizes and colours were hung, and a temporary high stage was constructed and adorned with bright colours. Programmes included somersaults, a tight-rope display, acrobatic dance on the top of a bamboo pole, puppet plays and various mixed forms of masked dance drama (*sandae-japgŭk*).

Another ritual of this period, *narae*, was performed to drive evil spirits out of the palace. Later the purpose of *narae* changed as it came to be performed for the public by professional male actors, *kwangdae*, probably the first actors in the history of Korean theatre to earn their living as performers. Some actors of this period belonged to the court, where they could be called upon to perform at any given time. Other actors maintained a livelihood entertaining wealthy and petty merchants. All actors were considered social outcasts and forced to reside in segregated areas, apart even from the residences of common people. When they were not performing, they engaged in such lowly professions as butcher, hunter and basket weaver.

In the following period of the Chosŏn court (1392–1910), cultural activities were heavily influenced by Confucianism. Popular literature, fine arts and theatre blossomed, gaining increasing support from commoners, particularly merchants and craftsmen. The Confucian court, strongly anti-Buddhistic, refused to sanction the Buddhist religious festivals of Koryŏ. From past dynasties, however, the inherited masked forms of *narae* and *sandae-japgŭk* continued, and contributed to the development of masked *sandae-gŭk*. Unmasked performances were also known. Some apparently were comic-satirical dramas in which perverse officials or tyrannical rulers were targets of ridicule. This type of theatre was referred to as *chaphui*, indicating plays performed by actors as distinguished from masked *sandae-gŭk* performed by dancers.

P'ANSORI, a solo narrative sung to drum accompaniment, was developed by professional *kwangdae* actors during the latter part of the Chosŏn period. The origin of this art is not clear. Some scholars trace it back to short songs sung by shamans in rituals of the early 18th century. As a kindred of shamans, the early *p'ansori* singer-actor belonged to the lowest class in society. If any member of that class was talented and possessed the necessary powerful quality of voice, he was given training to become a *p'ansori* singer-actor. A special hoarse vocal timbre was acquired after years of arduous training. In time *p'ansori* was taken over by itinerant professional *kwangdae* actors,

in search of material with which to entertain their popular audiences. Probably they replaced the short lyrics with longer popular songs derived from well known stories. In the 19th century, Shin Jae-hyo (1817–84) set down in writing the six stories of the repertoire which had existed until then in the oral tradition.

The performance of *p'ansori* requires no more than a singer-actor, a drummer and a small mat. This simplicity allows performances to be given anywhere, for any size audience and under almost any circumstance, and is responsible for *p'ansori* being one of the most popular entertainments for people of all classes during the past two centuries. Today *p'ansori* is frequently performed, not only live but also on television and radio reaching a mass audience.

Korean masked dance drama can be classified into two main types: village-festival plays (*purakje*) and various forms that derive from the court, collectively known as *sandae-gŭk*. Major village-festival masked forms include HAHOE PYŎLSIN-GUT, *kwanno, pŏm-gut* and *t'al-gut* of the east central region of the country. All other known forms of masked dance drama are related to court forms: PYOL-SANDAE plays of Yangju and Songp'a; T'ALCH'UM plays of Pongsan, Unyul, Haeju and Kangnyong; OGWANGDAE plays of T'ongyong, Kosong and Kasan; and YARYU plays of Tongnae and Suyong. Whether originating in folk or court surroundings, it is notable that masked dance plays took root in many regions of the country.

Of the village-festival plays, *Hahoe pyŏlsin-gut* is the best-known. Performance traditionally occurs once every ten years, on the 15th day of the first lunar month, as part of the Hahoe village festival. The play calls for twelve masks. Today, nine of the original wooden masks – the most refined among Korean theatre masks – remain. There is no record of the whereabouts of the other three. When they were not in use, the masks were traditionally kept in the village shrine. In Hahoe village the task of mask-making was supposedly accomplished only by a man instructed by divine message in a dream. The identity of the mask-maker and the date of carving the Hahoe masks are unknown today.

Village performers preserve and orally transmit knowledge of performance and the main action of the play without a written script. Rather than being built around a central plot, the play is made up of independent scenes held together by a common theme – satire of monks guilty of transgression, of corrupt aristocrats and of insensitive local officials.

During the early period of the Chosŏn dynasty, masked drama was organized at the royal court under the direction of a court official, the Master of Revels (*sandae-togam*). Performances served official functions – to entertain visiting Chinese envoys, to exorcise evil spirits, to welcome newly appointed provincial governors. However, in 1634 official support was withdrawn with the abolition of the Master of Revels position and during the last half of the Chosŏn period performers left the court and brought their theatre into the countryside. Different variations of masked drama were naturally developed in different regions, by village folk performers and by professional itinerant *kwangdae* troupes. This history explains why there are so many similarities as well as regional differences among the various masked drama forms in Korea.

Performance elements common to all *sandae-gŭk* forms include masking, dance, singing, music, pantomime, the exchange of witticisms and dialogue. Prime emphasis is placed on dancing, singing and music. Performance is held outdoors, avoiding the need for stage settings. Grotesque masks and colourful costumes may be intensified by blazing torchlights at night. Dance movement patterns, numbering more than a dozen, are complicated and difficult to decipher. In the Yodaji dance, for example, the player moves forward, placing both hands on the upper front of his body and, extending them forward, pantomimes the opening of his chest while his feet kick forward. Some dances are used for a humorous purpose: for example, the Horijapi dance, which requires lifting the player's leg while resting his hands on his waist, is designed to tease the other player.

With few exceptions, characters in *sandae-gŭk* are masked. The masks, made of dried gourds or paper, were traditionally burned at the end of each performance. Around the edge of the mask a dark cloth (*t'alpo*) is attached to cover the back of the head; dark strips of cloth are also used to tie the mask around the player's neck.

The musical ensemble generally consists of six instruments (*samhyŏn-yukgak*): a transverse flute (*chotdae*), two fifes (*p'iri*), a two-stringed fiddle (*haegŭm*), an hourglass-shaped drum (*changgo*) and a barrel drum (*puk*). A small gong (*kkwaenggwari*) may be added. Three tunes are played most frequently: 'Kutkori', 'T'aryong' and 'Yombul'. 'Kutkori' is a flowing tune with a twelve-beat pattern, 'T'aryong' has a twelve-beat pattern with an accent on the ninth beat, and 'Yombul' is a rhythmical six-beat pattern. The songs, which are interlaced with dance and dialogue, are mostly derived from popular folk songs and shamanistic incantations of the Chosŏn period. Because a song has come from a source outside the play, it may have no bearing on the plot at all.

The costumes make an important contribution to the theatrical spectacle. In particular, the costumes worn by the servants and the women of questionable morality are bright, even gaudy.

Being collaborative works and transmitted orally, the masked plays do not have identifiable authors. Only recently have performances been recorded and their texts transcribed and published. Each performance depends upon the village actors spontaneously improvising from a rough synopsis of the plot. The generally episodic nature of the plays can be illustrated by examples drawn from the masked play of Yangju (*Yangju pyŏlsandae*). Act I is about Sangjwa, a monk, while Act II consists of an exchange of nonsensical dialogue between two other characters. The transgressions of a second monk, unrelated to Sangjwa, are the subject of Act V. Characters introduced in one scene will not appear again. What is common to most of the masked plays is the satirical representation of four privileged character types: the corrupt local official who steals someone else's woman; the apostate Buddhist monk who engages in lascivious conduct with women; the aristocrat who blindly exercises his power; and the tyrannical husband who mistreats his wife. In the Confucian ethical system these male authority figures – monk, official, aristocrat, husband – should command total respect. The plays take the villagers' point of view, completely subverting the system by holding up their crudely excessive behaviour to contempt and ridicule. Dramatic language ranges from poetic expression in *Pongsan t'alch'um* to rough, bawdy vernacular in *Yangju pyŏlsandae*.

Traditionally, players are local farmers and petty town officials. In the past all performances took place at night and could last until dawn. Now, daytime performances are also given, sometimes in conjunction with a government cultural event or as a tourist performance.

Traditional puppet theatre, KKOKTU KAKSI, is believed to be the descendant of puppetry introduced into Korea

Kkoktu kaksi, traditional Korean puppet theatre.

during the 7th century by wandering players from the Asian continent. These groups of itinerant players, 'song-and-dance people' (*namsadang*), being nomads and social outcasts like *kwangdae*, never belonged to the mainstream of society, and developed and preserved puppetry in society's margins.

The Korean PUPPET, *kkoktu*, combines aspects of the hand puppet, the rod puppet and the MARIONETTE. The body of the puppet is held by the hand. The arms, somewhat like a marionette's, are manipulated by strings from below. And the stiff arm movements remind us of a rod puppet. During the performance a puppeteer manipulates a single puppet at a time, while delivering dialogue or singing songs to accompanying music.

A number of orally transmitted versions of the plays exist, ranging from seven to ten scenes. Although different in detail, they deal with a common pool of humorous subjects which are mercilessly ridiculed: the apostate monk; the triangular relationship between husband, wife and concubine; the unethical high official; the corrupt upper-class man. Generally, a different subject is treated in each scene. The structure of puppet plays is more tightly organized than masked plays because the main puppet character appears in each scene, serving as the narrator who links actions together.

Until the beginning of the 20th century, urban and rural audiences alike were greatly entertained by both the masked dance drama and puppet theatre. Modern audiences, however, find these art forms contain shortcomings: performance time is too long; because performances are outdoors lines often cannot be heard and, when delivered by the players behind their masks, are unintelligible; being entertained by masks and puppets seems old-fashioned. In addition, after 1910, these folk arts were faced by a stronger enemy, the occupying Japanese military who were determined to wipe out Korean culture and language completely. As part of its general cultural policy of forbidding Korean cultural expression, performances of masked dance drama and puppet theatre were banned by the Japanese colonial administration between 1930 and 1945.

Since the end of the Second World War, the folk theatre of Korea has not only been resurrected but also revitalized through performance, study and publication of the plays. The government of the Republic of Korea has designated these art forms as Important Intangible Cultural Properties. In contrast, the government of the Democratic People's Republic of Korea discourages the performance of folk theatre in its normal village environment. Traditional masked dance drama and the puppet theatre are considered not only backward but also not sufficiently revolutionary.

Modern theatre At the beginning of the 20th century, two types of modern drama were introduced into Korea: *shinp'a*, an imitation of Western sentimental MELODRAMA, and SHINGŬK, influenced by Western realistic drama. For a time, the folk theatre co-existed with these modern forms. But soon the popularity of the folk theatre began to decline.

The people of the folk theatre who were the first to respond to the influx of modern theatrical forms were *p'ansori* performers. They established the first modern, indoor theatre in Korea, the Hyopyul Theatre, in 1902, where they staged dramatized stories in *p'ansori* musical style. This reformed style of *p'ansori* was a kind of opera or music drama and was called *ch'anggŭk* ('song and drama'). The important difference between *p'ansori* and *ch'anggŭk* was that in the latter multiple singers enacted specific roles. The five basic stories of *p'ansori* make up the basic repertory, although other dramas are also written for *ch'anggŭk* staging. Despite the attempt at modernization, *ch'anggŭk* lost its popularity due to a limited repertoire. Occasional performances of the genre are seen today, mostly at the National Theatre. They appeal to the audience through sentimental lyrics and music.

Early Korean *shinp'a* artists were strongly influenced by the Japanese theatre of the same genre, SHINPA. A prominent pioneer actor and leader of the Hyoksin Troupe was Im Song-gu (1887–1921). Some of Im's performances and productions were extremely popular, but relying on third-rate touring Japanese troupes for his model and trusting to improvised dialogue, he was unable to raise the quality of *shinp'a* theatre. One of the artists most responsible for developing higher-quality plays and productions was Pak Sung-hi, a prolific playwright and director, who led the noted Earth and Moon group (Towolhoe) for approximately 20 years. Pak was the first person to use completely developed play scripts for his productions.

Most plays were set in the present time and dealt with contemporary events in Korean life. There are three main types of plays: military plays, detective plays and domestic plays. In the military plays patriotic soldiers who defend the Korean nation against the invading enemy are glorified as national heroes. *The Battle in the Snow* (*Chinjungsol*, ?1908) portrays youthful patriotic soldiers fighting the invading enemy whose identity is not clearly defined, but vaguely suggests the Japanese military. Producing this type of play was still possible until a harsh CENSORSHIP policy was enforced following the Samil Independence actions of March 1919. A very popular hero was the young policeman who relentlessly pursues the robber, disregarding personal wounds, to restore law and peace in the community in a detective play. Domestic plays, the soap operas of the time, deal with love, hatred, injustice, revenge, filial piety and the conflicts between legitimate and illegitimate children. Domestic plays became the predominant category in *shinp'a* and typically the Japanese occupation is shown to be the cause of individual and national suffering. In *Arirang Pass* (*Arirang-goge*), by Pak Sung-hi, the lovers are forced to part because of family bankruptcy due to Japanese exploitation. Korean audiences of the time responded enthusiastically to this theme because the misfortune of the dramatic characters in such plays reflected their own personal sufferings and their nation's tragedy.

In 1921, a group of Korean students studying in Tokyo formed the Society of Comradeship (Tongwuhoe) and performed first modern drama, or *shinguk*. Under the leadership of Kim U-jin, the group toured throughout Korea during the summer vacation, producing such important new plays as *The Death of Kim Yong-il* (*Kim yong-il ui chugum*) by Cho Myong-hi. The plays they chose dealt with the principle of self-determination and the freedom of man, ideas newly advocated by Woodrow Wilson after the

First World War. They staged plays by IBSEN, O'NEILL, ČAPEK and PIRANDELLO, thus introducing European and American drama to Korean audiences. After 40 performances the group was ordered to dissolve by the Japanese police. Despite its short existence, the Society of Comradeship made significant contributions to Korean theatre: it pioneered serious modern drama in contrast to shinp'a; it forced other companies to raise their production quality; it demonstrated that modern drama could be an educational tool to teach new ideologies.

The Society of Comradeship had no immediate successors. A decade later, in 1931, a group of young intellectuals organized the Theatre Arts Research Society (Kugyesul Yonguhoe) devoted to popularizing the new realistic drama through staging performances, playwriting, criticism, audience education and the translation of foreign plays. They established an experimental stage, where they produced the plays of CHEKHOV, Ibsen, GOGOL and GALSWORTHY. A number of notable young playwrights influenced by REALISM and NATURALISM emerged during the 1930s. Their plays exposed the true suffering Koreans endured under harsh Japanese military rule. *The Earthen Hut (T'omak)* by Yu Ch'i-jin depicts the misery of an aged farmer whose sole hope for regaining his farm ends in anguish when he learns that his only son, fighting for national independence, has been killed by the Japanese police.

During the 1930s modern Korean theatre was largely divided into two camps: popular commercial theatre represented by shinp'a and nationalistic, realistic shingŭk. Interestingly, some shinp'a artists were left-wing sympathizers who attempted to include Marxist ideas in their productions. Censorship and oppression directed against shingŭk by the Japanese military, which began in the early 1920s, became harsher still. Artists active in nationalistic theatre were targets of arrest, torture and detention. In 1939 the Theatre Arts Research Society was finally ordered to dissolve by the Japanese. With the suppression of this group, Korean theatre was once again dominated by shinp'a for a short period until it too was suppressed. The Japanese military, seeing the possibility of using Korean theatre to serve their policies, proposed to form a single theatre organization in 1941 that would be under direct Japanese control. Nine troupes were allowed to join, and all other companies and individuals were banned from performing. Playwrights, too, were required to write plays glorifying Japanese military policy.

Korea's liberation from Japanese domination at the end of the Second World War resulted in the division of the nation into two parts, North and South, and the splitting of the theatre people into two vehemently opposing factions. For those in the leftist group, theatre became a tool for political propaganda. The majority of the left-wing theatre people came from the shinp'a troupes, while the right-wing theatre was organized by the nationalistic theatre people of shingŭk. When the governments of North and South Korea were separately established in 1948, a large number of the left-wing theatre people went to the North where they became the nucleus of theatre in the Democratic People's Republic of Korea. Since the end of the Second World War, the theatre of North Korea has been utilized to propagate official government policies and Communist ideology. Until 1950 the dominant subject of drama was the struggle during the 1930s against the Japanese led by General Kim Il-sung, the present leader. The plays of this period were written to proselytize Kim's political message, especially *juche*, placing man at the centre. During the 1950s, the so-called 'great revolutionary works' emerged, such as *The Great River Is Flowing (Taeha-nun hunrunda)*, *The Young Vanguards (Ch'ungnyon junyu)* and *The Communist Guerrilla (Kongsan ppalchisan)*. These spectacular productions were a modern version of shinp'a, devoted to political ideology.

Since the 1970s three types of theatre dominate the stage in North Korea: 'revolutionary opera'; 'music and dance drama'; and 'epic drama of music and dance'. The major characteristics of the 'revolutionary opera' are songs, chorus, music, exaggerated scenic settings and colourful costumes. The difference between this theatre and the 'music and dance drama' is that the latter places a heavier emphasis on dance. In 'epic drama of music and dance', a series of grand, epic scenes containing political messages are performed through dance, song, chorus and music. In the musical ensembles used in the theatre Western instruments predominate. Almost all the theatrical productions presented on the major stages in P'yongyang today place great emphasis on spectacle with large casts, elaborate scenery, colourful costumes and dazzling lighting. To accommodate this type of production, the government has built large-scale theatres: P'yongyang's Mansudae stage can hold a cast of 5000. Because of tight ideological control, only a few approved themes may be used in the drama, and these occur again and again: the struggle against Japanese imperialism in the 1930s; the war against United States imperialism and the South Korean puppet government; commendation of Kim Il-sung; and praise for the glorious life under Communism. The collapse of Communist governments in Russia and Eastern Europe, 1989–91, has had no effect on these themes in North Korea.

In the five years following the Second World War, theatre in South Korea was marked by two significant events: the founding of the Theatre Arts Association (Kugyesul Hyophoe) in 1947 and the establishment of the National Theatre in 1950. The former was organized by shingŭk artists under the leadership of Yu Ch'i-jin to counter left-wing theatre. The National Theatre was created by the government to promote nationalistic theatre and to advance theatrical exchange with foreign nations. Two resident companies were attached to the National Theatre, the New Association (Shinhyop) and the Theatre Association (Kughyop). In two months 50,000 people attended the opening productions, *Wonsulrang* by Yu Ch'i-jin and *The Thunderstorm* by the Chinese playwright CAO YU, but this promising beginning was cut short by the outbreak of the Korean War. The staff of the National Theatre moved to Taegu and most theatrical groups barely continued. With the end of the war in 1953, the National Theatre returned to Seoul and resumed production. The Shinhyop troupe, now independent, achieved success in the war-ravaged capital staging recent works by ARTHUR MILLER, TENNESSEE WILLIAMS, WILLIAM INGE and Korean authors. Another notable event was the opening of the Wongaksa Theatre in 1958, a small theatre with 306 seats, constructed by the government to promote the Little Theatre movement. Unfortunately this theatre burned down in 1960.

The 1960s were marked by the emergence of numerous new theatre troupes. In 1960 the Experimental Theatre (Silhom-kugchang) opened with a production of IONESCO's *The Bald Prima Donna*, an obvious rebellion against the dominance of Shinhyop and its realistic production style. The ambitious Drama Center, founded by Yu Ch'i-jin, opened in 1962 with the great expectation that it would stimulate a new Korean theatre and provide a home for new Korean plays. Built with initial funding from the Rockefeller Foundation, the Center contained a flexible theatre seating 450, classrooms for a theatre school, and a library. It did not meet these expectations, however, and five of its first six productions were foreign plays. Furthermore, audiences were increasingly drawn to American films and able theatre artists migrated to television.

If the 1950s were marked by the production of contemporary American drama, the 1960s were the period in which the plays of DÜRRENMATT, FRISCH, ANOUILH, BECKETT and other modern European authors were introduced. A score of plays belonging to the THEATRE OF THE ABSURD were produced, often using the outmoded, and misunderstood, realism of the STANISLAVSKY method. Young Korean playwrights began to treat new subjects: contemporary economic–political systems; the absurdity of modern society; and the problems of urban life. Notable authors of this period are O Yong-jin (1916–74), Ch'a Pom-sok (1924–) and Yi Kun-sam (1929–).

During the decade of the 1970s a return to Korean roots in playwriting and directing can be seen. Playwrights experimented with subject-matter drawn, not from daily life, but from ancient legends, shamanistic rites, and classical literature. Others included traditional folk songs in plays on modern subjects. Authors in this period include Yun Tae-song, O T'ae-sok, Yi Jae-hyon, and Ch'oe In-hun (1936–). Energetic directors emerged such as Kim Chong-ok (1932–), Im Yong-ung and Yu Tok-hyong who attempted to apply the production techniques of total theatre.

Among many new initiatives of the 1980s were an experimentation with SURREALISM; updating the PUPPET theatre to meet the demands of today's audience; infusion of BRECHTian EPIC THEATRE into playwriting; and modernizing the old theatre of exorcism (*gut*). Potentially the most significant is the creation of a new form of masked dance drama, *madang-guk*, or 'yard play', designed to be performed in the street or open field for a large popular audience. Plays deal with present-day subject-matter, especially social–political events, in satirical fashion, thus returning to the folk tradition of social SATIRE in masked drama. It gained fashion among college students during the 1980s.

The Seoul Theatre Festival (originally the Korean Theatre Festival, begun in 1978) and the Regional Theatre Festival have been annual venues for supporting new productions and encouraging new plays. In an attempt to further encourage modern theatre, the Ministry of Culture proclaimed 1991 the 'Year of Theatre' and sponsored international and national conferences and performances. The objectives of the 'Year of Theatre' were to increase the audience; to exchange productions among domestic and foreign companies; to open new performing spaces. For Korean theatre, the 1980s were a decade of struggle to attract audiences in the South and to create new works in the North. The two governments are beginning to allow relations between the two Koreas, and in the distant future it may be possible again to speak of one Korean theatre. It is urged that theatre people in the South and the North cast aside ideological differences to exchange theatre productions. Recently troupes from eastern Europe have performed in Seoul (for example, in 1991 the Leningrad Bolshoi Drama Theatre and the Wybrzeze Theatre of Poland) and Seoul theatre artists welcomed the visit of a director of Korean descent from Kazakh in the former USSR, a happy result of the lessening of political tensions in the world. (See also ASIAN AND PACIFIC ISLAND THEATRE.) OKC

See: J. R. Brandon (ed.), *The Cambridge Guide to Asian Theatre*, Cambridge, 1993.

Kornblit, A.Y. see TAIROV, ALEKSANDR

Korneichuk, Aleksandr (Evdokimovich) 1905–72 Prolific and administratively eminent Ukrainian dramatist, whose optimistic and heroic socialist-realist MELODRAMAS made him extremely popular with the government and earned him honorary Russian status among Soviet historians, officialdom and the theatregoing public. With the exception of *The Truth* (1937), which offers one of the first dramatic depictions of Lenin on the Soviet stage, *Bogdan Khmelnitsky* (1939), a paean to the Ukrainian people's courage in repelling invaders, and several war plays featuring Ukrainian characters and settings, his plays eschew regional for national issues. His most famous works include *The Wreck of the Squadron* (1933), a historically based, monumentalist account of heroic Red seamen during the Revolution; *Platon Krechet* (1934, revised 1963), which offers a dedicated young surgeon as a symbol of the intelligent and humane new Soviet man; and *Front* (1942), an extremely popular, patriotic drama, growing out of the Soviet Union's early defeats in the Second World War, which argued that the old guard in the military must be replaced by younger officers with the necessary training to fight and win in a modern war. Korneichuk's *Why the Stars Smiled* (1957) and *Where the Dnieper Flows* (1960) are more intimate, comic and romantic treatments of the trials and entanglements of parents and their offspring, better suited to the climate of the post-1953 Thaw period in Soviet culture. SG

Körner, Theodor 1791–1813 German playwright. Körner's promising career was cut short by his death while fighting in the Napoleonic wars. His most successful play was the tragedy *Toni* (1812). He was briefly official dramatist to the BURGTHEATER. SW

Kornfeld, Paul 1889–1942 Austrian dramatist, born in Prague. His plays *Die Verführung* (*Seduction*, 1918) and *Himmel und Hölle* (*Heaven and Hell*, 1920) are prime examples of ecstatic, visionary EXPRESSIONISM. His key essay *The Man of Soul and the Psychological Man* proclaims that acting should reveal the energies of the soul and not just human psychology. He later wrote comedies:

Palme oder der Gekränkte (*Palme, or a Man Insulted*, 1924), *Kilian oder die gelbe Rose* (*Kilian, or the Yellow Rose*, 1926). He died in a concentration camp. HR

Kortner, Fritz 1892–1970 Austrian actor and director. His performance as the hero of TOLLER's *Transfiguration* in 1919 established him as a leading interpreter of EXPRESSIONISM, and he went on to play villains and heavies for JESSNER – Gessler in *Wilhelm Tell*, WEDEKIND's Marquis von Keith, and Richard III. He played Dr Schön to Louise Brooks's Lulu in G.W. Pabst's Wedekind film, *Pandora's Box*. After returning from US exile in 1948, though he was never given a theatre of his own, his meticulous, emotionally truthful productions of the classics in Munich (where PETER STEIN was his assistant), Berlin, Düsseldorf and Vienna were influential. He introduced BECKETT's *Waiting for Godot* to Germany. HR

Kotopoúli, Maríka 1887–1954 Greek actress who was virtually born into the theatre, as both her parents were actors. Kotopoúli's range was wide, for she could play tragic roles as well as VAUDEVILLE. For more than 30 years she managed her own theatrical group, Elefthéra Skiní (Independent Stage), after a successful start at the Greek Royal Theatre (1901–8) hosting a variety of plays from classical and modern theatre. Towards the end of her career, Kotopoúli helped revive ancient Greek drama (see GREECE, ANCIENT) by playing Electra, Clytemnestra and other heroines of tragedy. She was likened to SARAH BERNHARDT, and her bust guards the entrance of the Theatrical Museum of Athens. GT

Kott, Jan 1914– Polish theatre critic. His book *Shakespeare, Our Contemporary* (1964) argues exactly what its title suggests, and many directors – PETER BROOK among them – have taken Kott's ideas about the power of the fool in periods of change into the dimension of theatrical action. MB

Kotzebue, August von 1761–1819 German playwright. Although Kotzebue spent much of his life in the political service of the Russian Tsars, he was also an extraordinarily prolific writer. His early work, *Misanthropy and Repentance* (1798), was adapted by Benjamin Thompson as *The Stranger* (1798) to become one of the most popular plays of the 19th century in England. Equally popular in Germany were *The Two Klingsbergs* (1801) and *The Small-Town Germans* (1803), plays that might still receive the odd revival today. Several of Kotzebue's widely performed plays had historical settings. His work, deliberately written to appeal to as broad a cross-section of the populace as possible, reflects the transition from sentimentalism to melodrama. SW

Kraus, Karl 1874–1936 Austrian critic and dramatist. Kraus was the publisher of the radical journal *Die Fackel* (*The Torch*) from 1899 to 1936, and the first to promote WEDEKIND. His plays *The Last Days of Mankind* (1919) and *The Unconquerable Ones* (1928) present a satiric panorama of the era. CI

Krejča, Otomar 1921– Czech director, whose career has spanned six decades. He was an actor for celebrated directors E. F. BURIAN and Jiří Frejka in the postwar years before joining the National Theatre in 1951, where he began to direct a few years later. He established his own production team, soon drawing attention with stagings of CHEKHOV and SHAKESPEARE, as well as the work of new playwrights (Hrubín, Topol, Kundera). In 1965 he left the National Theatre to establish his own Gate Theatre, which soon gained international acclaim. While maintaining fidelity to a text, Krejča would subject it to exhaustive analysis, define his concepts and interpretations meticulously to his cast, and encourage his designers (e.g. SVOBODA) to create bold stage embodiments of their shared vision. Increasing political pressures eventually forced the closing of his theatre in 1972, and by 1976 his only outlet for work was abroad. In 1990 he returned to Prague to reactivate Gate Theatre II. Especially dedicated to the works of Chekhov, he has also shaped powerful productions of SOPHOCLES, Shakespeare and BECKETT. JMB

Krio theatre Highly popular theatre tradition in SIERRA LEONE. Krio, which is the lingua franca in Sierra Leone – a country in West Africa of approximately 4 million people – is an English-based Creole language which developed out of interchange between freed slaves settled in the capital Freetown, their European colonial masters, and the indigenous people of the region. Krio, though largely an urban language, is the language of the home and of commerce, and is spoken by approximately 60 per cent of the population.

Krio theatre was pioneered by Thomas Decker, who mounted a campaign spanning several decades for the use of Krio in literary endeavours. The breakthrough came in 1964 when his translation of SHAKESPEARE's *Julius Caesar* was performed in the grounds of State House by the National Theatre League, an umbrella organization for theatre in the 1960s and early 70s. Decker later wrote an adaptation of Shakespeare's *As You Like It*, which he called *Udat Di Kiap Fit*. These plays, combined with his writings in newspapers and radio plays, provided the impetus for the flowering of Krio drama. Juliana John took Decker's experiment a stage further by writing original plays in Krio, using a theme song and dance sequences. Her work started the process of popularizing Krio theatre. Dele Charley, YULISA AMADU MADDY and a host of other playwrights carried this process of popularization to fruition. Today, Krio theatre operates side by side with theatre in English.

Perhaps because Krio is the language of the urban masses, Krio drama is peopled by characters drawn from this social sector, and deals with issues common to them in a down-to-earth way. Krio theatre is therefore popular theatre which, although appreciated and patronized by a wide cross-section of society, draws the bulk of its audience from the working classes.

The unique feature of Krio theatre is the dance-drama, which came into existence in 1977 with Dele Charley's creation of *Fatmata*. Krio dance-drama usually takes the form of storytelling theatre in which theme and action are welded together through dance, music, MIME, choral speaking and narration. Not a dance-drama in the true sense of the term, it relies on a narrator and a chorus to present the story verbally but the individual characters, except for occasional songs, perform in a non-verbal mode through dance and mime. All verbal presentations (apart from the songs) are structured with a distinctive beat, thus facilitating their rendition to the steady rhythm of drums. JS

krishnattam Religious dance drama performed at the famous Guruvayur Temple in the pilgrimage town of the same name in the coastal region of Kerala state, south INDIA. The form was conceived by a Zamorin king, Raja Manaveda, in the mid-17th century as a means of glorifying the name of Krishna, one of Lord Vishnu's most beloved incarnations. *Attam* is 'story' in local Malayalam language, hence *krishnattam*, 'dramas of Krishna'.

A legend says that Manaveda, a devout follower of Krishna, prayed that he might see the god, who had been seen by a seer at Guruvayur Temple. To his amazement Krishna appeared before him as a small boy playing in the temple courtyard. When Manaveda reached out to touch the boy the vision vanished and a peacock feather in Krishna's hair was left behind. Thereafter generations of actors who portrayed Krishna wore this feather in their crown until it was destroyed by fire several decades ago.

The legend continues that, inspired by his miraculous vision, Manaveda wrote *Krishnagita*, recounting incidents from the life of Krishna. Based on the *Bhagavata Purana*, it serves as the basis for the eight plays comprising the entire dramatic repertory of the form.

Given the fact that Kerala possesses a long history of notable forms of theatre, such as KUTIYATTAM and KATHAKALI, it is not surprising that *krishnattam* shares many features with them, while retaining its own individual characteristics. As in *kutiyattam* and *kathakali*, dancer-actors interpret a text in performance through a highly sophisticated code of gesture language. Nonetheless, preliminary studies reveal that the meaning of many of the shared gestures and their execution is different from that of all the other Kerala performing arts. The dance movements closely resemble those of *kathakali* but they have their own definite character which stresses a lyrical, feminine quality of group movement rather than the masculine vigour of *kathakali* or the more abstract angularity of *kutiyattam*.

Make-up patterns for mythological characters – humans, demons and animals – reveal striking similarities to those of *kathakali* while, at the same time, they display their own flair. To a sophisticated theatregoer, the make-up, costumes and ornaments, which, at a casual glance, seem the same as those of *kathakali*, have shapes and patterns which could only belong to *krishnattam*.

The actors of the one troupe which performs *krishnattam* are all male devotees of the god. Many were offered in grateful service to god and the temple when they were small boys, in exchange for a boon that was granted to their parents. Others came freely to devote their lives to Krishna's service. The high level of devotion of the participants is echoed by the religious fervour of pilgrims who watch the performances.

Traditionally pilgrims, who come from all over India to worship at the temple, pay temple authorities to have a *krishnattam* performed as a part of their RITUAL sacrifice.

The devotee may choose to have any of the eight stories enacted. Favourite stories are associated with requests for particular boons. The play which includes Krishna's marriage is auspicious for a devotee celebrating a marriage; the story which depicts Krishna's miraculous birth ensures the birth of a male child to barren parents; and the story which shows the destruction of the wicked King Kamsa will ward off the evil eye. If all eight plays are performed in sequence, they must be followed by the re-enactment of the first night's play showing the birth of Krishna (it is inauspicious to end a sequence with Krishna's death).

Performances are generally held in the courtyard of the temple, northeast of the main shrine; however, a special proscenium-arch stage has been constructed outside the temple compound so that non-Hindus who have a desire to see *krishnattam* may do so. In recent years, *krishnattam* has been played in towns and cities elsewhere in India and in Europe and the United States. Any open space about 15ft square with room around it for spectators may serve as an appropriate place for performance. Scenery is not used and a simple stool symbolizes a throne, mountain or bench. A 4ft-high bell-metal oil lamp provides a flickering glow to the performance. In the proscenium house, two scoop lamps situated on the floor to the right and left of the oil lamp illuminate the space. This lighting deadens and flattens out costumes and ornaments which were designed to be seen under lamp light.

A performance takes place between 9 p.m. and 3 a.m. It may only be presented after the temple rituals are concluded and before the doors of the *sanctum sanctorum* have been opened for the morning prayers. The reason for the strict time frame is explained in a charming story. Many years ago, when the doors of the temple shrine were inadvertently left open, the effigy of Krishna was so moved by the music that it came to life and danced with the actors causing considerable dismay to the temple priests. Care is now taken not to allow the same incident to happen again.

Texts of the plays are sung by two chief singers in the *sopana* style of singing popular in Kerala. The actor-dancers do not speak. Basic rhythmic patterns are played on two *maddalam* drums struck at both ends and suspended around the waist of the drummers, an hourglass drum (*idakka*) played at the drummer's side, and bell-metal cymbals. A harmonium provides the pitch around which the singers weave their intricate melodies. A conch shell is played during auspicious dramatic actions.

In recent years, owing to the continual flood of pilgrims that come to the temple to perform austerities, *krishnattam* is performed nearly every night of the year. The performers are now unionized and the company divided into two groups that alternate in performing and thus no one is exploited. Experts complain that the death of the older generation of artists has led to a serious decline in the quality of *krishnattam*. The performance of the same material over and over again has led to a lethargy among artists whose work has become routinized. No new work may be added to the repertory and only on rare occasions is the full cycle of plays performed. FAR

Krleža, Miroslav 1893–1981 Croatian playwright; born in Zagreb, where he spent most of his life. Krleža was educated in military schools of the Austro-Hungarian Empire, in whose army he served in the First World War. He was an early supporter of the idea of a Yugoslav state, and of socialism. As an embattled intellectual and modernist, Krleža belongs to the same Central European orbit as KRAUS, Musil, HORVÁTH and Canetti. His early plays, written in symbolist and expressionist manner (see SYMBOLISM; EXPRESSIONISM) – *The Legend* (1913), *Salome* (1913), *Kraljevo* (1915), *Christopher Columbus* (1917), *Michelangelo Buonarroti* (1918), *Adam and Eve* (1922) – were initially considered unstageable and, if published at all, were largely ignored. They were successfully staged in Yugoslav theatres only after 1955.

Between the two world wars, Krleža was editor of several leftist literary reviews, and a productive novelist, poet, essayist and polemicist. As a playwright, he became established only after a gradual transition to REALISM, as marked by *Vučjak* (1923) and his trilogy *The Noble Glembays, In Agony* and *Leda* (1928–31). Isolated from the left for his early critique of Stalinism, and persecuted by the right for his leftist ideas, Krleža was a lonely figure from the late 1930s until Yugoslavia's break with Stalin in 1948; then he emerged as the towering figure of the domestic cultural scene, instrumental in rejecting socialist realism and inaugurating aesthetic pluralism. In the last three decades of his life he established and led the Yugoslav Lexicography Institute in Zagreb; edited the *Encyclopaedia Yugoslavica;* revised and published many of his old manuscripts, especially essays and diaries; and wrote a long novel but only one new play, *Aretheius* (1958), whose prophetic value became evident only with the recent demise of the Yugoslav state: in it, intellectuals are forced to emigrate, and savage violators of human rights clash in an oneiric time frame fusing Roman and contemporary epochs.

Krleža's plays, often loaded with his erudition and marked by vibrant intellectual discourse, have been translated into all major Slavic languages, as well as German, French and Hungarian. They have been performed in Central and Eastern Europe, but remain practically unknown in the English-speaking world.   DK

Kroetz, Franz Xaver 1946– German dramatist whose early one-acters were sequences of brief naturalistic scenes (see NATURALISM) from the lives of the underprivileged, with minimal dialogue in Bavarian dialect. Finding an authentic voice for the unskilled who eked out an inarticulate existence on the fringe of the German 'economic miracle' was Kroetz's contribution to the new VOLKSSTÜCK. His explicit treatment of sex and other bodily functions initially caused uproar. His 1971 double bill *Homeworker* and *Hartnäcking* (*Pig-Headed*) showed masturbation, attempted abortion and child murder. *Wildwechsel* (*Game Crossing*, 1971), which was filmed by FASSBINDER, shows an affair between a young factory hand and a minor, who murder the girl's fascistic father. *Stallerhof* (1972) and its sequel *Ghost Train* (1975) handle with great sensitivity the love between a retarded teenage girl and a repressed farm labourer four times her age. In 1972 Kroetz joined the Communist Party, and with *Oberösterreich* (*Morecambe*, 1972) and its sequel *Das Nest* (1975) plot and ideology enter his work, which now focuses on average urban workers struggling to keep up their standard of liv-ing. Aspiring to bigger plays, Kroetz has tried his hand at SYMBOLISM, with pieces like *Bauern sterben* (*Peasants Die*, 1985), and adaptation, with *Agnes Bernauer* (1977) after Hebbel, *Fear and Hope in the FRG* (1984) after BRECHT, and *Der Nusser* (*The Gelding*, 1986) after TOLLER. He left the CP in 1978 and has taken to acting in TV soaps.   HR

Krog, Helge 1889–1962 Popular Norwegian dramatist and essayist. Krog is the author of 16 sometimes playful social problem plays that owe at least an initial debt to IBSEN and GUNNAR HEIBERG. A recurrent theme is the unliberated position of women in modern society, especially in his most powerful plays *The Conch Shell* (1929) and *Break-Up* (1936). Krog is particularly admired for the wit and subtle dexterity of his dialogue, which may owe something to SHAW, and the ironic (sometimes satirical) tone that qualifies his treatment of human nature.   HL

Krones, Therese 1801–30 Austrian actress. For the few years in which she acted in the company of the Theater in der Leopoldstadt, Krones was the most celebrated actress in Vienna. Admired for her grace of movement and for the harmony of her performance, she was one of the first great interpreters of RAIMUND's plays. She is commonly considered to have embodied the spirit of the Old Viennese theatre, though some in her audiences were offended by the way in which she frankly exploited her sex-appeal on stage.   SW

Kruchonykh, Aleksei (Eliseevich) 1886–1969 Russian-Soviet futurist poet, dramatist and theorist, an extremist and 'the father of *zaum*', or transrational, universal language based solely upon expressive sounds and bypassing cognitive poetic thought. This marked an attempt to jettison Russia's romantic poetic past (exemplified by PUSHKIN), to forestall the philosophical influence of SYMBOLISM and to capture directly the confused sensory impulses of the moment, which was a cornerstone of futurist poetics. Along with his fellow futurists, Kruchonykh exploded grammar and syntax, invented new words, made purposeful omissions of phrases and punctuation, played with typography and 'textures' to stress certain words and sounds, and generally cultivated dissonance and 'primitive coarseness' in his art.

Kruchonykh became attached to cubo-FUTURISM in 1912, co-signing with painter David Burlyuk and VLADIMIR MAYAKOVSKY the manifesto *A Slap in the Face of Public Taste*, and participating in the poetic groups Hylaea (1910–13), 41° (1918–19) and Mayakovsky's Lef (the Left Front of Art Group; 1923–5). His work, which was strongly erotic, drew upon folk and children's art and the overall primitivist trend. He was librettist for the first and only pre-revolutionary futurist OPERA *Victory over the Sun* (1913) – music by Mikhail Matyushin, sets by Kazimir Malevich, prologue by Velimir Khlebnikov – which alternated over four nights (2–5 December 1913) with Mayakovsky's 'tragedy' *Vladimir Mayakovsky* at the Union of Youth in St Petersburg's Luna Park. The libretto, representing 'a complete break between concepts and words', and the music, suggesting 'a distorted Verdi', combined with the abstract sets, 'inept chorus', hastily assembled and rehearsed amateur actors – pausing after every syllable, according to Kruchonykh's instructions – and the out-of-tune piano to create the desired anti-aesthetic effect and elicit a satisfactory outpouring of hisses, hurled fruit and laughter. At the play's end the futurist Strong Men 'are victorious over the sun of cheap appearances and have lit their own inner light', thus assuring the continued progress of futurism beyond the earth's demise. SG

Krylov, Ivan (Andreevich) 1769–1844 Dramatist and journalist; best known as the greatest Russian fabulist, a conservative middle-class philosopher noted for his masterful aphoristic language and his satirical barbs aimed at political and literary enemies, the arrogantly stupid and the self-satisfied inept of all classes and professions. Before most of his nine volumes of *Fables* were written (1809–20), Krylov was a dramatist and satirical journalist of some note. His malicious but largely accurate portrayal of rival dramatist YAKOV KNYAZHNIN as an embezzler and plagiarist and his wife, SUMAROKOV's daughter, as an adulteress kept his coarse COMEDY *The Bombastics* (written 1787, produced 1793) from the stage until after Knyazhnin's death.

In his comedies Krylov also attacked the Russian literary vogue for sentimental heroines perpetrated by Karamzin (*The Pie*, 1802); Russian classical TRAGEDY's weakness for depicting enlightened monarchs (*Trumpf; or, Podshchipa*, a mock tragedy, 1799); and the abuses of serfdom – but, in something of a common sell-out, via the person of an overseer rather than a landowner (*The Fortune-Teller*, a Knyazhnin-like comic OPERA, 1783). His prose comedy *The Fashionable Boutique* (1805) captures the growing anti-French feeling following Louis XVI's execution and Russia's breaking off of diplomatic relations. On the other hand, his most popular play *A Lesson to Daughters* (1806) reflects MOLIÈRE's continued influence on Russian comic dramatists, extending from situations and devices such as disguisings to play titles. Despite his nationalist sympathies and his substantial contributions to the creation of a highly colloquial national literature, Krylov's satirical comedies and comic operas received no public performances in St Petersburg, the seat of government, during his lifetime. SG

Kubo Sakae 1900–58 Japanese playwright. He succeeded in developing Japanese social REALISM into a mature dramatic form through skilful characterization. Closely identified with OSANAI KAORU and the Tsukiji Little Theatre, Kubo was a translator of German drama, rendering over the course of his career some 30 plays into Japanese, ranging from GOETHE's *Faust* to works by KAISER, WEDEKIND and HAUPTMANN. Kubo's magnum opus is *Land of Volcanic Ash* (*Kazanbaichi*, 1937–8; trans. 1986), a monumental seven-act work that depicts life in a small agricultural community in Hokkaido in the 1930s. Kubo continued to write engaged, positivistic works in the postwar period and influenced major postwar playwrights like KINOSHITA JUNJI and FUKUDA YOSHIYUKI. DGG

kuchipudi South Indian theatre form named after a village in the Krishna River delta of Andhra Pradesh: the religious dance drama performed by male Brahmins of that village, as well as solo concert dances performed by men or women in this style.

The village of Kuchipudi was granted in perpetuity to Hindu actor-devotees by Abdul Husan Qutab Shah, the Muslim Nawab of Golconda, sometime between 1672 and 1687. As early as 1505–9, the Brahmin artists had performed before King Vira Narasimha Raya of the Vijayanagar Empire. Some authorities claim *kuchipudi* began even before this because it is similar to *bharata natyam*, the oldest surviving form of Indian classical dance. In the 17th century Siddhendra Yogi, called the father of *kuchipudi*, composed important dance dramas for players and required all male Brahmins of Kuchipudi village to take an oath to perform the role of Satyabhama, Krishna's jealous wife, in his drama *Bhamakalapam*, at least once during their lifetime. The practice continues today and the Brahmin men and boys of Kuchipudi village who practise the art are the direct descendants of ancestors who received Siddhendra Yogi's instruction three centuries ago.

Kuchipudi is the best-known 'classical' form of dance drama in the Telugu language. Like BHAGAVATA MELA, its plays deal with the incarnations of the god Vishnu. The following dance dramas are part of the *kuchipudi* repertory: *Prahlad Charitram*, *Usha Parinayam*, *Sashirekha Parinayam*, *Mohini Rukmangada*, *Harishchandra Nataka*, *Gayopakhyanam*, *Rama Natakam* and *Rukmini Kalyanam*. The dramas *Bhamakalapam* and *Gollakalapam* have become so popular that they are now regarded as separate performance forms (see BHAMAKALAPAM, GOLLAKALAPAM).

Kuchipudi performance style is similar to *bhagavata mela* but is executed with more sophistication and more attention to the classical hand gestures (*hasta*) described in the *Natyasastra*. *Kuchipudi* performers exhibit considerable feats of physical skill, executing intricate foot work and using difficult hand gestures while dancing on the sharp edge of a metal plate with a round-bottomed water pot balanced on their heads.

Kuchipudi performers tour constantly. Usually the troupe improvises an acting area in an open space before a temple, such as the Ramalingeshwara Temple of Kuchipudi village. Four poles are firmly planted at the corners of the playing area and a thatched roof is stretched overhead. The spectators sit around the area and witness performances through the night. A curtain is used for entrances of characters and illumination is provided by torches fed by castor oil and held by village washermen. Resin powder is thrown on the torches to produce spectacular flashes of light which accentuate the entrances of important characters.

The performance begins with a prayer to the goddess Amba. Following this, a young boy enters carrying the flagstaff (*jarjara*) of Indra. Then the lamp and incense are carried on and a dancer performs sacrifices. Another dancer, carrying a pitcher of sacred water, sprinkles and sanctifies the acting area. The stage manager (*sutradhara*) enters carrying a crooked stick and announces the title of the play. He joins the musicians and then he accompanies them by playing cymbals during the performance. These sacrifices and preliminaries are in direct imitation of practices described in the *Natyasastra* that are some two millennia old.

Stage attendants hold a curtain behind which a dancer enters wearing a mask of Ganapati, the elephant-headed god of good fortune. The curtain is removed and a dance follows. The curtain is brought forward once again and the chief character performs an elaborate dance entrance using the curtain to tease the audience. Eventually he tosses it aside and is fully exposed to the waiting spectators. Special dances (*patra pravesha daru*) follow, some emphasizing abstract form and style, and some requiring elaborate gesture-language coordinated with the precise meaning of the songs. Songs and dances form part of major scenes in the play being performed, adding variety and emphasizing dramatic moments. Humorous and witty remarks are also interspersed in Telugu, which is the regional language.

Music in classical Karnatic style is played on instruments such as the *mridangam* drum, the violin played in the south Indian manner, transverse bamboo flute, *tutti*, brass cymbals and harmonium.

Rich costumes and ornaments are characteristic. Occasionally, artists attempt to incorporate wing-and-drop settings, but traditionally performance takes place without scenery and properties, allowing for total focus on the performers and permitting the free play of the spectator's imagination. Should a particular performer excel, he is rewarded with necklaces of fresh flowers. Enthusiastic spectators will stop the dramatic action to honour a favourite artist.

On the concert stage, dances adapted from the dance-drama repertory are now performed as solo items. Master-teachers have also choreographed new items using themes from a variety of sources while retaining the fundamental characteristics of the form.

Owing to its popular reputation as a branch of classical Indian dance, few members of urban audiences are aware that *kuchipudi* is still practised as a full-scale dramatic performance in the villages of Andhra Pradesh. Nor are they aware of *kuchipudi*'s close association with the religious convictions of rural performers and the RITUAL significance of the dance drama in village life.   FaR

Kugel, Aleksandr (Rafailovich) [Homo Novus] 1864–1928 Russian literary and theatrical critic (under his pseudonym), editor of the influential journal *Theatre and Art* (1897–1918), member of the directorate of St Petersburg's Theatrical Club (1908); and dramatist and co-founder, with his wife Z. V. Kholmskaya, of the Crooked Mirror Theatre, where he served as director and *de facto* spokesman (1908–28). A knowledgeable man with strong opinions, Kugel argued in his articles and editorials for an actor's theatre to counter the directorial dominance of MEYERHOLD and EVREINOV and the 'anarchic individualism' of the new dramatists. Although he at first criticized MOSCOW ART THEATRE REALISM and embraced the primitivist trend of his day, supporting in theory if not always in practice Evreinov's experiments at the Ancient Theatre, and although he hired Evreinov to become artistic director at the Crooked Mirror (1910), he was opposed to extremism in the arts. Evreinov later hired Kugel to help stage the grotesque buffoonery of the bourgeoisie and the provisional government in the Soviet mass spectacle *The Storming of the Winter Palace* (1920). After 1920 Kugel briefly headed the Petrograd People's Theatre, which during his tenure produced historical plays; and he published

some notable books, including *Affirmation of the Theatre* (1923), *Literary Reminiscences* (1923), *Theatrical Portraits* (1923), *Shadows of the Theatre* (1926), *Leaves from Trees* (1926), *Profiles of the Theatre* (1929) and *Russian Dramatists* (1933).   SG

Kukolnik, Nestor (Vasilievich) 1809–68 Perhaps the best-known Russian reactionary romanticist writer of patriotic historical plays during the reign of Tsar Nikolai I. His contemporary, dramatist-critic F. A. Koni, likened Kukolnik to ALEXANDRE DUMAS *père*, who relied on 'over-involved plots, affectation, historical coloration, interpolated scenes and horrible theatrical effects'. His characters are unchanging declamatory figures who deliver themselves of rhetorical eulogies of king, country and the good old days. Nevertheless, they served as colourful starring vehicles for two of the great actors of Kukolnik's day, V. A. KARATYGIN and PAVEL MOCHALOV. Kukolnik's most famous blank verse historical epic was *The Hand of the Almighty Has Saved the Fatherland* (1833), set during the election of the first Romanov to the throne (1613) and given an elaborate staging for its monarchist sympathies. Critical and popular response to this play became an acid test of loyalty to the state, and it was revived even in the succeeding reign, to reawaken patriotic feeling. The title and its author have become synonymous in the annals of Russian drama with artist compliance to state demands. Kukolnik's other historical plays with Russian settings and themes include *Prince Mikhail Vasilievich Skopin-Shuisky* (1835), *Ivan Ryabov* and *Archangel Fisherman* (1839) and *Prince Daniil Vasilievich Kholmsky* (1841). At the same time, Kukolnik composed a series of dramatic verse 'fantasies', most notably *Torquato Tasso* (1833) and *Giulio Mosti* (1833), which treated the theme of the suffering artist with which he perhaps could, or at least imagined he could, identify.   SG

Kummer [*née* Beecher]**, Clare (Rodman)** ?1873–1958 Prolific American writer who created a BROADWAY play almost annually, beginning with her greatest hit, *Good Gracious Annabelle!* (1916). In addition to several original plays – such as *Be Calm, Camilla* (1918), *A Successful Calamity* (1917, written as a vehicle for WILLIAM GILLETTE), *Rollo's Wild Oat* (1920), *Pomeroy's Past* (1926) and *Her Master's Voice* (1933) – she also successfully adapted foreign plays and wrote a FLORENZ ZIEGFELD adaptation of *Annabelle!* called *Annie, Dear*. Although her plays were criticized for their weak plots and contrived situations, audiences enjoyed her humorous dialogue and her pleasant, rather eccentric characters.   FB

kundhei nata see GOPALILA; SAKHI KUNDHEI

kunqu Early Chinese musical style which gave rise to a theatre genre of the same name. *Kunqu* originated in the Kunshan area dominated by the town of Suzhou in Jiangsu province. The singer-composer WEI LIANGFU and his collaborators transformed the original music into a more refined and sophisticated style by drawing upon other current southern regional modes. Liang Chenyu, who had worked with Wei, composed *Washing the Silk Yarn* (*Huansha ji*), widely acclaimed as the debut of this literary-musical genre. Early developments in stage performance became manifest in two schools of thought concerning dramatic composition. One led by Shen Jing (1553–1610), a theorist first and playwright second, sought to codify a theory of prosody in relation to rhyme, tone and their correlation with the sung text. The second was dominated by playwright TANG XIANZU who advocated poetic licence and free rein to the imagination at the expense of rigid musical theory. *Kunqu* became the preoccupation of scholarly writers during the 17th and 18th centuries.

In its elemental form *kunqu* is performed as chamber music accompanied by a seven-holed horizontal bamboo flute (*dizi*), wooden clappers and a small hardwood drum slung on a tripod. On stage, stringed and percussion instruments are added and singing is synthesized with dance, gesture, song and speech. Monody and monologue are common devices. The pitches of the seven-holed flute, a key instrument in *kunqu*, set the tonics for keys and modalities which animate the versification and general structure of a play. Solo song passages are characterized by extremely intricate ornamentation and lengthy melismatic effects. Dance movements have great fluency of line extended through airy control of sleeve movements. Plays emphasize romantic love.

Kunqu began to lose ground in the late 18th century and by the end of the 19th century it had been superseded in popularity by the more robust theatricality of PIHUANG-

style theatre, which nonetheless drew upon the older form. Some revival of *kunqu* has been seen in this century. In the 1920s a school was set up in Shanghai that produced talented performers, some of whom are teachers today. Excellent young performers have been trained since 1961 at the Shanghai School of Dramatic Art under the leadership of YU ZHENFEI. *Kunqu* troupes have performed in the United States and Europe on several occasions, their repertoire including the widely acclaimed fusion production, *Kunqu Macbeth* (1987).   ACS

See: E. Henry, *Chinese Amusement, The Lively Plays of Li Yü*, Hamden, Conn., 1980; J. Huang Hung, *Ming Drama*, Taipei, 1966.

Kunst, Johann (Christian) (d.1703) A leading German actor-director of his time who was approached in 1701 by an emissary of Peter the Great to found the first national public theatre in Moscow as part of the Tsar's overall cultural programme. Accepting the charge in 1702, Kunst and a company of seven German actors undertook the training of Russian performers and presented three comedies at the palace of General Lefort in Moscow's foreign quarter. Before a separate wooden theatre in Moscow's Red Square facing the Kremlin could be completed for the company, Kunst died. He was succeeded by another German, Otto Fürst, who continued to draw upon the native population for actors. On 31 May 1706 the compa-

Entrance of Ravana, centre, the demon king of Lanka, with his minister (right) and charioteer (left), in a *kutiyattam* version of a Sanskrit play.

ny, which since its conception had encountered some opposition, was disbanded; and the theatre itself was dismantled because of obstreperous behaviour on the part of the audience and the performers. The theatre's failure has been attributed to the absence of Russian plays in its repertoire and of a literary language into which foreign plays could be translated. The 450-seat theatre averaged 25 admissions per performance. SG

kuravanji [*kuram; kuluva natakam*] Indian theatre form: literally, the 'dances' (*anji*) of the Kurava people, a nomadic clan of hunters who inhabit the hilly regions of Andhra Pradesh, whose women are said to be excellent fortune tellers. *Kuravanji* originated in the 17th century, perhaps as an offshoot of dance and song entertainments presented at holy shrines in Andhra Pradesh by bands of actors during festival seasons.

Performances in Tamil Nadu state begin with a procession in praise of Sri Vighneswara, the elephant-headed god. Then the clown (*kattiakaran*, also a character in *THERUKOOTHU*) announces the gist of the story to be enacted. During the proceedings, the heroine appears with her maids and, after being announced, she dances to depict her yearnings and sufferings. Her companions, usually spritely maidens, tease her as she tries to persuade them to convey her love messages. She implores the clouds, the wind, birds and the moon to act as intermediaries, but to no avail. The lover she is pining for never makes an appearance in any of the plays. Then a gypsy woman (*kuratthi*) appears and boasts of her expertise. At the request of the young heroine she reads her palm. The heroine denies that she is in love but eventually admits that she is. The gypsy is richly rewarded for her efforts. Then a hunter (*kurava*) enters the scene in search of his wife, the gypsy. She accuses him of infidelity but he convinces her of his innocence. The play comes to a happy conclusion.

The form has been used for modern stories as well. Maharaja Serfoji II (1798-1833) taught students world geography through *kuravanji*: the gypsy's song and dance presented the scientific material in an entertaining way. S. D. S. Yogi, a distinguished contemporary poet of Tamil Nadu state, recently composed a *kuravanji* entitled *Bhavani*, centring on the gifts of the river Bhavani after the construction of a dam. FAR

Kurbas, Aleksandr (Stepanovich) [Les] 1887-1937 Ukrainian actor and director who sought to move his native theatre away from conservative ethnographic REALISM and 'star'-driven production towards European-influenced (REINHARDT, CRAIG, FUCHS) stylization and ensemble and socialist political awareness. Educated in the relatively free Western Ukraine and at the University of Vienna, Kurbas worked at the prestigious Ruska Besida and Sadovsky Theatres (1910, 1916) in Kiev before organizing that city's Young Theatre (1917-19), where he staged European classics and contemporary plays in Ukrainian. In 1922, the Young Theatre became the Berezil [the month of March in Ukrainian] Artistic Association, which Kurbas directed until 1933, organizing six studios for the technical training and humanistic education of the new 'universal' actor. The Berezil, with leading actors Amvrosy Buchma, Natalia Uzhvi and Gnat Yura, produced AGIT-

PROP MIME-dramas (*Ruhr, October*) and expressionist (see EXPRESSIONISM) plays (KAISER's *Gas I*; a stage adaptation of Upton Sinclair's socialist novel *Jimmie Higgins*, 1923), which featured proto-BRECHTian 'transformed gesture', PISCATOR-like scene titles projected on screens and interwoven stage and film action, MEYERHOLDian *prozodezhda* (uniform costuming) and human machines constructed from group movement. Kurbas's tragi-farcical staging of *Macbeth* concluded with the crowning and stabbing of a 'line of kings'. His 1928 staging of Ukrainian playwright Mikola Kulish's *The People's Malakhy*, about a would-be reformer who is declared insane, foreshadowed Kurbas's arrest (1934) and execution for 'formalism'. He was belatedly credited with conceiving the SERGEI RADLOV-directed *mise en scène* for *King Lear* at the Moscow State Jewish Theatre (1935). SG

Kushner, Tony 1957- American playwright, brought up in Louisiana, and a graduate of Columbia with a graduate degree from New York University. Although Kushner is the author of only one major play ('a gay fantasia on national themes'), the two-part *Angels in America* (*Part One: The Millennium Approaches*; *Part Two: Perestroika*), no American playwright of the past twenty years has received as much attention for a work as he has. More significantly, his work marked a possible new direction for BROADWAY, what the *New York Times* termed a sign of a 'youthquake waiting to happen'. *Part One*, which began its development as result of a commission by San Francisco's Eureka Theatre's former director, Oskar Eustis, in 1987, received all major awards after its 1992 opening in New York (directed by GEORGE C. WOLFE), including the Tony (it received the most nominations in history), and the Drama Critics' Circle and Drama Desk Awards for Best Play. Its earlier productions in London (at the Royal NATIONAL THEATRE, directed by Declan Donnellan (see CHEEK BY JOWL)), and Los Angeles (the Mark Taper Forum, directed by Eustis), where a version of both parts was staged, also received accolades, including the 1992 London Critics' Circle Award as Best Play and for the L.A. production the Pulitzer Prize for Drama (the first gay-centred play to be so honoured). This daring play, focusing on three households in turmoil, also deals with the politics of sexuality, and through the central character of the historical figure, lawyer Roy Cohn (in a critically acclaimed, Tony-winning performance by Ron Leibman), who died of AIDS while denying his homosexuality to his deathbed, it also deals with power ('power *is* sex'). *Part Two* joined the earlier play in repertory on Broadway in autumn 1993. Kushner is also the author of *A Bright Room Called Day* (1985), *Slavs* (1993/4, from material not used in part two of *Angels*), and adaptations of CORNEILLE's *L'Illusion comique* (*The Illusion*), *The Good Person of Setzuan* and *The Dybbuk*. DBW

kutiyattam Perhaps INDIA's oldest continuously performed theatre form, and one of the few surviving art forms of the ancient world. *Kutiyattam* is unique to the state of Kerala, a lush tropical region located on the southwestern coast of the Indian subcontinent. As early as the 10th century, *kutiyattam* seems to have been 'reformed' by King Kulashekara Varman. A high stage of development, at this early point in its history, suggests an origin linking it with the traditions of ancient Sanskrit theatre.

Kutiyattam preserves a tradition of performing plays in Sanskrit, the classical language. Plays by well known playwrights of ancient drama – Bhasa, Harsha and Mahendra Vikrama Pallava – are popular in the *kutiyattam* repertory. In addition to using Sanskrit, actors use the Prakrit language and an old form of Malayalam, the regional language of Kerala, to convey the contents of the plays, much as ancient actors are thought to have used various regional dialects in their performances.

The artists who have preserved this unique theatre form with such dedication over ten centuries are members of the Cakyar caste, a sub-branch of temple servants. Traditionally, it has been their duty to perform *kutiyattam* as a RITUAL sacrifice to the chief deity in selected temples and to entertain the spectators who assemble there to pay their homage. Musicians who play the *mizhavu*, a large pot-shaped drum peculiar to *kutiyattam*, are traditionally of the Nambiyar communities, while women of the same social group, the Nangyar, act female roles, as well as play the small bell-metal cymbals which sustain the basic tempo of production. Today members of other castes may study *kutiyattam* and appear on stage. Members of other castes may not act in temple performances, however, because that would violate agreements made between temple authorities and the hereditary caste artists.

Kutiyattam has developed the only permanent traditional theatre structures (*kuttampalam*) in India. About nine theatres have been built in various temples in Kerala since the 16th century, the largest and most impressive in Vatukumnathan Temple in Trichur. The interior of this impressive structure is about 72 x 55ft and, like all existing structures, it is rectangular in shape. According to traditional practice, the theatre building is a separate structure located in the walled compound of the temple and situated in front and to the right of the main shrine. From the solid base of the building, pillars support a high central roof. The stage of the Vatakumnathan Temple is a large, square, raised, stone platform, the front edge of which divides the whole structure in half. Clusters of three pillars extend upward from each of the four corners of the stage to support an interior roof reminiscent of those used for NŌ stages in Japan. A back wall separates the dressing room from the stage. A narrow door in the wall upstage left is used for entrances and a door upstage right is reserved for exits. Downstage, between the doors, the large pot-shaped drums are suspended in heavy wooden stands. The surface of the stage, in all but a few of the theatres, is convex which allows easy drainage of the stage after washing. Intricate wooden carvings of decorative floral motifs, deities and mythological characters are all but unseen to the spectators who watch the performance under the flickering but weak light of a large bell-metal lamp placed downstage centre.

A typical *kutiyattam* performance extends over a period of several days. During the first few days, the characters in the play are introduced to the audience and historical incidents about them are explored in considerable detail. On the final day of the performance the entire action of the play is performed in chronological order from beginning to end, just as it was written. Performance begins around 9 p.m., after the final rituals have been performed before the deity in the *sanctum sanctorum* of the temple. Segments of the performance finish between midnight and 3 a.m., just before the morning rituals are performed in the *sanctum*. On the last day the performance lasts until 5 or 6 a.m.

Elaborately dressed actors with fantastical make-up and headdresses perform the various roles of mythological characters, gods and demons. They use an elaborate code of gesture-language, chanted speech and exaggerated facial and eye expressions. Much of the action is accompanied by the *mizhavu* drums, small bell-metal cymbals, a small hourglass-shaped drum (*idakka*), a wind instrument resembling an oboe (*kuzhal*) and a conch shell (*sankha*).

Ritual actions occur before and during performances, reflecting the sacred character of performance and the great respect for religion shown by the actors. Ancient manuals of instruction are consulted by the actors in order to ensure that correct procedures are followed.

Kutiyattam is performed once a year at Vatukumnathan Temple and nearby Irinjalagauda Temple. Other temple performances are rare owing to the decline in interest and the fluctuating fortunes of the large temple complexes. Measures have been taken by the state and national government and private institutions and individuals to support *kutiyattam* through performances in theatres outside the temple compounds, in various towns and cities in Kerala and elsewhere in India, as well as tours to Western countries, where non-Hindus may see performances of this ancient art form.

Instruction in the art is provided in Kerala at three schools – the famous Kerala Kalamandalam in Cheruthuruthy village, a school run by Madhavan Cakyar at Irinjalagauda and that run by Margi in the capital city of Trivandrum. Although much effort has been made to bring local, national and international attention to *kutiyattam*, its importance to the history of theatre has still not been fully realized in India or outside the country.   FAR

Kuwait see MIDDLE EAST

Kuzmin, Mikhail (Alekseevich) 1875–1936 Dandyish, decadent aesthete, Russian symbolist (see SYMBOLISM) and later acmeist (clarist) poet, prose writer, composer and dramatist, who played a diverse and significant role on the CABARET and the 'theatre of small forms' scene in pre-revolutionary St Petersburg. Educated in music by Rimsky-Korsakov, well travelled, an avowed homosexual and a supreme ironist, Kuzmin embodied many of the ideas and tendencies of his day: a transcendental-sensual aesthetic; an attraction to paradox and taboo, exoticism and eroticism; a sense of life as tragic *balagan* (puppet show) and self-created work, and of theatricalist art and of art as festive, transformative RITUAL. His period of major output, 1907–21, includes contributions to the symbolist journal, the *Scales* (1904–9); unofficial membership of VYACHESLAV IVANOV's Tower apartment literary circle (1905–7); controversial poetry and prose on homosexual themes – *Wings* (a novella, 1907), 'Alexandrian Songs' (poem cycle, in *Nets*, 1908), *Lakes in Autumn* (poetry collection, 1912); and his multi-faceted work in the theatre.

This last category includes early attempts to realize a Wagnerian *Gesamtkunstwerk* combining music, dance, poetry and the visual arts, galvanized by World of Art aestheticism; an epic quest-for-truth play, the 'dramatic poem' *The History of the Knight d'Alessio* (his first published work, 1905); music for MEYERHOLD's production of BLOK's *Puppet Show* (1906), which influenced Kuzmin's thinking about puppet theatre; numerous *divertissements* – pantomimes, OPERETTAS, comic OPERAS, mimic and mythological ballets, children's plays, puppet shows, pastorales and masquerades, some written for Meyerhold's 'Doctor Dapertutto' experiments around St Petersburg (c.1910) and others for the Stray Dog cabaret; three lyrical 'mysteries', which are variants on the voguish harlot–saint theme – *The Comedy of Alexis, Man of God, the Comedy of Eudoxia of Heliopolis*, which Blok called the most perfect Russian lyrical drama, and *The Comedy of Martinian* (1908); and his major play, *The Venetian Madcaps* (1912; produced 1914), a dark *COMMEDIA* piece on a temptress's destruction of a male friendship, possibly influenced by Meyerhold's production of LERMONTOV's *Masquerade* (1911) for which Kuzmin composed the original music. Despite the appealing theatricality of his plays, and even though Meyerhold named him one of the dramatists who had created the 'new theatre' in Russia (1911), Kuzmin continues to be known primarily as a poet.   SG

Kyd, Thomas 1558–94 English playwright, remembered for a single masterpiece, *The Spanish Tragedy* (c.1589). The details of Kyd's life are obscure, and even his authorship of this immensely popular play is in some doubt. His association with MARLOWE seems to have led to his arrest for heresy in 1593, and he died not long after his release from torture and imprisonment. *The Spanish Tragedy* adapted several features of SENECAN tragedy for the more visual taste of the Elizabethan stage. It was a primary influence in the development of REVENGE TRAGEDY, but it is far too good a play to be thought of primarily as a predecessor of *Hamlet*. Kyd's other known play, *Cornelia* (c.1594), is a version from the French of ROBERT GARNIER, and the ascription to him of a lost *Hamlet*, used as a source by SHAKESPEARE, is the product of scholarly speculation. PT

Kynaston, Ned [Edward] c.1640–1706 English boy actor, who specialized in women's roles – probably the last of his profession. He was a favourite on the Restoration stage and, after he had grown beyond female portrayal, played effectively in other roles.   MB

kyōgen Traditional Japanese theatre genre consisting of a repertory of some 260 short plays, celebratory and usually comic, that are performed by specialist *kyōgen* actors on a NŌ stage normally as part of a joint *nō–kyōgen* programme. *Kyōgen* humour arises in part from poking fun at human foibles – greed, lust, chicanery, cowardice. Characters are not idealized as they are in *nō* but rather their social weaknesses are shown – a priest is ignorant or useless (*Mushrooms, The Crow*), a wife domineering (*Fortified Beard*), a servant dishonest (*Poison Sugar*), a

A modern *kyōgen* comedy, but performed on a traditional nō stage and using traditional movements.

demon witless (*Head-pulling, Spring Evening*). Humour also arises from punning, onomatopoeia, and physical action. Plays such as *Monkey Quiver* begin seriously – a lord plans to kill a pet monkey to make a quiver from its hide – but conclude in felicitous celebration. Reflecting Shintō beliefs, *kyōgen* plays are fundamentally joyous and affirm the goodness of the natural order.

Language is vernacular prose of the 15th and 16th centuries and easily understood by today's audiences. Actors perform with a high energy level in controlled, clearly articulated vocal and movement patterns which, while stylized, are derived from daily speech and actions. *Kyōgen* is one of the few traditional theatre genres in Asia that is unaccompanied by music. A character may urge a companion 'let's sing a song together' at a play's climax, thus lifting the characters out of their particular, plebeian circumstances and transporting them into a universal state, described by Sakaba as 'rapture'. A handful of plays contain dances accompanied by a *nō*-style musical ensemble (*hayashi*) and a chorus (*ji*). MASKS

are worn for animals and special characters, but usually the actor performs without mask or make-up. Costume is based on the real clothing people wore in medieval times and is plain in comparison with the gorgeous and expensive silk brocades worn in *nō*. Tarōkaja, the stock servant character, wears a large-checked underkimono, sleeveless vest, bold-patterned bloused trousers and yellow socks. A landowner is identified by trailing trousers and sword.

Major acting families are the NOMURA and Miyake families within the Izumi school (*ryū*) of *kyōgen* and the Yamamoto, Shigeyama and Zenchiku families within the Ōkura school. Most actors live in Tokyo, Kyoto and Nagoya, but perform throughout the country.   JRB

See: D. Kenny, *A Guide to Kyogen*, Tokyo, 1968, and (comp.), *The Kyogen Book: An Anthology of Japanese Classical Comedies*, Tokyo, 1989; R. N. McKinnon (tr.), *Selected Plays of Kyogen*, Tokyo, 1968; S. Sakanishi, *Japanese Folk Plays: The Ink-Smeared Lady and Other Kyogen*, Rutland, Vt., 1960 (1938).

La Chaussée, Pierre-Claude Nivelle de 1692–1754 French dramatist and man of letters, who after a life of dissipation turned to producing edifying material for the theatre. Although he wrote other plays, he was most successful in his day and is still associated above all with his *comédies larmoyantes*, tearful comedies in which the influence of the contemporary sentimental novel is manifest. In them pathos is all-pervading, to the virtual exclusion of comic elements, and the audience are invited to sympathize with the domestic misfortunes and agonies of their recognizable counterparts on stage, particularly in the field of conjugal relations. While the proposed moral uplift is estimable enough, the emotions tapped are disproportionate to the situations created, characterization is woefully simplistic and tears have to be jerked by rhetorical artifice and stock theatrical devices. *Mélanide* (1741) is commonly regarded as his best play, but two others on the subject of unhappy marriage, *La Fausse Antipathie* (*The False Antipathy*, 1733) and *Le Préjugé à la mode* (*The Fashionable Prejudice*, 1735), are worthy of note, as is his adaptation of Richardson's novel, *Paméla* (1743). They were widely translated in their day, and as symptoms of 18th-century sensibility and forerunners of the *drame bourgeois* or fully fledged domestic drama they retain a precise historical value. La Chaussée was elected to the Académie-Française in 1736.   DR

La Grange [Charles Varlet] 1635–92 French actor, friend and devoted assistant of MOLIÈRE, whose company he joined in 1659 soon after their arrival in Paris and never left. A good-looking man of refined manners, he played the young lover in most of the repertoire, though his creation of parts like Don Juan and Acaste in *The Misanthrope* (1666) suggests that he was more than a simple *jeune premier*. In 1667 he took over from Molière as company 'orator', responsible for the formal address to the audience and announcement of the forthcoming performance. He was also its secretary and archivist and kept a daily register of all plays performed, together with a record of takings and comments on other company matters, which is an invaluable source of information. After Molière's death he was instrumental in rebuilding the company and ensuring its survival, and he became the first orator of the newly constituted COMÉDIE-FRANÇAISE in 1680. In 1682 he brought out the first collected edition of Molière's plays, to which he contributed a prefatory *Life* of the author. His wife Marie, daughter of the pastrycook-actor Cyprien Ragueneau, acted with him after their marriage in 1672.   DR

La MaMa (New York City) OFF-OFF BROADWAY theatre founded in 1962 by Ellen Stewart, a self-described Cajun who arrived penniless in New York in 1950 and became a successful fashion designer. With her earnings, she began Café La MaMa in a cramped, decrepit Manhattan basement, and moved several times before settling on East 4th Street in 1969, where the theatre now operates two large performance spaces and a CABARET. The Café became La MaMa ETC (Experimental Theatre Club), and Stewart still functions as artistic director, fund-raiser, tour manager and maternal spiritual guardian. Having produced more than 1000 plays, La MaMa introduced such American playwrights and directors as ROCHELLE OWENS, Megan Terry, Jeff Weiss, SAM SHEPARD, Harvey Fierstein, H. M. Koutoukas, LANFORD WILSON, Julie Bovasso, ADRIENNE KENNEDY and Tom O'Horgan, also presenting works by avant-garde directors RICHARD FOREMAN, MEREDITH MONK, PING CHONG, and others. In addition, La MaMa has taken to America such artists as JERZY GROTOWSKI, ANDREI SERBAN, PETER BROOK, EUGENIO BARBA and TADEUSZ KANTOR. In 1980 La MaMa established the Third World Institute of Theatre Arts and Studies (TWITAS). Through the 1980s and well into the 90s – despite dire financial problems in the early 90s – the La MaMa cabaret has provided a venue for new experimentation in COMEDY and performance art.   AS

La Rue, Danny [Daniel Patrick Carroll] 1928– British actor, born in Ireland, who has made his reputation in CABARET, PANTOMIME (*Queen Passionella and the Sleeping Beauty*, 1968) and VARIETY shows (*Danny La Rue at the Palace*, 1970) as the leading female impersonator (see FEMALE IMPERSONATION).   CI

La Taille, Jean de c.1535–c.1608 French dramatist and poet. Of his two tragedies on biblical subjects, *Saül le furieux* (*Saul Enraged*), published in 1572, and its sequel *La Famine, ou Les Gabéonites* (*The Famine*, 1573), the first is the more effective in dramatic terms and is prefaced by a treatise on the art of TRAGEDY which, in recapitulating the observations of ARISTOTLE and HORACE, stressing the importance of the three unities and condemning the presentation of violence on stage, offers a convenient résumé of the DRAMATIC THEORY of 16th-century humanist scholars. In *Les Corrivaux* (*The Rivals*, 1574) La Taille wrote the first French COMEDY in prose.   DR

Laberge, Marie 1950– Quebec playwright, actress, director and novelist. Laberge first came to national attention in 1981 with the award-winning play, *C'était avant la guerre à l'Anse à Gilles*. Sensitively depicting the inferior status of women in rural Quebec society of the 1930s, it was a striking success also in its English translation, *Before the War, Down at L'Anse à Gilles*, and won a Governor General's Award. Her eloquent, reasoned feminism pervades other notable successes, such as *L'Homme gris* (*The Tipsy Man*, 1984; published in English as *Night*, 1988), which brought her membership of France's Ordre des Arts et des Lettres after its remarkable two runs in Paris in 1986. *Jocelyne Trudelle, trouvée morte dans ses larmes* (*Jocelyne Trudelle, Discovered Dead in Her Tears*, 1986) is a haunting study of a woman's suicide. Other plays of note are *Le Night Cap Bar* (1987), featuring a murder, drug addiction and betrayal; *Oublier* (1987), first staged in Brussels and translated as *Take Care* (1988); *Aurélie, ma* *soeur* (*My Sister, Aurélie*, 1988), and *Le Faucon* (*The Falcon*, 1991). LED

Labiche, Eugène 1815–88 French dramatist. Labiche was one of the more prolific authors of the 19th century and, like many of those who saw themselves essentially as entertainers, generally worked with a collaborator, the most important of these being Marc Michel. Of his 175 plays, 57 were published in his *Complete Plays*. The majority of these are light comedies, or *vaudevilles*, but a few are more serious comedies of manners. The *vaudeville*, itself generally a one-act COMEDY with songs, was the most popular form in the 19th-century theatre. Labiche turned initially in his craft to the master of the *vaudeville*, EUGÈNE SCRIBE, but gradually transformed the genre itself into the 'French FARCE' that FEYDEAU would bring to perfection.

Labiche's heyday was the Second Empire, and his plays were written for the entertainment of the bourgeoisie of that period. This same bourgeoisie forms the basic subject-matter for all the plays, and is closely observed and constantly caricatured by Labiche in the tradition of Henri Monnier and Honoré Daumier. Labiche's career as a dramatist began in 1838, with his first real success in 1848, *Un Jeune Homme pressé* (*A Young Man in a Hurry*), for which he defined *vaudeville* as 'the art of making the girl's father, who first said no, say yes'. *An Italian Straw Hat* (1851) was one of his most popular plays (and survived into the 20th century with René Clair's classic film). A full-length play, it takes a popular device of farce and MELODRAMA, the chase, but instead of keeping it for the end of the play uses it as a leitmotif running throughout, as the hapless hero is pursued by an entire wedding party. The play abounds in wickedly accurate observations of the bourgeoisie, and moves at breakneck speed from situation to situation and misunderstanding to misunderstanding.

Le Voyage de Monsieur Perrichon (*Monsieur Perrichon's Holiday*, 1860) showed a more developed sense of characterization, its hero being the epitome of the Second Empire bourgeois. Much of the action hinges on the simple psychological mechanism that we are much more grateful to those we help than to those who help us. In *Célimare le bien-aimé* (*Célimare the Beloved*, 1863), a play that seems to anticipate the work of ANOUILH, the hero causes consternation to two husbands he has cuckolded when he decides to get married. This theme of the *ménage à trois*, previously thought of more as the subject for a drama, was fully developed by Labiche in one of his last plays, *The Happiest of the Three* (1870), in which the husband is the happiest (and ultimately prefers domestic bliss with the wife's lover rather than the wife). In 1864 Labiche was accepted into the COMÉDIE-FRANÇAISE with his harsh comedy about an egotist, *I*, but this was not one of his more successful pieces. *Three Cheers for Paris* (*La Cagnotte*, 1864) is the *Italian Straw Hat* in a darker vein, bringing a group of provincials to Paris, where they experience a variety of discomforts. Labiche was admitted to the French Academy in 1880 and spent his last years on the estate purchased with the proceeds of his plays. JMCC

Labou Tansi, Sony 1947– Prolific Congolese poet, novelist, dramatist and theatre director. Born in Zaire,

Labou Tansi was an English teacher for several years, before founding in 1979, from the amateur theatre group Moni-Mambou, what has since become his country's leading theatre company: the Rocado Zulu Theatre. It is also beginning to gain an international reputation, with its regular participation in the annual Limoges Festival of Francophone Theatre in France, where some of its collective creations, produced by various French directors in collaboration with Labou Tansi himself, have been well received. But with seven plays and five novels to his name, it is as a writer that he is best known.

His plays highlight the dictatorships, the material and moral misery, that characterize post-colonial Africa. With their cohorts of corpses, hallucinatory shadows and Ubuesque characters, his plays create a grotesque world where events seem to conform to no logical pattern: *Conscience de tracteur* (*The Conscience of a Tractor*, 1979), *La Parenthèse de sang* and *Je soussigné cardiaque* (*Blood Parenthesis* and *I, the Undersigned Cardiac Patient*, 1981), *Qui a mangé Madame D'Avoine Bergotha?* (*Who Has Eaten Madame D'Avoine Bergotha?*, 1984), *Moi veuve de l'empire* (*I, Widow of the Empire*, 1987); *Antoine m'a vendu son destin* (*Antoine Sold Me His Destiny*, 1986). Among plays already performed but not yet published are his *La Rue des mouches* (*The Street of Flies*, 1985) and an adaptation of *Romeo and Juliet* produced by Migrations Culturelles Aquitaines in Bordeaux in 1990 under Guy Lenoir. JCM

Lackaye, Wilton 1862–1932 American actor, who began his professional career in 1883 as Lucentio in LAWRENCE BARRETT's revival of BOKER's *Francesca da Rimini*. During a very active career he played hundreds of roles for many managements. In 1886 he supported FANNY DAVENPORT at the Union Square Theatre, New York City. In 1906 he adapted Hugo's *Les Misérables* into the play *Law and the Man*, in which he played Jean Valjean and M. Madeleine. He is remembered, however, as the original Svengali in Du Maurier's *Trilby* (1895), which he revived frequently. A devout Catholic, he founded the Catholic Actors' Guild and assisted with the organization of the Actors' Equity Association. DBW

Lacy, James 1696–1774 English actor and manager, who began acting in 1724 but soon realized that his talents were as a theatre manager. Arrested in 1737 for attempting to evade the Licensing Act, in 1744 he joined the partnership running DRURY LANE and in 1747 persuaded GARRICK to take a half-share in the company. Drury Lane had been in severe decline, but the huge success of the Lacy–Garrick partnership enabled them to recoup their investment within four years. Lacy played a major part in the success through his great determination and good business sense, though inclined to try to lord it over Garrick. PH

Lacy, John 1615–81 English actor and playwright. Apprenticed as a dancer, he was acting in the 1630s. At the Restoration he joined WILLIAM BEESTON's company at SALISBURY COURT and then the King's Men, playing Ananias in JONSON's *The Alchemist*. He was a major shareholder in the building of the Theatre Royal in London's Bridges Street and was soon co-managing the company for

KILLIGREW with Mohun and Hart. In 1667 he was arrested for mocking the court in his role as a rustic in *The Change of Crowns*. He was a brilliant CLOWN, particularly famed as Teague, an Irish footman, in SIR ROBERT HOWARD's *The Committee*, in the title role of his own *Sauny the Scot* and as MOLIÈRE's Sganarelle. His own plays included FARCES like *The Old Troop* and adaptations of SHAKESPEARE. He was painted in three of his roles, commissioned by Charles II. PH

Lacy, Thomas Hailes 1809–73 British publisher. Beginning as an actor in 1828 in London and the provinces, Lacy turned his hand to theatre management and playwriting, but made his name as publisher of cheap dramatic texts. Lacy's Acting Edition virtually cornered the market, absorbing many of his older rivals (like John Duncombe and G. H. Davidson), to become the largest and arguably the most important theatrical publisher of the 19th century. He began publication in 1849 from 17 Wellington Street, off the Strand, London, moving in 1857 to 89 Strand, where he remained until his retirement in 1873. His business was bought by Samuel French of New York, who continued to expand the series, which under Lacy had run to 99 volumes, numbering 1458 plays.

Lacy cultivated a rather Dickensian figure: F. C. Burnand, then a youthful victim of his sometimes cavalier attitude to authors' COPYRIGHT, remembered him grubbing about in his rather grimy shop in the early 1860s. The DRAMATIC AUTHORS' SOCIETY estimated on his death that he owed authors £700 – they settled for £250 – but the acting profession at least benefited by more than £8000 in the bequest he left to the charitable Royal General Theatrical Fund, on the board of which he had served for many years. JRS

Ladipo, Duro 1931–78 Nigerian musician, dramatist and performer; a notable composer of Yoruba folk opera, and founder of the Duro Ladipo Theatre. Born in Oshogbo in what was then the Western Region of NIGERIA, Ladipo discovered his theatrical inspiration in the oral tradition of Yoruba history, and in the Oshogbo masquerades and festivals (see MASQUERADES IN AFRICA), which rubbed against the grain of his stern Christian upbringing. He established the Mbari-Mbayo Centre (1962) in Oshogbo, with a performance of his first opera *Oba Moro* (*The Ghost Catcher*, published 1964). Aided by Chief Ulli Beier and Suzanne Wenger, Mbari-Mbayo became a hothouse for young Yorubas talented in the arts, some of whom went on to achieve international fame as painters, sculptors or performers. Ladipo's most famous opera, *Oba Ko So* (*The King Did Not Hang*, 1964), concerns the religio-mythic figure of Sango, god of lightning in the Yoruba pantheon. The opera, with Ladipo as Sango, remained in the repertory of his company for more than 12 years and was performed in many parts of the world, always with great success. Other operas which appealed to Yoruba audiences and achieved critical acclaim were *Oba Waja* (*The King Is Dead*), based on an incident in Nigeria's colonial period when a British district officer tried to stop a sacred ritual suicide; *Moremi*, based on the legend of a Yoruba woman who allowed herself to be captured so that she might learn the secret of the success of her people's enemy; and *Eda*, his

adaptation of HOFMANNSTHAL's *Jedermann* (*Everyman*). Ladipo also composed sketches for television, and made a series, *Bode Wasinmi*. He was a gifted musician; and this talent was enhanced by a strong visual sensibility. His work derived from Yoruba history, and indeed his art was more concerned with a specifically Yoruba aesthetic, as part of a wider Nigerian theatre aesthetic. His early death was a tragedy for Nigerian theatre. CD

Lafayette Players 1915–32 African-American STOCK COMPANY, organized by actress Anita Bush to provide dramatic entertainment for the Harlem community in place of VAUDEVILLE and MINSTREL SHOWS that often ridiculed blacks. On a weekly schedule the company presented at the Lafayette Theatre in Harlem at 132nd Street and Seventh Avenue (during 1935–9, home for the Negro Theatre Unit of the New York City FEDERAL THEATRE PROJECT) abridged versions of popular BROADWAY comedies and melodramas, hoping to demonstrate that black actors could play dramatic roles as well as song-and-dance clowns. As these productions gained popular support, the Players formed road companies for touring. In 1928 they moved to Los Angeles, where they played successfully to mixed audiences. Overall, they compiled a production record of 250 plays over 17 years before becoming a casualty of the Depression. Among well recognized players are CHARLES GILPIN, Clarence Muse, 'Dooley' Wilson, Inez Clough, Evelyn Ellis and Abbie Mitchell. EGH

Lagerkvist, Pär 1891–1974 Swedish playwright, novelist and poet, winner of the 1951 Nobel Prize for Literature. Best-known in the English-speaking world as a novelist, Lagerkvist was also recognized in Scandinavia as an innovative dramatist who relentlessly explored new dramatic forms. His concern with form was proclaimed in his essay 'Modern Theatre: Points of View and Attack' (1918), in which he dismissed NATURALISM (especially IBSEN's plays) as untheatrical and applauded the theatricalism of STRINDBERG's later plays. His own plays are exploratory variations on a central theme, that of evil as an abstract force in life and as an irrepressible instinct in the individual mind. His early plays, especially the one-act trilogy *The Difficult Hour* (1918) and the short *The Secret of Heaven* (1919), are grotesque expressionistic fantasies (see EXPRESSIONISM), showing humanity trapped within and poisoned by a meaningless, ferocious world. In the 1920s his faith in humanity seemed to increase, as in *He Who Lived His Life Over* (1928), but with the rise of Fascism in the 1930s his plays focused with increasing urgency on the dangerous religion of brutality, often contrasting it with some feminine figure representing motherly protection. Certainly, his most forceful and imaginative play of the period was *The Hangman* (1933), given productions all over Scandinavia by PER LINDBERG, Lagerkvist's most understanding director. His most popular play in the theatre was his most accessible, the moral parable *The Philosopher's Stone* (1947), which uses the story of a medieval alchemist to examine the complexities of faith. HL

Lahr, Bert [Irving Lahrheim] 1895–1967 American comic actor. After an apprenticeship in juvenile VAUDE-

VILLE acts, Lahr broke into BURLESQUE as a Dutch comedian. His first feature part, a punch-drunk fighter in *Hold Everything* (1928), won him critical acclaim and starring roles in musical comedies: *Flying High* (1930), *Hot-Cha!* (1932) and *The Show Is On* (1936). Lahr's stock-in-trade included a grimace like that 'of a camel with acute gastric disorder' and a laryngeal bleat 'like a lovesick ram'. His style was too broad for film, although he is immortalized as the Cowardly Lion in *The Wizard of Oz* (1938). He returned to BROADWAY in *Du Barry Was a Lady* (1939). Lahr considered the turning point in his career to be Estragon in *Waiting for Godot* (1956), an association with the avant-garde that brought him roles in SHAW, MOLIÈRE and SHAKESPEARE (Bottom). He enlivened five roles in S. J. PERELMAN's *The Beauty Part* (1962). Lahr never retired but died during the shooting of *The Night They Raided Minsky's*. LS

Lahr, John 1941– American drama critic and author. Born in Los Angeles, Lahr studied at Yale and Oxford Universities. He worked as a dramaturg for the GUTHRIE THEATRE (1968) and for the Repertory Theatre of Lincoln Center (1969–71; see VIVIAN BEAUMONT AND MITZI E. NEWHOUSE THEATRES). He has served as contributing editor of *Evergreen Review*, theatre editor of Grove Press, drama critic of the *Village Voice* and, since 1992, of the *New Yorker*. Lahr asks that theatre be socially responsible and forge new images to 'revitalize the imaginative life of its audience'. Such theatre, he feels, must be 'shocking, violent, and unpredictable'. He is the author of 15 books, including a masterful biography of his father, comedian BERT LAHR (*Notes on a Cowardly Lion*) and a biography of playwright Joe Orton, *Prick Up Your Ears* (1978). His stage version of *The Manchurian Candidate* (updated to 1996) premiered at London's LYRIC THEATRE, HAMMERSMITH, in 1991 and was first seen in the USA in 1994. TLM

Lamarche, Gustave 1895–1987 French Canadian playwright, director and poet; Catholic priest. Lamarche's collected works comprise 34 plays in six volumes. In the 1930s and 40s the plays which he wrote and directed, generally staged outdoors, attracted huge crowds, sometimes estimated at more than 100,000 for a single performance. They are vast pageant plays, medieval in format and inspiration (see MEDIEVAL DRAMA IN EUROPE), usually based on biblical themes. Best-known are *Jonathas* (1935), *La Défaite de l'Enfer* (*Hell Defeated*, 1938), *Notre-Dame-des-Neiges* (*Our Lady of the Snows*, 1942) and *Notre-Dame-de-la-Couronne* (*Our Lady of the Crown*, 1947). In conjunction with Father ÉMILE LEGAULT, Lamarche succeeded in making theatre, long suspect to the Catholic Church in Quebec, a respectable and worthwhile occupation. LED

Lamb, Charles 1775–1834 English essayist and critic, a long-term employee of the East India Company and an inveterate theatregoer. He included many theatrical subjects in his *Essays of Elia*, helping in particular to preserve the memory of JOSEPH MUNDEN, ROBERT ELLISTON and FANNY KELLY, for whom he cherished an unrequited love. His influential *Specimens of English Dramatic Poets who Lived about the Time of Shakespeare* (1808) raised awareness of the great age of English drama, and the *Tales from Shakespeare* (1807), written with his sister Mary, was a children's classic. Lamb was far from being the gentle angel of posthumous portraits, though he is rightly admired for his lifelong protection of his brilliant but unbalanced sister. His theatrical CRITICISM was robust. He was, for example, a vigorous opponent of the greedy taste for vast theatres, in which broad effects ousted subtlety and which he considered inappropriate for the performance of SHAKESPEARE's plays. When his own FARCE, *Mr H — —* (1806), was hissed off the DRURY LANE stage, he covered his chagrin by joining in the hissing. He was the author also of a remorse-laden TRAGEDY, *John Woodvil* (published 1802), which JOHN PHILIP KEMBLE declined to present, though it is no worse than some that he did. PT

Lang, Matheson 1879–1948 British actor-manager, born in Canada. Lang toured in F. R. BENSON's company and with LILLIE LANGTRY and ELLEN TERRY, before appearing in GRANVILLE BARKER's productions of IBSEN and SHAW at the ROYAL COURT THEATRE. From 1910 he toured Australia and South Africa and India with his own company, until 1913 when he returned to London in the title role of *Mr Wu* – a melodramatic part he became identified with, which he revived repeatedly all over the world – and in 1914 he directed and acted in the first SHAKESPEARE season at the OLD VIC. CI

Långbacka, Ralf 1932– Influential Finnish director, active internationally, especially in SWEDEN. He has worked primarily within institutional theatres, as either artistic director or guest director, but with a mission to renew their artistic and sociopolitical relevance. Långbacka was the first in Scandinavia to articulate in the 1960s and 1970s the need for *artistic theatres* of totally committed artists, rejecting outworn ideology and methods and presenting to renewed audiences coherent, purposeful repertoires dealing with fundamental issues; he was particularly successful at Turun Kaupunginteatteri, Finland, in 1971–7 (with co-director Kalle Holmberg). In Sweden his brilliant work at GÖTEBORGS STADSTEATER in 1967–9 inspired directors like PETER OSKARSON, Lennart Hjulström, and Ragnar Lyth, and companies like FOLKTEATERN I GÖTEBORG. His productions of BRECHT, SHAKESPEARE and CHEKHOV have been especially important in revealing the contradictory forces at work in their texts. HL

Langdal, Peter 1957– Danish director. Langdal quickly became known in the mid-1980s for his boldly conceived and often wildly playful productions of classics, including SCHILLER's *The Robbers* (1984) and HOLBERG's *Erasmus Montanus* (1984) and *Jeppe of the Hill* (1986). With the frequent collaboration of scenographer Karin Betz, his productions are often visually breathtaking and make extraordinary use of space, as in *The Robbers* in Gladsaxe Teater's huge arena and SHAKESPEARE's *A Winter's Tale* (1990) in Centraltreatret, Oslo. The CLOWN has been a recurrent figure in his work, and in 1986 he and Betz inaugurated Copenhagen's former East Gasworks as a theatre with a CIRCUS-like production of *A Midsummer Night's Dream*. Langdal has worked frequently at Betty Nansen Teatret, and became its director in 1992. HL

Lange, Harmut 1937– German dramatist, who escaped to the West after early work such as his ironic verse celebration of collective farming, *Marski* (1963; first performed 1968), was banned in the GDR. His best-known play *The Countess of Rathenow* (1969) attacks German traditionalism, but his characteristic style is political allegory (*Hercules*, 1968; *The Murder of Ajax*, 1971). CI

Langham, Michael 1919– English director, who began his theatre career directing *Twelfth Night* at Coventry's Midland Theatre Company (1946). In the next decade, Langham became a reputable classical director in England and Scotland, but North American work has comprised most of his career. After productions at Toronto's Crest Theatre (1955), he was appointed TYRONE GUTHRIE's successor as artistic director of the STRATFORD (Ontario) FESTIVAL in 1955. Langham enjoyed great success expanding the Festival to include touring, film and television projects, a training programme and school performances. Though praised by the critics, he was criticized often for employing too many Britons. After departing in 1968, he directed in English and American venues until 1971, when he was appointed artistic director at the GUTHRIE THEATRE, Minneapolis. Again following in his predecessor's footsteps, Langham used his Stratford techniques to pull the Guthrie from financial near-disaster. In 1979 he left to become director of drama at the Juilliard School, where he was responsible for all training and theatrical productions until 1992. Freed from this responsibility, he ventured into more freelance directing, beginning in 1993 with *Saint Joan* for the National Actors Theatre and *Love's Labour's Lost* OFF-OFF BROADWAY; then in autumn 1993, as artistic adviser of the NAT, with *Timon of Athens* and *The Government Inspector*. KN

Langner, Lawrence 1890–1962 One of the most enlightened producers in American theatre history. Langner grew up in London and studied to be a patent lawyer. In 1911 he emigrated to New York and established himself in that profession, later heading a large international firm. In 1914 he helped organize the WASHINGTON SQUARE PLAYERS and wrote several one-act plays for the group. After it disbanded because of the war (1917), he brought together members of the group in late 1918 to form the THEATRE GUILD. The most important of these was THERESA HELBURN, who together with Langner managed the organization throughout much of its active life. They pursued artistic aims and built a subscription audience of 25,000 by 1925. The success of their second production, *John Ferguson* (1919), established them artistically and commercially. Langner encouraged the production of foreign plays, including works by TOLLER, KAISER, MOLNÁR and PIRANDELLO. He obtained for the Guild SHAW's *Heartbreak House* (1919), *Back to Methuselah* (1921) and *St Joan* (1923), and he persuaded the Guild to stage O'NEILL's *Strange Interlude* (1928). With his wife, Armina Marshall (1895–1991), Langner built the Westport County Playhouse, Connecticut, in 1931 and formed an acting company. In the early 1950s he founded the AMERICAN SHAKESPEARE [THEATRE] Festival at Stratford, Connecticut. Called by BROOKS ATKINSON 'one of the most articulate men alive', Langner, whose memoirs were published in 1951, brought an able business mind to bear upon the American theatre for almost 50 years. TLM

Langtry, Lillie 1853–1929 British actress and society beauty, born in Jersey, of which her father, the Very Reverend William le Breton, was Dean. She made her London social debut in 1877, three years after her marriage to an Anglo-Irish landowner, and her theatrical debut under the BANCROFTS at the HAYMARKET in 1881, when she played Kate Hardcastle in a charity matinée performance of *She Stoops to Conquer*. Her amorous conquests had, by then, included the future Edward VII and Prince Louis of Battenberg, and her notoriety had been enhanced by Millais's portrait of her, holding a Jersey lily. It was as 'the Jersey Lily' that she continued to draw audiences in England, South Africa and, most of all, in the USA until her retirement in 1918.

At best a competent actress and a shrewd company manager, she numbered Rosalind in *As You Like It* and Lady Teazle in *The School for Scandal* among her most effective roles, but it was in SYDNEY GRUNDY's *The Degenerates* (1899) that she tempted and scandalized her public by offering glimpses of autobiographical sin in high society. Lillie Langtry was part-author, with J. Hartley Manners, of an unsuccessful play called *The Crossways* (1902). She also wrote a novel (as Lady de Bathe, her title by a second marriage), *All at Sea* (1909), and an evasive autobiography, *The Days I Knew* (1921). She died at her villa in Monte Carlo. PT

Languirand, Jacques 1931– French Canadian playwright, essayist and producer. Much influenced by the dramatists and plays encountered during his studies in Paris, 1949–51, Languirand became on his return Canada's most important exponent of the European THEATRE OF THE ABSURD. Several of his dramatic texts were performed on radio before his first stage play, *Les Insolites* (*The Unusual Ones*), was awarded the prize for best Canadian play at the Dominion Drama Festival in 1956. The same year *Le Roi ivre* (*The Drunken King*) was performed with success in Montreal, followed by his best-known work, *Les Grands Départs* (*Great Departures*), televised in 1957 and staged in 1958. Languirand continued to write and produce plays for the next dozen years, principally *Les Violons de l'automne* (*Violins of Autumn*, 1961), the multi-media *Man, Inc.* (1970) and the MUSICAL COMEDY *Klondyke* (1970), but despite performances in France and Great Britain his work had lost its appeal for Canadian audiences. Since 1970 he has abandoned the theatre in favour of philosophic essays, continuing as host of the popular radio programme, 'Par Quatre Chemins'. LED

Lansbury, Angela (Brigid) 1925– London-born actress and singer who went to the USA for a career in films, under contract to MGM (1943–50), for whom she performed mostly supporting roles. In 1957 she made her BROADWAY debut in *Hotel Paradiso*; subsequently she appeared as the mother in *A Taste of Honey* (1960). Lansbury made her MUSICAL debut as the Mayor in the ill-fated *Anyone Can Whistle* (1964) before winning the first of her four Tonys as the madcap 'Auntie Mame' Dennis in *Mame* (1966). Her other Tonys were for performances as the eccentric

Countess Aurelia in *Dear World* (1968), the compulsive Mama Rose in a revival of *Gypsy* (1974) and the maniacal Mrs Lovett in *Sweeney Todd* (1979). She brought a powerful singing voice, a flair for comedy, and a rare depth of characterization to her musical roles. An actress of considerable versatility, she has also appeared with the ROYAL SHAKESPEARE COMPANY and at the Royal NATIONAL THEATRE in London. Since the mid-1980s she has starred as a quirky and personable writer and crime buff in the popular TV series 'Murder, She Wrote'. MK

Lao She [Shu Qingchun] 1899–1966 Chinese dramatist and novelist of Manchu nationality. Born and educated in Beijing, he left for England in 1924 and taught at the London School of Oriental Studies. He lived in the United States (1946–9) and, on his return to China, wrote *HUAJU* plays and participated in literary committees and organizations under the new PRC government. His 1950 play *Dragon Beard Ditch* (*Longxu gou*) about the successful rehabilitation of a Beijing slum area earned him the title of People's Artist. In 1957 he published the highly regarded *Teahouse* (*Chaguan*), a three-act, slice-of-life naturalist drama. In it he demonstrates his knowledge and love of the old Beijing institution of the teahouse, his sensitivity to the disintegration of society in the half-century separating 1898 and 1949 and his skilful command of colloquial language. He is perhaps best known for his novel, *Camel Xiangzi*, plagiarized in English as *Rickshaw Boy*, a tragic story of corruption of the innocent. He drowned himself in 1966 following ill treatment by Red Guards during the Cultural Revolution. ACS CPM

Laos The population of this Southeast Asian country bordering on Thailand, Cambodia, Burma and Vietnam is comprised primarily of Lao peoples who are closely related to the Thai. The artistic traditions of the four million national Lao are shared by the 13 million Lao living in northern THAILAND. Three kinds of performance are important: (1) prototheatrical, indigenous forms; (2) court forms which since their 14th-century inception have emulated Khmer-Thai models; and (3) modern, popular genres created during the 20th century by combining folk forms with elements from popular Thai theatre, especially *likay*.

Prototheatrical, indigenous forms These forms can be divided into three categories according to the functions they serve: (1) storytelling; (2) courting; and (3) curing. The format of the performance and the personnel needed devolve from the function.

Sung storytelling, *lum pun*, is an old, now rare tradition in which a male chanter, accompanied by a *kaen* (bamboo panpipe) musician, sings *Jataka* (tales of Buddha's previous lives), local epics or historical tales. One popular story is the defeat of the Lao kingdom of Wiangjun by the Thai in 1827. The stories, told over one to three nights, are in *glawn*, a verse form with four lines to a stanza, seven or more syllables to a line, and using specific tones from the tonal Lao language for set words. The singer is called *mawlum* (*maw*, 'expert'; *lum*, 'melody derived from word tones'). In *lum luang* the singer acts out all the parts, changing his costume and movement for each character. Other performance forms which relate to storytelling are

an nungsu ('reading a book'), in which men read tales from palm-leaf manuscripts during wakes, and the sung recitation of *Jataka* tales or the delivery by Buddhist priests of sermons, *tet*. All are solo, male genres which tell a story.

It takes two to flirt; hence, the forms that relate to courting customs involve a male–female dialogue. *Pa-nyah* is a courting game in which boys and girls engage in a sung poetic dialogue, testing each other's wit and skill. A more theatrical form which alternates a male and female voice is the popular *lum glawn* presented at temple festivals and family celebrations. *Kaen* playing accompanies two professional singers who use memorized passages of poetry, improvising the order according to the needs of the presentation, or compose new verses in performance guided by the constraints of the poetic tradition. Performance begins about 9 p.m. with the male singer praising the beauty of the woman. It intensifies as she admits a reciprocal attraction, but fears betrayal, and concludes shortly before dawn when the pair sorrowfully part. Rhythm and musical scale as well as content of the poetry help create the different moods of the 'affair', and dance interludes (*fawn*) break up the singing. The charismatic singers may address the suggestive verses to audience members of the opposite sex, rather than their partner. Courting poems (*glawn gio*) have contributed heavily to the theatrical repertoire of *lum glawn*.

Performers customarily learn their art by studying music and poetry with a *mawlum* or a Buddhist monk. Many performers come from families that have a tradition of singing. The form may be called by a different name in each area of the country, but the pattern and personnel are constant. *Lum ching choo* ('competing for a lover') is a related courting form in which two males seek the hand of one lady. The courting forms customarily involve a member of each sex, and a contest of wits characterizes the subtle, procreant struggle of the sexes.

Curing is the aim of *lum pee fah* ('sky spirit singing'), in which old women contact this powerful, benevolent spirit to counteract illnesses caused by lesser sprites. Ecstatic dance, spirit possession and oracular statements about the identity of the disease-producing spirit are customary. Predominance of females in this form may be evidence of the importance of women as spirit mediums in pre-Buddhist, indigenous RITUAL, a pattern repeated in Burma in *nat kadaw* (literally, 'spirit wife' – that is, female medium). In Laos, men are the storytellers, but women dance divination, healing and spirit rites.

Court forms Court forms of dance theatre were established as Lao kings copied customs of powerful neighbouring monarchs. Tradition holds that Cambodian (Khmer) court dance, along with the *Ramayana* and *Jataka* repertoire, was introduced to Laos by Prince Fa Nguan in 1353. During the 14th century the Lao kingdom of Lan Sang ('Million Elephants') was established and in this time the Khmer monarchs with their troupe of female wives-dancers were the epitome of potent kingship in the region. Keeping up with the Khmer meant establishing female court dance with movement and repertoire modelled on Khmer practice. The Lao kings were never as rich as the rulers of Angkor. Nor could the Lao compete later in the 15th century with Thai rulers who, first at Ayutthaya and later in Bangkok, emulated Khmer practice (see CAMBODIA and THAILAND). Just as Lan Sang in the early period aped Ankgor, the small courts established by partition in 1700 – Luang Prabang, Wiangjun and Chapassak – imitated Thai models: Thai female court dance *lakon fai nai*, male masked dance drama *khon* and shadow play *nang yai* were taught and performed at court. The Lao chose not to alter the forms: the Royal Lao Ballet of the 1960s in Luang Prabang included only female dancers, the best of whom had trained in Bangkok. Rather than staging full dance dramas like the Thai and Cambodians, this smaller court favoured solo and small-group dances.

Modern, popular forms Drama which involves multiple performers playing characters in an extended narrative is largely a phenomenon of the last 60 years, occurring first in Lao-speaking areas which are a part of Thailand. Thai *likay* troupes began touring to these northern provinces in the 1920s, and soon local Lao groups started mixing *likay* features with indigenous ideas. From *likay* came flashy costumes, wing-and-drop scenery, repertoire and stock character types; from *lum pun* came *kaen* playing and *mawlum*-style singing. This mixed genre came to be called by different names, including *likay lao* ('Lao-style *likay*'), *mawlum moo* ('group *mawlum*'), *mawlum plun* ('spontaneous *mawlum*'), *lum moo* ('group singing'), and *lum luang* ('sung story').

Miller found two variants developed in the 1950s most popular during his fieldwork in the 1970s. *Mawlum moo* was more comic and added lute and Western drums to the *kaen*, while *mawlum plun* performance was more serious in tone and traditional in musical accompaniment. The staging, musical focus and repertoire, consisting of *Jataka* stories, Thai legends and Lao historical tales, were common to both forms.

Performances generally take place on temporary outdoor stages about 30 x 15ft. Electric bulbs hang above the wooden stage providing light for the nightlong performance. Scenery mounted on bamboo poles represents general locales such as a court, a forest or a town. Immovable microphones, which make the singing audible to the audience standing or sitting in the open air, are the focal points of the performance and the slight staging of action that is attempted never takes the actors far from one.

A troupe averages twenty or so members. Thousands of performers are part of such troupes in Laos and northeast Thailand. Since the 1970s these forms have increasingly shown the impact of Western popular culture – rock music and mini-skirted go-go girls becoming standard.

A form of Thai shadow theatre (see SHADOW PUPPETS), *nang talung*, has been adapted by Lao living in Thailand to create *nang daloong*. This shadow theatre appeared in the north as early as 1926, when amateurs began performing the Thai version of the *Ramayana* to the accompaniment of xylophones, finger cymbals and drums. Currently troupes perform Lao tales as well as stories from the Thai repertoire and they incorporate *kaen* playing and *mawlum*-style singing to win local audiences.

Laos proper tends to be more conservative than the Lao-speaking area of Thailand to the south. Here prototheatrical folk forms prevail, and theatre proper is less developed. The court forms evolved with Khmer and Thai influence. It is in the areas where Lao arts have freely interacted with Thai theatrical stimuli that a unique Lao-speaking theatre has emerged in the last 50 years. Everywhere singing skill remains the prime requisite for a good performer, and acoustics, rather than dramatic factors, govern the staging. What is heard, not what is seen, matters most to Lao theatregoers. (See also ASIAN AND PACIFIC ISLAND THEATRE.) KF

> *See*: J. R. Brandon (ed.), *The Cambridge Guide to Asian Theatre*, Cambridge, 1993.

Larivey, Pierre de c.1540–1619 French dramatist of Italian descent, his name being a French pun on the family name of Giunti. Inspired by the performances of itinerant *COMMEDIA DELL'ARTE* players visiting France, he wrote a number of comedies based on Italian models but transposed to a French milieu, of which six were published in 1579 and a further three in 1611. Employing the type characters and familiar plot devices of *commedia*, they abound in imposture, deceit, seduction and other characteristic forms of unscrupulous behaviour, and derive additional comic thrust from the racy, colourful idiom in which they are written and the opportunities they provide for stage business. They were widely performed and republished several times in Larivey's lifetime, infusing the French comic tradition with transalpine vitality. The most interesting, *Les Esprits* (*The Ghosts*, 1579), was adapted from an original by Lorenzo de' Medici which itself was indebted to PLAUTUS and TERENCE, and strong echoes of it can be found in plays by MOLIÈRE and REGNARD. DR

Larochelle [Boullanger], **Henri** 1827–84 French theatre manager. Larochelle studied as an actor at the Conservatoire, played with SÉVESTE's troupes and was accepted by the ODÉON in 1848. In 1850 he became manager of the Théâtre Montmartre for the Sévestes, and in 1851 he bought the ailing Théâtre Montparnasse, followed by the Théâtre de Grenelle. In 1851 Larochelle ran four troupes, and actors often had to commute between theatres in the course of the evening. Within a short time he found himself in control of some eight or ten suburban theatres. In 1856 he rebuilt the Montparnasse, increasing its size to 700 seats, and in 1866 opened a new theatre in Paris, the Cluny, where he aimed at a repertoire of higher quality, often doing plays rejected by other managements, such as Erckmann-Chatrian's *Le Juif polonais* (*The Polish Jew*; in England, *The Bells*).

In 1869 he built the Théâtre des Gobelins, to replace the Théâtre Saint Marcel, and invited an unknown sculptor called Rodin to provide statues for the façade. After 1870 he turned his attention to larger theatres. The Montparnasse was taken over by Hartmann in 1874, and rebuilt in 1886 (it was this theatre that was used for some of the Théâtre Libre performances, including TOLSTOI's *The Power of Darkness* (1888), and the Théâtre d'Art of Paul Fort also performed there in 1891 and 1892). Larochelle became director of the Porte-Saint-Martin (see BOULEVARD) in 1872, mounting HUGO's *Marie Tudor*, with the aged FRÉDÉRICK LEMAÎTRE; DENNERY and Cormon's *Les Deux Orphelines* (*The Two Orphans*); and the vastly successful *Around the World in Eighty Days*. In 1877 he took on the direction of the Ambigu. In 1878 he 'retired', taking on the management of the Gaîté, where one of his most spectacular productions was Paul Meurice's adaptation of Victor Hugo's *Quatre-vingt-treize* (*Ninety-three*). JMCC

L'Arronge, Adolf 1838–1908 German director, playwright and musician. A successful writer of light comedies, L'Arronge is best known as a founding member of the DEUTSCHES THEATER in Berlin and as its first director, from 1887 to 1894. SW

Lassalle, Jacques 1936– French director who has been particularly associated with the work of MICHEL VINAVER and who has been successful in combining the discovery of new playwrights with that of neglected classics. From 1983 until 1990 he was director of the Théâtre National de Strasbourg and of its theatre school, a post he used to encourage the growth of young companies, as well as putting on notable productions of his own, such as MOLIÈRE's *Tartuffe* with Gérard Depardieu. In 1990 he was appointed to direct the COMÉDIE-FRANÇAISE on the death of ANTOINE VITEZ, but he did not survive the intrigues of the right-wing government elected in 1993, when he was dismissed. DB

Lateiner, Jacob see HURWITZ, MOISHE

laterna magika System that integrates live performance with film projections of the performers themselves on multiple screens, devised by the Czechs ALFRED RADOK and JOSEF SVOBODA. It premiered in the Czechoslovakian pavilion at the Brussels Expo in 1958. Subsequently it degenerated into tourist entertainment, but occasionally its principle appeared in serious drama: e.g. *The Last Ones* (1966), a Radok–Svoboda collaboration. Svoboda has continued to explore scenographic applications of the system, as in the large-scale spectacle of *The Odyssey*, in 1987, *Minotaur* in 1991 and *Magic Flute* in 1993. The operation now has its own independent state theatre, the Laterna Magika. JMB

Latin America (See also individual countries.) To deal with the theatre of Latin America as a unit is to presuppose that a homogeneity exists with certain common denominators. As with all generalizations, this one contains both truth and fiction. The Spanish conquest began with Columbus's arrival in 1492, and the Portuguese explorers who claimed the territory of Brazil followed soon after. The geographic size and population diversity render a comprehensive term somewhat unsatisfactory, but despite its limitations, 'Latin America' acknowledges common historical, linguistic and cultural developments.

Theatre, or at least theatrical forms, existed in the Americas before the arrival of the Spanish and Portuguese. For the most part, these manifestations were not well documented by the conquerors; in fact, from the perspective of a religious conquest of the New World, their 'heretical' nature generally caused them to be suppressed. Some indigenous forms are described in the early Spanish chronicles, but the only authentic non-European work to survive is the *RABINAL ACHÍ* of the Maya-Quichés. *El baile de El Güegüence* and the *OLLANTAY* are both cited as early plays with indigenous flavour, but both are of dubious

origin and have European characteristics.

Early religious plays in the colonies, at a time when the Spanish theatre itself was still rudimentary, often drew on local traditions and customs to facilitate comprehension by the Native Americans. Performed in the church atriums and plazas, these plays soon shared with more secular manifestations in dramatizing important events in the colonies, such as the arrival or departure of a viceroy, or the saint's day of an important personage. Traffic between Spain and Portugal and their colonies was constant throughout the colonial period, and the advanced state of development of peninsular theatre during the Siglo de Oro (GOLDEN AGE), dominated by LOPE DE VEGA and CALDERÓN DE LA BARCA and their respective schools, contributed to the early transfer of theatrical interest from Spain and Portugal to Latin America. Both JUAN RUIZ DE ALARCÓN (born in Mexico) and TIRSO DE MOLINA spent time in the colonies, but neither had a significant impact on the development of national dramaturgy, in spite of critics' claims to the contrary. By the end of the 17th century, Mexico had produced one great playwright, the extraordinary nun Sor Juana Inés de la Cruz.

Throughout the colonial years the theatre tended to be either an imported phenomenon or an artistic form that paralleled closely the prevailing modes of the mother countries. During the 17th century the aesthetic trends ranged from early Renaissance to baroque, in tone, language and form. The *AUTOS SACRAMENTALes*, popular during the 17th century, were banned by Charles III in 1765, as religious drama became increasingly corrupted.

The period of independence in Latin America lasted from 1810 to 1825, but political independence did little to ensure cultural independence. Neoclassic and romantic plays characterized the first half of the 19th century, with strong influence of both French and Spanish literature and thought. Even though REALISM and the psychological theatre marked the latter half of the 19th century in Spain, a second wave of romantic influences impeded the development of a realistic, autochthonous theatre in the New World, and romanticism continued to prevail in many countries until about 1910.

Only in the 20th century did theatre in Latin America begin to find its own expression. The Golden Decade (1900–10) in Argentina sprang from the popular traditions of the CIRCUS and GAUCHO. From the late 1920s forward, the development of a vast movement of experimental and independent theatres, attuned to the latest techniques of staging, lighting, diction and direction in the European theatre – not to mention theatre architecture and construction – brought about a theatrical renovation and revolution in Latin America. These independent/experimental theatres paved the way for the introduction of serious, committed theatre from the 1950s forward, in contrast to the frivolous costumbristic comedies (see *COSTUMBRISMO*) that had often dominated the professional stage.

Massive problems continue to plague the development of theatre in Latin America. CENSORSHIP, social injustices, the lack of dramatic arts schools for the training of theatre professionals (directors, actors and technicians), impoverished and inadequate theatre structures poorly equipped to deal with modern plays – all are manifestations of wrenching sociopolitical and economic problems. In fact, much of the recent theatre reflects the deep-seated problems within the various societies, and, with pedagogical intention, it serves as a vehicle for ideological change. New forms of popular theatre can be found both in traditional theatre spaces and in manifestations of street theatre where a revolutionary spirit often prevails, invoking a process of change. The theatre in Latin America is responsive to world currents and at the same time it continues to develop its own themes and forms. In spite of the problems, therefore, the theatre continues to be a vital and dynamic medium of artistic expression in Latin America. GW

See: S. J. Albuquerque, *Violent Acts: A Study of Contemporary Latin American Theatre*, Detroit, 1991; J. J. Arrom, *Historia del teatro hispanoamericano: época colonial*, Mexico, 1967; P. Bravo Elizondo, *Teatro hispanoamericano de crítica social*, Madrid, 1975; F. Dauster, *Ensayos sobre el teatro hispanoamericano*, Mexico, 1975, *Historia del teatro hispanoamericano: siglos 19 y 20*, Mexico, 1973, and *Perfil generacional del teatro hispanoamericano (1894–1924)*, Ottawa, 1993; W. K. Jones, *Behind Spanish American Footlights*, Austin, 1966; G. Luzuriaga, *Popular Theatre for Social Change in Latin America*, Los Angeles, 1978; L. Lyday and G. Woodyard, *Dramatists in Revolt: The New Latin American Theatre*, Austin, 1976; P. Meléndez, *La dramaturgia hispanoamericana contemporánea: Teatralidad y autoconciencia*, Madrid, 1990; E. G. Neglia, *Aspectos del teatro moderno hispanoamericano*, Bogotá, 1975; R. Perales, *Teatro hispanoamericano contemporáneo (1967–1987)*, 2 vols., Mexico, 1989, 1993; G. Rojo, *Orígenes del teatro hispanoamericano contemporáneo*, Valparaíso, 1972; A. del Saz Sánchez, *Teatro hispanoamericano*, 2 vols., Barcelona, 1963, 1964; C. Solórzano, *El teatro latinoamericano en el siglo 20*, Mexico, 1964; D. Taylor, *Theatre of Crisis: Drama and Politics in Latin America*, Lexington, 1991; A. Versényi, *Theatre in Latin America: Religion, politics and culture from Cortés to the 1980s*, Cambridge, 1993; J. Villegas, *La interpretación de la obra dramática*, Santiago, 1971.

Laube, Heinrich 1806–84 German playwright and director. As a young journalist, Laube was closely associated with the Junges Deutschland (Young Germany) movement and was briefly imprisoned for his writings in 1837.

A photomontage showing Harry Lauder as 'the Tailor's Wife' and 'the Saftest o' the Family'.

After his release he turned to playwriting, producing several dramas in the fashion of SCRIBE, who was then enjoying an immense vogue in Germany. Among Laube's most frequently performed plays were *Monaldeschi* (1841), *Rococo* (1842), *Struensee* (1845), *Gottsched and Gellert* (1845) and *The Karlschüler* (1846). Despite his liberal views, in 1849 Laube was appointed director of the BURGTHEATER where, over the next 18 years, he developed the ensemble style of the company to its zenith. After his resignation in 1867, he took over the direction of the Leipzig Town Theatre. He returned to Vienna in 1871 to found a Town Theatre there, which he directed until 1880. Laube's memoirs on his career and his histories of German theatre are major sources for the historian. SW

Lauder, Harry [Henry MacLennan Lauder] 1870–1950 Scottish MUSIC-HALL performer, who worked in a flax mill and in coalmines for 10 years, before playing in concert parties as an Irish comic. His London debut in 1900 as an extra turn made him a star overnight, and he soon became the highest-paid British performer of his time. His repertory originally contained a whole gallery of Scottish types, but eventually he settled into a cosy, chuckling caricature of the canny Scot, invariably singing 'I Love a Lassie' and 'Roamin' in the Gloamin''. He made 22 tours of the USA between 1909 and 1932, organized the first frontline entertainment units during the First World War and was knighted in 1919. He was also the most prolific recording artist of the music-hall. He authored three autobiographies: *A Minstrel in France* (1918), *Between You and Me* (1919) and *Roamin' in the Gloamin'* (1928). LS

Laughton, Charles 1899–1962 British-born actor who, with his actress wife Elsa Lanchester (1902–86), became an American citizen in 1950. His first professional role, in *The Inspector General* (1926), was followed by parts including Hercule Poirot in *Alibi* and William Marble in *Payment Deferred*, the latter also marking his 1931 New York debut. At London's OLD VIC (1933–4) he played in seven productions, including leading roles in *The Cherry Orchard*, *The Tempest* and *Macbeth*. As the first English actor to perform at the COMÉDIE-FRANÇAISE (1936), he appeared in *Le Médecin malgré lui*. After a decade of film work, he returned to the stage in 1947 with *Galileo*, adapted with BRECHT and first performed in Los Angeles. For several years he toured the USA reading from the Bible, SHAKESPEARE and modern classics. As director of, and the Devil in, SHAW's *Don Juan in Hell* (1951), he earned critical acclaim. He played Bottom in *A Midsummer Night's Dream* and King Lear at Stratford-upon-Avon (1959). A revealing biography by actor-director SIMON CALLOW was published in 1988. DBW

Laurents, Arthur 1918– American screenwriter, director and dramatist. Although not a great success in the theatre, *Home of the Brave* (1945), concerned with a Jewish soldier's wartime problems, won Laurents the interest of critics and a reputation for insight into human nature and an interest in character development and language. In *The Time of the Cuckoo* (1952), *A Clearing in the Woods* (1957) and *Invitation to a March* (1960), he wrote about women whose psychological problems drive them towards disas-

ter. *The Bird Cage* (1950) builds upon the sexual frustrations of a vicious nightclub owner. Laurents is celebrated for writing the book for the musicals *West Side Story* (1957) and *Gypsy* (1959; revivals, 1974, 1989), *Hallelujah, Baby!* (1967) and the ill-fated *Nick and Nora* (1991; also directed). He wrote the screenplay for *Anna Lucasta* (1949) and *Anastasia* (1956). Laurents's later work – *The Enclave* (1973) and *Heartsong* (1974) – has been less appreciated. His most recent play, *Jolson Sings Again* (1995), premiered at the SEATTLE REPERTORY THEATRE. WJM

Lawler, Ray 1921– Australian playwright. As an actor in Melbourne he achieved fame when *Summer of the Seventeenth Doll* (1955), depicting two Queensland canecutters' annual holiday with their city girls, gained Australian and international success. After living in Britain and Ireland he returned to Australia in 1975, becoming literary adviser to the Melbourne Theatre Company. His plays include *The Piccadilly Bushman* (1959), *The Man Who Shot the Albatross* (1971), and *Kid Stakes* (1975) and *Other Times* (1977), depicting the characters of *The Doll* in earlier years and completing the *Doll* trilogy. MW

Lawrence, D(avid) H(erbert) 1885–1930 British novelist, poet and playwright. Lawrence's notoriety for the sexual explicitness of his novels prevented his plays from reaching the public stage until 1967–8 (see CENSORSHIP), though a biblical epic (*David*) was performed by the STAGE SOCIETY (1927), as was *The Widowing of Mrs Holroyd* (1926). This – like *A Collier's Friday Night* (written 1906), *The Daughter-in-Law*, based on the coal strike of 1912, and *The Fight for Barbara*, reflecting his own relationship with a married woman – superimposed the class struggle on the struggle of the sexes. Written from personal experience as the son of a miner and more starkly realistic than those of a contemporary like GALSWORTHY, these plays were well received when revived in repertory at the ROYAL COURT THEATRE in 1965–7, leading to performances of Lawrence's other social plays, *The Merry-Go-Round* (1973) and *Touch and Go* (1979). CI

Lawrence, Gertrude 1898–1952 British singer, dancer and comedy actress. From infancy 'Gertie' toured with her actress mother, making her own debut in 1910 as a dancer in *Babes in the Wood*. Her New York debut in *André Charlot's Revue of 1924* launched a brilliant American stage career in which *Lady in the Dark* (1941) and *The King and I* (1951) were high points. NOËL COWARD wrote *Private Lives* for her (she played Amanda), and they toured together in his *Tonight at 8:30* (1935). During the Second World War she entertained British and American troops. JOHN MASON BROWN described her as 'a MUSICAL COMEDY performer' who 'grew into an admirable actress'. Vivacity, warmth and a sense of fun characterized her remarkable stage presence. Her memoirs were published in 1945. FHL

Lawrence, Jerome 1915– and
Robert E(dwin) Lee 1918–94 Ohio-born American dramatists who joined in formal partnership in 1942, and have since written dozens of plays, many produced in New

York and most extremely popular with regional and amateur groups. Perhaps their best-received effort was *Inherit the Wind* (1955), a faithful, flashy, dramatic retelling of the story of the famous Scopes 'monkey trial'. Also extremely popular was their adaptation of *Auntie Mame* (1956) and the subsequent MUSICAL version, *Mame* (1966), for which they wrote the libretto. Their play, *The Night Thoreau Spent in Jail* (1970), a standard for several years with amateur groups, was an early offering of the American Playwrights' Theatre. This versatile and prolific team has also been responsible for many one-act OPERAS, screenplays, television plays and radio programmes. A research centre/archive at Ohio State University is named after them. LDC

Lawson, John Howard 1895–1977 American playwright who, in the theatre of the 1920s, was an anomaly: a dramatist of fiery left-wing convictions. Striking out against the convention-bound commercial theatre on the one hand and the ivory tower art theatre on the other, Lawson attempted to forge a new theatrical style, which he called 'political VAUDEVILLE'. His most successful experiment was *Processional* (1925), a staccato, fragmented series of sketches set in a West Virginia town during a coal strike. In 1926 he was a co-founder of the short-lived, politically radical New Playwrights' Theatre, for which he wrote a strident SATIRE of political campaigning called *Loud Speaker*. Lawson changed his style in the 1930s, replacing extravagance with a richly idiomatic REALISM that had a strong influence on CLIFFORD ODETS. The eloquently embittered, working-class anti-heroes of his *Success Story* (1932) and *Gentlewoman* (1934) speak a racy urban poetry. An active screenwriter (*Blockade*, *Action in the North Atlantic*) and a president of the Screen Writers' Guild, Lawson was imprisoned in 1948 for defending the Bill of Rights against the inquisition of the House Un-American Activities Committee. In 1949 he published a now standard work, *Theory and Technique of Playwriting and Screenwriting*. FH

Laya, Jean-Louis 1761–1833 French dramatist. Laya's reputation rests mainly on his political COMEDY, *L'Ami des lois* (*The Friend of the Laws*, 1793), which was staged at the Théâtre de la Nation (the COMÉDIE-FRANÇAISE) and vigorously attacked political extremists, in particular Marat and Robespierre. Laya ended up in prison and the play was hotly attacked by the Commune on the grounds that it could cause disturbances. It became a rallying point for former aristocrats, and the trial of Louis XVI was interrupted to discuss whether it should be banned. The play continued to be regarded as subversive well after the revolutionary period. In 1819 Laya wrote a pamphlet on the abuses of theatre CENSORSHIP. His son Léon Laya (1809–72) was also a dramatist, best-known for *Duke Job* (Comédie-Française, 1859). JMCC

Lazarenko, Vitaly (Efimovich) 1890–1939 Russian CLOWN, son of a coalminer and a seamstress. He began in Kotlikov's CIRCUS as a trapeze gymnast at the age of eight; in Nikitin's circus in Moscow (1914), he developed a vein of satiric comedy, influenced by ANATOLY DUROV and Richard Ribot, and established a world record by leaping over three

elephants. After the Revolution, he came into his own as a proletarian star, playing in many satirical pantoMIMES, including two pieces written for him by VLADIMIR MAYAKOVSKY: 'The Universal Class Struggle Championship' and 'ABC'. He performed for soldiers at the Western Front in 1918 and 1921 and at the Eastern Front in 1938. His proletarian costume of overalls impressed MEYERHOLD, who cast him as the devil in his second staging of Mayakovsky's *Mystery-Bouffe*. LS

lazzo (plural, *lazzi*; possibly a corruption of *l'azione*, action) An important constituent element in improvised Italian COMMEDIA DELL'ARTE. A *lazzo* may be a play on words, a quid pro quo, a piece of comic business, a sleight-of-hand trick or a pantomimic joke, usually intended to prompt laughter independent of the plot. Often sadistic and scatological, employing clysters and razors, some *lazzi* became traditional, such as HARLEQUIN's fly-catching or JOHN RICH's hatching from an egg. Latterly, the more extended version, the *burla*, did serve a dramatic function, as in the dinner scene in GOLDONI's *Servant of Two Masters*. LS

Le Fartere, Roland [Rolland le Pettour] French or English or Anglo-Norman popular performer. In c.1250 he is recorded as holding land in Hemmingstone, Suffolk (England), on condition that he appear before the king every Christmas Day to perform the jump, whistle and fart ('*unum saltum et unum siffletum et unum bumbulum*'). Farting is well attested as an amateur performing art to the present day, and artists such as LE PÉTOMANE has occasionally achieved success with it on the commercial stage; in the Middle Ages it seems to have belonged to the repertory of skills of the professional minstrel, whom, perhaps, Roland was emulating in a ritual of abasement – though the nickname which stuck as his surname suggests a recognition of his skill which puts it outside the realm of the semi-professional. AEG

Le Gallienne, Eva 1899–1991 Best known as an actress, but also director and producer. The London-born Le Gallienne participated in every aspect of American theatre. Her New York debut was in *Mrs Boltay's Daughter* (1915), but her first big success was as Julie in *Liliom* (1921). For the next 60-plus years Le Gallienne played most of the major female roles in Western drama, receiving critical acclaim for performances in plays by IBSEN, CHEKHOV and SHAKESPEARE, as well as for her Queen Elizabeth in both SCHILLER's *Mary Stuart* and MAXWELL ANDERSON's *Elizabeth the Queen*. She described her acting technique as 'getting rid of "Me"' in order to become the part'.

Le Gallienne's contribution to American theatre included more than her considerable acting skill. She introduced audiences throughout the country to Ibsen, Chekhov and French playwrights through her translations and productions of their plays. A lifelong proponent of repertory theatre, she founded the CIVIC REPERTORY THEATRE (1926–33), where she produced, directed and starred, offering quality theatre at bargain ticket prices. The Civic presented 1581 performances of over 30 plays, including many of the classics, GLASPELL's *Alison's House*, *Peter Pan* (in which Le Gallienne was the first actress to 'fly') and *Alice in*

Wonderland (adaptation by Le Gallienne and Florida Friebus). In 1946, Le Gallienne, CHERYL CRAWFORD and MARGARET WEBSTER founded the AMERICAN REPERTORY COMPANY, which lasted only one season.

Le Gallienne directed and acted for the National Repertory Theatre (1961–6), and acted in a revival of *The Royal Family* (1976), *To Grandmother's House We Go* (1981), the brief revival of *Alice in Wonderland* (1982; her last stage appearance) and the film *Resurrection* (1980). She also published her translations of Ibsen and Chekhov, a biography of ELEONORA DUSE, and two autobiographies – *At 33* (1934) and *With a Quiet Heart* (1953). In addition, she garnered most of the major awards in American performing arts, including Woman of the Year (1947), AMERICAN NATIONAL THEATRE AND ACADEMY awards (1964, 1977), a special Tony (1964), an Emmy (1978) and the National Medal of Arts (1986). A 1992 biography by Robert Schanke explores her sexual orientation as well as her theatrical career. FB

Lebanon see MIDDLE EAST

LeCompte, Elizabeth 1944– American director and playwright and, since 1979, artistic director of the experimental theatre COLLECTIVE known as the WOOSTER GROUP. With SPALDING GRAY and other members of the Group, she co-wrote and directed *Sakonnet Point* (1975), *Rumstick Road* (1977) and *Nayatt School* (1978), a trilogy called *Three Places in Rhode Island*; in 1979 LeCompte and the Group created an 'epilogue' (without dialogue) to this trilogy called *Point Judith*. She was also instrumental in the creation of *Route 1 & 9* (1981) and *L. S. D.* (1984), and participated in the creation of such pieces as *Frank Dell's The Temptation of St Antony* (1987), *... Just the High Points ...* (1988–9) and *Brace Up!* (1991), the last an epilogue to the company's *The Road to Immortality*. In 1984 she was appointed associate director of the short-lived American National Theatre (under PETER SELLARS) at the JOHN F. KENNEDY CENTER FOR THE PERFORMING ARTS. In the 1980s and early 90s she has been a leader in the nourishing of a sometimes radical avant-garde theatre in New York. DBW

Lecoq, Jacques 1921– French actor, director, MIME artist and teacher. After early work as an actor, Lecoq spent time in Italy, discovering and researching the MASKS of the *COMMEDIA* and helping to found the theatre school of the Piccolo Teatro (see GIORGIO STREHLER) in Milan. He returned to Paris in 1956 and set up his international mime school, which has attracted students from all over the world. Here he developed a teaching technique centred on the physical expressivity of the actor, but not insisting on pure mime. He has also run his own theatre company and has taught in the faculty of architecture, stressing always the importance of considerations of space for the art of theatre. DB

Lecouvreur, Adrienne 1692–1730 French actress, the outstanding tragedienne of her day. She first attracted attention with an amateur company in Paris and then spent some years in the provinces before making her debut at the COMÉDIE-FRANÇAISE in 1717 in the title role of CRÉBILLON's *Électre*. Its success rapidly won her the position of *sociétaire* and with it a series of leading roles in the classical repertoire of PIERRE CORNEILLE and RACINE as well as in contemporary TRAGEDY. Though not a great natural beauty, she was an instinctive performer with an imposing stage presence and the power to move an audience deeply. Owing to a frail constitution her vocal range was limited but this was turned to advantage by the control and emotional nuance of her delivery, which appeared to subsume the actress within the character played. Indeed, contemporary reports credited her, as they did MLLE CLAIRON a generation later, with an altogether simpler, less declamatory style of playing than was the norm, and an innovative regard for propriety in stage COSTUME. After a fêted career she died suddenly in somewhat mysterious circumstances, and the Church's refusal of Christian burial followed by the disposal of her body in open ground under cover of darkness prompted VOLTAIRE to write an angry lament deploring the hypocrisy of current attitudes to the acting profession. A century later, in 1849, she became the subject of a play by SCRIBE and Legouvé which afforded a prime role for RACHEL and subsequently SARAH BERNHARDT. DR

Lee, Canada [Leonard Canegata] 1907–52 African-American actor whose successful boxing career was halted by an eye injury, yet whose fighting spirit was manifested in several memorable roles. He played Blacksnake in the 1934 revival of the anti-lynching drama *Stevedore*, Banquo in the FEDERAL THEATRE PROJECT's 'voodoo' *Macbeth* (directed by ORSON WELLES, 1936), and the emperor Christophe in *Haiti* (1938). His finest performance was as Bigger Thomas in Richard Wright's *Native Son* (1941). Lee played Caliban in MARGARET WEBSTER's 1945 production of *The Tempest* and a whiteface Bosola in *The Duchess of Malfi* (1946). He was a powerful actor of animal-like grace who was committed to a theatre of social relevance. EGH

Lee, Eugene 1939– American set designer, unique among US designers in both concept and execution. Approaching each production without preconceived ideas, Lee treats the whole space of the theatre – not only the stage – as a place to be designed. From the late 1960s onward (except for 1989–90) he has been resident designer for the TRINITY REPERTORY COMPANY in Providence, Rhode Island, and for seven years head of design at the DALLAS THEATER CENTER. Together with director Adrian Hall he created iconoclastic, often environmental, settings, including the 1992 *As You Like It* in Central Park, New York. He took environmental design to OFF-BROADWAY and BROADWAY with *Slaveship*, *Alice in Wonderland* and *Candide*. Even with more conventional productions his sets tend to be large and use moving parts and real materials. Lee has worked with PETER BROOK in Shiraz and Paris and with HAROLD PRINCE on several shows, including in New York *Sweeney Todd* and *Grandchild of Kings* and, in Toronto and New York, *Show Boat*. He has been production designer for television's 'Saturday Night Live' at its inception and again later, and has designed several TV specials as well as concert tours for Paul Simon. AA

Lee, Gypsy Rose [Rose Louise Hovick] ?1914–70 American BURLESQUE artist and writer. After performing a child act with her sister June in VAUDEVILLE (1922–8), she starred in MINSKY's Burlesque by the age of 17. Her act comprised more 'tease' than 'strip', tantalizing with suggestive silk stockings, lace panties and a rose-garter tossed into the audience as a coda. H. L. Mencken coined the term 'ecdysiast' to label her speciality, and her sophisticated pose was parodied in the MUSICAL *Pal Joey* (1940). Seen in the *ZIEGFELD Follies of 1936*, at nightclubs, fairs and CARNIVALS, she was the first celebrity stripper (see NUDITY). Her writings include a play, *The Naked Genius* (1943); some murder mysteries; and a memoir, *Gypsy* (1957), turned into a popular MUSICAL COMEDY (1959). Her final major creative effort was a one-person show called *A Curious Evening with Gypsy Rose Lee* (1958), though in the 1960s she appeared frequently on television. LS

Lee, Ming Cho 1930– Generally considered the current doyen of American set designers. Lee's style and technique have significantly influenced the look of OPERA and theatre design since the mid-1960s. He was born in Shanghai and studied Chinese watercolour before emigrating to the USA in 1949. In 1954 he became an assistant to Jo MIELZINER, to whose poetic realism Lee's trademark spare, minimalist, emblematic style – best exemplified in the 1964 production of *Electra* at the NEW YORK SHAKESPEARE FESTIVAL – was, in part, a response. Lee is usually associated with pipe-work scaffolding, textured surfaces and collage; but since the late 1970s, his work has turned to detail and ultra-REALISM, as in the production of *K2*, for which he created a mountain on the stage. He is constantly working with new materials and new approaches. Despite his importance, he has designed little on BROADWAY: much of his work has been with the New York Shakespeare Festival and regional theatres, as well as for opera – most notably, the New York City Opera. Since the mid-1980s Lee, who heads the design programme at the Yale School of Drama, has devoted more time to teaching. AA

Lee, Nathaniel c.1650–92 English playwright. After graduating from Trinity College, Cambridge, he moved to London in 1671. A brief career as an actor led to his beginning to write plays. *Nero* was performed in 1674. *The Rival Queens* (1677) was a substantial success and its brilliance as a vehicle for two actresses playing Roxana and Statira ensured its frequent revival. In 1678 Lee collaborated with DRYDEN on a version of *Oedipus* of spectacular bloodthirstiness. *Lucius Junius Brutus* (1680), a careful study of ideological conflict and tyranny and the best political play of the Restoration, was banned after a brief run. In its intensity and restraint it is remarkably unlike the verbal and visual extravagances of his other work, with their frequent scenes of torture and speeches of ranting passion. Lee's only comedy, *The Princess of Cleves*, turns the calm feeling of Mme de la Fayette's novel into a vicious SATIRE on the sexual excesses of Restoration society. In 1684 Lee went mad and spent the next four years in an asylum. He died in obscurity. PH

Lee, Robert E. see LAWRENCE, JEROME

Legault, Émile 1906–83 French Canadian director, playwright and essayist. A Catholic priest, Legault studied theatre briefly on a bursary in Paris, and on his return to Montreal in 1937 assumed direction of the Compagnons de Saint-Laurent, making of it the most influential stage company in French Canada for the next 15 years. Initially a college troupe providing basic instruction in theatre arts, Les Compagnons evolved from an early emphasis on religious theatre towards a more eclectic, contemporary repertoire, in the process training the actors, directors and theatre professionals that would provide leadership over the next three decades. Legault also composed dramatic texts, but his reputation rests mainly on his role as director and manager. LED

'legitimate' theatre see THEATRICAL MONOPOLY

Leicester's Men The first of the great Elizabethan household companies was formed in 1559, enjoyed a period of high prosperity from c.1570 to 83, and had already dwindled into comparative insignificance by the time the Earl of Leicester died in 1588. The fluctuation owed something to Leicester's favour, or lack of it, at court, something to the new spirit of professionalism in London following the opening of the THEATRE in 1576, and much to the challenge of QUEEN ELIZABETH'S MEN, which commandeered many of the country's best-known performers on its foundation in 1583. JAMES BURBAGE, who built the Theatre, and WILL KEMPE, who became its star attraction, were both members of Leicester's Men in the early stages of their very different careers. PT

Leigh, Mike 1943– British director and playwright, who studied acting at RADA and became associate director of the Midlands Art Centre in Birmingham. His distinctive contribution to the British stage (and to TELEVISION DRAMA) has been the plays that he has devised together with the actors involved. Leigh's technique is to offer actors a basic idea and to encourage them to develop characters and situations which he then shapes into the final product. Significant successes have included *Abigail's Party* (1977) and *Goose-Pimples* (1981). For television his credits are longer. The strength of his group-created plays is in their acute observation, the weakness in the tendency of that observation to become petty and malicious. *Smelling a Rat* (1988) and *Greek Tragedy* (1989), about a Greek-Australian family living in self-imposed exile, were effective but somewhat shapeless studies of social behaviour, lacking the wit of his earlier works. His feature film, *High Hopes* (1988), won awards at the Chicago and Locarno Film Festivals. MB JE

Leigh, Vivien [Vivian Mary Hartley] 1913–67 British actress. Married to LAURENCE OLIVIER, Leigh played with him in a number of striking Shakespearian performances: in *Hamlet* at Elsinore (1937), *Romeo and Juliet* in New York (1940), *Antony and Cleopatra* in London (1951) and *Titus Andronicus* at Stratford-upon-Avon (1955). Her success in *The Doctor's Dilemma* (1942) prompted SHAW to suggest she play Cleopatra in the film of *Caesar and Cleopatra* (also staged with Olivier, 1951), and it is as a film actress that she is perhaps best-remembered – for her roles in *Gone with the Wind* and *A Streetcar Named Desire* (re-creating her acclaimed 1949 theatrical performance). The sensitivity and precision of her acting were widely admired. After touring with the OLD VIC and in GIRAUDOUX's *Duel of Angels*, she gave her final performance with GIELGUD in CHEKHOV's *Ivanov* (New York, 1966). CI

Leipzig style Formal, wooden style of acting of the early 18th century, encouraged by JOHANN GOTTSCHED in an effort to elevate the way in which tragic drama was acted. It was practised initially by the NEUBER troupe. Although such acting was highly unsubtle, based as it was on misconceptions of classical gesture and French tragic acting, it was for many a suitable alternative to the rough improvisation that, until the time of the Neubers, was standard on the German stage. The Leipzig style remained the dominant mode of acting until the rise of the *BÜRGERLICHES TRAUERSPIEL* required a quieter realism. SW

Leis, Raúl 1947– Panamanian playwright, journalist, sociologist, essayist, poet and popular educator. In addition to several children's plays, Leis is the author of *Viaje a la salvación y otros países* (*Journey to Salvation and Other Countries*, 1973) and *Viene el sol con su sombrero de combate puesto* (*The Sun Comes Up with its Combat Helmet On*), dealing with sovereignty issues over the Panama Canal. *María Picana* (1979) captures the inherent violence in Latin America through a woman torturer, raised as a child by animals. *El nido de Macúa* (*The Nest of the Macúa*, 1981) treats syncretism and magic in Panamanian social issues. Recent works include *Lo peor del boxeo* (*The Worst of Boxing*), *Primero de mayo* (*First of May*) and *El señor Sol* (*Mr Sun*, 1983). GW

Lekain [Henri-Louis Kain] 1729–78 French actor, who was first noticed and encouraged by VOLTAIRE. In 1750 he made his debut at the COMÉDIE-FRANÇAISE, where despite the enmity of his professional relationship with MLLE CLAIRON he gradually established himself as the company's foremost tragedian. His modest stature and bow legs were more than compensated for by a majestic bearing and forceful, passionate playing, a quality well suited to the plays of Voltaire, many of whose tragic heroes he was the first to portray. The thoughtful, responsible attitude that he took to his profession was reflected in his rejection of the tradition of conventional stage COSTUME, a process he began by adopting an approximation to ancient Greek dress as Oreste in RACINE's *Andromaque* and some hints of *chinoiserie* in Voltaire's *Orphelin de la Chine* (*The Chinese Orphan*). His encouragement of movement on stage and contempt for the long-cherished practice of delivering big speeches downstage centre was of a piece with his campaign for the removal of audience seating on the stage, a century-old institution favoured by fashionable theatregoers which was finally abolished in 1759 to make room for the introduction of changeable scenery occupying the entire playing area. He also drew up plans for an acting school associated with the Comédie-Française, for which royal patronage was obtained with the accession of Louis XVI in 1774, though failing health compelled him to relinquish its direction. Perennially in financial difficulties, he undertook many provincial tours to supplement his income, and these may well have undermined his delicate constitution and contributed to his premature death. He was widely admired by contemporary critics and often likened to GARRICK, but perhaps the most eloquent testimony to his theatrical genius was provided by Voltaire's epigram that it was not he but Lekain who had created his tragedies. DR

Lemaître, Frédérick 1800–76 Arguably the greatest, and certainly the most flamboyant and colourful French actor of the century. Frédérick began his career humbly at the tiny Variétés Amusantes of Boulevard du Temple in 1815 wearing a lion skin in a pantomime, *Pyrame et Thisbé*. He graduated to the nearby THÉÂTRE DES FUNAMBULES, where he performed in harlequinades and, in 1816, was noticed, recommended for the Conservatoire, and offered work in the *mimodrames* of the CIRQUE OLYMPIQUE. He stayed there from 1817 to 20, playing Mallorno (alias Iago) in their version of *Othello* in 1818. Accepted by the ODÉON in 1820 to play minor roles, he was dismissed in 1823 and moved to the Ambigu (see BOULEVARD), where he replaced Frénoy in the part of Vivaldi in PIXÉRÉCOURT's *L'Homme à trois visages* (*The Man with Three Faces*).

The turning point in his career came in 1824 when, together with the actor FIRMIN, he sent up a particularly pathetic MELODRAMA, *L'Auberge des Adrets*, turning it into a hilarious PARODY of the genre and creating the unforgettable silhouette of Robert Macaire with a costume picked up from rag-and-bone merchants. The subversive quality of the performance did not go unnoticed, and after 85 performances the piece was suddenly banned. The character of Robert Macaire took on an independent existence, especially through broadsheets and the lithographs of Daumier, and later became a means of attacking the government and society of Louis Philippe. Lemaître remained at the Ambigu until the fire of 1827, playing some 25 parts. He went to the Porte-Saint-Martin, which he saw as the new temple of romanticism, and found one of his greatest roles (one which he would play for over 40 years), that of Georges de Germany in *Thirty Years of a Gamester's Life*. At the Porte-Saint-Martin, he also met an ideal partner in MARIE DORVAL. He was tempted back to the Ambigu, with offers of both an actor's and a stage director's salary, and thus lost the opportunity of playing the original Marino Faliero (the part was taken by LIGIER, but Lemaître obtained it in the revival). In 1830, he joined HAREL at the Odéon, playing DUMAS *père*'s Napoléon, Ambrosio in *The Monk*, and Concini in *La Maréchale d'Ancre*. From 1831 to 33 he was back at the Porte-Saint-Martin, which Harel had now acquired, and here he created Dumas's Richard Darlington with enormous success, following it with Gennaro in HUGO's *Lucrèce Borgia* (MLLE GEORGE played Lucrèce and Hugo was delighted with his interpreters).

After a row he left the Porte-Saint-Martin and went on tour. On returning to Paris in 1834 he took a new piece, *Robert Macaire*, by the same team of authors as *L'Auberge des Adrets* – though he claimed to be the sole author – to the Folies Dramatiques (Harel had managed to shut the doors of most of the theatres to him). This satirical piece of indulgent buffoonery became the fashionable play to see, and Lemaître, ever extravagant, bought himself a country house out of the profits. In 1836, this time at the Variétés, he had another triumph, in a play which seemed almost tailor-made for him, Dumas's *Kean*. In 1838 Victor Hugo finished writing *Ruy Blas* for him – yet another success – and this was performed at the Théâtre de la Renaissance. In 1840 he gave the first performance of Balzac's *Vautrin* at the Porte-Saint-Martin, and the play was immediately banned (possibly because Lemaître made himself up to look like the king). He went from theatre to theatre, playing BOUCHARDY's made-to-measure role in *Paris le bohémien* (*Paris the Gypsy*) in 1842; Jacques Ferrand in the stage adaptation of Sue's *Mysteries of Paris* and Don César de Bazan in 1844; PYAT's *Le Chiffonnier de Paris* (*The Ragpicker of Paris*, 1847) and *Toussaint l'Ouverture* and *Paillasse* in 1850. All the time he was touring. In 1852, the re-establishment of CENSORSHIP hit his major roles, including Robert Macaire and Ruy Blas. During his last years he revived his earlier successes. In 1862 he gave the second performance of *Vautrin*, which was a flop. By the 1870s he was in a state of near destitution, playing the suburban theatres. JMCC

Lenderby, Nora fl.1590s Perhaps the first of the famous English theatrical landladies. It was at Mistress Lenderby's that SHAKESPEARE lodged when, as a young man, he went to London (and where he probably had his brief but unsatisfactory relationship with Mandy Lightsnot). His more substantial lodgings seem to have been with Toby Ornott. Toby is sometimes thought to have offered Shakespeare training as an actor, but this remains open to question. MXI

Leñero, Vicente 1933– Mexican playwright and novelist. Leñero was born in Guadalajara, trained as a civil engineer at the UNAM (1958), and won various literary prizes and a Guggenheim Fellowship. His first serious novel, *Los albañiles* (*The Bricklayers*, 1964), was a major contribution to the revitalization of Latin American letters. His introductory piece is *Pueblo rechazado* (*Rejected People*, 1968), a controversial documentary work based on a Cuernavaca monastery that promulgated psychoanalysis for its monks instead of slavish attention to prayer. Most of his subsequent plays are also documentaries: *Compañero* (*Companion*, 1971), based on Che Guevara; *El juicio* (*The Trial*, 1971), on the trial of the assassin of Mexican president elect Obregón in 1928; *Los hijos de Sánchez* (*The Children of Sánchez*, 1972), on the Oscar Lewis socioanthropological study of a Mexican village; plus several others including *El martirio de Morelos* (*The Martyrdom of Morelos*, 1981), about the Mexican national hero, and *La noche de Hernán Cortés* (*The Night of Hernán Cortés*, 1990), a version of the Conquest. His *Vivir del teatro* (*Life in the Theatre*, two volumes) recounts the vicissitudes encountered in staging his several plays. GW

Leno, Dan [George Galvin] 1860–1904 Generally regarded as the greatest British VARIETY artist. In a short lifetime, which ended in mental and physical collapse, he brought to maturity the achievements of his predecessors in MUSIC-HALL and PANTOMIME.

The son of minor London music-hall artists, by his own testimony he first went on stage at the age of three, and long before he reached manhood had acquired an impressive range of skills – contortionist, clog-dancer, Irish com-

edian, character vocalist – and a veteran's experience of the exhausting provincial tour and the challenging performance conditions of the minor halls. To the end of his days he employed the attention-grabbing entrance described by fellow comedian Harry Randall as 'a quick run down to the footlights, a roll like a drum with his feet, his leg raised, and brought down with a loud clap from the foot'; after which he would relax into an attitude of confidential friendliness to create a colourful character sketch, deliver a tortuous monologue or patter song, and impart the latest gossip of his fictitious neighbour Mrs Kelly.

His solo London debut came in the East End in 1885. He was an immediate hit with his first recorded appearance in drag as a 'Dickensian nurse-maid' who was 'off to get milk for the twins', rapidly transferred to the WEST END, and got his first London pantomime engagement as dame in *Jack and the Beanstalk* at the Surrey the following year – the beginning of an illustrious run of Christmas shows, including 15 consecutively at DRURY LANE from 1888. By 1897, when he made his first American appearance, he was billed hyperbolically as 'the funniest man on earth', and in 1898 Milton Bode wrote the BURLESQUE revue *Orlando Dando* specifically as a vehicle for his talents. In 1901, after a Command Performance at the royal residence Sandringham, he was presented with a diamond cravat-pin of the royal monogram, and became known (to the press at least) as 'the King's Jester'. It was the nearest he got to the honour bestowed on his younger contemporaries HARRY LAUDER and GEORGE ROBEY.

Leno's studio sound-recordings are disappointing, for he lacked the vocal strength and subtlety of MERSON and Robey. But some elements of his genius can be defined. Observers paid tribute to his infectious energy, and he had been trained in physical techniques since he could walk; it seems likely that he applied these to the creation of the multitude of vivid caricatures that throng his career. These imply, too, a fertile imagination, manifest again in his peopling the stage with non-existent characters with whom he conducted a one-sided dialogue. MARIE LLOYD noticed the distressing effect of his eyes, large and deep-set beneath steeply arched brows (and she might have mentioned his mouth, which in repose turned down slightly at the corners), and there are hints in his script (mainly written for him by Herbert Darnley) of the laughter that fights back tears. Physical objects take on a life of their own – an egg is 'awfully artful' and a cake may look as if it has 'an extremely obstinate nature'. Human relationships are predatory: landladies advertise 'Young men taken in and done for', and even friends meeting at Christmas are probably wondering who is going to stand the first drink. 'You can't get away from facts', Leno was fond of saying; inescapably, his ambiguous comic vision was of a recalcitrant physical world inhabited by unreliable people.

The burlesque autobiography, *Dan Leno, Hys Book*, is now known to have been ghosted by T. C. Elder. AEG

Lenormand, Henri-René 1882–1951 French playwright. Lenormand's work became associated with the PITOËFF company, who performed many of his plays between the wars. They employed techniques pioneered by CHEKHOV and PIRANDELLO to convey the psychological life, drawing on the insights of Freudian psychoanalysis.

His plays have not been revived since the war but his *Confessions d'un auteur dramatique* (*Confessions of a Playwright*, 1952) gives insight into both the period and his profession of playwright. DB

Lenya, Lotte [Karoline Blamauer] 1900–81 Vienna-born actress and singer, who went to Germany to begin an acting career. In 1928 she appeared in the Berlin premiere of the BRECHT-Weill *The Threepenny Opera*. After emigrating to the USA with her husband, composer KURT WEILL, she made her BROADWAY debut in *The Eternal Road* (1937). She appeared in several plays and MUSICALS, but is remembered for the OFF-BROADWAY production of *The Threepenny Opera* (1954), the REVUE *Brecht on Brecht* (1961) and the musical *Cabaret* (1966). MK

Lenz, Johann (Michael Reinhold) 1751–92 German playwright. Among the most prominent of the STURM UND DRANG dramatists, Lenz is best known for his comedies of contemporary life, *The Soldiers* (1776) and *The Tutor* (1778), which are two of the first German plays of genuine quality to exhibit the influence of SHAKESPEARE. His essay 'Observations on the Theatre' (1774) is among the most perceptive documents of the important German Shakespeare criticism of the 18th century. Lenz's creative career was cut short by a severe decline in his mental faculties, which led to his early death. SW

Leonard, Hugh [John Keyes Byrne] 1926– Irish playwright. ABBEY productions of *The Birthday Party* (1956) and *A Leap in the Dark* (1958) established Leonard, who honed his dramatic craft while writing for Granada Television. In *The Poker Session* (1963) edgy menace intrudes into suburban family comedy. *Mick and Mick* (1966) and the most politically suggestive of Leonard's plays, *The Au Pair Man* (1968), followed, interspersed with superb stage adaptations of Joyce (*Stephen D*, 1962, and *Dublin One*, 1963) and Flann O'Brien (*When the Saints Go Cycling In*, 1965).

While Leonard often satirizes Irish middle-class social and political life (*The Patrick Pearse Motel*, 1971, *Time Was*, 1976, and *Kill*, 1982), his best work has become more humane and personal: both *Da* (1973), in which memories and ghosts subvert the mock sophistication of a writer returning home for his father's funeral, and *A Life* (1976), which retraces the desiccation of an astute but emotionally crippled man, are based on autobiographical material. By repeating a basic story in two time frames, his recent comedy, *Moving* (1990), explores the ironies of social 'progress'.

Leonard's writing often marries darker or satirical tones to familiar comic genres from commercial theatre; but, while his craft and wit occasionally suggest glibness, in his best work – original or adapted – they serve to explore with humour the more complex areas of ordinary self-deception. DM GF

Leonardo da Vinci 1452–1519 Italian artist, scientist and stage designer. Little is known of Leonardo's work for the theatre, but extant designs suggest a keen interest in scenic decoration and stage machinery; from these, several attempts have been made to construct models of the machinery and stages he intended, like those for Isabella of Aragon's entry into Milan (1489) and the scene and revolving stage prepared for Poliziano's *Orfeo* (c.1495). KR

Leonov, Leonid (Maksimovich) 1899–1994 A prolific, Lenin Prize-winning Soviet novelist and dramatist, important for his efforts to make psychological and social REALISM the bases for the new Soviet literature. His work, which tends to be symbolic and even in places allegorical, consciously evokes Dostoevsky, CHEKHOV, GORKY and other predecessors in its treatment of the moral, emotional and psychological crises precipitated in individuals of various social classes, especially the 'little man', by societal change. His 13 plays include dramatizations of two of his novels, *The Badgers* (1927) and *Skutarevsky* (1934). The former, like his first original play, *Untilovsk* (1928), employs a Siberian setting. The latter, a character study of an old-guard scientist converted to Bolshevism, reflects the familiar Soviet conflict between 'altruism and egoism, self-sacrifice and self-love' – i.e. between service to the collective and to the individual, a question about which Leonov is more philosophical than dogmatic. His best-known play, *The Orchards of Polovchansk* (1938), embodies a Chekhovian sense of place, milieu and history – society on the brink of change. Written during the purges of 1936–8, under official pressure it was transformed by its author from a psychological character study to a sociopolitical tale with a clearly identifiable anti-Soviet villain. His most popular play, *Invasion* (1942), like *Lyonushka* (1943), is a patriotic picture of war-time heroism. It is notable for demonstrating the character-building potential of war. SG

Léotard, Jules 1838–70 French aerialist, son of a gymnastics instructor; he abandoned his law studies to become a trapeze artist, winning almost immediate success on his debut at the Cirque Napoléon, Paris, on 12 November 1859. Léotard perfected the trapeze act, inventing the *salto mortale* (see ACROBATICS) through the moving apparatus and lending his name to the tight-fitting garment he wore; and, after an engagement at the London Alhambra, inspiring the song 'The Daring Young Man on the Flying Trapeze'. His career was an unbroken series of triumphs, and in 1959 a commemorative plaque in his honour was dedicated at the Cirque d'Hiver. LS

Lepage, Robert 1957– Canadian theatre artist. Lepage studied with Alain Knapp in Paris, returning to Quebec in 1980 to help found Théâtre Repère, a company based on the creative style developed by Anna and Lawrence Halprin, in which a production takes shape from an initial focus on a single, tangible 'resource' object.

The distinctive hallmark of Lepage's creations is their collaborative shape, which encompasses all aspects of theatre. His experiences with improvisational acting taught him the necessity of having a peripheral consciousness that allows writing, acting, set design and stage direction to evolve 'globally'. For his one-man shows, *Vinci* (1986) and *Needles and Opium* (1991), this resulted in a sense of playfulness and freedom of movement in an atmosphere of stylistic multi-media effects. Moreover, the shape of a production evolves with changes in cast or venue: *La trilogie des dragons* began as a 90-minute piece (1985), grew to a three-hour performance (1986), and reached its final form as three autonomous two-hour shows (1987). Each version was not a work-in-progress, but a completed production at a particular stage in its process. Likewise, his *Plaques tectoniques (Tectonic Plates*, 1988) underwent the process of re-creation for its production in Glasgow (1990) to reflect the intercultural interaction between Canadian and Scottish cast members. A similar evolution is planned for *Seven Streams of the River Ota*, which opened in its initial form at the 1994 EDINBURGH FESTIVAL.

To create his 'global' theatre, Lepage frequently explores this type of intercultural collaboration on the levels of both theme and structure. His bilingual production of *Romeo and Juliet* (1989) recast SHAKESPEARE's story in the light of the tensions between the French and English cultures in his native Canada. His *Midsummer Night's Dream* (1992) at London's NATIONAL THEATRE was heralded as the only production to rival the originality of PETER BROOK's 1970 version. His upcoming film, *Le Confessional*, draws together Alfred Hitchcock, Quebec culture, and film companies from Canada, England and France.

Seeking to encourage an active, rather than passive, theatre experience, Lepage expects a collaborative effort from the audience, relying on them to appropriate the production and make their own meaning from what he presents. DAH

Lermontov, Mikhail (Yurievich) 1814–41 Russia's greatest romantic poet after PUSHKIN; a somewhat lesser novelist and dramatist in the same vein. He wrote under the influence of SHAKESPEARE, BYRON, SCHILLER, Pushkin, GRIBOEDOV, Scott and HUGO, as well as at the promptings of a melancholic, self-dramatizing, rebellious temperament. His career as an artist and military man described a cycle of sin, redemption and willed death, which he achieved in a duel with a former schoolmate.

Lermontov's five dramas palely reflect his life. *The Spaniards* (written 1830, published 1880, produced 1924) employs the romantic locale of Spain during the Inquisition as a metaphor for the repressive reign of Tsar Nikolai I. It is replete with poisonings, abduction, pathos, frenzy and a semi-autobiographical protagonist at odds with himself and society who murders the thing he loves. His best play, *Masquerade* (written 1836, censored production 1852, uncensored production 1862; see CENSORSHIP), is a Russian *Othello* by way of Pushkin which combines romanticism and social REALISM. The languor of its 'superfluous man' protagonist Arbenin masks a tormented soul, much as the court society which victimizes him and his wife masks cruelty and hypocrisy with gaiety and fashion. The play received an opulent mounting at the Aleksandrinsky Theatre in 1917 by MEYERHOLD, with sets by Golovin and music by Glazunov. Lermontov's remaining plays include *Men and Passions* (written 1830, published 1880); *The Strange Man* (written 1831, published 1860), a rewritten version of the former; and *The Two Brothers* (written 1836, produced 1915), which he reworked as the psychological novel *Princess Ligovskaya*. His celebrated novel, *A Hero of Our Time* (1840), features the fatalistic hero Pechorin, whom CHEKHOV spoofs via

Solyony in *Three Sisters*.

As a dramatist Lermontov continued the progressive romantic tendencies begun by Pushkin, mixing extreme subjectivism with a socially minded anti-tyrannical stance. His eccentric social SATIRE suggests Griboedov, and his grotesque social realism, SUKHOVO-KOBYLIN. His theatricalized fatalism, dandyism and eroticism, primarily in *Masquerade*, have something of the flavour of the symbolist-influenced dramatists of the early 20th century, especially ANDREEV, SOLOGUB and KUZMIN (see SYMBOLISM). SG

Lerner, Alan Jay 1918–86 and
Frederick Loewe 1904–88 American lyricist, and composer. Loewe, a classically trained composer born in Vienna, and Lerner, who had studied at Juilliard and Harvard, collaborated on their first MUSICAL score, *What's Up?*, in 1943. Four years later the team had its first major success with *Brigadoon*, a fantasy set in a magical Scottish village. Their next show, *Paint Your Wagon*, achieved a modest run. In 1956, Lerner and Loewe wrote the score for *My Fair Lady*, a musical version of GEORGE BERNARD SHAW's *Pygmalion*. One of the most successful musical comedies ever produced, *My Fair Lady*'s score was a perfect blending of Loewe's OPERETTA music with Lerner's pseudo-Shavian lyrics. Their next show, *Camelot* (1960), was generally conceded to be inferior to its predecessor. Lerner and Loewe collaborated on only one other BROADWAY musical, a 1973 adaptation of their film *Gigi*. After Loewe's retirement, Lerner worked with other composers on a number of shows.

Loewe's music successfully combined the older operetta tradition with more modern Broadway musical idioms. Lerner's versatility as a lyricist was demonstrated in songs whose styles ranged from the sophisticated verbal trickery of LORENZ HART to the simple treatment of OSCAR HAMMERSTEIN II. MK

Lesage, Alain-René 1668–1747 French novelist and dramatist. A near-penniless orphan in his teens, Lesage subsequently supported himself and his own family by his pen alone. His earliest plays, based on Spanish models, were unremarkable but it was a Spanish romance that inspired his first truly original work, *Le Diable boiteux* (*The Devil on Two Sticks*, 1707), a novel painting a realistic picture of contemporary French society and social types. The same year saw his first theatrical success with the COMEDY *Crispin rival de son maître* (*Crispin Rival of his Master*), which reflects a similar impulse to depict the true manners of the age in its portrayal of an opportunistic valet who impersonates his master in order to usurp the marriage settlement to which he considers himself no less entitled, and who acquits himself so well as almost to succeed. In his next play, *Turcaret* (1709), the central character, a financier or tax-farmer who is exploited by the fashionable people of his circle as mercilessly as he exploits others, is clearly drawn from contemporary life, and Lesage takes a sardonic view of a society motivated entirely by greed and self-interest. The play met with fierce opposition from financial quarters and despite its success at the COMÉDIE-FRANÇAISE was withdrawn after only seven performances, though it has remained in the classic repertoire until the present day.

Thereafter Lesage devoted himself almost entirely to the fair theatres, and between 1712 and 1744, when he left Paris to live in Boulogne, he produced over 100 *vaudevilles*, comic OPERAS, *pièces à écriteaux* (placard plays) and suchlike, many of them in collaboration with FUZELIER, d'Orneval and PIRON. His best-known work, however, is the picaresque tale of *Gil Blas de Santillane*, published in 12 books between 1715 and 1735, which profoundly influenced the evolution of the European novel. Despite his disapproval two of his sons became professional actors, the eldest, René-André (1695–1743), with some distinction under the name of Montménil. DR

lesbian theatre A term used to describe theatre made by or for lesbians, and to differentiate this from work by gay men.

Examples of lesbian work in the theatre before 1968 are rare. Lesbians in a theatre context are triply invisible: as women, as homosexual, as women in a male theatre tradition. Lesbian theatre history has focused on texts and figures 'readable' as homoerotic – e.g., the 18th-century cross-dressing actress Charlotte Charke, daughter of COLLEY CIBBER – and has found evidence there of the occasional lesbian presence or voice. The dominant view (from Michel Foucault), however, is that the social (and thus representable) identity of the 'lesbian' was not created until the late 19th and early 20th centuries, through sexology and psychoanalysis. Key figures in the British feminist theatre of the period were undoubtedly lesbian. EDITH CRAIG (daughter of ELLEN TERRY) founded the Pioneer Players (1911–20), a theatre company dominated by women and feminist ideas; her partner Christopher St John (Christabel Marshall) co-authored plays for the Actresses' Franchise League with Cicely Hamilton, whom a recent biographer proposes as lesbian. St John wrote novels and other plays with discernible lesbian narratives.

The first British play in which female homoeroticism can clearly be read is Edith Ellis's *The Mothers* (1915), a one-acter which uses the contemporary feminist image of the heroic mother to figure women's erotic bonding. Edith Ellis's husband was the British sexologist, Havelock Ellis, and one of the interesting features of the play is its opposition to his depiction of the 'mannish' lesbian.

Feminism as a movement declined after the First World War, and with it women's theatre and the potential for a lesbian drama. (This contrasts with the history of gay men's theatre: the 1920s and 30s in Britain saw the 'homosexualization' of the theatre.) The first plays containing recognizable 'lesbian' characters were produced in this period. German playwright Christa Winsloe's *Children in Uniform* (1932) and US playwright LILLIAN HELLMAN's *The Children's Hour* (1934) are two well known examples; others are documented in K. Curtin's *We Can Always Call Them Bulgarians*. But none was written by a lesbian, and the lesbian characters are presented within the descriptions of the sexologists or psychoanalysts. It was against these 'negative images' of lesbianism as hysteria, or failed heterosexuality, or masculinity complex, that the first phase of a truly lesbian theatre protested, in the USA and in Britain, in the 1970s and 1980s.

Lesbian theatre in Britain developed as part of the alternative political theatre movement. In its early phase it was allied to gay men's theatre. Gay Sweatshop, Britain's first GAY THEATRE company, was founded in 1975 and presented its first lesbian piece, *Any Woman Can* by Jill Posner, in 1976. Like many first lesbian and gay plays this tells the story of 'coming out', the first lesbian RITE OF PASSAGE. Fairly soon, however, the alliance with gay men was challenged by an increasingly radical lesbian feminism. Although lesbians continued to work with Gay Sweatshop, for some time there were separate male and female companies, and other, specifically lesbian, theatre companies developed. *Care and Control* (devised by the company and scripted by Michelene Wandor, 1977) was the Gay Sweatshop women's company's first production. A documentary account of the problems faced by lesbian mothers in custody cases, it inaugurated the feminist phase of lesbian theatre. There were further plays about lesbian mothers (*AID Thy Neighbour*, Michelene Wandor, 1978; *Neaptide*, Sarah Daniels, 1986); plays challenging male violence (*Curfew*, Siren Theatre, 1981) and patriarchal control of women's bodies and sexuality (*Basin*, Jacqueline Rudet, 1985; *Byrthrite*, Sarah Daniels, 1986); and plays celebrating the 'lesbian continuum' (*The Fires of Bride*, Ellen Galford/Red Rag, 1990; *Twice Over*, Jackie Kay, 1988).

Lesbian theatre expanded throughout the 1970s and 80s. Specifically lesbian companies were formed: in Britain; Hormone Imbalance, Siren, Hard Corps, Parker and Klein, Character Ladies, Red Rag, Dramatrix Productions and Shameful Practice. Lesbian playwrights were commissioned by other companies, including the Women's Theatre Group, the English Stage Company at the ROYAL COURT and – astonishingly, given its poor record for producing women's plays – the NATIONAL THEATRE. And venues particularly or exclusively associated with lesbian theatre developed: Oval House and the Drill Hall in London, and the WOW Café in New York. In London encouragement was given in the first half of the 1980s by the radical left administration of the Greater London Council and its generous funding for gay and lesbian work. Lesbian theatre was part of an expanding gay and lesbian cultural scene, alongside publishing houses, bookshops, bars and cafés, music and visual arts, much of which was also funded by the GLC.

That the audience for lesbian theatre is drawn from a metropolitan lesbian community raises questions about the point of address of lesbian theatre. Some, at least, of the 'issue-based' lesbian feminist theatre implied a (male) heterosexual spectator as recipient of protest about heterosexism or of new 'positive images' of lesbians. Although these plays were important in promoting lesbian audiences' sense of community, in its most recent phase, from the late 1980s, lesbian theatre seems to be turning away from political protest towards a celebration of the specificity of lesbian difference and desire. From address to undress ...

Not that sex was absent from earlier lesbian theatre. The British lesbian comedy duo Parker and Klein, and Hard Corps, the company with which they worked, were dedicated, in Debby Klein's phrase, to 'putting the sex back into sexual politics'. In Klein's 1986 comedy *Coming Soon* taboo figures (the nun and the butch) play havoc with the heroine's political correctness. Siren Theatre and Tasha Fairbanks's plays *Pulp* (1985) and *Hotel Destiny* (1987) use the *noir* thriller and Country and Western images respectively to represent lesbian desire. Dramatrix Productions' annual lesbian PANTOMIMES at the Drill Hall have been popular for their cross-dressing and flagrant transgression of classical heterosexual narratives. They began in 1987 with Cheryl Moch's *Cinderella*, which premiered in 1985 at the WOW Café, followed by lesbian versions of *Peter Pan* by Bryony Lavery, and *The Adventures of Robyn Hood* and *The Snow Queen*, both by Nona Shepphard.

Generally, however, these have been stories *about* sex, in which the erotic exchange between performer and audience has been rather coyly acknowledged. Recent work by US performers Split Britches (*Split Britches*, 1981; *Beauty and the Beast*, 1982; *Upwardly Mobile Home*, 1984; *Little Women*, 1988; *Anniversary Waltz*, 1989; *Lesbians Who Kill*, by Deborah Margolin, 1992) and Holly Hughes (*The Well of Horniness*, 1983; *The Lady Dick*, 1985; *Dress Suits to Hire*, with Split Britches, 1987; *World without End*, 1990; *No Trace of the Blonde*, 1992) is much more – to use the title of Gay Sweatshop's 1994 lesbian show – In Your Face. Their work is saturated with sexuality. The banished figures of lesbian culture and desire, the butch and the femme, have been reinvested with desire; erotic power and play have returned as *the* lesbian performance. A new aesthetic of lesbian theatre eschews 'representation' for a live/now performance of the lesbian body. Dressing, undressing, cross-dressing, PARODY, allusion, self-reverentiality and camp mark this theatre. In 1991 Split Britches collaborated with the British drag company Bloolips on *Belle Reprieve*, a butch/female/drag version of *A Streetcar Named Desire* which played on both sides of the Atlantic; one half of Split Britches, Lois Weaver, is now also joint artistic director of Gay Sweatshop, and Peggy Shaw, the other half, with US performer Pamela Sneed, opened a double bill of butch performance pieces – *Two Big Girls* – at London's Institute of Contemporary Arts in February 1994.

In the mid-1990s the term 'lesbian theatre' seems to be becoming outmoded. Having moved away from feminism (and from presenting as real/nice girls), what is now drawing lesbian audiences is Queer performance – Queer as something outside, disruptive, excessively sexual, incapable of assimilation; and the performance of the lesbian as neither real nor nice, nor girl. JD

See: S. E. Case (ed.), *Performing Feminisms*, Baltimore, Md, 1990; J. Davis (ed.), *Lesbian Plays* and *Lesbian Plays: 2*, London, 1987 and 1989; L. Hart (ed.), *Making a Spectacle*, Ann Arbor, Mich., 1989; L. Hart and P. Phelan (eds.), *Acting Out*, Ann Arbor, Mich., 1993.

Lescarbot, Marc ?1570–1642 French historian, poet and playwright, author of the first dramatic text composed and performed in French in the New World, the verse play *Le Théâtre de Neptune en la Nouvelle-France* (*The Theatre of Neptune in New France*), enacted on the waters before Port Royal, Acadia (today's Annapolis Royal, Nova Scotia), in November 1606. It portrays Neptune and his Tritons, who along with four American Indians (played by Frenchmen) welcome the colony's leaders on their return from a dangerous exploration, and ends with an invitation to all present to share a celebratory banquet. Replete with neoclassical allusions, this slender text, first

published in 1609, is a good-humoured example of the dramatic sub-genre known in France as a *réception*, a form that would long remain popular in French Canada. It was performed again on the same spot in 1956, marking the 350th anniversary of the birth of the theatre in North America. LED

Leslie, Fred [Frederick Hobson] 1855–92 English actor, the greatest star of early MUSICAL COMEDY. He made his professional debut in 1878, but it was a musical version of BOUCICAULT's *Rip Van Winkle* at London's Comedy Theatre in 1882 that made him a star. Employed by GEORGE EDWARDES at the GAIETY in 1885, he played opposite NELLIE FARREN in the BURLESQUE *Little Jack Sheppard* (1885) and *Monte Cristo, Jr* (1886) as well as in his own *Ruy Blas; or The Blasé Roué* (1889), and it was he above all who sustained the fortunes of the Gaiety in the aftermath of Nellie Farren's retirement in 1891. His untimely death of typhoid robbed the English theatre of a remarkable talent. PT

Lesotho see BOTSWANA, LESOTHO AND SWAZILAND

Lessing, G(otthold) E(phraim) 1729–81 German playwright and critic. Although Lessing's career in the theatre might seem to lack stature, because he so frequently deprecated his own work, his writings were in fact crucial to the German theatre at an important phase in its development. He was a journalist, critic and dramaturge during the short-lived Hamburg National Theatre project, and his essays consistently brought to his contemporaries' attention the shortcomings of the French drama, then still widely admired and imitated in Germany. Lessing was also among the first to recognize the strengths of SHAKESPEARE and the English dramatic tradition, in particular for the warm humanity expressed in their plays. In the *Hamburg Dramaturgy* (1768) especially, Lessing attempted to rid the German stage of its dependence on the French and in so doing engaged in radical interpretation of ARISTOTLE, focusing in particular on the nature of pity and fear. The end of drama, as conceived by Lessing, is compassion; by arousing compassion, the drama fulfils its important social function, as the audience becomes more aware of the humanity of those around it.

Lessing wrote several plays, the most notable of which are *Miss Sara Sampson* (1755), a domestic tragedy, highly popular in its day, that owed much to GEORGE LILLO and the novels of Samuel Richardson; *Minna von Barnhelm* (1767), widely regarded as the first major comedy in the German language; *Emilia Galotti* (1772), a tense, disturbing and theatrically effective tragedy that contains much criticism of the egoism and venality of the rulers of contemporary petty states; and *Nathan the Wise* (1779), a moving and noble plea for religious tolerance. Though Lessing claimed that he did not create with the spontaneity of the true artist, these four plays were among the first works of enduring quality written for the German stage. SW

Levental, Valery (Yakovlevich) 1938– A leading Russian designer of the 1970s–90s, responsible for the MEYERHOLDian tracking set which drove EFROS's celebrated production of GOGOL's *Marriage* (1974) in Moscow, and the revised scenography for the American version at the GUTHRIE THEATRE (1978). Levental designed an all-white revolving graveyard set for Efros's Taganka Theatre production of *The Cherry Orchard* (1975), a near-scale model locomotive for ALEKSANDR GELMAN's *We, the Undersigned* (1979), and a Levitan-like landscape with mobile gazebo for EFREMOV's production of *The Seagull* (1980), both at the MOSCOW ART THEATRE.   SG

Levin, Hanoch 1943– Israeli satirical playwright. The thesis of all his plays has been defined as 'I humiliate and/or am humiliated, therefore I am.' His plays depict petit-bourgeois life in Tel-Aviv as the antithesis of the idealism of the pioneers. His irreverent and pessimistic debunking of society has earned him the reputation of misanthropist and decadent writer. But he has won recognition and popularity for his unflinching naturalism of speech and his satirical barbs. In the greatest of his plays, *The Passion of Job* (1981), he created the Jewish equivalent of the Gentile myth. Among his other plays are *You and I and the Next War* (1969), *Queen of the Bath* (1970), *Hefetz* (1972), *Yaacobi and Leidental* (1972), *Vardaleh's Youth* (1974), *Shitz* (1975), *Krum* (1975), *The Patriot* (1982), *The Suitcase Packers* (1983) and *The Child Dreams* (1993). Although admired at home, Levin's plays have not found favour with audiences abroad, perhaps because of the highly local idiom of his SATIRE.   HAS

Lewes, G(eorge) H(enry) 1817–78 English critic and playwright, the grandson of an actor. Lewes was a man of many parts – philosopher, linguist, actor, dramatist, novelist, biographer and dabbler in the law, business and medicine. He had 14 plays, mostly adaptations from the French, performed in his lifetime, the most successful of which, *The Game of Speculation* (1851), provided CHARLES JAMES MATHEWS with one of his best parts, that of Affable Hawk. Lewes's dramatic CRITICISM has lasted better than his plays. The earliest examples were written for the *Leader* (1850–4), of which he was joint editor with LEIGH HUNT's son, Thornton. The campaign he conducted there against CHARLES KEAN was extended into the longer essays, written for the *Pall Mall Gazette*, some of which were collected in *On Actors and the Art of Acting* (1875). There is very little finer writing on the art of the actor than Lewes's essays on EDMUND KEAN, RACHEL and Charles James Mathews. They are eloquent and penetrating. Lewes was one of the many distinguished amateurs who delighted to act for CHARLES DICKENS at Tavistock House – he had had some professional experience in Manchester in 1849. It is a pity that his own distinction as a writer has been engulfed by interest in his long liaison with George Eliot.   PT

Lewis, Leopold 1828–90 British playwright, whose single claim to fame was his adaptation as *The Bells* of *Le Juif Polonais* by Erckmann and Chatrian. The role of the guilt-stricken Mathias was superbly played by IRVING in 1871. Lewis was a solicitor, volatile to the point of instability. Of three later plays staged in London, none succeeded.   PT

Lewis, Robert 1909– American director, producer and actor. Lewis first appeared with the CIVIC REPERTORY THEATRE during the 1929–30 season. From 1931 to 41 he worked with the GROUP THEATRE, for whom he directed

the road company of *Golden Boy* in 1938. He made his first appearance in London in the same year. After the war he directed extensively on BROADWAY; among his hit productions were *Brigadoon* (1947) and *The Teahouse of the August Moon* (1953). With ELIA KAZAN and CHERYL CRAWFORD he founded the ACTORS STUDIO in 1947. Lewis has also appeared in many films, taught acting and theatre at New York's Sarah Lawrence College and Yale, and is the author of *Method – or Madness?* (1958), an explication of the STANISLAVSKY system of acting. In 1984 he published his autobiography, *Slings and Arrows*. Kent State University, which houses Lewis's papers, initiated the Robert Lewis Medal for Lifetime Achievement in Theater Research in 1991.   SMA

Lewis, Saunders 1893–1985 Perhaps the only contender for the title of Wales's leading playwright. Born in Wallasey and educated at Liverpool University, where he gained a first in English, he lectured in Welsh at Swansea University from 1926 to 1939 and became president of the newly formed Nationalist Party (Plaid Cymru). During this period he was gaoled for his political activity (a token act of arson against the RAF bombing school at Penyberth), lost his university post, and from 1939 to 52 was a freelance writer and lecturer, becoming the most distinguished Welsh literary critic of the period. He returned to lecturing at the University of Wales, Cardiff, in 1952 and remained there until his retirement.

His first essay in playwriting was the English play *The Eve of St John* (1921), but his greatest plays are undoubtedly *Blodeuwedd* (1923–5, completed 1948) and *Siwan* (1956), both of which show Lewis exploring the older Celtic mythological tradition within the constraints of strict metre verse form. Born into a Calvinistic Methodist family, he nevertheless rejected the Nonconformism which had so powerfully influenced 19th- and 20th-century Welsh writing: he was received into the Roman Catholic Church in 1932, and the powerful exploration of both personal and larger themes in his drama is strongly influenced by his profound sense of the European Catholic tradition.   MA

Leybourne, George 1842–84 British MUSIC-HALL star, born in Stourbridge. As a 'buffo vocalist' under the name Joe Saunders he honed his skills at Tyneside concert rooms and made his London debut around 1863 working with a mechanical donkey. Imposingly tall (6ft 4in) and handsome, Leybourne perfected the image of the *lion comique*, the free-spending, hard-drinking sport. His most famous number was 'Champagne Charlie', a persona he carried into private life, treating all and sundry. He was rivalled by Arthur Lloyd, Alfred Vance and G. H. Macdermott, but he excelled them all in the breadth of his repertory and the magnetism of his personality. Alcoholic, debilitated and impoverished, he was still at the top of the bill when he made his final appearance in 1884, at the Queens, Poplar, London.   LS

Li Yu 1611–80 Chinese dramatist, drama theorist and director. He trained and directed a theatre troupe of actresses, travelling round the country to perform at homes of high officials. He was a talented and versatile playwright and director. His work reveals a profound knowledge of stage practices and dramatic composition based on first-hand experience. In a rare book on Chinese dramatic theory, *A Temporary Lodge for My Leisure Thoughts* (*Xianqing ouji*, 1671) Li described his own theatre practice in detail and rejected the stigma laid upon theatre by officials and scholars. ACS

Libya see MIDDLE EAST

Liebler, Theodore A. 1852–1941 American producer of nearly 240 plays in association with GEORGE TYLER, beginning with *The Royal Box* (1897). He also produced the riot-plagued US tour (1911) of Ireland's ABBEY THEATRE. Many of the greatest hits of Liebler and Company, such as *The Christian* (1898), *Alias Jimmy Valentine* (1910) and *The Garden of Allah* (1911), were adapted from popular fiction. Liebler's greatest hit was BOOTH TARKINGTON's chauvinistic *The Man from Home* (1908), which ran for 496 performances. He retired when a series of expensive failures after the First World War caused the collapse of Liebler and Company. WD

Lifshits, A. M. see VOLODIN, ALEKSANDR

lighting see STAGE LIGHTING

Ligier 1796–1872 French actor of large voice, small stature and a considerable talent for make-up. Ligier made his debut at the COMÉDIE-FRANÇAISE in 1820 as Néron in *Britannicus*. In 1824 he was allowed to play heavies. His argumentative temperament led to his departure from the Comédie for the ODÉON. In 1829 he created DELAVIGNE's Marino Faliero at the Porte-Saint-Martin (see BOULEVARD), following this with parts in the new repertoire at the Odéon, notably in DUMAS's *Christine, ou Stockholm et Fontainebleau* and VIGNY's *La Maréchale d'Ancre*. Re-admitted to the Comédie-Française as a *sociétaire* in 1831, he continued his line of sinister historical figures with *Louis XI* (1832), created Triboulet for the one performance of *Le Roi s'amuse*, Glocester in *Les Enfants d'Édouard*, Savoisy in *Charles VII et ses grands vassaux*, Caligula (1837) and, one of his greatest roles, Frédéric in HUGO's *Les Burgraves*. His last role was that of Antoine in *Caesar's Will* (*Le Testament de César*, 1847). He retired in 1851, but continued to appear at the Porte-Saint-Martin for a time, then returned to his native Bordeaux, where he acted in local performances until the age of 75. JMCC

Lillie, Beatrice (Gladys) [Lady Robert Peel] 1898–1988 Canadian comedienne, who appeared in VARIETY as a child. Her debut in London REVUE came in *Not Likely* (1914), singing lachrymose ballads, and she did not find her niche as a comic until André Charlot's revues of 1917 and 1924. The latter took her to the USA; her New York successes included *This Year of Grace* (1929) with NOËL COWARD, *The Show Is On* (1936) with BERT LAHR, *Set to Music* (1939) when she introduced Coward's 'I've Been to a Mahhhvelous Party', and *Inside USA* (1948). Lillie was the consummate revue performer, wielding the slapstick with a raised pinky, puncturing her own poses of sophisticated grandeur with lapses into raucous vulgarity. She

performed in the one-woman show *An Evening with Beatrice Lillie* (1952), in a revival of the ZIEGFELD Follies (1957), in the title role of *Auntie Mame* (1958) and as the medium Mme Arcati in *High Spirits* (1964). She also wrote an autobiography, *Every Other Inch a Lady*. LS

Lillo, George ?1691–1739 English playwright. Very little is known of his life. He worked as a partner in his father's jewellery business and seems to have died a fairly wealthy man. He began writing plays in 1730. His reputation is based on two works: *The London Merchant* (1731) and *Fatal Curiosity* (1736). The former, also known as *The History of George Barnwell*, is a rare example of English domestic TRAGEDY, recounting the fall of an apprentice lured to steal from his master by his passion for an evil woman. The genre's antecedents in Elizabethan forms like ARDEN OF FEVERSHAM (which he also adapted) are turned by Lillo into drama much more dominated by pathos. The apprentice as tragic hero was highly influential in the development of European 'bourgeois' tragedy by ROUSSEAU, DIDEROT and LESSING, all of whom praised Lillo's play highly. *Fatal Curiosity*, set in Cornwall and recounting an impoverished old couple's desperate decision to murder a wealthy stranger who turns out to be their long-lost son, is far more fatalistic and profoundly affected the development of the German SCHICKSALTRAGÖDIE. PH

Lincoln Center, repertory theatre of see VIVIAN BEAUMONT AND MITZI E. NEWHOUSE THEATRES

Lincoln's Inn Fields Theatre (London) In March 1660 WILLIAM DAVENANT leased Lisle's Tennis Court and enlarged it for use as a theatre. It opened in June 1661 with performances of his play *The Siege of Rhodes*, the first production in England to use changeable scenery in a permanent professional theatre. Davenant's company used it until November 1671, when they moved into DORSET GARDEN. In January 1672 a fire gutted the Theatre Royal at Bridges Street and KILLIGREW's company, the King's Company, moved into Lincoln's Inn Fields in February, opening with a performance in the presence of the king, with the company 'discovered on stage in melancholic postures'. They used the theatre until March 1674, when they moved to the rebuilt Theatre Royal. It reverted to use as a tennis court until 1695 when BETTERTON's company, seceding from the United Company, refurbished it and opened there in April 1695 with CONGREVE's *Love for Love*. From 1705 until 1714 it was not used, but JOHN RICH then relicensed it and rebuilt it into a theatre with a capacity of 1400. His company used it until 1732 and it was in occasional use until 1744. PH

Lindau, Paul 1839–1919 German journalist, playwright and director. Lindau's comedies enjoyed some success in his lifetime. In 1895 he directed the MEININGEN COMPANY, after it had concluded its tours. In 1904, he was briefly director of the DEUTSCHES THEATER before MAX REINHARDT took it over. SW

Lindberg, Per 1890–1944 Swedish director, who introduced to Scandinavia the non-illusionistic principles of such modernists as CRAIG, REINHARDT and MEYERHOLD. With the designer Knut Ström he made an early breakthrough at Lorensbergsteatern, Göteborg (1918–23), with theatricalistic productions of SHAKESPEARE, STRINDBERG and modern European plays. He dreamed of establishing a broadly based People's Theatre, inspired by German and Soviet models, with a socially relevant repertoire, inexpensive subscriptions and the physical unification of stage and auditorium. These ideas were later pursued in Stockholm at the huge Concert Hall theatre (1926–7 and 1931–2) and at the club theatre he created at DRAMATEN. He advised on the design of MALMÖ STADSTEATER, but died before its opening. Lindberg's work was always politically informed, but during the 1930s it was increasingly employed against Fascism, especially in his productions in Bergen (1934) and Oslo (1935) of *The Hangman* by LAGERKVIST, with whom he shared a long and close collaboration. HL

Lindsay, Howard 1889–1968 American playwright, director, actor and producer. Born in Waterford, NY, Lindsay attended Harvard University for one year and the AMERICAN ACADEMY OF DRAMATIC ARTS for six months before launching his acting career in 1909. Numerous stage appearances followed in VAUDEVILLE and BURLESQUE, on tour with ARTHUR MCKEE RANKIN, and as a member of MARGARET ANGLIN's Company (1913–18). After military service in the First World War he returned to the stage, and in 1921 directed as well as acted in *Dulcy*. In the 1920s Lindsay established himself on BROADWAY as both director and actor. He married actress Dorothy Stickney in 1927, and starred with her in *Life with Father* (1939), a play he co-wrote with RUSSEL CROUSE. Other collaborations with Crouse included the book for *Anything Goes* (1934); *State of the Union* (1945), which won the Pulitzer Prize; the book for *Call Me Madam* (1950); *The Great Sebastians*, which featured ALFRED LUNT AND LYNN FONTANNE; and the books for *The Sound of Music* (1959) and *Mr President* (1962). Lindsay's most popular role, Father in *Life with Father*, drew praise from BROOKS ATKINSON for its 'rare taste and solid heartiness'. He was a craftsman more than an artist, able to 'pull together' stageworthy theatrical pieces with his collaborators. TLM

Linney, Romulus 1930– American director, educator and playwright, trained at the Yale School of Drama. Linney's career has been nurtured primarily by the RESIDENT NON-PROFIT PROFESSIONAL THEATRE outside New York and by OFF-BROADWAY, as well as by repertory theatres of Great Britain (see REGIONAL THEATRE (BRITAIN)), Canada, Germany and Austria. His critically acclaimed plays include *The Sorrows of Frederick* (1967), *The Love Suicide at Schofield Barracks* (1972), *Holy Ghosts* (1976), *Childe Byron* (1978), *Tennessee* (1979; Obie, 1980), *Laughing Stock* (1984), *Woman without a Name* (1985), *Pops* (1986), *Three Poets* (1989) and *Unchanging Love* (1991). Critic Martin Gottfried has called Linney 'a playwright of true literacy, a writer in the grand tradition', and Mel Gussow terms him 'poet of America's heartland'. In 1984 he received the Award in Literature from the American Academy and Institute of Arts and Letters. In 1991 he was appointed the first playwright-in-residence at New York's Signature

Theatre, which opened its first full season with *The Sorrows of Frederick*, directed by Linney, and devoted the 1991–2 season to his plays (concluding with a new one, *Ambrosio*, in April). In 1992 he was awarded an Obie for sustained excellence in playwriting. His daughter, actress Laura Linney, won a Theatre World Award for *Sight Unseen* (1992) and the Callaway Award in Classical Acting for her Thea in *Hedda Gabler* (1994). DBW

Lipman, Maureen 1946– British actress, who has become a household name in Britain by her appearances as the prototype Jewish mother Beattie in a series of 35 television commercials for British Telecom. She studied at the London Academy of Music and Dramatic Art during the late 1960s and from then on, as one of her friends put it, her career 'plummeted upwards'. Whilst attractive, she rarely played juvenile leads, despite carving out a name for herself as the only known Jewish Princess of France in *Henry V*. Her gift for comedy was immediately apparent, although her versatility was less obvious. She played a demanding, fur-coated camp follower in Richard Harris's cricket comedy, *Outside Edge* (1979), and a single woman with a thirst problem in Philip King's FARCE, *See How They Run* (revived in 1984), two memorable comic performances; although she also appeared in two more sombre plays, Martin Sherman's *Messiah* (1981) and ALAN PLATER's roughish, leftish biographical drama about Old Mother Riley, *On Your Way, Riley* (1981), at the Theatre Royal, Stratford, London. Her first major WEST END success came in 1986, when she played Ruth, the journalist from Ohio, trying to take New York (or parts of Greenwich Village) by storm in a revival of LEONARD BERNSTEIN's *Wonderful Town*. In 1988 her one-woman show, based on the songs and sketches of JOYCE GRENFELL, *Re-Joyce*, was an immediate hit at the Fortune Theatre in the West End and successfully revived in subsequent years. Her three books of memoirs, *How Was It for You?*, *Something to Fall Back On* and *Thank You for Having Me*, provide an endearing insight into the life of an actress whose zest for fun spreads from her career to her friendships and marriage (to the dramatist Jack Rosenthal), and even to the embarrassment of TV chat shows. JE

Liston, John 1776–1846 English comic actor, born in London and an early specialist in cockney parts. Liston made his undistinguished debut in London in 1799, but earned his reputation in the provinces before returning to star at the HAYMARKET in 1805. His first major success was as Caper in J. T. Allingham's *Who Wins?* (1808). Vanity, stupidity and cowardice were traits of Caper and of many of Liston's later successes, among them Apollo Belvi in Theodore Hook's *Killing No Murder* (1809) and Lubin Log in James Kenney's *Love, Law and Physics* (1812).

Snub-nosed, red-cheeked and enormously broad-bottomed, Liston provoked laughter by his very appearance as well as by the shrewd way in which he costumed himself to heighten the comic effect. He was a low comedian, given to extempore gags, but also to exploiting a contrast between the extravagance of his appearance and the comparative restraint of his performance style. That the management of COVENT GARDEN, where he acted from 1805 to 22, wished to keep him a buffoon is implicit in the

Shakespearian parts he was allotted – Ophelia in JOHN POOLE's *Hamlet Travestie* (1813), Bottom (1816), Pompey Bum (1816), Cloten (1817), Dromio of Syracuse (1819), Sir Andrew Aguecheek (1820) and Launce (1821). It was at the Haymarket that Liston created his greatest role, that of Paul Pry in Poole's play of that name (1825). Liston had left Covent Garden for DRURY LANE in 1823. There he became an established star, the most highly paid comic actor in the history of English theatre. His own hankering for more subtle performance led to the surprise move to the OLYMPIC under MADAME VESTRIS (1831–7), and it was there that he spent his last active years, acknowledged as one of the greatest of the age's many 'personality actors'. He retired in 1837.   PT

Little Theatre movement see COMMUNITY THEATRE/ LITTLE THEATRE MOVEMENT

Little Tich [Harry Relph] 1867–1928 Diminutive British character-comedian, patter-singer and eccentric dancer. Initially a 'nigger MINSTREL' (billed as Little Tichborne after the notorious claimant), in which role he perfected the big boot dance which became his trademark, he went solo in 1884, and made his PANTOMIME debut in Glasgow the following year. One of the most internationally minded and linguistically gifted of British VARIETY artists, he worked with great success in the USA and Europe, particularly in France where he played the Olympia and the FOLIES-BERGÈRE to such effect that in 1910 he was made an officer of the Académie-Française for his service to French theatre. He was a master of surrealistic patter: his caricatures of the Territorial, the Gas Inspector, the Ballerina and others trod a delicate line between the realistic and the bizarre. He appeared in the first Royal Command Charity Performance at London's Palace Theatre in 1912, along with CINQUEVALLI, LAUDER, ROBEY, TATE, TILLEY and others, and was an important influence on Chaplin.   AEG

Littler, Prince 1901–73 and Sir **Emile Littler** 1903–85 Two brothers who became the leading impresarios in popular theatre after the Second World War. Prince Littler began by staging major PANTOMIMES in the WEST END, such as *Jack and the Beanstalk* at DRURY LANE in 1936, and continued for more than 20 years with light entertainment, bringing over MUSICALS like *Brigadoon* (1950) and *Carousel* (1951) from the USA. His great talent, however, lay as a businessman who became chairman and managing director of Stoll Theatres Corporation, chairman of Moss Empire and, through Prince Littler Consolidated Trust, came to own or control nearly half the West End theatres and 57 of the main out-of-London touring theatres. When Prince Littler turned his attention to, and diverted some of his assets into, commercial television in 1955, the effect was to cause a major slump in regional theatre.

His younger brother, Emile, who was knighted in 1974, was a more orthodox impresario who had worked his way through the profession from being BARRY JACKSON's assistant stage manager at the BIRMINGHAM REP in the 1920s to his debut as a producer in 1934. He excelled in comedies, pantomimes and musicals, producing *Annie Get Your Gun, Son of Norway, Zip Goes a Million* and many other hits. From 1964 to 1967 he was president of the Society of West End Theatre Managers, and a governor of the ROYAL SHAKESPEARE COMPANY until he retired in 1973. From 1946 to 1983 he controlled the Palace Theatre in London, where many of his successes were staged.   JE

Littlewood, (Maudie) Joan 1914– British director, who was the driving force behind the establishment of the Theatre Workshop company at the Theatre Royal, Stratford, East London. Although she trained at the Royal Academy of Dramatic Art, she was always contemptuous of WEST END theatrical values and accordingly left London to go to Manchester as a radio producer. In 1935 she met the folk-singer and playwright Ewan MacColl (Jimmy Miller), whom she married, and together they founded an adventurous, left-wing touring company, Theatre Union. This became a pioneering example for the FRINGE companies of the 1960s, using AGIT-PROP techniques borrowed from German theatre and compensating for the lack of technical resources by the vigour of performance.

In 1953, after years on the road playing in village halls and community centres, Littlewood took her small company to a decaying music-hall in London's East End. The ambitiousness of her programmes, combining contemporary documentary drama with classic productions of little-known plays, attracted interest from the EDINBURGH FESTIVAL in 1955, where her productions of *ARDEN OF FEVERSHAM* and BEN JONSON's *Volpone* were hits. The next five years saw Littlewood's work and energy invested in the Theatre Workshop, Stratford. New plays (BRENDAN BEHAN's *The Quare Fellow* and *The Hostage*, SHELAGH DELANEY's *A Taste of Honey*), new MUSICALS (FRANK NORMAN and Lionel Bart's *Fings Ain't Wot They Used T'Be*) and, above all, new character actors and actresses emanated from her theatre, often to the despised West End.

Despairing at the inadequacy of her grants and her inability to keep her team together against the financial lures elsewhere, she tried to launch a 'fun palace' in Lea Valley, which never reached even the trial stage. After visits to Tunisia, more receptive initially to her schemes, Littlewood returned to the Theatre Workshop in 1963 to direct her greatest success *Oh, What a Lovely War!*, a documentary SATIRE about the First World War, set within a seaside concert party framework. Subsequently, although she directed the successful *Mrs Wilson's Diary* (1967) and *The Marie Lloyd Story* (1967) at the Theatre Workshop, of which the first transferred to the West End, she lost her old energy and passion for people's theatre. Her last Stratford production was *So You Want To Be in Pictures?* (1973), but her influence on other British directors and companies has been profound. In 1994 she published her autobiography, *Joan's Book.*   JE

liturgical drama Narrowly viewed, the drama that developed from the liturgy or services of the Christian Church in Western Europe and remained part of that liturgy. Since with surviving texts it is sometimes impossible to be sure whether they are part of the liturgy or not, however, it is better to use the term somewhat more inclusively. The plays developed in the monasteries, later spreading to other churches, and were performed by members of the community and sung in Latin.

The earliest known is the *Quem queritis?* (*Whom do you*

seek?) dialogue (10th-century), associated with the early-morning services of Easter day, in which the visit of the three Maries to the sepulchre and their conversation with the angel(s) is represented. Elaborate forms of this incident (the *Visitatio Sepulchri*) developed and new plays appeared from within the liturgy of the Christmas season, most importantly those centring on Herod and the Magi (*Officium Stellae*), though there are a few representing the visit of the shepherds to the manger, and there is also the *Ordo Prophetarum*, a dialogue series of prophecies of Christ's birth. Later developments include SAINTS' PLAYS, plays on incidents from the lives of Old Testament characters (e.g. Daniel, Isaac), plays relating to Mary (one of the most extensive is the *Presentation of Mary in the Temple* of Philippe de Mézières, 14th-century), and extensions of the earlier Gospel scenes into PASSION and Nativity plays.

There has been considerable scholarly debate about when liturgical ritual becomes liturgical drama – a matter that is still unresolved, and perhaps unresolvable.   PM

Liverpool Playhouse Britain's oldest continuously operating repertory theatre (excluding war years). Inspired by the achievements of the GAIETY company in Manchester, theatre enthusiasts in Liverpool organized a trial season in 1911, the success of which led to the setting up of a company, financed by 900 shareholders from the city, which in turn bought the old Star Theatre and reopened it later that year as the Liverpool Repertory Theatre (from 1916 known as the Playhouse), with BASIL DEAN as artistic director. Perhaps less adventurous than its sister theatres in Manchester and Birmingham, it has had a more stable history than either, benefiting from the consistent support of its shareholders and audiences, a more cautious choice of plays, the long stays of director William Armstrong (from 1922 to 1940) and general manager Maud Carpenter (1923–62), and the reputations of the actors it has nurtured (such as Robert Donat, MICHAEL REDGRAVE and REX HARRISON). Improvements and extensions to the theatre (including a studio theatre) were made in 1966–8. A marked change of course occurred in 1981 with the appointment of four writers as joint artistic directors (ALAN BLEASDALE, Chris Bond, BILL MORRISON and WILLY RUSSELL). The consequent emphasis upon new and recent writing did not prove popular with audiences, however, and the directorship and repertoire have since reverted to more traditional practice.   AJ

living newspaper Although antecedents can be identified, this term is most frequently associated with the FEDERAL THEATRE PROJECT (USA). A documentary methodology was used, defining a problem and then calling for specific action. Bringing together both unemployed newspaper men and theatre personnel, presentations were written on such varied problems as housing, health care, labour unions, public utilities, cooperatives, natural resources, Negroes, and even motion pictures. Six examples were produced by the New York unit, although the first – *Ethiopia*, on the war in Abyssinia – was cancelled under pressure from the US State Department. The three most successful attempts were by Arthur Arent: *Triple-A*

Living newspaper scene from the Federal Theatre Project's *Triple-A Plowed Under*.

Plowed Under, on the need for farmers and consumers to unite for improved incomes and cheaper food, which was a great success in 1936; *Power* (1937), a plea for public ownership of utilities; and *One-Third of a Nation* (1938), an exposé of urban housing conditions. Less successful were *1935*, a SATIRE of the public's indifference to social issues, and *Injunction Granted* (1936), an account of workers' treatment in the courts. Units in other cities developed living newspapers on local problems, though few were produced. The techniques have been applied to more contemporary didactic theatre, such as the so-called Theatre of Fact begun in the 1950s.   DBW

living picture [*tableau vivant*] Mute, immobile arrangement of performers to reproduce a scene from art, literature or the imagination. Displayed by the medieval Church on the Feast of the Resurrection to reproduce episodes from the Gospels, such pictures were often borne in procession on a float; similar, allegorical *tableaux* were staged at Renaissance banquets. In 1760 CARLO BERTINAZZI recreated Greuze's painting *The Village Betrothal* in *Les Noces d'Arlequin*, and shortly before the French Revolution Mme de Genlis used *tableaux historiques*, arranged by the painters David and Isabey, to instruct the children of the Duc d'Orléans. The *tableau*, as a device enabling the spectator to take in clearly visible signs of emotional and moral states, was promoted as an important dramatic device by DIDEROT and became a component fixture of the MELODRAMA, especially at the ends of acts.

The *pose plastique*, in which the performer purports to imitate classical statuary, introduced a sensual note, originating in Naples with Lady Emma Hamilton, and, throughout the 19th century, was an allegedly artistic means of exhibiting nudes. Such shows provided finales at the song-and-supper rooms of Regency London and the Judge-and-Jury Society revels organized by 'Chief Baron' Renton Nicholson, as well as the private gatherings of courtiers at the Tuileries and Fontainebleau under Napoleon III. More respectable showings included the Court of Beauties, arranged at the OLYMPIC in 1835 by MADAME VESTRIS, based on portraits by Peter Lely, and the operatic *tableaux vivants* to be seen at the Royal Victoria Coffee Music Hall (OLD VIC). The European troupes that toured England, like the Rudolphs and the Kellers, were highly respectable and often played at private parties, but the tinge of immorality still clung and their audiences were exclusively male. The *pose plastique* as 'living statuary' found a home in turn-of-the-century MUSIC-HALLS, its exponents, like La Milo (Pansy Montague), whitened down with pearl powder. The spectacular REVUE made much of sumptuous *tableaux*, such as those arranged by Ben Ali Haggin for the ZIEGFELD Follies.

As Martin Meisel has recently demonstrated, the principle of the living picture underlay much 19th-century staging, and paintings by Wilkie and Frith were enacted as climactic moments in melodrama. The 'picturesque' quality was pursued in the productions of CHARLES KEAN, the Duke of Saxe-MEININGEN, HENRY IRVING and the young STANISLAVSKY, as a primary responsibility of the director. The most noteworthy recent artistic employment of the *tableau vivant* has been in STEPHEN SONDHEIM's musical *Sunday in the Park with George* (1983), in which Seurat's *Sunday on the Isle of La Grande Jatte* gradually comes to life on stage. (See also NUDITY.)   LS

See: J.W. McCullough, *Living Pictures on the New York Stage*, Ann Arbor, Mich., 1979; M. Meisel, *Realizations: Narrative, Pictorial and Theatrical Arts of the Nineteenth Century*, Princeton, NJ, 1983; K. G. Holmström, *Monodrama Attitudes: Tableaux Vivants*, Stockholm, 1967.

Living Theatre (USA) When Julian Beck (1925–85) and his wife, Judith Malina (1926–), founded the Living Theatre in 1948, they inaugurated the experimental OFF-OFF BROADWAY movement in New York. With one of the most influential and long-lasting avant-garde companies in American history, the Becks became the prophets of the burgeoning theatrical experimentation that was to explode during the 1960s.

From the very beginning, the Living Theatre sought the marriage of a political and aesthetic radicalism. 'We insisted,' Beck said, 'on experimentation that was an image for a changing society. If one can experiment in theatre, one can experiment in life.' This principle took a variety of shapes as the LT developed, but the Becks' anarchist-pacifist viewpoint remained a constant.

The Theatre began producing plays by Paul Goodman, Gertrude Stein, GARCÍA LORCA, PIRANDELLO, COCTEAU and BRECHT, seeking an anti-REALISM that could match the contemporary fervour in the visual arts and music. The group did not find a permanent performance space until 1959, and they lost it four years later when the Internal Revenue Service evicted them for non-payment of taxes. Early landmark productions before being closed were profoundly influenced by ARTAUD's *The Theatre and Its Double*, including Jack Gelber's *The Connection* (1959), about heroin addicts awaiting a promised fix; Brecht's *Man Is Man* and Kenneth Brown's *The Brig* (1963), a detailed documentary of daily brutal routine in a US Marine Corps brig in Japan, which was the company's last New York production. Having defied IRS orders to leave its building, the LT gave its final performance of *The Brig* in a padlocked theatre; the audience had to enter by climbing through the windows.

From September 1964 to August 1968 the LT performed only in Europe, concentrating on works made up of exercises and improvisations, and created collectively. This experimentation culminated in *Paradise Now* (1968), a 'spiritual and political voyage for actors and spectators'. A tour to the USA in 1968 helped convince the Becks that they no longer wanted to perform for a middle-class audience, but preferred to work in the streets with the people. After a brief return to Europe, the company went to Brazil in 1970 and stayed 13 months experimenting with COLLECTIVE creation before returning to the USA to work with coal miners and steel mill workers in Pittsburgh. They went back to Europe for further exploration of dramatic form and acting.

In 1984 the LT settled once again in New York. Since Julian Beck's death, the company has continued under the direction of Judith Malina and Hanon Reznikov. After more than 25 years, the LT found a home in Manhattan, a garage-like theatre on East 3rd Street, yet in 1993, after three and a half years, it was forced to vacate its East

Village home because of occupancy regulations, and once more took to the road. The company had been presenting plays based on poetry, collaborations with homeless people from the neighbourhood, and annual street theatre spectacles.

The Becks' works and ideas are described in Beck's 1972 book, *The Life of the Theatre*, and Malina's *Diaries 1947–57* (1984). AS

Livings, Henry 1929– British dramatist, who was once an actor with JOAN LITTLEWOOD's Theatre Workshop company. The anarchic cheerfulness of his plays, his sympathy with the underdog and his feeling for Lancashire and for northern England in general were all aspects of his writing encouraged by Littlewood. His first stage play, *Stop It, Whoever You Are* (1961), memorably featured Wilfred Bramble as a downtrodden lavatory attendant in a factory, plotting the downfall of all bosses. His heroes have usually been underdogs, such as Stanley the TV mechanic in *Big Soft Nellie* (1961), the cook in *Nil Carborundum* (1962) and Valentine Brose in *Eh?*, although Kelly in *Kelly's Eye* (1963) is someone who believes in punching first, to teach the others a lesson. A prolific writer, Livings has many television and radio plays to his credit, as well as more than 30 stage plays; and with ALAN PLATER and PETER TERSON he has established a tradition of northern playwriting which flourished in the 1980s with JOHN GODBER, WILLY RUSSELL and ALAN BLEASDALE.

Livings's reputation, meanwhile, has declined, partly because the improvising energy, once a feature of Littlewood's style, on which his humour relied, is now only rarely to be found in British theatre. He translated GARCÍA LORCA's play about sexual identity, *The Public* (1988), for the Theatre Royal, Stratford, East London; and wrote *Stop the Children's Laughter* (1992) based on a true Victorian story about foster-children and the homes to which they were sent, which was produced at the Octagon Theatre, Bolton. JE

Lizárraga, Andrés 1919–82 Argentine playwright and television writer. Although he wrote more than 20 plays, Lizárraga is known primarily for his historical plays that used national themes to speak to contemporary issues. In 1960 *Tres jueces para un largo silencio* (*Three Judges for a Long Silence*), *Santa Juana de América* (*Saint Joan of America*) and *Alto Perú* (*High Peru*) constituted a 'May trilogy', based on moments and figures of the Revolution and counter-revolution. The BRECHTian techniques fit well with the development of social themes throughout his dramatic production. GW

Lloyd, Marie [Matilda Alice Victoria Wood] 1870–1922 'Our Marie', most legendary of British MUSIC-HALL stars. Born in Hoxton, London, the daughter of a waiter, she made artificial flowers before her debut in 1885 at the Royal Eagle in City Road, as Bella Delmare. After choosing the name Marie Lloyd (from *Lloyd's Newspaper*), she rose to prominence at the Star Music Hall, Bermondsey, London, with Nelly Power's song 'The Boy I Love Is Up in the Gallery'. As early as 1888 she was known for saucy songs, such as 'Then You Wink the Other Eye' and 'She'd Never Had Her Ticket Punched Before', delivered with an

assortment of winks, ogles and chuckles. Soon she was earning £600 a week, but was so carelessly charitable that she was seldom solvent. She married three times, unhappily, and it was her reputation for bawdiness and her divorce from coster comedian Alec Hurley (1911) that kept her from being invited to the first Royal Command Variety Performance of 1912; on the other hand, she was active in the music-hall war against the managers, and entertained troops and factory workers during the Boer War and the First World War. Ageing rapidly, she switched her stage persona from knowing clothes-horse to cheerful harridan, in such numbers as 'Don't Dilly Dally' and 'One of the Ruins that Cromwell Knocked About a Bit'. Max Beerbohm named her, with Florence Nightingale and Queen Victoria, one of the three greatest women of the age, and T. S. ELIOT praised her as a true voice of the people; at least three unmemorable musical comedies have been based on her life. LS

Lloyd Webber, Andrew 1948– British theatre composer, whose first major success came when he was only 20, with *Joseph and the Amazing Technicolour Dreamcoat*, with lyrics by TIM RICE. *Jesus Christ Superstar* (1970), *Evita* (1976), *Cats* (1981), *Song and Dance* (1981) and *Starlight Express* (1984) provided an unparalleled sequence of hit MUSICALS, which not only established him as the leading theatre composer of his time, against some competition from such American composers as STEPHEN SONDHEIM, but also transformed the respective roles of London and New York as centres for musicals. In the 1980s London became the major centre for new musicals, greatly aided by TREVOR NUNN's direction of *Cats*, *Starlight Express* and other non-Lloyd Webber musicals, such as *Les Misérables*. Lloyd Webber's gift for lilting tunes provides one ingredient of his success, but he is also an astute businessman and producer, responsible for such WEST END productions as *Daisy Pulls It Off*. *The Phantom of the Opera* (1986) and *Aspects of Love* (1989) were hits on both sides of the Atlantic and there have already been major revivals of earlier Lloyd Webber successes. In 1993 he ventured a musical based on the Hollywood film, *Sunset Boulevard* (1993). JE

loa A short theatre piece, of sacred origin, normally with music; common in Spain and Latin America during the years of conquest and colonization. The principal object was to praise high-level officials on special occasions. These pieces were popular with audiences and served to introduce full-length works. GW

Loesser, Frank 1910–69 American composer and lyricist. After contributing songs to *The Illustrators' Show* (1936), Loesser spent 12 years in Hollywood writing the lyrics for numerous motion picture MUSICALS. He returned to BROADWAY with the score for *Where's Charley?* (1948), a musical version of *Charley's Aunt*. Two years later he wrote his most memorable songs for *Guys and Dolls*, a musical based on Damon Runyon's short stories about tough but soft-hearted New York gamblers and their girlfriends, revived to acclaim in 1992. He then devoted four years to writing the score for *The Most Happy Fella* (1956; successfully revived on Broadway in 1992), an ambitious musical whose 30 songs ranged from operatic ARIAS to typical Broadway speciality numbers. After a failure with *Greenwillow* (1960), Loesser wrote his last Broadway score for *How to Succeed in Business without Really Trying* (1961), a SATIRE on corporate politics and chicanery. He also operated a musical publishing house, through which he furthered the careers of several young composers. A biography by his daughter Susan was published in 1993. MK

Loew, Marcus 1870–1927 American theatre owner and impresario, dubbed 'the Henry Ford of show biz'. Considered an honest and generous showman, Loew joined with DAVID WARFIELD and, briefly, Adolph Zukor, in the penny arcade business. In 1904 Loew and Warfield formed their own company, and Loew emerged as a pioneer in the nascent film industry. Subsequently, he added low-price VAUDEVILLE between pictures. At his death he controlled 300 entertainment venues, headed Metro–Goldwyn–Mayer Pictures, and was president of numerous vaudeville and booking companies. DBW

Loewe, Frederick see LERNER, ALAN JAY

Logan, Joshua 1908–88 American director, producer and playwright. Logan is associated with many of BROADWAY's most successful plays and musicals as director, co-producer or co-author (frequently all three): *South Pacific* (1949), for which he and co-author OSCAR HAMMERSTEIN II received the Pulitzer Prize (1950); *The Wisteria Trees* (1950), based on CHEKHOV's *The Cherry Orchard* and written by Logan; *Wish You Were Here* (1952); and *Fanny* (1954). He was director and co-producer of *John Loves Mary* (1947) and *Picnic* (1953). *Mister Roberts* (1948) was directed by him and written with Thomas Heggen. Other plays and MUSICALS exhibited Logan's skill as an inventive director: *On Borrowed Time* (1938), *Knickerbocker Holiday* (1938), *Morning's at Seven* (1939), *Charley's Aunt* (1940), *By Jupiter* (1942), *Annie Get Your Gun* (1946) and *Happy Birthday* (1946). He also directed the motion pictures *Bus Stop* (1956), *South Pacific* (1958) and *Camelot* (1967).

His apprenticeship began with the Triangle Club at Princeton and continued with the University Players. He married Nedda Harrigan (daughter of EDWARD HARRIGAN) and wrote two volumes of autobiography: *Josh* (1976) and *Movie Stars, Real People, and Me* (1978). RM

Logan, Olive 1839–1909 American actress, lecturer, playwright, daughter of Cornelius Logan (1806–52), a popular comedian and author of YANKEE plays. Like her sisters Eliza and Celia, Olive won respect as an actress, but she left the stage in 1866 to concentrate on writing. Having lived in England and France during 1857–63, she drew upon her experiences abroad in novels like *Chateau Frissac* (1862), memoirs like *Photographs of Paris* (1866), and in certain topics during her dozen years of the nationwide lecture circuit. AUGUSTIN DALY employed her to translate French plays and produced her *Surf* (1870) and *Newport* (1879). In lectures, articles and pamphlets she called for equal rights for women while deploring 'the leg business', which put scantily clad women on stage. Her major books were

Apropos of Women and Theatre (1869), *Before the Footlights and Behind the Scenes* (1870) and *The Mimic Men* (1871). FHL

Lohenstein, (Daniel) Caspar von 1635–83 German baroque dramatist. Lohenstein's plays contain much overt violence and are written in an extremely florid style. They have rarely been performed. SW

Lomonosov, Mikhail (Vasilievich) 1711–65 Russian grammarian, literary critic, poet and playwright; the lawgiver of Russian literature, a true Renaissance man of the peasant class and among the best-educated and most influential men of his generation. Trained primarily at the Imperial Academy of Sciences in St Petersburg, where he later taught, and in Germany by philosopher-mathematician Christian Wolff and others, Lomonosov mastered the disciplines of classic and modern literature, literary criticism and translation, grammar, rhetoric and language theory, chemistry, physics, astronomy, geology, mining and metallurgy, mathematics and philosophy. He published a major study of Russian grammar (1757), virtually defined the high, middle and low styles of Russian literary language, and set forth the principles of the syllabotonic system of versification which has more or less dominated Russian poetry since the 18th century. In his two verse tragedies for the stage, *Temira and Selim* (1750) and *Demophon* (1752), he made significant adjustments in the courtly classical style of SUMAROKOV. He transformed the classical opposition of love versus duty into a politico-moral consideration of the natural man forced to endure unnatural forms such as tyranny. Sumarokov attempted unsuccessfully to spoof the more original artist. Lomonosov is also noteworthy for having helped to found Moscow University (1755), which today bears his name. SG

Long Wharf Theatre (New Haven, Connecticut) Founded in 1965 by Jon Jory (now with ACTORS THEATRE OF LOUISVILLE) and Harlan Kleiman, this RESIDENT NON-PROFIT theatre, playing to more than 160,000 patrons annually, is now under the leadership of artistic director Arvin Brown (since 1967) and M. Edgar Rosenblum. Known as an actors' theatre, Long Wharf, with two intimate performance spaces (484 and 199 seats) in the New Haven Meat and Produce Terminal, emphasizes the production of new and established, home-grown and foreign works that explore human relationships (25 world and 36 US premieres among its 211 productions during its first 25 years). Although transference to New York is not a priority at LWT, many important productions have made the move virtually intact, including *Shadow Box*, *Streamers*, *The Changing Room*, *Sizwe Banzi Is Dead*, *The Gin Game*, *Quartermaine's Terms*, *Broken Glass* and revivals of *Ah, Wilderness!*, *All My Sons*, *A View from the Bridge* (1982) and *American Buffalo* (1984). LWT has won praise and numerous awards, including the MARGO JONES Award for production of new works, a special citation from the Outer Critics' Circle, the Jujamcyn Theaters Award (1986), and a special Tony (1978) for the quality of its productions as well as the stability of its organizational structure. DBW

Lonsdale, Frederick 1881–1954 British dramatist, who began his career with a series of librettos for MUSICAL COMEDY including *The Maid of the Mountains* (1917). After *Madame Pompadour* in 1923, he turned to social comedies dealing ironically with polite manners and modern marriage, which at the time were compared with MAUGHAM. Epigrammatic wit and neatly constructed, near-farcical situations made his work highly successful, and the best of his eleven plays, *The Last of Mrs Cheney* (1925) – where the maid in a gang of burglar-servants gives up her criminal career to marry into the aristocracy – still retains its popularity. CI

Loos, Anita ?1893–1981 American actress, screenwriter and playwright noted for her satiric comedies. Loos, who wrote some 200 scripts for both silent and sound films, created the art of writing film captions, beginning with D. W. Griffith's silent films, such as *Intolerance* (1916). In 1926 she and her husband, John Emerson, dramatized her successful novel, *Gentlemen Prefer Blondes*. Noted for Lorelei Lee, the stereotypical 'dumb blonde', the play was made into a MUSICAL in 1949 by Loos and Joseph Fields. Throughout her career Loos wrote plays (*Happy Birthday*, 1946) and screenplays (*San Francisco*, 1936; *The Women*, 1939); adapted French plays into hit American shows (*Gigi*, 1951); and wrote witty, gossipy memoirs of her career in Hollywood (*A Girl Like I*, 1966; *Kiss Hollywood Goodbye*, 1974; *Cast of Thousands*, 1977). FB

Lope de Vega see VEGA (CARPIO), LOPE (FÉLIX) DE

López Rubio, José 1903– Spanish playwright, scenarist, film director and fiction writer. Following his first stage success, *De la noche a la mañana* (*Overnight*, 1929), he moved to Hollywood, where he wrote screenplays for Spanish-language films and became a member of Chaplin's inner circle. His highly metatheatrical *Celos del aire* (*In August We Play the Pyrenees*, 1950) has been translated into several languages and was successfully revived in Spain in 1990. Other major plays are *La venda en los ojos* (*The Blindfold*, 1954), in which characters employ unabashed theatricality to achieve more authentic lives, and *La otra orilla* (*The Other Shore*, 1954), in which the four principal characters are killed in the opening moments only to remain as witnesses to the revelations of their survivors. In the 1970s he created a series of short, ironic teleplays and longer teledramas demythologizing famous women of history. MPH

López, Willebaldo 1944– Mexican playwright, TV producer, actor and director. After studies in theatre at the Mexican Institute of Fine Arts, López held a fellowship at the Mexican Writers' Centre in 1971–2. Many of his plays have dealt with problems of Mexican youth – adolescents facing multiple problems of drugs, sex, unemployment and social pressures. His *Los arrieros con sus burros por la hermosa capital* (*The Muleteers with their Animals in the Beautiful Capital*, 1967) is a study in provincial/urban prejudices; *Cosas de muchachos* (*Kids' Things*, 1968) dramatizes the ubiquitous tensions and frustrations of adolescence. Other major works include *Yo soy Juárez* (*I am Juárez*, 1972), *Pilo Tamirano Luca* (1973) and *Vine, vi y*

mejor me fui (*I Came, I Saw, and I Should Have Gone*, 1971). López has won major prizes for his plays; in recent years he has devoted most of his creative efforts to television (see TELEVISION DRAMA). GW

Loquasto, Santo 1944– American set and COSTUME designer; master of both realistic detail and conceptual and theatricalist productions. Early BROADWAY and regional successes, such as *That Championship Season* and *American Buffalo* and later work including *Café Crown*, are almost photorealist in their painstaking detail. His work in the 1970s with the NEW YORK SHAKESPEARE FESTIVAL, especially at the outdoor Delacorte Theater, and his extensive work for dance, notably with Twyla Tharp and Mikhail Baryshnikov, emphasized sculptural and emblematic design and often included angular, large-scale, constructivist-like designs. Many of these tendencies came together in Broadway's *Grand Hotel: The Musical*, which won him a 1990 Tony. His costumes possess the same detail, sense of colour, and texture as his sets, and for dance he often designs costumes alone. Loquasto has worked frequently on films, notably with Woody Allen. AA

Loranger, Françoise 1913– Quebec playwright and novelist. She began writing for radio in the 1930s, and for national television from its inception in 1952. Her first stage play, *Une Maison ... un Jour* (*One House ... One Day*, 1965), was well received at home and abroad. A psychological drama, it was followed by *Encore cinq minutes* (*Five More Minutes*, 1967), one of the first Canadian plays to raise feminist concerns. The author's growing political commitment is evident in *Le Chemin du roy* (*The King's Highway*, 1968) and *Médium saignant* (*Medium Rare*, 1970). The former, a savage SATIRE written in collaboration with Claude Levac, depicts, in the guise of a violent hockey game between Quebec and Ottawa, the diplomatic fiasco resulting from President de Gaulle's provocative behaviour on his 1967 visit to Quebec; the latter focuses on the struggle for francophone rights in the atmosphere of Quebec's controversial Bill 63, which sought to legislate those rights. *Double jeu* (*Double Game*, 1969) reverts to her earlier psychodramas, but in an experimental vein that requires audience participation in the resolution of its romantic plot. LED

Lorca see GARCÍA LORCA, FEDERICO

Lord Chamberlain's Men The finest of Elizabethan theatre companies was founded in 1594 under the patronage of the Lord Chamberlain, Lord Hunsdon. Most of its senior members had been previously together in STRANGE'S MEN, and it is likely that friendship as well as financial interest united the men, who agreed to share the risks and profits of the enterprise. The original sharers were Cuthbert and RICHARD BURBAGE, Thomas Pope, AUGUSTINE PHILLIPS, JOHN HEMINGES, WILL KEMPE and WILLIAM SHAKESPEARE. The Chamberlain's Men took up residence at JAMES BURBAGE'S THEATRE and quickly gained a highly prized access to the court. Of the 20 recorded royal commands from 1594 to 97, 13 went to them and 7 to the ADMIRAL'S MEN.

When the theatres of London were threatened with closure in the wake of the *Isle of Dogs* scandal of 1597, these two companies were specifically exempted by the Privy Council. Licensed to 'use and practise stage plays', the Chamberlain's Men faced the threat of homelessness when the lease on the Theatre expired in 1597. James Burbage died in the February of that year, bequeathing the problem to his son Cuthbert. To his other son, Richard, he left his interest in the indoor BLACKFRIARS. But the company's access to the Blackfriars was blocked by a residents' petition, which included their new patron among its signatories. (Lord Hunsdon died in 1596, passing his title, his office and his theatre company to his son.) Using the CURTAIN as a stop-gap home, the Chamberlain's Men sought out and purchased a new site, south of the Thames and close to the Admiral's Men at the ROSE. The building of the GLOBE was completed in 1599, and it was there that the Chamberlain's Men confirmed their supremacy in a repertoire that included work by JONSON, WEBSTER, TOURNEUR, MIDDLETON, MARSTON, BEAUMONT, FLETCHER and the finest of Shakespeare's plays. They continued to use the Globe after the delayed occupation of the Blackfriars was at last complete in 1608–9.

Their theatrical leadership had been openly acknowledged in 1603, when the new king, James I, adopted them as the King's Men, and they maintained it throughout the reigns of the first two Stuart kings. With the exception of Kempe, who left the company and sold his share before the opening of the Globe, and Shakespeare, who seems to have retired in c.1613, all the leading actors of the King's Men remained active members until death or the 1642 CLOSURE OF THE THEATRES halted them. Having carried the major responsibilities of management from c.1611 until his death, Heminges was succeeded by JOSEPH TAYLOR and JOHN LOWIN. Shakespeare's place as 'ordinary' playwright was taken successively by Fletcher and MASSINGER. The company's hold at court, though sometimes challenged, was never surrendered. It was probably largely for their use that Charles I authorized the conversion of the COCKPIT-IN-COURT. PT

Lorde, André de see GRAND-GUIGNOL

Lortel, Lucille 1902– American producer. Born in New York, Lortel attended the American Academy of Dramatic Arts (1920) before studying in Germany with Arnold Korff and MAX REINHARDT. After a year in stock (1924; see STOCK COMPANY), she made her BROADWAY debut in a minor role. Upon her marriage in 1931, she gave up the stage until 1947, when she offered her Westport, Connecticut, barn for a dramatic reading. After two seasons of readings, she remodelled the White Barn Theatre into a functioning theatre that served as a showcase for new talent and continues summer seasons. Lortel acquired New York's Theatre de Lys in 1955 as a transfer venue for worthy White Barn productions. Her first Theatre de Lys production, *The Threepenny Opera*, ran for seven years. In 1956 she began offering a Matinée Series, which continued for 20 years. At both theatres she has presented lesser known plays by BRECHT, IONESCO, GENET, Mario Fratti and ATHOL FUGARD. The more successful presentations at the Theatre de Lys (rechristened the Lortel in 1981) include *Dames at Sea, A*

Life in the Theatre, Buried Child, Getting Out, Cloud Nine and *Woza Albert*. She is a co-founder of the AMERICAN SHAKESPEARE [THEATRE] Festival, and a recipient of the MARGO JONES Award for her dedication to new plays and of the DRAMA LEAGUE's 1993 Unique Contribution to Theatre Award. She is the subject of a documentary film, *The Queen of Off-Broadway*. The OFF-BROADWAY Lucille Lortel Prizes are given annually in her honour. TLM

Louis, Victor 1731–1802 French theatre architect, the most influential of the late 18th century. His Bordeaux theatre, generally considered the finest in France, opened in 1780. It is known for its grand staircase, which GARNIER would borrow a century later for the Paris opera house. With its 12-column façade, the Grand Theatre is a magnificent piece of urban landscaping. Louis used a circular auditorium, slightly opening out towards the stage, with a ceiling held up by four massive columns, two of them framing the stage. The proscenium was shallower than that of previous 18th-century theatres and the auditorium had indirect lighting rather than the conventional chandelier.

In 1781, after a fire at the Opéra in Paris, the Duke of Orleans commissioned Louis to build a new Opéra in his palace. By the time the theatre was built (1790) it was not needed for this purpose and was taken over by two theatrical entrepreneurs, Gaillard and Dorfeuille, who ran it briefly as the Variétés Amusantes. In 1799, this became the permanent home of the COMÉDIE-FRANÇAISE. Louis had to cope with a more limited site than at Bordeaux. He solved this problem by supporting the auditorium on 32 columns in the ground-floor vestibule. The auditorium was longer than Bordeaux, with parallel sides, which allowed for a wider proscenium (also imitated by Garnier). In 1791, MLLE MONTANSIER, who had a small theatre (originally built for PUPPETS) in the PALAIS-ROYAL, asked Louis to transform this, which he did in a matter of two weeks, increasing the seating to 1300 and doubling the stage dimensions to make the staging of tragedies, dramas and even operas possible. In 1792, Mlle Montansier acquired a site opposite the Bibliothèque Nationale and commissioned Louis to build her a theatre. The Théâtre National de Montansier was completed in 1793. Less monumental externally, it had a magnificent auditorium, with a stage 75ft square and 100ft high. There were no stage boxes, which emphasized the growing separation between actor and audience. The Opéra engineered the arrest of Mlle Montansier and took over the theatre, where it remained until 1820, when the Duke of Berry, heir to the throne, was assassinated there and the theatre had to be demolished. Louis's much admired auditorium was reconstituted for the new Opéra in the rue Lepeletier. JMCC

Løveid, Cecilie 1951– Norwegian playwright. Although her stage plays have been produced with lamentable infrequency in Norway, Løveid's fragmentary, imagistic writing is richly textured, and has been appropriately compared to that of BOTHO STRAUSS and HEINER MÜLLER. Among several important radio plays (see RADIO DRAMA), her *Seagull Eaters* won the 1983 Prix Italia. Stage plays such as *The Ice Breaks Up* (1983), *Tightrope-Lady* (1984), *Rational Animals* (1986) and *Double Delight* (1990) were produced to mixed critical receptions by institutional the-atres in Bergen and Oslo. Since 1989 she has found more sympathetic audiences in her collaborations with project theatres like Verdensteatret (*The Bath House*, 1989) and performance groups like Lilith (*Time between Times*, 1990, and *Baroque Frieze*, 1991).   HL

Lowin, John 1576–c.1659 English actor, who probably abandoned the trade of goldsmith for the stage. He is first heard of with Worcester's Men at the ROSE in 1602, and from 1603 until the CLOSURE OF THE THEATRES was a mem-ber of the King's Men, for whom he may have become busi-ness manager after the death of HEMINGES. Among the parts Lowin is known to have played are Falstaff, Volpone, Morose in JONSON's *Epicoene* and Bosola in WEBSTER's *The Duchess of Malfi*. His longevity made him an important link in the evolution of acting styles. In *Roscius Anglicanus* (1708), Downes claims that Lowin advised DAVENANT on SHAKESPEARE's ideas for the playing of Henry VIII and that Davenant then instructed BETTERTON. After some years as landlord of the Three Pigeons in Brentford, Lowin died in poverty.   PT

Lubwa, Cliff p'Chong 1946– Ugandan playwright, actor and producer. Lubwa was educated at Sam Baker School, Gulu, the National Teachers' College, Kyambogo, and at Makerere, Durham and Exeter Universities. He was Creative Writing Fellow at the University of Iowa in 1987, and lectures in drama-in-education at the Institute of Teacher Education, Kyambogo. His plays (published in English) are *Generosity Kills* and *The Last Safari* (1975), *The Minister's Wife* (1983) and *Kinsmen and Kinswomen* (1986). He has also published poems and other writings. MMAC

Lucas, Craig 1951– American playwright and actor. Born in Atlanta and educated at Boston University, Lucas, after singing in BROADWAY MUSICAL choruses for seven years, was one of the most produced American dramatists during the 1980s. *Reckless* (1983) and *Blue Window* (1984) both premiered at New York's Production Company, and *Three Postcards* (1986) and *Prelude to a Kiss* (1987) at the South Coast Repertory in California. Each has had subse-quent professional productions, including a Broadway run for *Prelude*. He wrote the words for an OPERA, *Orpheus in Love* (music by Gerald Busby) seen at CIRCLE REPERTORY COMPANY in 1992. Lucas has won numerous prizes, includ-ing Guggenheim and Rockefeller grants and the GLAAD [Gay and Lesbian Alliance against Defamation] Award for his screenplay *Longtime Companion* (1990), the first main-stream American film to deal directly with AIDS.   BBW

Lucie, Doug 1953– British dramatist, whose hard-bit-ten, amusing and brittle comedies satirized and then came to symbolize Mrs Thatcher's yuppies. His early plays, *John Clare's Mad Nuncle* (1975), *Rough Trade* (1977), *We Love You* (1978), *The New Garbo* (1978) and *Heroes* (1979), were certainly satirical, but he gave the impression of being a trainee marksman looking for a target. *Hard Feelings* (1983), about a group of Oxford graduates living in cynical self-indulgence in Brixton in the midst of the 1981 riots, began his sequence of plays about the seemier

sides to privilege. After *Strangers in the Night* (1981) and *Progress* (1984), in which Lucie provided a comedy of trendy people talking about trendy ideas against a back-ground of trendy violence, he turned his attention to the ad-man's world in *Fashion* (1988), produced by the ROYAL SHAKESPEARE COMPANY, with Brian Cox playing an adver-tising executive in search of lucrative political accounts. In *Grace* (1992), Lucie attacked the millionaire evangelists of the US religious missions. His satirical wit is his great asset, but also his liability, in that it tends to reduce his characters and his themes to a point where there does not seem to be any mileage in attacking them further. His writing could be supercilious in its attacks on Thatcherism, leading to a political glibness which at one time suited the house style of the RSC very well.   JE

Ludlam, Charles 1943–87 American actor, director and playwright. Ludlam was an early member of John Vaccaro's Play-House of the Ridiculous, an OFF-OFF BROADWAY theatre that presented his *Big Hotel* (1967) and *Conquest of the Universe* (1967). Splitting with Vaccaro in 1967, Ludlam started his own theatre, the RIDICULOUS THEATRICAL COMPANY, where his plays included *Bluebeard* (1970), *Camille* (1973; revived 1990), *Stageblood* (1975), *Professor Bedlam's Punch and Judy Show* (1975), *Der Ring Gott Farblonjet* (1977), *Le Bourgeois Avant-Garde* (1982) and *The Mystery of Irma Vep* (1984). These plays combined popular and high art forms, mixing colourful staging, scatological humour and FEMALE IMPERSONATION with plots and styles drawn from dramatic and operatic litera-ture. Ludlam's treatments of *Hamlet*, Wagner's *Ring* and *Camille* went beyond mere spoofing; his depth of involve-ment, he explained, gave rise to independent works that transcend PARODY. The Ridiculous Theatrical Company, one of the first New York theatres to deal explicitly with homosexual themes, often featured Ludlam in female roles – which he didn't necessarily play camply. In 1984 Pittsburgh's American Ibsen Theatre invited Ludlam to play Hedda Gabler. *The Complete Plays of Charles Ludlam* was published after his death from AIDS in 1987 and a col-lection of his essays and opinions in 1992.   AS

Ludlow, Noah (Miller) 1795–1886 American actor-manager who, with SOL SMITH, brought the legitimate the-atre to the Ohio and Mississippi valleys. First employed by SAMUEL DRAKE in 1815 to barnstorm in Kentucky, Ludlow formed his own company, playing New Orleans and remote corners of the South and West. In 1828 he joined THOMAS A. COOPER as manager of the Chatham Theatre in New York, but failed financially. With Smith, Ludlow formed the Ludlow and Smith Company (1835–53), build-ing and operating theatres in Mobile, New Orleans, St Louis and other cities, engaging many of the leading stars of the day. The partnership dissolved in hostility: Smith's journals never mention his partner. Ludlow's autobiogra-phy, *Dramatic Life as I Found It* (1880), although bitter in condemnation of Smith, offers an unequalled factual account of the FRONTIER THEATRE in America.   SMA

Ludwig, Otto 1813–65 German playwright and theo-rist. Ludwig was prevented by ill-health from achieving the eminence he coveted as a dramatist. Although he had a theoretical rather than a creative bent, *The Hereditary Forester* (1850) is an effectively MELODRAMATic tragedy, while *The Maccabeuses* (1852), a romantic verse TRAGEDY set in ancient Rome, has some power. Ludwig's most durable writings are probably his *Shakespeare Studies* (published 1871). SW

Lugné-Poe, Aurélien [Aurélien Lugné] 1869–1940 French actor and director. Remembered as the leader of the symbolist reaction (see SYMBOLISM) against NATURALISM, Lugné-Poe started as an actor under ANTOINE, but soon moved to Paul Fort's Théâtre d'Art, becoming its director in 1893 and renaming it the Théâtre de l'Oeuvre. The characteristic style of Oeuvre performances was a stylized or abstract decor, artificial intonation of dialogue and a pervasive dream-like atmosphere. Here he produced IBSEN (e.g. *Brand*, *Rosmersholm*), MAETERLINCK, HAUPTMANN and D'ANNUNZIO. Forced to close by financial pressures in 1899, he reopened the theatre in 1912 with CLAUDEL's *The Tidings Brought to Mary* and continued, with interruptions, to direct work of a symbolist tendency until he withdrew in 1929. He is remembered especially for *Ubu Roi* (1896), which he produced against his better judgement and which had only two performances. His *Cocu magnifique* by Crommelynck (1920) was influential. DB

Lully, Jean-Baptiste 1632–87 Italian musician, dancer and composer whose entire career was spent in France and who was naturalized French in 1661. Appointed composer to Louis XIV in 1653 and superintendent of music at court eight years later, he came to dominate French musical life for three decades. Apart from arranging and conducting instrumental concerts, he acted as impresario/composer for all court entertainments of a theatrical nature and collaborated with leading playwrights in their preparation, notably with Benserade on ballets, with MOLIÈRE on *comédies-ballets* and with QUINAULT on operas or *tragédies en musique*. In 1672 control of the French Opéra, which had been founded by letters patent from the Crown three years earlier, was transferred to Lully under the title of Académie Royale de Musique, and he continued to direct it successfully until his death, inducing other dramatists (THOMAS CORNEILLE, CAMPISTRON) to take advantage of the opportunities it afforded for spectacular scenic presentation. An able if autocratic administrator, Lully enjoyed the zealous favour of the king and amassed a considerable personal fortune as well as a title. DR

Lunacharsky, Anatoly (Vasilievich) 1875–1933 The intelligent, cosmopolitan and humane Soviet First People's Commissar for Education (1917–29), as well as a dramatist and critic involved largely with repertory questions. Lunacharsky's enthusiasm for the theatre (he was married to an actress) helped to save a good many artists and institutions in the years following the October Revolution. A revolutionary from 1897 and a Bolshevik from 1904, with a record of arrests and exile for Party activity and an on-and-off relationship with Lenin, he helped to create the 1919 decree of the Council of People's Commissars (Sovnarkom), which nationalized all theatres in regions under Bolshevik control.

He proceeded cautiously in his official capacity, moving to preserve what was best in Russian and European culture while the new Soviet culture was evolving. At the same time he was actively involved in giving Soviet art the opportunity to develop without undue pressure or overreaction. Thus, he was generally fair-minded and in some cases even protective of artists as diverse as STANISLAVSKY, MEYERHOLD, VAKHTANGOV and TAIROV (although he was decidedly ambivalent towards Meyerhold and Tairov), but he never confused tolerance for the avant-garde with loyalty to the Party or to the spirit of the Revolution. He proclaimed 'Back to October!' (1923) in protesting against directorial corruption of the classics, urged the theatres to adopt the new Soviet drama, championed REALISM and proletarian art and encouraged new theatres built since the Revolution, including the First State Theatre for Children (Moscow, 1920), which he directed. He opposed Meyerhold's plan as head of the Theatre Division of the People's Commissariat for Education (1920) to 'revolutionize' the MOSCOW ART THEATRE, and closed the director's RSFSR [Russian Soviet Federated Socialist Republic] Theatre 1 over his radical production of Émile Verhaeren's symbolist play (see SYMBOLISM) *The Dawns* (1920), which had displeased Lenin's wife.

Lunacharsky was the author of 14 somewhat fustian plays in which historical or legendary themes were contemporized so as to gain revolutionary resonance. These include *Faust and the City* (1918), *Oliver Cromwell* (1920), *Foma Campanella* (two-thirds of a trilogy, 1921) and *The Liberated Don Quixote* (1921). His historical plays were attacked by Marxist extremists, who saw his dimensionalized character portraits as emphasizing the role of the individual in history. SG

Lunt, Alfred 1892–1977 and
Lynn (Lillie Louise) Fontanne 1887–1983 American actors. Alfred Lunt became a star as the oafish lead in BOOTH TARKINGTON's *Clarence* in 1919. Lynn Fontanne's first major role was as a dizzy matron addicted to clichés in KAUFMAN and CONNELLY's 1921 SATIRE, *Dulcy*. It wasn't until they appeared together, two years after their marriage, in the THEATRE GUILD's sparkling 1924 production of *The Guardsman*, MOLNÁR's droll comedy of sexual intrigue, that their reputations and the future course of their career were ensured. From then on they were known as the Lunts and, until their farewell in *The Visit* in 1958, had what was probably the most successful American acting partnership of the 20th century. Audiences, critics and fellow actors were delighted by the charged intimacy of their dual performances; their good friend NOËL COWARD quipped that they were really one person. Though every gesture and fraction of a pause was scrupulously intentioned, the Lunts created the illusion of spontaneity. To later generations they came to represent an outmoded stylized tradition, over-deliberate and genteel, but in their heyday they were thought to have introduced a new American style. They broke with old-fashioned BROADWAY acting techniques by playing comedy in a conversational way, their love scenes were startlingly physical, and their overlapping method of speaking their lines – at times they seemed to be talking simultaneously – surprised audiences of the 1920s.

Individually, each had a few notable achievements in dramas: Fontanne was the original Nina Leeds in *Strange Interlude* (1928), a role she professed not to understand, and Lunt was memorable when cast against type as a tough-talking bootlegger in SIDNEY HOWARD's *Ned McCobb's Daughter* (1926); but it was in high COMEDY that they excelled. Their favourite playwrights, ROBERT E. SHERWOOD and S. N. BEHRMAN, provided them with vehicles in which the war between the sexes is a duel of wit and sly, charming manipulation. Highlights of their career include Behrman's *The Second Man* (1927), *Amphitryon 38* (1937) and *I Know My Love* (1949); Sherwood's *Reunion in Vienna* (1931), *Idiot's Delight* (1936) and *There Shall Be No Night* (1940); Sil-Vara's *Caprice* (1928); a rollicking *Taming of the Shrew* (1935), noted more for its vaudevillian spirits than for its poetry; *The Seagull* (1938); and Coward's *Design for Living* (1933). They became so closely identified with cosmopolitan comedy that producers as well as audiences were reluctant to let them try anything else; at the end of their career the Lunts expressed regret that they hadn't been asked to do such plays as *Death of a Salesman* and *Long Day's Journey into Night*.

The Lunts were renowned among actors for their dedication (holding rehearsals for minor adjustments on the last day of a run) and for their career-long devotion to 'the road' (playing more one-night stands in remote towns than any other stars). They were also remarkable for their lack of greed: unlike other stage stars, they resisted Hollywood except for one unhappy venture in 1931, when they made a film of *The Guardsman*; and when they could have commanded higher salaries from independent producers, they maintained their loyalty to the Theatre Guild. In 1958 a theatre on New York's West 46th Street, originally built in 1910 by producer Charles Dillingham, was named after them. FH

Lupino family English performers and designers. Historians have been unable to substantiate the family's claim to descend from an Italian puppeteer who settled in London in the reign of Elizabeth I. The first member of the tribe to make a mark in the theatre was **George Richard Estcourt** Luppino (*sic*) (1710–87) who, according to tradition, played in PANTOMIME with JOHN RICH, designed scenery and costumes for Galuppi's opera *Enrico* (1743) and was a ballet master in Dublin and Edinburgh. His son **Thomas Frederick** (1749–1845) painted pantomime scenery at the King's Theatre (1784–5) and COVENT GARDEN (1786–9, 1792–1803), a trade carried on by his son **Samuel George** (d.1830). The modern branch of the family, which shortened the name to Lupino, is descended from Samuel's son (possibly adopted) **George Hook** Luppino (1820–1902), a HARLEQUIN. Of his progeny, **George** (1853–1932) was the best CLOWN, a stalwart of the Britannia Theatre pantomimes, who allegedly is depicted in Frith's painting *Derby Day*; **Henry Charles** (1865–1925), an eccentric dancer, married into the Lane family that managed the Britannia; and **Arthur** (1864–1908) created the role of Nana in *Peter Pan* (1904).

George's sons **Barry** (1882–1962) and **Stanley** (1893–1942) both entered the theatre as children, and were stalwarts in pantomimes and musical comedies for many years. Barry specialized in dame roles (see FEMALE

IMPERSONATION) and wrote over 50 musical comedies, making his last appearance in *Dick Whittington* (1954). Stanley was seen in *So This Is Love* (1928) and *Love Lies* (1929). He starred in several works co-written with Arthur Rigby, one of the which he also directed (*Room for Two*, 1932), as well as in numerous plays of his own composition, the most popular of which was *Crazy Days* (1937). His daughter **Ida** (b.1914), after graduating from RADA, became a Hollywood star. Their cousin **Lupino Lane** (Henry George Lupino, 1892–1959) made his debut in infancy as Nipper Lane, and later created Nipper Productions to film his routines; he toured widely in MUSIC-HALL, MUSICAL COMEDY and pantomime before enjoying his greatest success as Bill Snibson in *Me and My Girl* (1937), in which he introduced the Lambeth Walk; he also popularized the songs 'Chase Me, Charlie' and 'Knees Up, Mother Brown'. An expert tumbler, he was often seen with his brother Wallace (1897–1961) and his son Lauri, who went into film. LS

LuPone, Patti 1949– American actress. Born in Northport, New York, LuPone studied acting at the Juilliard School, graduating in 1972. A founding member of the ACTING COMPANY, she demonstrated her versatility in a variety of roles before her portrayal of the title character in *Evita* (1979) won her a Tony and praise from WALTER KERR for 'rattlesnake vitality'. Her last major New York stage role was as Reno Sweeney in the 1987 revival of *Anything Goes!*. In recent years she has largely devoted her time to television, although in 1993 she returned to the stage in ANDREW LLOYD WEBBER's *Sunset Boulevard* in London. TLM

Lyceum Theatre (London) The first building on the site in Wellington Street, just off the Strand, was intended as an exhibition hall by the architect James Payne, who erected it in c.1765. It was probably first used for live entertainment by CHARLES DIBDIN and, a little later, by the ubiquitous PHILIP ASTLEY, and it was the musician Samuel Arnold who converted it into a theatre in 1794. There followed a period of struggle against the Patent theatres, during which freak shows, exhibitions, concerts, Madame Tussaud's first waxwork display (1802) and lectures alternated with occasional performances.

Arnold was clearly stating his own preferences by calling it the English Opera House. As long ago as 1765, he had been the chief composer for *The Maid of the Mill*, BICKERSTAFFE's popular challenge to the Italian OPERA. But the new name was not endorsed until 1810, under the management of Arnold's son, and then only because the DRURY LANE company had used it for a season after the burning of their own theatre. The younger Samuel Arnold was granted a licence for summer performance, and in 1815–16 he rebuilt the theatre to Samuel Beazley's design, incorporating an elegant saloon 72ft long and 40ft wide. FANNY KELLY made her London reputation here in 1816, the year before gas was installed on the stage and two years before CHARLES MATHEWS presented the first of his annual *At Homes*. The building was destroyed by fire in 1830 and rebuilt, again to Beazley's design, in 1834. Under the KEELEYS (1844–7) and MADAME VESTRIS and CHARLES JAMES MATHEWS (1847–55), the renamed Lyceum established its place in a London scene freed from restrictions by the 1843 Theatres Act. CHARLES FECHTER attracted adulation and controversy during his seasons of management (1863–7), but it was not until HENRY IRVING made his first appearance in *The Bells* (1871), under the management of HEZEKIAH BATEMAN (1871–5), that the Lyceum entered on its period of unique greatness. Under Irving's inspired management (1878–99), it became virtually a national theatre, the standard of dramatic excellence in Britain.

Forced by financial losses to enter into a syndicate in 1899, Irving made his last Lyceum appearance in 1902, still with ELLEN TERRY at his side, and the theatre fell into disuse. It was demolished in 1904. A new theatre, designed by Bertie Crewe for use as a MUSIC-HALL, opened later the same year. Under the management of the brothers Walter and Frederick Melville (1909–38), it was known as a home for MELODRAMA and PANTOMIME. It was scheduled for demolition in 1939 and JOHN GIELGUD presented six performances of *Hamlet* there as a symbolic farewell, but the war intervened, the London County Council changed its plans and the Lyceum became a Mecca dance hall in 1945. PT

Lyceum Theatre (New York City) Originally known as the New Lyceum to distinguish it from manager DANIEL FROHMAN's earlier playhouse on Fourth Avenue and 23rd Street, the theatre opened on West 45th Street on 2 November 1903 with a performance of *The Proud Prince*, starring E. H. SOTHERN. Under Frohman's management, the Lyceum was the home of first-class productions; it suffered a serious decline during the Depression, however, and was in danger of being torn down in 1939 when it was purchased by a group of investors that included playwrights GEORGE S. KAUFMAN and MOSS HART and producer MAX GORDON. The investors sold the Lyceum in 1945, and it is presently owned by the SHUBERT ORGANIZATION. During the late 1960s it was leased to the APA [Association of Producing Artists]–Phoenix Repertory Company, and today is the home of the National Actors Theatre.

The Lyceum seats approximately 900 and contains the most extensive complex of scene shops of any BROADWAY theatre, as well as an elaborate penthouse apartment. The penthouse is currently the home of the Shubert Archive, a collection of materials related to the history of the Shubert Organization. The Lyceum, which is the oldest Broadway theatre still in operation, was declared a landmark in 1975. BMCN

Lyly, John c.1553–1606 English playwright, whose entry into court circles after periods of study at both Oxford and Cambridge was facilitated by the patronage of the influential Burleigh family. Lyly made his literary reputation with the prose romance, *Euphues* (1578), which set a fashion for ornate English and donated the word 'euphuism' to the language. His plays were all written for BOYS' COMPANIES, and had in mind a sophisticated audience, familiar with the principles of rhetoric and with classical mythology. His use of prose in refined COMEDY was innovatory, although it is the verbal display that is more likely to impress or fatigue a modern reader.

Lyly became formally involved in the management of the BOYS OF ST PAUL'S by 1584, the probable year of performance of his first two plays, *Campaspe* and *Sappho and Phao*. It may be that the original audience was dissatisfied with the allusiveness of his third, *Galathea* (c.1585), and that the choice of an English folk theme in *Mother Bombie* (c.1587) was intended to soften opposition. Lyly's best-known play, *Endimion* (c.1588), includes a transparently flattering portrait of Elizabeth I as Cynthia. We can assume that contemporary audiences were alert to Lyly's allegorical references to figures and incidents at court. He was a vocal supporter of the established Church and the author of a pamphlet which took the episcopal side in the Marprelate Controversy. When he involved the Paul's Boys in the debate, probably by allusive costuming, Archbishop Whitgift was among those alarmed by the vulgarizing of the issues, and the theatrical activities of London's choristers were halted. Lyly's work was already old-fashioned in the fast-moving theatre and his last play, *The Woman in the Moon* (c.1593), may never have been performed. PT

Lyric Theatre, Hammersmith (London) Originally the Lyric Opera House, opened in 1890 and specializing in MELODRAMA and PANTOMIME, in 1918 it was taken over by Nigel Playfair, who had previously acted with F. R. BENSON, BEERBOHM TREE and GRANVILLE BARKER. With ARNOLD BENNETT and the designer Lovat Fraser, Playfair established a distinctive style of simplified REALISM, stylized gesture and formalized composition in a brilliant series of elegant productions, in many of which he also performed together with young actors of the stature of GIELGUD and EDITH EVANS. Although it opened with A. A. MILNE's first play, *Make Believe*, a Christmas entertainment especially written for Playfair, the production that really established the theatre's reputation was his revival of GAY's *The Beggar's Opera*. Its unprecedented run of 1463 performances reawakened interest in Restoration and 18th-century drama; and it was followed by other BALLAD OPERAS by Gay and BICKERSTAFFE, together with outstanding revivals of CONGREVE, FARQUHAR, SHERIDAN and GOLDSMITH, as well as classic productions of CHEKHOV and WILDE and contemporary light COMEDY by A. P. Herbert and CLIFFORD BAX. Knighted in 1928, Playfair left the theatre in 1933, after which it declined. Despite a period of renewed popularity with further revivals by the Company of Four after 1945, PETER BROOK's production of *The Brothers Karamazov* (1946) and a season under Gielgud (1952–3), the theatre closed in 1966. It was demolished in 1972, although the name was transferred to a new, smaller theatre built nearby. CI

Lytton, Edward Bulwer, Lord see BULWER LYTTON, EDWARD

Lyubimov, Yury (Petrovich) 1917– Soviet director. Until his firing as artistic director of the Moscow Theatre of Drama and Comedy on Taganka Square ('the Taganka') in April 1984 and his subsequent expulsion from the USSR, Lyubimov was perhaps the greatest and certainly the most controversial and socially important director of the later Soviet period. Called 'the theatrical conscience of his nation', he is a moral artist in the 19th-century tradition of GOGOL, LEV TOLSTOI and Dostoevsky and a theatricalist innovator in the Meyerholdian vein.

Born in the year of the October Revolution, he has always shown a strong AGIT-PROP element in his work, an attempt to bridge the gap between stage and audience and to address the issues of his day. He was trained at the Second Moscow Art Theatre Studio until its closing in 1936 and then at the Vakhtangov Theatre School, graduating into the war and thereafter into the Vakhtangov Theatre's acting company. His celebrated production of BRECHT's *The Good Person of Setzuan* with his third-year acting class at the Shchukin Theatre Institute, where he was teaching (1962), earned him the artistic directorship of the moribund Taganka Theatre (1964). For the next 20 years, with MEYERHOLD, STANISLAVSKY, VAKHTANGOV and BRECHT as his spiritual guides, Lyubimov eschewed Soviet drama for the more imaginative worlds of poetry and narrative fiction, which he dramatized, and the classics, which he broke apart, reconstituted and presented from a pronounced critical perspective. His carefully orchestrated *mises en scène* are masterfully focused in mobile, tactile and transformative scenic metaphors, Meyerholdian 'machines for acting', most often co-created with his brilliant designer DAVID BOROVSKY.

Lyubimov's productions feature a complex lighting plan which he designs; detailed, precisely timed music and acoustic sound scores; interpolated poetry and songs, performed by a highly musical company; direct audience address and presentational play, which often originates and culminates in the theatre lobby. His productions include John Reed's *Ten Days That Shook the World* (1965), an exercise in Eisensteinian agit-prop, cinematic montage produced through a light curtain; Chernyshevsky's *What Is to Be Done?* (1971), performed on a tracking, 19th-century tiered wooden school seating unit; and Boris Vasiliev's sentimental patriotic tale of female heroism in the Second World War, *And Here the Dawns Are Silent* (1971), realized via a wooden military transport which transforms into showers, rafts, trees, walls and coffins. His poetry-based 'recital' presentations extend from Andrei Voznesensky's and Evgeny Evtushenko's impressions of their visits to America, *Antiworlds* (1965) and *Under the Skin of the Statue of Liberty* (1972), respectively, to meditations on the lives of the poets themselves: *Listen!* (1967), in which five MAYAKOVSKYS cavort upon outsized children's alphabet blocks; *Comrade, Believe!* (1973), in which an overhead tracking black leather carriage and an opulent stationary carriage illustrate five PUSHKINS' flight from Tsarist persecution; and the rarely produced *Death of a Poet* (*Vladimir Vysotsky*), commemorating the Taganka's leading actor and legendary folk singer who died in 1980, performed in a white-shrouded theatre auditorium mock-up. Among his socially minded productions are two adapted from Yury Trifonov novellas, *The Exchange* (1976), on urban moral blight evoked via an overstuffed apartment collage of real objects, and the controversial Stalinist guilt memory piece *The House on the Embankment* (1980), in which a glass 'wall of silence' separating stage from audience reveals the inner workings of Soviet life; and Boris Mozhaev's *Alive*, banned in 1968, on the errors committed in 1930s collectivization by bureaucrats who, in performance, descend via lighting battens into the pristine clarity of a birch-pole forest.

Representative radical stagings of the classics include *Tartuffe* (1969) on MOLIÈRE's play in crisis, under attack by Church and state, performed before a puppet king and cardinal through life-size character portraits; *Hamlet* (1974), featuring a huge mobile woven rope curtain, representing a redemptive theatrical life force; BULGAKOV's *The Master and Margarita* (1977), composed of recycled theatrical props and scenic pieces, including the *Hamlet* curtain and a large pendulum from Ezi Stavinsky's *Rush Hour* (1969) which swings between Christ and the Devil; *The Inspector's Recounting* (1978), in which the GOGOL *oeuvre* is presented phantasmagorically through holes in a giant overcoat being stitched on machines which sound like clerks' abacuses, located on top of spectrally moving elevator platforms; and Dostoevsky's *Crime and Punishment* (1983), in which a murderous Raskolnikov, rather than the Soviets' victimized proto-revolutionary hero, is pursued by a blood-stained door. Lyubimov has recently staged this abroad, as well as Dostoevsky's *The Possessed*, and has written an autobiography, *The Sacred Fire*. SG

maach Form of sung folk theatre, popular in villages of central India. *Maach* is thought to have originated in Rajasthan about 300 years ago; today it is found principally in villages of Madhya Pradesh state. The form was introduced to the Malwa area of Rajasthan by Sri Gopalji Guru, who is reputed to have composed several *maach* plays and who served as the first of a long line of rural playwrights.

Originally *maach* was associated with the holiday festivals surrounding Holi, a spring celebration. Today it may be performed on any festival occasion, usually on a raised stage approximately 15 x 12ft built at the end of an open space in a village. A curtain at the back serves as scenery and a 1.5ft-wide border stretches across the front of the stage, masking the feet of the actor-dancers.

Maach is a sung drama into which some dialogue may be introduced and folk dances added for spice and variety. Performance is accompanied by *sarangi*, the classical north Indian stringed instrument, *dhol* drum, and harmonium.

Traditionally men have played all roles, although today some women distinguish themselves in the female parts. Well known performers earn their reputations because of their excellent singing voices.

Performance usually begins around 10.30 or 11 p.m. and continues until dawn. It begins with a sung *bhisti raag* which, like similar RITUAL overtures in other Indian theatre forms, is meant to sanctify the proceedings and call villagers to the playing area. Next, a set of preliminary dances and songs (*bhisti-farrasan samvad*) provide an overture to the drama.

Among the important characters is the *bidhab* or *shermarkhan*, a comical adviser or consultant to the chief character, frequently a king. The clown enlivens the performance. He knits together the various threads of the complicated plot and he converts songs into dialogue, thus interpreting their meaning to the spectators. Historical, social and religious plays satisfy the taste of village audiences for romantic sentiment charged with strong morals. FAR

Mabou Mines (USA, Europe) A collaborative, experimental American theatre company, founded formally in 1970 after years of collaborative work among founding members JoANNE AKALAITIS, LEE BREUER and RUTH MALECZECH in San Francisco, and later in Europe with Philip Glass and David Warrilow. The company has developed a formal performance style that synthesizes traditional motivational acting, narrative techniques and mixed media – revealing the influence of the group's regular collaboration with painters, sculptors, video artists, film-makers and composers. Though this distinctive acting style is always evident in Mabou productions, the group's directors leave their own particular stamps. Breuer's *The Red Horse Animation* (1970), *The B. Beaver Animation* (1974) and *The Shaggy Dog Animation* (1978) are theatrically clever and inventive, funny and self-reflexive; as opposed, for instance, to Akalaitis's ironically

romping *Dead End Kids* (1982) or her hyper-real production of KROETZ's *Through the Leaves* (1984). In addition to creating original works, Mabou is considered one of the foremost interpreters of SAMUEL BECKETT: its influential productions of *The Lost Ones*, *Play*, *Come and Go*, *Cascando* and *Company* combine narration and elaborate visual spectacle. More recent productions include Linda Hartinian's *Flow My Tears, the Policeman Said* (1988), a gender-reversed *King Lear* (1990), and Frederick Neumann's *Reel to Real* (1994). In residence for three years at LA MAMA, Mabou has performed at the NEW YORK SHAKESPEARE FESTIVAL and elsewhere since 1975. In 1986 they received an Obie for sustained achievement. AS

MacArthur, Charles 1895–1966 American playwright. A Chicago newspaperman who collaborated with BEN HECHT, another Chicago newspaperman, on their most famous play, *The Front Page* (1928), a farcical caricature of newspaper life. Before this, he had collaborated with EDWARD SHELDON on *Lulu Belle* (1926), about a black courtesan, and with SIDNEY HOWARD on *Salvation* (1928), about a woman evangelist; both are weak MELODRAMAS. The partnership with Hecht also produced *Twentieth Century* (1932), a broad COMEDY on theatre people; *Jumbo* (1935), a CIRCUS MUSICAL; *Ladies and Gentlemen* (1939), a murder mystery that served as a vehicle for his wife, HELEN HAYES; and *Swan Song* (1946), a suspense melodrama. Alone, he wrote *Johnny on a Spot* (1942), a political SATIRE. He also did some screenwriting. TP

Macauley, Barney 1837–86 American actor and manager. Beginning his career as an actor in Buffalo, NY (1853), he became a leading actor in the Ohio Valley in 1861, and made his New York City debut opposite MATILDA HERON during 1864–5. He entered management in partnership with John Miles of Cincinnati (1868–72), and in 1872 assumed solo management in Louisville, Kentucky, where he had always been popular. He built his Macauley's Theatre there in 1873; in 1878 he turned the management over to his brother, John, spending the rest of his career as the star of his own combination playing a rural MELODRAMA, *The Messenger from Jarvis Section*. DMCD

McCabe, Eugene 1930– Irish playwright, educated at University College, Cork. The subjects of McCabe's work range from his *Swift*, another attempt to illuminate Swift's complex nature, to a television trilogy about the contemporary Northern Irish violence (*Cancer, Heritage, Siege*, 1976). His first stage play remains most impressive. Bringing 1960s rural Ireland into a view of its past, *The King of the Castle* (1964) makes remarkably coherent the domestic tragedy of Scober – the King – public hard man and ageing husband privately, the dispersed peasantry whose vagabond contemporary heirs we see, and the Big House vandalized by Scober's improvements. McCabe's novel *Death and Nightingales* was published in 1992. DM

McCarthy, Lillah 1875–1960 British actress and theatre manager. After touring with BEN GREET and WILSON BARRETT's companies, McCarthy became closely associated with SHAW's work, playing in the first productions of *Man and Superman* (1905), *The Doctor's Dilemma* (1906) and *Androcles and the Lion* (1913) under her first husband GRANVILLE BARKER, for whom she also created the title role in JOHN MASEFIELD's *The Tragedy of Nan* (1908). In 1911 she took over the Little Theatre in London, playing a repertoire of IBSEN, Shaw and SCHNITZLER under her own management, and after repeating some of her most famous roles in New York she became manager of London's Kingsway Theatre in 1919. CI

McClendon, Rose 1884–1936 African-American actress, who became totally committed to theatre after winning a scholarship to the AMERICAN ACADEMY OF DRAMATIC ARTS. Playing her first professional role in GALSWORTHY's *Justice* (1919), she advanced steadily to the top of the profession, holding lead roles in PAUL GREEN's 1926 Pulitzer Prize play *In Abraham's Bosom* and in DOROTHY AND DUBOSE HEYWARD's melodrama *Porgy*, in which she was called 'the perfect aristocrat of Catfish Row'. Known on BROADWAY as the 'Negro race's first lady', she used her influence with the union to promote the needs of fellow black actors. In 1935 she appeared as Cora in LANGSTON HUGHES's long-running MELODRAMA *Mulatto*, from which she withdrew in ill health and died the following year. EGH

McClintic, Guthrie 1893–1961 American actor, director and producer. Born in Seattle, McClintic studied acting at the AMERICAN ACADEMY OF DRAMATIC ARTS before making his first stage appearance in 1913, and his New York debut a year later. During the 1915–16 season, he appeared in numerous roles with Grace George's Company at the PLAYHOUSE THEATRE, followed by a 10-year association with producer WINTHROP AMES. McClintic began his career as a director and producer in 1921 by presenting A. A. MILNE's *The Dover Road*. In the same year he married actress KATHARINE CORNELL and began a long professional association with her as the director of her major successes. Recognized as one of the most distinguished directors in the American theatre, McClintic staged more than 90 productions, including the Pulitzer Prize-winning *The Old Maid* (1935) and *Winterset* (1935), which won the New York Drama Critics' Circle Award. His other major credits include *The Barretts of Wimpole Street* (1931); *Yellow Jack* (1934); *Ethan Frome* and *The Wingless Victory* (1936); *High Tor* and *Candida* (1937); *No Time for Comedy* and *Key Largo* (1939); *The Doctor's Dilemma* (1941); *You Touched Me* (1945); *The Playboy of the Western World* (1946); *Antony and Cleopatra* (1947); *Life with Mother* (1948); *Medea* (1949); *The Constant Wife* (1951); and *Bernadine* (1952). He was known for casting his shows wisely and knowing how to get the most out of his actors. BROOKS ATKINSON called McClintic 'one of our most accomplished directors, especially for plays that depend on taste and elegance'. TLM

McCowen, Alec [Alexander] **(Duncan)** 1925– British actor, who played in reps in Birmingham and York from 1943 to 50, before his first major London appearance as Daventry in *Escapade* (1953). He played Claverton-Ferry in T. S. ELIOT's *The Elder Statesman* (1958) and joined the OLD VIC company in 1959. In the early 1960s, he became an established actor with major classical companies and also appeared in contemporary plays in the WEST END; but his first major international success came in Peter Luke's *Hadrian VII*, where he played the man-who-would-be-pope with an unforgettable irony and wit. Sheer intelligence has been a feature of his acting, shining through his Hamlet in Birmingham in 1969, and it led him towards roles of intellectuals and academics, notably in CHRISTOPHER HAMPTON's *The Philanthropist* (1970), as Alceste in *The Misanthrope* and Dysart in SHAFFER's *Equus* (two outstandingly successful NATIONAL THEATRE productions), and as Higgins in the 1974 West End revival of SHAW's *Pygmalion*.

In 1978, McCowen devised his remarkable solo performance of St Mark's Gospel, with which he toured widely in Britain and the USA. He returned to the National Theatre to play Crocker-Harris in the revival of RATTIGAN's *The Browning Version*, and in 1984 devised a new solo production, *Kipling*. His autobiographical writings include *Young Gemini* (1979) and *Double Bill* (1980). He appeared with MICHAEL RUDMAN's group at the NT in BRIAN FRIEL's version of IVAN TURGENEV's *Fathers and Sons* (1987) and as Vladmir in *Waiting for Godot* (1987); and achieved notable West End successes in two modern Irish plays, Friel's *Dancing at Lughnasa* (1991) and FRANK MCGUINNESS's *Someone Who'll Watch Over Me* (1992). In 1972, he was awarded an OBE. JE

McCullough, John 1832–85 Irish-born American actor, who made his stage debut at the ARCH STREET THEATRE in Philadephia in 1857 in *The Belle's Stratagem*. He subsequently toured with E. L. DAVENPORT (1860–1) and EDWIN FORREST (1861–5). A tall, classically handsome man in the heroic mould, McCullough had a volatile, physically robust acting style that resembled Forrest's. After the latter's death in 1872, he assumed several of Forrest's major roles, including Spartacus in *The Gladiator*, Virginius and Jack Cade. He also excelled as Othello, King Lear, Coriolanus and Mark Antony. During 1866–77 he managed the CALIFORNIA THEATRE in San Francisco, for the first four years in association with LAWRENCE BARRETT. A heavy financial loss forced his retirement from management, and he spent the rest of his career as a successful touring star. In 1881 he made a brief starring engagement at London's DRURY LANE, appearing as Virginius and Othello. In 1883, his health declined; in the summer of 1885, he was placed in a mental institution. DJW

McCullough, Paul see CLARK, BOBBY

MacDonagh, Donagh 1912–68 Irish playwright. MacDonagh wrote three verse plays: *Happy as Larry* (1946), *God's Gentry* (1951) and *Step-in-the-Hollow* (1957). Rather in the manner of JOHN GAY's *Beggar's Opera*, MacDonagh combines song and street ballads with an easily spoken, at times doggerel, verse. In its period his work was associated with the supposed revival of verse drama represented by FRY and ELIOT. DM

McGee, Greg 1950– New Zealand playwright who achieved immediate prominence with his first play, *Foreskin's Lament* (1980), a treatment of violence and cultural obtuseness, ostensibly within the context of rugby football. Various television plays have followed, as well as two notable stage plays: *Out in the Cold* (1983) and *Tooth and Claw* (1982). HDMCN

Macgowan, Kenneth 1888–1963 American producer and critic. For years Macgowan wrote reviews chiefly for the *New York Globe* and *Theatre Arts [Monthly]*, sometimes whimsically reviewing plays he produced for New York's Experimental Theatre, Inc., which he founded with ROBERT EDMOND JONES and EUGENE O'NEILL (1924). There he produced six of O'Neill's plays, including *All God's Chillun Got Wings* (1924), *Desire Under the Elms* (1924) and *The Great God Brown* (1926), as well as the first New York production of STRINDBERG's *Ghost Sonata* (1924) and a popular revival of MOWATT's *Fashion* (1924). Although he produced into the 1930s, perhaps his greatest contributions were his books on masks and modern theatrical practice. The most influential of these were *The Theatre of Tomorrow* (1921), *Footlights across America* (1929), *Continental Stagecraft* (1922) with Robert Edmond Jones and *Masks and Demons* (1923) with Herman Rosse. RHW

McGrath, John (Peter) 1935– British writer and director for stage, television and film. As a BBC television director in the early 1960s, he was one of the originators of the influential 'Z Cars' series, co-wrote *Diary of a Young Man*, and contributed to many of the stylistic innovations of the time. While McGrath's early plays (such as *Events While Guarding the Bofors Gun*, 1966; filmed 1968) were written in a social drama idiom, combining event-packed story with a strong message of sympathy for society's underdogs, after 1968, as the political climate changed, he developed a style of popular theatre that incorporated songs, GAGS and dance into a loose 'EPIC' play structure. Several of these plays were written for the Everyman Theatre, Liverpool – most notably *Soft, or a Girl?* (1971) and *Fish in the Sea* (1973). But the most successful were written for the company he formed in 1971 to tour theatre to working-class audiences, 7:84 (the name deriving from the statistic that 7 per cent of the population owned 84 per cent of the wealth). The company was later split into two, one to tour Scotland and the other England, McGrath continuing to direct, commission and write for both.

Plays from this period, such as *The Cheviot, the Stag and the Black, Black Oil* (1973), *Little Red Hen* (1975) and *Blood Red Roses* (1980; televised 1986), are characterized by their energy and humour and their consistency in exposing English (capitalist) exploitation of Scotland. In addition to some 40 plays, poems, songs and scripts for several feature films, McGrath's writing includes the seminal *A Good Night Out* (1981), in which he argues the case for a theatre that is both socialist and popular, reaching working-class audiences in their own venues and helping to articulate the need for social change, and *The Bone Won't Break* (1990). Other significant plays are *John Brown's Body* (1990), *Watching for Dolphins* (1991) and *The Long Roads* (BBC TV, 1993). AJ

McGuinness, Frank 1953– Irish playwright. Since the ABBEY THEATRE produced *The Factory Girls* (1982), McGuinness has written seven full-length plays, eight new versions of European classics (including a splendid *Peer Gynt*), THEATRE-IN-EDUCATION pieces, one-acters and television plays. The award-winning *Observe the Sons of Ulster Marching towards the Somme* (1985) ritualistically explores the blood loyalties of a group of Northern Irish Protestant men facing the Battle of the Somme. *Innocence* (1986), centred on Caravaggio, probes creativity and exploitation in increasingly nightmarish style, and McGuinness's anti-naturalist energy explodes in *Mary and Lizzie* (1989), a comic/poetic dream journey through 19th-century Irish and British politics. By contrast, *Someone Who'll Watch over Me* (1992) treats the plight of three hostages in an unnamed Middle-Eastern country with surprising naturalistic understatement. McGuinness is undoubtedly the most daring and productive Irish playwright for many years. GF

Machiavelli, Niccolò 1469–1527 Italian political theorist, historian, military strategist and dramatist. Born into the Florentine nobility, he served in that city's state diplomatic service within and beyond Italy until the return to power of the Medici family in 1512 forced him into premature retirement. Most of his writings, including *Il principe* (*The Prince*, 1513) and *I discorsi* (*The Discourses*), were a product of that retirement, as probably were versions he made of TERENCE's *Andria*, PLAUTUS' *Aulularia*, and the play by which he is best remembered, *La mandragola* (c.1518) – generally considered to be the finest COMEDY of the Italian Renaissance. A witty, sharp, cold-eyed view of the more provincial aspects of Florentine society, it has been variously interpreted as a social comedy exposing the hypocrisy of pseudo-Christian values, a light *jeu d'esprit* expressive of the high summer of Renaissance confidence, and a deep, cunning and admonitory political allegory. It was probably first produced in Florence in 1518, and was later accorded further elaborate scenographic settings-out which, along with its observance of the unities of time, place and action, Machiavelli mocked in his prologue. In 1524 he wrote his last play, *La Clizia*, closely based on Plautus' *Casina*. An early piece, based on ARISTOPHANES' *The Clouds* and apparently written about 1504, is now lost.

His classical adaptations and emulations nicely reflect the humanistic preoccupations of his age, but in *La mandragola* he transcended classic models and, working as much from the example of Boccaccio and the *novelle* tradition, produced a work richly of its own time and place and neatly expressive of the amoral pragmatism more rigorously formulated in *Il principe*. That work, if more by repute and the vulgarization of its ideas than by any considered understanding of its arguments in context, exerted considerable influence on foreign, particularly Elizabethan and Jacobean, dramatists' conceptions of Italian court life and political intrigue – the devious Machiavellian schemer becoming a stock figure in many plays. LR

McIntyre, James 1857–1937 and
Thomas Heath 1852–1938 Two-man blackface act, the

longest-lasting (1874–1924) of all major minstrel–VAUDE-VILLE (see MINSTREL SHOW) duos. Though born elsewhere, both grew up in the South, where they learned to mimic blacks. McIntyre, a former clog dancer and small-time actor, was the comic; Heath, the straight man, was an ideal feeder for his partner, leading him into preposterous predicaments in sketches such as 'The Georgia Minstrels', 'The Man from Montana', 'Chickens' (with McIntyre in drag) and 'The Ham Tree' (the last becoming a full-length piece presented by producers Klaw and Erlanger, first in 1905). In 1916 the *New York Dramatic Mirror* carped that 90 per cent of their act was tedium, 10 per cent laughs; yet they persisted for almost a decade longer. Rumour that they did not speak to each other for 25 years was vehemently denied. DBW

MacIntyre, Tom 1933– Irish playwright. After the relatively realist *Eye-Winker, Tom-Tinker* (1972), centred on the self-absorbed rhetoric of a vacillating Irish revolutionary, and *Kitty O'Shea*, based on the Parnell story, MacIntyre turned towards a theatre of non-naturalistic physical and aural effects. *The Great Hunger* (1983), loosely based on Patrick Kavanagh's poem, develops extravagant improvisations out of word and gesture. *Rise Up Lovely Sweeny* and *The Bearded Lady* (1984) push the method further, the latter transforming figures from *Gulliver's Travels* into images of Swift's own tormented psyche. *Chickadee* (1993) is more accessible, a surreal (see SURREALISM) satirical romp centred on the Pope. DM GF

MacKaye, Percy 1875–1956 American playwright, whose grand dramatic visions resembled those of his father, STEELE MACKAYE. He wrote *St Louis Masque* (1914), celebrating the 150th anniversary of the city's founding; *Caliban by the Yellow Sands* (1916, in Central Park, New York), to commemorate the tercentenary of SHAKESPEARE's death; and his tetralogy, *The Mystery of Hamlet* (1949), which explored 30 years of the Hamlet saga prior to Shakespeare's play. His best-known plays were *The Scarecrow* (1909), adapted from Hawthorne's *Feathertop*, and *Jeanne d'Arc* (1906). He crusaded for 'a theatre for the people' in *The Playhouse and the Play* (1909), *The Civic Theatre* (1912) and *Community Drama* (1917), wrote 13 other plays and seven MASQUES, six volumes of stories and poems and an OPERA, *Rip Van Winkle* (1919, music by REGINALD DE KOVEN). RM

MacKaye, (James Morrison) Steele 1842–94 American actor, playwright, teacher, architect and inventor; a brilliant, if erratic, dreamer. MacKaye's innovations in stage mechanics and his crusade for REALISM in acting and 'true-to-life' dialogue marked him as 'the most unsuccessful successful figure in the American theatre'. His early dreams of becoming an actor and artist, supported by unrestricted family funds, permitted him to study painting with George Inness and acting with François Delsarte (in Paris, 1869), and to found a 'school of expression' in New York (1871) for propagating the Delsartian system. He made his professional debut as actor, playwright and manager with *Monaldi* (New York, 1872), played Hamlet in London (Crystal Palace, 1873) and then achieved success as a playwright with *Rose Michel* (1875)

and *Won at Last* (1877). Of his 30 plays, *Hazel Kirke* (1880), presented in his MADISON SQUARE THEATRE, was the best: it ran for over a year and was repeatedly revived during the next two decades; but MacKaye had unwittingly contracted to assign the profits to his financial backers, the Mallory brothers.

The Madison Square Theatre, MacKaye's first venture into architecture, had an elevator stage that changed scenes in two minutes, a lighting system devised by Edison, folding seats and an ingenious ventilating system. His second theatre, to be combined with a hotel, never progressed beyond the blueprint stage. His third, New York's LYCEUM (1885), incorporated new stage machinery, firefighting equipment, an orchestra pit on an elevator and quarters for America's first dramatic school. His ultimate theatrical dream, a spectatorium (480ft long, 380ft wide and 270ft high) for the Chicago World's Fair (1893) to house his chronicle of Columbus's adventures, *The World Finder*, was disrupted by the national financial panic and was reduced to a scaled-down scenitorium. A detailed account of his life and work was written by his son, playwright PERCY MACKAYE (*Epoch*, 1927). RM

McKellen, Ian (Murray) 1939– British actor, whose first London appearance in JAMES SAUNDERS's *A Scent of Flowers* (1964) led to a season at the NATIONAL THEATRE and major roles in Donald Howarth's *A Lily in Little India* (1966) and ALEKSEI ARBUZOV's *The Promise* (1967). He first emerged as a major classical actor, however, through the Prospect Theatre Company, and his twin performances as SHAKESPEARE's Richard II (1968) and MARLOWE's Edward II (1969) established his reputation as one of the most sensitive and intelligent actors in Britain. He was a founder member of the touring acting cooperative, the Actors' Company, playing both leading and small character parts with equal panache. He joined the ROYAL SHAKESPEARE COMPANY in 1974 where, despite several major roles in the main theatre, he will be best remembered for an outstanding studio Macbeth with JUDI DENCH as Lady Macbeth.

He led the small-scale touring RSC company in 1978, playing major roles in *Three Sisters* and *Twelfth Night*. In 1979, he appeared as one of two homosexuals imprisoned in a Nazi concentration camp in Martin Sherman's *Bent* (see GAY THEATRE), which transferred to the WEST END, and in 1980 took the part of Salieri in the New York production of PETER SHAFFER's *Amadeus*. In 1984 he joined the National Theatre as an associate director, playing Coriolanus in a major PETER HALL production. His association with the NT continued under RICHARD EYRE, who directed him in the title role of *Richard III* (1990) where he played the hunchback as a Fascist war veteran, as Kent in *King Lear* (1990), in Peter Tinniswood's version of EDUARDO DE FILIPPO's *Napoli Milionaria* (1991) and as Vanya in *Uncle Vanya* (1992); but one memorable performance took place in an RSC studio production, *Othello* (1989), directed by TREVOR NUNN, in which he played Iago as a punctilious NCO to Willard White's Othello. JE

McKern, Leo (Reginald) 1920– Australian actor. Initially a Sydney actor, he appeared with the London OLD VIC in 1949 and has since played many classical and modern roles at the Old Vic, at Stratford-upon-Avon and in the WEST END, including Peer Gynt, Iago and Toad of Toad Hall; he directed the London production of *The Shifting Heart* (1959). He returned to Australia with the 1952–3 Shakespeare Memorial Theatre tour, and to play in Douglas Stewart's *Ned Kelly* (1955) and RAY LAWLER's *The Man Who Shot the Albatross* (1971). His best-known television role is as 'Rumpole of the Bailey'. MW

Mackintosh, Cameron (Anthony) 1946– British producer and impresario, who became stage-struck at the age of eight, having seen Julian Slade's *Salad Days*. His interests drew him towards MUSICALS, and after serving an apprenticeship in stage management he produced his first London musical, *Anything Goes*, in 1969. He gained experience with small-scale touring productions (*Side by Side with Sondheim*, 1976) and revivals (*Godspell*, 1975; *My Fair Lady*, 1979), before producing a sequence of ANDREW LLOYD WEBBER musicals in the 1980s, all but one of which became smash hits – *Cats* (1981), *Song and Dance* (1982) and *Phantom of the Opera* (1986). In addition, he went into partnership with the ROYAL SHAKESPEARE COMPANY to produce *Les Misérables* (1985) and with the NATIONAL THEATRE for a revival of *Carousel* (1993); and produced two other major hits, *Miss Saigon* (1989) and *Five Guys Named Mo* (1990), which he took to the WEST END from the Theatre Royal, Stratford, East London.

Mackintosh was a prime force behind the revival of West End musicals in the 1980s, drawing on the expertise of the national theatres, the various skills trained at the Guildhall School of Music and Drama, and a new generation of singers and dancers who dispelled the old belief that British actors were 'talking heads'. He succeeded in turning the tables on BROADWAY, in that the West End became the place where the most ambitious and lavish musicals were usually staged. While his greatest successes may have been with British writers, he promoted STEPHEN SONDHEIM's musicals as well, including *Follies* (1987), and Sondheim was the first occupier of a chair of musical drama that Mackintosh endowed at St Catherine's College, Oxford University. In 1991 he received a Laurence Olivier Award for Outstanding Achievement, and in 1993 was named among the top ten richest men in Britain. JE

Macklin, Charles 1699–1797 Irish actor, manager and playwright. After an apprenticeship touring, Macklin began to establish himself in London in the 1730s. In 1739 he was convicted of the manslaughter of an actor after a quarrel over a stage wig. In 1736 he scored his first major success as Peachum in GAY's *The Beggar's Opera*. He was at this stage a remarkably versatile actor with a massive repertory. In 1740 he played Shylock, turning him from the comic character of tradition into a fierce, harsh and powerful figure, while keeping the stock accessories of red hair, hooked nose and *pantalone* costume. It was a huge success, even though played opposite KITTY CLIVE's Portia: Pope praised it – 'This is the Jew/That Shakespeare drew'.

By 1742 Macklin was widely involved in the teaching of actors, helping GARRICK learn the role of King Lear. The following year when the actors revolted against the management, the terms of the agreement that resolved the dispute specifically excluded Macklin, who could not for-

give Garrick for his part in it. When Garrick took over DRURY LANE in 1747, Macklin's Shylock opened the first season. His increasing reputation as a teacher and an unsettled relationship with the companies led him to retire in 1753 to run a coffee-house and school of oratory, but bankruptcy led him back to the stage. In 1759 his seventh play, *Love à-la-Mode*, gave him his first success as a playwright. When he returned to play Macbeth in 1774 he was unable to persuade the company to adopt an authentically researched ancient Scots setting, but his own costume was 'the old Caledonian habit'. In his eighties he starred as Sir Pertinax Macsycophant in his own play *The Man of the World*, and finally retired in 1789 when he realized that his memory was failing. His plays are marked by an uncommon recurrent attempt at colloquial dialogue and realistic detail as well as a fascination with the nature of dramatic illusion. His own acting style and his influence as a teacher were heavily weighted towards a restrained NATURALISM. PH

Mackney, E(dmund) W(illiam) 1825–1909 The first important English blackface performer; of a theatrical family, he made a debut in PANTOMIME at the age of nine. Mackney commenced in London VARIETY at the Royal Standard, Pimlico, offering a one-man show in the style of THOMAS. D. RICE, accompanying himself on piano, banjo, bones, guitar and violin, the last providing farmyard imitations. However, he was better at ballad parodies and topical songs than as an interpreter of Negro life, and only after many vicissitudes as a burnt-cork comedian and tavern-keeper did he achieve success, when he was booked by CHARLES MORTON at London's Canterbury Hall. Thereafter he divided his time between the MUSIC-HALLS and touring the provinces with his own concert party, playing at town halls and mechanics' institutes for a public that regarded theatres as immoral. He retired in early middle age to devote himself to rose-growing, but returned to the stage after suffering financial reversals. (See also MINSTREL SHOW.) LS

McMahon, Gregan 1874–1941 Australian director. Initially an actor with Robert Brough, in 1911 he founded the Melbourne Repertory Theatre to stage serious drama and promising Australian works. Throughout his career he moved between commercial and amateur theatre, working with the J. C. WILLIAMSON and Tait managements, and establishing the Sydney Repertory Society in the 1920s and the semi-professional Gregan McMahon Players in the 1930s, both known for high standards and a serious repertoire; but an attempt to create a professional repertory theatre under Tait sponsorship proved unsuccessful. McMahon was awarded a CBE in 1938. MW

McNally, Terrence 1939– Texas-born American playwright, whose first produced script was *And Things That Go Bump in the Night* at the GUTHRIE THEATRE in 1964 and on BROADWAY the following year. *Bad Habits*, a double-bill of *Ravenswood* and *Dunelawn*, was produced OFF-BROADWAY and moved to Broadway in 1974. Other Broadway productions include *The Ritz* in 1975 and *Broadway* in 1979. Other plays include *Where Has Tommy Flowers Gone?* (1971, New York's Eastside Playhouse), *It's*

Only a Play (1982, 1986 at MANHATTAN THEATRE CLUB), *Frankie and Johnny in the Clair de Lune* (1987, Off-Broadway and subsequently a popular regional play), *The Lisbon Traviata* (1985, 1989 at MTC), *Lips Together, Teeth Apart* (1991, MTC) and *The Perfect Ganesh* (1993, MTC), the latter his most eloquent, capacious and true play to date, according to most critics. His book for *Kiss of the Spider Woman* won a 1993 Tony. McNally has also written drama for television and radio. His initial plays involved the major concerns of the late 1960s and early 70s – assassination, the Vietnam War, rebellion and the sexual revolution. Although he began as an angry and outraged playwright, his more recent work is in contrast more lyrical and positive, offering unsentimental hope for intimacy at a time when fear and death rule. His most recent work in progress, *L'Age d'Or*, dealing with Vincenzo Bellini's relationship with rival diva sisters (reflecting McNally's great love of OPERA, as does *Master Class*, which premiered in 1995), and *Love! Valour! Compassion!*, concerned with the fortunes of seven men in an isolated country home, had 1994 New York productions. In 1993 a new playwriting programme at the Juilliard school began under his tutelage.   SMA DBW

Macready, W(illiam) C(harles) 1793–1873 English actor, the son of the well known manager of the Bristol theatrical circuit. Sent to Rugby School and intended for the law, Macready had to leave school at 15 on his father's sudden bankruptcy and imprisonment for debt. Reluctantly, he plumped for the immediate financial prospects of the stage and made his debut as Romeo in Birmingham in 1810. The bitterness remained close to the surface throughout his 40-year career, emerging often in the angry, fascinating *Diaries* he kept from 1833 to 51. (A pruned selection was first published in 1875.)

In 1816, with JOHN PHILIP KEMBLE newly retired and EDMUND KEAN reigning supreme at DRURY LANE, Macready was hired as a new attraction at COVENT GARDEN. Poorly used there, he made little impact until 1819, when he risked all in a part that was virtually the property of Kean, Richard III, and was the first Covent Garden actor to be summoned for a curtain call by an enthusiastic audience. He followed up his success with the first of many parts in which he could display his skill in the portrayal of a favourite 19th-century emotion, paternal love. This was in SHERIDAN KNOWLES's *Virginius* (1820), and it marked the beginning of a mutually advantageous link between playwright and actor. Not until 1834 did Macready first play Lear, SHAKESPEARE's paternal tragedy and, by some accounts, Macready's finest role. Industrious and observant rather than charismatic, he aimed always to make passion intelligible. Knowles was the first of many contemporary playwrights through whom Macready hoped to raise the standards of the English drama. Others were Talfourd, Barry Cornwall, DICKENS, Browning and, more successfully, BULWER LYTTON, whose most effective plays he helped to create.

If the stage was to be his life, he was determined to make it worthy of him, and there is some pathos in his growing fury at others' refusal to measure up to his high standards. Well enough established to confine his London appearances to Covent Garden, Drury Lane and (in the summer)

the HAYMARKET, Macready also made regular tours to provincial theatres and three to the USA (1826, 1843 and 1848), the last of which was scarred by the enmity of EDWIN FORREST and the tragic conclusion of the ASTOR PLACE riot. His spells as manager of Covent Garden (1837–9) and Drury Lane (1841–3) had, for all their high endeavour, left him bankrupt, and he spent his last years on the stage saving towards his retirement. He took his farewell in 1851, in his favourite part of Macbeth, concluding his diary with the exclamation 'Thank God!'.   PT

McVicker, James H(ubert) 1822–96 American actor and theatre manager, who first achieved national recognition as an actor of YANKEE characters in the 1850s. In 1857 he settled in Chicago and built his McVicker's Theatre, a commodious clapboard version of an Italianate palazzo on Madison Street, which he managed successfully until his death. Although the theatre was destroyed in the great Chicago fire of 1871 and burned again in 1890 (the last legitimate theatre on the site was razed in 1922), it was rebuilt on both occasions in less than a year. McVicker was a highly regarded manager, noted for the quality of his STOCK COMPANY and for his carefully mounted revivals of *The School for Scandal*, *A Midsummer Night's Dream* and *The Tempest*. His adopted daughter Mary Runnion McVicker married EDWIN BOOTH in 1869, and McVicker managed one of Booth's starring tours, including an engagement at the LYCEUM THEATRE in New York in 1876.   MCH DJW

Madách, Imre 1823–64 Hungarian dramatist. His masterpiece, the dramatic poem *The Tragedy of Man*, written in 1860, is a panoramic, epic statement about mankind's destiny, in the genre of GOETHE's *Faust*, BYRON's *Cain* and IBSEN's *Peer Gynt*. It rejects Hegel's view of history as linear progress, and anticipates Spengler's view of history as cyclical. In a dream Lucifer leads Adam through episodes in human history, past and future, culminating in the demise of civilization and of life itself. The work ends with an enigmatic affirmation of faith in the need to struggle on against all odds. Its unity derives from the alternation of scenes pitting individual rights against collective ones and vice versa, and from the fact that Adam, Eve and Lucifer play the historical figures throughout. Madách's scepticism can be traced to the collapse of the traditional religious world outlook, induced by advances in the natural sciences, and to defeat in Hungary's War of Independence (1848–9). *The Tragedy of Man* was premiered in 1883 at the National Theatre, and remains one of Hungary's most enduring theatrical successes. It has been translated into more than 20 languages, produced numerous times in Germany, Austria and Czechoslovakia, and broadcast as a radio play in France and Switzerland.   EB

Madagascar Until 1895 when it became a French possession, Madagascar was ruled by the indigenous Merina monarchy, which presided over a rigidly stratified society of nobles, freemen and slaves. The island remained a French colony until 1967, when it obtained its independence. Its theatrical activity can be divided into three categories: traditional performance, a written theatre in Malagasy, and one in French.

One traditional yet contemporary Malagasy display is the *Hira-Gasy*: a spectacle of song, dance and improvised sketches that originally took place during ceremonies. Its cast of twenty or so peasant actors known as *Mphihira-Malagasy* highlight social problems for which, on the occasion of ceremonies, the community tries to find solutions. But, reflecting the island's history, this display has undergone changes in costume, movement and dance. Originally a spectacle by villagers for villagers, it was annexed in the 18th century into the service of the monarchy. Queen Ranavalona invited *Hira-Gasy* performers to her court to entertain her European visitors. The more enthusiastic among these sometimes joined in the dancing, and to this day their steps and movements, parodied, are an integral part of *Hira-Gasy* displays, as is their outfit, which incorporates wide stripes for the soldiers and religious decorations for the missionaries, and long dresses and sometimes gold-capped teeth for the ladies. The *Hira-Gasy* remained in the service of successive governments (the French after the Malagasy monarchy, then the independent nation's) until the mid-1970s when, after a Marxist revolution, it seems to have returned to its roots as a people's theatre.

Madagascar's theatre in the Malagasy language thrived in the 19th to early 20th centuries. Intensely moralizing, this theatre (compared by its exponents to a sermon) has a three-part structure: a prologue where a chorus states in song the play's theme and moral, a dramatic representation proper, and an epilogue in which chorus and actors return on stage to restate in song the play's lesson. A few of its many representatives are Justin Rainizablolona, Tselatra Rajaonah and Arthur Rodlish, two of whose plays – *Ramoniody* (*The Rumour*, 1926) and *Sangy Mahery* (*Violent Games*, 1926), both on the theme of love thwarted because of caste differences between the lovers – were among the most popular. Another form of theatre in Malagasy is the *Konserta Masina*, a religious kind of play in the Togolese *kantata* tradition, on biblical subjects.

With French colonial rule emerged a modest theatre in that language, practised by the poet Jean-Joseph Rabéarivelo with his dramatized legend *Imaitsoanala* (1935), and especially by JACQUES RABÉMANAJARA. It is a highly literary theatre whose subjects are borrowed from Malagasy myths and lore. Over the last ten years, this theatre in French has grown and also become less wordy, with playwrights like David Jaomanoro (*Le Dernier Caiman* (*The Last Caiman*, 1988) and *La Retraite* (*The Retirement*, 1988)); Michèle Rakotoson (her prize-winning *Sambany* (1979), *Un Jour ma mémoire* (*One Day My Memory*, 1989) and *La Maison morte* (*The Dead House*, 1991)); Charlotte Rafenomanjata (*La Pécheresse* (*The Fisherwoman*, 1988), *Le Prix de paix* (*The Price of Peace*, 1986) and *Le Troupeau* (*The Flock*, 1990)); and Susan Ravoaja (*Fanano*, 1989). Although Malagasy lore provides setting and subject for these plays, these elements are mostly interpreted in the light of contemporary social and political issues. JCM

See: R. Cornevin, *Le Théâtre en Afrique noire et à Madagascar*, Paris, 1970; D. de Saivre, 'De Madagascar, un théâtre populaire: L'Hira-Gasy', *Recherche, Pédagogie, Culture*, 49, 1980; C. Wake, 'Madagascar', *The Cambridge Guide to World Theatre*, ed. M. Banham, Cambridge, 1988.

Maddy, Yulisa Amadu 1936– Sierra Leonean playwright, theatre director and novelist; founder of the Gbakanda Afrikan Tiata theatre group. Maddy was educated in Freetown and at the Rose Bruford College of Speech and Drama in Kent, England. He has made a powerful impact on theatre in SIERRA LEONE, as well as in other African countries. He has also promoted black theatre and African performing arts during lengthy sojourns in Denmark, Britain and the USA. Although he is an imaginative and experimental director – his production of Alem Mezgebe's *Pulse* at the EDINBURGH FESTIVAL in 1979 won a FRINGE award – his greatest contribution to African theatre is probably as a playwright.

Maddy comes out of the urban Creolized context of Freetown. Increasingly, he writes in Krio, an urban language suitable for a theatre depicting the West African urban milieu, and bases his dramas within a class analysis. He has always written about the oppressed and their sense of a collectivity within communities which have lost hope. The humanist overview within the plays is always a complex one. The characters rarely find easy solutions to their oppression, as they struggle towards a fairer society within the scope of their limited resources. *Yon Kon* (published 1968) is about a criminal in gaol who is top dog amongst the other prisoners. Inside and outside the prison an amoral world is created through the language of conventional morality. The drama is developed, through a series of short scenes, to its ironic conclusion. Another early play – one with SARTREAN overtones – is *Life Everlasting*, in which recognizable Sierra Leonean types arrive dead in Hell, and are organized by 'Big Boy'. An anthology of his plays (1971) includes *Obasai* and *Gbana Bendu*. *Obasai*, about community renewal being spearheaded by the least likely people in that community, is a quasi-naturalistic play (see NATURALISM) with emotive songs and some vivid theatrical imagery. *Gbana Bendu*, a wholly integrated piece of 'total theatre', breaks new ground. It enters into the penumbra of the masquerade (see MASQUERADES IN AFRICA) and the secret cult, in order to explore alternative paths to social justice.

Big Berin, which Maddy produced in the early 1970s in Sierra Leone, is set in a compound of multiple occupancy among the urban poor. It explores the secret desires of its occupants; relates these desires, surrealistically (see SURREALISM), to the hegemony of the state; and shows the immoral implications of individualistic materialism. Since his production of this play, Maddy's work seems to have stagnated. Perhaps his imprisonment by the Sierra Leone government, as a result of his outspoken criticism of the corruption prevalent in the society of the 70s, has embittered him. Since the early 1980s, his productivity both as playwright and as director has diminished.

Forced to live in exile after his release from detention in the late 1970s, Maddy returned home periodically in the late 80s and early 90s, and has attempted to re-establish himself in the local theatre. ME JS

Madison Square Theatre (New York City) When the FIFTH AVENUE THEATRE burned down and its manager AUGUSTIN DALY moved to another theatre, the house was not immediately rebuilt. Four years later, in 1877, it was resurrected to become Minnie Commings's Drawing

Room with an open stage. In 1879, with financial backing from the Mallory brothers, STEELE MACKAYE gutted and redesigned the house, installing his famous double stage, experimenting with atmospheric lighting, relocating the orchestra above the stage and improving the comfort of his patrons with his invention of the folding chair. The theatre was renamed the Madison Square. In 1880, he had his greatest triumph with *Hazel Kirke*; the play brought about a falling-out with the Mallorys, and MacKaye left the playhouse. In 1884, A. M. PALMER was asked to take over, and his businesslike methods and his policy of presenting stars in imported and stageworthy plays brought great prosperity to the house. In 1891, CHARLES HOYT secured the lease to showcase his own plays and eventually changed the name to Hoyt's Theatre. On his death, it was rented on a run-of-the-play basis; but in 1908, obsolete and too far downtown, it was razed to make way for an office building. MCH

Maeterlinck, Maurice 1862–1949 Belgian poet, playwright, essayist and Nobel Prizewinner (1911). Maeterlinck wrote in French and reached international fame through plays like *La Princesse Maleine* (1889), *Les Aveugles* (*The Blind*, 1890), *L'Intruse* (*The Intruder*, 1890) and *Pelléas et Mélisande* (1892; performed in Paris by LUGNÉ-POE; inspired Debussy's opera of 1902). Maeterlinck represents the victory of SYMBOLISM over NATURALISM. He was fascinated by dimensions that make life elusive, such as mysterious forces and blindness. Only through contemplation, absolute silence and inactivity could these be made visible. His plays are characterized by their lack of action or conflict, and by their suggestive force. Especially his early work made him, in the eyes of some, a precursor of absurdism (see THEATRE OF THE ABSURD). The mysterious forces evoke an atmosphere resembling early PINTER. Later work included three *drames pour marionnettes* (*Alladine et Palomides*, *Intérieur* and *La Mort de Tintagiles* (*The Death of Tintagiles*, 1894)); a 'classical' tragedy, *Monna Vanna* (1902); a theatrical fantasy, *L'Oiseau bleu* (1908; first performed in Moscow and filmed several times); *La Princesse Isabelle* (1935), *L'Ombre des ailes* (*The Shadow of the Wings*, 1937), *L'Autre Monde, ou Le cadran stellaire* (*The Other World, or The Star System*, 1941) and *Jeanne d'Arc* (1943). MG WH HS

Maffei, Francesco Scipione 1675–1755 Italian dramatist and antiquarian. Of aristocratic birth and Jesuit education, he spent most of his life in his home town of Verona dedicated to the study of its antiquities and publishing extensive materials on the subject, including the important *Verona illustrata* (*Verona Illustrated*, 1732). His verse TRAGEDY *Merope* (1713) ranks as one of the major Italian plays of the century and was admired and imitated by VOLTAIRE and ALFIERI, but was indifferently received when staged by LUIGI RICCOBONI as part of his attempt to reform, and raise the standards of, the Italian literary theatre. LR

Magaña, Sergio 1924–91 Mexican playwright. Magaña achieved early success with his popular *Los signos del zodíaco* (*Signs of the Zodiac*, 1951), a play with sometimes simultaneous action in various settings of a lower-class

neighbourhood. Later plays include *Moctezuma II* (1953) with its view of pre-Hispanic Mexico and an emperor destined to fall, and *Los argonautas* (*The Argonauts*, 1967), which presents a jaundiced view of Cortés and the conquest of Mexico. His last major play was *Los enemigos* (*The enemies*, 1990), a moving reinterpretation of the RABINAL ACHÍ, the only surviving pre-Colombian play. GW

Maggi, Carlos 1922– Uruguayan playwright, novelist and lawyer. One of Uruguay's best, he has utilized absurdist techniques (see THEATRE OF THE ABSURD) to uncover the social and political problems of the national situation. His black humour, sharp dialogue and inventive techniques were evident in his earliest plays: *La trastienda* (*The Backstore*, 1958), *La biblioteca* (*The Library*, 1959) and *Esperando a Rodó* (*Waiting for Rodó*, 1961), the latter an obvious play on BECKETT's title, but with Maggi's particular vision of national corruption that foiled the great Uruguayan essayist's dream of an American utopia. *Las llamadas* (*The Calls*, 1965) decried the loss of national identity through the dehumanizing effects of television, with a resulting imbecilic language. *El patio de la Torcaza* (*The Patio of the Torcaza*, 1967) is a complex analysis of the disintegration of the national welfare state. After a long silence during the dictatorship, Maggi returned with *Frutos* (1985) and *Un cuervo en la madrugada* (*A Crow at Morning*, 1988). GW

magic (Europe; USA) In the guise of sleight-of-hand, magic had long been a fairground and street amusement before it entered the theatre in the mid-18th century: Isaac Fawkes (or Faux) worked the Bartholomew and Southwark Fairs in England, and was succeeded by Christopher Pinchbeck. During the Enlightenment, conjurors often used the paraphernalia and ambience of the Egyptian Rites of Freemasonry, founded by Alessandro Cagliostro; the American JACOB PHILADELPHIA and the French optical illusionist ROBERTSON played on these associations and this style had its effect on Mozart's *Magic Flute*, itself a forerunner of the Austrian *Zauberposse* or magical FARCE, so popular in the 19th century. (Much spectacular theatre of the period was predicated on technical magic, the instantaneous transformations of scenery and the tricks of the harlequinade.) Many magic acts posed as scientific demonstrations, like those of the quack Katterfelto, or centred on ingenious automata that played chess and performed lightning calculations.

With the peace that followed Napoleon's defeat, solo conjurors criss-crossed Europe, among them the great cup-and-ball artist Bartolomeo Bosco (1793–1863), Ludwig Leopold Döbler (1801–64) who caught a chosen card from a flung pack on the tip of a sword, and J. H. ANDERSON 'the Great Wizard of the North'. This school generally performed surrounded by the detritus of witchcraft, using flowing robes and intricate draperies for concealment. It was ROBERT-HOUDIN and Wiljalba Frikell (1816–1903) who first worked on a stage denuded of apparatus and supernatural frills, lending their acts the respectable charm of a drawing-room entertainment.

A fresh impetus was given by the spiritist movement that gained popularity in the 1860s. Mediums like the DAVENPORT BROTHERS (IRA ERASTUS, 1838–1911, and

WILLIAM HENRY HARRISON, 1841–77) claimed to effect miraculous escapes from knots and locked cabinets with the aid of ectoplasmic assistants; in turn, debunkers like J. N. MASKELYNE made an evening of demonstrating how such tricks could be accomplished naturally. Although exclusive magic theatres such as those of Robert-Houdin and HENRI ROBIN in Paris and Maskelyne's Egyptian Hall in London offered a full performance of a carefully structured series of illusions, the rise of VARIETY required conjurors to dazzle an audience in 20 minutes. Once again, touring magicians like Robert Heller (William Henry Palmer, 1826–78) and the HERRMANNS (Carl or Compars (1816–87), his brother ALEXANDER (1843–96), Alexander's widow Adelaide Scarcez (1853–1932) and his cousin Leon (1867–1909)) won international reputations. Innovations such as mentalism or mind-reading (invented by the Chicago newspaperman John Randall Brown and later performed over the radio by Joseph Dunniger) arose, and there were vogues for Chinese or Hindu conjurors – not uncommonly Europeans in masquerade, such as the Great Lafayette (Sigmund Neuberger, 1871–1911) and William Ellsworth Robinson known as Chung Ling Soo (1861–1918), who was killed in his own catch-the-bullet act. Since card tricks and simple prestidigitation did not carry over well in palatial *fin-de-siècle* music-halls and variety theatres, flashy and gigantic illusions, vanishing acts and mid-air transformations became popular as devised by BUATIER DE KOLTA, DAVID DEVANT, P. T. Selbit (Percy Thomas Tibbles, 1879–1939), KELLAR, THURSTON and HORACE GOLDIN. Not untypically, HARRY HOUDINI began as a card and coin manipulator before gaining fame as an 'escapologist', capable of keeping an audience in suspense for several minutes as it watched a static tank in which he was encased.

Ironically, cinematic trickery which seemed to outdo the feats of stage magicians was introduced by the stage conjuror GEORGES MÉLIÈS, and, with the decline of live variety entertainments, the more lavish acts folded. There were still flamboyant throwbacks like the Dane Dante (August Harry Jansen, 1883–1955), who updated the spirit cabinet routines, and Harry Blackstone (1885–1959), who perpetuated and perfected classic illusions like levitation and sawing a woman in half. Magicians continued to play wherever variety shows were offered; the German Kalanag (Helmut Ewald Schreiber, 1893–1963), the Bengali Protul Chandra Sorcar (Sarcar, 1913–71), and the Russian Kio (Émil Renard, 1900–65) maintained an international stardom; but in America, conjurors often drifted into chautauquas (lecture meetings of an educational or religious nature; see CHAUTAUQUA AND LYCEUM), CIRCUSES and fairgrounds. Television provided a new arena for old techniques, and there was a stage resurgence of sorts in the 1970s. BROADWAY, which had proved cool to Houdini in 1926 and Dante in 1940, warmed to the MUSICAL *The Magic Show* (by Bob Randall and Stephen Schwartz, 1974) in which the Canadian Doug Henning (b.1947) performed Houdini's water torture cell in blue jeans and T-shirt and vanished a tiger; he and colleagues like David Copperfield have invigorated the magic act with 'show biz' glamour and cunning lighting techniques. CABARET and casinos are now common venues for conjurors: the Las Vegas-style REVUE makes a congenial setting for the wild-beast illusions of Siegfried (Fischbacker) and Roy (Horn).

The fantastic aspects of the magical tradition have influenced much avant-garde theatre, particularly the surrealist obsession (see SURREALISM) with the *insolite*: COCTEAU's *Orphée* (1926) is a knowing adaptation of illusionism to a poetical conceit. John Vaccaro's transvestite production *The Magic Show of Dr Ma-Gico* (by Kenneth Bernard, LA MAMA, 1973) exploited the structure of the magic act for anarchic audience-bashing, a technique more subtly and amiably wielded by JÉRÔME SAVARY's Grand Magic Circus shows. LS

Magnani, Anna 1908–73 Italian actress. In the 1930s and 40s Magnani worked in both the 'straight' and REVUE theatres, notably in the early 1940s with the comedian TOTÒ, while developing a career in cinema that increasingly kept her from the stage but brought her international status, first in Italian neo-realist films like Rossellini's *Roma città aperta* (*Rome, Open City*, 1945) and *Amare* (1948), then in VISCONTI's *Bellissima* (1951) and Renoir's *La Carosse d'or* (*The Golden Coach*, 1952). In 1955 she won an Oscar for her performance in the Hollywood-made *Rose Tattoo*, from TENNESSEE WILLIAMS's play. Of her later film work, perhaps most memorable was the role she played in Pasolini's *Mamma Roma* (1962), a characteristically witty, volcanic and engaging performance in which she transcended the kind of 'woman of the people' typecasting of her later film work. She made occasional postwar stage appearances, notably in O'NEILL's *Anna Christie* (1945) and VERGA's *La lupa* (1965). KR

Mahelot, Laurent fl.1620s–30s French scene designer. Mahelot was resident designer and machinist of the Comédiens du Roi at the HÔTEL DE BOURGOGNE. He compiled a manuscript *Mémoire* listing all 71 plays in the company's repertoire in the early 1630s. The document also gives an often detailed description of the scenery, machinery and other effects required for their performance, together, in 47 cases, with a sketch of the resultant stage setting. The scenic pieces illustrated, which include palaces, fortresses, prisons, shops, fountains, forests, grottos, mountains and hermitages, are sometimes practicable and clearly derive from the tradition of multiple staging associated with medieval religious drama (see MEDIEVAL DRAMA IN EUROPE), though arranged in a semi-ellipse around a central acting area to fit the shape of an indoor stage. Mahelot's use of perspective foreshortening and concern for symmetry, however, betray a debt to the influence of Italian Renaissance scenography and his designs therefore mark an interesting transition between two distinct staging traditions (see THEATRE DESIGN). The *Mémoire*'s index was continued by another hand, giving the titles of plays in the repertoire in the mid-1640s, and two further supplements, added by Michel Laurent and others, contain a list and brief description of the decor of plays performed by the company in the late 1670s and by the COMÉDIE-FRANÇAISE in the 1680s. As a whole the manuscript represents a unique record of 17th-century stage practice. DR

Maillet, Antonine 1929– French Canadian playwright and novelist, the leading voice of francophone Acadia.

Maillet's career as dramatist began with performances of her unpublished texts *Entr'acte* (*Intermission*, 1957) and *Poireâcre*, which won first prize in the 1958 Dominion Drama Festival. The play *Les Crasseux* (*The Unwashed*, 1968) and her scripts for Radio-Canada led to her greatest success, *La Sagouine* (*The Slattern*, 1971), performed in French and English on national television and in theatres across Canada. In 16 monologues the titular character, an unlettered Acadian washerwoman, reflects philosophically on the injustices she and her people have suffered. She does so in the archaic dialect of New Brunswick, home of the majority of Acadians. *La Sagouine*'s themes and language return in most of Maillet's subsequent works, such as *Gapi et Sullivan* (1973), *La Veuve enragée* (*The Mad Widow*, 1977), *La Contrabandière* (*Smuggler Woman*, 1981); but most notably in her other critical and popular success, *Évangéline Deusse* (*Evangeline the Second*, 1976), in which she sets out to replace Longfellow's tragic heroine, too long the symbol of a passive Acadia. She is a major novelist; her *Pélagie-la-Charrette* was awarded France's prestigious Prix Goncourt in 1979.   LED

Mairet, Jean 1604–86 French dramatist, who occupies a significant place in the evolution of 17th-century TRAGEDY. His early work, written in the irregular vein then current, is unremarkable (if successful in its day), but in *Silvanire* (1629) he created a PASTORAL TRAGICOMEDY which faithfully observed the three unities and went on to advocate their universal application in a preface to the published text. His tragedy *Sophonisbe* (1634) was a model of classical regularity and decorum, and its success contributed substantially to the acceptance of classical rules. Predictably, he took part in the critical attack on PIERRE CORNEILLE's *Le Cid* in 1637, though his later work adopted a cavalier attitude to his own professed criteria. He enjoyed the favour of RICHELIEU, being one of the five dramatists commissioned to write plays for him, and was attached for some years to MONTDORY's company at the MARAIS before abandoning the theatre for a diplomatic career in 1640.   DR

Malawi Theatre in Malawi has been said to 'lack the quantity and vitality of its counterpart in West Africa'. The development of drama in this region has indeed been much slower than in West Africa. Such a situation, the critic Adrian Roscoe has suggested, may have arisen out of historic, political or social causes, if not all three together. Nevertheless, there is evidence of growth, which he has attributed to 'a blend of forces: political independence, a burgeoning of new schools, colleges, and universities; the desire to repatriate the syllabus, increasing economic prosperity, the spread of radio ... and the printed word; the desire to encourage popular and effective modes of crystalising distinctly national identities, and finally the catalytic example of West Africa'.

There are two groups involved in theatre work in Malawi: expatriate amateur dramatic societies and African drama groups. This division springs from the politics of colonialism, which encouraged development, of whatever sort, along racial lines. When Africans took power after independence (1964), expatriates created their enclaves, which became their cultural reserves. Even as late as 1992 expatriate theatre groups existed in the same clubs that had housed them in the colonial days. The repertoires continue to be aimed at expatriate audiences.

'Western' African theatre has learnt nothing from expa-

An outdoor production of Steve Chimombo's *Wachiona Ndani*, Malawi.

triate amateur theatre. One needs to establish where influences on the former came from. As early as 1950 concerts and VARIETY shows were common features in Malawi. Black South African life has played a big part in this type of recreation: Malawians have been going to work in South African mines as migrant labourers since the turn of the century. Usually such people have returned home completely changed, bringing with them not just habits, but items like record-players and bicycles, and a love for a particular type of life common amongst the city dwellers of South Africa. By the 1950s, South African blacks had already developed a popular theatre tradition which married music, dance and improvisation. The 'concert and variety show' common in Malawi in the 1950s is a by-product of this kind of theatre. Concert groups existed everywhere in the country – not just in large urban centres but also in remote mission schools and their neighbouring villages.

With the coming of independence and the consequent emphasis on promoting the indigenous cultural heritage of the people, Malawians have sought to be original in their theatre. Work is being spearheaded by particular cultural institutions, amongst which theatre groups are but one. The efforts of such institutions reveal not just the extent to which success has been achieved in theatre work, but an explanation of the way it is growing. There are now vigorous annual festivals and active travelling theatres, and good use is made of radio. The background to these operations may be found in cultural policy, education and CENSORSHIP.

If an official statement regarding government involvement in the development of theatre in Malawi is sought one may refer to the Arts and Crafts Department in the Ministry of Education and Culture, whose main functions have been given as: 'to awaken, preserve and develop Malawi's culture, tradition, art, music, drama and dances; to enrich the social, cultural and material life of Malawi; to project most effectively Malawi's cultural heritage; to assist in the teaching of music, drama, and dances by holding specific demonstrations from time to time as need arises; to provide public entertainment of the highest quality'.

Of drama specifically, the department says that it is 'predominantly a secondary school and university form of entertainment'. None the less, it considers drama to be a medium through which 'the norms, values, traditions and customs of the people are easily brought to the public'. Whether this reflects the department's expectation of what drama ought to be doing, or its conception of what it is actually doing, as promoted by secondary schools and university, is not clear. Certainly, as far as effort by the department itself is concerned, the function it describes here remains to be fulfilled. If cultural activities have been promoted in the country, it has been largely at the people's own initiative.

Drama in Malawi schools is organized by the Association for Teachers of English in Malawi (ATEM). Formed in the 1960s to coordinate and encourage efforts aimed at improving the teaching of English in the country's secondary schools and teacher training colleges, its main function at first was to organize conferences for teachers of English throughout the country. From time to time it set up workshops on English-language teaching methods. Then the association started to involve students directly in its work. It organized the National Oral English Competition for secondary schools, comprising recitations of poetry and prose readings, as well as interviews conducted in English by a panel of native English speakers.

In 1969, however, this competition was dropped, and instead a drama festival was established, open to all secondary schools and post-primary educational institutions, as well as teacher training colleges and technical colleges (but not the colleges of the University of Malawi). In order to ensure that the festival still contributed to the improvement of English-language teaching, its organizers sent out rules to all schools regarding how they should prepare for it. But these rules were concerned only with the running of the festival itself and with ATEM's basic aim of improving the spoken English of participants; any potential audience did not feature at all. It was merely assumed that the audience would be students, either from secondary schools involved in the festival directly or from schools near the venue of the festival. As it turned out, the audience included people other than students – people from the town or city where the festival was taking place who were more than ready for entertainment of this kind. And while the organizers thought of their festival as an exercise in English-language teaching, their audience was seeing it as theatre. Since the festival was public, it was the latter who were to direct the course of events in schools drama. It was not long before people started talking of adapting plays not just for student actors, but for expected audiences.

Most teacher-producers in the schools did not know the mechanics of producing a play, so they turned to ATEM to help them, either through workshops or by supplying notes on play production. Until recently English-language teaching in Malawi secondary schools and teacher training colleges has been dominated by expatriate teachers, so it is not surprising that suggestions such as the following were made: 'the producer looking for material to adapt ... should have a look at European plays from the medieval or Renaissance periods ... the periods in Europe when society most resembled society in Malawi today. The peasant population lived much the same sort of life as the Malawian villager, and you had the rapidly growing sophisticated town population that you also find here. So the situations and characters in these plays should be meaningful to our students.' The limitations of such a line of thought are obvious. The analogy holds only in so far as a large rural community is common to both. The history of the people, the experiences that they live through, and their political as well as cultural consciousness, offer no basis for comparison.

The effect of this advice has been to encourage writers to look at life in a determinist way, resigning themselves to the belief that things will happen exactly as they did in Europe hundreds of years ago, that no enhancement is called for. Thus playwrights do not write with the hope of changing the world they live in, nor are they inclined to commit themselves to particular dogmas. They are socially passive. The bulk of the plays that derive from the drama festival show a clear lack of interest in the immediate present. Instead of dealing with the lives, problems, dreams, worries and hopes of their audience, they continue to harp on themes of pre-industrial village days and ways. ATEM has claimed: 'Although the schools drama festival has been our major activity over the past few years, it is not the main aim of the association as it was established.' This perhaps indicates how popular drama has become. It also shows what pressures the demand for drama has brought to bear on the Association for Teachers of English in Malawi, whose drama work has now been taken over by the university in a more sympathetic, if academic, manner.

The Malawi government's Department of Arts and Crafts recognizes the work of the University of Malawi in the promotion of drama in the country. This work is spread over four of the five campuses making up the university – namely, Chancellor College (Zomba), Bunda College of Agriculture (Lilongwe), Zamuzu College of Nursing (Lilongwe) and the Polytechnic (Blantyre). The most active of these is Chancellor College, where there is a Department of Fine and Performing Arts under whose aegis comes the Chancellor College Travelling Theatre. Before 1981 there was no such department at the college, and all drama teaching was the responsibility of the English Department. Most of this work concerned dramatic literature rather than drama as performance. The only practical course offered was a two-hour session in 'practical drama and film' to third-year majors of English, in which students were introduced to the arts of theatre and filming. It is through this course that the Chancellor Travelling College Theatre really came into being. Although the Theatre was the responsibility of the English Department, it was an extra-curricular appendage, and thus open to staff and students from all departments of the college.

The first production to be put on there was WOLE SOYINKA's *The Trials of Brother Jero*, followed by *The Crucible* by ARTHUR MILLER. In 1969 the British actor and teacher John Linstrum was appointed lecturer in drama, and during his two years' stay at the college he directed two plays, *The Chalk Circle* (an adaptation of BERTOLT BRECHT's *The Caucasian Chalk Circle*) and *Everyman* by Obotunde Ijimere. Together with a Malawian, Mupa Shumba (a veteran of the first Makerere College Travelling Theatre in Uganda), in 1970 he formed and organized the first travelling theatre in Malawi, whose first tour was confined to nearby towns. When Linstrum's term of office came to an end, James Gibbs, a British teacher with extensive experience in West Africa, took over his work (1972–8). It was during this period that the Travelling Theatre really took root, reaching almost every district in the country. The bulk of the Theatre's work remained the presentation of plays in English in schools and urban centres (never in villages). When Gibbs left, Chris Kamlongera took over, and was subsequently joined by David Kerr, from the University of Zambia. Now the company's repertoire includes vernacular plays, and tours have been extended to include drama workshops in rural areas.

The affiliation of the Travelling Theatre to the English Department at Chancellor College has had particular consequences. The department was already changing its syllabuses to include more material from Malawian oral tradition and black aesthetics – which was to have phe-

nomenal results. Students now took to playwriting, producing plays and acting. From such activity came in 1979 the first anthology of Malawian plays in English, *Nine Malawian Plays*, edited by James Gibbs. Gibbs's concern with establishing theatre in Chancellor College was hampered only by a lack of space.

The Travelling Theatre constructed an open-air theatre, which became the home of all college productions until December 1982, when the Great Hall complex, with two theatres within, was opened on campus. The new open-air theatre received an unprecedented welcome from both students and staff. Now the Travelling Theatre had its own base.

Theatre life on Chancellor College campus includes visits from outside groups who perform in the open-air theatre. One such visit – which was to be memorable for the insight it offered the Travelling Theatre – was by the Zomba Community Centre Drama Group in the 1970s. They brought with them two plays: an adaptation of *The Pardoner's Tale* (in English) and *Kambale: The Famous Boy* (in Chichewa, a vernacular, and the national, language). The latter, the story of a young trickster who fools everyone around him by his antics, is the one that aroused discussion amongst theatre enthusiasts. And in spite of being merely primary school children with no formal training in drama, performers won the hearts of the audience. One critic, marvelling at the work of these children, speculated on the reasons for their success. His comments have remained at the heart of the Chancellor College Travelling Theatre's work: 'The fact that the play was in Chichewa is the most important factor: it was the language best suited to the theme, the setting, the characters, and ... the audience ... The playwright in Malawi should always decide beforehand what audience he wants to amuse and educate. If he is sensible he will first and foremost think of the man in the street most of the time; and hence use the language that best suits that man.' The Theatre's slogan is now 'Taking theatre to the people'.

It took five years to put this slogan into practice. The first time the Travelling Theatre worked with ordinary villagers was when the company went to Mbalachanda Rural Growth Centre in the Northern Region. Following the success of this tour, the Theatre has swung the weight of its work in favour of vernacular plays. Steve Chimombo's second play, *Wachiona Ndani* (1982), marks the firm establishment of Chichewa plays in the Theatre's repertoire, as well as a turning-point for Chimombo himself, who is also well known for his English verse, short stories and his first play, *The Rainmaker*.

The question of what language to use is central to any moves towards taking theatre to the people. Although Malawi is fortunate in having one national language, Chichewa, when it comes to working, for instance, in the Northern Region, it is necessary to know the local language.

Taking theatre to the people brings its own problems. First, there is the question of finance. Although the Travelling Theatre comes under the Chancellor College Department of Fine and Performing Arts, there is no money earmarked for its operations. From time to time it has thrived on support from outside bodies like the Schimmelpenninck Fund, the Morel Trust Fund, the

British Council and the Christian Service Committee. Of late it has taken to charging a fee for its shows – although this in fact goes counter to its stated aims.

Because the Travelling Theatre is semi-autonomous, in that there is no financial support from the department that houses it, some organizational problems arise. Left very much to himself, the Theatre's artistic director, David Kerr, relies heavily (if not totally) on the goodwill of enthusiastic students. The extra-curricular nature of the Theatre only emphasizes this reliance! Kerr has identified a number of problems in running the Theatre: shortage of directors, narrow choice of plays, lack of indigenous dance groups on campus. The problem of choice, he says, is complex: 'One complexity is the Censorship Board.' The involvement of the Malawi Censorship Board is crucial to the development of theatre in Malawi. It is required by law to approve all prospective scripts before any theatre group performs them.

Moves to stop indigenous culture from disappearing in African countries usually involves proclamations by politicians, encouraging the masses to revive and take pride in their own cultural heritage on the one hand, and advocating government-controlled conservation and protection of the people's cultural heritage on the other. Governments have established departments of cultural affairs and CENSORSHIP procedures in order to monitor cultural development. Theatre work is often encompassed by such censorship.

The duties of the Malawi Censorship Board include keeping a check on all theatrical activity. Before any play is performed in public, it must be passed, then previewed, by the Board. Censorship in Malawi can be political or social. Sex and nude pictures, for instance, are out. And books with a substantial political content of the 'wrong sort' will be banned outright. Describing the Censorship Board as he knew it between 1973 and 1978, the former director of the Travelling Theatre has said: 'My impression is that the Board is ignorant and confused, but that it can tell a direct attack when it encounters one. My conclusion is that, although the Malawian writer suffers severely under the Censorship Board, the devices it forces on him are not in every way detrimental to the shaping of his work.'

When the Board was set up it determined that: 'A publication, picture, statue or record shall be deemed to be undesirable if any part thereof (1) is indecent or obscene or offensive or harmful to public morals; or (2) gives offence to the religious convictions or feelings of the public; or (3) brings any member or section of the public into contempt; or (4) harms relations between sections of the public; or (5) is contrary to the interests of public safety, or public order.' The Board has banned books, plays, newspapers and magazines. It sees part of its job as being to 'protect' Malawians from books about the anti-colonial struggle, about socialism, religious dissent and birth control, and books that deal with corruption in post-independence Africa.

In theatre, this censorship focuses on the script rather than on the performance. This is because the latter has been found difficult to censor. Although the Board insists, publicly, on a preview of all shows, distances prohibit it from visiting all theatre venues in the country. Plays submitted have been rejected on all sorts of grounds: for 'inclusion of direct and indirect sex discussion', for showing 'a woman ... deceiving her husband', for promoting political 'subversion'; for pressing the 'European way of life ... on ... African youth'; for '[making] fun of the Police and the Church by showing that the rich, the law and the Church exploit the poor'. Thus the Malawian theatre would appear to depend, for its survival, on playwrights who avoid the central problems of their society and concern themselves with the now virtually exhausted themes of traditional versus Western life, and on plays that service a conservative national ideology by offering models of chiefly wisdom, marital stability and acquiescent labour. The activities of the Board are critical in determining the way theatre will develop in Malawi.

RADIO DRAMA also offers opportunities for Malawian writers and actors. Sewero (Kapalepale) is a 30-minute programme broadcast at 6.30 p.m. on Saturdays – a peak period in the Malawi broadcasting day – by the Malawi Broadcasting Corporation. Its producer-writer is Smart Likhaya Mbewe, and all the work is in Chichewa. The programme is popularly known as Kapalepale, which derives from the name of the leading character, who is always the centre of controversy in the drama.

Most of the episodes depict life in urban centres where the rural and the modern are in constant conflict. It would seem that Mbewe always aims at establishing, through comedy, an amicable solution to the problems that such a conflict breeds. Each presentation ends in a chief's home, where matters are sorted out to the satisfaction of all. One result of this is that the plays are heavily didactic – perhaps in keeping with the meaning of the word kapalepale itself, which is Chichewa for 'weeding a garden'. No scripts are written for this drama: Mbewe creates scenarios which he explains to his actors, and then, together, they improvise the dialogue.

His work has been described as: 'a weekly comedy about an urban trickster [Kapalepale himself] who lives by his wits'. 'The aim behind my plays is to teach good manners as well as to entertain people,' Mbewe has said. The initial 'trickster' idea has, over the years, given way to a more overtly didactic and moralist one. The reformed Kapalepale can no longer be seen as a man apart from his society. As Joyce Kumpukwe has pointed out: 'As playwright, Mr Mbewe can be compared to an artist in a traditional African society who functions as spokesman for the society in which he lives, sharing its prejudices and directing its dislikes against what is discountenanced.' But calling Kapalepale 'spokesman for his society' would be to romanticize. Rather, he is an artist who casts himself in the role of society's moral raider. And, working within a government-owned and controlled radio station, his morality must reflect the government's views.

Mbewe's plays are carefully calculated to produce a particular effect on Malawian audiences. The story is organized to illustrate an idea or teach a moral, and a common moral element unites the plays from week to week. The ideological element is linked to the concept of 'nation-building'. A high proportion of the Malawi Broadcasting Corporation's programmes deal with such subjects as literacy, public health, agricultural improvement, cultural traditions and social guidance.

'Theatre of the Air' is the other established MBC drama

programme. Modelled on the BBC World Service's 'African Theatre', the programme is in English and broadcast at around 9.30 p.m., by which time most rural people are already in bed. It can be safely assumed that this programme is aimed at urban listeners rather than country people, who do not have the necessary electricity to continue life into the late evenings. Like most of the work emanating from the MBC, 'Theatre of the Air' carries plays aimed at projecting the culture of the country. Such plays are likely to be tragedies, handled lightly but with a serious underlying tone; material will probably be drawn from rustic society; there will be between two and six characters, and programmes will run for 30 minutes.

MBC radio drama recognizes that radio is one of the mass media that has the capacity to surmount the major obstacles to developing countries' illiteracy. This fact is used as its springboard for all drama work. The dramatization of information is gaining the upper hand and radio drama has thus, in a modest way, kindled the desire in the general public for this means of propagating information. Because of the popularity of its drama, the MBC is flooded with requests from government ministries and departments to dramatize information. The Chancellor College Travelling Theatre has been taken as an example by almost all Malawian amateur theatre groups. Once formed, a group arranges a tour of some sort; but without adequate funding to meet the logistics involved, such tours are confined to very short distances. Only three groups, apart from the Chancellor College company, have attempted nationwide tours – Lonjezo Travelling Theatre, Wakhumbata Theatre Ensemble and Kwathu Drama Group. This last, led by Charles Severe, is the most successful and the oldest. The repertoires of this group and the Lonjezo ones, like those of most Malawian amateur groups, consist of Chichewa plays only, but Wakhumbata Theatre Ensemble has mostly English plays in its repertoire. The use of Chichewa, the national language, by the Chancellor College Travelling Theatre and by the other amateur groups has been crucial in popularizing theatre in the country. Chichewa plays are crucial to the development of drama in Malawi, since most of the country's population does not speak English.

Theatre is certainly active in Malawi, but what is still lacking is a willingness on the part of publishers to dare to publish the many scripts that companies are producing, either through group improvisation or through individual playwrights like Du Chisiza Jr, James Mg'ombe, Enoch Timpunza Mvula, Innocent Banda, Steve Chimombo, Vipya Harawa, Mvundula and Garton Kamchedzera. So far only a handful have been published. CK

See: S. Chimombo, *Wachiona Ndani*, Blantyre, 1983; J. Gibbs (ed.), *Nine Malawian Plays*, Limbe & Lilongwe, 1979, and 'Of Kamuzu and Chameleons: Experiences of Censorship in Malawi', *Literary Half-Yearly*, 23, 2, 1982; A. Horn, 'African Theatre – Docility and Dissent', *Index on Censorship*, 9, 3, 1980; C. F. Kamlongera, 'Theatre for Development: The Case for Malawi', *Theatre Research International*, 7, 3, 1982, and 'Problems in the Growth of a Popular Art: The Relationship between Drama and Society in Malawi and Zambia', PhD thesis, Univ. of Leeds, 1984; D. Kerr, 'Travelling Theatre: Problems and Pseudo-Problems', *Muse*, 60; J. Kumpukwe, 'S. M. Mbewe, Creator and Producer of Malawian Radio Plays', *BALAZA*, 1, June 1983; V. Mdovi, 'Censorship in Malawi', *Index on Censorship*, 8, 1, 1979; A. Roscoe, *Uhuru's Fire: African Literature East to South*, Cambridge, 1977.

Malaysia This Southeast Asian nation has a population of 18 million people of Malay, Chinese, Indian and Negrito heritage. The small Negrito population has music, dance and trance performance. The Malays have had a lively performance tradition for at least the last 500 years, and their theatre shows a distinctive reworking of pan-Southeast-Asian patterns. The Malay genres, discussed here, fall into four categories: (1) prototheatrical customs; (2) Hindu–Islamic folk and court genres; (3) popular, urban theatre of the last century; and (4) modern drama developed since the Second World War. The overseas communities from CHINA and INDIA largely transplanted practices from their homelands after British colonial rule began in 1824, and the many performances of these groups may be better understood in the context of those cultures. Notable genres found among the Chinese community are glove- and SHADOW PUPPET plays; Hokkien, Teochew and Cantonese opera; and spirit mediumship. Common genres of the South Indian community include *bharata natyam* dance, Karnatic music and the yearly Thaipusam festival, in which Hindu devotees pierce their bodies with metal skewers and dance in processions.

Prototheatrical customs As throughout Southeast Asia, prototheatrical customs, including epic recitation, poetry games and spirit mediumship, contributed much to Malay theatrical development. The singing of epics, *penglipur lara*, is still found. Stories are based on the *Ramayana* or Malay legends (*hikayat*). In a variant called *awang batil*, the performer accompanies himself on a brass bowl. Early storytelling traditions, like this, may have paved the way for the shadow-puppet tradition.

Songs and games that involve dialogues provide a base for folk theatricals. *Pantun* singing is poetry in which singers present memorized or newly composed octosyllabic lines in quatrains. The first two lines create a sound pattern and the final lines reveal the true message. Similar poetry is associated with courting games throughout the Malay world.

Call and response singing forms another base for Muslim theatricals. For example, *dikir barat* is a village entertainment, originally based on Sufi chanting (compare THAILAND's *likay* and INDONESIA's *dikir*). Two teams of men present improvised texts: a leader inaugurates the song, and the group repeats his line. Verses can be satiric or ribald, and mimed interludes are included. *Boria* is a comic sketch followed by a call and response processional.

Though epic and poetic traditions may generate the techniques, the deep need for theatre may rise from the employment of performance to communicate with spirits. Music, dance, and drama are generally practised in the context of seasonal ceremonies and RITES OF PASSAGE when spirits must be placated, and, hence, performances of all types normally open with mantras addressed to the spirits. Clear links with spirits occur in trances in which dancers become the medium for spirits. In *ulek bandul*, danced by seven girls and two boys, the featured female

Kuda kepang horse dance performers of Malaysia and Indonesia may eat lightbulbs while in a trance.

dancer communicates with the rice spirit; in *ulek meyang*, a man holding an areca-nut root enters into a trance to the chant of a male chorus; in *tari labi labi* a turtle spirit enters the dancer. *Kuda kepang* is a possession rite in the states of Johore and Selangor in which men possessed by horse spirits perform amazing feats: firewalking or eating glass, fire or hay. And in *dabus* performers may dance *silat*, the martial-arts dance, then pierce their skin with knives, without pain or lasting wounds. The latter two forms may be related to genres found in Indonesia.

Probably the most important of these trance-related forms is *main puteri*, which supposedly receives its name – 'play of the princess' – from the legend that it was first established to cure a melancholic princess. In performances, which are found in Kelantan and Trengganu states, two male curers (*bomoh*), using trance dances, diagnose and then treat patients, usually females. Since illnesses are believed to be caused by spirits, the main SHAMAN, *to'puteri*, allows the spirits to enter his body. His assistant, *to'mindok*, plays a *rebab* to facilitate his trance. The assistant converses with the spirits who speak through the *to'puteri* to reveal the cause of illness. Clownish, refined and rough spirits may alternately possess the medium's body, making the form a lively entertainment. Once the illness is identified the cure may be effected by a performance of the related female dance drama, *mak yong*.

Likewise, major celebrations required performances to keep good relations with the spirits. *Puja pantai* ('ritual of the shore') is a three-day ceremony involving various performances meant to placate sea spirits. *Berjamu* are exorcisms whereby those in danger of angering spirits may regain their favour. For example, puppetmasters in the *wayang siam* ('shadow theatre') or *mak yong* dancers require such RITUALS every few years. Such ceremonies are focused at a spirit audience, but also entertain human audiences.

Folk and court theatricals Some early folk or court theatre forms developed in old Malay states, like Patani, that are now part of Thailand. Hindu and Buddhist thought emanating from Indian and Indonesian sources affected this area – hence the *Ramayana* and *Jataka* (Buddhist birth tales) are standard stories. Indonesian influences seem to be especially important for understanding theatrical developments in Malaysia. Currently scholars hypothesize that the similarities in story patterns and theatre genres in island and mainland Southeast Asia and the variance of these from standard Indian models is due to the influence of the Indonesian Sriwijaya kingdom over both areas during the 7th–13th centuries. Sriwijaya's power declined, but its arts including female dance and puppet theatre prevailed in the courts of the new mainland states emerging in what is now Malaysia and southern Thailand. Islamicized re-interpretations of dance and puppetry may have again flowed from Indonesia in the 15th–16th centuries, carried by a network of Muslim traders and Sufi mystics. More recent emigration from Indonesia has established Javanese, Sumatran and Buginese communities in Malaysia with their arts intact. Many centuries of intercommunication have created similar, but distinctive theatre genres in Indonesia and Malaysia today.

The puppet tradition and the female dance drama remain relatively strong in the northern part of Malaysia in states that bordered on the former Malay kingdom of Patani. *Nang talung*, shadow-puppet theatre of southern Thailand, and *nora*, the masked dance drama, developed in the Patani area, perhaps as early as the 12th century. A tradition of female court dance was extant in 1611–13, when the European traveller Peter Flores visited there. From Patani *wayang siam* shadow theatre was supposedly brought to neighbouring Kelantan state by a female *dalang* ('puppetmaster'), about 400 years ago, and court dance and female dance drama in Kelantan and Trengganu states developed under Patani influence as well.

Wayang siam (compare INDONESIA's *wayang*) of the east coast is probably the oldest of the three puppet genres currently found in Malaysia. The most important traditional theatre of the country, it depends on a solo puppetmaster (*dalang*) who controls all the puppets, speaks the dialogue and delivers the narration. He also regulates the accompanying musicians. This puppet art, which has strong ritual and exorcistic aspects, focuses on *Ramayana* material and was very popular on the east coast prior to this generation. Of special significance is the clown puppet, Pak Dogol, a local variant of the pan-Southeast-Asian god-clown. Legends hold that Pak Dogol first brought the shadow play to men from heaven, and puppeteers treat this figure with special ceremony.

Traditions are changing in current *wayang siam*. Puppets, traditionally made of water-buffalo hide, may now be fashioned of translucent plastic. Performances that traditionally took place all night now generally last from only 8.30 p.m. to 12.30 a.m. Kerosene or electric lamps have largely replaced the flickering flames of old. Formerly, performances were given in the context of life-cycle ceremonies and were paid for by a single sponsor, but most current performances are played for a paying audience that comes specifically to attend the show. The added importance of clowning is highlighted in the proliferation of new clown characters in current performances. Wright noted two major groupings of *dalang* in the late 1970s – those who tend toward more traditional practice, as represented by Hassan Omar and Ghani Jambul, and those who incorporate new clown characters, puppets in modern dress and tunes from pop music, as represented by Abdullah Baju Merah and his emulators.

Wayang malayu, a more recent import to Malaysia, is a variant on the *wayang kulit purwa* of Central Java, and was created by Javanese who have settled in Malaysia. Meanwhile *wayang gedek* is a variation on the *nang talung* tradition of Thailand, and also a recent import. All these puppet genres face significant competition from modern media and puppeteers face considerable odds in keeping their sponsors and audiences.

Scholars debate the age and origin of the female dance drama *mak yong* which thrived in the Kelantan palace in the first quarter of this century. It appears that the form originated in the folk tradition, was elevated to a court art by a princely patron, and returned after his death with newly acquired polish to the folk sphere. From 1912 to the 1920s the prince in Kota Baru, Temenggong Ghaffar, supported a *mak yong* troupe which carried out performances as we currently know them. The largely female troupe adds two male clowns, who serve shaman-like functions.

The women performed opening dances and stories in dance-drama style, playing all the refined male and female roles while the males played the clown roles. The three major roles are the refined hero, the heroine and the clown.

The form corresponds to female dance drama of Thailand, Indonesia and Cambodia. Three sources probably contributed to its genesis: *nora*, female court dance, and trance medium rites. The Thai *nora* thrived in Patani and is still found to some extent in Kelantan. Though *nora* supposedly began as a three-person male genre, similar stories, character types and auras of magic power animate it and *mak yong*. Likewise, *mak yong* relates to the female court dance adopted by Malay kingdoms, perhaps in emulation of ritual court dancers of the Indonesian archipelago. *Asik*, the graceful female dance of the Patani palace, shared movement, costume and dance features with *mak yong*. *Mak yong*'s clearest connection is with trance-medium forms: *ulek bandel*, like *mak yong*, calls for a configuration of seven women and two men, and *main puteri* creates business for *mak yong* troupes. Current *mak yong* clowns often double as the shaman-like *bomoh* of *main puteri*. At the conclusion of a seance they will recommend that as a cure the patient play out the hero's part in a *mak yong* story with the assistance of experienced actresses.

Perhaps drama therapy is the original impulse behind many Southeast Asian female dance drama forms. Women who had healed themselves under the guidance of *bomoh*-clowns, turned their experience to curing and entertaining others. Since the forms were ways of communicating with powerful spirits, aristocrats might have desired groups of medium-wives who could maintain a firm connection with the other world. Such a model may lie behind these forms and explain the evolution of female drama in BURMA, Cambodia and Thailand.

Popular theatre Modern genres are developments of the more economically developed, urban west coast of Malaysia where traditional theatre forms have largely been abandoned. *Bangsawan* developed at the end of the 19th century in emulation of touring INDIAN Parsi troupes that performed Indian, Arabian and Shakespearian tales in the 1870s. By 1885 Mohammed Pushi had created the first local Malaysian *bangsawan* company in Penang. *Bangsawan* played for commercial audiences, and actresses and actors mingled freely on the stage. Groups found audiences everywhere in the Malay-speaking world, touring to Java, Sumatra and Borneo (Kalimantan) in Indonesia and influencing Thai theatre. The troupes were actress-centred, used Western-influenced drop-and-wing sets and bright costumes, and created orchestras comprising both indigenous and Western instruments. Troupes improvised stories to enthusiastic audiences. *Bangsawan* flourished until the Second World War, but then declined; fighting with communist insurgents in the postwar period prevented groups from reforming. In 1972 a government-sponsored troupe was recreated, and later PESBANA (National Bangsawan Art Organization) was founded.

As *bangsawan* passed, a new more Westernized theatre appeared. *Sandiwara*, popular into the 1950s, for the first time used a written script, amateur actors and a director. Arising first in schools, it appealed to Westernized, educated viewers. Authors treated historical and contemporary themes. Though *sandiwara* plays still appeared on a mixed bill with dance dramas and pantomimes, the productions were more realistic than *bangsawan* offerings. *Sandiwara* represents a transitional link between popular *bangsawan* and present-day modern drama.

Courses in drama are offered at Malaysia's two major universities – at the University of Malaysia where contemporary theatre director-critic Krishen Jit is professor, and at the Malaysian University of Science in Penang where Gulam-Sawar Yousof directs a programme of research into traditional theatre. Government support of performance includes competition prizes and sponsorship of festivals.

Modern drama Who wrote the first scripted Malay spoken drama, and when, are questions yet to be resolved. But the consensus is that the schoolteacher and playwright-director, Shahrom Hussain, was among the pioneers of the early modern-drama period (1940s to early 1960s). All but two of his plays are *purbawara*: plays based on the exploits and achievements of historical and mythical personages. Written mostly by students, teachers and journalists with a literary bent, *purbawara* plays re-enacted the glory and might of the Malay sultanate on stage. Offstage, however, Malay power had been progressively dissipated by British colonial rule. By highlighting the contrast between ideal and reality, *purbawara* plays contributed to post-Second World War Malay nationalism.

Immediately after independence in 1957, some *purbawara* playwrights reversed course, and critically scrutinized the orthodox feudal values glorified by their predecessors. The spirit of rational inquiry was manifested, for example, in Shahrom's later works, particularly in his emblematic play, *The Hunchback of Tanjung Puteri* (*Si Bongkok Tanjung Puteri*, 1961), which introduced the blatantly ugly, aggressive but probing anti-hero, Si Bongkok. The poet, playwright and journalist Usman Awang elicited the modern rebel, garbed in the guise of the 15th-century warrior-'traitor', Hang Jebat, in the intense and compact verse drama *The Death of a Warrior* (*Matinya Seorang Pahlawan*, 1964; trans. 1988). Usman's Jebat, presented in the play as the champion of truth and justice, was repeatedly resurrected as the archetypal rebel in the 1970s theatre.

In 1963, Mustapha Kamil Yassin, a teachers'-training-college lecturer and later a university professor, pronounced that, thematically and aesthetically, poetic dramas clung too much to the past. In the next decade he launched a vigorous campaign promoting the 'dynamic', Western-influenced realistic drama (see REALISM), called *drama moden*, 'modern drama'. His mostly comic plays, of which the best is *Brick House, Nipa House* (*Atap Genting Atap Rembia*, 1963), are crowded with social types and reconcile conflicting forces in post-independent Malaysian society: rural versus urban values, old versus young generation, Malay versus Chinese. Mustapha and his colleagues, Usman Awang, Awang Had Salleh, Aziz Jahpin and A. Samad Said, drew the newly urbanized Malay literati towards acceptance of *drama moden*.

The ethnic riots of May 1969, which gripped the major cities of peninsular Malaysia, undermined the optimist themes of current *drama moden*. The profound impact of this event justifies recognition of a 'post-1969' perspective on the arts, including theatre. Some Malay playwright-directors set about reviewing the Malaysian past, in order to better understand the disturbing present. Significantly, political trauma did not provoke Malay theatre practitioners to take a radical course as they did elsewhere in the region. One of the earliest results of these steps towards 'self-apprehension' was Noordin Hassan's *It Is Not the Tall Grass that Is Blown by the Wind* (*Bukan Lalang Di Tiup Angin*, 1970), partly allegorical and replete with oblique references to May 1969. Nonlinear and surreal (see SURREALISM), it uncovered the ironies and ambiguities that lurk behind the mask of harmony, peaceful co-existence and progress in multi-ethnic Malaysian society. Through an interaction between traditional and Western-modern performance modes and aesthetics, the piece strove to mediate between past and present in Malay experience. Audiences thought the play confusing and out of a deep need to communicate to the many, Noordin simplified his next two plays, *Five Braided Pillars* (*Tiang Seri Tegak Berlima*, 1973) and *Door* (*Pintu*, 1976) without compromising on his multi-channelled approach to performance, nor on his mission to inculcate a Malaysian identity.

What was to be called *teater kontemporari* assumed the proportions of a movement by the mid-1970s, with the rise of playwright-directors Syed Alwi, Dinsman, Bidin Subari, Johan Jaafar and Hatta Azad Khan, a performing arts graduate of the Malaysian University of Science in Penang. Syed's *Tok Perak* (1975), the first multimedia event in Malaysian theatre – and arguably the best play of the era – juxtaposed folk theatre events, images from film and slides, and an intricately textured realistic theatre. The mixed-means performance was an analogue of the protagonist's condition: the middle-aged street medicine seller, Tok Perak, is trapped in the transition between tradition and modernity, in the end choosing the latter.

The troubled and ruminating self was also exalted in sensational theatrical images by the University of Malaya graduate, Dinsman, the only genuine cult figure of 1970s theatre. Dinsman created startling personae – Jebat in *Jebat* (1973), Adam in *Not Suicide* (*Bukan Bunuh Diri*, 1974), and Ana in *Ana* (1976) – who echoed a young generation restive with traditional values, but uncertain about the modern persuasion. Dinsman's partially absurdist performances (see THEATRE OF THE ABSURD) found the measure of the post-book television generation, and were frequently performed in the 1970s.

Nevertheless, the unceasing experimental zeal of contemporary theatre began to wear down the audience. Simultaneously, a resurgent Islam in Malaysia caught contemporary theatre practitioners unawares and defenceless against attacks that they were harbouring the sins of polytheism and nihilism in their plays. For most of the 1980s, the Malay avant-garde attack was blunted and transferred to local English drama, as demonstrated by the performances of K. S. Maniam's *The Cord* (1984) and *The Sandpit* (1991), Kee Thuan Chye's politically controversial *1984 – Here and Now* (1985), and Leow Puay Tin's *Three Children* (1988). Noordin Hassan continued to experiment, exploring an Islamic mode of theatre in *1400* (1981), and *Don't Kill the Butterflies* (*Jangan Bunuh Rama-Rama*, 1983).

The American impersonator Ella Wesner (1841–1917) as the dude Captain Cuff in her variety act.

Stirred by the threat of Malay political and religious divisiveness, other Malay-language theatre practitioners have turned to the presumably exemplary period of nationalist struggle of the 1940s and show a self-conscious empathy with popular *bangsawan* performers who also fought for race and country. This nostalgia is directly depicted in Normah Nordin-Najib Nor's MUSICAL, *My Nostalgic Song* (*Nostalgia Laguku*, 1989) and in Zakaria Arifin's *Opera Players* (*Pemain Opera*, 1989). Popular theatre, including *boria*, is resurrected by Noordin Hassan in *Son of Penang* (*Anak Tanjung*, 1987) and Sayed Alwi in *The Servant of God* (*Hamba Allah*, 1989). Perhaps unexpectedly, some of the deepest and most troubling questions about the Malay psyche in political and moral crisis are posed by these senior playwrights. (See also ASIAN AND PACIFIC ISLAND THEATRE.)   KF

See: J. R. Brandon (ed.), *The Cambridge Guide to Asian Theatre*, Cambridge, 1993.

male impersonation Unlike FEMALE IMPERSONATION in the theatre, women dressing as men has had little sanction from ancient religion or folk tradition; it has usually been condemned as a wanton assumption of masculine prerogative. When women first came on to the Western stage, costuming them in men's garb was simply a means to show off their limbs and provide freedom of movement. This was certainly the case during the Restoration, when PEPYS remarked of an actress in knee-breeches, 'She had the best legs that I ever saw, and I was well pleased by it.' NELL GWYN, Moll Davis and others took advantage of these BREECHES PARTS, but few could, like ANNE BRACEGIRDLE, give a convincing portrayal of a male. Often, the part travestied was that of a young rake– Sir Harry Wildair in *The Constant Couple* and Macheath in *The Beggar's Opera* – providing a thrill from the pseudo-lesbian overtones of the plot's situations.

The leading 'breeches' actresses of the early 19th century, MADAME VESTRIS and MARY ANN KEELEY, noted for their delicacy, made an impression less mannish than boyish. The same holds true for the first 'principal boys' in English PANTOMIME, and as Aladdins and Dick Whittingtons became more ample in flesh throughout the Victorian period, no real effort was made to pretend they were men. JENNY HILL on the music-halls and Jennie Lee as Jo in various adaptations of *Bleak House*, Vernet in Paris and Josefine Dora and Hansi Niese in Vienna, represented the proletarian waif, a pathetic or cocky adolescent, not a mature male.

True male impersonation was first introduced on the American VARIETY stage by the Englishwoman Annie Hindle (b. c.1847) and her imitator Ella Wesner (1841–1917) in the guise of 'fast' young men, swaggering, cigar-smoking and coarse. They performed in the English MUSIC-HALL as well, but there an edulcorated portrayal aimed at a more genteel audience was effected by Bessie Bonehill. With her mezzo-soprano voice, she blended the coarse-grained fast man with the principal boy into a type that could be admired for its lack of vulgarity. Her example was followed by the celebrated VESTA TILLEY, whose soprano voice never really fooled any listener; her epicene young men-about-town were ideal types for the 1890s, sexually ambiguous without being threatening. Even so, at the Royal Command Performance of 1912, Queen Mary turned her back on Tilley's act.

After the First World War, with radical changes in dress and manners, the male impersonator became a relic, although the tradition persisted in ELLA SHIELDS ('Burlington Bertie from Bow'), Hettie King and, in black VAUDEVILLE, Gladys Fergusson. Ironically, contemporary FEMINIST THEATRE groups have revived the type for political reasons, as in Eve Merriam's REVUE *The Club* (1976), TIMBERLAKE WERTENBAKER's *New Anatomies* (ICA Theatre, 1981), and German ensembles like Brühwarm. In a work like CARYL CHURCHILL's *Cloud Nine* (1979), sexual cross-casting is an important aspect of the play's inquiry into gender identity.

Another aspect of male impersonation is the assumption of Shakespearian men's roles by actresses. It was long a practice to cast women as such children as Mamillius, the Princes in the Tower and Prince Arthur, as well as supernatural beings like Puck and Ariel. More ambitious was the usurpation of leading parts. The powerful American actress CHARLOTTE CUSHMAN played Romeo to her sister's Juliet and later aspired to Cardinal Wolsey. Women have undertaken Shylock and Falstaff on occasion, but Hamlet has proven to be irresistible. The most distinguished female Dane was SARAH BERNHARDT, who, according to MOUNET-SULLY, lacked only the buttons to her flies, but according to Max Beerbohm, came off *très grande dame*. In our time, JUDITH ANDERSON and Frances de la Tour have tried the experiment, but this has proved less acceptable to a contemporary audience than the all-male *As You Like It* attempted by the ROYAL SHAKESPEARE COMPANY.

Both as a legacy from 18th-century *castrato* singing and for reasons of vocal balance, breeches parts have persisted in OPERA, and it takes little time for an audience to adjust to sopranos impersonating libidinous youths like Cherubino and Octavian. Less successful are antiquarian attempts to revive past dramatic practices: although Christopherl the apprentice in NESTROY's *Einen Jux will er sich machen* (1842) is always played in the German-speaking world by a woman (ELISABETH BERGNER did it for REINHARDT), Felicity Kendal was sadly adrift in TOM STOPPARD's version *On the Razzle*. On the other hand, *Peter Pan* (1904), incarnated from its premiere by a series of formidable actresses including Pauline Chase, MAUDE ADAMS and MARY MARTIN, benefited in the NATIONAL THEATRE revival of 1981 by being conferred on a young man.

During the last decades, male impersonation has been used to explore sexual politics and wider gender issues, as at the WOW Café in New York's Greenwich Village, where both heterosexual and homosexual roles have been shuffled continuously. The LESBIAN Split Britches company, founded there in 1981 by Lois Weaver and Peggy Shaw, specialized in gender-bending, and in 1991 linked up with the gay male Bloolips to stage *Belle Reprieve*, a PARODY of *A Streetcar Named Desire*. San Francisco nurtured Elvis Herselvis, Leigh Crow's exposé of impersonators; the hard-edged macho caricatures of Shelly Mars; and the lesbian transsexual Kate Bornstein whose shows (*Hidden: a Gender*; *The Three-Dollar-Bill Opera*) thoroughly deconstruct assumptions about gender identity.   LS

Maleczech, Ruth 1939– American co-founder of MABOU MINES, actress and director. Maleczech worked with the Actors Workshop and the SAN FRANCISCO MIME TROUPE in the 1960s, then studied in Europe with GROTOWSKI and the BERLINER ENSEMBLE before returning to New York in 1970 to form the experimental COLLECTIVE Mabou Mines with LEE BREUER, David Warrilow, JoANNE AKALAITIS and Philip Glass. Her acting – direct, distanced, economical – has earned acclaim (and several Obies) in Mabou Mines productions such as *The Shaggy Dog Animation* (1978), *Hajj* (1983) and *Through the Leaves* (1984). In 1990 she played the title role in Mabou's gender-reversed production of *Lear*. As a writer-director, Maleczech has collaborated on the music-theatre works *Suenos* (1988), about dictatorship, and *Fire Works* (1987), about CENSORSHIP.   AS

Mali Modern Mali, the French Sudan in colonial times but independent since 1960, is a country with an ancient history and rich theatrical traditions both old and new. Among the many oral performances of its people are the *Do* and the *Kotéba* of the Bambara. Described as sacred theatre, the *Do* takes place every seven years and marks the end of the initiation ceremony of young adolescents into the society of the same name. It takes a little over three months to perform and is open only to initiates. Its performers are masked men (see MASKS) and their language is esoteric.

The secular version of this theatre is the *Kotéba* of central and southern Mali, which means a giant (*ba*) snail (*kote*). The shape of this animal is reproduced in the *Kotéba*'s dance formations, where a chorus of female singers in a middle circle is surrounded by five concentric circles of dancers, musicians and instrumentalists. Performed in public, unlike the *Do*, and at popular feasts, it presents satirical sketches on stereotyped subjects and characters. Its performers are young *Do* initiates and their spectacle combines MIME, dialogue, song and puppetry (see PUPPETS) to produce what is widely agreed to be the most total art form of the Bambara people.

Among the people of northern Mali, two interesting theatrical displays are the *Tendé* of the Tamasheq and the *Takouba* of the Bella. The first is a spectacle mounted on popular occasions, in which men and children on horse or camel back and on the ground engage in spectacular ACRO-BATICS and dances; this display is followed by dramatic sketches. The *Takouba*, or 'dance of the brave', is described as a dance of piety, with intricate steps sustained by warrior songs. The plot is sung and the action mimed.

But Mali also has a significant modern theatre in French, and several troupes such as the Nyogolon, the Kotéba National and the Troupe des Marionettes, that are engaged in building a performance style that has roots in tradition. The origins of Mali's modern theatre go back to the dramatic compositions of Malian students at the École William Ponty in SENEGAL, such as *La Ruse de Diégué* (*The Cunning of Diégué*, 1947) on the 13th-century founder of the Mali empire, Sunjata Keita. These sketches' penchant for epic history has been continued in post-colonial Mali with, for example, Sory Konaké's *Le Grand Destin de Soundjata* (*Soundjata: A Great Destiny*, 1973), Massa Makan Diabaté's *Une si belle leçon de patience* (*So Great a Lesson in Patience*, 1972) and Séydou Badian's *La Mort de Chaka* (*The Death of Chaka*, 1962). Malian dramatists use history to kindle nationalist feelings and to justify political options (as when Badian contrives a parallel in *Chaka* between the vision of the illustrious Zulu chieftain and that of the socialist government of Modibo Keita, in which he was a minister). It is also a reflection of the strong epic traditions of their country.

Other themes dramatized are traditional practices such as RITUAL sacrifice or death – Alkaly Kaba's *Mourir pour vivre* (*Die to Live*, 1976), Amadou Koné's *Le Respect des morts* (*Respect for the Dead*, 1980) – and social problems, such as Moussa Konaté's *L'Or du diable* (*The Devil's Gold*, 1985). Symbolic drama also finds favour in Gaoussou Diawara's *L'Aube des béliers* (*The Dawn of the Sheep*, 1975) and Diama and Alkaly Kaba's *Les Hommes du bakschich* (*Baksheesh Men*, 1973). JCM

> See: M.-J. Arnoldi, *Bamana and Bozo Puppetry of the Ségou Region Youth Societie*s, Lafayette, Ind., 1977; J. Brink, 'Bamana Koté-tlon theatre', *African Arts*, 4, Jul. 1977; G. Diawara, *Panorama critique du théâtre malien dans son évolution*, Sénégal, 1981, and 'Tende et Takouba: théâtres Tamasheq et Bella', *Notre Librairie*: *Théâtre Théâtres*, 102, Jul./Aug. 1990; M. Maiga, 'Le Kotéba', *Notre Librairie: La Littérature Malienne*, 75–6, Jul./Oct. 1984; A. Sonfo and O. Kanouté, 'Le théâtre historique', *Notre Librairie: La Littérature Malienne*, ibid.; C. Wake, 'Mali', in *The Cambridge Guide to World Theatre*, ed. M. Banham, Cambridge, 1988.

Malina, Judith See LIVING THEATRE

Malkovich, John 1953– American actor and director. As a member of Chicago's STEPPENWOLF THEATRE COMPANY since its founding in 1976 he became both its most famous actor and the one whose physically engaging approach best typified the company's appeal to audiences locally and abroad. Malkovich's extraordinary ability to generate a menacing physical presence was evident when he played the violent brother in SAM SHEPARD's *True West*, a performance that won him a Joseph Jefferson Award (Chicago, 1982) and Clarence Derwent and Obie awards (1983), and a protean villain in the 1993 film *Line of Fire*. At the opposite end of the emotional spectrum, his tearful vulnerability in a flashback scene as Biff (opposite DUSTIN HOFFMAN) in *Death of a Salesman* helped earn him a Drama Desk Award (1984) and an Emmy (1986). Malkovich's work as a director includes dynamic revivals of LANFORD WILSON's *Balm in Gilead*, for which he won Jefferson (1981), Obie (1985) and Drama Desk (1985) awards. Beginning in the mid-1980s, he appeared in a series of films, including *Places in the Heart*, *Making Mr Right* and *Dangerous Liaisons*. Recent stage appearances include a 1991 London run in Wilson's *Burn This* and a new Shepard play in New York; directing assignments include a 1994 staging of his adaptation of Don De Lillo's *Libra* for Steppenwolf. SF

Malleson, Miles 1888–1969 British actor and dramatist, one of Nigel Playfair's company at the LYRIC THEATRE, HAMMERSMITH (London). Malleson made his name in Shakespearian and Restoration COMEDY, and after 1950 helped to win popularity for MOLIÈRE on the English stage in his own adaptations. CI

Malmö Stadsteater Opened in 1944, this Swedish city theatre was an attempt to create a 'people's theatre'. Inspired by REINHARDT's Grosses Schauspielhaus, its fanshaped main auditorium seats 1695 people around a shallow thrust stage, backed by a wide proscenium. Movable walls modify its size, but this cumbersome system has been rarely used, with spoken drama increasingly relegated to a smaller auditorium, leaving the main stage more to OPERA, MUSICALS and ballet. One of the few to use it successfully for spoken drama was INGMAR BERGMAN, whose productions of STRINDBERG, IBSEN, GOETHE and MOLIÈRE made it the centre of theatrical Scandinavia during the 1950s. The company declined badly in quality from the late 1970s, but was resuscitated with great optimism in 1992–3 as a tripartite organization comprising Malmö Dramatiska Teatern (led by Staffan Valdemar Holm), Malmö Musikteatern (led by Lars Rudolfsson), and an orchestra. HL

Mamet, David 1947– One of the most important and highly regarded American dramatists to emerge from the 1970s. Mamet first attracted attention with such one-acts as *Sexual Perversity in Chicago* and *Duck Variations*. The 1977 production of *American Buffalo*, which marked his BROADWAY debut, offers a minimal plot; subtle character development emerges in its place. A similarly minimal script, *A Life in the Theatre* (1977), presents an elderly and a youthful actor, both on- and backstage, contrasting their different attitudes towards their work. While many traditionalists have been hostile towards or bewildered by Mamet's work, or offended by his liberal use of profanity and sexual language, the 1983–4 London and New York productions of *Glengarry Glen Ross* led to a Pulitzer Prize for Mamet. His most recent successes are the Lincoln Center production of *Speed-the-Plow* (1988) and the provocative *Oleanna* (1992), a play built on the theme of sexual harassment and seen as the first production of Boston's Back Bay Theater Company (then presented in New York and London). *The Old Neighborhood*, a work inspired by Mamet's Jewish background, premiered at Los Angeles's Mark Taper Forum in 1995. Much of Mamet's attention since the late 1980s has been devoted to filmwriting, directing, CHEKHOV adaptations and nonfiction efforts such as *Writing in Restaurants* (1986).

The American Academy of Arts and Letters in 1993 awarded him its Award of Merit Medal for outstanding work over the course of a career SMA

Mamoulian, Rouben 1897–1987 Russian-born American director. While preparing for a law career at the University of Moscow, Mamoulian attended VAKH-TANGOV's Studio Theatre. After graduation he went to London, and in 1922 successfully staged *The Beating on the Door* at the ST JAMES'S THEATRE. In 1923 he was invited to Rochester, NY, by George Eastman, and for the next three years headed the Eastman Theatre. In 1926 he became a teacher at the THEATRE GUILD in New York, and a year later made his BROADWAY directing debut with *Porgy*, gaining a reputation for integrating music, drama and dance into a rhythmic whole. He staged six plays in 1928, including O'NEILL's *Marco Millions*; two plays in 1929, including KAREL ČAPEK's *R.U.R.*; and four in 1930, including *A Month in the Country*. He divided his time between Hollywood and New York during the 1930s, and his theatrical output declined. His other outstanding stage credits include *Porgy and Bess* (1935); *Oklahoma!* (1943); *Carousel* (1945); and *Lost in the Stars* (1949). His 16 films include *Applause* (1929), *Dr Jekyll and Mr Hyde* (1932), *Golden Boy* (1939), *Blood and Sand* (1941) and *Silk Stockings* (1957). TLM

Manaka, Matsemela 1955– South African poet, playwright, musician and graphic artist. Born in the township of Alexandra, Manaka now lives in Diepkloof, Soweto. He first achieved prominence in 1980 when his play *Egoli* (*The Golden One*, literally: 'Johannesburg') was performed at the Erlangen Festival in Germany – the first time a black playwright had presented work there. A founder member of the Allahpoets, a group of 'performance poets', and founder of the Soyikwa Africa Theatre group, he is a prominent figure in the black theatre movement on the Witwatersrand. He has also published some poetry and a number of critical articles on the theatre, and exhibited his graphics both locally and internationally.

For a time employed by Ravan Press in Johannesburg, Manaka was the editor of the literary magazine *Staffrider*. Influenced in his early work by GIBSON KENTE, the first attempt he made at writing a play resulted in a MUSICAL called *The Horn* (1977), inspired by Kente's *How Long?*. The play was based on a theme to which Manaka would return: the dispossession of the migrant worker. In 1979 he produced *Egoli* in Cape Town; later it transferred to the Market Theatre in Johannesburg, and was invited to West Germany. After its staging at the Erlangen Festival the play toured to Frankfurt, Augsburg, West Berlin and other cities. Also in 1979 Manaka created, out of improvisation, the play *Imbumba* (*Unity*) – the first production of his newly formed Soyikwa Africa Theatre. Later plays were *Pula* (1982), *Vuka* (1982) and *Children of Asazi* (1984). As the organizer of the Drama Committee of the Funda Centre in Soweto in 1984, Manaka coordinated a vigorous theatre programme for aspirant young black theatre practitioners. IS

Manhattan Theatre Club (New York City) OFF-BROADWAY company founded in 1970 to develop new work. Under artistic director (since 1972) LYNNE MEADOW, MTC's goal is 'to present well crafted, bold, challenging plays by major writers from America and around the world'; but, according to Meadow, 'we don't do non-linear plays'. MTC's productions have included McNALLY's *Bad Habits* (1973–4); Corinne Jacker's *Bits and Pieces*; FUGARD's *The Blood Knot* (Obie, 1976); DAVID RUDKIN's *Ashes* (Obie, 1976, with NEW YORK SHAKESPEARE FESTIVAL); *Ain't Misbehavin'* (Tony, 1978); BECKETT's *Play, That Time* and *Footfalls* (1978); Bill C. Davis's *Mass Appeal* (1980); HENLEY's *Crimes of the Heart* (Pulitzer Prize, 1981) and *The Miss Firecracker Contest* (1984); VAN ITALLIE's new translations of CHEKHOV's *The Seagull* (directed by JOSEPH CHAIKIN, 1975) and *The Three Sisters* (1982); *Loot* (1985); *Frankie and Johnny in the Clair de Lune* (1987); *Hunting Cockroaches* (1987); Richard Greenberg's *Eastern Standard* (1988); McNally's *The Lisbon Traviata* (Lucille Lortel Award, Directing, 1989); FRIEL's *Aristocrats* (Lucille Lortel Award, 1989); AUGUST WILSON's *The Piano Lesson* (1990, with YALE REPERTORY THEATRE and CENTER THEATRE GROUP); AYCKBOURN's *A Small Family Business* (1991–2); Donald Margulies's *Sight Unseen* (1992); McNally's *A Perfect Ganesh* (1993), and the operas *Little Mahagonny* (1973) and *The Breasts of Tiresias* (1974). MTC received a 1977 Obie for Sustained Excellence and a 1989 Drama Desk Award for 'setting high standards, encouraging new playwrights and importing unusual plays from abroad'. REK

Mannheim Court Theatre The most important years of the Mannheim Court Theatre were its initial ones when, under the direction of Baron Heribert von Dalberg (1750–1806), it exercised much influence on the development of German theatre. Dalberg hired many of the actors from the Gotha Court Theatre after EKHOF's death in 1778. Among them was IFFLAND. For the next 12 years Dalberg encouraged them to develop a moderate, idealized REALISM in acting that became known as the Mannheim style. He also developed a wide repertoire and insisted on his actors being educated and capable of playing together in a unified whole. SW

Mansfield, Richard 1854–1907 American actor-producer. Hailed by many as America's answer to HENRY IRVING after the death of EDWIN BOOTH, this strong personality generated critical controversy whenever he performed. He played his first important role of Baron Chevrial in *A Parisian Romance* in 1883 after a series of minor roles in England and the USA. In 1886 he launched a production with himself as the star in the title role of *Prince Karl*; with this role, he began his successful career as a star and producer. Each year, Mansfield would arrange to occupy theatres in New York and on the road to present a repertory consisting of one or two new characters and revivals of his more successful previous vehicles. A compelling, intense actor and skilful producer, his notable roles and productions included the dual role *Dr Jekyll and Mr Hyde* (1887); *Richard III* and *Henry V*; CLYDE FITCH's *Beau Brummell* (1890); Bluntschli in *Arms and the Man* (1894, the first production of SHAW in the USA); the title role in *Napoleon Bonaparte* (1894); Dick Dudgeon in Shaw's *The Devil's Disciple* (1897); *Cyrano de Bergerac* (1889); BOOTH TARKINGTON's *Beaucaire* (1901); and IBSEN's *Peer Gynt* (1907). Mansfield also produced, but did not play in, *A Doll's House* in London (1888) and in New York (1889), with Beatrice Cameron (whom he was to marry in 1892) as Nora. His productions were characterized by lavish spectacle and a meticulous attention to realistic detail. Mansfield was a forceful transitional figure on the American stage at the turn of the century, representing the waning traditions of the old era and the emerging tendencies of the new.   MR DJW

Mantegna, Joe 1948– Chicago-born American actor. His work has been closely identified with the plays and films of DAVID MAMET (critic Jack Kroll described Mantegna in 1988 as 'gloriously Mametic'), a long-time friend and associate. He appeared in premieres at the GOODMAN THEATRE of Mamet's *A Life in the Theatre*, *The Disappearance of the Jews* and *Glengarry Glen Ross* (the role of Richard Roman), winning a Tony on BROADWAY for the latter in 1984. He also appeared in Mamet's *Speed-the-Plow* (1988) and his films *House of Games* (1987), *Things Change* (1988) and *Homicide* (1991). He was active early with Chicago's Organic Theatre Company; his career has focused increasingly on films in recent years.   DBW

Mantell, Robert (Bruce) 1854–1928 Scottish-born actor who trained in England under some of the leading late-19th-century practitioners of 'classical' acting, such as Barry Sullivan and SAMUEL PHELPS. He went to America in 1878 as a member of HELENA MODJESKA's touring company. He returned to England, but went back to the USA to play in support of FANNY DAVENPORT in *Fedora* in 1883. In 1886 he made his first star appearance in *Tangled Lives*, a modern domestic MELODRAMA. A series of starring tours in modern heroic melodramas outside of New York were only limited successes until he began to incorporate the tragedies of SHAKESPEARE and the 'classical' romances of BULWER LYTTON into his repertory in the 1890s. In 1904 he made a triumphant return to New York and established himself as the last remaining representative of a robust, passionate 'old school' of tragic acting in America, generating much discussion over the merits of this system. Among his more celebrated roles were Othello, Shylock, King John, King Lear, Macbeth, Richard III, Richelieu and Louis XI.   MR DJW

Mantle, (Robert) Burns 1873–1948 American drama critic and annalist. Trained as a printer, Mantle turned to dramatic criticism in 1898 for the *Denver Times*, moved to the *Denver Republican* in 1901, and during the same year left for Chicago and a six-year stint as critic for the *Inter-Ocean* (1901–7). In 1907 he spent a year as reviewer for the *Chicago Tribune* before becoming that paper's Sunday editor. In 1911 he accepted the dramatic post for the *New York Evening Mail*, and changed jobs one last time in 1922 when he moved to the *Daily News* (1922–43). A strong supporter of the American drama, Mantle wrote in a bright and newsy style. His 'Best Play' series, which he edited from 1919 until 1947–8, remains his most enduring contribution to the American stage.   TLM

Manzoni, Alessandro 1785–1873 Italian novelist and dramatist whose best-known novel, *I promessi sposi* (*The Betrothed*, 1840–2), has several times been adapted for stage and screen. He wrote two plays, *Il Conte di Carmagnola* (*The Count of Carmagnola*, 1815–19) and *Adelchi* (1820–2), both essentially literary works in the tradition of romantic poets like Shelley and BYRON; they are rarely performed today, although versions of the second have been given interesting stagings by VITTORIO GASSMAN (1960) and CARMELO BENE (1984), the last in the style of an oratorio. Manzoni was much influenced by SHAKESPEARE and helped to establish the English dramatist's reputation in Italy in the early decades of the 19th century.   LR

Maori theatre The culture of the pre-European population of Aotearoa/New Zealand was rich in RITUALized performance, generally without using impersonation. This century, Maori theatre retains a strong collective tradition, sometimes aggressively AGIT-PROP, as in the touring *Maranga Mai* (*Wake Up*, 1980). Theatrically, this was a reaction to the elasticity of 'biculturalism', which could refer to anything from the showcasing of Maori elements in English drama (like the *hui* in BRUCE MASON's *Awatea*) to the politically committed work of Paul Maunder in his Amamus collective and his Theatre of the Eighth Day. Maunder's groups, influenced by GROTOWSKI, worked from Wellington with *Song of a Kiwi* (1977), *Electra* (*Thoughts during the Tour*) (1982), *Ngati Pakeha* (1985), and the bilingual *Encounter at Te Puna* (1984), dealing with Maori reactions to European contact; these included Maori actors such as Jim Moriarty and Roma Potiki who, without questioning Maunder's artistry or commitment, have since preferred a less overtly intellectualized biculturalism controlled by Maori.

Many individual playwrights have recently emerged, including Rore Hapipi, Riwia Brown, Hone Tuwhare, Selwyn Muru, Rangimoana Taylor, Samson Samasoni, Rena Owen, John Broughton and Potiki. Much of their (often bilingual) work has been fostered by Wellington's Depot Theatre, which has served as a base for Te Ohu Whakaari (Young Maori in Performance) and was in 1991 renamed Taki Rua (Weaving with Two Threads) – biculturalism on Maori terms. Riwia Brown has commented that 'Taki Rua is almost a *tapu* place, almost a *marae* [sacred meeting place]'. 'Marae Theatre' is a term that Moriarty has used for Taki Rua, and with Broughton he has expanded the concept to performances in 'non-theatrical' public places, contextualized by protocols of greeting, reply, and display of cultural items such as carving and weaving before performance begins. This structure facilitates participation performance, which is at the root of Maori tradition, and its flexibility relates well to climatic features. Also, *marae* ceremony allows the drama to fuse with traditional RITUAL such as *tangi* (funeral), which might be improper in a commercial theatre. Broughton's *Te Hara* (1988) fades out into a *waiata tangi* (lamentation), Tuwhare's *In the Wilderness without a Hat* (1985) and Potiki's *Whatungarongaro* (1990) both include *tangi*, while the end of Hapipi's *Death of the Land* (1976) dissolves again into the wailing that has contained the other dramatic action; in each case, a Maori performance form has the last word.

The *tangi* play may be related to the *utu* (revenge) play, a term Muru has used for his own *Get the Hell Home Boy* (1982), but applicable also to the tone of anger underlying Maranga Mai or Hapipi's television play *The Protesters*. Since traditional ceremonial performance has never ceased – although urbanization has separated many people from it – the objective of contemporary cultural groups is continuation rather than retrieval. However, Maori theatre also acknowledges its place in the 20th century, and hybridity through Westernization is explored to articulate not only anger and grief but also SATIRE and broad COMEDY. Satirical subtlety is particularly apparent in the work of Hone Kouka, who questions not only the heroes of the past but also the available icons of the present, including media figures. Cultural denial and displacement, central to Rena Owen's work, provide the core of Kouka's first solo play, *Mauri Tu* (1991), about a young man out of touch with his culture but nevertheless wanting to be judged on a *marae*. Widely praised as a personal statement, the play is also metonymical for the dynamic of Maori theatre itself. HDMCN

Maponya, Maishe 1951– South African playwright, actor and director, born in the township of Alexandra. When Maponya was 11, his family was forcibly removed under apartheid legislation and resettled in Diepkloof, Soweto, where in 1975, when he was an insurance clerk in one of South Africa's giant corporations, he began writing plays. His writing career took off when he joined Medupi Writers' Association, which, along with many other organizations including newspapers, was banned in October 1977 (see CENSORSHIP). That year he founded the Bahumutsi Drama Group, and in 1978 he co-founded the Allahpoets, a group of 'performance poets'.

His first play, in 1976, was *The Cry*, written before the political uprising of 16 June; this was followed by *Peace and Forgive* in 1977, first performed in various townships and later at the Market Theatre in Johannesburg. In 1981 his play *The Hungry Earth* left South Africa for a lengthy tour of Britain, Switzerland and West Germany. As an example of a Sowetan drama created by Maponya independently of white managements, it was invited to perform in community centres, universities and FRINGE THEATRES and also at the EDINBURGH FESTIVAL, which it did to critical acclaim. The play toured to Germany again in May 1983, along with Maponya's new play *Umongikazi* (*The Nurse*, about health and working conditions in hospitals); both plays were enthusiastically received. Harassment from police and political organizations did not prevent him from creating two further plays in 1984: *Gangsters* and *Dirty Work* interrogated the methods and tactics of the South African security police. In 1986, in *Jika* (written when he was taking a postgraduate degree in theatre studies at Leeds University) he explored the potential for political change in his country, and in 1987 he co-authored with Amani Blackwood a play about the Incas in South America, *The Valley of the Blind*. Maponya is a lecturer in drama at the University of the Witwatersrand in Johannesburg. IS

Marais, Théâtre du (Paris) Originally built as an indoor tennis court in the rue Vieille-du-Temple, the Marais was rented, like other covered courts, by itinerant actors visiting Paris until a company led by MONTDORY and Charles Le Noir settled there permanently in 1634, acquiring a reputation with their performances of PIERRE CORNEILLE's plays which threatened to eclipse the Comédiens du Roi at the HÔTEL DE BOURGOGNE. It was destroyed by fire in 1644 but reconstructed as a fully fledged theatre and reopened in the same year, subsequently serving as a model for structural improvements at other playhouses. It was larger than most, with a raked stage offering a playing area of approximately 38ft by 32ft, a smaller upper stage and a well appointed auditorium capable of holding an audience of up to 1500. After the departure of FLORIDOR in 1647 its fortunes declined somewhat, and were sustained only by the perennial popularity of JODELET in COMEDY and FARCE and by a fashion for plays with elaborate machinery and spectacular scenic effects. In 1673 the leading actors from the Marais were amalgamated by royal decree with the rump of MOLIÈRE's former company and moved to a theatre in the rue Guénégaud, before a further fusion with the Hôtel de Bourgogne in 1680 gave birth to the COMÉDIE-FRANÇAISE. DR

Marble, Danforth 1810–49 American actor, who began a successful career in 1832 telling Yankee stories. In competition with GEORGE HANDEL HILL and J. H. HACKETT, Marble developed a distinctive YANKEE character with broad American idiosyncrasies. His vehicles included *The Forest Rose*, *The Vermont Wool Dealer*, *Yankee Land* and *The Backwoodsman; or, The Gamecock of the Wilderness*, but his particular success was in *Sam Patch; or, The Daring Yankee* (1836). The real Sam Patch made a career of jumping from high places: his last jump was from the top of the Genesee Falls in 1829, a distance of 125 feet. Marble made his jumps in theatres as spectacular as possible. A consummate teller of tales and strikingly costumed, he enjoyed a successful visit to England in 1844, playing before the king and queen; he sponsored a playwriting contest for new material in 1845 and toured America extensively. He died of cholera on the night of his benefit – the play, *A Cure for the Cholera*. WJM

Marbury, Elisabeth 1856–1933 American agent, producer and playwright. First dramatists' agent in the USA, Marbury developed an international clientele of writers and performers, including Frances Burnett, SHAW, WILDE, BARRIE, SARDOU, FEYDEAU, FITCH, CROTHERS, Vernon and Irene Castle and ROSTAND. An astute socialite and businesswoman, she convinced international authors to negotiate royalties rather than one-time fees. She sometimes influenced casting and script development, and lobbied for improved conditions for actors. With John W. Rumsey, she founded the American Play Company in 1914, a worldwide agency. She produced the Princess Theatre MUSICALS (New York, beginning 1915), developing the story-focused musical. Decorated for war services, she was politically active. Her memoirs were published in 1923. TH-S

Marceau, Marcel 1923– French MIME artist. The most influential and best-loved of modern mimes, Marceau was a student of DECROUX and DULLIN, and made his debut in 1947 at the Théâtre de Poche, Paris. Inspired by both silent-

Marcel Marceau at the Old Vic, London, 1984.

March, Fredric [Frederick McIntyre Bickel] 1897–1975 American actor. Educated at the University of Wisconsin, March made his theatrical debut (under his real name) in 1920 in SACHA GUITRY's *Deburau*, and followed it closely in GEORGE ADE's *County Chairman* (1921). His first major role was in WILLIAM A. BRADY's production of *The Law Breaker* (1922). After an assortment of juvenile leads, he performed in MOLNÁR's *The Swan* in Denver with actress FLORENCE ELDRIDGE (1926). They were married a year later and worked together for the rest of their careers. After spending most of the 1930s in Hollywood, March returned to the stage in 1938, co-starring with his wife in *Ye Obedient Husband*. Working in both media, he created for the stage the roles of Mr Antrobus in *The Skin of Our Teeth* (1942); Major Victor Joppolo in *A Bell for Adano* (1944); Nicholas Denery in *The Autumn Garden* (1951); and James Tyrone in *A Long Day's Journey into Night* (1956), which won him a Tony. He appeared in 69 films, including starring roles in *Dr Jekyll and Mr Hyde* (1935), which won him an Oscar; *Les Misérables* (1935); *A Star Is Born* (1937); *The Best Years of Our Lives* (1946), which won him an Oscar; *Inherit the Wind* (1960); and *The Iceman Cometh* (1973). March considered the role of James Tyrone his finest work. BROOKS ATKINSON wrote: 'As the aging actor who stands at the head of the family, Fredric March gives a masterly performance that will stand as a milestone in the acting of an O'Neill play.' TLM

Marcos, Plínio 1935– Brazilian playwright. Of humble beginnings, lacking formal education but trained in the world by experiences as a manual labourer and soccer player, Marcos entered the theatre world as actor and administrator and eventually became a playwright. *Dois Perdidos numa Noite Suja* (*Two Lost Men in a Dirty Night*, 1966) scandalized the São Paulo public for its brutally realistic treatment of the marginal society of two 'bums', who attempt to victimize society as they have been victimized and eventually destroy each other. *Navalha na Carne* (*Knife in the Flesh*, 1967) shows the brutal world of a prostitute, a pimp and a homosexual, a subculture elevated in lyrical terms through human suffering and psychological understanding. Other plays include *Homens de Papel* (*Paper Men*), *Quando as Máquinas Param* (*When the Machines Stop*, 1967), *Jornada de un Imbécil até o Entendimento* (*Journey of an Imbecile to Understanding*, 1968), and *Balbina de Iansã* (1970), the latter dealing with *umbanda* (São Paulo style voodoo). Marcos experienced serious problems with CENSORSHIP during the 1970s. As political restrictions were lifted in the 1980s, he returned to the stage with *Madame Blavatsky* (1985), a work based on the life of the Ukrainian mystic which, after his earlier scandalous pieces, shocked the critics for its religious asceticism. GW

Marcus, Frank 1928– British actor, director, dramatist and critic, who was born in Germany and emigrated to Britain in 1939. His German background helped him to produce a thoughtful translation/adaptation of ARTHUR SCHNITZLER's *Reigen*, presented in London as *Merry-Go-Round* (1952), and some traces of Schnitzler's cool analysis of sexual behaviour appeared in his first WEST END success, *The Formation Dancers* (1964), and in *Cleo* (1965),

film comics and the *COMMEDIA DELL'ARTE*, his character Bip, recognizable by his striped jersey, whiteface and the red rose in his top hat, was adaptable to all kinds of pantomime. Starting with simple stylistic exercises ('The Tug of War', 'Chasing Butterflies'), he moved on to such philosophical and elliptical mimodramas as 'The Cage' and 'The Mask Maker', and with his company (1948–60) could even expand into an adaptation of GOGOL's 'The Overcoat'. Marceau's international standing was confirmed at the Berlin Festival of 1951, where he won the friendship of BRECHT, and tours of 66 countries disseminated his abstract style throughout the world. In 1974 he presented a retrospective of his work and in 1978 founded the École de Mimodrame de Paris. LS which is like a female version of Schnitzler's *Anatol*. *The Killing of Sister George* (1965) established his reputation as one of Britain's leading writers of serious comedies, describing how the BBC got rid of a leading radio star because of her lesbian proclivities. His subsequent plays, which include *Mrs Mouse, Are You Within?* (1968) and *Notes on a Love Affair* (1972), were less successful, and from 1968 until 1980 Marcus was best known as the perceptive theatre critic of the *Sunday Telegraph*. JE

Mardzhanov, Konstantin [Kote Mardzhanishvili] 1872–1933 Soviet Georgian director who, after acting and directing in his native republic (1893–1909), Russified his name and established himself in Moscow. As artistic director of the Nezlobin Theatre (1909), he co-founded the Georgian Drama Studio with A. I. Yuzhin. At the MOSCOW ART THEATRE (1910–13), he staged works by Hansum and IBSEN and assistant-directed the NEMIROVICH-DANCHENKO *Brothers Karamazov* (1910) and the CRAIG *Hamlet* (1911). He organized the Sukhodolskys' Free Theatre (1913–14), where, along with the actress KOONEN and directors TAIROV and A. A. Sanin, he staged OPERA, OPERETTA, drama and pantomime and sought to develop a singing, dancing actor. In Kiev (1919), he staged a notable production of *Salome*, designed by Isaak Rabinovich; a May Day presentation of LOPE DE VEGA's *Fuenteovejuna*, in which rebellious villagers overthrow oppressive royals; and Vasily Kamensky's *Stenka Razin*, about a peasant rebel. Mardzhanov's experiments with festive staging in Rostov-on-Don (1914–15) and Petrograd (1916–17) prepared him to coordinate the mass spectacle *Toward a Worldwide Commune* (co-directed by Nikolai Petrov, SERGEI RADLOV, Vladimir Solovyov and Adrian Piotrovsky, 1920).

He returned to Georgia (and his Georgian name) to head Tblisi's Rustaveli Theatre, where he restaged *Fuenteovejuna* with a Georgian cast and mounted a Craigian *Hamlet*. Criticized for attempting to 'Europeanize' the troupe, he and part of the company left to found the Second State Georgian Theatre (after 1933, the Mardzhanishvili Theatre). He worked in films (1916–28) and directed at Moscow's Korsh, Maly and Operetta Theatres (1931–3). SC

Maréchal, Marcel 1937– French actor and director. Maréchal became known as the director of the avant-garde Théâtre du Cothurne in Lyon in the 1960s when PLANCHON had moved to Villeurbanne. His productions of AUDIBERTI and VAUTHIER gave new life to these dramatists, who had been associated with the Parisian absurdist theatre of the 1950s (see THEATRE OF THE ABSURD). In 1968 he inaugurated the Théâtre du Huitième with *La Poupée* (*The Doll*) by Audiberti and also commissioned a new play by Vauthier, *Le Sang* (*Blood*), first performed in 1970. He has also produced work by BRECHT, WEISS, BECKETT and YACINE, but is best known for an exuberant style well exemplified in *The Three Musketeers* (1980). In 1975 he became director of the new Théâtre National de Marseille. DB

Margalit, Meir 1906–73 Hebrew actor. Born in Poland, he went to Palestine as a pioneer in 1922, where he joined the Ohel Theatre. His performance as the brave soldier Schweik in Hašek's play (1936) established him as the greatest comic actor in the country. The play was performed over 800 times. Margalit is especially remembered for the lead roles in MOLIÈRE's *L'Avare*, *Le Bourgeois Gentilhomme* and *Le Malade Imaginaire*, and as Falstaff in *The Merry Wives of Windsor*. (See also HEBREW THEATRE.) HAS

Marinetti, F(ilippo) T(ommaso) 1876–1944 Italian poet, dramatist and polemicist. Founder and most active publicist of the futurist movement, Marinetti moved for some time in the French literary world, publishing one of his first plays in Paris, *Le Roi Bombance*, in 1905, and announcing the principles of the new art he championed with 'The Futurist Manifesto' in *Le Figaro* of 20 February 1909. Three years later his ideas were further developed in 'The Technical Manifesto of Futurist Literature'. Indeed, he pioneered a new literary form, the manifesto, and in the next few years many of these poured from his pen, concerned with all the arts that FUTURISM embraced, including theatre, of which the most important were *Il teatro di varietà* (*The Variety Theatre*, 1913) and *Il teatro sintetico futurista* (*The Synthetic Theatre*, 1915); later manifestos, prepared alone or with others, amplified early ideas or extended into new areas, like *Il teatro della sorpresa* (*The Theatre of Surprise*, 1921), *Il teatro anti-psicologico astratto di puri elementi* (*The Anti-Psychological Abstract of Pure Elements*), *Il teatro tattile* (*The Manifesto of Tactile Theatre*, 1924) and *Teatro totale per masse* (*Total Theatre for the Masses*, 1933).

Marinetti's dramatic output was basically of two kinds: the syntheses, which were among the movement's best, and full-length plays, including *Poupées électriques* (*Electric Puppets*, 1909, later adapted under various titles), *Il tamburo di fuoco* (*Fire Drum*, 1922), *Luci veloci* (*Rapid Light*, 1929) and *Simultanina* (1931), the last three of which combine spectacular effects with an empty verbosity. A champion of scientific modernity, Marinetti was interested too in the possibilities of radio and television, issuing futurist pronouncements on both in the early 1930s. The futurist exaltation of machines and technology, of man dominating the natural world through science, had latent Fascist elements in it from the beginning, and these came to the fore with the rise to power of Mussolini. In 1924 Marinetti lauded the new political nationalism in *Futurismo e fascismo* (*Futurism and Fascism*), became a propagandist for Fascist values and remained true to the regime even in its last stage, the Republic of Salò. In the postwar years his work was understandably neglected, but was rediscovered in the late 1960s and 70s and exerted a brief, general influence. LR

marionette Type of puppet hanging from a cross-piece or stick, whose articulated limbs are worked from above by strings or wires. The name may derive from medieval French: *mariotes*, *mariettes*, *mariolettes*, little statues of the Virgin Mary; it is used that way in the 13th-century PASTORAL play *Le Jeu de Robin et de Marion*. Marionettes were known as well to the ancient Greeks as *neurospasta*, wooden figures on strings; Xenophon cites a Syracusan puppeteer performing at a banquet of Kallias, and ARISTOTLE refers to them as a metaphor for the methods of a supreme being. According to Athenaeus, the puppeteer

Potheinos, a contemporary of EURIPIDES (485–406 BC), was so popular that the archons made the theatre of Dionysus available for his performances.

During the Middle Ages, marionettes recurred both as playthings and as performance tools. The 12th-century *Hortus Deliciarum* shows two knight-dolls manipulated by cords across a table. The Church employed marionettes to illustrate Bible stories, especially the nativity, and in Spain they played an important part in religious processions. The Council of Trent (1563) banned their use in church, but to little effect.

In Italy in c.1500 the *magatelli* were said to 'play, fight, hunt, dance, blow the trumpet and cook very skilfully'; in the next century, the term became *fantoccini*. In Sicily, the prolonged *opera dei puppi*, adventures of the Paladins drawn from ARIOSTO's *Orlando Furioso*, require 300 characters, nearly life-size figures, and go on for weeks; they have been successfully transferred to New York by the Manteco family. Between the 17th and 19th centuries marionettes enjoyed their most widespread popularity in Europe, often replacing live actors. Each major Italian city had its own theatre devoted to the favourite local character: Cassandrino in Rome, Girolamo in Milan, Gianduja in Turin. Ambulant showmen used lightweight and easily portable booths. The Teatro Fiando in Milan specialized in fairy plays and even operas. In Spain the *títeres* dramatized saints' legends and chivalric romances, as in the case of Maese Pedro, whose Saracenic display was devastated by Don Quixote.

Marionettes appeared in Germany as early as the 10th and 12th centuries as *Tokkespill*, animated statuettes employed by itinerant minstrels. German and Dutch marionettes were greatly influenced by the ENGLISCHE KOMÖDIANTEN (English Comedians) who toured in the 16th and 17th centuries, mingling them with live actors. The influence was mutual; a German chapbook of the life of Dr Faust by Johann Spiess (1587) inspired CHRISTOPHER MARLOWE, and his *Dr Faustus* (c.1589), played in Germany by the English Comedians, was in turn adapted as a marionette show, which was seen by the young GOETHE in Frankfurt-am-Main. After travelling through Saxony, Bohemia, South Germany and Austria (where KASPER would become the leading comic figure), marionettes came to court. In 1669 Johann Peter Hilverding, chamberlain of the Archbishop of Salzburg, performed 50 comedies and operas with figures about one metre long, and this tradition was maintained well into the 20th century. Joseph Haydn wrote music for five puppet OPERAS (1773–8) on classic themes, sung at the Court of Prince Esterházy. Such technical perfection inspired HEINRICH VON KLEIST's essay on marionettes (1810), wherein the puppet's judgement is praised for being never distorted by human prejudice.

A well established marionette theatre existed in Paris c.1590, when the classic characters Polichinelle and La Mère Gigogne were created. During the early reign of Louis XIV, the leading impresario was Jean Brioché (Giovanni Briocci) on the Pont-Neuf in Paris, who was paid 1365 livres for a performance before the Dauphin, and had the honour of being attacked from the pulpit by Bossuet; his son François, known as Fanchon, kept up the business. The legitimate theatre found the competition too great

and in 1710 statutes forbade marionettes to sing; they gradually removed to the fairs, where LESAGE wrote for them.

The usual terms in England were 'mammet' and 'puppet' for the figure, and 'motion' and 'drollery' for the show. From 1562, marionettes performed all sorts of plays, from *The Prodigal Son* to *Julius Caesar* in fairground showbooths, and managed to escape the proscription of the playhouses in 1642 (see CLOSURE OF THE THEATRES) and 1647; when the theatres reopened they sought (1675) the closure of the puppet-shows, unsuccessfully. The leading exhibitors were Martin Powell, whose PUNCH show (1710–13) became a byword; Pinkethman, who portrayed the gods of Olympus; and Crawley, who staged the Creation of the World with a very wet Deluge.

Marionettes were somewhat displaced in popularity during the 19th century, for many of the local types – Punch, GUIGNOL, Kasper – could be readily performed in the streets by hand-PUPPETS. A revival occurred in artistic circles in the early 20th century. Kurt Schmidt experimented with them at the Bauhaus and many famous writers and musicians created especially for marionettes. An American renaissance was promoted by Tony Sarg and Remo Bufano, and later by Bil Baird. The Czech Josef Skupa (1892–1957) invented the character Spejbl, a naive, prejudiced man-in-the-street; Gustav Nosek developed his alert and active son Hurvinek: the two puppets became vehicles for anti-Nazi SATIRE, even appearing in concentration-camp pyjamas, leading the Gestapo to confiscate the original figures. The Nazi regime also put a temporary end to UNIMA (Union Internationale des Marionettes), founded in Prague in 1929; it resumed in 1959, and since 1960 has been a member of the INTERNATIONAL THEATRE INSTITUTE. Czechoslovakia has remained in the forefront of developments, led by Jan Malik and Jiri Trncka.

In modern stage aesthetics, marionettes have played an influential role. MAURICE MAETERLINCK's propaganda in their favour was followed by GORDON CRAIG's desideratum of an *Über-Marionette* as the ideal actor. JARRY's *Ubu* cycle was conceived as a marionette spectacle, ANTONIN ARTAUD prescribed gigantic marionettes for his Theatre of Cruelty, and MICHEL DE GHELDERODE and GARCÍA LORCA (in the tradition of GOZZI's *Love of Three Oranges*) composed plays specifically for them. On the contemporary scene, DARIO FO has suggested marionettes as agents in the proletarian revolution, Takuo Endo has applied them to performance art, and the allegorical figures of the BREAD AND PUPPET THEATRE can be seen as a logical extension. LS

See: A. Altherr, *Marionetten*, Zurich, n.d.; J. Chesnais, *Histoire générale des marionettes*, Paris, 1947; G. Le Bolzer, *La Marionette*, Paris, 1958; J. Malik, *Les Marionettes tchécoslovacques*, Prague, n.d.; 'The Marionette' special issue of *Theatre Arts Monthly*, New York, July 1928.

Marivaux, Pierre Carlet de Chamblain de

1688–1763 French playwright, novelist and versatile man of letters. After studying law in Paris he turned to writing and became an habitué of salon and café society, where he associated particularly with Fontenelle and HOUDAR DE LA MOTTE and seconded their staunch advocacy of the Moderns against the Ancients in that lingering aesthetic debate. His earliest published works were novels and magazine articles, but in 1720 he produced three plays – two comedies, *L'Amour et la vérité* (*Love and Truth*) and *Arlequin poli par l'amour* (*Harlequin Refined by Love*), for the COMÉDIE-ITALIENNE and a tragedy, *Annibal* (*Hannibal*), for the COMÉDIE-FRANÇAISE. Thereafter he divided his time between writing for both these theatres and active journalism, becoming editor of several literary-cum-philosophical periodicals. It was for the Italian players that the greater part, and certainly the best, of his dramatic output was provided, presumably because he found them more responsive to the nuances of his dialogue, in which young love and the self-discovery it occasions are analysed so sensitively, often obliquely through subtle changes in linguistic register which betray an emotional sub-text, especially in the female roles.

Marivaudage was the term coined, at first pejoratively, for these delicate exchanges between young lovers by spectators who found the turgid sentimentality of LA CHAUSSÉE's *comédie larmoyante* more to their liking. But unlike the latter Marivaux's work has survived and is now widely performed. Amongst his most successful Italian plays were *La Surprise de l'amour* (*The Surprise of Love*, 1722), *La Double Inconstance* (*The Double Inconstancy*, 1723), *Le Prince travesti* (*The Prince in Disguise*, 1724), *Le Jeu de l'amour et du hasard* (*The Game of Love and Chance*, 1730), *Les Fausses Confidences* (*The False Confessions*, 1737) and *L'Épreuve* (*The Test*, 1740), while *La Seconde Surprise de l'amour* (*The Second Surprise of Love*, 1727) and *Le Legs* (*The Legacy*, 1736) were well received at the Comédie-Française. He published further novels in the 1730s and was elected to the Académie-Française in 1743. DR

Marlowe, Christopher 1564–93 English playwright and poet, born to a Canterbury shoemaker and educated at Cambridge University. He may still have been an undergraduate when he first worked as an agent for Francis Walsingham, Elizabeth I's scheming minister. Certainly Thomas Walsingham, Francis's brother, was Marlowe's patron at a time when the cult of friendship was strong at court. We have no knowledge of secret missions undertaken by Marlowe, and it is only speculation that links his violent death in a Deptford (London) tavern with his activities as an agent. What is known is that he took his BA in 1584 and his MA, after some hesitation from the university authorities, in 1587, and that almost at once he changed the course of English drama by presenting the still-emergent professional theatre of London with the startlingly original first part of *Tamburlaine the Great* (1587).

There is presumptive evidence that the play was first performed by the ADMIRAL'S MEN, with EDWARD ALLEYN in the title role. It certainly became, together with Marlowe's later plays, a popular feature of that important company's repertoire. Its rhetoric, the self-proclaimed 'high astounding terms', were superbly handled by Alleyn, and the second part (1587) matched the success of the first. Marlowe had probably already collaborated with NASHE in writing *Dido, Queen of Carthage* for the CHILDREN OF THE CHAPEL ROYAL – the chronological order of his work cannot be precisely established – but it was *Tamburlaine* that made him famous. The notoriety of his private life, which led to accu-

sations of atheism, blasphemy, subversion and homosexuality, added spice to his reputation. Certainly he was free-thinking and indiscreet. But *Dido*, for all its shortcomings, demonstrates a serious application to the playwright's craft. Like the translation of Lucan's *Pharsalia* (published 1600, but possibly completed at Cambridge) and of Ovid's *Elegies* (published 1595, but probably also student work), it shows a careful apprenticeship in the classics. Whilst the play is drawn mainly from Book Four of Virgil's *Aeneid*, it suggests a confident familiarity with the whole poem.

After *Tamburlaine*, Marlowe continued to dramatize the careers and aspirations of overreaching heroes whose titanic defiance of social, political and religious taboos commands admiration at the same time as it invites condemnation. *The Jew of Malta* (c.1589), described as a tragedy on the title-page of its first edition (1633), is better understood as a grotesque comedy, in which murderous excess and inflated rhetoric PARODY statesmanship and the posturings of Christian authority, but we do not know how much Marlowe's text had been revised by a later hand, perhaps that of THOMAS HEYWOOD. As in *Tamburlaine*, interest (and most of the best lines) centres on the utterly unscrupulous villain-hero, Barabas. *The Massacre at Paris* (c.1589), which has survived in a manifestly corrupt text, is similar in tone. Its central figure, the Duke of Guise, adopts with gusto a self-conscious villainy not unlike Barabas's. That the horrific St Bartholomew massacre of 1572 should be treated so sardonically in the theatres of Protestant England must have been shocking to contemporary audiences. So, in a different way, was Marlowe's most accomplished play, *Edward II* (c.1592), in which the defeat and eventual murder of a homosexual king by powerful barons are depicted with a new plainness of style. *Edward II* carried the crude chronicle play a long step towards its sophistication in the mature HISTORY PLAYS of SHAKESPEARE. It is a tragedy, in which the focus shifts subtly from Edward to his lover Gaveston, to his queen Isabella and to her lover Mortimer.

Whilst each of these characters provokes fate by defying propriety, the Marlovian overreacher comes to what, in retrospect, seems to be a logical conclusion in the title-role of *Doctor Faustus*, and this sense of logic has contributed to the belief that this is the last of Marlowe's plays. It survives in two unsatisfactory texts (1604 and 1616), each of which shows the marks of playhouse accretion and adaptation, but Faustus himself and his increasingly symbiotic relationship with Mephistopheles remain magnificently unaffected. The poetry of Faustus's despair as the Devil is about to claim him is particularly fine. *Doctor Faustus*, even more than *Tamburlaine*, *The Jew of Malta* and *Edward II*, has proved its power in many 20th-century revivals. PT

Marlowe, Julia 1866–1950 British-born American actress. From 1904, when E. H. SOTHERN and Julia Marlowe first appeared together, until her retirement in 1924, American theatregoers identified SHAKESPEARE with Sothern and Marlowe. They were an established team even before their marriage in 1911. The roles of Rosalind, Viola, Juliet, Ophelia and Portia became her property, and she captured the critics who praised her feminine loveliness, magnetic warmth and admirable grace. When they appeared in England in 1907, Arthur Symons wrote: 'No actors on the British stage could speak English verse so beautifully.'

Marlowe had a long and steady apprenticeship. Her family emigrated from England when she was five and settled in Cincinnati, Ohio, where she appeared with a juvenile company and was tutored in the 'classic' repertoire by Ada Dow, a retired actress. In 1884 Miss Dow brought her to New York, securing touring engagements for her in roles such as Lady Teazle and Miss Hardcastle, and (in 1886) as Lydia Languish with JOSEPH JEFFERSON III's touring company. Her first New York triumph came in 1899 in the title role in CLYDE FITCH's *Barbara Frietchie*. RM

Marmion, Shakerley 1603–39 English playwright and poet, educated at Oxford University. After serving as a soldier in the Netherlands, he settled in London, where he enjoyed the patronage of BEN JONSON and the friendship of Sir John Suckling. Marmion wrote three plays, the first two for Prince Charles's Men at the SALISBURY COURT THEATRE and the third for Queen Henrietta's Men at the PHOENIX. The chivalric main plot of *Holland's Leaguer* (1631) is less interesting than the scenes depicting Elizabeth Holland's notorious Southwark brothel. *A Fine Companion* (1633), like Marmion's first play, is a Jonsonian COMEDY OF HUMOURS, less effective than *The Antiquary* (c.1635), in which the follies of old age are wittily displayed. PT

Marowitz, Charles 1934– American-born director and critic. Marowitz directed his first London production in 1958, after which he worked with PETER BROOK on a series of productions that included *King Lear* (1962), an experimental Theatre of Cruelty season based on ARTAUD and GENET (1964), and the first of his 'collage' versions of SHAKESPEARE (*Hamlet*, 1965; *Macbeth*, 1970; *Othello*, 1972; *The Taming of the Shrew*, 1973; and *Measure for Measure*, 1975). In 1968 he founded the Open Space Company, introducing avant-garde drama by contemporary North American writers (John Herbert, *Fortune and Men's Eyes*, 1968; SAM SHEPARD, *The Tooth of Crime*, 1972) as well as his own plays (*Artaud at Rodez*, 1975) and adaptations (*Woyzeck*, 1973; *Hedda*, 1980); but their London stage closed in 1979, and the company disbanded in 1981. Since then he has established himself as a director in Los Angeles, recouping his earlier experimental work as well as presenting Elizabethan and commercial productions, and has gained a reputation for his theoretical writings. CI

Marqués, René 1919–79 Puerto Rican director, playwright, short story writer and novelist. Born in Arecibo, he studied agronomy, a career he abandoned after studying literature in Madrid. On his return to PUERTO RICO, he founded a little theatre group in Arecibo. A Rockefeller Foundation grant in 1949 allowed him to study at Columbia University and in PISCATOR's Dramatic Workshop; a Guggenheim in 1957 was used to write a novel. In 1951 he helped establish the Teatro Experimental del Ateneo in San Juan, and directed the group for three years. Devoted to maintaining the Hispanic traditions of Puerto Rico, he actively opposed the US economic and cultural invasion of the island, favouring independence instead of commonwealth status. His plays reflect great experimentation, ranging from REALISM/NATURALISM (*La carreta*, *The Cart*, 1952) to the absurd (see THEATRE OF THE ABSURD) (*El apartamiento*, *The Apartment/Alienation*, 1964) to a biblical trilogy including *Sacrificio en el Monte Moriah* (*Sacrifice on Mount Moriah*, 1970). His best are *Los soles truncos* (*The Fanlights*, 1958) and *Un niño azul para esa sombra* (*A Blue Child for that Shadow*, 1970), both complex psychological works on Puerto Rican identity problems. GW

Marron, Hanna 1923– Israeli actress. Born in Germany, where she started acting at the age of four, she emigrated to Israel at ten and grew up in Tel-Aviv. She trained at the HABIMAH studio, and joined the British army in 1941; she later performed in army troupes. Marron was one of the founders of the Cameri Theatre. She lost a leg in the 1970 terrorist attack at Munich airport, but returned to the stage. Among her famous roles are the leads in IBSEN's *Ghosts* (1990), *Hedda Gabler* (1966) and *A Doll's House* (1959), in Leah Goldberg's *The Lady of the Manor* (1959), Moshe Shamir's *He Walked the Fields* (1948), SENECA's *Medea* and SHAW's *Pygmalion* (1954); she played Arkadina in CHEKHOV's *The Seagull*, Winnie in Beckett's *Happy Days* and Queen Elizabeth in SCHILLER's *Mary Stuart* (1961). (See also HEBREW THEATRE.) HAS

Mars, Mlle [Anne Françoise Hippolyte Boutet] 1779–1847 French actress. Daughter of the actor Monvel, she made her first appearance at Versailles as a child, then followed MLLE MONTANSIER to Paris. At 16 she was part of the troupe of the COMÉDIE-FRANÇAISE at the Théâtre Feydeau, and with the reunification of the troupe she was admitted with three-eighths of a share. Physically an ugly duckling, she had an attractive voice and good eyes. She attracted attention in the role of a deaf mute in *L'Abbé de l'épée* because of the simplicity of her expression, and this led to a series of ingénue roles, especially those of MOLIÈRE. By the age of 30 she was perceived as attractive. She managed to bring back MARIVAUX to the Comédie-Française repertoire, being an incomparable Sylvia in *The Game of Love and Chance*, and it was at her instigation that all of Molière's great comedies were brought back to the stage. From 1795 to 1839, she created 109 roles at the Comédie-Française, including a number of romantic ones: the Duchesse de Guise in *Henri III et sa cour* (1829), Desdémone in *Le More de Venise*, and, not without some resistance, Dona Sol in *Hernani*. Her later roles included Clarisse Harlowe, Elisabeth in *Les Enfants d'Édouard* (1833), Tisbé in *Angelo* (1835), and Mademoiselle de Belle-Isle (1839) – her last new part, created at the age of 60. Mars became the model of fashion for Parisian ladies for 30 years. In her final illness the Comédie-Française published a daily bulletin. When she died, she lay in state for three days and 50,000 people attended her funeral. JMCC

Marsh, Ngaio 1895–1982 New Zealand director and novelist. Educated as a Fine Arts student at Canterbury University College, she began a notable series of student SHAKESPEARE productions there, with *Hamlet* in 1943, and continued to work with her students and ex-students until *Henry V* in 1972. An attempt at a more ambitious touring professional company in 1951, the British Commonwealth Theatre Company, failed. Marsh also achieved an international reputation as a writer of crime fiction.   HDMCN

Marshall, Norman 1901–80 British director, theatre manager and critic, who joined TERENCE GRAY at the Cambridge Festival Theatre in 1926. After managing the company in 1932, when he staged the first English production of O'NEILL's *Marco Millions*, he took over the Gate Theatre in London, where he directed a series of new and to some extent experimental plays. After 1942 he formed his own repertory company in association with CEMA, touring Europe and India for the British Council from 1949 to 1951, and in 1952 directed *Volpone* for the Cameri Theatre in Israel. As head of drama for Associated-Rediffusion (1955–9) he encouraged the development of theatrical programming for television (see TELEVISION DRAMA), and later played an active role in planning the NATIONAL THEATRE.   CI

Marston, John 1576–1634 English playwright, the son of a Shropshire lawyer. Marston entered the Middle Temple after graduating from Oxford, but abandoned the law after his father's death. He made his literary debut with acerbic verse SATIRES, and much of his dramatic work expresses his combative anger at a world in moral disorder. Marston's talent for the unpredictable is already evident in his first plays, written for the BOYS OF ST PAUL'S. The dark COMEDY of *Antonio and Mellida* (1599) is followed with wilful logic into the hysterical violence of its sequel, *Antonio's Revenge* (1599–1600). *Jack Drum's Entertainment* (1600) and *What You Will* (c.1601), also written for the Paul's Boys, are comparatively good-humoured satires of the follies of contemporary would-be gallants. But Marston became embroiled, as BEN JONSON's adversary, in the ill-tempered WAR OF THE THEATRES, reworking an unknown author's play, *Histriomastix*, to include a mocking portrait of Jonson, and perhaps sharing with DEKKER in the clumsy *Satiromastix* (1601). In *Poetaster* (1601), Jonson gave rather better than he got.

Within a few years, the volatile Marston had dedicated his finest play, *The Malcontent* (published 1604), to Jonson, and collaborated with him and CHAPMAN in the lively and controversial PARODY of CITIZEN COMEDY, *Eastward Ho* (1605). The central figure of *The Malcontent*, Malevole, is a usurped and alienated duke, whose bitter commentary on courtly corruption is eloquently representative of contemporary disaffection. *Parasitaster; or, The Fawn* (c.1604) is no less outspoken and probably more directly critical of James I and his court, as was *Eastward Ho. The Dutch Courtesan* (c.1604), a more exuberant comedy, is nonetheless censorious. For reasons unknown, Marston was imprisoned in 1608, and on his release he renounced the theatre and took holy orders.   PT

Marston, (John) Westland 1819–90 British playwright and dramatic critic whose best-known play, *The Patrician's Daughter* (1842), was one of many verse tragedies promoted and performed by the actor W. C. MACREADY. Marston's intelligent theatrical reviews for the *Athenaeum* in the 1860s and his retrospective book *Our Recent Actors* (1888) are substantial contributions to theatrical literature.   PT

Martin, Karlheinz 1886–1948 German director. Martin founded the Tribune in Berlin, where he staged TOLLER's *Transfiguration* in 1919, and the Proletarian Theatre, which influenced PISCATOR. He is best-known for his film of KAISER's *From Morn to Midnight* (1920), and for a cycle of 'revolutionary classics' produced in the Grosses Schauspielhaus constructed by REINHARDT, with whom he worked after 1921.   CI

Martin, Mary 1913–90 American singer and actress. Martin made her BROADWAY debut in *Leave It to Me* (1938), in which she stopped the show with her teasing rendition of 'My Heart Belongs to Daddy'. Her first starring role was as a statue come to life in *One Touch of Venus* (1943). Three years later, she played the faithful wife in *Lute Song*, a musical version of a traditional Chinese play. In 1947 she headed the national company of *Annie Get Your Gun*. Martin had the greatest success of her career as Nellie Forbush, a native nurse from Little Rock, Arkansas, in RODGERS and HAMMERSTEIN's *South Pacific* (1949). Among the songs she introduced in the show were 'A Cockeyed Optimist', 'I'm Gonna Wash That Man Right outa My Hair', and 'I'm in Love with a Wonderful Guy'. The role was ideally suited to her sunny temperament and buoyant singing style, and also gave her an opportunity to demonstrate her skill as an actress during the show's more serious scenes. In 1954 she appeared in a musical version of J. M. BARRIE's *Peter Pan*, a role she repeated in two television versions of the show. Although she was rather mature for the part of a young novice, Martin's performance in *The Sound of Music* (1959) was a favourite with audiences. Her next show, *Jennie* (1963), was a failure. She starred in the London company of *Hello, Dolly!* before appearing with Robert Preston in *I Do! I Do!* (1966), a two-character musical that followed a couple through 50 years of married life.

In most of her MUSICAL THEATRE roles Martin portrayed a warm-hearted idealist who ultimately triumphs over the problems she faces. Her clear singing voice, winning personality and high spirits contributed greatly to the success of the shows in which she appeared. Her final stage role was in *Legends* in 1986 with CAROL CHANNING. Her autobiography (*My Heart Belongs*) was published in 1976; a museum devoted to her career has been established in her home town of Weatherford, Texas.   MK

Martin-Harvey, John 1863–1944 British actor-manager, one of the last of his kind. After an extended apprenticeship in IRVING's LYCEUM company (1882–96), during which his only real opportunities came when Irving was away on tour, he played Pelléas to MRS PATRICK CAMPBELL's Mélisande in MAETERLINCK's poetic drama (1898) – to moderate notices – and Sydney Carton in a commissioned version of *A Tale of Two Cities* at the Lyceum during another of Irving's tours (1899). Hacked out of the novel by two forgotten clergymen, *The Only Way* became Martin-Harvey's staple diet for 40 years (he made his farewell tour in it in 1939), though it was not until his second provincial tour in it that he began to make money. He established his own company around it and, like many actor-managers, made his fortune in the provinces (and in Canada) rather than in London.

Like Irving on whom he modelled himself, Martin-Harvey was less interested in drama than in theatre. *The Breed of the Treshams* (1903), written under the pen-name of John Rutherford by two Bostonian ladies, is histrionic hokum as surely as was *The Bells*, and it became another stock piece in a company repertoire that also included *Hamlet*, *Richard III*, *Henry V* and *The Taming of the Shrew*. Martin-Harvey's critical reception might have been better if his wife, Nina de Silva (1869–1949), had been as good an actress as he thought she was. His Oedipus, in REINHARDT's spectacular production of *Oedipus Rex* (1912), gave full value to GILBERT MURRAY's translation. It played for three weeks at COVENT GARDEN in 1912 and was the finest thing he ever did. Knighted in 1921, Martin-Harvey held on to his Victorian vision, risible to some and magnificent to others, until the eve of the Second World War. PT

Martinelli family Italian actors. **Drusiano** (d.1606/8), a famous Arlecchino, took the first important COMMEDIA DELL'ARTE troupe to England (1577–8), and travelled to Spain in 1588. His wife **Angelica** Alberigi (or Alberghini; fl.1580–94) had her own company, the UNITI. As an actor Drusiano was overshadowed by his brother **Tristano** (c.1556–1630), the most famous Arlecchino before DOMENICO BIANCOLELLI, who boasted of numbering kings and queens among his 'gossips'. Owing to his domineering pugnacity, he shifted from company to company, appearing with the ACCESI in 1601 and in Paris with the ANDREINI (1611–13), who accused him of undermining their authority. His business acumen was as exceptional as his wit and acrobatic skill, and he was able to leave considerable property to his heirs. LS

Martínez, José de Jesús 1929–91 Panamanian playwright, director, poet, and professor of philosophy and mathematics at the University of Panama. Born in Managua, Nicaragua, and educated in Mexico, Madrid and Germany, Martínez held Panamanian citizenship. His first works included *La mentira* (*The Lie*), *La perrera* (*The Doghouse*) and *La venganza* (*The Vengeance*), all published in Spain in 1954. His doctoral work in metaphysics clearly influenced these plays as well as *El juicio final* (*Final Judgement*, 1962), a monologue of contemporary human anguish. *El mendigo y el avaro* (*The Beggar and the Miser*, 1963) questions the false aspects of charity. *Segundo asalto* (*Second Assault*, 1968) and *Cero y van tres* (*Zero and There Go Three*, 1979) are penetrating studies of personal domination and destructiveness. In *La guerra del banano* (*Banana War*, 1974), he attacked capitalist intervention in the banana industry with a play constructed on metatheatrical and collective techniques. GW

Martínez Queirolo, José 1931– Ecuadorian dramatist and poet; winner of various national prizes for his theatre. In addition to adaptations and translations of several works (CERVANTES, OSCAR WILDE, MROŻEK and others), Martínez Queirolo has written more than twenty plays. His principal works are *Réquiem por la lluvia* (*Requiem for the Rain*, 1960), a dramatic monologue; *Los unos vs. los*

otros (*Some against Others*, 1968), designated as a 'sensational open-air encounter' in which socio-economic family differences are disputed within a boxing match environment; and *Q.E.P.D.* (*R.I.P.*, 1969), with its descriptions of death and burial by two participants. GW

Marx Bros (their preferred billing) American comedy team. The first to perform were **Gummo** (Milton, 1897–1977) and **Groucho** (Julius, 1895–1977), with material written by their uncle Al Shean of GALLAGHER AND SHEAN; **Chico** (Leonard, 1891–1961) and **Harpo** (Adolph, 1893–1964) joined later. Shean wrote their act 'Fun in Hi Skool' (1912) with Groucho as a Dutch-accented schoolmaster, and 'Home Again' (1914), directed by their formidable mother Minnie Palmer. When Gummo was drafted into war service, **Zeppo** (Herbert, 1901–79) stepped in. By the time they topped the bill at the PALACE in 1920, they were commanding 10,000 dollars a week for their hilarious mayhem. By then, their distinctive characteristics were in place: Zeppo the handsome, bemused straight-man; Harpo the uninhibited curly-headed mute, honking his horn, goosing show-girls and taking every metaphor literally; Chico, the saturnine Neapolitan, interrupting his con-games only to crack bad puns and play ragtime piano; and Groucho with his greasepaint moustache and eyeglasses, stooping lope and unflagging cigar, confuting reason on every plane. They played London in 1922 but, tiring of VAUDEVILLE, moved to REVUE with *I'll Say She Is* (Casino, 1924), with its famous Napoleon scene in which Groucho ordered the band to strike up 'The Mayonnaise'. Their next shows, *The Cocoanuts* (Lyric, 1926) and *Animal Crackers* (44th Street, 1928), were co-written by GEORGE S. KAUFMAN, who, with S. J. PERELMAN, was largely responsible for perfecting their verbal style. With the filming of these productions, the brothers moved successfully to Hollywood, although during their MGM period they continued to make stage appearances to try out the comic scenes in their screenplays. Not so much satirists as anarchists, they flouted normality whenever they confronted it. Their film career petered out in the 1940s; Groucho became the star of a television quiz programme and did a one-man show at New York's Carnegie Hall. LS

Masefield, John 1878–1967 British poet laureate, dramatist and novelist. Masefield's verse tragedies progressed from depictions of social alienation in contemporary settings (*The Campden Wonder*, 1907; *The Tragedy of Nan*, 1908) and historical subjects (*The Tragedy of Pompey the Great*, 1910; *Philip the King*, 1914), to biblical themes (*Esther*, an adaptation of RACINE, 1921; *A King's Daughter*, based on the story of Jezebel, 1923) and religious affirmation (*The Trial of Jesus*, 1927; *Easter: A Play for Singers*, 1929). Relying on verbal imagery rather than dramatic action, they indicate some of the difficulties in finding appropriate theatrical forms for modern poetic drama, which led Masefield to experiment with Japanese models (*The Faithful*, derived from KABUKI) and older European traditions (*The Empress of Rome*, based on a French MIRACLE PLAY, 1937). CI

Maskelyne family A dynasty of English magicians. **J(ohn) N(evil)** Maskelyne (1839–1917), trained as a watchmaker, was an expert plate-spinner; he gained celebrity by exposing the psychic phenomena of the spiritualist DAVENPORT BROTHERS as tricks that could be replicated. With his aide George Alfred Cooke, he staged exhibitions of illusionism at London's Crystal Palace and ST JAMES'S THEATRE (1867, 1873) that were so successful that he took over Egyptian Hall, making it England's first 'home of MAGIC' (1873–1904). His sketch 'Will, the Witch and the Watch', using a 'cabinet of Proteus' to effect lighting transformations and disappearances, played over 11,000 times. An ingenious mechanic, Maskelyne invented the coin lock, the automatic ticket-dispensing machine, a keyboard typewriter and a cash register, as well as air-driven automata, the whist-playing 'Psycho' and the sketching 'Zoë'. His wife ELIZABETH, sons **Archie** and **Nevil** (d.1924), and grandsons **Clive** (1895–1928), **Jasper** (1903–73), **John** and **Noel** carried on the tradition.   LS

masks Masks serve to conceal, depersonalize or protect the wearer; they also serve to transform the identity of the masker by presenting an alternative set of features. They may cover the whole head, the face, or a part of the face; may be worn above the head of a performer or be part of a larger COSTUME covering the entire body; may be outsize or miniature. Whatever form they take, though, masks are distinguished from PUPPETS and from other sculptural treatments of the head by their essential incompleteness: the complementary presence of the human body is always implicit; the phenomenon of the mask establishes an active field of play between notions of presence and absence. The masked dancer is an amalgam of the inanimate and the animate, the other and the self, the static and the dynamic, matter and energy.

The liminal and uncanny nature of the mask has led to its frequent use as a link between the quick and the dead. From Meso-America to Melanesia – as far back as 5000 BC in Jericho – skulls thought to contain the life force of the deceased have been preserved, decorated with turquoise, clay, shells or painted designs, and sometimes used as puppet heads in mortuary rites; the intricate wooden *malanggan* masks of New Ireland in the South Pacific may be traceable to this practice. Death masks of beaten gold have been found in the Mycenae of Homeric Greece, the pre-Incan Empires of South America and ancient Egypt. Commemorative masks of striking dignity have been made and honoured by the Ife and Ashanti of West Africa, as well as in ancient Rome. This widespread association of the mask with the ancestral past has been important to the theatre: the masks of classical Greek tragedy (see GREECE, ANCIENT), of *NŌ* in Japan and of *topeng* in Indonesia have all represented human faces from history and myth for communal celebration and reflection.

The wearing of animal masks – in initiatory or shamanic ceremonies, in CARNIVAL masquerades or in the performances of fables designed to entertain and instruct – is a particularly ancient and widespread practice. The oldest probable evidence of masking is a palaeolithic cave painting of a dancing man with a stag's head at Trois Frères, France (c.13,000 BC). In the rock art of Bhimbetka, India (c.10,000 BC), human beings are depicted wearing masks of deer, antelope, buffalo, tigers and rhinoceroses; similar evidence of antiquity has been found from Wyoming to

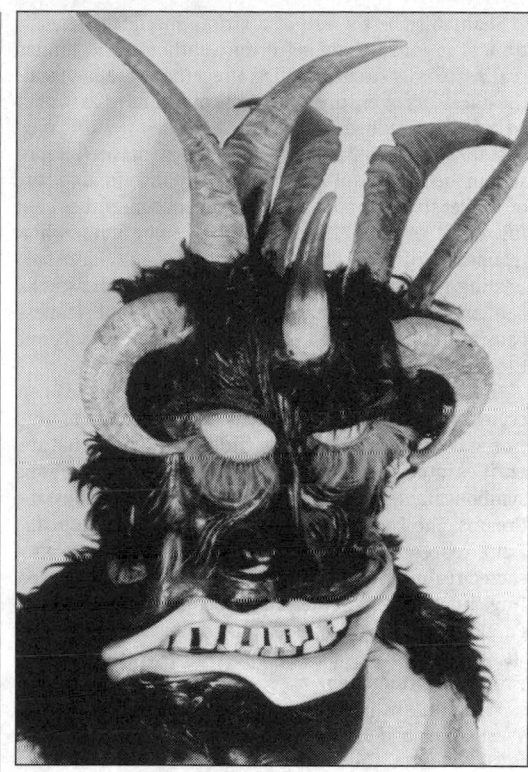

German medieval devil mask.

Algeria. Strikingly realistic masks of birds and of pigs from c.5000 BC have been discovered in the former Yugoslavia, and more recent examples include buffalo masks of the Mandan Indians, monkey and bird masks in theatricalizations of the Hindu *Ramayana*, bear masks used in the seasonal rites of Bavaria and Eastern Europe and in Inuit ceremonies, jaguar masks for sacred and secular performance in Mexico and Guatemala and – in a broad band stretching across West and Central Africa – a vast menagerie depicted with varying degrees of abstraction.

Sometimes, the man/beast duality implicit in theriomorphic cave paintings is emphasized: masks which simultaneously show human and animal faces are featured in Mexico, the Arctic Circle and the Pacific Northwest, where one mask may also spring open to reveal another. Two of the most frequently masked figures in India are Narasimha – Vishnu's furious man/lion avatar – and Ganesh, the elephant-headed god solicited at the start of most performances. Variants of the lion involving two or more performers are found in China, Korea, Japan, India, Indonesia and Nepal – all areas strongly affected by Buddhist tantric traditions. Paraded through the streets and thrust into theatrical and ritual performances, the frolicking, jaw-snapping lion has become the protector of mankind, exemplifying another tendency common among masked traditions: the apotropaic use of the mask as a way of harnessing, containing and placing into the service of humanity all that is threatening and uncontrollable outside the realm of artistic play.

Shamanism – the use of a RITUAL specialist (often in trance) to journey among divine, chthonic and human realms in order to cure the sick, affect the weather, placate the ancestors or ensure the success of a hunt – has provided a fertile seedbed for theatrical masked performance. The SHAMAN (or an assistant) may take up masks to represent or 'become' a spirit helper (usually an animal), a Lord of the Beasts sought out as a mediator, or some other helpful deity or troublesome demon. Sometimes whole troupes participate, as in the cacophonous 'false face' healing traditions of the Iroquois and the exorcistic Sri Lankan *sanniya yakuma*, in which an array of sickness-causing demons are tricked into the performing space and then robbed of their power through laughter.

Masks often function as revelatory devices, giving concrete form to divine and chthonic forces. They may function as conduits to draw the spiritual force of supernatural entities into a possessed dancer's body, or mimetically and symbolically represent images derived from visions and dreams. The *kachina* and *shalako* masks of the Hopi and Zuñi represent fantastic supernatural figures from a sacred realm associated with the past, while the bug-eyed, huge-lipped *kavats* of the Baining people of New Britain in Papua New Guinea represent phantasmagorical tree spirits, who enter the bodies of dancers in order to stamp out fires lit to attract them.

While masks have been used in medieval Europe, in West Africa and elsewhere to represent benign deities in idealized form, the terrible and grotesque faces of supernatural power have received even more attention, as have various demonic antagonists. The devil of medieval theatre is still represented in the *Fastnacht* celebrations of southern Germany (see *FASTNACHTSPIEL*), in the *pastorelas* of Mexico and in the *diablada* of Bolivia; and demonic masks appear frequently in Japanese rituals, *BUGAKU* and *nō*, as well as in dramatizations of Hindu epics and *Puranas*.

The capacity of the mask to obscure the identity of the wearer has been utilized by enforcers of civic virtue in the Congo and by flirtatious lovers at European masquerade balls, as well as by bandits the world over. This same capacity has facilitated theatrical transformations of age and gender. Classical Greek masks (worn by male dancers) frequently depicted women, as do some of the most expressive masks of Seraikella *chhau* in India and Japanese *nō*. While these traditions often represent women as victims, the *gelede* masks of the Yoruba allow male dancers to pay homage to female power, and *shakti* mask traditions in India, Nepal and Bali invoke terrifying female entities in order to placate (and perhaps ultimately control) the feminine energy frequently subordinated in social structures. The *tubuan* mask in the *duk duk* ceremony of New Britain is a more playful variant on this theme, and the *hexe* witch masks from the German Black Forest and the familiar hags of Hallowe'en are less respectful ones, with precedents in the gorgons of ancient Greece. While most traditions of masked transformation have been restricted to men, there are important exceptions, including the women's initiation ceremonies of the Mende of West Africa, *topeng* performances in the Cirebon region of Java, and the salacious skits performed for and by women after weddings in rural Rajasthan.

Grotesque comic masks arrest and expose character flaws, revealing men and women as conniving, stupid, vain, or otherwise disfigured in body and soul. Apostate monks and avaricious landlords of Korean *SANDAE-GŬK*, the burlesque characters of Old Comedy in ancient Greece, and the rogues, pedants, braggarts and superannuated lovers of the Italian *COMMEDIA DELL'ARTE* have all, through their masks, presented living, comic monuments to humankind's shortcomings. Treated with greater sympathy are the tricky servants *(eirons* of Greek New Comedy) and old people with vital hearts (such as the *viejitos* of Mexico), found in many masked traditions.

Heroic and beautiful masks are also made throughout the world, idealizing the human face and revealing spiritual grace; examples include certain *nō* masks, masks of refined characters in Javanese and Balinese *topeng*, and dance masks of the Dan and Bajokwe in Africa. Such masks often seem to change expression with subtle movements of the dancer's head. Both grotesque and idealized human masks refashion the individual in accord with a type, and represent the type in individuated form. The mask thus provides a theatrical means of simultaneously universalizing the particular and particularizing the universal.

Masks have been made of stone, clay, wood, gourds, leaves, husks, roots, shells, feathers, basketry, paper, leather, rubber, bone, plastic, dung, and probably numerous other substances. Sometimes, make-up can constitute a mask. Performance traditions using such 'pliant masks' have included *KUTIYATTAM* and *KATHAKALI* in India, *JINGXI* (Beijing opera) in China, courtship dances of Massai males in East Africa, Aboriginal rituals in Australia, CIRCUS CLOWNING in Europe and MINSTREL SHOWS in the United States, while 'street make-up' has frequently taken on a mask-like quality, as for example, among European dandies in the 17th and 18th centuries and American women in the 1950s.

In the post-Renaissance West, although the mask has remained emblematic of theatre, it has received more honour than use. Despite the rhetoric of ARTAUD and CRAIG and sporadic efforts by YEATS, O'NEILL, MEYERHOLD, BRECHT, CLAUDEL and others, the stress on a positivist world view inherent in a dominant NATURALISM and the emphasis on the psychologically complex fictional subject as the focus of the modern stage left little room for the mask's imaginative and metaphysical range, for its ability to portray emotions and epistemological approaches to the world in essentialized forms, for its innate and undisguised theatricality, or for its tendency to identify characters in reference to fixed typologies. The mask was relegated to history and ethnography, with limited use as a child's toy, in carnival processions, for pedantic re-creations of historical theatre, or as an occasional 'stylistic device' in 'experimental' productions.

Recently, the mask has reasserted itself in Western theatre, first in connection with a revived interest in MIME and movement training which, starting in France, came to feature both 'neutral' and character masks. This impulse reinforced the revival of *commedia* and *commedia*-like SATIRE in European theatres and among such politically oriented American troupes as the SAN FRANCISCO MIME TROUPE and EL TEATRO CAMPESINO. Peter Schumann and the BREAD AND PUPPET THEATRE took a different tack, drawing upon medieval, Asian and Latin American traditions to fashion giant masks and puppets for shows devoted to contemporary religious and political concerns. Recent multicultural and intercultural works by such directors as PETER BROOK and ARIANE MNOUCHKINE have frequently featured the mask as an integral element of production. As the postmodern Western theatre grapples with slippery aspects of human identity and of the perception/creation of reality, the mask is again becoming a vital element. JEM

See: L. Appel, *Mask Characterization*, Carbondale, Ill., 1982; O. Aslan and D. Bablet (eds), *Le Masque: du rite au théâtre*, Paris, 1991; M. O. Bihalji-Merin, *Masks of the World*, London, 1971; E. A. Dagan, *The Spirit's Image: The African Masking Tradition*, Montreal, 1992; J. Emigh, *Masking and Playing*, Philadelphia, 1995; J. B. Esser (ed.), *Behind the Mask in Mexico*, Santa Fe, 1988; W. N. Fenton, *The False Faces of the Iroquois*, Norman, Okla., 1992; E. Fergusson, *Dancing Gods: Indian Ceremonials of New Mexico and Arizona*, Albuquerque, 1931; M. Gimbutas, *The Goddesses and Gods of Old Europe 6500–3500 BC*, London, 1982; A. Hammoudi, *The Victim and Its Masks*, Chicago, 1993; B. Kapferer, *A Celebration of Demons*, Bloomington, 1981; A. Lommel, *Masks: Their Meaning and Function*, tr. N. Fowler, London, 1972; P. McFarren (ed.), *Masks of the Bolivian Andes*, Seattle, 1994; J. Mack (ed.), *Masks and the Art of Expression*, New York, 1994; E. Malin, *A World of Faces: Masks of the Northwest Coast Indians*, Portland, Oreg., 1978; Ministry of Information and Culture (ed.), *Masks of Korea*, Seoul, 1981; D. A. Napier, *Masks, Transformation and Paradox*, Berkeley, 1984; J. Nunley and J. Bettelheim (eds), *Caribbean Festival Arts*, Seattle, 1988; J. Pani, *World of Other Faces: Indian Masks*, New Delhi, 1986; J. Rudlin, *The Commedia dell'Arte: An Actor's Handbook*, London and New York, 1994; C. Schmitz, *Oceanic Art*, New York, 1969; J. Slattum, *Balinese Masks*, San Francisco, 1992; S. H. Smith, *Masks in Modern Drama*, Berkeley, 1985; R. Teele (ed.), *Nō/Kyōgen Masks and Performance*, Claremont, Calif., 1984; R. F. Thompson, *African Art in Motion*, Los Angeles, 1974; Tokyo National Research Institute of Cultural Properties (ed.), *Masked Performances in Asia*, Tokyo, 1987; D. Wiles, *The Masks of Menander*, Cambridge, 1991; D. Yupho, *Khon Masks*, 4th edn, Bangkok, 1971.

Mason, Bruce 1921–82 New Zealand playwright and actor, whose early experience at Wellington's amateur Unity Theatre led him into realistic one-act plays which caustically analysed New Zealand society. Association with Richard Campion led him to write a series of plays on MAORI themes: *The Pohutukawa Tree* (1957), *Awatea* (1965), *Swan Song* (1967), *The Hand on the Rail* (1967) and *Hongi* (1968). Mason also achieved celebrity with his solo works for his own performance, notably *The End of the Golden Weather* (1959; filmed 1992), *Men of Soul* (1965), *Not Christmas but Guy Fawkes* (1976) and *Courting Blackbird* (1976). His last major work was *Blood of the Lamb* (1980); several television plays have been premiered since his death. HDMCN

Mason, Marshall W. 1940– American director, and a co-founder and former artistic director of the CIRCLE REPERTORY COMPANY in New York. Trained at the ACTORS STUDIO, Mason specializes in the production of new American plays, especially those of LANFORD WILSON (most notably *The Hot l Baltimore*, 1973; *Fifth of July*, 1978; *Talley's Folly*, 1979; *Angels Fall*, 1983; *Burn This*, 1987; *Redwood Curtain*, 1993). In 1985 his award-winning Circle Rep production of William M. Hoffman's *As Is*, one of the first American plays to deal with the disease AIDS, was transferred to BROADWAY. In 1992 he directed Larry Kramer's award-winning AIDS play, *The Destiny of Me*, OFF-BROADWAY. He is the recipient of an Obie for Sustained Achievement. In 1986 Mason resigned from Circle Rep, replaced in 1987 by Tanya Berezin. Although he continues to direct at Circle Rep, in recent years he also has worked at such theatres as STEPPENWOLF and South Coast Repertory in California. DBW

masque It is not difficult to trace the derivation of the English masque from the RITUALS devised to celebrate the presence of welcome visitors in a resident community. Such rituals involved the ceremonial distribution of gifts and concluded with a dance in which guests joined with their hosts. Already formalized in the elaborate disguisings of the 15th- and 16th-century courts, these rituals became increasingly the pretext for display, in which music and dance were punctuated by florid speeches and rivalled by lavish COSTUME and inventive MASKS. During the latter half of the 16th century, these masks were sufficiently notable to give their name to the ceremonies they adorned. It was not, however, an idle whim of BEN JONSON's to prefer the French spelling, 'masque', to the English, since the court entertainments which he and INIGO JONES provided for James I owed much to the Continental precedent.

It was from his travels in France and Italy that Jones developed an interest in the scenes and machines which distinguished his work on Jacobean and Caroline masques. The famous collaboration of Jonson and Jones lasted, despite differences, from 1605 to 34, and included *The Masque of Blackness* (1605), *Oberon, the Faery Prince* (1611) and *Pleasure Reconciled to Virtue* (1618) among its particular splendours. The musician Thomas Campion was another notable exponent of the masque, as, after Jonson's angry severance from Jones, were SHIRLEY and DAVENANT. Charles I and his queen were greater devotees even than James I, and it was for them that Jones designed the Whitehall Masquing House (1637). The court masque, still characterized by dance, music, lavish costume and measured poetry, was embellished at the Stuart court by Jones's perspective scenery (viewed perfectly only from the monarch's central throne) and varied by the excitement of his mechanical scene changes, movable shutters and occasional scenes in relief. For *The Masque of Queens* (1609) Jonson introduced the boisterous contrast of antimasque, in which the urgent need for harmony was signalled by the enactment of disharmony.

The public theatres could not rival the splendours of the court masque, but there are many examples of masques used as devices within plays, often to startling effect, as in KYD's *The Spanish Tragedy* (c.1589), TOURNEUR's *The*

Revenger's Tragedy (c.1606) and MIDDLETON's Women Beware Women (c.1625). The English court masque was brought to a sudden end by the outbreak of the Civil War, and its significant influence is recognizable only in such scenic innovations as the proscenium arch, changeable scenery and the further deployment of stage machinery. (See also THEATRE DESIGN.)   PT

masquerades in Africa 'Masquerade' refers both to a performance given by masked characters and to the masked performer. The term 'masquerade' will be used to denote the performance, and 'masker' will refer to the performer. 'Mask' refers specifically to the face-covering.

The most important masquerades are those through which spirits enter the human world. In these, the human performer is not simply hidden from view, but is the embodied spirit. This supernatural and secret ability makes the mask, the masker and the masquerade sacred and powerful. The ambivalent visibility (there/not there; seen/not seen; concealed/revealed) is a visual mediation between the known world and the unknown world, legitimating temporary boundary-crossing between normally discrete categories of beings. Powerful masquerades such as the *egungun* ancestral masquerade of the Yoruba people of Nigeria, or the *dama* funeral and commemorative masquerade of the Dogon people of Mali, or the *nyau* initiation masquerade of the Chewa people of Zambia and Malawi are not performed often, and then only surrounded by considerable RITUAL and ceremony.

Masquerades assume many forms and can appear as spirits coming from the untamed bush into the domestic sphere, as feared and harmful spirits threatening death or destruction, or as benevolent spirits associated with abundance and the fertility of women or of crops. Whilst the majority of masquerades are specific to the people and area of their performance, some newer spirit masquerades such as *mammiwata* have a more widespread popularity.

Other categories of masquerade represent humans and animals who are typically in marginal or temporary states. For example, foreigners such as traders from other areas, neighbouring people, the cattle-herding nomadic people, or Europeans are popular categories for poking fun at. Other masquerades such as the Yoruba *gelede* represent older women as 'witches' who must be appeased, but women are also represented as ideal wives, as prostitutes and as mothers. In all of these masquerades, it is male performers who represent female characters. Only rarely, as among the Sande (or Bundu) women's secret societies mainly of Sierra Leone and Liberia, do women wear MASKS. Other masquerades, such as those of the Idoma of Nigeria, represent diseased persons (e.g. victims of smallpox or goitre) as a gesture of support, placing them visibly at the centre of the society's concern. There are also many wild or imaginary animals, and while the sacred masquerades arouse awe and fear in the spectator, human and animal masquerades often contain a high degree of entertainment, comedy and informality and are valued for their play qualities. Masquerades can be used as a form of social control, and sometimes a masked figure will publicly reprimand an individual. Antisocial characteristics such as sexual profligacy, meanness, drunkenness or laziness are singled out and the culprit made the butt of jest and mock-ery. Masked figures often chase women and children to reinforce what is considered to be appropriate submissive behaviour.

The masked figure may be costumed in grasses or leaves or else in fabrics ranging from sumptuous and new to ragged and scruffy, depending on the character. The mask itself is made of wood, grasses or leaves, or of textile. Sometimes the whole body is costumed in one piece, as with the basketry masks of the Chewa. Where the primary purpose of the masquerade is to comment on social change, topical elements such as aeroplanes, motorbikes, policemen and soldiers are carved as part of the masks. Carvers, who are sometimes also the performers, develop their own style and may experiment with bold colours in gloss paint.

Almost all masquerades are performed to music, and the individual performance of any masked figure is judged and appreciated by a skilled and critical audience both for the appropriateness of the movements to a character and for the degree of skill in matching rhythm to movement. Masked figures may move in a measured and stately way, as in the sacred ancestral masquerades, or may dart about and change their shape suddenly – as, for example, in the *ekong* masquerade of the Annang people or the Tiv *kwagh-hir*, or like the *onidan* performers in the Yoruba *egungun* masquerades. To be able to change shape is not a human characteristic, so such movements emphasize the masked figure as non-human. Great skill is needed by the performer in order to effect a transformation aesthetically, and how well it is achieved is one criterion of excellence. Similarly, the masker on stilts must negotiate the crowd without falling over, for his skill reflects the ability of the community to negotiate the difficulties in the times ahead. During a performance both comic and fierce masked figures may dash up to members of the audience, startling them with their sudden attention and making the crowd laugh with excitement and admiration of their control.

Powerful masquerades whose roles arise from religious or political beliefs change little in appearance and performance over decades, but new social and economic conditions create new concerns, and so in response new masks and masquerades are created or old ones revived such as the *ode-lay* masquerades of Sierra Leone. Some, like *mammiwata* – concerning a water goddess associated with sexuality and wealth – are popular in several countries of Africa, but nevertheless develop local usage, meanings and appearance, whilst others like the Tiv *kwagh-hir* continually develop new acts and characters but remain performed only by Tiv people.

Masquerades are performed by men even when they are representing female characters. All masquerades are a demonstration of supernatural power and, with few exceptions, men monopolize the performing. Strict rules govern the appearances of all masquerades, and some sacred masks cannot even be seen by any adult who is a woman. Most masked figures cannot be touched by women, nor should women know the identity of the mask-wearer, for to do so would acknowledge the presence of the human performer in the masquerade. Theoretically, transgressions can be punished severely – previously, even by death – but in practice women frequently do know all there is to know, and yet continue to provide the supportive role of audience and chorus in the masquerade. The threat of physical and spiritual sanctions is enough to ensure that most women publicly collude in maintaining the secrecy surrounding the masquerade – a *théâtre de complicité*.

It seems likely that, in performance, masked performers enter a state of altered consciousness; and ritualized preparations such as fasting, sexual abstinence, prayer and sacrifice, as well as drinking alcohol, costuming and covering the face, all combine to free the performer from personal and social constraints. Sacred masquerades are performed only by ritually appropriate groups such as a specific lineage or age set, but initiation into the more secular masquerades is open to most young men.   FHA

Massey, Raymond (Hart) 1896–1983 Canadian-born actor and director, who became a US citizen in 1944. From 1922, when he made his debut in London as Jack in O'NEILL's *In the Zone* at the Everyman Theatre, until 1931, when he made his BROADWAY debut in NORMAN BEL GEDDES's unorthodox production of *Hamlet*, he acted in England in several dozen plays and directed numerous others. Subsequently his career, largely limited to the USA, ranged from SHAKESPEARE, STRINDBERG, SHAW, O'CASEY and O'Neill in the theatre, to a wide range of villains and heroes in films (over 70), and the role of Dr Gillespie in the television series 'Dr Kildare'. His most memorable role was Lincoln in ROBERT E. SHERWOOD's *Abe Lincoln in Illinois* (1938), which suited his imposing presence, craggy handsomeness and vibrant voice. Other notable roles included Ethan Frome in an adaptation of Edith Wharton's novel (1936), Harry Van in *Idiot's Delight* (1938), Sir Colenso Ridgeon in *The Doctor's Dilemma* (1941), James Morell in *Candida* (1942), Higgins in *Pygmalion* (1945), Mr Zuss in *J. B.* (1958) and Tom Garrison in *I Never Sang for My Father* (his return to the London stage in 1970). Massey was the author of two autobiographies, *When I Was Young* (1976) and *A Hundred Different Lives* (1979). His children Daniel and Anna, born in England, have had successful careers in the theatre.   DBW

Massinger, Philip 1583–1640 English playwright, uncommonly prolific both collaboratively and singly. Massinger's father was an agent to the Earl of Pembroke, prosperous enough to send his son to Oxford University, which he left without a degree. He settled in London in 1606 and may have earned his living as an actor. The first reference to his writing in HENSLOWE's *Diary* dates from 1613, and his earliest known plays, *The Queen of Corinth* and *The Knight of Malta* (both c.1617), were collaborations with FLETCHER and NATHAN FIELD. He was to work with Fletcher regularly until the latter's death in 1625. About 15 of the plays once ascribed to BEAUMONT and Fletcher are, in fact, the work of Fletcher and Massinger. They include *The Custom of the Country* (c.1619), *Sir John Van Olden Barnavelt* (1619), *The False One* (c.1620), *The Double Marriage* (c.1621), *The Spanish Curate* (c.1622), *The Beggar's Bush*, *The Sea Voyage* and *The Prophetess* (all 1622). These were written for performance by the King's Men, with whom Massinger had a nearly continuous association from 1613 to 40.

He was a man of strong views, savage against the new rich of the city and bold enough to risk sympathetic portraits of Catholics in *The Virgin Martyr* (c.1620), a collaboration with DEKKER, and, most notably, in *The Renegado* (1624). *The Maid of Honour* (c.1621) dared to attack the Elector Palatine and *The Bondman* (1623) satirized the powerful Duke of Buckingham, whilst the anti-Spanish *Believe As You List* (1631) was licensed only after considerable cosmetic alterations. Massinger's own favourite among his works was *The Roman Actor* (1626), an ambitious TRAGEDY about the Emperor Domitian, which has proved less durable than *A New Way to Pay Old Debts* (c.1621), a COMEDY based on MIDDLETON's *A Trick to Catch the Old One*, and *The City Madam* (c.1632), a reworking of *Eastward Ho* whose original authors, CHAPMAN, JONSON and MARSTON, had infuriated the newly crowned James I. Both plays gain their peculiar power from Massinger's creation of central characters, respectively Sir Giles Overreach and Luke Frugal, whose monstrous appetites threaten to divert comic harmony into tragic chaos. Overreach was brilliantly played in the 19th century by EDMUND KEAN and in the 20th by DONALD WOLFIT.   PT

Master of the Revels This title for the official of the royal household responsible for the king's entertainment was first used in 1494, under Henry VII of England. The first full-time Master was Sir Thomas Cawarden, whose patent was issued by Henry VIII in 1545. Fears of Counter-Reformation under Edward VI and the enforcement of Catholicism under Mary I tended to extend the responsibilities of the office, but the Master's role remained formally confined to courtly entertainment.

It was the development of a professional theatre in London under Elizabeth I that increased the office's complexity. The long-lived Edmund Tilney, Master from 1579 to 1610, was alert to the possibilities of augmenting his meagre income by charging the professional companies for the protection his licence might afford them. It is, unsurprisingly, the rare examples of CENSORSHIP that have featured in historical studies. More generally, though, successive Masters maintained good relationships with the actors on whom much of their income depended. Tilney's practice of charging acting companies for each new play he licensed and playhouse owners for each licensed PUBLIC THEATRE was followed by his successors, Sir George Buc (1610–22), Sir John Astley (1622–3) and Sir Henry Herbert (1623–73). Although there were notable lapses in their effective control of the London companies, the paucity of such lapses is more striking than their occurrence.

In an era of factional politics, the Masters of the Revels seem to have escaped unscathed even when their political overlords were most offended. The tensions of the office may, however, have contributed to Sir George Buc's mental breakdown and to Sir John Astley's preparedness to sell it to Sir Henry Herbert for £150 shortly after the Lord Chamberlain's warrant of 1622 had asserted his control of theatrical performances throughout the kingdom. There is no clear evidence of the effectiveness of this warrant in the office-books of his successor. Our knowledge of Herbert's lost office-books comes from passages transcribed variously from the late 18th century and collected by Joseph Quincy Adams in 1917. They record a busy practice, sufficiently profitable to impel Herbert to fight to retain the Mastership when (see CLOSURE OF THE THEATRES) the theatres were re-opened under Charles II. In the event, he retained the title but surrendered, after a negotiated settlement, most of the power to Charles II's appointed patentees, THOMAS KILLIGREW and WILLIAM DAVENANT. The Mastership of the Revels was no longer of great significance. PT

Mathews, Charles 1776-1835 English actor who owed most of his contemporary fame to his gift for mimicry. He made his professional debut in Dublin in 1794 and was a leading low comedian with TATE WILKINSON on the York circuit from 1798 to 1802, after which he was engaged by GEORGE COLMAN THE YOUNGER for the HAYMARKET in London. Less troubled than Wilkinson had been by Mathews's lopsided mouth, Colman wrote parts to suit his new comedian. His double act with JOHN LISTON was particularly popular – Mathews playing the sharp, quick-thinking comic and Liston the slow, gullible one. He was already popular enough to take his pick of COVENT GARDEN or DRURY LANE in the winter months, using the summer to play at the smaller Haymarket or tour the provinces, when he decided to test out the idea, learned from JACK BANNISTER, of a one-man entertainment.

The Mail Coach Adventure (1808), in which his second wife played a small part, was tried out in Hull and repeated on provincial tours for the next two seasons. During 1811–12 he toured a second show, *The Travellers*, this time with the singer Charles Incledon, and then, from 1813 to 17, a reshaped *Mail Coach Adventure* for himself alone. This evolved into the famous series under the title *Mr Mathews at Home*, which was an annual feature of his acting year from 1818 until his last months, the lameness resulting from a coaching accident in 1814 notwithstanding. A combination of mimicry, storytelling, quick-change artistry, comic songs and improvisation, his *At Homes* were equally popular in England and the USA, which Mathews toured in 1822–3 and 1834. PT

Mathews, Charles James 1803-78 British actor, the son of CHARLES MATHEWS. He trained as an architect and became an actor only after his father's death. Having written some of the material for his father's *At Homes*, he wrote, or helped to write, over 30 dramatic pieces, of which *Patter versus Clatter* (1838) was the most successful. It allowed him to express his versatility as an actor in five contrasting parts. He had made his debut at the OLYMPIC in 1835 and quickly became a popular member of the excellent company there. The manager was MADAME VESTRIS, whom Mathews married in 1838, the year in which they toured the theatres of New York and Philadelphia.

Together they managed COVENT GARDEN (1839–42), where BOUCICAULT's *London Assurance* (1841) provided Mathews with one of his most characteristic parts as the light-tongued Dazzle. He was a new style of gentleman-comedian, relaxed and urbane, who spoke his lines without the conventional histrionic pauses. Contemporary audiences heard it as a rapid rattle and named it 'patter' after the character in which he regularly appeared. Boucicault would later provide him (though Mathews claimed the credit for much of the writing) with another

favourite part, as Sir Charles Coldstream in *Used Up* (1844). The Covent Garden management ended in bankruptcy and a brief imprisonment for debt.

The story at the LYCEUM (1847–55) was similar. Madame Vestris died in 1856, a few days after her improvident husband's release from a second term of imprisonment. He found his salvation in a second American tour (1857–8), which culminated in a second marriage, this time to a woman of means. Mathews combined acting with writing and travelling for the rest of his life. His autobiography was completed and edited by Charles Dickens Jr (1879). PT

Matkowsky, Adalbert 1857-1909 German actor. Matkowsky began his career in 1877 at the DRESDEN COURT THEATRE; then, after a few years spent in Hamburg, he was hired in 1889 by the BERLIN ROYAL THEATRE. He stayed here until his death. He had a herculean stage presence that best suited roles such as Coriolanus, Macbeth and Karl Moor. He was widely regarded by contemporaries as the last 'romantic' actor. SW

Matsui Sumako 1886-1919 First important Japanese *SHINGEKI* actress. Originally a member of TSUBOUCHI SHŌYŌ's Literary Arts Society (Bungei Kyōkai) where she created a sensation as Nora in IBSEN's *A Doll's House*, Matsui went on to help establish the Art Theatre (Geijutsuza) with her lover, Shimamura Hōgetsu, an important literary critic and also a former member of Tsubouchi's group. An important force in the 1910s, the Art Theatre tried to balance commercial success and artistic integrity. In despair over Shimamura's death from influenza in November 1918, Matsui took her own life on 5 January 1919. DGG

Matthews, (James) Brander 1852-1929 American educator, scholar, critic and playwright. Born in New Orleans to wealthy parents, Matthews grew up in New York and was educated at Columbia University. He entered law school in 1871, but became more interested in French drama and in writing novels and plays. From 1875 to 95 he wrote for the *Nation*; in 1878 he penned his first original play, *Margery's Lovers*, and from 1891 until his retirement in 1924 he taught drama at Columbia. In 1902 he was given the title of professor of dramatic literature, the first such post in American universities. His wide knowledge of French, English and American theatre is reflected in his 24 books; the best-known are *The French Dramatists of the Nineteenth Century* (1882), *Development of the Drama* (1903) and *Principles of Playmaking* (1919). He also wrote two volumes of memoirs: *These Many Years* (1917) and *Rip Van Winkle Goes to the Play* (1926). His view that a play is intended primarily to be performed rather than read brought credibility to theatre as an academic subject. TLM

Matura, Mustapha 1939- Trinidad-born playwright of East Indian ancestry, who moved to England in 1960 and is considered a major British dramatist. His first full-length play, *As Time Goes By*, produced at the TRAVERSE THEATRE in Edinburgh and at the ROYAL COURT in London, won the George Devine and John Whiting awards in 1971. Since then he has written 20-odd plays and has enjoyed productions in London, Manchester, Edinburgh, Chicago, Washington, DC, and in TRINIDAD. In 1978 he founded, and is now director of, the Black Theatre Co-operative in London, which has toured Holland, Denmark and Germany.

Matura's plays are set in Trinidad and among Caribbean communities in Britain. They examine the political and psychological effects of colonization on both the colonizer and the colonized. Thus *Play Mas'* (1974) shows how an unpopular government in Trinidad uses carnival (see TRINIDAD CARNIVAL) to entrap revolutionaries; *Rum and Coca Cola* (1976) reveals the dependency and secret hostility of calypsonians as they await tourists on a beach; and *The Coup* (1991) gives a farcical treatment of an attempted Black Power takeover of government, suggesting the impotence of a newly independent country to cope with world politics. Matura is skilful in his use of dialect, which he often employs to comic effect – especially notable in *Playboy of the West Indies* (1984; published in New York 1988), his adaptation of SYNGE's *Playboy of the Western World*. By contrast, the transformation of CHEKHOV's *Three Sisters* into *Trinidad Sisters* (1988) exposes the emptiness at the heart of the colonial's reputed love for the 'mother country'.

Matura has also written extensively for British television, notably for the Channel Four series *No Problem* (1983) and the BBC's *Black Silk* (1985; see TELEVISION DRAMA). He has published his plays in pairs or groups: e.g. *As Time Goes By* and *Black Pieces* (1972); *Nice, Rum and Coca Cola* and *Welcome Home, Jacko* (1980); *Play Mas', Independence* and *Meetings* (1982).   EGH

Maugham, (William) Somerset 1874–1965 British novelist and playwright. Maugham qualified as a surgeon. His early light comedies – from *Marriages Are Made in Heaven* (staged in Berlin, 1899) and *A Man of Honour* (produced by the STAGE SOCIETY, 1903) to *Caroline* (performed as *The Unattainable*, 1916) – reflect his view that drama is a craft of the order of woodcarving or dancing, rather than an art. Designed to appeal to a wide audience, the combination, in his plays, of tight construction, wit and unpretentious absence of any serious theme was so successful that in 1908 he had four running simultaneously in London: *Lady Frederick*, *Mrs Dot*, *Jack Straw* and *The Explorer*. With *Our Betters* (1917), in which adultery reveals apparent upper-class respectability as an empty façade, Maugham's comedy began to focus on social issues; and his masterpiece *The Circle* (1921) deals with repeated behaviour patterns over two generations, setting up expectations, in the satiric depiction of manners, and uses ironic reversal to expose the gap between conventional morality and personal fulfilment. The combination of cynicism and polished wit in these plays has been not unjustifiably compared to WYCHERLEY and CONGREVE. However, the serious commentary on sexual relationships, continued in *The Constant Wife* (1926) and *The Breadwinner* (1930), was extended into less comfortable and unconventional areas like miscegenation (*East of Suez*, 1922) and euthanasia (*The Sacred Flame*, 1928).

His work became increasingly didactic, and after the failure of *Sheppey* (1933), which portrays the martyrdom of a common man who is condemned as insane when he attempts to live according to Christ's teaching, Maugham abandoned drama in disgust at the public response to his plays. Although his reputation as a dramatist may have declined, the serious comedies of his middle period have been frequently revived since GIELGUD's production of *The Circle* in his outstanding 1944–5 season at the HAYMARKET Theatre.   CI

Mauritius Mauritius, a small island in the Indian Ocean, has been independent since 1968. During French rule (1722–1810) slaves were brought to the island from Africa, and when slavery was abolished in 1834 under British rule (1810–1968) indentured labourers were brought in from India. The population (1 million) is thus multi-ethnic and multilingual. English is the official language, but French is more widely spoken; there are several ancestral languages of Asian origin, and Creole is the lingua franca.

Both formal and non-formal theatre have always been an integral part of the cultural scene. The slaves brought with them from Africa a type of happening known as *sega*, the Indian immigrants came with their folk-drama, and the Europeans at a very early stage of settlement showed their interest in formal theatre. According to the historian Antoine Chelin, the first theatre building was fitted up in 1754. From then onwards theatrical activities with a heavy bias towards lyrical drama, performed by French artists for a francophone elite, thrived. Although Mauritius was formally ceded to Britain in 1814, the first English play was not staged until 1823. And it was only in 1932, with the founding of the Mauritius Dramatic Club, that theatre in English really started to develop.

We have to wait for the late 1930s to see the emergence of notable Mauritian performing artists like Amédée Poupard, Max Moutia and Yves Forget. During the Second World War, as a result of shortage of films from India, a new form of entertainment in Hindustani was created: *natak* (dance-drama). The postwar and pre-independence period saw the development of other new trends. First, several local writers tried their hand at playwriting in French and Hindi. Second, since the organization of the first Youth Drama Festival in 1951 the interest in theatre activities has substantially increased, to reach a much wider audience and to motivate young talents. Another boost came with the founding of the Société des Metteurs en Scène (Producers' Society, 1966).

Since independence, through stage, radio and television local writers in different languages have been able to reach an ever wider audience. The Youth Drama Festival, which originally accepted only entries in English, is now open to all the languages of Mauritius. The most spectacular development is perhaps the rise of Creole as a powerful vehicle of dramatic expression. It seems that in order to address as many people as possible and to be in a position to catch the mood and to express the major preoccupations of Mauritius, playwrights and directors have opted for Creole as the most effective language for dramatic experiment.

Asize Asgarally, who struck the imagination in the 1960s by writing and staging several plays in English, switched in the 1970s to Creole. His last play *Ritsitatane* is the first history play in a language that was until quite recently considered unfit for anything but cheap comic sketches. Henri Favory, too, has written and staged several plays in Creole, of which *Tras* is the best-known. The director Rajoo Ramana has successfully translated and adapted several plays to fit the current mood and taste. Over the last decade, the Mauritian public has been able to see and read works of SHAKESPEARE in the new theatre language. Besides direct translation of such plays as *Othello* and *The Merchant of Venice*, Shakespeare has also inspired original creation, or re-creation. *Macbeth* has become *Zeneral Makbef*, and *The Tempest*, *Toufann*.

Non-formal theatrical activities still enliven important occasions such as weddings, anniversaries and end-of-the-year parties, but technological progress in the field of entertainment (particularly television and video) has considerably reduced their importance. Formal theatrical activities are dynamic, thanks to the dedication of a handful of artists (writers, actors, directors). The most original contribution of dramatic art to social and cultural growth in Mauritius is probably in the field of language. Be it original creation or re-creation through translation, dramatic literature has greatly enhanced the process of promotion and standardization of Mauritian Creole.   DV

See: A. Chelin, *Le Théâtre à l'Île Maurice*, Mauritius, 1954; G. A. Decotter, *Le Plaza*,

Mayakovsky, Vladimir (Vladimirovich) 1893–1930 Grandiloquent Soviet futurist poet and dramatist, the self-dramatizing 'loud-mouthed Zarathustra' of his day. His noisy hooliganism and eccentric individualism served an intellectual anarchism which hopefully forecast a new age of freedom. A Georgian by birth and a Bolshevik from 1908, Mayakovsky co-signed the futurist manifesto (see FUTURISM) *A Slap in the Face of Public Taste* (1912) with his 'real teacher', painter-poet David Burlyuk, and launched his literary career. In his poetry, which includes *Me* (his first collection, 1913) and the narrative poems *A Cloud in Trousers* (1915), *The Backbone Flute* (1915), *War and Peace* (1916) and *Man* (1917), he cultivated a concrete, unpoetic, dissonant style of writing, consisting of staccato rhythms and coarsely colloquial speech – meant to counteract the refinement of the previous generation's SYMBOLISM and to embody the Russian futurist poetic. The poems likewise manifested soon-to-be familiar Mayakovskian themes: love's pain and disappointment; the poet's loneliness and alienation from the bourgeois world; the concordance of art, religion and revolution.

Although he never officially joined the Communist Party, never read Lenin's works (Lenin in turn found his art incomprehensible) and was on uneasy terms with GORKY, Mayakovsky, in his *Directive to the Army of Art* (1918), called for futurism to join forces with Bolshevism. In the latter he saw the faith in man as conqueror of history and nature, the breaking with the past and sense of moment, which the futurists extolled. Throughout the 1920s he created effective propagandist art: verse-captioned cartoons (*Windows of the Russian Telegraph Agency*, 1919); poetry (*Left March*, 1919; *Vladimir Ilyich Lenin*, 1924); advertising jingles for state stores (1923–5); the avant-garde journals *Lef* (1923–5) and *New Lef* (1927–8); and a series of plays and playlets mixing Russian folk idioms and Party slogans, moving-poster imagery, farcical and CIRCUS techniques – *And What If?*, *May First Daydreams in a Bourgeois Armchair*, *A Small Play about Priests Who Do Not Understand What Is Meant by the Holiday*, *How Some People Spend Time Celebrating Holidays*, *The Championship of the Universal Class Struggle* (all written 1920) and *Moscow Is Burning* (1930). His major dramatic works embody his preoccupation with time and its effects on personality (primarily his own), sociopolitical structures and the fate of the human race. *Vladimir Mayakovsky, A Tragedy* (1913), which he produced and acted in (in a programme with the futurist OPERA *Victory Over the Sun*), is a monodrama depicting

Set design by K. S. Malevich for Mayakovsky's carnivalesque political allegory, *Mystery-Bouffe*, 1918/21. Pictured is the earth, and the proletarian (Unclean) and bourgeois (Clean) survivalists who have fled it.

the transformation of the author as solitary artistic genius into saviour of the people. It reflects the recurring Mayakovsky-as-Christ theme, the author's interest in cinema (he wrote 13 film scenarios) and the influence of EVREINOV. *Mystery-Bouffe* (1918, revised version 1921) is a neo-mystery-fantasy-SATIRE in which the people establish paradise on earth. The premiere production was co-directed by Mayakovsky and MEYERHOLD and designed by Malevich.

His two greatest plays, *The Bedbug* (1929) and *The Bathhouse* (1930), are GOGOLIAN social satires which sharply criticize the petty bourgeoisie and the communist bureaucracy and grotesquely parody the promised future utopia, while expressing nostalgia for the romantic revolutionary past. Both plays were given coolly received theatricalist stagings by Meyerhold at his Moscow theatre, a fact which may have contributed, along with Mayakovsky's disappointment in love and in the course that the Revolution had taken, to his suicide in 1930. Stalin's rehabilitation of the poet in 1935 led to the republication of work banned since 1930. Until 1954 he was glorified as the 'drummer of the Revolution', but after de-Stalinization he was admired for his artistic merit.   SG

Mayfest This event (1983 to the present day) presents a programme of international popular music and drama in Glasgow during the first two weeks of May each year.   LM

Mayne, Rutherford [Samuel Waddell] 1878–1967 A successful Irish ULSTER LITERARY THEATRE actor and playwright. Except for *Peter* (1930), the action largely its protagonist's dream, Mayne's plays are much of their period, influenced by his experiences with the Land Commission. *The Troth* (1909) and *Red Turf* (1911) turn on landlordism and land rivalry. *The Drone* (1908) was probably the most popular Ulster comedy of its time.   DM

Mayo, Frank 1839–96 American actor and manager. Born and educated in Boston, Mayo made his stage debut in 1856 at the American Theatre in San Francisco; served as leading man at Maguire's Opera House during 1863–5; and took a similar position at the BOSTON THEATRE during 1865–6. He was competent in roles such as Hamlet, Iago, Othello and Jack Cade, but garnered critical and popular acclaim for his Badger in *The Streets of New York*. Making his New York debut in 1869, Mayo remained an outsider, touring as a star in his own company. In 1872 he first acted the frontiersman in the play *Davy Crockett*, a part he would perform over 2000 times. He wrote several plays in the 1880s but none was successful. In 1895 he adapted Mark Twain's *Pudd'nhead Wilson* for the stage and played the title role to popular acclaim until his death the following year. In his day he was thought a 'natural' actor because he underplayed the emotional scenes. While a versatile actor, Mayo found success only in roles that promoted YANKEE individualism or the myth of the American FRONTIER.   TLM

Mayol, Félix (Ludovic) 1872–1941 French MUSIC-HALL performer, originally from Toulon. He attained stardom at the Paris Scala in 1902, with 'Viens poupoule'. Mayol's distinctive blond quiff, lily-of-the-valley buttonhole and elo-

quent, if over-illustrative, hand gestures were widely publicized and imitated. He ennobled the *caf' conc'* (*café concert*; see CAFÉ CHANTANT) style by substituting gesticulatory MIME for the usual frenetic movements, and his repertory was extensive, ranging from gooey sentimentality to sly innuendo. He managed his own Concert Mayol from 1909 to 1914; it remained an important venue for singers until it was turned into a porno cinema and then closed in 1979. Mayol aged into a self-caricature who staged seven farewell appearances and finally retired in 1938.   LS

Mazurier, Charles-François 1798–1828 French acrobatic MIME artist and dancer; already a star in Lyons when he made his Parisian debut at the Porte-Saint-Martin (1824 see BOULEVARD) in *Polichinelle vampire*, which presented the French PUNCH as a greedy, hyperactive, ebullient type. His masterpiece was *Jocko, or The Brazilian Ape* (1825), a grotesque amalgam of pantomime, knockabout and MELODRAMA; audiences in Paris and London wept copiously over the death of a monkey. Mazurier's performances influenced the RAVELS, the Prices, the HANLON-LEES and the KIRALFYS, who preserved his repertory to 1893. When he died of consumption aggravated by fatigue, his body was denied Christian rites.   LS

Mbogo, Emmanuel 1947– Tanzanian playwright. He has published two plays in Swahili, *Giza Limeingia* (*The Dawn of Darkness*, c.1980) on the advantages of *Ujamaa* villages, and *Tone la mwisho* (*The Last Drop*, 1985), on the liberation struggle in Zimbabwe. Mbogo is a Research Fellow at the Institute of Kiswahili Research at the University of Dar es Salaam, but presently is working at Moi University, Kenya, where his playwriting activities continue.   PMM

Mbowa, Rose fl.1970– Ugandan playwright and academic. Educated at the Universities of Makerere and Leeds, where she gained a BA and MA and a diploma in drama, Professor Mbowa now heads the Department of Dance and Drama at Makerere. She has collaborated with JIMMY KATUMBA in overseas tours. Her play *Mother Uganda* (1987) links music and dance from all parts of Uganda with a simple story in which 'Mother Uganda' attempts to bring all her warring children into harmony. The play has toured in Europe as well as Uganda. Mbowa and her students are deeply engaged in community-based theatre projects. Her plays are usually written in response to a particular need, involve all the theatrical arts and, while written in English, translate easily.   MMAC

Mda, Zakes 1948– South African playwright, writer on theatre, poet and painter. Mda was born in the Eastern Cape Province of South Africa, and educated in Lesotho, Switzerland, the USA and South Africa. His first prominent play was *Dead End*, produced in 1979. In the previous year he had won an Amstel Merit award for his play *We Shall Sing for the Fatherland*, and in 1979 he won the Amstel Playwright of the Year award for *The Hill*. These three plays dealt, respectively, with the relationship between prostitution and apartheid, the betrayal of liberation fighters by post-independence politicians, and the effects of South African race policies on labour migrants in the subcontinent. *Dark Voices Ring* (1979) and *The Road* (1982) similarly deal with labour and politics. Mda differs from the major South African theatre exponents of his time in that he never foregrounds political debate, but rather focuses his action upon the interplay of characters who happen to be formed by their political context. More recently, he has concentrated on the uses of theatre-for-development (see THIRD WORLD POPULAR THEATRE), and in 1993 published a major scholarly treatise on the subject, *When People Play People*. He also works as a UNICEF consultant on rural development. IS

Meadow, Lynne [Carolyn] 1946– American director, who has served as artistic director of the MANHATTAN THEATRE CLUB since 1972. Her recent directorial work includes DAVID RUDKIN's *Ashes* (Obie, 1976), DAVID EDGAR's *The Jail Diary of Albie Sachs* (1979), SIMON GRAY's *Close of Play* (1981), AYCKBOURN's *Woman in Mind* (1988), Lee Blessing's *Eleemosynary* (1989) and Ayckbourn's *A Small Family Business* (1992). Her style is described as 'smooth and unobtrusive', aimed at 'getting something reduced to its essence'. A Yale School of Drama graduate, Meadow received 1981's MARGO JONES Award, 1989's Drama Desk Award for Outstanding Achievement and Torch of Hope Award, 1990's Distinguished Woman's Award from the Northwood Institute and 1992's National Theatre Conference's Person of the Year Award. She has served on advisory panels of the National Endowment for the Arts, New York State Council on the Arts, and Fund for New American Plays, and taught in the CIRCLE IN THE SQUARE Theatre School, Yale University, New York University and State University of New York–Stony Brook. REK

Meckler, Nancy British director, whose productions with the touring Freehold Theatre Company, notably *Antigone* (1969) at the Round House in London and *The Duchess of Malfi* (1970), were acclaimed by the national critics. Meckler directed *Kiss Me Kate* (1975) for the Oxford Playhouse, but became better known for her productions at HAMPSTEAD THEATRE (PAM GEMS's *Dusa, Fish, Stas and Vi*, 1976; and SAM SHEPARD's *Buried Child*, 1980) and at the ROYAL COURT (Shepard's *Starving Class*, 1977). In 1987 she took over from Mike Alfreds, the founder director from the Freehold, but with a home in London's Soho acquired in 1985. As Alfreds developed a gentle approach to the audience and a story-telling style which relied more on MIME and imagination than on props, so she directed *The Bacchae* (1988), *Heartbreak House* (1989) and *The Birthday Party* (1990) with a similar economy of means; but the production which most reflected the company's continuity was *Anna Karenina* (1992), a Meckler production of LEV TOLSTOI's novel to rank with Alfreds's famous version of CHARLES DICKENS's *Bleak House*. JE

Medebach, Girolamo 1706–90 Italian actor and manager. An actor from his early teens, in his thirties he joined a company of rope dancers led by Gasparo Raffi, married Raffi's actress daughter Teodora, took over the direction of the company, trained its performers in the methods of the 'straight' theatre, and established them in the little San Moisè Theatre in Venice. In 1748 he signed up CARLO GOLDONI as house dramatist to his troupe at Venice's Sant' Angelo Theatre: the playwright was contracted to write eight comedies and two operas a year, for 450 ducats. The bargain ensured Medebach an important place in Italian theatrical history, for while he was with him Goldoni drove through his reform of the Italian comic stage and wrote some of his most enduring plays, the actor-manager creating the lead male roles in many of them – e.g. Don Marzio in *La bottega del caffè* and the Cavaliere di Ripafratta in *La locandiera*. His wife similarly benefited from the Goldoni connection, and was, according to Goldoni's account in his *Memoirs*, an excellent if temperamental actress. A sharp businessman, Medebach claimed the publication rights to Goldoni's work, and when the dramatist left him for the rival San Luca Theatre in 1752 he replaced him with his arch-rival, the abbot CHIARI. In the late 1750s Medebach joined the service of the Duke of Mantua as master of the court theatre. KR

medicine show Working from caravan wagons, itinerant pedlars of patent medicines – the North American descendants of the mountebanks of Renaissance Europe – enlivened their sales pitch with VARIETY acts, ranging from simple card tricks and banjo solos to the elaborate pow-wows and war dances of the turn-of-the-century Kickapoo shows. To meet competition from VAUDEVILLE, the medicine show began to offer an idiosyncratic form of variety only occasionally broken by a commercial message. The performances, often changed nightly, were dominated by a blackface comedian generically called Sambo or Jake, a hybrid of MINSTREL endman and hobo CLOWN. The shows themselves, a mixture of ventriloquism, chalk talks, BURLESQUE comedy, prestidigitation and banjo-picking, usually lasted two hours, the eight or ten numbers interrupted by a few lectures with their medicine 'pitches'. The afterpiece, an audience favourite, was a chaotic FARCE involving a sheeted ghost. Certain medicine men like Fred Foster Bloodgood and Tommy Scott continued to play their routes well into the late 20th century, and in 1983 *The Vi-Ton-Ka Medicine Show*, a reconstruction with original performers, was staged at the AMERICAN PLACE THEATRE, New York. LS

medieval drama in Europe It is worth remembering that the medieval period – over 600 years – is far longer than the period of modern drama, but that until the 14th century (roughly two-thirds of the way through) there is insufficient evidence to give an overall idea of the forms and shapes that drama took, because we are dependent upon what has happened to survive and what happened to be recorded. The sections which follow (except for Eastern Europe and Scandinavia) are divided by country, but these headings should be taken in a very general sense of areas where a language or a group of related languages were spoken, since boundaries were often not fixed until very much later, or varied over the course of the period.

Much of the drama that has survived was written to teach; that is, to familiarize people with the stories of the Bible and apocrypha (Old and New Testaments) as well as to inculcate Christian doctrine and encourage good moral behaviour. But medieval playwrights, whether writing for the Church in Latin or in the vernacular for towns or private patrons, were as aware as anyone of the need to entertain in order to teach. Entertaining in the Middle Ages often means spectacle – entertaining the eyes – but not exclusively so; COMEDY, SATIRE, knock-about horseplay, music, ACROBATICS, dancing, all have their part to play.

The earliest recorded drama in all parts of Western Europe is the LITURGICAL DRAMA of the Church. Ecclesiastical prohibitions suggest the presence of other forms, and there is no doubt that MIMES, JUGGLERS, acrobats, illusionists and dancers existed; but how widespread or exactly what their activities were is unknown, since they have left almost no records. Equally it is likely that early folk drama existed, but again there is no evidence. The earliest liturgical drama (and this includes texts and a description of the action) is mid- to late 10th century; the earliest indication of FOLK DRAMA is 12th century. Though it is right to stress the early appearance of liturgical drama, it would be wrong to see it as the source of all later drama. It remains largely itself – drama celebrating the central Christian mysteries, influencing in some cases but by no means directing the course of the later vernacular plays. PM

Eastern Europe Medieval drama in the eastern half of Europe developed in two quite different ways, depending in the first place on whether the region was converted to Christianity by missionaries from the Latin or the Greek Churches, and in the second on the frequency and nature of the invasions and dynastic changes which continued to disrupt the area right through the period. This dichotomy is exemplified in the Balkans: in Croatia, which was Catholic and closely linked with the Holy Roman Empire in the north, and with the Italian states, especially Venice, to the west, both liturgical and vernacular drama flourished; while in Orthodox Serbia, invaded by the Turks in the 14th century when vernacular drama was emerging in the towns of England or France or Croatia, there is no medieval dramatic tradition at all.

In the countries of the Catholic group – Poland, Hungary, Croatia and Bohemia (western CZECHOSLOVAKIA) – Latin and Old Church Slavonic manuscripts of the traditional liturgical Christmas and Easter plays have survived in considerable numbers, while vernacular drama developed in different ways. In Bohemia it was short-lived: there are four liturgical plays in mixed Latin (sung) and Czech (spoken) and a few fragments of 14th-century vernacular plays including two incomplete versions of a FARCE, *The Quackdoctor*, featuring the merchant from whom the Three Maries buy their spices. The speeches of the Maries are, like the liturgical plays, partly in Latin. The absence of later vernacular plays in Bohemia may be attributed to the importance of the Hussite movement in encouraging the development of the native Czech culture in the early 15th century. Hus, like Wyclif in England, was opposed to all kinds of popular entertainment.

POLAND possesses a considerable number of vernacular religious plays dating mainly from the 16th and 17th centuries. The most notable is the *History of the Glorious Resurrection* of 1590, probably based on earlier material and including some information about performance. It is possible also that the traditional Polish Nativity plays using PUPPETS, performed for several centuries to an accompaniment of Christmas carols in Polish and which often include contemporary satirical characters, have medieval roots.

HUNGARY, despite the threat from the pagan Tartars to the east and pressure from the German-speaking Holy Roman Empire to the west, managed to create and maintain a national identity and express it in vernacular drama, though the surviving evidence is mainly in the form of performance records rather than texts. The earliest plays were similar to the Italian *laude*, and there are also many references in the 15th century to the presentation of plays linked with sermons and preaching. A number of MORALITY PLAYS are also extant, mainly debates of allegorical figures (cf. the Italian *contrasti)* or based on the theme of the Dance of Death. A short Latin morality dialogue of c.1388 is painted on the wall of a church in Zseliz. HROTSVITHA's newly rediscovered *Dulcitius* was adapted into Hungarian at the very end of the 15th century, with a Turkish ruler replacing the Roman seducer of the 9th-century original. In some of the religious plays, as well as in the court festivals and the performances of the travelling minstrels or *regös*, there are elements of secular and satirical humour or folk traditions such as the three birds, eagle, owl and peacock, who greet the newborn Christ in the fourth part of the Bucsu *regös* mystery, which combines survivals of pagan winter rites with the Christmas story and a legend of the founder king of Hungary, St Stephen.

Croatia's vernacular drama was first performed by religious confraternities in the Italian tradition. Later a separate national drama was developed whose major surviving text, the *Muka (Sufferings)*, is a PASSION PLAY some 3500 lines long, dating from the end of the 15th century and extant in several manuscripts including one in Glagolitic. The growing domination of the Dalmatian coast by Venice produced in the 16th century a renewed Italian influence on the Croatian drama, both religious and secular.

The development of drama in the countries christianized from the Greek-speaking Byzantine Church follows a very different pattern. The elaborate ritual of the Orthodox liturgy and the eremitical nature of much Eastern monasticism did not encourage the sense of community celebration and festival which nurtured the earliest Latin drama. Moreover, since there is no substantial difference between the Greek of the liturgy and of the laity, the Western European distinction between Latin and vernacular drama is hardly applicable. However, although the evidence for church drama in the Eastern Empire is uncertain and inconclusive it is not wholly lacking. Early this century an Italian scholar put forward the theory that a group of homilies (preserved in 9th–11th-century manuscripts) which contain dramatic scenes and dialogues, especially on the Annunciation, the Baptism of Christ and the Harrowing of Hell, represent the relics of an early and substantial Byzantine liturgical drama.

The main group of such Byzantine sermon plays is those on the Annunciation, which include dialogues between Mary and the Angel or Mary and Joseph. In the former, the Virgin treats Gabriel as a youth who threatens her reputation and warns him not to incur her husband's wrath. Joseph too is outspoken on the subject.

Whatever the purpose of these homilies – dramatic, liturgical or didactic – the combination of drama and sermon is found in many countries of both Eastern and Western Europe, while the pseudo-Augustinian sermon (perhaps originally composed in Greek) is an acknowledged source of the Latin prophet plays. Moreover, the reality of Greek drama, outside the extant homiletic form, is attested by two Passion plays, both surviving in 13th-century manuscripts (though one may be much older).

Christ's Passion (*Christos Paschon*) is attributed in the earliest manuscript (c.1260) to the 4th-century Greek Father, Gregory of Naziansus. Critical opinion on this attribution – which would make the play the oldest Christian drama in Europe – has been divided ever since it was first questioned in the 16th century. The play narrates the events of Good Friday from the point of view of the Mother of God. The text comprises the lamentations of the Mother, St John and a classical-style chorus of wailing women, while the action is narrated by a Messenger. This pattern is broken by the central dialogue between the Mother and the Son while he hangs on the cross. There are no stage directions but the play is certainly susceptible of performance.

In contrast, the other surviving Passion play, a 13th-century text from Cyprus, is a director's copy with detailed instructions for performance and only the opening words of the speeches. An important prologue spells out the director's duties and responsibilities for the preparation and rehearsal of the actors, including warnings against allowing either gestures or costumes which might give rise to laughter. In the 16th century another island, Crete, produced a Greek play of the *Sacrifice of Abraham* which shows affinities with the medieval versions of the subject in French and English, though the closest analogue is the Italian *Lo Isach* by the Venetian, Groto, published in 1585.

The relationship between the Eastern and Western Churches, especially in the Mediterranean, makes it very difficult to determine how far their drama was mutually influential, but the closest links would certainly seem to have been through Italy which, by trade and travel, linked the eastern Mediterranean with the more northerly areas of the west   LRM

England, Scotland and Ireland; Cornwall and Wales It is customary to think of the English medieval theatre in terms of LITURGICAL DRAMA, MYSTERY PLAYS (civic cycles), SAINTS' PLAYS, MORALITY PLAYS and INTERLUDES, and though the actual variety is far greater than this implies, it is convenient to use these terms as a starting point.

The liturgical dramas centring on Easter which are found in the *Regularis Concordia* (c.965–75) are amongst the earliest in Europe. They are of particular importance because they consist of descriptions and texts of the Good Friday ceremonies of laying the cross in the sepulchre, and of an extended *Quem queritis?*, or visit of the Maries to the sepulchre, on Easter Day. All the parts were performed by monks of the monastery. After this time there are very occasional texts and a large number of references to sung Latin drama in churches (mainly at Easter) from a variety of places up until the Reformation, the most important of which is from the nunnery in Barking of the later 14th century. It consisted of an elaborate Easter ceremony, including a Harrowing of Hell, performed by the priests serving the nunnery and the nuns themselves.

A variety of plays performed in churches are recorded (e.g. plays of the Magi, the Annunciation, the Pilgrims to Emmaus, as well as saints' plays). Associated with the Church too are the semi-dramatic Boy Bishop and Feast of Fools celebrations of the Christmas season of misrule, and the more serious representations of the prophets (including Caiaphas) during the Palm Sunday procession. Two rather unusual texts have survived from the drama of the Church. The Shrewsbury fragments (15th-century manuscript) are a single actor's part from three plays, a Shepherds, a *Quem queritis?* and a Pilgrims, with sung and spoken Latin as well as spoken English texts. They are clearly in some sense liturgical. The other unusual text is a pair of English plays, the *Burial* and *Resurrection of Christ* (early-16th-century manuscript). They deal with the events of Good Friday and Easter Day and are strongly devotional in tone. The manuscript was written in a Carthusian monastery.

Plays based on the Bible and the apocrypha, especially on the life of Christ, non-liturgical and in the vernacular, survive from early in the period, if the 12th-century Anglo-Norman *Adam* and *La Seinte Resurreccion* are English plays. If not, there is only the reference to a performance of a Resurrection play at Beverley (c.1220), played in the churchyard by masked actors, to indicate early development. The earliest surviving text of an English play of this sort is the fully fledged York Mystery Play, the first records of which date from 1376 and the text from 1463–77. This is one of the four extant plays of this type: York (over 13,000 lines), Chester (over 11,000), Towneley (over 12,000) and N. town (nearly 11,000). York and Chester are closely linked in many ways. Both provide the whole story of mankind from Creation to Last Judgement (as do Towneley and N. town); both were civic plays; both plays were divided into a number of shorter 'pageants', performed by different craft guilds or companies; both were performed on wagons at a series of 'stations' or stopping-places around the city. There are, however, also considerable differences. The York text is divided up into 48 pageants, Chester into 24; York was played on a single day, Corpus Christi, Chester on three – the Monday, Tuesday and Wednesday of Whitsun week; and the subject-matter does not exactly match.

Information about the staging of the York play is derived from the civic archives and from two series of guild records: the Mercers', by far the most extensive, and the Bakers'. The guild records provide information about repairs to the wagon and about props and costumes. The civic archives provide very full information about the route and stations of the play, its earlier (1415) content, the organization by mayor and council, and the varying responsibilities of the guilds for pageants. The Chester records are in some ways very different. The route and stations are far less well documented but there is far more about such things as rehearsal, props and especially actors – their names (in some cases) and their wages. Whereas the Mercers' records at York, however, begin in the early 15th century, for none of the Chester companies are there records earlier than 1546.

Towneley (manuscript of the late 15th or early 16th century) is in many ways similar. It consists of a series of separate pageants and its time-span is the same. Moreover it includes six pageants which are the same as, or based on, York ones. It lacks, however, the backing of any civic or guild records. It is associated with Wakefield, but even if this can be taken as certain the town records add little information about its staging. The Towneley cycle contains the work of the so-called Wakefield Master, a playwright with a remarkable dramatic range. His work represents one of the many examples of revision apparent in the cycles.

The N. town group of plays (late-15th-century manuscript) stands apart from the cycles. It contains a number of pageants, but also two unique plays: a play on the early life of Mary (c.1600 lines) and a two-part PASSION PLAY (c.3000 lines). The stage directions in both groups, pageants and plays, which are unusually full, indicate place and scaffold staging; and the Proclamation for the pageants, leaving space for the insertion of the place of performance, hints at performance by a group of smaller towns and villages (therefore not a civic play) and indicates Sunday as the day of performance (and therefore not a feast day). The subject-matter is also unusual, not only in the presence of the early life of Mary (unique to English drama), but also in including such episodes as the Trial of Mary and Joseph, the death of Lamech, and a Jesse tree of prophecies of Christ's birth.

Fragments of cycles survive from Coventry, Newcastle and Norwich, and there is a list of pageants from Beverley. At Hereford, Ipswich, or somewhere like Louth in Lincolnshire, however, the records are too scanty to allow certainty about the form or performance of the CORPUS CHRISTI PLAY.

The wagon-staged or processional cycles tend to dominate the picture of English vernacular theatre, but it is important to remember that besides the extant N. town Passion there are quite full records of a Passion play on fixed stages at New Romney in Kent in the 16th century, and of what sounds like place and scaffold staging of a full-scale civic play at Clerkenwell in London; quite apart from all the recorded performances about whose staging we know nothing. The London play, first recorded in 1384, was performed over a number of days (from three to seven) like the great French Passions, but it covered the same time-span as the English cycles, Creation to Last Judgement. There are no records of the play after 1410–11.

The N. town Mary Play may well have been written for a religious guild or a parish celebration, and other short plays may have had the same purpose. Certainly the Killing of the Children (566 lines) was intended as one in a series of New Testament plays performed each year in honour of St Anne. Plays were also staged as fund-raisers for the Church. The epilogue for such a play is preserved in the 15th-century commonplace book of Robert Reynes of Acle in Norfolk. Far larger were the two religious guild plays from York: the Creed and Paternoster plays. The former was the property of the Corpus Christi guild and the latter of the Paternoster guild. No texts survive but since both were sometimes played instead of the York cycle play, and were apparently staged in a similar way, they were clearly of considerable extent. The Paternoster Play is first heard of in 1388 and the Creed Play in 1446.

Equally possible as guild, church or town celebration are the SAINTS' PLAYS. References to saints' plays occur from all over England, from the single early-12th-century example of St Katharine at Dunstable to the multifarious 15th-century ones. They are not, however, as varied or as numerous in their survival as the French, and there are only two extant texts to give an idea of the genre: Mary Magdalen (2139 lines), and The Conversion of St Paul (662). Both are late 15th or early 16th century and come from East Anglia. Like the N. town plays, Mary Magdalen has a series of full stage directions which indicate place and scaffold performance and various special effects, like the collapsing idol, the burning of the temple, and the constantly voyaging ship. St Paul, like the N. town Mary Play, and the Killing of the Children, is introduced and the episodes linked by an expositor (in this case Poeta). The two plays suggest something of the variety of possibility within the saint's play genre.

Like the saints' plays, the moralities are enormously varied. What they have in common is the presentation, usually through allegorical figures, of the struggle of good and evil for the soul of man. Apart from the fragmentary Pride of Life (15th-century manuscript but perhaps as early as the beginning of the 14th century), the earliest morality to have survived is also the one with the largest scope, the Castle of Perseverance (3700 lines; 15th-century manuscript with stage plan). It opens before Mankind's birth and closes after his death. It contains a wide range of allegorical characters, including the seven deadly sins, the seven virtues, and the three enemies of mankind – the World, the Flesh and the Devil, each with his own scaffold. Of the other surviving moralities, two appear in what is now the same manuscript as the Castle, though written much later. Wisdom is a dignified but spirited depiction of the corruption of the three constituent parts of the soul and their ultimate purification. It includes three sets of elaborate dances. Mankind contains exuberant and linguistically inventive comedy while still depicting the struggle of good and evil

Everyman (first printed c.1510–25), the best-known today of all the moralities, is a translation from the Dutch play Elckerlijc. It is not so much a presentation of the struggle for man's soul as a picture of a man's realization in the last moments of his life of what is necessary for salvation. Earlier than Everyman but printed at about the same time was HENRY MEDWALL's Nature, a morality still on the universal medieval pattern. JOHN SKELTON's Magnyfycence, also printed at about the same time, shows the beginning of the shift towards a more specific satirical purpose which gives rise to the polemical moralities of religious controversy.

The use of the term 'interlude' in the Middle Ages is both varied and vague. The earliest surviving piece called an 'interlude' is The Clerk and the Girl (Interludium de Clerico et Puella; early-14th-century manuscript). Its plot is close to that of Dame Sirith, a dramatic monologue of a secular, comic and amorous nature (late-13th-century), and it is the nearest play in English to a French farce. Dame Sirith may give some slight idea of one side of the minstrel's repertoire – marginal letters in the manuscript indicate different speakers, perhaps for a change of voice by the reciter. The next surviving interlude, Medwall's Fulgens and Lucrese (c.1495), was almost certainly written for performance in Cardinal Morton's hall in Lambeth Palace, London. Its main subject is the true source of nobility and its most striking feature, the comedy, is mainly confined to the subplot. After the turn of the century the word 'interlude' embraces all the variety of the short plays of the early Tudor period.

The only true MIRACLE PLAY surviving is the *Croxton Play of the Sacrament*, dealing with the attempted desecration of the eucharistic wafer by a group of Jews and the consequent manifestation of its miraculous powers. The play includes an interpolated quack doctor scene similar in many ways to those of the later folk plays.

Whether by chance survival or frequency of performance, certain areas stand out for their theatrical activities. East Anglia is the source of extant texts of every kind of play: mystery, saint's, miracle, liturgical. Yorkshire was the home of at least three mystery cycles. Equally striking is the survival of Celtic drama from Cornwall. Not only is there probably the earliest mystery play manuscript surviving from Britain, the *Ordinalia*, but also a full-scale saint's play, *Beunans Meriasek* (*The Life of Meriasek*; manuscript 1504), and the first part of another mystery play, *Gwreans an Bys* (*The Creation of the World*; manuscript 1611). *Meriasek* and the *Ordinalia* both contain circular staging diagrams similar in many ways to that of the *Castle of Perseverance*, and in this case interestingly related to the Cornish 'rounds' or 'playing-places' (*plen-an-gwary*), examples of which still survive at St Just and near Perranporth. The *Ordinalia* were performed over three days: the first, Old Testament including the legend of the cross; the second, Passion, and the third, Resurrection and Ascension. All the Cornish plays contain extensive stage directions in Latin or English.

The only other Celtic plays to have survived in Britain (there are some Old and New Testament plays surviving from the late 16th century in Breton) are some Welsh biblical and morality plays and fragments of the late 15th and early 16th centuries, and a late-16th-century play of *Troelus a Chresyd* (*Troilus and Cressida*) partly based on Chaucer.

From Ireland and Scotland there are records and some extant texts of liturgical plays and plays in English. Dublin, capital of the English Pale, had a *Quem queritis?* (14th-century manuscript), and there are lists of pageants for Corpus Christi and St George's Day from the 15th century. Kilkenny may have had earlier plays, but records survive only from the second half of the 16th century: JOHN BALE's productions in 1553 of his Protestant polemical plays, and Corpus Christi and Midsummer plays from 1580. *The Pride of Life*, the earliest English morality, may stem from Ireland or have been copied there. Scotland has a great variety of records from the 16th century, including a surprising number of ROBIN HOOD entertainments. The only town with a record of theatrical activity stretching back to the early 15th century is Aberdeen, with its *Play of the Holy Blood*, the abbot of Bonaccord, pageants of Candlemas and Corpus Christi; but Edinburgh, with Sir David Lindsay's morality, *Ane Satyre of the Thrie Estaitis* (first version performed in Linlithgow, 1540), is the only city whose drama is represented by a text. *The Thrie Estaitis* was given an elaborate open-air performance in Edinburgh in 1554. The city also had its royal entries and

court disguisings. Perth, St Andrews and other places have isolated early references. There is in fact no reason to suppose that the variety of theatrical activity was any less in Scotland than in England in the later Middle Ages.

It is impossible to tell when most of the plays mentioned ceased to be performed. Only the civic cycles have sufficiently regular records and frequency of performance for the effect of the Reformation to be traced, sometimes in some detail. It was not until quite late in Elizabeth's reign (after a brief late-flowering under Mary) that the plays finally succumbed to government and ecclesiastical pressure. The same year as the abortive pro-Catholic Rising of the Northern Earls, 1569, saw the last performance of the York Play. The Chester one survived until 1575, despite injunctions from the Archbishop of York to prevent its performance. Coventry was 'brought forth' for the last time in 1579. Various substitutes were tried. At Coventry the costly *Destruction of Jerusalem* still used the guild organization and their individual pageants, but it was certainly performed only once, in 1582. At York one of the other medieval plays, the Paternoster Play, was performed in 1572, but not again. At Chester the emphasis seems to have shifted to the Midsummer Show, and at Lincoln the play of *Tobit*, performed over two days in 1564, replaced the old St Anne's Day show and its pageants. All this time, records of the visits of groups of travelling companies attached to noblemen's households increase in frequency.

The rather more formal dramatic pieces that have so far been described need to be seen in their context of theatrical and semi-dramatic entertainments and celebrations throughout the latter part of the period. Civic and religious processions, tournaments, triumphal entries, mummings and disguisings, *pas d'armes* and entertainments at feasts, folk celebrations and entertainments – all were an opportunity for spectacle and theatrical activity. PM

France Medieval drama in France differs from that of its European neighbours not only in the survival of some very early texts, but also in its richness and variety. Though its origins are no doubt the same as those of the drama of the rest of Western Europe, and reflect the influence of Latin LITURGICAL DRAMA and of popular dramatic modes, it is difficult to prove that the earliest religious plays derive directly from Latin liturgical dramas, since in the case of France complex religious plays in the vernacular precede, or at least are simultaneous with, the complex Latin church dramas.

The earliest examples of these latter plays are the two 12th-century versions of the story of Daniel, one from Beauvais and the other by the wandering scholar, Hilarius, who also wrote plays on the Raising of Lazarus and a Miracle of St Nicholas. A 13th-century manuscript from St-Benoît-sur-Loire, known as the Fleury Play-book, contains ten plays. Six of these are biblical: plays of the Magi and the Slaughter of the Innocents, the Raising of Lazarus, a *Visitatio* and a Pilgrims to Emmaus, and a unique play of the Conversion of St Paul. Four Miracles of St Nicholas (the only post-biblical saint to feature in early Latin drama) complete this unusual and important collection. Two elaborate Easter plays also survive: one from Tours, and one from the convent at Origny-Sainte-Benoîte which has a Latin text and French rubrics. All these plays are in Latin and intended to be sung, and are therefore liturgical in mode if not in context of performance.

Two of the three earliest vernacular plays are clearly linked to the liturgy. The *Sponsus* of the late 11th century, a 100-line sung drama in stanzas of varied metres, some in Latin and some in French, is a dramatization of the parable of the Wise and Foolish Virgins; though not part of the liturgy proper, the play was probably associated either with Advent or with the Easter Vigil ceremonies, dealing as it does with the arrival of Christ and the Day of Judgement. The *Ordo Representationis Ade*, usually known as the *Play of Adam* (*Le Jeu d'Adam*) and dating from the 12th century, is in effect a dramatized sermon based on the responses in the Septuagesima liturgy; it consists of the Creation and Fall of Adam and Eve, the Cain and Abel story, and a series of Old Testament prophecies of the coming of the Redeemer. After the reading of the first chapter of Genesis, the choir sings the responses, each of which is followed by a loose translation and expansion in dramatic form in Anglo-Norman verse. The *Play of Adam* is a remarkable achievement; it is unique in its structure and composition, and its anonymous author's sense of the dramatic and his penetrating psychological insight, especially in the Temptation scenes, prove that the oldest medieval plays are often among the best. The third play, the incomplete Anglo-Norman *Seinte Resurreccion*, though dealing with the Burial and Resurrection of Christ and thus based on the same material as the expanded *Visitatio Sepulchri* ceremonies, has no connection with the liturgy; its dramatic form and writing are more typical of later Passion plays.

The most striking feature of the six surviving 13th-century plays is that all but one were composed near Arras, then a thriving city, in north-east France. The two plays dating from the beginning of the century both present a religious message in a partly comic guise. *Courtois d'Arras* takes the parable of the Prodigal Son and places it in the realistic setting of 13th-century Artois, whereas Jehan Bodel's 1500-line *Jeu de Saint Nicolas*, the first French MIRACLE PLAY, dramatizes the legend of the saint's supernatural power to protect treasure entrusted to him, in the anachronistically juxtaposed worlds of Arras taverns and Saracen battlefields, the result being a totally original blend of low comedy and Christian commitment. Towards the end of the 13th century Adam de la Halle, equally well known as a composer of music and as a lyric poet, wrote two contrasting secular, comic plays. The *Jeu de la Feuillée* is a kind of student review in which SATIRE on contemporary religious and political issues springs from discussion of the author's wish to leave Arras for Paris. It is unique in that the characters on stage include not only the author's inventions, but also real people (and indeed the author himself) presumably acted by themselves. The *Jeu de Robin et de Marion*, often described as the first musical, is a dramatization of the lyric genres of the *pastourelle* and the *bergerie* (in the same way as his other play dramatizes the *congé*), in which the contrast between courtly and peasant cultures is demonstrated in a series of scenes interspersed with popular songs.

The 14th century sees not only the earliest French PASSION PLAY, the 2000-line *Passion du Palatinus*, but also the further development of the miracle play, attested by the *Miracles de Nostre Dame par personnages*, a collection of 40 plays whose lengths vary between 1000 and 3000 lines, preserved in one illuminated manuscript now in Paris. These plays were performed annually at the meetings of the Paris Guild of Goldsmiths between 1339 and 1382. All the texts take the form of an action in which the dramatic tension is resolved by the miraculous intervention of the Virgin Mary; however, this formula is but a framework within which the playwrights contrive to dramatize a vast range of narrative material which often has nothing miraculous or even religious about it. Thus the collection contains 'miracle plays' based on secular romances and *chansons de geste*, as well as saints' lives, the Nativity of Christ and true Marian miracles. Although comedy is rare in the *Miracles de Nostre Dame*, it is clear that during the 13th and 14th centuries the divisions between religious and secular, comic and serious, are not strictly observed, and that the labels attached to plays, both then and now, may be misleading.

This appears to be less true in the following centuries. From the beginning of the 15th century, and especially after the end of the Hundred Years War, there was a great expansion in dramatic activity, attested not only by the large numbers of texts that have survived, but also by other archival documentation which reveals widespread and frequent performances. The expansion is reflected, moreover, in a clearer differentiation in the types of play – MYSTERY PLAYS, morality plays, FARCES, *sotties* – and, most notably, in the increasing length of religious plays. Although texts between 1000 and 2000 lines were still written, by the middle of the 15th century many plays exceeded 10,000 lines and their performance, of necessity, spread over three, four or more days (*journées*). By the early 16th century, plays of 50,000–60,000 lines had been written, their performance extending over 30 or 40 days. Even the major Passion plays of the mid-15th century were often 30,000 lines long and took four full days to perform. And these texts were not as a rule broken down into small easily manageable units, as was the case in England. The exception to the rule was the tradition that existed in Lille in the latter half of the 15th century. A recently rediscovered manuscript contains 73 mystery plays of between 300 and 1700 lines each, mostly dramatizations of single Old or New Testament episodes, which were performed, exceptionally for France, on pageant wagons during religious processions.

The texts of over 250 mystery plays have survived, mostly in manuscript form, though from the late 15th century many early printed editions were published. The manuscripts are extremely varied in nature and function; though some are elegantly written and illuminated, clearly items of luxury, most are hastily written records of the text, with frequent stage directions, marginal additions and corrections. There are also a few examples of actors' roles (long strips of paper sewn together vertically, containing the lines of just one actor, which were wound around the actor's finger during rehearsals), such as those found at Fribourg, and of producers' texts, like that used for the Passion performed at Mons in 1501, where the stage directions are numerous but only the first and last line of each speech is given.

Mystery plays were in essence historical plays, in that

ne sa maniere ne pris·τ· fil de lice
ndrai pas ma feme qui au cuer me delice

Forms of juggling from the margin of an early 14th-century French manuscript.

they recreated on stage events that were perceived by the audience as being historically true. Virtually all mystery plays had religious subject-matter, and one can break them down into two groups: those based on the life of a saint and those based on biblical material, in particular the life of Christ, commonly referred to as Passion plays.

The earliest Passion plays date from the 14th century, the *Passion du Palatinus* and the 4500-line *Passion Nostre Seigneur* in the Paris Sainte Geneviève Library; these early texts are limited to the events of Passion week. Later Passion plays cover much more – the childhood of Christ, the life of John the Baptist and the Virgin Mary, Old Testament episodes and so on. The sources of these plays are not only the Bible or the Canonical Gospels, but also the many apocryphal Gospels and other Christian legends that circulated widely during the Middle Ages in non-dramatic literature and in contemporary art. The earliest Passion plays were based on the narrative *Passion des Jongleurs*, which is a 3000-line conflation of a number of sources, relating in a lively manner the events of Holy Week. But later Passion plays drew on much wider and more learned sources.

Although hundreds of Passion play performances took place, new texts were not written for each occasion. Obviously, many original texts were composed, but more often than not, when a Passion play performance was planned, an existing text was adapted – lengthened, shortened, modified, restaged – to suit the circumstances. The effect of this is that the surviving texts can be grouped into loose families, often attached to a particular region or

province of France. For example, the *Passion du Palatinus* can be linked to several other texts which are associated with Burgundy, including the 9000-line *Passion de Semur*; there are two manuscripts of Passion plays originating from Auvergne. All members of these families have certain distinctive features in common: e.g. length, external structure, order of episodes, absence or presence of certain characters' names. The two best-known French Passion plays illustrate this state of affairs. Arnoul Gréban's *Mystère de la Passion*, composed probably in Paris around 1450, dramatizes not only the life of Christ but also some Old Testament material as well. Its 35,000 lines, mostly octosyllabic but containing occasional stretches of more complex versification, are divided into four days. The first day starts with an abbreviated version of the Creation, then jumps to the Annunciation and continues up to the episode of Jesus among the Doctors; Day 2 takes us from the coming of John the Baptist to Peter's Denials; Day 3 contains the Passion up to the Entombment; Day 4 deals with the Resurrection and the Appearances. The success of this play is attested not only by the fact that it survives in several virtually identical manuscripts – very unusual for a play – but also by how much it was used by other *fatistes* (mystery play adapters). The second and third days of this play were copied and greatly expanded by Jehan Michel in his equally famous play, printed in 1486; another revision survives in the *Passion de Troyes*, produced in Troyes c.1490. It was also used in parts of the Passion plays performed at Mons in 1501 (along with Michel's text) and in the *Mystère du Viel Testament* of the early 16th century.

Yet many critics maintain that Gréban himself was greatly indebted to the *Passion d'Arras*, a play composed in Arras c.1420–30 probably by Eustache Marcadé; this play too was in four days, 25,000 lines long, and contained most of the subject-matter later appearing in Gréban.

The mystery plays based on the lives of saints were less subject to this continual adaptation, since the saints chosen were often those whose cult was limited to a particular area or town or group of people. For example, in the mid-15th century the shoemakers of both Paris and Rouen produced the same play on the lives of their patron saints Crespin and Crespinien; Saint Martin plays were performed in Burgundy and Maurienne, and at least two different plays were devoted to each of Saints Barbe, Christofle, Fiacre, Laurent, Louis and Sébastien. Almost 40 such plays have come down to us, from all corners of France.

Though the Passion plays and SAINTS' PLAYS have the primary religious function of illustrating and reinforcing the beliefs of the audience, it would be wrong to see them as uniformly serious in tone. Indeed, it is the great contrasts in register that disturbed many churchmen during the Reformation and critics in the 19th century. Next to solemn scenes like a sermon or the Crucifixion, the audience would witness action which was vulgar and violent, comic and scabrous. The best mystery plays catered for all tastes and all moods; they were microcosms of the real world.

The real world – at least that of the peasant and the bourgeois – appears to be reflected in the farces, of which over 150 survive, mostly in one of the four main collections. Typically, these are short (300–400 lines) comic plays involving three or four characters and based on the device of some sort of trick or deceit, played by one character on another; frequently the action concludes with a reversal, so that the outcome shows the deceiver deceived. The setting is often the *ménage à trois*, or the world of commerce or of law; the characters are given real names and a lifelike setting. However the realism is more apparent than real, owing to the stylization of the genre. The careful symmetry of the plots, the often very self-conscious use of language, the stereotyped characters and action are all artificial features, but the very features that make the farces so amusing. This is well proven in the case of *Maistre Pierre Pathelin*, which is usually held to be the masterpiece of the genre, in spite of its untypical length and complexity.

Closely linked to the farce was the *sottie*, which was also a short comic play; indeed some surviving texts were entitled *Farce et sottie* ... But the typical farce is clearly different from the typical *sottie*. The characters in the *sotties* were usually unnamed *sots* or fools, and often wore the identifying costume of cap with ass's ears, particoloured dress and staff with bells. Many *sotties* had no real plot, but just consisted of lively exchanges of banter based on word-play and misunderstandings, as well as acrobatics and slapstick comedy. The titles of the following examples reveal the nature of the *sottie*: *la Sottie des Menus Propos*; *la Sottie des Sots Triumphants Qui Trompent Chascun*; *la Sottie des Sots Fourrés de Malice*; *la Sottie des Sots Ecclesiastiques Qui Jouent Leur Benefice au Content*. The aim was to produce riotous laughter, and the means was

A glove puppet booth from the margin of an early 14th-century French manuscript.

often satirical allegory directed at social, political or religious abuses. In this latter respect at least, the *sotties* resembled the morality plays, which also survive in great numbers (about 70) from the later 15th and early 16th century.

Traditional criticism views the MORALITY PLAYS as a comic genre, but their fundamental aim was undoubtedly didactic, even if their method was to '*instruire en amusant*'. In their scope the morality plays were much closer to the mystery plays, in that some were as long as 20,000 lines, and most of the best-known were of considerable length. The essence of the morality play is the illustration of a lesson by means of a dramatic action enacted by a number of allegorical characters. The vices attacked may be gluttony (as in *La Condamnation des Banquets*), poverty (*Moralité de Charité*), or blasphemy (*Les Blasphémateurs du Nom de Dieu*). The characters may represent vices or virtues, social groups, institutions, or 'moral types', e.g. the Sinner, the Rich Man. In addition to the more usual moral allegories, there were also a small number of political morality plays, like the *Concile de Basle*. The 15th- and 16th-century comic plays were usually composed and performed by societies set up for the purpose. Groups of professional entertainers, often called *Les Enfants sans soucy*, appeared all over France; one especially famous group was the Basochiens, a society of law clerks, originally attached to the Paris high court.

All of these genres – mystery play, farce, morality and *sottie* – flourished well into the middle of the 16th century. Mystery plays were performed as late as the 17th and 18th centuries in some of the distant southeastern provinces. Even in Paris the 1548 Edict of the Paris *parlement* forbidding the performance of *mystères sacrés* was not immediately respected. Thus, in France, for many years in the middle of the 16th century 'medieval' plays were performed at the same time as 'Renaissance' plays. It was the former which appealed more to the general, uneducated public.

Producing plays was expensive and time-consuming and required the financial and personal commitment of patrons. In France the type of patron seemed to evolve along with the plays themselves. The early religious plays obviously owed much to the church authorities; but the Arras plays, some saints' plays and the *Miracles de Nostre Dame* were commissioned and financed by religious confraternities and trade guilds. Mystery plays, being the most complex of all, needed the support of whole towns and cities, and were usually planned and subsidized by the local authorities. Although most performances of mystery plays sprang from religious convictions, several were clearly designed to be lucrative in themselves, or even 'loss-leaders' attracting trade to the town. In France, there is only one example of an individual who financed large numbers of plays, both farces and mystery plays, and that is the pleasure-loving but spendthrift René d'Anjou.

There is little doubt that the theatre in medieval France

Tree of Jesse, one of the floats in the Brussels ommenganc of 1615, with children as the ancestors of Christ in the branches. The painting is by Denis van Alsloot.

was the most popular of all the literary genres. Not only did it reach beyond the literate public and appeal to the masses, but it flourished and evolved rapidly from the 11th to the 16th centuries in all parts of France; this is attested not only by the vast numbers of recorded performances, but also by the survival of over 500 texts reflecting the widest possible range of dramatic experiences.   GAR

Germany, Switzerland, etc.; Scandinavia The medieval theatre of the German-speaking countries divides clearly into 'religious' and 'secular', with separate origins and relatively little cross-fertilization between the two.

Religious theatre includes plays in Latin, in German and in a mixture of the two languages. Easter and Christmas plays derive in some way from the Latin celebrations associated with the Mass, but details of the development are entirely unclear. Recent scholarship rejects the notion of a straightforward line of development from Latin to mixed to German plays. At least some of the mixed Latin–German plays are now seen not to fit chronologically, and are regarded rather as a late development confined to specific contexts. Whereas the original celebrations were part of 'divine service' offered as praise to God, the vernacular plays are concerned with teaching the people the Christian message of salvation through faith in Christ's death and resurrection. Such non-liturgical plays are to be found in the German-speaking area from the 13th century onwards, reaching their peak in the 15th and early 16th, with isolated examples surviving into the early 17th century.

Of all the extant texts and the performances about which evidence – but no text – survives, over two-thirds are in some way related to the Easter story. The majority deal in some way with the Easter story itself. What scholars today refer to as 'Easter plays' (German *Osterspiele*) were in the Middle Ages often called 'Resurrection plays' (*spil von der urstend*) and, as that title implies, began with Easter morning; what are now called PASSION PLAYS (*Passionsspiele*) were often called 'Easter plays' (*Osterspil*), though the word *passion* (masc. gender) does occur, and these included scenes from the whole of Christ's life and ministry besides in many cases a number of Old Testament scenes, especially those thought to have a prefigurative significance for the New Testament action. These Passion plays and the CORPUS CHRISTI PLAYS (*Fronleichnamsspiele*), which deal with the same material but differ in the manner of presentation, occur only later in the Middle Ages, from the 13th century onwards. Amongst the best-known of the earlier Passion plays is the *Benediktbeurer Passionsspiel* (*Benediktbeuern Passion Play*) of c.1120, which like the *Carmina Burana* poems from the same manuscript contains both Latin and German text. The *Künzelsauer Fronleichnamsspiel* (*Künzelsau Corpus Christi Play*) from Künzelsau in Württemberg was performed at least between 1479 and 1522.

The remaining one-third of the plays are spread fairly evenly between four groups: Nativity plays; SAINTS' PLAYS, eschatological plays and MORALITY PLAYS. Nativity plays in German, with the sole exception of the *St Galler Kindheit Jesu* (*St Gall Childhood of Jesus*) of c.1330, occur only in the 15th and 16th centuries. Amongst saints' plays only those concerning St Catherine, St Dorothy and St George occur

in significant numbers. Eschatological plays include plays on the Wise and Foolish Virgins (*Zehnjungfrauenspiele*) surviving in late-15th- and early-16th-century versions; Antichrist plays, of which the only true extant text, the Latin *Ludus de Antichristo*, belongs to the 12th century and the only other two surviving examples occur in a form close to the Nuremberg FASTNACHTSPIEL (see below); and Judgement plays, the commonest of these subgroups. The morality play occurs almost exclusively in the Low German-speaking north and west, closest to those countries where this genre occurs most frequently.

Confusingly, the great majority of medieval German plays are known by titles which relate to the place where the manuscript was found rather than to the area in which the play was performed. Therefore recent scholarship refers to 'the Rhenish-Hessian Passion play from the Berlin manuscript' rather than, as previously, to 'the Berlin Passion play' (manuscript dated 1460). It has nevertheless long been recognized that the extant texts, where they are numerous enough to allow broader comparison – i.e. especially among the Easter, Passion and Corpus Christi plays – seem to belong to a number of areas where such plays were more common than elsewhere. Most notable are the Hessian group, for which several texts are known, and the South Tyrolean group from the area south of the Brenner Pass around the towns of Bolzano (formerly Bozen) and Vipiteno (Sterzing) which, though German-speaking, is now part of Italy. However, it may well be that such ideas of concentration of medieval religious drama in a number of areas are illusory, based on no more than the chances of the origins of the surviving manuscripts. Recent work by B. Neumann reveals a much wider set of references for performances of all kinds of plays than had hitherto been supposed.

The Passion plays, which sometimes lasted several days, were staged in the open air using 'simultaneous or multiple staging'; all those involved in the day's performance entered together and took up their basic positions in fixed locations, called 'house' or 'stall' (*domus* or *hof*), allocated to their group. They remained there throughout the performance, for up to 12 hours, seated except when involved in the action. This single large location, occupying the principal square of the town, allowed spectators to be all around, behind the stalls of the performers. This involved both the construction of spectator 'stands' and the use of the frontages of surrounding buildings to provide vantage points. These structures, required for both performers and spectators, were a major expense regularly paid for by the town council. There is, however, no evidence of admission charges.

Corpus Christi plays were processional, allowing performances at a number of locations along a route, and incorporated *tableaux vivants* (see LIVING PICTURE) as well as dramatic scenes. The surviving material, including texts, from Freiburg im Breisgau and Künzelsau shows the transition from procession to dramatic performance.

Open-air performance to large audiences allowed little subtlety in acting style. This, presumably, fitted well with the fact that all the actors were amateurs, members of the local community who vied with one another to obtain a part. Lists of actors' names are known from Alsfeld, Bozen, Sterzing, Lucerne and Zurzach and show participation by a wide range of social groups, though members of the local administration are particularly well represented. Participation also cost money, since each actor provided not only his own costume but also small props associated with it or with the scene. There is also some evidence of a further cash levy towards costs being made on a sliding scale according to the importance of the part to be played – cash to be handed over before the actor received the separate text of his part. A note also survives from Lucerne that nobody worthy of a part should be omitted if genuinely unable to pay.

The Passion plays do not divide properly into separate acts or scenes, though the term *Actus* is used in some plays; the simultaneous staging allows the possibility of one scene with dialogue going on at the same time as a piece of mimed action elsewhere on the acting area. The action is often interspersed with music, which can either further the action or accompany the walking about which signifies moving between locations. Such music was largely vocal but included instrumental music; paid musicians were the only participants from outside the local community involved in such a performance.

Such plays were almost invariably anonymous. The clergy had a significant role as censors of the theological soundness of the doctrines incorporated into the text and may often have been authors. Names of directors (*Regent/regens ludi* ...) are recorded more frequently; we know of Benedikt Debs (d.1515) in Bozen, Vigil Raber (d.1552) in Sterzing, and in Lucerne during the 16th century of Hans Salat, Zacharias Bletz and Renward Cysat.

Details of the staging of such Passion play performances are known from various kinds of document. First, some textual manuscripts, especially those which served as the director's prompt copy (e.g. the surviving first quarter of the 1583 Lucerne text), contain details of how stage effects were achieved. A similar purpose lies behind documents such as the *Frankfurter Dirigierrolle* (Frankfurt Director's Roll), dating from the early 14th century, a series of incipits and explicits plus a number of stage directions on a series of seven pieces of parchment glued together to form a narrow roll 172in (436 cm) long. Various details about staging and performance matters, e.g. costume, appear in other extant documents, sometimes surviving fortuitously but occasionally by deliberate effort, as at Lucerne where Cysat collected his own and his predecessors' notes.

To him we owe also the most detailed and most famous stage plans from the medieval German theatre, which he drew for the 1583 Lucerne performance and used again for the next performance in 1597. These show the positions all round the Lucerne Weinmarkt occupied by the groups associated with the various important characters. But even these plans, like those from Alsfeld and Villingen, are not unambiguously clear in all the details they appear to state, and must be read with more understanding of all the known details concerning the relevant performances than has sometimes been the case in the past. In particular, they do not give details of the relationship between the stalls for performers, the grandstands for spectators and the buildings behind them.

The great flowering of religious drama in the German-speaking countries comes right at the end of the medieval period. It ended with the Reformation in the areas which became Protestant, and in areas which remained Catholic it continued throughout the 16th century and in subliterary folk theatre even longer (see OBERAMMERGAU).

There is an unjustified tendency to label all medieval secular drama in German *Fastnacht(s)spiel* (Shrovetide Play or Carnival Comedy). Though this label is valid for the majority of extant plays and those known about, it is not applicable to all.

One small group is made up of the plays of demonstrably literary origin representing the clash between Spring and Autumn (*Mai und Herbst* in the titles). These represent ultimately the clash between courtly elegance and refinement and uncourtly excess and self-indulgence. The Neidhart Plays (*Neidhartspiele*) attach themselves to the historical poet Neidhart von Reuental (c.1190–1245) whose works reveal his aristocratic hatred of *nouveau riche* peasants who ape aristocratic fashion and knightly behaviour. Some of the manuscripts and the *Sterzinger Szenar* (Sterzing Scenario), which is akin to the *Frankfurter Dirigierrolle,* contain elaborate stage directions. These plays are, however, critical not only of the peasants but also of the degenerate and effete nobility. The concern of their plots with faeces and the provocation of a fight bring them close to the *Fastnachtspiel,* in which form two texts survive.

Since the medieval term *vasnachtspil* covers all kinds of pre-Lenten entertainment, it is difficult to make accurate statements about the extent and frequency of *Fastnachtspiel* as a dramatic genre. The largest corpus of texts, contained mainly in a handful of 15th-century manuscript compendia, comes from Nuremberg, where the origin of the genre seems to be in the telling of bawdy and scatological tall stories, in turn, in a limited verse form of two or three rhymed couplets per speaker. In these *Reihenspiele* or revue pieces each speaker starts afresh, and only by the implicit seeking to outdo the others does each speech refer indirectly to what has preceded it. The narrated exploits of these grotesquely unsuccessful lovers are often presented in the mouths of peasants, establishing the possibility of connection with the personnel of the *Neidhartspiele.*

The *Fastnachtspiel* is, like the religious drama, an urban genre. Its performers were apparently the journeymen members of the guilds who, during this time of celebacy imposed on them by guild regulations, relieved themselves of tensions at Shrovetide by at least verbal sexual excesses. Small groups went about between houses and inns during the days of pre-Lenten festivity, making a space for their performance on the floor amidst the other revelries – many texts begin with a claim on the attention of those present and end by passing the action back to the wider celebration.

Whilst the simplest revue pieces are scarcely dramatic and are only just emerging from the subliterary folk culture, as the 15th century develops plays incorporating a plot, *Handlungsspiele,* begin to appear, often relating to tales known in contemporary German *Mären* and French *fabliaux.* The only known authors of these *Fastnachtspiele* are Hans Rosenplüt (mid-15th century) and Hans Folz (c.1440–1513). This material brings into German drama for the first time the notion of stock comic characters, e.g. the unpleasant old woman, the cunning maid and the wise fool, as well as for the first time introducing the concept of dramatic intrigue. These plays, like the associated *Lügenmärchen* (tall stories), do not represent reality but use the licence of Shrovetide to turn contemporary society topsy-turvy and present it – as these texts might well say – 'arse over tits'. The effect is not merely intended *pour épater les bourgeois*, but more subtly to remind the audience that the world is not as it should be. If we bear this strand of concern in mind, it is less surprising to find the Nuremberg *Fastnachtspiel* in the 16th century in the hands of Hans Sachs essentially moralizing in tone. A small number of the 15th-century *Fastnachtspiele* from Nuremberg show clear tendencies to social criticism, as the citizens of the Free Imperial City rail at the shortcomings of territorial princes and high-ranking clergy and the venality of secular and clerical office-bearers.

Other centres with a tradition of Shrovetide Plays were Eger (now Cheb in the Czech Republic), with 25 known performances between 1442 and 1522 but no surviving texts, and South Tyrol, where Vigil Raber copied over 20 pieces as well as acting in these and other plays. Serious moralizing Shrovetide plays, performed by a patrician fraternity (*Zirkelbruderschaft*) in the open air, took place in Lübeck between 1430 and at least 1537. An incomplete Basel manuscript dated 1434 contains parts of a serious Shrovetide Play involving social criticism; a scene involving Lucifer sending out his devils into the world provides one of the few clear points of interrelationship between religious and secular drama. JET

There is considerable evidence for liturgical drama in medieval Scandinavia, as there is in most of the countries of Western Europe. There are few texts before the 16th century but many references to plays or ceremonies, and the trappings of plays sometimes survive (the very elaborate Easter sepulchre from Kerteminde, Denmark, for example, or the very early (1250–1300) Ascension figure from Visby, Gotland). There is also the extensive, suggestive but uncertain evidence of wall paintings. Besides the remains of liturgical dramas, there are some texts of saints' plays (e.g. the *Ludus de Sancto Kanuto Duce* (*Play of the Saint Lord Canute*, probably late 15th century), a miracle of the Virgin play (*De uno peccatore qui promeruit gratiam*), and secular plays on the lines of the *Fastnachtspiel* such as *Den Utro Hustru* (*The Unfaithful Wife*). From the 16th century there are a number of plays on Old Testament subjects (e.g. Susanna, Samson), moralities, saints' plays and farces, as well as revivals of classical plays (e.g. TERENCE). Many of these were school dramas. PM

Italy The earliest Italian drama, the sung Latin liturgical plays, comprises traditional representations of the Nativity and Resurrection as well as a number of more unusual and interesting subjects. The oldest extant manuscript of a PASSION PLAY, the 12th-century Latin text from Montecassino, is unfortunately incomplete at the beginning and the end, breaking off after three lines of a vernacular *Planctus* (Lament) of the Virgin Mary. The text has directions for movement and action but no indication of the location or time of the performance – in contrast to the 14th-century *Planctus Marie et aliorum in die Parasceven* (*Lament of Mary and others on Good Friday*) from Cividale, in which each of the Maries and Disciples lamenting

round the Cross has prescribed gestures written above nearly every line of the sung text. In Padua in 1244 the Passion and Resurrection were staged out of doors, at Easter, '*solemniter et ordinate*' (in a solemn and orderly way). The Padua text has not survived but the same events – from the Arrest of Christ to the Crucifixion – are included in a 14th-century manuscript from Sulmona of the role (speeches and cues only) of the Fourth Soldier (*Quartus Miles*). Many lines in this actor's copy are identical with lines in the 12th-century Montecassino play.

Very few Latin Old Testament plays have survived, but evidence of a Creation play in the 13th century is provided by performances recorded from Cividale in 1298 and 1303. In both years the plays were staged on Whitsunday and the two following days, by the city clergy in the courtyard of the episcopal palace in the presence of ecclesiastical and civic dignitaries. The *Representation of the Play of Christ* in 1298 comprised only the Passion, Resurrection, Ascension, Pentecost and Last Judgement, but in 1303 these episodes were preceded by scenes of the Creation, Annunciation, Nativity 'and many others'. A play of Antichrist was also added, making a sequence – Creation to Judgement – very similar to that of the English and German cycle plays. The Cividale texts have not survived but it seems probable, given the strongly clerical nature of the occasion, that they were performed in Latin. However, sung plays in the vernacular including all the Old and New Testament incidents represented at Cividale were already being composed and performed in Italy by the end of the 13th century.

The impetus for the creation of a sung vernacular drama closely linked with the liturgical year was given by the flagellant movement which arose in Umbria in the second half of the 13th century, when groups of laymen – inspired particularly by the preaching of Joachim of Fiore – banded together to do public penance on behalf of the sinful world and alternated the singing of praises (*laude*) to God with periods of self-flagellation (*disciplina*). The first company of *disciplinati* under a certain Raniero Fasano was formed in Perugia, whence the movement spread rapidly throughout Umbria; appropriate *laude* were composed for the different Sundays and feastdays of the church calendar, some of them merely lyrical, others in simple dramatic form. The most famous of the early *laude* is the *Donna del Paradiso* (*Queen of Heaven*) by Jacopone da Todi, a vernacular development of the Latin *Planctus* in which the weeping Virgin speaks in turn with Christ, John and, finally, the Cross itself. Of lesser poetic stature but of considerable importance in the history of Italian drama are the texts of the *Libro de Laode* or *Laudario* (*Book of Praises*) from Perugia. The performance of these texts was genuinely theatrical, as can be seen from the records of costumes and properties belonging to the Confraternity of Saint Augustine in Perugia whose *Libro di Prestanze* (*Book of Loans*) lists cloaks, MASKS for devils and death, curtains, painted cloths and so on.

By the end of the 14th century the *laude* had passed through a series of changes, the most important being that from sung to spoken drama. The plays, now called *laude*, *devozioni* or even *rappresentazioni* interchangeably, used a mixture of verse forms including six- and eight-line stanzas as well as quatrains, triolets and even whole sonnets. The subject-matter is also more varied and less closely tied to the liturgical year. The Orvieto *Laudario* includes a play on the Creation and Fall of the Angels and Man which demands both choral movement and singing; at the end, the *devoti* (members of the confraternity) pray to God to save Man.

Both the Franciscan and the Dominican friars were influential in the development of this vernacular drama. The former used stanzas and scenes from the Holy Week *laude* (including the *Donna del Paradiso*) to illustrate their sermons, as well as creating semi-dramatic presentations like the *Passio Volgarizzata* (*Vernacular Passion*) from Abruzzo which combines the '*Dic et tu*' (Now you speak) technique of the pseudo-Augustinian sermon with the practice of dramatizing the Passion lections on Good Friday and Holy Saturday. The Dominicans used plays as a means of more general instruction: their 14th-century *Laudario* from Aquila contains a long and elaborate three-day dramatization of the life of their fellow Dominican, St Thomas Aquinas, involving numerous scene changes, a large cast and much realistic detail in the presentation of secular life in court and castle. Both these theatrical forms, the Passion play and the biographical SAINTS' PLAY, were to be developed further in the 15th century, which in Italy, as in other parts of Europe, was the golden age of the medieval drama.

The most celebrated of the many Passion plays recorded is probably that performed annually from 1460 by the Gonfalonieri di Santa Lucia (Banner-bearers of St Lucy) in the Coliseum in Rome. The surviving text and records suggest a conflation of a number of short plays covering incidents from the Ministry, Passion and Resurrection, using multiple staging and performed, according to the German pilgrim Arnold von Harff who watched it on Good Friday morning 1494, 'by young gentlemen of good family'. After 1500 the performances became less regular and the play was finally banned by the Pope in 1539.

Among the many imitators of the Gonfalonieri was the Confraternity of St John in Velletri who, lacking a ready-made theatre, constructed early in the 16th century a permanent stone-built stage (the *palcoscenico*) for their Passion play. Set against the city walls, it occupied the whole of the west side of the Piazza San Giacomo so that there was shade for the afternoon performance. The stage was raised up six feet and access was through two doors in the front of the structure, from which steps led up to a passageway for the actors behind the façade whose archways were adorned with Corinthian columns and pediments. The Passion was staged there until 1563, and the structure was finally demolished in 1765 by order of the town council – though fortunately not before Cardinal Stefano Borgia had had an engraving made of it.

It was probably on a multiple stage, perhaps similar to that at Velletri, that the community of the Alpine town of Revello presented their three-day Passion play in the French style in 1494. Other notable performances include those in Ferrara under the Este family. In 1481, the duke had the Passion performed in the palace chapel on a stage specially constructed over the altar, with a wooden serpent's mouth which opened and closed for the scene of the Harrowing of Hell. In Holy Week of 1489, scaffolds for both performers and spectators were erected in the main square of Ferrara (leaving access to the houses and shops), where the events of Maundy Thursday and Good Friday were re-enacted on the appropriate days. These plays, sung by the choir from the ducal chapel, were in Latin except for four scenes in the vernacular, including the Lament of the Virgin Mary.

Mixtures of processions and plays are recorded from several towns, and the extant text from Bologna includes plays on the Temptation of Adam, the Trial in Heaven and the Nativity as well as lists of walking figures. Florence also had processional drama. A Greek visitor to the Ecumenical Council of 1439 has described the magnificent array of mounted and walking figures, biblical, legendary and fantastic, with which the Florentines celebrated the feast of their patron, St John the Baptist. In 1454 the St John's Day procession included a series of wagon-plays.

Although plays were performed in many different towns and communities, the outstanding contributor to the later religious drama is undoubtedly Florence. In the early 15th century plays were presented in many Florentine churches for the liturgical feasts, some of them with complex machinery, music and lights: VASARI describes a paradise and angels designed by Brunelleschi, and elaborate flying and lifting machinery is recorded by the Russian patriarch, Abramio of Sousdal, who watched plays of the Annunciation and Ascension during his visit to Florence for the Ecumenical Council of 1439.

The special contribution of Florence to the religious drama, however, was the *sacra rappresentazione,* a development of the later, spoken *lauda* but written by an individual and performed on any suitable occasion outside the liturgical calendar. The earliest known writer is Feo Belcari (1410–64), who wrote a number of these plays for the youths of the Company of St John the Evangelist, the *vangelista*, whose principal patron, Lorenzo da Medici himself, wrote for them a play on *SS Giovanni e Paulo.* More than a hundred *sacre rappresentazioni* have survived in manuscripts or printed texts; all are Florentine in origin, though many were subsequently reprinted and perhaps performed in other towns and regions throughout the 16th century. Subjects appropriate to the mainly youthful performers predominate in these plays: stories of Isaac, Ishmael (an example to be shunned), Joseph and the Prodigal Son. The didactic force of the plays is sometimes enhanced by a framework of contemporary scenes involving youthful characters: a group of good and bad boys, a father with a good and a bad son, and so on. Many details of production and staging can be gleaned from these scenes, which may even show their characters talking to the performers of the main play. There are also quite frequent stage directions in the body of the text. Not all the *sacre rappresentazioni* were written for boys; many do not specify performers or audiences, while some appear to be written for religious houses: the framework scenes of the play of *Santa Teodora* (*St Theodora*) show the nuns arguing about their roles, costumes and the number of lines they have to learn. A few of the framework sequences were printed independently of their centrepiece under the name of *frottole* (dialogues), thus forming a bridge between the religious and secular theatre.

Comic scenes are rare in Italian religious drama, and

there is not a great deal of humour in the medieval secular plays either, though some of the semi-dramatic debates, *contrasti*, have an element of visual comedy such as the mock battle in the *Debate of Carnival and Lent*. *Dialogues* (*frottole*) between stereotype characters – husband and wife or a blonde and a brunette – together with a few genuine FARCES make up the brief tally of humorous 'medieval' theatre. Nor is this paucity surprising in a period when the classical comedies of PLAUTUS and TERENCE were already inspiring the new generation of Renaissance dramatists. The semi-dramatic *giostre* (jousts), which like the English tournament or the French *pas d'armes* were often the occasion for pageants and maskings as well as combats, also show classical influence. The printed text of the *Giostra di Giuliano da Medici* consists of a series of verses followed by the *Favola d'Orfeo* (*Play of Orpheus*), the first neoclassical drama of the end of the 15th century.

Examples of serious secular drama are the Florentine plays on the stories of *Santa Uliva* or *Regina Rosana*. Although as Miracles of the Virgin they technically belong with the religious theatre, yet in subject-matter and treatment they owe more to the biographical romances than to hagiography, for scenes of everyday life (such as were used in the *lauda* of St Thomas) alternate with marvellous adventures, while in the *Santa Uliva* the action is divided by INTERLUDES involving mythical and allegorical figures. Like all the Florentine plays, these romantic dramas were continually reprinted throughout the 16th century, so that on paper at least the medieval drama in Italy survived long after it had been effectively superseded by the new genres of TRAGEDY and COMEDY. I.RM

The Low Countries The development of drama in the Low Countries ran parallel to that in the surrounding countries, especially France, and the range of religious and secular drama was as extensive. Town and church accounts contain many references to dramatic events such as pageantry or processions with *tableaux vivants* (see LIVING PICTURE), or to drama proper with action and speech, often with music as an essential element as in liturgical drama, or as an incidental element as in other dramatic genres.

Much of the evidence comes from the Southern Netherlands, from the wealthy provinces of Flanders and Brabant with their powerful trading towns; but the Northern Netherlands, in particular the provinces of Holland, Zeeland and Utrecht, had their share of drama. Judging from the many references to Easter, Christmas and Epiphany plays, liturgical drama was important and widespread. Two 12th-century Utrecht antiphonaria contain the *Quem queritis*? trope; slightly more elaborate is the 13th-century Haarlem Easter Play, which ends with the *elevatio* accompanied by the singing of 'Christus Dominus surrexit' and 'Deo gratias', then the *Te Deum*. The most extensive surviving church drama, the Maastricht Easter Drama of c.1200, was performed annually in the Church of Our Lady in Maastricht on the first day of Easter. The role of the ointment-seller survives from an Easter Play performed in Delft in 1496 and 1503. The properties and the helpers needed are recorded in the church accounts and show it to have been an elaborate affair.

The largest collection of early vernacular plays is that in the Van Hulthem manuscript (c.1410). It contains more than 200 literary texts, most important amongst which are four serious secular plays, the *Abele Spelen*, and six farces or *Sotterniën*. Each of the *Abele Spelen* treats of love. The first three, *Esmoreit*, *Gloriant* and *Lanseloet van Denemarken*, are romances; the fourth, *Vanden Winter ende Vanden Somer* (*Of Winter and Summer*), is an elaborate debate. The six farces too are variations on a theme: that of the wicked woman.

The serious plays and their accompanying farces were not conceived as a unity, but grouped together gradually, perhaps selected for their thematic similarities. By the time they were incorporated into the manuscript, the plays had been welded together, *Abel spel* to farce, by additions and changes in the prologues, the epilogues and the rhyme. The Van Hulthem manuscript was probably used in a *scriptorium* as a collection from which customers could choose pieces. There is no record of the performances of these plays, except for a mention of the play *Lanseloet* being performed in Aachen on 14 August 1412 by the Company of Diest, a town in Brabant. The plays could be performed by a small company, and there is a slender chance that amongst groups of minstrels – such as those employed, for example, by the Count of Flanders in 1378 – there were not only musicians who sang and recited but also performers of plays. The *Abele Spelen* and the farces are probably much older than the Van Hulthem manuscript; *Esmoreit*, indeed, may date from as early as c.1340.

It is impossible to discuss any of the drama produced in the 15th century without giving some attention to the *Rederijkerskamers* (Chambers of Rhetoric), whose presence is first recorded in the early years of the century and which were to become such a dominant feature in the literary life of the Low Countries, in particular towards the end of the 15th and during most of the 16th century. These amateur literary guilds were in origin not a special feature of the Low Countries. Non-aristocratic brotherhoods, *confréries* or guilds made their appearance in Western Europe in many places, as a third class of traders, merchants and craftsmen began to conceive of themselves as a separate and valuable part of society. The origins of the Chambers of Rhetoric go back in part to secular devotional brotherhoods which sometimes acted as an aid to the clergy in religious processions and drama. Some brotherhoods became converted into Chambers of Rhetoric. The element of mutual social and economic aid, so strong in the craft and religious guilds, can he perceived in the Chambers too: for instance, in the care they took to ensure that their members were given proper funerals. Whereas in spirit, the Chambers long retained the devotional element of the religious brotherhoods, in their organization they were very akin to the Archers' Guilds. These were common in the Low Countries, originally formed as local defence guilds by the fortified towns. The Chambers developed and made independent an element that was already present in such guilds, that of dramatic activities. Important archery competitions, for instance, were accompanied by other festive events such as the performance of drama or the antics of fools, and members of an Archers' Guild could form an independent organization.

The tamed dragon of St George (a two-man beast) led by the princess in the Brussels ommenganc of 1615, painted by Denis van Alsloot.

Rhetoricians are also known to have accompanied the archers to competitions.

In their activities the Chambers of Rhetoric resemble societies that were numerous in the French-speaking provinces in the Burgundian Netherlands before the Chambers appeared – the so-called *puys*. Poetry and drama, specifically in honour of Our Lady and the Saints, were their main activities and there was a strong competitive element, just as in the case of the Chambers of Rhetoric. In the Flemish-speaking provinces similar societies spread like wildfire. In the 15th century about 60 Chambers were established, and the number grew to about 180 in the 16th. They varied in size, from about 16 to 150 members.

Their dramatic activities consisted of the writing and the production of plays, religious and secular, serious and comic. The Rhetoricians also played an active part in all manner of pageantry and processions. In religious processions, often held on an important feastday such as Palm Sunday, Easter, Corpus Christi or Shrove Tuesday, they often organized *tableaux vivants* or wagon-plays with biblical or historical subject-matter. On secular occasions, too, the Rhetoricians had important contributions to make, and, indeed, were expected by the town to add lustre to such occasions as the celebrations of a peace, royal or ducal entries, weddings, coronations, and funerals of their immediate overlords or members of the ducal or royal family. A very specific item on such occasions was the triumphal arch, the development of which influenced the stage façades of the Rhetoricians. Instead of the simple platform with a curtained-off booth, 16th-century pictures show architectural façades with elaborate classically inspired decoration, with a number of entrances and compartments behind the screen which could be incorporated into the available acting space in a number of different ways.

An important part of the Rhetoricians' activities was their participation in local or regional literary competitions. A competition was an occasion which involved and affected the whole town. After the ceremonial entries came the declamation of the Prologue on a set theme, and then the actual plays: the *esbatement*, the *spel van sinnen* (MORALITY PLAY) and the *factie*, a short comic piece of street theatre. Prizes were given for all these aspects of the competition as well as for the best actor, the best fool, and the most splendid celebration afterwards.

Strict rules were laid down for the length and subject-matter of the entries, and in particular for the allegorical *spelen van sinnen*. Bound as they were to answer particular moral, religious, social or ethical questions, they are often somewhat stiff and stilted. The *esbatementen*, however, were often comic and displayed verve and lively dramatic action. They were not printed, but used as exchange material, and were copied out by other Chambers and played again, sometimes till well into the 18th century.

The *spelen van sinnen*, the moralities, were the most distinctive form to be created by the Rhetoricians, but from the beginning of the 15th century there is evidence to indicate that the guild members were involved in religious drama very akin to that, for instance, in France. The Low Countries had their MYSTERY and MIRACLE PLAYS, and the few surviving texts are witnesses to what must have been a lively and fully developed tradition. In fact, it is not easy to find 15th- and 16th-century drama in the Low Countries without the implicit or explicit involvement of the Rhetoricians.

The Chambers of Rhetoric produced a great deal of religious drama, and they are connected with the performing of the only surviving mystery plays. *The First Joy of Mary* (*Die Eerste Bliscap van Maria*) and *The Seventh Joy of Our Lady* (*Die Sevenste Bliscap van Onser Vrouwen*) are the only remnants of a cycle of seven plays; they relate, respectively, the events leading up to the Annunciation and to the Death and Assumption of Our Lady. The first recorded performance of *The First Joy* took place in Brussels in 1448, the last known performance of *The Seventh Joy* in 1566. In 1556 *The Fourth Joy* was staged, as we know from an eyewitness account by a member of the retinue of the Emperor Charles V. These mystery plays were part of the celebration of a local legendary event linked with Our Lady, which was commemorated by a very elaborate procession or *ommeganc*. It took place on the Sunday before Pentecost and its organization was in the hands of the Guild of the Crossbowmen who, possibly aided by members of the Chambers of Rhetoric in the town, also took part in the organization and performance of the mystery plays.

Much more is known about this procession, from the meticulous description given by the courtier mentioned above, than about the mystery plays. It took place in the morning and the mystery plays followed in the afternoon – one *Joy* every year – until the cycle was completed. In 1559 and 1566 the Chamber of Rhetoric called the Cornflower was responsible for the performance of the *Seventh Joy* and the two manuscripts of the *First* and the *Seventh Joy* are both annotated by the producer, the town poet of Brussels. The stage on that occasion was built 'in the form of the Coliseum'. The *First Joy* contains a list of players, including two women, and shows that the players sometimes had more than one role. The plays have a number of stage directions. One frequently used is that of *pausa*, a moment when the stage is empty, although action in some cases is implied behind closed curtains, and music is often played. The term *selete* indicates another moment when the stage is empty or the actors are silent or miming. It can also indicate a change of characters or a shift to a different location, and on such occasions music often had an important place.

The Play of the Holy Sacrament of Nyeuwervaert (*Het Spel vanden Heilighen Sacramente vander Nyeuwervaert*) is the oldest surviving miracle play in the Low Countries. Its author is unknown; its date of origin must have been shortly after 1463, when a Brotherhood of the Holy Sacrament of Nyeuwervaert was founded in Breda, to honour

the miracles performed by a Host found in a marsh in a village in the same diocese as Breda . The only known performance was organized by the Breda Chamber of Rhetoric on 24 June, St John's Day, 1500. A Sacraments Procession on the Sunday before St John's Day was a regular feature in Breda which continued into the 16th century, and it may be that the play was performed for a number of years in the same week. The procession was accompanied by various dramatic events and dancing; *tableaux vivants* are possibly indicated by 'a play of St Hubert, of St George, of St Barbara, of Herod, a shepherds' play, a play of the Four Sons of Aymon versus the King of France'. There were also sword-dancers and a savage. The performance of the play took place on a stage in or in front of an inn in the market square in Breda, and needed only six players. The play required a hell-mouth and was set in three different places. The liveliness and the dramatic tension are entirely due to the *sinnekens*, devilish tempters of mankind.

Possibly dating from the end of the 15th century is the only other surviving mystery play in the Low Countries, the *Play of the Five Wise and the Five Foolish Virgins* (*Het Spel van de V Vroede ende van de V Dwaeze Maeghden*). Both the Old and the New Testaments, and the parables in particular, became very popular subject-matter in the Rhetoricians' drama in the 16th century. Another characteristic feature in the *Play of the Virgins* is its allegorical nature and didactic emphasis. The Foolish Virgins, for example, have names symbolic of Man's forgetfulness of the Day of Judgement: Waste of Time, Recklessness, Pride, Vainglory, Foolish Chatter. The play has a processional ending, the only one extant in Dutch drama.

The true and very miraculous history of Mariken van Nieumeghen who lived more than seven years with the devil shows its problematic status already in its title. In form it hovers between narrative and dramatic text. It survives as a printed book (c.1515) in which the dramatic dialogues are interspersed with elaborate descriptive chapter headings in prose. It is an extraordinarily rich text. Particularly interesting from a theatrical point of view is Mariken's moment of true insight into her situation and her repentance, which occurs when she watches a play on a wagon performed in her native town of Nijmegen, in which our Lady pleads for forgiveness for Mankind from God. This play-in-a-play is not unique in the drama of the Low Countries in so far as a number of Rhetoricians' plays have inner and outer plays, but this is a particularly effective example of that and of a Trial in Heaven.

The Mirror of the Bliss of Everyman (*Den Spieghel der Salicheit van Elckerlijc*) has gained fame in world literature in its English translation *Everyman*. Its author and date of origin are unknown. It survives in three printed versions (oldest 1495) and one manuscript (c.1595). Whether the printer, who introduced this text as 'a beautiful booklet made in the manner of a play or playlet', left out any stage directions is uncertain; the four surviving versions do not contain any. One of its Latin translations, *Homulus*, claims that *Elckerlijc* was performed at a competition of Brabant Chambers of Rhetoric in Antwerp where it won first prize. Though *Elckerlijc*'s allegorical presentation is entirely in keeping with the Rhetoricians' didactic mode, there is no evidence to corroborate this statement.

Individual playwrights have made names for themselves; the best known of these are the Bruges poet and playwright Anthonis de Roovere (c.1430–82); the Brussels poet Jan Smeken (c.1450–1517); and the Flemish Rhetorician Matthys Casteleyn (1485–1550), poet, playwright, composer and author of the first extensive *art poétique* in Dutch *De Conste van Rhetoriken* (*The Art of Rhetoric*), written in 1548 and published in 1555. The only survivor of his plays, reputedly numbering 106, is the delightful *spel van sinnen Pyramus and Thisbe*, which presents the Ovidian material in an orthodox Catholic and moralistic manner.

Other significant playwrights include Cornelis Everaert (Bruges, early 16th century), the Zeeland Rhetorician Job Gommersz (writing c.1565), Jan van den Berghe (d. Brussels 1559), the Haarlem poet Louris Jansz, the Antwerp poet Willem van Haecht (c.1530), the Antwerp poet and translator Cornelis van Ghistele (b.1510), and JACOB DUYM (1547–?1612/20). ES

Spain Since the reconquest of Spain from the Moors was a gradual process, taking several centuries, the LITURGICAL DRAMA in the peninsula developed first in the northeast, in Catalonia, the earliest province to return to Christian rule. For more than two hundred years after the introduction there of the Roman–French rite, the Catalan dioceses were placed under the metropolitan see of Narbonne. Liturgical drama was widespread and popular in Catalonia as in France, the oldest surviving texts (early 12th century) being from the monastery of Ripoll, which had close links with St Martial de Limoges. In addition to numerous texts of Christmas and Easter plays (the merchant scene in the *Visitatio* from Ripoll is the earliest known) the Catalan material also includes dramatizations of the prose work *Victimae Paschale*, within the Mass, found in the customaries from Gerona and Mallorca (that from the latter being in the vernacular).

A small number of liturgical texts are found in the provinces of northern Spain – Aragon, León and Galicia – carried there perhaps by pilgrims en route to the shrine of St James at Compostella. Castile, however, has almost no liturgical texts apart from a handful of *Quem queritis?* tropes. It is generally accepted that this dearth results from the fact that after the expulsion of the Moors in the 12th century Castile came under the influence of Cluniac monks, and liturgical drama was almost unknown in Cluniac houses. Church drama is also unknown in Portugal, with the solitary exception of a brief shepherds' play of the 14th century from the monastery of Coimbra, which from its foundation in 1132 followed the customs of Avignon.

The only religious dramatic ceremony found widely and uniquely in the peninsula is the Monologue of the Sibyl on the Fifteen Signs of Judgement. Scenes of performances are recorded from all the provinces, but it is unknown outside Spain except as part of a prophet play.

The *Auto de los Reyes Magos* (*Play of the Royal Magi*), probably dating from the end of the 12th century, is the only pre-15th-century extant Castilian vernacular play. It covers the meeting of the three Kings, and their decision, on seeing the star, to go to Bethlehem and, by offering gifts to the newborn child, to try to discover if he is man, king or God. Recent investigation has pointed to the probability of Gascon authorship, and it has been suggested that it may have been written by a Gascon priest who intended it for the Epiphany services in Toledo. If this view is accepted, the *Auto* cannot be taken as evidence of an earlier dramatic tradition in Castile.

Few other vernacular texts are known before the 14th century, but from then on biblical pageants were included in the Corpus Christi processions in Barcelona and Valencia, and details from the accounts in Valencia in 1414 indicate how the floats – *rocas* or *entramesos* – were refurbished year by year; the cost of building, adorning and storing these pageant wagons was shared between the religious houses and the trade guilds. A description of the Barcelona procession from 1424 suggests the presence of MIMEd action, but the earliest evidence of full dramatic plays with dialogue comes from the island of Mallorca in 1442. One of the major surviving play manuscripts in Catalan is also from the island – the 49 plays contained in it, written in the 16th century, were performed in and staged by the cathedral in Palma. Variously referred to as *consuetas*, *representacións* and *misteris*, they depict incidents from the Old and New Testaments and saints' lives. Many of them have elaborate staging directions indicating that they were performed on scaffolds (*cadefals*), from three to five in number, set in the transept of the cathedral, with action taking place on and between the different locations. Special effects and machinery for raising and lowering are also described.

This use of multiple staging in the French mode is also found in some of the mainland plays, such as those from Valencia, which were, however, normally performed out of doors. An exception to this practice is the group of Assumption plays of the 16th century found in a number of towns, including Valencia and Prades, and usually presented in a cathedral or large church where the *ara-celi*, the machine used to lower actors from Heaven to Earth and raise them again, is often described. In the Elche play, still performed regularly today, the *ara-celi* and its machinery were built into the structure when the church was reconstructed after a fire in the 18th century.

By the end of the 15th century, Corpus Christi processions with floats and *tableaux* are found in many parts of Spain: the records from Toledo are particularly detailed and interesting. Although the trade guilds were involved in these celebrations, they never achieved the dominant position in play production of, say, England; the feast and its activities, processional and theatrical, remained very much in the hands of the Church. Details of the *tableaux*, of the floats and of the numerous walking figures, allegorical, biblical and fantastic, show some similarities to Italian practice.

Sacred and secular themes overlapped frequently in religious processions and royal entries; dancings and disguisings, jousts and processions, were common in the different courts. The first use of the name *entramesos* for the floats occurs in 1373, and the accounts of the coronation of Martin I at Saragossa in 1399 show sieges, battles and hunting scenes being enacted on such wheeled floats between the tables at the banquet.

Both music and dance were a regular part of plays: in some, especially the Mallorcan texts, the dialogue was sung rather than spoken and, despite the frequent Councils forbidding dancing inside the church, dance plays remained a very popular part of Spanish religious festivals. This can be seen from the 1540 contract from Seville for a danced representation of the Magi in the Corpus Christi procession, or the 16th-century play of the Nativity by Suárez de Robles in which the action is danced throughout.

The *momos* (mumming) played an important part in court entertainment, with ever more elaborate machinery being employed. Many references to *momos* can be found from the middle of the 15th century onwards, and in all parts of Spain and Portugal. Mock battles also play a part in court entertainment of the time. No clear distinction can be drawn between aristocratic entertainment and religious drama; there is evidence that religious plays were performed at court. Many Christmas ones are extant, often mainly PASTORAL in form, and in the 1460s Christmas and Epiphany Gospel scenes were arranged for performance in Jaén (Granada) by Miguel Lucas de Iranzo.

From the second half of the 15th century come four dramatic texts from Castile by Gómez Manrique; however, only the fourth, the *Representación del Nacimiento de Nuestro Señor* (*Representation of the Nativity of Our Lord*), is clearly written for performance. Based on the *officium pastorum* (shepherds' play), it adds an opening scene in the medieval tradition of St Joseph as a comic figure, in which he is rebuked by an angel for his excessive suspiciousness. Despite the existence of some plays, there is no evidence of a strong vernacular tradition before the second half of the 15th century.

The end of the 15th and the beginning of the 16th centuries saw the appearance as court dramatists of JUAN DEL ENCINA in the Duke of Alba's court in Salamanca (Castile) and of GIL VICENTE at the royal court of Portugal. Both have been described as the 'fathers' of their respective national dramas. The production of plays for both court and church festivities continued throughout the 16th century, with professional writers and producers becoming ever more involved in their preparation. *AUTOS SACRAMENTALES* (sacred plays) were composed on a wide variety of religious subjects, many of them including scenes of allegorical or typological significance such as the 16th-century *Farsa del Santísimo Sacramento* (*Play of the Most Holy Sacrament*), which describes the Feast of Corpus Christi itself. The use of the term *Farsa* even for a serious play is typical of the intermingling of the different strands of drama, religious and secular, which in the Iberian peninsula, unhindered by Reformation or Puritanism, continued to evolve smoothly into the 17th-century drama of the GOLDEN AGE of Spanish theatre.   PN LRM

Staging in the Middle Ages The wealth and variety of dramatic and theatrical activity in Europe in the Middle Ages is echoed in its staging. Everywhere was potentially a theatre: the street, the private hall and the guild hall, the church, the open field, the market square, the churchyard. Evidence, however, like that for theatrical activity, is variable in its frequency and its fullness. Information comes from a variety of sources besides texts and stage directions: church, guild and city accounts, carpenters' and other workmen's contracts, stage plans, descriptions, pictorial representations. These suggest a broad division into multiple and single-focus staging. The most important sources of evidence for multiple (or simultaneous) staging are stage plans, especially those of Lucerne (though late 16th century) and the *Castle of Perseverance*. The information contained in the Lucerne plans is supported and extended by the remarkable collection of notes and descriptions made for and by the director, Renward Cysat, and by the surviving texts and stage directions. The *Castle* plan is important as the centre of a cluster of information drawn from plays with apparently similar staging (*Mary Magdalen* and the *N. Town Passion*), from the stage plans of the Cornish plays, and from the Fouquet miniature of the martyrdom of St Apollonia. Though it should be stressed that the stage plans are specific to their own plays and their own times, and that the Fouquet miniature is an imaginary creation and not a documentary stage painting, nevertheless they can be used to clarify the often brief and enigmatic references that appear elsewhere

Basically, both sets of evidence show an open central area surrounded by a number of specific locations. In the case of the *Castle* these are all apparently raised as in the Fouquet miniature, but unlike the miniature and like *Mary Magdalen* and the *Passion*, action takes place on these 'scaffolds' as well as in the 'place'. At Lucerne the locations are divided between those which are merely 'stalls' or waiting-places for the actors, and those in which part of the action occurs, e.g. Heaven, Hell, the Temple, Mount Sinai. Some are raised (e.g. Heaven, the Nativity Hut), some are at ground level (e.g. most of the stalls, the Temple, Hell). In the *Castle* there is a central fixed scaffold, the castle itself, and similarly in one of the plans for the Cornish *Beunans Meriasek* there is a central chapel; at Lucerne there are a number of scaffolds or stage properties which are moved in, around or out of the *platz*, either during the day's performance (the sacrifice scaffolds) or between the two days (Moses' water rock, the Pool of Siloam). Mount Sinai is shifted across the upper end of the square to become the Mount of Olives on the second day.

The vocabulary used to describe multiple staging varies somewhat from play to play, though there are recurrent words, mainly everyday ones given a specific application. To what extent these were felt to be technical terms it is difficult to say. 'Place' (English), *platea* (Latin), *place*, *champ*, *parc* (French), *platz* (German) are all used with some frequency for the open playing area; *domus* (Latin), *lieu*, *mansion* (French), *hof* (German), for the surrounding locations. When no plan or supporting documentation exists it is hard to be sure what these terms mean, and it is possible that in some cases they are merely intended as indicators of a general mode of staging: the open playing area and the individual waiting or playing locations. On occasion the individual location will be decorated or will become a structure, perhaps a raised one (words like the English 'scaffold', French 'eschaffaut' and Spanish 'cadafal' imply this). Often such a structure will be called what it represents – Heaven, Hell, Paradise, the Temple – but it is only through the description of the staging structure or from the financial accounts of their construction that we can be sure what form they took: as, for example, from Mons (1501) and Romans (1509), in France, and from Lucerne in Switzerland.

This kind of staging is adaptable in shape and size, from the semicircle to the square and from the dimensions of a church to those of a city square. It can adapt itself to a quarry (as at Shrewsbury) or an amphitheatre (as at Bourges) or the Coliseum in Rome, and it offers scope for the most spectacular effects, like the Flood at Mons. The 'place' can be ground surface, as at Lucerne, or a raised stage, as at Mons or Romans. Structures can remain fixed around the edge or in the middle, as apparently with the *Castle*, or be movable, as with the scaffold for Abraham's sacrifice at Lucerne. The structures can be merely scaffolds, as shown in the Fouquet miniature, or elaborately decorated sets, like the Paradise of *Adam* with curtains and silk cloths, foliage and flowers; or the Hell at Mons, plastered, painted and stuck with stumps of willow trees.

The multiple set arranged in a straight line – the linear stage – is represented by the Hubert Cailleau miniature of the 1547 Valenciennes *Passion*, and perhaps also by the stage specially built for the Passion at Velletri. In the former the individual structures appear as representative buildings, from the tumble-down castle of Hell and Limbo to the classical lines of the palace and the temple.

The single-focus set also has its variants in the Middle Ages: e.g. movable, as in the pageant wagon, or fixed, as in the booth stage. With the pageant wagon the levels of the place and the scaffold are maintained through the use of wagon floor and street, but the wagon is used as a visual focus for the most significant action. The booth stage appears to restrict the action to the stage structure itself. The Rhetoricians' stages of the Low Countries in some ways resembled the booth stage, but they made considerable use of different levels and of inner stages behind the elaborate façades. Though these are sometimes divided into three separate 'compartments' at stage level, almost becoming mini-Valenciennes stages at times, they are still best considered as single-focus sets since the divisions were not permanent and the three could very easily be merged into a single inner stage.

Despite problems of movement in narrow streets, and possibly of non-steering wagons, the pageant could become very elaborate. No illustrations of performing pageant wagons survive, but the wagons of the *ommeganc*, or procession, of the Low Countries reveal how spectacular processional wagons could be. They range from the house on wheels for the Nativity or the Annunciation, to the fully rigged ship, to the astonishing Tree of Jesse with its child prophets and kings perched precariously in its branches (as shown in the van Alsloot paintings of Brussels in 1615), and to the towering structures of the late-16th-century *ommeganc* at Leuven; though late in date, the pictures often show structures which survive from an earlier period. In Spain agreement for the renovation of floats shows that the Creation at Barcelona (1453) contained a heaven of clouds on top of pillars, with two angels and a throne for God, while suspended beneath was an elaborately decorated revolving globe, and at floor level a 'revolve' on which four singing angels stood while four more stood and sang at the feet of the pillars. The Bethlehem float was divided into two structures, each roof supported by four pillars with angels on top and a vaulted heaven spanning the inner four pillars. There was clearly a common tradition of elaborate wagon and float decoration. The 1454 description of the St John's Day pageants at Florence confirms that the elaboration extended to the wagons intended for performance.

The Rhetoricians' stages, too, appear from the many surviving illustrations to have been often highly decorative, though the decoration is concentrated on the façade. They may well have been influenced in the first place by the complex scaffolds of the royal entries, which were at their most splendid in the Low Countries of the late 15th century. Nothing is known of the more ordinary booth stages beyond what can be deduced from pictures such as the Brueghel *Village Festival*. The stage is above the heads of the spectators, usually rests on large barrels or trestles, and sometimes has what appears to be a protective barrier around it (compare the railings attached to some fixed stages, e.g. at Romans, and the wagons, e.g. at Alcalá, 1568). In many cases the purpose was no doubt purely decorative, but that there was sometimes need for protection is shown by the performance in Florence (1454) when the actor playing the emperor Octavian was seized and flung down from his wagon by an apparently enraged German who had clambered up from the street.

Both fixed and movable forms of staging frequently made use of complicated machinery. Possibly the most remarkable of all was the revolving heaven peopled with angels, constructed by the architect and designer Brunelleschi in the roof of the church of San Felice in Piazza in Florence for an Annunciation play. Some idea of the effect of this church machinery can even now be gained from the play of the Assumption of the Virgin still annually performed in the church at Elche in southeastern Spain, where the most striking effect is the opening of the leaves of the 'pomegranate' to reveal the angel inside, all within a few feet of the ceiling of the dome. Raising and lowering of figures, real and artificial, to and from the ceilings of churches and halls was a common spectacle. Such raising devices were used also in outdoor performances; at Bourges (1536) a mechanism was required for 'flying' Simon Magus and also the apostles. Here, as almost inevitably elsewhere, this is associated with clouds – no doubt for appropriately concealing the mechanics. Even on the English pageant wagons some kind of raising mechanism was required for certain episodes (e.g. the Ascension or the Assumption), though the only documented one is that for the Mercers' pageant of the Last Judgement at York (1433).

The fixed stages frequently made use of the space underneath for surprise appearances and disappearances through trap-doors, and for removing altogether actors whose parts were over or who were changing roles. At Bourges, St Matthew moves to a position near a trap-door so that a dragon can appear near him spouting fire and be subdued by him. Characters are frequently said to 'vanish' and 'go underground', to reappear in another part of the stage. At Lucerne many of the dead are buried in the 'general burying place', to re-emerge later as other characters. Stages set up in a town square allowed not only scaffolds to be used but also the buildings around the square. The movement of the star and the dove representing the Holy Spirit at Lucerne was controlled by one of the stage crew from an upper room in the Haus zur Sonne at the upper end of the square. The eclipses of sun and moon at Christ's death were also managed from there. Musketeers were stationed on the roofs of certain houses to echo the divine thunder. At Mons the roofs were used to set up large barrels from which leaden pipes carried the waters of the Flood before they descended upon the stage below. The town walls and the walls of surrounding buildings were also used to support scaffolds (Alençon, 1520) or a covering awning (Romans).

The large multiple set created considerable problems of control for the director (indeed, made an overall director a necessity). Cysat at Lucerne made endless notes of the positioning and timing of processions, crowd scenes, the doubling of parts, entries and special effects, even at times making a note to be there himself – including the famous 'Director, go to hell.' At Mons the thunder-makers had separate cue-sheets to which they were urged to pay close attention so that they stopped when Christ said to the storm: 'Peace, be still!' A strong sense of the complexities of such a play in action is given simply by the cues in the director's copy. For instance, in the middle of the Transfiguration, 258 lines and a considerable amount of complicated action before he is due to appear with smoke and explosions, the devil Fergalus is warned to go to the trap-door beneath the Canaanite woman's daughter from whom he is to burst.

At Lucerne and at the large-scale French plays the most elaborate provision for audiences is found, though clearly the windows of surrounding houses, where they existed, were still the most prized viewing places. At Romans, stands with rows of separate lockable rooms were constructed with safety railings in front and privies at the ends of the rows. At Autun (1516) an 'amphitheatre' was made with all the seating covered by awnings as a protection against the sun, as in Romans. The provision of spectator scaffolds was a feature of tournaments from a very much earlier period, though nothing as complex as those for the plays is recorded. Here besides the audience's comfort there is some concern with being able to see; but even so it must frequently have been difficult both to see and hear in an open space like the Weinmarkt at Lucerne. To some extent in other types of staging this is overcome by having a mobile audience, thereby making sight-lines the individual concern of each spectator. But this in itself could cause problems with the more adventurous: the boy who fell from the triforium at Beverley (c.1220), or the roof collapsing at Bautzen in 1413 because of the weight of spectators on it. Sometimes the audience was conducted from stage to stage, as in the *Conversion of St Paul*.

The advantage for the organizers of a play of fixed audience accommodation was the revenue. There is considerable evidence from France of a concern with financial success, or at least with making as little loss as possible (e.g. Valenciennes, Mons, Issoudun); but these were one-off performances, not regularly recurring ones. There is no evidence of organized payment of this kind in England, though certain enterprising York citizens took advantage of the pageants stopping outside their houses to set up scaffolds and charge for access to them, and later the city council too made house-owners pay for the privilege of having the pageants stop outside. None of this was direct recouping of the expenses of the play, however. The civic cycles in England were financed by members of the guilds,

with no hope of return.

One of the most costly and cherished features of many of the French plays was the *feintes* or special effects. The list for the Bourges *Acts of the Apostles* (1536) fills several pages of the printed account. The provision for the Flood at Mons has already been mentioned. There also the stage was turfed over and contained a Sea of Galilee (perhaps like the sea in the Cailleau painting) upon which real boats floated, as well as the usual series of trap-doors for a variety of appearances and disappearances. Firework effects were the work of experts who were called in specially to organize them. This is evident in the contract for the Modane *Anti-Christ* play (1580), but was clearly also true very much earlier (e.g. Mons). Special effects were varied and ubiquitous. There is the polished bowl used to reflect the sun on to Christ's white robes for the Transfiguration at Revello (1483), the painting of the bloody sweat on to Christ's face as he prostrates himself on the Mount of Olives by a painter concealed underneath (Lucerne and Revello), Balaam's talking ass at Chester, or the extraordinary illumination of the church at Florence for the Annunciation play of 1439.

Other forms of special effects were the exotic animals, giants and other figures that were made mainly for processions but which were also used in plays. Representations of such creatures survive in, for example, the paintings by van Alsloot of the Brussels *ommeganc* or the *Liber Boonen* sketches from Leuven (late 16th century). Those referred to in Chester were made for the Midsummer Show, those in Valencia for the Corpus Christi procession (including lions, an eagle and dragons), while those in Lucerne (camel, elephant and dromedary) were for the entry of the three kings in the Passion. In France the *monstre*, or pre-performance parade, often included elaborate floats and figures (Bourges).

A frequent feature of these and all other displays and entertainments is the use of elaborate MASKS which fulfil a variety of purposes: in the courtly mumming (the early Revels accounts abound in mask references) for tantalizing concealment, in all mummings as a manifestation of the exotic or the frightening, or in plays symbolically to show disease or to express attributes of a character, especially extremes. The golden face of God or the hideous head of the devil recur throughout Europe. The golden mask was not only a feature of God in glory but also of Christ in his manhood on earth, mingling masked with unmasked actors in a single theatrical context. A symbolic effect of a similar kind is also created by certain kinds of costuming. Characters will be marked for what they are by a symbol: the young Mary with a crown to show that she is also Queen of Heaven, the apostle Peter with keys to show his saintly and papal role. Only later in the period is there a move towards a semi-historical costume (e.g. Aaron in the Lucerne play dressed as an Old Testament priest). If there is symbolic there is also literal detail: the painting on of Christ's bloody sweat in the garden of Gethsemane, or, in props, the use of real birds, animals and fish in the Creation (as at Mons).

Realism did not extend as a rule to the playing of women by women on the public stage, though it could clearly happen in nunneries (e.g. at Barking, and probably the *Santa Teodora* play from Italy). There are early-16th-century examples in France (at Romans, a few roles at Mons, and Valenciennes; Françoise Buatier at Grenoble in 1535), in the Tyrol (Bozen in 1514), but, except perhaps as dancers, women seldom appear earlier – or perhaps it would be more accurate to say that the available evidence points to the playing of most female roles by men and boys. Understandably REALISM did not extend to nudity, only to body-stockings (*lybkleidern* at Lucerne). Some directors clearly had trouble even ensuring appropriate costume, since there are prohibitions on people wearing the best costumes available regardless of what role they are playing.

At Lucerne there is concern with finding the right actor for the part; in York, for the general proficiency of all available players. Nowhere is there the suggestion of a casual attitude to the final effect, whether regarding the skill of the actor, the efficiency of the stage staff, or the ability of the painter or mechanist. The notes made by Cysat, the Lucerne director (and also town clerk), show the painstaking care that went into the smallest details. Cysat was an 'amateur' and almost all the plays referred to in this section were performed by 'amateur' actors. The 'professional' – in the sense of someone who earns his living solely by acting – seems to put in an appearance only during the late 15th century. Some actors were paid for their performances (at Chester, for example); some had to pay to perform (at Lucerne). They were drawn from all walks of life – the idea of medieval drama as the working man's drama is a totally false one. The only real 'professionals' were the musicians, brought in for their specialist training. Certainly, music played an important part in the plays. It could echo or emphasize the magnificence of Heaven, establish or symbolize through the singing of angels or mortals the harmony of Heaven or earth, or simply accompany a movement or a pause in the action (in France and elsewhere both *silete* and *pause* came to be music cues).

It is almost impossible to posit any one acting style for a drama as varied as that of the Middle Ages. Even in church drama there is a wide range of possibility, from the ritual movements of the Maries to the horseplay of Herod hurling spears down the church and beating the choir with a bladder (Padua, 13th century). It is sometimes said that a carrying voice, broad gesture and movement are essential elements, and for many plays this must have been true. But there is no reason to suppose that a medieval actor was unable to adapt himself to a more confined space such as a hall or narrow street might offer. Where evidence exists it points to a rhetorical style of broad gesture and open speaking, but it would be wrong to rule out other styles suggested by the text. The fixed tiered seating used for many of the big civic plays must have distanced the audience to some extent, whereas a mobile standing audience could be used as a crowd to hide in, move through, attack or harangue – almost as a part of the action.

In a formal way involvement with the audience was the essence of mummings. Though use of the audience seems likely in the plays, there is not a lot of evidence of it. There are forays by the devils in *Adam* (perhaps like the devils in the van Alsloot paintings); there is the concealment of *Bien Naturel* (Natural Goodness) in the audience in Jean Parmentier's *The Assumption of Our Lady* (1527); but more relevant to a style of acting is the presence of servants A and B in the audience of *Fulgens and Lucrece*. By far the most common actor–audience contact is direct address; that of A and B is intimate and colloquial, though still verse. Audience address is common in a wide variety of plays for a wide variety of purposes and with a comparable variety of tone: teaching, making a collection, gaining sympathy or simply chat. At all levels it is one of the most effective devices for involving the audience in the meaning and emotions of the play.

Plays in the Middle Ages were part of a broad use of drama and theatre which penetrated every level of society and grew within a wide variety of non-theatrical events. Interaction took place not just among dramatic and theatrical activities themselves but between them and the semi-theatrical, like tournaments, and the non-theatrical, like feasts and festivals. The church liturgy produced its own drama, and its music and RITUAL as well as some of its texts influenced the vernacular plays. The tournaments provided a model for audience accommodation and outdoor performance, as well as providing an opportunity for display and costumed role-playing. Mumming exploited the use of masks at the winter feasts and festivals in hall; royal entries enriched the single-focus stage of the streets; processions revealed the possibility of movement combined with elaborate staging, and provided the occasion for it. Theatrical forms interpenetrated. How much awareness of the tradition of one country influenced that of another is very difficult to tell. It is hard to believe that an Englishman present at one of the great French Passions would remain unimpressed, but being impressed is not necessarily followed by imitation. For a final suggestive piece of evidence we come back to Cysat at Lucerne. Worrying about the smoke at the Ascension and Pentecost, he notes: 'In Milan they have artificial fire in the plays which goes up quickly, produces much smoke, and yet neither burns nor stinks.' Did he discover the secret and use it at Lucerne?

The 20th century has seen a notable revival of interest in medieval theatre. Scholars in many countries have turned back to the records of performance, and in some cases whole projects have been set up for the purpose, like that of Records of Early English Drama (REED) in Toronto. There has also been practical experiment in the form of historical reconstructions of the staging of a number of the plays: processional staging on pageant wagons of the York and Chester cycles at Leeds (1975 and 1983) and Toronto (1977 and 1983); fixed 'place and scaffold' staging of the Cornish *Ordinalia* in St Piran's Round (1969), and the *Castle of Perseverance*, the *N. Town Passion* and the Towneley cycle in Toronto (1979, 1981 and 1985), and *Mary Magdalen* at Durham (1982). Impetus was given to these historical reconstructions by the many productions of individual plays and groups of plays which began early in the century in many parts of Europe. A professional company, the Medieval Players, was formed in Britain devoted to the performance of medieval and Renaissance plays, and the NATIONAL THEATRE in London has had enormous success with its promenade adaptation by TONY HARRISON of the cycle plays, *The Mysteries* (1985). In 1977 an international society was formed devoted to the study of medieval theatre, the Société Internationale pour l'Étude du Théâtre Médiéval. PM

MEDIEVAL DRAMA IN EUROPE

See: R. Axton, *European Drama of the Early Middle Ages*, London, 1974; D. Bevington (ed.), *Medieval Drama*, Boston, 1975; E. Simon (ed.), *The Theatre of Medieval Europe: New Research in Early Drama*, Cambridge, 1991; C. Stratman, *Bibliography of Medieval Drama*, 2nd edn, New York, 1972; R. W. Vince (ed.), *A Companion to the Medieval Theatre*, New York, 1989.

LITURGICAL DRAMA

See: W. Lipphardt (ed.), *Lateinische Osterfeiern und Osterspiele*, 6 vols. to date, Berlin and New York, 1975– ; K. Young, *The Drama of the Medieval Church*, 2 vols., Oxford, 1933.

EASTERN EUROPE

See: A. C. Mahr (ed.), *The Cyprus Passion Cycle*, Notre Dame, Indiana, 1947; G. E. Szönyi, 'European Influences and National Tradition in Medieval Hungarian Theater', *Comparative Drama*, 15, 1981; A. Tuilier (ed.), *Grégoire de Nazianze: La Passion du Christ*, Paris, 1969; J. F. Veltrusky, 'Medieval Drama in Bohemia', *EDAM Review*, 15, 1993.

ENGLAND, SCOTLAND AND IRELAND; CORNWALL AND WALES

See: R. Beadle (ed.), *The Cambridge Companion to Medieval English Theatre*, Cambridge, 1994; S. E. Berger, *Medieval English Drama: An Annotated Bibliography of Recent Criticism*, New York and London, 1990; E. K. Chambers, *The Mediaeval Stage*, 2 vols., London, 1903; H.-J. Diller, *The Middle English Mystery Play: A Study in Dramatic Speech and Form*, Cambridge, 1992; G. Jones, *A Study of Three Welsh Religious Plays*, thesis, University of Minnesota, 1918; I. Lancashire, *Dramatic Texts and Records of Britain to 1558*, Toronto, 1984; A. J. Mill, *Medieval Plays in Scotland*, St Andrews Publications 24, Edinburgh and London, 1927; *Records of Early English Drama* (York, Chester, Coventry, Newcastle upon Tyne, Norwich, Cumberland/Westmorland/Gloucestershire, Devon, Cambridge, Herefordshire/Worcestershire, Lancashire), Toronto, 1979, 1979, 1981, 1982, 1984, 1986, 1986, 1989, 1990, 1991; *Revels History of Drama in English*, vol. 1 (A. C. Cawley et al.) and vol. 2 (N. Saunders et al.), London, 1983 and 1980. Malone Society Collections, especially vols. 7, 8 and 11, Oxford, 1965, 1969, 1980/81; *Medieval English Theatre*; *Records of Early English Drama Newsletter*.

FRANCE

See: M. Accarie, *Le Théâtre sacré de la fin du Moyen Âge: Étude sur le sens moral de la Passion de Jehan Michel*, Genève, 1979; J.-Cl. Aubailly, *Le Théâtre médiéval profane et comique*, Paris, 1975, and *Le Monologue, le dialogue et la sottie: Essai sur quelques genres dramatiques de la fin du Moyen Âge et du début du 16e siècle*, Paris, 1976; R. Axton, *European Drama of the Early Middle Ages*, London, 1974; R. Bossuat, *Manuel bibliographique de la littérature française du Moyen Âge*, Paris, 1951, and supplements; G. Cohen, *Histoire de la mise en scène dans le théâtre religieux français du Moyen Âge*, Paris, 1951; *Dictionnaire des lettres françaises (le Moyen Âge)*, Paris, 1992; G. Frank, *The Medieval French Drama*, Oxford, 1954; H. Lewicka, *Bibliographie du théâtre profane français des 15e et 16e siècles*, 2nd edn, Paris, 1980; 'Medieval French Drama: A Review of Recent Scholarship', *Research Opportunities in Renaissance*

Drama, 21–3, 1978–80; L. Petit de Julleville, *Les Mystères*, Paris, 1980, and *Répertoire du théâtre comique en France*, Paris, 1986.

GERMANY, SWITZERLAND, ETC.; SCANDINAVIA

See: R. Bergmann, 'Spiele, mittelalterliche Geistliche', in *Reallexikon der deutschen Literatur*, vol. 4, Berlin and New York, 1979; M. B. Evans, *The Passion Play of Lucerne: An Historical and Critical Introduction*, New York and London, 1943, reprint 1977; H. Linke, 'Das volkssprachige Drama und Theater im deutschen und niederländischen Sprachbereich', in *Neues Handbuch der Literaturwissenschaft*, vol. 8, *Europäisches Mittelalter*, Wiesbaden, 1978, and 'Germany and German-speaking Central Europe', in *The Theatre of Medieval Europe: New Research in Early Drama*, E. Simon (ed.), Cambridge, 1991; W. F. Michael, *Das deutsche Drama des Mittelalters*, Berlin and New York, 1971; B. Neumann, *Zeugnisse mittelalterlicher Aufführungen im deutschen Sprachraum*, vol. 1, Cologne, 1979, and *Geistliches Schauspiel im Zeugnis der Zeit*, 2 vols., Zurich and Munich, 1987. G. D. Caie, 'Scandinavia', in *A Companion to the Medieval Theatre*, New York, 1989; S. Wright, 'Iconographic contexts of the Swedish *De uno peccatore qui promeruit gratiam*', *Comparative Drama*, 27, 1993.

ITALY

See: A. D'Ancona, *Origini del teatro italiano*, 2 vols., 1891, reprint Rome 1966; V. De Bartholomaeis, *Origini della poesia drammatica italiano*, 2nd edn, Turin, 1952; A. Cioni, *Bibliografia delle Sacre Rappresentazioni* (includes MSS, early printed editions and modern collections of texts), Florence, 1961; N. Newbegin (ed.), *Nuovo corpus di sacre rappresentazioni fiorentini del Quattrocento*, Bologna, 1983.

LOW COUNTRIES

See: W. M. H. Hummelen, *Repertorium van het Rederijkers-drama, 1500–c.1620*, Assen, 1968, 'Tekst en toneelinrichting in de Abcle Spelen', *De Nieuwe Taalgids*, 70, 1977, and 'Types and Methods of the Dutch Rhetoricians' Theatre', in *The Third Globe: Symposium for the Reconstruction of the Globe Playhouse, Wayne State University 1979*, ed. C. W. Hodges, S. Schoenbaum and L. Leone, Detroit, 1981; G. R. Kernodle, *From Art to Theatre: Form and Convention in the Renaissance*, Chicago, 1944; J. J. Mak, *De Rederijkers*, Amsterdam, 1945; J. A. Worp, *Geschiedenis van het drama en het toneel in Nederland*, Groningen, 1904.

SPAIN

See: R. B. Donovan, *The Liturgical Drama in Medieval Spain*, Toronto, 1958; J.-F. Massip, *Teatre religiós medieval als països catalans*, Barcelona, 1984; N. D. Shergold, *A History of the Spanish Stage*, Oxford, 1967; R. E. Surtz, *El teatro en la edad media*, Madrid, 1983.

STAGING

See: C. Davidson, *Illustrations of the Stage and Acting in England to 1580*, Kalamazoo, Michigan, 1991; E. Konigson, *L'Espace théâtral médiéval*, Paris, 1975; P. Meredith and J. Tailby (eds), *The Staging of Religious Drama in the Later Middle Ages: Texts and Documents in English Translation* (EDAM Monograph Series 4), Kalamazoo, 1983; H. Rey-Flaud, *Le Cercle magique*, Paris, 1975; W. Tydeman, *The Theatre in the Middle*

Ages, Cambridge, 1978; G. Wickham, *Early English Stages 1330–1660*, vols. 1 and 2, London, 1959 and 1963. *Early Drama, Art, and Music Review*; *Medieval English Theatre*; *Research Opportunities in Renaissance Drama*.

Medina, Louisa c.1813–38 Unique in her day as a successful American woman dramatist. Medina is credited with 34 plays between 1833 and 38; however, only 11 have been documented and only three are extant. All of her plays were written for Thomas S. Hamblin, manager of the BOWERY THEATRE and possibly her husband, and probably all were dramatizations of historical and adventure novels. Medina's talent for increasing the dramatic and spectacular elements of the novels made her plays successful and profitable MELODRAMAS, the staple of the Bowery. Her dramatization of BULWER LYTTON's *Last Days of Pompeii* had 29 performances in 1835 – the longest run on a New York stage to that date; and her dramatization of ROBERT MONTGOMERY BIRD's *Nick of the Woods* (1838) remained a consistent draw for most of the century. Other successes include *Rienzi*, *Norman Leslie* and *Ernest Maltravers*. FB

Medwall, Henry 1461–? English playwright. Born in Southwark, London, he was educated at Eton and King's College, Cambridge, where he studied law, but was no doubt also introduced to household drama. His two known plays, *Fulgens and Lucres* (printed c.1512) and *Nature* (printed c.1530), were probably written for performance in the household of his patron and employer (as a notary public) Cardinal John Morton, Archbishop of Canterbury. The former, a wholly secular play, presented within the context of a banquet, is remarkable for its comic invention and its ingenious theatrical use of a subplot involving two servants, A and B, appearing at first as members of the audience. *Nature* is a rather more traditional MORALITY PLAY. When Morton died in 1500 Medwall was not yet 40 but no other records of his life have so far been discovered. PM

Mei Lanfang 1894–1961 Chinese JINGXI star actor and teacher. Born into a traditional Beijing opera family, he was trained in women's roles (*dan*) like his father and grandfather before him. He was idolized by the theatre-going public. He created new dance plays based on historical literary themes that gave new dimensions to the repertoire. He innovated roles in which song, dance and combat techniques were combined in solo performance. Mei was active in breaking down prejudices against women and many actresses became his disciples. He collaborated with theatre scholar and adviser-impresario-playwright Qi Rushan (1876–1962). Mei refused to perform during the Japanese occupation of China, remaining secluded in Shanghai. After 1949 he was active on the stage and in teaching, carrying out an extremely heavy programme urged upon him by the new government. His former home in Beijing has been made into a commemorative museum in honour of his achievements. ACS

Meilhac, Henri 1831–97 and **Ludovic Halévy** 1834–1908 French dramatists. Although they did some work alone or with other collaborators, the names of Meilhac and Halévy are firmly linked as entertainers of the Second Empire and, above all, as librettists for the work of JACQUES OFFENBACH. Meilhac began his career as a caricaturist, later transferring this skill into the creation of amusing dramatic figures. From 1855 he had a series of *vaudevilles* staged at the Théâtre du Gymnase. In 1861 he collaborated for the first time with Halévy on a piece for the Variétés (see BOULEVARD), *Le Menuet de Danae* (*Danae's Minuet*), and would continue to work with him for most of his career. In 1883 he and Philippe Gille wrote *Mam'zelle Nitouche*, a delightful MUSICAL COMEDY about a respectable school music teacher who also writes naughty OPERETTAS. In 1888 he was elected to the French Academy.

Halévy, son of the dramatist Léon Halévy, worked as a librettist, his first great success being *Orpheus in the Underworld* (1861). He also wrote novels and was elected to the Academy in 1884. Together Meilhac and Halévy provided librettos for Offenbach's *La Belle Hélène* (1864), *Bluebeard* (1866), *The Grand Duchess of Gerolstein* (1867) with the talented Hortense Schneider (this show was the first thing the Emperor Alexander wanted to see when he visited Paris for the Great Exhibition), and *La Périchole* (1868). There are some parallels to be drawn between their work and that of W. S. GILBERT. Meilhac and Halévy also wrote one of the most successful light comedies of the Second Empire, *Froufrou* (1869), which would later provide a popular role for SARAH BERNHARDT. Meilhac was more given to the fantastic and the grotesque, whereas Halévy preferred realistic detail and close observation of contemporary life and mores. JMCC

Meiningen company German court theatre. During the last decades of the 19th century, the Meiningen Court Theatre was possibly the most widely admired and imitated company in Europe. It was developed out of the existent Meiningen Court Theatre by Georg II, Duke of Saxe-Meiningen (1826–1914), his wife Ellen Franz (1839–1923), and the director Ludwig Chronegk (1837–91). It was financed by the duke's private money. In 1874, during their first guest appearance in Berlin, the Meininger (i.e. the company members) achieved national prominence with their performances of *Julius Caesar*, *Twelfth Night* and other plays. From then until 1890, the company performed both in Meiningen and on tour in 38 German and European cities. One of the most arresting aspects of their productions was the extreme accuracy with which the historical sets and costumes were designed. The actors were also directed with a meticulous eye for the whole stage picture. The company was celebrated for the individuality of its crowd members. A rigorous standard of ensemble was constantly striven for. Although some critics felt that the plays suffered from overproduction, too much attention being paid to the physical elements of the stage, it was the duke's ambition that each production should provide only sufficient means to support the dramatic text effectively. The Meininger were seen on tour by ANDRÉ ANTOINE and KONSTANTIN STANISLAVSKY; both claimed that the company had a profound influence on their own work. SW

Meisl, Karl 1775–1853 Austrian playwright. Although Meisl wrote for the Viennese popular theatre, where entertainment was always the prime consideration, many of his 184 plays express disquiet at the way in which the contemporary preoccupation with luxury undermined the integrity of family life. However, while his plays consistently dramatize the precarious nature of economic life in Vienna, they are not bitter, though their slight plots mean they have not worn well. Meisl was a skilled writer of travesties and ended his career writing scripts for NESTROY. His play *1722, 1822, 1922* (1822), one of the peculiarities of dramatic literature, foretells the advent of planes and cars. As a young man he joined the Austrian army, and remained in military administration until 1844. A dramatist who outlived his time, he died in total obscurity. SW

Meisner, Sanford 1905– American actor, teacher and director. As an original member of the GROUP THEATRE, Meisner appeared in most of their productions throughout the 1930s. He co-directed, with ODETS, *Waiting for Lefty* (1935), and had roles in all the other Odets plays, from *Awake and Sing!* (1935) to *Night Music* (1940). Before joining the Group, he acted in several productions at the THEATRE GUILD. In 1935 he began teaching the Group's Method acting at the NEIGHBORHOOD PLAYHOUSE School of Theatre, and became its head the following year. He continued in this position until 1959, then taught in Los Angeles for two years at Twentieth Century-Fox before returning to New York City and his headship in 1964. During the 1940s and 50s he directed several plays, including a revival of *The Time of Your Life* (1955). He continued to act occasionally. TP

Melanesia see OCEANIA

Méliès, Georges 1861–1938 French conjuror and film-maker, the first showman to conceive of the importance of cinema as entertainment. He took over the Théâtre Robert-Houdin, Paris, in 1888, giving a series of 'fantastic evenings'. This illusionism led to lantern-slide FÉERIES; he transformed the theatre into a projection room and founded the first film studio (1896), Star Film, using MUSIC-HALL singers and underpaid chorus girls from the Théâtre du Châtelet, since legitimate actors refused at first to appear in such a low medium. Between 1895 and 1910 he produced 4000 reels of standard pantomime subjects and cinematic trickery, the most famous being *A Trip to the Moon* (1902). Méliès is also important for taking the first live-action films in a theatre; using 30 arc lamps, he captured PAULUS in his act. LS

Mélingue, Étienne Marin 1807–75 French actor. One of the most attractive, picturesque and original of the BOULEVARD, his career was particularly associated with the great cloak-and-dagger parts of DUMAS *père*. Having studied drawing and sculpture at Caen, he made his stage debut at Belleville in 1829. In 1832 he was a *grand utilité* at Rouen, where DORVAL noticed him and introduced him to Alexandre Dumas. He was taken on at the Porte-Saint-Martin, where he played lead roles until 1840, when he moved to the Ambigu, creating the title role in BOUCHARDY's *Lazare le pâtre* (*Lazarus the Shepherd*), and built his reputation with the plays of SOULIÉ. In 1847 he joined Dumas at his newly opened Théâtre Historique, where one of his great parts was Edmond Dantès in *Monte Cristo* (1848).

After the collapse of Dumas's venture, Mélingue was not attached to any one theatre. His most popular roles included Fanfan-la-Tulipe and Benvenuto Cellini. As the latter he had to carve a statuette on stage every night (Napoleon III gave him a gold snuff-box set with diamonds for one of them). In the last 15 years of his career he mainly revived earlier parts. His last major role was that of Don César de Bazan in the 1872 revival of *Ruy Blas* (ODÉON). Mélingue was the idol of popular audiences, extremely handsome and gifted with a very powerful voice. He paid great attention to details of COSTUME and make-up in preparing his parts. His wife, Mlle Théodorine, was also an actress and was chosen by HUGO for the role of Guanhumara in *Les Burgraves* (1843). JMCC

melodrama Like FARCE, melodrama is a popular form of theatre which has been denigrated by critics, so that it is associated with sensationalism and implausibility. These features make for lively theatre, however, and they sustain the mass media today.

The word 'melodrama' (*melos*, Greek, means 'a song') comes from France, where ROUSSEAU coined it for his *Pygmalion* (1766) in which music served as background for dialogue (in contrast to OPERA, where music is joined to dialogue). Since the COMÉDIE-FRANÇAISE had a monopoly on plays with spoken dialogue, the new genre in many variants was seized upon by other theatres along the Boulevard du Temple, and became the staple fare of the appropriately named Théâtre de l'Ambigu-Comique (see BOULEVARD). There, at the convenient date of 1800, *Coelina* by GUILBERT DE PIXÉRÉCOURT was performed, in which innocent young lovers suffer at the separation engineered by a scheming villain. All ends well, with assistance from a tell-tale scar, a conspiracy overheard and a helpful comic. Within two years, in that pre-COPYRIGHT age, the play crossed the Channel as *A Tale of Mystery* by THOMAS HOLCROFT, the first English play to be labelled 'melodrama'. In the rapidly industrializing capitals of London, Paris and Berlin, melodrama played triumphantly in large theatres to illiterate audiences. Necessarily, it was a *large* genre with spectacular settings, large casts gesturing broadly, and loud music to accompany the predictable emotions.

Each of the major European capitals sported its playwright of melodrama – Pixérécourt in Paris, KOTZEBUE in Berlin and BOUCICAULT in London (and New York). These three men led such melodramatic (adventure-filled) lives that they may well have thought they were inventing realism in their plays, were it not that they so often stole their action-filled plots, usually from novels. By mid-century, the genre was less formulaic: crime was popular on both sides of the Channel, so that the Paris theatre row was called Boulevard du Crime; patriotism was exhibited in battles on stage; social protest took the harmless form of equating poverty with nobility and virtue; the dastardly villain (the choice role) persecutes the defenceless heroine, who is rescued by an intrepid hero aided by a benevolent and colloquial comic, against increasingly spectacular dangers. Coelina had merely to survive a raging storm, but her progeny gasped through near-drowning, burning, devouring by wild beasts – all thrillingly palpable in the large theatres packed with thousands of spectators. Boucicault, especially, had a gift for 'sensation scenes' – designing prison escapes, avalanches, explosions – but his colleagues soon introduced icebergs, air balloons and speeding trains. With technical sophistication came more sophisticated plots; innocence does not triumph in *Uncle Tom's Cabin*, and virtue is tainted in *East Lynne*.

By the turn of the 20th century melodrama had merged into REALISM in England and France, but American melodrama was revitalized by DAVID BELASCO, who insisted on careful writing for a basic plot of poor heroine facing assorted calamities, plus weak hero, resourceful comic who was the star of the show, and a sequence of heavies who kept the plot speeding along. After the First World War AGIT-PROP plays adopted the structure, but no longer the settings, of melodrama.

Historians of melodrama stress its democratic and humanitarian substratum. ERIC BENTLEY in *The Life of the Drama* (1964) and Robert Heilman in *The Iceman, the Arsonist, and the Troubled Agent* have both defended melodrama as a different genre from TRAGEDY, which should be evaluated by its own attributes. Bentley finds melodramatic elements in most great tragedies of the anglophone tradition, and he dubs O'NEILL a successful melodramatist rather than tragic playwright. Heilman distinguishes between the divided protagonist of tragedy and the whole protagonist of melodrama; the first contributes to his own undoing, whereas the second is crushed by external forces. This necessitates reclassifying some classical tragedies as melodramas – *Romeo and Juliet*, *The Duchess of Malfi*. On the other hand, the righteous-victim-triumphant of socialist realism and of Chinese opera (revised to support the Revolution) abjure the name of melodrama but adopt its all-or-nothing ethic. RC

mélodrame French term, signifying one of the many ways of manipulating speech and music in the service of drama. Spoken words are uttered either unaccompanied during intervals between instrumental movements, or against a background of instrumental music. A most influential and perhaps the most famous *mélodrame* is *Pygmalion* (1770), with text by JEAN-JACQUES ROUSSEAU and music by Horace Coignet (1735–1821). This text was also set in 1779 by Georg Benda (1722–1821), who composed several *mélodrames*, notably *Ariadne auf Naxos* (1775) to words by JOHANN CHRISTIAN BRANDES and *Medea* (1775) to words by Friedrich Wilhelm Gotter (1736–97).

The *mélodrame* never established itself as an independent form, but passages of *mélodrame* are to be found in many OPERAS, notable examples being in Mozart's *Zaide* and in the dungeon scene of Beethoven's *Fidelio*. Brief snatches of spoken dialogue in otherwise completely sung operas (e.g. the few words of Ellen and Balstrode in Benjamin Britten's *Peter Grimes*) can only be pedantically referred to as *mélodrame*. GH

Menander c.342–c.291 BC Greek comic playwright. Menander was the most celebrated poet of the Athenian New Comedy (see GREECE, ANCIENT). He wrote over 100 plays (the first probably performed in 321), but won first prize at the Great Dionysia only eight times. After his death, however, he became one of the most popular and influential of all Greek poets.

Until this century, knowledge of his work rested only on the numerous lines quoted by later authors, generally for their edifying content, and on the fact that three plays by PLAUTUS and four by TERENCE were known to be adaptations of Menandrean originals. The position has been transformed, however, by the publication of ancient texts, generally on papyrus, which have been excavated in Egypt. These publications began in 1905 and still continue. We now have one virtually complete play, *Dyscolus* (*The Bad-Tempered Man*, performed in 316 BC, published in 1959), more than three acts of *Samia* (*The Girl from Samos*), substantial portions of *Aspis* (*The Shield*), *Epitrepontes* (*The Men Who Went to Arbitration*), *Perikeiromene* (*The Girl Who Had Her Hair Cut*), *Sicyonius* (*The Sicyonian*) and *Misoumenos* (*The Bête Noire*), and smaller fragments of several others.

While some of Menander's characters and themes have precedents in Old Comedy, his is a very different world from that of ARISTOPHANES – a world of bourgeois families and their servants, striving to act decently according to their lights (except for the occasional villain, like the wicked uncle Smicrines in *Aspis*), their lives bounded by the same laws of nature and the same social conventions as the Greeks of Menander's audience. Unity of place and time are carefully observed. Dramatic illusion can be toyed with, through sly references to COMEDY or TRAGEDY, but is not broken, except by the formal 'prologue speech', in which a character or god addresses the audience directly to explain the situation. This is a convention borrowed, not from earlier comedy, but from the tragedy of EURIPIDES, who also provides precedents for the aside, the moralizing soliloquy and the recognition scene (which often involves foundlings recognized by tokens, as in Euripides' *Ion* and some lost tragedies). There are five acts, usually in a single metre, with little music or singing (except between the acts, in choral performances that are not part of the text). Language, though colloquial, is never indecent.

Plots were ingeniously worked out, with the audience well able to predict the essentials of the denouement but kept in suspense as to how it could be accomplished. The plot of *Dyscolus* is simple enough – the resolution comes when the misanthropic Cnemon, who has refused to let his daughter marry her wealthy suitor, is made to repent by being rescued after falling down a well. But this was an early play, and evidently the complexities were greater elsewhere.

There is a limited range of stock character types – stern fathers, lovesick youths, innocent girls, worldly courtesans, fawning parasites, cunning slaves, clownish cooks, and so forth – though there is room for variation within each type, and the dramatist can play with the expectations which the types create. Plot motifs too are drawn from a fairly restricted repertory of deceptions, misunderstandings, estrangements and recognitions, and the happy ending often depends on a coincidence that would be highly unlikely in real life. All this has made it difficult for some modern critics to discern the realism for which Menander was famous in antiquity. But by ringing the changes on his types and motifs Menander is able to confront his characters with any number of socially delicate situations, and the realism, as well as the humour, lies largely in their reactions to these. And it is because he works on a relatively small canvas that such subtleties can capture the audience's attention.

The moral sentiments which take up so much of Menander can often be seen, when the context is known, to be ironically undercut by the situation in which they are spoken. While he doubtless intended them to be remembered and quoted for their wisdom and elegant expression, he ensures that they always contribute to the comedy, never interrupt it. ALB

Mendes, Sam 1965– British director, whose technical competence, amounting almost to virtuosity, was revealed while he was still in his early 20s and working in FRINGE theatres. In 1989 he won the Critics Circle Award as director of the Minerva Studio in Chichester. The clarity of his productions led to his first WEST END engagement to stage *The Cherry Orchard* at the Aldwych, with JUDI DENCH as Mme Ranevskaya, in 1989. This was a commercial venture, backed by MICHAEL CODRON, but it quickly led to invitations for Mendes to direct at the ROYAL SHAKESPEARE COMPANY. His *Troilus and Cressida* with Simon Russell Beale as Thersites, at the Swan Theatre in 1990, was hailed by IRVIN WARDLE as restoring 'the full glory of verse-speaking to the Stratford stage', although his skills seemed to lie more towards clear presentation and forceful thematic development than in textual interpretation.

In 1991 he directed SEAN O'CASEY's *The Plough and the Stars* at the YOUNG VIC and EDWARD BOND's *The Sea* for the NATIONAL THEATRE, while his *Richard III* (1992) with Beale in the title role toured the British Isles after its RSC premiere at the Other Place in Stratford-upon-Avon. In the same year, his production of JIM CARTWRIGHT's *The Rise and Fall of Little Voice* transferred from London's Cottesloe Theatre to the West End. Mendes celebrated the reopening in London of Donmar Warehouse under his management in 1992 with the British premiere of STEPHEN SONDHEIM's *Assassins*, which had a mixed response from both press and public. In 1993 there were guest visits to the Donmar from ATHOL FUGARD's company from Johannesburg and CHEEK BY JOWL, while Mendes's own contribution to its programme included a memorable revival of BRIAN FRIEL's *Translations.* JE

Mengistu Lemma 1925–88 Ethiopian poet and playwright. The son of a senior priest, Mengistu received an Orthodox Church education, then spent seven years studying in England before his mildly socialist writings led to a summons to return to Ethiopia. He took up playwriting in order to occupy his mind, when forced to join the Ethiopian diplomatic corps in India. His two pre-revolutionary comedies in Amharic, *Telfso Bekisse* (*Marriage by Abduction,* 1962) and *Yelecha Gebecha* (*Marriage of Unequals,* 1963), looked critically at accommodations between tradition and modernity, and were hugely successful. After the revolution Mengistu produced several more comedies, which took a critical look at changes in society. Both *Balekabara Baledaba* (*The Mighty and the Lowly,* 1974) and *Shumiya* (*Office Scramble,* 1985) examine how power corrupts. His most powerful work was probably *Kassa* (1980), a play which drew on his own child-

hood memories of the Italian occupation. In his later years Mengistu Lemma worked for the Theatre Arts Department of Addis Ababa University. JPL

Menken, Adah Isaacs [*née* Ada C. McCord or Adèle Theodore] ?1835–68 American actress and poet, born near New Orleans; after the deaths of her stepfather and her first husband, Alexander Isaacs Menken, a conductor, she supported herself as a dancer and circus rider, before making her acting debut at Shreveport as Pauline in *The Lady of Lyons* (1857). A bigamous marriage to the pugilist John Heenan (1859) ended in scandal, which she topped by appearing in flesh-coloured tights and minimal drapery, bound to a 'wild horse of Tartary' in Milner's MELODRAMA

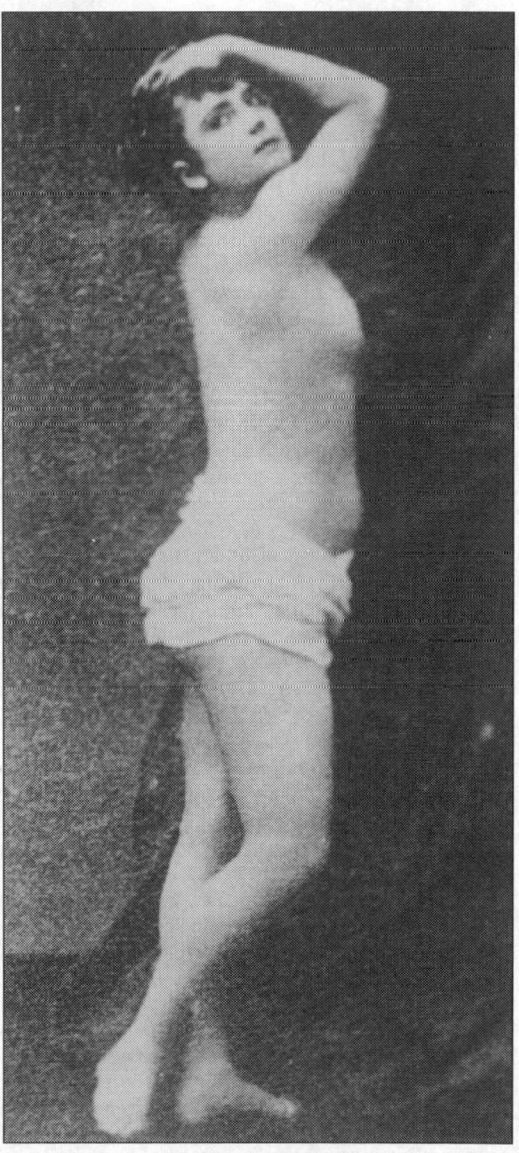

A pin-up of Adah Isaacs Menken in her 'Naked Lady' guise.

Mazeppa (Green Street Theatre, Albany, 1861). This role, which she performed throughout America, won her renown as the 'Naked Lady' and made her a star. A marriage to R. H. Newell (Orpheus C. Kerr) brought her popularity with New York's Bohemia, and a tour to San Francisco repeated this with the literati of the Far West. In London, at ASTLEY's (1864), she played in *Mazeppa* and *The Child of the Sun* for £500 a performance, the highest salary yet earned by an actress, and was lionized by DICKENS, Rossetti and Swinburne. After a fourth marriage, the last phase of her career took place in Paris, in a silent equestrian role in *The Pirates of the Savannah* (Théâtre de la Gaîté); she was rumoured to have had an affair with DUMAS *père*. Her last performance was at SADLER'S WELLS, 1868, before her sudden death from peritonitis. LS

Mercer, David 1928–80 British dramatist, who wrote prolifically for the stage, television and films during the 1960s and early 1970s. Throughout his life, he retained an individualistic Marxist faith which he tried to reconcile with the circumstances around him as a writer from Northern working-class roots who became successful in the middle-class South. That was the theme of his first WEST END play, *Ride a Cock Horse* (1965), in which the successful writer, Peter, reverted to infantilism. Madness, usually but not invariably caused by social circumstances, was the subject of his screenplay, *A Suitable Case for Treatment* (1965), and *In Two Minds* (1967), while Mercer's plays also featured rebellious eccentrics, such as Flint the agnostic vicar who runs away with a pregnant Irish girl in *Flint* (1970). This eccentricity could be caused by the tug of loyalties between love and economic necessity, between class backgrounds, or by other factors; but Mercer's heroes are usually in retreat from societies which appal them. In *After Haggerty* (1970), a critic dislikes the new world of theatre almost as much as he rebels against the narrow-minded fundamentalism of his father's generation, while in *Cousin Vladimir* (1978) a refugee from Soviet Russia finds himself appalled by the degeneracy of modern Britain. Mercer's dialogue was usually witty, handling profound ideas and complicated themes with energy and grace; but his more abstract style of writing, as in *Duck Song* (1974), worked less well in the theatre. JE

Mercier, Louis-Sébastien 1740–1814 French dramatist, critic and man of letters, deputy to the revolutionary Convention of 1792. As befitted a friend and disciple of DIDEROT and an admirer of contemporary English authors, the bulk of Mercier's work for the stage consisted of domestic dramas and comedies, with characters and incidents drawn from everyday middle-class life but often unduly sentimental or declamatory in tone, earnest and moralizing in their espousal of social issues. Notable are *Le Déserteur* (*The Deserter*, 1770), a remonstrance against war, and *La Brouette du vinaigrier* (*The Vinegar-man's Barrow*, 1775), which through a misalliance between a rich girl and a boy from the working class presents a plea for equality and the dignity of labour. Mercier was also the author of historical dramas and adaptations of SHAKESPEARE which domesticated Lear's troubles and gave Romeo and Juliet a happy ending. His critical writing not only reiterated Diderot's arguments for an extension in the normal subject-matter of drama but anticipated the attack on classical values mounted by the romantics and some of their preoccupations. DR

Mercury Theatre (London) 150-seat theatre opened by ASHLEY DUKES in 1933. The combination of poetic drama and dance in its first production (*Jupiter Translated*, an adaptation of MOLIÈRE's *Amphitryon* with an interpolated ballet by Rupert Doone) marked the two lines that have characterized the work presented there. From the beginning the Mercury served as the London base of the Ballet Rambert, while its early successes included E. MARTIN BROWNE's 1935 production of ELIOT's *Murder in the Cathedral* (originally intended as part of a Poets' Theatre season that was to have included works by YEATS and AUDEN) and the 1937 premiere of *The Ascent of F6* by Auden and ISHERWOOD. Its reputation for verse drama was re-established by the Pilgrim Players' 1945–7 seasons under Browne's management, with productions of contemporary religious plays – Norman Nicholson's *The Old Man of the Mountains*, Ronald Duncan's *This Way to the Tomb*, Anne Ridler's *The Shadow Factory* – which were followed by two popular poetic comedies, CHRISTOPHER FRY's *A Phoenix Too Frequent* and DONAGH MACDONAGH's *Happy as Larry*.

Although used solely as a studio for the Ballet Rambert from 1952 to 1966, its suitability for avant-garde work, demonstrated by the London premieres of SAROYAN's *The Beautiful People* (1947) and GENET's *The Maids* (1952), has more recently made it a base for visiting companies like the International Theatre Club, the Café LA MAMA and the Other Company. CI

Mercury Theatre (New York City) Repertory company, established in 1937 by ORSON WELLES and JOHN HOUSEMAN. The brief but historically significant two-year history – from the Welles–Houseman withdrawal from the FEDERAL THEATRE PROJECT over the refusal by Washington bureaucrats to produce MARC BLITZSTEIN's proletarian drama with music *The Cradle Will Rock*, to the final production of *Danton's Death* (1938) – is told vividly in Houseman's *Run-Through* (1972). Other imaginative productions were *The Shoemaker's Holiday*, *Heartbreak House* and a modern-dress *Julius Caesar* intended as an anti-Fascist tract – though, in fact, Welles's cutting of the text led to confusion. The ensemble included Norman Lloyd, Joseph Cotten, Martin Gabel, Vincent Price, Ruth Ford, Hiram Sherman and GERALDINE FITZGERALD. The Mercury Theatre of the Air was responsible for the infamous broadcast of 'The War of the Worlds' (1938), and many of the company members appeared in Welles's film *Citizen Kane* (1940). DBW

Merezhkovsky, Dmitry (Sergeevich) 1866–1941 Russian mystical symbolist (see SYMBOLISM) and historical dramatist and novelist parodied in BLOK's *The Puppet Show* (1906). Merezhkovsky and his poet wife Zinaida Gippius propounded theatre as temple and drama as liturgy. His plays include *Return to Nature* (1890), an adaptation of CALDERÓN DE LA BARCA's *Life Is a Dream*; *The Storm Has Passed* (1893), a symbolist variant of *A Doll's House*, which parallels conjugal and poetic liberation; *The Red*

Ethel Merman in *Annie Get Your Gun*.

Poppy (co-written with Gippius and Dmitry Filosofov, 1908), dealing with revolutionary disillusionment, the role of the artist and the nature of art; the historical dramas *Pavel I* (1908, successfully revived in 1989) and *Tsarevich Aleksei* (1920); the utopian *There Will Be Joy* (1916); and *Romantics* (1917) on the radical Bakunin as a young man. Merezhkovsky's translations of SOPHOCLES' *Oedipus* cycle and EURIPIDES' *Hippolytus* played at the Suvorin and Aleksandrinsky Theatres, 1902–7.   SG

Merman [*née* Zimmerman]**, Ethel** 1909–84 American singer and actress. Merman made an auspicious stage debut in *Girl Crazy* (1930), where her renditions of two GERSHWIN songs, 'I Got Rhythm' and 'Sam and Delilah', stopped the show nightly. She was soon typecast as a brassy, big-hearted nightclub singer, a role she played, with slight variations, in *Take a Chance* (1932), *Anything Goes* (1934) and *Red, Hot and Blue* (1936). Although she appeared in secondary roles in these shows, Merman was often given the best songs to sing because of her powerful voice and exemplary diction. She received her first solo star billing for *Panama Hattie* (1940), in which she again portrayed a nightclub singer. After a change-of-pace role as a defence worker in *Something for the Boys* (1943), she appeared in IRVING BERLIN's *Annie Get Your Gun* (1946). The part of Western sharpshooter Annie Oakley gave Merman a rare opportunity to portray a character that differed significantly from her own personality. Four years later she was back in another Berlin show, *Call Me Madam*, in which she portrayed a Washington hostess appointed ambassador to a tiny European kingdom. Her next MUSICAL, *Happy Hunting* (1956), gave her a similar role – as a Philadelphia socialite seeking a husband for her daughter. In 1959 she capped her career with her performance as

Rose, the quintessential stage mother, in *Gypsy*. Both her singing and her acting received superlative reviews from the critics. A decade later Merman made her last BROADWAY appearance when she took over the title role in *Hello, Dolly!*.

Although most of the shows in which she appeared were haphazard assemblages of stale MUSICAL COMEDY formulas, their major appeal lay in Merman's electrifying interpretations of songs by such important musical comedy composers as the Gershwins, COLE PORTER and Irving Berlin. She published autobiographies in 1955 and 1978 (with George Eells).   MK

Merrick, David 1912– American producer. Beginning with his first success, *Fanny*, in 1954, Merrick produced or co-produced over 80 plays, including many imported foreign hits. Some of his more successful have been *The Entertainer* (1958), *Gypsy* (1959), *Becket* (1960), *Stop the World – I Want to Get Off* (1962), *Luther* and *One Flew over the Cuckoo's Nest* (1963), *Oh What a Lovely War!* and *Hello, Dolly!* (1964), *Marat/Sade* (1965), *I Do! I Do!* (1966), *Rosencrantz and Guildenstern Are Dead* (1967), *Play It Again Sam* (1969), *Travesties* (1975) and *42nd Street* (1981).

Merrick's publicity stunts for his shows are legendary on BROADWAY. To publicize *Fanny*, he commissioned a nude statue of Nejla Ates, the show's belly-dancer, and had it placed in Central Park, opposite a bust of SHAKESPEARE; *Life* covered the story, and *Fanny* ran for 888 performances. Of such stunts, Merrick said, 'Other things being equal, using promotion stunts would allow me to get ahead of my competitors. I'd say that's been a big factor in my success.'

In 1983 he suffered a stroke that rendered him incapable of administering his $50–70 million estate; but in

1985 the New York Supreme Court ruled him sufficiently recovered to manage his affairs. His first production since recovery (his 88th overall) was an unsuccessful all-black revival in 1990 of the MUSICAL *Oh, Kay!*, which had originated in 1989 at the Goodspeed Opera House in Connecticut. SMA

Merry [*née* Brunton]**, Anne** 1769–1808 British-born actress and manager noted for appearances on the American stage, where, according to her biographer Gresdna Doty, she was the artistic pace-setter. Daughter of John Brunton, provincial English actor-manager, she followed her successful debut at Bath in 1785 with an engagement at London's COVENT GARDEN for the next season, remaining there until her retirement in 1792 after her marriage to minor poet Robert Merry. Soon Merry lost his money, and Anne accepted an offer in 1796 from THOMAS WIGNELL to join the CHESTNUT STREET THEATRE company in Philadelphia. Widowed four years, she married Wignell in 1803. When he died seven weeks later, she co-managed the Chestnut Street. In 1806 she married WILLIAM WARREN THE ELDER; two years later she died in childbirth at 39. As an actress she was known for her excellence in tragic roles and especially for the sweetness of her voice, her gentleness, simplicity and grace on stage. Her brother John and sister Louisa were also actors. DBW

Merson, Billy [William Thompson] 1881–1947 English PANTOMIME and VARIETY artist. Chiefly remembered as composer and singer of 'The Spaniard that Blighted my Life', this versatile Nottingham-born performer illustrates neatly the range and skill of the MUSIC-HALL professional. After an apprenticeship as half of a double act, working under various pseudonyms as Irish comedian, eccentric equilibrist and circus CLOWN, he went solo under his best-known billing in 1908. A successful career in MUSICAL COMEDY culminated in 1925 in his creation of the role of Hard Boiled Herman in *Rose Marie* at DRURY LANE. His craft is perhaps best appreciated from a recording of 'The Night I Appeared in *Macbeth*'. Studio recording was an unkind medium to many variety artists, including some of the greatest such as DAN LENO, because it deprived them of the relationship with their audience that was at once structure and nourishment. Merson transcends it, conveying through the recording not only his finely controlled natural baritone, impeccable diction and delicate use of *SPRECHSTIMME*, but also his ability to create instantly a rich characterization. His interpretation of an ageing and unsuccessful thespian of the old school – 'They made me a present/of Mornington Crescent,/They threw it a brick at a time' – is a classic example of the music-hall comedian's ability to evoke laughter and sympathy simultaneously. AEG

Meskin, Aaron 1898–1974 HABIMAH's greatest actor. Born in Russia, the son of a poor shoemaker, he joined the collective in 1918 and remained with it all his life. He was of large stature and deep voice; his most famous role was that of the man of clay in Leivik's *The Golem* (1925). Meskin played Willy Loman in ARTHUR MILLER's *Death of a Salesman* (1951) and the father in O'NEILL's *Anna Christie* (1957). He was noted for his characterizations of Othello

(1950), Macbeth (1954), King Lear (1955) and, especially, Shylock (1936, 1959). (See also HEBREW THEATRE.) HAS

Messel, Oliver 1905–78 British stage and film designer, and artist. Messel started his career designing for C. B. COCHRAN's annual *REVUES* from 1926 to 1931. Known as a colourist who frequently employed classical rules of perspective in his designs, Messel designed for the ballet such works as Frederick Ashton's and Ninette de Valois's *Sleeping Beauty* (1946) and Ashton's *Homage to the Queen* (1953). His efforts in play design are highlighted by *A Midsummer Night's Dream* (1938), *The Lady's Not for Burning* (1949) and *Roshomon* (1959). His versatility is exemplified in his designs for such films as *Caesar and Cleopatra* and *Suddenly Last Summer*. In addition, Messel is the author of a text on scene design entitled *Stage Designs and Costumes* (London, 1934; see THEATRE DESIGN). TM

Metastasio [Trapassi]**, Pietro** 1698–1782 Italian poet, dramatist and librettist. His literary gifts were early recognized and, though of modest social background, Metastasio was given an intensive private education in which the study of classical literature and theory was prominent and left a lasting influence on his writing. Prolific of verse and plays from his youth, in his mid-twenties he found his true forte, the opera libretto – his first *OPERA SERIA*, *Didone abbandonata* (*Dido Forsaken*), being performed in Naples in 1724. Among composers who later set this sentimental drama, drawn from Virgil's *Aeneid*, was Handel, and to his music it quickly achieved a European-wide celebrity. Metastasio became the most popular and successful OPERA librettist of his age, enjoying an international reputation as a major poet. Vivaldi, Albinoni and Mozart were among the scores of composers eager to set his work.

In 1729 he was called to Vienna, where he remained official court poet for the rest of his life. Most of his subject-matter was taken from Graeco-Roman history, mythology and literature, and his later critical writings indicate the extent to which he deliberately sought to emulate the austerity and elevation of Greek tragedy, while eschewing its elemental realism in favour of a formality, dignity and pathos more in tune with his temperament and acceptable to his age. Benefiting from the turn-of-the-century reform of Italian *opera seria*, he wrote at a time when music was still subordinate to text, and thus his work could enjoy a literary status *sui generis* and influence writing for the non-musical stage. His strengths lay in his instinct for the theatrically effective, his ability to produce fluent and mellifluous verse, and his consummate skill at wedding the needs of dramatic action and character delineation, on the one hand, with those of music, vocal delivery and stage spectacle on the other. In large measure, his reputation passed as his subject-matter (and even more the social and moral assumptions underpinning his treatment of it) ceased to appeal. But in recent years his theatrical skills and the extent of his influence on the drama of his age have come increasingly to be appreciated. KR

Methling, Finn 1917– Prolific Danish playwright and essayist, who has written extensively for radio and television, but also for the theatre, most distinctively in his modernist monologue *Journey to the Green Shadows* (1952), which presents a woman's life from the womb to her death. It gave Methling an important breakthrough at the KONGELIGE TEATER and on television in 1957, and has been widely performed. Another successful stage play is *Neighbours* (1979), with its triple action, allowing for overlapping and simultaneous staging.   HL

Method see STRASBERG, LEE

Mexican-American theatre see CHICANO THEATRE

Mexico With the longest sustained tradition in all of Latin America, the theatre in Mexico has passed through many stages of development. Hernán Cortés led his band of *conquistadores* against the flourishing culture of the Aztecs in 1519, and despite overwhelming odds was able to defeat Moctezuma. Using as a point of departure the Aztecs' natural inclination towards music and dance that was evident in their own dramatic productions, the early missionaries used drama to convert the indigenous peoples to Catholicism. These pieces later showed refinements, but the initial purpose of the theatre was closely related to religious instruction. For the diversion of those accustomed to the delights of the Continental theatre, a secular theatre was not long in developing in the New World. With regular routes of communication established with Spain, the influence of the Madrid theatre made itself apparent throughout the region. A developing Creole theatre emphasized local themes. Juan Pérez Ramírez (1545-?) is considered to be the first dramatist born in America; his contemporary Fernán González de Eslava (c.1534-c.1601) arrived in Mexico at an early age and wrote *coloquios*, *entremeses* (see GÉNERO CHICO) and *LOAS*, pieces with a strong religious orientation and graceful style that overcame their dramatic defects.

During the 17th and 18th centuries, the Mexican theatre continued to reflect the literary traditions of the Continent. JUAN RUIZ DE ALARCÓN was born in Mexico but made his most significant contributions to the Spanish theatre. Known as the moralist of his age, he valued human dignity in his works, combining the didactic with the entertaining. His best plays, *Las paredes oyen* (*The Walls Have Ears*, 1617) and *La verdad sospechosa* (*The Doubtful Truth*, 1621), presented the vices of inherent character faults with dramatic formulae adopted later by CORNEILLE and MOLIÈRE. The other important writer of the period was Sor Juana Inés de la Cruz (1651-95), the inimitable and precocious nun whose poetry, essays and theatre rivalled in quality the European masters. Unequalled in the American baroque, her theatre corresponds to the cycle of CALDERÓN. *El divino Narciso* (*The Divine Narcissus*, c.1680) was a prime example of the AUTO SACRAMENTAL destined for the festivities of Corpus Christi. *Amor es más laberinto* (*Love Is a Greater Labyrinth*, c.1668) was a typical cloak-and-dagger play, and *Los empeños de una casa* (*The Obligations of a Household*, c.1680) parodied the title of Calderón's play, *Los empeños de un acaso* (*The Obligations of Chance*).

By way of contrast, the 18th-century theatre, born in Spain and in Mexico and overshadowed by the earlier GOLDEN AGE masterpieces, produced a derivative and exaggerated style. In Mexico, the secular theatre competed unsuccessfully with the dominant Church as a locus for public meetings and as the vehicle for transmitting ideas and customs. Spanish plays that had already proved themselves in the peninsula were favoured over local dramatic productions. The century in Mexico is represented primarily by Eusebio Vela (1688-1737), the impresario of the insolvent Coliseo de México (Mexican Colosseum). Only three of his plays have survived, all of which show the baroque taste which mark him as one who tried to sustain the traditions of LOPE DE VEGA and Calderón de la Barca.

During the first quarter of the 19th century the disruptive influence of the wars of independence produced a general state of decay in the Latin American theatre. In Mexico the famous 'cry of Dolores' rang out on 16 September 1810, the day recognized as Independence Day when Father Hidalgo led the charge against the Spanish. Fighting continued until 1821, but even after that date the cultural bonds with the mother country remained strong. The neoclassical tendencies in vogue in Spain at the time continued to dominate, although romanticism was by then prevalent in the rest of the Continent. Joaquín Fernández de Lizardi (1776-1827), known as the 'Mexican thinker', captured the picaresque tradition in the first novel written in Spanish America, *El periquillo sarniento* (*The Itchy Parrot*, 1816), but his theatre was less innovative and also less moralizing, with plays ranging from allegorical and religious topics to contemporary historical events. The major playwright of the period is Manuel Eduardo de Gorostiza (1789-1851), who was born and died in Mexico but was educated and spent most of his life in Europe during the height of romanticism. He was not induced to follow the romantic currents, however, and his masterpiece, *Contigo pan y cebollo* (*Bread and Onion with Thee*, 1833), presented first in Madrid and shortly after in Mexico, satirized the exaggerations of the movement. Gorostiza used a mildly didactic tone to ridicule excessive sentimentalism and the idealization of standards.

Romanticism was nourished primarily by themes and techniques from Europe. The indigenous elements lacked a coherent expression, although some writers turned their attention to local matters which gave rise to the *costumbrista* theatre (see COSTUMBRISMO). Also, the awakening of national consciousness coincided with independence, and the new political and literary freedom generated innumerable works barely worthy of mention. The principal exponent of Mexican romanticism was Fernando Calderón (1809-45), whose dramas portrayed a desire to escape temporal and spatial boundaries in search of European themes, especially chivalrous themes of the Middle Ages. His only play with a Mexican setting is *A ninguna de las tres* (*None of the Three*, 1839), a satiric comedy written as a reply to Bretón de los Herreros's *Marcela o ¿a cuál de las tres?* (*Marcela, or Which of the Three?*, 1831). The works of Ignacio Rodríguez Galván (1816-42) reflected his romantic existence, but unlike his contemporary Calderón, instead of seeking inspiration in the tales of medieval Europe he looked to the traditions and legends of the New World. His dramatic production is scanty because of his premature death, but one play - *Muñoz, Visitador de México* (*Muñoz, Inspector General of Mexico*,

1938) – was an early historical drama.

Later in the century, as realistic and naturalistic aesthetics (see REALISM; NATURALISM) signalled the advent of a technological, scientific and psychological society, a post-romantic momentum controlled the theatre with little sign of evolution. José Peón y Contreras (1843–1907) has been compared with Lope de Vega for his prolific production and with the Spanish romanticist ZORRILLA for his facile verses. *El pasado* (*The Past*, 1872), a play with monologues and asides, reserved a place in Mexican theatre history for its young author, Manuel Acuña (1849–73), who committed suicide. Manuel José Othón (1848–1906), a classical poet of some renown, reflected the romantic influence of JOSÉ ECHEGARAY in two important works, *Después de la muerte* (*After Death*, 1883) and *Lo que hay detrás de la dicha* (*What's beyond Happiness*, 1886). The first pieces of children's theatre appeared during this period, works by José Rosas Moreno (1838–83), a melancholic poet and playwright whose *Sor Juana Inés de la Cruz* (1882) dealt with the apocryphal love of the illustrious nun for the Count of Mancera. At the end of the century, there was a great deal of theatre activity, although the quality was uneven at best.

The 20th century The peace, order and economic progress proclaimed by Porfirio Díaz during the early part of the century did little to foment the development of Mexican theatre, which was still closely tied to the Spanish tradition. The outbreak of the Mexican Revolution in 1910, following by exactly 100 years the wars of independence, brought some insignificant political drama, but for the most part the period was little more than a prolongation of the previous century. Many travelling foreign companies stopped off in Mexico, where they helped with the efforts of such playwrights as Federico Gamboa (1864–1939), Marcelino Dávalos (1871–1923) and Antonio Mediz Bolio (1884–1957).

After the constitutional consolidation at the end of the Revolution, coinciding with the end of the First World War, the nationalist current became stronger, and the period of the 1920s was characterized by a desire for reconstruction and reforms. Popular customs of local life and colour were captured in the light forms of the *sainete* (see *GÉNERO CHICO*) and ZARZUELA. The Teatro Folklórico (Folkloric Theatre, 1921) and the Teatro del Murciélago (Theatre of the Bat, 1924) fostered typically indigenous dances, songs and RITUAL ceremonies from all of Mexico. The struggling Sociedad de Autores Dramáticos (Playwrights' Society), founded in 1902, was re-established in 1923 as the Unión de Autores Dramáticos (Playwrights' Union) to organize the reading of plays and translations. This impetus prepared the way for the formation of the more important Grupo de los Siete Autores (Group of Seven Authors) in 1925, whose members were Francisco Monterde, José Joaquín Gamboa, Carlos Noriega Hope, Víctor Manuel Díez Barroso, Ricardo Parada León and the brothers Lázaro and Carlos Lozano García. This group started the process of modernization by discarding some quaint procedures such as asides and by accepting Mexican Spanish instead of Madrid Spanish for stage dialogue – tendencies also adopted by the Comedia Mexicana (Mexican Comedy, 1927). Carlos Díaz Dufóo's *Padre mercader* (*Father Merchant*, 1929), a realistic social piece about the dismal economic situation of a Mexican family, was the first Mexican play of the century to achieve 100 performances.

The renovation lacking in the professional companies was fostered by a series of experimental groups. In 1928 XAVIER VILLAURRUTIA and SALVADOR NOVO established the TEATRO DE ULISES (Ulysses Theatre) under the patronage of Antonieta Rivas Mercado. This vanguard theatre experiment lasted only two seasons, but it presented six plays, all foreign, to counteract the outmoded influence of the Mexican Comedy. Other groups followed, of which the most influential was the TEATRO DE ORIENTACIÓN (Theatre of Orientation, 1932–4, 1938–9), founded by CELESTINO GOROSTIZA with government sponsorship. These groups relied on intimate settings and the most recent concepts of European directors and artists – CRAIG, REINHARDT, STANISLAVSKY, PISCATOR and others – to achieve the greatest plasticity. With translations of plays by the world masters – SHAKESPEARE, Molière, LENORMAND, CHEKHOV, IBSEN, SHAW and O'NEILL, to name a few – they brought new concepts to the Mexican theatre, which in turn stimulated national works. Julio Bracho and the Escolares del Teatro (Theatre Scholars) produced the first play in the new movement in 1931, *Proteo* (*Proteus*) by Francisco Monterde. Although the play did not have long-range influence, it was now important for the director to take responsibility for balancing multiple aspects of a performance.

These groups also encouraged the construction of small theatres with a capacity of 200 or less. Seki Sano, the Japanese director trained in Stanislavsky techniques, arrived in Mexico in 1939 and participated in actor training and the creation of new groups, including Proa (1942), La Linterna Mágica (the Magic Lantern, 1946), Teatro de Arte Moderno (Modern Art Theatre, 1947) and his own group, the Teatro de la Reforma (Theatre of Reform, 1948). The major writers included Xavier Villaurrutia (1903–50), a brilliant poet who wrote short philosophical and intellectual plays such as the *Autos profanos* (*Profane Pieces*, 1933–7) and other works dealing with generational conflicts and the Mexican middle class. Salvador Novo (1904–74) and Celestino Gorostiza both made major contributions to theatre over many years as directors, critics and playwrights.

The exceptional case was RODOLFO USIGLI, who criticized Mexican reality in family and class relations but without moralizing. Usigli was a diplomat, theatre historian and prolific playwright; two of his plays have become modern classics. *El gesticulador* (*The Impostor*) is a complex, provocative examination of hypocrisy in Mexican life portrayed by a history professor who adopts the identity of a revolutionary general. *Corona de sombra* (*Crown of Shadow*, 1943) revises history to study the ill-begotten empire of Maximilian and Carlota in Mexico (1864–7) and to penetrate the lessons imparted by Carlota's long years of madness. The play is part of his *Corona* trilogy that also focused on Cuauhtémoc and the Virgin of Guadalupe. Usigli was a major experimenter in the Mexican theatre, although he did not affiliate with any experimental group. Among other features, the nationalistic movement of the 1920s focused new interest on the rising middle class, a new source of dramatic conflict, with plays implicitly or explicitly critical of social situations and revealing an increased interest in psychological examination.

The experimental cycle begun in 1928 ended in 1947 with the demise of the Teatro de México (Theatre of Mexico), and a new era of professionalism was marked that year by the formation of the Instituto Nacional de Bellas Artes (National Institute of Fine Arts). The INBA was established to foment national art through actor training, professional theatre seasons, and practical courses for theatre personnel in artistic centres. Annual drama festivals were sponsored by INBA, with prizes for new plays. For the most part, the post-Second World War theatre in Mexico concerned with psychological or character studies developed along two lines: a realistic tendency of the costumbristic theatre, and the fantasy tendency of an expressionistic theatre (see EXPRESSIONISM). Of this generation EMILIO CARBALLIDO was the most prolific and innovative. His theatre was marked by the dual inclinations towards both the realistic and the fantastic, the former in provincial settings such as *Rosalba y los Llaveros* (*Rosalba and the Llavero Family*, 1950), a play that penetrates the psychological contrast between a young city girl and her provincial cousins, and the fantastic in such plays as *La hebra de oro* (*The Golden Thread*, 1955), *Yo también hablo de la rosa* (*I Too Speak of the Rose*, 1965) and *Las cartas de Mozart* (*Mozart's Letters*, 1974). Carballido's creative spirit led to innovative forms in psychological, ontological and even political issues. In addition, he promoted a younger generation of writers through classes in directing and playwriting, and through the publication of a major theatre journal, *Tramoya*, and various editions of plays by the younger generation.

Carballido's contemporary, LUISA JOSEFINA HERNÁNDEZ, inherited Usigli's position as professor of theatre history at the National University; her plays showed careful structure and solid character development, always tempered by a Mexican reality. Other major writers of the period included Federico S. Inclán, Luis G. Basurto (1920–90), SERGIO MAGAÑA, Wilberto Canton (1925–79), JORGE IBARGÜENGOITIA and Hugo Argüelles (b.1932). Héctor Azar (b.1930) promoted theatre training through CADAC, his centre for actor training and for performing his own plays and adaptations. A number of women writers were particularly active – Margarita Urueta (b.1913), María Luisa Algarra (1916–57), Maruxa Vilalta (b.1932) and Pilar Campesino (formerly Pilar Retes). The most outstanding internationally is ELENA GARRO, whose poetic works bordering on fantasy were promoted by POESÍA EN VOZ ALTA (Poetry Out Loud). CARLOS SOLÓRZANO was born in Guatemala, but as theatre director, critic, historian and playwright his career belonged to Mexico. Affiliated with CAMUSian existentialism, the main currents in both of his short plays as well as his full-length works – *Doña Beatriz* (1952), *El hechicero* (*The Wizard*, 1954) and *Las manos de Dios* (*The Hands of God*, 1956) – were aspects of individual freedom.

During the 1950s the theatre in Mexico was strongly realistic in conception, design and staging. Both the INBA and the theatre programme of the National University staged translated plays by such authors as ARTHUR MILLER and TENNESSEE WILLIAMS. Between 1956 and 1963, Poetry Out Loud sought to bring a new intellectual and imaginative dimension to the Mexican theatre. Comprising Mexico's leading poets and most creative people, the mainsprings in the initial years included Juan José Arreola and Octavio Paz. In the eight programmes of its eight years of existence, the group presented plays ranging from Greek and Spanish classics to modern contemporary works, always with the intention of uplifting and renovating the theatre. The critics were often hostile to what was perceived as an elitist movement, and fiscal support was difficult, but many talented actors and directors contributed and thrived from the association. Héctor Mendoza, Juan José Gurrola, José Luis Ibáñez, Nancy Cárdenas and Julio Castillo were principal directors whose work continued to show the influence of Poetry Out Loud – which constituted an interesting chapter in Mexico's theatre history – long after the group's demise.

In the late 1960s a new generation of authors, many of them the products of Carballido's theatre workshops, began to emerge – in spite of the difficulties of staging new plays by unknown authors. OSCAR VILLEGAS challenged theatrical conventions with thematically and technically daring pieces: *La paz de la buena gente* (*The Peace of the Good People*, 1967), *Marlon Brando es otro* (*Marlon Brando Is Another*, 1967) and his major play, *Atlántida* (*Atlantis*, 1976). JOSÉ AGUSTÍN, an engaging novelist as well, also helped set the tone of a generation influenced by rock music with his *Abolición de la propiedad* (*Abolition of Property*, 1969), an experimental work incorporating technological elements (such as closed circuit TV, tape recordings, slides) and reflecting thematically the ontological uncertainty of the generation. Felipe Santander (b.1934) arrived late but with a huge success, *El extensionista* (*The County Extension Agent*), although his later efforts to establish an independent theatre with *Los dos hermanos* (*The Two Brothers*) and *El milagro* (*The Miracle*) were less successful.

The young writers reflected the problems of their age: specifically, the political, social and economic issues facing Mexico, and the interpersonal relationships of her youth. The generation included JESÚS GONZÁLEZ DÁVILA, Tomás Espinoza (b.1943), WILLEBALDO LÓPEZ, Damte del Castillo (b.1946), Carlos Olmos (b.1947), Gerardo Velázquez (b.1949), VÍCTOR HUGO RASCÓN BANDA, Antonio Argudín (b.1953), SABINA BERMAN, Alejandro Licona (b.1953), Miguel Angel Tenorio (b.1954) and GUILLERMO SCHMIDHUBER DE LA MORA. Two novelists who have enjoyed great success in the theatre are CARLOS FUENTES and VICENTE LEÑERO. Leñero was particularly attracted to the documentary, which he exercised with plays on Che Guevara, Morelos and other figures from the Mexican past. Fuentes, after two plays in 1970, returned to theatre in 1982. *Orquídeas a la luz de la luna/Orchids in the Moonlight* was written simultaneously in Spanish and English, and deals with the changing values and realities in the world of two ageing Mexican film stars.

Following on the heady years of the 1960s and 70s, which featured such directors as Ignacio Retes and Julio Prieto, and a brilliant group of actors including Ignacio López Tarso and others, the López Portillo regime sponsored an ambitious theatre project through the social security agency. Called Teatro de la Nación (National Theatre) and organized by Carlos Solórzano, the project consisted of five cycles (classical, Mexican, theatre of the Americas, experimental and lyrical) plus invited companies. When the economic promise of the early 1980s took a downward turn, the impact on theatre groups and institutions was notable and they did not recover until the early 90s under the presidency of Carlos Salinas de Gortari. In spite of the difficulties, the familiar names continued to be seen and were joined by a new generation that included Hugo Salcedo, Jaime Chabaud, Estela Leñero, Sergio Galindo and others.

Although Mexico City can still claim an estimated 85 per cent of all theatre activity, with its hundreds of plays and scores of playwrights and directors, there is increasing evidence of good material in the provinces. Before his untimely death, Oscar Liera (1944–90) not only wrote and directed some of Mexico's best plays but also launched a social theatre movement in Culiacán. Sonora, Veracruz, Puebla, Morelos, Guadalajara and Querétaro have active theatre as well.   GW

See: R. D. Burgess, *The New Dramatists of Mexico, 1967–1985*, Kentucky, 1991; A. De Kuehne, *Teatro mexicano contemporáneo (1940–62)*, Mexico, 1962; A. Magaña Esquivel, *Medio siglo de teatro mexicano (1900–61)*, Mexico, 1964; R. S. Lamb, *Breve historia del teatro mexicano*, Mexico, 1958; J. B. Nomland, *Teatro mexicano contemporáneo (1900–50)*, Mexico, 1967; C. Solórzano, *Testimonios teatrales de México*, Mexico, 1973; R. Unger, *Poesía en Voz Alta in the Theatre of Mexico*, Missouri, 1981; R. Usigli, *México en el teatro*, Mexico, 1932.

Meyerhold, Vsevolod (Emilievich) [Karl Theodor Kasimir Meyerhold; Dr Dapertutto] 1874–1940 The genius among Russian-Soviet theatricalist directors. Meyerhold's career describes the full trajectory from idealistic aestheticism through revolutionary experimentalism to prescriptive socialist REALISM that spans one of modern theatre history's most significant chapters (c.1898–1939). He trained in music and law before embarking on NEMIROVICH-DANCHENKO's drama course at the Moscow Philharmonia (1896–8). He and classmate OLGA KNIPPER were invited to join the newly founded MOSCOW ART THEATRE (MAT, 1898), where he first played the roles of Treplev and Tuzenbach in CHEKHOV's *The Seagull* and *The Three Sisters*, respectively. In 1902 he and other MAT company members formed the Fellowship of the New Drama, which toured the provinces for two years with typical realistic MAT fare. His growing interest in symbolist drama (see SYMBOLISM) – MAETERLINCK, Przbyszewski, ANDREEV, BLOK – coincided with STANISLAVSKY's, who invited him to test new staging methods at the MAT Studio on Povarskaya Street (1905).

Like GORDON CRAIG, GEORG FUCHS and the oriental theatre masters, Meyerhold came to believe in the primacy of movement in the theatre and in the essential difference between the rhythms of drama and of life. This resulted in what Stanislavsky considered to be puppet-like acting in Meyerhold's stagings of Maeterlinck's *Death of Tintagiles* and HAUPTMANN's *Schluck und Jau*, which Stanislavsky refused permission to open. The following year Meyerhold became artistic director of VERA KOMISSARZHEVSKAYA's Theatre (1906–7), where his experiments with stylized methods – bas-relief, rhythmic movement and intonation – applied to such symbolic and symbolist plays as IBSEN's *Hedda Gabler*, Maeterlinck's *Sister Beatrice*, Andreev's *The Life of Man*, and Blok's *The Puppet Show* (with innovative designs by Sudeikin and Sapunov), combined with the under- and misuse of his lead actress-employer, again led to his dismissal.

His official work as director at St Petersburg's Imperial opera and drama theatres (1908–18), which included sumptuous mountings of MOLIÈRE's *Don Juan* (1910) and LERMONTOV's *Masquerade* (1917), both designed by Golovin, was paralleled in time by experimental work at various small theatres and studios – the St Petersburg House of Interludes, the Tower and Strand Theatres – under the pseudonym of Dr Dapertutto. He continued the COMMEDIA DELL'ARTE research begun with *The Puppet Show* in his production of SCHNITZLER's *Columbine's Scarf* (1910), the first important event in the area of theatrical pantomime, and in his journal *Love for Three Oranges* (1914–16), in which were published scenarios and related articles. Meyerhold was now developing his theory of the actor-*cabotin*, a combined singer-dancer-juggler-tumbler, whose precise physicalization and mask-like presence would unite primordial and contemporary forms in a new, universal theatre. His experiments in scenic reconstructivism (paralleling EVREINOV's), begun with *Sister Beatrice*, *Tristan and Isolde* (1909) and *Don Juan*, continued with his staging of CALDERÓN DE LA BARCA's *The Adoration of the Cross* (Tower Theatre, 1910). Meyerhold embraced Bolshevism and, with the rallying cry 'Put the October Revolution into the Theatre' (1920), initiated a personal programme to make his art accessible to political themes and to the new proletarian audience.

In 1920 LUNACHARSKY named him head of the Theatre Division of the People's Commissariat for Education. His productions at the Theatre of the Revolution (1922–4) and at the Meyerhold Theatre (1923–38) fall into two categories. The first discovered new forms for old and old-style plays, beginning with his production of Crommelynck's *The Magnanimous Cuckold* (1922), which utilized the first pure constructivist set (by POPOVA) – a 'machine for acting' – and biomechanics, his system of kinetic, reflexive acting derived from sports, CIRCUS ACROBATICS, Pavlovian association and industrial time–motion studies. He composed complex and exact 'directorial scores', based upon a playful and grotesque ('the schematization of the real') musical and rhythmic restructuring of space, text and perspective, for SUKHOVO-KOBYLIN's *Tarelkin's Death* (with a famous design by STEPANOVA, 1922), OSTROVSKY's *The Forest* (1924), GOGOL's *The Inspector General* (1926) and GRIBOEDOV's *Woe from Wit* (which he retitled *Woe to Wit*, 1928). His AGIT-PROP-derived political productions include MAYAKOVSKY's *Mystery-Bouffe* (1918, 1921), Verhaeren's *The Dawns* (1920), SERGEI TRETYAKOV's *Earth Rampant* (1923) and *Roar, China!* (1926) and M. Podgayetsky's *D. E.* (1924). He also staged impressive productions of such new Soviet plays as Mayakovsky's *The Bedbug* (1929) and *The Bathhouse* (1930), ERDMAN's *The Mandate* (1925) and *The Suicide* (closed at dress rehearsal, 1932), OLESHA's *A List of Blessings* (1931) and Tretyakov's *I Want a Child* (refused permission to open, 1927–30).

Accused of formalism, Meyerhold lost his company and

the 'total theatre' that was being built for him. After some OPERA stagings, including a stint at the Stanislavsky Opera Theatre in Moscow (1938–9), his anger and frustration over his situation and the influx of untalented socialist realism into the Soviet theatre led to a brave but futile tirade at a theatrical congress (1939), which sealed his fate. He was immediately arrested and was executed in a labour camp (1940). His wife and lead actress Zinaida Raikh was butchered in their apartment, and Meyerhold officially became a 'non-person'. He was rehabilitated in 1955 and since then has exerted a tremendous influence on Soviet-Russian and Western directors, most notably on YURY LYUBIMOV, the Taganka Theatre's former artistic director. SG

Michell, Keith 1928– Australian actor. After acting in Adelaide, he joined the YOUNG VIC Company in 1950, and has since played many leading roles at Stratford-upon-Avon, the OLD VIC, and in the WEST END and New York. He was artistic director of the CHICHESTER FESTIVAL THEATRE in 1974–8; appeared in Australia with the Shakespeare Memorial Theatre tour of 1952–3, in *The First Four Hundred Years* (1964), *Othello* (1978) and *La Cage aux Folles* (1985); and acted with the Queensland Theatre Company (1982). His most famous television role is Henry VIII in the BBC's *The Six Wives of Henry VIII* (1970). MW

Mickery-theater Founded in 1965 by Ritsaert Ten Cate in Amsterdam, the Mickery-theater was the Dutch institution that consistently chose to present theatrical productions from abroad that stood for new developments and trends in theatre. Performances were originally held in Ten Cate's farmhouse in Loenersloot, a village close to Amsterdam. Having been a private enterprise for five years, Mickery received subsidy for the first time in 1970 and moved to Amsterdam. Its building there (a former cinema) had no fixed area for either audience or actors. Mickery-theater's aim was to give to Dutch actors and theatre a new direction. In cooperation with foreign companies, it stimulated and developed theatrical initiatives that were difficult to stage elsewhere. There were a few regulars amongst the visiting companies: TRAVERSE THEATRE (Edinburgh), LA MAMA (New York), the Pip Simmons Theatre Group (London), Tenjo Tsukiji (Tokyo) and the PEOPLE SHOW (London).

Projects produced by Mickery itself showed an increasing interest in the relationship between the theatre and reality, and between theatre and audio-visual means. The use of movable cubicles, which, supported by air-cushions, would allow the audience to drift past several scenes during a performance, was particularly spectacular. Projects that made use of such cubicles were *Fairground* (1975), *Cloud Cuckooland* (1979, with Tenjo Sajiki), *Outside* (1979) and *Fairground '84* (produced for the HOLLAND FESTIVAL). During the 1984–5 and 85–6 seasons, research into the relationship between the theatre and video/television took a central place in the initiatives undertaken by Mickery-theater – for instance, in Pip Simmons's *La Ballista*.

Mickery's activities ceased in 1991. The last project was *Touchtime*, a kind of festival in which the company presented a mix of groups. On the one hand were those that became classics of the FRINGE, such as the WOOSTER GROUP and BREAD AND PUPPET THEATRE; and on the other, new initiatives representing new directions in the theatrical landscape such as *Hula Kahiko* by Hawaiian hula dancers and the Arena Teatro from Murcia in Spain. HS MG

Mickiewicz, Adam 1798–1855 Polish romantic poet and playwright, who from 1823 lived in Russia, Germany, Italy and France as a political exile dedicated to the cause of Poland's freedom. His visionary work on the suffering and messianic destiny of Poland, *Forefathers' Eve* (1823, 1832; fully staged, 1901), is the national sacred drama, dreamlike in structure. His ideas for a monumental theatre based on Greek tragedy, medieval mysteries (see MYSTERY PLAY) and primeval folklore have had enduring influence on Polish directors. DG

Micronesia see OCEANIA

Middle East It has long been assumed that theatre is a recent import to the Middle East and North Africa from the Western world. Modern scholarship is rapidly demonstrating that this is a misconception. While it is certainly true that Western plays and production styles were imported to most urban areas of the region from Europe for the first time in the late 19th and early 20th centuries, earlier indigenous theatrical traditions have existed in the Middle East continuously for many centuries. The richness and importance of these earlier traditions, which have played an important role in the cultural life of the region for so long, have only recently begun to be appreciated. According to some theorists, Middle Eastern traditional theatre may even have influenced the development of theatre in the West, particularly comic theatre.

The rediscovery of traditional theatre in the Middle East has become an important cultural feature of the overall development of art in the region as playwrights and writers attempt to develop new modes of artistic expression which move away from imitation of Western tradition, and attempt to develop new theatre which speaks to the cultural roots of modern Middle Eastern peoples.

Most of these historical forms of Middle Eastern and North African theatre escaped the attention of orientalist scholars because they existed primarily as folk theatrical tradition with little in the way of formally recorded text. Today it is not possible to reconstruct the exact forms of the earliest historical traditions. Researchers must rely on comparisons of existing folk traditions, and historical accounts by travellers and local chroniclers, to come to an understanding of the earliest theatrical forms.

The ancient past Evidence exists which suggests that dramatic performances were held in Pharaonic Egypt in temple settings. Ancient Pharaonic texts dating to as early as 2500 BC exist which suggest dialogue, stage directions and dramatic conventions. Particularly notable are the coronation 'dramas' of ancient Egypt, which were enacted in processional style, each scene being presented at a separate station along the route. Another well known text, the Memphite Creation Drama, deals with the death and resurrection of Osiris, and was probably enacted on the first day of spring. These early works suggest that ancient

Egyptian drama probably consisted of enactment of legends and religious stories which were well known by spectators. No attempt seems to have been made to produce 'catharsis' or emotional reaction in the audience. Nevertheless, comic dialogues also exist which show that humour was present in these early performances.

Theodore Gaster, in his comprehensive study, *Thespis: Ritual, Myth and Drama in the Ancient Near East*, suggests that RITUAL and drama have a common religious origin in the Near East. He deals not only with the ancient Egyptian texts mentioned above, but also with ritual poems and texts from Canaanite, Babylonian and Hittite sources. While many of the sources cited by Gaster are not written in contemporary dramatic form, these mythological texts were probably enacted in ritual context before a public audience.

From Alexander to the Moghul empires There is little mention of indigenous theatrical activity in the Middle East during the period from the 3rd century BC to the establishment of the great Moghul empires throughout the region in the 13th century. What is known about traditional theatre can only be surmised from indirect evidence. Greek and Roman civilization (see GREECE, ANCIENT; ROME) penetrated into most areas of Mesopotamia, Asia Minor and North Africa during the early centuries of this period on the heels of the conquests of Alexander the Great, and through the establishment of the Eastern Roman Empire at Byzantium. The ruins of ancient theatres and colosseums are found throughout North Africa, in Syria, and as far East as the central part of present-day Turkey, and it must be presumed that Greek and Roman spectacles, including dramatic presentations, were performed in them.

It is also undoubtedly the case that performance traditions of the Indian subcontinent were known in parts of the Middle East, particularly in the Sassanian Empire of Iran (c.AD 225–652). Numerous historical sources document the migration of gypsies across the Iranian plateau during this period. The Iranian poet Ferdowsi, in his epic *Shāhnāmeh*, notes that Bahrām-Gur (AD 420–38), the legendary Sassanian king, ordered the importation of ten thousand musicians, dancers and performers from INDIA to Iran during his reign. Another Sassanian ruler, the grand patron of the arts Khosrow Parviz (AD 591–628), is likewise said to have supported performers in his court.

The Islamic conquest of the region beginning in the 7th century AD marks a period with little mention of any dramatic or theatrical activity. Orthodox Islam tended to view dramatic presentation as suspect, since it involved the depiction of personages who were imaginary or deceased. Thus the most conservative religious officials labelled it idolatry, an illicit attempt to create an alternative reality to that created by God. Just as images of human beings and animals were banned from plastic and pictorial arts under Islam, human images were banned from depiction in public performance.

Nevertheless, the verbal arts of poetry, storytelling and recitation continued to be practised widely throughout the Islamic world. Many of these arts, such as the public recitation of epic poetry or of religious stories, took on the quality of dramatic art. These practices continued down to

modern times, and served as the basis for the development of more modern theatrical forms. Several forms of Middle Eastern traditional performing arts probably came into being in the centuries between the advent of Islam and the great 16th-century empires. These were (1) puppet drama, particularly shadow puppet drama; (2) narrative drama and dramatic storytelling; (3) religious epic drama; (4) comic improvisatory drama.

Shadow puppet theatre similar to that found today throughout East and Southeast Asia was probably introduced to the Middle East at the time of the Mongol invasion in the 13th century. Even before this time a rotating magic lantern with shadow figures propelled by hot air generated by the light inside the lantern was known in the region. Omar Khayyām (?1021–1122) mentions it in one of his quatrains, calling it *fanus-e khayāl*, 'lantern of fantasy' or 'lantern of dreams'. SHADOW PUPPETS are found from Japan to Greece, and vary little in their basic form of manufacture. Their method of manufacture helped them deal with basic orthodox Islamic objections to their existence. Shadow puppet makers were able to circumvent these objections by pointing out that since the figures were perforated with holes, they no longer represented animate beings. Even so, tradition dictates that angels cannot enter houses that contain these questionable images. Therefore during religious holidays it is desirable to hold performances in gardens or courtyards.

Although there is very little record of shadow puppet drama in Iran, it was known throughout the Turkish, Greek and Arabic world first as *khayāl az-zill*, then by the Turkish word *karagöz*, or '*ara-'uz* in Arabic – 'black-eye', in reference to the chief comic character, KARAGÖZ, who had a black eye.

Other forms of puppet drama in the Middle East are also very old. Khayyām mentions them in his quatrains:

> We are the puppets [*lo'bat*]
> and destiny is the puppeteer.
> We play on the spread of life
> and go again into the trunk of death.
>
> (after Gaffary, 1984:365)

The poet Farīdu'd-dīn 'Attar (d.1221) also deals at length with the puppet theatre in his *Oshtor Nāme* (*Book of the Camel*). The poet Nezami mentions puppets in his *Makhzen ul-Esrār* (*Treasure-house of Secrets*, 1165/6).

Metin And, the renowned Turkish folklorist, maintains that shadow puppet theatre first appeared in the Middle East as a borrowing from INDONESIA. Arabic traders brought the entertainment to Egypt during the medieval period, where it was first witnessed by the Ottoman sultans in the 16th century. Adopted by the Ottoman court, it soon assimilated themes from human and puppet drama already in existence.

Narrative drama may have originated in religious preaching, but it also has pre-Islamic precedent in the Parthian storytelling practice known as *gōsān*. The epic folk tale is very ancient throughout the Middle East, and is found in all languages. The episodic organization of long epics such as the *Thousand and One Nights* suggests the storyteller's art may have served as the principle of their organization. Already at the end of the 9th century, a celebrated Arabian storyteller, ibn al-Magazili, had begun to introduce dramatic elements and characterization into his performances. By the 11th century it had crystallized into a literary genre, the *maqama* ('assembly'), at the hands of Badi 'az-Zamān al-Hamadāni, and expanded by al-Ḥariri.

Whatever its origin, it is certain that narrative drama was given impetus by the sermons and public recitations occasioned by Islam. It was a natural step for eulogizers and panegyrists to begin recitation of popular drama. The fact that these narratives became associated with the Islamic month of religious fasting, Ramadan, gives further support to the idea that they may have had a religious origin. In the Ottoman world narrative drama was known as *meddah*, 'eulogy'. In Iran it came to be known as *naqqāli*, 'recounting', for coffee-house recitation of secular epics such as Ferdowsi's *Shāhnāmeh pardeh-dāri* – literally, 'screen-keeping' – for narration of religious stories with large illustrated screens which contained visual images of the stories being presented; and *rowzeh-khāni*, for recitation of the events surrounding the death of the 7th-century AD Shi'a martyr, Imam Husain (d.680).

Religious epic drama was limited to Shi'a communities, and, like *rowzeh-khāni*, concerned the events surrounding the death of Imam Husain. Known variously as *shabih* (simulation) or *ta'ziyeh* (mourning), religious epic drama may also have had its origins in pre-Islamic practices of mourning for the legendary prince Siyāvosh, a blameless hero, killed unjustly by his father-in-law. These mourning practices were noted in the 10th century, by the historian Narshakhi, as having taken place for many centuries in the city of Bukhara. They were still practised in some parts of Iran until as recently as 1974. Present day *ta'ziyeh* probably grew out of public mourning ceremonies for Imam Husain, which were seen as early as the Buyyid Empire (c.AD 940–76). These ceremonies began as processions and later took on enactment of the story in dramatic form.

Comic drama was known throughout the Middle East generically as *taqlid* (also *taklid* or *taklit*), 'imitation'. However, in local areas it became better known by specific names. In the Ottoman Empire it was *orta-oyunu*, 'play in the middle', referring to the open square, or *meidan*, where it was usually performed. In many Arab countries itinerant players presented *fuṣūl mudhika* (comic scenes). In Iran the same dramatic form came to be known by many names, but one common appellation in modern times is *ru-howzi* or *takht-e howzi* theatre, referring also to the place of performance: *ru* 'on' the *howz* 'pool', referring to the pool commonly found in the courtyards of large homes, over which a platform (usually a plank bed – a *takht*) was often placed for the performance.

In eastern Afghanistan, in and around the city of Herat, Magadi theatre – named after the social group which performs it, the Magads – is directly related to *orta-oyunu* and *ru-howzi* traditions. Many theatrical forms of the Indian subcontinent, such as BHAVAI in Gujarat, *bhand pater* in Kashmir, KHYAL in Rajasthan and *sang* in Uttar Pradesh, are clearly related to these forms as well, suggesting for the traditions a long history of migration. Indeed, these traditions are almost certainly also linked to European *COMMEDIA DELL'ARTE*, raising the possibility that this European form may once have had Asian roots. *Orta-oyunu* performances were first recorded during the Seljuq dynasty (11th–12th centuries AD) in the city of Konya.

Similar performances are not noted in Iran until several centuries later. Nevertheless, given its extraordinarily wide distribution throughout South and Southwest Asia, it is likely that improvisatory comic theatre was performed in Iran on a regular basis long before it was first recorded in historical accounts.

Traditional theatre from the 16th to 19th centuries

Following the Mongol invasion, two great empires arose in the Middle East – the Ottoman, centred in Istanbul (1498–1926), and the Safavid in Iran (1501–1723). The Safavids were succeeded after a short interim by the Qājar dynasty (1779–1924). Except for extreme Northwestern Africa, all of the present-day Middle East was contained under the reign of these empires until the First World War.

Court life dominated the wealthy classes, and all manner of entertainments were found in the capitals of the empires. For the most part the shahs of Iran and the sultans of the Ottoman Empire were interested in patronizing the arts. They maintained performers, including actors and artists, in their courts despite general Islamic disapproval of these entertainments. At the same time, the theatrical arts flourished on a popular level outside court settings, although the historical record of these more popular forms is much less complete.

Puppet drama fared better in the Ottoman Empire than in Iran, where shadow puppet drama seems to have disappeared completely, the last vestigial performance recorded in 1926. *Karagöz*, by contrast, spread throughout the Ottoman Empire and adjacent lands. It was found at its peak in Egypt, Syria, Morocco, Algeria, Bosnia-Herzegovina and Greece, as well as throughout Asia Minor.

The Ottoman sultans were great patrons of *karagöz*. The form first flourished under the reign of Bayazid Yildirim (1389–1402), especially at the hand of one of the sultan's servants, one Kör Hasan. Shadow puppetry was especially encouraged by Selim I, who was greatly impressed by a performance he witnessed in Egypt in 1517. Under Suleiman the Magnificent (1520–66) shadow puppet theatre was shown on ceremonial days, such as celebrations of the circumcision of royal princes. The plays were called *haial* (compare Persian and Arabic *khiyāl*, 'dream', 'fantasy') and the puppeteers, *haialdji*, the suffix -*ji* signifying a practitioner of any trade.

The 17th-century Turkish traveller, geographer and historian Evliya Chelebi describes *karagöz* extensively in his *Siyahet Nāme*, or *Book of Travels*. In this he describes the artist Kör Hasan Zade Mehmed Chelebi, descendant of Kör Hasan, the famous puppeteer who served under Bayazid Yildirim. Mehmed Chelebi gave performances twice a week in the court of Sultan Murad IV (1623–40). Most of the characters were those of modern *karagöz*, and many of the plays presented are still known today. By the reign of Sultan Ibrahim (1640–8) puppet drama had reached unprecedented popularity. It was at the sultan's coronation on 23 February 1640 that the first European, the French traveller Thévenot, witnessed the shadow theatre, which he called *carageuz*.

Numerous famous *haialdjis* dot Ottoman cultural history. Of particular note were Hafiz Bey in the reign of

Selim III (1789–1807), and Said Efendi (1808–39). Royal patronage continued unabated until the early 20th century. By this time, *karagöz* was being performed in coffeehouses throughout Constantinople and was a lucrative form of popular entertainment among the masses as well as at court. Although shadow puppetry was never widespread in Iran during this period, glove PUPPETS and MARIONETTES gained a degree of popularity. The German traveller Adam Oléarius provides an account of a strolling puppeteer in Iran in the first half of the 17th century. It is interesting that puppeteers in Iran traditionally used glove puppets during the day, and marionettes during the evening when their strings would be less noticeable. Puppet drama in Iran was commonly called *kheimeh shabbāzi* ('tent-play in the night'). There is no historical record of royal patronage, though individual strolling players existed up until the revolution of 1978–9.

Narrative drama was well established by the 13th century among the Arab populations of the Middle East. At this time the storytellers of Baghdad organized themselves into a guild headed by a sheikh.

Storytellers were already popular at the beginning of the Ottoman Empire. They were greatly revered in the Ottoman court and are mentioned continually in accounts of the reigns of the sultans, from Bayazid Yildirim in the 15th century down to the First World War. *Meddahs* (eulogizers) in the Ottoman Empire were ingenious parodists and satirists (see PARODY; SATIRE). Because of their tendency to burlesque political affairs, they were subject to rigorous CENSORSHIP, particularly in the 19th century. They could not use the word 'sultan' nor mention riots, revolutions or insurrections, even those of other countries. They were also prohibited from mocking the clergy.

The *meddahs* performed most often in coffee-houses in large cities. Financial arrangements varied. Occasionally tickets were sold, and the coffee-house owner was paid rent for the use of the room. Often the proprietor would be content with the additional income brought in by the large number of customers attracted by the performance. The Iranian *naqqāl* operated in a similar fashion, working from coffee-houses, or occasionally from private homes. His stock in trade was almost exclusively Ferdowsi's *Shāhnāmeh* (*Book of Kings*), although he would occasionally narrate other epics for the pleasure of the crowd. The art of the *naqqāl* was codified in a 17th-century work, *Tarāz al-Akhbār* (*The Adornment of Narrative*). One unusual setting for the Iranian storyteller even today is the *zurkhāneh* ('house of strength'), a traditional athletic club. In this setting, a professional chanter, called a *murshed*, accompanies the traditional athletic exercises with drum beat, and recitations of deeds of bravery from Ferdowsi's epic.

The history of *pardeh-dāri* (screen-keeping) is lost to us. Similar narrative techniques exist throughout Asia and the Middle East, however, suggesting great antiquity. The *pardeh-dar*'s episodes from Islamic religious drama were illustrated using a giant rolled screen which was often handed down from father to son. The *pardeh-dars* would ply their trade in public markets and bazaars, collecting money as free-will public offerings for their stories. They most often would recite the events of the martyrdom of Imam Husain at Kerbala, and are occasionally seen even today.

Rowzeh-khāni would not be called entertainment by strictly religious persons in Iran, but it was so classified in Safavid and Qājar Iran. The *rowzeh-khāns* even had a guild at one time. These reciters of the events of Kerbala are often Islamic clergymen, but they need not be. They receive fees for their services when reciting outside normal prayer services at public mosques, at funerals, private family memorial services, or occasionally at private devotions. Since Safavid times, on principal Shi'a religious holidays the most famous *rowzeh-khāns* have been in heavy demand. Many became both rich and famous for their performances. In recent years, their recitations have even been sold as audio tape cassettes. *Rowzeh-khāni* is noteworthy as the one narrative tradition open to women, but only for consumption by all-female audiences.

Religious epic drama in Iran most likely evolved under the patronage of the Safavid shahs. They themselves had origins as a religious brotherhood, and were particularly interested in encouraging religious ritual. Mourning ceremonies for Imam Husain were patronized by them on a grand scale. During their reign enormous processions of mourners in groups, called *dasteh*, would congregate in the streets during the first ten days of the Islamic month of Muharram, scourging themselves with chains, and cutting themselves with swords and knives while they chanted rhythmic dirges of mourning. As the size of the processions grew, they became more elaborate, with depictions of the events of the martyrdom enacted by players on 'floats' situated at intervals among the mourners.

Early travellers noted these processions. The first fully fledged account was given by the English traveller William Francklin in 1787, though the Russian voyager Gmelin noted the ceremonies and used the word 'theatre' to describe them in 1770; and two other travellers, Salamons and Van Goch, had seen the processions – without calling them 'theatre' – sometime between 1722 and 1735. By the 19th century, *ta'ziyeh* was being performed as a fully fledged dramatic form. Adrian Dupré, who was attached to the scientific body accompanying the French mission to Persia in 1807–9, gives an account which is essentially a description of the dramatic form as it is seen today. Manuscripts of *ta'ziyeh* dramas held privately in Iran date from the late 18th century, suggesting that the form was already well established when Dupré saw it.

Ta'ziyeh was lavishly patronized by the Qājar shahs. Huge open-air arenas called *tekiyeh* were built for royally patronized performances featuring thousands of actors and an equally large number of live animals. Members of the foreign community were regularly invited to attend, and Naser od-Dīn Shah (1848–96) had a *ta'ziyeh* 'director' as part of his royal household. Gradually the dramas began to be performed nearly all year, not only in the court, but in cities and villages throughout the country. Shi'a communities in Lebanon and Bahrain also enacted *ta'ziyeh*, though not on such a grand scale. The processional form of the mourning ceremony continues today in Shi'a communities in INDIA and PAKISTAN.

Comic improvisatory theatre was also supported by the courts. Shah 'Abbās of Iran (1588–1629) had a famous jester, Kal 'Enāyat (Bald Enāyat), who performed comic entertainments in court. A miniature painting by Soltan Mohammad Naqqāsh from this period (1621) shows performers entertaining in what seems to be a court setting. One of the clowns is wearing a tall hat, and others are clothed in goat-skins. Bezā'i reports that musicians from this period used to give comic performances when called on to entertain in the homes of the wealthy:

> Entertainers in *taqlid* would normally imitate the accents and personal characteristics of well known people in the towns and villages in which they performed. These people would be seen meeting and greeting each other. After a short while they would fall to arguing and making fun of each other's accents and behaviour, and the story would end with the two characters fighting and chasing each other.
>
> (Bezā'i 1965:55)

Orta-oyunu was active throughout the duration of the Ottoman Empire, and served as an important form of social protest. In true *taqlid* style (*taklid* in Turkish), performers in *orta-oyunu* would imitate the attitudes and accents of persons of different trades and nationalities and make fun of them. The sultan maintained a troupe at court which performed on Imperial holidays, such as the birth of a prince, his circumcision, coronations and other state occasions. A band of actors accompanied the sultan into war, where they served to divert him from the difficulties of battle. Bands of actors also accompanied ambassadors, provincial governors and foreign legations, thus spreading theatrical practice into the provinces and other lands where Ottoman influence was felt. Local nobles in Egypt, Walachia, Moldavia and other provinces wishing to imitate the sultans likewise organized theatrical performances.

The advent of Western theatre During the 19th century, the Qājar and Ottoman Empires began to come under the influence of European culture. Although many European travellers had journeyed to Middle Eastern lands in the 16th and 17th centuries, it was only in the 18th that Middle Easterners began to tour Europe with any regularity. Most cultured travellers were greatly impressed by European theatre, as well as by OPERA. It was at this point that European-style drama began to be performed.

It is difficult to ascertain who staged the first Western-style drama in a Middle-Eastern language, but a strong claim may be made for Mārūn Mikhā'il al-Naqqāsh, a Maronite Christian with musical and literary talents born in Sidon in 1817. He was trained as a book-keeper and, as a member of the Beirut Chamber of Commerce, travelled throughout the Ottoman Empire. In 1846 he travelled to Italy, where he was greatly struck with the theatre and opera. On returning to Beirut he determined to stage a theatrical performance with the help of his family and friends, and in 1847 wrote an original drama in Arabic heavily inspired by MOLIÈRE's *L'Avare*, entitled *al-Bakhīl* (*The Miser*).

The play was produced in al-Naqqāsh's home and was enthusiastically received, prompting him to stage another play, *Abū al-Ḥasan al-Mughaffal aw Hārūn al-Rashīd* (*Abū al-Ḥasan the Fool*, or [*the Caliph*] *Hārūm al-Rashīd*, a story adapted from the *Thousand and One Nights* (known in the West as The *Arabian Nights*), in

1848–50. The British traveller David Urquhart witnessed this performance in 1850, and declared it technically weak but artistically successful.

These successes encouraged al-Naqqāsh to stage a third drama, after obtaining permission from the Ottoman authorities to build a theatre adjacent to his home. The third and last production was staged in 1853, *al-Salīṭ al-Ḥasūd* (*The Sharp-Tonged Envious Man*).This drama is almost entirely original, but al-Naqqāsh borrows from Molière in places, particularly from *Le Misanthrope* where Molière's character Alceste became al-Naqqāsh's model for his own Sam'an, a handsome and vain youth whose contempt for everyone around him in fact conceals consuming envy. In his characterization of the simple-minded Jirjis, Al-Naqqāsh also includes the famous passage from Molière's *Le Bourgeois Gentilhomme* where M. Jourdain discovers to his surprise that he has been speaking prose all his life.

Al-Naqqāsh died of a fever in 1855, but he had inspired a number of younger men. His nephew Salīm later took his theatrical troupe to Egypt, where *Abū al-Ḥasan al-Mughaffal* was staged in Alexandria in 1876.

The first Western-style Arabic production in Cairo was not that of al-Naqqāsh but the play *Operette* by Ya'qūb Ṣannū' (1839–1912), staged in 1870 in the garden of a coffee-house at Azbbakiyya, which had been built, along with the Cairo Opera House, by Khedive Ismail, who had an interest in transforming Egypt into a Europeanized state.

Ṣannū', known also as James Sanua, was a Cairene of Italian-Jewish parentage. At the age of 13 he was sent to Italy to study at the expense of a member of the royal family. Besides mastering Italian (so well, we are told, that he composed plays in it), he studied the theatre and was particularly fond of the Italian opera (elements of which would later creep into his Arabic plays). Upon his return to Egypt, he began teaching at the polytechnic in Cairo and supplemented his income by becoming a private tutor of foreign languages to children of wealthy families. He was later dismissed from his teaching position – allegedly because of his theatrical activities and his criticism of the Khedive.

He wrote and staged a number of humorous plays in the Egyptian colloquial, full of songs and satirical musical sketches, much like the Turkish *orta-oyunu* and reflecting the influence of the Italian opera which greatly fascinated him during his year in Italy. Some of the plays are comedies of manners, centring on stock characters such as the Nubian servant (al-Barbari), the talkative maid, and the European with faulty classical Arabic. Like al-Naqqāsh's, Ṣannū''s plays were influenced by Molière – full of scheming lovers, intrigues, mistaken identities and pedants who abuse and misuse language, and taking love and greed as common themes.

His first play was favourably received by Khedive Ismail, and as a result he was dubbed by him 'the Molière of Egypt'.The text of this play is lost; what we know about it is based on a summary left to us by Ṣannū'. It is about the Egyptian harem and is aimed at fighting European stereotypes – subject-matter typical of the time was the moral laxity of women in the Egyptian harem. It tells the story of a European prince who bets a member of the Egyptian nobility one thousand pounds that, if he is given a few weeks in Cairo, he will be able to have his way with a woman in the harem. It appears, some time later, that the European has won the bet, when he manages to sneak into the chamber of a harem woman who has been sending him secret messages through her eunuch. Discovered by the head of the household, he is captured and ordered to be put in a sack, along with the woman, and thrown into the Nile. After pleading on his part, his life is spared by the head of the household, who is in fact the Egyptian nobleman in disguise. The whole affair turns out to be a trick played by the Egyptian nobleman and a male friend, who had disguised himself as the harem woman. The play ends happily with a dinner party.

Between 1870 and 1872 Ṣannūʿ wrote and acted in over ten plays, one of which, entitled (aḍ-Durritĕn (The Co-Wives), was for a non-Muslim a daring attack on Islamic-sanctioned polygyny. It is said that in 1872 the Khedive Ismail became so upset after watching the play that he ordered Ṣannūʿ's theatre to be closed down. Ṣannū's then began a career as a journalist. He directed biting SATIRE against the Khedive Ismail, and, as a result, was exiled to France in 1878. He continued his attacks on Khedive Ismail and later on Khedive Tawfīq in the form of sarcastic dialogues and cartoons. According to his – probably exaggerated – count, he wrote and produced 32 plays. Only eight have been discovered; they were published by Yūsuf Najm in 1963.

Salīm al-Naqqāsh's productions in Alexandria were highly successful, developing some remarkable actors, including Yusuf al-Khayyāṭ. When Salīm al-Naqqāsh himself became embroiled in political controversy through his journalistic writings in 1878, Khayyāṭ moved the troupe to Cairo where the sturdy Abū al-Ḥasan al-Muḡaffal was once again produced with success before the Khedive. Another play, Salīm al-Naqqāsh's al-Ẓalūm (The Tyrant), angered Ismail, who imagined that the tyrant of the play was a veiled reference to his oppressive rule. He therefore forced the troupe to perform outside of Cairo in Alexandria and in provincial towns, where it enjoyed enormous success. Khayyāṭ was responsible for introducing a number of excellent actors to the stage, including the singer and actor Salāma Ḥijāzi.

Sulaymān al-Qurdāḥī was another player in Khayyāṭ's troupe who went on to found his own company. Al-Qurdāḥī's troupe was established in Alexandria in 1882. He toured Egypt, Syria, Europe and North Africa, eventually settling in Tunisia until his death in 1909. Al-Qurdāḥī is credited with introducing to North Africa the first Western-style theatre produced in Arabic.

The first professional theatre in Syria (after the amateur productions of Mārūn al-Naqqāsh) was established by Aḥmad Abū Khalīl al-Qabbānī (1833–1902), born in what is present-day Turkey and raised in Damascus. Al-Qabbānī first produced his own amateur plays, including Salīm al-Naqqāsh's Arabic adaptation of Verdi's Aida. The Ottoman government officials in Damascus, particularly the ruler Midḥat Pacha, bent on modernization, supported al-Qabbānī and ordered construction of a theatre; but religious officials, objecting to theatre, forced the troupe to leave the country in 1884 for Alexandria in Egypt.

He and his troupe eventually moved to Cairo, where they achieved enormous success, employing the best per-

fomers of the period. Unfortunately a fire in his Cairo theatre ruined al-Qabbānī financially, and he lived out his days in Damascus on a government stipend. One of his actors, Iskandar Faraḥ, formed yet another troupe, which was reputedly even better than al-Qurdāḥī's. Faraḥ's troupe achieved such renown that it was able to attract the famous actor Salāma Ḥijāzī. Faraḥ commissioned a number of new plays in Arabic from promising writers of the day.

A thorny problem facing the early drama writers was the choice between literary Arabic and the spoken idiom of everyday life. It was difficult to abandon literary Arabic for the pedestrian language of the market-place, but it was unnatural to make both the peasant and the intellectual speak terse literary Arabic. A compromise, not totally satisfactory, was reached, whereby the dialogue in comic plays was rendered in colloquial Arabic, whereas the dialogue in serious and historical plays would be in literary Arabic (also used for stage directions for all plays – a convention that continues to the present day).

Further to the east another early pioneer of Western-style theatre was Mirzā Fatḥ ʿAli Ākhundzādeh (1812–78). Though living in the Russian Caucasus, Ākhundzādeh wrote in Āzeri Turkish, the dialect of Āzerbāijān. He composed six plays between 1850 and 1855: Mollā Ibrāhim Khalil Kimiyāgar (Mullah Ibrahim the Alchemist); Musir Jordān, Hakim-e Nabātāt (Monsieur Jordan the Botanist); Vizir-e Khān-e Sarāb (The Vizier of the Khān of Sarab); Khers-e Qoldorbāsān (The Thief-catching Bear); Sargozasht-e Mard-e Khasis (The History of a Miser); and Vokalā-ye Morāfeʿe-ye Tabriz (The Rich Lawyers of Tabriz). He translated some of these plays into Russian and performed them in large cities of the Caucasus. A collection of these works, Tamsilāt (Proverbs), was published in Āzeri Turkish in 1859 and later became the first Western-style dramatic literature published in Persian in a translation by Mirza Mohammad Qarāje-dāghi in Tehran (1974).

The first original plays in Persian were written by Mirzā Āqā Tabrizi, a literary government bureaucrat who visited Constantinople and came in contact with Ākhundzādeh's writings. Ākhundzādeh asked Mirzā Āqā to translate his works into Persian, but the latter preferred to write original works. His comedies – Ashraf Khān Hokzumat-e Zamān Khān (The Rule of Zamā Khān), Kerbalā Raftan-e Shāh Qoli Mirzā (The Pilgrimage to Kerbalā of Shāh Qoli Mirzā) and ʿĀsheq Shodan-e ʿĀqā Hāshem (Āqā Hāshem's Love Affair) – are extremely amusing and surprisingly modern. Until recently many of Mirzā Āqā's works were attributed to Malkām Khān, a literate, rebellious politician who lived abroad. Because of the satirical nature of many of the plays, Mirzā Āqā may have been content to allow this mistake to stand.

Western-style theatre in Istanbul was first introduced during the regime of Abdül Mecit I. By 1839 there were two theatres in the Ottoman capital, one for Italian opera and one for orta-oyunu plays. The earliest drama may have been the comedy Şair Evlenmesi by Ibrahim Şinasi (1859). The father of Western-style theatre in Turkish was Agop Vartovyan, later known as Güllü Agop, an Armenian who later converted to Islam. Agop established the Ottoman Theatre Company at Gedikpaşa Theatre in Istanbul. The first play produced there was César Borgia, a translation from French to Turkish, in April 1868. This was not a success, and in 1869 Agop produced a tragedy by Mustafa Efendi based on the well known Middle Eastern romance, *Leyla ve Mecnun* (*Leila and Majnun*). This successful production fostered much original Turkish theatre in the decade to come, by such playwrights as Raciazade Ekrem, Namĩk Kemal, Ali Bey, Ahmet Mithat Efendi, Ahmet Vefik Paşa and Ebûzziya Tevfik.

The Grand Vizier Ali Paşa granted Güllü Agop a ten-year monopoly on all theatrical productions in Istanbul in 1870, which somewhat limited the growth of Turkish theatre. Would-be producers started in cities in the provinces – Adana, Trabazon and Bursa being the most prominent. Ahmet Vefik Paşa, who founded the theatre in Bursa, translated nearly all of Molière into Turkish and trained his own company of actors.

Güllü Agop's monopoly only covered theatre 'with a prompter', i.e. with written scripts. Therefore *orta-oyunu* actors claimed exemption from the monopoly, and challenged him for audiences in Istanbul. The result, improvised theatre based on daily news and political occurrences, was known as *tulûat tiyatrosu*. This revived *orta-oyunu* tradition stood somewhere between Western-style theatre and the traditional improvisatory styles.

The Young Turk revolution of 1908 ushered in a new era of interest in Western cultural institutions. In 1913–14 Cemil Paşa, the mayor of Istanbul, invited ANDRÉ ANTOINE, then director of the Paris Odéon, to found a municipal theatre and school of drama, the Darülbedaye (Academy of Dramatic Arts). It is still in existence as a training school for young artists, and runs four theatres and an opera house. In 1918 the first female student was admitted. Audiences would not accept women on the stage at first, but gradually their reticence was overcome and by 1923 women were seen regularly in dramatic productions in Turkey.

The father of modern Turkish theatre, Muhsin Ertugul, began his stage career in 1908. In 1920, following a period acting and stage-managing in the German film industry, he was appointed head of the Darülbedaye. In 1925 he studied in Russia with STANISLAVSKY and MEYERHOLD, and returned to reform acting and production in Turkey. Ertugul gradually introduced the latest techniques in staging and direction. He promoted the production of Western classic plays alongside original Turkish productions by new playwrights, such as Müsahipzade Celâl (1870–1959), Vedat Nedim Tör (b.1897) and Nazim Hikmet (Ran) (1902–63).

An important development in Turkish dramatic life was the establishment of a National Conservatory (Devlet Konservatuari) in 1936 in Ankara. The founder was the composer Paul Hindemith. A dramatic section for the training of actors, singers and dancers was established under the direction of Carl Ebert. State subsidies for both playwrights and actors have encouraged a continuing stream of Turkish dramatic productions. Many private companies began to develop, starting in 1930, including the Milli Sahne (National Stage), Türk Tiyatrosu (Turkish Theatre) and Türk Akademi Tiyatrosu (Turkish Academy Theatre). Following the Second World War many other small theatres opened. In 1951 Ertuğul resigned from the state theatre and opened a small art theatre, Küçük Sahne

(Little Stage). Other similar ventures followed, until by the mid-1970s there were six municipal theatres and over 20 private municipal theatres in Istanbul alone.

The principal trend in Turkish theatre in the post-1945 period was towards the production of more native Turkish drama. Nearly 200 new plays in Turkish were produced in the years following the war on an enormous variety of themes and styles. Traditional theatre has served as the inspiration for much of the modern period. The trend towards theatre integrated with music and dance has been very strong, particularly in the emergence of *operet*, a form of musical theatre, before the Second World War. Two of the most popular writers in this style were Ekrem Reşit Rey (librettist) and Cemal Reşit Rey (composer), whose popular pieces included *Uç Saat* (*Three Hours*, 1932), *Deli Dolu* (*Crazy*, 1934) and *Lüks Hayat* (*High Life*, 1934). The Rey brothers paved the way for highly successful MUSICAL THEATRE in the 1960s and 1970s.

Although the development of the Turkish film and television industry has slowed the growth of theatre somewhat, the future seems very good for a rigorous modern Turkish theatre tradition. Among the most prominent modern playwrights are Orhan Asena, Güngör Dilmen, Refik Eduran, Turgut Özakman, Hidayet Sayĩn and Haldun Taner.

Popular theatre in the 20th century Traditional theatre forms have declined greatly in the 20th century, but have continued to influence theatrical development in all countries in the Middle East and North Africa. An assessment of their form today is also a key to understanding something of their artistic structure in the past.

Puppet drama Although marionette and glove-puppet theatre has nearly disappeared in the Middle East, shadow-puppet theatre, *karagöz* (see KARAGÖZ), is still actively performed in Turkey, Greece and several of the Arabic-speaking countries. The stage for *karagöz* consists of a frame covered with white, translucent cloth. The puppets are constructed of fine, thin leather, traditionally camel-skin, through which light can shine. They range between 25 and 35cm in height, with some special figures ranging to nearly 60cm. The leather is coloured, so the figures likewise appear in colour on the screen. The puppets differ from oriental SHADOW PUPPETS in that they are held by a horizontal rod extending at right-angles from the back of the puppet, as compared with the vertical rods used by East Asian puppeteers. The puppets are hinged, and have a second rod which allows the puppeteer to manipulate the body parts. Other devices allow the puppets to swivel, or allow more than two puppets to be held against the screen at one time. Some puppets contain special devices, such as second heads, which can be flipped up by the puppeteer for special effects.

There are three parts to a *karagöz* performance: the prologue (*mukaddeme*), dialogue and interlude (*muhavere* and *muhaveresi*), and the main story (*fasil*). As in Asian shadow-puppet drama, a screen ornament appears against the cloth before the drama begins.

A whistle, *nareke*, introduces the prologue. One of the main characters, Hacivat, appears first, and often gives a religious invocation and a long speech. Then Karagöz himself appears and has an argument with Hacivat, where he is beaten. He in turn hits Hacivat every time he appears on stage. The dialogue which then ensues may have nothing to do with the main plot of the performance. It may be a humorous battle of wits, or a trading of insults in 'duelling rhyme' form, something also practised by children on the streets of Turkey, and thus greatly appreciated by them. Then the main story unfolds, involving many ethnic and linguistic types, including women both young and old; a juvenile character, Çelebi, who is always in love with a princess or girl of high family; various odd characters, such as an opium addict, dwarf or drunkard; and numerous other ethnic types – Persians, Jews, Balkans, Greeks, Armenians, Kurds and Arabs.

Much of *karagöz* involves PARODY of various occupations or ethnic groups. One stock plot involves Çelebi falling in love with a young girl of good family and having various obstacles put in his way before being allowed to marry her. In this, Karagöz and Hacivat are always implicated in some manner. There are dozens of stock stories presently performed by puppeteers. These have been passed down for generations, and are largely improvisatory in nature, although over time some of the scripts have been transcribed. Among some of the better known are *Kanli Kavak* (*The Bloody Poplar*), *Timarhane* (*The Madhouse*), *Yazici* (*The Public Scribe*) and *Kanli Nigâr* (*Bloody Nigâr*).

Throughout the 19th and 20th centuries, *karagöz* has served not only as entertainment, but also as a focus for political protest. In Greece, where *karagöz* was established as an art form in 1860 by John Vrahalis, *karagöz* performances ironically served as the meeting place for anti-Turkish revolutionary leaders. In the Greek shadow theatre, Karagöz becomes Karaghiozis, and Hacivat, Hatziavatis, but it is clear that these characters originally come from Turkish tradition.

Improvisatory comic theatre The two principal forms of comic improvisatory theatre in the Middle East, *ru-howzi* and *orta-oyunu*, are very similar, and probably related historically. In the 20th century they still bear a clear resemblance to each other, sharing many common features.

Comic improvisatory troupes in both *ru-howzi* and *orta-oyunu* traditions are generally actors and musicians. All members of the troupe generally play one or more musical instruments, and are able usually to perform a full musical programme in addition to, or in lieu of, a theatrical performance. Many troupe members, especially those who specialize in women's roles, are also adept dancers.

Troupes have largely hereditary recruitment patterns. That is, most troupe members are recruited from the families of other members. They tend to 'grow up in the tradition', taking minor roles when young and graduating to major roles such as 'clown' or 'king' when older. In the past, troupes were highly itinerant. They would leave home for months on a performance circuit that would take them hundreds of miles from home. In the past it was possible for them to support themselves entirely from their work as performers. Troupes also existed in urban areas throughout Iran and Turkey, performing in commercial theatres.

They handle their financial arrangements using division according to importance of role in the total performance. The total proceeds obtained by the troupe for an evening are divided into shares, major performers and principal musicians receiving more than minor performers. Also, equipment, such as the costume trunk or amplification equipment, may receive a 'share'. Proceeds for a performance are typically divided after the performance. The troupe leader may be morally obliged to support members during slack seasons, or to loan them money to be paid back when the troupe is working.

Performers use a 'secret language', with a number of vocabulary items in Romany (Gypsy), mixed with disguised speech (on the model of pig-Latin) known primarily to musicians in many cases.

All comic traditions in South and Southwest Asia emphasize the clown as a central figure, and *ru-howzi* and *orta-oyunu* do the same. He may be thought of as the central figure around whom the 'text' of the performance is constructed. In *ru-howzi* the clown has no fixed name, but 'Rajab' seems to be a common personal name assigned to him, especially when he is cast in the role of a servant. He is dressed in blackface, and so is regularly referred to by performers as the *Siah*, or Black. Similarly, playing the clown is called *siah-bâzi*, or 'black-playing'. In *orta-oyunu* the clown is called Pişekiar (as well as, often, Tosun Efendi). He is dressed in a yellow gown and red trousers, with a multicoloured cap. There is always a second principal figure in both *ru-howzi* and *orta-oyunu*. In *ru-howzi* it is the *hajji*, an elderly merchant who represents conventional morality and respectability. In *orta-oyunu* the second figure may be a merchant, but he is also often a companion of Pişekiar. He is called Kavuklu, 'large hat', as well as often being called by the name Hamdi. He frequently wears a turban or fez.

The performance also depends on stock characters in addition to the clown. The most important of these are the juvenile 'dandy' – called Zampara in *orta-oyunu* – female figures, nobles, court figures, and a whole range of ethnic characterizations. Parallels here with *karagöz* are very clear, and have led to speculation that live comic improvisatory drama may have developed from puppet drama.

Performances are not entirely improvisatory; perhaps they would better be characterized as semi-improvisatory. Although in *orta-oyunu* texts have been recorded, in *ru-howzi* there is no written text. In both traditions, stock plots are most commonly transmitted through rehearsal and oral transmission and learned by troupe members. These plays are refined over years of performance, and acquire slightly different realizations for each individual troupe.

One important feature of performance is that the individual play storylines are interlaced with set comic routines – *schtiks*, or, using a term from COMMEDIA DELL'ARTE, *lazzi* (see LAZZO). These routines are set pieces often involving pratfalls, acrobatics, visual or verbal humour. Many involve satirizing other groups and dialects, and skill as a performer is often linked to the ability to mimic other language and ethnic groups. Performance is expandable or contractable at will. Troupes can perform the same play in half an hour or three, depending on necessity. The active repertoire consists of from 10 to 20 pieces. Many more are known by troupe members, but are not in active use. These can be resurrected if requested by patrons.

Plays given by *ru-howzi* troupes bear a close relationship to the concerns of the patrons they serve. They involve a great deal of SATIRE, and they favour broad mockery of groups and individuals typically seen as oppressive of the communities served by the troupes. Thus many authority figures are mocked in the performances.

Another important source of humour is based on sexual reference. In this regard troupes are able to approach topics which are extremely sensitive in society at large. The clown is typically the vehicle for approaching the topics of authority and sexuality. By serving as a surrogate for the audience, the clown is able to provide that audience with a vicarious method of dealing with these vital areas of their own life. His use of paradox, mockery and distortion to create humour makes these potentially dangerous areas manageable. He is able to dispel their danger in laughter.

The performance in both traditions has a fixed form. Following music and a dance by all members of the troupe except the two principal comic figures, the clown enters. He engages in comic dialogue with the musicians, exits, and the performance begins, often with a dialogue between the two comic characters. Then the comic story begins in earnest. Many plots are common to both traditions. A few follow:

1 A master has a girlfriend, and doesn't want his wife to know about it, so he persuades his servant, the clown, to sleep in his place so that his wife will not detect that he has gone to his girlfriend's house. The wife discovers the ruse, and decides to teach both the master and the clown a lesson by pretending to make sexual advances to the clown.

2 Two thieves, one quick-witted, one slow-witted, proceed to rob a house in the dark. They divide the spoils, which turn out to be a large number of ridiculous or sexually suggestive objects. The quick-witted clown manages to get the best booty for himself.

3 A clown persuades his companion, a merchant, to balance a bowl of yoghurt on his head as a cure for an ailment. The yoghurt eventually ends up all over the companion's head and face.

4 A master suspects his wife of being unfaithful. His servant the clown persuades him to pretend to be dead to see what his wife will do. Her lover immediately arrives on hearing of the master's death, and puts on his clothes, talks about using his money to go abroad, and so on. The clown then resurrects the master from the dead, to scare the couple.

A second set of plots are based on literary, historical and legendary events which are illustrated through performance. Here, actual historical figures, such as Harun-al-Rashid or Moses, are seen, as well as legendary figures drawn from epics such as Ferdowsi's *Shāhnāmeh* or other literary works such as the *Haft Peikar* of Nezami.

Some examples:

1 The Three Riddles The king's daughter declares that she will only marry a clever man, so each suitor must answer three riddles. The *hajji*, his son and the clown all go to the court with the purpose of obtaining the princess for the son. On seeing the princess, the *hajji*

decides he wants her for himself, as does the clown. They bandy words with court officials, and finally give silly answers to the riddles. The son gives the correct answers, and the *hajji* and clown are admonished to seek more suitable wives.

2 Moses and the Pharaoh The clown is servant to Moses, and harasses the Pharaoh in the traditional story of the Children of Egypt.

3 Rostām and Sohrāb The clown is servant to Rostām, and is present at the famous epic unwitting battle between father and son. He manages to make fun of all and sundry, as well as of the event itself, finally announcing to the hapless Rostām, 'Oh, now you've done it – you shouldn't have killed that poor boy, you know.'

Religious epic theatre Religious epic theatre, *ta'ziyeh* or *shabih*, continues to be performed in areas of the Middle East with large Shi'a populations: Iran, Iraq, Southern Lebanon and Bahrain. But the most elaborate, full-blown performances of *ta'ziyeh* continue to be performed in Iran.

Performances of *ta'ziyeh* are given both by 'professional' troupes of players and by villagers in amateur performances. Many small towns and villages have erected special buildings – *hoseinieh*– specifically for the performance of mourning ceremonies during the month of Muharram. It is most often in these buildings that *ta'ziyeh* is performed, although an open-air playing space may also be constructed to accommodate large crowds, live animals and dozens of players, some on horseback.

Whether the performers are hired for the occasion, or amateur, the staging of *ta'ziyeh* is a community affair, with cooperative funds committed for the purpose. Performances may be long or short, but they often take place all day, particularly on the ninth and tenth days of the Islamic month of Muharram, called *Tasuā* and *Ashurā* respectively, the latter being the day of the martyrdom of Imam Husain. A noon meal may be provided for spectators, and the performance may be preceded or followed by communal mourning ceremonies, consisting of processions, religious chanting, and self-flagellation. Often persons leave a bequest in their wills to contribute to the annual support of these rituals.

Participants and spectators do not view *ta'ziyeh* as theatre, but rather as part of RITUAL mourning. Nevertheless, it has many theatrical conventions. The players do not, by convention, memorize their roles (though many have memorized them through years of repetition); rather, they read them from strips of paper held in their hands. The parts are not welded together in a common script, but are maintained as separate scripts with cue lines for each role. The 'good' characters, on the side of Imam Husain, chant their lines in classical Persian musical modes, and wear the colour green. The 'bad' characters declaim their lines in stentorian tones and wear the colour red. Women's roles are taken by men, who wear black, and veil their faces. The performances offer a number of roles for children, played by young boys, who are also dressed in black, but are unveiled.

Several forms of staging exist, but most observe the convention of having one area for the camp of Imam Husain, and another area in the same open playing space for the camp of the enemies. A third space may represent Damascus, the seat of the governor Yazid, who ordered the death of the martyrs. A fourth area usually contains props. When characters are not 'on stage' they often do not leave the playing area, but merely retire to their playing space, drink tea, and converse. When moving in the playing area, spaces traversed in circles or arcs represent long distances, and straight lines are short distances.

Each of the first ten days of Muharram is the occasion for the staging of a different performance depicting the death of each of the relatives and supporters of Imam Husain. Typically on the day of *Ashurā* a synoptic performance is given where all of the martyrs' deaths are presented in a single recounting.

Over the years a number of 'secular' *ta'ziyeh* performances developed around other religious or even political themes, including events preceding or following the martyrdoms at Kerbala, and also other religious or even secular themes including Moses and the Pharaoh, and Solomon and the Queen of Sheba. These included even 'comic' *ta'ziyeh* performances, such as 'The Binding of the Thumbs of the Demon' which has a masked figure playing the demon's role. All of these performances eventually turn back to the events of Kerbala, however.

Ta'ziyeh performances have suffered a decline in the 20th century. Immensely popular, they are none the less suspect from both a religious and a political standpoint. Religious officials were always uncomfortable with the depiction of actual historical figures on stage. Political officials did not like huge gatherings of people mourning injustice. Nevertheless, the performances continue unabated in many parts of the Shi'a world. The influence of these traditional forms is deeply felt in the modern theatrical tradition of the Middle East. Despite the importation of Western-style theatre to the region in the 20th century, when native writers have attempted original work the most successful productions have always contained elements of these traditional performance genres.

The 20th-century rise of national theatres The great 19th-century empires came to an end with the First World War. The Ottoman Empire was split into a dozen small states, and modern Iran emerged under the leadership of Mohammad Rezā shah Pahlavi. All of the resulting new nations looked towards Europe and the United States as models for development. The theatre was no exception. Traditional theatre forms declined rapidly in favour of Western-style theatre. Film and later television became important entertainment media, further speeding the decline of traditional performance forms. For the most part the national theatres arising in 20th-century Middle Eastern nations have been pale imitations of Western theatre. It has been only in the last 20 years that new experimentation combining traditional forms of past centuries with modern directorial and acting styles has yielded a revitalized theatre in the Middle East.

Turkey, Egypt, Syria, the Maghreb and Iran have remained central in theatrical development in the 20th century. A brief review of principal trends for each nation follows.

Turkey Theatre in Turkey in the 20th century continued the trend towards political commentary and SATIRE present in traditional *karagöz, meddah* and *orta-oyunu*. In the last days of the Ottoman Empire, a number of writers turned to political drama as a means of expressing new feelings of protest. Namik Kemal (1840–88) felt that drama could be used as a means of awakening people and inspiring them to greater political sensibility. His play *Vatan yahut Silistre* (*Fatherland or Silistre*) was produced at the Gedikpaşa theatre in 1873, and was partially instrumental in the theatre's closing the next year. Popular sentiment against the sultan aroused by the play was so great that Namik Kemal was put in prison, and the play censored. Abdülhak Hamit (1852–1937), a diplomat and poet, wrote some 20 plays which circulated as literature, but were never produced during his lifetime because of their political content. Social reform was also represented in the works of a number of playwrights. Ahmet Mithat (Efendi) railed against polygamy and superstition in his plays *Eyvah* (*Alas*, 1873) and *Çengi* (*Dancing Girl*, 1884).

Egypt Egypt has dominated the theatre of the Arabic-speaking world for the entire 20th century. The foundation for this domination was laid in the 19th century with the establishment of a number of successful theatrical troupes, within which actors of excellent quality developed, who then established their own troupes. Theatre was additionally aided by the talents of a number of prominent literary figures who directed a significant part of their energy to writing for the stage.

For the first 20 years of the century the most important troupe was that established by Jūrj Abyaḍ, born in Beirut and trained in acting at the Paris Conservatoire under a government scholarship. He is reputed to have been tutored by the famous actor Sylvain. Abyaḍ returned to Egypt in 1910 (he had first moved to Alexandria in 1898, where he had joined an amateur drama society). He brought with him a troupe of French actors which performed a number of French plays such as *Tartuffe, Horace* and *Andromaque*. He was encouraged by Sa'd Zaghlūl, Egypt's Minister of Education at the time, to stay and form an Arabic-speaking troupe, drawing from the actors of the troupes of al-Qurdāhi and Farah which had begun to decline. Abyaḍ was an excellent dramatic actor, and specialized in both COMEDY and TRAGEDY. He performed original Arabic works as well as a number of European works in translation, such as MOLIÈRE's *Tartuffe* (Arabized by 'Uthmān Jalāl under the title *Shaykh Matlūf*), SHAKESPEARE's *Othello* (translated by the famed poet Khalil Muṭran as *'Uṭayl*) and GEORGE BERNARD SHAW's *Caesar and Cleopatra*, among others.

In 1914 he joined forces with Salāma Ḥijāzī, who had formed his own troupe. Ḥijāzī's skills as a singer and dancer complemented Abyaḍ's dramatic skills, and the resulting troupe was an enormous critical and financial success. In typical fashion, it engendered yet other troupes, such as those of Yūsuf Wahbī, Fāṭima Rushdī and Najīb al-Rīhānī (1892–1949).

Al-Rīhānī was born in Cairo in 1892. He acted with Abyaḍ's troupe in 1914, having worked earlier with a small troupe in Alexandria. He became employed with a Greek *karagöz* theatre, the Abbaye des Roses, in 1916 and there developed his most famous character, Kish Kish Bey, a turbaned village *'umda* (headman) – a naive, good-hearted yokel with a pronounced weakness for women. Plays involving Kish Kish Bey had a stock plot. He would invariably be tricked by Europeanized city slickers, but would always outsmart them in the end. A whole series of stock characters accompanied him, making Kish Kish Bey dramas a strong depiction of an Egyptian Everyman in his natural social setting.

Al-Rīhānī later turned to more serious satire. The struggle was long and difficult, since the public wished only to see more of Kish Kish Bey, but finally in the 1930s and 1940s he was able to achieve success with his more serious comic work, such as *Al-Gineh al-Miṣrī* (*The Egyptian Pound*, 1931) and *Ḥukm Qarāqūsh* (*Qarāqūsh's Rule*, 1935). He also toured extensively and appeared in films, making his popularity greater than ever.

The development of dramatic literature in Egypt has paralleled the development of the theatrical institutions. Although the number of dramatic writers has increased in the 20th century, eight individuals can be singled out for their outstanding contributions to playwriting. These are Ahmad Shawqī, Ibrāhīm Ramzī, Tawfīq al-Ḥakīm, Mahmūd Taymūr, Nu'mān 'Āshūr, Yūsuf Idrīs, Alfred Faraj and Rashad Rushdī.

Ahmad Shawqī (1868–1932) achieved success first as a poet and only secondarily as a playwright. He wrote six historical dramas, five of them in verse, and one comedy. He was influenced by an early education in law in France, where he wrote his first tragic drama, *'Ali Bey al-Kabir* (*'Ali Bey the Great*). His other dramas include *Majnūn Layla*, his own version of the Leila and Majnūn story; *Maṣra' Kilyūbatrā* (*The Fall of Cleopatra*), a tragedy dealing with Cleopatra and borrowing from Shakespeare; *Qambiz*, a historical version of the story of Cambyses; *Amīrat al-Andalus* (*The Princess of Andalusia*), a story set in early Islamic Spain and his only prose play; *'Antara*, about the pre-Islamic poet, 'Antara b. Shaddād; and the largely ignored comedy *al-Sitt Hudā* (*Lady Hudā*).

Shawqī was considered a fine versifier, and paid great attention to historical detail. He was less successful in the construction of character and plot. Almost all of his characters are killed by the end of his tragedies, a feature which at times seems strained and artificial. He adopted the innovative device of changing the poetic metre to accord with the character and subject. While acknowledging his contributions to Arabic drama, critics generally have found him to be a better poet than playwright. In fact it was his own prestige as a neoclassical poet laureate, rather than his actual plays, that gave much respectability to the developing Arabic dramatic art.

Ibrāhīm Ramzī (1884–1949) became familiar with Western theatre during his study years in England. He wrote 12 plays, varying from the historical to the comical. His desire was to create a truly Egyptian theatre; his serious historical dramas, such as *Abṭāl al-Manṣūra* (*The Heroes of Mansura*, c.1915), centre on Egyptian history and nationalism; and his comedies, such as the one-act *Dukhūl al-Hammām Mish Zayy Khurūguh* (*Admission to the Baths Is Not as Easy as Coming Out of Them*, c.1915), composed in the Egyptian colloquial, reflect a peculiarly Egyptian setting and sense of humour. This last tells the story of a village headman who, much like al-Rīhānī's character

Kish Kish Bey, goes to Cairo loaded with the profits from the sale of his cotton harvest. He ends up in a public bath where he is conned into proposing to a coquette there, who turns out to be none other than the wife of the manager of the bath. The wife deceives the headman into believing that, in order to marry her, she must first be divorced from her husband, who abandoned her seven years earlier. The woman's real husband, disguised as a judge, grants her divorce and orders the headman to pay her an enormous amount of money as her rightful compensation (for delayed portion of dowry, alimony for seven years and so forth). Having lost all of his money, the village headman is grateful to escape. *Admission to the Baths* is considered to be the first fully developed Egyptian social comedy.

The Heroes of Mansura deals with the events of the sixth Crusade of the French monarch Louis IX and the way Egyptians valiantly defended their country and jealously guarded their freedom against the autocratic ways of their then ruler. The play resonates with many echoes of the contemporary situation in Egypt; it was written during the First World War, when Egyptian nationalism against the British occupiers was soaring. *The Heroes* is considered the first historical drama of great literary merit.

Tawfīq al-Ḥakīm (1898–1988) has been called the father of modern Egyptian drama. Like Shawqī, he was trained in France in law in the 1920s. Through this he developed a close acquaintance with European literature and cultural life; among European writers he admired Shaw. Al-Ḥakīm was a prolific playwright. He completed more than 80 literary works, most of them plays written in a number of different styles.

His works divide into three periods. The first consists of those written during his schooling in France, such as *'Ali Bābā* (1926). The second period starts after his return to Egypt in 1928. He wrote a number of what he called 'plays of the intellect': these specimens of *drame à thèse* draw on historical or religious subjects. During this period he wrote the successful *Ahl al-Kahf* (*People of the Cave*, 1933). The play presents the Qur'anic version of the Christian legend of the Seven Sleepers of Ephesus. But al-Ḥakīm places the events of the story in Tarsus – unlike the Christian legend – and makes the period of their sleep 300 years instead of 200; moreover, the seven sleepers are reduced to three. They are surprised to realize that they have slept for 300 years, and are made to feel alien and unwanted. Overwhelmed by this sense of being out of place, they find themselves unable to adapt to the changed world around them and so they return to their cave, lie down and die. The play was the first to be performed by the Egyptian National Troupe, formed in 1935.

Many of al-Ḥakīm's 'plays of the intellect' indeed seemed to have been written more to be read than to be produced. His 1936 play on the life of Muhammad, *Muhammad*, is so long that it is doubtful that he ever intended it to be performed on stage.

The third period is his modern phase, after the overthrow of the Egyptian monarchy. He engages in gentle social criticism in plays such as *Al-Aydī al-Nā'ima* (*The Soft Hands*, 1954) and *Al-Sulṭān al-Ḥā'ir* (*The Sultan Who Could Not Make up His Mind*, 1960). He also shows traces of THE-ATRE OF THE ABSURD, as in his 1962 play *Yā Ṭali' al-Shajara*

(*O Tree Climber!*). In this, as in all of his plays, al-Hakīm emphasizes the conflict between two opposing forces: compromise and heroism; tradition and modernization; idealism and realism. Whether pursuing these ideas in classical or absurdist dramatic format, his work has been continually provocative and influential.

Mahmūd Taymūr (1894–1973) is another playwright who has had extensive influence on contemporary Arabic drama. Taymūr, who came from a family of talented writers and scholars, was a prolific literary figure, writing short stories and literary criticism in addition to a dozen plays of varying quality. Like al-Hakīm's, Taymūr's plays seem to work better as literary efforts than as stage productions; they are largely comic, but with an overlay of social criticism. He sought to reflect everyday society in Egypt – indeed, to create genuine Egyptian drama, and towards that end he composed his plays in the Egyptian colloquial, as did a number of playwrights before him, notably his brother Muhammad, and Ibrāhīm Ramzī.

One of Taymūr's more important works is *Al-Makhba' Raqm 13* (*Shelter Number 13*, 1941) which deals with a socially diverse group of people caught in an air-raid shelter. Their sense of social difference is gradually eroded, and they reveal their genuine selves as the fear of death takes hold of them. Then they re-acquire their sense of difference, once the threat of death recedes. Curiously, this play, as well as others (e.g. *Kidhb fī Kidhb* (*A Pack of Lies*, 1953), was written in both the Egyptian colloquial and classical Arabic – presumably in order to gain access to educated Arab readers outside Egypt. Another of his plays, *Haflat Shāy* (*A Tea Party*, 1943), takes a heavily satirical look at the snobbism and affectation of the emerging Egyptian middle classes, who ape foreign customs while forgetting essential elements of human interaction.

Nu'mān 'Āshūr (1918–87) deals with Egyptian social themes and with the exploration of human foibles and frailty. Unlike his French-influenced contemporaries, 'Āshūr was most heavily influenced by the work of ANTON CHEKHOV. His well known works *Il-Nās illi Taht* (*The People Downstairs*, 1956) and *Il-Nās illi Fō'* (*The People Upstairs*, 1957) deal with the difficulties of reconciliation between different socio-economic classes. *Bilād Barrah* (*Europe*, 1967) deals with the state of society during the post-1952 revolution which overthrew the monarchy. It is a mordant SATIRE on the socialist sloganeering of those in power, the mindless imitation of European ways and fads concomitant with the immoderate desire to procure European consumer goods and fashions, and the defeatism of those who leave Egypt to its crises and emigrate to the West. But 'Āshūr seems unable to contain all of these themes in a coherent structure, and the result is an episodic work that suffers from lack of unity.

Yūsuf Idrīs (1927–91), a physician turned playwright, is equally famous for his short stories. His most famous play is *al-Farāfīr* (literally, 'Small Fry', translated as *Flipflap and His Master*, 1964). The play, according to him, was a culmination of his ceaseless search for a genuinely Egyptian drama, drawing on native folk drama (shadow theatre, the comic character of Juhā, the wise fool, and the improvisatory village *al-Sāmir* night entertainment). He also appropriates elements from European drama, such as the deliberate breakdown of the illusion of reality as in

BRECHT's plays and some of PIRANDELLO's. The result is an impressive work that had a tremendous impact on Egyptian, and indeed on all Arab, drama.

Al-Farāfīr is a disturbing view of power relations, depicting a servant and his master locked in their perpetual roles with no hope of freedom for the servant, so that even their deaths result only in turning the servant into an electron spinning around the proton of his master. The play shows that nothing can change this power relation, not even the author of the play who is a character in it. The author character eventually disappears, thereby presenting the idea that we live in a world divested of its own author/creator, and that there is no escape from the execrable power relations that chain us. This gloomy outlook is tempered, however, by some humorous episodes. In similar vein, Idrīs's later *al-Mukhattatīn* (*The Striped Ones*, 1969), an absurdist play that attacks the lack of freedom in a totalitarian state, is an overt SATIRE on the Nasser regime.

Alfred Faraj (b.1929) draws heavily on Arabic folklore – with the *Arabian Nights*, once again, as the fountainhead, along with medieval romances. He composed both COMEDY and TRAGEDY; his fame rests to a large extent on his use of satire as manifested in *'Alī Janāh al-Tabrīzī* (1964). The play tells the story of 'Alī Janāh, a young prince who, having squandered his wealth by his extravagant living, journeys to a faraway land, accompanied by one of his faithful subjects. They pose as a wealthy merchant and his servant who arrive ahead of their caravan. In the new land the prince acquires a reputation for generosity, handing out money and gifts to people; in fact, he has been giving away his subject's life savings. The merchants of the city are impressed by him – even the king, who allows the princess to marry him. Everyone believes that he is awaiting his goods-laden caravan, but when no caravan arrives he is revealed as a cheat and sentenced to death. He escapes, however, accompanied by the princess, who has discovered some lovable qualities in him.

The play deals with issues of political and philosophical significance: what is the dividing line between reality and fantasy? What is the difference between deception and self-deception? Is a lie still reprehensible if it benefits others, and if it is not, what will then be the difference between prophets and impostors? The character of 'Alī Janāh is believed by some critics to bear a striking resemblance to Nasser: both are 'dream-vendors', who may or may not be blamed for hawking fantasies to self-deceiving buyers.

Rashād Rushdī (1912–83) is primarily a dramatist whose works are not just literary products, but created specifically for the stage. Many deal with issues related to the Egyptian woman, as in *Al-Farāsha* (*The Butterfly*, 1959), *Lu'bat al-Hubb* (*The Game of Love*, 1962), *Nūr al-Zalam* (*Light of Darkness*, 1964) and *Halawat Zamān* (*The Sweetmeats of Yesterday*, 1967), and a few tackle political themes. He was able to survive CENSORSHIP during the Nasser era – which has caused some commentators to see his work as less socially relevant than that of other writers.

Others worthy of note include 'Alī Sālim (b.1936) and Salāh 'Abd al-Sabūr (1931–81). The plays of 'Alī Sālim are primarily political satires on bureaucracy, corruption and tyranny. In both *al-Būfēh* (*The Buffet*, 1967 or 68), a gloomy

Kafkaesque work about being a writer under a totalitarian regime, and *Bakalūrriyūs fī Ḥukm al-Shu'ūb* (*B.A. in Ruling the Masses*, 1979), Sālim aims his telling blows at autocratic rulers who are all too familiar to his audience/readers. The accomplished verse dramas of Ṣalāḥ 'Abd al-Ṣabūr, such as *Ma'sāt al-Ḥallāj* (*The Tragedy of al-Ḥallāj*, 1965) and *al-Amīra Tantaẓir* (*The Princess Waits*, 1971), are both well structured and powerfully evocative.

The years following the 1967 war with Israel and the assassination of Anwar al-Sādāt in 1981 were not good for the development of the serious theatre in Egypt. Difficult economic conditions during the war years were followed by an upsurge in Islamic fundamentalism which hampered, and still hampers, stage productions. During this period television and film became more prominent as vehicles for dramatic art. The growing market for Egyptian TV soap operas and frothy films throughout the Arabic-speaking world gave these forms an economic and artistic prominence at the expense of the serious theatre. The commercial theatre, however, has continued to stage plays, of varying degrees of popularity. These are more often than not composed by lesser-known writers, such as Lenin al-Ramli and Samir 'Abd al-'Aẓim, but performed by popular actors and actresses such as 'Ādil Imām, Sa'id Ṣāliḥ, Suhayr al-Bābili and Muḥammad Ṣubḥi. The most popular productions of the commercial theatre in recent years have been *Madrasat al-Mushāghibīn* (*The School for Mischief-Makers*), *Shāhid Ma-Shafsh Ḥāga* (*An Eye-Witness Who Did Not Witness a Thing*), *al-Mahzūz* (*The Man Who Vacillates*), and *il-Wād Sayyid il-Shaghghāl* (*Young Sayyid, the Servant*). Unlike those of serious drama, the texts of these plays, and others, are often not published. But like the dramas of the 19th and early 20th centuries, the plays are full of song and dance and slapstick.

It is perhaps too early to assess the impact of Islamic religious fundamentalism on the development of Arabic drama in Egypt, or elsewhere in the Arab world. But Muslim fundamentalists in Egypt are reported to have attacked entertainment establishments including theatres, and have threatened the lives of actors. Some valiantly defy these threats – such as the popular comedian 'Ādil Imām. Others, especially actresses, succumb, and even renounce their acting careers, donning the Islamic dress and giving rise to the new phenomenon *al-fannānāt al-tā'ibāt* (the repentant woman artist). This trend constitutes yet another chapter in the ongoing struggle between conservative religious forces and dramatic artists.

Iran The first Western-style playing space in Iran was not constructed until 1886 at the Dār al Fonun secondary school in Tehran. Because of religious opposition, performances there of translations of Molière and other European authors were patronized only by the court. Nevertheless, there was an increased interest in drama during this period, and Mirza Aqa Tabrizi's example prompted many writers to experiment. Among these were Morteza Qoli Khan Fekri, Ahmad Mahmudi, Abdolrahim Khalkhali, Afrasiyab Azad, Ali Mohammad Khan Oveysi, Taqi Raf'at and Abolhasan Foroughi.

The constitutional revolution of 1906–11 ushered in a new cultural era. The Teātr-e Melli (National Theatre), built in 1911, staged the first public performances of Western-style theatre – some in public parks. Gradually, other theatres began to appear in Tehran. A number of writers began to translate European stage works and a few original plays were produced.

Aḥmad Maḥmud Kamāl al-Vezāreh (1875–1930) wrote a number of dramas, including *Ostād Nowruz-e Pineduz* (*Master Nowruz, the Cobbler*, 1919), in which the colloquial Persian of south Tehran was used for the first time. Mirzādeh Eshqi (1893–1925) wrote six historical patriotic works including *Rastākhiz-e Salātin-e Irān* (*The Resurrection of Iranian Kings*, 1916), which conjures up the spirits of the pre-Islamic Achamenian kings of Iran. Ḥasan Moqaddam (1896–1925) wrote a mocking satire, *Ja'far Khān az Farang Amadeh* (*Ja'far Khān Has Returned from Europe*, 1922), which makes light of pretentiously Europeanized Iranians speaking French-spattered Persian on their return from abroad and putting on Western airs. Unlike the satirical works of Tabrizi, which remained buried for many years, this play was an immediate success and was highly influential in Iranian drama for many years.

Rezā Shāh Pahlavi's reign (1925–1941) proved difficult for the Iranian theatre because of heavy CENSORSHIP. Few writers of fiction turned their talents to the stage, although the novelist Sādeq Hedāyat did write two plays: *Parvin Dokhtār-e Sāsān* (*Parvin, the Daughter of Sāsān*, 1928) and *Māzyār* (1933), both concerned with the Arab invasion of Iran in the 7th century AD. During the reign of Rezā Shāh women appeared on the Iranian stage for the first time.

It was only after the end of the Second World War that Western-style theatre became established on a fully professional basis. 'Ali Nasiriān and 'Abbās Javanmard began to stage productions in a small theatrical company, the Goruh-e Honar-e Melli (National Art Group), brought into being by Shāhin Sarkissiān (1912–66). Both Nasiriān and Javānmard later worked with the Office of Dramatic Arts of the Ministry of Culture and Arts after its establishment in 1964. In its early days the Goruh-e Honar-e Melli produced stage adaptations of Hedāyāt's stories, including *Mohallel* (*The Temporary Husband*, 1957) and *Mordeh Khorhā* (*Eaters of the Dead*, 1957). Nasiriān was the first serious Iranian writer to be inspired by traditional performance forms in writing for the modern stage. He has written several successful plays including *Af'i-ye Talā'i* (*The Golden Serpent*, 1957) and *Bolbol-e Sar-gashteh* (*The Wandering Nightingale*, 1959). The latter, based on a folk tale, was the first Iranian play to be produced in Europe (Paris, 1960); he also wrote *Siyāh* (*The Black One*, c.1962), a play depicting the deep sadness of the blackfaced clown of *ru-howzi* comedy, and *Bongāh-e Theatrāl* (*The Theatre Company*, 1974), a straight scripted version of a *ru-howzi* comedy.

The finest dramatic writer of the post-Second World War years was also one of Iran's greatest novelists and short-story writers, Gholam-Hosein Sā'edi (1935–85), who often wrote under the pen name Gohār Morād. Like many Iranian writers, Sā'edi avoided censorship by couching his work in heavy symbolism. His early plays were direct in their political comment – e.g. his collection *Panj namāyeshnāmeh as enqelāb-e Mashrutiyyat* (*Five Plays from the Constitutional Revolution*), which depicts the plight of citizens of the city of Tabriz victimized by an uncaring upper class around the turn of the 20th century. His later plays grew more subtle and simpler. *Chub-be-dast-hâ-ye Varazil* (*The Club-wielders of Varazil*, 1965) told the story of villagers threatened by hunters who first befriend them; the villagers eventually take refuge in an Islamic shrine which offers them no protection. In *Kârbâfakhâ dar Sangar* (*Workaholics in the Trenches*, 1960) he focuses on the conflicts that arise from rapid industrialization. Of his other plays, perhaps the best-known are *Ây bi kolâh, Ây bâ kolâh* ('A' *without a Hat*, 'A' *with a Hat* (referring to the long A – â – in the Persian alphabet which has a 'hat' over it, and also to an idiom: to have a cap put on one is to be fooled), 1967); *Vây bar Maghlub* (*Woe to be Vanquished*, 1971); and *Mah-e Asâl* (*Honeymoon*, 1978).

Bahrâm Bezâ'i (b.1938) has had a varied career as a theatre scholar, film director and playwright. His *Nimâyesh dar Irân* (*Performance in Iran*, 1965) remains the definitive work on Iranian traditional theatre. His plays are highly symbolic, and often draw on folkloric sources. The traditional puppet theatre inspired his influential play *Arusakha* (*Marionettes*, 1962, published 1963), in which an unwilling hero is inspired to fight a demon in a final battle to the death for the love of a woman. The puppet theatre also inspired his *Ghorub dar Didyâri Gharib* (*Evening in a Strange Land*, 1963) and *Qesse-ye Mâh-e Penhân* (*The Story of the Hidden Moon*, 1963). Traditional Iranian wrestling furnished the background for *Pahlavân Akbar Mimirad* (*Akbar the Champion Dies*, 1965). Bezâ'i has gradually included more political allegory in his writing. In *Chahâr Sanduq* (*Four Boxes*, 1967) he presents four characters representing different factions of society in different colours: yellow, the intellectual; green, the clergy; red, the merchant; and black, the labourer. In order to protect themselves from some unknown threat, they construct a scarecrow, who comes to life and forces them to live out their lives in separate boxes, thus preventing them from uniting to overthrow him. The clear analogy to the Pahlavi regime prevented this play from being produced during the reign of the Shah. Similarly, *Marg-e Yazdigerd* (*The Death of Yazdigerd*, 1979) deals with the death of the last Sassanian king, and by extension the death of any despot.

Sadeq Chubak (b.1916) is one of Iran's best-known modern writers. Most famous for his short stories depicting the life of villagers and poor urban residents, he also wrote several influential plays, including *Hafkhat* (*Sly*, 1960) and *Tup-e Lastiki* (*Rubber Ball*, 1949/50). His novel *Sang-e Sabur* (*The Patient Stone*, 1966) contains several sections in dramatic format, including a myth of creation.

Nader Ebrahimi (b.1936) is a prolific writer who has produced short stories, novels, screenplays and dramatic works, many of which seem to be literary works rather than stage pieces. Two of his plays, *Nafs-e Entezâr* (*The Essence of Waiting*, 1976) and *Entezâr-e Kur* (*Blind Expectation*, 1976), have been translated into English.

Several institutions formed the backdrop for dramatic work in Iran in the 1960s and 1970s, as the regime of Mohammad Rezâ Pahlavi attempted to develop the arts along European lines. A School of Dramatic Arts was founded, and a major national theatre, the 25th of Shahrivar Hall, was opened with a regular theatre season in both the main theatre and a smaller studio space. A good deal of experimental theatre work was produced here.

National Iranian Radio–Television also served as a major source for support of theatre. The Kâr-gâh-ye Namâyesh (Performance Workshop) was opened in 1969, and served as a training school for actors. Within this framework a number of plays were written and given outstanding productions by a group of talented young writers and directors. Arby Ovanessian (b.1942) produced several plays by 'Abbâs Na'lbandiân (b.1947), including *Pazhuheshi Zharf* (*Profound Research*, 1968) a surrealist drama (see SURREALISM) in BECKETT style about a number of persons waiting for an 'answer', and *Nâgâhân* (*Suddenly*, 1972), concerning the murder of an 'outsider' by a group of fanatics. Bizhan Mofid wrote *Shahr-e Qesseh* (*A City of Tales*, 1968), which mocked Iranian society, using actors in the guise of animals, and used traditional storytelling methods and music; and *Jân-Nessâr* (*Soul-sacrificer*, 1972), a satirical FARCE which preserves the style of traditional *ru-howzi* comedy. Esmâ'il Khalaj wrote several plays dealing with village life, including *Hâlet Chetowr-e Mash Rahim* (*How Are You?, Mash Rahim*, 1977) and *Goldune Khânom* (1977). Ashurbanipal Bâbella's *Emshab Shab-e Mâhtâb-e* (*Tonight Is Moonlight*, 1974) is a *ru-howzi*-inspired satire.

The most important contribution of National Iranian Radio–Television to theatrical life in Iran was perhaps the establishment of the Festival of Arts in Shiraz. Under the direction of the writer and film-maker Farrokh Gaffary, the Festival was a major international showcase for avant-garde Western drama and for the traditional performance arts of Asia, Africa and Latin America.

All major postwar Iranian actors and directors produced works at the Festival. Additionally, the world's major avant-garde directors also produced new works, including PETER BROOK, JERZY GROTOWSKI, ROBERT WILSON, Shuji Teriyama, Peter Schuman, TADEUSZ KANTOR and ANDRE GREGORY. One important consequence of the Festival was the artistic cross-fertilization it produced. Iranian actors and directors had the opportunity to see daring new works, such as Brook's *Orghast* (1971) and Wilson's *Ka Mountain and GUARD-enia Terrace* (1972). These directors in turn had the opportunity to be exposed to traditional performing arts, such as *ta'ziyeh* and *ru-howzi* theatre, both of which were produced extensively at the Festivals. *Ta'ziyeh* was first produced at the 1967 Festival by director Parviz Sayyâd in conjunction with theatre scholar Kojasteh Kiâ. Sayyâd had presented an earlier production in Tehran in 1965. In 1976 a series of ten *ta'ziyeh* performances were held at the Festival under the direction of actor, director and theatre researcher Mohammad Bâgher Ghaffâri.

Ru-howzi was presented in several 'modernized' forms during the 11 years that the Festival was in existence. In 1977, Mohammad Bâgher Ghaffâri assembled existing traditional troupes from throughout the country for a series of highly successful performances held in a garden in Shiraz.

The revolution of 1978–9 halted much of the theatrical activity that had taken place under the Pahlavi regime, making the future of theatre much less certain. Theatrical training schools and regular performance in public virtually ceased in Iran. National Iranian Radio–Television, its name changed to the Voice and Vision of the Islamic Republic of Iran, on occasion produced dramas on revolutionary themes for television, but stage drama was viewed with great suspicion. Sa'id Soltānpur, a leftist writer, staged *'Abbās Aqā Kārgar* (*'Abbās Aqā, Worker*) in 1980 but was executed by the authorities in 1981. Many Iranian writers, actors and directors emigrated, producing works in Persian abroad. Director Parviz Sayyād toured the United States with two successful plays, *Khar* (*The Donkey*, 1983) and *Samad be Jang Miravad* (*Samad Goes to War*, 1984), both dealing with Iran after the revolution. Gholam Hosein Sa'edi published two plays in Paris before his death: *Pardehdārān'e A'inehafruz* (*Mirror-Polishing Chamberlains*, 1986) and *Otello dar Sarzamin'e Ajāyeb* (*Othello in Wonderland*, 1986). Mohammad Bāgher Ghaffāri staged an updated version of a traditional *ta'ziyeh*, *Moses and the Wandering Dervish* (1989), in the United States.

In Iran traditional theatre forms are reportedly making a comeback. Sturdy *ru-howzi* seems to have survived the revolution by turning its satire on the former Pahlavi regime; and *ta'ziyeh*, despite scepticism from some clerics, has undergone a full-blown revival. A government-sponsored troup toured France in 1991, and *ta'ziyeh* performances with modern sound amplification are now seen widely in Iran.

Other Middle Eastern countries Significant theatrical development has taken place in other Middle Eastern countries, particularly following the First World War. Three principal areas can be singled out: North Africa, Syria and Lebanon, and Iraq. Some theatrical activity has also been seen in recent years in Kuwait.

In Tunisia, Algeria and Morocco before the First World War the court traditions of the Ottoman Empire, including *karagöz and orta-oyunu* performances, were supported. Although a Viennese troupe visited Tunis in 1826, and many foreign-language plays were performed throughout the 19th century, the first Western-style play presented in Arabic in North Africa was *Al-'Ashiq al-Muttaham* (*The Accused Lover*), presented by the Egyptian troupe of Sulaymān al-Qurdāhi on their visit to Tunis in 1908. Al-Qurdāhi settled in Tunis, and died there a year later. An Egyptian–Tunisian trouped was formed, and staged the Egyptian play *Şidq al-Ikhā'* (*Genuine Friendship*). After 1911, two Tunisian troupes were founded: Al-Ādāb al-'Arabiyya (Arabic Literature) and al-Shahāma al-'Arabiyya (Arabic Pride). On 7 April 1911 the Al-Ādāb troupe produced the first Arabic play by a native company, *Salah ad-Din* (*Saladin*) by Najib Hasddad. In 1922 the two companies merged. Four companies were formed in 1932, and more by 1959, including the well known al-Masrah al-Ḥadith headed by al-Munṣif Sharaf al-Din. In 1954 the creation of al-Firqa al-Baladiya, the Municipal Troupe of Tunis, added impetus to the development of theatre. The troupe was widely associated with the director, Aly Ben Ayed, who continued to present it in festivals throughout Europe and the Middle East until his death in 1972.

It is estimated that between 1966 and 1971 more than 500 Tunisian plays were performed. By 1970 the first national Tunisian playwright, 'Izz al-Din al-Madani, had appeared on the scene. Like other Arab playwrights, al-Madani has been preoccupied with the attempts to create a genuine Arabic theatre, and towards this end he too draws on Arab folklore, which he uses critically. He also looks critically at Arab heritage, in which he finds examples of Third-World-style revolutionaries who at first stood triumphantly against tyrannical rulers but who then tended to abort their own revolution; this can be seen in his *Thawrat Şāḥib al-Ḥimār* (*The Revolution of the Donkey Owner*, 1970), *Diwān al-Zanj* (*The Poetry Collection of the Zanj*, 1972), *Riḥlat al-Ḥallāj* (*Al-Ḥallāj's Mystical Journey*, 1973) and *Mawlāy al-Sulṭān Ḥasan al-Ḥafsi* (1977).

The first permanent regional company was started by Moncef Souissi in Kef in 1967. By the end of the 1970s there were eight permanent professional troupes throughout Tunisia, a number of festivals, and a healthy audience for theatre which has continued to the present day.

Algeria, of all North African countries, was most widely influenced by *karagöz* and *orta-oyunu*, which was performed in colloquial dialect. Serious stage drama had difficulty becoming established because of the disparity between the classical Arabic of the stage and the language understood by the audience. Even visiting Egyptian troupes, such as that of Jûrj Abyaḍ which performed there in 1921, had difficulty being accepted.

Eventually two troupes were formed which emphasized comedy performed in native Algerian dialect: Rashid Ksentini's (1887–1944) and Bāshtarzi Muhi'l-Din Ksentini's troupes produced farces in the provinces, starting in 1926, but later wrote comic plays which attracted urban crowds as well. Muhi'l-Din produced musical theatre, weaving simple plots with songs. Later he wrote more complex plays including adaptations of MOLIÈRE and SHAKESPEARE. KATEB YACINE (see also FRENCH-SPEAKING NORTH AFRICA) ranks as one of the principal literary figures of Algeria, having composed a number of compelling dramas, although he wrote in French. But it is the folk idiom that characterized early developments in drama in Algeria that continues to hold sway today. Improvisation and audience participation are characteristic of the popular plays of Kâki Wild 'Abd al-Raḥmān, who draws on folk tales and popular entertainment.

Morocco was introduced to the theatre by an enthusiastically received visit from a Tunisian company in 1923. The first Moroccan troupe was formed in 1924 by a group of amateurs (mostly high school students from Fez); in 1956 drama institutes were established by the state, and in 1957 two drama companies. The most important figures among Moroccan playwrights are Aḥmad al-Ṭayyib al-'Ilj (b.1928) and al-Ṭayyib al-Şiddiqi (b.1939). An impressively Morrocanized version of Molière's *Tartuffe* under the title *Waliy Allāh* was written by al-'Ilj, who has gained both popular admiration and critical acclaim. Al-Şiddiqi draws on Arab heritage in both his *Diwān Sidi 'Abd al-Rahmān al-Majdhūb* (*The Poetic Record of Sidi 'Abd al-Rahmān al-Majdhūb*, 1966) and *Maqāmāt Badi 'al-Zamān al-Hamadhāni* (*The Seances of Badi al-Zamān al-Hamadhāni*, 1971), a satirical treatment of the Arabic *maqāma*.

Interest in the theatre began in Libya after visits from Egyptian troupes. Beginning with the 1970s, native Libyan plays were written and staged: e.g. *Zari'at al-Shaytān* (*Satan's Implant*, 1973) by Mahdi Abū Qurayn, which tells the story of the downfall of a corrupt contractor; *Sa'dūn* (1974) by 'Abd al-Karīm al-Dannā', which deals with the national struggle against the Italian colonizers; and *al-Aqni'a* (*Masks*) by Muhammad 'Abd al-Jalīl al-Qunaydi, about the nature of tyranny and the dream of universal justice. Theatrical activities in Libya are generally low-key, and there has not yet appeared a major national playwright; this may be because Libya's population is small and the Islamic fundamentalist orientation of its government is not known for its patronization of the dramatic arts.

The theatre in Lebanon has been held hostage to the country's political vicissitudes. The civil wars in 1958 and throughout the 1970s and 80s disrupted life there, and with it the theatrical arts. Between 1960 and 1974 there were five companies staging world drama. These productions, overlooking the desire of the common folk to watch plays that deal with issues relevant to their social and political realities, seemed to appeal mostly to intellectuals. One such company was the Beirut School for Contemporary Drama, headed by Munīr al-Dibs.

Other companies emerged and performed plays which dealt with real social and political issues; one such was the Beirut Studio, run by Roger 'Assāf and Nidāl al-Ashqar. One of the good plays it staged was *Idrāb al-Haramiyya* (*The Thieves on Strike*, 1971), a BRECHTian work that reveals how both thieves and the authorities – supposedly out to catch the thieves and protect the people against them – derive benefit from each other.

The Rahbāni brothers and the famous singer Fairūz staged numerous operettas, extolling the goodwill of the Lebanese peasants and the beauty of rural life. But no major Lebanese plays of merit can be singled out, with the exception of 'Isām Mahfūz's *al-Zanzalakht* (*The China Tree*, 1968). Ziad Rahbāni, son of Fairūz and 'Assi Rahbāni, wrote a number of plays with music in the 1970s and 80s, including *Nazl Assouroor* (*The Inn of Joy*, 1974), *Bin'nisbeh Laboukra Sho* (*What About Tomorrow?*, 1978) and *Film Amirki Tawil* (*A Long American Movie*, 1980). In 1993 his play *Concerning Dignity and the Stubborn People* was staged in Beirut. This is an ultimately pessimistic prediction of the fate that awaits the Lebanese people if current attitudes towards language, technology and religion are not resolved. A sequel, *If There Were No Hope* ..., was presented in 1994. Rahbāni's work, and the emergence of other companies in Beirut, point to the revival of serious theatre in that strife-torn country.

After promising beginnings, dramatic arts in Syria initiated by Ahmad Abū Khalīl al-Qabbāni were reduced to popular puppet performances of the *karagöz* type, storytelling by a folk storyteller, *hakawāti*, and dance, all put on at coffee-houses. Syrian theatre was then boosted by the appearance on the scene of two French-trained dramatists, Rafiq al-Sabbān and Sharīf Khazandār. Both staged plays from world drama; al-Sabbān formed a drama group called Nadwat al-Fann wa al-Fikr (Thought and Art Club). In 1959 the National Theatre Company was formed by the state, drawing to itself actors and directors trained in America and at the Institute of Dramatic Arts in Cairo. One of the most talented Syrian dramatists is Sa'dallāh

Wannūs. It was the Arab defeat at the hands of the Israelis in the 1967 war that prompted Wannūs to compose his powerful play, *Haflat Samar min ajl Khamsa Huzayrān* (*An Evening Party to Celebrate the 5th of June*, 1968), a dramatic presentation of the agony and soul-searching that gripped the Arabs in the aftermath of their crushing defeat. In his *Mughāmarāt Ra's al-Mamlūk Jābir* (*The Adventures of the Head of Jābir the Mamlūk*, 1969), Wannūs draws on folk theatre and the world of the *Arabian Nights*. He continued to appropriate material and techniques from folklore, perhaps most effectively, and not without humour, in *al-Malik huwa al-Malik* (*The King Is the King*, 1977), a serious look at the nature of oppressive regimes and rulers and at the futility of disposing of individuals when the corrupt regime is allowed to live on.

It was the Egyptian troupe of Jūrj Abyad that introduced the Iraqis, too, to theatrical arts. The performances of the troupe in 1926, in Baghdad and Basra, inspired some Iraqis and prompted one Haqqi al-Shibli to form a troupe that employed both Iraqi and Egyptian actors. After some years of training in the theatrical arts in French, al-Shibli returned to Iraq and worked in the Arts Academy to train actors and directors.

One of the major Iraqi dramatists is Yūsuf al-'Āni (b.1927), who wrote a number of competent plays such as *Anā Ummak Yā Shākir* (*I Am Your Mother, Shakir*, 1955), a MELODRAMATic piece about despotic rule and its effects on the Iraqi citizens; in *al-Miftāh* (*The Key*, 1967–8) and *al-Kharāba* (*The Waste Land*, 1970) elements from Arabic folklore (songs, puppet shows, tales from the *Arabian Nights*) are effectively utilized.

Kuwait had had theatrical activities since the 1940s in the form of comic improvisations staged by Muhammad al-Nashmi. Between 1956 and 1962 al-Nashmi produced about 20 such plays. More serious and competent works, which deal with the theme of fathers and sons and the problems created by the generational gap, were written and directed by Saqr al-Rashūd. The impact of the oil wealth on Kuwaiti society is treated in the plays of 'Abd al-'Azīz al-Surayyi – such as his *Fulūs wa Nufūs* (*Money and Souls*, 1969–70). From the early 1960s, theatrical activities in Kuwait have been shaped by Egyptian directors and artists.

In 1912 a performance of an Egyptian play by a group of Egyptian instructors at the Gordon College in Khartoum fired the imagination of many Sudanese. Twenty years later, Khālid Abū al-Rūs wrote the first Sudanese play (*Tājūj and al-Muhalliq*, 1932), a drama that revolves around the theme of tragic love. It was performed in a sports club. In 1964 the Abad Amak company was formed. By 1967 the National Theatre was already in existence, headed by the British-trained al-Fakki 'Abd al-Hamid, and later a department for drama was established. Civil war between the north and south, famine, political instability, and the establishment of an Islamic fundamentalist regime (in power currently, 1994), have had adverse effects on the development of the Sudanese theatre and may have delayed the emergence of a national Sudanese playwright.   WOB KA-M JG

See: M. H. al-Khozai, *The Development of Early Arabic Drama 1847–1900*, London, 1984; 'Ali al-Ra'i, *Funun al-kumidiya* (*The Craft of Comedy*), Cairo, 1971; 'Adel Abu-

Shanab, *Karakûz*, Damascus, n.d; M. And, 'Origins and Early Development of the Turkish Theatre', *Review of National Literatures*, 4, 1973, and *A History of Theatre and Popular Entertainment in Turkey*, Ankara, 1963–4, and *Karagöz, Turkish Shadow Theatre*, Istanbul, 1979; Badr el din Aroudiki, 'Theatre in Syria', *Lotus: Afro-Asian Writings*, Cairo, 19, 1974; L. Awad, 'Problems of the Egyptian Theatre', in R. C. Ostle, *Studies in Modern Arabic Literature*, Warminster, England, 1975; H. Baghban, 'The Context and Concept of Humour in Magadi Theatre', PhD thesis, Indiana University, Bloomington, Indiana, 1977; T.-A. Bedi, 'Modern Turkish Theatre', *Review of National Literatures*, 4, 1973; W. O. Beeman, *Culture, Performance and Communication in Iran*, Tokyo, 1982, and 'A Full Arena: The Development and Meaning of Popular Performance Traditions in Iran', in E. Bonine and N. R. Keddie (eds.), *Modern Iran: The Dialectics of Continuity and Change*, Albany, 1981, and 'Why Do They Laugh? An Interactional Approach to Humour in Traditional Iranian Improvisatory Theatre', *Journal of American Folklore*, 94, 374, 1981; H. Ben Halima, *Un Demisiècle de théâtre arabe en Tunisie (1907–1957)*, Tunis, 1974; Bahrâm Bezâ'i, *Namâyesh Dar Irân (Performance in Iran)*, Tehran, 1965; I. J. Boullata (ed.), *Critical Perspectives on Modern Arabic Literature*, Washington, DC, 1980; P. J. Chelkowski, 'Bibliographic Spectrum', in P. Chelkowski, (ed.), *Ta'ziyeh: Indigenous Avant-Garde Theatre of Iran*, New York, 1979; E. Drioton, *Le Théâtre égyptien*, Cairo, 1942; Farrokh Gaffary, 'Evolution of Rituals and Theatre in Iran', *Iranian Studies* 17, 4; T. H. Gaster, *Thespis: Ritual, Myth and Drama in the Ancient Near East*, 2nd edn, New York, 1959; A.-A. Hammouda, 'Modern Egyptian Theatre: Three Major Dramatists', *World Literature Today*, 53, 4, 1979; G. Jacob, *Geschichte des Schattentheaters in Morgen- und Abenland*, Hannover, 1925; Abu al-Qâsem Jannati-Atâ'i, *Bonyâd-e Namâyesh dar Irân (The Institution of Performance in Iran)*, Tehran Châp-e Mihan, 1955; A. Krymsky, *The Persian Theatre: Its Origin and Development*, Kiev, 1925; J. Landau, *Studies in the Arab Theatre and Cinema*, Philadelphia, 1958; I. Lassy, *The Muharram Mysteries among the Āzerbāijān Turks of Caucasia*, Helsingfors, 1916; Hassan Mniai, 'Connaissance du théâtre marocain', *Europe: Revue Littéraire Mensuelle*, 602–3, 1979; M. Moosa, 'Naqqâsh and the Rise of the Native Arab Theatre in Syria', *Journal of Arabic Literature* 3, 1972; R.C. Ostle (ed.), *Studies in Modern Arabic Literature*, Warminster, England, 1975; L. Pelly, *The Miracle Play of Hasan and Hussein*, 2 vols., London, 1879; M. Rezvani, *Le Théâtre et la danse en Iran*, Paris, 1962; S. E. Siyavuşgil, *Karagöz, Its History, Its Characters, Its Mystic and Satiric Spirit*, Ankara, 1955; A. Tietze, *The Turkish Shadow Theatre and the Puppet Collection of the L. A. Mayer Memorial Foundation*, Berlin, 1977; N. Tomiche and C. Khaznadar (eds.), *Le Théâtre arabe*, Paris, 1969.

Middleton, Thomas c.1580–1627 English playwright, the son of a master bricklayer. He may have spent some time at Gray's Inn in London after leaving Oxford University. He is first identified as a working playwright in HENSLOWE's *Diary* in 1602. His earliest known play, *The Phoenix* (1603–4), was written for the BOYS OF ST PAUL'S, as were the citizen comedies (see CITIZEN COMEDY), *A Trick to Catch the Old One* (c.1604), *Michaelmas Term* (c.1605) and *A Mad World, My Masters* (c.1605). *Your Five Gallants* (1607) was produced by the rival CHILDREN OF THE CHAPEL ROYAL. It says much about Middleton's industry that he should, at the same time, have been providing material for Henslowe and the adult ADMIRAL'S MEN. Two collaborations with DEKKER, both superior catchpenny comedies, frame the plays written for boys. They are *The Honest Whore* (1604) and *The Roaring Girl* (c.1610). In common with Middleton's own comic masterpiece, *A Chaste Maid in Cheapside* (1611), these collaborative works rely on the ingenious interweaving of multiple plots, but Middleton's individual voice, objective and quizzical, is discernible. His moral observations on mercantile values and manners are strangely uncorrective. A similar ambivalence marks the collaborations with WILLIAM ROWLEY, *A Fair Quarrel* (c.1616), *The World Tossed at Tennis* (c.1619) and the extraordinary TRAGICOMEDY, *The Changeling* (1622), one of the most fluent and unerring of Jacobean plays, and *The Spanish Gipsy* (1623).

Middleton was an unfussy poet, with a fine ear for dialogue. That he was also tough-minded is suggested by the steady control of his insistently unsentimental plays, and by the professional opportunism that dictated his choice of themes in such plays as *The Witch* (c.1612), *More Dissemblers Besides Women* (c.1615) and the controversial anti-Spanish SATIRE, *A Game at Chess* (1624). He was certainly admonished and may have been imprisoned as a result of this play. His appointment as City Chronologer of London (1620–7) would not have protected him, though it did reward his achievements as a writer of MASQUES and pageants. His last known play is the remarkable tragedy *Women Beware Women* (c.1625), which concludes mischievously in an almost comic scene of slaughter. It is not surprising, in view of this piece, that Middleton is seen by many critics as a more likely author for *The Revenger's Tragedy* than TOURNEUR. PT

Mielziner, Jo 1901–76 The most dominant figure in American set and lighting design (see STAGE LIGHTING) from the mid-1920s until his death. Mielziner created the sets for virtually every major American drama and MUSICAL in the 1930s, 40s and 50s, exerting a great influence not only on the field of design but on the plays themselves. Dramas such as *A Streetcar Named Desire* and *Death of a Salesman* were in part shaped by his designs, and their success was to some degree dependent upon them. His use of scrims and a painterly style created a visual counterpart to the poetic realism of the plays of the period, notably the works of TENNESSEE WILLIAMS. The scrims, together with fragmented scenic units, allowed a cinematic transformation from one scene to the next through the manipulation of light rather than the shifting of scenery; this was in keeping with the trend in playwriting towards a cinematic structure. He was equally capable of REALISM, as demonstrated by his set for *Street Scene* (1929), in which he re-created the façade of a tenement and a New York City street. His designs for musicals such as *Carousel, Annie Get Your Gun* and *Guys and Dolls* captured the vibrancy of the American musical at its peak. The power of Mielziner's designs is demonstrated by the fact that some have outlasted the plays or are integrally entwined with them: his design for MAXWELL ANDERSON's *Winterset* – a soaring panorama of the Brooklyn Bridge receding into the fog – is better remembered than the play itself; and designers today trying to re-create *Death of a Salesman* must compete with the ghost of Mielziner's set. Mielziner also lit most of his own plays in order to control light, mood and colour. Working together with Edward F. Kook, he was responsible for many improvements in lighting instruments. Mielziner also worked as a THEATRE DESIGNer and consultant on many theatres, including the somewhat controversial VIVIAN BEAUMONT THEATRE in New York. AA

Mihura, Miguel 1905–77 Spanish playwright, director, humorist, and founder in 1941 of *La Codorniz*, a satirical magazine featuring lampoons and cartoons on Spanish life during the most restrictive years of the Franco dictatorship. His first and most admired play, *Tres sombreros de copa* (*Three Top Hats*), was written in 1932 but not staged until 1952. This tragicomic FARCE about a young man's short-lived flirtation with the unconventional has been translated into several languages and is frequently revived.

Although some critics maintain that none of Mihura's subsequent plays equals his first, he did write other innovative and thought-provoking comedies. Both *Sublime decisión* (*Sublime Decision*, 1955) and *La bella Dorotea* (*The Enchanting Dorothea*, 1963) deal persuasively with a young woman's assertion of her own identity in defiance of ingrained male superiority and the expectations of a conservative society. In *Carlota* (1954), the best of his several crime plays, he thwarts audience expectations as he exploits and inverts the conventions of the murder mystery, providing a totally enigmatic ending and anticipating the theatrical sleight of hand of TOM STOPPARD. Many of his plays served as vehicles for the influential actress Isabel Garcés, and more often than not Mihura himself was the director of the brisk and stylish productions. MPH

Mikhoels, Solomon 1890–1948 Yiddish actor. Leading actor and later director of the MOSCOW STATE JEWISH THEATRE, Mikhoels was one of the favourite actors of the Soviet public until his death in mysterious circumstances immediately after the enforced closure of his theatre in 1948. His greatest roles were King Lear, for which he received international acclaim, Reb Alter in *An Evening of Sholom Aleichem*, Benjamin in Mendele Mocher Sforim's *The Voyage of Benjamin III* and Hostmach in GOLDFADN's *The Witch*. (See also YIDDISH THEATRE.) AB

Miles, Bernard (James) 1907–91 British actor and director. His career as an actor flourished from the 1930s onward, but it is as the founder of the Mermaid Theatre, London, that he made his greatest contribution to the British theatre. Miles had always wished to establish a resident theatre company within the City of London, and after several temporary 'Mermaids' had tested the ground, the permanent building, created largely through the enthusiasm and effort of Miles and his wife Josephine,

opened on the north bank of the River Thames at Puddle Dock in May 1959. The first production was his own adaptation of FIELDING's *Rape upon Rape*, called *Lock up Your Daughters* – a rumbustious play with music. At the Mermaid he built a repertoire of classics and directed and performed in many of them. In more recent years the theatre has come under financial pressure, but in 1987 the ROYAL SHAKESPEARE COMPANY temporarily made it the London base for productions created at the Swan Theatre in Stratford-upon-Avon. Miles also appeared in a large number of British films, and created a radio character whose monologues of rural life made him a nationally known figure even before the Mermaid venture. He was knighted in 1969. MB

Miller, Arthur 1915– American playwright and director. Following the death of TENNESSEE WILLIAMS in 1983, and in spite of the paucity of his own recent output, Miller remains relatively unchallenged as America's greatest living playwright. His first produced play, *The Man Who Had All the Luck* (1944), was a consummate failure, but *All My Sons* (1947) proved that Miller could create powerful scenes and believable characters. His next play, *Death of a Salesman* (1949), won him both the Pulitzer Prize and the Drama Critics' Circle Award. Shifting neatly between REALISM and EXPRESSIONISM, this piercing study of an ageing 'drummer' (commercial traveller) elicited highly praised, prize-winning efforts from the entire original production company and has subsequently been performed all over the world. His adaptation of IBSEN's *An Enemy of the People* (1950) was a thematic prelude to *The Crucible* (1953), a drama of the Salem witchcraft trials written in passionate response to Senator Joseph McCarthy's investigations of alleged subversives. This spellbinding drama of real conflict and impassioned action, revived on BROADWAY in 1991, has outlived the immediacy of its inception and may yet prove to be Miller's finest work. *A View from the Bridge* (1955), which played in New York the year Miller married Marilyn Monroe, continued his exploration of the tragedy of the common man. This time his hero is a hard-working Sicilian longshoreman who is killed because he breaks the community's law of silence about some illegal immigrants.

Miller's stage voice was silent for the next eight years, during which time he divorced Monroe (1961) and married photographer Ingeborg Morath (1962). He returned to the stage in 1964 with *After the Fall*, apparently a highly personal play based on his life with beautiful filmstar Monroe. *Incident at Vichy*, an examination of the Nazi–Jewish conflict during the Second World War, followed in the same year. *The Price* (1968), a heart-wrenching confrontation between two brothers, became the last Miller play to achieve anything like a popular success. *The Creation of the World and Other Business* (1972) and *The American Clock* (1980) failed and were hastily withdrawn. In recent years Miller's plays have been given significant revivals or premieres in England, where he seems more popular today than in the USA. (In 1989 the University of East Anglia opened the Arthur Miller Centre for American Studies; London revivals of *After the Fall* and *The Crucible* occurred in 1990.) In 1987 two new one-acts were presented at Lincoln Center as *Danger: Memory!*, though the bill was more successful in London. *The Archbishop's Ceiling* was staged by the ROYAL SHAKESPEARE COMPANY in 1986 and has yet to be seen in New York. Likewise, his *The Ride down Mount Morgan* also opened in London in 1991 without a New York production, though in 1992 *The Last Yankee* was seen both in New York City and London and a new work, *Broken Glass*, was staged at the LONG WHARF THEATRE, New Haven, Connecticut, in 1994, and then on Broadway.

Throughout his career Miller has produced a rich collection of essays about the craft of playwriting, especially the nature of modern TRAGEDY. These pieces, published as *The Theatre Essays of Arthur Miller* (edited by Robert A. Martin, 1971), remain the closest thing to a complete 'poetics' yet written by an American playwright. LDC DBW

Miller, Gilbert (Heron) 1884–1969 American producer, director and theatre manager; son of actor HENRY MILLER and actress Bijou Heron. Miller produced a half-century career. He was known for his elegant staging of high COMEDY by such writers as PHILIP BARRY, SOMERSET MAUGHAM and other masters of literate dialogue. He introduced to the American stage such British actors as CHARLES LAUGHTON, ALEC GUINNESS and Leslie Howard. From 1918 until its demolition in 1958 he owned the ST JAMES'S THEATRE, London; from 1929 until his death, the LYRIC THEATRE, London; and during 1926–68 the Henry Miller Theatre in New York. His greatest success was *Victoria Regina* (1936) with HELEN HAYES. Other significant productions included Maugham's *The Constant Wife* (1927), SHERRIFF's *Journey's End* (1928), ELIOT's *The Cocktail Party* (1950) and DYLAN THOMAS's *Under Milk Wood* (1957). DBW

Miller, Henry 1859–1925 London-born actor and manager who emigrated with his parents to Canada, where he made his debut in 1876. He quickly became a juvenile leading man in America opposite a variety of young actresses, including Bijou Heron, whom he married in 1883. In 1893 he became leading man of CHARLES FROHMAN's new EMPIRE THEATRE Stock Company. During 1905–8 he and MARGARET ANGLIN starred under their own management, notably in *The Great Divide* by WILLIAM VAUGHN MOODY. Though he continued to act until after the First World War, Miller's principal occupation after 1908 was as a producer for others. He launched the career of ALLA NAZIMOVA, and became manager and producer for WALTER HAMPDEN, Laura Hope Crewes and Ruth Chatterton, among others. As an actor, Miller personified the American ideal of honest, sympathetic, taciturn masculinity. DMCD

Miller, Joaquin [Cincinnatus Hiner Miller] 1839–1913 American writer, whose early life among the miners and Indians of California and Oregon is confused by his autobiographical embroidery. In 1863 he settled as a newspaper editor in Oregon. When his early poems and stories were favourably received, he moved to San Francisco (1870), but his Byronic appearance, behaviour and writing were most popular in England. His best works were the books *Songs of the Sierras* (1871) and *Life among the*

Modocs (1873). He also wrote four plays, and *The Danites in the Sierras* was performed in a heavily revised version by ARTHUR McKEE RANKIN (1877–81). DMCD

Miller, Jonathan (Wolfe) 1934– British actor and director, who was part of the original *Beyond the Fringe* team which added, in 1960, a new note of political SATIRE to intimate REVUE. He qualified as a doctor at Cambridge University and his career has combined medical research with his contributions to stage and television. In 1962, he was invited to direct JOHN OSBORNE's one-act play *Under Plain Cover* at the ROYAL COURT, and he subsequently worked as a director in New York, at the Mermaid Theatre (see BERNARD MILES) in London and elsewhere. His 1969 production of *King Lear* with MICHAEL HORDERN introduced a scientific understanding of the ageing process and established him as a director of originality and insight.

He was invited by LAURENCE OLIVIER to direct at the NATIONAL THEATRE, notably *The Merchant of Venice* with Olivier as Shylock, which led to an eventual appointment as associate director from 1973 to 75. His relationship with PETER HALL, who succeeded Olivier at the National Theatre, was less happy, and he left to direct a season of 'family' plays, including *Hamlet* and *Ghosts* at Greenwich Theatre in 1974, and subsequently freelanced among several regional repertory theatres, including the Yvonne Arnaud Theatre in Guildford, Surrey, where he directed a memorable production of CHEKHOV's *Three Sisters*.

Miller preferred to work within relaxed conditions where no large sums of money or national prestige were at stake, and where he could develop his remarkable gifts at encouraging actors to pursue accurate interpretations. He has also directed OPERA with great success, including a remarkable *Rigoletto* for the English National Opera in 1984, set among the Sicilian Mafia in New York during the 1930s. In 1987, he was appointed director of the Old Vic and immediately launched two ambitious seasons, including Racine's *Andromache*, N. F. SIMPSON's *One Way Pendulum*, GEORGE CHAPMAN's *Bussy D'Ambois* and LEONARD BERNSTEIN's *Candide* in 1988, and *King Lear* and PIERRE CORNEILLE's *The Liar* in 1989. The attempt was brave, but failed to attract enough box office revenue to sustain it. JE

Miller, Marilyn [Marilyn; *née* Mary Ellen Reynolds] 1898–1936 American dancer and singer. As a child she appeared in VAUDEVILLE, and was dancing in a London club when she was discovered by LEE SHUBERT. She made her BROADWAY debut in *The Passing Show of 1914*. Miller was a featured performer in two editions of the ZIEGFELD Follies (1918, 1919). In *Sally* (1920), she was given her first starring role, as a poor dishwasher who becomes a star of those same *Follies*. Critics found her performance enchanting, complimenting her on her graceful dancing, her delicate beauty and her buoyant personality. After a long run and national tour in *Sally*, Miller returned to Broadway in *Sunny* (1925), where her weekly salary was reported to be $3000, making her the highest-paid MUSICAL COMEDY performer of the 1920s. Her next shows, *Rosalie* (1928) and *Smiles* (1930), were not as successful as the previous two. In 1933 she made her final Broadway appearance in *As*

Thousands Cheer, a REVUE with a score by IRVING BERLIN. Although her singing voice was so weak as to be inaudible at times, Miller's radiant beauty and elegant dancing made her the reigning queen of musical comedy in the 1920s. MK

Miller, Max [Thomas Sargent] 1895–1963 The most celebrated British comedian of the heyday of VARIETY; 'the Cheeky Chappie'. Born in Brighton, he began work as a motor mechanic, but soon took to popular entertainment, initially with amateur concert-parties in his home town, then professionally with the original Billy Smart's Circus. Although his CIRCUS career was interrupted by the outbreak of the First World War, he was drafted into an army entertainments unit in which he seems to have had his first solo experience. After demobilization, three years touring provincial venues was followed by his London debut in 1922. Though not an overnight success, by 1924 he was working steadily under his subsequently famous solo billing, and by 1926 was top of the bill at the Holborn Empire, a position he maintained for three decades until his retirement.

A brashly colourful figure in white trilby, two-tone shoes, kipper tie and multicoloured plus-four suit, he was accurately summed up by a reviewer as 'vulgar, loud, earthy and blue'. Though his act was mainly concerned with sex, and was generally regarded by contemporaries as rather daring, his material was no bawdier than that of many comedians before and since. What made it seem so was his stage persona, and his relationship with his audience.

The dandified appearance, preening gestures and physical display – which so easily imply effeminacy –expressed total sexual confidence, the more so as his numerous asides were invariably addressed familiarly to ladies. His stories were often in the first person. Furthermore, Miller told everybody that he was dirty, and drew them into complicity. 'I'm filthy with money,' he confided, flashing his gross dress-ring, and adding as an afterthought, 'I'm filthy without it.' Complimenting himself on the quality of his suiting, he would invite a lady in the front row to have a feel. To draw the whole house into his conspiracy, he would display the White and Blue Books which allegedly contained clean and dirty jokes, and make the audience choose. Hobson's choice. Thereafter, the audience were looking for trouble even when none existed, and of course they always found it, encouraged by the comedian's simple but beautifully handled technique of not completing his punch-line or of omitting the end rhyme of his mildly saucy ditties. The inevitable laughter would be punctuated by pained appeals of 'Here, listen' (a proletarian version of GEORGE ROBEY's injunction to 'desist'), challenges to the audience to 'make something of that', and his famous complaint, 'You're the kind of people who'll get me a bad name.' They did, they would, and they were.

His handling of an audience (there for all to hear in a 1957 recording of one of his last bookings, at the Metropolitan in London's Edgware Road) was masterly. His timing was superb; his ability to prompt laughter and encourage it to grow by saying virtually nothing was unrivalled; above all, he exuded personal and professional self-confidence, while approaching his audience (not to mention the band-leader) with a relaxed and conversational intimacy. While Miller was on stage, they were all 'pals'. AEG

Mills, Florence 1895–1927 African-American comedienne, singer and dancer who became the idol of Harlem. At age five she appeared in Williams and Walker's MUSICAL COMEDY *Sons of Ham* (see BERT WILLIAMS), and at 15 joined her two sisters in a musical trio, *The Mills Sisters*, that toured the country in VAUDEVILLE shows. Her first major billing came when she replaced Gertrude Sanders as leading lady in the hit MUSICAL *Shuffle Along* (1921) at New York City's 63rd Street Theatre. The next year Mills was on BROADWAY in *Plantation Revue*, which extended her fame internationally. Performances followed in Paris and London in *From Dover to Dixie* (1923–4) and as the star of *From Dixie to Broadway* (1924) back in the USA. In Lew Leslie's *Blackbirds* (1926), written specially for her, she again toured Paris and London, leaving the show because of ill health. A pixie of a woman, delicate and stunningly attractive on stage, she was beloved by the 150,000 people who followed her funeral procession in Harlem. EGH AEG

Mills, John [Lewis Ernest Watts] 1908– British actor and director, who first appeared on the stage in 1929. A popular actor in the 1930s, who appeared in light comedies and MUSICALS and played a season at the OLD VIC in 1938, Mills became best known as a film-star during the 1940s and 1950s, appearing in many patriotic war films as well as such epics as *Scott of the Antarctic*, *The Colditz Story* and *Around the World in Eighty Days*. For at least two generations of film audiences, Mills represented the figure of a cheerful, stocky Englishman whose fundamental decency could always be relied on, especially in a crisis. He took few unsympathetic or character roles.

His stage career, however, indicates an acting range beyond that of his films. He appeared in the New York production of RATTIGAN's *Ross* (1961) and in CHARLES WOOD's *Veterans* at the ROYAL COURT in 1972, a SATIRE on ageing film actors on location. His roles in the musical version of *The Good Companions* (1974), in *Separate Tables* (1977) and *Goodbye Mr Chips* (1982) can be regarded as within his familiar range, but he astonished audiences at the NATIONAL THEATRE in 1986 with his performance as General Sir Edmund Milne in Brian Clark's *The Petition*, an elderly right-wing hawk distressed to find that his wife after many years of marriage is a dying dove. Mills is an actor who has a wide emotional range, from light COMEDY to TRAGEDY, within an apparently limited stage and film personality. His autobiography, *Gentlemen Please*, was published in 1980. He received the CBE in 1960 and was knighted in 1976. JE

Milne, A(dam) A(lexander) 1882–1956 British children's author and dramatist. Of his many light comedies written after 1918, his satiric demolition of conservatism *Mr Pim Passes By* (1919), and *The Dover Road* and *The Truth About Blayds* – in which run-away couples are brought to realize that escape to Paris is not the path to happiness and a revered poet is discovered to be a fake (both 1921) – all became popular repertory pieces. Their whimsical fantasy and sentimental humour mark Milne as the successor to BARRIE, and his best-known play *Toad of Toad Hall* (1929, based on Kenneth Grahame's *The Wind in the Willows*) is still revived almost every Christmas in London. CI

Milwaukee Repertory Theater (USA) Organized in 1954 as the Fred Miller Theater Company, a professional STOCK COMPANY, in Milwaukee, Wisconsin. After seven years in the Miller Theater (a converted cinema) and the production of 71 plays with well known guest stars, the governing board employed a resident ensemble, turning first to the Association of Producing Artists, then to the AMERICAN CONSERVATORY THEATRE for brief seasons. The organization became the Milwaukee Repertory Theater in 1964, and has since featured its resident professional acting company. Three artistic directors have been outstanding: Tunc Yalman (1966–71), who managed the company's move to the Todd Wehr Theater in Milwaukee's Performing Arts Center and the growth of the group's subscription base to 16,000; Nagle Jackson (1971–7), who added productions at the Court Street Theater in 1974 and at the historic Pabst Theatre; and John Dillon (1977–93), who included resident playwrights in the company, conducted international tours with the group, and, in 1987, moved it to a new three-theatre facility on the east bank of the Milwaukee River. Typical of Dillon's productions was a non-traditionally cast *Our Town* (1991). Dillon was succeeded by Joseph Hanreddy, formerly at the Madison Repertory Theatre. WD

mime, pantomime (See also PANTOMIME, ENGLISH) Two terms that have altered in meaning and become confused over the centuries. Today they are used interchangeably to signify wordless, gestural performance; but in classical times they referred to distinct and different phenomena. Mime, from the Greek *mimos*, originally meant a form of comic folk play and then the actor who performed it (see GREECE, ANCIENT). Dorian or Megaran in origin, the plays at first parodied mythological characters, but later were sketches of contemporary life; the two or three characters were masked and phallephoric and featured a gluttonous slave. Epicharmus (c.530–c.440 BC) packed his mimes with puns; Herodas turned out vignettes of everyday life, introducing the schoolmaster, the inveterate shopper and the quack doctor as standard types. Sophron of Syracuse (c.430 BC) brought the genre to a literary pitch that influenced the idylls of Theocritus and Moschus.

Among the Romans, the mime changed in both form and content (see ROME). It gradually usurped the popularity of the Atellan farces, and could be distinguished from regular comedy by the fact that women (*mimae*) performed, and masks and cothurnoi were not worn. Homogeneous companies of various sizes were led by an *archimimus* or *archimima*, an actor-manager who played the lead role. The comic types usually included the *stupidus*, a bald-headed, soot-smeared lout, and the *sannio* or face-maker; a common item of costume was the *centunculus*, a variegated cloak which some scholars have seen as an ancestor of HARLEQUIN's piebald jacket. In the tradition of the Floralia, when prostitutes appeared naked, the *mima* was often required to undress before the public.

Officially, mimes were on the lowest rung of the social ladder, but their popularity was such that many of their names have been preserved, and in time they toppled TRAGEDY and COMEDY from their pedestals. Their plays were slices of life, often highly satirical and earthily obscene, with an emphasis on adulteries, swindles and rough-housing.

Political SATIRE, which thrived under the Republic, was less independent under the Empire: the most popular and frequently revived mime between AD 30 and 200 was *Laureolus* by Quintus Lutatius Catullus, which demonstrated by the fate of its bandit-hero that the government knows best. (The emperor Domitian replaced the actor with a condemned criminal in the final scenes, so that the audience might enjoy genuine torture and execution.) Comic Christians were a frequent butt, with much byplay made of the rite of baptism. In the late classical period, mimes of a high literary quality were written by Decimus Laberius (106–43 BC) and his contemporary Publilius Syrus. But the greater the mime's popularity, the less important the written script became; actors gesticulated and improvised their own dialogue, while the GRAND-GUIGNOL recourse to real bloodshed increased.

The Roman pantomime, on the other hand, whose name derives from the Greek *pantomimos* (meaning 'imitating everything'), was a male dancer who single-handedly interpreted classical literature, especially tragedies, to the accompaniment of chanted recitation and flute music, and by changing MASKS. These one-man shows were supported by factions and associated with court intrigue, subject to imperial favour or displeasure by turns. The most famous were Pylades (c.20 BC), who introduced a large choir in place of the solo singer, and Bathyllus, whose racy performance of *Leda and the Swan* was mentioned by Juvenal. They too were censured for lasciviousness.

Mimes and pantomimes alike composed the bridge that brought the tradition of professional acting into the medieval world, although condemned by church councils and outlawed by monarchs. The mime thrived in Byzantium, and certain ecclesiastics like Gregory of Nazianzus (?330–390?) tried to adapt it to sacred subjects. Choricius (6th century AD) defended the mimic performer as an imitator of life, but these proponents were in the minority. Eventually, the excommunicated *mimi* were lumped with all itinerant jugglers, minstrels and showmen, and renamed *ioculatores*, goliards or VAGANTES. The miscellaneous nature of the mime's performance is clear in the description Theodoric, King of the Visigoths, made of the mime he sent to King Clovis of France: 'a skilful man who joins the art of expressing feelings by gestures and facial movements to the harmony of voices and sounds of instruments'. This all-purpose entertainer excelled at FARCE and was employed to interlard more serious presentations with 'dainty morsels' of his fooling: in French, *entremets*; in Spanish, *entremeses*.

One curious cognate is the Elizabethan DUMB SHOW, best remembered for its appearance in *Hamlet*. Descended from the allegorical 'mummings' on festive occasions, it was never used as an interlude but always related to the play in which it was inserted. It served both to prefigure action to come and to endow that action with a more symbolic meaning. Besides SHAKESPEARE, MARSTON, MIDDLETON and WEBSTER all used it to pungent effect.

The preservation of the mimic tradition in continental Europe devolved upon the *COMMEDIA DELL'ARTE*, whose comedy was physical but also highly verbal. The association with mute expressiveness may result from the first introduction of Italian troupes into France: not knowing French, they fell back on the universal language of gesture.

Modern mime and pantomime emerged in the 18th century from French fairgrounds and minor theatres, where the dramatic monopoly constrained 'illegitimate' performers to avoid dialogue and develop a primarily physical means of expression. At the Saint-Germain fair in 1710, Pierre Alard (d.1721), whose troupe was forbidden to speak, played *pièces à la muette*, in which the actors mimed to scrolls pulled out of their pockets and, later, signboards let down from the flies. Such mimic shows, accompanied throughout by music, were brought to London, and soon became acclimatized as the English pantomime, which developed its own idiosyncratic conventions.

DIDEROT, vexed by the static nature of conventional acting, argued for gestural action to be made equal to the words in legitimate drama; and Marmontel in the *Encyclopédie* deemed pantomime especially necessary for 'the most impassioned movements of the soul ... There it seconds the words, or takes their place entirely.' Mimic gesture became an important principle of late-18th-century acting theory: Johann Jakob Engel (1741–1802) in his *Ideas towards a System of Mimicry* (1785–6) suggested that mimic gesture in rituals functioned as natural signs, as colour does in painting; but the actor had to provide the strongest, most animated expressiveness to jolt the audience's awareness of what was being imitated. Ultimately, he concluded, mime was imperfect because it had to convey both ideas and feelings.

The *philosophes* were seeking a primal universal language, but the fairground *pantomimes dialoguées* and *pantomimes historiques*, cross-pollinating the increasingly popular *ballets d'action*, evolved in other ways. Preromantic ballet was dominated by fairground performers like Grimaldo Nicolini, who was approved by LESSING, and the line between dance and pantomime was hard to draw. After the French Revolution, for a newly proletarian audience, gestural acting became a dominant partner of dialogue in melodrama, while *mimodrame*, as practised at the CIRQUE OLYMPIQUE, eschewed language altogether.

Throughout the 19th century, the spectacular pantomime was subjugated to the style of its leading actors. MAZURIER bequeathed his acrobatic style to the immensely popular RAVELS who popularized pantomime in the USA. JEAN-GASPARD DEBURAU made PIERROT the indispensable pivot of the pantomimes at Paris's THÉÂTRE DES FUNAMBULES, a whey-faced Everyman whose loose smock garbed historical characters and modern types, no matter what the plot; this tradition was upheld by his son Charles and by the more robust Paul Legrand (1816–98). The whiteness of costume and make-up put attitudes, gestures and facial expressions in relief. However, since this form of pantomime dispensed with words and used music only as an auxiliary, it required a conventionalized dramatic sub-ject. Charles Nodier, JULES JANIN and THÉOPHILE GAUTIER all wrote scenarios for it, but the chief purveyor was Champfleury.

This genre declined as its favourites died out, and was replaced in popularity by the violent, so-called American pantomimes of the HANLON-LEES. But the older style enjoyed a brief and fashionable revival with the foundation of the amateur Cercle Funambulesque in 1888, when music played a preponderant role: Paul Margueritte's *Pierrot assassin de sa femme*, Catulle Mendès's '*Chand d'habits*, and *L'Enfant prodigue* by Michel Carré *fils* (1890) were widely performed, not to popular audiences but to a middle-class public in quest of novelty. The great mimes of this period are Louis Rouffe and his student Séverin, noted for refinement, delicacy and precision. In *Mains et masque*, the latter reduced Pierrot to a silent mask and eloquent hands.

In the 20th century, the silent film's ability to present a convincing representation of reality compelled the theatre to re-examine its own roots in search of inspiration. François Delsarte had already tried to classify and categorize the possibilities of emotional expression by the human body. GORDON CRAIG with his concept of the *Über-Marionette* (1905, 1911), YEATS with his demand for an aristocratic Western *nō* theatre, and other anti-realists called for symbolic gesture. The dance reforms of Isadora Duncan and the eurhythmic exercises of Jaques-Dalcroze were regarded as potential sources for a new theatrical art. JACQUES COPEAU, who had always seen the *commedia dell'arte* as a fountainhead of the actor's art, founded a school in 1921 where exercises with masks worked to isolate the body as a tool of expression in preparation for the spoken drama.

What had been a means for Copeau became an end in itself for his student ÉTIENNE DECROUX. Decroux formulated 'pure mime' or *pantomime de style*, an independent art form whose (usually solo) performer creates a circumambient world and its objects wholly through movement. Hand gestures were reduced to a minimum, the face to a neutral mask, and narrative elements discarded in favour of an abstract distillation of a symbolic essence. Decroux viewed man as a struggling worm, with a right to unhappiness. This aspect of his teaching was emphasized by his disciple JEAN-LOUIS BARRAULT, whose mimodramas usually depicted a struggle against time and death. Jacques Lecoq (b.1921), who studied mask work with Copeau's son-in-law JEAN DASTÉ, founded a school in 1956, whose two-year course deliberately excluded this austerity to embrace more psychological situations, theatrical styles, sound, colour and lighting effects.

Decroux's teaching was in part widely popularized by yet another student, MARCEL MARCEAU. As early as 1947, Marceau's character Bip of the white face and striped jersey appeared at the Théâtre de Poche, Paris, a sophisticated throwback to Deburau's Pierrot. Although fascinated by death, Marceau diluted his melancholy with wistful comedy and did not disdain to tell a story. His influence has been phenomenal, not only on such professionals as the Israeli Samy Molcho, the Czech LADISLAV FIALKA, and (in opposition) the American Adam Darius, but also on the cohorts of street performers who perpetuate his exercises of the cage and walking against the wind *ad infinitum* and *ad nauseam*.

A new direction in mime was taken by the Pole Henryk Tomaszewski, who founded the Wroclaw Pantomime Theatre in 1956. Distrustful of the sterility of 'pure mime', Tomaszewski creates elaborate ensemble pantomimes inspired by painting, sculpture, architecture and Oriental theatre, and based on such cultural archetypes as Gilgamesh, Dionysus, Hamlet, Faust and Woyzeck. Offering an absurdist view of the universe, his sumptuous mélange of mime and dance raises questions about human existence but leaves the meaning sufficiently ambiguous to force the spectator to interpret the dreamlike and sensuous spectacle.

Contemporary mime has also been invigorated with injections of choreography and CLOWNING. The German *Ausdruckstanz*, or expressive dancing, of the 1920s had given rise to VALESKA GERT, whose dance-pantomimes explored the type of the whore; in America, ANGNA ENTERS practised a similar art with avatars of the Madonna. Gert's work was carried on by the grotesque Lotte Goslar, and, recently, a resurgence of this dance-pantomime can be discerned in the work of Pina Bausch and her Wuppertal Tanztheater.

Bausch's exploration of sexual roles indicates the more serious ends to which modern mime has been adapted. The SAN FRANCISCO MIME TROUPE split from the Actors' Workshop in 1959 to play *commedia dell'arte* scenarios in public parks; its broadly humorous collective creativity has always served radical political ends. The same holds true of the BREAD AND PUPPET THEATRE. A more Jungian approach is taken by the Swiss trio Mummenschanz (literally, Game of Chance), founded in 1972 by Andrés Brossard, Bernie Schürch and Floriana Frassetto. Its use of masks made of vacuum-cleaner hoses and toilet rolls creates a nightmarish, abstract and chilling view of the human predicament, reminiscent of the paintings of Paul Klee. The most recent experiments in mime have been omniclusive, admitting words and whatever might prove expressive to expand its potential.

Typical exponents of this trend are the Decroux-trained groups of Montreal, Omnibus (founded by Jean Asselin and Denise Boulanger, 1977) and Carbonne 14 (founded by Gilles Maheu), reliant on evocative imagery and text. A similar synthesis of all the actor's means to communicate is evident in such disparate artists as the Czechs Boleslav Polivka and Ctibor Turba who combine buffoonery and existential messages; the Russian group Ilkhom with its nightmarish evocation of constricted lives; and American performance artists, who range from the anarchic Ronlin Foreman to the bemused manipulator of objects, Paul Zaloom. LS

See: J. Dorcy, *The Mime*, London, 1975; M. Felner, *Apostles of Silence: The Modern French Mime*, London, 1985; P. Hugonnet, *Mimes et Pierrots*, Paris, 1889; T. Leabhart, *Modern and Postmodern Mime*, New York, 1989; D. Mehl, *The Elizabethan Dumb Show*, Cambridge, Mass., 1966; A. Nicoll, *Masks, Mimes and Miracles*, London, 1931; B. Rolfe (ed.), *Mimes on Miming*, Los Angeles, 1982; M. H. Winter, *The Pre-Romantic Ballet*, London, 1974.

mimodrame see MIME

mimos see MIME

Minetti, Bernhard 1905– German actor who from 1930 to 1945 at the Berlin State Theatre lent villains like SCHILLER's Franz Moor (*Die Räuber*), GOETHE's Mephisto, and Angelo in *Measure for Measure* a lean, evil intelligence. After the war he played heroic roles such as Julius Caesar (Düsseldorf) and Schiller's Wallenstein (Ruhr Festival). At the Berlin Schillertheater from 1965 until its closure in 1993 he favoured new writers. He was a fine Max in PINTER's *Homecoming*, and his glittering eye and jutting jaw in BECKETT's *Krapp's Last Tape* were unforgettable. A friend of THOMAS BERNHARD's, he created many of his manic heroes, notably himself in *Minetti* and Caribaldi in *The Force of Habit*. Still active, his one-man show *Grimm's Fairy Tales* was selected for the Berlin Theatertreffen in 1991. HR

Minsky brothers Synonymous with post-1920s stock BURLESQUE in New York, in particular the popularization of the strip-tease (see NUDITY). **Billy** [William] **(Michael)** (?1887–1932), the showman of the family, was soon joined by **Abe** [Abraham] (1881–1949), **Herbert Kay** (?1892–1959) and, by the early 1920s, **Morton** (1902–87) in running their father Louis's National Theatre and Winter Garden (1912). The theatre ran the gamut of entertainment ventures until 1923–4, when it emerged as the National Winter Garden, a paradigm for all burlesque theatres in the country, including a dozen subsequent Minsky houses (in particular, the Republic, 1931). Innovations included illuminated runways; slim, attractive and scantily clad Minsky girls, such as GYPSY ROSE LEE and Margie Hart; and good comics (such as Steve Mills and Phil Silvers). Some feel the Minskys caused burlesque's downfall, for as they developed dirty, escapist shows that attracted sizeable patronage, censors also took notice (see CENSORSHIP). Mayor Fiorello LaGuardia helped effect the closing of their operation in 1937, although a legal ban did not exist until 1942. DBW

minstrel show American medley of sentimental ballads, comic dialogue and dance interludes, ostensibly founded on Negro life in the South. Its origin is attributed to THOMAS D. RICE, who copied the eccentric mannerisms of an elderly black in Baltimore in 1828 and adopted blackface and banjo to produce the wildly popular 'Jim Crow'. At first a solo act, minstrelsy grew to four performers – on violin, banjo, bones (a rhythm instrument) and tambourine – with the Virginia Minstrels, founded by Dan Emmett (1842–3); despite the burnt cork, their repertoire drew heavily on traditional English choral singing and lugubrious parlour ballads. The same held true of the troupe of E.P. Christy, who invented whitefaced master-of-ceremonies Mr Interlocutor and the semicircular arrangement of performers; his troupe had 30 members and gave 2500 performances in New York in a single year. By the early 1850s Christy had evolved what was to be the standard tripartite programme: in the first part, the performers would enter in the 'walkround' until told, 'Gentlemen, be seated.' Vocal numbers, both lively and sentimental, would be sung, interspersed with comic chat from the 'endmen' (in England, 'cornermen'), Mr Tambo and Mr

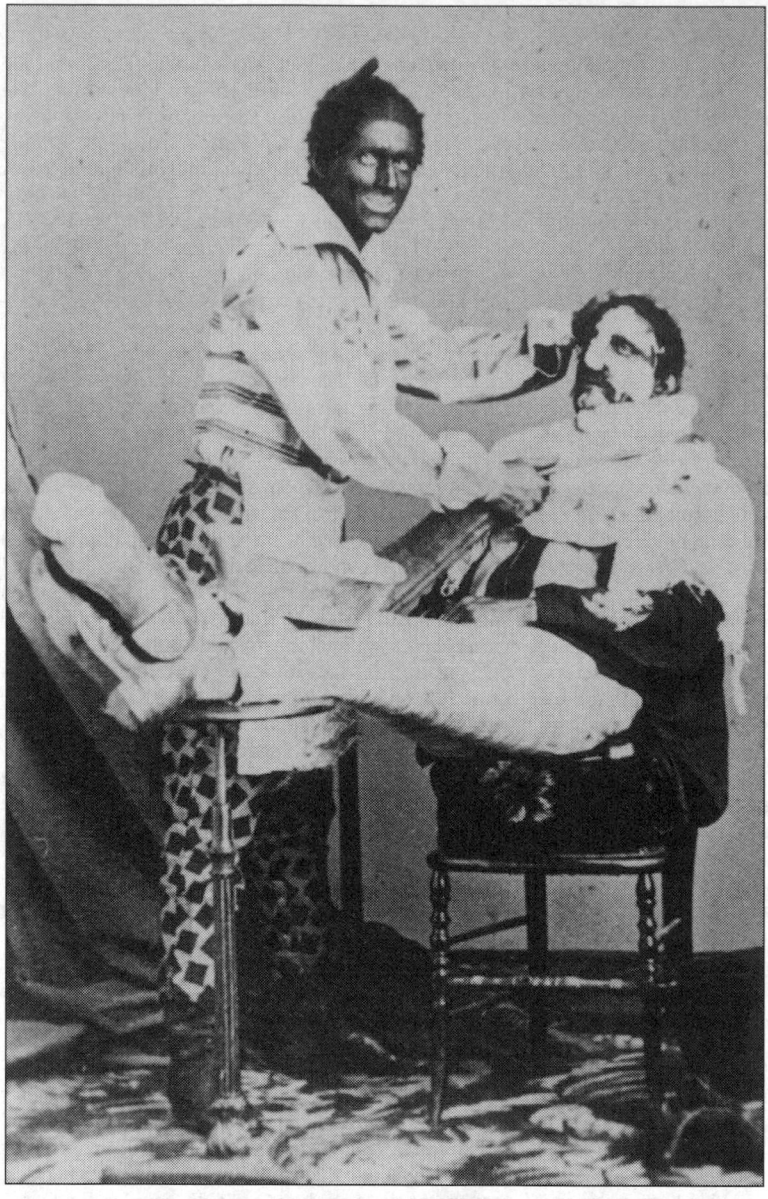

Dan Bryant, a blackface
Figaro, shaving Eph Horn
in an American minstrel act
of the 1860s.

Bones. Part two, the olio, was a fantasia of speciality acts before the drop curtain; these included the stump speech, perfected by James Unsworth, and the wench impersonation, originated by George N. Christy (Harington). Part three comprised a sketch, either a plantation scene with dancing 'darkies' or BURLESQUES of Shakespearian plays and MELODRAMAS. Originally most of the performers and composers were white Northerners who, like Stephen Foster, had little first-hand acquaintance with Southern life; consequently the blacks they portrayed (like Zip Coon, the urban dandy) were extravagant fictions, and blackface comprised a theatrical MASK not unlike HARLEQUIN's.

After the Civil War, competition from other popular forms, especially VARIETY and MUSICAL COMEDY, compelled the minstrel show to expand and change its homely char-

acter. In 1878 J.H. Haverly combined four troupes in his United Mastodon Minstrels with his slogan, 'Forty – Count 'Em – Forty'. Sumptuous costumes and lavish scenery became the rule. Primrose and West even omitted the blackface and dressed their minstrels in 18th-century court dress. From 1880 the traditionalists complained loudly about such changes.

A more significant factor was the presence in troupes of AFRICAN-AMERICANS themselves. As early as the 1850s, black troupes, such as the Luca family, toured the Eastern states, often performing for abolitionist societies. These black-owned companies were popular throughout the Civil War years, but in the 1870s were taken over by white managers. Thus, Callender's Georgia Minstrels, featuring the great comic Billy Kersands, was sold to Haverly, who then claimed falsely to have launched 'colored minstrels'. A major component of black shows, whatever the race of the management, was female performers: Sam T. Jack's Creoles even had an all-black female first part. By adopting such stereotypes as the loyal uncle, warm-hearted mammy and shifty lazybones, black performers perpetuated the notion that these caricatures were true to life. Nevertheless, the minstrel show provided a valuable training ground for such talents as Sam Lucas, Billy McLain and composer James Bland.

The minstrel show was one of the few truly indigenous American entertainments, and made a profound impression worldwide. Its influence can be traced in much American popular music and theatre, and many outstanding performers, including EDDIE CANTOR, AL JOLSON and BERT WILLIAMS, owed a great deal to its traditions. Great Britain took rapidly to minstrelsy, sending its own troupes as far afield as India and Australia. Anglo-Saxon blackface artists were well entrenched throughout the British Empire long before the first minstrels arrived in strength in the 1870s; as a result, the ingrained stereotypes were even more remote from African-American reality than in the USA. LS

miracle play A term now used for plays about the miracles of the Virgin Mary or the saints after their deaths, or about miracles of other kinds (e.g. of the sacrament). In the Middle Ages in England the word 'miracle' was used of any religious play. An attempt was made by modern scholars to revive this general use in the phrase 'miracle play', but because of its apparent inappropriateness the phrase MYSTERY PLAY (not a term used in England in the Middle Ages) was and is generally preferred. PM

Mirren, Helen 1946- British actress, who was discovered through the NATIONAL YOUTH THEATRE for whom she played, at the age of 19, a fiery Cleopatra in *Antony and Cleopatra*. She joined the ROYAL SHAKESPEARE COMPANY, where she was chosen for such roles as Cressida in *Troilus and Cressida* and STRINDBERG's Miss Julie, which demanded her voluptuous good looks and capacity to convey a wayward temperament. She was, however, too intelligent to be easily typecast as a temptress, and in 1972 joined PETER BROOK's International Centre of Theatre Research, touring North African desert villages in a mainly improvised story, *The Conference of Birds*. She returned to the RSC to play Lady Macbeth in 1974, while her first major part in a contemporary play came when she played an alcoholic lead singer in DAVID HARE's *Teeth 'n' Smiles* (1975). She also appeared in BEN TRAVERS's *The Bed before Yesterday* (1975) and BRIAN FRIEL's *The Faith Healer* (1981), but her maturity as an actress has been distinguished by her performances in major classic roles for a variety of companies, in the title role in WEBSTER's *The Duchess of Malfi* (1980) for the ROYAL EXCHANGE Company in Manchester, and as Cleopatra in the RSC's studio *Antony and Cleopatra* (1983). In 1989, she appeared with Bob Peck in the YOUNG VIC premieres of two short plays by ARTHUR MILLER, *Some Kind of Love Story* and *Elegy for a Lady*. She has appeared in many films. JE

Mistinguett [Jeanne-Marie Bourgeois] 1873–1956

Fabled queen of the Parisian music-hall (see *CAFÉ CHANTANT*) and REVUE, who escaped her French middle-class upbringing by going on the stage, first as Miss Helyett, then Miss Tinguette, and finally Mistinguett. Her debut at the Trianon-Concert (1885) was followed by a long tenure at the Eldorado (1897–1907). Her double-jointed mimicry made up for her thin voice, as she moved from singing to eccentric comedy to revue. The success of the *valse chaloupée*, danced with MAX DEARLY at the MOULIN-ROUGE (1909), made her a star, and she confirmed her status with the *valse renversante* (1912) with MAURICE CHEVALIER, who was for a time her partner, lover and model for all her subsequent leading men. From 1919 to 1923 she flourished in tours of both Americas, introducing 'My Man'. When she appeared in *Ça c'est Paris* (1926), Colette called her a 'national treasure' and COCTEAU described her 'poignant voice' as the symbol of Paris. Her shapely legs and buck teeth were godsends for caricaturists, and even at the end of her long career, audiences gladly accepted her in the role of a little flower girl. LS

Mitchell, Adrian 1932- British novelist, playwright and poet. Although he is best known as a poet and performer of poetry, Mitchell started to write plays in the early 1960s (*The Ledge*, 1961, with music by Richard Rodney Bennett) and adapted PETER WEISS's *The Marat/Sade* (1964) for PETER BROOK's famous ROYAL SHAKESPEARE COMPANY production. He contributed to Brook's Vietnam play, *US* (1966), and wrote a celebration of William Blake's life and works for OLIVIER's NATIONAL THEATRE, *Tyger* (1971). It proved to be less of a celebration than a wake, and while he has written amusing children's plays, REVUE sketches and fragments of poetic dramas, Mitchell has yet to write a full-length play which matches up to his skill with word-play, his left-wing convictions and his star quality as a performer. For the director Declan Donnellan (see CHEEK BY JOWL) in RICHARD EYRE's NT, he provided a useful version of LOPE DE VEGA's *Fuente Ovejuna* (1989), but his attempt to conflate two plays from the Spanish GOLDEN AGE, de Vega's *A New World* and Bartolomé de las Casas's *The Tears of the Indians*, to commemorate Columbus's voyage, went badly off course when it was produced in 1992 at the Nuffield Theatre, Southampton. JE

Mitchell, Billy [William] 1798–1856 English-born actor, playwright and theatre manager. A distinguished comedian in London and English provincial theatres since 1831, Mitchell appeared first in the USA at the National Theatre in New York in 1836. His particular achievement was his management of Mitchell's Olympic on BROADWAY in New York (built in 1837) from 9 December 1839 to 9 March 1850, the year of his retirement. Advertising the production of 'VAUDEVILLES, Burlesques, Extravaganzas, Farces, Etc.', Mitchell made the Olympic a popular success when other theatres were failing. As an actor he was a favourite as Vincent Crummles in a FARCE created from DICKENS's *Nicholas Nickleby* entitled *The Savage and the Maiden*. A staff of actor-playwrights – Henry Horncastle, Charles Walcot, Alexander Allen and BENJAMIN BAKER – provided him with novelties. *1940; or, Crummles in Search of Novelty* was repeated as *1941; or, Crummles in Search* and

1942; or, Crummles in Search. Catching the topic of the day was the clue to Mitchell's success. When BOUCICAULT's *London Assurance* reached New York, he responded with *Olympic Insurance*; he BURLESQUEd Dickens's visit to the USA in *Boz* and the EDWIN FORREST–W. C. MACREADY feud in three sketches; he starred in and wrote *Billy Taylor*, a local extravaganza. The greatest event at Mitchell's Olympic, however, was Baker's *A Glance at New York*, 1848, with Mose the fire b'hoy.   WJM

Mitchell, Julian 1854–1926 American director. After an early career as a performer, Mitchell served as assistant director on several of CHARLES HOYT's FARCE comedies. He directed a number of BURLESQUES for WEBER AND FIELDS, after which he turned to the staging of elaborate comic OPERAS such as *The Wizard of Oz* (1903) and *Babes in Toyland* (1903). During 1907–14 he directed the ZIEGFELD *Follies*, and is credited with creating the chorus of beautiful, lively and individualized girls that became the hallmark of those shows. He continued to be in demand as a director of MUSICALS up to the time of his death.   MK

Mitchell, (Charles) Julian (Humphrey) 1935– British novelist and playwright, educated at Winchester and Wadham College, Oxford. He began his career by writing novels, including *Imaginary Toys* (1961), *A Disturbing Influence* (1962), *As Far As You Can Go* (1963), *The White Father* (1964), *A Circle of Friends* (1966) and *An Undiscovered Country* (1968). His first plays seen in the WEST END were adaptations of novels by Ivy Compton-Burnett, notably *A Family and a Fortune*; and Compton-Burnett's mannered evocations of Edwardian life, with their dry wit and cool observation of human behaviour, provided him with an effective and original genre with which to begin his new career as a dramatist. His best-known play, *Another Country* (1981), which feels somewhat like an adaptation from a novel, concerns the links between homosexuality and political treachery, fostered by the British public school system. It was subsequently filmed. His other stage plays, *Half-Life* (1977), *The Enemy Within* (1980), *Francis* (1983) and *After Aida* (1986), reveal a sensibility which sometimes seems to be offended by theatrical compromises. *After Aida* is a more thoughtful, accurate and learned account of Verdi's relationship with Boito than is PETER SHAFFER's account of Mozart and Salieri, *Amadeus*, with which it was immediately compared; but it did lack the impact of *Amadeus* when it was first performed at the OLD VIC.

Curiously, Mitchell writes exceptionally well for television (see TELEVISION DRAMA), where even more compromises usually have to be made, and the subtlety of his reasoning has distinguished many episodes of several series, including *Morse*.   JE

Mitchell, Langdon (Elwyn) 1862–1935 American playwright. Educated at St Paul's in the USA, Mitchell studied in Dresden and Paris, attended law school at Harvard and Columbia, was admitted to the New York bar in 1886 and in 1892 married English actress Marion Lea, who appeared in his *The New York Idea*. Son of the eminent physician and novelist Silas Weir Mitchell, he is principally known for this one play (1906). A witty SATIRE on easy

divorce and easy marriage, defined as 'three parts love and seven parts forgiveness of sin', it prompted critics to call him 'the American SHAW'. 'What I wanted to satirize,' Mitchell once wrote, 'was the extreme frivolity of our American life.' Written for MINNIE MADDERN FISKE, the play was revived by Grace George (1915), and produced by MAX REINHARDT in Berlin (1916). Mitchell also wrote *In the Season* (1893); *Becky Sharp* (1899), an adaptation of *Vanity Fair* and a vehicle for Mrs Fiske; *The Kreutzer Sonata* (1906), an adaptation from the Yiddish of JACOB GORDIN; *The New Marriage* (1911); and *Major Pendennis* (1916), adapted from Thackeray's novel.   RM

Mitra, Tripti Indian actress. Considered one of the great women performers of 20th-century INDIA, Mitra was born in West Bengal and made her reputation performing in the Calcutta amateur theatre. She was attracted to the theatre as a college student during the mid-1940s because of its political and social potential during this time of great social unrest and famine. Appearing in the Indian People's Theatre Association's original production of *New Harvest (Nabanna)* in 1944, she later gained fame for her sensitive portrayals of TAGORE's heroines in *Red Oleanders (Raktakarabi)* and *King of the Dark Chamber (Raja)*, as well as Nora in IBSEN's *A Doll's House*. Most recently she has appeared in one-woman shows, designed by herself, which have successfully toured India, Europe, Russia and the United States.   FAR

Mitterwurzer, Friedrich 1844–97 German actor. An unusually restless man, Mitterwurzer was hired on three different occasions by the Vienna BURGTHEATER –1871 to 1874, 1875 to 1880, and 1894 to 1897. He was renowned for his ability to play what LAUBE called 'broken characters'. His staccato acting, which revealed inconsistencies in characters, went against the general idealist interpretation of classic roles, but was eminently suited to IBSEN. Mitterwurzer was a celebrated Consul Bernick, Hjalmar Ekdal and Alfred Allmers. Some historians claim his acting foreshadowed EXPRESSIONISM.   SW

Mitzi E. Newhouse Theatre see VIVIAN BEAUMONT AND MITZI E. NEWHOUSE THEATRES

Mlama [Muhando], Penina 1948– Tanzanian playwright and director. All her published plays are in Swahili and include *Haitia (Guilt*, 1972); *Tambueni Haki Zetu (Recognize Our Rights*, 1973); *Heshima Yangu (My Respect*, 1974); *Pambo (Decoration*, 1975); *Talaka si Mke Wangu (I Divorce You*, 1976); *Nguzo Mama (Mother the Main Pillar*, 1982); *Harakati za Ukombozi (Liberation Struggles*, 1982), with A. Lihamba and others, and *Lina Ubani (There Is an Antidote for Rot*, 1984). Like other Tanzanian playwrights, Mlama deals with the problems of the struggle for liberation and a just society, as in *Tambueni Haki Zetu*, *Harakati za Ukombozi* and *Lina Ubani*. She also explores more personal problems, as in her treatment of the effects of divorce on children in *Talaka* and hypocrisy in *Heshima Yangu*. She is concerned with women's rights, and her *Nguzo Mama* shows the conflicts and contradictions in the Tanzanian struggle for the liberation of women. She is active in the theatre-for-development movement (see

THIRD WORLD POPULAR THEATRE). Her book *Culture and Development: The Popular Theatre Approach in Africa* (1991) discusses theatre-for-development programmes and strategies. Mlama heads the Department of Art, Music and Theatre at the University of Dar es Salaam. PMM

Mnouchkine, Ariane 1939– French theatre director, known for her successful use of *création collective* (collaboratively devised productions) and shared responsibility within her theatre group, the THÉÂTRE DU SOLEIL. After studies at the Universities of Paris and Oxford, where she was involved in student theatre, she travelled to the Far East, returning to found the Soleil in 1964. Inspired by the ideas of COPEAU and the work of VILAR, she sought to extend research into the theatrical resources and implications of a people's theatre. Like ARTAUD she wanted to use the whole range of expressive means available to theatre, but like BRECHT she wanted to develop an idiom appropriate for dealing with social process as well as private drama.

The choice of WESKER's *Kitchen* (1967) was a first move in this direction, but it was only after the upheavals of 1968 that she felt the group must create its own plays. Her influence was strongly evident in the recourse to popular CLOWN traditions in *The Clowns* (1969). But she felt this had been essentially a set of individual creations. She wanted a *collective* creation, something the company achieved in *1789* (1970), *1793* (1972) and *L'Âge d'or* (*The Golden Age*, 1975). After this, she drew on her father's experience as a film director to make a remarkable film of MOLIÈRE, in which she confronted the problems of how a theatre company can live and work together. She returned to theatre production with her adaptation of Klaus Mann's *Mephisto* (1979) and then embarked on a cycle of SHAKESPEARE plays: *Richard II* (1981), *Twelfth Night* (1982) and *Henry IV Part 1* (1984). These were followed by two epic plays, one about Cambodia, the other about India, by HÉLÈNE CIXOUS: *Norodom Sihanouk* (1985) and *L'Indiade* (1987). Mnouchkine has declared, following Artaud, that 'theatre is oriental', and her productions of these plays attempted to bring the influence of oriental theatre to bear on epic-historical material in the Shakespearian mould. Mnouchkine's tendency to return to origins asserted itself once again in the early 1990s with a cycle of ancient Greek plays, again borrowing elements from oriental performance styles. DB

Mochalov, Pavel (Stepanovich) 1800–48 Son of a former serf actor; the 'Russian KEAN', the greatest Russian tragedian of the early 19th century. In the debate over the question of genius versus craft, Mochalov's inspired but uneven performances at Moscow's Maly Theatre were favoured by merchants, students and literati such as SHCHEPKIN, PUSHKIN, Herzen, Belinsky and SEMYONOVA over those of his St Petersburg rival, the coolly technical tragedian KARATYGIN. He was hindered in his career by a lack of discipline engendered in part by his father, a tendency to play to his audiences at the expense of the role, and by a shrewish wife who drove him to alcoholism and self-destructiveness. He paid little attention to costumes and make-up, relying instead upon the power of his imagination and his physical attributes to transform him.

Although MELODRAMA and neoclassical TRAGEDY by KOTZEBUE, VOLTAIRE, OZEROV, POLEVOI and KUKOLNIK were staples of his repertoire, he succeeded in the roles of SCHILLER's Don Carlos (1829), Karl and Franz Moor (1828 and 1844) and Mortimer (1835), and as SHAKESPEARE's Othello (1837), Lear (1839) and Richard III (1839). The high and low ends of this spectrum were his romantic Hamlet (1837), much praised by Belinsky, in Polevoi's translation, and Romeo which he played at the age of 41. He thought himself miscast as Chatsky in the original Moscow production of *Woe from Wit* (1831). Mochalov was a revolutionary romantic icon, much loved and admired by the people, in the reactionary Nikolayen era. His tours helped to promote Shakespeare and Schiller in the provinces. He also wrote a romantic drama, *The Circassian Girl* (produced 1840), some lyric poetry and a theoretical treatise on acting (published 1953). SG

Modena, Gustavo 1803–61 Italian actor whose career is inextricably linked with the Italian struggle for independence. After studying law at Bologna, Modena worked in a number of acting troupes before forming his own company, in association with his father Giacomo, in 1829. Political events obliged him to leave Italy in 1832, and he spent several years in exile in Switzerland, France, Belgium and England. In London, under the patronage of Mazzini, and to advance the national cause, he gave a public reading from Dante's *Divina commedia* at the Queen's Theatre. In 1843, after his return to Italy, he formed a company of young actors that included TOMMASO SALVINI and LUIGI BELLOTTI-BON, and through them his insistence on a natural, unemphatic style and uncluttered scenic decoration profoundly affected stage presentation in Italy for several decades. He was a champion, too, of the stage as a means of debating social and political issues. Off-stage his social commitment involved him in the 1848 Risorgimento. The acting roles with which he was best associated were the stock pieces in the mid-19th-century Italian actor's repertoire: ALFIERI's Saul, DELAVIGNE's Louis XI and DUMAS's Kean. He made an unsuccessful attempt, in a much adapted version, to introduce Italian spectators to SHAKESPEARE's Othello; the failure of this venture in 1847 led him to abandon his plan to do *Hamlet*. LR

Modjeska [Modrzejewska], **Helena** [*née* Jadwiga Benda; Jadwiga Opid] 1840–1909 Polish-born actress, daughter of the widowed Madame Benda, she used the name of the family guardian Michal Opid until she married Gustave Sinnmayer Modrzejewski in 1856 and made her stage debut as Helena Modrzejewska in 1861. Managed by her second husband Count Bozenta, she became an international star before emigrating to the United States in 1876. She learned English and made her American debut in 1877 in SCRIBE's *Adrienne Lecouvreur,* one of her great roles, along with Camille and SHAKESPEARE's Rosalind, Viola, Beatrice and Portia. The tall, comely actress was noted for her charm, naturalness and, in WILLIAM WINTER's words, 'exquisite refinement and grace'. Her memoirs were published in 1910. FHL

Moeller, Philip 1880–1958 American director, producer and playwright. Born in New York, Moeller graduated from Columbia University and joined the WASHINGTON

SQUARE PLAYERS in the winter of 1914. His one-act plays, *Two Blind Beggars and One Less Blind* and *Helena's Husband*, were produced by the group and attracted critical attention; but Moeller made his reputation as a director, and was regarded by LAWRENCE LANGNER as one of the most brilliant directors of COMEDY in the USA. A founder and director of the THEATRE GUILD, he staged their first production, *Bonds of Interest*, in 1919. He was especially adept in directing the plays of EUGENE O'NEILL. His Guild credits include *Strange Interlude* (1928), *Dynamo* (1929), *Mourning Becomes Electra* (1931) and *Ah, Wilderness!* (1933). BROOKS ATKINSON called his direction of *Strange Interlude* a 'tremendous achievement' because he found a way to distinguish between the speeches and the asides. Atkinson also praised Moeller for finding the 'exact tempo and style' in *Mourning Becomes Electra*. Moeller thought of himself as an inspirational director. After directing films for RKO Radio in the early 1930s, he went into virtual retirement. TLM

Mogulesco, Sigmund fl.1880–90 Romanian-born actor of the YIDDISH THEATRE, who started his career with GOLDFADN's company before moving to America in 1886. A natural clown, he specialized in comic roles besides being an accomplished musician. AB

Moiseiwitsch, Tanya 1914– British-born set and COSTUME designer noted for her collaborations with director TYRONE GUTHRIE and the bold thrust stage and innovative auditorium she designed for the STRATFORD [Shakespeare] FESTIVAL Theatre, Ontario (1957), and the similar GUTHRIE THEATRE in Minneapolis (1963). Moiseiwitsch began her career in London in 1934. The following year she went to the ABBEY THEATRE in Dublin, where she designed over 50 productions until 1939. She subsequently designed for London's OLD VIC, beginning in 1944, and at the Shakespeare Memorial Theatre in Stratford-upon-Avon from 1949, as well as commercial theatre in London and theatres in Italy, the USA and Australia. She is most closely associated with the plays of SHAKESPEARE, but notable productions include *Oedipus Rex* at Ontario (1954; film 1957) and *The House of Atreus* in Minneapolis (1968), both of which contain what is perhaps the most successful use of MASKS in the 20th century. Beginning with her work at the Abbey, Moiseiwitsch's designs have been typified by simple, direct, presentational sets that embody the visual metaphor of the play. Since she generally designed costumes as well there was a strong visual unity in her productions. With the polygonal, stepped stages at Ontario and Minneapolis that jutted into the steeply banked auditoriums, she was able to eliminate most scenery and provide a space in which her highly textured costumes could be sculpted by light. A major retrospective of her work was seen at Stratford, Ontario, in 1992. AA

Moisiu Aleksandër [Alexander Moissi] 1879–1935 Albanian actor, born in Kavaja (Albania), the youngest child of émigré Albanian forwarding agent Moisi Moisiu and his Italian-Albanian wife Amalia (*née* De Rada). He had his first speaking role in Prague in 1902, and in 1904 joined MAX REINHARDT's company in Berlin, where he quickly distinguished himself by his deep, psychological interpretations of the roles he played, by his expressive, melodious voice, and by his mobile features and body. He normally performed without make-up. Fluent in English, French, German, Greek, Italian and Spanish, he attained international fame, performing in Argentina, Austria, Britain, Czechoslovakia, Egypt, France, Germany, Greece, Holland, Hungary, Italy, Japan, Mexico, Romania, Russia, Sweden, Switzerland and the USA. He also appeared between 1910 and 1935 in 12 films, including three sound films. He was the author of a play about Napoleon, *The Prisoner*, first performed in Hamburg. His most famous stage roles were those of SHAKESPEARE's Hamlet and Othello, GOETHE's Faust, IBSEN's Oswald (in *Ghosts*), SHAW's Dubedat (in *The Doctor's Dilemma*) and LEV TOLSTOI's Fedya (in *The Living Corpse*). He married in 1919 the German actress Johanne Terwin (1884–1962). Having become an Albanian citizen in 1934, he died the next year in Vienna. In 1962 he was posthumously awarded the highest Albanian award in the artistic field, the title of People's Artist; a theatre in Durrës (Albania) is named after him. WBB PI

Molander, Olof 1892–1966 Swedish director, who had considerable impact on Swedish perceptions of direction, scenography and acting style, particularly during his leadership of DRAMATEN (1934–8). As a reformer, he was more cautious than his visionary contemporary, PER LINDBERG; for example, Molander's plan for a 'people's theatre' was a compromise with the existing function of Dramaten. As a director, he followed GORDON CRAIG's concept of the director's need to coordinate scenography and acting around a central idea. Molander established the predominant mid-century Swedish approach to STRINDBERG, particularly with late plays like *A Dream Play*, *The Ghost Sonata* and *The Great Highway*, by rejecting REINHARDT's forcefully expressionistic style (see EXPRESSIONISM) for a blend of fantasy and selective REALISM that emphasized the plays' autobiographical content. Dramaten's international reputation for producing O'NEILL (including several European and world premieres) owed much to Molander's productions of *Mourning Becomes Electra*, *The Iceman Cometh* and *A Moon for the Misbegotten*. HL

Molière [Jean-Baptiste Poquelin] 1622–73 French actor-manager and dramatist, one of the theatre's greatest comic artists. Well educated son of a prosperous Paris merchant, he forsook the family's upholstery business at the age of 21 to throw in his lot with a group of friends and young professional actors and found a new theatre company, the Illustre-Théâtre. Unable to compete with the established HÔTEL DE BOURGOGNE and MARAIS, it went bankrupt within two years and in 1645, after a short spell in a debtors' prison, Molière left Paris with MADELEINE BÉJART and other erstwhile colleagues to join an itinerant company led by the actor Charles Dufresne. There followed almost 13 years of constant peregrination in the southern provinces, a period of strenuous but invaluable apprenticeship which allowed him to discover and refine his gifts as a comic actor and to develop into a resourceful company leader. During this period he also wrote his first plays, *L'Étourdi* (*The Blunderer*, 1653) and *Dépit amoureux* (*Lovers' Quarrel*, 1656), and the brief, partly improvised FARCES *La Jalousie du Barbouillé* (*The Jealousy of Barbouillé*) and *Le Médecin volant* (*The Flying Doctor*), inspired by the work of COMMEDIA troupes encountered on his travels and tailormade for his fellow actors.

In 1658 he took them north, and through the patronage of the king's brother secured a command performance before Louis XIV comprising PIERRE CORNEILLE's *Nicomède* and his own farce *Le Docteur amoureux* (*The Doctor in Love*). The young king was so amused by the latter that he granted Molière the use of the PETIT-BOURBON in alternation with the *commedia* company of FIORILLI and it became the scene of his first successes with the Parisian public, *Les Précieuses ridicules* (*The Affected Ladies*, 1659) and *Sganarelle, ou Le Cocu imaginaire* (*Sganarelle, or The Imaginary Cuckold*, 1660). Following its demolition Molière was installed at the refurbished PALAIS-ROYAL, where in 1661 the failure of his 'heroic comedy' *Dom Garcie de Navarre* was quickly redeemed by *L'École des maris* (*The School for Husbands*) and by his first *comédie-ballet*, *Les Fâcheux* (*The Bores*), initially performed at Fouquet's residence at Vaux. In the following year the 40-year-old Molière married the teenage ARMANDE BÉJART and produced his first great comedy of character, *The School for Wives*, a reflection on the role of women and the incompatibility of youth and age. So huge a success did it enjoy both in Paris and at court that it provoked accusations of immorality from churchmen, and its author found himself scurrilously pilloried in the plays of jealous rivals.

Molière counter-attacked vigorously and amusingly in *La Critique de l'École des femmes* and *L'Impromptu de Versailles* (both 1663) and emerged from this first skirmish with his enemies more securely placed than ever, the king even agreeing to act as godfather to his firstborn in 1664. The same year brought commissions for royal entertainments, *Le Mariage forcé* (*The Forced Marriage*) at the Louvre and *La Princesse d'Élide* at Versailles, while in 1665 as a tangible mark of this favour Molière's company was awarded a regular pension from the Crown and took the title of the Troupe du Roy. Thereafter Molière, with LULLY, became the accredited purveyor of *divertissements* to the court: *L'Amour médecin* (*Love's the Best Doctor*, 1665), *Mélicerte* (1666), *La Pastorale comique* (1667), *Le Sicilien, ou L'Amour peintre* (*The Sicilian, or Love Makes the Painter*, 1667), *Monsieur de Pourceaugnac* (1669), *Les Amants magnifiques* (*The Magnificent Lovers*, 1670), *The Bourgeois Gentleman* (1670) and *La Comtesse d'Escarbagnas* (1671), mostly couched in the form of *comédie-ballets*, and *Psyché* (1671), a *tragédie-ballet* written in collaboration with Corneille and QUINAULT, were all initially performed at royal *fêtes* before being transferred with modifications to his public theatre in Paris.

Meanwhile, the comedies intended for the Palais-Royal had encountered a mixed reception and in some cases powerful opposition. His study of religious hypocrisy, *Tartuffe*, after its premiere at Versailles in 1664 was withheld from public performance until a revised version was acted once in 1667, only to be denounced for its impiety by the Church and proscribed by the Parlement, the ban not being finally lifted until 1669. *Don Juan* (1665), too, doubtless because it was considered to present its cynical, free-thinking hero in too favourable a light, was abruptly

withdrawn despite public success and never re-staged in Molière's lifetime. *The Misanthrope* (1666) was received with only cool interest, while *The Miser* (1668) was an outright failure and *Les Fourberies de Scapin* (*The Tricks of Scapin*, 1671) little more. Contrariwise, there was an enthusiastic response to *A Doctor in Spite of Himself* (1666) and *Amphitryon* (1668), though of the later comedies of character only *The Learned Ladies* (1672) could be accounted an unequivocal success. At the same time Molière's over-exertion was taking its toll, illness having already forced him to give up acting for several months in 1667. His last play proved to be *The Imaginary Invalid* (1673), another *comédie-ballet* evidently designed for presentation at court but actually created at the Palais-Royal, presumably in the wake of some fall from royal grace. During the fourth performance Molière, ironically playing the hypochondriac Argan, was seized with a genuine coughing fit and died later that night.

In the course of 14 years of ceaseless activity in Paris as performer and playwright Molière transformed French COMEDY. His comic method, mastered during the preliminary years of touring, is an intensely physical one in that it has little recourse to technical resources and gives full scope to the prowess of the actor, aided only by COSTUME, an almost emblematic use of personal properties and a skilful patterning of dialogue which encourages specific movement and visual display on stage. With these deceptively simple means Molière's text breathes new life into the traditional situations of French farce and the stock masks and devices of the Italian *commedia*, by which he was so deeply impressed, to produce a satiric commentary on the society of his time and a penetrating exploration of eternal human foibles and obsessive attitudes of mind. In his hands their absurdity never ceases to amuse, but equally their potential for mischief and harm is clearly perceived by a comedian of genius whose view of life is imbued with a sense of philosophical resignation.   DR

Molina, Tirso de   see TIRSO DE MOLINA

Molloy, M(ichael) J(oseph) 1917– Irish playwright. Molloy abandoned training for the priesthood through illness, then farmed near his birthplace. His foremost works are his first play, *The Old Road* (1943), *The Visiting House* (1946), *The King of Friday's Men* (1948), *The Wood of the Whispering* and *The Paddy Pedlar* (1953).

The King of Friday's Men has claims to greatness. Set in western Ireland in 1787, it mourns the passage of a feudal *modus vivendi*, freshly evoking a bygone world, ignoring neither the landlord's careless autocracy nor, among the peasants' thriving folkways, the savage sport of mass shillelagh fights.

Molloy deals less certainly with the contemporary residue of those folkways, but *The Visiting House* effectively dramatizes the dying institution where country districts were regaled with songs and stories, real life in the play having to compete with the Master's beguiling games and eccentric accomplices. Molloy's dialect speech at its fluent best carries his often knotty plots. Though more restricted by his region than either SYNGE or FITZMAURICE, he is the last remarkable exponent of their folk drama.   DM

Molnár, Ferenc 1878–1952 Hungarian playwright, born in Budapest. He gained an international reputation for his plays, which exhibit technical mastery and sophisticated dialogue and depict the minor pitfalls that threaten but never seriously damage the bourgeois morality of his characters. His use of light and clever SATIRE is tempered by sincere sentiment and pathos. Many of his plays, including *The Devil* (1907), *Liliom* (1909), *The Guardsman* (1910), *The Swan* (1920) and *The Play's the Thing* (1926), were produced in Vienna, London, Paris and on BROADWAY, as well as in HUNGARY. In 1928 Molnár's collection, *Twenty-five Plays*, appeared in English. *The Play's the Thing* is continually revived the world over, and the famous MUSICAL *Carousel* (1945) by RODGERS and HAMMERSTEIN is based on *Liliom*.   EB

Moncrieff, Gladys 1892–1976 Australian MUSICAL COMEDY star. As a child in Queensland she sang with her parents' travelling picture show, and later in suburban VAUDEVILLE. She appeared in musicals with the J. C. WILLIAMSON management, first starring in *Katinka* (1918), and until 1959 appeared in numerous musicals and OPERETTA, including *The Maid of the Mountains* (1921), the London production of *The Blue Mazurka* (1926), *Rio Rita*, in which she toured Australia in 1928–30, the Australian MUSICAL *Collit's Inn* (1933), and various productions of *The Merry Widow*. To her Australian public she was affectionately known as 'our Glad'.   MW

Moncrieff, W(illiam) T(homas) 1794–1857 English playwright and theatre manager, lessee at various times of the Queen's, ASTLEY's Amphitheatre, the Coburg, Vauxhall Gardens and the City Theatre (all in London). Moncrieff was a hack writer who turned out plays to suit the time. Adaptations of novels by Scott, BULWER LYTTON and DICKENS were entrusted to him by managers eager to cash in on the latest vogue. *The Lear of Private Life* (1820), from a novel by Mrs Opie, has some interest as a 19th-century domestication of SHAKESPEARE. *The Shipwreck of the Medusa* (1820) exploited the excitement created by Géricault's picture, which was being exhibited in Bullock's Egyptian Hall in 1820 (nearly 50,000 people paid to see it). *Tom and Jerry* (1821) was a particularly zestful adaptation of Pierce Egan's documentary novel, *Life in London*. *The Cataract of the Ganges* (1823) was the sensation of its season at DRURY LANE, less for the script than for the use of David's horse troupe (see HIPPODRAMA) and the lavish sets (there was real water in the cataract for the finale) of CLARKSON STANFIELD and David Roberts. Moncrieff, who wrote over 100 plays, was evidently willing to accept the modest standing of contemporary playwrights.   PT

Monk, Meredith 1942– American choreographer, composer, director, performance artist and leading innovator in the so-called Next Wave (since the mid-1960s) and in her association with the Judson Dance Theatre (New York City). Her dances have evolved into multimedia, nonverbal theatre pieces, such as *Vessel* (1971–2) and *Quarry* (1975–6), both termed 'opera epics'. In the early and mid-1970s she also created several chamber theatre works: the 'travelogue' series (*Paris, Chacon, Venice/Milan*) in collab-

oration with PING CHONG, and the 'archaeology' pieces (*Small Scroll, Anthology, The Plateau Series, Recent Ruins*). In the late 1970s she began to concentrate on musical composition and performance, having begun to 'distrust the theatre a little bit', although by the early 1980s two multimedia theatre pieces had been added to her canon: *Specimen Days* (1981) and *The Games* (1983), the latter commissioned by PETER STEIN's Schaubühne repertory theatre in West Berlin, with its US premiere at the Brooklyn Academy of Music's Next Wave Festival the following year. In the early 1990s she devoted attention to her unique form of OPERA, such as *Atlas* (1991), most notably with commissions from the Houston Opera, and to additional performances pieces, such as *Facing North* (1991) with Robert Eden, and *Volcano Songs* (1994), a solo piece.   DBW

monopoly, theatrical   see THEATRICAL MONOPOLY

Montansier, Mlle [Marguerite Brunet] 1730–1820 French actress who forsook the boards to pursue a long and colourful career in theatre management. Having opened a playhouse at Versailles in 1777 she was invited to present performances at court and, with the help of her able business manager and devoted lover Neuville, another ex-actor, proceeded to widen her base by acquiring a chain of provincial theatres before establishing herself in Paris in 1790 at a theatre in the PALAIS-ROYAL, to which she gave her own name. After the Revolution she presided over a salon frequented by literary and theatrical personalities and built a large new theatre under the name of the Théâtre National. Always suspect for her previous Royalist associations, she was finally denounced in 1793, imprisoned and narrowly missed the guillotine. Despite this and severe financial setbacks she persisted, opening the Salle Olympique in 1801 and the celebrated Théâtre des Variétés on the boulevard Montmartre in 1807, while running her Palais-Royal theatre as a house for acrobats and puppeteers. Predictably, her resilient career was later to become the stuff of several popular plays.   DR

Montdory [Guillaume des Gilberts] (1594-1653/4) French actor-manager, the most powerful tragedian of his day. First heard of as a member of VALLERAN LE CONTE's company in 1612, he spent more than a decade touring the northern provinces and Holland in the plays of HARDY before bringing a new company to Paris, where he played in a number of tennis court theatres in succession but settled for good at the MARAIS in 1634, thanks to the munificence of CARDINAL RICHELIEU. It was here, playing the central role of Don Rodrigue, that he presented *Le Cid* with huge success in January 1637, having already created *Mélite* and other early plays of PIERRE CORNEILLE. But his triumph was to be short-lived, for in August of that year he was seized by a partial paralysis of the body and tongue while playing Herod in TRISTAN L'HERMITE's *La Mariane* (*Mariamne*) and was obliged to retire from the stage, whereupon Richelieu awarded him a handsome pension. This mishap suggests that there was an element of rant or physical exaggeration in his playing, but with his strong voice and well proportioned physique he must have possessed an impressive presence on stage, for no less a critic than D'AUBIGNAC called him 'the greatest actor of our time'. DR

Monteiro, (Luís de) Sttau 1926– Portuguese playwright. Also a left-wing journalist and novelist, Sttau Monteiro came to the theatre in 1961 with *Felizmente Há Luar* (*Luckily We Still Have the Moonlight*) to attack contemporary abuses and institutions in a historical drama based on the Portuguese people's struggle against the 'liberating' English rule of Beresford in the period immediately after the Peninsular War campaigns in Portugal. *A Estátua* (*The Statue*, 1966) ridicules the hero-worship sought by and accorded to Salazar, while the *Auto da Barca do Motor Fora da Borda*, of the same year, updates VICENTE's *Auto da Barca do Inferno* by providing the boat with an outboard motor and redirecting the SATIRE against latterday capitalists. LK

Montez, Lola [*née* Maria Dolores Eliza Rosanna Gilbert] 1818–61 Irish-born adventuress, who, when her first marriage failed, went on stage as a dancer (London, 1843), performing in Europe, America and Australia. Her beauty and charm compensated for her lack of talent and musical sense. Her liaison with Ludwig I of Bavaria (1847–8) culminated in his forced abdication, and she went to the USA, making her New York debut (1851) in *Betley the Tyrolean*; a biographical play, *Lola Montes* [*sic*] *in Bavaria* by C. P. T. Ware (1852), capitalized on her sensational past. She toured to the gold rush country, performing a spider dance that shocked San Francisco audiences, and took the child actress LOTTA CRABTREE under her tutelage. After 1856 she appeared as a spiritualist and lecturer, speaking on fashion, gallantry and Roman Catholicism. She underwent a religious conversion and became a recluse after 1859. LS

Montfleury [Zacharie Jacob] c.1600–67 French actor who first appeared at the HÔTEL DE BOURGOGNE c.1638 and remained there until the end of his career, excelling in both TRAGEDY and COMEDY, according to CHAPPUZEAU. Despite this testimony, his excessive corpulence and capacity for mannered, self-indulgent acting attracted the wicked jibes of Cyrano de Bergerac and more particularly MOLIÈRE in *L'Impromptu de Versailles* (1663), where he is described as 'roaring' his lines and signalling when the audience is to applaud. This provoked a bitter exchange with Molière, whom he publicly accused of having married his own daughter. In reality Montfleury may have been guilty of no more than an exaggeration of the rhetorical delivery then associated with tragedy, but he certainly seems to have been a physically assertive performer to judge by the reputed manner of his death, occasioned by bursting a blood vessel while playing Oreste in RACINE's *Andromaque* (1667). In his one play, *La Mort d'Asdrubal* (*The Death of Hasdrubal*, 1647), he wrote an inferior tragedy with a leading part for himself. DR

Montherlant, Henry de 1896–1972 French writer. Montherlant came to the theatre late in life, his first big success being *La Reine morte* (*The Dead Queen*) at the COMÉDIE-FRANÇAISE in 1942. This was inspired by Guevara's *Reinar después de morir* and was the first of a number of plays in which Montherlant attempted to celebrate the values of the Spanish GOLDEN AGE. A great literary stylist, as his novels show, Montherlant was never interested in theatre production, seeing drama as above all literary and psychological. His better plays attempt to deal with religious subjects along French neoclassical lines, e.g. *Le Maître de Santiago* (1948), *Port-Royal* (1954). His one generally acknowledged masterpiece is *La Ville dont le prince est un enfant* (*The Town Whose Prince is a Child*). This semi-autobiographical play was written in 1951 but he did not allow a production until 1967 (directed by Michel). It depicts the passionate relationships between boys and priests in a Catholic seminary with considerable truthfulness, restraint and force. DB

Monti, Ricardo 1944– Argentine playwright. As a participant in the vanguard theatre of the 1970s, Monti sought new forms for exposing old problems of the bourgeoisie through symbols and allegories. For the Laboratory Theatre he wrote *Una noche con el señor Magnus e Hijos* (*A Night with Mr Magnus and Sons*, 1970), and for the Payró Theatre in 1971, *Historia tendenciosa de la clase media argentina* (*Tendentious History of the Argentine Middle Class*). Later plays include *Visita* (*Visit*, 1977), *Marathón* (*Marathon*, 1980) and *Una pasión sudamericana* (*A South American Passion*, 1989). As a workshop director Monti has had a major influence in forming a new generation of Argentine playwrights. GW

Montigny, Adolphe Lemoine ?1812–80 French actor, dramatist and theatre manager. Montigny began his career as an actor at the COMÉDIE-FRANÇAISE in 1829. Conscientious rather than gifted, he moved to the BOULEVARD theatres, scoring a success in an adaptation of Balzac's *Les Chouans* at the Nouveautés and moving on to play more important parts at the Ambigu. He became a director of the Gaîté, with Meyer, in 1841, and in 1844 took over the ailing Théâtre du Gymnase, which he brought back to fashionable popularity with the talents of his wife, Rose Chéri, and the repertoire of EUGÈNE SCRIBE. He ran the Gymnase for over 30 years and achieved official recognition in 1865, when he was decorated. A very able theatre manager and play director, he specialized in the French equivalent of 'cup and saucer' drama and moved the French theatre strongly in the direction of a more intimate NATURALISM. In the 1830s he wrote a number of *vaudevilles* and dramas usually in collaboration; these include *Le Doigt de Dieu* (*The Finger of God*, 1834), *Amazampo; ou La Découverte de quinquina* (*Amazampo, or The Discovery of Quinine*, 1836), *Zarah* (1837), *Samuel le marchand* (*Samuel the Merchant*, 1838), *Le Fils* (*The Son*, 1839). In 1847, Montigny published his *Observations on the Théâtre-Français and the Secondary Theatres*, in which he attempted to diagnose the current ills of the Comédie-Française. JMCC

Moody, William Vaughn 1869–1910 Indiana-born American dramatist, who took a degree in English at Harvard (1893) and taught there and at the University of Chicago (1895–1902). He co-wrote a standard history of English literature, and was widely regarded as the best lyric poet of his generation. With Harriet Brainard, whom he married (1909), he was active in Donald Robertson's New Theatre. He experimented with two verse plays, but turned to prose when he dramatized a story about a woman kidnapped by a band of drunken cowboys. *The Great Divide* was premiered by Margaret Anglin at a matinée in Chicago (April 1906). It was easily the finest American play of its time, successfully blending realistic motivation with poetic treatment of the national myth. His last play, *The Faith Healer* (1909), was a failure in performance, and Moody died of a brain tumour soon after. DMCD

Moore, Edward 1712-57 English playwright. Moore turned to writing plays when his business as a linen draper failed. His first play, *The Foundling* (1748), was a serious and sentimental comedy, full of feeling and devoid of humour. He adapted Lesage's *Gil Blas* in 1751 as an energetic disguise comedy. His major contribution was a domestic tragedy heavily influenced by Lillo, *The Gamester* (1753), where the hero, overwhelmed with gambling debts, commits suicide moments before he would have heard he had inherited a fortune. The play was adapted by Diderot and was a strong influence on the development of the *drame bourgeois*. PH

morality play Term used in English for any play presenting through allegorical personages the struggle between good and evil for man's soul (e.g. *Castle of Perseverance*, *Mankind*, *Wisdom*). The usage in the rest of Western Europe, though referring to allegorical action, is not so precise, and the parallel terms can cover debates or moral teaching generally (French, *moralités*; Dutch, *spelen van sinnen*; Italian, *contrasti*). PM

Moratín, Leandro Fernández de 1760-1828 Spanish playwright and translator of Shakespeare and Molière. A representative figure of the 18th-century stage, he was influenced by neoclassicism. His five original comedies are social satires marked by impeccable structure and didactic intent. *El sí de las niñas* (*The Maidens' Consent*, written 1801 and staged 1806) has become part of the Spanish repertoire. Using stock devices of classic farce, it entertainingly argues against planned marriages, particularly between young women and old men. It received a memorable revival at the Teatro Español in 1969, directed by Miguel Narros and starring Ana Belén. Less successful was a 1988 musical version, written by Enrique Llovet and directed by Gustavo Pérez Puig. His other major work, *La comedia nueva* (*The New Comedy*, 1791), has not been revived recently. *El barón* (*The Baron*, 1786), however, was staged professionally in Madrid in 1983. PZ

Morecambe, Eric [Eric Bartholomew] 1926-84 and **Ernie Wise** [Ernest Wiseman] 1925- British comedy double act. Unlike many, Morecambe and Wise survived the transition from the last days of variety into television to become the longest-standing and best act of their kind. Wise was already an established juvenile performer when he met Morecambe in 1943. Basing their routines as much on American as on British models, their early career included provincial tours with Lord John Sanger's Circus and Variety and on the Moss Empire circuit, and a stint at London's Windmill Theatre providing unwelcome comic relief between the notorious nude tableaux. After early failures in the medium, it was their work on television from the early 1960s until Morecambe's death that brought them to the peak of their popularity (one Christmas show attracted an unprecedented 26 million viewers), though they maintained a theatrical presence in clubs, pantomime and summer season. Their television series reflected their variety training, the format comprising stand-up, sketches and pastiche song-and-dance numbers. A particular feature was the gentle humiliation of celebrity guest stars (including a serving prime minister). Although they worked from stock characters – Wise vain, mean and self-important, Morecambe vulnerable, naive, yet devious and cunning – they never operated simply as feed and comic, but from a more complex, shifting relationship where 'one doesn't know the other doesn't know who the boss is'; their act, Morecambe insisted, was always motivated by fear. Their career was already winding down when Morecambe died, but they remain a real, if unexpected, influence on a later generation of 'alternative' comedians. RPB

Moreno, Rita 1931- Puerto Rican-born American actress, who initially worked as a Spanish dancer and nightclub entertainer. She appeared in *The Sign in Sidney Brustein's Window* (1964) and several other plays before winning a Tony for her supporting role in *The Ritz* (1975). In 1985 she toured in a female version of Neil Simon's *The Odd Couple*. Moreno is the only performer to have won an Academy Award, a TV Emmy, a Broadway Tony and a Grammy (recording). MK

moresca Dance drama of the eastern Adriatic, the northern Mediterranean littoral and some of the islands, Iberia and Central America. Sometimes associated with carnival, sometimes with a local feast (as on Korčula, where until recently it was performed in July, largely to tourists), *moresca* reflects the political and commercial interplay between Christian and Muslim (in Spain it is explicitly entitled *Cristianos y moros*). Though its form varies little – a spoken prologue, sometimes with character interaction, to a spectacular sword dance – aetiological legends, inside or outside the text, frequently refer it to a particular local event. The name may have given us 'morris dance'; there is otherwise no resemblance. AEG

Moreto y Cabaña, Agustín 1618-69 Spanish playwright, born in Madrid, who studied in Alcalá and became a priest assigned to a charitable fraternity in Toledo. Considered the best and the last talented dramatist in the cycle of Calderón in the Golden Age, he is known for his witty, urbane comedies, his sense of decorum, his incisive portrayal of female characters and for his *comedias de figurón* (plays of ridiculously amusing character types) of which his *El lindo Don Diego* (*Don Diego the Dandy*) is best. His recasting of earlier dramatic plots (in this case, that of Castro y Bellvís's *El narciso en su opinión*) has not diminished his reputation for originality.

El desdén con el desdén (*Scorn of Scorn*, 1654), his comic masterpiece about a disdainful heroine won over to love by the feigned scorn of the pretender, was the model for

MOLIÈRE's *La Princesse d'Élide* and was revived by the Spanish National Classical Theatre Company in 1991. This company also presented *No puede ser el guardar una mujer* (*There's No Guarding a Woman*) in 1986, a comic thesis play showing woman's dignity and capacity for self-determination. Although Moreto wrote more serious works, it is his comedies that have retained their popularity. ELB

Morley, Robert 1908–92 British actor and playwright. Morley made a reputation playing eccentric extroverts like OSCAR WILDE, a part he first played under NORMAN MARSHALL at the London Gate Theatre in 1936 and later repeated in a film version of Wilde's life; Professor Higgins in SHAW's *Pygmalion* at the OLD VIC in 1937; and Sheridan Whiteside in *The Man Who Came to Dinner* by GEORGE S. KAUFMAN and MOSS HART, which he played for two years after his first appearance in the part in 1941. As the author of several light comedies, including *Edward, My Son* (with Noel Langley, 1947), *Hippo Dancing* (adapted from André Roussin, 1954), *Hook, Line and Sinker* (1958) and *A Ghost on Tiptoe* (with Rosemary Sisson, 1974), he specialized in roles written by himself as well as appearing in FARCES by Peter Ustinov, ALAN AYCKBOURN and BEN TRAVERS. CI

Morocco see FRENCH-SPEAKING NORTH AFRICA; MIDDLE EAST

Morosco, Oliver (Mitchell) 1876–1945 Utah-born American manager and producer, who moved to San Francisco at an early age and appeared as an acrobat in the troupe of Walter Morosco. After adopting his mentor's name, he managed several theatres in the Bay area, later acquiring on his own at least six theatres in Los Angeles. He began producing in 1909, and later offered in New York *The Bird of Paradise* (1912) and *Peg O' My Heart* (1912), both starring LAURETTE TAYLOR; and in 1915, *The Unchastened Woman* with Emily Stevens. The SHUBERTS built the Herbert J. Krapp-designed Morosco Theatre for him in New York on West 45th St (1917), an intimate 1000-seat venue which he opened with his own play, *Canary Island*. The author of numerous plays, all undistinguished, Morosco went bankrupt in 1926 in a scheme to build a motion picture settlement in California. The Morosco Theatre, however, took its place in history in 1920 when EUGENE O'NEILL's first full-length play, *Beyond the Horizon*, was presented there at a matinée. MCH TLM

Morris [*née* Morrison], **Clara** 1846/8–1925 American actress. Born in Canada, possibly of a bigamous union, Morris received her early training in JOHN ELLSLER's STOCK COMPANY in Cleveland (1861–9). For years she sustained a reputation as one of America's greatest emotionalistic actresses, although her career is one of incongruities. In the 1870s she was praised as realistic, though by the 80s she was denounced by many as the queen of spasms and the mistress of the tricks of the acting trade. In 1870 she began her New York career as a member of AUGUSTIN DALY's company, excelling in plays like *Man and Wife*, *Divorce* and especially Daly's *Article 47*, in which she played Cora the Creole. She left Daly in 1873 and spent most of her remaining career as a travelling star, appear-

ing in popular roles such as Camille and Miss Moulton (in a version of *East Lynne*). Although she attempted classical roles, she was always more successful when playing pathetic girls in MELODRAMA, which allowed her to use her 'tearful' voice and to loose a veritable flood of emotion on her audience. She appeared in VAUDEVILLE in the 1900s and made her last appearance in Washington, DC, in 1906. She wrote three unreliable autobiographies (1901–6). Her diary (54 volumes), 1867–1924, is housed at Radcliffe College. DBW

Morrison, Bill 1940– Irish playwright. Apart from numerous adaptations, radio and television plays, Morrison's best-known work is the award-winning *Flying Blind* (1977), in which Northern Irish terrorists are downfaced by their victims' threat to sexually seduce them. He has written MUSICALs and adapted for theatre novels by Hardy, Chandler and Brian Moore, much of this work for the LIVERPOOL PLAYHOUSE. *A Love Song for Ulster* (1993), a most ambitious trilogy allegorically exploring the history of the North of Ireland, was staged at the Tricycle Theatre, London. GF

Mortimer, John 1923– British dramatist, journalist and, by profession, a barrister. Mortimer was educated at Harrow and Brasenose College, Oxford; and worked with the Crown Film Unit during the Second World War as a script-writer. During the 1950s he wrote one-act plays for radio: one of these, *The Dock Brief*, was staged with another short play, *What Shall We Tell Caroline?*, in 1958. He thus emerged as a playwright in those pivotal years when a new generation was starting to transform British theatre, but he was not an angry young man. His tone was cool, witty and professional, though more suited to shorter than to longer plays. *The Wrong Side of the Park* (1960) and *Two Stars for Comfort* (1962) were enjoyable, but felt like extended sit-coms. He adapted plays from abroad for the NATIONAL THEATRE, including *A Flea in Her Ear* (1966, from FEYDEAU) and *The Captain of Kopenick* (1971, from ZUCKMAYER); and his evenings of one-acters include *Come As You Are* (1970) and *Heaven and Hell* (1976). His one full-length play to achieve both critical and box-office success was *A Voyage Round My Father* (1970), a semi-autobiographical study of his own father. In it, he revealed an understanding and emotional warmth which could hardly have been predicted from his other plays. Since then, he has adapted other plays from Feydeau (*The Lady from Maxim's*, 1977, and *A Little Hotel on the Side*, 1984); and written two popular TV series, *I, Claudius* (1971, adapted from the novels by Robert Graves) and *Rumpole of the Bailey* (from his own stories). He is well known as a barrister for liberal causes, but his skill at making debating points may be his weakness as a writer, concealing other, and deeper, truths less easy to express. JE

Morton, Charles 1819–1904 British waiter and publican who rose to become 'the Grand Old Man of the Music Hall'. Around the age of 21, he opened a small tavern in Pimlico, London, that featured 'harmonic meetings', and in 1849 the Old Canterbury Arms in Westminster Bridge Road, Lambeth. His elegant Canterbury Hall (1852, rebuilt 1854) was the first MUSIC-HALL to appeal to a broad middle-class public, with its mixture of classical and popular music. A master of publicity, Morton initiated music-hall advertising in *The Times* and presented Sunday evening performances. He later managed the Oxford, the Philharmonic Theatre and the GAIETY, expanding into comic OPERA and minstrelsy; his longest tenure was at the Alhambra (1877–81, 1883–90). LS

Morton, Martha ?1865–1925 'The dean of America's women playwrights'. Morton, also a director, was the first to crack the gender barrier on BROADWAY, with her many commercial, if not critical, successes. In 1891 she wrote *The Merchant*, followed by *Geoffrey Middleton* (1892), *A Fool of Fortune* (1896), *A Bachelor's Romance* (1896), *The Triumph of Love* (1904) and others. In 1907 she organized the Society of Dramatic Authors because the American Dramatists Club refused to accept women. FB

Morton, Thomas 1764–1838 English playwright, born in County Durham, but orphaned at the age of four and brought up by an uncle in London. He was sent to Lincoln's Inn, but showed no interest in the law, preferring cricket and the theatre. His first play, *Columbus* (1792), like most of the other 25, was staged at COVENT GARDEN, though he owed his first successes to the patronage of GEORGE COLMAN THE YOUNGER at the HAYMARKET. These were the sentimental OPERETTA *The Children in the Wood* (1793) and the preposterous *Zorinski* (1795). There followed a sequence of five-act comedies for Covent Garden, of which the best are *The Way to Get Married* (1796), *A Cure for the Heartache* (1797), *Secrets Worth Knowing* (1798) and the splendid *Speed the Plough* (1800), avowedly a COMEDY but embodying many of the features of later domestic MELO-DRAMAS.

Speed the Plough deserves to be remembered for much more than the invention of MRS GRUNDY, a character who never appears, but whose possible disapproval clouds the Ashfield home. As famous in Morton's lifetime, largely by virtue of JOHN EMERY's comic mastery of the Yorkshire dialect, was the character of Tyke in *The School of Reform* (1805). Towards the end of his active writing life, Morton became successively Reader of Plays for Covent Garden and DRURY LANE. His son John Maddison Morton (1811–91) was a prolific writer of short FARCES, many of them adroitly adapted from French originals. The best known began as *The Double-Bedded Room* (1843), was rewritten as *Box and Cox* (1847) and transformed, by the addition of Sullivan's music, into *Cox and Box* (1867). PT

Moscow Art Theatre (MAT) Soviet-Russian theatre's original 'house of art', a realistic ensemble based upon a home-grown system and paralleling European models (the MEININGEN troupe, Théâtre Libre, FREIE BÜHNE), dedicated to aesthetic and social idealism. On 21 June 1897 KONSTANTIN STANISLAVSKY, an amateur actor-director with the Moscow Society of Art and Literature, and VLADIMIR NEMIROVICH-DANCHENKO, a playwright-teacher at the Music and Drama School of the Moscow Philharmonia, joined contrasting backgrounds (industrialist's son and noblewoman's husband), temperaments and skills (theatrical and literary) as well as acting pupils – OLGA KNIPPER, VSEVOLOD MEYERHOLD, IVAN MOSKVIN – to form a

theatre based upon new principles. These included a conscious, craft-like realistic approach to acting to counter the lazy and artificial 19th-century conventions that still reigned – artificial declamation and falsely inspired emotions; a harmonious ensemble dedicated to art, and not to themselves or to the idea of a 'star system'; the blending of the new acting style with a scenic approach, newly and fully conceived for each individual drama, utilizing in-depth research into historical detail; a lengthy and systematic rehearsal to allow the actors to realize the essence of the play; education of the public to appreciate the new art and the theatre as a 'temple of art', via the elimination of the footlights, by taking a unified, sober approach to the theatre's decor (see THEATRE DESIGN), by barring latecomers from entering the auditorium until intermission, and by dispensing with curtain calls until the play's end.

MAT took its role as social educator seriously, and hoped to take the pulse of contemporary Russian life. The company opened on 14 October 1898 at the Hermitage Theatre on Carriage Row, with a production of A. K. TOLSTOI's history play *Tsar Fyodor Ioannovich*, which proved to be an exercise in archaeological reconstruction featuring Meiningen-like crowd scenes. The theatre took wing on CHEKHOV's *The Seagull* (1898), which gave the company its logo and identity and began a legendary association with the playwright – *Uncle Vanya* (1899), *The Three Sisters* (1901), *The Cherry Orchard* (1904). V. A. Simov's textured, varied realistic settings and Stanislavsky's innovative staging – including actors with their backs to the audience and a detailed sound score – helped to realize the 'theatre of mood'. In 1902 MAT began its long association with GORKY, after whom the theatre would be named in 1932. His *The Lower Depths* together with LEV TOLSTOI's *The Power of Darkness*, both produced in 1902, brought the inner lives of the lower classes to the stage and testified to the theatre's social consciousness. MAT was aesthetically more committed to lyrical REALISM than to NATURALISM and even made tentative forays into SYMBOLISM, as its varied and significant work of the next 30 years would prove: productions of IBSEN, HAUPTMANN, Hamsun, MAETERLINCK, ANDREEV and SHAKESPEARE; production and studio work by master teacher Leopold Sulerzhhitsky and by anti-realist directors Meyerhold, VAKHTANGOV, MICHAEL CHEKHOV, KONSTANTIN MARDZHANOV, ALEXANDRE BENOIS and GORDON CRAIG (the famous 1911–12 monodramatic *Hamlet*); and innovative design work by Benois, M. V. Dobuzhinsky and N. K. Roerikh.

This anti-realistic approach proved unpopular with the public and with Stanislavsky, who reapplied himself to developing an acting system, the first results of which were seen in his 1909 production of TURGENEV's *A Month in the Country*. Nemirovich-Danchenko's more mystical stagings of Dostoevsky's *The Brothers Karamazov* (1910) and *Nikolai Stavrogin*, from the novel *The Devils* (1913), elicited the charge of negativism from Gorky. Overall, the theatre's aesthetic and ideological profile was moderate. MAT survived the ravages of the October Revolution and the Civil War – company attrition due to voluntary defections abroad and involuntary detainment by White Guard troops – and was named an academic theatre (1920), largely through the good offices of Lenin and LUNACHARSKY. While the theatre publicly committed itself to reinforcing Bolshevik themes in its work, its directors privately disagreed philosophically over what artistic course it should follow.

The first post-revolutionary production, BYRON's *Cain* (1920), was politically anomalous. Anti-realistic experimentation continued under Vakhtangov at the Third Studio (1920) and at the Fourth Studio (1931). Stanislavsky applied his acting techniques at the Bolshoi Theatre's OPERA studio, while Nemirovich-Danchenko opened his Musical Studio at MAT. Simultaneously, the theatre produced the new Soviet drama. BULGAKOV's *The Days of the Turbins*, despite its White sympathies, proved a favourite of Stalin's and thus was successful, as was VSEVOLOD IVANOV's *Armoured Train 14-69* (1927) and VALENTIN KATAEV's comedy, *Squaring the Circle* (1928). The 1920s also saw influential MAT tours of Europe and the USA (1922-4), and richly visualized productions (sets by Golovin) of OSTROVSKY's *The Ardent Heart* (1926) and BEAUMARCHAIS's *Marriage of Figaro* (1927). In the 1930s new productions of Russian classics by GOGOL and Lev Tolstoi were staged, Chekhov's *Three Sisters* was ideologically reworked (1940), socialist realism (1934-53) was solidified and more of the new Soviet drama produced (AFINOGENOV, KIRSHON). In 1938 Stanislavsky died.

The Thaw (1954-6) was the training period for a new generation of directors, including Nemirovich-Danchenko's former student and Sovremennik Theatre head OLEG EFREMOV, who in 1972 reluctantly became MAT's new artistic director. As founder of the Sovremennik Theatre (1958), the Soviet theatre of the 1960s, Efremov and his young company had tried to speak for and to their generation via new drama and styles. In 1973 MAT moved to its new, modernly equipped 1370-seat facility on Tverskoi Boulevard, complete with an updated 'seagull' act curtain and prompter's box, while running productions concurrently in the original and the off-spring theatre buildings. Although he staged a weak production of *The Seagull* in 1980 and failed to develop a new performance style for the company, Efremov has guided the Chekhov MAT more successfully than actress Tatyana Doronina has led the Gorky MAT, the original theatre's rival subdivision. In the 1980-1 season, Efremov opened MAT's Little Stage for the development of a new generation of plays, playwrights and directors. The Chekhov MAT's successes include Efros's MARX BROS-inspired staging of *Tartuffe* (1981); ROSHCHIN's patriotic war play *Troop Train* and his satirical comedy *Mother-of-Pearl Zinaida*; Rozovsky's *Kafka, Father and Son*; SHATROV's revisionist Lenin play *Blue Horses on Red Grass*; and Kama Ginkas's staging of Nina Pavlova's *The Club Car*, which concerns female juvenile delinquency. In 1990, the Chekhov MAT began housing Roman Kozak's Fifth Studio, formerly the Theatre-Studio Chelovek, which has produced MROŻEK's and PETRUSHEVSKAYA's plays. SG

Moscow State Jewish Theatre Founded as the Jewish Theatre Studio in 1919 in Petrograd, under the leadership of ALEKSEI GRANOVSKY. After a period of intensive training of its young members, including Marc Chagall and Nathan Altman as designers and Alexander Krein as composer, and actors like SOLOMON MIKHOELS and Benjamin Zuskin, the company soon created a unique style and was desig-

nated a state theatre. The problem of finding plays reflecting both the company's ethnic quality and its political fervour was solved by ruthlessly adapting the classic Jewish plays of such writers as SHOLOM ALEICHEM, Mendele Mocher Sforim and GOLDFADN. The company was particularly successful with SHAKESPEARE's plays - *King Lear*, directed in 1935 by SERGEI RADLOV with Mikhoels as Lear and Zuskin as Fool, was a triumph. The theatre was closed down by an edict of Stalin in 1948 along with all other Jewish theatres. AB

Mosher, Gregory (Dean) 1949- American director, best known as the first director of works by DAVID MAMET. Mosher is also the first artistic administrator to have had popular success with the theatre programme at New York's Lincoln Center. Having studied theatre at Oberlin, Ithaca and Juilliard, he went to Chicago's GOODMAN THEATRE in 1974 to direct its Stage 2 programme. As Goodman artistic director (1978-85), he concentrated on new works by such authors as Mamet, JOHN GUARE, DAVID RABE, MICHAEL WELLER, WOLE SOYINKA, TENNESSEE WILLIAMS and EDWARD ALBEE, a policy that met with some resistance from subscribers. Ironically, Mosher's tenure at Lincoln Center (1985-91) was criticized for being *too* popular, for blurring the line between non-profit and commercial production. He left Lincoln Center in 1991 to pursue independent film and theatre work, including a 1992 revival of *Streetcar Named Desire*. SF

Moshinsky, Elijah 1946- British director, who was chosen by PETER HALL to be his assistant on *Hamlet* (with ALBERT FINNEY), the production which opened the NATIONAL THEATRE's Lyttelton Theatre in 1976. He also directed THOMAS BERNHARD's *The Force of Habit* (1976) at the Lyttelton and *Troilus and Cressida* in the YOUNG VIC studio for the NT, before widening his range of interests to include opera and television. For the BBC's TV SHAKESPEARE series he provided two of the better productions, *Coriolanus* (with ALAN HOWARD) and *All's Well that Ends Well*. Moshinsky is one of the most able, if underrated, directors of his generation, capable (like TREVOR NUNN and TERRY HANDS) of mounting spectaculars for large stages as well as interior dramas for small ones. He has been a more-than-reliable director of classical revivals for the WEST END, including *Much Ado about Nothing* (1989), *Ivanov* (1989) and *Cyrano de Bergerac* (1992) with Robert Lindsay in the title role. But his true skills have perhaps been better revealed in two modern plays, both with tender, tragic plots - RONALD HARWOOD's *Another Time* (1989) and particularly William Nicholson's *Shadowlands* (1989), about C. S. Lewis's late-life marriage to the poet Joy Davidman. While his staging of the MUSICAL *Matador* (1991) was admired, this Spanish mixture of guitars, castanets and a rags-to-riches biography of a bull-fighter was hailed with more bricks than roses in the West End. His revival of JEAN ANOUILH's *Becket* (1991), with Robert Lindsay and DEREK JACOBI, fared better. JE

Moskvin, Ivan (Mikhailovich) 1874-1946 One of the best Russian-Soviet character actors of his generation, who specialized in portraying native types from the subclass of the 'insulted and the injured'; director of the

MOSCOW ART THEATRE (1943). Following stints with GLIKERIYA FEDOTOVA'S (STANISLAVSKY's teacher) touring company at Z. A. Malinovsky's theatre in Yaroslav (1896), where he played 77 roles in one season, and at Korsh's Theatre in Moscow (1897–8), Moskvin was invited to become a charter member of the MAT (1898). There he was reunited with VLADIMIR NEMIROVICH-DANCHENKO, who had been his acting teacher at the Moscow Philharmonia (1893) and who now helped secure him the title role in MAT's premiere production, A. K. TOLSTOI's historical drama *Tsar Fyodor Ioannovich* (1898). From this success Moskvin went on to play a wide variety of roles at MAT, where he spent his entire professional career. These included Luka in GORKY's *The Lower Depths* (1902), Epikhodov in CHEKHOV's *The Cherry Orchard* and Snegiryov in Nemirovich-Danchenko's dramatization of Dostoevsky's *The Brothers Karamazov* (1910).

Moskvin was noted for the deft comic touch and the sharply individualized idiosyncratic detail, betokening a richly imagined inner life which he brought to his roles. In the Soviet period he appeared in the dramas of TRENYOV, KORNEICHUK and Kron and played a leading role in POGODIN's *Kremlin Chimes* (1942), about Lenin. His career also extended to film acting and stage directing. He helped stage the MAT productions of MAETERLINCK's *The Blue Bird* (1908), GOGOL's *The Inspector General* (1908) and TURGENEV's *A Month in the Country* (1909). SG

Mostel, Zero (Samuel Joel) 1915–77 American actor. Trained as an artist, Mostel became an immensely talented comic actor, noted for his sagging jowls and large paunch but dancer's grace, acrobat's control and his enormously expressive face. After appearing in sketches at a New York City Greenwich Village nightclub in 1942, he made his BROADWAY debut the same year in *Keep 'Em Laughing*. Subsequent roles of note included Shu Fu in *The Good Person of Setzuan* (1956), Leopold Bloom in *Ulysses in Nighttown* (1958, 1974), Jean in *Rhinoceros* (1961), Pseudolus in the MUSICAL *A Funny Thing Happened on the Way to the Forum* (1962) and his greatest popular triumph, Tevye in *Fiddler on the Roof* (1964, 1976). In 1965 his memoirs were published. He died in Philadelphia rehearsing Shylock in ARNOLD WESKER's *The Merchant*. His son Josh is also an actor (Milo Crawford in *Texas Trilogy*, 1976; Norman in *The Boys Next Door*, 1987). DBW

Moulin-Rouge, Bal du In 1889 a former butcher named Charles Zidler, with Joseph Oller, opened a dance-hall-cum-*café-concert* (see CAFÉ CHANTANT) in the Place Blanche, Paris, intending to convey the boisterous cancan of the amateur MUSIC-HALLS to more respectable premises. The entrance was surmounted by a giant windmill designed by Willette, and a hollow stucco elephant stood in the garden to house intimate performance. The *quadrille naturaliste* with its *porte d'armes* (the uplifted ankle held by the dancer's hand) and *grand écart* (splits), as danced by LA GOULUE and her squalid colleagues, and the insinuating songs of YVETTE GUILBERT gave the house a reputation that enhanced the erotic prestige of Montmartre. The dance floor was reduced in 1903 to make way for a music-hall stage; after the building burned in 1915, it

reopened to offer dinner shows of cancan and ballet. Between 1925 and 1929, Jacques-Charles revived the old glories with eight spectacularly novel REVUES; then it was converted into a cinema and not reopened as a place of live entertainment until 1953. LS

Mounet, Paul 1847–1922 French actor. Like his more celebrated brother, MOUNET-SULLY, Paul Mounet came to the theatre relatively late, making his debut at the ODÉON in 1880 as the young Horace in PIERRE CORNEILLE's play. He joined the COMÉDIE-FRANÇAISE in 1889, appearing as Don Salluste in *Ruy Blas*. He excelled in older and character parts and his deep and resonant bass voice suited him not only for tragic roles, but also for more sinister ones such as Iago. Other memorable parts were in *Le Juif polonais* (*The Polish Jew*) and as an imposing Hercules in *Alkestis*. In 1908 he appeared, with SARAH BERNHARDT, in a silent film of *La Tosca*. JMCC

Mounet-Sully [Mounet], **Jean** 1841–1916 The major French tragic actor of the late 19th century. Mounet-Sully originally trained to be a Protestant pastor. He left the Conservatoire in 1868 and managed to find work at the Montmartre Theatre, where he was noticed by CHILLY who needed an actor with a strong voice for the ODÉON. He added Sully to his name and first appeared there as Cornwall in *King Lear*. After the 1870 war he joined the troupe of the COMÉDIE-FRANÇAISE, making his debut in 1872 as Oreste in RACINE's *Andromaque*, followed by Rodrigue in *Le Cid*. Like RACHEL in 1838, he was immediately seen as the perfect actor for the classical repertoire, audiences being overwhelmed by his passion, conviction and sheer dramatic power. His greatest roles were Hamlet, Orestes and Oedipus. His vocal and physical means and his majestic attitudes made him the definitive Oedipus of the period (1881). His range included the 19th-century repertoire, notably the plays of VICTOR HUGO: his Didier in *Marion de Lorme* (1873) led to his becoming a *sociétaire*, and he played a particularly fine Hernani opposite SARAH BERNHARDT. In 1889 he was decorated with the Légion d'Honneur. In 1909 he appeared as Jesus in a silent film, *The Kiss of Judas*. JMCC

Mowatt [Ritchie], **Anna Cora (Ogden)** 1819–70 American playwright and actress. She had read all of SHAKESPEARE by age ten; at 14 she translated, staged and acted in Voltaire's *Alzire* in the family parlour; wrote her first play, *Pelayo*, when she was 17; and became a regular contributor to *Graham's Magazine* and the *Columbian*. She married James Mowatt when she was 15, and after his death (1851) married William F. Ritchie. Although now best known for *Fashion* (1845), a SATIRE on the nouveaux riches who make themselves ridiculous by aping foreign manners, in her own time she was also known as a public reader and actress. Encouraged by Longfellow, she began her readings in Boston (1841) and the following year in New York. After the success of *Fashion*, she toured for 200 nights as Lady Teazle, Juliet and Pauline in BULWER LYTTON's *The Lady of Lyons*; she toured again in 1852, and performed in England (1847, 1851). As an actress she was admired for her grace, radiant smile and naturalness, which Edgar Allan Poe found 'so pleasantly removed from the customary rant and cant'. Her second play, *Armand* (1847), was also well received, and she wrote two vivid accounts of theatrical life: *Autobiography of an Actress* (1854) and *Mimic Life; or, Before and Behind the Curtain* (1856). RM

Mozambique see PORTUGUESE-SPEAKING AFRICA

Mrożek, Sławomir 1932– Polish playwright, essayist, cartoonist, short story writer and film-maker, who left Poland in 1963 and has lived in Italy, France and Mexico. Using slapstick techniques of VAUDEVILLE and CABARET, he transforms concepts into model theatrical situations. *The Police* (1958) and early one-act parables – *Out at Sea* (1960), *Striptease* and *Charlie* (1961) – reveal the mechanisms of power by pushing absurd premises to logical extremes. Using SATIRE and the grotesque, he mocks national myths and parodies different theatrical styles and genres, notably the Polish romantic tradition. *Tango* (1964) traces European civilization from liberalism to totalitarianism in the form of family drama. *Vatzlav* (1970) and *Émigrés* (1974) offer ironic views of exiles from tyranny confronting paradoxes of freedom. Later plays include *On Foot* (1981), apocalyptic panorama of dislocated lives during the Second World War; *Portrait* (1988), painful reckoning with the fatal legacy of Stalinism; *Widows* (1990), allegorical dance of death; and *Love in the Crimea* (1993), CHEKHOVian variations. DG

Mugo, Micere (Githae) 1942– Kenyan educationalist, playwright and poet (*Daughter of My People, Sing!*, 1976), who was co-author with NGUGI WA THIONG'O of *The Trials of Dedan Kimathi* (1976). Micere Mugo's contribution to this major work of the Kenyan theatre may well be seen in its strong representation of women's role in the independence struggle and in a free society. *The Long Illness of Ex-Chief Kiti* (1976) is set during the emergency in colonial Kenya, with the leading character a collaborator rejected by his children. *Disillusioned* (1976), a radio play, concerns colour prejudice in a Christian mission. Micere Mugo now lives in exile. KG NWAM

Mukulu, Alex fl.1980s–90s Ugandan actor and performer, playwright and director. Mukulu first drew attention in the early 1980s with a group which paid more attention to competent presentation than most companies, performing plays that incorporated plenty of dance and music, in the pattern of BYRON KAWADWA and ROBERT SERUMAGA: most recently *Wounds of Africa* (1990) and *Thirty Years of the Banana* (1991). As well as writing the plays and directing, Mukulu usually takes the leading role and is reported to maintain rigid discipline within the company. His songs are dramatically topical and often satirical, and, while there is a bias towards the Luganda language, his plays appeal over the language barrier, through MIME, dance and music. MMAC

Müller, Heiner 1929– German playwright and director. *The Scab* (1958) and *The Peasants* (1961) were socialist-realist treatments of the Communist reorganization of industry and agriculture respectively. Müller's REALISM was deemed too objective, and he was expelled from the GDR

Writers' Union in 1961.

A utopian Communist, he turned to antiquity, making his verse *Philoctetes* (1968) a critique of Stalinist expediency and *The Horatian* (1968) an oblique attack on manipulated historiography. In *Mauser* (1975) Müller takes issue with BRECHT's *The Measures Taken*. *The Battle* (1975) and *Germania – Death in Berlin* (1978) were plotless montages of disparate scenes – workers on a building site, clowns enacting a Frederick the Great anecdote, a wordless MIME with a bandaged, brutalized puppet – which exposed German history as a catalogue of barbarism and internecine brutality from Roman to Nazi times. *Life of Gundling Lessings Sleep Dream Scream* (1979) is a similar exposure of the German Enlightenment. Müller adapted *Macbeth* (1972) and *Titus Andronicus* (1985), and translated *Hamlet* (1977) and *As You Like It* (1968). *The Hamlet Machine* (1979), a short arabesque on the theme of treachery, combines Hamlet's story with the agonies of the Marxist intellectual after Berlin, Budapest and Prague. This and other enigmatic, fragmentary pieces, like *Der Auftrag* (*The Mission*), *Verkommenes Ufer* (*Desolate Shore*) and *Medea-Material* (all 1983), show Müller moving towards Western avant-garde forms.

By the 1980s he was tolerated in his native GDR, lionized in the FRG and widely if selectively performed in both. He collaborated with ROBERT WILSON on the *CIVIL warS*. Müller's sensational 1988 DEUTSCHES THEATER production of *The Scab* exposed, unwittingly inscribed in the text, the flaws that were soon to bring down the GDR. Unscrupulous efforts have nonetheless been made to link him with the Stasi. Since 1992 he has been a director of the BERLINER ENSEMBLE. HR

Munday, Anthony 1560–1633 English playwright, pamphleteer, actor and government agent, engaged in anti-Catholic espionage. Munday was a prolific journeyman-writer and translator, who could turn his hand as readily to anti-theatrical tracts as to writing plays for the PUBLIC THEATRES or pageants for the city of London. Francis Meres, in *Palladis Tamia* (1598), surprisingly calls him 'the best for comedy' and 'our best plotter'. For the Elizabethans, the latter skill defined the dextrous division of a given story into appropriate dramatic episodes. It is not particularly evident in Munday's extant plays, *Fedele and Fortunio* (c.1584), *John a Kent and John a Cumber* (1594) and the two parts of *The Downfall* and *The Death of Robert, Earl of Huntingdon* (1598), written with HENRY CHETTLE. However, his collaborative skills may have been appreciated by fellow writers in many lost plays as well as in the revisions of *Sir Thomas More* (c.1596) and in Part 1 of *Sir John Oldcastle* (1599). PT

Munden, Joseph (Shepherd) 1758–1832 English comic actor, derided by his detractors as a 'mugger' but celebrated, for the same reason, by his admirers as one who 'literally *makes faces*'. After several years in the provinces, Munden made his debut at COVENT GARDEN in 1790 as the low-comedy replacement for John Edwin, and retained his place on the London stage until his retirement in 1824. 'Out of some invisible wardrobe he dips for faces,' wrote CHARLES LAMB, whose essays have immortalized Munden in 'the grand grotesque of FARCE'. PT

Munford, Robert c.1737–83 American playwright and politician. One of Virginia's more influential elected representatives, both before and after the Revolution, Munford wrote two plays that are outstanding examples of America's early comic drama and its interest in SATIRE. *The Candidates; or, The Humours of a Virginia Election* (1770) satirizes the methods by which politicians win elections. *The Patriots* (1779) attacks half-hearted and hypocritical patriots as well as Tory and Whig politics. Not interested in a playwriting career, Munford wrote mainly to air his views, showing some skill in contriving plots and creating amusing scenes with stereotypical characters. Both plays were published in 1798. WJM

Muni, Paul [Muni Weisenfreund] 1896–1967 American actor who started in the YIDDISH THEATRE at the age of 12 as Weisenfreund, playing old men's parts, quickly establishing himself as a superb character actor and master of make-up. After 18 years as a leading Yiddish actor he moved to BROADWAY in English-speaking roles, and then to a distinguished career in Hollywood. AB

Munk, Kaj 1892–1944 Danish writer and Lutheran pastor. Munk was the author of some 35 plays vigorously exploring issues surrounding faith, human will and the creation of identity through courageous action; his debt to Kierkegaard and IBSEN is frequently clear. Some early plays reveal a fascination with 'strong leaders', such as Herod in *An Idealist* (1924) and Henry VIII in *Cant* (1931), anticipating his brief but real attraction to Nazism's apparent promise to lead mankind to a new age of faith. Very different views emerge in the explicitly anti-Nazi *He Sits at the Melting Pot* (1938) and in the parable of Danish resistance *Niels Ebbesen* (1940–2); its suppression began a process that ended with Munk's murder by the Gestapo. His most enduring play is *The Word* (1925), about the power of faith and the will to free humanity from prejudice. HL

Murdoch, Frank H(itchcock) 1843–72 American actor and playwright. An actor of comedy roles who borrowed his last name from his uncle, JAMES MURDOCH, Murdoch spent his entire career with Mrs John Drew's (see DREW–BARRYMORE FAMILY) ARCH STREET THEATRE Company in Philadelphia. He wrote *Davy Crockett* (1872) for FRANK MAYO, who, after its early discouraging reception, helped create the popular version that emphasized the gentle side of the Westerner in scenes of spectacle and romance. His other plays include *Light House Cliffs* (1870?); *Bohemia; or, The Lottery of Art* (1872), a SATIRE on critics; and *Only a Jew* (1873). WJM

Murdoch, James (Edward) 1811–93 American actor. Murdoch's debut was in 1829 at the ARCH STREET THEATRE in Philadelphia as Frederick in KOTZEBUE's *Lover's Vows*. In 1833, he supported FANNY KEMBLE during her appearance at the CHESTNUT STREET THEATRE. For the next decade he appeared in various theatres in New Orleans, Mobile, Pittsburgh, Philadelphia, New York and Boston. For two years, he retired from the stage and lectured on Shakespearian characters and 'The Uses and Abuses of the Stage', and gave elocution lessons. He returned to the stage in 1845, and for the next 15 years established a reputation as both a tragedian and a light comedian. In 1856, he appeared at London's HAYMARKET THEATRE for 110 nights and was also engaged briefly in Liverpool. He retired again in 1861 and 1879, but appeared intermittently until 1889. Among his more acclaimed roles were Hamlet, Charles Surface in SHERIDAN's *The School for Scandal*, Benedick, Orlando and Mercutio. His reminiscences, *The Stage; or, Recollections of Actors and Acting from an Experience of Fifty Years*, were published in 1880. DJW

Murphy, Arthur 1727–1805 Irish playwright. Dissatisfied with his career as a clerk in a banking house, he turned to journalism as a columnist in the *Gray's Inn Journal* in 1752. He began writing plays in 1753, through friendship with SAMUEL FOOTE but, resisting GARRICK's attempts to improve his play, he rewrote it as *The Apprentice* (1756). He was an actor briefly from 1755, playing Othello, but recognized that he would never be particularly successful and returned to journalism as well as training in law, practising as a barrister until 1788; he continued to write plays. He translated VOLTAIRE's tragedy *The Orphan of China* (1759) but, after disputes over his tragedy *The Grecian Daughter*, his best work was in comedy, including a study of married life and its attendant boredom in *The Way to Keep Him* (1760) and the more sentimental *Know Your Own Mind* (1777), his later plays being presented at COVENT GARDEN. He retired both from the law and the theatre in 1788 and was given a royal pension in 1803. PH

Murphy, Tom [Thomas] **(Bernard)** 1935 Irish playwright. Following the success of *A Whistle in the Dark* (1961), concerning the self-destructive brutality of an Irish immigrant family in Coventry, Murphy wrote television and film scripts for a period in London. Outstanding among his subsequent plays are *Famine* (1968), *A Crucial Week in the Life of a Grocer's Assistant* (1969), *The Sanctuary Lamp* (1975), *The Gigli Concert* (1983), *Conversations on a Homecoming* (1985) and *Bailegangaire* (1985).

His plays range widely in style and material. *Famine* is an epic, based on the Irish famine of the 1840s; *A Crucial Week* surrealistically presents (see SURREALISM) the 'coming-of-age' of a harassed, small-town adolescent; in *The Gigli Concert* – an unnerving marriage of *Faust* and deadpan comedy – a manic-depressive Irish businessman, bent upon singing like Gigli, 'consults' an English 'philosophical dynamatologist'. In *Too Late for Logic* (1989) a university philosopher interrogates those elements of his own life that led to his suicide.

Conversations is a genre piece – a drunken reunion during which old friends shred each other's illusions – but underlying its meandering, slice-of-life REALISM is a fugue-like structure that lifts it into a tragicomic lament for individual and communal lost ideals. The magnificent *Bailegangaire* seems almost YEATSian by comparison: a senile crone, distracted by imaginary hens, sits up in bed reciting an old tale of journey, contest, death and loss, while her two grand-daughters tend her and muddle through their own traumas, helped by vodka and birthday cake. Miraculously, the story gets told, the grand-daughters find an accommodation, and this battered remnant of a 'fambly' finds its own form of salvation.

The operatic range of Murphy's theatre is grounded in specifics: precisely localized individual voices; the characters' moral and psychological bewilderment, violence and delicacy; the still-potent emblems of Catholic liturgy. Underlying those is his irreducible theatricality, his unerring sense of the cultural contradictions of modern Ireland, and his tragicomic vision of a secularized world where individuals mourn and bitterly celebrate their loss of faith.   DM GF

Murray, (George) Gilbert (Aimé) 1866–1957 British classical scholar, philosopher and dramatist, who provided SHAW with the model for Cusins in *Major Barbara*. After writing two original plays, *Carlyon Sahib* (1889) and *Andromache* (1900), Murray turned to verse translations of Greek tragedy (see GREECE, ANCIENT) which had a significant influence in the first decades of the century. His versions of EURIPIDES were staged by GRANVILLE BARKER for the STAGE SOCIETY at the ROYAL COURT THEATRE (*Hippolytus*, 1904; *The Trojan Women*, 1905; *Electra*, 1906) and at the Savoy Theatre (*Medea*, 1907), while his translation of SOPHOCLES' *Oedipus Rex* was staged by REINHARDT at COVENT GARDEN in 1912. He later turned to COMEDY, with adaptations of ARISTOPHANES and the first reconstructions of MENANDER: *The Rape of the Locks* (*Perikeiromene* 1914) and *The Arbitration* (*Epitrepontes*, 1945).   CI

Murray, T(homas) C(ornelius) 1873–1959 Irish playwright. With LENNOX ROBINSON, Murray was one of the 'Cork realists', in the ABBEY's early years, whose work determined the theatre's characteristic style. In *Birthright* (1910), his first play, a father's jealous care for the disposition of his land becomes a mortal issue between his two sons. It is a theme typical of Murray's sombre vision of a small-farming society obsessed by ownership of their harsh land, 'with more o' the rock, an' the briar, an' the sour weed than the sweet grass'. Marriage and careers come equally under its sway.

Murray's most successful later plays are *Aftermath* (1922), *Autumn Fire* (1924) and *Michaelmas Eve* (1932). In none of them does anyone win: the mother of an idealistic young teacher forces him into a 'practical' marriage with a woman who could 'buy and sell them that talk like angels'; an ageing man marries a young girl who falls in love with his son. In a society bound by strict Catholic teaching, which Murray approved, his characters must simply endure within the restrictions. From the tension between extreme emotional conflicts and their enforced suppression, his plays derive their intense, claustrophobic atmosphere.   DM

Murrell, John 1945– Canadian playwright and director. Born in the USA, Murrell began a teaching career in Calgary, Alberta, before turning to playwriting. His first major play, *Waiting for the Parade* (1977), about the lives of five women during the Second World War, remains one of the most frequently produced plays in Canadian theatre. He quickly followed this success with *Memoir* (1977),

a fictionalized account of the last days of SARAH BERNHARDT, which has received even wider acclaim. It has been translated into 15 languages and performed in more than 35 countries since its premiere at Canada's Guelph Spring Festival, with Siobhan McKenna in the lead role. His next plays, *Farther West* (1982) and *New World* (1984), did not entirely live up to these early successes, despite their premiere productions by ROBIN PHILLIPS. Murrell directed the premiere of *October* (1988), a fictionalized meeting between ELEONORA DUSE and Isadora Duncan, which failed utterly to recapture the dramatic balance of *Memoir*. *Democracy* (1991), a Civil War conversation between Ralph Waldo Emerson and Walt Whitman, was again directed by Phillips. In addition to his original plays, Murrell has also created fine translations of such classics as *Uncle Vanya*, *The Seagull*, *The Master Builder* and *Oedipus Rex*.   DAH

Musco, Angelo 1872–1937 Italian actor and company manager. Beginning in the Sicilian MARIONETTE theatre, he later joined the company of GIOVANNI GRASSO as an actor in the 'straight' theatre. Although he was eventually established in Milan and elsewhere with his own company, much of his most important work looked back to his Sicilian roots; CAPUANA's *Il paraninfo* (*The Marriage Arranger*, 1915) was an early success, and he was a noted interpreter of PIRANDELLO's plays, like the one-act piece *La giara* (*The Jug*), and the full-length *Pensaci, Giacomino!* (*Think, Giacomino!*) and *Liolà*.   LR

music-hall English Victorian term for VARIETY theatre, with earlier analogues (so-called 'music-halls' had opened in Bolton and Manchester in 1832). Under the patents system (see THEATRICAL MONOPOLY), because dialogue was forbidden them, minor theatres had perforce to offer musical entertainments. But music was available elsewhere: the public-house bar parlour or 'free-and-easy' with its weekly sing-songs (the Georgian catch or Comus clubs), performed by amateurs, with a chairman and some professionals; the assembly-room entertainments at hotels; and the suburban London tea garden, a middle-class version of the pleasure gardens, where aristocratic patronage had fallen off by 1830, and which exhibited singers on a small stage. All three forms were licensed under the liberally interpreted Music and Dancing Act of George II. In London, these places of mixed entertainment, smoking and light refreshment included the Britannia in Hoxton, the Bower in the Lower Marsh (Lambeth), and the Grecian in the City Road, whose pleasure garden was also known as the Eagle Tavern, described by DICKENS in *Sketches by Boz*.

The Theatres Act of 1843, which distinguished sharply between legitimate playhouses under the Lord Chamberlain's control where no smoking or drinking was allowed in the auditorium, and tavern concert-rooms under the jurisdiction of local magistrates where such practices were allowed, compelled many of the lesser resorts to make an evolutionary choice. Saloon theatres opted either to go legitimate or carry on as miscellaneous entertainments with no permission to stage plays. Typically, the Mogul tavern in Drury Lane transmuted into the Middlesex or 'Old Mo' music-hall and eventually became the grandiose Winter Garden Theatre.

Harry Tate in his sketch
'Golfing'.

The old bohemian singing-rooms in night cellars gradually disappeared, among them the Cyder Cellars in Maiden Lane and the Coal Hole in the Strand. These had been all-male resorts, featuring hearty suppers and strong drink, bawdy songs and blood-curdling performers like W. G. Ross as Sam Hall. Evans's in Covent Garden, the last to go, survived by turning into a respectable music-hall that admitted ladies (1854). Respectability was the touchstone for success with many early 'halls: CHARLES MORTON, the intelligent manager of the Canterbury Hall in Lambeth (1852), opened it to ladies at all times and presented the first English performance of Gounod's *Faust* as an oratorio, although bookmakers still shouted odds on the premises. Morton's Oxford near St Giles's Circus, the London Pavilion in Piccadilly Circus and the Tivoli in the Strand were other important WEST END houses.

At first, music-hall programmes copied the repertory of the 'harmonic meetings', mingling madrigals and glees with lengthy BURLESQUE ballads, such as SAM COWELL's 'Villikins and his Dinah' and 'The Ratcatcher's Daughter', SAM COLLINS's Irish ditties, and E. W. MACKNEY's 'Ethiopian' delineations. In the 1860s, the type of the *lion comique*, a free-spending swell, was made popular by

GEORGE LEYBOURNE, 'The Great Vance' (Alfred Peck Stevens) and Arthur Lloyd, while women excelled at dramatic renditions. JENNY HILL, the 'Vital Spark', was typical in coming from a background of poverty, achieving fame and fortune, and retiring early because of ill health and exhaustion. Drawn from the working classes, performers shared common experience with their audiences, who were boisterous and fond of joining in the chorus and 'giving the bird'.

In 1878, the Metropolitan Board of Works required a Certificate of Suitability, which caused some 200 halls, unable to meet new standards, to close. In reaction, STOCK companies formed to float luxurious, well appointed houses, designed by outstanding architects like Frank Matcham. The first palatial hall was the Great Variety Theatre in Leicester Square, whose neo-Moorish building, burnt down and rebuilt as the Alhambra Palace under E. T. Smith, became famous for its ballets, managing to survive a lawsuit citing them as dramatic performances. Variety theatres continued to advance in number and importance, with improved ventilation, comfort and decoration, as well as higher prices. Admission rose from 1s at the London Tivoli in the 1860s to 3s in the 1890s; the top price at the Liverpool Palace was 5s. Soon every London neighbourhood had its local, and the journalist F. Anstey could discern four distinct levels of quality and audience in London alone: the aristocratic variety theatre in the West End, the small West End house, the large bourgeois music-hall in the outlying areas and suburbs, and that of the poor and squalid districts. In the provinces, most halls clustered in the centres, even in Manchester, Liverpool and Glasgow.

From 1879, the infusion of music-hall stars into PANTOMIME accustomed the family audience to variety material and persuaded it to attend. The middle classes took to visiting halls as the managers strove successfully to dispel the public-house image, banning sales of drinks in the auditorium, replacing tables with rows of seats, cleaning up artistes' material and taking measures to control audience behaviour. The chairman, a holdover from the singing-room, eventually disappeared, replaced by numbers slotted into the proscenium arch and cued to a printed programme. Since sanitation, elegance and safety were totems of the middle-class ethos, the music-hall sought to embody them. It was aided by new access through public transport and improved street-lighting that made it safer to venture out at night. Prominent managers who sponsored changes were, in London, OSWALD STOLL, Edward Moss and Richard Thornton; the Livermore Brothers and James Kiernan in Liverpool; Joseph Smith in Rochdale; and William Morgan in Bradford. The Empire and Alhambra in London's Leicester Square and the Palace in Cambridge Circus became the models for halls all along the new circuits organized by agents and managements.

The average single turn seldom lasted more than 20 minutes, enabling popular performers to play several halls a night. However, to meet the increased costs, Henry de Frece in Liverpool and George Belmont in London instituted the notorious 'twice-nightly' arrangement (1885). These costs now included star salaries, for the 1890s were the heyday of the music-hall star. MARIE LLOYD with her artful innuendo, ALBERT CHEVALIER, a legitimate actor who excelled at coster impersonations, LITTLE TICH the eccentric pygmy, DAN LENO, greatest of the comedians of humble life, HARRY LAUDER with his Scottish ballads, the male impersonator VESTA TILLEY, blackface artistes G. H. CHIRGWIN and Eugene Stratton, GEORGE ROBEY of the outraged eyebrows and outrageous *double entendre* were all expensive performers to maintain.

This period of consolidation also saw some last-ditch assaults on the institution. Prostitution on the premises had always been an outrage to reformers, and Mrs Ormiston Chant attacked the London Empire for its flagrant promenade in 1895. In Manchester a combination of reform groups opposed the licence for the new Palace, and in Liverpool disputes over licensing were conducted along class lines. In the wake of the Local Government Act of 1888, anti-music-hall forces were backed by newly elected town councils, bodies more susceptible to public pressure than local magistrates had been. Another attack came from the Lord Chamberlain's office, as sketches began to play a prominent part in the music-hall bill. Parliamentary commissions of 1866 and 1892 both recommended more liberal changes in licensing, but these were not followed up until 1912, when half an hour of dialogue

was permitted. One result was the appearance of legitimate stars like HERBERT BEERBOHM TREE on the variety stage.

The old intimate relationship between the performer and the audience began to disappear as colossal halls like Moss's London HIPPODROME with its water-tank for aquatic spectacles and the Stoll COLISEUM with its triple revolving stage were built. Programmes became filled with acrobats, trained seals and elephants, living statuary, 15-minute MELODRAMAS, mentalists and adagio dancing, edging out though not entirely displacing the solo comedian and singer who had been the music-hall's staple. In 1906, the Variety Artists Federation, a trade union, was formed and the next year held a strike for paid matinées and abrogation of the 'barring clause' that prevented contracted performers from appearing at neighbourhood houses after a term of contract ended. The strike resulted in a compromise.

A token but important recognition of the music-hall came with the Royal Command Performance in 1912. A kind of resurgence occurred in the 1920s with the introduction of American jazz and ragtime and singers like SOPHIE TUCKER, who were already known to the public through their recordings. But it could not compete with the talking pictures, the wireless, or the wartime air raids that made going to the theatre a danger. The music-hall was still capable of fostering such talents as MAX MILLER and GRACIE FIELDS, and throve at the Palladium in London till 1961. But television put paid to the process of diminution by featuring most of the surviving music-hall types on its variety programmes, and the microphone reduced the camaraderie between performer and public. Most of the extant buildings were wantonly demolished or restored for other purposes. Ironically, the tavern concerts that spawned the music-hall thrive as working men's clubs in industrial areas, whereas ersatz 'olde-tyme' music-halls forcibly demonstrate the obsolescence of the original form.

But the spirit long infused British drama, not only thematically as in JOHN OSBORNE's *The Entertainer* (1957) and TREVOR GRIFFITHS's *Comedians* (1975), but in the dialogue rhythms in BECKETT, O'CASEY, PINTER and PETER NICHOLS, as well as in performance style. A comedian like MAX WALL, excelling in *Krapp's Last Tape*, is a perfect example of this cross-fertilization. LS

See: P. Bailey (ed.), *Music Hall: The Business of Pleasure*, Stony Stratford, 1986; J. S. Bratton (ed.), *Music Hall: Performance and Style*, Stony Stratford, 1986; D. Cheshire, *Music Hall in Britain*, Newton Abbott, 1974; H. Scott, *The Early Doors*, London, 1946; L. Senelick, D. Cheshire and U. Schneider, *British Music Hall 1840–1923: A Bibliography and Guide to Sources*, Hamden, Conn., 1981; C. D. Stuart and A. J. Park, *The Variety Stage*, London, 1895.

music-hall, French see *CAFÉ CHANTANT*; REVUE

musical see MUSICAL THEATRE, AMERICAN

musical comedy Term whose limits are somewhat indefinite, and a British and American phenomenon that was probably at its height between the 1890s and 1918.

Writing about *A Gaiety Girl* (1893), WILLIAM ARCHER commented, 'There is no doubt that this class of play has become a social institution, the history of which will one day form a curious study. This is the real New Drama.' Archer applauded the usurpation of BURLESQUE by musical comedy.

From the providers' point of view musical comedy was a matter of showbusiness; from the consumers', a thrilling, titillating, amusing, tuneful affair making little call on credibility. What was hoped would be a box office success was cobbled together by a story deviser, a lyric writer and a composer, often with collaborators. The original material was frequently much altered during rehearsals – dialogue changed, musical numbers dropped or added, and characters eliminated or introduced. Even after the opening night, alterations were made from time to time according to audiences' reactions. *The Lucky Star* (Savoy, 1899) was advertised as 'Founded on a French original by Leterrier and Vanloo, adapted by J. Cheever Goodwin and Woolson Morse, with new dialogue by Charles H. Brookfield and new lyrics by Adrian Ross and Aubrey Hopwood, the whole revised and assembled by H. L., and with music by Ivan Caryll.' No mention was made of the fact that some of the music was borrowed from the 'French original'. A couple of months after the show opened, the *Monthly Musical Record* observed, 'The libretto has been brightened up on every page and Mr François Cellier has done wonders in touching up the music.' Such tinkering was the true but often unacknowledged fate of most musical comedies.

The 'books' of musical comedies were strung together by writers who had an eye to what would keep a far from intellectual audience attentive throughout. This included a simple central feature such as the love of the highly placed for the humble (who often turned out to be not so humble after all) or luck arising from a windfall, and there had to be plenty of occasions for laughter and for the admiration of elegant females – everything set, if possible, in a modern context. The lyrics were often platitudinous and sometimes sheer nonsense. Catch phrases were eagerly sought after. Nevertheless, some of the rhymesters displayed considerable talent, notably Adrian Ross (1859–1933) who, in Archer's opinion, was 'easier and more fluent' than W. S. GILBERT. Adrian Ross was the pseudonym of Arthur Reed Ropes, who had distinguished himself as a scholar at Cambridge and who wrote both musical comedy lyrics and serious literature. Musical comedy was full of pseudonyms, many of which plumbed the depths. James Davis (1854–1907) called himself OWEN HALL, which was complemented by Arthur Roberts's (1852–1933) assumption of 'Payne Nunn'.

The music of each work was newly written by one or two composers, but this did not prevent the later interpolation of previously written numbers either by these or by other composers. This music was calculated to have an immediate appeal and was hoped to have a hit tune in it somewhere. The composers were often highly trained musicians whose craftsmanship was of a high order and whose facility guaranteed an instant response to a request for a new number.

The cult of 'the girl' in musical comedy is obvious from the very titles of the works. A short selection of British musical comedies from the years 1893 to 1913 (with the number of performances each achieved on its first appearance) could include *The Casino Girl* (196), *The Circus Girl* (497), *A Country Girl* (729), *The Earl and the Girl* (371), *A Gaiety Girl* (413), *The Girl from Kay's* (432), *The Girl from Utah* (195), *The Girl in the Taxi* (385), *The Girl in the Train* (340), *My Girl* (183), *The Pearl Girl* (254), *The Quaker Girl* (536), *The Shop Girl* (546), *The Sunshine Girl* (336) and *A Runaway Girl* (593). (A similar list could be made for the USA, e.g. *The Motor Girl*, *The Yankee Girl*, *The Wall Street Girl*, *The Charity Girl*, and so on.) Although 'the girl' appears so frequently, the tendency was to emphasize 'the lady'. In contrast to the tights and short skirts of Victorian burlesque, costumes were expensive and elegant. This elegance, and sometimes a studied simplicity, is well illustrated in the mass-produced photographs eagerly purchased by the public. The ladies of musical comedy are picture postcard beauties *par excellence*. Not infrequently their lives had outcomes like their roles. The Baroness Churston, the Countess of Dudley, the Countess of Drogheda, Countess Poulett, the Marchioness of Headfort and others were recruited to the peerage from the musical comedy stage.

The promoters of musical comedy aimed at long runs and big profits. The performance figures noted above are not exceptional. It is true that some shows did not achieve 183 performances, but others exceeded 729, notably *A Chinese Honeymoon* (1901) with 1075 and the remarkable *Chu-Chin-Chow* (His [Her] MAJESTY'S THEATRE, London; 1916) with 2238. As well as these initial runs there were frequent revivals and there were touring versions playing not only in Britain but in America and Australia as well. GEORGE EDWARDES, whose principal London theatres were the GAIETY and Daly's, is regarded as the prime architect of musical comedy – if someone whose sole gift seems to have been spotting what would keep the paybox busy can be called an architect. He is said to have had as many as 16 touring companies roaming Britain. The distinctions between musical comedy and OPERETTA on the one hand and REVUE on the other are often very blurred. A European operetta that was transmogrified into a most successful English musical comedy was *The Merry Widow* (Daly's, 1907) by Franz Lehar (1870–1948). This was followed by further adaptations of Lehar's, and he was only one of the Continental composers upon whom English musical comedy fastened.

But the years after the First World War saw the gradual decline of musical comedy of the distinctive Edwardian kind. The cinema began to vie with the theatre in spectacle, the cult of the film star replaced that of the picture postcard beauty, up-to-the-minute references became the province of revue, and the somewhat effete melodiousness of the old music was challenged by jazz. These influences were markedly American. America and England had had a musical comedy import-export relationship. Now America was growing in independence. Composers such as JEROME KERN and GEORGE GERSHWIN added lustre to the musical theatre, and native American librettists adopted an increasingly contemporary American outlook. In England the old style was a long time a-dying, but after the Second World War the influence of the vitality, coherence, wit, seriousness and even political awareness to be found in American MUSICAL THEATRE had an overwhelming effect and the old kind of musical comedy was gone, replaced by what was merely called 'the musical'. Musicals such as *Cabaret* (1966) and *Evita* (1978) belong to the same family as musical comedies such as *A Gaiety Girl* (1893) and *The Belle of New York* (1897), but their relationship is not the closest, nor is it free of the bar sinister.   GH

musical theatre, American The first musical performances on the American stage occurred during the colonial period, when BALLAD OPERAS were presented by touring companies of English actors. After the Revolution (1776–83), resident composers and writers created the first American comic OPERAS. Notable among these was *The Archers*, with book and lyrics by WILLIAM DUNLAP and music by Benjamin Carr.

By the 1840s several types of European entertainment were contributing to the growth of American musical theatre. Burlesque reached the USA in the 1830s, and by the 1850s there were numerous American burlesques on native subjects, such as JOHN BROUGHAM's *Po-ca-hon-tas; or, The Gentle Savage* (1855). Another imported form that proved popular with American audiences was the spectacle, which made use of lavish scenery and special effects as well as music and dance to tell its story. Meanwhile, the MINSTREL SHOW brought a uniquely American form of musical entertainment to its audience.

Theatre activity in the USA was retarded by the Civil War. After the war, pantomime reached the height of its appeal in America with *Humpty Dumpty* (1868) starring GEORGE W. L. FOX, while BURLESQUE received a boost from periodic visits by the English star LYDIA THOMPSON and her troupe of 'British Blondes'. Minstrelsy continued to be popular, with several companies establishing permanent theatres in the larger cities in addition to taking advantage of the expanding railways to tour the country.

Despite the existence of this lively and diverse assortment of musical forms, the event most often singled out as

Backstage during *The Black Crook*, 1866. Ladies of the ballet preparing to 'fly'.

the starting point of American musical theatre is the production of *The Black Crook* in 1866. This show, created when a MELODRAMA on Faustian lines was augmented with dances by a French ballet company stranded in New York, is viewed as a primitive example of MUSICAL COMEDY because of its use of music, dance and spectacle, as well as scantily clad chorus girls, in the telling of its story. *The Black Crook* was successfully revived a number of times during the 19th century, and spawned a host of imitators. Other spectacles combined elaborate settings with a burlesque of some classical or current literary work in a form called 'extravaganza'. *Evangeline*, the most popular show of this type, opened in 1874 and toured the country in various revivals for the rest of the century.

OPÉRA BOUFFE, particularly the works of Jacques Offenbach, had a vogue on the American stage in the 1870s and 80s, when noted French singers were imported to the USA by impresario Maurice Grau. Also available to audiences were native entertainments such as the Mulligan Guard series of musical plays, created and performed by EDWARD HARRIGAN AND TONY HART, depicting life among New York's Irish, Germans and blacks.

The triumphant American premiere of GILBERT and Sullivan's *HMS Pinafore* in 1879 made British comic opera the dominant musical form for the rest of the century. Most distinguished of the American composers of comic opera was REGINALD DE KOVEN, whose *Robin Hood* (1891) was frequently revived. Since comic opera plots typically combined high-flown romantic fantasy with comic horseplay, star billing often went to comedians such as JEFFERSON DE ANGELIS, DE WOLF HOPPER, FRANCIS WILSON and EDDIE FOY.

Most musical theatre librettos in this period were constructed in such a way as to allow for interpolations of unrelated songs and dances by members of the company. This taste for unrelated specialities – also found in the olio portion of the minstrel show and the second act of FARCE comedies such *The Brook* (1879) – led to the development of the REVUE, a form of musical theatre in which songs, dances, comedy sketches and elaborate production numbers were loosely connected by a plot or recurring theme, such as a 'review' of the year's events. The first American revue was *The Passing Show* (1894).

In the last decade of the 19th century, comic opera and *opéra bouffe* declined, while burlesque was given a temporary reprieve in the shows of WEBER AND FIELDS, many of which featured comic opera soprano LILLIAN RUSSELL. As the 1890s progressed, signs of change began to appear on the musical stage. In 1894, the Bostonians (the BOSTON IDEAL OPERA COMPANY) presented the comic opera *Prince Ananias*, which contained the first full score by VICTOR HERBERT, destined to be one of the most important composers of OPERETTAS for the American stage. Also appearing in 1894 was *A Gaiety Girl*, a British musical that abandoned the exotic locales and stilted language of comic opera in favour of a contemporary setting and more topical humour. In 1898 two musicals written and performed by AFRICAN AMERICANS made their appearance: BOB COLE and Billy Johnson's *A Trip to Coontown*, and Paul Laurence Dunbar and Will Marion Cook's *The Origin of the Cakewalk; or, Clorindy*. Despite the warm reception these two shows received, few black artists were seen on the BROADWAY stage before the 1920s.

Comic opera, operetta, musical comedy and revue were the dominant forms on the American musical stage at the dawn of the new century. While New York was now the theatre capital of the country, the vast national system of railways made possible extensive tours for shows that had been a success on Broadway. The most successful show of the decade was *Florodora* (1900), a British comic opera. Victor Herbert continued to compose operettas such as *Babes in Toyland* (1903), *Mlle Modiste* (1905), *The Red Mill* (1906) and *Naughty Marietta* (1910). The increasing prestige of American operetta lured European opera stars such as Fritzi Scheff on to the musical stage.

With the arrival of Franz Lehár's *The Merry Widow* in New York in 1907, a vogue for Viennese operetta was launched that lasted until the advent of the First World War. In the same year, FLORENZ ZIEGFELD produced the *Follies of 1907*, the first in a series of annual revues that diverged from the traditional topical humour towards a greater emphasis on elaborate scenery, beautifully costumed chorus girls and star comedians and singers such as FANNY BRICE, BERT WILLIAMS and WILL ROGERS. The native comic tradition of Harrigan and Hart was continued by GEORGE M. COHAN in a series of musical comedies, such as *Little Johnny Jones* (1904), that emphasized contemporary characters and settings, wisecracking humour and a generous dose of patriotic sentiment.

Some significant innovations took place in the American musical stage during the First World War. Several of the shows written during that era rejected European styles in favour of American musical idioms, most notably ragtime. Developed by black musicians, ragtime was first heard on the musical stage in the form of individual songs interpolated into shows. In 1914 IRVING BERLIN composed a ragtime score for the revue *Watch Your Step*. Although it has been argued that many of Berlin's songs were not true ragtime, the success of his work brought ragtime to the forefront of musical styles for the legitimate stage.

Meanwhile, composer JEROME KERN and librettist GUY BOLTON (later joined by lyricist P. G. WODEHOUSE) were experimenting with small casts, simple settings and recognizable characters and situations in their Princess Theatre (New York) shows, such as *Very Good Eddie* (1915) and *Oh, Boy!* (1917). In the years immediately following the war, such musicals as *Irene* (1919) and Kern's own *Sally* (1920), which starred MARILYN MILLER, demonstrated that contemporary American plots and settings and fresh musical styles could be effectively employed in more elaborate shows.

Despite the changes being wrought in American musical comedy, the demand for operetta did not abate. A new generation of European-trained composers, most notably RUDOLF FRIML and SIGMUND ROMBERG, joined Victor Herbert in the creation of operetta for the American stage. Friml's scores during the 1920s included *Rose-Marie* (1924), *The Vagabond King* (1925) and *The Three Musketeers* (1928). Among Romberg's best works were *Maytime* (1918), *The Student Prince* (1924), *The Desert Song* (1926) and *The New Moon* (1928). American singers such as Vivienne Segal and Robert Halliday starred in many of these new operettas.

In the early postwar years a number of new revue series appeared, including the *Greenwich Village Follies*, GEORGE WHITE's *Scandals*, the *Music Box Revues*, the *Grand Street Follies* and EARL CARROLL's *Vanities*. The early 1920s also marked the reappearance of the black musical on the American stage: although there had been a few isolated efforts since the turn of the century, including *In Dahomey* (1903), *Abyssinia* (1906) and *The Shoo Fly Regiment* (1907), African Americans had their greatest impact on the Broadway musical stage in the 1920s. Beginning with SISSLE AND BLAKE's *Shuffle Along* (1921), a succession of black book musicals and revues popularized a form of jazz that replaced ragtime as the dominant musical comedy style, and also introduced many new dance steps, such as the Charleston, to the musical stage. In addition, a number of black performers, including BILL ROBINSON, Adelaide Hall and FLORENCE MILLS, were featured in shows created by whites.

During the 1920s a new generation of composers began to make their mark on the Broadway stage. Writing in the jazz-influenced style that had evolved in the years following the Princess Theatre shows, GEORGE AND IRA GERSHWIN had a series of successes with *Lady, Be Good!* (1924), *Tip-Toes* (1925), *Oh, Kay!* (1926) and *Funny Face* (1927). The Gershwins' tricky rhythms and sophisticated lyrics ideally suited the talents of GERTRUDE LAWRENCE and dancers FRED AND ADELE ASTAIRE. As the 1930s dawned, the Gershwins moved into political SATIRE with *Strike Up the Band* (1930) and the Pulitzer Prize-winning *Of Thee I Sing* (1931). Matching the Gershwins in sophistication were the new song-writing team of RICHARD RODGERS and LORENZ HART, whose successes in the 1920s included *The Garrick Gaieties* (1925), *Dearest Enemy* (1925), *A Connecticut Yankee* (1927) and *Present Arms* (1928). Other composers writing musical comedies in the 1920s included VINCENT YOUMANS and DESYLVA, BROWN AND HENDERSON.

Jerome Kern, who had pioneered the style of contemporary MUSICAL COMEDY so popular in the 1920s, took musical theatre in another direction when he composed *Show Boat* (1927), an operetta that used both traditional and contemporary musical idioms in depicting the lives of a family of showboat performers from the 1880s to the 1920s. With lyrics by OSCAR HAMMERSTEIN II, *Show Boat* pointed the way to the serious musical plays of the 1940s and 50s.

The 1927–8 season, with some 250 shows, was a quantitative high point in the history of the BROADWAY stage. Events outside of the theatre, including the advent of sound films and the stock market crash of 1929, would prevent it from ever again reaching that level of production. By the 1930–1 season there was a marked decline in the number of shows produced on Broadway, and those that did appear were usually presented on a more modest scale. Although Florenz Ziegfeld, George White and Earl Carroll were able to mount a few more spectacular editions of their trademark shows, most revues now emphasized singing, dancing and satiric comedy rather than expensive sets and costumes.

The musical theatre was invigorated at the end of the 1920s by the appearance of some new composers and lyricists. COLE PORTER wrote insinuating melodies and clever lyrics for a number of frothy musical comedies, including *Fifty Million Frenchmen* (1929), *The New Yorkers* (1930) and *Anything Goes* (1934), while the song-writing team of Arthur Schwartz and Howard Dietz brought a new, more subdued and melodic sound to their scores for the revues *The Little Show* (1929), *Three's a Crowd* (1930) and *The Band Wagon* (1931). Despite the appearance of these new contributors to the musical theatre, two of the more impressive musicals of the 1930s were created by composers, lyricists and librettists who had begun their careers in the previous decade: *Porgy and Bess* (1935) by the Gershwins (with DUBOSE HEYWARD) and *On Your Toes* (1936) by Rodgers and Hart (with choreography by GEORGE BALANCHINE).

As the Depression worsened, musicals began to reflect the country's growing unrest. In 1936 the GROUP THEATRE produced *Johnny Johnson*, a musical with an anti-war message; the following year the International Ladies' Garment Workers Union presented a 'socially significant' revue called *Pins and Needles*, with songs by Harold Rome; and in 1938 the MERCURY THEATRE offered MARC BLITZSTEIN's controversial capitalism versus labour parable, *The Cradle Will Rock*. This interest in the issues of the day was short-lived, however, for with the advent of the Second World War the musical theatre once again turned its back on political and social commentary in favour of escapist shows with flimsy plots. Nevertheless, a few musicals of the early 1940s demonstrated that the seriousness of the 30s had not entirely dissipated. Rodgers and Hart's *Pal Joey* (1940) had an amoral gigolo, played by Gene Kelly, for its hero, while the KURT WEILL–Ira Gershwin musical *Lady in the Dark* (1941) dealt with a mentally disturbed magazine editor (GERTRUDE LAWRENCE) whose problems were solved through psychoanalysis.

Musical theatre experienced another change in direction in 1943 as a result of the unprecedented popularity of *Oklahoma!*, the first musical by the new partnership of Richard Rodgers and Oscar Hammerstein II. *Oklahoma!*'s affirmation of the simple values of an earlier America gave it a broad and lasting appeal. Although it adhered in many ways to the traditions of operetta, its departures from standard musical theatre practice – such as allowing a murder to take place on stage and using a 'dream ballet' to amplify the dramatic action – made *Oklahoma!* the most influential and widely imitated musical of its day. Among the subsequent 'musical plays' created by Rodgers and Hammerstein were *Carousel* (1945), *South Pacific* (1949), *The King and I* (1951), *Flower Drum Song* (1958) and *The Sound of Music* (1959). MARY MARTIN, whose winsome personality and good humour made her an ideal Rodgers and Hammerstein heroine, starred in both *South Pacific* and *The Sound of Music*.

Despite the pervasive influence of Rodgers and Hammerstein, the formulaic musical comedy continued to flourish in the 1940s and early 50s. *Annie Get Your Gun*, with a score by Irving Berlin and a bravura performance by ETHEL MERMAN as backwoods sharpshooter Annie Oakley, opened to critical acclaim in 1946. FRANK LOESSER received enthusiastic notices for *Guys and Dolls* (1950), a musical about Broadway gamblers and their perennial girlfriends. *Wonderful Town* (1953), by the team of LEONARD BERNSTEIN and COMDEN AND GREEN, dealt with life in New York's Greenwich Village in the 1930s. *Pajama Game*, a musical about management–labour strife in a pyjama factory, introduced the song-writing team of Richard Adler and Jerry Ross to Broadway in 1954. A year later *Damn Yankees*, also by Adler and Ross, combined the Faust legend with baseball, and elevated dancer GWEN VERDON to stardom.

In 1956, ALAN JAY LERNER AND FREDERICK LOEWE adapted BERNARD SHAW's comedy *Pygmalion* into the musical *My Fair Lady*. Like *Show Boat* and *Oklahoma!* before it, *My Fair Lady* changed the course of musical theatre: its opulent OLIVER SMITH setting and CECIL BEATON period costumes inspired a vogue for operettas set in bygone eras; the matchless performance of REX HARRISON as Henry Higgins inaugurated a trend towards hiring actors rather than singers for important musical theatre roles; and the skill with which Lerner converted the Shaw play into a musical led other librettists to concentrate on adapting already successful plays, films and novels rather than creating original librettos.

Although they had changed greatly in the past two decades, the two basic threads of musical theatre, operetta and musical comedy, continued to flourish from the mid-1950s until the mid-60s. As usual, the operettas tended to be the more elaborate and ambitious works. Leonard Bernstein, ARTHUR LAURENTS, STEPHEN SONDHEIM and JEROME ROBBINS based *West Side Story* (1957) on the Romeo and Juliet legend. The song-writing team of JERRY BOCK AND SHELDON HARNICK caught the flavour of European operetta with *She Loves Me* (1963; successfully revived in 1993), and in the following year created one of the most popular of all American musicals, *Fiddler on the Roof*. *Man of La Mancha*, based on Cervantes's *Don Quixote*, received excellent reviews when it opened in 1965.

The creators of musical comedy tried to vary the traditional formulas by exploring new settings and subjects. *Gypsy* (1959) was based on the life of stripper GYPSY ROSE LEE. *Fiorello* (1959) followed the career of New York mayor Fiorello La Guardia. *How to Succeed in Business without Really Trying* (1961) satirized corporate back-stabbing and in-fighting. *Hello, Dolly!*, while blazing no new trails in subject-matter, made more extensive use of dance than was the custom in musical comedy. *Cabaret* (1966) was set in the decadent Berlin of the 1930s. *Hair* (1968) brought a more authentic rock sound and nudity to the Broadway musical stage.

Music, particularly rock, was an integral part of many ALTERNATIVE THEATRE pieces of the 1950s and 60s, such as Megan Terry's *Viet Rock* (1966). Traditional notions of musical theatre were challenged by a number of OFF-BROADWAY and OFF-OFF BROADWAY artists, notably composer-lyricist-librettist Al Carmines, who created several experimental musicals, including *Peace* (1968) and *Promenade* (1969), the latter with book and lyrics by MARIA IRENE FORNÉS. Several more traditional shows produced Off-Broadway, such as *The Fantasticks* (1960; still running in 1993) and *Dames at Sea* (1968), demonstrated anew that elaborate spectacle was not a necessary component of the musical stage; and several modest shows produced in nightclubs and Off-Broadway theatres by Ben Bagley and Julius Monk continued the revue custom of emphasizing satire and topical humour.

By the beginning of the 1970s, however, it had become clear that the musical theatre was failing to develop new artists and audiences. The Off-Off Broadway revolution was fading away, having contributed relatively few new performers, composers or choreographers to the mainstream theatre. On Broadway an increasing number of revivals of older shows, coupled with revues created out of the songs of veteran composers, held the stage. The only new composer-lyricist to contribute importantly to the musical theatre in the 1970s was Stephen Sondheim. His brilliant but often controversial shows of the 1970s and 80s included *Company* (1970), *Follies* (1971), *A Little Night Music* (1973), *Pacific Overtures* (1976), *Sweeney Todd* (1979), *Merrily We Roll Along* (1981), *Sunday in the Park with George* (1984) and *Into the Woods* (1987). Aided by orchestrator Jonathan Tunick, Sondheim created a unique sound using electronic instruments and tempered rock rhythms. His lyrics were often cerebral, unflinching and cynical.

The Sondheim shows produced and directed by HAROLD PRINCE popularized the 'concept musical', a show in which the director and designers, instead of attempting to translate a pre-existing libretto and score into theatrical terms during rehearsals, collaborate with the composer, lyricist and librettist during the creation of the show, so that every element is conceived in terms of production. Because of the emergence of the concept musical – and because so few new composers, lyricists and librettists of stature appeared during the period – the musical theatre of the 1970s and 80s was dominated by the choreographer-director. Such shows as BOB FOSSE's *Pippin* (1972), *Chicago* (1975) and *Dancin'* (1978), MICHAEL BENNETT's *A Chorus Line* (1975) and *Dreamgirls* (1981), and TOMMY TUNE's *Nine* (1982) and *The Will Rogers Follies* (1991) benefited immeasurably from the imaginative and energetic staging that their director-choreographers created for them. The concept musical went out of fashion in the 1980s as its most talented practitioners died or retired; by the end of the decade and into the 1990s only Tommy Tune (MICHAEL KIDD returned to direct *The Goodbye Girl* in 1992) was still actively creating shows for the Broadway stage. Producers turned instead to shows with librettos based on vintage Hollywood films, such as *Grand Hotel* (1989), *City of Angels* (1989), *Nick and Nora* (1991, a disappointing $4.3 million failure that had been under development for several years), *Red Shoes* (1993, an $8 million loss), and ANDREW LLOYD WEBBER's *Sunset Boulevard* (1993, London; 1994, New York).

The period of the 1970s and 80s was a time of reassessment of the musical theatre in the light of rising production costs and prohibitive ticket prices. Many artists and producers preferred to work in the more relaxed surroundings of Off- or Off-Off Broadway, some of their more successful creations eventually finding their way to the Broadway theatre. Also contributing shows to Broadway were regional theatres, notably the Goodspeed Opera House in East Haddam, Connecticut, where *Annie* premiered, and South Coast Rep in California, where the revised version of the rock musical *Tommy* was developed. Since relatively few American musicals were produced each year, writers, directors and performers often worked more frequently in film and television than in live theatre.

The current generation of musical theatre stars, such as Mandy Patinkin and Bernadette Peters, appeared only sporadically on the Broadway stage. The dearth of American musicals led producers to look to Europe and Great Britain for new shows: *Les Misérables* and *Miss Saigon* were created by a French song-writing team, while Andrew Lloyd Webber took to New York a number of his London successes such as *Cats*, *Phantom of the Opera* and, in 1994, *Sunset Boulevard*. Even the KANDER AND EBB *Kiss of the Spider Woman* had success in Toronto and London before it opened on Broadway in 1993 (and won the Tony for Best Musical).

Sometimes called the only uniquely American contribution to world theatre, the Broadway musical faces some severe economic and artistic tests in the years to come. MK

See: G. Bordman, *American Musical Theatre: A Chronicle*, 2nd edn, New York, 1992; D. Ewen, *New Complete Book of the American Musical Theatre*, New York, 1970; M. Gottfried, *Broadway Musicals*, New York, 1979; M. Gottfried, *More Broadway Musicals*, New York, 1991; S. Green, *Encyclopedia of the Musical Theatre*, New York, 1976; S. Green, *Broadway Musicals: Show by Show*, Milwaukee, Wis., 1985; A. J. Lerner, *The Musical Theatre*, New York, 1978; G. Mast, *Can't Help Singin'*, Woodstock, NY, 1987; J. Mates, *The American Musical Stage Before 1800*, New York, 1962, and *America's Musical Stage: Two Hundred Years of Musical Theatre*, Westport, Conn., 1985; S. L. Porter, *With an Air Debonair: Musical Theatre in America 1785–1815*, Washington, DC, 1991; T. L. Riis, *Just before Jazz: Black Musical Theater in New York, 1890 to 1915*, Washington, DC, 1989; C. Smith and G. Litton, *Musical Comedy in America*, New York, 1981; J. P. Swain, *The Broadway Musical: A Critical and Musical Survey*, New York, 1990; A. Woll, *Black Musical Theatre from Coontown to Dreamgirls*, Baton Rouge, La., 1989.

Musser, Tharon 1925– American lighting designer (see STAGE LIGHTING). Musser began her career as designer and stage manager for the José Limon Dance Company and made her BROADWAY debut with the premiere production of *A Long Day's Journey into Night*. By the late 1960s she was probably the dominant lighting designer on Broadway. Her versatility is apparent from her credits, which include several seasons with the AMERICAN SHAKESPEARE [THEATRE] Festival, all of NEIL SIMON's plays since *Prisoner of Second Avenue* (1971) and MUSICALS such as *Mame*. From 1975 she teamed up with designers ROBIN WAGNER and THEONI ALDREDGE and the late director MICHAEL BENNETT to design *A Chorus Line*, *Dreamgirls* and several others. Her style ranges from flashy production numbers to painstakingly researched re-creations of specific light qualities and moods (such as *A Little Night Music*, 1973). AA

Musset, Alfred de 1810–57 French poet and dramatist. For a long time thought of as a poet, Musset's stature as a dramatist has increased steadily since the beginning of the 20th century. His earliest plays appeared in a volume of verse, *Tales of Spain and Italy* (1830). After the failure of his first performed work, *La Nuit vénitienne* (ODÉON 1830),

he published his plays as armchair theatre. In 1837 his one-act dramatic proverb *Un Caprice* was performed in St Petersburg by a French actress, and the play entered the repertoire of the COMÉDIE-FRANÇAISE in 1847. From this date Musset wrote with the theatre directly in view, and created new stage versions of earlier plays, published in editions of his work after 1851. After his death his brother Paul also reworked some of the plays.

Musset's main creative period extends from 1833 to 1837 – with *André del Sarto* and *Les Caprices de Marianne* (1833), *Fantasio*, *On ne badine pas avec l'amour* (*Love Is Not to Be Trifled With*) and *Lorenzaccio* (1834), *La Quenouille de Barberine* (*Barberine's Distaff*) and *Le Chandelier* (1835), *Il ne faut jurer de rien* (*Nothing Is Certain*, 1836) and *Un Caprice* (1837). This period corresponds largely with his traumatic relationship with George Sand, and its aftermath. The best of his later plays are *Il faut qu'une porte soit ouverte ou fermée* (*A Door Must Either Be Open or Shut*, 1845) and *Carmosine* (1850). Most of the plays, especially the dramatic proverbs, concern conflicts between the sexes, with detailed psychological observation and an emphasis on sub-text. Musset's women are usually idealized or regarded as false and heartless. The young Musset stated that he wanted to be SHAKESPEARE or SCHILLER. The structure of his plays, not written with specific production in mind, has a fluidity reminiscent of the Elizabethans, with a number of short scenes focusing on different groups of characters, rather than the traditional French construction in long unbroken acts. *Lorenzaccio*, often called the French *Hamlet*, has 34 scenes and an army of characters. Here the emphasis is on the identity of the central figure, who ceases to be able to distinguish between his 'real' self and the mask he wears (the double is a favourite Musset theme).

The morality of Musset's plays worried the censors. The end of *André del Sarto* had to be rewritten, and *Le Chandelier* had to be taken off at the Comédie-Française in 1852 (see CENSORSHIP). *Lorenzaccio*, with its overt attacks on the monarchy of Louis Philippe and on the bourgeoisie, was unperformable in the 1830s, forbidden under the Second Empire, and only reached the stage, much adapted and reduced, with SARAH BERNHARDT in 1896. Since then a number of actresses have tried the role of the hero, including Marguerite Jamois in BATY's famous production of 1945, which, played with properties against a black background, restored the original rhythm and fluidity of the play. It became an established classic of the THÉÂTRE NATIONAL POPULAIRE repertoire with GÉRARD PHILIPE's more muscular performance at Avignon in 1952. Musset was particularly interested in the actress RACHEL, to whom he dedicated an important essay on TRAGEDY, and for whom he wrote an abandoned play, *La Servante du roi* (*The King's Handmaid*). JMCC

mystery play A term in general use in English; but its meaning (a play with biblical or apocryphal subject-matter) unfortunately varies when used as a translation of the French *mystère*. Unlike the English usage the French dates from the Middle Ages and can refer to any 'historical' narrative: biblical, apocryphal or hagiographical. In English, because of the nature of the surviving texts, the term often has overtones of a series (or 'cycle') of short plays ('pageants'): the York and Chester plays, for example, are often referred to as 'mystery cycles'. *The Mysteries* was the title chosen for TONY HARRISON's NATIONAL THEATRE adaptation of the plays (1985). The term can loosely cover the French *mystère, passion*; German *Osterspiel, Passion*; Italian *sacra rappresentazione*; Spanish AUTOS SACRAMEN-TALES – but it is not really helpful to straitjacket different national traditions.   PM

nadagama Form of SRI LANKAN folk theatre, said to have been introduced by Catholic missionaries from south INDIA in the early 19th century. Although its original intention seems to have been to proselytize the religion, it soon added non-religious stories to its repertory and thrived along the whole western coastal region of the island. The plays, many of which are available in script form, are long and episodic. They deal with the exploits of heroic characters who encounter numerous dramatic challenges in love and war. The Tamil and Sinhalese languages mix freely in the works, indicating that they were particularly popular among the Tamil-speaking minority of the region.

Phillipu Sinno is regarded as the author of many of the works and the legendary father of *nadagama*. Little is known about the man except that he was a popular versifier and a blacksmith born in Colombo in the late 18th century. No less than 13 plays are attributed to him.

Nadagama performances take place in a village and are acted on a semicircular raised platform. A roof shelters the acting area and painted scenery separates acting from dressing areas. No front curtain is used. Entrances are made from the side of the stage near which the Presenter (Pote Gura) stands and sings verses to introduce each character. The Presenter is joined by two other musicians who serve as a chorus, repeating each line of the song. Seated on the floor at the opposite side of the stage are two drummers, the *horana* and cymbal players. In recent times a violin and a harmonium have been added to the musical ensemble. A unique feature of the *nadagama* is the use of musical techniques adapted from south India and later from the more popular Hindustani music of north India. The audience gains entrance to the performance area by paying a small price for seating space on the ground or a slightly higher price to sit in a chair.

A performance begins when the Presenter chants introductory stanzas paying homage to the deities and asking their protection for a successful performance. Then he describes the plot of the story and craves the audience's indulgence. Next he introduces the stock characters, one by one, beginning with the jester. Punctuating the jester's dances, the Presenter asks questions which provoke humorous responses. The next character to be introduced is the Sellan Lama, a wise man who is learned in the 64 arts and sciences. Then come two Desanavadi, characters who foretell the future, and by doing so give insight into the story to be enacted. Next the drummers employed in the royal court enter and announce in a declamatory tone the arrival of the king. Last the king's criers enter making way for the king. He summons various characters of his court who make ceremonial entrances in dance and song. Finally the dramatic action gets under way.

A traditional *nadagama* play takes a week to enact, each night's episode lasting from about 9 p.m. until midnight. FaR

Nakamura Utaemon VI 1917– Japanese actor; second son of Utaemon V (1866–1940), the most esteemed living KABUKI actor of female roles. He is a Living National Treasure and President of the Japanese Actors Association. He took the name Kotarō at 5, Fukusuke VI at 16, Shikan VI at 24, and his present name at the age of 34. He projects a willowy elegance and, overcoming a physical handicap, he excels in dance roles, as in *Sumida River* (*Sumidagawa*) and *Maid of Dōjō Temple* (*Musume Dōjōji*). His mature performances retain youthful delicacy while projecting powerful emotion. JRB

naluyuks Inuit Twelfth Night mummers of northern Labrador, literally 'heathens'. Groups of MASKed young men, disguised in bear skins or sacking, visit houses where there are children, interrogating them on their behaviour and distributing presents. In return, the children are required to sing a Christmas carol. Formal behaviour inside turns to boisterousness outside: spectators are chased and harassed, special attention being devoted to social undesirables, with the encouragement of the crowd. The tradition has both indigenous and European elements. AEG

Nansen, Betty 1873–1943 Danish actress and director. In 1917 Nansen transformed a small Copenhagen playhouse (later renamed Betty Nansen-Teatret) into an art theatre specializing in IBSEN, BJØRNSON, STRINDBERG and contemporary European and American drama. She introduced PIRANDELLO's *Six Characters in Search of an Author* to Denmark, as well as plays by TOLLER, the ČAPEKS, O'NEILL and SHAW; she also presented new Danish plays rejected by other theatres, such as MUNK's *The Word*. Her work as an actress echoed the 19th-century grand manner, but had focus, authority and psychological complexity. Among her major roles were Hedda Gabler and Mrs Alving, which she also played in Paris. HL.

Napier, John 1944– British stage designer primarily associated with the ROYAL SHAKESPEARE COMPANY, who studied sculpture in art school before receiving THEATRE DESIGN training under RALPH KOLTAI at London's Central School. Rejecting decorative, pictorial design conventions, his early work revealed highly selective realism and a sculptor's sense of space. More recently, he has become known for found-art and pop-art assemblages with which he creates unusual stage environments frequently involving complex mechanisms and basic reconstructions of stage and auditorium. Representative productions include *Nicholas Nickleby* (1980), *Cats* (1981), *Les Misérables* (1985), *Miss Saigon* (1989) and *Sunset Boulevard* (1993). JMB

Nash, 'Jolly' John 1830–1901 British MUSIC-HALL artist; former Gloucestershire metal-worker, billed as 'the Laughing Blacksmith'. An early protégé of CHARLES MORTON, Nash appeared at the Oxford Music Hall in London in 1861, was the first music-hall artist to perform at royal command, and one of the first British VARIETY performers to tour the USA, in 1874. He was a musician and a specialist in silly walks; his act centred on laughing songs such as the famous 'Little Brown Jug'.   AEG

Nashe, Thomas 1567–c.1601 English pamphleteer and playwright, known as one of the UNIVERSITY WITS and associated with LYLY, ROBERT GREENE and MARLOWE, with the last of whom he collaborated on *Dido, Queen of Carthage* (c.1587). The vigour and exuberance of Nashe's prose are splendidly displayed in the pamphlet, *Pierce Penilesse* (1592), and the picaresque tale, *The Unfortunate Traveller* (1594). His surviving play, *Summer's Last Will and Testament* (c.1593), is comparatively subdued. It is a courtly entertainment, probably presented before Archbishop Whitgift. The punning title refers not only to summer's yielding to autumn, but also to Henry VIII's famous jester, Will Summers. Evidently more characteristic of the combative Nashe was *The Isle of Dogs* (1597), a collaboration with BEN JONSON. This lost play so offended the authorities when performed at the SWAN that a Privy Council order for the destruction of all London's theatres was issued. For unknown reasons, the order was not obeyed, but neither the Swan nor Pembroke's Men, who had performed the play, ever recovered.   PT

Nathan, George Jean 1882–1958 American critic. Born of wealthy parents in Fort Wayne, Indiana, Nathan graduated from Cornell University in 1904 and studied abroad for a year at the University of Bologna (1905). In 1906 he worked as a reporter for the *New York Herald*, after which he reviewed plays for *Outing* and the *Bohemian*. He became drama critic of *Smart Set*, in 1909 joining H. L. Mencken, who had been hired in 1908 to review books. The two served as co-editors during 1914–24 and made *Smart Set* a cult publication among young intellectuals. Their irreverence and iconoclasm seemed to epitomize a generation attempting to rid itself of the Genteel Tradition. They founded the *American Mercury* in 1923 but quarrelled in 1924, with Nathan continuing only as drama critic until 1932. He founded and edited the *American Spectator* (1932–5), then reviewed for numerous publications including *Newsweek*, *Theatre Arts [Monthly]*, *Saturday Review* and *Esquire*. Influenced by JAMES G. HUNEKER and GEORGE BERNARD SHAW, Nathan wrote in a lively, impressionistic style and fought for a drama of ideas. He became a champion of EUGENE O'NEILL, publishing his early plays in *Smart Set*, and arranging for professional productions of his work. He reviewed musical REVUES, noting that 'Good drama is anything that interests an intelligently emotional group of persons assembled together in an illuminated hall.' His reputation declined after his death because his 'hot' impressionistic style cooled with age, and many of his opinions after 1930 proved to be erroneous.

Nathan reworked his criticism into books, which appeared almost every year during 1915–53. From 1943 to 51 he published an annual *Theatre Book of the Year*. In 1955 he married actress Julie Haydon, the original Laura in *The Glass Menagerie*, and in his will left a provision for the George Jean Nathan Award for Dramatic Criticism to be given annually.   TLM

National Theatre (Britain) The long struggle to establish a national theatre began in the 18th century with calls from DAVID GARRICK, but received widespread support only in 1848 with the appearance of a proposition from the publisher, Effingham Wilson, for a theatre and drama school to be built at Stratford-upon-Avon in the name of SHAKESPEARE, 'the world's greatest moral teacher'. This proposal won the support of the dramatist-MP BULWER LYTTON, HENRY IRVING and Alfred Lyttelton, the father of the National Theatre's first chairman, Oliver Lyttelton (Lord Chandos). Matthew Arnold was converted to the cause when in 1879 he saw the COMÉDIE-FRANÇAISE for the first time. His essay 'The French Play in London' in the magazine *Nineteenth Century* concluded with a much quoted clarion call, 'The theatre is irresistible, organize the theatre!'

The first serious attempts to establish a national theatre, however, came in 1907 with the publication of a detailed scheme, with financial estimates, prepared by the critic WILLIAM ARCHER and HARLEY GRANVILLE BARKER, then at the height of his influence as a director and dramatist. This led to the formation of a Shakespeare Memorial National Theatre committee, with broad support within the acting profession, which raised £100,000 in five years. A Private Member's Bill was introduced into the House of Commons in 1913 to 'crown' this sum with money from the public exchequer – and was passed, though not with a sufficiently large majority to make it effective. A site was bought in Bloomsbury, London, but all future plans were halted by the First World War.

Between the wars, the cause was upheld by the British Drama League through the efforts of its general secretary, Geoffrey Whitworth, and its president, Granville Barker. The Bloomsbury site was sold and another bought in Kensington. Sir Edwin Lutyens designed an imposing building which would have faced the Victoria and Albert Museum. But the funds were never forthcoming, either from private or from public sources, and supporters of the OLD VIC, including LILIAN BAYLIS, actively opposed the SMNT campaign. During the Second World War, a reconciliation took place between Geoffrey Whitworth of the SMNT committee and Sir Reginald Rowe of the Vic–Wells Trust, which cleared the way for eventual London County Council and parliamentary support. A bill was passed in 1948 which allocated one million pounds from public funds to build a national theatre on the south bank of the Thames. A design was commissioned from a fresh architect, Brian O'Rorke, and in 1951, in a third ceremonial laying of a foundation stone, Queen Elizabeth, deputizing for King George VI, laid a trough of mortar in what afterwards turned out to be the wrong place.

These plans were for various reasons delayed, until LAURENCE OLIVIER lent his support to the cause. He was appointed the National Theatre's first director and it was decided to form a National Theatre company which could operate at the Old Vic until its new theatre building was completed. The National Theatre opened at the Old Vic with a production of *Hamlet* in 1963 and the first seasons were triumphantly successful, with Olivier's Othello, PETER SHAFFER's *The Royal Hunt of the Sun* and FARQUHAR's *The Recruiting Officer* providing highlights. Meanwhile, a new architect, Denys Lasdun, was chosen to design a major new complex which contained three theatres – the open-stage Olivier, the proscenium-arch Lyttelton and the experimental 'black-box' Cottesloe – together with large foyers, workshops, restaurants and dressing rooms. The stage technology was considered to be in advance of its time.

The costs rose beyond those anticipated by parliament and the delays were considerable. The new National Theatre complex eventually opened piecemeal in 1976–7. Olivier had given way as director to PETER HALL in 1973 and the company found itself surrounded by controversies. Some issues were short-lived, occasioned by the high costs of running the new building. Others were more fundamental, in that high subsidies to the National Theatre were regarded with envy by grant-aided REGIONAL managements and with distrust by WEST END commercial companies. Furthermore, the National Theatre had deviated from the original intention of providing a classic repertoire along the lines of Continental theatre companies and was venturing into deals with commercial theatre companies. The bulk of the profits from the Peter Shaffer hit, *Amadeus*, launched at the National Theatre in 1979, went to the SHUBERT ORGANIZATION in the United States, which owned the rights. This was far from the original scheme proposed by Archer and Granville Barker.

Despite some loss of the original idealism, Hall managed to bring together a talented team of writers, directors and designers to work at the National Theatre, including PETER GILL, DAVID HARE and BILL BRYDEN. Under Richard Eyre, who succeeded Hall as director in 1988, the Theatre went through another transformation. Eyre had been responsible for one of the NT's greatest hits, the revival of *Guys and Dolls* (1982), and while classic plays still formed a large part of the Theatre's repertoire, as they do with almost any repertory company, the emphasis was upon teams of mainly young writers and directors who were given the opportunity to use the resources of the big and small stages as they thought fit. This led to some exciting (*Angels in America*, 1992) and not-so-exciting (*Square Rounds*, 1992) experimental theatre, some strange readings of Shakespeare (ROBERT LEPAGE's *A Midsummer Night's Dream*, 1992) and several popular hits, although it would have astonished Matthew Arnold and most NT pioneers to have found a revival of a 1940s MUSICAL playing for six months on one of the NT's main stages (*Carousel*, 1992). They would have been equally surprised by the virtuosity of the young directors, such as NICHOLAS HYTNER and STEPHEN DALDRY, who learned to take advantage of the technically advanced stage equipment. Daldry's productions of *An Inspector Calls* (1992) and *Machinal* (1993) transformed old-fashioned WELL MADE PLAYS into expressionist extravaganzas (see EXPRESSIONISM).

In one sense, the logic which brought the NT into existence was turned into reverse. It had been intended that it should be a living academy for British theatre, retaining the old theatrical skills in an atmosphere of scholarship; but it became a different kind of research centre, where professionals learned, among other matters, the tricks of computerized lighting systems. Eyre's NT demonstrated the virtues of a postmodern National Theatre, putting on glittering productions of a wide range of plays and similar theatrical happenings, where no distinctions were made

between high and low art, and the various less-than-modest claims for actors' and director's theatres were scrupulously avoided. It became a lively, unpompous and cheerful playground on the South Bank, where SHAKESPEARE, ALAN BENNETT and RODGERS and HAMMERSTEIN could meet on equal terms before (mainly) large and enthusiastic audiences.   JE

National Theatre (Washington, DC) In 1834, the first National Theatre opened its doors through the financial support of six Washington businessmen, who decided that the city needed a new place of entertainment. Fires destroyed the house in 1845, 57, 73 and 85, and all but obliterated the early features in the rebuilt versions. In 1885, the theatre was completely redesigned, and is the structure that still stands. The fortunes of the National followed the pattern typical of the 19th-century playhouse, beginning with a resident STOCK COMPANY and ending as a theatre for booked-in performances. During long periods in the 20th century the house was not used. Owned and renovated in 1984 by the Pennsylvania Avenue Development Corporation, it is leased to the SHUBERT ORGANIZATION, which manages the theatre and books its touring BROADWAY attractions.   MCH

National Youth Theatre (Britain) The actor, novelist and schoolmaster Michael Croft (d.1986) founded this organization in 1956, primarily to give his young school actors a chance to take part in a SHAKESPEARE play, directed to professional standards, during the summer holidays. At first the actors came from Alleyn's School in Southeast London where Croft taught and Dulwich College nearby, but after the NYT successes at the EDINBURGH FESTIVAL and in London, students from all over Britain went to audition.

During the 1960s, the NYT summer seasons which were held in various London theatres, such as the Jeannetta Cochrane in Holborn, began to include contemporary plays. The NYT produced DAVID HALLIWELL's *Little Malcolm* in 1965 and, with spectacular success, gave the premiere of PETER TERSON's *Zigger Zagger* in 1967, in which the songs of the football terraces mingling with a gentle warning against soccer hooliganism provided the structure for the most popular school play that has yet been written. Terson wrote several other plays for the NYT, as did Barrie Keefe in the 1970s; but the fortunes of the company were changed when they moved into the Shaw Theatre in Marylebone Road, owned by Camden Council. Here they launched the Dolphin Company, a professional group which played in the theatre when it was not wanted for the NYT seasons. In 1981, when the NYT's small grant from the ARTS COUNCIL was withdrawn, the company received sponsorship from the oil company, Texaco. Among the many famous actors to have emerged from the ranks of the NYT, DEREK JACOBI and HELEN MIRREN were shortly to be seen at the NATIONAL THEATRE and the ROYAL SHAKESPEARE COMPANY.   JE

Nationale Scene (Bergen) The National Stage, founded in 1876, is one of Norway's national theatres, with traditions beginning with the Norske Theater (1850–63), where IBSEN was resident playwright and stage director. Although the company endured poor premises until 1909, it was always aggressively innovative, premiering important plays before their Oslo productions: *The Wild Duck* (1885), *Rosmersholm* (1887), *The Master Builder* (1894) and *Little Eyolf* (1895). It has also been a training ground for important actors such as JOHANNE DYBWAD, Egil Eide, Ingolf Schanche and TORE SEGELCKE. Artistic directors have included GUNNAR HEIBERG (1884–8), HANS JACOB NILSEN (1934–8), STEIN BUGGE (1946–48) and KJETIL BANG-HANSEN (1982–6); Nilsen's and Bang-Hansen's tenures were especially distinguished. Since 1985, artistic director Tom Remlov has foregrounded new Norwegian plays. The main theatre has three stages, and the company collaborates with Bergen Internasjonale Teater in using the Teatergarasjen building, as in its celebrated 1992 adaptation of Amelie Skram's *The People of the Hellemyr.* HL

Nationaltheatret (Oslo) Norway's National Theatre opened in 1899, replacing the originally Danish-speaking Christiania Theater, founded in 1827. Its first director, BJØRN BJØRNSON, fought for its construction and assembled a first-rate company, despite the theatre's uncertain economic basis; it remained a private company until 1927, but is now fully state-subsidized. Its history has been one of brilliant acting rather than overall artistic importance, which partly reflects the decentralized nature of Norwegian theatre. In 1977 it opened the suburban Teatret på Torshov, where its most innovative work was done, especially under the direction of STEIN WINGE. An international Ibsen Festival was originated in 1990, but Nationaltheatret began the 1990s plagued by financial, administrative and artistic crises, including the closure of Teatret på Torshov. HL

Native-American ritual/theatre Native-American theatre is rooted in communal celebrations and ancient RITUALS reflecting the religious outlook and shared values of the indigenous nations that created it. Unlike Western drama, it is charged with cosmic significance that sets it apart from events in the ordinary world, and the 'audience' are participants rather than passive spectators. Because the native population contains many distinct nations, Native-American drama is diverse, ranging from the polished one-person dramas of storytellers and the improvisations of the SHAMANS to the Navajo chantways: 100-hour-long celebrations involving the entire community, in which no costume, word, gesture, movement or song is left to chance.

Native-American theatre encountered enormous difficulties. Conquest by whites destroyed entire nations, including, of course, their drama. The confinement of native peoples to reservations and the increasing dominance of Western culture often had a negative influence on the drama of nations that survived. The potlatch drama of the coastal Northwest, for example, in which the wealthy distributed gifts, degenerated from a mechanism for cementing the interrelationships of family and village into ostentatious displays of hierarchy and privilege. Nevertheless, many dramas, such as the Plains sun dances, the Cheyenne sacred arrow ceremony, the Iroquois false face drama and the Navajo chantways, survived into the 20th century and continued their time-honoured functions of uniting their communities and reinforcing traditional beliefs. In the 1970s Hanay Geiogamah's Native-American Theatre Ensemble used 'Western'-style drama to transmit Native-American traditions, values and aesthetics. Despite isolated attempts to encourage Native-American theatre and drama, there is only a small body of contemporary literary plays written by Native Americans, and performances by Native Americans about themselves and their native culture are infrequent. Annual powwows and ritualistic enactments continue, however.

Most frequently, Native Americans have been depicted and conceived by white writers for predominantly white audiences, contributing little to the understanding of the problems and frustrations of Native Americans. As one of a number of Native-American types seen on the American stage, the 'Indian' has been represented in over 600 plays from 1606 to the present (both South and North American aborigines). Most of these representations have inevitably been stereotyped, ranging from the noble savage to ruthless, varmint redskins or lazy, drunken, dissipated rascals, and from Indian princess to the squaw on the fringe of white society. MS DBW

naturalism Although naturalism and REALISM are often assumed to be synonymous, it is useful to distinguish between them. The term 'naturalism' refers to the scientifically based extension of realism propounded by ÉMILE ZOLA in the 1870s and 1880s. In naturalistic writing, medical and evolutionary theories of 19th-century science inform readings of human character and social interactions, which are seen as genetically and historically determined. The struggle of the individual to adapt to environment and the Darwinian idea of the survival of the fittest become central concerns of naturalistic fiction and drama.

Although naturalism in the arts is like realism in being a mimetic genre, it takes more explicit cognizance of environment, not merely as a setting but as an element of the action of drama. If the key play of realism is IBSEN's middle-class *Ghosts*, that of naturalism is LEV TOLSTOI's peasant *The Power of Darkness*, forbidden in Russia but played in Paris in 1886.

Among the plays often heralded as classics of naturalism are *The Selicke Family* of HOLZ and Schlaf, HAUPTMANN's *Weavers*, GORKY's *Lower Depths*, the minetown plays of D. H. LAWRENCE and the sea plays of EUGENE O'NEILL. These dramas depict a group in a hostile environment that is visible and sometimes palpable on stage; the group belongs to a distinctly less fortunate class than the usual bourgeois audience. Although such plays continued to be written – e.g. ARNOLD WESKER's *Roots* – the adjective 'naturalist' has fallen into disuse, replaced in English by 'kitchen-sink drama', in French by *théâtre du QUOTIDIEN*, in German by 'new realism'. RC

Naughton, Bill 1910–92 British dramatist, who started to write novels and short stories in the 1940s, after working as a lorry driver and weaver in Lancashire. His upbringing in Bolton provided the background for two gentle, ironic comedies, *All in Good Time* (1963) and *Spring and Port Wine* (1964). He became the natural successor to the dramatists of the Manchester school, HOUGHTON, BRIGHOUSE and later Walter Greenwood. But his range was wider than that of Lancashire comedy, for *Alfie* (1963), which provided JOHN NEVILLE with one of his best roles, concerned a Cockney 'wide boy' with a gift for 'pulling the birds'. Alfie's philandering was presented not in a censorious spirit, but with a cool sense of tragic waste, and the play became a parable for the 'swinging sixties', a sobering retort to JELLICOE's *The Knack*. Naughton also attempted Orwellian SATIRE, *He Was Gone When We Got There* (1966), and wrote his autography, *Pony Boy*, in 1966. JE

naumachia (Greek, meaning 'naval battle') Mimic sea combat, devised by the ancient Romans as a spectacular entertainment, staged by constructing basins in amphitheatres which were then flooded. The first on record was presented by Julius Caesar on a lake in the Campus Martius (46 BC), as a fight between a Tyrian and an Egyptian fleet, involving 2000 combatants and 4000 rowers; the brutality was striking. The Emperors Augustus and Titus also patronized such diversions, and under Claudius (AD 52) a crew of 19,000 gladiators and condemned criminals, costumed as Rhodians and Sicilians, fought and manoeuvred to their deaths. In later efforts, volunteers took part and crocodiles were employed for special effects. During the Renaissance, the *naumachia* was revived for both popular festivals and noble *divertissements*, especially at weddings. The marriage of Cosimo II Medici (1608) was celebrated by an *Argonautica* staged on the Arno; and a production of SENECA's *Hercules Furens* at Düsseldorf in 1585 was enhanced by such a show. One final efflorescence can be seen in the aquatic dramas produced by CHARLES DIBDIN at SADLER'S WELLS, London (1804–17). LS

nautanki One of the most beloved and popular forms of theatre, until recently, in the heavily populated central Indo-Gangetic plain of north INDIA (primarily Uttar Pradesh, Punjab, Rajasthan, Hariyana and Bihar states). A musical play entitled *The Story of Princess Nautanki* (*Shehzadi Nautanki*) may provide the origin of the name. It was popular in the 19th century, and evidence solidly suggests that it was closely related to SVANGA and *bhagat*.

Nautanki's popularity is due in part to the strong singing voices of its actors, who train to reach audiences sometimes numbering in the thousands, and to catchy rhythms produced on kettle drums (*nakkara*). It is said that spectators make up their minds to attend a *nautanki* performance on the basis of the reputation of the singers and the drummers. A typical company consists of 10 to 12 actors. Actors are generally Hindus of various lower castes; musicians are Muslims.

Nautanki may take place virtually anywhere, in an open space of a village, in a farmer's field, in the courtyard of a patron, in an enclosed proscenium theatre or under a tent (*shamyana*). A raised stage 3 to 4ft high is erected. Actors may commandeer the balcony or veranda of a nearby house or a tree in the village if needed. In early times the site was demarcated by a special post of wood inserted with great ceremony by the company head several days before the stage was erected. Performance is hired to celebrate a special occasion – a wedding, birth of a male child, festival occasion or fair.

The usually serious and highly moralistic dramas stress MELODRAMA and romantic love. They draw on mythology, history, semi-history, popular folklore and original sources. They are either epic or narrative in form. The stage manager (*ranga*) links diverse elements of the plot together. Following preliminary RITUALS, he informs spectators that they are going to see a particular story and the dramatic action commences.

Music is provided by small and large drums (*nakkara*). A *dholak* drum, bell-metal cymbals and harmonium may be added. *Nautanki* music is a blend of classical, folk and film music. Under the influence of film songs, musical style has changed enormously in recent years. The wooden *sarangi*, the classical north Indian stringed instrument, for example, is now often replaced by wind instruments, such as the clarinet. The dominant element of singing is broken by dialogue, simple dances incorporating film and folk elements, and improvised comic skits.

With the introduction of women performers after the 1930s, the predominantly male audiences demanded actions and dances which are somewhat provocative. In traditional companies young boys always play the female roles. Whatever the sex of the players, enthusiastic patrons make donations of money to the singers during the performance. The women take the welcome gift and stick it in their blouses and repeat the song or dance to please the adoring follower. In other companies the stage manager takes the money and names the donor loudly to the public, indicating how much he gave to the player. Today, *nautanki* players find it difficult to survive in a society in which films dominate the public imagination and where television is on the verge of becoming readily accessible to millions of rural patrons. Troupe leaders usually hold odd jobs and assemble available players when commissioned to give a performance.

Two styles of *nautanki* dominate today. The style of the city of Hathras is regarded as the older and was popularized by Indarman and his pupil Natharam in the 19th century. They established a training centre (*akhara*) for disciples. The leaders of the group (*khalifa*) established strict discipline and as master-teachers exercised enormous control over the form. Natharam printed and distributed *nautanki* scripts to the voracious reading public of peasants and lower-caste townspeople, gaining for the style a wide popular following. Artists of the Hathras style sing in a high pitch and ornament their songs with elaborate flourishes. Performers work on simple raised platform stages with little or no scenic decorations, inviting the audience to use its imagination.

The second style, of the city of Kanpur, was created by Sri Krishna Pahalvan after 1913. His goal was to crack the tight *akhara* system which admitted no one other than those who adhered to the dictates of its teachers. He replaced the opening prayers with a chorus in simple metre sung by the entire cast, which proved popular with audiences. He accepted performers who demonstrated promise and inspiration in singing, regardless of length of training. Kanpur-style singing is in a lower pitch and the dramatic story line is emphasized over vocal ornamentation. Typically the style incorporates great scenic detail. Wings and drops are used to set locale. 'The garden' and 'the court' are typical stock set pieces. This has forced audiences into a frontal juxtaposition to the acting area, virtually abandoning the three-sided or arena performance spaces with their neutral acting area typical of the Hathras style. FAR

Nazimova, Alla [Alla Yakovlevna Leventon] 1879–1945 Russian-born actress. Nazimova studied with VLADIMIR NEMIROVICH-DANCHENKO, acted with the MOSCOW ART THEATRE and became leading lady of a St Petersburg theatre. She toured Europe and America in 1905. In New York in 1906 she presented, in English, matinée performances of IBSEN's *Hedda Gabler*, *A Doll's House* and *The Master Builder*. She appeared different from the popular personality actresses of the day, since she could transform herself externally into different characters. She remained in America, but by 1918 her fame had faded, and she was considered another personality actress capitalizing on her sensuous exoticism. After 10 years starring in Hollywood films such as *Camille* and *Salome*, she performed with the CIVIC REPERTORY THEATRE and the THEATRE GUILD. In 1935 she directed and starred in her own version of *Ghosts*, after which she returned to filmmaking. RAS

Ndao, Cheik (Sidi Ahmed) 1933– Senegalese dramatist and English teacher, educated in Senegal and at the University of Swansea, Wales. The author of a volume of poetry, short stories and a novel, Ndao has also written five plays in French including one of the earliest francophone history plays and winner of the first prize in the 1969 Algiers Art Festival: *L'Exil d'Albouri* (*Albouri's Exile*, 1967). This play has the distinction among French-language history plays of being more than just a picturesque spectacle of song, dance and movement. It presents a unified plot with a solid core of moral dilemmas and individualized characters. His other plays include *Le Fils de l'Almamy* and *La Case de l'homme* (*The Almamy's Son* and *The Hut of Manhood* (on the practice of circumcision), 1973); *L'Île de Bahila* (*The Island of Bahila*, 1975); *Du Sang pour un trône* (*Blood for a Throne*, 1983) and *La Décision*, on the problems of race in the USA. Ndao's plays mostly deal with the resistance of African princes to French imperial conquest in the 19th century. He has also published two in English: *Tears for Tears* (1977) and *Love but Educate* (1978). JCM

Nederlander, James 1922– Scion of an American family prominent for three generations in producing and in the operation of theatres. Born in Detroit, Nederlander was a member of the Air Force staff, producing *Winged Victory* in New York in 1943. One of the major forces in the BROADWAY theatre, the Nederlander Organization owns or operates 10 Broadway theatres and runs a large chain of legitimate theatres, including some in Detroit, Chicago, San Francisco, San Diego, Los Angeles and London. Representative Broadway productions include *Nicholas Nickleby*, *Whose Life Is It Anyway?*, *Orpheus Descending*, *La Cage aux Folles*, *Me and My Girl*, *Shadowlands* and revivals of *Peter Pan* (two), *Sweet Charity*, *Hello, Dolly!* and *Porgy and Bess*. Robert E. Nederlander (1933–), one of five brothers, serves as president of the organization, but is less involved in legitimate theatre activities than James. The Nederlander Theatre on West 41st Street in New York, built originally in 1921 as the National (subsequently the

Billy Rose and Trafalgar), was named after David, the founder of the dynasty who died in 1967. SMA MCH

Negro Ensemble Company (USA) Established in 1967 in racially troubled times with a generous Ford Foundation grant, the predominantly African-American company (see AFRICAN-AMERICAN THEATRE) inhabited the OFF-BROADWAY St Mark's Theatre. Under DOUGLAS TURNER WARD's inspired leadership, it began an ambitious programme of training young theatre aspirants and producing plays relevant to black Americans. The company was initially criticized for locating outside the black community and producing foreign plays, but its successful nurturing of black writers, performers, directors and technicians and the sustained excellence of its productions have brought it national and international renown. In over 25 successive seasons, through good times and lean, it has presented over 50 major productions of new plays, with twice that number of workshop presentations and staged readings. It has undertaken national tours and performed abroad in London, Rome, Bermuda, Munich and on tour in Australia. Among its many awards are the 1982 Pulitzer Prize for *A Soldier's Play*, Tonys both for Special Achievement and for *The River Niger* (1973), and 13 Obies for outstanding new plays, performances and productions such as *Dream on Monkey Mountain* (1971), *The First Breeze of Summer* (1975) and *Eden* (1976). In 1980 the company relocated its offices in New York City's theatre district and its productions in Theatre Four (West 55th Street); but since 1988 it has been renting various Off-Broadway theatres while searching for a more permanent home. In 1993 the first mainstage production in two years was staged, following a period of financial uncertainty. EGH

Neighborhood Playhouse (New York City) Like the PROVINCETOWN PLAYERS and the WASHINGTON SQUARE PLAYERS, the Neighborhood Playhouse (1915–27) was a pioneering OFF-BROADWAY theatre. Remote both geographically and temperamentally from the commercial theatre, the Playhouse, located on New York's Lower East Side, was an experimental outpost connected with the Henry Street Settlement House, a social agency for the area's immigrant population. The Playhouse's major interest was in exploring through folk drama the theatre's ritual, lyric, mystical roots. Among its celebrated offerings were an ancient Hindu comedy entitled *The Little Clay Cart* (1924), *The Dybbuk* (1926), a 14th-century French MYSTERY, a Japanese *Nō* drama, a dance drama based on Celtic legend, a Norse fairy tale and a medieval INTERLUDE, as well as more conventional fare such as GALSWORTHY's *The Mob* (1920), O'NEILL's *The First Man* (1922), JAMES JOYCE's *Exiles* (1924) and five editions of a musical REVUE called *The Grand Street Follies*.

Organized as an educational and philanthropic enterprise, the Playhouse achieved a renown that its amateur patrons Alice and Irene Lewisohn had never envisaged. ELLEN TERRY, YVETTE GUILBERT, Ethel Barrymore (see DREW–BARRYMORE FAMILY) and RICHARD BOLESLAVSKI, among others, offered their services. The theatre provided an important impetus to Martha Graham and to scene designers ALINE BERNSTEIN and DONALD OENSLAGER, and generated both the Neighborhood Playhouse School of the Theatre, begun in 1928 and still flourishing (for over 50 years under the direction of SANFORD MEISNER), and the Costume Institute of the Metropolitan Museum, founded in 1937. In 1959 Alice Lewisohn Crowley published *The Neighborhood Playhouse: Leaves from a Theater Scrapbook*, a modest and charming memoir.   FH

Neilson, Adelaide [Elizabeth Ann Brown] 1848–80 British actress. Born in Leeds, she ran away to London under the name Lizzie Ann Bland and worked as a SHAKESPEARE-reciting barmaid near the Haymarket. She played Julia in *The Hunchback* for her stage debut at Margate in 1865; and Juliet for her London debut that same year and for her New York debut in 1872. A highly regarded Juliet and Viola, she was praised for her intelligent conception of the role as well as her genuine acting talent, fresh beauty and 'deliciously musical' voice. Slender, dark-eyed and 'ravishingly pretty', she projected a commingling of gleeful, childlike vitality and deep womanly pathos. Her other outstanding roles were Shakespeare's Rosalind, Beatrice and Isabella; and Amy Robsart in *Kenilworth* and Rebecca in *Ivanhoe*. She played return engagements in America in 1874, 1876 and 1879–80. She died suddenly in Paris.   FHL

Nekrosius, Eimuntas 1952– Lithuanian director whose physically expressive stagings reflect the influence of his teacher ANATOLY EFROS. His production of *Love and Death in Verona* (after *Romeo and Juliet*) was one of several extremely popular punk-style rock MUSICALS he staged at the Lithuanian Youth Dramatic Theatre, which he founded in 1985. Between 1989 and 91 he staged V. Korastylev's *Prosmani*, *Pirosmani*, dealing with a naive Rousseauesque Georgian painter, Chingiz Aitmatov's *A Day Lasting More Than a Century*, and an eccentric *Uncle Vanya* (featuring Russian ZANNI and a choral Waffles) whose imagery derived in part from non-textual actor improvisations and expressed unseen realities. His Moscow production of GOGOL's *The Nose* (designed by Nadezhda Gultyaeva), which opened in the month separating the failed Soviet coup and the assertion of Lithuanian independence (September 1991), transformed a castration fantasy into a farcical allegory on the dismemberment of the Soviet Union and the irreconcilability of Russia and Lithuania. SG

Nelson, Richard 1950– American playwright and dramaturge, born in Chicago and educated at Hamilton College, Clinton, New York. Nelson was America's most prolific dramatist during the decade of the 1980s, with such productions as *Rip Van Winkle or 'The Works'* (1981), *The Return of Pinocchio* (1983), *Between East and West* (1984) and *Principia Scriptoriae* (1986). He won Obies for *Vienna Notes* (1978) and for his 'innovative programming' while literary manager at the Brooklyn Academy of Music. He has adapted a number of classics, such as *The Suicide* (1980), *The Marriage of Figaro* (1982) and *The Three Sisters* (1984); was dramaturge for the GUTHRIE THEATRE; and wrote the book for the MUSICAL *Chess* (1988). His plays have a wide following in England, where he has written radio dramas for the BBC; both *Americans Abroad* (1989) and

Two Shakespearean Actors (1990) debuted at the ROYAL SHAKESPEARE COMPANY prior to Lincoln Center productions. A commissioned play, *Misha's Play*, written in collaboration with Russian dramatist Alexander Gelman, also premiered at the RSC (1993) prior to production at the MOSCOW ART THEATRE (autumn 93). *Life Sentences* (1993) was produced in New York, and New England premiered at the RSC in 1994.   BBW

Nelson [Lewysohn]**, Rudolf** 1878–1960 German VARIETY manager. He began as a child prodigy pianist, and by 1904 was running the elegant CABARET Roland von Berlin. Later he founded the German Chat Noir (1907) and the Metropol-Kabarett (1910), both supplanted by the Nelson-Kunstlerspiele (1919). A gifted OFFENBACHIAN composer, he wrote the music for several OPERETTAS, and toured with his troupe during 1926–32. The rise of the Nazis exiled him to Amsterdam, where he founded La Gaieté (1934). After the war, he returned to West Berlin and undertook experimental REVUES. Nelson was instrumental in providing a style of cabaret that was not particularly satiric or political, but had sophistication and high tone.   LS

Nemirovich-Danchenko, Vladimir (Ivanovich) 1858–1943 Russian-Soviet dramatist-teacher-director, and co-founder with STANISLAVSKY of the MOSCOW ART THEATRE (MAT, 1897), where as its literary manager and dramaturge he manifested a superior sensitivity to playwrights and their plays. In 1877 he began contributing theatre criticism to various journals and in 1881 initiated his career as a writer of narrative fiction. He wrote 11 plays, mostly conventional light comedies and MELODRAMAS, which achieved popular success in productions at the Aleksandrinsky and Maly Theatres. His *The Worth of Life* (1896) won the prestigious Griboedov Prize as the season's best play, an honour he felt should have gone to CHEKHOV's innovative *The Seagull*, which had been savaged by actors, critics and audience in its Aleksandrinsky Theatre premiere.

From 1891 to 1901 Nemirovich-Danchenko taught in the Music and Drama School of the Moscow Philharmonia, whose prize acting students – OLGA KNIPPER, VSEVOLOD MEYERHOLD and IVAN MOSKVIN – he took with him to the Moscow Art Theatre (1898). On MAT's behalf he coaxed permission from Chekhov to revive *The Seagull* and enlisted GORKY to write *The Petty Bourgeoisie* and *The Lower Depths* (1902), even assisting in their creation. With Stanislavsky he co-directed *The Lower Depths* and Chekhov's plays, save for *Ivanov*, which he staged alone. As a dramatist he was especially sensitive to realizing the author's intentions and the play's essence, and sought to educate Stanislavsky (who was prone to sentimentality and extraneous detail in his staging) in Chekhov's special lyricism.

A number of his MAT productions reflect his penchant for poetry and mysticism: IBSEN's *When We Dead Awaken* (1900), *Pillars of Society* (1903), *Rosmersholm* (1908) and *Brand* (1906); SHAKESPEARE's *Julius Caesar* (1903); ANDREEV's *Anathema* (1909), *Ekaterina Ivanovna* (1912) and *Thought* (1914); Dmitry Merezhkovsky's *There Will Be Joy* (1916); and, especially, his productions of Dostoevsky – the two-evening long *The Brothers Karamazov* (about whose pessimism Gorky protested, 1910) and *Nikolai Stavrogin* (from the novel *The Devils*, 1913). In 1919 he organized MAT's Musical Studio, which in 1926 became the Vl. I. Nemirovich-Danchenko Musical Theatre. He brought MAT principles of performance to his OPERA work, replacing the conventional singer with the 'singing actor', rethinking the role of the chorus and striving to capture the music's essence as he did a play's. One of his most important productions was of Dmitry Shostakovich's *Lady Macbeth of Mtsensk District* (*Katerina Izmailova*, 1934). He was named a People's Artist of the USSR in 1936 and became sole director of MAT following Stanislavsky's death in 1938. His book *My Life in the Russian Theatre* (1937) offers personal opinions about and memories of MAT's halcyon days. SG

Nestroy, Johann (Nepomuck) 1801–62 Austrian actor and playwright. After several years as an opera singer and then as an actor in various provincial theatres, Nestroy made his debut in Vienna at the Theater an der Wien in 1831. From then until his retirement in 1860 he was consistently the most visible and controversial figure of the Viennese theatre, as improvisational actor, as actor-manager and as playwright. His penetrating wit and fearless attitude towards the Viennese censor (see CENSORSHIP) ensured that he was continuously in conflict with authority, which almost landed him in gaol.

Nestroy wrote over 80 plays: these indicate a shift of interest in the Viennese VOLKSSTÜCK from magic to consistently secular matters. The most enduring are *The Evil Spirit Lumpazivagbundus* (1833); *Zu ebener Erde und im ersten Stock* (*On the Ground Floor and the First Storey*, 1835), which employs a split stage to demonstrate class differences; *The Talisman* (1840); *The Girl from the Suburbs* (1841); *Einen Jux will er sich machen* (*He Will Go on a Spree*, 1842), best known to English audiences in THORNTON WILDER's adaptation, *The Matchmaker*; *Der Zerrissene* (*The Torn One*, 1844); and a political SATIRE that borders on greatness, *Freedom in Krahwinkel* (1848). Nestroy was also a master of PARODY; *Judith and Holofernes* (1849), a travesty of HEBBEL's *Judith*, is his masterpiece in this genre.

Although Nestroy's reputation went into steep decline after his death, the 20th century has seen a vigorous and probably permanent revival of interest in his work. This was initiated by KARL KRAUS, who enthusiastically brought it to public attention. However, this interest is likely to remain confined to the German-speaking world as, because of Nestroy's dependence on Viennese dialect and his extraordinarily complex verbal play, his comedies are almost impossible to translate accurately. SW

Netherlands (see also MEDIEVAL DRAMA IN EUROPE (The Low Countries) The origins of Dutch theatre are generally assumed to lie in the liturgy of Catholic worship at the beginning of the 12th century. It is presumed that ritual drama, spoken in the vernacular, developed from here. It seems likely that a parallel tradition grew from RITUALS that marked the beginning of a new season and from festivities held at annual fairs. Thus far, theatrical development in the Netherlands bears a close resemblance to that of other Western European countries.

The 17th century is the Netherlands' Golden Age of dramatic art. Under the influence of the classics, the distinction between TRAGEDY and COMEDY took on a renewed importance. The master of Dutch comedy is GERBRAND ADRIAANSZ BREDERO, who wrote a number of FARCES. They stand out for their faithful reproduction of everyday life in 17th-century Amsterdam, particularly as concerns the language – for instance, in *The Farce of the Cow* and *The Spanish Brabanter*. The outstanding representative of 17th-century Dutch baroque is JOOST VAN DEN VONDEL. His *Gijsbrecht van Aemstel* marked the opening of the municipal theatre of Amsterdam, the AMSTERDAMSE SCHOUWBURG, in 1638. Next to Vondel, P. C. HOOFT occupies a special place. Going back to the classics, notably SENECA, Hooft developed his individual, self-assured Dutch neoclassicist style.

The 18th century marks the transition from a declamatory style of acting to a relatively realistic style – although, measured by modern standards, it can still be considered rather artificial. Jelgerhuis (1770–1836), an actor, graphic artist and painter, has left us a textbook on the art of acting whose instructive illustrations give a good idea of the standards and style of 18th-century acting.

In the 19th century it was mainly *vaudevilles* that were performed, in which the comic element was predominant. In 1874, in reaction to this state of affairs, a group of interested citizens started a drama school, a drama magazine and a theatrical company, all with the aim, similar to that of the COMÉDIE-FRANÇAISE, of re-establishing drama as an art. To this end, the Koninklijke Vereeniging Het Nederlandsch Tooneel (Royal Dutch Drama Society) was founded. Acting with this company, Louis Bouwmeester (1842–1925) as Shylock and his sister Theodora Mann-Bouwmeester (1850–1934) gave highly acclaimed performances. Its director, Willem Pieter de Leur, was a disciple of MEININGEN's. After 1870, in imitation of the Théâtre Libre (see ANDRÉ ANTOINE) and the FREIE BÜHNE, the Nederlandsche Tooneelvereeniging (Dutch Drama Society) was founded, under the leadership of Louis Henry Chrispÿn (1854–1926), who produced plays by IBSEN, HAUPTMANN and MAETERLINCK.

Around 1900, HERMAN HEIJERMANS appeared before the footlights as a playwright and producer of distinction. He wrote his realistic plays (see REALISM), which show a deep concern and solidarity with the poorest in society, for the Nederlandsche Tooneelvereeniging. In the age of literary NATURALISM, it was Eduard Verkade (1878–1961) and Willem Royaards (1867–1929) who, opposing the literary taste of their time, stepped forward as theatrical leaders. Royaards appreciated the aesthetic innovations that were taking place and, being a student of REINHARDT's, set out to parallel poetic language with theatrical equivalents. He realized his aesthetic ideals in performances that were defined by a refined and immaculate taste in colour, style and costumes, set against a spacious and sober background. It was a prerequisite that the actors worked together as an ensemble. Verkade, on the contrary, inspired by GORDON CRAIG, strove for stylization and SYMBOLISM, an approach which was occasionally seen as clashing with the theatrical requirements of a performance.

Van Dalsum (1889–1971) and Defresne (1893–1961), both taught by Verkade and Royaards, bear witness to a humanitarian sense of life. In their productions truth prevails over beauty. *De beul* (*The Hangman*, 1935) by PÄR LAGERKVIST has a clear anti-Fascist moral; the NSB (the Dutch equivalent of the National Socialist German Workers' Party) rioted against the performance. The NSB's action and the reaction of the government, which clung convulsively to a political course of neutrality, point to a changing climate, even to the extent that during the Second World War the development of drama reached a temporary standstill. The Kultuurkamer (Chamber of Culture), established by the Germans, led to a controversy amongst actors. To become a member, a person had to sign a declaration stating that he or she was an Aryan. The actors who signed entered German employment; others refused to sign on principle. Secret plans were made in preparation for the postwar period. After 1945 Van Dalsum, Sternheim and Defresne, actors who had all gone underground, were given free access to the municipal theatre. Where it was deemed necessary, those actors who had played through the war were hit by punitive measures dealt out by a committee established especially for the purpose. The government soon became directly involved in the theatre by supplying subsidies. In the big cities, repertory companies were formed that received a guaranteed subsidy on the condition that they perform outside their own theatres as well. The aim was to reach a wide audience throughout the country. In practice, this meant that the companies had to travel a great deal.

Just after the war it was Sjaroff, a student of STANISLAVSKY's, who as a guest director left his mark upon performances of plays by OSTROVSKY, GOGOL and CHEKHOV. Through Sjaroff, Stanislavskian acting methods became known in the Netherlands.

During the 1960s, much attention was given to Dutch playwrights; their plays, however, differed widely in quality, and thus failed to provide a solid basis for a tradition of playwriting. New locations were tried out in search of an alternative for the proscenium arch theatre. Notably, the MICKERY-THEATER and, somewhat later, the Shaffy-theater were in the forefront of new developments. Later in the decade, AKTIE TOMAAT (the Tomato Campaign) created a considerable stir in the Dutch theatre world. It masterminded a fierce campaign against traditional repertory drama, attacking it for its lack of any form of social involvement and protesting vehemently against the authoritarian status of the director. From 1970 onwards, this resulted in a reformation within repertory companies. Some disappeared altogether, and new companies emerged.

This development created the financial opportunity for the establishment of new small companies like the Onafhankelijk Toneel (Independent Theatre, founded 1974), an organization in which practitioners of the plastic arts work jointly with theatre producers, the Appel (founded 1972, director Erik Vos) which has given new form to classical repertory (AESCHYLUS, *Oresteia*; SHAKESPEARE, *King Lear*), and the WERKTEATER, which was set up as a kind of laboratory for practical theatre research. But some repertory theatre performances were controversial, notably those directed by Gerard-Jan Rijnders for Globe. The political VORMINGSTONEEL (educational drama), which made use of drama to educate and to emancipate its audience, flourished: companies like Sater and Proloog (1964–83) were part of the official theatre circuit. And it was in the 70s that the repertory company Centrum (1961–87, director Peter Oosthoek) devoted itself to producing new Dutch plays (e.g. by Gerben Hellinga, Gerard Lemmens, Ton Vorstenbosch and Wim Schipper).

Outside the official circuit, 1975 marks the birth of the Festival of Fools. An initiative taken by 'fool' Jango Edwards, it is intended to be held every other year. Run virtually without subsidy, the Festival provides a stimulus to FRINGE THEATRE, performed in regular theatres and in the streets of Amsterdam as well. The 'fool' stands for the basic idea behind the festival: he is the jester, who comments upon life and draws attention to its ironies.

In the 1980s an extreme diversity in theatrical aesthetics became the main characteristic of the Dutch theatrical landscape, coloured by a still increasing number of subsidized and non-subsidized small companies. Their repertory varies from the very traditional to performances in which new environments are explored (e.g. in warehouses or in locks, such as Hollandia's performance, *La Paloma*, 1986). Hundreds of new performances take place each year; the new national theatre festival, which started in 1987, shows the highlights of the former season.

In the 1980s and 90s innovative theatre is no longer the trademark of the fringe groups. Gerardjan Rijders, since 1987 artistic director of the highly subsidized Toneelgroep Amsterdam, has brought innovation within the walls of the Municipal Theatre of Amsterdam, e.g. with his montage performances *Bakeliet* (1987), *Ballet* (1990) and *Count your Blessings* (1993), which use non-linear narration techniques. Noteworthy is his collaboration with directors and actors who do not belong to the established theatre groups (e.g. Nieuw West and Hollandia). As in Flanders, also in Holland, young directors with small but powerful theatre groups present their views on modern society and theatre. Frans Strijards founded Art and Pro and directed – from 1986 (*Hensbergen*) up to 1992 (*Sporen*) – six of his own plays himself, presenting his individual anger about theatrical forms. A collective anger against understatement and against lack of feeling is displayed in the emotional acting of the Trust (a group founded in 1988), directed by Theu Boermans and performing in a former swimming pool in Amsterdam.

Immigrant theatre is another new development. Immigrant workers, who have been entering the country since the 1950s, have brought their cultural heritage with them. Since 1983 the Stagedoor Festival, where migrant theatre companies from Surinam, Morocco, Turkey and other countries are offered the opportunity to present themselves before an audience, has been held annually. Multicultural groups such as Cosmic Illusion and the Nieuw Amsterdam have consolidated their position within the theatre system. Even theatre for children is becoming an established element. Many new Dutch plays are produced for this audience by groups such as Teneeter, Huis aan de Amstel and Artemis.

A recent development in the Netherlands and Flanders is a move towards internationalization of theatre production. In particular, links between Frankfurt (Theater am Turm), Berlin (Hebbel Theater), Brussels (Kaaitheater), Vienna (Wiener Festwochen) and Amsterdam (Felix

Meritis) promote a lively exchange of ideas about the new theatre. From this has emerged the journal *Theaterschrift*, in four languages, promoting discussion about new aesthetics within theatre.   HS MG WH

See: B. Albach, *Helden, draken en comedianten: Het Nederlandse toneelleven voor, in en na de Franse tijd*, Amsterdam, 1956, and *Duizend jaar toneel in Nederland*, Bussum, 1965; E. Alexander, 'For Holland a New Beginning: Royaards (1867–1929) and Verkade (1879–1961)', *Theatre Research/Recherches théâtrales*, 10, 2, 1969; H. Becker, 'Divine Love as the Unifying Principle in Vondel's Lucifer', *Modern Language Review*, 54, 3, 1959; G. W. Brandt and W. Hogendoorn (eds), *German and Dutch Theatre, 1600–1848*, Cambridge, New York, Melbourne, 1993; A. Brine, 'Amsterdam. Europe Newsletter', *Plays and Players*, 14, 1, 1968; B. Gascoigne, 'The Low Countries and Amsterdam', in *World Theatre*, London, 1968; A. S. Golding, *Classicistic Acting: Two Centuries of a Performance Tradition at the Amsterdam Schouwburg*, New York, London, 1984; W. M. H. Hummelen, *Repertorium van het rederijkersdrama 1500ca. 1620*, Assen, 1968; B. Hunningher, 'The Nederlandish Abele Spelen', *Maske und Kothurn*, 10, 1964; K. Hupperetz and P. Kapteyn (eds), 'Niederländisches Gegenwartstheater', *Tijdschrift voor Theaterwetenschap*, 9, 34/35, 1993; J. Jelgershuis, *Theoretische lessen over de gesticulatie en mimiek*, reprint of 1827 edn, Amsterdam, 1970; G. R. Kernodle, *From Art to Theatre: The Rederijkers Stage in the Netherlands*, Chicago, 1944; P. King, 'The Sacramental Thought in Vondel's Drama', *Modern Language Review*, 51, 2, 1956; H. H. J. de Leeuwe, 'Das Theater in den Niederlanden', in *Das Atlantisbuch des Theaters*, ed. M. Hürlimann, Zurich, 1966; J. J. Mak, *De Rederijkers*, Amsterdam, 1944; J. M. Manly, 'Elckerlijc-Everyman: The Question of Priority', *Modern Philology*, 8, 1910; G. Rekers, 'Avant-Garde Theatre in the Netherlands', in *International Theatre Information*, 1971; J. G. Riewald, 'New Light on the English Actors in the Netherlands, c.1590–c.1660', *English Studies*, 11, 1960; M. B. Smits-Veldt, *Het Nederlandse Renaissancetoneel*, Utrecht, 1991; B. Stroman, *De Nederlandse toneelschrijfkunst: Poging tot verklaring van een gemis*, Amsterdam/Antwerp, 1973; H. Traver, 'Religious Implications in the Abele Spelen of the Hulthem Manuscript', *Germanic Review* (New York), 26, 1951; G. J. de Voogd, *Facetten van vijftig jaar Nederlands toneel: 1920–1970*, Amsterdam, 1970; J. A. Worp, *Geschiedenis van het drama en van het tooneel in Nederland*, 2 vols., Groningen, 1904, 1908; W. Zweers and L. Welters, *Toneel en publiek in Nederland*, Rotterdam, 1970.

Nethersole, Olga 1870–1951 British actress and manager. Born in London, she made her first stage appearance in Brighton, at age 17, and performed for 26 years, touring Britain, America, Australia and France. Her 1888 London debut was in *The Union Jack*; she first appeared in America in 1894 in Chicago in *The Transgressor*. In 1895 she visited the USA with *The Wife of Scarli*, and returned in 1899 with *The Second Mrs Tanqueray*. For the next six years she toured America. Later successes included *Mary Magdalene*

and *Camille*. In 1900 she excited considerable controversy with a production of *Sappho*, which was closed by the New York police as immoral. The courts cleared Nethersole; she took the show to London for a huge success. Upon the outbreak of the First World War she retired and became a nurse, appearing only for a single performance in 1923 in London.   SMA

Neuber, Caroline 1697–1760 German actress. With her husband Johann (1697–1756), Caroline Neuber served as leader of the most successful troupe of travelling players in Germany during the 1720s and 1730s. In cooperation with GOTTSCHED, she attempted to raise the standards of contemporary theatre by abolishing improvisation and by introducing into the repertoire 'regular' tragic drama, translated from or modelled on French tragedy. She had much initial success, though her fortunes declined after breaking with Gottsched in 1741, and her final years were spent in obscurity. As an actress Neuber was most successful in comedy, to which she brought much personal grace. SW

Neville, John 1925– British actor and theatre director. After some years in repertory he achieved national distinction at the OLD VIC (1953–9) as an actor in the classical mould, giving memorable performances as Romeo, Mark Antony and (alternating with RICHARD BURTON) Othello and Iago. In 1961 he joined the Nottingham Playhouse and, in 1963, at the opening of the new Playhouse, became its artistic director. After five energetic years there in which he firmly placed the theatre in the forefront of REGIONAL THEATRES (aiming at creating a 'national theatre' for the area), he resigned amidst a controversial dispute with the ARTS COUNCIL and the theatre board over matters of funding and artistic control. While at Nottingham he had demonstrated the range and depth of his acting in roles as diverse as Oedipus and the homosexual barber in Charles Dyer's *Staircase*. Neville eventually moved to Canada, where he was appointed director of the Citadel Theatre, Edmonton, in 1973 and artistic director of the Neptune Theatre in Halifax in 1978. In 'retirement' he has made several notable apperances in films and television plays, the most recent being in DAVID STOREY's *Home* (BBCTV, 1994).   AJ

New Dramatists American service organization for playwrights. Founded in New York in 1949 by Micaela O'Harra with assistance from ROBERT W. ANDERSON, RICHARD RODGERS and HOWARD LINDSAY, New Dramatists exists to 'encourage and develop playwriting in America'. After a screening process, accepted members are provided with a cast and director for readings of their plays. A critique session with other playwrights and professionals gives the writer a frank evaluation and suggestions for rewriting. Members may also be assigned to review a BROADWAY production from first rehearsal to opening. New Dramatists informs members about current writing opportunities; provides classes on the craft of writing; solicits tickets to current theatre productions; maintains a library of current periodicals and trade journals; and provides loans for members with plays in production. Successful alumni include JOHN GUARE, LANFORD WILSON,

WILLIAM INGE, ED BULLINS, Megan Terry, MARIA IRENE FORNÉS, Paddy Chayefsky, Horton Foote, Eric Overmyer and AUGUST WILSON. TLM

New Theatre New York's first major art theatre, at Central Park West and 62nd Street – a stone's throw from the present Lincoln Center complex. The New Theatre had an auspicious dedication ceremony (6 November 1909) with speeches by J. Pierpont Morgan, Woodrow Wilson, GEORGE PIERCE BAKER, WILLIAM DEAN HOWELLS, Thomas A. Edison and WILLIAM ARCHER, preceding the performance of *Antony and Cleopatra* with E. H. SOTHERN and JULIA MARLOWE. The idea for the New Theatre originated with Heinrich Conried, director of the Metropolitan Opera. Funds were subscribed by 30 wealthy opera patrons to build an elegant Italian Renaissance structure with magnificent staircases and lobbies, a roof garden, a spacious orchestra pit and the latest stage equipment, including the first electrically operated revolving stage. WINTHROP AMES from Boston's Castle Square Theatre was appointed director.

The New got off to a poor start. The production was not ready, the house (seating 2500) was too large and the acoustics were abominable. Clearly, the plan to stage operas and plays in the same theatre had been a mistake. In two seasons only GALSWORTHY's *Strife*, EDWARD SHELDON's *The Nigger* and Mary Austin's *The Arrow Maker* could properly be called 'new'. The lessons from its brief life (1909–11) were clear: an art theatre could not be bought with dollars. The new theatre movement demanded intimate quarters.

The SHUBERT BROTHERS acquired the building and renamed it. As the Century (1911–30), it housed an assortment of MUSICALS by VICTOR HERBERT, Offenbach, ROMBERG and Oskar Straus; MORRIS GEST's production of REINHARDT's *The Miracle* (1924), for which NORMAN BEL GEDDES transformed the theatre into a massive Gothic cathedral; and, that same season, ELEONORA DUSE in 11 matinées of five plays, including *Lady from the Sea* and *Ghosts*. It was demolished in 1930 . RM

New Vaudeville Sprawling category of American performers who harness traditional popular entertainment skills and a carnival spirit to a postmodern aesthetic. The versatility of such actor-athletes as CLOWN, MIME and eccentric dancer BILL IRWIN, dancer and master JUGGLER Michael Moschen, musician and puppeteer Bruce D. Schwartz (see PUPPETS), monologuist SPALDING GRAY, tabletop puppeteer and political satirist Paul Zaloom, is a hallmark. Ensemble groups such as the Pickle Family and Big Apple CIRCUSES can be considered part of New Vaudeville. Unlike the players of old-time VARIETY shows, New Vaudevillians are mostly college-educated children of the middle class. While acknowledging forebears from COMMEDIA DELL'ARTE to the Three Stooges, these are the thinking man's clowns, whose physical talents serve thematic and stylistic agendas with roots in the anti-establishment theatres of the 1960s (themselves in debt to such diverse influences as BRECHT, MEYERHOLD, dada and BUNRAKU).

While each is unique, New Vaudevillians share a number of traits. Most reject the conventions of realistic theatre, substituting physical virtuosity and violating the fourth wall with direct address and audience interaction: slack-wire acrobat and silent clown Avner 'the Eccentric' Eisenberg brings audience members on stage; crackerjack banjo player and storyteller Stephen Wade pitches ballpoint pens to the house; and during Bill Irwin's *In Regard of Flight*, the quintessential New Vaudeville show, players invade the auditorium, as they do in Irwin's and David Shiner's 1992–3 show, *Fool Moon*.

Despite their avant-garde affinities, New Vaudevillians forsake elitist aspects of experimental theatre for populist perspectives, and expose the mysteries of their entertainment specialities. Disillusionistic MAGICians Penn and Teller unmask their own tricks; the Flying Karamazov Brothers, a four-man (originally five) juggling team, maintain an ironic, mid-act commentary on their craft. Together with their self-reliance, such egalitarian attitudes constitute a reaction against the modern technological world, demonstrating, as Ron Jenkins puts it, 'an affirmation of what a human being can accomplish without the aid of machines'. In recent years New Vaudevillians have obtained mainstream popularity, suggesting the appeal and staying power of the fresh theatrical visions that they have created using familiar means. CLJ

New York City theatres From its inception, New York – or, more specifically, the island of Manhattan – was blessed with an air of cosmopolitanism. Settled by the Dutch at the toe of the island early in the 17th century, its population grew to include English, French, Irish, German and Jewish inhabitants plus Black slaves. If, when the English took over the settlement later in the century, the Anglican Church dominated its religious life, the tone had been set by the fundamentalism of the Dutch Reformed Church. The arrival of the Presbyterians and Methodists served to strengthen the conservatism of the early population, which found its entertainment within the family and home and in simple outdoor pursuits and sports.

The creation of a miniature English court at the beginning of the 18th century, plus the growing prosperity of the colonials, brought people out of their homes and into society. Early records suggest amateur theatrical entertainment in and around the colonial court and, perhaps, itinerant performers in the early taverns. Then, in 1732, a newspaper advertisement referred to a theatre owned by 'the honourable Rip Van Dam'; later a map (1735) showed a playhouse close to the English fort, the site of the governor's residence. Both theatres were probably rudimentary and makeshift, but they point to a greater interest in theatrical activity among the colonial population.

By the mid-18th century, two theatrical companies visited New York, the second of which was composed of professional actors from London. They settled in a theatre on Nassau Street, which may well have been the Rip Van Dam warehouse theatre used by the amateurs some 20 years before. Although it still encountered religious opposition, a company assembled by DAVID DOUGLASS in JAMAICA from the remnants of the old HALLAM company returned to New York in 1758, and was emboldened by a palpable interest in theatrical entertainment to build three theatres in the next nine years. One of them, the JOHN STREET THEATRE built in 1767, was to serve Douglass until his withdrawal from the mainland before the Revolution, and was later used by the occupying English troops during the war. When Lewis Hallam Jr returned to New York in 1785, he reopened the theatre and used it until 1798.

The first substantial playhouse to be built in New York was subscribed by the city's important and wealthy citizens and located on a site destined to become an early municipal centre: at a place where Broadway was to merge with the Bowery, the main road to Boston from the city. Here, in 1798, theatre was established as a necessary concomitant of urban living. Designed by French architect Joseph Mangin, the playhouse, which came to be known as the PARK THEATRE, had an ugly exterior but provided reasonable comfort for its patrons in the auditorium; it represented a distinct improvement over the old unattractive and uncomfortable wooden John Street house.

While the Park dominated theatrical activity through the early years of the 18th century, it provided the spur for the building of other theatres in the burgeoning city. To the east and north of it, a more elegant theatre was built on the BOWERY, but quickly fell out of favour with the fashionable class and survived into the 20th century as a 'neighborhood house', catering for the tastes of its shifting and immigrant population. For the sixth and last time, it was destroyed by fire in 1929.

By 1825, New York had emerged as the premier theatre city of America. Theatres dotted the urban landscape, but they never strayed too far from BROADWAY, the principal thoroughfare of the city. Stars from England and Europe generally made New York the first stop on their lucrative tours. When the fortunes of the Park waned, other theatres arose to take its place. Comedian BILLY MITCHELL made Mitchell's Olympic Theatre the most popular theatre on Broadway in the late 1830s and early 40s. Another comedian, WILLIAM E. BURTON, turned a little opera house into Burton's Chambers Street Theatre, dispensing his merry entertainment to enthusiastic audiences. Theatres tended to get bigger and more comfortable, culminating in the 4500-seat Broadway Theatre, modelled on London's HAYMARKET.

As the city pushed northward, so did the theatres. By mid-century, Broadway was no longer residential, but mixed factories, office buildings, shops and department stores together with theatres along its way. Playhouses purveyed everything from MINSTREL SHOWS to OPERA to urbane English COMEDY, and became more attractive architecturally as they reflected the trends from Europe. NIBLO's Garden had a grand foyer for its patrons, and most theatres included refreshment stands. Seats were upholstered in the National Theatre (northwest corner of Leonard and Church Streets), and the pit was rendered into the orchestra and made respectable, as the gallery became the family circle – to combat the rowdyism of its early denizens. The familiar tiers of boxes atrophied into ceremonial sidewall appendages, as the stage was pulled closer to the curtain line.

In the last decades of the 19th century, following the process of urbanization, a theatre district began to form around Union Square, at the junction of Broadway and Fourth Avenue at 14th Street. The Academy of Music, WALLACK'S THEATRE, the Union Square and TONY PASTOR's all offered different entertainment, forming a core around which a small support industry of agents, costumers, photographers, managers, restaurants, theatrical boarding-houses and hotels sprang up. More theatres were built above Union Square, reaching to Herald Square and beyond, to satisfy an entertainment-hungry population. In 1869, EDWIN BOOTH built his elegant BOOTH'S THEATRE at the corner of Sixth Avenue and 23rd Street and provided a new look in theatres: gone was the raked stage and, with it, the wing-and-drop setting; in their place, illusory walls of canvas and lath were fastened to the stage floor to create rooms and scenes of extraordinary realistic detail.

In 1893, CHARLES FROHMAN built his EMPIRE THEATRE on Broadway at 40th Street, and OSCAR HAMMERSTEIN I crossed 42nd Street to build his OLYMPIA at 44th Street just two years later. Both structures signalled the development of a new theatre district around Longacre (later Times) Square. During 1900–28, an unprecedented boom in theatre building ensued, providing New York's population with more playhouses than it could support. The new theatres reflected the change in theatrical production. The 19th-century STOCK COMPANY resident in its own theatre was supplanted by the 'combination system', the assembling of a cast for the presentation of a single play to be produced at a rented theatre. Consisting of a stage, dressing rooms, a box office, an auditorium and a small lobby, 20th-century playhouses served the new system; with fewer than 2000 seats, they were well suited for the plays and MUSICALS presented on their stages.

Some 80 theatres were built during this era and filled Broadway from 39th Street to 54th Street, and its side streets. Some erected on odd-shaped parcels of land; others had proper façades designed in a variety of styles from Egyptian to Georgian; all were proscenium theatres. They were largely the architectural work of J. B. McElfatrick and Company and Herbert J. Krapp. Beginning with the Depression and extending into the years beyond the Second World War, more than half of them fell victim to the competitive effects of films and television and the rise of New York's ALTERNATIVE THEATRE, OFF-BROADWAY and OFF-OFF BROADWAY. Some were torn down, others were converted to cinemas (those lining 42nd Street), and a few were rebuilt to serve other purposes.

With the recognition that New York's theatres were rapidly becoming an endangered species, a succession of the city's mayors began to take steps to protect the standing playhouses while stimulating the erection of others. Zoning laws were changed to permit the incorporation of theatres within tall office buildings, which resulted in the GERSHWIN (1972) and Minskoff (1973) theatres and two smaller playhouses in the early 1970s. Only a few have been protected by the landmark law, and the fate of the others depends heavily on the availability of plays and musicals suitable for production and the willingness of investors to wager ever greater sums of money to mount them. In 1982, an advisory panel was appointed by the then Mayor Edward I. Koch to study the situation and to make recommendations for the preservation of the remaining theatres; but as of the mid-1990s, the project is just beginning to move forward, with plans announced for renovation of the Victory Theatre (to be the New Victory) and the New Amsterdam, both on 42nd Street. MCH

New York Shakespeare Festival New York's busiest company, founded in 1954 by JOSEPH PAPP 'to encourage and cultivate interest in poetic drama with emphasis on ... SHAKESPEARE ... and to establish an annual summer Shakespeare Festival'. Every summer, NYSF performs free productions in Central Park's Delacorte Theater, built for it in 1957. Bernard Gersten became associate producer in 1960 (until 1978). In 1967, NYSF established the Public Theater in the East Village. During 1973-7, Papp directed Lincoln Center's VIVIAN BEAUMONT AND MITZI E. NEWHOUSE THEATRES. In 1982, NYSF started the Festival Latino de Nueva York, and in 1983 adopted the Young Playwrights Festival (until 1985) and established an exchange with London's ROYAL COURT THEATRE. In 1986, NYSF launched a short-lived project, directed by actress Estelle Parsons, to present Shakespeare on BROADWAY for schoolchildren, and in 1987 inaugurated a six-year plan to produce all of Shakespeare's plays. In 1990, JoANNE AKALAITIS was appointed artistic associate and after Papp's death in October 1991 artistic director, but without Papp's title of 'producer'. Fired abruptly in 1993, Akalaitis was replaced by GEORGE C. WOLFE, who did assume this title. Actor-director KEVIN KLINE became artistic associate.

NYSF has not limited itself to classics but has also staged new American plays, including *Hair* (1967), *No Place to Be Somebody*, Galt MacDermot's MUSICAL *Two Gentlemen of Verona* (Tony, 1971), *Sticks and Bones* (Tony, 1971), *That Championship Season* (Tony and Pulitzer, 1972), *A Chorus Line* (Tony, 1975, and Broadway's longest-running show), *For Colored Girls Who Have Considered Suicide When the Rainbow Is Enuf* (1976), Elizabeth Swados's *The Haggadah* (1982), *The Marriage of Bette and Boo* (1985), Larry Kramer's *The Normal Heart* (1985), Rupert Holmes's *The Mystery of Edwin Drood* (1985), Wallace Shawn's *Aunt Dan and Lemon* (1986), Larry Shue's *Wenceslas Square* (1987), George C. Wolfe's *The Colored Museum* (1986), Harry Kondoleon's *Zero Positive* (1988) and Elizabeth Egloff's *The Sun* (1993).

NYSF also hosts visiting companies and artists, such as MABOU MINES, MEREDITH MONK, RICHARD FOREMAN, JOSEPH CHAIKIN and ANDREI SERBAN, and produces American premieres of foreign works, including VÁCLAV HAVEL's *The Memorandum* (1968) and *Largo Desolato* (1986), Roberto Athaye's *Miss Margarida's Way* (1977), DAVID HARE's *Plenty* (1983), CARYL CHURCHILL's *Top Girls* (1983), *Fen* (1984) and *Serious Money* (1987), and Louise Page's *Salonika* (1985). Over the years NYSF productions have won over 150 awards, including Tonys, Obies, Pulitzers, Drama Desk and New York Drama Critics' Awards. As of the end of 1993, 17 shows had been transferred to Broadway.   REK

New Zealand Pioneer theatres, mostly hotel annexes, began to appear with systematic European colonization (from 1840 onwards), and the gold rush economy of the 1860s saw the establishment of substantial theatres in most towns. Until the turn of the century, these generally housed touring professional companies covering the Australasian circuit, although resident STOCK companies also occurred. A few locally written MELODRAMAS were presented, including George Darrell's *Transported for Life* (1876) and *The Pakeha* (1890) and George Leitch's *The Land of the Moa* (1895), only the last of which has survived.

Just as a national railway system began to facilitate touring, which had previously depended on coastal shipping, the advent of motion pictures effectively destroyed it; a vacuum was created, to be partially filled by repertory theatres (large amateur groups, sometimes with a professional director) in most cities in the late 1920s. A New Zealand branch of the British Drama League, established in 1932, coordinated an extensive amateur movement that reached smaller towns with festivals and playwriting competitions. One-act plays by Alan Mulgan, J. A. S. Coppard, Eric Bradwell, Violet Targuse and NGAIO MARSH were thus promoted, while full-length works by expatriates such as Merton Hodge, Austin Strong and Reginald Berkeley were also seen. Marsh, better known for her crime fiction, began a notable series of student SHAKESPEARE productions at Canterbury University College in 1943 and continued until 1972, failing in an attempt to establish a touring professional troupe, the British Commonwealth Theatre Company, in 1951.

Tours by various J. C. WILLIAMSON professional companies (operating from Australia since 1881) continued intermittently after the Second World War, generally presenting MUSICALS and polite COMEDY, but the only comparable New Zealand companies to achieve a significant duration were the NEW ZEALAND PLAYERS and the COMMUNITY ARTS SERVICE THEATRE. The Players, founded by Richard and Edith Campion in 1953, toured the major centres from Wellington several times a year with a repertoire and style reflecting their OLD VIC training, until their collapse through lack of state subsidy in 1960. CAS toured mainly in the North Island, including minor centres, between 1947 and 1962; based in the Adult Education Centre of Auckland University, it offered a literary repertoire, but, like the Players, very little New Zealand writing. A few idiosyncratic amateur groups encouraged local scripts, notably Unity Theatre, Wellington (1944-78), Elmwood Players, Christchurch (1949-), and the Globe Theatre, Dunedin (1961-); BRUCE MASON, JAMES K. BAXTER and Craig Harrison were major playwrights who emerged through this context.

However, the main stimulus for local dramatic writing in the late 1950s and early 60s was the national radio (NZ Broadcasting Service, later Corporation, now Radio NZ). Government subsidy on a significant scale came with the Queen Elizabeth II Arts Council's foundation in 1964; this has supported various professional and semi-professional companies, some of which have also engaged in limited touring: the Southern Comedy Players (Dunedin, 1957-71), Central Theatre (Auckland, 1962-76), Downstage Theatre (Wellington, 1964-), Mercury Theatre (Auckland, 1968-92), Four Seasons Theatre (Wanganui, 1970-92), the Court Theatre (Christchurch, 1971-), Gateway Theatre (Tauranga, 1972-7), Fortune Theatre (Dunedin, 1973-), Theatre Corporate (Auckland, 1973-86), Centrepoint Theatre (Palmerston North, 1974-), Circa Theatre (Wellington, 1976-), Taki Rua/Depot Theatre (Wellington, 1983-), and Bats Theatre (Wellington, professional since 1989). The Association of Community Theatres (ACT) represented many of these theatres and the New Zealand Drama School, also supported by the Arts Council, offers a two-year course which trains many of the actors entering them. Playmarket has supported the 'presenter model venue', a much more flexible theatrical structure, such as has recently flourished in Auckland (Maidment, Watershed) and in the Christchurch Arts Network coalition.

In the 1960s, as a restaurant theatre, Downstage was prominent as the patron of local writers, producing Bruce Mason, Peter Bland, Robert Lord and Joseph Musaphia; Downstage's Hannah Playhouse (1974) is unique as a contemporary theatre building in New Zealand, and its potential has been demonstrated by directors like Sunney Amey and Colin McColl. In the 1970s other theatres became equally important in promoting New Zealand playwrights: MERVYN THOMPSON was first produced at the Court, and GREG McGEE at Theatre Corporate, at the time Auckland's most adventurous theatre. Circa has premiered much of the most popular recent satirical comedy, such as Roger Hall's *Glide Time* (1976) and *Middle Age Spread* (1977), and Robert Lord's posthumously produced *Joyful and Triumphant* (1992), although Stephen Sinclair and Anthony McCarten have elsewhere widened the popular base of New Zealand theatregoing with *Ladies' Night* (1987) and its spin-offs.

The establishment of the community theatres in the 1970s has stimulated alternative forms such as MAORI THEATRE, the collectives of Francis Batten and Paul Maunder, and many women's theatre groups. Renée, the leading feminist playwright, is best known for her trilogy (*Wednesday to Come*, 1984; *Pass It On*, 1986; and *Jeannie Once*, 1990), but emerged as a theatre writer through the REVUE collective associated with the feminist *Broadsheet* magazine. Maori writers have orientated towards less formal venues such as Taki Rua, although John Broughton has written for Fortune and Downstage, which took his *Michael James Manaia* to the 1991 EDINBURGH FESTIVAL. The vitality of contemporary New Zealand theatre has attracted numerous writers already established in other genres; most notable recently has been Vincent O'Sullivan (*Shuriken*, Downstage, 1983; *Jones & Jones*, Downstage, 1988; *Billy*, Bats, 1989), whose work interrogates national identity and post-coloniality, and indicates a growing audience acceptance of intellectually complex scripts. Similarly, a willingness to transgress the boundaries of 'authorized' history is shown in the popularity of Michelanne Forster's *Daughters of Heaven* (Court, 1991) and *Larnach: Castle of Lies* (Court, 1993), the former about lesbian schoolgirls convicted of murder, the other about the country's most bizarre parliamentarian. HDMCN

New Zealand Players Touring professional company founded by Richard and Edith Campion in 1953, in association with another graduate of the OLD VIC Theatre School, the designer Raymond Boyce; G. H. A. Swan was administrator. Touring the major centres from Wellington several times a year, the Players offered a repertoire popular enough to compensate for the lack of subsidy, until economic factors conflicted with their elaborate style, leading to collapse in 1960; a quartet, touring schools, continued through the 1960s. Boyce and the Campions have made notable contributions to other Wellington theatres, such as Downstage and Unity, particularly in mounting New Zealand plays (few of which were done by the Players). HDMCN

Ngahyoma, Ngalimecha fl.1970s Tanzanian playwright, working with the Audio-Visual Institute in Dar es Salaam. He has published two Swahili plays: *Huka* (1973), which portrays the problems of a young schoolgirl trapped and destroyed by the evils of city life, and *Kijiji Chetu* (*Our Village*, 1975), which deals with some of the social problems arising from the creation of *Ujamaa* villages. PMM

Ngema, Mbongeni 1955– South African playwright, actor and director. Ngema first attracted international attention with his performance in the play *Woza Albert!* in the early 1980s. Spending much of his youth in Zululand, he drew upon traditions of Zulu music and dance which, using his experience as an actor in the township MUSICALS of GIBSON KENTE, he incorporated into his later work. His play *Asinamali!* (1985), influenced by the work of the Chicano American group EL TEATRO CAMPESINO, exemplifies his approach to performance. Depicting the experiences of black prisoners in apartheid South Africa, it utilizes MIME, dance, song and rhythmic movement and gesture to create powerful theatrical images of political oppression and resistance. Later plays have focused on music and singing, *Sarafina* (1987) and *Township Fever!* (1990) being praised in New York as musical representations of the black struggle against apartheid; and *Magic at 4.00 am* (1993), a spectacular musical mounted in Johannesburg's Civic Theatre, heralding Ngema's now central role in professional theatre in South Africa. He has established a company called Committed Artists, which is both a training school and a production company, focusing on the presentation of what he calls 'theatre of liberation'. IS

Ngugi wa Thiong'o 1938– Kenyan novelist, playwright and polemicist. His plays in English include *The Black Hermit* (1962), *This Time Tomorrow* (1968) and *The Trial of Dedan Kimathi* (with MICERE MUGO). With Ngugi wa Mirii he wrote the draft script of Kamiriithu (see KENYA) Community Educational and Cultural Centre's Gikuyu play, *Ngaahika Ndeenda* (*I'll Marry When I Want*, 1982), and following that, also in Gikuyu, *Maitu Njugira* (*Mother Sing to Me*, 1986). Ngugi's work is characterized by a consistent development of early nationalist positions into an anti-imperialist commitment to the cause of peasants and workers in Kenya today. His work in theatre shows a parallel development – from individual authorship to collective authorship in Gikuyu and other Kenyan languages. Ngugi was detained by the Kenyan government from 1977 to 1978 and now lives in exile. Critical essays, which address issues of language and culture in theatre and literature, are contained in *Decolonising the Mind* (1986) and *Moving the Centre* (1993). KG NWaM

Niblo, William 1789–1878 American victualler and businessman. Niblo opened the Sans Souci Park in 1828, a restaurant garden containing a 1200-seat concert hall. Under various managers (including Charles Gilfert, Joseph Sefton and J. W. WALLACK), it became home to VAUDEVILLE and light entertainment. Niblo's Garden, on the northeast corner of Broadway and Prince Street, expanded in 1839 to include a conventional theatre catering to musical events and standard fare. In 1848, after the complex burned down, Niblo took the lease of the ASTOR PLACE OPERA HOUSE, which he held during the riot that year. The Garden's theatres reopened in 1849 and continued to feature stars of music, COMEDY, dance, pantomime and extravaganza. Niblo retired from management in 1861, although the theatre, which had been rebuilt after a 1872 fire, survived until 1892. It is remembered for 30 years of appearances there by the RAVEL FAMILY and the 1866 production of *The Black Crook*. RKB MCH

Nicaragua Nicaragua's early claim to drama lies in *El baile de Güegüence* (*The Dance of the Old Man*), a folkloric piece combining ballet and dialogue whose origins belong to the Nahuatl pre-Columbian period. By the time it was recorded, certain Spanish elements had been integrated into the story of an old man, el Macho Ratón, in a family exchange with the regional governor. Less pure than the *RABINAL ACHÍ*, the Mayaquiché play from the Guatemalan region, it nonetheless conserves vestiges of the indigenous dramatic tradition.

The colonial years left few traces of theatre in Nicaragua. Through the 19th century travelling companies visited the country and several expatriate writers, such as the Cuban-Dominican Alejandro Angulo Guridi (1826–1906) and the Salvadoran Francisco Gavidia (1864–1955), settled there. Rubén Darío (1867–1916), Latin America's modernist poet *par excellence*, presented two plays in Managua, one comedy and one tragedy, but both texts are lost.

The 20th century Sporadic theatre activity continued in the 1900s. Santiago Arguello (1871–1940), Marcial Rios Jerez (b.1897) and Hernán Robleto (1895–1968), who spent most of his life in Mexico, tried varieties of tragedy mixed with religious and romantic dramas, but without great aesthetic success. It was the creation of the literary journal *Vanguardia* (*Vanguard*) in 1928, followed by a homonymous theatre group in 1935, that began to bring to Nicaragua a sense of world styles and techniques. Joaquín Pasos (1915–47) and José Coronel Urtecho (b.1906) exaggerated the popular figures of Nicaraguan folk tales into grotesque caricatures with popular poetry in their *Chinfonía burguesa* (*Bourgeois 'Chymphony'*; written in 1932 as a poem, rewritten as a dramatic FARCE in 1939). PABLO ANTONIO CUADRA also utilized traditional and popular religious forms. His major play *Por los caminos van los campesinos* (*Along the Roads Go the Peasants*, 1937) focused on a farmer's struggle to retain his land and his dignity in the face of adversity, aggression and injustice. Other plays of psychological bent are *El árbol seco* (*The Dry Tree*) and *El avaro* (*The Miser*). Other playwrights include ROLANDO STEINER, whose major works are *Judit* and *La puerta* (*The Door*), and Alberto Ycaza (b.1945), the author of surrealistic plays (see SURREALISM) based on a pre-Hispanic tradition, such as *Ancestral 66*.

Nicaragua has one of the most modern theatre buildings in all of Latin America, the Rubén Darío Theatre, completed in 1969 and located on the shores of Lake Managua. Its 1300-seat main stage and a small experimental theatre below (named after Edgar Munguía) offer attractive space for both local productions and visiting troupes. Before the

fall of the Somoza dynasty in 1979, several amateur theatre groups were operational, including Jaime Alberdi's Teatro Experimental de Managua (Managua Experimental Theatre). With the advent of the Sandinista Revolution (1979), these groups were displaced by a new revolutionary theatre based largely on the Cuban model. Socorro Bonilla made the transition with the Comedia Nacional de Nicaragua (Nicaraguan National Comedy), established in 1965. Under the direction of the Ministry of Culture, this movement generated new groups throughout the provinces that concentrated on popular theatre with liberationist themes embedded in folkloric music and dance. With only rudimentary props and costumes, the people used theatre to express their culture, their joys and sorrows, and the process of change in a revolutionary society. Groups include the Nixtayolero, Teatro Investigación de Niquinohomo, Xipaltomal and others. Hernán Robledo and Alan Bolt are primary writers and directors in this movement, which is reinforced by the annual festivals and meetings sponsored regularly by the government. GW

See: O. Ciccone, 'Il muestra nacional de teatro (Managua)', *Latin American Theatre Review*, 16, 2, Spring 1983; N. Miller, 'Il encuentro de teatristas latinoamericanos y del Caribe (Nicaragua, 1983)', *Latin American Theatre Review*, 17, 2, Spring 1984; C. Morton, 'The Nicaraguan Drama: Theatre of Testimony', *Latin American Theatre Review*, 17, 2, Spring 1984; O. Rodríguez Sardiñas and C. M. Suárez Radillo, *Teatro contemporáneo hispanoamericano*, Madrid, 1971; C. Solórzano, *Teatro breve hispanoamericano*, Madrid, 1970.

Nichols, Anne c.1891–1966 American playwright. Nichols wrote numerous forgettable plays, VAUDEVILLE sketches and MUSICALS before and after the phenomenal success of her recording-breaking *Abie's Irish Rose*. The story of the mixed-up marriage between a Jewish boy and an Irish girl, the play ran for 2327 consecutive nights on BROADWAY (1922–7), even though critics found it cliché-ridden. The play made a fortune for Nichols, was revived in 1937 and 54, filmed in 1928 and 46, and became a radio show in the 1940s and the basis of a 1970s TV sitcom. FB

Nichols, Mike [Michael Igor Peschkowsky] 1931– American actor, director and producer. Born in Berlin, Nichols fled to New York with his parents to escape the Nazis. He attended the University of Chicago for two years, after which he studied with LEE STRASBERG at the ACTORS STUDIO. He began his professional career in Chicago performing with a comedy group that included Elaine May. In 1957 Nichols and May developed their own act, which comprised regular satirical sketches and improvisations. They gave two New York concerts in 1959, followed by *An Evening with Mike Nichols and Elaine May* on BROADWAY in 1960, establishing both performers as major stars. Nichols turned to directing in 1963 with NEIL SIMON's *Barefoot in the Park*, followed by *The Knack* (1964), *Luv* (1964), *The Odd Couple* (1965), *The Apple Tree* (1966), *Plaza Suite* (1968) and *The Prisoner of Second Avenue* (1971). His comic inventiveness made him one of the most sought-after directors in New York. Beginning in the 1970s he turned to more serious fare, including *Streamers* (1976),

Comedians (1976), *The Gin Game* (1977), *The Real Thing* (1983), *Hurlyburly* (1984), *Waiting for Godot* (1989), *Elliot's Loves* (1990) and *Death and the Maiden* (1992), demonstrating skill and vitality in shaping complex dramatic works. Richard Schickel (*Time*) praised his 'uncanny sense of modern body language' in communicating the shapeless lives in DAVID RABE's *Hurlyburly*. Nichols produced the musical *Annie* (1977) and *The Gin Game*. His major films include *Who's Afraid of Virginia Woolf?* (1965), *The Graduate* (1968), *Catch-22* (1970), *Carnal Knowledge* (1971), *Postcards from the Edge* (1990) and *Wolf* (1994). Winner of five Tonys and one Oscar, Nichols remains one of the most successful American directors of the contemporary theatre. TLM

Nichols, Peter (Richard) 1927– British dramatist, who worked as an actor and schoolteacher, before starting to write TV plays in the early 1960s. His first stage success came with *A Day in the Death of Joe Egg*, about how two parents coped (or not) with their spastic child, a 'vegetable'. This showed his ability to take a painful theme, to handle it with a humour that did not minimize the despair and with a directness that became his hallmark as a writer. His plays fall with deceptive ease into two categories: those with expansive themes and messages for our time, and those with intimate or domestic stories. The first category would include *The National Health* (1969), about hospital life where a ward for the incurably sick becomes a symbol for Britain, *The Freeway* (1974) where Britain grinds to a halt in a monstrous traffic jam (both staged by the NATIONAL THEATRE) and *Poppy* (1983), a Victorian panto about the opium wars in China, staged with inappropriate lavishness by the ROYAL SHAKESPEARE COMPANY. The second includes such plays as *Down Forget-me-not Lane* (1971), *Chez Nous* (1974), *Born in the Gardens* (1980) and *Passion Play* (1981), in which the alter egos of the partners in an adulterous marriage are given a chance to speak. *Privates on Parade* (1977), a comedy based upon his experience and his assessment of imperial decline, could be an exception to prove this categorizing rule; but he is a writer who moves easily from the general to the particular and back again. Depressed by *Poppy* and convinced that writers were mistreated by directors' theatre, he wrote a *cri de coeur* against the system in *A Piece of My Mind* (1986), which was not well received, even by those whom it did not criticize. JE

Nicolet, Jean-Baptiste 1728–96 Parisian showman who inherited his father's puppet shows at the fairs of St Germain and St Laurent, and soon added live actors, playing the roles of HARLEQUINS and bankers himself. In 1759 he removed to a building in the Boulevard du Temple, amplifying his offerings of PANTOMIMES with comic opera and pieces from the repertory of the COMÉDIE-ITALIENNE. He made an instant success, and for 30 years had to placate the jealousies of the legitimate theatres and the scrutiny of police inspectors. Outside, the theatre performed *scènes à la Momus*, farcical skits; inside, saucy plays were interspersed with acrobats, rope dancers and trained animals: the ape Turco made all Paris laugh with his PARODY of the indisposed Molé. In 1772 Louis XV was amused by the troupe and dubbed it the Théâtre des Grands Danseurs

du Roi. Deemed by his rivals illiterate and churlish, Nicolet managed by his intuition of popular taste to amass a fortune and could boast a company of 30 actors, 60 dancers, 20 musicians and 150 works in his repertory. 'To go from strength to strength as at Nicolet's' became a proverb. After the Revolution he renamed his house the Théâtre de la Gaîté and added classics, enjoying a huge success with MOLIÈRE's *Georges Dandin*. LS

Nietzsche, Friedrich 1844–1900 German philosopher and aphorist. Nietzsche's most substantial contribution to the theatre, his essay *The Birth of Tragedy* (1872), argues that Greek TRAGEDY came about through the eruption of irrational, Dionysian forces into the serenity of Apollonian culture (see GREECE, ANCIENT). Tragedy declined, Nietzsche argued, when it was reduced in scope by EURIPIDES and clarified by Socratic rationalism. Nietzsche's version of Greek drama has often been questioned and may more correctly be regarded as an argument in support of RICHARD WAGNER's music drama, which, to Nietzsche's mind, exercised a 'Dionysian' influence in the modern 'Socratic' world. Later, Nietzsche was to repudiate both Wagner and the ideas expressed in *The Birth of Tragedy*. SW

Nieva, Francisco 1927– Spanish playwright, director and designer. He began writing plays in the 1950s during a long residence in Paris, but did not achieve professional stagings for more than a decade after returning to Spain. The 1976 production of *Combate de Opalos y Tasia* (*The Battle of Opalos and Tasia*) and *Carroza de plomo candente* (*The Carriage of White-Hot Lead*) won the prestigious Mayte Prize. Other prize-winning productions include his adaptation of CERVANTES's *Los baños de Argel* (*The Baths of Algiers*, 1979), written, directed and designed by Nieva; *La señora Tártara* (*Woman from the Nether Land*, 1980); and *Coronada y el toro* (*Coronada and the Bull*, 1982), staged at the TEATRO NACIONAL MARÍA GUERRERO, with direction and design by the author.

In 1986 he was elected to the Royal Spanish Academy, and in 1992 became the first playwright honoured by the Prince of Asturias Prize for Literature. His plays are noted for their verbal and visual imagination and for their spirit of transgression. Highly metatheatrical and theatricalist, often erotic and always wildly funny, they are anti-realistic and anti-illusionist, reminiscent of SURREALISM. PZ

Niger An inland republic which before its independence in 1960 was part of the French West African Federation, Niger has few concrete achievements in the field of modern theatre. What existed during the colonial period was limited to a few troupes: the Amicales des Fonctionnaires de Niamey, the Elmina Renaissance and the Amis de Niamey; a couple of plays by the ex-École William Ponty graduate Mahamane Dandobi: *L'Aventure d'une chèvre* (*The Adventure of a Goat*, 1955) and *La Légende de Kabrin Kabra* (*The Legend of Kabrin Kabra*, 1957), both published in *Traits d'Union*, the cultural organ of French West Africa; and performances by William Ponty (see SENEGAL) students on tour. Although visiting French theatre troupes, under the direction of Pierre Ringel, brought MOLIÈRE to supplement this scant activity, because of the language used – French – this cultural offering was accessible only to the Western-educated minority.

But theatrical activity in French has fared no better after independence, with only one full-length play in that language published to date: the historian André Salifou's *Tanimoune* (1973). Set in the 19th century, it dramatizes the successful struggle of Tanimoune, ruler of Damagaran, to overthrow the tutelage of a Bornu king and to set up an independent Hausa state.

What has flourished, however, since independence is a popular theatre in the national languages known as *teyatur* in Hausa (from the French *théâtre*) – the language most widely spoken in Niger and used in these plays. Student theatre groups, *samariyas* (mostly uneducated youth groups involved in community projects), and radio and television groups are the greatest practitioners of this genre, which also includes dance-dramas known as 'ballets'. Arts festivals at regional and national levels, and radio and school competitions, provide a forum for the various troupes and act as a stimulus to creation. This theatre has been actively encouraged by successive governments, which provide money for the troupes, construct *maisons des jeunes* (youth centres that house theatres), and programme festival plays on radio and television.

Drawing from the many play and imitative activities of traditional Hausa culture, as well as from its religious theatrical displays such as the *Kora* and the *Bori* (exorcism and spirit-possession cults, respectively), and using their resources of song, dance, MASK and MIME, Niger's popular theatre improvises on themes that range from history through developmental issues to contemporary social ills. But because of extensive government support for it, popular theatre sometimes presents little more than the government's point of view. JCM

See: J. Beik, *The Hausa Theatre in Niger*, New York and London, 1987; R. Cornevin, *Le Théâtre en Afrique noire et à Madagascar*, 1970.

Nigeria Nigeria, with over 90 million people, is the most populous country in Africa. It became independent from Britain in 1960, within boundaries created during the 19th century by European rivalry, which ignored existing African societies. The British legacy of a tripartite regional division within the country was singularly misconceived as a starting-point for Nigeria's future national political development. Relations of domination and disadvantage between ethnic groups remain a serious political problem, despite the failure of the civil war (also called the Biafran War) to split the country into independent states at the end of the 1960s. To some extent, though, inter-ethnic division has been eroded by the abandonment of the regional structure and the creation of states (30 by 1993) under a federal system, and by the gradual creation of a governing elite and strong interest groups that cut across ethnic lines.

During the 1970s and the so-called oil boom, Nigerians were able to use massive oil revenues to create both spectacular consumption and a large-scale internal market (though the country failed to exploit these revenues to industrialize and to create a more dynamic economy). Much of this spending was channelled through the states – which proved significant for the development of drama, as each state sought to establish its own arts council and television station. In addition, there was a huge expansion in the university system, at both federal and state levels: by the early 1990s the country boasted more than 40 such institutions. This has led to a significant stimulus in publishing, including that of drama texts for study as literature. A number of universities (including Ibadan, Jos, Ahmadu Bello, Ife (Obafemi Awolowo), Calabar, Ilorin, Benin, Nsukka, Port Harcourt, Abuja) have established degree courses in theatre and performing arts, and graduates from these courses initially found many new opportunities for employment in the newly founded state arts council troupes and television stations. Since the early 1980s, however, the drastic reduction in oil revenues and therefore in Nigeria's GNP has arrested the development and even the consolidation of this establishment.

There are regional variations to this general picture of substantial commitment to theatre from the Nigerian

A Nigerian Travelling Theatre company on the road.

public purse. While all the states, without exception, are conscious of their heritage in the traditional performing arts, contemporary theatre is more actively encouraged by the southern states, and is most vigorous in the largely Yoruba states (Ondo, Oyo, Osun, Ogun, Lagos and Kwara). This is true both of indigenous-language drama and of drama in English, of which perhaps as much as three-quarters of Nigeria's very substantial output has been written by Yoruba playwrights. Nevertheless, theatre is neither weak or necessarily retarded in the largely Muslim Hausa and Fulani states in the north. Traditional performance there is dynamic and complex, though different from the southern masquerade traditions (see MASQUERADES IN AFRICA); modern drama is developing in rural villages in innovative and political ways; and some young northerners, such as Sadiq Balewa, are notably channelling their dramatic talents into film-making and television. States like Benue, whose peoples are not part of the large groupings (Hausa, Yoruba, Igbo), have supplied a disproportionately large number of talented drama graduates who have become actors, teachers and recorders of rich performance traditions which have received national recognition.

The states within the Nigerian federation have not entirely taken over the patronage of traditional performance. Many traditional rulers remain the ultimate authority for seasonal and religious rituals and cults. Nevertheless, the sponsorship by each state of a regional cultural identity has created the necessary conditions for contemporary drama to grow out of traditional performance, because dances, music, masquerades, festivals, storytelling, minstrelsy – all part of the oral tradition – have survived the years of colonial rule to offer now a richer historical view than that drawn from written colonial records. This forms the basis of both discourse and aesthetic in the emerging Nigerian theatre.

For example, J. A. Adedeji's pioneering study of *Alarinjo* theatre in the Oyo Yoruba empire shows how that theatrical art evolved in the 14th century out of the *egungun* masquerade, becoming eventually both court MASQUE and professional popular travelling theatre. This research is complemented by other studies of *egungun*, exploring, for example, the mimetic satire of the *gelede* masquerade which imposes animated wooden puppetry upon the mask. *Egungun* is given a complex metaphysical significance by the playwright WOLE SOYINKA, both in his writing and in his aesthetic theory. In fact, many Yoruba playwrights, writing either in Yoruba or in English, find both content and style in *egungun*, the popularity of which is, if anything, on the increase. A later outcome of the professional popular travelling theatre *Alarinjo*, itself an outgrowth of the *egungun* masquerade, was the YORUBA TRAVELLING THEATRE, and this in turn has developed into a prolific and commercially successful Yoruba television and film drama.

The *Ozidi* saga of the Ijo people is an example of a full-scale dramatic performance, still put on today, within the tradition. It takes a number of years to rehearse, and three nights and days to perform. It engulfs the whole village in which it takes place (see J. P. CLARK- BEKEDEREMO). Similar in dramatic scope is the drama *Ekong* (Ibi), which takes six years to rehearse and involves in the enactment of its narrative every aspect of performance. Scholars like D. Adelugba, J. Amankulor, M. Echeruo, O. Enekwe, M. Nzewi, O. Ogunba and N. Ugonna have variously and extensively researched and analysed the relationship between theatre and drama on the one hand, and trance, festivals, masquerades and RITUALS on the other – for example, in the Igbo Ekpe dance-drama which occurs in December at the close of the Ekpe cycle within the religious-ritual year.

These ancient traditional performances can still extend their scope and are able to represent modern Nigeria; one vividly contemporary yet traditional theatrical display is the *kwagh-hir* of the Tiv people in Benue state, which consists of highly complex animated PUPPETS, either in tableaux on mobile platforms depicting modern Tivland, or as giant bestiary and SHAMANesque MASKS. They are non-affective and are presented in a night of competition between villages. Each village's puppet team is backed up by a chorus of women singers and a large orchestra of traditional instruments. The playlets performed by these teams frequently use SATIRE in a biting depiction of contemporary social custom. The assessment, by a team of judges, is an aesthetic one and seeks to relate the depiction of modern Tivland to established traditional aesthetics, especially in song and music.

In the north, there are nascent theatrical elements in the grand spectacle of the Fulani emirs' *Sallah* processions on the high feast days of Islam. Hundreds, sometimes thousands, of people take part in each *Sallah*, either on caparisoned horses and camels or on foot, costumed and in armour. In the midst of this pomp, and often ridiculing it, are the *'yankama*, whose entertainment, *'yanka-manchi*, is made up of satirical skits, songs and scurrilous SURREALISM. The *'yankama* are travelling minstrels who entertain both at the emir's court and in the market-place. They belong to guilds, and are sometimes protected and patronized by an emir; they are an accepted part of the cultural life of the emirates. Not so *Bori* (researched variously by D. Adelugba, A. Horn, M. Onwuejeogwu), which is an ancient Hausa ritual-possession cult, pre-Islamic, practised by women who live sequestered within their own compound. *Bori* has an affective healing context with access to the spirit world; it also has a pure entertainment mode, the enjoyment of which derives from a complex aesthetic. *Bori* is not acceptable to Islam, or to the traditional rulers. Yet another sort of traditional performance among some Hausa villages is the lord-of-misrule festival, an example of which is *Kalankuwa* in Zaria, Kaduna state, organized by the young male farmers. There is a strong contemporary satire in the mimetic role-play, with people in naturalistic costume acting the parts of national and local rulers and bureaucrats, in the context of 24 hours of total licence within the village.

The years of the struggle for independence were accompanied by a flowering of dramatic talent at all levels in society, which has not abated in the 35 years since independence was achieved. Inspiration comes from many directions, though the traditional arts are dominant. The main legacy of performance traditions to new Nigerian drama is the concept of 'total theatre'. This applies whether the play is performed in English or, say, Yoruba, or in pidgin, or even in a mixture of languages and language registers. The linguistic dimension is itself a part of total theatre which also includes significant non-naturalistic idioms: masks, masquerades, music, dance, rhythm and movement, incantation and word-play. Many of these elements are fused to create surrealist physical imagery. Plays which vividly demonstrate total theatre are the Yoruba operas developed in the 1950s by people like HUBERT OGUNDE and at the Mbari Clubs at Oshogbo and Ibadan, where DURO LADIPO's great success *Oba Ko So* (1964) was created. Other important examples of total theatre are Soyinka's *A Dance of the Forests* (1960) and WALE OGUNYEMI's *Langbodo* (1980).

Some playwrights deal with the supernatural as content, but avoid its direct meaning through symbolism in the style of the play. Sonny Oti's *The Old Masters* (1977) deals naturalistically with the clash between Church and cult; and the brilliant actor E. K. Ogunmola, in his adaptation of Amos Tutuola's *The Palmwine Drinkard*, retreats from Tutuola's surrealism. Since the mid-70s, a new generation of dramatists has emerged whose work inclines towards a radical appreciation of the problems of society. Here again the principle of total theatre is still highly valued, and plays such as FEMI OSOFISAN's *Morountodun* (1982), OLA ROTIMI's *If* (1983) and BODE SOWANDE's *Ajantala-Pinocchio* (1992) stimulate audience consciousness through a rich and constantly modulating range of theatre resources.

Many dramatists promote a serious debate on Nigeria's social formation, though re-creating traditional performance modes. Folklore, myth, magic and ritual become the framework for engaging in rigorous analysis of the class structure and polarities inherent in the neo-colonial state. Notable works of this mode are Osofisan's *The Chattering and the Song* (1976), KOLE OMOTOSO's *The Curse* (1976) and *Shadows in the Horizon* (1975), Olu Obafemi's *Suicide Syndrome* (1987) and Akanji Nasiru's *Our Survival* (1982). Ben Tolomoju, Stella Oyedepo, TESS ONWUEME (*The Desert Encroaches*, 1985; *Legacies*, 1988, among others), Bode Osanyin and Fred Agbeyegbe (e.g. *The King Must Dance Naked*, 1990) also belong to this emergent radical theatrical tradition.

The synthesizing, multi-referential nature of much of the most challenging Nigerian drama is seen also in the way playwrights draw on quite diverse models from world theatre: Ladipo's *Eda* from HOFMANNSTHAL's *Jedermann* (*Everyman*); the Zaria Performing Arts Company's *Lawal Kung Fu Kaduna* from UDALL's *Ralph Roister Doister*; Rotimi's *The Gods Are Not to Blame* from SOPHOCLES' *Oedipus the King*; Osofisan's *Who's Afraid of Solarin?* from GOGOL's *The Government Inspector*. All these have become distinctly Nigerian plays. Their audiences neither know nor care about the originals; they receive the plays as yet further contribution to the rich texture of Nigerian theatre today.

Other plays of social criticism are far more exclusively reliant on (often didactic) dialogue. Writers and performers are influenced by NATURALISM, on television and in the cinema as well as in the theatre. A direct representation of contemporary life on stage appeals to actors as well as to audiences, who take pleasure in the acute observation of human behaviour at a time of extensive social change. Naturalistic drama is exemplified in the plays of James Ene-Henshaw, such as his *Dinner for Promotion* (1967).

Plays concerned with personal morality in sexual and social relationships among upwardly mobile Nigerians tend also to be crafted and performed naturalistically: Meki Nzewi's *Two Fists in One Mouth* (1976), 'Laolu Ogunniyi's television plays (see TELEVISION DRAMA) such as *Candle in the Wind* (1977), ZULU SOFOLA's *The Sweet Trap* (1977), and Rasheed Gbadomosi's *Echoes from the Lagoon* (1972) all exemplify this. Naturalism, though still present, is less obvious in a number of theatrically effective historical dramas, like *Ovonramwen Nogbaisi* by Rotimi, as well as in some pidgin plays such as 'Segun Oyekunle's *Katakata for Sofahead* (1978) – about a group of petty criminals who, in gaol, act out the poverty and petty thieving of the latest convict to join them. Tunde Lakoju's *Moonshine Solidarity* (1980), a political satire on the 1979 civilian government elections in Nigeria which uses the newspaper cartoon strip character Pappy Joe, is read naturalistically by Nigerian audiences – as are pidgin adaptations of BRECHT.

If there is an underlying aesthetic in contemporary Nigerian theatre, it is the way in which quite disparate styles are effortlessly combined in performance. Life is presented on the stage, directly; but it is mediated by symbolic representations of a further, or 'other', reality. This may result from performing to eager audiences with eclectic tastes.

A significant extension of Nigerian theatre is seen in the work of Nigerian playwrights living in the USA or Britain. Tess Onwueme has been based in the USA since 1990; Biyi Bandele-Thomas, living in London, continues to address that central concern of Nigerian drama, the state of the nation state (*Marching for Fausa*, 1993). Nigerian myth may still provide core thematic material for an Anglo-Irish–Nigerian playwright such as Gabriel Gbadamosi (*Eshu's Faust*, 1992).

Practitioners in Yoruba-language theatre (Ladipo, Ogunde, MOSES OLAIYA ADEJUMO) were able to form professional, commercial theatre companies from the outset. From the 1960s onwards there were also many attempts by university-based practitioners to form performance companies: Soyinka and the Orishun Theatre, Rotimi and the Ori Olokun theatre (Ife), Onuora Enekwe, Kalu Ika and Meki Nzewi with the Oak Theatre in Nsukka.

With the end of the oil boom and the ever deepening economic crisis of the 1980s and 90s – exacerbated, as throughout Africa, by government's adherence to World Bank/IMF-imposed economic programmes – theatre might have been expected to decline through lack of audience support. Yet Nigerian theatre continues to attract a substantial audience, a tribute to its entertainment value as well as to its ability to speak to popular perception of current realities. Furthermore, even though the audience for Nigerian theatre is still often centred on universities and/or is made up of members of the elite (productions sponsored by banks and other organizations are now a familiar feature of Lagos social life, for example), there are signs of an interaction between popular and literary theatres and of the existence of a broad-based audience for companies prepared to perform outside prestige venues. The last 15 years have seen a growth in the establishment of fully professional and commercial theatre companies, often formed by formerly university-based dramatists: J. P.

Clark-Bekederemo's PEC Repertory Theatre (Lagos) has been joined in the 1990s by Bode Sowande's Odu Themes Meridian (Ibadan) and Ola Rotimi's African Cradle Theatre (Ife). Other significant companies include the Dasuku Living Theatre (Port Harcourt) and the Ayota Community Theatre, based in a low-income area of Lagos. CD

See: D. Adelugba (ed.), LACE Interview series, Univ. of Ibadan; *Nigerian Magazine* (Lagos); *Nigerian Stage* (Univ. of Ilorin); M. Banham and C. Wake, *African Theatre Today*, London, 1976; E. Clark, *Hubert Ogunde: The Making of Nigerian Theatre*, London, 1979; J. P. Clark, *The Ozidi Saga*, Ibadan, 1977; B. Crow, *Studying Drama*, London, 1983; H. J. and M. T. Drewal, *Gelede: Art and Female Power among the Yoruba*, Bloomington, Ind., 1983; C. Dunton, *Make Man Talk True: Nigerian Drama since 1970*, London, 1992; M. Etherton, *The Development of African Drama*, London, 1982; B. Jeyifo, *The Yoruba Popular Travelling Theatre of Nigeria*, Lagos, 1984, and *The Truthful Lie: Essays on a Sociology of African Drama*, London, 1985; Z. Kofoworola and Y. Lateef, *Hausa Performing Arts and Music*, Lagos, 1987; O. Ogunbiyi (ed.), *Drama and Theatre in Nigeria: A Critical Source Book*, Lagos, 1981; W. Soyinka, *Myth, Literature and the African World*, Cambridge, 1976.

Nilsen, Hans Jacob 1897–1957 Norwegian director and actor, crucial in the development of modern Norwegian theatre; head of the NORSKE TEATRET (1933–4 and 1946–50), the NATIONALE SCENE (1934–9) and the Folketeatret (1952–5); during the war he joined the Fri Norsk Scene (Free Norwegian Stage) in Sweden. Like his associate PER LINDBERG, Nilsen sought to create a socially committed theatricalistic people's theatre. Among his achievements were frequently controversial productions of important new plays, such as GRIEG'S *Our Power and Our Glory* (1935), the ČAPEKS' *Insect Comedy* (1939), and radical revisionings of classics such as his 'anti-romantic' *Peer Gynt*, with himself as Peer (1948), and his cartoon-like *Jeppe of the Hill* (1934). As an actor he achieved particular success as Hamlet, Peer Gynt and Masterbuilder Solness. HL

Nina Vance Alley Theatre see ALLEY THEATRE (Houston, Texas)

Ninagawa, Yukio 1935– Japanese theatre director. Ninagawa trained as an actor in the Seihai Theatre Company, where SHINGEKI (modern Japanese theatre) orthodoxy based on NATURALISM and REALISM was promoted. He began directing studio productions with the company, but when the ANGURA (underground) theatre movement took place in Tokyo in the late 1960s, reflecting the political campaign against the renewal of the Japan–USA Security Treaty, he left the STC in order to find a new style of staging: he formed Gendaijin Gekijyō (Contemporary People's Theatre, 1967–72) and then Sakura Sha (the Sakura Troupe, 1972–4). With these companies he staged several plays by Shimizu Kunio, including *Shinjyō afururu keihakusa* (*Silliness Filled with Sincerity*), for the late-night show at the Shinjyuku Art Theatre (the fringe base). The play succeeded in portraying the confused state of mind of the young people of the time and became a milestone of contemporary Japanese theatre.

In 1974 Ninagawa was invited to direct *Romeo and Juliet* by Tōhō, one of the largest commercial companies in Japan, and began work in both commercial and *shingeki* arenas. In 1983 he formed the Ninagawa Studio Theatre. Productions from the European classical theatre included *Macbeth* (Ninagawa's '"cherry-blossom" *Macbeth*'), *Medea* (taken to the EDINBURGH FESTIVAL in 1985 and 1986 respectively), *Oedipus Rex* and *The Tempest*. From the Japanese repertoire major productions included AKIMOTO MATSUYO's *Chikamatsu Shinjyū Monigatari* (*The Tale of Chikamatsu's Love Suicide*, 1989), Yukio Mishima's *Sotoba Komachi* (1990) and – for the NATIONAL THEATRE in London in 1991 – Shimitzu Kunio's *Tango at the End of Winter* (Ninagawa's first production in English). In 1994 his production of *Peer Gynt* was staged in Oslo on the occasion of the Winter Olympics, and then at the ROYAL SHAKESPEARE COMPANY's Barbican Theatre and in Manchester.

Ninagawa's belief is that the theatre is a place where the audience should see and experience the unusual – reflected in the vast theatrical scale of many of his productions. MY

Nō Serious and subtle Japanese dance drama that evolved in the 14th century out of earlier songs, dances and sketches. It was originally performed by priest-performers attached to Buddhist temples. In performance, movement, music and words create an ever-shifting web of tension and ambiguity. The combined repertories of the five schools of performing – Kanze, Hōshō, Kongō, Komparu and Kita – consist of c.240 plays.

A play text (*utaibon*, 'song book') contains prose (*kotoba*) and poetry (*utai*) sections. Prose is delivered in a sonorous voice that rises gradually and evenly in pitch, then drops at the end of a phrase. This typically repeating pattern is heard in all plays and varies only slightly by character type. The male actor does not attempt to reproduce the female voice but uses the normal male register when portraying a woman. Verse sections, which make up the bulk of the text, are sung (indicated by the musical term *fushi*, 'melody') by the Doer (*shite*), Sideman (*waki*), or Chorus (*ji*). The singing voice moves flexibly, with many melismas and slides, on and around base notes (three in soft style, *yowagin*, and five in strong style, *tsuyogin*). Verse composed in lines of 12 syllables, each line divided into a first phrase of 7 and a second phrase of 5 syllables, is known as normal rhythm (*hira nori*). This is the metre of the central, narrative song (*kuse*), sung by the Chorus, in which the major character dances a crucial event from his or her past. The vocal pattern of 7–5 syllables is overlaid on an 8-beat rhythm played by hip drum (*ōtsuzumi*), shoulder drum (*kotsuzumi*), and a bamboo flute (*nōkan*). The resulting syncopation produces an inherent musical tension. In contrast, verse in 8-syllable lines (*ō nori*) and 16-syllable lines (*chū nori*), are rhythmically congruent with the musical beat. These rhythms are used to accompany strong dances at the climax of a play, with a stick drum (*taiko*) adding to the rhythmic effect.

Voice, action and music are never precisely congruent, for that would be bare and uninteresting. Tempo continually fluctuates within a play, a scene or a phrase of movement or sound, following the basic Japanese aesthetic principle of *jo-ha-kyū* ('beginning, break, fast'). Each strand of the performance can be perceived separately; the spectator senses a continual advancing and receding of one performance element *vis-à-vis* the others. The well known finesse of *nō* performance rests on the Buddhist view that the world is in a state of continual flux. This view is exemplified in concrete performance characteristics. Acceptance of change underlies ZEAMI's admonition that the *nō* actor always seek newness or freshness (*hana*, 'flower') in performance. The actor should never do what is expected, but rather, by analysing the performance situation – the audience, the season, the time of day, previous plays on the bill – he should choose a play and an interpretation that will elicit audience interest by being unexpected and therefore novel and interesting.

The 240 or so plays in the current repertory are categorized into one of five play types according to the nature of the *shite* role. Representative plays of each type are the God (*kami*) play: *The Twin Pines* (*Takasago*), *Chikubu Island* (*Chikubu shima*), *The Crane and the Tortoise* (*Tsurukame*); Warrior (*asura*) play: *Atsumori*, *Kiyotsune*, *Sanemori*; Woman (*katsura*) play: *The Well Curb* (*Izutsu*), *Pining Wind* (*Matsukaze*), *The Feather Robe* (*Hagoromo*); Living-person (*genzai*) plays: *The Ataka Barrier* (*Ataka*), *The Sumida River* (*Sumidagawa*); and Demon (*kichiku*) plays: *The Earth Spider* (*Tsuchigumo*), *Benkei in the Boat* (*Funa Benkei*).

The dramatic development of a play can be analysed into five units according to *jo-ha-kyū* progression (*ha* is divided into *jo-ha-kyū* as well): Sideman's entrance (*jo*), Doer's entrance (*jo* of *ha*), Doer and Sideman conversation (*ha* of *ha*), Doer's main narrative (*kyu* of *ha*), and conclusion of Doer's narrative (*kyū*). Each of these scenes is made up of smaller modules (*shōdan*, 'small scene'), identifiable by function or form. The typical modules in a play are the opening music and Chorus song (*shidai*), Sideman's speech of self-introduction (*nanori*), travel song (*michiyuki*) and arrival speech (*tsukizerifu*), Doer's arrival song (*issei*), Doer–Sideman conversation, either spoken (*mondō*) or sung (*kakeai*), Doer's opening narrative song (*kuri* and *sashi*) leading into Doer's main narrative dance (*kuse*), interlude by Villager (*ai kyōgen*), Sideman's song waiting for Doer's return (*machi utai*), and Doer's final dance (*mai*) and Chorus song (*kiri*). High-pitched songs (*age uta*), low-pitched songs (*sage uta*), Doer–Chorus songs (*rongi*) and other modules are used where needed.

Around 1600 the stage became standardized as a raised dancing platform about 19ft square; it was made of polished cyprus wood and covered by a temple-like roof which was supported by pillars at the four corners. The roof protects the outdoor stage from the elements and demarcates the performance area visually, thus helping to focus audience attention on the performing area. A bridgeway (*hashigakari*) 20–40ft long runs from upstage right diagonally back to the dressing room and serves as an entrance and exit passage.

Role types have conventional locations on the stage. The Sideman sits beside the Sideman pillar, down left, the flautist is beside the flute pillar, up left, and the Doer is either centre stage or near the Doer pillar, up right. Players of the interlude (*kyōgen kata*) sit on the bridgeway, musicians (*hayashi kata*) sit rear centre (*ato za*), stage assistants (*kōken*) wait upstage right, and the Chorus sits in two rows of four or five singers on the left side stage (*waki za*). The Chorus became standard in *nō* after Zeami; its seating area is usually covered by a separate roof.

Today festival performances occur on traditional free-standing outdoor stages maintained by temples and shrines. Nighttime performance by torchlight (*takigi nō*) in late summer became popular in the 1980s, in part for tourist promotion. Contemporary urban *nō* stages are constructed within modern buildings where they can be used daily for training, rehearsal and performance without regard to weather. Major stages include the Kanze, Hōshō, Umewaka, Tessenkai and Kita theatres owned and run by these groups, and the National Noh Theatre, funded by the national government, all in Tokyo, the Kanze and Kongō theatres in Kyoto, and the Yamamoto theatre in Osaka. New plays and fusion productions occasionally occur. JRB

See: J. R. Brandon, (ed.), *Nō and Kyōgen in the Contemporary World*, Honolulu, 1996; J. Goff, *Noh Drama and The Tale of Genji*, Princeton, N.J., 1991; T. B. Hare, *Zeami's Style: The Noh Plays of Zeami Motokiyo*, Stanford, Calif., 1986; D. Keene, *Nō: The Classical Theatre of Japan*, Palo Alto, Calif., 1966, and (ed.), *Twenty Plays of the Nō Theatre*, New York, 1970; K. Komparu, *The Noh Theater: Principles and Perspectives*, Tokyo, 1983; Nippon Gakujutsu Shinkokai (ed.), *Japanese Noh Drama*, 3 vols., Tokyo, 1955, 1959, 1960; P. G. O'Neill, *A Guide to Noh*, Tokyo, 1954, and *Early Nō Drama: Its Background, Character, and Development, 1300–1450*, London, 1959; E. de Poorter (tr.), *Zeami's Talks on Sarugaku*, Amsterdam, 1986; T. Rimer and M. Yamazaki (tr.), *On the Art of the Nō Drama: The Major Treatises of Zeami*, Princeton, N.J., 1984; R. Tyler, *Pining Wind: A Cycle of Nō Plays*, Ithaca, N.Y., 1978, and *Granny Mountains: A Second Cycle of Nō Plays*, Ithaca, N.Y., 1978; K. Yasuda, *Masterworks of the Nō Theater*, Bloomington, Ind., 1989. JRB

Noah, Mordecai M(anuel) 1785–1851 American playwright. Noah was an active Zionist who sought his livelihood in politics (surveyor of the Port of New York, judge of the Court of Sessions) and journalism (New York *Enquirer*, the *Commercial Advertiser*, the *Times and Messenger*) and his diversion in the theatre. He was an inveterate theatregoer, an intimate of the managers (PRICE, Edmund Simpson, DUNLAP and SOL SMITH), and an occasional playwright. His ardent patriotism was reflected in his documentary-like plays: *She Would Be a Soldier* (1819), based on the Battle of Chippewa (1814) and written for Catherine Leesugg; *The Siege of Tripoli* (1820), the piratical menace with which Noah had had first-hand experience as Consul to Tunis; *Marion; or, The Hero of Lake George* (1821), based on the Battle of Saratoga; *The Grecian Captive* (1822), on the Greek Revolution; and *The Siege of Yorktown* (1824), set in the Revolutionary War. *She Would Be a Soldier* became a popular patriotic piece for national holidays for over 40 years. RM

Noble, Adrian (Keith) 1950– British director, who studied at Bristol University and the Drama Centre in

London, before becoming an associate director of the BRISTOL OLD VIC (1976–9). He was a guest director at the ROYAL EXCHANGE THEATRE, Manchester, in 1980–1, where his productions of *The Duchess of Malfi* (1980, with HELEN MIRREN) and *A Doll's House* (1981) won critical acclaim, particularly when they transferred to the Round House in London. From 1980 to 82, Noble was resident director with the ROYAL SHAKESPEARE COMPANY, becoming an associate director in 1982; here his productions of *King Lear* (1982) and *Henry V* (1984) attracted particular attention within a range of other ambitious Shakespearian and Jacobean works.

Noble is an imaginative, original director, whose weaknesses are related to his strengths. To present Lear and the Fool, played by MICHAEL GAMBON and ANTONY SHER, as a BECKETT-like couple from a Shakespearian *Waiting for Godot* was a bold gamble which nearly worked at Stratford-upon-Avon; but to offer a version of *Mephisto* (1986), without much in the way of a devil, was less happy. Noble has also directed *Antony and Cleopatra* (1982), *The Comedy of Errors* and *Measure for Measure* (1983), *The Winter's Tale* (1984) and *As You Like It* (1985) for the RSC; and *Don Giovanni* for Kent Opera. His compression of the three parts of *Henry VI* and *Richard III* into a trilogy, *The Plantagenets* (1988), was outstanding during the two difficult RSC seasons preceding TERRY HANDS's departure in 1990. Noble took over from him as the RSC's director, staging the two parts of *Henry IV* (1991) and three plays by SOPHOCLES – *Oedipus Tyrannus, Oedipus at Colonus* and *Antigone*, collectively known as *The Thebans* (1991). This trilogy, which grouped together plays of various themes and written at different times in Sophocles' life, gave a chronological narrative but little internal logic. It was said to be his answer to ARIANE MNOUCHKINE's *Les Atrides*.

More exciting and rewarding was his production of *Hamlet* (1992), with a virtually uncut text and KENNETH BRANAGH as the Prince. During the 1993–4 season this production, as well as those of *King Lear* with ROBERT STEPHENS and *Macbeth* with DEREK JACOBI, could be seen on the main RSC stages, indicating his eagerness to tackle the demanding heights of Shakespearian drama, together with his revivals of *The Winter's Tale* and of TOM STOPPARD's *Travesties*. With the tragedies, Noble's ability to provide a clear if rather uncomplicated reading of the text, allowing for an uncluttered central performance to emerge, was demonstrated with particular success in *King Lear*. JE

Noda Hideki 1955– Japanese playwright, director and actor. Noda's theatre company Yume no Yūmin Sha (Dream Theatre Company, 1976) was born of the drama society of the University of Tokyo, where he was a student of law. His first play performed outside the university, *Run Merusu* (*Hashire Merusu*, 1976), was written for the young theatre groups competition sponsored by VAN 99 Hall Theatre. Since then most of his plays – such as *Hunting Boys* (*Shōnen Gari*, 1979), *The Capture in Zenda Castle* (*Zenda-jyō no Toriko*, 1981) and *The Fallen Beasts* (*Nokemono Kitarite*, 1982) – have attracted large audiences. He is a third-generation member of the ANGURA (underground) theatre movement of the 1960s, but his predecessors' influences are found only remotely in his work.

His theatre is described as 'larger than life' because of its athletic, dynamic style of acting, spacious and spectacular design, and absurd and fantastic story lines from both Eastern and Western historical novels and classics. While Noda's theatrical language is stunningly rich and fluent, his 'playing with words' is the aspect that keeps his plays light-hearted and fast-moving. His theatre is very much like children's fantasy. As this suggests, his heroes and heroines are often adventurous children who live through different times and spaces. Yume no Yūmin Sha was invited to the EDINBURGH FESTIVAL in 1987 and to the New York International Art Festival in 1988. MY

Noguchi, Isamu 1904–88 Los Angeles-born sculptor and designer, who moved to Japan with his Japanese mother at age two, returning to the USA in 1917. Although he designed almost solely for dance, his abstract design, use of objects and ability to focus the cubic volume of the stage space had a significant effect on mid-20th-century design. In 1926 he went to Paris as assistant to the sculptor Brancusi, and also that year designed MASKS for actress Ito Michio in YEATS's *At the Hawk's Well*, his first theatre work. In 1935 choreographer Martha Graham asked him to design a set for *Frontier*; it was the first set she had ever used, and it began a collaboration that lasted until 1966 and included *Appalachian Spring* (1944) and *Seraphic Dialogue* (1955). Drawing on the tradition of N\O(¯,O) and the vocabulary of his own sculptures, his designs were simple distillations of images creating psychological rather than literal space. He has also designed for GEORGE BALANCHINE, Erick Hawkins, Merce Cunningham and the ROYAL SHAKESPEARE COMPANY (*King Lear*, 1955). AA

Nomura Manzō 1898–1978 Major 20th-century Japanese KYŌGEN actor of the Izumi school. A Living National Treasure, noted for his powerful and formal style of acting, he raised the social and artistic status of kyōgen, established kyōgen programmes separate from NŌ, and brought new audiences to this medieval theatre form. His successors are two brilliant sons, Nomura Mannojō (1930–) and Nomura Mansaku (1931–). JRB

non-profit theatre (USA) see RESIDENT NON-PROFIT PROFESSIONAL THEATRE

Norén, Lars 1944– Prolific Swedish playwright. Norén explores with disturbing frankness (underpinned by comedy) the perversions in relationships that have become brutal struggles to escape. Many of his plays focus on family gatherings, in which unresolved Oedipal tensions (often involving an absent or ineffective father) are reopened in futile attempts to find relief through speaking and hearing truths. Among the most important of his stage plays are *The Smile of the Underworld* (1980), *A Terrible Happiness* (1981), *Munich–Athens* (1982), *Night Is the Mother of Day* (1982), *Chaos Is God's Neighbour* (1983), *Holy Communion* (1984), *Autumn and Winter* (1989), *Dragonflies* (1989), and his play about EUGENE O'NEILL, *And Grant Us the Shadows* (1991). In 1992 Norén expanded his concerns and dramaturgy in the rather CHEKHOVIAN

Time Is Our Home, in which family tensions are contextualized and partly mediated within a summer-holiday gathering of family, friends and neighbours.   HL

Norman, (John) Frank 1930– British dramatist, who was brought up in a Dr Barnado's home from 1937 to 46. He worked as a farm labourer and with a travelling fair; and served several short prison sentences for minor crimes. His two autographical accounts of prison life, *Bang to Rights* (1958) and *Stand on Me* (1961), were published by Secker & Warburg, earning him a reputation as an authority on low life and cockney slang. With Lionel Bart he wrote the successful MUSICAL, *Fings Ain't Wot They Used T'Be* (1959), set in London's Soho, which was produced by JOAN LITTLEWOOD at the Theatre Royal, Stratford East, and had a long run in the WEST END. Further musicals with Joan Littlewood's company followed – *A Kayf Up West* (1964, with music by Stanley Myers), and *Costa Packet* (1972, with Lionel Bart and Alan Klein); but they were less successful. In 1969, his play *Insideout* was produced at the ROYAL COURT THEATRE; but since the early 1970s he has mainly written novels, reminiscences and studies of London's underworld.   JE

Norman, Marsha 1947– American playwright, whose realistic characters confront some devastation in their past to determine whether and how to survive. *Getting Out* (1978) reveals the internal conflict of a woman parolee in her choice of a new beginning – dramatized by two actresses who simultaneously portray her violent, younger self and her present, numbed self. In 1983 Norman won the Pulitzer Prize for *'night, Mother*, a wrenching enactment of the last night in the life of a hopeless young woman as she prepares herself and her mother for her suicide, and of the mother's desperate attempts to prevent it. Other works include *Third and Oak: The Laundromat (and) The Pool Hall* (1978), *The Holdup* (1983), *Traveler in the Dark* (1984), *Winter Shakers* (1987), *Sarah and Abraham* (1988, a MUSICAL with Norman L. Berman), *Loving Daniel Boone* (1993), several television plays, and the screenplay for *'night, Mother*. An eight-year absence from BROADWAY ended with *The Secret Garden* (1991), a musical based on Frances Hodgson Burnett's classic novel, with book (Tony Award) and lyrics by Norman (as part of an all-female creative team), followed in 1993 with *The Red Shoes* (lyrics and book), music by Jule Styne.   FB

Norske Teatret (Oslo) The Norwegian Theatre is one of Norway's national theatres; it is devoted to performance in Nynorsk ('New Norwegian'), one of two official forms of the language. Derived from provincial dialects, in contrast to the Danish-derived Norwegian of the capital, Nynorsk remains part of an ongoing movement to strengthen indigenous culture. Founded in 1913 by Arne and Hulda Garborg, the theatre also established traditions of touring and performing new drama, and became one of the most avant-garde in Scandinavia. From the start it attracted superb actors: Lars Tvinde, Edvard Drabløs, Alfred and Tordis Maurstad, LIV ULLMANN. Important directors have included Agnes Mowinckel, HANS JACOB NILSEN, Tormod Skagestad, STEIN WINGE and KJETIL BANG-HANSEN; for some 40 years its scenographer was the modernist Arne

Walentin. In 1985 it moved to one of Europe's most elaborate theatres, with three stages, huge workshops and advanced equipment. It has expanded its musical traditions by staging megaMUSICALS like *Cats* and *Les Misérables*, but remains a leading innovator in spoken drama.   HL

North Africa, French-speaking see FRENCH-SPEAKING NORTH AFRICA; MIDDLE EAST

Norton, (William) Elliot 1903– Boston-born American critic who attended Harvard University, where he studied with George Lyman Kittredge and GEORGE PIERCE BAKER. After graduation in 1926, he worked as a reporter for the *Boston Post*, taking over as drama critic when Edward Harold Crosby retired in 1934. With the demise of the *Post* in 1956, he switched to Hearst's *Record American*, retiring in 1982, though he remains visible in Boston theatre circles. Norton acquired the reputation of being honest and reliable about new shows that were BROADWAY-bound. MIKE NICHOLS and JOSHUA LOGAN thought that he had a 'smell for the public' and for 'what the public is feeling'. He was not a great stylist, nor did his reviews break new critical ground; but New York producers respected his opinion and made changes in their shows based upon his reviews. He received the first GEORGE JEAN NATHAN Award for Dramatic Criticism in 1964, and a special Tony in 1971.   TLM

Norton, Thomas see SACKVILLE, THOMAS

Norway Primarily because its union with Denmark (1397–1814) made Danish the language of government and literature, Norway lacked permanent playhouses, using Norwegian actors, until the 1800s. The country's first great dramatist, LUDVIG HOLBERG, was educated in Copenhagen and helped found the *Danish* theatre.

Although the Sagas suggest court entertainments from the 12th century, the earliest firm evidence of acting comes in 1539. Nevertheless, historians believe that there were medieval liturgical plays (see LITURGICAL DRAMA), and Epiphany plays that survived to this century may have derived from them. By the mid-1500s Bergen certainly had humanist school dramas, such as the 1562 *Fall of Adam*, and the city encouraged them as morally improving. In the mid-1600s German companies toured popular HAUPT- UND STAATSAKTIONEN, followed by Danish companies offering similar fare. In 1771 the German actor Martin Nürenbach obtained permission for a permanent Norwegian company to present Danish plays in Christiania (now Oslo); the venture rapidly folded. More successful were the amateur dramatic societies that flourished from 1780, often with permanent playhouses like Bergen's Comoediehuset (1800) and the Trondhjem Theater (1816). Their success increased audiences for professional companies and in 1827 Johan Peter Strömberg opened Christiania Theater, the city's first permanent playhouse. Its Norwegian actors were so scornfully criticized that they were rapidly replaced by Danes, beginning the company's 'Danish period'.

Theatre was central in the 19th-century struggle between the so-called 'Danomanes', led by J. S. Welhaven,

Botho Strauss's *The Time and the Room*, directed by Flemming Weiss Andersen, Rogaland Teater, Stavanger, 1989.

and the nationalistic 'patriots', led by Henrik Wergeland. The nationalists' first victory in the theatre was Ole Bull's founding of Bergen's Norske Theater in 1850; IBSEN joined it in 1852 as resident playwright and stage director. Meanwhile, Christiania Theater had accepted its first Norwegian-born performers and in 1852 Kristiania Norske Theater opened with a completely Norwegian-speaking company, directed by Ibsen from 1857 to 1862. His colleague BJØRNSTJERNE BJØRNSON had meanwhile led a campaign against Danish domination of Christiania Theater and in 1863 the two theatres combined, with a predominantly Norwegian company. Bjørnson himself directed it from 1865 to 67, creating distinguished productions of SHAKESPEARE, Holberg, Ibsen and his own social-problem plays.

Bergen's Norske Theater folded in 1863, but was revived as the NATIONALE SCENE in 1876, and the century's final decades witnessed rapid growth in Norwegian theatre generally. Christiania Theater flourished under the leadership of the Swede Ludvig Josephson in 1873-7; his many premieres of Norwegian plays included *Peer Gynt* (1876), with Grieg's music. Both theatres succeeded in the 1880s, with GUNNAR HEIBERG in Bergen (1884-8) and BJØRN BJØRNSON in Christiania (1885-91), both determined to achieve naturalistic performances of the plays they were premiering: *The Wild Duck* at both theatres, 1885; *Rosmersholm* in Bergen, 1887; *The Lady from the Sea* in Christiania, 1889. Although actors trained in the older declamatory style experienced difficulty, new actors like JOHANNE DYBWAD emerged to lead the way.

At the close of the century, several new playhouses opened: Stavanger Theater (1883); Centralteatret, Christiania (1897); and in 1899 the present Nationaltheatret, led by Bjørn Bjørnson. The fine company he assembled indicated how rapidly Norwegian acting had developed: Dybwad, Sophie Reimers, Ragna Wettergren, Egil Eide, August Oddvar and Halfdan Christensen – to be joined by Ingolf Schanche and many more. Despite precarious financing (it remained a private theatre until 1927), Bjørnson's company gave an impressive series of premieres (including Ibsen, Bjørnstjerne Bjørnson and Heiberg) until he resigned in 1907.

By 1913, the development of Nynorsk ('New Norwegian'), one of Norway's two official language forms, was sufficient to enable Arne and Hulda Garborg to found the NORSKE TEATRET, devoted to performance in Nynorsk. It also emphasized touring, employing important actors such as Edvard Drabløs and Lars Tvinde, later joined by Agnes Mowinckel, HANS JACOB NILSEN and Tordis and Alfred Maurstad. Dramatists' demands for a stage dedicated to new drama led to the opening of the Nye Teatret (1929), which later combined with Folketeatret to become the city-owned Oslo Nye Teater. In Bergen, STEIN BUGGE introduced modernism to the Nationale Scene, and with Nazism on the rise in Europe, Nilsen increased its political profile with productions of LAGERKVIST and GRIEG. During the German occupation (1940-5), audiences boycotted Nazi-run theatres, while many actors fled to the Fri Norsk Scene (Free Norwegian Stage) in Sweden.

With the Liberation came further growth. Claes Gill opened Studiotheatret (1945-50), a Stanislavskian (see STANISLAVSKY) studio ensemble; the Norske Teatret flourished again under Nilsen, a period highlighted by his 1948 'anti-romantic' *Peer Gynt*. Trondheim's Trøndelag Teater (1937) and Stavanger's Rogaland Teater (1947) quickly grew in stature, re-emphasizing the decentralized nature of Norwegian theatre. Riksteatret (1949), the national touring theatre, began by touring other theatres' productions but later created its own; ironically, its success encouraged development of regional and local theatres, making its own function uncertain.

The 1960s brought impressive consolidation: Tormod Skagestad confirmed the Norske Teatret's avant-garde role with adventurous programming and guest directors like PETER PALITZSCH and Henryk Tomaszewski (see MIME); Erik Pierstorff made Trøndelag Teater an academy for today's leading directors, such as KJETIL BANG-HANSEN, Thea Stabell and STEIN WINGE.

The contemporary scene The 1970s saw tremendous expansion: five subsidized regional theatres opened, in Tromsø (1971), Molde (1972), Skien (1975), Forde (1977) and Mo i Rana (1979); new free groups included Tramteatret (1976–86), Musidra (1971–), Perleporten (1975–84) and Grenland Friteater (1976–). Many groups joined Teatersentrum (1978–), a promotional organization that in 1985 opened the Black Box theatre. Many companies were politically active, including Nationaltheatret, where projects such as Klaus Hagerup's SATIRE *Alice in the Underworld* and the documentary group creation *The Black Cat* featured. Out of this activity developed Teatret på Torshov (1977–92), an experimental theatre in an Oslo suburb where much of Nationaltheatret's best work was done.

The 1980s began as a decade of optimistic expansion, but suffered a harsh reversal during the economic downturn of its last years. Important group theatres were founded, including Bikuben Musikkteater (1981–9), Beljash (1981–9), Lilith, Sampo, and Totalteatret (all 1983–), Boreas Teater (1984–) and the SAMI company Beaivvás, state-supported since 1987. In 1985 the Norske Teatret moved into a huge, new building that partly encouraged it to stage megaMUSICALS like *Cats* and *Les Misérables*, while still continuing its experimental work on its smaller stages. But generally the late 1980s witnessed increasing commercialism within institutional theatres, which responded to shrinking budgets by taking fewer risks with challenging Norwegian plays. Norway has remarkable dramatists, such as CECILIE LØVEID, Edvard Hoem, Bjørg Vik and Knut Faldbakken, but their plays are staged less frequently than they deserve. The Åpne Teater opened in Oslo in 1985 specifically to workshop new scripts.

In the 1980s interest grew in visual performance, based on dramaturgical equivalence between visual, textual and musical elements, in the manner of ROBERT WILSON and Denmark's former Billedstofteater. Internationally focused project theatres (engaging artists for specific projects, rather than permanent companies), including Baktruppen in Bergen and Passage Nord and Verdensteatret in Oslo, have led this movement. Through links with other European performance companies, Bergen Internasjonale Teater arranges exchanges and collaborations between Norway and avant-garde Europe.

Although Norway's state theatre school began teaching directing only in 1983, outstanding directors are numerous, including Bentein Baardson, Kjetil Bang-Hansen, CARL JØRGEN KIØNIG, Terje Mærli, Thea Stabell and Stein Winge. Among the country's innovative scenographers are Rolf Alme, John-Kristian Alsaker, Kari Gravklev, Helge Hoff Monsen and Tine Schwab. A few of its countless remarkable actors are Mona Hofland, Kjersti Holmen, Lars Andreas Larsen, Sverre Anker Ousdal, Espen Skjønberg, Bjørn Sundquist, Liv Ullmann, Anneke von der Lippe and Øystein Wiik.

In 1993 the government subdivided state-supported theatres into three categories: (1) national theatres, which are funded 100 per cent by central government (Nationaltheatret, Norske Teatret, Nationale Scene, Riksteatret and Beaivvás Sami Theater); (2) major regional theatre centres, which are funded primarily by central government, and partly by the county and municipality (theatres in Stavanger, Trondheim and Tromsø); (3) regional theatres, whose funding comes from the county. While this formula apparently honours Norway's traditional decentralization of resources and authority, it also formalizes a hierarchy of theatres that some consider unNorwegian. HL

See: K. O. Arntzen, T. O. Svendsen and M. Moi (eds), *Kunnskapsforlagets Teater- og Filmleksikon*, Oslo, 1991; P. Brask (ed.), *Drama Contemporary: Scandinavia*, New York, 1989; J. Garton, *Norwegian Women's Writing 1850–1990*, London, 1993; J. Garton and H. Sehmsdorf, *New Norwegian Plays*, Norwich, 1989; L. Lyche, *Norges teaterhistorie*, Oslo, 1992; F. J. and L.-L. Marker, *The Scandinavian Theatre*, Oxford, 1975; *Nordic Theatre Studies*, Copenhagen, 1988– ; *På norske scener* (annual), Oslo, 1987– ; L. Senelick (ed.), *National Theatre in Northern and Eastern Europe, 1746–1900*, Cambridge, 1991; *Spillerom* (journal), 1981– ; C. Waal, *Johanne Dybwad Norwegian Actress*, Oslo, 1967.

Nouvelle Compagnie d'Avignon French theatre company, which has worked together in the Théâtre des Carmes at Avignon since 1963 under the influence of its director André Benedetto, who writes many of its plays. Its work employs a broad range of techniques from the traditions of FARCE, and open-air performance. Its stance is extremely radical, challenging not only political orthodoxies but cultural ones as well, and identifying with problems of the Occitan community. DB

Novelli, Ermete 1851–1919 Italian actor and company manager, who began acting at 17 and rose to prominence in the company of BELLOTTI-BON in the early 1880s before establishing his own companies from 1884. Novelli was very much a 'personality' player; his repertoire consisted largely of stock pieces, in which he showed the wide range of his talent, from GOLDONI to DUMAS. It was for his versatility, indeed, that he was perhaps most noted. He occasionally attempted SHAKESPEARE, most successfully with *King Lear* and *The Merchant of Venice*, and toured widely in Europe and South America. He was involved in turn-of-the-century attempts to raise the standards of Italian theatre by the establishment of *teatri stabili*; his own semi-permanent company, the Casa di Goldoni, based at the Valle Theatre in Rome in 1900, met with little success and he soon returned to regular touring. LR

Novo, Salvador 1904–74 Mexican playwright. Novo was instrumental in founding the TEATRO DE ULISES with his friend XAVIER VILLAURRUTIA, thereby launching the independent theatre movement in Mexico in 1928. A serious director, actor and critic, Novo held important positions in the Mexican Institute of Fine Arts and wrote several major plays, many of them based on classical Greek or Mexican characters. Of special note are *Yocasta, o casi* (*Jocasta, or Almost*, 1961), *Ha vuelto Ulises* (*Ulysses Has Returned*, 1961), *In Pipiltzintzin o La guerra de las gordas* (*The War of the Large Ladies*, 1963) and *In Ticitezcatl o El espejo encantado* (*The Enchanted Mirror*, 1965).   GW

Nowra, Louis 1950– Australian playwright. His plays, often with exotic or historical settings, depict the private worlds of illusion, obsession and madness under pressure from external power structures, and are characterized by episodic construction, heightened language and powerful, even lurid, theatrical effects. They include two radio plays, *Albert Names Edward* (1975) and *The Song Room* (1980); *Inner Voices* (1977), *Visions* (1978), *Inside the Island* (1980), *The Precious Woman* (1980) and *Sunrise* (1983); and a television drama, *Displaced Persons* (1985). Recently he has completed two plays of a semi-autographical trilogy – *Summer of the Aliens* (1992), set in an outer-suburban housing estate in the 1960s, and *Cosi* (1992), about an attempt to stage Mozart's opera with a group of mental patients – as well as a SATIRE on big business, *The Temple* (1993); and *Radiance* (1993), for three Aboriginal women performers.   MW

nudity For prurient effect nudity on stage was already common in the Roman pantoMIME or *mimus*, which provided undressing scenes for female performers. In the presentations of the Floralia the *mima* was often shown naked by the end of the performance, and Apuleius describes a nude *Judgement of Paris*. The *mimus* also preserved the leather phallus of Greek comedy as late as the 5th century AD, long after it had lost its religious significance.

Christianity was scandalized by both nakedness and the theatre, and the emperor Justinian imposed drawers on all mime artists, tumblers and acrobats. The medieval Church banned public nudity, so that the Adam and Eve of the MYSTERY PLAYS were clad in form-fitting doeskin. Yet, according to Marc de Montifard, the cleavage was so deep on the three Marys in one PASSION PLAY that, gazing down from the cross, Christ suffered a conspicuous erection. Princely pageants were exempt from the ecclesiastical strictures: at the entry of Charles VII into Paris in 1437 three naked girls swam in an ornamental fountain; when Louis XI entered Paris in 1461 several unclothed beauties portrayed mermaids. Allegorical nudes occasionally turned up in the festivals and MASQUES of the Renaissance.

With the common acceptance of women as actors, the exposure of breasts and legs became a popular allurement, and was equated by the authorities with full nudity. The French Church censured the Italian GELOSI troupe for emphasizing the female bosom in its pantomimic business, but many plays of the 17th century made the denuding of the bosom a climactic moment in the denouement. After Mme de St Huberty appeared as a nymph in 1783 with one bared breast and naked legs, the government forbade her appearance. Yet 'historical accuracy' demanded

looser draperies on dancers, so tights (invented by the Opéra milliner Maillot) became *de rigueur* c.1780, soon to be followed by trunks and the tutu (conceived by Duponchel). The Pope allowed such garb on the Roman stage, provided the tights were sky-blue rather than pink.

In the early 19th century a static display of female nudity was available in 'the hymns to nature' and 'living statuary' to be seen at the Hall of Rome in London. These developed into LIVING PICTURES and *poses plastiques*, in which several naked or semi-clothed women would hold an artistic pose for some moments, often in imitation of a well known painting or sculpture. FRÉDÉRIC SOULIÉ applied the principle of static nudity to drama in *Christine à Fontainebleau* (ODÉON, 1829) by showing a naked woman on a dissecting table, a gimmick twice repeated in Naples, but soon abandoned owing to the hostility of the audience. The accepted definition of nudity was elastic, and not infrequently ballet dancers with brief skirts or 'leg show' performers who wore tights without skirts would be accused of brazenness. The fleshings of ADAH ISAACS MENKEN won her the billing of 'the Naked Lady', and LOLA MONTEZ created a scandal by omitting tights during her dances. But most of what passed for flesh on stage was cunningly dyed fabric: Cassive in FEYDEAU's *The Lady from Maxim's* (1899) appeared in bed in flesh-coloured tights under a corset and still managed to scandalize.

The strip-tease, a ritual wherein various garments are serially discarded leaving the performer more or less totally undressed, was, according to legend, first performed by a certain Mona at an art students' ball at the MOULIN-ROUGE on 9 February 1893. It was definitely exhibited by Mlle Cavelli at Le Divan Fayouau on 13 March 1894 in a sketch entitled 'Le Coucher d'Yvette'; this was much imitated and even repeated at the World's Fair by Renée de Presles in 'Le Coucher de la Parisienne'. In America legend related that it was introduced by the trapeze artist Charmian, who inadvertently lost her tights during a performance; by 1920 it had become a BURLESQUE attraction offered by Millie de Leon, and was later perfected as a 'dance' by GYPSY ROSE LEE and ANN CORIO. Originally, at the climax a blackout or fall of the curtain supervened; certain wardrobe items, the 'pasties' that covered the nipples, would often be flung to the audience, but the *cache-sexe* or G-string usually stayed in place. Later, the performers at such tourist traps as Paris's Crazy-Horse Saloon (opened 1953) would leave nothing to the imagination.

Five stark-naked beauties were seen at a REVUE at the Variétés (1901; see BOULEVARD) Colette Willy appeared stripped to the waist in the pantomime *La Chair* (1907); and an undressed dancer first appeared at the FOLIES-BERGÈRE in 1912. The MUSIC-HALL dancer Maud Allan and her imitators were censured for their abbreviated Salome costumes, but the biblical theme was the chief cause for objection. After 1918, in reaction to pre-war prudery, taboo-breaking and voyeurism combined to produce the *Naktballett* that originated in Berlin. It was first danced by Celly de Rheydt (Cäcilia Schmidt) in 1919, to be immediately rivalled by a naked Salome ballet; by 1922, it had become widespread throughout Germany, its principal star the notorious Anita Berber (1899–1929). Influenced by Isadora Duncan, by the physical culture movement and by sports, undraped dancing based on classical art remained popular in CABARETS until about 1927. SALLY RAND's fan dance, first seen at the Chicago Exposition in 1933, became a byword.

In the Anglo-Saxon world, however, stage nudity was permissible only if it was inert as in the lavish *tableaux* that Ben Ali Haggin staged for ZIEGFELD. The Lord Chamberlain's ruling on the Revuedeville at the Windmill Theatre, London, in 1931 – 'If it moves, it's rude' – became a guiding principle followed by the theatre's wartime manager Vivian van Damm (1889–1960) who could boast, 'We never closed.'

In the 1960s, nudity became a tactical weapon of the ALTERNATIVE THEATRE, a direct assault on middle-class sensibilities and an alignment with 'Nature'. 1968 was its *annus mirabilis*, when the rock MUSICAL *Hair* displayed its unclad cast frontally; the LIVING THEATRE's players were arrested in San Francisco for disrobing ('We can't take off our clothes in public', was one of their opening plaints, until, at the London Round House, an audience member undressed to confute them); and Sally Kirkland became the first New York dramatic actress to appear fully nude throughout an entire play, in TERRENCE MCNALLY's *Sweet Eros*. The commercial theatre was quick to adopt this licence in *Oh, Calcutta!* (1969), whose company, male and female, shed its bathrobes in the first moments. Soon full-frontal nudity could be seen in London in DÜRRENMATT's *Meteor*, in Paris in Panizza's *Council of Love* and in Frankfurt in HANDKE's *Self-Accusation*. German directors have been particularly active in defoliating their lead actresses. That male nudity, at least in motion and at a state theatre, still had the power to shock was clear from the flustered over-reaction to HOWARD BRENTON's *The Romans in Britain* (1980).

Frontal male nudity soon turned from a token of stage REALISM (as in DAVID STOREY's *The Changing Room*, 1971) to a touchstone of gender identification (David Henry Hwang's *M. Butterfly* (1989). Having become a convention of homosexual drama, as in Robert Patrick's *Mercy Drop* (1973) and *T Shirts* (1978) and Terrence McNally's *The Lisbon Traviata* (1985), used both to shock a straight audience and appeal to a gay one, it was carried over into JOHN GUARE's mainstream comedy *Six Degrees of Separation* (1990).

A 1991 US Supreme Court decision permitted communities to ban nude dancing for reasons of 'public morality'. Such a resurgence of CENSORSHIP creates a chilling climate that compels actors to put their clothes back on. However, performance artists like KAREN FINLEY and Annie Sprinkle exaggerate and abuse their own naked bodies for galvanic effect, to make political statements about sexual exploitation, while certain contemporary choreographers have attempted to abstract nudity as a formal element of composition.   LS

Nuevo Grupo (New Group) Venezuelan theatre group created in 1967 and headed by a triumvirate, ISAAC CHOCRÓN, ROMÁN CHALBAUD and JOSÉ IGNACIO CABRUJAS. Instrumental in establishing the standards for the contemporary theatre movement in Venezuela, the group operated two theatres and provided regular programming of the best international and national plays. Alternating as authors, directors and actors, this 'Holy Trinity', as they have been called, was at the forefront of the Nuevo Grupo until it closed in 1988.   GW

Núñez, José Gabriel 1937– Venezuelan playwright. Born in Carúpano, trained as an economist, Núñez has been an active force in Venezuelan theatre and television since he began to write in 1967. With more than 25 original plays and various adaptations, he has won several prizes. He also writes for literary reviews and regular columns. Principal works are *Parecido a la felicidad* (*Similar to Happiness*, 1969), *El largo camino del Edén* (*The Long Road to Eden*, 1970), *Madame Pompinette* (1981) and *María Cristina me quiere gobernar* (*María Cristina Wants to Govern Me*, 1984).   GW

Nunn, Trevor (Robert) 1940– British director, who started to direct plays with the Marlowe Society at Cambridge University. After a spell as a trainee director with the Belgrade Theatre, Coventry, he joined the ROYAL SHAKESPEARE COMPANY in 1965 and succeeded PETER HALL as the RSC's artistic director in 1968. In 1978, he became chief executive and joint artistic director with TERRY HANDS at the RSC, which helped him to take some time away from the company to direct in commercial theatre, where in 1981 he staged the hit musical, *Cats*, and in 1984, *Starlight Express*.

Nunn can be regarded without too much challenge as the best all-round director currently working in British theatre. His first RSC success came with TOURNEUR's *The Revenger's Tragedy* in 1966 which, with ALAN HOWARD as Lussurioso, exactly captured the play's voluptuous yet macabre obsessions. His range of classical productions at the RSC is unequalled for its richness and variety – SHAKESPEARE's 'Roman' plays in 1972, his musical version of *The Comedy of Errors* (1976), the studio *Macbeth* (1976) and his Edwardian *All's Well That Ends Well* (1981). In 1980 he collaborated with John Caird, DAVID EDGAR and the RSC to bring together *Nicholas Nickleby* in two substantial evenings, which presented a vivid picture of CHARLES DICKENS's London and paraded the wealth of acting talents at the RSC.

Nunn possesses most directorial skills. He works well with individual actors, encouraging them to explore new possibilities in the text, but he is also excellent with large companies. He has a fine eye for scenic pictures on the stage, a sound instinct for style and historical appropriateness. He is sensitive to music and dancing, and has rivalled American directors at their prized skills in staging MUSICALS. He has proved to be an excellent administrator of the RSC. He is not, however, an intellectual's director, unlike PETER BROOK, nor can he be regarded, in European terms, as an innovator. Under his guidance the RSC became a world-renowned company, but in 1986 he became the target with Peter Hall of some *Sunday Times* articles, accusing him, among other matters, of spending more time in directing WEST END musicals than running the RSC. He handed over to his co-director, Terry Hands, but was as prolific as a freelance director as he had been at the RSC. His studio Shakespeares have included *Othello* (1989) and *Timon of Athens* (1991); his musicals have included *Aspects of Love* (1989), *The Baker's Wife* (1989) and the revived *Starlight Express* (1992); and his star-studded classical revivals have included *Heartbreak House* (1992) at London's HAYMARKET. In 1992, he had no less than six shows in the West End. JE

nurseries Under patents granted to them, WILLIAM DAVENANT and THOMAS KILLIGREW in 1660 acquired the right to establish in London 'nurseries', training companies for young actors. The precise location and span of existence for these companies are unclear but there were at least three. One was established by Killigrew in 1667 in Hatton Garden and operated until 1669. One was set up by Lady Davenant, Sir William's widow, in the Barbican in 1671. One was run by John Perin at Bun Hill in Finsbury Fields in 1671. It was a site of trouble, the Secretary of State warning the king that 'If the nurseries be not taken away in a year, expect a disorder.' At various times GEORGE JOLLY was involved in the running of the nurseries. Few of their actors appear to have graduated to the professional adult stage. PH

Nušić, Branislav 1864–1938 Serbian playwright, born and educated in law at Belgrade, whose comedies have been part of the national repertory for almost a century. Nušić's career as a humorist was interrupted by imprisonment for writing an antidynastic poem at the time of his first theatrical success, *A Suspicious Person* (1887). Later, he served as a Serbian consular officer in Kosovo, still under Turkish rule, and as a ministry official and head of theatres in Belgrade and other cities. His patriotic historic tragedies and his heavily moralistic domestic dramas have remained completely overshadowed by his popular comedies, in which figures of a patriarchal Serbian mentality are shown in transition from an agrarian, oriental state towards urban and European aspirations. Nušić is rarely and only marginally a satirist, and his humour is mostly verbal. His incompetent bureaucrats, corrupt politicians, town gossips and con-men, his *nouveau riche* merchants and their quasi-Westernized offspring, have served as effective vehicles for generations of comic actors. Recent attempts to transcend in staging the realistic pattern of Nušić's plays have usually failed. Often performed in the Slavic world and in Germany, Austria and Hungary, his most significant plays are *The Cabinet Minister's Wife* (1929) and *The Bereaved Family* (1934). DK

Nuyorican theatre (USA) The term 'Nuyorican' refers to Puerto Rican culture in New York, which typically is bilingual, bicultural and working-class in socio-economic orientation. Moreover, 'Nuyorican' or 'Rican' is used by the children of working-class Puerto Rican migrants to the city. During the ethnic revivalist and civil rights movements of the 1960s, young Puerto Rican writers and intellectuals began using the term as a point of departure in affirming their own cultural existence and history as diverging from that of the island of Puerto Rico and that of mainstream America. A literary and artistic flowering in the New York Puerto Rican community ensued in the late 1960s and early 70s as a result both of greater access to education for Puerto Ricans brought up in the USA and of the ethnic-consciousness movement. Nuyorican Theatre has included such diverse theatrical manifestations as street theatre, as collectively created and performed by Teatro Orilla, Nuevo Teatro Pobre de América, Teatro Jurutungo, Teatro Guazabara and Teatro Cuatro; but it is also exemplified by a wide range of works by individual playwrights, produced in prisons, at small non-profit HISPANIC THEATRES such as Teatro Repertorio Español and the Puerto Rican Traveling Theatre, at the Henry Street Settlement's New Federal Theatre and at JOSEPH PAPP's NEW YORK SHAKESPEARE FESTIVAL, and even at large commercial houses on BROADWAY.

Although the term was first applied to literature and theatre by playwright-novelist Jaime Carrero in the late 1960s, and finds some stylistic and thematic development in his plays *Noo Jall* (a play on the Spanish pronunciation of New York and the word 'jail') and *Pipo Subway No Sabe Reír*, it was a group of playwright-poets associated with the Nuyorican Poets' Café and Joseph Papp that first defined and came to exemplify Nuyorican Theatre. Included in the group were Miguel Algarín, Lucky Cienfuegos, Tato Laviera and Miguel Piñero, all of whom focused their bilingual works on the life and culture of working-class Puerto Ricans in New York. Two members of the group, Cienfuegos and Piñero, were ex-convicts who had begun their writing careers while incarcerated, and they chose to develop their dramatic material from prison, street and underclass culture. Algarín, a university professor and proprietor of the Nuyorican Poets' Café, created a more avant-garde aura for the collective, while the virtuoso bilingual poet Tato Laviera contributed a lyricism and a folk- and popular-culture base. It was Piñero's work (and life), however, that became most celebrated, his prison drama *Short Eyes* having won an Obie and the New York Drama Critics' Award for best American play in the 1973–4 season. His success – coupled with that of fellow Nuyorican writer and ex-convict Piri Thomas, and that of Pedro Pietri who developed the persona of a street urchin – often resulted in Nuyorican literature and theatre becoming associated with a JEAN GENET-type NATURALISM and the themes of crime, drugs, abnormal sexuality and generally aberrant behaviour, thus leading to a reaction against the term by many writers who were, in fact, affirming Puerto Rican working-class culture in New York.

Today there is a new generation of New York Puerto Rican playwrights who were nurtured on the theatre of Piñero and the Nuyoricans, and who have also experienced greater support and opportunities for developing their work. They quite often repeat and re-evaluate many of the concerns and the style and language of the earlier group, but with a sophistication and polish that has come from drama workshops, playwright residencies and university education. Among these are Juan Shamsul Alam, Edward Gallardo, Federico Fraguada, Richard Irizarry, Yvette Ramírez and Cándido Tirado. NK

See: J. Antush, *Recent Puerto Rican Theatre: Five Plays from New York*, Houston, Texas, 1991; N. Kanellos (ed.), *graphical Dictionary of Hispanic Literature in the United States*, Westport, Conn., 1989; J. Miller, in *Hispanic Theatre in the United States*, ed. N. Kanellos, Houston, 1984.

Oberammergau When, following a severe outbreak of the Black Death in 1633, the inhabitants of this Upper Bavarian village vowed to perform a Passion play every ten years if they were spared from further deaths, the late medieval PASSION PLAY tradition in the south of the German-speaking area was still alive. Their original play was based on the 15th-century manuscript from Augsburg known as the 'Augsburg Passion Play' and on the Passion play by Sebastian Wild from the same city. The version of the text currently used was written originally for the 1810 performance by the Benedictine priest Othmar Weis from the nearby Ettal monastery, and the music was composed at the same time by the village schoolmaster Rochus Dedler. The text has been revised several times since; recently this has involved removal of anti-Jewish statements. The current version consists of two sessions, each of some three hours' duration performed in the morning and in the late afternoon, and includes 17 *tableaux vivants* (see LIVING PICTURE) of the Glorified Christ.

The regular performance in 1980 was followed by a 350th anniversary production in 1984, when performances on five days per week ran from late May to end September. Several major roles, most notably Christ, Virgin Mary, Prologue, Peter, John and Judas, were played at alternate performances by two actors; unmarried women played all the women's roles. JET

Obey, André 1892–1975 French playwright associated with the work of COPEAU's disciples, who formed the COMPAGNIE DES QUINZE and commissioned and staged five of his plays at the VIEUX-COLOMBIER theatre. These included his first and best play *Noah* (1931), later staged with equal success by the group's director, MICHEL SAINT-DENIS, when he moved to London (1935). Other plays included a new version of the Don Juan story, twice rewritten and staged by Copeau in 1937 as *Le Trompeur de Séville* and by the COMÉDIE-FRANÇAISE in 1949 as *L'Homme de cendres*. He was director of the Comédie-Française for one year (1946/7). His plays combine mythical archetype with modern setting in a manner reminiscent of GIRAUDOUX, his contemporary, but with less verbal preciosity and more sense of what is effective in performance. DB

Obraztsov, Sergei (Vladimirovich) 1901–91 Russian actor and puppeteer. After studying painting, Obraztsov made his acting debut at the MOSCOW ART THEATRE Musical Studio in 1922, and only the next year appeared as a solo puppeteer. He alternated careers until 1931, when he became artistic director of the newly founded State Central Puppet Theatre, Moscow, premiering with *Jim and Dollar* (a new building was opened in 1970). He staged more than 50 puppet plays, made documentary films and wrote several books, including *The Actor and the Puppet* (1938). He tried to introduce Javanese rod PUPPETS to the West in 1945, and toured Europe (1950/51, 66, 70), demonstrating his virtuosity with satirical sketches and magical fantasies. LS

O'Casey, Sean 1880–1964 Irish playwright. O'Casey was the youngest child of a lower-middle-class Protestant family, severely impoverished when his father died in 1883. He worked as a labourer, interesting himself at nights in Irish culture, and active in the Republican and Labour movements. Disillusioned by the shift from socialism to Catholic nationalism, O'Casey withdrew acrimoniously from political and militant organizations, separating himself particularly from Padraic Pearse's cult of violence. He remained a lifelong 'proletarian Communist'.

Afflicted by poor eyesight, O'Casey nonetheless read omnivorously: SHAKESPEARE and the Elizabethans, Shelley and SHAW; and shared the working-class folklore of patriotic oratory, ballads, the poems of Burns, Tom Moore's songs. He appeared occasionally in amateur theatricals, when he could afford it attended plays, and submitted his own work to the ABBEY.

In 1923 the Abbey accepted *The Shadow of a Gunman*. Its period is the Anglo-Irish war which led to the 1921 Settlement. *Juno and the Paycock* (1924), set in the Civil War after the Settlement, and *The Plough and the Stars* (1926), an anti-heroic version of the 1916 Rising, completed his 'Dublin trilogy'. *The Shadow* and *Juno* were popular successes and repaired the Abbey's rocky finances. *The Plough* attracted riotous abuse. 'You have disgraced yourselves again,' YEATS told the audience, alluding to a similar response to SYNGE's *Playboy*.

In 1928 the Abbey directors refused *The Silver Tassie*, O'Casey's pacifist play about the First World War, objecting unpersuasively to its expressionist second act, its distance from O'Casey's own experience and the absence of strong comic characterization. Yeats's distaste for the war as a subject may have been influential. Disturbed by the reception of *The Plough*, O'Casey, now living in England, was outraged by this rejection. He broke with the Abbey and despite some fragile reconciliations never established a permanent relationship with it or any other theatre.

O'Casey's later work is in its attitudes didactic, informed by his communist beliefs, and in its forms symbolic, stylized, experimental: *Within the Gates* (first production, 1934), *The Star Turns Red* (1940), *Red Roses for Me* (1943), *Purple Dust* (1945), *Oak Leaves and Lavender* (1947), *Cock-a-Doodle-Dandy* (1949), *The Bishop's Bonfire* (1955), *The Drums of Father Ned* (1958).

O'Casey's relatively realist Dublin trilogy used to be viewed as his masterpiece, which he never equalled. Despite structural disunities and conventional plotting, the plays refute complaint by their brilliant comic invention, their MUSIC-HALL knockabout and rhetorical extravagance, their moments where tragic, often brutal, action collaborates with farce. More recent criticism has reunified his work, re-evaluating the later plays and discerning latent EPIC THEATRE elements in the early ones.

Of the later plays only *Red Roses* and *The Star* are set in Dublin. Though *Red Roses* suffers from 'fine writing' and overplays the vernacular, it movingly evokes the 1913 lockout, effectively using song, dance and MIME. *The Star*,

Gates and *Dust* are political allegories, restlessly seeking form appropriate to 'message'. With more theatrical vigour than literary subtlety, *Bonfire*, *Cock-a-Doodle* and *Father Ned* return to Irish villages, where clerical/mercantile oppression battles with a liberating, sexual life-force.

Although O'Casey also wrote (1939–54) a remarkable autobiography, his achievement is in drama. His disastrous estrangement from the Abbey robbed the developing Irish tradition of its most theatrically adventurous and politically engaged playwright. Nevertheless, his major plays, embodying his disputatious scepticism and great warmth for the antic human pageant, continue to be among the most powerful and enduring works of the Irish dramatic movement.   DM GF

Oceania The Pacific region is customarily divided into three groupings based on linguistic, ethnic and cultural features: Melanesia, Micronesia and Polynesia. At the same time certain features bind together performances of this area as a whole. Firstly, a combination of music, dance and poetry and improvised comic skits are, traditionally, significant arts – rather than theatrical pieces in which actors portray another persona in an extended narrative. Secondly, the expertise of artists is high, although few are full-time, professional specialists in these small, geographically isolated communities. Thirdly, much performance takes place in the context of festivals, life-cycle ceremonies or communal feasts which celebrate the social life of the community. Large groups of dancers, most often of a single sex, participate: hundreds of dancers may join in a running dance at a New Guinea *sing-sing* ('communal feast'), long lines of women or rows of men perform unison dance movement in a Fijian *meke*, a Hawaiian hula or an *ur* on the Micronesian island of Ifaluk. This tendency is not new: in the 1790s, just 16 years after the first European landfall, George Vancouver described a Hawaiian performance in which 200 women danced in astounding unison.

The talents of singing and dancing are traditionally thought to be common to all rather than reserved to a few. Precision and uniformity of the group are cultivated in preference to self-expression on the part of a solo performer. Songs are often thought to be the gift of the spirits, communicated in dream or vision to the composer-choreographer. Performance is an activation of group cohesiveness.

The social change wrought by contact with the West and Christianization in the 19th and early 20th centuries was profound. In almost every area arts as previously practised were deprived of their social context and attacked as 'heathen' by early missionaries. In some cases the indigenous language was largely replaced by that of the colonial power and audiences lost the ability to understand both text and context of traditional performance. Only in the last 30 years have religious festivals and government holidays increasingly become a venue for traditional performance due to altered church policy and growing local political autonomy.

Current performances are reflections of contemporary culture, showing the changing tastes of the indigenous peoples and interplay with performance generated for tourist entertainments. Music, dance and dramatic performance clearly maintain traditional elements, but the

Dance postures of the Micronesian performers in a Kiribati *ruoia* emulate the flight of the frigate bird, an old religious symbol.

adaptation of European musical instruments is common. Dance movements, once indigenous to a specific island, can be found throughout the region. Often performances have changed from outdoor, nightlong, torchlit entertainment at communal feasts, to two-hour presentations on electrically lit proscenium stages. Current attempts to create 'professional' companies of full-time, paid performers that emphasize individual creativity or solo dancing have come in the wake of Western influence and urbanization. Governments feel the need to articulate an ethnic image to both a national and an international audience, by creating a national company (Papua New Guinea, the Cook Islands and Fiji).

Though artists often state that their aim is to recapture the forms which existed prior to European contact, they recognize that the context is dramatically changed. What they seek is a reaffirmation of the arts as the arena for exploring and defining community values. In this context, current performance becomes a modern political statement documenting the search for indigenous alternatives to the pervasive pop culture and mass media of the First World. These exciting experiments show that dance and drama remain important modes of integrating the societies concerned.

A brief survey of the three major areas can help clarify some of the variations and reveal continuities or disjunctures with the past. Two strains of performance can be noted: first, forms which develop out of indigenous music, dance and mime traditions and, second, forms which derive from Western models. The former include traditional dances and dance MIMES. The latter include religious plays presented by the Christian churches and modern drama which has been introduced through the schools. A growing tendency of religious and modern drama to reintegrate traditional music, dance and themes shows the current blending of these two strains.

Melanesia Melanesia includes Papua New Guinea, Irian Jaya, Vanuatu (New Hebrides), New Caledonia and the Solomons. These islands are largely inhabited by people of considerable linguistic and cultural diversity who cultivate democratic societies in which leadership is achieved rather than inherited. Leaders, called 'big men' in pidgin, traditionally held feasts involving mass killings of pigs (which represented wealth) with concomitant public donations to bind supporters to them. Performances of music, dance and clowning were a regular part of such feasts.

Dance mimes are common throughout the Melanesian area. While Micronesians and Polynesians often act out fishing or hunting from the human viewpoint, Melanesian performance tends to adopt the perspective of the prey. MASKS are common throughout the region, and are often thought to represent spirits. Drama is thus an important mode of understanding the others, animal and spirit, that round out the world. This mimetic bias makes drama an important feature of Melanesian society to the present.

The relative autonomy and variety of ethnic groups have resulted in a wealth of distinctive artistic choices within Melanesian societies. This brief survey can only mention selected genres and hint at the creative usage of elements like time, space and costuming. Many of these performances, linked to previous religious beliefs, are now extinct.

One performance that used time expansively was documented by F. E. Williams in the 1930s. The Orokolo of Papua conducted a cycle of ceremonies that took decades to enact. The cycle culminated in dancing with huge masks from the men's club house to the sea amid general rejoicing. Modernization and social change has since then enervated the men's organizations by undercutting their myths, and this ceremonial cycle is now defunct. The performance systems of other Melanesian groups have been substantially altered by changes in religion and social practices that have ended or greatly modified initiation rites, traditional warfare and secret societies.

The elaborate feather headdresses, penis coverings, leaf or tapa coverings, body painting and tattooing that are found in Melanesian performance show the human body in unique splendour. Masks of wood, gourds, bark-cloth and other natural materials are often presented in performance and RITUAL. The spatial usage is often striking: societies which use trees as stages (as in a New Ireland form of women's song) and allow masked images suddenly to materialize in front of a hut from the surrounding jungle (as in *duk-duk* dances of the Tolai of New Britain) show impressive use of the environment. On Vanuatu's Pentecost Island men dive from high platforms only to be caught by vines attached to their feet, a performance which is said to commemorate how a woman foiled a persistent suitor by sending him plummeting to death while she saved herself by this ruse.

The entire village can be involved in a performance, blurring the line between audience and performers. In a Papua New Guinea *sing-sing*, the whole community may join in the nightlong dancing. Perhaps as a result of this, the dance steps tend to be simple, consisting of a running hop-step or a side-to-side swing for women. Nevertheless some divisions between performers are significant. Men and women often dance in separate groups, reaffirming the importance of sex differentiation, and only a few performers tend to take central roles, often by wearing the masks that are the centrepieces of the event.

Exactly who takes the central roles varies significantly, but in New Guinea it is often initiated men. Many performance objects – bull-roarers, gongs, masks – are the property of a village men's club. Traditionally, boys learn the method of using these objects, said to represent spirits, as part of their initiation into manhood while separated from their mothers. Via performance, initiated men display their superior understanding of the spirit world to the audience of women and children.

In New Guinea performers may gain prime roles by making certain sacrifices. Gell noted that, among the Umeda, men who wore the main masks of a bowman and cassowary (a running bird) were required to undertake difficult fasts. In other areas, blood-letting ceremonies or beatings are inflicted on those learning songs or steps. Bought with pain, the songs and dances were apt to be remembered. Suffering has a part in the *gisaro* performance of the Papuan Kaluli peoples: singers try to make the audience members cry by making songs that remind people of their dead. The emotionally aroused audience members then seize torches and brand the singer, and the skilled performer is known by his wealth of burns the morning after a presentation. Such performers who suffer can, perhaps, be compared to 'big men' within the political sphere. Performance is democratic in that it is open for all men to participate, but those who sacrifice more gain the admiration of the community.

Performance in Melanesia serves recognized social functions. The conical masks of the *duk-duk* society of New Britain's Tolai people are 'spirit' manifestations, worn by initiated members of the group to frighten and control those who flout social mores or gain members' anger. Currently they may appear in less charged situations like a government celebration. Funeral rites in New Ireland, the buying of a higher grade in a secret society in Vanuatu, the dedication of slit gongs in the Solomon Islands, or the marking of male initiation ceremonies or a killing in battle in traditional Papua New Guinea, all require performances. In each case, something irreversible happens and the performance notes the new status. Currently a wedding or local festival ceremony might be celebrated with dances borrowed from these older rites.

In this century church theatricals were introduced by missionaries. Since then they have absorbed some of the energy of earlier men's house mimesis. Plays about the martyrdom of early missionaries were common and choirs and marching bands were widely introduced. Current officials are more open to incorporating traditional dance and music in the context of church events.

Modern drama is an innovation dating from the late 1960s, introduced by European teachers and reworked by local artists to inculcate social change. Students at the University of Papua New Guinea studied creative writing and literature under Ulli Beier, a German, in a programme aimed at creating political and cultural awareness. Students wrote plays which agitated for independence and portrayed the conflict between traditional values and those inculcated by Western education. An early play, Leo Hannet's *Ungrateful Daughter*, placed emphasis on text, and lent itself to realistic staging. It showed an adopted Papua New Guinea girl rejecting the values of her European parents in favour of indigenous standards. Produced in Port Moresby and abroad, this play advocated independence from colonial rule which was achieved in 1975. John Kasaipwalova's *Kanaka* showed the problems a villager encounters returning to his hamlet from a sojourn in the city. John Kaniku's *Scattered by the Wind* dealt with the disruptions that Christianity, modern schooling and government regulations introduced into village life. Authors, a number of whom were subsequently to take prominent posts in the Papua New Guinea government, found writing was a way to make political statements with relative impunity.

In New Caledonia as well, modern drama was a seedbed for political activism. The first modern theatrical experiment was *Kanaka*, given at an exhibition entitled Melanesia 2000 in 1975. The text drew on pre-Christian ceremonies as recorded by the missionary-anthropologist, Maurice Leenhardt. The sound and light performance presented by actors-dancers moving to a prerecorded tape showed the invasion of the islands by missionaries, slavers and merchants as Kanak, local tribesmen, struggled to carry out death ceremonies for the old chief and prepare for the election of a new leader. The performance – created by Jean Marie Tjibaou, who spearheads anti-colonial activism, and George Dobbelaere – was a rehearsal for Kanak attempts to reassert control over the nickel-rich French colony.

As independence has come to some areas of Melanesia, more experimentation with traditional models has begun. Recent work in Papua New Guinea de-emphasizes text and initiates more lyrical, myth-based presentations which involve music, traditional dance and masks. These tendencies are evident in the plays of Arthur Jawadimbori, head of the Papua New Guinea National Theatre in Port Moresby, and the work of the Raun Raun Theatre in Garoka whose work has been influenced by Greg Murphy, an Australian director. These troupes have been funded by the Papua New Guinea government since 1975. In 1980 the former group presented *Eberia*, a rock opera by William Takaku, and the latter a dance-mask play using visual and music elements of different ethnic groups to present John Kasaipwalova's *Sail the Midnight Sun*. Both performances were seen at the 1980 Pacific Arts Festival, a quadrennial event which since its inauguration in 1972 has prompted some of the best theatre productions in the pan-Pacific area. Both plays took indigenous myths and explored new theatrical avenues. The sound–movement emphasis of these productions may be a sign that the text-based modern drama of the 1970s is returning to more indigenous mime for a base.

SATIRE is a developing genre in Papua New Guinea. Indigenous clown traditions are evoked by the Raun Raun players who play improvised comedies in the open air at village gatherings. Political satire is exploited by Nora Vargi Brash, author of *Which Way Big Man* (1977) which mocks the pretensions of the new government elite. RADIO DRAMA is another lively outlet for writers in Papua New Guinea, a leader in modern theatrical activity in the Pacific.

Micronesia Micronesia is composed of the Federated States of Micronesia (Yap, Truk, Ponape and Kosrae – formerly the Carolines), the Mariana Islands, Marshall Islands, Beleu (Palau), Kiribati (formerly Gilbert Islands) and Nauru. The people are related to Malays and speak Austronesian languages. Societies acknowledge hereditary chiefs, in moderately hierarchical systems. Matrilineal patterns can be seen in traditional society and this may contribute to the importance of girls and women as performers. Research and documentation of the performing arts of this region is not extensive, but based on the information currently available, the following generalizations seem to hold true.

For Micronesians the beginning is the word: song texts are considered the most important element in a presentation. Songs are usually delivered in conjunction with group or solo dances, and most gestures are abstractly decorative. Mimetic role-playing exists, but is not emphasized. Poetry, as represented in the writings of Micronesian authors published in *Mana*, a journal of arts issued by the University of the South Pacific in Fiji, can be considered a livelier genre than mimetic drama.

Impersonation is found in: (1) representation of creatures, often a frigate bird or iguana; (2) mimes of fishing, canoeing, battling or lovemaking; and (3) possession trances in which a spirit enters a performer. Possession, *per se*, in performance is rare, yet the nature of some dance movements – the quivering movements of the frigate bird and the convulsive movements of the iguana – are possible evidence of a venerable link between possession and dance. Both animals are associated with old religious practice.

Dances are performed sitting or standing. Canoe paddles or sticks are used as props. Musical instruments are traditionally few and the human voice the major accompaniment. In group dances one or two dancers may parody the movements of the group, adopting a clown persona. Performances occur in village assembly halls or outdoors. Traditional contexts for performance include religious worship and female initiation rites, courting practices (including lovers' trysts) and group celebrations such as performance contests between villagers, entertainments at village feasts, and welcoming visitors from another island at the beach.

Islands such as Beleu, Guam and Ponape, which have served colonial governments as capitals, exhibit less of the traditional performance practices that were noted by early European visitors. Marching bands, church choirs, and 'Micronesian' dances of relatively recent vintage are common. More removed islands, like Ifaluk and Kiribati, have more conservative performance practice. On both islands danced poetry dealing with themes like the sea, spirits and love remains of great significance.

In Kiribati, traditionally, the composer-choreographer role has SHAMANIC overtones, for he often receives songs from the spirit world in trance and then teaches these *ruoia* ('dance-songs') to villagers. One or two dancers may clown during performance, thereby distinguishing themselves from the group. A woman is often the dance leader. This practice may come from older sitting dances called *te bino*, which feature a female and have movements said to be inspired by the flight of birds. In *ruoia* some performers will suddenly cease the group dance and emulate a frigate bird, associated with old religious belief. Small girls have prominence in some dances. The special status of prepubescent performers in societies as distant from each other as Bali and Kiribati may indicate this is an old practice common to Malayo-Polynesian groups.

On Ifaluk, Burrows reports old religious chant-dances. In *gapengpeng* the single-sex, seated chorus calls on the god to take possession of a dancer. In *ur*, a group standing dance done by either sex, dancers emerge from the group to 'become' a frigate bird. Women are also notable performers on Ifaluk. Their compositions, called *bwarux*, are primarily solo dance-songs meant for private performance by the female for her lover as sole audience. The association of these songs to female fertility may explain their traditional performance for female initiation ceremonies which mark a girl's first menstruation, rites honouring male visitors from other islands and ceremonies to welcome shoals of fish in the harbour.

Performance in Micronesia generally promotes group solidarity under the direction of the composer-choreographer, who may himself be thought to be directed by spirits. A performer may emerge from the group, primarily when the signs of the old god – possession or bird impersonation – occur. Traditionally performers do not seize the group focus for self-expression, but to act out the spirit world. Individual love songs, in theory at least, are for the ears of the loved one alone.

Polynesia Polynesia is divided by specialists into two separate groups: West Polynesia includes Tonga, Samoa, Uvea (Wallis), Futuna, Niue, Tuvalu (Ellice), Tokelau, and Fiji; and East Polynesia includes the Society Islands (Tahiti), Marquesas Islands, Austral Islands, Mangareva, Tuamotu Islands, Cook Islands, Easter Island, New Zealand and Hawaii. In the Eastern area, as Kaeppler notes, movement of the lower body, especially hips and knees, is a strong feature of dance, while this is not the case in the Western area. Performance in Polynesia traditionally involves music and dance interpretation of poetic texts that are rich in metaphor and allusion. Rather than decorative dance, as in Micronesia, the Polynesian tends to use the hands and arms to signify selected words of the text via an elaborate gestural language. Movements of the legs and hips are abstract and relate to the rhythm of the music. The dancer is a storyteller, delivering the narrative in his own persona and not by becoming the characters in the text. Mimetic interludes between these poetic dance-songs can include short skits. Men, or sometimes older women, improvise dialogue on pre-arranged themes, usually satirical in nature.

Polynesian societies were traditionally class-stratified and genealogy determined rank and power. Texts often were in praise of important individuals and presentations were at events that reiterated the power of the aristocracy. Solo chants were often reserved by and for the noted chanter who might him- or herself be a high aristocrat. Large-scale performances needed extensive resources. Performance specialists included composer-choreographers and dancers trained under them.

Kaeppler notes that performances were largely a reaffirmation of social structure: large groups of men, women or occasionally men and women might perform dances in unison with the choreography directed toward the most important viewers – that is, the chief and his guests. Placement of dancers in the configuration might also reflect the hierarchy of rank and age, and obedience to the composer-choreographer was likewise strict. Satirical interludes seem to have served as a release from these customary constraints, and impromptu dialogue and the free use of space, language and subject matter delighted the audiences. A brief consideration of some Tahitian, Samoan, Hawaiian and Fijian performance gives examples of traditional and contemporary performance in Polynesia.

Perhaps the most elaborate performance system reported by early European visitors was that of the *arioi* on Tahiti. This group worshipped Oro, the god of fertility, and as part of his service became specialists in dance-chant. Poetry was a major element in the performances of dramas enacting serious myths. Clowning and female actors are reported. Their 'lewd' dance which included much hip and pelvis articulation, the raising of skirts and facial contortions distressed Europeans. The sexual licence of members, who did not marry and were normally required to kill any children that they might bear, caused the missions effectively to outlaw the sect. It remains difficult to assess the parameters of pre-contact practice based on the fragmentary evidence remaining.

In current Tahitian practice as reported by Moulin, hip movement is still important. However churches now foster the dance as a mode of bringing congregations together. As in Hawaii where the indigenous language has been largely replaced by a European tongue, the emphasis on poetry is greatly diminished and the gestural language is more limited. In contrast to the past group dances, virtuoso solo or couple dances receive focus. These are indications that the current societal values may vary significantly from former ones. Emphasis on decor and spectacle was noted by Victor Carrell in recent Bastille Day competitions. Since their inauguration at the end of the last century Bastille *fêtes* have become the major dance event in Tahiti, and the audience is apt to be treated to innovations such as that prepared by Coco, a major troupe leader, who had his dancers fall on their stomachs and mime swimming in the ocean in a 1985 piece that departed freely from traditional dance.

One group which presents a traditional version of dance is the Cook Islands National Theatre under Ota Joseph. The group is traditional in its preference for precision and group dancing. Still, theatricalization of folk culture is evident in their work. In addition to traditional group standing and sitting dances, the troupe stages mimes of kite-flying, coronation ceremonies, and dance dramas such as one exploring the coming of the Bible to the Cook Islands. These works, based on careful research, are conscious attempts to recycle traditional material in modes that will suit modern audiences.

Examples of how the comedy works in the total context of Polynesian traditional performance can be seen in Samoa. Performers of *fale aitu* ('house of the spirit') are called *fa'aluma*. Traditionally a chief might take along a pair of these clowns as part of his dance group when he went travelling to other islands. Supposedly, spirits (*aitu*) could be invoked by the best performers, and, under the protection of these ghosts, the *fa'aluma* might be allowed to mock the highest chief. The clown skits occurred between dance-chants by the larger ensemble of dancers. Performances that mix group dance by 50–200 performers and such clowning are now usually presented at church fairs. Skits show traditional comic figures, such as transvestites or homosexuals and Europeans, or explore Samoan economic difficulties. Petelo, from Western Samoa, is a noted exponent of this form.

In Samoa, church theatricals on religious themes are also popular, especially on children's day, White Sunday. Experiments in biblical opera, such as Ueta Solomona's *Jeptha* presented at the 1972 Pacific Arts Festival, are products of this tradition. In recent years there has been some experimentation in Samoa in modern spoken drama by authors like John Kneubuhl.

In Hawaii the power of performance is in the poetry. Chant or *mele* was the single most important cultural expression, chronicling history, genealogy and emotion. *Mele* are divided into two categories: ones that have no musical accompaniment, are performed solo and may be on a religious theme (*mele oli*), and ones performed with dance movements, sometimes accompanied by musical instruments (*mele hula*). Divine inspiration was often considered the mode whereby the chanter (*kumu*) gained his songs. Male hula was associated with worship in the temples and martial-arts training (*lua*). Use of weapons and a strong physicality mark male style. Female hula was a more graceful art. Hips and feet elaborate the rhythm while the hands interpret the lyrics through mime and stylized gesture-language. Supported by the nobles, training took place under the teacher in a school (*halau*) which housed a temple to the goddess of dance, Laka. Students trained in religious dances, which were accompanied by the drum (*pahu*), and in dance that told the achievements of nobles, praised gods or recounted historical epics, and which were accompanied by the gourd (*ipu heke*). Comic dance and improvisation provided comic relief. In 1819 traditional religion was outlawed and public performance of hula largely discouraged, until King David Kalakaua (1836–91), a noted musician and patron of the arts, encouraged both revival of traditional chant-dance and innovations which incorporated Western instruments. Films, tourism, television and adopting English as the major language led to *hapa haole* ('half white') versions of hula in this century. Since the 1970s a strong revival of Hawaiian chant and hula has been spearheaded by many Hawaiian artists such as Winona Kapuailohia Beamer.

Fiji lies on the border of Melanesia and Polynesia culturally and ethnically. It exhibits the strengths derived from each of these areas in its theatrical arts. Traditional dance and the highly formalized *kava* drinking ceremony are to be found at church fairs. The traditional *meke* (dance-songs) include war, club, spear, fan and other standing and sitting dances. The most important member of a group is the composer (*dau ni vucvu*) who may receive inspiration from the sprite-like *veli*, spirits who teach dances with quick unpredictable movement, or stillborn children, who teach more sedate songs. Other tunes are composed without such spirit helpers.

The Dance Theatre of Fiji is an innovative group under Manoa Rasignatale, a former pop star who began researching his island heritage after the 1972 Pacific Arts Festival. Performances of the company re-enact village life. Top-spinning contests or the spirit-inspired creation of a *meke* may be acted out. This theatrical presentation of indigenous practices is comparable to the choices of Cook Islands National Theatre and conforms to folkloric theatre-dance companies that have emerged in many Third World countries. The Dance Theatre has found popularity both at home and abroad.

Modern drama is written and presented at the University of the South Pacific in Fiji by Joe Nacola. In Hawaii, too, university theatre programmes have resulted in a wealth of modern spoken drama and given rise to groups like the professional Honolulu Theatre for Youth, which plays to child audiences, and the Kuma Kahua players dedicated to the production of new plays by playwrights who live in Hawaii.

It is notable that in Polynesia, as in Melanesia, spoken drama is being utilized to vent criticism of Western culture or remoulded to reflect the cultures that make up the multi-ethnic and multitalented population of the Pacific basin. Film and television are becoming areas of experimentation. Films written and directed by Papua New Guineans are beginning to be made and the islands are experimenting with television programming. Pacific universities have distinctive features, including choirs that perform traditional dance-chant (University of the South Pacific) and give degrees for courses of study that focus on Asian Theatre or Pacific Dance (University of Hawaii). The excitement that permeates the annual Merrie Monarch hula competition in Hawaii, Bastille Day performances in Tahiti, and the pan-Pacific fervour that erupts as each island prepares to send dances and dramas to the South Pacific Arts Festival shows that the arts are changing, and remain vital to the peoples of Oceania. (See also ASIAN AND PACIFIC ISLAND THEATRE.) KF

See: J. R. Brandon (ed.), The Cambridge Guide to Asian Theatre, Cambridge, 1993.

October Group French AGIT-PROP theatre company working between 1933 and 1936. Many of its short plays were scripted by Jacques Prévert and were distinguished by a combination of playful wit and biting SATIRE. An example is The Battle of Fontennoy (1933), which presented the First World War as a spectator sport in which lives were sacrificed in the name of hypocritical idealism while the population (the spectators) bayed for blood. The Group's work was supported by the French Workers' Theatre Federation, which selected them to represent France at the Moscow Theatre Olympiad of 1933, where they won first prize. As Prévert began to work as a film script writer, many members of the Group followed him and can be seen at their best in Renoir's The Crime of Monsieur Lange (1935). DB

Odéon, Théâtre de l' (Paris) 1900-seat theatre in the Latin quarter, constructed by the architects Peyre and Wailly to house the COMÉDIE-FRANÇAISE in 1782. It was the first to introduce benches into the pit. BEAUMARCHAIS's Marriage of Figaro was first produced there in 1784. In 1789 the more revolutionary members of the troupe, including TALMA, moved to the Théâtre de la République, which became the Comédie-Française in 1799. From 1794 to 97 the theatre closed, then opened under the name Odéon. Burnt in 1799, its actors rejoined the rest of the troupe at the 'new' Comédie-Française. It reopened in 1808, suffered another fire in 1818, when it became the Second Théâtre-Français. Here the first plays of CASIMIR DELAVIGNE were performed. Under HAREL (1829–32) this 'Siberia' of dramatic art saw productions of AUGIER's Le Ciguë (Hemlock) and a move towards REALISM with George Sand's François le champi. MUSSET's Une Nuit vénitienne had its disastrous first night there in 1830, and his Carmosine was shown there for the first time in 1865.

In 1866 SARAH BERNHARDT became one of the leading actresses of the theatre, notably with the role of Zanetto, the young musician in François Coppée's The Passer-by (1869), and during the siege of Paris in 1870 she turned the theatre into a field hospital. In 1872 she played the queen in a very successful revival of VICTOR HUGO's Ruy Blas (banned during the Second Empire). Major managers were La Rounat (1872–80) and Porel (1884–92). Duquesnel turned resolutely to more ambitious mise-en-scène, his production of Newsky's Les Danicheff (1878) providing the

longest run in the history of the theatre. Porel made a success of Alphonse Daudet's L'Arlésienne (1885), with a chorus and orchestra of 150 and Bizet's music. He also staged a number of SHAKESPEARE plays, with much attention to music and spectacle, kept in touch with the naturalist (see NATURALISM) movement (in 1887 he produced the Théâtre Libre play, Jacques Damour). Porel left the theatre thriving. He introduced electric lighting in 1888 (one of the last theatres in Paris to install it).

In 1896, ANDRÉ ANTOINE became director of the Odéon, in collaboration with Paul Ginisty. Seventeen days after the opening of the new directorate, Antoine resigned; the more conservative Ginisty remained in control for a decade. In 1906 Antoine returned as sole director, installing an up-to-date lighting system and getting rid of the old chandelier which had remained lit throughout performances. In the years leading up to the First World War his company set new standards of truth to life and quality of ensemble playing.

The next major figure at the Odéon was FIRMIN GÉMIER, who took over in 1921 and used his position as director in his campaign to establish an effective National People's Theatre (the THÉÂTRE NATIONAL POPULAIRE). Gémier had steps installed joining the stage to the auditorium so that actors could enter through the audience. Towards the end of the 1920s Paul Abram became co-director and, from 1930, sole director, a post he retained till the occupation of Paris by the German army. Abram continued Gémier's policy of trying to present a repertoire of broad appeal, with a judicious mixture of classic revivals and new plays; for a while Saint-Georges de Bouhélier was resident dramatist. In 1946 the theatre was annexed by the Comédie-Française and became its second house, used particularly for modern works, while the classics remained at the Salle Richelieu. In 1959 this arrangement was cancelled by André Malraux, Minister of Culture under de Gaulle, who installed the Renaud-BARRAULT company there instead. Here they performed some of the key plays in the recent history of French theatre, including Rhinoceros by IONESCO (1960) and The Screens by GENET (1966), an event which provoked riots both inside and outside the theatre. From 1967 to 1970 the performances of the THÉÂTRE DES NATIONS were given at the Odéon and it was after one of these, on 15 May 1968, that the theatre was occupied by students. They used it as a debating forum until they were expelled on 14 June. Barrault was dismissed by Malraux for having displayed too much tolerance in dealing with the occupation. From 1971 onwards, the company again came under the administration of the Comédie-Française. Companies of the DECENTRALIZATION MOVEMENT also use it as a Paris showcase for their best productions. In 1983 the theatre became, for six months of each year, the Théâtre de l'Europe under the direction of GIORGIO STREHLER; in 1990 this new arrangement became full-time, and Strehler was succeeded by LLUÍS PASQUAL. JMCC DB

Odets, Clifford 1906–63 The one true company playwright in the entire sweep of American theatre history. In the early days of the GROUP THEATRE, as he listened to HAROLD CLURMAN's orations and followed LEE STRASBERG's formulations of the basic principles of Method acting, Odets was absorbing the elements of a theatrical style that erupted on 14 January 1935, when the Group presented *Waiting for Lefty*, his incendiary play about taxi drivers driven to call a strike. In a series of short, jabbing scenes and in language alive with the rhythms and inflections of urban folk idiom, he expressed the fury, passion and sorrow of the dispossessed working class. With this play the Group discovered its voice: *Lefty* released the full potential of the new realistic acting style that its members had been investigating for four years (see REALISM).

Later in the same year the Group produced two other Odets plays, *Awake and Sing!* and *Paradise Lost*, family dramas whose contemporary but archetypal Jewish sufferers speak in a language of their own, a dense idiom of metaphor and incantatory repetition that alternates irony with exultation and brief, stabbing sentences with longer speeches of operatic intensity. When Odets left for Hollywood at the end of his triumphant year, his Group colleagues felt betrayed. As if in compensation, Odets presented them with a new play, *Golden Boy* (1937). In it, his hero's hard choice between being a violinist and a prizefighter expresses Odets's own conflict about whether to serve art or commerce. Though this central premise is spurious, the play proved to be the Group's biggest moneymaker. Odets's final works for the Group, *Rocket to the Moon* (1938) and *Night Music* (1940), are diminished in their thematic scope and vitality. By 1940, when the Group itself had lost its focus, Odets had also apparently reached a creative impasse. Despite their ripe language and strong conflict, his four remaining dramas – *Clash by Night* (1941), *The Big Knife* (1949), *The Country Girl* (1950) and *The Flowering Peach* (1954) – don't have the same sense of occasion as even the least of the Group efforts. To accomplish his most vibrant work Odets seemed to require a Depression background; he is now regarded as the quintessential 1930s playwright, who transmuted working-class pressures into timeless theatrical eloquence.   FH

Odin Teatret (Nordisk Teaterlaboratorium for Skuespillerkunst; Nordic Theatrical Arts Laboratory) International theatrical community founded in Oslo in 1964 by the expatriate Italian EUGENIO BARBA, who had just returned from three years with GROTOWSKI in Opole. The company's first production, *Ortofilene*, toured Scandinavia with such success that the town of Holstebro, Denmark, invited them to create a permanent theatre there. Since 1966 this has been the company's base, though it also tours extensively.

The Holstebro company opened in September 1967 with *Kaspariana* (based on the strange life of Kaspar Hauser, 1812–33), and followed this in 1969 with *Ferai*, scripted by Peter Seeberg on the basis of Scandinavian mythology and EURIPIDES' *Alcestis*. Shown at the THÉÂTRE DES NATIONS in Paris, it brought them the international reputation that they have enjoyed ever since. These early productions were strongly Grotowskian, and his ideas and training methods remain central to the company's work: a community of actors living under a strict regime of taxing physical and vocal exercise, and at the same time involved in policy and organization; creating performances which arise from their personal confrontation with source materials, techniques and each other; appearing before the public, often to deliberately small audiences, only when they feel that they have something to show. This notion remains fundamental.

Odin Teatret performing *Anabasis* in Peru, 1978.

At the same time, during the early 1970s Barba began to mistrust the fetishistic devotion to skills within a highly protected environment; and partly as a result of experiencing less reverential and more vocal audience responses while touring Sardinia with *Min Fars Hus* (*My Father's House*, based on the life and work of Dostoevsky), the company began to mount CLOWN shows, street parades and improvised musical performances, and developed its 'barter-principle', whereby, instead of paying in cash for a performance, the audience offer in return their own performance or a commitment to some local project. During the 1980s and 90s, as well as continuing to mount resolutely anti-naturalistic productions such as *Brecht's Ashes* (1982) and *Oxyrhincus Evangeliet* (1985), Odin has been a leading contributor to the work of the International School of Theatre Anthropology. AEG

Oenslager, Donald 1902–75 American set designer and educator. His influences include GEORGE PIERCE BAKER; the work of APPIA and GORDON CRAIG, which he saw in Europe in 1921; and ROBERT EDMOND JONES, whom he assisted in the early 1920s. Oenslager designed some 250 productions, including *Anything Goes*, *You Can't Take It with You* and *The Man Who Came to Dinner*. Although he emphasized the need to find the proper style for each play, his designs were frequently decorative and elegant. His greatest influence, however, was as a teacher: he was a professor of design at Yale University for nearly 50 years (1925–71), and many of the major figures in American design were trained by him. He is author of *Scenery Then and Now* (1936) and *Stage Design: Four Centuries of Scenic Invention* (1975), the latter illustrated with drawings from his extensive private collection; a collection of his own designs was published in 1978. AA

Off-Broadway Term, coined in the 1950s, both for New York City productions or theatres outside the so-called BROADWAY area surrounding Times Square – including several houses along THEATRE ROW – and for an Actors' Equity Association contract for theatres with 100–299 seats. (Other unions adopted Equity's designation.) Critic Stuart Little notes, however, that 'Off-Broadway is a state of mind ... a way of looking at theater at every point at odds with Broadway's patterns'.

Off-Broadway began in the early 1900s as the 'Little Theatre movement' (see COMMUNITY THEATRE/LITTLE THEATRE MOVEMENT). Offering artistically significant plays in an inexpensive, non-commercial atmosphere, groups such as the WASHINGTON SQUARE PLAYERS and the PROVINCETOWN PLAYERS staged, in small, out-of-the-way theatres, plays that Broadway ignored. Other companies included the NEIGHBORHOOD PLAYHOUSE, Cherry Lane Theatre, CIVIC REPERTORY COMPANY and GROUP THEATRE. Many were not only experimental but amateur as well, lasting only a few years before falling victim to their own success as artists parlayed triumphs into jobs in commercial theatre and, later, Hollywood. After the Second World War, however, Off-Broadway attracted critical attention. Several successes transferred to Broadway, beginning with New Stages' production of SARTRE's *The Respectful Prostitute* (1948).

In the 1950s and early 60s, several companies had an impact on American theatre. With untried, non-commercial or experimental plays or productions, using then-unknown talent and shoestring budgets, Off-Broadway became an artistic magnet. Serious attention started with the 1952 revival of TENNESSEE WILLIAMS's *Summer and Smoke*, launching the careers of JOSÉ QUINTERO and GERALDINE PAGE. Such companies as the LIVING THEATRE, Phoenix Theatre, NEW YORK SHAKESPEARE FESTIVAL, AMERICAN PLACE THEATRE, NEGRO ENSEMBLE COMPANY, Roundabout Theatre Company, Chelsea Theatre Center, CIRCLE REPERTORY and MANHATTAN THEATRE CLUB presented failed commercial or neglected plays. Over the years, a split developed between commercial Off-Broadway houses such as the Astor Place, LUCILLE LORTEL, Orpheum, Westside Arts, Perry Street, Promenade, Minetta Lane and Criterion Center – represented by the League of Off-Broadway Theatres and Producers – and non-profit companies like the WPA, Jewish Repertory, Pan Asian Repertory Theatre, Brooklyn Academy of Music, RIDICULOUS THEATRICAL COMPANY, Hudson Guild, Lincoln Center Theatre Company, Second Stage and Negro Ensemble Company that still foster new works and US productions of European plays. Mostly, however, real experimental and avant-garde theatre has moved to OFF-OFF BROADWAY.

Off-Broadway theatres have presented such works as BECKETT's *Endgame*, EDWARD ALBEE's *The Zoo Story*, Jack Gelber's *The Connection*, Tom Jones and Harvey Schmidt's *The Fantasticks* (America's longest-running play, opening in 1960), GENET's *The Blacks*, ORTON's *What the Butler Saw*, Bernard Pomerance's *The Elephant Man*, CHARLES FULLER's *A Soldier's Play*, CARYL CHURCHILL's *Cloud 9*, MBONGENI NGEMA's *Sarafina!*, Alfred Uhry's *Driving Miss Daisy*, MICHAEL BENNETT's *A Chorus Line*, BROOK's *Mahabharata*, FUGARD's *The Road to Mecca*, Harling's *Steel Magnolias*, HENLEY's *Crimes of the Heart*, Larrry Shue's *The Foreigner*, Harvey Fierstein's *Torch Song Trilogy* and Howard Ashman and Alan Menken's *Little Shop of Horrors*. Other writers have included KOPIT, Murray Schisgal, BARAKA, VAN ITALLIE, LANFORD WILSON, GUARE, BULLINS, Kurt Vonnegut, RABE, MAMET, Paul Zindel, Albert Innaurato, Eric Bogosian, DURANG, FORNÉS, GURNEY, David Henry Hwang, Larry Kramer, SHEPARD, WASSERSTEIN and ROBERT WILSON.

The talent in these productions included directors Anne Bogart, QUINTERO, SCHNEIDER, GROTOWSKI, Tom O'Horgan, SERBAN, ZAKS and GROSBARD, and actors JASON ROBARDS JR, COLLEEN DEWHURST, GEORGE C. SCOTT, JAMES EARL JONES, JULIE HARRIS, DUSTIN HOFFMAN, Meryl Streep, KEVIN KLINE, STACY KEACH, RUBY DEE, CLAIRE BLOOM, Kathy Bates, Adolph Caesar, Morgan Freeman, Paul Hecht, Edward Herrmann, Swoosie Kurtz, JOHN MALKOVICH, Bernadette Peters, Christopher Reeve, Danitra Vance and AL PACINO. Off-Broadway is also a place for established actors to try unfamiliar roles, including that of director. Recent productions have been directed by actors GERALDINE FITZGERALD (*Mass Appeal* and an all-black *Long Day's Journey into Night*), George C. Scott (*Present Laughter* and *Design for Living*) and Kevin Kline (*Hamlet*). Off-Broadway stages have also lured film and television actors such as Demi Moore, Richard Thomas, Malcolm-Jamal Warner, Molly Ringwald and Robert De Niro, and singers such as Linda Ronstadt and Rex Smith. In 1955, the *Village Voice* established the Obies to recognize accomplishments in this arena. The Lucille Lortel Awards are also given for excellence Off-Broadway. REK

Off-Off Broadway Term coined in the early 1960s to distinguish professional, commercial theatre (BROADWAY and OFF-BROADWAY) from non-commercial theatre presented in coffee houses, churches, lofts and storefronts in New York's Greenwich Village and Lower East Side. Technically, the term also refers to productions that fall under Actors' Equity Tiered Non-Profit Theatre Code for performances with limited runs that feature unsalaried union actors in non-contractual theatres of not more than 100 seats.

Often perceived as a movement, Off-Off Broadway encompasses a wide spectrum of theatrical activity so diverse in impulse, conception, method and intent that no common objective characterizes it. Off-Off Broadway has spawned works of numerous types and terms to go with them: experimental, COLLECTIVE, ALTERNATIVE, environmental, radical, guerrilla and Theatre of Images. Off-Off Broadway is usually considered an alternative theatre grounded in exploration and experimentation, and questioning the limits of performance. The initial impulse was to generate new approaches and methods in a climate free from the demands of popular taste that inform commercial theatre artistically and economically. Frequently, though, Off-Off Broadway productions mirror commercial theatre values and standards.

CAFFE CINO became the first Off-Off Broadway theatre when Joe Cino began to present plays in his one-room coffee house in 1959. By 1965 there were several small producing organizations; the major ones include Judson Poet's Theatre, formed in 1961 by Al Carmines; Café LA MAMA, founded by Ellen Stewart in 1962; and Theatre Genesis, founded in 1964 by Ralph Cook. Devoted primarily to producing work of new American playwrights, these houses mounted plays by writers like Julie Bovasso, ED BULLINS, Rosalyn Drexler, Tom Eyen, MARIA IRENE FORNÉS, Paul Foster, ISRAEL HOROVITZ, ADRIENNE KENNEDY, H.M. Koutoukas, Ruth Krauss, CHARLES LUDLAM, TERRENCE MCNALLY, Leonard Melfi, ROCHELLE OWENS, SAM SHEPARD, Ronald Tavel, Megan Terry, John Vaccaro, JEAN-CLAUDE VAN ITALLIE, Jeff Weiss and LANFORD WILSON.

The term quickly expanded to include a new breed of theatrical work as Off-Off spawned a visually oriented, non-linear, non-narrative – some might even say, non-dramatic – type of performance by such companies as the WOOSTER GROUP, Manhattan Project (see ANDRE GREGORY), MABOU MINES, RIDICULOUS THEATRICAL COMPANY and Split Britches, and by individual artists who mount their own productions, like MEREDITH MONK, RICHARD FOREMAN, ROBERT WILSON and Stuart Sherman. In the 1980s and 90s, as theatrical techniques once associated with Off-Off Broadway have become commonplace in commercial Broadway venues (e.g. the autobiographical and spare nature of *A Chorus Line*, the cross-dressing theme in David Henry Hwang's *M. Butterfly*, or the postmodern mixing of stage and filmic perspectives in the musical *City of Angels*), the boundaries between Broadway, Off-Broadway and Off-Off Broadway have become more and more slippery.

Off-Off still, however, evokes experimental or alternative theatre. That rubric has expanded to include not only the collectives and performance spectacles that developed in the 1970s, but also the explosion in the late 80s of performance art – small-scale pieces, often combining abstract movement or visual elements with non-linear, often autobiographical text, usually performed by its author (e.g. SPALDING GRAY, HOLLY HUGHES, Eric Bogosian, KAREN FINLEY and Robbie McCauley). AS

Offenbach, Jacques [Jakob Eberst] 1819–80 French composer, born in Cologne, Germany, son of a cantor. After a successful career as cellist and conductor, in 1855 he took over the Théâtre des Champs-Élysées, Paris, as the Bouffes-Parisiens, where his first OPERETTAS (hence, *OPÉRAS BOUFFES*) were produced, and then ran the Théâtre de la Gaîté (1872–6). A long stream of hits ensued, including *Orphée aux Enfers* (1858, revived 1874), *Geneviève de Brabant* (1859), *La Belle Hélène* (1864), *Barbe-Bleue* (1866), *La Vie Parisienne* (1866) and *La Grande-Duchesse de Gérolstein* (1867). With librettos by Hector Crémieux, HENRI MEILHAC and Ludovic Halévy, they effervesced with satiric verve, voicing Second Empire cynicism and hedonism. Their influence was worldwide, far beyond the musical sphere: NIETZSCHE, STRINDBERG and CHEKHOV all testified to their liberating effect.

In England, saucy productions at London's Gaiety starring EMILY SOLDENE and Selina Dolaro fired GILBERT and Sullivan to provide chaste alternatives. In Austria, JOHANN NESTROY adapted them as star vehicles for his own comedy and KARL KRAUS gave solo readings of them with shrewd commentary. In the USA, Offenbach's operettas formed a bridge between the loosely knit extravaganza and the modern MUSICAL COMEDY. In Japan, they were media for the earliest performances by Europeans. In Russia, *La Belle Hélène* was the most frequently performed play in the 1870s and 80s. Offenbach's only serious opera, the posthumous *Les Contes d'Hoffmann* (1881), served as the basis for one of the most successful experiments at Prague's Laterna Magika theatre (see LATERNA MAGIKA). LS

Ogilvie, George 1931– Australian director. An actor in the 1950s, he first directed with the Union Theatre Repertory Company, Melbourne, before studying at the LECOQ MIME school in Paris and becoming a tutor at the Central School of Drama, London; he also conducted workshops for the ROYAL SHAKESPEARE COMPANY. Returning to Australia in 1966, he has directed with several major companies, including the South Australian Theatre Company, Melbourne Theatre Company, the Australian Opera and the Australian Ballet, as well as for television. His most notable recent production is John Waters's musical evocation of John Lennon, *Looking through a Glass Onion*, first performed in 1992, which toured Australia with great success in 1993 before being staged in London. MW

Ogunde, Chief Hubert 1916–90 Nigerian playwright and musician, founder of the Ogunde Theatre, and of the Association of Theatre Practitioners of Nigeria (with a membership of over one hundred professional travelling theatre companies). Ogunde is sometimes described as the father of Nigerian theatre, or the father of contemporary

Yoruba theatre. His work was mainly in Yoruba, and reveals some largely Yoruba influences: the traditional *Alarinjo* theatre which derived from the *egungun* masqueraders, the Lagos concert parties, and the (Lagosian) Church of the Lord. Yet for nearly 40 years he travelled the length and breadth of Nigeria, developing a national view in the years before independence. He began his theatre career in 1944, when he was a poorly paid policeman, with his first folk-opera *The Garden of Eden and the Throne of God*, to raise money for his Church. The following year he resigned from the police to start his own professional travelling theatre company. During the next 35 years he composed over 50 operas, plays and MELODRAMAS. During a full life he took titles, reputedly became a millionaire, and was in his later years a film-maker and arts entrepreneur. His productions over the years are a record in performance of a popular perception of all the major events in Nigeria's recent history.

Between 1946 and independence in 1960 he identified closely with the political struggle, and his plays were banned by the colonial authorities: *Tiger's Empire* (1946), *Strike and Hunger* (1946), *Bread and Bullet* (1950). He was commissioned to write a play for the independence celebrations, *Song of Unity* (1960). His almost AGIT-PROP operas were interspersed with other folk-operas based on myths and love stories. After independence he became embroiled in the political turbulence in the Western Region, as the country began to slide towards civil war, and his most famous political play, *Yoruba Ronu!* (*Yoruba Awake!*, 1964), resulted in his being banned from performing in the Western Region (see CENSORSHIP). He produced *Otito Koro* (*Truth Is Bitter*), records his biographer Ebun Clark, 'as a biting answer to this ban'. He composed and produced the opera *Muritala Mohammed* in 1976, after the traumatic assassination of that Nigerian head of state.

He always worked hard to remain in touch with popular sentiment; and he subjected himself as well as his company to gruelling touring schedules, even when it was no longer financially necessary for either himself or his company to reach so many distant audiences. In turn, Ogunde always sought to increase a national awareness among his largely Yoruba audiences. He was a superb entertainer: able to catch the mood of an audience and then suddenly heighten it – thus transforming rather bland tales of love, heroism and evil politicians into exciting theatrical performances that were observant, witty, and full of meaning for their enraptured audiences. Ogunde was the first of the YORUBA TRAVELLING THEATRE practitioners to see the commercial possibilities of full-length film-making. In films like *Aiye* (1980) and *Jaiyesimi* (1981) he was able to use the resources of cinema especially to emphasize the supernatural aspects of his plots. Shortly before his death he worked with Bruce Beresford as casting director for the film of Joyce Cary's *Mister Johnson* (1990), and also played the role of Johnson's father-in-law. CD

Ogunyemi, Chief Wale 1939– Nigerian playwright, director and actor. Ogunyemi was born in Igbajo, Osun state. He worked with WOLE SOYINKA as a member of Orisun Theatre. Particularly in the late 1960s and 70s, the University of Ibadan provided a focal point for productions of his work by, amongst others, Soyinka and Dapo Adelugba. These productions, of plays dealing with Yoruba history and myth, made considerable impact on younger Nigerian dramatists, especially because of their vigorous pursuit of 'total theatre', employing music, dance, song and dialogue.

A versatile actor and director, Ogunyemi is one of the most prolific dramatists in Nigeria, freely admitting that he can no longer list all the plays he has written and that he no longer has copies of some! His plays can be broadly divided into three categories. The first deal with traditional and mythical themes, with the intervention of gods in human affairs and with disputes amongst the gods themselves. These plays, which offer vivid insight into Yoruba conceptualization of the religious pantheon, include *The Scheme* (1967), *Obaluaye* (1968) and *Eshu Elegbara* (1970). Closely associated with these are two adaptations: a fiercely effective condensation of *Macbeth* entitled *Aare Akogun* (1969), and *Langbodo* (1980), a dramatization of D. O. Fagunwa's novel *Ogboju Ode* (first translated by Soyinka as *The Forest of a Thousand Daemons*). The latter, in Adelugba's production, was Nigeria's FESTAC entry for the London Commonwealth Arts Festival, 1976. It exemplifies both the spectacular brilliance of Ogunyemi's stagecraft and his radical conservatism. The second category embraces such historical plays as *Ijaiye War* (1970) and *Kiriji* (1976), both of which explore the fratricidal conflicts among the Yorubas in the 18th and 19th centuries. Here Ogunyemi brings a fresh, raw vigour to a subject treated by other Nigerian playwrights, including OLA ROTIMI and Adebayo Faleti. The third category comprises satirical comedies such as *Business Headache*, a pidgin work from the early 1960s, and *The Divorce* (1977), one of the most frequently performed of all English-language plays in Nigeria.

Based at the Institute of African Studies, University of Ibadan, since 1967, Ogunyemi is now Senior Executive Officer there. CD

ogwangdae (literally, 'five performers') Generic term for several traditional masked dance plays (SANDAE-GŬK) unique to Kyongsang-namdo province in the southwest of South Korea, especially the towns of T'ongyong, Kasan and Kosong. The term probably refers to RITUAL performance to the deities in 'the five directions'. The plays are generally made up of five scenes. OKC

Ōida Yoshi 1933– Japanese actor and director. Ōida was a member of the Bungaku-za Theatre Company, and later joined the Shiki Theatre Company, before going to Paris in 1968 to take part in the work of PETER BROOK's International Centre of Theatre Research. Although he was an actor in SHINGEKI, at the same time he trained himself as a NŌ actor – which has contributed to the depth and distinctiveness of his performances in his work with Brook. He has acted in most of Brook's productions, such as *The Tempest* (1968), *The Ik* (1975), *The Conference of Birds* (1979), *Mahabharata* (1985) and *The Man Who* (1994). His book *An Actor Adrift* (1992) discloses the hardship and satisfaction that Oida experienced in his work in international theatre. He also gives acting workshops based on his own method in many countries, and stages his own productions. MY

O'Keeffe, John 1747–1833 Irish playwright. Born in Dublin, he began acting in 1764, working with companies touring Ireland as actor, singer, writer of PANTOMIMES and plays. His first plays, including *The Shamrock*, later successful as *The Poor Soldier* (1783), were produced in Ireland from 1767. From 1777, through friendship with GEORGE COLMAN THE ELDER, he began to establish a reputation as a playwright, particularly with *Tony Lumpkin in Town*, and moved to London in 1781. Most of his plays of this period depend heavily on songs and incidental music, turning them into a form between musical farce and comic opera – for example, *The Castle of Andalusia* (1782). By far his best play, *Wild Oats*, an often sentimental and genial farce with a brilliant portrait of a strolling player, Rover, was produced in 1791. Though he continued to be prolific, writing more than 60 plays, a long series of failures in the 1790s left him withdrawn and reserved. He retired in 1798, publishing his collected plays. In 1803 he sold the copyrights for all his plays in return for an annuity and settled in Sussex, writing his energetic autobiography, *Recollections* (1826). PH

Okhlopkov, Nikolai (Pavlovich) 1900–67 Post-revolutionary Soviet actor-director, important primarily for his cinematic productions at the Realistic Theatre in the 1930s, in which he experimented with flexible stage–auditorium configurations. The success of his 1921 mass spectacle, *The Struggle between Labour and Capital*, which he staged with a cast of 30,000 Siberians in his native Irkutsk, and his 1922 Youth Theatre production of MAYAKOVSKY's *Mystery-Bouffe*, propelled him to Moscow and the State Institute of Theatrical Art (GITIS). Here he studied with MEYERHOLD, at whose theatre (1923) he became the ideal biomechanical actor, in full control of his body.

Meyerhold taught him about COMMEDIA DELL'ARTE, KABUKI and NŌ theatre techniques, about ancient and folk theatres, APPIA and FUCHS. Theatrical co-worker Sergei Eisenstein, who would direct Okhlopkov in *Aleksandr Nevsky* (Okhlopkov was a film actor from 1924), helped teach him about cinematic montage. This was reinforced by Okhlopkov's work as a film director, following his departure from Meyerhold's theatre (1926) in a disagreement over the actor's role. His productions at Moscow's smallest theatre, the Realistic, of which he was artistic director (1930–7), embodied the stage dynamism, strong emotionalism, cinematic, improvisatory and Eastern techniques he had absorbed. Replacing the stage with mobile platforms and rearranging audience seating for each new production, he brought the immediacy of the outdoor theatre indoors. For Stavsky's *The Start* (1932) he utilized arena staging, a ramp half-surround of the audience and overhead circular bridge. For GORKY's *The Mother* (1933), he effected montage via light shifted among small square platforms surrounding the audience. For Serafimovich's *The Iron Flood* (1933) he replaced the stage with a landscape, as he would in his 1953 production of OSTROVSKY's *The Thunderstorm* at the Moscow Theatre of Drama, in which the mountains actually moved. His production of POGODIN's *The Aristocrats* (1935) drew upon oriental staging techniques and pointed towards the full-scale CARNIVALIZATION of ROSTAND's *Cyrano de Bergerac* (1943), which featured giant, silent PUPPETS as choral presences and the

milling audience as a Parisian crowd. The latter was Okhlopkov's second production for the Vakhtangov Theatre, following his departure from the Realistic, which had been forcibly merged with TAIROV's Kamerny Theatre in 1938. His famous *Hamlet* (1954) at the Mayakovsky Theatre (formerly the Moscow Theatre of Drama) was set in and around a huge pair of iron gates, symbolizing the prison that Denmark and the world had become. In both A. P. Shtein's war play, *Hotel Astoria* (1956), and ARBUZOV's *Irkutsk Story* (1960), Okhlopkov employed variants on the Japanese bridge or *hanamichi*. For his production of EURIPIDES' *Medea* (1961), in which the protagonist was presented as a social victim, the director made over the interior of the Tchaikovsky Concert Hall (originally built as Meyerhold's theatre) to resemble a Greek amphitheatre.

After Okhlopkov's death, Soviet critics judged rather harshly his post-1930s work and his insistence on cultivating multiple perspectives in the theatre. SG

Okuni [Izumo no Okuni] fl.1600–10 Japanese actress-dancer who founded KABUKI. 'Okuni from Izumo' is reputed to have been a priestess of the Grand Shrine of Izumo. Ticket-buying audiences of commoners were captivated by her popularized version of a Buddhist Prayer Dance (*nenbutsu odori*) and a new dance play, *kabuki odori*. The swaggering dandies she portrayed were known in Kyoto as *kabuki mono* ('far out, outrageous fellows') and Okuni's performance took that name. She was called 'Best in Japan', and she danced for the first Tokugawa Shogun, Ieyasu, in Edo Castle in 1607. Okuni's performances were copied by scores of female performers whose troupes toured throughout Japan, thus assuring the continuation of *kabuki* after her death. There is no evidence that Okuni was a prostitute, but her successors were. The prohibition against their performances, first promulgated in 1629, continued to bar women from Japanese stages until the 20th century. JRB

Old Tup Traditional British comic ballad drama, centred on the slaughter of its eponymous animal hero, first recorded c.1845, though the ballad as such is documented earlier and a proverbial reference may indicate its existence as early as 1739. It is impossible to know whether the play is a dramatization of a pre-existing song or the song derived from the play. Performed by teenage boys and girls during the Christmas and New Year period, generally in pubs and clubs, its distribution is largely restricted to an area bounded by Chesterfield, Mansfield and Sheffield in northern England. It is a very lively and popular tradition: fieldwork during the 1970s (*Folk Music Journal*, 3, 1979) located 41 groups of actors from 14 communities, collecting substantial sums for their performances. AEG

Old Vic Theatre (London) Built on the unfashionable south bank of the Thames, not far from Waterloo Bridge, the Old Vic was originally called the Coburg. It opened in 1818. Derided as the home of vulgar 'transpontine' MELODRAMA by critics who preferred the smarter and safer theatres north of the river, it played to packed houses when most other London theatres were struggling to make ends meet. After extensive redecoration in 1833, the Coburg was renamed the Royal Victoria and was soon affectionately familiarized as the Old Vic. By mid-century it had declined into a notoriously rough house, was closed in 1871, reopened as the New Victoria Palace, then closed again in 1880 and bought by a temperance reformer called Emma Cons.

Having supervised the reconstruction of the interior, Cons opened it as a concert hall in late 1880 under the indicative name of the Royal Victoria Hall and Coffee Tavern. She was joined in 1898 by her niece, LILIAN BAYLIS, who took over and transformed the enterprise in 1912. Baylis was an eccentric, whose first love was OPERA and who was utterly unafraid of big schemes. The first such scheme led to the presentation at the Old Vic (1914–23), at popular prices, of all the plays in the SHAKESPEARE First Folio. From 1915, BEN GREET was the director of most of these productions and SYBIL THORNDIKE the star. Extensive repairs and refurbishing were needed in 1927, but from then on and throughout the 1930s the Old Vic remained a centre of excellence. GIELGUD, OLIVIER, WOLFIT, LAUGHTON, ASHCROFT, RICHARDSON, EDITH EVANS and FLORA ROBSON were among those who acted there, and TYRONE GUTHRIE and MICHEL SAINT-DENIS among the directors. Lilian Baylis died in 1937, having run the Old Vic and SADLER'S WELLS in tandem since 1931, and the war closed the theatre in 1939. Damaged by bombs in 1941, it was not fully repaired until 1950, though it housed the influential Old Vic School, under Saint-Denis, from 1947 to 52. Michael Benthall, as artistic director of the renovated Old Vic, repeated the achievement of presenting plays in the Shakespeare First Folio as part of an announced five-year plan (1953–8).

In 1963, after further extensive alterations, the Old Vic became the first home of the NATIONAL THEATRE Company under Laurence Olivier. Among its outstanding productions during this period were *Othello* (1964), PETER SHAFFER's *The Royal Hunt of the Sun* (1964) and *Equus* (1973), STOPPARD's *Rosencrantz and Guildenstern Are Dead* (1967) and *Jumpers* (1972), SENECA's *Oedipus* (1968), directed by PETER BROOK, and TREVOR GRIFFITHS's *The Party* (1973), which brought Olivier's management to an end. PETER HALL became director in 1974 and led the company to its new home in 1976. After a spell as the London base of the touring Prospect Theatre Company (1977–81) was brought to an end by the cutting of the ARTS COUNCIL subsidy, the Old Vic was left empty until 1983, when it was bought by a commercial speculator, and embarked on a programme of repertory (see REGIONAL THEATRE (BRITAIN)). PT

The Tin man from the original production of Yuri Olesha's *The Conspiracy of Feelings*, 1929.

buried in Westminster Abbey, though with no monument because of her two illegitimate children.   PH

Oldfield, Anne 1683–1730 English actress. She is said to have been discovered by FARQUHAR, who overheard her reading aloud. VANBRUGH introduced her to Christopher Rich, who employed her at DRURY LANE in 1692. She began to take new roles from 1700 but her career was slow to reach success. In 1703 her worth was recognized by COLLEY CIBBER who cast her in *The Careless Husband*, and that ensured her reputation. As a result ANNE BRACEGIRDLE retired and Mrs Oldfield triumphed over her rival Mrs Rogers. Farquhar was in love with her but she did not marry. She was frequently cast in star roles by Cibber and ROWE, and she proved equally good in COMEDY and TRAGEDY, e.g. as Andromache in PHILIPS's *The Distressed Mother*. She continued acting until her death and was

Olesha, Yury (Karlovich) 1899–1960 Soviet novelist, short story writer, poet, dramatist, essayist, journalist, translator and film scenarist, in whose work was manifested the fatal ambivalence of the intelligentsia towards the communist regime. The son of Polish Catholic monarchists, Olesha embraced Bolshevism and enlisted in the Red Army (1919), but he grew disillusioned with the curtailments of artistic freedom under the new order. He wrote satirical verse (published collections, 1924, 1927) for the Moscow railway newspaper *Gudok*, whose writing staff included BULGAKOV, Ilf and Petrov and VALENTIN KATAEV. He transformed his famous novel *Envy* (1927) into the play *The Conspiracy of Feelings* (1928) at the suggestion of the Vakhtangov Theatre, where it received a controversial expressionist (see EXPRESSIONISM) staging by Sergei Eisenstein (1929). Here Olesha externalized his conflicting feelings via two brothers – a pro-Soviet rational pragmatist and a retrograde, impractical dreamer, who fails in his attempt to destroy him.

Olesha's one original play, *A List of Blessings* (1931), was staged by MEYERHOLD (whom the author admired) at his theatre as a contemporary Soviet tragedy. In it an egotistical Russian actress, celebrated for her Hamlet, is ambivalent about Soviet society's treatment of the artist, until exposure to the crass materialism of Parisian society leads her belatedly to embrace, and martyr herself to, the communist cause. Meyerhold's wife Zinaida Raikh played the actress, said to be based on MICHAEL CHEKHOV, whose interpretation of Hamlet as victim of his own and society's ills aroused the ire of the communist press (1924–5). At STANISLAVSKY's and NEMIROVICH-DANCHENKO's suggestion, Olesha adapted his fairy tale *The Three Fat Men* (1922) for the stage, and it became a Soviet classic, spawning opera, ballet and film versions. It depicts the overthrow of the titular autocrats by a band of circus performers-revolutionaries. *The Stern Young Man* (1934), a short scenario for a film by Abram Room that was never released into general circulation; *The Black Man* (1932), a fragment featuring another divided self; *Play on an Execution Block*, a 'little drama' in rhymed alexandrines; and dramatizations of ANTON CHEKHOV's short story 'Late-Blooming Flowers' and of Dostoevsky's novel *The Idiot* (1958) – round out the author's writing for the stage. SG

Olivier, Laurence (Kerr) 1907–89 British actor, director and manager, who was a matinée idol in the 1930s, regarded as the finest classical actor of his generation in the 1940s, a patron of new-wave theatre in the 1950s, the first director of the NATIONAL THEATRE in the 1960s, and the first actor to receive a life peerage in 1970. At school, Olivier proved to be a fine, natural actor, and SYBIL THORNDIKE described his performance as Katharina in *The Taming of the Shrew* when he was only 14 as 'the best Kate I ever saw'. He joined BARRY JACKSON's BIRMINGHAM REP in 1926, then the best training ground for acting talent in the country, and gave up the chance to play Stanhope in R. C. SHERRIFF's *Journey's End* (1928) in the WEST END, a part he created, for the chance to star as Beau Geste in a commercial version of P. C. Wren's story, which turned out to be a glossy failure.

This lapse of judgement can be seen as characteristic, in that Olivier excelled in dashing, adventurous roles and seemed temperamentally less suited to the quieter, monochromatic qualities of Sherriff's play. After playing second fiddle to NOËL COWARD in *Private Lives* (1920) – impatiently but fruitfully, for it brought him his first experience of success in London and BROADWAY – he joined JOHN GIELGUD at London's New Theatre to alternate with him the parts of Romeo and Mercutio in *Romeo and Juliet* (1935). The fascinating duel, in a production directed by Gielgud which also offered PEGGY ASHCROFT's Juliet and EDITH EVANS's Nurse, immediately began to upset conventional theories about the correct playing of SHAKESPEARE. Gielgud's Romeo was a superbly controlled, musical performance, but Olivier's had more daring and virility, though his verse-speaking was considered rough. He

joined the OLD VIC in 1937 where, under TYRONE GUTHRIE's direction, he played Hamlet, Sir Toby Belch, Macbeth and Henry V in his first season, and Iago (to RALPH RICHARDSON's Othello) and Coriolanus in his second.

In 1939 he went to Hollywood where, through such films as *Wuthering Heights* and *Lady Hamilton*, he became an international film star, and he married another star, VIVIEN LEIGH, at the height of her fame from *Gone with the Wind*. Despite the glamour of their life in Hollywood, Olivier returned to England in 1941 to enlist in the Royal Navy Volunteer Reserve, but his patriotism was indispensable on the screen. His films, *The Demi-Paradise* (1943) and *Henry V* (1944), which he also directed, encouraged a national pride without lowering artistic sights. In 1944–5, he joined Ralph Richardson to lead the Old Vic company at the New Theatre; and those seasons in which he played Richard III, Hotspur and Justice Shallow, Oedipus and Astrov in *Uncle Vanya* have entered into the legends of British theatre – acting of the finest quality to be seen in a London ravaged by the blitz.

The Old Vic after the war contained the elements of a National Theatre, with an acting school attached to a heroic company; but in a grotesque miscalculation, the Old Vic governors decided not to renew the contracts of Olivier and Richardson, while they were away on tour in Australia. For a few years, he made films with Vivien Leigh and entered into theatrical management in London. But his marriage was deteriorating, and Olivier quickly realized that the theatre of the 1930s was no longer suitable in postwar Britain. After appearing in PETER BROOK's production of *Titus Andronicus* (1956) with Vivien Leigh at Stratford-upon-Avon, which was taken on a triumphant European tour, he returned to films, partly to escape from a theatre in which he no longer believed. In 1957 he allied himself with the new wave of British dramatists, which was then barely a ripple, by appearing in JOHN OSBORNE's *The Entertainer* as the seedy comic, Archie Rice; and in the following years he played Berenger in IONESCO's *Rhinoceros*, Becket and then Henry II in ANOUILH's *Becket*, and Fred Midway in David Turner's satirical comedy, *Semi-Detached* (1962). His marriage to Vivien Leigh was dissolved in 1960 and he married JOAN PLOWRIGHT, his third wife, whom he had met at the ROYAL COURT, in 1961.

He was appointed director of the first CHICHESTER FESTIVAL in 1962, which he partly used to prepare a repertoire for the newly formed National Theatre company which opened at the Old Vic in 1963. His years as the first director of the National Theatre were courageous, in that he battled against building delays, state parsimony, cancer and other major illnesses; and still managed to offer such daring acting performances as his Othello (1964), Edgar in *The Dance of Death* and James Tyrone in *Long Day's Journey into Night* (1971). In 1970 he was created a life peer, Baron Olivier of Brighton. In 1971, the governing board of the National Theatre decided to approach PETER HALL as Olivier's successor without consulting him, and it was several months before he heard of their decision. In 1973 he resigned as director, two years before the new National Theatre complex opened on the south bank of the Thames, with an auditorium that bears his name. After that, he appeared in films and on television, notably as King Lear in 1984. JE

Ollantay A Quechua-language play from Peru that vies with the *RABINAL ACHÍ* as an authentically pre-Columbian work. Padre Antonio Valdés directed a performance around 1780 near Cuzco in the presence of Tupac Amaru II, the Inca chieftain who rebelled against the Spanish. The dispute centres on whether Valdés wrote the play down as the oral tradition dictated, or whether he constructed it out of the myths and legends that existed from pre-Columbian times. Its GOLDEN AGE structure favours the latter interpretation. The post-Second World War period has produced adaptations by César Miró and SEBASTIÁN SALAZAR BONDY, as well as a translation by José María Arguedas. GW

Olympia (New York City) OSCAR HAMMERSTEIN I officially launched the new theatre district BROADWAY at Longacre (Times) Square with the opening of the Olympia in 1895, an entertainment centre that was to include three theatres, a roof garden, billiard rooms, a bowling alley, a turkish bath and restaurants, all for one admission. He completed only two theatres, which he lost to creditors within three years. His MUSIC HALL became the New York Theatre for VAUDEVILLE, and CHARLES FROHMAN changed the Lyric to the Criterion for legitimate fare. Under Klaw and Erlanger, the roof garden became the Jardin de Paris, where the prototype of FLORENZ ZIEGFELD's *Follies* was presented in 1907. The theatres quickly succumbed to films and were razed in 1935. MCH

Olympic Theatre (London) Situated in the meanness of Wych Street, off Drury Lane, the Olympic was one of London's most successful minor theatres during the 19th century. The first theatre on the site was erected by PHILIP ASTLEY in 1805, chiefly from the wood of a French warship. Because of its tent shape, it came to be known as the Olympic Pavilion. Finding it too small for effective HIPPODRAMA, Astley sold it to ROBERT ELLISTON in 1813. The flamboyant Elliston installed gas there in c.1815, rebuilt it in 1818 and, in 1819, bought the lesseeship of DRURY LANE on his profits. A lean period in the theatre's fortunes was ended by the brilliant management of MADAME VESTRIS (1830–9), who made the Olympic the genteel home of tastefully presented light entertainment, with PLANCHÉ as her resident dramatist and with an unrivalled company of comic actors, including LISTON, the KEELEYS and, after 1835, CHARLES JAMES MATHEWS.

When Madame Vestris left, the Olympic soon lost its fashionable audience, briefly recalled by Gustavus Brooke's sensational playing of Othello (1847), and was destroyed by fire in 1849. Walter Watts, having rebuilt it to seat 1750 and reopened it within nine months, was found, three months later, to have embezzled money for the venture (he hanged himself rather than face transportation), and the comedian William Farren took over as manager (1850–3). It was under Farren that the extraordinary FREDERICK ROBSON made his first Olympic appearance in 1853, but it was under the next manager, Alfred Wigan (1853–7), that Robson became a star attraction, making the Olympic famous again in a sequence of bizarre BURLESQUES. Robson was joint manager (with John Emden) from 1857 until his death in 1864, during the run of TOM TAYLOR's *The Ticket-of-Leave Man* (1863). Subsequent managers included Horace Wigan (1864–9), Henry Neville (1873–9), GENEVIÈVE WARD (1883) and WILSON BARRETT (1890–1), for whom the theatre was rebuilt to accommodate 3000, but the Olympic had, by then, a reputation as an unlucky house. It closed in 1897 and was demolished in 1904. PT

ombres chinoises see SHADOW PUPPETS

Omotoso, Kole 1943– Nigerian playwright, novelist, essayist, actor, critic and journalist. Omotoso was born in Akure, studied French and Arabic at Ibadan University, and took his doctoral degree in Edinburgh in 1968. Committed to a specific socialist ideology, his plays include the part-absurdist (see THEATRE OF THE ABSURD) and part-political *The Curse* (1976) and *Shadows in the Horizon* (1975), in which he explores the vulgarity of bourgeois wealth and the essence of revolutionary action by the oppressed. In the former work a servant revolts against his greedy master, kills him and his erstwhile colleague and takes over the estate. Professional praise-singers who praised their first master return to laud their new one, and the cycle continues. The play states explicitly that a revolution that aims at achieving the values of those removed will bring no change but perpetuate evil in greater proportion. Between 1981 and 1982 Omotoso produced for the Nigerian Television Authority 30 serial episodes entitled *Life Off the Course*. CD

O'Neal, Frederick 1905–92 African-American actor and theatre administrator. O'Neal performed in St Louis and organized the IRA ALDRIDGE Players before moving to New York City, where he attended the New Theatre School in 1936–40. With Abram Hill he founded the AMERICAN NEGRO THEATRE (1940–50), and in 1944 he appeared as Frank in its BROADWAY production of *Anna Lucasta*. Subsequently he played a variety of roles on and OFF-BROADWAY (*Lost in the Stars*, 1949; *Take a Giant Step*, 1953), on television and in films. O'Neal held several important positions, such as president of the Negro Actors Guild (1961–4) and of Actors' Equity Association (1964–73). His many awards testify to his achievements as actor and leader in the theatrical profession. EGH

O'Neil, Nance 1874–1965 American actress, who joined the ARTHUR McKEE RANKIN company in San Francisco in 1893. Rankin soon built her into a star, booking her into several national tours, and in 1900 sponsored her world tour of *Magda*, *Fedora*, *La Tosca* and *Camille*. In 1903 she added IBSEN's *Lady Inger of Ostrat* to her repertoire and played it in San Francisco and Boston. Two years later she began performing *Hedda Gabler* and eventually took it to New York. Billed as the great tragedienne, she was usually considered to stand in the shadow of other great emotional actresses. RAS

O'Neill, Eliza 1791–1872 Irish actress, who was greeted on her COVENT GARDEN debut as Juliet in 1814 as a second SARAH SIDDONS. Other successes during her remarkable five-year career at Covent Garden included Lady Teazle in *The School for Scandal* and the title role in Richard Lalor Shiel's tragedy, *Evadne* (1819). Shelley wrote *The Cenci* with her in mind, as well as EDMUND KEAN. She retired in 1819 to marry a Mr (later Sir) William Becher.   PT

O'Neill, Eugene (Gladstone) 1888–1953 The first American playwright of major talent, the only one ever to win the Nobel Prize for Literature (in 1936), and still universally regarded as America's finest. Also, having written his autobiography not only in *Long Day's Journey into Night* but also piecemeal, under lesser or greater disguise, in most of his works, he is among the most subjective of dramatists. Probably only AUGUST STRINDBERG, whom he called his mentor, was as obsessed with his own life and family history. The son of actor JAMES O'NEILL, Eugene used to deride the sentimental and melodramatic theatre of his father's day, yet he stood on his father's shoulders in attaining his pre-eminent position. Immersed in a theatrical milieu from birth, he unconsciously absorbed, as though by osmosis, the basics of stagecraft and playwriting. In youth and early manhood, however, there was virtually no indication that he would ever, in any field, amount to much: it appeared, rather, that he, like his self-destructive older brother, Jamie, would become a hard-drinking wastrel.

Perhaps the key to understanding him is that he suffered from lifelong feelings of guilt, born apparently of the fact that his mother, a shy, devout Catholic, innocently became a drug addict as a result of his birth. Recalling how wretched he felt on learning of her addiction to morphine and of his role in her downfall, he says through his counterpart in *Long Day's Journey*: 'God, it made everything in life seem rotten!' Turning against his ancestral faith, the apostate began to question all orthodoxies, all authority. Despite his familiarity with the ancient Greeks and SHAKESPEARE, his sense of tragedy grew from his own life, not from the classics. He was an emotional haemophiliac whose family-inflicted wounds never healed. Here, then, we find the original of his sombre outlook on life, the major source of the power and anguish pounding throughout his writings.

After an unimpressive record at Catholic and secular schools, he sought the lower depths, intent on experiencing 'real life'. He went to sea, drifted on the waterfronts of Buenos Aires and New York, and once became so depressed that he attempted suicide. O'Neill often said that he never thought of being a writer till his health broke down, in his mid-20s, confining him to a TB sanatorium for months. While recuperating, he 'really thought' about his life for the first time and resolved to become a playwright. After his recovery in 1913, plays began to pour out of him, most of them tales of the sea and of the underside of life; what, in other words, had seemed misspent years, proved to be a major part of his working capital as a writer.

In a move beneficial to both parties, Eugene in 1916 joined a group of amateur playmakers on Cape Cod, who became known as the PROVINCETOWN PLAYERS on moving to Greenwich Village, with O'Neill as their most imaginative and gifted writer. When he made his BROADWAY debut in 1920 with *Beyond the Horizon* (written in 1918), a story of defeat on a farm with the sea beckoning in the background, most of the critics, though faced with something novel in their experience – an American tragedy – were enthusiastic; but several complained that the play was too

long, while another criticized its many changes of scene. The harsher critics failed to realize that the author, who eventually would ignore most stage conventions, was determined to hack out his own course. The play enjoyed a good run for so sombre a work and won for O'Neill the first of his four Pulitzer Prizes. The others were for *Anna Christie* (written in 1920), *Strange Interlude* (1926–7) and *Long Day's Journey into Night* (1939–41).

A veritable Proteus of the drama, O'Neill kept changing his style. Starting as a realist (see REALISM), with occasional returns to the genre, he also wrote expressionistic works (see EXPRESSIONISM; *The Emperor Jones*, 1920; *The Hairy Ape*, 1921), costume drama (*The Fountain*, 1921–2; *Marco Millions*, 1923–5), Strindbergian views of marriage (*Welded*, 1922–3), biblical fables (*Lazarus Laughed*, 1925–6) and even a comedy (*Ah, Wilderness!*, 1932). As though set on avenging his father's bondage to plays pandering to popular taste, he made demands on his audiences with extra-long works, namely *Strange Interlude*, nine acts; *Mourning Becomes Electra* (1929–31), a trilogy in 13 acts; and *The Iceman Cometh* (1939), twice the standard length. Again, testing what the public would accept, he wrote *The Great God Brown* (1925), a bewildering work in which the characters constantly mask and unmask; *All God's Chillun Got Wings* (1923), a poignant story ahead of its day about a white girl married to a black; and *Desire under the Elms* (1924), a drama of greed, incest and infanticide. In writing some 30 long works and nearly a score of short ones in so many different styles, O'Neill almost exhausted the stage's nonverbal resources through his use of song, pantomime, dance, masks, imaginative scenic devices and novel sound effects. In the end, though, after all his imaginative flights, realism proved his forte, as was demonstrated by *The Iceman Cometh* and *Long Day's Journey into Night*, his masterpieces.

In the 1930s he worked for years on his most ambitious project, a cycle entitled 'A Tale of Possessors Self-Possessed' that would span a large part of the American past in dramatizing highlights in the history, generation after generation, of a 'far from model' family. In the work, first envisioned as five plays (then seven, next nine, and, for a time, 11), O'Neill aimed to show that materialism and greed had corrupted America. Unfortunately, a number of factors, particularly ill health and his despair as the Second World War loomed, prevented him from achieving his goal. After he had destroyed most of his cycle writings, all that survived was one finished play, *A Touch of the Poet* (1935–42), and, by chance, a rough draft of another, *More Stately Mansions* (1935–40), which was staged posthumously in truncated form.   LSH

O'Neill, James 1846–1920 Irish-born American actor. Despite his great popularity in the late 19th century, he is primarily remembered today as the father of EUGENE O'NEILL. For a time, appearing opposite such stars as CHARLOTTE CUSHMAN, ADELAIDE NEILSON and EDWIN BOOTH, it appeared that he would attain similar stature, that he would become Booth's successor. His promise faded, however, particularly after he had, as his son said, 'the good bad luck' to find a gold mine in CHARLES FECHTER's dramatization of DUMAS *père*'s *The Count of Monte Cristo*. Initially O'Neill, who had suffered a hungry childhood, rejoiced in his prosperity as the Dumas hero, but as the decades piled up and the audiences flocked to see him only when he played Edmond Dantès, the role became a straitjacket that gradually diminished his talent. Fragments of his history are woven into his son's devastating family portrait, *Long Day's Journey into Night*. LSH

onnagata see FEMALE IMPERSONATION

Ōno Kazuo 1906– Japanese dancer. Having graduated from the School of Athletics, Ōno became a gymnastics teacher. In 1933 he started studying modern dance with Ishii Baku and later began dance classes with Eguchi Takaya, who had studied dance in Germany with Mary Wigman. After the Second World War he began his recitals of short pieces, and in 1959, with *The Old Man and the Sea* (based on the novel by Hemingway), he collaborated with Hijikata Tatsumi (1928–86) for the first time.

Their new dance movement, *ankoku butō* ('dance in the darkness'), started when Hijikata performed *Kinjiki* (*Forbidden Colours*, based on a novel by Mishima Yukio) early in the same year. *Bara Iro Dance* (*Rose-coloured Dance*, 1965) and *Anma* (*The Masseure*, 1963) are also works that he has performed with Hijikata. *Ankoku butō* is a postmodernist Japanese dance form, free of the constraints of both Western-style modern dance and traditional Japanese dance. It is a provocative form of social criticism and strongly influenced the *ANGURA* (underground) theatre movement in the 1960s. The dancers of the second and third generations of *ankoku butō* are now called Butō after their style, and dance companies such as Dairaku-kan, Sankaijyuku and Byakko Sha, and dancers such as Ishii Mitsutaka, Nakajima Natsu and Iwana Masaki, are known internationally. Ōno astonished the dance world by his solo performance of *Celebrating la Argentina* (1977), which he gave when he was 71 years old. He still performs on stage and gives lessons to young dancers. MY

Onwueme, Tess 1955– Nigerian playwright, director and critic. Onwueme was born in Ogwashi-Uku, Bendel state. She studied at the Universities of Ife and Benin, completing a doctoral thesis on the work of FEMI OSOFISAN. As a lecturer at the Federal University of Technology, Owerri, she founded an innovative theatre group whose members comprised junior (non-academic) staff and science students, and which was responsible for the first performances of many of her early plays. Onwueme's work is notable for its constant experimentation with form, language and theatrical technique. *A Hen Too Soon* (1983) and *The Broken Calabash* (1984) are essentially realistic domestic dramas on familiar themes in Nigerian theatre, such as parental opposition to love partnerships. *The Desert Encroaches* (1985) and *Ban Empty Barn* (1989) are extremely ambitious animal allegories, audacious in their use of language, exploring political and economic oppression both within the authoritarian African nation-state and at an international level. These early plays achieved high prominence, with productions at the National Theatre and on Nigerian television. *Cattle Egret versus Nama* (1989) is a short play of ferocious impact set in a Nigerian prison cell. Two much longer works, *The Reign of Wazobia* and *Legacies* (both 1988), scrutinize traditional value systems and structures of government: the two plays focus, respectively, on women's organization and on the relationship between African and African-American communities. Since 1990 Onwueme has been teaching in the USA. CD

Open Theatre (New York City) An experimental, influential OFF-OFF BROADWAY acting company during 1963–73. JOSEPH CHAIKIN left the LIVING THEATRE after playing Galy Gay in BRECHT's *Man Is Man* to establish a study group for exploring new styles of acting. This collection of actors, writers and dramaturges came to be known as the Open Theatre. Chaikin believed that the creative intervention of the performer could lead to a new dramatic expression, and he developed a technique based on the ideas of *presence* (focusing on the performer, not the character) and *transformation* (the actor changing from one role to another before the audience's eyes). This approach is described in Chaikin's book, *The Presence of the Actor*. Open Theatre workshops combined vigorous physical, vocal, breathing and improvisational exercises with discussions led by critics Gordon Rogoff and Richard Gilman. Gradually the group began to work on ensemble creations shaped by a single writer, resulting in *Viet Rock* by Megan Terry (1966), *The Serpent* by JEAN-CLAUDE VAN ITALLIE (1968) and *Terminal* by Susan Yankowitz (1969). The Open Theatre gave these works full productions and then created some chamber works, including *The Mutation Show* (1971) and *Nightwalk* (1973); but as it edged away from being an acting workshop towards becoming a producing company, it decided to close – in Rogoff's words, it was 'doomed to succeed'. AS

opera In order to avoid speculation about such early and such exotic examples of music drama as could by some highly debatable definition be considered to be opera, and about very recent examples of music drama that may be reaching beyond the limits of what is generally called opera, what follows has been made consistent with John Drummond's statement, 'Opera is, strictly speaking, one particular child in the family of music drama. Born in Western Europe at the end of the sixteenth century, it is now, according to some, fast approaching its demise. It is essentially a regional art-form, although it has been exported along with other trappings of Western civilization to many parts of the globe.'

An opera is not, as many rough and ready definitions claim, a play with music, nor is it a play set to music or a sung play. Opera is a form of theatre in which music provides a dramatic and aesthetic predicate to the situations in which the characters find themselves. The words, supplied by the libretto, that are sung in opera are usually in themselves of rudimentary dramatic and of slight aesthetic significance. If they had such significance in any marked degree they would resist musical setting; it would be a case of gilding refined gold, or painting the lily. The words indicate a focus for the feelings aroused in the audience by the music, or, the music arouses the feelings that are to be fused with the import of the words. The gaiety or the melancholy aroused by a passage in a Mozart symphony is general. The gaiety is not specifically that of a child at play nor the melancholy that of someone bereaved, yet either could be the case. In a Mozart opera such feelings are part of an organic whole whose other elements are particular characters in particular situations. WAGNER's image of male and female creating a child is very apt. The words are the male element, the music the female, and opera the child. Both male and female are autonomous beings. They come together and the result is a child which is not the mere addition of male and female but a creation from them. Features of both father and mother will be discernible in the child, who nevertheless will itself have a distinct identity. Although Wagner's image arose in a particular 19th-century context, the central idea is applicable to all opera, the nature of its applicability varying at different periods of opera's history.

Music, with its immediate sensuous appeal, affects the feelings. The effect on the feelings of the two bars during which the hero sings 'Venere splende' ('Venus is shining') at the end of the first act of Verdi's *Otello* is not merely due to the information conveyed by the two words in the context of what has happened so far in the opera. It is also due to the effect of the music, both of the orchestral accompaniment and of the singing. An actor in a play both supplies information and affects feelings by means of spoken words. He chooses his manner of utterance according to one of the several possible interpretations of his part. Although the score cannot specify his utterance with absolute precision, the actor in opera is much more restricted. His pitch, his inflections, his emphases, his pauses are under the rigorous control of the composer.

Theatre is an art that exists in time. One of its more important characteristics is its exploitation of time in the form of rhythm. Much of the impact of a play is due to the rhythm of its performance, the changes of pace in utterance and movement. Although the speeds at which various sections of a play are performed may not be wholly determined by the director and the actors, under the influence of a particular audience, they are largely so. The paces of the various sections of an opera are very much less at the discretion of the director, the conductor and the performers, or under the influence of the audience. Again, the score does not rule with absolute authority, but it exercises great control. The composer indicates whether a passage is to be delivered quickly or slowly. He specifies the rhythm of the words, indicating the location of pauses and their lengths and the relative lengths of syllables. When, in the second act of SHAKESPEARE's *A Midsummer Night's Dream*, Helena says, 'O wilt thou darkling leave me? Do not so', the performer may speak the line at any one of various speeds, give the syllables various relative emphases, introduce various pauses, make various inflections. The utterance chosen will accord with one of the several legitimate interpretations of the play as a whole. Although it cannot be said that there is a unique legitimate interpretation of Benjamin Britten's opera *A Midsummer Night's Dream*, the performer singing the same words as Helena is by no means as free as the actress in Shakespeare. The speed at which she is to sing is indicated by a metronome marking. The relative lengths of the syllables are set down: e.g. the proportions of the first five syllables are 2, 3, 1, 2, 2. There must be a substantial pause

after 'darkling' and another of equal length after 'me'. The voice at the end of the line has to be a major third lower than it was at the beginning.

Music's fundamental control of pace, pitch and emphasis may, from one point of view, be restrictive; from another it is liberating. In a particular situation in a play several characters may simultaneously be reacting quite differently but equally forcibly. They cannot be allowed equal status in the expression of their reactions. All cannot speak at once and be individually understood. Usually one speaks and the others are restricted to movements and gesture. If all speak at the same time a significant feature in the unfolding of the drama will occur – confusion. Opera is at an advantage. It is a commonplace for several lines of music to be clearly perceptible when sounded simultaneously, and for their simultaneity to produce a further clearly perceptible effect. Several characters in an opera can express forcible and sustained yet distinct reactions at the same time, and if the manner of expression is not absolutely equal for all of the characters it is very much more nearly so than could ever occur in a play. This is admirably illustrated by the famous quartet to be found towards the end of Verdi's *Rigoletto*. The Duke and Maddalena are in a room in Sparafucile's lair. Gilda and Rigoletto are outside. We hear the Duke protesting his love and at the same time, to quote Ernest Newman, 'Maddalena laughing it all off ironically, Gilda bemoaning her lover's perfidy and her own sad lot, and Rigoletto assuring her with grim persistence that she shall soon be avenged'. VICTOR HUGO, when he heard the opera (which after all is derived from his own play *Le Roi s'amuse*), commented wistfully on the advantages music sometimes has over poetry or prose, opera over spoken drama: 'What would the ordinary dramatist not give,' he asked, 'to be able to make four people animated by different sentiments speak all at the same time, each in character, and each fully intelligible to the audience!'

It is often objected that opera is essentially ridiculous. Particular manifestations of it may be so; but this is true of any activity, theatrical or otherwise. The English have a long tradition of scoffing at opera. Although guilty of travesty of meaning and misattribution of source, they frequently claim that DR JOHNSON defined opera as 'an exotic and irrational entertainment'. Such sentiments have always had wide popular approval. In PLANCHÉ's burletta *The Deep, Deep Sea* (1833) Perseus exclaims,

Run – fly – the dreadful sacrifice delay
Till my arrival. I will only stay
To sing a song – as opera heroes choose
Always to do, when they've no time to lose.

In 1874, 18 years after Verdi's *La Traviata* had been first performed in England, a critic writing in the *Athenaeum* referred to that opera's heroine as 'the consumptive lady, who coughs *pianissimo* and sings *fortissimo* in her death scene'.

Theatre is not actuality. Even in a play by ZOLA the actors do not live their lives on the stage: they act. Objects are not there to serve the actors but to serve the characters, and whether or not the objects are those of everyday life is a matter of style, not of essence. It has been well pointed out that actors do not need to consume real food during a meal in a play (see STAGE FOOD). Their responsibility is to act, not to eat. And such actuality as is introduced by drinking glasses of real wine is immediately confounded when characters are required to take poison. Opera is exotic, at least in origin, as far as the English are concerned. It is also irrational in the way that plays are irrational, dealing with personae divorced from persons. Dr Johnson was right when, in his *Preface to Shakespeare* (1765), he claimed, 'It is false, that any representation is mistaken for reality; that any dramatic fable in its materiality was ever credible, or, for a single moment, was ever credited.' Planché was right in noting that a character in opera who has no time to lose may sing at length. The dramatic objective of the singing will be the anguish that the character feels in his harassed situation. The *Athenaeum* critic's comment must be similarly interpreted. *La Traviata* is not concerned to present a clinically accurate simulation of the heroine's death. It conveys the feelings that are appropriate to the character desperately aware of imminent death. In real life a consumptive lady *in extremis* may be capable of no more than a faint whisper. The intensity of her feelings may call for powerful expression. It is with these feelings that opera is concerned.

Opera, like all forms of art, requires the acceptance of convention. Many people are quite unable to cope with the convention of opera. People do not pause to sing when they are beset by hostile pursuers. Frail people do not sing loudly at the point of death. In fact people do not carry out their lives in song at all. If you cannot accept the fundamental conventions of opera you can have no access to it. There is no point in someone who cannot understand Chinese dismissing a book written in Chinese as rubbish, and anyone who thinks that a portrait must be as closely as possible identical with a colour photograph will be cut off from much art. Opera gives access to experience that cannot be had otherwise, an experience in which the main elements are feelings integral to situations. Like all conventions, the convention of opera is a means; and opera, like all art, requires the means to be as unobtrusive as possible. The convention is the blind man's stick. The blind man does not pay attention to his stick, but to what his stick reveals to him – information to which he would have no access were it not for his stick. Different kinds of stick will give access to different kinds of information and the effective use of any kind of stick must be learned. Opera is a particular kind of stick and its use must be learned.

The music in opera is not confined to the performers on the stage. Much of it may be located in the orchestra pit, and the contribution of the orchestra may have a considerable effect on the drama. The orchestra may act as commentator or as dramatic memory. While a character expresses his overt reaction to a particular situation, the orchestra may introduce irony, pathos or other feelings as it plays passages heard earlier in the work that set what is now being uttered on the stage in the context of past happenings or feelings. It was in relation to this possibility that APPIA commented that a character can leave the orchestra to express his suffering while he himself expresses what his situation immediately calls for. The matter had been noted a century earlier by the Belgian composer Grétry: 'I soon grasped that music has resources that declamation alone certainly has not. For example, a girl assures her mother that she is ignorant of love, but while she affects indifference by means of a simple and monotonous melody, the orchestra expresses the torment of her amorous heart.'

Music is essential to opera, but so are words. An opera libretto is on its own incomplete. It requires music for its completion. If a libretto were merely performed in speech and movement it would make a bad play. Considerable skill is needed to write a good libretto. The librettist must not try to write a play, yet inability to write a play is by no means a guarantee of skill as a librettist. The rhythm of an opera, in detail and overall, is dictated by the music. The feelings evoked by opera are at the behest of the music, not of the words. Unlike words, music cannot cope with elaborate factual information. Music has its own formal structure to which words must submit. BERNARD SHAW has pointed out that however impressive words may be when read silently, they are unsuitable for a play unless they can be spoken effectively. Similarly, words are unsuitable for opera unless they can be sung effectively. Wagner claimed that the ideal situation occurs when composer and librettist are the same person, a combination achieved by himself and certain others. Many composers have not provided their own librettos. Some have worked to a libretto they have been presented with. Some have been fired by a play, a novel, a historical incident, and have required a writer to base a libretto on it. Many composers have insisted on the revision of the structure of librettos with which they have been presented, and many have insisted on verbal alterations. How an opera came to have a particular libretto is of interest; but how good an opera results from the fusion of libretto and music is the essentially important matter.

Many operas are based on plays, and frequently not on the best plays. Verdi's *La Traviata* originated in *La Dame aux camélias* by DUMAS *fils*, PUCCINI's *Tosca* in SARDOU's *La Tosca*. Both of these plays are highly melodramatic. MELODRAMA is a kind of theatrical puppetry. It is when music infuses feelings into the characters and the situations of melodramatic plays that the works cease to be theatrical manipulation and become drama. Of course, some operas, Verdi's *Otello* for instance, are not based on inferior plays; but examination always shows marked differences between the librettos and the original plays. It is because *Otello* and *Othello* are both great theatrical works that audiences attribute to them a degree of similarity greater than is justified by sober comparison. Whilst the foregoing is almost universally true, two exceptions must be noted. Berg's opera *Wozzeck* and Britten's *A Midsummer Night's Dream* are settings of the almost unaltered plays by BÜCHNER and Shakespeare.

Othello was written in English, the libretto of *Otello* in Italian. The music of *Otello* is as accessible to an English audience as are the words of *Othello*: the words of *Otello* are not. The English audience has no difficulty with the music of Wagner's *Ring* cycle, but it has with the original words. Audiences ignorant of Russian attend performances of Mussorgsky's *Boris Godunov*. Those with no familiarity with Central European languages patronize operas by Smetana and Janáček. Such people are in danger of treating operas not as dramas but as concerts in costume. Short of requiring audiences to learn several languages, what is to be done? The obvious answer is to provide translations. But faithful translation, difficult in any event, is notoriously difficult in opera. As well as being faithful to the import of the original words, the translation of a libretto must make as accurate a fit as possible with the music, and this was written in conjunction with totally different words. To consider the matter at the simplest level it is sufficient to remember that in different languages words of equivalent meaning frequently differ in their numbers of syllables. For example, an English monosyllabic word common in opera, 'hope', becomes in Italian, French and German, *speranza*, *espoir*, *Hoffnung*. The Italian, French and German vocal lines may have different notes for each syllable. How are these notes to be managed if a monosyllabic translation is attempted?

Accuracy in detail in libretto translation is virtually impossible, especially in view of the fact that a great number of opera books, as they are sometimes called, are in rhyming verse. In Verdi's *Aïda* the words 'Numi pietà' are in one translation rendered as 'Merciful gods' and these words fit the music; but in the original mercy is not attributed to the gods – it is sought from them – and the sustained note for the fourth syllable emphasizes 'pity', not 'gods'. The most successful libretto translations provide words that make a good fit with the music and that express the import of the original as closely as this fit will allow. When in Mozart's *The Magic Flute* Tamino gazes at the medallion portrait of Pamina, he sings, 'Dies Bildnis ist bezaubernd schön' – literally, 'This likeness is enchantingly beautiful.' Edward Dent has rendered this as 'O loveliness beyond compare', not achieving accuracy in detail but commendable fidelity in general. Translations do not only reduce the risk of operas becoming concerts in costume. As Dent put it in his address to the Musical Association in 1935, 'translation is a necessity if opera is to receive any popular encouragement'. It will have been noted that *Aïda* and *The Magic Flute* have been referred to, as is common, as Verdi's and Mozart's and not as Ghislanzoni's and SCHIKANEDER's, the writers of the librettos. This is a sharp illumination of the status of the libretto in comparison with the music of an opera.

The foregoing has been a broad description of matters relevant to opera in general. Particular operas, especially those written at different historical periods, exhibit certain features more vividly than others. The earliest operas are distinguished by their preoccupation with classical subjects. This arose because opera originated in deliberate attempts by Florentine *camerate* (groups of noblemen, musicians and men of letters) to re-create what they assumed ancient Greek theatrical performance to have been. The first of all operas was *Dafne*, with words by Ottavio Rinuccini (1562–1621) and music by Jacopo Peri (1561–1633). It was played in 1597 to a private audience in the palace of Jacopo Corsi, who may have contributed some of the music. Unfortunately the score has disappeared, except for a couple of fragments. The earliest opera whose music we still have is *Euridice*. Its libretto is by Rinuccini and there are two settings, one by Peri and one by Giulio Caccini (?1545–1618). Peri's version was first performed in the Pitti Palace in 1600. Caccini's had to wait another two years. In the early operas, again because of their aim of reproducing Greek drama, the words tend to

dominate the music, and the music's form is very much what is known as RECITATIVE. This state of affairs was much altered by Claudio Monteverdi (1567–1643) whose *Orfeo* was produced in 1607 and his *L'Incoronazione di Poppea* in 1642. As Donald Jay Grout has written, 'The doctrines of the Camerata had emphasised poetic values at the expense of music. Monteverdi, by means of organising the recitative, deepening its content, and introducing arioso or ARIA forms at critical points in the action, had made the music an equal partner with the text.' Opera henceforth sees constant attempts to integrate words and music, both of which aspire to self-sufficiency, into a unity whose justification is dramatic effectiveness, and it falls under a new influence with the establishment of public as against private performances. The words and music are disposed in such a manner that information-giving is accommodated by recitative, and feelings by arias and ensembles.

Opera spread from the Italy of its origins to other countries in Europe and fell under the spell of already existing activities, e.g. in France the ballet, in England the MASQUE. Italian opera had always been associated with spectacle. Association with ballet and masque reinforced the tie. Gradually the river from the Italian spring divided into many streams. As Italian, French, German and English music and spoken drama took on particular identities, so did their styles of opera; and by the end of the 19th and beginning of the 20th centuries there were recognizably Russian and Czech opera.

The history of opera, especially from the 18th century, has been treated exhaustively in many authoritative and readily available books. There is not space to summarize it adequately here. Nevertheless mention should be made of a few very significant figures. CHRISTOPH WILLIBALD GLUCK (1714–87) reinvested opera that was tending towards the purely decorative with powerful drama, purity and nobility. Wolfgang Amadeus Mozart (1756–91) demonstrated a high degree of perfection in the various styles – formal, relaxed, comic, serious – that had emerged by the second half of the 18th century. Giacomo Meyerbeer (1791–1864) was, in spite of his Italian-German name, responsible for French GRAND OPERA, which exploited purely theatrical values to the full. Richard Wagner (1813–83) was more seriously concerned with and more thoroughly understood theatrical effectiveness in the service of powerful drama than any other creator of opera. He claimed to write 'music dramas' rather than operas, was his own librettist, and wrote extensively on the nature of opera and of the theatre. He abandoned the practice of recitative and aria, writing works of close-bound unity that follow an uninterrupted dramatic flow and in which the orchestra plays an equal, not subordinate, part. Originally adulated by some composers and audiences and vilified by others, his work split the world of opera into Wagnerians and anti-Wagnerians. The passage of time has shown Wagner's operas to be of intrinsic worth and to have had profound influence on the general development of opera.

The operas of Giuseppe Verdi (1813–1901) have the distinction of enjoying more performances than those of any other composer. They range from traditional Italian-style works in which vocal considerations take precedence to intensely romantic operas in which both voices and orchestra are used equally powerfully. It has been said that the two greatest of all love operas are Wagner's *Tristan und Isolde* (1865) and Verdi's *Otello* (1887), and indeed in many ways these works typify the musical-dramatic achievements of their composers. In the 20th century various types of opera have emerged: some developments of Wagner, some of Verdi, some experimental under the influence of twelve-tone music or of naturalist, surrealist or expressionist drama (see NATURALISM; SURREALISM; EXPRESSIONISM), some arising from renewed interest in old forms. Most recently there have been manifestations of what is called 'music theatre', which attempts to bring theatre into the concert hall or use the concert hall as a kind of theatre.

A note on opera in England is called for. Italian opera did not establish itself as firmly in England as it did in France and Germany. Henry Purcell (1659–95) wrote a very fine *Dido and Aeneas*, but in spite of its title it is not Italianate. From the early 18th century the Italianate operas of George Frederick Handel (1685–1759), a German who became a naturalized Englishman, were much patronized in London, and the cultivation of foreign opera by the aristocracy became both a fact and an object of satire, lasting until the early years of the 20th century. It was assumed that only foreign musicians were of any worth and that Italian was the only language suitable for opera; hence the assumption of foreign names by English singers and performances of, say, *Die Zauberflöte* neither in its original German nor in the English spoken by the audience, but in Italian as *Il Flauto Magico*. The ridiculous situation was made fun of by many English writers and was most effectively satirized in *The Beggar's Opera* (1728) by JOHN GAY (1685–1732) and John Pepusch (1667–1752), in which songs are sung to well known tunes, there is much spoken dialogue, the characters are contemporary and from the gutter not from the palace, and references are made to contemporary manners, not to eternal verities. The 19th century saw many attempts by British composers and librettists to write operas comparable in achievement to those of Continental works, but the composers produced at best imitations of Italian and German models and they succumbed to publishers' demands for 'shop ballads' – that is, detachable songs that could be sold to amateurs over the counter, rather like the 'hit songs' of 20th-century musicals. Some composers sold detached numbers from operas they were yet to compose. The librettists churned out drivel that was frequently nonsensical. In spite of sustained efforts no English composer was significant in the field of opera until Benjamin Britten (1913–76). Only the comic works of Arthur Sullivan (1842–1900) to librettos by W. S. GILBERT (1836–1911) achieved both immediate and lasting success.

With *Dulcamara, or the Little Duck and the Great Quack* (1866), a travesty of Donizetti's *L'Elisir d'Amore*, and his first stage work to be performed, Gilbert entered the crowded field of operatic BURLESQUE that occupied a huge amount of theatrical space in Europe during the 18th and 19th centuries. Sometimes incorporating the burlesqued works' original music, sometimes using borrowed or specially written music, these travesties varied from the rather clever to the downright inane. Their heavy reliance on punning is illustrated even by their titles. Meyerbeer's *Le Prophète*, which is about Anabaptists, was guyed in Paris in 1849 as *L'Âne à Baptiste* and bore the surprising subtitle *ou le berceau de socialisme*. In 1867 Gounod's *Roméo et Juliette*, first performed on 27 April, was followed on 9 July by Jallais's *Rhum et eau en juillet*, a title whose punning utterly defies translation. Germany, Austria and Italy also had their complements of operatic burlesques; but one suspects that England enjoyed, or endured, most: for example, between 8 and 20 October 1866 three different burlesques of Weber's *Der Freischütz* were put on in London. That such an occurrence is nowadays inconceivable says much about changes in theatrical taste and in popular familiarity with opera.

Opera is European in origin. Countries outside Europe tended to enjoy opera to the extent that they were settled by Europeans concerned to preserve the ways of life of their original countries. As immigrants and natives forged a new nation, characteristic music and drama, and hence opera, slowly emerged. In the USA, for example, English, French, Italian and German operas were presented in the 18th and early 19th centuries, and American operatic activity was much like that in European countries. The first work by a Native American to be acknowledged as a 'real' opera was *Leonora* (1845), with music by William Henry Fry (1813–64), who was not a professional musician. *Leonora* resounded with European echoes. In later years American operas were written by very professional musicians and the European echoes became fainter but were still clearly audible. The influences of Black and Latin American cultures and of the social, political and economic climates have all contributed to the emergence of American opera. *Treemonisha* (1911) by Scott Joplin (1868–1917) is historically significant, although it was not performed during the composer's lifetime. *Porgy and Bess* (1935) by GEORGE GERSHWIN (1898–1937) has proved a lasting characteristically American opera. The works of MARC BLITZSTEIN (1905–64) exhibit social and political awareness and those of Gunther Schuller (b.1925) are notable for their jazz. Many Americans have written many operas, but not many have created truly American operas. This may in part be due to the great success of the American MUSICAL which the USA seems to find a more vital form than opera – although where on the musical-theatrical continuum opera ends and the musical begins is highly debatable. Such successful works as *West Side Story* (1957) by LEONARD BERNSTEIN (1918–90) and *Sweeney Todd* (1979) by STEPHEN SONDHEIM (b.1930) seem to be as much operas as, say, *The Beggar's Opera*.

Australasia is further than the USA from Europe and it has not been so subject to direct influences. Isaac Nathan (1790–1864), who went to Australia from London, promoted opera of the old-world type. Neville George Barnett (1854–95), born in London, wrote an opera called *Pomare*, 'on a Tahitian legend', which was performed privately in Auckland. Australians who have written operas – e.g. Arthur Benjamin (1893–1960), Malcolm Williamson (b.1931) – have not tended to produce anything characteristically Australian.

Since the middle of the 20th century opera composers outside Europe have been subjected to two powerful influences: that of the music and manners of their countries, which gives rise to individuality, and that of a world shrinking because of advances in communications, which tends to produce a marked uniformity.

Operas are not an undifferentiated collection. They are usually assigned to a variety of types, although accurate classification is often difficult and frequently pointless. GH

opéra bouffe Denotes a form of opera that was extremely popular during the Second Empire in France and that was vigorously exploited by JACQUES OFFENBACH (1819–80). Farcical rather than comical, and often satirical, it included spoken dialogue, stage spectacle and both gay and sentimental music of immediate appeal. Its librettos and manner of performance were thought by the Victorian English to be indecent – markedly so in comparison with GILBERT and Sullivan. GH

opera buffa A form of comic opera, which had its heyday in 18th-century Italy. It included no spoken dialogue. In contrast to those of OPERA SERIA its characters were distinguished by ordinariness and truth to life, and its action tended to be bustling rather than restrained. GH

opéra comique Not necessarily comic, in spite of its name. Derived from 18th-century French *vaudevilles*, its characteristic is having spoken dialogue. The comicality from the *vaudevilles* declined; the speech remained. *Carmen* (1875) by Georges Bizet (1838–75), a far from comic work, is an authentic *opéra comique*. GH

opera seria Literally 'serious opera' – an 18th-century opera of great stylistic formality. Its subjects are drawn from mythology and ancient history. It is closely associated with the librettos of PIETRO METASTASIO (1698–1782) which were widely set, some achieving musical treatment by upwards of 20 different composers. GH

operetta Distinguished by its tone rather than by its length, although the word means 'little opera'. Any seriousness tends towards sentimentality and the overall effect is one of pleasantness, if not of unalloyed gaiety. An operetta's construction may vary from a close resemblance to that of a full-blown OPERA to a close kinship with a play enhanced by songs. Spectacular staging is almost inevitable. The expression 'light opera' is often used as an alternative to operetta which, in turn, is often extended to include OPÉRAS BOUFFES and MUSICAL COMEDY. GH

Opitz, Martin 1597–1639 German writer. Opitz translated Latin and Italian plays and wrote a book of poetics, published in 1624. His work helped turn the German theatre towards classicism, which was to dominate it until the middle of the 18th century. SW

Oregon Shakespeare Festival (USA) Founded in 1935 by Angus L. Bowmer in Ashland, Oregon, to produce SHAKESPEARE'S plays in an Elizabethan-style setting. Beginning on a rough, wooden platform, the Festival built the present stage in 1959, modelled largely on John Cranford Adams's reconstruction, with a seating capacity of 1173 and standing room for 115 (as of 1993 enclosed by the $7.6 million Allen Pavilion). In 1970 the Festival opened the new 600-seat indoor Angus Bowmer Theatre to house modern works; and in 1977 the 140-seat Black Swan for more experimental productions. Today, in addition to an eight-month season (10–11 plays) at Ashland, there is also a five-play, six-month season in Portland. Noted for a house style that emphasizes the clarity and beauty of the text, the Festival has completed the Shakespeare canon twice: for the first time in 1958 with *Troilus and Cressida*; and for the second time in 1978 with *Timon of Athens*. A budget of over $12 million per year supports 16 productions in the three theatres before an audience of more than 350,000. Artistic directors have included Angus L. Bowmer (1935–71), Jerry Turner (1971–91) and Henry Woronicz (1991–). TLM

Orionteatern Formerly Modellteatern, a children's touring company based in Eskilstuna, Sweden, Orionteatern was founded in 1983, when it acquired a disused foundry in south Stockholm. Lars Rudolfsson, its director until 1993, employed the vast performance space in spectacular ways to stage inventive productions of modern classics by STRINDBERG, BÜCHNER, CHEKHOV and SHAW. The company generally favours lengthy rehearsal periods, followed by long runs. Rudolfsson's 1985 *Pygmalion* (which ran for two years) was very much a signature production, with its ensemble acting, strong visual emphasis and playful incorporation of music and popular entertainment forms. In 1993 Rudolfsson moved to MALMÖ STADSTEATER and PETER OSKARSON became Orion's director. HL

Örkény, István 1912–79 Hungarian playwright. Drawing upon his dehumanizing experiences in the Second World War, he began writing naturalistic stories. By the mid-1960s his characteristic grotesque style emerged. Örkény's work has exerted enormous influence over the development of modern Hungarian drama. *The Tóth Family* (1967), the first Hungarian absurdist play to be staged (see THEATRE OF THE ABSURD), examines with black humour the ambiguous relationship between tyrant and victim. *Stevie in the Bloodstorm* (1969) is a grotesque panorama of modern history, in which the title character, played by four actors, is a Hungarian Everyman: executioner and condemned, oppressor and oppressed, in one person. *Screenplay* (1979), a multi-layered approach to the Stalinist show trials, pays homage to film, CIRCUS and theatre. Örkény's other plays, *Catsplay* (1971), *Blood Relations* (1974) and *Keysearchers* (1977), present the clash of inner and outer truth, reality and illusion, while examining aspects of the national character. *The Tóth Family* and *Catsplay* established Örkény's international reputation. EB

Orlenev [Orlov], **Pavel (Nikolaevich)** 1869–1932 Russian actor, known for his tempestuous nature on stage and off. A star of the private theatres of Korsh in Moscow (1893–5) and Suvorin in St Petersburg (1895–1902), he combined a matinee idol's magnetism with a sense of mission. Orlenev specialized in tormented psyches like Raskolnikov in *Crime and Punishment*, Mitya in *The Brothers Karamazov*, the title character in IBSEN's *Brand* and Oswald in *Ghosts*, and A. K. TOLSTOI's Tsar Fyodor (which he imbued with contemporary political references). In 1904–5 he took a scratch company, the St Petersburg Players, to Berlin, London and New York, introducing the West to the intense, psychologized playing of himself and his mistress-disciple ALLA NAZIMOVA. After the Revolution, alcoholism and erratic behaviour reduced him to playing excerpts from his best roles on the concert stage, at factories and collective farms. LS

Orton, Joe 1933–67 British dramatist, who specialized in high camp comedy, whose excesses were expressed in a delicate verbal wit. His first stage play, *Entertaining Mr Sloane* (1964), caused a *succès de scandale* when it was first produced at the Arts Theatre Club in London. A violent young man is blackmailed into becoming the sexual pet of a respectable brother and sister whose father he has murdered. *Loot* (1966) is like an updated black FARCE from the 1950s, with a comic detective who will stop at nothing, the corpse of a recently deceased mother, and tons of money. His funniest play, *What the Butler Saw* (1969), succeeds on several levels – as a French farce, as a BURLESQUE on psychiatry, and as an Edwardian comedy with the same dandified use of language. A one-act play, *Funeral Games* (1970), and two short plays, *The Ruffian on the Stair* (1967), originally written for radio, and *The Erpingham Camp* (1967), complete the short list of Orton's stage works, although his television play, *The Good and Faithful Servant* (1964), was performed at the King's Head, Islington, London. In 1967 Orton was brutally murdered by his homosexual friend, Kenneth Halliwell, who then committed suicide. JE

Osanai Kaoru 1881–1928 Influential Japanese director who helped establish a modern, realistic theatre in Japan. In 1909 Osanai founded the Free Theatre (Jiyū Gekijō) with Ichikawa Sadanji II, a *KABUKI* actor. Unsatisfied with the results of his experiments in training *kabuki* actors to perform the realistic works (see REALISM) of IBSEN and CHEKHOV, Osanai established the Tsukiji Little Theatre (Tsukiji Shōgekijō) in 1924 with the help of HIJIKATA YOSHI, which created a completely new production system for modern theatre in Japan. DGG

Osborn, Paul 1901–88 American playwright. Educated at the University of Michigan and Yale, Osborn's best-remembered plays are *On Borrowed Time* (1938; revived in 1991 with GEORGE C. SCOTT) and *Morning's at Seven* (1939; Tony revival, 1980). The former was a touching study of an old man's attempt to cheat death. The latter, although praised by some critics after its brief original production and kept alive in anthologies, had to wait until a 1980 revival to achieve wide acclaim. It took a nostalgic and sometimes bittersweet look at the life of four sisters in a small American town. Most of Osborn's works to reach BROADWAY were adaptations of novels, such as *A Bell for Adano* (1944), *Point of No Return* (1951) and *The World of Suzie Wong* (1958). His plays provide a mélange of characters drawn with skill and affection. LDC

Joe Orton's *Entertaining Mr Sloane*, Lyric Hammersmith, London, 1981.

Osborne, John (James) 1929–94 British dramatist and actor, who started his theatrical career spear-carrying in Northern reps. He sent his third play, *Look Back in Anger*, to the newly formed English Stage Company at the ROYAL COURT THEATRE, where it received its premiere on 8 May 1956, a date often taken to signify the start of the postwar British theatre revival. The hero (or anti-hero) was Jimmy Porter, from a relatively poor background, educated at university but who afterwards found himself unable to find a job which matched his self-esteem. Jimmy's tirades against British society led to his becoming a role model for other 'angry young men', including Osborne himself who wrote vituperative articles against British society in the press.

Look Back in Anger was the English Stage Company's first outright hit, and in 1957 Osborne wrote an equally successful play, *The Entertainer*, which provided LAURENCE OLIVIER with the part of Archie Rice, a tatty comic and heir to a once noble music-hall tradition, who now toured in sleazy nude REVUES. In the 1960s, and particularly before the death of his mentor, GEORGE DEVINE, Osborne wrote plays with strong parts for major actors, notably *Luther* (1961, which starred ALBERT FINNEY), *Inadmissible Evidence* (1964, with NICOL WILLIAMSON) and *A Patriot for Me* (1965, with Maximilian Schell, which featured Devine as a drag queen in his final role). Osborne's adaptation of LOPE DE VEGA's *La Fianza Satisfecha* (*A Bond Honoured*, 1966) was, however, scrappy, and his later plays showed how easily his old and energetic anger could dwindle to a routine tetchiness. *Hotel in Amsterdam* (1968) and *West of Suez* (1971) had some wit; but *A Sense of Detachment* (1972) began the decline into his not-so-attractive angry middle-aged man status. *Watch It Come Down* (1976) was staged at the NATIONAL THEATRE, and in 1992 he came out of what had seemed to be a retirement to provide an angry backward look at life, *Dejavu*. His autobiography, *A Better Class of Person*, was published in 1981. JE

Oskarson, Peter 1951– Swedish director. Oskarson has sought to establish the 'art theatre' in Sweden, first at Skånska Teatern from 1973 to 1982, then at Folkteatern in Gävleborg (1982–7), and since 1993 at ORIONTEATERN. As set out in the manifesto he drafted for GÖTEBORGS STADSTEATER in 1981, the art theatre prioritizes art over administration, puts acting at the centre of production, and demands total collective commitment from all participants. It aims to restore theatre as a source of understanding and stimulus for the enrichment of spectators' lives. This potential has been demonstrated with insight, daring and great beauty in Oskarson's own remarkable productions, especially *A Dream Play* (1984), *The Hairy Ape* (1986), *Hamlet* (1989) and *The Great Wrath* (1988), a dramatization of myths of Northern Sweden, which the company spent an entire year preparing. HL

Osofisan, Femi 1946– Nigerian playwright, poet, novelist and critic. Osofisan was born in Iloto, Ijebu-Ode, Ogun state. He studied French at Ibadan University, then pursued postgraduate studies at the Universities of Dakar and Paris. He took his doctorate at Ibadan, and after lecturing there in French and theatre arts was appointed professor of theatre arts at the University of Benin in 1983. After a period in journalism, helping to found the most reputable daily in Nigeria today, the *Guardian*, he returned to Ibadan where he is now professor of theatre arts.

Osofisan's critical writing reflects his exposure to some of the Marxist criticism and structuralist philosophy in French intellectual circles in the 1960s and 70s. With fellow Nigerian playwrights like KOLE OMOTOSO and left-wing critics like Biodun Jeyifo, Osofisan has helped shape a new discourse which places contemporary political class analysis at the centre of the literary and theatrical enterprise. This has involved a critique of the work of established writers such as WOLE SOYINKA and J. P. CLARK-BEKEDEREMO. Two of his plays, *No More the Wasted Breed* (1981) and *Another Raft* (1989), are direct replies to Soyinka's *The Strong Breed* and Clark-Bekederemo's *The Raft*, respectively. Osofisan rejects the older playwrights' metaphysics and what is regarded as their unreconstructed view of myth and African history. Yet he does not simply ignore or discard myth: rather, as the critic David Richards has noted, 'he subjects tradition to scrutiny and reinterpretation'. He admits the persuasiveness of Soyinka's drama, a legacy it is impossible for him not to engage with, however critical that engagement may be.

Osofisan's own vigorous analysis of materialism and culture in Africa appeals to many Nigerian students and young writers in the post-oil-boom, SAP (Structural Adjustment Programme)-ridden 1990s. In the later 1970s the discourse was publicly extended in the periodicals *Afriscope* and *Positive Review*. Taking up where Soyinka's *Ch'Indaba* (formerly *Transition*) left off, it attempted to situate art, history and literature in a class-based analysis of Nigeria's social formation. At the same time, Osofisan's writings on culture are profoundly concerned to analyse the aesthetic. This binary emphasis obtains in his plays also: as Jeyifo has said, 'a consummate *artistry* [exists] side by side with a passionate advocacy of social justice'.

Performances of Femi Osofisan's plays on Nigerian university campuses have reinforced his popularity among radical students and intellectuals. *Red Is the Freedom Road* (1969) is a play on the Yoruba wars of the 19th century, a subject also tackled by OLA ROTIMI and WALE OGUNYEMI. This was followed by the publication of a satirical novel, *Kolera Kolej* (1975; later dramatized and produced at Ibadan by Dexter Lyndersay); and then by a widely performed version of GOGOL's *The Government Inspector* entitled *Who's Afraid of Solarin?* (1978). This brilliantly transforms Gogol's satirical model to dissect the behaviour of Nigeria's governing elites.

In 1976 appeared the first of three plays that established Osofisan's reputation as one of Nigeria's foremost dramatists, *The Chattering and the Song*. This complex and subtle play explores the relationship of a number of intellectuals towards a revolutionary movement – and towards each other as their real affiliations emerge. This was followed in 1978 by the first production of *Once upon Four Robbers*, an attack on the Nigerian military government. Niyi Osundare has commented: 'The play revolves around a magnificent irony: the real armed robbers [the soldiers] are those set to catch the four robbers.' In 1979 his most ambitious work to date, *Morountodun*, was premiered: the first version had a running time of four to five hours. The play combines the myth of the heroine Moremi with the 1969 uprising of farmers in western Nigeria. The synthesis is made in the context of an enactment of the latter by a 'Theatre Director' and 'Actor', in order to show 'the urgent necessity to deploy the energies of the past to struggle against and defeat the forces of oppression and injustice that ensnare our people in the purgatory of poverty and insecurity' (*Positive Review*).

Osofisan's satirical flair was shown again in *Midnight Hotel* (1982), his adaptation of FEYDEAU's farce, *Paradise Hotel*. In his later plays he addresses his major themes – the gaining of self-knowledge, the contestation of oppression, the ability to achieve an undistorted reading of history – through a remarkable range of different storytelling techniques, always thoughtful and yet never ponderous or too wordy. Music and the imaginative use of role-play episodes are primary resources for his theatre, as is comedy, though the latter arguably sometimes clouds his work's critical pungency. Most of his plays are published and some are amongst the most frequently performed in Nigeria (especially *Once upon Four Robbers* and the short play *The Oriki of a Grasshopper*).

Among the most important of Osofisan's later plays are three that occupied him through the 1980s: *Farewell to a Cannibal Rage* (published 1986), *Esu and the Vagabond Minstrels* and *Aringindin and the Nightwatchmen* (both 1991). *Esu*, a highly entertaining piece that has gained a popular audience, uses Yoruba myth to explore individual conscientiousness; *Aringindin* is a grim investigation of the nurturing of violence as a method of, and pretext for, totalitarian government. *Yungba Yungba and the Dance Contest* (1993), which has an all-female cast, is a display piece for Osofisan's stagecraft; it also exemplifies, as Chris Dunton has said, his 'firm, sober confidence in the value of debate and reflection'. After this play, Osofisan's theatre seems likely to head in new directions: during the early 1990s he began work on an ambitious project, a trilogy on Nkrumah, Sékou Touré and Cabral. The first part, a massive play on Nkrumah in exile, was completed in 1993. CD

Osten, Suzanne 1944– Swedish director and playwright; artistic director of Unga Klara, the celebrated children's theatre company within Stockholms Stadsteater. Osten was a founder of the free group Fickteater from 1967, before joining Stockholms Stadsteater in 1970. She founded Unga Klara in 1975, to write, produce and direct plays for children, and plays for adults *about* childhood. Her work insistently incorporates the perspective of childhood, and a determination to learn from young audiences. Outstanding productions include *Medea's Children* (exemplifying 'children's tragedy', 1975), *Hitler's Childhood* (1984), *The Piggle* (1991) and *The Dolphin* (1992). She has also been acclaimed as a film director (for example, of *The Mozart Brothers*, 1986, and *Speak Up! It's So Dark*, 1993). HL

Ostrovsky, Aleksandr (Nikolaevich) 1823–86 Russian dramatist and administrator at the Maly Theatre, who charted the course of 20th-century Russian stage REALISM, based upon questions of social class, environment and ethics. A native Muscovite and son of a govern-ment clerk turned merchant-lawyer, he became Russia's most prolific painter of mercantile society and the common people, writing well over 50 plays, mostly comedies, for the stage. His first COMEDY, *The Bankrupt* (1847), later revised as *It's a Family Affair – We'll Settle It Ourselves* (1849), exposed fraudulent business practices for which it was banned from production for 11 years. His best-known comedy in the West, *Diary of a Scoundrel* (or *Enough Stupidity for Every Wise Man*, 1868), dealt with a double-dealer in the tradition of GOGOL's Khlestakov and SUKHOVO-KOBYLIN's Krechinsky.

While he translated plays by PLAUTUS, TERENCE, SHAKESPEARE, CERVANTES, GOZZI and MACHIAVELLI for his own education as a dramatist, Ostrovsky saw his chief role to be the furthering of a native dramatic tradition. He embraced a less dogmatic Slavophilism and aligned himself with publisher M. P. Pogodin's *Moskvityanin* circle of journal editors and associates (such as poet-critic Apollon Grigoriev, actor PROV SADOVSKY, dramatist ALEKSEI PISEMSKY), which conducted ethnographic and historical inquiries into Russian folk poetry and ritual. This folk quality can be found in the most famous of his three tragedies, *The Thunderstorm* (1859), derived in part from information gathered while on a literary tour of the Volga in 1886. Ostrovsky here dramatized in characteristic fashion the struggle between oppressor and oppressed, and the corruption of innocence, with nature participating as an agent of fate in the outcome. His dramatic fable, *The Snow Maiden* (1873), drew upon his knowledge of Russian folk songs, proverbs and popular poetry, blending romanticism with realism.

These plays, *An Ardent Heart* (1869) and others furnished Russian actresses with strong roles through which to further their craft. Ostrovsky created characters with specific performers in mind, rewriting roles often as the play's director, while in rehearsal, to suit the individuals cast. While SHCHEPKIN had difficulty realizing these roles, Sadovsky and a new generation of actors built their careers upon them. Ostrovsky's understanding of the actor's world is reflected in such comedies as *The Comedian of the Seventeenth Century* (1872), on the founding of the first Russian theatre in Moscow, and *The Forest* (1871), which features a pair of itinerant performers. The latter received a controversial non-realistic staging by MEYERHOLD in 1924. Ostrovsky was less sympathetic towards the nobility and fashionable society, whom he ridiculed as idlers, hypocrites and petty tyrants. This made him popular in progressive circles and throughout the nation after the 1917 Revolution, when he became the most frequently performed classical Russian dramatist. He founded and was president of the Society of Russian Dramatic Writers and Opera Composers (1874), which awarded the Griboedov Prize for playwriting and secured for its members production royalties. In 1882 he helped to break the monopoly of the Imperial theatres, beginning with the establishment of the Korsh Theatre in Moscow, which set tradition for the MOSCOW ART THEATRE, to follow in 1897. In 1885 he was appointed director of the artistic department of the Moscow Imperial Theatres and head of the Moscow Theatrical School.

Ostrovsky the dramatist tended towards the sentimental and MELODRAMATIC; his plotting was often structurally weak and his endings contrived. He lacked GRIBOEDOV's and Gogol's talent for abstraction and mastery of language. What he had was a genius for concreteness – a clear sense of environment conditioning behaviour, idiomatic expression tailored to individualized characters, and a broad view of the social stratification, socio-economic relationships and native traditions which contribute to the formation of a national consciousness. SG

Ōta Shōgo 1939– Japanese playwright and director. He first joined the theatre troupe Hakken no Kai (Discovery Troupe) and in 1968 became a founder member of Tenkei Gekijyō (the Tenkei Theatre Company), where he continued his major theatrical work until the company was dissolved in 1988. Ōta's main interest lies in exploring the power of language and of silence in relation to the presence of actors' bodies. For this he attempted to stage a series of plays without words. The first of the series was *Komachi Fūden* in 1977, in which he used the NŌ stage and an old woman reliving her memories from the past – a situation from an original *nō* play. All the lines for the part of the old woman were scripted, but on stage the actress performed the role without actually saying them. The words were only for her to establish the inner drama within herself – which succeeded in giving a sense of reality to the silence in the performance.

Ōta's trilogy of silent plays – *Mizu no Eki* (*The Water Station*, 1981; English translation 1990), *Chi no Eki* (*The Earth Station*, 1985) and *Kaze no Eki* (*The Wind Station*, 1986) – have been performed in both Japan and abroad; *The Water Station* was presented as part of the New York International Festival of Arts in 1988. Ōta has experimented with using mounds of scrap materials, sand and running water on stage, exploring the relationships between people and the objects surrounding them. Thus his theatrical concept is quite close to the idea of THEATRE OF THE ABSURD, or anti-theatre. MY

O'Toole, Peter 1932– British actor, born in Ireland, who made his reputation with the BRISTOL OLD VIC from 1955 to 1958. He was spotted by London managements at the ROYAL COURT THEATRE in *The Long and the Short and the Tall* (1959). He joined the Shakespeare Memorial Company in 1960, where he was a memorable Shylock and Petruchio; and played Hamlet in the inaugural production of the NATIONAL THEATRE company at the OLD VIC in 1963. Increasingly, however, he was drawn towards films, and starred as Lawrence in the epic, *Lawrence of Arabia* (1962). His stage appearances became infrequent, although he appeared as the novelist Peter in DAVID MERCER's *Ride a Cock Horse* (1965) and in Dublin as Jack Boyle in O'CASEY's *Juno and the Paycock* (1966). His blond hair, gaunt face and idiosyncratic vocal delivery could be compelling in the right part, but his screen career seemed to magnify his mannerisms when he returned to the stage. He was unfortunate enough to appear in a disastrous *Macbeth* for the Prospect Company at the Old Vic in 1980, although he redeemed his reputation with a forceful John Tanner in a WEST END production of *Man and Superman* two years later. His most memorable comic performance was as the low-life Soho journalist in KEITH WATERHOUSE's *Jeffrey Bernard Is Unwell* (1989), where his haggard looks

gave the appearance of a dissipated corpse in hiding from God the Father. JE

Otto, Teo 1904–68 German stage designer. Educated at the Academy of Fine Arts, Kassel, and at the Bauhaus, Otto began designing AGIT-PROP plays for the Proletkult Kassel in 1926. Otto Klemperer engaged him in 1927 for the Kroll Opera, Berlin. In 1931 he became chief designer at the Berlin State Theatre, where he worked until he emigrated to Switzerland in 1933. His association with the Schauspielhaus in Zurich led to a collaboration with BRECHT on the premiere productions of *Mother Courage* (1941), *Galileo* (1943) and *The Good Person of Setzuan* (1943). Also in Zurich he designed premiere productions of plays by DÜRRENMATT and MAX FRISCH. During the 1950s his designs could be seen in major opera houses and theatres in Austria and Germany. The most important of these productions was GRÜNDGENS's revival in Hamburg of *Faust, Part 1 and Part 2* (1957), which was transferred to New York's City Center in 1961. While in New York Otto designed productions of *Nabucco* and *Tristan und Isolde* (1960) for the Metropolitan Opera. Professor of stage design at the Academy of Fine Arts in Düsseldorf until his death, he wrote two books on design theory: *Nie wieder* and *Meine Szene*. His designs were noted for economy of architectural detail, sparse and symbolic use (see SYMBOLISM) of properties, decorative screens and atmospheric lighting. AJN

Otway, Thomas 1652–85 English playwright. Educated at Winchester and Oxford University, he moved to London, failing as an actor when, as the King in APHRA BEHN's *The Forced Marriage*, he suffered badly from stage fright. His first play, *Alcibiades* (1675), gave a leading role to ELIZABETH BARRY, with whom Otway became hopelessly and unrequitedly in love. He followed *Alcibiades*' success with further heroic tragedies, *Don Carlos* (1676) and *Titus and Berenice* (1676), a version of RACINE's *Bérénice*, performed with his adaptation of MOLIÈRE's farce *The Cheats of Scapin*. Realizing his talent for bitter comedy, he wrote *Friendship in Fashion* (1678). At about this time he served briefly in the Duke of Monmouth's regiment in the Netherlands, making some use of his experience as a soldier in his comedy *The Soldier's Fortune* (1680) and its sequel *The Atheist* (1683). He also adapted SHAKESPEARE's *Romeo and Juliet* as *The History and Fall of Caius Marius* (1679). But Otway's enormous reputation in the 18th century was based on the two tragedies that led to his being praised as 'next to Shakespeare': *The Orphan* (1680) and *Venice Preserv'd* (1682). *The Orphan* is a tearful tragedy of the innocent woman caught between love for two men, both equally virtuous. *Venice Preserv'd* combines a similarly pitiable love with a remarkable analysis of a conspiracy to overthrow the corrupt Venetian state and contains a vicious mockery of Shaftesbury's sexual tastes in the caricature of Antonio. Otway died in penury. PH

Ouellette, Rose(-Alma) [La Poune] 1903– French Canadian actress, comedian and theatre manager. Ouellette began her stage career as a child singer in VARIETY shows, then as a comic in early American-style BURLESQUE. In the 1920s she worked with Olivier Guimond, then considered the outstanding practitioner of burlesque. In a genre that required great improvisational ability and little or no prepared text, La Poune rapidly became the best-known stage personality of her day. She directed Montreal's Cartier Theatre, 1928–36, and the National, 1936–53, during the golden age of burlesque in Canada. When television brought burlesque into disfavour she moved easily into the new medium, playing in dramas and serials such as *Dix sur dix, Rue des pignons,* and *Les Coqueluches.* She is the author of a book of memoirs. LED

Ouyang Yuqian 1889–1962 Chinese modern drama actor, director, theatre educator and dramatist. As a student in Japan in 1907 he acted in *The Black Slave's Cry to Heaven* (*Heinu yutian lu*) and hence took part in the origins of HUAJU. Over a long career he wrote 40 modern plays, directed 50, and adapted or revised some 50 dramas in traditional style. An excellent JINGXI performer of female roles, he was deeply engaged in integrating Chinese tradition with foreign influences. One instance of this was his *Pan Jinlian* (1928). First written as a spoken drama, it was also performed as a Beijing opera, Ouyang Yuqian himself playing the leading female role, Pan Jinlian. Ouyang portrayed an intelligent, passionate rebel against conventional morality. JRB

Owen, Alun (Davies) 1926– British dramatist, who began his stage career as an actor with the BIRMINGHAM REP (1943–4). A prolific writer for television and radio, Owen adapted his first play, *The Rough and Ready Lot* (1958), for the stage from the original radio script. It concerned four soldiers of fortune in South America after the end of the American Civil War, and illustrated Owen's easy command of dialogue and his gift of characterization. *Progress to the Park* (1959) was a vivid portrait of his birthplace, Liverpool, and was given a characteristically lively production by JOAN LITTLEWOOD at the Theatre Workshop, Stratford, East London. *A Little Winter Love* was produced in Dublin in 1963 and in London two years later; and he collaborated with the song-writer, Lionel Bart, in an ambitious MUSICAL about a Liverpool legend, *Maggie May* (1964). Owen's stage plays never matched the popular success of his television writing, partly because his stories seem to lose their shape when extended to a full evening. At best, his language has a poetic quality of its own, combining unforced imagery, a keen ear for dialect and a love of the unusual phrase. JE

Owens, John E(dmond) 1823–86 Liverpool (England)-born actor and manager who went to Philadelphia in 1828, began as a supernumerary at WILLIAM E. BURTON's National Theatre (1841), quickly graduated to speaking roles and then played in all the principal American cities and in London (1865). He bought and managed the Baltimore Museum (1849–52), made his New York debut (1851) as Uriah Heep in JOHN BROUGHAM's adaptation of *David Copperfield,* and in 1864 appeared as the YANKEE Solon Shingle in JOSEPH S. JONES's *The People's Lawyer* – the role for which he became best known and which prompted the critics to speak of his 'merry temperament, his exuberant and incessant glee'. His memoirs, edited by his wife, appeared in 1892. RM

Owens, Rochelle 1936– American playwright and triple Obie-winner, who creates her own cultural anthropology complete with myths, RITUAL, chants and symbols in her experimental OFF-OFF BROADWAY plays. Her highly controversial play *Futz* (1967, Obie; revived in 1991 at LA MAMA) is a TRAGICOMEDY relating the sexual love of a man and his pig and the violent, demented response of his repressed neighbours to his sodomy. Owens continued to explore perversity, violence and sexuality as responses to the conflict of individual primal impulse with a self-righteous society in such plays as *Beclch* (1967) – an example of Theatre of Cruelty with its depiction of savagery and depravity; *Istanbul* (1965); *Kontraption* (1970); *He Wants Shih* (1975); *Chucky's Hunch* (1981); and two surreal historical biographies – *The Karl Marx Play* (1973) and *Emma Instigated Me* (1977). FB

Oyono Mbia, Guillaume 1939– Cameroonian bilingual playwright, civil servant and university teacher. Born in Mvoutessi, Oyono-Mbia was educated at the Collège Évangélique of Libamba and Keele University, England. His plays have been widely produced in Cameroon and on British and French international radio services, where two of them – *Until Further Notice,* 1968 (*Jusqu'à nouvel avis,* 1970) and *Notre fille ne se mariera pas* (*Our Daughter Will not Get Married,* 1971) – won the BBC African Service and Radio France Internationale drama competitions, respectively. But his most popular play to date is the village comedy *Trois prétendants ... un mari* (*Three Suitors ... One Husband,* 1964). In 1978 he published a fourth play, *Le Train spécial de son Excellence* (*His Excellency's Special Train*).

Oyono-Mbia's plays, mostly concerned with the disruptive effects of modern values on traditional society, are constructed principally as dramatic entertainment. Their material is not so much built on the elaborate literary effect of 'high comedy', with a properly integrated plot, as on the comic personality of stock characters that rely on MIME and slapstick to perform typical numbers. Language as a source of the comic is a resource also exploited in his plays. Oyono-Mbia is also the author of three volumes of stories. JCM

Ozerov, Vladislav (Aleksandrovich) 1769–1816 Russian dramatist who wrote neo-classical tragedy which in the conventions of its form imitated CORNEILLE, RACINE and VOLTAIRE, but which in its linguistic style and heightened subjectivism pointed towards the developing sentimental and pre-romantic schools of playwriting. Compared with his contemporaries ALEKSEI SUMAROKOV and YAKOV KNYAZHNIN, Ozerov adopted a more conversational tone and posited more complex psychological motives and more realistic limitations for his heroes. Nevertheless, his plays were still largely contrived, and the declamatory acting style and emotional demands which they required made them favourites of such star performers as A. S. YAKOVLEV, E. S. SEMYONOVA, Ya. E. Shucherin and V. A. KARATYGIN.

The plays which followed his initial, strictly classical TRAGEDY *Yaropolk and Oleg* (1798) enjoyed a brilliant albeit short-lived success for the cleverness with which their author drew parallels between historical and contemporary political events. *Oedipus in Athens* (1804), a reworking of *Oedipus at Colonus*, was based on a French rather than the original Greek model, which accounts for its relatively happy ending. *Fingal* (1805) was inspired by the Ossianic poems. *Dmitry of the Don* (*Donskoi*, 1807) was by far his most popular work, bolstering Russians' patriotic spirit during their struggle with Napoleon by reminding them of their stirring victory over the Tartars in 1380. The play, which became even more popular after 1812, was no more highly regarded by Ozerov's peers than was the author himself, in general. GRIBOEDOV penned a parody entitled *Dmitry of the Trash* (*Dryanskoi*), and PUSHKIN would say ,'I dislike Ozerov not because I envy him but because I love art.' Ozerov's best play, *Polyxena* (1809), which dramatized the eponymous heroine's tragic love for Achilles, met with some oppposition from the censor and was not a success (see CENSORSHIP). Depression over financial matters, partly related to the poor box-office performance of this play, prompted Ozerov to destroy the manuscript of his last complete tragedy, *Medea*, and to sink into an irreversible state of paralysis and catatonia. SG

Pacino, Al 1940– American actor, who studied with LEE STRASBERG and is a member of the ACTORS STUDIO. Pacino made a strong impression on stage in the late 1960s playing jittery, violent low-life New Yorkers, OFF-BROADWAY in *The Indian Wants the Bronx* (1968) and in his BROADWAY debut as a drug addict in *Does a Tiger Wear a Necktie?* (1969). His naturalistic style (see NATURALISM) proved ideal for film (*The Godfather, Serpico, Scarface*). In his periodic returns to the stage, Pacino has tried with limited success to overcome the typecasting of his films. His *Richard III* (1973) was brave though unavoidably contemporary. He was more comfortable as TENNESSEE WILLIAMS's Everyman in the 1970 Lincoln Center revival of *Camino Real*; as the nonentity swept up by the Vietnam War in the 1977 revival of RABE's *The Basic Training of Pavlo Hummel* (Tony); and as a wheezing, shuffling, pinch-voiced crook with a battery of tics in a revival of DAVID MAMET's *American Buffalo* (1982). In summer 1992 he appeared in two plays in repertory at CIRCLE IN THE SQUARE: WILDE's *Salomé* and Ira Lewis's *Chinese Coffee*.   FH

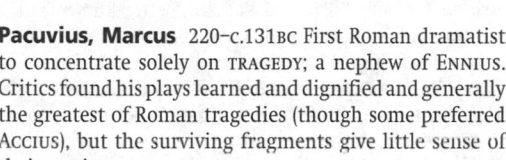

Pacuvius, Marcus 220–c.131BC First Roman dramatist to concentrate solely on TRAGEDY; a nephew of ENNIUS. Critics found his plays learned and dignified and generally the greatest of Roman tragedies (though some preferred ACCIUS), but the surviving fragments give little sense of their merits.   ALB

Page, Geraldine 1924–87 Missouri-born American actress. Page attended the GOODMAN THEATRE Dramatic School (1942–5) in Chicago before making her New York debut in the Blackfriar's Guild production of *Seven Mirrors* (1945). JOSÉ QUINTERO cast her as Alma in the OFF-BROADWAY production of *Summer and Smoke* at the CIRCLE IN THE SQUARE (1951–2) to rave reviews, establishing her career. Her BROADWAY debut as Lily in *Midsummer* (1953) again received critical acclaim; Wolcott Gibbs in the *New Yorker* praised her 'charm and pathos and almost matchless technique'. Her later work included Lizzie in *The Rainmaker* (1954); Alexandra del Lago in *Sweet Bird of Youth* (1959); Olga in *The Three Sisters* (1964); Baroness Lemberg in *White Lies* and Clea in *Black Comedy* (1967); Marion in *Absurd Person Singular* (1974); and Mother Miriam Ruth in *Agnes of God* (1982). From 1983 she was a member of the Mirror Theatre Company. Her husband was actor Rip Torn.

While Page appeared too often in neurotic roles, she was a versatile actress capable of a wide emotional range. Her Alexandra del Lago provoked BROOKS ATKINSON to eloquence: 'Loose-jointed, gangling, raucous of voice, crumpled, shrewd, abandoned yet sensitive about some things that live in the heart, Miss Page is at the peak of form in this raffish characterization.' Her numerous film appearances included *Summer and Smoke* (1961) and Woody Allen's *Interiors* (1978). In 1986 she won an Academy Award for her portrayal of Carrie Watts in *The Trip to Bountiful* (her eighth Oscar nomination).   TLM

Pakhomushka Russian folk FARCE, performed by young men or women at village parties, or during collective sedentary work such as sewing-bees. It concerns the humped and fanged idiot Pakhomushka and his sexually frustrated wife Pakhomikha. The hero's attempt to find a bride among the girls in the audience develops into a BURLESQUE marriage and wedding-night, and finally into a farce of cuckoldry and revenge. Organization and performance are informal: roles are distributed and costumes and props improvised on the spot, by-play between actors and audience is the norm.   AEG

Pakistan The modern states of Pakistan and INDIA were created in 1947. Pakistan's two parts, East and West Pakistan, were separated by more than 1000 miles of Indian territory. In 1971 East Pakistan became the independent state of BANGLADESH.

The history of the theatre of modern Pakistan is the history of the Urdu-language theatre which started in 1853 with the composition of Mirza Amanat's *Inder Sabha*, performed at the court of Wajid Ali Shah of Oudh in the city of Lucknow in north central India. Pakistan is an Islamic state and like neighbouring countries of the MIDDLE EAST has not, for religious reasons, condoned or encouraged the production of plays. It is not surprising that theatre in this region of the subcontinent has been relatively slow in developing and only recently became a part of the cultural heritage of the people. In Pakistan, there was no classical tradition on which a theatre could be built and what folk heritage there may have been is obscure, except performances of the *bhand* of the Punjab, recitation of dramatic poetry and the PUPPET theatre.

Inder Sabha was not intended to be a landmark production but was designed to satisfy the cravings of a lavish court ruled by an extravagant composer-king. The play is in verse and requires musical accompaniment, dance and elaborate costumes to be fully realized. In 1856 the kingdom of Oudh came to an abrupt end when the British deposed the Shah and exiled him to Calcutta. However, for at least two generations after that, actors and musicians of Oudh sang the songs of *Inder Sabha* and kept alive the potential of an Urdu-language theatre.

The next major dramatic activity in Urdu occurred in an entirely different region of the Indian subcontinent when some Parsi entrepreneurs of Bombay, motivated no doubt by economic gain, set about developing a form of theatre in Urdu which was to captivate the public imagination, not only in the whole of India but even in Sri Lanka and Malaysia, as well. Producers such as Pestonji Framji and Khurshidji Balliwalla developed a popular form of theatre known as the 'Parsi musical'. In 1870, assisted by several Muslim poets, they composed Urdu plays which were set to music. After 1880, Raunaq Banarsi, Mian Zarif, Vinayak Prasad Talib, Ahsan Lucknowi, Narain Prasad Betab and Agra Hashr Kashmiri are among the better known writers of Parsi musicals staged by the Victoria Theatrical Company, the Alfred Company and the New Alfred Company.

The plays were designed exclusively to entertain and thus satisfy the taste of audiences of the day. Themes of romantic love, chivalry and generosity, from a wide array of literary sources – Hindu and Muslim classics, history and legends – were elaborated upon in the plays. Even some Shakespearian plays were re-assembled and the characters provided with Indian names while the bard's dialogue was transformed to Urdu verse. Two distinct plot lines – one humorous and the other serious – were made to correlate and interweave in each play.

From the outset, dancing girls were a part of every show. This led to an expression of outrage in 1914 when the New Alfred Theatrical Company visited Lahore to stage Betab's *Mahabharata*, based on the Hindu epic of the same name. The audience reacted negatively to characters with religious names such as Rukmini and Draupadi when they were played by women whom they considered of questionable morals. As a consequence, the company refrained from presenting the show.

Some authors of the time demonstrated a social consciousness by attacking social evils of the day, such as child marriage and the rigidity of the purdah system. Others expressed an interest in political subject matter by addressing issues such as the controversy over the formation of Punjab state and border disputes.

With the development of the film industry in the 1930s, audiences quickly shifted their allegiance to the cinema and many of the most successful companies closed their doors for good and their personnel went into the film industry. Only the smaller groups and minor companies remained as a testament of an active past.

Scattered activity in modern theatre began in the western half of the country soon after independence in 1947, with the formation of dramatic clubs in colleges and universities. The dramatic club of the Government College of Lahore was managed by students under the supervision of interested staff members. At first both Urdu and English plays were presented. The Urdu plays were mostly translations from Western dramas. Some of the plays staged between 1951 and 1957 were *Swan Ran Ka Sapana*, a Punjabi version of SHAKESPEARE's *A Midsummer Night's Dream*, an Urdu version of GOGOL's *The Inspector General* and adaptations of one-act plays by MOLIÈRE. Many of the students who were part of this early activity have since entered the professional field of films and television.

In 1956 the Pakistan Arts Council opened a small theatre in the council building and invited productions by Government College students. For the next three years the citizens of Lahore found an alternative theatre outside the college environment. Among the better-known productions were PRIESTLEY's *An Inspector Calls* and IBSEN's *A Doll's House*, both of which were presented in Urdu. After 1960 the production of comedies drew larger and more regular audiences.

In 1964 the Arts Council attempted to turn the Alahamra Theatre into a year-round theatre rather than an occasional place for performance. By 1966 plays were running on a regular basis and a campaign was begun to produce original plays in Urdu. In 1967 the theatre in Lahore was broad-based and had gained considerable momentum.

After independence, theatre in Karachi still clung to the old theatrical traditions inherited from Bombay and Calcutta. Then, in 1950–51, the Osmania University Old Boys produced Khwaja Moinuddin's *Zawal-e-Hydrabad*, a tense drama portraying the conditions of the Kashmiris under Indian Army rule. The play had touching lyrics and music which helped make it a popular success. His *Naya Nishan* was produced in the same year and gained even greater public recognition; it was banned by the government for probing a sensitive political issue at the very time the Indian and Pakistan governments were attempting to negotiate a treaty over Kashmir.

In 1953 Moinuddin wrote *Lal Qile Se Lalukhet*, which revolved around the trials of a family that had to migrate to Pakistan from India after partition. It was produced in the K. M. C. Stadium and the four-hour drama set a record attendance by drawing nearly 10,000 people. It was later staged in Karachi at the Katrak Hall and ran for 140 performances. Later it played in Lahore, Hyderabad and Mirpurkhas and was revived in 1956 in Karachi and Lahore.

Numerous productions were staged by various groups formed in Karachi between 1952 and 1955. Some of these were supported by the oil companies that encourage dramatic activity under their welfare programme for the benefit of employees. Throughout this entire period the British Amateur Society of Karachi, better known as the Clifton Players, produced a number of drawing-room comedies in English.

In 1956 the Karachi Theatre was formed. It was born of the Theatre Group of the Arts Council headed by Sigrid Nyberg Kahle, German wife of a diplomat, the playwright Khwaja Moinuddin and the actor Zia Mohyeddin, whose work in the film *A Passage to India* and the television series *The Jewel in the Crown* later gained him world-wide recognition. Productions included Molière's *School for Wives*, *Gas Light*, *Our Town*, *Antigone* and Khwaja Moinuddin's *Lal Qile Se Lalukhet*, among others.

When Ms Kahle left the group to go abroad, the Avant Garde Arts Theatre came into being, presenting Urdu versions of GORKY's *The Lower Depths*, Molière's *Perfect Gentleman*, BECKETT's *Waiting for Godot* and COWARD's *Hay Fever*. Much of the success of the group was due to the work of Meherji and Pervez Dastur, who later broke away from the AGAT and formed the Seekers.

In 1967–8 many of the theatre organizations in Pakistan's cities began to tour the country, much as groups do in India, in order to sustain their activities through revenues earned in the smaller towns of the countryside. During this period, theatre came to the attention of the central government when it exempted plays from paying a small but annoying entertainment tax. Similarly, state awards by the president of Pakistan helped to bring greater national recognition to theatre. Then, too, the period saw many plays published in Urdu, the formation of a number of small semi-professional theatre companies, and an increase in the number of men and women interested and skilled in theatre, television and film. (See also ASIAN AND PACIFIC ISLAND THEATRE.) FaR

Palace Theatre (New York City) The legendary Mecca for VAUDEVILLE performers, built by Martin Beck, who then had to turn over 75 per cent of the stock to EDWARD F.

ALBEE for permission to use KEITH circuit acts. Albee in turn paid OSCAR HAMMERSTEIN I 225,000 dollars for the rights to offer Keith acts in that neighbourhood. Located at Broadway and 47th Street, the 1800-seat theatre opened on 25 March 1913 and, after a slow start, gained popularity with the booking of SARAH BERNHARDT. 'Playing the Palace' was the ambition of every American VARIETY act, although names did not go up in lights until 1928. The record bill was for a nine-week teaming of EDDIE CANTOR and George Jessel in 1931. On 7 May 1932 the Palace became a four-a-day theatre, the live performance mingled with newsreels and cartoons, and on 16 November turned into a five-a-day cinema; this date marks the official death of vaudeville as a dominant entertainment form. After a period as a BURLESQUE house and a brief revival of vaudeville in 1950, the Palace was converted into a theatre for MUSICAL COMEDY in 1965. In 1987 it closed for extensive renovations, reopening in April 1991 with the MUSICAL *The Will Rogers Follies*.   LS

Palais-Royal, Théâtre du (Paris) Originally known as the Palais-Cardinal, it was built by the architect Jacques Lemercier as a small private playhouse in RICHELIEU's palace and inaugurated in January 1641 with a performance for Louis XIII. Designed to emulate the aristocratic theatres of Italy, it boasted a permanent proscenium arch and drop curtain, machinery for scene changes and an elegant auditorium with two balconies at either side and 27 rows of tiered seating in the centre. Reverting to the Crown after Richelieu's death, it was occasionally used for court entertainments, Luigi Rossi's opera *Orfeo* being mounted there in 1647 by TORELLI, who demolished the existing stage walls to accommodate more sophisticated machinery. In 1660 it was made available to MOLIÈRE's company following the loss of the PETIT-BOURBON, and substantially refurbished and re-equipped in 1670 for the presentation of spectacular 'machine-plays'. After Molière's death it was acquired by LULLY as a home for his Académie Royale de Musique, and with further structural modifications by VIGARANI it remained in use as an OPERA house until 1763 when it was destroyed by fire and rebuilt. A further fire in 1781 caused the whole site to be redeveloped and a number of theatres were subsequently built there under this name.   DR

Palitzsch, Peter 1918– German director; an assistant to BRECHT at the BERLINER ENSEMBLE, where with WEKWERTH he directed *Arturo Ui* (1959) and BAIERL's *Frau Flinz* with WEIGEL. He introduced Brecht's plays and techniques to the West German stage after leaving the GDR in 1961. As director in Stuttgart (1966–72) he supported new writing, directing the premieres of WALSER's *Der schwarze Schwan* and *Überlebensgross Herr Krott*, and DORST's *Toller*. His *Wars of the Roses* (1967) brought to SHAKESPEARE the clarity and political intelligence which are his hallmark. He joined the directorate of the Berliner Ensemble in 1992 alongside HEINER MÜLLER.   HR

Palladio, Andrea [Andrea di Pietro Monaro] 1509–80 Italian architect. Most of his work was done in Venice and Vicenza, where he was a member of the Accademia Olimpica, founded by his patron, TRISSINO. Palladio was one of the greatest of Italian Renaissance architects. His work was rooted in a close study of Roman remains and the writings of Vitruvius, and in the ideas of Alberti on the correspondences between architectural and musical forms. In execution, however, his work was profoundly original in the fluency, purity and harmony of its lines, and his influence throughout Europe in the 17th and early 18th centuries was considerable. In 1561 and 1562 he built theatres within the hall of the Basilica at Vicenza, the second being used for the production of Trissino's *Sofonisba*. His most famous theatre is the Teatro Olimpico at Vicenza, begun in the year of his death and finished by SCAMOZZI in 1585, essentially on the basis of his plans. It represents the triumph of Renaissance academicism – a beautifully conceived and completed structure for all that its Roman *scaenae frons* had by the time of its conception been made obsolete by the development of the proscenium stage with changeable settings.   KR

Pallenberg, Max 1877–1934 Intuitive Austrian comic actor with the popular touch, whose consummate technique enabled him to fill a role while at the same time criticizing it. Found by REINHARDT in the provinces in 1914, he became the highest-paid actor in the Weimar Republic. He played the title role for PISCATOR in *The Adventures of the Good Soldier Schweik in* 1927, and Mephistopheles in Reinhardt's 1933 Salzburg *Faust*.   HR

Palmer, A(lbert) M(arshman) 1838–1905 American theatrical manager, who first entered the business in 1872 as co-manager of the Union Square Theatre with Sheridan Shook. Although trained as a lawyer and without theatrical background or experience, he established a reputation as one of the leading managers of his time, with a keen business sense and cultivated theatrical tastes. During his 10-year tenure at the Union Square, he improved both the quality of the acting company and production standards. He also fostered the production of contemporary (particularly American) drama, often commissioning new plays, translations and adaptations. In 1883, following a dispute with Shook, he left the Union Square; however, he subsequently managed the MADISON SQUARE THEATRE during 1884–91. In 1888, he secured control of WALLACK's THEATRE, renaming it Palmer's, and in 1891 he moved his famous Madison Square STOCK COMPANY to this theatre.

Unlike DALY and FROHMAN, Palmer was not a 'star maker', but he did promote the careers of numerous actors and actresses, including Agnes Booth, RICHARD MANSFIELD, WILLIAM H. CRANE, Maurice Barrymore (see DREW–BARRYMORE FAMILY), CLARA MORRIS and JAMES O'NEILL. Among his more notable productions of American plays were BRONSON HOWARD's *The Banker's Daughter* (1878), BARTLEY CAMPBELL's *My Partner* (1879), CLYDE FITCH's *Beau Brummel* (1890), JAMES A. HERNE's *Margaret Fleming* (1891) and AUGUSTUS THOMAS's *Alabama* (1891). He also produced plays by HENRY ARTHUR JONES, OSCAR WILDE, W. S. GILBERT and a popular dramatization of DU MAURIER's *Trilby* (1895). Palmer was among the first American managers to pay foreign authors royalties for the performance of their plays, and he was a major force in the founding in 1882 of the Actors' Fund of America.   DJW

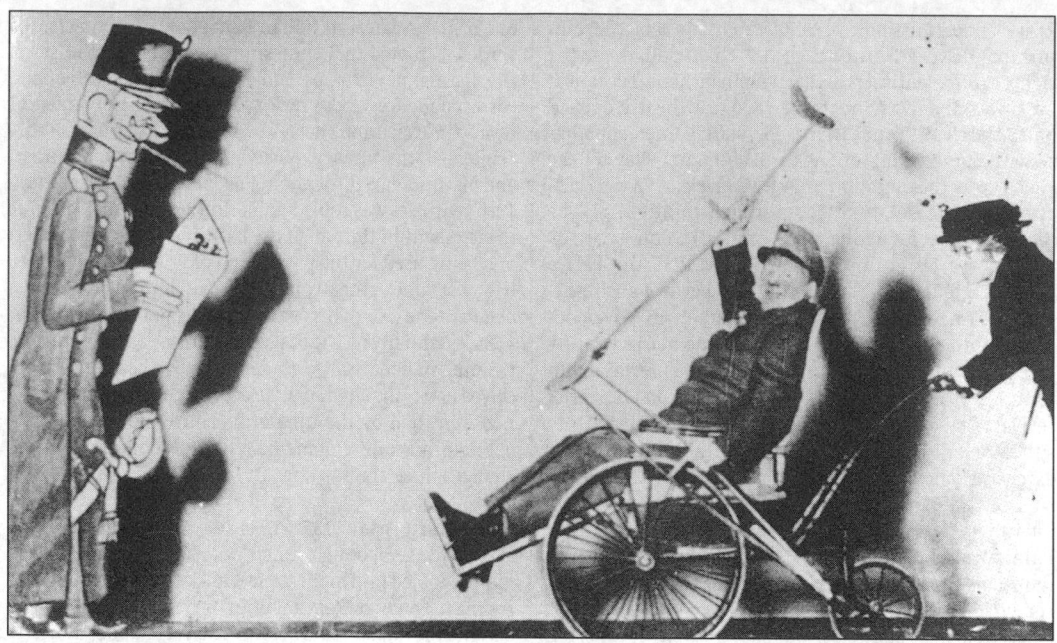

One of Max Pallenberg's most famous roles was as Schweik in Piscator's 1928 production. Parallel conveyor belts on the stage carry Schweik and the Officer-marionette past each other.

Palsgrave's Men see ADMIRAL'S MEN

Panama The possibility of constructing a canal across Panama to facilitate traffic between the oceans surfaced during the years of the Conquest, but the Panama Canal did not become a reality until 1914. In the intervening years, the territory of Panama was assigned first to the viceregency of Peru, later to New Granada (Colombia), and it finally became a separate nation in 1903 when the US interests in building the Canal supported the insurgents' claim to independence. Panamanian interests and economics during the 20th century have been closely related to the Canal.

Cultural life in the colony and even into the 19th century was quite limited. The first play written and performed in Panama was by Víctor de la Guardia (1772–1824); his *La política del mundo* (*World Politics*, 1809) was a classical Roman play with references to the Napoleonic invasion of Spain. References to other performances in the 19th century are infrequent, and no plays of substance have survived, although the indigenous populations and country folk traditionally developed popular theatrical forms that mixed their customs and religious elements.

The 20th century The economic boom produced by the construction of the Canal permitted Panama to build the National Theatre in 1920, which has served to house visiting troupes. In 1937 the poet ROGELIO SINÁN launched a children's theatre movement with a musical farce – *La cucarachita mandinga* (*The Impish Little Cockroach*) – a trend followed later by Eda Nela, among others, who wrote *La fuga de Blanca Nieves* (*Snow White's Flight*) in 1950. Plays deriving from Panamanian folklore, myths

and legends became popular in the 1940s during the regime of President Dr Arnulfo Arias. Some of these plays had a moralizing message designed to improve living conditions for poor peasants. In 1942 the government established the Ricardo Miró award to stimulate national interest in fiction and poetry. The competition was extended to theatre in 1952, and Renato Ozores (b.1910) won the first award with *Un ángel* (*An Angel*). Daniel Guigui established the Teatro de Arte (Art Theatre) in 1953, and the University Theatre was created in 1959. Other major writers from this period include Mario Augusto Rodríguez, Mario de Obaldía (1891–1951), Moisés Castillo (b.1899) and Juan O. Díaz Lewis (b.1916).

In the postwar period the theatre began to acquire higher levels of social commitment. Mario Riera Pinilla (1920–67) advocated peasant revolt in *La montaña encendida* (*The Burning Mountain*, 1952). The Nicaraguan-born JOSÉ DE JESÚS MARTÍNEZ (1929–91), long-time Panamanian citizen, was a major force in the theatre as playwright, director and organizer of theatre programmes for underprivileged areas. His early plays, such as *La mentira* (*The Lie*, 1955) and *El juicio final* (*Final Judgement*, 1962), reflected his doctoral training in philosophy and metaphysics. The urgency of individual freedom turned towards social concerns in his later plays, such as *La guerra del banano* (*The Banana War*, 1974). The cultural impetus generated by the nationalist period of Omar Torrijos, and the anti-imperialistic struggle of the Panamanian people, brought forth another major voice – that of RAÚL LEIS. An outspoken revolutionary, author of such plays as *María Picana* (1979) and *El nido de Macúa* (*The Nest of Macúa*, 1981), he writes plays that intercalate folklore and magic with political protest and even violence. Since 1981 Danny Calden, a director and actor, has sponsored an intense project of popular theatre and collective creations in the poorer regions of the country. A popular theatre group, Oveja Negra (Black Sheep), directed by Ileana Solís Palma, presented its first collective work, *El gran circo requeterrojo* (*The Big Red Circus*) in 1982.

Throughout the 1980s the level of activity continued to be limited primarily to foreign productions of BRECHT, PINTER, GARCÍA LORCA, and several Latin American writers. The Panamanian authors of note include Agustín del Rosario, Ernesto Endara, Jarl Ricardo Babot, Alfredo Arango and Soberón Torchía. The American invasion of Panama in 1989 has not yet produced evidence of improved theatre conditions in this small country.   GW

p'ansori KOREAN one-person, sung folk narrative, often called an 'operetta' in English translation. The solo performer, originally a man but often a woman today, is accompanied by a seated drummer (*kosu*) who plays the double-headed barrel drum (*pug*). The singer-actor's performance includes three theatrical elements: singing (*sori*), dialogue and narration (*aniri*), and acting and pantomime expressing joy (*ballim*). The performer may also employ gestures (*ch'umsae*). Of these elements, singing is the most important. The narrative is so composed that dialogue alternates with songs, so that the singer-actor need not sing continuously. The professional's voice is notably hoarse, a quality that is aesthetically desired and is the result of years of training and performing. Performers memorize scripts and performance can last several hours. *P'ansori* is still popular today.   OKC

pantomime see MIME

pantomime, English Form of entertainment so indigenous that its conventions have to be interpreted to non-Britons. It originated in the early 18th century under the influence of French fairground performers, who put on 'night scenes' with COMMEDIA DELL'ARTE characters in London. John Weaver, a dancing-master, copied these in short ballets staged at DRURY LANE in 1716, and was in turn imitated by JOHN RICH at LINCOLN'S INN FIELDS, with *A New Italian Mimic Scene between a Scaramouch, a Harlequin, a Country Farmer, his Wife and Others*. Rich played HARLEQUIN under the name Lun, and in Weaver's *The Cheats of the Tavern Bilkers* (22 April 1716) transferred the action to a contemporary setting, thus creating a truly native pantomime. His first outstanding success was *The Necromancer or Harlequin Dr Faustus* (1723), which prompted imitations at Drury Lane and the HAYMARKET.

Soon pantomime settled into its customary format: the opening was drawn from classical mythology and, following a transformation of characters into such types as Harlequin, Pantaloon and Columbine, the second half devolved into a knockabout harlequinade. Rich was lavish with mechanical devices, such as a coiling serpent, and his own mimic agility became proverbial. When theatrical CENSORSHIP was applied to the spoken word in 1737, there was more recourse to pantomime; even GARRICK had to comply with the popular taste, featuring Henry Woodward as his Harlequin. In *The Genius of Nonsense*

(1780), GEORGE COLMAN THE ELDER effectively altered the mythological opening to a fairy tale, which became standard.

By the early 19th century, these afterpieces had swollen to fill the major portion of a bill and accrued a number of traditions: the 'dame roles' were played by men (see FEMALE IMPERSONATION), the old Harlequin costume had been transformed by James Byrne into a skin-tight suit of spangled lozenges, and the entertainment predominated at Christmas and Easter. CARLO DELPINI had already shifted the comic emphasis from Harlequin to PIERROT, and this moved to CLOWN via the genius of JOSEPH GRIMALDI. Grimaldi came to prominence in Thomas Dibdin's *Harlequin Mother Goose, or The Golden Egg* (COVENT GARDEN, 1806), a panto which also set a pattern with its 'big heads' MASKING the characters in the opening prior to their transformation. Joey the clown with his introductory cry of 'Here we are again!', his singing of 'Hot Codlins' and 'Tippitiwitchet', his tricks of construction turning household utensils into animated figures, his greediness and exuberance were Grimaldi's legacy to future generations, who faithfully imitated his costume, make-up and behaviour (Tom Matthews added the frills, but allowed a stand-in to perform the acrobatics). This style of panto was carried to America by Charles Parsloe in 1831, but it enjoyed only a limited period of popularity, culminating in GEORGE W. L. FOX at the BOWERY THEATRE, New York (1850–67), and his *Humpty Dumpty* (1868).

In the Victorian age, pantomime, as scripted by J. R. PLANCHÉ and E.L. Blanchard, was alloyed with elements from the French FÉÉRIE, the BURLESQUE and the OPERETTA; the hero became the 'principal boy', played by a woman in tights (MADAME CÉLESTE may have been the first, in 1855) and backed up by a stockinetted chorus line. Certain stories proved to be worth repeating, such as *Cinderella*, *Puss in Boots*, *The Babes in the Wood*, *Dick Whittington* and *Aladdin*, and standard characters like the Widow Twankey (first seen in H. J. BYRON's burlesque *Aladdin*, 1861), Baron Hardup and Buttons in *Cinderella* (a descendant of Dandini in Rossini's opera by way of the Dandy Lover in Regency pantomime), the Broker's Men, and Whittington's Cat were carried over from year to year. It became exclusively a Christmas-time amusement aimed primarily at a juvenile audience, a seasonal source of employment for minor craftsmen, performers and children used to play fairies and animals. Some theatres, like the Britannia, Hoxton, and the Grecian, City Road, in London were famous for the excellence of their pantos. Elaborate trickwork, utilizing traps, hinged properties, instantaneous transformations dazzling with Dutch metal and gilt, were expected at the climactic moments.

The second half of the 19th century beheld the rise of the spectacular pantomime with its sumptuous processions, ballets and flying corps, the star status of the principal boy (see MALE IMPERSONATION), and the decline of the harlequinade. It became a speciality of actor clans like the CONQUESTS, the LUPINOS and the Vokeses, who monopolized it at Drury Lane (1869–80) with their indefatigable high-kicks. But they were ousted by Augustus Harris Jr (known as Druriolanus), who was eager to attract middle-class audiences who attended only pantomime by familiarizing them with the stars of the less respectable

MUSIC-HALL and burlesque. Hence, from 1879, the introduction of Fannie Leslie, Herbert Campbell, Arthur Roberts, MARIE LLOYD and DAN LENO, causing critics to complain of non-juvenile GAGging and topical songs, as well as speciality acts imported from VAUDEVILLE which held up the action.

After the First World War, pantomime was banished from Drury Lane by MUSICAL COMEDY until 1929, and from Covent Garden by opera and ballet until 1938. It survived as 'rep-theatre panto', domesticated and formulaic with its obligatory kitchen, schoolroom and dressing-for-the-ball scenes, and such audience-participation devices as the 'Oh, no, it isn't' – 'Oh, yes, it is' interchange, the shouts of 'Look behind you!' and the sing-along chorus. It was reinstituted at the London Palladium (1948–60); in 1961 Norman Wisdom played principal boy, an innovation repeated for a decade with male pop and rock stars until Cilla Black resumed the female prerogative in 1971. The substitution of RODGERS and HAMMERSTEIN's 'book musical' *Cinderella* at the COLISEUM (1957) was an ill portent which had no serious after-effects. The conventional pantomime returned to favour, albeit with some curious alterations, such as the Dame taking centre stage as a glamorous drag queen (DANNY LA RUE) and the NATIONAL THEATRE adding panto to its repertory in 1983. In 1984–5 there was only one WEST END panto, but 30 in the London suburbs, 70 in the provinces and 22 in Scotland, Wales and Ireland. On the dramatic stage, the conventions of the panto have often been adopted for special effect: in *The Fairy's Dilemma* (1904), W. S. GILBERT staged a topsy-turvy transformation scene; G. B. SHAW (not a fan) brought Harlequin and Columbine on in the last act of *You Never Can Tell* (1899); and PETER NICHOLS's *Poppy* (1983) attacked imperialism through a pantomime about the Opium Wars. (See also MIME.) LS

See: G. Frow, *'Oh, Yes It Is!' A History of Pantomime*, London, 1985; R. Mander and J. Mitchenson, *Pantomime: A Story in Pictures*, London, 1973; D. Mayer, *Harlequin in His Element*, Cambridge, Mass., 1969.

pantomimos see MIME

Papp [Papirofsky], **Joseph** 1921–91 American director and producer; founder of the NEW YORK SHAKESPEARE FESTIVAL in 1954. Starting as a BROADWAY and CBS-TV stage manager (1952–60), Papp began the Shakespeare Theatre Workshop on New York City's Lower East Side in 1953. After *Cymbeline* (1954) and *The Changeling* (1956), he continued to direct occasionally for NYSF: *Twelfth Night* (1958, 63, 69), *Hamlet* (1964, 67, 68, 83), RABE's *In the Boom Boom Room* (1973), Thomas Babe's *Buried Inside Extra* (1983), and *Measure for Measure* (1985). For television, he directed *The Merchant of Venice* (1962), *Antony and Cleopatra* (1963) and *Hamlet* (1964). During 1973–7, Papp ran Lincoln Center's VIVIAN BEAUMONT AND MITZI E. NEWHOUSE THEATRES. In 1990 he appointed JOANNE AKALAITIS his artistic associate and hired three young staff directors, easing away from the Festival's daily operation. By mid-1991 he had retained the title 'producer' but was no longer involved with the actual running of the NYSF, having appointed Akalaitis artistic director several months before his death in October 1991.

In 1958, 'driven ... to create theater without regard for ... cost or human interference', Papp received a Tony for Distinguished Service to Theatre. That year, he refused to identify left-wing artists for the House Committee for Un-American Activities, causing problems later when he proposed taking productions into city schools. Frequently taking chances, Papp advocated creative freedom, saying, 'If this theatre isn't being criticized for being too extreme, there's something wrong.' In 1990 he rejected $748,000 from the National Endowment for the Arts because of its restrictive anti-obscenity pledge. In 1988 he became the first recipient of the William Shakespeare Award for Classical Theatre from the Shakespeare Theatre at the Folger in Washington, DC. He also received Equity's 1987 PAUL ROBESON Award. A biography by Helen Epstein was published in 1994. REK

Paraguay The territory of Paraguay was largely ignored during colonial times after the capital city, Asunción, was founded in 1537, and the Spanish barely protested when Paraguay declared independence in 1811. In the interim, the Jesuit missionaries were active in education, religion and agriculture from their arrival in 1588 until expulsion in 1767. In addition to the occasional travelling company that brought Spanish classical fare, the Jesuits promoted local productions in both Spanish and Guaraní, the two dominant languages of the area.

Since independence Paraguayan politics have been marked by a series of repressive dictatorships. The cruel regime of Francia was followed by that of Carlos Antonio López, who contracted with the Spaniard Ildefonso Antonio Bermejo (1820–92) to bring journalism, education and theatre to Paraguay. His productions of Larra, ZORRILLA and Ramón de la Cruz brought more acclaim than his own plays. Marshal Francisco Solano López continued his father's tradition during his brief term (1862–70), and even started work on a theatre modelled after Milan's La Scala, but construction was interrupted by the devastating War of the Triple Alliance (1865–70) with Brazil, Argentina and Uruguay, which left Paraguay and its male population nearly decimated.

The 20th century Until the War of Chaco with Bolivia (1932–5) somewhat restored Paraguay's shattered image, theatre in the capital and outlying parts consisted primarily of visiting Spanish and Argentine troupes and an occasional local play. Writers such as Alejandro Guanes (1872–1925), Leopoldo Centurión (1893–1922), Eusebio Aveiro Lugo and Leopoldo Ramos Jiménez were the 20th-century pioneers, writing works with historical and social themes that suffered generally from MELODRAMAtism and flamboyancy. With so little importance given to local productions, many plays were actually lost during a period when the general public preferred the cinema or imported plays. Julio Correa (1890–1953) is the major playwright, director and actor of the period. With his own company he traversed the provinces with psychological plays in Guaraní that dealt directly but gracefully with the problems of the country folk or the working class, who suffered social, economic or psychological disruption during the period after the wars. Two émigrés, Arturo Alsina (1897–1984) from Argentina and JOSEFINA PLA from the

Canaries, brought talent to their adopted country. Pla is a prolific writer, Paraguay's best-known playwright internationally. She has often collaborated with Roque Centurión Miranda, who established the Municipal School of Dramatic Art in 1948. José María Rivarola Matto (b.1917) is known for rural social plays and his work as a critic.

Without state support the Paraguayan theatre struggles for survival in modern times. Paraguay's artistic subservience to Argentina has tended to eclipse local talent, and the repressive Stroessner regime that controlled Paraguay for 35 years forced many intellectuals into exile. Groups have been stimulated to some extent by the national theatre festivals and participation in international festivals, although the scarcity of decent theatre space is a serious problem. In 1989 the Theatre Festival of May, sponsored by José Luis Ardissone's Teatro Arlequín, brought new excitement in the months following the return to democracy, although the event was marred by the censorship of *San Fernando* by Alcibíades González Delvalle.

Some theatre groups have disappeared; others have been formed. The longstanding Ateneo Paraguayo (Paraguayan Athenaeum), one of Paraguay's oldest groups that regularly staged Greek, French and Paraguay theatre, folded after 50 years. The short-lived Tiempoovillo used collective techniques in staging collages and national works, and the Aty Ne'e (Assembly) was effective for nearly 15 years (1975–90) in promoting community theatre in the provinces. La Farándula, the Taller Paraguay Teatro (Paraguayan Theatre Workshop) and the Arlequín (Harlequin) all ceased to exist. In their place arise MSZ Productions and the Teatro Estudio Libre (Free Theatre Studio).

The currently active Paraguayan writers continue to deal with the massive problems that confront present-day Paraguay: social injustices, class differences, discrimination and CENSORSHIP. The younger generation of writers includes Ramiro Domínguez (b.1930), Alcibíades González Delvalle (b.1936), Ovidio Benítez Pereira (b.1939), Tadeo Zarratea (b.1947) and Néstor Romero Valdovinos. The Guaraní theatre continues to be a major force, and plays in Guaraní and Spanish are often translated into the other language. Actores Asociados (Associated Actors) presents an annual Guaraní production; in 1990 Tadeo Zarratea's novel *Kalaíto Pombero* was adapted for the stage by Antonio Escobar Cantero. Mario Prono and Antonio Pecci are important directors. Josefina Pla in 1984 won the Ollantay Prize, offered by CELCIT in Venezuela, for her research on four centuries of Paraguayan theatre. *Yo el supremo*, an adaptation of Augusto Roa Bastos's novel, won critical acclaim in 1991. Paraguayan theatre is still largely concentrated in the capital city of Asunción, although there is sporadic activity in provincial areas. GW

See: A. Pecci (ed.), *Teatro breve del Paraguay*, Asunción, 1981; J. Pla, *Cuatro siglos de teatro en el Paraguay*, Asunción, 1966.

Parigi, Giulio 1580–1635 Italian architect and scene designer. Parigi was a student and assistant to BUONTALENTI, whom he succeeded in 1608 as architect at the Medici court. Like his mentor, he became responsible for the decor for court festivities, the most important of which he designed in 1606, 1608, 1615 and 1616. In addition to influencing the work of German architect JOSEF FURTTENBACH, he became the teacher of the English designer INIGO JONES, thus disseminating the technology of stage machinery and movable scenery to Germany and England. His most important designs included *Il giudizio di Paride* (*The Judgement of Paris*, 1608), a PASTORAL with intermezzi and NAUMACHIA in honour of Prince Cosimo's marriage to Archduchess Maria Magdalena; *Eros and Anteros* (1613); *The Liberation of Tyrrhenus* (1616), an intermezzo performed at CARNIVAL time before the Medici court; and *La guerra d'amore* (1616), an equestrian ballet (see HIPPODRAMA) for which a wooden amphitheatre had to be constructed. In 1620 he was replaced as designer for the Medici by his son Alfonso (d.1656). AJN

Park Theatre (New York City) In 1795, tired of the deteriorating and déclassé JOHN STREET THEATRE, a group of prominent New Yorkers subscribed money to erect a new theatre in an area that promised to become the heart of the early-19th-century city. Three years later, it opened as the New Theatre in an unfinished state. The unattractive exterior belied a comfortable and handsome interior, which was designed European-style with three tiers of boxes overhanging a U-shaped pit, and a gallery above the highest tier. The first managers were actors JOHN HODGKINSON and LEWIS HALLAM JR, who moved their John Street company into the new house. WILLIAM DUNLAP was added to the management, and he succeeded them as sole manager for several years until forced into bankruptcy in 1805. The house, by then known as the Park, was bought by John Jacob Astor and John Beekman, who eventually leased it in 1808 to STEPHEN PRICE. Credited with introducing the 'star system' to American theatre practice, Price bolstered flagging box office receipts by importing English stars and managing their tours. In 1810, he brought over GEORGE FREDERICK COOKE, and in 1820 lured EDMUND KEAN to America. Because he spent so much time in England, Price left actor Edmund Simpson in charge of the theatre during his absences. In 1820, the Park burned to its exterior walls, but was rebuilt the following year. For more than a decade, it established itself as the first theatre in the land with an outstanding resident company. In addition to English stars, it helped to create such American stars as EDWIN FORREST and CHARLOTTE CUSHMAN. In its last decades, the high status of the Park was eclipsed, and Simpson was forced to place meretricious fare on its stage. In 1848, fire again consumed the house, and the Astor heirs replaced it with commercial buildings. MCH

Parker, L(ouis) N(apoleon) 1852–1944 Dramatist, composer and pageant-master, born in France. Parker's light comedies, MELODRAMAS and historical plays were staple popular fare for the English stage between 1890 and 1919. Between 1892 and 1905 he regularly had as many as four plays produced in London during a single year, and he also wrote specifically for the American stage (*The Mayflower*, 1897; *The Woman and the Sheriff*, 1911). The popularity of his plays was largely due to the strong acting parts they offered, the best of which, *Disraeli* with GEORGE

ARLISS in the title role, was revived several times and had a long run in New York. In addition, he gained a reputation as a deviser and producer of civic pageants throughout England as well as in the Lord Mayor's procession (1907, 1908), and on patriotic themes in London during the First World War, culminating in *The Pageant of Drury Lane* at the DRURY LANE Theatre in 1918. CI

Parker, Stewart 1941–88 Irish playwright. The bittersweet humour of Parker's work often centres on the meeting between well-meaning naivety and violent absolutism. The musical *Spokesong* (1975) presents the bicycle as the answer to the North of Ireland's sectarian disputes; *Catchpenny Twist* (1977) tells of two naive popmusicians who, by writing for both sides, become terrorist targets; in *Northern Star* (1984) a pastiche of Irish writers forms a commentary on the 1798 rebellion. *Nightshade* (1980), centred on a magician-undertaker, explores death as illusion. *Pentecost* (1987), literally set between warring sides, finds jazz and love to be almost sacramental ways for individuals to transcend the horrors around them.

Parker's wit often enunciates the 'instinct for play itself', but underlying his stage and television work is a whimsically tragicomic vision of human decency incorrigibly persisting in the face of surrounding brutalities. DM GF

parody BURLESQUE, parody and SATIRE are often treated as synonyms for ridicule through distortion, but it is useful to suggest distinctions between them. Parody is a form of mimicry. At one end of the spectrum parody may approach burlesque by exaggerating mimicry into caricature. At the other end, it may approach satire by enfolding a critique of social behaviour into its ridicule of an artistic form.

None of the three words refers exclusively to drama; yet all have been applied to drama. The word 'parody' is the first to enter European languages, deriving through the French from the Greek, where it means a song by the side, or a mocking of another song. Setting AESCHYLUS against EURIPIDES, ARISTOPHANES parodies both of them in a famous scene in his comedy *The Frogs*. Caricature of a particular person does not necessarily consign the entire work to the genre of parody. BRECHT's *Threepenny Opera* and *Arturo Ui* may be considered examples of parody embracing whole works, the one parodying GAY's *The Beggar's Opera*, and the other both *Richard III* and GOETHE's *Faust*. RC

Parry, Gwenlyn 1932–91 Welsh playwright. Born and educated in North Wales, he developed an interest in the theatre while teaching in London; on his return to Wales he continued teaching until appointed to a post with BBC Wales in 1966, after having won prizes for his writing at the National Eisteddfod. As well as writing for the stage he wrote and produced for Welsh television; in plays like *Y Tŵr* (*The Tower*, 1978) he introduced the conventions of the THEATRE OF THE ABSURD to Welsh audiences and, perhaps more importantly, encouraged Welsh actors and directors to explore alternatives to the domestic REALISM which had been the dominant convention of Welsh theatre. MA

Pasadena Playhouse (USA) Founded in California in 1917 by Gilmor Brown and incorporated in 1918, the Pasadena Playhouse grew into an important theatre institution. Brown depended upon amateur talent and volunteer help. He built a new theatre in 1925, adding a school for training actors in 1928 and an intimate Playbox Theatre in 1929. Premieres of new works, including EUGENE O'NEILL's *Lazarus Laughed* (1928), and revivals of seldom produced classics made the Playhouse famous. Beginning in 1935 it offered a series of Midsummer Drama Festivals that attracted wide attention. The theatre gained a reputation as a showcase for aspiring film actors, with Randolph Scott, TYRONE POWER and Robert Young among the stars discovered. Brown served 31 years as president and retired as director of the Playhouse in 1959. After it closed in 1970, the Playhouse was designated a historical landmark, renovated and reopened in 1985, with Paul Lazarus III as artistic director since 1990. The building was heavily damaged by a 1991 earthquake. TLM

Páskándi, Géza 1933– Hungarian playwright. As a member of the Hungarian minority in Romania, he studied at Bolyai University in Kolozsvár, and was imprisoned for political reasons (1957–63); he has lived in Budapest since 1974. His coinage, 'absurdoid', characterizes his drama, in which absurdity (see THEATRE OF THE ABSURD) is presented as an *aspect* of life: in the creation of his characters, or as something that unexpectedly visits itself upon them. In his historical dramas, e.g. *Sojourn* (1970), *The Hiding Place* (1972) and *Residents of the Windmill* (1981), Páskándi seamlessly combines psychological REALISM with the absurdity elicited by external and internal constraints. His plays have been performed in theatres throughout Hungary, including the National. His *oeuvre* includes poetry, short stories and essays. His work has appeared in seven other languages. EB

pasku Roman Catholic Sri Lankan PASSION PLAY. *Pasku* originated in the Catholic areas of Jaffna in northern SRI LANKA in the late 19th century. Soon after, it was performed in the Sinhalese-speaking Catholic regions of the western coastal region as well. The play began in Passion Week and lasted for the entire Holy Week. In some congregations, the actors are replaced by life-size statues depicting the central characters in the episodes of Christ's death and resurrection. The statues move and create stage pictures above and behind 6-ft-high temporary walls. Painted scenes ascend to nearly 20ft behind the figures. A reciter stands between the audience seated on the ground and the statues, interpreting each scene of the well known biblical stories. In some locales actors wear historical costumes of the period. Whether statues or live actors are used, performances incorporate Christian church music and sometimes Western musical instruments, such as the organ.

Several notable plays were written and produced by K. Lawrence Perera of Boralessa whose ambition was to imitate the famous OBERAMMERGAU Passion Play. He created the Shridhara Boralessa Passion Play in 1923 which drew together unschooled actors from among virtually every humble profession of the area. Over a hundred performers participated to create the epic. The stage consisted of five sections arranged like the RUKADA puppet theatre with a central acting area and side wings stretching out to the right and left. A sensation occurred in 1939 when it was announced that all the female roles would be played by women. The Archbishop of Colombo banned the performance on the grounds that women acting on the same stage as men would have violated the decorum of the country. Although they were not pleased, the actors gave in to church pressure and used only men.   FAR

paso see *GÉNERO CHICO*

Pasqual, Lluís 1951– Spanish theatre and OPERA director. A major figure in CATALAN THEATRE, he studied in Poland and Italy, where he worked under GIORGIO STREHLER. In 1976, with Fabià Puigserver, he founded Teatre Lliure in Barcelona; this prize-winning resident company has featured international classical and modern theatre (BRECHT, CHEKHOV, GENET, SHAKESPEARE). In 1983 he was named director of the National Drama Centre, housed at Madrid's TEATRO NACIONAL MARÍA GUERRERO. Among his internationally acclaimed productions were *Luces de bohemia* (*Bohemian Lights*) by VALLE-INCLÁN, and *El público* (*The Audience*) and *Comedia sin título* (*Play without a Title*), avant-garde works by GARCÍA LORCA that were long considered unperformable. Since 1990 he has headed the Théâtre de l'Europe at the ODÉON in Paris. In France he has recreated his productions of Genet's *Le Balcon* (*The Balcony*) and Lorca's *Sans titre*.

In conjunction with Quincentennial activities, he was instrumental in introducing Spanish authors to the French stage: his own version of Valle-Inclán's novel *Tirano Banderas* and LOPE DE VEGA's *Le Chevalier d'Olmedo* (*The Knight of Olmedo*), which was a featured production at the 1992 AVIGNON FESTIVAL. Outstanding among his opera credits are works by Verdi performed in Spain, Italy, France and Belgium.   PZ

Passion play A term with different meanings in different language areas. (The 'Passion' refers specifically to the sufferings of Christ between his taking in Gethsemane and his death on the cross, though the period is sometimes extended.) The French *passion* can be used of a series of events starting with the Creation and ending with the Resurrection. The German *Passion* can be used as an alternative to 'Easter play' (*Osterspiel*). In England, with only one Passion play extant, it is used fairly narrowly. Passion plays can vary enormously in length (of lines and the number of days of performance), and in style from sung Latin (Monte Cassino) to spoken vernacular (Semur, Sterzing, N. town, Rome).   PM

Pastor, Tony [Antonio] 1837–1908 American VARIETY performer and manager, called 'the Father of Vaudeville'. The son of a theatre violinist, he made his professional debut in 1846 as an infant prodigy at BARNUM'S AMERICAN MUSEUM. He later travelled as a circus CLOWN, minstrel and ballad-singer, with a repertory of some 1500 songs, arranging concerts in small towns. He first booked variety into the rowdy American Theatre at 444 Broadway, New York (1861), and, determined to attract a respectable audience, took over the Volksgarten at 201 Bowery in 1865. Renaming it the Opera House, Pastor advertised it as 'the Great Family Resort' and invited women and children to special matinées, but even door prizes of turkeys, hams and barrels of flour were insufficient to attract a God-fearing public. The fat man with the waxed moustache and mincing step moved his clean bill of variety to 585 Broadway in 1875, where he introduced the theatre checkroom, and then to 14th Street in 1881. There he finally succeeded in promoting clean VAUDEVILLE to a family audience, paving the way for KEITH and ALBEE; performers he sponsored include NAT GOODWIN, LILLIAN RUSSELL and WEBER AND FIELDS. A devout Catholic who kept a shrine backstage, he continued to pay low salaries, lost his stars to sharper managers and died a relatively poor man.   LS

pastoral The pastoral form found its way into drama by way of poetry. Theocritus and Virgil provided a classical precedent, carried into Renaissance Italy not least in the dramatic work of Poliziano and Beccari. TASSO's *L'Aminta* (1573) is generally regarded as the first true pastoral play, but the genre is not easily defined. Pastorals generally depict the happy outcome of faithful love in a removed, rural setting. GUARINI's *Il Pastor Fido* (1596) influenced one of the finest English examples, FLETCHER's *The Faithful Shepherdess* (1608). LYLY's *Love's Metamorphosis* (c.1589) looked to Spanish as well as Italian models. PHILIP SIDNEY's influential prose romance, *Arcadia* (published 1590), was avowedly inspired by the Spanish Jorge de Montemayor's *Diana* (c.1560), and itself became the source of JAMES SHIRLEY's play *The Arcadia* (c.1630). In much the same way, SHAKESPEARE built *As You Like It* out of Thomas Lodge's pastoral romance *Rosalynde* (1590). The rudimentary dramatic form of the dialogues that comprise Spenser's *The Shepherd's Calendar* (1597) is a closer formal model for JOHN DAY's *The Parliament of Bees* (written c.1595), which was intended for recitation rather than theatrical performance, but which indicates the ease with which the charms of pastoral poetry could be accommodated in the language of the court MASQUE.

Pastoral plays had a longer life in the French theatre, above all in the work of JEAN MAIRET, than they did in England, though Milton's *Comus* (1634) belongs to the genre as securely as had PEELE's masterpiece, *The Old Wives Tale* (published 1595), and BEN JONSON left an unfinished pastoral, *The Sad Shepherd*, at his death.   PT

Paterson, Bill 1945– Scottish actor, whose performance as the cramped writer in John Byrne's *Writer's Cramp* (1977) was the hit of that year's EDINBURGH (FRINGE) FESTIVAL and transferred to the BUSH THEATRE in London. This may have been a mixed blessing for his career, in that while it established his presence in the public eye it did so as a character actor, with a thick Scots accent, a swagger, a stoop and an air of cunning. It took nearly ten years for his range as an actor to emerge on stage and TV. He played Andrei in the TRAVERSE version of ALEKSANDR GELMAN's *A Man with Connections* (1989), which transferred to the ROYAL COURT, and was a memorable Wang the Water-Seller in *The Good Person of Setzuan* (1989) at the NATIONAL THEATRE. In 1991 he played in HAROLD PINTER's *The New World Order*, and as Gerardo the husband in Ariel Dorfman's award-winning play, *Death and the Maiden*.   JE

Paulding, James K(irke) 1778–1860 American man of letters. Paulding is significant in American theatre for two reasons. Writing about 'American Drama' for the *American Quarterly Review* (1827), he urged a carefully supported 'National Drama'. His play, *The Lion of the West* (1830), won a prize from J. H. HACKETT. From its conventional plot involving lost relations and international characters, as revised by JOHN AUGUSTUS STONE, Hackett created a substantial vehicle with Colonel Nimrod Wildfire, a humorous imitation of Davy Crockett. William Bayle Bernard adapted the play for English audiences as *A Kentuckian Trip to New York in 1815*, in 1833. Paulding also wrote *The Bucktails; or, American in England* (1847). WJM

Paulus [Jean Paulin Habans] 1845–1908 One of the earliest stars of the French music-hall (see *CAFÉ CHANTANT*), the first to earn a huge salary (400 francs a night in 1888) and to rely heavily on publicity. His career was a series of ups and downs in Paris and Marseilles, quarrels with managers, broken contracts and attacks by the censors (see CENSORSHIP). Then, in 1886, he won glory by adding a topical verse about General Boulanger to the song 'En revenant de la revue', which became epidemic. A strenuous performer with a stentorian voice, he founded and edited the *Revue des Concerts* (1887) as a vent for his vindictiveness; toured to London and America (1891–2); and managed the Ba-ta-clan and the Marseilles Alhambra unsuccessfully, before retiring in 1903. LS

pavai kathakali Glove-puppet play of Kerala state, India, in which wooden dolls imitate various characters in the repertory of *KATHAKALI* dance drama. The figures are 1–1.5 ft tall. Their faces are painted and bodies costumed in the distinctive patterns and colours of *kathakali*. A puppet is operated by a manipulator who sticks his middle finger into the head of the figure while thumb and little finger move its hands. At least four puppeteers are needed in performance, standing behind a curtain stretched between poles. They hold the glove PUPPETS above their heads to perform.

Stories are drawn from the *Mahabharata* and follow the *kathakali* pattern of organization. Musical accompaniment is by bell-metal cymbals and *cenda* drum. The artists come from the village of Kavadi Parambu in Palghat district and are relatively secretive about their art form, which they generally show only on religious occasions. FAR

pavai koothu Glove-PUPPET theatre form performed in Thiruchendoor city in Tamil Nadu, India. It may have originated in the 16th century. The language of performance is Tamil.

Plays centre on Vali, a female attendant of Shiva, and her love for Subramanya, one of Shiva's sons. Hence the name of the form: *pavai*, 'woman', and *koothu*, a 'play'. On Shiva's advice Vali was born to a deer in the forest. A hunter found her and he and his wife reared her. Seeing the beautiful maiden one day in the forest, Narada, divine troublemaker, hastened to tell Lord Subramanya. Infatuated by Narada's description, Subramanya disguised himself as an old bangle-seller and came to the

hunter's cottage in the forest. Through a ruse, he took Vali far from her home and then revealed himself in his heavenly form. They embraced and received the blessings of Ganesha, who appeared to them in the form of an elephant, an auspicious sign.

Puppets are about a foot tall. Heads and arms are made of papier mâché. Costumes are constructed of cloth and garlanded with coconut fibre or paper. Performance is given by a single manipulator who sits cross-legged behind a wooden box which masks him from view. (This can be compared to *wayang* (see SHADOW PUPPETS) in INDONESIA and MALAYSIA.) He is accompanied by an *idakka* drummer and a singer who keeps time with bell-metal cymbals. Popular tunes are sung, liberally borrowing from folk melodies of the region. FAR

pavaikuthu [*tholpavaikuthu*] Shadow-puppet theatre of Kerala state, south INDIA; *pava* means 'figure of a shadow' and *kuthu* means 'play'.

Plays are based on a Tamil version of the *Ramayana* called *Kamban Ramayana*, named after Kambar, its author, and written for a Chola king in the 9th century. It has unique characteristics which distinguish it from other forms of shadow-puppet theatre in south India, including the fact that the people of the region in which the performance takes place speak Malayalam not Tamil, the language of the drama. *Pavaikuthu* is usually performed near the *sanctum sanctorum* of a Kali temple as a RITUAL form of entertainment for the goddess. Processions and general celebrations are part of every programme.

The short, stout silhouettes, as small as 4in and as large as 3ft tall, are made of thick, opaque antelope-doe skin, thought to be holy. The silhouettes projected on the screen appear as almost solid black, for only minimal perforations in the leather delineate costume and ornament, and unlike other SHADOW PUPPETS in India, they are not translucent. The puppets are held tightly against the screen by a thorn pin or spike. The shadows are articulated by movable heads, arms and hands. Puppets of less important characters have no movable parts. The puppets (*ola pava*) are similar to Javanese *wayang* (see INDONESIA).

Performance is held in a specifically constructed enclosure (*kuthumadom*) which is about 42ft long, 9ft deep and 4ft above ground level. These special stage houses are placed at an elevated end of a broad stretch of temple compound. The shadows face south, or in the direction the temple deity faces. The long narrow opening in the *kuthumadom* is completely draped to create a screen about 18ft long and 5ft high, the upper portion of which is white and the lower portion black.

Below the white screen a long strip of bamboo is stretched horizontally in which grooves are cut, and coconut halves or small earthen vessels are placed in the holes to serve as lamps to cast shadows on the screen. Manipulators squat below the white portion of the screen masked by the black curtain and operate the puppets from behind the lamps.

A performance usually begins when drums are played and a wick from the *sanctum sanctorum* of the Kali temple is brought in procession to the *kuthumadom* to light the wicks of the oil lamps. This ritual is called *kotti kayattam* which means 'installing the puppets to the sound of the drums'. Next a special ritual sacrifice is offered to Ganapati, the elephant-headed god of success and beginnings. After the installation ceremony, all but two of the puppets are removed from the screen.

Gangayati Patter and Muther Patter, the remaining characters, praise the master-teachers of *pavaikuthu*, past and present, invoke the blessing of specific gods and, if patronized by a family, bless the household. Then they provide a summary of the previous night's story which serves as a prologue to the events about to take place. The episodes of the local version of the *Ramayana* are enacted in sequence.

The conclusion to the story is the grand coronation of Rama. On this night a procession takes place, beginning from the innermost part of the temple to the *kuthumadom*, to pay homage to Rama whose spirit is worshipped in the puppet. The performance ends when the sacrifice to Ganapati is again performed, the clown puppet (*kirita pava*) performs a ritual, and finally Rama appears wearing his crown. FAR

Pavlovsky, Eduardo 1933– Argentine playwright, actor and director. Also a medical doctor, a specialist in psychoanalysis, Pavlovsky studied in New York, and in Buenos Aires founded a specialized theatre group. Protesting against the absurd political situation, he considers himself a representative of what he calls 'exasperated realism'. From the psychoanalytic position of early plays, such as *La espera trágica* (*Tragic Wait*, 1964), he turned to more committed sociopolitical plays with *La mueca* (*The Grimace*, 1971), *El Señor Galíndez* (*Mr Galíndez*, 1973), *Telarañas* (*Spiderwebs*, 1976), and *El Señor Laforgue* (*Mr Laforgue*, 1982). *Galíndez* and *Laforgue* are particularly outspoken about brutality, torture and repressive political actions in Argentina and Haiti, respectively. *Potestad* (*Power*, 1985), *Pablo* (*Paul*, 1987) and *Paso de dos* (*Pas de deux*, 1989) continue the same exposées; the latter play has usually been acted by Pavlovsky as a male monologue that reveals both political and sexual repression. Later plays include *Cardenal* (*Cardinal*, 1991), *La ley de la vida* (*The Law of Life*) and *Alguna vez* (*Some Time*), both from 1992. GW

Pavy, Salathiel (Solomon) c.1590–c.1603 English boy actor, who may have begun with the BOYS OF ST PAUL'S before joining the CHILDREN OF THE CHAPEL ROYAL, for whom he acted in JONSON's *Cynthia's Revels* (1600) and *Poetaster* (1601). It is to Jonson's touching epitaph that Pavy owes his immortality. Though 'scarce thirteen' when he died, he was, Jonson claims, the 'stage's jewel' for 'three fill'd zodiacs', so skilled in the playing of old men that even sophisticated spectators thought him one. PT

Payne, Ben Iden 1881–1976 British director, educator and actor. Payne's experience as an actor with F. R. BENSON's company and as stage director at the ABBEY THEATRE in Dublin directly contributed to the success of ANNIE HORNIMAN's repertory company in Manchester (see REGIONAL THEATRE (BRITAIN)), which he managed from its inception in 1907 until 1911. From 1913 until 1934 he was active in American theatredirecting in Chicago and New York, being appointed artistic director of the Little

Theatre, Philadelphia (1914), and of the GOODMAN THEATRE, Chicago (1926). In charge of the School of Drama at the Carnegie Institute from 1919, he directed for the THEATRE GUILD in 1928–9, and in 1934 became director of the Shakespeare Memorial Theatre at Stratford-upon-Avon. Returning to America in 1943, again at the Carnegie Institute and the Theatre Guild, he inaugurated a summer Shakespeare Festival in San Diego (1949–52) and directed productions of SHAKESPEARE at the OREGON SHAKESPEARE FESTIVAL (1956 and 1961) and in Alberta (1958–60 and 1962). He was given the Rodgers and Hammerstein Award for distinguished services to the theatre in 1962. CI

Payne, John Howard 1791–1852 American actor and playwright. Now remembered for the lyrics to 'Home, Sweet Home!' (music by H. R. Bishop) in his *Clari, the Maid of Milan* (COVENT GARDEN, 1823), Payne wrote or translated and adapted from the French some 60 plays. Among the best-known are *Brutus; or, The Fall of Tarquin* (with EDMUND KEAN, DRURY LANE, 1818; with EDWIN FORREST in New York, 1829); *Thérèse; or, The Orphan of Geneva* (Drury Lane, 1821; with Forrest in New York, 1829); *Clari*; and two collaborations with Washington Irving – *Charles II; or, The Merry Monarch* (Covent Garden, 1824); and *Richelieu* (Covent Garden, 1826). In spite of close friendships with Irving, Coleridge, LAMB and (in Paris) TALMA, who encouraged him to translate French MELODRAMAS – and in spite of his occasional appearances as an actor and one season as manager of London's SADLER'S WELLS (1820) – Payne's years abroad (1813–32) were marked by financial distress: twice he was confined to debtors' prison.

He made his acting debut as Young Norval in JOHN HOME's *Douglas* (New York's PARK THEATRE, 1809), appeared as Hamlet and Romeo, quickly became known as 'Master Payne, the American ROSCIUS', and was favourably compared with 'Master BETTY'. His writing debut had come earlier with little magazines: *The Fly* (co-edited with SAMUEL WOODWORTH, 1804); *Thespian Mirror* (1805); and his first play *Julia; or, The Wanderer* (1806).

In 1842 President Tyler appointed Payne consul at Tunis (a reward for his crusade on behalf of the Cherokee Indians), where he served until 1845 and again from 1851 until his death. RM

Peele, George 1558–96 English playwright, son of a salter. Having graduated from Oxford University, Peele became associated with other UNIVERSITY WITS, GREENE, NASHE and MARLOWE among them, in the uncertain world of professional writing. Two civic pageants survive from an unknown number, as well as several interesting examples of court-ceremonial verse. Peele's earliest extant play, *The Arraignment of Paris* (1581–4), was written for performance by the CHILDREN OF THE CHAPEL ROYAL before the queen. It is a lifeless debate play, distinguished only by the beautiful songs so characteristic of Peele. *The Battle of Alcazar* (c.1598) provided EDWARD ALLEYN with a role reminiscent of Marlowe's Tamburlaine. *Edward I* (c.1593) deploys historical characters in apocryphal adventures. *The Love of King David and Fair Bethsabe* (c.1594) is much more unified in style and moral purpose, but Peele is better remembered for *The Old Wives Tale* (published 1595), a unique play which combines good-hearted PARODY of contemporary dramatic styles with a lyrical delight in story-telling. PT

Pene du Bois, Raoul 1914–85 American set and COS-TUME designer, who began his career at the age of 14 designing costumes for the *Garrick Gaieties*. From the 1930s on he designed many shows and MUSICALS ranging from *DuBarry Was a Lady* and *Jumbo* to *Wonderful Town* and *No, No, Nanette*. He also designed for films, ballets, ice shows and the Rockettes. His designs are typified by a strong sense of colour, and a certain whimsicality of line. AA

penny gaff see PENNY THEATRES

penny theatres Cheap minor playhouses which arose in Regency London and which allowed amateurs, on payment of a fee, to play roles of their choice; DICKENS penned a classic description of them in *Sketches by Boz*. First known as 'dukeys', the earliest was an unnamed booth at the back of the Westminster Theatre in the Broadway; it was copied by Hector Simpson's Vine Yard, Tooley Street, which specialized in dog drama (see ANIMALS AS PERFORM-ERS), and Bryant's Varieties, New Road, Sloane Square, where Richard III cost a fiver and the Lord Mayor six shillings to enact. Performing without a licence, these houses were frequently closed: the Bower Saloon, Stangate, which presented a PANTOMIME three times daily was suppressed in 1838. But the Theatres Act of 1843 spawned a spate of low-priced professional houses; their emphasis on gruesome true-crime MELODRAMAS like *Maria Marten* was another nuisance to the authorities, who put down the Dust Hole in Tottenham Court Road in 1858 for its staging of *The Bloodspot, or The Maiden, the Miser and the Murderer*. Legally, spoken dialogue was not permitted, but the statute was honoured more in the breach than the observance.

Henry Mayhew, who visited several 'penny gaffs', as they had come to be known, in the early 1860s, found them a crude descendant of the fairground booth, pandering to a juvenile public with obscenity and horseplay. The Rotunda in the Blackfriar's Road was the largest, seating 1000, and giving two performances an evening at a top price of threepence; but the average might offer six performances of 'flash' singing and dancing in a converted warehouse.

The New York equivalent was the Grand Duke's Opera House, located in a Baxter Street cellar and operated by street boys, with tallow candles as footlights, wash-tubs as private boxes and a six-cent admission fee. Throughout the 1870s it was a favourite Bohemian resort, and WEBER AND FIELDS got their start there. LS

People Show (Britain) A small loosely knit touring company, formed in 1966, whose first shows in the basement of the booksellers Better Books in London's Charing Cross Road won them a cult following. While the company members may have changed over the years – although Mark Long, Jeff Nuttall, Allan Hill and George Khan have regularly appeared – the People Show has stayed constant to its original plan. In its shows, which are largely improvised, a theme or popular genre (such as a TENNESSEE WILLIAMS's

Deep South play in *People Show 95*) is developed to its anarchic limits. The company depends upon a free association of ideas and its own friendly spirit in order to generate the fun which typifies its evenings, but this does not mean that its shows are not well planned. The company takes over its venues to deluge its public in all the paraphernalia that go with gas-lit Edwardian London or palm-trees-on-a-desert-island, which turns out to be a traffic crossing in Camden Town (*People Show 93*). The People Show can claim to be one of the most influential FRINGE companies of the 1960s, touring Europe and contributing to the beginnings of modern performance art, to a post-modern SURREALISM and to alternative comedy. It also deserves a special award, since it is approaching its 100th production, for sheer survival. JE

People's National Theatre (London) Founded in 1930 by the actress Nancy Price, who had begun her career with F. R. BENSON's company in 1899, the People's National Theatre was based on similar ideas to the Scottish National Theatre Society or the New York THEATRE GUILD. Its first production was a revival of Anstey's *The Man from Blankley's* at the FORTUNE THEATRE, and in 1932 a permanent home was found at the Little Theatre, a 309-seat house until then mainly identified with GRAND-GUIGNOL and REVUE. There an extensive programme of non-commercial drama was presented, ranging from EURIPIDES to PIRANDELLO, though Price also staged (and acted in) Mazo de la Roche's *Whiteoaks*, which ran for two years. The venture came to an end when the Little Theatre was destroyed in 1941. CI

Pepper's ghost A theatrical effect, whereby an actor standing at a 90° angle in the orchestra pit below the level of the stage is lit so that his reflection is cast on a sheet of glass mounted between the audience and the stage, thus producing the impression of a phantom. The illusion was invented by a retired civil engineer named Henry Dircks, who sold it, as the Aetheroscope, in 1862 to John Henry Pepper, director of the Polytechnic Institution, London. It was first used there for a dramatic reading of DICKENS's *The Haunted Man* on Christmas Eve of that year, and the many theatres that pirated it were soon forced to pay Pepper a royalty, so that 'Pepper's ghost' became current as the term for any trick effect for raising stage spectres. It was introduced to the USA by Harry Watkins in a MELO-DRAMA, *True to the Last*, at WALLACK'S THEATRE, New York (1863), and for the next two months New York managers presented horror shows teeming with ghosts. The illusion eventually was superseded by the use of back-lit scrim. LS

Pepys, Samuel 1633–1703 English diarist. He began writing his great *Diary* in 1660, as a rising young civil servant working in the Navy Office. He gave it up in 1669, believing that he was going blind. Throughout its nine years, Pepys recorded his impressions of his great love, the theatre, providing the earliest English account of regular play-going. If some of his critical comments are notoriously dogmatic – e.g., announcing that *A Midsummer Night's Dream* was 'the most insipid ridiculous play that ever I saw in my life' – his tastes were broad and his pleasure in theatre is infectious. In his numerous comments on the

Henri Robin menaced by his own version of the Pepper's Ghost illusion.

players, the scenery, the other members of the audience and the plays he vividly records the Restoration theatre. PH

Perelman, S(idney) J(oseph) 1904–71 Humorist, occasional playwright, and one of the USA's greatest erudite wits. After two MARX BROS screenplays in the 1930s, he collaborated with Ogden Nash on the book for WEILL's *One Touch of Venus* (1943) and wrote his only well known BROADWAY play, *The Beauty Part* (1962). DBW

Peretz, Isaac (Loeb) 1852–1915 Polish-born playwright who directed the Hazomir Group in Warsaw. The most notable of Peretz's plays are *The Sisters* (1904), dealing with the extreme poverty of the Jews in Poland, and *Night*

in the Old Market, an eerie, atmospheric, poetic fantasy first produced by ALEKSEI GRANOVSKY for the MOSCOW STATE JEWISH THEATRE (1925) and offering a challenge to art theatres ever since. AB

Performance Group (USA) One of the most controversial and visible of the environmental theatre groups of the 1960s and 70s; formed in New York City in 1967 by Richard Schechner, critic, director, and editor of the *Drama Review*. Although in practice the work of the Group often seemed amateurish and self-indulgent, Schechner broke through traditional barriers of a text- and stage-bound theatre with productions such as *Dionysus in 69* (1968), *Makbeth* (1969), *Commune* (1970) and GENET's *The Balcony* (1979). Schechner's ideas were codified somewhat in his book *Environmental Theatre* (1973). Though only partially successful, his group, performing in the Performing Garage in Wooster Street, was notable for its risk-taking, its concern with social issues and (with some direct influence from GROTOWSKI) its investigation into RITUAL and the use of other cultures in the development of a new performance art. Schechner left the Garage in 1980, and the Group, renamed the WOOSTER GROUP, has continued under the nominal leadership of ELIZABETH LeCOMPTE. DBW

Perkins, Osgood 1892–1937 American stage and film actor, noted for his versatility and polish. Perkins graduated from Harvard in 1914 after having participated in some of the GEORGE PIERCE BAKER plays. After serving in the First World War, he formed the Film Guild, a cinematic production company, and appeared in several of its productions. WINTHROP AMES then cast him as Homer Cady in *Beggar on Horseback*, his BROADWAY debut; JED HARRIS next hired him for *Weak Sister*. Perkins later starred as Walter Burns in *The Front Page* (1928) and played Astrov in *Uncle Vanya* (1930). He also appeared in films such as *Scarface* and *Madame Du Barry*. He was described as 'wiry, nervous, unerring in his attack'. Perkins's son, the late Anthony (Tony) Perkins (1932–92), of *Psycho* fame, enjoyed a highly successful stage and film acting career, including stage appearances in *Look Homeward, Angel, Greenwillow, The Star-Spangled Girl, Equus* and *Romantic Comedy*. SMA

Perlini, Memé 1940– Italian actor and director who made a major reputation as an innovative director in experimental work during the mid- and late 1970s, with productions like *Candore giallo* (1974), *La partenza dell'Argonauta* (1976) and *Grand Hôtel des Palmes* (1978), in alternative venues and at festivals. Although Perlini's early work included a version of SHAKESPEARE's *Othello* (1974), it was only with a production of ARISTOPHANES' *Birds* (1980) that he turned more to staging classic plays in regular theatres, including his own translation of *The Merchant of Venice* (1980) and IBSEN's *John Gabriel Borkman* (1981). He has had an enduring interest in the work of PIRANDELLO, writing and staging *Pirandello chi?* (1973), and giving imaginative reorchestrations to plays like *All'uscita* (*To the Exit*, 1989) and *Lazzaro* (*Lazarus*, 1989–90). Another recurring interest has been classical drama, as in *Ifigenia in Aulide* (1992). KR

Perry, Antoinette 1888–1946 American actress, producer, director and activist. Following her 1905 Chicago debut, she acted in New York until her 1909 marriage to socially prominent businessman Frank Frueaff. After his death, she returned to the stage in 1924, acting under Brock Pemberton, then assisting him, and finally directing such successes as *Harvey* (1944). As chair of the American Theatre Council's Apprentice Theatre (1937–9), she inaugurated and conducted 5000 auditions to encourage young talent. In 1941 she was president of the Experimental Theatre. She held leadership positions with the Stage Relief Fund, the Actors Thrift Shop and the American Theatre Wing and its Stage Door Canteen. The annual Antoinette Perry (Tony) Awards, named after her,

commemorate her extraordinary service to the theatre. FHL

Peru Accounts of the legendary riches of the Incas reached the Spanish even before the Spanish reached Peru. Atahualpa filled rooms with silver and gold but was nonetheless betrayed by his conqueror Pizarro, an act that symbolized the treachery of the Spanish in dealing with these cultured Native Americans. The Inca Garcilaso de la Vega (1539–1616) wrote in his chronicles of both tragedies and comedies performed by the 'Indians' as well as the *tarquis*, RITUAL festivals set to music representing nature's sacred cosmovision. As early as 1546, Cuzco, then the capital, was the usual site of the religious and secular works offered on feast days of the church or in celebration of a secular event (the crowning of a king, the arrival of a viceroy).

The first theatre building constructed in Lima in the late 16th century served for performances of the GOLDEN AGE plays in vogue as well as an occasional local work. Arequipa, located on the route from Lima to Potosí, also boasted early theatrical productions, but Lima, as the major cultural centre in all of South America, fomented the most theatre. The early writers included the satirical poet Juan del Valle y Caviedes (1652–94), who wrote LOAS and *entremeses*, (see GÉNERO CHICO), as did Lorenzo de las Llamosas (1665–1705) and others. The major figure was Pedro de Peralta Barnuevo (1664–1743), who wrote historical plays with French and Greek motifs, as well as folkloric works with prototypes of colonial society. An internationally known actress of the time was Michaela Villegas, known as La Perricholi, who captivated Lima with her talents (and apparently the heart of the Viceroy Amat as well, a man fascinated with French encyclopaedism).

The tempo of dramatic activity increased in the latter part of the 18th century, even though the century was not on the whole a productive time for the arts. Around 1780 the growing resentment with Spain produced rebellions led by Tupac Amaru II, the great Inca leader whose exploits and heroism were recaptured in 19th- and 20th-century drama. In his presence Padre Antonio Valdés directed a performance near Cuzco of the OLLANTAY, an allegedly pre-Columbian play in the Quechua language that recounts love and war among the Native Americans before the arrival of the Spanish.

After General San Martín withdrew to the south in 1822, Bolívar imposed independence on Peru in spite of the lack of enthusiasm of the local citizenry. The theatre during the 19th century was dominated by two major playwrights whose styles are quite different from each other. Felipe Pardo y Aliaga (1806–68), perhaps because his formative years were spent in Spain, followed the Hispanic tradition, writing elevated, lightly satirical pieces such as *Frutos de la educación* (*The Fruits of Education*, 1830), considered to be the first dramatic work of independent Peru. With a neoclassical posture and technique, the play examined the value of education. Pardo's counterpart, Manuel Ascencio Segura (1805–71), on the other hand, was more lively and spontaneous in his efforts to capture local colour and life in a popular vein. His *Ña Catita* (1856), the portrait of a Lima matchmaker, is still the best-known, most played Peruvian work.

The 20th century The early part of the century witnessed a continuation of the romantic and costumbristic theatre (see *COSTUMBRISMO*) of the previous century. Among others, José Chioino (1898–1960) was representative of this period in which few plays were written and few groups were active. In 1938 the creation of the Asociación de Artistas Aficionados (Association of Amateur Artists) as a private institution dedicated to the promotion of the arts, including ballet and music, was a first major step in renovating the moribund theatre. Bernardo Roca Rey (1918–84) evolved as its principal director, and the AAA theatre now carries his name.

In the years immediately following the Second World War, when a new excitement about the world community was growing in Lima, several events helped the theatre to prosper. The Compañía Nacional de Comedias (National Drama Company) was created in 1945, and the ENAE (Escuela Nacional de Arte Escénico, National School of Dramatic Art) was formed the same year, later reorganized as the Instituto Nacional de Arte Escénico (National Institute of Dramatic Art). The ubiquitous MARGARITA XIRGÚ toured Peru with her exciting versions of GARCÍA LORCA, and three new playwrights appeared in response to the national theatre contest of 1946–7: Percy Gibson Parra (b.1908) wrote *Esa luna que empieza* (*The Crescent Moon*), a successful poetic and metaphysical play; Juan Ríos (b.1914) with *Don Quixote* and SEBASTIÁN SALAZAR BONDY with *Amor, gran laberinto* (*Love, the Great Labyrinth*) launched overlapping careers with different styles. Ríos followed a more traditional and universal format while Salazar Bondy, more experimental and nationalistic, established a sense of a new Peruvian drama, and became Peru's best-known playwright on an international scale. GRÉGOR DÍAZ collaborated with the Club de Teatro (Theatre Club) and wrote strong social protest plays such as *La huelga* (*Strike*, 1966). *Collacocha* (1958) by ENRIQUE SOLARI SWAYNE set the tone for high-level national tragedy in its treatment of a civil engineer defeated by the powerful forces of nature.

Other major writers of the period include Julio Ramón Ribeyro (b.1929), Edgardo Pérez Luna (b.1928) and Víctor Zavala (b.1932), who deals especially with problems of peasant classes. Two exiled playwrights took university positions in the USA: Julio Ortega (b.1942), author of 18 short plays including the documentary/drama *Mesa pelada* (1972), and ALONSO ALEGRÍA, former director of the Teatro Nacional Popular (National Popular Theatre) and author of *El cruce sobre el Niágara* (*Niagara Crossing*, 1969), a prize-winning rendition of existential values predicated on the 19th-century French tightrope artist, BLONDIN. Peru's internationally known novelist of the 'boom', Mario Vargas Llosa (b.1936), turned to theatre in 1981 with *La señorita de Tacna* (*The Girl from Tacna*), an excellent play dramatizing the process of story-telling, followed in 1983 by *Kathie y el hipopótamo* (*Kathie and the Hippopotamus*). *La Chunga* (1986) is an adapted scene from one of his novels that touches on female power, with overtones of lesbianism in a provincial setting.

Although Peru has produced important writers and some major plays, the theatre has not developed as an organic, cohesive national phenomenon. The government is unable and/or unwilling to patronize the arts, and the 20 or more theatre groups that operate in and around Lima maintain a precarious existence. Theatre fare is sparse for a city of four million inhabitants, and young playwrights do not receive much encouragement or support. Theatre groups appear and disappear. One of the oldest is the TUSM (Teatro de la Universidad de San Marcos, San Marcos University Theatre), originally established in 1941. Directed by Guillermo Ugarte Chamorro from 1968 until 1991, it sponsors an active season and maintains an ambitious publication programme devoted to all aspects of theatre. The most significant and transcendent group is the Club de Teatro (Theatre Club), established by Salazar Bondy in 1953 with the Argentine Reynaldo D'Amore (b.1923), who introduced the STANISLAVSKY system. The Club inaugurated the first school of independent theatre art in Peru and gave respectability to the independent theatre movement. Histrión, established soon after, promoted high-quality work during its lifetime (1956–77). SARA JOFFRÉ, creator of Homero, Teatro de Grillos (Homer, Cricket Theatre), directs, writes and publishes, especially in children's theatre. Efforts by Miriam Reátegui and Ernesto Ráez, editors of *Creart*, a monthly newsletter about cultural events in Lima, to organize the disparate groups and coalesce the Peruvian theatre movement coincide with the sponsorship of an international festival of children's theatre held in Lima in 1985. Jorge Chiarella's Alondra (Lark) is another major group.

In recent years the depletion of Peru's rich natural resources (mines, guano, fisheries, to name a few) and a depressed economy have encouraged the development of revolutionary theatre groups, although some contend that the popular theatre forms scattered throughout the Peruvian provinces – the famous Devils of Cajabamba, the fiestas of Buldibuyo and the Magi plays of Huavilillas – are the true antecedents of the recent impetus. The ideological positions expressed by such groups as Cuatrotablas (Four Sides) and the TIT (Taller de Teatro, Theatre Workshop) speak to the urgency of social reform. Yuyachkani (1971) is a lively musical group with an ideological position that has achieved an international reputation for its vibrant popular theatre. Ensayo, Asociación de Estudio y Producción Teatral (Rehearsal, Theatre Study and Production Association) was established in 1983 by graduates of the Catholic University theatre programme: Alberto Isola, Jorge Guerra and Luis Peirano. The Muestras Nacionales (National Showcases), the first four of them organized by Homero, provided exposure for several playwrights, directors and groups, and a major festival in Ayacucho in 1978 attracted international participation on revolutionary themes. Other groups that were active throughout the 1980s include Telba, Abeja, Piqueras (MIME theatre), Yego, Quinta Rueda, Teatro del Sol and many others. Most conventional theatre is now located in the suburban areas of Miraflores, San Isidro and Barranco (and not in downtown Lima), the result of years of violence during the Sendero Luminoso (Shining Path) period. Especially during the 1980s the theatre, along with virtually all other manifestations of daily and cultural life, was imbued with direct or indirect aspects of violence. Street theatre is popular in Lima and especially in the poorer districts around the city.

After Quechua was recognized as an official language in

Peru in 1975, the TUSM sponsored the first national contest for dramatic works written in Quechua. Nevertheless, Quechua theatre is not yet a major force, in comparison with the importance of the Guaraní theatre in Paraguay, for example. Even so, many Peruvian plays written in Spanish deal with themes and figures from the indigenous national past, such as Tupac Amaru, Ayar Manko and Ollantay. GW

See: R. J. Morris, *The Contemporary Peruvian Theatre*, Lubbock, Texas, 1977; C. M. Suárez Radillo, 'Poesía y realidad social en el teatro peruano contemporáneo', *Cuadernos Hispanoamericanos*, 269, Nov. 1972.

Peruzzi, Baldassare 1481–1536 Italian painter and architect. Peruzzi is important in theatre history as a pioneer of stage perspective and decoration, and for his use of original research on the archaeology of classical theatre buildings. VASARI devotes one of his *Lives* to him, and in that indicates the range of his contribution to the early development of stage settings, theatrical machinery, and the devising and execution of festival entertainment and triumphs. His designs provided the models for SERLIO's influential tragic, comic and pastoral settings. KR

Peshkov, A. M. see GORKY, MAKSIM

PETA see PHILIPPINES

Petit-Bourbon, Salle du (Paris) A lofty, well appointed hall in the former palace of the Dukes of Burgundy, adjacent to the Louvre and frequently used for court entertainments in the 16th and 17th centuries. Equipped at either side with balconies divided into boxes, it was long enough to accommodate a spacious stage, approximately 50ft square, at one end, while the flat floor afforded a convenient space for court ballets and MASQUES. Over the years it was temporarily occupied by a variety of visiting companies from Italy and Spain, and in 1645 the backstage area was reconstructed by the designer-machinist TORELLI for his productions of Italian OPERA. In 1658, following his successful command performance before the young Louis XIV, MOLIÈRE was given use of the theatre in alternation with the COMMEDIA troupe of TIBERIO FIORILLI already established there, and it became the scene of his earliest successes with the Parisian public. Two years later it was demolished, VIGARANI appropriating the scenery and stage machinery installed by Torelli, and Molière being allowed to take the boxes and other fittings with him to his new base at the PALAIS-ROYAL. DR

Petitclair, Pierre 1813–60 French Canadian dramatist, author of the first published play by a native Canadian, *Griphon, ou La Vengeance d'un valet* (*Griphon: or A Valet's Revenge*, 1837), a comedy visibly influenced by MOLIÈRE. It was never performed, but was followed by two others staged with repeated success: *La Donation* (*The Legal Donation*, 1842), the first French Canadian MELODRAMA and first staged play by a native Canadian; and *Une Partie de campagne* (*A Country Outing*, 1857), an engaging COMEDY of manners, portraying the dangers of mimicking British speech and customs, and remarkable for its authentic use of rural Québécois speech. LED

Petito, Antonio 1822–76 Italian actor and dramatist. Born into the profession, Petito worked mainly in Naples, and although he early acted in a wide variety of drama, including playing Iago in an adaptation of *Othello*, he was best-known for his performances in the MASK of Pulcinella and as the unmasked character Pascariello in Neapolitan farces, many of his own devising. He first acted Pulcinella at Naples's San Carlino Theatre in 1853, and later wrote many pieces for the FARCE player, SCARPETTA. LR

Pétomane, Le [Joseph Pujol] 1857–1945 French music-hall (see CAFÉ CHANTANT) artist, whose billing means 'the man mad about farts'. A star at the MOULIN-ROUGE (1906–10), he earned 20,000 francs by vibrating his sphincter to imitate the characteristic eructations of a mother-in-law, various animals, and a bride on her wedding night. He also used it to smoke a cigarette, produce music on the ocarina and blow out a candle at a distance of 20 centimetres. LS

Petrolini, Ettore 1886–1936 Italian actor, entertainer and playwright. Petrolini began his career in the *caffè-concerto* world of Rome when in his late teens, specializing in comic patter and songs and also acquiring wide experience abroad in the Americas. Although established nationally before the First World War, after it his art matured and took new directions, becoming sharper, more bitter and satirical, in a series of self-devised sketches including *Nerone*, *Romani de Roma*, *Mustafà* and *Gastone*. He formed his own company specializing in his sketches and improvisations, adaptations of comedies by dramatists like Testoni and Novelli, and embracing one-act pieces by PIRANDELLO; some critics have found a Pirandellian influence in his caustic, questioning humour. LR

Petrushevskaya, Lyudmila [Stefanovna or Iosifovna] ?1938– Soviet Russian playwright. Raised in a Siberian orphanage, she studied journalism at Moscow University, served as a nurse and wrote short stories before turning to drama. Her early plays, influenced by VAMPILOV and ARBUZOV in whose studio she worked, were written years before they were allowed production. Fame came with the screenplay for the award-winning *Tale of Tales*. Hers is a disillusioned, painfully honest yet comic vision of a sleazy world; her exhilarating and seemingly spontaneous dialogue has been dubbed a 'tape-recorder effect'. Her plays, variations on domestic tribulations, feature middle-aged, middle-class failures. *Three Girls in Blue* (Lenin Komsomol, Moscow, directed by MARK ZAKHAROV) presents a woman caught between responsibility to her sick child and aged mother and an affair with a married man. *Cinzano*, an all-male trio of layabouts, became world-famous in the Chelovek Studio production (1987); in his directorial debut, Roman Kozak turned its sullen REALISM into a 'bruitistic' concert. Musical analogies can also be traced in such plays as *Music Lessons*, a study of moral and environmental kitsch; *Andante*, about a drug-taking *ménage à trois*; *Twentieth-Century Songs*, concerning a displaced youth living on the porch of a dacha; and *Moscow Chorus*, in which choirs from Moscow and Dresden sing a joint Miserere. In 1987, ROMAN VIKTIUK staged *Love*, *Stair Landing* and *Columbine's Apartment* as a trilogy on the theme of blighted affections. Petrushevskaya has since turned to novel-writing. LS

Peymann, Claus 1938– German director. Sympathetic to the 60s protest movement, he pioneered HANDKE (*Offending the Audience*, 1966) and BERNHARD (*Ein Fest für Boris*, 1970). As Intendant at Stuttgart, Bochum and Vienna, Peymann has commissioned and staged much new writing, and has personally premiered most of Bernhard's and MÜLLER's plays. He applied a light, irreverent touch to classics like KLEIST's *Das Käthchen von Heilbronn* and *Die Hermannsschlacht* (*Hermann's Battle*), LESSING's *Nathan the Wise* and SCHILLER's *Wilhelm Tell*. His 1976 production of GOETHE's *Faust 1 and 2* in two evenings ranged over the Stuttgart theatre's stage and foyer and achieved a fascinating balance of kitsch and style, whimsy and seriousness. Peymann is an outspoken critic of residual Fascism in Germany and Austria. HR

Pezzana, Giacinta 1841–1919 Italian actress. Pezzana first appeared on the stage in 1859, rising quickly to become lead actress in the company of Cesare Dondini, playing opposite ERNESTO ROSSI in a wide variety of drama, from romantic stock pieces to SHAKESPEARE. From 1870 she led her own company, touring abroad to South America, Egypt and Russia. She achieved a notable success as the mother in ZOLA's *Thérèse Raquin* (1879) at the Teatro dei Fiorentini in Naples, acting with EMANUEL and the young DUSE. LR

Phelps, Samuel 1804–78 British actor, whose career as a leading Shakespearian began during the supremacy of MACREADY and ended during the supremacy of IRVING. He was, in fact, more devoted to SHAKESPEARE than either of his more illustrious lives. He made his debut in the York circuit in 1826 and his first London appearance as Shylock at the HAYMARKET in 1837. This challenge to the memory of EDMUND KEAN was sustained throughout his Haymarket engagement, when he appeared exclusively in parts that Kean had favoured – Hamlet, Othello, Richard III and Sir Edward Mortimer in COLMAN THE YOUNGER's *The Iron Chest*.

Playing opposite Macready at COVENT GARDEN (1837–8) taught Phelps a lesson about theatrical rivalry. After playing Iago to Phelps's Othello, Macready relegated his new employee to minor parts. Only at the Haymarket and in the provinces could he play leads. His opportunity came with the abolition of the Patent monopoly (see THEATRICAL MONOPOLY) in 1843. He became joint lessee of the highly unfashionable SADLER'S WELLS, where from 1844 to 62 he staged all but four of Shakespeare's plays. Not only that; he

Samuel Phelps as Henry IV.

also showed a rare respect for the text. His was the first serious production of *Antony and Cleopatra* (1849) for over two centuries and the first London *Pericles* since the Restoration. Temperamentally austere, Phelps was the finest Lear of his generation, and although not at ease in comedy, widely admired as Bottom, Falstaff and, less surprisingly, Jaques in *As You Like It*. After leaving Sadler's Wells, he continued to act, making his last appearance as Cardinal Wolsey in the year of his death.   PT

Philadelphia, Jacob [Jacob Meyer] 1721–c.1800 American conjuror, the son of Polish Jews, and the first US-born MAGICIAN to gain international acclaim. He acted as a scientific jester for William Augustus, Duke of Cumberland, performing mathematical and physical experiments. After the duke's death in 1765 he went public, travelling through Europe billed as 'an Artist of Mathematics', and played before Catherine the Great, Sultan Mustafa III and Frederick the Great, who was very fond of him. Philadelphia, a member of a secret Rosicrucian society and anti-monarchical, was eventually expelled from Berlin. Meanwhile, he had gained the reputation of a true sorcerer who could pass through doors, grow a second head and read minds.   LS

Philipe, Gérard 1922–59 French actor who made his name in the title role of CAMUS's *Caligula* (1945), followed by numerous film roles. In 1951 he played Rodrigue to VILAR's Don Diègue in *Le Cid* at the AVIGNON FESTIVAL. After this he joined the THÉÂTRE NATIONAL POPULAIRE team and until his death played leading roles, e.g. Lorenzaccio and Friedrich Prince of Hamburg. He was unique among French actors in achieving at one and the same time acclaim from the theatre critics and adoration from young theatregoers, who reacted to him with the kind of hysteria normally reserved for pop stars.   DB

Philippines In this Southeast Asian island nation of 62 million, the tribes that follow indigenous religion retain performance traditions which probably were widespread in precolonial times. The 5 per cent of the population who are Muslim have traditions related to MALAYSIA and INDONESIA, and the 90 per cent who are Christian have theatre forms developed under Hispanic and American colonial influence. The major performance categories are (1) prototheatrical forms; (2) Islamic dances; (3) Hispanic-influenced theatre genres, and (4) American-influenced forms, including modern drama.

Prototheatrical forms In attempts to reconstruct the parameters of early Filipino entertainments, scholars have turned to the performance of the tribes that have not accepted the Christian or Islamic religion. Though performances themselves may have changed in the hundreds of years that Muslim and Christian influences have dominated lowland areas, their categories have probably remained stable. Spirit mediumship, epic recitation, dances and games involving improvised poetry, are widespread in Southeast Asia and part of the common heritage of Malay peoples, including inhabitants of the Philippines. The first European reports noted such forms in the 16th and 17th centuries.

Music and dance are traditionally used for curing, courting, entertainment and RITE OF PASSAGE ceremonies. Dances may be abstract or mimetic. Examples of the latter include the honey-gathering dance of the Negritos and the boar-hunting dance of the Igorots. Courting and war dances are widespread. The *pinanyo-wan* ('veiled'), for example, is a wedding dance of the Bontok, in which a boy and girl dance with the boy's foot movements emulating a cock attracting a hen. The *tchugas* ('exorcism') of the Kalinga is a victory dance over ghosts of a slain enemy in which two young men and a priestess re-enact a war dance, whereupon the priestess asks the ancestral spirits to give her the names of glorious headhunters.

RITUALS were undertaken by local SHAMANS, called *babaylan* among the Visayan peoples and *catalonan* among the Tagalog. Performances were frequently part of curing, and possession trance was common. A present-day example is the Tagbanwa female shaman who, dancing while in trance, communicates with spirits and may be possessed by them.

The singing of epics is found in all layers of Filipino culture, and it may be that Muslim and Hispanic variants are cultural adaptations that allowed older oral narrative practices to continue with a new content. Epics might be sung for one to three nights in celebration of a wedding, at gatherings for guests or as entertainment for villagers. Among the Mandaya, Mansaka and Bagobo, heroes like Agyu, Tuwaang and Ulahingan were praised. *Tutol* are epic songs treasured by the Muslim Magindanao. They tell of the exploits of heroes like Radya Indara Patra, a noble who flies to the palace of the clouds and fights mythical monsters to save his people. Epic singing may also be related to *pasyon*, a chanted narrative of the Passion and other biblical events sung during Lent, and to metrical romances, including the duodecasyllabic line *awit* and octosyllabic *corrido*. The latter are Filipino narratives, written in quatrains and published in the early 19th century. Based on European tales, they gave rise to corresponding folk theatricals.

Games involving dialogue between two or more voices are another indigenous theatrical impulse. In the *badiw* of the Ibaloi a singer improvises riddles in a strict verse form. The chorus repeats the last lines, giving the singer a chance to compose the next verse. Performing during ceremonies for the dead, the singer might invite spirit relatives to drink rice wine, praise the host or comment on the properties of the deceased. In *kaharian*, a king (*hari*) makes an accusation – 'You stole the roses from my garden!' – and the accused must improvise a defence or accuse another in quatrains full of riddles and poetic devices. The player who fails to provide an acceptable response is found guilty as charged. Frequently the dialogue games involve a male and a female voice and may be part of old courting practices. As early as 1668 the Jesuit Alzina reported observing *bikal*, verbal jousts in song between boys and girls, each sex amusingly finding fault with the other. The rather functional *pamanhikan* asks for a girl's hand in marriage. One singer represents the groom and the answering voice sets out the demands of the girl. Although cast in game framework, this sung dialogue forms the substructure of indigenous drama, and shows that Filipino performance relates to a pan-Southeast Asian

An Easter-season *moriones*, or *pugatan* drama on Marinduque Island. Longinus is beheaded for his fealty to christ.

pattern of courting games between male and female groups, found in CAMBODIA, LAOS and Indonesia.

Islamic dances Muslim performance, believed to have come to the southern Philippines via Borneo, shows similarity to dance and music traditions of the Islamized peoples of Indonesia and Malaysia. Theatrical aspects, however, are little developed. Dances are generally performed to the *kulintang*, a gong-chime ensemble related to the Indonesian *gamelan*. The subtle grace of dancers who may impersonate princesses and slave girls and the curving gestures of the lower arm correspond to the movement of refined characters in Indonesian dance drama. There is some evidence that Muslim sword dances, probably related to Indonesia's horse-trance dance and *dabus*, contributed to the evolution of the Christian *moro-moro* folk theatricals. No evidence links the Filipino *carillo*, the shadow theatre using rough cardboard figures, with the intricately developed shadow theatre of the Malay world. SHADOW PUPPETry in the Philippines, presented since 1879, emulated, perhaps, European experiments, which were themselves shadows of Asian models.

Hispanic-influenced genres Major theatre traditions that developed during Spanish colonization and Christianization continue to the present. These include (1) religious spectacles; (2) *komedya* or *moro-moro*; and (3) *zarzuela*. Spanish (see ZARZUELA) and indigenous elements fuse in these forms.

Religious customs including dramatizations were introduced by the Spanish in an attempt to displace folk rituals. Popular performances intended to promote Christianity included the Lenten play (*senakulo*), Christmas theatricals (*panunuluyan*), the digging for the true cross by St Helena (*tibag*), and the lives of the saints. *Senakulo*, for example, takes its name from the cenacle where the Last Supper took place. Produced during Holy Week all over the Philippines, these plays, which re-enact the death of Christ, may have evolved from the *pasyon* narrative singing. Plays are in verse, and major religious figures maintain slow, decorous movement and declamation. Peter, old and absent-minded, added comic touches, while Mary Magdalene, dancing and seducing her soldier, helped make the action more stimulating. Self-flagellations and real crucifixions of devotees, undertaken in fulfilment of vows, tableaux and processions, made performances powerful events in community life. *Senakulo* performances continue to the present, especially in rural areas.

Komedya, the major genre of the 17th to the 20th centuries, is believed to have developed from religious plays based on Spanish models. In 1598 a priest, Vincente Puche, wrote a Latin play presented by schoolboys in Cebu. In 1609 the first play in the vernacular concerning St Barbara reportedly prompted many religious conversions in Bohol. By 1619 there were five-day programmes presenting plays on Old and New Testament events and more recent themes, like the martyrs in Japan. The dramas were rehearsed for church celebrations by the sons of the native aristocracy.

The most famous play was supposedly written in 1637 to celebrate a victory of the local Christians over the Muslim leader Kudarat (Corralat). The event was probably first played out in Cavite province by boys, of whom the one playing the Muslim leader was actually wounded. Fr Jeronimo Perez saw the enactment and was inspired to write on this theme, creating the first play known as *moro-moro* or *komedya*. These are plays, affected by Spanish COMEDIA models, centred on the struggle of Christians and Muslims resulting in the marriage of the hero with a princess. Open-air performance at festivals was common and inclusion of clown characters was standard.

Although most scholars trace the form to European models, some counterarguments should be noted. The fight of the boys inspiring the first author could have been a hobby-horse dance, related to the *kuda kepang* trance dances of Indonesia that combine stylized battle with self-mutilation. This argument is strengthened by the fact that some sources cite furious battle dances by six Muslim soldiers at the baptism of a Sultan of Jolo in 1750 as the true source of *komedya*: such dances sound like *dabus*, martial dances still found in Sufi sects of the Malay area. Evidence becomes more convincing if we consider that plots which may involve princesses and heroes marrying after a ritual battle are commonly found after Muslim influence appears in areas as far apart as England, Spain, East Java and the Philippines. The persistence of the name – *moro-moro* ('play of the Moors'), morris dance, morisco – is notable. It is possible that Eurocentric biases are blinding scholars to a significant drama that grew from dances of Sufi mystics and entered the Philippines and other areas with Islamic, as well as Christian, influences.

Likewise, the use of set characters, stylized movement, the popularity of clown characters (*pusong*), the open-air production scheme, and the enactment in the context of a fiesta are features that relate to widespread Southeast Asian theatre practice, not just European models. The belief that the omission of a *komedya* presentation might cause rain and trouble fits a Southeast Asian use of performance to placate supernatural powers. Perhaps even the puzzling lack of scripts prior to the 19th century may hint that like most Southeast Asian performance, scenario rather than text was the generative principle, and indigenous rhyming improvisation games paved the way for actors to create dialogue. Jose de la Cruz and his pupil Francisco Baltazar were prolific *komedya* authors during the form's heyday.

Late-19th-century, middle-class educated Filipinos gave birth to a more literary theatre. Indoor proscenium theatres lit by gaslight appear from the beginning of the 1800s and become numerous around the end of the century. The Zorrilla Theatre (1893) with 400 orchestra seats and 52 boxes was the most noted of these structures. Spanish genres, such as *entremés* ('interlude') and *sainete* (short comic piece written in octosyllabic verse; see GÉNERO CHICO), and Italian OPERAS caught the audiences' attention.

In the 1880s a Spanish actor Alejandro Cubero, the 'Father of Spanish Theatre in the Philippines', and his mistress, actress Elisea Raguer, brought the Spanish-influenced *zarzuela* to the fore. These musical plays on contemporary themes first appeared in the mid-18th century. Spanish remained the language of performance until the United States took over the colony in 1898. By the turn of the century *komedya* had retreated to the *barrios* as a folk performance, and Severino Reyes (1861–1942), a Tagalog playwright, wrote the satirical *zarzuela* play *R.I.P.* (*Requiescat in Pace*, 1902), showing actors burying the old *komedya* form and taking up the new, more 'realistic' musical genre.

Among the new musical plays came performances characterized by nationalistic fervour: Reyes's *Without a Wound* (*Walang Sugat*, 1902) was a stringent attack on Spanish dominance. Foreign heroes and locales were soon replaced with scenes of Filipino domestic life. Most plays were MELODRAMATic entanglements where true love eventually triumphed, yet indigenous characters and scenes were considered a commitment to nationalism and realism. Wing-and-drop scenery and contemporary costuming were prized, and songs became hits of the period. Atang de la Rama was the most noted of performers in the first quarter of this century.

American-influenced genres VAUDEVILLE, called *bodabil* or *vodavil*, made its debut around American bases by 1916. Louis Borromeo, who arrived from the United States in 1921, made the genre important. Troupes included torch singers like the noted Katy de la Kruz, CLOWNS like the Chaplinesque Canuplin, and rockette-like chorus girls. During the Japanese occupation in the Second World War *bodabil* shows, which had long included skits, expanded to include plays. The Barangay Theatre Guild under Lamberto Avellana, one of the foremost groups currently presenting modern drama, began working in this format. *Bodabil* itself later devolved into BURLESQUE-like girlie shows.

Modern spoken drama, too, arose at the time of American intervention in the Philippines, although as early as 1878 the didactic domestic drama *The Ideal Woman* (*Ang Babaye nga Huaran*) was written by Cornelio Hilado in Iloilo vernacular. The first English-language play, *A Modern Filipina*, by Jesus Araullo and Lino Casillejo was written in 1915, and English was an important medium during American rule. In the 1970s the theatre returned to the vernacular: *komedya* and *zarzuela* texts were researched and performed and dance troupes like Bayanihan (founded 1958) and Filipinescas researched indigenous dances and rechoreographed them into dance dramas for modern, urban audiences. The importance of indigenous music, dance and folk arts in contemporary performance and the search for solutions to the dichotomy between young Filipinos' aspirations and reality, is exemplified in such productions as *Oath to Freedom* (*Panata Sa Kalayaan*) which the Peryante company opened on Human Rights Day, 10 December 1984. The injustices of the past (government corruption, unfair labour practices, education atuned to American rather than indigenous models) were explored through song, mime, choral recitation, and visual theatre. The piece demanded that the audience pledge to build a just and free nation that would break for ever with the past. Further, the play has been done in several other countries, either touring or with local casts.

Modern theatre Contemporary Philippine theatre of the 1990s is the direct outgrowth of a century of struggle to shape an indigenous theatre out of the people's colonial past. The first scripted spoken dramas in all of Southeast Asia were written by Filipinos. The so-called 'seditious plays' of 1902–6 emerged while the Philippines was engaged in brutal guerrilla warfare with the United States, and caused its creators to be harassed, if not imprisoned. These Tagalog dramas were written by *ilustrados* (elite) who regarded themselves as heirs to the committed literature tradition of Balagtas and Rizal. Couched in allegory, their inflammatory plays struck a responsive chord with the politicized Filipino populace. Juan Abad's 1902 play, *The Golden Chain* (*Tanikalang Ginto*), is considered typical of the genre. It tells of the persecution suffered by the damsel, Liwanang or 'Light' (the Philippines), at the hands of Maimbot or 'Greedy' (America), and the rescue attempt by her sweetheart, K'Ulayaw (Revolutionary Filipinos). Also suppressed were *I Am Not Dead* (*Hindi Aco Patay*) by Juan Matapang Cruz and *Yesterday, Today and Tomorrow* (*Kapahon, Ngayo, at Bukas*) by Aurelio Tolentino (?1867–1915). Despite its short duration, the revolutionary drama period left a legacy of allegorical theatre and 'people's art' that is vivid with Philippine contemporary theatre practitioners.

Once the fury of the Filipino Revolution had been contained by the Americans, spoken dramas and *zarzuela* sputtered into innocuity, and appeared in the 1920s as domestic tales of bourgeois romance and moral persuasion. The *ilustrados* switched their allegiance to the new rule, and with the coming of 'the second American occupation' – the American education system – they also turned from the vernacular to English. The result was doldrums in modern Filipino drama. American-sponsored educators thought of drama as efficacious only for speech and moral training. The ensuing self-conscious literary homilies could hardly compete with the increasingly popular vaudeville (*bodabil*) and movies of the 1930s.

Even after the Philippines achieved independence in 1946, the urban Filipino elite continued to write their plays in English. Psychological and social REALISM was essayed by playwrights such as Wilfrido Ma Guerrero, Alberto Florentino, Severino Montano, Estrella D. Alfon, and Nick Joaquin who wrote mainly for magazines. Theatre was primarily based in schools, which staged BROADWAY MUSICALS and Western classics. Theatre companies rose and fell with equal rapidity. By their Western-influenced standards, the indigenous product was found wanting. The introduction of playwriting competitions did not make a substantial dent in these attitudes, and plays languished while 'in search of a stage'. However, Joaquin's play, *The Portrait of the Artist as Filipino* (1952), became the most popular English-language play of the 1950s and 60s. While flawed by overwriting, the tragicomic paean to a lost Hispanic-Filipino age of nobility and to human compassion is often lyrical. The presence of the narrator-character, and the (to the audience) unseen painting looming in spiritual potency during the course of the play, were clever and innovative images for its time.

Apart from Guerrero, who was the leader of the University of the Philippines Dramatic Club for three decades, and Joaquin, the work of only a few theatre directors, particularly that of Rolando Tinio, lent lustre to a theatre era (1946–66) that Fernandez describes as 'short-lived, merely transitional, and with an unfortunate alienating effect'. The maverick director, Tinio, anticipated a new age of theatre with his unconventional staging of conventional Western plays.

Two features in Philippine theatre since 1966 set it apart from the other contemporary theatres of Southeast Asia. The first difference is that metropolitan Filipinos had to make a traumatic language change in theatre, from English to Tagalog. This was the initial Filipino route to a 'self-apprehension' that everywhere in Southeast Asia has been the wellspring of decolonization in contemporary theatre. Secondly, the intense and prolonged politicization of contemporary Philippine theatre is also uncommon. The process began with the student demonstrations in the late 1960s, and accelerated with the imposition of Martial Law in 1972. Since then, there swelled a sense that, as Fernandez writes, 'The present has too much urgency. It pressed on the playwright's consciousness too insistently. He had to respond.'

These unique sensibilities were foreshadowed even before Martial Law was declared. Beginning in 1966, Manila audiences were 'shocked' by the 'bold' Tinio translations and adaptations of ARTHUR MILLER, TENNESSEE WILLIAMS and GARCÍA LORCA. In 1967, the Philippine Educational Theatre Association (PETA) inaugurated its 'national theatre' performances of indigenous and avant-garde foreign works in Tagalog vernacular. Theatre took to the streets and other open and crowded places in support of the students' demands for an end to 'American imperialism, feudal corruption, and bureaucratic capitalism'.

The exposure of injustice and the enactment on stage of kinship with the masses surfaced as persistent themes in contemporary Philippine theatre. By digging into themselves, Filipino playwrights and directors exhumed seemingly limitless theatre resources which they reshaped to suit their pressing needs. The resources excavated ranged from *ur*-dramas and epic plays of the pre-Hispanic period, to Spanish-influenced religious and secular dramas, and to the *zarzuela* musical and even its death knell, *bodabil*. One of the earliest deconstructions of indigenous and indigenized performance texts was the play *Monster* (*Halimaw*, 1971) written by Isagani Cruz and staged by PETA. Reviving traditional *zarzuela*, Cruz fused it with a variety of epic, absurd and Broadway-musical devices to convey his dire warning on tyrannical power. Passion plays (*senakulo*) were also refashioned for contemporary purposes by the revival-conscious Babaylan Theatre in the 1970s. This company's *senakulo* series was climaxed in 1977 with the appearance of a radical Christ taking up arms against his imperialist persecutors. A Mass calling on the Filipino clergy to join 'the life-and-death struggles of the nation' was written by Bonifacio Ilagan. Called *The Nation's Worship* (*Pagsambang Bayan*), it was reconstructed street theatre, persuading the audience into communion through the RITUALS of collection, readings and singing. The performance led to investigation of the play-wright by the Martial Law authorities, and detention (for a second time) for the director, Behn Cervantes.

Conventional Western forms were not entirely rejected; instead they were selectively borrowed to serve indigenous ends. The constraints of Martial Law impelled naturalistic playwrights to camouflage their true intentions by 'sticking to the facts'. One of the best-received plays of this genre was Orlando Nadres's *Square Paradise* (*Paraisong Parisukat*, 1974) about a female shoe-store employee. Rediscoveries of neglected and hitherto maligned personalities of the Filipino past provoked a spate of history-based dramas.

In the quest for effective and directly communicable forms of theatre, the University of the Philippines Repertory Company, led by Cervantes, created the 'play-poem' (*dula-tula*). Asian in its suppleness, minimalism and strategies of transformation, this didactic form requires only three performers: a narrator, principal actor and a 'common man' playing multiple roles. Amelia Lapeña Bonifacio in her *The Journeying of Sisa* (*Aug Paglalakbay ni Sisa*, 1976) grafted Japanese *nô* drama techniques to *pasyon*, or 'passion', style chanting to poetically express the anguish of Sisa, a character taken from José Rizal's famous 1886 novel, *Touch Me Not* (*Noli Me Tangere*).

The spirit of the age is perhaps best encapsulated by PETA. A polyfunctional and private theatre organization, it is unique in Southeast Asia. PETA is a performing company and a training centre reaching out to the provinces and to some other Asian countries. As a political action group, PETA is intent on creating political awareness among the masses. Founded and guided by Cecile Guidote, PETA in 1967 built a challenging 'environmental' theatre, the Raha Sulayman, encompassing the ruins of Manila's Fort Santiago. PETA's recent 'nuclear' rock operas sum up its means and ends. *Nukleyar I* (1983) and *Nukleyar II* (1984), performed in song, dance and MIME, blended indigenous and empathetic Western dramaturgies, particularly the anti-bourgeois mischief of SURREALISM, the grotesque of the absurd (see THEATRE OF THE ABSURD), and the 'learning' devices of BRECHT. The outcome was exhilarating theatre designed to transform the audience into active participants in the anti-nuclear cause.

Even before the Marcos regime ended in February 1986, disillusionment was expressed over the blatantly political theatre sponsored by Cervantes and PETA, but more especially that of the latter's clones in the provinces. Beginning in 1984, influential detractors argued that while the radical theatre kept the issues and the struggle against Marcos alive, it had now reached a state of fossilization. They asserted that the politics of committed theatre people were too narrow, the dramas predictable, and the experiences they generated stale and counterproductive. The ending of the Marcos dictatorship found such issue-oriented theatres without a cause and ideologically leaderless.

On the other hand, the poetic voices of the best realistic and expressionist playwrights (see EXPRESSIONISM) – Tony Perez, Paul Dumol, Rene Villaineuva, Jose Dalisay – and directors – Chris Millardo, Nonon Padilla – were discovering supporting echoes within Filipino theatre. One of the most evocative of Perez's works, staged in New York in 1986 and Singapore in 1991, is *Trip to the South* (*Biyahang Timog*) written in 1984. An existential drama, it subtly interweaves the real and metaphorical in exposing the debilitating effects of Filipino feudalism, as embodied by the power wielded by the dead father over his grown children journeying to his funeral.

After a short period of rejoicing and repose following the departure of Marcos, some theatre people were induced to delve deeper into the regional arts, in part so as to develop folkloric aptitude that could be applied to fusion performances. Theatre pieces that emerged veered toward dance drama, as exemplified by the confident works of the Mindanao group, Sinambayok, and PETA's production of Marilou Jacob's *Macli-ing* (1988) that expressed, with anguished rage, the continuing tragedy of the Cordillera people of the north.

Some of the inspiration and financial and moral support for the retrieval in living contemporary form of the regional folk arts, stemmed from the revamped Cultural Centre of the Philippines (CCP), artistically led since 1986 by the theatre scholar and playwright, Nicanor Tiongson. The shining emblem of elite Manila culture under the stewardship of Imelda Marcos, the CCP was restructured, after 1986, into a mini-ministry of the the arts, leading the way toward the Filipinization, democratization and decentralization of the arts. The economic crisis of 1991–92 has forced retrenchment of these ambitions; neverthless, the CCP no longer functions as a 'First World institution in a Third World country'. (See also ASIAN AND PACIFIC ISLAND THEATRE.) KJ

See: J. R. Brandon (ed.), *The Cambridge Guide to Asian Theatre*, Cambridge, 1993.

Philips, Ambrose 1674–1749 English playwright. He was educated at St John's College, Cambridge, where he became a Fellow. His *Pastorals* were first published in 1706. In 1712 his first play, an adaptation of RACINE's *Andromaque*, retitled *The Distressed Mother*, was extraordinarily successful, a surprisingly good neoclassical tragedy. It continued to be popular through most of the 18th century. His later plays, *The Briton* (1722) and *Humphrey, Duke of Gloucester* (1723), were less noticed and he gave up writing plays when he became an Irish MP in 1727. He was nicknamed 'Namby-Pamby' by Swift, undeservedly. PH

Phillips, Augustine d.1605 English actor, one of the original sharers in the LORD CHAMBERLAIN'S MEN, with whom he remained from 1594 until his death. From the slender surviving evidence, we can guess that Phillips was at the social centre of SHAKESPEARE's company of players, that he was a musician and an athlete as well as an actor, and that he was the performer as well as the author of his own *Jig of the Slippers* (1595). In his will he left 30 shillings to Shakespeare and CONDELL and silver bowls worth £5 to HEMINGES, SLY and RICHARD BURBAGE. These were not negligible bequests. PT

Phillips, Robin 1942– British-born director who has established a reputation as Canada's leading director of classical theatre. Phillips came to Canada in 1974 to assume the artistic directorship of the STRATFORD FESTIVAL, where his meticulous rehearsal style and his establishment of the Festival's first Young Company resulted in many innovative and artistically exhilarating productions. Since his controversial resignation from Stratford in 1980, he has directed at several of Canada's major theatres, returning to Stratford in 1986 for one season as director of the Young Company. Another attempt at artistic directorship, at the Grand Theatre in London, Ontario (1983–4), again produced a brilliant repertoire, but its box-office failure resulted in his dismissal after only one season. His exacting artistic standards and need for absolute control, and his tendency towards financial extravagance have, not surprisingly, frequently set him at odds with boards and administrators. In 1991 he was named director general of the Citadel Theatre in Edmonton, Alberta.

Phillips is known as an actors' director, who works through a rehearsal process that first carefully establishes a context from which the actions and the text can emerge, rather than imposing an external directorial idea. His productions are known for their brilliant visual impact – a result of his cinematic style which guides audience perception as though through the lens of a camera – and for his brilliant staging of visual tableaux. DAH

Phillips, Stephen 1864–1915 English playwright and poet, who acted in his cousin F. R. BENSON's SHAKESPEARE company from 1885 to 92. His *Poems* (1898) earned him the prestige of a literary prize and there was briefly an extravagant vogue for his sonorous poetic dramas. TREE staged *Herod* (1900) and *Ulysses* (1902) at HIS [HER] MAJESTY's and GEORGE ALEXANDER produced the pick of the bunch, *Paolo and Francesca* (1902), at the ST JAMES's. But *Nero* (1906) and *Faust* (1908) limped at His Majesty's and *Iole* (1913) and *The Sin of David* (1914) failed without the theatrical flair of Tree or Alexander to back them. Having made and squandered fortunes, Phillips died destitute. PT

Phiri, Masautso fl.1970s Zambian playwright, director, novelist and poet. Active in theatre since 1963, he co-founded with Stephen Moyo the Bazamai Theatre Group in 1970 while a student, and Tikwiza Theatre in 1975. He has written and directed a number of plays including a trilogy on Soweto, plus novels and poetry. RK

phlyax play see GREECE, ANCIENT

Phoenix Theatre (London) The first theatre of this name is better known as the COCKPIT. A second, on the corner of Charing Cross Road and Phoenix Street, was opened in 1930. PT

Phrynichus 6th–5th centuries BC Greek tragedian; an older contemporary of AESCHYLUS, and his most prominent rival. He is chiefly remembered for two tragedies on historical subjects: the *Capture of Miletus*, which according to Herodotus so upset the Athenians that Phrynichus was heavily fined, and the *Phoenician Women*, which influenced Aeschylus' *Persians*. Few fragments survive. ALB

Piaf, Édith [Édith Giovanna Gassion] 1915–63 French singer and song-writer. The daughter of street performers, she began singing in the streets at 12 and, by 17, already a mother, was well ensconced in the Pigalle milieu of whores and pimps. In 1935 she was hired to sing at a chic club by Louis Leplée, who dubbed her *la môme Piaf* (Kid Sparrow). An appearance at the ABC in 1937 made her a star, not least because of the way she used emotion and emotion used her. The brassy voice blaring out of the frail, black-clad body sang of hopeless love and intense suffering, and sounded as if it meant it. With her best numbers, 'L'Accordéoniste' and 'La Vie en rose', she became the darling of the intellectuals, their emblem of tormented devotion. Successful tours of the USA (1949, 1955) and a triumphal return to France in 1956 with 'Milord' and 'Je ne regrette rien' were vitiated by her increasing reliance on drugs. Her addiction and ill health grew until she collapsed during a concert in 1959. After surviving three hepatic comas, she died four years later. JEAN COCTEAU, who had written the monologue *Le Bel Indifférent* for her, succumbed the following day. A biographical play by PAM GEMS, *Piaf* (1980), enjoyed a good run in London and New York. LS

Picard, Louis B. 1769–1828 French dramatist, actor and theatre director, best known as a writer of comedies during the Empire and Restoration. His first play, *Le Badinage dangereux* (*Dangerous Trifling*), was staged at the Théâtre de Monsieur in 1789, and *Encore des Menechmes* (*The Nephew as Uncle*, 1791) established him. He appeared as an actor at the Feydeau and Louvois Theatres in 1796 and at the Odéon in 1798, excelling in the roles of comic valets. His play *The Parasite* (*Médiocre et Rampant*), a COMEDY of manners, was performed at the Théâtre Louvois in 1797 after the burning of the Odéon. In 1799 he made a huge success playing the lawyer, Pavaret, in his own play *Le Collatéral*. In 1801 he set up his company at the Louvois and became known for casting actors according to their physical qualities and defects, rather than according to stock *emplois*. Picard himself tended to shout on stage, and his actors also. However, his plays themselves were praised for their lively sense of observation. In 1805 he staged *Bertrand et Raton*, and in 1806 *Les Marionettes*, considered one of his best plays.

In 1807 he gave up acting, and was made director of the Opéra, which he left in 1815 for the Odéon. He continued to write for the Louvois company, which was not doing very well, but after 1815 he had a series of successes at the Odéon, notably *Les Deux Philibert*, *Le Capitaine Belronde*, *Une Matinée d'Henri IV*, *Vaugelas* and *La Maison en loterie*. With the Odéon fire of 1818 he moved temporarily to the Favart. In 1820 he retired and in the same year his *Les Deux Ménages* (*Two Households*) was successfully staged at the Odéon, and subsequently taken into the COMÉDIE-FRANÇAISE repertoire. His last play, written in conjunction with Mazères, *L'Enfant trouvé* (*The Foundling*), was put on at the Odéon in 1824. JMCC

Picasso, Pablo 1881–1973 Spanish painter and sculptor, who worked primarily in France; perhaps the most significant figure in 20th-century art. Although much of his early work included theatrical motifs, he did not turn to

Fred Pullan's Yorkshire Pierrots, a typical Pierrot troupe, photographed in 1909.

THEATRE DESIGN until his cubist period, when he was asked by Serge Diaghilev, probably at the suggestion of JEAN COCTEAU and Léonide Massine, to design the Ballets Russes production of *Parade* (1917). Over the following eight years he designed seven more ballets and a play, including *Le Tricorne* (1919), *Pulcinella* (1920) and *Mercure* (1924). In all of these he sought to find a means of combining the thematic aspects of the dance with his artistic aesthetics. *Parade*, for example, combines a colourful, whimsical act-curtain reminiscent of his early work, and the cubistic COSTUMES of the Managers that were intended to connect the three-dimensionality of the dancers with the non-illusionist images of the decor. This tendency reached its peak with *Mercure*. Picasso continued to provide designs for the stage as late as 1962 (Honneger's *Icare*), but the later works were generally backdrops or simple scenery adapted from existing drawings. He also wrote two plays: *Desire Caught by the Tale* (1941) and *The Four Little Girls* (1965).   AA

Piccolo Teatro   see STREHLER, GIORGIO

Picon, Molly 1898–1992 American entertainer who began performing as a child in Philadelphia, where her mother sewed costumes for Yiddish actresses. After a stint in VAUDEVILLE, she starred internationally in YIDDISH THEATRE, CABARET and films with husband Jacob Kalich as producer, writer or co-performer. Known for her saucy but innocent gamine charm, through much of her life she was associated with the roles of very young women and even mischievous schoolboys. She also starred in English-language plays and films, such as *Milk and Honey*, *A Majority of One* and *Come Blow Your Horn*, and on television and radio. Her autobiography, *So Laugh a Little*, appeared in 1962. Active well into her 80s, in 1979 she wrote and performed in the REVUE *Those Were the Days*.   NS

Pierrot   An unrivalled illustration of the complexities of a popular stereotype, in its protean nature, its association with particular performers, its tendency to lend and borrow characteristics to and from its figurative neighbours (notably HARLEQUIN), and its capacity to provide inspiration for the avant-garde.

Possibly related to the COMMEDIA DELL'ARTE character Pedrolino, particularly as played by Giovanni Pellesini (1576–1614) – who is recorded as performing in France as well as in Italy – Pierrot appears in France in the second half of the 17th century. MOLIÈRE's appropriation of a rustic figure from French popular literature in *Dom Juan, ou Le Festin de Pierre* (1665) was taken up in 1673 by Giuseppe Giaratone, when the COMÉDIE-ITALIENNE revived its own Don Juan scenario, to create a character at once naive and mischievous. The characteristic loose white costume and unmasked, whitened face seems to have been established by this point.

During the Italians' exile from Paris (1697–1716), their repertory was appropriated by the showmen of the Théâtre de la Foire, where Pierrot became a central figure in the hands of the actor Jean-Baptiste Hamoche and the playwright ALAIN-RENÉ LASAGE, in whose scripts we see the beginning of the sentimentalization of the role.

For most of the 18th century – when the *comédie larmoyante* held the French stage, and even Harlequin, theatrical anarchist *par excellence*, became domesticated in the works of Florian – the Gallicized *commedia* 'masks' took on a new existence in English PANTOMIME, with Pierrot finding a particularly strong interpreter in DELPINI. After the Revolution, the English-trained French actors the Laurent brothers took them back to the THÉÂTRE DES FUNAMBULES, where they were joined (c.1819) by the most influential interpreter of Pierrot, the MIME JEAN-GASPARD DEBUREAU. His exploration of the role's ambiguities, together with the work of his successor Paul Legrand, prompted the post-romantic and modernist fascination with Pierrot which influenced Laforgue, PICASSO, ELIOT, BLOK and Schoenberg, and gave rise to eccentricities such as Margueritte's pantomime *Pierrot assassin de sa femme* (1881). AEG

Pierrot show English seaside entertainment which at the turn of the 20th century successfully supplanted the 'nigger minstrels' who had hitherto dominated the sands. Around 1890 small groups of concert singers from London would perform at houseboat parties in MASKS; in 1891 Clifford Essex introduced a song-and-dance group costumed as PIERROTS in loose blouses with ruffs and pompons in Southern Ireland and the Isle of Wight. These innovations were rapidly taken up, the leading entrepreneurs being Carlton Frederick (Weymouth, 1894), Will Catlin (Scarborough, 1894) and Edwin Adeler (Southport, 1898). In a later format, the Pierrot costumes would be exchanged in the second half for blazers, boaters and holiday attire. The Pierrots' freshness and exuberance were conveyed to the WEST END by H. G. Pélissier's REVUE *The Follies* (Apollo Theatre, 1908, 1910) and the 'Pierrotic entertainment', *The Co-optimists* (Royalty Theatre, 1921–7). Ben Popplewell's *Good Companions* at Bradford inspired J. B. PRIESTLEY's eponymous novel, and several popular comedians, such as Arthur Askey, Fred Emney, Leslie Henson, and Elsie and Doris Waters, served their apprenticeships on the piers. By the time JOAN LITTLEWOOD ironically garbed the players of her anti-militaristic revue *Oh, What a Lovely War!* (1963) in Pierrot costumes, the conventions of the seaside show were regarded as fey and antiquated. LS

pihuang xi Chinese drama (*xi*) using the *pihuang* musical system. *Pihuang* is a telescoping of *xipi* and *erhuang*, two musical styles with a complex history and controversial origin, quite likely in Hubei and Jiangxi Provinces respectively. In 1790 performers from Anhui brought the *pihuang* musical style to Beijing where it became very popular. *Pihuang* style has been freely adapted in many regions, as well as Beijing, forming the musical basis of numerous opera forms. Beijing opera (*JINGXI*) and Guangdong opera (*YUEJU*) are important types of *pihuang xi*. CPM

Piñera, Virgilio 1912–79 Cuban playwright, poet and fiction writer. Piñera studied at the University of Havana and lived in Argentina from 1946 to 58. His first play, *Electra Garrigó* (1948), set off a heated scandal for its bold Cuban treatment of a classical myth. His theatre is characterized by absurd (see THEATRE OF THE ABSURD) black humour and a depiction of reality in intellectual and, on occasion, abstract terms. On the other hand, his *Aire frío* (*Cold Air*, 1962), considered a classic Cuban play, is a

totally realistic vision of a middle-class family before the Revolution. Among his most significant works are *El flaco y el gordo* (*The Thin Man and the Fat Man*, 1949), *Jesús* (1950), *El filántropo* (*The Philanthropist*, 1960) and *Dos viejos pánicos* (*Two Old Panics*), the latter a recipient of the Casa de las Américas prize in 1968. GW

Pinero, Arthur Wing 1855–1934 British playwright. Born in London and frugally educated there, Pinero left his father's law office to become an actor in 1874. He had written 15 plays before 1884, when he abandoned acting to commit himself wholly to authorship, and the work that established him as the leading playwright of his period postdates that critical decision. He was successful in two distinct styles, that of FARCE and that of the social 'problem' play. Of the first kind are *The Magistrate* (1885), *The Schoolmistress* (1886) and *Dandy Dick* (1887). *The Cabinet Minister* (1890) is less sure-footed. Pinero had, by the time he wrote it, established a new reputation as a writer of COMEDY with the outrageously sentimental *Sweet Lavender* (1888), and he risked that reputation with *The Profligate* (1889), controversial in its time simply because its plot hinged on seduction.

Without radically criticizing contemporary moral values, Pinero proceeded to write a succession of social dramas highlighting the plight of women in an unforgiving world. They include the sensationally successful *The Second Mrs Tanqueray* (1893), with its unctuous ending in the wayward heroine's socially expedient suicide, *The Notorious Mrs Ebbsmith* (1895), *The Benefit of the Doubt* (1895), *Iris* (1901), *Letty* (1903), *His House in Order* (1906), *The Thunderbolt* (1908) and *Mid-Channel* (1909). A preparedness to examine, if not quite to challenge, conventional morality is present also in two effective comedies, *The Princess and the Butterfly* (1897) and *The Gay Lord Quex* (1899). Pinero's best comedy, *Trelawny of the 'Wells'* (1898), is a nostalgic celebration of the mid-Victorian theatre, already lost in the era of the long run. Pinero was knighted in 1909. He continued to write plays for the rest of his life, seeking to maintain a hold in a theatre that changed too fast for him. PT

Pinski, David 1872–1959 Yiddish playwright who, like many of his contemporaries, began writing in Eastern Europe (Warsaw) and died in Israel. In 1899 he arrived in America, where he wrote most of his 38 plays, as well as novels, short stories and articles. *Isaac Sheftl* (1896) is a naturalistic TRAGEDY. *The Tsvi Family* (1904) and *The Eternal Jew* (1906) are serious symbolic dramatizations of Jewish history, past and contemporaneous. *Yankl the Smith* (1906), eventually filmed, is a domestic drama about love and jealousy. *The Treasure* – staged first in German by REINHARDT in 1910, then in YIDDISH, and then in English by the THEATRE GUILD – is a COMEDY about poverty and human greed. NS

Pinter, Harold [David Baron] 1930– British dramatist, actor and director, who once acted under the stage name of Baron. His early plays, *The Room* (1957) and *The Party* (1958) which received a short London run, were condemned by most critics as obscure, although Harold Hobson and J. C. Trewin recognized that he was 'a natural

Harold Pinter in his own play, *No Man's Land*, London, 1992.

dramatist'. He clearly possessed an acute ear for dialogue and his plays undeniably contained suspense, even if they did not seem to lead anywhere. Pinter was labelled a writer of the absurd and placed in that loose category (see THE-ATRE OF THE ABSURD) which contained such dramatists as N. F. SIMPSON, EUGÈNE IONESCO and SAMUEL BECKETT. In fact, his only affinity here was with Beckett, whose novels and plays he absorbed with an intuitive understanding. Pinter's one-act play, *A Slight Ache* (1959), has marked similarities with the second part of Beckett's novel, *Molloy*, while the tramp in Pinter's *The Caretaker* (1960) has more than rags in common with the tramps in *Waiting for Godot*. The ambiguity of his writing can be compared with the self-contradiction of Beckett's creatures, but at this point the similarities begin to peter out. Beckett establishes a sense of metaphysical isolation in which nothing is or can be precisely known, whereas Pinter is more influenced by the naturalistic tradition (see NATURALISM), particularly by his Jewish childhood in Hackney in the 1930s during the Fascist demonstrations.

The bullies, Goldberg and McCann, in *The Birthday Party*, are not abstract creations but physical tormentors, whose threats emerge through their studied politeness and speech rhythms. The settings in *The Caretaker* and *The Homecoming* (1965) are precisely evoked and belong to unfashionable London. Pinter likes (if not exactly to confuse) to allow his themes to accumulate layers of possible meanings. *The Homecoming* is ostensibly about a don who returns from a civilized US university campus to his childhood home in North London, bringing his wife Ruth to meet his working-class father, uncle and brothers. But Ruth also brings a feeling of home to the all-male house-

hold, while her internal fantasies are aroused by the surrounding sexual longings. She too comes 'home' to her instincts. While the play's final scene may seem to be far-fetched, where Ruth accepts with alacrity the prospect of being established as a call-girl in Soho, there are clues in the action to make it seem plausible, and the impact was shocking at the time and remains so. Other plays of this time were less complicated, such as *The Lover* (1963), and Pinter, often tempted by minimalism, wrote some powerful sketches which seem misplaced in their context of intimate REVUE.

As his idiom became more familiar and the term 'Pinteresque' was coined to describe anything menacing and enigmatic, Pinter seemed to tire of his former themes and territory. He started to play with notions of time, as in *Landscape* and *Silence* (1969), a double bill produced by the ROYAL SHAKESPEARE COMPANY, which also staged his memory play, *Old Times* (1971). His long association with PETER HALL, which began with *The Homecoming*, continued when Hall went to the NATIONAL THEATRE, where Pinter became associate director. Hall directed JOHN GIELGUD and RALPH RICHARDSON in *No Man's Land* (1975), *Betrayal* (1978), a study of adultery in retrospect, and a triple bill which included *A Kind of Alaska* (1982), in which a patient suffering from sleeping sickness recovers her memory-lopped mind with the help of the drug L-Dopa. His writing became more politically urgent in the 1980s, without losing its minimalist power, and his short plays, *One for the Road* (1984), *Mountain Language* (1988) and *Party Time* (1991), all warn of the dangers of Fascist dictatorship. Pinter has directed several of SIMON GRAY's plays, and in 1992 he played the part of Hirst in a revival of *No*

Man's Land, challenging the still-glowing memories of Ralph Richardson in its premiere seventeen years before.
JE

Pirandello, Luigi 1867–1936 Italian dramatist, novelist and short-story writer. Pirandello was born into a prosperous middle-class Sicilian family, and after studying at the Universities of Palermo and Rome and taking a doctorate in philosophy at Bonn he settled into a comfortable, mildly Bohemian literary life in Rome's café society of the 1890s. During that decade he published several volumes of poetry, wrote short stories, and in 1893 produced his first novel, *L'Esclusa* (*The Outcast*). In 1894 he married, and in the mid- and late 1890s his wife, the daughter of his father's business partner, bore him three children. But the comfort and equanimity of his domestic and literary life were shattered when the family sulphur mines in Sicily were destroyed by floods, leaving his father and father-in-law bankrupt. Hitherto financially dependent on them, now in order to support himself and his family Pirandello was dependent upon a university lecturing post. His wife's mental health gradually deteriorated, and she became prey to suspicions and rages which led eventually to her being confined to an asylum. Pirandello gave up teaching only in 1922. By that time he had begun to acquire international status as a dramatist.

Pirandello turned to playwriting late in his career, after establishing his reputation in Italy with novels, short stories and two critical works, *Arte e scienza* and *L'umorismo* (both 1908). His *Weltanschauung* was sceptical, pessimistic and emotionally deep-rooted, and his fraught domestic life may well have reinforced it. Perhaps the most important of his novels, *Il fu Mattia Pascal* (*The Late Mattia Pascal*) appeared in 1904, and treated of themes he was later to explore in his plays: the elusiveness of personal identity; the relativity of all values; the dependence of the individual on social forms and conventions for self-definition; and the relationship between art, characterized by its fixity, and life, subject to constant flux. Such motives recur, too, in the short stories, some 28 of which he later adapted into plays.

It was his plays which first won for Pirandello an international reputation. Encouraged by the Sicilian actor ANGELO MUSCO, shortly before and during the First World War he wrote a number of one-act pieces for Sicilian dialect companies, then followed these with a series of full-length plays crafted for Italian bourgeois audiences including *Pensaci, Giacomino!* (*Think, Giacomino!*, 1916), *Liolà* (1916), *Così è (se vi pare)* (*It Is So, If You Think So*, 1917), *Il piacere dell'onestà* (*The Pleasure of Honesty*, 1918) and *Il giuoco delle parti* (*The Rules of the Game*, 1918) – plays which made contemporary critics associate him with the *TEATRO DEL GROTTESCO*. By the end of the war his national reputation as a playwright was secure. Perhaps the most influential of all his plays, *Sei personaggi in cerca d'autore* (*Six Characters in Search of an Author*, 1921) provoked uproar when first performed in Rome but quickly came to be recognized as seminal, expressing the early-20th-century crisis in bourgeois social and cultural values and encapsulating the 'modernist' assault on traditional theatre forms. It was the first of his three so-called 'theatre in the theatre' plays which all explored the rela-

tionship between appearance and reality, life and the theatre, private accommodations and social role-playing. The other two, *Ciascuno a suo modo* (*Each in His Own Way*, 1924) and *Questa sera si recita a soggetto* (*Tonight We Improvise*, 1929), have never enjoyed the success or influence of *Sei personaggi*, the PITOËFF production of which in 1924 made an impact in Paris comparable to that of BECKETT's *Waiting for Godot* in the early 1950s.

Throughout the 1920s and 30s Pirandello was remarkably prolific, although the quality of his work was uneven. Among the best-known plays are *Vestire gli ignudi* (*To Dress the Naked*, 1922), *Enrico IV* (1922), *La vita che ti diedi* (*The Life I Gave You*, 1923), the one-act *L'uomo dal fiore in bocca* (*The Man with the Flower in His Mouth*, 1923), *Diana e la Tuda* (*Diana and Tuda*, 1926), *Bellavita* (1927), *La nuova colonia* (*The New Colony*, 1928), *Lazzaro* (*Lazarus*, 1929), *Trovarsi* (*To Find Oneself*, 1932), *Quando si è qualcuno* (*When One Is Somebody*, 1933), *Come tu mi vuoi* (*As You Desire Me*, 1936) and *I giganti della montagna* (*The Mountain Giants*, 1937, posthumously). Some of these were written for, and were performed by, Pirandello's own company, the Teatro d'Arte, established in 1925 with Marta Abba and RUGGERO RUGGERI as lead players, and with which he travelled extensively throughout Europe and Latin America. The company was formed with financial support from the new Mussolini-led government, and many commentators have felt that Pirandello's later years were unhappily compromised by his association – real, but fluctuating and often uneasy – with the Fascist regime, notwithstanding his own attempts to divorce writing from politics by insisting on the irreconcilability of the aims of art and propaganda, and by cultivating – some would say retreating into – a mythological dimension in some of his later work. In 1934 he was awarded the Nobel Prize for Literature, and two years later died in Rome.

Together with IBSEN and BRECHT, Pirandello has been one of the most influential of modern dramatists, yet the extent of his achievement remains peculiarly hard to calculate. The sheer range of his output – plays, novels, short stories, critical and theoretical writings – has militated against any easy classification and assessment. Much of what was once strikingly innovative in his work has now been so thoroughly assimilated as to leave the plays themselves historically stranded: even in his most overtly experimental 'theatre in the theatre' plays, his mockery of directorial authoritarianism and the conventions of bourgeois drawing-room NATURALISM is now rather jarringly *passé*, for all that the objects of his mockery are still evident in much contemporary theatre. His plays dominate the repertory today in Italy and several regularly hold the stage internationally. Yet when revived, outside Italy at least, they invariably provoke a mixed critical response. One problem is that even the finest, like *Sei personaggi* and *Enrico IV*, can today appear irritatingly prolix, marred by excessive discussion and explanation, and by an overly insistent irony.

Pirandello questioned received assumptions about individual personality, the nature of 'reality', the status of theatrical illusion and the relationship between art and life. By stripping away what he saw as self-constructed deceptions he sought to expose the essential 'nakedness' of man in a condition of things subject to constant flux. He opened up the abyss of the absurd. But he never wholly escaped from the pull of the traditions he rejected as he sought to turn the drama of middle-class drawing rooms, character psychology and domestic conflict to serve his 'modernist' perceptions. Striking as many of his theatrical situations are, he still tends to trust verbal discourse more than the theatrical image. As far as English response is concerned translation has proved a problem: not all the plays have yet been made available, nor has much of his occasional writing, letters and such like, been translated. Again, the validity and pertinence of his quasi-philosophical arguments remain contentious, generating suspicions that he traffics meretriciously in melodrama and showmanship. Yet the sheer theatrical power of his best work, in its bitter humour, emotional drive and storytelling power, is undeniable: Pirandello, like STRINDBERG, can disturb and persuade in ways not readily definable by critical explication. And like Strindberg he remains challengingly elusive and a still potent force.   LR

Pires, José Cardoso 1925– Portuguese playwright and novelist. The first of two plays to date, *O Render dos Heróis* (*Relieving the Heroes*, 1965), deals with a historical event, a reactionary peasant revolt of the 1840s that failed, showing it up as an illusory or mythical episode that was marginal to the machinations of those in real power. The approach and techniques employed are highly BRECHTian, with 'alienating' cutting from scene to scene, the mix of 'real' named characters with stock characters as old as drama itself – e.g. Coronel Matamundos (Col. Kill-'em-all), and a blind man who signifies when he wishes to be blind and when he does not by turning over a placard with the appropriate labelling hung round his neck. *Corpo-Delito na Sala de Espelhos* (*Body of Evidence in the Hall of Mirrors*, 1979), Brechtian and absurd (see THEATRE OF THE ABSURD), with more than a touch of the GENET of *Le Balcon*, frighteningly and unforgettably brings the nightmare of the PIDE (Salazar's secret police) to the boards.   LK

Piron, Alexis 1689–1773 French dramatist and poet. His first success came as a regular purveyor of *vaudeville* and operatic parodies to the Paris fair theatres in the 1720s, before he turned to the legitimate stage with a series of plays for the COMÉDIE-FRANÇAISE. Of these, *Gustave Wasa* (*Gustavus Vasa*, 1733), a historical TRAGEDY, and *L'École des pères* (*The School for Fathers*, 1728), a tearful middle-class COMEDY, are of some interest, but it is for *La Métromanie* (*Metromania*, 1738) that he is justly remembered. This is a lively, original comedy on the subject of poetry and poets and has as its central character a young provincial poet with recognizable affinities to Piron himself. He was also famous as the author of witty epigrams directed against contemporary literary figures, especially VOLTAIRE of whom he was a persistent antagonist.   DR

Pisarev, Aleksandr (Ivanovich) 1803–28 In his short career, known as the best Russian *vaudeville* dramatist, combining farcical situations with effective characterization and even some early social criticism. GOGOL condemned the *vaudeville* for 'its light mockery at the funny side of society without a glance at the soul of man'.

However, during the reactionary reign of Nikolai I when freedom of speech and of the press was largely curtailed, the disarming medium of the *vaudeville* became one of the few avenues for superficial criticism into which the audience could read its own deeper meanings.

In spite of his talent for *vaudeville* and verse COMEDY, most of Pisarev's 23 plays were translations or adaptations of French neo-classical models. Basically a conservative in literary matters, Pisarev aligned himself with the classically minded SHAKHOVSKOI circle in its attack of *Moscow Telegraph* editor NIKOLAI POLEVOI, and with Shakhovskoi and IVAN KRYLOV he founded the classicist (anti-romantic) journal the *Diplomatic Courier* (1808). MIKHAIL SHCHEPKIN, the father of Russian realistic acting (see REALISM), took a serious approach to the playing of roles in Pisarev's *vaudevilles The Tutor and the Pupil* (1824) and *The Busybody* (1825), although he preferred to play in the comedies of MOLIÈRE, which also formed part of the standard repertory. *The Tutor and the Pupil* is also noteworthy for its satirical portrait of a stupid pedant named Schelling, a topical reference to the vogue in certain Russian circles for the German philosopher of the same name. Two of Pisarev's works, *The Caliph's Amusements* (1825) and *The Magic Nose, or the Talisman and the Dates* (1825), were dubbed 'vaudeville-operas', indicating a greater emphasis on spectacle-scenic transformations, COSTUMES and dances, well suited to their oriental stories. The first play also offered some criticism of judicial corruption.   SG

Piscator, Erwin (Friedrich Max) 1893–1966 German director, and the leading exponent of political theatre in the Weimar Republic after espousing Communism in the trenches in 1917. His Proletarian Theatre Company (1920–1) developed a no-frills, AGIT-PROP style for working-class venues in Berlin's East End. This led to the CP-sponsored *Red Revue*, a contrapuntal demonstration of Communist vitality and bourgeois decadence, for the 1924 elections; followed during the CP conference in 1925 by *In Spite of Everything*, a documentary REVUE of events from the outbreak of the First World War to the assassinations of Karl Liebknecht and Rosa Luxemburg in 1919.

The script was pasted up from newspapers, parliamentary speeches and memoirs, and backed up with clips from films and newsreels. After using still projections and film clips at the VOLKSBÜHNE to give A. Paquet's *Flags* (1924) and E. Welk's *Storm over Gotland* (1927) a Communist slant, he was forced to resign from the organization. A politicized production of SCHILLER's *Robbers* at the Prussian State Theatre in 1926 brought him private backing for a season at the Theater am Nollendorfplatz, where he developed elaborate machinery for TOLLER's *Hoppla, Such Is Life*, TOLSTOI/Shchegolev's *Rasputin* in 1927, Hasek's *Adventures of the Good Soldier Schweik* and Lania's *Boom* in 1928.

Hoppla presented a cross-section of Weimar society on a four-storey set with back-projected decor. *Rasputin* showed the historical process that replaced the Tsar with Lenin. The set was a revolving hemisphere made of gas-piping and balloon silk which symbolized the world. Segments opened for live scenes, screens were lowered for illustrative projections, and social, political and military data derived from a carefully researched chronology of events was projected on side screens. *Schweik*, which used two conveyor belts as treadmills, had cartoon projections by G. Grosz to satirize Austro-Hungarian officialdom in the First World War. The project went bust after seven months. In *The Political Theatre* (1929) Piscator defines his EPIC THEATRE as expanding the text to expose its sociopolitical context. He resented the later appropriation of the term by BRECHT, who worked on the scripts for *Schweik* and *Boom* and acknowledged Piscator's influence on him.

Piscator went to the Soviet Union in 1931 to make a film. He moved to the USA ahead of Stalin's purges, and set up the Dramatic Workshop in 1938 in New York. He returned to West Germany in 1951, where after lean years as a freelance director he became head of the Freie Volksbühne in West Berlin in 1962. Here he applied the techniques he had devised for adapting conventional plays in the 1920s to develop the documentary plays of the 1960s – in productions of HOCHHUTH (*The Representative*, 1963), KIPPHARDT (*In the Matter of J. Robert Oppenheimer*, 1964) and WEISS (*The Investigation*, 1965). In England Piscator's work influenced JOAN LITTLEWOOD's Theatre Workshop, and in America the LIVING NEWSPAPER productions of the FEDERAL THEATRE PROJECT. HR

Pisemsky, Aleksei (Feofilaktovich) 1821–81 Russian writer-dramatist (non-ideological, sceptical, realistic-naturalistic) who, with his friend OSTROVSKY, brought the common people on to the Russian stage. His play *A Bitter Fate* (1859) is sometimes called the first Russian realistic tragedy (see REALISM). Antecedent in plot, character and theme to LEV TOLSTOI's *The Power of Darkness*, Pisemsky's dramatization of a provincial *ménage à trois* with fatal consequences is largely devoid of Tolstoi's moral didacticism. It was preferred by such knowledgeable critics as INNOKENTY ANNENSKY and D. S. Mirsky. His later plays were mostly historical MELODRAMAS and SATIRES on incipient capitalism in the 1860s and 70s – e.g. *Baal*, 1873, which suggests SUKHOVO-KOBYLIN's *The Case* in theme and intensity. An unallied spokesman for the objective representation of reality, he wrote narrative works including the novels *The Muff* (1850), *A Thousand Souls* (1858) and *Troubled Seas* (1863). He continued the GOGOLIAN tradition of exposing the baser side of humanity and shared with this author a malady that was the subject of his first stage comedy, *The Hypochondriac* (1852). SG

Pitoëff family Russian-French producers and actors. **Georges** (1884–1939) and **Ludmilla** (1895–1951) Pitoëff left Russia, where they had known STANISLAVSKY and MEYERHOLD, for Switzerland (1915–21) and then Paris, where Georges's productions were some of the most significant of the interwar period. A member of the CARTEL, Georges was an outstandingly inventive director in spite of having to work with constant financial difficulties. He is particularly remembered for his productions of PIRANDELLO (*Six Characters in Search of an Author*, 1923) and CHEKHOV, but his repertoire was enormously wideranging and thoroughly international. He was important in bringing both LENORMAND and ANOUILH to public notice. Ludmilla, his wife, was an outstanding actress and something of a mystic. As well as in Chekhov, she tri-

umphed in SHAW's *St Joan* (1925) and in CLAUDEL's *L'Échange* (1937 and 1946). Their son, **Sacha** (b.1920), set up his own company in 1949, which excelled in productions of Pirandello and Chekhov. A powerful actor who exudes a sense of mystery, he has also performed in films, notably Resnais's *Last Year at Marienbad* (1961). DB

Pittsburgh Playhouse (USA) A COMMUNITY THEATRE, established in 1933, that presented its first productions at the Frick Training School for Teachers, Pittsburgh. It occupied the Hamlet Street Theatre (formerly a speak-easy) in 1935 and attempted professionalization. The community withdrew its support, but returned it under the general management (1937–63) of Frederick Burleigh. The Playhouse acquired the Craft Street Theatre in 1952 and edged again towards greater professionalization. Concerted efforts during 1963–8 to establish a RESIDENT NON-PROFIT PROFESSIONAL company brought the organization to the brink of collapse. Point Park College assumed operational control in 1968, making the Playhouse and its personnel its performing arts department and continuing to offer a professional mainstage season. WD

Pix, Mary 1666–1709 English playwright. Her first plays appeared in 1696, a TRAGEDY *Ibrahim* and a lively FARCE *The Spanish Wives*. By the following year she had become well enough known to be mocked with other female playwrights in *The Female Wits*. Her fast-paced COMEDY *The Deceiver Deceived* (1698) was plagiarized by the actor George Powell for his play *The Imposture Defeated*, performed by the rival company. Her friendship with CONGREVE began in 1700. In all she wrote 12 plays, tragedies of heroic sentiment and comedies of witty intrigue; all her work displays a similar concern to defend the independence of her heroines. PH

Pixérécourt, (René Charles) Guilbert de 1773–1844 French dramatist. Pixérécourt, son of a noble family, destitute at the Revolution, turned to the theatre to make a living, his first performed play being *Selico; ou Les Nègres généreux* (*Selico; or The Generous Negroes*, Nancy, 1796). Within a few years he had become the acknowledged father of the newly emergent genre, the MELODRAMA. He also wrote *vaudevilles* and comic OPERAS, but the most successful of his 120 works were melodramas, some of which ran for hundreds of performances. He generally directed his own plays, attaching much importance to the *mise-en-scène*. From 1825 to 35 he managed the Gaîté (see BOULEVARD). His last play, *Bijou; ou L'Enfant de Paris* (*Bijou, or The Parisian Child*), was performed in 1838.

Pixérécourt's triumphal career began with a work originally intended for the Opéra Comique and adapted from the popular novelist Ducray-Duminil (whose novels provided sources for many early melodramas), *Victor; ou L'Enfant de la forêt* (*Victor, or The Child of the Forest*, 1797). The play, with its theme of a virtuous youth discovering his father to be a brigand, shows clearly Pixérécourt's fondness for sentimental moralizing and his view of the theatre as a school for virtue for the popular classes. *Coelina; ou L'Enfant du mystère* (1800; adapted into English by HOLCROFT as *A Tale of Mystery*) set the pattern for melodrama. It exploits the idea of a mutilated 'hero', has an innocent persecuted heroine, a good comic role, an exciting chase and conflict above a ravine, and the final triumph of virtue. It also exploits the pathetic fallacy, the mood of the action being reflected in the scenery and the behaviour of nature. *L'Homme à trois visages* (*The Man with Three Faces*, 1801), with its Venetian setting, conspiracies, and hero who is obliged to play three different roles, established another much followed pattern in the early melodrama. *Tékéli* (1803) was one of Pixérécourt's favourite plays, and one of his most heroic. *Robinson Crusoe* (1805) owed little to Defoe, made much of the noble savage theme, and borrowed Birnam wood from *Macbeth*. *The Forest of Bondy; or, The Dog of Montargis* (1814) owed its appeal to the use made of a dog to prove the innocence of the hero about to be falsely executed. *Christophe Colomb; ou La Découverte du Nouveau Monde* (*Christopher Columbus*, 1815) made an interesting move in the direction of local colour with its savages speaking a language from a dictionary of Caribbean. Over a dozen stage adaptations were made of d'Arlincourt's best-seller novel, *The Solitary*. One of the better versions was Pixérécourt's for the Gaîté, *Le Mont sauvage; ou Le Solitaire* (*The Wild Mountain; or The Solitary*, 1821), with its striking scenic effects by Gué, including a famous vision scene. His *Château de Loch Leven; ou La Captivité de Marie Stuart* (*Castle of Loch Leven, or The Captivity of Mary Stuart*, 1822) managed to have a happy ending.

After 1830 he joined in the flood of Napoleonic pieces now permitted with *Malmaison et Sainte Hélène*. His last major play, and one of his most important, *Latude; ou Trente-cinq ans de captivité* (*Latude, or Thirty-five Years of Captivity*, 1834), was based on a real event, an unjust imprisonment, and the action illustrated well the episodic nature of many melodramas. Pixérécourt had an excellent sense of theatre, but his dialogue was little more than a support for the action, and after his death most of his plays rapidly disappeared from the repertoire. He was one of the founders of the Committee of Authors and did much to ensure the payment of proper royalties. JMCC

Pla, Josefina 1909– Paraguayan dramatist, poet, journalist and critic . Pla was born in the Canary Islands, but has been a Paraguayan resident since 1927, later naturalized. She has written more than 40 plays, some in collaboration with Roque Centurión Miranda, with whom in 1948 she created the Municipal School of Dramatic Art in Asunción. Her best-known play is *Historia de un número* (*Story of a Number*, 1949), an expressionistic (see EXPRESSIONISM), sentimental farce; other plays range from local themes, written in Guaraní (the non-official language) to classical tragedies such as *Alcestes*. She was the winner of the 1984 CELCIT prize for scholarship in recognition of a massive four-volume work on Paraguayan theatre. GW

Placide family Famous actors, less known but equal in American theatrical importance to the BOOTHS or JEFFERSONS. The US Placides begin with **Alexander** Placide (?–1812), a French rope dancer and pantomimist of some distinction, who fled from France during the Revolution. He emigrated to the USA, and first appeared in America at New York's JOHN STREET THEATRE in 1792. He married a Miss Wighten, the daughter of a celebrated London actress. For a time, Placide managed theatres in Charleston and Richmond, and was scheduled for a benefit on 26 December 1811, the day of a disastrous Richmond theatre fire.

Of Placide's many children the best-known was **Henry** Placide (1799–1870), considered one of the finest character actors of the American stage. After appearing as a child actor in 1814, he made his adult debut in 1823 at the PARK THEATRE as Zekiel Homespun. He remained at the Park for 20 years, acting more than 500 roles, 200 of which he created. He attempted one London engagement, unsuccessfully. American audiences considered him best in traditional English comedy, Sir Peter Teazle being among his most successful parts.

Henry Placide's older sister Caroline (1789–1881) married WILLIAM RUFUS BLAKE, and his siblings **Eliza** (?–1874) and **Thomas** (1808–77) both had theatrical careers, Thomas managing the Park Theatre for some years. **Jane** (1804–35), another sister, made her debut in Norfolk, Virginia, in 1820, and in 1823 she appeared in New Orleans, playing there almost exclusively for a decade. At that time she appeared as a singer, as well as a dramatic and comic actress. She was said to be the most polished actress in the South in her time, and was referred to as the 'Queen of the Drama in New Orleans', her Lady Macbeth and Cordelia being especially admired. She appeared at London's COVENT GARDEN in 1834 and died shortly after her return to the USA. SMA

Planché, J(ames) R(obinson) 1795–1880 English playwright, antiquarian and musician whose autobiographical *Recollections and Reflections* (1872) is uniquely informative about 19th-century theatre practice. Planché had his first play produced in 1818, but it was an adaptation from the French of *The Vampire* (1820) at the London LYCEUM that brought him into prominence, not least for its introduction of the 'vampire trap'. For CHARLES KEMBLE at COVENT GARDEN he designed accurate historical COSTUMES for a revival of *King John* (1823), and his research in this field culminated in the publication of *The History of British Costume* (1834). Almost single-handed, Planché had transformed the theatre's view of 'wardrobe'. Already a Fellow of the Society of Antiquaries (1829), he became a member of the British Archaeological Association in 1844 and a Somerset Herald in 1866.

All these activities had outlets in his theatrical practice. Planché wrote over 150 plays and librettos. His libretto for Weber's *Oberon* at Covent Garden (1826) contributed to the opera's phenomenal success. It was written during his year as director of music at Vauxhall Gardens. Planché's most original dramatic work, however, was written for MADAME VESTRIS at the OLYMPIC during 1830–9. *Olympic Revels* (1830) was the first of a rich sequence of charming extravaganzas, tailor-made for the talented and ambitious actress-singer. Wittily rhymed and prettily costumed, these extravaganzas, based on classical mythology, significantly altered the development of English PANTOMIME. Planché maintained the style after Madame Vestris had left the Olympic. In 1845, he embellished her HAYMARKET season with one of his best, *The Golden Fleece*, and ten years later he matched the very different genius of FREDERICK ROBSON with the part of Prince Richcraft in *The*

Discreet Princess. Planché stands as an exemplary figure of the 19th-century British theatre – a man of high standards only too prepared to lower them.   PT

Planchon, Roger 1931– French director, actor and playwright. Planchon is of working-class origins and largely self-educated in the theatre; all his work is marked by the originality and vigour of the young man discovering the great theatre classics for himself, not through the classroom. His first company was founded when he was 21 in a disused printing works in Lyon. In this small (110-seat) auditorium he alternated ebullient musical comedies (mostly scripted by himself and his company) with avant-garde plays by ADAMOV and IONESCO. One of the first directors to produce BRECHT in France (*The Good Person of Setzuan*, 1954), he and Adamov together evolved a Marxist theatre style of great social and theatrical complexity. He coined the term *écriture scénique* (scenic writing) to express the importance of the director's work which should complement that of the author, which he called 'dramatic writing'.

His first production to be shown in Paris was Adamov's *Paolo-Paoli* (1957), which divided the critics, some praising its brilliant mix of theatricality and social detail, others complaining at this production's demystification of the *belle époque*, which made the French capitalism of the period look both ludicrous and murderous. In 1957 he moved to the large municipal theatre in Lyon's workers' suburb of Villeurbanne, where he has remained ever since. Here his work has been particularly characterized by Marxist reinterpretations of plays by SHAKESPEARE (*Henry IV*, 1957; *Troilus and Cressida*, 1964; *Richard III*, 1966), MOLIÈRE (*George Dandin*, 1958; *Le Tartuffe*, 1962 and 1973 (new version); *Dom Juan*, 1980), MARIVAUX (*La Seconde Surprise de l'amour*, 1959) and RACINE (*Bérénice*, 1966; *Athalie*, 1980).

Since 1962 he has written over a dozen plays of his own, many of which he has directed and performed in, notably *La Remise* (1962), *Bleus blancs rouges, ou Les Libertins* (1967), *L'Infâme* (1969), *Le Cochon noir* (1973), *Gilles de Rais* (1976), *Fragile forêt* and *Le Vieil Hiver* (1991). These often present images of peasant life in which clashing ideological concepts are dramatized in realistic scenes of great theatrical force. In 1972 Planchon's theatre received the title THÉÂTRE NATIONAL POPULAIRE and so the mantle of VILAR passed to him. His style is much richer than Vilar's and he does not share Vilar's vision of culture as a uniting force, but by remaining in Villeurbanne he has placed a similar emphasis on making the best of modern theatre available to working-class audiences. Much of his success is due to his ability to retain a small group of fine actors together, notably Jean Bouise, Isabelle Sadoyan and Claude Lochy, who also wrote the music for the company's productions. René Allio designed most of his productions in the 1960s and he has worked regularly with others e.g., André Acquart, Luciano Damian and Ezio Frigerio. He has also encouraged other directors and helped them to establish themselves, e.g. Jacques Rosner, PATRICE CHÉREAU and Georges Lavaudant. In the 1980s and early 90s he devoted most of his energies to trying to launch a new career as a film director. In 1995 he was dismissed from his post at the TNP.   DB

Plater, Alan (Frederick) 1935– British dramatist, born in County Durham, who became in 1970 a co-founder of the Hull Arts Centre. He began writing television plays (see TELEVISION DRAMA), several of which he adapted for the stage. *A Smashing Day* (1965) received a brief London run in 1966 and concerned the problems of a young man who did not know what he wanted to do with his life or whom he should do it with. *See the Pretty Lights* (1970) is a tender love-story between a middle-aged man and a teenage girl. But Plater's true vitality as a writer only emerged when he started to work with song-writers such as Alex Glasgow and in a style of regional 'epics' which owed much to JOAN LITTLEWOOD, combining songs, MUSIC-HALL sketches and comedy GAGS into what were often serious social themes. The most successful of these local documentaries was *Close the Coalhouse Door* (1968), based on stories by Sid Chaplin, which described the history of coalmining as seen through the eyes of the Milburn family. Plater has written mainly for television in recent years, but has provided two plays for the Theatre Royal, Stratford, East London: *Rent Party* (1989), a jazz MUSICAL set in Harlem during the 1930s, and *I Thought I Heard a Rustling* (1991) about *agents provocateurs* in a threatened local branch library.   JE

platt Elizabethan theatrical term for the outline or 'plot' of a play. The Elizabethan platt was not an abstract but a concrete reality. Because plays had to be prepared in haste and performed in repertoire, the BOOK-KEEPER was entrusted with the task of writing out the detail of the plot and hanging it where it could be consulted by actors and stage hands. A few such platts have survived. Written on foolscap, divided into two columns, with marginal notes on properties and sound effects, they generally noted the names of the actors as well as the characters they were to impersonate against the episodes in which they were to appear. The platts were then pasted on to a thin wood pulp board, pierced at the top for hanging.   PT

Plautus [Titus Maccius Plautus] d. c.184 BC The first Roman dramatist to specialize solely in COMEDY, and the first whose work survives. The legends concerning his life are of little value, though it could be true that he worked as a stage-hand or actor before starting to write plays. Not even his name is certain; it is usually given as Titus Maccius Plautus, but all three may be nicknames.

Nor do we know how many plays he wrote. After his death there were said to be 130 circulating in his name, but Roman scholars were agreed that many were spurious. The scholar Varro drew up a list of 21 that were universally regarded as authentic, and these doubtless correspond to the 21 preserved, completely or partly, in medieval manuscripts. The authenticity of all of these is accepted by most modern scholars.

Of the 21, one (*Vidularia, The Wallet Play*) is a mere fragment. Only two are firmly dated, *Stichus* to 200 BC and *Pseudolus* to 192. The others are *Amphitruo*, *Asinaria* (*The Ass Play*), *Aulularia* (*The Jar Play*), *Bacchides* (*The Bacchises*), *Captivi* (*The Prisoners*), *Casina*, *Cistellaria* (*The Casket Play*), *Curculio*, *Epidicus*, *Menaechmi* (*The Menaechmuses*), *Mercator* (*The Merchant*), *Miles Gloriosus* (*The Braggart Soldier*), *Mostellaria* (*The Spook*

Play), *Persa* (*The Persian*), *Poenulus* (*The Wretch from Carthage*), *Pseudolus*, *Rudens* (*The Rope*), *Trinummus* (*Threepence*) and *Truculentus*. All are adapted from Greek originals: three by MENANDER, two by Diphilus, two by Philemon, one probably by Alexis, one by a certain Demophilus, the rest by unknown authors.

There has been much scholarly discussion of the extent to which Plautus departed from these originals. Our increased knowledge of Menander's work has made this easier to assess, but brings dangers, for Menander had a distinctive style of his own which was not simply representative of New Comedy; and there is evidence that some character-types which to us seem peculiar to Roman comedy (such as the braggart soldier) were deliberately avoided by Menander, not unknown to him.

Certainly Plautus' style is far more jokey than that of his models, being full of puns, alliteration, coinages, bizarre imagery and other tricks of language. Even the more serious figures are allowed to come out of character for the sake of a joke, though more often it is the slaves and other low-life figures who joke at their expense. The role of the cunning slave – a likeable rogue who solves all his master's problems with his trickery – is built up enormously, and this character may give his name to a play (*Epidicus*, *Pseudolus*, *Stichus*) as he never does in Greek. Obscenities and topical allusions are not particularly common, but are far more so than in Greek New Comedy. Address to the audience is frequent, especially from the cunning slave; sometimes this is thinly disguised as soliloquy, but Plautus is quite prepared to break the 'dramatic illusion' altogether by acknowledging the audience's presence. The pathos and moral delicacy of Menander are abandoned or undercut, as the cynicism and deceitfulness of the cunning slave prevail over all (though there is some moral edification in *Captivi*). Metres are far more varied than in Menander, large sections of most of the plays being written for musical accompaniment.

Names of persons and places are Greek (or sometimes a comic PARODY of Greek), but Greek institutions and customs are generally Romanized – sometimes merely to avoid puzzling the audience, but sometimes to create deliberate incongruity. *Amphitruo* is the only ancient comedy to survive on a mythical theme, but even here the focus is on intrigue and deception and the characters are familiar Plautine types.

In some plays, such as *Aulularia* and *Menaechmi* (the source of SHAKESPEARE's *Comedy of Errors*), the plot is well sustained and more or less consistent; in others, such as *Stichus*, it is ragged and unimportant beside the element of FARCE and slapstick. No doubt the former plays are closer to their Greek models than the latter. The only case in which we can make a direct comparison, however, is that of *Bacchides*, adapted from Menander's *Dis Exapaton* (*The Double Deceiver*), of which a fragment has been discovered. Here it can be seen that Plautus has altered the structure considerably, amalgamating two speeches, which were separated by an act division, into one. Sometimes, however, the positions of act divisions in the original remain obvious in the adaptation.

The formal prologue, which Menander had used to set the scene, is sometimes abandoned altogether (and some of the prologues we have are probably not by Plautus himself). When it is retained, it not only sets the scene but attracts the audience's attention by means of jokes and direct advertisement of the play's merits. Sometimes it is delivered by an anonymous person who has no other function, rather than by a god or a character in the ensuing action.

Plautus can have had no conception (unlike TERENCE, perhaps) that he was writing literature, to be studied by readers who would criticize the loose ends of his plots, the incongruity of his jokes, and the repetitiveness of his farcical scenes. He was writing scripts for theatrical performance, and it is obvious that he knew his theatre and his audience intimately, and provided exactly what was wanted. ALB

Plavilshchikov, Pyotr (Alekseevich) 1760–1812 Russian dramatist, actor and teacher, who helped to forge the Russian national theatre envisioned by Lukin. After graduating from Moscow University in 1779, he taught history, literature and rhetoric and then embarked on an acting career in Moscow and St Petersburg (early 1780s). As a former student of the famous actor-teacher IVAN DMITREVSKY, he continued the tradition of coolly reasoned playing. Added to this were athletic good looks and a noble countenance, which made him ideally suited for the impersonation of positive heroes, kings and moralizers in TRAGEDY. His search for original ideas in everything he essayed may have been responsible for the assortment of tricks which he employed in such roles as Oedipus in OZEROV's tragedy – all of a sudden lurching and freezing, shrieking and whispering, for effect.

His real talent was expressed in roles drawn from bourgeois drama and *bytovoi* (daily life) comedies. Here he manifested a degree of simplicity, naturalness and sincerity of feeling and expression which in a sense belied his training but revealed his instincts. These works were closer in style and tone to his own bourgeois dramas and doleful comedies on Russian historical, patriotic and colloquial themes. He rejected Lukin's compromise method of transforming foreign plays to a Russian context, and regarded the unities as inconsequential. His comic OPERA, *The Miller and the Mead-Seller as Rivals* (1782), a sequel to KNYAZHNIN's *The Mead-Seller* and Ablesimov's comic opera *The Miller*, favours the miller for his more total Russianness. His comedy *Kuteikin's Agreement* (1789) is a sequel to FONVIZIN's classic Russian national comedy, *The Minor*. *The Landless Peasant* (1790), on the other hand, violates Fonvizin's fiercely satirical spirit by sentimentally depicting the relationship between master and serfs. *The Shopman* (1804) offers a satirical treatment of the Russian merchant class in a state of moral decline under French influence, which foreshadows OSTROVSKY's comedies of the latter half of the 19th century.

Plavilshchikov was also a man of great administrative talents. In 1781 he succeeded Dmitrevsky as supervisor of the Russian theatre in St Petersburg. Leaving for Moscow two years later as a result of a contract dispute with Prince Yusupov, he taught declamation at the Noblemen's Boarding School and trained companies of serf actors, one of which was acquired by the directorate of the Imperial theatres. Everywhere he worked he tried to enhance the standard repertory with new dramatic offerings. In a case of life imitating art, he died in 1812 in a remote province while fleeing the French invaders.   SG

play Play is central to the health and the growth of individual and community. Through play human beings both celebrate and shape their world. It is a dynamic which permeates culture; more a process, a relationship and an attitude than a thing in itself. Play is a free activity, intrinsically self-motivated and non-utilitarian, where attention is voluntarily limited. For the player, absorption may lead to an altered sense of time and/or space, a fusion of action and awareness, and an enhanced feeling of competence, energy and discovery. The activity is often felt to be different, set apart, from everyday life, and in Protestant cultures this division has been rigidified in the opposition of work and play. The uselessness of play is an irritant to a moralistic work ethic, and this rigidity has nurtured a considerable anti-theatrical prejudice.

In many languages the word or words used to express play are at root associated with swift movement, with leaping, dancing, joking. Motion through space and time, fun and make-believe, the flow of appearance and experience, are constituent elements of theatre, and from an early period in England the Anglo-Saxon words *pleg* and *gamen* were used to describe theatrical events of all kinds. Throughout medieval and Tudor times the live performance, that unique meeting between actor and spectators, was known in the vernacular as a play or a game. For this sport, a 'play-ground' or 'play-house' was required and usually, along with other 'play-stuff', a 'play-book' (sometimes with separate 'rolls' for individual players). Many of the artifacts needed for the practice of theatre took on terms related to the central activity. A play in the sense of a literary text is a late and special use of the word.

A play as a script can take many forms. It may be a record written down after the event, like numerous British folk plays transcribed in the 19th and 20th centuries by enthusiastic collectors. It may be an elaborate narrative written down, after a period of oral transmission, in order to stabilize the story but with little concern for the way it is staged, like the manuscripts of Tibetan harvest festival dramas. It may be a schematic aid to performance – outlining plot, characters, entrances and exits, and the disposition of 'props' – like the scenarios or *canovacci* of the *COMMEDIA DELL'ARTE*. Or it may be a literary composition in dialogue form with either implicit and explicit instructions for the players or, as with SHAW and O'NEILL, lengthy novelistic stage directions intended primarily for the reader. This preparation of a text for a reading public alongside the principal aim of notation for performance creates a double focus. Rules and conventions alien to the play as event shape the play as script. For example, the notion of the division of playing time into five acts comes from the world of reading. The performances of PLAUTUS and TERENCE were continuous. In England, the Renaissance interest in this pattern at first affected the printing, far more than the playing, of plays. However, the development of scenic illusion, and the gradual division of actors and audience into separate acoustic spaces, meant that act structure became a substantive part of the play as experienced.

This double focus can lead in literate societies to an undue emphasis on 'interpretation', to a conviction that the play is in essence literature, and, more seriously, to a division of labour which excludes the living writer from direct involvement in theatre-making. Early records in Britain refer to 'devisers', 'doers' and 'makers' of plays and games. These unnamed creators share with most great dramatists, many of whom were actors, a common interest and involvement in the actual activity of play. A playwright is one who works play. That is both the craft and the essence of theatre.   LSR

Playfair, Nigel see LYRIC THEATRE, HAMMERSMITH

Playhouse Theatre (New York City) In 1911, BROADWAY producer WILLIAM A. BRADY built the small Playhouse on West 48th Street for his own productions, which often starred his wife Grace George. With an auditorium seating fewer than 1000, the theatre also contained his own offices and those of other producers, press agents and the League of New York Theatres and Producers. At the age of 81, Brady sold his theatre, which eventually passed to Rockefeller real estate interests in 1967; a year later, it was demolished. Its most notable tenants included the first Broadway production of SHAW's *Major Barbara* (1915), the Pulitzer Prize-winning *Street Scene*, and *The Miracle Worker* (1959). On its stage LAURETTE TAYLOR played her last and greatest role, Amanda Wingfield, in *The Glass Menagerie*.   MCH

Playwrights Horizons American writers' theatre, founded in 1971 in New York by Robert Moss to develop and produce new scripts. Working in two small theatres on THEATRE ROW, the organization – through readings, workshops and full-scale productions – has presented more than 250 new plays, including *Kennedy's Children*, *Gemini*, *Sister Mary Ignatius Explains It All for You*, *The Dining Room*, *Sunday in the Park with George*, *Driving Miss Daisy*, *The Heidi Chronicles*, *March of the Falsettos* and *Later Life*. André Bishop (artistic director, 1981–91) and Paul S. Daniels (managing director) worked with a stable group of resident playwrights that included CHRISTOPHER DURANG, A. R. GURNEY JR, Albert Innaurato, Ted Talley and WENDY WASSERSTEIN. Bishop was succeeded in 1992 by Don Scardino, director of the 1990 BROADWAY success, *A Few Good Men*.   TLM

Pleasants, Jack 1874–1923 British comedian, 'the Bashful Limit'; the *ne plus ultra* of the shy comedian, the beauty of whose act lies in the spectacle of one so ostensibly ill at ease and tongue-tied exhibiting himself solo before a packed house (at the other end of the spectrum lies the brash persona of a MAX MILLER). Discovered at the Scarbrough Taps, Leeds, then the talent-spotting venue for the City Varieties (both still exist, though there is no longer a business connection between them), he opened his professional career at the Varieties in 1884. Following a big success in PANTOMIME at the Theatre Royal in his native Bradford in 1906, he expanded his career outside his northern stamping ground to become a nationally known dialect comedian. He 'wore a costume suggestive of the charity boy who had outgrown his clothes', and carried or sported in his buttonhole his whimsical trademark, a large white daisy. Remembered chiefly for the naive gaiety of 'Twenty-one Today' and the sexual gaucheness of his keynote song 'I'm Shy, Mary Ellen, I'm Shy', he contributed to the longstanding and questionable tradition of regional gormlessness on the English stage. AEG

Pleasence, Donald 1919–95 British actor, who made his first stage appearance in Jersey in 1939. After serving with the RAF during the war, and after being shot down and taken prisoner, he returned to the theatre in 1946, playing in *The Brothers Karamazov* at the LYRIC THEATRE, HAMMERSMITH, and in *Huis Clos* at the ARTS. He joined the BIRMINGHAM REPERTORY THEATRE (1948–50) and the BRISTOL OLD VIC in 1951; and in 1953 he wrote and appeared in his play, *Ebb Tide*, which transferred from the EDINBURGH FESTIVAL to the ROYAL COURT. His voice, soft and expressive, and his slightly plump appearance brought him into demand as a character actor throughout the 1950s, in plays by ANOUILH and PIRANDELLO which received respectable reviews and London runs; but it was not until he played the tramp in HAROLD PINTER's *The Caretaker* (1960), alternately cringing and sinister, that he became a star, repeating his London success in New York. Two other major roles followed, in Anouilh's *Poor Bitos* and as Eichmann in Robert Shaw's play, *The Man in the Glass Booth* (1967), for which he won the London Variety Award for Stage Actor of the Year (1968).

His film and television appearances were numerous, often as sinister German officers in war dramas or mastercriminals; and this stereotyping tended to conceal the range of his acting abilities, which became too rarely seen on stage. In 1991, he played Davies again in a memorable revival of *The Caretaker*, directed by Harold Pinter, which achieved almost as much of the power, if not the unexpectedness, of its premiere 30 years before. JE

Plowright, Joan (Anne) [Lady Olivier] 1929– British actress, who trained at the OLD VIC Theatre School in the late 1940s and joined GEORGE DEVINE's original English Stage Company in 1956. Despite her successes as Margery Pinchwife in WYCHERLEY's *The Country Wife* and as the Old Woman in IONESCO's *The Chairs* (1957), it was only when creating the part of Beatie in WESKER's *Roots* in Coventry and London in 1959 that she emerged as a leading actress of her generation. She met LAURENCE OLIVIER at the ROYAL COURT and played Daisy in Ionesco's *Rhinoceros* (1960), opposite Olivier's Berenger, in an English Stage Company production directed by ORSON WELLES. She joined the NATIONAL THEATRE company when it was formed in 1963, playing a variety of major roles there in subsequent years, including Joan in SHAW's *St Joan*, Hilde in IBSEN's *The Master Builder* and Portia in *The Merchant of Venice* (1970). Her particular quality lies in down-to-earth directness showing few mannerisms and little fuss, but good technical control and much emotional warmth – assets which were particularly helpful in two plays by EDUARDO DE FILIPPO, *Saturday, Sunday, Monday*, produced at the National Theatre in 1973, and *Filumena*, which opened in the WEST END in 1977. She appeared in BEN TRAVERS's last comedy, *The Bed before Yesterday* (1975), in ALAN BENNETT's *Enjoy* (1980) and as Poncia in *The*

House of Bernarda Alba (1987). She married Laurence Olivier in 1961. JE

Plummer, (Arthur) Christopher (Orme) 1929– Toronto-born actor who, after playing nearly 100 roles with the Canadian Repertory Theatre, beginning in 1950, made his New York debut in 1954. In the 1950s and 60s his speciality was SHAKESPEARE; he appeared at the AMERICAN SHAKESPEARE THEATRE (1955), the STRATFORD (Ontario) FESTIVAL (1956, 57, 60, 62) and with the ROYAL SHAKESPEARE COMPANY (1961). Roles included Mark Antony, Henry V, Hamlet, Sir Andrew Aguecheek, Benedick, Leontes, Mercutio and Richard III. In 1981 he returned to the American Shakespeare Theatre as Iago and in the title role and as Chorus in *Henry V*. He was Nickles in MacLeish's *J. B.* (1958), Pizarro in *The Royal Hunt of the Sun* (1965), won the Tony as Best Actor in a MUSICAL version of *Cyrano de Bergerac* in 1973, played Chekhov in NEIL SIMON's *The Good Doctor* (1973), and was praised as Spooner in the 1994 New York revival of *No Man's Land*. In London he played King Henry in *Becket* (1961) and joined the NATIONAL THEATRE at New York's NEW THEATRE in 1971. In 1990 he received the third William Shakespeare Award for Classical Theatre from the Shakespeare Theatre at the Folger, Washington, DC.

His daughter, by actress Tammy Grimes, is actress Amanda Plummer (*Agnes of God*, 1982, Tony), who appeared on the New York stage some nine times during 1979–91, including as Bess Johnson in BETH HENLEY's *Abundance* (1990). DBW

Plyuchek, V(alentin) N(ikolaevich) 1909– Soviet director. Plyuchek was one of MEYERHOLD's pupils in the latter's experimental studio (1926–9), and worked as an actor at the Meyerhold Theatre (1929–32) while simultaneously organizing a Theatre of Young Workers (TRAM). In 1939 he co-founded with ALEKSEI ARBUZOV an experimental Moscow studio where, in 1940, a production entitled *A City at Dawn* was co-created by Arbuzov and the studio's students and directed by Plyuchek. In 1941 the studio became a front-line theatre, and in 1942 Plyuchek was made director of the Theatre of the Northern Fleet. He directed the Moscow Touring Theatre (1945–50) and staged plays at the Moscow Theatre of Satire (1950–7), where he has been artistic director since 1957.

Founded in 1925 on the site of BALIEV's former Bat CABARET, the Theatre of Satire at first duplicated that organization's VARIETY-sketch format. Its search for good domestic satirical comedies, difficult enough in the 1920s, became even harder for its artistic director N. M. Gorchakov during the period of socialist realism (1934–53), when SATIRE was regarded with suspicion. Plyuchek's arrival at the theatre coincided with the Thaw, the new order being announced by his productions of MAYAKOVSKY's now classic satires, *The Bathhouse* (1954, with Nikolai Petrov and Sergei Yutkevich), *The Bedbug* (1955, with Yutkevich) and *Mystery-Bouffe* (1957).

Plyuchek's controversial constructivist stagings *à la* Meyerhold remained in the repertory, thanks largely to Mayakovsky's rehabilitated reputation. Plyuchek became a specialist in staging the hyperbolic satirical grotesque and has produced plays by Russian satirists Ilf and Petrov, poet-editor Aleksandr Tvarkovsky, G. B. SHAW, BEAUMARCHAIS, BRECHT (who received the Stalin Prize in 1954 and thereafter became 'performable' in the Soviet Union), OSTROVSKY, Aleksandr Shtein, ERDMAN and ROZOV. In 1964 Plyuchek was named a People's Artist of the Russian Soviet Federated Socialist Republic. SG

Poel [Pole], William 1852–1934 British actor and director and pioneer polemicist of the return to the bare Elizabethan stage. Poel abandoned office work in 1875 to follow his idol, CHARLES JAMES MATHEWS, into the theatre. It was the beginning of a strangely obsessive and initially piecemeal career. In the early days he was, for a while, manager for Emma Cons of what became the OLD VIC and, during the first half of 1884, F. R. BENSON's stage manager. But his real direction was already evident in his staging of the bad quarto of *Hamlet* on a bare platform in London's St George's Hall (1881). It was an isolated and, with Poel himself as Hamlet, probably an excruciating event, but it heralded his lifetime's mission to rescue SHAKESPEARE and his contemporaries from the restrictions of the picture-frame stage (see THEATRE DESIGN). An 1893 production of *Measure for Measure* was plain and impressive, and Poel's work for the Elizabethan Stage Society (1895–1905) was not only original in itself but also immediately influential on HARLEY GRANVILLE BARKER and, through him, on theatrical ideas through the 20th century.

Beginning with *Twelfth Night* (1895), and including a notable production of *Everyman* (1901) as well as neglected work by FORD, MARLOWE, FLETCHER, JONSON, MIDDLETON, and even CALDERÓN, Coleridge and Swinburne, this unique venture ended with *Romeo and Juliet* (1905). It was not in theatres, but in halls, lecture rooms and courtyards that the Elizabethan Stage Society performed. Critical recognition might have been swifter if Poel had not added to his love of austerity some quirkily fanatical views on voice production. Too often the outcome was risible and Poel increasingly barricaded himself behind his ideas. His voluminous writing is fairly represented by the selection in *Shakespeare in the Theatre* (1913), and his startling combativeness by his rejection of a knighthood, proffered in 1929, because 'it was inconceivable to me that my name could be added to the long list of theatrical Knights not one of whom was in sympathy with an Elizabethan method of presentation'. PT

Poesía en Voz Alta (Poetry Out Loud) Mexican theatre group (1956-63), founded by Juan José Arreola, Octavio Paz, Juan Soriano and Leonora Carrington, all writers and painters; an experimental and controversial theatre project dedicated to the importance of language and poetry in the theatre. Its eight programmes in eight years, with total or partial support from the National University, conceptualized theatre as a game. Despite its stormy trajectory, the movement inspired experimentation in other formats, and produced a new generation of talented directors, including Héctor Mendoza. GW

Poetomachia SEE WAR OF THE THEATRES

Pogodin [Stukalov], Nikolai (Fyodorovich) 1900–62 Soviet journalist and prolific (almost 30 plays) and much decorated (e.g. Stalin and Lenin Prizes) conformist playwright, who embraced socialist realism and myth-making monumentalism as opposed to psychological and social veracity. His unabashedly schematic, 'conflictless' plays demonstrate the inevitable conversion of recalcitrant types to the noble cause of 'socialist construction'. They reflect his own experiences as a labourer and *Pravda* correspondent (1922–30) who travelled to construction sites throughout the USSR. *Tempo* (1929), his first play, attempts via earthy humour and the use of a sympathetic American engineer protagonist to depict the inspiring construction work of the First Five-Year Plan (1928–33). *Aristocrats* (1934), produced by OKHLOPKOV at the Realistic Theatre, depicts the reclamation for Soviet society of prison camp inmates, who became inspired by their work on the Baltic–White Sea Canal project.

Part of Pogodin's creative programme to glorify and humanize the Soviet leadership is his Lenin cycle – *The Man with a Gun* (1937), *The Kremlin Chimes* (1942), *The Third, Pathétique* (1959) – of which the middle drama is the best. Set during Lenin's drive to electrify Russia, it shows the sensitive leader's effect on a disaffected Jewish engineer, who finally agrees to repair the chimes so that they will again play the 'Internationale'. Pogodin's most atypical play, *A Petrarchan Sonnet* (1957), concerns the corruption of a platonic affair by hypocritical busybodies and broaches the subject so relevant under Stalin of the individual's right to the privacy of his emotional life. Its theme, its call for humanism and its attack on the 'new philistinism', and its open-ended conclusion – the antithesis of socialist realism's 'happy endings' – identify this as a drama of the 'year of protest' (1956). SG

Poisson, Raymond [Belleroche] c.1630–90 French actor and playwright, founder of a minor theatrical dynasty. After some years as a provincial actor in the 1650s, he made his debut at the HÔTEL DE BOURGOGNE under the stage name of Belleroche in about 1660 and remained there until 1680, whereupon he became a member of the first COMÉDIE-FRANÇAISE company until his retirement in 1685. He was renowned above all for developing the character of Crispin as a comic type, using his considerable bulk, his large mouth and even his tendency to stutter to advantage, and he became a great favourite of Louis XIV. He was also the author of a number of farcical comedies, the most interesting of which, *Le Baron de la Crasse* (1661), concerns a performance for an audience of country gentry given by some itinerant actors whose leader has been taken to be a caricature of MOLIÈRE. Of the six children he had by his actress wife, no fewer than four took to the stage, notably his elder son Paul (c.1658–1735), who inherited his father's roles when he entered he Comédie-Française in 1686, even preserving the speech defect; while two grandsons also became actors, the elder soon retiring to write plays, and one granddaughter was a dramatist. DR

Polaire [Émilie-Marie Bouchard] 1877–1939 French actress and singer, born in Algeria. Her singing career began in Paris at the age of 14, and her minuscule waist, doe's eyes and bobbed hair (20 years ahead of its time) caught the public's attention. She introduced 'Ta-ra-ra-boom-de-ay' to France, and was taken up by Colette whose *Claudine à Paris* she played (1906). She was also seen in London and New York (1910), billed cruelly as 'the ugliest woman in the world'. After the First World War, she devoted herself exclusively to acting. LS

Poland Theatre in Poland has always occupied a special place in the life of the nation. Constant threats to its very existence have made theatre the guardian of national consciousness. In the unending struggle against censorship and political controls, Polish theatre remains a vital institution. Denied other outlets for the discussion of national issues, Poles find in theatre a public forum where, in response to poetic metaphor and allusion, they may express their feelings and reassert their sense of identity as a people. Even though there has been little Polish political drama, all theatre in Poland becomes political because of the expectations of audiences who look to the stage for what they can find nowhere else. For Polish artists, creating theatre in opposition to the powers that be, under circumstances of adversity, in exile, or underground, has often been a common fate.

The earliest form of Polish theatre was liturgical drama in Latin growing out of the Easter Mass and performed by the clergy. By the 16th century these ritual dramas had already been replaced by mystery plays dealing with the life of Christ and other biblical stories, written in the vernacular and performed in market-places by guild members and paid student actors. Two celebrated Polish mysteries are *The Story of the Most Glorious Resurrection of Our Lord* (1570) by Mikołaj of Wilkowiecko, a Pauline monk, and *The Life of Joseph* (1545) by the Calvinist poet Mikołaj Rej. Combining music, pageantry and spectacular stage effects, the mystery plays often contained farcical episodes and extraneous folk materials, and reflected contemporary manners and dress. Nativity plays spread throughout Poland and served as the basis for the *szopka*, a popular form of puppet theatre presented at Christmas time, which survives today.

Under the influence of Renaissance humanism, the Polish school theatres in the 16th century introduced the plays of SENECA, PLAUTUS and TERENCE, which were given at the court and by University of Cracow students, in both Latin and vernacular adaptations. Jesuit school theatre flourished for over two hundred years – from 1566 to 1773 – staging plays in Latin, Greek and Polish, and using drama as propaganda in the battle against Protestantism.

Court theatre produced a masterpiece in *The Dismissal of the Greek Envoys*, a humanist tragedy by the greatest Polish Renaissance poet, Jan Kochanowski (1530–84). The play was performed by amateur actors for a royal wedding in 1578. Divided into five acts (although only slightly over 600 lines), and with a chorus and messenger, Kochanowski's blank-verse tragedy dramatizes portions of Book III of the *Iliad*, but is actually concerned with topical political issues addressed to the audience of the time. Companies of actors were established at the court theatres, where Italian opera and COMMEDIA DELL'ARTE enjoyed a vogue and foreign plays, particularly French works, were translated, adapted and performed. Italian, French and German companies played at the Polish court throughout the 16th century; and in the private theatres

of the leading nobles, the lords and ladies themselves, their guests, and the servants and serfs (who became the earliest professional actors in Poland) took part in performances on festive occasions.

By the early 17th century, strolling players and buffoons gave public performances in market-places and at fairs, and foreign troupes toured the country. In 1611 a company of English comedians led by John Greene went to Poland with SHAKESPEARE's plays. Native itinerant theatre produced a popular form of drama known as *komedia rybałtowska*, which gave a satirical picture of manners and morals and featured typical characters such as priests, bailiff, merchant and beggar. A good example of the genre is *Peasant Turned King*, written in 1637 by Piotr Baryka.

The evolution of the Polish theatre was disrupted in the mid-17th century by the decline of town life and of the middle class, and by the Swedish invasion. It was not until 1765 that Stanisław August Poniatowski, the last king of Poland, founded the National Theatre in Warsaw and created the first professional company acting in Polish for the general paying public.

Under WOJCIECH BOGUSŁAWSKI's directorship from 1783 to 1814, the National Theatre achieved a high level of excellence and began to develop a repertory of original Polish plays. Because of his prestige as a nobleman, Bogusławski was able to change the status of the actor and make the profession respectable. His leadership of the National Theatre came at the time of Poland's loss of independence due to the three partitions – in 1722, 1793 and 1795 – at the hands of Russia, Prussia and Austria, resulting in the country's total disappearance from the map until 1918. Bogusławski's plays reflect his involvement in the patriotic cause of resistance. Because of its sympathetic portrayal of peasants and mountaineers, *The Cracovians and the Mountaineers* – a national comic opera with music by Jan Stefani – was stopped by the occupying powers in 1794 on the eve of Kościuszko's insurrection against the Russians. After the suppression of the revolt, the National Theatre was closed, and Bogusławski forced to flee to Lwów.

In the course of the 19th century, unsuccessful uprisings – against Russia in 1831, Austria and Prussia in 1846, and Russia again in 1863 – were suppressed and followed by harsh reprisals. Yet the theatrical life continued even under conditions of material and political duress. In fact, Polish theatre acquired new importance for its role in maintaining the cultural, national and linguistic identity of a people which had lost all its own institutions. Although theatres in all sections of the divided country were subject to CENSORSHIP and under constant surveillance, the level of cultural repression in the three occupied zones differed markedly. In the first half of the 19th century, conditions were least favourable in the Prussian-ruled western territory, where a programme of Germanization was in effect and no permanent Polish theatre was allowed. Under Tsarist domination, which encompassed over half the country, including Warsaw, and brought about the closing of Polish universities, some Polish theatre was permitted under severe restrictions. New plays were often forbidden and old ones drastically cut to remove any episodes that might excite thoughts of rebellion. Authors, actors and audiences grew skilful at the game of allusion, and even the most oblique references to Poland, the fatherland or persecution were greeted with applause.

The southern portion of the country, under Austrian rule, known as Galicia and containing the provincial cities Cracow and Lwów, enjoyed more cultural freedom, and it was there that the most interesting theatrical developments occurred. Poland's major comic dramatist, ALEKSANDER FREDRO (1793–1876), came from Galicia and wrote many of his finest works for the theatre in Lwów. His plays bring to perfection the genre of verse comedy that evolved from Polish neoclassical comedy and the French tradition going back to MOLIÈRE.

The most significant event for the future course of Polish theatre was the November Uprising in 1830, begun by Polish army officers. As a result of its defeat more than 10,000 Poles – leaders in politics, the military and the arts – left the country in the Great Emigration. Among those seeking refuge in the West were Poland's two outstanding romantic poet-playwrights, ADAM MICKIEWICZ and JULIUSZ SŁOWACKI, who wrote their dramas in exile without a thought for the practicalities of the stage, knowing that they could not be performed for political reasons.

Romantic drama characteristically exists outside the reigning conventions of performance; modelled after GOETHE'S *Faust* and BYRON'S *Manfred*, the plays of Mickiewicz and Słowacki – and of their politically conservative contemporary Zygmunt Krasiński – share certain traits with the 'dramatic poems' of the 19th-century European literary tradition. Polish romantic drama differs from its counterpart in the West in the power and originality of its theatrical form and in the resonance of its social and political vision. These seemingly unstageable works have in the 20th century become the classics of the Polish repertory and the basis of modern theatrical practice and innovation. Writing as seers about martyred Poland's messianic destiny as the Christ of nations, the Polish romantic poets were able to create an imaginary stage that transcended the narrow conventions of the 19th-century playhouse. In his 16th lecture at the Collège de France in 1843, on the future of Slavic drama, Mickiewicz forecast a theatre that would encompass the various arts, appeal to all classes, emulate the medieval mysteries and draw on primeval rites, and yet utilize the most modern scenic techniques of Italian opera and the Parisian CIRQUE OLYMPIQUE.

The masterworks of Polish romantic drama – Mickiewicz's *Forefathers' Eve* (1832), Słowacki's *Kordian* (1834) and Krasiński's *The Undivine Comedy* (1833) – were called forth by the November Uprising, the first in a long series of lost causes in which Poles have fought unsuccessfully to regain their freedom. In *Forefathers' Eve* Mickiewicz draws upon ancient Lithuanian folklore and primitive religion, and fulfils two of the principal goals of modern theatre: the return to myth and RITUAL and the creation of a total spectacle. Słowacki intended *Kordian* as a counterstatement of *Forefathers' Eve* in an ongoing debate about the role of the artist-intellectual in the struggle for Poland's freedom; it thus introduced what would become a characteristic procedure in the Polish dramatic tradition: response to an earlier work as a springboard for new creativity (an artistic practice not unlike BRECHT'S

Gegenstück). *The Undivine Comedy*, written when Krasiński was 21, theatricalizes the dynamics of violent class revolution (conceived in almost Hegelian terms) in an unspecific European setting, rather than in the context of Polish history, making it a work of universal and prophetic application.

In partitioned Poland, a hidebound theatre lagged behind the other arts and produced results on a par with Western Europe only in ballet and OPERA. The National (a dangerous word) Theatre, which became the Warsaw Theatre on orders from the Russian government that financed it, was known for its drama school and high standard of acting; the repertory was mediocre, consisting mainly of translations, adaptations and imitations of French melodrama. The Tsarist censor was reluctant to allow any plays of social significance, or even Shakespeare's dramas, which showed too many crimes in high places and conspiracies and rebellions. In retaliation the Polish theatres (run by Poles but administered by a Tsarist official) refused to present Russian plays, and guest appearances by Russian companies from Moscow and St Petersburg were boycotted by the Polish public.

Only in the second half of the 19th century, under the influence of the French WELL MADE PLAY and the trend to REALISM, was there a change towards the portrayal of manners and character types. High comedy became the dominant genre, and Warsaw attracted many celebrated actors and actresses, such as HELENA MODJESKA. The cult of the performer and intense public interest in the art of acting were encouraged by the authorities in order to fill the vacuum left in the absence of any political life. Despite the visit in 1885 of the MEININGEN Theatre, the Warsaw stage remained an old-fashioned actor's showplace in which the role was more important than the play or production.

The situation was different in Austrian-ruled Galicia, where a semi-independent Polish administration made possible an advanced repertory, including many plays forbidden by the Prussian and Russian occupations. WAGNER and IBSEN were first performed in the late 1870s in Lwów, the capital of the province, where a new audience of bourgeois intellectuals with progressive political views was receptive to innovations. Always a centre of the fine arts, Cracow, with its small elite public, developed a distinct visual approach to stage production, which it has retained to the present; noted painters such as Matejko and Kossak worked on settings and produced elaborate historical reconstructions.

Throughout much of the 19th century, Polish-language companies toured and sometimes found permanent homes in Lithuania, Belorussia and the Ukraine, and at the same time foreign-language theatres competed for different audiences within Polish society. A German-language stage existed in Cracow, Jewish theatre in Yiddish enjoyed success in both Galicia and the Russian sector, and an Italian opera company played for several months each year in Warsaw.

Modern Polish theatre begins with the movement in the arts known as Young Poland, which flourished in Cracow and Lwów from the early 1890s until the outbreak of the First World War. Drawing upon Western European NATURALISM and SYMBOLISM, the Polish modernist movement in theatre was a brilliant adaptation of foreign influences to the Polish tradition of romantic drama, which finally became realizable on stage. A quieter, more nuanced acting style permitted subtle characterization and revelation of inner life; electric lighting, a painterly approach to design, and a strong directorial hand, all led to the creation of harmonious stage pictures and powerful scenic effects. All subsequent Polish theatre is the result of an alliance between a nationalistic romantic movement and modernist stagecraft and design (see THEATRE DESIGN).

Polish modernism attracted poets, novelists and artists to the theatre. Stanisław Przybyszewski (1868–1927) revealed the torments of the naked soul in lurid dramas of the battle between the sexes; GABRIELA ZAPOLSKA (1857–1921) introduced naturalism to the Polish stage in biting comedies and brutal MELODRAMAS. The most exciting Polish theatrical figure at the turn of the century was STANISŁAW WYSPIAŃSKI (1869–1907), a painter and playwright who continued the work of the Polish romantics and anticipated the ideas of APPIA and CRAIG. Designing costumes, properties and sets for the theatre in Cracow, Wyspiański worked on the staging of his own and others' plays, including the first complete production of *Forefathers' Eve* in a condensed version presented in 1901.

Using Greek theatre and Wagner's music-drama as his models, and drawing upon folk arts, village customs, popular ceremonies, processions and the *szopka*, Wyspiański created a total theatre uniting many arts. The production of his play *The Wedding* (1901) ends with an extended wordless scene, characteristic of Polish theatre at its best. At dawn the drunken wedding guests, weary of waiting for the great revolution that never comes, put down the scythes with which they have armed themselves and begin a slow, somnambulistic dance, a striking theatrical image of stagnation and hopelessness that will be taken up again and again by later Polish writers, film-makers and directors. Because of Russian censorship, *The Wedding* could not be performed in Warsaw, although there were clandestine stagings in private apartments.

After the Revolution of 1905 brought some liberalization to the Russian sector, the authorities allowed private entrepreneurs to establish new theatres. When Arnold Szyfman opened the Teatr Polski in Warsaw in 1913, it was the most modern and best-equipped stage in Poland, with an excellent acting ensemble and directors. Audiences for theatre constantly expanded. To meet the need, state-supported theatre for the urban lower classes was provided, but under strict police control. Regional amateur theatres in the countryside, devoted to preserving local customs and language, specialized in staging huge pageants for mass audiences. Cracow was the inspiration for all the provincial theatres in the period before 1914; it also gave birth to the Green Balloon, a CABARET (modelled on the Parisian Chat Noir) which functioned as a miniature satirical theatre and drew upon the traditions of the *szopka* and its puppets. During the First World War actors from the different sectors were scattered throughout Europe and established Polish theatres in Vienna, Kiev and Moscow.

From 1918, when Poland regained her independence, until 1939, Polish theatre enjoyed a brief but unstable interlude in which it tried to stand on its own feet. Because the government was too poor to subsidize the arts, the bur-

den of financing fell on the cities, but the economic crisis of 1929 made the situation increasingly difficult. Censorship and government interference in the arts continued, but were now directed against anything suspected of being Bolshevik or anarchist, which included almost all forms of artistic experimentation. Writers were harassed and arrested, magazines confiscated and theatres raided. But despite the general mood of hostility to innovation in the arts, avant-garde theatres sprang up in the interwar years. In 1919 Juliusz Osterwa, an actor recently returned from Moscow where he had become acquainted with STANISLAVSKY's work, founded the actors' studio Reduta, which was to be an outpost in the battle against theatrical falsity and conventionality. The company's guiding principles were monastic dedication to truth in art, scrupulous psychological realism and communal effort.

The representative man of the theatre in the interwar years was LEON SCHILLER (1887–1954), who began his career as a proponent of Wyspiański's theatre, made his reputation as a reinterpreter of the Polish classics, and survived war and imprisonment to become the teacher of a new generation of directors. The Ateneum, established by actors from the Reduta, including Stefan Jaracz (1883–1945) who managed the theatre in the 1930s, was known for its repertory of modern plays on social issues. Attempts to establish a revolutionary workers' theatre in Poland in the 1920s ended in disaster. Witold Wandurski (1891–1937), known for *Death on a Pear Tree* (1925), and Bruno Jasieński (1901–37), author of *Ball of the Mannequins* (1931), fleeing persecution and arrest, escaped to the Soviet Union where they perished in concentration camps during Stalin's purges.

The most colourful and controversial figure in the Polish avant-garde between the wars was STANISŁAW IGNACY WITKIEWICZ (1885–1939), whose plays and theories enjoyed little success until after 1956. Another writer who suffered neglect was Stanisława Przybyszewska (1901–35), author of a trilogy about the French Revolution, of which only *The Danton Case* was staged in her lifetime. Innovative Polish dramatists did not find encouragement in the interwar years – from theatres, public or critics.

With the outbreak of the Second World War in September 1939, Poland was again divided and threatened with extinction. Theatre continued to exist in Lwów under Soviet rule until all of Poland came under German occupation in 1941. Collaborationist light entertainment persisted, but most Polish actors refused to appear publicly. Instead, clandestine performances (as during the partitions) were given in private homes, actors secretly trained and theatres set up conspiratorially – most notably, in Cracow, TADEUSZ KANTOR's Independent Theatre (1942–4) and Mieczysław Kotlarczyk's Rhapsodic Theatre (1941–67), in which Karol Wojtyła (later Pope John Paul II) appeared. (He also wrote plays – *Our God's Brother* (1950), *The Jeweller's Shop* (1960) – and essays on theatrical theory.) Wartime theatre also existed in military units and prisoner-of-war and concentration camps.

The first period in postwar theatre under the new communist government (1945–9) was devoted to reconstruction. Not a single theatre had been left standing in Warsaw; devastation elsewhere was great. No centralized control yet existed to impose ideological conformity. The repertory consisted of Polish classics, including some Słowacki (although no *Kordian*, *Forefathers' Eve* or *Undivine Comedy*), Shakespeare and recent Western drama. Once power was consolidated by the Communist Party, Stalinism descended on Poland. In January 1949, at the Congress of the Polish Writers' Union in Szczecin, socialist realism was proclaimed as the only style for all the arts. At the end of the year a festival of Russian and Soviet plays (in which 47 Polish theatres took part) was organized to teach Polish playwrights how to portray 'the building of socialism', and young artists and intellectuals made an effort to adopt the new dogma. In 1951, at the New Theatre in Łódź, Kazimierz Dejmek – whose career has mirrored all the vicissitudes of modern Polish theatre – staged a productivity play, *Grinder Karhan's Team* (by the Czech Vašek Kána), in which an entire factory was faithfully reproduced.

Soviet-dictated socialist realism proved so alien to the Polish tradition of metaphoric, poetic drama that even Leon Schiller, now an active party member, resigned from the directorship of the Teatr Polski in 1951 because he was denied the possibility of staging the national romantic repertory. In late 1954, when the abuses of Stalinism were about to be exposed, Dejmek presented MAYAKOVSKY's *Bathhouse* at the New Theatre as a scathing attack on bureaucracy. In 1955 *Forefathers' Eve* – always a talisman of incalculable power – returned to the stage at the Teatr Polski in Warsaw, attracting audiences from all over the country.

With the thaw in 1956 allowing more cultural autonomy, the great period of modern Polish theatre began. The avant-garde became the mainstream, officially sanctioned and lavishly subsidized, with no restrictions on form, although censorship of content continued, ruling out truthful presentation of everyday social reality, criticism of the USSR and its relations to Poland, and treatment of religious or sexual issues that might offend the Catholic hierarchy and upset the delicate Church–state balance. Given these limitations, the repertory was immense and varied, consisting of 400 new productions a year, the majority contemporary foreign plays.

BECKETT, IONESCO, DÜRRENMATT, FRISCH and the entire Western avant-garde were quickly assimilated and widely performed, after being first published in translation in the new drama magazine *Dialog*. There were also the triumphal stagings, often for the first time, of Polish works from the interwar years, such as WITOLD GOMBROWICZ's *Ivona* in 1957, and especially the plays of Witkiewicz, although CENSORSHIP kept his most political drama, *Shoemakers*, from being publicly performed until 1970. Among new playwrights in the later 1950s, SŁAWOMIR MROŻEK and TADEUSZ RÓŻEWICZ have proved the most enduring, dominating the Polish stage for more than a quarter of a century.

After 1956 theatres became municipally financed and controlled (by local planning committees), with general supervision by the Ministry of Culture and Art. Different functions, audiences and repertories were assigned to each theatre, which presented two or three plays a week, with a yearly offering of eight to ten works which might stay in the repertory four or five years. The artistic director of the theatre chose the repertory in consultation with his literary manager and board of actors. Actors from major theatres appeared in TELEVISION DRAMA. Theatre reviews in newspapers had no effect on the success or failure of a play.

Among outstanding directors are Aleksander Bardini, Erwin Axer, JÓZEF SZAJNA, Andrzej Wajda, Jerzy Jarocki, Zygmunt Hübner, Janusz Warmiński, Wanda Laskowska, Konrad Swinarski, Adam Hanuszkiewicz, Kazimierz Dejmek, Kazimierz Braun, Jerzy Grzegorzewski and Janusz Wiśniewski. Leading theatres are the Stary in Cracow, the Contemporary in Wrocław, the Ludowy in Nowa Huta, the Nowy in Łódź, and the Ateneum, Dramatic, Studio, Polski, Powszechny, Contemporary and National in Warsaw. Landmark productions include Mickiewicz's *Forefathers' Eve* (1973) by Swinarski, Dostoevsky's *Possessed* (1971) by Wajda, and Witkiewicz's *Mother* (1964 and 1972) by Jarocki at the Stary; Mrożek's *Tango* (1965) by Axer at the Contemporary (Warsaw); *Replica* (1972), about the Holocaust, created by Szajna at the Studio; Przybyszewska's *Danton Case* (1975) by Wajda at the Powszechny; *The Story of the Glorious Resurrection* (1962) and *Forefathers' Eve* (1967) by Dejmek at the National, the latter stopped by the authorities for inciting anti-Soviet demonstrations and resulting in Dejmek's dismissal as manager of the theatre.

Other professional theatres of a special nature include the Wrocław PANTOMIME Theatre, directed by Henryk Tomaszewski since 1955, and the Warsaw Jewish Theatre, from 1955 to 1968 led by IDA KAMIŃSKA (whose parents ESTHER and Aleksander headed a Jewish theatre from 1913 to 1939). PUPPET theatres such as the Groteska in Cracow, Lalka in Warsaw and Marcinek in Poznań, draw on both folk and avant-garde sources.

Two outstanding theatre artists, JERZY GROTOWSKI and Tadeusz Kantor, moved outside the official structure in the 1950s, established their own theatres, trained their own actors and created their own texts or radically reshaped existing ones. By the late 1970s both were working abroad. Other alternative forms of theatre have played a role in developing an artistic medium independent of state financing and supervision. The poet Miron Białoszewski set up his Theatre Apart in his apartment, where from 1953 to 1961 he and his friends performed his radical linguistic experiments.

Polish student theatres have been a powerful force for freedom and renewal, leading the struggle against socialist realism in the early 1950s. Part of the university system and financed by student organizations, early groups such as STS, Stodoła and Hybrydy in Warsaw, Pstrąg in Łódź, Bim-Bom in Gdańsk and Kalambur in Wrocław, were not connected to the regime's cultural apparatus and could offer spontaneous commentary on social issues. Some staged plays (including works banned elsewhere); others worked with CABARET, poetry or song. A semi-independent world of culture grew up around the student theatres, with competitions, festivals, workshops, galleries and actors' studios. In the 1970s the Ministry of Culture gave professional status and financing to groups of long standing, so that they could be more effectively controlled. Principal companies are Teatr STU (Cracow), Teatr 77 (Łódź) the Academy of Movement (Warsaw), playing in the streets of urban centres; Gardzienice (near Lublin), recovering folk culture in rural communities; and Theatre of the Eighth Day (Poznań), utilizing the methods of Grotowski's Laboratory (largely ignored by the professional theatre).

During the triumph of Solidarity (1979–81), official theatre was not able to keep pace with the changes taking place in society, although there were staged readings of previously censored poetry. After the military takeover and martial law in December 1981, all theatres were closed. When they reopened in spring 1982, some managers lost their jobs in reprisal for association with Solidarity, and because of the boycott of television theatre the actors' union was dissolved. Censorship, greatly relaxed during Solidarity, was reinstated. Having tasted greater freedom, many artists were not content with the return of restrictions, and performances outside the sanctioned theatres became common.

Clandestine theatre by professional actors and directors using banned texts appeared in homes and apartments. In March 1982, with the curfew still in effect, Jarocki staged ELIOT's *Murder in the Cathedral* at St John's Cathedral in Warsaw, the Four Knights armoured like Polish security forces. Wajda, who in 1984 had staged a highly politicized *Antigone*, for the Easter season the following year presented Ernest Bryll's MYSTERY PLAY, *The Cenacle*, at the church on Żytnia Street in a topical production that equated the plight of earliest Christians and modern Poles through devices such as screaming police sirens. The Theatre of the Eighth Day, denied official status in 1984, found a patron in the Church. In this time of crisis, the Polish theatre reverted to the traditions of underground performance established during the 19th-century partitions and Nazi occupation; by going back into the churches, the stage reaffirmed the atavistic power of its national religious roots.

Despite these acts of defiance on the part of theatre artists, who often risked loss of employment and imprisonment, the mainstream 'official' Polish theatre of the 1980s proved unable to break out of the closed circle of allegory and allusion or to move beyond the accustomed themes of persecution and martyrology presented in the guise of historical drama. In Poland as in other Eastern European countries, the lavishly financed, bloated and overly privileged communist state theatres no longer filled a pressing need; they could not address contemporary social issues or respond to the rapid political developments already producing a more open society. Dissatisfied with the solemn repertory, audiences dwindled. Despite efforts made to offer MUSICALS and light entertainment, younger generations preferred the videos and discos of a burgeoning consumer society. As subsidies were cut, technical and acting standards fell. The once vital Polish theatre deteriorated and sank into stagnation.

Paradoxically, at the same time that it was losing its unique role as a public forum and bulwark of national identity in a disintegrating totalitarian society, Polish theatre achieved increasing recognition abroad and showed signs of influencing Western avant-garde. An effect of martial law, political oppression and economic hardship had been to disperse Polish artists throughout the world, and by the mid-1980s many leading theatre practitioners were working outside Poland. Grotowski closed his

Laboratory Theatre in 1982 and went abroad to pursue his research on the roots of theatre. Until his death in 1990 Kantor constantly toured with Cricot II, creating many of his later works abroad. Because of government censorship and harassment, half of the Theatre of the Eighth Day went into exile. Mrożek moved to the West in 1963, although his plays continued to be a mainstay of the Polish stage. In playwriting no major new talent emerged after the 1960s.

The important productions of alternative Polish theatre in the 1980s – inspired by Grotowski and Kantor – were collective creations. Foreign theatre artists and students made contact with Polish theatre primarily through performing groups at international festivals and workshops or through study with Grotowski and his interpreters. An enduring legacy of Polish theatre to the West has been in the conception of the actor's vocation as a quest for authenticity and technical excellence.

After the collapse of communism in 1989, leading to the abolition of censorship in June 1990, Polish theatre achieved the freedom for which it had so long struggled. But with its oppositional role suddenly removed, the new democratic Polish theatre found itself without clear function or direction. The challenges of surviving under market conditions in an open capitalist society surpass those previously faced when Polish theatre had only to resist a repressive but weak communist regime that paid all the bills. Polish cultural identity is in the process of radical redefinition; the theatre must now find a place in a competitive world in which its own centrality can no longer be taken for granted, as had been the case throughout Poland's troubled history when the stage embodied the national spirit. DG

See: K. Braun, 'The Underground Theater in Poland under Martial Law During the Last Years of Communism (1981–1989)', *Polish Review*, 2, 1993; K. Cioffi, 'Alternative Theatre in Poland, 1954–1989', PhD diss., New York University, 1993; E. Csató, *The Polish Theatre*, Warsaw, 1963; W. Filler, *Contemporary Polish Theatre*, Warsaw, 1977; D. Gerould, Introduction, *Twentieth-Century Polish Avant-Garde Drama*, Ithaca, 1977; A. Grodzicki, *Polish Theatre Directors*, Warsaw, 1979; A. Grodzicki and R. Szydłowski, *The Theatre in People's Poland*, Warsaw, 1975; Z. Hübner, *Theater and Politics*, Evanston, 1992; J. Marek, 'Theatre', in *Polish Realities: The Arts in Poland, 1980–1989*, ed. D. Pirie, Glasgow, 1990; T. Kudliński, *Rodowód polskiego teatru*, Warsaw, 1974; S. Marczak-Oborski, *Teatr czasu wojny 1939–1944*, Warsaw, 1967, and *Życie teatralne w latach 1944–1964*, Warsaw, 1968; K. Puzyna, Prologue, *Theatre in Modern Poland*, Warsaw, 1963; Z. Raszewski, *Krótka historia teatru polskiego*, Warsaw, 1977; H. B. Segel, Introduction, *Polish Romantic Drama*, Ithaca, 1977; M. Semil and E. Wysińska, *Słownik współczesnego teatru*, Warsaw, 1980; Z. Strzelecki, *Współczesna scenografia polska/Contemporary Polish Stage Design*, Warsaw, 1984; B. Taborski, 'Poland', in *Cromwell's Handbook of Contemporary Drama*, New York, 1971; *Teatry studenckie w Polsce*, Warsaw, 1968.

Polevoi, Nikolai (Alekseevich) 1796–1846 Russian critic and journalist. A self-educated son of the merchant class, he brought an unjaded eye but sometimes erring and paradoxical sensibility to his roles as editor-critic of the progressive journal the *Moscow Telegraph* and contributor to the 'officially nationalistic' drama of the Nikolayen era, which glorified the oppressive rule he otherwise opposed. He undervalued two of the century's most significant plays, PUSHKIN's *Boris Godunov* and GOGOL's *The Inspector General* (although they were equally misunderstood by liberals and conservatives in their time). His translation of *Hamlet,* staged in 1837 in Moscow and St Petersburg with PAVEL MOCHALOV and V. A. KARATYGIN in the title role, respectively, was praised by many but attacked for its sentimentalism. The charge of 'Kotzebuism' (see KOTZEBUE), or plagiarized sentimentalism, was levelled against virtually all of the 38 plays that he hastily composed over the last eight years of his life. Of these negligible works, which enjoyed audience and official popularity to match their critical disfavour, the most characteristic was *The Grandfather of the Russian Fleet* (1838). This specimen of time-serving reactionary romanticism was of the same type as KUKOLNIK's *The Hand of the Almighty Has Saved the Fatherland* (1833). Ironically, Polevoi's savaging of the latter helped lead to the closing down of his journal in 1834. While his art was attacked from such diverse quarters as the liberal critic Belinsky and the *vaudeville* playwright PISAREV, his politics were applauded by Herzen and Chernyshevsky, and Belinsky as well. SG

Poliakoff, Stephen 1952– British dramatist, who started to write plays as a teenager and contributed at 19 to a group play about pornography and rape, *Lay-By* (1971), at the ROYAL COURT with such writers as HOWARD BRENTON and DAVID HARE. Three plays produced by London's BUSH THEATRE, *The Carnation Gang* (1973), *Hitting Town* (1975) and *City Sugar* (1975), together with *Heroes* (1975, staged by HAMPSTEAD THEATRE), established his name as a prolific writer with an instinct for depicting the urban deserts of modern Britain, where (as in *City Sugar*) a middle-aged DJ can provide a radio friendship for a teenager to compensate for the loneliness in her (and his) life.

He was appointed writer-in-residence to the NATIONAL THEATRE in 1976–7, during which time he wrote *Strawberry Fields* (1977); but *Shout Across the River* (1978, staged by the ROYAL SHAKESPEARE COMPANY) was a more telling play, in which an agoraphobic mother failed to protect her daughter from the delinquencies of big city life but became cured herself. This play revealed his strengths and weaknesses as a dramatist – a fine sense of urban panorama but a loose writing technique. *American Days* (1979) and *Favourite Nights* (1981), about a girl addicted to gambling, seemed to have been hurriedly written; but *Breaking the Silence* (1984), based on his grandfather's experience as an inventor on the run with his family from the effects of the Russian Revolution, was more tightly constructed, providing ALAN HOWARD with a strong part. *Coming in to Land* (1987) and *Playing with Trains* (1989) had more interesting themes than the results suggested. *Sienna Red* (1992), directed by PETER HALL for his own company, was an experience that both may want to forget. JE

Polichinelle see Punch

Polin [Pierre-Paul Marsalès] 1863–1927 French music-hall performer (see *CAFÉ CHANTANT*), for 20 years a favourite comic singer at the Paris Scala. He popularized the type of the ingenuous private, his cap at a rakish angle, and his songs 'Ah, Mademoiselle Rose' and 'La Petite Tonkinoise' became classics. The originality of Polin's technique lay in standing still, using only a checked handkerchief to make his effects, and in slurring his words to compel the audience's attention. His subtle style had a great effect on Raimu and Fernandel. After the First World War he appeared on the legitimate stage, playing the title role in *The Imaginary Invalid* at the Opéra in 1922. LS

Pollock, Sharon 1936– Canadian playwright, actress and director. Pollock received her early theatre experience in her native New Brunswick, where she returned for a brief tenure as artistic director at Theatre New Brunswick (1988–9), but her main work is associated with theatres in western Canada. Her early plays enact a definite polemical stance: *Walsh* (1973), *The Komagata Maru Incident* (1976) and *One Tiger to a Hill* (1980) use historical situations to oppose condoned systemic racism and injustice. With *Blood Relations* (1980), her version of the Lizzie Borden story, she began to focus on personal conflicts; and subsequent plays, including *Generations* (1980), *Whiskey Six Cadenza* (1983), *Doc* (1984) and *Fair Liberty's Call* (1993), have explored more closely the effects of socio-historical forces on the development of individual subjectivity. In 1993 Pollock became director of Calgary's Garry Theatre. DAH

Polynesia see OCEANIA

Ponnelle, Jean-Pierre 1932– French opera director and designer. Ponnelle studied philosophy and art history at the Sorbonne, music at the Paris Conservatory, and painting with Fernand Léger. He began his design career with Hans Werner Henze's OPERA *Boulevard Solitude* (1952), and continued to design ballets and operas in Europe and in San Francisco for the next decade. His 1962 production of *Tristan and Isolde* in Düsseldorf marked the start of a dual career as director and designer of opera. Together with FRANCO ZEFFIRELLI, Ponnelle is now considered one of the foremost director-designers of opera in the world. Some prominent examples of his work include *Il barbiere di Siviglia* (Salzburg, 1968), *La cenerentola* (San Francisco, 1969), *Pelléas et Mélisande* (Munich, 1973), *Le nozze di Figaro* (Salzburg, 1976) and *Lear* (San Francisco, 1981). His design style is metaphoric and suggests the historical context as the internal mood of the operas. This is perhaps best typified by his controversial *Tosca* at the San Francisco Opera, in which the showy façades of the church were shown as unfinished shells. AJN

Ponsard, François 1814–67 French dramatist. At a time when romantic drama was going out of fashion, Ponsard was seen as a champion of the revival of neoclassical TRAGEDY with *Lucrèce*, inspired by RACHEL and staged at the ODÉON in 1843. In 1846 *Agnès de Méranie* returned to more fashionable medieval themes and in 1850, with *Charlotte Corday*, often regarded as his best work, he was accepted by the COMÉDIE-FRANÇAISE. The play explores different approaches to the Revolution. In 1853 and in 1856 he produced two important satirical comedies on contemporary life, *L'Honneur et l'argent* (*Honour and Money*) and *La Bourse* (*The Stock Exchange*). The first of these ran for nearly a hundred performances at the Odéon and opened the doors of the French Academy to its author. *Le Lion amoureux* (*The Lion in Love*, 1866) returned to the revolutionary period and was an attempt to write a new 'scientific' tragedy. JMCC

Poole, John 1786–1872 English playwright, whose first dramatic work, the *Hamlet Travestie* (1811), established a fashion for BURLESQUE versions of SHAKESPEARE. Only with *Paul Pry* (1825) did Poole again rise above the journeyman level of other hack dramatists, and the credit for that play's extraordinary success must be shared with the actor JOHN LISTON, who played the name part. PT

Popov, Aleksei (Dmitrievich) 1892–1961 Russian-Soviet director and theorist, and teacher of Boris Shchukin and MARIYA BABANOVA, among others. Popov was STANISLAVSKY's pupil and VAKHTANGOV's disciple, acting with the latter at the MOSCOW ART THEATRE's First Studio (1912–18) and directing BLOK's *The Unknown Woman* for his Mansurov Studio (1916). After installing the Stanislavsky system at the Kostroma Theatre of Studio Productions (1918–23), he directed MAT's Third Studio (1923–30; from 1926 the Vakhtangov Theatre) and the Theatre of the Revolution (1930–5), where his productions of *Poem about an Axe* (1931), *My Friend* (1932) and *After the Ball* (1934) established POGODIN's playwriting career. He also staged BULGAKOV's New Economic Policy SATIRE *Zoya's Apartment* (1926), *Romeo and Juliet* (1935, 1948) and *The Taming of the Shrew* (1937), in the last two stressing the social issues underlying blood feuds and anti-authoritarian behaviour. Popov won three State Prizes (1943, 1950, 1951) and in 1948 was named a People's Artist of the USSR. SG

Popov, Oleg (Konstantinovich) 1930– Russian CLOWN, who, after mastering ACROBATICS and juggling, excelled at parodies of circus acts and naive spectators. His type embodies the simple-minded booby Ivanushka of Russian folklore, with his blond Dutch-boy haircut and checked cap. Although adept at satiric sketches, he prefers to fill the pauses between acts, rather than create elaborate numbers. LS

Popova, Lyubov (Sergeevna) 1889–1924 Innovative Russian-Soviet scene and COSTUME designer (see THEATRE DESIGN) who, for MEYERHOLD's production of Crommelynck's *The Magnanimous Cuckold* (1922), designed what is considered to be the first pure constructivist stage set. Influenced in her early career by the mystical Russian painter Mikhail Vrubel and by Renaissance art, her commitment to modern art was strengthened and focused at Vladimir Tatlin's studio (1912–15). She progressed through several creative phases before constructivism, in which she confronted the problems of form (cubism), movement and colour (FUTURISM), abstraction of the object, 'displacement' or 'shift' (related to futurist 'transrationalism'), construction of form and line (post-cubism)

and colour (suprematism). Her talent for thinking austerely, concretely and three-dimensionally led to a series of 'plastic paintings' (1915), reliefs, graphics and lino-cuts (1920–1), in which she explored the creative function of space in art and anticipated her *Magnanimous Cuckold* design. This was a configuration of moving wheels – one large black wheel, bearing the letters CR-ML-NK, and two small red and white wheels – ramps, slides, ladders, stairways and platforms, which interpreted the actions in the script kinetically, in keeping with Meyerhold's 'biomechanics' approach to the acting. This design greatly influenced VARVARA STEPANOVA's for the Meyerhold production of *Tarelkin's Death* (1922) and Aleksandr Vesnin's for G. K. Chesterton's *The Man Who Was Thursday*, directed by TAIROV at the Kamerny Theatre (1923).

Popova's less successful design for SERGEI TRETYAKOV's *Earth Rampant* (1923), also directed by Meyerhold, was an agitational mass-spectacle-inspired montage of real objects – such as vehicles, weapons, telephones, a screen on which were projected slides and films – all set against a huge gantry crane and illuminated by searchlights. Popova's other theatrical designs include costumes for a children's puppet play at the Theatre of Marionettes (1919) and for LUNACHARSKY's play *The Locksmith and the Chancellor* (Korsh Theatre, 1921); fantastic pictorial sets and costumes for Tairov's *Romeo and Juliet* (Kamerny Theatre, 1921) of which the director disapproved, replacing her with Aleksandr Vesnin; and an unrealized collaborative design with Meyerhold and Vesnin for the mass spectacle *Struggle and Victory* (1921). SG

pornographic theatre Participants graphically depict sexual acts, allying exhibitionism with voyeurism. It is only when eroticism has been divorced from any religious, poetic or symbolic significance (or American law's 'redeeming social value') that a performance can be deemed truly pornographic, though moralists have tried to apply that label to erotic manifestations in the theatre throughout history. The Romans of the Empire solicited such exhibitions from their MIME artists, and the Byzantine empress Theodora gave public displays of genital acrobatics during her early days as a circus girl (5th century AD).

Although the Restoration stage has enjoyed a reputation for licentiousness, its one wholly pornographic play, *Sodom, or The Quintessence of Debauchery* (c.1684), a medley of fornication, buggery and incest couched in heroic couplets and attributed erroneously to John Wilmot, Earl of Rochester, was probably never staged. Throughout the 18th century brothels were the usual arenas for sexual exhibition in London: the Rose Tavern in Russell Street offered 'posture women' who posed naked (see NUDITY) on a large platter manipulating a lighted candle (the preparations can be seen in the third plate of Hogarth's *Rake's Progress*). Mrs Charlotte Hayes in King's Place, Pall Mall, invited clients to see a facsimile of a Tahitian fertility rite performed by 12 'beautiful nymphs' and 12 'athletic youths'. Similar shows were provided in Berlin by Mme Schwitz and at De Fontein in Amsterdam. The first exclusively pornographic theatre may have been that run by the Parisian brothel-keeper Lacroix in 1741, but private erotic theatres soon became a fad of the French nobility and their actress mistresses.

The Regent, Philippe d'Orléans, opened one in Montmartre in 1749, where, following the tradition of fairground *parades*, the smut was purely verbal. The best was that of Duc d'Hénin, whose stars were Sophie Arnould and the Comte de Grammont; the realistic Priapées of the house-dramatist Delisle de Sales (Jean B. C. Isoard, b.1745), known as 'the Sade of the drama', required sexual athletes to perform them, and included *L'Air de Mirza*, staged in the actress's bathroom. Other such theatres were the primarily scatological playhouse built by Grandval *fils* for Dumesnil; and those in Paris and Auteuil managed by Geneviève and Marie Verriers (Riteau), the latter the great-grandmother of George Sand. The Prince de Soubise built a superb secret theatre for Marie-Madeleine Guimard, the Opéra dancer and patron of the painter David; the pornographic plays of Collé were cast from ballet girls and directed by the choreographer Dauberval. In Russia, a rougher equivalent was the erotic shows put on by dissolute landowners in their serf theatres.

Times of social upheaval are particularly ripe for this sort of exhibition, and in 1791, after the outbreak of Revolution, a pair of so-called savages did the deed of kind in the PALAIS-ROYAL as a public show. (Similarly in Berlin in 1919 a married couple staged a *Schönheits-abend*, performing the sex act behind a muslin curtain.) But the 19th century returned such displays to the brothel, where Guy de Maupassant's obscene play ambiguously titled *À la feuille de rose, Maison Turque* (*At the Sign of the Rose Petal, Turkish House*) was performed for the Goncourts and Flaubert, who remarked, 'Mon Dieu, this *is* entertaining.' The Theatron Erotikon or Théâtre Érotique of the rue de la Santé founded by Henry Monnier and Albert Glatigny in 1862 was a PUPPET-show playing smutty one-acts for a similarly select gathering. In England, such plays were circulated *sub rosa* but not put on; *The Sod's Opera*, once attributed for no good reason to GILBERT and Sullivan, and the cod PANTOMIME *Harlequin Prince Cherry Top and the Good Fairy Fairfuck*, jokingly advertised as produced at the Theatre Royal Olimprick in 1879, remained closet reading in an age when IBSEN's *Ghosts* was attacked by conservatives as pornographic.

Secret erotic theatres sprang up in Germany after the First World War as part of the black market, but it was not until the so-called 'sexual revolution' of the 1960s that ordinary titillation was augmented by programmatic exploitation of 'deviant' practices. FERNANDO ARRABAL used taboo-breaking simulation of sadism and *bestialité érotique* to rouse audiences from their torpor, and the works of Sade himself were dramatized. Michael McClure's play *The Beard* (1967) which ends with Billy the Kid performing cunnilingus on Jean Harlow was merely a tame prelude to Lennox Raphael's *Che!* (1969), featuring a nude Uncle Sam whose involvement in oral sex and sodomy caused the whole cast to be arrested by the New York police. Much of this blatant sexuality was performed in the name of theatrical experimentation and dadaism; much in protest, as with Tuli Kupferberg's anti-war spectacle *Fuck Nam*. But a good deal was purely commercial, like the clubs that sprang up in West Germany to show simulated sexual acts, while the real thing was offered in US nightspots.

KENNETH TYNAN's revue *Oh, Calcutta!* (1968) garnered contributions from BECKETT, Gore Vidal, Jules Feiffer and others in its celebration of copulation; imitations like *Let My People Come* had less pretence to wit. The boundary lines between Underground and Establishment were entirely effaced, with orgies a commonplace in GRAND OPERA, as in PETER HALL's production of Schoenberg's *Moses and Aaron* (COVENT GARDEN, 1969) and Swinarski's production of Penderecki's *Devils of Loudon* (Stuttgart, 1969); but the buggering of a naked druid in HOWARD BRENTON's *The Romans in Britain* (NATIONAL THEATRE, 1980), though meant as a metaphor for imperialist rape, proved too literal for many. Some sort of climax was reached with the happenings of Austrian Otto Muehl, who slaughtered a pig over the body of a naked woman and then proceeded to abuse her in other less imaginative ways. The prevalence of pornography in film and video-tape has somewhat reduced its allure in the live theatre, freeing playwrights to use the sexual act or leave it alone as dramatic need arises.

Throughout the 1980s, actual rather than simulated copulation took place in the Times Square sexual emporia Show World and Playland; mildly comic REVUE sketches were pretexts for graphic entertainment. The two styles of porno presentation popular in Tokyo during the 1970s and early 80s, *nudo gekijo*, a strip-tease theatre in which the voyeurs were invited to become participants during the 'open stage' segment, and *honban manaita* (chopping board) shows of genital acrobatics, are now illegal but carry on in suburbs and spas. When the AIDS epidemic jeopardized promiscuity, sexual congress was replaced by sado-masochistic demonstrations encouraging audience participation, such as those offered by the Project and Belle de Jour at private New York clubs. Backroom S and M games have now filtered into the plays of Catherine Harrison and Robert Chesley, the performance work of Ruven Hannah and Victoria Baker, and even revivals of Jacobean drama.

Whether or not material is taken to be pornographic depends in part on cultural climate, in part on artistic handling. When ARNOLT BRONNEN tried to depict bestiality in *Die Exzesse* (1918–21), he had to shatter dramatic discourse to express extreme behaviour, whereas ROCHELLE OWENS in *Futz* (1965) simply treated the practice as a cartoon. In both cases, the critics were put off. Feminists are divided between condemning pornography as a degradation of women and promoting it as a life-enhancing liberation. The latter attitude prevails in the performance art of KAREN FINLEY, Annie Sprinkle and others who PARODY standard responses by grotesque caricature. This approach has been misconstrued by conservatives who take the parody to be the real thing, and in the USA neo-Puritanism has even demanded the CENSORSHIP of simulated masturbation on the radio. LS

See: 'Sex and Performance' issue, *Drama Review*, Mar. 1981; *Drama Review*, Spring 1989; A. M. Rabenalt, *Mimus Eroticus*, 5 vols., Hamburg, 1965, *Theater ohne Tabu*, Emsdetten, 1970, and *Voluptas Ludens*, Emsdetten, n.d.

Porte-Saint-Martin, Théâtre de la see BOULEVARD

Porter, Cole 1891–1964 American composer and lyricist. Born into a wealthy Midwestern family, Porter abandoned his plans for a legal career to study at the Harvard University School of Music. He contributed songs to the BROADWAY MUSICAL *See America First* in 1916. After a stint with the French Foreign Legion, he lived in Europe for most of the 1920s. At the end of the decade he wrote songs for two Broadway shows with French settings: *Paris* (1928) and *Fifty Million Frenchmen* (1929). In the 1930s Porter wrote the scores for a series of frothy musical comedies, including *The Gay Divorce* (1932), *Anything Goes* (1934), *Red, Hot and Blue!* (1936), *Leave It to Me!* (1938) and *Du Barry Was a Lady* (1939). His songs for these shows, generally characterized by ingenious lyrics and unusual rhythms, placed him in the forefront of MUSICAL COMEDY composers.

After his legs were crushed in a riding accident in 1937, Porter's creativity seemed to wane. His shows of the early 1940s were financially successful but artistically undistinguished. However, in 1948 he created what many consider to be his most theatrically effective and versatile score: *Kiss Me, Kate*, a musical version of SHAKESPEARE's *The Taming of the Shrew*. During the 1950s he wrote his last two hit shows: *Can-Can* (1953) and *Silk Stockings* (1955).

For most of his career Porter was content with providing sophisticated songs for shows with trivial librettos. As a consequence, although his songs still remain popular, few of his shows are revived in their entirety.   MK

Portugal There are no extant texts of works written expressly for performance before VICENTE's 1502 *Monólogo do Vaqueiro*. There are many references to performers over the medieval period, probably strolling players; and to miming and mimics (see MIME), dating from 1193, where the Latin word *arrimidilum* – *arremedilho* in Portuguese – seems to indicate a playlet or 'turn' in which the actors poked fun at people, often no doubt at butts indicated for them by their royal employers.

Far better documented are the *momos*, a genre linked to the French *momerie*, the Venetian *momarie* and English mummery, at least in the emphasis on DUMB SHOW. The Portuguese term is wide, embracing fairly simple pieces with a handful of masked actors and highly elaborate and luxurious COSTUMES, staging and special effects. The court was the principal patron and the ambient for these productions. We have reference to a princess bequeathing her MASK to a brother in 1276, and a 1413 reference to the existence of a permanent corps of court tailors and weavers specially for such spectacles. There are detailed descriptions of many of the more famous *momos* associated with royal weddings, major feastdays of the Church, and royal entries into such cities as were perforce the temporary hosts of the highly peripatetic court. There was little authentic dialogue in the *momos*: the overwhelming pageantry was accompanied at best by stilted speeches of a formal or diplomatic nature and emblematic and allegorical content. The *momo* developed into much more of a play in the hands of Vicente, who injects life into the dialogue and allegory to produce MASQUES which are highly readable (if too expensive to stage) today – e.g. *As Cortes de Jupiter* (*Jove's Parliament*, 1521), put on for a royal wedding. Apart from *arremedilho* and *momo*, there was a slender tradition of medieval debate and poetic contest, including improvisation, which whiled away many a *serão* (soirée) in the long evenings at court, with the occasional pieces to be found in the anthologies that can be considered as embryonic dramatic monologues or duologues.

For lack of texts from these early four centuries, Gil Vicente, court playwright from 1502 to about 1536, is usually taken to be the father of the Portuguese theatre. His plays, created at a historical and cultural turning point, put everything on stage, in a repertoire that comprises a summation of European medieval theatre and the first Renaissance theatre in the country: SAINTS' PLAYS, MYSTERY and MORALITY, dramatized chivalresque episodes, elaborate allegories on real ceremonial events; *farsas* which are far closer to MOLIÈRE than to his models, the Italians and the Spaniard TORRES NAHARRO; *tragicomédias* which are the truest inspiration for Spanish GOLDEN AGE theatre, and *pastoril* (shepherd) plays in which the early abysmally unlettered shepherds evolve into sophisticated pastoral characters versed in the casuistry of love.

The resources upon which Vicente could call were considerable, and there is much internal evidence of elaborate sets for some plays. There is none, surprisingly, whether internal or secondary, to suggest the building of a permanent theatre within any of the royal palaces or houses, as happened in the courts of other countries. Nor is there any stage direction anywhere to suggest there existed a raised platform, even though many plays cry out for separate stage levels.

On the death of Vicente, court theatre died too. Vicente, with his genius and strong political position at court, overshadowed those of his contemporaries and successors known collectively as 'the School of Gil Vicente'. There are indications that he protected his post jealously, even overzealously, from possible competitors. He had no successor as court playwright. The increasing puritanism of the court and the growth in power of the Inquisition in the middle and late 1500s militated against the emergence of a robust theatrical tradition. Nevertheless, some of the obvious disciples of Vicente had considerable flair. Anrique da Mota (dates not known, alive still in 1544) wrote a number of proto-playlets, of which the *Trovas do Alfaiate* (*The Tailor's Tale*) is the most dramatic. António Prestes (?–1587) wrote about legal affairs, as in the *Auto do Procurador* (*The Attorney's Play*, post-1563) and the *Auto do Desembargador* (*The High Court Judge's Play*); but also, importantly, transferred theatrical interest to the four walls of a bourgeois domestic setting. Jerónimo Ribeiro (dates unknown), with four plays surviving, is best-remembered for his *Auto de S. Aleixo* (*Saint Alexius*, published 1537), the story of a nobleman who for love of Christ forsook home and kin and returned as a beggar to die at his family's door, told with a moving dignity and poignancy.

With António Ribeiro Chiado (?–1591), the theatre effectively goes public, finding its audience in the squares of Lisbon (one of the most central is named after him). Two plays with *Prática ...* (*Conversation ...*) in their titles evince his enormous talent for creating character linguistically; the *Auto das Regateiras* (*The Fishwives' Play*) is racy lower-class comedy – mothers scheming to marry off their daughters, who then, like Vicente's Inês Pereira, give free rein to their sensuality with a variety of suitors. *The Auto* da Natural Invenção (*The Play of Native Wit* – Chiado's – performed between 1545 and 1557) depicts the antics of a band of the by-then familiar travelling theatricals. They put up at a boarding house, whose landlord rashly decides to have them put on a show and even pay them for the performance. He repents too late ...

A neoclassical school, initiated by the poet Sá de Miranda (?1481–1558) on his return from Italy in 1527, naturalized the new comedy in Portuguese. *Os Estrangeiros* (*The Foreigners*, 1528) and *Os Vilhalpandos* (a family name, 1538) were both given first performances in Coimbra. They are five-acters, respect the three unities and have a deal of wit, but not quite the verve of Vicente. Sá de Miranda's lead in the comedy was followed by ANTÓNIO FERREIRA in two plays: *A Comédia do Franchono* (also, perhaps, more commonly known as *O Bristo*, 1564), about two friends, rivals in love, and two braggart soldiers who owe much to PLAUTUS' *milites gloriosi*; and *O Cioso* (*The Jealous Man*), a TERENCE-like treatment of a twice-cuckolded husband.

The neoclassical tragedy was a genre cultivated at the university, and largely the province of humanists and men of letters. A version of the *Electra* dates from 1537, to be followed by a spate of versions of Greek and Roman plays, with some originals, from 1547 onwards at Coimbra University. The high point in this theatre is António Ferreira's *Castro*, a tragedy on national history, with a Christian dimension of free will and action that depends less on fatality than on the clash of individuals' options – a formula that was not to be used again with such success until RACINE.

Luís de Camões (1525–80), the country's greatest epic and lyric poet, created three hybrid plays in which the classical plot and theme, faithfully followed, are set in contemporary Portugal and couched in a language closer to Vicente and the colloquial usage. *O Auto dos Enfatriões* (performed between 1543 and 1549 at Coimbra) is one of the worthiest plays from the long line stretching from Plautus' *Amphitruo* to GIRAUDOUX's *Amphitryon 38*. *El-Rei Seleuco* (*King Seleucus*, also 1543–9) also deals with a classical episode, from Plutarch. *Filodemo* (*Philodemus*), a PASTORAL drama on love themes, had its first performance in Goa in 1555 and would stand revival, at least before an academic audience.

With the Philippine (Spanish) annexation of the Portuguese state from 1580 to 1640, and increasingly harsh Inquisition CENSORSHIP, the theatre went into almost total eclipse. The Jesuits monopolized the national stage with their doctrinal expositions of biblical, dogmatic and classical themes, characterized by an excess of rhetoric and a corresponding lack of dramatic dialogue and contact with real life – this from the late 1500s to the late 1700s! Lacking in dramatic vigour, these plays were strong on spectacle, and do provide a link between the lavish *momos* and the richly spectacular Italian OPERA which came to dominate taste in the 1700s. Both needed large amounts of money for their staging: a 1619 play about the discoveries in the East featured 300-odd actors, and over 5000 precious stones adorned the principals in homage to Philip II (III of Spain); the 18th-century Brazilian bonanza permitted Lisbon to become one of opera's most munificent patrons.

The only 17th-century play worth (and well worth) revival is the comedy-farce *O Fidalgo Aprendiz* (*The Apprentice Nobleman*, 1646), in which D. Francisco Manuel de Mello (1608–66) brings together the tight construction of the Spanish cloak-and-dagger drama and the native tradition. A boorish minor provincial nobleman comes to Lisbon and, the better to get embroiled in amorous intrigue, takes lessons from a *maître d'armes*, a dancing master and a versifier. A transparent (if unproven) model for *Le Bourgeois Gentilhomme*, the play not only exploits specific situations, with comedy of movement as well as of language, but also delivers a swingeing attack on those aspects of Portuguese society life – most – that Mello found wanting. The 18th century, too, is fairly devoid of truly dramatic activity. Opera ruled, and the common people had to be content with puppet theatre. But they had their own venues, theatres in Lisbon's Bairro Alto, and commissioned their own plays. The best writer of these plays, ANTÓNIO JOSÉ DA SILVA, used PUPPETS, interpolated operatic ARIAS and used weird and wonderful stage machinery for 'magic' effects. The dialogue is fanciful and incisively witty. Silva's successors wrote more for the reader than for the playgoer, combining their own armchair theatre with the conscientious translation of French plays and dramatic criticism, Racine and BOILEAU more particularly, and later the Italians. Self-titled Arcadians, their theatre was academic.

The man who made the leap between, or more properly combined, neoclassical and romantic was JOÃO BAPTISTA DE ALMEIDA GARRETT, first director and resident dramatist of the National Theatre, inaugurated in 1846. After him, reacting to outside influence, the native bent of the Portuguese for SATIRE found a voice in the theatre of the REVISTA (from 1859 to the present), a pantechnicon genre eschewing little but strictly legitimate theatre. Drama went somewhat morbidly naturalistic (see NATURALISM) and vaguely socialistic in thesis or problem plays, especially those of Gomes de Amorim (1827–91), with giveaway titles like *Ódio de Raça* (*Race Hatred*, 1854) and *Aleijões Sociais* (*Society's Deformities*, published 1870, previously performed as *A Escravatura Branca*, *White Slavery*). Mendes Leal (1818–86) was the most successful of these dramatists, but even his best work, e.g. *Pobreza Envergonhada* (*The Shame of Poverty*, 1864), is oversentimental and unconvincing in psychology, and points a doubtfully valid moral.

At the turn of the century, we find dramatists of greater refinement. Júlio Dantas (1876–1962) attracted much personal opprobrium, seen as he was as the regime's official author and playwright, but his 20-odd plays were extremely popular, especially *A Ceia dos Cardeais* (*The Cardinals' Supper*, 1902). Three cardinals – one Italian, one French and one Portuguese – meet for supper in the Vatican, and over a pheasant stuffed with truffles discuss the amours of their youth, in so doing portraying their national way of being madly in love. Nostalgic, anodyne, it was, and is, nevertheless a marvellous vehicle for virtuoso acting, an important factor in the play's long success. More substantial as a middle-class dramatist was D. João da Câmara (1852–1908), who, starting by writing somewhat romantic historical dramas, then graduated through a poetic REALISM to tentative essays in symbolist (see SYMBOLISM) and verse drama. His best-known play, *Os Velhos* (*The Old Folk*, 1893), set in 1874, deals with the expropriation of the peasants' land for the spreading railway network, but concentrates more on the loving portrayal of character than on the happenings. His later plays were ahead of public taste.

Legitimate theatre became esoteric in the First World War years and in the 1920s, with much experimentation by poets open to the European influences – FUTURISM and dada, for example. None of these major lyric poets, however – Eugénio de Castro (1869–1944), Fernando Pessoa (1888–1935), Mário de Sá-Carneiro (1890–1916) – left a lasting mark on the theatre.

Alfredo Cortez (1890–1946), no poet, is one of three writers with a truly theatrical talent. With 11 plays to his credit, he more than any contemporary brought new theatrical experiences to his public. His *Zilda* (1921) is a portrayal of a self-willed, narcissistic and essentially empty woman, a free agent in the IBSEN mould, or amoral – according to the eye of the beholder – and, simultaneously, the unmasking of a society that has lost its bearings. Another play, *Gladiadores* (*Gladiators*, 1934), is a 'caricature of the age in which we live', using techniques learned with PIRANDELLO (ten male and ten female characters reacting fluidly to successive situations) and from SURREALISM and EXPRESSIONISM. RAÚL BRANDÃO, also ahead of his time, wrote of cripples, physical and social, and grotesques in existential dramas that allowed him great scope for arousing compassion and understanding in his audience. JOSÉ RÉGIO, like Cortez, underwent the strong influence of Pirandello, sharing the Italian's questioning of reality and appearances, and has an affinity with the 'spiritual' theatre of such writers as CLAUDEL. These three are the founders of contemporary Portuguese theatre, and their influence has been as strong as their individual achievements.

The Salazar regime (1928–74) dealt very repressively with theatre and intellectual freedom, suspecting theatre, rightly, of being subversive – the *revista* often cocked a snook at government shortcomings. Serious theatre, when not overtly concerned with social and political matters, survived, but the censorship of police closure or the self-censorship of theatre managers denied wide public airing of any politically motivated drama attacking the regime. There *were* plays mounting frontal attacks, but they usually closed down rapidly. The would-be audience would just as rapidly buy copies of the play before the police circulated the booksellers. A prime example of this overt activist theatre, BERNARDO SANTARENO's *A Traição do Padre Martinho* (*Father Martin's Treason*, 1969), depicts a priest disciplined for attempting to apply principles of Catholic social justice and charity. His superiors, abjectly supporting the New State, ordain his transfer. The people rally to him, the situation gets tenser and the paramilitary police eventually fire on a demonstrating crowd, killing a young girl. The audience is drawn into the action because the order to disperse comes from behind them. More often, though, authors resorted to the time-honoured devices of using historical situations to treat of the present – the case of CARDOSO PIRES's *O Render dos Heróis* (*Relieving* [as of sentries] *the Heroes*, also, punningly, *The Surrender of the Heroes*, 1960) and STTAU MONTEIRO's

Felizmente Há Luar (*Luckily We Still Have the Moonlight*, 1961); and a 'fabular' method of distancing in space, e.g. Sttau Monteiro's A *Estátua* (1966) is ostensibly any dictator's statue. In Alves Redol's (1911–69) *O Destino Morreu de Repente* (*Destiny Died All of a Sudden*, 1967), the action is supposed to take place and to be played in a circus arena. The audience is swept in imagination to the Land of Destiny. The ringmaster cracks the whip and all the cast have to jump to it. Things go desperately wrong because there is a vast bureaucracy between whip-crack and jump which ensures that they do. Destiny of this imposed kind is itself doomed to collapse when faced by the human longing for freedom.

Since the 1974 coup, there has been a great expansion of interest in the theatre. Lisbon had 15 theatres in 1984 instead of 10 in 1974, Oporto seven instead of one, and all over the country semi-professional and amateur groups have sprung up. The most radical theatres have probably been the Lisbon Teatro da Comuna (the Commune) and A Barraca (literally the Shed, but also 'the Flop'). Portuguese theatre as a whole has continued to revive classics and present foreign plays, as well as giving recognition to the plays suppressed prior to 1974 and welcoming new experimental plays by established and new authors. Productions are lively, imaginative, original, and the audience has grown – and grown to appreciate all kinds of theatrical experience.

In the last four or five years there has been continued growth. In a typical week in March 1994 there were 27 plays on in Lisbon, in 22 theatres, including Vicente's *Breve Sumário da História de Deus* and Silva's *Guerras do Alecrim e Manjerona*, both plays calling on considerable theatrical ingenuity for effect. There have also been 'celebratory' occasions (see REVISTA; TEATRO D. MARIA II). In 1994 it was Lisbon's turn to be Cultural Capital of Europe. There has latterly been much more in the way of official and private firm sponsorship and publicizing of theatre – e.g. the 1991 slogan painted large on Lisbon's municipal transport: 'Don't make a drama out of life, go to the theatre!' LK

See: *Bulletin d'histoire du théâtre portugais*, Lisbon, 1950–4; L. W. Keates, *The Court Theatre of Gil Vicente*, Lisbon, 1962 (Portuguese trans., Lisbon, 1987); F. Mendonça, *Para o Estudo do Teatro em Portugal*, 1946–1966, Assis, Brazil, 1971; L. S. Picchio, *Storia del Teatro Portoghese*, Rome, 1964; C. Porto and S. T. de Menezes, 10 *Anos de Teatro e Cinema em Portugal*, 1974–84, Lisbon, 1985; L. F. Rebello, *História do Teatro Português*, Europa-America, Mem Martins, 1967.

Portuguese-speaking Africa European theatre was introduced very early on, by missionaries, into the Portuguese colonies. The plays were religious in character, their objective being the propagation of Catholicism. The religion of the Africans was not taken into consideration: the settlers imposed on them their own religion and culture. The literary genre of drama, as seen from a Western point of view, appeared much later than poetry and prose in the Portuguese-speaking African countries. This can be explained by the fact that the colonialists provided very little in the way of facilities needed to perform a play, and that poetry could more freely express the violence experienced by the colonized peoples.

When independence was declared in 1975 in Angola, Cape Verde, Guinea-Bissau, Mozambique and São Tomé e Príncipe, illiteracy was higher than 90 per cent. This had affected both literary production and the people's interest in drama. It was very difficult to publish at all, and as writers had little incentive to do so anyway there came about a cultural stagnation. Portuguese colonialism had imposed severe CENSORSHIP on newspapers and books: any expression of opinions contrary to those held by the ruling power would not be published. The principles of negritude and Pan-Africanism had formed the political and cultural background that had led to the armed struggle for liberation in 1961 in Angola, in 1963 in Guinea-Bissau and in 1964 in Mozambique. This anti-colonial war had led to their independence, after a coup in Portugal in 1974 that had overthrown the oldest dictatorship in Europe.

Negritude and Pan-Africanism influenced in part the dramatic production of these territories. Although some plays performed before independence directly challenged the ruling values, the majority were *vaudeville* pieces that came from metropolitan areas, their objective being mainly to amuse the white spectators. After independence Marxist regimes were formed, aiming to make good the damage done by colonialism and to build a classless society. Drama was often used as a means of politicizing people, as an instrument of the principles of socialist realism.

Angola As elsewhere in Portuguese-speaking Africa, the subjects of the plays performed by the missionaries related to Catholicism. And as critic Carlos Vaz notes, 'the roles of the Infant Jesus, of the Angels and of Joseph and Mary could only be performed by white people, while the roles of Judas, Satan and even sometimes Herod were only performed by the blacks'. The *vaudeville* pieces staged mainly by theatre groups from the cities offered the only light relief.

Important 20th-century plays include Domingos Van-Dúmem's *Auto de Natal* (*Christmas Play*), performed in Luanda in 1972 and written in Quimbundo, a native language, as a reaction against the language imposed by the settlers and as a revalidation of the African culture; two plays by Orlando de Albuquerque, published in 1974, *Ovibanda* and *O Filho de Zambi* (*Zambi's Son*), on Angolan religious themes; and the children's play *Os Pioneiros do Futuro* (*The Pioneers of the Future*, 1974), by Júlio de Almeida and Elsa de Sousa.

A month after Angola became independent in 1975, the Union of Angolan Writers was formed. They promulgated:

At this moment when our people have just taken over full responsibility for their future as a free and sovereign nation, Angolan writers take their stand at the forefront, facing the enormous tasks of national liberation and reconstruction.

Our literary history bears witness to the generations of writers who were able in their own time to keep alive the process of our liberation by expressing the deep longings of our people, mainly those of its most exploited classes. Thus Angolan literature emerges not merely as an aesthetic need but also as a weapon for the affirmation of the Angolans.

The first step of direct armed struggle against colonialism has been made. Angolan writers in many different ways answered the call to arms, and some gave their lives on the field of honour for their fatherland.

Today, our people have entered into a new battle in this centuries-old war for our self-assertion as a free nation, in Africa and in the world. Once more, as is their duty and tradition, Angolan writers are present at the heart of this popular resistance, joining the battle on the cultural front.

This statement encapsulates the themes that dominated literature in Angola during the first years of independence. Confirming this, the then president of the republic, Agostinho Neto, himself an eminent poet, declared that 'literature in this independent country of Angola, which is marching towards a superior form of social organization – socialism – must necessarily reflect this new situation'. However, two years later, realizing that art had merely served politics, had no autonomy, and had often been reduced to political pamphleteering, Neto qualified the principles of the cultural policy thus: '… we cannot be schematic or follow stereotypes as the theoreticians of socialist realism once did'.

After the fall of the dictatorship in Portugal and during the period of transition that led to independence, a spontaneous theatre that reflected the social contradictions of a colonial society in open disintegration flourished in Angola. The plays *As Duas Caras do Patrão* (*The Two Faces of the Boss*), *A Província de Angola* (*The Province of Angola*), *Manifestação no Jardim da Celeste* (*Demonstration in Celeste's Garden*), *Combate de Box* (*Boxing Match*) and *Uma Lição de Portugalidade* (*A Lesson in Portugueseness*) were performed by students and workers.

After independence, the aim of the Angolan theatre was to awaken the political consciousness of the people. In 1975, *Poder Popular* (*Popular Power*) was performed by the Tchingange Group. In accordance with its didactic, political and doctrinal approach, it was presented in schools, factories and hospitals in Luanda and in rural areas. In 1976, the National School of Theatre was created. One of the groups belonging to it performed *Africa Liberdade* (*Africa Freedom*). In 1977, the group Xilenga-Teatro was formed, which resurrected four narratives from the rich, vast repertory of the oral tradition of the Tchokwe people. The Ngongo group were experimenting at this time in the field of the PUPPET theatre.

Other plays took the same political line: *A Pele do Diabo* (*The Devil's Skin*, 1977) by Manuel Santos Lima; *A Corda* (*The Rope*, 1978) by Pepetela; *O Círculo de Giz de Bombó* (*Bombó's Chalk Circle*, 1979) by Henrique Guerra, adapted from BERTOLT BRECHT's *The Caucasian Chalk Circle*; *No Velho Ninguém Toa* (*The Old Man is Untouchable*) by Costa Andrade; and *A Revolta da Casa dos Ídolos* (*The Revolt in the House of the Idols*, 1980) by Pepetela. This last shows a formal and thematic depth that contrasts with the naive spontaneity that was common in the vast majority of the plays of the time.

Cape Verde The first known play, *Terra de Sôdade* (*Land of Nostalgia*), was written in the 1940s by Jaime de Figueiredo. It is a sentimental four-act ballet on the theme of emigration. The only theatre group of note before independence was run by the Adriano Moreira Grammar School in the capital, Praia. After independence, theatre became a means of politicizing the people, as in the other Portuguese-speaking African countries. Using as his theme an incident in the history of Cape Verde – an uprising of slaves against colonial domination – Oswaldo Osório, heavily influenced by Brecht, wrote *Gervásio*.

Seeking to reveal the origins of the culture of Cape Verde, and combining acting with music and dance, Kwame Konde founded the theatre group Korda Kaoberdi. In 1977 he staged *Os Disanimados para os Infernos* (*To Hell with the Pessimists*) by Kaoberdiano Dambará. Later this group performed AUGUSTO BOAL's *A Lua Muito Pequena e a Caminhada Perigosa* (*The Very Small Moon and the Dangerous Journey*), which dealt with the political activity and theory of Che Guevara. In 1979 Donaldo Pereira de Macedo's play *Descarado* (*Shameless*) was published in the USA. Its importance lies in its being the first play from Cape Verde to appear in book form, and in its being written in Creole.

The present situation is not very encouraging. There are few incentives to create or produce theatre, and previous experiments are not being followed through. Some directors, such as Leão Lopes, occasionally experiment in combining the traditional dramatic features – dance, masks, and so on – with audio-visual techniques, taking as their themes old tales, poetry and national literature.

Guinea-Bissau Besides the traditional theatre and the *vaudeville* shows based on the everyday life of the settlers that flourished before independence, plays for children, based on fables, also used to be staged. Traditional dances that are still performed, such as the *dança do boi* (the dance of the ox) and the *danças dos bíjagós* (bijagós dances), use underlying dramatic features. After independence, no dramatic activity has been reported in this country.

Mozambique As in the other Portuguese-speaking African countries, before independence the most popular form of entertainment was the *vaudeville*. Notable among them were: *Crime Anica, Madalena, As Aventuras de um Herói* (*Adventures of a Hero*), *Sua Alteza o Criador* (*His Highness the Creator*), *Os Cavaleiros do Arcabuz* (*The Knights of the Arquebus*) and *Era Eu* (*It was I*) by Carlos da Silva; *Polana Azul* (*Blue Polana*) and *Sete de Março* (*The Seventh of March*) by Fernando Baldaque and Carlos Queirós de Fonseca – all written in the first 20 years of this century; *Ponta Vermelha* (*Red Point*, 1931) by Fernando Baldaque and Arnaldo Silva; *Ice-cream Today* (1932) by António Alonso Moreira, Fernando Baldaque and Arnaldo Silva; *Renúncia* (*Resignation*, 1932) by Alexandre Cabral Campos; *A Palhota de Moçambique* (*The Thatched Hut of Mozambique*, 1937) and *Zona Perigosa* (*Danger Zone*, 1941) by Fernando Baldaque and Arnaldo Silva; *Africa Menina e Moça* (*Africa Young and Lovely*) by Ruy Sant'Elmo, *Latitude Sul* (*Southern Latitude*) by Luna de Oliveira, *Amor à Vista* (*Love on the Way*) by José Mendonça and Fausto Ritto, *O mato* (*The Forest*) by Caetano Montez, and *Infortúnio* (*Misfortune*) by Felisberto Ferreirinha – these last performed in the 1940s.

Since CENSORSHIP controlled all literary production in

the years before independence, it was difficult to write plays with clear political themes. Some, however, dared to denounce the claustrophobic colonial status quo. In 1959, Afonso Ribeiro wrote *Três Setas Apontadas para o Futuro* (*Three Arrows Pointing to the Future*). Two characters face each other all through the play: a poet, who symbolizes an alternative future, and his boss's son, who represents colonial values. Out of the conflict between these two philosophies emerges a movement towards a new society which will be more aware of universal human values.

Lindo Lhongo's *Os Noivos ou Conferência Dramática sobre o Lobolo* (*The Engagement, or The Dramatic Discourse about the Purchasing of a Bride*) follows the same theme of confrontation with colonial ideology. It was performed in 1971; an excerpt was published in the literary magazine *Caliban*, and banned soon afterwards by the political police. The play emphasized the renewal and re-evaluation of a genuinely African culture.

Not long before independence, other politically and culturally engaged plays were written: *As Trinta Mulheres de Muzelini* (*The Thirty Wives of Muzelini*), also by Lhongo; *Filhos da Noite* (*Children of the Night*) by António Francisco, and *O Feitiço e a Religião* (*Sorcery and Religion*) by João Fumane.

According to the regime that emerged after 1975, the principal task was then to 'heal colonial wounds' and build a fairer society. As in the other Portuguese-speaking countries, drama was a means of propagating the ideology of the party in power. The model followed was Soviet AGIT-PROP. These pragmatic principles were displayed in the plays of Orlando Mendes: *Um Minuto de Silêncio* (*One Minute of Silence*) and *Na Machamb de Maria – Sábado às Três da Tarde* (*On Maria's Small Farm – Saturday Afternoon at Three O'clock*, 1975); in the radiophonic theatrical experiment elaborated by Alvaro Belo Marques, a Portuguese voluntary worker, in 1978; in *A Estrada* (*The Road*, 1979) by Leite Vasconcelos; in *O Destino Inimigo do Povo* (*Destiny: Enemy of the People*), performed by a workers' collective; in *A Comuna* (*The Commune*, 1979), created by the students of the University Eduardo Mondlane and Mozambique railway workers; in *A Sagrada Família* (*The Holy Family*) written and performed by the Grupo Cénico das Forças Populares de Libertação de Moçambique.

Other dramatic activities include the adaptation of Luís Bernardo Honwana's tale *Rosita até Morrer* (*Rosita to My Dying Day*) by a group of Brazilian voluntary workers; Sant'Anna Afonso's *Eu não Sou Eu Outras Peças* (*I Am Not I and Other Plays*); *Memórias de um Projecto* (*Memories of a Project*) by the Cuban voluntary workers Maité Vera; and Pedro Paulo Pereira's *Tempo de Mudança* (*Time for a Change*). Theatre for children, with a basically didactic aim, is represented by *Chiquinho malandrinho* (*Naughty Chiquinho*) by Mwaparra, and *Coisas que só Acontecem na flor de lótus* (*Things that Only Happen in the Lotus Flower*) by Álvaro Belo Marques.

São Tomé e Príncipe Of first importance is *Tchiloli ou Tragédia do Marquês de Mântua e do Imperador Carloto Magno*, brought to São Tomé e Príncipe by the Portuguese settlers: it consists of a Portuguese text to which were added African features – music, MASKS, dances and costumes. *O Auto de Floripes*, performed in the island of Príncipe, was also brought over from Portugal. In 1965 and 1969 two plays by Fernando Reis were performed: *Os Mangas de Alpaca* (*The Red-Tapists*) and *D'Jambi*. DP

See: J. M. Abrantes. 'A procura de um Reencontro com a Realidade', *Africa*, 3, Jan./Mar. 1979; C. Andrade, *Literatura Angolana* (*Opiniões*), Lisbon, 1980; M. E. O. Assumpção, 'A identidade nacional na dramaturgia angolana. A revolta da casa dos ídolos e a pele do diabo', *Les Littératures Africaines de Langue Portuguaise. Actes du Colloque International*, 28, 29, 30 Nov., 1 Dec. 1984, Paris, 1985; M. Ferreira, *Literaturas Africanas de Expressão Portuguesa*, vols. 1, 2, Lisbon, 1977; R. G. Hamilton, *Literatura Africa Literatura Necessária*, vols. 1, 2, Lisbon, 1981, 1984; F. Reis, *Povô Flogá – O Povo Brinca*, São Tomé, 1969; B. Traoré, 'Le Théâtre négro-africain et ses fonctions sociologiques', *Présence Africaine*, 14/15, June/Sept. 1957; C. Valbert, *Le Tchiloli de São Tomé. Un Exemple de subversion culturelle. Les Littératures Africaines de Langue Portuguaise. Actes du Colloque International*, 28, 29, 30 Nov., 1 Dec. 1984, Paris, 1985; C. Vaz, *Para um Conhecimento do Teatro Africano*, Lisbon, 1978.

pose plastique   SEE LIVING PICTURE; NUDITY

Potier, Charles 1774–1838 French actor. One of the great comic performers of the 19th century, Potier has been called a major actor in a minor genre. Of noble origin, he first appeared on the stage of the Délassements, then worked in the provinces, including Bordeaux. He drew maximum advantage from a weak voice and an emaciated build. His debut at the Variétés (see BOULEVARD) in 1809 led to his becoming that theatre's chief comic actor. In 1812, he showed he could appear in three different plays in the same evening and give the impression of three different actors. He brought all Paris to the Variétés in such plays as *Les Anglaises pour rire* (*English Ladies for a Joke*, 1814). In 1818 he moved to the Porte-Saint-Martin, where he created the role of Père Sournois in *Les Petites Danaïdes* (*The Little Danaides*). In 1825 he returned to the Variétés, in 1826 he spent two months in England, and in 1827 his health forced him to give his farewell performance. In 1829 he was invited to the new Nouveautés, where he showed his versatility once more in *Antoine, ou Les Trois Générations*. One of his most popular roles was in *Le Ci-devant Jeune Homme* (*The Young Man from the Old Regime*, 1812). JMCC

Potter, Denis (Christopher George) 1935–94 British stage and television dramatist, who started his career as a journalist and was a member of the BBC's current affairs staff from 1959 to 61. His first TV play, *Vote Vote Vote for Nigel Barton* (1965), about a miner's son who fights as a parliamentary candidate for the Labour Party but discovers too late that power corrupts, was turned into a stage play for the BRISTOL OLD VIC in 1968; and prompted a sequel, *Stand Up, Nigel Barton* (1965). *The Son of Man* (1969) was a life of Christ, interpreted as a self-doubting rebel against Roman oppression, and was staged (with FRANK FINLAY as Christ) and screened in the same year, an appropriate time for its subject when there were many would-be Christs determined to save the world, following the events of May 1968.

Potter was undoubtedly a better and more inventive writer for TV than for the stage, where his relatively weak dialogue and failure to sustain the presences of several characters let him down; but on TV his shorter scenes, with evocative songs, resulted in several memorable series, including *Pennies from Heaven* (1978), *Blue Remembered Hills* (1979) and *The Singing Detective* (1986), in which MICHAEL GAMBON played a patient in a hospital suffering from a skin disease who sees himself as Raymond Chandler's Philip Marlow in a dream-like evocation of a MUSICAL film noir. Nostalgia, loneliness and sexual longing were themes in *Blackeyes* (1989), which was poorly received; but *Lipstick on Your Collar* (1993) proved a welcome return to form. Potter wrote a novel, *Hide and Seek* (1973), and adapted novels by Thomas Hardy, Angus Wilson and Edmund Gosse for television. By the time of his death he had completed two four-part serials, *Karaoke* (for the BBC) and *Cold Lazarus* (for Channel 4), due to be screened in 1996. The first is a classic thriller about a writer who finds that his literary inventions start to happen in his own life; in the second, the writer dies of cancer (as Potter did), is scientifically frozen for 400 years and then brought back to life. (See also TELEVISION DRAMA.) JE

Power family Actors, originally from Ireland, most of whom spent large portions of their careers in the USA. The first, **Tyrone** Power (1795–1841), successfully played stage Irishmen in London and wrote a number of comedies before going to the USA in 1840. A great success there, he returned often and was drowned at sea on a transatlantic trip. His 1836 *Impressions of America* offers a sympathetic and detailed view of the American theatre at the time. Power's son **Maurice** (?–1849) was also an actor. Another son, Harold, sired **(Frederick) Tyrone (Edmond)** Power (1869–1931), a leading man and member of DALY's company, with whom he appeared in London. Frederick first appeared successfully with FANNY JANAUSCHEK, and for a time acted with MINNIE MADDERN FISKE, his Lord Steyne in *Becky Sharp* being especially well received. In later life, he appeared almost exclusively as major support in Shakespearian revivals.

In turn, his son **Tyrone** Power (1914–58) was for some time on the stage, but won his most substantial reputation as a film actor. He made his debut as Benvolio in KATHARINE CORNELL's production of *Romeo and Juliet*. After his film career began he appeared in *John Brown's Body* and *The Dark Is Light Enough*. In the 1980s his son, **Tyrone** Jr, also became an actor. SMA

Praga, Marco 1862–1929 Italian dramatist and critic. After a modest success with *La moglie ideale* (*The Ideal Wife*, 1891), in which DUSE appeared, Praga was prolific of pieces in the 1890s, written either alone or in collaboration, treating middle-class psychology and manners and more particularly the woman with a past. His work is marked by considerable technical skill and some mordant social comment, but his morality was too conventional seriously to question the values of the society he depicted in plays like *L'innamorata* (1894), *La crisi* (*The Crisis*, 1905), *La porta chiusa* (*The Closed Door*, 1914) in which Duse scored a great success, and *Divorzio* (1915). His theatrical criticism in *L'Illustrazione Italiana* was highly influential. LR

prahlada nataka Indian theatre form: literally, the 'play' (*nataka*) of Prahlada. Some 40 village companies in the district of Ganjam in Orissa state in eastern INDIA preserve a style of performing this play demonstrating the faith of the child-prince Prahlada, who worships the name of Vishnu despite the evil machinations of his wicked father-king. The play is thought to have been adapted from a classical text popularized by Raja Ramakrishna Deva Chotterai, a local ruler of the mid-19th century. A special MASK endowed with great power is worn by the actor who plays Narasimha, the man-lion incarnation of Lord Vishnu, who ultimately destroys the wicked king.

Troupes enact the play on special festival occasions on a bleacher-like platform placed in an open field. The performing style includes dialogue and song, accompanied by the music of *mridangam* drums, harmonium, wind instrument (*mukha veena*), cymbals and conch shells. At the climax of the dramatic action, the actor dons the mask of the man-lion, becoming possessed. He must be forcibly restrained by attendants from inflicting harm on the person of the actor playing the king. Symbolically, when the king is killed by Vishnu, order is restored to the universe. FaR

Prampolini, Enrico 1894–1956 Italian painter, sculptor, stage designer and director. An early member of the futurist movement, with MARINETTI he wrote many of its major manifestos, and advanced the movement through the exhibitions he organized and the journals he edited, like *Noi* and *Stile Futurista*. From 1921 he was particularly active in theatre, designing scenes and COSTUMES first for the Teatro Sintetico Futurista, then collaborating with BRAGAGLIA's Teatro degli Indipendenti. The grand and visionary range of his ideas for art work outside the theatre is well seen in his *Manifesto dell'aeropittura* (1929). Avoiding many of the political associations that FUTURISM had in the 1920s and 30s, he remained committed to its artistic principles throughout his life. LR

Pratinas active early 5th century BC Greek playwright, from Phlius in the Peloponnese, active at Athens. He is said to have written 50 plays of which 32 were satyric, and to have been the first to write satyr plays (see GREECE, ANCIENT). No doubt there were traditional precedents, but Pratinas may have been the first to give satyr plays a written text and/or to produce them at Athens. ALB

Prehauser, Gottfried 1699–1769 Austrian actor, who inherited and cultivated the role of HANSWURST. He made his debut in 1716 with an itinerant troupe in the Viennese suburbs, and in 1720 first played Hanswurst in Salzburg. STRANITZKY acknowledged him as his successor and Prehauser became the Hanswurst of the Vienna Kärntnertortheater from 1725, refining the type into a polished Viennese gallant. According to EDUARD DEVRIENT, he was a better comic and mimic than his predecessor: 'His caricatures always remain recognizable human beings and never sink to BURLESQUE.' LS

Preston, Thomas ?16th century English playwright. His TRAGICOMEDY *Cambyses King of Persia* illustrates the bridge in English drama from the medieval to the Elizabethan periods, offering a historical tale rather than a MORALITY. The play was written around 1569 and Preston wrote others, but details are unreliable. Certainly, he wrote with a flourish that gave this work contemporary popularity. MB

Prevelákis, Pantelís 1909–86 Greek playwright. Like his mentor KAZANTZÁKIS, Prevelákis was a versatile author who wrote for the theatre as well as translating into Greek a number of Spanish, Italian and French dramas. He displays a concern for ethical issues. His main characters are people posing existential questions, in search of their better identity. The early and the late plays are set in Greece and the time is the present, while the trilogy 'The Sickness of the Century' (referring to the moral crisis of Western civilization) combines biblical, Renaissance and modern settings and times. In the first part of the trilogy, *The Holy Sacrifice* (1952), the protagonist Juliano de'Medici walks to his death knowingly in order to purge, through his sacrifice, both himself and those around him. *The Hands of the Living God* (1952) treats a theme drawn from Dostoevsky. The play leads again to a catharsis. *Lazarus* (1954), which concludes the trilogy, was meant to recall, structurally, an ancient Greek tragedy (see GREECE, ANCIENT) and delves deeply into the spiritual aspect of a physical miracle. *The Volcano* (1962) develops a heroic theme from Crete's struggle of liberation from the Turkish yoke. Prevelákis shows good knowledge of the practical side of theatre and aims at a classical type of expression. GT

Price, Stephen 1783–1840 The first successful American theatre manager who was neither a playwright nor an actor. Price began gaining control of the PARK THEATRE in New York in 1808, and in 1810 started importing English stars; this practice gradually destroyed the resident repertory tradition in America. Price, with Edmund Simpson, managed to keep the Park open during the War of 1812, and after the war went frequently to London to recruit new talent. In 1816 he imported Mrs John Barnes from DRURY LANE, beginning an especially prosperous period for the Park. From 1826 to 30 Price managed the Drury Lane Theatre in London, gaining a monopoly over English stars, thus forcing other American managers to deal with him for their services. This power caused Washington Irving to refer to Price as 'King Stephen'. Price drained the London stage of its talent to supply visiting stars for the Park; other managers were forced to employ his visiting stars on his terms in order to compete. Price was shrewd, even unscrupulous in his dealings, but he read audiences' tastes and preferences accurately on both sides of the Atlantic. SMA

Priestley, J(ohn) B(oynton) 1894–1984 British dramatist, novelist and critic. After the success of the dramatization of his best-selling novel *The Good Companions* (1931, adapted with Edward Knoblok), a sentimental comedy about an acting troupe, Priestley began to develop his characteristic themes in *Dangerous Corner* (1932). The idea of relativity, encapsulated in two alternative sequences of events following from the same incident, was transferred to time in two 1937 plays, one contrasting hopes for the future and the actualities of 20 years later (*Time and the Conways*), the other presenting actions as conditioned by unconscious patterns established in previous incarnations (*I Have Been Here Before*). Though viewed as strikingly original at the time, the concepts are used as dramatic devices, rather than posing serious intellectual questions. In 1938 he took over the Westminster Theatre with his own company, the London Mask Theatre, which performed his more experimental works like *Music at Night* and the modern MORALITY PLAY, *Johnson over Jordan* (both 1939), four-dimensional dramas using expressionistic techniques (see EXPRESSIONISM). During the same period he wrote a series of comedies, such as *Laburnum Grove* (1933) satirizing middle-class suburbia and *When We Are Married* (1938) bordering on FARCE, and in 1943 a socialist allegory, *They Came to a City*.

After the war, during which he became a popular radio broadcaster, he continued the same mixture of dramas based on relativity and the spirit world (*An Inspector Calls*, 1946) or exploring political attitudes (*The Linden Tree*, 1947), experimental works (*Dragon's Mouth*, 1952, a play for voices written with Jacquetta Hawkes) and comedy. One of the last of his 49 plays, a dramatization of Iris Murdoch's novel *A Severed Head* (written in collaboration with her, 1963), ran for two years in the WEST END and his work has continued to be a staple of English repertory theatre (see REGIONAL THEATRE (BRITAIN)).   CI

Prince, Harold 1928– American producer, director and playwright. Launching his career as a producer in partnership with Robert E. Griffith and Frederic Brisson, Prince had immediate success with *The Pajama Game* (1954) and *Damn Yankees* (1955). With Griffith he produced *West Side Story* (1957) and *Fiorello!* (1961), and on his own he produced *Fiddler on the Roof* (1964). Beginning with *She Loves Me* (1963), he served as both producer and director of a number of successful MUSICALS. Prince's most notable contribution to the musical stage was the series of 'concept musicals' he produced and directed in conjunction with composer-lyricist STEPHEN SONDHEIM: *Company* (1970), *Follies* (1971), *A Little Night Music* (1973), *Pacific Overtures* (1976), *Sweeney Todd* (1979) and *Merrily We Roll Along* (1981). In recent years he has devoted considerable attention to the direction of OPERA, in the USA and abroad; his most successful musical theatre production of the past few years has been the spectacular LLOYD WEBBER *Phantom of the Opera* (London, 1986; New York, 1988). Current projects have included the adaptation of O'CASEY's autobiographies (the first part staged in 1992); a new production of *Show Boat* (Toronto, late 1993; BROADWAY, autumn 1994); and the development of *Kiss of the Spider Woman* (begun in 1990; London, 1992; Broadway, 1993). Winner of seven Tonys for direction of a musical, in 1991 Prince received the Richard Rodgers Award for excellence in musical theatre (which had been given previously only to MARY MARTIN (1988) and Julie Andrews (1989)) and in 1994 he was a JOHN F. KENNEDY CENTER Honoree. Late the same year he directed a musical, *The Petrified Prince*, OFF-BROADWAY.

Foster Hirsch, author of a 1989 study of Prince, believes Prince and his collaborators 'have altered the popular idea of what a musical can be', and another author, Carol Ilson, concludes that risk-taker Prince's greatest contribution has been 'his unwillingness to repeat himself'. His largely autobiographical book, *Contradictions*, was published in 1974.   MK

Prince Henry's Men see ADMIRAL'S MEN

Prince of Wales's Theatre (London) Built in 1772 as a concert room, this small theatre in Tottenham Court Street had so declined that by the mid-19th century it was familiarly known as the 'Dust Hole'. Determined on management, MARIE WILTON, a popular star of burlesque at the Strand, bought it in 1865. Having completely redecorated it and made it the most comfortable theatre in London, she renamed it, with royal permission, the Prince of Wales's. By a mixture of luck and good judgement, she proceeded to bring to the theatre 15 years of unparalleled prosperity. Wilton had intended, in partnership with H. J. BYRON, to provide a mixed fare of BURLESQUE and COMEDY, but it was the series of plays by T. W. ROBERTSON, beginning with *Society* (1865), that made her fortune and that of the actor, SQUIRE BANCROFT, whom she married in 1867. They were already rich by 1880, when they left the Prince of Wales's for the HAYMARKET. Two years later, the theatre was found to be structurally unsound, and because the necessary repairs were never made it ended up as a Salvation Army hostel. It was demolished in 1903, except for the portico, which became the stage door of the Scala, an undistinguished theatre which was itself demolished in 1972. Another theatre, originally the Prince's but renamed the Prince of Wales's in 1886, was built in Coventry Street in 1884. It was demolished in 1937 and replaced by the present building in the same year.   PT

Princess's Theatre (London) The original building opened in Oxford Street in 1828, when it housed a diorama by CLARKSON STANFIELD and David Roberts. It was adapted as a theatre in 1836 and named the Princess's in 1840. Its most distinguished period was that of CHARLES KEAN's management (1851–9), during which it became London's most fashionable theatre. Kean mixed gentlemanly MELODRAMA with grandly pictorial productions of SHAKESPEARE and LORD BYRON. The subsequent management of Augustus Harris (1859–63) was most notable for the unsuccessful London debut of HENRY IRVING and the phenomenally successful one of the French actor, CHARLES FECHTER. The rest of the theatre's history is patchy. It was at the Princess's that Charles Warner gave his startling version of the physical effects of alcoholism in CHARLES READE's *Drink* (1879), and in the rebuilt and enlarged house (1880) that WILSON BARRETT had his most successful years in London management (1881–6). The Princess's ceased to be used as a theatre in 1902, stood empty for several years and ended its life as a warehouse. It was demolished in 1931.   PT

principal boy see PANTOMIME, ENGLISH; MALE IMPERSONATION

Pritchard, Hannah 1711–68 English actress, who was a leading member of GARRICK's company at DRURY LANE from 1748 almost to her death. Pritchard's most acclaimed performance was as Lady Macbeth to Garrick's Macbeth. Before then she had mainly been associated with comedy roles, and contemporary reports indicate an actress of charm and gentleness, wit and intelligence. They also unkindly draw attention to her stoutness, against which she fought a losing battle in her later years. MB

private theatres (London) The indoor playhouses of Elizabethan, Jacobean and Caroline London were, and still are, sometimes called 'private theatres' to distinguish them from the open-air public theatres. The title embodies a fiction which was a useful defence against interference from the civic authorities. They were, in fact, open to the public on the payment of an admission charge which was generally higher than that of the public theatres. But the first actors to use private playhouses were choristers, and it was convenient for their managers to claim that what the public witnessed were private rehearsals of plays in preparation for presentation at Court. The title stuck long after it had lost all conviction. The main private theatres were the unknown home of the BOYS OF ST PAUL'S (c.1575), the first BLACKFRIARS (1576), the second Blackfriars (1600), the WHITEFRIARS (1605–8), the COCKPIT or Phoenix (1616) and the SALISBURY COURT (1629). More genuinely private were the court theatres. PT

Proctor, F(rederick) F(rancis or Freeman) [Fred Levantine] 1851–1929 American VAUDEVILLE manager ('dean of vaudeville') and theatre owner. Maine-born Proctor began his career touring the USA and Europe as Fred Levantine, an equilibrist. In 1886 he bought an interest in an Albany theatre; in 1889 he opened the 23rd Street Theatre, a legitimate house, in New York City. By the 1890s his focus was clean, continuous vaudeville, first at New York's Proctor Pleasure Palace (1894), then with the first vaudeville circuit and ultimately controlling a group of 25 eastern theatres. Proctor joined his rival B. F. KEITH in 1906 as head of the United Booking Office, a virtual monopoly of first-class vaudeville; his theatrical holdings were taken over by the Radio–Keith–Orpheum circuit in 1929. DBW

producer In the professional theatre (as in television and film) the producer brings together the financial and artistic resources that are necessary to create a production. The producer may have the original idea for a production, or commission others to develop an idea. In amateur theatre the term is often used to describe the function of the person more correctly known as the director. MB

Prokopovich, Feofan 1681–1736 Ukrainian clergyman and classical humanist who, via his brilliant sermons and orations, historical and literary-theoretical treatises (*De arte libri tres*, written 1705, published 1786) and political school dramas, championed Peter the Great's programme of reform against reactionary obscurantism. Educated at the Kiev Academy, then in Poland and Rome, he brought a mastery of theology, philosophy, classical literature and poetics, mathematics and the natural sciences back with him to the Ukraine where he assumed monastic orders. He became a teacher at, then rector of, Kiev Academy (1710),

bishop of Pskov (1718), archbishop of Novgorod (1720) and vice-president of the Synod, co-organizer of St Petersburg's Academy of Sciences and from 1715 ecclesiastical adviser to Peter's reform programme.

His TRAGICOMEDY *Vladimir, Duke and Ruler of Slavic Russian Lands Led by the Holy Ghost from the Darkness of Unbelief to Evangelical Light, in the Year 988 after the Birth of Christ* (1705), a 13-syllable verse drama on the introduction of Christianity into Old Russia, is actually allegorical propaganda glorifying the valiant struggle of the reform-minded Tsar Peter (who is praised in the prologue) against unenlightened opposition. In an effort to secularize the school drama, Prokopovich introduced into his play comic characters, musical interludes, more natural dialogue and satirical commentary on daily life. His satirical treatment of the priestly caste was borrowed from the folk theatre, where this was commonplace. This marks another early unsuccessful attempt to devise a dramatic literature for a national theatre. SG

Prolet-Buehne A New York workers' theatre group formed in 1925 by immigrant German workers. Led by John E. Bonn in 1928–9, they introduced AGIT-PROP techniques into their performances to promote socialist and workers' class-consciousness and political activism similar to groups in Berlin (see PISCATOR) and Moscow. They influenced the performance style of the Workers' Laboratory Theatre, and eventually the LIVING NEWSPAPER. The group disbanded in 1934, and Bonn was later appointed to the German section of the FEDERAL THEATRE PROJECT. RE

Provincetown Players (USA) Led by George Cram Cook, an enthusiastic visionary from Iowa who revered the ancient Greek drama. In the summer of 1915 a band of amateurs staged several of their own plays in Provincetown, Massachusetts. The following year, after EUGENE O'NEILL joined the group and contributed the outstanding work *Bound East for Cardiff*, Cook – backed by O'Neill and journalist John Reed, among others – decided to move their playmaking to Greenwich Village, New York City. Launched in a brownstone building at 139 Macdougal Street on 3 November 1916, the Provincetown Players initially featured short works, with O'Neill and SUSAN GLASPELL as their leading writers. After two years, the Players moved into larger quarters at 133 Macdougal Street. Though Cook gave unstintingly of himself for O'Neill's writings, most notably for *The Emperor Jones* (1920), he himself had literary ambitions and envied the other's growing fame. In 1922 he and his wife Susan Glaspell sailed for Greece, where he died two years later. After a hiatus (1922–3), the Players were headed by a triumvirate of O'Neill, KENNETH MACGOWAN and ROBERT EDMOND JONES, who in turn were succeeded by James Light as director. A casualty of the stock market crash and the Depression, the Players folded in 1929. LSH

Prowse, Philip 1937– British designer-director, long associated with the Glasgow CITIZENS' THEATRE. Trained in THEATRE DESIGN at London's Slade School of Art, he subsequently gained experience as a design assistant at COVENT GARDEN before moving on as stage designer at Watford

(1967–9) and Glasgow (since 1969). Although primarily a designer of plays, he has also worked in OPERA and ballet with other companies and abroad. Prowse's stage settings are marked by their highly expressive, architectonic character. Rather than merely indicating the place where action occurs, his sets tend to function dramatically during the course of the action. Since the mid-1970s he has combined designing with the direction of his own productions, notable examples being *Phèdre* (1984) and *The Duchess of Malfi* (1985), both of which were produced in London, and the following in Glasgow: *Anna Karenina* (1978), *Mother Courage* (1990) and *Edward II* (1992).   JMB

Pryce, Jonathan 1947– British actor. Repertory at Liverpool Everyman Theatre and Nottingham Playhouse established his reputation as one of Britain's most exciting younger actors. At Nottingham he played Gethin Price in TREVOR GRIFFITHS's *Comedians* (1975), a production that went on to tour internationally. His Hamlet at the ROYAL COURT was made remarkable by the manner in which he also played the Ghost as a regurgitated voice from within Hamlet, and his Macbeth for the ROYAL SHAKESPEARE COMPANY (1986) gave further evidence of his fierce power. Pryce has worked in film, television and as a director. He played Macbeth as a hearty soldier in ADRIAN NOBLE's RSC production of *Macbeth* (1987), and Astrov in MICHAEL BLAKEMORE's production of *Uncle Vanya* (1988). In *Miss Saigon* he scored a personal triumph as the Engineer, a Vietnamese pimp, whose dreams hold this large-scale MUSICAL together – a casting decision challenged (but successfully resisted) when the musical transferred to BROADWAY in 1990.   MB JE

Prynne, William 1600–69 English campaigning Puritan and pamphleteer, whose long *Histriomastix* (1632) is one of the most famous of anti-theatrical tracts. Because it was seen by Archbishop Laud to contain attacks, albeit veiled, on the king and queen, Prynne was fined and pilloried, had his ears cut off and was sentenced to life imprisonment. Freed by the Long Parliament in 1640, he became a leading Puritan and a vigorous Member of Parliament. PT

Public Theater (New York City) In 1966 JOSEPH PAPP, founder of the NEW YORK SHAKESPEARE FESTIVAL, acquired a large Italianate building on Lafayette Street for its permanent home. The building dates from 1854, when the Astor family dedicated it as a library for New Yorkers. After two additions, it was completed in 1881, becoming part of the city's public library system until 1911. In 1920, the building was sold to the Hebrew Immigrant Aid Society, which had intended to sell to a developer until the Landmarks Preservation Commission designated it a landmark in 1960. Papp originally assigned Giorgio Cavaglieri and MING CHO LEE to convert it into theatres. Struggling to keep as much of the original building intact as possible, the designers during the next few years created the Newman Theater (proscenium, 299 seats), Martinson Hall (flexible, 190 seats), LuEsther Hall (flexible, 150 seats), Susan Stein Shiva Theater (flexible, 100 seats) and Anspacher Theater (three-quarter arena, 275 seats). In 1992 (on 23 April, Shakespeare's birthday), the building's name was officially changed to the Joseph Papp Public Theater in honour of the late producer.   MCH

public theatres (London) The open-air theatres of Elizabethan, Jacobean and Caroline London were, and still are, sometimes called 'public' playhouses to distinguish them from the equally public but more exclusive indoor 'private theatres'. They are, in approximate chronological order, the THEATRE (1576), the CURTAIN (1577), a theatre of unknown name in Newington Butts (c.1580), the ROSE (c.1587), the SWAN (1595), the GLOBE (1599), the BOAR'S HEAD (c.1599), the FORTUNE (1600), the RED BULL (1605), the second Globe (1614), the HOPE (1614) and the second Fortune (1623).   PT

Puccini, Giacomo 1858–1924 Italian composer, born into a musical family. The first of Puccini's pieces to attract attention was the one-act *Le Villi*, which the librettist Arrigo Boito was instrumental in getting produced at Milan in 1884. His mature work, beginning with *Manon Lescaut* (1893), is characterized by powerful, if at times sentimental, melodic lyricism and a highly developed theatrical sense, particularly in the depiction of character psychology and the handling of ARIAS. Several of his finest OPERAS were taken from stage plays, and indeed have survived triumphantly on the stage as the plays themselves have not: *Tosca* (1900) from SARDOU, and *Madame Butterfly* (1904) and *La fanciulla del West* (1910) from the American dramatist, DAVID BELASCO. His *Turandot*, begun in 1921, was unfinished at his death.   KR LR

Puerto Rico Until the 19th century only sporadic theatre activity existed on this eastern island in the Antilles chain. From the time of the Spanish conquest, the rivalries among the Spanish, French, English and Dutch for possession of the Caribbean islands resulted in invasions and raids that left little time for cultural development and entertainment. Through the 18th century the scant records showed the performance of an occasional GOLDEN AGE or religious play to mark special occasions. Although researchers have documented some 130 plays during the 19th century, few are of transcendental value.

For the most part the century was still dominated by foreign imports. Spanish, Italian, Mexican and Argentine travelling companies staged OPERAS, OPERETTAS, ZARZUELAS and plays from the classic Spanish repertory, or the romantic pieces of JOSÉ ZORRILLA, for example. The principal themes of the emerging Puerto Rican theatre ranged from the fanciful, escapist works following the romantic model to regionally oriented works with historical or sociopolitical overtones. The acknowledged founder of the Puerto Rican theatre, Alejandro Tapia y Rivera (1826–82), was censured for trying to humanize the English royal family in *Roberto D'Evreux* (1854). Other plays dramatized historical figures, and his *La cuarterona* (*The Quadroon*, 1867) dealt with racial issues on the island. *La parte del león* (*The Lion's Share*, 1880) anticipated later concerns about woman's role in the society. The other important 19th-century author is Salvador Brau (1842–1912), whose romantic play *La vuelta al hogar* (*Return Home*, 1877) teemed with pirates and adventures, but is only one of his many successful plays. Carmen

Hernández de Araújo (1832–77) was the island's first woman playwright, and Eugenio Astol (1843–1904) was Puerto Rico's outstanding actor of the romantic period. In the final decades of the century, the costumbristic theatre (see *COSTUMBRISMO*) also gained importance through plays such as *El jíbaro* (*The Farmer*, 1878) by Ramón Méndez Quiñones (1847–89).

Before the first theatre houses were built, it was customary to arrange provincial sites to present plays in the model of the Spanish *corral*. In 1823 the Teatro de Amigos del País (Theatre of Friends of the Country) staged several plays, and in 1834 the first theatre opened in Puerto Rico, not with a theatre itself but with operatic performances – an indication of the importance of music in the local culture. (The municipal theatre was subsequently remodelled and renamed the Tapia Theatre in 1950 (in honour of Tapia y Rivera) and restored in the 1970s to its colonial grandeur.) Throughout the century the strong hand of the Church and an active CENSORSHIP programme discouraged free expression, but was not able to suppress the construction of new theatres in San Juan, Ponce, Mayagüez, Arecibo and other towns scattered across the island.

Ruben Figueroa in Carlos Canales's *Maria del Rosario*, Puerto Rico, 1985.

The 20th century In the War of 1898, Spain ceded control of Puerto Rico to the USA. Until the Commonwealth was created in 1952, Puerto Rico was governed by a series of American-imposed governors. The changes resulting from this new political status did little to promote theatre on the island, although *El grito de Lares* (1914) by Luis Lloréns Torres (1878–1944) signalled the first of a long series of plays that examined and protested against American intervention. The stimulus for new theatre came in 1938 when EMILIO BELAVAL, as president of the Ateneo Puertorriqueño (Puerto Rican Atheneum), called for the creation of a national dramaturgy. The three plays honoured in the contest sponsored by the Ateneo were by Manuel Méndez Ballester (b.1909), author of *El clamor de los surcos* (*Cry of the Land*), Gonzalo Arocho del Toro (1898–1954), with *El desmonte* (*The Clearing*) and Fernando Sierra Berdecía (1903–62), whose *Esta noche juega el jóker* (*Tonight the Joker Plays*) broke new ground in dealing with the painful issue of the Puerto Rican immigrant in New York.

Belaval's theatre group, Areyto, created in 1939, lasted only two seasons but succeeded in establishing the basis for other groups and for a new sense of identity in the Puerto Rican theatre. FRANCISCO ARRIVÍ's Tinglado Puertorriqueño (Puerto Rican Stage, 1944) captured the same spirit and was followed by RENÉ MARQUÉS's Teatro Nuestro (Our Theatre, 1950) and the Ateneo's Experimental Theatre (1951), both in conjunction with José Lacomba (b.1924). The Puerto Rican Cultural Institute, established in 1955, sponsored its first Puerto Rican theatre festival in 1958, an unparalleled event for encouraging new playwrights and fostering theatre in Puerto Rico. The University of Puerto Rico, unable to present Puerto Rican plays from 1944 (Enrique Laguerre's *La resentida*) to 1956 (Arriví's *El murciélago* and *Medusa en la bahía*) because of political compromises, contributed to the training of new directors, actors, designers and technical crew.

Belaval, Arriví and especially René Marqués set the standards for the new theatre. Their plays dealt with life and death, philosophical and political issues; Arriví's works were often lyrical and metaphysical, such as *María Soledad* (1947). Marqués experimented with social commitment, absurdism (see THEATRE OF THE ABSURD) and biblical motifs, all within vanguard techniques incorporating light and sound. His *Los soles truncos* (*The Fanlights*, 1958) is still the classic Puerto Rican play because of the effective combination of its theme of psychological, cultural and political distress with techniques of poetic staging. The common denominator throughout Marqués's plays is his opposition to American encroachment on Hispanic values.

Some of the later generation of writers, such as Myrna Casas (b.1934), followed Arriví's lyrical patterns. Others echoed the sociopolitical commitment of Marqués, especially LUIS RAFAEL SÁNCHEZ in *La pasión según Antígona Pérez* (*The Passion according to Antígona Pérez*, 1968). Piri Fernández (b.1925), working for the Institute of Puerto Rican Culture, wrote and staged plays such as *De tanto caminar* (*So Much Walking*, 1960), depicting with double planes of action the religious doubts of a nun.

Between 1966 and 1975 collective theatre achieved new

levels of popularity and influence, as seen in such groups as El Tajo del Alacrán (the Scorpion's Sting, 1966), headed by Lydia Milagros González (b.1942), Unamu, Teatro de Guerrilla (Guerrilla Theatre, 1969), Morivivi (1972) and others – all with the function of raising the consciousness of political theatre of protest. Jaime Carrero (b.1931) dealt with the Vietnam War and the Puerto Rican in the USA (see NUYORICAN THEATRE) in his plays *Flag Inside* (1966) and *Pipo Subway no sabe reír* (*Pipo Subway Does Not Know How to Laugh*, 1971); his *Prohibido el silencio* (*Silence Forbidden*) is from 1987. Pedro Santiliz (b.1938) arranged works especially for street theatre. The younger writers include José 'Papo' Márquez (b.1950), Abneil Morales (b.1958), and others who struggled against bourgeois influences in the theatre. Major productions of the 1980s include Pedro Cabrera's *La verdadera historia de Pedro Navaja* (*The True Story of Mack the Knife*, 1980) and Myrna Casas's *El gran circo Eukraniano* (*The Great Ukrainian Circus*, 1988). The most active of the younger generation may be ROBERTO RAMOS-PEREA, whose plays are brutal and closely tied to a strong critique of the reality of contemporary Puerto Rico.

In addition to the festival sponsored by the Puerto Rican Cultural Institute (1985 was the 26th), other events raised the level of theatre consciousness. The International Theatre Festival (created in 1956) staged the best foreign plays. In the 1970s the *muestras* (showcases) sponsored by the Spanish-born Luis Molina promoted a consciousness of Third World theatre and provoked a political storm, testing allegiances among theatre groups vying for funding. A host of independent theatre groups was formed in the 1960s and 70s, some of them short-lived: El Cemí, Teatro Yukayeke, Teatro La Máscara, Cimarrón, Proscenio, Nuestro Teatro and others. Teatro del Sesenta has functioned for more than 20 years and owns the Sylvia Rexach Theatre. Travelling groups such as Teatro Rodante and Farándula Universitaria generate interest in the theatre across the island. Ironically, the oldest existing theatre group is still the English-speaking Little Theatre, created in 1931.

The mixture of Anglo and Hispanic culture on the island remains anomalous. In spite of programmes like Operation Bootstrap designed to encourage the Puerto Rican economy, New York has lured millions of Puerto Ricans over the years, although many have returned disillusioned to the island. Political positions in Puerto Rico range from pro-independence to pro-statehood, with the present Commonwealth status in the middle. The threat of annexation by the United States provokes groups such as the Comité de Defensa de la Cultura Puertorriqueña (Puerto Rican Cultural Defence League) to use theatre as a weapon for defending the Hispanic identity. GW

See: F. Arriví, *Areyto Mayor*, San Juan, 1966; J. A. Collins, *Contemporary Theatre in Puerto Rico*, San Juan, 1979, and *Contemporary Theatre in Puerto Rico: The Decade of the Seventies*, Río Piedras, 1982; N. González, *Bibliografía de teatro puertorriqueño* (*siglos 19 y 20*), Río Piedras, 1979; A. Morfi, *Historia crítica de un siglo de teatro puertorriqueño*, San Juan, 1980; E. J. Pasarell, *Orígenes y desarrollo de la afición teatral en Puerto Rico*, Santurce, 1969; J. B. Phillips, *Contemporary Puerto Rican Drama*, New York, 1972; E. H. Quiles Ferrer, *Teatro puertorriqueño en acción (dramaturgia y escenificación) 1982–1989*, San Juan, 1990; R. Ramos-Perea, *Perspectiva de la nueva dramaturgia puertorriqueña: Ensayos sobre el nuevo teatro nacional*, San Juan, 1989.

Pulcinella see PUNCH

Punch The most celebrated of English PUPPETS; the name is short for Punchinello, itself from the Italian Policinella, whose etymology is disputed. The character's hooked nose and hump may derive from the Maccus of the Roman Atellan FARCES, although these attributes are more changeable in the Neapolitan *COMMEDIA DELL'ARTE* figure, Pulcinella, than in the Northern European puppet. The former, according to some claims, was invented by the actor SILVIO FIORILLO and then perfected by Andrea Calcese, alias Ciuccio (d.1656). His Pulcinella was a peasant of Acerra, shrill, cowardly, oafish and given to mischief and sententiousness. At the Teatro San Carlino, Naples, the character became acclimatized as a kind of HARLEQUIN clad in a loose white smock and black half-MASK, and was a constant participant in all public ceremonies there and in Venice.

The French Polichinelle first appears as a MARIONETTE in the 17th-century show of the tooth-drawer Jean Brioché; cleverer than his Italian counterpart, this 'little wooden Aesop, moving, turning, spinning, dancing, laughing, talking, farting', as he was described in *Le Combat de Cyrano de Bergerac* (1649), was soon adapted to political SATIRE. A puppet Polizinell crops up in Nuremberg in 1649 and a Don Cristóval Pulichinella in Spain of the same period. The flesh-and-blood Polichinelle played in an intermezzo to MOLIÈRE's *Imaginary Invalid* (1673), but EVARISTO GHERARDI dropped the character from the Théâtre Italien for being too scurrilous a villain. After a lapse in popularity, the early 19th century saw a Polichinelle revival: the dancer MAZURIER imitated the puppet and the MIME artist Vautier made him a major character at the THÉÂTRE DES FUNAMBULES.

The English Punch probably came over during the Restoration, for the word was in common use by 1669 to describe something short and thick. PEPYS and Evelyn both witnessed a marionette Punch and as early as 1678 OTWAY in *Friendship in Fashion* mentions Punch's characteristic voice, later produced by the 'swazzle' or 'swatchel', a device of metal and silk held in the showman's mouth. The English Punch inherited many of the traits of the medieval Vice and was linked with all sorts of traditional themes: he took part in the creation of the world (Bartholomew Fair, 1703) and the Deluge (1709) and, as the hero of Martin Powell's puppet-show at COVENT GARDEN (1710), he associated with paladins and danced a minuet with a pig.

By 1780, the glove puppet Punch had become a familiar street show, played in a curtained booth either solo or with a commentator and 'bottler' who collected the audience's coins. A conventional scenario had taken shape: Punch, a kind of anarchic Falstaff, lying, bragging and bullying, in a series of confrontations with representatives of the social order – wife, beadle, doctor, executioner, devil – wins out by sheer egoistic brazenness. His dog Toby, first wooden, then real, is a silent observer of the mayhem. The first 'swatchel omi', as Punchmen are known in street performer slang, to be taken up by the literati was Giovanni Piccini (d.1835), whose script was published by John Payne Collier with engravings by George Cruikshank in 1828. Percy Press is the best-known of the modern showmen, though other dynasties, like the Maggs and the Codmans, still thrive, playing chiefly at seaside resorts. In 1962, the 300th anniversary of Punch's advent in England (dated from Pepys's *Diary* entry) was celebrated at St Paul's Cathedral, London; but of late he has been under attack by feminists and educationists for his wife-beating and child abuse. LS

puppets Dolls or figures which imitate human behaviour, often in a parodic or alienated manner. Live manipulators animate the figures dexterously to produce an impression of life upon the spectators; the paradox is that the puppeteer remains hidden or obscured, while his creation takes centre stage as a vivid individual. The art may have arisen out of MASKed religious ceremonials, and the use of miniature human figurines for magical purposes. The earliest to develop were the stringed puppets or MARIONETTES, which appear to have been known to the early Egyptians, Hindus and Greeks. Other common types are hand or glove puppets, SHADOW PUPPETS and rod puppets.

Hand puppetry, in which the puppeteer cannot see the public's reaction, is portrayed as early as 1340 in the Oxford MS *Li romans du bon roi Alexandre* by the Fleming Jehan de Grise, but is probably much older. Three, rarely five, fingers are used, and the stage concealing the manipulator is a booth with three walls, known in the Romance languages as *castelet*, *castillo* and *castello*. The 'motions' of Elizabethan and Jacobean England, reproduced in BEN JONSON's *Bartholomew Fair* (1614), presented anachronistic legends, chock-full of slapstick, violence and bawdry. Hand puppets were a favourite instrument of the Russian *SKOMOROKHI*, being easily portable and wielded by one man, and devolved into the popular figure Petrushka. Indeed, the most enduring national types of puppet – PUNCH in England, GUIGNOL in France, KASPER in Germany and Austria – were portrayed most commonly by hand puppets. The leading 20th-century performer was SERGEI OBRAZTSOV.

Rod puppets, more characteristic of the Orient, may have been created in Bengal and, with the spread of Hinduism, became the popular *wayang golek* of Sunda, Java and Thailand. In China, the *tiexian kuilei* are first mentioned at a mourning service during the Tang era (618–906), but gained popularity during the Sung dynasty. The three leading types are the big heads from Sichuan, the medium-sized from Hunan, Shanxi and Beijing, and the miniature variety from Shandong. Except for the clowns, most have no feet and the faces are painted in the style of Beijing Opera, the colour combination indicating the complexity of the character. Occasionally, in an intricate action like a swordfight, the puppeteer will use his hands as well as the rods.

In Japan, the *BUNRAKU* is a separate genre of the drama, with its own repertory. The large but lightweight figures are moved by a principal operator, assisted by two hooded auxiliaries, by means of a control stick and various levers manipulating arms, fingers, eyes, eyebrows, mouth, and so on. The voices are provided by a *joruri* reciter, who spins the narrative to samisen accompaniment. This style arose in the early 17th century and flourished during the Tokugawa period (1600–1868), by which time it had the masterpieces of CHIKAMATSU MONZAEMON to perform.

In the 19th century, puppets engaged the imagination of the literary world. George Sand created a Théâtre des Amis for hand puppets at her estate at Nohant; Henry Monnier opened a pornographic puppet theatre in 1862; and Count Franz Pocci, intendant of the Munich court theatre, composed plays for Kasper. The notion of the actor as puppet gained ground among the European avant-garde. In 1888, Henri Signoret opened a Petit Théâtre des Marionettes, which presented ARISTOPHANES, CERVANTES and SHAKESPEARE. MAURICE MAETERLINCK wrote three plays for puppets in 1894 (*Alladine et Palomides*, *Intérieur*, *La Mort de Tintagiles*), claiming that actors were too obtuse to convey his metaphysical concerns. The Russian symbolist FYODOR SOLOGUB argued that actors should simply perform what the playwright reads aloud, thus emblematizing the relationship of the helpless human being to fate. JARRY's *Ubu Roi* was performed at the Théâtre des Pantins in 1898 with puppets of the painter Bonnard, and GORDON CRAIG hoped in 1905 and 1911 that the actor would acquire the technique and egoless grace of an *Über-Marionette*. ERWIN PISCATOR staged *The Adventures of the Good Soldier Schweik* with figures devised by Georg Grosz (1928). Such oversized manikins became a popular AGIT-PROP device, taken to heights of ingenious creativity in the USA during the anti-Vietnam War protests by the BREAD AND PUPPET THEATRE. LS

> *See*: M. Batchelder, *The Puppet Theatre Handbook*, New York, 1947; S. Benegal, *Puppet Theatre around the World*, New Delhi, 1961; M. Byron, *Punch in the Italian Puppet Theatre*, London, 1983; J. Buch and A. Lehmann, *Das Puppentheater*, 4 vols., Leipzig, 1923–31; P. McPharlin, *The Puppet Theatre in America: A History 1524–1948*, with a supplement by M. B. McPharlin, New York, 1969; G. Speaight, *The History of the English Puppet Theatre*, London, 1955.

Purim play Purim, a Jewish festival held on Adar 14 and 15 (late March and early April), celebrates the thwarting by Esther and Mordecai of Haman's planned massacre of the Jews in Persia under Artaxerxes (Ahasuerus). From earliest times, it constituted a Jewish equivalent to CARNIVAL, with masquerades and cross-dressing. At first, Haman was burnt in effigy and the story retold in the bosom of the family; by the late 15th century, jesters and mummers were performing more public enactments and selecting a 'King of Purim'. This gave rise to the only true Jewish folk drama. Significantly, the first Judaeo-Spanish play is *Esther* by Solomon Usque and Lazara Gratiano (1567); and an anonymous COMEDY, *Haman and Mordechai*, was published in Leyden in 1699. *Purimspiele* were of long standing among the German Jews; a *Spil von Tab Jaklein mit Sein Weib* was performed every Purim in Tannhausen throughout the 16th century. The first of these to be published was *Ahasweroshspiel* (Frankfurt, 1708). The Rabbinical authorities frequently forbade performances and burnt the texts, because they parodied serious portions of the ritual.

The Mekirat Yosef, a recounting of the tale of Joseph and

his brethren by Baermann of Limburg (c.1711), was enacted by Jewish theological students of Prague and Hamburg with the author as their stage manager. It created a sensation, but was banned as soon as Christians began to attend. (It could be seen in Minsk as late as 1858.) An *Esther and Ahasuerus* acted in Prague by rabbinical students in 1774 was later rewritten by Itsik Manger in the 1920s, with the action translated to a small Eastern European village; this version played in both America and Tel Aviv. Ephraim Lauter's 1925 Purim play initiated the first YIDDISH THEATRE in the Ukraine. By this time, it had become a vehicle for the *badchen*, the improvising master of ceremonies of Jewish weddings and celebrations; the term 'Purim play' had become synonymous with crude Yiddish productions and 'Purim author' with a hack playwright. (See also HEBREW THEATRE.) LS

Purimspiel see HEBREW THEATRE; PURIM PLAY

Purvis, Billy c.1781–1853 British showman, CLOWN, conjuror, dancer and virtuoso of the Northumbrian pipes. Though born near Edinburgh he was brought up in Newcastle upon Tyne, where he became a call boy at the Theatre Royal. In 1818 he established a fit-up company (a small and minimally equipped travelling outfit that played at non-theatre venues), subsequently and grandly known as the 'Victorian Theatre', which toured the fairs and races of the north of England and lowland Scotland presenting 'PANTOMIME plays full o' reed an' blue fire', MELODRAMAS and cut versions of SHAKESPEARE; interspersed with local songs, dances and music, and introduced by Billy himself, grotesque in clown's pantaloons, skull cap and round glasses, who would invite the public to walk up across the forestage of his booth, or, if they proved diffident, to 'get in by Billy's backside' (the rear entrance). At his death his former employee NED CORVAN penned an affectionate elegy which refers to a number of Billy's skills and GAGS, notably his routine of 'stealing the bundle', a simple LAZZO with improvised asides to the audience in which the clown robbed an unsuspecting bumpkin of his possessions. AEG

Pushkin, Aleksandr (Sergeevich) 1799–1837 Russia's greatest national poet, formulator of her literary language, and dramatic theorist of note. Despite his admiration for the verse comedies of FONVIZIN, KNYAZHNIN, SHAKHOVSKOI, KHMELNITSKY and GRIBOEDOV, Pushkin pioneered the historical, romantic, pre-realistic drama in opposition to the prevailing French neo-classical model. His dramatic output, while not large and somewhat diffuse, is ambitious, novel and experimental, progressive and even revolutionary technically and ideologically. He drew upon contemporary parlance, literary sources and native folklore to forge a purposely hybrid Russian literary language suitable for comic and tragic scenes and character-specific for individuals of every class and profession. His inspiration for this was SHAKESPEARE, whom he read in the translations and criticisms of A. W. SCHLEGEL and François Guizot.

The direct result was his dramatic *magnum opus, Boris Godunov* (written 1825, produced 1870), an episodic blank-verse TRAGEDY about the Time of Troubles (1604–13)

patterned after Shakespeare's historical chronicle plays. It illustrates Pushkin's thesis that the object of tragedy is 'man's fate and the people's destinies'. Ever watchful of Boris, the Slavic Macbeth, are the people 'always clandestinely leaning towards sedition', in what is the most celebrated instance of the collective hero in Russian drama. Here, as elsewhere in his work, Pushkin reveals insight into the poignant, seductive and above all tragic relationship between ruler and ruled, the struggle against tyranny and the yielding to power. A publication and performance ban, together with a long-standing myth concerning its unstageability, has kept the play from assuming a place in the dramatic repertoire equal to that occupied by Mussorgsky's operatic treatment of it (1873).

In his *Little Tragedies* (written 1823–30, published 1832–9), Pushkin presents history writ small via a series of short, self-contained character sketches of familiar European literary types – the miser (*The Covetous Knight*), the artistic genius and his rival (*Mozart and Salieri*), and the legendary Don Juan as a tragic romancer (*The Stone Guest*). These dramatic variations on three of the deadly sins together with an allied piece, *The Feast in Plague-Time* (after John Wilson), are seldom performed. The MOSCOW ART THEATRE, recognizing the opportunities afforded here for psychological REALISM, in 1915 presented a programme of all save *The Covetous Knight*, with sets by BENOIS, and with STANISLAVSKY and KACHALOV in major roles. Pushkin's *Rusalka* (1831), a REVENGE TRAGEDY on a fairy-tale theme which provided tragedienne MARIYA ERMOLOVA with an artistic success, and *Scenes from the Age of Chivalry* (1835), an unfinished historical-dramatic meditation on peasant rebellion and impoverished nobility, round off his playwriting career. Several theatres in Moscow and St Petersburg today bear his name. SG

putul nautch Form of rod-puppet theatre in Bengal state in eastern INDIA: literally, 'dancing dolls'. In the past PUPPETS 2 to 3ft in height were constructed of plaster on a bamboo frame covered by banana leaves to give shape to the different parts of the body. Nowadays dolls are carved from wood, hollowed to reduce weight and to allow rods and strings to pass through the body.

Manipulators work the dolls from below. To their waistband they tie a cup in which they support a long rod which goes through the centre of the puppet to its head. Through a system of strings connected to various parts of the figure they manipulate and dance the puppets, giving life to the figures.

Today performances are presented in connection with fairs and festivals, though not as frequently as in the past. Some plays centre on events from the *Mahabharata*. Other plays draw on local folk tales, such as that of Manasa, the snake-goddess sister of Sesha, the serpent-king, and stories concerning Radha and Krishna. FaR

Pyat, Félix 1810–89 French journalist and dramatist. A prominent utopian socialist, hostile to the government of Louis Philippe and later to Napoleon III (during most of whose reign he had to remain in exile), he became an important figure in the Commune of 1871 and was obliged to return to exile for a further ten years. He made three brief incursions into government in 1848, 1871 and 1888.

Pyat saw himself as a socialist dramatist and as having a role to play in the creation of a popular theatre. He subscribed to the moral virtues of the MELODRAMA and most of his ten principal plays, with the exception of *Diogène* (1846), are cast in this form. *Ango*, written in collaboration with Auguste Luchet in 1835, was a virulent attack on the monarchy in the person of François I. The censors demanded modifications after the first performance, and the play was definitively banned a few days later following the Fieschi attempt on the life of the king (see CENSORSHIP). With *Les Deux Serruriers* (*The Two Locksmiths*, 1841) and *Le Chiffonnier de Paris* (*The Rag-Picker of Paris*, 1847), starring FRÉDÉRICK LEMAÎTRE, he turned to a drama of modern society where the villains are bankers and where it is clearly shown that there is one law for the rich and another for the poor. *Le Chiffonnier de Paris* was his most popular work and contains the common opposition between poverty and virtue in a garret and wealth and corruption in an affluent drawing-room. The tone is at times close to that of the novels of Eugène Sue, whose *Mathilde* he had dramatized in 1841. JMCC

pyolsandae Traditional masked dance plays (*SANDAE-GUK*), performed in villages of central KOREA, near Seoul. Literally, 'separate stage performance', the term indicates folk performances 'separated' from the original, now defunct, masked plays of the Seoul court. The *pyolsandae* from Yangju town, about 15 miles northeast of Seoul, is one of Korea's major cultural treasures. Performances are given several times a year; that celebrating Buddha's birthday on the 8th day of the fourth lunar month is the most splendid. The entire town is lit up with colourful lanterns and the night-time performance lit by torches lasts until dawn. The playing area is an open field at the foot of a hill, with the costume room (*kae-bokch'ung*) installed at one side. Musicians playing transverse flute, two-stringed fiddle, hourglass-shaped drum, barrel drum and two fifes, take positions at one end of the circular playing area while the audience stands or sits at the other end. Actors make their entrances and exits through two doors in the costume rooms. A momentary pause in the action indicates a change of scene. The language is frank, the down-to-earth colloquial conversation of country people. Actors perform more than a dozen types of dances: including 'Yodaji', 'Kopsawi', and 'Kkaeki' dances. The faces of the MASKS are made of curved sections of large, dried gourds. Exaggerated features are glued and painted to the surface. No old masks of this theatre exist since they are burned as part of the religious ceremonies marking the end of each performance. OKC

Q Theatre (London) Opened by Jack de Leon in 1924, Q Theatre gained a reputation for trying out new plays, among which were TERENCE RATTIGAN's earliest work *First Episode* (1934) and PRIESTLEY's *Bright Shadow* (1950), as well as for the number of actors who made their first appearance on its stage – including Max Adrian, ANTHONY QUAYLE and Dirk Bogarde. The death of de Leon in 1956 ended a campaign for funds to modernize the building, which had been refused a performance licence a year earlier, and it was demolished in 1958.   CI

Quayle, (John) Anthony 1913–89 British actor and director, who was a stalwart member of the OLD VIC company in the 1930s without ever becoming one of its stars. He joined the Royal Artillery during the war, and when he left in 1945 he took a leading part in the reconstruction of British theatre in the postwar years. He succeeded BARRY JACKSON as the director of the Shakespeare Memorial Theatre at Stratford-upon-Avon and stayed there for eight years, during which time he built up its financial resources and earned the company an international reputation with such productions as *Titus Andronicus* (1956), directed by PETER BROOK and starring LAURENCE OLIVIER, in which he played Aaron. His Stratford policy was criticized for being too star-orientated, but under difficult conditions he nevertheless provided a succession of worthwhile Shakespearian productions and acted in many of them himself, notably as Falstaff in *Henry IV Parts 1 and 2* (1951), in *Coriolanus* (1952) and in *Othello* (1954). On leaving Stratford in 1957, he was in continual demand as an actor in contemporary plays, and scored a personal triumph in François Billetdoux's *Chin-Chin* (1960), playing opposite Celia Johnson. He appeared as Sir Charles Dilke in *The Right Honourable Gentleman* (1964), as Galileo in BRECHT's play in New York in 1967, and directed Dostoevsky's *The Idiot* (1970) for the NATIONAL THEATRE.

Quayle appeared in numerous films, usually in major supporting roles, and his normally restrained acting style was not one which commanded centre-stage attention. With PEGGY ASHCROFT as his partner, he provided a memorable account of ALEKSEI ARBUZOV's *Old World* in 1978. That year he joined the Prospect Theatre Company to direct *The Rivals* and play King Lear, and when Prospect eventually collapsed as Britain's major touring classical company, he formed an unsubsidized alternative, Orbit, in 1981, which took leading actors in classical productions to many regional theatres.   JE

Queen Elizabeth's Men It was a sign of the growing power of the theatre in England that Elizabeth I granted the patronage of her name to a new company, formed primarily for the purpose of performing at court, in 1583. That it had a bias towards COMEDY and extempore entertainment is suggested by the prominence in it of RICHARD TARLTON and ROBERT WILSON. The company's best days ended with Tarlton's death in 1588, and it was disbanded in 1594.   PT

Questors Theatre (Ealing, West London) A leading British amateur theatre group since its foundation in 1929. Its tireless leader for the first 40 years of its existence was Alfred Emmet (d.1990), who distrusted commercial theatre and wanted to present intellectually stimulating plays in competent productions. From 1933 until the late 1950s the company used a disused chapel in Mattock Lane, but it acquired the site and built a new 400-seat theatre, adaptable in its staging, although its best configuration is as an open stage, with the audience sitting on three sides.

Questors Theatre has facilities beyond the range of most amateur companies; but it also has a proud reputation for discovering new plays and dramatists, JAMES SAUNDERS being perhaps the best-known. For 17 years, from 1960 to 1977, it ran an annual Festival of New Plays. It is also internationally known, a founder member (1952) of the International Amateur Theatre Association (IATA), and has acted as host to amateur companies from Europe, North America and the Third World. Alfred Emmet retired in 1969, leaving behind a professionally run administration, a membership of 3000 and a training school for actors in the West London region, in addition to Questors Theatre itself. Right up to his death he remained actively involved. Members of his family are still active in what has been for half a century, and remains, an amateur group for all kinds of theatre artists, amateur and professional.   JE

Quin, James 1693–1766 English actor, known as 'Bellower Quin'. Contemporary records show that in matters of costume and vocal projection Quin favoured the grand style. At LINCOLN's INN FIELDS from 1718 to 1732 he played the major Shakespearian tragic heroes. He remained working in London, at COVENT GARDEN and finally DRURY LANE, until 1751, his manner of playing becoming less and less fashionable – but a powerful reminder of the heroic tastes of the Restoration theatre.   MB

Quinault, Philippe 1635–88 French dramatist and librettist. From a humble background, he went into service with TRISTAN L'HERMITE who encouraged his natural ability and helped him make his way in literary and fashionable society. He was only 18 when he adapted *Les Rivales* (*The Rivals*) from a comedy by ROTROU and went on to produce a series of plays for the HÔTEL DE BOURGOGNE and the MARAIS, all cleverly contrived and popular with the public, though occasionally owing more than a little to the work of other writers. The most successful were the TRAGEDY *Astrate, roi de Tyr* (*Astrates, King of Tyre*, 1664) and the COMEDY *La Mère coquette* (*The Flirtatious Mother*), which opened at the Hôtel de Bourgogne in 1665 in direct opposition to VISÉ's play of the same name at the Marais. Writing the libretto for LULLY's court *divertissement*, *La Grotte de Versailles*, in 1668 enabled him to discover his most distinctive talent, and with the foundation of the Paris Opéra in 1672 he became

Lully's accredited collaborator, producing librettos for a dozen large-scale works which delighted Louis XIV and were to dominate operatic tradition for many years. He also collaborated with MOLIÈRE and PIERRE CORNEILLE on the lyrics for the *tragédie-ballet Psyché* in 1671, the year after his election to the Académie-Française. DR

Quintero, José 1924– Panamanian-born American director specializing in the plays of EUGENE O'NEILL. Having begun directing in 1949, Quintero helped launch CIRCLE IN THE SQUARE in 1951. Attracted by theatre's passion, he firmly believes 'the collective product more important than any individual contribution'. His O'Neill productions include the definitive *The Iceman Cometh* with JASON ROBARDS JR (1956; Vernon Rice Award), *Long Day's Journey into Night* (1956; Tony), *A Moon for the Misbegotten* (BROADWAY, 1973; Tony and Drama Desk Award), *Strange Interlude* (ACTORS STUDIO, 1963) and *A Touch of the Poet* (Broadway, 1977). In 1980 he directed *Ah, Wilderness* at Mexico's National Theatre. Awarded the 1981 O'Neill Birthday Medal, Quintero, a member of the Theatre Hall of Fame, toured a 1985 revival of *Iceman* with Robards, which won the HELEN HAYES and Los Angeles Drama Critics' Circle Awards and the O'Neill Gold Medal.

Other Quintero productions include the revival of TENNESSEE WILLIAMS's *Summer and Smoke* (1952), BEHAN's *The Hostage* (1954) and *The Quare Fellow* (1958), Jules Feiffer's *Knock Knock* (1976) and COCTEAU's *The Human Voice* (1978, Melbourne, Australia; 1979, Broadway). After the Broadway failure of Tennessee Williams's *Clothes for a Summer Hotel* (1980), Quintero left New York and now works primarily in Texas and Florida. He won the 1986–7 Drama League Award for 'bringing to renewed life the plays of O'Neill'. His autobiography, *If You Don't Dance, They Beat You*, was published in 1974. REK

quotidien, théâtre du Style of theatre, influenced partly by German-language playwrights such as FASSBINDER, KROETZ, SPERR and HANDKE and pioneered in the 1970s by the Comédie de Caen and the Théâtre National de Strasbourg. The plays characteristically show inarticulate people in everyday situations presented with a heightened realism so that powerful theatrical images express, often brutally, the desires and needs which they are unable to express in spoken language. Behind the ordinariness of these people's lives the hidden violence of modern European social structures emerges with great force. Plots are fragmentary and characters are often controlled by language that is imposed upon them from outside, e.g. the language of the sports business in René Kalisky's *Skandalon* (1970), about a champion racing cyclist controlled entirely by the interests of others. Georges Michel is often seen as the first of these playwrights, though his success *La Promenade du dimanche* (*The Sunday Walk*, 1966) also owes much to the THEATRE OF THE ABSURD. Michel's work was encouraged by SARTRE, who published his first play, *Les Jouets* (*The Toys*), in *Les Temps modernes* in 1963. He has since written several more plays on the theme of alienation in the consumer society, of which the best is *Un Petit Nid d'amour* (*A Little Love Nest*, 1970).

The major *quotidien* playwrights of the 1970s were Michel Deutsch and Jean-Paul Wenzel. During this period Deutsch worked as dramaturge for the Théâtre National de Strasbourg under JEAN-PIERRE VINCENT and some of his plays were commissioned for that theatre, for example, *Convoi* (*Convoy*, 1980), which depicts the relationship between a young Jewish girl and the old French peasant woman who tries to shelter her during the Occupation. Their relationship becomes a battleground for conflicting ways of articulating experience, mirroring the larger national conflict. Wenzel has directed the work of Deutsch as well as writing his own plays, the most successful being *Loin d'Hagondange* (*Far from Hagondange*), partly thanks to a brilliant production by PATRICE CHÉREAU at the THÉÂTRE NATIONAL POPULAIRE (1977). DB

Rabe, David 1940– Iowa-born American playwright and screenwriter, known for his work about the Vietnam War. Rabe, a Loras College graduate (1962), also attended Villanova University, Philadelphia, where a number of his early plays were performed. Drafted in 1965, he was then sent to Vietnam. His big break came when, discovered by JOSEPH PAPP, five of his early plays were staged by the NEW YORK SHAKESPEARE FESTIVAL. In 1971 *The Basic Training of Pavlo Hummel* and *Sticks and Bones* ran simultaneously, *Pavlo* at the PUBLIC THEATER and *Sticks* (Tony) on BROADWAY. Far less successful were *In the Boom Boom Room* (1973–4), about the victimization of a Philadelphia go-go dancer, and *The Orphan* (1974), Rabe's adaptation of the *Oresteia*. *Streamers*, the third play in his Vietnam Trilogy (*Pavlo* and *Sticks* being the others), was staged in 1976. Rabe, however, is more than a Vietnam War playwright: *Goose and Tomtom* (1982, 86) is an existential comedy about a bizarre robbery; *Hurlyburly* (1984) is about Hollywood image-making and failed dreams. A prequel to *Hurlyburly*, entitled *Those the River Keeps*, premiered in 1991 (revived in 1994). Rabe's screenplays include *I'm Dancing As Fast As I Can* (1981) and *Casualties of War* (1990). His plays, filled with violence, racism, betrayals, foolish heroism and male tribal customs, combine grotesque COMEDY, surrealistic fantasy and bitter SATIRE. PK

Rabémanajara, Jacques (Félicien) 1914–89 Malagasy poet and playwright, closely associated with the negritude movement and its cultural organ *Présence Africaine*. Born in Maroantsetra, Rabémanajara was educated in Paris, where he lived from 1938 to 45. After the Second World War, he returned to Madagascar and became involved in the nationalist politics of his day. He was accused of complicity in the 1947 Malagasy rebellion against French rule, detained for more than a year, then sentenced to 20 years' hard labour; he was released from gaol in 1956. He held political office in the first government of independent Madagascar until 1972 when, after the regime's overthrow in a coup, he went to live in France.

Rabémanajara was above all a poet, but he also wrote three plays: *Les Dieux malgaches* (*The Malagasy Gods*, 1964) on the period leading to the conquest of the island; *Les Boutriers de l'aurore* (*The Boatmen of the Dawn*, 1957) on the arrival of its early Southeast Asian settlers; and *Agapes des dieux, Tritriva* (*Reunion of the Gods, Tritriva*, 1962), on a tragic love story in which a father's attempt to prevent his daughter's marriage to the man of her choice ends with the death in Lake Tritriva of the lovers and of the girl's aunt. The fatal passions in these plays, presented in verse and in a context of legend and history, lend a distinct French classical tonality to Rabémanajara's theatre. JCM

Rabinal Achí The only indisputably authentic dramatic work of the pre-Columbian New World. (The *OLLANTAY* of Peru and the *Güegüence* of NICARAGUA have later influences.) Created as the *Dance of Tun* by the Maya-Quichés, it shows no European influence. Music and spectacle are integral to the repetitious, stylized dialogue involving two primary characters, the Quiché Warrior and the Rabinal Warrior, engaged in ceremonial battle over death with honour. Preserved through oral tradition, the play was first recorded in 1850, and subsequently translated into French, Spanish and English. A part of the rich folkloric tradition of GUATEMALA, the play is still performed annually at the end of January in the city of Rabinal. GW

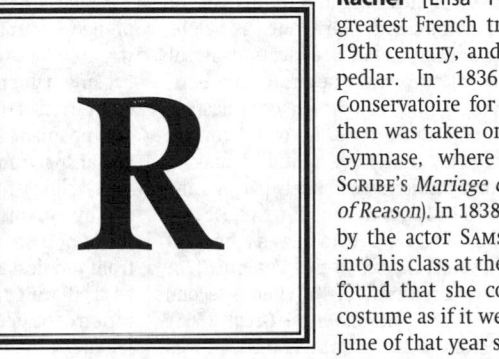

Rachel [Élisa Félix] 1820–58 The greatest French tragic actress of the 19th century, and the daughter of a pedlar. In 1836 she joined the Conservatoire for a few months but then was taken on at the Théâtre du Gymnase, where she appeared in SCRIBE's *Mariage de raison* (*Marriage of Reason*). In 1838 she was discovered by the actor SAMSON, who took her into his class at the Conservatoire and found that she could wear classical costume as if it were made for her. In June of that year she made her debut at the COMÉDIE-FRANÇAISE as Camille in PIERRE CORNEILLE's *Horace*. By September audiences were flocking to that theatre.

Rachel rapidly became extremely demanding, prompted by a family who were not slow to exploit her. The rest of the troupe had to put up with her caprices and, as the years went by, her increasingly frequent absences on personally lucrative tours. In 1849 she had her contract as a *sociétaire* annulled, and then had herself re-employed at a salary of 42,000 francs as a *pensionnaire* (which gave her six months' leave a year). She had visited England in 1841, 1843 and 1846, when the Comédie-Française had refused to prolong her leave. In 1850 she spent four months touring, in 1851 six months. In 1855 she resigned from the Comédie-Française, paid a final visit to England, went to New York with her own troupe in August, but began to suffer from tuberculosis and had to dissolve her troupe in January 1856.

Rachel's greatest roles were in the classical repertoire, and in 1838 she played Hermione in *Andromaque*, Émilie in *Cinna*, and Roxanne in *Bajazet*. ALFRED DE MUSSET became one of her lovers in 1841 (others were Véron, who included her in his harem at the Opéra, the Prince de Joinville, and Napoleon's son, Count Walewski, and nephew, Prince Napoleon). He wrote a review of Rachel's first season, which is virtually a manifesto for a new type of TRAGEDY on neoclassical lines using themes from French history. Musset also wrote a celebrated description of a visit to Rachel, *A Supper at Rachel's*.

Rachel was an inspired natural performer, with an ability to give to the text a strong human quality and to make it sound as if it were being heard for the first time. She also had very clear diction, a sense of musical rhythms and an economy of gesture (particularly striking at a period when the larger gestures of MELODRAMA were the norm). Although she was to play Bérénice (1844), Athalie (1847) and, less successfully, Agrippine in *Britannicus* (1848), her greatest triumph in the Racinian repertoire was as Phèdre, first performed in 1843, when it ran for an unprecedented 74 successive performances. Rachel also appeared with some success in the modern repertoire in Scribe's *Adrienne Lecouvreur*, but her last new part in his *The Czarina* at the Comédie-Française in 1855 was a failure. In her later years, when her talent was declining, she was often compared unfavourably to the Italian actress RISTORI by those who preferred a more romantic style. JMCC

Racine, Jean 1639–99 French poet and dramatist, the most gifted tragedian of his century. Orphaned as a child, he received an outstanding classical education at the Jansenist schools of Port-Royal, where he wrote some early religious verse. Having vainly sought an ecclesiastical living through his uncle's influence, he opted for the worldly pleasures of Paris and endeavoured to make a career in literature, dedicating verse to likely patrons and becoming friendly with La Fontaine and BOILEAU. He also made the acquaintance of MOLIÈRE, who agreed to present his first play, *La Thébaïde, ou Les Frères ennemis* (*The Thebaïd, or The Enemy Brothers*, 1664). When a second TRAGEDY, *Alexandre le Grand* (*Alexander the Great*, 1665), again premiered by Molière at the PALAIS-ROYAL, proved successful, he promptly transferred it to Molière's competitors at the HÔTEL DE BOURGOGNE, who were the recognized performers of tragedy. Further evidence of his ambition and lack of scruple was provided by an offensively personal attack on Pierre Nicole, his erstwhile teacher at Port-Royal, for the latter's condemnation of dramatic authors. Racine may also have engineered the defection from Molière's company of his current mistress, the talented tragic actress Mlle du Parc, so that she could play the lead in his next tragedy *Andromaque* at the Hôtel de Bourgogne. It was a triumph there in 1667, and was followed by a period of intense creativity for Racine. In addition to the COMEDY *Les Plaideurs* (*The Litigants*, 1668), derived partly from the *Wasps* of ARISTOPHANES, he produced six tragedies in only ten years, all of them masterpieces: *Britannicus* (1668), *Bérénice* (1670), *Bajazet* (1672), *Mithridate* (1673), *Iphigénie en Aulide* (1674) and *Phèdre* (1677).

It was also a period of growing antagonism with the ageing PIERRE CORNEILLE, whose *Tite et Bérénice* was presented by Molière only one week before Racine's version at the rival theatre and whose reputation as a tragic dramatist Racine was soon acknowledged to have outstripped. His Bérénice, and new mistress, was MLLE CHAMPMESLÉ, who scored some of her greatest successes in this and the following plays. Having now reached the pinnacle of his career, he could count on protection in the highest places, above all from the king, and he was elected to the Académie-Française in 1673. But inevitably he had made enemies, and in 1677 an organized cabal ensured not only that a tragedy entitled *Phèdre et Hippolyte* by Pradon opened in direct opposition to his own play on the subject but also that it was more favourably received. This experience may have contributed to his abrupt decision to retire from the theatrical scene, as must assuredly his appointment as historiographer-royal in the same year. He married, became reconciled with Port-Royal and took his duties as courtier seriously enough to be made a secretary to the king. He subsequently relented only to write a court *divertissement* to music by LULLY, *Idylle sur la paix* (*Idyll on Peace*, 1685), and, at Mme de Maintenon's request, two tragedies on biblical subjects, *Esther* (1689) and *Athalie* (1691), for performance, with music, by the young ladies of the school she had founded at Saint-Cyr. Although different in inspiration and form, they have since taken their place alongside his earlier work in the classic French repertoire. Other spiritual writings occupied his last years, when his ties with Jansenist circles grew even closer.

Racine's *oeuvre* offers a vindication of the principles of neoclassical dramaturgy, but in observing its constraints he transcended them. In his hands tragedy became a highly refined, sophisticated vehicle for the expression of tragic feeling which is all the more powerful and poignant for being confined within a defined emotional spectrum, a precise convention of language and a fairly rigid structural form. Decorum and the unities combine to displace the centre of interest from the incidents of a story towards their effect on the characters, from physical action towards what goes on in their weak or vacillating minds and this begets a remorseless exploration of profound psychological depths, most of all in his female roles, which have attracted leading actresses of every generation, though difficulties of translation have conspired to deny Racine his due attention in English-speaking countries. DR

Radio City Music Hall (New York City) Built in 1932 by S. L. 'Roxy' Rothafel with Rockefeller money, the 6200-seat, art deco theatre was originally intended to present popular-priced VAUDEVILLE, but policy and leadership changed quickly: the new formula of showing a film in combination with a stage show highlighted by the Rockettes, a precision tap-dancing chorus, endured for many years. When the supply of 'family-type' films fell off and the attraction of the stage show wore thin, the theatre seemed doomed; but it was declared a landmark in 1979, and was thoroughly renovated to reopen as a showplace for large spectacles and star appearances. In 1985 it earned its first profit since 1955. MCH

radio drama If radio comes, can drama be far behind? Immediately after the end of the First World War, radio began to establish itself internationally as a medium of mass communication, and its potential for drama was quickly appreciated by the pioneers of broadcasting. Indeed, some theorists of the media believe that it is in the nature of both radio and television to aspire to the condition of drama. What this means is that much more of the non-musical output of radio is 'dramatic' than would be the case if this word were thought to designate only productions emanating from drama departments. For one thing, fiction is not the preserve of these departments: what is labelled 'light entertainment' includes a considerable amount of material that is essentially dramatic and that descends from popular theatre, such as the English MUSIC-HALL and American VAUDEVILLE traditions, involving stand-up comedians and humorous sketches. Comedy series and sitcoms, including such major BBC ones as Tommy Handley's ITMA in the 1940s, *Hancock's Half Hour* and *The Goon Show* in the 1950s, and the more recent

Dad's Army and *Yes, Minister*, are undoubtedly dramatic in their employment of narrative and character creation. Several students of radio have argued that *The Goon Show* has claims to be one of the most dramatically innovative programmes in the history of sound broadcasting, since it exploits the representational possibilities and limitations of radio to the full.

If, as Martin Esslin (a former head of BBC Radio Drama) has argued, theatre is what happens when exhibitionists confront voyeurs, 'theatre' encompasses an enormous range of performances from strip and sex shows to productions of the *Oresteia* and *King Lear*. Similarly, radio drama, like Walt Whitman, contains multitudes, and academic attempts to reserve the term for the more serious and highbrow end of the radio-drama spectrum soon founder on the impossibility of clear-cut demarcations when analysing a popular mass medium reaching millions. Is the BBC's long-running daily serial in fifteen-minute instalments, *The Archers*, radio drama or not? If not, what is it? During the interwar years, a substantial amount of fictional programming on American radio took the form of serialized soap operas, and to separate the 'soaps' (together with comedy series) from 'radio drama' would be to reduce the American experience to a marginal rump. But the problem of definition is not restricted to manifestly fictional output, from dramatized readings, through comedy series and thriller serials, to new one-off plays and productions of stage classics. If radio really does have in-built tendencies towards the dramatic, this would apply to factual or at least non-fictional areas of broadcasting as well as to what would be widely acknowledged to be variants of drama proper. The most obvious case is documentary, which slides very easily into what has become known as docudrama, but quiz programmes, confrontational discussions and interviews, actuality reportage, and even illustrated accounts of yesterday's proceedings in parliament (a non-stop theatre with a cast of hundreds) or language-instruction programmes with interpolated episodes of typical conversational situations do develop dramatic momentum and tension, helping to sustain listeners' interest.

The history of British radio is particularly relevant to the problem concerning the boundaries between fact and fiction and between the dramatic and non-dramatic. From the 1930s, the Features Department of the BBC existed alongside the Drama Department before they were eventually merged in the mid-1960s, and credit for exploring the unique dramatic potential of radio during the 1930s, 40s and early 50s is rightly accorded to Features, under the brilliant leadership of Laurence Gilliam, rather than to Drama, which in its earlier days concentrated on conventional, theatre-like plays.

The word 'feature' suggests a factual basis as opposed to an entirely fictional construct, but in practice the BBC Features Department blurred any clear-cut distinction between fact and fiction. Long before the word 'faction' was coined to describe a mode of writing in which the techniques of fiction were applied to real-life stories (non-fiction novels such as Truman Capote's *In Cold Blood* and Thomas Keneally's *Schindler's Ark*, and documentary drama of the kind associated with PETER WEISS and various South African groups), this is precisely what Features

specialized in, although it did other things too. Among the principal writer-producers of radio features were a number of poets, notably Louis MacNeice, and 'highly imaginative' is the best way of describing their work, whether documentary or non-documentary. Some of the most famous and seminal productions by Features, including D. G. Bridson's *The March of the '45* (1936) and MacNeice's *Christopher Columbus* (1942), resemble Elizabethan chronicle history plays in existing as both dramatized history and poetic drama, documentary and fiction. Yet Features also produced entirely fictional work, including two of the most renowned radio plays in the history of broadcasting, MacNeice's *The Dark Tower* (1946) and DYLAN THOMAS's even more revered *Under Milk Wood* (1954). Such works were the province of BBC Features rather than Radio Drama because they totally violate conventional ideas of well made realistic drama and accord with the free, radiogenic form of the feature. MacNeice shapes his work as a poetic, saga-like quest with rapid shifts from episode to episode, while Thomas uses a narrative structure with dramatized inserts involving numerous characters.

Although broadcasting organizations and their histories differ widely from nation to nation, and what happened at the BBC has not been exactly paralleled elsewhere, the fluidity of 'radio drama' and the concomitant problem of fixing frontiers has been an almost universal phenomenon. In some countries, such as Australia, this indeterminacy is virtually institutionalized in the official nomenclature: the ABC has a Radio Drama and Features Department, a name simultaneously acknowledging a distinction and closely linking the two modes under one umbrella, with the same production staff. The most famous American radio broadcast ever – and probably in the world – illustrates radio's uncertainty principle in a way that remains startling nearly 60 years later. At Hallowe'en in 1938, one of the Columbia Broadcasting System's radio-drama series, 'Mercury Theatre on the Air', put out an adaptation by ORSON WELLES of H. G. Wells's novel, *The War of the Worlds*. Not only did this occupy a regular drama slot that should have established it as fiction; it was also science fiction, a fantasy about a Martian invasion of the Earth. Yet millions of Americans reacted to it as though it were actually happening; there was widespread mass hysteria, and people fled from their homes and cities in panic and terror. The truth proved to be much stranger than the totally fabricated and far-fetched fiction that caused it, a fiction interpreted by many listeners as fact.

Although a newcomer to radio, Welles grasped the actuality techniques characteristic of American radio drama in the 1930s, which were designed to promote REALISM and conviction, and were identical to those employed in radio journalism and other factual investigations; in *The War of the Worlds* he employed them to give as much authenticity as possible to a highly improbable story. Welles and his colleagues did not for a moment imagine that the broadcast would have the extraordinary effect it did, and many books and essays have been written by students of the media, social history and mass psychology to account for what happened, but the 'Mercury Theatre' production demonstrates how powerful an illusion of reality radio can create, and how different radio drama is from drama with a visual dimension, whether stage, television or big screen. None of these media could have produced an equivalent response; in Welles's hands, the 'blindness' of radio turned out to be its greatest asset.

This much discussed 'blindness' is the most significant factor in distinguishing radio drama from any other dramatic form. Historically, most drama from the Ancient World onwards has been intended for performance in visual as well as aural terms. Some poets, including Milton, Shelley and Matthew Arnold, have written works in dramatic form aimed at the silent reader, not the stage, but such dramatic poems are exceptions. SENECA has been claimed as a forerunner of radio drama because his plays were performed by readers as sound plays, not by actors as stage plays; but in this respect Seneca had no significant predecessors or successors until 20th-century technology made possible the widespread dissemination of sound plays. As a former head of BBC Radio Drama, Val Gielgud, liked to point out, we do not talk of going to hear or listen to plays but to see them.

Indeed, in the recent past a number of influential theorists have stressed the visual side of theatre at the expense of other elements, which has in turn provoked other theorists to reassert the primacy of language. If the extreme case that drama is an essentially visual medium were true, mime would be far more central and popular than it is, and the 'talkies' would not have supplanted the silent – more precisely, speechless – cinema as easily as they did. Nevertheless, the everyday use of 'show' as a synonym for 'theatrical presentation' emphasizes an experience for the eye, although the fact that radio-drama producers use the same word to refer to what they are creating is a reminder that 'showing', or ostension (to use the technical term), can be an entirely aural experience and, except for totally silent mime, always involves the ear, however lavish the visual spectacle may be. On radio, ostension is achieved largely through language, which is why radio drama is thought of as more of a writer's medium than theatre itself: somewhere between an entirely verbal form, such as the novel, and stage drama. It is possible for radio drama to dispense with speech altogether and rely solely on sound effects, as in Andrew Sachs's pursuit play *The Revenge*, which caused a considerable stir when broadcast by BBC Radio 3 in 1978; but however interesting an occasional experiment of this kind is, its self-imposed limitations as a narrative consisting of nothing but noises make it a curiosity, not a feasible model for further development.

The sightlessness of radio makes impossible a number of elements we take for granted in drama on stage: in addition to scenery, costumes, lighting and visual symbols, there are proxemics and kinesics – the positioning and movement of actors as well as their physical gestures and facial expressions. Stereophonic and quadrophonic productions on radio can create some illusion of space, but they do so at the price of sacrificing monophonic radio's symbolic reality (its spacelessness, its sense of being located in the listener's head rather than 'out there') for an imaginatively impoverished iconic one. In the very early days of radio, attempts were made to broadcast live stage performances, from both 'straight' theatre and music-hall, but these were disastrous because in unadapted form

they proved to be very difficult to follow or even downright incomprehensible without visual definition. On radio, settings, including the time of day, have to be conveyed principally through language; without a verbal context, the usefulness of sound effects is severely restricted owing to their inherent imprecision and ambiguity. The notorious BBC seagull implies water but does not, in itself, tell us whether the setting is on land or at sea, a beach or a small sailing boat, a dockside or a luxury liner. Even a clock chiming twelve can mean midday or midnight, so that speech or a qualifying sound effect (a traffic jam, an owl hooting) is needed to clarify the exact time. This is why Elizabethan and Jacobean drama, with its verbal scene painting and other descriptive devices necessitated by the theatrical conventions of the time, transfers to radio much more easily than some stage plays in the naturalistic and expressionistic traditions (see NATURALISM; EXPRESSIONISM), which rely heavily on visual presentation.

An actor on radio is a voice – no more, no less – and identification by an audience is entirely aural. This makes it difficult to mount plays with large casts on radio, especially if there are a number of equally important characters using roughly the same linguistic register, because the unaided ear (at least in sighted people) cannot recognize and keep track of more than a few voices, unless there are frequent and possibly awkward reminders in the form of name dropping, either by the characters themselves or by an intrusive narrator. Effects entirely natural to the stage, such as the counterpointing of words and actions, are not feasible on radio, which accounts for the notorious difficulty experienced in adapting CHEKHOV for the medium. Whereas a silent character on stage can have a powerful visual presence, a silent character on radio is an absence and simply does not exist. 'I speak, therefore I am' is the appropriate neo-Cartesian formulation for radio. Pauses and hesitations can be extremely expressive in stage plays (Chekhov, BECKETT), but only because we can see the characters. On radio, an unfilled break in the dialogue is more likely to be interpreted as a fault in transmission than a meaningful silence.

There are a number of ways in which radio obviously cannot compete with the stage, television or cinema as a medium for drama, but the comparison is by no means to its disadvantage. Marshall McLuhan, who was fond of perverse paradoxes, described television as a tactile medium because it appeals to the sense of touch, and radio as a visual medium because it stimulates the inward eye by denying the eye itself anything to hold its attention. Much has been made of the imaginative possibilities of radio and of listeners' active involvement in creating a fictional reality from the acoustic information provided by a broadcast play. In this respect, the process more closely resembles the reading of fiction than the viewing of drama in any of its visual forms, although listeners, like members of a theatre or cinema audience and unlike readers of the printed page, have to respond to the spoken word and a variety of other acoustic signals, sometimes including music as well as effects.

Radio's stage is in the mind, and each listener, like each reader of a novel, constructs his or her own imaginary world without having it fixed, as in any visual form, by the physical appearance of the actors, the decor, and the sequence of images decided by the director. It is easy to overlook how imaginatively restricting theatrical productions can be, which explains why many people find reading such open texts as the great dramatic classics (*King Lear, Hamlet*) a more satisfying and complete experience than seeing them, however heretical this may be at a time when orthodoxy decrees that *on stage* the play's the thing. There is a sense in which all productions of *Hamlet* and all interpretations of the prince himself by actors, whether good, bad or indifferent, original or stale, illuminating or perfunctory, are reductive, since certain possibilities are necessarily developed at the expense of others. A reader, on the other hand, is not dictated to by visual presentation, and is more capable of holding a multiplicity of interpretations than a captive audience in a theatre. In a radio play, unlike a novel, narration and dialogue are, of course, fixed aurally through the actors' voices – direct speech really is speech – but the human ear is much less of a tyrant than the eye and does indeed leave a lot to the imagination.

Early producers of radio in the 1920s soon realized its positive advantages as an imaginative medium, and how important the difference is between drama *on* radio and drama *for* radio, a distinction disguised by the term 'radio drama'. The German word *Hörspiel*, stressing the mode of sensory apprehension (hearing) rather than the mode of transmission (radio), is more exact in designating a work written for the medium, but unfortunately there is no English equivalent: the word 'earplay', coined by the outstanding Canadian producer Fletcher Markle as a radio-drama series title for American National (Public) Radio in 1978 as part of the attempt to revive the form in the USA during the 1970s, comes very close, but like TYRONE GUTHRIE's much earlier term 'microphone play' it has not entered the critical vocabulary. *Hörspiel* is *le mot juste* for the first play written for the new medium to be broadcast by the BBC, Richard Hughes's *Danger*(1924), which is set in total darkness, a coalmine following an accident that has literally put out the light. Because there is nothing to see, *Danger* is unstageable: it is 'a play for voices', to use the phrase Dylan Thomas attached to *Under Milk Wood*, which can be staged though never without a considerable degree of awkwardness (even more than Chekhov on radio).

Unlike *Danger* and *Under Milk Wood*, many broadcast plays fall into the category of 'drama on radio' (stage plays and plays written in the hope of stage and television production but not achieving it), but there is also a considerable body of 'drama for radio', exploiting its ability to go places and do things either impossible or unsatisfactory in live theatre or even the more visually flexible media of film and television. *Danger*, about trapped miners in a blacked-out pit, is a good example, but Andrew Crisell has recently drawn attention to a single BBC effects track that illustrates, in a particularly startling and succinct way, radio's ability to enter places with zero visibility. Called 'premature burial', this presents the experience of a supposedly dead person inside a coffin returning to consciousness after an interment ceremony and attempting to escape in a state of extreme panic. Being totally 'blind', this piece of Poe-like Gothicism would be impossible to convey visually but can be vividly evoked in sound.

'Premature burial' is an extreme case, but sound effects can suggest with great ease, compared with any visual medium, such events and experiences as large-scale catastrophes (the destruction of Pompeii, the fire-bombing of Dresden) and, at the other end of the scale, inner states of mind such as mental anguish (noises in the head). In COMEDY, too, invisibility can be a great help rather than a hindrance, especially when it comes to sound effects. The surreal humour of *The Goon Show* (see SURREALISM), which perfected this technique, depends on hilarious patterns of sound that have no exact visual analogues and could function in no other medium.

In discovering what was radiogenic and what was not, early producers were influenced, strangely enough, by the methods of the silent cinema. For a short time in the 1920s, drama in a new medium that could be seen but not heard coincided with drama in an even newer medium that could be heard but not seen. Radio writers borrowed from cinema many of the techniques that distinguished it from theatre, including montage and superimposition, and adapted them to suit a presentation in sound alone. The visual flexibility of cinema, moving from scene to scene with a single cut, sliding between past and present with a dissolve, and placing characters in situations impossible in theatre (Charlie Chaplin in the precariously balanced hut in *The Gold Rush*), has its counterpart in the aural flexibility of radio. Even moving from long shot to close-up can be paralleled in sound since radio can create a sense of distance and also enter the minds of characters, the latter much more readily than any visual medium. Such devices as the soliloquy and aside are, of course, entirely satisfactory in small doses on an Elizabethan thrust stage, however clumsy they may appear in a proscenium-arch picture frame, but radio focuses very naturally on the interior workings of consciousness and can relay mental processes at length without any sense of strain. The invisibility of the radio actor makes the dramatic convention of speaking thoughts aloud particularly appropriate to the medium, in a way that it is not in cinema, television and realistic stage plays; since we do not see the actor speaking, the words seem to come straight from the mind, not the mouth. This accounts for the great intimacy of radio drama, the paradoxical sense of immediacy and proximity produced by actors physically at a considerable distance from the listener.

Arguably the best of the three 'microphone plays' Tyrone Guthrie wrote within a couple of years while working for the BBC, *The Flowers Are Not for You to Pick* (1930), exemplifies how gifted writers in the early days of radio seized on a cinematic method that could readily be adapted for radio, while also indulging to the full the new medium's novelistic ability to render the inner lives of people. Guthrie's play is all in the mind of its central character, who as a drowning man in the middle of an ocean is located realistically in a position unrealizable in the theatre, except in a highly stylized way. To capture the man's dying review of his entire life, Guthrie employs a sequence of flashbacks, a collage of memories involving fast transitions in time and place. The result is unstageable drama but seminal radio. Even more unstageable are the contemporary 'radiophonic' experiments by Lance Sieveking, notably *Kaleidoscope I* (1928), a decidedly original montage of speech and sound owing little to theatrical tradition but indebted to the principles of cinematic editing. What makes the achievement of these avant-garde figures so remarkable is that their complex works were broadcast live without benefit of magnetic tape, in conditions and using equipment that now seem primitive.

An important feature of radio drama that seems to be completely uncinematic is narration, a method largely eschewed by film and television and relatively rare in Western theatre, in spite of the importance of the chorus in Greek TRAGEDY and BRECHT's influence on recent drama. What makes narration so natural on radio is, as with some other aspects of the genre, the invisibility of the speaker. Excessive reliance on narration in radio drama did lead to a reaction against it by the new writers of the 1950s and 1960s, such as GILES COOPER and Samuel Beckett, but abuse of an essentially radiogenic technique does not invalidate it, and it has been making a strong comeback since the heyday of the absurdists. Narration can certainly be an over-easy way of solving problems, but handled with skill, as in *Under Milk Wood*, it functions as a verbal camera, suggesting another, though oblique and unexpected, cinematic analogue. On radio, a narrator can establish with a few words a fictional reality that might cost a fortune to provide visually: mention ancient Rome or an elaborate sci-fi super-city in space, add appropriate effects, and they exist in sound.

In his enormously popular radio-drama serial, *The Hitch-Hiker's Guide to the Galaxy* (1978), which acquired cult status and seduced the young into thinking of radio as a source of something other than non-stop pop music, Douglas Adams made brilliant use of narration. This self-reflexive cosmic fantasy, accommodating a major character with two heads, numerous time warps, visits to a number of bizarre planets, a variety of weird life forms, not to mention chatty computers, presented radio with marvellous opportunities rather than problems. Such is life today, however, that its triumphant success led to a television adaptation, which was vastly inferior to the point of embarrassment, not because it was badly done, but because what was imaginatively stimulating on radio inevitably became gauche when translated into visual images. Perhaps the ultimate comment on the hazards inherent in converting radio codes into visual ones is a famous joke from *The Goon Show*. Bloodnok asks Eccles to climb on his shoulders and then reach down and pull him up, to which Eccles replies with devastating acuteness as he performs this physically impossible but radiophonically simple task, 'I'd like to see them do this on television.'

Radio excels in creating fantasy and symbolic worlds, indeterminate characters who may or may not be real, and interior monologue. Although Mervyn Peake was a gifted painter and his prose is strongly visual, a dramatic adaptation of his grotesque *Gormenghast* novels into theatrical or filmic terms would be fraught with near-insoluble difficulties, whereas the BBC radio version was among the Drama Department's triumphs of the 1980s. John Huston's famous film of *Moby Dick* is far from contemptible, but it reduces the allegorical dimensions of Melville's novel to a thin realism, the white whale being no more than a white whale, an artificial one to boot. Henry Reed's 1947 radio adaptation, on the other hand, is

among the masterpieces of radio. Among the imaginary worlds that radio has no problem in establishing are the ones giving speech to voiceless things, whether animate or inanimate: in Don Haworth's *On a Day in a Garden in Summer* (1975), for example, the speakers or 'characters' are plants. The nearest visual equivalent would almost certainly be whimsically twee and his serious purpose completely subverted. The ghosts of Elizabethan and Jacobean tragedy, such as Hamlet's father and Banquo, present a radio producer with none of the hard decisions a stage director has to make about whether they should be represented physically, even if through a glass darkly or as electronic flickerings. Similarly, Macbeth's hallucinatory dagger, made visible in Polanski's film although normally invisible on stage, is, on radio, what Macbeth says it is, 'a dagger of the mind'.

A celebrated example of a character having an uncertain existence on radio is the mute match-seller in HAROLD PINTER's *A Slight Ache* (1959). In stage productions, the match-seller has either to be shown (in which case he exists independently) or not shown (in which case he exists only in the minds of the two 'real' characters). Radio does not have to make this choice and can sustain an uneasy ambiguity without, to cite Keats on Negative Capability, 'any irritable reaching after fact and reason'. Pinter's match-seller may lack body and consciousness, but disembodied consciousness might be called 'the stuff of radio', to borrow the title of Lance Sieveking's pioneering study of the medium (1934). Because it presents six disembodied consciousnesses rather than six characters, Virginia Woolf's most abstract work of fiction, *The Waves*, probably defies transformation into a visual medium more than any major novel apart from *Finnegans Wake*, but her six voices might almost have been designed for radio, as MacNeice's celebrated adaptation reveals. *Finnegans Wake* itself was given the full radio treatment by that least inhibited or artistic experimenters, John Cage, in his extraordinary *Roaratorio*, subtitled 'an Irish Circus' on James Joyce's novel.

The fate of radio drama in different countries during its short history of only two-thirds of a century has depended on their vastly different broadcasting structures as well as on internal and external political pressures. In various parts of Europe, radio got off to an enterprising start during the 1920s, but with the spread of totalitarian regimes, both right and left, it increasingly became a propaganda tool and an instrument of state control. As a mass-medium art form, radio drama inevitably suffered badly. Germany was in the forefront of radio-drama development during the post-First World War Weimar period, thanks to the innovative work of such writers as Bertolt Brecht and Walter Benjamin, but Hitler's rise to power in 1933 put an end to this momentum and stifled experiment. It was some time after the Second World War before German radio recaptured something of its early imaginative energy, by which time it was under pressure from television. Today, Germany is one of the main producers of radio drama, and the *Hörspiel* probably has a higher artistic status there than radio drama does in any other country. The *Hörspiel* continues to attract the literary avant-garde in a way that barely survives outside the German-speaking world. At Westdeutscher Rundfunk in Cologne, Klaus

Schöning has been responsible for creating a particularly fine and internationally renowned centre of radio-drama production, which encourages a wide range of acoustic possibilities, including sound poetry. The German *Hörspiel* is characterized by a more radical break with traditional dramatic forms than its British equivalent. For historical reasons Germany is one of a number of countries conspicuously lacking in the so-called Golden Age of radio (including drama) in the anglophone world, the period from the early 1930s to the early or mid-1950s.

This Golden Age in such nations as Australia, Britain, Canada and the USA depended on the stability and continuity of democratic institutions, something denied to continental Europe except for non-combatant Sweden and Switzerland. Ironically, the Second World War was a crucial factor in the making of the Golden Age since it effectively postponed the domination of television for more than a decade. Television transmissions began in the 1930s, well before radio had even come of age, but the war curtailed these experimental broadcasts, and in Britain, for example, the television audience did not overtake the radio audience until the televising of Elizabeth II's coronation in 1953, an event that encouraged millions of people to buy television sets. In some countries, radio drama did not have to compete with television for considerably longer because the introduction of the latter was delayed for political reasons. This explains why radio drama remains a viable form in South Africa whereas in the USA it is again on the extreme edge of extinction after receiving a temporary reprieve in the 1970s.

The ability of radio drama to withstand the assault of television varied according to the broadcasting system involved. From the beginning, the American system was based on commercial sponsorship, and the bulk of radio drama was unashamedly popular: soap operas, variety series, mystery and detective series. What happened with the advent of television was that all such forms deserted radio for the newer medium, leaving a vacuum to be filled by pop music. Although the output of serious radio drama in the USA was relatively small, the work of the three directorial giants of the 1930s and 40s, Norman Corwin, Arch Oboler and Orson Welles, was of a consistently high quality and was widely appreciated. Nevertheless, even in the Golden Age, serious drama led a fairly embattled existence, with worthwhile series being set up and dropped almost at whim, and there was no structure to save it from the tidal wave of television. American radio drama did limp on throughout the 1950s, but was apparently laid to rest about 1960, only to be tentatively resurrected by Elliot Lewis and a few others in the mid-70s. This was not exactly a new dawn, but the example of Earplay in the 1970s, broadcasting ambitious work nationwide on public radio stations, encouraged others to keep the genre alive and even to explore its potential in the style of the German *Hörspiel*. Chief among these have been Everett Frost with Voices International in New York and Erik Bauersfeld with BARD (Bay Area Radio Drama) in Berkeley, California. It is in a handful of large urban centres, including Boston, Chicago and Los Angeles, that radio drama can be said to survive in the USA.

The American experience of a rapid rise and an equally rapid decline in the fortunes of radio drama has been partly paralleled in countries such as Australia and Canada, where commercial sponsorship has had an important, sometimes dominant, role in broadcasting alongside a public-service sector akin to the BBC (in Australia, the ABC; in Canada, the CBC). It has been estimated that fewer than one in ten of the Australian population ever tune in to an ABC radio broadcast; the CBC, however, commands considerably greater loyalty from Canadians. In both Australia and Canada, television arrived later than in the USA, its spread was slower, and consequently its impact was not so immediately overwhelming. Indeed, Howard Fink has argued that the Golden Age of radio drama in Canada did not begin until the mid-1940s, when television arrived in the USA, and lasted until the mid-1960s, by which time American radio drama was little more than a memory. Yet despite the commitment of both ABC and CBC to maintain drama as a presence on radio, output has declined steadily although not dried up altogether. Audiences have shrunk, and in enormous countries with small populations this absence of listeners is more conspicuous than in much smaller European countries with much larger populations, such as Britain and Germany. The conditions that encouraged the poet Douglas Stewart, a New Zealander by birth but Australian by adoption, to write in verse one of the finest radio plays ever broadcast, *The Fire on the Snow*, first produced by the ABC in 1941, no longer appertain. Yet some young writers in Australia and Canada were attracted to radio during the 1970s and 80s, partly as a reaction against television. The celebrated intimacy of radio and its existence as spoken language still have appeal for literary artists, and the ABC and CBC continue to provide a limited outlet for them. In addition to mainstream radio drama, both organizations continue to encourage a small amount of radical innovation in the vein of the *Hörspiel*.

The reasons for Britain's pre-eminence in radio drama should now be clear: on the one hand, political stability, continuity and openness; on the other, the BBC's monopoly in nationwide broadcasting as a public-service institution. Whereas commercial television began transmissions in 1955 on a national basis, commercial radio stations were not allowed to operate until 1973, and then only to serve strictly circumscribed localities. Proposals for national commercial radio were not seriously put forward until well into the Thatcher era (mid-1980s) and as yet have come to nothing. During the 1960s and 70s, it was fashionable to sneer at the Reithian doctrines enshrined in the theory and practice of the BBC from the 1920s to the 50s as elitist and patronizing, but it is now obvious that without such commitment to excellence in all areas of broadcasting and to disseminating high culture as well as popular entertainment the BBC would not enjoy its international reputation as, arguably, the most reliable and most imaginative broadcasting institution in the world.

The idea of radio being a national theatre of the air, in the absence of a bricks-and-mortar national theatre, developed early in BBC history: radio could bring the theatre to the people in their homes, making available the masterpieces of world drama from AESCHYLUS to IBSEN to millions who either had no access to live theatre or lacked the theatregoing habit, especially when it came to the classics. The BBC has undergone several major reorganizations since the Second World War, but its policy for serious radio drama, as opposed to light-entertainment drama, has survived more or less intact; although audiences have declined considerably, output has remained remarkably buoyant. Despite cutbacks during the 1980s, plenty of stage classics and adaptations of classic novels are still broadcast, as are plenty of new plays. Radio-drama production may be relatively expensive by the standards of radio, but it is absurdly cheap by the standards of television, and radio can therefore take risks and attempt experiments that would be totally out of the question in television. Indeed, as TV drama becomes more and more anodyne, with a plethora of stereotypical soap operas and mini-series, and as older viewers yearn nostalgically for the good old days of TV drama in the 1960s and 70s, the virtues of radio drama are increasingly obvious in the 1990s.

The BBC's strong tradition of radio-drama and feature production has been a vital factor in enabling these forms to survive so well in the television era, despite all the talk about a dying art during the past 30 years. One crucial change, following the recommendations of audience research, has been to move drama away from prime-viewing times (previously peak listening times) to afternoon and early evening slots, and even morning and late-at-night ones. Yet developments in drama itself helped to give radio a new lease of life as a dramatic medium when television was taking over as *the* mass medium in the 1950s. Several critics have argued that radio is the natural home for the THEATRE OF THE ABSURD, and there was something approaching a revolution in radio drama between the mid-1950s and the mid-60s, with Giles Cooper, Samuel Beckett, Rhys Adrian, Frederick Bradnum, Harold Pinter, JAMES SAUNDERS, Barry Bermange, JOE ORTON and TOM STOPPARD. Until this time, there was a tendency for some of the best radio writers to compensate for its blindness by providing rich verbal textures, colours for the ear, as in *The Dark Tower* and *Under Milk Wood*. The new writers demonstrated that radio drama could function just as well without such compensation, that minimalism could be as radiogenic as the work of poets such as MacNeice and Thomas. Indeed, radio proved to be the training ground for a new generation of British playwrights, who subsequently made their names in the theatre, television and film. Radio continues to do this, but the momentum of the 1960s is now something to be recollected in tranquillity. Yet plays of the stature of DAVID RUDKIN's *Cries from Casement As His Bones Are Brought to Dublin* (1973), JOHN ARDEN's *Pearl* (1978), Robert Ferguson's *Transfigured Night* (1984) and HOWARD BARKER's *Scenes from an Execution* (1984) are reminders that, if radio is a dying or dead art in some countries, it is still thriving in others, notably in Britain and Germany. There, at least, it is dying by millimetres if it is dying at all. PL

See: D. G. Bridson, *Prospero and Ariel: The Rise and Fall of Radio*, London, 1971; A. Crisell, *Understanding Radio*, London and New York, 1986; J. Drakakis, *British Radio Drama*, Cambridge, 1981; A. P. Frank, *Das Hörspiel*, Heidelberg, 1963; V. Gielgud, *British Radio Drama 1922–1956*, London, 1957; P. Lewis (ed.), *Papers of the Radio Literature Conference 1977*, Durham, 1978, and (ed.), *Radio Drama*, London and New York, 1981; D.

McWhinnie, *The Art of Radio*, London, 1959; H. Priessnitz, *Das englische 'radio play' seit 1945: Typen, Themen und Formen*, Berlin, 1977, and (ed.), *Das englische Hörspiel: Interpretationen*, Düsseldorf, 1977; I. Rodger, *Radio Drama*, London, 1982; L. Sieveking, *The Stuff of Radio*, London, 1934.

Radlov, Sergei (Ernestovich) 1892–1958 Russian-Soviet director, a leader in the post-revolutionary movement to unite folk theatrical forms with modern 'urban eccentrism' in order to create a new popular theatre. His techniques derived primarily from COMMEDIA DELL'ARTE, CIRCUS and silent screen COMEDY, and demonstrated his belief that the actor's art consists of 'pure sound + pure movement + pure emotion – correctly disposed in time and space'. He received his early training from MEYERHOLD during the latter's *commedia* period at the Studio on Borodinskaya Street and on the journal *Love for Three Oranges* (1913–17). As part of two projects sponsored by the People's Commissariat for Education – the mobile First Communal Troupe, which played the Civil War front, and the Petrograd Theatre Studio (with K. Tverskoi and K. Landau, 1918–19) – Radlov worked with improvisation, children's and puppet theatre. In 1920 he co-directed with Nikolai Petrov, Vladimir Solovyov and Adrian Piotrovsky the mass spectacle *Towards a World Commune*, and founded with Solovyov the Theatre of Popular Comedy, which operated until 1922. The latter utilized circus performers, as had YURY ANNENKOV in his 1919 production of *The First Distiller*, in a series of 'circus comedies' and 'circus pantoMIMEs' on anti-capitalist themes: *The Corpse's Bride* and *The Monkey Who Was an Informer* (1919), *The Sultan and the Devil* and *The Adopted Son* (1920), and *Love and Gold* (1921).

Drawing upon the speed and ingenuity of American popular forms such as detective and adventure serials, Radlov experimented with multiple and simultaneous staging in order to create a sense of continuous flow. He employed similar means to contemporize and dynamize comedic classics – MOLIÈRE, Hans Sachs, CALDERÓN DE LA BARCA, LABICHE and especially SHAKESPEARE. In 1922 Radlov opened the Laboratory for Theatre Research and thereafter directed at a series of theatres and studios in Petrograd (1929–42) and in Latvia (1953–8). He staged a number of notable productions of Shakespeare in the 1930s – *Romeo and Juliet* (1934, 1939), *Othello* (1932, 1935), *Hamlet* (1938) and his most celebrated, *King Lear* (1935) at the Moscow State Jewish Theatre, designed by Aleksandr Tyshler and starring the great SOLOMON MIKHOELS. Radlov also taught (1922–35) and wrote *Ten Years in the Theatre* (1929), and several works on staging Shakespeare. SG

Radok, Alfred 1914–76 Innovative Czech director, whose successes were frequently interrupted by political pressures. An assistant to E. F. BURIAN in the late 1930s, he was a founder of the postwar Theatre of the Fifth of May, which produced provocative new versions of established drama and musical theatre. Essentially an apolitical artist with an innate genius for theatrical metaphor and multimedia, he struggled to survive in the ideological minefields of a dogmatic regime, often being shunted from one position to another at the National, the Municipal and provincial theatres, while directing landmark productions for the stage (*The Entertainer*, 1957; *Marriage*, 1963; *Game of Love and Death*, 1964), in film (*Distant Journey*, 1949), and for the mixed media – above all the hybrid form of LATERNA MAGIKA (1958), a technically sophisticated offspring of Radok's talent for juxtaposing realistic elements in theatrically striking, often poetic configurations. The Soviet bloc invasion of CZECHOSLOVAKIA in 1968 triggered his self-exile, and he worked in more limited fashion abroad, chiefly Sweden, until his death.   JMB

Radrigán, Juan 1937– Chilean playwright. A late bloomer in the recent Chilean theatre, Radrigán is affiliated with theatre of the marginal classes. His plays are brutal and violent portrayals of contemporary society, written in the vernacular but with poetic imagery. Since he burst on the theatre scene with *Testimonios sobre la muerte de Sabina* (*Testimonies on the Death of Sabina*) in 1979, he has become one of Chile's most prolific writers. Other major plays are *Viva Somoza* (*Long Live Somoza*) written in collaboration with Gustavo Meza in 1980, *El loco y la triste* (*The Crazy One and the Sad One*, 1980), *Hechos consumados* (*Accomplished Deeds*, 1981), *El toro por las astas* (*The Bull by the Horns*, 1982) and *Las voces de la ira* (*Voices of Anger*, 1984).   GW

Radzinsky, Edvard (Stanislavovich) 1938– Russian dramatist of the postwar generation, whose plays (14 to date) present the philosophical dilemmas of the native intelligentsia past and present and of youth in conflict with the values of their elders. The son of a well known man of letters, Radzinsky graduated from the Moscow State Historical-Archival Institute in 1960. His first popular success was the bittersweet romance *104 Pages about Love* (1964), one of five of his works staged by the director ANATOLY EFROS. A largely comic play with an unexpected tragic ending, and representative of the 1960s trend towards personal dramas, it has been staged in 120 Soviet theatres and made into a ballet and a film. *Making a Movie* (1965) deals with a no longer young film director's difficulties in maintaining his integrity in art, love and life. This theme is broadened and deepened considerably in Radzinsky's historical plays of conscience – *Conversations with Socrates* (1975), *Lunin* (1977, about a Decembrist conspirator) and *Theatre in the Time of Nero and Seneca* (1980).

Utilizing all manner of theatrical devices, from ancient Greek MASKS and *cothurni* to *tableaux vivants* (see LIVING PICTURE), romantic prison house metaphor and hallucinatory visions, Radzinsky focuses on teacher–pupil/master–servant relationships and suggests various sources and traditions vying for pride of place in the collective memory of the Russian intelligentsia: CHEKHOV's meditations on the price of survival and the pathos of extinction; GOGOLian and BULGAKOVian theatrical grotesque, to render the former's sense of Russia's moral failure and the latter's crisis of freedom in the thrall of patrimony and the nightmare of exile; Western metafictional heroes – Hamlet, Quixote and Robinson Crusoe – as free creators; and DIDEROT and the *encyclopédistes* as symbols of national inquiry and honest discourse. Radzinsky's heroes struggle to escape the myth-making apparatus which rewrites history in the manner of the Soviets to conform to a prescribed end (e.g. the path to the October Revolution). In *The Seducer Kolobashkin* (1968) and *Don Juan Continued …* (1979), he employs the idea of time travel to suggest the eternal flight of the creative persona from false and banal reality.

With the highly popular *She, in the Absence of Love and Death* (1980), Radzinsky returned to the difficulties of the young, bereft of the great romantic 19th-century literary themes, in reconciling their ideals and fantasies with contemporary reality. Following the 1986 premiere of *Jogging* (*Sporting Scenes*, 1981), a four-character battle-of-the-sexes exposé of the children of the ruling elite, Radzinsky became one of the most frequently produced native playwrights in modern Russia. His 1986 play *Let's Kill the Man* was staged in Kiev in 1991. *An Old Actress in the Role of Dostoevsky's Wife*, a Pirandellian battle of wits and realities between a role-playing man and woman in an institution for the aged, had its US premiere in 1992. Radzinsky's *The Last Tsar* (1992), a historical study of the final days of the Romanov family in Russia, became a US best-seller. SG

Raikin, Arkadi (Isaakovich) 1911–88 Soviet Russian CLOWN, who began his career as an actor and mime with the TRAM group, and in 1938 shifted to CABARET, becoming the director of the Leningrad Theatre of Miniatures. There he combined drama, OPERETTA, VARIETY and pantomime into an idiosyncratic style. Despite the bluntness of his SATIRE and his Jewish ancestry, Raikin managed to avoid persecution because of his immense popularity. His range extended from full-length shows such as *Around the World in 80 Days* (1951) to one-man quick-change concerts. He was seen in London in 1964.   LS

Raimund, Ferdinand 1790–1836 Austrian actor and playwright. After an unsuccessful start as a tragic actor, Raimund won acclaim in the comic roles that he played at Vienna's Theater in der Josefstadt in 1814. After moving to the Theater in der Leopoldstadt in 1817, he started to write plays that represented a sustained attempt to employ the Viennese VOLKSSTÜCK, especially in the *Zauberstück*, to express serious romantic themes. They represent the high point of that Austrian dramatic tradition, originating in the JESUITENDRAMA, that explored the interrelationship of spiritual and secular spheres of being. Of the nine plays Raimund wrote, *The Peasant as Millionaire* (1826), *The King of the Alps and the Misanthrope* (1828), and the ambitious, serious comedy written after his retirement from the Theater in der Leopoldstadt, *The Spendthrift* (1834), have proved to be remarkably durable, though with his contemporaries his earlier, lighter comedies were more popular. Raimund shot himself, believing he had contracted rabies after being bitten by a dog. It has been speculated that his suicide may have been caused by his apprehension at the growing reputation of NESTROY, whose caustic wit and social SATIRE were more to the public taste than his own poetic style.   SW

Rajatabla Venezuelan theatre group, subsidiary of the Ateneo de Caracas (Caracas Atheneum), created in 1971

Ferdinand Raimund as Aschenmann.

and headed for years by Carlos Giménez (1945–93), Argentine director long established in Venezuela. Rajatabla is a major force in experimenting with vanguard theatre in Caracas. GW

Rame, Franca 1929– Italian actress and dramatist. Rame was born into the profession; her early experience was on the VARIETY stage. From 1953 her career has been inseparably entwined with that of her husband, DARIO FO, with whom she worked on television in the late 1960s, in nearly all of whose plays she has appeared, and with whom she has collaborated as playwright. That fruitful collaboration, however, has not obscured her own very distinctive acting and writing talents, evident in her performances in the plays of other dramatists, like SHAW's *Mrs Warren's Profession* (1981), and in her own work, expressive of vigorously held feminist views – notably *Parti femminili* (*Female Parts*, 1988) and *Coppia aperta, quasi spalancata* (1991). LR

ramlila An all-India phenomenon: celebration of Lord Rama, hero of the epic *Ramayana*, through depiction of dramatic episodes from his life. At no time is it more prevalent than September–November, and nowhere is it celebrated with greater verve than in north INDIA. Activities leading up to the destruction of evil, symbolized in effigies

built for the Dassahra Festival, provide the opportunity for the Hindu community to express its renewed faith in the restoration of world order. Following soon after Dassahra is Diwali, the Festival of Lights, which welcomes Rama home from his self-imposed exile from Ayodhya, his kingdom and his home. Millions of tiny oil lamps that decorate the exteriors of countless village homes throughout the north symbolically light Rama's path. This great public outpouring of faith over a three-month period is accompanied by public performances of the devotional theatre form, *ramlila*. Although performances in different localities share the same subject matter, they differ considerably in the manner of their execution and length.

Lila means 'play' or 'sport'; *ramlila* is the 'play of Rama'. The generic term applies to a variety of different theatre events performed on festival occasions that centre on Rama's life. Historical evidence places the beginning of *ramlila* in the 17th century when a version of the story was staged, based on the poet Tulsidas' famous Hindi version of the *Ramayana*, entitled *Ramcharitmanas*.

Two centres for large-scale *ramlila* spectacles are the cities of Ramnagar and Delhi. In Ramnagar alone, over a million pilgrims arrive annually for the vast processions and performances organized by the Maharaja Vibhuti Narain Singh (commonly known as the Maharaja of Benares). The Ramnagar festival is supported by a grant of public money which helps the upkeep of the temples in the great pilgrimage city of Varanasi, across the river from the Maharaja's palace.

The usual procedure for establishing small-scale versions of the *ramlila* begins with the formation of committees, often democratically elected, by constituents of an area of a town or city. Although members of the *ksatriya* caste are thought to dominate the committees in many areas, in Mathura and Allahabad members of the merchant community control the organization. Obviously, besides expressing his religious devotion through public service on a *ramlila* committee, a merchant might reap profits from the festival occasions, especially since people purchase new clothing and prepare special sweets and foods, as well as increasing their charitable contributions, at this time of year. The bulk of the money to support festival activities is raised by small subscriptions collected from thousands of eager patrons.

Ramlila is performed by amateurs drawn from the community. In some areas actors have come from the same Brahmin families for centuries. It is customary for the roles of the five chief characters – Rama, his three brothers, Lakshmana, Bharata and Satrugna, and his wife, Sita – to be played by Brahmin boys who have not yet reached the age of puberty. Normally the youths are required to live in the house of the head of the *ramlila* committee prior to the opening of the performance because they are thought to take on the aspects of the gods they represent, to become *svarups*, embodiments of divinities.

The person who trains the boys and who heads the entire *ramlila* performance inherits the right to instruct the amateur players in proper stage deportment, to lead the singing and to make sure that correct procedures are followed in the preparation of scenery, costumes, make-up and music.

The stage space varies depending on the city where a

performance is held and the community that prepares the festivities. In Ramnagar, which literally means 'Rama's city', 30 days are assigned to the *ramlila*, each day's events occurring in their own particular locations in the city and surrounding area. The Maharaja often travels from one event to another in his horsedrawn carriage or rides atop his elephant to better see the activities. During the great battle scenes between the monkey soldiers of Rama and the demon soldiers of Ravana, the symbolic representation of evil, hundreds of youths take part. The spectacle ends in the burning of the effigies of Ravana and his demon brothers. The effigies are four to five storeys tall. At the conclusion of the evening they are shot with burning arrows and they burst into flames and explode with fireworks falling in a heap at the feet of the actor playing Rama, as the crowd fervently chants, 'Victory to Rama'.

In village performances, an earthen platform 3 to 4ft off the ground topped by a colourful canopy will serve as the stage on which all the dramatic events are enacted. Processions of floats (*chauki*), separate chariots designed for Ravana and Rama, and processions of elephants and camels represent various events in the story. Microphones and loudspeakers carry the songs, music and dialogue in some performances. In others the actors must project their voices valiantly in open spaces, but are rarely heard by the thousands of participants who jam the area just to be a part of the RITUAL occasion.

People from many walks of life participate in the *ramlila* – Hindus, Muslims, Christians, Sikhs, and Parsis; rich and poor; maharajas and beggars – whoever comes to witness the events may participate. Those who consider the events sacred often reverently touch the feet of Rama and Sita when the boy *svarup* draw near.

Costumes differ considerably among the various groups. Because hundreds of actors typically participate in the major performances, costume houses in the area specialize in *ramlila* costumes which they rent out for the duration of the season. The make-up of the five central characters is usually a pinkish-white base over which stencil designs in the shapes of flowers and stars are drawn. Sequins and mica are added to provide a glittering, colourful and unrealistic appearance. The moment the actor playing Rama wears his crown, he is thought to be invested with the spirit of the god-man he portrays.

The actor who plays Ravana wears a MASK depicting the ten heads that mark the demon king. His brothers usually have various distorted and deformed features, as do his demon hordes, many of whom smear black make-up on their faces to symbolize their evil nature.

The music of *ramlila* follows the folk-music tradition of the area with the addition of religious tunes as well as classical pieces. Bell-metal cymbals, drums and harmonium are the chief musical instruments. Chanting of the whole of the *Ramcharitmanas* is a part of the ritual activities in many areas, and priests capable of excellent recitation regard this as a ritual obligation, no matter what the hour of the day or night.

In Andhra Pradesh state a popular form of presenting the *Ramayana* is *chiratala ramayanam*. The actors, mostly amateurs from different communities, wear make-up and costumes appropriate to the characters they portray and gather in an open place for the celebration. They stand in a circle and dance, keeping time with *kartal*, a pair of wooden pieces with small metal discs held in the hand and struck against each other. *Kartal* are associated with devotional music (*bhajans*). The musicians sit in the centre of the circle and accompany the performers with *tabla* drums and harmonium. When a passage of music is used for dance, the clown, who keeps a whistle in his mouth, blows it in time to the rapidly accelerated music. He governs the performance and moves the action forward.   FAR

Ramos-Perea, Roberto 1956– Puerto Rican playwright, essayist and short story writer. Born in Mayagüez, Ramos-Perea studied in Mexico and Puerto Rico, and has been an actor and director in several Puerto Rican theatre groups. In addition to *Los 200 no* (*The 200 Noes*, 1983), a violent encounter between a university student and a professor, and *Ese punto de vista* (*That Point of View*, 1984), his work includes a major historical trilogy: *Revolución en el infierno* (*Revolution in Hell*), based on the Ponce massacre of 1937; *Módulo 104, revolución en el purgatorio* (*Module 104, Revolution in Purgatory*), based on the Puerto Rican penal system during the years 1980–2; and *Cueva de ladrones, revolución en el paraíso* (*Thieves' Cave, Revolution in Paradise*), based on the radical student movement. Later plays include *Obsesión* (*Obsession*, 1988) and *Llanto de luna* (*Moon Lament*, 1989).   GW

Rand, Sally [Helen (or Hazel) Gould Beck] 1904–79 American dancer, who scandalized America in 1933 by performing a fan dance at the Chicago World's Fair. Born in Hickory County, Missouri, she worked as an acrobat in CIRCUSES and CARNIVALS, then went to Hollywood in the mid-1920s to appear in such silent films as *King of Kings* and *Getting Gertie's Garter*. After the Depression she changed her name and began working Chicago speak-easies. She then toured the VAUDEVILLE circuit, headlining at the PALACE THEATRE in 1928, there reviewed as 'indifferently pleasant'. After breaking in the fan dance in 1932 in a Chicago nightclub, her World's Fair appearance made her a star, and she worked steadily almost till her death. Rand also appeared nude as Lady Godiva – she called it her form of social protest during the Depression – and also developed a 'bubble dance'. Critics called her 'saucy, piquant ... a cute, lithesome charmer ... [who] radiates personality'.   SMA

Randolph, Thomas 1605–35 English playwright and poet, who owed his contemporary esteem to the work he produced while at Cambridge University. The facility with which he wrote is well illustrated by 'An Ode to Master Anthony Stafford', which is a charming poem in praise of country life. His PASTORAL play, *Amyntas* (1630), is enlivened by its comic scenes, but his other full-length piece, *The Jealous Lovers* (1632), is dramatically insipid. Randolph was better suited to the writing of dramatic sketches. *Aristippus: or, The Jovial Philosopher* (c.1626) proposes that study of the philosophy of drinking should be added to the university syllabus, a theme pursued with variations in *The Drinking Academy* (c.1626). *The Conceited Pedlar* (1627) is an ephemerally witty monologue. *The Muses' Looking-Glass* (1630), in which an actor out-argues Puritan opposition to the theatre, is

Randolph's most interesting work. It reflects the influence of BEN JONSON, of whom Randolph was a favoured 'son'. PT

Rankin, Arthur McKee 1841–1914 A dashing actor-manager, Canadian-born. Rankin was a theatrical gambler whose charm usually kept him one step ahead of disaster. Acting with his wife, Kitty Blanchard (1847–1911), he achieved his greatest success as the stalwart miner Sandy McGee in *The Danites* (1877), a tale of Mormon revenge in a gold mining town. Other roles included another miner, ''49', in a play of that title (1881) and a Canadian hero in *The Canuck* (1891). In 1883–4 Rankin managed the Third Avenue Theatre, and in the 1890s he coached actress NANCE O'NEIL, who would not perform without his assistance. Rankin's legal and marital problems were legend; in 1904 he declared bankruptcy. His oldest daughter, Gladys, married Sidney Drew and another daughter, Doris, married Lionel Barrymore (see DREW–BARRYMORE FAMILY). RAH

Rascón Banda, Víctor Hugo 1948– Mexican playwright, whose portrayal of middle- and working-class situations and problems has brought popularity, even when the plays are melodramatic or unrealistic. Major successes include *Las armas blancas* (*White Arms*, 1982) and *Máscara vs. Cabellera* (*Mask versus Head of Hair*, 1985), the latter an apotheosic look at a wrestling idol. GW

raslila Generic term throughout INDIA for various dances and dance dramas dedicated to Krishna, seventh incarnation of the god Vishnu. *Ras* refers to Lord Krishna's joyous, melodious, circular dance with the wives of Brahmin cowherds of Vrindavan, a holy city in north India, described in mythological sources. *Lila* means 'play' and implies the god's playful tryst with man and earthly beings. Because they are devoted to Krishna, KRISHNATTAM of Kerala and ANKIYA NAT of Assam are also *raslila*. *Ras* dances in Gujarat and other states are not included here because they do not have a significant dramatic structure.

The *raslila* performed in Vrindavan is perhaps the best-known in India. Vrindavan is in the Braj region along the Jumna River, a 90-mile-square area south of Delhi. The present form probably came into being in the 16th century on the crest of the devotional (*bhakti*) movement dedicated to Vishnu-Krishna which swept this part of north India.

Krishna is said to have been born in the city of Mathura, a few miles from Vrindavan where he spent his childhood and youth. Thus, the whole area is considered holy ground and enactment of *raslila* is an extension of the religious fervour of the inhabitants and the hundreds of thousands of pilgrims who flock to the area every year to join in the holy-day celebrations and to walk the very ground which Krishna is reputed to have trod. To witness *raslila* is tantamount to experiencing *darshan* (revelation of god).

Performance centres on aspects of Krishna's earthly life and the miraculous experiences of lovers and devotees in association with him. The first part of a performance begins with a tableau: Krishna is seated enthroned, with Radha, his beloved chief consort (*sakhi*), on his left, and less important consorts arranged on lower steps of a platform to his right and left. The chief singer and other musicians reverently touch the feet of the divine couple, at that moment regarded as incarnations of god requiring respect. Ritual prayers are sung in praise of them and other deities. A tray with a lighted lamp is waved in a circular motion in front of them (*arati*), the same ritual which is performed in the temple before idols. Then Krishna and Radha perform a series of dances (*nitya ras*), joined in some by Krishna's consorts. Songs accompanying the dances move through different rhythmic patterns, slowly raising the level of religious fervour of the spectator-devotees. When particular sections are well executed the spectators shower verbal praise on the gods, not on the artists. Sometimes fervent devotees are moved by an action or moment in the performance and stand and sway to the infectious rhythms or make their way to the playing area and reverently bow down and touch their heads to the ground in front of the actors. When the latter have returned to their throne decorated with sumptuous fabrics, other songs and a short discourse by Krishna may follow.

After a short interval, the second part of the *nitya ras* begins in which songs predominate and dance plays a secondary role. Group singing involves the spectators in the emotional fervour which climaxes in a duet sung by Krishna and Radha, particularly relished by the crowd. Then Krishna, Radha and the *sakhi* perform a final group dance which culminates in a tableau. At this point devotees surge forward to touch the feet of the divine couple. After they have prostrated themselves before the god-actors, they leave gifts of money, the musicians singing popular hymns all the while. Curtains close on the tableau and a short interval follows.

The final part of the evening's performance is a short play (*lila*) based on an episode in Krishna's life. The plays are composed primarily of dialogue and song, with relatively little dance. The particular audience, season or holiday will often dictate which *lila* out of the nearly 150 that have been composed is appropriate for performance. Plays concern episodes connected with Krishna's birth, his mischievous childhood, his sport with the young milkmaids of Vrindavan and his adult life. At the conclusion of the *lila*, devotees shout 'Victory to Krishna of Vrindavan!' and the performance and rituals end.

Performance lasts about two and a half hours. Unlike many forms of rural theatre, *raslila* must be completed before midnight. Since it is regarded as a religious RITUAL, shoes must be removed outside the performance area, spectators must sit on the ground and may not presume to sit or stand above the heads of the actors who play Radha and Krishna, and smoking and talking are strictly forbidden.

The proper place for a *raslila* performance is in a temple, a private garden, a bungalow or holy resting place for travellers. It is not considered appropriate to perform such a sacred event in the street.

A *raslila* performance area is a circle (*mandal*), echoing the circle dance of the *nitya ras*. A throne is placed at one side with several platform steps leading down to the ground. A curtain strung on wire masks the platform from spectators sitting opposite. A rectangular area (about 15 x 20ft) is marked out on the playing area in front of the throne. To one side of the playing area and facing the throne, the musicians (*samaji*) arrange themselves. The musical party consists of two singers, each with a harmonium, a *tabla* drummer and a cymbal player. The musicians act as a chorus and the chief singer (*rasdhari*) takes the lead and controls the progress of the performance.

A *raslila* party consists of 10–18 males. Only boys who have not yet reached the age of puberty may play the divine couple and consorts, and Radha and Krishna are carefully chosen from among sons of traditional Brahmin families of Braj. When the young actors wear the crowns of Krishna and Radha they are thought to be the gods and are treated with great deference. They are carried on the back of the troupe leader to the playing area so that their feet do not touch the ground. Adults who have distinguished themselves for their playing skill take the roles of adults in the *lila*.

The young boys study with a teacher (*swami*) who serves as the leader of the troupe. The texts of the songs and the various *lila* are taught verbally to those who are not literate. The chief singer (*samaji*) acts as the prompter. He may correct the actors or jump in to aid them to speak a line properly or support them when they fall out of character or forget a particular section of dance. In performance, actors often seem to drop out of character, staring at the audience indiscriminately. No standard of excellence exists, even though the companies are professional. The religious fervour of the experience seems to outweigh aesthetic considerations.

The high season for *raslila* performance in Vrindavan is the monsoon season and the holy days connected with Krishna's birth and special events in his life. FAR

Rastell, John c.1475–1536 English playwright. Brother-in-law of Sir Thomas More, father-in-law of JOHN HEYWOOD, Rastell is regarded not as a particularly good writer, but as an important one in terms of the movement of English drama away from moralities (see MORALITY PLAY) to more secular themes. Plays believed to be by him include *The Nature of the Four Elements* (c.1517), in which the leading character is offered the benefits of the new Renaissance education, despite alternative temptations; *The Dialogue of Gentleness and Nobility* (c.1527); and *Calisto and Melibea* (c.1527), taken from FERNANDO DE ROJAS's *Celestina*. Rastell and his son William were printers, and published the INTERLUDES of other writers including Heywood. MB

Rastelli, Enrico 1896–1931 Italian JUGGLER, born in Samara, where his CIRCUS family was on tour. He trained for the slack-rope, trapeze and ACROBATICS, for his father had forbidden him to juggle; but he practised in secret and made his debut at the Circo Gatti in 1922, breaking a world record by juggling ten rubber balls in one hand and ten table mats in the other. Unequalled for accuracy and number in balancing spheres, he usually performed in football shorts and ended his act with a one-man soccer game that sent the balls into the audience. A victim of leukaemia, he hastened his death by over-rehearsal. LS

Rattigan, Terence 1911–77 British dramatist. Although his early output was somewhat uneven, Rattigan established a reputation for light COMEDY with *French without*

Tears (1936), which ran for more than 1000 performances, *While the Sun Shines* (1943) and *Love in Idleness* (played by the LUNTS in 1944, and in New York as *O Mistress Mine*, 1946). The autobiographical play about his wartime experiences *Flare Path* (1942) began to introduce serious themes, which became the keynote of social dramas that made him the leading playwright of the immediate post-war period. These ranged from dramatizations of notorious miscarriages of justice in *The Winslow Boy* (1946), dealing with the Archer–Shee trial where a schoolboy was accused of theft, and *Cause Célèbre* (1977) based on a murder case, and provocative moral issues – *Ross* (1960) dramatizing homosexuality through the life of T. E. Lawrence, and *A Bequest to the Nation* (1970) on the relationship between Nelson and Lady Hamilton – to sensitive studies of psychological domination in *The Browning Version* (performed together with *Harlequinade* under the title of *Playbill*, 1948) and *Separate Tables* (1954). He also continued to write comedy, with *The Sleeping Prince* (1956), and contributed a number of successful film scripts.

By the time Rattigan was knighted in 1971, his works were already being criticized as conventional 'problem play' treatments catering to unsophisticated popular taste – the 'Aunt Ednas' of his prefaces – but his skilful craftsmanship and subtle characterization have been recognized in revivals of *Playbill* (at the NATIONAL THEATRE, 1980) and *Separate Tables* (at the Ontario STRATFORD FESTIVAL, 1984). CI

Raucourt, Françoise [Marie Antoinette Josephe Saucerotte] 1756–1815 French actress. Endowed with a fine voice, noble bearing and considerable beauty, she made her debut at the Théâtre-Français (see COMÉDIE-FRANÇAISE) in 1772 in the role of Dido. Her popularity with the public was mitigated by her strong masculine tendencies and scandals associated with her private life. In 1776 she made a fine appearance as the statue in ROUSSEAU's *Pygmalion*, and then spent some time in Russia, returning to the Comédie-Française in 1779. She played roles of mothers and queens and was magnificent as Athalie and Cléopâtre (*Rodogune*), but less good in roles requiring the depiction of motherly love. An ardent royalist, she was imprisoned, and nearly executed in 1793. In 1796 she grouped together a company for a second Théâtre-Français at the Théâtre Louvois. This company included Molé, PICARD, LAROCHELLE and other more conservative elements. With the closure of the Louvois in 1797, she moved to the ODÉON in 1798, and rejoined her former colleagues in 1799. In 1807, Napoleon gave Raucourt the task of organizing a French company for Italy, performing in Milan, Turin, Genoa and Venice, which lasted until 1814. One of her last roles was Cathérine de Médicis in *Les États de Blois* (*The Parliament at Blois*, 1814). Fifteen thousand people attended her funeral, but the curé of the Église Saint Roch would not accept her body into the church until the king gave orders that she receive full Christian burial. JMCC

Raupach, Ernst 1784–1852 German dramatist. Referred to by LAUBE as 'the SHAKESPEARE of triviality', Raupach was by far the most popular and fertile dramatist of his day. He wrote several MELODRAMAS, but was most celebrated for his skilfully constructed history plays, of which the 16-play cycle, *The Hohenstaufens* (1837), was the best-known. SW

ravana chhaya Form of shadow-puppet theatre in Orissa state in eastern INDIA: literally, 'shadow' (*chhaya*) play of 'Ravana', the demon king of Lanka, Prince Rama's foe in the *Ramayana* epic. The puppet of Ravana is interesting and large in size. Some scholars see the influence of the Jain religion and Buddhism in naming this genre after the reputed villain of *Ramayana*. In the Jain version of the *Ramayana*, Ravana assumes considerable dignity. Or it may be that players were hesitant to speak of Rama as a shadow, for he is the incarnation of Vishnu, a popular and important figure of worship and respect.

The one story in its repertory concerns the life of Rama and his struggles with Ravana as described in the *Vichitra Ramayana*. This Oriyan-language version of the Sanskrit epic was written by Viswanath Khuntia sometime between 1692 and 1720. Episodes have been drawn from this work to make up seven plays.

The simple SHADOW PUPPETS are 6–8in tall. About seven hundred puppets are required to perform the seven plays in the repertory. A character requires more than one puppet to depict its various moods. Besides the characters of the epic, there are stock characters of village barber and his grandson, and numerous properties and scenic items which lend interest to the story.

Puppets are made of deerskin mounted between strips of bamboo. Unlike other shadow figures in India, they have no movable parts. After they are created, life is breathed into them through a simple RITUAL sacrifice. When they can no longer be used due to excessive wear, they are symbolically cremated and reverently disposed of in a nearby river.

Performance is a simple affair and may be arranged at any convenient location where two poles can be fixed in the ground six or seven feet apart. An oil lamp casts the puppets' shadows on a white curtain about four feet wide that is stretched between the poles. Straw mats threaded together provide masking for the puppeteer who squats behind the screen.

Performance begins when a coconut is broken and a *puja* invokes the blessings of the elephant-headed god Ganapati and Rama. The leader of the troupe steps to the side of the acting area in view of the audience and offers a prayer to Rama. Then he introduces the story in a prose narrative. The puppets of the village barber and his grandson enter on the screen and the play begins.

The narrator speaks the parts of all characters, joined only by two singers. A blend of Oriyan folk and classical melodies set to lively rhythmic patterns accompanies dialogue and songs.

Although the action is limited by the static construction of the puppets, the religious atmosphere of the event and the magical transformation of the screen coupled with poetic language and music heighten the effect of the evening performance. FAR

Ravel family French MIME artists and dancers, arguably the most popular and influential performers in early-19th-century America. **Gabriel** (1810–82), an excellent pantomimist and rope dancer, was the chief businessman of the troupe; **Jérome** (1814–90) wrote such durable scenarios as *The Green Monster*, *Mazulme, or The Night Owl*, *Pongo the Intelligent Ape* and *Raoul, or The Magic Star*. The other siblings were **Angélique** (1813–95), **Antoine** (1812–82) and **François** (1823–81). After training in Italy, they had earned fame in Paris by 1828 and created a furore at DRURY LANE in 1830 with pantos, inspired by MAZURIER, that combined skilled ACROBATICS, graceful dance and advanced trickwork. They appeared at the PARK THEATRE, New York, in 1836–7, and then became a fixture at NIBLO's Garden in 1842–6, 1849–50 and 1857–60, where they were much admired by the boy HENRY JAMES. In 1850 the troupe divided, with Jérome and Antoine touring the USA and François and Gabriel playing in Europe; throughout their career they were closely associated with the Martinettis, the Marzettis, the Lehmans, the Zanfrettas, LÉOTARD, and the dancers Paul Brilliant and Josephine Bertin. They returned to France to retire in 1866. Angélique's children Marietta (Mrs Martin Hanley) and Charles Winter Ravel preserved the family tradition for many years, and the pantomimes were revived by the KIRALFYS in spectacular versions. LS

Ravenscroft, Edward 1643–1707 English playwright. He followed his father, a successful barrister, in becoming a member of London's Inner Temple in 1659 and Middle Temple in 1667; but with the success of his first play, an adaptation of MOLIÈRE's *Le Bourgeois Gentilhomme* as *The Citizen Turned Gentleman* (also known as *Mamamouchi* in its revivals) in 1672, he gave up the law for a career in the theatre. Ravenscroft tried most genres, including one of the first plays to use characters from COMMEDIA DELL'ARTE in England, *Scaramouche a Philosopher* (1677), and a good farce, *The Anatomist* (1697) – a favourite play of GARRICK's – as well as a SHAKESPEARE adaptation, *Titus Andronicus* (1686). By far his most successful play, *The London Cuckolds*, a bawdy mockery of the sexual ambitions of citizens, proved to be so popular with the citizens themselves that it became traditional to perform the play on the Lord Mayor's Day every year until Garrick stopped the practice at DRURY LANE in 1751. PH

Raznovich, Diana 1945– Argentine poet, novelist, essayist and playwright, with more than a dozen plays. From *Buscapiés* (*Fireworks*, 1968), a prize-winning first effort, and *Plaza hay una sola* (*There's Only One Plaza*, 1969), a collection of eight short plays under one title, to *Jardín de otoño* (*Autumn Garden*, 1983), her best-known play – with its two women madly enamoured of a television personality – she has maintained her commitment to serious theatre. Her *Casa matriz* (*Mother Centre*, 1991) shows the depths of consumerism through a 'rent-a-mother' agency that assuages basic emotional needs. GW

Reade, Charles 1814–84 British playwright and novelist, most often remembered as the author of the historical novel, *The Cloister and the Hearth* (1861). Reade managed to combine a cloistered life as a Fellow of Magdalen College, Oxford, with a vigorous and often litigious career as a social campaigner. Fascinated by the theatre, he wrote plays before he wrote novels. Early performed work included *The Ladies' Battle* (1851) at the OLYMPIC and a highly successful collaboration with TOM TAYLOR on *Masks and Faces* (1852) at the HAYMARKET. He based his first novel, *Peg Woffington* (1853), on the latter. The relationship was reversed in the case of *It Is Never Too Late to Mend*, which Reade published as a novel in 1856 and dramatized in 1868. It is a typically pugnacious criticism of the brutality of the British penal system. *Foul Play* (1868), a collaboration with BOUCICAULT, and *Griffith Gaunt* (1867) were other works to appear as both novels and plays, the latter under the preferred title of *Kate Peyton*. Reade's adaptation of ZOLA's novel, *L'Assommoir*, as *Drink* (1879) provided the actor Charles Warner with a virtuoso role as a man drawn into alcoholism. *The Lyons Mail* (1854), an effective adaptation from the French, passed from the repertoire of FECHTER to that of IRVING and on to MARTIN-HARVEY. A lifelong bachelor, Reade was a close companion of the actress Laura Seymour and a friend of ELLEN TERRY, whom he persuaded back to the professional stage in 1874, to take over a part in his play, *The Wandering Heir* (1873), a story based on the celebrated case of the Tichborne claimant. PT

realism Although realism and NATURALISM are often assumed to be synonymous, it is useful to distinguish between them. The term 'realism' was first used in France in the 1850s to characterize works concerned with representing the world as it is rather than as it ought to be. What realism and naturalism share is an allegiance to an art of representation or imitation of unheroic everyday contemporary life. It is now clear that realism is a style, no closer to reality than the several movements that rose in reaction against it, each claiming to approach reality more closely.

The 19th-century European novel is a bastion of realism, but its techniques entered the theatre gradually. Towards the middle of the 19th century came real objects on a stage that resembled a room with the fourth wall removed – the so-called picture-frame stage. T. W. ROBERTSON introduced real bread and real tea to the London stage of the 1860s. ANDRÉ ANTOINE founded the Théâtre Libre in Paris in 1887, where he provided authentic settings with real objects – most famously, a side of beef – for slice-of-life dramas that eschewed the tight, suspenseful structure of the WELL MADE PLAY. Inspired by him, OTTO BRAHM founded the FREIE BÜHNE in Berlin in 1889, and J. T. Grein his INDEPENDENT THEATRE SOCIETY in London in 1891. For these three avant-garde theatres, Ibsen's *Ghosts* was the key realistic play. Realism as a dramatic movement spanned the 30 years between IBSEN's first socially realistic play *The Pillars of Society* (1877) and SHAW's *The Doctor's Dilemma* (1906).

Variously ill received in their day, realistic plays are now acknowledged as the beginning of the modern repertory. After NEMIROVICH-DANCHENKO and STANISLAVSKY founded the MOSCOW ART THEATRE in 1898, an understated, psychologically based style of acting accommodated realistic plays; through STRASBERG's 'Method' adaptation of Stanislavsky, such acting now dominates film. The impact of the realistic movement was powerful and is still evident: realism is the dominant style of modern drama, recognizable in verisimilitude of setting, coherence of character, modernity of problems and prosaic quality of dialogue. RC

Reaney, James 1926– Canadian poet and playwright. Reaney began his writing career by publishing several award-winning volumes of poetry before turning to serious attempts at drama. His early poetry often exhibits tendencies towards the dramatic, taking the form of monologues or dialogues. In turn, his dramas rely heavily on his sense of the poetic in their densely symbolic structure, rich image patterns and vocal rhythms. The plays are dominated by his sense of the mythic and archetypal, often incorporating local history and folklore into his storytelling, and almost always experimenting (to varying degrees of success) with different forms of theatrical presentation.

Beginning with *The Killdeer* in 1960, he embarked on a versatile and prolific career as a playwright. Much of this early work was in theatre for young audiences; various plays for performance by live actors, PUPPETS and MARIONETTES (which he often created himself in abstract and unusual forms), or combinations of both, allowed him to develop his sense of fun and childish play on stage. Even the 'adult' dramas are permeated with a sense of childhood innocence, usually in conflict with the forces of corrupted experience. Reaney achieved his best integration of the worlds of childhood and adulthood in *Colours in the Dark* (1967), produced by JOHN HIRSCH at the STRATFORD FESTIVAL.

His subsequent plays have shown a greater focus on local history and myth. He is probably best-known for his trilogy, *The Donnellys*, about a bitter blood feud that climaxed in the 1880 mass murder of an entire Irish immigrant family a few miles from Reaney's birthplace. The *Donnelly* plays – *Sticks and Stones* (1973), *The St Nicholas Hotel* (1974) and *Handcuffs* (1975) – were developed in workshops, a favourite Reaney method. All three premiered at Toronto's TARRAGON THEATRE before touring nationally. More recently, he has written for OPERA and begun work in video and film.

In addition to his writing, Reaney maintained an active teaching career, retiring from the English faculty at the University of Western Ontario in 1992. DAH

recitative OPERAS, like PLAYS, involve passages that convey necessary information about the action and passages that express characters' states of feeling. Recitative copes with the first, ARIA with the second. Recitative approximates to the rhythms and inflections of ordinary speech. In the style known as *recitativo secco* ('dry' recitative) the voice is accompanied only by a harpsichord and string basses that provide a kind of punctuation by means of fairly infrequent chords and arpeggios. In *recitativo stromentato* or *accompagnato* ('instrumented' or 'accompanied' recitative) the accompaniment is orchestral. Rather than strictly following the composer's indication of the length of notes in recitative, singers have always allowed themselves some discretion, on the grounds that they are coping with a quasi-speech that cannot be accurately notated. Once recitative became accompanied by the orchestra its musical significance increased and the singer's discretion decreased. This, together with the increased flexibility of the aria and the growing concern for the organic rather than the aggregative work of art, ultimately resulted in operas in which there is a continuous flow of music rather than a number of arias connected (or separated) by recitative. In the 20th century some opera composers have used SPRECHSTIMME as a device for the effective utterance of the words. GH

Red Bull Theatre (London) One of the many London inns used for occasional theatrical productions, the Red Bull was converted into a distinctive theatre by Aaron Holland in 1605. It was situated on St John Street in Clerkenwell, close to the site of the modern City University. The yard was almost certainly square, surrounded by galleries on all four sides. Dimensions are not known, but the Red Bull was reputed to be 'big'. During the significant years of its occupation by Queen Anne's Men (1605–19) it was certainly notorious for the boisterousness of its audiences and for its ready recourse to specious effectiveness and to the popular appeal of JIGS and drolls. THOMAS HEYWOOD provided much of the most successful material. After the death of Queen Anne in 1619 and the defection of CHRISTOPHER BEESTON, the Red Bull housed a number of companies. Renovations in 1625 did little either to raise its status or deter its audience. Even during the Interregnum, the Red Bull could attract people to illegal productions and to puppet-plays (see PUPPETS). After the Restoration it quickly lost its place, and seems to have been demolished in 1665. PT

Red Lion Theatre (London) The discovery, in 1983, of legal documents relating to the building of a 'scaffold or stage for INTERLUDES or plays' in the Red Lion in Stepney has revised our knowledge of the enterprise. We now know that it was a farmhouse, not an inn, and that the conversion work in the yard was more substantial than had been supposed. The enterprise was financed by JOHN BRAYNE, brother-in-law of JAMES BURBAGE. His instructions were for a stage 5ft high, 3ft deep and at least 40ft wide. There was to be a trap-door and a 'turret' or tower 30ft high, presumably to serve as a TIRING HOUSE. Nine years before Burbage, Brayne envisaged a specialized structure, dedicated to the performance of plays. There is, however, no solid evidence that it was ever used, or even completed. PT

Redgrave, Michael (Scudamore) 1908–85 British actor from a long-established theatrical family, who worked as a schoolmaster before joining the LIVERPOOL PLAYHOUSE company in 1934, where he met and married the actress, Rachel Kempson. In 1936 they went to the OLD VIC, then under the direction of TYRONE GUTHRIE, where Redgrave played such roles as Orlando in *As You Like It*, Horner in WYCHERLEY's *The Country Wife* and Laertes in *Hamlet*. He was a member of JOHN GIELGUD's repertory company at the Queen's Theatre in 1937, and played Harry in T. S. ELIOT's *The Family Reunion* in 1939, his first major part in a contemporary play. His handsome presence, polite but somewhat studious manner and gentle speaking voice were equally well suited to stage and screen; and in the 1940s he starred as Charleston in Robert Ardrey's *Thunder Rock* (1940), a wartime hit, and in Alfred

Hitchcock's comedy-thriller, *The Lady Vanishes*. He joined the Royal Navy during the war, but also appeared in several discreetly patriotic wartime films. He created the part of Crocker-Harris in TERENCE RATTIGAN's *The Browning Version* (1948) and joined the Shakespeare Memorial Company in 1951, playing Richard II and starting an association with that company which led to notable performances as Prospero, Hotspur, Antony and King Lear. In 1959, he appeared in his own adaptation of HENRY JAMES's *The Aspern Papers*.

In 1962 he joined LAURENCE OLIVIER's company in the first CHICHESTER FESTIVAL season, playing the title role in *Uncle Vanya*, a production which entered the first repertoire season of the NATIONAL THEATRE at the Old Vic. Subsequently, he played Hobson in *Hobson's Choice* and Solness in *The Master Builder* at the National Theatre, before ill-health forced him to leave the company. He returned in 1972 to play the silent ageing academic in SIMON GRAY's *Close of Play*, but he suffered in later years from fears about memory lapses. Redgrave's two books on acting, *The Actor's Ways and Means* (1955, revised 1979) and *Mask or Face* (1958), reveal his intelligent, almost too self-aware, approach to his craft; and he was knighted in 1959. The repertory theatre in Farnham, Surrey, was named after him in 1965 and he was appointed the artistic director of the Yvonne Arnaud Theatre, Guildford, for a season. His autobiography, *In My Mind's Eye*, was published in 1983. His three children, VANESSA (b.1937), Corin (b.1939) and Lynn (b.1943), all became successful actors, as are two of his grandchildren by Vanessa Redgrave (Richardson). JE

Redgrave, Vanessa 1937– British actress, daughter of MICHAEL REDGRAVE and Rachel Kempson, who first appeared in the WEST END with her father in N. C. HUNTER's *A Touch of the Sun* (1958). Her Rosalind in MICHAEL ELLIOT's production of *As You Like It* (1961) at Stratford-upon-Avon was acclaimed, and she appeared in other Elliot productions including as Ellida in *The Lady from the Sea* (1982). She played Nina in *The Seagull* (1964), directed by Tony Richardson who was then her husband, and in 1966 achieved a triumphant success as Miss Brodie the Scottish schoolmistress in the stage version of Muriel Spark's novel, *The Prime of Miss Jean Brodie*. Her membership of the WRP (Workers' Revolutionary Party) and her passionate advocacy of political causes have attracted much publicity; but her dedication and sincerity, two outstanding qualities also of her acting, have rarely been questioned. Her tall, willowy appearance, expressive voice, and, not least, her marvellous comic sense have made her one of the leading actresses of her time, internationally as well as nationally. In recent years she has specialized in roles from modern US drama, including EUGENE O'NEILL's *A Touch of the Poet* (1988), TENNESSEE WILLIAMS's *Orpheus Descending* and two plays by Martin Sherman, *A Madhouse in Goa* (1989) and *When She Danced* (1991). In 1989 her company, Vanessa Redgrave Enterprises, brought over to London from Moscow the powerful Vakhtangov Theatre version of MIKHAIL SHATROV's *Peace of Brest*, banned for many years in the Soviet Union for portraying Lenin as a political wheeler-dealer. JE

Pit Prop Theatre in *Brand of Freedom*, a participation theatre-in-education programme in Wigan schools in 1984.

Régio, José 1901–69 Portuguese playwright. With only four dramas and three further one-act plays to his credit, Régio is nevertheless his country's greatest dramatist of the mid-century. His theme is essentially the same as that explored in his non-dramatic writing, and recurs poetically and dramatically over the 20 years between the mystery *Jacob e o Anjo* (*Jacob and the Angel*, 1941; performed in 1952 in Paris) and the one-act *Mário ou Eu-Próprio-o Outro* (*Mário/or/Myself-the Other Person*, 1957): the theme of duality, either of identity, or that of living in a dualistic world between spirit and matter, between God and the Devil, which in turn leads to conflicts of conscience or ambiguities in the apprehension of reality. Régio's protagonists are characteristically 'fools' in the Erasmian sense, or Pirandellian, believing in an ideal or an illusion that sets them apart from their fellows; but possessed nevertheless of an otherworldly lucidity and higher understanding. Often criticized for being too 'literary', Régio's works have in fact been well received in performance; one in particular, *A Virgem Benilde* (*The Virgin Benilde*, 1947), has recently (as *A Virgem-Mãe – Benilde, the Virgin Mother* – 1974) been filmed by the Leone de Oro director Manoel de Oliveira, with great lyrical and dramatic impact.   LK

regional theatre (Britain) The history of regional theatre this century has been dominated by two main trends: the decline of the commercial touring circuit from its peak in the Edwardian period, and the growth of the repertory movement from campaigns and experiments at the turn of the century to its establishment now as the major provider of theatre in the regions. Recent years have seen interesting and lively variations of the pattern: the partial revival of the touring circuit with the help of public subvention, and the emergence of small-scale community theatre touring to non-theatre venues.

The touring theatre At the beginning of the century dramatic entertainment outside London – in the towns, cities and suburbs – was provided mainly by theatres that were part of a complex series of touring circuits: the larger, more opulent and more strategically placed houses able to attract the finest companies; the smaller attracting the lesser, second-, third- and even fourth-rate companies. The rapid expansion of road and rail links in the second half of the 19th century had allowed the actor-managers to transport complete productions – elaborate sets and entire acting companies – with relative ease, and in the face of such competition the old resident STOCK COMPANY had all but disappeared. Long-running, well proven WEST END productions (mostly of MELODRAMAS, musical comedies and VARIETY, with some leavening of SHAKESPEARE) could thus be seen in their original spectacular form in Manchester, Newcastle and Glasgow. Likewise, new plays could be tried out in the regions before transferring (if successful) to the West End. There were, too, the companies devoted wholly to touring, with repertories ranging again from melodrama to Shakespeare (F. R. BENSON's company being the most notable example of such a troupe exclusively dedicated to the classics).

The confidence in, and profitability of, the touring

system was evidenced in the boom in new theatre building that occurred between the mid-1890s and 1914. Frank Matcham, that most prolific of theatre architects, was responsible during this period for almost 100 new or rebuilt provincial theatres. By 1914, Liverpool was able to boast seven theatres (of varying size and status) and Birmingham five, while the increasingly popular seaside resorts such as Blackpool and Brighton equally found new theatres a profitable investment. Only in the late 20s, with the arrival of the 'talkie' to boost still further the rise of cinema in the public's affections, did theatre building virtually cease. Thereafter the impact of cinema upon the touring system was profound. In 1914 there had been 170 or so touring companies; 20 years later there were less than 40. The old actor-manager system was by this time almost a thing of the past: DONALD WOLFIT's company (started in 1937), touring Shakespeare and the classics, was one of the few exceptions to the rule.

Another symptom of the sea-change undergone by the commercial theatre during these early decades was the marked shift in the patterns of theatre ownership. Although this had begun before the First World War it became most noticeable in the post-1918 years and undoubtedly was to contribute further to the wane of touring. Wartime profits from the entertainment industry had led business combines to take control of many of the London theatres, and the suburban and regional theatre circuits likewise increasingly became 'chains' run by a small but powerful number of commercial enterprises. Artistic control both of the buildings and of the products staged inside them passed steadily out of the hands of actors and into those of business managers representing limited liability companies. Later, in the face of stiff competition from cinema, 'business sense' by and large dictated a policy of hasty retreat from the risks of live, large-scale theatre.

The decline of touring continued unabated after the Second World War, the next blow being the rapid growth in the 50s of television and especially, with the inauguration of commercial television in 1955, of the sheer range of entertainment it offered. The touring houses themselves shrank in number during the 50s and 60s through demolition or conversion to cinemas and, later, bingo halls. By 1970 the number of touring and variety theatres had been reduced from 130 in 1930 to about 30. The quality and availability of shows for tour had likewise dwindled. Actors were increasingly loath to leave London as work opportunities in television multiplied; and the actor whose aspirations lay primarily in the field of live theatre was more likely to find fulfilment in the subsidized regional or national companies than on tour. In fact, more and more of the touring product that was available had originated within the subsidized sector – the ARTS COUNCIL-sponsored tour of *Oklahoma!* (in 1980) for example, and the national tours of the major OPERA, ballet and theatre companies.

While there was still a need for the touring theatre, at least in key geographical areas of the country, it became increasingly clear during the early 1970s that the commercial sector was now so entwined with the subsidized that complete separation was no longer feasible nor desirable. In order that the large, costly and mostly antiquated

buildings could go on providing the kind of service that the repertory theatres could not, rejuvenation was essential. With Arts Council encouragement and financial support, the big city municipalities – and a number of smaller ones too – actively sought business sponsorship and public subscription and themselves invested considerable sums in renovating and rebuilding. As a result there now exists a greatly reduced but healthier network of restored and vastly improved touring theatres in such towns and cities as Nottingham (the Theatre Royal), Buxton (the Opera House), Leeds (the Grand Theatre and Opera House), Manchester (the Palace), Newcastle (the Theatre Royal), Glasgow (the Theatre Royal) and Belfast (the Grand Opera House) – all serving large populations and capable of receiving a wide variety of dramatic and musical productions. This in turn helped to generate an increase in both the quality and the quantity of touring shows compared with the situation in the early 1970s, and audience figures rose correspondingly, until dented by the impact of the recession in the early 1990s.

The repertory movement It was primarily against the commercial touring system and all that went with it that the early pioneers of repertory rebelled. The actor-managers, the 'stars', the long runs, the domination of London, the priority of profit over experiment and new work – all these features were seen as stultifying and a hindrance to the healthy development of theatre as a social force. Looking back to the days of the resident stock companies and abroad to the accomplishments of the well endowed national and state theatres (the COMÉDIE-FRANÇAISE in particular), men such as HARLEY GRANVILLE BARKER and WILLIAM ARCHER, during the early years of the century, argued forcefully for the establishment of a National Repertory Theatre in London, to be followed later by regional theatres on similar lines if smaller in scale. In its ideal form, a Repertory Theatre would offer to the public a wide variety of the very best of drama, old and new, British and foreign, popular and minority interest. Commercial considerations ought not to govern the repertoire and for this reason, it was claimed, the theatre would need to be well-funded, either by private benefactors or, preferably, by national or local government (just as were museums and libraries). A large stock of productions would be maintained and presented on a regular, rotating basis by a permanent, resident company of actors able to play as an ensemble and to keep plays fresh in performance, freed from the deadening constraints of the long run. Barker's famous seasons at the ROYAL COURT THEATRE, 1904–7, were an early attempt to put some of the ideas to the test and certainly inspired others to carry the movement forward. But with London entrenched in the very system that repertory was endeavouring to oppose, it was in cities outside the capital that the establishment of full-scale repertory companies was to come. The repertory movement was henceforward essentially *regional* in character and in philosophy.

Within a space of just seven years, five repertory ventures had been initiated: at Manchester in 1907 (ANNIE HORNIMAN's company, which based itself in the refurbished GAIETY THEATRE from 1908); at Glasgow in 1909 (under Alfred Wareing); at Liverpool in 1911 (the first such theatre to be run by a trust rather than a wealthy patron); at Birmingham in 1913 (under BARRY JACKSON); and, briefly, at Bristol in 1914. These early repertory companies set the pattern for future growth, successfully building reputations for their high-quality ensemble playing, for their provision of a varied repertoire and for their encouragement of new writers (HOUGHTON, BRIGHOUSE and Drinkwater, to name only a few).

After the First World War, the movement in many respects lost momentum. It diversified: in many towns and seaside resorts small *commercial* repertories were started, as were a number of *touring* repertories – both contradictions in terms, both playing only the most easily digestible of repertories (FARCES and thrillers in the main) and giving rise to the common association of repertory with the third-rate. At the other end of the spectrum there was the adventurousness of TERENCE GRAY's Cambridge Festival Theatre (1926–33) and his experiments in 'presentational' stage design. Birmingham and Liverpool, however, continued to be the twin beacons of the movement and provided the inspiration for the founding of a dozen more genuine repertory theatres across the country. It was the work of the handful of outstanding companies – in Bristol, Oxford, Cambridge, Sheffield and Northampton especially, in addition to Birmingham and Liverpool – that helped to ensure a firm (if uncoordinated) basis on which could be built the stronger national network of repertory theatres after the Second World War.

The massive process of renewal of towns and cities which began in 1945 was accompanied by new attitudes to the role of the arts at both national and local government level. The whole idea of civic theatres, for so long an objective of Barker, Jackson and others, now grew in official acceptability, evidenced by the schemes that emerged, slowly at first but surely, for new repertory theatre buildings at Coventry, Nottingham, Birmingham and elsewhere – to be heavily financed by the local authorities, often with additional money from the Arts Council and public subscription. Coventry's Belgrade Theatre (1958) was the first purpose-built repertory theatre for 20 years. By 1980 some 40 new theatres (or major conversions of pre-existing buildings) had been completed, most of which were designed for regional repertory. The buildings were often prestigious in character, sometimes too large (and costly to run) but sometimes imaginative and exciting in design: Sheffield Crucible Theatre's thrust stage, the Manchester ROYAL EXCHANGE's in-the-round auditorium and the spacious foyers and auditoria of the West Yorkshire Playhouse (Leeds) are good examples.

Arts Council money, though it was eventually made available for capital building projects, was first channelled into an even more pressing cause – the freeing of companies from the tyranny of 'weekly rep' (the dominant practice of weekly changes in the bill to maximize box-office income). With the help of subsidy more and more theatres were able to change to two- and then three-weekly runs, increase rehearsal time and so improve their standards. At the same time ticket prices could be kept at reasonable levels and new or experimental work risked more frequently. The common causes, from the 1960s onwards, were less to do with opposition to the commercial theatre that, in the provinces at least, was on its knees,

and more to do with the very survival of a vital regional theatre in the face of television and a fast-changing, increasingly complex, urban society. Subsidy helped, but even more crucial has been the imagination, energy and enterprise of dozens of directors, actors and administrators and, not least, the moral and financial support of many theatre trusts. Of special note have been the seasons directed by JOHN NEVILLE, Stuart Burge and RICHARD EYRE at the Nottingham Playhouse (between 1963 and 1978); Peter Cheeseman's series of local documentaries at the VICTORIA THEATRE, Stoke-on-Trent; and the unique, assertively theatrical style pursued at the CITIZENS' THEATRE, Glasgow, since 1970.

The repertory concept had, by the mid-60s, begun to widen out, to take on a more strategic, 'audience-centred' significance – less associated now with providing a varied selection of plays for regular, traditional theatregoers, more with the function of *regional* theatres serving a multiplicity of interests and tastes, communities and age groups, and in a multiplicity of ways, inside and outside the building, on the main stage and in studio theatres – and as such claiming and earning public subsidy for a public service. Community touring and THEATRE-IN-EDUCATION units made significant strides in bringing theatre to new audiences, while the buildings themselves became more accessible and pleasing venues as befitted the theatres' own changing perceptions of their role in society.

Not all the aims of the original proponents of repertory have been achieved. The permanent acting company can rarely be afforded by theatres other than the NATIONAL and the ROYAL SHAKESPEARE, and rarely are plays presented in 'true repertory' (i.e. on the rotational basis): actors are now usually cast play by play, and short runs are the norm. Nonetheless, since the war, artistic standards have undoubtedly been raised, the repertoire broadened, much new work generated, the principle of subsidy (if not its correct level) agreed and a decentralized network of some 60 regional theatres firmly established. But, having become the establishment, it was inevitable, in the cycle of things, that they should be challenged and alternatives sought.

Community theatre Whereas in the USA COMMUNITY THEATRE usually refers to amateur theatre, in Britain the term refers essentially to professionals, based in and working for and with the local community. With roots in the work of some of the more locality-minded repertories (notably Cheeseman's Victoria Theatre in Stoke), in LITTLEWOOD's Theatre Workshop, Stratford East, and in WESKER's Centre 42, community theatre emerged in the late 1960s and early 70s alongside the political and YOUNG PEOPLE'S THEATRE movements and the growth of 'community arts'. The first of the community theatre groups (as distinct from political and general 'fringe' companies) was Professor Dogg's Troupe formed by Ed Berman as part of his INTER-ACTION community arts schemes in 1968 in north London. The group performed in the streets and on play sites, ran play schemes for children, and was soon joined by OATS (Old Age Theatre Society) and the Fun Art Bus, all part of the same overall operation and all aiming to involve different sections of the community in activities beyond the actual performances: helping, for example, parents and others to create and run their own play schemes and perform their own plays. OATS was short-lived but in every other respect Inter-Action expanded, moving in 1977 into its new centre in Kentish Town which housed some 14 different community projects. Its success in becoming part of, and a stimulus within, its locality provided a model for many similar if smaller-scale ventures elsewhere.

Community theatre since has tended to be of three main kinds: first, the companies whose primary role is *performance*, usually of original plays written with the locality in mind which are toured to non-theatre venues *within a distinct geographical area* – to community centres, schools, play schemes, trade union clubs, and so on. Often such companies combine this work with theatre-in-education or children's theatre. Examples include Theatr Powys in mid-Wales, Pentabus Arts Ltd serving the West Midlands, Medium Fair in south and east Devon, Solent People's Theatre in Hampshire and North West Spanner in Manchester and Salford, the latter specializing (until the early 1980s) in taking plays into factories and labour clubs. Some repertory theatres also have attached community theatre units, such as Theatre About Glasgow (based at the Citizens' Theatre). Second, there are the *community arts* companies, who see the theatre as just one part of a larger operation in which 'animating' the community, getting people to become involved in a whole range of activities, from drama to silk-screen printing or video-making, is just as important as the group's own performances. Such groups are Interplay in Leeds, Hoxton Hall Theatre Project (London) and WELFARE STATE INTERNATIONAL (based in Cumbria but frequently commissioned as theatre animateurs by communities across Britain and beyond). Also deserving of attention here are ANN JELLICOE's experiments in large-scale community productions in Devon and Dorset involving professionals and amateurs, adults and schoolchildren. Then, thirdly, there are the companies who gear themselves less to geographical areas than to serving specific *communities of interest* – women's groups, racial minorities, gays and so on – and who will often tour nationally. Such companies include the Women's Theatre Group, the Asian TARA ARTS group, Age Exchange (specializing in 'reminiscence' theatre), Graeae Theatre Company (of and for the disabled) and Gay Sweatshop. (See also FRINGE THEATRE.)

Despite their manifold differences of purpose and strategy, all of these companies (of which there were in 1992 over 50) tend to operate within communities that are theatreless and in other ways underprivileged. Almost without exception, too, their work is underpinned by a concern for social improvement and a belief in the power of theatre to help effect change, though few these days are inclined to ally their work with overt political campaigning. Their repertoires can be as much celebratory as critical and the best companies have succeeded – despite invariably low levels of public subsidy – in creating theatre that is at once entertaining, directly relevant to the concerns of its audiences, challenging, unpatronizing and, in its standards of performance, easily comparable to (if it does not surpass) most mainstream theatre.

In the late 1980s and early 90s, recession, subsidy standstills and the increasingly market-driven economy have taken a severe toll on all levels of regional theatre work, but on the more precariously based community theatre companies most of all.   AJ

See: S. Craig (ed.), *Dreams and Deconstructions*, 1980; G. Rowell and A. Jackson, *The Repertory Movement: A History of Regional Theatre in Britain*, Cambridge, 1984.

Regnard, Jean-François 1655–1709 French playwright, son of a wealthy merchant, who after an adventurous youth devoted to pleasure and travel took up writing largely as a leisure pursuit. His first efforts were farces and light comedies, some written in collaboration with Dufresny, for the COMÉDIE-ITALIENNE which he always admired. Appropriately, his later, more substantial comedies for the COMÉDIE-FRANÇAISE retain the same Italianate spirit laced with some palpable echoes of MOLIÈRE. *Le Joueur* (1696), concerning an incurable gambler, and above all *Le Légataire universel* (*The Residuary Legatee*, 1708), in which love and the finer feelings are all subordinated to a naked profit motive, are particularly interesting in their refusal to moralize about the most callous, unsavoury behaviour. Regnard's detached, uncomfortably realistic view of human nature is saved from an indigestible cynicism only by the sheer verve of his writing and some buoyant comic plotting.   DR

Rehan [Crehan], **Ada** 1860–1916 American actress whose family migrated to Brooklyn, New York, from Ireland when she was five. She made her debut at age 13, and at 15 became a member of Mrs John Drew's (see DREW–BARRYMORE FAMILY) ARCH STREET THEATRE company in Philadelphia. In 1877 AUGUSTIN DALY spotted her in Albany and engaged her to appear in New York in his own play *Pique* (1878). He was so impressed with her talents that he persuaded her to join him permanently, and from then until his death (1899) she was his leading lady.

During her 31 years on stage in the USA and in England, Rehan played over 200 roles, ranging from the title role in Daly's *Odette* (1882) to Lady Teazle in *The School for Scandal* (1894), and a host of Shakespearian roles: Katherina, Rosalind, Viola, Beatrice, Miranda and Portia. She appeared in London at TOOLE's Theatre (1884), played Katherina at the Shakespeare Memorial Theatre (1888), and opened Daly's Theatre (just off Leicester Square in the WEST END) as Viola (1893); she made a cross-country tour of the USA (1896) and finally after Daly's death toured again with OTIS SKINNER in *The Taming of the Shrew* (1904–5).

Critics called her 'sweetly reckless', 'ardently impetuous' and 'piquantly alluring'. ELLEN TERRY described her as 'the most lovely, humorous darling I have ever seen on the stage'.   RM

Reicher, Emanuel 1849–1924 German actor. After several years acting in Vienna, Munich and Hamburg, in 1887 Reicher was hired by the Berlin Residenztheater. Here his performance as Pastor Manders in *Ghosts* established him as a leading naturalistic actor. From 1895, he acted under BRAHM at the DEUTSCHES THEATER. Here he was celebrated for the minute psychological accuracy of his roles, especially in IBSEN's plays. From 1917, he directed at the Garden Theatre in New York.   SW

Reid, Christina 1942– Irish playwright. Reid came to critical notice as a television writer with *Did You Hear the*

One about the Irishman? (Ulster Television, 1980), later adapted for theatre. Theatre work includes *Tea in a China Cup* (1982) and *Joyriders* (1986) – realist, idiomatic presentations of Belfast working-class characters. *The Belle of Belfast City* won the George Devine Award in 1986, and was followed in 1989 by *My Name? Shall I Tell You My Name?* and *Lords, Dukes and Earls.* GF

Reid, (J.) Graham 1945– Irish playwright. Reid's plays centre on the violence, actual and threatened, in the North of Ireland: *The Death of Humpty-Dumpty* (1979) and *The Closed Door* (1980) show ever-widening circles of loss occasioned by terrorist murders; *The Hidden Curriculum* (1982) explores the inadequacies of a teacher faced with sectarian violence among his pupils; the terrorism, rape and torture in *Dorothy* (1980) proved too strong for Reid's main venue, the ABBEY THEATRE. *Remembrance* (1984) is somewhat gentler, exploring sectarian family pressures on middle-aged lovers from opposite sides of the political divide. His most recent stage work is the 1990 adaptation of his television trilogy *Billy* (1982). His consistent engagement with the Northern troubles make his plays, in STEWART PARKER's phrase, pungent with 'the thick and acrid' air of Belfast. DM GF

Reid, Kate 1930–93 Canadian stage and screen actress. She studied at Toronto's Royal Conservatory of Music and with UTA HAGEN in New York before appearing in productions at Toronto's Hart House Theatre and Crest Theatre, as well as in numerous CBC radio and television roles (see RADIO DRAMA; TELEVISION DRAMA). Following her 1959 debut as Celia in *As You Like It*, she frequently appeared at the STRATFORD FESTIVAL, playing roles that included Emilia in *Othello* (1959), Kate in *The Taming of the Shrew* (1962), Lady Macbeth (1962), and Ranevskaya in *The Cherry Orchard* (1965).

In New York she played Martha in the matinée cast of *Who's Afraid of Virginia Woolf?* (1962), and in 1964 was nominated for a Tony for her performance opposite ALEC GUINNESS in Sidney Michael's *Dylan*. Her reputation as one of North America's finest theatre artists led to roles created specifically for her, by TENNESSEE WILLIAMS (*Slapstick Tragedy*, 1966), EDWARD ALBEE (*A Delicate Balance* – she played only in the film version, 1973), and ARTHUR MILLER (*The Price*, 1968, in which she played for almost two years in New York and London). During the 1970s Reid appeared at numerous major theatres throughout North America. Her repertoire during this decade included Gertrude in *Hamlet*, Juno in O'CASEY's *Juno and the Paycock*, Lily in FRIEL's *The Freedom of the City*, Kitty Warren in SHAW's *Mrs Warren's Profession*, and Big Mama in a highly successful New York revival of *Cat on a Hot Tin Roof*. In 1985 she gave a brilliant performance as Linda Loman opposite DUSTIN HOFFMAN in a major revival of *Death of a Salesman*.

Throughout her career, Reid frequently returned to the Stratford stage, displaying her versatility in both modern and classical roles. In 1992, despite ailing health, she took on three roles for her final Stratford season. DAH

Reinhardt, Max 1873–1943 Austrian director. Reinhardt's early years in the theatre were spent as an actor, mainly of old men's roles, first at the Salzburg Town Theatre, then at the DEUTSCHES THEATER in Berlin under the direction of OTTO BRAHM. In 1903 he gave up acting to concentrate on directing, and over the next decade became the most celebrated stage director in Europe. Although Reinhardt was able effortlessly to absorb the latest developments in scenic design, employing designers such as GORDON CRAIG and Ernst Stern (1876–1954), and fully to exploit advances in actorial training and technique, he always maintained an illusionistic stage (see THEATRE DESIGN). This illusionism is the unifying element in his work that otherwise appears to be unusually eclectic, ranging from intimate chamber drama through vivid productions of SHAKESPEARE and the classics, to vast spectacles staged in arenas throughout Germany and Europe.

During these years Reinhardt was director of the Deutsches Theater, a post he kept until 1933. From 1917 on, he was closely involved with running the newly established Salzburg Festival; here he employed both theatres and extra-theatrical settings such as churches and the cathedral square for his productions. During the 1920s, his style of theatre came to seem slightly dated as a result of the rise of an anti-illusionistic stage, especially in Berlin. Because of this and for political reasons, his career increasingly became centred on Salzburg and Vienna, where he was, for several years, director of the Theater in der Josefstadt. In 1933, with the coming to power of the Nazis, Reinhardt gave the Berlin theatres that he owned and directed to the German people. While he kept a foothold in Salzburg, from then on more and more of his time was spent in the USA, where he worked both in Hollywood and on BROADWAY. His most significant work in these later years was his film of *A Midsummer Night's Dream* (1935). He died in New York. SW

Reinshagen, Gerlind 1926– German dramatist who came to the theatre late, after writing radio drama. Her scrupulously observed plays invest the structure and mechanisms of everyday life with an unobtrusive significance.

Doppelkopf (*Rummy*, 1968) shows the fall of a careerist during an office party, and *Eisenherz* (*Ironheart*, 1982) exposes emotional tensions behind the professional rivalries of office life. *Leben und Tod der Marilyn Monroe* (*Life and Death of Marilyn Monroe*, 1971) dramatizes the legend of Reinshagen's film heroine from slums to suicide, using 'at least' three actresses for the lead. In *Himmel und Erde* (*Heaven and Earth*, 1974) a waitress's reflections on the men she has served are terminated by a heart attack. Her best play is *Sonntagskinder* (*Sunday's Children*, 1976), an evocation of childhood during the war years in Germany, showing the domestic impact of distant carnage. Like *Das Frühlingsfest* (*Spring Festival*, 1980), which looks at the shady side of the German 'economic miracle' in the 1950s, it places a young woman of integrity in an atmosphere of casual corruption. Both plays are in part autobiographical. HR

Réjane [Gabrielle Réju] 1856–1920 French actress. The daughter of a refreshment-seller at the Ambigu, Réjane, after a difficult beginning, became one of the most brilliant actresses of the BOULEVARD. If she excelled in light and polished COMEDY, her range included much broader popular roles, such as SARDOU's Madame Sans-Gêne (1893), as well as the carefully observed NATURALISM of her interpretation of the pathetic and grotesque servant, Germinie Lacerteux, based on the Goncourt novel (1888). She was associated with a number of theatres, but the most important period of her career was spent at the Vaudeville, whose director, Porel, she married in 1893 (they divorced in 1905). The Porel management opened with the triumph of *Madame Sans-Gêne*, which was followed by Réjane in BECQUE's *La Parisienne*. In the following year she was the first French Nora in IBSEN's *A Doll's House*. One of her greatest parts was in Paul Hervieu's *Course au flambeau* (1901). In 1905 she left the Vaudeville and in 1908 she took on the Théâtre Nouveau and baptized it the Théâtre Réjane. It was here that she staged *John Gabriel Borkman*. She was also involved in the making of films, notably *Madame Sans-Gêne* and, a few weeks before her death, *Miarka, la fille à l'ours* (*Miarka, the Girl with a Bear*). JMCC

Remizov, Aleksei (Mikhailovich) 1877–1957 Russian

modernist prose writer and dramatist; a superb literary craftsman known variously as the 'sacrist' and the PICASSO of the Russian language. His novels, stories and plays reflect his interest in ancient RITUALS and folklore, children's games and fairy tales, dreams, etymology and Old Russia. Although he was attracted to SYMBOLISM, his work embodies a more individual tragic sense of life's mysterious causality and man's incomprehensible suffering, balanced by a mischievous and at times blasphemous playfulness in tone and literary devices. He served as literary manager of MEYERHOLD's Fellowship of the New Drama in Kherson, South Russia (1903–4), and wrote several plays – contemporary stylizations of ancient legends and forms, reflecting his belief in theatre as 'a cult, a mass, in the mysteries of which perhaps the Redemption is concealed'.

The Devil Play (1907) is a modernization of a medieval Kievan legend, featuring commentary, stylized gestures and the onstage transport, via a serpent, of a newly extracted soul to hell. Although it may come closest of all the Russian symbolist neo-mysteries to capturing the spirit and style of the original, Remizov was booed off the stage when the play was produced. *The Tragedy of Judas, Prince of Iscariot* (1909) combines an apocryphal Judas legend, the Oedipus myth and Russian folkloric imagery and stylization. *Tsar Maximilian* (1919) is Remizov's version of a well known and much rewritten Russian folk drama. His prose works formed the bulk of his writing and include a major critical work on Russian literature, *The Fire of Things* (1954). He emigrated to Berlin in 1921 and to Paris in 1923. SG

Rene, Roy [Harry van der Sluys; 'Mo'] 1892–1954

Australian comedian. Born in Adelaide, as 'Master Roy' he sang and appeared in PANTOMIME, and later in suburban MINSTREL SHOWS, from which he adapted Mo's characteristic black-and-white make-up. Partnered from 1916 to 28 by Nat Phillips ('Stiffy'), he dominated Australian VAUDEVILLE in the 1920s–30s with a distinctive earthy humour and outrageous innuendo; his catch-phrase 'Strike me lucky!'

became a household term. In the 1940s he appeared in the RADIO comedy series McCackie Mansions; his last stage appearance was in *Hellzapoppin'* in 1949–50. MW

Rengifo, César 1915–80 Venezuelan playwright, direc-

tor, professor, historian, politician and journalist. Another career took him into painting and muralism. Author of more than 60 plays (from 1942), Rengifo wrote trilogies on VENEZUELAN history and the petroleum industry. Chronologically, the periods that he dealt with are the Conquest, pre-independence, the wars of federation and the petroleum period. A revisionist historian, he made strong critical statements about injustices in contemporary society. His leftist political orientation led him to experiment with BRECHTian techniques, balancing aesthetics against ideology to avoid outright propaganda. His *Manuelote* (1952) is widely known; other major plays include *El vendaval amarillo* (*Yellow Wind*, 1959), *Lo que dejó la tempestad* (*What the Storm Left*, 1961) and *Las torres y el viento* (*Towers and Wind*, 1970). GW

repertory theatre (Britain) see REGIONAL THEATRE

(BRITAIN)

resident non-profit professional theatre (USA)

This movement, which gained its greatest momentum in the 1960s, has variously been called the regional, repertory or resident theatre movement. Although its initial impetus was the creation of an alternative, decentralized US theatre network outside of New York, the movement's most current nomenclature is 'resident', so as not to exclude New York City's not-for-profit theatres. Its nonprofit status is significant in that box office income is not of prime concern; rather, the focus is on the art of the theatre, the development of theatre artists, craftsmen and administrators dedicated to establishing a new American theatre, the production of classical and innovative contemporary drama, and often, community service.

Most resident theatres have a set season with subscribers, and are established in their own building. From a handful of theatres three decades ago, today there are more than 300 playing to well over 16 million people annually, forming a complex network and comprising the nearest thing in the USA to a national theatre institution. Today these theatres – which by 1966 employed more actors than BROADWAY and the road combined – are the chief originators and producers of significant theatre in America. According to a 1991–2 Theatre Communications Group survey of 182 theatres, more than 27,630 artists, administrators and technical and production personnel are currently employed by these theatres. Surviving on the basis of both public and private subsidy, the theatres have been in jeopardy since the mid-1980s because of the erratic pattern of contributed support that has failed to close the growing gap between income and expenses, intensified by the recession of recent years. Since 1980 over 40 theatres, including at least two that have existed for more than 30 years, have ceased operation (one was New York's Chelsea Stage, which as the Hudson Guild dated back to 1896), and 23 companies went under during the five years up to 1993. Nonetheless, as a result of this movement, most major American cities, such as Chicago,

Los Angeles, San Francisco and Seattle, today are important centres of theatre activity.

Claiming as antecedents the amateur COMMUNITY THEATRE/LITTLE THEATRE movement of the 1920s, the GROUP THEATRE of the 1930s and the FEDERAL THEATRE PROJECT of the Depression, the movement most frequently marks its beginning with the founding of the CLEVELAND PLAY HOUSE in 1915 (still in existence), although its impetus and inspiration is credited to MARGO JONES, who in the 1940s devised the prototype for the regional theatre with her Theatre '47 in Dallas, Texas. In her book on arena staging (1951), which was the manifesto for the movement for many years, she proposed a network of regional theatres. Following Jones's lead, Nina Vance founded Houston's ALLEY THEATRE in 1947 and ZELDA FICHANDLER co-founded the ARENA STAGE in an old Washington, DC, cinema in 1950. With Jones and Vance deceased, Fichandler, who has left Arena, is now considered the prime representative of the movement's beginnings and still a visionary voice for its future, though the earlier cohesiveness of the movement has dissipated.

From these beginnings other theatres followed in quick succession: the MILWAUKEE REPERTORY THEATER and the NEW YORK SHAKESPEARE FESTIVAL (1954); the DALLAS THEATER CENTER (1959); Baltimore's Center Stage, the SEATTLE REPERTORY THEATRE and the GUTHRIE THEATRE (founded by TYRONE GUTHRIE, Olivier Rea and Peter Zeisler) in Minneapolis (all 1963); in 1964, the ACTORS THEATRE OF LOUISVILLE, New York City's AMERICAN PLACE THEATRE, the HARTFORD STAGE COMPANY and EUGENE O'NEILL MEMORIAL THEATRE CENTER (both in Connecticut), South Coast Repertory (Costa Mesa, California) and TRINITY REPERTORY COMPANY (Providence, Rhode Island); San Francisco's AMERICAN CONSERVATORY THEATER and New Haven, Connecticut's LONG WHARF THEATRE (1965); New Haven's YALE REPERTORY THEATRE and the Arizona Theatre Company (1966); Los Angeles's Mark Taper Forum and San Francisco's Magic Theatre (1967); and Atlanta, Georgia's Alliance Theatre and NYC's CIRCLE REPERTORY COMPANY in 1969. During the 1970s the number of theatres established increased appreciably, only to ebb during the 80s and early 90s. The movement was helped extensively early in its history by the Ford Foundation (under the dynamic leadership of W. McNeil Lowry) and Rockefeller Foundation, and later by the National Endowment for the Arts – though under recent administrations this source of support failed to increase as it had during the 1960s and 70s – and state arts agencies.

As theatres associated with specific communities, these resident non-profit institutions have attempted to serve their specific areas in terms of individual needs and profiles. In addition to preserving the classics as exciting living theatre for their patrons, these theatres have the potential to achieve the ensemble acting possible only in companies that work together in numerous productions over many years (though, in practice, only a few companies have been successful in this regard). They can also be educational resources for their communities, create professional theatre training programmes, and – perhaps their major mission – develop new texts without restrictions on theme and content, as is often not true of the commercial theatre. However, regional audiences are often more conservative than those in New York, and as more varied philosophies and programmes develop, some companies are, in fact, less concerned with new plays or traditional classics.

Though not as large as it might be, the number of playwrights who owe allegiance to the resident theatre is impressive. For example, Chicago's GOODMAN THEATRE (founded in 1925) devoted much of its energy to the development of early plays by DAVID MAMET (who had previously worked extensively at Chicago's now defunct St Nicholas Theatre) and JOHN GUARE. Jon Jory's Actors Theatre of Louisville has demonstrated an intense interest in new plays, with an annual new play festival; playwrights such as MARSHA NORMAN and BETH HENLEY have emerged from this programme. Writers as diverse as SAM SHEPARD, AUGUST WILSON and CHARLES FULLER have been nurtured by the non-profit theatre. It is significant that 16 of 17 Pulitzer Prize-winners (1976–93) premiered in non-profit theatres before being transferred to commercial New York theatres, although such a trend predates 1976 (one of the first was Arena Stage's 1968 production of Howard Sackler's *The Great White Hope*) and continues today. Indeed, the non-profit theatre has been accused of becoming nothing more than a try-out institution for the commercial theatre, a charge that ignores the natural desire to prolong the life of and give greater visibility to significant plays. It is, therefore, noteworthy that David Mamet's *Glengarry Glen Ross* (1984 Pulitzer) began at the Goodman, that Marsha Norman's *'night, Mother* (1983 winner) went to New York from the AMERICAN REPERTORY THEATRE, that a play like TONY KUSHNER's *Angels in America* (1993 Pulitzer) developed at London's Royal NATIONAL THEATRE and Los Angeles's Mark Taper Forum, and that AUGUST WILSON's plays to date were developed at Yale Repertory Theatre. Other examples of plays first presented regionally include FUGARD's *A Lesson from Aloes* and *Master Harold and the Boys* (Yale), DAVID RABE's *Hurlyburly* (Goodman), HERB GARDNER's *I'm Not Rappaport* (Seattle Rep) and the Steinbeck–Frank Galati *Grapes of Wrath* (Chicago's STEPPENWOLF THEATRE). In 1990 *A Chorus Line*, produced by the non-profit New York Shakespeare Festival, closed after a significant 15-year BROADWAY run; this and other transfers, and the considerable profits accrued as a result, allowed JOSEPH PAPP to produce dozens of less profitable or more risky plays and MUSICALS.

Unquestionably, in today's non-profit resident theatre there is a true danger of allowing artistic product to take second place to the institution, of creating a regional theatre that moves away from indigenous needs to a more traditionally commercial, conservative and safe product that appeals to a mass audience and guarantees the box office needed to supplement other sources of income for survival. It is certainly a fact, with notable exceptions, that little avant-garde or true experimentation has taken place in the regions. Since the mid-1970s, in fact, the lines between commercial and non-commercial theatre have blurred. However, as long as the American resident theatres allow themselves to be operated by strong personalities with vision and sensitivity, they will remain more individual than similar. In this regard, however, it is significant that a true network is beginning to emerge that perhaps stresses important similarities of goals and aspirations. For example, one of the most popular resident theatre plays of the 1980s, Sam Shepard's *Fool for Love*, originated at San Francisco's Magic Theatre before it played at New York's Circle Repertory Company – both non-profit theatres. Michael Cristofer's *The Shadow Box* (1977) went from the Mark Taper to New Haven's Long Wharf to Broadway. CHRISTOPHER DURANG's *A History of the American Film* was staged in different productions at the Hartford Stage Company, the Arena Stage and the Mark Taper Forum before it was presented in New York. Emily Mann's *Execution of Justice* (about political assassination) was seen at the Arena Stage in 1985 after an earlier production at the Actors Theatre. Such a pattern of movement within the regional network is becoming more commonplace, as are co-productions with two or more theatres sharing production costs and extending the life of productions.

The US non-profit theatre network is served by dozens of organizations, although two are of special importance. Theatre Communications Group, founded in 1961, serves as a communications network for its institutional members and individual artists. Among their goals is 'to foster cross-fertilization and interaction among different types of organizations and individuals that comprise the profession'. One of TCG's services is the annual publication of *Theatre Facts*, which provides a statistical guide to the finances and productivity of the non-profit professional theatre in America. Recent reports underscore the increasing number of large deficits of major institutions since 1980, and the ominous news that 'the costs of doing business have grown faster than available income' and that long-range planning efforts 'are increasingly hampered by the shifting philanthropic terrain'. In 1992 nearly half of the nation's non-profit theatres ended the year with deficits brought on by the recession; in 1991 attendance declined for the first time since 1973 and in 92 almost two-thirds of theatres surveyed reported subscription declines. The second vital organization, the League of Resident Theatres (LORT), represents about 80 non-profit professional theatres, is active in labour relations, and concerns itself with the artistic and management needs of its members.

What seems clear from all available evidence is that the non-profit professional theatre is being forced to re-examine its structure and product in order to ensure stability, throughout the 1990s, of what in the early 90s was a $366 million industry. Thus far action has included reducing the number of plays produced in a season, making administrative cuts and changes, and frequently seeking a balanced season that restricts the size and scope of productions while minimizing changes in artistic integrity and vision. The future of small to mid-size theatres is especially in jeopardy as support continues to decline. Although the future for the non-profit theatre sector is uncertain, what is clear is that it has entered a new phase requiring creative and imaginative adjustments. DBW

See: G. M. Berkowitz, *New Broadways: Theatre across America 1950–1980*, Totowa, NJ, 1982; M. Jones, *Theatre-in-the-Round*, New York, 1951; J. Novick, *Beyond Broadway: The Quest for Permanent Theatres*, New York, 1968; L. Ross et al. (eds.), *Theatre Profiles*, New York, published annually by TCG; J. W. Zeigler, *Regional Theatre: The Revolutionary Stage*, Minneapolis, Minn., 1973.

Reumert, Poul 1883–1968 Danish actor. Reumert was engaged at Dagmarteatret and the Ny Teater, where his speciality included OPERETTA. In 1936 he began a long and glorious career at the KONGELIGE TEATER, most of it in a legendary partnership with Bodil Ipsen. He specialized in complex tragicomic roles, contrasting well with her exuberant, provocative style; they were especially successful as Edgar and Alice in *The Dance of Death* and Ill and Madame Zachanassian in *The Visit*. Perfectly fluent in French, Reumert had a special affinity to the plays of MOLIÈRE, whose *Précieuses ridicules* he translated. An outstanding Scapin, a very sensual Tartuffe and a controversially grave Alceste, he acted Molière throughout Scandinavia and in Paris, where he also lectured at the Sorbonne. HL

Reutter, Otto [Otto Pfützenreuter] 1870–1931 German MUSIC-HALL singer and song-writer; after a commercial education, he gained experience as a walk-on at minor theatres and as a folk-singer, before launching his real career at Berlin's Apollo Theatre in 1895. Basically a minstrel of the proletariat, conservative and patriotic, occasionally topically satirical, he displayed a wit and feeling in his reflections on the workaday world that taught volumes to more sophisticated song-writers. He played all the major music-halls in Germany, and wrote the words and music to thousands of numbers, the most famous being 'Ick wundre mir über gar nischt mehr' ('Nothing Surprises Me No More') and 'In fünfzig Jahren ist alles vorbei' ('It'll All Be Over in Fifty Years'). LS

revenge tragedy The fashion for revenge tragedy in Elizabethan and Jacobean England was sparked off by the success of KYD's *The Spanish Tragedy* (c.1589). Strictly speaking, a revenge tragedy begins with the appearance of the ghost of a wronged and/or murdered man to a still-living descendant or associate. Having heard the ghost's story, the listener assumes the role of avenger and the play pursues the story through to the completion of the revenge. Rarely adherents of strict form, the Elizabethan playwrights incorporated those features that best suited them whilst re-ordering or abandoning others. SHAKESPEARE's two revenge tragedies, *Titus Andronicus* (c.1592) and *Hamlet* (c.1601), exhibit almost the full range of their kind. Other notable examples come from TOURNEUR – *The Revenger's Tragedy* (c.1606) and the clumsy *The Atheist's Tragedy* (published 1611); WEBSTER – *The White Devil* (c.1612) and *The Duchess of Malfi* (c.1613); MIDDLETON – *The Changeling* (1622) and *Women Beware Women* (c.1625); MARSTON – *Antonio's Revenge* (1600); and SHIRLEY – *The Traitor* (1631). But the theme of revenge so dominated the tragedies of the period that the list could be vastly prolonged. PT

revista The Portuguese *revista* is somewhat wider in definition than its immediate translation 'review' would suggest, ranging from intimate sketch to mini-MUSICAL. Characteristically, it has played in the larger theatres, more particularly in Lisbon. The first *revista*, an imitation of the early-19th-century REVUE, *Fossilismo e Progresso* (*Fossil-Worship and Progress*, 1859), started a tradition of one annual *Revista do Ano* (*Review of the Year*), which was just that. Initially with no real plot, just a series of brief sketches, they were the theatrical equivalents of lampoon and caricature: the queen might be depicted squawking out a *fado*, the government furtively picking the lock of the Treasury. By the end of the century the *revista* had acquired the framework of a story, usually mythological in theme, for its political SATIRE, a chorus line and an orchestra; and could have long runs: *Sal e Pimenta* (*Salt and Pepper*, with the actress Palmira Bastos at the beginning of a half-century's career in the lead) ran for more than 200 performances.

The satire was often vitriolic and usually near to the bone. It was fired against the dictator Franco in the first decade of the new century, and against over-heavy policing under the Republic. The *revista* gained great popularity and importance under the Estado Novo (Salazar's corporatist regime, c.1928–74) because, in spite of having somehow to accommodate the rigours of CENSORSHIP, it was the only political theatre with any continuity in the nation's life. In the five decades following 1920, there was a high of 122 new shows in the 30s and a relative low of 68 in the 60s.

From May 1991, Felipe la Féria's *Passa por Mim no Rossio* (*It's All There, in the Rossio* – Lisbon's central square, where the theatre is), an *antologia de revista à portuguesa* in two acts and 41 scenes, celebrated 150 years of *revista* (from 1851; *Fossilismo e Progresso* has the first surviving complete 'book') with lavish staging, re-creation of high moments, the catchiest songs, and updating of satire: e.g. inclusion of the prime minister's call for an overall majority in country and Assembly, or he would resign – with its echo of Salazar – at the October 1991 elections. Over three hours long, on eight or nine times a week, the show played to packed houses over three years in the TEATRO NACIONAL D. MARIA II, as if to confirm *revista* as Portugal's favourite genre. LK

revue Episodic programme of songs, COMEDY sketches, MIME, dance and instrumental music, ostensibly organized around topical and satirical subject-matter, occasionally connected by a single theme or a master of ceremonies. Topical humour is as old as ARISTOPHANES and elements of revue may be discerned in Adam de la Halle's *Jeu de la feuillée* (c.1262), but the term first appears at a French fairground theatre with *La Revue des théâtres* by Romagnesi and Dominique (1728). The end-of-year survey became an annual Parisian feature at the Théâtre de la Porte-Saint-Martin during 1828–48 (*L'An 1841 et l'an 1941* by the brothers Cogniard is an early example of the contrast structure), and Berlin continued the tradition at the Metropol-Theater during 1903–14. In London, J. R. PLANCHÉ experimented with allegorical entertainments (1838–55) and JOHN BROUGHAM staged a revue in New York in 1869, but these bore no fruit. The small-scale topical revue was later absorbed into CABARET and chamber-theatre.

At the turn of the century, the spectacular revue arrived, a dance-dominated form that substitutes nostalgia, sentimentality and visual effects for SATIRE. The *revue*

à grand spectacle is built on cumulative effects and sensual contrast, each tableau contributing to an overwhelming sense of glamour. The first was *Place aux jeunes* (1886) at the FOLIES-BERGÈRE, Paris, which became a leading purveyor of this form, ever increasing in splendour: by 1906, the show boasted 18 tableaux and 600 costumes; by 1928, 80 tableaux, 500 performers, 1200 costumes. Other Parisian theatres making it a speciality were the Casino de Paris, Bobino, Alhambra and Ba-ta-clan.

In Germany and Austria, the revue became the second half of VARIETY programmes and occasionally transmuted into OPERETTA. Eric Charrell and James Klein were its leading producers there, and jazz bands, nude women and light shows regular features after the First World War. The form's loose-knit structure attracted the theatrical avant-garde. MAX REINHARDT's pantomimic spectacles *Sumurun* (1910) and *The Miracle* (1911) owed much to it, and ERWIN PISCATOR's *Revue Rote Rummel* (1924), which employed hundreds of lay actors, effectively adapted it to leftist political ends, inspiring ERNST TOLLER's *Trotz Alledem* (1925) and the AGIT-PROP Red Revues of the German Communist Party. BRECHT in Berlin, MAYAKOVSKY and MEYERHOLD in Moscow, VOSKOVEC AND WERICH in Prague, and Constantin Tanase in Bucharest also took it as a structural model.

Despite earlier attempts like *Under the Clock* by SEYMOUR HICKS and Charles Brookfield (1893), the revue did not catch on in England until 1912 with Albert de Courville's *Hullo, Ragtime*; the wartime thirst for light entertainment confirmed its success, when OSWALD STOLL imported French revues to London's HIPPODROME. The impresarios André Charlot and C. B. COCHRAN specialized in more intimate showcases for such talents as NOËL COWARD, BEATRICE LILLIE and GERTRUDE LAWRENCE (*Cheep*, 1917; *London Calling*, 1923; *Charlot's Revue*, 1924; *On with the Dance*, 1925; *Words and Music*, 1932). The basic unit became the 'black-out' sketch, a short comic scene ending with a punchline and a rapid lights-out. The smart WEST END revue flourished well into the 1960s and proved to be a nursery for comedians, singers and dancers whose personalities admirably suited the cosily saucy style of the genre: Binnie Hale, Cicely Courtneidge, Jack Hulbert, Cyril Ritchard, Hermione Gingold, Dora Bryan, Max Adrian and JOYCE GRENFELL. Eventually it succumbed to television and a blacker brand of satire, more akin to cabaret.

In New York some 200 revues opened between 1900 and 1930, often originating in the after-hours roof gardens of legitimate theatres. These included both the spectacular – the ZIEGFELD Follies (1907–31, 1933, 36, 43), the SHUBERT BROTHERS' *Passing Show* (1912–34), GEORGE WHITE's *Scandals* (1919–29, with music by GEORGE GERSHWIN and Paul Whiteman; 1931, 36, 39) and Earl Carroll's *Vanities* (1923–32) – and the intimate – *Greenwich Village Follies* (1919–28), *Music Box Revue* (1921–4, with music by IRVING BERLIN) and *Garrick Gaieties* (1925). *As Thousands Cheer* (1933) was the first intimate revue to feature a female black star, ETHEL WATERS, in a white cast (BERT WILLIAMS had already appeared for Ziegfeld). The decline of the intimate revue is due in part to the disappearance of a homogeneous audience that is reliably *au courant*, shares similar tastes and possesses a certain level of urbanity.

After 1945, the spectacular revue diversified into nightclub shows (Las Vegas, the Paris Lido), floor shows, striptease (the Crazy Horse Saloon, Paris; see NUDITY), ice shows and fashion shows. Much of its function had already been usurped by the revue film, exemplified by the work of Busby Berkeley. The topical revue became a feature of television, while the intimate revue was narrowed to a survey of a single composer's work (*Oh, Coward!*, 1972; *Side by Side by Sondheim*, 1976). It throve in OFF- and OFF-OFF BROADWAY theatres and cabarets well into the 90s, spinning off such parodic treatments of its own fare as *Forbidden Broadway* and CHRISTOPHER DURANG's *Das Lusitania Songspiel*. Economic necessity has reduced many revues to the format of a one-person show, featuring the talents of an outstanding piano performer or song stylist. In the 1960s, revue techniques once more inspired experimental theatre, while writers like N. F. SIMPSON and HAROLD PINTER provided sketches for commercial revues (*Pieces of Eight*, *One to Another*, both 1959). Poland's LATERNA MAGIKA, JOAN LITTLEWOOD's *Oh, What a Lovely War!* (1963), PETER BROOK's *US* (1966), JEAN-LOUIS BARRAULT's *Rabelais* (1968), LUCA RONCONI's *Orlando Furioso* (1969) and ARIANE MNOUCHKINE's *1789* (1970) have drawn on the revue format; much contemporary radical street and ALTERNATIVE performance (e.g. Bloolips; see FEMALE IMPERSONATION) is organized as a deliberate perversion of the revue's more outmoded traditions. LS

See: R. Baral, *Revue*, New York and London, 1962; J. Damase, *Les Folies du music-hall de 1917 à nos jours*, Paris, 1960, London, 1962; W. Jansen, *Glanzrevuen der zwanziger Jahre*, Berlin, 1987; F.-P. Kothes, *Die theatralische Revue in Berlin und Wien 1900-1938*, Wilhelmshaven, 1977; R. Mander and J. Mitchenson, *Revue: A Story in Pictures*, London and New York, 1971.

Reyes, Carlos José 1941- Colombian playwright and director. After his initiation to theatre with the Independent Theatre Club, Reyes joined El Buho (the Owl) from 1959 to 1962 as a member of the governing board, directing GARCÍA LORCA, ELIOT, and his own children's theatre. Affiliated with several other groups (including the Experimental Theatre of the Industrial University of Santander and the Popular Art Theatre), he collaborated with SANTIAGO GARCÍA to establish the Casa de Cultura de Bogotá, later the Teatro La Candelaria. He has operated his own theatre, El Alacrán, which merged in 1984 with the Popular Theatre of Bogotá. A committed writer, he has a wide range of plays to his credit, including many pieces of children's theatre and extensive historical dramas written exclusively for Colombian television (see TELEVISION DRAMA). Among his major plays are *Soldados* (*Soldiers*, 1967), a gripping account of COLOMBIAN violence based on a chapter of Alvaro Cepeda Zamudio's novel, *La casa grande* (*The Big House*); *Los viejos baúles empolvados que nuestros padres nos prohibieron abrir* (*The Dusty Old Trunks Our Parents Forbade Us to Open*, 1968), and *Variaciones sobre la Metamorfosis* (*Variations on Metamorphosis*), a play structured around Kafka's work *Metamorphosis*. Later examples include *La voz* (*The Voice*, 1990) and *Función nocturna* (*Night Function*, 1991). A formidable director, he is arguably Colombia's major spokesperson for the theatre. GW

Reynolds, Frederick 1764-1841 English playwright, exact contemporary of THOMAS MORTON. In his autobiography (1827) Reynolds boasted that during his professional career to date he had made over £19,000, 'a sum, hitherto unequalled in the history of dramatic writing'. He realized early that tragedy did not pay - claiming that modern dramatists had to write for money, not reputation - and most of his income came from a series of successful comedies, including *The Dramatist* (1789), *Laugh When You Can* (1798), *Folly as It Flies* (1801) and *The Delinquent* (1805). Up to about 1812 he was regarded by the Patent houses as a reliable author in a period when box-office receipts generally began to decline. Later he turned to comic opera, including several adaptations of SHAKESPEARE. He became adviser to Henry Harris at COVENT GARDEN, and in the 1820s reader of plays at DRURY LANE. In retirement he wrote PANTOMIMES for the same theatres, completing nearly 60 years' service to the drama at his death. Ten of Reynolds's plays were still in print (in Dicks's Standard Plays) at the end of the century. JRS

Ribeyro, Julio Ramón 1929- Peruvian novelist and playwright. Ribeyro is principally known for *Santiago, el pajarero* (*Santiago, the Bird Dealer*, 1970), inspired by a *tradición* of Ricardo Palma: the play criticizes governmental systems in an 18th-century setting. Other plays include *El sótano* (*The Basement*, 1959), *Fin de semana* (*Weekend*, 1961), *Los caracoles* (*The Snails*, 1964) and *Atusparia* (1979), based on an indigenous revolt in 1885. GW

Riccoboni family Italian actors. The founder of the dynasty, **Antonio** (fl.1655-95), was seen in London as Pantalone in 1679. His son **Luigi (Andreas)**, known as Lélio (1676-1753), sought in 1699 to establish a theatre in the French taste in northern Italy, in opposition to a decadent COMMEDIA DELL'ARTE; in 1716, under the protection of the Duc d'Orléans, he reopened the COMÉDIE-ITALIENNE, which, ironically, he gallicized to suit the taste of Paris and where he won acclaim for his expressive acting, especially in MARIVAUX's plays. He toured to London in 1727-8; served as a majordomo at the court of Parma in 1729-31; and returned to Paris in 1733. His works include a history of the Italian theatre (Paris, 1728, 1731) and a study of European acting (1738); and calls for theatre reform (1738, 1743) in support of sentimental comedy. He married, first, Gabriella Gardellini, known as **Argentina**; and second, Elena Balletti (1686-1771), known as **Flaminia**.

His son **Antoine-François-Valentin**, known as Lélio *fils* (1707-72), worked with the Comédie-Italienne during 1726-50 as first lover, dancer and choreographer; his acting was judged to be cold and pretentious, and he left because the Duc de Richelieu insulted him during the FAVART affair. He wrote several comedies, a discourse on PARODY (1746) promoting opera over tragedy, and *L'Art du théâtre* (1750), which raised questions of the actor's emotional involvement in his role. His wife Marie-Jeanne de La Boras, known as **Madame Riccoboni** (1713-92), was a friend of DIDEROT and wrote comedies in the style of Marivaux. LS

Rice, Dan [McLaren] 1823-1900 American CLOWN, son of a New York provision merchant. Rice led a chequered career as a jockey, strong man, blackface minstrel (see MIN-STREL SHOW) and (he alleged) agent for the Mormon leader Joseph Smith, before setting up his own show in 1841 with 'Lord Byron', 'the most sapient of pigs'. His debut as clown was ostensibly made in Galena, Illinois, in 1844, and he was soon a favourite for his native American humour with its heavy-handed mockery of local politicians. His red-and-white striped costume, top hat and chin-whiskers later became attributes of Uncle Sam. Rice popularized the term 'one-horse show', originally an insult flung at him by a competitor; and, as the 'Great Shakespearian clown', rival to the English jester William Wallett, he bandied mangled quotations with his audience. He was half-seriously proposed for president in 1868; alcoholism undermined his abilities before he made a comeback as a temperance lecturer in the 1870s and 80s (evil tongues claimed that the water jug on the podium contained gin). His final CIRCUS appearances were made in and around New York City in 1891-2. Feisty and quarrelsome, alternately populist and genteel, Rice neatly suited the tastes of an adolescent nation.   LS

Rice [Reizenstein]**, Elmer** 1892-1967 American playwright. Rice's career started in 1914 with *On Trial*, an experimental play that used flashbacks to reveal aspects of the crime being tried. A New Yorker who graduated from law school before becoming a playwright, Rice used his legal knowledge in several plays, in various disputes with theatres, and in the causes he served – from Marxism in the 1930s to the American Civil Liberties Union. A wise and fearless man, he wrote with considerable skill on subjects both popular and unpopular. When his efforts with the FEDERAL THEATRE PROJECT were threatened with government CENSORSHIP, he was outraged and resigned his administrative post. Responding to the high-handed methods of the THEATRE GUILD, he and four other playwrights – ROBERT E. SHERWOOD, S. N. BEHRMAN, SIDNEY HOWARD and MAXWELL ANDERSON – founded the Playwrights' Company in 1938. He later vigorously opposed Senator Joseph McCarthy's attacks on theatre artists.

Rice's plays reflect his various interests in theatrical experiments, realistic scenes and protest drama. His best work, *The Adding Machine* (1923), an expressionistic play (see EXPRESSIONISM) about the dehumanization of humankind, was followed by further experiments – *The Subway* (1929) and *Dream Girl* (1945). Man's social condition both fascinated and angered Rice, who exclaimed through a character in *Street Scene* (1929): 'Everywhere you look, oppression and cruelty!'. *We, the People* (1933), a bitter attack on Depression times, ended in an AGIT-PROP call for democratic ideals. In *Judgment Day* (1934) he scourged Nazi Fascism, and in *Between Two Worlds* (1934) he contrasted the political systems of Russia and America. Finally, in *American Landscape* (1938), he maintained his support for American idealism but, disillusioned with both Marxism and American commercial theatre, threatened to stop writing plays. Post-Second World War theatre brought him little satisfaction. *The Grand Tour*, a romance in Europe (1951), *Winners*, a crime MELODRAMA (1954), and *Cue for Passion*, a weak story of a California Hamlet (1958), did little for his reputation. He recounted

his experiences in *The Living Theatre* (1959) and *Minority Report* (1963), where, always a liberal idealist, he preached individual freedom from all tyranny.   WJM

Rice, Thomas D(artmouth) ['Daddy'] 1806-60 Blackface performer ('Ethiopian delineator'), considered the 'father of American minstrelsy (see MINSTREL SHOW)'. Between 1828 and 31 Rice, according to tradition, observed a crippled Black stableman (possibly in Louisville, Kentucky) sing a refrain and dance with a jerky jump – thus 'Jump Jim Crow', after the slave's name. From this single song and dance Rice developed full-length entertainments called 'Ethiopian operas'. He toured the British Isles in 1836, 38 and 43, leaving his stamp on the English stage. In 1858, he played the title role at the BOWERY THEATRE in *UNCLE TOM'S CABIN* (1850), though generally he remained a solo entertainer throughout his career.   DBW

Rice, Tim(othy Miles Bindon) 1944- British lyricist and author, who teamed up with ANDREW LLOYD WEBBER while still at school to write *Joseph and the Amazing Technicolour Dreamcoat*, which was eventually seen in London in a professional production in 1968. Rice is a skilful if unconventional lyricist, whose off-rhymes and unusual rhythms contributed to the success of two further Lloyd Webber MUSICALS, *Jesus Christ Superstar* (1970) and *Evita* (1976); but *Blondel* (1983), written with Stephen Oliver, received only a short run at London's Aldwych Theatre. *Chess* (1986), with music by Benny Andersson and

Thomas 'Daddy' Rice as the original Jim Crow, c.1830.

Björn Ulvacus, told a love story against a background of Cold War politics in sport; and, like *Evita*, revealed an earnest if somewhat raw world outlook. He has written lyrics for such composers as Paul McCartney and Marvin Hamlisch; and written and edited books on cricket, including the *Lord's Taverners Sticky Wicket Book* (1979). He is also well known in Britain as a TV presenter.   JE

Rich, Frank 1949– American theatre critic. Born in Washington, DC, and educated at Harvard in American history and literature (1971), Rich was co-founder, reporter and editor of the *Richmond* [Virginia] *Mercury* (1972–3); the senior editor and film critic of *New Times Magazine* (New York City, 1973–5); film critic of the *New York Post* (1975–7); film and television critic of *Time* magazine (1977–80); and chief drama critic of the *New York Times* (1980–94). He is author of *The Theatre Art of BORIS ARONSON* (co-written with Lisa Aronson, 1987). As daily critic of the *New York Times*, Rich is arguably the most powerful drama critic in the USA. Intelligent, demanding and generally knowledgeable about theatre and popular culture, he writes for the literate reader with style and authority but with a hard intellectual edge and – in the estimation of the New York theatre community – little sympathy or affection for the theatre.   TLM

Rich, John [John Lun] ?1682–1761 English actor and manager. He was the son of Christopher Rich, the unscrupulous manager who had secured the patent for DRURY LANE Theatre and, when expelled, took over the LINCOLN'S INN FIELDS THEATRE. Christopher Rich died before the theatre was ready to reopen, but his son inherited the patent and opened in 1714 with a cast of actors from Drury Lane. In 1716 he began producing PANTOMIMES with extraordinary success, starring himself as HARLEQUIN, under the stage name of John Lun. The tradition of the annual pantomime continued until his death. In 1728 he was persuaded to accept GAY's *The Beggar's Opera*, which made 'Gay rich and Rich gay'. In 1730 he raised money by subscription to open a new theatre in COVENT GARDEN, and he used it intermittently until 1732 when it began to be fully used by his company. Illiterate and with the affectation of never remembering names, he used his business acumen to ensure the commercial profitability and popularity of his theatres.   PH

Richards, Lloyd 1923– African-American actor, director and educator. Richards began his professional career as an actor OFF-BROADWAY and as resident director at regional theatres. His major directorial opportunity came with *A Raisin in the Sun* (1959), whose success is legendary. Richards then turned his attention to directing and teaching, accepting assignments at colleges and opening the Lloyd Richards Studio (1962–72). In 1968 he was appointed artistic director of the National Playwrights' Conference at the EUGENE O'NEILL MEMORIAL THEATRE CENTER in Waterford, Connecticut, for the development of new plays. Appointed dean of the Yale Drama School and artistic director of the YALE REPERTORY THEATRE in 1979, he used his strategic positions of leadership to promote the work of contemporary playwrights, the most prominent being Lee Blessing, AUGUST WILSON and the South African

ATHOL FUGARD. He produced seven of Fugard's plays and, while at Yale, directed all five of Wilson's, working collaboratively with the author. He won a Tony as Best Director for Wilson's *Fences* (1987). In 1990 Richards was elected to the Theatre Hall of Fame, and he recived the 1993 PAUL ROBESON Award from Actors' Equity. His term at Yale expired in 1991.   EGH

Richardson, Ian 1934– British actor, born and trained in Scotland. His substantial reputation rests on his Shakespearian work. He played Hamlet at BIRMINGHAM REPERTORY THEATRE in the 1958–9 season, and in 1960 went to the Shakespeare Memorial Theatre (later the ROYAL SHAKESPEARE COMPANY) in Stratford-upon-Avon. For the next 15 years he performed across the range of the repertoire, including Sir Andrew Aguecheek (1960), Oberon (1962), Edmund (in PETER BROOK's *King Lear*, 1964), Chorus in *Henry V* (1966), Richard II (1973) and Richard III (1973). He had notable successes in *The Duchess of Malfi* (Count Malatesti, 1960) and in WEISS's *Marat/Sade* (1965). He has also worked extensively in film and television, and developed his work as a director of SHAKESPEARE and modern classics. His best-known TV appearances were in the productions of John Le Carré's *Tinker, Tailor, Soldier, Spy* and Michael Dobbs's *House of Cards*, in which he played a conspiratorial politician whom everyone trusted. It was screened in November 1990 (and had a sequel in 1993) at a time when, to many people's surprise, Margaret Thatcher was ousted as the British prime minister; but this was a strange coincidence.   MB JE

Richardson, John see RICHARDSON'S SHOW

Richardson, Ralph (David) 1902–83 British actor, who joined the BIRMINGHAM REPERTORY THEATRE company in 1926 where he made his early reputation, playing the Stranger in SOPHOCLES' *Oedipus at Colonus* (1926). In 1930 he joined the OLD VIC company, where he showed his versatility as an actor in roles which ranged from Caliban in *The Tempest* to Henry V. He was not, however, ideally suited to the major classical parts, having neither the exceptional musicality of JOHN GIELGUD nor the dynamic sex appeal of LAURENCE OLIVIER, his two great contemporaries. Richardson's qualities emerged through his performances in contemporary plays, by MAUGHAM (*For Services Rendered*, 1932, and *Sheppey*, 1933) and J. B. PRIESTLEY (*Eden End*, 1934, and *Cornelius*, 1935). As Johnson in Priestley's *Johnson over Jordan* (1939) he gave a memorable performance as a modern Everyman, recollecting at the moment of death the vagaries of his life.

Richardson excelled as the ordinary man with a natural decency and even innocence; his Othello (1938), partnered by Olivier's homosexual Iago, was a notable example of miscasting. He joined the Fleet Air Arm during the war but was invited to lead a revitalized Old Vic company at the New Theatre in 1944. With Olivier, he provided four outstanding Old Vic seasons, in which his personal successes came as Peer Gynt, Falstaff and Inspector Goole in J. B. Priestley's *An Inspector Calls*. He was knighted in 1947, but with Olivier was shabbily treated by the Old Vic governing board in 1948. But his career did not suffer from the uncertainties and sharp changes of direction which characterized that of Olivier. In the 1950s, he continued to play major roles at the Shakespeare Memorial Company, such as Prospero in *The Tempest* (1952) and Volpone, and at the Old Vic as Timon in *Timon of Athens* (1956); while also finding suitable starring roles in contemporary WEST END successes, such as Cherry in ROBERT BOLT's *Flowering Cherry* (1957).

He was not fully in tune with the new wave of British drama and was notably ill-at-ease in JOE ORTON's *What the Butler Saw* (1969); but where the writers were taking notice of his particular skills, he became a fine interpreter. For WILLIAM DOUGLAS HOME he became a latter-day A. E. Matthews, enjoying a bumbling eccentricity in *Lloyd George Knew My Father* (1972) and *The Kingfisher* (1977). With John Gielgud, he starred in DAVID STOREY's *Home* (1970) and in HAROLD PINTER's *No Man's Land* (1975), in which he played the elderly wealthy writer, Hirst, for PETER HALL's NATIONAL THEATRE production. As a member of the National Theatre company he played in *The Wild Duck* and the title role in *John Gabriel Borkman* (1975), but his last major role came as the elder statesman contemplating his political career without much affection in David Storey's *Early Days* (1980).   JE

Richardson's Show English fairground theatre most responsible for spreading popular drama beyond London in the early 19th century. A former workhouse boy, itinerant actor and publican, John Richardson (1766–1836) opened his first show-booth at Bartholomew Fair in 1798 with scenery from DRURY LANE and three blind Scotsmen as musicians. At its zenith, the widely touring show consisted of a large booth with an elevated platform lined at the back in green baize; the interior stage boasted crimson curtains. The narrow theatre (100ft long by 30ft wide) was said to contain 1500 lamps and a thousand spectators. The average offering presented an overture, a MELODRAMA (with three murders and a ghost, according to DICKENS), a PANTOMIME, a comic song and incidental music in the space of 25 minutes. James Barnes the Pantaloon and the young EDMUND KEAN both worked there at one time. Taciturn but charitable, Richardson tried to auction off his show in 1826, but owing to low bids carried on until his death, when it was taken over by Nelson Lee, who finally sold the property in 1853.   LS

Richelieu, Armand-Jean du Plessis, Cardinal (de) 1585–1642 Chief minister of Louis XIII, and generous patron of the arts who exerted a strong influence on 17th-century French literature. From the circle of writers and scholars with whom he surrounded himself he formed the Académie-Française in 1634, whose prescribed role as guardian of French language and culture led to the dissemination of their prestige throughout Europe. His patronage extended particularly to the theatre, on which he doted: also in 1634, he helped to establish MONTDORY's company on a permanent footing at the MARAIS, and in 1641 was the inspiration behind a royal decree authorizing the legal 'rehabilitation' of professional actors upon certain conditions. He also commissioned a group of five dramatists (Boisrobert, Colletet, PIERRE CORNEILLE, Claude de l'Estoile and ROTROU, all but the last sometime academicians) to write plays at his suggestion and to the greater glory of the French stage, perhaps intending them ultimately for performance in the well equipped private theatre he built within his palace, later to be known as the PALAIS-ROYAL. It opened in January 1641 with *Mirame*, a TRAGICOMEDY by Desmarets de Saint-Sorlin in which Richelieu himself is reputed to have had a hand.   DR

Ridiculous Theatrical Company (New York City) OFF-OFF BROADWAY theatre founded by the late actor, director and playwright CHARLES LUDLAM after he split off from John Vaccaro's Play-House of the Ridiculous (see THEATRE OF THE RIDICULOUS) in 1967. The Ridiculous was one of the first American theatres to deal explicitly with homosexual themes. Known for their flamboyant style, high camp and combinations of the lofty and the lowly, plays at the Ridiculous are often based on classical dramatic and operatic texts, which are then both spoofed and celebrated with cross-dressing, scatological humour, visual GAGS and puns. Ludlam starred in many of his own plays, among them *Bluebeard* (1970), *Camille* (1973, revived 1990), *Der Ring Gott Farblonjet* (1977) and *The Mystery of Irma Vep* (1984). Since Ludlam's death from AIDS in 1987, the Ridiculous has continued under the directorship of his life-partner Everett Quinton, a long-time actor and designer with the theatre. The company has been reviving Ludlam works as well as developing new pieces, such as Quinton's giddy adaptation of *A Tale of Two Cities* (1988) and his country-western MUSICAL, *Linda* (1993), inspired by Trollope's *Linda Tressel* and the Baron Von Sacher-Masoch's *Venus in Furs*, Georg Osterman's *Dr Jekyll and Mr Hyde* (1989) and *Brother Truckers* (1992), Quinton's one-person show, *Movieland* (1994), and a camp production of *A Midsummer Night's Dream* (1994–5).   AS

Ridley, George 1835–64 English (Gateshead-born) performer and composer of comic songs, notably 'Blaydon Races', who took to the stage after a serious accident at the local coalpit. In his naturalistically costumed and highly characterized performances he belonged to the new and growing tradition of the MUSIC-HALL; his penny songbooks, effectively chapbooks (complete with crude woodcuts), look back to an older tradition of ballad publication.   AEG

Rigg, Diana 1938– British actress, who joined the Shakespeare Memorial Company in 1959 and remained with the company until 1964, by which time it had become transformed into the ROYAL SHAKESPEARE COMPANY. She became a popular television star through *The Avengers* series in which she played Emma Peel, returning to the stage in 1966 to appear as a memorable Viola in the RSC's *Twelfth Night*. She joined the NATIONAL THEATRE in 1972, to appear in TOM STOPPARD's *Jumpers* (1972), as Lady Macbeth to Denis Quilley's Macbeth and with particular success in MOLIÈRE's *The Misanthrope* (1973), updated to the court of de Gaulle's France by TONY HARRISON, where she played Célimène to ALEC McCOWEN's Alceste, directed by JOHN DEXTER. The same Rigg–McCowen–Dexter team appeared in a WEST END production of *Pygmalion* (1974), while in 1975 she returned to the National Theatre in another Harrison modernization, this time of RACINE's *Phèdre – Phaedra Britannica*.

A strikingly attractive actress, Rigg excels in roles which

bring out her gift for ironic comedy, usually under-stressed, revealing a natural gift for timing. In 1978 she starred in Tom Stoppard's play, *Night and Day*. Despite her early successes at the NT, she has rarely appeared within the national companies in recent years, despite West End appearances in *Wildfire* (1986) and in STEPHEN SONDHEIM's *Follies* (1987), and as a 'mesmerizing' Cleopatra in a revival of JOHN DRYDEN's *All for Love* at London's Almeida Theatre (1991). The Almeida production of *Medea*, with Rigg in the title role, moved to the West End in 1993. In 1994 she was made a DBE. JE MB

Ring, Blanche 1876–1961 American singer-actress, born in Boston, Massachusetts; a great VAUDEVILLE star, master of the sing-along (which she probably introduced into vaudeville) and an accomplished monologuist of Irish characters. No single act topped hers for over two decades. Ten years earlier, she had made her debut in a small role opposite RICHARD MANSFIELD in *The Defender* (1902), in which she introduced 'In the Good Old Summertime'. In 1909 she first sang what became her theme song, 'I've Got Rings on My Fingers', in *The Midnight Sons*. When she introduced 'Yip-I-Addy-I-Ay' to a vaudeville audience in 1913, she was encouraged to repeat it five times. She debuted her most famous role, *The Yankee Girl*, in 1909 (filmed 1915; she appeared in two additional films (1926, 1940) and made a number of early recordings). Other hit MUSICALS included *The Jersey Lily* (1903), *About Town* (1906), *The Wall Street Girl* (1911) and *The Passing Show of 1919*. DBW

Ringelnatz, Joachim [Hanns Bötticher] 1883–1934 German poet and CABARET artist, formerly a sailor, shop clerk and window-dresser before entering the Munich cabaret Simplicissimus as 'house poet' in 1909. The hard-featured Bohemian was renowned as a reciter at Berlin's Schall und Rauch during the 1920s, performing his poetry, particularly the scurrilous exploits of the mythical sea-man Kuttel Daddeldu. His style lies somewhere between nonsense verse and topical SATIRE, and influenced BRECHT. In 1933 his performances were declared 'undesirable' by the Nazis, and he died the following year of tuberculosis. LS

Ristori, Adelaide 1822–1906 Italian actress, who was born into the profession and appeared on the stage at an early age, entering the major Compagnia Reale Sarda at the age of 15 and in a few years becoming its leading actress. In the 1840s Ristori was *prima attrice* to many of the prominent actor-managers of the day, like Domeniconi and Coltellini, before retiring for several years following her marriage to an Italian nobleman.

To this point her reputation had been won largely in native Italian drama, from GOLDONI, through ALFIERI to contemporary writers and adapters of French plays. In 1853 she returned to the stage, again with the Reale Sarda, and the mid-1850s saw her established as an actress of international standing. In 1855 she triumphed in Paris, benefiting from French critical hostility to the waning star, RACHEL; this success she repeated in 1856, adding Lady Macbeth to her repertoire. In 1857 she appeared for the first time in London, winning acclaim for her power-fully 'realistic' interpretation of Legouvé's Medea and SHAKESPEARE's Lady Macbeth, notwithstanding that the latter role dominated a much truncated version of the play. She was now launched on a long international career as 'star' actress and company manager, which took her to North and South America, North Africa and most of Europe. The plays in her repertoire were likewise interna-tional, including Alfieri's *Mirra*, SCHILLER's *Maria Stuart*, RACINE's *Phèdre* and GIACOMETTI's *Elisabetta regina d'Inghilterra*, as well as the roles of Medea and Lady Macbeth. After first performing the sleep-walking scene from *Macbeth* in English as a finale to her London perfor-mances of 1873, in 1882 she undertook the whole part in English – with commendable success for so ambitious a venture (elsewhere she did the sleep-walking scene in French and Spanish, as well as in Italian).

Ristori's great strength lay in her combination of classi-cal appearance, pose and deportment, and acute psycho-logical REALISM. In common with her younger contemporary, TOMMASO SALVINI, she studied her parts in depth, developing a subtle, emotionally powerful charac-terization through the accumulation of small but signifi-cant detail: her extant prompt books for the sleep-walking scene show how meticulous was her working-out of moves, gestures and delivery. Her memoirs and occasional writings on theatre reveal the seriousness of her approach to her art, and her comments on the strengths and weak-nesses of her contemporary rivals, like those for example on DUSE, are measured and perceptive. KR

rite of passage RITUAL to celebrate and effect the tran-sition of an individual from one social position to the next. Naming ceremonies, puberty rites, weddings and funerals are typical and virtually universal examples, but occupa-tional rituals such as degree ceremonies and the transfor-mation of an apprentice into a craftsman are also included. Their structure is invariably tripartite: the sepa-ration of the individual from his/her existing network of relationships, a liminal period during which he/she stands outside normality, and his/her incorporation into a new network of rights and obligations. AEG

Rittner, Rudolf 1869–1943 The naturalistic German actor (see NATURALISM) who most completely fulfilled OTTO BRAHM's conception of acting. He created many of HAUPTMANN's leading roles under Brahm's direction at the FREIE BÜHNE, the DEUTSCHES THEATER and the Lessingtheater in Berlin. He retired in 1907 to take up farming. SW

ritual Ever since Jane Ellen Harrison's classic studies of ancient Greek religion, the relationship between ritual and theatre (and even the derivation of the latter from the former) has been one of the keystones of theatre history and dramatic analysis, and an important element in cer-tain forms of 20th-century dramatic practice as diverse as the work of GROTOWSKI and WELFARE STATE INTERNATIONAL. There is undeniably a danger in pressing the relationship to the point where the two become syn-onymous, and in the related process of treating a relation-ship of analogy as one of chronological and generic evolution. The latter, all too common in theatre history, is seen at its clearest in the analysis of FOLK DRAMA (see also FOLK THEATRE, ASIAN), where every manifestation of traditional working-class theatrical activity, especially if rural in provenance, is likely to be seen, not as a phenomenon with its own – possibly quite brief – history, but as a corrupted remnant of an ancient religious or magical act. At the same time, there is lasting value in Harrison's Aristotelian observation that both ritual and drama are 'the things done', which places the emphasis, in both, on the action rather than the agent, and directs our attention to the concrete and actual rather than the metaphysical and putative.

At bottom, both drama and ritual deal with social relationships, and both do so in the most direct way possible, through the enactment of those relationships by living people. God may be held by believers to be present in the wafer and wine; everyone can agree immediately that a priest holding a chalice is present as a focus of attention. Similarly, it may be a matter of endless debate whether or not the spectator in a theatre suspends his/her disbelief, willingly or otherwise, and what exactly that might mean; it is not a matter of debate that an actor representing a murderer mimics the assassination of an actor representing a victim. Further, in both modes, social relationships are given very high definition. As the anthropologist Edmund Leach has observed, the very notion of 'social relationships' is an abstraction; they are not something that can be observed. What we observe are forms of greeting, expressions of deference, gestures of affection.

Most of these, if not all of them, are 'ritualistic' in the sense that their form and meaning are culturally determined and inherited, not spontaneously generated. This fact is not altered merely because we take them for granted: one function of cultural determinism is precisely to get things taken for granted. However, even the simplest of routine actions will shift its meaning according to context. In Western cultures, to hold a door open and let somebody pass through is, at its simplest, merely a routine courtesy, and, where total strangers of the same sex and similar age are concerned, who holds the door depends on nothing more significant than who gets there first, or which has the more commitment to good manners. If, however, one is a man and one a woman, whether they are acquainted or not, a different significance is present which derives from a whole bundle of notions about the roles of men and women and which puts on the man a quite strong obligation to hold the door. Finally, if the woman is also the queen of England, it is virtually unthinkable that the man would not give her precedence. Here, status is involved as well as sex. Both ritual and drama take these routine acts and their contextually determined meanings – the small change of social currency – exaggerate them, stylize them, refine them, and set them into a pattern of expressive sequences of visual and auditory symbols.

There, however, the identity between them stops; the means they have in common are applied to divergent ends. Overlap is likely to remain in practice as well as principle – community theatre companies invoke the notion and structures of communal celebration in framing their performances, and the professional Balinese SHAMAN offers his trance dance as an entertainment for tourists –

but ritual and theatre lie at the opposite poles of a functional continuum. While theatre confines itself to saying things about social relationships, ritual also does things with them; and what it does is to reinforce or change them.

This function, and the distinction between theatre and ritual, are clearly seen in the RITE OF PASSAGE, such as the wedding ceremony. The young woman who dresses in ceremonial clothes to play Hippolyta in the final act of *A Midsummer Night's Dream* is clearly an actress representing a bride, and she will do so repeatedly during the run. Enactment is infinitely replicable (and as such is a useful laboratory for the inspection of social relationships). The young woman who dresses in ceremonial clothes on the morning of her wedding day *is* a 'bride', from that moment, and will remain so until she and her 'groom' are pronounced 'man and wife'. Nor, in principle, is her action replicable. The change in status and role which has been effected by the ritual of marriage cannot be reversed. A legal or ecclesiastical nicety may define the ritual itself as having been invalid, thus in effect not to have occurred; otherwise, a woman whose husband dies becomes a 'widow', and a woman whose marriage is dissolved becomes a 'divorcée'. No woman who has participated in a valid ritual can revert to the status of 'maiden' or 'spinster'. The linguistic and social embarrassments suffered by the divorced are a powerful indicator of the ritual's ability not merely to describe a change in status and role, but to constitute it. 'With this ring I thee wed' is not a descriptive but a performative utterance. Further, not only the bride and groom are involved in an event which changes their relationship to each other; so, if less radically (and without any necessary accompanying status change), are their kinsfolk, and even their friends. Not just two individuals but two extended families are conjoined in a relationship not previously existing, and certain obligations will follow (even if they are subsumed in a conveniently symbolic exchange of Christmas cards). Even 'friendship' (that ultimate in voluntary and loosely defined associations) may find itself subject to obligation, as the accidental welding of two individuals into a new social unit necessitates meeting and mixing with acquaintances not of one's own choosing.

The interest of such a ceremony is that it creates new social arrangements in an actual sense (real people are redeployed and redefined within the social network) while reinforcing an existing structure of relationships (a woman is 'given' by one man to another, a 'son' and 'daughter' take on the additional, publicly recognized roles of 'husband and wife', the nature of their new relationship is defined in traditional terms); and that it does this by theatrical means. For it is crucial to the event, and its constitutive power, that there be not merely protagonists and a master of ceremonies, but an audience, whose presence as witnesses ratifies the validity of the ceremony and the specific redeployment that is taking place. Further, just as in the theatre the audience contracts to accept a fiction, so in the wedding ceremony the congregation condones *en masse*, both by its silence and by its vocal participation when called upon, not merely the particular act but a whole framework of values within which it exists. A liberal agnostic wedding congregation witnessing the enactment of a marriage through the English *Book of Common Prayer* agrees that marriage was ordained for the procreation of children, to be brought up in the fear of the Lord; that it is a permanent and metaphysical state not subject to human dissolution; that a man may endow a woman with all his worldly goods but not vice versa; and so on. Very little of which the average wedding guest, as an individual, is likely to believe. Yet, as a congregation, whether they suspend their disbelief or not, they silence it, and their silence gives consent. This it is that makes ritual such a powerful conservative force, even while it effects pragmatic change.

Ritual is never an unambiguously progressive force. Its effectiveness depends on the public acceptance of a status quo, whatever the participant's private reservations may be; its symbols, though often complex and diffuse, are never avant-garde (a dual consideration which might give pause to exponents of 'ritual' theatre). The Kwakiutl Indian, Quesalid, who set out to expose witch-doctors as fraudulent and to his surprise achieved fame as a practitioner, did not become a shaman because he was a skilled healer; he became a skilled healer because he was a shaman. His patients were unimpressed when he disclosed the tricks of the trade; they had never taken them wholly seriously anyway. Their concern was that they were ill and he was able to cure them. Prestidigitation with pebbles and bloody feathers was merely a technique through which the end was achieved. Similarly, a Queensland Kanaka who sickens and even dies as a result of a sorcerer's bewitchment does not get ill because a bone has been pointed at him – a merely indicative action – but because he believes in the sorcerer's power to damage him. The effects either way, for healing or harming, are broadly psychosomatic and medical attempts have been made to explain them, with some success. The symbolism is no more than a trigger-mechanism which releases powerful psychosocial forces to work on the organism.

This should not surprise us. For all man's long history of evolving cultural systems which adapt, harness and even override nature, still men and women are biological organisms and subject to the same internal rhythms as other living things. This is one of the things which life-cycle rituals celebrate, and which the magician can exploit for good or ill. It is a commonplace that rituals are often tied to seasons and cycles, whether those of the natural world or of the many sacred and secular calendric calibrations of it; harvest celebrations depending for both their content and their timing on season and weather spring readily to mind, as does, from a calendric point of view, the pre-Lent festival of CARNIVAL.

But the idea of seasonality is more deeply embedded in culture, and specifically in its ritual expression, than these simple examples show. Annual festivities mark out time as signposts and fences mark out space; their recurrence, usually in a form which changes only slowly and gives the impression of not changing at all, at once lends a comforting air of continuity to human life and reminds participants that their own time is passing. Laid over this inexorable terrestrial rhythm is the changing of the human seasons, the movement from the cradle to the grave celebrated in the life-cycle rituals. The two kinds of seasonality come together in the fact that, although it is in

itself no rite of passage, any annual festivity may involve people not previously present (the baby's first Christmas, the first involvement in masquerade of a newly initiated age grade), and suffer the absence, through death, of former participants. It is important to note here a further distinction between ritual and theatre: whereas the latter almost always sets its action in fictional time, the action of the former always exists in real time, and it is arguable that it would otherwise lose its point.

These, then, are the two axes at whose intersection the ritual act stands: the passage of time, both terrestrial and human, and the cyclic recurrence of crucial biological events within it; and the interplay of the human group through its inevitable losses and replacements and necessary redeployments, as manifest in the actions of ritual protagonists and the bearing witness of, in principle, the whole reference group (or, in practice, enough members of it to constitute an undefined but recognizable quorum). In any given ritual, one axis may be the more strongly marked but the other is there vestigially, and shows a tendency to claim greater prominence even when the immediate function of the ritual seems not to require it.

This is clear in those rituals concerned with the administration of justice. Certain 'ritualistic' elements in court proceedings have often been noticed: the elaborate formal courtesies, the use of a specialized language, the stylization of the presentation of evidence into a FLYTING between 'prosecution' and 'defence', the vital role of the citizenry – as represented by 12 good men and true – in redefining the status of the 'accused', who occupies a liminal position for as long as he or she bears that name. Clearly, the event is structured so as to declare the accused to be or not to be a fit person to retain his or her position in society. Less frequently noted is the element of time. In English courts this is manifest in the partly archaic dress worn by the legal specialists. Just as a priest's vestments give him an identity beyond the personal one, going back in mythological terms to Melchizedek, so the robes and wigs of judge and counsel declare them to be representatives of the Law, an abstract value and an institution whose existence stretches back beyond their birth (and by implication forward beyond their death) and which preempts any personal views they may have on the matter in hand. And this is important; for the evidence which counsel presents, and the judgement given by the judge on the basis of the jury's finding, will result in an atomization of the accused's time: to be left untouched if not guilty; if guilty, a series of carefully graduated sentences, up to and including the judgement that on a given day the condemned criminal will have no more time left.

The latter sentence is an extreme example of ritual's ability to manage social time and space; and it is no surprise that, until a growing distaste for public violence and a concern for the discreet management of public order led to their abolition, the public execution was a popular and complex event all over Europe. As DR JOHNSON said, in a famous objection to the abolition of public hangings, 'If they do not draw spectators they don't answer their purpose'; and vast crowds flocked to witness the 'morality play' of public justice, in which the crimes of the condemned were re-enacted on his own body, in which public confessions (sometimes in verse) were given from the scaffold (and ballad-sellers distributed their substance at a penny a sheet), and the condemned might be harried beyond death in the ghastly practices of quartering and decapitation. The gibbeted body or the head displayed on a spike would remain as an eerie puppet-like image of the consequences of wickedness. At the same time, the event has a strangely festive air, and not merely because the throngs of spectators, ballad-singers, street vendors, pickpockets and colourfully uniformed military made it look a cross between a grand parade and a chartered fair. In 18th-century London, a condemned man would often dress as a bridegroom for his final ride to Tyburn, and, depending on public sentiment concerning himself and his offence, might find himself the recipient of nosegays rather than brickbats. GAY's 'The youth in his cart hath the air of a lord/And we cry, "There dies an Adonis"' was no mere literary conceit. A condemned man might indeed be a hero to a proletarian populace suffering under increasingly draconian property laws; and if, doubtless in most cases, the popular view was more ambiguous than that, still he was a hero in the theatrical sense, and the events of the day the last act of his tragedy. His white-trimmed garments declared him to be about to be wedded to death, and ironically evoked the idea of human seasonality explicit in the rite of passage.

Less extreme in its effect on the individual, but in consequence even clearer as evidence of the force of the ritual imagery, is the widespread juridical ritual of the CHARIVARI, organized not by the state but by the community, and applied not to criminal offences but to antisocial acts such as sharp practice in trade, marital disharmony, or unsuitable marriages such as that between an old widower and a young virgin. Characteristically the community or its representatives (often the peer group of young adult males, no doubt encouraged by their elders) would express their disapproval by a procession with rough music (the beating of pans and kettles and so on) to the dwelling of the wrong-doer, usually early in the morning or late at night so as to cause maximum embarrassment to the offender. In more elaborate forms, the procession would include an effigy of the offender, riding backwards on a donkey or mounted on a pole, which would subsequently be hanged or burned. The offender had two choices: either to correct his or her behaviour, or, if this was impossible (e.g. the old widower), to buy the rough musicians off – effectively a fine or even, in this case, financial compensation for their loss of a potential bride. Either way, re-incorporation into decent society would follow.

Usually a charivari would occur as occasion demanded; but not infrequently we find it associated with seasonal festivities such as 5 November in England (in Horsham, Sussex, the effigy, known as the 'Crispin', would be displayed between 25 October, St Crispin's Day, and Bonfire Night, when it was carried in procession and ceremonially burned on a public bonfire) and, in continental Europe, Carnival. Again, a clear expression of the tendency of ritual to locate social relationships and values in time, as conventionally defined.

To ritual, convention is all. Though a crowd at a public execution may express sympathy with the condemned through floral tributes, that very expression is conventional, even though the sentiment expressed be unortho-

dox, as far as the state's rulers are concerned. The unconventional act would be to rescue the condemned, or to rescue the corpse before it was mutilated or displayed. Both happened; and both disrupted the ritual as surely as if a wedding guest were to stand up and show just cause. There are rituals which invert status – the common practice of army officers serving a celebratory dinner to other ranks is a simple case – or turn normal values inside out in a more comprehensive sense – the 12-day Christmas period of Misrule in medieval and early modern Europe springs to mind. But in both examples normality reasserts itself as soon as the defined period of licence comes to an end. Carnival, because more open-ended in its time span and its expressive activities, and because by definition it involves large numbers of people the worse for drink, has sometimes got out of hand; so that over the six centuries which separate *böse Fastnacht* (see *FASTNACHTSPIEL*) in Basle from London's Notting Hill Carnival in the 1970s, participants have tried to make a reality out of the idea of the world turned upside-down. But without exception Lent returns and triumphs; the authorities, temporarily shaken, reassert their control, break a few heads, gaol a few ringleaders and clear the streets of broken glass. And what happens is not revolution, but a reversion to status quo for another year. Misrule may be subversive as an idea; as a practice, there is no evidence that it has ever done other than provide a safety-valve for the pressure on existing arrangements. AEG

See: W. B. Cannon, '"Voodoo" Death', *American Anthropologist*, 44, 1942; M. Foucault, *Discipline and Punish*, London, 1977; M. Gluckman (ed.), *Essays on the Ritual of Social Relations*, Manchester, 1962; E. R. Leach, 'Ritual', in D. Sills (ed.), *International Encyclopedia of the Social Sciences*, vol. 13, 1968; R. Rappaport, 'Obvious Aspects of Ritual', *Cambridge Anthropologist*, 1, 1974; A. Smith, *The Seasons*, London, 1970; E. P. Thompson, *Customs in Common*, Harmondsworth, 1993; V. Turner, *The Ritual Process*, London, 1969; A. Van Gennep, *The Rites of Passage*, London, 1960.

Rivel, Charlie [Josep Andreu i Lasserre] 1896–1983 Catalan CLOWN, born into an old CIRCUS family. In 1929 he won world fame at the London Olympia and the Cirque d'Hiver, Paris, in a parody of Charlie Chaplin on the flying trapeze. At the age of 16, he joined two of his brothers; as the traditional august with the Three Rivels, his standard outfit was an ankle-length, sleeveless red jersey, a bald pate and a square red nose. Like GROCK, a musical-acrobatic clown of few words, he emitted at regular intervals the cry: 'Akrobatschööööön!' He inspired some clown dynasties – e.g. the Charlirivels. LS

Riverside Studios (London) Arts centre in Hammersmith, occupying premises beside the Thames which were once television studios belonging to the BBC. It was founded as an independent trust in 1975 with PETER GILL as its first artistic director, and for ten years, under Gill, Jenny Stein and David Gothard, it was the most adventurous centre of its kind in Britain, bringing over avant-garde companies from abroad (such as TADEUSZ KANTOR's Cricot 2) and providing a London venue for such British touring companies as Joint Stock. Gill staged several notable productions in the main studio, of *The Changeling, The Cherry Orchard* and *Measure for Measure*, but when he moved to the NATIONAL THEATRE in 1980 the Riverside Studios came under threat from the local authorities. David Lefeaux joined David Gothard in 1982 and directed several ambitious plays there, including EUGENE O'NEILL's *A Moon for the Misbegotten*, which transferred to BROADWAY, but in 1984 their long rearguard campaign to protect the Studios from the twin evils of shortage of funds and interference from the local authorities came to an end with their departures. After this, Riverside Studios became less of a producing management or an entrepreneurial one, and more of a receiving house for a wide variety of companies and artists, ranging from DEBORAH WARNER's *Electra* (1992) and *Hamlet* with Alan Rickman (1992) to ROBERT LEPAGE's *The Dragon Trilogy* (1991). JE

Rix, Brian 1924– British actor-manager, under whom London's Whitehall Theatre established a reputation for FARCE between 1950 and 1967 that rivalled the Aldwych farces of the 1930s. The first of these, Colin Morris's *Reluctant Heroes* (previously toured with his own company and with Rix in the lead role), ran for four years, as did *Dry Rot* (1954), which was followed by *Simple Spymen* (1958, both by John Chapman) and by Ray Cooney's *One for the Pot* (1961) and *Chase Me, Comrade* (1964). After a further series of successful farces at the Garrick and Cambridge Theatres in London, he left the stage for charity work with the mentally handicapped in 1980, for which he was honoured with a life peerage in 1992. CI

Robards, Jason, Jr 1922– American actor, praised for his rich voice and intense characterizations. Robards made his debut as Nick in the AMERICAN ACADEMY OF DRAMATIC ARTS' production of *Holiday* (1946). His BROADWAY debut was in D'Oyly Carte's *Mikado* (1947), after which he stage-managed for a time. He attracted considerable attention as Hickey in a now legendary production of *The Iceman Cometh* (1956) at the CIRCLE IN THE SQUARE. Robards secured his stardom as James Tyrone in *Long Day's Journey into Night* (1956), in which he was noted as 'an actor of tremendous dynamic skill'. Another triumph was as Quentin in ARTHUR MILLER's *After the Fall*, for which critics lauded him as 'brilliant', 'magnificent' and 'beyond praise'. In 1988 he appeared with COLLEEN DEWHURST in revivals (in repertory) of O'NEILL's *Long Day's Journey* and *Ah, Wilderness!*. His most recent New York stage appearances were in HOROVITZ's *Park Your Car in Harvard Yard* (1991–2) and the 1994 revival of *No Man's Land* with CHRISTOPHER PLUMMER. His distinguished film and television career includes *Long Day's Journey* and *A Thousand Clowns*, as well as film scripts in which he has played various curmudgeons and outcasts. SMA

Robbins, Carrie 1943– American COSTUME designer, who began her professional career in the late 1960s and has become one of the busiest in the theatre. Although she has done contemporary costumes, her best work is in detailed yet theatrical period costumes, such as the 1971 *Beggar's Opera*, or lavish operatic ones, such as for the San Francisco Opera's *Samson et Dalila*, which combined a

19th-century sensibility with a biblical epic style. Her work is typified by rich textures and bold lines, and her sketches are detailed and almost frenetic, creating a sense of energy and movement. She has frequently collaborated with set designer DOUGLAS SCHMIDT, notably on *Grease* and *Frankenstein*. AA

Robbins, Jerome 1918– American choreographer and director. Trained in the techniques of classical ballet, Robbins joined the American Ballet Theatre in 1940 and danced in several of its programmes. In 1944 he choreographed *Fancy Free*, a ballet with music by LEONARD BERNSTEIN. Later the same year Robbins repeated his role as choreographer when *Fancy Free* was transformed into the BROADWAY musical *On the Town*. For *High Button Shoes* (1947) he created a hilarious Keystone Kops ballet that remains one of the few masterpieces of comic choreography in the American MUSICAL THEATRE. Among his other memorable dances of the period was the 'Small House of Uncle Thomas' ballet for *The King and I* (1951). For the teenage gang members of *West Side Story* (1957) Robbins created a restless, explosive, yet balletic style of movement. He directed and choreographed two other acclaimed musicals: *Gypsy* (1959) and *Fiddler on the Roof* (1964). In 1989 he re-created his most successful numbers in the retrospective *Jerome Robbins' Broadway* (Tony for Best Musical). He was given the Common Wealth Award of Distinguished Service in Dramatic Arts in 1990. MK

Robert-Houdin [Jean-Eugène Robert] 1805–71 French conjuror, who utterly transformed the performance of MAGIC. Wed to the daughter of a watchmaker named Houdin, he built automata, created surgical and optical instruments and the first pneumatic clock, while privately practising illusionism. In 1845 he gave up watchmaking and opened the Théâtre des Soirées Fantastiques de Robert-Houdin, in the Palais-Royal, Paris, where for seven years he played to full houses. There he turned what had been a fairground amusement into a salon entertainment by doing away with obvious fakery, macabre decorations and verbose commentary. He is also said to have invented the matinée performance. During the conquest of Algeria, the French government employed him to overawe the rebels and diminish the prestige of the marabouts with his Invincible Man act, in which he seemed impervious to bullets. In 1853 he moved his theatre to the Boulevard des Italiens and retired; the building survived until 1925 when it was demolished. LS

Robertson [Étienne-Gaspard Robert] 1763–1837 Belgian illusionist, the first to present animated projections using the *fantascope*, a MAGIC lantern on wheels (1798). Starting in Paris at the Pavillon de l'Échiquier, he moved to a deconsecrated Capuchin monastery (where Franconi's first CIRQUE OLYMPIQUE would be installed in 1807). There he terrified audiences with 'supernatural' evocations of François Villon, William Tell, VOLTAIRE, ROUSSEAU and Marat, who seemed to approach and withdraw. The atmosphere was thickened by fake bats, clouds forming on the ceiling and performers in white sheets and masks surging through the hall lit by hidden lamps. SHADOW-PUPPET techniques allowed Robertson to give the illusion of legs moving and other rudimentary actions. LS

Robertson, T(homas) W(illiam) 1829–71 British playwright, the eldest of 22 children born into a family of provincial actors. Robertson travelled the Lincoln circuit with his parents and siblings, acting, writing and making himself useful about the stage. He was 16 when his *The Chevalier de St George* (1845) was staged at the PRINCESS'S in London, to be followed by *Noémie* (1846), both adaptations from the French, but this gives a misleading impression of precocious success. It was by drudgery and industry that Robertson made his scanty living in London after the collapse of his uncle's Lincoln-based company in 1848–9. Until 1864, when the personality actor E. A. SOTHERN chanced to select the previously unperformed *David Garrick*, a perfunctory adaptation from the French, for performance at the HAYMARKET, Robertson was known, if known at all, as a journalist – prolific contributor to, among many other journals, the *Illustrated Times*, which housed the bitter comedy of his gallery of 'Theatrical Types', and *Fun*. After prolonged struggles as a bit-player, prompter and stage manager, during which SAMUEL PHELPS and MADAME VESTRIS were among his employers, he had retired from the theatre in c.1859.

It was probably his friend, the playwright H. J. BYRON, who persuaded MARIE WILTON to stage Robertson's *Society* (1865) at the PRINCE OF WALES'S, where her adventurous management had just begun. The content of *Society* would have been familiar enough to contemporary theatregoers, but the detail of its conduct, under Robertson's own meticulous supervision, had the freshness of revelation. The production saw the birth of what came to be known as 'cup-and-saucer drama', the faithful-seeming reproduction on stage of the indoor customs of Victorian England. It is, by any reckoning, extraordinary that a playwright as conventional and intellectually drab as Robertson should have had so radical an influence on the English theatre, and some credit must be given to the innovative ensemble playing of the company. But it was Robertson who perceived the potential purchase on the public imagination of a style of writing and acting that would replace the blatantly theatrical with the persuasively accurate.

The making of a roly-poly pudding in *Ours* (1866), immediate successor to *Society* at the Prince of Wales's, is a brilliant domestic adaptation of the MELODRAMATIC sensation scene supremely exploited by Robertson's chief rival among mid-century playwrights, BOUCICAULT. The tea-and-sandwiches of Act I of *Caste* (1867) are a comic *tour de force* in the genre. In his brief remaining lifetime, Robertson never matched *Caste*, though *Play* (1868), particularly *School* (1869) and *M.P.* (1870) all had successful runs at the Prince of Wales's, and Robertson's modest innovations admitted a new REALISM to the writing and acting of plays in the last decades of the 19th century. Historians of early-20th-century theatre, whilst celebrating SHAW, GORDON CRAIG and the ROYAL COURT seasons of 1904–7, have overlooked the remarkable summer season of 1910, when the impresario Robert Arthur staged eight of Robertson's comedies in repertoire at the Coronet Theatre, Notting Hill. PT

Robeson, Paul 1898–1976 African-American actor. A Columbia Law School graduate, Robeson opted for a stage career and gained prominence in 1924–5 when he appeared in the PROVINCETOWN PLAYERS' revival of *The Emperor Jones* (1925) and as Jim Harris, the black lawyer who marries white in O'NEILL's controversial play, *All God's Chillun Got Wings* (1924). Robeson took the lead in *Black Boy* (1926), played Crown in *Porgy and Bess* (1927) and was Joe in the London performance of *Show Boat* (1928), in which he sang 'Ol' Man River', the song he refashioned into a lifelong protest against oppression. With his commanding physique, deep, resonant voice and humane spirit, Robeson was a magnificent Othello, a role he played three times: in London (1930), in New York for a record-breaking run (1943) and at Stratford-upon-Avon (1959). He was also renowned as a concert artist and film actor. Robeson's outspoken opposition to racial discrimination, his embrace of leftist causes worldwide and his communist sympathies led to professional ostracism at home and the withdrawal of his passport. In failing health, he retired from public life in the 1960s. His life was dramatized in Philip Hayes Dean's 1978 monodrama *Paul Robeson*, which starred JAMES EARL JONES. An annual award in his name is presented by American Actors' Equity to someone committed to the struggle for justice, equality and the principles to which Robeson was devoted. EGH

Robey [Wade]**, George** 1869–1954 'The Prime Minister of Mirth'; English comedian, London-born son of a civil engineer, whose work took him to Germany, where George spent his early teens. In 1885, his father's financial circumstances preventing his further education, George took a job as a clerk with the company constructing Birmingham's new cable tramway, and began to appear at the city's smoking concerts as a musician and comic vocalist. His rise to stardom was rapid: a first London professional appearance at a smoking concert in April 1891 was followed by his WEST END debut at the Oxford in July of the same year; by the end of 1892 he was top of the bill, and there he stayed through a long and varied career in MUSIC-HALL, VARIETY, PANTOMIME, REVUE, OPERETTA and MUSICAL COMEDY. At the age of 66 he tried his hand at SHAKESPEARE, appearing to critical acclaim as Falstaff in *Henry IV, Part 1* at His [Her] MAJESTY'S THEATRE. In addition to live theatre, he worked extensively in radio, television and film, played Sancho Panza opposite Chaliapin in Pabst's *Don Quichotte* (1932), and made a brief retrospective appearance as the dying Falstaff in OLIVIER's film of *Henry V*. He was still touring in variety and revue at the age of 82.

His solo work pursued two music-hall traditions: that of the buffo vocalist's unchanging persona (though for the classic frock-coat Robey substituted a simple black costume suggesting rather than representing the clerical, with bowler hat and swish cane); and the newer mode, associated with DAN LENO and JENNY HILL, of character monologue and patter-song, in which he ranged widely from the Prehistoric Man to contemporary figures such as the District Nurse.

Fundamentally a high-status comedian, he employed an orotund but crystal-clear middle-class diction, eschewed the egalitarian matiness of a CHIRGWIN and the low-status bashfulness of JACK PLEASANTS, and constantly ordered his audience to 'desist' from laughing – an injunction utterly undermined by his exaggerated air of dignity, his mobile face and his famous raised eyebrows. His superb handling of a song, his impeccable diction and timing, and his ability to lend dignity to cheap material are manifest in the well known recording, with Violet Loraine, of 'If You Were the Only Girl in the World' (originally from *The Bing Boys Are Here*, 1916).

Created CBE for his charitable work during the First World War, Robey was knighted in the year of his death. AEG

Robin, Henri [Henrik Joseph Donckel] 1811–74 Dutch illusionist. As early as 1847 he displayed a 'Living Phantasmagoria' in Paris, using the plate-glass principle to conjure up phantoms which he then fought; this well established trick later prevented PEPPER'S GHOST from getting a French patent. Robin performed in England during 1850–3 (with a command performance at Windsor Castle), and in 1861 gave the first full evening's show of MAGIC at the Egyptian Hall, London. He successfully managed his own theatre in the Boulevard du Temple in Paris (1862–9). His famous illusion here was 'The Medium of Inkerman', a drum on a tripod which, allegedly beaten by the spirit of a slain drummer, tapped out answers to questions from the audience. LS

Robin Hood plays Popular dramatizations of episodes from the life of the great English outlaw, related to and possibly derived from ballads about him, and associated with May Games. Allusions to the playing of Robin Hood exist in the 15th and 16th centuries, and two (possibly three) texts are extant: 'Robin Hood and the Friar' (c.1560), which may be an amalgamation of two plays, and the fragmentary 'Robin Hood and the Sheriff' (c.1475). References cease early in the 17th century: later 'Robin Hood plays' are ecotypes of the HERO-COMBAT. AEG

Robins, Elizabeth 1862–1952 Kentucky-born American actress and author. Robins made her acting debut with the BOSTON MUSEUM Stock Company in 1885 and subsequently toured with EDWIN BOOTH, LAWRENCE BARRETT and JAMES O'NEILL. She visited London in 1889, remaining there rather than return to New York. Soon she was playing Martha Bernick in *Pillars of Society* (1889); two years later in a revival of *A Doll's House* she played Mrs Linde. Ultimately, Robins became identified with the introduction of Ibsen to the English stage, appearing as Hedda (1891), Hilda in *The Master Builder* (1893), Rebecca West in *Rosmersholm* (1893), Agnes in *Brand* (1893), Astra in *Little Eyolf* (1896) and Ella in *John Gabriel Borkman* (1897), and holding the stage rights to many of these plays. With the exception of starring in the short-lived US premiere of IBSEN's *Hedda Gabler* (1898), she never performed again in her native land. She retired from the stage in 1902 and devoted herself to writing. Using the nom de plume C.E. Raemond, she published several novels as well as the suffragist play *Votes for Women* (1907). In later years she wrote *Ibsen and the Actress* (1928), *Theatre and Friendship* (1932) and *Both Sides of the Curtain* (1940). A biography by Joanne E. Gates was published in 1994. RAS

Robinson, Bill 'Bojangles' 1878–1949 African-American dancer and singer who, after many years as a star of VAUDEVILLE, made his MUSICAL THEATRE debut in *Blackbirds of 1928*, where his seemingly effortless tap dancing helped the show become a hit. Robinson was next seen in *Brown Buddies* (1930), *Blackbirds of 1933* and *The Hot Mikado* (1939), a jazz version of the GILBERT and Sullivan classic. Unlike the 1920s, when a number of black musicals had been successful on BROADWAY, the shows of the 1930s were unable to garner long runs, even when featuring popular stars like Bill Robinson. In the 1940s he appeared in two other failures, *All in Fun* (1940) and *Memphis Bound!* (1945), the last a jazz adaptation of Gilbert and Sullivan's *HMS Pinafore*. Although few of Robinson's shows were big successes, his performances were uniformly praised for the matchless ease and grace of his tap dancing. MK

Robinson, (Esmé Stuart) Lennox 1886–1958 Irish playwright. The year after his first play – *The Clancy Name* (1908), a gloomy exercise in the 'Cork realist' manner – Robinson became the ABBEY THEATRE's play director. Disagreements with LADY GREGORY and an unprofitable American tour led to his resignation in 1914. Reappointed in 1919, he founded the DUBLIN DRAMA LEAGUE and was the Abbey's main play director until 1934, when HUGH HUNT succeeded him. Joining the Abbey board of directors in 1923, he remained until his death.

Robinson was a skilful, at times a facile, craftsman. His early plays are unremittingly cheerless, as he acknowledged: *Harvest* (1910) manages to turn a situation promising comic development into bitter despair. His talent was in fact for satiric comedy, as he demonstrated in *The Whiteheaded Boy* (1916) and *Drama at Inish* (1934). Yet he ranged widely: *The Big House* (1926) movingly chronicles the fortunes of an Ascendancy family; *Church Street* (1934) draws effectively on PIRANDELLO, as a young Irish dramatist invents plots for his family's lives.

Though much criticized in the 1940s and 50s for the Abbey's doldrums, Robinson served the theatre well, as administrator and one of its liveliest writers. DM

Robinson, Richard c.1598–1648 English actor, one of the few known to have made a successful transition from boy to adult in the Jacobean theatre. Robinson may have been apprenticed to RICHARD BURBAGE, whose widow he married, when he first appeared with the King's Men in c.1611. In that year he played the Lady in *The Second Maiden's Tragedy* and possibly Fulvia in JONSON's *Catiline*. Jonson praises his female impersonation in *The Devil Is an Ass* (1616), but he had probably by then graduated to male roles. He is known to have played the Cardinal in a revival of WEBSTER's *The Duchess of Malfi* and to have remained with the King's Men until the CLOSURE OF THE THEATRES in 1642. PT

Robson, Flora 1902–84 British actress. A consistently fine actress who whilst never dominating the great female roles always offered sensitive, witty and intelligent portrayals in a wide range of styles. For the OLD VIC in 1933 she played Gwendoline in WILDE's *The Importance of Being Earnest*, and over 30 years later, in 1968, played Miss Prism in the same play in London's WEST END. She worked extensively in America (including Hollywood), playing Lady Macbeth in New York in 1948, a part she had previously played in 1933. Her Shakespearian roles were few, but for JOHN GIELGUD's production of *The Winter's Tale* (1951) she created what many critics describe as her best performance, typically in a 'supporting' role, Paulina. Her full list of credits is impressive and her status in the British theatre was confirmed when she was made a Dame of the British Empire in 1960. She effectively retired from the stage in 1969.   MB

Robson, Frederick [Thomas Brownbill] 1821–64 English actor, whose years at the OLYMPIC (1853–63) were among the most astonishing success stories of the 19th-century theatre. Robson was only five feet tall and had no choice but to make his lack of inches a feature. J. R. PLANCHÉ, for example, wrote for him the title role of Gam-Bogie in *The Yellow Dwarf* (1854), exploiting both his diminutiveness and his unrivalled ability to combine COMEDY and terror. It was Robson's sudden transitions from hilarity to horror that delighted Olympic audiences. TOM TAYLOR provided him with an ideal vehicle in *A Blighted Being* (1854) as the suicidal Job Wort, who swallows what he believes to be poison and only then discovers, to his consternation, that he is in love and enjoying life. Playing for laughs at first, Robson would suddenly silence spectators by betraying Job Wort's anguish.

This trick of grounding extravagant comedy on a base of pathos was Robson's source of power, but it had discomforting parallels in his private life. Having trained as an engraver, he had made his first theatrical appearances (1842–4) as a singer of comic songs, and was a regular performer at the Grecian from 1844 to 50 before 'coming out' as an actor in Dublin in 1850. It was his singing of 'Vilikens and his Dinah' in the character of Jem Bags in Henry Mayhew's revived *The Wandering Minstrel* that turned him into a star at the Olympic in 1853. Until then, he had been considered a BURLESQUE actor merely – a comically inappropriate Macbeth and an exaggeratedly Jewish Shylock in Talfourd's travesties (1853). From early on, and increasingly, acting was an ordeal for Robson, and he drank to give himself courage. Critics frequently alluded to the Dickensian quirkiness of his character creations, but Robson was more like the dying clown of *Pickwick Papers* than they knew.   PT

Robson, Stuart [Henry Robson Stuart] 1836–1903 American actor. Robson made his stage debut as Horace Courtney in *Uncle Tom's Cabin as It Is*, a dramatic retort to UNCLE TOM'S CABIN, at the Baltimore Museum in 1852. Subsequently he appeared with numerous stock companies (see STOCK COMPANY), including those of LAURA KEENE's Theatre in New York, Mrs John Drew's (see DREW–BARRYMORE FAMILY) Theatre in Philadelphia, and the Globe Theatre in Boston. From 1877 to 89 he teamed with WILLIAM H. CRANE, starring in such FARCES as *Our Bachelors* and *Our Boarding House*, but also in *A Comedy of Errors* as the two Dromios, and *The Merry Wives of Windsor* as Falstaff (Crane) and Slender (Robson). BRONSON HOWARD's *The Henrietta* was especially written for them. After 1890, Robson starred on his own, most notably as

Tony Lumpkin in *She Stoops to Conquer.*   DJW

Roche, Billy 1949– Irish playwright. Roche's televised Wexford trilogy originated as stage plays: *A Handful of Stars* (1988), *Poor Beast in the Rain* (1989) and *Belfry* (1991). In strongly localized dialect he proclaims the tension between rebellious individual desire and the comfortable miseries of small-town life. *Amphibians* (1992) uses similar characters to explore the masculine search for mythic rites. *The Cavalcaders* (1993) is a highly accomplished exploration, through the fragmentation of a working men's early-1970s singing group, of the complex betrayals of friendship and heterosexual desire.   GF

Rodgers, Richard 1902–79 American composer. After studying music and writing scores for amateur musicals, Rodgers teamed up with lyricist LORENZ HART in 1919. Their songs were heard in *A Lonely Romeo* (1920) and *Poor Little Ritz Girl* (1920). After their first successful score for *The Garrick Gaieties* (1925), they created an almost unbroken stream of hit MUSICALS, including *Dearest Enemy* (1925), *The Girl Friend* (1926), *Peggy-Ann* (1926) and *A Connecticut Yankee* (1927). In the early 1930s Rodgers and Hart wrote the songs for several Hollywood musical films, then returned to BROADWAY to create some of the most popular scores of the late 1930s and early 40s, including *Jumbo* (1935), *On Your Toes* (1936), *Babes in Arms* (1937), *I'd Rather Be Right* (1937), *I Married an Angel* (1938), *The Boys from Syracuse* (1938), *Too Many Girls* (1939) and *By Jupiter* (1942). *Pal Joey* (1940), a musical chronicling the adventures of an amoral nightclub owner, was initially unpopular with critics and audiences, but more successful in its 1952 revival. Early in his career Rodgers had composed bouncy, jazz-influenced music that complemented the clever lyrics of Lorenz Hart. After demonstrating that he could compose on a grander, more sweeping scale with the 'Slaughter on Tenth Avenue' ballet for *On Your Toes*, Rodgers wrote dramatic, emotionally expansive scores for his 'musical plays' of the 1940s and 50s.

In 1943 Rodgers initiated his partnership with lyricist-librettist OSCAR HAMMERSTEIN II. Their first show was *Oklahoma!*, one of the most popular and influential of all American musicals. The Rodgers–Hammerstein partnership was responsible for some of the longest-running shows of the 1940s and 50s, including *Flower Drum Song* (1958) and *The Sound of Music* (1959). Their shows were noted for the care with which music and dance were integrated with the libretto. After Hammerstein's death in 1960, Rodgers served as his own lyricist for *No Strings* (1962), then collaborated with other lyricists on *Do I Hear a Waltz?* (1965), *Two by Two* (1970), *Rex* (1976) and *I Remember Mama* (1979). His autobiography, *Musical Stages*, was published in 1975.   MK

Rodrigues, Nelson 1912–81 Brazilian playwright, known for sensational and provocative topics. His first major success, *O Vestido de Noiva* (*Wedding Gown*) in 1942, was the play that marked the renovation of the contemporary Brazilian theatre through an ingenious staging by Zbigniew Ziembinski, a Polish émigré director whose knowledge of European vanguard expressionistic staging (see EXPRESSIONISM) enabled him to capture the three levels of a complex play. Rodrigues's plays often range through taboo topics such as incest, homosexuality and adultery, with MELODRAMATIC treatments – seen in *Album de Família* (*Family Album*), *Anjo Negro* (*Black Angel*), *Toda Desnudez Será Castigada* (*Nudity will be Punished*) and *O Beijo no Asfalto* (*Kiss on the Pavement*). He is now BRAZIL's most widely staged playwright. The 1981 production of *O Eterno Retorno* (*The Eternal Return*) by Antunes Filho triggered a resurgence of interest in professional productions of his works which continued into the 1984 production *Nelson 2 Rodrigues*, also by Filho and his Grupo Macunaíma. GW

Rogers, Will(iam Penn Adair) 1879–1935 This warm, gum-chewing American folk hero began in WILD WEST EXHIBITIONS billed as 'the Cherokee Kid, the wonderful Lasso-Artist', making $20 a week. At the St Louis World's Fair in 1904 he dazzled audiences by circling a horse and rider with a lasso in each hand. He made his first appearance in New York in 1905 with a trick roping and riding company (Madison Square Garden) and gradually evolved his technique of commenting drolly on current events in his slow Oklahoma drawl while he played with his lariat. His stage personality, which used no make-up or comic properties, was basically an extension of his own, winning the audience's trust and affection. Rogers appeared in MUSICALS, the ZIEGFELD *Follies* of 1916, 17, 18, 22 and 24, on the VAUDEVILLE stage and in 24 films. In 1934 he played the father in O'NEILL's *Ah, Wilderness!*; the next year he disappeared flying over Alaska with the aviator Wiley Post. In 1991, a MUSICAL COMEDY, *The Will Rogers Follies* (book by Peter Stone, music by CY COLEMAN, lyrics by BETTY COMDEN AND ADOLPH GREEN), opened successfully in New York. LS

Rojas Zorrilla, Francisco de 1607–48 Spanish GOLDEN AGE playwright. Born in Toledo, he lived in Madrid where he wrote mainly for an aristocratic audience. His poetic language reflects the baroque style of Góngora (1561–1627), and his dramatic practices place him in the cycle of CALDERÓN. His originality is characterized by exaggerated dramatic situations, which produce intense emotional effects, and by his unconventional treatment of the honour theme and its resolution, which often feature spirited female characters.

The violence of tragedies such as *Lucrecia y Tarquino* recalls neo-SENECAN models. His comedies, particularly *Entre bobos anda el juego* (*The Fools' Game*), excel at the presentation of ridiculous comic types anticipating the *COMEDIA de figurón* of MORETO. *Del rey abajo ninguno* (*None But the King*) is one of his several plays on the popular theme of peasants' honour. ElB

Rolland, Romain 1866–1944 French novelist and playwright, one of the first to advocate the *théâtre populaire*. His essay on *Le Théâtre du peuple* (1903) was a major reference point for subsequent practitioners and he also attempted to put theory into practice with plays about the French Revolution, notably *Danton* (1900) and *Le 14 juillet* (1902). But these melodramatic and rather worthy dramas did not have the same force as *Le Théâtre du peuple*. DB

Romains, Jules 1885–1972 French novelist and playwright, influenced by unanimism, but whose most important plays were social SATIRES on the themes of imposture, propaganda and trickery. His unanimist play *Crommedeyre le vieil* (*Old Crommedeyre*) was produced by COPEAU in 1920, but JOUVET acted in and produced his

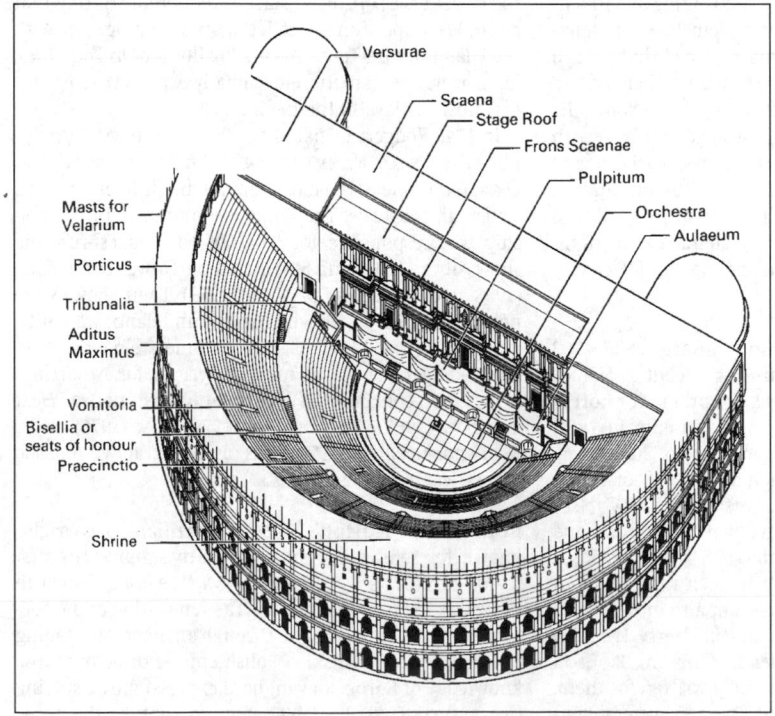

The Theatre of Marcellus, Rome, 13–11 BC.

most successful play *Dr Knock, ou Le Triomphe de la médecine* (*Dr Knock, or The Triumph of Medicine*) in 1923, a comedy satirizing the mystificatory tendencies of medicine with a verve that recalls MOLIÈRE. He also adapted JONSON's *Volpone* (from Stefan Zweig's version), one of DULLIN's major successes, and wrote a series of plays based on a self-important Professor Le Trouhadec, the first of which were also produced by Jouvet.   DB

Roman theatres and amphitheatres The earliest Roman theatres were temporary wooden constructions, erected when needed at the different sites of the various festivals. The scenic resources required by the plays of PLAUTUS and TERENCE are very simple: the stage has merely to be backed by a building with up to three doors, representing entrances to different houses. Plautus' *Amphitruo* shows that it was possible to climb to the roof of the building. Similar resources were presumably used in TRAGEDY and FARCE.

As powerful Romans competed to impress the populace with lavish spectacles, theatres, even while remaining temporary, became more ornate, and we hear of elaborate scenic decoration. Certain wall paintings found in private houses at Rome, Pompeii and Boscoreale look very much like pictures of stage sets, though their value as evidence for actual sets is uncertain.

Attempts to build a permanent theatre at Rome were opposed as a danger to public morals until Pompey the Great, celebrating his eastern conquests, overrode the opposition on the thin pretext that his stone theatre, which was surmounted by a shrine, was really a temple. It probably resembled the better preserved Theatre of Marcellus, erected later under Augustus, and held about 17,500 people. It was opened in 55 BC with shows of unparalleled magnificence, including tragic performances (of a sort which, from Cicero's description, sound more like the spectaculars of Cecil B. de Mille than classical tragedy) as well as gladiatorial contests, athletics and wild-beast shows. It remained in use until the 6th century AD.

Under the emperors stone theatres became widespread throughout most of the Empire. Those which survive are among the most impressive of all Roman monuments; there are particularly well preserved examples at Aspendus in Turkey, Orange in France, and Sabratha and Leptis Magna in North Africa. It comes as a disappointment to realize that all these were built at a time when COMEDY and tragedy had been largely replaced by MIME and pantomime; indeed there is no proof that any surviving Roman play was ever performed in any surviving theatre. Often the theatres must have been used merely for public assemblies or (in place of amphitheatres) for gladiatorial contests and wild-beast shows. One writer complains that even the Theatre of Dionysus at Athens has been subjected to this indignity.

In a Roman theatre the *scaena* (scene building) rises to the full height of the *cavea* (seating) or higher, and is integrally connected to it. Thus the *parodoi* leading to the *orchēstra* from outside consist of vaulted passages. While Greek theatres had to be built against hillsides, the engineering skills of the Romans enabled them to build freestanding theatres on level ground. The stone-floored *orchēstra*, no longer used for dancing, was reduced to a small semicircle, and might be occupied by additional seating. The wood-floored stage was broader, deeper and lower than that of Hellenistic Greece. Behind it rose the imposing façade, the *scaenae frons*, richly ornamented with pillars, niches and statues.

A stage curtain (*aulaeum*) was commonly used. Though the evidence is confusing, it appears that the normal arrangement was to lower the curtain for the duration of the performance, storing it in a slot at the front of the stage, and to raise it at the end. There might be a roof over the stage, and an awning (*velarium*) might be spread over the entire theatre. Small theatres, called *odea*, were completely roofed, and were housed in rectangular buildings.

VITRUVIUS, writing in the Augustan period, gives instructions for the design of a Roman theatre, distinguishing it from the Greek type. He also describes painted scenery, with perspective effects, for tragedy, comedy and satyr play (see GREECE, ANCIENT). Vitruvius and the later Greek writer Pollux describe various scenic devices such as *periaktoi* – prism-shaped wooden constructions painted

The theatre at Aspendus, Turkey.

with three different scenes, any one of which could be turned to face the audience. It is unclear, however, in what theatres these were actually used, and it does not seem to have been usual at any period to provide appropriate scenery for individual plays.

Amphitheatres were used for gladiatorial contests and wild-beast fights, and some could be flooded to accommodate mock sea battles. They consisted of an oval arena (beneath which there might be concealed pits to house equipment and animals) completely surrounded by seating. Thus, as the name implies, the shape was roughly that of two theatres facing each other (but the story that there once existed two theatres which could *actually* be combined to form an amphitheatre is surely fictional). Greatest of all was the Flavian Amphitheatre or Colosseum at Rome, which was built in the first century AD and could seat about 45,000 spectators.   ALB

See: R. C. Beacham, *The Roman Theatre and Its Audience*, London, 1991; W. Beare, *The Roman Stage*, 3rd edn, London, 1964; M. Bieber, *The History of the Greek and Roman Theater*, 2nd edn, Princeton, 1961.

Romania Thracian tribal ceremonials, classical Greek drama, Roman gladiatorial contests, Slavic funeral rites and Byzantine MIMES mark the history of theatrical performance in the Romanian lands – Wallachia, Moldavia and Transylvania – from antiquity to the early Middle Ages, when the structural elements of the Romanian folk theatre – its MASKS, symbolic accessories, mimetic dances and pantomime scenes – are believed to have taken shape. In the following centuries, these elements gave rise to a number of noteworthy late-medieval FOLK plays including the *căluşarii* (in modern form, the most celebrated of all Romanian folk dances), in which male transvestite magical dancers carried naked swords at Whitsuntide, and the *turca* or *brezaia* (which became the still-popular winter goat pageant, *capra*), whose protagonists were a mythical beast and a droll old man.

Considering such performances an undesirable pagan tradition, the Romanian Orthodox Church tried either to suppress them or to graft them on to its own theatrical forms, of which the most important was the two-part pageant of the *vicleim*. Performed between Christmas and Epiphany from the beginning of the 19th century until well into the 20th, this pageant began with the *irozii*, a vivid dramatization of biblical and apocryphal stories about Herod and the three Magi, and it ended with the *jocul păpuşilor*, a farcical puppet show in which the PUPPETS, coarsely carved in wood and colourfully dressed, were made to enact plotless plays on the candle-lit miniature stage of the *chivot*, a portable chest in the shape of a church and richly adorned with Nativity scenes. To build up these plays, the puppeteer, accompanied by a fiddler, brought to life a wide range of such diverse episodes as the amorous misadventures of Vasilache the gypsy and his jealous wife Gagiţa, or of the Gallicized lady Mariţa, or the beheading of the Turk by the Cossack (an echo of the Russo-Turkish wars), or the naive song of a mouse who ends up being eaten by a cat. Much of the humour of these puppet shows, whose uninhibited SATIRE sometimes prompted local authorities to prohibit them, resulted from the hilarious use of picturesque and foreign words, a technique

which was to have notable reverberations in the Romanian literary establishment. If the *irozii* was most probably an adaptation of a Transylvanian German MYSTERY PLAY, the puppet theatre of the *vicleim* owed much to *hayali zil*, the Turkish SHADOW show which was so popular with Romanians that to this day the word *caraghios* (ludicrous) is descriptive of attributes of the farcical Turkish character KARAGÖZ.

First mentioned in 1652 as a court entertainment, the shadow show remained a favourite with the Romanian aristocracy until well into the 18th century, when Western observers expressed astonishment at its lack of decorum. For most of the late Middle Ages, which in Romania lasted into the 19th century, a taste for low comedy characterized the court and the boyars (nobles), whose chief theatrical *divertissements* included *măscărici*, jesters who could be killed by anyone with impunity; *pehlivani*, travelling acrobats who, joined by the *măscărici*, performed CIRCUS numbers at wedding ceremonies; and *soitari*, gaudily dressed retainers who, in the vein of Turkish *orta-uyunu* farces, enacted resourceful, topical and obscene improvisations in Romanian, Turkish and Greek. But in the late 18th century and especially in the first quarter of the 19th, a period in which an increasing number of foreign troupes – French, Italian, German, Russian and Polish – came to the Ottoman-dominated principalities of Wallachia and Moldavia, preferences changed rapidly in favour of Western theatrical forms.

In Bucharest, the capital of Wallachia, the beginnings of legitimate theatre are linked to the activities of the Hetairia, a Greek secret society seeking national emancipation. To spread their anti-despotic ideas, the Hetairists encouraged student representations in Greek of Greek, French and Italian plays – I. R. Nerulos, VOLTAIRE and ALFIERI were favourite authors. These pioneer theatrical endeavours proved successful and, in 1818, their influential patron, Ralu, the youngest daughter of Prince Ioan Caragea, provided the first permanent theatre building in Wallachia, located at Cişmeaua Roşie, for the enthusiastic actors – exclusively men at the beginning, but later women also acted. In 1819 this theatre had its first Romanian-language production: emulous Romanian students staged *Hecuba* by EURIPIDES. The performance opened with a memorable Prologue by Iancu Văcărescu which, urging the implementation of the moral, educational and patriotic functions of theatre, gave quintessential expression to the overriding concerns of the early Romanian theatrical promoters and practitioners, members of the intelligentsia for the most part.

In 1833, with a view to training actors and musicians for the much desired national theatre, Ion Heliade Rădulescu and Ion Cîmpineanu founded the first conservatory in Wallachia, the Philharmonic Society. Its initial repertory relied largely on plays by MOLIÈRE and Voltaire which, however, were soon to yield to plays by KOTZEBUE, the favourite author of the time. Under the guidance of Costache Aristia, their professor of declamation, the students performed, alternately with German players of opera, at the Momolo Theatre, built by an Italian cook and entrepreneur in 1833; when political suspicion and rowdy personal disputes put an end to the Philharmonic in 1837, the first generation of Romanian actors disbanded.

Their staging and often fiery acting style were for the most part a response to an eclectic body of French ideas about theatre, which included those of BOILEAU, Voltaire and HUGO. Of the former students the only one who pursued a theatrical career was Costache Caragiale. His activities as an actor, impresario and playwright reinforced the general wish for a state-subsidized theatre in Bucharest on the model of those in other European capitals; and, when the 1000-seat Great Theatre opened in 1852, he assumed the leadership of the Romanian troupe, which was to share the facilities with an Italian opera company. By that time a number of Wallachian plays, chiefly satiric comedies, had been published, of which some were also successfully performed (notably Costache Bălăcescu's *A Good Education*, 1845, and Costache Caragiale's *A Soirée in Suburbia*, 1847); but, written in the spirit of Ion Heliade Rădulescu's famous dictum 'Write, boys, just write', they are now of only historical interest.

Theatrical developments in Jassy, the capital of Moldavia, differed from those in Bucharest in few, but significant, respects. While in Jassy student representations were less important, the participation of the aristocracy in the theatre arts produced superior results; it also imprinted a characteristic Bohemian quality on the theatrical life of that city. Although young boyars had begun to perform plays in Romanian in their parents' manor houses as early as 1816, it was only in 1834 that a Moldavian production took place on a public stage, that of the elegant Théâtre des Variétés, built in Jassy in 1832 for the French Fouraux troupe. There, amateur actors played *The Moldavian Shepherds' Festival*, a historical PASTORAL by Gheorghe Asachi, Moldavia's distinguished theatrical promoter. Other occasional performances followed, and, in 1836, the Philharmonic Dramatic Conservatory was established. Its activities were similar to, yet less intense and more conservative than, those of the Philharmonic Society. It closed in 1839 owing to financial difficulties, but Romanian-language theatre revived during the sojourn in Jassy of the Wallachian Costache Caragiale. In 1840, the successful Romanian troupe he had assembled was united with the French troupe under a single subsidized directorship to which, in 1846, Prince Mihail Sturza offered his houses at Copou for Moldavia's Great Theatre.

Official theatrical patronage, however, was hardly magnanimous and CENSORSHIP was ironhanded – the playwright Alecu Russo and three leading actors ended up in monasteries to fast, pray and repent for the political liberties they had taken in the production of *Provisioner Vadră* (1846), a satire on the popular violent MELODRAMAS of the day. Yet that eventful period saw the glory of Moldavian drama – the *vaudevilles*, farces and comedies of Vasile Alecsandri, a French-educated aristocrat, whose plays about the adventures of Chiriţa, an upstart provincial lady who has many of the traits of the puppet lady Mariţa, still fill the theatres in both Romania and former Soviet Moldavia (the eastern half of Moldavia). Essential to Chiriţa's success was the interpretative art of that comic master of women's parts, Matei Millo, a boyar who became Moldavia's foremost actor. Trained in Paris, he brought a new, more natural style to Romanian acting, and his rising star soon eclipsed that of Costache Caragiale. Millo also wrote plays: his 'OPERETTA-witchery' *Hîrca* (*The Old Hag*,

1848) was probably the single most successful Romanian play in the 19th century.

After Wallachia united with Moldavia to form Romania in 1859, Bucharest, the capital and largest city, emerged as the theatrical centre of the new country. Led by prominent literati and politicians, the Great Theatre of Bucharest, renamed the National Theatre in 1875, operated as a subsidized concessionary enterprise until 1877, when the Romanian parliament voted to reorganize it on the model of the COMÉDIE-FRANÇAISE. Similar changes were subsequently made for the theatres of Jassy and Craiova. Thus, at the beginning of the 20th century there were three state-subsidized theatres in Romania, the only ones allowed to bear the name of National Theatre. In addition to these there were numerous private and municipal theatres. There, as well as in hotels and outdoor cafés, itinerant troupes produced melodramas, operettas, *vaudevilles*, comedies and REVUES, along with a few serious dramas. Despite some attempts by Romania's first director, Paul Gusty, an admirer of OTTO BRAHM, to implement naturalist production methods at the National Theatre of Bucharest, rigidly conservative practices and regulations threatened to freeze this foremost Romanian theatre in outmoded traditions. To address this problem, Alexandru Davila, who led the National Theatre of Bucharest during 1905–8 and 1912–13, introduced a series of reforms aimed at modernizing stagecraft and at allowing more room for contemporary plays, chiefly French. Davila also founded the first important Romanian private acting company in 1909 – it played at the Modern Theatre.

Although Romanian acting, having by now established its own traditions, was rapidly raising its standards, it was also losing some of the éclat it had had at the end of the 19th century. The greatest names among the actors of that period are Grigore Manolescu, the most celebrated Romanian Hamlet; Aristizza Romanescu, renowned for her 'silver bell' voice; and Constantin I. Nottara. Trained in Paris, these star performers, all from the National Theatre at Bucharest, were also influenced by their older colleague Mihail Pascaly, Romania's chief romantic actor. An important Romanian actress who acquired international fame was Agatha Bârsescu, a stately tragedienne who played in Austria, Germany, and the USA.

Encouraged by officials and drawing on the talent of a number of literary figures, Romanian drama flourished between the Union of the Principalities (1859) and the First World War. Even though it generally echoed trends in the playwriting of the day, it achieved considerable originality, at least in spirit if not necessarily in form, in the brilliant dramatic work of ION LUCA CARAGIALE, Costache Caragiale's nephew, whose caustic farcical comedies present, in a style reminiscent of LABICHE's, a grotesque picture of hopelessly degraded and ridiculous humanity – their characters, without exception, are both amoral and, in one way or another, mentally defective. Most of the other enduring plays of the period are historical pieces, especially attractive in a country whose national identity had long been denied (Romania proclaimed its independence from the Ottoman Empire only in 1877). It was Bogdan Petriceicu Haşdeu who gave the Romanian theatre its first important historical play, and probably its best romantic verse drama, *Răzvan and Vidra* (1867), in which a medieval gypsy brigand, Răzvan, spurred by Vidra, the so-called Romanian Lady Macbeth, ascends to and dies tragically on the throne of Moldavia. The same Hugo-inspired spirit marks *Prince Despot* (1879) by Vasile Alecsandri, who, in a new burst of creativity, went on to write two gracefully sensual and melancholic 'Roman plays', *The Fountain of Blandusia* (1883) and *Ovid* (1885).

More in line with the romantic tradition of Romanian historical drama are Alexandru Davila's sober and gripping verse play *Prince Vlaicu* (1902) about an obscure episode at the beginning of Wallachia's history, and the monumental (over 100 characters) prose trilogy *Sunset* (1909), *The Storm* (1910) and *The Morning Star* (1910) by Barbu Ştefănescu Delavrancea. Naturalistic touches serve as a counterpoint to the lyrical tone of the best part of the trilogy, *Sunset*, which centres on the figure of the ageing Stephen the Great, Moldavia's most famous medieval ruler. While I. L. Caragiale, Haşdeu, Alecsandri, Davila and Delavrancea have come to be considered Romania's classic dramatists, other playwrights popular at the time are no longer in fashion. These include Vasile Urechiă, most successful as an author of historical melodramas (*Minister Bucioc*, 1867); Grigore Ventura, of note for his topical and colourful war melodrama *Curcanii* (1878); I. Bengescu-Dabija, whose melodramatic verse TRAGEDY *Pygmalion, the King of Phoenicia* (1886) was highly praised by contemporary critics; Haralamb Lecca, a leading writer of IBSENite bourgeois dramas (*The Card Players*, 1899; *The Dogs*, 1902); and Ronetti Roman, a talented Romanian-Jewish playwright who, in his compelling *Manasse* (1900), a *pièce-à-thèse* about interracial marriage, addressed the controversial issue of the integration of Jews in Romanian society. More enduring in popularity has been Mihail Sorbul, the author of the naturalistic drama *The Red Passion* (1916).

Of particular interest is Lucian Blaga, an important philosopher-poet who wrote mystical, existentialist plays (e.g. *Zamolxes* (1921), a 'pagan mystery' in blank verse). Also deserving of mention are the early-20th-century symbolic verse plays (see SYMBOLISM) *The Gossamer Legend* (1907) by Şt. O. Iosif and Dimitrie Anghel; *String Yourself, Pearl!* (1911) and *The Black Rooster* (1913) by Victor Eftimiu; and *The Red Roses* (1915) by Zaharia Bârsan.

In 1918, following the dissolution of the Austro-Hungarian Empire, Romania acquired Transylvania, a province where large Hungarian and German minorities had been politically and culturally dominant since the early Middle Ages. The pre-eminent Hungarian-language theatre (founded in 1792) was at Cluj (Koloszvár), and the principal German-language theatre (founded in 1787) was at Sibiu (Hermannstadt). Partly because of cultural oppression, partly because of frequent tours by professional troupes from Romania, the Romanians in Transylvania (the majority of the population) did not develop a significant theatre of their own until 1919, when Romania's fourth National Theatre was established at Cluj.

The period between the wars saw a considerable and fruitful diversification of Romanian theatrical life, due largely to the rapid expansion of the commercial theatre. In Bucharest, which remained the theatrical centre of the country, the foremost private acting company was the Bulandra, led by a team of actors of whom Tony Bulandra,

his wife Lucia Sturdza Bulandra, and Ion Manolescu were the most important. Among the other great Bucharest actors of the period were George Calboreanu at the National Theatre, Maria Filotti at the Sărindar, and Constantin Tănăse, the undisputed master of Romanian revue, at the Cărăbus. Eclectic for the most part, Romanian directing was best represented by the work of Aurel Ion Maican; of the nonconformist Ion Sava, whose 1946 production of *Macbeth* with masks made history on the stage of the National Theatre in Bucharest; of the exigent Victor Ion Popa; and of Soare Z. Soare, a disciple of MAX REINHARDT. Another distinguished director was Iacob Sternberg, who, together with scene designer M. H. Maxy, painter Marcel Iancu (Tristan Tzara's former collaborator and one of the founders of dadaism) and others, championed the avant-garde theatre movement in Bucharest in the 1920s. Sternberg was also the chief promoter of Bucharest's YIDDISH theatre, which he led back to the VARIETY tradition begun by AVROM GOLDFADN.

Of the important and often revived dramatists of the period Camil Petrescu is notable for his intellectual dramas, *The Fairies' Dance* (1919) and *Danton* (1925); George Mihail Zamfirescu (also known as a director) for his 'tragic comedy' with songs, *Miss Nastasia* (1927), a masterpiece which blends melodrama, NATURALISM and EXPRESSIONISM; George Ciprian for the mystic comedy, *The Man with the Jade* (1927); Alexandru Kiriţescu for his comedy of manners, *The Jays* (1930); Tudor Muşatescu for *Titanic Waltz* (1932) and *... Escu* (1933), two satirical comedies; Victor Ion Popa for *Take, Ianka, and Cadîr* (1933), a comedy on racial prejudice; and Mihail Sebastian for the lyrical comedies, *The Nameless Star* (1943) and *Stop News* (1945).

After the Second World War the Romanian stage entered a period of increased material prosperity brought about by the nationalization of the theatres in 1948. For a time the prescriptions of socialist realism, the official artistic doctrine, were strictly followed, but in the later 1950s a number of young directors and scene designers, of whom the most influential was LIVIU CIULEI, began to call for a theatre of visual metaphor and allusion, more in tune with current Western theatrical trends.

Romanian theatrical art opened itself to 're-theatricalization' and to international theatre during the 60s. International recognition followed quickly after. Ciulei, David Esrig, Lucian Pintilie, Radu Penciulescu, Vlad Mugur and Lucian Giurchescu, through significant performances, also made themselves well known abroad. The excellent designers Ion Popescu-Udriste, Miruna and Radu Boruzescu, Dan Nemteanu, Ion Oroveanu and Paul Bortnovschi, and leading actors like Tom Caragiu, Octavian Cotescu, Gina Patrichi and Radu Beligan, should also be mentioned, together with the Bucharest theatres they served – the National, the Bulandra, the Comedie, the Nottara and the Mic.

The flowering lasted up to 1971, when Ceauşescu's notorious doctrinaire ideas put a stop to cultural evolution. A lot of Romanian artists emigrated. The gradual impairment of the social-political climate, the catastrophic state of the economy, the cultural isolation, the CENSORSHIP – all of these factors generated an open or implicit oppositional theatre whose characteristic is that particular paralinguistic dialogue with the audience, communication between the lines. Allegorical writing, allusive messages, and performances in a parabolic baroque style dominated the period. In spite of the unpropitious times, directors such as György Harag, Cătălina Buzoianu and Alexa Visarion still created, and theatre survived.

In contemporary Romanian drama, which has ranged from socialist realism to the abstract but has eschewed such themes as eroticism, violence and alienation, the well known playwrights are Aurel Baranga, whose *The Rabid Lamb* (1954) is a satire against bureaucracy; Horia Lovinescu, the author of *The Boga Sisters* (1959), in which, unlike its model, *The Three Sisters* by CHEKHOV, poetic justice prevails; Ecaterina Oproiu, whose popular romantic comedy *I Am Not the Eiffel Tower* (1965) signalled a movement away from socialist realism; and Marin Sorescu, who wrote a number of innovative plays including *Jonah* (1969), a symbolic monodrama, and *The Third Pale* (1978), a metaphorical historical drama about the medieval Wallachian prince, Vlad the Impaler (Dracula).

The fact that theatres were obliged to eliminate foreign plays (out of ideological considerations) led to a certain quantitative expansion of Romanian dramaturgy between 1970 and 89. However, high quality remains characteristic of some playwrights: Dumitru Radu Popescu (serious, profound drama), Dumitru Solomon (philosophical parables), Romulus Guga (allegorical comedy) and Theodor Mazilu (absurd comedies; see THEATRE OF THE ABSURD).

The revolutionary events of December 1989 brought about spectacular changes, even in the cultural field. The most important Romanian stage directors returned from their exile, in order to be appointed artistic directors: ANDREI SERBAN (National Theatre of Bucharest), Ciulei (the Bulandra), Mugur (the Odeon), Giurchescu (the Comedie). Their new performances put Romania in touch with the European theatrical experience, after so many years of isolation. *The Ancient Trilogy* staged by Serban at the National Theatre is looked upon as the moment of rebirth of the Romanian theatre, proposing a 'return to sources'. The National Theatre of Craiova is also noteworthy on both a national and an international scale, especially through Silviu Purcărete's performances (Ubu-Rex and Titus Andronicus). In Bucharest, a National Theatre Festival takes place every November; at Piatra Neamtz, the first International Theatre Festival of Romania is being arranged; the first private theatre companies are being founded. But theatre continues to be mainly subsidized by the state. A number of playwrights are being reintroduced into the repertoire after more than 20 years (e.g. EUGÈNE IONESCO). Romanian playwrights in the diaspora are frequently staged (Matei Visniec, Gheorghe Astalos). A process of a genuine cultural reintegration is in train. AP

See: S. Alterescu (ed.), *Istoria teatrului în România*, 3 vols., Bucuresti, 1965–73, and (ed.), *An Abridged History of Romanian Theatre*, Bucuresti, 1973; V. Brădăteanu, *Istoria literaturii dramatice românesti si a artei spectacolului*, Bucuresti, 1982; T. T. Burada, *Istoria teatrului în Moldova*, Bucuresti, 1975; G. Călinescu, *Istoria literaturii române*, Bucuresti, 1982; M. Florea, *Scurtă istorie a teatrului românesc*, Bucuresti, 1970; V. Mîndra, *Istoria literaturii dramatice românesti*, vol. 1, Bucuresti, 1985; A. Mititelu, *Teatro romeno*, Milan, 1960; D. C. Ollănescu, *Teatrul la români*, Bucuresti, 1981.

Romans (France) Town on the Isère, 50 miles west of Grenoble, which provides our best documented example of a CARNIVAL which became assimilated to social conflict, and ended in bloodshed. In 1580, against a complex background of economic and political tensions, the town's patricians and plebeians mobilized the traditional carnival societies as paramilitary power bases, and transformed the processions into political demonstrations. In what they afterwards represented as a pre-emptive strike, on the evening of *lundi gras* the bourgeois party murdered the moderate craftsmen's leader, Jean Serve (whose worst proven offence was to sit in Council wearing a zoomorphic costume), and arrested and hanged the 'ringleaders' of an alleged popular uprising. The intricate behaviour of both parties before the MASKS came off and the weapons out shows clearly that, under the *ancien régime* at least, symbolism may be disingenuous but is rarely innocent. AEG

Romberg, Sigmund 1887–1951 Hungarian-born musician, who went to the USA as a young man and became one of the prolific composers of OPERETTA and MUSICAL COMEDY scores. In 1914 he began a long association with the SHUBERT BROTHERS when he wrote the score for *The Whirl of the World*. As the Shuberts' staff composer, he wrote songs for their REVUE series *The Passing Show*, and also turned out scores for dozens of commonplace musicals. In 1921 he adapted Franz Schubert's melodies for the musical biography *Blossom Time*, whose phenomenal success gave him greater freedom in choosing projects. As the 1920s progressed, he wrote the operettas by which he is most remembered: *The Student Prince* (1924), *The Desert Song* (1926) and *The New Moon* (1928). He continued to write operettas and musicals up to his death, though with less success. MK

Rome

1 The origins of drama Patriotic Romans such as Livy and HORACE liked to claim that Rome possessed an indigenous dramatic tradition, which had developed from certain religious ceremonies and from the ritual abuse ('Fescennine verses') which accompanied them. It is difficult, however, to relate these claims to the types of drama actually known to have existed in Republican times. Certainly the festivals of the Roman calendar, at which aristocratic magistrates vied with each other to finance shows that would win the favour of the electorate, provided good opportunities for drama to develop and flourish. From an early date, however, Rome was in contact with the Greek colonies of southern Italy, and these colonies (notably Tarentum) had a thriving tradition of drama, both literary and subliterary. And even the most popular and informal types of drama at Rome seem to have had non-Roman origins.

These types were the MIME and the Atellan FARCE, both of which were established at Rome by the late 3rd century BC. The mime was a Romanized version of a widespread Greek form (see GREECE, ANCIENT) – a vulgar, often improvised low-life episode performed by a small group of unmasked actors. The Atellan farce (*fabula Atellana*) was believed to be an import from the Oscan town of Atellae in Campania, which would itself have had close connections with the Greek colonies. It was a boisterous entertainment performed by a stock troupe of MASKED clowns – Maccus, Pappus, Bucco, Dossenus and others – somewhat reminiscent of the *COMMEDIA DELL'ARTE*.

Literary drama at Rome probably dates from 240 BC, when the Romanized Greek LUCIUS LIVIUS ANDRONICUS first produced a Latin adaptation of a Greek play at the Ludi Romani (one of the annual festivals). Such adaptations became popular, and the conventions of Roman drama were quickly established. Andronicus and his immediate successors, Naevius and QUINTUS ENNIUS, differed from the Greek dramatists in writing both TRAGEDY and COMEDY, as well as non-dramatic works.

2 Tragedy, historical drama and pantomime We possess only fragments and play titles from the work of the great tragedians of the Roman Republic – the 3rd-century pioneers Andronicus and Gnaeus Naevius, and the 2nd-century classics Quintus Ennius, MARCUS PACUVIUS and LUCIUS ACCIUS. Tragedies were almost always based on Greek originals. Ennius favoured the plays of EURIPIDES as models, but Pacuvius seems to have preferred SOPHOCLES; and Accius may occasionally have taken his material direct from epic poetry, showing the same degree of originality as the Greek tragedians themselves. There was a general preference for warlike and melodramatic themes. The interest in the supernatural (ghosts, dreams and portents) and in madness, which is prominent in SENECA, can be traced back to this period. Though the Greek mythical settings were retained, the values expressed and celebrated – courage, endurance and piety, especially in the service of the state – were distinctively Roman; and Stoic philosophy became influential at an early date. Above all, Roman tragedy was strongly rhetorical, and increasingly so as it developed; and the rhetoric, clothed in elaborately ornate diction, seems to have aimed more at solemn grandeur than at the intellectual stimulation and provocation found in the best work of Euripides.

The metre of spoken dialogue, the iambic *senarius*, was adapted from the main dialogue metre of Greek tragedy, but was less strict. Large sections of the actors' parts, however, were sung, chanted or declaimed to the accompaniment of the pipe or *tibia* (the Greek *aulos*). The Chorus was retained, but no attempt was made to imitate the complex metres of Greek choral songs.

From the time of Naevius onward, the tragedians occasionally wrote plays on subjects from Roman history, whether legendary or recent. These *fabulae praetextae* (plays performed in the *toga praetexta*, the bordered toga of Roman magistrates) had a precedent in Greek historical tragedies such as AESCHYLUS' *Persians*, but the plots naturally had to be freely invented by the Roman dramatists.

In the 1st century BC, revivals of existing Latin tragedies continued to be popular, but we hear less of the composition of new works for the stage – perhaps largely because the subjects which appealed to Roman taste had already been treated. At the same time poets started to write tragedies merely as literary exercises, intended for declamation (like other Roman poetry), not for staged performance. The *Thyestes* of Varius Rufus, performed in 29 BC, is the last tragedy known to have been produced on stage; the *Medea* of Ovid (43 BC to AD 17) was evidently not pro-

duced. By the time of Seneca the stage was regarded with contempt by respectable Romans, but the word 'tragedy' had a lofty sound and the form was one in which the contemporary taste for blood, rhetoric and melodrama could be indulged to the full.

One reason for the decline of staged tragedy was doubtless the rise of the pantomime, which was introduced in the reign of Augustus. This was a performance in dumbshow by a masked dancer (the *pantomimus* himself) to the accompaniment of a kind of cantata sung by a chorus. The subject was normally taken from Greek myth, but the libretto was unimportant; what mattered was the grace of the dancer and his skill in mimicking the actions described. Sometimes the *pantomimus* used more than one mask in the course of his performance, and sometimes two or more *pantomimi* might perform together.

The earliest *pantomimi* at Rome were two freed slaves from the Greek east, Pylades and Bathyllus, who seem to have fashioned the genre on Greek models, and who gained immediate popularity by their own virtuoso dancing. While the performances of Bathyllus were burlesque in character, it was the serious, 'tragic' pantomime of Pylades that had lasting influence.

This curious form of entertainment was despised by the best-educated Romans, but remained extremely popular as long as the Western Empire lasted, and survived in the East well into the Byzantine period. We also hear of performances by solo singers (including the Emperor Nero) on tragic themes; references to 'tragedies' acted in late Imperial and Byzantine times probably mean performances of this type.

3 Comedy, farce and mime The most admired writers of Roman comedy were PLAUTUS, CAECILIUS STATIUS and TERENCE. Like Livius Andronicus, Naevius and Ennius, they adapted their plays from the New Comedy of 4th- and 3rd-century Greece (unless Plautus' *Amphitruo* is adapted from Middle Comedy). The characters' names and the nominal settings were Greek, and comedies of this kind are known as *fabulae palliatae*, plays performed in the *pallium* or Greek cloak. The action usually takes place in a city street, and always in front of one, two or three houses, each with a visible door.

The Greek plots were handled with considerable freedom, although the *kind* of freedom varied from one dramatist to another. The complexity of the intrigue was often increased by Terence, often reduced or casually treated by Plautus. The Chorus, already vestigial in MENANDER, was dropped altogether (though a trace remains in Plautus' *Rudens*). This meant that the action of each play was continuous, and, while the act divisions of the Greek originals are sometimes easy to detect, they are sometimes concealed (the act divisions in our texts are an editorial addition). Those Greek institutions and customs which would have puzzled the Roman audience are either Romanized (especially in Plautus) or played down (especially in Terence). The Prologue may serve to advertise the coming play as well as (Plautus), or instead of (Terence), setting the scene. The practice of adding scenes or characters from one Greek original to a play mainly based on another is particularly associated with Terence, but he himself claims (in the Prologue to *Andria*) to have precedents for this in the work of Naevius, Plautus and Ennius. Plautus constantly enlivens his plays with jokes, puns, topical allusions, audience address, and vulgarities of various kinds (but not political SATIRE, which was restricted by libel laws, and for which Naevius had been prosecuted). These elements, however, were perhaps reduced by Caecilius, and certainly much reduced by Terence.

The verse forms are much more varied than those of Greek New Comedy, and similar to those of Roman tragedy, showing that large sections of each play were accompanied on the *tibia*. The accompanied passages are usually referred to as 'recitative' (blocks of a single iambic or trochaic metre) or 'song' (in varied metres), though the actual modes of delivery are uncertain. Even the 'songs' (which are rare in Terence) are not divided into stanzas, and contribute to the action in much the same way as 'recitative' and unaccompanied dialogue.

The writing of *palliatae* continued for a time after the death of Terence, but came to an end with the work of Sextus Turpilius, who died in 103 BC. Revivals of the old plays remained popular in Cicero's day (mid-1st century BC), but are not heard of thereafter.

The increased refinement and Hellenization of the *palliata* at the hands of Terence left room for a more popular form of comedy that would inherit the more boisterous and Roman side of Plautus' work. Hence, probably, the *fabula togata*, or drama in Roman dress, of Titinius, Afranius and Atta. This was set among the lower classes in Italian towns, but otherwise the fragments suggest that the plays resembled Plautus', with much vulgar abuse between the characters and with plot motifs of love, intrigue and misunderstanding borrowed from the *palliata*. The writing of *togatae* seems to have come to an end with Atta, who is said to have died in 77 BC, though we hear of later revivals.

In the late Republican period attempts were made to give literary form to the Atellan farce and the mime. Atellans were written in the early 1st century BC by Pomponius and Novius, and mimes were written rather later by Decimus Laberius and Publilius Syrus. Both forms seem to have been used as tailpieces after more serious plays. The authors borrowed verse forms, and perhaps plot motifs, from the *palliata*, but the plays evidently retained the crude and simple character of their subliterary prototypes. Atellan titles such as *Maccus as Soldier*, *Bucco as Gladiator*, *The Pig*, *The Farmer*, show how the stock troupe of clowns could be put to various uses, and evoke the plays' homely and rustic settings. Adultery was a frequent theme of the mime, which by now employed actresses as well as male actors; and mime-actors might also indulge in ribald political satire, which could not be risked in respectable types of drama.

Though the literary farce and mime were short-lived, their improvised counterparts continued. Atellans survived until the 1st century AD, while the mime, which was patronized in the Republican period by the dictator Sulla, survived through the Empire and indeed through the Byzantine period, persisting even after Justinian's official closing of the theatres in the 6th century. Its vulgarity was constantly denounced by moralists, especially after the rise of Christianity, and no doubt many mimes consisted simply of pornography; but allowance should be made for the snobbery of most Roman writers, and the more sympa-

thetic attitude of a few, such as Pliny, shows that some mimes could rise to a certain sophistication. In any case, the form proved too informal and popular to be suppressed.

4 Shows and spectacles From the earliest times the Romans used shows of various kinds to mark the annual religious festivals, as well as special events such as triumphs and important funerals. Dancing, acrobatics and gymnastic contests must always have existed, but in 264 BC such harmless entertainments were supplemented by the introduction of gladiatorial fights from Etruria. Gladiators were prisoners, condemned criminals or otherwise desperate men, who, having nothing to lose, were prepared to fight to the death in the hope of winning fame and popularity if they survived. Various kinds of specialized equipment were used to lend variety and excitement to the spectacle. As early as Terence we read (in the prologues to *Hecyra*) of audiences being distracted from watching comedy by the rival attractions of tightrope-walkers, boxers and gladiators.

By the end of the Republic the main types of spectacle were well established: the gladiatorial fight, the wild-beast show (all manner of exotic animals being pitted against men or against each other – see BAITING), the mock sea-battle (see NAUMACHIA) and the chariot race. As the population of Rome grew, as wealth flowed in from wars of conquest and an expanding empire, and as struggles for power among the nobility grew more and more desperate, greater and greater sums were spent on buying the favour of the Roman mob. Under the emperors this expenditure continued, since the largely unemployed populace of Rome and other cities had to be kept quiet by being given the entertainments which it had come to expect.

Such spectacles might be performed in the theatres themselves (see ROMAN THEATRES AND AMPHITHEATRES), and dramatic performance was inevitably influenced by the public taste for lavish expenditure and crude realism. We hear of a *fabula togata* of Afranius, concerning a fire, being revived in the time of Nero for the sake of showing a building burnt to the ground on stage. Less reliable, perhaps, are the claims of salacious Roman writers that condemned criminals might be executed on stage as part of a dramatic performance.

5 Actors and musicians The usual word for 'actor', *histrio*, apparently derives from an Etruscan word for a masked dancer. The earliest Roman dramatists are said to have acted in their own plays, like the earliest Greek ones. By the time of Plautus and Terence, however, there were permanent troupes of professional actors, each led by an actor-manager, and a dramatist had to win the patronage of one of these if his plays were to be staged. Plautus sometimes alludes to one of these actor-managers, Titus Publilius Pellio, and some of Terence's prologues are written to be delivered by another, Lucius Ambivius Turpio, in his own person. Turpio is presented as a man proud of his artistic calling and of his discernment in championing the unpopular work of Terence, as he earlier championed that of Caecilius Statius. He and Pellio had aristocratic names, and were evidently men of consequence. They in their turn had to win the favour of the *aediles* (magistrates responsible for the administration of the festivals), by whom they and their fellow actors were paid.

There is no evidence for any restriction on the number of actors in any one play. Plautus' *Poenulus* requires six actors on stage at once; other plays could be performed with four or five, given some doubling. The *tibia*-player was evidently an important figure, for many of the surviving production notices give us his name and tell us what kind of *tibia* he used. The plays were delivered to an audience of both sexes and all social classes, and production notices often tell us whether a play 'pleased' or not, . though it is unclear how this was judged.

At the end of the Republic acting was still a respectable enough profession for QUINTUS ROSCIUS GALLUS, a famous actor who performed in both tragedy and comedy, to be the friend and protégé of Cicero. In the next generation, however, Livy writes contemptuously of actors, apparently thinking mainly of performers in mimes and pantomimes, who were always of low social class, being debarred from citizenship and placed under other legal restrictions.

This did not, however, prevent successful *pantomimi* under the Empire from winning all the wealth and adulation accorded to stars of opera and ballet today. They figure remarkably often in the scandals of the Imperial court: Mnester, a favourite of Caligula's, was later executed by Claudius for adultery with Messalina; Paris, a favourite of Nero's, was executed by Nero himself as an artistic rival.

6 Masks and costumes Some Roman writers claim that MASKS were not worn on the Roman stage until the time of Roscius, but it is generally agreed that this must rest on a misunderstanding and that they were worn from the first (except in the mime), as they had always been in Greece. Surviving representations and descriptions of actors and masks date only from the time of the late Republic and Empire, but indicate that the Romans followed, or exaggerated, the practice of the Hellenistic Greek theatre.

Thus tragic actors had their height increased by means of raised soles to their boots (*cothurni*) and a raised forehead (*onkos*) on the mask, and wore padding under their robes so that their build was proportional to their height. The mask of the *pantomimus* had a closed mouth. Comic actors wore the costume of everyday life, whether Greek (for the *palliata*) or Roman (for the *togata* – which cannot often have required actual togas – and the *Atellana*). Masks of slaves, old men and other figures of fun had gaping mouths and comically exaggerated features, while those of young men and maidens were more realistic.

Representations of tragic and comic actors and, in particular, masks continue to be common in painting, sculpture and mosaic throughout the Imperial period. The masks are often grotesquely distorted for comic or horrific effect. It is uncertain, however, how much these representations owe to contemporary dramatic performances (for which there is little other evidence) and how much to artistic convention. ALB

See: W. G. Arnott, *Menander, Plautus and Terence* (*Greece and Rome: New Surveys in the Classics*, 9), Oxford, 1975; R. C. Beacham, *The Roman Theatre and Its Audience*, London, 1991; W. Beare, *The Roman Stage*, 3rd edn, London, 1964; R. L. Hunter, *The New Comedy of* *Greece and Rome*, Cambridge, 1985; E.J. Kenney and W. V. Clausen (eds.), *The Cambridge History of Classical Literature*, vol. 2, Cambridge, 1982; D. Konstan, *Roman Comedy*, Cornell, 1983; F. H. Sandbach, *The Comic Theatre of Greece and Rome*, London, 1977.

Romeril, John 1945– Australian playwright. Romeril was initially a writer for La Mama and the Pram Factory, Melbourne; his plays, often with strong political or social content, range from the surreal absurdity (see SURREALISM; THEATRE OF THE ABSURD) of *I Don't Know Who to Feel Sorry For* (1969) and the REALISM of *Bastardy* (1972) to cartoon-like EXPRESSIONISM in *Chicago Chicago* (1971) and *The Floating World* (1974), and the musical adaptation of a novel, *Jonah Jones* (1985). He now works chiefly with the Melbourne Workers Theatre, creating performances related to workplace issues, and was script consultant for the MUSICAL *Snugglepot and Cuddlepie* (1993). MW

Romero, Mariela 1949– Venezuelan playwright and essayist. Her major plays include *El juego* (*The Game*, 1977), the bifurcated experiences of two characters named Ana. *Rosa de la noche* (*Rose of the Night*, 1980) takes place in the seedy Caracas underworld of pimps and prostitutes. In *El vendedor* (*The Salesman*, 1981), the world of a lonely woman without love is invaded by an aggressive type pretending to be a salesman. GW

Ronconi, Luca 1933– Italian actor and director. After drama school training he acted with a number of major companies before turning to direction with a version of GOLDONI's *La buona moglie* (*The Good Wife*) in 1963. During the mid- and later 1960s he evolved a distinctive and highly theatrical production style with mountings, particularly, of Renaissance drama, including SHAKESPEARE's *Measure for Measure* and *Richard III*, BRUNO's *Il candelaio* (*The Candle Maker*) and TOURNEUR's *The Revenger's Tragedy*. Perhaps his most ambitious work of the 1960s was an inventive and stunningly spectacular stage treatment in 1968 of ARIOSTO's epic poem *Orlando Furioso*, which he co-scripted with the poet Eduardo Sanguinetti. The range of his work in the 1970s and 80s was considerable, including productions of AESCHYLUS' *Oresteia*, MIDDLETON's *A Game at Chess* and IBSEN's *Ghosts*, plays which reflect an apparent preference for classic or neglected drama, of a kind both intellectually challenging and likely to permit the highly imaginative stage re-orchestration that is a hallmark of his work. He has had a distinguished career, too, in the lyric theatre, his work there including productions of Gounod's *Faust*, WAGNER's *Siegfried*, GLUCK's *Orpheus and Eurydice*, Rossini's *William Tell* (La Scala, 1988) and Mozart's *Idomeneo* (La Scala, 1990). Outstanding recent stage productions have included a version of Georges Bernanos's *Dialogues des Carmélites* (1988), CHEKHOV's *The Three Sisters* (1989), EUGENE O'NEILL's *Strange Interlude* (1990 and 91), a further production of Shakespeare's *Measure for Measure* (1991) and a brilliant staging of TASSO's Renaissance PASTORAL play, *Aminta* (1994). In 1992 he established under his personal supervision a School of Theatre attached to the Teatro Stabile of Turin, of which he has been director since 1988. LR

Roscius Gallus, Quintus c.120–62 BC Roman actor. His reputation in plays by PLAUTUS and TERENCE was of the highest, and it is suggested that he took great care in the preparation of his roles. His name has been conferred as an accolade of virtuosity on a number of more recent actors, not always with good cause. For instance, SAM COWELL was dubbed the Young American Roscius, and IRA ALDRIDGE, the black American actor, the African Roscius. MB

Rose, Billy [Samuel Wolf Rosenberg] 1899–1966 Flamboyant American showman ('I sell ballyhoo, not genius') and lyricist ('Barney Google', 'Without a Song', 'Me and My Shadow', and so forth). His ventures ranged from nightclubs and theatre-restaurants (Back Stage Club, Casino de Paree, the Billy Rose Music Hall in New York during the 1920s and 30s; Casa Mañana in Fort Worth in the 1930s; New York's Diamond Horseshoe, 1939–52) to epic spectacles such as *Jumbo* (1945) and the aquacades at the 1939–40 New York World's Fair and the San Francisco Golden Gate Exposition (1940), as well as 11 legitimate BROADWAY productions, including *Carmen Jones* (1943) and *The Immoralist* (1954). In the 1950s and 60s he owned two New York theatres. Among Rose's five marriages was one to FANNY BRICE (1929). The Billy Rose Theatre Collection of the New York Public Library was funded by his foundation (organized in 1958). DBW

Rose Theatre (London) The foundations of this playhouse, built in 1587 close to the south bank of the Thames, were uncovered and excavated in 1989. We now know that the inner yard had a diameter of about 49ft, that the stage (built at the northern end of the yard) was about 38ft wide along the TIRING HOUSE façade (tapering to perhaps 25ft at the front) and 18ft deep, and that the front half of the yard sloped down to the stage, presumably to improve sightlines for the standing audience. This precious and unique evidence of the physical dimensions of one Elizabethan playhouse has, after a vigorous public campaign, been preserved. The Rose was built and owned by PHILIP HENSLOWE, whose 1592 alterations to the interior can be traced in the foundations. From 1592 to 94, STRANGE'S MEN were the main users, but after 1594 it was the London base of the ADMIRAL'S MEN under the leadership of EDWARD ALLEYN. The plays of MARLOWE belonged to this company and were favoured fare at the Rose. The probability is that the nearby GLOBE stole much of the audience after 1598, and the Admiral's Men moved to the FORTUNE (north of the river) in 1600. For a while the Rose was occupied by Worcester's Men, but when Henslowe's lease ran out in 1603 it was soon demolished. PT

Rosencof, Mauricio 1933– Uruguayan playwright, journalist and short story writer. Rosencof's first play was presented by the theatre group El Galpón in 1960, but it was *Las ranas* (*The Frogs*) in 1961 that brought him public attention for its realistic presentation of the human misery that permeates a working-class neighbourhood. In a brief incursion into children's theatre he also dealt with social themes, and *La valija* (*The Suitcase*, 1964) has been frequently anthologized and translated. His major work is *Los caballos* (*The Horses*, 1967), in which he follows the formal and stylistic REALISM of his earlier plays but experiments with elements of fantasy with considerable success. During the period of military repression in URUGUAY in the 1970s–80s, Rosencof was imprisoned for his writings and activities. GW

Rosenthal, Jean 1912–69 American theatre, architectural and industrial lighting designer who virtually invented the field of lighting design (see STAGE LIGHTING). When she began working with ORSON WELLES and JOHN HOUSEMAN in the FEDERAL THEATRE PROJECT there were no lighting designers; the job was done by the set designer or electrician. In 1938 she began working for Martha Graham as lighting and production supervisor (and continued until her death). Aware of the dependence of dance on light, Rosenthal was able to develop the new art of lighting design. A common element in all her designs is an evocative sense of mood. Critics and directors commented on her apparent ability to work magic with her effects. Her hundreds of theatre designs include *West Side Story* and *The Sound of Music*. She also designed the architectural lighting for theatres and projects ranging from airline terminals to hotels. Her ideas and techniques are presented in her book *The Magic of Light* (1972, with Lael Wertenbaker). AA

Roshchin, Mikhail 1933– A member of the postwar generation of Soviet-Russian playwrights which includes RADZINSKY and VAMPILOV, and a practitioner of the 1960s 'new lyricism' applied to personal romantic themes by ROZOV, VOLODIN and ARBUZOV. Roshchin lived a peripatetic early life as a result of dislocation caused by the war, the need to support his family at age 16 following his father's death, and his job as an editor of the journals the *Banner* and *New World* during the 1950s and 60s. He published his first book at age 23 and his first play, *The Seven Feats of Heracles* on the cleaning of the Aegean Stables, seven years later. In 1968 he wrote both the very popular *A Rainbow in Winter* and the more problematic *The Old New Year*. The latter, the first Soviet SATIRE for some time, was produced at the MOSCOW ART THEATRE in 1973, largely owing to the success of Roshchin's 1971 youth play, *Valentin and Valentina*, performed in some 60 Soviet theatres and in America at San Francisco's AMERICAN CONSERVATORY THEATRE (1977), where it failed.

In this Soviet *Romeo and Juliet*, which utilizes 1950s and 60s theatricalist devices, the young lovers are not so much star-crossed as impeded by abandoned mothers and a divorced older sister (representing different social classes) who discourage young marriage. Other features are crowded living conditions which permit no privacy – the spatial logistics of three generations of a family living together reinforcing the theme of generational conflict; a society which has overlooked personal problems in favour of social ideology and productivity; youth's own confusion over the possibility and proper place of romantic love in contemporary life; and the lack of paternal guidance, many fathers having been lost in the Second World War. *Troop Train* (1975), Roshchin's emotional commemoration of the 30th anniversary of the Second World War and of his mother's personal experience aboard a crowded troop train, is noteworthy for its cast of almost entirely female types, its creation of environment via a box-car setting and stage effects and its deeply felt tone. It was successfully staged by ANATOLY EFROS at the Moscow Art Theatre and at the Sovremennik by Galina Volchyok, who was taken to Houston's ALLEY THEATRE in 1978 to replicate her Moscow production.

Other plays by Roshchin include *Husband and Wife*, a *Valentin and Valentina* update on the problems of young marrieds; *The Galoshes of Happiness*, a censored adaptation of Hans Christian Andersen's tale of a man who encounters unhappiness and similar problems in the past, present and future; *Mother of Pearl Zinaida*, a satirical COMEDY about a writer named Aladdin; *Hurry to Do Good*, and an adaptation of TOLSTOI's *Anna Karenina*. SG

Rossi, Cesare 1829–98 Italian actor and company manager. A solid player of the middle rank, in the 1850s and 60s Rossi rose slowly through the profession, acting with many leading companies including those of ERNESTO ROSSI and LUIGI BELLOTTI-BON until in the mid-1870s he formed his own company, attempting to establish it on a semi-permanent basis in Turin. Perhaps his most sustained and distinguished period as a company manager was that between 1881 and 1884, when his troupe included the young ELEONORA DUSE and her leading man Flavio Andò. In association with Duse, Rossi made a tour of Latin America in 1885–6. Although never himself an outstanding player, he was sound in second-rank roles, a model of careful study and an excellent manager. Many younger players, like Duse and ZACCONI, learned much from their work with him. KR

Rossi, Ernesto 1827–96 Italian actor-manager, who began his career in companies run by the leading players of the period, GUSTAVO MODENA and ADELAIDE RISTORI. It was with Ristori that he made his first appearances outside Italy, when she played in Paris in 1855. From the 1860s to the end of his career Rossi acted mainly with his own companies in a large repertoire that included the major Italian stock pieces of the century. SHAKESPEARE figured prominently in his list of lead roles, which included Othello and Hamlet – of which he gave the first textually significant performances in Italy in 1856. His other Shakespearian roles included Macbeth, King Lear, Richard III, Shylock, Romeo and Coriolanus. He translated and adapted *Julius Caesar* for his own stage interpretation, and had some knowledge of English stage versions of the other Shakespeare plays he staged.

In the manner of 19th-century 'star' actors Rossi spent much time performing abroad, travelling to North and South America and throughout Europe. In 1876 he took several of his Shakespeare productions (including *Hamlet*, *King Lear* and *Macbeth*) to London, where he was in the main well received, particularly as Romeo. But he never enjoyed the same success as his contemporary SALVINI, and a return visit in 1882, when he performed King Lear in Italian with English players acting the rest of the play in English, was a disaster. This experiment he had attempted the previous year in New York, during the last of his visits to the USA, with no greater success. When he first toured there in 1865, Henry James noted his reliance on tricks and technique, and while acknowledging his great histrionic skill thought him, and perhaps with justice, not an actor

of the first rank.

His contribution in the area of direction (or, more properly, stage-management), and in acclimatizing Shakespeare to the Italian stage, is rather underrated, in part perhaps because he himself makes too much of the last in his informative, if somewhat pompous, memoirs. Of solid, rather stocky appearance and of limited vocal range, he had a lively, demonstrative mode of playing that well suited him to romantic roles, and a fondness for interpolating engaging, if often extraneous, stage business. Sensibly, he was not reluctant to adapt Shakespeare to the tastes of his Italian audiences: a practice that won him contemporary success in the theatre, and the lasting suspicion of academe. KR

Rostand, Edmond 1868–1918 French dramatist. At a time when NATURALISM was the dominant orthodoxy, Rostand's plays seem to look back to the romantic period in spirit. At the same time, a part of their appeal lay in their explicit or implicit patriotic sentiment, most noticeable in *Cyrano de Bergerac* (1897) and *L'Aiglon* (1900). A one-act play, *Les Deux Pierrots*, was turned down in 1891 by the COMÉDIE-FRANÇAISE, but the same theatre accepted his charming comedy *The Fantasticks* (*Les Romanesques*, 1894), which had many of the qualities of the comedies of ALFRED DE MUSSET, notably a light and witty dialogue. *La Princesse lointaine* (*The Distant Princess*, 1895) provided a role for SARAH BERNHARDT, as Mélissinde, the princess of its poet hero's idealized dream. Sarah again played the lead role in *La Samaritaine* (*The Woman of Samaria*, 1897), a biblical piece based on the meeting of Christ and the Woman of Samaria. *Cyrano de Bergerac*, created by COQUELIN at the Porte-Saint-Martin (see BOULEVARD), was his most popular play, combining nostalgia for the *grand siècle* (scenes include a reconstruction of the 17th-century HÔTEL DE BOURGOGNE theatre in Paris) with swashbuckling heroism and panache and a strongly romantic theme of a love which can never express itself to its object. Audiences loved its swordsman-poet hero and were carried along by the strongly lyrical quality of Rostand's verse. *L'Aiglon*, a play about the Duke of Reichstadt, son of Napoleon, was less strong, but depended even more heavily upon stirring up patriotic fervour, and offered another major role to Bernhardt as the sickly prince.

Rostand's career was cut short by ill health, but he did write one other major play, *Chantecler* (1910), with Lucien Guitry in the role of the cock. It was based on the *Roman de Renart* and the actors wore cumbersome costumes as farmyard animals. Like VICTOR HUGO, Rostand was often more poet than dramatist, but his romanticism was always tinged with a streak of clear-sighted realism, whether in the character of Cyrano or in the satirical comment on contemporary politics and literature contained in *Chantecler*. JMCC

Rostovsky, St Dmitry [Danylo (Savych) Tuptalo; Dmitry of Rostov] 1651–1709 Ukrainian ecclesiastic poet and dramatist, appointed metropolitan of Rostov by Peter the Great although he neither supported (like FEOFAN PROKOPOVICH) nor opposed his reforms. His popular school dramas, based on medieval MYSTERY and MORALITY PLAYS, mixed biblical and allegorical characters with low comic types and demonstrated his gift for poetic and dramatic language. These include *Nativity Play* (produced 1702, Rostov), *The Dormition Play*, *Esther and Ahasuerus*, *The Resurrection of Christ* and *A Sinner's Repentance*. The last, performed at court by FYODOR VOLKOV's company (1752), featured the future famous actor IVAN DMITREVSKY, and established Volkov's Yaroslavl troupe in St Petersburg – an important step in the development of the formal Russian theatre. Tuptalo was canonized in 1757. SG

Rote Sprachrohr, Das 'The Red Megaphone', the first and most important AGIT-PROP troupe in Weimar Germany, was founded in 1927 by M. Vallentin, using members of communist youth groups. It performed choral works, didactic plays and REVUES at workers' gatherings. *Hallo, Kollege Jungarbeiter* (*Hello, Young Colleagues*, 1928) depicted workers struggling against exploitation in episodic scenes, and a choral piece *Dritte Internationale* (*Third International*, 1929), with songs by Hanns Eisler, toured the USSR. After 1930, the group moved towards EPIC THEATRE techniques with *Song of the Red United Front* and *General Strike* (both 1931). Several brigades continued to perform for a few weeks after the Nazi seizure of power, but their members either were arrested or emigrated. LS

Rotimi, Ola 1936– Nigerian playwright and theatre director. Born in Sapele in the Niger delta, in what is now Bendel state, Rotimi went to Boston and Yale Universities in the USA. He returned to Nigeria to a research fellowship at Ife University, where he founded the Ori Olokun Acting Company (later the Ori Olokun Players). The popularity of this theatre in the late 1960s and early 70s was the result not only of the talents of Rotimi as writer and director, but also of the considerable musical talents of the composer Akin Euba. Rotimi began writing plays in America. *Our Husband Has Gone Mad Again* was premiered at Yale, directed by Jack Landau, in 1966 (although it was published only in 1977, after Rotimi had made his theatrical reputation in Nigeria). A comedy, set in a Nigeria in the throes of a general election, it concerns a retired Nigerian army major who has made money in cocoa farming and is now determined to get himself and his party elected to power – so that he can make more money.

The comedy arises mainly out of the major's marital condition: he has two Nigerian wives about whom he has failed to tell his 'abroad' wife. She unexpectedly flies in to Lagos as the election is in progress. The play has an earthy wit, often appropriately communicated through pidgin phrases. This work is especially interesting in the light of Rotimi's play *If*, which was first performed in Port Harcourt, Nigeria, in 1979 (published in 1983). In *If* the action takes place in the middle of a general election but, unlike *Our Husband* of 13 years before, *If* has a serious political intent and is wholly concerned with a group of ordinary working-class Nigerians. The electoral candidate, who is also their oppressive landlord, is depicted as an evil figure (seen only at the beginning and end of the play) against whom good people struggle and fail. The racy dialogue, as in *Our Husband*, reflects the linguistic texture of Nigeria.

However, the difference in tone between the two plays

A libation scene in Rotimi's *Kurunmi*, 1973.

could not be more striking. The transition is perhaps an indication of Rotimi's disillusionment with the political processes in Nigeria and the increasing politicization of his dramatic art. The play also contains a number of elements characteristic of his craft as a playwright: a strong theatricality combined with touches of MELODRAMA (such as the death of the little boy from asthma, and the use of music to heighten emotion), which builds to a tragic and moving climax.

One of Rotimi's best-known plays is *The Gods Are Not to Blame*, a Nigerian version of SOPHOCLES' *Oedipus the King*. It was the first production of the Ori Olokun Acting Company in 1968, and published in 1971. Rotimi has hinted that the play is an allegory of the Nigerian civil war: the ethnic pride of Nigerians, and not fate or 'the gods', was responsible for the slide into war in 1966. Its first performance during the civil war might well have been read in this way; its later success comes from its appealing theatricality.

Rotimi then turned to creating Nigerian history on stage, and from a Nigerian perspective. *Kurunmi* (premiered by Ori Olokun in 1969; published in 1971) depicts an aspect of the internecine wars amongst the Yorubas in the mid-19th century, and creates an Aristotelian (see ARISTOTLE) tragic hero out of the Yoruba commander Kurunmi. This was followed in 1971 by *Ovonramwen Nogbaisi*, enacting the sack of Benin by the British in 1897 and the exile of the eponymous Oba. Again, the playwright's vision is tragic, though historically the central figure, the Oba, is less susceptible to this heroic treatment.

Rotimi moved from Ife to Port Harcourt, to become head

of drama at the university there; and he formed a new company of players to stage his work. Here *If* was premiered, preceded by *Holding Talks: An Absurdist Drama* (published in 1979), which was popularly received. *Hopes of the Living Dead*, produced in Ibadan in 1985, is based on the life of Ikoli Harcourt-Whyte, who was a leper from the age of 19: 'Leprosy ... is a grand metaphor for a social, political and psychological disease which, though daunting and stigmatising, can be tackled,' the critic Osundare has noted. One of the most striking features of Rotimi's drama has been his development of a 'trans-Nigerian idiom' through the use of indigenous theatre means such as music, specific musical instruments, gesture, dance, chant. In *Hopes of the Living Dead* this takes on a new dimension, as he saturates the play with dialogue in a dozen Nigerian languages. As the lepers strive to communicate with each other, to achieve effective solidarity, Rotimi creates a powerful image for group commitment.

In 1991 he left the University of Port Harcourt to found, the following year, a professional theatre company, African Theatre Cradle, based in Ife. The group gave performances of a number of his plays in prestige venues in Lagos. ATC folded in 1993 through lack of funds.   CD

Rotrou, Jean de 1609–50 French dramatist, contemporary of PIERRE CORNEILLE and his only serious rival in stature. His first play was produced at the HÔTEL DE BOURGOGNE when he was only 19, and he seems to have become the theatre's resident playwright in succession to HARDY: certainly many of his plays were in its repertoire in the early 1630s and their staging requirements were noted by MAHELOT in his *Mémoire*. Rotrou's total output may have been well in excess of the 35 plays that survive, of which the majority are good examples of the freewheeling TRAGICOMEDY then popular, compounded of multiple incident and an almost total disregard for the three unities. One of them, *La Bague de l'oubli* (*The Ring of Forgetfulness*, 1629), which is a translation from LOPE DE VEGA, reflects an interest in Spanish literature which he shared with Corneille. He also wrote a number of comedies, the best of which is a version of the Amphitryon story entitled *Les Sosies* (*The Doubles*, 1636), and several tragedies, amongst them *Hercule Mourant* (*Hercules Dying*, 1634), which along with the work of MAIRET and Corneille helped to introduce a more regular neoclassical form of tragedy.

Rotrou was sufficiently esteemed by RICHELIEU to become one of the group of five dramatists who wrote plays under the Cardinal's aegis, though his most mature work was produced in the last decade of his life after he had returned to take up a post in his native Dreux. It included the tragicomedy *Venceslas* (1647), the regular tragedy *Cosroès* (1648) – both of which continued to be performed for many years, the former until the 19th century – and his most imaginative tragedy *Le Véritable Saint Genest* (1645), also derived from Lope de Vega, which depicts the conversion of the Roman actor Genesius while playing the part of a Christian martyr and his own condemnation to martyrdom in consequence.   DR

Rousseau, Jean-Jacques 1712–78 Philosopher and man of letters of Swiss birth and French culture. Although the author of several OPERATIC works, notably *Le Devin du village* (*The Village Soothsayer*, 1753) and *Pygmalion* (1770), and a comedy *Narcisse* (1752), presented at the COMÉDIE-FRANÇAISE, Rousseau condemned the theatre in his philosophical writings, seeing it as a baleful social influence. In his *Lettre à d'Alembert* (1758) challenging the proposal to establish a playhouse in Geneva, he widens the argument into a general indictment of the theatre, whose aim is solely to please, not to instruct, and far from stimulating moral sentiments exploits them in the service of mere diversion. Both TRAGEDY and COMEDY are equally guilty of interesting us in characters who, in their excessive heroism, villainy or foolishness, are disproportionate to our own experience; both give an undue prominence to love and often present vice in an attractive or sympathetic light, thus exciting our sensibilities unhealthily. Moreover, theatregoing itself encourages a taste for extravagance and indolence, while the very company of actors, whose art depends on dissembling and flouts natural modesty, is suspect. In essence his ideological position is the direct antithesis to that of DIDEROT.   DR

Roux, Jean-Louis 1923– French Canadian director, playwright and actor. Roux studied theatre in Paris, 1947–50, and on his return helped found Montreal's enduring THÉÂTRE DU NOUVEAU MONDE (1951), becoming its artistic director, 1966–82, and guiding it towards a modern, diversified repertoire. Director of the École Nationale du Théâtre, 1981–7, he has been awarded many national honours. His brilliant career as an actor has included major stage, radio and television plays. Roux has also adapted many works for Quebec audiences, notably SHAKESPEARE's *Julius Caesar* (1971), and is the author of *Rose Latulippe* (1951), dealing with a popular Canadian legend, and *Les Bois-brûlés* (*Halfbreeds*, 1967), a historical drama dealing with the armed revolt of French-speaking Métis under Louis Riel against federal authority in 1885.   LED

Rovina, Hanna 1889–1980 Russian-born first lady of the Hebrew stage. Together with NAHUM ZEMACH and Menahem Gnessin she founded the original HABIMAH Studio, emigrated with it to Palestine in 1931 and remained an active member of the Habimah Theatre all her life. Her dedication to her art and to the collective was absolute: 'My family is Habimah.' The role that brought her international fame was that of Leah, the possessed bride in ANSKI's *The Dybbuk*. She played memorable mother roles in *The Eternal Jew* by DAVID PINSKI (1923), *The Mother* by KAREL ČAPEK (1939), *Mirele Efros* by JACOB GORDIN (1939), *In the Wastes of the Negev* by Yigal Mossinson (1949) and *Hanna Szenes* by Aaron Megged (1958). Among her great roles were also EURIPIDES' Medea (1955) and the Old Lady in DÜRRENMATT's *The Visit* (1959). (See also HEBREW THEATRE.)   HAS

Rovinski, Samuel 1932– Costa Rican playwright, whose motivation derives from a sense of justice and the need to raise the consciousness of those responsible for intolerable situations. His plays focus on social and political issues, for the most part, and include *Gobierno de alcoba* (*Bedroom Government*, 1971); *Las fisgonas de Paso*

Hanna Rovina in the original Habimah production of
The Dybbuk, 1922.

Ancho (*The Busybodies of Paso Ancho*, 1971), a caricature of a wide variety of social ills; *Un modelo para Rosaura* (*A Model for Rosaura*, 1974); and *El martirio del pastor* (*Pastoral Martyrdom*, 1984), which dealt with the assassination in El Salvador of Monsignor Romero. GW

Rovner, Eduardo 1942– Argentine playwright, and director of the General San Martín Municipal Theatre in Buenos Aires. Rovner is the author of a dozen or so plays, beginning with a realistic style in *Una pareja* (*A Couple*, 1976) and *Último premio* (*Last prize*, 1981). Within the so-called 'satiric absurd' (see THEATRE OF THE ABSURD) are *¿Una foto...?* (*A Photo...?*, 1977) and *Cuarteto* (*Quartet*, 1991). Plays that function as comic FARCES include *Compañía* (*Company*, 1989) and *Volvió una noche* (*She Returned One Night*, 1990). GW

Rowe, Nicholas 1674–1718 English playwright and actor. He gave up law on inheriting the family estate in 1692 and began writing plays. His first play, *The Ambitious Stepmother* (1700), established his serious neoclassical style, larded with political allegory in *Tamerlane* (1701) which celebrated William III. He adapted MASSINGER's *The Fatal Dowry* as *The Fair Penitent* (1703) and began to write in a style much influenced by the 'she-tragedies' of BANKS, centring the drama on the plight of a virtuous woman and aiming at pathos and tears. His best play in this form, *The Tragedy of Jane Shore* (1714), was explicitly written 'in imitation of SHAKESPEARE's style' and combines *Richard III*

with a more Restoration style of political and pathetic tragedy. His drama of pity and moral warning was markedly unsentimental. In 1709 Rowe published his edition of Shakespeare in six volumes. The first serious attempt to edit Shakespeare since the First Folio (1623), the edition attempted to remove textual corruption and add scene and stage directions, as well as regularizing act and scene divisions and act numberings according to Rowe's belief in neoclassical five-act form. For all its indications of the gulf between Rowe and Shakespeare, it is significant for inaugurating the work of editing Shakespeare afresh. PH

Rowley, Samuel c.1575–1624 English actor and playwright, who was a leading member of the ADMIRAL's MEN from at least 1597 to 1613. As an 'attached playwright' to his company, Rowley probably agreed not to publish his work. The only known survival, *When You See Me, You Know Me* (1603), is a rambling chronicle play about Henry VIII. His name is associated with the lost *The Taming of a Shrew* (c.1589), which SHAKESPEARE knew, and HENSLOWE records a payment to him in 1602 for 'additions' to MARLOWE's *Doctor Faustus*. PT

Rowley, William c.1585–1626 English actor and playwright, who was a leading member of Prince Charles's Men and, on occasions, of the King's Men from 1610 to 25. To judge from the parts he is known to have played – Plumporridge in MIDDLETON's *Masque of Heroes* (1619), the Fat Clown in his own muddled tragedy, *All's Lost by Lust* (c.1620), the Fat Bishop in Middleton's *A Game at Chess* (1624) – Rowley made comic capital out of his size. He was a force in the Jacobean theatre, not only as actor and writer, but also as a company manager after the fashion of JOHN HEMINGES with the King's Men. Best remembered as a playwright for his collaboration with Middleton on *The Changeling* (1622), Rowley worked with Middleton on several other plays and was much influenced by him in his own citizen comedies (see CITIZEN COMEDY), *A New Wonder: A Woman Never Vexed* (published 1632) and *A Match at Midnight* (published 1633). He collaborated with DEKKER and FORD on *The Witch of Edmonton* (1621) and with FLETCHER on *The Maid in the Mill* (1623). PT

Royal Court Theatre (London) The present theatre, extensively renovated after bomb damage in 1940, opened in 1888 to replace a Chelsea theatre demolished for road-widening. After an undistinguished decade, it staged a major hit in PINERO's *Trelawny of the 'Wells'* (1898), and made its most distinctive early contribution to the advance of the English theatre under the joint management of J. E. VEDRENNE and HARLEY GRANVILLE BARKER (1904–7). It was these seasons that established SHAW as a major force and introduced the English public to recent work by the Continental avant-garde. Its location, away from London's theatreland, and its modest capacity (642 when first opened) made management of the Royal Court a financial hazard and, after challenging post-1918 seasons under J. B. FAGAN, BARRY JACKSON and, for three Shaw-filled years, the Madonna Players, it was converted into a cinema in 1932. It was not in regular use as a theatre again until 1952.

A second great period in the history of the Royal Court

began in 1956, when the English Stage Company appointed GEORGE DEVINE as its artistic director. His commitment to the staging of new, and if necessary controversial, plays was triumphantly vindicated by the success of *Look Back in Anger* (1956), which introduced JOHN OSBORNE to a startled public and involved the previously disengaged drama in the abrasive cultural spirit of the times. That the Royal Court was much more than a home for 'angry young men' was amply illustrated by a repertoire that stretched from BRECHT to IONESCO by way of WESKER, N. F. SIMPSON and JOHN ARDEN. Devine died soon after the renovations of 1964 had been completed, but the Royal Court maintained its leadership of the 'new' drama under his successor, WILLIAM GASKILL (1965–72). Under Gaskill, in regular association with LINDSAY ANDERSON, the theatre gave prominence to plays by DAVID STOREY and EDWARD BOND as well as reviving the neglected work of D. H. LAWRENCE, and it has maintained its challenging lead under Oscar Lewenstein (1972–7), Stuart Burge (1977–9) and Max Stafford-Clark.

The additional provision of the Small Theatre Upstairs in 1969 has enabled the staging of low-budget new plays, sustaining the hopes for London performance of many young playwrights. Still no stranger to controversy, the Royal Court notably raised hackles in 1987, first by determining to stage Jim Allen's *Perdition*, a play proposing the historical complicity of certain Zionist Hungarian Jews in the Holocaust, and then by withdrawing it at the eleventh hour. PT

Royal Exchange Theatre (Manchester) One of the premier REGIONAL THEATRES in Britain. The building itself is a remarkable piece of theatre design: a theatre-in-the-round built of steel tubing and glass, suspended within the vast hall of Manchester's old Royal Exchange – a unique combination of new and old. The company began life as the 69 Theatre Company, based in the Manchester University Theatre (1968–73), and eventually, with a change of name, transferred to the new theatre when it opened in 1976. High-quality productions especially of the classics and modern classics, often with star names in the cast, have been the hallmark of the policy, notable productions including *The Rivals* (1976), *The Duchess of Malfi* (1980), *The Dresser* (1980) and *The Three Sisters* (1985). There has never, apart from one season, been a resident acting company, but continuity is provided by the multiple artistic directorship which has included MICHAEL ELLIOT, Braham Murray, James Maxwell and Gregory Hersov. A recent innovation has been the Mobil/Royal Exchange International Playwriting Competition, with winning entries (such as Ian Heggie's *A Wholly Healthy Glasgow*) guaranteed a first production at the Exchange. AJ

Royal Shakespeare Company (RSC) The first Shakespeare Memorial Theatre at Stratford-upon-Avon, England, was opened in 1879 and destroyed by fire in 1926. The present building, designed by Elizabeth Scott, opened in 1932. It was renamed the Royal Shakespeare Theatre in 1961. The present theatre incorporates the surviving elements of the first theatre; it has a 29-ft proscenium stage and can accommodate 1500 spectators. The transformation of what had been a seasonal festival theatre at

Stratford-upon-Avon, the Shakespeare Memorial Theatre, into the home for Britain's first *de facto* national theatre company can be largely credited to the determination of two men, Fordham Flower and PETER HALL. Fordham Flower was a member of the family of Stratford brewers who had been the chief patrons of the theatre from the beginning. His great-uncle, Charles Flower, had raised the money and launched the theatre in 1879, and appointed F. R. BENSON as the first director of its festival seasons. Fordham Flower followed his father, Archibald, and his grandfather, Edgar, as chairman of the board, a post which he held from 1944 until his death in 1966.

Fordham Flower led the theatre through the difficult postwar years to its comparative prosperity and expansion during the 1950s. In 1946, he appointed BARRY JACKSON as director, in an attempt to graft new ideas on to what had previously been regarded as an unadventurous tradition, and Jackson had responded by introducing such young directors and actors as PETER BROOK and PAUL SCOFIELD. When Jackson retired in 1948, he turned to ANTHONY QUAYLE, the actor-director, who brought in stars from London, such as the Oliviers. Quayle exploited the relative decline in the fortunes of the OLD VIC; and such spectacular successes as Peter Brook's *Titus Andronicus*, with LAURENCE OLIVIER as Titus, in 1955 established the Stratford theatre as a Mecca for Shakespearian production. When Quayle resigned in 1957, to be succeeded briefly by Glen Byam Shaw who had joined him in the leadership of the company in 1953, the Shakespeare Memorial Company was comparatively wealthy, with many gifts and assets at Stratford (apart from the theatre) and with a useful surplus in the bank.

In 1958, while the company was on tour in Leningrad, Fordham Flower discussed the company's future with Peter Hall, then 28 years old, who had successfully directed *Love's Labour's Lost* (1956), *Cymbeline* (1957) and *Twelfth Night* (1958) at Stratford. They shared the same vision of a theatre modelled along the lines of the major European repertory companies, with resources and a permanence previously unknown in Britain. Hall was appointed to succeed Shaw as director in 1960, but even before he took over some of his radical proposals were being widely discussed. These included establishing a large semi-permanent company, with actors on two- or three-year contracts, who would be encouraged to stay with what was then a provincial company by the prospect of also playing in a second theatre, in London, the Aldwych Theatre eventually being chosen. The Stratford programmes would concentrate on the work of SHAKESPEARE and his contemporaries, while those at the Aldwych would include modern plays from Britain and abroad, together with transfers from Stratford. Not least among the assumptions was that the days of private patronage were over and that the new company should actively pursue state support at a level appropriate to its planned national status. To that end, the old pious but somewhat funereal title was dropped and replaced in 1961 by the Royal Shakespeare Company, and the royal charter of 1925 was amended to this effect.

This dramatic transformation was praised but also criticized, by Brook among others, for putting expansion of the company before the raising of its standards – and by some members of the board for gambling away the company's hard-won resources. The company's trading position revealed that following the start of the RSC's residency at the Aldwych Theatre in 1960 a small surplus in 1959–60 had become a deficit in 1960–1, and, despite the first annual subsidy from the ARTS COUNCIL in 1963, the deficits and the grants continued to grow in future years. By the time of Hall's departure, the deficit had risen to £161,126 despite an increase in its grant-funding to £226,500 (1968/9); but the audiences had trebled, and in addition to running its two theatres the RSC ran experimental seasons at smaller theatres, such as the influential Arts Theatre season in 1962 and the Theatre of Cruelty collage at LAMDA (the London Academy of Music and Dramatic Art) in 1964. The company's reputation had soared, led by such Peter Brook productions as PETER WEISS's *The Marat/Sade* (1964) and *US* (1966) and by the Hall–JOHN BARTON adaptation of Shakespeare's early HISTORY PLAYS, *The Wars of the Roses* (1963). A rivalry developed between the RSC, regarded as a 'directors' theatre', and the newly formed NATIONAL THEATRE under Laurence Olivier, an 'actors' theatre' with higher subsidies.

Like the National Theatre, the RSC sought a new London theatre as its metropolitan home, which eventually opened in 1982 as part of the Barbican Arts Centre. Hall, frustrated by the delays and dispirited by the death of Fordham Flower whom he regarded as 'a second father', handed over the RSC's directorship in 1968 to TREVOR NUNN, who was as young as Hall had been when originally appointed. In 1978, TERRY HANDS became with Nunn joint artistic director, a post made necessary by the continuing expansion of the company. Notable among Nunn's achievements was the establishment of two studio theatres in London and Stratford, where vigorous programmes of new and experimental productions could be pursued. In London, the studios were at The Place, then at the Donmar Warehouse and then, after the move into the Barbican, the Pit; while at Stratford, a converted store and rehearsal room became known as The Other Place (1974).

Despite the record of new plays by EDWARD BOND, HOWARD BARKER and DUSTY HUGHES, among other contemporary writers, the studio productions of *Hamlet* (1975) and *Macbeth* (1976) were particularly memorable and reflected a growing dissatisfaction with over-decorated versions of Shakespeare. In 1977 the RSC opened a six-week season at Newcastle upon Tyne, part of its growing regional responsibilities which also included small-scale touring productions. The RSC also became internationally known for the bold scale of its ventures, such as the cycle of Roman plays directed by Trevor Nunn in 1972, the *Henry VI* trilogy directed by Terry Hands in 1977 and the collective efforts at historical reconstruction reflected in *Nicholas Nickleby* (1982) and *Les Misérables* (1985).

In 1986 an anonymous benefaction made possible the opening of a third theatre in Stratford, the Swan – an open-stage playhouse in the shell of the auditorium of the old Memorial Theatre. Formally opened before Queen Elizabeth II with HEYWOOD's *The Fair Maid of the West*, directed by Trevor Nunn, the Swan is dedicated to exploring the work of Shakespeare's contemporaries.

Late in 1986 Trevor Nunn stepped back from the leadership of the RSC and his co-director, Terry Hands, took over.

The RSC found itself in an awkward dilemma. Its 'empire', with five theatres in its control and some major MUSICALS in the WEST END, greatly outstripped its resources from grant-funding; but it could not operate on a commercial basis and the margins for financial error became slim. Some doubtful musicals, including *A Clockwork Orange* (1990) and a revival of JEROME KERN's *Showboat* (1990), led to the questioning of their artistic standards, while their financial plight led to the closing of the Barbican Theatre for four months in 1990. Hands resigned and ADRIAN NOBLE became director, whose initial impact was to pull the RSC back from its more speculative schemes and to return to star-studded classic repertoire, such as *Henry IV, Parts 1 and 2*, (1991, with ROBERT STEPHENS as Falstaff), *The Theban* (1991) and *Hamlet* (1992, with KENNETH BRANAGH).
JE MB SS

Royce, Edward (William) 1841–1926 British actor and dancer, who was the least obtrusive of the famous GAIETY Quartette (NELLIE FARREN, KATE VAUGHAN and EDWARD TERRY were the others) from 1876 to 83. He had been trained, and made his London debut, in ballet, but it was as what was known as a 'character dancer' that he achieved his brief fame. After a breakdown in health, Royce returned to the theatre and remained active as a choreographer as well as an actor long after the rest of the Quartette was dead.   PT

Rozenberg, Lev see BAKST, LÉON

Rozenmacher, Germán 1936–71 Argentine playwright, who dealt with Jewish values and traditions in such plays as *Réquiem para un viernes a la noche* (*Requiem for a Friday Night*, 1964). He collaborated with COSSA, SOMIGLIANA and TALESNIK in the creation of *El avión negro* (*The Black Airplane*, 1970), a play that in various scenes anticipated Perón's return to Argentina.   GW

Różewicz, Tadeusz 1921–90 Experimental Polish playwright, poet and prose writer. Judging both traditional and avant-garde drama as obsolete, Różewicz considered himself a poetic realist who created plays out of fragments of daily life, newspapers and conversational clichés, as collages from the refuse heap of modern civilization. Practising open dramaturgy in which director and actors were invited to collaborate, he mixed genres and created extensive stage directions that are arguments with the theatre. Major plays are *The Card File* (1960), fragmentary biography of a disaffected Everyman; *The Old Woman Broods* (1968), post-apocalyptic journey through the detritus sustaining humankind; *White Marriage* (1974), multi-layered pastiche of *fin-de-siècle* sexual repression and feminine revolt; *Dead and Buried* (1979), torment of a brutish young peasant tried and executed for rape by his Second World War partisan unit; and the *The Trap* (1982), about Kafka's erotic relations and family life, prefiguring the Holocaust.   DG

Rozov, Viktor (Sergeevich) 1913– Extremely popular and prolific Soviet social dramatist who, despite a penchant for conventional and sentimental plotting, is important as part of the movement beginning in the late

1950s to demythologize and rehumanize the Soviet theatre by focusing on real, often anti-heroic, contemporary personalities and their problems. A student at MEYERHOLD's school affiliated with the Moscow Theatre of the Revolution (1934–8), Rozov acted and directed at the Front until he was wounded. His first play, *Her Friends* (1949), written in the year he entered Moscow's Gorky Literary Institute, initiated a long association between the author, the Central Children's Theatre and the director ANATOLY EFROS.

The majority of Rozov's plays deal with the painful necessity of taking stock of one's life, making legitimate compromises and divesting oneself of unrealizable dreams, while maintaining personal integrity, moral strength and a belief in the power of love. His characters' successes are measured on the basis of personal fulfilment rather than in terms of professional advancement or ideological correctness, which means that some of society's ostensible losers are actually winners in his plays. Rozov often focuses upon a single family or an organized social device – a wedding, a reunion – to provide a theatrical microcosm of the world at large. Some of his many plays which conform to these themes and models are *Good Luck!* (1954), *On the Wedding Day* (1964), *The Reunion* (1967) and *From Night to Noon* (1969). *Alive Forever* (1956), a revised version of his 1943 play *The Serebrisky Family*, treats the small-scale human dramas which occur around the edges of war and extols the sensitive and committed individual and the sustaining force of Russianness without embracing ideological positions. This was the opening production, and remains the signature piece, of Moscow's Sovremennik Theatre (1957); it was made into the popular and critically acclaimed film *The Cranes are Flying*.

His 1979 family drama, *The Nest of the Woodgrouse (Meet My Model Family)*, is a generational-conflict play which confronts the problems of careerism and moral decay among top-level bureaucrats, and the collision of material, social and spiritual values, precipitating a sense of longing and renewed religious consciousness, especially among the young. Originally denied permission to be produced in Moscow, it was eventually staged at the Moscow Theatre of Satire (1981) and later at the NEW YORK SHAKESPEARE FESTIVAL's Public Theatre. Rozov continued this somewhat tougher trend in his playwriting with *The Back of Beyond* (1983), based on an actual incident, in which the corrupt officials of a small town not far from Moscow out of self-interest covered up a father's murder of his son. SG

Rozovsky, Mark (Grigorevich) 1937– Russian director, dramatist and teacher. A graduate of Sergei Yutkevich's Student Theatre at Moscow State University, where he founded the theatre studio Our House (1958–69). There he helped launch the playwriting career of Viktor Slavkin (*Cerceau*, *The Grown-up Daughter of a Young Man*), as well as the studio theatre movement of the 1960s–90s. In 1983 he established the Nikita Gates Theatre Studio, which blends theatrical amateurs and professionals, conducts institutes for foreign students and tours outside of Russia. Rozovsky's play *Strider: The Story of a Horse* (1975), a musical adaptation of a LEV TOLSTOI short story, played in New York at the Chelsea Theater Center (1979)

and on BROADWAY, as well as at London's NATIONAL THEATRE. His other plays include *The Red Corner*, *The Concert by Vysotsky*, *Murderer* (after *Crime and Punishment*), *Kafka*, *Father and Son*, *The Lounge* and the MEYERHOLD tribute *Triumphal Square* (Nikita Gates production, 1992), which includes scenes of the late director's interrogation by the NKVD (the People's Commissariat of Internal Affairs). The most recent of Rozovsky's three books is *Theatre Out of Nothing* (1989). SG

Rudkin, (James) David 1936– British dramatist whose first play, *Afore Night Come* (1960), revealed his instinct for high tragedy and myth. The story concerned an itinerant Irish tramp, murdered by a gang of fruit-pickers on a Midlands farm, but the heightened language evoked ritual slaughter, infertility and the suppression of the imagination (and Ireland) by imperialism. The relationship between Ireland and England is the subject of *Cries from Casement as His Bones Are Brought to Dublin* (1973) and *Ashes* (1974), about a Belfast couple whose infertility is linked to the struggle in Ulster. In *Sons of Light* (1976) Rudkin moves away from a specific political situation towards an allegorical assessment of contemporary man, part-fable, part-science-fiction and partly an attempt to realize on-stage some teachings of the Reichian therapist Dr Robert Ollendorf, to whom the work is dedicated.

Rudkin has written widely for radio and television (see RADIO DRAMA; TELEVISION DRAMA), is an accomplished linguist and a musician whose translation of the libretto to Schoenberg's *Moses and Aaron* was performed in 1965. *The Triumph of Death* (1981) concerned the way in which organized Christianity loses its idealism through its association with temporal powers, mainly capitalistic. He adapted EURIPIDES' *Hippolytus* for the ROYAL SHAKESPEARE COMPANY in 1978, and his more recent plays include *Space Invaders* (1983), *Will's Way* (1984) and *The Saxon Shore* (1986). JE

Rudman, Michael (Edward) 1939– American-born theatre director who moved to Britain to study at Oxford University and was president of OUDS from 1963 to 64. After gaining experience as an associate director at the Nottingham and Newcastle Playhouses (1964–8) and at the ROYAL SHAKESPEARE COMPANY (1968), he became artistic director of the influential TRAVERSE THEATRE Club in Edinburgh from 1970 to 73, where his international outlook and championship of such Scottish dramatists as C. P. TAYLOR and EVELING became a major feature of the annual EDINBURGH FESTIVAL. He moved to a London theatre club of similar size, HAMPSTEAD, in 1973 where he stayed for five years, producing and directing such plays as HANDKE's *Ride across Lake Constance*, Taylor's *The Black and White Minstrels* and Eveling's *Union Jack (and Bonzo)* (both previously seen at the Traverse), FRAYN's *Clouds*, *Alphabetical Order* and *Donkey's Years*, and PAM GEMS's first play, *Dusa, Fish, Stas and Vi*. He joined the NATIONAL THEATRE in 1979, being appointed director in charge of the Lyttelton Theatre, where he directed *Death of a Salesman*, *Measure for Measure* and *The Second Mrs Tanqueray*. Other National Theatre productions include *Watch on the Rhine*, a black *Measure for Measure* and *On the Razzle*, the TOM STOPPARD version of a NESTROY comedy. He left the NT in 1988 and after some less-than-convincing WEST END productions, such as Jeffrey Archer's *Exclusive* (1989), and an unhappy period as the director of the CHICHESTER FESTIVAL THEATRE (1990), he was appointed director of the Crucible Theatre, Sheffield (1992). JE

Rueda, Lope de c.1509–65 Spanish actor-manager and playwright. Born in Seville, he toured with his company throughout Spain, performing in courtyards, squares and palace halls. CERVANTES praised his comic acting, and he achieved commercial success by combining elements of popular Spanish humour with fashionable Italian drama. His works were published posthumously in 1567 by Valencian playwright Juan de Timoneda. Although he also wrote several longer plays he is remembered for his short and witty *pasos*, which continue in the tradition of rustic FARCE. The best of these is the gently ironic *Las aceitunas* (*The Olives*). CL PZ

Rueda, Manuel 1921– Dominican Republic poet, musician, playwright, fiction writer and critic. Born in Monte Cristi, Rueda is considered one of the most important writers of his country. His play *La trinitaria blanca* (*The White Flower*) won the National Prize in 1957, and was anthologized in 1968 along with *Vacaciones en el cielo* (*Vacations in Heaven*), *La tía Beatriz hace un milagro* (*Aunt Beatriz Works a Miracle*) and *Entre alambradas* (*Inside Fences*), the latter a work dealing with the US occupation of the Dominican Republic in 1965. Rueda's theatre is characterized by his balance in form, poetic language, humour and dramatic action. *El rey Clinejas* (*King Clinejas*) won the National Prize for Theatre in 1979, and as an example of popular theatre has enjoyed good public reaction for its poetry and fantasy. GW

Ruggeri, Ruggero 1871–1953 Italian actor. Ruggeri first appeared on the stage in 1888 and had a long professional career working with many of the major players of his day including NOVELLI, TALLI and Grammatica. A forceful actor with a striking presence, he is best-remembered for his acting in the plays of PIRANDELLO, playing lead roles in, among others, *Il giuoco delle parti* (*The Rules of the Game*, 1918), and *Sei personaggi in cerca d'autore* (*Six Characters in Search of an Author*, 1921) *Enrico IV* (1922). A member of the company that Pirandello took to Paris in 1925, he acted there with spectacular success the lead role in *Enrico IV*. LR

Ruiz de Alarcón (y Mendoza), Juan 1580–1639 Spanish dramatist born in Mexico, who trained as a lawyer and settled in Madrid. After TIRSO DE MOLINA, he is considered to be the most important playwright in the cycle of LOPE DE VEGA. His relatively limited number of plays are highly structured and polished and stand out from those of his contemporaries for their emphasis on the ethical and moral bases of dramatic conflict; his best plays are socially critical comedies of manners. His attention to the notion of personal worth and merit as a determinant of true nobility and honour, as against that which is inherited or unearned, is often ascribed to his treatment by contemporaries as an outsider, both as a Mexican and as physically deformed.

His *La verdad sospechosa* (*The Truth Made Suspect*, 1619) condemns the vice of lying. It is the source of PIERRE CORNEILLE's *Le Menteur*, of the Italian GOLDONI's *Il Bugiardo*, and of several English plays. It was revived by the Spanish National Classical Theatre Company in 1991. *Las paredes oyen* (*Walls Have Ears*) inspired a French metatheatrical performance by Eduardo Manet in 1976. Three plays on national heroic subject-matter, *Ganar amigos* (*Winning Friends*), *Los pechos privilegiados* (*Privileged Nobles*) and *La crueldad por el honor* (*Cruelty for Honour's Sake*), show protagonists whose exemplary heroism is based more on their sense of virtue and personal integrity than on blood lines and worldly values, thus confirming Alarcón's consistent moral vision. CL ElB

rukada SRI LANKAN doll-puppet theatre, practised almost exclusively in the city of Ambalangoda on the southwestern coast. Three- to 4-ft-high PUPPETS are manipulated by strings. Performances are presented on an acting area divided into three sections. The central area occupies the back of a raised platform. Side stages extend out towards the audience to the right and left. The centre stage symbolizes the audience chamber of the king. All three divisions have dark back curtains and drops. A front curtain is used to mask scene changes while action occurs in one of the other acting areas. Puppeteers stand on a ledge above the stage and manipulate the puppets below.

The orchestra is composed of harmonium player, violinist and *tabla* drummer who sit facing the stage with their backs to the audience. The form probably developed after NADAGAMA. *Rukada*'s songs and stories are derived from this live theatre form and puppeteers were former players of *nadagama*. The songs and stories are set to Hindustani tunes rather than in the more traditional Karnataka musical style of south INDIA. FaR

Russell, Annie 1864–1936 English-born actress who, two years after her New York stage debut in 1879, established her career with a brilliant portrayal of the title character in *Esmeralda*. Ill health forced her from the stage for three seasons (1891–4), but she returned to regain her popularity and invite comparison with ELEONORA DUSE for her simplicity and naturalism. She was effective especially in emotional and comic roles. In 1905 she created SHAW's heroine in *Major Barbara*, and gave memorable performances as Puck in *A Midsummer Night's Dream* (1906), Viola in *Twelfth Night* (1909), Beatrice in *Much Ado* (1912) and Lady Teazle in SHERIDAN's *The School for Scandal* (1914). Her charming stage presence made her the ideal ingénue. She retired from the stage in 1918 to head the dramatic programme at Rollins College, Winter Park, Florida. TLM

Russell, Henry 1812–1900 British entertainer and songwriter, of Jewish descent; after studying music with Rossini and Bellini, he became an organist and choral director in Rochester, New York. In 1837, he made a debut as a ballad singer at the Brooklyn Lyceum; in a short time he became a hugely popular performer, offering the first solo vocal programmes in America aimed at the common man. He not only sang in a pleasant baritone and accompanied himself on the piano, but composed his entire

Annie Russell as Esmeralda, a role she first played in 1881.

repertory. This included such warhorses-to-be as *Cheer, Boys, Cheer!, Woodman! Spare That Tree, A Life on the Ocean Wave* and *The Old Armchair*, as well as temperance, anti-slavery and humanitarian ballads. His appearance in London at the Hanover Square Rooms, 1842, was a triumph; he performed in England and America until the early 1860s. LS

Russell, Lillian [née Helen Louise Leonard] 1861–1922 American singer and actress whose name is synonymous with one of her show titles, *An American Beauty*. Rising from obscurity in Clinton, Iowa, she became a much sought-after star in comic OPERA, BURLESQUE, VAUDEVILLE and drama. TONY PASTOR billed her as 'The English Ballad Singer' at his BROADWAY variety theatre in 1880. Cross-country tours and engagements in New York and England followed. She was applauded for her physical and vocal charms in such vehicles as *The Pie Rats of Penn Yan* (Pastor's burlesque of *The Pirates of Penzance*), *The Snake Charmer, The Sorcerer, The Princess of Trebizonde, Iolanthe* and *The Princess Nicotine*. She enjoyed five seasons (1899–1904) with WEBER AND FIELDS's celebrated troupes. Roles in *Lady Teazle* (musical version of SHERIDAN's *The School for Scandal*), *The Butterfly* and *Wildfire* furthered her already flourishing reputation. She died in Pittsburgh, survived by her fourth husband and a daughter. DBW

Russell, Willy [William] **(Martin)** 1947– British dramatist, born near Liverpool, whose career was supported in its early days by the local Everyman Theatre which com-

missioned several of his plays, including his first hit, *John, Paul, Ringo and ... Bert* (1974). This was, unsurprisingly, a MUSICAL based on the lives of the Beatles. Russell, also a singer and a song-writer, often likes to add songs to a straight play or to write musicals. *Blood Brothers* (1981) was written as a straight play, with a story about twins brought up separately in different class settings – a modernized version of BOUCICAULT's *The Corsican Brothers* – but he added songs and it became better known, and successful, as a musical (1983). Not a sophisticated writer of musicals, he rarely attempts to write complicated scores or lyrics. His directness is one of his assets, as a good-humoured, straightforward and usually very funny chronicler of human experiences.

Educating Rita (1979) is a two-handed play about a working-class girl seeking education from a male tutor, who becomes more knowing than her mentor; while *Shirley Valentine* (1986) concerns a woman approaching middle age who succeeds in breaking away from her humdrum life. Both were successful as stage plays and as films; and, from his early plays, *Breezeblock Park* (1975), *One for the Road* (1976) and *Stags and Hens* (1978), to *Shirley Valentine*, he clearly has developed the knack of allowing audiences to enjoy interesting and recognizable characters in plausible situations. Russell does not put on airs, nor does he seem to tolerate those who do; but he is gifted in arousing familiar emotions, sometimes sentimental and often comic, but rarely boring. JE

Russia and the republics of the former Soviet Union Despite Russian Orthodox Church opposition and that of the absolutist Tsar, the largely illiterate general populace and the affected, unsympathetic aristocracy, Russian theatre and drama had developed from a pagan, animistic, oral base into a full-fledged institution by the 18th century – a good deal later than their European counterparts. Russia's earliest semi-professional entertainers were the *SKOMOROKHI*, itinerant and (from 1572) court-attached jesters-musicians-singers-storytellers, who often performed with bears and PUPPETS. Their performances, the profane evolution of what may have been priestly rites before 988 (when Russia converted to orthodox Christianity), were too shocking and their presences too charismatic – the people credited them with magical powers – to be tolerated by either Church or state, and they were officially proscribed by Tsar Aleksei Mikhailovich in 1648. They died out as a profession in the late 18th century.

Not so easily suppressed was a tradition of seasonal and occasional theatrical plays which could be found at fairs (*gulyaniya*); Christmas and Shrovetide CARNIVALS, featuring animal-human transformations and impersonations and a schedule of games, feasts, revels and processionals; birth and puberty rites with mimetic dances (*igrovye*); and 'performed' weddings, with town-wide participation in 'scenes' and interludes, clowning, mock battles and round dances (*khorovody*). These RITUALS inspired parodic folk plays which often satirized the ignorant and corrupt rural clergy. Non-ritual FOLK DRAMAS, offering sociopolitical commentary and protest, had developed by the 17th century, the most popular of which were *The Ship* (*Lodka*) and the scenic assemblage *Tsar Maksimilian*, which dealt with the pagan ruler's conflict with and murder of his Christian son, Adolph. These were performed in the late 18th century in temporary wooden structures called *balagany* (from the Persian *balakhan*, an upper chamber or balcony), originally built at markets and fairs during Shrovetide and Easter week, and most often associated with comic interludes and harlequinades. Puppet theatre, especially the Ukrainian *vertep*, performed on a medieval-type two-tiered, trapped stage, may also have influenced the live folk theatre tradition from the 17th century.

The origins of Russian theatre and drama were, then, folkloric and not liturgical, although the Church exerted considerable positive and negative influence on their early development. Russian bishop Avraamy of Suzdaal left an enthusiastic written account of the spectacular stage effects achieved in performances of two *sacre rappresentazioni* in Florence (1437–9). A church-produced 'Fiery Furnace' show, in which Chaldeans (townspeople) burned three Israelite youths (choirboys) in a cauldron (the pulpit), was staged in Novgorod before 1548. School dramas, designed to teach Latin and religion via stories about the Nativity, the Resurrection of Christ and Lives of the Saints and Martyrs, entered Russia from POLAND via the Kiev (Mohyla) Academy (1615, 1632), established to counter Polish attempts to convert Russia to Catholicism during and after the Time of Troubles (1604–13). Theological students tailored these dramas to popular tastes by converting them to the vernacular and to Church Slavonic, and by introducing comic interludes which eventually toured independently. Three clerics associated with the Kiev Academy – SIMEON POLOTSKY, Danylo Tuptalo (Metropolitan DMITRY ROSTOVSKY) and FEOFAN PROKOPOVICH – helped establish a formal Russian dramatic repertory in the late 17th and early 18th centuries with their plays on biblical and historical themes, expressing pro-Tsarist sympathies and incorporating realistic elements, songs and dances.

The Russian court theatre was founded in 1672 under reformed theatre-hater Tsar Aleksei Mikhailovich, who invited Lutheran pastor JOHANN GREGORY of Moscow's foreign quarter to stage a play in honour of his son and heir's (the future Peter the Great's) birth. The ten-hour presentation of *The Comedy of Esther, or The Play of Artaxerxes*, featuring a cast of 64, mainly merchants' sons, led to the development of a dramatic repertory composed of biblical and adapted Elizabethan dramas and tragicomedies for a theatre which remained open only until the Tsar's death in 1676. Peter I ('the Great', reigned 1682–1725), introduced to theatre while abroad and cognizant of its propaganda value, sponsored the first secular public theatre, under the leadership of German actor-manager JOHANN KUNST, and encouraged attendance via several methods: by introducing the ceremonial spectacle, a musical and special-effects extravaganza on mythical and allegorical themes expressing partisan politics; staging performances in Russian as well as in German, which only the court spoke; eliminating road taxes on performance days; offering free admission; issuing Imperial decrees. The theatre lasted only from 1702 to 1706, and although comic interludes remained popular, a formal theatrical tradition had yet to be established.

During the reigns of Empresses Anna (1730–40) and Elizabeth (1741–61), visiting Italian artists introduced OPERA (Francesco Araia); *COMMEDIA DELL'ARTE*, whose MASKS were absorbed into the Russian interludes accompanying the *vertep* and the school dramas; perspective scenery techniques (Giovani Buon); and an acrobatic form of ballet (Antonio and Giulia Fusano), which was replaced by a more graceful style devised by Frenchman Jean Baptiste Landet. German actress CAROLINE NEUBER, a disciple of JOHANN GOTTSCHED, established classical TRAGEDY at the Russian Court (1739–40). Unfortunately, the lavishness of theatrical spectacle, much of it the work of foreigners, reinforced the Russians' sense of theatre as being something alien to their culture.

The first permanent professional public theatre in Russia was founded in 1756, at the behest of Empress Elizabeth, by the Yaroslavl actor FYODOR VOLKOV, his brother Grigory and director-dramatist ALEKSEI SUMAROKOV, Russia's first professional man of letters. His Russified neo-classical Voltairian tragedies – e.g. *Khorev* (1747) and *Dmitry the Pretender* (1771) – written for Russia's first great tragedian, IVAN DMITREVSKY, and his MOLIÈRE-based comedies helped free Russian theatre of its dependency upon translations of foreign works and remained repertory staples for the next two decades. This lustreless neo-classical tradition was continued by Sumarokov's son-in-law, YAKOV KNYAZHNIN, and by Vasily Maikov, Aleksei Rzhevsky, Nikolai Nikolev, Mikhail Kheraskov and the father of Russian science, MIKHAIL LOMONOSOV.

Empress Catherine II ('the Great', reigned 1762–96) regarded the Russian theatre as a 'national school' and herself – the author of forgettable historical plays, satirical comedies and comic operas aimed at her enemies, the freemasons and the theosophists – as the senior teacher. While theatrical enterprises multiplied, the drama remained didactic, and Catherine's liberality waned following the French Revolution (1789). During Catherine's reign, German manager Karl Knipper and English circus performer Michael Maddox founded short-lived theatres. More importantly, in 1771 Catherine ordered the building of the Petersburg Bolshoi Theatre and in 1779 added the Imperial Theatre School for the training of Russian actors, singers and dancers. Catherine's 1762 charter freeing the nobles from many of their state obligations led to the beginning of the serf theatre, a microcosm of Tsarist patriarchy in which indentured performers were treated as gifted children and had bestowed upon them monetary and amorous favours alternating with torture and public humiliation. Eventually numbering 173 venues, the serf theatres of Prince Yusupov, COUNT NIKOLAI SHEREMETIEV and others were the best-equipped and most lavishly appointed facilities in the land. In the 1840s the combination of rising Imperial municipal theatres' fortunes and falling rural landowners' profits brought their closure, or their absorption into professional and amateur provincial touring companies, the latter precipitating the birth of the provincial repertory system. The spectre of serfdom, abolished in 1861, haunts CHEKHOV's plays, and the lot of the provincial actor is well described by OSTROVSKY.

From 1710 to the late 1740s (the advent of Russian neo-classicism), the chivalric romance play, adapted from French and Italian poetic sources and produced by Princess Natalya (Peter the Great's younger sister) at her private theatre, was the most popular form of secular drama in Russia. By the end of the century, the Russian aristocracy, following Europe's lead and desirous of casting a glow of moral goodness, embraced sentimentalism and especially the work of AUGUST VON KOTZEBUE, who became the most frequently performed foreign dramatist in 19th-century Russia. Dramatist NIKOLAI POLEVOI became the leading Russian theorist of Kotzebuism and Nikolai Ilyin its most influential interpreter, with his popular BALLAD OPERA *Liza, or the Triumph of Gratitude* (1802). Like Vasily Fyodorov's highly successful *Liza, or the Consequence of Pride and Seduction* (1803), it derived from Nikolai Karamzin's sentimental novella *Poor Liza*. The ballad and the comic opera, the bourgeois drama (*drame*) and the sentimental comedy (*comédie larmoyante*) – all part of an effort to democratize the stage via SATIRE and moralizing in the manner of DESTOUCHES, DIDEROT, BEAUMARCHAIS, LILLO and LESSING – were exceedingly popular in early-19th-century Russia. Comic opera authors included actor PYOTR PLAVILSHCHIKOV; former serf Mikhail Matinsky; minor journalist Nikolai LVOV; Aleksandr Ablesimov, whose *The Miller, the Magician, the Deceiver and the Matchmaker* (1779) was a popular success; and Vladimir Lukin, whose campaign to Russify the stage was reinforced by intensified anti-French feeling after the French Revolution and during Napoleon's reign.

While Lukin's call for a people's theatre was not immediately heeded, sentimental drama – e.g. Nikolev's *Rozanna and Lyubim* (1776) and Mikhail Popov's *Anyuita* (1772), the first Russian comic opera – extolled the people's moral values and aroused empathy for the difficult conditions of the peasant serf's life without actually questioning the institution of serfdom itself. Sentimentalism was also applied to neo-classical tragic formulas to produce the patriotic, Tsarist-propagandist history plays in mythological and historical settings of VLADISLAV OZEROV (*Oedipus in Athens*, 1804; *Dmitry of the Don*, 1807) and NESTOR KUKOLNIK (*The Hand of the Almighty Has Saved the Fatherland*, 1833). DENIS FONVIZIN's *The Brigadier* (1769) and *The Minor* (1781) established the Russian satirical comedy of manners, which, although neo-classical in form, constituted the first step towards a national comedy of social realism with its native character, linguistic and topical elements. VASILY KAPNIST's *Chicane* (1789), which satirized judicial corruption, deepened Russian COMEDY's social role while synthesizing the earlier prose comedy conventions of Lukin and Fonvizin.

However, it was the *vaudeville* genre, adapted from the French prototype and from Russian comic opera, commencing with PRINCE ALEKSANDR SHAKHOVSKOI's *The Cossack Poet* (1812) and intensifying during the reactionary reign of Nikolai I (1825–55) which offered the most pointed social commentary. Its Russian practitioners included ALEKSANDR PISAREV, its 'father'; poet Nikolai Nekrasov; Nikolai Khmelnitsky, who elevated its social setting; Pyotr Karatygin, the great tragedian Vasily's brother; Mikhail Zagoskin; theatrical journalist Fyodor Koni; Dmitry Lensky, author of the extremely popular *Lev Gurych Sinichkin*; and Russia's greatest moral fabulist, IVAN KRYLOV, who invented 'Aesopian language' (a term later coined by SALTYKOV-SHCHEDRIN) – i.e. the allegorical, circumlocutory expression of satirical and ironic criticism

of and commentary on the status quo which became the currency of Soviet drama after 1917. ALEKSANDR GRIBOEDOV's comic verse masterpiece *Woe from Wit* (1824) became the basis for Russian national comedy and the most commonly quoted Russian literary source. Griboedov refined and complicated plot and psychological character, streamlined exposition and introduced philosophical content, relating to the Decembrist movement. His protagonist, Chatsky, an inveterate truth-teller and a victimized, uncompromising spirit imprisoned in a soulless society, became a variously interpreted paradigm in Russian and Soviet drama.

The first two decades of the 19th century saw the Imperial Theatre Directorate gaining a monopoly over the Moscow and St Petersburg stages which lasted until 1882. The first CENSORSHIP law (1804) led to Imperial censorship control over all provincial and capital theatres in 1842 and to the hegemony of Nikolai I's secret committee after 1848. The acting profession ascended in craft and prestige during this century, despite the overall weakness of the repertory, the limitations of *emploi* and the general lack of enlightenment among administrators, audiences and actors themselves. In the first third of the century, Dmitrevsky and Shakhovskoi trained many of the best actors: Moscow's craft-conscious Y. E. Shusherin; the more emotional and incipiently realistic A. S. YAKOVLEV and E. S. SEMYONOVA, PUSHKIN's favourite; coolly technical Y. G. Bryansky; and the great Petersburg tragedians V. A. KARATYGIN and I. I. SOSNITSKY. The Imperial Maly Theatre became 'the house of the actor', and former serf actor MIKHAIL SHCHEPKIN that theatre's and Russian REALISM's patriarch. His pupil and STANISLAVSKY's teacher, GLIKERIYA FEDOTOVA, the popular MARIYA ERMOLOVA, romantic tragedian PAVEL MOCHALOV and Ostrovsky specialist PROV SADOVSKY all helped earn the Maly the mantle of 'a second Moscow University'. Directing lagged behind in the Russian theatrical consciousness, with the protean Shakhovskoi receiving credit as being the first *régisseur*. Although stage scenery followed the lead of the 'natural school' of the 1830s–50s and the box set (see THEATRE DESIGN) and specialized decor for opera and ballet were developed, dramatic productions relied on a handful of stock sets and the designer's role was ill-defined and ill-appreciated until the advent of the MOSCOW ART THEATRE and the World of Art Group in the late 1890s.

Russian romanticism (1815–40), adapted from English, French and German sources (especially from fabulist E. T. A. HOFFMANN) and from native folkloric, historical and traditional sources, initiated linguistic experimentation and genre cross-fertilization, as well as several themes – man's and reality's doubleness, woman's infernality, urban paranoia – which resonated primarily in poetry and secondarily in drama until 1917. Its leading exponent and Russia's national poet, Aleksandr Pushkin, attempted to found a school of national tragedy with *Boris Godunov* (1825), a sprawling, misunderstood and seldom staged account of the Time of Troubles, embodying the influences of SHAKESPEARE, KHMELNITSKY and Griboedov, whose final image of the strong but silently suffering people fired the Bolsheviks' imagination nearly a century later. His four psychological miniatures, collectively entitled *The Little Tragedies* (1830), were reclaimed by the Moscow

Art Theatre in 1915 and were made into operas by Dargomyzhsky, Rimsky-Korsakov and Rakhmaninov. Pushkin's literary criticism included useful commentary on dramatic genres and on the educational purpose of dramatic repertory, but the most important 19th-century Russian literary criticism, written by Vissarion Belinsky, Nikolai Chernyshevsky and Nikolai Dobrolyubov, was socially utilitarian. The great lyric poet, MIKHAIL LERMONTOV, wrote several BYRONIC dramas, of which only the *Othello*-inspired *Masquerade* (1836) is remembered – and that owing more to the sumptuously designed (by Aleksandr Golovin), MEYERHOLD-directed Imperial Aleksandrinsky Theatre production (1917) than to the intrinsic merit of the play.

Despite the significant anti-aristocratic, popular biases of Griboedov's, Pushkin's and Lermontov's plays, they were banned in their own day and did not exert nearly the influence of NIKOLAI GOGOL's *The Inspector General*, Russia's greatest comic masterpiece since *Woe from Wit*. A brilliantly eccentric mix of a traditional premiss suggested by Pushkin – a town duped by its own avarice and paranoia in the form of a self-dramatizing nonentity – the *vertep*, *commedia dell'arte*, Plautine farce (see PLAUTUS), medieval allegory and apocalyptic tale, it has been variously interpreted as social satire, moral parable and pure theatrical hyperbole. Gogol, who publicly disapproved of farce and *vaudeville*, wrote several, as did IVAN TURGENEV, although the latter is remembered for *A Month in the Country* (1850), a psychological study of 'superfluous' gentry lives, redolent with proto-Chekhovian ambiance. Disgraced nobleman ALEKSANDR SUKHOVO-KOBYLIN's dramatic trilogy – *Krechinsky's Wedding* (1854), *The Case* (1861) and *Tarelkin's Death* (1869) – combined the Gogolian satirical grotesque with the author's personal experience of bureaucratic hell to evoke the sense of imminent dehumanization, vampirism, loss of faith and innocence that awaited the Comtean–Darwinian world of the future and the modernist art that followed. Monstrous merchant and peasant milieux were depicted in satirist Mikhail Saltykov-Shchedrin's *Pazukhin's Death* (1857) and in ALEKSEI PISEMSKY's *A Bitter Fate* (1859), respectively, the latter antecedent to LEV TOLSTOI's better known but less skilled peasant tragedy *The Power of Darkness* (1888) and part of the realistic peasant drama tradition initiated by Aleksei Potekhin's plays of the 1850s–70s.

The so-called first Russian tragedy, *The Thunderstorm* (1859), was written by 19th-century Russia's consummate professional dramatist, ALEKSANDR OSTROVSKY, best known for creating the quotidian (*bytovaya*) drama of merchant life, beginning with *Don't Get into Another's Sleigh*, the 1853 Maly Theatre production which established his reputation and solidified his relationship with this producing organization. Ostrovsky also wrote historical dramas, as did L. A. Mei, whose *The Tsar's Bride* (1849) and *The Maid of Pskov* (1859) were transformed into operas by Rimsky-Korsakov; D. V. Averkiev; I. Lazhechnikov; and above all, A. K. TOLSTOI, whose trilogy – *The Death of Ivan the Terrible* (1866), *Tsar Fyodor Ioannovich* (1868) and *Tsar Boris* (1870) – provided the Moscow Art Theatre with the chance of realizing psychologically detailed, strongly contrasting characters (the rapacious Ivan and Boris; the gentle Fyodor).

KONSTANTIN STANISLAVSKY's and VLADIMIR NEMIROVICH-DANCHENKO's Moscow Art Accessible Theatre, as it was originally called, was the culmination of a century's progress towards REALISM. Inspired by the Russian tours of the MEININGEN troupe (1885 and 1890) and by the new dramaturgy of IBSEN, HAUPTMANN and MAETERLINCK, it increased the public's theatrical awareness, elevated the acting profession and set new production standards, largely through its collaborations with successful short story writer and previously failed dramatist Anton Chekhov and with self-made prose writer and social icon MAKSIM GORKY, after whom MAT was named in 1932. In his comedies of uneventful, stunted lives – *The Seagull* (1896), *Uncle Vanya* (1899), *The Three Sisters* (1901), *The Cherry Orchard* (1904) – Chekhov deconstructed the artificially closed and logical structure of the WELL MADE PLAY and the orderly world it reflected, recycled 19th-century farce-*vaudeville* types and conventions and achieved a world of concrete mystery related to SYMBOLISM, but with greater humour and less pretence. The majority of Gorky's dramas, which marginally resemble his mentor Chekhov's, embody his ingrained sense of class distinctions and social inequities and his hatred for the self-satisfied philistinism of the intelligentsia and the bourgeoisie. His best-known play in the West, the somewhat atypical, philosophically ambiguous tramp drama *The Lower Depths* (1902), is drawn from his own early life experience. Gorky encouraged both realistic writers – Evgeny Chirikov, Semyon Yushkevich and Sergei Naidyonov – and anti-realists BLOK and ANDREEV through his publishing house Znanie (Knowledge, founded 1900), as well as protecting countless others after the Revolution from his unequalled position of cultural eminence. Aid came as well from the sympathetic First People's Commissar for Education, ANATOLY LUNACHARSKY, a theatre aficionado and author of politically conceived historical dramas.

The anti-realist movement began in the 1890s with the cultural aestheticism of such World of Art group painters as ALEXANDRE BENOIS, LÉON BAKST, Mstislav Dobuzhinsky, Nikolai Sapunov and Serge Soudeikine, whose decorative work graced their own highly refined journal (founded 1898), the related Ballets Russes productions of Sergei Diaghilev and numerous theatre projects by STANISLAVSKY, MEYERHOLD, EVREINOV and others. They were particularly important to the Petersburg-based cultural retrospectivism movement, centred in Evreinov's and Baron Nikolai Drizen's Ancient Theatre, and to the CABARET-'theatre of small forms' – e.g. the Bat, the Crooked Mirror Theatre, the Stray Dog, the Comedians' Rest – specializing in literary and theatrical PARODY, harlequinade, pantomime and VARIETY acts, in the capital cities. Low art, which gained sustenance from primitive and folkloric forms, entered the official theatres primarily via Meyerhold and bridged the gap between pre-revolutionary decorative aestheticism and post-revolutionary dynamic functionalism, in which *vaudeville*, CIRCUS and cinema were employed in mass actions and AGIT-PROP presentations. The 'high art' of Russian symbolism (1890–1917) combined the philosopher Vladimir Solovyov's apocalyptic theories, FRIEDRICH NIETZSCHE's ideas on the Dionysian origins of the drama, RICHARD WAGNER's *Gesamtkunstwerk*, Baudelaire's theory of correspondences, and the philosophical-symbolic, folk and subjectivist dramatic visions of Ibsen, Maeterlinck, Hauptmann and STRINDBERG.

The Russian symbolists' erudite, static and visionary dramas, beginning with Nikolai Minsky's *Alma* (1900), reflected their self-dramatizing personalities and ruling concepts; included here are Dmitry Merezhkovsky's and his wife the poet Zinaida Gippius's God-seeking; VYACHESLAV IVANOV's theatre of congregate action; VALERY BRIUSOV's *uslovny* (self-conscious, conventional) theatre; ANDREI BELY's neo-MYSTERY PLAYS; INNOKENTY ANNENSKY's and ALEKSEI REMIZOV's mythic and Russian folkloric themes; FYODOR SOLOGUB's fatalism and author-centred 'Theatre of One Will'; and MIKHAIL KUZMIN's darkly dandyish *commedia*. The greatest symbolist dramatist, Aleksandr Blok, posited theatricalism as an alternative faith to symbolist mysticism in his epochal harlequinade *The Puppet Show* (1906); so too did such marginally symbolist writers as NIKOLAI EVREINOV, in his monodramas and in his major play *The Chief Thing* (1921), and Leonid Andreev, in his Poe-like romantically horrific, allegorical meditations on death's proximity and life's vacuity (e.g. *He Who Gets Slapped*, 1915).

While the symbolists faltered as aesthetic saints, the most talented of their director-contemporaries – Evreinov at the Ancient Theatre and the Crooked Mirror, Meyerhold, TAIROV and VAKHTANGOV – succeeded as theatricalist visionary showmen. Vsevolod Meyerhold's career embraced all of the foregoing aesthetic trends, as well as constructivism, his 1922 constructivist-designed production of Crommelynck's *The Magnanimous Cuckold* coinciding with Aleksei Gan's manifesto stating that 'art is dead'. The 'new machine art' of constructivist designers LYUBOV POPOVA, Vladimir Tatlin, ALEKSANDRA EKSTER, Aleksandr Rodchenko, Vladimir Stenberg and others, derived in part from cubo-FUTURISM and modelled on industrial design, posited a new, demystified, scientific basis for art, the glorification of proletarian man and the 'truth' and organization of materials. This new democratization of the stage was opposed by Aleksandr Tairov at his aesthetically elitist Kamerny (Chamber) Theatre (founded

1914), which featured balletic, cubist- and *commedia*-influenced productions (e.g. RACINE's *Phaedra*, 1922; Hoffmann's *Princess Brambilla*, 1920) and aspired to the ideal of musical sculpture and a complete synthesis of the arts. Evgeny Vakhtangov synthesized the Stanislavskian and Meyerholdian theatrical approaches in his 'fantastic realism', whereby he alternately carnivalized (*Princess Turandot*, 1922) and ritualized (*The Dybbuk*, 1922) the stage and sounded a note of harmonious creation in the final days of 'war communism's' (1917–22) optimistic experiments.

This period saw a theatrical explosion – over 3000 professional troupes in Russia alone, the nationalization of all theatres in regions under Bolshevik control (1919), and attempts by the innovators Meyerhold, Evreinov, SERGEI RADLOV, YURIY ANNENKOV and Sergei Eisenstein to create a uniquely Soviet popular theatre of montage-like mass spectacles and agit-prop presentations, performed by circus artistes, gymnasts, military personnel and participants in the actual historical events being dramatized. These tendencies were continued by the Proletkult (1917–23) and BLUE BLOUSE movements (1923–8), the latter numbering 484 professional and 8000 amateur companies nationwide in its final year of operation. Its 'montage of attractions' approach – film, animated poster, agit-prop cabaret and so on – owed much to Italian futurist MARINETTI's 'Variety Manifesto' of 1913. The advent of the New Economic Policy (NEP, 1921–8) engendered a Soviet brand of satirical grotesque which focused upon careerists and financial speculators, as well as a theatre, the Moscow Theatre of Satire (founded 1924), at which to perform them. The futurist poet VLADIMIR MAYAKOVSKY, whose neo-mystery *Mystery-Bouffe* (1918) has been called the first Soviet play, summarized and transformed NEP SATIRE in *The Bedbug* (1928) and *The Bathhouse* (1929), which projected anti-utopian images drawn from cartoons, cinema and science fiction.

This pessimistic experimentalism was countered by the 'factographic' MELODRAMAS of SERGEI TRETYAKOV and by the Civil War paeans of VLADIMIR BILL-BELOTSERKOVSKY,

The finale to Meyerhold's production of Ostrovsky's 1871 comedy, *The Forest*, 1924. The acting, like the set, embodied a strong sense of rhythm.

VSEVOLOD IVANOV, KONSTANTIN TRENYOV, LEONID LEONOV and Boris Lavrenyov, whose *The Break-up* (1927), in a not unfamiliar scenario, was rewritten at Stalin's direction. From these followed the epic, romantic monumentalist plays of the 1930s – VSEVOLOD VISHNEVSKY's *An Optimistic Tragedy* (1933), ALEKSANDR AFINOGENOV's *Fear* (1931), ALEKSANDR KORNEICHUK's *Platon Krechet* (1934) and NIKOLAI POGODIN's Lenin trilogy, beginning with *The Man with a Gun* (1937). The best plays of the 1920s–40s were branded 'formalist' and went largely unproduced until after Stalin's death. The dramas of MIKHAIL BULGAKOV (such as *The Days of the Turbins* (1926), *Flight* (1927), *A Cabal of Hypocrites* (*Molière*, 1930)), of NIKOLAI ERDMAN (*The Mandate* (1925) and *The Suicide* (1928)) and of YURY OLESHA (*The Conspiracy of Feelings* (1928) and *A List of Blessings* (1931)) presented common-man dreamers, artistic 'egoists', 'class enemies' and 'former people' alienated from the Soviet ideal of progress and the new personality-less society. The Serapion Brothers (1921–9) – EVGENY ZAMYATIN, et al. – and the OBERIU (the Association for Real Art, 1927–30), led by Aleksandr Vvedensky and Daniil Kharms, rejected ideological art in favour of modernist, allegorical, neo-futurist and proto-absurdist forms whose impact did not register until the 1960s. The children's theatre movement (see SOVIET CHILDREN'S THEATRE), whose flagship institution, the Moscow Central Children's Theatre (its name after 1936), was founded in 1920 by Natalya Sats, and which was compelled to stage Stalinist parables in the 1930s, produced one dramatic master of 'Aesopian language', EVGENY SHVARTS (*The Naked King*, 1934; *The Shadow*, 1940; *The Dragon*, 1943).

In 1934 a Party spokesman and 'culture specialist', Andrei Zhdanov, speaking at the First All-Union Congress of Soviet Writers, proclaimed the doctrine of 'socialist realism', which resulted in the greying out of Soviet art and literature until after Stalin's death in 1953. Finding recent precedents in the policies of the First Five-Year Plan (1928–32), it fused Russia's belief in its messianic mission, the mission of its proletariat and its penchant for separating the 'useful' from the 'superfluous'. History was reconceived as the inexorable path to revolutionary communism, whose material accessibility made it a suitable spiritual replacement for Christian paradise. Scientists were dubbed 'soldiers of the mind' and artists 'engineers of the soul' in the war against egoism, mysticism and self-doubt, and in the ideological transformation and education of workers. The implicit moral superiority and final victory of communism led Nikolai Virta to posit the theory of 'conflictless drama', which featured the 'positive hero', new slogans involving 'Party spirit' (*partinost*) and 'national character' (*narodnost*), and pursued a new mythic egalitarianism which glorified labour and produced common-denominator art – 'plays about whether to plant wheat or to plant corn' (Viktor Rozov). The patriotic war plays of KONSTANTIN SIMONOV, Korneichuk and Leonov, the anti-capitalist dramas of Simonov and Lavrenyov and the historical rewrites of A. N. TOLSTOI and Vishnevsky put these themes into practice.

Stalin's death and Krushchev's de-Stalinization speech at the 20th Party Congress (1956) ushered in the 'Thaw' period in the arts, which precipitated a 'new lyricism' and 'rehumanization' in the theatre. The first generation of post-Thaw dramatists – VIKTOR ROZOV, ALEKSANDR VOLODIN and ALEKSEI ARBUZOV – created a new form of intimate play of conscience and crisis, presented in a diversified theatricalist style composed of interpolated music, songs, dances, pantomime and poetry, choruses, flashbacks, split focus and montage, borrowed in part from the 1920s. While the results in drama were sometimes overly schematic and sentimentally monumentalist, these experiments suited a new generation of stage directors seeking to dramatize narrative fiction and to revitalize and gain critical perspective on classic and contemporary plays. YURY LYUBIMOV made the *mise en scène* the star at the Taganka Theatre, whose direction he assumed in 1964, and perfected a style which combined agit-prop, minstrelsy and revisionist historical and cultural criticism. The equally controversial and peripatetic ANATOLY EFROS sought in his productions to capture the essence of contemporaneity by internalizing the *mise en scène* in the actor as iconographic feeling man. GEORGY TOVSTONOGOV, from 1956 director of Leningrad's Bolshoi Dramatic Theatre, brought a more sober but humanitarian sensibility to his productions. He also helped to popularize and adapt the American MUSICAL, along with younger directors Vladimir Vorovyov and Efim Padve (his former students), Gennady Yudenich, Vyacheslav Spesivtsev, Mark Rozovsky and MARK ZAKHAROV.

OLEG EFREMOV's youth-oriented Sovremennik (Contemporary) Theatre embodied the first flush of post-Thaw optimism and self-criticism, some of which was directed at the moribund 'realism' of the Moscow Art Theatre, which Efremov now heads. The Sovremennik's production of Chingiz Aitmatov's and Kaltai Mukhamedzhanov's *The Ascent of Mount Fuji* (1973), within a month of the 20th anniversary of Stalin's death, symbolized the new standard for self-criticism, not only in its subject-matter – collective guilt over compliance with Stalinist tyranny – but in its materials, drawn from the biographies of poet-folksinger Bulat Okudzhava and dissident novelist Aleksandr Solzhenitsyn, and in its means – a reunion and the 'truth' game from Dostoevsky's *The Idiot*. While Arbuzov reinvented the 19th-century farce-*vaudeville*, ANDREI AMALRIK updated OBERIU drama to modern absurdism (see THEATRE OF THE ABSURD), VASILY AKSYONOV reclaimed NEP satire and EDVARD RADZINSKY extended the Gogolian-Bulgakovian line of satirical grotesque and philosophical inquiry to expose the mythic fallacy of Soviet history, Soviet drama closed out the 1960s and entered the 1970s and 1980s on a youthful note. By the time of his accidental death at the age of 35, ALEKSANDR VAMPILOV had become the voice of his generation, and with his play *Duck Hunting* (1967) he initiated the genre of the 'urban grotesque' – i.e. realistic dramas in claustrophobic, modern urban settings. Practised by older writers such as Arbuzov, Volodin, Rozov and the late Yury Trifonov, whose work Lyubimov adapted for the Taganka stage, it became the preserve of such younger playwrights as Semyon Zlotnikov, MARK ROZOVSKY, Viktor Slavkin, Aleksei Kazantsev and, especially, LYUDMILA PETRUSHEVSKAYA, whose hyper-realistic plays intimately and somewhat ambiguously focus upon male–female relationships and mundane contemporary reality.

Since the 1970s dramatists have been treating the prob-

A scene from Yury Lyubimov's 1965 adaptation of John Reed's *Ten Days that Shook the World*. Despite accusations from the Soviet press and officialdom of irreverence toward the Revolution, this became one of Lyubimov's longest running productions at the Taganka. It is a characteristic (for him) cinematic montage of light, shadow, carnival mask and grotesque in the service of revolutionary agit-prop.

lems of youth, the family and social relationships progressively more realistically, and even clinically. Teenage pregnancy, alienation, brutality, rebellion and failure at personal commitment, often in the light of the negative examples set by their elders, are being closely and objectively examined by Alla Sokolova, Andrei Kuternitsky, Olga Kuchkina-Pavlova, Galina Shcherbakova, Nina Pavlova, Lyudmila Razumovskaya and Viktor Slavkin, as well as by Aleksandr Gelman, who with Ignaty Dvoretsky helped promulgate the industrial plays of the 1970s; Radzinsky who, in *She, in the Absence of Love and Death* (1980), returned to the intimate scale of his 60s plays; and Arbuzov and Rozov, whose *Cruel Games* (1978) and *The Nest of the Woodgrouse* (1979), respectively, are their most controversial plays in recent years. In January 1985, after more than a decade of struggle, EDWARD ALBEE's corruscating *Who's Afraid of Virginia Woolf?* premiered at the Sovremennik Theatre, which in 1973 had produced DAVID RABE's devastating 'family play' *Sticks and Bones* under the title *As Brother to Brother*. Youth's voice was heard in the extremely popular Soviet rock musicals of the late 1970s and early 1980s which Mark Zakharov, artistic director of the Moscow Lenin Komsomol Theatre, derived from Western themes and cinematic influences and exported to the West for limited runs.

Mikhail Gorbachev's policies of *glasnost* and *perestroika* (from 1985) and his ousting and eventual replacement by Boris Yeltsin in 1991 hastened the reconfiguration of the theatrical landscape. CENSORSHIP's disappearance from the Russian theatre brought forth a flood of new images and the echoes of many more that had long been suppressed. Russian playwrights created unsympathetic Lenins and sympathetic tsars, as well as singing and dancing Stalins, Brezhnevs and Berias, revising and retrieving history and, for some, the true communist faith. Jewish, republican, gay, erotic and pluralistic themes and sensibilities were openly depicted and discussed. The Moscow public read and saw previously banned works by and about Erdman, Bulgakov, Meyerhold, Aleksandr Galich, Andrei Platonov, Mariya Tsvetaeva, proto-absurdists Daniil Kharms and Aleksandr Vvedensky, Velimir Khebnikov, Western absurdists BECKETT and IONESCO and

exiles Vladimir Nabokov, Joseph Brodsky and Aleksandr Solzhenitsyn. Strong female if not precisely feminist playwrights like Petrushevskaya, NINA SADUR, Lyudmila Razumovskaya, Valeria Vrubevskaya, Mara Zalite and Leia Stumbre were published and produced, and even the most sensitive subjects like the Chernobyl nuclear plant meltdown of April 1986 were examined in the theatre. Directors like ROMAN VIKTIUK, Anatoly Vasiliev and Kama Ginkas returned to the formalism of the 1920s, often drawing upon Meyerholdian rehearsal and staging techniques, improvised action and audience participation. Eros and Thanatos entered the stage through productions of WILDE's *Salome*, Nabokov's *Lolita*, GENET's *The Maids* and Hwang's *M. Butterfly*.

The triumph of human irrationalism over state propaganda led to a resurgence of the spiritually based psychophysical acting theories of MICHAEL CHEKHOV and JERZY GROTOWSKI, which were previously subjects mainly for underground study. A combination of elements led the Russian theatrical profession to reorganize somewhat according to the more efficiently managerial American model. Theatres became more independent, selecting their own repertory, often with a sharper eye turned towards box-office success (and self-determined ticket prices), which after 1991 replaced to varying degrees government subsidies in supporting operations. This change led to more frequent touring and performances, to all-star casting of short-term productions, and to private, sometimes foreign, corporate underwriting. In 1986, the Union of Theatre Workers replaced the All-Russian Theatre Society, instituting (after 1989) such Western-style reforms as actor pension funds and unemployment benefits. The break-up of what had been since 1939 the universal Soviet repertory theatre system began in the early 1980s, as actors and directors sought out new colleagues, audiences and materials, and independent careers. Even the venerable Moscow Art Theatre split into two halves, named after Chekhov and Gorky. Non-subsidized theatre studios became ubiquitous after 1987, successors to the various little or alternative stages for intimate, experimental and workshop productions opened by artistic directors of major theatres in the 1960s in order to satisfy their own and company members' (including actors as first-time directors) creative yearnings.

By 1989, there were nearly 200 studio theatres in Russia and the various republics and countless amateur dramatic circles (in comparison to 650 state-supported theatres). Young and old moonlighting amateurs and theatre professionals brought varied life experiences, work ethics and performance styles to experimental, sometimes autobiographical, dramatic fare staged in converted basements, communal apartments, rehearsal halls, museums, factories, palaces of culture, collective farms, schools and universities. They performed for small audiences of 30–100 spectators, following lengthy rehearsal periods organized around work schedules. These often unadvertised performances employed a 'poor theatre' aesthetic of minimal scenic, prop and costume elements, defined informal and interactive stage–auditorium relationships and included post-show discussions. New and revitalized, uncensored theatres and theatre studios paraded (neo-)Stalinist henchmen, corrupt *apparatchiki*, the spoiled children of the *nomenklatura*, drug addicts and mafiosi before audiences who proved increasingly difficult to shock.

Since 1988, theatregoers in the West have had the opportunity to see Lev Dodin's Maly Dramatic Theatre productions of Aleksandr Galin's *Stars in the Morning Sky* and Abramov's epic *Brothers and Sisters*; Eimuntas Nekrosius's Lithuanian State Theatre production of *Uncle Vanya*; Vasiliev's staging of Slavkin's *Cerceau* and *Six Characters in Search of an Author*; Robert Sturua's Rustaveli (Georgia) Theatre productions of *Richard III* and *King Lear*; Roman Kozak's Theatre–Studio 'Chelovek' interpretation of Petrushevskaya's *Cinzano*; Yury Yeremin's Pushkin Theatre staging of Chekhov's *Ward Number Six*; Zakharov's Moscow Lenin Komsomol rock musical *Juno and Avos: The Hope*; Lyubimov's *mises en scène* (performed by different companies) of *Crime and Punishment* and *The Possessed (The Devils)*. In return, the USA has sent Russia theatre directors (including Mark Lamos, Nagle Jackson and Theodore Mann) to stage American classics (e.g. Eugene O'Neill and Tennessee Williams), along with children's theatre companies and university and acting institute students. In 1992, Moscow's first Anton Chekhov International Theatre Festival included eleven productions from outside the former Soviet bloc, as well as performances from Georgian, Ukrainian, Armenian, Turkmenistanian and Tajik theatres. In 1993, Lithuania hosted its first International Theatre Festival. Republican histories and sensibilities have increasingly taken the stage at home, in Russia and for export abroad, at a time when the idea of a national culture is rapidly eroding. SG

ENGLISH-LANGUAGE SOURCES

See: A. Bakshy, *The Path of the Modern Russian Stage and Other Essays*, London, 1916; A. Bates, *The Drama: Its History, Literature, and Influence on Civilization*, vol. 18, *Russian Drama*, London, 1903; J. E. Bowlt, *Russian Stage Design: Scenic Innovation, 1900–1930*, coll. Mr and Mrs N. D. Lobanov-Rostovsky, Jackson, Miss., 1982, and *The Silver Age: Russian Art of the Early Twentieth Century and the 'World of Art' Group*, Newtonville, Mass., 1982; W. E. Brown, *A History of Seventeenth-Century Russian Literature*, Ann Arbor, Mich., 1980; M.

A. S. Burgess, 'The Early Theatre' and 'The Nineteenth- and Early Twentieth-Century Theatre', in R. Auty and D. Obolensky (eds.), *An Introduction to Russian Language and Literature*, Cambridge, 1977; H. Carter, *The New Spirit in Russian Theatre 1917–28*, London, 1921; J. D. Clayton, *Pierrot in Petrograd: Commedia dell'-Arte/Balagan in Twentieth-century Russian Theatre and Drama*, Montreal, 1993; H. W. L. Dana, *Handbook on Soviet Drama*, New York, 1938; R. Füllöp-Miller and J. Gregor, *The Russian Theatre*, New York and London, 1968; G. Gibian (tr.), *Russia's Lost Literature of the Absurd*, Ithaca, 1971; S. Golub, *The Recurrence of Fate: Theatre and Memory in Twentieth-century Russia*, Iowa City, 1994; N. Gorchakov, *The Theatre in Soviet Russia*, New York, 1957; L. Hecht (ed.), *Newsnotes on Soviet and East European Drama and Theatre*, Fairfax, Va., 1981–5; N. Houghton, *Moscow Rehearsals*, New York, 1936, and *Return Engagement*, New York, 1962; C. V. James, *Soviet Socialist Realism: Origins and Theory*, New York, 1973; G. Kalbouss, *The Plays of the Russian Symbolists*, East Lansing, Mich., 1982; S. Karlinsky, *Russian Drama from Its Beginnings to the Age of Pushkin*, Berkeley, Calif., 1985; J. Kennedy, The *'Mir Iskusstva' Group and Russian Art 1898–1912*, New York and London, 1977; A. H. Law and C. P. Goslett (comp. and ed.), *Soviet Plays in Translation: An Annotated Bibliography*, New York, 1981; R. Leach, *Revolutionary Theatre*, London, 1994; C. Lodder, *Russian Constructivism*, New Haven, Conn., 1983; V. Markov, *Russian Futurism: A History*, 1968; H. Marshall, *The Pictorial History of the Russian Theatre*, 1977; D. S. Mirsky, *A History of Russian Literature*, New York, 1973; C. and E. Proffer (eds.), *The Silver Age of Russian Culture: An Anthology*, Ann Arbor, Mich., 1975; S. E. Roberts, *Soviet Historical Drama: Its Role in the Development of a National Mythology*, The Hague, 1975; 'Russian Issue', *Drama Review*, 17, Mar. 1973; H. B. Segel, *The Literature of Eighteenth-Century Russia*, 2 vols., New York, 1967, and *Twentieth-Century Russian Drama from Gorky to the Present*, New York, 1979; L. Senelick, *Russian Dramatic Theory from Pushkin to the Symbolists*, Austin, Tex., 1981; M. Slonim, *Russian Theatre from the Empire to the Soviets*, New York, 1962; A. van Gyseghem, *Theatre in Soviet Russia*, London, 1943; B. V. Varneke, *History of the Russian Theatre*, New York, 1951; E. A. Warner, *The Russian Folk Theatre*, The Hague and Paris, 1977; L. Warner, *Russian Folk Drama*, The Hague, 1978; D. J. Welsh, *Russian Comedy 1765–1823*, The Hague and Paris, 1966; P. Yershov, *Comedy in the Soviet Theatre*, New York, 1956; R. Zguta, *Russian Minstrels: A History of the Skomorokhi*, Pittsburgh, 1978.

RUSSIAN-LANGUAGE SOURCES

See: A. A. Anikst, *Teoriya dramy v Rossii ot Pushkina do Chekhova*, Moscow, 1972; B. N. Aseyev, *Russkii dramaticheskii teatr 17–18 vekov*, Moscow, 1958; P. N. Berkov, *Russkaya narodnaya drama 17–20 vekov*, Moscow, 1953; A. O. Boguslavsky and V. A. Diev, *Russkaya sovetskaya dramaturgiya 1917–35. Osnovye problemy razvitiya*, Moscow, 1963, and *Russkaya sovetskaya dramaturgiya*, 3 vols., Moscow, 1965–8; A. O. Boguslavsky, V. A. Diev and A. S. Karpov, *Kratkaya istoriya russkoi sovetskoi dramaturgii*, Moscow, 1966;

V. Churakov (ed.), *Dramaturgiya Znaniya*, Moscow, 1964; N. N. Chushkin et al. (eds.), *Moskovskii khudozhestvennyi teatr*, vol. 1, *1898–1917*, Moscow, 1955; S. S. Danilov, *Ocherki po istorii russkogo dramaticheskogo teatra*, Moscow–Leningrad, 1948; S. S. Danilov and M. G. Portugalova, *Russkii dramaticheskii teatr 19 veka*, 2 vols., Leningrad, 1974; O. Z. Derzhavina, K. N. Lomunov and A. N. Robinson (eds.), *Rannaya russkaya dramaturgiya 17–pervoi poloviny 18 v.*, 5 vols., Moscow, 1972–6; V. Frolov, *Zhanry sovetskoi dramaturgii*, Moscow, 1957; *Istoriya russkogo dramaticheskogo teatra*, 7 vols., Moscow, 1977– , in progress; A. R. Kugel, *Russkie dramaturgii*, Moscow, 1923; L. Lotman et al. (eds.), *Istoriya russkoi dramaturgii 17–pervaya polovina 19 veka*, Leningrad, 1982; P. A. Markov, *O teatre*, 4 vols., Moscow, 1976; S. S. Mokulsky et al. (eds.), *Teatralnaya entsiklopediya*, 5 vols., Moscow, 1961–7; Y. Osnos, *Sovetskaya istoricheskaya drama*, Moscow, 1947; M. Paushkin (ed.), *Strarii russkii vodvil 1819–1849*, Moscow, 1937; *Pesy sovetskikh pisatelei*, 6 vols., Moscow, 1972–5; V. F. Pimenov (ed.), *Pervye sovetskie pyesy*, Moscow, 1958, and *Sovetskie dramaturgi o svoyom tvorchestve. Sbornik statei*, Moscow, 1967; M. Polyakov (ed.), *Russkaya teatralnaya parodiya 19–nachala 20 veka*, Moscow, 1976; *Rossiskii teatr*, 43 vols., St Petersburg, 1786–94; K. Rudnitsky, *Portrety dramaturgov*, Moscow, 1961; *Russkaya dramaturgiya 18 v.*, 2 vols., Moscow–Leningrad, 1959; *Russkie dramaturgi 18–19 vv. Monograficheksie ocherki*, 3 vols., Moscow, 1959–62; T. Shantarenkov (ed.), *Russkii vodvil*, Moscow, 1970; *Sovetskaya dramaturgiya 1917–1947*, 6 vols., Moscow–Leningrad, 1948; L. Tamashin, *Sovetskaya dramaturgiya v gody grazhdanskoi voiny*, Moscow, 1961; *Teatr. Kniga o novom teatre*, St Petersburg, 1908; V. Vsevoldsky-Gerngross, *Istoriya russkogo teatra*, 2 vols., Leningrad, 1929, *Russkii teatr ot istokov do serediny 18 v.*, Moscow, 1957, and *Russkii teatr votoroi poloviny 18 v.*, Moscow, 1960; M. O. Yankovsky (ed.), *Stikhotvorenaya komediya kontsa 18–nachala 19 v.*, Moscow–Leningrad, 1964; A. Z. Yufit (ed.), *Sovetskii teatr: Dokumenty i materialy 1917–67*, Leningrad, 1968; E. A. Znosko-Borovsky, *Russkii teatr nachala 20 v.*, 2 vols., Prague, 1925; D. Zolotnitsky, *Zori teatralnogo oktyabrya*, Leningrad, 1976.

Rustaveli Theatre see STURUA, ROBERT

Ruzzante [Ruzante; Angelo Beolco] ?1502–43 Italian amateur actor, whose plays in the Paduan dialect paved the way for the COMMEDIA DELL'ARTE. The head of a travelling company, which performed chiefly in Padua but also at Venice and Ferrara at CARNIVAL time from 1520, (Il) Ruzzante ('the Chatterbox') incarnated the type of garrulous, grumbling peasant, pungently criticizing princes, citizens and war. The members of his ensemble, which spoke the vernacular, always impersonated the same characters: M. A. Alvarotto as Menato, G. Zanetti as Vezzo. Ruzzante's comedies united the experiments of court theatre such as the PASTORAL eclogue and the Terentian comedy (see TERENCE) with the indigenous *momarie* of urban Venice and the *mariazi* of the Paduan countryside. In his own time, his reputation as an actor overwhelmed his fame as a playwright, for his sensual, surly, anti-idealistic Ruzzante was a striking natural. He has been rediscovered at regular intervals in the 20th century: JACQUES COPEAU revived his *Ancontana* (1522?) in 1927; the Teatro Stabile of Turin staged his *Moschetta* (1528) in 1960; and in England *Il Reduce*, his caustic anti-war monologue, has occasionally been revived. LS

Ryga, George 1932–87 Canadian playwright, poet and novelist, whose plays are known for their technical innovations and experimentation. Stylistically diverse, Ryga's plays nonetheless focus on a common theme: the conflict between the ideological status quo and those who are defined by their alienation from it and who strive to maintain their integrity in the face of their dispossession and destruction. *The Ecstasy of Rita Joe* (1967) examines the difficulties faced by Canada's native people in their attempts to define a space for their culture within the social and legal structures of white society; it remains one of the most important works in the development of Canadian theatre. *Captives of the Faceless Drummer* (1971), about the relationship between a revolutionary and his diplomat hostage, bore such close resemblance to contemporary political events that its initial production was abandoned. *Captives* typifies Ryga's dedication to radical political art: his plays, not written to gain easy public acceptance, often debate on a thematic or structural level concerns about political involvement and artistic success. This stance led to his alienation from mainstream theatre in Canada and ultimately his return to non-dramatic writing. DAH

Sabbattini, Nicola 1574–1654 Italian architect and engineer, and author of *Pratica di fabricar scene e machine ne'teatri* (1638). Sabbattini was born and died in Pesaro, and for many years was architect for the Duke of Urbino. Although most of his work was on civil and military projects, he also designed and built theatres – which at the time meant transforming great halls – and scenery. The one theatre specifically attributed to him is the Teatro del Sol at Pesaro, built in 1637 for the production of *L'Asmondo*. His importance lies in his book, which documents the theatre machinery and technology of the day with special reference to perspective (see THEATRE DESIGN) and *intermezzi*. It was widely read and influenced theatre practice throughout Europe. AA

Sacco [Sacchi], **(Giovanni) Antonio** 1708–88 A famous Truffaldino, who travelled with his COMMEDIA DELL'ARTE troupe throughout half of Europe (1738–62). In Venice he played at the Teatro Sant' Angelo, where, at his urging, GOLDONI wrote for him *The Servant of Two Masters* (1745), *Truffaldino's 32 Mishaps* (1738–40) and *Truffaldino's Son Lost and Found* (1746). GOZZI followed suit with *The Love of Three Oranges* (1761), an enormous success. GARRICK and Casanova spoke highly of Sacco's talents, especially in improvised COMEDY. LS

Sackville, Thomas 1536–1608 English playwright. With Thomas Norton he wrote *The Tragedy of Gorboduc* (1561) – usually considered the first English tragedy, drawing upon classical precedent in some respects (chorus, reported action) but otherwise showing an inclination to freer form and to political comment that was to be a feature of classic Elizabethan TRAGEDY. MB

Saddler, Donald 1920– American ballet dancer and theatre choreographer who, before joining the company of *High Button Shoes* (1947), was a soloist with Ballet Theatre (1940–3, 46–7). He was a featured dancer along with BOB FOSSE and Joan McCracken in *Dance Me a Song* (1950). Saddler's choreographic career began with *Wonderful Town* (1953) and *JOHN MURRAY ANDERSON's Almanac* (1953). From the unsuccessful *Shangri-La* (1956), he went on to choreograph *Milk and Honey* (1961), *Tricks* (1973) and *No, No, Nanette* (1971 BROADWAY revival), for which he received critical and popular acclaim: capturing the spirit of the show, he had his dancers performing on beach balls. Saddler was also recognized for his work in industrial shows as a producer and choreographer. LF

Sadler's Wells Theatre (London) Sadler (there is dispute about whether his first name was Dick or Thomas) was a surveyor of highways by profession and a theatrical impresario by inclination. He opened a Musick-House in 1683 on a site in Finsbury, aiming to provide cheap entertainment in the northern fringes of London. The discovery of a medicinal spring on the same site either just before or just after the opening of the Musick-House turned the gardens of Sadler's Wells into a popular resort, but the prestige of both hall and gardens had sunk by 1746, when the lease was bought by Thomas Rosoman. Under Rosoman, the old wooden hall was replaced with a brick theatre in 1764–5 (capacity 2600) and Sadler's Wells was recognized as one of London's effective 'minor theatres', a home for PANTOMIME and illegitimate drama in addition to music and acrobatic displays.

Tom King, who had made his name as an actor at Smock Alley and DRURY LANE, was the active lessee from 1772 to 85. Under his shrewd control, the theatre earned a fashionable reputation for patriotic spectacle, musical innovations (particularly through the work of CHARLES DIBDIN) and good wine. The infant JOSEPH GRIMALDI began his long association with Sadler's Wells in 1781, and his precocious dancing was one of many bids to preserve for the theatre its reputation for novelty over the next 60 years of its history. King and his managerial successors would try anything, from dancing dogs to feats of arms and even a staging of the storming of the Bastille (August 1789). From 1799 to 1819, the driving force was the enterprising and ambitious Charles Dibdin the younger. He it was who exploited the theatre's aquatic potential in 1803 by installing a large water tank (90ft x 25ft) on the stage, but the opening success of *The Siege of Gibraltar* (1804) proved hard to follow. It was above all Grimaldi who sustained Sadler's Wells during the difficult years from 1807, when panic following a false alarm of fire caused 18 deaths, until his retirement in 1828. By then, MELODRAMA was the rage and, having lost its confidence in novelty, Sadler's Wells followed the lead of other minor theatres. A thorough renovation in 1838 failed to halt the slide. It was SAMUEL PHELPS's decision, in the wake of the Theatres Act of 1843, to take a lease on Sadler's Wells that raised the theatre to new heights.

Between 1844 and 1862, Phelps staged a classical repertoire, including 31 of SHAKESPEARE's plays, and attracted by far the most discerning audience in London. The supremacy of Sadler's Wells did not survive his retirement, and by 1878 the theatre was virtually derelict. After a full interior reconstruction, it was reopened in 1879 by MRS SIDNEY BATEMAN, former lessee of the LYCEUM, and struggled through in a variety of guises until 1906. Despite the pleas of conservationists, London's oldest surviving theatre was allowed to deteriorate, and it was in a new building on the site, designed by F. G. M. Chancellor to seat 1550, that LILIAN BAYLIS opened her north London operations, in association with the OLD VIC in south London, in 1931. The original plan was to alternate productions at the two theatres, but by 1934 Sadler's Wells was devoted almost exclusively to OPERA and ballet. The policy continued after wartime closure (1940–5) until the ballet company moved to COVENT GARDEN in 1956 to provide the nucleus of the Royal Ballet. In 1968, the opera company, under similar financial pressure, moved to the Coliseum

The interior of Sadler's Wells Theatre, showing the water tank, c.1809.

as part of the English National Opera. After a period of uncertainty, the theatre became the home of the Sadler's Wells Royal Ballet in 1977.   PT

Sadovsky [Ermilov]**, Prov (Mikhailovich)**   1818–72 Russian actor. Scion of a century-old family of actors at the Maly Theatre, Sadovsky was the primary interpreter of OSTROVSKY and he succeeded SHCHEPKIN in developing naturalness, simplicity and psychological veracity as the cornerstones of Russian realistic acting. Shchepkin discovered, advised and promoted the provincial actor, arranging for his Moscow debut in 1839. Although Sadovsky appeared in foreign MELODRAMAS and *vaudevilles* and acted with some success in MOLIÈRE's comedies, he was most believable playing Russians or characters like the gravedigger in *Hamlet* whom he could transform into earthy Russian types. Apart from the 29 roles he had in 28 plays which helped to establish Ostrovsky on the Russian stage, he performed works by GOGOL, D. T. Lensky, PISEMSKY, TURGENEV and SUKHOVO-KOBYLIN. The latter rejected Sadovsky's interpretation of Rasplyuev in *Krechinsky's Wedding*, in spite of its popular success, as being too vulgar. This very commonness made Sadovsky's Osip in *The Inspector General* (1845) so believable that observers thought he had become the role. Sadovsky, along with Ostrovsky, belonged to POGODIN's Slavophile *Moskvityanin* circle of journal editors and associates, which championed native culture over Western influences.   SG

Sadur, Nina (Nikolaevna)   1950– One of the new wave of Russian women dramatists. Sadur's work offers apocalyptic mystery, folklore and SURREALISM as an antidote to the mundaneness of contemporary Russia and as a summons to a reawakened spiritual life. Her plays, especially *The Swallow, or Caught in the Act, Nose, Mongrel and Moonwolves*, the GOGOLIAN *Panochka* (her most popular play, produced at the Theatre Studio Chelovek, 1988) and the historically absurdist (see THEATRE OF THE ABSURD) *Red Paradise* (1988), offer eerily sexual women, aggressive, unenlightened men, town and country myths and Pirandellian (see PIRANDELLO) inversions of illusion and reality. Banned in the 1970s, a number of these plays were published in Russia in 1989 and have since been staged abroad.   SG

sainete   see *GÉNERO CHICO*

St Charles Theatre   (New Orleans) Built by JAMES H. CALDWELL in 1835, the St Charles, with 4000 seats, a 55-ft proscenium opening and a central chandelier with 23,000 cut-glass drops lit by 250 gas jets, was the largest, handsomest and probably the most expensive theatre built in America to that date. The original STOCK COMPANY included CHARLOTTE CUSHMAN and JAMES MURDOCH. In 1842, it burned to the ground and was replaced by a lesser structure, which eventually passed to the management of Caldwell's rivals, NOAH LUDLOW and SOL SMITH. During its highwater years, most American and English stars played at the theatre, and the last known performance of JUNIUS BRUTUS BOOTH occurred on its stage. In 1899, it burned down again and was rebuilt in 1901 as a VAUDEVILLE house, which changed to films in the movie era. For a number of years, it served as a rehearsal hall for the New Orleans Symphony Orchestra because of its excellent acoustics, but was torn down in 1966. MCH

Saint-Denis, Michel 1897–1971 French director; nephew of COPEAU. Saint-Denis's first directing work was with the COMPAGNIE DES QUINZE, a group of Copeau's former pupils. In 1935 he left France to direct GIELGUD in an English version of the Quinze's success: *Noah* by OBEY. He stayed on in London to found the London Theatre Studio, a theatre school modelled on Copeau's ideas. Out of this he hoped to develop an art theatre similar to those of the Paris CARTEL, but the venture failed. However, his production of CHEKHOV's *Three Sisters* in 1939 is still remembered. During the war he worked for the BBC and then helped, with HUGH HUNT and GEORGE DEVINE, to revive the OLD VIC and establish its theatre school. Disagreements with the governors led to his departure in 1951, and in 1952 he became director of one of the new decentralized theatres (see DECENTRALIZATION MOVEMENT), the Comédie de l'Est. He founded the first theatre school outside Paris and moved theatre and school to Strasbourg in 1953, where both have since acquired an international reputation. In 1957 he went to America to advise on theatres and theatre training, later becoming co-director of the Juilliard School at the Lincoln Center, New York. He also served as artistic adviser to the ROYAL SHAKESPEARE COMPANY and to the Canadian National Theatre School. In 1960 he published *Theatre: A Rediscovery of Style*, in which methods and approaches derived from Copeau are set out. DB

St James Theatre (New York City) Intended to be a personal monument to its builder, Abraham Erlanger, a partner in the infamous THEATRICAL SYNDICATE, the theatre was named the Erlanger for the first five years of its existence. Opening in 1927 with a lesser GEORGE M. COHAN MUSICAL, the theatre reverted to the Astor estate in the early Depression. It was then leased to a succession of producers until it was bought by the SHUBERTS, who were later forced to relinquish it to comply with the terms of a consent decree limiting the number of theatres in their control in 1957. It was bought by and has remained a property of the Jujamcyn Organization. Built as a musical house with more than 1600 seats, BROADWAY history has been made on its stage. Starting in 1943, the RODGERS and HAMMERSTEIN musical *Oklahoma!* occupied it for five years. *The King and I*, another Rodgers and Hammerstein production, opened in 1951, and did not close for three years. Their *Flower Drum Song* followed in 1958. Other notable musicals have included *Hello, Dolly!* (1964), *Barnum* (1980), *My One and Only* (1983), *The Secret Garden* (1991) and *The Who's Tommy* (1993). MCH

St James's Theatre (London) Designed by Samuel Beazley for the famous tenor, John Braham, this theatre opened close to Piccadilly in 1835 and earned itself a reputation as an unlucky house. Despite occasional successes, like the appearances of the French actress, RACHEL, between 1846 and 1855, this reputation held good until 1879, when it was taken over by JOHN HARE and the KENDALS. After renovations the house held 1200 in unrivalled comfort. Hare and the Kendals tempted fashionable society with comedies about fashionable society, including several of PINERO's early plays. They left in 1888.

LILLIE LANGTRY took the St James's for a season in 1890, but its most brilliant years began in 1891 with the management of GEORGE ALEXANDER. Until his retirement in 1917, the theatre and Alexander were identified with each other. His best known productions include Pinero's *The Second Mrs Tanqueray* (1893), WILDE's *The Importance of Being Earnest* (1895), HENRY JAMES's *Guy Domville* (1895), STEPHEN PHILLIPS's *Paolo and Francesca* (1902) and Pinero's *His House in Order* (1906). Alexander was an excellent manager and his choice of plays appealed to the intelligent middle-class audience of his day by its judicious mixture of audaciousness and reassurance. Alexander was succeeded in management by Gilbert Miller, an American impresario whose method was to sublet the St James's to interested, and often interesting, companies. LAURENCE OLIVIER and VIVIEN LEIGH took it in 1950–1, opening with CHRISTOPHER FRY's *Venus Observed* and then alternating *Antony and Cleopatra* with SHAW's *Caesar and Cleopatra*. BARRAULT and Renaud presented a fine season of French plays in 1951. RATTIGAN's *Separate Tables* (1954) broke the theatre's long-run record. All was in vain. Despite a vigorous campaign, the St James's was closed in 1957 to be replaced by an office block. PT

St Lucia see EASTERN CARIBBEAN STATES

saints' play [saint's play; saint play] Term that can cover all European plays on the lives (as opposed to the miracles after death) of the saints. Length varies – from the English *Conversion of St Paul*, 662 lines, to the 40-day *Acts of the Apostles* from Bourges, France. PM

Sakata Tōjūrō 1647–1709 The most popular Japanese KABUKI actor in Kyoto–Osaka during the period of Genroku culture (1688–c.1730). Little is known of his early life except that he was the son of an actor. In 1678 he created a sensation playing Izaemon, the romantic lover of the prostitute Yūgiri, in *New Year's Remembrance of Yūgiri* (*Yūgiri nagori no shōgatsu*). Yūgiri was an actual prostitute from Osaka who had died the month before and this 'overnight pickles' (*ichiyazuke*) play capitalized on town scandal about this event. Tōjūrō revived the play 18 times in his career, gaining the nickname Sakata Izaemon. In this and similar 'disguised lover' (*yatsushi*) roles in plays about contemporary commoners (*sewamono*) he developed a gentle, humorous, 'soft' (*wagoto*) acting style. For five years he was actor-manager (*zagashira*) of the Mandayū Theatre in Kyoto, acting in similar plays written by his staff playwright CHIKAMATSU MONZAEMON.

He based his acting on close observation of merchant life. His colleagues, including Chikamatsu, praised his egoless acting, careful attention to the dramatic requirements of the script and 'realistic' approach to directing other actors, insisting that the actor study the actual details of a character's circumstances. His comments on acting were set down by others in *The Actors' Analects* (*Yakusha rongo*, 1776; trans. 1969). The tradition of *wagoto* acting is continued today by Nakamura Ganjirō III (1931–) and a small number of other actors.   JRB

sakhi kundhei *[sakhi nata; kundhei nata; gopa lila]* Form of string-puppet performance found in Orissa state in eastern India: literally, 'doll dance'. Puppet heads and hands are made of light wood and paper. Their costumes follow those of *JATRA* actors of the region, especially in the well known character roles. Some PUPPETS are made with movable legs, others have a skirt, like their Rajasthani counterparts, covering the legless torso. Animal puppets include tigers, elephants, goats and horses. Stories centre on events in the life of Lord Krishna.

The stage, like that of *kathputli* of Rajasthan, may be decorated with colourful cloth pieces of the region, depending on the wealth of the players. Itinerant families of four or five performers work fairs and festivals, collecting what they can in donations from villagers.

Musicians sing folk tunes and adaptations of film songs to narrate the story. A cymbal player, *pakhavaj* drummer and harmonium player provide the basic rhythm for the narrator-singer.   FaR

Saks, Gene 1921– American director and actor, former president of the US Society of Stage Directors and Choreographers. Born in New York City and educated at Cornell University (1939–43), Saks studied acting at the ACTORS STUDIO and Dramatic Workshop. He made his New York debut in 1947 as Joxer in O'CASEY's *Juno and the Paycock*. During the next decade he appeared mainly in supporting roles before attracting critical attention in 1962 as Leo Herman in *A Thousand Clowns*. He turned to directing in 1963, establishing himself as one of BROADWAY's premier directors of comedy, known for his inventiveness and attention to detail. His major directing credits include *Nobody Loves an Albatross* (1963), *Generation* (1965), *Mame* (1966), *Sheep on the Runway* (1970), *How the Other Half Loves* (1971), *Same Time, Next Year* (1975), *I Love My Wife* (1977, Tony), *Supporting Cast* (1981), *Special Occasions* (1982), *Brighton Beach Memoirs* (1983), *Biloxi Blues* (1984, Tony) and *Lost in Yonkers* (1991). He is married to actress Beatrice Arthur. Numerous films include *Barefoot in the Park*, *The Odd Couple*, *Last of the Red Hot Lovers* and *Mame*.   TLM

Salacrou, Armand 1899–1989 French playwright who made a small fortune in advertising but sold up to devote himself to writing. His first success was *Patchouli* produced by DULLIN in 1930, and Dullin was to direct many of his subsequent plays, notably *Atlas-Hotel* (1931) and *La Terre est ronde* (*The World Is Round*, 1938). He was influential in the late 1940s, partly because of BARRAULT's fine staging of *Les Nuits de la colère* (*Nights of Anger*) in 1946, a play about resistance and collaboration which was chosen by STREHLER the year after to open his Piccolo Teatro. *L'Archipel Lenoir* (*The Lenoir Archipelago*; directed by Dullin, 1947) satirized the bourgeoisie and *Boulevard Durand* (directed by Reybaz, 1961) was a documentary drama about Jules Durand, a trade union activist of Le Havre sentenced to death in 1910 for a murder he did not commit.

Salacrou was a fine craftsman, using the well tried devices of plot and character. Some of his plays explore themes later developed by SARTRE, and his *L'Inconnue d'Arras* (*The Unknown Woman of Arras*, 1935) has been seen as a source for *In Camera*. He anticipated the social drama that flourished in the DECENTRALIZATION MOVEMENT after the Second World War, but his work was neither so bold theatrically nor so clear politically as that of BRECHT and his successors, who became the mainstay of those theatres. His major contribution to the movement was *Boulevard Durand* performed in Le Havre by the Centre Dramatique du Nord in 1961. His earlier plays show men and women who cover their sense of the meaninglessness of life with a commitment to action, however futile.   DB

Salazar Bondy, Sebastián 1924–65 Peruvian playwright and poet. Salazar Bondy studied at the University of San Marcos, and later at the National Conservatory in Paris. He founded the Club de Teatro (Theatre Club) in Lima in 1953 with Reynaldo D'Amore. In 1947 he obtained first prize in a national theatre contest for his first play, *Amor, gran laberinto* (*Love, the Great Labyrinth*), that revealed his affinity for satirical FARCE. *Rodil* (1952) and *Flora Tristán* (1958) dealt with aspects of Peruvian social history. *El fabricante de deudas* (*The Debt Arranger*, 1962), inspired by Balzac, used humour and BRECHTian techniques to uncover bourgeois economics. His masterpiece was *El rabdomante* (*The Diviner*, 1965), a play that incorporated his earlier techniques of SATIRE, social commentary and humour into an absurdist mould (see THEATRE OF THE ABSURD). His several one-act plays, which he called 'games' and 'toys', are also important.   GW

Salisbury Court Theatre (London) This indoor theatre, built of brick and stone, was the last to be erected before the English Civil War. It was opened in 1630 as a home for the Children of the King's Revels under the management of an actor-playwright, Richard Gunnell, and with the King's MASTER OF THE REVELS as a shareholder. An INIGO JONES drawing at Worcester College, Oxford, of a previously unidentified theatre may be his design for the Salisbury Court. It housed a semicircular stage in a rectangular frame 53ft by 37ft, a typically intimate 'private' Caroline theatre. Prince Charles's Men and Queen Henrietta's Men were among prominent companies to play there before the CLOSURE OF THE THEATRES. During the Interregnum, the lease of the Salisbury Court was purchased by WILLIAM BEESTON, perhaps for surreptitious performance by a children's company which provoked a military raid in 1649. The dismantled theatre was refurbished by Beeston in 1660 and continued to house plays until its destruction in the Great Fire of 1666.   PT

Salle des Machines (Paris) Large theatre in the Tuileries palace, built by the architect Le Vau and lavishly equipped by GASPARE VIGARANI for the entertainments arranged to celebrate the marriage of Louis XIV in 1660. It remained in use for many years for court performances, notably of OPERA and similar spectacles, under the successive direction of the younger Vigarani, BERAIN and ultimately SERVANDONI. It housed the Opéra between 1763 and 1770 and the COMÉDIE-FRANÇAISE for a short period after 1770.   DR

Salom, Jaime 1925- Spanish playwright from Barcelona whose first major success was the metatheatrical *El baúl de los disfraces* (*The Trunk of Disguises*, 1964) His highly charged Civil War drama, *La casa de las Chivas* (*The House of the 'Chivas'*, 1968), broke Madrid records by running for 1343 performances. In the 1970s Salom adopted liberal stances on social issues and experimented with fluid episodic structures. *La piel del limón* (*Bitter Lemon*, 1976) highlights the need for divorce reform. *El corto vuelo del gallo* (*The Cock's Short Flight*, 1980) offers a sympathetic portrait of General Franco's liberal and libertine father. His historical drama about Bartolomé de las Casas, *Una hoguera al amanecer* (*Bonfire at Dawn*, 1991), premiered in Mexico and was performed in Washington during the 1992 Quincentennial. This portrayal of the defender of the New World's indigenous people is made more poignant by the protagonist's enduring homosexual love for a young Indian.   MPH

Saltykov-Shchedrin, Mikhail (Evgrafovich) [N. Shchedrin] 1826–89 Russian satirist, novelist, dramatist and radical journalist, who exposed hypocrisy, petty tyranny, and spiritual and moral bankruptcy at all levels of Tsarist society. A long-time civil servant and one-time provincial governor, he became a colleague in the liberal press of Chernyshevsky, Dobrolyubov and Nekrasov, writing for the *Contemporary* and editing its successor, *Notes of the Fatherland*. His major narrative works include *Provincial Sketches* (1856), an anti-bureaucratic SATIRE; *History of a Town* (1869), a PARODY of Russian history and an attack on Tsarist tyranny via the study of a mythical town named Stupidville; *The Golovlyovs* (1880), a gloomy chronicle of a family's gradual self-destruction; and *Fables* (1869–86), which employs the traditional Russian device of Aesopian language to criticize the status quo. His writings, rich in dialogue and character sketches, were staged during his lifetime not always to the author's satisfaction. His two plays met with some resistance. *Pazukhin's Death* (1857), which depicts another monstrous family, received its provincial and Moscow premieres in 1889 and 1893, respectively. It was revived by NEMIROVICH-DANCHENKO at the MOSCOW ART THEATRE in 1914. *Shadows* (1862–5), another satire on the world of clerks and bureaucrats, was first staged in 1914. Saltykov's satire was tentatively embraced by the Soviet regime, blessed by GORKY as an indictment of the past and staged in recent years by TOVSTONOGOV, LEV DODIN and others.   SG

Salvini, Tommaso 1829–1915 Italian actor-manager. Born into the profession, Salvini acted professionally from an early age and was a prominent member of the new young company formed in 1843 by GUSTAVO MODENA, whose stage reforms in favour of simplicity, naturalness and psychological truth greatly influenced his development. By his late teens he was playing lead roles opposite the principal actresses of the age, including RISTORI. In 1856 he gave one of the first significant performances of a SHAKESPEARE play in Italy when he played Othello at

Vicenza (ERNESTO ROSSI undertook the part at about the same time); shortly afterwards he appeared as Hamlet.

His repertoire was never large and these roles (to which he later added Macbeth, King Lear and Coriolanus) – along with a handful of Italian parts, like Corrado in GIACOMETTI's *La morte civile* (*Civil Death*) and the title role in ALFIERI's *Saul* – formed the cornerstone of his later foreign touring repertoire. He became the most internationally celebrated actor of his age, enjoying a triumphant histrionic progress from 1869 onwards to his retirement, through North and South America, Western Europe and Russia. The opening performance of his Othello at the Boston Conservatoire in 1873 was an unqualified triumph, and that success he repeated two years later in London, where the gradually unleashed savage animality of his Moor astonished critics and public alike.

Endowed with rich physical attributes – a powerful, sonorous voice, striking and muscular figure, stage presence, and perfect command of gesture and movement – he brought intelligence and imaginative perception to his preparation and execution of roles, on occasions retiring from the stage for months at a time in order to study a new piece. Although none of his Shakespearian roles equalled his Othello in public favour, all commanded admiration in part or in whole, particularly his Hamlet, which G. H. LEWES thought the most satisfying interpretation he had ever seen. Critics and practitioners, from HENRY JAMES and THÉOPHILE GAUTIER to BERNARD SHAW, from Ristori to BERNHARDT to STANISLAVSKY, were unanimous in his praise. The success of his British tour in 1876 through a dozen provincial cities is witness to the spell he could exercise on spectators wholly ignorant of the language in which he performed. For all that his productions were meticulously thought out and respectably, if simply, mounted, his performance was always the dominant attraction: he was perhaps the consummate 'star' actor of the century.   KR

Sam S. Shubert Theatre (New York City) In 1913, LEE and JACOB J. SHUBERT, their position as producers and theatre owners ensured, bought a site that ran through the block from West 44th to West 45th Street behind the Hotel Astor. There they built two theatres, one of which they named after their brother Sam S. Shubert, who had been killed in a railway accident in 1905. It was to become the flagship of the Shubert enterprises and their headquarters, which it has remained. Ultimately, with the BOOTH THEATRE, it formed the western wall of Shubert Alley. For most of its history, the Shuberts have presented their own brand of MUSICAL drama and comedies. In 1975, JOSEPH PAPP moved *A Chorus Line* to the Shubert, where it broke all standing records as the longest-running production (6137 performances) on a BROADWAY stage.   MCH

Sami theatre The Sami (sometimes referred to as 'Lapps') are a people of about 60,000, indigenous to northern Norway, Sweden, Finland and Russia. After over a century of suppression of their language, religion and customs, and industrial destruction of their reindeer-grazing lands, Sami have begun to succeed in their demands for protection and cultural expression. Norway, Sweden and Finland have Sami parliaments, although only advisory in status, and there has been a cultural revival in which theatre has played a significant though ephemeral role. Productions are important for their use of the Sami language, drumming and chanting, and dramatization of Sami mythology and contemporary social problems. Dálvadis Theatre started in Jokkmokk, Sweden, in 1971, and lasted until 1993, performing in Sami, but also in Swedish and English. Beaivvás began in Guovdageaidnu (Kautokeino), Norway, in 1981, growing directly out of the protest movement against a proposed hydro-electric dam at Alta. Beaivvás has been state-supported since 1987, and one of Norway's national theatres since 1993; it performs in Sami, but has staged not only Sami works but plays by BRECHT and GARCÍA LORCA. Other companies have included Samiska Teatern and Hiwak, which worked in Sweden in the early 1990s, and Ravgos, an ambitious Finnish amateur group. There is discussion of starting a Sami theatre school in Finland.   HL

Samson, Joseph Isidore 1793–1871 French actor. Samson's career was particularly associated with the COMÉDIE-FRANÇAISE, of which he became *doyen* in 1840. Admitted to the Conservatoire in 1810, he was advised to try COMEDY rather than TRAGEDY because of his nasal voice and undistinguished appearance. He worked in the provinces, especially Rouen, until PICARD took him to the reconstructed ODÉON in 1819. In 1826, the Comédie-Française, using a right granted it in 1818, co-opted him. In 1831 he moved to the PALAIS-ROYAL for a brief period, but was forced to return to the Théâtre-Français, where he had his first successes in the repertoire of SCRIBE, with Bertrand de Rantzau in *Bertrand et Raton* (1833) and the doctor in *L'Ambitieux* (*The Ambitious Man*, 1834). He wrote a number of plays, of which the most successful was *La Famille Poisson* (1845). Together with Baron Taylor, he founded the Society for Dramatic Artists. His major later roles included André in *Le Chandelier* (*The Candleholder*, 1852) and the marquis in *Mlle de Seiglière* (1851), a role in which he was unequalled. He had a particularly fine reputation as a teacher at the Conservatoire, and RACHEL was one of his pupils and protégés.   JMCC

San Francisco Mime Troupe (USA) In embryonic form since 1955, but founded in 1962 by R.G. Davis, who had moved to San Francisco in 1958 after several years of mime study in Paris. Over the years it moved from silent MIME to avant-garde happenings to outdoor COMMEDIA DELL'ARTE-styled performance and on to radical politics. This theatre COLLECTIVE, an expression of the members' social and political concerns, is based on the highly physical expression of *commedia dell'arte* and R.G. Davis's dance and mime training. This amplified aesthetic perfectly suits the outdoor venues in which the troupe performs for part of every year. Davis left the troupe in 1970; Joan Holden has been the chief resident playwright since 1967. In recent years the troupe has undertaken extensive touring in the USA as well as in Europe and in Central America, including the successful *I Ain't Yo' Uncle*, an AFRICAN-AMERICAN deconstruction of *UNCLE TOM'S CABIN*.   TL

Sánchez, Florencio 1875–1910 Self-taught journalist and playwright, Uruguayan-born but later settled in ARGENTINA. His plays captured the essence of a period of social turbulence in the River Plate region. An admirer of IBSEN and HAUPTMANN, Sánchez wrote with a realistic, at times naturalistic, language and technique (see REALISM; NATURALISM) faithful to his region in portraying problems endemic to both rural and urban settings. His nearly 20 plays staged between 1901 and 1909, the so-called 'Golden Decade' in the River Plate, dealt with such issues as racism, poverty, alcoholism, the *gaucho*, and man *vis-à-vis* nature. Major dramas include *La gringa* (*The Foreigner*, 1904) and *En familia* (*In the Family*, 1905); his masterwork is *Barranca abajo* (*Down the Valley*, 1905), in which Don Zoilo, the old *gaucho* victimized by family, neighbours and society, finds no recourse but suicide. Sánchez died of tuberculosis at an early age, but left a rich legacy of *sainetes* (see *GÉNERO CHICO*) that inspired others such as Gregorio de Laferrère and Armando Discépolo in renovating the national theatre.   GW

Sánchez, Luis Rafael 1936– Puerto Rican playwright, novelist and professor. Sánchez was influenced by IONESCO and by his compatriot RENÉ MARQUÉS in the early stages. His *Sol 13, interior* (*Sol 13, Inside*, 1961) consisted of a suite, *La hiel nuestra de cada día* (*Our Daily Gall*) and *Los ángeles se han fatigado* (*The Angels Are Tired*), plays thematically linked in contemporary working-class Puerto Rican settings to classical motifs. *O casi el alma* (*Or Almost the Soul*, 1964) posits Christ in a theological discussion on PUERTO RICO. *La pasión según Antígona Pérez* (*The Passion according to Antígona Pérez*, 1968) is an 'American chronicle' of Latin American revolution using BRECHTian techniques and the Antigone dilemma. *Quíntuples* (*Quintuplets*, 1984), played by two characters, consists of six monologues (by the father and five siblings) that reveal the often sordid details of their lives with ingenious and humorous techniques.   GW

sandae-gùk Korean dance drama. The literal meaning, 'mountain or hillside ritual', may be interpreted as indicating either a formal performance, that is, one given on a high stage, or a folk performance that uses a mound of earth for a stage. *Sandae-gùk* is now a term which broadly includes most forms of traditional MASKED dance drama in Korea (none today are performed on a built stage, however). They are folk forms preserved by local performers through oral tradition, and performed as a rule for RITUAL and ceremonial occasions specific to each village or area. Important regional varieties of masked drama are: *OGWANGDAE*, *PYOLSANDAE*, *T'ALCH'UM* and *YARYU*.   OKC

Sandow, Eugen [Ernst Friedrich Möller] 1867–1925 German strong-man, the first stage Hercules to parlay his physique into a commercial property. As a boy he was influenced by classical statuary and developed a system of body-building through attention to individual muscle groups. At his London debut at the Royal Aquarium (1889), he wrestled the champion Samson and lifted weights, including, later, a 312lb dumb-bell and a 600lb cart-horse (1891). At the Chicago Columbian Exposition of 1893, FLORENZ ZIEGFELD glorified him with spectacular publicity, abbreviated costumes and such stunts as having him lift his pianist with the grand piano. Sandow advertised

Eugen Sandow in a typical pose which led contemporaries to debate how the fig-leaf was kept on.

products like corsets and health oils and promoted several physical culture magazines. He retired in 1907. LS

Sangallo, Bastiano da [Aristotile] 1481–1551 Italian architect and stage designer, and a crucially influential figure in the evolution of perspective staging and scenic effects. BUONTALENTI and VASARI were his pupils and learned much from him, although few examples of his scenic work have survived. KR

Sanger, 'Lord' George 1827–1911 British showman, who began as a child spieling outside his father's show-booth. He created a sensation using naphtha lamps in London's Mile End Road, and moved on to limelight with lantern shows in the midlands. His first CIRCUS opened at Charter Fair, Kings Lynn, and in 1860 he originated the first three-ring circus at Plymouth Hoe but, finding it did not pay, reverted to one ring. In 1871 he bought ASTLEY's Amphitheatre, enlarged it and opened it as Sanger's Grand National Amphitheatre with the PANTOMIME *Lady Godiva*. There and at Royal Agricultural Hall he staged mammoth spectaculars that earned him a fortune. In 1893 Sanger let the Ecclesiastical Commissioners pull down Astley's, but carried on his gigantic TENT SHOW until 1905. The dapper bald man with the handlebar moustache was married to the lion-tamer Ella Chapman and, in 1911, was murdered by a berserk farmhand wielding an axe. LS

Sanquirico, Alessandro 1777–1849 Italian scene designer. From 1817 to 1832 Sanquirico was the sole designer and chief scene painter for La Scala in Milan. He designed operas by Bellini, Donizetti, Mozart, Meyerbeer and Rossini, thus exerting great influence on the development of GRAND OPERA. Among the hundreds of OPERAS and ballets designed for La Scala, the most important included the premieres of Rossini's *La gazza ladra* (1827), Bellini's *Norma* (1831) and Donizetti's *Lucretia Borgia* (1834). His settings were on a vast scale, using a richly decorated architectural foreground and opening out to a broad landscape view painted with a single-point perspective. He used the qualities of gas lighting to create the correct atmosphere against his painted scenery. His designs epitomized the 'grand opera' style and became published and circulated, creating a standard for opera design in Italy and elsewhere in the mid-19th century. AJN

Santana, Rodolfo 1944– Prolific Venezuelan playwright. Santana has written more than 50 plays, most of them performed and/or published. An early period was dominated by metaphysical, absurdist (see THEATRE OF THE ABSURD) and science-fiction plays. In a later period he used Kafkaesque techniques to examine cruelty, violence, sex and revolution in contemporary society: *La muerte de Alfredo Gris* (*The Death of Alfredo Gris*, 1968) and *El sitio* (*The Siege*, 1969) are examples. A third, more eclectic, period included experimentation with historical materials (*Barbarroja*, 1970) as well as sociopolitical issues. Santana's plays have won prizes in many of the national drama festivals. Other works include the monologue *La empresa perdona un momento de locura* (*The Company Allows a Moment of Madness*, 1979), *El animador* (*The MC*, 1980) and the boxing piece *Fin del Round* (*End of the Round*, 1981). GW

Santareno, Bernardo [Antonio Martinho do Rosario] 1920–80 Portuguese playwright. Driven by *saeva indignatio* against all forms of exploitation and injustice, Santareno was the dramatist most closely and constantly in touch with the most intimate and passionately cherished aspirations of the people in the Salazar era. In the theatre he developed a highly naturalistic and compelling dramatic construction and dialogue, from *A Promessa* (*The Promise*, 1957), over most of the 18 plays he wrote up to the unpublished *O Punho* (*The Fist*). *A Promessa* was first performed in the Teatro Experimental do Porto; many subsequent plays were banned or withdrawn after short runs (see CENSORSHIP). His *Crime de Aldeia Velha* (1959) shows, every bit as powerfully as MILLER in *The Crucible*, superstition, rural backwardness and mass hysteria leading to a 'witch' trial and burning. *O Judeu* (*The Jew*, 1966) is a harrowing reconstruction of the infamous Inquisition trial of the 18th-century dramatist SILVA, and of the society which could countenance such an institutional crime. LK

São Tomé e Principe see PORTUGUESE-SPEAKING AFRICA

Saqui, Madame [Marguerite-Antoinette-Sévère Lalane; La Belle Nini] 1777–1866 French rope dancer, the greatest of her age; the daughter of gymnasts. As La Belle

Nini, she played juvenile roles and at 15 made a thunderous debut at the CIRQUE OLYMPIQUE. In 1809 she married the acrobat and impresario Saqui. Her exploits included vaulting over 24 armed soldiers and dancing on a cord stretched between the towers of Notre Dame. When she performed before Napoleon, she was set ablaze by the fireworks. In 1816, she performed quick-change roles in her own booth on the Boulevard du Temple, which she maintained till 1830. Penniless, she returned to touring, amassing 32,000 francs which were stolen by highway robbers when she was 75. She returned to Paris and could be seen in the Champ de Mars pushing a child in a wheelbarrow across the tightrope.   LS

Sarcey, Francisque   1827–99 French critic. Sarcey began his career as a teacher, but was dismissed for his liberal beliefs. In 1860 he gave public lectures at literary matinées at the Athénée and Gaîté theatres (see BOULEVARD). Under various pseudonyms he contributed to a number of newspapers. From its foundation in 1860 he was drama critic for the *Opinion Nationale* and in 1867 he took on Sainte-Beuve's Monday column in the *Temps*, which he continued until his death. His criticisms were published by Adolphe Brisson as *Quarante Ans de théâtre* (1900–2). Sarcey was much respected by actors, who knew him as 'uncle' Sarcey, and noted for his impartiality. His tastes were basically conservative and he placed great emphasis on common sense and professionalism. He believed that the critic should go with the current of popular opinion and try to shape it, rather than offer absolute principles; that the voice of the critic was that of the audience and that a play should be judged according to its own conventions.   JMCC

Sardou, Victorien   1831–1908 French dramatist. Like SCRIBE, to whom he is often compared, Sardou was a master-craftsman of the theatre. He developed the WELL MADE PLAY, using a wide arsenal of effective devices. Like much popular, but secondary, 19th-century dramatic writing, his work depends on the exploitation of successful formulae. It was this aspect of his work that led G. B. SHAW to coin the term 'Sardoodledom' (he refers to the Napoleon of Sardou's *Madame Sans-Gêne* as 'nothing but the jealous husband of a thousand fashionable dramas, talking Buonapartiana'). Sardou had a good sense of stage business. Every exit and entrance had a distinct purpose for the development of the plot. The dialogue is basically naturalistic, avoiding long monologues and generally slipping exposition into casual remarks.

Sardou ranks with AUGIER and DUMAS *fils* as one of the successful dramatists of the Second Empire and Third Republic, despite the frequently meretricious quality of his plays. The major areas exploited by Sardou are the large-scale historical play and comedies reflecting French society towards the end of the Second Empire. His first play, *La Taverne des étudiants* (*The Students' Tavern*, 1854), was a failure, and he could not get another play staged until VIRGINIE DÉJAZET put on his *Les Premières Armes de Figaro* (*Figaro's First Arms*) at her theatre in 1859. *A Scrap of Paper* (*Pattes de mouches*, 1860), at the Théâtre du Gymnase, established his reputation as a master of stagecraft, this COMEDY being a very clever piece of

skilfully manipulated intrigue.

He is at his best in his comedies, notably in early works such as *La Famille Benoîton* (1865) and *Nos bons villageois* (*Our Good Villagers*, 1866), in the hard-hitting political SATIRE of *Rabagas* (1872) or in the extremely amusing vaudeville, *Let's Get a Divorce* (1880). He embarked on the large-scale historical drama with *Patrie* (*Fatherland*, 1869) and *La Haine* (*Hatred*, 1874). These plays are partly an excuse for an imposing *mise-en-scène* and generally involve a mixing of dramatic genres. Characterization is schematic and the more serious of them leave a sense of MELODRAMA with pretensions. This is particularly true of a series written as vehicles for a star, SARAH BERNHARDT: *La Tosca* (1887), *Cléopâtre* (1890) and *Gismonda* (1894), or his historical comedy *Madame Sans-Gêne*, played first by RÉJANE in 1893. The latter illustrated how much more at home he was in historical comedy than in more serious works, where the hollowness of the psychology is only too evident. Two of his late plays, *Robespierre* (1899) and *Dante* (1903), were written to be staged by IRVING. *L'Affaire des poisons* (1907) was his last play and exploited a particularly seamy side of the court of Louis XIV.   JMCC

Saroyan, William   1908–81 Californian Armenian, who made his debut as a playwright with *My Heart's in the Highlands* (1939). Both the GROUP THEATRE and the THEATRE GUILD had a hand in its production, and although most playgoers were baffled by its loose allegorical form, the play received enough critical acclaim to establish Saroyan as the leading avant-garde playwright of the day. His next play, *The Time of Your Life* (1939), solidified his critical reputation by winning the Pulitzer Prize and the Drama Critics' Circle Award (the first time the two groups ever agreed on a choice). Saroyan rejected the Pulitzer Prize on the grounds that material awards were debilitating to the recipient. Now a modern American classic, *The Time of Your Life*, revived periodically in New York, has appeared on the bill of almost every professional regional theatre, pleasing audiences with its originality, imagination, wit, humanity and local San Francisco colour. Continuing to write for the stage through the late 1950s, Saroyan never again achieved the success of his first two plays, although amateur groups everywhere have produced his uncharacteristically conventional one-act play, *Hello Out There* (1942). *The Beautiful People* (1941), directed by the playwright, and *The Cave Dwellers* (1957) found a brief audience and are occasionally revived, but his other works including *Love's Old Sweet Song* (1940) and *Get Away Old Man* (1943) were quick failures. Much of Saroyan's later years were spent writing novels and autobiographical remembrances.   LDC

Sartre, Jean-Paul   1905–80 French philosopher, novelist and playwright. Sartre rejected psychological theatre, defining his as a 'theatre of situations' in which characters are defined not by their psychological states, but by their choices and actions. Sartre's existentialism posits a world of interpersonal relations in which each person struggles to control the other, and this makes for exciting dramatic situations especially well exemplified by *Huis clos* (*In Camera*, 1944), which has become an acknowledged masterpiece of the modern theatre.

Sartre's career as a playwright began with *Les Mouches* (*The Flies*; directed by DULLIN, 1943), a modern version of the Electra story which was seen in occupied Paris as a call to resistance. His reputation was high throughout the late 1940s, when he wrote many plays, several of which were performed at the Théâtre Antoine (which otherwise specialized in BOULEVARD comedy). These included *Les Mains sales* (*Dirty Hands*, 1948) about political expediency and *Le Diable et le bon Dieu* (*The Devil and the Good Lord*, 1951), which JOUVET had been directing when he died. In 1954 Sartre made a successful adaptation of DUMAS *père*'s *Kean* in which Pierre Brasseur scored a big success, but *Nekrassov* (1955) was a failure with the boulevard public because of its caustic anti-capitalist SATIRE. In *Les Séquestrés d'Altona* (*The Condemned of Altona*, 1959) he came nearest to writing a tragedy of modern times with the story of a young German whose attempts at free choice during the Hitler period were falsified by the subsequent turn of historical events. In 1965 he wrote a fine adaptation of EURIPIDES' *Trojan Women* (directed by Cacoyannis, THÉÂTRE NATIONAL POPULAIRE).

Despite his lifelong interest in Greek tragedy, Sartre's imagination was essentially melodramatic. The model for his dramaturgical practice was Alexandre Dumas, whose work he so brilliantly adapted. Like SALACROU, he attempted to articulate themes of existential despair and political commitment without ever elaborating a fully adequate dramatic form.   DB

Sastre, Alfonso 1926– Spanish playwright and dramatic theorist whose first major play, the existentialist *Escuadra hacia la muerte* (*The Condemned Squad*, 1953), was closed by official CENSORSHIP after three performances for its anti-militarism. Thus began a long period of conflict with the Franco regime, culminating in imprisonment two decades later.

His plays, banned in Spain, were frequently staged in France and Italy. In the 1950s he concentrated on a socially committed SARTREan theatre, centring on revolution and the moral ambiguity of terrorism and violence. By the early 1960s he had abandoned Aristotelian concepts of tragedy and moved to EPIC THEATRE. Among his most performed plays internationally are *Guillermo Tell tiene los ojos tristes* (*Sad Are the Eyes of William Tell*, 1962), an ironic inversion of the historical tale, and *Historia de una muñeca abandonada* (*Story of an Abandoned Doll*, 1964). This charming reworking as children's theatre of BRECHT's *The Caucasian Chalk Circle* was successfully revived in 1989 at the TEATRO NACIONAL MARÍA GUERRERO. Dating from the mid-1960s are his 'complex tragedies', which combine elements of classical TRAGEDY with Brechtian techniques and a use of the grotesque reminiscent of VALLE-INCLÁN. Two historical plays from this group, *La sangre y la ceniza* (*Blood and Ashes*, 1967) and *Crónicas romanas* (*Roman Chronicles*, 1970), have been performed successfully abroad. Sastre's long-awaited integration into mainstream Spanish theatre came finally in 1985, when he was awarded the National Theatre Prize for *La taberna fantástica* (*The Fantastic Tavern*, 1966).   PZ

satire BURLESQUE, PARODY and satire are often treated as synonyms for ridicule through distortion, but it is useful to suggest distinctions between them. None of the three words refers exclusively to drama; yet all have been applied to drama. Although sometimes confused with the Greek satyr play, the word 'satire' is of Roman origin, meaning a dish of mixed fruit, and the long poems first called satires mixed several literary techniques. Satire as ridicule with a meliorative intention did not, however, await the invention of the Latin word, for the technique of satire is virulently evident in the comedies of ARISTOPHANES. Sometimes claimed as a genre distinct from COMEDY, satire can vary from the gentle mockery of SHAKESPEARE or MOLIÈRE to the bitter thrust of JOHN MARSTON or LESAGE. Perhaps the most celebrated modern satirist is SHAW, but BRECHT also draws upon its long tradition in such plays as *Man Is Man*.   RC

Satoh Makoto 1943– Japanese playwright and director. The product of a complex intellectual background that included affinities with the ultra-nationalist right, the revolutionary left, Christianity and existentialism, Satoh received his theatre education at the Actors' Theatre Training School, graduating in 1965. He was a founder of the Black Tent Theatre (Kuro Tento) in 1968. Satoh won the Kishida Prize for Playwriting in 1970 for *Nezumi Kozō: The Rat* (*Nezumi Kozō Jirokichi*, 1969; trans. 1986), and the plays he wrote between 1966 and 1976, from *Ismene* (*Isumene*, 1966; trans. 1992) to *The Murder of Blanqui, Spring in Shanghai* (*Buranki-goroshi Shanhai no haru*, 1976), are among the most challenging and rich of the post-SHINGEKI period. In recent years, he has written less and devoted himself increasingly to directing, particularly for the opera.   DGG

satyr play   see GREECE, ANCIENT

Satz, Ludwig 1895–1944 Much loved leading 'star' comedian of the American YIDDISH THEATRE from 1918 until his death. Billed as 'the man who makes you laugh with tears and cry with a smile', he was a master of characterization, improvisation and make-up.   AB

Saunders, James 1925– British dramatist, whose early plays were influenced by English poetic drama and the French absurdists (see THEATRE OF THE ABSURD). His IONESCO-inspired duologue, *Alas, Poor Fred*, was produced in Scarborough in 1959 and in London seven years later, but his first stage success came with *Next Time I'll Sing to You* (1963). It was suggested by the life of an Essex hermit, Jimmy Mason; the actors, who discuss the recluse, act episodes from his life and sometimes wonder what they are supposed to be doing, are themselves presented as lonely individuals, not too far removed from Mason's seclusion. Loneliness is also a theme in *A Scent of Flowers* (1964), about a young girl who died from lack of love. Literary experiment is a feature of Saunders's prolific output, with frequent echoes of PIRANDELLO, BECKETT and even BEAUMONT and FLETCHER (in *The Borage Pigeon Affair*, 1969). He collaborated with Iris Murdoch in adapting her novel, *The Italian Girl* (1968), for the stage. He has worked widely among the little theatres around London and is a strong supporter of Britain's leading amateur theatre, QUESTORS, in Ealing, West London; but his major

WEST END success was *Bodies* (1978), about two middle-aged couples facing crises in their lives. *Making It Better* (1992), about a World Service radio producer at the time of the Velvet Revolution in Czechoslovakia, was an intelligent comedy chosen to reopen London's Criterion Theatre after four years' restoration. JE

Savary, Jérôme 1942– French actor, director and dramatist. Savary's theatre career began with the writing and production of a 'musical tragedy' in 1965 and the founding (with ARRABAL) of the Grand Théâtre Panique. This became the Grand Magic Circus in 1968 and produced a series of highly successful shows, part CABARET, part social SATIRE, usually performed in unconventional theatre spaces. In 1981 he applied his irreverent performance techniques to MOLIÈRE's *Le Bourgeois Gentilhomme*, and in 1982 he became director of a new Maison de la Culture at Béziers. He has directed OFFENBACH in Germany and made several films. In 1988 he returned to Paris as director of the CHAILLOT THEATRE. DB

Savina [Podramentsova]**, Mariya (Gavrilovna)** 1854–1915 Russian actress, best known for her epistolary relations with IVAN TURGENEV. After seven years on the provincial stage, in 1874 she joined the Imperial Alexandra Troupe in St Petersburg where she remained until her death. Throughout the 1870s her roles constituted a portrait gallery of Russian girlhood, and she excelled as the Mayor's daughter in *The Government Inspector*. In 1879 she created Verochka in Turgenev's *A Month in the Country* and would age into the role of Nataliya Petrovna (1903), the pinnacle of her achievement. Other parts include Katharina in *The Taming of the Shrew*, Nastasya Filipovna in a dramatization of Dostoevsky's *The Idiot*, Akulina in LEV TOLSTOI's *The Power of Darkness*, Sasha in CHEKHOV's *Ivanov* and Nora in the first Russian *Doll's House*. Her acting, based on French models, was highly polished but somewhat shallow, and Chekhov thought her wooden in comparison with DUSE. Nevertheless, Tolstoi deemed her 'clever' and Turgenev valued highly her judgement and her contributions to his plays. LS

Savits, Jocza 1847–1915 German director. Savits pioneered the 'SHAKESPEARE stage' in the Munich Court Theatre between 1888 and 1906. With this stage he attempted, without much success, to re-create the non-illusionistic playing conditions of the Elizabethan theatre. Despite the incompleteness of his achievement, Savits's experiments pre-dated those of the Englishman WILLIAM POEL and also influenced GEORG FUCHS in his founding of the Munich Artists' Theatre. SW

Savoy, Bert [Everett McKenzie] c.1888–1923 Female impersonator (see FEMALE IMPERSONATION). 'Chair dancer' in a Boston dime museum, chorus boy, and passing as a female singer from Montana to Alaska, Savoy wound up in New York where he teamed up with Jay Brennan (c.1913). In their double act Brennan played a fey 'feed' to Savoy's flamboyant red-haired tart, always talking about her girlfriend Margie. Savoy's brassy style and catchphrases – 'You musssst come up', 'You slay me', 'You haven't heard the half of it, dearie' and 'I'm glad you ast me' – may have inspired MAE WEST. The act, an eruption of homosexual subculture into the mainstream, earned $1500 a week in VAUDEVILLE and REVUE: *The Passing Show of 1915*, *The ZIEGFELD Follies of 1918* and *The Greenwich Village Follies* (1920–3). After Savoy was killed by a lightning bolt on Long Island beach, Brennan continued the act with other partners. LS

Saxe-Meiningen, Duke of see MEININGEN COMPANY

Scamozzi, Vincenzo 1552–1616 Italian architect and stage designer. From the school of PALLADIO, on the latter's death Scamozzi completed the Teatro Olimpico at Vicenza (1585), and was himself responsible for the Teatro Olimpico at Sabbioneta, completed in 1590. His work on both theatres shows his original and imaginative borrowing from classical models, and both are supreme examples of late Renaissance theatrical architecture, although they look back, rather than forwards, to theatre and stage structures determined by developments in stage scenography and mechanics. KR

Scaparro, Maurizio 1932– Italian director. Scaparro began his career as a theatre critic for the socialist newspaper *Avanti?*, moving on to practical stage work in Bologna. A highly informed director – with a literary as well as a theatrical instinct, and a talent for drawing out in production the social implications of the plays he directs – he has always displayed a keen interest in recovering neglected work from the Italian repertory, including lesser known GOLDONI pieces and rarely performed Renaissance plays such as ARIOSTO's *La Lena* and the anonymous *La Venexiana* (staged first in 1964, and then at the Teatro Argentina in Rome in 1984). He has also directed pieces from the modern repertory, such as PIRANDELLO's *Liolà* (1992). His major SHAKESPEARE productions have included *Hamlet* and *Richard II*. From 1982 he has been co-director, with GIORGIO STREHLER, of the Paris-based Théâtre de l'Europe, and in 1983 succeeded LUIGI SQUARZINA as the director of the Teatro Stabile in Rome, where he has essayed a wide range of classic and modern plays, including an adaptation of Marguerite Yourcenar's *The Memoirs of Hadrian* (1989). KR

Scarpetta, Eduardo 1853–1925 Italian actor and dramatist. At an early age he rose to fame in the Neapolitan theatre with a farce character type, Don Felice Sciosciammocca. Engaged by the San Carlino Theatre, he met there the actor-writer ANTONIO PETITO, who for the next few years worked closely with him in writing and staging pieces in Neapolitan dialect. After Petito's death he formed his own company, performing in several Neapolitan theatres but based particularly at the San Carlino from 1881, and producing work like *Lo Scarflietto* (*The Bed Warmer*, 1881), *Il romanzo di un farmacista povero* (*The Story of a Poor Chemist*, 1882) and, particularly, *Miseria e nobilità* (*Poverty and Nobility*, 1888). Although much of his work was a Neapolitanization of French FARCE, he did much to reform the theatre by eliminating the gratuitous LAZZI of the old tradition and rooting comedy in recognizable local life. He retired in 1914, having dominated the Neapolitan stage for some 40 years.

His successor as a master of Neapolitan comedy, EDUARDO DE FILIPPO, was a member of his company in its last years. LR

Scarron, Paul 1610–60 French dramatist and man of letters, whose long disablement by rheumatism gave him a capacity for self-mockery and an amused view of the world. Literary recognition came initially with the publication of collections of BURLESQUE verse, and a similar manner informed his first play, *JODELET, ou Le Maître-valet* (*Jodelet, or The Master-Servant*), a vehicle for the comedian of that name and a great success at the MARAIS in 1645. More comedies in the same vein followed, some of them adapted from Spanish originals, including *Don Japhet d'Arménie* (1647), which was often revived by MOLIÈRE and is regarded as his best work for the stage, and *L'Écolier de Salamanque* (*The Student of Salamanca*, 1654), which popularized the character of Crispin later associated with members of the POISSON family. Nowadays their mixture of verbal wit and stylistic incongruity makes them more difficult to appreciate, and Scarron is best known for *Le Roman comique* (*The Comical Romance*), a long picaresque romance in two parts (1651 and 1657), which recounts the adventures of a troupe of strolling players and tempers its fantasy with some realistic details of theatrical and provincial life. DR

scenic design see THEATRE DESIGN

Schechner, Richard see PERFORMANCE GROUP; THEATRE DESIGN

Schembartläufer Masked figures of the Bavarian and Austrian CARNIVAL, particularly associated with Nuremberg. Their name, as well as denoting obvious attributes of their appearance and behaviour (they are bearded (in German, *Bart*), and 'run' (*Läufer*, runner) through the streets), also suggests that they are phantoms. Their MASKS, though always bearded, are female as well as male, they carry staves or lances, and their behaviour is wild and threatening. They are recorded as throwing ashes, and sometimes burning embers, into the crowd. AEG

Schicksaltragödie ('fate tragedy') Form of play, popular in Germany during the romantic period, that represents *in extremis* the Sophoclean concept of fate (see SOPHOCLES) as an inescapable force. The most celebrated *Schicksaltragödie* was ZACHARIAS WERNER's *The 24th of February* (1810), which owed much to GEORGE LILLO's *Fatal Curiosity* and itself influenced ALBERT CAMUS's *Le Malentendu*. Werner's play was also widely imitated in its time, most notably by Adolf Müllner (1774–1829) in *The 29th of February* (1815). GRILLPARZER's first play *The Ancestress*, though of a far higher standard than most *Schicksaltragödien*, owed its success partially to its affinity with some popular plays of this genre. SW

Schikaneder, Emanuel 1751–1812 Austrian actor and singer. Schikaneder, a highly successful impresario in the Viennese popular theatre, is best known today as the librettist for Mozart's *The Magic Flute* (1791). Partly as a result of the immense popularity of this opera, he was able to build the Theater an der Wien. SW

Schiller, Friedrich 1759–1805 German playwright, historian and aesthetician. Schiller's contribution to the development of German drama is equal in quality and importance to that of GOETHE, with whom Schiller was closely associated during the last nine years of his life. Schiller's first play, *The Robbers* (1781), written while he was a deeply disaffected recruit in the military academy in Württemberg, must be considered to be among the greatest of all first plays. Though dependent on SHAKESPEARE and imitative of the STURM UND DRANG movement of the previous decade, in its depiction of the Moor brothers – one of whom is a monster of malice, the other of titanic disaffection – *The Robbers* has a unique power. Of his next two plays, written while he was house dramatist at Mannheim, *Fiesko* (1781–2) and *Love and Intrigue* (1782–3), the latter is still stageworthy because Schiller's intense sense of outrage at the injustice of the class system can be viscerally felt, despite the play's strident tone. *Don Carlos* (1787) took Schiller several years to write, which is reflected in the unwieldy and complex plot and in a radical change in tone halfway through the play. While the first part, involving Don Carlos's fear and hatred of his father Philip II, belongs to *Sturm und Drang*, the second part, with its ironic view of the idealist Posa and the surprisingly humane characterization of Philip, elevates the tragedy to a more complex plane.

The next ten years Schiller devoted to the study of history, philosophy and aesthetics, in 1789 becoming professor of history at Jena University, close to Weimar. When he returned to the drama with his trilogy on the Thirty Years War general, Wallenstein – *Wallenstein's Camp*, *The Piccolomini* and *Wallenstein's Death* (all 1799) – Schiller produced a TRAGEDY on the strength and fallibility of the tragic hero that belongs to the rank of world drama. His next play, *Maria Stuart* (1800), he labelled a 'romantic tragedy', possibly because of the disquieting appeal of his beautiful heroine and his dispassionate portrayal of the political forces to which she falls victim. His next major play, *The Bride of Messina* (1803), was a deliberate revival of Greek tragedy (see GREECE, ANCIENT). His final completed work, the ever-popular *Wilhelm Tell* (1804), while demonstrating a thorough knowledge of current romantic philosophies and a fine grasp of romantic dramaturgy, in fact throws doubt upon the viability of the romantic personality as embodied in the enigmatic figure of Tell.

Schiller possessed a surer understanding of the practical stage than Goethe, and his tragedies, in which the influence of Greek, Shakespearian and French neoclassical forms can be found, have proved more durable than much of Goethe's dramatic work. As a result, Schiller is widely regarded as the national dramatist of Germany. SW

Schiller, Leon 1887–1954 Polish director, manager, composer, author and teacher. As a young man he came under the influence of GORDON CRAIG, whose views he assimilated into the Polish tradition of MICKIEWICZ and WYSPIAŃSKI. He began directing in his mid-30s, staging old Polish nativities and mysteries (see MYSTERY PLAY). He founded the Bogusławski Theatre (1924–6), where he developed a monumental style based on the Polish romantic repertory and combining elements of EXPRESSIONISM, constructivism and cubism with the use of large crowds, PISCATOR'S technique of montage, and revolutionary themes. In the 1930s he moved to radical political theatre and neo-REALISM. After the war, he created the State Theatre Institute. Major productions are Miciński's *Revolt of the Potemkin* (1925), Wyspiański's *Achilleis* (1925), Krasiński's *Undivine Comedy* (1926), BRECHT'S *Threepenny Opera* (1929), SŁOWACKI's *Kordian* (1930), Mickiewicz's *Forefathers' Eve* (1932) and TRETYAKOV's *Roar, China* (1932). DG

Schlegel, A(ugust) W(ilhelm) 1767–1845 German literary historian and translator. Schlegel's work did much to familiarize the public with the ideas of the romantics. In particular, his *Lectures on Dramatic Art and Literature*, first delivered in Vienna in 1808, covered the whole field of Western drama, creating an awareness of how genuinely popular the theatre had been in past ages. The ideal of such a theatre was shared by many romantics. Schlegel was also a translator of genius, and his versions of 17 of SHAKESPEARE's plays, published between 1797 and 1810 (the series was completed by Dorothea Tieck and Wolf von Baudissin in 1833), are regarded by some as being as close in quality as can possibly be to the original. Schlegel also adapted EURIPIDES' *Ion*, which was produced by GOETHE at Weimar in 1802. SW

Schlegel, J(ohann) E(lias) 1719–49 German playwright and aesthetician. Although he was associated with JOHANN GOTTSCHED, Schlegel had a strong appreciation of SHAKESPEARE and of his works as an alternative to the neoclassical tradition. However, as a playwright he is known as 'the German RACINE'. Of his several neoclassical tragedies, *Canute* (1746) is possibly the most original. SW

Schlemmer, Oskar 1888–1943 German sculptor, painter and designer, and head of the Bauhaus stage workshop from 1923 to 1929. Like many designers of the era, Schlemmer sought to unite the human figure with the three-dimensional space of the stage, but he approached it from the standpoint of making the human form abstract. Basing his work upon mathematical analysis of the geometric shapes that the body (or parts of the body) makes as it move through space, he created MASKS and COSTUMES that suggested, in WALTER GROPIUS's words, 'moving architecture'. Schlemmer also sought to create a modern vocabulary of visual symbols. These explorations were best realized in his *Form Dance*, *Gesture Dance* and *Space Dance*. The most complete integration of his ideas was achieved in the *Triadic Ballet* (1912–22), a highly structured and schematized series of dance scenes. His work with the Bauhaus was an influence not only on postwar design but on modern dance. He also designed for the commercial theatre and dance – notably the KOKOSCHKA–Hindemith opera, *Mörder, Hoffnung der Frauen* – creating settings in the style of the expressionist painters (see EXPRESSIONISM) with broad swaths of rich and subtly shaded colours. AA

Schmidhuber de la Mora, Guillermo 1943– Mexican playwright. With degrees in engineering and business, Schmidhuber de la Mora for years managed the Alfa Technological Museum in Monterrey, before earning a doctrate in the USA and returning to Guadalajara. In a country where theatre activity tends to concentrate in the capital, he continues to write diligently and to win national prizes. Of his dozen or more plays, the major items include *Los herederos de Segismundo* (*Segismundo's Heirs*, 1981), with its attribution to CALDERÓN's *Life Is a Dream*; *El día que Monalisa dejó de sonreír* (*The Day Mona Lisa Stopped Smiling*, 1987), examining the myths of Da Vinci; and *El quinto viaje de Colón* (*Columbus's Fifth Voyage*, 1992), written for the 500th anniversary of Columbus's exploration. A major coup was Schmidhuber's discovery of a long-lost manuscript which was attributed to the colonial genius Sor Juana Inés de la Cruz. GW

Schmidt, Douglas 1942– American set and COSTUME designer, most closely associated with large-scale, kinetic, multi-scene MUSICALS and OPERAS that evoke an almost 19th-century sensibility. Schmidt is also capable of sculptural scenery and realistic detail. After graduating from Boston University he assisted MING CHO LEE and also designed at Cincinnati Playhouse in the Park. Lee's influence is very clear in his early work. He was resident designer for the Repertory Theatre at Lincoln Center during 1969–73. Schmidt has collaborated frequently with directors RICHARD FOREMAN, Des McAnuff, Tom Moore and Jack O'Brien. His productions include *Grease* and *Over Here!*, as well as several productions with the San Francisco Opera and other opera companies. AA

Schneider, Alan [Abram (Leopoldovich) Schneider] 1917–84 Russian-born director, known as BECKETT's American interpreter. Schneider worked at Washington's ARENA STAGE (artistic director, 1952–3; acting producer, 1973–4), New York's NEIGHBORHOOD PLAYHOUSE and elsewhere across the USA. Director of the Juilliard Theater Center (1976–9) and, at his death, a co-artistic director of the ACTING COMPANY, he headed the graduate directing programme at the University of California at San Diego and was president of the Theatre Communications Group, which initiated the annual Alan Schneider Director Award in 1986.

Schneider, who believed his main function was 'to serve as the intermediary between the playwright and the actual stage production', directed premieres of Beckett's *Waiting for Godot* (1956), *Endgame* (1958), *Happy Days* (1961), *Play* (1964) and the movie *Film*, starring Buster Keaton (1964). He received an Obie for *The PINTER Plays* (*The Collection* and *The Dumb Waiter*, 1963), a Tony for EDWARD ALBEE's *Who's Afraid of Virginia Woolf?* (1963), and a Drama Desk Award for his direction of Preston Jones's *Texas Trilogy* (1976); he was nominated for Tonys for Albee's *Tiny Alice* (1965) and *A Delicate Balance* (1967) and ROBERT W. ANDERSON's *You Know I Can't Hear You When the Water's Running* (1968). Schneider, killed in a traffic accident in London, left an autobiography, *Entrances: An American Director's Journal*, published in 1986. REK

Schnitzler, Arthur 1862–1931 Austrian playwright and short story writer. Schnitzler's training as a doctor is often considered to have influenced fundamentally his attitude as a dramatist. His plays are for the most part stringently ironic analyses of life in contemporary Vienna. *Anatol* (1893) and *La Ronde* (1900), both cycles of one-act plays that disclose the anxieties lying behind the gracious appearance and easy sexual mores of the city's life, are best-known internationally. But his greatest achievement probably lies in his full-length plays – in the moving and tragic VOLKSSTÜCK *Liebelei* (*The Game of Love*, 1895), the melancholy drama *The Lonely Way* (1904), the bitterly satirical survey of Viennese society *The Vast Country* (1911), and the powerful play on anti-Semitism in Vienna, *Professor Bernhardi* (1912). Though he was only slightly acquainted with Freud, there is a remarkable concordance between Freud's and Schnitzler's perceptions of the human condition, one Freud himself acknowledged. SW

Schönemann, Johann (Friedrich) 1704–82 German actor. Schönemann took over the leadership of the Neuber troupe after CAROLINE NEUBER had broken with GOTTSCHED. He continued for several years to perpetuate the LEIPZIG STYLE of acting, though his pre-eminence in the profession declined as a result of the rise of REALISM in acting, associated with EKHOF. Schönemann's mismanagement of his finances eventually led to his early retirement in 1757. SW

Schönherr, Karl 1867–1943 Austrian playwright. Schönherr was best known for his grim and powerful realistic dramas about peasant life in the Tyrol. Among the most successful of his plays are *The Picture Carvers* (1900), *Midsummer Day* (1902), *Carnival People* (1905) and *Faith and the Homeland* (1910). SW

Schreyvogel, Josef 1788–1832 Austrian director. From 1815 until close to his death, Schreyvogel was artistic director of the BURGTHEATER. During this time he established the famous ensemble style of the company, translated and produced important Spanish plays, and introduced the plays of GRILLPARZER. SW

Schröder, Friedrich (Ludwig) 1744–1816 German actor and playwright. The stepson of KONRAD ACKERMANN, Schröder spent most of his childhood and adolescence as a comic, improvisational actor in Ackermann's troupe. He took over the leadership on his stepfather's death in 1771. In 1776, he established the troupe on a permanent basis at the Hamburg Town Theatre. In 1780 he left to join the Vienna BURGTHEATER, where he stayed until 1784. Then he returned to Hamburg to direct his old theatre until his retirement in 1798. As an actor, Schröder was famous for his unvarnished realism, powerful climaxes and distinct characterization, which embraced a broad emotional compass. Such acting was referred to as the HAMBURG STYLE, and was later regarded as antithetical to the WEIMAR STYLE. In Hamburg he introduced to the stage several STURM UND DRANG plays and, most importantly, many of SHAKESPEARE's works: some of his adaptations of Shakespeare enjoyed wide popularity in Germany until the early 19th century. His production of *Hamlet* in 1776,

with BROCKMANN as Hamlet and himself as the Ghost, was a landmark in the introduction of Shakespeare to the German stage.

Schröder was a skilled playwright and adapted the work of several other English dramatists, including SHERIDAN, for German audiences. As leader of the Hamburg Town Theatre, he accumulated an unprecedentedly large stock of sets and costumes, doing much to improve the quality of physical production. Schröder was the original for the figure of the actor-manager Serlo in Goethe's novel *Wilhelm Meister's Apprenticeship*. SW

Schröder, Sophie 1781–1868 German actress. The most important years of Sophie Schröder's career were between 1815 and 1829 when she was a leading actress at the BURGTHEATER under SCHREYVOGEL. Here she gave the first performance, in 1818, of GRILLPARZER's Sappho and, in 1821, of his Medea. In these and in classic roles, her acting was regarded as the epitome of romanticism. SW

Schwartz, Maurice ?1890–1960 Yiddish actor, producer and director. At age one, en route from the Ukraine to America, he was separated from his family and remained in London; as a young boy he supported himself and attended the new Yiddish theatre. In America he became an amateur actor and then a professional, soon making a name for his fire and panache. In 1919 in New York he organized the YIDDISH ART THEATRE and managed to keep it going, most seasons, until 1950. Among its most successful productions were *The Brothers Ashkenazi* and *Yoshe Kalb* (1932), both by I.J. Singer, and *Shylock's Daughter* (by Zahav), as well as Yiddish classics and translations of classics from other cultures. Not only was Schwartz personally famous as an actor – in Sholom Aleichem's *Tevye the Dairyman*, for example, onstage and in film – he was also an institution through his Yiddish Art Theatre, which, whether on Second Avenue, on tour, or in temporary disarray, seemed the last bastion of YIDDISH THEATRE's energy, colour and sustained intellectual aspirations. Schwartz was still touring till the year he died. NS

Scofield, (David) Paul 1922– British actor. His first substantial work was developed at the BIRMINGHAM REPERTORY THEATRE under the direction of BARRY JACKSON, where Scofield went after a period in local repertory in 1942. He followed Jackson to Stratford-upon-Avon and the then Shakespeare Memorial Theatre in 1946, and this brought Scofield a series of Shakespearian roles in which he has distinguished himself over the years. These have included one of his most renowned performances, Lear in PETER BROOK's production of *King Lear* in 1962 (subsequently filmed, 1969) for the ROYAL SHAKESPEARE COMPANY, and portrayals of Macbeth (RSC, 1967), Prospero in *The Tempest* (Leeds Playhouse, 1974), Othello (NATIONAL THEATRE, 1980) and Oberon (National Theatre, 1982). But Scofield has not been limited to Shakespearian roles. His Sir Thomas More in BOLT's *A Man for All Seasons* (Globe Theatre, London, 1960; filmed, 1966) remains one of the great performances in postwar British theatre, and his work in plays by contemporary playwrights (OSBORNE's *Hotel in Amsterdam* (1968), HAMPTON's *Savages* (1973),

SHAFFER's *Amadeus* (1979), for instance) has given evidence of his power, range and versatility. He starred in Jeffrey Archer's Fleet Street drama, *Exclusive* (1989), and played Shotover in TREVOR NUNN's production of BERNARD SHAW's *Heartbreak House*. MB JE

Scotland Scotland has a rich theatrical tradition, which has played a significant part in the country's cultural development but which has been neglected for a number of reasons. One complicating factor is that in the past Scots themselves have sometimes refused to acknowledge the existence of their own theatre tradition. As late as 1932, Murray McClymont bewailed the fact that 'theatrically we are and have been for four hundred years a conquered nation'. Scots have also laboured under the misapprehension that (as a people) they are not theatrically inclined. WILLIAM HAZLITT first expressed this view when he contrasted the Irish and Scottish temperaments in terms of their theatricality.

The views of Hazlitt and McClymont can be explained by the fact that the Scottish theatre tradition has developed in an irregular, spasmodic fashion – often in the face of considerable opposition – and this irregularity has made it extremely difficult for succeeding generations to see themselves working within a discernible tradition. Yet neither view is borne out by the facts, least of all Hazlitt's, for the Scottish people have at all times retained a basic love for popular forms of theatrical and musical entertainment, from the BALLAD OPERA in the 18th century to music-hall and pantomime in the 19th, not forgetting the ceilidh, the Burns Supper and the village concert. Moreover, at various times recourse to these forms of entertainment has assisted the country's dramatic development.

Another complication lies in the fact that, having sometimes denied or belittled their native theatre tradition, Scottish theatre historians have also tended to look at it somewhat askance, placing too much emphasis on Scottish drama at the expense of other forms of theatrical entertainment, as well as (in the 20th century) on a professional drama tradition at the expense of amateur activities, and on middle-class repertory drama at the expense of popular or working-class initiatives.

During the past four hundred years, periods of intense activity have been followed by long years of inertia. There are three periods in which Scottish drama can be seen to have developed apace. The first of these spans the mid-15th to the end of the 16th century, when travelling players performed a series of MORALITY PLAYS which were highly critical of the pre-Reformation Church. The high point of theatrical achievement in these years came with Sir David Lindsay's *Ane Satyre of the Thrie Estaites*, which was performed before King James V of Scotland at Linlithgow Palace in 1542.

The second period of development occurred in the 18th century, in the wake of the Scottish Enlightenment when the first theatres were built in Scotland – notably in Edinburgh, the Athens of the North – and new Scottish plays were written and performed, including Allan Ramsay's *The Gentle Shepherd* (1725) and JOHN HOME's *Douglas* (1756). The latter caused great consternation: it was condemned by the Kirk but cheered enthusiastically by its audiences, one member of which was heard to give vent to Scottish drama's celebrated battle cry, 'Whaur's yer Wullie Shakespeare noo?'

These growth periods were interspersed with periods of decline in the 17th and 19th centuries. Such lapses are difficult to account for in full. Many different theories have been put forward over the years. Scottish drama's demise in the 17th century has been attributed both to the loss of patronage following the removal of James VI and I's court to London, and to the artistic, cultural and moral rigidity imposed by the Scottish Reformation and the consequent spread of Calvinism and Presbyterianism. Similarly, the 19th-century decline has been attributed to English cultural dominance in the British Empire's heyday, during which time the Scottish arts as a whole withdrew into Celtic myth, the kailyard and tartanry.

It is important, before moving on to look at subsequent developments, to take a closer look at Scottish theatre in the 19th century. During this period of English cultural hegemony, Scottish cities and towns became largely dependent on English actor-manager touring companies for their dramatic fare, while Scottish villages depended on the pennygeggie's Victorian MELODRAMAS, such as *Burke and Hare*. At this time the MUSIC-HALL came to the fore, offering weekly VARIETY programmes and long-running, annual PANTOMIMES that starred such celebrated Scottish comedians as HARRY LAUDER, Will Fyffe, Harry Gordon, Tommy Lorne, Tommy Morgan and George West. These variety programmes and pantomimes (as LEWIS CASSON first pointed out) formed the national theatre of Scotland, in the absence of an indigenous drama tradition. Their legacy has been mixed for, like the kailyard novels of the 19th century, they were inclined to lapse into stifling sentimentality and tartanry. Nonetheless, many 20th-century drama companies (notably, 7:84 Scotland) have made extensive use of the music-hall's form and style, and actors from Duncan Macrae to BILL PATERSON have readily acknowledged their debt to the music-hall tradition.

Scottish drama's third period of development began in the early 20th century, on the heels of the Scottish Literary Renaissance, and its evolution since has been rapid and sustained. It can be said to have developed not one, but two, complementary traditions. First, there is a more conventional mainstream repertory tradition, founded by the Scottish Repertory Theatre (1909–14) and revived after the First World War by the Scottish National Players (1921–48). Scottish drama's development in the interwar years was assisted by the Perth and Dundee Repertory Theatres; as well as a series of little theatres including the Byre Theatre in St Andrews and the Curtain Theatre (1930–9), the Tron Theatre Club (1931–2), the MSU Theatre in Rutherglen (1939–44) and the Park Theatre (1940–9), all based in Glasgow. Its progress was also enhanced by the activities of a series of other small, amateur clubs including the Torch and Pantheon Theatre Clubs that took part in the Scottish Community Drama Association's annual one-act play festivals.

These early companies prepared the way for Scotland's postwar repertory theatres, including the Glasgow CITIZENS' THEATRE (1943–), Pitlochry Festival Theatre (1951–) and Edinburgh's Gateway and Royal Lyceum

Theatre Companies (1953–65 and 1965–). They also paved the way for a series of postwar theatre clubs which specialized in a more intimate style of theatre. These include Edinburgh's TRAVERSE THEATRE Club (1963–) and Glasgow's Close Theatre Club (1965–73), which burned down and was eventually replaced by the new Tron Theatre Club (1981–).

The early 20th century also saw the emergence of a Scottish popular or working-class theatre tradition, based in the industrial urban centres of Scotland. During the 1920s, 30s and 40s hundreds of amateur working-class drama groups were formed, some as the offshoots of two British theatre movements of the day, the Workers Theatre Movement (WTM) and the UNITY THEATRE Society, others as the scions of other, local, working-class organizations – the Scottish Labour College, branches of the Labour and Independent Labour Parties, the Clarion Society, Cooperative Societies and Socialist Sunday Schools, in addition to local Burns Clubs and Miners' Welfare Institutes. The most important of these theatre companies were the Bowhill, also called the Fife Miner Players (1926–31); the Glasgow Workers' Theatre Group (1937–40); and Glasgow Unity Theatre (1941–51) – which can all be seen to have laid the foundations for more modern popular theatre companies, particularly 7:84 Scotland and Wildcat Stage Productions.

Scottish drama's development in the 20th century has been influenced by a number of factors, not least the country's geography. Scotland has a small population, concentrated in a number of large towns and cities but otherwise scattered in remote rural communities. Theatre companies from both traditions have resisted the impulse to establish a single national theatre based in Edinburgh or Glasgow, and have demonstrated a strong interest in touring their productions. Early in the century the Scottish National Players, the Fife Miner Players and Glasgow Unity Theatre set a precedent. During the 1970s and 80s, the Scottish Theatre Company, 7:84 Scotland, Borderline and Wildcat followed suit.

During the Second World War, the Glasgow Citizens' Theatre Company received help form CEMA. Since the war, Scottish drama has been assisted by state subsidies. The Scottish Committee (1947–67) of the ARTS COUNCIL OF GREAT BRITAIN gave financial support to other middle-class repertory theatres and theatre clubs, but their popular, working-class counterparts – in particular, Glasgow Unity Theatre – were less fortunate. During the 1970s, following the creation of the more autonomous Scottish Arts Council, this balance was at last redressed. There followed a period of unprecedented growth in Scottish theatre, which continued despite the more austere financial climate of the 80s and 90s.

Drama in Scotland has been dominated by two major concerns. First, there is the Scots' desire to create an indigenous, native drama, which is matched by a simultaneous desire to assert their independence of English dramatic development. This has led Scottish playwrights, directors, designers and performers either to turn inward to their own culture and experience, or to turn outwards to alternative, international models for inspiration. While the Scottish National Players turned to the ABBEY THEATRE in Dublin, Scottish popular drama groups turned further afield to the BLUE BLOUSE troupes of the Soviet Union, or the American FEDERAL THEATRE PROJECT, performing the works of a host of international socialist authors including ODETS, O'NEILL and ELMER RICE, GARCÍA LORCA, O'CASEY and ERNST TOLLER. During recent times the Citizens' Theatre, under the artistic directorship of Giles Havergal, has pursued a similarly eclectic, internationalist artistic policy, while the EDINBURGH [International] FESTIVAL of Music and Theatre (1947–) and Glasgow's MAYFEST (1983–) have ensured that Scottish theatre-makers and theatregoers continue to be brought into close and regular contact with contemporary developments.

Secondly, there is the matter of Scottish playwriting. At the turn of the 20th century it was possible to count all the Scottish plays of note on one hand, with the result that in modern times the Scots have been particularly conscious of the need to produce a body of indigenous dramatic literature, and this in turn has led to a proliferation of playwrights and plays. Indeed, many Scottish writers, specializing in other literary forms – poetry or the novel – have turned their hand to playwriting. These include Hugh MacDiarmid and Neil Gunn and, more recently, Liz Lochhead and Alan Spence. J. M. BARRIE and JAMES BRIDIE remain Scotland's best-known playwrights. Revered in their homeland, they stand in a rather odd relation to Scottish drama's overall development, primarily because their plays were first performed not in Scotland, but in London. As a result, neither has had a very strong influence on the development of Scottish playwriting as a whole.

The Scottish Repertory Theatre was the first Scottish company to encourage native playwrights. During the interwar years its mantle was taken up by the Scottish National Players and other amateur theatre companies, notably the Curtain Theatre. These companies inherited two particular kinds of play – the Scottish history play and the kailyard COMEDY – which were both deeply flawed and which they consequently sought to rehabilitate. While the best Scottish history plays – including Robert McLellan's *Jamie the Saxt* (first performed in the Curtain Theatre in 1936) – strove to come to terms with Scotland's beleaguered past, many sank to the level of sentimental costume drama, returning with remorseless regularity to the same well worn episodes in Scottish history, notably the '45 Rebellion and Bonnie Prince Charlie's flight to Skye.

The kailyard comedy first came into vogue in the 19th century; J. M. Barrie's *The Little Minister* and Graham Moffat's *Bunty Pulls the Strings* (1906) are good examples of the genre. These kailyard dramas were rural romances or comedies portraying minor events in the lives of rather two-dimensional Lowland village folk – the local minister, an elder of the Kirk, the village schoolteacher. They were parochial and excessively sentimental. The Scottish National Players, inspired by the Scottish Literary Renaissance, sought to provide the first real alternative to the kailyard romance or comedy, but succeeded only in extending the genre's scope and territory. They presented plays about Highland rather than Lowland folk, but these plays remained firmly attached to rural domestic life and were as couthy as their predecessors. The Scottish Community Drama Association (1926–) further broadened the range of the kailyard, introducing the kitchen comedy which portrayed domestic incidents in the lives of humble working-class folk in a similarly comic, not to say banal, fashion.

It was the Scottish popular working-class theatre companies that offered the first new kind of play in the early 20th century. They produced a series of plays about contemporary industrial urban working-class life, including JOE CORRIE's *In Time o' Strife* (first produced by the Fife Miner Players in 1927), Robert McLeish's *The Gorbals Story* and Ena Lamont Stewart's *Men Should Weep* (first produced by Glasgow Unity Theatre in 1946 and 1947, respectively).

Today, Scottish playwrights write about an increasingly broad range of subjects. Those that continue to write directly about Scottish experience like to think that the kailyard tradition has finally been laid to rest. Some continue to draw on Scottish history, including JOHN McGRATH, who treated the history of the Highland clearances in his play, *The Cheviot, the Stag and the Black, Black Oil* (first performed by the 7:84 Scotland in 1973). Other writers have continued to explore contemporary urban working-class experience, whether on the stage or, increasingly, in films like Bill Forsyth's *Gregory's Girl*; or in TELEVISION DRAMAS, such as John Byrne's *Tutti Frutti*, and a flood of successful drama series, notably Scottish Television's *Taggart* and BBC Scotland's *City Lights* and *Rab C. Nesbitt*. Most writers address the subject in a genuinely exploratory way, but there is a danger that this preoccupation will lapse into a new 'urban kailyard', in which the values and way of life of Scotland's urban working class become a source of the same kind of humour or sentiment that permeated the kailyard comedy and the Scottish music-hall, with its annual panto.

Drama has dominated Scottish theatre's development. But Scotland has also made important contributions to OPERA and ballet in the 20th century. Scottish Opera presents a wide international repertoire, including some new Scottish work. Scottish Ballet (1970–), which traces its origins back to Margaret Morris's Celtic Ballet (1947–58) and the Scottish National Ballet (c.1960), has likewise been immensely active. LM

PRE-20TH CENTURY

See: P. Baxter, *The Drama in Perth*, Perth, 1907; W. Baynham, *The Glasgow Stage*, Glasgow, 1892; F. Boyd, *Records of the Dundee Stage from Earliest Times to the Present Day*, Dundee, 1886; J. M. Bulloch, *The Playhouse of Bon Accord: A Short Survey of the Actor's Art in Aberdeen*, Aberdeen, 1906; J. C. Dibden, *Annals of the Edinburgh Stage*, Edinburgh, 1888; J. Jackson, *History of the Scottish Stage*, Edinburgh, 1793; R. Lawson, *The Story of the Scots Stage*, Paisley, 1917; D. MacKenzie, *Scotland's First National Theatre: A History of the First Theatre Royal, Edinburgh*, Edinburgh, 1963; A. Robertson, *History of the Dundee Theatre*, London, 1949.

20TH CENTURY

See: W. Bannister, *James Bridie and His Theatre*, London, 1955; M. Coveney, *The Citz*, London, 1990; V. Devlin, *Kings, Queens and People's Palaces: An Oral History of the Scottish Variety Theatre, 1920–70*, Edinburgh, 1991; D. Hutchinson, *The Modern Scottish Theatre*, Glasgow, 1977; W. Isaac, *Alfred Wareing*, London, 1951; J. H. Littlejohn, *The Scottish Music Hall,*

1880–1990, Glasgow, 1990; A. D. Mackie, *The Scottish Comedians from the Music Hall to Television*, Edinburgh, 1973; J. McGrath, *A Good Night Out: Popular Theatre: Audience, Class and Form*, London, 1981, and *The Bone Won't Break: On Theatre and Hope in Hard Times*, London, 1990; E. MacLennan, *The Moon Belongs to Everyone: Making Theatre with 7:84*, London, 1990; J. MacMillan, *The Traverse Theatre Story, 1963–1988*, London, 1988; H. Murdoch, *Travelling Hopefully: The Story of Molly Urquhart*, Edinburgh, 1981; T. Paterson, *Citizens' Theatre, Gorbals, Glasgow: Its Story from the Beginning to the Present Day*, Glasgow, 1970.

Scott, George C.

Scott, George C. 1927– American film and stage actor and director, noted for a strong artistic integrity and intense acting style. His first stage appearance was at the University of Missouri after the Second World War. After playing some 150 roles in STOCK companies, Scott made his New York debut as Richard III in the NEW YORK SHAKESPEARE FESTIVAL (1957). He received excellent response to *Children of Darkness* (1958). Alternating stage work with an outstanding film career, he appeared as Ephraim Cabot in *Desire under the Elms* (1963). More recent successes on BROADWAY include *Sly Fox* (1976), based on BEN JONSON's *Volpone*. Although noted for his dramatic intensity, Scott directed and starred in NoËL COWARD's *Present Laughter* in 1982, directed *Design for Living* in 1984 and directed and starred in OSBORN's *On Borrowed Time* in 1991, all at CIRCLE IN THE SQUARE. He refused in 1971 to accept the Academy Award for Best Actor in the title role of *Patton*. Scott has also appeared with the NYSF playing Antony and Shylock. Campbell Scott, the son of Scott and the late COLLEEN DEWHURST, is also an actor (Pericles, 1991, at the PUBLIC THEATER). SMA

Scribe, (Augustin) Eugène

Scribe, (Augustin) Eugène 1791–1861 French dramatist and librettist. One of the most prolific writers of the 19th-century theatre, Scribe is generally thought of as the creator of the WELL MADE PLAY. A master of his craft, he was much imitated by his successors, notably by LABICHE and SARDOU. Scribe's favourite genre was the *vaudeville* (nearly 250 pieces, accounting for well over half of his total output). His primary material was the bourgeoisie of his day, which he observed with great accuracy. Again and again he showed, especially in the one-act *vaudeville*, how something could be made of nothing. His characters are not highly developed, but are sustained by the sheer force of the dramatic action. Each play is built around a central situation, but in addition to this there is normally a 'situation' in every scene. Scribe understood the art of preparing a situation, prolonging it, and finally sorting it out, and it is this very neatness that has always impressed.

Initially trained for the law, Scribe had his first play performed at the Variétés (see BOULEVARD) in 1810. He tried his hand at almost every genre, but the *vaudeville* was that in which he excelled. His first success came in 1815 with *Une Nuit de la Garde Nationale* (*A Night of the National Guard*), written in collaboration with Delestre Poirson. A large part of his writing would be in collaboration, a widespread 19th-century practice. His popular *vaudeville*, *L'Ours et le pacha* (*The Bear and the Pacha*, 1820), added a proverbial expression to the French language. In 1820, the

Théâtre de Madame, which would become the Gymnase, opened as a 'fashionable' boulevard theatre, patronized by the Duchess of Berry. The repertoire of this theatre was to be light comedies and *vaudevilles*. Scribe was contracted as a house dramatist to the Gymnase in 1821 and, over the next ten years, alone or in collaboration, turned out some 150 plays for it. *L'Héritière* (*The Heiress*, 1823), written with G. Delavigne, became one of the classics of the Gymnase repertoire. *Bertrand et Suzette; ou Le Mariage de raison* (1826), whose theme is that of a girl turning her back on the man she loves in favour of a mercenary marriage, created a scandal, but it is one of his best plays. He explored this theme further in a play for the COMÉDIE-FRANÇAISE, *Le Mariage d'argent* (*The Mercenary Marriage*, 1827), where the hero sacrifices his own happiness in order to keep his fortune. The play, which refused to idealize society, was poorly received, but remained in the repertoire.

It is often felt that Scribe's best work was produced for the Gymnase, but the Comédie-Française represented a form of consecration, and it was for this theatre that his major plays were written (usually without collaborators). He developed a new type of political-historical COMEDY, often based on the thesis that great effects are the result of trivial causes. In the plays for the Comédie-Française greater attention is given to characterization than in the *vaudevilles*. These plays include *The School for Politicians* (*Bertrand et Raton; ou L'Art de conspirer*, 1833), *La Camaraderie* (1837), *La Calomnie* (1840), *The Glass of Water* (1840), *Une Chaîne* (1841), *Adrienne Lecouvreur* (1849), specially written for RACHEL, and *The Ladies' Battle* (1850). Scribe was also librettist for some 28 OPERAS as well as nearly 100 OPÉRAS COMIQUES. Amongst these are *La Dame blanche* (1825), *Masaniello; or The Dumb Girl of Portici* (1828), *Fra Diavolo* (1830), *Robert the Devil* (1831), *The Jewess* (1835), *The Huguenots* (1836), *The Black Domino* (1837), *La Favorite* (1840), *The Crown Diamonds* (1841) and *The Prophet* (1849). When he died in 1861 he was working on the libretto for Meyerbeer's *L'Africaine*. JMCC

Scudéry, Georges de 1601–67 French dramatist and poet who after service as a soldier, on which he subsequently capitalized, laid down the sword in favour of the pen and in 1629 began to frequent the Paris salons, publishing books of verse and providing a quantity of plays to both established theatre companies, at the HÔTEL DE BOURGOGNE and the MARAIS. Tragedies, tragicomedies and comedies, irregularly constructed, stronger on rhetorical eloquence than characterization and full of extravagant or violent incidents, they hold little interest now, with the exception of *La Comédie des comédiens* (*The Actors' Comedy*, 1635), which presents on stage the company of actors under MONTDORY who performed it. In 1637 Scudéry initiated the influential literary controversy over PIERRE CORNEILLE's *Le Cid* by publishing his adverse comments on the play. Later he collaborated with his sister Madeleine in the composition of her successful romances and was elected to the Académie-Française in 1649. DR

seaside entertainment see PIERROT SHOWS
Seattle Repertory Theatre (USA) Founded in Seattle

in 1963 by Stuart Vaughan in a building erected for the 1963 World's Fair. The company met financial difficulties in its early days; by 1969–70 their deficit was over a quarter of a million dollars. W. Duncan Ross was appointed managing director at that time; six years later the company had 22,000 season subscriptions.

In 1974 SRT leased a second building, called Stage 2, to house a second season of five plays. In 1979 Ross accepted a position elsewhere and was replaced by Daniel Sullivan; two years later Sullivan became artistic director. Sullivan continued previous policy, but added a New Plays workshop (four scripts each spring) and began to employ more local actors. In 1983 the company opened the 850-seat Bagley Wright Theatre at the Seattle Center, which also contains a 140-seat PONCHO (Patrons of Northwest Cultural, Civic and Charitable Organization) Forum for new works. The Wright Theatre annually presents a six-play season, balancing classics, contemporary works and premieres of new plays; Stage 2 offers three productions. In early 1994 the SRT presented the West Coast premiere of MAMET's *Oleanna*. SMA

Sedaine, Michel-Jean 1719–97 French dramatist and poet, a former stonemason by trade and largely self-educated. He became a friend of DIDEROT and seems to have shared his views on widening the subject-matter and social range of contemporary drama. In *Le Philosophe sans le savoir* (*A Philosopher without Knowing It*), his most progressive play, Sedaine wrote a good example of Diderot's projected genre of the serious bourgeois COMEDY, with adequate touches of domestic realism to leaven the prevailing sentiment and special pleading, and certainly better than Diderot's own attempts to dramatize his theory. The play was well received at the COMÉDIE-FRANÇAISE in 1765, as was his engaging one-act comedy *La Gageure imprévue* (*The Unforeseen Gamble*, 1768), but the bulk of his output consisted of OPÉRAS COMIQUES, or comedies with songs and musical accompaniment, which he wrote in collaboration with Grétry, Monsigny and other composers for performance at the COMÉDIE-ITALIENNE and the theatres of the Paris fairs. DR

Segelcke, Tore 1901–79 Norwegian actress. With her colleagues Gerd Egede Nissen and Aase Bye, Segelcke dominated the female repertoire at NATIONALTHEATRET from the 1930s to the 1950s. Specializing in roles demanding both inner strength and emotional spontaneity, she was particularly successful in O'NEILL (Nina Leeds, Lavinia Mannon and Josie Hogan) and IBSEN. Her Nora was admired for its clear through-line and she was an especially strong Agnes in *Brand*. The later successes of this remarkable actress included Mrs Alving and BRECHT's Pelagea Vlassova. She was much acclaimed during her 1956 tour of the USA. HL

Seibel, Beatriz 1934– Argentine critic, director and playwright. Seibel has had success with children's theatre – *De gatos y lunas* (*Of Cats and Moons*, 1965) – and with adult theatre such as *Siete veces Eva* (*Seven Times Eve*, 1982) and *Canto latinoamericano* (*Latin American Song*, 1985). A serious researcher, she often incorporates historical and literary items into her theatre. GW

Seldes, Marian 1928– American actress, director and teacher; daughter of critic Gilbert Seldes (d.1970). A member of the theatre and dance faculties at the Juilliard School since 1969, Seldes, an award-winning actress trained in her teens at the NEIGHBORHOOD PLAYHOUSE, appeared in the complete BROADWAY runs of *Equus* and *Deathtrap*. Originally a dancer, the tall, regal, articulate Seldes is considered an actor's actor. Leadings roles in TINA HOWE's *Painting Churches* (1983–4), Win Wells's *Gertrude Stein and a Companion* (1985–6), and ALBEE's *Three Tall Women* (1994) have brought her acclaim. She is the author of an unusual theatre memoir, *The Bright Lights* (1978; revised 1984), a superb analysis of the chemistry of acting. In 1990 she married actor-playwright GARSON KANIN. DBW

Sellars, Peter 1957– Controversial American director. Sellars had staged over 100 productions by the age of 27 and first came to prominence as a Harvard undergraduate when he directed *The Inspector General* for the AMERICAN REPERTORY THEATRE (1980–1). After one year as artistic director of the Boston Shakespeare Company (1983–4), Sellars became head of the short-lived American National Theatre (ANT) Company at the JOHN F. KENNEDY CENTER in Washington, DC, a post which he left in 1986, becoming head of the Los Angeles Festival and serving as artistic adviser of the Boston Opera Theater, both in 1990. Among Sellars's ambitious and controversial productions have been Handel's *Orlando* (1982), BRECHT's *The Visions of Simone Machard* (1983), a GORKY–GERSHWIN mélange at the GUTHRIE called *Hang On to Me* (1984), *The Count of Monte Cristo* (1985) for the ANT in Washington, SOPHOCLES' *Ajax* (1986), featuring a Rambo-type Vietnam general gone cuckoo, Mozart's *Magic Flute* at Glyndebourne (1990) in a contemporary American setting, AESCHYLUS' *The Persians* at the Los Angeles Festival (1993) in a new translation by Robert Auletta, and an updated and transplanted *The Merchant of Venice* (to the multicultural world of Venice, California) at Chicago's GOODMAN THEATRE (1994). After being fired as the original director of BROADWAY's *My One and Only* in 1983, he received the same week an unsolicited grant for $136,000 from the MacArthur Foundation. Since the late 1980s he has concentrated on OPERA, on both sides of the Atlantic, including premiere productions of the contemporary operas *Nixon in China* and *The Death of Klinghoffer*, an iconoclastic 1989 Mozart trilogy (*Don Giovanni* set in a crime-ridden ghetto, *Figaro* in the Trump Tower and *Cosi fan tutte* in Despina's Cape Cod diner); and a *Tannhäuser* in Chicago staged as the sexual scandal of a television evangelist. DBW

Semyonova, Ekaterina (Semyonovna) 1786–1849 The greatest Russian actress of her day, a favourite of PUSHKIN and Decembrist youth, often compared to MLLE GEORGE, whose singsong, declamatory delivery she emulated in a rich contralto voice. The daughter of a landowner and one of his female serfs, Semyonova was trained by the heroic, neo-classical actor DMITREVSKY and, beginning in 1803, excelled in the roles of tragic heroines to which she brought sincerity and ardent emotionalism. Her career is closely linked with those of PRINCE SHAKHOVSKOI and dramatist-translator N. I. Gnedich, who advised her

professionally, and with that of 'the unfortunate OZEROV' whose plays Pushkin said she 'ennobled' in the 1810s. Although she played Sofiya in the original St Petersburg cast of *Woe from Wit* (GRIBOEDOV also translated Barthe's *Feigned Infidelity* for her), her career suffered when classical TRAGEDY gave way to romantic drama on the Russian stage. She and her famous fellow St Petersburg company member A. S. YAKOVLEV straddled the line between two acting traditions – one artificial, the other more realistic. During 1820–2 she temporarily retired from the stage. In 1826 she married Prince S. Gagarin, thereafter using her power to terrorize her enemies and rivals, especially young actresses. Her notable roles include RACINE's Clytemnestra and Phaedra, VOLTAIRE's Mérope and SCHILLER's Mary Stuart. SG

Senda Koreya [Itō Kunio] 1904–94 Japanese actor and director; brother of Itō Michio, dancer in YEATS's productions in London, and stage designer Itō Kisaku. Senda began his acting career at the Tsukiji Little Theatre in 1924 but left the troupe in 1926 to participate more actively in the proletarian theatre movement. He spent the years 1927 to 1931 in Germany, where he remained active in left-wing theatre. In 1932 he produced an adaptation of Brecht's *Threepenny Opera*, and he continued to translate BRECHT's work throughout his career. Imprisoned for his leftist affiliations for much of the war, he founded the Actors' Theatre (Haiyūza) in 1944. He was a pillar of the SHINGEKI movement; in the 1950s and 60s under Senda's direction the Actors' Theatre pioneered actor training and produced the work of young playwrights like Abe Kōbō (1924–93). DGG

Seneca [Lucius Annaeus Seneca; Seneca the younger] c.4 BC–AD 65 Roman orator and Stoic philosopher; and playwright. After a period of exile, Seneca was made tutor to the young Nero. When Nero became Emperor in AD 54, he remained his adviser, and was able for some years to exercise a benign influence on him, while amassing immense wealth for himself. He retired from public life in 62, and in 65 was accused of complicity in the Conspiracy of Piso and forced to commit suicide.

Ten plays are ascribed to Seneca in medieval manuscripts. The ascription has been doubted, but is now generally accepted, except for two plays thought to be by a later hand. The probably authentic plays are *Hercules Furens*, *Troades* (*Trojan Women*), *Phoenissae* (*Phoenician Women*), *Medea*, *Phaedra*, *Oedipus*, *Agamemnon* and *Thyestes*. *Oedipus* is based on SOPHOCLES (*Oedipus Tyrannus*), *Agamemnon* on AESCHYLUS, *Thyestes* on an unknown (perhaps Latin) source, the rest on EURIPIDES. The adaptation, however, is always free, as Seneca selects only those scenes of the original plays which suit his purpose, and makes many additions and rearrangements.

Of the plays considered spurious, one, *Hercules Oetaeus*, is merely a ponderous imitation of Senecan TRAGEDY, but the other, *Octavia*, is of interest as the only surviving *fabula praetexta*, or play on a historical subject (see ROME). It concerns events in AD 62, when Nero divorced his wife Octavia and then ordered her execution, and was evidently written after Nero's death, which it prophesies.

It is disputed whether the plays were written for stage performance or merely (like most non-dramatic Latin poetry) for recitation to a small private audience. They contain nothing that *cannot* be staged, given a theatre with some stage machinery (see ROMAN THEATRES AND AMPHITHEATRES) and an audience with some imagination. But dramatic realities are persistently neglected; often, for instance, it is impossible to determine when a character enters, as he turns out to be present only when he starts to speak. It is anyway probable that the haughty and wealthy Seneca would have thought it beneath his dignity to write for the theatre. Passages of rapid dialogue could not easily have been delivered by a *single* reciter, but it is possible to imagine a small group of reciters, and perhaps some kind of semi-staged performance.

Certainly Seneca's main concern is with the rhetoric of speeches. He portrays the most heightened extremes of passion throughout, while striving at the same time for neatness and cleverness in his epigrams and rhetorical conceits. These purposes work against each other, giving, to modern tastes, an extremely artificial effect, and eliminating all possibility of subtle characterization. The epigrams and conceits are often striking and memorable; but every idea, whether striking or banal, is invariably flogged to death, often with a long list of mythical or geographical examples.

Each of the tragedies has five acts. Between the acts the Chorus utters general reflections loosely inspired by the action, but it hardly seems to occupy the same world as the characters, and is itself barely characterized. From *Phoenissae*, as we have it, choral songs are for some reason missing.

Stoic ideas are sometimes expressed, and the plays in general are Stoic in their portrayal of the evils stemming from passion and ambition. But evil always prevails, and there is no sign that human beings can ever attain the wisdom of the ideal Stoic sage. Every tragedy builds up to a violent climax, related in a messenger-speech towards the end. The violence, like everything else, is evoked in the most extravagant terms, and to read some of these messenger-speeches requires a strong stomach, even by today's standards.

Senecan tragedy came into its own in the Renaissance, when the plays were assumed to be meant for performance, and were sometimes performed at universities. Among the tragedies of Elizabethan and Jacobean England Senecan influence is most obvious in inferior plays, such as SHAKESPEARE's *Titus Andronicus*; but without that influence, the tragedy of the period could not have existed at all. ALB

Senegal Senegal, formerly the capital of the French West African Federation and independent since 1960, has the longest tradition of modern theatre in French West Africa. And until the late 1970s, when the centre of dramatic production and theatre research moved to countries such as Côte d'Ivoire, the Congo and Mali, it was also the strongest.

Theatrical activity in Senegal goes back to before the First World War, when visiting troupes, on their way to South America, staged performances in Dakar to a mostly French expatriate audience. The subsequent founding in that country of the École William Ponty, and the large part that it devoted to theatrical activity, made of that school and, by extension, Senegal – as the drama historian Robert Cornevin has noted – the 'great laboratory of African drama'. Through the school's annual *fête d'art indigène* (festival of indigenous art), in particular, which presented

A scene from Diop's *L'Os de Mor Lam*, Senegal, 1967.

dramatic works by student groups based on the history or folklore of their countries, Senegal became the centre of theatre activity in the Federation.

This role was reinforced in 1954 with the construction of the modest Théâtre du Palais, replaced in 1965 with the grand Théâtre Daniel Sorano, complete with a Conservatory of Dramatic Arts, an African ballet troupe, a theatre company proper and a traditional ensemble of *griots*. Under the direction of Sonar Senghor and with the collaboration of the French theatre producer and former pupil of JACQUES COPEAU, Raymond Hermantier, and of the Haitian playwright Gérard Chenet, the Daniel Sorano mounted performances as varied as the Senegalese CHEIK NDAO's *L'Exil d'Albouri* (*Albouri's Exile*, 1967), SHAKESPEARE's *Macbeth* and GOGOL's *The Government Inspector* (1836), adapted by Senghor as *Monsieur Pots-de-vin et consorts* (*Mister Bribery and Company*). The 1966 first World Festival of Negro Arts in Dakar consecrated that city's reputation as a leading sub-Saharan capital of the modern arts and, with its cohorts of visiting troupes and their productions, acted as a stimulus to the creative activity of its theatre practitioners.

Senegal has given some notable works to French-language African dramatic literature, among them Amadou Cissé Dia's *Les Derniers Jours de Lat Dior suivi de la mort du Damel* (*The Last Days of Lat Dior Followed by the Death of The Damel*, 1966); Abdou Anta Ka's *Amazoulou* (1972); Cheik Ndao's *L'Exil d'Albouri* and *Le Fils de l'Almamy* (*The Son of the Almamy*, 1973); Thiérno Ba's *Bilbassy* (1980); Seyni Mbengue's *Le Procès de Lat Dior* (*The Trial of Lat Dior*, 1971); Ibrahim Sall's *Le Choix du Madior* (*The Choice of the Madior*, 1981), and not least Léopold Senghor's dramatic poem for two voices and a chorus, *Chaka* (1956). What these plays have in common is a preoccupation with the African past. But their treatment of it is not uniform; not only are there differences in technique, but there is also a sharp difference in the vision of the past presented in plays like Cissé Dia's and Anta Ka's written before independence, on the one hand, and the rest written after. Where the former's folklorish vision is consistent with that of official colonial history, the latter's is robustly nationalistic, idealizing ancient kings like Lat Dior (whom Cissé treats rather negatively), Albouri Ndiaye, Chaka and Samory Touré.

Some of Senegal's plays are technically distinguished. Ndao's *L'Exil d'Albouri*, for example, stands out in its epic quality created by the movement of crowds and the use of vast open spaces and battle scenes. It also conveys a high sense of drama in its handling of situation and character. Ba's *Bilbassy* is striking in its music, which functions as an integral part of the action and not just as an exotic extra, while Abdou Anta Ka excels in the poetry of his works and in the theatricality of their language.

If Senegal's long cultural contacts with France enabled it to produce a leading modern theatre in the immediate pre-independence years and for almost a decade and a half later, it is those contacts that are also responsible for a certain sterility currently present in that theatre. While elsewhere in French-speaking Africa creative energy is being channelled into ways of evolving a truly African theatre aesthetic derived from the traditional performing arts, Senegal, the home of negritude, continues paradoxically to produce historical dramas that merely nod politely at the African arts. JCM

See: R. Cornevin, *Le Théâtre en Afrique noire et à Madagascar*, Paris, 1970; M. Diouf, 'Un baobab au milieu de la brousse: le théâtre de langue française', *Notre Librairie: La Littérature Sénégalaise*, 81, Oct./Dec. 1985; C. Wake and M. Banham, *African Theatre Today*, London, 1976.

Serban, Andrei 1943– Romanian-born and -educated American theatre director, singled out while still a student for his exceptional gifts. His first productions established his renown. In 1968, when his staging of SHAKESPEARE's *Julius Caesar* stirred up vigorous polemics, he decided to stay on in the USA, thus gaining undisputed recognition abroad. He made his debut in the USA at Ellen Stewart's LA MAMA in 1970.

Unconventional and imaginative, Serban, whose greatest influence has been PETER BROOK, soon became one of the prominent figures in contemporary American theatre. Among his most notable productions were *The Cherry Orchard* at Lincoln Center (1977), *Sganarelle* at the YALE REPERTORY THEATRE (1978), *The Umbrellas of Cherbourg* (MUSICAL) at the PUBLIC THEATER, New York City (1979), *The Marriage of Figaro* at the GUTHRIE THEATRE (1982), *Uncle Vanya* with F. Murray Abraham at La MaMa (1983), *The King Stag* (1985) and *The Miser* (1989) at the AMERICAN REPERTORY THEATRE, Massachusetts. Operas he stage-directed include Tchaikovsky's *Eugène Onegin* (Welsh National Opera, 1980), Mozart's *Magic Flute* (Nancy, 1980), Verdi's *Traviata* (Juilliard American Opera Centre, 1981) and *Rigoletto* (La Fenice, 1982), Borodin's *Prince Igor* (Covent Garden, 1989), Donizetti's *Lucia di Lammermoor* (Chicago, 1990), Prokofiev's *Fiery Angel* (Amsterdam and Opéra Bastille, 1991).

In 1990 Serban was appointed general manager of the National Theatre of Bucharest, where he spends two or three months every year. He has renewed the ensemble and demonstrated that a traditional and academic theatre company can be regenerated through its enthusiastic devotion to a modern guiding spirit. Romanian productions include *An Ancient Trilogy* ('a great achievement not only in the context of Romania or Eastern countries, but for the European and world's theatre' – John Elsom), *Twelfth Night* and *The Cherry Orchard*. Since 1992 he has been teaching at the Columbia University, New York. BM REK AP

Serlio, Sebastiano 1475–1554 Italian architect. Born in Bologna, Serlio worked as painter and architect before going to Rome in 1525 to work with BALDASSARE PERUZZI. Before moving to Paris in 1541 to work on the palace at Fontainebleau, he designed a temporary wooden theatre in Vicenza, said at the time to be the world's largest, the only specific theatre architecture Serlio is known to have produced. *Architettura* (1537–51), his seven-volume commentary on VITRUVIUS' *De Architectura*, was probably the most influential and significant Renaissance work on architecture. Book 2 of his treatise, published in 1545, contained a short section on theatre architecture and design which formed the basis for theatre practice throughout Europe for the next two centuries (see THEATRE BUILDINGS;

THEATRE DESIGN).

Serlio's significance lies in the way he combined his study of antiquity with Renaissance aesthetics and technology, thereby creating the foundation for the development of the proscenium stage and illusionistic scenery. His theatre plan included a long, narrow stage and semicircular arrangement of seats taken from the classical Roman theatre (see ROME). But he also assumed that the theatre would be contained in a rectangular space, so that the seating plan was truncated. More importantly, the main stage was backed by a deep, raked, scenic stage that contained stock perspective scenery on flat frames enhanced by 'wooden relief'. The three scenes were the tragic, comic and satyric. The first, which bore a striking resemblance to Peruzzi's 1514 scene for *La Calandria*, contained a street with stately houses, statuary and the like. The comic was a street containing houses of ordinary citizens and was to include a tavern, courtesan's house and a church. And the satyric depicted a pastoral setting. By 1620 his writings on theatre were translated into five languages. When François I died in 1547 Serlio fell into disfavour and destitution. He spent a few years in Lyon, but was able to return to Paris before he died. AA

Serreau, Jean-Marie 1915–73 French director. Having trained with DULLIN, Serreau became one of the directors responsible for the success of the THEATRE OF THE ABSURD, directing plays by ADAMOV, GENET, IONESCO and BECKETT. But he also directed one of the first plays by BRECHT to be performed in France (*The Exception and the Rule*, 1947) and in the 1960s became identified with the post-Brechtian political theatre of writers such as CÉSAIRE and YACINE. In reality the consistent guiding thread in Serreau's work was an experimental approach and in the 1960s he conducted a series of experiments in multimedia performance, attempting to find a synthesis between science and poetry. His widow, Geneviève Serreau, also works as a theatre producer and adapter and wrote one of the best accounts of the theatre of the absurd: *Histoire du Nouveau Théâtre* (1966). DB

Serulle, Haffe 1947– Dominican Republic fiction writer and playwright, with a socially committed tendency. Serulle has written two historical plays: *Duarte* (1975) and *El hatero del Seybo* (*Pedro Santana*, 1976). His other plays denounce a variety of secular evils: *La danza de Mingó* (*Mingó's Dance*, 1977), *Prostitución en la casa de Dios* (*Prostitution in God's House*, 1978), *Testimonio de un pueblo oprimido* (*Testimony of an Oppressed People*, 1980), *Miriam la buena* (*The Good Miriam*, 1982) and *Bianto y su señor* (*Bianto and his Master*, 1984). GW

Serumaga, Robert 1940–81 Ugandan playwright and producer. Educated at Trinity College, Dublin, Serumaga trained at the BBC and in theatre in Europe before returning to Uganda in 1966. He founded Theatre Ltd, later known as the Abafumi Players, gathering together outstanding actors and backstage personnel from existing dramatic societies (largely expatriate in the beginning) to form a semi-professional group. After producing several plays by other writers he concentrated on producing his own. Subsequently he gathered together a group of school-leavers whom he trained as professional performers and with whom he travelled widely, creating two notable dance dramas: *Renga Moi* (1972) and *Amerykitti* (1974). He held the senior Creative Writing Fellowship at Makerere University for one year. In the last two years of the Amin regime (1977–9) he found it easier to operate his company from Nairobi. He was briefly (1979) Minister of Commerce in the Lule government. He returned to the Abafumi Players in Nairobi, where he died. His published works are *A Play* (1967), *The Elephants* (1970) and *Majangwa* (1971). MMAC

Servandoni, Giovanni (Niccolò) [Jean Nicolas Servan] 1695–1766 Italian architect, painter and stage designer who moved to Paris in 1724 and subsequently spent most of his working life in France. From 1728 he was principal designer at the Opéra and was frequently commissioned to devise the decorations for official court functions and those of the aristocracy. Between 1738 and 1742 and again in the 1750s he mounted at the SALLE DES MACHINES a number of performances with non-speaking actors, which were little more than a pretext for displaying spectacular changeable scenery, machines and lighting effects to a scenario written by himself. In later years he worked in several other European capitals. In 1749 COVENT GARDEN imported him to paint scenes for their operas and plays and in 1763 he was hired for one year by Duke Karl Eugen as a scene painter for the court at Württemberg. Servandoni's designs, with their impressive perspectives and diagonal vistas, mark the high-point of illusionistic scenery as an autonomous element in the stage picture. DR AJN

Settle, Elkanah 1647–1724 English playwright. Educated at Westminster School and Trinity College, Oxford, he began writing plays in 1666. His tragedy *The Empress of Morocco* (1669) was the first play published in England with illustrations of the performance. It was BURLESQUED by Thomas Duffett for the rival company and fiercely attacked in a pamphlet by DRYDEN, CROWNE and SHADWELL. He wrote numerous heroic tragedies, including *The Female Prelate* (1680), a play on Pope Joan, and adaptations of earlier plays before turning to OPERATIC spectacle. His adaptation of *A Midsummer Night's Dream* as *The Fairy Queen* with music by Purcell was first performed in 1692 and contains spectacular scenes of music and dancing for monkeys and Chinamen. In 1679 his comedy *The World on the Moon* was performed with the most extravagant machine effects yet tried in England. From 1683 onwards Settle also wrote drolls, shortened comic versions of his own and others' plays, for performance in booths at Bartholomew Fair and Southwark Fair. He may have acted in these as well. In 1691 he became city poet and produced city pageants for London until 1708. From 1718 he lived in Charterhouse, a poorhouse. PH

Séveste, Pierre-Jacques 1773–1825 French theatre manager. A former dancer and actor in the BOULEVARD theatres, Séveste set up one of the first dramatic agencies in France c.1810. With the Restoration of the monarchy he acquired special favour by helping to find the burial place of Louis XVI and Marie Antoinette, and in 1817 was granted a licence to erect theatres in the suburbs and to perform plays which had recently been performed at the theatres in Paris. His first theatre was the 348-seat Théâtre Montparnasse (1819), and this was followed by the larger Théâtre de Montmartre (1822). His actors were usually badly paid, and often of semi-amateur status. After the death of Pierre-Jacques, his widow and sons Edmond and Jules continued the business, adding the theatres of Belleville (1827) and Grenelle (1830), and taking over, with compensation, the Batignolles theatre, 'illegally' built by Souchet in 1830.

The Séveste monopoly of suburban theatres in a rapidly expanding city was the subject of much jealousy and opposition. They maintained it, without making their fortune, until 1851. The most important of the theatres was Montmartre, built largely from the demolished Château de Cramagel (whence came much of the original scenery), and which was described as 'ideal for a provincial town of 8–10,000 inhabitants'. Prices at Montmartre ranged from 2 francs to 50 centimes in 1845 and by the mid-century these theatres were becoming the real 'popular' theatres of Paris. JMCC

Sewell, Stephen 1953– Australian playwright. His plays, written from a Marxist perspective, share an episodic structure, powerful theatrical effects and a preoccupation with the tension between political commitment and private emotion. They include *The Father We Loved on a Beach by the Sea* (1976), *Traitors* (1979; staged at HAMPSTEAD THEATRE CLUB, London, in 1980), *Welcome the Bright World* (1982), *The Blind Giant Is Dancing* (1983), *Dreams in an Empty City* (1986); a grotesque allegorical fantasy of corporate greed, *King Golgrutha* (1991), and a TELEVISION DRAMA, *The Long Way Home* (1985). His less overtly political recent work focuses on family relationships in *Sisters* (1991) and *The Garden of Granddaughters* (1993). MW

Seydelmann, Karl 1793–1843 German actor. One of the greatest virtuosi of the 19th century, Seydelmann acted in companies in Prague, Cassel, Darmstadt, Stuttgart (from 1828 to 1837) and, during the final years of his life, at the BERLIN ROYAL THEATRE. Chronic sickness and nervous disorders made him a lonely and difficult man. His interpretation of classic roles, especially Carlos in *Clavigo*, Mephistopheles, King Philip in *Don Carlos*, and Shylock, were distinguished for the dryness and individuality of his approach. For some of his critics, Seydelmann acted with little attention to the role's context within the play; for others, he was the epitome of the 'thinking' intellectual actor. His letters and occasional writings are an invaluable source for the theatre history of the time. SW

Seymour, William 1855–1933 American actor, director and stage manager. A child actor in New Orleans until 1865, when he went to New York, Seymour served as a call-boy at BOOTH'S THEATRE and performed with EDWIN BOOTH, JOSEPH JEFFERSON III, CHARLOTTE CUSHMAN and EDWIN FORREST. Among Seymour's many management positions were the Union Square Theatre, the MADISON SQUARE THEATRE, the Metropolitan Opera House and CHARLES FROHMAN'S EMPIRE THEATRE in New York, and a

decade (1879–88) at the BOSTON MUSEUM. In 1882 he married May Davenport, daughter of E. L. DAVENPORT and younger sister of FANNY DAVENPORT. His theatrical memorabilia and personal library form the nucleus of the extensive Princeton University Library theatre collection (integrated, sans curator, into other Princeton holdings in 1992–3). FHL DJW

shadow puppets, shadow theatre A form of entertainment in which flat figures of a non- or semi-transparent material reflect stylized shadows against a screen, and are moved to music or chant. All oriental shadow theatres began as illustrations to narration. In INDONESIA (Java and Bali) the figures of the *wayang* (i.e. silhouette) theatre are usually of water-buffalo hide: the *wayang klitik* figures are flat with one movable arm; those of the *wayang golek* are three-dimensional with movable heads and arms. The forms of the characters are traditional, the differences in size indicating their type. Some tales of gods, heroes and demons are drawn from south INDIAN myth and ritual, with an admixture of topical and sexual matters. The *dalangs*, or showman-reciters, perform only by invitation and are used to spread religious and dynastic propaganda; they now present drawing-room versions of traditional plays. The play is performed on a screen 13ft long and 5ft high set up in an inner verandah; it begins at sundown after a long musical introduction, and goes on into the night (in Bali up to 1 a.m., in Java until 4 or 5 a.m.). It is a common diversion for the night after a wedding.

The Thai version, *nang*, still performed by a few troupes, is not technically a shadow play since the leather puppets which can represent a single character or a whole scene are in direct view. They are moved according to the choreography of the Siamese dance, and a troupe may comprise 10 to 20 players.

The *piyingxi* of China is a form of miniature OPERA. The translucent figures of coloured parchment (or leather in Sichuan) cast coloured shadows in this synthesis of painting, song, music and manual choreography. The technique originated in the Sung era (960–1279) as depictions of the folkloric tales *shuo-shu*, but soon evolved a distinct repertory of historic and Buddhist themes. It declined after 1911, but in the 1930s Tang Jiheng proposed its revival as competition for the Western cinema. During the Japanese occupation, it was used for Resistance propaganda, and during the Korean War the communist government exploited it in training soldiers. For a short period in the 1950s it was influenced by the American comic strip, but has reverted to the traditional love stories, criminal cases and battles.

Oriental shadow puppets first came to Central Europe in the 17th century, as an auxiliary to the use of the magic lantern. In France they became known as *ombres chinoises*, especially as popularized by Dominique Séraphin (1747–1800), and were later sophisticated by Henri Rivière at the Parisian CABARET the Chat Noir (after 1887) with crowd scenes, incandescent colour shifts and scored music. They greatly influenced the Austrian artist Richard Teschner (1879–1948), whose Golden Shrine Theatre (1912) featured a synthesis of Indonesian and Viennese Secession elements. Alexander von Bernus also brought it to a high degree of artistry in his Schwabing

Shadow Plays (1907–12). In the early 1920s Lotte Reininger (b.1899) brought shadow puppets to the screen in her classic animated films, such as *Prince Achmet* (1926).   LS

See: W. Grube, *Chinesische Schattenspiele*, Munich, 1915; R. Long, *Javanese Shadow Theatre*, Ann Arbor, 1982; I. C. Orr, 'Puppet Theatre in Asia', *Asian Folklore Studies* 33 (1974); J. Pimpaneau, *Les Poupées à l'ombre*, Paris, 1977; J. and P. Remise and R. Van de Walle, *Magie lumineuse*, Tours, 1979.

Shadwell, Thomas   c.1642–92 English playwright. Most famous as the target of DRYDEN's SATIRE *MacFlecknoe* (1678), an attack avenged when Shadwell succeeded Dryden as Poet Laureate and Historiographer Royal after the Revolution of 1688. He was educated at Caius College, Cambridge, and at the Middle Temple in London, and began writing plays with an adaptation of MOLIÈRE's *Les Fâcheux* as *The Sullen Lovers* (1668). Shadwell quickly defined himself as the inheritor of the style of JONSON in *The Humorists* (1670) and *Epsom Wells* (1672). He transformed Dryden and DAVENANT's version of SHAKESPEARE's *The Tempest* into an OPERA in 1674, as well as adapting Molière's *The Miser* (1672) and collaborating with William Cavendish, Duke of Newcastle, on *The Triumphant Widow* (1677). Of his original plays, the best of his satiric comedies are *The Virtuoso* (1676) which incorporates mockery of the pseudo-science of the Royal Society, *The Squire of Alsatia* (1688) with its virtuoso display of the language of the criminal underworld, and *Bury Fair* (1689) which explores provincial aping of London manners. His dark comic version of the Don Juan story, *The Libertine*, was performed in 1675 and his version of Shakespeare's *Timon of Athens*, in part turned into a contemporary political satire, in 1678.   PH

Shaffer, Peter (Levin)   1926– British dramatist who worked as a coalminer, librarian and music critic before his early play, *Five Finger Exercise*, was successfully produced in 1958. This demonstrated a command of the skills of drawing-room drama, but his television scripts, *The Salt Land* (1955) and *Balance of Terror* (1957), suggested an imagination drawn towards religious and philosophical subjects.

The first stage play to combine his craftsmanship with his wider interests was *The Royal Hunt of the Sun* (1964), about the destruction of the Inca civilization in Peru by the Spanish conquistadores led by Pizarro. The contrast between the Inca god-king, Atahuallpa, and Pizarro represented the battle between Inca and European values, passion and intellect, the soul and the mind. *The Royal Hunt of the Sun* demanded unusual MIME and vocal disciplines, but under JOHN DEXTER's direction and with ROBERT STEPHENS and COLIN BLAKELY in the main parts, it became the NATIONAL THEATRE's first success with a new and untried play. His FARCE, *Black Comedy* (1965), in which the stage characters grope around apparently in darkness while the audience watch them in full light, was another NT hit, and later matched with *White Lies* (1968) to form a double bill in the WEST END.

The Battle of Shrivings (1970) was less successful, but Shaffer's subsequent plays, *Equus* (1973) and *Amadeus* (1979), are considered to form the core of his high interna-

tional reputation. In *Equus*, a psychoanalyst attempts to grapple with the mysterious Dionysian faiths of a delinquent youth, Alan Strang, while in *Amadeus* the composer Salieri bitterly watches the progress of his divinely inspired rival, Mozart. Both plays contrast reason with faith, common sense with inspiration; and both decide in favour of inspiration, which is indeed a favourite Shaffer theme – from *The Royal Hunt of the Sun* even to his comedy, *Lettice and Lovage* (1987), where a romantic historical tour guide, exuberantly played by MAGGIE SMITH in the West End, settles down with and converts her opposite, a pedantic fact-bound historian. *The Gift of the Gorgon* (1992) about a dead Dionysian playwright and his Apollonian widow attracted reviews which were also at extremes, ranging from 'amazingly awful' to 'brilliant'; and this reception revealed a characteristic of his plays. If their theatricality can be accepted at its face value, the drama can seem to be rewarding, even profound; but if they are watched with a trace of irony, they can easily seem to be melodramatic or rather absurd.   JE

Shakespeare, William   1564–1616 English playwright. In a flamboyant age and a notoriously flamboyant profession – he was an active member of a theatre company for at least 20 years – Shakespeare was abnormally reticent. As a result, researchers have had painstakingly to piece together the story of his life from surviving scraps of evidence.

He was born in the market town of Stratford-upon-Avon, Warwickshire, where his father was a prosperous glover and one of the town's 14 principal burgesses. In 1565, John Shakespeare was promoted to the rank of alderman, and he became Chief Alderman in 1571. It is a reasonable assumption that such a man would send his son to the local grammar school, though there is speculation that the boy did not complete his course there, owing to the decline in his father's fortunes after 1576. The years before Shakespeare's marriage to Anne Hathaway in 1582 are blank. Within six months of the wedding, the couple had a daughter. She was the Susanna who later married John Hall, a local physician, and lived prosperously in Stratford. The family was completed with the birth of twins, Judith and Hamnet, in 1585. Hamnet died in 1596 and was buried in Stratford, where Judith remained until her death in 1662.

Virtually nothing is known of Shakespeare's life from 1585 to 1592. It may be that he left home and family to tour with a group of London players. Certainly his name was sufficiently familiar in the London theatres by 1592 to invite ROBERT GREENE's jibe at him as an 'upstart crow'. Greene was one of the university men who resented the rivalry of the new breed of professional playwrights, and he had probably in mind Shakespeare's part in the writing of the three *Henry VI* plays. This early collaboration suggests that Shakespeare served his apprenticeship alongside some of the growing number of dramatic aspirants seeking advantage in the demand for plays from the emergent professional theatre. Other surviving texts from the 1590s, however, suggest that Shakespeare preferred to work alone. Only in *Sir Thomas More* (c.1595) has his collaborative hand been confidently detected. We do not know how Shakespeare came by the money to purchase a share in the newly formed LORD CHAMBERLAIN's MEN in

1594. His likeliest patron, Henry Wriothesley, Earl of Southampton, was in financial straits of his own at this time, but he cherished the role of Maecenas and may have helped the young man who had already dedicated to him his narrative poem, *Venus and Adonis* (1593). By 1594 Shakespeare had also written at least three comedies, *The Comedy of Errors*, *The Two Gentlemen of Verona* and *The Taming of the Shrew*; and two corpse-laden tragedies, *Titus Andronicus* and *Richard III*, the latter of which provided a brilliantly original conclusion to the three parts of *Henry VI*, as well as a second narrative poem, *The Rape of Lucrece*. The Lord Chamberlain's Men must have perceived in him not simply an actor, but also a potential resident writer for their London base, the THEATRE in Shoreditch.

Living close to Bishopsgate and the Theatre, Shakespeare continued to write plays at the rate of approximately two per year. The period 1594–8 may have seen the first productions of *King John* (sometimes dated as early as 1589); the middle comedies, *Love's Labour's Lost* (scholars continue to argue about *Love's Labour's Won*, ascribed to Shakespeare by Francis Meres in *Palladis Tamia* (1598)), *A Midsummer Night's Dream* and *The Merchant of Venice*; the outstandingly popular tragedy *Romeo and Juliet*; and the cycle of English HISTORY PLAYS comprising *Richard II*, the two parts of *Henry IV* and *Henry V*. That Shakespeare also had aspirations as a gentleman, and sufficient means to support them, is apparent in the application, on his father's behalf, for a coat of arms. The award was made in 1596. In the following year, Shakespeare bought New Place, one of the finest houses in Stratford. Early in 1598 he made a small investment in malt (malting was Stratford's principal industry). The London theatres were under threat of permanent closure at this time, and he may have been contemplating the life of a country gentleman. If so, the plan was shelved when, at the end of 1598, the company responded to the landlord's threat of eviction from the Theatre by transporting its timbers to the south bank of the Thames and re-erecting them as the GLOBE.

Shakespeare wrote most of his greatest plays during the first decade (1599–1608) of his company's occupation of the Globe. They include the mature comedies, *Much Ado About Nothing* (which may shortly pre-date the move), *As You Like It* and *Twelfth Night*; the darker comedies, sometimes called 'problem plays', *All's Well that Ends Well*, *Measure for Measure* and *Troilus and Cressida*; a pot-boiler, *The Merry Wives of Windsor*, written in response to demands for more of Falstaff; and the major tragedies, *Julius Caesar*, *Hamlet*, *Othello*, *King Lear*, *Macbeth*, *Antony and Cleopatra*, *Coriolanus* and *Timon of Athens*. It was a period that saw the Lord Chamberlain's Men honoured by the new monarch with the title of King's Men and confirmed in their ascendancy at court.

Shakespeare had moved his London lodgings to Southwark, in closer proximity to the new theatre, and maintained his financial interests in Stratford. A small investment in land (1602) was followed by a larger one (1605). He may have feared the continuing insecurity of his profession, threatened by authority, by the regular outbreaks of plague and by the faddish interest in boy actors. Facile younger dramatists, BEAUMONT and FLETCHER in particular, were challenging his supremacy by the readiness of their response to Jacobean taste for sensation and spectacle. It was a taste more easily satisfied in the indoor BLACKFRIARS, which the King's Men added to the outdoor Globe in 1608. Shakespeare's last plays, *Pericles, Prince of Tyre* (on which he collaborated, probably with George Wilkins), *Cymbeline*, *The Winter's Tale* and *The Tempest*, take account of the revived interest in romance, magic and improbable resolutions whilst giving scope to a new 'indoor' fondness for scenic spectacle. At the end of his career, Shakespeare returned to the collaborative composition with which he had begun, working with Fletcher on *Henry VIII*, *The Two Noble Kinsmen* and the lost *Cardenio*. By 1613, when the Globe was destroyed by fire, his hold on the London theatre was slipping. He had just purchased the upper floor of one of the Blackfriars gatehouses and may not have wished to contribute more to the rebuilding of the Globe. It is possible, though not certain, that he relinquished his share in the old theatre, now under reconstruction, and spent his last years in Stratford.

Texts Less than half of Shakespeare's plays were published during his own life, and this is not at all surprising. Not only were plays held in low esteem as literature, but also acting companies were unwilling to make their possessions available to others and to the public at large. The single known example of a playwright's contract, RICHARD BROME's with Queen Henrietta's Men at the SALISBURY COURT THEATRE (1635), specifies that Brome shall publish none of the plays written for the company. Authorized publication of plays often followed unauthorized, 'pirated' publication of unreliable texts, like the famous 'bad' Quarto of *Hamlet* (1603). It was, then, an act of singular homage when two of the King's Men, JOHN HEMINGES and HENRY CONDELL, oversaw the publication in lavish Folio form, of 36 plays by their late colleague. The First Folio (1623, reprinted 1632, 64 and 85) includes 20 plays which might otherwise never have been published. It was, by any reckoning, a remarkable printing achievement. Various facsimiles have been subsequently published. Subsequent editors, even of the 16 plays published in earlier Quartos, have always to refer to the Folio.

The first critical edition was that of NICHOLAS ROWE (1709), who used the Fourth Folio as his authority. Himself a playwright, Rowe respected Shakespeare's text more than was common in the theatre of his time, but he sought to regularize the plays' division into scenes and acts in a way that the Folio editors had considered unnecessary. Later 18th-century editors, including Alexander Pope (1725), LEWIS THEOBALD (1734), SAMUEL JOHNSON (1765) and Edmond Malone (1790), followed Rowe's pattern. Malone's exemplary scholarship is commemorated in the reprints of dramatic texts and documents by the Malone Society (founded 1907). Modern editors are served, not only by the textual studies of W. W. Greg and his successors, but also by the Variorum editions pioneered by H. H. Furness in 1871. Reliable single-volume collections include those edited by Peter Alexander, W. J. Craig and C. J. Sissons. Untroubled by the anxieties that led Thomas Bowdler to produce an expurgated 'Family Shakespeare' (1818), 20th-century editors seek to establish as perfect a text as possible, explaining their decisions in copious notes. Even so, discrepancies remain, and no two editions of the same play will ever be identical. Outstanding among 20th-century series are the variously edited Arden, New Cambridge, Penguin and Oxford Shakespeares.

Shakespeare in performance There can be little certainty about the conditions in which Shakespeare's plays were first performed. We know that RICHARD BURBAGE'S acting was greatly admired and that he played Richard III, Hamlet, Lear and Othello, but we do not know how he played them, nor even how well he knew his lines. There is some contemporary evidence, particularly in the case of comic roles, that Elizabethan actors sometimes substituted their own words for the playwright's. We cannot assume that Shakespeare's own company performed his plays 'straight' and word-perfect. What we can say is that the actors walked out on to the platform to deliver their part of a story, since it was as a storytelling art that the drama made its bid for audiences. It is a mistake of which many scholars have been guilty to suppose that there was a single style of playing – formal and rhetorical, say some, natural and direct, say others. On the contrary, the variety of verbal styles in which the best Elizabethan plays were written indicates the expectation of a variety in the acting. Play days in the open-air theatres were probably boisterous and certainly colourful – an extravagant delight in clothes was shared by actors and audiences. Rich gowns turned boy actors into acceptable women, one of many conventions on which effective staging relied. The Elizabethan theatre was not a haven for purists, and the more 'correct' taste of the late 17th century found fault with it. Even Shakespeare's admirers, like DAVENANT and DRYDEN, admitted the need to improve him.

From the early days of the Restoration theatre until well into the 19th century, it was normal practice to hack, reshape and plunder Shakespeare's texts to suit prevailing tastes or to ease the task of leading actors. NAHUM TATE'S *King Lear* (1681) and COLLEY CIBBER'S *Richard III* (1700) are only the best remembered of the cobbled versions in which the plays reached Restoration audiences. THOMAS BETTERTON, whose playing of such contrasting parts as Hamlet and Falstaff brought Shakespeare's name into a new prominence, did his own doctoring of the texts, setting a precedent which would be followed by later actor-managers from DAVID GARRICK through JOHN PHILIP KEMBLE, W. C. MACREADY, CHARLES KEAN and HENRY IRVING to BEERBOHM TREE and the 20th century. The manifest leader of his profession, Betterton unwittingly established the rule that the greatness of English actors would be measured by their achievement in Shakespearian roles. His versions had to take account of the new delight in changeable scenery, a sophistication which ran counter to the fluidity of scene changes on the bare Elizabethan stage. The re-ordering of scenes may not be the most offensive of the alterations of Shakespeare, but it is one of the most enduring. The director of the ROYAL SHAKESPEARE COMPANY'S 1977 revival of the *Henry VI* trilogy, TERRY HANDS, for example, laid stress on the decision 'not to do even our own usual reshaping of a few corners'. A programme note for the same company's 1974 *King John* confessed that 'the text for this production incorporates lines from *The Troublesome Reign* and BALE'S *Kynge Johan*, and some

additions by John Barton'. It would be a mistake for 20th-century audiences, confident of the respect in which Shakespeare's text is now held, to neglect the continuing theatrical urge to bend what cannot easily be made to fit.

Betterton's formally cadenced delivery of Shakespeare's lines was copied by JAMES QUIN. They stood, probably firm-footed and facing front, on the proscenium in the full light of the candelabra, enacting through gesture the passions expressed in their lines. Garrick's memorable debut as Richard III (1741) was an energetic, and eventually decisive, challenge to the old-school conventions, as, earlier in the same year, was CHARLES MACKLIN'S vividly serious Shylock. But Shakespearian acting was changed also by external forces. The increasing size of the major London theatres throughout the 18th century demanded a broader style. Only a presence as imposing as that of SARAH SIDDONS or as charismatic as that of EDMUND KEAN could command an audience of over 3000. With the development of gas lighting during the second decade of the 19th century came another significant change. The greater visibility allowed actors to play inside, rather than in front of, the scenery. One significant outcome was the increasing hold of 'pictorial Shakespeare', to which designers contributed almost as much as actors. The various regimes of Macready, MADAME VESTRIS, Charles Kean, Irving and Tree brought the visual elements of Shakespearian production into parity with the aural. The splendour of the crowded 19th-century stage was a new convention which few actor-managers – SAMUEL PHELPS outstandingly at SADLER'S WELLS (1844–62) – were bold enough to challenge before WILLIAM POEL began his sequence of bare-stage productions for the Elizabethan Stage Society in 1894.

It is the replacement of the actor-manager by the director that distinguishes 20th-century Shakespearian production. GRANVILLE BARKER'S innovatory work at London's Savoy (1912–14) demonstrated how the text could be released by the clearing of the cluttered stage. The new approach was further strengthened during LILIAN BAYLIS'S years at the OLD VIC, where the young TYRONE GUTHRIE was one among many directors who dared radically to reinterpret Shakespeare's plays. At the rebuilt Shakespeare Memorial Theatre (opened 1932), Komisarjevsky (KOMISSARZHEVSKY) offended purists with a series of unconventionally designed productions (1933–9), bringing Stratford into new prominence as a centre of Shakespearian performance. That prominence was firmly established by 1960, when PETER HALL became the managing director of the newly named Royal Shakespeare Company. Most of the major English actors and directors have worked at Stratford, or at the company's London bases, the Aldwych (1960–82) and the Barbican (since 1982). The conventions of modern Shakespearian production – that the director should discover the leading idea or ideas of a play and reinforce them through design (see THEATRE DESIGN) and COSTUME on a stage that permits the free flow of scenes – have been authorized by the Royal Shakespeare Company. PT

Shakespeare festivals (USA) In the USA, the modern idea of a festival of Shakespearian plays seems to have been initiated by Angus L. Bowmer, who founded the OREGON SHAKESPEARE FESTIVAL in 1935, still the oldest surviving American Shakespearian festival. The San Diego National Shakespeare Festival can also trace its origins back to 1935, although it did not offer a summer festival of plays until 1949. In the 1950s and 60s several other important festivals were founded, including the AMERICAN SHAKESPEARE [THEATRE] Festival (Stratford, Connecticut) in 1955, the NEW YORK SHAKESPEARE FESTIVAL (as the Shakespeare Theatre Workshop) in 1954, and the Great Lakes Shakespeare Festival in 1961. Although initially confined to summer seasons, most of the major festival theatres have gradually extended their seasons and expanded their operations. The Oregon Shakespeare Festival, for example, went from a two-month summer season to a virtual year-round operation. In 1970 the modern, indoor Angus Bowmer Theatre was built adjacent to the outdoor Elizabethan Theatre modelled on John Cranford Adams's Globe reconstruction. The present Elizabethan Theatre opened in 1959, replacing two earlier outdoor theatres. Typically, the Oregon festival also operates a small 'studio' theatre named the Black Swan. In the late 1960s and 70s, the San Diego and New York festivals also expanded into additional theatres and longer seasons. In 1984, the Alabama Shakespeare Festival moved into a new two-theatre, multimillion-dollar complex in Montgomery. With such expansion, these major festival theatres have also stretched their repertoires well beyond SHAKESPEARE's plays. A typical season will now include not only two or three Shakespearian plays, but also revivals of international classics and productions of contemporary comedies, dramas and MUSICALS. As an indication of its less restricted repertoire, the Great Lakes festival has recently dropped 'Shakespeare' from its name.

Although Shakespeare's plays present producers with formidable artistic and financial challenges, a Shakespearian festival remains an attractive concept, particularly for theatres operating mainly in the summer. Almost every American region has at least one summer Shakespearian festival; in fact, in the early 1990s there were over 80 Shakespeare festival theatres operating in the USA. Among the principal ones, in addition to those noted above, are the California Shakespeare Festival in Orinda, Shakespeare at Santa Cruz, the Utah Shakespeare Festival, the New Jersey Shakespeare Festival, Shakespeare & Company at Lenox (Massachusetts), the Shakespeare Festival of Dallas, the Three Rivers Shakespeare Festival in Pittsburgh, the Colorado Shakespeare Festival and the North Carolina Shakespeare Festival. The quality of presentation can vary widely from festival to festival and season to season, but the various festivals do offer thousands of theatregoers the opportunity to experience Shakespeare on the American stage. Moreover, they also provide Shakespearian performance and production opportunities for numerous aspiring and accomplished American actors, directors and designers. Many festival productions are usually reviewed annually in issues of *Shakespeare Quarterly* or *Shakespeare Bulletin*. Glen Loney and Patricia MacKay's *The Shakespeare Complex* (New York, 1975) provides an excellent if somewhat out-of-date overview of both year-round and summer festivals. An international guide to Shakespeare festivals (and companies) edited by R. Engle, F. Londré and D.J. Watermeier promises a more comprehensive survey. In 1991, the Shakespeare Theatre Association of America was founded to facilitate communication among the various Shakespearian producing organizations.   DJW

Shakhovskoi, Prince **Aleksandr (Aleksandrovich)**
1777–1846 An indefatigable force in the 19th-century Russian theatre: conservative director of the repertory section of the Imperial Theatre (1802–26); author of over 100 plays, including tragedies, melodramas, *vaudevilles*, opera librettos, patriotic historical dramas and, most notably, satirical comedies of manners; a demanding acting teacher, whose famous pupils included E. S. SEMYONOVA, V. A. KARATYGIN and I. I. SOSNITSKY; translator-adapter from French, German and English (SHAKESPEARE and Walter Scott); one of Russia's first serious *régisseurs*; and a member of the Russian Academy (1810).

Physically unprepossessing and vocally limited – fat with a long, pointed nose and unable to pronounce 'r' and 'sh' – Shakhovskoi forged an acting style in part from his observations of Monvel and TALMA while in Paris to engage a French company (1803). He began writing plays under the influence of MOLIÈRE and at the instigation of the actor DMITREVSKY, *A Woman's Jest* (1796) being his first, and the COMEDY of manners *The New Sterne* (1805) making him famous. He was engaged in several conservative literary enterprises, including A. S. Shishkov's Forum of the Friends of the Russian Language (1811–16), which attempted to preserve old forms, and, along with IVAN KRYLOV and ALEKSANDR PISAREV, publication of the *Dramatic Courier*, in which neo-classicism was defended against the onslaught of sentimentalism and early romanticism. These last two trends, together with Gallomania and the *neo-philosophes* (*umniki*), were ridiculed in his most controversial comedy, *Lesson for Coquettes, or The Lipetsk Spa* (1815), via a character said to have been modelled on the poet V. A. Zhukovsky. This was also the first five-act Russian play to set its entire action out of doors.

Shakhovskoi eventually embraced romanticism, co-authoring a comedy, *All in the Family, or the Married Fiancée* (1817), with GRIBOEDOV, whose early work he had influenced, and KHMELNITSKY. He also freely adapted Shakespeare's *The Tempest* (1827), brought PUSHKIN's 'Queen of Spades' to the stage (1836) and was the author of 'magical' comedy-ballets, replete with spectacular stage effects. In *Seigneurial Pursuits, or Home Theatre* (1808) Shakhovskoi characterized the serf theatre and introduced the stage type of the upstart landowner, reprised in his *Tranchirin's Boast* (1822) which marked the acting debut of MIKHAIL SHCHEPKIN. Shakhovskoi's *The Cossack Poet* (1812) is generally considered to be the first Russian *vaudeville*. His longest-running play, *The Bigamous Wife* (1830), was an early attempt to portray the merchant class on stage. While not a superior playwright, the suppleness of his verse, naturalness of his dialogue and individualism of his characters prepared the way for Griboedov, who in *Woe from Wit* (1824) transformed the Russian satirical comedy of manners into truly social comedy.   SG

shaman Tungus word now in general use to mean a witch-doctor, medicine man, cunning person or professional sorcerer. His (less frequently her) skills are various: human and veterinary medicine, the location of lost goods and people, the identification of witches and counter-measures against them, the ability to harm an enemy magically. The method of work is usually a RITUAL performance employing literary, musical, dramatic or choreographic techniques. Typically, the shaman is one whose own affliction has been cured by a shamanic ritual.   AEG

Shange, Ntozake [*née* Paulette Williams] 1948– African-American playwright. Born in Trenton, New Jersey, Barnard College graduate Shange's first play, *For Colored Girls Who Have Considered Suicide When the Rainbow is Enuf* (1976), brought immediate acclaim to an exciting and innovative playwright. The play called for seven women in individual recitations to recount life experiences. More conventional was *A Photograph: A Study in Cruelty* (1977), followed by *Spell #7* (1978), an extended choreopoem of character revelations using poetry, song, dance and MASKS; *Boogie Woogie Landscapes* (1980); a revisionist adaptation of BRECHT's *Mother Courage* (1980); with Emily Mann and Baikida Carroll, a rhythm-and-blues MUSICAL, *Betsey Brown* (1991), based on her 1985 novel; and for CROSSROADS THEATRE company in 1992, *The Love Space Demands*. Shange's free-form theatre pieces give her a distinctive voice on the contemporary stage. In 1993, to recognize this uniqueness, she received a three-year grant (a Lila Wallace–Reader's Digest Writers' Award) for over $100,000 to create a theatre piece with the Freedom Theatre of Philadelphia. In 1994 Shange published her third novel, *Liliane*.   EGH

Shank, John   d.1636 English actor, who was a member of several companies before joining the King's Men (see LORD CHAMBERLAIN's MEN) at some time between 1613 and 1619. His links with an older tradition of gagging CLOWNS are supported by his liking for JIGS, at least one of which, *Shank's Ordinary* (1624), he wrote. He is known to have maintained, and perhaps trained, several apprentices during his membership of the King's Men. The most provocatively interesting of the parts allotted to him is that of the waiting-woman Petella in a revival of FLETCHER's *The Wild Goose Chase*. We do not know how often a company would exploit the broad comic potential of the clown in female roles.   PT

Sharaff, Irene   1910–93 American theatre and film COSTUME designer. Sharaff began as an assistant to ALINE BERNSTEIN and by the early 1930s was designing major BROADWAY plays and (primarily) MUSICALs such as *As Thousands Cheer* and *On Your Toes*. Through the 1960s she designed many significant musicals, including *The King and I* and *West Side Story*. Her Hollywood career began in 1944 with *Meet Me in St Louis* and later included *An American in Paris*, *Cleopatra* and *Who's Afraid of Virginia Woolf?*. Although this last film demonstrated her ability to create pedestrian costumes, she is best known for stylish design and her use of colour. She also had the unusual ability to translate stage productions into film. Her last Broadway show, of 60, was *Jerome Robbins' Broadway* in 1989.   AA

Sharman, Jim   1945– Australian director. Graduating from the National Institute of Dramatic Art in 1965, he was based in London in the early 1970s, working at the ROYAL COURT THEATRE and directing large-scale productions, including *Hair*, *Jesus Christ Superstar* and *The Rocky Horror Show* in London, America and Japan. Returning to Australia in 1975, he specialized in staging PATRICK WHITE's work and has directed with several major companies, including the South Australian Theatre Company, the Sydney Theatre Company and the Australian Opera. He was director of the Adelaide Festival in 1982. In 1992 the Queensland Theatre Company staged his epic drama *Shadow and Splendour*.   MW

Shatrov [Marshak], **Mikhail (Filippovich)**   1932– The most influential Soviet Russian dramatist of the early Gorbachev period, whose works range from traditional psychological plays to comedy to documentary drama. He abandoned his position as mining engineer on the success of his first play *Clean Hands* (1953). Shatrov is best known for his revisionist dramas of Soviet history, the first of which, *In the Name of the Revolution* (1957), was one of nine to deal with Lenin; written chiefly in the 1960s, CENSORSHIP kept them off the stage until the 1980s. *The Peace Treaty of Brest-Litovsk* (1962 as a film script) showed Trotsky and Bukharin as Lenin's henchmen, and so was forbidden production at the MOSCOW ART THEATRE. It was finally staged by ROBERT STURUA at the Vakhtangov Theatre in 1987, with half the text cut and Mikhail Ulyanov playing an unorthodox Lenin who flops on to the floor. *The Sixth of July* (1964) dealt with the Mirbach assassination which split the Bolsheviks and left socialist-revolutionaries; Lenin is constantly discussed but never appears. *Bolsheviks* (1966), about an attempt on Lenin's life and White terror, received an excellent production from OLEG EFREMOV at the Sovremennik. *Blue Horses on Red Grass* (1977) concerned the end of the Civil War and anti-illiteracy campaigns; Sturua's irreverent Tbilisi production was banned when it went to Moscow in 1980. *We Are Bound to Win!* (1981–2), a retrospective about Lenin's last days, was written for the Moscow Art Theatre to honour the 26th Communist Party Conference. *Onward, Onward, Onward!* (1987), a product of *glasnost*, abandons documentary drama to create a debate over Stalin's reign.

For all their attempts to destroy traditional clichés and to show Lenin's opponents as serious and intelligent, Shatrov's plays are tendentious and conservative, with little appeal for Western audiences.   LS

Shaw, George Bernard   1856–1950 Irish-born playwright, critic and polemicist. Shaw's uneasy childhood and youth were spent in Dublin, which he left in 1876 to accompany his mother, a singer, to London. There he developed his largely self-taught interest in the arts and in politics, declaring himself a socialist in 1882 and joining the Fabian Society in 1884. He was already writing prolifically and the pull of the theatre is evident in the serialized novels of the early 1880s, from *Immaturity* to *Cashel Byron's Profession*. It was, however, as music critic for the *Star* (1888–90) and the *World* (1890–4) that he began to develop the witty iconoclasm that was to characterize his finest writing. Shaw had abandoned novel writing by the time he undertook to provide J. T. Grein's INDEPENDENT THEATRE with a play. The work began as a collaboration with WILLIAM ARCHER, whose interest in IBSEN Shaw shared and had quirkily expressed in *The Quintessence of Ibsenism* (1891), but Shavian social analysis was too over-whelmingly individualistic for the well intentioned Archer. *Widowers' Houses* (1892), by its diagnosis of slum-landlordism, exposes the collaboration of the aristocracy and the 'respectable' bourgeoisie against labour, announcing, however clumsily, the dramatic intentions of the fledgeling playwright whose mental agility was to disturb the placid surface of the English theatre for 50 years.

Not only Shaw's themes, but also the jesting stance he took towards the craft of playmaking, made it virtually impossible for the contemporary theatre to accommodate his work. He had to rely on readings, private productions and publication to mount his attack on the entrenched actor-managers and the traditional deceits of the received drama. Shaw's combativeness is exemplified in the titles he chose for the three published collections of his first ten plays. *Plays Unpleasant* (1898) contained *Widowers' Houses*, the much more proficient and highly controver-sial *Mrs Warren's Profession* (first performed 1902) and *The Philanderer* (first performed 1905). More palatable, though rich with tongue-in-cheek challenges to conven-tional dramatic values, were the *Plays Pleasant* (1898), *Arms and the Man* (1894), *Candida* (1897), *The Man of Destiny* (1897) and *You Never Can Tell* (1899). *Three Plays for Puritans* (1901), *The Devil's Disciple* (1897), *Captain Brassbound's Conversion* (1900) and *Caesar and Cleopatra* (1907), are often-impish illustrations of the Shavian dic-tum that 'decency is indecency's conspiracy of silence'.

These early plays are all fed by Shaw's perception of the intellectual flabbiness of the English 19th-century theatre and can usefully be read alongside the dramatic CRITI-CISMS he contributed to the *Saturday Review* (1895–8), col-lected in *Our Theatre in the Nineties* (3 vols., 1932). Incisive, irreverent and always suspicious of anything nor-mally taken for granted, Shaw's writing on drama has the liveliness and eye-opening rhetoric of the published *Prefaces* to his plays (collected in a single volume in 1934, with revisions and additions in 1938 and 1965). Throughout his long life, he sustained his mischievously boyish delight in outstripping the ponderous intellectual establishment, which responded by underrating him as effectively as it could manage. But the stifling or misrep-resentation of Shaw's talent was brought to an end during the seasons at the ROYAL COURT THEATRE (1904–7) under HARLEY GRANVILLE BARKER and J. E. VEDRENNE. They not only revived several of the earlier plays, but also mounted the first performances of major new plays in which Shaw's genius for dramatizing debate on social and political issues of national importance was fully revealed. *John Bull's Other Island* (1904) drew attention to the persistent Irish question. In *Man and Superman* (1905), a socialist hero can outmanoeuvre all his political adversaries but surrenders to the rival life force of a woman. *Major Barbara* (1905) displays Shaw's debating talents at their most dazzling, pitting social conscience against con-scienceless social reform. Two decades later, this play would excite BERTOLT BRECHT to call Shaw a 'terrorist' and to complement Shaw's original with his own *Saint Joan of the Stockyards*. Beside *Major Barbara*, *The Doctor's*

Dilemma (1906) seems barrenly clever.

Shaw's hold on the London theatre was maintained, though not greatly enhanced, by further discussion plays like *Getting Married* (1908) and *Misalliance* (1910), as well as by the controversy aroused when the Lord Chamberlain banned performances of *The Shewing Up of Blanco Posnet* (1909) on the grounds of blasphemy. Shaw was no stranger to the risks involved in contrasting Christian forms with the substance of Christ's teaching, and conversion is a major theme in his plays from *Candida* to *Androcles and the Lion* (1913) and beyond, but it was the satirical account of a thoroughly secular conversion that brought him his first and greatest popular triumph, *Pygmalion* (1914). Staged by one of the last great actor-managers, HERBERT BEERBOHM TREE, and starring MRS PATRICK CAMPBELL as the flower seller who conquers society through elocution, *Pygmalion* established Shaw as England's leading play-wright. It was a reputation soon tarnished amid the jingo-ism of 1914 by the publication of the brilliantly rational essay *Common Sense about the War* (1914).

Between the outbreak of the First World War and his death in old age, Shaw would write upwards of 30 new plays, but only a few of them have established a place in the theatrical repertoire. They include his most complex discussion play, *Heartbreak House* (1920); the extraordi-nary and eccentric philosophical 'pentateuch', *Back to Methuselah* (1922); the startlingly original historical tragedy, *Saint Joan* (1923); three plays which he termed 'political extravaganzas', *The Apple Cart* (1929), *Too True to Be Good* (1932) and *Geneva* (1938); and a frequently underrated comedy, *The Millionairess* (1936). There has been a recent revival of interest in *In Good King Charles's Golden Days* (1939), 'a true history that never happened', but Shaw's command of the English-speaking theatre has significantly weakened in recent years, not least because of the birth of a modern political drama to reinforce what used to be his lonely voice. Scholars have come increasing-ly to recognize the contribution he made to the develop-ing art of the director and to the serious study of acting, of which there is much evidence in the many selections from his voluminous correspondence. PT

Shaw Festival (Canada) An annual summer festival in Niagara-on-the-Lake, Ontario, devoted to presenting the works of GEORGE BERNARD SHAW and his contemporaries, and home to one of the finest acting ensembles in North America.

In 1962 playwright and retired Niagara Falls lawyer Brian Doherty organized 'A Salute to Shaw', presenting eight performances of *Candida* and the 'Don Juan in Hell' sequence from *Man and Superman*, under the direction of Maynard Burgess, over four successive weekends in the historic court-house building at Niagara-on-the-Lake. The success of these productions encouraged Doherty, Calvin Rand and others to incorporate the theatre as a non-profit organization in 1963. Andrew Allan was named first artis-tic director, and he spent the next three seasons nurturing a theatre company in a building so small that sets had to be built and painted in an adjoining parking lot.

Allan was succeeded in 1966 by Barry Morse, who assem-bled a superb company of actors, attracting national atten-tion for a nine-week season that included productions of

Man and Superman, Misalliance and *The Apple Cart.*

In 1967 Paxton Whitehead succeeded Morse and began a decade-long tenure as artistic director, during which the Shaw Festival experienced significant growth. For the first time it went on the road, touring a post-season production of *Major Barbara* to Expo '67 in Montreal, the first of many successful touring productions. Whitehead also expanded the season to 21 weeks and added contemporary plays to the repertoire. While the productions attracted audiences in unprecedented numbers, critics often accused Whitehead of sacrificing dramatic worth for commercial success.

By 1969 the company had outgrown the cramped quarters in the Court House Theatre, and chose architect Ron Thom to design a new theatre. His elegant red-brick Shaw Festival Theatre opened for the 1973 season, housing an 847-seat cedar-lined proscenium theatre, administrative offices, and carpentry, props and wardrobe shops.

After Whitehead's resignation in 1977 and two transitional years under Richard Kirschner and Leslie Yeo, the Festival appointed Christopher Newton as artistic director in 1980. Newton quickly established an innovative leadership, hiring Cameron Porteous as the first permanent head of design, and adding music and dance programmes, establishing the lunch-time series to showcase Shaw's one-act plays in the newly acquired Royal George Theatre; adding the 'Risk' series to present lesser-known plays of daring appeal; initiating the Toronto Project to explore more contemporary scripts for younger audiences; and fostering the Academy of the Shaw Festival, a workshop initiative for the creative stimulation and development of members of the Shaw Festival company. Under Newton, the Festival season once again expanded dramatically, using three theatres (the Festival Theatre, the Royal George and the original Court House Theatre) to present 10 or 11 productions over a five-month season.

Newton interprets the Festival's mandate as presenting works 'about the beginning of the modern world', and has added many plays by Shaw's contemporaries to the company's repertoire. In fact, a typical Shaw Festival season now contains only three or four plays by Shaw, the remainder being selected from works written during his considerable lifespan. Perhaps Newton's greatest contribution, however, has been his dedication to assembling and nurturing one of the premiere acting ensembles in North America. A strong core of well established actors is augmented by promising younger actors, who are encouraged to return to the Festival for successive seasons, allowing the company to develop a unique familiarity and style. Younger members frequently rise through the ranks to make their mark as leading actors or directors at the Shaw or at other theatres throughout the country. Members of Newton's ensemble have included Geraint Wyn Davies, Frances Hyland, Heath Lamberts, Barry MacGregor, Marti Maraden, Tom McCamus, Duncan McIntosh, Douglas Rain, Goldie Semple and Susan Wright. DAH

Shaw, Fiona British actress. Shaw was part of a group of striking and individualistic actresses (among them JULIET STEVENSON and Lindsay Duncan) who first attracted public acclaim during the 1980s. Slightly gawky and not conventionally pretty, she grew in stature through roles to which she could bring her qualities of passion and nervous intelligence. She was a demandingly free-thinking Mary Shelley in HOWARD BRENTON's play, *Bloody Poetry* (1984), for the touring company Foco Nova, and a less than submissive Celia in *As You Like It* for the ROYAL SHAKESPEARE COMPANY (1985). She was teamed with Stevenson and Duncan in CHRISTOPHER HAMPTON's version of *Les liaisons dangereuses* (1986), playing Mme de Volanges in a style likened to JOYCE GRENFELL.

By 1986, with her performances in two other productions, GORKY's *Philistines* and MNOUCHKINE's *Mephisto*, Shaw was established as a strong RSC company member without having emerged as a star; but in 1988, three performances – as Mary Stuart in SCHILLER's play of the same name at London's Greenwich Theatre, as Katherine in JONATHAN MILLER's production of *The Taming of the Shrew* for the RSC and, above all, as Electra in DEBORAH WARNER's version of Sophocles' play – removed any doubts about her outstanding ability. Prowling the stage with a haggard ferocity, her Electra commanded the kind of emotional power that is associated only with great actors. It gave her the authority to tackle the most demanding role for an actress, Hedda Gabler, in a Deborah Warner production of IBSEN's play for the ABBEY THEATRE (1991) in Dublin – a detailed and harrowing account of someone who lives frustratingly below her self-imagined station in life.

Shaw has come to represent women angry at their own inferior statuses in a man's world, feminists in the making, which was how she played Mistress Carol in JAMES SHIRLEY's *Hyde Park* for the RSC in 1988 and Rosalind in Tim Albery's *As You Like It* at the OLD VIC in 1989; but her greatest triumph in the battlefield of the genders came with STEPHEN DALDRY's revival of a little-known play by American playwright SOPHIE TREADWELL, *Machinal*, at the NATIONAL THEATRE in 1993, in which she played a Young Woman, convicted and sent to the electric chair, for murdering her husband to spare him the pains of a divorce. JE

Shchepkin, Mikhail (Semyonovich) 1788–1863 The Ukrainian former serf-actor who became the acknowledged father of Russian realistic acting and a major influence upon STANISLAVSKY via the education of the latter's teacher, GLIKERIYA FEDOTOVA. Shchepkin's professional career, which began in the provinces in 1805 and later moved to Moscow (1822) and the Maly Theatre (1824), was partially shaped by amateur actor Prince P. V. Meshchersky and Slavophile writer-critic S. T. Aksakov. The former demonstrated natural stage speech in opposition to the declamatory approach exemplified by DMITREVSKY. The latter improved his tastes in foreign literature, translating MOLIÈRE's *The Miser* for him to perform, and encouraged the development of a more intelligent native drama.

A political conservative and 'closet democrat', Shchepkin counted a wide assortment of artist-intellectuals among his social equals and personal friends, a situation unheard of since Dmitrevsky's day. These included radical writer-critics Herzen, Belinsky and Nekrasov, as well as dramatists GRIBOEDOV, PUSHKIN, TURGENEV, SUKHOVO-KOBYLIN and, especially, fellow Ukrainian GOGOL. Shchepkin supplied these inventors of the modern

Russian drama with anecdotes that were incorporated into their plays and served as the models from which a number of their characters were conceived. This collaboration helped to end the hegemony of foreign comedies, farces, tragedies, melodramas and operettas on the Russian stage, and to educate the Russian critics and audience, especially the intelligentsia, to accept and appreciate Russian plays. Shchepkin, whose squat, rotund physiognomy, large head and natural exuberance targeted him from youth for the 'comic old man' *emploi*, applied his natural warmth and humour, facility with verse, simplicity and emotional expressiveness, profound humanity, personal dignity and moral strength to the social SATIRES and dramas of the 'little man' which now began to appear.

By the 1840s he had won acclaim as Famusov in *Woe from Wit* (1830) and the Mayor in *The Inspector General* (1836). By the 1860s, however, the House of Shchepkin, as the Maly was called, became the House of OSTROVSKY, in honour of the dramatist whose brand of photographic REALISM achieved great success via the performances of a new generation of actors headed by PROV SADOVSKY. In 1897 the Shchepkin legacy passed to the MOSCOW ART THEATRE in the form of the following ideas: the sacredness of theatrical art and the selflessness of acting in a role as part of an ensemble; the need for extensive rehearsals; strict discipline, careful observation, self-knowledge, imagination and emotion as the cornerstones of the actor's craft. The systematizer of these tenets, Stanislavsky, was born in the year of Shchepkin's death. SG

Shean, Al see GALLAGHER AND SHEAN

Sheldon, Edward (Brewster) 1886–1946 American playwright. A graduate of GEORGE PIERCE BAKER's Workshop 47 at Harvard College, Sheldon was an early proponent of social REALISM in America with *Salvation Nell* (1908), in which a girl avoids a repulsive 'profession' by joining the Salvation Army; *The Nigger* (1909), concerned with the struggle of a Southern governor who discovers that his grandmother was an octoroon slave; and *The Boss* (1911), a drama of labour–management conflicts. However, his romantic conclusions in these plays (with the exception of *The Nigger*) suggest his true interests: as revealed in *The High Road* (1912), a search for beauty, and in *Romance* (1913), as an American clergyman explains his love for an Italian diva. When poor health apparently incapacitated Sheldon, he collaborated with such dramatists as SIDNEY HOWARD (*Bewitched*, 1924) and CHARLES MACARTHUR (*Lulu Belle*, 1926). Although none of his later works was outstanding, he remained a source of inspiration and help on dramaturgical problems for a number of prominent dramatists. WJM

Shepard, Sam [Samuel Shepard Rogers] 1943– American playwright (as well as film actor and screenwriter) who, though lacking a major commercial BROADWAY success, is arguably the most critically acclaimed, if the most obscure and undisciplined, US dramatist of the past 20 years. *New York Magazine* called him 'the most inventive in language and revolutionary in craft', as well as the 'writer whose work most accurately maps the interior and exterior landscapes of his society'. Uniquely American and contemporary in his subject-matter – ranging from myths of the American West, American stereotypes, the death or betrayal of the American dream, the travail of the family, to the search for roots – Shepard defies easy classification. Influenced by rock and roll, the pop and countercultures beginning in the 1950s, the graphic arts and dance, the West of Hollywood, hallucinatory experiences and a dozen other eclectic forces, his path as a writer is hard to plot. Richard Gilman suggests that it is best to accept the volatility and interdependence of Shepard's plays – 'they constitute a series of facets of a single continuing act of imagination'.

Of his more than 40 plays, 11 of which have received Obies (beginning with the Theatre Genesis (New York City) productions of *Cowboy* and *The Rock Garden* in 1964), the following are major works: *La Turista* (1966); *The Tooth of Crime* (1972), a rock drama written during a four-year period in London; *Curse of the Starving Class*, written in 1976 and produced first in 1978 at the NEW YORK SHAKESPEARE FESTIVAL with a successful New York revival in 1985; *Buried Child* (1978), for which he won the 1979 Pulitzer Prize; *True West* (1980) and *Fool for Love* (1979), both originally staged at the Magic Theatre in San Francisco, where he was playwright-in-residence for several years; and *A Lie of the Mind* (1985). In 1991, *The States of Shock*, his first drama in six years and his ambiguous look at post-Vietnam America, played a brief season at the AMERICAN PLACE THEATER, and in late 1994 he directed his play *Simpatico* at New York's PUBLIC THEATER. Shepard has also co-authored three pieces with JOSEPH CHAIKIN – one, *The War in Heaven* (1985), was also revived in 1991 at the American Place.

Shepard has appeared in several successful films, including his own *Fool for Love*, and for his screenplay *Paris, Texas* won the Golden Palm Award at the 1985 Cannes Film Festival. DBW

Sher, Antony 1951– South African-born British actor. He trained in London and Manchester, and after a period in repertory established his reputation with a series of roles between 1975 and 1981, especially as Klestakov in GOGOL's *The Inspector General* (Edinburgh, 1975) and as Muhammad, the confused Arab businessman, in MIKE LEIGH's *Goose-Pimples* (1981). He joined the ROYAL SHAKESPEARE COMPANY in 1982, and his Fool in *King Lear* was the first of his brilliantly theatrical creations of Shakespearian characters. Richard III in 1984 and Shylock in 1987 were others. He is a truly exciting actor to watch in action, taking risks that are usually triumphantly vindicated. His starring appearances with the two British national companies include (for the RSC) those in PETER BARNES's *Red Noses* (1985), *The Merchant of Venice* (1988) and *Tamburlaine the Great* (1992), and (for the NATIONAL THEATRE) in STEVE BERKOFF's *The Trial* (1991) and BERTOLT BRECHT's *The Resistible Rise of Arturo Ui* (1991). MB JE

Sheremetiev, Count **Nikolai (Petrovich)** 1751–1809 Owner of the largest and most sumptuous serf theatres in Russia, which set the standard for others to follow. Educated at the University of Leiden, he spent the period

1769–73 familiarizing himself with theatre in England, Switzerland and the Netherlands. Upon his return to Russia, he inherited his father Count Pyotr Sheremetiev's serf company on his estate at Kuskuvo, a Moscow suburb. What had been the site of occasional entertainments honouring state visits and the like, hosting as many as 30,000 persons, became under the son a fully fledged theatrical enterprise rivalling St Petersburg's court theatres and far surpassing Moscow's public theatres.

Sheremetiev imported leading Moscow actors such as IVAN DMITREVSKY and PYOTR PLAVILSHCHIKOV to instruct his company of serf actors, which numbered as many as 95. Senior musicians were imported from abroad to train his serf orchestra. A scenic designer (see THEATRE DESIGN) and translator were on staff. Ballets, comedies and *vaudevilles* were staged, but OPERAS were the favourite and received the most attention. This was especially true after 1801, when the count married his leading lady, the serf actress Praskovya Ivanovna, to whom he gave the stage name Zhemchugova ('the Pearl'). In order to remove his new wife from her serf environment, he moved his company to the Moscow suburb of Ostankino. There, using the latest information on theatre architecture secured from abroad, two serf architects erected a theatre with a seating capacity of 300, a removable parquet floor to allow for balls and banquets and a large stage equipped with trapdoors, *periaktoi*, flying machines and all manner of special effects. The count treated his serf actors better than those belonging to other landowners and far better than his other serfs. His wife, around whom his productions were built, died in 1803, 20 days after giving birth to their son. SG

Sheridan, Richard Brinsley 1751–1816 Irish playwright and theatre manager. Born in Dublin, educated at Harrow, he lived in Bath with his family, his father running a school of elocution. After marriage to a singer he moved to London and in 1775 his first three plays were produced. *The Rivals* made brilliant use of Sheridan's experiences of Bath as a setting for a tangled plot, contrasting mockery of sentimentalism in Lydia Languish against apparent admiration for it in the serious lovers, Faulkland and Julia. Sheridan's verbal dexterity is at its best in his creation of Mrs Malaprop. The other two plays of 1775 were a FARCE, *St Patrick's Day*, and a very successful comic OPERA, *The Duenna*. In 1776 he took over as principal manager of DRURY LANE Theatre, though his ambitions, his difficulties in dealing with his colleagues and successive financial crises never made him a success as manager. In 1777 his adaptation of VANBRUGH's *The Relapse* as *A Trip to Scarborough* appeared, as well as his best play, *The School for Scandal*. Sheridan's attack on scandalmongers returns to the satiric methods of Restoration comedy while finding in the reconciliation of the Teazles, after Lady Teazle's flirtation with adultery, a distinctive optimism. His affectionate but sharp mockery of the foolishness of much contemporary drama, *The Critic* (1779), continues the tradition of BUCKINGHAM's *The Rehearsal*. In 1780 he became an MP, was appointed Secretary to the Treasury in 1783 and was extremely active in the parliamentary proceedings in the impeachment of Warren Hastings. He was still closely involved in running Drury Lane, opening the rebuilt theatre in 1794, though he wrote few plays other than adaptations of KOTZEBUE. He finally gave up management not long after the disastrous fire that destroyed Drury Lane in 1809, a fire that he watched in an armchair in the street, 'by his own fireside' as he said. PH

Sherriff, R(obert) C(edric) 1896–1975 British dramatist and novelist. Sherriff's bitterly realistic depiction of the pressures on front-line soldiers in a dug-out preparing for an attack, *Journey's End*, was performed by the STAGE SOCIETY in 1928 and had a wide international impact. It still provides an effective anti-war statement, but the conventional NATURALISM of his later work has dated. Although providing impressive roles for an actor like RALPH RICHARDSON and dealing with similar psychological themes, the immediacy and public commitment were missing in his treatment of historical subjects like the last years of Roman Britain or Napoleon (*The Long Sunset*, 1955; *St Helena*, 1935), his study of amnesia (*Home at Seven*, 1953) and his rustic comedy about village cricket (*Badger's Green*, 1930). CI

Sherwood, Robert E(mmet) 1896–1955 American playwright, screenwriter, essayist, historian and propagandist; a man of strong emotions and goodwill who preached simplistic solutions to complicated problems. His career started with *The Road to Rome* (1927) and continued with *Waterloo Bridge* (1930) and *Reunion in Vienna* (1931), sentimental and frivolous comedies about emotional problems. With *The Petrified Forest* (1935), a story of frustrated idealism, *Idiot's Delight* (1936), an anti-war play, and *Abe Lincoln in Illinois* (1938) Sherwood won three Pulitzer Prizes. During the 1930s he also wrote screenplays, served as president of the US Dramatists Guild, and helped found the Playwrights' Company (1938).

With the advent of war in Europe, Sherwood dramatically changed his thinking about conflict and the purpose of drama. Having complained that his plays started with a message and ended only as good entertainment, he wrote *There Shall Be No Night* (1940), a militant condemnation of American isolationism, trumpeted across the land by actors LUNT AND FONTANNE. Having shown his ability to write brilliant propaganda, and his hatred of Hitler, he became a speech-writer for President Roosevelt, who appointed him director of the overseas branch of the Office of War Information. Sherwood's postwar plays – *The Rugged Path* (1945) and *Small War on Murray Hill* (1957) – were failures. Only in his history *Roosevelt and Hopkins* (1948) did he again show his considerable writing skills. WJM

Shields, Ella 1879–1952 American (Baltimore-born) singer, comedienne and male impersonator (see MALE IMPERSONATION). Shields was initially a coon singer, in which role she began a 25-year career on the British VARIETY stage in 1904. She rapidly moved into PANTOMIME, and in 1910 at the London Palladium made her first appearance in top hat and tails, à la VESTA TILLEY. Many of her songs became popular classics, notably 'If You Knew Susie' and the celebrated 'Burlington Bertie from Bow', written by her husband William Hargreaves. AEG

Shiels [Morshiel], **George** 1886–1949 Irish playwright.

Crippled in a railway accident in Canada in 1913, Shiels took to writing. His earliest plays, one-acters, were produced by the ULSTER LITERARY THEATRE. The ABBEY presented his first full-length play, *Paul Twyning* (1922). Thereafter Shiels supplied the Abbey with a string of box-office successes whose popularity owed much to the theatre's broadly farcical interpretation of them. They include *Professor Tim* (1925), *Cartney and Kevney* (1927), *The New Gossoon* (1930), *The Passing Day* (1936), *The Old Broom* (Group Theatre, Belfast, 1944), *Tenants at Will* (1945) and *The Caretakers* (1948).

From the earliest work, where the comic machinations are light-hearted, Shiels's plays take place in a deceitful, even vicious, world. In *The Passing Day* a dying man manipulates and is manipulated by his family and business circles. *Tenants at Will*, 'a comedy in three acts', is a bitter play of decent poverty seduced by possessions. Feelings are professed but not felt; work, money and property appear to be the real determinants of relationships. In Shiels's funniest scenes, the laughter does not conceal the ironic reserve noted and disliked by YEATS. Although his range is narrow, with recurring situations and characters, contemporary Northern Irish settings and a prose holding close to common speech, Shiels's dispassionate observation of human meanness and folly conveys unsettling but not depressing truths.   DM GF

shingeki Literally 'new drama', the generic term for modern theatre and drama in JAPAN. The term is used to distinguish modern theatre from traditional forms like NO and KABUKI. At the same time and more narrowly, *shingeki* also refers to one kind of modern theatre: the realistic, Western-based modern drama (see REALISM) performed by companies like the People's Art Theatre, the Literary Theatre and the Actors' Theatre. Today in its broadest meaning, *shingeki* refers to the entire gamut of non-traditional theatre performed in Japan.   DGG

shinguk Literally, 'new performance', in contrast to traditional theatre, within the context of South Korean theatre (the term is not used to describe North Korean theatre, although perhaps it could be). In general, *shinguk* is all theatre that is recognizably cast in the mode of Western 'literary' or high theatre. This includes Western 'literary' plays (classic and modern) in Korean translation, plays by Korean authors written under the influence of IBSEN, SHAW, BECKETT or other Western models, Stanislavskian (see STANISLAVSKY) and BRECHTian acting styles, as well as proscenium theatre buildings and an audience of educated elite. Ideologically, *shinguk* implies modernity and Western values (democracy, individualism, socialism and so on), as well as Korean nationalism. Most new theatre and drama is created today in KOREA within this theatrical milieu.   OKC

shinpa Genre of modern Japanese commercial theatre (see also KOREA). The name literally means 'new wave [drama]'. It was one of a number of experiments to 'modernize' KABUKI around the turn of the century. The form was in every respect transitional. It reintroduced actresses to the Japanese stage but retained female impersonators (see FEMALE IMPERSONATION) as well. It took up contemporary themes but treated them with a jejune, 'train-whistle REALISM'. Its style is characterized by a cloying sentimentality. Although it is performed today by one troupe, *shinpa* has had virtually no influence on the evolution of SHINGEKI, the mainstream of Japanese modern theatre. Kawakami Otojiro (1864–1911) and his wife, actress Sada Yakko (1872–1946), are frequently cited as the founders of *shinpa*. They experimented boldly in a variety of areas, including the training of actresses, the use of pyrotechnics to represent scenes of modern warfare, the production of theatre for children and the use of everyday speech to replace stylized *kabuki* diction. They performed in Europe and the USA and attempted to incorporate their experiences abroad into a modern Japanese theatre. When Kawakami died, he was planning a production of IBSEN's *Enemy of the People*, but his work had already been superseded by the nascent *shingeki* movement. It was the work of Ii Yoho (1871–1932) who had worked with Kawakami in 1891, that prefigured *shinpa* as we know it today. His dramatization of popular novels written for an upper-middle-class female audience and his commercial acumen, bringing *shinpa* under the aegis of the Shochiku Theatrical company in 1917, are the real source of today's *shinpa* drama.   DGG

Shirley, James 1596–1666 English playwright, born in London and educated at the Merchant Taylors' School and the Universities of Oxford and Cambridge. Shirley took holy orders, and in 1623 was appointed headmaster of the grammar school in St Albans, a post which he forfeited in 1625 by his conversion to Roman Catholicism. He returned to London to make money by writing and had completed at least 36 plays before the CLOSURE OF THE THEATRES in 1642, at which time he had few rivals as the leading working dramatist in London. Having sided with the Royalists during the Civil War, Shirley could count himself lucky to find a post as a schoolmaster during the Interregnum. He did not long survive the Restoration, dying of exposure in the Great Fire of London. Shirley was an uncomplicated writer, an admirer of JOHN FLETCHER whose fondness for contrivance he emulated in the multiple plots of such comedies as *The Witty Fair One* (1628), *Hyde Park* (1632), *The Gamester* (1633), *The Lady of Pleasure* (1635), *The Imposture* (1640) and *The Sisters* (1642). The social values and witty dialogue anticipate elements of Restoration comedy. Shirley's tragedies look rather to the past, bringing REVENGE TRAGEDY to a moral end. They include *The Traitor* (1631), *The Politician* (c.1639) and *The Cardinal* (1641). A few of his MASQUES survive, among them *The Triumph of Peace* (1634), one of the showiest of its kind, as well as a modest volume of *Poems* (1646).   PT

Sholom Aleichem [Solomon Rappaport] 1859–1916 The most treasured of Yiddish writers, whose homely plays, filled with lovable philosophical comic characters, provided artistic and financial successes for theatre companies all over the world. *Tevye the Milkman* (made into the American MUSICAL *Fiddler on the Roof*) is probably the best-known. *200,000*, albeit a most amusing play (sometimes called *The Big Win*), is filled with social significance, whilst in *Hard to Be a Jew* two students, one Jewish and one not, change places for a year to find out whether it is

Spalding and Rogers's
Floating Circus Palace.

indeed hard to be a Jew. Other plays include *Scattered and Dispersed*, about the dissemination of the Jewish people at the turn of the century, and many dramatizations of his novels. (See also YIDDISH THEATRE.)   AB

showboats From the early 19th century, flatboats, then steamers and paddle-wheelers, plied the Mississippi and Ohio rivers, offering entertainment to the residents along the banks. Although NOAH LUDLOW, JOSEPH JEFFERSON II and SOL SMITH dabbled in such amusements, the first intentionally designed showboat was that of William Chapman Sr, launched at Pittsburgh in 1831. The Chapman family in their *Floating Theatre*, a rude shed set on a barge and poled downriver, soon became a familiar sight, making annual tours of the major waterways with a repertory of KOTZEBUE, SHAKESPEARE and musical FARCES. Before Chapman's widow sold out in 1847, they had set the style for similar enterprises, although imitators tended towards song-and-dance and lecture entertainments and sometimes lacked the respectable domestic veneer of the Chapmans. The crafts ranged from ramshackle scows to grandiose arks. CIRCUS boats, led by Spalding and Rogers's *Floating Circus Palace* (1851), were capable of seating up to 3400 spectators and offered MINSTREL SHOWS and a museum of curiosities in addition to sawdust acts.

After the disastrous hiatus of the Civil War, a new period of prosperity came to the showboat. The leading entrepreneur was Augustus Byron French, a riparian BARNUM who operated five boats from 1878 to 1901; he pioneered the use of marching bands on shore to advertise his lavish VARIETY bills, and launched both the apt term and the luxurious vessel, the 'floating palace'. His double-decker *Sensation No. 2* sat 759, but the only full-length drama ever offered was UNCLE TOM'S CABIN. French's main rival was E.A. Price, whose press agent Ralph Emerson came up with sensational innovations in publicity, using calliopes, billboards and postcards to herald the boat's arrival.

The reliance on variety was challenged by the Eisenbarth–Henderson *Temple of Amusement*, which purveyed drama exclusively; these 'moral amusements', which included *Faust*, were lit by electricity. As *The Cotton Blossom* under Emerson's management, it featured BROADWAY hits and spectacular MELODRAMAS until 1931. Drama was also the fare provided by Norman Thom, 'the John Drew [see DREW-BARRYMORE FAMILY] of the Rivers', the first actor since Chapman to own a boat; for *The Princess*, he shrewdly chose plays of regional interest. The Bryants specialized in lurid melodrama, offered in direct competition to the rival silent pictures.

More than 76 verifiable showboats (as they had come to be known) have existed. There were 26 active in 1910, 14 in 1928 and 5 in 1938. (The last recorded by Philip Graham was *The Goldenrod*, tied up in St Louis in 1943 (recently refurbished and moved to St Charles, Missouri), although the *Majestic*, built in 1923, operates May–September on the Cincinnati city landing.) The decline can be attributed to the closure of the frontier: unable to compete with the urban entertainments that sprang up in the wake of civilization, the owners suffered greatly from the Depression of 1929. Behind the fashion even in their heyday, the boats became a nostalgic artefact, and imitations were much in use by society promoters in the 1930s. It was JEROME KERN and OSCAR HAMMERSTEIN II's MUSICAL adaptation of *Show Boat* (1927), a novel by EDNA FERBER, that simultaneously immortalized the phenomenon and encased it in an aura of quaintness. Once a unique product of westward expansion, showboats are now adjuncts of tourism and municipal festivals.   LS

Shubert brothers American theatre owners and producers. The family business was founded by three brothers – **Sam S.** (?1877–1905), **Lee** (?1875–1953) and **Jacob J.** (?1879–1963) Shubert – who began their careers in Syracuse, NY, in the late 19th century. The brothers moved to New York City in 1900 and began producing and acquiring theatres, including the Herald Square and the Casino. Among the stars who worked in Shubert shows during the early years were RICHARD MANSFIELD, SARAH BERNHARDT and LILLIAN RUSSELL. Sam Shubert died in a train crash in 1905, but his brothers continued to operate the business on an increasingly lavish scale, often coming into conflict with the THEATRICAL SYNDICATE, a rival group of theatre owners and managers that dominated American theatrical activity in the early 20th century. By 1916, however, the Shuberts had broken the Syndicate monopoly and had themselves became the nation's most important and powerful theatre owners and managers. During the 1910s and 20s, the Shubert brothers built many of BROADWAY's theatres, including the WINTER GARDEN, the SAM S. SHUBERT and the Imperial. In addition, they came to own or operate more than 100 theatres across the country and to book more than 1000 others. Among their major stars of the period were AL JOLSON and EDDIE CANTOR, both of whom were great successes at the Winter Garden. The Shuberts were especially well known for their productions of OPERETTAS by SIGMUND ROMBERG, among them *Maytime* (1917), *Blossom Time* (1921) and *The Student Prince* (1924). They were also known for their popular annual REVUES – *The Passing Show*, which appeared regularly during 1912–24, and *Artists and Models*, produced in a number of editions from 1923 to 43.

Although the Shuberts' business was badly hurt by the Depression, they continued to produce throughout the 1930s and 40s, presenting a number of well known MUSICALS and revues, including the later editions of the *Ziegfeld Follies,* COLE PORTER's *You Never Know* (1938) and Olsen and Johnson's *Hellzapoppin'* (1938), as well as such popular straight plays as *Ten Little Indians* (1944) and *Dark of the Moon* (1945). During the 1950s the US government brought an anti-trust suit against the Shuberts, who were forced to divest themselves of a number of their theatres in 1956. During the 1950s and early 60s the company was run by Jacob J. Shubert's son John (1909–62), and after his death by a great-nephew of the founders, Lawrence Shubert Lawrence Jr (1916–92). The most recent studies of the brothers are by Brooks McNamara (1990), director of the Shubert Archive, and Foster Hirsch (1995). BMCN DBW

Shubert Organization American theatrical property and producing company, founded in the late 19th century by the SHUBERT family. Since 1972 its chief operating officers have been two former Shubert lawyers, Gerald Schoenfeld and Bernard B. Jacobs. Jacobs serves as president of the Shubert Organization and Schoenfeld as chairman of the board. In addition, they are respectively president and chairman of the Shubert Foundation, a related philanthropic institution that provides support to many non-profit theatre and dance producing groups. The Shubert Organization currently owns and manages 16 of the operating BROADWAY theatres, including the Ambassador, Ethel Barrymore, BELASCO, BOOTH, Broadhurst, Broadway, Cort, John Golden, Imperial, Longacre, LYCEUM, Majestic, Plymouth, Royale, SAM S. SHUBERT and the WINTER GARDEN. In addition, the company has a half-interest in the Music Box Theatre. Outside New York City, it owns and operates the Shubert and Blackstone in Chicago, the Forrest in Philadelphia and the Shubert in Boston. It leases and manages two other theatres, the Shubert in Los Angeles and the National in Washington, DC. Although the company was not active in theatrical production during the 1950s and 60s, in recent years it has once again become involved in Broadway producing. Its representative productions have included *Sly Fox* (1976), *Gin Game* (1977), *Ain't Misbehavin'* (1978), *Dancin'* (1978), *Amadeus* (1980), *Children of a Lesser God* (1980), *Dream Girls* (1981), *Nicholas Nickleby* (1981), *Cats* (1982), *Glengarry Glen Ross* (1984), *Sunday in the Park with George* (1984), *The Heidi Chronicles* (1989) and *Someone Who'll Watch over Me* (1992). The Shubert Organization has also produced a highly successful OFF-BROADWAY show, *Little Shop of Horrors* (1982).

The company has been influential in the revitalization of the Times Square theatrical district and has pioneered a number of innovative theatre business practices, among them the introduction of telephone and charge ticket sales and a computerized ticket system. BMCN

shund theatre (Literally, 'rubbish theatre') Term used to describe the popular sentimental and MELODRAMATic YIDDISH THEATRE in America, designed to please the mass audience of unsophisticated immigrants from 1890 onwards. AB

Shvarts, Evgeny (Lvovich) 1896–1958 Soviet dramatist, the son of liberal Jewish intellectuals in Kazan; writer of witty and wise adult fairy tales that were transparent yet evocative sociopolitical SATIRES, unique during the period of socialist realism (1934–53). Shvarts's legal studies at Moscow University were interrupted by his father's conscription during the war. He toured as an actor with P. K. Veysbrem's amateur theatre troupe from Rostov-on-Don (1917–22) and eventually settled in Leningrad, where he built his life and career.

His work for the publishing house and children's magazines *Canary* and *Hedgehog* of writer-poet-editor-translator Samuil Marshak led to Shvarts's producing his first short story, 'The Tale of the Old Balalaika' (1925), and his first play, *Underwood* (1929), about a witch who steals a typewriter and the orphan who retrieves it. In the late 1920s he became friendly with the Serapion Brothers and the Oberiuty, whose work ranged from the realistic (see REALISM) to the absurd (see THEATRE OF THE ABSURD) and whose formalist experiments appealed to Shvarts – as did the fairy tale which was then regarded with suspicion. Shvarts was influenced by fabulists Hans Christian Andersen, E. T. A. HOFFMANN and Charles Perrault, as well as by the symbolists (see SYMBOLISM), who believed in life's doubleness and in the possibility of creating a philosophical drama, and by VAKHTANGOV, whose 'fantastic realism' manifested a joyful theatrical dualism.

Shvarts eschewed the straight allegory, preferring to mix or texture his sources to achieve a rich ambiguity. While these plays have had a troubled production history, they were not condemned outright, for two main reasons. First, they are written in Aesopian language, making their exact satirical meanings somewhat flexible – thus, Shvarts's studies in militarism, tyranny, racism, xenophobia, the humanness of animals and the bestiality of man could be applied as easily to Hitler (as Shvarts openly did), who invaded Russia in 1941, or to the Soviets' recalcitrant capitalist allies, as they could to Stalin. Second, Shvarts wisely balanced his fantasy output with realistic, patriotic plays extolling the courage and resourcefulness of the Russian people, which as a civil defence warden during the Nazi blockade of Leningrad he knew about at first hand. Such plays include *The Treasure* (1933); *Brother and Sister* (1936); *Our Hospitality* (1939), which went unproduced because it showed a plane penetrating Soviet borders; *One Night* (1941), about the bombing of Leningrad; and *Far Land* (1943), dedicated to the Leningrad children separated from their parents during the evacuation.

The first of his major fairy-tale satires, *The Naked King* (1934), drawn from several Andersen stories, exposes the pettiness and fakery in all dictators, and was banned from the stage until 1960 when the Sovremennik Theatre produced it. His best and most philosophical play, *The Shadow* (1940), based on Andersen's 'Peter Schlemeil', contemplates man's doubleness, his capacity for good and evil, his repressed power fantasies, the relativity of truth and reality which makes simple solutions unwise if not impossible, and the precariousness of life, art and even history which, as in several of Shvarts's plays, is transformed into a fairy tale. There are even veiled references in the play to recently 'rehabilitated' Soviet writers; it was beautifully realized by designer-director NIKOLAI AKIMOV in 1940 at the Leningrad Theatre of Comedy. *The Dragon* (1944), his most political play, is based on Perrault's legend of Lancelot and attacks the conspiracy to tyranny between ruler and ruled. Like Shvarts's work in general, it posits the need for constant vigilance of self and society, thus rejecting the traditional happy ending of fairy tales and socialist-realist literature. Staged by Akimov in 1944, it was banned until 1960, the same year in which *The Naked King* and *The Shadow*, which had been removed from the stage shortly after their premieres, were revived. *An Ordinary Miracle* (1956), Shvarts's *Tempest*, about a senior magician who learns that love is the real magic, was also staged by Akimov, in 1956.

Shvarts's remaining work includes the fairy-tale plays *Adventures of Hohenstaufen* (1932), *Little Red Riding Hood* (1937), *The Snow Queen* (1938) and *Two Maples* (1954), which preach the value of the collective and the dangers of capitalism; screenplays, including *Cinderella* (1947), which has been adapted for the stage, and *Don Quixote* (1957), based on the 1938 BULGAKOV adaptation and filmed by Kozintsev with Nikolai Cherkasov in the title role; and a number of puppet plays.   SG

Shverubovich, V. I.   see KACHALOV, VASILY

Sibenke, Ben 1945– Zimbabwean playwright and actor, founder member of the People's Company, and author of, among other plays in both English and Shona, *My Uncle Grey Bhonzo*, a COMEDY on the need for cultural roots, and *Chidembo Chanhuwa* (*The Polecat Stank*), a play set in the rural areas after independence.   RK

Siddons, Sarah 1755–1831 English actress – probably the greatest English actress in tragedy. The eldest child of Roger Kemble, a touring theatre manager, she was educated on the road and was soon acting as a child star, an infant phenomenon. Arguments over her love for William Siddons, a young actor, led to her being sent away as a lady's maid but she married him in 1773. In 1775 she was engaged by GARRICK to play at DRURY LANE, but she failed completely and left the company. She learnt her art in Manchester, touring on TATE WILKINSON's circuit in Yorkshire and in Bath, returning to London to triumph on her debut as Isabella in Garrick's version of SOUTHERNE's *The Fatal Marriage* in 1782. Her declamatory delivery was offset by the eloquence of her face so that, as Davies noted, 'her eye is so full of information that the passion is told from her look before she speaks'. She was instantly admired for the unremitting concentration of her performances. In 1784 she was painted by Sir Joshua Reynolds as 'The Tragic Muse'. She toured to Dublin and Edinburgh with equal success, and returned to London where her brother JOHN PHILIP KEMBLE was now acting. In 1785 she played Lady Macbeth for the first time, perhaps her greatest role. By 1790 she was acting only occasionally at Drury Lane, moving to COVENT GARDEN in 1801.

In June 1812 she retired, playing Lady Macbeth in her last performance, the play stopping after the sleep-walking scene, though she appeared occasionally thereafter at charity performances. She found retirement difficult. Apart from her Lady Macbeth, she was famous as Jane Shore in ROWE's play, as Belvidera in OTWAY's *Venice Preserv'd* and in other classical English roles. Wilkinson's tribute to her dignity exemplifies her style: 'If you ask me "What is a queen?" I should say Mrs Siddons.'   PH

Sidney, Philip 1554–86 One of the outstanding figures of Elizabethan England. Sidney died too young to witness the golden age of drama, and his doubts about the status of plays as literature are evident in *The Apology for Poetry* (c.1580), which nonetheless provides important evidence of the cultured scepticism soon to be challenged by the work of MARLOWE and the UNIVERSITY WITS.   PT

Sierra Leone Sierra Leone, in West Africa, has been independent since 1961. The land on which its capital, Freetown, now stands was first settled in 1787 by a group of freed slaves from Britain. In 1792, about 1100 freed slaves, mostly from Nova Scotia, landed on the peninsula and founded Freetown. Christian with European acculturation, in the 19th century they later intermixed with much larger numbers of men and women whom British anti-slavery patrols had freed from illegal slave ships. Together, this group of settlers came to be known as the Creoles (now called Krios). They acquired formal education and were very British in outlook, but developed a language which has become the lingua franca of Sierra Leone: Krio.

The published drama of Sierra Leone largely reflects the urban black settler culture of the Freetown Krios. There is, first of all, a less secure base in the traditional roots of drama than obtains in NIGERIA or GHANA. However, a vibrant traditional performance culture persists among the indigenous ethnic groups. The Mende, for instance, have a vigorous storytelling tradition. But the character of the independence struggle precluded the emergence of the traditional culture as the means of expressing black aspirations. A Europeanized Krio culture was already in place.

Modern theatre in Sierra Leone has its origins in the

19th-century Church, which used drama as a means of elucidating Bible passages. This activity developed into a kind of VARIETY-concert performance that came to be known as the 'pleasant Sunday afternoon gathering', with a drama sketch as its centrepiece. Up to the 1950s, it was the most popular form of entertainment in Freetown.

Apart from this, pre-independence Sierra Leone theatre was dominated by performances of published European and American plays. Notable exceptions were the works of Sierra Leonean writers including Gladys Caseley-Hayford and Professor N. J. G. Ballanta-Taylor in the 1930s, and John Akar in the 1950s. Caseley-Hayford dramatized folk-tales, while Ballanta-Taylor wrote 'African' operas. Akar wrote and produced plays which had distinctive African themes, enhanced by his use of song and dance. The production of his play *Valley without Echo* by the Hans Crescent Society in London in 1954 was described by one critic in *West African Review* as 'the first significant play about African village life'. Akar was also instrumental in setting up the Sierra Leone National Dance Troupe in 1963.

A moralizing critique of post-independence Sierra Leonean society is presented by the plays of the Freetown medical practitioner, R. Sarif Easmon: the prize-winning *Dear Parent and Ogre*, and *The New Patriots* (both 1965). The plays explore the private lives of the new Sierra Leonean political elite. Love affairs, corruption and matters of state are combined in tight plots with obvious moral lessons. A high-art reaction against what might be seen as a limiting NATURALISM is reflected in Gaston Bart-Williams's *The Drug*, an experimental drama which owes something to the influence of PETER WEISS's contemporary experimentation in German theatre, and was first broadcast on West German radio in 1972.

Perhaps the most important development in post-independence theatre in Sierra Leone is the emergence of KRIO THEATRE. This is the product of the pioneering work of Thomas Decker, whose translation of SHAKESPEARE's *Julius Caesar* into Krio in 1964 marked the watershed in Sierra Leone theatre. Although Decker pioneered the introduction of Krio drama, it was Juliana John, Dele Charley (d.1993) and YULISA AMADU MADDY who spearheaded its development as an alternative class-based theatre. John wrote the first original full-length plays in Krio – *Na Mami born Am* and *I Day I nor Du* in 1966. Both had unusually long runs for the time, playing to packed houses in Freetown. Charley founded the Tabule Experimental Theatre in 1968, the group responsible for the popular Krio play *Titi Shine Shine* (1970) and the even more successful *The Blood of a Stranger*, performed more than 20 times between 1975 and 77 and entered for FESTAC in 1977. Maddy founded the group Gbakanda Afrikan Tiata in Freetown in 1969, but because he then went to Zambia to train the new Zambian National Dance Troupe, it did not really take off until he returned to Freetown in 1974. He was head of RADIO DRAMA before going to Zambia, and became acting Director of Culture on his return. But he has had a stormy relationship with the Sierra Leonean government, and has been imprisoned for his outspoken criticism of it, both on and off the stage.

The 1980s witnessed the flowering of theatre in Sierra Leone. With the building of the city hall in 1978, which could seat over a thousand people, groups found that they could make money out of theatre. The theatre now became popular in both outlook and structure; plays assumed an episodic plot structure, and contemporary and commonplace themes and situations could be used. The popularity of the theatre eventually caused it to fall foul of government, and, spurred by Kolosa John Kargbo's production of his sociopolitical SATIRE, *Poyo Tong Wahala*, in 1979 it introduced CENSORSHIP.

Although the city hall was closed to theatre in 1986, the popularity of the theatre did not wane. Theatre groups proved very resilient, and took their art on to the streets, hotel courtyards, bars, nightclubs and community halls. This period saw the rise to prominence of the Freetong Players, a group led by Charlie Haffner, which has been largely responsible for popularizing street theatre and giving it respectability, and of Spence Productions, directed by Julius Spencer. JS

See: M. Banham and C. Wake, *African Theatre Today*, London, 1976; D. Cosentino, *Defiant Maids and Stubborn Farmers: Tradition and Invention in Mende Story Performance*, Cambridge, 1982.

Sieveking, Alejandro 1934– Chilean playwright and director. After initial studies in architecture at the University of Chile, Sieveking studied acting and presented his first play, *Encuentro con las sombras* (*Meeting with Shadows*), at an amateur festival in 1955. His work tends towards realistic psychological drama, as in *Mi hermano Cristián* (*My Brother Christian*, 1957), presenting the case of a man victimized by his invalid sibling. *Parecido a la felicidad* (*Akin to Happiness*, 1959) was a successful tour show about intimate personal relations, a pleasant touch before the violence of *La madre de los conejos* (*Mother Rabbit*, 1961), a family study in sibling rape with two suicides. During the 1960s he continued to explore folkloric and poetic tendencies – in *Animas de día claro* (*Fair Weather Souls*, 1962), a successful MUSICAL *La remolienda* (*The Carousing*, 1965), and *La mantis religiosa* (*The Praying Mantis*, 1971). Like his contemporaries, he has also dealt with sociopolitical issues, as in *Tres tristes tigres* (*Three Sad Tigers*, 1967). An accomplished, versatile and prolific writer and director, Sieveking normally works within a realistic framework. From 1974 to 84, during the post-Allende period in Chile, he and his wife Bélgica Castro, the lead actress for whom he often writes, maintained the Teatro del Angel in San José, Costa Rica. GW

Sigurjónsson, Jóhann 1880–1919 Icelandic playwright, who wrote in both Icelandic and Danish, and was internationally acclaimed just before the First World War. In 1905 BJØRNSTJERNE BJØRNSON helped Sigurjónsson get *Dr Rung*, his first play, published in Denmark, but his first success came with the 1908 production in Reykjavík of *The Hraun Farm*, which marks the beginning of an era of Icelandic playwriting. His next play was his masterpiece, his excellent neo-romantic tragedy *Eyvind of the Mountains* (1911) – with a female hero worthy of classical TRAGEDY – which was produced and published in Copenhagen in 1912, only a few months after the Reykjavík premiere. GEORG BRANDES hailed the play as the best new work of the season. It was subsequently produced in 12 countries on both sides of the Atlantic, ranking

Sigurjónsson with major European playwrights of the period; it was filmed by Victor Sjöström as *The Outlaw and his Wife* (1917). The heroic-poetic *The Wish* (1914), based on Icelandic legend with Faustian overtones and owing something to *Hamlet*, is frequently performed in Iceland but it has never been as popular as *Eyvind of the Mountains*. Although within a year of the Reykjavík premiere the play was produced by the KONGELIGE TEATER (the Royal Theatre), Copenhagen, the war prevented it from reaching audiences outside Scandinavia at the time. His last play, *The Liar* (1917), based on *Njál's Saga*, was commissioned by the Kongelige, but failed to regenerate interest outside Denmark.

Sigurjónsson is considered by his countrymen the great Icelandic playwright. His plays deal with the heroes' unbridled ambition to rise above the common crowd and their quest for an ideal, which leads to their fall.   AI

Silva, António José da 1705–39 Portuguese playwright, probably the most noteworthy between VICENTE and FERREIRA and the 19th-century figure of GARRETT. He was burned by the Inquisition for his being allegedly a practising Jew, an iniquitous event dramatized in SANTARENO's *O Judeu* of 1966. Da Silva's seven plays made great use of stage machinery and effects and incorporated quasi-operatic ARIAS. The first, *Vida do Grande D. Quixote e do Gordo Sancho Pança*, had the knight, his squire and the supporting cast played by puppets. The best, *As Guerras do Alecrim e da Manjerona* (*The Wars of Rosemary and Marjoram*), contrasts the preciousness of the higher classes with the racy earthiness of the common people and is finely observed.   LK

Simeon Polotsky [Samuil (Emelyanovich) Petrovskii-Sitniyanovich] 1629–80 Russia's first court poet-playwright and founder of its didactic, civic-minded school drama. A native of White Russia, he graduated from the Kiev Academy in 1650, entered a monastery and, having settled in Moscow, became tutor to Tsar Aleksei Mikhailovich's children. He revised JOHANN GREGORY's dramatic repertoire and in the 1670s wrote two plays of his own, ostensibly on biblical themes after the Jesuit school drama (see JESUITENDRAMA): *The Comedy-Parable of the Prodigal Son* (published 1685) and *Of Nebuchadnezzar, the Golden Calf, and the Three Youths Who Were Not Burned in the Furnace*, a new version of the fiery furnace show which was said to have entered Moscow from the West via Novgorod. The first play employed ecclesiastical trappings to criticize the contemporary practice of young nobles travelling abroad to secure an education and giving themselves over to drinking, carousing and sometimes expatriation. In the second, a wise and just king, meant to resemble Aleksei Mikhailovich, opposes a tyrant, who is the cause of national suffering. Simeon Polotsky was not above enlivening his plays with music, dancing and scenic effects.   SG

Simon, John 1925– Yugoslavian-born drama and film critic. Educated at Harvard (PhD, 1959), Simon has been regarded as a brilliant stylist who demands that the theatre be intelligent and articulate. He wrote about drama for *Hudson Review* (1960–81); about films and drama for

New York Magazine since 1969; and about films for the *New Leader* since 1962. He is author of at least eight books, including *Singularities: Essays on the Theatre, 1964–73* (1976). Simon believes that the critic is responsible first to himself then to his audience, and that a piece of criticism should be both pleasurable to read and philosophical in nature. A penchant for invective and harsh personal comments, however, has put him at odds with the theatre community and his colleagues.   TLM

Simon, (Marvin) Neil 1927– American playwright. Critical acclaim has come slowly for Simon, who has had more smash hits than any other American playwright. Even with almost a hit a year since 1961, he fights a reputation of being a gag writer who caters to the moral hang-ups and material greed of middle-class America; however, his recent hit, *Lost in Yonkers* (1991), won both the Tony for Best Play and the Pulitzer Prize.

Born in New York, Simon learned his craft by writing comic material for radio and television personalities. With his brother Danny, he wrote sketches for BROADWAY shows, *Catch a Star* (1955) and *New Faces of 1956*. His first full-length COMEDY, *Come Blow Your Horn* (1961), was a hit, followed closely by the musical FARCE *Little Me* (1962, with CY COLEMAN and Carolyn Leigh). After *Barefoot in the Park* (1963), he penned one of the funniest and wisest plays in 1965, *The Odd Couple*; and a year later he added both *The Star-Spangled Girl* and the musical *Sweet Charity*. With four shows running simultaneously on Broadway, Simon was the most successful playwright of the 1960s. He added *Plaza Suite* to his list of smash hits in 1968 together with the musical *Promises, Promises* (with Burt Bacharach and Hal David). After *Last of the Red Hot Lovers* (1969), he wrote *The Gingerbread Lady* (1970), which attempted to deal honestly with alcoholism. While audiences rejected it, the playwright seemed more willing to attempt serious themes, and two bittersweet comedies followed: *The Prisoner of Second Avenue* and *The Sunshine Boys* (both 1972).

Following the death of his wife in 1973, Simon reached a low point in his career, with two failures: *The Good Doctor* (1973), adapted from short stories by ANTON CHEKHOV; and *God's Favorite*, adapted from the Bible (1976). However, a move to California resulted in another hit, *California Suite* (1976), a Beverly Hills version of *Plaza Suite*. His marriage to actress Marsha Mason resulted in *Chapter Two* (1977), regarded by some critics as his finest play to that point in his career. His fourth musical, *They're Playing Our Song*, proved popular in 1979, but his next three efforts were not successful: *I Ought to Be in Pictures* (1980), *Fools* (1981) and a revised version of *Little Me* (1982). Simon then returned to his own past for a charming *Brighton Beach Memoirs* (1983) and the Tony-winning *Biloxi Blues* (1984); and by recasting the two major roles in *The Odd Couple* for women, he found himself with three hits in 1985, and new respect from the critics. The following year, *Broadway Bound* proved to be another popular success, followed by two failures (*Rumors* (1988) and *Jake's Women* (1990), the latter initially seen only in San Diego but revised for Broadway (1992) with Alan Alda). *Lost in Yonkers* (1991; film version, 1993) has proved to be his most critically acclaimed play to date. The musical version of his film, *The Goodbye Girl*, had a modest Broadway run in 1993; of his most recent plays, *Laughter on the 23rd Floor*, which harks back to his days as a young comic writer for TV's 'Your Show of Shows', opened in autumn 1993 on Broadway, and *London Suite* premiered at the SEATTLE REPERTORY THEATRE in autumn 1994. TLM

Simonov, Konstantin (Kirill Mikhailovich) 1915–79 Soviet prose writer, poet and dramatist who survived Stalinism, achieved international repute and a long list of government posts and prizes (Hero of Socialist Labour, six Stalin Prizes, one Lenin Prize) by composing patriotic war stories and anti-capitalist partisan tales, strong on romance, heroism, sentiment, and strict adherence to the Party line. His prolific literary career began in 1934, and in 1938 he graduated from Moscow's Gorky Literary Institute. A second career in journalism, begun in 1939, included stints as a war correspondent for *Red Star*, as editor-in-chief of *New World* (1946–50, 1954–8), where he replaced the condemned Aleksandr Tvardovsky and proposed a more flexible reading of socialist-realist doctrine; and as editor of the *Literary Gazette* (1938, 1950–3). His romantic poetry and novels – *Comrade in Arms* (1952) and the trilogy consisting of *Days and Nights* (1943–4), *The Living and the Dead* (1959–71) and *Soldiers Are Not Born* (1963–4) – all relate to the war and were of great importance to the Russian people during the 1940s and 50s.

The same can be said of his 10 plays, which include *A Fellow from Our Town* (1940–1), a Stalin Prize-winner about a tank driver; *Wait for Me* (1942), a dramatization of one of his romantic poems about a Russian pilot shot down behind enemy lines trying to return to his beloved wife; his best-known war play, *The Russian People* (1942), whose message of solidarity among Russians and the heroic potential of ordinary people appealed to CLIFFORD ODETS, who prepared an American acting edition for New York's THEATRE GUILD; *Under the Chestnut Trees of Prague* (1945), a postwar play demonstrating the necessity of Soviet guidance in the democratization of its satellite countries; and *The Russian Question* (1947), an anti-capitalist piece set in New York City, which argues that the inherent goodness and Soviet sympathies of the American people are being undermined by corrupt Wall Street speculators. Simonov served as secretary of the Union of Soviet Writers and as a Deputy of the Supreme Soviet. SG

Simonson, Lee 1888–1967 American set designer; a founding member and director of the THEATRE GUILD. Simonson studied for three years in Paris and, like ROBERT EDMOND JONES, returned to the USA with great excitement about the New Stagecraft. He advocated simplified REALISM: while creating sets that were based in realism, he stripped away all scenic elements that were unnecessary for mood or information. As resident designer for the Theatre Guild he designed over half their productions, including *Heartbreak House*, *Liliom* and *Green Grow the Lilacs*. His designs for *The Adding Machine* were among the most successful examples of EXPRESSIONISM on the American stage. He authored several important books, including *The Stage Is Set* (1932) and *Part of a Lifetime: Drawings and Designs, 1919-1940* (1943). AA

Simpson, N(orman) F(rederick) 1919– British dramatist. His most successful plays were written in the late 1950s (*The Resounding Tinkle*, 1957; *The Hole*, 1958; and *One Way Pendulum*, 1959) and were staged at the ROYAL COURT THEATRE. These plays, distinguished by anarchic comedy, were seen as peculiarly British versions of the THEATRE OF THE ABSURD. Later work (*The Cresta Run*, 1965; *Playback 625* in collaboration with Leopoldo Maler, 1970; and *Was He Anyone?*, 1972) failed to make the impact of the earlier plays, but Simpson continued a writing career in television and film. He translated EDUARDO DE FILIPPO's *Napoli milionaria* from which Peter Tinniswood adapted the acting version for RICHARD EYRE's NATIONAL THEATRE production (1991), an example of how close some modern practices are coming to the notorious group authorships of Hollywood. MB JE

Sinán, Rogelio [Bernardo Domínguez Alba] 1904– Panamanian poet, playwright and fiction writer. Sinán revolutionized Panamanian poetry with his vanguardist collection, *Onda* (*Wave*, 1929). He is the author of such children's plays as *La cucarachita mandinga* (*The Impish Little Cockroach*) and *El desquite de Caperucita Roja* (*The Revenge of Little Red Riding Hood*). *Lobo Go Home* (*Wolf Go Home*, 1978) deals with the political, economic, cultural and military intervention of the USA in Panama through a retelling of the Little Red Riding Hood story. GW

Sinden, Donald (Alfred) 1923– British actor. His distinctive vocal qualities and broad style have emphasized Sinden's reputation as a fine comedy actor, though this has sometimes meant that he has worked in plays of slight merit. But as a classical actor he has produced exciting and often adventurous performances, as, for instance, in his role as Richard Plantagenet in JOHN BARTON's *The Wars of the Roses* (ROYAL SHAKESPEARE COMPANY, 1963). He has played Lear and Othello for the RSC (1977 and 1979 respectively) as well as creating witty character studies in such roles as Lord Foppington (VANBRUGH's *The Relapse*, RSC, 1967) and Sir Peter Teazle (SHERIDAN's *The School for Scandal*, 1983). His skills in demanding, naturalistic roles have been shown in appearances as Vanya in CHEKHOV's *Uncle Vanya* (1982) and Doctor Stockmann in IBSEN's *An Enemy of the People* (1975). He appeared in the comedy-thriller *Over My Dead Body* (1989) and in NOËL COWARD's *Star Quality* (1989), and directed a revival of *The Importance of Being Earnest* (1987), which reopened the Royalty Theatre in London; but his most challenging part in recent years was perhaps as the Duke of Altair in the CHICHESTER FESTIVAL THEATRE's revival of CHRISTOPHER FRY's *Venus Observed* (1992), tackling LAURENCE OLIVIER's well remembered part in an attempt to revive a prominent local dramatist's reputation. A keen theatre historian, Sinden has been a strong advocate and worker for the establishment of the British Theatre Museum (which opened in London's Covent Garden in 1987). MB JE

Singapore Singapore has four official languages: Malay, Mandarin, Tamil and English. The plural linguistic-cultural system of Singapore has led to the formation of four separate enclaves or 'streams' of theatre. Until recently, rapprochement between streams was rare. Each stream looked to outside sources for inspiration and models to help shape its aesthetics and repertory: Mandarin theatre to CHINA, Tamil to INDIA, and English theatre to the West.

Singapore Malay theatre, however, was an integral and, occasionally, leading part of Malaysian Malay theatre until Singapore's separation from Malaysia in 1963. (Singapore was a part of The Federation of Malaysia for four years from the time of independence from the British in 1959, following more than a century of British rule.) For more than a decade after the Japanese occupation, Singapore was the virtual centre of Malay literary activities on both sides of the Causeway. The era spawned the durable Malay theatre company, Sriwana. Led by the idiosyncratic theatre professional, Kalam Hamidy, its eclectic performances encompassed *purbawara*, dramatized tales of legendary figures, and *drama moden*, realistic drama (see MALAYSIA). The separation from Malaysia in 1963 left Singapore Malays as a political and cultural minority in a Chinese-dominated society. Sriwana assumed the role of bastion of a beleaguered theatre culture. Recent efforts to encourage an experimental sensibility in the Sriwana troupe, particularly by Nadi Putra, Sriwana's leader, have so far been thwarted by the group's conservatism. Significantly, Nadi's contemporary vision of the legendary Malay rebel Jebat, *Ivory Tower* (*Menara Gading*, 1986), was staged by Teater Kemuning, a young theatre company drawn to Indonesian–Malaysian contemporary theatre. Directing the play was Lut Ali, an informal leader of the young-turk elements in Singapore Malay theatre.

Tamil theatre, also the product of a distinct cultural minority, turned from its traditional historical-mythological plays to a reformist realistic theatre in the 1950s. Since then, it has not felt any urgency radically to change its aesthetic direction, although of late Tamil audiences are responding to home-grown dramas.

The firm foundations of a Mandarin-based realistic theatre were laid by the teachers and journalists leading the Singapore Amateur Players in the early 1950s. Their painstaking groundwork was rudely shaken by the local reverberations of the Cultural Revolution in China (1966–76). What ensued was a Singapore version of the Cultural Revolution's militant non-realistic theatre of heroic gestures and images exalting the common man. KUO PAO KUN, a playwright-director trained in Australia's National Academy of Dramatic Arts, injected strong doses of professionalism and artistic responsibility into the revolutionary theatre. His epic-type plays, improvised and conceived collectively, demystified Mandarin playwriting in Singapore. Staged by the students, workers and clerks enrolled in the Practice Performing Arts School which he directed, his performances expounded on the social dislocations brought on by foreign investment and urban redevelopment in an increasingly corporate Singapore. In 1976 Kuo was detained during the government's massive anti-leftist drive. Upon his release in 1980, he immediately returned to the stage, disclosing a human and reflective dimension in his partially expressionist theatre. In 1985 he began the writing and directing of a successful series of Mandarin-English one-man theatre pieces, inspired by the Chinese oral storytelling tradition. Gently satirical and in convincing Singlish (Singapore English), *The Coffin Is Too*

Big for the Hole (1985), and *No Parking on Odd Days* (1986) rue the excessive homogenization and bureaucratization of contemporary Singapore society. These plays also gave witness to his new-found role as bridge-builder between the polarized theatre societies.

The early 1960s generation of Singapore playwrights in English was a politicized, nationalist-minded, university-trained literary elite, represented by Lim Chor Pee and Goh Poh Seng. The indifferent response to their pioneering plays was followed by a drought in local English drama, relieved only by the 1970s political plays of the poet and novelist Robert Yeo. At the end of the decade, an identity crisis was perceived by the theatre director and university lecturer, Max LeBlond, who lent his zest for the local *patois* of Singlish to resourceful adaptations of foreign works in the early 1980s. Along with Kuo's monodramas, LeBlond's staging of Stella Kon's *Emily of Emerald Hill* (1985) elevated the status of the Singapore English play in the national estimation. Kon's Asian treatment of time and space in her bitter-sweet eulogy of the disappearing culture of the local 'Straits-born Chinese' (*peranakan*) was a rare experience for the ethnically dispossessed middle-class audience. An alternative theatre, directly influenced by the Philippine Educational Theatre Association (PETA) (see PHILIPPINES) was proposed by Third Stage, which presented 'learning plays' on the ills of Singapore society to the young, 'high-rise' generation. The May 1987 detention of Third Stage leaders by the Singapore government has led to paralysis of the company.

If current trends prevail, English promises to be the dominant language of Singapore. Presently, the Singapore government has launched a rational support system for theatre, by way of providing physical infrastructure, grants and tax rebates, annual and biannual national and international festivals and playwriting competitions. The continually expanding middle class has responded by filling the theatres, causing the internationally-minded government and business agencies to be aggressive about sponsoring a 'cultural' Singapore.

One of the results of the expansionist drive was that in 1990 Kuo founded the Substation, a privately financed and managed all-purpose arts centre that acts as a channel for creative fellowship between ethnically and/or aesthetically diverse art forms and artists. In his own theatre, Kuo has been persuaded to take a deeper look at the usability of Asian dramaturgy. Indeed, the most concrete sign of the breakdown of audience resistance to presentational theatre was exposed by Kuo's performance of *Mama Looking for her Cat* (1988), a multilingual ensemble piece that aspired to bridge the generation gap.

Traditions of Asian theatre are also explored by William Teo's Asian Theatre Research Circus, unashamedly inspired by PETER BROOK's intercultural performance methods. In 1988 the law graduate Ong Keng Sen took over artistic leadership of Theatreworks, Singapore's first professional theatre company, where he executed fusions of Chinese opera, tai chi and Western theatre in directing Leow Puay Tin's Malaysian play, *Three Children* (1988), David Hwang's *Dance and the Railroad* (1990) and Henry Ong's *Memories of Madame Mao* (1991). While also launching the first major BROADWAY-style MUSICAL, *Beauty World* (1988), written by Michael Chiang and Dick Lee, the

27-year-old Ong convened the first 'Retrospective of Singapore Plays in English' in 1990.

Singapore theatre is burgeoning and the idea and practice of the 'Singapore play' has gained momentum, so much so that the frequency of indigenous English drama performances from 1986 to the present is unprecedented. Even so, the new plays have not been able to match the moral resonance and/or the eclectic performance strategies of Kon's *Emily at Emerald Hill* or Kuo's *Coffin* and *Mama Looking for her Cat*. Also the pull of Asian theatrical images on the highly Westernized young generation remains uncertain. (See also ASIAN AND PACIFIC ISLAND THEATRE.) KJ

Singspiel A popular form of musical drama that arose in Germany during the mid-18th century – as a result, it has been argued, of the popularity of GAY's *Beggar's Opera* (1728). Most *Singspiele* have a popular setting and comprise light, tuneful songs connected by dialogue that is spoken, not sung. Several dramatists wrote *Singspiele*, most notably GOETHE, but the most consummate achievements in the genre are Mozart's *The Abduction from the Seraglio* (1782) and *The Magic Flute* (1791). The OPERETTA of the 19th century evolved in part from the *Singspiel*. SW

Sircar, Badal 1925– Indian playwright and director. Born in Calcutta, he studied to be a civil engineer and town planner. He began his theatre career in 1953 as a director and actor. In 1956 his first original script was produced in Calcutta. In 1957 he went to London for further education in his original profession. National recognition came with *And Indrajit* (*Evam Indrajit*), composed while he was abroad. Between 1966 and 1967 he worked in Nigeria as a town planner. Shortly after returning to India in 1967 he formed his theatre group Satabdi, and shortly thereafter toured the USSR, Poland and Czechoslovakia where he saw productions by LYUBIMOV and GROTOWSKI. Tiring of structured plays, he returned to INDIA and restructured his group in 1969, beginning a period of experimentation requiring little of the scenery and lighting elements characteristic of urban theatre in Calcutta. Among his notable recent productions are *Spartacus*, *Bhoma* and *Procession*. Today he teaches workshops in creative process throughout India and has inspired several generations of contemporary artists with his ideas. FaR

Sissle, Noble 1889–1975 and
Eubie Blake 1883–1983 American singer-lyricist and pianist-composer. Blake met Sissle in 1915. For several years they performed in VAUDEVILLE in an act featuring their own songs. In 1921 they joined with the vaudeville comedy team of Flournoy Miller and Aubrey Lyles to create the first black MUSICAL to play a major BROADWAY theatre during the regular theatrical season: *Shuffle Along*. With a book by Miller and Lyles, who also starred in it, *Shuffle Along* was a big hit both in New York and on tour. Critics and audiences delighted in the vitality of the score and the lively dancing of the chorus.

Sissle and Blake went on to write the scores for several other musicals, including *The Chocolate Dandies* (1924) and *Shuffle Along of 1932*, but without the success that had been achieved by *Shuffle Along*. On his own, Blake wrote the music for several other shows. A revival of *Shuffle Along* in 1952 was a failure, but with the rediscovery of ragtime in the 1960s and 70s Sissle and Blake songs were again heard on Broadway in *Doctor Jazz* (1975), *Bubbling Brown Sugar* (1976) and *Eubie* (1978). MK

sitcom see TELEVISION DRAMA

Sjöberg, Alf 1903–80 Swedish director, whose 50-year career at DRAMATEN was decisive in broadening the company's repertoire and increasing its artistic standards. He combined a belief in the moral and intellectual function of theatre in a confused, unjust world with an impressive mastery of modern staging. An accomplished designer, he used light and space with creative fluidity. He is best known for his productions of SHAKESPEARE, STRINDBERG, BRECHT and IONESCO, as well as dramatists he introduced into Sweden such as GOMBROWICZ and WITKIEWICZ. Typically he combined analysis of a play's historical context with emphasis on its relevance to the present. Some of his most inventive work, such as his adaptations of C. J. L. Almqvist's novels *Amorina* and *The Queen's Jewel*, was done within the limited resources of Dramaten's second stage, Lilla Scenen. HL

Skármeta, Antonio 1940– Chilean novelist, short story writer and playwright. His single but stunning play, *Ardiente paciencia* (*Burning Patience*, 1982), demythifies the life of Pablo Neruda, Nobel laureate, through the eyes of his young postman. GW

Skelton, John c.1460–1529 English poet and dramatist. Large quantities of his poetry have survived, but among his plays only *Magnyfycence* (printed c.1530 by JOHN RASTELL). Before 1500 he was made a poet laureate by Oxford, Louvain and Cambridge Universities, was tutor to the young Henry (later VIII), and by 1503 was rector of Diss in Norfolk and out of the king's service. Though classed as a MORALITY, *Magnyfycence* is not concerned with the struggle of good and evil for the soul of a generalized mankind but with good and evil counsel struggling for power over the ruler, the Magnyfycence of the title. PM

Skinner, Cornelia Otis 1901–79 American actress, monologuist, humorist and author; daughter of actor OTIS SKINNER, with whom she made her professional debut in 1921 in *Blood and Sand*. Skinner established her reputation as a fine actress, beginning in the 1920s touring the USA and Britain in monodramas that she wrote and staged herself. These included *The Wives of Henry VIII* (1931), *The Empress Eugenie* (1932), *The Loves of Charles II* (1933) and *Paris '90* (1952). In more traditional theatre she appeared in *Candida* (1939), *Theatre* (1941), *Lady Windermere's Fan* (1946) and *The Pleasure of His Company* (1958), the last co-authored with Samuel Taylor. She also wrote memoirs, light verse, essays and three critically acclaimed theatrical biographies: *Family Circle* (1948), the story of her famous family; *Madame Sarah*, a life of SARAH BERNHARDT (1967); and *Life with LINDSAY and CROUSE* (1976). She is probably most remembered for the 1942 travelogue she co-wrote with Emily Kimbrough, entitled *Our Hearts Were Young and Gay*. DBW

Skinner, Otis 1858–1942 One of America's most versatile actors who, by his own account, played over 140 roles during 1877–9 with the resident companies of the Philadelphia Museum and the WALNUT STREET THEATRE. Between 1879 and 92, Skinner played in the companies of EDWIN BOOTH, LAWRENCE BARRETT, AUGUSTIN DALY, HELENA MODJESKA and JOSEPH JEFFERSON III, and occasionally starred as romantic hero, classical tragedian, comedian and character actor. From 1892, he was a confirmed and popular star who continued to play a varied repertory. In his own time and for later generations he was best-remembered for the role of Hajj, the beggar, in *Kismet*, which he created in 1911, played exclusively for three years, and preserved in two film versions. Skinner, and his actress daughter, CORNELIA OTIS SKINNER, were both prolific writers, the former the author of *Footlights and Spotlights* (1924), *The Last Tragedian* (1939, on Edwin Booth) and *One Man in His Time: The Adventures of Harry Watkins, Strolling Player, 1845–1863* (1938, with his wife, Maud). MR

skomorokhi Itinerant players of Old Russia. The Byzantine chronicler Theophanes mentioned Slavs playing guzlas as early as 583, but the first clear reference was a condemnation of them by the Primary Chronicle in 1068. Musicians, boxers, and dancers with long hair and tunics had been portrayed in the frescos of the Sophia Cathedral in Kiev in 1037; however, the Church opposed them as anti-ascetic vestiges of paganism and propagandists for immorality. Their antics at Easter with made-up faces and old clothes, and their disguises as women or animals on New Year's Eve, proclaimed the *skomorokhi*'s heathen origins. By the late 16th and early 17th centuries they had become hugely popular, some troupes consisting of over 100 men. They dressed in ordinary peasant clothing, ornamented with ribbons, and excelled as puppeteers, bearleaders, dog and rat trainers and storytellers. The most famous, Foma and Erema, entered folklore. Following an uprising in Moscow, Tsar Aleksey Mikhailovich, first of the Romanovs, banned them 'and all manner of devilish sports' (1648); this ban was strictly enforced and they were exiled to the northern hinterlands, where the traditions were long upheld. Some became private jesters, some entertainers at weddings and parties. They exercised an immeasurable influence on the Russian puppet theatre (see PUPPETS) and the fairground booth, and, through them, on Russian CIRCUS and VARIETY. LS

Slabolepszy, Paul 1948– South Africa's most prolific new playwright. Slabolepszy has a performer's diploma from the University of Cape Town. His carefully textured plays seldom refer directly to the political context which determines the action, but inscribed in every one is dialogue which reveals the damage wrought by apartheid politics. His work is characterized by accurate representation of the idiosyncrasies of poor whites, primarily with respect to language. All of his plays employ a rich multilingual dialogue, and his comic characterizations of apartheid's children have made his works extremely popular. Major plays are: *The Defloration of Miles Koekemoer* (1980), *Saturday Night at the Palace* (1981), *Karoo Grand* (1983), *Under the Oaks* (1984), *Over the Hill* (1985), *Boo to the Moon* (1986), *Making like America* (1986), *Travelling Shots* (1988), *Smallholding* (1989), *The Eyes of Their Whites* (with David Kramer, 1990), *One for the High Jump* (1990), *Braait Laaities* (1991), *The Return of Elvis du Pisanie* (1992), *Mooi Street Moves* (1992), *Pale Natives* (1993) and *Victoria Almost Falls* (1993). His plays have been translated into German, Swedish and Hebrew. IS

Slavkin, Viktor 1935– Soviet Russian construction engineer turned dramatist, whose first efforts in the late 1960s were one-act plays staged at Our House, the theatrical studio of Moscow State University. These were grotesque, metaphoric pieces: *A Rotten Apartment*, whose inhabitants live in a shooting gallery; *Frost*, whose hero never leaves his house; *The Orchestra*, in which a musician cannot open his instrument case. With *The Painting* and work in ALEKSEI ARBUZOV's studio for young playwrights, he moved to a more realistic mode. His best work is associated with the director ANATOLY VASILIEV, who staged *A Young Man's Grown-up Daughter* (1979) at the STANISLAVSKY Theatre, Moscow. Reflecting the fate of the 60s generation, this play contrasts a father living a life of illusions about a fantasy America with his cynical, disillusioned offspring. *Cerceau* (1985–6), directed by Vasilicv at the Taganka, became an international success; it received its first English-language production at the ARENA STAGE, Washington, DC, before being seen in Holland, Germany and London. A CHEKHOVian ensemble piece about inevitable loss and the treachery of memory and hope, written during the uncertain Chernenko period, it is infused with pessimism and a longing to escape. LS

Slovakia see CZECHOSLOVAKIA

Slovenia see YUGOSLAVIA; MEDIEVAL DRAMA IN EUROPE (Eastern Europe)

Słowacki, Juliusz 1809–49 Polish romantic poet and playwright who from 1831 lived in political exile in Switzerland, Italy and France. He wrote over 20 verse dramas dealing with European and Polish history and legend, folklore and fairy tale, which blend the mystical and cruel, the cosmic and grotesque, in loose, fragmentary scenes. Major works are *Maria Stuart* (1832), *Kordian* (1834), *Beatrix Cenci* (1839), *Balladyna* (1839), *Mazeppa* (1840) and *Fantazy* (1841). DG

Sly, William d.1608 English actor, first heard of in 1590, when he was with STRANGE'S MEN in TARLTON's *The Seven Deadly Sins*. After a spell with the ADMIRAL'S MEN, he joined the LORD CHAMBERLAIN'S MEN, perhaps from the company's foundation in 1594, becoming a sharer after the death of AUGUSTINE PHILLIPS. A surviving portrait in the Dulwich Picture Gallery, London, shows a dark, strong face, turned slightly sinister by the curl of the lips. It is not known what parts Sly played, though he may have served an apprenticeship with Phillips and inherited his role as actor-athlete in the company. PT

Smit, Bartho 1924–86 Arguably the most prominent Afrikaans playwright; also a theatre critic. Smit was a controversial figure, his plays frequently censored in South Africa (see CENSORSHIP). He was active in professional theatre for many years, directing for the National Theatre Organization and the performing arts councils. His work spans three decades, from *Moeder Hanna* (*Mother Hanna*, 1959), a drama about the futility of war, through *Don Juan onder die Boere* (*Don Juan among the Boers*, 1960), *Die ver-minktes* (*The Maimed*, 1960) and *Putsonderwater* (*Well without Water*, 1962), an absurdist study (see THEATRE OF THE ABSURD) of religious bankruptcy in modern life, to *Bacchus in die Boland* (*Bacchus in the Highveld*, 1974), in which Bacchus visits a wine estate and makes the white farmer switch roles with his black staff. *Die Keiser* (*The Emperor*, 1977) adapts the Hans Christian Andersen story *The Emperor's New Clothes* to present a satirical look at the absurdities of social mores. His best-known play is *Christine*, commissioned for the opening of the Nico Malan Theatre in Cape Town in 1971, but then cancelled and produced two years later in the Transvaal. It is a richly allusive play focusing on Nazi Germany and developing themes of Calvinist guilt and racial prejudice. A young and an old Christine appear simultaneously on stage, as the play moves through past and present exploring its central character's existential anxieties and guilt. His plays have frequently been censored, yet he has also been recognized through the *Encyclopedia Britannica* Award (for *The Maimed*) and a number of local prizes.   IS

Smith, Albert Richard   1816–60 English writer and entertainer. Smith was already a popular humorist and journalist, with some theatrical success accruing to his extravaganzas and dramatizations of DICKENS, when in 1850 he presented his panorama-lecture *The Overland Mail*, studded with songs, anecdotes and impersonations at Willis's Rooms, London. Aided by his brother Arthur (1825–61), the bluff, bearded Smith took over London's Egyptian Hall for the entertainment, *The Ascent of Mont Blanc* (1852), complete even to the sound effects of pop-ping champagne corks. It was one of the greatest hits of the Victorian amusement scene and ran for 2000 performances, shocking the German actor LUDWIG BARNAY that a gentleman should so exhibit himself. It was followed by *Mont Blanc to China* (1858–9). In 1859 Smith married a daughter of the comedian Robert Keeley.   LS

Smith, Anna Deavere   1951– American actress and playwright. Since 1983 Smith has been developing a series of one-person performance pieces collectively called 'On the Road: A Search for American Character' (based on interviews about controversial events or subjects), yet her work was not widely known until May 1992 when *Fires in the Mirror: Crown Heights, Brooklyn, and Other Identities* (based on the 1991 stabbing of a Hasidic scholar by a group of young black men), the 13th in this series, was presented at the JOSEPH PAPP PUBLIC THEATER in New York. Her human collage of over 20 individuals won her wide acclaim and multiple awards, including a special OFF-BROADWAY Obie. Her most recent work, *Twilight: Los Angeles, 1992*, first produced at the Los Angeles Mark Taper Forum in spring 1993 and Off-Broadway (later trans-ferred to BROADWAY) in 1994, likewise won her numerous awards and accolades.   DBW

Smith, Harry B(ache)   1860–1936 American librettist

and lyricist. Smith's first connection with the theatre was as a dramatic and musical editor for a Chicago newspaper. For composer REGINALD DE KOVEN he created the libretto and most of the lyrics for the most beloved American comic OPERA of the late 19th century, *Robin Hood* (1891). Although much of his writing was mediocre by modern standards, Smith's ability to adapt to changing styles and tastes in MUSICAL THEATRE ensured him a long and prolific career, in the course of which he was reported to have writ-ten some 300 librettos and 6000 lyrics. His autobiography appeared in 1931.   MK

Smith [Sultzer], **Joe**   1884–1981 and
Charlie Dale [Charles Marks]   1881–1971 Comic VAUDE-VILLE team (for 73 years); inspiration for NEIL SIMON's *The Sunshine Boys*. Smith and Dale began in 1898 as a black-face act (see MINSTREL SHOW), singing and dancing in Bowery saloons while working as hash-slingers at the Child's Restaurant chain. New names were adopted when calling cards for another team, who then chose to change their names (to Moran and Mack), were used by a theatre owner to advertise them. In 1901 they joined the Imperial Vaudeville and Comedy Company. When the company folded they stayed with two other members (Will Lester and Jack Coleman) to form the Avon Comedy Four, devel-oping such classic sketches as 'Hungarian Rhapsody', 'Dr Kronkhite', 'The New School Teacher' and 'Venetian Knights'. Numerous comics served with the Avon troupe before 'Smith and Dale' became headliners in the 1920s, featuring their 'Dr Kronkhite' sketch (Smith the patient, Dale the doctor), thereafter inseparably associated with them. In their sketches Smith, lanky with a pencil mous-tache, received the punch lines while Dale, smaller and deadpan, was his foil. BROOKS ATKINSON characterized them as 'professional performers, acting two low-comedy parts with style, authority and abandon'.   DBW

Smith, Maggie [Mrs Margaret Natalie Cross]   1934– British actress, who appeared briefly in the New York REVUE, *New Faces*, before starring with Kenneth Williams in the Bamber Gascoigne revue, *Share My Lettuce* (1956). Her attractive wit and lively personality gave her a consid-erable WEST END success; but she wisely chose not to stay with intimate revue but to gain experience as an actress elsewhere. She joined the OLD VIC company for the 1959–60 season, playing in *As You Like It* and *Richard II*; and then appeared in ANOUILH's *The Rehearsal* (1961) and PETER SHAFFER's *The Private Ear* and *The Public Eye* (1962), two parts in a double bill which brought her the *Evening Standard*'s Best Actress Drama Award for 1962. She was invited to join OLIVIER's NATIONAL THEATRE company for the opening seasons, playing in *The Recruiting Officer*, *Miss Julie*, *Hay Fever* and memorably as Desdemona to Olivier's Othello.

She began her film career in 1963 mainly playing light comedy parts, but with *The Prime of Miss Jean Brodie* (1968), which won her an Oscar, she became a major film star. Her sensitive face, husky voice and ironic delivery helped her to excel in comedies of manners from all peri-ods: in NOËL COWARD's plays (*Design for Living*, 1971; *Private Lives*, 1972) and in CONGREVE's *The Way of the World*, as Millamant (1984), which brought her her sixth major acting award. Her skills as a tragic actress, however, have been questioned, although her Hedda Gabler (1970) was much admired. In 1976, after her first marriage to the actor ROBERT STEPHENS was dissolved, she joined the STRATFORD (Ontario) FESTIVAL company in Canada, where she stayed for several seasons, giving the premiere performance there of *Virginia* (1981), a study of the life of Virginia Woolf. She provided another in her list of wildly eccentric characters, as a flamboyantly romantic historical guide in Peter Shaffer's *Lettice and Lovage* (1987). In 1970 she was awarded the CBE, and in 1982 became a director of United British Artists. In 1975 she married the playwright, Beverley Cross. Her biography by Michael Coveney was published in 1992.   JE

Smith, Oliver 1918–94 American set designer, theatrical producer and educator. Smith designed some 400 theatre, dance, OPERA and film productions from 1941, and also served as co-director of American Ballet Theatre (1945–81). He began his career designing for dance, notably *Rodeo* and *Fall River Legend* for AGNES DE MILLE, and *Fancy Free* for JEROME ROBBINS. Starting with the 1944 production of *On the Town* (which he also co-produced), he designed a steady stream of long-running MUSICALS, including *My Fair Lady*, *West Side Story* and *Hello Dolly!*. Smith believed that scenery for musicals should be bright and entertaining, and change quickly and unobtrusively. He talked about scenery in terms of choreography: in *Fall River Legend*, the scenery is, in fact, an integral part of the choreography. In terms of style he frequently mixed painterly backgrounds with sculptural scenic elements. He also had an almost formulaic approach to the arrangement of scenic elements and space, which meshed well with the musicals of the 1940s and 50s and contributed to his prodigious output. He also taught design at New York University.   AA

Smith, Richard Penn 1799–1854 One of many American intellectuals who wrote fiction and poetry and edited journals, Smith created some 20 plays, five of them staged in 1829. Of these, *The Eighth of January* celebrated Andrew Jackson's victory, while *William Penn* reveals Smith's talent for COMEDY. *Caius Marius* (1831), a TRAGEDY based on this Roman's love of country, was selected as a Prize Play by EDWIN FORREST, who performed the title role only a few times. Although Smith enjoyed some success, his interest in the theatre was momentary.   WJM

Smith, Sol(omon Franklin) 1801–69 American theatre manager and actor, especially noted for his pioneering work on the frontier. He began his theatrical career in Vincennes, Indiana, in 1819, and by 1823 had organized his own company, which he managed for four years. He then toured the Mississippi valley with JAMES H. CALDWELL, and in 1835 entered into a partnership with NOAH LUDLOW. They dominated the FRONTIER THEATRE of their time, but ended the partnership in 1853.

As an actor, Smith, affectionately known as 'Old Sol', was particularly effective as a low comedian in such roles as Mawworm in *The Hypocrite*. He eventually went into law and became a Missouri state senator. His three autobiographical volumes, *Theatrical Apprenticeship* (1845), *The*

Theatrical Journey-work and Anecdotal Recollections of Sol. Smith (1854) and *Theatrical Management in the West and South for Thirty Years* (1868), are flawed but valuable insights into theatrical conditions of the time.   SMA

Smith, William Henry Sedley 1806–72 American playwright, actor and stage manager. Born in Wales, Smith began acting with the Theatre Royal, Lancaster (1822), joined Philadelphia's WALNUT STREET company (1827), the TREMONT THEATRE in Boston (1828) and the BOSTON MUSEUM (1843) as stage manager and actor. His *The Drunkard; or, The Fallen Saved* (1844) was the first successful temperance drama and the most enduring. After the initial 100-performance runs in Boston and New York, the play blanketed the country. His later career was spent in San Francisco as manager of the CALIFORNIA THEATRE.   RM

Smithson, Harriet (Constance) 1800–54 British actress, born in Ireland, where her father managed theatres. She made her debut at DRURY LANE in 1818, but her impact on London audiences was slight. In Paris, by contrast, where she played Juliet, Ophelia and NICHOLAS ROWE's Jane Shore in the company of CHARLES KEMBLE in 1827, she was a sensation. The frantic adulation of youthful Frenchmen, including Sainte-Beuve, GAUTIER, DUMAS *père* and HUGO, contributed to the rise of the French romantic theatre. Extravagantly courted by Berlioz, Smithson eventually married him in 1833. She retired from the stage in 1836 and spent the rest of her life in increasingly brandy-soaked isolation and misery as the neglected Madame Berlioz.   PT

Smoktunovsky, Innokenty (Mikhailovich) 1925–94 Soviet Russian actor. A prisoner in Germany during the Second World War, then from 1946 on the provincial stage in Norilsk, the gaunt figure with thinning blond hair and an otherworldly voice exploded into the Leningrad playgoer's awareness in 1957 as Prince Myshkin in Dostoevsky's *The Idiot* at the Bolshoi Gorky Theatre, a performance of stunning spontaneity and sensitivity. GEORGY TOVSTONOGOV directed him in this and as Sergei in ARBUZOV's *It Happened in Irkutsk*. From 1960, Smoktunovsky concentrated on film, most notably as Hamlet (directed by G. Kozintsev, 1965) and Uncle Vanya. He returned to the stage in 1973 as A. K. TOLSTOI's Tsar Fyodor Ioannovich (Moscow Maly Theatre), but in 1975 transferred to the MOSCOW ART THEATRE. There he played CHEKHOV's Ivanov as an extraordinary man stricken with spiritual paralysis, and 'Little Judas' Golovyov in LEV DODIN's adaptation of SALTYKOV-SHCHEDRIN's *The Golovyov Family* (1984) as an incarnation of the monstrous bombast which overwhelmed Russia. He also recreated his Vanya in a production by OLEG EFREMOV.   LS

soap-opera see TELEVISION DRAMA

Sofola, Zulu 1935– Nigerian playwright and director. Sofola was born at Isele-Uku in Bendel state, and studied at the Catholic University, Virginia, USA, and at the University of Ibadan, researching into traditional Nigerian religious and political systems. Her plays employ elements of magic, myth and RITUAL to examine conflicts between traditionalism and modernism in which male supremacy persists. Her most frequently performed plays are *Wedlock of the Gods* (1972) and *The Sweet Trap* (1977). In the former, the heroine experiences a sense of liberation after the death of a husband she has never loved. She and her new lover are hunted down after breaking their society's marital taboos. *The Sweet Trap* has a contemporary setting, but again examines a conflict of authority in marital relations. Sofola's treatment of women's rights and of class difference here have sharply divided critical opinion: does her work offer a blueprint for liberation, or is it inherently conservative? *King Emene* (1974), *Old Wines Are Tasty* (1981), *Memories in the Moonlight* (1986) and *Song of a Maiden* (1991) all examine traditional values and conflicting notions of authority. Other plays range outside her primary interest in traditional value systems. *The Wizard of Law* (1975) is a highly skilful adaptation of the medieval French play, *Maistre Pierre Pathelin*. *The Operators* (unpublished) deals with a familiar theme in Nigerian theatre – armed robbery. Sofola is professor of performing arts, University of Ilorin, NIGERIA.   CD

sokari Devotional performance, perhaps the oldest form of theatre in SRI LANKA. It is staged after the Sinhalese New Year in the months of Vesak and Poson which end around September. It is performed as a votive offering to the goddess Pattini, chief among the deities who are worshipped through RITUAL with the object of blessing human undertakings and granting immunity from disaster. Performances are confined to remote hilly regions, and performers, who are all male peasants, undergo training by elder performers in preparation for their devotional duties. Any open spot in the village, usually the threshing ground, may be used for an all-night show. Dancing and music punctuate the lively events and full-face MASKS are often used by performers.

As in so many ritual performances, one story is enacted here, the story of Sokari. The story differs in various details from group to group and place to place, with some performers even integrating popular music to enliven the original story line.

In essence, the episodic events centre on the following story: Guru Hami, a north Indian, and Sokari, his wife, along with Paraya, their comic servant, are disenfranchised, build a boat and sail to Sri Lanka where they experience various comic adventures. Sokari, who is young and seductive, elopes with, or is seduced by, a local doctor who has been summoned to treat Guru Hami for a dog bite. Eventually Sokari returns and delivers a child. The ending, along with the recurrent sexual symbolism and ribaldry that appear throughout the performance, suggest that *sokari* may be a dramatic elaboration of an archaic fertility ritual.

Among its unique features, *sokari* makes elaborate use of MIME in which the players depict various actions described in song.   FaR

Solari Swayne, Enrique 1915– Peruvian playwright. Solari Swayne studied in Germany, and was professor of psychology at the University of San Marcos in Lima. He is known primarily for *Collacocha* (1955), a play that epito-

mized the tragic struggle of an engineer, Echecopar, to conquer the forces of nature. *La mazorca* (*The Corn*, 1964) echoed similar telluric concerns in a Peruvian jungle plantation setting. *Ayax Telemonio* (1969) used a classical motif to criticize current national sociopolitical issues.   GW

Soldene, Emily 1840–1912 The most shining star in British OPÉRA BOUFFE. Soldene began her career in the Oxford music-hall, then moved to the Alhambra and the Philharmonic. She sang OFFENBACH, Hervé and Lecocq, her greatest successes being in *Geneviève de Brabant*, *Chilpéric* and *La Fille de Madame Angot*. She directed productions and formed her own company. She toured extensively in Britain and made several wide-ranging tours of the USA, as well as performing in Australia and New Zealand. Although aiming at the highest standards, she had no illusions about the corner-cutting and makeshifts of show business. Of the premiere of *Madame l'Archiduc* in New York she recalled: 'A friend ... brought over a vocal score, and in one week it was translated, scored, studied, learnt, rehearsed and produced'; and of Bessie Sudlow's valiant effort in *Fleur de Thé*: 'She studied the part in 24 hours ... She sang songs she did not know to tunes she had never heard, wedded to words improvised as she went along. But she was alright ... pulled through ... by the conductor.'   GH

Soleil, Théâtre du see THÉÂTRE DU SOLEIL

Sologub, Fyodor [Fyodor Kuzmich Teternikov] 1863–1927 Russian decadent poet, novelist, short story writer and dramatist preoccupied with these concomitant themes: Platonic Idealism and perverse sensualism; the possibility and impossibility of communion between the real and ideal worlds; beauty and banality; love – death as preferable to life – suffering; art as transcendent medium; and the artist as insensitive, unsuccessful discoverer of life's hidden beauty ('the uncrowned Dulcinea'). A repressed, obsessive pessimist bordering on nihilism, Sologub envisioned an inverted cosmos in which God rules an evil world of matter and desire, while Satan governs a calm realm of beauty and death. Although man's inner world is good, its commerce with the outer world via naive projection precipitates the romantic irony of life.

Sologub's art, in the manner of the symbolists (see SYMBOLISM), remythologizes ancient legends, transforming them into highly private scenarios which in his case revolve around sex, sadism and the humiliation of the very beauty he seeks. His idea of theatre, as expressed in the essay 'The Theatre of One Will' (1908), is similarly contradictory and self-referential, as well as vaguely suggestive of EVREINOV's theory of monodrama. Via the self-conscious, subjective expression of the author's 'I', theatre may achieve the focused spirituality of the Russian icon and effect a congregant mystery between stage and audience. Although he advocated a bare stage and presentation of the text by the author or a single reader, Sologub's 18 plays offer theatrical levels and devices, interesting shifts in perspective, focus and pacing, which attracted theatricalist directors. MEYERHOLD achieved a rare success for symbolist drama with his CRAIGIAN-set staging of *The*

Triumph of Death (1907), his last production at Vera Komissarzhevskaya's Theatre. To this ironic, quasi-MAETERLINCKian treatment of a medieval tragedy involving cruel romantic deception, suffering and death, Sologub wrote a special prologue, meant to parody the symbolist mystery's pretentiousness, for Meyerhold as the Poet to deliver.

Meyerhold's symbolic-realist staging of *The Hostages of Life* (1912), a mystical variation of IBSEN's *The Master Builder*, marked the first production of a symbolist play at a traditional theatre, the Aleksandrinsky. Evreinov presented *Nocturnal Dances* (1908), with choreography by Mikhail Fokine, at his Merry Theatre for Grown-up Children (1909). The play is a fairy-tale-based, tragicomic rendering of Sologub's 'poet as blind defiler of beauty' theme; its central image of princesses ecstatically dancing suggests the author's attraction to Isadora Duncan's 'frolic dance' as metaphor for the non-cognitive, transformative potential of art. Sologub and Evreinov were both less successful with *Vanka the Lackey and Jean the Page*, at Vera Komissarzhevskaya's Theatre (1909), a rapidly shifting, self-conscious and highly stylized presentation of parallel tales of seduction in medieval Russia and France. Of his other dramatic remythologizations, Sologub's *Gift of the Wise Bees* (1907) treats the Laodamia legend (also essayed by ANNENSKY and BRIUSOV). Sologub's most popular play was a dramatization of his novel *The Petty Demon* (1907) for Nezlobin's Theatre (1910). SG

Solórzano, Carlos 1922– Guatemalan-born playwright, critic and professor. Solórzano has been resident in Mexico since 1939, where he studied architecture and literature; he received a doctorate at the National University of Mexico with a thesis on Miguel de Unamuno. With a Rockefeller grant he spent 1948–50 in Europe, where he met ALBERT CAMUS, MICHEL DE GHELDERODE and existentialism. In Mexico he was named artistic director of the Professional University Theatre and later professor at the National University. His major plays are *Doña Beatriz* (1952), *El hechicero* (*The Sorcerer*, 1954) and his masterpiece, *Las manos de Dios* (*The Hands of God*, 1956), plus several one-act plays. He actively fomented theatre and theatre criticism with several books on Latin American theatre and a weekly column in a major Mexican journal. During the regime of López Portillo (1976–82) he served as executive director of an ambitious project under the social security department to organize the Teatro de la Nación (Theatre of the Nation). In 1994 he was honoured by the National Autonomous University of Mexico for his years of service to the university and for his work in the theatre. GW

Somigliana, Carlos 1932–87 Argentine playwright, lawyer and journalist. Somigliana was a figure in the realistic generation (see REALISM) of Argentine theatre of the 1960s. His major plays include *Amarillo* (*Yellow*, 1965), *El avión negro* (*The Black Airplane*, 1970), written in collaboration with COSSA, ROZENMACHER and TALESNIK, and short plays for TEATRO ABIERTO in 1981 and following years. GW

Sondheim, Stephen 1930– American lyricist and composer. After an apprenticeship with OSCAR HAMMERSTEIN II and some early writing for television, Sondheim created the lyrics for *West Side Story* (1957) and *Gypsy* (1959). In 1962 he received his first opportunity to write both music and lyrics for *A Funny Thing Happened on the Way to the Forum*. After a failure with *Anyone Can Whistle* (1970), he startled the MUSICAL THEATRE world with the scores for a series of highly experimental shows. *Company* (1970) was a collage of musical vignettes about married life in contemporary New York. *Follies* (1971) used a reunion of musical comedy performers to examine the effects of middle age on love and marriage. *A Little Night Music* (1973) had a score written entirely in three-four time. *Pacific Overtures* (1976) employed the conventions of Japanese KABUKI theatre and an all-Asian cast to tell of the opening of Japan to the West. *Sweeney Todd* (1979) adapted Victorian MELODRAMA to modern sensibilities by suggesting the tormented soul behind the 'demon barber of Fleet Street'. *Merrily We Roll Along* (1981) examined the myth of the American success story by tracing the lives of its central characters backwards from middle age to youth. *Sunday in the Park with George* (1984) explored the process of artistic creation by bringing to life the work of French painter Georges Seurat. *Into the Woods* (1987) explored the darker Freudian aspects of classic fairy tales. Sondheim's scores for each of these shows were characterized by brilliant, often cerebral lyrics and driving, unsentimental music.

Of his recent work, only *Assassins* (1991), which probed the minds of those who had attempted to assassinate US presidents, has failed to succeed, though it has fared better outside of New York. A compilation of Sondheim songs, *Putting It Together* (with Julie Andrews making her first New York appearance in 33 years and directed by Julia McKenzie), ran briefly OFF-BROADWAY in spring 1993 following its debut in Oxford, England (1992). A new musical with James Lapine, *Passion*, opened on BROADWAY in spring 1994, for which Sondheim won the 1994 Tony for Best Musical Score. He is generally considered to have been the most distinguished composer-lyricist in the musical theatre since the 1970s. In the late 1980s and early 90s several major revivals of his shows demonstrated anew his brilliance as lyricist and composer. MK

Sonnenfels, Josef von 1733–1817 Austrian critic. Strongly influenced by GOTTSCHED, Sonnenfels's *Letters on the Viennese Stage* (1768) attacked the local, improvised comedy and advocated a more decorous, scripted theatre. Although he did not succeed in dislodging the popular theatre, he had considerable influence on the founding of the BURGTHEATER and on the development of its ideals of ensemble. SW

Sophocles c.496–406/5 BC Greek tragedian from Colonus, near Athens. As a boy Sophocles is said to have led the singing of a paean to celebrate the Greek victory at Salamis (480). He produced his first set of plays in 468, and won first prize in the Great Dionysia (see GREECE, ANCIENT) although he was competing against AESCHYLUS. He is said to have given up acting in his own plays because of a weak voice, but had a remarkably long and successful career as a dramatist. He is said to have produced 132 plays (we know the titles of over 110) and never to have been placed third in the competitions. He probably won 18 victories at the Great Dionysia (making 72 victorious plays) and others at the Lenaea. It is doubtful whether any of his plays belonged to connected tetralogies; certainly, most did not. He is said to have been responsible for introducing the third actor (though this is also attributed to Aeschylus) and for increasing the size of the tragic Chorus from 12 to 15. He took an active part in public life, and his offices included a generalship (an elective one-year post) in 440/1 as a colleague of the statesman Pericles. In later times he had a reputation for piety, illustrated by various anecdotes.

The chronology of the seven surviving plays is uncertain. There is evidence dating *Antigone* to c.442, and some reason for thinking that *Ajax* and *Trachiniae* (*Women of Trachis*, concerning the death of Heracles) are earlier than this. *Oedipus Tyrannus* (*King Oedipus*) perhaps dates from the 420s. *Philoctetes* is securely dated to 409, and *Electra* may not be much earlier. *Oedipus at Colonus* was not produced until 401, after Sophocles' death. Thus even the earliest surviving plays may not have been written until Sophocles was in his 50s, and he seems to have written the latest – still assured masterpieces like the rest – when well into his 80s. We also possess about half of a satyr play, *Ichneutae* (*Trackers*, concerning the childhood of Hermes), and various shorter fragments.

Any reader of the seven plays senses common themes and purposes running through them. One constant factor is a concern with plot, regarded as a complete and coherent sequence of events, linked together by principles of cause and effect and of plausible human motivation. While critics have found problems in the construction of some of the plays – notably *Ajax*, *Trachiniae* and *Antigone*, in all of which a central character dies some time before the end – the importance of plot as a shaping and unifying principle is certainly greater than in Aeschylus or EURIPIDES (hence the admiration which Sophocles inspired in ARISTOTLE, who regarded *Oedipus Tyrannus* as the ideal TRAGEDY). With this goes the importance of prophecy: by the end of a play it generally turns out that the prophecy of an oracle or seer has been fulfilled, in a way that at least some of the characters did not expect or intend. This concern is paralleled in the work of the historian Herodotus, whom Sophocles probably knew, and no doubt reflects the dramatist's actual beliefs; but it also helps to shape the plays by making the denouement seem inevitable, and to make possible the pervasive dramatic irony.

Each of the plays is concerned with death (at least the possibility of it, though in *Philoctetes* no one actually dies); with human suffering (sometimes acute physical suffering, evoked in harrowing detail); and with abrupt changes of fortune, whether for good or ill (the mutability of fortune being a staple theme of Sophoclean moralizing). There is fruitful tension between this grim material and the harmonious form of the plays. While the effect of death, suffering and change is not softened by any real compensation or consolation, these things are seen to form part of a pattern; and this pattern reflects the working of the gods in human affairs. The gods do not act justly in any human sense (indeed, the characters may complain bitterly of their injustice, notably at the end of *Trachiniae*); nor do they act arbitrarily and unintelligibly.

Their perfect knowledge is set against the inevitably limited knowledge of mortals, who may bring disaster on themselves while acting with the best of motives (*Trachiniae*, *Oedipus Tyrannus*), and may deceive each other with lying messenger-speeches that are as plausible as any truthful ones (*Trachiniae*, *Electra*, *Philoctetes*).

Schematic attempts to make each play centre on a single 'Sophoclean hero' have not been successful (in *Trachiniae*, *Antigone* and *Philoctetes* they have led to sterile arguments as to who 'the hero' is). Nevertheless, each play contains a major character who, while he may be less attractive morally than those around him, wins our respect by his uncompromising adherence to some purpose, whatever the opposition and whatever the cost. Thus Ajax insists on suicide, Heracles on making outrageous demands on his son (though this case is rather different from the rest), Antigone on burying her brother, Oedipus (*Tyrannus*) on learning the truth about the killing of Laius and his own identity, Electra on opposing her father's murderers, Philoctetes on refusing to come to Troy, Oedipus (*at Colonus*) on remaining at Colonus and on cursing his sons. When this intransigence is set against the forces of change and illusion, the result is often the death of the 'hero'; but, as he remains morally undefeated, his courage attains a paradoxical value which transcends death itself. There is further paradox in the fact that two of these characters are women (the defiance of Antigone and Electra must have startled the Greek audience) while two others are destitute outcasts (Philoctetes and Oedipus (*at Colonus*)), who are granted power over other men's lives through the will of the gods, and whose inner strength enables them to resist manipulation by those men.

Characterization is always strong enough to provide a criterion by which actions may be judged plausible, but does not extend to psychologically detailed portraiture. The Chorus, while less central than in Aeschylus, is resourcefully used for various purposes. It often draws a moral lesson from the action that it witnesses, but such lessons are there for the sake of the play, not as ends in themselves; and, as it always remains within the framework of the drama, it often contributes to the dramatic irony by sharing the misapprehensions of the characters. In the choral odes Sophocles' style can be almost as ornate and elaborate as that of Aeschylus; in dialogue it is simpler, combining dignity and elevation with great suppleness and vigour. ALB

Sorge, Reinhard (Johannes) 1892–1916 German dramatist and poet, whose visionary play *The Beggar*, written in 1911 and produced posthumously by MAX REINHARDT in 1917, inaugurated lyrical EXPRESSIONISM. It has the subjective intensity, episodic structure, father–son conflict and mystical plea for the spiritual regeneration of mankind that typified idealistic expressionism. HR

Sorma, Agnes 1865–1927 German actress. Sorma was a woman of quite extraordinary grace and beauty, whose poetic style on stage complemented exactly the acting of JOSEF KAINZ, with whom she was a colleague at the DEUTSCHES THEATER from 1883 to 1899. Later she worked with MAX REINHARDT, specializing in both classical and contemporary leads. Her last years were spent in the USA. She died on her ranch in Arizona.   SW

Sosnitsky, Ivan (Ivanovich) 1794–1872 Along with KARATYGIN, one of the two leading St Petersburg (Russian) actors of his day. Trained by DMITREVSKY and later SHAKHOVSKOI, he was an attractive, elegant, charming and popular actor, who often paid more attention to polish than to feeling. He excelled as lovers, officers, rakes and dandies in light comedies and *vaudevilles*, and was noted for his skill in playing multiple roles in a single play via external transformation. SHCHEPKIN helped turn him into a more serious realistic actor, with the result that he inherited some of the 'old man' roles that had been his friend's staple since youth. Sosnitsky and Shchepkin each played the role of the Mayor in *The Inspector General* in the St Petersburg and Moscow premieres, respectively. The latter's portrayal was realistic, whereas the former's was in the spirit of *vaudeville*. The rivalry undermined their friendship. Other rogues in his gallery included Figaro, Tartuffe and Repetilov (*Woe from Wit*).   SG

Sothern, E(dward) A(skew) 1826–81 and **E(dward) H(ugh) Sothern** 1859–1933 American actors. Beginning his career as an eccentric comedian on English stages, the elder Sothern made his American debut as Dr Pangloss in *The Heir at Law* in 1852. He achieved sudden star status with LAURA KEENE's company when he assumed the role of Lord Dundreary in TOM TAYLOR's *Our American Cousin* in 1858 for an uninterrupted run of five months. In 1861, after 400 consecutive performances, Londoners indulged in frequent 'Dundrearyisms', and his distinctive side-whiskers, known as 'Dundrearies', became popular. Other Sothern roles included Dundreary's Brother Sam in the play of that name (1862), and the title roles in T. W. ROBERTSON's *DAVID GARRICK* (1864) and H. J. BYRON's *The Crushed Tragedian* (1878). Excelling in original comic business, the British-born actor remained popular on both sides of the Atlantic and died in London.

In 1879, Sothern provided the opportunity for his American-born son, E. H. Sothern, to make his debut in New York in a small role in *Brother Sam*. Playing in England and America, the younger Sothern gained experience in the companies of JOHN MCCULLOUGH, Helen Dauvray and others. In 1887 DANIEL FROHMAN engaged Sothern for the newly formed company at New York's LYCEUM THEATRE. Sothern quickly established himself as a dashing romantic hero in such roles as Prince Rudolph in *The Prisoner of Zenda* (1895). Still under Frohman's management, Sothern broadened his range to poetic drama in 1900 as the hero in HAUPTMANN's *The Sunken Bell* and as Hamlet. Under the management of CHARLES FROHMAN, Sothern first appeared with JULIA MARLOWE (whom he married in 1911) in *Romeo and Juliet* in 1904. Together, until Marlowe's retirement, they reigned for a decade as America's foremost Shakespearian players. Sothern wrote his memoirs in 1916 and retired in 1927.   MR

sottie see MEDIEVAL DRAMA IN EUROPE (France)

Soulié, Frédéric 1800–47 French dramatist and novel-

E. A. Sothern as Lord Dundreary in Tom Taylor's *Our American Cousin*.

ist. Soulié's reputation as a dramatist rests on the plays written during the 1840s. His early plays, written for the ODÉON, were mostly historical with some literary pretension. An adaptation of *Romeo and Juliet* (1828) was the first to be performed, followed by a disastrous *Christine à Fontainebleau* (1829), which had to be replaced by DUMAS père's rather more successful play on the same theme. His interest in a more socially committed type of drama could be seen in *L'Homme à la blouse* (*The Man in a Smock*), at the Porte-Saint-Martin (1832; see BOULEVARD). In the later 1830s he published a series of novels, most of them in *feuilleton* form, which he subsequently adapted for the theatre.

The short-lived Renaissance Theatre (1838–41), which aimed at a high-quality repertoire under the direction of Antenor Joly, with the collaboration of HUGO and Dumas, was temporarily saved from closure by the success of Soulié's *Diane de Chivri* (1839), which together with *Le Fils de la folle* (*The Son of the Madwoman*) and *Le Proscrit* formed a trilogy on French history from the Revolution to the reign of Louis Philippe. The MELODRAMA theatres gave Soulié the outlet he really needed. Starting with *Le*

Proscrit (*The Workman*, 1840), he wrote a series of highly profitable plays for the Ambigu-Comique. The populist appeal was strong, with villains, robbers and virtuous workers amongst the dramatis personae. With *Gaetan, Il Mammone* (1842) he turned to a complex Neapolitan plot and provided an excellent role for the popular boulevard actor, MÉLINGUE. *Eulalie Pontois* (1843) was pure melodrama, heavily dependent upon complicated plot and Gothic castles. *Les Amants de Murcie* (1844) was a rather more romantic Spanish version of *Romeo and Juliet*. *Les Talismans* (1845) exploited a contemporary fashion for the diabolical, and the cast included good and bad angels in a variety of guises. His much lighter piece, *Les Étudiants* (*The Students*, 1845), anticipated Henri Murger's presentation of student life.

Soulié's last, and major, work was *La Closerie des genêts* (1846), adapted by BOUCICAULT as *The Willow Copse*, which contained material from two of his novels, *The She-Tiger of Paris* (*La Lionne*) and its sequel *The Countess of Monrion*. The play ran for hundreds of performances and took five hours to play. It is often regarded as one of the best plays of the reign of Louis Philippe. Its interest is in the wide range of carefully studied social types and in the interaction of different traditions in post-Napoleonic France. The complicated plot looks seriously at social attitudes to illegitimacy and also introduces a particularly unpleasant villainess, Leona, with an unsavoury past, anticipating such characters in the plays of the latter half of the century.   JMCC

sound in the theatre

Sound effects In the days before microphones, gramophone records and tape recorders, sound in the theatre depended upon mechanical and live effects. The creation of these was a great art and was usually the domain of the property department. Even in the mid-1950s, although gramophone records had very much taken over, live effects were still employed. Rather than hire expensive sound equipment and records, producers would insist, say, that mechanical wind or wave machines, clock chimes or metal thunder sheets be used.

Certain sounds will probably be more convincingly produced 'live', or manually. For example, a pistol shot with a real gun and a blank cartridge has a sharpness and imme-

Taped sound effects at the Theatre Royal, Drury Lane, London, 1957.

diacy difficult to achieve with an electronic sound system. The sounds of door bells, phone bells, door chimes and door knockers are usually more easily achieved live. Glass and crockery crashes are also better with the real thing. One of the most famous of all sound effects sequences was for *The Ghost Train* by Arnold Ridley. First produced at the St Martin's Theatre in London in 1925, it is still a firm favourite with repertory and amateur companies. The stage directions in the original script call for an assortment of tubular bells, garden rollers, galvanized iron tanks, thunder sheets, drums, air cylinders, whistles, milk churns, mallets and wire brushes, and require six carefully rehearsed stagehands to create the various train sounds.

During the late 1940s and into the 1950s the use of 78rpm sound effects discs was prevalent. The sounds were selected from specialist libraries and transferred to lacquer disc. Usually only two or three items were recorded on each single side, to allow for maximum flexibility during replay. Music was still obtainable only on 78rpm commercial discs, since the new long-playing record (at that incredibly low speed of $33\frac{1}{3}$rpm) was only introduced in the mid-50s.

The turntable units for the 78rpm effects discs were rugged affairs, incorporating large valve (or tube) amplifiers and loudspeaker switching. Each pick-up arm had a lowering device and some form of patent groove-locator. In Britain, these large gramophones were called 'panatropes', and instead of 'sound cues' stage managers used to write 'pan cues' in their prompt scripts. A selection of sound effects discs was very convenient during rehearsals because the director could call for any combination, sequence and balance of effects *in situ*. Because of this flexibility, the BBC radio drama department still uses sound effects discs if rehearsing and broadcasting a play on the same day.

American theatre was a few years ahead of Britain with the transition from disc to tape. The first major production in London to use reel-to-reel tape machines was *My Fair Lady*, which transferred from BROADWAY to the Theatre Royal, DRURY LANE, in 1957. From around this period UK theatres began to employ recording tape, although the use of 78rpm discs was not uncommon well into the 1960s.

Standard tape *cassette* recorders have not proved very successful in the theatre because of the inaccurate nature of the tape counter which makes it impossible to locate the start of an effect with any degree of certainty, the relatively slow mechanical start, and the impossibility of editing. Tape *cartridge* recorders, on the other hand, have been popular in the professional theatre since the early 1980s because they are compact, mechanically silent and extremely accurate in operation. These machines were developed particularly for use in radio stations for the convenient handling of jingles and commercials. The thin tape is contained on a single spool within an enclosed plastic cartridge, with the tape exposed at the front like a standard cassette. The cartridge slots into an opening in the machine rather like a video recorder.

However, against any advantages a cartridge player might have in terms of accuracy and flexibility in playing in effects, there are a number of drawbacks. For example, there is no fast rewind facility and the forward wind (to return to the start of the recording) is relatively slow. This can be very frustrating in a rehearsal situation. Editing is not really feasible on a cartridge, and the quickest way to modify an effect is to revert to the standard reel-to-reel master tape, make the changes, and record the result on to a new cartridge. There is also a cost factor, in that it is still necessary to have reel-to-reel machines for making up the original sound tracks, and one usually needs a number of cartridge players for playing the sound sequences in the theatre. As with the old 78rpm lacquer gramophone records, it is common practice, for maximum flexibility, to have a separate cartridge for each effect.

DAT cassette recorders (digital audio tape) are suitable for theatre use, although not widely employed. The quality of this digital recording process is of the highest; moreover, each cue can be identified with a number or by an accurate clock read-out. When the pre-programmed cue number is dialled, the machine will run to the beginning of a sound sequence and be ready for an almost instantaneous start.

Advances in computer technology, combined with ever-increasing memory power and the ever-decreasing cost of micro-chips, means that the larger subsidized theatre companies, such as the ROYAL NATIONAL THEATRE in London, have since the mid-1980s been moving towards solid-state digital *tapeless sound*.

Digital samplers coupled with MIDI (Musical Instrument Digital Interface) control keyboards are ideal systems for playing back sound in the theatre. There are no moving parts, there is instantaneous access, and there is high-quality sound. Sounds can be recorded (sampled) in mono or stereo into the sampler, where they can easily be edited with the aid of a screen showing the wave form. When the beginning and end of an effect have been cleaned up and any other unwanted material has been edited, the effect is assigned to a key on the keyboard. Thus, every time this key is touched, the sound will play.

It is also possible to shift the pitch of a particular effect (e.g. to make a bell sound lower and a more sonorous or a large hound sound like a yappy dog), to add reverberation or other processing, and to assign other properties such as routing and volume level. The sound designer, having built up a sequence of different effects on the keyboard, is able to sit in the auditorium and 'play sounds'. The touch of a key in rehearsal or performance will retrieve a particular sound with the predetermined amount of processing and the chosen pitch at the correct volume level routed to the selected loudspeaker.

Most of the everyday sounds of weather, traffic, birds, animals, aircraft, bells, people and so on can be obtained on commercial recordings. However, these recordings are limited both in their range and in the duration of the tracks. With portable recording equipment, many natural sounds can be captured. But be warned – it can be a very time-consuming exercise and sometimes impossible to capture the desired effect without unwanted background noises; and in the theatre it is essential to have clean sound effects. Therefore it is often necessary, and sometimes even preferable, to simulate effects in front of a microphone where extraneous noises can be eliminated altogether.

Sound effects are used in the theatre for a variety of reasons:

1 to establish (a) locale (b) time of year (c) day or night (d) weather conditions;
2 to evoke atmosphere;
3 to link scenes;
4 to provide an emotional stimulus;
5 to reproduce physical happenings: e.g. cars arriving, babies crying, clocks striking.

Because one is usually putting a single sound on to a single loudspeaker, theatre recordings are more often than not monaural. But there are exceptions. For example, in most cases music is enhanced by stereo. Stereo can also be useful for providing breadth and perspective to scenes involving crowds, battles, traffic, sea effects, and so forth. Travelling sounds like cars, aeroplanes and trains can, of course, be recorded in stereo, but will be fixed in their timing. It is much more flexible to have the same mono sound on twin tracks fed separately to two loudspeakers. Then, when the relative gains are adjusted, the effect can be moved between the loudspeakers at will. Twin tracks may also be used for two different continuous effects of indeterminate length: e.g. rain on one track and wind on the other. This leaves a second tape machine free for superimposing other effects.

Sound reinforcement and public address Public address systems were originally, as implied, functional systems for addressing the public where quality of sound was secondary to the clear transmission of information. A significant improvement in quality did not come about until the explosion of the pop music scene during the 1960s. A new breed of high-performance sound equipment was developed so that recording artists like the Beatles and the Rolling Stones could present themselves in concert to vast audiences. Sound reinforcement systems, on the other hand, were originally conceived to present the listener with an amplified yet natural sound, with the microphone (or microphones) not necessarily near the performer.

Modern musicals more often than not call for a combination of the close and distant microphone techniques to produce louder than natural sound – in other words, a cross between reinforcement and public address. This requirement has arisen partly because audiences have become used to the electronic sound of broadcasting, films and pop concerts and are less prepared to concentrate in the theatre than was once the case; and partly because modern technology has made it possible to produce a larger-than-life sound for a live performance. Another factor is that composers, knowing that a sound system will be available, feel freer to write orchestration which once would have been appropriate only in a recording studio. Also, the style of acting has changed: a large percentage of actors have either lost the art of projection or are content to rely upon the sound system to reach the audience at the back of the room.

From the 1930s to the late 1960s a theatre speech reinforcement system would normally consist of a set of microphones on raised stands along the front edge of the stage, two or four (probably column) loudspeakers on the proscenium driven by one or two power amplifiers, and a simple mixer with rotary master volume and treble and bass controls. The operating procedure was to turn the master control up for the songs and down for the dialogue. This is a far cry from the sophisticated mixing desks that are now installed in theatres, where the balance engineers often have to control 60 or more microphones. The first musical in London to use a recording-studio style of mixing desk was STEPHEN SONDHEIM's *Company*, first produced on Broadway in 1970 and later that year transferred to London. It is interesting to note that the Broadway production was still employing a number of the old-style rotary fader mixers.

Around this period it became the practice to site the mixing desk within the body of the auditorium, for balancing the sound of musicals. Before this, microphone controls plus disc and tape playback units would be located somewhere on the side of the stage, where the sound operator could only guess at what the audience was hearing.

Loudspeakers Whether we are dealing with reinforcement or PA, a suitable location has to be found for the loudspeakers, and their positioning and angling are critical. The basic requirements are that they should be sited as near to the stage as possible to maintain the illusion of the sound coming from the actors; they should be on the audience side of the microphones to minimize acoustic feedback; and they should be angled to provide direct sound to every seat in the house.

In theory, a single sound source in the centre above the proscenium will give the 'cleanest' sound, as the number of sound paths and therefore the chances of unwanted reflections will thereby have been reduced to a minimum. Furthermore, the sound source is not in close proximity to any one section of the audience. One of the drawbacks to this solution is that often there is a sightline cut-off from overhanging balconies. If there are seats in the house where it is not possible to see the top of the proscenium the people sitting there will not receive direct sound. And, of course, these are the areas which normally require the most help from a sound system. A solution might be to add some small loudspeakers to 'fill in' the dead areas. But if this is attempted it will be necessary to incorporate some form of electronic time delay; otherwise, because electricity travels faster than airborne sound, the audience at the back would hear the sound from the nearer 'fill-in' loudspeakers a fraction of a second before the main loudspeakers and the natural sound from the stage. This can be a disconcerting effect, certainly destroying the realism and often actually hindering intelligibility. A correctly delayed sound can be surprisingly loud (up to 10dB louder than the source at the listening point) without sacrificing realism. This is because the human brain always registers the initial sound received as being the source.

Acoustic feedback, or 'howlround' Caused by the signal from a loudspeaker being picked up by a microphone, then going round through the system and out of the loudspeaker again *ad infinitum*. Sound reflecting off walls, ceilings and balcony fronts back to the microphone can be a prime cause of feedback. For this reason we tend to use loudspeakers with directional characteristics, so that the sound is delivered to where it is required and reflections back to the microphones from walls and balcony fronts are kept to a minimum. So an overhead loudspeaker array in an auditorium might consist of one or a number of bass units (which will not be very directional) plus some mid- and high-frequency reproducers which will have directional properties.

Sometimes additional loudspeakers are installed at the sides of the proscenium in order to cater for stereo music reproduction and, perhaps, to bring the 'image' of the sound down from the overhead loudspeaker array. Where a central loudspeaker position is not suitable or not desired, then the side proscenium locations become the prime source.

Microphones In a reinforcement system where the requirement is for maximum pick-up with minimum potential feedback, we deal almost exclusively with directional, or 'cardioid' (so called because of their heart-shaped pick-up pattern), microphones. The most obvious and usually the most important position for reinforcement microphones is along the front edge of the stage, being directly in the firing line between the actors and the audience. We call microphones in this position 'foot mics' or, more commonly in Britain, 'float mics'. (This is because all theatres once had lights in this position called 'footlights', which were originally known as 'floats' because they consisted of lighted wicks floating in wax.)

It used to be the object of every sound engineer to raise the float microphones as near as possible to the source of sound – that is, the actor's head. But in the late 1960s some American engineers were testing out a large installation and discovered that one of the microphones appeared to perform more efficiently than all the others. Upon closer inspection they were surprised to find that the microphone in question had fallen from its stand and was resting on the floor.

Subsequent experiments with test equipment produced the explanation that when a microphone is raised in the air it will receive direct sound plus reflections from the floor, and these reflections will not only make for a less clean sound but the short time lag will mean that certain groups of frequencies will arrive at the microphone out of phase with those of the original signal. This produces a cancelling effect in those frequencies. Thus the quality of sound is impaired. If the microphone is placed at floor level the direct and reflected sound waves arrive at the microphone at almost the same instant, producing a tighter sound with no audible cancellation effect. And there are additional benefits, in that not only does the floor act as a radiator but the microphone in this low position is more shielded from the sounds emanating from the orchestra pit.

'Pressure zone' or 'sound field' microphones, which are especially designed to be placed on hard, reflective surfaces, have been commonly used as float microphones since the late 1970s. Transmitted foot noise is checked by correct shock mounting to insulate the microphone from floor vibrations. Shock mounts especially designed for float microphones are now available. If the action takes place at some distance from the front of the stage or upon raised platforms, it may be necessary to employ overhead microphones. These will normally be of the very directional 'shotgun' variety.

It has become common practice for leading performers in musicals each to be equipped with a wireless microphone. The kit comes in two or three parts: the microphone and transmitter, which can be separate or integral, and the receiver. The receiver with its aerial (or antenna) simply plugs into an input on the mixer, like an ordinary microphone. The transmitter pack, tuned to the same frequency as the receiver, is secreted somewhere in the actor's clothing, usually fixed securely to a belt around the waist. The associated microphone will ideally be a miniature unit only a little larger in circumference than the narrow-gauge wire to which it is attached. The optimum position for the microphone is just within the hair line at the centre of the forehead. The wire is brought from the transmitter up to the actor's body and over the head, taped as necessary with medical sticking plaster or similar.

If the microphone is too large for mounting in this manner, it can be fixed to the clothing so that it is approximately 4in (100cm) below the chin in a central position. It is vital to ensure that the head of the microphone is completely exposed or, at most, covered by only a thin piece of material. The microphone will be of the omnidirectional variety, providing a general pick-up to cope with all the head movements. Since it is so near the source of sound there are unlikely to be serious feedback problems.

For the cabaret or concert performer and for some musicals, hand-held microphones are called for. They may be either wireless systems or conventional microphones with trailing leads. If the musical backing is on stage it will be necessary to use a very directional microphone (hyper-cardioid) and one which is designed to be used close to the mouth. Both of these factors will help exclude the orchestral sounds and allow the voice to predominate. This type of microphone will have a built-in 'windshield' or 'pop-gag' to stop explosive breath sounds. Other microphones designed for close work under less stringent conditions – either on a stand or in the hand – will be straightforward cardioids with, perhaps, optional windshields for use as necessity dictates. Some performers find a very directional microphone difficult to handle because one can so easily move 'off-mike'.

Amplifying musical instruments There are different techniques for amplifying musical instruments, but most of these employ a directional microphone placed as near the source of sound as possible: e.g. near the bridge of a violin, the bell of a wind instrument, the struck surface of a drum or cymbal, the loudspeaker of an electric guitar or organ. There are available 'contact microphones' which are actually attached to the sounding boards of instruments like pianos, harps and double basses, where the microphone reacts to the vibrations of the sounding board. The main advantage is the exclusion of pick-up from other instruments.

With electronic instruments there is an excellent way of ensuring a 'clean' sound. This is with the use of a little plugging unit called a direct-injection box. This box accepts the feed at the pre-amplifier stage from the guitar or keyboard and splits it two ways: one into the instrument's own amplifier in the normal way, and the other straight into the mixer. So a microphone is not used at all because the signal is directly injected into the mixer. Some instrument amplifiers incorporate a suitable output for sending direct signals to the mixer. There are also 'microphone inserts' of different types especially designed to be inserted into various wind instruments. The object is to obtain as clean a sound as possible.

The control position It is as important for the sound technician to hear what the audience is hearing as for the lighting switchboard operator to see what the audience is seeing. It can even be argued that with a complicated sound balance it is much more important. For, whereas lighting levels when plotted will remain the same for every performance, sound levels will vary. The number of people in the auditorium, even the clothes they are wearing (whether lightweight or heavy and absorbent) will have an influence. The amount of humidity in the air also has an effect. When one is working with microphones the changes can be quite dramatic. Every performance will need a slightly different balance. A particular performer may be 'giving' more or less or may be at a different distance from the microphone; or the orchestra may be playing louder or softer, and so on.

If a theatre has a permanent sound control room, it should be located in the auditorium at the centre rear of the main floor or first tier. (The central position is particularly vital for balancing stereo.) It should be soundproofed to the auditorium but have a very large window, which opens easily and quietly, affording an unrestricted view of the stage and orchestra pit. The control room should have a space for the mixing desk, two or more tape machines, disc turntable and other playback devices, processing equipment, and plug patch panels for microphone and line level signals. The ventilation system should be adequate and *silent*. Heat dissipation from power amplifiers should be taken into consideration.

For balancing a multi-microphone set-up for a musical, it is essential for the operator to be within the acoustic environment of the auditorium, where the combination of the original sound from the stage, the amplified sound from the loudspeakers plus the natural reflections from walls, ceilings and other surfaces can be assessed. An alternative plug-in point in the auditorium, with all the necessary microphone lines and tie-lines to power amplifiers and so on, will facilitate the movement of a portable mixer from the control room, as required.   DC

See: D. Collison, *Stage Sound*, London, 1976.

South Africa Political relations in a racially heterogeneous population of nearly 40 million people have produced fundamental cultural tensions in South Africa in the latter half of the 20th century. In the mid-1990s. it strives for identity as a non-racial democracy.

These tensions have found expression for decades in a multiplicity of theatrical forms and traditions, mainly dealing with race and politics. As a result of colonization and the subsequent control of the means of production and distribution of resources, nearly 5 million 'white' people of European descent wielded political power over the rest of the population, of whom nearly 30 million were disfranchised blacks of African descent.

This latter group comprises descendants of the Bantu-speaking aboriginal peoples who had settled in the sub-continent before the arrival of European settlers in the 17th century. These Africans of the pre-colonial period practised various forms of dramatic enactment – in, for example, songs and storytelling narratives. Some of these, like the Xhosa *intsomi* and the Zulu *inganekwane*, would be invoked by later dramatists and theatre practitioners as important models for 'authentic' African theatrical dialogue and action. In addition, the Zulu *izibongo* tradition of 'praise poetry' employed mimetic narrative and dance in a form which incorporated oral communication as well as broadly gestural enactment. Religious RITUALS and military and political ceremonies also called for dramatic enactment through movement, speech and singing. The occasion of such performance was a major determinant of form and theme: the pieces were functional in relation to the tribal social structure or to religious custom.

These indigenous performance traditions are by no means based upon merely archaic forms: they are still constantly practised and re-created, changing in theme and style in relation to historical developments. They have continued into the present in two ways. First, many of them have been commodified. The most obvious arena for their contemporary performance is the gold-mining compound, where tribal groupings are often maintained. In some cases traditional forms have undergone metamorphosis in accordance with the changed circumstances of the migrant labourer. One such contemporary form of oral poetry is *sefela*, which enacts the life and experience of the migrant labourer temporarily uprooted from his rural home. Second, some of the aspects of visual and oral communication derived from narratives and praise poetry have been incorporated into contemporary theatrical forms. Many plays, especially in the 1980s, relied heavily in performance on the traditions of narration and solo enactment that have their roots in the early indigenous forms: in the 1980s, for example, Mbongeni Ngema's *Asinamali!* and the workshop-produced *Woza Albert!*

Apart from these modes of performance among the Bantu-speaking peoples, there is evidence of other modes in the cultural traditions of other ethnic groups: e.g. in the games and ceremonies of the nomadic Bushman communities which roam over vast areas of semi-desert terrain in the Cape Province are found the *Khoi-San* traditions of dance, MIME and narrative enactments whose history goes back more than six thousand years. Thus, many roots of African performance were already firmly established when the European settlers arrived.

As part of the strategy to maintain white hegemony, authoritative accounts of South African cultural history for decades largely ignored these indigenous African traditions and focused instead on the European influence. Thus a performance of BEAUMARCHAIS's *The Barber of Seville* given in 1783 by French troops at the military barracks in Cape Town (at that time an important refreshment station on the sea route to the East) was commonly considered to be the earliest recorded instance of theatrical performance in South Africa. From this event one can trace the growth and development of European tradition in South African theatre – although alongside this tradition there were always alternative indigenous and syn-

The Market Theatre Company's production of Mbongeni Ngema's *Asinamali! (We have no Money)*. The prisoners' story is related through a kaleidoscope of song, dance and mime.

cretic forms – one of the earliest of which was the Anglicized Dutch dramatic poem *Kaatje Kekkelbek*, in the first decade of the 19th century.

The dominant cultural influence from the beginning of the 19th century coincided with British rule over the Cape Colony. After the founding in 1801 of the first theatre – the African Theatre in Cape Town – visiting professionals and entrepreneurs imported European plays and players. Actor-managers and impresarios arriving from England and elsewhere in Europe developed theatre under the influence of European theatrical models. Then the discovery of diamonds in 1867 and of gold in 1886 brought an influx of immigrants, which in turn determined the growth of amateur theatre in the different European languages to cater for the needs of a new cosmopolitan audience. By the end of the century, Afrikaans drama had appeared. The first Afrikaans play, S. J. du Toit's *Magrita Prinslo*, was produced in 1897. After the Anglo-Boer War in 1902 Afrikaans nationalism found expression in a wave of patriotic writings such as C. J. Langenhoven's drama *Die Hoop van Suid-Afrika (The Hope of South Africa)* in 1912, and in numerous other Afrikaans plays which were toured by companies to the rural areas – at that time dominated by Afrikaans farming communities.

By the beginning of the 20th century the large cities boasted numerous well equipped theatre buildings modelled on London's WEST END theatres, and during the first quarter of the century both Afrikaans and English companies established an infrastructure for professional theatre. In addition, again in both languages, there was a thriving amateur theatre industry. Perhaps less influential in the development of South African theatre, but nonetheless an important strand in the spectrum of performance styles and forms, were equestrian spectacles (see HIPPODRAMA), PANTOMIME and MELODRAMA, VAUDEVILLE and MUSIC-HALL, the CIRCUS and popular entertainments from France, Germany, England and the USA. Anglo-European political dominance was reinforced by cultural activities in which the theatre played an important role.

While the second quarter of the century witnessed the consolidation of this process, important developments were taking place in theatre among black communities. In 1927 the first published Xhosa drama was G. B. Sinxo's *Debeza's Baboons*; and in 1935 HERBERT DHLOMO became the first black person to publish a play in English, with his drama about the Xhosa legend, *The Girl Who Killed to Save: Nongqause the Liberator*. The black middle class began to assert a taste for theatre based on European models of dramatic literature, and elitist clubs were formed, such as the Johannesburg Bantu Dramatic Society in 1932. Meanwhile, a popular form of theatre among working-class blacks began to make an impact. Mthethwa's Lucky Stars was founded in Natal in 1927 as the first professional black troupe, and toured the country with plays based on Zulu legends and customs, performing in the vernacular to popular acclaim.

During the 1930s and 40s the urbanization of Africans, gathered in slum yards and communities in and near the big cities, produced syncretic forms of music and theatre. The synthesis of tribal and traditional with Western models of performance, especially from the USA, would lead eventually to the important point when, in 1959, the black MUSICAL *King Kong*, about the rise and fall of a heavyweight boxer, brought African musicals and actors to the attention of theatregoers in Johannesburg, London and New York.

Meanwhile, English and Afrikaans theatre profited from a number of developments. The growth of professional and amateur theatre until the end of the Second World War was rapid but eclectic, and some cohesion was necessary. In 1938 a nationwide coordination of amateur theatre groups had been achieved when P. P. B. Breytenbach founded the Federation of Amateur Theatrical Societies of South Africa. Then in 1947 emerged the National Theatre Organization, and Breytenbach soon became chairman of this first state-funded body for professional theatre. During the 1950s the NTO provided important training and experience for a new generation of actors and directors, and in 1963 the process of consolidation was crystallized with the formation of provincial performing arts councils. This coincided with the entrenchment of rigid racial segregation in theatres, and a consequent international playwrights' boycott. As it came of age, the state-funded theatre found itself symbolizing the political system that had brought South Africa international disrepute.

In opposition to this theatre, alternative forms emerged among practitioners determined to defy government policies on racial segregation. One important group was Union Artists, which coordinated activities on behalf of black musicians and actors. This was the group which produced *King Kong*. It also gave encouragement to an important generation of theatre practitioners, among them ATHOL FUGARD and GIBSON KENTE. Both were to forge independent careers in the 1960s, 70s and 80s – Fugard as a white liberal exploring on stage the relationships of South Africans frustrated by social and political pressures, and Kente as a black entrepreneur creating popular musicals about life in the black townships. While, for two decades after 1963, Afrikaans theatre was confined almost totally within the performing arts councils, a number of English writers emerged to present their work in FRINGE THEATRES, though none achieved the sustained success of Fugard's work. Far more important for English-language theatre after 1963 was the training and experience gained in the performing arts councils by a number of theatre practitioners who would make an important contribution in the 1970s. The experimental theatre that emanated from the Arena Company, under the auspices of the performing arts council of the Transvaal in Johannesburg, and from the Space Company, in Cape Town, provided arguably the most innovative theatre amongst English-speaking whites in the 1970s.

At the same time, an important development occurred with the growth of black nationalism. The Black Consciousness movement began in the universities and quickly spread to other sectors of the black populace. Black Consciousness led to radical changes in black politics, and black cultural expression became one way of asserting an alternative South African cultural identity.

Militant political theatre emerged from groups like the People's Experimental Theatre and the Theatre Council of Natal. Both were cited in the charge sheet at a trial under the Terrorism Act for their involvement in the dissemination of 'subversive' plays and literature. Significantly, the groups involved in what was defined as 'black' theatre in the 1970s comprised, in addition to Africans, the other population groups categorized by the state as 'Indian' and 'coloured'. Throughout the country, among all three population groups, theatre became a means to assert black nationalism. Even Gibson Kente introduced a more pronounced political theme into his musicals, and the title of his play *How Long?* attained a symbolic importance in the revolutionary action which developed among schoolchildren in the townships in 1976. Meanwhile, one of the most radically innovative groups, Workshop 71, began its work. Creating plays in 'workshop', this non-racial group challenged the conventions of South African theatre, making plays out of the experiences of its participants, and produced an impressive range of forms and themes, in plays such as *uNosilimela*, *Survival* and *Crossroads*.

These workshop techniques, as well as the wave of black political militancy, did not fail to influence white theatre practitioners, and in the 1970s fringe groups emerged, producing plays about South African politics and race relations. The Market Theatre in Johannesburg and the People's Space Theatre in Cape Town were two of the most innovative, providing venues for many of Fugard's works as well as for works by a number of other young writers and directors. The extraordinary international success of John Kani and Winston Ntshona, the actors who created *Sizwe Bansi Is Dead* (1972) with Fugard, inspired many groups to adopt improvisatory methods in the creation of theatre, and by the end of the 1970s South African theatre had rejected many of its European and American models and discovered its own voice.

After 1976 the home for most of this new work was the Market Theatre, which focused on developing theatre about the cultural contradictions of South African life. In the 1980s one of the most successful plays to emerge was *Woza Albert!*, created in workshop by director Barney Simon with actors Percy Mtwa and MBONGENI NGEMA. Four other factors were related to the developing political crisis in the 1980s. First, as various black trade unions produced plays about working conditions and union solidarity as one way of educating workers about these important issues, trade union workers' theatre emerged. Second, the township musical, which remained the dominant form of theatre in the townships in the hands of people like Kente, began to be supplemented by political plays. Major exponents of black political drama included Dukuza ka Macu, MATSEMELA MANAKA, MAISHE MAPONYA, Mzwandile Maqina, Percy Mtwa and Ngema. Third, a new wave of white Afrikaans playwrights appeared. These included Deon Opperman and Reza de Wet, whose work was innovative with regard to forms and techniques, and frequently involved experimental pieces dealing with sexual and psychological taboos related to political anxiety. Fourth, English-speaking playwrights began to recognize the importance of multilingualism in South African theatre, and a new generation of playwrights like PAUL SLABOLEPSZY, Sue Pam and Opperman exemplified these discoveries by creating plays which provided insights into the fears and anxieties, the hopes and aspirations, of the younger generation of South Africans facing a post-apartheid society.

Apart from politically committed theatre there also existed a popularly supported commercial theatre. In the 1970s African musicals, backed by white capital and marketing expertise, enjoyed lengthy seasons both in South Africa and abroad. Though popular with audiences, these were often criticized as inauthentic 'tribal musicals' exploiting indigenous culture for commercial gain – the visiting card of black Africa in Europe. Most prominent of the genre was the musical *Ipi-Tombi*, while *Umabatha*, a Zulu adaptation of *Macbeth*, achieved critical acclaim at the 1972 World Theatre Season in London. White commercial theatre also flourished in South Africa's major cities, despite (and perhaps partly because of) the introduction of television in 1976. From the 1950s to the 80s these commercial theatre enterprises relied almost exclusively on British and American FARCES and whodunnits. By the 1990s, however, the partial breakdown in racial exclusivity began to influence even these bastions of Anglo-American culture in South Africa, and some cross-over work began to find its way into the commercial theatres.

After 1994, when the country's first democratic elections had taken place and a non-racial government had been installed, the performing arts councils and the civic and commercial theatres began to reflect these developments by employing black artists in key positions. Not all of these appointments were cosmetic: many of the appointees were able to exert pronounced influence in some of the old bastions of apartheid theatre. At the same time, a new union, the Performing Arts Workers' Equity, an organization dedicated to eradicating all vestiges of race and gender discrimination in theatre in South Africa, effected major changes in policy within the theatre industry.

By the mid-1990s South African theatre has built up an impressive infrastructure. Political theatre and theatre based on the country's unique social problems has given birth to a new identity, after decades during which Eurocentric models predominated. Commercial success associated with the new forms of theatre has given rise to independent professional companies. Training facilities proliferate as universities and colleges offer courses in all aspects of the performing arts. The fledgeling television and film industries are providing new expanding outlets for graduates, and each of the major cities can boast impressively equipped theatre buildings. As the apartheid system has been steadily dismantled, the theatre appears to have arrived at full maturity. IS

See: D. Coplan, *In Township Tonight: South Africa's Black City Music and Theatre*, Johannesburg, 1985; A. Fuchs, *Playing the Market: The Market Theatre, Johannesburg, 1976–1986*, Chur, 1990; S, Gray, *South African Plays*, Johannesburg, 1993; T. Hauptfleisch and I. Steadman, *South African Theatre: Four Plays and an Introduction*, Pretoria, 1984, and (eds.), *South African Theatre Journal*, Univ. of Stellenbosch; International Defence and Aid Fund for Southern Africa, *Black Theatre in South African* London, 1976; R. Kavanagh (ed.), *South African People's Plays*, London, 1981, and

Theatre and Cultural Struggle in South Africa, London, 1985; A. von Kotze, *Organise and Act: The Natal Workers' Theatre Movement 1983–87*, Univ. of Natal, Durban, 1988; M. Orkin, *Drama and the South African State*, Manchester and Johannesburg, 1991; I. Steadman, 'Theatre beyond Apartheid', *Research in African Literatures*, 22, 3, 1991, and 'Performance and Politics in Process', *Theatre Survey*, 33, 1992.

Southerne, Thomas 1660–1746 Irish playwright. Educated at Trinity College, Dublin, he entered the Middle Temple in London in 1680. After writing two plays, *The Loyal Brother* (1682) and *The Disappointment* (1684), he joined the Army as an ensign in 1685 rising to captain in 1688, when he turned back to the theatre. Between 1690 and 1696 he wrote five plays and, though he continued to write plays infrequently until 1726, none of his later work was as successful.

Sir Anthony Love (1690) gave Susanna Mountfort a virtuoso role in a BREECHES PART as the disguised woman playing at being a rake. *The Wives' Excuse* (1691), Southerne's best play, is a large-scale depiction of the intrigues of society, placing at its centre a serious portrayal of the unfortunate wife who refuses to take the easy option advocated by Southerne's subtitle, 'cuckolds make themselves', as revenge of her foolish husband's treatment of her. In its representation of the complex interconnections of events in a closely knit community, the play is extraordinary. *The Maid's Last Prayer* (1693) is a similar though even more vicious SATIRE on some women's pursuit of 'any, rather than fail', this play's subtitle. Southerne's two tragedies from this period were both long-lasting successes and both based on novellas by APHRA BEHN: *The Fatal Marriage* (1695) from *The Nun* points forward to a more sentimental form of tragedy; *Oroonoko* (1695) is a fine example of the sentimental noble-savage play, combining noble actions with exotic locations. Throughout his career Southerne was admired by all other writers and gained a particular reputation for his attempts to help younger dramatists with their first plays. PH

Southwark Theatre (Philadelphia) In 1766, DAVID DOUGLASS erected America's first substantial theatre just outside Philadelphia's city limits to avert official interference; it was to remain active for 51 years. On its stage, Douglass presented the first play by an American-born playwright, Thomas Godfrey's *The Prince of Parthia* (1767). Closed by the Continental Congress in 1774, it was used briefly as a hospital, then reopened by British occupation troops for entertainments to benefit widows and orphans. A drop curtain attributed to Major John André continued to be used until the theatre closed. The playhouse was two and a half storeys high, painted red, brick in its lower storey and surmounted by a cupola. In 1784, LEWIS HALLAM JR reoccupied the theatre, skirting the laws against playacting by presenting 'moral lectures'. In 1789 the ban was lifted, and the Southwark was in full operation. Outmoded as newer theatres were built and better companies assembled, the playhouse closed its doors in 1817. When the structure was damaged by fire a few years later, a brewery was built on its foundations and survived until 1912. MCH

Soviet children's theatre A child of the October (1917) Revolution, sired by the director-dramatist Natalya I. Sats (b.1903) and the director-theorist Aleksandr A. Bryantsev (b.1883) and assorted members of the intelligentsia, with the support of Soviet First People's Commissar for Education ANATOLY LUNACHARSKY, acting in the name of Lenin. Today there are well over 50 Children's Theatres and Theatres for Young Spectators (TYUZs) in the 15 former Soviet republics. They account for 400–500 plays annually in the various national languages, encompassing traditional and modern fairy tales, Russian, ethnic and foreign classics, historical and psychological dramas, comedies, MUSICALS, MELODRAMAS and dramatizations of poetry, biography and other narrative forms. The Soviet children's theatre constituted the most ambitious and successful enterprise of its kind in the world. Audience growth (23 million in 1974) far outstripped new theatre construction, with the result that adult companies had to include a certain percentage of children's theatre productions in their repertoires or lose their government subsidies. It was not always so.

Russia has a rich folkloric heritage. School dramas and children's literature were introduced in the 17th and 18th centuries (the former by SIMEON POLOTSKY and FEOFAN PROKOPOVICH). However, the scattered attempts to create professional children's theatres prior to 1917 stalled through lack of commercial success. Children's theatrical fare, with rare exceptions like the MOSCOW ART THEATRE's productions of OSTROVSKY's *The Snow Queen* (1900) and MAETERLINCK's *The Blue Bird* (1908), was mainly relegated to matinées in the adult theatres. Few adult actors specialized in children's or 'travesty' roles, and adolescents were perceived as being 'first-draft' adults. The government's decision to invest in children's theatres after 1917 was largely political. Lenin's wife, Nadezhda K. Krupskaya, saw them as a means of making youth sensitive to the beauty of the new society's ideals and the unprecedented act of creative imagination that building such a society necessitated. STANISLAVSKY called for a children's theatre independent of and superior to the adult theatre, what Bryantsev named a 'theatre of special commitment'. Children's writer Kornei I. Chukovsky counselled that the child's emotional education was paramount. What evolved was a children's theatre aesthetic balanced precariously between fantasy and reality, classical humanism and revolutionary idealism.

In 1918 the Commissariat for Education organized mobile children's theatre performances in Moscow, Petrograd and Saratov. The Moscow venture became permanent in October 1918, the first anniversary of the Revolution, under the direction of N. I. Sats (daughter of Moscow Art Theatre composer Ilya A. Sats), N. Ya. Efimov, V. A. Favorsky, composer A. N. Aleksandrov and ballet-master K. Ya. Goleizovsky. The theatre presented puppet shows, concerts and ballets. The First State Children's Theatre was opened in 1920 (renamed the State Central Theatre for Young Spectators in 1931) under Lunacharsky's direction. He was succeeded by G. M. Paskar, Yu. M. Bondy and G. L. Roshal. Here the first Soviet plays for children on contemporary themes were presented. Bryantsev founded Petrograd's TYUZ in 1921, which after 1963 (as Leningrad TYUZ) was directed by Zinovy Korogotsky. In 1936 Moscow's Central Children's Theatre (founded 1921), under the direction of N. I. Sats, moved to Sverdlov Square, near the Bolshoi Theatre. Here Sats pioneered 'synthesized theatre' – a combination of music, dance, ACROBATICS, drama and multimedia – which has become a dominant style of children's theatre production.

Children's theatres opened in the republics during the Civil War (1918–21) and thereafter. The Ekaterinodarsky (Krasnodar) Children's Theatre (1920–4) was the first to develop its own children's dramatic repertoire, featuring the plays of poet Elena N. Vasilyeva and of influential children's writer and children's literature publisher Samuel Ya. Marshak. The Kharkov Children's Theatre (founded in the early 1920s as the Fairy Tale; now the Lvov TYUZ) was the first and is now the oldest continuously existing Ukrainian children's theatre. Ukrainian TYUZs were later created in Kiev – Russian (1924) and YIDDISH (1928) – and in Odessa (1930). Important children's theatres also opened in Riga (Latvia), Tbilisi (Georgian and Russian, 1927–8), Alma-Ata (Kazakhstan), Tashkent (Uzbek and Russian) and throughout the Central Asian republics (1938–40). By the beginning of the Great Patriotic War (the Second World War, 1941–5), there were 71 children's theatres (and 120 puppet theatres (see PUPPETS)) in the Soviet Union, drawing an audience of five million. By the war's end, only 20 children's theatres remained, but 21 were rebuilt, and new theatres were created. The war years saw a preponderance of children's plays on historical and contemporary patriotic themes. Overall, the period of socialist realism (1934–56) shifted the balance in children's theatres' dramatic repertoires towards REALISM. Natalya Sats disappeared into a labour camp for 26 years. The Thaw (1956) brought the character of Lenin to the stages of Moscow's TYUZ (M. F. Shatrov's *In the Name of the Revolution*, 1957) and Central Children's Theatre (*Popov's Family*, 1960). VIKTOR ROZOV introduced the adolescent as a viable stage character in *Her Friends* (1949) and *A Page from Life* (1953), and in a succession of plays directed by ANATOLY EFROS at the Central Children's Theatre, including *Good Luck!* (1954), *In Search of Happiness* (1957), *Unequal Battle* (1960), *Before Supper* (1962) and *On the Day of the Wedding* (1964). The 1960s saw the founding in Moscow of the First State Museum of Children's Theatre (1964) and the first State Children's Musical Theatre (1965), both under the direction of Natalya Sats, as well as of the Soviet Centre of the International Association of Theatre for Children and Youth (ASSITEJ, 1965). After 1966, the Centre, governed by representatives from all the republics, sponsored trips by Soviet children's theatres to international festivals, and from 1968 it hosted children's theatre practitioners from abroad.

'The stage for young audiences,' Bryantsev had stated, 'must be a collaboration between artists who think like educators and teachers with the perceptions of artists.' Under the Soviet system, the task of introducing and conditioning the child to the theatre was approached scientifically by each theatre's pedagogical department (headed by a trained teacher, the 'chief pedagogue'), which met with teachers, parents and Komsomol (Young Communist) organizations; advised on script selection and production style appropriate to particular age groups (7–10, 11–14 and 15–18) – unambiguous and highly theatrical fare for the youngest, more complex and real material for the oldest; consulted at rehearsals and on script rewrites; observed audience members and tracked them for a time after the performance to gauge the psychological effects of theatrical productions; sponsored production-related art and essay contests; provided class study guides; visited classrooms; and ensured that the theatre's repertory reflected what was being studied in the schools. Among the more famous pedagogues were: N. N. Bakhtin, S. Ya. Gorodisskaya and N. A. Litvinovich.

The first dramatic literature staged in the children's theatres consisted of adaptations of fairy tales and popular children's stories with romantic subjects and heroic protagonists by such authors as Longfellow, HUGO and Jack London. In the 1920s and 30s there developed a body of contemporary Soviet plays for young spectators by S. G. Rozanov, N. I. Sats, S. A. Auslender, S. S. Zayaitsky, V. A. Selikhova, N. Ya. Shestakov and Aleksandra Ya. Brushtein, Bryantsev's collaborator at Leningrad's TYUZ. These theatres have regularly performed Russian and Soviet classics by FONVIZIN, PUSHKIN, GOGOL, Ostrovsky, LEV and Λ. N. TOLSTOI, CHEKHOV, GORKY, MAYAKOVSKY, ALEKSANDR AFINOGENOV, A. A. Kron, KONSTANTIN SIMONOV, KONSTANTIN TRENYOV, VLADIMIR BILL-BELOTSERKOVSKY, A. A. Fadeev, VALENTIN KATAEV, ALEKSEI ARBUZOV, Viktor Rozov, MIKHAIL ROSHCHIN, LEONID ZORIN, I. V. Shtok, L. A. Kasill, G. Mamlin, A. Aleksin, MIKHAIL SHATROV and others. Leading authors of fairy tales written for or adapted by the children's theatres include Pushkin (*The Fisherman and the Little Goldfish*, *The Golden Cockerel*); S. Ya. Marshak (*Carousel*; *The Luckless One*; *Twelve Months*); EVGENY SHVARTS (*The Two Maples*; *The Snow Queen*); A. N. Tolstoi (*The Little Golden Key*, adapted from *Pinocchio*); V. P. Kataev (*The Seven-Petal Magic Flower*); L. E. Ustinov (*The City without Love*); P. P. Ershov (*The Little Humpbacked Horse*).

Foreign authors represented in the children's theatre repertoire include SHAKESPEARE, CERVANTES, GOZZI, MOLIÈRE, Hugo, GOETHE, BRECHT, Maeterlinck, KAREL ČAPEK, DICKENS, SHAW, KIPLING, Jules Verne, Hans Christian Andersen, Charles Perrault, Mark Twain, Harriet Beecher Stowe, Poe, Faulkner, and LILLIAN HELLMAN. Among the leading artists from adult theatres who have worked in the children's companies are (actors and directors) I. V. Ilyinsky, N. K. Cherkasov, M. O. KNEBEL, A. D. Diky, R. N. Simonov, GEORGY TOVSTONOGOV, B. V. Zon, Yu. P. Kiselev, G. L. Roshal, A. Ya. Shapiro, K. Ya. Shakh-Azizov, OLEG EFREMOV and Anatoly Efros; (designers) V. F. Ryndin, N. A. Shifrin and I. V. Shtenberg; (composers) D. B. Kabalevsky, Krennikov and M. R. Rauthverger; and the puppeteer SERGEI OBRAZTSOV.

Among the most innovative and controversial Soviet children's theatre productions of the 1970s and 80s were several by Vyacheslav Spesivtsev, who, in *Stenka Razin*, showed young actors engaged in violence, drunkenness and debauchery, and in *Romeo and Juliet* featured multiple actors in the roles of the two protagonists in the style of LYUBIMOV's Taganka Theatre productions, for which he once staged MIME. Spesivtsev's production of *The Train of My Memory*, adapted from Gadarev's novel, took place on board an actual train in transit. In 1983 he lost his artistic director's position. In the 1980s, EIMUNTAS NEKROSIUS filled houses and set off mass hysteria with his punk-rock musical on the Romeo and Juliet theme, *Love and Death in Verona*, at the Vilnius (Lithuania) Youth Dramatic Theatre. SG

ENGLISH- AND OTHER-LANGUAGE SOURCES

See: M. Goldberg, 'The Pedagogue in the Eastern European Children's Theatre', *Educational Theatre Journal*, 24, Mar. 1972; H. Marshall, *The Pictorial History of the Russian Theatre*, New York, 1977; M. Morton (ed. and tr.), *Russian Plays for Young Audiences*, Rowayton, Conn., 1977, and (ed. and tr.), *Through the Magic Curtain: Theatre for Children, Adolescents and Young Adults in the USSR*, New Orleans, 1979; H. Pascar, *Mon théâtre à Moscou*, Paris, 1930.

RUSSIAN-LANGUAGE SOURCES

See: V. F. Ashmarin, M. E. Koltsov, A. Y. Tairov and Y. V. Pisarenko, *Natalya Sats: Desyat let sredi detei*, Moscow, 1928; A. Bryantsev, *Khudozhnik v teatr dlya detei*, Leningrad, 1927; S. N. Lunacharskaya, *Teatr dlya detei kak orudie kommunisticheskogo vospitaniya*, Moscow, 1931; L. Makarev, *Gosudarstvenny teatr yunykh zritelei*, Leningrad, 1929; N. Sats, *Nash put: Moskovsky teatr dlya detei i ego zritel*, Moscow, 1932; and *Deti prixodyat v teatr*, Moscow, 1960; N. Sats and S. Rozanov, *Teatr dlya detei*, Leningrad, 1925; L. Shpet, *Sovetsky teatr dlya detei*, Moscow, 1971; E. Vasilyeva and S. Marshak, *Teatr dlya detei*, Krasnodar, 1922.

Sowande, Bode 1948– Nigerian playwright, director and novelist. Sowande was born in Abeokuta, and studied at the Universities of Ife, Nigeria and Sheffield. He was a founding member of the Ori Olokun Players and a scriptwriter in WOLE SOYINKA's Orisun Theatre. The first work of Sowande's to gain widespread attention was the trilogy comprising *The Night Before*, *Farewell to Babylon* and *Flamingoes* (produced 1972–82). These plays deal with the totalitarian state and with problems of leadership and loyalty amongst a radical group, first seen as students, who contest oppressive authority. Increasingly through the 1980s Sowande's plays embraced BRECHTian techniques of dislocation, which readily graft on to the Nigerian theatre's convention of mixing song, music, dance and role-play episodes. These techniques are seen in *Afamako – the Workhorse* (1978), a play dealing with the exploitation of labour, and even more in the satirical *Monkey's Gold* (1993). *Tornadoes Full of Dreams* (1990) is a powerful, large-scale treatment of the Haitian revolution, commissioned by the French Cultural Centre in Lagos to commemorate the bicentenary of the French Revolution. The same organization commissioned *Arede Owo* (1990), a free adaptation of MOLIÈRE's *The Miser*. Sowande's increasingly bold stagecraft and growing use of song and dance are seen in *Mammy-Water's Wedding* and *Ajantala-Pinocchio* (both 1992, unpublished). He taught at the University of Ibadan until 1990, when he resigned to devote more time to Odu Themes Meridian, which was transformed in 1993 into a fully professional and commercial theatre company. CD

Soyinka, Wole 1934– Nigerian playwright, poet and novelist; generally recognized as Africa's greatest living playwright, and considered by some critics to be one of the

Peter Adegboyego Badejo
as praise singer in the
British premiere of
Soyinka's *Death and the
King's Horseman*, 1990.

foremost writers of his generation. Soyinka was born in Aké, in what was then the Western Region of Nigeria, the son of a canon in the Anglican Church. He has recreated his childhood in a reminiscence, *Aké: The Years of Childhood* (1981). The tensions between the Christian home and the Yoruba *egungun* masqueraders (see MASQUERADES IN AFRICA) among the people have helped create the dynamic of his poetic vision. He treated the conflict early in his career in a radio play about an adolescent emerging into a tense world of confused adults, *Camwood on the Leaves*, broadcast on Nigerian radio in 1960 and on the BBC World Service in 1965. *Aké* is more the sustained recollection, in maturity, of the writer's youth.

Soyinka went to University College, Ibadan, and then to Leeds University, England, in 1956. He became involved in the new drama at the ROYAL COURT THEATRE, London, where he became a playreader in 1957–9. With a company of actors whom he had brought together, he developed three experimental pieces there. While he was still in England, two of his plays were produced in Nigeria: *The Swamp-Dwellers*, about the moral realignment necessary to make the land productive and the community whole in rural Nigeria; and *The Lion and the Jewel*, a comedy in which a village chief and the schoolteacher vie with each other for the hand of the village belle. Soyinka returned to Nigeria in 1960 and founded the 1960 Masks, which presented his first major play, *A Dance of the Forests*, for the independence celebrations. The play was not what was

expected. It offered a critique of pre-colonial history while diminishing the cultural significance of the colonial period. Many of the themes of Soyinka's later plays are present in this complex work: the notion of the three parallel and interlocking worlds of the past, the present and the future (the dead, the living and the unborn); Nature, conceived metaphysically in a romantic vision of the moral imperative laid upon the questing hero; the need for sacrifice; the role of the artist in society; the presence of the god Ogun.

The theatre company the 1960 Masks acted as an umbrella, administratively, for the younger, fully professional Orisun Theatre Company, whose actors Soyinka trained between 1962 and 1965. The company premiered two series of sketches containing some pungent political SATIRE: *The New Republican* and *Before the Blackout*. During these years some of his major plays appeared in print, following performances in Nigeria. Their publication acted as a spur to young dramatists in other countries in anglophone East and West Africa: *The Trials of Brother Jero*, a satirical comedy recounting the adventures, sexual and otherwise, of a mendicant Christian preacher on Lagos's Bar Beach; *The Strong Breed*, an ironical exposition of the context for human sacrifice today; and *The Road*, also concerned, metaphysically, with sacrifice, but in the context of wanton death on Nigeria's roads and the rubbishing by society of a lumpen working class. *The Road* suggests that in modern Nigeria the *egungun* masquerade can offer a Nigerian audience a more contemporary discourse than can a naturalistically presented materialism. The mask can discover a meaning for those at the base of society for their wasted lives and random deaths – even though the class-based nature of their oppression remains 'hidden' in the play.

In 1965 Soyinka published his first novel, *The Interpreters*, about, again, meaning in the lives and deaths of a group of young Nigerian artists and intellectuals. He also had two plays broadcast by the BBC, London (see RADIO DRAMA). Then, in the October, he was arrested for allegedly seizing the Western Region radio studios and making a political broadcast disputing the published results of the recent elections. He was acquitted in December. His next play, *Kongi's Harvest*, about the abuse of power and the tyrant's ability to corrupt a whole people, was performed at the Dakar Festival of Negro Arts in 1966. It was published in 1967, as was his collection of poems *Idanre and Other Poems*.

Nigeria slid into civil war. In August 1967 Soyinka was detained without trial, and released only in October 1969. He made notes during this period of incarceration, secretly, and was able to publish them on his release under the title *The Man Died* (1972) – 'The man dies,' he wrote, 'in all who keep silent in the face of tyranny.' This work forms a quartet: with his next major play, *Madmen and Specialists* (premiered in Connecticut, USA, 1970); with another collection of poems, *A Shuttle in the Crypt* (1971); and with the novel, *Season of Anomy* (1973). *Madmen and Specialists* is set in the civil war – also known as the Biafran War – and is an intensely moral play about man's responsibility to his fellow men, in his control both of his own nature and of an external Nature. The quartet shows how Soyinka's intense vision of people corrupted and debased by power-play transcends any single genre, moving vividly through them all.

After his release in 1969, Soyinka went into exile. He became editor of the cultural and political magazine *Ch'Indaba* (formerly *Transition*), which he intermittently edited from Ghana between 1970 and 1975. He was appointed professor of comparative literature at the University of Ife, but was not able to take up the position. He wrote for the NATIONAL THEATRE in London a version of *The Bacchae of Euripides* (the title of his play), which was performed in London in 1973. He had a visiting professorship at Sheffield University and a fellowship at Churchill College, Cambridge. Out of his reaction to this last experience came a collection of essays, *Myth, Literature and the African World* (1976), a theorizing of African aesthetics. This important text develops, among other things, the relationship of myth to performance today. Soyinka has a vision of the transformation of the physicalities of space and time in the act of performance. In particular, he explores the significance of Ogun – the god of iron, war and creative fire – in the Yoruba pantheon. He is seen by Soyinka as the embodiment of contradiction; he is the original sacrifice, the one who dares chaos and the abyss. In connection with the concept of the co-existence of the three worlds of the dead, the living and the unborn, Soyinka emphasizes the importance of the masquerade for a new moral consciousness: through the RITES OF PASSAGE there is 'movement of transition' between these worlds, which open upon each other. The MASK – and, by extension, the modern actor – can actualize this metaphysic.

While at Cambridge Soyinka also wrote *Death and the King's Horseman* (1975). This play reworks a moment in Nigeria's colonial past from inside the Yoruba metaphysic: it is about the halting of the ritual suicide of the equerry of the Alafin of Oyo by the local British district officer, in 1946. The incident had already been handled in an opera by DURO LADIPO. The play in performance is the praxis of Soyinka's theory. Together, theory and drama are a summation of his work up to his return to Nigeria. Many of the plays of this period require the dialogue to carry the burden of the playwright's philosophical preoccupations. The writing is dense and Soyinka has been criticized for overloading the language – through his play on words, control of rhythm and assonance, and with metaphor piled on brilliant metaphor. His own sensibility often seems to outstrip his audience's.

He returned to Nigeria, to Ife, in 1976. After directing a production of *Death and the King's Horseman* there in the same year, he set about generating a new drama. The Guerrilla Theatre Unit, based at the University of Ife, presented plays and sketches attacking corruption and political oppression; eschewing formal stage presentation, the Unit operated on a 'hit-and-run' basis, mounting its satirical playlets in car parks and markets and at street corners. Soyinka has always seen this type of theatre as a necessary activity, parallel to the metaphysical explorations of plays such as *The Road* and *Death and the King's Horseman*. A related production is his recording 'Unlimited Liability Company' (1983), which satirizes the corruption and hypocrisy of the Shehu Shagari regime. One song in particular, the caustic 'Etiko Revo Wetin?', became a popular hit.

In December 1977 Soyinka produced *Opera Wonyosi*, a Nigerian amalgam of GAY's *The Beggar's Opera* and BRECHT's *Threepenny Opera*. The play is a full-frontal satirical attack on Bokassa, the self-crowned emperor of the short-lived Central African Empire, and, at the same time, an attack on the values of the Nigerian petty bourgeoisie who benefit materially from such tyrants. The onslaught was continued in his next work, *A Play of Giants* (1985). Using GENET's *The Balcony* as a model, Soyinka parodies some of Africa's worst modern tyrants – in particular, Idi Amin of Uganda. The play also attacks the Superpowers and the United Nations, which he sees as sanctioning the megalomania and butchery of these dictators. *Requiem for a Futurologist* (1985) is a Swiftian satire on the cult of bogus fortune tellers and astrologers, with a witty exposure of false prophets – who make Jero (of *The Trials of Brother Jero* and *Jero's Metamorphosis* (1973)) seem positively benign – manipulating a gullible public. These plays, and the work of the Guerrilla Theatre Unit, are complemented by Soyinka's film *Blues for a Prodigal* (1985), in which he attacks the power-play and corruption of the civilian government of Shagari. Banned in Nigeria (see CENSORSHIP), the film was screened privately in London in 1985 on the occasion of his Herbert Read Memorial Lecture, in which he reaffirmed his commitment to a political praxis in his dramatic art.

Soyinka was awarded the Nobel Prize for Literature in

1986. The occasion provided a fresh opportunity for those critics who see his art as elitist to condemn him for 'writing for the West', but it also generated considerable and widespread national pride that Nigeria had 'bagged' Africa's first Nobel. Soyinka has retained a high profile in Nigerian public consciousness ever since, with his work (until 1993) as chairman of the Road Safety Corps and with his frequent public comments on human rights abuses on the part of Babangida's military regime. Since the mid-1980s, Soyinka has written little new work for the theatre. His major publications have been the poetry collection *Mandela's Earth* (1990) and a fictional extension of *Aké*, a study of his father's circle of friends entitled *Isara: A Voyage around Essay* (1989). *Art, Dialogue and Outrage* (1988) is a major collection of his essays on drama, literature and criticism, which offers many insights into the world-view that underlies his theatre. A new play for radio, *A Scourge of Hyacinths*, was broadcast by the BBC in 1991; *From Zia with Love*, first performed in Siena, Italy, in 1992, is an expansion from this play. Here Soyinka focuses once more on corruption and on civil rights abuses under Nigeria's military regime: in common with many other Nigerian plays – notably Segun Oyekunle's masterly *Katakata for Sofahead* – the action takes place in a prison cell.

Soyinka is a political playwright; but, rather than being didactic, his work demonstrates the dialectic within the term 'political art'. He thinks politically, and can see no other way of thinking as an artist in Africa today. Thus, the greater Soyinka's commitment to his art, the more political it becomes; and the greater his commitment to praxis, the more artistically compelling are the plays which come out of his experience.   CD

Spain (See also CATALAN THEATRE; MEDIEVAL DRAMA IN EUROPE (Spain).) The Renaissance in Spain roughly coincides with the unification of Aragon and Castile resulting from the marriage of Ferdinand and Isabella in 1469. By the mid-15th century, LITURGICAL DRAMA flourished throughout the northeastern and central regions. A written version in Catalan of the anonymous medieval MIRACLE PLAY of the Assumption, *Misteri d'Elx* (*Mystery of Elche*, c.1492), added references to the New World and the forced conversion of the Jews. The work is still staged each August in Elche. The most gifted writer of religious plays, or *autos*, was Portugal's GIL VICENTE, who also wrote in Spanish; his theatre blends lyric and dramatic qualities.

In the same period, secular drama developed new currents, separate from both the crude and often obscene medieval farces deplored by the Church and the superficial courtly pageants. The masterpiece from the late 15th century is FERNANDO DE ROJAS's *La Celestina*, an enormously influential work that combines medieval and Renaissance elements, Spanish and foreign influences, TRAGEDY and COMEDY, earthy lower-class figures and romanticized aristocrats. In his eclogues, JUAN DEL ENCINA adapted classical PASTORAL poems to dramatic form. TORRES NAHARRO created the prototype for GOLDEN AGE cape-and-sword dramas. These two major Renaissance playwrights lived for extended periods in Italy and were familiar with classical texts.

By the mid-16th century Spain had a thriving public the-atre, and professional acting companies, both Italian and Spanish, toured the country. The former emphasized classical, Renaissance, and the new COMMEDIA DELL'ARTE styles. Foremost among Spanish actor-managers of itinerant troupes was LOPE DE RUEDA. His sketches, or *pasos*, introduced comic types and colloquial language found throughout Spain's later GÉNERO CHICO, and his *bobo* (buffoon) prefigures the stock GRACIOSO who serves as the humorous counterpart to aristocratic protagonists of the full-length Golden Age COMEDIA.

Permanent open-air playhouses, called CORRALES and simulating courtyards, were established first in Madrid (1579) and then in other cities; they attracted audiences of all social classes and both sexes, and the noisy response of the groundlings had a great effect on the development of Spain's national theatre. Except for a brief period in the 1590s, women were allowed to perform on stage, in contrast to England and France where boys continued to play female roles until the second half of the 17th century.

In 1517 Torres Naharro had already published a dramatic theory based on HORACE's classic principles, including the five-act structure. Juan de la Cueva and CERVANTES, important exponents of neoclassical drama, nevertheless deviated from classical norms. Cueva, who lived in Seville, wrote violent tragedy inspired by SENECA. He favoured four acts and metric forms varied to reflect action and character, and incorporated Spanish history in his plots. Cervantes's historical *El cerco de Numancia* (*The Siege of Numantia*), despite its four acts and epic effect, is considered Spain's best neoclassical tragedy. Several of his *entremeses*, comic interludes that build on the tradition of Lope de Rueda's *pasos*, have also entered the international repertoire, but the most successful and prolific writer of short comic pieces in the 17th century was Luis Quiñones de Benavente.

The creative flourishing of the Golden Age stage effectively begins with LOPE DE VEGA. In his *Arte nuevo de hacer comedias* (*The New Art of Writing Plays*, 1609), Lope established norms for Spain's national theatre: plays should be written in three acts and polymetric verse and should combine plots and subplots, upper- and lower-class characters, serious and comic elements. Above all, plays should entertain. Although in his hundreds of plays he drew on a wide range of subjects, much of his theatre consists of cloak-and-sword comedies, historical drama (with emphasis on medieval Spain), and religious AUTOS SACRAMENTALES. His masterpiece, *Fuenteovejuna*, anticipates late-19th-century theatre in its use of a collective protagonist and its call for social justice.

Written with performance in mind, Golden Age plays were action-oriented and enormously popular with audiences of all classes. Numerous playwrights adopted Lope's dramatic formula and many attempted to rival his productivity. Foremost among Lopistas are TIRSO DE MOLINA, author of *El burlador de Sevilla* (*The Trickster of Seville*), and the Mexican-born RUIZ DE ALARCÓN, who excelled at satirical comedies of manners. *El esclavo del demonio* (*The Devil's Slave*) by the Andalusian author Mira de Amescua presents a Faust-like pact with the devil. Guillem de Castro contributed *Las mocedades del Cid* (*The Young El Cid*), source of PIERRE CORNEILLE's *Le Cid*.

A second cycle of Golden Age drama developed under

the baroque genius of CALDERÓN DE LA BARCA, whose works generally reflect greater development of character and a more self-conscious artistry, polished structure and complex ideology than those of the spontaneous and innovative Lope. Calderón's masterpiece is the philosophical *La vida es sueño* (*Life Is a Dream*). He created superb *autos sacramentales* and wrote in a range of sub-genres, but, because of a trilogy of wife-murder tragedies, his name has also become associated with a vengeful code of honour. Major authors in the Calderonian school include ROJAS ZORRILLA and MORETO. His last important follower, after his death, was Francisco Antonio de Bances Candamo, whose treatise on the court play, *Teatro de los teatros* (*Theatre of the Theatres*, 1689–93), promoted theatre with a political message.

The establishment of the Bourbon dynasty in the 18th century brought the Enlightenment to Spain, but popular audiences preferred the baroque style and structure of the Calderonian school to neoclassical restraint. They demanded spectacular stage effects made possible by elaborate machinery at new, enclosed theatres. The few successful neoclassical tragedies – by Nicolás Fernández de Moratín, Vicente García de la Huerta and Ignacio López de Ayala – liberalized the French mould and dealt with Spanish history.

The most enduring works of the period are comedies. The masterpiece of Spanish neoclassicism is a satirical FARCE by Nicolás's son LEANDRO FERNÁNDEZ DE MORATÍN: *El sí de las niñas* (*The Maidens' Consent*), a work noted for its impeccable structure and witty, natural dialogue. Popular theatre for much of the 18th century was dominated by Ramón de la Cruz; his prolific output of *sainetes* (short SATIRES of Madrid society and customs) form an essential part of Spain's long tradition of *género chico*.

Two new sub-genres, sentimental plays and national heroic dramas, date from the late 18th century, thus anticipating romantic drama, but because of the repressive policies of Ferdinand VII romanticism did not truly reach the Spanish stage until after the tyrant's death in 1833. Intellectuals returning from exile in England and France brought with them revolutionary attitudes towards art, society, politics and religion. While romanticism blossomed belatedly in Spain and lasted only a decade, from 1834 to 44, paradoxically the country's passionate image had inspired romantic drama elsewhere in Europe. Moreover, in Spain the rejection of neoclassicism was in some ways a return to Golden Age conventions.

Francisco Martínez de la Rosa's *La conjuración de Venecia* (*The Conspiracy in Venice*), Mariano José de Larra's *Macias*, and Juan Eugenio Hartzenbush's *Los amantes de Teruel* (*The Lovers of Teruel*) are dramas of ill-fated love with medieval settings. *Don Alvaro o la fuerza del sino* (*Don Alvaro, or The Force of Destiny*) likewise highlights fatal love and a prototypical romantic hero. This masterwork by Angel de Saavedra, Duque de Rivas, was the source of a Verdi opera, as were Antonio García Gutiérrez's historical dramas, *El trovador* (*The Troubadour*) and *Simón Bocanegra*. ZORRILLA also wrote interesting history plays, but he is best-remembered for his exuberant version of the Don Juan myth, *Don Juan Tenorio*.

Even when romanticism prevailed, comedy did not disappear. Writing in the style of Moratín or SCRIBE, Larra, Manuel Bretón de los Herreros and Ventura de la Vega used comedy to satirize middle-class society. The first major woman writer of the Spanish stage, Cuban-born GÓMEZ DE AVELLANEDA, excelled at both biblical tragedies and entertaining comedies. The 1860s and 1870s brought a kind of realistic high comedy. Typified by works of Adelardo López de Ayala and Manuel Tamayo y Baus, the new form concentrated on serious political and economic concerns. Tamayo's masterpiece, however, is the metatheatrical, melodramatic *Un drama nuevo* (*A New Drama*).

Although *Juan José* by Joaquín Dicenta and *Terra baixa*

La taberna fantástica (*The Fantastic Tavern*) by Alfonso Sastre, directed by Gerardo Malla in 1985.

(*The Lowlands*) by the Catalan writer GUIMERÀ were excellent examples of realistic social drama, in the last decades of the 19th century the Spanish stage was dominated by the exaggerated neo-romanticism of ECHEGARAY (Nobel Prize, 1904). Even Echegaray's best-known work, the thesis drama *El gran Galeoto* (*The Great Galeoto*, 1881), verges on MELODRAMA, and his plays elicited a bombastic acting style.

Novelist Benito Pérez Galdós and BENAVENTE (Nobel Prize, 1922) attempted to break Echegaray's influence and reform the Spanish stage by fostering realistic, representational theatre. Galdós's *Realidad* (*Reality*, 1892) scandalized bourgeois spectators by its daring themes, everyday language and natural acting. Galdós's novels have been successfully adapted for the stage, but Benavente was clearly the superior theatrical craftsman. For 50 years he so dominated the bourgeois stage with formula dramas that the adjective 'Benaventine' became synonymous with the WELL MADE PLAY. His masterworks – the metatheatrical farce *Los intereses creados* (*The Bonds of Interest*) and the rural tragedy *La malquerida* (*The Passion Flower*) – are atypical of his theatre.

In the late 19th and early 20th centuries, ZARZUELA (light opera) and comedy retained their traditional appeal. Authors whose comedies are still being staged include the ALVAREZ QUINTERO brothers, ARNICHES and Pedro Muñoz Seca; they contributed to the thriving *género chico* as well as writing full-length plays.

Two of Spain's greatest playwrights, VALLE-INCLÁN and GARCÍA LORCA, belong to the pre-Spanish Civil War period. The former's *esperpentos* (grotesque tragicomedies), long considered unstageable, are now recognized as innovative links with expressionistic, BRECHTian and absurdist theatre (see EXPRESSIONISM; THEATRE OF THE ABSURD). Lorca's international fame following his assassination at the outbreak of the war in 1936 stems largely from his trilogy of poetic tragedies: *Bodas de sangre* (*Blood Wedding*), *Yerma* and *La casa de Bernarda Alba* (*The House of Bernarda Alba*). Recently his stature has been enhanced by long-delayed staging of daring surrealistic works.

In the 1920s and 30s many Spanish authors and theatre practitioners experimented with new currents of the Western stage, but the war and its aftermath stifled their efforts. CASONA, for example, treated reality/fantasy themes in a way reminiscent of PIRANDELLO and EVREINOV; during a quarter-century of political exile, he was active in the Argentine theatre.

Postwar Spanish theatre was hampered by CENSORSHIP, but nevertheless produced works of lasting interest. The first new playwright of the 1940s was Víctor Ruiz Iriarte; his mildly satirical comedies of theatricalized life, such as *El landó de seis caballos* (*The Six-Horse Landau*, 1950), were box-office successes but dismissed by liberal critics as escapist fare. On the other hand, the humorist MIHURA was well received across the political spectrum; his *Tres sombreros de copa* (*Three Top Hats*, 1952) was recognized by IONESCO as innovative absurdist theatre. Other talented writers of comedy had worked in Hollywood as scenarists in the 1930s. They include JARDIEL PONCELA, author of wildly ingenious parodies, and LÓPEZ RUBIO, noted for his clever metaplays.

The premiere in 1949 at Madrid's historic TEATRO ESPAÑOL of *Historia de una escalera* (*Story of a Stairway*) introduced both BUERO-VALLEJO, Spain's foremost contemporary playwright and only real tragedian, and a renewed current of socially committed drama. Buero later also established the prototype for historical plays that demythologize the past while commenting obliquely on the present and, in works like the masterful *El sueño de la razón* (*The Sleep of Reason*, 1970), refined an immersion technique that plunges the audience into the inner world of blind, deaf or insane protagonists.

Buero's first production was followed by the works of a 'realistic' generation, playwrights born in the 1920s who were often in conflict with the Franco regime. SASTRE's *Escuadra hacia la muerte* (*Condemned Squad*, 1953) was quickly banned; for decades his fame was greater outside Spain than at home. Lauro Olmo's landmark *La camisa* (*The Shirt*, 1962), dealing with the economic emigration of Spain's working poor, met with such acclaim that the censors were forced to extend its initial limited performance. Some of the best realistic works were not staged until after Franco's death in 1975. These include José Martín Recuerda's *Las arrecogías del Beaterio Santa María Egipciaca* (*The Inmates of the Convent of St Mary Egyptian*) and José María Rodríguez Méndez's *Bodas que fueron famosas del Pingajo y la Fandanga* (*The Famous Nuptials of Pingajo and Fandanga*).

The difficulties faced by these writers resulted from their sharp criticism of Spain's political and social history, not from their REALISM/NATURALISM. Psychological dramas, particularly ones probing moral questions, were among the longest-running plays of the 1950s and 60s. Examples are Joaquín Calvo-Sotelo's *La muralla* (*The Wall*) and SALOM's *La casa de las chivas* (*The House of the 'Chivas'*), both dealing with the Civil War.

Writers of anti-realistic, experimental works found the Franco-era stage virtually closed to them. ARRABAL in the 1950s chose voluntary exile and gained international fame via French theatre. NIEVA, now one of Spain's most celebrated authors, did not achieve a professional production of his imaginative and transgressive brand of SURREALISM until 1976. Starting in the 1960s, 'underground' authors of political allegories and absurdist tragicomedies – a group that includes Antonio Martínez Ballesteros, Luis Matilla, Manuel Martínez Mediero, Luis Riaza, Eduardo Quiles, José Ruibal and many others – won prizes at festivals in Sitges and elsewhere but were more likely to be staged abroad than in Spain. Under democracy their works have generally not had wide enough box-office appeal to enter mainstream theatre.

Two authors who achieved fame in the late Franco era and continue to enjoy commercial success are ANTONIO GALA and Ana Diosdado. Gala is a brilliant stylist who excels in all literary genres; typically his works combine surface humour with a plea for personal and political freedom. Since the triumph in 1970 of *Olvida los tambores* (*Forget the Drums*), Diosdado has been Spain's major woman playwright. She combines impeccable theatrical structure and sparkling dialogue with an underlying criticism of political divisiveness and materialism.

By the early 1970s, innovative theatre movements had developed in various regions of Spain in reaction to the dominant culture. These included acclaimed CATALAN

Sèmola Teatre production of *Hibrid*, directed by Joan Grau at the Catalan Theatre.

troupes like ELS JOGLARS, and small independent companies in Madrid. Two important new authors to emerge under democracy, ALONSO DE SANTOS and Fermín Cabal, came from the independent movement. Their works are noted for their creative use of contemporary slang and cinematographic codes. Among major stage hits of the 1980s are *Bajarse al moro* (*Going Down to Marrakesh*) by Alonso de Santos, *Las bicicletas son para el verano* (*Bicycles Are for Summer*) by Fernando Fernán Gómez, and *¡Ay, Carmela!* by the Catalan playwright and director José Sanchis Sinisterra.

In the late 1970s, the TEATRO NACIONAL MARÍA GUERRERO premiered works by living Spanish authors, but in the past decade that function has been shifted to the FRINGE National Centre for New Tendencies of the Stage. Increasingly young writers, shut out of both commercial and government showcase theatres, have created their own alternative theatres and theatre schools, and have sought to reach younger audiences with colloquial language and contemporary subjects. Among new talents emerging from these efforts are Ernesto Caballero, Ignacio del Moral and Paloma Pedrero. PZ

See: G. Bleiberg, M. Ihrie and J. Pérez (eds), *Dictionary of the Literature of the Iberian Peninsula*, 2 vols., Westport, Conn., and London, 1993; M. T. Halsey and P. Zatlin (eds), *The Contemporary Spanish Theater: A Collection of Critical Essays*, Lanham, Md, 1988; M. P. Holt, *The Contemporary Spanish Theater (1949–1972)*, Boston, 1975; M. McKendrick, *Theatre in Spain: 1490–1700*, Cambridge, 1989; C. Oliva, *El teatro desde*

1936, Madrid, 1989; J. Rubio Jiménez, *El teatro en el siglo 19*, Madrid, 1983; F. Ruiz Ramón, *Historia del teatro español (desde sus orígenes hasta 1900)*, Madrid, 1967, and *Historia del teatro español, siglo 20*, Madrid, 1975; N. D. Shergold, *A History of the Spanish Stage from Medieval Times Until the End of the Seventeenth Century*, Oxford, 1967; A. Valbuena Prat, *Historia del teatro español*, Barcelona, 1956; G. Wellwarth, *Spanish Underground Drama*, University Park, Penn., and London, 1972.

Spencer, Gabriel d.1598 English actor, who joined the ADMIRAL'S MEN after the dissolution of Pembroke's Men in 1597. There is no record of the parts he played, though HENSLOWE is known to have valued him. Spencer is remembered only for his death – 'slain in Hogsdon fields by the hands of Benjamin Jonson bricklayer', as Henslowe wrote to EDWARD ALLEYN. In 1596 Spencer had killed a man who attacked him with a candlestick. We do not know the cause of his quarrel with JONSON. PT

Sperr, Martin 1944– German dramatist whose *Jagdszenen aus Niederbayern* (*Hunting Scenes from Lower Bavaria*, 1966), in which a homosexual is hounded by Bavarian villagers, inaugurated the VOLKSSTÜCK revival in the 1960s. *Landshuter Erzählungen* (*Tales from Landshut*, 1967) shows two rural entrepreneurs fighting for control of a local monopoly. HR

Sprechstimme The possible relations of music with words have always preoccupied composers of opera (see RECITATIVE and MÉLODRAME). *Sprechstimme* (literally, 'speech voice') has been used in the 20th century to bring the singer's utterance closer to speech than was the case with traditional recitative. The rise and fall of the voice is indicated, but there is no precise pitch indication. There has always been a tendency for singers to move towards *Sprechstimme* at intense moments during the action of an opera: e.g. Tosca's last words at the end of Act 2 of PUCCINI's opera. Notable use of *Sprechstimme* proper occurs in *Wozzeck* (1925) and *Lulu* (1937) by Alban Berg (1885–1935) and in *Moses and Aaron* (1957) by Arnold Schoenberg (1874–1951). Sometimes a distinction is made between *Sprechstimme* and *Sprechgesang* (literally, 'speech song'), but essentially both signify singing that approaches speech. GH

Spurling, John 1936– British dramatist, whose innovative plays have sought to examine historical themes from several points of view. *MacRune's Guevara* (1969), which was produced by the NATIONAL THEATRE, gives an account of the life of the Bolivian revolutionary hero Che Guevara, as interpreted by the dead Scottish artist MacRune, a Marxist, and the narrator who deciphers MacRune's drawings, Edward Hotel. This multi-viewpoint approach allows Spurling to discuss the nature of political myths; and *In the Heart of the British Museum* (1971) extends this technique into the consideration of three kinds of cultural revolution – in China during the 1960s, in Ovid's Rome, and in the Aztec Empire, when Quetzalcoatl was succeeded by Texcatlipoca as god. *The British Empire, Part One* (1980), which was staged in the studio theatre of the BIRMINGHAM

REP, vividly contrasted different episodes of British colonial history by placing them on side platforms, with a promenade audience. Spurling has likened his ideal theatre to an art gallery. A witty and sophisticated writer, he has trouble in conveying information to audiences who are less well informed than he is: and his plays, which include *Shades of Heathcliff* (1971), *Death of Captain Doughty* (1973), *Coming Ashore in Guadaloupe* (1976) and *Antigone through a Looking Glass* (1979), have been staged mainly in studio and FRINGE theatres. JE

Squarzina, Luigi 1922– Italian director and playwright. Trained at the Academy of Dramatic Art in Rome, since the late 1940s he has been one of the most active and versatile directors in the Italian theatre for both classic and modern drama. Between 1962 and 1976 he was artistic director of the Teatro Stabile in Genoa, and from 1976 to 1983 of the Teatro Stabile in Rome. His work on classic texts, in particular those of GOLDONI, PIRANDELLO and SHAKESPEARE, has been marked by an intelligent and sensitive orchestration that both serves and illuminates the text. He was one of the first to re-explore the stage possibilities of D'ANNUNZIO's plays after their postwar neglect. Among his notable productions of Shakespeare are *Timon of Athens* (1983) – only the second time the play had been given a professional production in Italy – and *The Merchant of Venice* (1992), from his own translation. Among his many productions of Pirandello are *Ciascuno a suo modo* (*Each in His Own Way*, 1984) and *Come prima meglio di prima* (*As Before, Better than Before*, 1990). He has written a number of plays on social and political themes and is a perceptive commentator on the contemporary Italian stage. His sophisticated comedy, *Siamo momentaneamenti assenti* (*We Are Temporarily Absent*) won the Premio IDI in 1991 and was highly praised when staged in Milan and toured the following year. KR

Sri Lanka Sri Lanka is an island nation inhabited primarily by Buddhist Sinhalese, with a large Hindu Tamil minority, the descendants of Indian immigrants. The theatre of Sri Lanka has originated in various rituals and ceremonies of folk religions that are practised throughout the island. Unlike their counterparts in INDIA – representing the dominant culture of the region, which had a classical tradition of drama on which to build later dramatic forms – Sinhalese writers had no indigenous classical model, except that provided by the neighbouring Sanskrit tradition. A possible explanation for the absence of a classical tradition of drama in Sri Lanka is that Buddhist monks were the principal writers in ancient times and they considered drama a taboo art form and so confined their efforts to poetry and narrative stories.

The elaborate ceremonies connected with the worship and propitiation of numerous folk deities of the island seem to have inspired the dramatic impulse. In RITUAL form alone, a strong dramatic character is evident. For example, the *rata yakuma* ceremony, which is performed to ensure the safe delivery of a child, to protect the child in the womb, to ensure the health of the infant already born or to make a barren woman conceive, contains elements of mimesis and theatre. The ceremony begins with performance offerings of chanted invocatory stanzas, drumming and dancing before sacrificial altars dedicated to the Seven Barren Queens. Three exorcists dressed in female attire are questioned by the chief exorcist or a drummer in order to reveal the purpose of the ceremony. The exorcist chants the legend of the Seven Barren Queens, wraps a white cloth around his head and after chanting verses spreads the cloth on the altar and throws incense on the flames of a torch which causes the whole altar to seem to burst into flames. This is an enactment of the legend of the demons' birth. Then follows the Twelvefold Ritual in which the seven daughters present a cloth to the Dipankara Buddha and thus attain permission to cause illness to human beings. Eventually, through sacrificial offerings, they agree to relinquish their control.

At the conclusion of the Twelvefold Ritual, the exorcist depicts in mime how the Barren Queens wore a cloth to be offered to the Dipankara Buddha. During the action which follows a man comes forward and the exorcist leads him around the performance area and mimes the Origin of the Mat, a symbolic fertility rite. Through song and mime, the exorcist relates the birth and swaddling of a child. Eventually he symbolically places the child in the arms of the parent and pronounces blessings on the mother. In turn, he presents the child to relatives and to spectators who have gathered to watch the ceremony.

Ceremonies such as these often require either 'patient' or exorcist to dress in the supposed likeness of the 'afflictor'. He will be costumed, wear elaborate make-up or a mask and brandish various weapons. In the process of introduction, which may include dancing to musical accompaniment, the patient or exorcist may become possessed and speak in the voice of the demon when replying to the priest's numerous questions. These transitions, beginning and ending with rituals, closely resemble dramas in the structure of the acts that occur within the ritual framing elements. During the ceremonies, offerings are made to appease the demon, sometimes in the form of a cock whose blood is either symbolically or actually shed or in the form of human sacrifices depicted through effigies, dolls or their symbolic representations. Ceremonies usually begin in the evening and continue the entire night without reaching a conclusion until midday.

In some ritual events, dramatic interludes using MIME and comic dialogue have been added for ritual purposes or to entertain an audience. They break up the tedium of the long hours of the ceremonies and serve to entertain the participants.

Perhaps one of the most interesting and popular of these interludes is that of the 'Brahmins from the Port of Vadiga' which occurs in a ritual intended to dispel evil influence that may accrue to a person who is suspected of having evil charms performed against him. The interlude depicts the arrival in Sri Lanka of some Brahmins who are versed in the ritual. When they enter they see a ceremony being performed and begin to question what is going on. Because they cannot speak Sinhalese they have trouble communicating with the exorcist, a situation which results in a great deal of humour. Finally it is discovered that the Brahmins speak Pali, the Buddhist language of Sri Lanka, and a dialogue commences between them and one of the exorcists in a kind of pseudo-Pali which is considered very amusing. At the conclusion of the ritual, they dance, bless the patient and exit, allowing the ritual ceremonies to proceed.

Among the specific forms in which ritual and drama are almost equally balanced are masked SOKARI and KOLAM. Kolam's connection to religious ritual is clear in the structure of performance and is suggested by the fact that the large MASKS probably descended from ritual use. The date of their origin has not yet been determined. NADAGAMA is a full-scale form of FOLK THEATRE with a considerable body of dramatic literature. Its plays concerning royalty and fortune-telling were exceptionally popular during the late 18th and 19th centuries. Nadagama, in turn, became the source of RUKADA puppet theatre. In the late 19th century, PASKU, or the PASSION PLAY, was born and popularized among the Christian population.

Modern theatre Modern drama, designed to appeal to urban audiences, began during the last decade of the 19th century in Colombo. It was inspired by the immense success of a touring Parsi musical troupe from Bombay – Baliwallas' Elphinstone Dramatic Company which appeared in the 1880s. The Parsi musical of that time appealed to audiences by combining popular Hindustani music with techniques borrowed from the amateur English theatre of India – proscenium-arch stages, painted changeable scenery, elaborate COSTUMES, declamatory acting, Western-style auditorium seating and the permanent enclosed theatre designed exclusively for the purpose of performance. The popularity of the Parsi musical prompted Colombo writers to imitate the Parsi models, writing Sinhalese dialogue and lyrics for the Hindustani tunes. The resultant form was known as nurti, 'new drama', and it soon ousted nadagama as the city's most popular theatre.

Nurti became a popular medium of expression and low-cost play editions were published and widely sold. Among the best-known writers was John de Silva (1857–1922), whose popularity eventually led to the construction of a theatre named in his honour. He borrowed ideas from Indian classical Sanskrit drama and combined them with elements of Parsi musicals. His plays were staged by the Arya Subadha Natya Sabha and later by the Vijaya Ranga Sabha. The first Sinhalese nurti was C. Don Bastian's Romeo and Juliet staged in 1884 and published in 1885. It was based on an adaption of SHAKESPEARE's work by D. J. Wijesingha.

Actresses performed in nurti, thus introducing women on to the stage for the first time. Educated middle-class spectators of Colombo were therefore hesitant to patronize this theatre. Nurti's real popularity was realized among the working-class people of the smaller towns and cities and it is still preserved today by amateur theatrical organizations which present performances in these environs during major Buddhist religious festivals. Although these activities are not called nurti today, they maintain a similar amalgam of MELODRAMA and COMEDY, song and declaimed dialogue and the same loose episodic structure. The performances are enacted during festival nights. In Colombo nurti declined and disappeared with the advent of the films in the 1930s. Symbolically, its death knell was sounded with the conversion of Colombo's Tower Hall Theatre to a cinema.

During the 1920s and 30s nurti was replaced by a brand of playwriting known by the name of an actor who made the plays successful – Eddie Jayamanna. Jayamanna plays satirized the middle and upper middle classes of Colombo. They maintained a pretence of using literary language and the characters sometimes burst into song. Besides the acting of Eddie Jayamanna, the plays are also remembered for the singing of Rukmini Devi. Eventually, jayamanna plays were adapted into films and have long since disappeared from the stage.

In the 1940s and 50s students of the Sinhalese Society of University College (now the University of Sri Lanka) in Colombo wrote straight plays in colloquial prose dialogue. These were Sinhalese translations and adaptations of Western dramatic classics by MOLIÈRE, WILDE and CHEKHOV. They were written by the intelligentsia for the intelligentsia.

In 1956 Ediriweera Sarachchandra's dramatization of a Buddhist Jataka tale, entitled Maname, broke new ground by attempting to formulate an indigenous style of writing using nadagama, sokari, thovil and folk dance music coupled with a serious theme meant for intellectuals. This led to a split between those writers favouring REALISM and those favouring folk-related theatre. By the mid-1960s the paths of the writers began to converge.

Today, modern theatre in Sri Lanka is still a part-time occupation for most of those engaged in it. Short-term workshops and symposia provide the only training for practitioners outside of their own performances. By custom, playwrights usually serve as directors and producers, and groups of actors in urban centres generally disband after a show has been completed. Theatre facilities are minimal, except in Colombo. But a large and loyal following for modern theatre has developed outside the urban centres as a result of touring companies who carry their lighting equipment and scenery with them and who set up their shows in makeshift facilities in cinema houses and schools.

Interest in drama has been stimulated in the young by island-wide drama competitions which showcase young talent. They are sponsored by the Department of Cultural Affairs. Drama and theatre have recently been adapted as part of the school curriculum and the training of drama teachers has proved quite successful at the University of Sri Lanka. (See also ASIAN AND PACIFIC ISLAND THEATRE.)
KJ

stage food The decorum of the classical theatre relegated to offstage both the celebratory feasts that conclude the comedies of ARISTOPHANES and the cannibal banquets of Thyestes and Atreus that entail tragic aftermaths. The bloodthirsty Elizabethans had no such qualms: as for tragedy, in Titus Andronicus (1594) Tamora feeds on her sons, 'baked in that Pie'. And the hunger of menials, which looms so large in European comedy, reaches the Gargantuan excesses of the starveling jongleur reconstructed by DARIO FO, who devours himself piecemeal before the eyes of the audience (SEE HUNGER ARTIST).

English theatrical tradition had Audrey in As You Like It munch a raw turnip, and Pistol in Henry V gnaw on compulsion a leek carved from an apple. Most commonly when Elizabethan actors were shown consuming food, the comestible was marchpane. Real marchpane was an elegant almond-paste spice-cake made for such special occasions as Juliet's nuptials; the stage version seems to have resembled hardtack, for BROME's *City Wit* (1629) refers to 'your player's marchpaines – all shew and no meat'. The standard stage meal was a Barmecide feast of empty pasteboard goblets and wooden fruit, just as the foodstuffs tossed about in harlequinades were of painted canvas stuffed with sawdust, 'ham' sandwiches filled with red blotting-paper, and custard pies confected of lather.

The danger and expense of supplying the real article are attested by the exceptions. Whincop tells us that, in Higden's comedy *The Wary Widow, or Sir Noisy Parrot* (1693), 'the author contrived so much drinking of punch that almost all the actors got drunk and the audience was dismissed at the end of the third act'. Things were better managed in Scotland, where, in Murray's MELODRAMA *Cramond Brig* (1826), it was an unwritten law to introduce a real sheep's head and trotters, which would afford the company a meal of broth one night and meat the next. Allan Ramsay's *The Gentle Shepherd* (1725) called for a real haggis, usually replaced by a dish of oatmeal; and a hot boiled leg of lamb and turnips made the centrepiece in Hoare's musical FARCE *No Song, No Supper* (1790). On the OPERATIC stage, it was customary to serve hot macaroni in *Masaniello* (1825) and genuine champagne in *Don Giovanni* (1787); but niggardly managers like Joe Cave of the Victoria Theatre frequently fined actors for eating the properties.

G. B. SHAW noted in 1894 that 'pasteboard pies ... are being banished from the stage by the growth of that power of accurate observation which is commonly called cynicism'. Certainly, at the dress rehearsal of *Cyrano de Bergerac* (1897) ROSTAND's wife felt compelled to compensate for the property-master's frugality by garnishing Ragueneau's *pâtisserie* with purchases from a local delicatessen. With the rise of dramatic NATURALISM, onstage cooking became the rage, so that the scenes of roly-poly pudding making and leg-of-mutton roasting in T. W. ROBERTSON's *Ours* (1866) were pronounced 'irresistibly droll' (G. A. Sala). When ZOLA dramatized his novel *Le Ventre de Paris* (1887) with one episode in a *charcuterie* kitchen, it proved impractical to manufacture blood pudding *in situ*, so a simpler galantine was substituted. The display of culinary techniques continues even now. ARNOLD WESKER's *The Kitchen* (1959), showing a day in the life of a restaurant staff, wisely chose PANTOMIME as its medium; but at London's NATIONAL THEATRE, JOAN PLOWRIGHT concocted and dished up a Neapolitan ragù in successive acts of EDUARDO DE FILIPPO's *Saturday, Sunday, Monday* (London production, 1973), while Cardinal Richelieu whipped up and ate an omelette in ROGER PLANCHON's *Trois Mousquetaires*. A classic recipe for potato salad was read aloud in DUMAS *fils*'s *Francillon* (1887), but in VIKTOR SLAVKIN's *A Young Man's Grown-up Daughter* (Stanislavsky Theatre, Moscow, 1979), the audience watched with bated breath as a potato salad was constructed on stage ('They forgot the mayonnaise' was a frequent comment). In TINA HOWE's *The Art of Dining* the locale is a cooking school in operation.

The rise of the society comedy reflected the table manners of a round of meals. F. Anstey's *The Man from Blankley's* (1901) was probably the first play to be completely structured around the grave sequence of a Victorian dinner party; but Shaw's *You Never Can Tell* (1898) had required a full-course lunch to be served and consumed in Act 2. William Collier's *Never Say Die* (1912) presented an afternoon tea in the first act, an elaborate dinner in the second (complete with freshly cooked lobster Newburg and asparagus tips) and breakfast for the finale. Less patrician feeding was also represented. The opening Bowery saloon scene in EDWARD's SHELDON's *Salvation Nell* (1908) had a fresh keg of beer tapped at every performance, and the counter was furnished with cheese and pretzels. DAVID BELASCO recreated a Child's Restaurant on stage in the last act of *The Governor's Lady* (1912), with the characters effecting a reconciliation while tucking into freshly made buckwheat cakes and coffee, whose aroma wafted into the stalls.

The use of real food sets serious pitfalls for performers. Although Lucien Guitry had no trouble polishing off thirty-five zakuski at each performance of *Le Grand Duc* (1921), an actress in GILBERT's *Engaged* (1877), required to eat three strawberry tarts in quick succession every night, soon went off that sweet. Rosetta Le Noire gained 23lb consuming chocolate mints in *Anna Lucasta* (1944). JOHN GIELGUD, sickened by bolting the muffins in *The Importance of Being Earnest*, slowed down and discovered that when they were partaken of with real solemnity the scene got more laughs.

This illustrates the problem of timing mastication to fit the lines. To enable actors to chew, swallow and speak with some dexterity, more manageable substitutes are usually provided. The last act of GALSWORTHY's *Old English* (1924) hinges on an epicurean dinner of oysters, Germaine soup, fillet of sole, sweetbreads, cutlet Soubise, rum soufflé and cheese, washed down with sherry, champagne, port and brandy. What GEORGE ARLISS actually ate for the sweetbread was lemon meringue, the cutlet was soft toast garnished with green pepper, and the soufflé portions of orange slices. Mashed potatoes or bananas can easily be moulded into fish or poultry fillets; ricotta cheese stands in for ice-cream; tinned stew is a versatile substitute, and more recently tofu has become a popular double. The much hated liver in NEIL SIMON's *Brighton Beach Memoirs* (1990) was actually steamed black bread. Champagne corks can be made to pop with a mixture of Alka Seltzer and ginger ale, which prolongs the fizz. Whisky may be cold tea, red wine cranberry juice, white wine diluted white grape juice, but it has proved difficult to come up with an ersatz beer.

The steam from a smoking tureen usually issues from dry ice, and the Cratchits' pudding in many *A Christmas Carol* is a gauze pad steeped in a mixture of ammonia and hydrochloric acid. Modern technology has aided the property-maker in devising convincing if inedible substitutes out of latex, foam rubber, spray paint, Plasticine moulds and vinyl. Durable and visually enticing, they have the drawback of bouncing when dropped.   LS

stage lighting Stage lighting, particularly in the 100 years since the first use of electricity in the theatre, has had a profound effect upon staging, scenery, styles of production and acting, and even upon the shape of the theatre building itself. But its impact must be seen against a continuum that takes us back centuries.

Sophisticated electric lighting now employs computers and precisely focused lighting instruments subtly to control the composition, intensity and colour of light. Such control allows atmospheric light to fill the theatrical space, to reveal the living actor and unify him with his stage environment. Its development has encouraged the new, specialist profession of the lighting designer.

Theatre has always used the technology of its period. Stage lighting did not begin with electricity. The important role of lighting in the theatre has been recognized since the 16th century. During the days of candle, oil lamp and gas, great ingenuity was employed to illuminate the stage and provide atmosphere and effects. Many principles concerning the placement of lighting, the basic types of instrument and even the intentions of the lighting designer were conceived a surprisingly long time ago. Theatre began outdoors: God said, 'Let there be light', and he liked what he saw. All religions have recognized light as a fundamental element, the one which enables us to see. From the most ancient times, light and its primeval influence on our every thought, emotion and action has been seen as a harbinger of things to come, as a messenger from the supernatural and as a constantly changing companion that shapes all life on earth.

The theatre evolved from religious RITUAL. The moving of the sun across the sky, the waxing and waning of the moon, the wheeling firmament of stars, the seasons, all played an important role in the life of early man. Primitive theatre used this natural light. As the open-air theatres of ancient Egypt, Crete and Greece developed and became more formalized, the cycle of natural light would play a part. The more comfort-loving audiences of ancient Rome were protected from the weather by coloured awnings that could be drawn over the semicircular auditorium. Presumably daylight was still the predominant light source, although after dark, torches, braziers, fires and oil lamps were put to theatrical use, for they were the only means of dispelling darkness. (Nero's 'concert lighting' became the stuff of legends.)

The earliest custom-built theatres of England were also open to the elements and to natural light. These theatres had a flexible, but usually thrust-shaped stage, surrounded by the audience. The stage roof space concealed the hoisting machinery for the descent of gods and visions, and the ceiling was painted to represent the heavens. (Light was also represented in this way in the surprisingly similar forms of theatre across the world in China.) The beauty of light has never been more exquisitely described in words than by SHAKESPEARE, but perhaps even he used flame to illuminate a gloomy winter matinée performance, or to enhance the drama.

In *Seven Deadly Sins of London* (1606), THOMAS DEKKER described a shuttered city 'like a private playhouse, when the windows are clamped down, as if some nocturnal or dismal tragedy were presently to be acted'. Indoor performances must also have taken place, and perhaps had done so since the cave dwellers. No doubt, light was admitted or shuttered and artificial light kindled or put out, according to the show, the time of day and the ingenuity of the ancient organizers.

The Church was highly organized. Religious ceremony has always employed the symbolism of light, but the 15th century marks a significant beginning to the employment of artificial light: a Russian bishop describes an incident concerning Brunelleschi's (1377–1446) *Annunciation* in the church of San Felice, Florence. From a revolving globe, surrounded by circles of light illuminating translucent clouds, which supported eight cherubim, was lowered another, internally lit globe, containing the Angel Gabriel. This could be darkened by remote control as he stepped out to speak to Mary. As the angel returned and rose into the air, the light blazed forth again. Other descriptions of the period reveal more spectacular effects, with over 1000 oil lamps, diagonal and tracking movements of tableaux and lighting, rays of fire, glistering fireworks and glowing clouds all re creating in three dimensions the wonders of

A candle-snuffer trimming the footlights.

Renaissance painting and pointing the way to the stage-craft that was soon to come.

But in the open-air MYSTERY PLAYS of more northern Europe, how was light evoked? The *mansion* or wagon depicting hell's mouth probably belched out real flame and smoke. But a stage direction of 1501 in the Mons PASSION PLAY reads: 'See to it that the painter goes to Paradise to paint Raphael's face red.' In the same play, Christ is described as having gold hands and feet – and 'Let there be a big sun behind him.' Painting the features, reflective metal haloes or even a brightly polished basin to reflect the sunlight were used, some indications of which are to be found in the Revello Passion of 1483.

The influence of Italy The Italian Renaissance theatre became the cradle of stage lighting. Artificial light must have possessed great power over people's imagination. For most of the population, darkness, which began as the sun set each day, was only occasionally broken by flame, torch or a guttering smoky candle.

The courts of 16th-century Italy provided the opportunity. First in 1514 is a description of PERUZZI's design of *La Calandria*, one of the earliest comments on the use of perspective on the stage. 'One cannot imagine how in so narrow a space he could build up so many places ... with great knowledge he also arranged the sources of light, the inner light that increases the perspective illusion.' In 1580 we find the author GUARINI extolling the virtue and economy of good lighting for his plays: 'Without artificial lighting, the scene will be deprived of its beauty ... besides, expenses will be reduced ... for the beauty that can be created by light can be made up only by great expense in adorning devices.'

A pupil of Peruzzi, SERLIO, built a theatre in Vicenza during the 1530s, and in 1545 published his *Architettura*, which describes contemporary theatrical methods. His drawings of a semicircular theatre with shallow perspective scenes are part of theatre history. His lighting descriptions, which are less well known, bring his woodcut renderings to life. He describes 'general stage light', which lights the whole stage; 'decorative light', ornamenting the perspective picture; and 'mobile light' that often simulates the sun or moon moving across the sky. General light is achieved by torches and chandeliers hung above and to the front of the stage, but the chandeliers have reflective glass vessels filled with liquid to aim the light towards the stage. 'It is better to illuminate the scene from the middle because of the greater power of a light hanging in the centre,' he states, but he also mentions that 'a large number of lights are placed leaning at the front of the scene' – the first mention of footlights?

The first recorded stage lighting instrument was the *bozze*. This was a glass vessel of various convex and concave shapes, filled either with oil and wick when used as a lamp, or with coloured liquids as a colour medium, lens or reflector. A number of these, fixed to boards behind holes in the scene, would light up the windows of the street or the many coloured silk transparencies of the pastoral scene. When a strong light was needed, 'you put a torch behind a glass and, behind, a barber's basin well burnished'. Thus the spotlight had also arrived. The stage, glowing with multicoloured, flickering light, shimmering

The Warsaw National Theatre, 1791; the stage, auditorium and orchestra pit are all lit by candles.

with encrusted and translucent scenery and jewel-bedecked costumes, must have been an astonishing and lovely spectacle.

In about 1565 LEONE DE' SOMMI, a dramatist and stage designer of Mantua, anticipated GORDON CRAIG by 350 years when he wrote *Four Dialogues on Scenic Representation* in which his protagonists discourse upon mood and atmosphere. From a stage expressing joy, brightness and life with brilliant and glowing colours, they discuss the onset of tragedy with much of the lighting dimmed or put out. 'This created a profound impression of horror ... and won universal praise.' De' Sommi pointed out that the coloured lens-like *bozze* not only coloured the light effectively but also reduced glare. He recommended the use of mirrors to amplify the lights, but also to allow them to be placed further from the stage, hidden from view behind the wings, to reduce obnoxious smoke. Smoke and heat were severe problems for hundreds of years. Finally, he championed the darkened auditorium: 'A man in the shade sees more distinctly an object illuminated from afar.' Further: 'You obviate smoke fumes and render the seeing clearer ... you save the Duke fifty ducats in respect of the torches usually set.'

Truly, stage lighting had begun! Angelo Ingeneri (1550–1613) was the scene designer for the famed Teatro Olimpico in Vicenza in 1585. He described lighting in 1598 as 'one matter of supreme theatrical importance'. He also said, 'The darker the auditorium, the more luminous seems the stage.' He wanted light sources concealed and was concerned that the actors' faces be well lit. To this end he proposed the first flown lighting position over the front of the stage: 'a valance ... on the inner side fitted with lamps having tinsel reflectors'. Ingeneri described the use of gauze to give an effect of mystery, and stressed the creative use of light and darkness to enhance the drama. Also in Italy, BERNARDO BUONTALENTI worked on a stage at the Uffizi, which used about 100 oil lamps with four wicks each, including footlights behind an ornamental balustrade. The lighting crew were told to take great care in trimming the wicks and refilling the lamps.

Stage lighting was by now becoming systematized, and SABBATTINI in his *Manual for Theatrical Scenes and Machines* (1638) describes that system in words and drawings. He evaluates the merits and problems of oil lamps and candles and sketches the fittings. He illustrates a method of remote dimming by lowering tin cylinders on cords over each light. He describes proscenium lights, footlights and sidelights behind the wings ('lights must be strongly fixed so they do not shake during the dances'). Sabbattini started a discussion on the problems of footlights that was to last over 300 years. 'The disadvantages outweigh the advantages. You believe that you make the stage brighter, but it actually becomes darker. Heat, dazzle and smell force the actors backward, their legs and costumes are brighter than their pale and haggard faces and a haze of smoke creates a barrier to clear vision.' He also mentions a concealed upstage row of lamps, parallel to the footlights, to light ground rows and backcloths. JOSEF FURTTENBACH, a German who studied in Italy and published *Architectura Recreationis* in 1640, gives a detailed description of lighting, which includes *bozzi* with reflec-

tors in a seven-foot-deep upstage pit, as well as, for the first time, rows of lamps overhead 'between the clouds'. This completed the repertoire of Renaissance lighting that created precedents for patterns of thought and practice that still pertain today.

As the Renaissance transformed itself into the elaborations of the baroque, Italian influence spread across Europe, with each country emphasizing one aspect or another according to its own theatrical tradition. In England, INIGO JONES bought and used some *bozzi* in 1609. He opened English theatre to Italian-style spectacle and employed multicoloured lights in profusion. He vividly used translucencies and produced extraordinary effects of nature, but his more old-fashioned flambeaux torches, used in the Whitehall Banqueting Room, damaged the ceiling paintings and theatrical performances there were stopped.

The Puritan revolution brought English theatre to a halt, but the future King Charles II, living in France, saw much of theatrical development in the French court. In 1660, Richard Flecknoe in *A Discourse of the English Stage* said, 'We in England are only scholars and learners yet ... especially not knowing how to place our lights, for the more advantage and illuminating of the scenes.' With the English Restoration, London theatres were built and restored, but were now indoors. The COCKPIT (1660) had two chandeliers and five pairs of sconces. In the Hall Theatre (1665) tin lanterns and reflectors are described, but a few years later these were supplanted by 130 candlesticks with reflectors. Footlights, too, are described in February 1670. The frontispiece to *The Wits*, 1672, shows an indoor stage but with an almost Elizabethan thrust, lit with chandeliers and footlights.

In France, it was the court that led the way to innovation. In 1581 the *Ballet Comique de La Reine* was performed. The famous sketch of this production shows a courtyard space with audience on three sides, but the settings are simultaneously spread through parts of the hall, like medieval *mansions*. Detailed descriptions tell of scenery glittering with gold and jewels, shining in the light of many lamps. Gauzes and glowing translucencies, transparent coloured glasses – all the techniques of Renaissance lighting – must have made a magical spectacle, which, sadly, only comes to us today through an inadequate black and white engraving.

In 1641 in Paris, CARDINAL RICHELIEU began the horse-shoe-shaped PALAIS-ROYAL theatre, where MOLIÈRE was later to perform. The width of the proscenium was only 9.5 metres and the stage depth 17.55 metres. In 1687 Nicodemus Tessin, a Swedish architect touring Europe, described the lighting. Footlights with 50 lamps, each with five flames, supplemented candles on vertical lighting poles at either side of the stage and chandeliers in the auditorium. The French theatre blazed with light throughout, unlike the Italian, where more frequently the auditorium was darkened so as to increase the impact of the stage. Tessin also wrote of his experiences in the Italian theatre. In Venice he visited the San Giovanni Grisostomo. Here the lighting had been developed on the principles of Sabbattini. The chandeliers at the front of the auditorium were hoisted out of sight to darken it, and the footlights could be gradually raised or lowered. Side lighting was now on turnable poles to enable the brightness to be varied and portable lighting strips could be attached to wing trolleys or set pieces.

The Italian stage rapidly grew in width and depth. A scene could be created up to 40 metres in depth. Wings, sliding in grooves, could be swiftly changed and backcloths could be flown in to vary the depth of the stage. Machines could move huge tableaux with performers and lights up and down and diagonally. Mirrors, glass and translucency made spectacular effects. Contrasts of light and shade enhanced the sense of depth of the stage, and asymmetry and oblique perspective scenery became increasingly popular. FERDINANDO BIBIENA and his family led the movement that produced astonishing vistas on the stage. Asymmetrical scenery with great columns or trees in the middle of the stage, behind which lights could be hidden, must have greatly improved the possibility of lighting the darker middle of the backcloth.

GIOVANNI SERVANDONI, an Italian who worked extensively in Paris, developed further the use of distorted perspective and transparencies to create the impression of vast distances and spectacle. In 1738 he opened his Spectacle d'Optique in the SALLE DES MACHINES, Paris, with a stage 40 metres deep. From a darkened auditorium, spectators watched performances depicting mythological events, which used live and painted figures in gigantic settings. 'A large number of lamps were so well arranged that it all resembled a tableau of a perfectly arranged chiaroscuro', was one observation. Servandoni himself observed that 'expenses for the lighting had been no less than 10,000 francs, but ... the admission-fees had yielded nearly 20,000 francs'. Outside the conventional theatre, such spectacles, under the direction of leading stage designers such as DE LOUTHERBOURG (in 1781) and Daguerre (in 1822), proved their popularity time and again. Their value as an occasion for experiment, which returns benefit to the theatre, has parallels for today, where high-budget, industrial theatre and rock-and-roll spectacle provide a similar opportunity for development.

England's great actor and director, DAVID GARRICK, travelled to the Continent in 1765 and returned determined to modernize the lighting at his Theatre Royal, DRURY LANE. A friend, Jean Monnet of the Paris Opéra-Comique, sent samples of stage lighting equipment to London. They were a success: 'The public were agreeably surprised to see the stage illuminated with a strong and clear light, and the rings removed that used to supply it.' Garrick introduced wing and footlights with reflectors and removed the overhanging chandeliers. His great scene designer, De Lutherbourg, a master of atmosphere creation, used colour-changing silks on his side lighting. At the COMÉDIE-FRANÇAISE Ferdinando Quaglio, a designer, stated that he needed one whole day to arrange the scenery and lighting: 'The illumination should be to my taste and regardless of expense, particularly during the first two or three nights.' He also stipulated his desire for billing on the posters. The management were grudging. They might provide billing, but the lighting would be arranged by the theatre 'as was habitual'. However, M. Quaglio 'could have access to the stage, provided no other performance was jeopardized'.

In 1790 George Saunders wrote *A Treatise on Theatres*. He recommended placing 'reverberators' on the front of the near-stage boxes, and mentions these front-of-house spotlights being used successfully at several theatres including Blenheim.

Stage lighting was continually growing brighter. At the Comédie-Française in 1719, 48 tallow candles were used in the footlights. In 1783 there were 128 of the more efficient, but more expensive, wax candles. In 1784 the Argand lamp was developed: this was an oil lamp but, for the first time, with a chimney. It was as bright as about a dozen wax candles. Used with reflectors it created new conditions on the stage, which contributed towards the reduction of make-up and towards new styles of costume – and, most importantly, it encouraged another step towards more naturalistic acting.

Gaslight In 1803 the LYCEUM THEATRE, London, was the scene of a historic demonstration: lighting by gaslight. It was not until 1817 that the stage of the same theatre was to be the first in England lit by the new substance. A month later the stage of Drury Lane blazed with the new light; but already across the Atlantic, the CHESTNUT STREET THEATRE, Philadelphia, had installed gas the year before. The owners 'flatter themselves that its superior safety, brilliance and neatness will be satisfactory'.

The gas burned with a bare flame, for the mantle would not be invented until the end of the 19th century. Albeit dependent on the quality of the gas, the light it produced was brighter and whiter than even the Argand lamp. It burned without changing intensity and required no trimming of wicks – and, most vitally, it was easier to control. The brightness could be varied by regulating the gas supply, and a 'gas table' that allowed control of separate parts of the stage became the first 'stage switchboard'. At the Paris Opéra in 1822 the former ballet-master wrote, 'This light is perfect for the stage. One can obtain gradation of brightness that is really magical.' But there were problems. The smell of gas could be offensive and the danger from heat was more serious than ever. Bare gas jets next to wood and canvas presented a major hazard. The Chestnut Street Theatre disappointed its owners and was one of the first of hundreds to burn down.

As the use of gas became more widespread, it was principally employed to replace the former oil lamps and candles. Perhaps the only significant change in lighting positions was the increase in overhead battens of light. High in the air, it was easier to light a row of gas jets than a great quantity of candles. But brightness again increased and opened up new possibilities. *The Corsair* at HER MAJESTY'S THEATRE, London, in 1856 removed the customary wings and employed a panoramic cyclorama. Once again styles of acting, scenery, costumes and make-up that had seemed acceptable under murky candle and oil lamp light now seemed overblown, vulgar and garish.

Gaslight could not provide a beam or shaft of light any better than its predecessors. But in 1826 a new light source, limelight, was invented. W. C. MACREADY tested it in his PANTOMIME *Peeping Tom of Coventry* at COVENT GARDEN in 1837. Limelight used a block of quicklime heated by a flame of oxygen and hydrogen to provide an intense point source that could be installed in a hand-operated spotlight. This, for the first time, was used to provide strong accents of light across the stage.

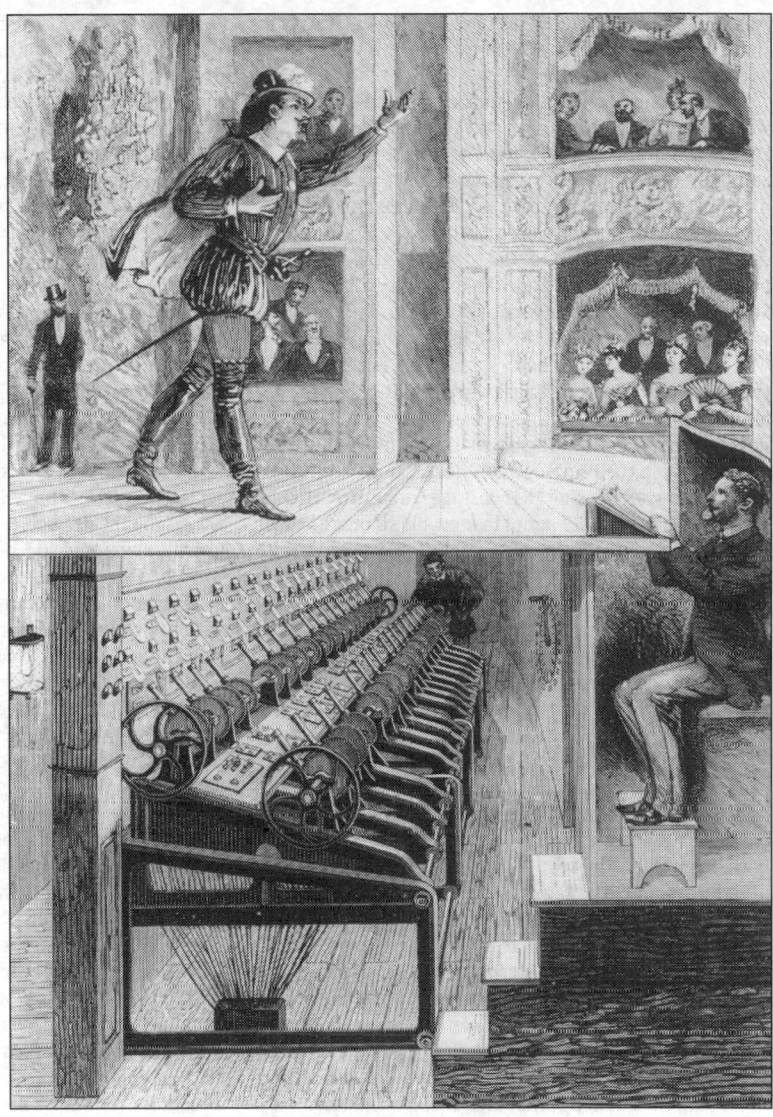

The electric switchboard of
the Paris Opéra, 1887.

The practice of darkening the auditorium during the performance was introduced by HENRY IRVING, who was a great innovator in stage lighting. 'Stage lighting and groupings are of more consequence than the scenery,' he said. He explored the subtleties of colour mixing and sought to enhance his productions with the imaginative use of light and shade. Bram Stoker, his lighting assistant, reported: 'It became an easy matter to throw any special part of the stage into greater prominence.' Irving had extensive lighting rehearsals, without actors but attended by the staff, which included his 30 gasmen and eight limelight operators. In 1889 the French director ANTOINE wrote of his admiration for Irving's lighting.

Stage lighting had spawned a service industry to the theatre. Walter Kerr (1809–93) became the 'king of limelight'. Employing dozens of technicians, his firm serviced most of the principal theatres of London with staff and equipment. On his death one of the crew said, 'He was the "father of limelight". At one time he used to do all the business. Contracted all the theatres, and laid by, they say, quite 30,000 pounds. Old Kerr was the grandfather of us all.' In 1857, Charles Garnier's new Paris Opéra had opened. It contained a lighting system with 28 miles of piping, feeding 960 gas jets from a gas table of 88 stopcocks. A Parisian lighting catalogue of 1877 contains details of many types of instrument, including carbon-arc spotlights which ranged from versions that could flood the whole stage to small hand-held follow spotlights. A multitude of special effects and projection apparatus was used. The climax of the age of gas employed massive resources, often to spectacular effect.

Electric light In 1881 the Savoy Theatre in London opened with an electric lighting installation. It used 1158 incandescent lamps, of which 824 were on the stage, controlled by six dimmers. Richard D'Oyly Carte appeared before the curtain and demonstrated the new safety of electricity by smashing a lit lamp wrapped in muslin. This was greeted with tumultuous cheers.

The electrical revolution quickly spread across the world. David Belasco tells us that the first theatre in the USA to be equipped with electricity was the California in San Francisco. However, for many years electric light was used only to replace the gas jets that preceded it. Footlights, battens and vertical strips at the side of the stage were converted to the new electricity. It was brighter, had no smell and was much safer. (A Captain Shaw noted that the temperature in the grid of the Savoy was 68 degrees while at the Alhambra, with gaslight, it was 105 degrees Fahrenheit.) It has been estimated that the electric lamp was perhaps a third brighter than the gas jet. Despite frequent criticism of excessive, harsh brightness, theatres rapidly increased the number of lamps used. By 1902, the Prinzregententheater in Munich had a four-colour system using 1542 onstage lamps in footlights, battens and wings, 770 lamps in movable standards (floor stands) and lengths (strip lights), and 12 arc lamps. Despite being cumbersome and often noisy, and flickering, arc lights were still required to give accent. It was many years before the spotlight, coupled to the dimmer, began to offer new opportunities. Even today the arc lamp is still in use as the brightest long-range follow spot, although newer light sources such as xenon increasingly replace the carbon arc.

Meanwhile, in reaction against the flat glare of early electric light, two men, GORDON CRAIG and ADOLPHE APPIA, were dreaming of a new stage lighting. Both rejected the increasingly realistic scenery of their time, and both, inspired by the beauty and evocative power of natural light, imagined a stage with the actor within an environment unified by being filled with three-dimensional light. Appia said, 'Light is to space what sounds are to time.' Craig wrote of a 'master of the art and science of the theatre', the stage manager, who would unify all the arts of theatre into a harmonious whole. Craig and Appia were more influential by their writings than by their all too few productions. Others, although perhaps without realizing it, took up the challenge that their inspiration posed.

In the USA, BELASCO was the first director of the 20th century to pay great attention to lighting. Lighting rehearsals for his productions could take weeks, and he established a lighting laboratory to plan the lighting in advance. His engineer was Louis Hartmann, who for 28 years worked with him and was responsible for the development of the first incandescent spotlights. They also introduced indirect overhead lighting by shining spotlights into reflective silver-coated bowls, which produced a soft, naturalistic impression of light from the sky. Today, a multiplicity of carefully focused spotlights creates an equally soft and potentially naturalistic impression, but with the advantage – we believe today – of more precise control.

Hartmann, a great innovator, was a true man of the theatre. 'Why should we suppose that a radical change is necessary in the theatre?' he wrote. 'The glory of a sunrise or sunset is just the same today as when the first human beheld it. Our emotions have not changed. Let us use our modern devices to enhance the value of the text; and

"hold, as 't were, the mirror up to nature".' In 1917 Hartmann's baby spotlights were first introduced in Britain by the director BASIL DEAN. He, like Belasco, was intensely concerned with stage lighting, and also introduced German equipment such as the acting-area flood. In 1923 he installed a Schwabe cyclorama system at the St Martin's Theatre, London, and in *R.U.R.* used scene projection in Britain for the first time. In 1939 he directed J. B. PRIESTLEY's *Johnson over Jordan*, devising with his electrician, Bill Lorraine, a British version of Hartmann's reflected light.

A giant of the German theatre, who shared Dean's conviction about the importance of lighting, was the director MAX REINHARDT. His versatility made him a master of the stage, in the tradition spoken of by Gordon Craig, with productions that ranged from the vast and spectacular *The Miracle* to the most intimate, such as his work at the Redoutensaal recital room in Vienna. 'Lighting must replace the decorations,' he wrote in 1901.

German theatres, since the mid-19th century, had been lavishly appointed, aided by substantial funding from the court or state. The practice of repertoire, with a different performance every night, led to large stages equipped with bridges hung over them to carry the lighting, which could thus be readily reached and reset by electricians. Equipment was large but finely engineered. High-quality optics and spacious stages encouraged developments in large-scale scene projection. Linnebach, Haseit and other German engineers developed a pattern of stage lighting which, from the 1920s, was to remain largely unchanged for many years. Meanwhile in the USA and later in Britain, lighting in the form of electric lamps in rows of battens (or X-rays) and footlights, imitating the soft overall lighting of the age of gas, began to change.

The oldest specialist stage lighting manufacturer is Kliegl Bros of New York, founded in 1896. Siemens of Germany and Clemançon in Paris are early pioneers, but counted the stage as only one of many activities. In England, Strand Electric was founded in 1914 and remained the leading British company in the field for over 80 years. Innovation for many years was largely under the direction of Frederick Bentham (b.1911). He led the development of many modern English instruments, but his major achievement was in the field of lighting control.

Intensity control of electric light was achieved with dimmers, variable resistances or auto-transformers, the operation of which was synchronized by increasingly sophisticated mechanical linkage systems. A grand master control allowed dimmers to be connected via shafts and clutches to a central lever or wheel. Bentham, inspired by a lifelong enthusiasm for 'colour music', mixing light to music, conceived that lighting should be controlled in a way that was analogous to music. He developed the light console, which employed a console derived from the cinema organ, driving remote motor-driven dimmers. An alternative way of miniaturizing lighting control, with multiple presets, was developed using thyratron valves. These were later replaced by silicon control rectifiers (SCRs). A skilled operator was able to play the lighting in a remarkably fluid manner. One man instead of many could control several hundred dimmers. This led to remote-control systems being installed by WEST END commercial managements a decade before such systems were adopted by BROADWAY in the USA. The emerging, and wealthy, TV industry in Britain adopted the principle of dimmer control for each light and installed similar control systems. The advent of the computer led to the first memory control.

In the USA, Ed Kook founded Century Lighting. He developed the compact ellipsoidal spotlight, often colloquially named the Leko, after himself and his partner Levy. More significantly, Kook supported the emergence of the new professional in the theatre, the lighting designer. While in England between the wars lighting was the province of the director, with men such as TERENCE GRAY and NORMAN MARSHALL working with their electrician Harold Ridge, in the USA lighting remained the designer's responsibility. LEE SIMONSON, NORMAN BEL GEDDES, ROBERT EDMOND JONES, DONALD OENSLAGER and JO MIELZINER all extended the use of lighting as an integral part of their scene designs.

Lighting design In 1925, Stanley McCandless was appointed to teach stage lighting at Yale University. In *A Method of Lighting the Stage* he formulated a structured approach to the new lighting. Specialists in lighting design – ABE FEDER, Peggy Clark and JEAN ROSENTHAL – emerged and began to establish a professionalism around the lighting process.

In Britain in the late 1930s, Joe Davis (1912–84) was an electrician with leading theatrical producers, H. M. Tennent. His lighting for hundreds of productions demonstrated a rare sensitivity, and his work reproducing American productions which transferred to London in the 1950s demonstrated the advances that had been effected by the professional lighting designer in the USA. In 1957

Richard Pilbrow founded Theatre Projects. He introduced into Britain American methods of pre-planning lighting and imported equipment from America and Germany, thus widening the spectrum of technology available. He also developed a team of lighting designers, and in so doing established the lighting design profession in Britain. This team included Robert Ornbo, Robert Bryan, John B. Read, David Hersey, Andy Bridge, Nick Chelton and others who were to have a profound influence upon British stage lighting. Through the 1980s, with the emergence of CAMERON MACKINTOSH as worldwide producer of the British 'mega-hit' MUSICAL, this lighting influence went international, particularly with Hersey (*Cats, Les Misérables* and *Miss Saigon*) and Bridge (*Phantom of the Opera* and *Sunset Boulevard*). These spectacular productions demonstrated dramatic stage lighting, employing all the resources of modern technology, but always aimed at enhancing and underpinning the drama of story and song.

Just as designers of the 18th century took their work outside the theatre, so today the lighting designer's skills find a wider audience. Designed lighting in architecture shows the significant impact of theatre practitioners, as does lighting for television. Rock-and-roll concert lighting and industrial theatre and exhibitions have been fruitful areas of operation for the designer, and have also offered much opportunity for technical experiment.

The increase in government financial support for REGIONAL THEATRE in the UK and for the NATIONAL THEATRE in London and the ROYAL SHAKESPEARE COMPANY in the 1970s and 80s led to considerable improvement in British stage design and lighting. And there were other factors that led to an explosion in lighting opportunity. Industrial theatre, trade shows and commercial presentations

Cheek by Jowl's *As You Like It* (Dir: Declan Donnellan; Des: Nick Ormerod; Lighting Des: Judith Greenwood). Lighting creates the Forest of Arden within a white set by the use of colour and gobos.

became increasingly theatrical and complex. The emergence of the popular music industry created a huge upsurge of lighting for concert tours. These often employed, by theatrical standards, amazingly elaborate resources involving much ingenuity on the part of the pioneer designers and technicians, who introduced techniques that were later to influence theatrical practice. New theatres with new sophisticated installations and new demands from directors and producers brought new designers to the forefront. By the mid-1990s the work of British-based designers such as Chris Parry, Paul Pyant, Benny Ball, Mark Henderson, Rick Fisher, Mick Hughes, Jean Kalman, Mark Brickman, Patrick Woodroffe and hundreds of others is seen all around the world. There has been a similar explosion in lighting equipment manufacture. In 1957 there were less than half a dozen companies in the field, whereas in 1994 nearly 200 firms were members of PLASA, the Professional Lighting and Sound Association, many of whose members are major equipment suppliers internationally.

In the USA, unlike Britain, major universities offer training in stage lighting design. Outstanding designers such as THARON MUSSER, Jules Fisher, JENNIFER TIPTON, Roger Morgan, John Gleason, Ken Billington, Richard Nelson, Howell Binkley, Paul Gallo and Marc Weiss lead a profession rich in both numbers and talent. As in Britain, the proliferation of regional theatre has led to a widening of opportunity for the lighting designer. The major regional theatres and opera companies utilize lighting of the highest quality, with designers such as Peter Maradudin, Pat Collins, Arden Fingerhut and Thomas Mann. Architectural lighting as a vital part of architectural design is more strongly established in the USA than elsewhere, in large part thanks to the early influence of theatre lighting designers such as Abe Feder and Jean Rosenthal, who have been followed by such outstanding practitioners as Paul Marantz, Howard Brandston and William Lam. Chip Mounk, Jeff Ravitz and James Moody are three of the pioneers of rock-and-roll lighting, which not only has had an important influence upon theatre techniques, but has also probably become the widest known market for theatrical lighting, opening the eyes of millions to the excitement of lighting through live concerts and television broadcasts.

A 1990 study by lighting designer Lee Watson estimated that there might be as many as 50,00 individuals worldwide in lighting or associated industries. Of these, some 260 were members of the United Scenic Artists Union (New York, Chicago, Los Angeles and Florida lighting designers); 400 were architectural lighting members of the International Association of Lighting Designers; and 200 were members of the Hollywood American Society of Cinematographers. The British Association of Theatre Lighting Designers had 120 members (up to 300 in 1994), British TV lighting associations have 400 members, Canadian TV 120 members, and Australian TV 120 members – to list but a selection. Altogether Watson estimated 3000 lighting designers worldwide, with others involved as educators, technicians, manufacturers or suppliers.

British and American techniques increasingly merged in the 1980s. Lighting is now achieved with a multiplicity of spotlights (largely ellipsoidal or profile spots that allow the beam of light to be shaped at will), which may be coloured with a choice of hundreds of different shades of plastic colour media. Accent light is usually provided by low-voltage beam projectors or PAR (parabolic reflector sealed-beam) reflector lamps. Instruments are still usually positioned overhead on pipes or trusses in rows across the stage and vertically at the side. In the 1950s, probably 200 instruments were commonplace, but in 1994 over 600–1200 units, of an average power of 1000 watts, were the norm. Swings of theatrical fashion seem to dictate whether or not the lighting should be hidden from the audience's sight, or be incorporated into the scenic design.

Until the late 1980s instrument design had advanced little since the principles were established in the 30s. In Britain, CCT was first to develop profile spots with a variable zoom beam angle. Advances in lamp manufacture and in reflector design continue to allow improvement in instrument efficiency in the incandescent lamp. The use of new light sources continues, but the theatre's need to have smooth dimming from full brightness to black-out is a restraint. Highly efficient discharge lighting sources using mechanical shutters to fade out the light are used most commonly in Germany.

From the concert music business new advances in remote-control focusing have become increasingly available. Since the early 60s, spotlights with motorized focusing and colour change have been developed, but usually at considerable cost. Led by innovations from Vari*Lite of Dallas, Texas, the world of rock and roll began successfully using computer-controlled remotely resettable spotlights and, helped by falling prices, this has spread to the theatre. Now fluid control is possible over not only the intensity of light, but also its movement about the stage and its colour, and all are capable of sudden or subtle change as the action unfolds. The brightness improvement of projection equipment, developed in Austria and France, has encouraged renewed interest in scenic projection in the USA and Europe. Projections of enormous size, almost able to compete with daylight, are now possible, together with computer control of the image changer.

Lighting and the computer The advent of the computer brought the ability to memorize at the touch of a button a complete lighting picture, initially by recording the level of dimmer channels, but later by recording the position of remote-controlled spotlights and colour changers. As theatre consultant to the NATIONAL THEATRE Richard Pilbrow designed Lightboard, a control that developed Bentham's 'playability' but with a new freedom to mix pre-recorded lighting images or 'groups'. It offered for the first time a control that combined intensity recording with remote-control focusing, and through the use of calculator keyboard channel and group access and multiple control wheels established a standard for most of the control systems that followed. Only in the mid-1990s, as a consequence of the constantly greater memory, speed and cheapness of micro-processors, does the prospect of another quantum leap forward in lighting control appear. Computer power will be used to handle the ever-increasing complexity of lighting systems, without the endless proliferation of numbers and digits and using graphics and computer modelling techniques to close the loop between the visual image on the stage and the mind processes of the designer.

The centuries-old argument over footlights and the need for light from the front and above the actor is long over. Front-of-house spotlighting was first mounted on the front of the balconies, then invaded the audience boxes, and now hundreds of instruments may be used. New theatres make elaborate provision, with bridges in the ceiling and slots in the walls, to allow light to reach the stage with the greatest possible freedom of angle.

In Europe (even in Germany), lighting design has generally been slower than in Britain and the USA to make creative advances, except in the work of some exceptional artists. WIELAND WAGNER, in directing his grandfather's operas at BAYREUTH, created memorable images with light. JOSEF SVOBODA, the Czech scenographer, with light (often low-voltage) and projection has opened new vistas. The emergence of the professional lighting designer has been slow to gain acceptance in central Europe, in part because of union traditions, but this is finally changing thanks to pioneer work of such as Munich's Max Keller, as well as to the influence of visiting British designers.

Jean Rosenthal in her book *The Magic of Light* wrote, 'Light is quite tactile to me. It has shape and dimension. It has an edge. It has quality and it is an entity. It is the one miracle of creation without which, to me, the others would be meaningless.' Today the stage is a space that can be filled with any shape, pattern, texture, feeling or atmosphere of light that the performance requires. Opera, ballet, dance, musicals, drama, popular music – each make particular demands on theatrical lighting. Each can be considered well, or poorly, lit. That judgement must be based on a summation of how expressively, purposefully and appropriately light has been used to illuminate the stage, and how successfully the performers are three-dimensionally revealed; and equally important are the composition of the lighting within the overall visual intent of the scenic picture, and the degree to which the stage is charged with the correctly evocative atmosphere. Each of these qualities will stem from the content and intended style of the production.

Each step of progress in lighting – candle to oil lamp, oil lamp to gas, gas to electricity – has brought change. More light, improved safety and greater facility for control have been achieved, and yet always accompanied by complaints of over-brightness. Each step has been followed by changes in acting technique, and ever more subtle and often more realistic scenery, costumes and make-up. By the 1980s the 20th century had seen the passing of many styles of production. REALISM had given way to many other -isms; and the wheel of style continues to revolve. But the new lighting, the ability to fill stage space with light of character, remote from its source, has had an effect perhaps more profound than ever before.

The actor's scenic environment has become more three-dimensional. Physical thickness, depth and texture, used with light, have replaced much of the painted detail of previous ages. Often scenic elements have become larger, and backstage areas have had to accommodate consequently bulkier scenery. But the most significant change has been in the theatres themselves and in the relationship between the actor and the audience. Throughout most theatrical eras the players performed amongst their audience and both were lit throughout the performance. As we have seen, every period produced innovators who wished to darken the auditorium, but only in the late 19th century did this become the norm. The desire for increased NATURALISM and audience concentration on the stage now made dimming the houselights the symbol of the play's commencement. But the actor had to perform upstage of the proscenium lighting in order to be seen, and a gulf grew between him and the darkened audience. Almost immediately, visionary directors realized that this broke the fragile bond of communication that lay at the heart of live theatre – which is the interplay between performer and spectator.

The coming of the spotlight, which illuminated space from a distance, not only allowed the actors' faces to be lit from the auditorium, but allowed the actor to work in lit space that could be placed within the audience. So a re-examination of antique and new forms of theatre began. Theatre-in-the-round, thrust, transverse, environmental, open stages – all became legitimate means of theatrical expression. All were enabled by lighting to place actor and audience in the same space, but allowed the proper focus of attention to remain with the performer. Once more the actor is able to be at the heart of his audience. Once more he can be seen as a live, three-dimensional human being in intimate communication with his living audience. At a period of theatre history where new, electronic means of storytelling challenge the live theatre as never before, this rediscovered intimacy, this living contact, continues to give theatre its uniqueness in a world of ever more dazzling media.

Lighting, as an element in the theatre, has had a long and often unrecognized history. Just as stained glass in a Gothic cathedral brought wonder to the beholder, so, since the Renaissance, lighting has played its part in bringing magic to the stage. Today the lighting designer has at his or her fingertips computer-controlled intensity, movement and colour. These things were imagined by our theatrical ancestors, but electronics has brought them within our grasp. The speed of technological change is still accelerating. The challenge of the future must be to match technical development with a creativity that is always sensitive to the theatre's essentially human needs, so that lighting plays its appropriate role in the service of the living theatre.   RP

See: W. F. Bellman, *Lighting the Stage: Art and Practice*, New York and London, 1974; F. P. Bentham, *Art of Stage Lighting*, London, 1980; G. M. Bergman, *Lighting in the Theatre*, New Jersey, 1977; D. Hays, *Light on the Subject*, New York, 1989; S. McCandless, *A Method of Lighting the Stage*, New York, 1958; R. H. Palmer, *The Lighting Art: The Aesthetics of Stage Lighting Design*, New York, 1979; W. O. Parker and H. K. Smith, *Scene Design and Stage Lighting*, New York, 1979; R. Pilbrow, *Stage Lighting*, London, 1979, and *Stage Lighting Design*, New York, 1995; T. Rees, *Theatre Lighting in the Age of Gas*, London, 1978; F. Reid, *Stage Lighting Handbook*, London, 1982; J. Rosenthal and L. Wertenbaeker, *The Magic of Light*, New York, 1972; H. D. Sellman and M. Lessley, *Essentials of Stage Lighting*, New York, 1982; T.

Streader and J. A. Williams, *Create Your Own Stage Lighting*, London, 1985; W. B. Warfel, *Handbook of Stage Lighting Graphics*, New York, 1974.

Stage Society, Incorporated (London) This successor to Grein's INDEPENDENT THEATRE SOCIETY was founded in 1899 to produce modern plays that had been refused a licence for public performance, in professional stage conditions on Sunday nights when the theatres were otherwise closed. It was the first to produce SHAW's early plays, opening with *You Never Can Tell* and successfully asserting its freedom from stage CENSORSHIP with *Mrs Warren's Profession* (1902). As well as opening the theatre to other new English works like GRANVILLE BARKER's *Waste* (1907), it introduced a whole range of major European dramatists – from the NATURALISM of HAUPTMANN, GORKY and TOLSTOI to forerunners of EXPRESSIONISM like KAISER and WEDEKIND. It provided the impetus for the influential 1904–7 ROYAL COURT seasons of VEDRENNE and Granville Barker, who gained his experience as an actor and director in early Stage Society productions. It also initiated the Phoenix Society. This was formed to continue the revivals of Restoration comedy that had been started in 1915, and was instrumental in bringing early English drama back to the public stage between 1919 and 1925 with a series of productions ranging from MARLOWE and JONSON to DRYDEN and WYCHERLEY.

In the interwar period the Stage Society continued its function of championing new and unlicensed works, including the plays of James Joyce, D. H. LAWRENCE, JOHN VAN DRUTEN and R. C. SHERRIFF, as well as drama by PIRANDELLO, COCTEAU, ODETS and GARCÍA LORCA (*Blood Wedding* being its final production in 1939), although by that time it was no longer unique and its role had been largely taken over by the GROUP THEATRE and by Peter Godfrey and NORMAN MARSHALL at the GATE THEATRE. CI

Stainless Stephen [Arthur Baynes] 1892–1971 British (Sheffield-born) comedian and ex-schoolteacher who built into his act both his regional identity – stainless steel shirt front and bowler hat band – and his former professional pedantry – through the technique of speaking the punctuation of his script (not to mention his own stage directions) as if giving dictation. He is included here by special request of the editor, whose childhood he greatly influenced. AEG

Stanfield, Clarkson 1793–1867 English scene-painter, responsible during a long and varied career for over 550 recorded scenes. Stanfield's father, an actor and former seaman, apprenticed his son to a heraldic painter, but the boy was at sea from 1808 to 1815. Seascapes remained a feature of his later painting. His first engagement was as a scene-painter at the East London Theatre in 1815 and, after a spell at the Coburg (see OLD VIC THEATRE), he was added to ELLISTON's team of painters at DRURY LANE in 1823. Elliston's object was to challenge the supremacy of JOHN HENDERSON GRIEVE's family at COVENT GARDEN. Stanfield remained at Drury Lane until 1834, dividing his time between theatre work and easel painting on his own behalf. Admired as a marine and landscape artist, even compared by some to Turner, he was elected to the Royal

Academy in 1835. MACREADY, who was a personal friend, persuaded Stanfield to paint scenes for him at Covent Garden, the 1839 diorama for *Henry V* being particularly famous. Among the finest of his many dioramas, spectacles in their own right though used to enliven Drury Lane PANTOMIMES, were his Plymouth Breakwater (1823) and his Venice (1831). He had no rival in the depiction of the subtle textures and colourings of water. His last theatrical work was an 1858 act-drop for the New ADELPHI THEATRE, a service to another friend, BENJAMIN WEBSTER. (see also THEATRE DESIGN.) PT

Stanislavsky [Alekseev], **Konstantin (Sergeevich)** 1863–1938 Russian-Soviet actor-director-teacher, creator of the most influential 'system' of acting in the Western world. The son of enlightened progressive art patrons – the rich industrialist Alekseev and his wife, descended from the French actress Varley – Stanislavsky (he adopted this stage name in 1885) was quickly introduced to ballet, theatre and Italian OPERA. This instilled in him a sense of plastique and musicality and an aversion to fustian stage conventions and disrespectful audience behaviour. His amateur theatrical career began at home (1877) with the Alekseev Circle's productions of FARCES and OPERETTAS and continued at the Moscow Society of Art and Literature (1888), which he co-founded with A. F. Fedotov and three others. Here Stanislavsky played a variety of roles from the Russian and European repertoire, and in so doing recognized his limitations – a poor memory, the result of rote training at school; a somewhat random approach to acting; and artificial playing. However, his self-critical temperament, physical endowments – height, handsomeness and grace – and good role models (the opera star Fyodor Shaliapin and actors such as TOMMASO SALVINI and FEDOTOVA) would eventually combine to create a first-class character actor. VLADIMIR NEMIROVICH-DANCHENKO, a popular playwright and teacher at the Moscow Philharmonia, was impressed with Stanislavsky's first directorial effort for the amateur society, LEV TOLSTOI's *The Fruits of Enlightenment* (1891), with future star VERA KOMISSARZHEVSKAYA in the cast.

In 1897 a lengthy discussion of common goals led to the founding of the MOSCOW ART THEATRE, dedicated to the highest ideals of ensemble art, good citizenship and public education. The bases of the company's approach were naturalness, simplicity, clarity, an end to the actor's traditional *emploi*, the alternation of large and small roles, and the detailed and individuated realization of the essence and world of the play. With staff director A. A. Sanin and designer V. A. Simov in tow, the company opened with an antiquarian-set, naturalistically staged production of A. K. TOLSTOI's historical drama *Tsar Fyodor Ioannovich* (14 October 1898), which featured sensitive acting and a rich overlay of sound, lighting and scenic effects (see THEATRE DESIGN) deemed necessary by Stanislavsky but extraneous and counterproductive by CHEKHOV. Stanislavsky's wife (since 1887), Mariya Petrovna Perevoshchikova (*née* Lilina), and Chekhov's future spouse, OLGA KNIPPER, scored personal triumphs as Masha and Arkadina, respectively, as did Stanislavsky as Trigorin.

Stanislavsky excelled in all of Chekhov's plays for MAT – Astrov in *Uncle Vanya* (1899), Vershinin in *The*

Three Sisters (1901), Gaev in *The Cherry Orchard* (1904) – as well as in the roles of Dr Stockmann in IBSEN's *An Enemy of the People* (1900); Satin in GORKY's *The Lower Depths* (1902), which helped launch a long association between the theatre and that author; Famusov in GRIBOEDOV's *Woe from Wit* (1906); Argan in MOLIÈRE's *The Imaginary Invalid* (1913); and in many others requiring in-depth preparation and total transformation of his physical appearance. He became interested in the new symbolist-decadent drama (see SYMBOLISM), which he as a director felt ill equipped (despite attempts) to realize, and in the possibility of finding alternative methods of staging the classics. He invited GORDON CRAIG to design and direct *Hamlet* (1912), ALEXANDRE BENOIS to perform the same tasks for Molière and GOLDONI (1913–14) and VSEVOLOD MEYERHOLD to stage MAETERLINCK's *The Death of Tintagiles* (1905), a production which, owing to the stylization of the acting, Stanislavsky refused to let open. Stanislavsky's frustration with these alternative approaches led to a reaffirmation of his own instincts, which he tested together with Leopold Sulerzhitsky at MAT's First Studio (1912), where the 'system' was developed and the theatre enjoyed its first post-revolutionary success – *Twelfth Night* (1917).

While new Soviet dramas – e.g. BULGAKOV's *The Days of the Turbins* (1926) and VSEVOLOD IVANOV's *Armoured Train 14–69* (1927) – were produced by younger company members, Stanislavsky sidestepped the effects of the Revolution by working at the Bolshoi Theatre's opera studio, continuing to supervise experimental studio work and administering MAT's European and American tours (1922–4). His productions of OSTROVSKY's *The Ardent Heart* (1926) and BEAUMARCHAIS's *The Marriage of Figaro* (1927) embraced the grotesque, even as he began to record the tenets of his realistic acting system (see REALISM). To publicize the American tour he hastily and somewhat carelessly assembled the autobiographical *My Life in Art*, which he revised in 1926 and 1936. While recuperating from a heart attack (1928), he worked on the first part of his text *The Actor's Work on Himself*, completed in 1937, at which point he began the second part. While housebound, he also continued to coach singers and opera singers, his last directing work being on Molière's *Tartuffe* (1935). He was named a People's Artist of the USSR in 1936 and, save for occasional lapses in popularity, his system has remained the basis of Russian acting.

Stanislavsky advocated a balance between the actor's inner experiencing of the role (*perezhivaniye*) and its precisely attuned physical and vocal expression. Using the imaginative 'magic if' and 'affective memory' (adapted from the ideas of the French experimental psychologist Théodule Armand Ribot) as bridges between actor and character realities, the 'circle of attention' for focusing the actor's powers, and 'the through-line of action', broken into units and objectives, to score the role, the system offers a clear and precise groundplan. The confused publication history of Stanislavsky's acting text in the USA, and Americans' penchant for self-analysis and self-expression, led to the psychologically and emotionally based and physically and vocally underfed 'Method' approach of New York's ACTORS STUDIO, which has been mistaken for the original system. SG

Starr [*née* Grant], **Frances** 1886–1973 American actress who made her debut in her home-town STOCK COMPANY (Albany, NY, 1901), and for the next four years worked in similar companies in San Francisco, Boston and New York City. BELASCO hired her as a replacement for the ingénue during the run of *The Music Master*, and then starred her as Juanita in *The Rose of the Rancho* (1906) and as Laura Murdock in EUGENE WALTER's *The Easiest Way* (1909). In the latter role she personified the dilemma of the modern woman, morally liberated but economically enslaved. She continued to act until 1940. DMCD

Steele, Sir **Richard** 1672–1729 Irish dramatist. Educated at Charterhouse, where he met JOSEPH ADDISON with whom he so often collaborated as essayist, and Oxford University, he became a soldier in 1694, writing his pious tract, *The Christian Hero* (1701), as an aid to fellow soldiers. He responded to the criticisms of JEREMY COLLIER by producing a drama that was both entertaining and moral. *The Funeral* (1701) was a FARCE mocking undertaking but *The Lying Lover* (1703) and *The Tender Husband* (1703) were serious, almost pious, studies of the success of virtue in a comic world. With their advocacy of repentance and their lack of realism in dramatic form they were strong influences on the development of sentimental comedy. But the plays were not successful and Steele began editing a series of periodicals, including the *Tatler* (1709–11), the *Spectator* (1711–12), the *Guardian* (1713), the *Englishman* (1713–15), *Town Talk* (1715) and the *Theatre* (1720), which were all frequently concerned to discuss theatre and drama, advocating new plays and new genres and satirizing staging and acting. In 1715 he was knighted and also took on the management of DRURY LANE Theatre. His fourth and last play, *The Conscious Lovers* (1722), was a fully fledged sentimental comedy, influential in the establishment of *comédie larmoyante* in Europe, a serious and unfunny play founded on middle-class morality and using TERENCE's *Andria* as source. PH

Stein, Peter 1937– German director, who established the Berlin Schaubühne on collective, egalitarian principles in 1970. His sympathies with East–West détente and the anti-Vietnam movement motivated his productions of WEISS's *Vietnam Discourse* (1968) and BRECHT's *The Mother* (1970), but at heart he is a conservative perfectionist. Dramaturgs Dieter Sturm and BOTHO STRAUSS and designer Karl-Ernst Herrmann, who re-configured stage and auditorium for each play, were essential members of his team. His projects were minutely researched by the cast and production staff, and the social, political and artistic findings were then fed into a long rehearsal process. For *As You Like It* (1977) the material became *Shakespeare's Memory*, a multi-media Elizabethan experience which ran in tandem with the play. His riveting productions of IBSEN's *Peer Gynt* (1971, with four different actors as Peer), VISHNEVSKY's *Optimistic Tragedy* (1972), KLEIST's *Prince of Homburg* (1972), GORKY's *Summerfolk* (1975), AESCHYLUS' *Oresteia* and CHEKHOV's *Three Sisters* (1984) and *The Cherry Orchard* (1989) exposed the roots of the present in the world of the plays.

The Schaubühne's pre-eminence faded in the 1980s, and German critics attacked Stein's 'aestheticism'. Since he

Elke Petri as Phoebe in
Peter Stein's production of
As You Like It.

resigned in 1985 he has directed twice for Welsh Opera. He became director of drama at the Salzburg Festival in 1992, producing *Julius Caesar* in his first season.   HR

Steiner, Rolando 1935– Nicaraguan playwright, journalist and critic. Steiner studied in Spain (1963–5) and returned to Managua to work for *La Prensa*, the major newspaper. His three one-act plays, *Judith*, *Un drama corriente* (*An Ordinary Drama*) and *La puerta* (*The Door*), were collected under the title *La trilogía del matrimonio* (*The Matrimonial Trilogy*) and published in 1970.   GW

Steinsson, Gudmundur 1925– Icelandic playwright. Steinsson's tragicomic *A Brief Respite* (1979) broke box-office records at Iceland's National Theatre, subsequently going on European tour. It has since been produced in eight countries, including Japan. Essentially a critique of the consumer society mentality, the play depicts an average urban family caught in the rat race, where there is no time for anything, not even for death. Another popular play is the farcical *Viva España* (1976), which describes holidaymakers in Spain, their boredom, alienation and sexual frustration under a veneer of marital bliss. Steinsson often deals in highly stylized SATIRE with alienation and self-deception, while some of his plays are large-scale allegories about man's self-inflicted fate. Important plays include *Matthew* (1975), *The Garden Party* (1982) and *The Wedding Portrait* (1986).   AI

Stepanova, Varvara (Fyodorovna) 1894–1958 One of the original group of Soviet scenic constructivist designers who, although overshadowed by colleagues LYUBOV POPOVA and husband Aleksandr Rodchenko, is remembered for her distinctive work on MEYERHOLD's production of SUKHOVO-KOBYLIN's *Tarelkin's Death* (24 November 1922). Indebted to Popova's design for *The Magnanimous Cuckold* (1922), which it tried to outdo (according to Meyerhold), the *Tarelkin* set consisted of a series of booby-trapped, white-painted wooden 'acting machines', each individually conceived – chairs with false spring seats, a stool that detonated a blank cartridge, a table whose legs collapsed, a tall box that served as a human jack-in-the-box and, most prominently, a large, barred cage and wheel resembling a meat grinder. Whereas Popova had designed the entire space, Stepanova simply inhabited hers with designed objects. Ironically, Stepanova complained that it was the director's and actors' insistence on playing through themselves rather than through the objects that had made the latter appear illusory and decorative, the exact opposite of what constructivist design intended. Stepanova's complaint ended her association with Meyerhold. Still, the single production – with its baggy costumes resembling prisoners' uniforms (also designed by Stepanova), its knockabout action, role reversals and CARNIVALesque tone – is representative of the 'eccentrist' trend of the day, begun with ANNENKOV's production of *The First Distiller* (1919), and of Meyerhold's CIRCUS phase. SG

Stephens, Robert 1931– British actor, who started his career with Caryl Jenner's Mobile Theatre before appearing at the ROYAL COURT THEATRE in *The Crucible* (1956) with the English Stage Company. He became a familiar member of GEORGE DEVINE's acting team, playing in OSBORNE's *The Entertainer* (1957) and *Epitaph for George Dillon* (1958); and he was often cast as a smooth young man, perhaps untrustworthy. He appeared in the WEST END in *Look After Lulu* (1959) and *The Wrong Side of the Park* (1960), and appeared in the film version of *A Taste of Honey* (1962); but the range of his talents was not recognized until after LAURENCE OLIVIER invited him to join the NATIONAL THEATRE company in 1963. He appeared in the NT's *Hamlet*, *St Joan* and *The Recruiting Officer*, but his first great success came as Atahuallpa in PETER SHAFFER's *The Royal Hunt of the Sun* (1964). Through arduous physical training and brilliant vocal and MIME control, Stephens transformed himself into an image of the Sun God of the Incas. Other major roles followed in such NT productions as *Armstrong's Last Goodnight*, *Trelawny of the 'Wells'*, *A Bond Honoured* and *The Dance of Death*. He continued his NT career under PETER HALL, appearing in *The Cherry Orchard* (1978) and *Brand* (1978), but by the mid-1970s he was equally well known as a television and film star.

While Stephens has not so far become a major star, either in Britain or the USA, the versatility and professionalism of his acting have strengthened two leading companies in postwar British theatre, Devine's Royal Court and Olivier's NT. He was a memorable Falstaff in ADRIAN NOBLE's ROYAL SHAKESPEARE COMPANY production of *Henry IV, Parts 1 and 2* (1992). His performance as Lear in Noble's RSC production of *King Lear* (1993) demonstrated his commanding stage presence, rarely used by the British national companies since the 1960s, while his interpretation stressed the sheer wilfulness of Lear's authority. JE

Steppenwolf Theatre Company (USA) The most celebrated group to emerge during Chicago's period of theatrical growth in the 1970s and 80s. Begun in 1976 in the basement of a suburban parochial school, Steppenwolf rapidly became the foremost exemplar of a highly physical, naturalistic approach to acting (see NATURALISM) often referred to as the 'Chicago Style'. By subordinating repertory to the needs of the actors, this company of recent college graduates (predominantly from Illinois State University) developed both a strong sense of ensemble and a number of powerful individual actors, many of whom found success beyond the company, including JOHN MALKOVICH, Terry Kinney, Laurie Metcalf, Gary Sinise, Joan Allen, Glenne Headly and John Mahoney. Since the mid-1980s, Steppenwolf has regularly toured successful productions to BROADWAY and other venues. Notable productions include *True West*, *Balm in Gilead*, *And a Nightingale Sang*, *Orphans*, *Coyote Ugly*, *Burn This*, and

company member Frank Galati's adaptation of *The Grapes of Wrath*. In 1991 it moved into its fourth home, a newly built $8 million facility including 500- and 100-seat houses.

The history of Chicago theatre is dotted with the corpses of companies that tried to increase revenue by moving into larger venues. As Steppenwolf settled into its new home, it faced both a national recession and the continual struggle of maintaining a cohesive ensemble combining new members with those who have increased commitments to other theatres and media. If past success is any indication, however, Steppenwolf's future looks bright. Among its many awards are four Tonys, including the 1985 award for regional theatre excellence. SF

Sternhagen, Frances (Hussey) 1930– American actress. After a Vassar education and a year of advanced study at Catholic University, Washington, DC, Sternhagen studied acting with SANFORD MEISNER and made her professional debut in 1948 as Laura in *The Glass Menagerie* and Mrs Manningham in *Angel Street* at Bryn Mawr Summer Theatre. Her New York debut was at the Cherry Lane Theatre (1955). Obies followed for performances as Lydia Carew in *The Admirable Bashville* (1956), Margery Pinchwife in *The Country Wife*, and roles in *The New PINTER Plays* (1965). For her several roles in NEIL SIMON's *The Good Doctor*, she received a Tony. Three other Tony nominations have complemented frequent critical recognition of her work, especially in *Equus* and Ernest Thompson's *On Golden Pond* and TERRENCE MCNALLY's *A Perfect Ganesh*. She is an actor's actor; CLIVE BARNES called her one of 'the great players of BROADWAY'. FHL

Sternheim, Carl 1878–1942 German dramatist, whose comedies 'from the heroic life of the bourgeoisie' have become modern classics. *The Knickers* (1911), *The Snob* (1914) and *1913* (1919) chronicle the ruthless rise of the Maske family from the petty bourgeoisie to the financial aristocracy in Imperial Germany. *The Casket* (1911) shows nationalism, family values, and even sex being abandoned when cash is in prospect. *Schippel* (1913) shows the assumption of Schippel, the singing plumber, into the bourgeoisie. The sequel, *Tabula Rasa* (1919), exposes the venality of trade unions and Social Democrats in Schippel's factory. Sternheim's satirical view of the rapacity and materialism of German society before the First World War – he is sometimes called a modern MOLIÈRE – is akin to WEDEKIND's. His language has the economy of the expressionists (see EXPRESSIONISM), but where they aspire to intensity, his clipped dialogue is dry and ironic. HR

Stevens, Roger (Lacey) 1910– Detroit-born American producer. Since producing *Twelfth Night* on BROADWAY in 1949, Stevens has worked steadily with great distinction in the American theatre and has been associated with many of the leading theatrical groups of the USA: the Producers Theatre, Phoenix Theatre, AMERICAN NATIONAL THEATRE AND ACADEMY (ANTA), Metropolitan Opera Company, ACTORS STUDIO Theatre, AMERICAN SHAKESPEARE [THEATRE] Festival and Academy, New Dramatists Committee and JOHN F. KENNEDY CENTER FOR THE PERFORMING ARTS. While Stevens was a member of the

Playwrights' Company (1951–60), that organization produced or co-produced 38 Broadway plays, including *The Fourposter* (1951), *Tea and Sympathy* (1953), *Ondine* and *The Bad Seed* (1954) and *Cat on a Hot Tin Roof* (1955). He chaired the National Council on the Arts during 1964–9.

As head of the John F. Kennedy Center, Stevens produced over 30 productions that went on to other theatres. In 1957 he received the Sam H. Shubert Foundation Award for the outstanding producer on Broadway; in 1971 he was given a special Tony; and in 1988 he received the Kennedy Center Honor and the President's Medal of Freedom. He has also been honoured by England (knighted in 1980), Sweden, Italy, Germany and Austria. His productions have won numerous New York Drama Critics', Tonys and Outer Critics' Circle awards. In 1988 he retired from the Kennedy Center to pursue his dream of a national theatre, undeterred by the failure of a similar effort in 1984, and to serve as president of ANTA. SMA

Stevenson, Juliet 1956– British actress, who emerged to stardom through the ranks of the Royal Shakespeare Company. In 1981–2 she played leading roles in three RSC productions – *A Midsummer Night's Dream*, *The Witch of Edmonton* and Edward Bulwer Lytton's *Money* – before moving to the Royal Court to appear in Robert Holman's *Other Worlds* (1983). She returned to the RSC to play Isabella in *Measure for Measure* (1983), which won her the *Drama* magazine award as Best Actress of the Year, and she appeared in Stephen Poliakoff's *Breaking the Silence* (1984). In 1986, she played La Présidente de Tourvel in Christopher Hampton's adaptation of Laclos's *Les Liaisons Dangereuses* in the RSC's studio, the Pit, where the cast (including Fiona Shaw, Lindsay Duncan and Alan Rickman) now reads like a summary of the acting stars of her generation. She played Cressida in the RSC's *Troilus and Cressida* (1986) as a feminist role-model, a cool, wary girl taking her chances among male wargames; while at the other extreme she was an anguished Yerma in a revival of García Lorca's play at the National Theatre's Cottesloe.

This experience of playing major roles with leading companies has left its mark on Stevenson's style. She is a precise actress with an element of surprise in her playing. She holds back her expressions of feeling until the point when they are so long-awaited as to seem inevitable; and then she erupts in fury or passion. Her performance as Hedda Gabler in the NT's production of Ibsen's play in 1989 provides one example, but her Paulina in Ariel Dorfman's *Death and the Maiden* (1991) offers a better one. The play is set in an unnamed Latin-American country, where Paulina was the victim of torture, imposed by the Fascist leaders of a previous regime. In a less experienced actress's hands the part would have veered towards melodrama, but Stevenson kept it under strict control. JE

Stewart, Nellie [Eleanor] 1858–1931 Australian actress. Daughter of the actress Theodosia Yates (Mrs Guerin), she appeared aged five with Charles Kean in Melbourne, and in childhood toured internationally in *Rainbow Revels*, written for the Stewart family. She first starred in the pantomime *Sinbad* in 1880, and was identified with many musical roles, including Griolet in *La Fille*

du Tambour Major, *Sweet Nell of Old Drury* and *Cinderella*. Her lifelong companion George Musgrove managed her career in Australia, England and America. An enchanting performer even in old age, she played Romeo in the balcony scene shortly before her death. MW

stock company Nineteenth-century play production in England and America was typified by the independent stock company of a permanent troupe of actors headed by an actor-manager and performing a number of different works in repertory rotation, either in a permanent house or on tour. Actors were cast according to type or 'line', which usually resulted in 'stock' characterizations, and productions were mounted from the company's meagre collection or 'stock' of scenery and props (actors furnished costumes).

Economically undermined by the advent of expensive, visiting international stars (mainly from England), American stock companies were further diminished by the 1880s when rail travel facilitated the growth of 'combination companies', which travelled complete with star, full cast, scenery and costumes. By century's end most professional American theatre production was centralized in New York City and most US theatres were controlled by the Theatrical Syndicate, an infamous booking outfit. SL

Stoll, Oswald (Gray) 1866–1942 British manager, born in Melbourne, Australia. He began by sharing the management of the Parthenon Music Hall, Liverpool, with his mother, and after various provincial successes took over the London Coliseum (1904), which in his hands became a home for giant circuses, gargantuan musicals and Max Reinhardt's epics. Other theatres under his control were the Hackney, Shepherd's Bush and Ardwick Empires, the Croydon and Manchester Hippodromes and the Leicester Palace. In 1911 he left Moss Empires and joined Walter Gibbons's Variety Theatres Consolidated, thereby gaining 29 halls with a capitalization of £2,000,000. A knighthood came in 1919. A follower of Herbert Spencer, Stoll was known as a cold and formal employer, and a shrewd dealer. LS

Stone, John Augustus 1800–34 American playwright and actor. Stone's *Metamora; or, the Last of Wampanoags* (1829) was the winner over 13 other entries in Edwin Forrest's first playwriting contest (judged by W.C. Bryant, William Leggett, Prosper Wetmore and others). The play became Forrest's property and his 'war-horse' piece, with over 200 performances. The Stone-Forrest Indian chief epitomized the natural goodness of the 'noble savage'. Stone's acting debut was as Old Norval in *Douglas* (1820), and through most of his career he played eccentric comics or 'rough and bluff' old men. He wrote nine other unsuccessful plays, among them *The Demoniac* (1831), *The Ancient Briton* (1833) and *The Knight of the Golden Fleece* (1834). RM

Stoppard [Straussler], **Tom** 1937– British dramatist, who was born in Czechoslovakia. His family emigrated to Britain, where they settled in 1946. After working on the *Western Daily Press* as a journalist, he began to write plays for radio and television; his first TV play, *A Walk on the Water* (1963), was later adapted for the stage as *Enter a Free Man* (1968). He translated and adapted MROŻEK's *Tango* (1968) for the ROYAL SHAKESPEARE COMPANY – and other plays from middle Europe, by NESTROY, SCHNITZLER and HAVEL, for a variety of companies, ranging from the NATIONAL THEATRE to FRINGE groups.

Throughout his work, the influence of the Polish and Czech absurdists (see THEATRE OF THE ABSURD) can be felt, but his first major success came with *Rozencrantz and Guildenstern Are Dead* (1966), which was originally produced by the Oxford Theatre Group on the EDINBURGH FESTIVAL fringe, but bought and staged six months later by the National Theatre. The story of *Hamlet*, seen through the eyes of two attendant courtiers, was a powerful myth for audiences in Britain, surrounded by world events (such as the Vietnam War) over which they had no control. The professor of moral philosophy in *Jumpers* (1972) is similarly out of touch with the politics of the brave new world, while Henry Carr in *Travesties* (1974) is a minor consular official in Zurich in 1917, a town visited by Lenin, James Joyce and Tristan Tzara, of whose significance Carr is sublimely unaware. Carr is a representative for Britain in more than consular ways, an Edwardian air-bubble, miraculously untouched by outside events.

Stoppard's sympathy with the underdog and his political scepticism led to his writing *Every Good Boy Deserves Favour* (1977), about those imprisoned by totalitarian regimes; and his liberal sympathies permeate *Night and Day* (1978), about politics and Western journalism in an African state. He is a writer whose zest with language and skilful plotting generate more fun than almost any other modern British dramatist, as his Whitehall farce *Dirty Linen* (1976), *Dogg's Hamlet* and *Cahoot's Macbeth* (1979) demonstrate; while his comedy about adultery, *The Real Thing* (1982), was a neat BOULEVARD play, successful on both sides of the Atlantic. *Hapgood* (1988) was a mixture of a John le Carré spy novel and a pun-ridden farce; *Artist Descending a Staircase* (1988), adapted from his 1972 radio play, was a comic homage to the surrealists. Stoppard's ingenuity, inventiveness and gifts at PARODY, coupled with his cosmopolitanism, have delighted theatre audiences for a quarter of a century. The complaint sometimes levelled against him is that his plays contain too much trickery and too little depth. His witty extravaganza on BYRON's strange disappearance from Britain in 1809 and other unanswered riddles of romanticism, *Arcadia* (1993), was his most intellectually ambitious play since *Travesties*, with which it shares an impressive range of riddles and arcane references. Behind this display of wit and erudition many tantalizing themes jostle to be expressed. JE

Storey, David (Malcolm) 1933– British dramatist and novelist, whose early novels (including *This Sporting Life*, 1960) describe the Yorkshire working-class background which permeates his later plays. He conceived his first play, *The Restoration of Arnold Middleton*, in 1959, but the first London production came at the ROYAL COURT THEATRE in 1967; and its study of a provincial schoolmaster, driven to madness in an unhappy mariage but also through homesickness for his lost Northern childhood, expressed eloquently Storey's understanding of class alienation. Although it transferred to the WEST END, *Arnold Middleton* was a somewhat clumsy play with brilliant individual tirades in the Jimmy Porter manner.

When Storey teamed up with his sympathetic director, LINDSAY ANDERSON, his plays gained in sharpness and dramatic effect. *In Celebration* (1969) ironically contrasts the lifestyles of two generations of the Shaw family, indicating that material and social success do not bring happiness. Storey's observation of working environments provided the framework for *The Contractor* (1969) in which a large wedding marquee is raised and lowered on stage, *The Changing Room* (1971) about a rugby team, *The Farm* (1973) and *Life Class* (1974), but he cleverly selects the details to reveal the emotional complexities of individual lives. *Home* (1970), in which JOHN GIELGUD and RALPH RICHARDSON appeared, ostensibly describes a rest home for the near-senile, but Storey hints that this place could be a model for Britain itself. This satirical, allegorical vein appears in *Cromwell* (1973), the curious black sex farce *Mother's Day* (1976) and *Sisters* (1978); but *Early Days* (1980) provided Ralph Richardson with a fine near-solo role as an elder statesman contemplating his past life, in a striking NATIONAL THEATRE production. Storey's studies of changing British working-class life and the loss of roots by those who have graduated or declined into the middle classes, have continued with *The March on Russia* (1989) and *Stages* (1992). JE

Strachan, Alan (Lockhart Thomson) 1946– British director, who joined BERNARD MILES's Mermaid Theatre in 1970 as associate director. This gave him the opportunity not just to direct such plays as *John Bull's Other Island* (1971) but also to devise useful, small-scale musical shows, such as *Cowardy Custard* (1972) and *Cole* (1974), based on the songs of NOËL COWARD and COLE PORTER. His sensitive, practical approach to the theatre stood him in good stead as a freelance director (1975–8), when he directed several WEST END successes including *A Family and a Fortune* (1975), based on the novel by Ivy Compton Burnett, ALAN AYCKBOURN's *Confusions* (1976) and *Just Between Ourselves* (1977). In 1978 he was appointed artistic director of Greenwich Theatre, where his blend of popular classics and intelligent new plays won high attendance figures for a London suburban repertory theatre whose audiences were always in danger of being drawn away by the West End. Several Coward plays transferred from Greenwich to central London, but Greenwich Theatre also became known as the theatre where Ayckbourn's plays were tried out before their London runs. Strachan directed MAUREEN LIPMAN in *Re:Joyce* (1988), an affectionate tribute to JOYCE GRENFELL, and *June Moon* (1992), Ring Lardner and GEORGE S. KAUFMAN's MUSICAL COMEDY about writing musical comedies. JE

Straiges, Tony 1942– American set and COSTUME designer best known for his sets for *Sunday in the Park with George* (1984), for which he won a Tony, and for *Into the Woods* (1987). Straiges has designed extensively at the ARENA STAGE, YALE REPERTORY THEATRE and several other regional theatres, as well as for OFF-BROADWAY companies. His sets often have a sparse elegance or sense of fantasy about them. AA

Strange's Men This prominent Elizabethan household company was active in the English provinces before its first recorded appearance at Elizabeth I's court in 1582. Its patron was the son of the Earl of Derby, who had a household troupe of his own, and the two companies caused confusion among contemporaries as well as later scholars. As was the case with all the early Elizabethan groups of players, Strange's Men often amalgamated with actors from other companies when performing in London's public theatres. They were with the ADMIRAL'S MEN at the THEATRE in 1590–1 and at the ROSE in 1592–3. A playhouse synopsis of the second part of TARLTON's *The Seven Deadly Sins*, which Strange's Men performed in London between 1590 and 1592, names the actors of this lost play. Among many prominent players are RICHARD BURBAGE, WILLIAM SLY and AUGUSTINE PHILLIPS. Although SHAKESPEARE is not named, his imminent association with these three in the formation of the LORD CHAMBERLAIN'S MEN in 1594 adds credibility to the claim that his early plays were in the repertoire of Strange's Men. When Lord Strange became Earl of Derby on his father's death in 1593, his company was touring the provinces, driven out of London by a virulent plague epidemic. On their return to London, they formed the nucleus of the incomparable Chamberlain's Men, of which Shakespeare was indubitably a member. PT

Stranitzky, Josef (Anton) 1676–1726 Austrian comic actor, creator of the character HANSWURST. He is first heard of in 1699 as an itinerant comedian in southern Germany, before he moved in 1705 to Vienna, where he set up as a tooth-drawer. Acting with Johann Baptist Hilverding's troupe at a fair-booth in the Vienna marketplace around 1705, he developed the part of a Salzburg peasant (Hanswurst), which became a leading role when he took over the company in 1706 and moved it to the new Kärntnertor Theatre in 1711. It was there that Lady Mary Montagu saw him in 1716 and was shocked by his smutty jokes and the dropping of his trousers. Stranitzky's Hanswurst was earthy and foul-mouthed, improvising irreverently even in the lofty *HAUPT- UND STAATSAKTIONEN* whose themes were drawn from Italian *OPERA SERIA*. He made a fortune and, as actor-author, founded a tradition that would descend to NESTROY. LS

Strasberg, Lee 1901–82 American director and acting teacher. Strasberg studied at the American Laboratory Theatre, acted with the THEATRE GUILD and in 1931 helped found and directed for the GROUP THEATRE, espousing the work of the Russian director, KONSTANTIN STANISLAVSKY. Among his directorial successes were *The House of Connelly*, *Night over Taos*, *Men in White* and *Clash by Night*.

In 1950 Strasberg became a director for the ACTORS STUDIO and emerged as the leading exponent of the Method, based on the Stanislavsky system. In 1965 he directed a highly controversial *The Three Sisters*, which played at the Aldwych Theatre in London during the World Theatre Season. A great many of America's leading film and stage actors studied with Strasberg, either privately or at the Studio, among them MARLON BRANDO, whose 'internal' style as Stanley in *A Streetcar Named*

Desire became popularly associated with Method acting. Among Strasberg's more famous students were Montgomery Clift, Ann Bancroft, Shelley Winters, Paul Newman and Joanne Woodward.

Although his methods and results excited great controversy, little doubt remains that Strasberg had a major effect on modern acting. His thoughts on the Method (*A Dream of Passion*) were published posthumously in 1987. SMA

Stratford Festival (Canada) One of the world's major theatrical organizations, it began in 1953 as a modest summer festival, founded by local resident Tom Patterson in the small Ontario town of Stratford. The first season, mounted by TYRONE GUTHRIE, featured *Richard III* and *All's Well that Ends Well*, performed in a tent seating 1477 people. The budget was $150,000. In 1994 the Festival's annual budget was $23,954,500 and featured ten productions in 497 performances during the six-month season (May to November). The permanent Festival Theatre, erected in 1957, seats 2276 in a 220-degree circle. The thrust stage, designed by TANYA MOISEIWITSCH and Guthrie, a recreation of the Elizabethan open stage, has been immensely influential on contemporary stage architecture, as may be seen in the GUTHRIE THEATRE, Minneapolis, and at the CHICHESTER FESTIVAL THEATRE, England.

Stratford's artistic directors include Guthrie (1953–5), MICHAEL LANGHAM (1956–67), JEAN GASCON (1968–74), ROBIN PHILLIPS (1975–80), JOHN HIRSCH (1981–5), JOHN NEVILLE (1986–9), David William (1990–3) and Richard Monette (1994–). Guthrie's use of minimal sets, opulent costumery and swiftly paced movement, especially in group scenes, has remained a characteristic of the Festival's productions. Langham's tenure was notable for its collaborative work with French-Canadian companies and actors (particularly, Gascon). Gascon complemented the mainly Shakespearian character of the Festival with European classics, especially the work of MOLIÈRE. Phillips, who directed 29 new productions and six revivals during his term as artistic director, used such stars as MAGGIE SMITH and Peter Ustinov to highlight his intensely stylized productions. Following a successful career as an actor, Monette first showed his directorial talents in a highly acclaimed 1988 *Taming of the Shrew*; his approach is governed by a keen intelligence in recreating SHAKESPEARE and by an engaging wit in his reading of comedic material – a refreshing change from the pedestrian if thorough workmanship displayed by William during his tenure.

In the 1980s and 1990s productions of GILBERT and Sullivan, directed by famed choreographer Brian Macdonald, were presented at the conventional proscenium Avon Theatre (1107 seats). Macdonald also began to present mainline American MUSICALS such as *Cabaret* and *Guys and Dolls* on the Festival Theatre stage, which had hitherto been reserved for classical theatre fare. That artistic programming should be so obviously influenced by box-office considerations has drawn protest. The Third Stage (493 seats), established by Jean Gascon for new and experimental work, was renamed the Tom Patterson Theatre in 1991.

While Canadian cultural nationalists have denounced

Bådteatret, Copenhagen, in Botho Strauss's *The Time and the Room*, 1991/2.

the Stratford Festival for not presenting more Canadian plays, it may be argued that the mandate of the Festival is to present works from the international theatrical repertoire, and not primarily Canadian work. The value of the Festival to Canadian theatre is that in the 1950s and 1960s it provided a professionalism not seen before in Canada, and that it helped train a new generation of theatre practitioners who continue to make the Festival the pre-eminent classical repertory theatre in North America. EBEN

Strauss, Botho 1944– German dramatist, novelist and essayist who was *Theater Heute*'s staff critic from 1967 to 1970, then PETER STEIN's dramaturg at the Berlin Schaubühne. Strauss's first plays, *Die Hypochonder* (*The Hypochondriacs*, 1972) and *Bekannte Gesichter, gemischte Gefühle* (*Known Faces, Mixed Feelings*, 1975), were ironic exercises in high style. His first success came with *Trilogie des Wiedersehens* (*Three Acts of Recognition*, 1977), whose fluid, interlocking conversations reveal the essential vapidity of a provincial arts society. *Gross und klein* (*Great and Small*, 1978) offers another cross-section of German society as its heroine seeks real human contact in a world of self-obsession. *Kalldewey Farce* (1982) marked a shift from comedy of manners to intellectual FARCE. *Der Park* (1984) transposed *A Midsummer Night's Dream* to a sordid urban park in present-day Germany. *Besucher* (*Visitors*), *Die Zeit und das Zimmer* (*Time and the Room*) and *Sieben Türen* (*Seven Doors*), three 'bagatelles' that

Strauss published in 1988, abandon plot but retain a surreal coherence (see SURREALISM). *Schlusschor* (*Final Chorus*, 1991), three one-acters deceptively disguised as a play, was his comment on German reunification.

With his ear for contemporary idiom, Strauss is an avid collector of contemporary emotional and intellectual poses. His literary and esoteric comedies – suave, enigmatic, pessimistic – with their surreal twists and mythological allusions, are played all over continental Europe; but not in Britain. HR

street theatre see FEMINIST THEATRE (USA); LIVING THEATRE

Strehler, Giorgio 1921– Italian director, and one of the major figures in post-Second World War theatre in Italy. Although Strehler began his career as an actor he soon emerged as a leading director, and in Milan, jointly with Paolo Grassi, established in 1947 the first fully fledged Italian *teatro stabile*, the Piccolo Teatro. A subsidized theatre with an acknowledged public service purpose, it tried to reach a socially more heterogeneous audience than had traditional urban theatre. Save for a period between 1968 and 1972, when the events of May encouraged Strehler to form the Gruppo Teatro e Azione and explore a more politically engaged theatre, it is at the Piccolo that he has been mainly based, although in the 1980s he was equally involved in the work of the Théâtre de l'Europe for which he has directed plays like BRECHT's *The Threepenny Opera*.

Strehler's work has been massively wide-ranging, running to more than 200 productions in the MUSICAL and regular theatre. He has brought a questing, lively intelligence and brilliant theatrical flair to so many and to such very different kinds of drama, that his career does not readily divide into clear periods. The early work, however, of the late 1940s and early 1950s, may be seen as exploratory mainly of the European classical and modern repertory, a focus reflective perhaps of the artistically uncertain bearings of postwar theatre as a whole. A seminal influence was the work of Brecht's BERLINER ENSEMBLE and its European tour of 1956. Strehler later mounted important Italian productions of *The Threepenny Opera*, *The Good Person of Setzuan*, *The Good Soldier Schweik* and *Galileo*, and Brechtian influence is felt in his work on other plays, such as SHAKESPEARE's *Coriolanus* (1957). Shakespeare has, indeed, been an ongoing interest, from 1948 when he mounted *The Tempest* in the Boboli Gardens in Florence, through the 1950s when he staged a number of the HISTORY PLAYS like *Richard III* (1950), *Henry IV* (1951) and *Julius Caesar* (1953), to the exploratory metaphysical and poetically evocative productions of *King Lear* (1972) and *The Tempest* (1978).

Strehler's work on the Italian repertoire has included notable reorchestrations and rediscoveries, among them FERRARI's 19th-century piece *Goldoni e le sue sedici commedie nuove* (*Goldoni and His Sixteen New Comedies*, 1958), turn-of-the-century plays by PRAGA and Bertolazzi, an influential revival of PIRANDELLO's *I Giganti della montagna* (*The Mountain Giants*, 1951) and a string of plays by GOLDONI: *Gli innamorati* (*The Lovers*, 1950), *L'amante militare* (*The Military Lover*, 1951), *La trilogia della villeggiatura* (*The Villeggiatura Trilogy*, 1954), *Le baruffe chiozzotte* (*The Chioggian Squabbles*, 1964) and several reworkings of *Arlecchino, servitore di due padroni* (*Arlecchino, Servant of Two Masters*, from 1947). In his productions of this last play he has sought to recuperate the MASKED tradition of the settecento for modern audiences; his work on several of the late Goldoni plays has brought out a note of melancholy to underscore the passing of a culture and its values. Strehler's fascination with the mid-18th century is evident too in his many productions of Mozart's operas, and the lighter comic pieces of Piccinni and Cimarosa. His current work straddles activity in Paris and Milan and points up the European, indeed international, emphasis of his engagement with the theatre.

A notable recent production, under the joint aegis of the Piccolo Teatro and the Théâtre de l'Europe, was Goldoni's *Le baruffe chiozzotte* (1992): this highly balletic staging, rich in visual echoes of Pietro Longhi's Venetian scenes, was seen at the British NATIONAL THEATRE. In the same year Strehler resigned from the directorship of the Piccolo Teatro, but continued to direct, making notable contributions to the Goldoni bicentenary in 1993 with further reorchestrations of *Arlecchino, servitore di due padroni* and *Il campiello* (*The Square*), as well as a piece devised from Goldoni's *Memoires* (1993). Exploration of drama and theatre through work that he has devised and adapted, like the two parts of the *Progetto Faust*, done in the Piccolo's Studio Theatre (1989–90), has been a feature of his recent activity, complementing a continued interest

in the lyric theatre, as in his staging of Beethoven's *Fidelio* at La Scala (1990), and in work from the modern Italian repertory such as DE FILIPPO's *La grande magia* (*The Great Sorcery*, 1990).   LR

Strindberg, August 1849–1912 Swedish playwright, novelist and essayist, whose first link with theatre was as a would-be actor. Two of his first plays, *In Rome* (1870) and *The Outlaw* (1871), both indebted to Oehlenschläger, were staged by DRAMATEN. Paradoxically, the same theatre rejected his first major play, the remarkable *Master Olof* (1872), which was finally performed in 1881 in August Lindberg's six-hour production – Strindberg's breakthrough in the Swedish theatre. Meanwhile, in the 1870s he had abandoned a university education, married Siri von Essen, and written his first novel, *The Red Room* (1879). His plays were more frequently staged in the 1880s; Dramaten produced *The Secret of the Guild* (1880) and Ludvig Josephson's Nya Teatern staged *Master Olof*, *Sir Bengt's Wife* (1882) and *Lucky Per's Journey* (1882).

Always eager to be at the forefront of new trends, Strindberg responded quickly to ZOLA's call for NATURALISM in the theatre, albeit in a typically personal way. *The Father* (1887) employed a naturalism that baffled Zola, but which Strindberg claimed was the French naturalists' real goal: 'the great naturalism', larger than real life, focusing on extraordinary, major conflicts, 'the struggles between natural forces'. While he gives his naturalistic plays a psychological basis, explained in the two essays 'On Psychic Murder' (1887) and 'On Modern Drama and the Modern Theatre' (1889), Strindberg points psychology to a level of symbolic, elemental action. *Miss Julie* (1888), especially in its 'Preface', seems an eloquent celebration of the tenets of naturalism, with its emphasis on heredity and environment, its vacillating characters and meandering, non-sequential dialogue. However, its schematic patterns and mythic references lift it beyond the literal to the symbolic.

Strindberg's dream of having his own theatre was briefly realized in Copenhagen in 1889, in his 'Scandinavian experimental theatre', modelled on ANTOINE's Théâtre Libre. The Danish censor (see CENSORSHIP) having banned *Miss Julie* (performed privately a few days later), the theatre's single programme consisted of *Creditors* (1889) and two new *quart d'heure* plays, *The Stronger* and *Pariah* (both 1889). Strindberg spent much of the 1890s in Berlin (where he met his second wife Frida Uhl), Austria and Paris, devoting himself obsessively to scientific experiments and occult studies. Between 1894 and 1896 occurred what is called the Inferno crisis, a sequence of psychotic episodes culminating in his hospitalization and eventual return to Sweden. His recovery was partly aided by his discovery of the 18th-century Swedish mystic, Emmanuel Swedenborg, who provided a religious explanation of his sufferings and a rationalization of apparently chaotic phenomena as 'correspondences' of a higher, coherent reality. Determined to be 'the Zola of the Occult', Strindberg assembled masses of esoterically connected phenomena in his *Occult Diary*; they provided much of the detail in his semi-fictional accounts of the crisis – *Inferno* (1897), *Legends* (1897) and *Jacob Wrestles* (1898) – and in his post-Inferno plays.

Revivals of earlier plays persuaded him to resume

dramatic writing, beginning in 1898 with Part 1 of *To Damascus*, the first of a new type of drama, exploring mankind's spiritual progress in a divine context. The 34 plays that followed in the next 14 years are remarkable for their diversity and innovation. Some, like the *Damascus* trilogy and *The Great Highway* (1909), are large psycho-spiritual pilgrimage dramas with dream-like settings and action. Others, such as *A Dream Play* (1902), use dream structure to reformulate experience. Harriet Bosse, his third wife, appeared in many of them. Strindberg resumed writing history plays, producing 11 on Swedish topics and several plans for *The Saga of Mankind*, an ambitious world-history cycle, of which four were actually completed.

From 1907, Strindberg was actively involved in running the tiny Intima Teatern, which the actor August Falck had opened, in imitation of REINHARDT's Kammerspielhaus. For it he wrote new 'chamber plays', attempting to create the dramatic equivalent of chamber music, 'intimate in form; a simple theme treated with thoroughness; few characters; vast perspectives'. Four of these – *Storm Weather*, *The Burned House*, *The Ghost Sonata* and *The Pelican* (all 1907) – explore death as a kind of painful awakening from a life of sleep-walking illusion. As a practising painter, he had a strong visual sense, and used the tiny stage to experiment with ways to 'dematerialize' settings. Projected scenery had been tried for productions of *To Damascus* (1900) and *A Dream Play* (1907) and had failed. Now he tried other solutions: drapery and tapestry settings; formal stages derived from his study of theatre history; coloured lighting.

Strindberg's entire career was marked by his urge to experiment, to redefine, and to transgress. He exploded Zola's concept of naturalism; his history plays established a new relationship between character and history; and his dream and fantasy plays anticipated and influenced surrealistic, expressionistic, and absurdist theatre (see SURREALISM; EXPRESSIONISM; THEATRE OF THE ABSURD).   HL

strip-tease   see BURLESQUE SHOW, AMERICAN; NUDITY

Stubbes, Philip c.1555–91 English printer and minor poet who is best known for his colourful attack on London's immorality in *The Anatomy of Abuses* (1583). Only a small portion of Stubbes's invective is directed against the PUBLIC THEATRES, but it was on this portion that NASHE concentrated in his answering *The Anatomy of Absurdity* (1589). Stubbes's book is ironically treasured for the information it gives on popular entertainments in Elizabethan England.   PT

Stukalov, N. F.   see POGODIN, NIKOLAI

Sturm und Drang ('storm and stress') Term used to denote the work of certain German dramatists and writers of the 1770s. *Sturm und Drang* drama represents a reaction to the rational drama of the Enlightenment. It was written under the influence of ROUSSEAU's natural philosophy and of the plays of SHAKESPEARE, which at that time were being translated into German and, very gradually, introduced on to the stage. In *Sturm und Drang* drama the rights of the individual are often unequivocally expressed,

the focus is frequently those aspects of personality and character that render the individual unadjusted to ordered society, and heroes may well be luminescent figures who attract a following by the sheer force of their personalities. Themes of the *Sturm und Drang* dramatists are often sensational, as they deal with incest, infanticide, extreme suffering and radical disaffection with the world. Dramaturgically their plays are indebted to the 'epic' form of Shakespeare rather than to the carefully composed work of playwrights such as LESSING.

GOETHE was a leader among these writers in the first half of the 1770s, his *Götz von Berlichingen* being one of the most accomplished and characteristic specimens of this type of drama. The plays of LENZ are also among the most durable works of *Sturm und Drang*. Other prominent writers in the movement were Heinrich Leopold Wagner (1747–79), who wrote two plays of considerable power, *Repentance after the Deed* (1775) and *The Child Killer* (1776), and Friedrich Klinger (1752–1831), who was known for *The Twins* (1776) and the play that has been used to give the movement its name, *Storm and Stress* (1776). The plays of the young SCHILLER, *The Robbers*, *Fiesko* and *Love and Intrigue*, although written in the 1780s, show many of the characteristic features of the movement. Several of the plays were given their first performances either by DÖBBELIN in Berlin or by FRIEDRICH SCHRÖDER in Hamburg. The acting of Schröder was especially suited to the jagged, harsh characterizations in these plays.   SW

Sturua, Robert (Robertovich) 1938 Georgian director, trained by Mikhail Tumanishvili, who since 1963 has run Tblisi's Rustaveli Theatre and who became a Deputy of the Supreme Soviet of the Georgian Soviet Socialist Republic. Sturua mounted spectacular, offbeat productions of *The Caucasian Chalk Circle* (1975), *Richard III* (London and Edinburgh, 1979–80) and *King Lear* (New York, 1990), starring comic actor Ramaz Chkhikvadze. Sturua's Richard, a casually murderous, clownish embodiment of totalitarian evil, defeated a slobbering, Brezhnev-like King Edward and duelled his omnipresent understudy Richmond through a giant map of Great Britain. Sturua's *King Lear* (1987) featured choral elements musically scored by Gia Kancheli, a punkish Cordelia and a theatre-in-ruins setting by Mirian Shevelidze, which ultimately collapsed. Sturua staged SHATROV's historically revisionist plays *The Peace of Brest-Litovsk* (as a near-vaudevillian spectacle in Moscow, 1987, and Chicago, 1990) and *Blue Horses on Red Grass*, which ran briefly in Moscow. His 1992 London production of CHEKHOV's *Three Sisters*, starring VANESSA, Lynn and Jemma REDGRAVE, was judged to be physically, emotionally and symbolically overbearing. SG

Suassuna, Ariano 1927– Brazilian playwright from the northeast (Pernambuco). Suassuna's *Auto da Compadecida* (*The Rogue's Trial*) in 1957 vaulted him into national prominence in Rio and São Paulo for its aesthetic and ingenious mixture of popular, religious and folkloric elements from the Brazilian northeast. Other plays in similar vein, although less successful, are *O Arco Desolado* (*The Desolate Arch*), *O Casamento Suspeitoso* (*The*

Suspicious Marriage) and *O Santo e a Porca* (*The Saint and the Pig*), the latter a treatment of the classical miser, borrowed freely from PLAUTUS and MOLIÈRE but with a uniquely Brazilian flavour. GW

Sudermann, Hermann 1857–1928 German playwright. At the height of his fame at the turn of the century, Sudermann was regarded by many as a playwright equivalent in stature to IBSEN. His naturalistic dramas (see NATURALISM) *Honour* (1889), *Sodom's End* (1890) and *Heimat* (*Homeland*, 1893 – known in English as *Magda*) were celebrated, the last mentioned because the powerful central role appealed to the prominent actresses of the time. As the naturalist movement ebbed, Sudermann moved unsuccessfully into poetic drama. Despite his dramaturgical expertise, his plays, though occasionally revived, are dated, because of his almost total dependence on Ibsen and the WELL MADE PLAY. SW

Sudraka c.5th century AD Playwright (INDIAN) of ancient Sanskrit theatre. He apparently produced a single work, *The Little Clay Cart* (*Mrcchakatika*), a complex and dynamic play about the love of a Brahmin and a courtesan and the overthrow of a despotic ruler. The preface to the play describes the author in considerable detail, indicating that he was a king, mathematician, knowledgeable in love and skilled in the training of elephants. According to the verse, he was a hundred years old when he committed suicide. Obviously it is impossible that a writer could discuss his own death in the preface of one of his plays; hence numerous questions about the authenticity of the preface and the author of the work. Whatever the circumstances, Sudraka certainly produced a masterpiece. FAR

Sukhovo-Kobylin, Aleksandr (Vasilievich) 1817–1903 Wealthy Russian noble, trained primarily in Hegelian philosophy, whom fate helped make a dramatist. Falsely indicted for the murder of his estranged French mistress, he was dragged through the Tsarist court system for seven years before being acquitted. His experiences of this period resulted in the writing of the dramatic trilogy which is his sole but major claim to fame. Published in 1869 under the collective title *Tableaux of the Past*, each of the three plays is written in a distinct style, furthers a sequential course of events and revolves around an interlocking set of characters. The monstrous petty bureaucrats, romantic deceivers and mercenary thieves herein depicted are reminiscent of GOGOL and SALTYKOV-SHCHEDRIN.

The plays describe a movement from apparent truth to blatant falsehood, from naive idealism to degenerate amoralism, via concentric philosophical, social and dramatic structures. *Krechinsky's Wedding* (written in prison, 1854) is a SCRIBEan WELL MADE PLAY whose romantic contrivance symbolizes an innocent world about to be corrupted. A Khlestakov-like gambler-poseur deceives a young girl and her family and is unmasked. *The Case* (1861) grimly chronicles the spiralling events that trap and ruin the girl and her father when they are dragged into the bureaucratic beehive of the Tsarist legal system. Here the tone is harshly satirical, the structure, language and environment more realistic. *Tarelkin's Death* (1869) is

a phantasmagoria featuring two petty-bureaucrat vultures who, having disposed of the hapless family in the previous play, now attempt to cheat one another. Here all is sham, including disguisings, feigned death and the charge of vampirism. This is fittingly the most self-consciously theatrical of the three plays, rooted in the tradition of the Gogolian grotesque and foreshadowing the THEATRE OF THE ABSURD.

While *Krechinsky* premiered in 1855, *Case* was not staged until 1882 as *Bygone Times* (stressing its pastness) and *Tarelkin* until 1900, as *Rasplyuev's Merry Days*. The entire trilogy was performed in 1901 on succeeding evenings. The most famous single production was MEYERHOLD's *Tarelkin* in 1922, which featured the director's experiments in biomechanics and CIRCUS play, utilizing constructivist sets by VARVARA STEPANOVA. Both *Krechinsky* (in the 1970s) and *Tarelkin* (in the 1980s) have been transformed into MUSICALS in Leningrad. Sukhovo-Kobylin was elected to the Russian Academy of Sciences in 1902. SG

Sumarokov, Aleksei (Petrovich) 1717–77 Russia's first modern tragic and comic dramatist, a poet and critic; 'the Russian BOILEAU', whose 'Epistle on Poetry' (1748) was the rough equivalent of *L' Art poétique*. He was (for his time) an enlightened noble and humanist, sensitive to the abuse of power by the Tsar and other hereditary nobility, dedicated to the concept of *noblesse oblige*, and convinced of the theatre's importance as an agent for social and moral education. He was one of the first graduates of St Petersburg's Noble College of Land Cadets (1740), where his best TRAGEDY, *Khorev* (1747), was played under his direction. This was the first Russian neo-classical play to be performed by Russians and, like his eight other tragedies, adhered to the three unities, the five-act play structure, and the rhetorical language and heroic tone of the French models.

Of some interest are his *Hamlet* (1748), based on French translations, and *Dmitry the Pretender* (1771), which previews the historical events treated by PUSHKIN in his superior *Boris Godunov*. His 12 comedies of character and situation, inspired by MOLIÈRE, attack the commonly depicted vices of his day: Gallomania, judicial corruption, ignorant and self-serving *philosophes*, dandyism, the idleness and cruelty of landowners, the abuses of serfdom and the problem of education. Of these, *The Odd Fellows, Nartsiss* and *Tresotinius*, all from 1750, are characteristic.

Although his situations were largely borrowed and his characters undeveloped, his comedies as well as his tragedies remained highly popular until the advent of sentimental comedy, bourgeois drama and FONVIZIN's more original and refined comedies of manners. Still, Sumarokov provided the necessary first step in introducing native elements and cultured language where before there had been only translations and adaptations. In 1756 he was appointed director of St Petersburg's Russian Patent Theatre, the first permanent Russian professional public theatre, at which FYODOR VOLKOV and IVAN DMITREVSKY performed. In 1761 he was relieved of his position and replaced by Volkov. Upon his death, the theatre passed over to the Imperial household, thus initiating the tradition of the Russian Imperial theatres. SG

Sunda see INDONESIA

surrealism After rejecting the word 'surnaturalism', the poet Guillaume Apollinaire in 1917 invented the word 'surrealism' in the preface to his play *The Breasts of Tiresias*: 'When man wanted to imitate walking, he created the wheel, which does not resemble a leg. He thus made surrealism without being aware of it.' And he – Guillaume Apollinaire – thus founded an art movement, without being aware of it.

The seed, as opposed to the name, of surrealism was planted in neutral Zurich in 1916. Young artists, refugees from the First World War, viewed all art with a jaundiced eye and voiced their disapproval raucously – especially in unmatrixed performances at the Café Voltaire. Romanian Tristan Tzara not only participated in these manifestations; he also established correspondence channels with a rebellious avant-garde among the futurists in Italy (see FUTURISM) and the cubists in Paris. Apparently choosing their name 'dada' by opening a dictionary at random, the temperamentally theatrical artists opposed dada to art, process to product. Nevertheless, Tzara penned a play, *The First Celestial Adventure of M. Antipyrine*, which was first performed in Zurich, and four years later in Paris, when Tzara moved to that bastion of the avant-garde.

Paris had seen not only Apollinaire's *Breasts* in 1917, but the PICASSO–COCTEAU–Diaghilev *Parade*, and the publication by André Breton and Philippe Soupault of their *Magnetic Fields*, a dialogue obtained by 'automatic writing'. Chance, spontaneity, deliberate shock were the tactics of the year 1920, with more or less collective participation. By 1924 the rivalry of Tzara and Breton was irremediable, and the latter, seizing upon the neologism of Apollinaire, 'the patron saint of surrealism' (dead in 1917), published the movement's first manifesto. An heir of SYMBOLISM in its opposition to reason and REALISM; a sibling of dada in its espousal of the unconscious, the erotic, the shocking – surrealism was, more ambitiously, a lifestyle that sought through images to pierce to man's deepest centre. Programmatically hostile to theatre, Breton expelled Artaud and VITRAC. If we exclude dada performances and the unreconstructed dadaist Georges Ribemont-Dessaignes, there were scarcely a dozen surrealist performances, but the emphasis upon spontaneity and imagery nevertheless was a lasting legacy of surrealism to the theatre. Above all, surrealism's impact on the theatre came through the mediacy of its first director of research, ANTONIN ARTAUD. RC

Sutherland, Efua T(heodora) 1924– Ghanaian playwright, director and researcher. Born in Cape Coast and educated in England and Ghana, Sutherland has dominated Ghanaian theatre since independence and over 30 years has made an incalculable contribution to the development of drama in Ghana. As a playwright she has written and devised a wide range of works in the Akan language and in English; as a director she has staged many kinds of performances, from traditional community music to modern experimental drama. She has also devoted her energies to the social production of dramatic art in Ghana. She has, for example, inspired the innovative *kodzidan* the 'story house', built by community effort in the village

of Atwia as a centre for musical and dramatic performances. In the 1960s she established the Ghana Drama Studio in Accra, which she helped design and for which she raised funds, and she has explored the scope of research into traditional performance, at the Institute of African Studies, University of Ghana. Through her position of influence she found the means to set up a programme of experimental theatre (1958–61), and subsequently to explore new plays for children – e.g. her 'rhythm plays' *Vulture! Vulture!* and *Tahinta*, which she later published as a text with photographs. She later developed *anansegoro* (drama extensions of *anansesem* – storytelling performances of Ananse, the spider man). *Anansegoro* were performed by a number of groups, mainly in Akan; an English text of Sutherland's own *The Marriage of Anansewa* (1975) was published together with a brief introduction to the theory and practice of the new dramatic form. Her own earlier stage plays, *Foriwa* (1962) and *Edufa* (1967), show eclecticism and an interest in Western dramatic modes. The economic problems in Ghana constantly postpone the realization of a National Theatre for Ghana, which Sutherland has consistently promoted. ME

Sütő, András 1927– Hungarian playwright, born in Transylvania, the leading writer of the Hungarian minority in Romania. Sütő's dramas probe the duty of the individual, confronted by arbitrary authority, to preserve his dignity and identity even at the cost of his life. *The Palm Sunday of a Horse Dealer* (1974), *Star at the Stake* (1976) and *The Wedding Feast at Susa* (1981) are historical dramas. *Cain and Abel* (1977) and *Advent on Mount Hargita* (1985) are based on myth and folklore; *The Dream Commando* (1987) is about the production of a play set in Auschwitz. His latest play, *The Barking Bird* (1993), is about Transylvania following the 1848–9 War of Independence. These works have had numerous productions in Hungary and Transylvania. Their success is due as much to the lyrical beauty of Sütő's language as to their subject-matter. Sütő is also well known for prose works, and his writings have appeared in ten other languages. He was awarded the 1979 Herder Prize (Vienna). EB

Sutro, Alfred 1863–1933 British dramatist, whose more than 50 works made him one of the most popular exponents of the WELL MADE PLAY after PINERO. He was also responsible for translating MAETERLINCK's plays. CI

Suzman, Janet 1939– British actress, born and educated in South Africa, the niece of a leading political opponent of apartheid, Helen Suzman. She moved to London to study drama at the London Academy of Music and Dramatic Art, which staged an experimental season in 1963 with the newly formed ROYAL SHAKESPEARE COMPANY. Suzman joined the RSC, playing Joan la Pucelle in *The Wars of the Roses* (1963–4), and for the next 15 years came to play major classical roles with the company, including Rosalind and Portia (1965), Ophelia (1965–6), Cleopatra (1972), and Clytemnestra and Helen in JOHN BARTON's cycle, *The Greeks* (1980).

Her most notable achievements, however, have come in more recently written plays, as an outstanding Hedda in

Hedda Gabler (1972), Masha in JONATHAN MILLER's production of *Three Sisters* (1976) and Hesta in ATHOL FUGARD's *Hello and Goodbye* (1973). She has been equally successful in films and television, notably in *The Draughtsman's Contract* (1981) and the TV serial *Clayhanger* (1975–6). Strikingly tall and attractive, Suzman nevertheless commands attention as an actress more through the subtlety of her voice inflexions and the intelligent ironies of her interpretations. She appeared in the title role of JEAN RACINE's *Andromache*, directed by Jonathan Miller in 1988, and in EURIPIDES' *Hippolytus* (1991) at the Almeida; but she has also directed Michael Hastings's *A Dream of People* (1990) for the RSC and *No Flies on Mr Hunter* (1992, from GEORGES FEYDEAU's *La Chasse*) for London's Chelsea Theatre Centre. JE

Suzuki Tadashi 1939– Japanese director and dramatic theorist. Suzuki originally established his reputation directing experimental works by post-*shingeki* playwrights like BETSUYAKU MINORU, KARA JŪRŌ and SATOH MAKOTO at the Waseda Little Theatre (Waseda Shōgekijō), which he founded with Betsuyaku and actor Ono Seki. In 1969, however, his fertile collaboration with actress Shiraishi Kayoko began, and he moved away from a text-centred to an actor-centred theatre. He assembled dramatic collages to showcase Shiraishi's talents, *On the Dramatic Passions, I* (*Gekiteki naru mono o megutte, I,* 1969) and *II* (1970), and out of these grew the actor-training method for which he subsequently became famous. In 1976 Suzuki moved his troupe out of Tokyo to the village of Toga in Toyama prefecture and later changed its name to SCOT (Suzuki Company of Toga). Since 1982, he has organized an annual international theatre festival at Toga. As a director, Suzuki's reputation rests on his renditions of Western classics. *The Trojan Women* (1974), *The Bacchae* (1978) and *Clytemnestra* (1983) are representative. Suzuki has taught at the University of Wisconsin–Milwaukee, the University of California–San Diego, and the Juilliard School. He has staged bilingual productions, using JAPANese and American actors, including *The Tale of Lear* (1988). In addition to his position as leader of SCOT, Suzuki has been artistic director of the Mitsui Festival since 1988 and artistic director for theatre at the regional Mito Art Tower since 1990. DGG

svanga [swang; sang; sangeet] Rural theatre form of Haryana, Uttar Pradesh and Punjab states in north India. *Svanga* is thought to have originated in the late 18th century. In urban as well as rural areas, Hindu festivals and family celebrations, especially marriages and the birth of a son, provide the occasion for *svanga* performance. Plays concern conflicts between rivals found in popular ballads and semihistorical tales. Stories of love, honour and duty abound.

Performance takes place in an open space of the village or on the veranda of a patron's house. Actors, all male, wear costumes which are simple village garments, exaggerated headdresses and brightly coloured cloth pieces. False hair and beards 'theatricalize' a performance to satisfy village tastes.

An evening's entertainment begins with songs in praise of Hindu deities, especially Ganapati, the elephant-headed god of good fortune. A strong plot line emerges in which characters express their feelings in vernacular dialogue and punctuate their emotions with songs which have a strong poetic line.

Svanga can also mean an act of a *KARIYALA* play. FAR

Svoboda, Josef 1920– Czech scenographer. Educated in Prague as an architect, he was for nearly 30 years chief designer and head of technical operations in the National Theatre; since the early 1980s he has been head of the *LATERNA MAGIKA* operation, now with its own independent state theatre, the Laterna Magika. Svoboda's work is based on a metaphoric rather than realistic approach to design, on the premise that stage setting and lighting form an organic, dynamic component of production rather than a static indication of place, and on the use of the widest range of contemporary equipment, materials and techniques in the scenography for a given production concept. Outstanding among his more than 600 international productions have been *Hamlet* (Brussels, 1958), *Carmen* (New York, 1972), WAGNER's *Ring* (London, 1974–6; Geneva, 1975–7; Orange, 1988), *Idomeneo* (Ottawa, 1983), CLAUDEL's *Partage de Midi* (Louvain, 1984), GOETHE's *Faust* (Milan, 1989) and *La Traviata* (Macerata, 1992). JMB

Swan Theatre (London) This undistinguished theatre, built in c.1595 by the parsimonious Frances Langley, is given a peculiar significance by the chance preservation of a sketch of its interior, made in 1596 by a visiting Dutchman, Johannes de Witt. Published in 1888, shortly after its discovery, this sketch, the only substantial visual evidence of the inside of an Elizabethan playhouse, caused a radical revision of assumptions about Elizabethan staging. De Witt shows us a round, or more probably polygonal, building with three galleries surrounding an open yard. An almost square stage, supported by stout timbers, occupies half of the yard. Access for actors is provided by two double doors, and the unadorned platform is backed by a gallery and partly roofed. The pillars which support the roof effectively break the stage into sections.

The Swan, built on the south bank of the Thames, was not a lucky theatre. A performance of *The Isle of Dogs* there in 1597 was largely responsible for a Privy Council ban on the performance of plays in London. One of the authors, JONSON, was imprisoned; another, NASHE, fled to the Continent; Pembroke's Men, who staged the play, disbanded, and the Swan itself sank into obscurity. It is known to have been used for amateur performances as well as, occasionally, by professional companies and promoters of prize fights. The only surviving play known to have been staged there is MIDDLETON's *A Chaste Maid in Cheapside* (c.1611). Probably disused after the death of James I in 1625, the Swan had already 'fallen to decay' by 1632, when Nicholas Goodman described it in his pamphlet, *Holland's Leaguer*.

In 1986 the ROYAL SHAKESPEARE COMPANY opened a new Swan Theatre, designed with an open stage, at Stratford-upon-Avon. This new Swan has, as its policy, the presentation of plays by Shakespeare's contemporaries and the playwrights of the Restoration stage. PT MB

Swanston, Elliard [Eyllaerdt] d.1651 English actor,

A scene from the Pistol Theatre's production of Molière's *Les Femmes Savantes* (*The Learned Ladies*), Stockholm, 1984.

who was a leading member of the King's Men (see LORD CHAMBERLAIN'S MEN) from 1624 until the CLOSURE OF THE THEATRES in 1642. As well as creating many of MASSINGER's main roles, Swanston is known to have played Othello, Richard III and CHAPMAN's Bussy d'Ambois in revivals. In SHADWELL's *The Virtuoso* (1676) he is remembered as 'a brave roaring Fellow, who would make the House shake'. Swanston was, unlike most actors, on the Parliamentary side in the Civil War, and is said to have turned jeweller during the Interregnum. PT

Swaziland see BOTSWANA, LESOTHO AND SWAZILAND

Sweden It is possible that Sweden had performances in the 6th century; it certainly had LITURGICAL DRAMA from the 13th century until the Reformation in 1521. However, Epiphany and Resurrection plays survived outside the churches until the 17th century, augmented by MIRACLE and MORALITY drama. The Lutheran Church encouraged school drama on moral grounds, both Latin comedies and indigenous hybrids like *The Play of Tobias* and *The Play of Holofernes and Judith*. The 17th century witnessed gradual secularization, as in the burlesque INTERLUDES in the morality *Judas Redivivus* (1614).

School drama declined in the 17th century, as royal patronage began its long domination of the Swedish stage. In 1628 Gustav II Adolf engaged a permanent court troupe, but Christina (1632–54) established elaborate temporary theatres, with complicated changeable scenery, foreign OPERA and *COMMEDIA DELL'ARTE* troupes, and *ballets de cour* and pageants for royal amateurs. Under her successors, theatrical activity continued to thrive. Charles XII

(1697–1718) engaged a permanent troupe of French actors, led by Claude Rosidor, and the royal tennis court was converted into a theatre in the French style, with scenery by JEAN BERAIN. They were followed by a French opera company and, in 1737, by the first Swedish troupe under royal patronage, 'the Royal Swedish Stage', performing a mixed French and Swedish repertoire. These lasted until 1753, when Queen Lovisa Ulrika, an enthusiast for French and Italian theatre, replaced them with yet another French company. She also commissioned the DROTTNINGHOLM SLOTTSTEATER, whose present building (1766) is the best-preserved baroque court theatre in the world.

Royal patronage reached a peak under Gustav III (1771–92), not only in Drottningholm's summer opera and ballet seasons and open-air pageants, but also in the refurbished tennis court and his new opera house (1782). Gustav hired leading designers, such as CARLO BIBIENA; he engaged the French actor Monvel to train rising Swedish stars like LARS HJÖRTSBERG; he himself wrote and promoted Swedish drama; and he established Kungliga Dramatiska Teatern (DRAMATEN), to perform new Swedish works, albeit in the French neoclassical style. Gustav's initiatives were crucial in developing a Swedish theatre, although his assassination in 1792 temporarily stopped theatrical activity. However, while Drottningholm gradually fell into neglect Dramaten eventually reopened, in the converted Royal Arsenal, with Gustav's last play *The Jealous Neapolitan*, whose gothic atmosphere signalled a trend away from French taste towards German and English; indeed, SHAKESPEARE finally reached Dramaten in 1819, with a production of *Hamlet*. When the Arsenal burned in 1825, Dramaten began an unsatisfactory shared tenancy of the Opera House, whose mere size may have influenced it to favour celebratory historical dramas about the Nordic past.

Stockholm's first private theatre, Nya Teatern, opened in 1842. By the 1880s, under Ludvig Josephson's direction, it became Sweden's most progressive theatre, staging BJØRNSON, IBSEN and STRINDBERG, who achieved his first success with *Master Olof* in August Lindberg's superb production. The end of the century brought other new theatres (many owned by Albert Ranft); Dramaten, meanwhile, was in crisis, deprived temporarily of its subsidy and attacked for its conservatism.

Although Dramaten premiered several of Strindberg's later plays, he was increasingly dissatisfied by the cluttered REALISM employed and was proud to collaborate with the experimental Intima Teatern (1907–10), for which he wrote his chamber plays. The breakthrough of modernism was to occur after Strindberg's death, prompted by visits from the REINHARDT and Michel Fokine companies and realized in Sweden by the innovative theatricalism of PER LINDBERG and Knut Ström at the Lorensbergsteatern, Göteborg. Lindberg's erratic but seminal work reached its climax in his productions of LAGERKVIST in the 1920s and 30s. He was Sweden's major proponent of the 'people's theatre' concept, which he fought to realize in the huge Konserthusteatern in the 1920s. Overlapping Lindberg's career was OLOF MOLANDER's. Under his leadership Dramaten developed the restrained, psychological acting style that supported both his Strindberg productions and the world premieres of several of O'NEILL's plays in the 1950s. Also at Dramaten from the 1930s to 1980 was ALF SJÖBERG, who directed some 130 productions, constantly exploring new styles and repertoire. At mid-century the company could boast a superb acting company, including LARS HANSON, INGA TIDBLAD, Tora Teje, Anders Ek and ALLAN EDWALL.

Theatre outside Stockholm entered a new phase with the opening of municipal theatres in Helsingborg (1921), Göteborg (1934), Malmö (1944) and Uppsala-Gävle (1951). Others followed in the 1960s, including Stockholms Stadsteater (1961), whose precise function in relationship to Dramaten has always been uncertain, although its children's theatre Unga Klara, led by SUZANNE OSTEN, has always maintained a distinctive (and distinguished) profile. Riksteatern (the national touring theatre) was founded in 1934, to send touring productions around the country; it also established regional ensembles, most of which subsequently became independent regional theatres. The municipal theatres' importance has fluctuated, depending on artistic leadership; for example, the young INGMAR BERGMAN's productions first boosted Helsingborg's reputation, then Malmö's. From 1963 to 1966 Bergman was head of Dramaten; he created some superb productions, but also initiated some timely reforms, decentralizing policy-making, raising salaries and sometimes holding public rehearsals.

During the 1960s, institutional theatres were often attacked for their conservative repertoires, aesthetics and audiences. Even within the institutions, there were attempts to change the ways in which theatre was made. At GÖTEBORGS STADSTEATER Lennart Hjulström staged a series of partly group-created social and political parables, beginning with Kent Andersson's *The Raft* (1967), using metaphorical settings (a drifting raft, an old people's home, a mental hospital) to expose a complacent Swedish welfare state that encouraged intolerance and ignored injustice. This methodology and politics were later pursued by FOLKTEATERN I GÖTEBORG, where Hjulström and Andersson subsequently worked. Dramaten's group projects included *Gypsies* (1968) and the steelworks docudrama *N.J.A.* (1969), performed by a group which then left to form the 'free group' Fria Proteatern.

The free groups were the 1960s' and 1970s' most lasting expression of distrust of institutional theatre. They were often collectively organized, consisting mostly of young artists who demanded freedom from establishment politics, structures and (initially, at least) funding. Inspired by various foreign models (LIVING THEATRE, LA MAMA, GROTOWSKI, DARIO FO), they sought to reassert theatre's relevance through experimental, physical and polemical performance strategies, sometimes with more enthusiasm than skill. Among the more important groups have been Pistolteatern (1964), which began by staging happenings, and then passed through several phases of political work; Fickteatern (1967), specializing in provocative children's theatre; Teater 9 (1969), combining politics with formal experimentation; Byteatern (1970), using PUPPETS and MASKS for children's theatre; the music theatre Oktober (1972); Skånska Teater (1973), artistically innovative in its treatment of classics and its 1982 Rudolf Värnlund trilogy; the laboratory theatre Schahrazad (1976); and Earth Circus (1977), originally specializing in political street theatre. In 1977 several free groups collaborated on the Tent Project, touring Sweden for four months in a huge circus tent, to present *We Are Thousands*, a musical docudrama about the Swedish labour movement. By 1969 there was need for a Theatre Centre to coordinate and promote the groups; today it has more than 60 members. Seventy-five per cent of Swedish children's performances are still given by group theatres.

The 1970s were also marked by the expansion of regional theatre, especially after the 1974 state cultural policy proclaimed the principles of universal accessibility and decentralization, including the establishment in each of Sweden's 24 counties of a subsidized regional theatre with touring responsibilities. Already in 1967 the collectively organized Norrbottensteatern had opened, serving Sweden's most northern county; its desire to treat local issues was reflected in *The Play of Norrbotten*, created with local amateurs in 1970. Other regional theatres followed, as well as regional ensembles established within the administrative structure of Riksteatern; several, such as the Västeråsensemble and Växjöensemble, subsequently became regional theatres. A SAMI theatre, Dálvadis, was started in Jokkmokk in 1971.

The contemporary situation In many ways, the 1980s were a decade of stagnation for most Swedish theatres. Audiences grew, and funding continued at high levels until the late 1980s. However, with a few exceptions, the political and artistic drive of the 1960s and 70s was greatly diminished. The free groups were particularly affected, and most have either become small institutions or disappeared. Some important alternative theatres began, such as Remote Control Productions (1981), the provocative Teater Galeasen (1982), ORIONTEATERN (1983), Folkteatern i Gävleborg (1983) and Allan Edwall's tiny Brunnsgatan 4 (1986). Some major institutions have endured particularly bleak periods. At Göteborgs Stadsteater, the defeat of a proposal to redefine the company as an art theatre caused enduring bitterness and uncertainty. (Its young people's company, Backa Teater, has flourished, largely because of the determination of its director, Eva Bergman.) Malmö Stadsteater continued its artistic decline until its reorganization in 1993. Dramaten has increased its activity, and promoted itself as the national standard-bearer of high quality, but many question its repertoire policies. Stockholms Stadsteater has finally moved into its own building, but has an uncertain identity, with the exception of its lunchtime 'soup theatre' and its brilliant children's company Unga Klara. Riksteatern's future is uncertain because it now partly duplicates the work of the many regional companies it helped to create. All Swedish theatre felt threatened financially by the recession of the early 1990s and by Sweden's political swing to the right.

Paradoxically, the number of significant Swedish playwrights has greatly increased during the 1980s. In addition to internationally known writers like PER OLOV ENQUIST, LARS FORSSELL and LARS NORÉN, important contemporary dramatists include Margareta Garpe, STAFFAN GÖTHE, Stig Larsson, Magnus Nilsson, Agneta Pleijel, Barbro Smeds and Staffan Westerberg. Several theatres, including Jönköpings Länsteater and Uppsala Stadsteater, have encouraged new writing by staging all-Swedish seasons. The number of outstanding directors includes not only established names like Ingmar Bergman, Lennart Hjulström, PETER OSKARSON, Suzanne Osten and Finn Poulsen, but also Eva Bergman, Wilhelm Carlsson, Karl Dunér, Hilda Hellwig, Staffan Waldemar Holm, Ragnar Lyth, Björn Melander, Lars Rudolfsson and Christian Tomner. The leading scenographers remain Sören Brunes, Lennart Mörk and Gunilla Palmstierna-Weiss, joined by Jost Assmann, Charles Koroly, Lars-Åke Thessman and Göran Wassberg. Sweden has countless remarkable actors, including Börje Ahlstedt, BIBI ANDERSSON, Anita Björk, Allan Edwall, Stina Ekblad, Agneta Ekmanner, Erland Josephson, Stellan Skarsgård, MAX VON SYDOW and Sven Wollter. HL

See: G. M. Andermann, *New Swedish Plays*, Norwich, 1992; K. O. Arntzen, T. O. Svendsen and M. Moi (eds.), *Kunnskapsforlagets Teater- og Filmleksikon*, Oslo, 1991; P. Brask (ed.), *Drama Contemporary: Scandinavia*, New York, 1989; P. G. Engel and L. Janzon, *Sju decennier: Svensk teater under 1900-talet*, Stockholm, 1974; *Entré* (journal), Stockholm, 1974– ; F. J. and L.-L. Marker, *The Scandinavian Theatre*, Oxford, 1975, and *Ingmar Bergman: A Life in the Theater*, Cambridge, 1992; *Nordic Theatre Studies*, Copenhagen, 1988– ; L. Senelick (ed.), *National Theatre in Northern and Eastern Europe, 1746–1900*, Cambridge, 1991; H. Sjögren, *Stage and Society in Sweden*, Stockholm, 1979; *Teaterårsboken* (annual), Stockholm, 1982– ; P. A. Tjäder, *Den allvarsamma lekplatsen*, Stockholm, 1984; C. Waal, *Harriet Bosse*, Carbondale, 1990.

Switzerland The geopolitical situation of Switzerland, turntable of Europe, has exerted a profound influence on its cultural life. On the one hand Switzerland enjoys rich and varied theatrical activity; on the other, it lacks a distinctive national drama.

The Middle Ages and the Renaissance (See also MEDIEVAL DRAMA IN EUROPE (Germany, Switzerland).) The Abbey of Saint-Gall, early in the 10th century, staged a Latin Easter play which is at the origin of the flowering of the tradition of PASSION PLAYS performed throughout Europe to the end of the 16th century. Early in the 13th century the first dramatic text in German appeared in Muri: *Osterspiel von Muri* (anon.). Lausanne staged its first Passion play in 1453 and the same year saw the beginning of the famous tradition of the *Osterspiele* on the Weinmarkt in Lucerne. During the 16th century, theatre was used to further the aims of Swiss political independence (*Urner Tellenspiel*, Altdorf, 1511–12), of the Reformation (Théodore de Bèze, *Abraham Sacrifiant*, Geneva, 1550), and of the Counter-Reformation (Jesuit drama (see JESUITENDRAMA) in Lucerne, Fribourg, Sion and, particularly, in Einsiedeln).

The 17th–18th centuries The theatre was under attack: autocratic governments banned plays in Lucerne (1616), Geneva (1623) and Zurich (1624). In 1692, the reformed city of Berne banned a play attacking Louis XIV's persecution of the Huguenots after a complaint from the French envoy. In the 18th century, the only activities in German as well as in French Switzerland were foreign tours of German, French and English companies, and shows put on by aristocratic amateur societies. The first permanent theatres were built in Baden (1673), Lucerne (1741), Solothurn (1755) and Geneva (1783). The most important event during the Enlightenment was the controversy opposing VOLTAIRE and ROUSSEAU: in his *Lettre à d'Alembert* (1758) Rousseau accused the theatre of immorality and of frivolity, and his intervention led to a total ban in Geneva. But the ruling families of the city flocked to Voltaire's house in Ferney (a few kilometres away, but in French territory) to applaud comedies ridiculing their philistinism and religiosity. Rousseau's letter, however, also had a positive effect: it reminded its readers of the lost medieval tradition of religious popular festivals, and called for the active creation of open-air civic festivities staged by the entire community for its own wholesome delight and true enlightenment. It so happened that the *Tellspiel* was revived at the end of the century in German Switzerland and that the wine-harvest feast of Vevey grew into a theatrical event, two developments which will bear fruit in the 20th century.

The 19th century A new freedom entered Swiss theatre with the arrival of Napoleon's armies. A call was heard for the creation of a National Theatre, comprising two companies, one German, one French. In 1837, Berne awarded the first (modest) official grant to a municipal theatre, and by the middle of the century Zurich was regarded as an important centre of German theatre.

Popular theatre The end of the 19th and the beginning of the 20th centuries witnessed a strong resurgence of an amateur and semi-professional theatre movement, creating new or reviving ancient festivals or *Festspiele*. The theme of these huge popular pageants was the commemoration of glorious events of Swiss history or folklore, or the celebration of the agricultural year, especially the harvest (grain or grape). Actors were, and still are, members of local choirs, sport societies and amateur drama companies. The *mise-en-scène* of the *Festspiele* consists of lavish and colourful sets, a profusion of rich and historically accurate costumes, many favourite country dances, music, songs and breath-taking crowd scenes. The renowned *Fête des Vignerons de Vevey* began modestly in the 17th century. It celebrates the four seasons and glorifies Bacchus. It is now staged every 25 years. For the *Fête* of 1977, Charles Apothéloz directed over 4000 unpaid amateurs, a small cast of professionals and an army of technicians. The production cost over 17 million Swiss francs and attracted 200,000 spectators. SCHILLER's *Wilhelm Tell* has been performed every two years in Altdorf since 1899 (Tellspielhaus) and annually, in the open, in Interlaken since 1912. In 1924 Einsiedeln harked back to its medieval past, presenting at irregular intervals CALDERÓN's *The Great Theatre of the World* (*Das Grosse Welttheater*).

Romansh and Italian theatre in Switzerland deserve a passing mention here, as Tschlin (in Engadine) organizes a popular festival, and in Ticino, Mendrisio perpetuates a 17th-century tradition by staging a religious procession, the *Sacra Rappresentazione*, during holy week. René Morax, author of the libretto of the *Fête des Vignerons* of 1905, created in 1908 the Théâtre du Jorat, dreaming of uniting nature, culture and society by setting a theatre in the middle of the countryside (Mézières). Inside the building, Morax abolished the separation between auditorium and stage with the addition of stairs linking the two. His best play, *King David*, was set to music by Arthur Honegger.

The 20th century On a smaller scale, but with the same aim of reaching a popular public, the novelist C. F. Ramuz wrote *The Soldier's Tale* (*L'Histoire du soldat*, 1918), which Stravinsky set to music. Two other Russians, LUDMILLA and GEORGES PITOËFF, passed briefly through Switzerland (1915–21). In Lausanne and Geneva they performed new authors: IBSEN, PIRANDELLO, SHAW and CHEKHOV, and were part of an avant-garde comprising the creator of eurhythmics Jaques-Dalcroze and the far-seeing designer APPIA. Unfortunately the burghers of Geneva failed to recognize their luck: the Pitoëffs settled in Paris in 1921, never to return. Similarly Appia, who rejected painted flats and naturalistic sets in favour of suggestive architectural construction and the use of atmospheric lighting adapted to the inner spirit of the work of art, was ignored, not only in Geneva but throughout the theatre world.

The first decades of the 20th century saw the establishment of municipal theatres in every major town: Basle, Zurich, Berne, Lucerne, Bienne, Lausanne, Geneva ... These theatres are used for plays, ballets, OPERAS and OPERETTAS and host mainly touring companies, especially in French Switzerland where, until the 70s, most professional shows were provincial tours of Parisian commercial successes. Only Basle and Zurich and, to a lesser extent, Berne had a resident company. OSKAR WÄLTERLIN was outstanding as a director in Basle, where he invited Appia in the 20s to design WAGNER's *Ring*, and then at the Zurich Schauspielhaus which he established as the main centre of German theatre from the 30s to the 60s. In 1938, returning from Frankfurt, he attracted to Zurich actors and directors fleeing Hitler's persecutions. Under his direction Leopold Lindtberg premiered BRECHT's *Mother Courage* (1941), to be followed by *The Good Person of Setzuan* (1947) and *Galileo* (1947). It was Wälterlin also who revealed the two foremost Swiss authors to the public of the Schauspielhaus: FRISCH and DÜRRENMATT. Basle (under Werner Düggelin) and Zurich (under Kurt Hirschfield) have retained their excellence, even if the true driving force is now to be found in the 'small theatre movement' and in regional touring companies. 'Pocket theatres' (*théâtres de poche*) are permanent amateur or semi-professional companies, specializing in new avant-garde and 'alternative' plays.

In Lausanne, Les Faux-Nez, under Apothéloz, presented IONESCO and BECKETT in the early 50s, plays by local authors, CABARETS and street theatre. Similar organizations sprang up in the 60s in, amongst other towns, Berne, Basle, Zurich, Bienne, Aarau and Neuchâtel. New authors emerged: Adolf Muschg, Hans Mühlethaler, Heinrich Henkel in German; Henri Deblüe, Walter Weideli, Bernard Liègme in French. They are regularly performed in Switzerland, and write mainly about the difficulty of being Swiss, although no author has yet emerged to challenge Frisch and Dürrenmatt.

In the mid-90s, Swiss theatre people speak of a profound crisis. The established theatres fail to attract new spectators and the little theatres have lost their early impetus. The arrival of BENNO BESSON in Geneva, where he was in charge of the Comédie from 1982 to 1989, welcome as it was, highlights the Swiss malaise: commentators of the Swiss cultural scene were quick to predict that his appointment (like Matthias Langhoff's at Lausanne/Vidy in 1989–91) would transform the situation for the better, ignoring that the two most important theatres, the Théâtre Populaire Romand (TPR) under CHARLES JORIS, and Das Theater für den Kanton Zürich (TZ) under Reinhart Spörri, are struggling for their survival and wasting a lot of their energies fighting bureaucracy instead of creating plays. These two theatres, founded respectively in 1961 and 1971, tour extensively and perform a rich mixture of world classics and indigenous plays (in the case of TZ often in German-Swiss dialect). Both theatres fulfil an important social as well as cultural role, taking their plays outside the main centres and encouraging theatrical activities in the communities. The TPR pursues the task of permanent training inside the company – which is of vital importance, as Switzerland has no policy of theatrical education and lags behind other European countries.

The overall picture, though, is far from bleak. If Switzerland lacks a theatre company of international stature, the country is full of amateur or semi-professional activity and also rich in German-Swiss dialect productions. Nevertheless, the overall output will remain very bland if new developments are stifled for lack of official and financial support – which is lavished on ballet and opera. CLS

See: Théâtre en Suisse/Theater in der Schweiz/Teatro in Svizzera/Theater en Svizra, annual publication of the Swiss Theatre Society, Basel; Adolphe Appia, *Œuvres complètes*, L'Age d'Homme, Lausanne, 1983–91; Bernard Bengloan, *La Muette. Le Théâtre en Suisse romande, 1960–1992*, L'Age d'Homme, Lausanne, 1994; Balz Engler and Georg Kreis, *Das Festspiel: Formen, Funktionen, Perspektiven*, Willisau, 1988; Louis Naef and Béatrice Perregaux, *Visions, Entwürfe, Prospettive, Ideas*, Annuaire du théâtre suisse, 53–4, Basel, 1992–3; Beat Schläpfer, *Sprechtheater in der Schweiz*, Pro Helvetia, Lausanne, 1992.

symbolism Symbolism in theatre is probably as old as theatre itself, but the widely symbolic must not be confused with the self-styled French symbolists of the last decade of the 19th century and the Russian playwrights of the first two decades of the 20th.

The French symbolist poet-playwrights admired a man of the theatre, RICHARD WAGNER, and a philosopher (of theatre, among other matters), FRIEDRICH NIETZSCHE. The major symbolist poet and thinker was Stéphane Mallarmé, who viewed *Hamlet* as a drama of the mind, and who urged the creation of a new drama that would reflect the mental or spiritual life rather than the crude world of the senses. Through Mallarmé the symbolists viewed art not only as expression, but primarily as a mode of cognition.

Disdaining everyday reality and the REALISM that reflected it, symbolism came to the theatre in reaction against ANTOINE's Théâtre Libre (whose repertory was not exclusively realist). The 18-year-old poet Paul Fort founded his Art Theatre in 1890 and committed it to symbolism the following year, notably with the production of MAETERLINCK's *Intruder* (death) and *The Blind* (who are blind to death) – short, static plays in which the interior life is conveyed mainly through atmospheric effect. Fort was fortunate in securing the services of actor AURÉLIEN LUGNÉ-POE (the Poe affixed in admiration for the American poet), but the young theatre manager was unable to sustain his symbolist theatre, which he dissolved before producing *Axel* by the recently deceased Villiers de l'Isle Adam. This operatic work presented sensitive aristocrats in a Gothic landscape of forest, moonlight and castle, which would also be found in the work of such symbolist playwrights as HOFMANNSTHAL, early YEATS and, with modifications, PAUL CLAUDEL. When Fort retired at age 20, Lugné-Poe raised the symbolist banner over his Théâtre de l'Oeuvre, which lasted till 1929.

The Russian symbolists' erudite, static and visionary dramas, beginning with Nikolai Minsky's *Alma* (1900), included VYACHESLAV IVANOV's theatre of congregate action; VALERY BRIUSOV's *uslovny* (self-conscious, conventional) theatre; ANDREI BELY's neo-mystery plays; INNOKENTY ANNENSKY's and ALEKSEI REMIZOV's mythic and Russian folkloric themes; FYODOR SOLOGUB's fatalism and author-centred 'Theatre of One Will'; and MIKHAIL KUZMIN's darkly dandyish *COMMEDIA*. The greatest Russian symbolist dramatist, ALEKSANDR BLOK, posited theatricalism as an alternative faith to symbolist mysticism in his harlequinade *The Little Showbooth* (1906); so, too, did such marginally symbolist writers as NIKOLAI EVREINOV, in his monodramas and in his major play *The Chief Thing* (1921), and LEONID ANDREEV, in his Poe-like meditations on death's proximity and life's vacuity (e.g. *He Who Gets Slapped*, 1915).

The symbolist theatre is noteworthy as the first modern Western theatre to look beyond the stage to occult powers – what Baudelaire in a famous sonnet called *correspondances* between the natural and the supernatural, the visible and the invisible, the material and the mystical.   RC

Syndicate, Theatrical see THEATRICAL SYNDICATE

Synge, J(ohn) M(illington) 1871–1909 Irish playwright. From 1895 he lived mainly in Paris, regularly visiting home. His permanent return in 1903 had been preceded by his journeys to the Aran islands, beginning in 1898, the last in 1902. In the west he also travelled through Mayo and Kerry, in the east in remote parts of Wicklow. But as YEATS had foreseen, when the two met in Paris in 1896, these awesome scenes were the inspiration which Synge's rather aimless pursuit of an artistic vocation had lacked.

The last seven years of Synge's life were intensely productive. In 1902 he wrote *In the Shadow of the Glen* (staged by Frank and Willie Fay, 1903) and *Riders to the Sea* (Irish National Theatre Society, 1904), and drafted *The Tinker's Wedding*, whose anticlericalism frightened the ABBEY THEATRE. (It went unproduced until 1971.) *The Well of the Saints* was produced in 1905; *The Playboy of the Western World*, which occasioned riots, in 1907; and his last play, *Deirdre*, posthumously in 1910.

Synge was robust, and a force in the Abbey directorate from 1905, but his body harboured Hodgkins disease, which killed him. David Greene, his biographer, ascribes Synge's fascination with death to a family disposition and his mother's evangelical religion. Intellectually, he was estranged from his family and his class: landowning, clerical, bourgeois Protestant. He abominated the organized Churches; his life acquired a Bohemian aura: Paris, the study of music, of Irish, his love for the Abbey actress Marie O'Neill. He was introspective, sometimes shy even with his friends, but on his rural travels convivial. These travels prompted his creative urge. He scorned the experimental drama of IBSEN and MAETERLINCK, but responded to a tragic joy in the endurance of the Aran islanders. The Aran experience precipitated Synge's private suffering into the healing lament of his tragicomic art, a delight in an almost pantheistic nature, elating and dangerous.

Synge's characters assert their destinies. Deirdre exalts her death into 'a story will be told forever'. In *The Well of the Saints* the blind and outcast Douls see in their 'own minds ... lakes, and broadening rivers, and hills are waiting for the spade'. The tramp's 'fine bit of talk' in *The Shadow* entices Nora from her husband's small-holding – 'each day and it passing you by' – to 'the south wind blowing in the glens' – and 'the cold and the frost'. Off they go together – to the outrage of the play's first audiences.

Berated for defaming the purity of Irish morals, Synge was also attacked on the grounds that his language travestied and coarsened Irish speech. He defended its authenticity, but his aim was not faithful transcription. His achievement was the greater one of forging a dramatic rhetoric from imaginative fidelity to its source. It is a splendid convention, as artificial as SHAKESPEARE's blank verse. The speech of Synge's plays invests their realist stage with a poetry both lyrical and mocking.　DM

Syria see MIDDLE EAST

Szajna, Josef 1922– Polish director, scenographer and artist. Szajna's theatrical activities started in Nowa Huta at the People's Theatre in 1955, where he designed such plays as *Princess Turandot* (1956) and *Of Mice and Men* (1956). He was its director from 1963 to 1966. After moving to Warsaw, he worked on many productions, the best known of which was GROTOWSKI's revival of WYSPIAŃSKI's *Acropolis* (1966). In 1971 Szajna became director-designer for the Studio Theatre in Warsaw. A total theatre artist in the spirit of GORDON CRAIG, he has been a playwright and dramaturge, developing scripts from sections of literary texts by such authors as Dante, GOETHE and SHAKESPEARE. His work in this realm includes productions of *Faust* (1971), *Dante* (1974) and *Cervantes* (1976), as well as *Macbeth* (1963, England). Szajna taught scenography at the Academy of Fine Arts in Cracow, published works on the subject, and lectured and toured such productions as *Death on a Pear Tree* (1978) throughout Europe and North America. In 1982 he retired, to confine his activities to directing and designing.　TM

Tabakov, Oleg (Pavlovich) 1935– Popular Soviet Russian actor, co-founder (1956) and producing director (1971–6) of the liberal Sovremennik Theatre, Moscow, where his roles mirrored the state of his society, moving from a lyrical hero like Misha in Rozov's *Alive Forever* (1958) to the cynical opportunist Aleksandr Aduev in a dramatization of Goncharov's *The Same Old Story* (1966). He also played Khlestakov in *The Government Inspector* in Russian in Prague (1968). In 1976, exasperated by intramural dissension and governmental interference, he resigned as the Sovremennik's producer and concentrated on film acting (*Oblomov*, 1978; *Moscow Does Not Believe in Tears*, 1980) and on directing his own Theatre-Studio (founded 1974), where he staged plays by VOLODIN, GALIN, GALICH, ANOUILH and NEIL SIMON. In 1983 he joined the MOSCOW ART THEATRE, playing Bouton in BULGAKOV's *Molière*, Salieri in *Amadeus* and Famusov in *Woe from Wit*. He also became a fabled teacher at the MAT school, and has toured his acting courses to British and American universities. LS

Tabarin [Antoine Girard] c.1584–1626 French CLOWN and FARCE-player about whose career the surviving evidence is scant and rather confused. After some provincial activity he settled in Paris, where in c.1618 he set up a booth stage in the Place Dauphine (and perhaps the adjacent Pont-Neuf) in company with his brother Philippe, who played the quack-doctor Mondor, and a few other performers. There the passing crowd were regaled with a free entertainment of cross-talk routines, comic monologues and short knockabout farces, designed to alternate with and promote the profitable business of selling nostrums and medicaments. Tabarin's stage name presumably derived from the short cloak (or *tabar*) which he wore over a belted smock and baggy, calf-length trousers, together with a wooden sword or slapstick and his most famous prop, a floppy felt hat capable of any number of metamorphoses for comic effect. So successful had he become by 1622 that rival publishers brought out two separate collections of his material, much of it probably improvised in performance after the manner of COMMEDIA, to which he was clearly indebted, and characterized by the most uninhibited, frequently scatological humour. Unlike other booth performers such as Jean Farine and BRUSCAMBILLE, who also published anthologies of his original material, Tabarin appears never to have acted with an orthodox theatre company; but he fired the popular imagination sufficiently to bequeath his name to the language in the sense of street performer and in the expression *faire le tabarin* (to play the fool). DR

tableau vivant SEE LIVING PICTURE; NUDITY

Tagore, Rabindranath 1861–1940 Perhaps INDIA's best-known modern playwright: winner of the 1913 Nobel Prize for Literature, author of India's national anthem, painter and poet. Tagore was born into a large family of wealthy and artistic Bengalis. He founded a unique school, Santiniketan, in 1901 in rural Bengal aimed at melding the best of Indian and Western culture, and in 1935 Visva-Bharati University dedicated to the arts. He travelled and lectured widely in Europe, America, China, Japan, Malaysia and Indonesia. Although his many plays are not frequently produced outside Bengal today, they are an important contribution to the world's dramatic literature. They include *Chitra* (*Chitrangada*, 1892), *The King of the Dark Chamber* (*Raja*, 1910), *The Post Office* (*Dakghar*, 1913) and *Red Oleanders* (*Raktakarabi*, 1924). FAR

Tairov [Kornblit], **Aleksandr (Yakovlevich)** 1885–1950 Russian-Soviet director, founder with his actress-wife ALISA KOONEN of the Moscow Kamerny (Chamber) Theatre (1941), a venue for highly sophisticated 'synthetic theatre' productions structured around the master-actor, composed along musical and rhythmic lines and featuring innovative cubist and constructivist designs (see THEATRE DESIGN). Tairov began his acting career in Kiev (1905), joining Vera Komissarzhevskaya's Theatre in St Petersburg for the 1906–7 season. Disillusioned with the artistic director MEYERHOLD's idea of the actor, he left and signed on with P. P. Gaideburov's touring company (1907–9), for which he directed *Hamlet* and *Uncle Vanya* (1908) as well as other plays. In 1913 he completed law studies and staged *Yellow Jacket* and the SCHNITZLER-Donani musical pantomime *The Veil of Pierrette* for KONSTANTIN MARDZHANOV's Free Theatre.

The Kamerny Theatre, which he founded next, owed much to the production work of Mardzhanov, who went on to create the modern Georgian theatre. Tairov's theatre was dedicated to the connoisseur, to theatrical art as self-contained reality, and to the creation of beauty. If Meyerhold's theatre often resembled a CIRCUS – purposely crude and gymnastic – Tairov's consistently suggested ballet – controlled, exquisite, lacking in rough edges. While Meyerhold sometimes made the actor anonymous in proletarian dress, Tairov geared his entire theatre to the actor's three-dimensionality, clothing him in dramatic, dynamic costumes which fitted like a second skin. As with APPIA and JESSNER, sets for Tairov were 'keyboards for the actors' playing', rhythmic assemblages of ramps, steps and platforms. All movement was choreographed, dialogue intoned. The acting was neither strictly representational nor presentational, but expressive. Rejecting Stanislavskian emotion-memory (see STANISLAVSKY) and transcending *perezhivaniye* (emotional experiencing), Tairov called for 'emotional saturation' – i.e. for the refilling of beautifully crafted actions with emotions generated during performance. Overall, the theatrical presentation was to strive to equal the purity of music.

While the Kamerny's opening production, the Pavel Kuznetsov-designed *Sakuntala* (1914), failed to realize Tairov's vision, ALEKSANDRA EKSTER's cubist-designed *Thamira, the Cither Player* (1916) by ANNENSKY and

Aleksandr Vesnin's severely constructivist *Phaedra* (1922) came closer. Tairov's contention that theatrical action hovers between two poles – the mystery and the harlequinade (he discounted the primacy of literature in the theatre) – was reflected in the Kamerny production of E. T. A. HOFFMANN's *Princess Brambilla* (1920), adapted by L. Krasovsky. Designed by Georgy Yakulov in a HARLEQUIN's motley of swirling colours, boldly defined shapes, 'dynamic decor' (moving banners and scenic pieces) and expressionist (see EXPRESSIONISM) lighting effects, which helped create a subjective, dream-like perspective, this 'capriccio for the theatre' embodied the pure joy of creativity. With music by Henri Forterre and choreography by Antonia Shalomytova, one of the Kamerny dancers, the production approached Tairov's synthesis of theatrical elements and forms. Yakulov went on to design the highly successful, circus-like *Giroflé-Girofla* (1922) for the Kamerny. The theatre also helped introduce Western classics to the Soviet stage, including WILDE's *Salome* (1917), whose premiere at Vera Komissarzhevskaya's Theatre (1908) had been banned; G. K. Chesterton's *The Man Who Was Thursday* (1923), with a Vesnin constructivist design; SHAW's *St Joan* (1924); and EUGENE O'NEILL's *The Hairy Ape* and *Desire under the Elms* (1926) and *All God's Chillun Got Wings* (1929).

Tairov's productions of Soviet plays ranged from BULGAKOV's *The Crimson Island* (1928) and Semyonov's *Natalya Tarpova* (1929), anti-establishment works which were quickly removed from the repertoire, to VISHNEVSKY's orthodox, romantically monumentalist *An Optimistic Tragedy* (1934), which helped win the director the honour of People's Artist of the USSR (1935). Tairov's ability to serve the state and his theatre earned him the Order of Lenin (1945), but is better dramatized by the fact that the Kamerny, despite periods of government intervention and supervision, remained open until shortly before the director's death. Tairov's *Notes of a Director*, chronicling his theatrical work and ideas, was published in 1921. SG

Taiwan Taiwan is a mountainous island of 13,885 square miles in the South China Sea, about 90 miles off the Chinese coast, with a population of some 19 million. The Chinese took control of Taiwan in the late 1600s and administered it as part of CHINA until 1895 when Japan gained control of the island as a result of the first Sino-Japanese War. China regained Taiwan after the Second World War. In 1949 the Chinese Communists defeated Chiang Kai-shek's Nationalist forces and took control of the mainland. Chiang moved the government of the Republic of China to Taiwan in December of that year.

A major local theatre form is *gozai xi*, or Taiwanese opera, a regional Chinese drama that first flourished in the southern Fujian province. Taiwanese opera shares with Beijing opera (see JINGXI) basic patterns of staging such as movement, costumes, make-up and the percussive accompaniment, while musically the two forms are distinct. *Gozai xi* literally means 'drama of songs', indicating the singing element is the most important. At first *gozai xi* was performed at street corners or country fairs without a stage; later a makeshift, open-air stage came into use and finally performances moved into theatre structures with the added elements of scenery, lighting and special effects. During the Japanese occupation this Taiwanese-language form was banned by the authorities. After the Second World War it gradually regained its audiences, and today it is the most popular form of theatrical entertainment in Taiwan. A popular actress who has done much to revive audience interest today is Yang Li-hua, who is the star of a widely seen television series featuring Taiwanese opera.

Other forms of Taiwanese theatre consist of the tribal dances of the Aborigines and PUPPET theatres of various kinds. Glove-puppet theatre, *budai xi*, is especially popular among peasants and fishermen. The 1-ft-tall puppets can be highly expressive in the hands of skilled puppeteers who also provide the narration and the dialogue of the characters. The typical stage is a highly ornate, if makeshift, structure erected twelve feet above the ground in a market place or on a street corner. A performance is often hired or commissioned and the casual audience attends free. The most respected living puppeteer is Li T'ien-lu, whose Yi Wan Ran troupe celebrated its 60th anniversary in 1991.

Although mainland Chinese make up only one tenth of Taiwan's population, their theatrical taste – mainly the appreciation of the much refined Beijing opera – has affected theatre development in Taiwan for nearly a century. In 1909 a Beijing-opera company from Shanghai played for two weeks in Taipei, and ever since troupes from the mainland have toured the island with varying degrees of success. Especially the performances, beginning in 1948, of the talented young actress Ku Cheng-ch'iu had a lasting effect on Taiwanese theatre. For four and a half years, she and her 60-member troupe performed at the Yung Lo Theatre in Taipei to an appreciative audience of wealthy mainlanders who had fled to the island to avoid the new Communist government. While Ku and her colleagues were forced to remain on the island, other Beijing-opera troupes also made their exodus to Taiwan. Some of these troupes were associated with the armed forces, most notably the Ta P'eng Troupe of the Chinese Air Force, personally initiated by Air Force Chief Wang Shu-min, an avid theatre-lover. For 40 years a training school attached to the troupe has nurtured many talented actors who are today mainstays of the stage.

Four major Beijing-opera troupes perform in Taiwan at present: the Ta P'eng troupe, the Lu Kuang troupe associated with the Army, the Hai Kuang troupe associated with the Navy, and the Fu Hsing troupe of the National Fu Hsing Dramatic Arts Academy, the leading institution training Beijing-opera and Taiwanese-opera actors and musicians. They perform in Taipei at the Armed Forces Cultural Activities Centre, a modestly equipped 950-seat theatre devoted to traditional opera, and the newly constructed National Theatre. Both Beijing opera and Taiwanese opera are featured on television in a government effort to develop a wider audience for traditional theatre. Paid attendance at regular Beijing-opera performances, however, is declining steadily. In the late 1980s and early 90s, ambitious productions of Beijing opera were staged at the National Theatre using lavish scenery and based on newly created scripts. One example was a free adaptation of SHAKESPEARE's *Macbeth*, which toured to the NATIONAL

THEATRE in London in 1990. Among contemporary Beijing-opera performers, two of the most popular and important, in terms of their impact on the theatre, are Hsu Lu, a skilled performer of leading female roles with a superb singing voice, and Kuo Shiao-chuang, known for her creation of new-style Beijing operas favoured by young audience members. Both Hsu and Kuo are graduates of the Ta P'eng training school.

Modern theatre, HUAJU, literally 'spoken drama', occupies a less important position than traditional theatre in Taiwan. The earliest performance activity can be traced to 1911 when a Japanese director came to stage several productions with local actors. Most of the actors recruited were ruffians in town, hence the term 'ruffian drama' (langren ju) for modern theatre. Over the next 20 years numerous local drama troupes were organized on an amateur basis and they staged works by well known mainland playwrights and by local authors dealing with Taiwan themes. Influential was Chang Wei-hsien, who studied dramatic arts in Tokyo in the 1930s and then returned to become an innovative director and acting teacher. Spoken drama was given a major impetus by the influx of 1.5 million mainland refugees when Chiang Kai-shek's Nationalist government moved to Taiwan in 1949. Among the new arrivals were playwrights, directors and actors of modern spoken drama, most of whom were attached to the entertainment units of the armed forces. They mounted productions and trained the next generation of theatre workers. They also contributed to the development of the film and television industries. Prominent among them was the playwright and legislator Li Man-kuei, who promoted the Little Theatre Movement in the early 1960s. In 1962 she organized the Committee on Spoken Drama Appreciation, which became the major producing agency (120 productions between 1961 and 1969) of modern dramas. She and the Committee also started a World Drama Festival in 1967 to present foreign plays in the original languages performed by language students in local universities, and a Youth Drama Festival in 1968 to present plays by local playwrights, both of which continue to foster modern drama today.

Modern theatre in Taiwan is modest in scale and quality in comparison with neighbouring China, JAPAN, KOREA or HONG KONG. The economics of performance do not support professional modern drama troupes; the active companies are either amateur or semiprofessional. Theatre facilities are scarce and the first adequately equipped theatre auditorium, Chung Hsing Hall in Taichung, was built in the mid-1970s. The theatre department of the University of Chinese Culture has long offered academic training in theatre, and since 1982 the National Institute of the Arts provides a full training programme in modern drama.

Among well known spoken-drama groups in Taiwan are the Lan Ling Ensemble and Performance Workshop. The Lan Ling Ensemble, an experimental group, was founded in 1980 by Wu Chin-chi, a psychology professor who had worked at LA MAMA Theatre in New York. Lan Ling productions are noted for their free adaptation of Chinese materials, simplicity of staging, and using the actor's voice and movement, rather than a dialogue text, as their chief means of communication. An early work, Ho Chu's New Match (Ho Chu xinpei, 1979), is a free adaptation of a Beijing opera in which conventions of the traditional theatre are used in hilarious, tongue-in-cheek fashion. This group disbanded in 1990 due to lack of leadership. The highly influential Performance Workshop was founded in 1984 by Berkeley-educated Lai Sheng-ch'uan. Lai's company emphasizes improvisation and group creation of productions that deal with current political and social issues.

In the mid-1980s the government of Taiwan started ambitious projects to advance modern theatre. The National Theatre and National Concert Hall complex constructed in the heart of Taipei opened in 1987. It contains a 1524-seat main theatre and a 300-seat experimental theatre. Modern theatres that meet international standards are planned for other cities on the island as well. In 1982 the National Institute of the Arts was inaugurated, offering training in four departments: music, fine arts, theatre and dance. A well equipped 400-seat theatre opened at its new campus in 1991. (See also ASIAN AND PACIFIC ISLAND THEATRE.) DSPY

See: J. R. Brandon (ed.), *The Cambridge Guide to Asian Theatre*, Cambridge, 1993.

Takemoto Gidayū 1651–1714 Japanese puppet chanter, who established the powerful musical style known by his given name, *gidayū*, which is used today in BUNRAKU performance. He studied under the older chanter Uji Kaga no Jō. In 1684 he co-founded with theatre manager Takeda Izumo I (?–1747) the important Osaka PUPPET theatre that takes his family name, the Takemoto Theatre. In the following year he created a 'new' style of chanting that displaced 'old' *jōruri* and all other musical styles in the puppet theatre. CHIKAMATSU joined the Takemoto Theatre as staff playwright in 1705. This remarkable artistic triumvirate put a human face on a didactic storytelling form and brought contemporary life into their plays. In domestic plays, such as *The Love Suicides at Sonezaki* (1703), Gidayū created reality in the tones of ordinary townsmen. Gidayū published scenes from plays he had chanted, at that time considered the property of the chanter, and a treatise on performance and playwriting that shows familiarity with ZEAMI's writings. JRB

t'alch'um (literally, 'masked dance') Generic term for traditional Korean masked dance plays (SANDAE-GŪK) originating in the towns of Pongsan, Haeju and Kangnyong in the northwest, presently in North Korea. Pongsan t'alch'um is especially noted for its poetry, songs, witty dialogue and punning. Pongsan MASKS are relatively small and portray grotesque faces. No longer performed in the North, this theatre has been preserved in South Korea by performers who escaped to the South during the Korean War (1950–3). OKC

Talesnik, Ricardo 1935– Argentine playwright, actor and director. After an auspicious beginning in television, he wrote *La fiaca* (*The Doldrums*, 1967), a dramatization of the lack of individual freedom experienced by a man suffering from Monday morning 'blahs'. The play was an instant success, was staged throughout Europe and Latin America and filmed in 1968. Major later plays include *Cien* *veces no debo* (*A Hundred Times I Ought Not*, 1970) and *Los japoneses no esperan* (*The Japanese Don't Wait*, 1973), both with anti-bourgeois postures. Talesnik has experimented with MUSICAL COMEDY, pantomime and one-person shows, and was a collaborator with ROZENMACHER, SOMIGLIANA and COSSA in *El avión negro* (*The Black Airplane*, 1970), a play based on myths regarding Perón's proposed return to Argentina. In later years he has been involved in skits and short comic pieces. GW

Talli, Virgilio 1858–1928 Italian actor and company manager. An able rather than an outstanding actor, his importance as an actor-manager lay particularly in his contribution to stage-management, in which his activities prefigured those of the director in the Italian theatre in concern for the unity of a production and insistence on subordinating the personality playing of lead actors to the requirements of the play. From 1885 he managed a number of fine companies and was responsible for the first stagings of plays like GIACOSA's *Come le foglie* (*Like the Leaves*, 1900) and D'ANNUNZIO's *La figlia d'Iorio* (*Iorio's Daughter*, 1904). LR

Talma, François Joseph 1763–1826 French actor – Napoleon's favourite. He contributed to a revival of interest in neoclassical TRAGEDY which accorded with Napoleon's own attempt to create an empire inspired by ancient Rome. More importantly, Talma, whose early years had been spent in England (where he trained to be a dentist), was interested in reforms in stage costume which he had seen there and introduced to France. In 1789, playing a small part in VOLTAIRE's *Brutus* at the COMÉDIE-FRANÇAISE, he delighted his audience and scandalized his colleagues by appearing in authentic Roman dress, with bare arms and a toga (instead of a periwig and breeches), designed by the painter David, and this led to a rapid COSTUME revolution at the Comédie-Française. Talma, who had been one of the first pupils of the newly founded Conservatoire in 1796, studied under the actors Molé and Dugazon. From Molé, who did not believe in the romantic idea of the actor being guided by nature, he received a firm grounding in technique. Dugazon, much interested in *pantomime*, trained him in the expressive use of his face and taught him to act when not actually speaking. His own experience of the English theatre led him towards a more natural style of delivery than the traditional declamation normally reserved for tragedy. His attention to detail in the preparation of his roles, costume and make-up was unusual for the period.

Talma made his debut at the Comédie-Française in Voltaire's *Mahomet* in 1787. In 1789 he played the title role in *Charles IX*, Marie-Joseph Chénier's violently anti-monarchical and anticlerical play. He took the part because no one else wanted it, and it allowed him to show his skill at portraying the darker passions of fury and despair, which he would use to advantage in the DUCIS adaptations of *Othello*, *Hamlet* and *Macbeth*, as well as in the roles of Néron in RACINE's *Britannicus* and Oreste in *Andromaque*. *Charles IX* was the occasion of a split in the Comédie-Française. Talma, although never really active in politics, espoused the revolutionary cause in what was a fundamentally royalist institution, and finally left with a group of other dissidents to take up residence at the former Variétés Amusantes, the Théâtre de la République (the present Comédie-Française), in 1791.

It was at this period that he came to know Napoleon, of whom he became a fervent admirer and who had a considerable interest in the theatre and a taste for neoclassical plays (notably those of PIERRE CORNEILLE, whose Cinna was to be one of Talma's great roles, being played by command before the famous parterre of kings at Erfurt in 1808). Talma once more became part of the Comédie-Française when the various factions were brought together in 1799. From 1802 to 1811 he frequently toured and was often attacked for this by the critic Geoffroy (with whom he finally had a punch-up in a box at the Comédie-Française in 1812). One of the few parts in which Geoffroy had liked him was as Manlius in Lafosse's *Manlius Capitolinus* (1806), Talma's most popular part after Oreste in Racine's *Andromaque*. In 1815 he left the Comédie-Française and continued to tour for the next few years. In 1816 the king renewed the pension that Napoleon had granted him. In 1819 Talma was the one person to vote for the admission of FRÉDÉRICK LEMAÎTRE to the ODÉON. He did not return to the Comédie-Française until his last role, significantly another historical role. Talma was almost a symbol of the Empire. He was also the actor who made the bridge between neoclassical tragedy and the romantic drama, to which his temperament and style of playing clearly drew him. It is significant that VICTOR HUGO had Talma in mind as he worked on *Cromwell* (1827), whose central part was tailor-made for him. JMCC

tamasha Major form of rural theatre in the state of Maharashtra, in west-central INDIA. Approximately 10,000 artists in some 450 *tamasha* troupes serve a population of about 62 million people. In sheer numbers alone, this makes *tamasha* among the more popular forms of theatre in India. Also, few of India's many forms of rural theatre stress humour as extensively. *Tamasha* satirizes and pokes fun at contemporary society, often at the expense of politicians and businessmen, priests and prophets, clothing its barbs in the guise of historical or mythological stories.

Evidence suggests that *tamasha* developed in the 16th century as a bawdy entertainment both for the Mogul armies that occupied the Deccan plain and among insurgent Maratha forces determined to free their people from their oppressors. The term itself is a Persian word meaning 'fun', 'play' and 'entertainment', and was probably introduced to the area by Urdu-speaking soldiers of the Mogul armies. The form that we call *tamasha* today is probably the amalgam of many different influences which may be traced back over many centuries. Some scholars have suggested that *tamasha* developed out of the decaying remnants of two short forms of classical Sanskrit entertainment – the *prahasana* and the *bhana*. Just how this transpired is not certain. Other scholars suppose that diverse pieces of musical, dance and dramatic entertainment coalesced to form *tamasha* sometime in the 16th century. There were certainly plenty of forms of entertainment available from which artists might draw inspiration – including classical *kathak* dance of north India, with its infectious rhythms and sensuous appeal; Muslim *kavali* and *ghazal* songs designed to assault the ear with rich melodies and exotic rhythm; DASHAVATARA musical plays and *bharud* dramatic poetry recitals; *lalit* religious plays and *gondhal* religious songs; *kirtan*, a one-man musical sermon; and *kal sutri* PUPPET shows.

The diverse elements found in *tamasha* performance indicate eclectic borrowing as suggested above. All *tamasha* performances open with a *gan*, a devotional song in praise of the deities, lustily sung by the chief male singer and musicians. This is followed by the *gaulan*, a dramatic segment in which Krishna and his clown attendant wittily converse with milkmaids on their journey to market. Songs and dances punctuate the raucous humour. Following this is the *vag*, a short dialogue play drawn from historical or mythological sources and laced with satirical incidents and broad slapstick humour. After the *vag* was introduced to *tamasha* in the 19th century, it quickly became the soul of the art form.

The performance practice above typifies *dholki-baari* FOLK drama troupes, who present one of two varieties of *tamasha* performance. *Dholki-baari* troupes get their name from the popular drum used in *tamasha*, the *dholki*. A troupe consists of a leading male actor, half a dozen male actor-singers, one or more female dancer-singers and several instrumentalists.

Sangeet-baari, or song troupes, represent an older style that emphasizes song and dance. They do not use the *vag* as part of their entertainment. *Sangeet-baari* troupes are relatively small in size, consisting of half a dozen dancers and singers and several instrumentalists. The clown character (*songadya*), whose improvised humour is so integral to the success of *tamasha* performance, is common to both varieties.

Tamasha's popularity is partially due to love songs (*lavani*) which are interpreted through singing and dancing. *Lavani* entered the form during Maharashtra's Peshwa period (1707–1818). Until the end of the 19th century, they were sung by male singers dressed as women. Today *lavani* are sung by professional dancing girls whose physical charms, as much as their vocal abilities, help to sell a song. Enthusiastic patrons pleased with particularly brilliant singing, or perhaps taken with the beauty of the singer, are encouraged to go to the performance area and offer a token of their esteem to the singer in the form of a rupee note. These special requests (*daulat-jadda*) are often honoured by the singer who repeats the song to the enchanted enthusiast. Poetic dialogues coupled with MIME (*chakkad*) are also honoured in this way. The songs themselves have provided the inspiration for many popular Hindi and Marathi film songs, while film songs popular with rural audiences are taken into *tamasha*.

In addition to the *dholki* drum, *tamasha* musicians play the *tuntuni*, a single-string drone instrument; the *manjeera* cymbals; the *daf*, a large tambourine-like instrument with a single leather surface; the *halgi*, a small version of the *daf*; the *kade*, a metal triangle; the *lejim*, an instrument resembling buttons strung like beads on a wooden rod, producing jangling sounds; and the harmonium. Many strings of *ghungrus*, or ankle bells, worn by the dancers accentuate the rhythm of the music.

Tamasha dance is an amalgam of *kathak* classical dance technique and indigenous folk dance, broadly described as 'filmic' by some local critics.

Historically, *tamasha* has been linked with two untouchable communities of Maharashtra – the Kolhati and the Mahar. Training has largely been kept within the confines of family units which have been long associated with the art. With the introduction of female dancers in the late 19th century, however, the general public assumed that the artists were little more than prostitutes; consequently they have continued to be the subject of censure by puritanical and conservative forces in Maharashtrian society.

During the 18th century, poet-singers (*shahir*) were chiefly responsible for raising the artistic level of the narratives and love songs. As company leaders they gained an enviable reputation with the rulers of the day and helped to lift the reputation of the *tamasha* artists. This tradition of *shahir* leadership brought the idea of freedom from British rule to the heartland of India during the independence movement in 1947. In the 1930s and 40s, some popular *shahir* became associated with communist causes. In response to the recent diminishing of *shahir* influence, an association of *shahir* was formed in 1969 to revitalize *tamasha*.

Tamasha is performed almost anywhere that there is a suitable open space. Throughout most of the year performances are presented out of doors; during the heavy monsoon rains indoor performances are given in urban, proscenium-arch theatres in Bombay, Pune, Nagpur, Nasik, Aurangabad and smaller cities. Troupes that perform in these theatres are regarded as 'raw' *tamasha* and are welcome at venues in working-class districts.

Loknatya, or 'people's theatre', companies play a more refined style of *tamasha*, cleansed of obscene remarks and actions typical of rural companies. They play in expensive urban playhouses for patrons who can afford the relatively high-price admission and who want wholesome family entertainment.

Like other forms of rural theatre, *tamasha* serves as a source of inspiration to modern urban directors and actors. Prominent productions developed in imitation of *tamasha* technique in recent years include Vijaya Mehta's Marathi versions of *The Caucasian Chalk Circle*, *The Little Clay Cart*; Jabbar Patel's *Ghashiram Kotwal*, written by Vijay Tendulkar; and *Teen Paishacha Tamasha*, also directed by Jabbar Patel and adapted from BRECHT's *Threepenny Opera* by P. L. Deshpande. FAR

Tamiris (Becker), Helen 1905–66 American modern dancer-choreographer and theatre choreographer. After establishing herself in modern dance primarily as a solo artist, she continued her concert work while choreographing for BROADWAY musicals. Initially, Tamiris worked with experimental theatre groups, including the PROVINCETOWN PLAYERS and the GROUP THEATRE. Her first MUSICAL THEATRE productions were *Annie Get Your Gun* (1946) and *Park Avenue* (1947). She directed *The Great Campaign* (1947) and choreographed the Jules Munshin–Pearl Bailey political REVUE, *Bless You All* (1950). Tamiris was highly regarded by her modern dance contemporaries, many of whom danced in the musicals she choreographed. Using trained dancers raised the standard of dance in musical theatre and made Tamiris's productions tremendously popular. LF

Tandy, Jessica 1909–94 British-born actress, who in 1954 became a naturalized American citizen. Trained in drama school (l924–7), Tandy made her London debut in *The Rumour* (1929) and before she was 25 had become a star. She made her debut on BROADWAY as Toni Rakonitz in 1930 in *The Matriarch*. Among her later outstanding roles were Ophelia to JOHN GIELGUD's *Hamlet* (1934) and Blanche Dubois (for which she was awarded a Tony) in *A Streetcar Named Desire* (1947). As Blanche she won rave reviews and achieved Broadway stardom; a critic called the role 'deeply moving ... acted gloriously ... [she gives] one of the most arresting and moving performances you are likely to thrill to in many a semester'.

Having divorced actor Jack Hawkins in 1940 after eight years of marriage, in 1942 Tandy married HUME CRONYN, with whom she subsequently appeared in six Broadway productions: *The Fourposter* (1951), *The Physicists* (1964), *A Delicate Balance* (1966), *Noël Coward in Two Keys* (1974), *The Gin Game* (1977) and *Foxfire* (1982). She won Tonys for the latter two. Tandy and Cronyn appeared regularly in American regional theatres, chief among them the GUTHRIE THEATRE, which they admired for its adequate rehearsal periods and superior facilities compared to most Broadway theatres. At the Guthrie, Tandy played such roles as Linda in *Death of a Salesman*, Gertrude in *Hamlet* and Madam Ranevskaya in *The Cherry Orchard*.

Tandy, one of the great ladies of the American stage, also appeared in numerous British and American television programmes, first appearing on British television in 1939. In later years she devoted more time to film acting, winning an Academy Award for *Driving Miss Daisy*, her first major film role, at age 80, and completing her career with a film role in *Nobody's Fool* (1994) with Paul Newman. SMA

Tang Xianzu 1550–1616 Chinese *KUNQU* dramatist. In 1598 Tang abandoned an official career and became a romantic, individualistic playwright. In contrast to his contemporary and rival Shen Jing (1553–1610), who adhered strictly to the traditional forms of metrical composition, Tang sidestepped the rigid rules of orthodox metrical usage in favour of a free, sensual use of diction and poetic expression. Tang's major work is a quartet of plays with a dream motif of which *The Peony Pavilion* (*Mudan ting*), in 55 scenes, is famous for its poetic excellence. The theme of romantic love expounded in a supernatural context has great emotional impact. Excerpts from this play are constantly performed on the traditional stage. ACS

Tanguay, Eva 1878–1947 Canadian-born singer, the 'oomph' girl of VAUDEVILLE's heyday, epitomized by her best-known song, 'I Don't Care', first sung in *The Chaperones* (1903). Beginning in VARIETY in 1886, she toured for five years with the Redding Company as a child actress, graduating to MUSICAL COMEDY roles (*The Merry World*, *My Lady*, *The Sambo Girl* and so forth). After *A Good Fellow* (1906), she entered vaudeville, becoming its leading star and leaving it only infrequently over the next 25 years. Described by one critic as 'not beautiful, witty or graceful', her appeal defies explanation; she claimed it was in the force of her personality. Flamboyant, a bit risquée in costumes (she said her 1908 Salomé costume

consisted of two pearls) and in songs (such as 'I Want Someone to Go Wild with Me'), and tempestuous on- and offstage, she seemed to her audiences perennially young. Financial reverses and poor health forced an early retirement. DBW

Tanvir, Habib Contemporary North Indian director. He began his theatre career in 1948 after his basic education in rural Madhya Pradesh. Between 1945 and 1953 he was a radio producer and writer, film actor and song writer in Bombay. Like other prominent contemporary performers in the late 1940s he became an active member of the India People's Theatre Association. In 1954 he moved to Delhi where he founded the Hindustani Theatre. In the late 50s, after studying at RADA and the British Drama League in London, he spent nearly a year with the BERLINER ENSEMBLE. His notable productions include *Agra Market* (*Agra Bazaar*, 1954), *The Little Clay Cart* (1958) and *Thief Charandas* (*Charandas Chor*, 1975). Between 1972 and 1978 he served as a Member of Parliament for Madhya Pradesh. Recent works include film and television appearances, as well as experimental productions which he has directed with rural artists from his home state. FAR

Tanzania Over 90 per cent of the 20 million inhabitants of Tanzania subsist on agriculture. The 123 ethnic groups are linguistically united by Kiswahili, the national language, which has greatly influenced the growing nationalist theatre movement, especially after the adoption of *Ujamaa* (socialism) in 1967.

The theatre of pre-colonial times was a conglomeration of many forms derived from a variety of pre-capitalist production modes and their resultant cultures. These can be broadly categorized into four types: RITUAL theatre, especially relating to initiation; celebration dances related to some social event such as weddings and harvest festival with the basic aim of reinforcing social values, e.g. *nindo*, which is found among the Wagogo; *mkwajungoma* (the Wazaramo), *maseve* (the Wangoni), *selo* (the Wazigua) and *hiari ya moyo* (the Wanyamwezi); storytelling, called *Simo* (a Wagogo tradition) and *Hadithi* (found among coastal groups); and heroic recitations.

Colonization by the Germans and later by the British brought about significant changes. Though the British – by means of missionaries, colonial educators and administrators – discouraged or prohibited traditional theatre performances, regarding them as 'barbaric' and 'uncivilized', most forms stubbornly survived. In 1948, however, colonial policy changed, and traditional theatre performances were encouraged at agricultural exhibitions and trade fairs as well as at colonial festivals such as Empire Day, to ensure wider publicity and to distract the people from their discontent with the colonial situation. This resulted in the formation of over 58 'dance associations' in the urban areas by 1954. The colonialists also encouraged certain new dances that were considered 'appropriate' for 'enlightened natives', e.g. *beni*, whose movement, costuming and music borrowed from colonial military bands, and *mpendoo*, which was devised especially to distract the Christian and 'educated' Wagogo people from their traditional *nindo* and *msun-yunho* dances. Later, however, the colonial government again discouraged these traditional dance groups because of their subversive potential.

Western theatre was introduced in the early 1920s, and by 1952 almost all schools were staging the works of, among others, SHAKESPEARE, SHAW, and GILBERT and Sullivan. In 1957 the British Council launched a school drama competition to foster British culture and to emphasize 'correct and proper' English speech. Because of their exposure to exclusively British bourgeois theatre, the Tanzanian colonial elite came to look upon this kind of theatre as the one and only. *Vichekesho*, an offshoot of Western theatre, was very popular in colonial times in the schools alongside the imported Western drama. Based on improvised sketches, directed and performed by students, *vichekesho* sought to 'cause laughter' among the audience by making fun of the 'uncivilized' and 'uneducated' masses for not being able to use such items of 'civilized' life as a fork, a sprung bed or a mirror.

Expatriate theatre was established in the form of two 'little theatres' – the Dar es Salaam Players (1947) and the Arusha Little Theatre (1953). These remain to this day oblivious of any theatre tradition inside or outside Tanzania other than that of BROADWAY and the WEST END. As a result, they have exerted no influence on the development of Tanzanian theatre.

The attainment of political independence in Tanzania in 1964 brought little change to the theatrical scene. The formation of the Youth Drama Association in 1966 under the patronage of expatriates and of the Tanzanian elite resulted in the emergence of original Swahili plays by Tanzanian playwrights, such as *Mukwava wa Uhehe* (*Mukwava of the Hehe People*) by M. Mulokozi. *Vichekesho* lived on, but the emphasis changed from laughing at the 'uncivilized' to rebuking the educated for looking down on their own people, as in *Zabibi* (*The Raisin*), a radio play, and *Martin Kayamba*, both by G. Uhinga.

More significant changes came with the Arusha Declaration, the blueprint for *Ujamaa*, in 1967. Plays by foreign dramatists were discouraged and theatre in Kiswahili gained the upper hand. More than 20 published Tanzanian playwrights emerged during this period. The plays written during 1967–77 portray a general enthusiasm and support for socialism, while pointing out hurdles in its implementation. Such works include *Kijiji Chetu* (*Our Village*) by NGALIMECHA NGAHYOMA, *Haitia* (*Guilt*) by P. Muhando (see MLAMA), *Mwanzo wa Tufani* (*Beginning of the Storm*) by K. Kahigi and A. Ngemera, and *Giza Limeingia* (*The Dawn of Darkness*) by EMMANUEL MBOGO. Plays produced after 1978 present a more critical analysis of the socialist construction process, portraying the disillusion and helplessness of the masses in the face of mounting corruption and exploitation by members of the ruling class: e.g. *Kaptula la Marx* (*Marx's Capital*, c.1985) by E. Kezilahabi; *Nguzo Mama* (*Mother the Main Pillar*) and *Lina Ubani* (*There is an Antidote for Rot*), both by P. Muhando, *Harakati za Ukombozi* (*Liberation Struggles*, 1982) by A. Lihamba and others, and *Ayubu*, c.1985, by the Paukwa Theatre Association. *Vichekesho* continued, to become the core of workers' theatre.

Another theatre form that developed during this period was *ngonjera*, based on traditional poetic forms and constituting a recital accompanied by dramatic movement and gesture, costumes and props. Commonly performed at Party functions, national festivals and other official occasions, *ngonjera* answered President Nyerere's call for poets to 'go out and publicize *Ujamaa*'. *Ngonjera* troupes now exist in all schools, and it is one of the most popular theatre forms. Traditional dance, too, has transformed itself into an appropriate bearer of the new messages of the *Ujamaa* era. Over 30 dance troupes, some professional, are active in Dar es Salaam alone. These groups also engage in slapstick improvised drama.

The search for a Tanzania-based theatre has been the preoccupation of the University of Dar es Salaam's Department of Art, Music and Theatre, the Bagamoyo College of Art and the Butimba Arts College of Education. Drawing on traditional and contemporary local resources as well as on foreign theatre traditions, they have produced performances and writings both based in Tanzanian cultural reality and of contemporary relevance, such as *Shing'weng'we* (*Monster*), *Harakati za Ukombozi* (*Liberation Struggles*) and *Nyani na Mkia Wake* (*The Monkey and its Tail*) (by the university), *Tunda*, *The Challenge and the Gap* and *Chakatu* (by Bagamoyo) and *Azota na Azenga* (*Azota and Azenga*) (by Butimba). The same trend is apparent in the writings of those who are the products of these institutions – Mlama, Lihamba, EBRAHIM HUSSEIN – and in the work of the amateur theatre groups such as Paukwa and Sayari, as exemplified in the former's *Ayubu* and *Chuano*.

In the 1980s the theatre-for-development movement emerged (see THIRD WORLD POPULAR THEATRE) in Tanzania, spearheaded by the university's Department of Art, Music and Theatre. Long-term projects and short-term workshops have been conducted in Malya (Manxwa Region), Mosoga and Bagamoyo villages in Coast Region, and Mkambalani in Morogoro Region. Other theatre-for-development workshops have been based at Namiyonga (Mtwara Region, 1989), and Misalai, Mbuyuni and Kisiwani villages in Tanga Region in 1990, 91 and 92 respectively. In 1993 the university embarked on a major theatre-for-development initiative in eight villages in Rukwa Region. Work of this nature has also been undertaken by a range of government and non-government development agencies, including the National Arts Council, UNICEF and the National Aids Control Programme. In addition, local communities have adopted theatre-for-development processes as a vehicle for local political and economic debate.

Theatre for children and youth is another important activity, promoted by the university's Art, Music and Theatre Department since 1978. A five-year programme (1991–6) of training for primary school teachers aims to provide the methodology and stimulus for theatre in schools. Arising from this programme is an annual festival of theatre for young people, presented by schools participating in the training programme and by children's theatre groups from Dar es Salaam, Bagamoyo College of Arts and Morogoro Region.   JM PMM FN

See: E. Hussein, 'On the Development of Theatre in East Africa'. PhD thesis, Humbolt Univ., 1975; A. Lihamba, 'Politics and theatre in Tanzania after the Arusha Declaration, 1967–1984', PhD thesis, Leeds Univ., 1985; L. Mbughuni, 'Old and New Drama from East Africa',

African Literature Today, 8, 1976; P. Muhando [Mlama], 'Traditional African Theatre as a Pedagogical Institution', PhD thesis, Univ. of Dar es Salaam, 1984, 'African Theatre – the Case of Tanzania', UDSM, unpublished paper, and *Culture and Development: The Popular Theatre Approach in Africa*, Scandinavian Institute of African Studies, Uppsala, 1991; M. Rugyendo, 'Towards a Truly African Theatre', *Umma*, 1, 2, 1974.

Tara Arts The first and foremost professional theatre company to be established and run by Asian immigrants in Britain. In 1976 a small group of Asian artists, led by Sunil Saggar, Ovais Kadri and Jatinder Verma, decided to found a small company from the Asian community in South London; their first production was of RABINDRANATH TAGORE's play, *Sacrifice* (1977). Tagore, the Nobel Prize-winner who died in 1941, represented what might be regarded as a Bengali classical tradition. But one of the first aims of Tara Arts was to establish a new tradition that would reflect its situation in Britain, as a community that was losing touch with the Asian languages and modes of thought but needed to assert its identity in what was still an alien country. It could be said that communal fear was one motive, for Tara Arts was formed in the wake of the brutal murder of Gurdip Singh Chaggar.

Tara Arts has described its evolution as having three stages – Alphabet (1977–82), in which the company was learning its trade and paying its performers on a part-time basis; Vocabulary (1982–5), where it was discovering its Asian theatre roots, inspired by Kirti Jain and the Pune Theatre Company from India; and Language (1985–), in which the company had succeeded in fusing classical traditions from East and West and developed its own form of AGIT-PROP community drama. Among contemporary plays, Tara Arts produced *Scenes in the Life of ...* (1982), about the experiences of a young woman migrating to Britain, and *Chilli in Your Eyes* (1984), about the problems of the Asian unemployed; but the company is best known for its work with Indian and Western classics, where it has provided a bridge between several traditions. Its productions have toured Britain and further afield, appearing in festivals around the world.

In 1990 its artistic director and founder member, Jatinder Verma, was invited to stage an Indian version of MOLIÈRE's *Tartuffe*, set in the court of the Mogul Emperor Aurangzeb; but an equally valuable contribution to the NATIONAL THEATRE's programme was of the little-known 8th-century Indian classic, SUDRAKA's *The Little Clay Cart* (1991). Tara Arts' other classical productions have included BHASA's *Broken Thigh*, GOGOL's *The Government Inspector* and SOPHOCLES' *Oedipus the King* (1991). Its most distinctive contributions have come not so much from its classical or its agit-prop productions, but from the fusion of Indian and Western techniques through Verma's imaginative leadership. *The Jackal's Cackle* (1991) told its story, derived from the *Panchatantra*, through classical Indian dance, MIME and MASKS. *Heer and Romeo* (1991–2) brought together *Romeo and Juliet* and Varis Shah's *Heer and Ranjha* into one play; while *Monsters and Minotaurs* (1992–3) used puppetry and dance to combine the Greek story of the Minotaur with tales from India.

It is perhaps inevitable that purists from both East and West have complained about the debasement of traditions, but Tara Arts' achievement has been to provide convincing proof that different cultures can be drawn together, and fused, with powerful and entertaining results. (See also REGIONAL THEATRE (BRITAIN).) JE

Tarkington, Booth 1869–1946 American novelist and playwright. Better known as a novelist, Tarkington was the author of 21 produced plays. Whether taking his theme from history or a contemporary event, he was a romanticist who enjoyed writing for actors: *Monsieur Beaucaire* (1900) for RICHARD MANSFIELD, *Master Antonio* (1916) for OTIS SKINNER, *Poldekin* (1920) for GEORGE ARLISS. When the success of *The Man from Home* (1907), written with Harry Leon Wilson, was followed by failures, Tarkington stopped writing plays for four years. Later, his most successful play, *Clarence* (1919), written for ALFRED LUNT and HELEN HAYES, showed the disruption caused in a normal household by a handsome, bumbling hero. Never feeling that he was taken seriously as a playwright, Tarkington distrusted the theatre as a place for serious art. A collection of his letters (*On Plays, Playwrights, and Playgoers*) was published in 1959. WJM

Tarlton [Tarleton], **Richard** d.1588 English CLOWN, who became a legend in his own lifetime. He is first heard of in 1570, as the supposed author of a ballad, and the Stationers' Register lists among his lost work *Tarlton's Toys* and *Tarlton's Tragical Treatises* (both 1576) and *Tarlton's Device upon this unlooked for great snow* (1579). The manuscript of *Tarlton's Jig of a horse loade of Fooles* is now assumed to be one of John Payne Collier's many forgeries, but Tarlton was almost certainly the author of the popular play, *The Seven Deadly Sins* (1585), of whose second part an outline plot (or PLATT) survives. It was performed by QUEEN ELIZABETH's MEN, which Tarlton joined on the company's formation in 1583. He had probably been one of LEICESTER's MEN before that date. There is every indication that Tarlton was more suited to solo or extempore performance than to the faithful recitation of other men's lines. The spirit, though not the letter, of his comic routines is probably present in the posthumously published *Tarlton's Jests* (1611), an important source-book of biographical information.

Tarlton specialized in JIGS, which were a popular feature of the playhouse programme. He was also a Master of Fence and a skilled musician. The well known drawing by John Scottowe shows him in a buttoned cap and short boots, playing a pipe while beating a tabor. It is the image of a rustic clown, with curly hair, broad nose flattened and bent, and simple suit, probably russet. The squint to which he confessed is not evident. That Tarlton's fame outlived him is not surprising. He was the finest popular entertainer of his generation as well as a favourite at court. It is something more than sentiment that reinforces claims that SHAKESPEARE had him in mind when he wrote Hamlet's reminiscence of Yorick. PT

Tarragon Theatre Toronto's most firmly established 'alternative' theatre. Since its founding in 1971 by Bill Glassco and Jane Gordon, Tarragon has demonstrated an admirable commitment to the development of Canadian plays and playwrights by establishing a playwright-in-residence programme and premiering a large number of Canadian plays by such major writers as DAVID FRENCH, David Freeman, SHARON POLLOCK, JAMES REANEY, JUDITH THOMPSON and GEORGE F. WALKER. In addition, Tarragon is largely responsible for bringing Québecois playwright MICHEL TREMBLAY to English Canada by regularly premiering his works in translation. In 1982 critic and dramaturge Urjo Kareda succeeded Glassco as artistic director, expanding Tarragon's commitment to developing playwrights with the establishment of a programme for promising writers. Kareda also oversaw the opening of the Extra Space in 1983, a 100-seat venue that has allowed Tarragon to expand its own programming and offer a low-cost rental space for independent productions.

Both an artistic and a commercial success, Tarragon has done more than any other theatre to bring Canadian drama into the mainstream of Canadian theatre. DAH

Tasso, Torquato 1544-95 Italian poet and dramatist. Most of Tasso's dramatic writing was done for court entertainment, celebrations, festivals and like theatricals. Among the many kinds of dramatic writing he produced two plays are particularly important: *Re Torrismondo* (*King Torrismondo*, 1578, but written earlier), a quasi-baroque verse TRAGEDY in emulation of SOPHOCLES that treats of the disastrous consequences ensuing from an illicit passion, and *Aminta*, the most celebrated and influential dramatic PASTORAL of the Renaissance, first performed at Ferrara in 1573 by the GELOSI company. He was one of the most admired of Italian poets abroad; his influence was strongly felt in the work of many 16th- and 17th-century English writers. LR

Tate, Harry [Ronald Macdonald Hutchinson] 1872-1940 Scottish comedian, on the British MUSIC-HALLS during 1895-1939. As the man who was 'always in control of the situation', he possessed the superb capability of reducing his environment to utter chaos. At golf, billiards, motoring, fishing, flying or broadcasting he was invariably defeated by the malice of objects, including his recalcitrant moustache, and by obstructive fellow creatures like his obnoxious son and mute, staring little boys. His sketches became classics and made catch-phrases of 'Goodbyeeee' and 'Isn't it annoying, Papaaaa!'. His influence on W. C. FIELDS was patent. LS

Tate, Nahum 1652-1715 Irish playwright. Born in Dublin and educated at Trinity College, he graduated in 1672. His poems began to be published in 1676. He began having his plays performed in 1678. In 1680 his adaptation of SHAKESPEARE's *Richard III* was banned for its study of usurpation and abdication (see CENSORSHIP): Tate disguised it as *The Sicilian Usurper*. In 1681 his version of *King Lear* was performed and, itself adapted, effectively kept Shakespeare's play off the stage until 1838. Tate's work is endlessly vilified for its elimination of the Fool, the introduction of a love plot between Edgar and Cordelia and its happy ending with Lear restored to the throne, but his changes are the result of an honest attempt to combine new conventions of probability and decorum with a work that he admired. Tate adapted Shakespeare again in the same year, turning *Coriolanus* into *The Ingratitude of a Commonwealth*. His farce, *A Duke and No Duke*, was performed in 1684; the second edition (1693) contains an important defence of FARCE by Tate. He also wrote the libretto for Purcell's *Dido and Aeneas* (1689). In 1692 he was appointed Poet Laureate and in 1702 Historiographer Royal. PH

Taylor, C(ecil) P(hilip) 1928-81 British dramatist, who once described his career as 'a gradual scaling down of ambition'. Throughout his life he kept faith with the socialism of his Glasgow Jewish childhood, but the revolutionary flavour of his early plays, such as his first *Aa Went to Blaydon Races* (1962), gave way to the warm humour of such plays as *Allergy*, a one-act comedy about the downfall of a Trotskyist paper with a very small circulation, or *The Black and White Minstrels* (1972) which went from Edinburgh to the HAMPSTEAD THEATRE CLUB in London.

Taylor was a prolific dramatist, adapting plays by STERNHEIM and IBSEN as well as writing for the stage and television; and for many years he stayed with regional companies in Newcastle, Liverpool and in Scotland, producing scripts for their needs rather than for the more financially rewarding theatres in the South. His *Schippel* (adapted from a Sternheim comedy) was seen as *The Plumber's Progress* (1975) in London with Harry Secombe, while *Bread and Butter* (1966), *Bandits* (1977), *And a Nightingale Sang ...* (1979) and his last play, *Bring Me Sunshine, Bring Me Smiles* (1982), had brief London runs. His most successful play, *Good*, about a liberal German professor in the 1930s whose moral cowardice leads to a military career and a job in Auschwitz, was first staged by the ROYAL SHAKESPEARE COMPANY at the Warehouse in 1981 and later transferred to the WEST END, starring ALAN HOWARD. Taylor's energy and charm were present in all his writing, giving life to even apparently casual scripts; but he sometimes lacked the disciplined concentration to ensure that his many talents lived up to their promise. In 1992, a major feature of the EDINBURGH FESTIVAL was devoted to a retrospective of his plays. JE

Taylor, Joseph 1586-1652 English actor, already famous in London when he joined the King's Men (see LORD CHAMBERLAIN'S MEN) probably to replace RICHARD BURBAGE, in 1619. After the death of HEMINGES in 1630, Taylor shared with LOWIN the business management of the company, as well as creating many of MASSINGER's leading roles and playing Hamlet, Iago, and Ferdinand in WEBSTER's *The Duchess of Malfi*. The fact that Burbage is known to have created Hamlet and Ferdinand strengthens the belief that Taylor was his successor as the company's leading tragedian. But he was versatile enough to be an outstanding Mosca in a revival of JONSON's *Volpone*. PT

Taylor, Laurette (Cooney) 1884-1946 American actress, who debuted as a child in Gloucester, Massachusetts, then went in 1903 to the Boston Athenaeum. She first appeared in New York the same year in *From Rags to Riches*. Her first substantial success came in 1910 in *Alias Jimmy Valentine*, but she achieved stardom in the title role of *Peg o' My Heart* in 1912, a script by J. Hartley Manners, who married Taylor in 1911. Later roles included Nell Gwyn in *Sweet Nell of Old Drury* and Rose Trelawny in *Trelawny of the Wells*. After her husband's death in 1928, Taylor retired from the stage, but she returned as Mrs Midgit in the 1938 revival of *Outward Bound*. She co-starred in *The Glass Menagerie* (1945), a smash hit that made her once more the toast of BROADWAY. SMA

Taylor, Tom 1817–80 British playwright, journalist and art critic whose phenomenal energy allowed him to cram several careers into less than 63 years. Taylor was born near Sunderland and educated at the Universities of Glasgow and Cambridge, at the latter of which he taught for two years before moving to London in 1844. He was professor of English in the University of London from 1845 to 47, during which time he was called to the Bar and had eight plays staged at the LYCEUM. After practice as a barrister on the northern circuit from 1847 to 50, he was appointed assistant secretary to the newly created Board of Health in London, continuing to serve the Board in various capacities until 1871. By this time he had written a further 60 plays (there were at least nine more to come); published a three-volume biography of the painter Benjamin Haydon (1853); and established himself as art critic of *The Times*, regular writer of leaders for the *Morning Chronicle* and the *Daily News* and popular contributor to *Punch*, of which he became editor from 1874 until his death.

Add to all that the fact that he was virtually house dramatist for the Wigans at the OLYMPIC from 1853 to 65 and for BUCKSTONE at the HAYMARKET from 1859 to 61, and some estimate of his productivity can be made. It is not surprising that most of Taylor's plays have proved as ephemeral as his journalism. He gratified the taste of the time with BURLESQUES, PANTOMIMES, even a HIPPODRAMA (*Garibaldi*, 1859), and, like most contemporary playwrights, he was a shameless thief of French plots. His most famous MELODRAMA, *The Ticket-of-Leave Man* (1863), is from the French, as is his probing moral COMEDY, *Still Waters Run Deep* (1855), whilst two of his best comedies, *The Contested Election* (1859) and *The Overland Route* (1860), are certainly derivative, though not tied to a particular source. Taylor's most ambitious work for the theatre was the succession of history plays, some in blank verse, which began with 'Twixt Axe and Crown* (1870) and ended with *Anne Boleyn* (1876). They have survived no better than *Our American Cousin* (1858), the outstanding popular success of Taylor's lifetime, which owed much more to the inventiveness of the creator of Lord Dundreary, E. A. SOTHERN, than it did to Taylor. There is finer stuff among Taylor's collaborative work – *Masks and Faces* (1852) with CHARLES READE and *New Men and Old Acres* (1869) with Augustus Dubourg, for example. It is a fair summary of Taylor's dramatic career to say that he took the styles he found – FARCE, comedy, melodrama, history play – and, without ever trying very hard, improved on them. PT

Tchelitchew, Pavel 1898–1957 Russian-American theatre designer and artist. Tchelitchew studied abstract art and stage design under ALEKSANDRA EKSTER, and in 1918

became an assistant to Soviet designer Isaac Rabinovitch. But Tchelitchew eventually renounced his cubist style and moved to Berlin in 1921, where he designed the OPERA *Le Coq d'Or* and met Serge Diaghilev. In Paris in 1923 he embraced a neo-romantic style and developed his controversial technique of multiple perspectives. This technique gave his representational painting a surrealistic quality (see SURREALISM) and brought him to the attention of Gertrude Stein. In 1934 he designed LOUIS JOUVET's production of *Ondine* in Paris, and subsequently moved to the United States where he eventually acquired citizenship. His designs for ballet included *Nobilissima Visione* (1938) and *Balustrade* (1940) for George Balanchine. By the 1940s Tchelitchew became disillusioned with stage design and he refused AGNES DE MILLE's offer to design the ballet *Rodeo* (1942), suggesting instead that she use OLIVER SMITH. Tchelitchew's works were frequently shown in galleries in Paris, the Museum of Modern Art in New York, and elsewhere. TM

Teatro Abierto (Open Theatre) Argentine theatre phenomenon organized by OSVALDO DRAGÚN and others in 1981 in response to an oppressive political regime. Designed to revitalize a stagnant stage, the first promotion in 1981 resulted in 21 new one-act plays by as many authors, staged by 21 directors, in a seven-day cycle with three plays each night. The Teatro Picadero mysteriously burned at the end of a week, but the fierce determination of the group, coupled with great public enthusiasm for the event, enabled them to continue in the Teatro Tabarís almost immediately. The 1982 cycle was overshadowed by the Falklands (Malvinas) War and by a diminished quality of the new scripts. Events scheduled for subsequent years have become less impelling because of the Alfonsín election of 1983 and the return to democratic procedures in Argentina. GW

Teatro Campesino, El see EL TEATRO CAMPESINO

Teatro de Orientación With objectives similar to those of the TEATRO DE ULISES, this Mexican theatre group (1932–4 and 1938–9) was established with a governmental subvention under the direction of CELESTINO GOROSTIZA. GW

Teatro de Ulises Mexican theatre group co-founded in 1928 by XAVIER VILLAURRUTIA and SALVADOR NOVO, with the patronage of Antonieta Rivas Mercado. The group broke with the old traditions of Castilian accent, prompter's box and full attention on the star of the show in order to stress the overall coordination role of the director. The objectives were a poetic, universal, conceptual theatre. New lighting and staging techniques were adopted from the European masters – CRAIG, REINHARDT, STANISLAVSKY, PISCATOR and others. Defunct by 1929, the group presented six plays, mostly French translations, and managed to give new impetus to the renovation of Mexican drama and new spirit to Mexican playwrights and directors. GW

teatro del grottesco The name given to a body of plays by Italian dramatists of the second and third decades of the 20th century. Never a movement, the 'theatre of the grotesque' sought an anti-naturalistic (see NATURALISM) renewal of the bourgeois theatre via the development of ironic, parodistic and grotesque situations; by the use of an author's spokesman or *raisonneur*; and by emphasis upon the public and private faces of dramatic characters. The best-known plays of this theatre included the widely translated and performed *La maschera e il volto* (*The Mask and the Face*, 1916) by LUIGI CHIARELLI, and Rosso di San Secondo's *Marionette che passione!* (*Puppets, What Passion!*, 1918). PIRANDELLO is considered by many to have written some of his early plays in this vein, and his essay on humour, *L'umorismo* (*Humour*, 1908), was a seminal influence. LR

Teatro Español Madrid's municipal theatre, built on the site of a *CORRAL DE COMEDIA*. The present building was modernized in the mid-1800s and restored after a 1975 fire, reopening in 1981. It celebrated its 400th anniversary in 1983. Its venerable history embraces Spain's greatest authors, actors and directors.

In the early 20th century Benito Pérez Galdós and BENAVENTE premiered major works there, and it witnessed the brilliant career of the María Guerrero–Fernando Díaz de Mendoza company. In the 1930s, MARGARITA XIRGU and artistic director Cipriano de Rivas Cherif administered it for an unprecedented five years, creating a model national theatre. Besides establishing an international repertoire of classical and modern works, they premiered GARCÍA LORCA's *La zapatera prodigiosa* (*The Shoemaker's Prodigious Wife*) and *Yerma*, VALLE-INCLÁN's *Divinas palabras* (*Divine Words*), and early Lope de Vega Prize-winners, including CASONA's *La sirena varada* (*The Stranded Mermaid*). In 1949 another Lope de Vega winner, BUERO-VALLEJO's *Historia de una escalera* (*Story of a Stairway*), announced the revival of the postwar stage. The Teatro Español has housed a children's theatre and a Franco-era national experimental theatre. Among important directors of recent decades are José Tamayo (1950s), Miguel Narros (1960s and 80s), Alberto González Vergel (1970s), José Luis Gómez (1980s) and Gustavo Pérez Puig (1990s). PZ

Teatro Nacional D. Maria II The Portuguese National Theatre is the most visible result of a very deliberate decision taken in 1836 by a newly formed and fragile Liberal regime and administration to further the dramatic and theatrical arts in the country. The locale eventually chosen was the premier site in the capital, at the head of the Rossio, the most topographically central and historically important square in Lisbon.

The first director, ALMEIDA GARRETT, concurrently Inspector-General of Theatres, supervised its building, provided its first successful plays, transformed the professional training of actors, set up the theatrical archives associated with the building and generally launched it as the 'decent home for the national drama' it was intended to be. As has been true of many national theatres, it was and is the goal of most aspiring dramatists and actors. Even during the Salazar regime, under the management of the actors Amélia Rey-Colaço and Robles Monteiro (1929–64), it strove to maintain high standards.

Portuguese and foreign classics alternated with foreign moderns from ANOUILH to VALLE-INCLÁN and native play-wrights who, in revival or first performance – achieved often enough through one laudable subterfuge or another – were remembered or introduced to the capital's and the country's theatregoing public. The prestige and imaginative direction of the company in the latter years enabled it to soar above the crasser CENSORSHIP and conformist social pressures, even if it tended to play safe.

Garrett's beautiful theatre was gutted by fire in 1964; but arose, like a phoenix from its ruins, to be reopened in 1978. To the more traditional main auditorium it has now added a *sala experimental* (workshop theatre). The theatre as a whole is extremely elegant and well appointed, but disappoints some by continuing to be too 'discreet' with its repertoire and montages. The criticism applies far less to the workshop theatre, where the contributor saw the first production of 1986, a telling performance, in translation, of Edna O'Brien's *Virginia*.

The theatre has recently been in celebratory mode, hosting both a magnificent REVISTA 'retrospective' and a special nostalgic show in which, after playing Dantas's *A Ceia dos Cardeais* (see PORTUGAL), with ballet interludes to Renaissance music, Portugal's three senior male actors reminisced in their own scripted words about life on the stage and on the road, before moving down to the auditorium to chat, and further blur the distinction between the two realities – of the stage and of the world.

1994 was Lisbon's turn to be cultural capital of Europe. This national theatre put on a half-dozen special productions, of which the most theatrically brilliant was F. la Féria's *As Fúrias* (*The Furies*). LK

Teatro Nacional María Guerrero Madrid theatre, originally called the Princesa, which opened in 1885. In 1915 the María Guerrero–Fernando Díaz de Mendoza company assumed ownership and made it famous for high-quality stagings and premieres of Spanish authors. In 1940 it became a national theatre, named in memory of the great actress (1868–1928). The outstanding Franco-era director was José Luis Alonso (1924–90). Under his leadership (1962–74) the theatre presented major productions of BRECHT's *The Caucasian Chalk Circle*, GIRAUDOUX's *The Madwoman of Chaillot* and *Intermezzo*, and PIRANDELLO's *It Is So, If You Think So*, as well as important revivals of VALLE-INCLÁN and the premiere of his 1908 *Romance de lobos* (*Ballad of Wolves*, 1970).

Since 1978 the María Guerrero has been the headquarters of the National Drama Centre, where lavish productions and low ticket prices attract large audiences. During PASQUAL's directorship (1983–9), the Centre achieved international stature by becoming associated with the Théâtre de l'Europe. Since 1989 it has been headed by José Carlos Plaza (b.1943), who is widely recognized for his innovative cinematographic stagings. His major accomplishment to date at the María Guerrero is his spectacular marathon production in 1991 of Valle-Inclán's trilogy, *Comedias bárbaras* (*Barbaric Comedies*). PZ

television drama Over most of the world today, more people are being exposed to more drama than ever before. This drama is not that of the theatre or even that of the

The priest on a mule in a
scene from *Gabriela*,
Brazilian TV.

cinema: it comes to them on the domestic screen in their own homes or – as is sometimes the case in Third World countries – in communal venues. This drama-in-the-home may reach them from terrestrial, cable or satellite sources; often it will be recorded on videocassette and played back at the viewer's leisure. This is an unprecedented invasion of the private sphere by a previously public activity.

Television may of course be merely a means of transmitting pre-existing material. The simplest form of electronic drama is obtained by putting one or more cameras in front of a stage and recording a theatrical event. At a more ambitious level, stage drama may be adapted for the specific interpretative possibilities of the medium. SHAKESPEARE has proved to be effective on the small screen in many countries. The BBC presented the entire 37-play canon in a six-year project begun in 1978 jointly with Time–Life Films, a prestige project massively backed by major US corporations. In France, the COMÉDIE-FRANÇAISE has presented MOLIÈRE, MARIVAUX, BEAUMARCHAIS and other classics on TV; in Greece, Channel ERT 1 has recorded some of the dramas of antiquity, including all the plays of ARISTOPHANES and EURIPIDES, in the theatres of Epidaurus and Herodes Atticus. The German ZDF network has shown not only German playwrights like LESSING, KLEIST, HAUPTMANN and BRECHT but also GOLDONI, STRINDBERG and SYNGE, among many others. Japan's public-service network NHK televises KABUKI plays as well as items from the more esoteric BUGAKU and NŌ repertoire.

Television may also be, and very frequently is, a channel for broadcasting films originally intended for the cinema.

Although it would be doctrinaire as well as unrealistic to object to stage plays or cinema films on the small screen, television has its own potential which is somewhat distinct from that of the other dramatic media. But drama written for TV, some negligible pre-war experiments apart, did not emerge until the late 1940s and early 50s. At that time such plays were exclusively produced in the studio. The difference between film and television studio production was that, whereas for film a single camera would take each shot discontinuously to be edited afterwards, for television two, three or more cameras would shoot the action in an unbroken run. TV plays, normally set indoors, would go out 'live', i.e. they were seen at the actual moment of performance. Exterior scenes, if needed at all, were filmed beforehand and then inserted into the transmission. In other words, television drama shared with theatre the element of 'real time' untouched by any editing process (other than the vision-mixer's switch from one camera image to another).

The coming of videotape in 1958 was to change all that. Plays could now be recorded and edited, first physically (by actually cutting the tape) and then electronically: this made a more cinematic construction possible. Indeed, in the 1960s many television writers and directors turned directly to film in order to break out of the studio. The fact that by the 80s lightweight video cameras had to quite an extent replaced film cameras has not affected this basic approach to production: single-camera operation of whatever kind retains the visual mobility and structural flexibility of the cinema film. From the viewers' standpoint, an even more visible change in the 60s and 70s was the introduction of colour (PAL or SECAM in Europe, with 625 lines per image; or NTSC in America and Japan, with 525 lines). These innovations have meant that television drama, even in the strict sense of a medium-specific form, can now draw on a wide range of techniques: studio and/or location, monochrome and/or colour, film (of different gauges) and/or videotape (of different formats), as well as a wide range of electronic special effects.

It follows that the defining characteristic of television

drama is not so much the mode of production as the mode of reception. The viewer does not make any special effort: drama is offered to him in the home, surrounded by everyday distractions. The play may at times even be resented as an intruder, breaching family taboos. Small screen size and imperfect image resolution make the television experience less overwhelming than that of the cinema: the viewer has the choice at any time to switch over or off. A television play then has to grab him quickly to retain his attention; the response is rarely going to be as compelling as that experienced by a crowd in the theatre or the cinema. TV drama speaks to its audience as individuals or at best as members of small groups.

But perhaps the significant point is not so much the impact of any one play as such but that of television drama as a whole. Embedded in a continuous stream of electronic information (news, weather reports and so on), it forms part of the viewer's alternative world, an extension or even a partial replacement of first-hand experience. Is this enriching or enfeebling? That will of course depend on the overall context of programming, the sense of social reality it conveys, the imaginative enrichment it brings. Even the advertising messages on commercial channels that punctuate plays will subliminally colour their reception. The sheer quantity of television drama available for consumption in itself becomes problematic. In the USA, somewhere between 30 and 70 channels may be available: the viewer is literally spoilt for choice.

It has been said that viewing conditions favour the close-up as against the long shot, the actor as against the environment, the narrow domestic vision as against the wider social insight. But technical circumstances are contingent. Larger screen sizes can enhance image impact; High Definition Television (with a standard of 1125 or 1250 lines) can drastically improve picture quality. The programming context will continue to evolve. We must therefore see the medium's seeming preference for domestic NATURALISM as a conditional rather than an unchallengeable fact. What will remain constant is the smallness of the domestic audience and the discourse arising from this premiss.

The social framework TV drama in different countries varies according to differing socio-economic, technological and cultural/political conditions. Some Third World countries cannot as yet afford television at all. Others are so poor, with thin network coverage and few sets in private ownership, as to make television – drama or whatever – a negligible influence. For instance, in India where regular broadcasts started only in 1965 and colour was not introduced until 1982, the impact of TV drama cannot begin to compare with that of its flourishing film industry, the world's largest. On the other hand, pay TV in some countries is able to cater for minority tastes, creating a class system among its viewing public.

The cultural/political climate cannot fail to be a major factor in the tone and quality of television drama. South African television, long hampered by divisive internal policies, has tended to rely on imports for the bulk of its programmes. In the former East European bloc the government line would carry more weight in broadcasting policy than would 'merely' pleasing the viewers, although in the various countries there were significant programming differences which reflected differing political nuances. Generally speaking, Western influence was kept at bay – though when the BBC's *Forsyte Saga* was shown on Soviet television in 1971 it was a great success. Much of Soviet television drama used to derive from stage plays. Official guidelines frowned on scenes of sex, violence and racism. Since the dissolution of the USSR in 1991, Western soap operas, including Latin American ones, have flooded Russian TV screens. The early period of Chinese TV drama – over 80 monochrome plays broadcast live between 1958 and 1966 – was terminated by the Cultural Revolution. For ten years only the eight revolutionary operas approved by Mme Mao were featured on Chinese television. The toppling of the 'Gang of Four' ushered in a new era, technologically as well as ideologically. Modern production methods came in: plays were at last recorded on tape in specialized drama studios; and production expanded at a dizzy rate. Since 1986, China's more than 500 stations have produced an average of 2000 plays per annum; in 1991 this figure rose to 5000. Here, too, Western dramas began to invade the screen, including the BBC's Shakespeare series.

In Thailand, the army-directed Channel 7 used the traditional operatic form of *mau-lum* for anti-communist propaganda. Israel Television's prize-winning *The Wordmaker* (1992), a biopic on the creator of modern Hebrew, clearly had an incidental political point to make, although the programme was not uncritical of its hero. The Canadian Broadcasting Corporation's mini-series *Conspiracy of Silence* (1991) came out boldly against victimization of Native Americans. Prevailing conditions will also determine what is not shown. In Japan, competition between the channels offers some flexibility in programming; nevertheless, in the 60s a good many socially critical plays in the *Hanketsu* (*Verdict*) series had to be rewritten or were cancelled altogether, because of political interference and sponsorship pressures.

Cultural factors which may not be directly political will also colour a country's TV drama output. Hong Kong is as addicted to martial arts programmes as Japan is to samurai epics. Among the latter the story of the 47 *ronin*, about an early-18th-century vendetta set among feudal retainers, has been as popular on the box as it has on the *kabuki* stage and in the cinema. And Britain's meticulously researched and expertly produced period dramas (which have a rich overseas sales potential) owe not a little to post-imperial nostalgia.

The actual organization of broadcasting institutions is bound to be crucial: out-and-out commercialism as in the USA; a state-run service as in Cuba or the former communist countries of Eastern Europe; a duopoly, partly a public service and partly independent, as in Great Britain, Sweden and Japan; stations run by special interest groups (Catholic and socialist) as in the Netherlands; or any of the possible range of variants of these, with regulations tough or permissive as the case may be – all make for very different kinds of drama output.

West German television, for instance, presents a unique and interesting organizational picture. Authority in the first channel (ARD) is vested in the regional (*Länder*) governments. The second channel (ZDF) is jointly controlled by federal government, *Länder* and various interest groups. This arrangement leaves an occasional space for delving into controversial areas. In the 60s there were quite a few plays dedicated to coming to terms with the Nazi past. In the early 70s the regional station WDR screened a number of telefilms dealing sympathetically with working-class topics, such as Klaus Wiese and Christian Ziewer's *Dear Mother, I'm OK* and *Snowdrops Bloom in September*, as well as Ingo Kratisch and Marianne Lüdcke's *Wages and Love*. R. W. FASSBINDER's five-part series *Eight Hours Don't Make a Day*, which examined the link in working-class life between work, home and leisure, managed to antagonize critics both left and right. A regular platform for experimental telefilms has been provided by ZDF's weekly slot, 'Das kleine Fernsehespiel' ('The Little Television Play'), which puts out work of minority interest.

The world's largest producer of TV drama, chiefly of the entertainment variety, is the USA. The domestic strength of the industry makes it the leading exporter, able to offer its programmes abroad at irresistible prices. An oligopoly of three networks – ABC, CBS and NBC – has dominated the numerous local stations, which get 70 per cent of their material from the Big Three. There is a solid home market: in 1979, 98 per cent of the population owned a set; in 30 million homes there were two, and in 10 million homes three or more sets. By 1992, average daily viewing had risen to the daunting figure of over seven hours. Since the purpose of commercial television is to sell air time to advertisers, the criteria of success are 'ratings' (i.e. viewer numbers) or, at a more sophisticated level, 'demographic profiles' (i.e. the socio-economic slice of the market reached). The networks produce only a fraction of their own material and buy in telefilms from six major Hollywood studios (Columbia, Paramount, MGM, 20th Century Fox, Universal and Warner Brothers) or independent – large and not so large – TV film production companies. The bulk of these productions comes from the West Coast; their style and ethos is that of Hollywood. Production values count for a great deal, cultural prestige for rather less. In the ceaseless competition for a slice of the market, the principle of Least Objectionable Programming is held in high regard. There have, of course, been notable exceptions to this generalization. For example, the *Hallmark Hall of Fame*, begun in 1952 and continued into the 1990s, mixed prestigious theatrical offerings with plays specially written for TV; associated for 27 years with NBC, this show switched in the 1979–80 season to CBS. The (privately supported) Public Broadcasting Service (PBS), which is dedicated to transmitting 'quality' work, only reaches some 2–3 per cent of American viewers; much of its material is of British origin.

At times ideological considerations do, of course, supplement purely commercial ones. When ABC's *Roots*, the dramatization of the Alex Haley novel which traced the progress of an African-American family over several generations from slavery to post-bellum Reconstruction, was shown for eight successive nights in January 1977, its impact was immense. This 12-hour indictment of white America's treatment of its black population struck a chord: the mayors of over 30 cities proclaimed a 'Roots Week', and some 250 colleges were to offer courses based

on the book and the mini-series. *Roots the Next Generation* (1979), which brought the family saga up to modern times, caused slightly less of a stir but still drew an estimated 110 million viewers. A comparable blockbuster with educational intent was NBC's *Holocaust* (1978), which won 107 million viewers in the USA and an estimated 220 million in 50 other countries. This story of the Nazi persecution of a family of Berlin Jews, shot wholly on location in Germany and Austria, was criticized by some on grounds of taste but undoubtedly brought home to many viewers, in Germany and elsewhere, genocidal horrors the memory of which had been repressed until then. On the other hand, the failure of ABC's 8-part, 12-hour serial *Amerika* (1987) – a Cold War fantasy of a Soviet take-over of the USA widely dismissed as 'warnography' – suggests the limits of audience manipulation.

Away from theatre In Britain, where the BBC, guided by the Reithian public-service ethos, used to enjoy a monopoly of the air, television drama tended at first to be little more than televised theatre. But in the early 1950s attempts were made to ginger things up; Nigel Kneale's science-fiction serial, *The Quatermass Experiment*, caused much excitement in 1953. This alarming preview of the dire consequences of space flight was followed in 1955 by the moon-rocket mystery *Quatermass II*, in 1958–9 by *Quatermass and the Pit* – diabolical forces unleashed by technology – and finally, as late as 1979, by *Quatermass 4* (produced on this occasion not by the BBC but by Thames Television).

The coming, after a vigorous debate, of commercial television in 1955 opened up British broadcasting to more popular tastes. The USA had shown the way. The American networks, originally broadcasting from New York, had encouraged a spate of fresh TV playwriting, probably to persuade people in the higher income brackets to buy receivers. The competition between 'The Philco Playhouse' (NBC) and 'Studio One' (CBS) in the late 40s and early 50s brought on what in retrospect glowed like a golden age of television drama. Writers like Gore Vidal and N. Richard Nash made their mark. Reginald Rose's court-room drama, *Twelve Angry Men* (CBS 1954), came out with a powerful liberal plea for even-handed justice. Paddy Chayefsky's *Marty* (NBC 1953) depicted an unglamorous butcher's longing for love; other plays of his such as *The Catered Affair*, *The Bachelor Party* and *Middle of the Night* all revelled in what he called 'the marvellous world of the ordinary'. A similar outburst of creativity took place in Canadian television around that time. Interestingly enough, the work of Rose and Chayefsky also had a deep influence on Japanese TV dramatists in the 1960s.

In seeking out more popular material, Britain – both the BBC and the drama-orientated independent company ABC – bought in a large number of North American scripts. ABC's 'Armchair Theatre' (sometimes derided as 'Armpit Theatre') changed the tone of drama on the small screen; writers like ALUN OWEN, Clive Exton and BILL NAUGHTON gave it a contemporary and British accent. Associated Television, ATV and Granada also promoted original TV playwriting. In 1964 the BBC started 'The Wednesday Play', a title changed in 1970 to 'Play for Today'. This became a platform for innovative (and to some timid souls, alarming) drama, presenting the work of MICHAEL FRAYN, SIMON GRAY, PETER TERSON and many other writers who were either already, or were destined shortly to become, well known. DAVID MERCER's *In Two Minds* (1967) questioned the conventional wisdom about schizophrenia. PETER NICHOLS's *The Common* (1973) mixed domestic with political intrigues. One of the instant hits was Jeremy Sandford's *Cathy Come Home* (1966), brilliantly directed by Ken Loach. This story of young Cathy and Reg, filmed on location in *cinéma-vérité* style, brought the plight of the homeless close to millions of viewers and implied, in the author's words, that 'our State is needlessly cruel'. The verisimilitude of *Cathy* and other documentary dramas (an ill-defined category that runs all the way from the biopic to personalized reportage) gave rise to some anxiety: would viewers be fooled into thinking the play was '*real*'? Curiously, such fears were aroused only by plays with a radical thrust.

It is not to underrate the contribution made by producers, directors, actors and designers to say that it was above all the writers who raised the prestige of British television drama from the 1960s onwards. Established literary figures like TERENCE RATTIGAN and J. B. PRIESTLEY were attracted to the new medium; authors like JOHN OSBORNE, JOHN MORTIMER and TOM STOPPARD were all to write for it. The success on the domestic screen of *A Night Out* (ABC, 1960) gave HAROLD PINTER a wider hearing than his first stage plays had commanded. John Hopkins's quartet, *Talking to a Stranger* (BBC, 1966), was described as 'the first authentic masterpiece written directly for televison'. The politically committed playwright and screenwriter TREVOR GRIFFITHS favoured the small screen – when granted access to it – as giving him the widest audience. His 11-episode *Bill Brand* looked at left-wing politics from the inside. Jim Allen's *Days of Hope* (BBC, 1976), a 4-part chronicle of British working-class history up to the General Strike of 1926, unleashed a storm of protest in the press: the issues raised were far from merely historical. Author-director MIKE LEIGH successfully transferred his improvisational playmaking technique to television with naturalistic and satirical pictures of English life. The Irish novelist William Trevor played variations on the theme of loneliness in his TV plays; Elaine Morgan showed great skill in dramatized biographies. The highly productive ALAN PLATER, initially inspired by Paddy Chayefsky, at first used his north-country background to create regional speech and characters of great authority, but then diversified in many directions; he has expertly dramatized many novels. His fellow Northerner ALAN BENNETT – actor, REVUE artist, writer for stage and screen – has created affectionate and shrewdly observed cameos of 'ordinary' people without disguising the melancholy beneath his laughter.

DENIS POTTER, originally a television critic, began a spectacular and highly productive TV playwriting career with *The Confidence Course* (BBC) in 1965. His work increasingly veered away from mainstream naturalism, most notably perhaps in the trilogy which employed popular music in a startlingly novel way: *Pennies from Heaven* (BBC, 1978); *The Singing Detective* (BBC, 1986) and *Lipstick on Your Collar* (Whistling Gypsy for Channel 4, 1993). The first of these serials harked back to the songs of the 1930s, the second to those of the 40s, the third to the 50s. The

irruption of songs into the action had the reverse effect of that of MUSICAL COMEDY: it was an alienating device which questioned, while at the same time sympathizing with, the very emotions being expressed.

This literary flavour of much British television contrasts with American television, where a script like ARTHUR MILLER's play set in Auschwitz, *Playing for Time* (CBS, 1980), tends to be the exception. In Britain the single play was long held to be the key to dramatic innovation; all the alarm bells would ring whenever that was in danger of being crowded out by the series or the serial. In fact it was not until the 1980s that the single play finally took a very modest back seat in programming,
with ratings looming ever larger in the more competitive climate of Thatcherism. Up to the 1970s, the BBC's freedom from commercial pressures allowed it to take risks (principally in the area of the single play) and to set standards that the independent companies had to acknowledge and follow. Even so, there were unstated limits as to how far drama might go. Peter Watkins's *The War Game* (1965), a by no means sensationalized vision of how Britain might fare in a nuclear war, was banned on the grounds that 'it had the power to produce unpredictable emotions'. If over the years the BBC was to become somewhat less enterprising, the creation in 1982 of Channel 4, with a brief to innovate, to cater for minority tastes and to commission rather than produce programmes itself, gave British television drama a new fillip. A number of production companies sprang up to fill the programming gap. The funding provided by Film on Four increasingly blurred the distinction between the telefilm and the cinema film: many of the films it commissioned were shown on the large as well as the small screen. By the end of the 1980s, Film on Four had been involved in over 150 full-length features, a godsend to the ailing British film industry.

Television genres Once American television play production had moved to the West Coast, the series replaced the single play. Commercially the change-over made sense: cast, location and sets can be used repeatedly, and captive audiences 'delivered' to advertisers with a high degree of certainty. A 'wasteland' (in the words of the chairman of the Federal Communications Commission) followed the era of creativity. But a crude ratings approach gave way in the early 1970s to demographic considerations: in order to retain upmarket viewers, networks had to provide something better than what one critic called 'mind candy'. Standards improved without actually departing from a broad consensus of taste.

Like Hollywood movies, series quickly took on genre patterns. The Western proved to be as popular on TV as it had in the cinema. *Wagon Trail* (NBC) began its long, largely studio-bound career in 1957, some of its episodes improbably inspired by *Pride and Prejudice* and *Great Expectations*. Owen Wister's 1902 novel, *The Virginian*, had spawned some films for the cinema; now NBC was to run a series under that title (1962–9), with guest performers like GEORGE C. SCOTT, Bette Davis and Robert Redford. *Bonanza* (NBC, 1959–71) was a sort of Western soap opera.

In the movies, crime had been depicted largely from the gangster's perspective. On television it is policemen or detectives who carry the action: long-term identification has to be with the side of law and order. ABC's *Dragnet* (begun in 1952) was based on actual case histories; Sergeant Joe Friday's 'Just the facts, ma'am' entered the language. The policemen Columbo, McCloud and Madigan were the eponymous heroes of the 'Mysterie Movie' cycle made by Universal for NBC (1971–7). *Kojak* (CBS, 1973–7) fought crime while licking a lollipop. *Hill Street Blues* (NBC, 1980–7) took a disenchanted look at a police station in a deprived East Coast city: law officers had drinking problems, their daughters were raped, urban warfare prevailed. The same company's *Miami Vice* (1984–9) stressed formal values, some sequences resembling pop promos.

Indeed, villainy has a worldwide appeal. A series on RadioTelevision Hong Kong dramatizing real crimes enjoyed the collaboration of the police. East German Television's crime series, *The Prosecutor Takes the Floor* and *Police Call 110*, had a very long run indeed. The Australian Broadcasting Corporation's *Phoenix* (1991) aimed to give a gritty look to its portrayal of the inner working of the Major Crime Squad. The British version of the genre was at first rather benign. *Dixon of Dock Green* (BBC), a cosy cop show devised by Ted (later Lord) Willis, ran from 1955 until 1976, by which time its avuncular lead Jack Warner was well beyond retirement age. But *Z Cars* (BBC, 1960–78), as well as its spin-off *Softly, Softly* (BBC, 1966–76), gave a more down-to-earth picture of police work. Thames TV's *The Sweeny* (1974–8) portrayed Scotland Yard's Flying Squad in action-packed mid-Atlantic terms. The BBC's *Juliet Bravo* (from 1980) featured a woman police officer – a breakthrough in a traditionally macho genre. *The Bill* (Thames TV, from 1985) has also included women police constables in its cast.

The detective – private eye or member of the force – is a television hero in many countries. Robert Taylor, his boyish good looks long since gone, starred in ABC's *The Detective* (1959–61). In the French series *The Last Five Minutes* (ORTF, 1958) Inspector Bourrel always solved his case just in the nick of time. In the late 50s the BBC's *Maigret* series, based on Simenon's famous sleuth, conjured up a satisfyingly French atmosphere; many of the scripts were by GILES COOPER. The lead created by Rupert Davies was reincarnated on the small screen some 30 years later by the versatile MICHAEL GAMBON.

The image of the British detective was to become increasingly differentiated – Taggart and Bergerac representing opposite ends of the UK, Glasgow and the Channel Islands respectively; there was even a Chinese detective. A number of British TV sleuths derive from crime fiction: Miss Marples out of AGATHA CHRISTIE, Chief Inspector Wexford out of Ruth Rendell, Commander Adam Dalgliesh out of P. D. James, Chief Inspector Morse out of Colin Dexter. The latter, played by John Thaw, was to become a cult figure. Made by Zenith for Central Television, *Morse* (1987–93) regularly played to 15 million UK viewers and a worldwide audience of 75 million in over 50 countries. Far from being the usual police detective, Morse – Oxford-based, literate and opera-loving – often barked up the wrong tree. The solution of the crime would leave him melancholy rather than elated. His landmark, a 1960 Mark Two Jaguar, has become famous.

The medical show, too, had a well established Hollywood history. MGM, which had made as many as nine films between 1938 and 1947 on Dr Kildare, a young intern under the mentorship of a crusty old doctor, went on to make a television *Dr Kildare* series for NBC (1961–6). In Britain, *Emergency – Ward 10* (often misread as *Emergency Ward 10*) kept ATV viewers tranquillized from 1957 onwards; with *Call Oxbridge 2000* followed by *General Hospital*, the treatment continued for an almost uninterrupted 21 years. *Casualty* (BBC, from 1986) has scored high marks for realism in situation as well as make-up: the gashes and contusions look clinically accurate.

Science fiction, a well established literary genre since the days of Jules Verne, had been popular in the cinema before it blasted off on the TV screen. *Star Trek*, NBC's sci-fi serial which started in 1966, has taken a positive view of space exploration, borne aloft by confidence in America's cosmic mission. Moral dilemmas tended to be confronted from a liberal perspective. The extraterrestrial Mr Spock's pointed ears and the simple but recurrent dematerialization effects endeared the programme to viewers in many countries. This long-running serial had been anticipated in Britain by the evergreen *Doctor Who*, launched by the BBC in 1963; originally aimed at children, this soon conquered audiences within a broad spectrum of age and status. The ongoing tale of an eccentric doctor who travels through time and space in the Tardis, his supertechnological spacecraft disguised as a police box, proved to be highly marketable around the world and built up a devoted following. Thus, a Doctor Who Convention held in Chicago in 1982 drew as many as 10,000 fans. Until its demise in 1986, the serial adapted to evolving audience requirements by periodic changes of writers and of actors playing the lead.

The most important of the lighter sorts of television drama is situation comedy – sitcom for short. Its format is based on the need to spin (often initially an unpredictable number of) episodes out of a more or less constant situation. Its ancestor is radio comedy with its weekly instalments. In a sitcom a group of people assembled within a fixed framework (family, workplace, pub, corner grocery shop or boarding-house) are made to strike sparks from each other: the performers' personalities are the key to success. Though normally close to reality, with some inevitable stereotyping, it may well verge on farce; John Cleese's misadventures as the manic hotel owner of *Fawlty Towers* (BBC, 1975–9) were pure latter-day FEYDEAU.

American sitcoms, usually backed by the deplorable device of the 'laugh track', have often been built around a female character. CBS starred the effervescent and indestructible Lucille Ball in *I Love Lucy* (1951–5), *The Lucy Show* (1962–8) and *Here's Lucy* (1968–73). The *Mary Tyler Moore Show* (CBS, 1970–4) focused on a bachelor girl working in a TV station newsroom; it produced two more woman-based series – *Phyllis* and *Rhoda* – among several other spin-offs. *The Golden Girls* (NBC, from 1985) are a group of irrepressible middle-class old-age pensioners in Miami; *Roseanne* (ABC, from 1988) features Roseanne Barr as an equally irrepressible working-class wife.

In Britain sitcom had its first flowering in the prickly (and alas, self-destructive) Tony Hancock. *Hancock's Half Hour*, scripted by Alan Simpson and Ray Galton, produced notable delights on radio as well as BBC television between 1954 and 61; *The Blood Donor* (1961) is a fondly remembered classic. In the same co-authors' *Steptoe and Son* (BBC, 1964–73), a rag-and-bone man bickered incessantly with his son and partner. In Johnny Speight's *Till Death Us Do Part* (BBC, 1966–74), the preposterous views of Alf Garnett, a working-class reactionary played by Warren Mitchell, were held up to ridicule. Archie Bunker, his counterpart in the American adaptation, *All in the Family* (CBS, 1971–9), though equally foul-mouthed was more of a wisecracker. At the other end of the social spectrum, Antony Jay and Jonathan Lynn's *Yes, Minister* (BBC, 1980–5) gave a rare view of the Whitehall corridors of power, allegedly very close to the real thing. In the sequel *Yes, Prime Minister* (1986–9), its politician hero Jim Hacker's rise in status allowed him to win the odd round against his antagonist, top civil servant Sir Humphrey Appleby – while still generally losing out as he had done before.

A subdivision of sitcom found on both sides of the Atlantic is the military comedy. *You'll Never Get Rich* (CBS, 1955–8) featured Phil Silvers as the tireless schemer Sgt Bilko. *Hogan's Heroes* (CBS, 1961–71) was set in a German POW camp during the Second World War. Jimmy Perry and David Croft's *Dad's Army* (BBC, 1967–77) poked fun at an ineffectual but lovable Home Guard platoon which went through the motions of guarding England against the Nazi invader. *M*A*S*H* (CBS, 1972–83), a medical-cum-army sitcom, was set in a medical army surgical hospital during the Korean War. The war lasted three years; *M*A*S*H* ran for 11. When the last of its 251 episodes went out in the USA it was watched by 125 million viewers. Its star Alan Alda allegedly earned $30 million from syndication alone. Robert Altman, the maker of the film on which the series was based, disapproved of it as 'the most insidious kind of propaganda'. However, *M*A*S*H* did manage at times to go beyond mere blood-and-guts comedy and strike a truly disturbing note.

A similar glorious finale in terms of viewing figures was scored by *Cheers* (Paramount Television for NBC, 1982–93). With a run as long as that of its military predecessor, this sharply written sitcom based on a group of regulars in a Boston bar collected as many as 26 Emmys.

The soap opera A genre of American derivation but of truly universal appeal is the soap opera, so called because its radio predecessor in the 1930s was mainly sponsored by soap powder firms. Its hold on the American public is such that addicts can read a *Soap Opera Digest* or dial a 24-hour 'Soap by Phone' service to bring themselves up to date on any episodes they might have missed. In 1979 there were as many as 12 soaps a day on tap. This family- or community-based type of narrative has a beginning but no end, and hence no middle: Aristotle would not have approved. A soap opera dies of inanition rather than for any dramaturgical reasons. Its tone is a mixture of the melodramatic and the mundane. Viewer identification is essential, hence narrative time and viewing time generally coincide: when it is Christmas in the story it is actually Christmastime. A common feature is the interweaving of several narrative strands in any one instalment so as to keep track of the group as a whole. Cliffhanger endings characterize not only the end of episodes but even the moment before the commercial breaks: the viewer must not be let off the hook.

With their Hollywood gloss, American soaps have lathered their way into the hearts of much of mankind. Perhaps none has had a greater impact than *Dallas*, made by Lorimar for CBS (1978–82), with an international audience of some 300 million viewers. The feuding among the Ewing family, Texan oil multimillionaires, kept the telemasses spellbound, unmoved by *Variety*'s judgement: 'Basically it has all the trashy elements people want from this kind of fare.' The shooting of the baddie, J. R. Ewing, hyped by a lavish publicity campaign, echoed around the world. Other soaps in tycoon country satisfied a similar appetite. *Dynasty* (ABC, 1981–9) was also set in an oil-rich family, British-born Joan Collins playing Alexis, the woman you love to hate. The show's weekly wardrobe budget alone came to $10,000. The battle for power in *Falcon Crest* (Lorimar for CBS, 1981–90) was located in the wine country of Northern California.

In Britain, too, soap opera had its roots in RADIO – serials like *Mrs Dale's Diary* (1948–69) and *The Archers*, broadcast daily since 1 January 1951. British soap opera keeps some grip on social and regional realities. While the suburban lower-middle-class *Grove Family* (BBC, 1953–6) led the way, quite the greatest success among British soap operas (though its makers reject the label) has been *Coronation Street*, the Granada serial with a Lancashire working-class setting. Launched on 9 December 1960, it was originally scheduled to run for a mere 13 weeks – but it just never stopped. The Rovers Return must be the best-known pub in the country; the fame of Bet Lynch, Elsie Tanner and Hilda Ogden rivals that of royalty. The biographies of the saga's characters are chronicled by an archivist for the benefit of succeeding generations of scriptwriters. Studiously contemporary in external detail, *Coronation Street* plays on nostalgia for older, more settled values. Throughout the 1980s, viewing figures oscillated around the 16 million mark; a matrimonial cliffhanger in February 1983 clocked up an audience of 29 million.

Crossroads (ATV/Central, 1964–87) also counted its followers in millions, but it never enjoyed the critical esteem of *Coronation Street. Emmerdale Farm* (Yorkshire TV, since 1972) combines studio work with location shooting in the country. The village where its exteriors are filmed has become a tourist mecca. Scottish Television joined the chorus in 1980 with *Take the High Road*. Merseyside Television's *Brookside*, broadcast on Channel 4 since 1982, has a decidedly topical look. Shot on location in an actual housing estate near Liverpool, it has confronted down-to-earth problems such as unemployment and rape. *EastEnders* (BBC, from 1985, created by Julia Smith and Tony Holland) has made Albert Square the Cockney equivalent of Coronation Street. The viewing figures of this serial rival those of its Northern elder brother.

Australia, too, has its soap operas. The middle-class appeal of *Neighbours* works its charm not only at home but overseas as well, e.g. on as many as 14 million viewers in Britain.

Soap opera is, of course, not confined to the English-speaking world. A soapy flavour is found in much of Egypt's TV drama. The more popular programmes are known as 'street cleaners' because crowds tend to disappear off the streets during transmission times. Though the Egyptian state broadcasting company ERT takes a good deal of foreign, chiefly American, material it also turns out or commissions from local independent producers a large volume of TV drama. The first country in Africa to have colour TV, which was introduced in 1971, Egypt enjoys a great advantage: it has had a fully established film industry since well before the Second World War, and television can draw on a pool of creative and technical talent. Being far and away the strongest producer of TV drama in the Arab world, it exports a great many programmes to other Arabic-speaking countries. Egyptian soap operas pose no political or moral challenges. In addition to tales of everyday life, ERT also presents serials with a patriotic or religious thrust: for several years it filled the screens during the month of Ramadan with 30-part serials on the lives of the prophets, ending the cycle with a lavishly mounted biography of Mohammed himself.

In some countries soap opera may be more than mere entertainment. Thus, *Cockcrow at Dawn*, broadcast by the Nigerian Television Authority since 1980, was the story of the Bello family, country folk who fail to adapt to city life and return to the land where they settle down as small farmers. Without being overtly didactic, the serial has slipped in practical hints about modern farming methods.

There is a vast and eager public for soap operas in Japan. NHK puts out a 15-minute 'novel serial' at 8.15 a.m. from Monday to Saturday – a form of breakfast television watched by nearly 50 per cent of the viewing audience. This daily dose of soap differs from the continuous serial *proprement dit* in that it normally runs for only six months at a time. The kind of Japanese serial termed 'home drama' frequently features plucky women who keep the family together – like *Mother Intrepid* (TBS, 1968–72), in which the owner of a noodle shop was felt to typify the warmhearted hardworking Japanese mother. *O-Shin* (1983) was not perhaps classical soap opera in that it was set in the Meiji era rather than in the present; but this MELODRAMA of a woman from a poor farming background who achieves success after countless tribulations became a national obsession quite in the manner of soap opera. The very name of the heroine came to stand for patience and endurance. This serial was exported to China and South East Asia; it made a particularly strong impact on Iranian TV. NHK's *taiga* drama shares with soap opera not so much a contemporary theme as an extended running time. Each play lasts for one whole year – from January to December in a regular 45-minute Sunday night slot. However, far from being the identification figures of

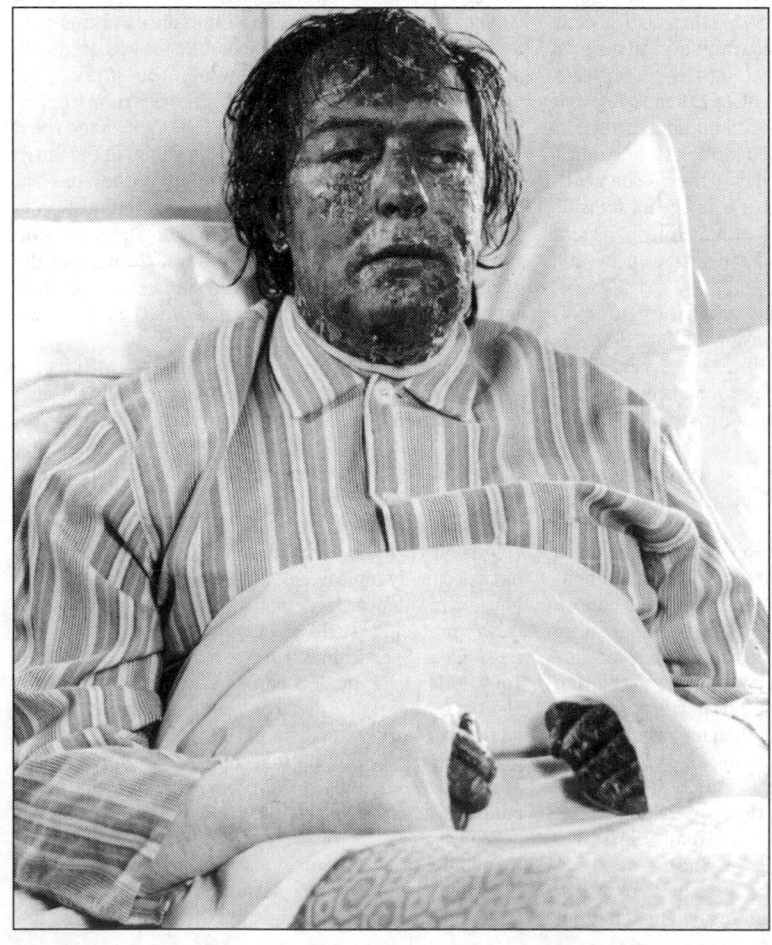

Michael Gambon as Philip Marlow in Dennis Potter's *The Singing Detective*, BBC TV.

home drama, the subjects tend to be characters who have played a leading role in Japanese history.

Televisa, the major private network in Mexico, has used the Latin American parallel to such long-running serials, the *telenovela* – but for very contemporary and indeed didactic purposes. *Come with Me* (1974–5) conducted a literacy campaign in story form; *Join with Me* (1977–8) advocated birth control, allegedly with tangible results. Other Mexican *telenovelas* have dealt with the status of women in a macho society and with teenage sex education.

Initially Mexico was the chief producer of *telenovelas*, exporting them to other Latin American countries; in the 1970s Brazil was to sprint into the lead. Brazil's high illiteracy rate has given a peculiar importance to television drama. TV Tupi, a São Paolo station which has since gone out of business, launched *Beto Rockefeller* in 1968, the tale of a poor man who makes his way to the top. Fantasies of social climbing were to be a major ingredient of the genre. *Telenovela* authors became national figures; the funeral of one of the best-known of these, Janete Clair, was a great public occasion watched by millions on television. The length of *telenovelas* is prodigious: Dias Gomes's *The Well Beloved*, the saga of politics in a town in Bahia, ran for 177 episodes, Gilberto Braga's *Dancin' Days*, which was set in a discotheque, for 174. Brazilian *telenovelas* are close to the traditional soap opera in that they are constantly evolving, new episodes being written in response to viewer reactions.

The chief purveyor of these is the Globo TV Network – the world's fourth largest. This family enterprise developed out of a newspaper founded in 1925 and a radio station started in 1944. Now the Globo TV Network, which began broadcasting in 1965, is part of an immensely powerful communications empire: it includes book and magazine publishing, music recording as well as home video production. With a TV drama output of feature-film proportions, Globo is far from indifferent to quality: it employs leading writers, directors, designers and musicians. It has as many as 500 actors on staff or under contract. In 1993 it opened Latin America's largest production centre in Rio de Janeiro. Its serials achieve viewing figures of up to 50 million – more Brazilians having access to a TV screen than to clean drinking water. Some of the subjects of these serials, not all of which can really be termed soap operas, boldly plunge into controversy. *Gabriela*, a feminist story based on a Jorge Amado novel, proved enormously popular not only at home but also in Portugal – where a bishop denounced it for subverting the family. *The Woman Malu* showed a middle-class divorcee who comes to question many of society's dominant values. The mini-series, *Rebel Years*, which dealt with the protest movements of the 1960s, inspired a new generation of students to take to the streets. The fact that Globo exports its telefilms to more than 80 countries suggests that US (and even UK) preponderance in the world market for TV drama is not written on tablets of stone.

Indeed, the American industry has been transformed rapidly in the last two decades of the 20th century. All the Big Three networks changed hands in the 1980s, their new ownership more attuned to a tough-minded corporate culture than ever; and a great many old-established media corporations went out of business. But this was merely part of a worldwide media revolution. The boundaries in which regulations used to flourish can easily be leapt over by satellite broadcasting; the use of videocassettes has meant that wider consumer choice has partially replaced drama seen only as and when broadcast. Interactive television-on-demand is a technical possibility. The interconnectedness of the various TV systems has more and more taken the shape of co-productions, at any rate in the case of high-budget prestige serials. This has obvious advantages, but it may well threaten the national flavour of drama.

'Quality' television Although British television was to find itself under increasing pressure during the 80s, partly from a worsening economic climate and partly from the attitude of a government unsympathetic to the public-service ethos, a good many outstanding programmes were achieved nevertheless. Financially strong enough to go in for large-scale prestige telefilms, Granada in 1981 presented a 13-episode adaptation (by John Mortimer) of Evelyn Waugh's *Brideshead Revisited*, which positively glittered with production values and stars of the calibre of CLAIRE BLOOM, JOHN GIELGUD and LAURENCE OLIVIER; it followed this up in 1984 with the equally dazzling 14-episode *The Jewel in the Crown*, based on Paul Scott's 'Raj Quartet'. The latter serial tackled a delicate subject, the last days of British rule in India, with considerable complexity and a wealth of narrative detail. The BBC's blockbuster reply to all this came in 1987 with *The Fortunes of War*, the adaptation (by ALAN PLATER) of Olivia Manning's 'Balkan Trilogy' and 'Levant Trilogy'. This serial, which brought the actors KENNETH BRANAGH and Emma Thompson to prominence, was, however, a co-production with two American companies.

Equally notable, though in a wholly different key, was ALAN BLEASDALE's 5-episode *Boys from the Blackstuff* (BBC, 1982). In this angry, compassionate study of a group of unemployed Liverpool workers and their families, each man in turn came to the fore in successive episodes. The style moved from naturalism to something almost surreal in a desolate picture of society in the 1980s. The death of a militant old worker while being pushed in a wheelchair through the ruins of Liverpool's dockland sounded a requiem for a whole era. The series was universally praised. Not so Bleasdale's next BBC serial, *The Monocled Mutineer* (1986), a First World War story denounced by the right-wing press as less than respectful of the British Army. Other dissident productions that stood out in an increasingly conformist decade were Troy Kennedy Martin's *Edge of Darkness* (BBC, 1985), a police thriller which developed into a story of nuclear skulduggery, and Alan Plater's adaptation of a novel by Chris Mullin MP, *A Very British Coup* (Skreba for Channel 4, 1988), in which Establishment machinations against a possible Labour victory at the polls were unmasked.

Undeniably, television drama is a significant social phenomenon; but is it aesthetically significant? The bulk of it may be trivial; but then so is the bulk of stage plays and films. A critical problem is that popular and minority tastes, regrettably perhaps, tend to diverge. Both levels have their separate justification; both should ideally be catered for in a mass medium such as TV drama.

An outstanding German example of a serial which did

manage to do this – and at the same time to straddle the divide between cinema and TV – was Edgar Reitz's *Heimat* (*Homeland*; WDR, 1984). This 11-part, 16-hour epic, which follows the history from 1919 to 1982 of the Simon family and their neighbours in a fictitious village in the Hunsrück district, has the sweep and amplitude of a 19th-century novel. The result of some two years' location shooting in the area, *Heimat* places personal destinies in the wider context of the nation's history. Technological, political and social transformations shape the lives of the villagers, who are moved from a patriarchal lifestyle into the modern age. The sequel, *Die Zweite Heimat* (*Leaving Home*, 1992), is set in the 60s: an even longer epic, with a total running time of 26 hours, this shows the adventures of the younger generation whose homeland is no longer the village but the wider world of art.

Television drama may at times threaten to become socially enervating by its very quantity. Its essentially domestic appeal may be stripping dramatic performances of their former sense of festive occasion. But against that, plays that enter virtually every home can, in ideal circumstances, have the power to move a whole nation, or indeed many nations together. Constantly evolving, television drama is an ineluctable fact of contemporary life: a possible danger, perhaps, but a great opportunity for imaginative enrichment and deeper self-understanding if, collectively, that is what we choose to have. GWB

> See: G. W. Brandt (ed.), *British Television Drama*, Cambridge, 1981, and (ed.), *British Television Drama in the Eighties*, Cambridge, 1993; R. Dyer et al., *Coronation Street*, London, 1981; J. Ellis, *Visible Fictions/Cinema: Television: Video*, London, 1982; S. Kalter, *The Complete Book of M*A*S*H*, Bromley, 1984; H. Kingsley, *Soap Box: The Papermac Guide to Soap Opera*, London, 1988; B. Millington and R. Nelson, *'Boys from the Blackstuff': The Making of a TV Drama*, London, 1986; R. W. Stedman, *The Serial*, Oklahoma, 1977; G. Tibballs, *The Boxtree Encyclopedia of TV Detectives*, London, 1992; J. Tulloch, *Television Drama: Agency, Audience and Myth*, London, 1990.

Téllez, Gabriel see TIRSO DE MOLINA

Templeton, Fay 1865–1939 Favourite American actress of the MUSICAL COMEDY stage at the turn of the 20th century. Born in Little Rock, Arkansas, on Christmas Day, she appeared on stage as a child. She toured extensively with her parents, then joined WEBER AND FIELDS for four seasons, making a hit of the song, 'Rosey, You Are My Posey'. In 1905 she appeared in COHAN's *Forty-five Minutes from Broadway* as Mary, singing 'Mary Is a Grand Old Name', a huge success. She later appeared in GILBERT and Sullivan, retiring from the stage in 1931 after performing in *HMS Pinafore*. Templeton lived for a time in the Actors' Fund Home in Englewood, New Jersey, and died in San Francisco. SMA

Tennyson, Alfred, Lord 1809–92 British poet who, if his teenage fantasy *The Devil and the Lady* is discounted, completed his first play at the age of 65. This was *Queen Mary*, staged at the LYCEUM in 1876, with IRVING as Philip of Spain. A second historical verse drama, *Harold*, remained

unperformed until 1928, when LAURENCE OLIVIER took the title role in a production by the BIRMINGHAM REPERTORY Company at the ROYAL COURT in London. A third, *Becket*, was in rehearsal at the Lyceum when Tennyson died. It opened early in 1893, and the part of Becket remained in Irving's repertoire until the night of his death in Bradford, scarcely an hour after the curtain had rung down on Tennyson's play. Irving also provided *The Cup* – a short play that is nonetheless too long – with a lavish Lyceum production in 1881. But Tennyson's remaining three plays were staged in lesser theatres: the one-act *The Falcon*, by William and MADGE KENDAL at the ST JAMES's in 1879; the domestic tragedy in prose, *The Promise of May*, at the GLOBE in 1882 (the production was a fiasco); and *The Foresters* in a production by AUGUSTIN DALY at his own New York theatre in 1892. Only BYRON, among 19th-century poets, had a stage life to rival Tennyson. PT

tent show American style of theatrical presentation in which plays or VARIETY shows are trouped from community to community and staged under canvas. One of the earliest entrepreneurs was Fayette Lodowick 'Yankee' Robinson, whose touring company performed in the river towns of Iowa and Illinois in 1851; prosperity led him to switch from drama to CIRCUS. By the late 19th century, travelling troupes with repertories extensive enough to provide a week's worth of entertainment had become popular in the summer, when local opera houses were too poorly ventilated to attract the public. The influence of the CHAUTAUQUA circuit (lecture meetings of an educational or religious nature), with its portable theatres lit by naphtha lamps, was strong after 1904; its tents were brown to distinguish its educational purpose from the white tops of the circus. In France, FIRMIN GÉMIER had commissioned an elaborate canvas structure to house the tours of the Théâtre Antoine in 1911, but the average American show tent was limited to a width of 50 or 60 feet, with bare benches or bleachers and a platform stage designed for portability.

The earliest repertories were imitations, often pirated, of the standard dramatic fare, primarily MELODRAMA; but as these grew stale and COPYRIGHT laws stricter, tent showmen composed their own plays, carpentered to a limited company and the familiar themes of rural life. The standbys of this repertory include Charles Harrison's *Saintly Hypocrites and Honest Sinners* (1915) and W. C. Herman's *Call of the Woods*, which pitted homespun virtue against urban corruption. The comic character TOBY, developed c.1911, became the popular hero of these works, often partnered with the tomboy Susie and the eccentric known as the G-string character, a sage descendant of the stage YANKEE.

After the First World War, motor vehicles replaced rail transport, and tent shows proliferated, doubling their admission rate to 1 dollar. Some 400 shows were travelling through the USA by 1927, playing to an estimated audience of 78 million. But the catastrophic effect of the Depression and dust storms on the agricultural population led to a decline in the 'rag opries'. Price-cutting and unionization, the competition from local cinemas and inability to organize were also contributory factors to the closure of hundreds of long-standing companies in the

1930s. The FEDERAL THEATRE PROJECT absorbed many of these entertainers, and in the 1950s only some dozen troupes survived. In 1976 a revival of the Harley Sadler Show, one of the most prosperous in its time, was staged at Texas Tech University, which houses a Tent Show Collection. Another archive is the Museum of Repertoire Americana in Mount Pleasant, Iowa. LS

Ter-Arutunian, Rouben 1920–92 Armenian-American set and COSTUME designer; born in Russia, educated in Berlin 1927–43, emigrated to the USA in 1951. BROADWAY credits included *New Girl in Town* (1957), *Redhead* (1959; Tony for Best Costumes), *Advise and Consent* (1960), *The Milk Train Doesn't Stop Here Anymore* (1964), *Eh?* (1966), *Exit the King* (1968), *All Over* (1971) and *The Lady from Dubuque* (1980). In addition to theatre and OPERA, Ter-Arutunian designed for television in the 1950s (*Twelfth Night*, 1957, Emmy). His work fell primarily into two categories: 'decorative' (or painterly), such as his famous *Nutcracker* for the New York City Ballet; and sculptural, such as *Riceracare* for American Ballet Theatre. Ter-Arutunian preferred the latter style, which allowed him to create space around a minimal amount of scenery. He said that he designed 'visual counterpart to drama, poetry, music and movement ... with simplicity, clarity, and a certain element of mystery' AA

Terayama Shūji 1935–83 Innovative and controversial Japanese playwright, director and film-maker. Influenced by Lautréamont, Breton and Fellini, he was a true advocate of European-style avant-garde iconoclasm in Japan. His plays, from *Blood Sleeps Standing Up* (*Chi wa tatta mama nemutte iru*, 1957) through *Heretic's Gate* (*Jashūmon*, 1971), *Knock: Street Theatre* (*Nokku*, 1975; trans. 1992) and *Directions for Servants* (*Nuhikun*, 1978), were meant above all to shock the bourgeoisie. In 1967 he founded the Upper Gallery (Tenjō Sajiki) troupe, which he directed in performances in Europe as well as Japan. DGG

Terence [Publius Terentius Afer] c.184–159 BC Roman comic dramatist. A number of alleged biographical details are preserved, but they must be treated with caution. He is said to have been a freed slave from Carthage; to have associated with aristocratic and cultured philhellenes in the circle of Scipio Aemilianus; and to have been killed in his 25th (or 35th) year on a journey to Greece or Asia.

The six plays which survive appear to be all he ever wrote. They are *Andria* (*The Girl from Andros*, 166 BC); *Hecyra* (*The Mother-in-Law*, performed unsuccessfully in 165, then once unsuccessfully and once successfully in 160); *Heauton Timoroumenos* (*The Self-Tormentor*, 163); *Eunuchus* (*The Eunuch*, 161); *Phormio* (161); and *Adelphoe* (*The Brothers*, 160). *Hecyra* and *Phormio* were adapted from plays by Apollodorus of Carystus, who was a follower of MENANDER, the others from plays by Menander himself.

The broad and farcical humour which PLAUTUS had introduced into his plays was largely eliminated by Terence, who sought to bring Menandrean restraint and refinement to Roman comedy. While *Eunuchus* and *Adelphoe* contain farcical scenes, and *Phormio* has a clever trickster as its central character, the humour of Terence's work is generally a subtle consequence of the interplay of character and situation. *Hecyra*, indeed, is a largely serious and realistic exploration of domestic difficulties, with little, apart from the happy ending, to qualify it as a comedy at all.

Terence was not a mere translator, however, but tried in various ways to improve on his Greek models. For one thing, he dispensed with the expository Prologue which Menander had used to set the scene. Thus some details of the initial situation are not revealed at all (so that the element of suspense and surprise is increased, at the expense of dramatic irony), while others are revealed through dialogue. All the plays do in fact possess prologues, but these were not always written for the first performance, and stand entirely outside the drama (two, indeed, are explicitly written for delivery by the actor-manager who championed Terence's work, Lucius Ambivius Turpio). They serve the special purpose of explaining Terence's aims, complaining of the audience's past failure to appreciate his work, and replying to the attacks of a jealous rival, one Luscius Lanuvinus. The prologues are thus of great interest as revealing a new artistic self-consciousness and affording a glimpse of the theatrical conditions of the period.

Luscius had alleged that Terence's style was thin; that he had plagiarized other Latin plays; that he had received help from aristocratic friends; and that he had 'spoiled' many Greek comedies by inserting scenes or characters from one into a play otherwise based on another. Terence's reply to the last charge is surprisingly defensive: in mixing his sources he is doing no more than Naevius, Plautus and ENNIUS had done (see ROME), and he prefers their 'carelessness' to pedantic fidelity to his source. The actual extent of the mixing has been much debated, for Terence's plays are certainly not the scissors-and-paste work which his prologues might suggest; and it is now generally agreed that the four Menandrean plays, at least, have been substantially reworked. A simple case, where Terence's motive is clear, is that of *Andria*: the play concerns a young man's efforts to marry the girl he loves instead of the wife his father intends for him, but Terence (unlike Menander) provides the latter girl with a suitor of her own, so as to give the play a rudimentary subplot and ensure a happy ending for all.

While self-conscious moralizing is avoided, the plays have a distinctly high-minded tone. Most characters try to act for the best; their problems are held up for sympathy rather than ridicule, and their foibles are exposed with genial tolerance. Terence shows insight and understanding in his portrayal of women, and has a particular interest in relations between fathers and sons. The 'humanity' for which he is famous can now be seen to be largely an inheritance from Menander, but it is at least an inheritance which he preserved intact, to be passed on to such admirers as MOLIÈRE.

Unlike Plautus, Terence has perhaps had more success with readers than with audiences. The wholesomeness of his plays and the purity of his Latin ensured that he was a favourite author for school use, both among the Romans and in more recent times. A commentary by the 4th-century grammarian Donatus preserves useful information about Terence's sources. ALB

Terriss, William [William Charles James Lewin] 1847–97 English actor, the son of a barrister. He made his professional debut in Birmingham in 1868 and was briefly with the BANCROFTS at the PRINCE OF WALES'S in 1869. Terriss found it difficult to choose between the stage and an outdoor life (he had been briefly a merchant seaman and a tea-planter in Assam), and from 1869 to 71 he was a sheep farmer in the Falkland Islands, where his daughter, the actress Ellaline Terriss (1871–1971), was born. The rest of his life belongs to the English stage, where his first significant success was as Squire Thornhill to ELLEN TERRY'S Olivia in W. G. WILLS's sentimental dramatization of GOLDSMITH's *The Vicar of Wakefield*. He repeated the part at the end of his five-year engagement with IRVING at the LYCEUM (1880–5), during which he also played Cassio in *Othello*, Laertes in *Hamlet*, Mercutio in *Romeo and Juliet* and Orsino in *Twelfth Night*. He returned to the Lyceum in 1892 to play the King in Irving's lavish production of *Henry VIII*. But Terriss found his natural home at the ADELPHI, where, after 1885, he featured in a succession of muscular MELODRAMAS, beginning with *The Harbour Lights* (1885), by George R. Sims and Henry Pettit. Terriss's swashbuckling athleticism earned him the nickname of 'Breezy Bill', and there was no subtlety about his acting. He was, however, immensely popular and widely mourned when a deranged fellow actor stabbed him to death outside the stage door of the Adelphi. PT

Terry, Edward (O'Connor) 1844–1912 British actor, who worked in the provinces from 1863 to 67 and who made his London reputation in BURLESQUE at the Strand from 1869 to 76. JOHN HOLLINGSHEAD took him to the GAIETY in 1876, and from then until 1883 he was NELLIE FARREN's rival as the leading member of the Gaiety Quartette (KATE VAUGHAN and EDWARD ROYCE were the others). In 1888 he opened Terry's Theatre in the Strand, creating there the part of the good-hearted drunkard Dick Phenyl in PINERO's immensely popular (and immensely sentimental) *Sweet Lavender* (1888). Terry was an eccentric comedian, famous for his self-transformations through make-up. Having sold his theatre for conversion to a cinema in 1910, he spent his last active years on a world tour in his most famous comedy and burlesque roles. PT

Terry, Ellen (Alice) 1847–1928 British actress, the second daughter of a theatrical family. Hurried into the theatre – she played Mamillius for CHARLES KEAN at the

PRINCESS's in 1856 and toured in a programme of sketches with her elder sister Kate in 1859–61 – she was also jostled into an unfortunate marriage with the artist George Frederick Watts in 1864. A contemporary photograph by Julia Cameron gives surer evidence than such canvases as Watts's *Choosing* of her extraordinary beauty (an unusual mixture of innocence and opulence) at this time. Sadly at odds with Watts, she returned to the theatre, playing, among other parts, the 'shrew' to IRVING's Petruchio at the Queen's (1867). Irving considered her charming but frivolous. She was already contemplating a liaison with the married architect E. W. Godwin, a deeper relationship than she achieved in any of her three marriages. They lived together in the Hertfordshire countryside from 1868 until 1875 and had two extraordinary children who came to be known in the theatre as EDITH CRAIG and GORDON CRAIG. Their different effects on Ellen Terry's life are a story in themselves.

Her return to the theatre was negotiated by CHARLES READE, who needed a replacement for MRS JOHN WOOD in his Tichborne claimant play, *The Wandering Heir* (1874). In 1875, she made her first major Shakespearian appearance, as Portia in the BANCROFTS' production of *The Merchant of Venice*. The apparent spontaneity of her verse-speaking, a natural ability to record the processes as well as the product of reflection, would continue to charm audiences for 50 years. In 1878, having just seen Terry playing the sentimental title role in W. G. WILLS's *Olivia* (this version of GOLDSMITH's *The Vicar of Wakefield* was still in her repertoire 30 years later), Irving hesitantly invited her to join him at the LYCEUM, where she remained for 25 years and was

Ellen Terry, 1864, photographed by Julia Margaret Cameron.

recognized as the leading actress of the English stage. She was Irving's Ophelia (1878), Portia (1879), Desdemona (1881), Juliet (1882), Beatrice (1882), Viola (1884), Lady Macbeth (1888), Queen Katharine (1892), Cordelia (1892), Imogen (1896) and Volumnia (1901), but never his Rosalind, since *As You Like It* had no satisfactory part for him. It was this imbalance, her agreement to play second fiddle, that antagonized GEORGE BERNARD SHAW and that underlay his long and loving correspondence with Terry (published in 1931). She would eventually play the part Shaw wrote for her as Lady Cicely Waynflete in *Captain Brassbound's Conversion* (1906).

By then Irving was dead, and Terry herself had tried a spell of management in her own right, at the Imperial, where she staged IBSEN's *The Vikings* (1903) in sets designed by her son, Gordon Craig. The production was a costly failure. Partly to recoup her losses and partly to keep the improvident Craig in pocket, Terry played Hermione for BEERBOHM TREE at His [Her] MAJESTY's (1906). It was her last Shakespearian role. In her retirement home in Smallhythe, she completed an autobiography, *The Story of My Life* (1908), and prepared the series of lectures on SHAKESPEARE's heroines that became a regular part of her programme from 1910 to 21. She also appeared, unflatteringly, in five silent films between 1916 and 1921. In 1925, when the Godwin scandal had died away, and four years after GENEVIÈVE WARD had been the first actress so honoured, Terry was appointed DBE. Few stage personalities have ever been so loved.

Benjamin Terry (1818–96) fathered a veritable theatrical dynasty. Three of Ellen's sisters, Kate (1844–1924), Marion (1852–1930) and Florence (1855–96), had distinguished stage careers, as did her brother Fred (1864–1932) and a multitude of great-nephews, -nieces and grandchildren, of whom JOHN GIELGUD is the best-known. PT

Terson [Patterson]**, Peter** 1932– British dramatist, who worked as a teacher for ten years before his first play, *A Night to Make the Angels Weep* (1964), was produced at the VICTORIA THEATRE, Stoke-on-Trent. This play, together with *The Mighty Reservoy* (1964), revealed him to be an amusing observer of life in the Midlands and the North, with the instinctive ability to seize on a symbolic idea, raising NATURALISM towards myth. He became resident dramatist at Stoke's Victoria Theatre in 1966 and wrote prolifically for that company, collaborating with Joyce Cheeseman to adapt ARNOLD BENNETT's novel, *Clayhanger*, for the stage in 1967. Several of Terson's plays transferred in the 1960s and 1970s to the little theatres around London, including *Mooney and his Caravans* (1968), and *Zigger Zagger* (1967), about football fans and hooligans, written for the NATIONAL YOUTH THEATRE where it was an instant and often-repeated success. *The Apprentices* (1968), *Spring Heeled Jack* (1970) and *Good Lads at Heart* (1971) were also written for the NYT. Terson's good humour and ability to conjure up well observed situations and settings have made him a popular writer in the North, but not so well received in London, where his only WEST END success has been with *Strippers* (1984), about unemployed women who take to stripping in pubs to earn some pocket money. JE

Tesfaye Gessesse 1937– Ethiopian playwright, actor and director. Tesfaye performed as an amateur actor in Ethiopia before studying drama in the USA. Returning in 1960, he worked as a director at the Haile Selassie I Theatre in Addis Ababa and at the University of Addis Ababa Cultural Centre. After the 1974 revolution he took charge of the AGER FIKIR Theatre, and in 1976 assumed control of the National Theatre. His efforts to improve actors' working conditions led to his being sacked in 1983. In 1989 he was appointed chairman of the Theatre Arts Department at Addis Ababa University, but was removed and imprisoned for a short time when the Marxist government was overthrown in 1991. Tesfaye has written several plays, including *Yeshi*, which brought the question of urban prostitution to the fore; and after the 1974 revolu-

tion, *Iqaw* (1975) and *Tehaddiso* (*Renaissance*, 1979), concerned with issues of state coercion. JPL

Teternikov, F. K. see SOLOGUB, FYODOR

Thacker, David 1950– British director, whose early Shakespearian productions, including a university *Pericles* which toured prisons before arriving triumphantly at the EDINBURGH FESTIVAL, established his reputation as a communicator and a fine interpreter of the text. He studied at the University of York, where he became the president of the Drama Society; and joined the Theatre Royal, York, as an assistant stage manager before being appointed assistant director in 1975. In 1978 he established the Rolling Stock Theatre company, a touring YOUNG PEOPLE'S THEATRE group, and was appointed director of the Duke's Playhouse in Lancaster in 1980. In 1984 he became the director of the YOUNG VIC in London, established by FRANK DUNLOP in 1968 as an experimental wing of the NATIONAL THEATRE company. The Young Vic had an eminent history and a ramshackle appearance; but under Thacker's leadership it became the best place in London to take students of all ages to see intelligent SHAKESPEARES. His own productions included *Othello* and *Macbeth* (1984), *Hamlet* and *Measure for Measure* (1985), *Julius Caesar* (1986) and *Romeo and Juliet* (1987). It was no coincidence that his theatre was chosen in 1986 to stage an International Association of Theatre Critics conference to celebrate the 25th anniversary of JAN KOTT's book, *Shakespeare Our Contemporary*.

Thacker is also adept at directing modern plays with challenging themes, particularly from the USA. His production of IBSEN's *Ghosts* (1986) with VANESSA REDGRAVE transferred to the WEST END and was nominated for the KENNETH TYNAN Outstanding Achievement Award from the Society of West End Theatres. His revival of ARTHUR MILLER's *The Crucible* (1985) led to a special relationship with the author. At the Young Vic, he directed the world premieres of *Two-Way Mirror* (1989) and *The Last Yankee* (1993), which transferred to the West End. His success at the Young Vic led to offers from the national companies. In 1989, he directed *Pericles* for the ROYAL SHAKESPEARE COMPANY's Swan Theatre at Stratford-upon-Avon, a production which won a Laurence Olivier Award in 1990 for the Outstanding Revival of the Year. This led to mainstage RSC productions of *As You Like It*, *The Merry Wives of Windsor* and *Two Gentlemen of Verona* in 1992. The latter production included popular songs from the 1930s and was a box-office hit.

Thacker was appointed director in residence at the RSC, where three of his productions were seen in the 1993–4 season – *The Merchant of Venice*, *Julius Caesar* (on tour) and *Two Gentlemen of Verona*. His handling of the texts sometimes seems to be compromised by the need to enlarge his productions to the scale required from big stages. But he has clearly demonstrated that his skills are not limited to small theatres and student audiences, and commands respect as a major European director. JE

Thailand Thailand (formerly Siam) is a Southeast Asian country bordering on Malaysia, Burma, Laos and Cambodia. Its population is a mixture of hill tribes and lowlanders. Malays of the southern provinces have been significant in shaping Thai dramatic practice, while Lao peoples in the northeast and Chinese Thais enjoy performances comparable to those found in LAOS and southern CHINA respectively.

Theraveda Buddhism was adopted by the early Thai. Today this belief, mixed with indigenous animism and Brahmanism-Hinduism, is held by 95 per cent of the population. Dance and dramatic performances may first have evolved in conjunction with religious practice at the village level, and rural performances continue to be a regular part of religious festivals. The emergence of the Thai as a political force on the peninsula began in the 13th century, but artistic ascendency came only after the capture of the Khmer (Cambodian) kingdom of Angkor in 1431, an event which cemented the Thai predilection for adopting Khmer arts. Expertly trained musicians and harem wives-dancers of the Khmer king's household were carried into exile. This ready-made performance tradition was developed in Thailand over following generations, with many monarchs and princesses becoming accomplished poets or performers of dance-drama texts. This expanded tradition became, in turn, the model for the Burmese court theatre (see BURMA), when the Burmese seized the Thai court wives-dancers and musicians during the sack of Ayutthaya, the Thai capital, in 1767. Later the Thais returned the CAMBODIAN loan of artistry with interest, for much of the repertoire which the Khmer court adopted in the 19th century seems borrowed from Thai court models of that time.

The current music, performance practice and repertoire of the Thai theatre are related to pan-Southeast-Asian patterns. The major theatre types are: (1) village animist-influenced performances; (2) court forms; (3) modern popular genres; and (4) modern spoken drama.

Village animist-influenced performances Dance offerings to the spirits have probably been carried out from the early period of Thai history. Even in modern Bangkok one can find temples where dancers regularly carry out performances commissioned by donors as offerings for some boon granted. Dancers emulate the costume and dance style of the court forms. Pure dance is standard and occasionally dramatic episodes or whole plays may be presented. A mixture of animistic, Hindu and Buddhist influences seems to underlie these practices. Although most performances discussed hereafter are for audience entertainment rather than such ritual purposes, it is significant that much theatre continues to be presented in the context of temple festivals.

The earliest known drama in Thailand, *nora* (also *mano-ra*), may have originated in village performances connected with animist–Buddhist practice in the ethnically Malay south around the 14th century. This early form is still extant in the area around Nakhon Sri Thammarat, the site of the old Malay Buddhist kingdom of Ligor, which became part of Thailand in the 14th century. The form seems to have evolved practices that affected later theatrical genres. The traditional all-male troupe included three actors: prince, princess and a clown who enacted the other roles, including ogres and monkeys, and often wore a mask for these characterizations. A performance included a musical prelude, an opening incantation, solo dances, songs, skits and finally a play.

The legendary origin of the form hints at a possible relationship with female spirit-mediums: a Thai princess, Nuensamli, was possessed by a god, and her crazed activity caused her family to cast her out. She gave birth to a son, who learned dance by watching *kinnari* (mythical bird-women); the son magically created a clown from a rock; and a god became incarnate to become the third performer of the genre. The Manora story, believed to be the only one presented in the early period of the form, may be further evidence of the relationship with spiritually empowered women. Manora is a bird-woman (*kinnari*), who takes off her wings to bathe and has them stolen by a hunter, Bun. He takes her to the prince, Suton, who marries her, but true love is complicated when a minister turns the people against her in the prince's absence. At the moment Manora is to be executed, she borrows her wings for one last dance, and thus escapes to her mountain home. Her faithful husband follows her there, proving his devotion.

This bird-woman story, seen in mainland Southeast Asia as a *Jataka* (tale of a previous life of the Buddha), is known in many cultures. Its pattern gains greater significance when seen in relation to later plots, such as *Rothasen*, in which a young prince strives to find a cure for his mother's blindness. He marries the stepdaughter of an ogress, who teaches him the cure, but then abandons the love-stricken maid to return home. She dies cursing him to be the lovelorn one when they meet in a future life.

Both plot patterns and the *nora* origin myth associate men with women who are possessed, powerful or semi-divine. They may be evidence that *nora* was originally a male performance form that evolved from female-spirit-medium dances of divination. Such trance dances are still found in Burma, where two princes emulating female mediums in the 1400s are the alleged origin of Burmese drama. The two reports may be variants on a theme: female mediums' trance rites become the model for male artists' performance practice.

In times past *nora* was commonly called *lakon jatri*. *Lakon* means 'play' and *jatri* 'sorcerer'; troupe heads were felt to have great spiritual power and were called on for exorcisms, ordinations and other ceremonies. It is said these sorcerers would enchant their audiences so that viewers would follow from performance to performance. Though magic still creates an aura around the form, changes have occurred. Current performers may be of either sex, a troupe is larger than three actors and a vaudeville format prevails. By 1972 this genre had been transformed: singers in Western costume crooned romantic lyrics to Western band accompaniment and skits and comic routines abounded.

If the tradition dies out, it will be the end of an art which may explain patterns which underlie human drama in Thailand. The three-person configuration may be the source of the role types that dominate Thai theatre. The male (*phra*), the female (*nang*), ogre (*yak*) and monkey (*ling*) are the types into which all traditional roles are divided. The first two correspond to the hero and heroine of the *nora*, and the last two in court dance are always masked (resulting, perhaps, from the fact that in *nora* they were performed by a single person alternating masks). More research might clarify how *nora* relates to mask dance genres like INDONESIA's *topeng* and how character types common to most theatres in the Southeast Asian region may be linked to these masked dance forms. The most important *nora* artist today is Thongbai Roungnon.

A now defunct theatre form which developed out of the *nora* and pleased audiences through the first decades of this century is *lakon nok* (literally, 'play outside [the palace]'). It originated in the same southern area, and was introduced in the Bangkok region. An expanded cast and orchestra, and more secular emphasis, characterized the form. As in *nora*, dance and music were components, but in *lakon nok* the dialogue, action and comedy gained in significance.

Initially *lakon nok* troupes were all-male, but by the mid-19th century women began playing female roles as women from the palace tradition were allowed to perform in public. Eventually the *lakon nok* repertoire of Buddhist birth stories, local histories and legendary tales was emulated in court theatricals, and this expropriation has saved the form from complete extinction. Performances in *lakon-nok* style are occasionally staged by the National Theatre in Bangkok today, in a style style less lively and risqué than in the past.

Court forms Court performance, consisting of *nang yai* ('large leather puppets'), *khon* ('mask dance drama'), and *lakon fai nai* ('female dance drama'), is derived from Cambodian court arts of the 15th century, but scholars debate the extent of Khmer impact. Cambodia currently boasts equivalents of all three forms, and origins of all Thai court genres might date from 1431, when the Thai captured Angkor. But many scholars feel that what was taken differed substantially from current practice, and that the close similarity of Thai and Khmer classical theatre in the current era results from Thai influence on Cambodian arts in the 19th century.

It seems reasonable to assume that the Khmer equivalent of *nang yai*, called *nang sbek thom*, was already in existence. Although the 1458 Thai Palatine Law is the first extant reference to the mutually shared form, the Khmer had been influenced by Indonesia where SHADOW PUPPETRY, masked dance and female non-dramatic dance were venerable court traditions.

Nang yai is a shadow and silhouette play performed with large, incised, two-dimensional leather puppets manipulated by dancing puppeteers who move in front of and behind a wide white screen 30ft long and 10ft high. Two narrators called *khon pak* recite an episode from the Thai version of the *Ramayana* (*Ramakien*) to the accompaniment of a *piphat* orchestra, composed minimally of a double reed (*pi*), xylophone (*ranat ek*), barrel drum (*klong that*), cymbals (*ching*), gong chime (*khong wong yai*) and another type of barrel drum called *taphon*. Eventually, other stories were presented using *nang yai* technique, but these stories did not rival the popularity of the Rama material, which was put into literary form by Thai kings, notably Rama I, who ruled 1782–1809.

The main outline of the story follows the Indian epic. Rama, an incarnation of the god Vishnu, with the assistance of monkey warriors wins back his wife Sita who has

been kidnapped by the lustful demon king Ravana (Thai, Tosakanth). Variations from Indian material are apparent: for example, Sita is Ravana's daughter, abandoned as a child, and many new episodes are interpolated. Especially popular in the repertoire are dramatizations of these new episodes that deal with the amorous and martial exploits of Hanuman, Rama's monkey general. Typically Hanuman meets and marries a demon's beautiful daughter.

Similarities in story patterns may link *nang yai* to Indonesian *wayang* ('puppet theatre'). (Bengali versions of the *Ramayana* may be the ultimate source of the story materials used by both.) The centrality of a narrator or storyteller, the mode of introducing satire via the clowns, and the function of the orchestra within the performance are comparable as well. At the same time many techniques are unique to the Thai-Khmer court puppet tradition: the huge 4ft x 5ft puppets dwarf the 1ft–3ft puppets of Java. The depiction of multi-character scenes in a single puppet, and the need for multiple puppeteers who dance on both sides of the screen each carrying a single figure, are quite unlike the solo, stationary puppeteer mode of Indonesia and MALAYSIA, and lead some scholars to look for Indian models. In south INDIA, puppet forms are found in which multi-character scenes are represented, and multiple puppeteers are common. However, the aesthetic which allows the dancing puppeteers to emerge from behind the screen has no known Indonesian or Indian precedent, and must be attributed to indigenous ingenuity.

The figures are impressive, being the largest shadow figures known in the world. The iconography of the puppets corresponds to images on temple walls, and most figures sport the distinctive crown-type headdress (*chada*) worn by classical dancers. The fine carving emulates the delicate patterns of the cloth of gold and jewel inlay of dance-drama costumes – outfits into which court dancers were sewn before each performance. The kings, including Rama I, Rama II and Rama IV, were responsible for writing the texts of the Rama story that were presented in the *nang* and masked dance. Unfortunately, performances of *nang yai* are rare today, but at least two temples maintain this tradition that fell into disarray when court support lapsed in the 1930s. The crown princess H.R.H. Mahachakri Sirinthorn has recently commissioned some new puppets.

Khon is a masked dance drama enacted by a male cast to the chanted narrative of a narrator (*khon pak*) accompanied by a *piphat* orchestra. Dancers MIME the action of the text, normally excerpted from literary versions of the *Ramakien*. *Khon* was supposedly first presented in the Thai court in 1515 when King Rama Thibodi II celebrated his 25th birthday. The original dancers are said to have been manipulators of *nang yai*. The basic square, flat stance of the dancers, and the tendency in *khon* to construct visual friezes as dancers assume poses, correlates well with the style of puppet manipulation aimed at enhancing the figure of the large puppet against a screen. Because of the puppet origin of the form, scripts are divided into 'sets' (*chut*), referring to sets of puppets used in *nang yai* episodes.

Khon luang ('royal *khon*') was supported by Thai rulers. Early court performances seem to have emphasized fight sequences and the recitation (*kampak*) of the narrator, making it close to the puppet theatre. In later periods, characters playing refined males and females have ceased to wear masks, and non-battle scenes and song have become more significant. The movement away from all-masked, martial theatre has probably come as a result of the popularity of the female dance-drama tradition, for females have increasingly taken over refined roles in which they do not wear MASKS.

The female dance tradition reportedly stems from 1431 when the Thai captured the Khmer court dancers. However, it seems likely that the Thai may have emulated the Khmer custom of coupling the role of queen or royal concubine and dancer prior to this date. Though it is difficult to pinpoint exactly when the custom originated and trace precisely when drama rather than abstract dance became the focus, the female court drama is clearly the most significant and innovative of Thai court arts. *Lakon fai nai* (literally, 'inner court play') is the most refined, poetic and slow-moving of the dance dramas. Female performers dance-act a story accompanied by a *piphat* orchestra and a chorus. The poetic texts are attributed to members of the nobility. Dialogue may be delivered by performers; much of the text is sung by offstage singers. Clowns who improvise their own dialogue are, traditionally, the only male performers.

The name of the form comes from the fact that it was performed by the ladies of the court and, hence, only played inside the palace. Dancers would traditionally be under the direction of one of the queens and serve as performer and king's lady for the duration of a reign. Upon the death of a king, this group would disband, and the new monarch would appoint one of the former king's dancers to teach his own group. Provincial lords might emulate this practice, but few groups could compete with the training, grace, exquisite costuming and delicate singing of the king's troupe. Other terms for the form are *lakon nai* and *lakon phuying*.

Lakon fai nai evolved from the early, non-dramatic dances of the Khmer court ladies, which served a semi-ritual purpose of linking the ruler with chthonic forces of earth and fertility. In Javanese, Balinese and Malay court performances female dancers have an analogous function, and the Khmer may have been emulating the practice of these southern courts where tantric Hindu-Buddhist thinking laid the groundwork for the arts. The Thai secularized this ritual function, and allowed the form to become more dramatically oriented, often incorporating story material from the Malay regions of Thailand.

Thai court dancers were presenting drama in daylong performance episodes in the late 1600s when the Frenchman de la Loubère visited Thailand. Around 1760 two royal princesses learned from their Malay maidservant the Prince Panji story, called *Inao* in Thailand, and they wrote their own versions as a basis for a female court dance drama. Though the princesses' versions were later superseded by the version of Rama II, who reigned 1809–24, their choice of subject was apt. The amorous exploits of this Javanese prince, creeping unbeknownst to fathers and husbands into the bedchambers of his beloveds, must have had resonance for the ladies of the king's entourage, who were themselves given to forbidden affairs. It became the favoured subject of the dance drama

and contributed to the dramatic enrichment of court dance.

The languorous, graceful dance style of the ladies fitted *lakon fai nai*'s emphasis on feminine concerns and characters. Some of the women were trained for the ogre and monkey roles needed for the *Ramakien* which was taken into its repertory, but episodes like 'Surpanakha's Pangs of Jealousy', which show the hopeless love of Ravanna's sister for Rama, and the 'Abduction of Sita', which depicts the helpless wife of Rama carried off by the ogre king, were preferred to the battles and monkey exploits presented in male-dominated mask and shadow plays. Other stories were introduced over time, including *Unaruth*, which tells of the loves of a grandson of Krishna. Rama II is said to have introduced six *lakon nok* stories, including the popular *Jataka* of *Sang Thong* about the prince born as a conch shell. The strange birth results in mother and shell being cast out of the palace. The conch prince steals magic accoutrements from his adoptive mother, an ogress, and disguises himself as a negrito. Despite his disguise, a princess marries him, braving persecution by her mortified family. Another popular story from the south is *Suwanna-hongse*, which tells how Prince Suwanna-hongse climbs a kite-string to find the princess of his dreams, an ogre king's daughter, but is killed by her sisters. The princess disguises herself as a Brahmin and, with the aid of an oafish clown-ogre, restores the prince to life. This last tale seems to have come to the *lakon nok* from *nora*. Its presence in the repertoire may hint at some link with the female court dance drama of Malaysia, *mak yong*, for the story is a version of the most significant and sacred story in the *mak yong* repertoire, *Dewa Muda*, or *The Magic Kite*.

Both the Panji story and *lakon nok* tales come to the female dance drama from the Malay south. Further research into the past dramatic practice of the southern provinces might clarify whether the importance of women as actors in a court dance drama could have been stimulated by practices of this area as well, perhaps in the court of Patani where a visiting European, Peter Flores, attended a 1613 banquet given by the queen and saw, 'A commedye all by women, to the manner of Java, which were apparelled very antikly, very pleasant to beholde'.

Development and innovation in *khon* and *lakon fai nai* traditions continued through the last century, first under royal direction and then under the government Department of Fine Arts (Krom Silpakon). After the reign of Rama IV (King Mongkut) (r.1851–68), division of the sexes in theatre forms disintegrated, as males were allowed to dance with the royal ladies and female dancers were allowed to perform and teach outside the court. Today women play in virtually all forms, often taking the refined male roles as well as female ones. Men customarily play ogres, clowns and monkeys and, perhaps, refined male roles. Clear distinctions between genres have blurred: *khon* has become more refined in its dance style and *lakon fai nai*, using males for ogre and monkey roles, probably lacks the delicate ambience of times past. The two forms are nowadays intermingled and the combined genre termed *khon* if masks are involved or *lakon ram* if masks are not.

Extensive experimentation has characterized the 19th and 20th centuries. Performances of classical plays were given using three-dimensional puppets, *hun*. The form is probably inspired by Chinese rod- and string-puppet theatres. *Lakon dukdamban* (literally, 'ancient story') was an innovation during the reign of Rama V (King Chulalongkorn) (r.1868–1910). Actors sang their own lines rather than merely pantomiming their parts, males played male roles, and the offstage chorus and descriptive passages characteristic of earlier court drama were eliminated. During the reign of Rama VI (King Vajiravudh) (r.1910–25) experiments proliferated. The king wrote examples of *lakon rong* (literally, 'a sung drama'), an all-female opera form developed in the 19th century. He also wrote spoken dramas, based on Western models. Meanwhile Prince Naradhip adapted plots from English musicals and European operas to present in Thai classical dance style.

Following the transition to a constitutional monarchy in 1932, sponsorship of theatrical activities was assumed by the government Department of Fine Arts, and expanded under the directorship of Dhanit Yupho, 1956–68. In 1934 a training school for music and dance was founded under the department's direction, and this institution eventually became the College of Dance (Witthayalai Natasin). Since 1971 seven new branch Colleges of Dance, training students in *khon*, *lakon fai nai* and traditional music, have been established outside Bangkok. There students are groomed to play one of the four major roles, studying carefully the 66 gestures (sometimes said to be 68) of the classical dance technique which were codified in the reign of Rama I (1782–1809) in the *Text for the Training of Dancers*. Outstanding graduates may become members of the National Theatre Company at the National Theatre in Bangkok.

At the National Theatre thousands of ticket-buyers now can see the forms which a hundred years ago were played only to an invited few in a hall of the royal palace. The company presents most of the previously noted genres, *khon*, *lakon fai nai*, *lakon dukdamban*, *lakon nok* and *lakon phantang* (mixed-genre experiments). The latter form combines local legends from the *sebha*, a rhymed story-telling tradition, with classical dance presentation.

Few performers can maintain themselves by performing classical arts. Performers at the National Theatre receive token payment, and most turn to tourist performance for additional income. Thammasat and Chulalongkorn Universities stage student, amateur productions of classical dramas. The puppet performances, in particular, are extremely rare. *Nang yai* players are mostly aged, with few students to take over when they die. The last rod-puppet troupe retired in 1975, and only an amateur group under the Bangkok painter, Chakrapand, does occasional performances.

Popular forms Thailand's most popular theatrical entertainments are *nang talung* and *likay*. Both trace their origins to the Malay south from whence *nora* and *lakon nok* came in generations past.

Little is known of the origin of *nang talung* (literally, 'shadow theatre of Pattalung province'). In its basic form it is related to the *wayang siam* of MALAYSIA and genres in Cambodia and Laos. A single performer, called a *nang nai*, manipulates translucent leather puppets whose iconography depicts the costumes of classical dance drama. Through dialogue and narration, the *nang nai* presents the story which may be based on *Ramakien*-derived stories, local histories or legends. Because it draws large rural audiences, in recent times it has been used for propaganda as well as mass-entertainment purposes.

Likay is a creation of the last hundred years. Remnants of court performance meet rock and roll in this popular, commercial drama that utilizes many elements of traditional forms (dance, singing and *piphat* music). All these elements fuse to suit the tastes of the middle-class housewives who form its prime audience. Actors are cast according to type. They improvise dialogue and song lyrics to play out the scenario. Stories are from the traditional repertoire and also modern inventions. Psuedo-classical dance melds with MELODRAMA. If the female court dancer was the mistress in times past, the *likay* male lead, gigolo to his middle-aged patroness, is the man of the present. The tastes of the bourgeoisie, rather than the courtier, create the style.

The name *likay* is a variant of *dikay*, a form of Islamic singing (compare INDONESIA's *dikir*) from the southern provinces, that originally preceded performance. Buddhist chanting for funerals, known as *suat phramalai*, may also have influenced the form in its early stages. As presently acted, it is far from these sources. In its combination of classical, rock and Indian popular singing and dancing it represents the mixture of influences that appeal to current audiences. Its popularity far surpasses the esoteric appeal of the court-derived and modern spoken drama (*lakon phut*) forms. It shows that drama which is sung and danced remains the preferred theatre of the Thai. Current actors such as Somsak Phakdee increase their popularity by performing on television and radio.

Other popular forms which exhibit some of the same flexibility as *likay* have maintained audiences outside Bangkok. *Mawlum luong* (compare LAOS's *mawlum*) in northeast Thailand uses Lao language for its Lao-speaking audience. Music is provided by a Lao mouth organ, called a *kaen*, rather than a *piphat*, while costumes, dancing and stories parallel *likay*. Some 3000 troupes were active in 1975. *Lakon saw* is found in northern Thailand: like *mawlum*, it is derived from a local storytelling tradition that has expanded into improvised theatre, perhaps in emulation of the *likay* model. Chinese operas performed by local troupes and by companies invited from Singapore and Hong Kong draw audiences from among the Chinese Thai population.

Different genres of Thai theatre enjoy varying popularity at present. In general, popular folk forms remain the most vigorous. Traditional mask dance and court dance drama retain an important place in government-supported training institutions and through the large-scale productions regularly produced at the National Theatre in Bangkok.

Spoken drama For a number of reasons, modern spoken drama (*lakon phut*) remains a singularly elitist enterprise in Thailand and has yet to develop more than a tenuous hold on the Thai theatrical imagination. The earliest spoken dramas were staged by and for the Western-educated aristocracy. Prince Vajiravudh (King Rama VI) produced the first spoken drama in 1904 in a 100-seat theatre he had built upon his return from study in Europe. During his reign, 1910–25, he wrote more than 100 plays, romantic and didactic melodramas that swelled with national pride and exorted loyalty to the crown, such as *King Ruang* (*Phra Ruang*, ?1914), as well as Victorian-type FARCES, light romances and drawing-room comedies. M. L. Pin Malakul was another pioneer of Western-style drama.

Benefiting from the strong policy of Westernization pursued during the Phibul Songkram military government (1938–44), modern theatre re-emerged in the decades following King Rama VI's death and moved beyond aristocratic circles. At this time, chauvinist poet, novelist and playwright Luang Wichit Wathakorn 'modernized' Thai classical dance drama by grafting it with modern music, contemporary dialogue and historically accurate costumes (an attitude not confined to Thailand, but paralleled in China, Japan and other Asian countries).

Western and modern elements were exploited by professional theatre companies such as Chalerm Thai during and immediately following the Second World War. Their syncretic musical dramas recaptured the time-honoured practice of mischievously fusing foreign music and dance styles into indigenous theatre, proving more accessible to audiences than elitist spoken drama. This popular style went into premature decline with the rise of films and, after 1955, television.

Both Thai classical and modern Western theatre were introduced into the university system, beginning in the 1960s. The programme at Chulalongkorn University, under the direction of UCLA-trained Sodsai Pantunkomal, has produced a generation of actors and directors trained in Western, and especially Stanislavskian (see STANISLAVSKY) dramaturgy. Since the 1970s Mattani Rutnin has synthesized Thai, Asian and Western techniques in productions at Thammasat University. Formal campus theatre, however, remains remote from the national consciousness.

A new-wave theatre appeared in the 1970s in the context of the 'American Era' (1963–73) and the 'Democracy Period' (1973–6). Emerging from a middle class that had experienced a decade of unprecedented economic development, an intelligentsia sought 'self-apprehension' in an era of consolidation of militarism and bureaucratic capitalism. The modest SURREALISM and absurdism (see THEATRE OF THE ABSURD) in the plays of Widhayakorn Chiengkul and Suthart Swardsri, leaders of the loose literary grouping, Crescent Moon (Phrajan Siew), were a prelude to a politically radical theatre of the short-lived Democracy Period. Like its Filipino counterpart, this radical theatre was saturated with American counterculture and Maoist ideals. Kamron Kunadilok, a Crescent Moon adherent, married Western contemporary dramaturgies, particularly BRECHT and GROTOWSKI, and Thai folk RITUALS, fun and games, and popular *likay* theatre music in a trilogy, *Country I*, *Country II*, and *Country III*, produced in Chiengmai. These 'impoverished' theatre pieces told how a farmer, rendered impotent by tradition and feudal corruption, gained strength through fellowship in the urban workers' association. AGIT-PROP theatre groups, such as Shakdao and Thawanplueng, struck postures of a street parliament in their productions in Bangkok.

The radical theatre officially died in the right-wing coup of 1976, but the concerns of decolonializing theatre are continued by Santi Chitrachinda and Samsak Kanha in their mobile children's theatre company, MAYA, founded in 1981. Concerned with empowering children in city slums and the depressed countryside, MAYA performances infuse Thai folk arts with the contemporary lyricism of comics, cartoons and caricature. The same strategy was employed to provoke social and political consciousness among adult middle-class audiences in their productions of *Phlae Kan* (1991), inspired by the Thai folk classic *Siddharta*, and *Fifty Ways to Torture Children* (1991). Group 28 was initiated in 1986 by Suchart Sawardsri and other Crescent Moon alumni. Guided by artistic director Yale-educated Rassame Paolungtong, Group 28 has gained a tenaciously loyal following with thought-provoking productions of Brecht's *Galileo* (1986), DÜRRENMATT's *The Visit* (1988) and Kafka's *The Fall* (1991).

Spoken drama is also performed for more popular audiences in commercial settings. The highest production values are achieved at the Montienthong Theatre in the Montien Hotel in Bangkok, whose audience comes from the prosperous upper middle class. Typically, the group's performers are well known actors in television drama (*lakon toratat*) and Thai-language films and earn their living from these media. Playwrights, too, usually support themselves by other professions: Somopop Chandaraprapa, author of *Noresuan the Great* (1973), earns his living as an engineer. During the 1980s Montienthong productions tended toward locally written social SATIRES. *Lady Amarapa* (*Khunying Amarapa*, 1986) showed a nouveau riche woman trying to use her fortune to buy a title. *Sorry, No Name Card* (*Khotot tee, mai mee fun un ying yai*, 1988) dealt with the love between a highborn girl and a lower-class boy.

Group 28's disdain of indigenous plays is symptomatic of the larger issue that, with few exceptions such as the work of MAYA and Kunadilok's ensemble pieces, serious modern theatre is nearly synonymous with the staging of Western plays for the educated elite. It appears that a sense of Thai national identity is adequately fulfilled by the symbolic presence of the nationalized traditional performing arts. (See also ASIAN AND PACIFIC ISLAND THEATRE.) KJ

See: J. R. Brandon (ed.), *The Cambridge Guide to Asian Theatre*, Cambridge, 1993.

Theatre, the The first dedicated public playhouse in England, situated in Shoreditch outside the city walls of London. Opened in 1576, as a bold commercial project, by JAMES BURBAGE, the Theatre became the favourite home of the LORD CHAMBERLAIN's MEN and provided the first stage for many of SHAKESPEARE's plays. When Burbage's lease ran out in 1597, the Theatre was hastily dismantled and its timbers carried over the Thames to provide building material for the GLOBE. It is from this evident compatibility that scholars have concluded that the otherwise unrecorded Theatre was, like the Globe, a polygonal building, with three galleries surrounding an open yard. Since James Burbage would have wanted his arena to be suitable for the popular spectacle of animal-baiting, we can reasonably assume that its scaffold stage was removable. PT

theatre buildings (Europe and anglophone nations) Theatre buildings are not essential for theatre performances. The roots of drama lie in the interaction between actor and audience, and there are regular pleas to return to these roots. But a common slogan of the fundamentalists – Two Planks and a Passion – includes recognition of some of the basic reasons for organizing theatre space. Planks assist the actor to project passion by enhancing visibility and audibility. And they also help to delineate the acting area.

Origins The form of today's theatre buildings was established during the 16th century, when the general cultural Renaissance included a surge of interest in drama which stimulated a simultaneous revival of theatre building throughout Europe. Although formal theatre buildings had disappeared during the Middle Ages, the art and craft of the actor had survived with the mimes, minstrels, acrobats, conjurors and ballad singers performing wherever the need arose. This was largely a time of passion without planks, except in the case of the mysteries, for which a series of *mansions* appropriate to each episode were built on temporary platforms around a market square, or built on wagons and moved from station to station around town. (See MEDIEVAL DRAMA IN EUROPE (Staging in the Middle Ages)). The 16th-century Italian humanists, wishing to restore to the stage the classical dramas of the ancients, looked back to the architectural forms of the theatres of antiquity. Combining a study of the architectural books of VITRUVIUS with observation of the remains of Roman theatres, they created temporary open-air theatres in courtyards on the Roman model (see ROMAN THEATRES AND AMPHITHEATRES; GREEK THEATRES).

The late-Roman model provided a positive starting point for the new theatres: it had evolved over many centuries and incorporated all the basic features of most subsequent theatres, including those of today. Sight and sound are enhanced by raising both actor and audience, whose respective areas are shaped to maximize contact between them yet provide a clearly delineated acting area. Once seating is provided within a structure, it is possible to control the audience by selective admission and selective seating – with an option of charging for tickets. After regulating the performance spaces for actor and audience, facilities such as dressing-rooms and foyers follow, the productions become more elaborate, and stage technology grows. This growth is often towards decadence: either long-term, as accompanied the decline and fall of the Roman Empire, or short-term, as in today's continuing cycles of reactionary return to the simplicities of the street, where success triggers an escalation into the provision of ever more elaborate planks for projecting the passion.

Temporary Renaissance outdoor theatres were followed by permanent indoor theatres, and in Vicenza we still have PALLADIO's Teatro Olimpico with its monumental *scaenae*

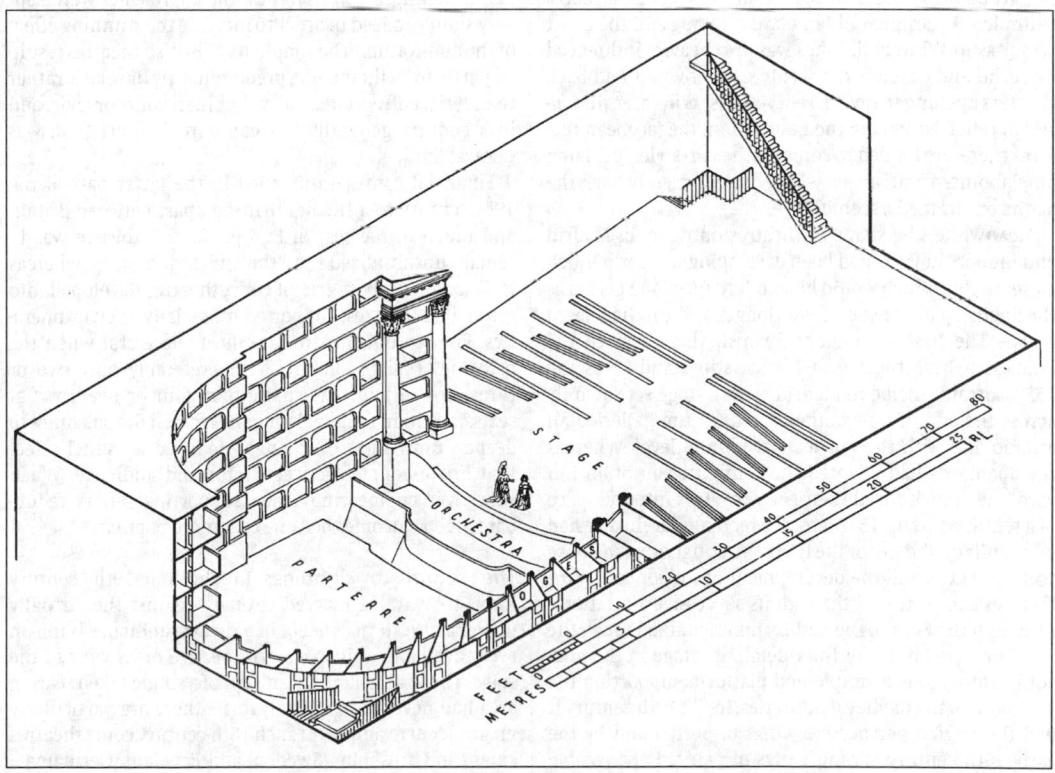

The Italian opera house has retained its basic form since the Teatro SS Giovanni e Paolo, Venice, of 1639, up to the present day.

frons backing an acting area which faces an orchestra, and an audience *cavea* whose semicircle has been flattened to fit the site. Beyond the five openings in the *scaenae frons* still stand the perspective scenes designed by SCAMOZZI for the opening performance in 1585 of SOPHOCLES' *Oedipus Tyrannus*. These represent the other line of Italian Renaissance development – the concept of perspective scenery developed by SERLIO, whose illustrated writings on theatre architecture, published in French (1545) and in English (1611) as *The Second Book of Architecture,* were probably the most influential source for Renaissance theatre builders.

Outside Italy there was less concern to seek inspiration from the ancient world and the new theatres were designed to accommodate the growth of indigenous drama. The surge of theatre growth that began in Elizabethan England and continued until the Commonwealth embargo in 1642 (see CLOSURE OF THE THEATRES), bred two forms of theatre building. Outdoor theatres such as the CURTAIN, SWAN, GLOBE and FORTUNE developed out of the methods used for temporary staging in inn yards and bear-baiting pits. A thrust stage in an encircling courtyard was surrounded for some 300° by an audience in galleries and on the ground. This was the theatre that SHAKESPEARE wrote for – a theatre based on the passion of words delivered from planks that might support some furniture and simple mechanics but virtually no representational scenery. The indoor theatres such as the COCKPIT had a Palladian-inspired *scaenae frons* resulting from INIGO JONES's 1613 visit to Vicenza's Teatro Olimpico. As designer of temporary stagings for the court MASQUES in Whitehall, Jones was also heavily influenced by Serlio and developed a scenic style of wings and back shutters opening to reveal 'relieves', vistas in three-dimensional relief. Following the Restoration, the Jacobean theatres therefore tended to combine the two styles, utilizing an elaborate frontispiece which did not merely back the actors but framed a scenic stage.

Meanwhile, the shape of theatres outdoors in Madrid and indoors in Paris had been developing in a form much closer to that which would be standard for a long period as the English playhouse and even longer as the Italian opera house. The first permanent Spanish theatre since the Romans (whose theatre in Merida still stands) was the 1582 Corral Príncipe in Madrid, with a stage set squarely across the end of a rectangular auditorium galleried all around and with rows of seats at ground level. Whereas the Spaniards had adapted the configuration of an inn yard, the French fitted their early theatres into the space of a tennis court. In 1548 a roofed rectangular theatre had been built on the site of the HÔTEL DE BOURGOGNE to house MYSTERY PLAYS, and the development of indoor courtyard theatres can be traced through its successive alterations. Although the Bourgogne auditorium remained much the same in spirit, if not in finer detail, its stage in the mid-16th century was a simple end platform supporting the *mansions* of the medieval mysteries; in the 17th century it had the angled perspective wings of Serlio, and by the early 18th century sliding wings of painted changeable scenery.

Italian concern with a revival of the ancient Roman dramatic traditions was short-lived: the growth of opera in

the 17th century moulded theatre building in the same basic form that was emerging everywhere – the proscenium-framed scenic stage facing a galleried auditorium. Indeed, auditorium shape across Europe, and in those countries colonized by Europeans, became relatively stabilized throughout the 18th and much of the 19th centuries. There were many variations in the geometry of the balconies (mostly boxed) that lined the walls, which were occasionally straight, but mostly curved on every possible inspiration from the bell to the horseshoe. English actors continued throughout the Georgian period to play in something of a residual tradition of the ancient theatre and its early Renaissance revival, by acting on an apron stage, thrust forward through a proscenium arch flanked by 'doors of entrance' and framing a background of changeable scenery. Although this forestage was gradually cut back, it lasted well into the 19th century, when public taste for a more spectacular entertainment forced the actors somewhat reluctantly back into a scenic environment.

Throughout the 18th and early 19th centuries the British playhouse remained relatively simple in structure and unadorned, with its architectural roots in the concept of a simple shell building furnished by a carpenter. Elsewhere in Europe, however, particularly in Italy and Germany, theatre auditoria became places for artists like the BIBIENAS to lavish the grandeurs of the baroque and the elegances of the rococo. Sometimes this spilled over into the foyers, but elsewhere, as in the extant Margrafentheater in Bayreuth, the approaches were kept very simple indeed in order to increase the stunning effect of the auditorium. The simplicity of British theatres resulted partly from their being predominantly dramatic rather than lyric, entrepreneurial rather than court or civic, and in a country generally less committed to art than was Central Europe.

Financial considerations led in the latter part of the 19th century to a further drifting apart between Britain and much of the rest of Europe. British theatre was to remain unsubsidized until the mid-20th century, whereas in Central Europe a grid of court theatres developed into municipal theatres, supported financially as civic amenities. Proscenium theatres are most successful when the balconies remain shallow with preferably only two or three, but certainly not more than four or five, rows of seats. In Britain financial pressures forced the balconies to deepen until their overhangs produced a tunnel effect that broke contact between actor and audience. When cantilever engineering made supporting pillars redundant, deep balconies became ever more popular.

The return to sightlines In the mid-19th century RICHARD WAGNER reacted strongly against the virtually universal Western concept of a theatre audience hung on every available wall space, irrespective of its view of the stage. The Graeco-Roman concept of a single raked seating area had never been entirely lost – there are particularly magnificent examples of such 18th-century court theatres extant in Gripsholm (Sweden) and Potsdam (Germany) – but this system of the ancients, revived briefly at the Renaissance, had mostly given way to the curved courtyards with tiers of boxes covering the walls and extending to the proscenium arch. Wagner called for universally perfect sightlines from every seat to a scenic stage, and in 1876 built his BAYREUTH Festspielhaus with a single wedge of raked seating. Blank side walls can be a problem in such a theatre, but at Bayreuth this was solved with a success that has eluded many later architects. Here they were broken up by a series of short pillared walls at right angles to the side walls, deepening towards the stage and focusing on it so that the actual proscenium seemed unstressed and less of a barrier than many a conventional frame. The result was excellent when applied to the new music drama deploying singers, orchestra and scenery on a particularly large scale to perform works dealing with themes of epic grandeur. However, it was less satisfactory for more intimate music theatre or for drama, even when scaled down. Nevertheless, preoccupation with sightlines became an increasing feature of the debate, particularly as the role of theatre in society became more and more a matter for philosophic agonizing. The suggestion that boxes enabled the audience to be seen rather than to see was an obvious battle cry for those who sought a new serious role for the drama and pursued a democratic theatre based on purity of sightline from all seats.

Technological influences Meanwhile, theatre technology was advancing. In nearly two centuries there had been only one really major development in the backstage area: the full-height flying towers that became standard in the second half of the 19th century. Most scenery had continued to move in one plane, parallel to the front of the stage whether it came down from the flies, up through sloats (slotes) or traps in the floor, or slid on from the sides. Here again there were differences between British practice and the rest of Europe, mostly attributable to their respective traditions of subsidized OPERA or commercial drama. In Central Europe the scenic wing flats were simultaneously changed by elaborate carriage systems running on rails in the basement under slots in the stage, whereas British wings moved in simple wooden grooves fixed to the stage and suspended from the flies. Towards the end of the 19th century a number of factors produced a shift away from perspective painting towards solid three-dimensional scenery. One was the introduction of electricity, which was less sympathetic to painted scenery than the soft gaslight that preceded it (even gas had seemed hard after the shimmering haze from candles and oil lamps, but this had been a difference that could largely be compensated for by painting techniques; see STAGE LIGHTING). But perhaps more important was that three-dimensional scenery was more appropriate to a new drama that pursued REALISM rather than rhetoric.

The growth in the use of three-dimensional scenery required new methods when it came to changing it. Complex technologies were developed in Germany, particularly. First the turntable stage enabled a sequence of scenes to be revolved towards the proscenium opening (first installed for *Don Giovanni* at Munich's Cuvilliestheater in 1896). Then came wagon stage systems whereby full-sized stage areas could be slid on from left, right or rear to fill the proscenium. Although a few revolves were installed in Britain, scene changing mainly remained a labour-intensive exercise involving breaking

down the set into small elements which could be stored as flat as possible against the walls or in a small 'dock' alongside. But Britain's Victorian theatre expansion had abandoned the repertoire system of its early Georgian growth phase, and based its organization on 'runs' or performances of the same play. This was unlike most of Europe, where the repertoire system remained, requiring sophisticated changing, storage, rehearsal and production manufacturing facilities of all kinds. The Italians stood aside from all this, continuing with simple stages and a system of scenery based on painted canvas stored in rolls and temporarily battened out on simple timber framing when required for a performance. However, because opera was (and still is) a matter of popular importance in Italy, the public areas were as extensive as in Germany and in other countries where a theatre was an important civic building. Indeed, in comparing plans of British and other European theatres in the late 19th century, the ratio of auditorium space to the rest of the building is very telling.

European concepts of theatre architecture were carried forth into the New World by colonists who sought, at least initially, only to create a theatre in the image that they knew. In the intensely colonized areas such as the Americas and the Antipodes, there was little indigenous drama; it was not organized to the point of requiring special housing; and settlers were more likely to suppress than to encourage it. Available resources tended to restrict theatres to the simpler models, although there were exceptions – Manaus, isolated up the Amazon, built an opulent opera house to demonstrate the wealth of its rubber economy to the world. The earliest American theatres were firmly based on the British Georgian playhouse, but by quite early in the 18th century the basic form was already showing signs of the widening of stage and auditorium that would in the early 19th and 20th centuries give a characteristic shape to BROADWAY and the road houses across America, which were fed with tours from the New York base. This configuration brought a higher proportion of the audience closer to the stage by adopting a short, wide format rather than the long, narrow shape more common in Europe. Colonization of the Antipodes came later, and so their early theatre tended to reflect the approach that was standard for much of the great surge of British theatre building during the later decades of the 19th century. These had deep galleries with two or three token side boxes to break up the side walls.

The 19th century Today, most of Britain's remaining stock of 'old' theatres dates from this period, which came to an end in the years leading up to the First World War. Outside London's WEST END, with its open-ended runs of the same play, these theatres were intended for a touring system of plays and musicals based on a weekly run (or multiples of one week) in each town. Their stage arrangements lacked storage and workshops, while their seating capacities were geared to a commercial system whereby a couple of reasonable houses on Friday and Saturday could comfortably clear the costs, leaving the rest of the week as profits. This required the sort of capacities (1000 was small) which could only be achieved by making the balconies deep and steep. Sightlines to the stage were often clear (after cantilevers had removed the need for pillars), but the view could be from far away and often funnelled by the overhang of the balcony above. The commercial basis of such theatres also required that they be built on a minimum site area, and the most prolific architect of the period, Frank Matcham, was renowned for his skill in extracting maximum usage from small irregularly shaped sites. He was also adept at contriving the rich decorative treatment which a popular theatre needed to offer as an escape from the social conditions of a rapidly developed industrialization.

The 20th century Art centuries rarely tally with neat spans of a hundred years: the 20th century for theatre architecture got under way in the 1920s and was, inevitably, heavily influenced by the cinema. Boxes on the side walls disappeared altogether, or became so vestigial that they were intended as decoration rather than for audience. Out went the plasterer's excesses of Victorian and Edwardian quasi-baroque and in came the new clean lines of modernity. The plasterer's art was redeployed to form coves in which the colour symphonies of the concealed indirect lighting replaced the earlier traditions of the Georgian painters and their successors who had pursued their art in gilt and plush. A single rake of auditorium

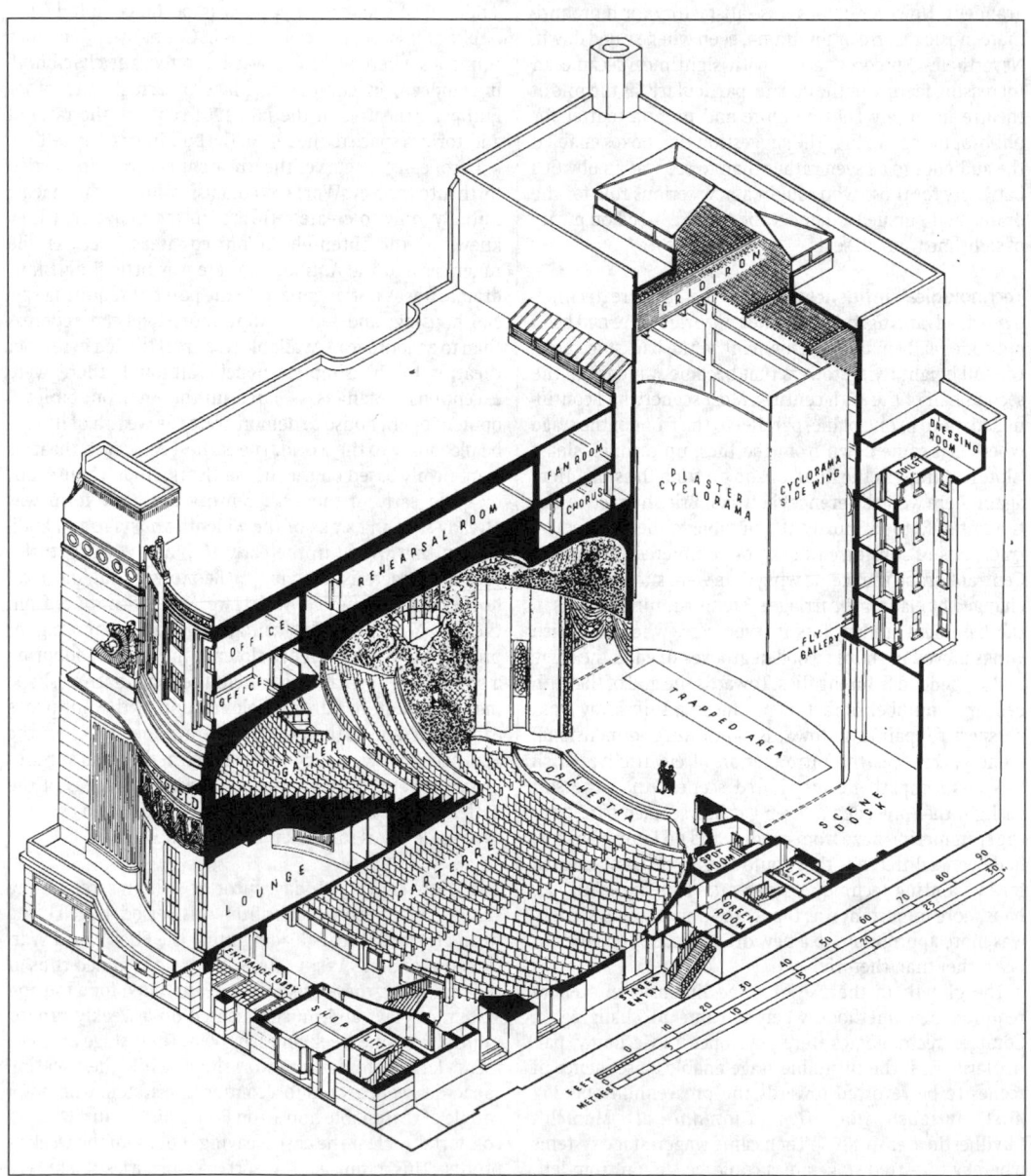

The Ziegfeld Theatre, New York (1926), combines an auditorium influenced by the cinema with a cyclorama to exploit the new developments in stage lighting.

seating with the possible addition of not more than one deep balcony became the norm. Everyone could see, from seats which became cheaper as the stage became ever more distant. Outside the majority of theatres built on this norm, there were many exceptions. Everywhere that MAX REINHARDT went, an interesting theatre seemed to emerge: in Berlin the Grosses Schauspielhaus wrapped its 3000 audience around a huge arena stage thrusting forward from a restrained proscenium; in London, Olympia became a cathedral, while in Salzburg the cathedral square became a theatre, as did the 17th-century rock-hewn riding school. On a smaller scale, COPEAU in Paris and TERENCE GRAY in Cambridge were amongst those who thrust through the proscenium arch and discarded it totally. Visionaries such as GROPIUS and NORMAN BEL GEDDES produced exciting schemes which were rather too advanced to build, and by the time that their philosophies were adopted some 50 years later a reaction had already set in. However, developments in lighting, particularly the limitless spatial backgrounds of Fortuny's cyclorama, helped to realize a stage design revolution sought by APPIA and CRAIG, whose visual concepts had initially been frustrated by the available technology.

By the time that the Second World War loomed, the age of agonizing was well established – it had been started by Wagner and gathered momentum until by the mid-20th century it had become a major conference topic. No magazine was complete without an article on adaptable theatres or the actor–audience relationship, and the correspondence columns were alive with anarchy. It even bred a new occupation, probably always in existence but now formalized as theatre consultancy, whose members endeavoured to establish the purpose of a proposed theatre and rationalize that purpose against the various current theories. Theatre consultants, although aiming for objectivity, tended to be people with strong, rather subjective ideas, and therefore they became a major influence, often sharing at least equal responsibility with the architect for the theatrical form of the building.

In 1945 Europe was devastated, with many theatres destroyed or disabled. In Germany particularly the rebuilding began almost immediately, with performances restarting in improvised theatres. (German opera house stages were so large that it was often possible to contrive an interim theatre of stage, orchestra pit and auditorium for more than 600 on the old stage, if the fire curtain had saved the backstage area.) In Britain, old theatres temporarily saved by the wartime surge in demand for entertainment now entered a downward spiral of decreasing quality, increasing costs and lack of maintenance. But the repertory movement (see REGIONAL THEATRE (BRITAIN)), slowly established between the wars, now blossomed with ARTS COUNCIL funding, and there was a growing demand for new theatres with their own resident acting companies in every town of consequence. In the USA the universities were developing drama faculties which needed housing, and each campus became the focus for a regional theatre movement that first complemented and then began to replace the old touring houses in all but the biggest centres of population. In the Antipodes the old theatres were coming down, to be rebuilt within new commercial developments, and there was a growing demand

for major opera-house-sized theatres in the major centres. Third World countries gaining independence often regarded a National Theatre as a desirable acquisition. Even Great Britain once again revived its long-smouldering NATIONAL THEATRE ambitions.

But what was to be the shape of the new theatres? Today's building techniques and regulations bring an inflexibility unknown to earlier theatre builders, who 'fitted out' a theatre by furnishing a shell which could expect to house a series of different fashions during a century of its lifetime. But concrete has finality, and this has helped to fuel demand for an adaptable theatre that can cope with every style of production – from intimate drama to grand opera, from proscenium via thrust to fully encircled theatre-in-the-round – and with audiences of widely varying sizes. A 1961 international conference in London on 'Adaptable Theatres', launching the new Association of British Theatre Technicians, appeared to reach a consensus that adaptability was a strictly limited concept: if a theatre tried to do too many things, it ended up doing none of them well. Nevertheless, experiments in flexible theatre have continued from time to time, often using complex expensive engineering to produce variations that were either nominal or, if significant, had become unfashionable by the time the theatre opened. More successful were the small theatres where flexibility could be achieved manually, but unfortunately frequently so expensively in terms of money and/or time that such theatres soon found their most comfortable format and stayed that way.

The new German opera houses generally opted to hang the audience on the walls, but adopted a fan-shaped auditorium so that the ascending tiers of boxes faced the stage. The main proscenium was often unstressed, but standardized technology produced an inner black-clad structure of bridge and towers to carry the lighting equipment. This provided a frame, adjustable in width and height, for the huge wagons and elevators for moving scenery. A *grosses Haus* usually had a *kleines Haus* attached and this tended to be a more flexible space, increasingly moving towards the neutral black box concept that represented an ideal for many people in the 1960s and 70s. In the USA, mainstream theatres got bigger and bigger: the perfect sightline was supreme. Australia built, in Sydney's Opera House, the only new theatre to be instantly recognizable by everyone across the world, whether or not they ever went to a theatre. During the fitting out of this magnificent shell, some unfortunate decisions led to the actual performance space being considerably less than ideal. The other main Australian cities then built simple, large theatre complexes which are probably the best of the world's pure sightline theatres. In Britain the new theatre building comprised almost entirely regional playhouses with seating in the 350–650 bracket, usually with a studio attached for about 100 people – the wedge-shaped single tier being the most popular and, at its most effective, capable of up to about 500 seats. The proscenium was unstressed, being formed by the natural termination of the walls and ceiling. It became standard to have a flexible area in front of the stage, which could be optional forestage, flat floor or sunken orchestra pit. The old theatres and their touring circuits were allowed to die away in the 1960s, but several (often ones that had been preserved by use as bingo halls) were refurbished during the 1970s to provide a national grid for opera, dance, musicals and star performers of all kinds. The National Theatre was finally built. Its largest auditorium, showing considerable resonances with pre-war Bel Geddes concepts, was the culmination of a growth in thrust staging that started with Tyrone Guthrie's improvised stage at the Edinburgh Festival in the late 1940s, continued by him in North America, and by the Chichester Festival Theatre and the Crucible in Sheffield. Its second auditorium was a straightforward proscenium house, serviceable but not particularly distinguished. However, it is the third and smallest (the Cottesloe) that has caught most imagination and stimulated an almost inevitable rediscovery of what has been labelled 'the courtyard form'.

The courtyard revival is a response to the isolation that can be experienced by an individual member of the audience in a theatre designed to give everyone a direct, clean, uninterrupted view of the stage. Indeed, it almost follows from defining a pure sightline that an individual will not be aware of fellow members of the audience. Hang some on the walls, and those in the central seats will be aware, out of the corners of their eyes, of the response of those

hanging over their balcony rails to see the stage. This may not be an ideal in a theatre with democratic aims, but many would hold that, for the cheaper seats, close contact is more important than a view that is clear but remote. Consequently an increasing number of theatres are being built to concepts against which Wagner started the reaction.

The future So where does theatre architecture go next? As we approach the end of the 20th century, a particularly hectic 50 years of intensive theatre building has slowed down. The postwar renewal-and-development phase is complete and economic stagnation has concentrated diminishing resources on maintaining performances on existing stages rather than creating new ones. When new theatres arise, they tend to be adaptations of existing non-theatre buildings, often organized in a very simple spatial way. The clue to the future may lie in the way in which alternative theatres, setting out as a reaction against the established theatre, become absorbed by it. This becomes a cycle of rediscovery: a theatre building and its technology grow until a reaction provokes allegations of decadence and demands for a return to the simplicities of street

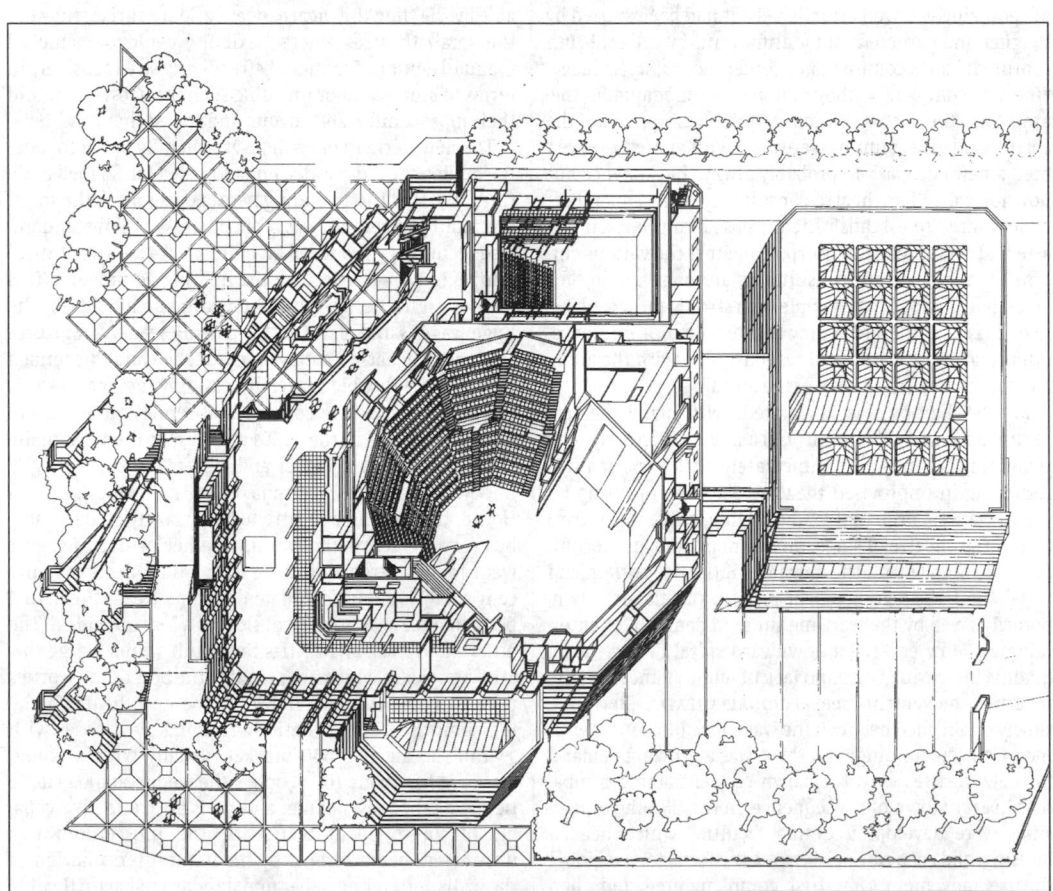

Britain's most recent major theatre building, the West Yorkshire Playhouse, Leeds, (1990), offers two auditoria, a large theatre with the audience wrapped round and above a ground-level stage, and a smaller flexible space allowing end-on, thrust, or in-the-round configurations. (Architects: Ian Appleton Partnership)

theatre. But success in the street builds an audience, and planks are again required to project the passion – the beginning of another escalation that will eventually provoke a reaction. In today's theatres there are so many overlapping cycles that all forms from the simplest to the most sophisticated coexist. There is no reason to suppose that this will change. A whole series of stylistic options for realizing a text in performance will require a similarly wide series of architectural options. Or is the adaptable theatre possible? Technology, which in its rigid systems of elevators and hydraulics seemed to offer only an option of fixed variables which turned out to be more restrictive than an empty space, is now offering, through the air castor, the possibility of moving huge chunks of building around on the hovercraft principle without tracks or other preconceived movement paths. Perhaps this will return architecture to the flexibility of the age of the carpenter.

Meanwhile, simple or complex, we would do well to bear in mind the definition that has been offered by John Orrell: 'The essence of theatre design is to bring players and audience together in a fruitful collaboration, never allowing the two elements to become remote from each other, nor yet so mingling them together that the audience loses its capacity for wonder.' FR

Théâtre de Complicité Founded in 1983 as a touring company, devoted to what was at first called 'physical theatre', influenced by the French MIME director JACQUES LECOQ. They have concentrated on athletic acting in which, as one critic remarked, an actor has to spend as much time on practising back-flips as on vocal delivery. The founder members include Simon McBurney and Kathryn Hunter, two actors whose performances veer towards the grotesque, and whose style pervades the company. *Help! I'm Alive* (1990) was an agile version of a 16th-century Italian FARCE by RUZZANTE, *Il Bilora*, but it was their brilliantly expressionist version (see EXPRESSIONISM) of FRIEDRICH DÜRRENMATT's *The Visit*, seen at the NATIONAL THEATRE in 1991, which established their reputation as an innovative force in British theatre. Their production of *The Winter's Tale* (1992), sacrificed text to tumbling, but McBurney's adaptation of short stories by the Polish writer Bruno Schultz, *The Street of Crocodiles* (1992), was a company triumph at the NT. JE

Théâtre des Funambules (Paris) As the name indicates, this theatre was licensed only for rope dancing and acrobatics when it opened in the Boulevard du Temple in 1813. Two years later it was allowed to stage harlequinades, provided that no word was spoken. It was still more a show-booth than a playhouse when it was taken over by Nicolas Michel Bertrand, who put on topical FARCES and pantoMIMES centred on HARLEQUIN as played by Bambochinet. The young and unknown FRÉDÉRICK LEMAÎTRE appeared there, as did MADAME SAQUI the rope dancer. JEAN-GASPARD DEBURAU joined c.1820 and soon his pale-faced PIERROT was attracting huge crowds. After the 1830 Revolution, Bertrand was enabled to add *vaudevilles* to his bill and rapidly became a millionaire.

The 500-seat theatre boasted a well trapped stage that could accomplish instantaneous scene changes; since there were no intervals (the proletarian public got too rest-less), an average of 15 changes took place in two hours. Bertrand's nephew Billion expanded the house to 773 seats but raised prices as well. When the popular Deburau died in 1846, he was succeeded by his son Charles and by Paul Legrand. The theatre was demolished in 1860 to make way for Baron Haussmann's 'improvements', but by that time it had become legendary as a temple of fantasy for the Parisian populace. LS

Théâtre des Nations Festival of international theatre held for two months of each year in Paris between 1957 and 1968. It had a strong influence on the development of European theatre styles, especially in France, where new discoveries are sometimes hailed with exaggerated enthusiasm. It had begun as the Festival de Paris in 1954, when the visit of the BERLINER ENSEMBLE, giving its first performance in the West, struck many with the force of a revelation. Other companies who visited were Theatre Workshop, the Piccolo Teatro (see GIORGIO STREHLER) and the LIVING THEATRE. Since 1968 international influences have continued to have a significant impact on theatre in France, outstanding examples being the work of OTOMAR KREJČA, GROTOWSKI, the BREAD AND PUPPET THEATRE, ROBERT WILSON and TADEUSZ KANTOR, but the Théâtre des Nations has become peripatetic and is managed by the INTERNATIONAL THEATRE INSTITUTE. DB

theatre design While the necessary ingredients for a theatrical event vary depending upon the needs and expectations of particular societies in particular eras, there are only two elements essential for theatre to occur: a performer and a spectator. But a performance must occur *somewhere*, and if there is space there is, inherently, design.

The design may range from a circular piece of ground surrounded by standing spectators – as in much street theatre, RITUAL performances, and, probably, pre-Aeschylean Greek dance and dithyrambs – to the lavish settings and computerized mechanisms of GRAND OPERA performed for spectators surrounded by baroque splendour. In both cases someone has made decisions about the space, about its delineation, about the relationship of the performer to the space and the space to the spectator, and about the role the space plays in the spectators' responses. All of this is design, and no theatre exists without it. Indeed, it can be argued that design is as essential to theatre as the performer. Theatre is, after all, a visual medium and the size, shape, colour, texture, arrangement and style of the sets, costumes and lights frequently determine the movement and rhythm of a performance and, in conjunction with the theatre space, significantly affect the spectators' responses, even if subliminally (see THEATRE BUILDINGS).

While there are periods in theatre history in which it is possible to talk about scenic design separately from stage architecture – the painterly style of, say, the romantic scenic artists, or the distorted and exaggerated sets of the German expressionists – in most cases there is an indivisible connection between the stage, the overall space of the theatre, and the elements that comprise the scenic design. And in most of the classic periods of theatre history – ancient Greece and Rome, the 15th-century NŌ of Japan, Elizabethan England, 17th-century France and Spain –

there is little scenery *per se*, but formal, architectural stages instead; platforms on which to act. Scenery, by which we normally mean some sort of stage decoration, tends to be either illusionistic – pretending to be something it is not, such as a room or a forest – emblematic, or evocative. Formal stages emphasize their own theatricality, constantly reminding the audience that what they are seeing is taking place in a theatre. Such stages also throw focus on to the performers and the language.

Theatre architecture or space is generally classified according to the relationship of the stage to the audience. Scenic design is usually categorized by its style. There are two broad categories of staging: frontal and environmental. In the former, the audience sees a performance directly in front of it; in the latter, the audience is surrounded to some degree by the performance space. Most theatre, of course, is frontal, and this category can be broken down to end stage – usually a raised stage at one end of a rectangular theatre, directly facing an audience; thrust – a stage surrounded on three sides by audience; and arena – a stage completely surrounded by the audience. Needless to say, there are many variants on this arrangement, most notably the booth or trestle stage generally associated with popular entertainment and certain forms of medieval staging. It consists of a raised stage, usually with a curtain or scenic backdrop at the rear creating a 'backstage' area for costume changes, storage and entrances. It differs from an endstage only in that it is most frequently used outdoors or as a temporary structure in spaces not normally used for theatre.

It might be noted that outdoor theatre (which includes most theatre throughout approximately the first 2000 years of both occidental and oriental theatre history) tends to blur the distinction between frontal and environmental staging. Many plays and theatre structures in such surroundings incorporate natural events and topography into the design and production in a way that indoor theatres rarely do, leading the spectator to perceive him or herself surrounded by the 'design'.

Design is broadly categorized as presentational or representational. Representational theatre tries to create an illusion of reality. Presentational theatre emphasizes theatricality and acknowledges the theatre as theatre – there is no illusion. This is perhaps best expressed in the *Natyasastra* of Bharata, the ancient Sanskrit treatise on theatre: 'Some accessories ... will be Realistic, while others will be conventional. Any thing following its natural form is called Realistic, while any deviation from the same will be known as Conventional.' Just as in the history of art, there are many individual styles too numerous to list here. There are, however, three general classifications that are worth noting: architectural, sculptural and painterly. Architectural stages – such as those of ancient Greece and Rome, Elizabethan England, and most of the permanent stages of classic Indian, Chinese and Japanese theatres – are the result of a marriage between design and architecture. The features of the stage – arches, platforms, doors, steps and so on – are permanently built into the stage space. While specific scenery and set pieces may be used within a production to transform the stage into a specific place, the designer and performers are limited by the basic architecture.

Sculptural settings see the stage space as a cubic volume and, like sculptures, emphasize the fact by organizing the space around themselves. They emphasize three-dimensionality of the stage space (rather than creating an *illusion* of depth) by the use of three-dimensional forms and the sculpting of space with light. This is largely a 20th-century phenomenon and is typified by the use of geometric forms, abstract structures, platforms and steps. It is sometimes referred to as a structural stage.

Painterly, as the name suggests, relies on painted images, usually to create an illusion of place, or to evoke a particular mood or sensibility. Painterly designs of one style or another dominated much Western theatre design from the Renaissance until fairly recently.

Greek theatre The method of presentation of Greek theatre apparently evolved from the dancing circle or *orchēstra* upon the threshing floor of the Agora (see also GREECE, ANCIENT). When the first Theatre of Dionysus was built on the hillside of the Acropolis a more formal orchestra was created by levelling part of the slope. Very little is known of the physical aspects of the early Greek theatre. The earliest version of the Theatre of Dionysus probably presented the spectators – who were seated on the hillside or perhaps on wooden benches – with no more than the orchestra and a view of the Temple of Dionysus behind it and the sea in the distance. All the extant plays prior to about 460 BC take place in the open countryside or in a barren place; there are no references to buildings of any kind. When the hillside was levelled, an embankment of some six feet was created at the rear of the orchestra. AESCHYLUS probably took advantage of this in *Prometheus Bound* and had Prometheus sink behind the embankment as if into the earth, presumably to rise again at the start of the second play of the trilogy, the fragmentary *Prometheus Unbound*.

This being an outdoor theatre, lighting, of course, came from the sun. But even so, the playwrights learned to utilize natural phenomena in the design. The performances commenced at dawn, and several plays incorporate the sunrise into the script. In Aeschylus' *Agamemnon*, for example, the play begins with the watchman waiting for a beacon that will announce the capture of Troy. In his speech he refers to the waning stars, the morning dew, and, if the timing was accurate, the sunrise. 'Oh hail, blaze of the darkness,' he cries, 'harbinger of the day's shining.' Similarly, the opening of EURIPIDES' *Iphigenia at Aulis*: 'That light/Shows the approach of morn, the harbinger/Of the sun's fiery steeds.'

Sometime in the mid-5th century a *skēne* or scene building was introduced. The evidence is so minimal that scholars cannot agree on its size or shape. In its earliest versions it was probably a temporary wooden structure which later became more elaborate and permanent. But whatever its form, the *skēne* provided playwrights and performers with greatly expanded possibilities. About two-thirds of the extant tragedies occur before a temple or palace which could, of course, be represented by the *skēne*. The door (perhaps three doors by the end of the 5th century) allowed for exits and entrances, and the possibility of concealment and surprise. The roof of the *skēne* provided a raised stage for certain scenes, particularly the appearance of gods.

Through the next century the emphasis shifted from the chorus to the actor, and hence the size of the orchestra shrank as the stage was raised higher.

Scholars have debated fiercely about the use of painted scenery in conjunction with the architectural stage. In the *Poetics* ARISTOTLE claims that SOPHOCLES introduced *skenographia* which has generally been taken to mean 'scene painting'. There is, however, no evidence or reference to scene painting, or to specific, illusionistic or changeable scenery in any other source except the writings of the Roman architect Vitruvius. Writing in the 1st century BC he says that Agatharchus first created scenery, but he implies that this was a permanent image depicting architectural perspective – in other words, a decoration or generic scene. Those who have tried to make a case for play-specific decor tend to be influenced by the general use of literal and realistic scenery of Western theatre in the 19th and 20th centuries. The Greek theatre was a theatre of convention; locale, by and large, was suggested through dialogue and actions in front of a bare façade or an unchanging stylized background as in the Japanese *nō* theatre.

There is evidence, however, for at least two mechanical scenic devices. One is the *mechane* or 'machine', probably a crane-like device for flying gods, chariots and the like – hence the phrase *deus ex machina*, or god from the machine. There is no evidence that Aeschylus or Sophocles used the device but it was used frequently by Euripides (and was parodied by ARISTOPHANES); the phrase came to signify a contrived ending. The other device is the *ekkyklema*, a rolling platform or wagon that was wheeled out through the door of the *skēne* to display a tableau or scene such as the end of *Agamemnon*, in which Clytemnestra is discovered with the bodies of Agamemnon and Cassandra. The fact that an 'interior' scene now intruded upon what had been an 'exterior' scene apparently did not trouble Greek audiences. The unities of time and place, so rigidly demanded by Renaissance interpreters of Aristotle, were unnecessary in a theatre of suggestion, imagination and convention.

It should be noted, however, that as Greek theatre evolved through the 5th century, there was an increasing tendency towards greater NATURALISM. Thus, in the plays of Euripides it is no longer sufficient to say that it is night; the performers must also carry torches. By the 4th century BC there were very likely more scenic devices such as the *pinakes* or painted panels set in niches or between supporting columns. Vitruvius suggests that these were made of wood and functioned as sound resonators as well as decoration. Vitruvius also speaks of *periaktoi* – prism-shaped scenic pieces with scenes painted on each of their three sides. When the *periaktoi* was rotated, a change of scene could be suggested.

Roman theatre The great period of Roman playwriting, the period of PLAUTUS and TERENCE, occurred in the 2nd century BC, but this was before the building of the first permanent theatres in ROME. The theatre of Pompey was not constructed until 80 BC. In Rome itself theatre was performed on temporary platform stages; elsewhere it could be done in existing Greek and Graeco-Roman theatres. Virtually all the extant comedies are set on a street in front of three houses, suggesting that even in the 2nd century the stage was probably a bare platform with three doors in the façade behind the stage. When Roman theatres were finally constructed the Greek *skēne* became the *scaenae frons*, a three-tiered façade of pillars, niches and statuary with three doors (and one door at either side of the stage). The Romans also used two kinds of curtains: the *aulaeum*, a front curtain, possibly decorated, that *lowered* into a trough in front of the stage; and the *siparium*, which was a relatively small painted drop or backcloth that covered part of the *scaenae frons* and was raised and lowered somewhat in the manner of a Venetian blind. The *siparia* were clearly used to suggest more specific locales, yet, ironically, the extant Roman plays tend to be less specific in their identification of place than the Greek.

A major difference between the Roman theatre and the Greek resulted from the Romans' architectural use of the arch. This device allowed free-standing structures of great size, and the theatre no longer had to be built into a hill. The *cavea* or auditorium of the Roman theatre was architecturally unified with stage or *proscenium*. (And the *cavea* was probably at least partially covered by a *velarium*, or awning.) For the spectator this meant being enclosed within a unified space, separated from the world outside. This differed from the Greek experience of a play as religious festival which was intrinsically set within the natural and religious surroundings. The early Greek theatre, was, in a sense, able to incorporate the physical world within the experience of the play. The Roman experience was one of escapism; the Greek, at least prior to the Hellenistic period, was one of communion.

Legitimate theatre atrophied in the period of the Roman Empire. But the spectacles and paratheatrical events which supplanted theatre, such as NAUMACHIA, gladiatorial games and *venationes*, also employed scenery ranging from the epic (Caesar's man-made lake and replicas of warships for *naumachia*) to the simple and suggestive that was used to give a sense of narrative story to many of the bloodthirsty events at the Colosseum. What survived the fall of Rome was the popular entertainer, the one constant throughout theatre history. Obviously, there is little information on such performances, but the little evidence and documentation that does survive indicates that the presentation has remained virtually unchanged from Greek times to the present. Performers who presented plays or skits (as opposed to simple CIRCUS skills) used a platform stage with a painted backcloth. It is this stage that became the basic scenic element of medieval theatre.

Medieval theatre Certain staging concepts predominated in the Middle Ages that may seem alien to modern audiences used to a more or less realistic approach to design (see MEDIEVAL DRAMA IN EUROPE). Of greatest significance were the ideas of *simultaneous setting* and *emblematic design*. Simultaneous setting involved the depiction of several discrete locations simultaneously, rather than sequentially, which is more common in contemporary theatre. In some cases the spectators moved from one scene to the next; but the scenes could also exist side by side on a raised stage. Emblematic design involves the suggestion of a place or idea by use of an image or device. For example, in certain medieval productions Jerusalem was depicted simply by a gate, and hell by an open-mouthed monster head spewing fire and smoke.

LITURGICAL DRAMA developed within the church, and it was to a great extent the architectural elements of the church – the balconies, aisles, tombs, altar – that provided the theatrical design. The basic arrangement and use of space is what has come to be called *mansion* and *platea* or (with raised mansions) place and scaffold. The *mansion* was an emblematic structure suggesting a location, person or idea (e.g. Bethlehem, Herod, Paradise); the *platea* was the neutral space in front of or surrounding the *mansion*. From the earliest records it is evident that the *mansion* could involve the making of a separate structure, but it is also clear that even in the 16th century some churches still simply used altar, rood screen or other pre-existing structure for performance. The most elaborate structures within churches for which descriptions survive are the Italian ones of the early 15th century (e.g. those of Brunelleschi, 1377–1446), where the *platea* appears to have become something akin to a raised stage and the older distinction between *mansion* and *platea* in many ways no longer exists.

Information about the early outdoor place and scaffold staging is very limited. There are the often detailed descriptions of the elaborate scaffolds and indications of *platea* action in the *Jeu d'Adam* (12th century), which is generally thought to be designed for outdoor performance, but most of the information comes from very much later: the BOOTH STAGES (in the paintings of Brueghel and others), the Dutch rhetoricians' stages, the Easter Play from Lucerne, the PASSIONS from Mons and Valenciennes – all are from the 16th century.

Most medieval theatres used some variant of the *mansion* and *platea* idea. The pageant wagons of English and Spanish mystery cycles were essentially rolling *mansions* with the street or square as *platea*. The raised stage and simultaneous setting of the MYSTERY PLAY at Valenciennes, for example, was a frontal version of the *mansion* and *platea*. Likewise, the presentation of secular FARCES at inn yards, palaces and market squares, and the 'in-the-round' staging of plays in the Cornish 'rounds', all employed the concept of *mansion* and *platea*.

The *mansions* (or *pageants*, as the wagons were often called) were not intended to contain the action, as this stage direction from the Coventry cycle shows: 'Here Herod rages in the pageant and in the street also.' By the act of stepping out of a *mansion* the actor transformed all the space through which he moved into an extension of the *mansion*, even if he performed in front of another scenic unit. The *platea* could also function metaphorically. The movement of performers or audience through the *platea* to another *mansion* functioned as a movement through time and space. A walk of a few yards could transport the spectators from Rome to Jerusalem, from Noah's Ark to Egypt.

In terms of the scenic elements, the medieval productions employed a seemingly contradictory mixture of realistic and emblematic devices. There are accounts of actors playing Christ or Judas who had to be removed from their respective crosses or nooses because they had nearly died in reality. Yet the parting of the Red Sea, not easily achieved on a rolling pageant, might be suggested by part-ing a red cloth which was subsequently draped over the 'Egyptians' to indicate their being swallowed up by the Sea. As with simultaneity, medieval audiences saw no con-tradictions in this style.

Classical Asian theatre Though some scholars have attempted to demonstrate that Greek theatre exerted an influence upon the development of Indian theatre, as it followed the conquests of Alexander the Great, no con-crete evidence supports this. Concrete evidence, in fact, is problematic for virtually all ancient Asian theatre. While Indian and Chinese theatrical forms were most likely flourishing by the 2nd century BC, and emerging in Japan by the 7th century AD, the temporary theatres in which performances were presented never transformed into per-manent stone structures as they did in Greece and Rome. Hence, they left no structures or ruins to help modern scholars to re-create the ancient theatre. Furthermore, pic-torial evidence of theatrical presentation is also lacking from the ancient eras in virtually all Asian cultures. Information on design and architecture must come from literary sources such as the *Natyasastra*, surviving the-atres, mostly from the 19th century, and illustrations, mostly from the 18th century onward, though there are some earlier examples.

All classical Asian forms employ architectural stages and some form of emblematic and symbolic scenery and decoration. Painted scenery and overt realism were virtu-ally unknown. As with the ancient Greek and medieval European theatre, many Asian forms emerged from or were associated with religious ceremonies. Thus, there is often a sense of the stage as a sacred or consecrated space even if an altar is no longer present. Such a sensibility rein-forces the idea of stage as stage, or emblematic stage, and is not conducive to scenic illusionism.

The *Natyasastra* gives elaborate instructions for the con-struction of various types of playhouses which, it says, 'should be made like a mountain cavern', but emphasizes a relatively intimate space as ideal. Within the theatre were to be four pillars representing each caste. The stage floor was to be inlaid with diamonds, gold, lapis lazuli, quartz and coral, each at a specific site within the stage. The woodwork was to have decorative designs including figures of elephants, tigers and snakes, while the plastered and whitewashed walls were to be painted with images of 'men, women, and their amorous exploits'. The back of the stage was delineated by the tiring house wall in which were two doors with screens overhead. This wall was by convention the east; the orchestra sat between the doors. The stage was divided into invisible zones that functioned somewhat as the *platea* of the medieval theatre of Europe. A character's placement within a zone would indicate locale, and movement through zones could suggest a change of time and place. The zones could represent any-thing from a house, garden, forest or city to the earth, sea, 'three worlds ... any one of the nine great divisions of the earth or its seven continents or any of the different moun-tains, the invisible world ... or the nether world'. Frequent changes of locale within a single scene are not uncommon in Sanskrit drama, and suggestion of place was often achieved through poetic reference rather than physical means.

Nonetheless, certain props and set pieces existed in the classical Indian theatre. While the *Natyasastra* notes that various weapons and architectural units cannot be made realistically, it suggests methods for constructing emblematic set pieces including hills, palaces, mountains, horses, elephants, 'aerial cars' and houses. It is very likely that these units functioned much in the way of medieval *mansions*, as representations of place or as embodiments of concepts such as kingship. The emblematic design of classical Indian theatre was reinforced through elaborate and colourful costumes, make-up and body paint.

While these classical practices survive in such forms as *KUTIYATTAM*, modern Indian theatre has been strongly influenced by European models since British colonial times. Interestingly, 18th-century changeable scenery and a wing-and-groove system of scene changing, introduced by the British, has survived in some Indian theatres long after it has disappeared in England.

Although many forms of drama have emerged in China over the past 2000 years, most evidence suggests that the stage unit was most often some variant of the booth or trestle stage – a raised bare stage with a curtained back wall and frequently a roof. The traditional Chinese stage may have had a carpeted floor and lacquered columns supporting the roof. Scenery, therefore, was primarily ornamental decoration within the theatre structure. Beijing opera (see *JINGXI*), which in its current form dates only to the late 18th century, employs nothing more than a few chairs and a table which, by convention, may represent, for instance, a throne, a mountain, a bridge, a tower or a bed (a cloth suspended between two chairs). Beijing opera is perhaps the most starkly emblematic theatre in the world: two yellow flags with painted wheels twirled by an actor represent a chariot; an actor running across the stage with a small black flag becomes the wind; a banner with a painted fish represents water, while the same banner rolled up on a platter becomes a fish. The true scenic design of the classical Chinese theatre, though, is to be found in the lavish costumes and make-up.

The classical forms of Japanese theatre, notably NŌ and *KABUKI*, likewise use formal stages, but even in the relatively austere nō the emblematic elements are rigidly prescribed, and the more popular *kabuki* employs decorative scenery and elaborate stage mechanisms. The current nō stage dates from the early 17th century. It consists of a rectangular stage with pillars at each corner, the *atoza*, or rear stage, where the orchestra sits, and the *hashigakari*, or bridge, that leads at an angle from the upstage right side of the *atoza* to the curtained dressing room. Even after the theatre moved indoors the stage and *hashigakari* continued to be covered by a roof in Shinto shrine style. Each pillar has a symbolic and conventional meaning and is named according to character association or spatial function. The upstage wall is painted with a pine tree and the upstage left wall is painted with bamboo. These paintings are not scenery *per se* but stylized reminders of the outdoor origins of the nō stage. Three real pine trees are planted along the front of the *hashigakari* representing heaven, earth and man. All nō drama is presented within this setting and, while props are used, no other scenery is introduced.

The *kabuki* stage evolved from the nō stage over a period of some 300 years. Most scholars feel it achieved its ideal form by about 1830, but it continued to change to accommodate larger audiences and Western architectural styles, notably the proscenium. The 20th-century *kabuki* theatre bears a strong resemblance to the modern European opera house. Its key components are the wide, relatively shallow stage with a revolve and trap lifts, and the *hanamichi*, a runway through or along the side of the audience by which performers make their entrances on to the stage.

The decor of the *kabuki* is illusionistic in that it depicts specific locales, but it is actually emblematic in that it is a scenic indication of place or spatial relationships which is set in opposition to the performer. Unlike European Renaissance perspective which created an illusion of a stage that was an extension of the auditorium, receding behind the performer, the *kabuki* scene emphasizes its painted flatness. Perspective painting was introduced into Japan in the 18th century, and this was adapted to theatrical use on sliding stage doors or panels by the 1760s. But the idea of the character existing within the decor is primarily a Western concept that is alien to Japanese performance. Perspective in the *kabuki* became a tool to indicate movement or to create psychological space. A character's departure from a house, for instance, could be indicated by opening a pair of sliding doors to reveal a smaller set of doors, which in turn could be opened to reveal a yet smaller set, and so on. Perspective in this case becomes not an illusionistic device but a sign system to convey the concept of departure. Opening screens to reveal a perspective vista is a means used on other occasions to suggest a greater sense of space on an otherwise crowded stage. As we will see, Renaissance perspective, too, existed in opposition to the performer because to enter into the scenic space of the stage was to destroy illusion, but it nonetheless suggested a unity with the actor. *Kabuki* scenography emphasizes the three-dimensionality of the actor and the theatricality of the stage space while semiotically indicating locale.

In addition to the painted backdrop the *kabuki* may also utilize a platform to indicate an interior or, occasionally, an exterior, scene. The latter may be further indicated through the use of scenic elements such as rocks or trees. Interiors may use three-dimensional or painted scenic units such as furniture. Simultaneous scenes suggesting interiors and exteriors are sometimes used. The height of the platform is also an indication of social rank – it may represent ordinary homes, samurai homes, and temples or palaces.

By the late 18th century, spectacle began to be an essential element of *kabuki*. Sudden and startling scene changes are characteristic of the form. Namiko Shozo is credited with the invention of both the trap lift (1727) and the revolving stage (1758). Trap lifts could range from small units for individual scenic pieces and later for actors, to large elevators for the sudden revelation of entire settings. The revolving stage could be used for changing scenery, of course, but was also employed for changing the point of view in a particular scene. Though temporary revolves were used in European Renaissance productions as early as 1602, the 'invention' of the revolving stage at the Munich Residenz Theater in 1896 owes a great deal to the *kabuki*.

The Renaissance The road to naturalistic design – the attempt to create an illusion of reality or verisimilitude – began in the Renaissance; and at the same time theory, design and architecture combined radically to alter the relationship between the stage and the auditorium. The three most significant developments in this period were the relocation of the theatre indoors, the discovery of techniques for creating perspective sets, and the evolution of changeable scenery.

The physical theatre of the period evolved as Renaissance scholars became aware of Vitruvius' *De Architectura*, which contained descriptions of Greek and Roman theatres, but no illustrations. SEBASTIANO SERLIO, the most significant designer and theatre architect of the period, first addressed the problems of design and architecture in his treatise *Architettura* (1545). Synthesizing the ideas of Vitruvius and others, he set forth a plan for a classical-style theatre, but one that would be temporary and housed in existing spaces – usually the rectangular great halls of palaces. As Serlio and others interpreted Vitruvius they inevitably devised a classical theatre that was informed by the technology, sensibilities and aesthetics of the Renaissance.

This can be seen in the early attempts at staging the rediscovered plays of TERENCE and PLAUTUS, for which *mansions* were placed on a raised end stage – the so-called Terence stages. Illustrations from that period, however, suggest that the *mansions* were placed side by side and architecturally unified; they were more like curtained sections of an arcade screen than the free-standing *mansions* of the Middle Ages or the doors of the *scaenae frons*. Whereas the medieval stage allowed the juxtaposition of seemingly incongruous scenery, and symbolic movement through time and space, the Renaissance sensibility moved towards unification and rationality in its attempt to maintain the ideal of verisimilitude.

The Teatro Olimpico at Vicenza, designed by ANDREA PALLADIO and VINCENZO SCAMOZZI, opened in 1585, is the most stunning example of the combination of classical and Renaissance ideas, as well as being the first permanent theatre of the Italian Renaissance. The theatre had to fit into an existing space, and thus the auditorium became elliptical rather than semicircular. But the long, narrow stage was backed by an elaborate *scaenae frons* with three arched openings and a doorway at either side. Behind the three arches, however, were five 'streets' lined by buildings constructed in perspective style, thus adding contemporary practice to classical design. This theatre, though, was unique and had little impact on the subsequent development of theatre architecture.

Another Teatro Olimpico, this one at Sabbioneta, was designed by Scamozzi alone. Opened in 1588, it was essentially a permanent adaptation of Serlio's design in which a scenic stage – a stage constructed for the purpose of displaying scenery – rather than an architectural stage was used. This small theatre was the true precursor of modern theatre architecture.

The rules of perspective – which enabled an object or scene to be painted which, when viewed from a particular point, achieved mathematically correct spatial relationships – were developed in the early 15th century. The first-known use of perspective scenery was for ARIOSTO's *La Cassaria* at Ferrara in 1508, designed by Pelligrino da Udine. The chief proponent of perspective design in the 16th century was BALDASSARE PERUZZI, whose work and ideas were enhanced and disseminated by Serlio, his student. The development of perspective design was facilitated by its use in the *intermezzi*, or spectacle performances, often staged by the Medicis (and others), for whom BERNARDO BUONTALENTI was chief architect, designer and machinist (inventing the machines that created the special effects).

Perspective scenery made possible the illusion of real space onstage. Now, rather than looking at discrete units of emblematic scenery, the audience saw a view of the stage that appeared to be a continuation of the auditorium – a vista of a street, perhaps, that seemed to disappear into the distance just as a real street would. Of course, the illusion was totally successful only from a fixed point in the auditorium directly opposite the stage.

Serlio, working from Vitruvius, devised three generic perspective scenes – one tragic, one comic, one satyric – that were to be used for all plays. The first two were city streets with buildings on either side that appeared to recede into the distance upstage, the tragic showing columns, pediments and stately buildings, and the comic showing private residences, shops and balconies. The satyric showed trees, caverns and rustic dwellings. The illusion was to be created through perspective-painted book flats diminishing in size on either side of a raked stage, converging towards a central vanishing point on a perspective-painted backcloth or back shutter at the rear of the stage.

Several things become apparent in considering these scenes. First, the offstage sides had to be concealed in order for the illusion to be believable; second, actors could not move within the scenic stage without destroying the illusion – they would be significantly larger than the scenery as they moved upstage; and third, there was no easy way to alter the location without disrupting the performance.

The problem of masking the wings was solved by framing the stage. The Teatro Farnese, built in 1618 and designed by GIOVANNI BATTISTA ALEOTTI, is the first-known example of a proscenium arch theatre. The proscenium – in essence an architectural picture frame – hid not only the offstage side of the flats, but the increasingly elaborate stage machinery being developed in order to change the scenes or create special effects. More significantly, the frame had a perceptual effect; it psychologically distanced the spectator, making the audience more of a voyeur than a participant. The irony of the Renaissance theatre was that, once the audience was architecturally separated from the stage by the proscenium arch, it was pictorially unified with it through perspective illusion.

It is worth noting at this point that scholars have debated the origin of the proscenium arch, attributing it variously to an expansion of the unifying frame of the Terence stages, to triumphal arches erected for public processions, to the central arch of the Teatro Olimpico of Vicenza, and to the method of framing paintings in that time. While these undoubtedly contributed to the general perceptions of art and performance, and may have provided a subliminal inspiration, the framing of the stage seems to be a logical response to the exigencies of presentation and the Renaissance ideal of unity.

The second problem, that of the actor, was solved by keeping the performance space in front of the scenery. Serlio's 1545 plan for a temporary theatre shows a semi-circular orchestra used primarily as a seating area for distinguished spectators, a raised, relatively shallow stage, and a raked, fairly deep scenic stage. In this arrangement, the performers could go no farther upstage than the first wing. In many of the early court theatres in Italy and elsewhere, however, the orchestra was replaced with an extremely deep thrust stage surrounded by a horseshoe-shaped auditorium with a raised scenic stage at the rear. The result was a theatre divided into three discrete sections: the auditorium, the performance stage and the scenic stage.

During the 16th to the 18th centuries, the baroque and rococo period, theatre architecture was dominated by the Italianate ideal and the trend was towards ever deeper scenic stages that facilitated more splendid and spectacular design while allowing the actors to step further and further into the scene. It was not until the mid-19th century, however, that the actor was totally enveloped within the environment of the proscenium stage. It is important to note that even with increasing depth, the full perspective illusion still worked only for that part of the audience seated directly opposite the stage.

Although neoclassical theoreticians interpreted Aristotle as demanding the unities of time, place and action – arguing whether a play could unfold in several locations or had to be confined to a single room – the audiences delighted in spectacle, and changeable scenery emerged to cater to this taste. Early attempts at changing scenes tended to be awkward, and it was suggested in all seriousness that the audience be momentarily distracted by staging a fight or blowing horns at the rear of the auditorium. In the early 17th century Aleotti developed a system of flat wings that could be slid on and off the stage in grooves. While this greatly simplified and improved changes it was still inefficient, and it was GIACOMO TORELLI, probably the most important designer of the 17th century – called *il gran stregoni* (the great wizard) – who developed the chariot-and-pole system at the Teatro Novissimo in Venice in the 1640s. By cutting slots in the stage floor, flats with rods descending through the slots to rolling wagons all attached to a single winch could be smoothly and easily shifted. Overhead borders were shifted in the same way. The changing of scenes, which created an impression somewhat like cinematic dissolves, became so fascinating that totally unnecessary shifts were made during the course of a production for the pure delight of seeing it.

While the performances of neoclassical drama tended to be played in front of an unchanging scene, intermezzi – allegorical scenes presented between the five acts of the drama or as part of court spectacles and performances – developed in Italy into lavish and wondrous displays of scenic technology. By the mid-1600s audiences could be awed by the sight of choruses of angels descending from the deepest recesses of the stage on cloud machines (scenic elements that looked like clouds and would unfold to reveal often scores of performers); gods arriving in flying chariots; rocky grottoes transforming into stormy seas complete with ships. Thus, by the 17th century an audience at such a spectacle was treated to the experience of a TRAGEDY or COMEDY in five acts in front of a single setting that was transformed at the close of each act into an allegorical scene of fantasy and splendour. Although the scenes depicted in the intermezzi were fantasy, they were done in perspective illusion – a sort of fantastic realism.

The design and technology of the intermezzi affected the development of OPERA in the 17th century. The ability easily to transform scenes – to travel through time and space – allowed the scenes of the opera to occur anywhere. The librettist was no longer confined by the limitations of a single setting. Also, the work of Torelli and his contemporary Alfonso Parigi (see GIULIO PARIGI) led to an increased ability to control light through the use of reflectors and lens-like devices. The theatre moved indoors in the Renaissance and developments in lighting control made it possible not only to illuminate the stage, but to contribute to the illusion and mood and enhance the effects of changeable scenery. Costumes for the opera tended to be lavish and embroidered in gold and silver – a perfect surface for the reflection of light that added even more spectacle.

While these developments occurred in Italy and had their greatest impact on the evolution of opera design and architecture, the theatre in England, France and Spain developed in somewhat different directions.

Although English culture and scholarship turned to Italy for inspiration, the English theatre of the Renaissance emerged organically out of the strong traditions of medieval theatre. The physical theatre combined the trestle stages and presentational style – MANSION and *platea* – of liturgical and popular theatre; the architecture of the great halls of manors and castles (generally rectangular rooms with an arcade screen against one end containing one to three doors and a balcony above) commonly used for the presentation of INTERLUDES; and existing structures such as bull- and bear-BAITING arenas and courtyards. Concrete evidence is frustratingly lacking, but the generally accepted view is that most of the thriving Elizabethan theatres were circular or polygonal three-tiered structures with audience galleries or boxes in each tier; a trestle-style stage thrusting into the arena or 'pit', behind which were one to three doors leading into the backstage area known as the TIRING HOUSE; a roof over the stage supported by two columns; and, perhaps, the second gallery continuing through this back wall to be used as a balcony if necessary (as in *Romeo and Juliet*) or for spectators at other times, thus creating an arena stage. The pit contained standing patrons. Scenery was minimal; existing records suggest some generic props including chairs, tables, thrones, rocks, trees and the like. There may have been some *mansion*-like scenic pieces, but these would have to have been placed upstage so as not to hamper sightlines. Thus, while the Italianate ideal of complex and illusionistic changeable scenery was spreading throughout Europe, English popular theatre achieved the same rapid changes of locale through language and imagination.

In the court theatre of James I and Charles I, however, the Italian style thrived. In the MASQUES designed by INIGO

A 'Glory' on stage at San Salvatore Opera House, Venice, 1675.

JONES, who had spent time in Italy and been influenced by the work of Palladio as well as the scenic artists, perspective illusion and clever machinery created lavish spectacle. But while the court and PUBLIC THEATRES coexisted, there was little, if any, scenographic influence of one upon the other until the Restoration.

The Italian ideal spread more rapidly in Paris. Through the mid-1630s staging was essentially medieval with simultaneous, *mansion*-like settings on a raised end stage. Many illustrations of these settings are preserved in a volume by the designer LAURENT MAHELOT. The illustrations suggest that certain scenes, especially those on the backcloth, may have been painted in perspective. The *mansions*, too, may well have bridged the two eras, as many of Mahelot's illustrations suggest that the *mansions* were painted on flats along either edge of the stage, thus combining a medieval concept with Italian techniques. It was CARDINAL RICHELIEU who first brought Italian staging to Paris. The Palais Cardinal (PALAIS-ROYAL after Richelieu's death in 1642) was designed by Le Mercier, and was the first French theatre to have a permanent proscenium arch and employ painted-perspective wings. It was built in a rectangular space with galleries along each side; the king and his special guests were seated in the orchestra or *parterre* section while the majority of spectators sat in the galleries facing each other and the king, rather than the stage. The theatre opened in 1641 with *Mirame*, designed by Georges Buffequin.

Cardinal Mazarin brought Torelli to Paris, where he grudgingly designed for the *COMMEDIA DELL'ARTE* troupe but also remodelled the PETIT-BOURBON as a chariot-and-pole theatre and staged *La Finta Pazzi* there in 1645. The opera was a huge success and firmly established Italianate staging in France. The marvels of the new scenography became so popular, in fact, that a genre emerged known as 'machine plays' which consisted essentially of a minimal plot that could be used as an excuse for scenographic wonders – opera without singing. GASPARE VIGARANI, brought to Paris by Mazarin in 1659, built the SALLE DES MACHINES on the site of the former Petit-Bourbon. When opened in 1662 with the opera *Hercules in Love*, it was the largest theatre in Europe, with a stage depth of 140ft (42.67m), a proscenium opening of only 32ft (9.7m) and a cloud machine capable of flying 300 people.

The French public theatres of the time – the HÔTEL DE BOURGOGNE, the MARAIS and others – were long, narrow theatres with raised end stages. The theatre form was determined to some extent by the royal tennis courts in which makeshift theatres were erected from time to time. The tennis courts had a seating gallery along one side – ideal for viewing the back-and-forth action of a tennis game, but singularly unsuited for theatre. Nonetheless, existing architecture and economics won over common sense.

Many of the etchings from the time showing productions by MOLIÈRE's troupe or the earlier farces at the Hôtel de Bourgogne depict what appears to be a very shallow architectural stage, sometimes with a single chair or throne as sole scenic element. In actuality, the 'architectural' façade was constructed scenery, but was placed in the first wing position, creating a very shallow stage and functioning as an architectural setting would. Many of the

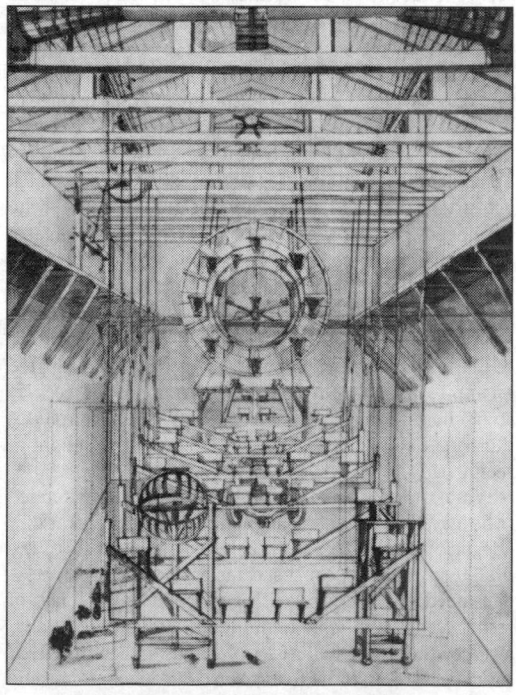

Stage machinery for the same, 1675.

plays of Molière and his contemporaries adhered fairly well to the unity of place, and the action was frequently set in a single room – a generic room whose specificity was unimportant. Acting in 17th-century Paris generally consisted of standing near the centre of the stage, rather estranged from the scenic background; the scene provided entrances and places of concealment and a vague suggestion of place. Even the tragedies were presented in front of stock scenes: the *palais à volonté* and a *chambre à quatre ports*. This isolation was reinforced by spectators who sat on the edges of the stage, essentially creating a thrust stage. Thus the scenery functioned as a medieval *mansion* – a suggestion of locale – with the stage as *platea*.

Although the size and complexity of Parisian theatres grew through the 18th century, the basic arrangement – rectangular auditorium, seating along sides of a *parterre*, and scenic end stage – remained constant.

The English theatre of the Restoration became a strange amalgam of the Elizabethan thrust stage and the Continental scenic stage that became familiar to English royalty and theatre practitioners exiled in Paris. As in France, the early Restoration theatres were built in converted tennis courts. In the early 1670s two theatres were built: DORSET GARDEN and DRURY LANE, both designed by Christopher Wren. The theatres were sometimes identified by the auditorium arrangement of 'box, pit, and gallery'. The gallery was the open seating of the upper balcony, the boxes were the private compartments along the sides and back of the theatre, and the pit was the floor level which in this case was filled with rows of benches. With the building of Drury Lane in 1674, Wren created a fan-shaped auditorium which has been the basis of much theatre architecture ever since.

The acting area consisted of a deep, raked stage *in front* of the proscenium. The upper tier of boxes extended along the side of this stage and entrances were made by doors – two on either side, and referred to as proscenium doors – beneath the boxes. Behind the proscenium were sliding wing-and-groove, perspective scenes (chariot-and-pole was seldom used in England). Somewhat as in the French theatres, the actor was thus isolated from the scenery. Entrances and exits were generally made through the proscenium doors, regardless of dramatic location; a door could lead to 'another part of the forest' as easily as to a palace room. Scenery tended to be stock scenes of rooms, palaces, parks and so on; and, of course, the perspective illusion allowed for little interaction between actor and scenery. The result was that the performers were intimately connected to the audience – surrounded on three sides by them and sharing the same architectural space – while the scenery was architecturally separated from the performers and spectators by the proscenium. Audience onstage, until removed by DAVID GARRICK in 1762, also contributed to the isolation of the performer.

Lighting was another factor in the use and perception of space (see STAGE LIGHTING). The auditorium remained lighted by chandeliers; and the lighting on the scenic stage was generally not as bright as that on the forestage. But through the 18th century, the control and brightness of light increased so that it was possible to illuminate the scenery more brightly than the forestage. This, in combination with increased skill at perspective scenery and the

desire of the managers to make more money by creating space for more spectators, led to the slow but ineluctable shrinkage of the forestage as the actors retreated into the scenery.

While Italy's importance to the world of drama rapidly declined through the 17th century, it still dominated design until well into the 18th. The main reason for this was the work of a remarkable family of designers and architects, beginning with Giovanni Maria Galli da BIBIENA and continuing through four generations to the end of the 18th century. Their work dominated court spectacle, performance, opera and ballet throughout Europe, from St Petersburg to London. The work of the Bibienas is the epitome of the triumphant and grandiose style of the baroque.

Ferdinando Bibiena is usually credited with the next major innovation in stage design, the *scena per angolo* or multipoint (angled) perspective in 1703. But evidence suggests that this technique was used as early as 1694 by Marcantonio Chiarini in *La Forza della virtù* at Bologna. Until this time, all perspective scenery had a single vanishing point – for a spectator seated in an ideal position, the scenery seemed to disappear at a single point in the distance. Because of this, the scenery appeared to be an extension of the auditorium; it was in the same scale as the spectators. Multipoint perspective, as the name implies, could have several vanishing points. The effect of this, apart from more varied possibilities, was to free the stage from the auditorium. The scene behind the proscenium no longer had to conform to the scale of the spectators; it could be larger than life. There was no need for symmetry; a scene could be shown from any point of view. The designs of the Bibienas in the 18th century were marked by soaring splendour, as seemingly vast rooms and colonnades disappeared in the heights above the proscenium and divergent corridors seemed to dissolve into the far depths of the stage. Now, not only did the proscenium create an architectural separation between spectator and performance, but the setting, too, depicted not merely a different time and place, but a different world.

Apparently, the Bibienas used the *scena per angolo* in conjunction with the standard sets of wings on either side of the stage, at least for the first decade or so of the 18th century. But an important step was taken by FILIPPO JUVARRA, who enhanced the perspective illusion by placing flats anywhere across the stage, though still parallel to the proscenium. This allowed a greater freedom to designers and laid important groundwork for the scenography of the 19th century.

The 18th century By the middle of the 18th century most of the elements of modern theatre were in place or were being developed. Most major cities had opera houses whose tiers of boxes resembled the interior of a beehive. Although the orchestra seating was still not the place of choice, neither was it the domain of groundlings or musketeers as it once had been. Orchestra pits were placed in front of elaborate proscenium arches; many opera houses experimented with devices for enhancing acoustics; a curtain across the proscenium would part at the start of the performance. The scenery was done in painted perspective on flats, drops, overhead borders, and shutters arranged so as to recede upstage, although some decor employed scene pieces at other positions. Depending on the theatre, the scenery might either be new and specific for the performance, or part of the theatre's stock. In most Continental opera houses the scenery was shifted by the chariot-and-pole method. The use of *scena per angolo*, improved lighting technology and other techniques allowed the performers further and further back into the setting, thus emphasizing the separation between auditorium and stage. The smaller public theatres that presented dramatic fare were generally rectangular with a proscenium end stage. The basic arrangements, technology and decor were essentially the same as at the opera houses, though on a smaller scale.

By the middle of the 18th century, a trend towards both realism and exoticism was apparent, as a fascination with history and distant cultures developed. Just as in the world of art, neoclassicism and a burgeoning romanticism vied for dominance. The neoclassicism manifested itself in terms of simplicity, symmetry and formal style as opposed to the lavish and complex decor of the baroque and rococo, while romanticism was apparent in terms of a fascination with nature, historical accuracy, local colour and mood.

Already, by the end of the 16th century, Italian playwright LEONE DE' SOMMI was calling for the use of historically accurate COSTUMES in tragedy. In 1741, German actor-manager CAROLINE NEUBER attempted such costumes in one of her productions, but was laughed off the stage. The great French actor TALMA met with derision from his fellow actors at the COMÉDIE-FRANÇAISE as late as 1789 when he recreated a Roman costume with help from the painter David for his small part in *Brutus*. But in England, at least, audiences and performers seemed more accepting of these trends. The actor CHARLES MACKLIN created detailed costumes for Macbeth and Shylock in the mid-1700s, while Garrick did the same for Lear in 1776.

Interest in antiquarianism, as it was called, was sparked off by the discovery and early excavation of Pompeii, which led to an 18th-century fascination with ruins. In terms of design this manifested itself in dark and moody scenes of ancient ruins, Gothic architecture and pastoral settings. One of the strongest influences at the time was the painter and designer Gian Battista Piranesi, whose sketches of prisons and ruins were suffused with shadows, dark recesses and a general sense of mystery. By the early 19th century, German designer Karl Friedrich Schinkel declared that a designer could no longer be a mere perspective artist but must also be an architect, archaeologist, sculptor and historian.

The most significant designer from this period was PHILIP DE LOUTHERBOURG, brought to London by Garrick in 1771. De Loutherbourg, in his stage designs and in the designs for his miniature theatre, the Eidophusikon, made important advances in lighting technology and scenic placement that allowed for greater detail and transformation than had ever been available before. His theatrical reproductions of actual places stimulated the vogue for local colour in design; and through the use of silk screens, gauze curtains and other means of controlling the amount and colour of light – including the intro-

duction of overhead lighting battens – he was able to suggest weather and the passage of time. A scene might begin in morning sunlight, transform into a thunderstorm, and finally transform from afternoon into night. By breaking up the stage with ground rows and free-standing set pieces he was able to achieve a greater sense of depth and reality, while avoiding the symmetricality of the wing-and-groove system. The invention of the Argand lamp at this time also made it possible to intensify the brightness and colour of light behind the proscenium and contributed to the retreat of the actors into the scenic stage.

Romanticism By the beginning of the 19th century, a standard design for historical dramas tended to consist of a scene in the foreground – constructed with flats, ground rows, set pieces and the like – that seemed to frame an accurate and detailed vista of a foreign or historical locale painted on a drop or shutter at the rear. Schinkel's design for *Die Jungfrau von Orleans* at Berlin in 1817, for instance, included an accurately reproduced vista of the cathedral and city of Rheims which was seen through the Gothic arches of a vaulted terrace during Joan of Arc's soliloquy.

In England, designer WILLIAM CAPON convinced actor-manager JOHN PHILIP KEMBLE to begin using historically correct costumes and scenery in his productions of SHAKESPEARE. This concept was carried further by J. R. PLANCHÉ in his work with CHARLES KEMBLE, and in the work of W. C. MACREADY. It would be more than half a century, however, before the antiquarian approach became consistent. Because new scenery cost money, and because performers were responsible for their own wardrobes, it was not unusual for a production to have one accurate set while the rest of the scenes were played in front of the stock scenery, or for one character to be dressed in historical costume while the other performers were dressed in contemporary finery. In the 1860s George II, Duke of Saxe-MEININGEN, sometimes considered the first modern director, imposed a consistent visual style based on painstaking historical and cultural research. As his theatre company toured Europe in the 1870s it had a profound influence on the development of theatre production and design.

However, it was neither theory nor romantic sensibilities that determined the course of theatre as much as economics. As the general public began attending the theatre in increasing numbers, it quickly became apparent to managers that larger theatres meant larger profits. In England, as the forestage was chipped away, the rest of the auditorium was expanded. By 1810, the Theatre Royal, COVENT GARDEN and the Theatre Royal, Drury Lane each held well over 3000 spectators and the farthest spectator might be 100 feet away. Under such circumstances, subtlety was utterly useless and a broad style of acting and a reliance on spectacle became dominant.

Spectacle could simply be the use of gimmicks, such as the 1820 production of *King Lear* at Drury Lane, in which the trees in the heath scene bent in the wind. Certainly it was apparent in the rising melodramatic theatre, which regularly depicted earthquakes, waterfalls, erupting volcanoes, shipwrecks and the like. Etchings and paintings of the productions as seen from the audience's perspective show marvels and wonders. Backstage sketches, however, suggest relatively simple and crude devices dependent on cut-outs, ground rows, free-standing set pieces, and even street urchins hired to create a stormy sea by crawling about under a blue ground cloth. More complex means, of course, were used and included stages divided into sections, each capable of rising above or sinking below the usual stage level; special traps to allow for the sudden appearance or disappearance of a character; and fairly sophisticated devices such as PEPPER'S GHOST – a means of suggesting an apparition by projecting an image from the orchestra pit on to a piece of tilted glass situated onstage. The same principle is still in use – perhaps a bit more sophisticated – in Disney World.

Just as the late-Renaissance theatre of France culminated in the creation of the Salle des Machines, so English MELODRAMA achieved a technological, if not aesthetic, peak with two early 19th century theatres: SADLER'S WELLS, with a water tank beneath the stage, and ASTLEY'S Amphitheatre that included a circus ring where the orchestra seats or stalls would normally be in addition to the proscenium stage. Equestrian melodramas (see HIPPO-DRAMA) were shown at Astley's – plays whose plots included a horse race or chase, or in some way incorporated equestrian acts. Sadler's Wells saw sea battles, mythological and allegorical scenes, and anything else that might conceivably make use of water.

By the mid-19th century, historical accuracy was often a euphemism for spectacle and pageantry. Processions, lavish weddings and feasts, elaborately staged battles, as well as natural disasters were incorporated to 'illustrate' the texts. On the Continent this was best exemplified in the designs of ALESSANDRO SANQUIRICO at La Scala in Milan. In England it reached a pinnacle of sorts with the mid-century productions of Shakespeare at the PRINCESS'S THEATRE by actor-manager CHARLES KEAN, who worked with designers Thomas Grieve, Frederick Lloyds, H. Cuthbert and William Telbin (who founded a family of scene painters that worked into the 20th century). Kean became known as the 'illustrator' of Shakespeare because he frequently cut Shakespeare's descriptive passages and replaced them with spectacle, processions, lavish feasts and PANTOMIME. Examples included the workshop of Quince the Carpenter in *A Midsummer Night's Dream*, and Bolingbroke's triumphal entry into London in *Richard II*.

As theatre moved in this direction, however, much of the scenery, rather than becoming more realistic in design and execution, turned towards painted images. The designer in the mid-19th century became more of a scene painter than a scenographer. The French poet THÉOPHILE GAUTIER declared that the 'age of purely visual spectacles [had] arrived'. The painted scene was well suited for creating the ethereal images of untrammelled nature and exotic locales that so typified the romantic era. The romantic atmosphere was further enhanced by the warm glow of the newly introduced gaslight (1816 in Philadelphia, 1817 at Covent Garden and Drury Lane, 1822 at the Paris Opéra). While much of the legitimate theatre of the period was devoted to melodramatic spectacle, the ballet became the home for the romantic scene painter. Nowhere was this better demonstrated than at the Paris Opéra in the designs of PIERRE CICERI for such ballets as *La Sylphide* and *Aladin ou la Lampe merveilleuse*.

Illustrations from the theatre of this period suggest a stage that was almost a parody of the Serlian perspective. Rather than having a series of wings receding upstage towards a painted perspective backshutter, the action was frequently brought downstage and a painted drop hung directly behind. While the drop itself may have been expertly rendered, the image came to an abrupt end where the bottom of the drop hit the undisguised stage floor. This may not have been entirely obvious to patrons in the orchestra seats, but it certainly was to the denizens of the boxes and galleries.

The quest for ever greater REALISM while maintaining a sense of visual interest led, by the last quarter of the century, to gimmicks now associated with films. Scenery would revolve or move to create the equivalent of reverse angles, tracking and dolly shots. A prime example was DION BOUCICAULT's *Arrah-na-Pogue* in which a character is shown escaping from a tower prison. He was first seen within the tower, climbing out of the window. The scene then revolved to show him climbing out from an exterior point of view; finally, climbing down the vine-covered wall was achieved by having the scenery rise towards the fly-space as he descended. It is no mere accident or coincidence that films were invented at the time that drama reached a realistic pinnacle. Earlier in the century the daguerreotype was invented in part as a result of Louis-Jacques Daguerre's attempts to create more realistic images in theatre design. Now, theatre seemed to have gone as far as it possibly could in terms of illusion – the film was the only possible solution.

While romantic drama of the period used some of this technology to create castles, mountain fortresses, ships at sea and so on, the melodrama was becoming increasingly sophisticated. The so-called 'gentlemanly melodrama' shied away from a reliance on visual and spectacular effects, and substituted instead realistic depictions of middle- or upper-class life with tasteful effects such as the vision scene in Boucicault's *The Corsican Brothers*, in which one brother sees his twin dying – achieved by use of a scrim allowing a scene to become visible upstage.

The primary development associated with this form was the *box set* – a depiction of a room with three walls and a ceiling, the fourth wall supposedly removed so that the audience could see in. The introduction of the box set is frequently attributed to MADAME VESTRIS, who worked with Planché at the OLYMPIC THEATRE in London from 1831 to 38. However, something like a box set may have been achieved as early as 1642 in Venice by Torelli, with the production of *Il Bellerofonte*. Painted perspective borders created an illusion of a ceiling, and it is possible that he also placed panels between the wings to achieve continuous walls. And by the early 18th century, the free placement of flats and the enclosure of space downstage practised by the Bibienas created at least the illusion, if not the actuality, of a box set. By the late 18th century box sets were not unusual, at least on the Continent. Through the middle of the 19th century the box set became increasingly realistic, as actual furniture, rugs, bookshelves, wall sconces, knick-knacks and the like were added to create the aura of the real world.

In order for the 'fourth wall' concept to work, the set and the performer had to be completely contained within the proscenium. While the proscenium doors of the London theatres were eliminated by the 1820s, the apron persisted. Beginning in 1867 at the PRINCE OF WALES THEATRE, the theatrical managers SQUIRE BANCROFT and MARIE WILTON strictly adhered to the fourth wall demarcated by the proscenium arch, and when they assumed the management of the HAYMARKET theatre in 1880 they extended the gilded proscenium arch across the bottom of the stage. The metaphoric picture frame was now a literal reality. The so-called peep-show stage had arrived.

The obvious concession to theatricality, of course, was that all action and all the furniture had to be placed so as to face the audience. Also, as more and more real props, furniture and set pieces were added, the more unbelievable became theatrical devices, props and scenic pieces. As late as 1888, well into the modern period, playwright AUGUST STRINDBERG, in his Preface to *Miss Julie*, complained of canvas walls that shook when doors were slammed, and painted pots and pans on the walls instead of real ones.

The rise of realism in the 19th century culminated with the birth of NATURALISM in the 1870s, led by ÉMILE ZOLA. In terms of scenographic practice, it was ANDRÉ ANTOINE's Théâtre Libre in Paris that took naturalism to its logical end. Antoine was one of the many theatre practitioners of the era to see and be influenced by the work of the MEININGEN troupe. In rehearsal Antoine would place the furniture and props as they would be in a real room and only later decide which wall was to be removed. Thus, even though the spectators saw a box set with an imaginary fourth wall, blocking and scenery made relatively few compromises to sightlines and visibility. Antoine also sought to have actual props and set pieces onstage. In his production of *The Butcher*, set in a butcher's shop, real sides of beef hung from hooks on the stage.

This approach was continued by KONSTANTIN STANISLAVSKY at the MOSCOW ART THEATRE in conjuction with such designers as Viktor Simov, Konstantin Korovine, Alexander Golovine and Mstislav Dobuzhinsky. Although the MAT, at least in the first decade of its existence, was associated with realism, the settings showed strange inconsistencies. While a room in a house was entirely decorated by furniture and props taken from an actual home, the exterior scenes were often created with obviously painted two-dimensional trees and a painted backdrop.

What became obvious to many within a few years of Zola's manifesto was that absolute realism was unattainable on a stage – the moment anything is framed (actually or metaphorically) on a stage, it loses its 'reality'; it becomes part of the theatricality of the performance. Further, the use of real items inevitably focused attention on the unreality of a stage performance. A prime example comes not from naturalism but from melodrama. In Boucicault's play, *The Colleen Bawn*, there is a scene in which a character jumps into a lake to save a drowning woman. In the original production in 1860, the lake was created by strands of silk cloth set at about waist height and surrounded by cut-out scenery, ground rows and papier-mâché rocks. The soft gaslight shimmering on the silk created an easily accepted illusion of waves as the actors moved through, apparently immersed in the water. Because all the scenery was of a single style, there was, in

Coleridge's famous phrase, a suspension of disbelief – the audience accepted the convention readily. In the 1890s, however, there was a revival of the play in which a lake containing real water was created. The actors, naturally, created real ripples and splashes and emerged dripping wet. Yet, because the audience knew, of course, that it was not a real lake, and because it was so obviously inconsistent with the scenery round it, the illusion, rather than enhanced, was completely shattered.

The later 19th century At the same time that realism in the theatre was moving into its ultimate phase of naturalism there were already movements in a different direction. The most significant theorist was the opera composer RICHARD WAGNER, who fundamentally altered the theatre auditorium and whose writings inspired future generations. Wagner's concept of *Gesamtkunstwerk* or 'total work of art' was based on the idea that all the elements of a production must be unified. While such an idea seems obvious, it was a radical notion in the mid-19th century when, as noted, there was generally no overriding artistic control over sets and costumes.

To house his operas Wagner had a new theatre constructed at BAYREUTH. Designed by Gottfried Semper, Wilhelm Neumann, Otto Bruckwald and others, the opera house opened in 1876. The major innovation was in the auditorium with its 'democratic' seating; the box, pit and gallery arrangement that had dominated theatre architecture for over two centuries was abandoned. There were no side boxes or central aisle. Rather, there were thirty rows of seats in the raked auditorium, each leading to a side exit. The auditorium was fan-shaped, approximately 50ft wide at the front and 115ft at the rear. There was a large box at the rear over which was a small balcony. The orchestra pit was hidden under the apron of the stage so that the illusion of the stage picture would not be broken. Wagner talked about a 'mystic chasm' between the stage and auditorium, created by a double proscenium, by which the 'ideal' world of the stage was to be separated from the everyday world of the spectators. The goal was, by means of the production and mythic elements of the opera, to create a communal experience that would unite the audience.

The most lasting contribution apart from the seating plan, however, was the darkening of the auditorium. For the first time in history it was possible to plunge the audience into darkness while illuminating the stage. Taken for granted today, the effect wrought profound changes upon the experience of theatre. The social interaction that had been as much a part of the theatrical experience as the play itself, and the sense of unity with the performers, if not with the scenic stage, was now eliminated. The separation of the stage and auditorium, begun with the invention of the proscenium arch and continued through the development of the *scena per angolo*, was now complete.

Ironically, for all his innovations, Wagner was strongly rooted in the scenography of the 19th century; his ideal was to be reached through total illusion. Rather than forging new ground, his productions were, in a sense, the epitome of romantic staging. It was the symbolists, inspired by Wagner's theoretical writings, who were to begin the reaction to naturalism in the late 1880s.

The symbolists' battle cry was 'de-theatricalize the theatre'. What they meant by this apparently contradictory aesthetic was a desire to bring the theatre back towards its original roots and impulses by stripping away the accumulated bulk of the naturalistic stage and replace it with an evocative theatre more dependent on the imagination and subconscious response. The symbolist theatre (see SYMBOLISM) emerged in the Théâtre d'Art founded by Paul Fort in 1890, which evolved into the Théâtre de l'Oeuvre in 1892 under the leadership of AURÉLIEN LUGNÉ-POE, whose motto was 'the word creates the decor'. The decor was certainly far simpler than that of the concurrent naturalist and melodramatic theatres, but scenery was not forsaken altogether. Scrims were a common aspect of the productions, frequently hung several deep across the stage, creating a soft-edged ephemeral image. Medieval and Gothic iconography were common in their attempt to create a 'forest of symbols' whose effect was evocative but nonspecific. The symbolists also experimented with synaesthesia, trying to relate sounds with colours and even smells. Among those who contributed to the theatre were future famous painters such as Édouard Vuillard, Maurice Denis, Pierre Bonnard, Odilon Redon, and Henri Toulouse-Lautrec.

Although many of the productions at these theatres were radically avant-garde and are little known today outside scholarly circles, symbolism quickly spread into mainstream theatre. Many of the visual ideals were furthered by the writings and works of Swiss designer ADOLPHE APPIA and British designer GORDON CRAIG. Attacking both the naturalistic and the pictorial approaches, these two men stripped the stage of its illusionistic clutter and detail and provided instead evocative masses of light and shadow, and three-dimensional forms, objects and masses. Their design harked back to the architectural stages of ancient Greece and the formal stages of the Orient.

Appia was strongly influenced by Wagner's writings, but felt that his staging of the operas did not coincide with his theories. Appia set out to resolve this contradiction. He saw a fundamental problem in 19th-century staging that juxtaposed the moving, three-dimensional actor with two-dimensional painted scenery and the flat, non-illusionistic stage floor. Beginning with the concept that the actor was the primary aspect of the theatre, Appia's solution was to create a plastic stage environment of suggestive scenery – including the stage floor – enhanced by a sculptural form of lighting. He was one of the first to realize the potential and possibilities of electric light, which had begun to be introduced in theatres in the 1880s. He realized that the appearance of three-dimensionality is created by the sculptural use of light and shadow, and described one scene, for instance, as 'Siegfried bathed in light and flickering shadow'.

Appia's sketches, generally done in shades of black, white and grey, were suggestive (but still recognizable) scenes bathed in moody and evocative light – but light, nonetheless, that clearly defined the sculptural space of the stage. He also saw light as the visual counterpart of music, which needed to be orchestrated to coincide with the moods of the play. These ideas led him towards a structural stage setting. For the music school of Émile Jaques-Dalcroze at Hellerau, whom he met in 1906, Appia created 'rhythmic' scenic units – steps, platforms, ramps – that were to function as the visual equivalent of the rhythm of the text. His approach to lighting became the basis for much 20th-century lighting practice, and his structural stage furnished the basic vocabulary for much 20th-century reaction to naturalism.

Gordon Craig also moved the stage setting away from literalism. But whereas Appia created suggestive but generally recognizable scenes, Craig developed an approach dependent on movable screens that created a theatrical space. By the movement of screens (in essence, flats), the stage space would be constantly redefined – closed in or expansive, cramped or soaring. Although some of Craig's sketches are vaguely suggestive of location – his sketch for a scene in *Macbeth*, for instance, shows a staircase winding around a massive column issuing up from some cavernous Gothic palace – basically, his sets emphasize their own theatricality.

Craig was attacked by some contemporary designers and critics as being impractical. And indeed, many of his designs, if built, could not fit into the space of any existing theatre. Furthermore, there was no technical means of creating the transformation of space smoothly; the screens were not meant to slide back and forth on parallel tracks as in the Renaissance, but to move gracefully and cinematically in any direction, including vertically. Those designs that Craig was able to execute seldom possessed the grandeur or kinetic energy of his sketches. Nonetheless, they served as inspiration for much 20th-century design, ranging from German EXPRESSIONISM of the 1910s to the musical of BROADWAY.

Alternatives to the proscenium Except for court theatres, in which vast sums of money could be spent to entertain an individual for perhaps a single time, theatre architecture, like all aspects of theatre, is public and must compromise with the dictates of economics (and the even more mundane dictates of public safety). Allardyce Nicoll has pointed out how, just at the time that reactions to the illusionistic stage were blossoming, the proscenium arch became even more structurally entrenched in turn-of-the-century theatres because of laws requiring fire walls and fire curtains between the stage and auditorium.

But many felt that with the encapsulation of the actor and setting within the proscenium, a sense of intimacy and communion that had once been an essential part of theatre was lost. They now sought to recapture that experience, and as early as the 1840s there was a definite movement toward other forms. In Germany, LUDWIG TIECK and KARL IMMERMANN both advocated an open stage based upon their understandings of Shakespearian staging. Tieck adapted the open-stage idea to the proscenium and the result, not surprisingly, was very similar to the English Restoration stage. Immermann's stage for an 1840 production of *Twelfth Night* resembled the Teatro Olimpico in many ways. These were, nonetheless, significant movements away from the pictorial realism of the proscenium stage that dominated at the time.

In the second half of the 19th century, a greater interest and knowledge of oriental theatre developed that reinforced this trend. One of the first elements borrowed from

V. Hofman's design for
Sophocles' *Oedipus*, Prague
National Theatre, 1932.

the East was the revolving stage of the *KABUKI* theatre, first used by Karl Lautenschläger in Munich in 1896. Ironically, it was put to use to speed up and simplify scene changes required by the detailed naturalism of the period. But the *NŌ* and *kabuki* of Japan also used thrust stages; runways into the audience; simple, stylized and emblematic scenery; a starkly presentational style; and a formal, minutely prescribed theatre architecture. Whether this had any direct effect on symbolist staging is not clear, but it most definitely influenced the major theoreticians and practitioners of 20th-century design and staging.

The reaction against the proscenium went in several directions. The most successful involved thrust stages and architectural stages (sometimes the two combined), but there were also fanciful projects involving annular stages, revolving auditoriums, stages or spectators suspended in the centre of spherical theatres and so on. Most of the latter, of course, were never built, but detailed plans and even models exist for such projects as WALTER GROPIUS's Totaltheater, the Spherical Theatre of his Bauhaus colleague Andreas Weininger, FREDERICK KIESLER's Endless Theatre, and the several projects of NORMAN BEL GEDDES. Of the theatres that were constructed, the most notable and influential were MAX REINHARDT's Grosses Schauspielhaus and the Redoutensaal, and JACQUES COPEAU's VIEUX-COLOMBIER THEATRE.

The Grosses Schauspielhaus in Berlin was adapted by Hans Poelzig from an existing circus in 1920. It was, in essence, a modern version of the Teatro Farnese. Three thousand five hundred spectators sat in a U-shaped auditorium surrounding a thrust stage some 60ft deep, behind which was a scenic stage with a revolve. The audience and the performers on the thrust, therefore, were architecturally united. The theatre worked well for Reinhardt's spectacles, but was totally inappropriate for more intimate fare. The Redoutensaal, converted from an 18th-century palace ballroom in Vienna in 1922, was also an architecturally unified space but, like Appia's theatre at Hellerau, enveloped the audience in a single intimate surrounding. The stage was a raised platform with an archi-

tectural-style setting of curved screens and a balcony.

But it was the architectural stage of the Vieux-Colombier that had the biggest influence on design and architecture in the post-First World War era. Copeau first simplified the proscenium stage of the converted music-hall in 1913, with the idea that the bare essentials of scenography would focus attention on the actors. In 1919 he renovated it again. The proscenium was eliminated and a concrete stepped arch was built at the back. The basic idea of the spare, non-illusionistic scene, architecturally united with the auditorium – traceable from Tieck and Immermann through the symbolists, Appia and Craig, and Reinhardt – seemed to have triumphed. But while the open stage gained popularity, the architectural stage was found to be too limiting. Even with the use of curtains, and scenic pieces that could plug into the arches and doorways of the stage, the basic groundplan and limited access could never be completely overcome and Copeau abandoned the theatre in 1924. But the open thrust stage slowly began to emerge, and by the 1950s the architectural thrust stage and the pictorial thrust stage (a combination of a scenic end stage with a thrust) seemed to be the standard for all new theatre spaces.

The 20th century Most of the various art movements of the early 20th century found counterparts in the theatre, but in terms of design there was little true innovation. Artists working in two-dimensional forms were rarely successful in translating these into the three-dimensional scenery of the stage. Most notably, PICASSO, who designed several dances for the Ballets Russes, seemed unable to find a vocabulary that allowed cubism to transform from a two-dimensional exploration of planes to the requirements of the stage. His sets were frequently painted backdrops – beautiful as works of art, but hardly innovative – and his costumes, as in *Parade*, seemed to mimic the look of cubism without actually achieving it.

Some artists, however, were successful at developing a painterly style for the theatre that was bold, striking and stimulating. At the same time that stage designers were moving towards simplification of the image, Serge Diaghilev, director of the Ballets Russes, brought artists such as LÉON BAKST, NATALYA GONCHAROVA and Mikhail Larionov to design for him. Bakst employed Byzantine and oriental splendour notable for its vivid use of colours and line. In contrast to the monochromatic and moody images of Craig and Appia, Bakst used rich colours in startling combinations, grotesque exaggeration of form, and a stark, theatrical false perspective. Goncharova and Larionov carried this a step further, virtually eliminating perspective, and painting, instead, flat images in the style of primitive painters and medieval icons. The result was the adaptation of the painterly style to the non-illusionistic stage. But for all the excitement this created when the Ballets Russes first performed in Paris in 1909, there was no form of dramatic theatre for which this style of design seemed appropriate. The immediate effect was to reinforce the movement away from realism towards theatricality but, by and large, stage design turned to non-painterly approaches.

Some of the most notable anti-illusionistic movements also came from Russia and were associated with the dynamic avant-garde art movements of the first three decades of the century. The most significant figure was director, actor and theoretician VSEVOLOD MEYERHOLD. Strongly influenced by Appia in his early years, Meyerhold was a central figure of FUTURISM and constructivism in the theatre but worked in many styles. Artists and designers who worked with him included Kazimir Malevich, Aleksandr Vesnin, LYUBOV POPOVA, Georgii and Vladimir Stenberg and El Lissitzky. Constructivism emerged about 1920, and was clearly influenced by futurism and cubism. This movement sought an art based on 'space and time' and using 'kinetic and dynamic elements'. This was manifested in skeletal sets of wood and metal with platforms, ramps, steps and various kinetic elements, often on stages otherwise stripped bare. Meyerhold called these sets 'machines for acting'.

Constructivist design was also the predominant form at the Kamerny Theatre of ALEKSANDR TAIROV, although the sets by ALEKSANDRA EKSTER, his primary collaborator, were seldom as stark or 'homemade'-looking as most constructivist design. Tairov also worked with Georgii Yakulov, Goncharova, Larionov and Vesnin. Other avant-garde artists who designed for the theatre at some time included YURY ANNENKOV, Aleksandr Rodchenko and Vladimir

Simov's design for Act III of *The Lower Depths*, Moscow Art Theatre, 1902. The play is regarded as one of the classics of naturalism.

Tatlin. As with so many other 'isms', pure constructivism in stage design lasted only briefly (although variations on the idea can be seen to this very day), but it was a major contributor towards theatricality over illusion and was especially notable for settings that sat like islands in the midst of the stage with no connection, literally or metaphorically, with the wings or flyspace.

The most dominant theatrical force during the early decades of the century was EXPRESSIONISM. Clearly influenced by Appia, expressionist design frequently reduced the stage to its bare essentials, often little more than a few scenic elements and black drapes on an otherwise bare stage. Light became the most important aspect of design. The movement of light reinforced the stream-of-consciousness imagery of many expressionist plays, and allowed the smooth transition through episodic scenes. The light frequently cut a swath through the dark void of black-curtained stages. The contrast of light and shadow, unusual angles and unrealistic colours of light contributed to the nightmare quality of the productions. Images were distorted and exaggerated; walls tilted at precarious angles; oversized set and prop pieces and bold blocks of colour wrenched the image out of objective reality into a subjective view of the world. Expressionist design is frequently associated with the work of director LEOPOLD JESSNER who, working primarily with designer Emil Pirchan, created architectural/structural settings of steps and platforms that changed through the use of lights and curtains. Jessner's reliance on this formula led to cliché, and quickly became known as *Jessnertreppen* (Jessner steps).

In the years before and after the First World War, many American designers and directors went to Europe and studied with these designers, or observed productions. The various ideas were distilled through Américan sensibilities and production needs and the result became known as the New Stagecraft. Led by designers ROBERT EDMOND JONES, LEE SIMONSON and Norman Bel Geddes, the practitioners of the New Stagecraft revolted against the 'Belasco realism' (so called because of director DAVID BELASCO's highly detailed, realistic productions) in favour of simplification and abstraction. Although examples of constructivism, expressionism and other specific movements cropped up on the American stage, most American theatre remained firmly rooted in realism and the new design substituted simplicity and suggestion – sometimes called selective realism – for naturalism.

This has remained, albeit with some changes, as the most dominant style of American design. The second generation of these designers, led by JO MIELZINER, evolved a style sometimes known as 'poetic realism' that relied on painterly images often rendered in a soft-edged, almost dream-like style – a style enhanced by Mielziner's use of scrim, which accommodated transitions from outside reality to scenes of memory and subjective experience typical of plays by ARTHUR MILLER, TENNESSEE WILLIAMS and others.

The closer one gets to one's own time, the harder it becomes to separate the small details from the overall developments. Several major directions in 20th-century design, none of which are mutually exclusive, can be identified. These include (1) a continuation of the trend already discussed – simplified or selective realism; (2) new directions in pictorial design; (3) sculptural design; (4) multi-media design; (5) environmental theatre; and (6) conceptual design.

The bulk of modern drama, especially in the English-speaking world, has remained realistically based, although much of it has included flashbacks, memory scenes, dream sequences, subjective perception, poetic imagery, cinematic transformations from scene to scene and other 'non-realistic' devices. Clearly, a purely naturalistic approach to design for such conventions would be cumbersome and inappropriate. Thus, fragmentary images, scrims, washes of coloured light, emblematic or exaggerated set pieces, isolated details or fragmentary sets placed in the midst of a theatrical void are some of the devices that designers have used to meet this challenge. Although the terms 'selective' or 'poetic realism' are the most common, the struggle between the forces of realism and theatricality is perhaps best captured in the term 'magic realism'.

The second movement of the modern era was a continuation of the still-thriving painterly style. In the 20th century this was, typically, lyrical and fantastic depictions of scenes. It is most evident in the mid-century designs for ballet, and its roots can be traced to ALEXANDRE BENOIS's sets for Diaghilev. Some of the finest examples can be seen in the work of CHRISTIAN BÉRARD, EUGENE BERMAN, George Sheringham, OLIVER MESSEL, Leslie Hurry, Nicholas Georgiadis, Lucien Coutaud, Gianni Polidori and CECIL BEATON.

The third style, sculptural design, deals with new conceptions of space on the stage. From the Renaissance until the end of the 19th century design was essentially pictorial – a two-dimensional image creating the illusion of depth or volume. Building upon the foundations of Appia and constructivism, however, many designers rejected any form of realism for sculptural design. The images themselves varied greatly. Geometric masses, architectonic structures, fanciful versions of classical columns, ramps, platforms and steps intersecting on a multitude of planes, scaffold-like structures – all found their way on to the stage. The work of TANYA MOISEIWITSCH, Nadine Baylis, MING CHO LEE, SANTO LOQUASTO and others typify much of this aesthetic.

The fourth tendency is the incorporation of technology, primarily in the form of film and projections. From a theoretical viewpoint, it was a logical extension of contemporary practices. Since it was impossible ever to re-create the outside world fully onstage, the argument went, why not acknowledge the fact while still using the image? In other words, project a picture of the real thing. The stage could become any place in the world at the push of a button. It was a photographic equivalent of the Renaissance-baroque scenic stage – an image that existed behind and separate from the performer, and that functioned as a visual reference point for the audience. The evolution of the projected scenery was somewhat more pedestrian than the theory. It was essentially ERWIN PISCATOR's response to necessity: his need to present performances on a limited budget on makeshift stages for factory workers. Projected images, of course, became a major element in BERTOLT BRECHT's subsequent epic theatre, and they reached their pinnacle in the work of Czech scenographer JOSEF SVOBODA in the 1960s and 70s.

There was, however, a reaction to this and to the poetic realism of the Americans. Building upon the ideas of constructivism and sculptural design, designers in the 1960s began to reject any form of illusion. This reaction began with stripping away the 'content' of scenic structures, leaving skeletal frameworks instead. Structures were dismembered, leaving fragments. A favourite device was to 'perforate' settings, thus allowing the 'reality' of the stage to penetrate the illusion of the decor. This was followed by settings composed of scaffolds, tubing, fabrics and 'real' objects and materials such as raw wood, erosion cloth and metal. Collage settings – frequently including photo blow-ups, junk and fabric sculptures – became popular. Significantly, the designers creating these new settings were using the vertical space of the stage in a way that had rarely been attempted before.

In some cases the stage was stripped down to bare essentials – planks, platforms and ramps with little or no objective scenery. The circle, in a sense, was completed: the designers of the 1960s and 70s had returned to the open stage of ancient Greece and Elizabethan England; to Molière's 'two boards and a passion'.

One manifestation of this response was environmental theatre. The concept of the spectator and performer sharing the space of the theatre, or the inclusion of the spectator within the performance space, had been current since at least the Middle Ages, but the term was coined by American director and theoretician Richard Schechner. The roots of modern environmental theatre can be traced to the productions in the 1930s of Szygmunt Tonecki in Poland and NIKOLAI OKHLOPKOV in the USSR. The most significant examples in the postwar era are the works of JERZY GROTOWSKI (and his sometime collaborator, JOSEF SZAJNA) in Poland, ARIANE MNOUCHKINE at the THÉÂTRE DU SOLEIL in Paris, LUCA RONCONI in Italy, and Schechner's PERFORMANCE GROUP in the USA.

Related to this is the movement in the 1970s and 80s often termed 'conceptual design' or 'theatricalism'. Primarily a European development, these tend to be designs for classical plays and operas created either by a director working closely with a designer, or a single individual assuming both roles, such as FRANCO ZEFFIRELLI or JEAN-PIERRE PONNELLE. In either case, one individual is generally responsible for all aspects of design, not just sets; and from this comes the term 'scenographer', which implies a more unified and far-reaching involvement than the term 'designer' does. Typically, the setting is a single image – or a single basic setting that can transform into variations of the single image – that embodies the central concept of the production. These are most often productions in which the directorial concept is more significant or more pronounced than the playwright's script – if, indeed, one exists. The impulse for this approach is traceable to Reinhardt and Meyerhold and the practices of Brecht. The productions of the BERLINER ENSEMBLE have been an acknowledged influence on many contemporary designers.

Although such designs may, of course, take any of the forms listed above, theatricalism has rediscovered the proscenium, as it were, and the designs tend to enclose the cubic space of the stage. Theatricalist sets are frequently distinguished by high walls that soar into the flyspace and seemingly overwhelm the performers; and by overwhelming images or emblems whose visual power suffuses the sets and costumes. Examples can be found in the work of Karl von Appen, Achim Freyer, ANDRÉ ACQUART, JOHN NAPIER, JOHN BURY, RALPH KOLTAI, EUGENE LEE and WIELAND WAGNER, and in the productions of BENNO BESSON, GIORGIO STREHLER, PATRICE CHÉREAU, LIVIU CIULEI, ANDREI SERBAN, PETER STEIN, ROBERT WILSON and RICHARD FOREMAN.

Thus, by the 1980s, theatre design seemed to be heading in two antithetical directions: conceptual design with its strong images, metaphorical use of line and space, and celebration of the stage on the one hand; and on the other hand, a rejection of standard or formal theatrical spaces altogether. The latter seems to be fading, however. Through the 1970s performance moved out of theatres and into streets, beaches, public spaces, city rooftops, old factories, ancient ruins, and almost any conceivable 'found' space. The major anthologies of design for those years, *Stage Design throughout the World Since 1960* and *Stage Design throughout the World 1970–1975*, exalted the revolution in production and the rejection of the bourgeois theatre.

But at the same time that this was happening, opera directors and designers were reclaiming the stage and moving towards what is now generally called postmodern design. Patrice Chéreau's production of Wagner's Ring Cycle at Bayreuth in 1976, with sets by Richard Peduzzi and costumes by Jacques Schmidt, is often cited as a landmark by many designers. Visually, the production alluded not to Teutonic mythology, but to a range of industrial, technological and sociopolitical references and images from the 19th and 20th centuries, thus grounding the production in Wagner's time and its historical aftermath. Whereas modern design sought an organic and aesthetic unity in which the stage picture functioned as a metaphor for the world of the play, postmodern design cries out that unity is impossible in the contemporary world. Postmodern design is a kind of pan-historical, omnistylistic aesthetic in which the world is seen as a multiplicity of competing, often incongruous and conflicting, elements and images. Using discordance, juxtaposition and even ugliness, postmodern design often makes reference to other productions, to other works of art and to the world beyond the play, with only the stage frame as a unifying element. This technique is often referred to as quotation or pastiche.

This approach has been exemplified in the designs of JOHN CONKLIN, Robert Israel, Adrianne Lobel and GEORGE TSYPIN in the USA; Richard Hudson in Great Britain; Yannis Kokkos and Peduzzi in France; and Bert Neumann, Karl Kneidl and Jochen Finke, among others, in Germany.

There is no question that the Western and even some Eastern theatre is still dominated by forms of realism, painterly design, and the kinetic stages of MUSICAL THEATRE. But, ironically, just as the scenic practices of the burgeoning opera of the 17th century helped shape the style and technology of theatre design throughout the 19th century, it may be doing so again, at a time when many thought opera was dying. AA

Théâtre du Châtelet see CIRQUE OLYMPIQUE

Théâtre du Nouveau Monde The most respected and influential of existing companies in French Canada, founded in Montreal in 1951. Under JEAN GASCON's direction it began staging French classics, especially works of MOLIÈRE. By the end of the decade it was offering at least one Canadian play each season, notably the works of MARCEL DUBÉ. The TNM has collaborated with the STRATFORD FESTIVAL (Ontario) and toured successfully in Europe. In 1966 Gascon was replaced by JEAN-LOUIS ROUX, under whose direction the company has moved towards a more varied repertoire, including experimental plays and musical REVUES. A subsidiary troupe, Les Jeunes Comédiens, trained many of the theatre professionals now active in Quebec. In the early 1980s economic and labour difficulties seriously circumscribed TNM's activities, however, and particularly its ability to experiment. After reaching crisis proportions in 1984–5, necessitating the cancellation of that season, the threat to its survival has receded and the company's future now seems assured. LED

Théâtre du Soleil French theatre company founded in 1964 by ARIANE MNOUCHKINE and a group of friends who had worked together in university theatre. They adopted a cooperative structure, sharing all the jobs of running the theatre and taking decisions collectively. After starting with a repertoire typical of the decentralized theatres (see DECENTRALIZATION MOVEMENT), including *The Kitchen* (1967), the first WESKER to be performed in France, they became committed to the system of *création collective*, or collaborative devising of productions, after taking part in the political upheavals of 1968. Their most famous production *1789* (1970) was devised by a combination of historical research and improvisation. It told the story of the French Revolution from the point of view of the people, employing a wide mixture of theatre styles. Its scenic inventiveness (it was performed in a large open space on stages placed around the audience, who were free to move about) contributed to the atmosphere of festivity and celebration which made the production so successful with audiences eager to pursue ideas thrown up in 1968.

The company set up home in a disused *cartoucherie* (cartridge warehouse) at Vincennes, and the very remoteness of the location contributed to the excitement of audiences. *1789* was followed by two further collective creations, *1793* (1972) and *L'Âge d'or* (*The Golden Age*, 1975). Both productions were attempts to press further the political lessons of *1789*, while continuing to search for an appropriate performance style. *L'Âge d'or* owed much to MEYERHOLD and the tradition of the *COMMEDIA DELL'ARTE*. In 1976 the company disbanded and a splinter group was formed under Jean-Claude Penchenat: the CAMPAGNOL. A film, *Molière, ou La Vie d'un honnête homme*, employed the energies of Mnouchkine and other company members until they regrouped for *Mephisto* in 1979, a dramatization of Klaus Mann's novel. This was followed in the early 1980s by a cycle of SHAKESPEARE plays, *Richard II, Henry IV, Part 1* and *Twelfth Night*, performed in a style giving maximum opportunity to physical expressiveness while also suggesting the remote, hieratic quality of Shakespeare's

nobles by borrowings from oriental theatre styles, costumes and so on. The purpose of the Shakespeare cycle was to permit the company to develop a contemporary play about Southeast Asia, *Norodom Sihanouk*, which opened in 1985. This and *L'Indiade* (1987) were written for the company by HÉLÈNE CIXOUS, who continues to collaborate with them. In the 1990s, with many new actors in the company, they once again returned to the classics with productions of EURIPIDES' *Iphigenia at Aulis* and AESCHYLUS' *Agamemnon* (1990), which continued in repertory as the other two plays of Aeschylus' Oresteian trilogy were added: *The Choephori* (1991) and *The Eumenides* (1992). The whole cycle was performed in a converted wool warehouse in Bradford in 1992, the company's first visit to Britain since their performance of *1789* at London's Roundhouse in 1971. DB

theatre-for-development see THIRD WORLD POPULAR THEATRE

Théâtre-Français see COMÉDIE-FRANÇAISE

Theatre Guild (USA) In 1915, a group of young actors and writers dissatisfied with the conventions of the commercial theatre organized the WASHINGTON SQUARE PLAYERS. For three seasons they presented a series of one-act plays distinctly modern in both content and form. After the war, in 1919, a patent lawyer and sometime playwright named LAWRENCE LANGNER restructured the Players as the Theatre Guild. Langner and his board – which included PHILIP MOELLER (who was to become the Guild's leading director), THERESA HELBURN (a playreader soon to be made executive director), actress Helen Westley, banker Maurice Wertheim and scene designer LEE SIMONSON – were determined to shed their amateur downtown status and present challenging full-length plays on BROADWAY.

In its first few years the Guild's notable achievements were with European EXPRESSIONISM (KAISER's *Man and the Masses*, 1924) and with the world premieres of several plays by SHAW (*Heartbreak House*, 1920; *Back to Methuselah*, 1922; *Saint Joan*, 1923; and *Caesar and Cleopatra*, 1925). Although the Guild was criticized for neglecting American writers, two American plays that it presented early in its history – ELMER RICE's *The Adding Machine* (1923) and JOHN HOWARD LAWSON's *Processional* (1925) – testify to the influence its productions of European plays had on native experiment. Later in the 1920s, and for the following three decades, the Guild produced the work of major American dramatists, including SIDNEY HOWARD (*They Knew What They Wanted*, 1924; *The Silver Cord*, 1926); S. N. BEHRMAN (*The Second Man*, 1927; *Biography*, 1932); ROBERT E. SHERWOOD (*Reunion in Vienna*, 1931; *Idiot's Delight*, 1936); and MAXWELL ANDERSON (*Elizabeth the Queen*, 1930; *Mary of Scotland*, 1933). In 1928, with *Strange Interlude* and *Marco Millions*, the Guild began regularly to produce the plays of EUGENE O'NEILL.

If in the 1920s the Guild had the lustre of an experiment conducted by idealistic upstarts, by the early 1930s it had begun to acquire the reputation of a theatrical dowager. In 1931 some of its younger members defected to form the

GROUP THEATRE, whose agenda of knitting systematically trained actors into a true ensemble and encouraging the development of socially relevant plays highlighted two areas where the Guild had failed. Throughout the 1930s and 40s, as it produced popular shows like *Philadelphia Story* (1939) and MUSICALS like *Oklahoma!* (1943) and *Carousel* (1945) – and depended over and over again on its in-house stars, the LUNTS, to rescue it from a financial abyss (thereby violating its original policy of starring the play rather than the player) – the Guild became little different from a commercial producer. Despite its lack of success in maintaining a repertory set-up or in developing a company of actors – and despite its concessions to popularity and its literary shortcomings (its predilection for airy comedies and stodgy historical romances) – the Guild's record is unique in the history of the American theatre. Through its subscription policy and its extensive national tours it brought more worthwhile, well produced plays to a greater number of people, and over a longer period of time, than any other theatrical organization. FH

theatre-in-education (TIE) (Britain) Professional theatre work for young people with explicit educational aims, providing a unique resource to schools and colleges. Although it has roots in the work of such pioneers as JOAN LITTLEWOOD, Peter Slade and Brian Way, the beginnings of theatre-in-education may be traced to the setting-up of a pilot educational project at the Belgrade Theatre, Coventry, in 1965. The aim was to forge new links between the theatre and local schools, and to this end a small unit of 'actor-teachers' was formed to take programmes of work into classrooms and school halls, utilizing both drama-teaching methods and performance skills. The objectives were educational and the means theatrical.

The success of the scheme, together with the availability of new money from the ARTS COUNCIL for YOUNG PEOPLE'S THEATRE (YPT), led over the next five years to the formation of similar teams at repertory theatres in Bolton, Leeds, Nottingham, Edinburgh and Glasgow. The scale and adventurousness of the work grew, and soon a number of education authorities set up TIE units of their own, the Cockpit team in London being the most notable example. In due course some repertory-based teams found their relationship with their parent theatre inhibiting and became independent YPT or community/YPT companies. In 1992 there were about 30 TIE companies, or YPT companies with a strong commitment to TIE. The early 1990s, however, saw a severe cut-back in the volume of work done and the number of companies operating, partly as a result of the government's radical shake-up of British education funding, partly because of the growing impact of the market economy upon the arts world as a whole, compounded by general reductions in subsidy for the arts. Only in two areas has there been growth in TIE work: in health education (especially in response to concern about drugs and AIDS) and in museum education.

Kinds of TIE work range from straight performance of a play – devised for children of a particular age; performed to one or, at most, two classes at a time; and followed by a workshop on its themes, discussion with the 'characters' of issues raised, or a follow-up programme of work organized by the teacher in collaboration with the company –

to full participation programmes. It is for the latter that TIE won its reputation as a pioneering force in education. Such programmes may last from one hour to a full day, or even to a series of visits made to each class over four weeks. The pupils are involved in an experience *with* the characters – for example, as witnesses or in role as factory workers within the narrative – and confronted with dilemmas, problems to be solved, decisions to be reached. Learning through experience is a crucial tenet of the work.

Subject-matter ranges from the conventional curriculum, such as local history or the study of themes from an examination text, to more general, sometimes sensitive, matters of social concern such as racial prejudice, drugs, AIDS or the environment. Always the aim is to inform, to stimulate interest and to challenge preconceptions. Particularly successful programmes are *Pow Wow* (Coventry Belgrade TIE), devised for 6- to 7-year-olds who participate in a 'Cowboy and Indian' story that deals with racial prejudice and initiates classroom study of the American West and Indian culture; *Brand of Freedom* (Pit Prop Theatre, Wigan), a two-visit programme about the Lancashire cotton famine of the 1860s and the American Civil War; *The School on the Green* (Greenwich (London) YPT), a programme that puts the children in an investigative role as they reconstruct the events of the Burston School strike of 1914 and confront key issues about education in the process; and *Trappin'* (M6 Theatre, Rochdale), a performance piece for older pupils about the breakdown of, and violence within, a marriage, followed by a workshop based on BOAL's forum theatre techniques.

The material presented is always the product of much careful research and discussion with teachers and education advisers, and schools are fully involved in follow-up work. But at the same time the efficacy of TIE at its best, and its power to stimulate, ultimately lie in its use of the theatrical medium and in its considerable measure of independence from the educational system.

While TIE originated as a British phenomenon, it was not long before its methods were taken up, adapted and developed in Australia, then in the USA, Eire, Scandinavia, Nigeria and Kenya; and interest in TIE continues to grow. AJ

See: A. Jackson, *Learning through Theatre: New Perspectives on Theatre in Education*, London, 1993; J. O'Toole, *Theatre in Education*, London, 1976; C. Redington, *Can Theatre Teach?*, London, 1983; P. Schweitzer, *Theatre in Education* (scripts), 3 vols., 1980.

Théâtre Libre see ANTOINE, ANDRÉ

Théâtre National Populaire (TNP) French National People's Theatre founded by FIRMIN GÉMIER in 1920 after years of campaigning by ROLLAND and other advocates of the *théâtre populaire*. Despite Gémier's success in persuading the French parliament to acknowledge the TNP as a state-subsidized venture, he was given only a theatre (see CHAILLOT) and not the means to run a producing company. His achievement was thus limited, and after his death in 1933 the TNP remained moribund until the appointment of VILAR in 1951. He brought to the enormous theatre (rebuilt 1937) the company and production style pioneered at the AVIGNON FESTIVAL, abolishing footlights, front curtain and painted scenery, making use of bold movement, lavish COSTUME and complex lighting (see STAGE LIGHTING).

Under Vilar's administrator, Jean Rouvet, the normal Parisian theatregoing ritual was simplified: evening dress and tipping were abolished, performances began on time with latecomers excluded, and the text of the play was sold in place of glossy programmes. Rouvet pioneered a network of supporter groups through trade unions and student organizations, which was soon copied by the decentralized theatres (see DECENTRALIZATION MOVEMENT). The repertoire combined vigorous productions of French classics, in a fluent style not frightened of heroics, with SHAKESPEARE, the German romantics and other world classics unfamiliar in the France of the 1950s. Vilar directed some of the first BRECHT to be seen in France – *Mother Courage* (1951) and *Arturo Ui* (1960) – as well as modern classics such as T. S. ELIOT's *Murder in the Cathedral*, but was not successful in his attempts to introduce contemporary plays.

Actors of the highest calibre were attracted to the TNP: e.g. GÉRARD PHILIPE and MARIA CASARÈS. One of these, Georges Wilson, succeeded Vilar in 1963. Wilson tried to follow the same policies as Vilar but was overtaken by a rapidly polarizing political situation in the late 1960s: young and committed audiences were looking for new formulae and Wilson's audience figures dropped disastrously. In 1972 the TNP crisis was solved by the expedient of transferring the title to PLANCHON's company in Lyon. The new title meant increased subsidy and touring obligations, but not a change of artistic direction for Planchon and his new co-director CHÉREAU. Their company continued its policy of adventurous revivals and new plays, often of a demanding nature. Against Gémier's view of the TNP as a place of commission and Vilar's as a 'public service', Planchon considers it must constantly remind people of the violent cultural divide in modern French society: 'Our job is to keep the wound open.' In 1986 Georges Lavaudant succeeded Chéreau as co-director. DB

theatre of the absurd Literally meaning 'out of harmony', absurd was ALBERT CAMUS's designation for the situation of modern humanity, strangers in an inhuman universe. Recognizing such strangers in stage characters of the 1950s, the critic Martin Esslin in 1961 published his influential *Theatre of the Absurd*. He defined plays of the absurd as those that presented man's metaphysical absurdity in aberrant dramatic style that mirrored the human situation. Never a formal movement, the playwrights of the absurd were centred in postwar Paris, but they soared to international fame with the unexpected success of BECKETT's *Waiting for Godot*. Journalists soon seized upon the label, confusing it with the everyday meaning of absurd as outrageously comic. Esslin's main absurdists are Beckett, ADAMOV, IONESCO and GENET, with less attention paid to ALBEE and PINTER.

Since then, almost every non-realistic (see REALISM) modern dramatist has had this label affixed. Certain absurdist techniques have, nevertheless, established themselves in the contemporary theatre, and it is in this formal sense, rather than in a philosophical one, that the idea of 'theatre of the absurd' has been maintained in crit-

ical currency. Among these techniques are the rejection of narrative continuity and character coherence and of the rigidity of logic, leading to ridiculous conclusions; scepticism about the meaning of language; and bizarre relationship of stage properties to dramatic situation. Such techniques have occasionally resulted in memorable stage images. Residual absurdism may be seen in such images as the Vampire in CARYL CHURCHILL's *Mad Forest* and the Angel in TONY KUSHNER's *Angels in America*. RC

theatre of the ridiculous (USA) In 1967 the Play-House of the Ridiculous opened on OFF-OFF BROADWAY with *The Life of Lady Godiva*, written by Ronald Tavel, directed by John Vaccaro, and featuring CHARLES LUDLAM as actor. Though these three men did not stay together long, they independently continued their 'ridiculous' work – a self-consciously wild dramaturgy full of witty wordplay, sexual *double entendre*, theatrical flamboyance, sexual ambiguity and bad taste. Tavel left the Play-House within a year to pursue a writing career, and in 1967 Vaccaro directed two Ludlam works, *Big Hotel* and *Conquest of the Universe*, before Ludlam left to become actor-manager of his own company. Vaccaro toured Europe with the Play-House and then operated it out of LA MAMA until 1972, when he closed his theatre. At the RIDICULOUS THEATRICAL COMPANY, Ludlam went on to write, direct and perform in plays such as *Turds in Hell* (1968), *Camille* (1973) and *Der Ring Gott Farblonjet* (1977). AS

Théâtre Ouvert Organization set up in France by Lucien Attoun in 1971 at the 25th AVIGNON FESTIVAL to promote new work by playwrights. Attoun's formula involved presentation through rehearsed readings with the possibility of broadcast on the radio programme he produced. In 1974 the *gueuloir* was introduced, a chance for an author to give a free public reading of his play, and in 1975 the possibility for an author to work on his play with actors was added. In 1978 *tapuscrits* were introduced: cheaply produced duplicated typescripts of new works to be circulated among theatre professionals. Gradually activities were extended to Paris and other parts of France. In 1981 the organization moved into a permanent studio theatre at the Winter Garden in Montmartre. Here authors are given a chance to try out plays with actors in a laboratory context which may or may not lead to public performance. A great many new authors have been helped in this way, and Théâtre Ouvert has been a significant force in encouraging new French playwriting. DB

Theatre Passe Muraille (Canada) An 'alternative' theatre in Toronto, Ontario. The company derives its name, 'Theatre without Walls', from its emphasis on a performance style that transcends both the imaginary fourth wall of the stage and the four walls of theatre buildings that enclose more traditional performances.

Founded in 1968 by Jim Garrard, it quickly gained notoriety for its provocative work in unconventional venues. Garrard left TPM in 1969; subsequent artistic directors have developed the company's commitment to collective creation and shaped many exciting productions with a particularly Canadian historical and sociological focus. Under the decade-long artistic directorship of Paul

Thompson (1972–82), the company put on some of its most successful collective productions, including *The Farm Show* (1972); *1837: The Farmers' Revolt* (1973), written with Rick Salutin; *I Love You, Baby Blue* (1975), which examined the sexual morals and mores of Toronto society; and *Maggie and Pierre* (1979), about Pierre Trudeau's relationship with his wife.

The financial success of *I Love You, Baby Blue* allowed TPM to purchase a theatre building, giving up the freedom of a moveable theatre for a permanent home that allowed for even greater freedom of experimentation. Since Thompson's retirement, subsequent directors and ensembles have reintegrated more scripted materials, relying less exclusively on methods of collective creation, but they have all maintained a strong commitment to new Canadian plays and experimental modes of theatrical expression. DAH

Théâtre Populaire de Lorraine One of a number of groups which formed in France in the 1960s as part of the DECENTRALIZATION MOVEMENT influenced by the ideals of *théâtre populaire*. This company began with performances by ADAMOV and 19th-century classics, then, like the THÉÂTRE DU SOLEIL, changed to *création collective* for a play about local steel mining, *Splendeur et misère de Minette la bonne Lorraine* (1969). Since 1970, many of its plays have been written by its artistic director Jacques Kraemer. DB

Théâtre Populaire Romand see JORIS, CHARLES

Theatre Row (New York City) In 1975, when Robert Moss, director of the OFF-OFF BROADWAY group PLAYWRIGHTS HORIZONS, found himself without a theatre, he rented a building on West 42nd Street – amid a neighbourhood of pornographic shops, BURLESQUE houses and massage parlours – and transformed it quickly and cheaply into a performing space. His success signalled the development of an alternative theatre district a few blocks west of BROADWAY for Off-Off Broadway companies. A quasi-governmental agency, the 42nd Street Redevelopment Corporation, was persuaded to buy the block from 9th to Dyer Avenues to begin phase one of the transformation; the created spaces were then rented out to companies, which accepted the responsibility to rebuild them into theatres and offices. In 1978, amid much official fanfare, Theatre Row was opened and comprised 10 working companies, all to be operated on a non-profit basis and representing diverse artistic goals as well as ethnic backgrounds. Phase two, which encompasses the block between Dyer and 10th Avenues, has added four other members and one west of 10th Avenue. Most companies have been upgraded to OFF-BROADWAY theatres.

In 1982, with most of the original companies struggling to survive under the weight of mortgages and escalating operating expenses, they decided collectively to rent out their theatres when they were not being used by themselves. This formula has worked for most of the theatres. Through a fortunate and generous donation, Playwrights Horizons has acquired its theatres outright.

The theatres and companies utilize a collective box office, Ticket Central, to serve their patrons and offer a variety of entertainment at relatively low cost. Theatre Row provides a testing ground for actors, directors, playwrights and designers, many of whom move their activities to Broadway, Off-Broadway and regional theatre. The presence of restaurants, shops and Manhattan Plaza, a subsidized housing complex for performing artists, has stabilized and revitalized the surrounding area.

The theatres and companies comprising Theatre Row are the Samuel Beckett, the Harold Clurman, the Judith Anderson, Playwrights Horizons (main stage and studio theatres), Theatre Row Theatre, INTAR Hispanic American Arts Center, the ACTING COMPANY, Alice's Fourth Floor, Theatre Arielle, the Douglas Fairbanks, Nat Horne Musical Theatre, the George S. Kaufman and the John Houseman Center. MCH

theatrical monopoly Under patents granted by Charles II to WILLIAM DAVENANT and THOMAS KILLIGREW in January and April 1662 respectively, which were interpreted as giving them and their successors the exclusive right to perform drama in London, this so-called monopoly beleaguered the theatre for well over 150 years. The precise nature of the rights granted was later much disputed, but the proprietors of DRURY LANE and COVENT GARDEN theatres, on whom the patents devolved, had their claims to privilege reinforced by the terms of the 1737 Licensing Act, which, in addition to the imposition of formal CENSORSHIP by the Lord Chamberlain, restricted plays to the city of Westminster and 'places of His Majesties residence'.

The patent holders, having invested substantially in their purchase, were staunch defenders of their so-called rights, especially as competition began to gnaw away at their exclusivity. The appearance of a theatre at SADLER'S WELLS in the 1780s was the first real challenge; later, as the Lord Chamberlain of the day became less disposed to defend patent privileges, a number of 'minor theatres' emerged to cater for the huge population increase in London in the early 19th century.

To avoid direct conflict with the patent rights of the 'majors' (which had by this time begun to include the HAYMARKET as a summer Patent theatre), these theatres restricted their performances to burlettas, loosely defined as plays with musical accompaniment – from this arose the distinction between 'legitimate' and 'illegitimate' drama. But even this ruse was gradually abandoned, and by the 1820s some theatres like the ADELPHI and OLYMPIC, which were tolerated by the Lord Chamberlain's Office, were in virtually open conflict with the Patent theatres' exclusivity, the former doing damage to box-office receipts at Covent Garden (it was claimed) to the tune of £2000 a year.

The Patent theatres' claim to be the upholders of Britain's dramatic heritage was by the 1830s a somewhat empty one – especially after performing animals were introduced to the Drury Lane stage – but the law was at intervals still invoked, often unsuccessfully, by the patentees in an attempt to crush any new minor theatre competitors. In 1832 a select parliamentary inquiry into the state of the drama chaired by EDWARD BULWER LYTTON concluded that the monopoly, having 'neither preserved the dignity of the Drama, nor, by the present Administration of the Laws, been of much advantage to the Proprietors of the Theatres themselves', should be abolished forthwith. In practical terms the monopoly was already in its death throes; but legislation guaranteeing free competition on the London stage was delayed another 11 years until the Theatre Regulation Act of 1843. JRS

Theatrical Syndicate (USA) The origins of the Syndicate lay in the combination system of producing. The expansion of railways after the Civil War made it possible to tour a production anywhere in America. This proved more profitable than the previous system of resident companies hosting visiting stars. Consequently, by 1885 nearly all the first-class STOCK companies had been replaced by combinations from New York City, and both producers and regional theatre owners had opened booking offices there to arrange these tours. In 1896 producer CHARLES FROHMAN joined the booking agency of Marc Klaw and Abraham Erlanger in a partnership with Alfred Hayman, who leased the most important theatres in the West, and with Fred Nixon and Fred Zimmerman, who controlled Philadelphia and the mid-Atlantic region. This arrangement was called the Theatrical Syndicate, and by 1903 it governed first-class theatrical production in America. The source of its power was its insistence upon exclusive representation: its clients had to agree to do business only with it, taking the attractions, routes and dates it specified, and paying the fees it levied.

Its monopoly was broken not by rebellious clients, but by even more ruthless monopolists. The SHUBERT BROTHERS, Sam, Lee and Jacob, were regular clients of the Syndicate, operating some 30 theatres in the Northeast. In 1905, concerned about potential rivalry, the Syndicate ordered them to stop acquiring theatres; instead, the Shuberts secured bank financing and declared war, and by 1913 controlled twice as many theatres as the Syndicate. The last Syndicate agreement expired in 1916; the Shuberts retained a national monopoly on theatres until 1930, and a BROADWAY one until 1950.

The Syndicate was a means of maximizing profit, not a vehicle for artistic innovation or social welfare; consequently, it was ruthless in its methods and rapacious in its charges. However, monopoly was the accepted way of doing business in the 19th century, and the Syndicate was only doing in theatre what Standard Oil, United States Steel, and American Telephone and Telegraph were doing in their industries. Furthermore, the Syndicate was only one theatrical monopoly: the so-called popular-price theatres were monopolized during 1900–11 by the Stair and Havlin Theatrical Management Syndicate. In 1906 B. F. KEITH and EDWARD F. ALBEE organized their United Booking Office, which monopolized all of VAUDEVILLE; and Samuel Scribner's Columbia Amusement Exchange virtually monopolized BURLESQUE after 1905. DMCD

theatrum mundi A mechanical theatre, whose figurines are moved horizontally by means of strings along a track in a flat wing-and-border set by a single performer or, in German, *Mechanikus*. This forerunner of the newsreel recreated current events, such as natural disasters, battles or scenes from everyday life. Brown's Theatre of Arts toured British fairs (1830–40) with miniatures of Napoleon's campaigns, while Clapton's featured Grace

Darling's heroic rescue. GOETHE owned such a theatre, and that in Berlin's Luisenstrasse in 1848 displayed 'The Battle of Genoa', 'The Battle of Schleswig-Holstein' and 'Bombardment by the First German Fleet'. LS

Theobald, Lewis 1688–1744 English playwright and critic. Trained as a lawyer, he undertook in 1714 a large and unfinished project to translate Greek drama. His adaptation of SHAKESPEARE's *Richard III* (1719) was not a success, but he wrote a number of innovative and entertaining PANTOMIMES for JOHN RICH throughout the 1720s, e.g. *Harlequin Sorcerer* (1725). In 1726 he attacked Pope's edition of Shakespeare in *Shakespeare Restored*, the first book ever published on Shakespeare alone. Though mocked, Theobald's attempts to emend and restore the text of Shakespeare's work were intelligent and effective. His own edition of Shakespeare was published in 1734. In 1727 his play *The Double Falsehood* was performed. Theobald claimed that it was an adaptation of Shakespeare's lost play *Cardenio* (written with JOHN FLETCHER and performed in 1613), but it seems unlikely. He adapted WEBSTER's *The Duchess of Malfi* as *The Fatal Secret* (1733). He was appointed Poet Laureate in 1730. PH

Thérésa [Eugénie Emma Valadon] 1837–1913 First star of the French music-hall (see CAFÉ CHANTANT). Daughter of a tailor, she made her stage debut in Paris in 1856 at the Théâtre de la Porte-Saint-Martin. Fame arrived in 1863 at the Alcazar; already known for sentimental ballads, she decided to PARODY one with a comic yodel and was cheered to the echo. For almost 30 years, this scrawny (later stout), swarthy woman with a mouth 'large enough to swallow the conductor' kept audiences in stitches with such favourites as 'Nothing Is Sacred to a Sapper' and 'The Bearded Lady'. She also appeared in FÉERIES and comic OPERAS (*La Reine des Halles*, 1881) before her retirement in 1893. LS

therukoothu Indian theatre form. *Theru* means 'street'; *koothu*, 'play'. As the name suggests, *therukoothu* has a rustic origin. It is usually performed by members of the Koothadi community and is most frequently seen in the north and south Arcot and Chingleput districts of Tamil Nadu state. Its players and audiences come from the lower strata of urban and rural society. Some scholars suggest it was inspired by YAKSHAGANA of Karnataka state, others by KATHAKALI of Kerala state. One thing seems clear: *therukoothu* is not like any other form of traditional theatre in south INDIA.

A troupe performs in an open space in a village. Four tall posts of bamboo or wood are fixed in the ground bounding the acting area. A large banner proclaiming the company name hangs above the musicians who assemble in the space upstage centre. Colourful banners are strung overhead between the remaining posts. The make-up of central characters is bright blue and red accentuated with white and black lines. Heavily waxed moustaches accentuate the virility of the heroic characters of the epics and *Puranas*. Colourful wooden ornaments decorate their chests and arms and impressive crowns adorn their heads. Special short grass skirts are worn under the outer cloth skirts. In some respects the make-up and ornaments resemble those of the *yakshagana* of Andhra Pradesh and south Kanara in Karnataka state, and the skirts resemble *kathakali* skirts of Kerala actors.

As part of large-scale ritualistic events in a village, the actors parade through its streets along with the temple deities. Following an all-night performance, they participate in the symbolic destruction of evil under the watchful eye of temple effigies and thousands of enthusiastic villagers. The ceremony concludes when they walk across beds of hot coals to prove their faith in god.

Plays centre on stories drawn from epic literature and concern events in the lives of famous epic characters. Among popular fun-loving figures is the *kattiakaran*, a clown figure who combines the functions of the fool with those of the stage manager.

Traditional *therukoothu* music is a blend of classical and folk music. Melodies are first sung by the actors and then repeated by musicians singing in chorus. About half of a performance is made up of songs and the other half is improvised prose dialogue spoken in Tamil. *Therukoothu* songs characteristically require a high shrill pitch demanding sustained vocal power.

The musicians' space is called the *pin pattu*, or 'back song'. When an actor is not in character, he joins the musicians and sings from the *pin pattu*. The harmonium provides the basic pitch. A reed instrument (*kurukuzhal*) provides melodic background. Small hand drums played on both ends and bell-metal cymbals complete the musical ensemble.

Dance steps are simple and violent, involving circular movements with quick turning leaps. There is no symbolic code of hand gestures. Dance provides an element of fast-paced spectacle demonstrating the emotional state of the character, or forms part of a battle scene.

Few companies remain today. Highly praised is the Raghava Thambiran Company, named after its founder. Other companies playing in and around the slums of Madras city have abandoned traditional costumes and use film music to attract people to their performances. FaR

Thespis 6th century BC Greek tragedian, the earliest whose name was known to ancient scholars (see GREECE, ANCIENT). He is said to have won a victory with a play produced c.534 and to have been the first to introduce an actor (the dramatist himself) conversing with the Chorus. He is also credited with inventing the MASK. Since none of his plays was preserved for posterity, no authentic fragments survive, and it is impossible to assess the value of the traditions concerning him. ALB

Thimig family Distinguished Viennese actors. **Hugo** (1854–1944) was a leading comic actor at the BURGTHEATER. His daughter **Helene** (1889–1974), a versatile actress, was married to MAX REINHARDT; she did much to perpetuate her husband's method of training actors. Hugo's two sons, **Hermann** (b.1890) and **Hans** (b.1900), also acted with the Burgtheater. sw

Third World popular theatre Theatre used by oppressed Third World people to achieve justice and development for themselves. There are now thousands of orga-nized groups of landless peasants, workers and threatened minorities, in Africa, the Americas and Asia, who use drama and theatre to confront the political, economic and social problems in their lives. These initiatives occurred quite separately in the late 1970s all over the Third World, as economic and social conditions worsened for the very poor. Some indigenous activists came to despair of any solutions to the growing misery via conventional development and political strategies. Their despair focused on the 'top-down' nature of these 'solutions', seen to be located in Super Power rivalry, a one-world economy, and the nuclear and conventional arms race. Theatre provided those at the base of society with their own voice. Drama, as a process of collective improvisation using existing cultural forms of expression, could offer the means of creating an analysis by very poor people of their material and cultural conditions.

Subsequently, these drama and theatre initiatives were discovered to have many objectives and strategies in common. Various local, regional and international networks were established during the 1980s, including the International Popular Theatre Alliance. However, this networking remains tenuous except at local levels. Regional and international workshops in the early 80s, funded by aid agencies responding to grass-roots Third World initiatives for radical development alternatives, exchanged drama and organizational skills at village level, and discussed new perspectives and insights. Since the essential characteristic of this grass-roots theatre is that it enables those making the drama to form their own analysis and strategies, a distinction is drawn between this drama for collective awareness and other political and popular theatre in the Third World which adopts a 'top-down' approach. This includes AGIT-PROP and sloganizing theatre; professional theatre companies used by governments and development agencies to put across specific messages (for example, encouraging people to dig pit latrines); and popular theatre which, because of commercial objectives, is unwittingly articulated into the hegemony of the ruling elites.

Instead, this grass-roots theatre grows out of collective thought, and the dramatic process carries that thinking further. It is also concerned with cultural identity among minorities threatened with the complete destruction of their societies: Native populations in the Americas (for example, the Inuit in Canada; the Caribbs in Dominica), and Aboriginal peoples in Australasia. Therefore, despite the common perspectives and intentions of these organized groups, there are also considerable differences resulting from the cultural and political forces of the particular region.

The following examples may indicate the scope of this Third World popular theatre.

In LATIN AMERICA, some groups, like Teatro Nixtayolero in Nicaragua, have developed among rural peasant farmers; others, like the theatre workshops of TAREA, a popular education support group in the *barrios* of Lima, Peru, have emerged among the dispossessed and landless peasants who have drifted into the cities. Some are Indian or Inca groups, like the Ayni Ruway, an indigenous people's movement in the Cochebamba Valley of Bolivia among the Aymara and Quechua people, whose spontaneous theatre at festivals and markets is part of their fight for justice and material improvement within their own historical identity. The cultural problems and material contradictions of colonialism and neo-colonialism in the region are reflected, for example, in the work of the gifted (black American) Panamanian dancer-actor, Danny Calden, who rejected his career and his background to work politically and artistically alongside Native Indians, the most ignored and deprived group in Panama. They draw on his skills and artistic expertise to help them work out for themselves possible strategies for survival.

In the Caribbean a quite different project is the theatre company of a group of working-class women in Kingston, JAMAICA: Sistren. This group has found a means through drama of enabling the most oppressed class of women in the Third World to articulate to large audiences of other classes, male and female, their growing consciousness and confidence. This brilliant theatre enterprise is now internationally known through tours of their plays, and more especially through workshops amongst black female workers in, for example, Canada and Britain.

In Africa, in the wake of the destruction of life at the base of society by dictatorial regimes inheriting the independent African states, there have been a number of attempts to involve peasant farmers in articulating a new order, using drama and theatre. Perhaps the most notable was the drama project of the people of Kamiriithu in KENYA. This involved the Kenyan playwright NGUGI WA THIONG'O. The government imprisoned him, banned the plays and bulldozed the theatre. But it is more often through lack of wider organizational structure that drama initiatives in Africa tend to lose momentum.

In parts of Asia, the scale of popular theatre is linked to successful economic and political organizations among the oppressed. The thousands of theatre groups in Mindanao, southern PHILIPPINES, have emerged through the church and popular education organizations, and in turn gave focus and momentum to the opposition to the oppressed of the Marcos regime in that country. The theatre groups have used the Catholic feast days and liturgical processions to communicate their thinking and growing confidence. Karl Gaspar, actor, poet, artist and lay secretary of the Church Conference in the area, was among many imprisoned without trial in 1983 for participating with these theatre groups.

In BANGLADESH there are now hundreds of groups of landless wage-labourers in remote rural areas who have formed themselves into economic organizations and who use drama as a means to action against local injustice. Such is their growing confidence that they have asked members of the student theatre company Aranyak to leave Dhaka, live with them in their poverty and contribute their drama skills as animateurs in the wider organizations.

It is in INDIA, however, that popular theatre is most diverse and effective. A significant example is the work among Harijans (so-called 'Untouchables') in Tamil Nadu by the Association for the Rural Poor and the Integrated Rural Development Society. These organizations, founded and run by Harijans, use drama to analyse issues, think through strategies, and 'rehearse' a particular line of action, which has then been carried out successfully.

This growing Third World theatre is subordinate to effective new social and economic initiatives amongst the very poor. It reflects the use of their culture by the people themselves to develop their own thinking and analysis. ME

Thoma, Ludwig 1867–1928 German playwright and novelist. Thoma wrote several comedies about life in rural Bavaria. The most popular is *The Local Train* (1902), which is still revived. SW

Thomas, Augustus 1857–1934 American playwright, who always dealt with well documented American scenes in such plays as *Alabama* (1891), *In Mizzoura* (1893) and *Arizona* (1899). *The Copperhead* (1918), which made Lionel Barrymore (see DREW–BARRYMORE FAMILY) a star, details the story of an Illinois farmer who, at the request of President Lincoln, pretends to be a sympathizer with the Confederacy. Many plays explored contemporary issues: capital and labour in *New Blood* (1894); politics in *The Capitol* (1895); hypnotism in *The Witching Hour* (1907); and mental healing in *As a Man Thinks* (1911). Even his FARCES, *The Earl of Pawtucket* (1903) and *Mrs Leffingwell's Boots* (1905), had a distinctively American flavour. The prefaces to many of his more than 60 plays provide a lively and intimate account of the dramatist at work. Thomas's autobiography, *The Print of My Remembrance*, was published in 1922. RM

Thomas, (Walter) Brandon 1856–1914 British actor and playwright, born in Liverpool, where he first attempted to make a career as a journalist, supplementing his income by writing and performing coon songs in MUSIC-HALLS. He made his London debut as an actor in 1879–80, and was a prominent member of the HARE/KENDAL company at the ST JAMES'S. SHAW, who saw him as Sir Lucius O'Trigger in an 1895 revival of *The Rivals*, thought he played the part 'agreeably and even with dignity, mainly by not doing what is expected of him', a characteristic which Thomas had significantly displayed in the writing of *Charley's Aunt* (1892), an immensely popular FARCE which describes the escapades of three Oxford undergraduates, the most vacuously obliging of whom is cajoled into playing the part of a rich woman in order to advance the marital ambitions of the other two. It is for *Charley's Aunt* alone that Thomas is remembered, though he is credited with at least a dozen more plays. PT

Thomas, Dylan (Marlais) 1914–53 Welsh poet and dramatist, at one time an actor in repertory theatre (see REGIONAL THEATRE (BRITAIN)). Thomas's expressionistic (see EXPRESSIONISM) radio 'play for voices' *Under Milk Wood* (first staged in 1953) has gained a wide reputation. (See also RADIO DRAMA.) CI

Thomashefsky [Tomashevsky], **Boris** 1868–1939 Yiddish actor (and producer). In 1882, newly arrived from Russia and still a 13-year-old soprano, Thomashefsky appeared in the first professional YIDDISH production in America (GOLDFADN's *The Witch*, on the Lower East Side). Later, his mellifluous tenor voice and florid good looks were especially suited to the costume OPERETTAS popular through the first half of his career, and his reputation as an irresistible ladies' man enhanced his romantic onstage image. He often produced and co-starred with his wife Bessie in New York (especially at the National and People's Theatres) or on tour. He also contributed to the writing of some MUSICALS, the best-known of which was Moshe Zeifert's *Dos Pintele Yid* (*The Little Spark of Jewishness*, 1909), and appeared in several Yiddish films. Late in life he ventured, mostly unsuccessfully, on to BROADWAY and into some non-theatrical enterprises.   NS

Thompson, Denman 1833–1911 New England-born American actor-playwright, who became a specialist in ETHNIC and eccentric COMEDY. He first played his sketch featuring Uncle Josh Whitcomb in 1875; by 1877 it had become a three-act play, and in 1886, with George Ryer, he completely revised it as *The Old Homestead*, which he played until 1910. A derivation of temperance MELO-DRAMA, *The Old Homestead* was the epitome of sentimental rural Americana.   DMCD

Thompson, Judith 1954– Canadian playwright whose plays blend NATURALISM and SURREALISM in a portrayal of the complex struggle between the conscious and the unconscious mind. The rich, psychologically complex texture of her work is augmented by her superb control of regional speech rhythms and voice, as well as by her manipulation of theatrical space. *The Crackwalker* (1980) presents a relatively ordinary regional setting that is repeatedly violated by repressed images of sordidness and madness. Thompson's second play, *White Biting Dog* (1984), received the Governor General's Award for Drama for its highly complex metaphorical portrayal of the relationships involving a mother and son. *I Am Yours* (1987) envelops characters and audience in a type of collective unconscious where they share a dream-like experience of demonic possession and maternal repression. In addition to these stage plays, Thompson has written several scripts for radio and television.   DAH

Thompson, Lydia 1836–1908 British-born actress. Fair-haired and sprightly, she had already made a name for herself as a dancer and comedienne in London, the English provinces and Germany when she took her troupe of

Lydia Thompson as Robinson Crusoe in H. B. Farnie's burlesque of that name, 1877.

British Blondes to New York (1868). Heralded by a barrage of publicity, her production of *Ixion, or The Man at the Wheel*, the first modern BURLESQUE in more than one act, did not so much introduce burlesque to America as combine it with pulchritude in tights to create the 'leg show'. A strict taskmistress to her underlings and a shrewd businesswoman, Thompson was the first actress to horsewhip a libellous newspaper editor. Teamed with Willie Edouin for a while, she toured the USA several times (1868–71, 77–8, 86, 88–9, 91), retaining her popularity on both sides of the Atlantic. Her last appearance was with MRS PATRICK CAMPBELL in *A Queen's Romance* (Imperial Theatre, London, 1904). LS

Thompson, Mervyn 1936–92 New Zealand playwright and director. Thompson was co-founder of the Court Theatre, Christchurch; artistic director of Downstage Theatre, Wellington, 1975–6; and drama lecturer at the University of Auckland, 1977–89. He was best-known for solo plays for his own performance – *Coaltown Blues* (1984) and *Passing Through* (1991); and for his unique form of 'songplay' – *O! Temperance!*(1972), *Songs to Uncle Scrim* (1976) and *Songs to the Judges* (1980). His last work was *Jean and Richard* (1992), a whimsical fantasy about the pioneer aviators Batten and Pearse. HDMCN

Thompson, Sam 1916–65 Irish playwright. A shipyard painter, Thompson began writing for BBC radio. The soberly observed realities of *Over the Bridge*(1960), denouncing mob bigotry and murder, outraged the Unionist establishment in the directorate of Belfast's Group Theatre. It was independently produced by James Ellis in Belfast, Dublin, Scotland and England. *The Evangelist*(1963), whose butt is commercialized religion, was very effective theatre in Hilton Edwards's Belfast Opera House production. In a posthumously discovered MS, *The Masquerade*, three characters act out Nazi fantasies in a London basement. Thompson's political and social themes were clearly encouraging him to new forms of expression. DM

Thorndike, (Agnes) Sybil 1882–1976 British actress. Thorndike joined ANNIE HORNIMAN's company in 1908 after touring America with BEN GREET in an extraordinarily wide variety of Shakespearian roles, male as well as female. She made her name in a number of modern plays – MAUGHAM's *Smith* (New York, 1910), GRANVILLE BARKER's *The Madras House*, HOUGHTON's *Hindle Wakes* (London, 1910 and 1912) and ST JOHN ERVINE's *Jane Clegg* (Manchester, 1912) – before joining the OLD VIC, where she not only played Shakespearian and Restoration heroines but also Prince Hal in *Henry IV, Part 1*, Ferdinand in *The Tempest*, the Fool in *King Lear* and Launcelot Gobbo in *The Merchant of Venice*. She extended her range still further with a repertoire of CLAUDEL and GILBERT MURRAY's translations of EURIPIDES (1919–20) and a season of GRAND-GUIGNOL (1920–2), but her major successes in the interwar period were in the title roles of SHAW's *Candida* (1920), *St Joan* (a part written specifically for her, 1924) and a revival of *Major Barbara* (1929). She also worked with the Phoenix Society, acted in several films and gave striking performances in plays by JOHN VAN DRUTEN, EMLYN WILLIAMS and PRIESTLEY.

During and after the Second World War she toured widely with the Old Vic company for ENSA. In the later part of her career she frequently appeared with her husband, LEWIS CASSON (notably in Priestley's *The Linden Tree*, 1949; JOHN HOME's *Douglas* at the EDINBURGH FESTIVAL, 1950; CLEMENCE DANE's *Eighty in the Shade*, specially written for them, 1959; COWARD's *Waiting in the Wings*, 1960, and CHEKHOV's *Uncle Vanya* at the first CHICHESTER FESTIVAL, 1962). She was appointed DBE in 1931 and Companion of Honour in 1970, and her final performance in 1966 inaugurated a new theatre in Surrey named after her. CI

Throckmorton, Cleon 1897–1965 American set designer. Throckmorton began his career with the PROVINCETOWN PLAYERS and designed many of EUGENE O'NEILL's early plays, including *The Emperor Jones* and *The Hairy Ape*. In the same way that O'Neill was experimenting with EXPRESSIONISM, Throckmorton employed stylized settings in the manner of various European movements. He designed several plays for the THEATRE GUILD, including *Porgy*. AA

Thurston, Howard (Franklin) 1869–1936 American MAGICian. The son of a carriage-maker, he began as a card manipulator, playing at TONY PASTOR's 14th Street Theatre, New York, but developed into a specialist in spectacular illusions. In his acts, he would make vanish an Arabian horse, a girl playing a piano, a Whippet automobile; in 'The Triple Mystery' he made a girl materialize in a nested box, suspended her in a mummy case above the stage, and then caused her to appear in a roped trunk above the spectators' heads. He was held over at the London Palace for six months in 1900, purchased HARRY KELLAR's show in 1907, and introduced his version of the Indian rope trick in 1926. Having lost millions, he toured a ghost play *The Demon* (1929), finally retiring in 1935. His autobiography, *My Life of Magic*, was published in 1929 (reprinted as *Our Life of Magic* in 1989, with augmentations). LS

Tian Han 1898–1968 Chinese dramatist. After study in Japan (1916–22), Tian helped found the literary Creation Society (1921) in Shanghai. In 1928 he was one of the organizers of the left-wing Southern Society and by 1932 had joined the CCP. When the PRC was established he was appointed to head the Drama Reform Committee under the Ministry of Culture (1950).

Tian Han wrote 24 dramas in traditional style, such as *The White Snake*(*Bai she zhuan*), and some 60 works in the modern genres, HUAJU and GEJU. Representative of his early left-wing period is *Moonlight Serenade of 1932* (*Yijiusanernian de yueguang qu*) about a bus-workers' strike against foreign capitalists that focuses on the class struggle.

Tian's best-known spoken drama, *Guan Hanqing*(1958), was chosen to represent the 700th anniversary of the great dramatist GUAN HANQING. The drama portrays Guan as a people's artist and fighter against tyranny, and revolves around Guan's composition of his famous play *Injustice to Dou E* (*Dou E yuan*). His last work was the tragic Beijing opera *Xie Yaohuan* (1961), named after the heroine, an official in the reign of Empress Wu Zetian. Tian died during the Cultural Revolution, one of numerous artists and intellectuals to come under fire from radical Maoists. In its early stages he had been branded one of the 'four villains' of the cultural world: *Guan Hanqing* was denounced and *Injustice to Dou E* was attacked as a 'poisonous weed' by the *People's Daily*. CPM

Tibetan drama Form of theatre popular in the Tibetan Autonomous Region and among other Tibetan communities, including those in Sichuan, Qinghai and Yunnan Provinces of CHINA, and in INDIA. Among the theatres of China's current minority nationalities it is the oldest and most important.

The origins of a real and developed drama in Tibet go back to the Buddhist monk Tang-ston rgyal-po (flourished 15th century), who formed a company of singers and dancers in which performers impersonated characters in stories based on Buddhist sutras. Only after the 17th century did Tibetan drama gradually split from religious RITUAL.

Tibetan drama is an integrated art form in which singing, dialogue, dance, ACROBATICS, MIME and extremely colourful COSTUMES all play a part. Musical accompaniment is confined to percussion instruments, drum and cymbal, and a chorus. Make-up is simple, but MASKS are an important feature. Traditionally Tibetan drama is performed with simple properties in a square, a temple or any open space, spectators on three or all four sides of the action. A favourite venue even now is the old Summer Palace of the Dalai Lama in Lhasa. A large tent is put up and the audience sits round the area where the drama is performed.

There are three sections of a Tibetan drama. The first is the prologue, a masked dance which among other functions explains the plot. Then comes the core, the drama itself. Finally a farewell blessing is given, used by the company to seek donations from the audience.

Tibetan drama was, and to some extent remains, an oral tradition. Many items were not written down and varied greatly from troupe to troupe and time to time. Over a dozen survive today. They concern Tibetan history and mythology, kings, queens and beautiful women. Several are based on Indian literary works. The characterization tends to be stark, with the positive and negative characters clearly delineated. The elements of love, magic, religion and comedy are strong. Most of the dramas were long and performed in the daytime only, extending over one or several days.

A well known and popular play is *The Historical Drama of King Srong-btsan sgam-po*. The great Tibetan king of the title, an actual historical figure (d. AD 650), sends an ambassador to China to seek marriage with the Princess Wencheng. With great ingenuity the ambassador performs difficult tasks set him by the Chinese emperor and wins the bride for his king. In contemporary China the story is considered to promote 'the unity of the nationalities'.

In the past performers held a very low social status. Usually men played female roles. Fully professional companies existed, but most were semi-professional, their members being mainly male peasants serving overlords and acting only part of the year. In late summer each year 12 famous troupes were selected from among these semi-professional folk groups to gather in Lhasa for a competitive drama season.

The Tibetan Drama Troupe of Tibet was set up in Lhasa in 1960 just after the 1959 rebellion against Chinese rule. It offers mainly traditional pieces in two- to three-hour performances. In line with PRC policy, the pieces are 'reformed', but they retain their traditional dance, costumes, singing style, offstage chorus and masked dance of the prologue, as well as the main elements of the older stories. Reformed performances by the Tibetan Drama Troupe of Tibet use an orchestra much enlarged to include wind and string instruments, not only Tibetan, but also Han Chinese and Western, and are staged in a theatre with properties and scenery. The troupe also performs 'unreformed' traditional items at festival time at the old Summer Palace of the Dalai Lama. In Tibet in the 1990s there are also numerous semi-amateur folk troupes, which perform traditional dramas completely unchanged from the past, except that women play female roles. The custom of gathering troupes in Lhasa for a summer festival was revived in 1984 and it is now again an annual event, opening with the exposition of the Buddha picture at the great Bras-spungs Monastery just outside Lhasa.

There have been occasional attempts since 1960 to adapt propaganda themes to Tibetan drama. On the whole the Tibetan people have not welcomed these experiments. In 1987, 1988 and 1989 there were demonstrations in Lhasa in favour of Tibetan independence, which were suppressed by the Chinese government and in the last year led to the imposition of martial law in Lhasa for over one year. The impact of these troubles on drama has been a return to an emphasis on unreformed traditional drama at the expense of reformed, let alone modern items. However, drama continues to play a major role in the social and cultural life of the Tibetan people.

There is a Tibetan Institute of Performing Arts in Dharamsala in the northern Punjab, India, which studies and performs the traditional Tibetan drama. CPM

Tidblad, Inga 1901–75 Important Swedish actress, particularly admired for roles in Shakespearian comedy (Rosalind, Viola, Beatrice and Portia) which she played with depth and subtlety. She never acted in major classical tragedy, but specialized in the psychological REALISM for which DRAMATEN was famous in the mid-20th century, especially in STRINDBERG, IBSEN and O'NEILL. Her Miss Julie (which she played in New York at 61) and Queen Christina were admired for their focused complexity, as were her roles in world premieres of O'Neill: Mary Tyrone in *Long Day's Journey into Night* (1956) and Deborah in *A Touch of the Poet* (1957) and *More Stately Mansions* (1962). HL

Tieck, Ludwig 1773–1853 German playwright, novelist and essayist. One of Tieck's earliest loves was the theatre, and his interest in it was sustained throughout his extremely fertile career as a writer and editor. His plays exhibit the same failings as those of other early romantic writers. While they are wonderfully inventive, and often idiosyncratic, they defy effective staging, though his comedies *Puss in Boots* (1797) and *The World Upside Down*

(1798) have done well in modern revivals. However, his vast dramatic fantasy, *Emperor Octavian* (1804), cannot be properly represented on stage.

Throughout his life, Tieck was profoundly interested in SHAKESPEARE and the Elizabethan playwrights. He translated some of the plays, notably *The Tempest* (1795), and was involved in the completion of A. W. SCHLEGEL's translations of Shakespeare. In his critical writings, he explored more thoroughly and richly than previous critics Shakespeare's imaginative world. As a result of a visit to England in 1817 to collect materials on the Elizabethans, he became interested in the physical arrangement of the Elizabethan theatre. In 1836, with the help of the architect Gottfried Semper, he reconstructed on paper London's FORTUNE THEATRE. In 1843 he produced *A Midsummer Night's Dream* in Berlin, utilizing many features of the Elizabethan stage. In 1824 he had been appointed dramaturge of the DRESDEN COURT THEATRE, where he laboured, not always with success, to improve standards of diction and to create, especially in the classics, a simpler approach to staging than the one then current. His writings on the theatre are collected in the four volumes of *Critical Writings* published in 1848. SW

Tilley, Vesta [Matilda Alice Victoria Powles] 1864–1952 The most popular male impersonator of the British MUSIC-HALL. Tilley made her stage debut at the Gloucester Theatre Royal at the age of three or four, and first appeared in trousers as the Pocket Sims Reeves. Her first London appearance was in 1878 at the Royal Holborn. Although she was a celebrated principal boy in PANTOMIME, famous for her waltz-tempo songs, her chief contribution was as an elegant young man-about-town, singing such numbers as 'Following in Father's Footsteps' and 'The Midnight Son'. Her natty masculine attire, specially tailored for her, set fashions, and her transvestism was made palatable for a newly genteel audience by the fact that the visual illusion was undermined by her soprano voice. During the First World War, she won greater popularity and some opprobrium for her aid in recruiting (dressed as a Tommy, she sang 'The Army of Today's All Right'). She retired in 1920 after her husband, the manager Walter de Frece, was knighted, and devoted the rest of her life to charity work. (See also MALE IMPERSONATION.) LS

Tingeltangel Generic term for a lower-class MUSIC-HALL in Berlin, deriving from a song the comedian Tange sang at the Triangel Theater. Ten or 20 female singers and a few comedians would sit on a small stage and come forward to deliver their numbers, accompanied solely by a piano. The verses were usually ribald and called for the almost exclusively male audience of artisans, small tradesmen and students to join in the chorus and goose-step round the platform. At the end of the 19th century the most famous were Moors Academy of Music, the Silberhalle and Elysium, the Kuhstall, Klosterstiebel and the Singspielhalle. LS

Tipton, Jennifer 1937– American lighting designer (see STAGE LIGHTING), director and teacher whose early interest in dance led to an appreciation of the potential of light

and its uses and impact on performance. She studied with lighting designer Tom Skelton, began her career designing for choreographer Paul Taylor, and since 1965 has designed every production by choreographer Twyla Tharp as well as productions for Mikhail Baryshnikov and Robert Joffrey. In theatre she has designed frequently for the NEW YORK SHAKESPEARE FESTIVAL, the GOODMAN THEATRE and many regional theatres. BROADWAY credits include *La Bête* and *Jerome Robbins' Broadway*. Her preference for more 'abstract' theatre has led to collaboration with MABOU MINES, ROBERT WILSON, ANDREI SERBAN and the WOOSTER GROUP. In 1991 she directed *The Tempest* at the GUTHRIE THEATRE. Tipton's work is typified by a sense of sculptured and textured space. AA

tireman Important member of Elizabethan theatre companies, since COSTUME was the most costly and colourful element in contemporary styles of performance. Whilst leading actors possessed their own costumes, the tireman (wardrobe master) would probably have checked their appropriateness as well as supplying women's clothes for the boys and fitting the hired men. What could not be supplied out of stock he would have to make or order, and we can assume that it was his task to maintain and replenish the wardrobe store in the TIRING HOUSE. PT

tiring house Name given to that section of Elizabethan theatre buildings directly behind and giving access to the stage, derived from one (the most important in a clothes-conscious age) of its many functions. It was there that the actors 'attired' themselves for performance. But the tiring house must also have accommodated a wardrobe and property store, the collection of plays in the care of the BOOK-KEEPER, and meeting-rooms for the company and privileged visitors. Its façade served as the upstage wall of the platform, so that actors entered directly from the tiring house on to the stage. PT

Tirso de Molina [Gabriel Téllez] c.1579–1648 Spanish playwright of the GOLDEN AGE, considered with LOPE DE VEGA and CALDERÓN the best of the period. Born in Madrid, he entered the Mercedarian religious order in 1620. Tirso combined, not without occasional conflicts, playwriting for popular audiences with successive appointments and promotions within the order, including a stay in Santo Domingo, heading several monasteries, and writing *The General History of the Order of Mercy* (1693). He wrote few plays after 1625, when the Council of Castile's Committee for Reform declared his playwriting activities scandalous for a monk.

Eighty of Tirso's plays are extant (he claimed to have written 300). He is best known for having composed the first fully developed play on the now mythological figure of Don Juan, *El burlador de Sevilla y convidado de piedra* (*The Trickster of Seville and the Stone Guest*). With notable charm, dynamism and malicious intent the protagonist brazenly tricks all of those with whom he comes into contact and receives poetic and divine justice as the notions of free will and divine grace are played out. These latter themes are also developed with singular craftsmanship in *El condenado por desconfiado* (*Damned for Despair*), combining Tirso's solid grounding in philosophy and theology with his instinct for dramatic entertainment.

He wrote plays based on biblical stories, saints' lives and historical sources, but the majority and the most popular are comedies of intrigue, manners and character in which love and jealousy are the motivating themes. An ardent defender of the new COMEDIA and of Lope de Vega, he challenges the audience's eyes and ears with complicated plots of deceit and disguise in which the individual triumphs over social restraints. Fascinated by role-play and illusion that destabilize identities, Tirso reveals human nature with psychological acuity. In *Don Gil de las calzas verdes* (*Don Gil of the Green Breeches*), an urbane COMEDY set in Madrid, the female protagonist, Juana, dresses as a man to search for and reclaim the young man who has won her heart and honour. This play expands the *comedia* convention of cross-dressing and features a young woman of intelligence, verve and imagination not uncommon in plays by Tirso. Here, as elsewhere in his work, the *figura del donaire* (comic figure) is also given greater dramatic range. Another comedy, *El vergonzoso en palacio* (*The Shy Man at Court*), was revived by the National Classical Theatre Company in 1989.   ElB

Toby Principal character of the North American TENT SHOW, a redhaired, freckle-faced farmboy. He appears to derive from the rustic low comedians of 18th-century FARCE; accepted tradition is that Fred Wilson of Horace Murphy's Comedians combined all his 'silly kid' roles under the blanket name Toby around 1909. His dramatic function resembles that of the 'comic man' in MELODRAMA, providing laughs while contributing to the happy ending. Wilson's Toby was still recognizable as a farmhand in his checked shirt and boots, but the character grew more grotesque. Harley Sadler turned him into a Texas cowpoke in woolly chaps and a phallic pistol, and Neil Schaffner into an awkward dude whose large freckles and blacked-out front teeth constituted a kind of COMMEDIA MASK. The female equivalent was Sis Hopkins, created by Rose Melville c.1898, an 'Indiana jay' in pigtails and a pinafore; the type became known as Susie. The growing predominance of Toby and his antics, to the detriment of the dramas in which he appeared, has been cited as a factor in the declining popularity of the tent show.   LS

Togo Togo was a German territory from 1884 to 1914. In 1919 it came under Franco-British control as a League of Nations mandated territory, with the British western third joining independent Ghana in 1957 and the French section becoming the independent Republic of Togo in 1960. The division of Togo's largest and most influential ethnic group, the Ewe, into Ghanaian and Togolese, and the irredentist feelings this has fostered, are at the heart of the distrust and disputes between the two affected countries.

Togo's triple colonial heritage has had a direct influence on its modern culture, especially the theatre. For it was the mid-19th-century work of early German missionaries (followed by the British) in standardizing the Ewe language for evangelical purposes that laid the foundations for the emergence of a modest Ewe literary theatre. This theatre is basically didactic and proselytizing, and its chief representatives are F. Kawasi Fiawoo, author of *Toko*

Atolia (*The Fifth Lagoon*, 1937) and winner of the International African Institute prize, and B. H. Setsoafia, playwright and translator of SHAKESPEARE into Ewe.

Ewe literary theatre went into decline partly as the result of an aggressive French policy which promoted literacy in French at the expense of Ewe, and was replaced in the 1940s by a church-based Ewe religious theatre, the *kantata*. Of missionary origins, the *kantata*, which spread from Ghana, dramatizes Bible stories and MORALITY PLAYS as in, for example, *La Vie de Daniel* (*The Life of Daniel*) and *Le Mariage d'Isaac et de Rebecca* (*The Marriage of Isaac and Rebecca*). Danced and sung to Christian music on the piano – notably in the hands of its first Togolese practitioner Morehouse Apedo-Amah – it later evolved to include dialogue. But some *kantatas* were lay, improvising on Togolese or oriental lore: examples are *Mille et une nuits* (*One Thousand and One Nights*) and the hugely popular *Ali Baba et les quarante voleurs* (*Ali Baba and the Forty Thieves*) which ran from 1947 to 1954. The lay *kantata*, unlike its religious counterpart, is sung and danced to traditional Togolese music and instruments. It also has a greater element of fantasy which, according to the theatre historian Alain Ricard, derives from its original subject-matter as well as from the influence of popular Indian films, aspects of whose scenography and choreography it reproduces.

It is this theatre which from the late 1960s gave rise to the only truly popular Ewe theatrical form to date, the 'concert party'. Resolutely oral, without (unlike the *kantata*) even a written outline and aimed at a mass audience (it is despised by the literate elite), the concert party, whose origins are also Ghanaian and Nigerian, is an evening of musical and theatrical entertainment. It comprises a warming-up session of 'highlife' music, a prologue of skits and storytelling, and an improvised play on topical and moral issues. It uses a mixture of Ewe and pidgin French and combines the comic, the burlesque and the satirical. The performers, untrained and mostly recruited from among the urban unemployed and petty employee class, invent the action as they go along, relying on their imagination and, in the tradition of the Pantaloons that they are, on their talents as mimics, dancers and singers. They depict stock characters like the prostitute, the houseboy and the trader, who are easily recognizable by their costumes.

Side by side with this popular activity go two types of official theatrical activity: a state-organized *théâtre d'animation culturelle* and a theatre in French. But in spite of the efforts of the French and the Togolese authorities to promote it, it has not produced any writers of note. The exception is SENOUVO ZINSOU. But even he integrates many concert-party and traditional performing arts techniques in his plays in French, such that he can be considered as continuing in the language the modern Togolese popular theatre tradition. However, over the last five years a few more Togolese have published successful plays in French: *Le Carrefour* (*The Crossroads*, 1990) and *Récupération* (*Recuperation*, 1992) by Koffi Efoui; *Gagio, ou l'argent, cette peste* (*Gagio, or Money, This Plague*, 1993) by Koffi Gomez, and *Chemins de croix* (*Stations of the Cross*, 1991) and *La Saga des rois* (*The Saga of Kings*, 1992) by Kangni Alemdjrodo.   JCM

See: S. Amégbléamé, 'Le Théâtre dans la littérature Ewe', *Afrique Littéraire et Artistique*, 51, 1979, and 'L'Influence biblique dans la littérature Ewe', in *Mélanges offerts à Albert Gérard*, ed. J. Riesz and A. Ricard, Tübingen, 1990; A. Ricard, 'Concours et concert: théâtre scolaire et théâtre populaire du Togo', *Revue d'histoire du théâtre*, 1, 1975, and *L'Invention du théâtre*, Lausanne, 1986.

Toller, Ernst 1893–1939 German dramatist – with KAISER, the most prominent expressionist playwright. *Die Wandlung* (*Transfiguration*, 1919) is a poetic distillation in 'stations' of the author's conversion from patriot to pacifist in the First World War. KARLHEINZ MARTIN's production at the Tribüne was Berlin's first taste of full-blooded scenic EXPRESSIONISM. His new fame catapulted the pacifist and socialist Toller into politics, as president of the abortive Munich Soviet Republic, which earned him five years in prison. There he turned his experience of politics into *Masse Mensch* (*Masses and Man*, 1920), in which utopian socialist realism clashes with Leninist revolutionary violence and triumphs in death. Real scenes alternate with dream scenes, both written in the same verse telegraphese. *Die Maschinenstürmer* (*The Machine Wreckers*, 1992) deals with the Luddite revolt. With *Hoppla, wir leben* (*Hoppla We're Alive*, 1927) Toller espoused 'new sobriety' and presented a contemporary political cross-section of Berlin. PISCATOR turned it into complex analysis of the failure of the 1919 German Revolution.

Toller went into exile in 1933. His last, anti-Nazi play *Pastor Hall* (1939) was filmed in England. He committed suicide in New York in 1939. Toller the poet-politician is the subject of TANKRED DORST's *Toller*. HR

tollu bommalu [*tholu bommalatta*] One of the best-known forms of puppetry in INDIA, and one example of the wonderfully varied forms of shadow-puppet theatre in Asia. It is found in several regions of Andhra Pradesh state in south India. *Tolu* means a 'doll' and *bommalu* means 'leather'. According to the oral tradition, the form originated in 200 BC when it was patronized by the rulers of the Satavahana dynasty. In the 16th century during the reign of King Kona Reddy, a ruler of the Vijayanagar Empire, a Telugu manuscript entitled *Ramayana Ranganathana* was composed specifically for the shadow theatre. Besides providing a dramatic text of the famous epic story, the manuscript includes instructions for the construction and decoration of SHADOW PUPPETS. Families of puppeteers even today jealously guard copies of the manuscripts from outside study.

Puppets are cut from various types of hide and processed in a special manner. Most puppets, including humans and saints, are made of goatskin. Demons are carved of buffalo hide, and gods and heroes of deerskin. Puppets are large, translucent and multicoloured. Their sizes depend upon the area of the state in which they are produced. For example, puppet figures from Madnapalli district are generally around 4ft tall and those from Kakinada as tall as 5ft.

The leather puppet is wedged into a split bamboo strip and tied along the length of the strip from the head to the crotch to provide support. Different emotional states of a character are depicted by separate puppets. Some puppets incorporate a scenic environment around the figure. For example, Rama's wife, Sita, is depicted beneath an Ashoka tree in King Ravana's garden.

Many puppets have movable hands and legs and some movable heads and necks. The hands are moved by sticks and the legs allowed to dangle from the trunk of the puppet. The skirt of a dancing girl is hinged at her waist and, through a clever device contrived with strings and knots, she may even turn her head and torso from side to side.

Refined characters have a delicate physiognomy, whereas demons have exaggerated and gross features revealing their excessiveness and crudity. Some puppets are delicately carved with traceries of fine perforations. Puppets are dyed black, red and green; for females and sages the dominant colour is yellow.

The colourful shadows are cast on a wide, white screen made of a sturdy cotton *sari* or cloth pieces stretched between two poles temporarily fixed in the ground about 6 to 12ft apart. The total height of the screen depends on the size of the puppets used, ranging from 5 to 7ft. The stage behind the screen is raised about half a foot above the ground and encased by thatch matting to provide privacy for the performers and their families during the long hours of the performance.

About 11in above the bottom of the screen a rope is stretched on which the puppets may be rested when they are on stage. Puppets are pinned in place on the screen with acacia-thorn pins. Traditionally the flickering mellow glow of oil lamps and torches produced the shadows on the screen. Nowadays companies use petromax lamps which give off a harsh blue-white glow that changes the true colour of the images. The chief manipulator stands pressing the large puppets firmly against the screen. With his free hand he manipulates the arms of the puppet. When big puppets are used for fight sequences, two people manipulate each puppet. Puppets are passed from hand to hand when they are moved across the wide screen. A manipulator wears a set of bells on one of his ankles which accentuates his dance steps. A loose elevated board on the floor of the performance booth provides additional sound effects when struck with his foot.

A typical troupe of between 6 and 10 people is composed of manipulators, singers, dancers and instrumentalists. Women speak the female parts and the stage manager manipulates the shadows during dance numbers.

While songs have a written text, dialogue sections are improvised and extend as long as the puppeteers can hold the audience's interest. Musicians play a *mridangam* drum, bell-metal cymbals, and sometimes harmonium and *mukavina*, an oboe-like wind instrument. A metal barrel is struck with long thin sticks, like a drum, and a piece of leather slapped by the hand provides special sound effects. Folk and classical melodies are integrated. Even film music has crept in because of its popularity.

During performance puppeteers chant and speak dialogue to each other rather than through the puppets. The puppets seem to act only as symbols of the characters portrayed to which the manipulators add their own highly effective emotional reactions.

Special effects delight the audience. For example, when

a character is shot with an arrow during a battle, a whizzing noise is produced by a small whistle as a leather arrow on a rod is whisked across the screen. When it strikes the victim, severing his head, the puppet head is detached quickly by a string and made to roll across the screen. Drummers accentuate the action with loud thuds.

Popular characters are the clowns – Katikayata, the drunken lecher and womanizer, and Bangavaka, his fat, scandalmongering wife. They provide comic interludes within the familiar stories of the *Ramayana*, the *Mahabharata* and the *Puranas*. A company has six to a dozen plays in its repertory, each of which takes four to eight hours to perform.

Lord Shiva is regarded as the god of puppeteers. During Shiva's birthday in May, some companies perform special nine-night programmes in his honour outside temples of the region. This tends to be one of their most lucrative engagements. The playing season extends between the monsoons which strike Andhra Pradesh twice a year.

Performance begins when the puppet of Ganapati, the elephant-headed god, is placed on the screen and songs of praise are sung in his honour. Then Saraswathi, goddess of learning, appears and is praised. A comic interlude takes place between the husband and wife. Jokes are made about local spectators. Then the stage manager introduces the subject of the play. Nearly two hours are devoted to pre-liminaries and introduction of characters. Finally, the drama based on an epic story is enacted. About sunrise performances end with songs of thanksgiving. FAR

Tolstoi, Aleksei (Konstantinovich) [Kozma Prutkov] 1817–75 Diplomat, poet, novelist and major Russian historical dramatist of the 19th century. He began his literary career in 1841 with one of three vampire tales, which may have provided source material for SUKHOVO-KOBYLIN's *Tarelkin's Death*. From 1853 to 63 he published nonsense verse, satirical prose and theatrical parodies with his cousins the Zhemchuzhnikovs in the person of pseudonymous author Kozma Prutkov, an arrogant clerk with literary pretensions. 'His' work influenced Vladimir Solovyov, Count Vladimir Sollogub and NIKOLAI EVREINOV in the late 19th and early 20th centuries. Tolstoi also wrote well regarded satirical and lyrical verse and ballads under his own name, some of which have been set to music by Tchaikovsky, Mussorgsky and Rimsky-Korsakov. His popular romantic historical novel, *Prince Serebryany* (1862), based largely on Karamzin's *History of the Russian State* (1818–26), is set during the reign of Ivan the Terrible.

Tolstoi's reputation as a dramatist rests on his popular blank verse historical trilogy on three of Russia's feudal monarchs (1533–1605): *The Death of Ivan the Terrible* (1864), *Tsar Fyodor Ioannovich* (1868) and *Tsar Boris* (1870). In each of these self-contained dramas, Tolstoi humanizes history à *la* SCHILLER by focusing upon the personal psychological and moral ramifications of the ruler-protagonist's political crisis. The first play received a lavish, antiquarian staging in 1867 at St Petersburg's Aleksandrinsky Theatre, owing to the author's court connections, but failed with a comic actor miscast in the title role. The second drama premiered in 1898 in St Petersburg and then at the MOSCOW ART THEATRE, whose production established the play in Russia's permanent dramatic

repertoire. The role of gentle, naive Fyodor is a favourite of actors, and has been interpreted memorably by IVAN MOSKVIN at the MAT premiere and by INNOKENTY SMOKTUNOVSKY at the Maly Theatre in the 1970s. SG

Tolstoi, Aleksei (Nikolaevich) 1883–1945 Soviet novelist, short story writer and dramatist (in that order of significance), whose works have become official classics. A nobleman by birth and an anti-Bolshevik at the time of the Revolution, Tolstoi, later known as the 'Red Count', accommodated himself totally to the new regime and became an apologist for Stalin following an interlude in Parisian exile (1918–23). Before 1917 he produced symbolist poetry (see SYMBOLISM) and some talented novels and short story collections. He wrote 28 plays, beginning in 1908. His pre-revolutionary plays are FARCES and comedies satirizing the landed gentry and the merchant class. Seven received Moscow stagings, and his dramatic fairy tale *The Sorcerer's Daughter and the Enchanted Prince* was produced at MEYERHOLD's 'theatre of small forms', the Strand (1908). In the 1920s Tolstoi was the co-author of three historical dramas with historian P. E. Shchegolev; and he wrote the science fiction play *The Revolt of the Machines* (1924) and the first part of his Peter the Great trilogy – *On the Rack* (1929), rewritten as *Peter the First* (first version, 1935; second, 1939) – which parallels his unfinished three-part historical novel *Peter the First* (1930, 1934, 1945), recipient of the 1941 Stalin Prize and thought by some to be exemplary of its genre. Tolstoi's evolving presentation of Peter as tyrant, modernizer and finally national hero reflects the shift in official perspective which was interested in likening Peter to Stalin. His two-part historical play *Ivan the Terrible (The Eagle and Its Mate*, 1944; *The Difficult Years*, 1946), which won him a third, posthumous Stalin Prize in 1946, is a somewhat idealized view of the Tsar which Soviet critics considered his best dramatic work. SG

Tolstoi, Lev (Nikolaevich) 1828–1910 A titled noble, one of Russia's greatest novelists and a social dramatist. Count Tolstoi rejected his class and justified art solely as a means of inculcating Christian doctrine and virtue and of changing the status quo. Following the success of his autobiographical writings of the 1850s, he turned to educational reform, founding a school for his serfs' children, studying European educational theory and practice and publishing his findings in the 1860s and 70s. In 1878, after the completion of his masterful novels *War and Peace* (1869) and *Anna Karenina* (1877), he underwent a celebrated spiritual crisis, resulting in his rejection of orthodox Christianity in favour of a partially self-devised code of non-resistance to evil.

This ethical philosophy manifests itself in all of his remaining work – three religious treatises (1880–3); social polemics exposing the inequalities of the class system, and the evils of alcohol, tobacco, war and patriotism; aesthetic essays; and dramas. About the latter, he had decidedly mixed feelings. He rejected theatre's sham and self-indulgence but embraced its potential for educating and uplifting a popular audience. He was particular as to how and by whom his plays were performed. His earliest – *A Contaminated Family* (1864), *The Nihilist* (1866) and *The*

First Distiller (1886), two SATIRES and a moral fable – treated such contemporary evils as women's rights, nihilism and alcoholism. In *What Is Art?* (1897–8), 'On SHAKESPEARE and the Drama' (1903–4) and other aesthetic and critical works, Tolstoi distinguished between true and counterfeit art. True art is universal, moral, affective but not excessive in emotional and scenographic detail. False art, which includes the works of Shakespeare, GOETHE, HUGO and others, violates these criteria and those relating purely to craft.

Tolstoi condemned his own naturalistic peasant tragedy, *The Power of Darkness* (1886), for wallowing in extraneous detail, but it remains a powerful indictment of the inhumanity and moral degeneracy brought on by the ignorance and squalor of Russian peasant life. Based upon a contemporary criminal case and echoing PISEMSKY's *A Bitter Fate*, it relates a tale of adultery and infanticide and features a typically meek Tolstoyan *raisonneur* and a climactic confession-conversion. Originally written for performance in the 'popular' theatres, it was banned from the Russian stage until 1895, premiering instead at ANTOINE's Théâtre Libre in 1888. *The Fruits of Enlightenment* (1889) satirized the unenlightened attitude of the Russian landed nobility towards the peasantry, despite the abolition of serfdom in 1861. *The Living Corpse* (1900), like *Power*, was based on an actual court case and, like *Fruits*, exposed the inadequacy of secular laws, this time governing marriage and divorce. *The Light Shines in the Darkness* (1900) is an unfinished autobiographical tale of an aristocrat whose adherence to a transparently Tolstoyan ethic puts him at odds with his family and society. *The Cause of It All* (1910) is another anti-alcohol tract.

While the plays suffer somewhat from the author's moral didacticism, they benefit from the emotional intensity generated by his convictions. His vision and the veracity of his language and characters align Tolstoi somewhat more closely with GRIBOEDOV's and GOGOL's psychological realism than with OSTROVSKY's contrived ethnographic REALISM. Much of his narrative writing has been adapted for the stage, including the short story 'Kholstomer' by playwright MARK ROZOVSKY and director GEORGY TOVSTONOGOV at Leningrad's Gorky Theatre (1975–6). This version was further adapted and produced as *Strider: The Story of a Horse*, in New York at the Chelsea Theatre Centre in 1979 and later on BROADWAY and in regional theatres. SG

'Tom show' see *UNCLE TOM'S CABIN*

Tomaszewski, Henryk see MIME

Toole, J(ohn) L(aurence) 1830–1906 English actor, the foremost low comedian of the 19th century's last decades. Toole made his professional debut in Dublin in 1852 and his London debut later in the same year. His famous friendship with HENRY IRVING began in Edinburgh in 1857 (Toole was the Artful Dodger and Irving Monks in a deplorable adaptation of *Oliver Twist*, which might have tested DICKENS's fondness for Toole, had he seen it) and blossomed into lifelong intimacy when they acted together in London in 1867. The relationship was a gift for cartoonists, the squat extrovert comedian and the gaunt introverted tragedian, but their performances together in their years of fame were limited to benefits.

Toole was the first to win public favour as a star of ADELPHI FARCES and BURLESQUES from 1859 to 67. Like FREDERICK ROBSON, whom he admired, Toole was at his best in roles combining eccentric COMEDY and pathos: Caleb Plummer in BOUCICAULT's *Dot* (1862) and Michael Garner in H. J. BYRON's *Dearer than Life* (1868). For JOHN HOLLINGSHEAD at London's GAIETY (1869–73) he revived *Paul Pry*, in conscious emulation of the great JOHN LISTON. In 1879, Toole bought the lease of the Charing Cross Theatre, which he rechristened Toole's Theatre in 1882. He was the first English actor confident enough of his standing with the London public to name a theatre after himself (it was not until 1888 that EDWARD TERRY became the second). He proved a shrewd manager, though his choice of plays (H. J. Byron and F. C. Burnand dominated the repertoire) was generally predictable. He was, however, the first to present J. M. BARRIE's plays – *Ibsen's Ghost; or, Toole Up-to-Date* (1891) and *Walker, London* (1892). Toole retired in 1895 and left a fortune when he died. PT

Topol, Haim 1935– Israeli actor, now resident in England. His great roles in Israel were Azdak in BRECHT's *The Caucasian Chalk Circle* (1962) and Sallah Shabbati in the film of that name (1964) by EPHRAIM KISHON. In London he rose to fame with his portrayal of Tevye the Milkman in the MUSICAL *Fiddler on the Roof* (1967), based on SHOLOM ALEICHEM's Yiddish novel. HAS

Torelli, Giacomo 1608–78 Italian architect, engineer and stage designer whose innovations became a standard part of Continental theatre practice. He was responsible for developing the chariot-and-pole system of changeable scenery which consisted of attaching wing flats through slits in the stage floor to rolling wagons in the cellar beneath: by an arrangement of pulleys and ropes wound on a common drum all the flats could move smoothly and simultaneously under the control of a single stage-hand, while overhead borders were similarly operated by counterweights. The result was a swift, magical transformation of one scene to the next, creating an illusion akin to a cinematic dissolve, which had a profound effect not only on design but on the evolution of theatrical forms, notably OPERA and intermezzi.

Torelli is said to have been a pupil of ALEOTTI at the Teatro Farnese, but he first became prominent in Venice where he designed the Teatro Novissimo and several of its earliest operatic productions, including *La Finta Pazza* (1641), *Bellerofonte* (1642) and *Venere Gelosa* (1643). Their use of machinery was so impressive that he was dubbed 'the great sorcerer'. Summoned to Paris by Mazarin in 1645, he re-equipped the PETIT-BOURBON where his designs for the performances of Italian opera, for PIERRE CORNEILLE's 'machine-play' *Andromède* (1650) and subsequently for a series of court ballets earned him an equal reputation with French audiences.

In 1659 the arrival in France of his fellow countryman GASPARE VIGARANI soon ousted him from royal favour, and shortly after supervising the staging of MOLIÈRE's *Les Fâcheux* (*The Bores*) for Fouquet in 1661 he was forced to return to his native Fano, where he continued to work until his death and produced some of his most interesting designs. With the demolition of the Petit-Bourbon the machinery he had installed there was removed and destroyed by the jealous Vigarani, but his drawings survived and were later reproduced in DIDEROT's *Encyclopédie* (1772) under 'Machines de Théâtre'. Torelli's achievement in revolutionizing French *mise-en-scène* established an Italianate tradition of spectacular staging for opera and ballet which was to be maintained by Vigarani, BERAIN and SERVANDONI. (See also THEATRE DESIGN.) AA DR

Toronto Workshop Productions TWP's founding in 1959 marked the beginning of Canada's 'alternative' theatre movement. Begun as an amateur theatre workshop in donated factory space, it gained professional status in 1963 and eventually moved into a downtown Toronto theatre building. The company's history was predominantly shaped by founding artistic director George Luscombe, an ardent iconoclast who had worked with Dora Mavor Moore and JOAN LITTLEWOOD. Luscombe fostered an ensemble company with a strong commitment to leftist politics and collective creation, and a flair for theatrically imaginative productions that provided a needed counterpoint to the realistic domestic dramas prevalent on the Canadian stage.

The collective creation technique drew on the expertise of playwrights, directors and actors to create some notable productions, including *Hey Rube!* (1961), *Mr Bones* (1968) – which shared the billing with Mario Fratti's *Che* when TWP represented Canada at the 1969 Venice Biennale – *Chicago '70* (1970) and *Ten Lost Years* (1974), a play about the Great Depression that became one of the most successful in Canadian theatre history.

Attempts to rescue TWP's theatre building from commercial developers led to the establishment of a board of directors in 1981; subsequent conflicts with that board forced Luscombe to leave his position as artistic director in 1986. TWP ceased productions in 1989, amid bitter legal battles over the future of the company and its theatre. DAH

Torres Naharro, Bartolomé de c.1480–1525 Spanish playwright, poet and dramatic theorist who wrote most of his nine plays in Rome. *Propalladia* (*First Fruits of Pallas*, 1517) includes plays, poetry and an influential prologue. This systematic dramatic formula favours a five-act structure and characters' speech and actions appropriate to their status. The plays separate out into the categories of realistic and imaginary. Placed on the 1559 Index for its bold SATIRE, an expurgated *Propalladia* was republished in Madrid in 1573. *Himenea* (*Hymen*), based on episodes from FERNANDO DE ROJAS's *La Celestina*, sets the pattern for GOLDEN AGE cape-and-sword plays. PZ

Totò [Antonio de Curtis] 1898–1967 Italian comedian and actor-manager. After an early career as a club entertainer he entered the 'straight' theatre, eventually becoming an actor-manager, specializing in COMEDY and REVUE which exploited his mimic genius, perfect timing of lines, and skill with frenetic stage 'business'. Often compared to screen comedians like Chaplin and Keaton, he was a brilliant improviser whose impact was more visual than verbal, not least thanks to his expressive face and hand gestures. In the 1950s, he rapidly became established as one of the most popular Italian film comedians, in films like *Napoli milionaria* (*Affluent Naples*, 1950), *Guardie e ladri* (1951) and *L'oro di Napoli* (*The Gold of Naples*, 1954), a reputation he enjoyed until his death. LR

Tourneur, Cyril c.1575–1626 English playwright. Tourneur's is the extraordinary case of a writer whose name is celebrated for a single play, *The Revenger's Tragedy* (c.1606), that is, in the view of many scholars, more likely to have been the work of MIDDLETON. The details of his life are obscure. He was probably, at various times, in the service of the Earl of Essex, the Veres and the Cecils, dying in Ireland as a result of wounds or illness after Sir Edward Cecil's ill-starred expedition against Cadiz. Tourneur is known to be the author of a lost play, *The Nobleman* (c.1607), and *The Atheist's Tragedy* (published 1611), a dismally mechanical REVENGE TRAGEDY. It is difficult to believe that the same man could also have written the sombrely ironic *The Revenger's Tragedy*. PT

Tovstonogov, Georgy (Aleksandrovich) 1915–89 Soviet director, part of the wave of new artists to emerge from the Thaw period (1954–6). He became artistic director of the Bolshoi Dramatic Theatre (BDT, or the Gorky) in 1956, and over the years transformed it into the best theatre in Leningrad, and its company – especially its mature actors – into perhaps the best in the former Soviet Union. Tovstonogov began his career in Tbilisi as an actor and assistant director (1931), and after attending the Moscow State Theatrical Institute (GITIS) in 1938 became artistic director of the Tbilisi Russian Theatre (the Griboedov Theatre, 1938–46). From 1946 to 49 he directed the Moscow Children's Theatre, and between 1950 and 56 he was chief director of Leningrad's Lenin Komsomol Theatre, where he developed the successful policy of mixing Soviet dramas, Russian classics and Western literature, which he took with him to the Gorky.

A STANISLAVSKY-based craftsman with a lush, romantic pictorial style, Tovstonogov did not so much radically reinterpret as carefully texture literature with new values. His orthodox Soviet productions include stagings in the later 1950s and 60s of works by Dvoretsky, KORNEICHUK, Shtein, Sholokhov and Rakhmanov; ALEKSANDR GELMAN's *Minutes of a Meeting* (1976), one of four plays by the author on industrial themes, whose static conference-table format Tovstonogov relieved by revolving the set periodically to force new perspectives; and V. Tendryakov's *Three Sacks of Wheat Tailings* (1974), a drama about a good collective farm chairman versus a corrupt Party official, staged to celebrate 'thirty years of victory over Fascism', and for some time watched closely by Moscow officials before formally being admitted into the theatre's repertoire.

Tovstonogov staged a number of examples of post-Thaw 'new lyricism' and intimate, human drama: VOLODIN's *Five Evenings* (1959) and *My Elder Sister* (1961); ARBUZOV's *Irkutsk Story* (1960) and *Happy Days of an Unhappy Man* (1968); and ROZOV's *The Reunion* (1964). Best were his tastefully different readings of classical texts, justly celebrated for their brilliant ensemble play: Dostoevsky's *The Idiot* (1957; London, 1966), with the exceptional INNOKENTY SMOKTUNOVSKY as Myshkin; GRIBOEDOV's *Woe from Wit* (1962), featuring another charismatic performer, Sergei Yursky, as an atypical Chatsky; CHEKHOV's *The Three Sisters* (1965), a production which was favourably compared to the MOSCOW ART THEATRE's; GORKY's *The Petty Bourgeoisie* (1967), which became the theatre's longest-running production; SHAKESPEARE's *Henry IV, Parts 1 and 2* (1969), condensed into a single evening – another repertory standard; GOGOL's *The Inspector General* (1972), compared with some exaggeration to MEYERHOLD's landmark production, and featuring a nightmarish Inspector in dark glasses played throughout as a manifestation of the Mayor's and contemporary Soviet paranoia; and *The Story of a Horse* (adapted from LEV TOLSTOI's narrative 'Kholstomer' by co-director MARK ROZOVSKY, 1975), an alternately ebullient and touching treatment of the man's-inhumanity-to-man theme from the perspective of a horse, beautifully enacted by Evgeny Lebedev, one of the theatre's stalwarts, and with folk-influenced songs and dances and a richly weathered-looking set by EDVARD KOCHERGIN. The play's immense popularity extended to America, where it has been produced on BROADWAY and in university and repertory theatres.

In 1984 Tovstonogov premiered a musical version of SUKHOVO-KOBYLIN's *Tarelkin's Death*. He was also responsible for producing such modern Western classics as Dreiser's *An American Tragedy* (at the Lenin Komsomol, 1951); BRECHT's *Arturo Ui* (directed by Erwin Axer, 1963); Steinbeck's *Of Mice and Men* (1966) and the BERNSTEIN–LAURENTS–SONDHEIM musical *West Side Story* (1968), in student productions at the Leningrad State Institute of Theatre, Music and Cinematography, where he trained Vladimir Vorovyov and Efim Padve, who continued their MUSICAL THEATRE experiments as artistic directors of the Leningrad Theatre of Musical Comedy and the Leningrad Youth Theatre, respectively; ARTHUR MILLER's *The Price* (1968); and EUGENE O'NEILL's *A Moon for the Misbegotten* (1968). The defection to other theatres of actors Yursky and Oleg Borisov and the age of others such as Lebedev, V. I. Strzhelchik, Oleg Basilashvili and Tovstonogov himself ended the theatre's artistic dominance. Tovstonogov's book *The Profession of the Stage Director* (1965) has been published in English (1972). In 1957 he was named a People's Artist of the USSR. SG

Towse, John Ranken 1845–1933 American drama critic. Born in England and educated at Cambridge, Towse went to New York in 1869 as a reporter for the *Evening Post*. In 1874 he was given the drama desk, a position he held until his retirement in 1927. Regarded as a scholarly and trustworthy critic, Towse fought to maintain Victorian tastes in drama and 19th-century standards in the theatre. Like his contemporaries, WILLIAM WINTER and HENRY AUSTIN CLAPP, he could not accept REALISM, especially the plays of IBSEN. His book *Sixty Years of the Theatre* (1916) provides a detailed account and analysis of 19th-century actors. TLM

toy theatre [juvenile drama] Toy theatre originated in early-19th-century London with the full-length coloured theatrical portraits of Robert Dighton. Possibly influenced by engraved pages of characters and scenery for the use of provincial managers issued by a French concern in 1806, sheets of characters from current London productions, 'a penny plain and tuppence coloured', began to appear. In line with earlier cut-out story books and turn-up harlequinades, sets of sheets providing all the major poses, scenery and properties, along with a book of words, enabled children to recreate the stage of their time. The images were cut out, pasted on cardboard and mounted on wire slides, and manipulated in miniature wooden playhouses, lit by candles or small oil-wicks. Often the characters' costumes would be ornamented with gilt and tinsel. The early sheets are of great historical importance, preserving the look of Regency MELODRAMA, OPERETTA and PANTOMIME; the most popular and frequently reprinted plays were M. G. Lewis's *Timour the Tartar* (1811), an equestrian spectacle (see HIPPODRAMA) and Isaac Pocock's *The Miller and His Men* (1813), with its climactic explosion of gunpowder stores. Since the publishers were highly conservative, these were copied again and again, lending what had once been authentic an aura of quaintness: W. S. GILBERT clothed the buccaneers in the first production of *The Pirates of Penzance* (1880) in garb appropriate to the toy theatres of the audience's childhood.

The leading publishers, beginning in 1811, were William West, J. K. Green, J. H. Jameson, and Hodgson & Co.; they were followed by Martin Skelt, W. G. Webb, Green's successor J. Redington, and Redington's son-in-law Benjamin Pollock. Germany was a late starter in the 1830s, but by mid-century dominated the English market with elegant sets, based on fairy tales and operas, designed by Trentsensky of Vienna. France, Spain and Denmark also produced toy theatres, but their repertory was not drawn from actual stage productions; the USA, with Seltz's American Boy's Theatre, was content to copy English models. A minor artistic revival of the form took place in the early 20th century with plays written and/or illustrated by Jack Yeats and Albert Rutherston. Alan Leen and George Speaight revived Pollock's business, and under Marguerite Fawdry it became the Toy Museum in London's Monmouth Street, then in Scala Street, and presently maintains a shop in Covent Garden. LS

tragedy Almost every culture offers an audience pleasure – paradoxically – through an art based on human suffering. In Western culture a significant form of such art is tragedy, a word whose meaning changes with time and place of text or performance. Through the centuries, too, the very word 'tragedy' has acquired a valorizing resonance, which is unique for an art form. Ancient and modern critics have contrasted tragedy with COMEDY; and more recently with MELODRAMA. Early critics – pre-eminently ARISTOTLE – focused on tragic action, whereas recent critics dwell on tragic vision. After centuries of commentary on Greek elements of tragedy (see GREECE, ANCIENT), more recent approaches have shifted to abstruse semiotics and ideological codes of tragedy.

'Tragedy' (*tragōidia*) means 'goat-song', but there is no caproic trace in what we know of Greek tragedy. Performed annually to celebrate the god Dionysus, Attic tragedy of the 5th century BC was based on Greek myth.

REDINGTON'S FAVORITE FOURS.

A typical tuppence-coloured toy theatre sheet, representing the leading characters in a Victorian harlequinade.

Formally, each tragedy was a verse exchange between a Chorus and a small number of actors (usually three). The episodes of the plot were punctuated by choral songs, and the ending was not necessarily unhappy. Of the three Greek tragic playwrights whose works are extant, only AESCHYLUS wrote tetralogies, i.e. three sequential tragedies followed by a satyr play. Between Aeschylus and EURIPIDES the scope of tragedy narrowed from cosmic moral questions to more personal passions.

It was Aristotle in the 4th century BC who first praised tragedy as the highest form of poetry. Preferring SOPHOCLES to other dramatists, and *Oedipus* to other tragedies, Aristotle began the comparative evaluation of works, which has since become a major tool of criticism. Although Aristotle was descriptive rather than prescriptive, he bequeathed to posterity terms that today elude exact definition – *hamartia* (error), *catharsis* (purgation) and *mimesis* (imitation), as well as the more familiar pity and fear. Aside from criticism, later homage to Greek tragedy was seen in imitation. SENECA (and see ROME) accomplished this so sensationally that his nine plays became the strongest influence upon subsequent European tragedy. To him later tragedy is indebted for the five-act structure, the violent catastrophic ending, and the clash of characters speaking *stichomythia* (under emotional stress, each character utters a line that is rhythmically matched to the one preceding it).

In the medieval dearth of theatre, tragedy came to mean the downfall of a person of high degree. During the Renaissance, this bleak fate entered the drama as *de casibus* tragedy. With the Renaissance, tragedy gained importance in both theory and practice. Italy and especially France looked back and up to the pagan classics. Senecan imitation (in Latin) began in the 14th century, but after the defeat of Constantinople in 1453 Greek tragedy gradually became the model, and a misunderstood Aristotle the rule. Thus GIRALDI, who proclaimed the superiority of Seneca to the Greeks, in 1543 set forth the unities of time and action; Scaligero in 1561 added that of place. The architect SERLIO in 1545 distinguished between tragic, comic and satyric settings. Italian Renaissance tragedy, as opposed to comedy, is of only scholarly interest, and not until ALFIERI in the 18th century did Italy produce a playable tragedy.

France took a similar path a century later, with MAIRET in 1630 prescribing the three unities. Other dramatists voluntarily donned this straitjacket. Since PIERRE CORNEILLE's *Cid* violated the unities, it gave rise to the *querelle du Cid*, which was terminated when the Académie-Française laid down the rules of tragedy. Self-consciously noble, neoclassical verse tragedy with its strict decorum dominated not only French but most other Continental drama for the next 150 years.

In England and Spain, however, popular traditions outweighed the learned, encouraging 'impure' tragedy. Although the first English tragedy, *Gorboduc*, is sternly regular, MARLOWE and SHAKESPEARE soon rattled the stage with their action-packed tragedies, towering protagonists, ironies, images and final catastrophes. KYD's *Spanish Tragedy* is usually cited as the first REVENGE TRAGEDY, a self-explanatory subgenre, of which *Hamlet* is the crowning achievement.

When James I succeeded Elizabeth, the tragic genre grew darker and more sceptical. Good and Bad Angels underline the moral conflict of Marlowe's *Dr Faustus*, but WEBSTER, TOURNEUR and CHAPMAN question the very basis of moral judgement in tragedy. Moreover, alongside these dramas of the unfortunate mighty, a few so-called domestic tragedies dramatized the suffering of common people, and this departure from the tragic tradition was to culminate in the 18th-century *London Merchant* (LILLO), a source of middle-class drama throughout Europe, so that noble tragedy suffered an eclipse. Before then, however, during the court-centred theatre of the Restoration, English tragedy briefly adapted the French form into heroic tragedy, a violence-filled struggle between Love and Honour, neatly encapsulated in couplets.

. With romantic bardolatry, tragedy returned loquaciously but untheatrically to literature, since almost every romantic poet of every European country tried his (left) hand at verse tragedy. Along with these efforts came a resurgence of theory, in the works of the SCHLEGEL brothers and LESSING and HUGO's preface to his *Cromwell*, with its blatant rejection of decorum. During the same period, the philosopher Hegel enunciated his view of tragedy as 'the collision of equally justified ethical claims'. Towards the end of the 19th century, NIETZSCHE rejected a moral approach to tragedy, and instead he praised the Dionysian irrational element that paralleled the spirit of music. Realists refused to limit tragedy to privileged protagonists, and the director ANTOINE found nothing incompatible between REALISM and tragedy, while STRINDBERG called his *Miss Julie* 'a naturalistic tragedy' (see NATURALISM). Whether or not they were preoccupied with genre, several modern playwrights have been labelled tragic – IBSEN, CHEKHOV, O'NEILL, GARCÍA LORCA and BECKETT.

In the voluminous 20th-century literature on tragedy, two major questions recur. First, is tragedy possible in our anarchic age that lacks a community of belief? Second, is the ordinary individual a fitting subject for tragedy in our democratic age? Perhaps the most resounding negative reply to the first question is George Steiner's *Death of Tragedy*, whereas ARTHUR MILLER has uttered as resounding an affirmative answer to the second question. Although contemporary dramatists may care little about genre designations for their plays, tragedy is still of deep concern to many contemporary critics – not only those of drama. RC

tragicomedy The word conjures a mixture of sadness and merriment, but the genre has meant different mixtures at different periods in the Western theatre. The word was coined by PLAUTUS in the Prologue to his *Amphitryon*; spoken by the god Mercury, it high-handedly designates a new genre in which kings (who frequent tragedy) mix with slaves (who frequent comedy). Another fissure of classical decorum had earlier been noted by ARISTOTLE, in the happy endings of several tragedies by EURIPIDES (seven extant to our time), but these plays were not called tragicomedies until the Renaissance, when Italian playwrights turned critics to justify their practice.

From late classical to late medieval times, genre terminology was loose, and we cannot recapture today the meaning of such sporadic labels as *tragicomoedia*, *comoedotragoedia* and *comoedia tragica*. Often unlabelled, popular drama mixed the funny and the sad, the common and the divine. The serio-comic *Second Shepherd's Play* was contemporary with Latin school plays of serious main plot and comic subplot. These different mixtures – neoclassical and popular – flourished indiscriminately in the playing spaces of England, France and the Low Countries, but Italian playwright-critics tried to systematize the amorphous practice. GIRALDI spurned the word 'tragicomedy' for his tragedies with happy endings, preferring 'mixed tragedy'. It was, however, GUARINI whose PASTORAL tragicomedy *Il Pastor Fido* (1590) and critical defence *Compendio della poesia tragicomica* (1601) raised a lively little storm. As playwrights, both men evolved labyrinthine plots that twisted their way to a happy and romantic ending, but those of Giraldi were solemn, whereas Guarini sounded an occasional comic note in such figures as a satyr. Both playwrights voluminously defended their respective practices, citing a host of classical authorities to justify the breach of classical decorum. The genre proved eminently exportable, and in the early 17th century tragicomedy (for the most part removed to court from pasture) bloomed happily in England, France and Spain, counting among its practitioners FLETCHER, SHAKESPEARE, HEYWOOD, MARSTON, MASSINGER, SHIRLEY; GARNIER, HARDY, MAIRET, CORNEILLE, ROTROU; LOPE DE VEGA, TIRSO DE MOLINA and ZORRILLA.

Renaissance tragicomedy, in verse form, was set exotically, plotted suspensefully, and resolved satisfactorily; as the 17th century rolled on, the violent action of tragicomedy departed more and more from the inner thrust of tragedy, while more or less comic elements provided entertaining distraction. Although lacklustre dramatists tried to prolong its life into the 18th century, prose popular theatre soon displaced it. The ghost of tragicomedy nevertheless infiltrated into Gothic melodrama of the 19th century.

Modern tragicomedy derives from a minor attribute of the Renaissance variety – comic elements in the basically serious action. There is, however, no clean lineage; there rarely is in theatre. If one seeks a history of a merry–melancholy genre, much depends on the mixture. Almost all English Renaissance tragedies have a comic component, but the mixture became programmatic in the romantic movements of France and Germany. MELODRAMA, the mass medium of the time, thrived on a comic character who helped the hero defeat the villain. Throughout the

19th century English verse drama tended towards solemnity, and perhaps for that reason rarely reached a theatre; but in prose and verse, comic notes sound increasingly loud in plays by Germans LENZ, GRABBE, BÜCHNER and even KLEIST.

With the advent of REALISM in the late 19th century, classical genre designations were all but forgotten, and most serious plays supported a comic component without reducing it formulaically, as in melodrama. SHAW recognized: 'IBSEN was the dramatic poet who firmly established tragicomedy as a much deeper and grimmer entertainment than tragedy.' Although neither Shaw nor Ibsen (who designated *The Wild Duck* as tragicomedy) defines the modern genre, it overlaps with such terms as irony, humorism, the grotesque and the absurd (see THEATRE OF THE ABSURD). Ironists and humorists tend to dramatize contradictions within a realistic world, whereas playwrights of the grotesque and the absurd tend to disorientate the spectator to the frontier of fantasy. Ibsen, STRINDBERG, Shaw, CHEKHOV and PIRANDELLO are masters of the first group; the second is larger, embracing the Spaniards VALLE-INCLÁN, GARCÍA LORCA and ARRABAL; Flemish GHELDERODE and Romanian Tzara; Swiss DÜRRENMATT and FRISCH; and most prolifically the Paris-centred playwrights of the 1950s – ADAMOV, BECKETT, GENET, IONESCO and Pinget. Dürrenmatt and Ionesco have reverted to the Italian Renaissance habit of rationalizing their practice with theory of tragicomedy, but the critic ERIC BENTLEY in *Life of the Drama* most instructively classifies modern tragicomedy into (1) tragedy transcended (as opposed to Renaissance 'tragedy averted') – for example, Strindberg's *Dream Play*; and (2) comedy with an unhappy or indeterminate ending – for example, Beckett's *Waiting for Godot*. Contemporary dramatists tend to express their tragic vision with comic devices, creating tragicomedy that is funny without being foolish, serious without being solemn. RC

Travers, Ben 1886–1980 British dramatist and novelist, who made his reputation with the ten 'Aldwych farces', a label given to his plays because they occupied the stage of London's Aldwych Theatre continuously – from *A Cuckoo in the Nest* (1925), *Rookery Nook* (1926) and *Thark* (1927), to *Dirty Work* (1932) and *A Bit of a Test* (1933). Combining absurdly improbable situations, eccentric characters and broad humour with social SATIRE, his work has stood the test of time well. Film versions, for which he provided the scripts, have helped to spread its popularity, and in 1970 he adapted seven of his farces for television. In 1976 there were three of his plays on the London stage: a revival of *Plunder* (1928) at the NATIONAL THEATRE; a revival of one of his later farces *Banana Ridge* (1938), with ROBERT MORLEY; and his last, *The Bed before Yesterday*, which opened in 1975 with JOAN PLOWRIGHT as an outspoken middle-aged woman who belatedly discovers the joy of sex. His autobiographies, *Vale of Laughter* (1957) and *A-Sitting on a Gate* (1978), provide many insights into the technical craft of FARCE. CI

Traverse Theatre (Edinburgh) Britain's first studio theatre. The Traverse (so called because its audiences were seated either side of the stage) was started in 1963 with the

aim of providing an experimental theatre club offering creative opportunities for theatre artists the whole year round and not merely during the EDINBURGH FESTIVAL. Its founder was Jim Haynes, an American director who subsequently went on to start the Arts Lab in London. His policy was to present new plays and explore new styles of performance: in the early years he was responsible for introducing to the British stage many of the plays of such international writers as ARRABAL, MROŻEK, WEISS, KROETZ, Bellow and SHEPARD, and soon established a reputation for commissioning new work from British playwrights too. This policy remains central to the theatre's work. In 1969 and then again in 1992 the Traverse moved to new premises. The current building is a purpose-designed theatre space housing two auditoria: the larger, able to deal with more epic pieces, seating 350; and the smaller, having a completely flexible seating system, 110. New work premiered at the Traverse has included Jimmy Boyle's and Tom McGrath's *The Hardman*, Clare Luckham's *Trafford Tanzi*, C. P. TAYLOR's *Bread and Butter* and STEVE BERKOFF's *East*. AJ

travesty role (sometimes called 'trouser role' or 'pants part') Male character in opera, written for and sung by a woman's voice. It is to be distinguished from male parts originally written for castrati but nowadays sometimes sung by women. The currently most frequently heard travesty roles are Siebel in *Faust* (1859) by Charles Gounod (1818–93), Nicklaus in *Tales of Hoffmann* (1881) by JACQUES OFFENBACH, Prince Orlofsky in *Die Fledermaus* (1874) by Johann Strauss II (1825–99), Octavian in *Der Rosenkavalier* (1911) and the Composer in *Ariadne auf Naxos* (1916), both by Richard Strauss (1864–1949). (See also CASTRATO; MALE IMPERSONATION.) GH

Treadwell, Sophie 1885–1970 Californian-born American playwright and journalist (war correspondent, 1916–18). Although other plays of hers were produced – *Gringo* (1922), *Plumes in the Dust* (1936) and *Hope for a Harvest* (1941) – Treadwell's reputation rests predominantly on her innovative *Machinal* (1928), revived successfully in New York (1990) and London (1993). In nine expressionistic scenes (see EXPRESSIONISM), the play perfectly combined form and content, as it told the story of a woman who is robotized by life. In 1933 it was performed in Moscow, and it has had several revivals in the USA, most recently a critically acclaimed one by the NEW YORK SHAKESPEARE FESTIVAL (1990). FB

Tree, Herbert (Draper) Beerbohm 1853–1917 British actor and theatre manager, the half-brother of Max Beerbohm. He made his professional debut, against stern parental opposition, in 1878. His first success was as the Rev. Robert Spalding in Charles Hawtrey's *The Private Secretary* (1884), a FARCE whose popularity went unchallenged until the appearance of *Charley's Aunt* (1892). Acting on his own principle that 'everything comes to him who doesn't wait', Tree entered into management in 1887, briefly at London's Comedy Theatre and then at the HAYMARKET (1887–96). The authority gave new scope to his flair for showmanship. Tree was no more a literary purist than IRVING. He liked plays with plenty of action and knew the value of a dash of scandal. HENRY ARTHUR JONES's *The Dancing Girl* (1891), WILDE's *A Woman of No Importance* (1893) and a matinée production of the still-shocking IBSEN's *An Enemy of the People* (1893) all endowed Tree's Haymarket with one or the other. His *Hamlet* (1892) was probably mistaken and anyway belittled by W. S. GILBERT's widely quoted view that it was 'funny without being vulgar'. (No one broadcast the comment more than Tree.) But the outstanding Haymarket productions were the last two, Paul Potter's dramatization of *Trilby* (1895), with Tree as Svengali, and *Henry IV, Part 1* (1896), with Tree as Falstaff.

He was one of the great make-up artists – like Irving before him – and a shameless dominator of the stage. His larger-than-life personality dominated and became identified with HIS [HER] MAJESTY's THEATRE, of which he was manager from 1897 to 1915. He had planned the theatre himself, from foyer to private penthouse, and, with 14 productions during his tenure, he earned for it a reputation as the home of lavish Shakespearian productions, the last surviving monument of pictorial Shakespeare. The repertoire contained little else of note. It was at His Majesty's that the stock of STEPHEN PHILLIPS rose (*Herod*, 1900; *Ulysses*, 1902) and fell (*Nero*, 1906); that Tree created in Fagin another of his great costume roles (1905); and, supremely, that SHAW's *Pygmalion* (1914) opened, with Tree as Henry Higgins partly obliterated by MRS PATRICK CAMPBELL's Eliza Doolittle. An Edwardian, even during the reign of Victoria, Tree was a witty and humane man, whose commitment to the theatre was rarely untouched by humour. Despite his major role in the foundation of the Royal Academy of Dramatic Art (1904), he was less a student of acting than a brilliant opportunist. He was knighted in 1907.   PT

Tremblay, Michel 1942– Quebec playwright and novelist. Tremblay first achieved national prominence with *Les Belles-Soeurs* (*The Sisters-in-Law*) in 1968, transposing to the stage the profound frustrations of Montreal's urban proletariat of which he is himself a product. In this play, set in one tawdry flat, his characters, all female, express their individual and collective despair in pure *joual*, the impoverished idiom of Quebec (the word itself is symbolic, a deformation of standard French *cheval*, 'horse'). Yet this stark setting and starker language are infused with great poetic feeling, enhanced by stylized monologues and choreographed choruses which transform a seemingly banal plot into poignant tragedy. The influence of this play has been remarkable, a whole generation of young dramatists following Tremblay's lead in the use of *joual* without, however, attaining his dramatic and poetic intensity.

In nine plays composed over the next decade he continued to portray this microcosm of social and economic despair, peopled by transvestites, homosexuals and misfits. Some characters reappear, in works such as *En pièces détachées* (*Like Death Warmed Over*, 1969); *À toi pour toujours, ta Marie-Lou* (*Forever Yours, Marie-Lou*, 1971); *Hosanna* (1973); *Sainte Carmen de la Main* (*Saint Carmen of Main Street*, 1976) and *Damnée Manon, sacrée Sandra* (*Damned Manon, Holy Sandra*, 1977). Tremblay's own literary and financial success has generally been used to explain the end of this first period, underlined by his move to Outremont, an affluent section of Montreal. But the election of the first Parti Québécois government in 1976 has also been an important factor in his personal evolution. A fervent separatist, he appeared to avoid embarrassing the government which, nominally at least, represented his cause. Plays such as *L'Impromptu d'Outremont* (*The Impromptu of Outremont*, 1980) deal with middle-class concerns, while *Albertine en cinq temps* (*Albertine, in Five Times*, 1984), considered by some to be his finest work, is timeless, portraying brilliantly the universal problem of ageing. A new departure was his OPERA *Nelligan* (1990), with music by André Gagnon, dealing with the tragically short career of Quebec's talented poet, Émile Nelligan.

His theatre has been performed successfully in France, Belgium, Switzerland and, in translation, in the Netherlands, England, Scotland (*Les Belles-Soeurs* was well received as *The Guid Sisters* in Glasgow in 1989), the USA, Germany, Chile, Japan and elsewhere. Tremblay is easily French Canada's outstanding dramatist to date. LED

Tremont Theatre (Boston, USA) In 1827, although they were hardly able to support the FEDERAL STREET THEATRE, Bostonians were presented with a second theatre, a handsome and elegant edifice built through the largesse of a group of wealthy and prominent citizens. For the next 16 years, the house struggled to survive as stars were lured to its stage and an excellent STOCK COMPANY was assembled. It was never able to pay for itself, and its managers resorted to a succession of novelties to keep it afloat. In 1835, CHARLOTTE CUSHMAN there made her first appearance onstage as a singer in *The Marriage of Figaro*. In 1843, the theatre was sold to the Baptist Church and transformed into the Tremont Temple; nine years later, it burned down and was rebuilt as a church.   MCH

Trenyov, Konstantin (Andreevich) 1876–1945 Soviet short story writer and dramatist who helped create the post-revolutionary Soviet drama. His playwriting, which began in 1907 with some GORKY-influenced one-act plays, became a career only with the MOSCOW ART THEATRE production of *Pugachyov Times* (1924). This monumentalist play was made controversial by the author's unexpectedly harsh depiction of the popular hero of the 18th-century peasant revolt. Trenyov's classic Civil War drama, *Lyubov Yarovaya* (1926), offered a gallery of clearly individuated characters on both sides of the conflict, set against an epic historical backdrop. The play's titular heroine, a strong-minded schoolteacher who sacrifices her beloved White Russian husband for her Bolshevik beliefs, became a prototype for revolutionary women in Soviet dramas (e.g. the lady commissar in VISHNEVSKY's *An Optimistic Tragedy*). Produced at Moscow's Maly Theatre (1926) and at the Moscow Art Theatre following a Stalin-induced revision (1936), it returned to the stage in its original form after 1956.

Trenyov's remaining plays were primarily anti-bourgeois SATIRES and Soviet problem plays grounded in psychological realism. *On the Banks of the Neva* (1937), set during the Revolution, marked an early appearance by

Lenin on the Soviet stage. Trenyov's final play, *The Commander* (1945), about General Kutuzov, hero of the War of 1812, represented his return to the epic historical drama. SG

Tretyakov, Sergei (Mikhailovich) 1892–1939 Soviet poet, journalist, translator and dramatist, best known for his post-revolutionary AGIT-PROP theatrical collaborations with MEYERHOLD and the latter's pupil, Sergei Eisenstein. An ego-futurist from just before the Revolution, Tretyakov became an aggressive spokesman for utilitarian, 'factographic' (agit-prop documentary) art and constructivist design and poetics via his involvement in MAYAKOVSKY's journals *Lef* (1923–5) and *Novy Lef* (*New Left*, 1927–8).

His first theatrical work with Eisenstein (at the Proletkult Theatre) was their 'annihilation' and 'CIRCUS-ization' of OSTROVSKY's *Enough Stupidity for Every Wise Man* (1923), staged as a 'montage of attractions' – an episodic, politically satiric REVUE featuring CLOWNING, ACROBATICS, caricature and film clips. Eisenstein's production of Tretyakov's *Gas Masks* (1923), about a German factory revolt, was actually staged in a Moscow gas-works, an extreme example of the contemporary trend to merge the factory and the theatre. Tretyakov's *Earth Rampant* (1923), an adaptation of Marcel Martinet's play *Night*, was a laconically and episodically conceived, constructivist-designed (by LYUBOV POPOVA) 'military-revolutionary action', dedicated to the Red Army and its leader Lev Trotsky on the fifth anniversary of its founding (23 February 1923). Staged by Meyerhold at his theatre on Sadovo-Triumfalnaya Street, it incorporated all of the elements of the mass spectacle – military transports and weaponry spilling out into the audience, propaganda slogans projected on to a screen (a 'machine-photo-poster'), declamatory acting, and grotesque characterizations of priests, the Tsar and his generals. Often performed in the open air, it played to an audience of 25,000 at the Fifth Congress of the Comintern in Moscow (June 1924), enlisting the participation of infantry and horse cavalry.

Roar, China! (1926), a great success at Meyerhold's theatre, was based on a real incident known to Tretyakov from his 1924 stint as a lecturer in Russian literature at Peking University. Meyerhold offered a naturalistic staging of colonialist brutalization of the Chinese, humanizing the victims and caricaturing the exploiters. Its effectiveness as a propaganda vehicle led to productions throughout Europe, and in New York by the THEATRE GUILD, in 1930. The author's *I Want a Child* recommended socially based eugenics to achieve perfect proletarian children in Soviet society, a thesis which he sought to make more palatable by first presenting in episodic fashion the sordidness of the worker's life – a technique later employed by Mayakovsky in *The Bedbug*. Meyerhold's production (1927–30), designed by El Lissitsky (pseudonym of Lazar Markovich Lisitsky), was denied permission by Glavrepertkom (the Main Repertory Committee), which considered the play to be ahead of its time. BRECHT, who met Tretyakov on the 1930 *Roar, China!* tour in Berlin, called him 'my teacher', found the factographic approach useful to his concept of EPIC THEATRE, and adapted *I Want a Child* for the German stage, where it never played. Tretyakov translated Brecht's *St Joan of the Stockyards*,

The Measures Taken and *The Mother* into Russian (1936).

Arrested and executed in 1939, Tretyakov was rehabilitated in the 1960s, when the influence of his collaboration with Meyerhold could be seen in YURY LYUBIMOV's staging of *Ten Days that Shook the World* and in other productions at Moscow's Taganka Theatre. SG

Triana, José 1931– Cuban playwright. Triana studied in Santiago de Cuba, wrote poetry in Spain and returned to Cuba to espouse revolutionary programmes. His first plays, *Medea en el espejo* (*Medea in the Mirror*, 1960) and *La muerte del ñeque* (*Death of the Strong Man*, 1963), both contain elements of classical Greek tragic figures integrated into a working-class Cuban environment, where violence and criminality prefigure the game SYMBOLISM in his later theatre. His masterpiece, and Cuba's best-known play internationally, is *La noche de los asesinos* (*The Night of the Assassins*, 1965), a brutal play with metatheatrical techniques that involves three adolescents in the myth, ritual and exorcism of killing their parents. No other plays appeared until Triana defected on a trip to Paris in 1980. *Ceremonial de guerra* (*War Ceremony*), written over the period 1968–73, and *Diálogo de mujeres* (*Women's Dialogue*, 1979–80) are both set in Cuba at the turn of the century. The ROYAL SHAKESPEARE COMPANY staged his *Worlds Apart* – a study of Cuba in the period 1894–1914 in 1986, at Stratford. His 1992 monologue, *Cruzando el puente* (*Crossing the Bridge*), was followed by *La fiesta, o Comedia para un delirio* (*The Party, or Comedy for a Delirium*) in 1993. GW

Trinidad and Tobago The sister islands of Trinidad and Tobago were placed by the British under a single administration in 1889. Before that date, their histories were markedly different. Trinidad, most southerly of the Caribbean rim, was seized by Columbus from the Arawak Indians on his third voyage in 1498, and for 300 years the island remained a Spanish possession. It was largely underdeveloped until 1783, when French planters from the northern islands were given land grants to settle on Trinidad with their slaves. In 1797 British forces took the island, which remained a British colony until 1962.

Tobago changed hands repeatedly between the Dutch, French and English in the 18th-century wars, finally becoming British in 1763. After the abolition of slaves, Trinidad sought to acquire an indentured labour force to replace the Africans who had left the estates. The country brought in Portuguese, Chinese and East Indians; this last group now represents 40 per cent of the population. Tobago remained predominantly African. It was first governed from BARBADOS, then from Trinidad, just 18 miles away. When the islands were united, Tobago's population was roughly 18,000, while Trinidad, with 200,000, became senior partner of the union. In 1962 they became independent of Great Britain and in 1976 they were declared the Republic of Trinidad and Tobago.

The most important national festival – encompassing original music, singing, masking, street parades, orchestral drumming and various forms of enactment – is the TRINIDAD CARNIVAL, an annual parade that has been in existence for some two hundred years. The Indian community also has a major street festival called 'Hosay', which commemorates the Muslim battle of Karbala and the deaths of the brothers Hasan and Husein. While Tobago participates in this carnival, it has its own equivalent called 'Speech Mas' or 'Speech Band'. These festivals, important as they are, do not overshadow achievements in the regular theatre.

Between 1826 and 1831 Port of Spain, capital city of Trinidad, contained five theatres (or halls converted into theatres), three amateur theatre companies (two English and one French), one professional English touring group and one professional French lyric company. The amateurs played once a month, the professionals twice or three times a week. Most important at this time was the emergence of a resident playwright, E. L. Joseph, a Scotsman who had made Trinidad his home. He wrote and produced a series of local plays that were performed by the Brunswick Amateurs. Among these were *Martial Law in Trinidad* (1832), a musical SATIRE on the militia; *Past and Present*, a FARCE on social climbers; and several dramatic sketches. Joseph's work is notable for its objective portrayal of both the Creole and the African, and its attempt to capture the different local dialects. He also translated German plays for local production and wrote a *History of Trinidad* (1838).

A period of decline followed, doubtless the result of uncertainty in the years after emancipation. The theatrical drought was relieved periodically by visiting troupers from North America, such as J. W. Lanergan's company in 1858 and E. A. McDowell's in 1886 and 1891. From time to time a locally written play would appear in print or in production. In 1845 *The Count del Santa Cruz* and *The Grand Seignor*, two farces by an unnamed author, were presented by amateurs. In 1847 the *Trinidad Spectator* printed a short play in French, its title taken from the Creole proverb: '*Ca qui pas bon pour z'oies, pas bon pour canards*' ('What's good for the goose is good for the gander'), in which the author defended the reinstatement of the carnival, banned by an outgoing governor. In the 1860s the distinguished Trinidad lawyer M. Maxwell Philip wrote an historical play entitled *Apodoca*, about the Spanish admiral who, defending the island, burned his ships rather than surrender them to a superior British fleet. Neither script nor production record has been traced.

To celebrate the centenary of British rule in the island, long-time resident Lewis Osborne Inniss, a pharmacist born in GUYANA, wrote and produced *Carmelita, the Belle of San José* (1897), followed the next year by *Mura, the Cacique's Daughter*, to mark the anniversary of 'Discovery Day'. These scripts survive – sentimental romances portraying Amerindians who are saved by the British from the cruel Spaniards. However, they completely ignore the existence of Africans, who were then the predominant racial group on the island.

In 1858 the press reported only one functioning theatre in Port of Spain. An attempt to make it into a permanent playhouse failed, and by 1866 there was 'no theatre, major or minor', in the city. To entertain two British princes who were cruising the islands, in 1861 the government had constructed the 'Princes' Building' opposite the Queen's Park Savannah. Though it had no proper auditorium, it was put into service to accommodate visiting theatre companies. When the Trinidad Drama Club was formed in 1897, it pressed immediately for a permanent civic theatre. It was suggested that the Princes' Building be converted into a theatre; but no plan was found acceptable, and the building was put to a multitude of uses until, decrepit, it burned to the ground in 1979.

The 20th century brought an influx of professional companies to the island. Among them were the F. R. BENSON Shakespeare Company in 1905, and, on repeated visits, the Harkins Dramatic Company, the Florence Glossop-Harris Company and the Empire Players – all English companies of the first order. They performed first at the Princes' Building and later at the Empire Theatre, a large cinema built with a commodious stage and superior acoustics. These visiting groups doubtless inspired the formation of local drama clubs. The Paragon Dramatic Club, launched in 1924 with its own playwright, Cecil Cobham, produced original plays whose titles, in the absence of surviving scripts, suggest the sentimental drama fashionable in an earlier age: among them *False Honeymoon*, *Sold But Not Lost* and *Retribution*. Later writers in this mode were Ethelbert Young of the Thalia Drama Club, Kate Bourne, and Errol Cherrie whose two musical comedies, *Among the Young* and *Chamber in the Moon*, were presented in 1943 and 1944 by the St Cecilia Music Club.

It was left to two schoolteachers, Arthur Roberts and De Wilton Rogers, to bring a sense of realism to the local stage. From 1932 for almost a decade, Roberts produced, with pupils from the Nelson Street Boys' Roman Catholic School, a series of sparkling farces on current affairs in Trinidad: *Divorce* (a controversial subject in Catholic Trinidad); *That Hospital*, about dissatisfaction with the public hospital; *Romance without Sanitation*, on the incidence of tuberculosis; *Obeah*, dealing with belief in the spirit world; *War Gossip*, on the danger of loose talk during the Second World War. Rogers, too, dealt with current topics, but he adopted a more serious approach. In plays such as *Blue Blood and Black* (1936) on the race problem, *Trikidad* (1937) on graft in high places, and *Silk Cotton Grove* (1942) on the uprooting of residents to make way for US military bases, he dramatized issues of grave importance to the ordinary citizen.

Outside the Caribbean, the Trinidadian historian and novelist C. L. R. James had his play *Toussaint l'Ouverture* (1936; later revised and retitled *The Black Jacobins*) presented by the Stage Society in London at the Westminster Theatre, with PAUL ROBESON in the leading role. Two Trinidad and Tobago writers who worked for the American stage were Donald Heywood (fl.1920s–30s) and William Archibald (fl.1940s–60s).

In the 1940s a movement arose towards recognizing folk expression as important to the development of a national culture. The calypso and steel band were defended as vigorous elements of indigenous expression. In 1943 the Trinidadian singer Edric Connor gave his celebrated lecture to the Music Association on West Indian folk-music, while Barbados-born Joseph Griffith, bandmaster of the police band, offered his own orchestral compositions at the Princes' Building. In 1948 Beryl McBurnie, dancer and choreographer, opened her Little Carib Theatre primarily to promote Caribbean dance; a national arts festival was inaugurated with 500 entries; and in 1946 the Whitehall Players was founded by Errol Hill and Errol

John. This group, merged in 1952 with the New Company into the Company of Players, is noted as much for its production record as for the number of outstanding artists it has nurtured.

The 1950s promised much for the theatre, not only of Trinidad and Tobago but of the entire anglophone Caribbean. The publication of Caribbean plays by the Extramural Department of the University of the West Indies (UWI) encouraged writers to write plays and theatre groups to perform them. For the first time audiences in Trinidad and Tobago were exposed to plays by DEREK WALCOTT of St Lucia, when *The Sea at Dauphin* and *Henri Christophe* were staged. Also presented at this time was Errol Hill's *Ping Pong*, the first play about the steel band, which attracted larger audiences than were usually seen then in the live theatre. In 1955 John Ainsworth, a professional actor from England who staged racially integrated productions of *Hamlet* and *Macbeth* (the former playing in Barbados, Trinidad and Guyana), attempted to form a professional theatre company but could not raise continuing financial support for it.

In 1955 the Drama Guild was founded in San Fernando, Trinidad's second town, where the preponderance of East Indians ensured their participation in the national theatre movement. About 1954 St Clair Wesley Dorant started his Merry Circle group in order to produce his own plays – a total of over 30. In 1957 Freddie Kissoon established the Strolling Players. The major event of the decade was the regional festival of arts held in 1958 to herald the inauguration of the West Indies Federation. The centrepiece was an open-air production of the epic drama *Drums and Colours*, written by Derek Walcott and directed by the Jamaican Noel Vaz, with actors and production personnel from other Caribbean territories. The festival ignited a rush of theatre activity in Trinidad and Tobago. Of several groups formed in the next few years, Walcott's Trinidad Theatre Workshop (1959) was to prove the most influential.

Once the carnival, the calypso and the steel band were accepted as vital elements of national expression, playwrights were drawn to the challenge. For the mammoth Dimanche Gras carnival show in 1963–5, attempts – generally unsuccessful – were made to structure the presentation around a dramatic story. Of these the most satisfying was the political satire *Whistling Charlie and the Monster*, written and directed by Errol Hill in 1964. The next year Hill's calypso verse MUSICAL *Man Better Man* represented the country at the Commonwealth Arts Festival in Britain. Of many other carnival-based plays, the best-remembered are: Marina Maxwell's *Play Mas'* (1968), Lennox Brown's *Devil Mas'* (1971), Ronald Amoroso's *The Master of Carnival* (1974), MUSTAPHA MATURA's *Rum and Coca Cola* (1976), Earl Lovelace's dramatization of his novel *The Dragon Can't Dance* (1984); Derek Walcott's *Steel* (1991), and Rawle Gibbons's *I Lawah* (*I Le Roi*, 1986) and his three calypso theatre pieces: *Sing de Chorus* (1991), *Ah Wanna Fall* (1992) and *Ten to One* (1993). In a unique experiment in 1980, the Trinidad Tent Theatre, working with playwright Felix Edinborough, created a number of original musicals in which all stage characters were based on traditional masquerades (see MASQUERADES IN AFRICA), identifiable by their COSTUME, movement, speech and behaviour.

To encourage development in the country areas, a Best Village Competition that included the arts was launched by the government in 1967. Although mostly at a rudimentary level, the competition in playwriting and production served to expand interest in the live theatre and, under skilled leadership, village groups could achieve a respectable standard. One such group, the Mausica Folk Performers, appeared in 1984 at the Amateur Theatre Festival in Los Angeles in the musical *Bitter Cassava* written and directed by Efebo Wilkinson. A secondary schools drama festival, organized in 1965 by James Lee Wah of San Fernando, had by 1972 adjudicated 98 plays, half of them by Caribbean playwrights.

Reinforcing the work of schools and amateur groups, the UWI Extramural Department (now School of Continuing Studies) has since 1964 conducted a summer school in the performing and visual arts. Employing trained and experienced professionals as tutors, the Department has contributed substantially to improving the skills of the younger theatre generation. In 1986 the UWI established a Creative Arts Centre on the Trinidad campus, so that students can now benefit from full-time training and gain academic credit towards their first degree for certain drama courses. In 1985 the National Drama Association of Trinidad and Tobago was established. By allocating productions to different centres during its annual festival, the Association ensures that the best work reaches the widest possible audiences.

With the growth in theatre activity has come a corresponding increase in performance spaces, along with the understanding that a formal proscenium-arch theatre is not necessary for staging plays. The auditoriums most often used include the Little Carib, Queen's Hall, the City Hall and Central Bank in Port of Spain, and the Naparima Bowl in San Fernando. Tobago has halls, but no central auditorium for use as a theatre.

Other kinds of theatre exist in Trinidad and Tobago. The Trinidad calypso, in which contemporary events are enacted in song, most often by a single performer, has long been accepted as a unique theatrical form. And speech theatre, a form of storytelling, has been revived in Trinidad and Tobago with notable success. The principal presenter is Paul Keens-Douglas, who acknowledges the influence on his work of Louise Bennett of Jamaica. Keens-Douglas is now a roving professional storyteller whose dramatized conversations in dialect prose and verse, published in six booklets, have inspired storytellers in other Caribbean countries.

The development of Caribbean dance owes much to the pioneering work of Beryl McBurnie, who introduced the themes to which she has devoted her life in the recital *A Trip through the Tropics*, staged in 1940 at the Empire Theatre, Port of Spain. Almost every creative dancer from Trinidad and Tobago has studied under McBurnie, including Percy Borde, Boscoe and Geoffrey Holder, and Molly Ahye. The outstanding performer of classical Indian dance is Rajkumar Krishna Persad, who has studied in India and now conducts a school in Trinidad. EGH

See: M. Ahye, *Cradle of Caribbean Dance: Beryl McBurnie and the Little Carib Theatre*, Port of Spain, 1983; K. Corsbie, *Theatre in the Caribbean*, London,

1984; E. Hill, 'The Emergence of a National Drama in the West Indies', *Caribbean Quarterly*, 18, 4, 1972; J. W. Nunley and J. Bettelheim, *Caribbean Festival Arts*, Seattle, Wash., 1988; K. Omotoso, *The Theatrical into Theatre*, London, 1982; G. Rohlehr, *Calypso and Society in Pre-independence Trinidad*, Trinidad, 1990.

Trinidad carnival In its 200-year history the pre-Lenten Trinidad CARNIVAL, essentially an annual parade of original costumes worn by bands of masked revellers (see MASKS), has encompassed many theatrical forms. To the carnival over the years have accreted exhibitions of music, song, dance, MIME and the spoken word that have made it a grand theatrical spectacle and a repository of the nation's performing arts.

Carnival was brought to Spanish-held Trinidad by French colonial planters in the 1780s. Under British rule it continued to be observed by the white elite as a European festival, the free coloureds and black slaves having no part in it. When slavery ended in 1834, the black and coloured masses took over the festival and transformed it into an expression of their new-found freedom. Among the principal 19th-century masquerades (see MASQUERADES IN AFRICA) were *canboulay* ('*cannes brûlées*', or 'burnt canes'), featuring revellers re-enacting scenes from slavery, dread stick-fighters whose music, dance and pungent argot survive on the contemporary stage, military bands that satirize the armed forces, indigenous creatures of myth and folk-tale, and the ubiquitous calypsonian who emerged as carnival songster and public commentator. During this period repeated attempts by government to

Adoration of Hiroshima by Hugh Bernard, Trinidad carnival, 1985.

suppress the masquerade as a rowdy and indecent exhibition were strenuously resisted, sometimes with rioting and loss of life.

In the 20th century conditions slowly improved, as English replaced French patois in song lyrics and the street parade gained respectability. Costumed bands like the Wild Indians and Burroquites would hold pre-carnival meetings in backyards. Before a growing audience they rehearsed speeches, dances, mimes and playlets, and on carnival eve installed the bands' kings and queens. Calypsonians, now universally recognized professional singers, gave nightly concerts which often ended with a comic sketch that recounted in song a recent topical event. On carnival streets traditional maskers like the Midnight Robber would harangue spectators with threats, in hair-raising encounters, until paid off. The Dragon Band would perform an elaborate street ballet, the Pierrot Grenade would give its version of a spelling-bee. Military bands would exhibit precise drills or make furious assaults on an imaginary enemy.

Carnival music kept pace with developments. When drum-beating was restricted, the skin drums and wooden clappers used to accompany *canboulay* trampers and stick-fighters gave way to the shack-shack (gourd rattle) and bottle-and-spoon ensembles. Then came the bamboo bands and finally the steel orchestras, using discarded petrol drums, which have extended their musical repertoire from calypsos to classics and have spread abroad. Maskers who could afford them hired string bands and later jazz ensembles to accompany their parade, but the bamboo bands and steel orchestras were the creative response of the indigent masquerader whose meagre funds would have been carefully garnered to pay for his costume.

In recent years traditional masquerades have dwindled, as new bands enroll thousands of revellers. Detailed ornamentation in costume and theatrical presentation has been replaced by massed colour effects. Competing carnival kings and queens, whose costumes used to be so extravagantly constructed as to encumber their free movement, have benefited from the designs of Peter Minshall, who employs traditional mask-making techniques in such a way as to free the performer to dance in his costume. In addition, Minshall has presented his masquerade bands as dramatic spectacles that PANTOMIME contemporary concerns such as environmental pollution and nuclear war. In recognition of his skill, the 1992 Olympic Committee in Barcelona invited him to stage the arrival of Columbus's ship in the stadium at the opening ceremony of the games.
EGH

Trinity Repertory Company (USA) Founded in 1964 in Providence, Rhode Island, by a group of local citizens, this ensemble became one of the more adventurous of the regional theatres in the USA (with over 27 world premieres). During 1965–89 its artistic director was Adrian Hall. Before moving in 1973 into their present complex (the Lederer Theatre, a converted vaudeville/cinema house), the company performed primarily in a converted church. A federal grant in 1966 (Project Discovery) covered many of the theatre's expenses for three years, allowing it to reach true professional stature. A major grant from the

National Endowment for the Arts allowed financial security for its theatre artists, beginning with the 1985–6 season. A varied bill of approximately 9–12 productions is staged annually in two theatres. In 1978 a training programme for actors, directors and playwrights was initiated, and in 1986 'Square' was removed from the theatre's original name. Anne Bogart, known primarily as a freelance avant-garde director, presented a controversial season (1989–90) after Hall's departure, and was succeeded by a long-time company actor-director, Richard Jenkins (1990–4), then Oskar Eustis (best-known for commissioning Kushner's *Angels in America*). DBW

Trissino, Gian Giorgio 1478–1550 Italian dramatist, academician and literary theorist. His two plays, the tragedy *Sofonisba* (1514–15) and the comedy *I simillimi* (1548), written under strong classical influence, were highly regarded in their day, especially the former which was widely imitated. LUIGI RICCOBONI tried unsuccessfully to revive Italian interest in tragedy by staging the play in Venice in 1713. Trissino was an active patron of the architect PALLADIO. LR

Tristan [François] **l'Hermite** c.1601–55 French poet and dramatist. His first, and perhaps best, play, a TRAGEDY entitled *La Mariane* on the subject of Herod's jealous love for his doomed wife, was performed with great success at the MARAIS only months before *Le Cid*, and many contemporaries considered him to be PIERRE CORNEILLE's equal at least; it remained in the repertoire until the end of the century. His later work, which included several tragedies, notably *La Mort de Sénèque* (*The Death of Seneca*, 1644), one of the plays staged by MOLIÈRE's ill-fated Illustre-Théâtre, a TRAGICOMEDY, a PASTORAL and an entertaining COMEDY, *Le Parasite* (1654), was also well received and he was elected to the Académie-Française in 1649. Of late a renewal of interest in his plays has led to several revivals. DR

Trotter, Catharine 1679–1749 English playwright. Trotter was highly educated and precocious: her first poems and novels were published in 1693 when she was 14. Her first play, *Agnes de Castro*, a romantic TRAGEDY with an unusually classical style and centred on a pathetic heroine, was performed two years later. She was mocked with MARY PIX and Mrs Manley in *The Female Wits* in 1696. By this time she was admired by DRYDEN and CONGREVE. Her plays, mostly 'she-tragedies' with a distressed heroine, were often revised with help from Congreve. In 1700 she became a friend of Bishop Burnet and John Locke, publishing a pamphlet defending Locke's *Essay on Human Understanding* in 1703. Her marriage to a clergyman in 1708 ended her career as a playwright. PH

Tsegaye Gebre-Medhin 1936– Ethiopian playwright. Tsegaye started writing plays in his youth, then won a UN scholarship to study theatre in Europe, returning to ETHIOPIA in 1960 to become director of the Haile Selassie Theatre. Here he put on a series of his plays, which won him fame both for their poetic use of Amharic language and for their new REALISM and oblique criticism of society. He became the country's foremost playwright with works

such as *Ye Kermasow* (*A Man of the Future*, 1965) and *Tewodros* (1966). In 1970 he left Ethiopia to study negritude theories in Senegal, but was brought back by actors' demand in 1974 to run the Haile Selassie Theatre again (renamed the National Theatre). Here he produced a series of highly popular plays in praise of the new regime. Most famous were *ABC in Six Months* and *Mother Courage*.

Tsegaye has also translated numerous SHAKESPEARE plays into Amharic, and has written four of his own in English: a version of his *Tewodros* (1966); *Azmari* (1966); and two plays about early Ethiopian history, *Oda Oak Oracle* (1965) and *Collision of Altars* (1975). His poor treatment of actors led in 1976 to demands for Tsegaye's removal from the National Theatre, and after a brief period in prison he was appointed adviser to the Ministry of Culture where he remained until 1993 when he retired. By the 1980s his work was increasingly critical of the Marxist government, and he was gradually forced into silence by the censors (see CENSORSHIP). In 1992 he produced a new play, *Ha Hu Weyim Pa Pu?* (*ABC or XYZ?*), celebrating the overthrow of the previous government but also making some criticism of the new, transitional, government of Ethiopia. JPL

Tsodzo, Thompson 1947– Zimbabwean playwright, novelist and writer on education. Formerly a teacher, he joined the government at independence. Many of his plays in Shona have been televised. He also produced his *The Storm* in 1982 with S. Chikwendere, commemorating Zimbabwe's struggle for independence. His published plays include *The Talking Calabash* (1976), *Tsano* (*The Brother-in-law*, 1982) and *Shanduko* (*Changes*, 1983). His focus is generally moralistic, though *The Storm* and *Shanduko* show an interest in modern political developments in ZIMBABWE. RK

Tsubouchi Shōyō 1859–1935 One of the fathers of modern Japanese theatre as well as a theoretician of the modern novel in JAPAN. Tsubouchi was a professor of English literature at Waseda University in Tokyo. A man of diverse talents, he wrote pieces for Japanese dance and staged pageants in addition to translating Shakespeare and founding *Waseda Literature* (*Waseda Bungaku*), an influential literary review. In 1906 he founded one of Japan's first modern theatre troupes, the Literary Arts Society (Bungei Kyōkai). His 40-volume translation of the complete works of SHAKESPEARE was completed in 1928. In 1926 his *En the Ascetic* (*En no Gyōja*), written in 1913, became the first play by a Japanese writer to be staged by the Tsukiji Little Theatre. DGG

Tsuka Kōhei 1948– Japanese playwright and director. Tsuka best represents the climate of the Japanese theatre of the 1970s, the period of the aftermath of the ANGURA (underground) theatre movement of the 1960s, which drastically changed the concept of modern Japanese theatre. He formed Tsuka Kōhei's Office in 1974, and staged his plays with Office actors. As the name of the company suggests, the productions presented were strongly influenced by Tsuka's own idea of theatre. Instead of giving a written script to his actors for rehearsals, he conveyed all the lines orally, by *kuchidate* (word of mouth), the method often used in traditional Japanese theatre. He also used improvisations to create the script of a play. This made it possible for his actors to swap their roles easily, and they were given their parts just before performances. His method also kept the tension of performances high and fresh, and was successful in nurturing actors who were flexible and responsive to the variable dramatic situations.

Tsuka uses a simple, bare stage. His plays include elements of discussion and ironic comment on political or social matters. The best-known include *For the Father Who Could not Kill Himself in the War* (*Sensō de Shinenakatta O-tōsan no Tameni*, 1972), *The Departure* (*Shuppatsu*, 1974), *Murder in Atami* (*Atami Satsujin Jiken*, 1973), *Stripper Story* (*Sutorippā Monogatari*, 1975) and *The Kamata March* (*Kamata Kōshin Kyoku*, 1980). MY

Tsuruya Namboku IV 1755–1829 Japanese dramatist. The dominant playwright of Edo KABUKI in the early 19th century, his nickname was Namboku the Great. His career is typical of traditional playwrights: apprenticed to an actor as a boy, apprenticed to playwright Sakurada Jisuke I at 22, promotion to third assistant playwright and to second assistant playwright, and finally success as staff playwright at the age of 46. He wrote vehicles for the great actors of his time: the *onnagata* Iwai Hanshirō V, Matsumoto Koshirō V and Onoe Kikugoro III.

His 125 plays encompass all genres. In an almost postmodern fashion, he excelled in rewriting (*kakikae*) familiar scenes from old plays and joining them to contemporary material, often with darkly parodic intent. He originated the 'raw' domestic play (*kizewamono*) about criminals and society's outcasts. Against this 'real' dramatic material, Namboku counterposed beautiful, stylized performance techniques: poetic elocution (*shichigochō*), quick costume changes (*hayagawari*), nighttime pantomime (*danmari*), stage tricks (*keren*) and dance scenes. His most often revived work is *The Ghost of Yotsuya* (*Tōkaidō Yotsuya kaidan*, 1825) in which the ghost of Oiwa torments her husband, Iemon, in revenge for having brutally disfigured and murdered her. JRB

Tsypin, George 1954– Soviet-born designer who studied at the Institute of Architecture in Moscow before going in 1979 to the USA, where he studied stage design at New York University with JOHN CONKLIN. Tsypin is the foremost practitioner of the postmodern school of design. Working frequently with directors PETER SELLARS and JOANNE AKALAITIS, he has designed startling settings for classic and new plays and OPERAS such as *The Death of Klinghoffer* (1991). The sets show a strong constructivist influence and often utilize metal, moving parts and an overlay of projected images; images from contemporary culture mingle with references to classical architecture and theatre. In addition to work at the NEW YORK SHAKESPEARE FESTIVAL, GUTHRIE THEATRE, GOODMAN THEATRE and other regional theatres, Tsypin has had a gallery show of his sculptures and did the art direction for Peter Sellars's film, *The Cabinet of Dr Ramirez* (1991). AA

Tucker, Sophie [*née* Sophia Kalish] 1884–1966 American VAUDEVILLE singer, born in Russia; known as 'the Last of the Red-Hot Mammas'. She made her professional debut at the 116th Street Music Hall, New York, in 1906 in blackface and won a reputation as a 'coon shouter', singing ragtime melodies. A brief moment in the 1909 *ZIEGFELD Follies* (from which she was ejected when NORA BAYES found the competition too daunting) was followed by stardom in vaudeville, where she capitalized on her girth and her innuendo in such songs as 'He Hasn't Up to Yesterday, but I Guess He Will To-night'. In 1911 she introduced 'Some of These Days', which became her theme song. She moved easily from ragtime to jazz, made a huge success in England beginning in 1922, appeared in the MUSICALS *Leave It to Me* (1938) and *High Kickers* (1941), and helped in organizing vaudevillians into the short-lived American Federation of Actors, which she served as president in 1938. LS

Tukak Teatret Founded in 1975 by the Norwegian actor-director Reidar Nilsson, this experimental theatre and theatre school (from 1980) is based in the remote village of Fjaltring on the northwest coast of Jutland, Denmark. Its early identity grew primarily from its mission to train Greenlandic actors and to rediscover and adapt to the modern theatre the lost paratheatrical forms (including drum dances, MASKS and storytelling) of Inuit Greenland before its colonization by Denmark. By the early 1980s, partly as a result of its successful international tours, it had broadened into an international theatre of and for Arctic native peoples in general, including North-American Indians and Inuit. It has particularly close links with Canadian and Alaskan native theatres, and has toured extensively. By the mid-1980s ex-company members were involved in establishing the first permanent theatre company in the Greenlandic capital, Nuuk. Among Tukak's major productions have been *Inuit*, *Tupilak*, *Man and the Mask* and *Sinnattoq/The Dream* (based on GEORGE RYGA's *The Ecstasy of Rita Joe*). HL

Tune, Tommy [Thomas] **(James)** 1939– American dancer, actor and choreographer. Tune made his BROADWAY debut in the chorus of *Baker Street* (1965), followed by MICHAEL BENNETT's *A Joyful Noise* (1966). Fabulous tap dancing in the film version of *The Boyfriend* was followed by his Broadway show-stopping clog dance in *Seesaw* (1973), co-choreographed with Bennett: the lanky, 6ft 6in Texan tap danced in clogs, travelling down a staircase on to a stage covered with balloons.

Tune's choreography of dance sequences has been enormously popular: the locker room dance in *Best Little Whorehouse in Texas* (1978); the 'dance of the feet' in *A Day in Hollywood/A Night in the Ukraine* (1980); the flirtatious water tap dance in *My One and Only* (1988); and Klingelein's ecstatic Charleston in *Grand Hotel: The Musical* (1989). Tune is the only person to receive Tonys in four different categories: featured actor (*Seesaw*); choreography (*Hollywood/Ukraine*); director (*Nine*, 1980); and leading actor, *My One and Only* (also winning in choreography with Thommie Walsh). He is also the first to win Tonys in choreography and direction of a musical for two consecutive years, with *Grand Hotel* and the spectacular extravaganza *The WILL ROGERS Follies* (1991). In 1991 he toured in *Bye Bye Birdie* and since 1992 has appeared frequently on tour and in New York in his own REVUE, *Tommy Tune Tonite*. LF

Tunisia see FRENCH-SPEAKING NORTH AFRICA; MIDDLE EAST

Turgenev, Ivan (Sergeevich) 1818–83 Russian writer and dramatist, whose subtle, lyrical character studies shifted the narrative focus to internal action and helped pave the way for CHEKHOV's psychological REALISM. A liberal and a Westernizer, Turgenev absorbed the romantic idealism of the 1840s without embracing its radicalism. Personal reticence and melancholia, conditioned by a sadistic mother, made him vulnerable to the exaltation produced by art and love and simultaneously prepared him for disillusionment. His narrative, *The Diary of a Superfluous Man* (1850), defined this as the characteristic literary type of his generation and one whose forebears he described in his essay 'Hamlet and Don Quixote' (1860). While his gentility, his 'female genius', made him suspect among his politically committed contemporaries – Belinsky, Bakunin and Stankevich were early friends – his anti-serfdom stance and harsh criticism of the nobility and other classes made him unpopular with the Russian censor (see CENSORSHIP).

With the publication of his great novel *Fathers and Sons* (1862), which alienated Slavophiles and Westernizers alike, Turgenev went into more or less permanent exile in France. He became the first Russian writer to find a large Western following for his work. Although he considered himself to be primarily a novelist, Turgenev came to drama first, writing a total of ten plays. His early efforts are Gogolian SATIRES, genre parodies and *vaudevilles* of no real distinction. A number of them, including *The Charity Case* (1845), *Where It's Thin, There It Breaks* (1847), *The Bachelor* (1849) and *The Provincial Lady* (1850), were written with his friend and GOGOL's favourite comic actor SHCHEPKIN in mind. They feature the 'insulted and injured' little man in whom are mingled the humour and pathos that were the actor's strong suit. His best play, the classic *A Month in the Country* (1850), is perhaps unfairly undervalued in relation to Chekhov's work, which it clearly foreshadows in its conversational misdirection, leisurely pacing, verbal and visual counterpoint half-revealing an inner action; in this inner focus creating a sense of *ennui* and uneventfulness, centred on a single non-event or a series of non-events; in an oppressive rural environment in which an ineffectual ensemble enacts a tangled roundelay, energy is contrasted with enervation, and change waits on the periphery. SG

Turkey see MIDDLE EAST

Turlupin see *TURLUPINADES*

turlupinades FARCES played at the HÔTEL DE BOURGOGNE, Paris, from 1618 to about 1630 by a famous trio of comedians. GROS-GUILLAUME, allegedly a former baker's boy, was round and fat, in white garments and a red cap, his belly cinctured with two belts to suggest a barrel, his face powdered with flour. He played a foul-mouthed, good-natured drunkard, and occasionally a corpulent harridan. GAULTIER-GARGUILLE was said to be the son-in-law of TABARIN; his character was a modified Pantalone in black and red: tall, scrawny, with a pointed beard, lensless spectacles and slippers. Although he published a collection of licentious songs (1632), he was praised as the first actor to lead a relatively thrifty and ordered private life. Turlupin (Henri Le Grand, c.1587–1637) may have begun in fair-booths; a witty and malicious improviser, he wore a brick-red beard and a striped costume like Brighella's (see COMMEDIA DELL'ARTE). All three played high comedy as well, Gros-Guillaume as Lafleur, Gaultier-Garguille as Fléchelles and Turlupin as Belleville. Legend has them renting a small tennis court at the Porte St-Jacques to give performances for schoolboys; when the actors of the Hôtel de Bourgogne protested to CARDINAL RICHELIEU, he was so delighted by the scene of an unfaithful wife pleading not to be killed that he enrolled the comedians in the official acting troupe. Dates do not support this: Gaultier-Garguille joined the Hôtel de Bourgogne in 1606 and teamed with Gros-Guillaume only from 1612, Turlupin from 1618. LS

Turrini, Peter 1944– Austrian dramatist. *Rozzenjogd* (*Rathunt*, 1971) and *Sauschlachten* (*Pigslaughter*, 1972) belong to the VOLKSSTÜCK revival, cynically showing an underclass degraded by the consumer society – in *Sauschlachten* a mute peasant lad is treated, then slaughtered as a pig by other villagers. These plays explore simple situations in crude but vigorous dialect. *Der tollste Tag* (*The Maddest Day*, 1972) is a coarsened, sharpened adaptation of BEAUMARCHAIS's *Marriage of Figaro*. To reach the '90 per cent of Austrians that theatre never touches', Turrini with W. Pevny turned to TV – with *Alpensaga*, the six-part story of the intrusion of politics and industry into an Alpine village between 1900 and 1950. He came back to theatre more objective, but still provocative, with *Der Minderleister* (*The Underperformer*, 1988), which explores the torment of a redundant steel worker with surreal stage metaphors (see SURREALISM), dream scenes and explicit sex. With *Tod und Teufel* (*Death and the Devil*, 1990) and *Alpenglühen* (*Alpine Glow*, 1993) he achieved BURGTHEATER status, though these plays, like *Grillparzer im Pornoladen* (*GRILLPARZER in the Porn Shop*, 1993), continue to scourge the establishment in flamboyant, anarchic vein. HR

Tussaud, Madame see WAXWORKS

Tutin, Dorothy 1931– British actress, who began her stage career in 1950. She joined the Shakespeare Memorial Theatre at Stratford-upon-Avon in 1958, and on their subsequent tour of Russia played Ophelia, Viola and Juliet. Her first major appearance in a contemporary play came in 1961, when she played the tormented Sister Jeanne in JOHN WHITING's *The Devils* at the Aldwych Theatre; and she stayed with the ROYAL SHAKESPEARE COMPANY to play Desdemona, Varya in *The Cherry Orchard*, Polly Peachum in *The Beggar's Opera* and to appear in JOHN BARTON's Shakespearian anthology on kingship, *The Hollow Crown*.

This grounding in classical theatre helped her in her first major WEST END success, as Queen Victoria in *Portrait of a Queen* (1965), which went to New York in 1968; and her cool, controlled timing was a memorable feature of HAROLD PINTER's *Old Times* at the Aldwych in 1971. As Lady Plyant in *The Double Dealer* (1978) she won the Society of West End Theatres Award, one of several roles played at the NATIONAL THEATRE in the late 1970s, including Madam Ranevsky in *The Cherry Orchard*. She played Hester in a revival of TERENCE RATTIGAN's *The Deep Blue Sea* (1981) and appeared in the West End production of Pinter's *A Kind of Alaska* (1985). Among her film parts, she won the Variety Club of Great Britain's Film Actress Award as Sophie Breska in *Savage Messiah* and appeared in *The Shooting Party*. In 1967, she was awarded the CBE. She has appeared in two recent Harold Pinter plays, *Mountain Language* and *Party Time* (1991), in a revival of STEPHEN SONDHEIM's *A Little Night Music* (1989), and as Arkadina in ANTON CHEKHOV's *The Seagull* in a revival at Theatr Clywd, Mold, Wales. JE

Tyler, George (Crouse) 1867–1946 Ohio-born American manager and producer, who managed his first theatre in Chillicothe at the age of 20. Afterwards, he moved to New York and worked as a dramatic reporter, advance agent and producer. In 1897, he joined forces with THEODORE A. LIEBLER to found Liebler and Company, which for the next 17 years produced some 300 plays, took to America MRS PATRICK CAMPBELL, ELEONORA DUSE, RÉJANE and the ABBEY THEATRE, and managed such stars as ARNOLD DALY, JAMES O'NEILL and GERTRUDE ELLIOTT. After the firm failed in 1915, Tyler was associated with Klaw and Erlanger until he became an independent producer in 1918. His best-known presentations include BOOTH TARKINGTON's *Clarence* (1919), EUGENE O'NEILL's *Anna Christie* (1921), KAUFMAN and CONNELLY's *Dulcy* (1921) and O'CASEY's *The Plough and the Stars* (1927). His revival of *Macbeth* in 1928 was designed by GORDON CRAIG. Tyler is noted for attracting European talent to the USA, and for preferring new works to revivals. His memoirs (with J. C. Furnas), *Whatever Goes Up*, were published in 1934. TLM

Tyler, Royall 1758–1826 American playwright, author of *The Contrast* (1787), the first script by an American to receive a successful professional production. Born in Boston and educated at Harvard, Tyler showed some early literary talent and wrote *The Contrast* in three weeks after seeing his first stage presentation, a New York production of SHERIDAN's *The School for Scandal*. The script contrasts the effete world of fashion and the more manly American types, and introduced the YANKEE character to the American stage. Tyler also wrote a FARCE, *May Day in Town; or, New-York in an Uproar* (JOHN STREET THEATRE, New York, 1787) and the COMEDY *A Georgia Spec; or, Land in the Moon* (Boston and New York, 1797), as well as four other plays, probably never performed. SMA

Tynan, Kenneth (Peacock) 1927–80 British theatre critic and literary adviser to the NATIONAL THEATRE (1963–9). After a flamboyant university career at Oxford, he briefly became the director of the Lichfield Repertory Company and an actor, appearing as First Player in a *Hamlet* (1951) in which ALEC GUINNESS played the Prince. He turned to journalism, where his wit and unorthodox left-wing views made a powerful impression in the *Evening Standard* and, from 1954 to 1958, the *Observer*, where his theatre columns were outstanding. His liveliest journalism dates from this period, although he also wrote eloquently for the *New Yorker* (1958–60), the *Observer* again (1960–3) and as a freelance commentator (until his death). LAURENCE OLIVIER invited him to join the National Theatre in 1963, when it was formed, and Tynan's influence was felt in the radical tone of the early seasons. He was an advocate of BRECHT and BECKETT, although he underrated the talents of HAROLD PINTER. He championed HOCHHUTH's *Soldiers*, to the annoyance of Lord Chandos, then chairman of the National Theatre's board of governors, for the play attacked Churchill, a friend and wartime colleague of Chandos.

From then on, Tynan's place at the National Theatre was insecure and, after co-producing *Soldiers* in the WEST END in 1968, he brought together an evening of 'elegant erotica', *Oh, Calcutta!*, the first and most successful sex REVUE which came in the wake of the abolition of CENSORSHIP in 1968. He published several essay and review collections, including *He That Plays the King* (1950), *Curtains* (1961) and *The Sound of Two Hands Clapping* (1975). JE

Überbrettl see CABARET

Udall, Nicholas 1505–56 English playwright. The most famous of Udall's plays is *Ralph Roister Doister*, a comedy about the amorous manoeuvrings of its broadly drawn characters, possessing the robustness of the comedies of TERENCE and PLAUTUS which it imitated and adapted to a truly English context. He wrote other plays, but only *Ralph Roister Doister* can be attributed to him with any certainty, and its date of performance is not fully established. He taught at both Eton and Westminster schools, and the play seems to have been written and performed by the boys at one of these. MB

Uganda Uganda became a unit in 1900 when the agreement which made it a protectorate was signed, uniting four separate kingdoms and several other separate societies. Although it is a multi-lingual society with two major ethnic groups, the country's pre-theatre traditions have common features from which a recognizably Ugandan theatre is developing. In the past, both religious and social occasions have employed dance and music in close conjunction, and in a dialogue which could be seen as dramatic. Whether within the northern and eastern Nilotic culture, or the western and southern Bantu tradition, the lead singer sets both chorus and musicians in motion with verbal commands, and the musicians then inspire the singers and dancers. All participate, and improvisation within a set rhythm is valued. Whether the occasion is an attempt to exorcize an evil spirit or the celebration of a marriage, the performance is a mass emotional experience. There is no audience – all are part of the happening. Basic steps are taught and sometimes rehearsed (as in the Masaba circumcision dances), and there is a set form of words for some traditional stories. Royal courts used to maintain a professional team of musicians and dancers (including a jester in the kingdom of Bunyoro), and there are still itinerant performers who can be invited to weddings and other celebrations, following the traditional pattern. Individual improvisation is still seen as a mark of excellence. Unlike in West Africa, storytelling was a family entertainment that took place around the evening fire rather than in the market-place, and while the narrator, often a senior woman, would grip the audience by her versatile role-playing, the form did not develop into theatre as we know it, although it provided a wealth of material for theatre treatment. These forms are still current in rural areas.

After 1877 Christian missionaries established schools, and British administrators concerned themselves with social welfare. Schools and colleges, while discouraging traditional forms of entertainment, began to present performances, before an invited audience, which were rehearsed and in which the spoken word was the major means of communication. Plays in English helped with learning set books, but the students also enjoyed improvised vernacular farces, usually of a topical nature. Later, in community centres, social welfare assistants and

Mothers' Union officers developed for didactic purposes the traditional form of cantor/response into a sung dialogue, with coordinated dance-MIME and gesture. With hindsight, this can be seen as the beginnings of real Ugandan dramatic communication. In the 1950s, the emergence of songs that were a reaction to current situations showed one way in which this mode could develop: for instance, the strike of Mulago nurses – who were objecting to being made to wear badges with identity numbers – produced the dramatic song 'Namba, Namba'.

The early missionaries had tried to suppress the indigenous entertainments, but by 1946 Mukono Theological College, like the medieval European Church, had seen the value of drama and was teaching its students to employ acting as a means of understanding. The major Bible stories were used to create plays drawn from the imaginations of the students and expressed in the mother tongue. The most notable was *Were You There?* (1949). A further development of this form later produced scripted plays from traditional stories – another step in the development of theatre (*The Cows of Karo* and *Kitami the Queen*, for instance).

Since 1946, all forms of theatre have been encouraged by organized competitions within and between youth groups, schools, colleges and adult groups, and at national level. At first drama was separated from other forms of theatre, but increasingly they have come together again. All the earliest-known writers first reached the public in festivals. The majority are graduates of Makerere University, which served all East Africa until the break-up of the East African Community. Its Department of Literature not only produced plays and encouraged writing but began a drama diploma course which has generated a full Department of Music, Dance and Drama, offering degree and postgraduate courses. A creative writing fellowship, financed for several years, was held largely by playwrights, including ROBERT SERUMAGA, BYRON KAWADWA, ELVANIA ZIRIMU and John Ruganda. Despite several attempts to establish professional groups, Ugandan theatre is still largely amateur, although the recent development of full-scale dramatic presentations by such professional musical groups as that of JIMMY KATUMBA may be a significant new feature. A national dance group has been formed from time to time, and schools and colleges are now often able to teach traditional dance and music from all parts of Uganda.

The National Theatre in Kampala was built in 1959, before independence, and in its first five years was used largely by expatriate groups. Stimulated by radio serials and, after 1962, by television, a local audience began to emerge and by 1966 more local than expatriate groups were performing: two landmarks were the premieres of *The Black Hermit* (1962) by NGUGI WA THIONG'O, the first full-length play in English by an East African, and *Gwosussa Emwani* (*The One You Despise*) (1963) by WYCLIFFE KIYINGI-KAGWE, the first full-length Luganda-language play produced and acted entirely by Ugandans in the theatre. A further notable development came with the collaboration of Byron Kawadwa and Wassanyi Serukenya in *Makula ga Kulabako* (*Kulabako's Wonderful Gift*, 1970), where original music in the Ugandan idiom was combined with a romantic story told in the form of a light opera. The number of original plays presented in the National Theatre grew impressive, but Luganda is so much the dominant language that critics suggest it is a regional rather than a national theatre.

There is a taste for theatre entertainment throughout the country. In Kampala the National Theatre is only one of many venues. This tiny theatre cannot satisfy demand; some groups have taken over cinemas and halls, and there are frequent outdoor performances in the capital. Elsewhere a similar increase can be observed. Every village provides an audience for travelling concert parties. Nearly all schools and colleges offer an appropriate venue, and presentation in community centres, market squares and churches is showing more versatility. Uganda is blessed with an equable climate, and in many parts a natural hill can provide an amphitheatre with minimum effort, although the increasing dependence of musical groups on electrical amplification for their instruments can be a complication. Transport is extremely expensive, but travelling groups now perform to full houses wherever they go. The first of the social welfare groups to attempt to tour villages were the Uganda Pilgrim Players, who from 1958 to 1960 took adaptations of medieval plays to parts of Buganda. The Makerere Travelling Theatre extended its itinerary to the whole of Uganda in the summer of 1965, and in its heyday travelled to Tanzania and Kenya as well. This kind of intracultural exchange is all too limited now.

The standard of performance of the current touring groups varies, and upcountry groups are seen too infrequently in Kampala, although the annual appearance of Namasagali Secondary School is a highlight in the theatre year. Dance-drama is increasingly popular. It both solves the language problem to some extent and builds on the traditional forms. There is a large audience for FARCE, which has been encouraged by the TV serials about office immorality, nagging wives, drunken husbands, corruption and trickery. Audiences like to escape from the problems of raging inflation, disease and inefficient administration into laughter. Performing groups can claim to have a didactic purpose – although how much effect their efforts have on attitudes is debatable. Some plays, scrappily scripted and naive in story line, are so heavily didactic that it is only the music, plus the ability and charisma of individual actors, that attract the audience. Many such performances, running for as long as four hours and sometimes changing direction in the middle, would seem interminable to a more sophisticated public. Rivalry and fear of plagiarism, and cost and difficulty of publication as well as the continued emphasis on improvisation, discourage literary development. Serious writers, producers and actors in the 1970s made their protests under cover of SATIRE, mostly in English, the language of the educated audience, and now are trying to educate by the same means.

There is no closet drama. All playwrights – including Elvania Zirimu, Nuwa Sentongo and Robert Serumaga – write for performance, usually by a specific group, and often working through to a final script via group improvisation. The most popular plays are in local languages, usually Luganda – used, for instance, by Byron Kawadwa and Kiyingi-Kagwe, for many years the best-known dramatists. Serumaga, whose aim was to build on traditional forms and appeal across language divisions, attracted limited 'intellectual' audiences in Uganda, although he was for some time the best-known Ugandan theatre practitioner overseas. For a few years he ran a professional group, developing a theatre form dependent on movement, sound, music and dance which looks as though it will become the dominant form – although not in the shape he envisaged. Serumaga has been followed in recent years by ALEX MUKULU, whose plays – such as *Twenty Years of the Banana* (1993) – are well shaped and presented; John Ruganda's influence in Uganda has been limited since he left the country, but his plays are published and studied in schools there and he is still attacking the evils of Uganda, if from a distance. Elvania Zirimu, a gifted actress and producer as well as lecturer in theatre arts, in the 1970s formed and led a group of graduate players and was a wider influence than her limited number of published plays suggests. CLIFF P'CHONG LUBWA, who was her husband, has been writing continuously as well as teaching and producing plays. He encourages the dramatization of traditional material as well as using comedy as a means of outspoken social criticism. He contributes to the raising of standards by his productions and his acting as well as by his writing. Eli Kyeyune, Zirimu's brother, writes didactic satire. Kiyingi-Kagwe has turned increasingly to writing series for television, where his work has always been most popular. But his plays have been published and are now on the Luganda school syllabus. His *Muduuma Kwe Kwaffe* (*Muduuma Our Home*, 1977) was originally an excellent stage play that has become a popular series. It was during the years of oppression (1971–86) that the majority of these writers learned the art of protest, instantly recognized as such by the target audience, but not by anyone else. Since 1986 it has been possible for criticism to be more explicit.

An interesting recent development has been the creation of the satirical story as a framework for the music of an increasing number of popular music groups, of which the best known and most dynamic has been Jimmy Katumba and the Ebonies. Making full use of recording studios, highly sophisticated equipment and technical knowledge, they led the way in the commercial theatre. But Katumba is now in the USA, and the raising of standards of composition and general performance is still hindered by the proliferation of largely amateur groups, exploiting the immense but unselective demand for theatre entertainment. The didacticism, reminiscent of medieval European MORALITY PLAYS, is often heavy-handed and unsubtle, but much current work is vigorous, there is an increasing sensitivity to the need for wit in both dialogue and music, and the combination of music, dance and drama would appear to point the way in which Ugandan theatre is going.

The present government and many international agencies have recognized the educative value of theatre and commission plays to be taken on tour to encourage awareness of AIDS and of the need to halt the spread of malaria.

Under the guidance of Professor ROSE MBOWA a community-based drama (theatre-for-development, see THIRD WORLD POPULAR THEATRE) is tackling similar problems from the grass roots. A leader goes to a village, gathers potential performers, discusses local problems and identifies the one considered most urgent. Then, under his guidance, together they improvise a play, lasting usually some 30 minutes, highlighting the problem and often suggesting a possible solution. The play is rehearsed until fixed, then performed in school, in church after a service, or in the market-place, with the audience summoned by drums. At the close the audience is asked to discuss the problem – role-playing moving easily into reality – and suggest solutions. The play is occasionally so successful that the players perform it in neighbouring villages.

At all levels of performance, interaction between actors and audience is of great importance. Most forms of theatre in Uganda, while sometimes using very sophisticated means of communication (video interpolation drawing on TV narrative forms, for instance), concentrate almost entirely on local subjects. A wider knowledge and experience of drama from elsewhere would give Ugandan theatre a greater resonance. MMAC

See: M. Banham and C. Wake, *African Theatre Today*, London, 1976; E. Breitinger, 'Popular Urban Culture in Uganda', *New Theatre Quarterly*, 8, 31, 1992; D. Cook, *In Black and White*, Nairobi, 1976; D. Duerden and C. Pieterse, *African Writers Talking*, London, 1972; R. Grandquist (ed.), *Signs and Signals: Popular Culture in Africa*, Umea, 1990; E. Jones, *African Literature Today*, 8, London, 1976; A. Roscoe, *Uhuru's Fire*, Cambridge, 1977.

Ullmann, Liv 1938– Norwegian actress. Ullmann's stage work is often mentioned as a footnote to her films (particularly those with INGMAR BERGMAN). However, she acted at Rogaland Teater, the NORSKE TEATRET and NATIONAL-THEATRET, playing Anne Frank, Juliet and Saint Joan, before her international breakthrough in Bergman's film *Persona*. Some of her most important work has been in BRECHT at the Norske Teatret, including Grusha in *The Caucasian Chalk Circle* and Mother Courage. While she has typically been cast in roles that emphasize suffering, she individualizes it with great intensity, and the remarkable range of work often incorporates a volatile anger. HL

Ulric [*née* Ulrich], **Lenore** 1892–1970 American actress who, like BLANCHE BATES, DAVID WARFIELD and MRS LESLIE CARTER, was a DAVID BELASCO creation. From her debut in 1916 as an Indian maiden in *The Heart of Wetona*, Belasco cast her as a temptress in a series of exotic potboilers. In *The Son-Daughter* (1919) she was a Chinese siren, in *Kiki* (1921) a Parisian chorus girl, in *Lulu Belle* (1925) a Harlem whore and in *Mima* (1928) a slinky mannequin. Raven-haired, with large dark eyes in an oval face, Ulric made a beguiling 1920s vamp, sultry and sharp-tongued, voluptuous and swivel-hipped. She received good notices even when the primitive, scenically spectacular Belasco vehicles she starred in were critical howlers. FH

Ulster Literary Theatre (from 1915, the Ulster Theatre) Founded in 1902 (with no encouragement from YEATS) by

Bulmer Hobson and David Parkhill (Lewis Purcell), both of whom contributed some plays. It proposed to enunciate a regional identity, a variant of the ABBEY THEATRE's work, often in good-humoured SATIRE. The company toured England and Ireland and gave the premieres of some 50 Northern Irish plays. Apart from RUTHERFORD MAYNE, it cultivated no important dramatist and remained amateur to the end, though working to professional standards. Its demise in 1934 was due to the lack of either private or government financing. DM

Uncle Tom's Cabin No other American play has had such a remarkable stage history. Mrs Stowe's novel, published in March 1852 (after its serialization), was first dramatized and performed in Baltimore (January 1852); another version played in New York in August, and a third, by GEORGE L. AIKEN (now the accepted version), with the HOWARD FAMILY in Troy, New York, in September. The Howards made a life's work of 'Tomming', as did a host of American actors. In the 1850s productions were seen also in London, Berlin and Paris.

'Tom shows' were on the road by 1854; by 1893 a national exchange for 'Tom' actors opened in Chicago, and in the 90s some 400 troupes were barnstorming across the country. Every season companies in the major cities called in the hounds to pursue Eliza across the Ohio River, a spectacle not included in the novel. Theatrical novelty became the 'Tommer's' stock-in-trade: bloodhounds, 'Jubilee Singers' and dioramas became featured attractions; some troupes carried as few as three actors. In 1901 WILLIAM A. BRADY's production dwarfed its predecessors with 200 buck-and-wing (tap) dancers and singers plus a transformation sequence of 21 scenes. A dozen companies were still on the road in 1927; in 1933 a Players Club revival featured OTIS SKINNER and Fay Bainter.

Thomas Gossett notes how strongly the play has affected American and international thinking on the character of African-Americans, the nature of life in the old South and the struggle between good and evil. Though not essentially anti-slavery, it served as propaganda for abolition. In this century the popular belief, as expressed by JAMES BALDWIN, has been that *UTC* spread the lie that 'black equates with evil and white with grace'. Few revivals have been seen since the 1930s; however, in 1978 TRINITY REPERTORY COMPANY offered a version, with some success. Moreover, as recently as 1990–1 three adaptations were developed: a MELODRAMATIC version by the SAN FRANCISCO MIME TROUPE and the LORRAINE HANSBERRY Theatre; an epic dance-theatre piece by the dancer-choreographer Bill T. Jones (*Last Supper at Uncle Tom's Cabin/The Promised Land*); and *Unkle Tomm's Kabin: A Deconstruction of the Novel by Harriet Beecher Stowe* by Seattle's Empty Space Theatre. Apparently, with racial tensions resurfacing in American society, *UTC* has once more emerged as one vehicle for investigating collective racial images and attitudes, as Misha Berson has suggested in *American Theatre* (1991). RM DBW

United States of America

1 To the Civil War The early history of the American theatre is largely one of the transference of European traditions, primarily those of provincial England, and a gradual development towards self-identity, which did not reach its full potential until after the First World War. Early settlers in the colonies, many representing the same anti-theatre element that existed in England, through the exigencies of the times diverted their energies into other and more complex channels than entertainment. As actors in the real-life drama of survival in hostile surroundings, colonists, with some notable exceptions, reflected Benjamin Franklin's attitude: 'After the first cares for the necessities of life are over, we shall come to think of the embellishments.'

The earliest records of theatre in the New World were not English in origin at all; indeed, the initial dramatic performances were the NATIVE AMERICAN RITUALS performed by Indians of the North and South. Early in the 16th century the Spanish discovered Aztec performances in Mexico that blended song, dance, comic byplay and animal imitations; warlike tribes in the US Northeast, though less inclined to organized theatricals, engaged in variegated revels; and tribes in the Pacific Northwest created elaborate stage effects for dramatizations of tribal mythology. More complex theatre, however, is tenuously documented as having occurred in Spanish as early as 1538 in the Southwest and Mexico and by 1606 in French, in what is now Canada.

With the establishment of the first settlement (Jamestown, Virginia, 1607) in what would become the USA, two traditions were quickly established among the English-speaking residents. The Southern colonies, especially the Royalist colony of Virginia, were more congenial to the theatre; Puritan New England and Quaker-dominated Pennsylvania were vehemently against this frivolous pastime, although William Penn's efforts were inevitably overturned by regal veto, the king and his court being strong supporters of the theatre in England. Nonetheless, in various colonies between 1700 and 1716 laws were passed against the theatre, with some effect. In Massachusetts, Increase Mather expressed the typical Puritan attitude when he wrote in 1687 that 'there is much discourse of beginning Stage-Plays in New England. The last year Promiscuous Dancing was openly practised.' Despite such outcries, there were local amateur theatricals from an early date. A non-extant piece called *Ye Bare and Ye Cubb*, the first recorded play in English presented in the colonies, was written by one William Darby of Accomac Country, Virginia, and performed in 1665 by Darby, Cornelius Wilkinson and Philip Howard in Cowles Tavern, though this is the last recorded performance in Virginia until 1702. In 1687 a Boston innkeeper named John Wing attempted to fit out a room in his establishment for theatrical use, but to no avail: attitudes like Mather's and the protests of Judge Samuel Sewall ended the brief experiment. There is evidence, however, that three years later a Harvard College student, Benjamin Colman, wrote the first play (*Gustavus Vasa*) by an American to be acted in the colonies. In Virginia students at William and Mary College offered in 1702 the recitation of a 'pastoral colloquy' before the governor. Other colloquies of this sort were offered at other institutions of higher learning. Between 1699 and 1702 a Richard Hunter petitioned for permission to produce plays in New York, then a town of 4436 people; it was granted, but no more is known. On 6 May 1709, however, the Governor's Council in New York forbade 'play acting and prize fighting', with no rationale provided.

Early evidence of professional efforts is scattered and imprecise. The British vagabond player ANTHONY ASTON is generally credited as the first professional actor in America; in 1703, in his early 20s, he acted in 'Charles Town', South Carolina, writing that he 'turn'd *Player* and *Poet*, and wrote one Play on the Subject of the Country'. He then claims to have gone to New York. His play is unknown, and in 1704 he returned to London. In 1715, the first known play written and published in America appeared. Written by Governor Robert Hunter of New York, *Androboros* is a SATIRE on the citizens of that city and the New York Senate. There is no record of a performance.

For the next 35 years theatrical activity was sporadic. In 1716, in Williamsburg, Virginia, the most advanced town in the colonies to promote theatre, William Levingston, who ran a dancing school, built a theatre that was operated by his indentured servants William and Mary Stagg until Levingston's death in 1729. In 1724 a makeshift playhouse (the New Booth) was built in the Society Hill section of Philadelphia, for 'roap dancing' and the traditional CLOWN pieces called Pickleherring. The 1730s mark the advancement of Charleston as a theatrical centre and the erection of a theatre in Dock Street in 1736. During the same period there was limited activity in New York: in 1730 an amateur production of *Romeo and Juliet* was presented, the first SHAKESPEARE on the American stage; in 1732 a space above a commercial establishment was turned into an acting space; and in 1735 at 'The New Theatre' (a converted warehouse in Pearl Street) a season of recent English plays, including *The Beaux' Stratagem*, was presented.

A sustained record of professional theatre in Philadelphia, which quickly became America's theatrical centre until about 1825, dates from 1749 and is associated with the activities of the first professional company known in the colonies, under Walter Murray and Thomas Kean, about whom we know virtually nothing. In August they performed in Plumstead's Warehouse, converted for use as a playhouse; by February they were performing in New York in a converted building in Nassau Street. In October 1751 they opened a new, crudely built wooden playhouse in Williamsburg, played in Maryland the following year as the Virginia Company of Comedians, and then drifted into obscurity. They had, however, as historian Hugh F. Rankin indicates, acted 'as an advance agent for those to follow, whetting the appetite of the colonials for the drama and upon occasion wearing down religious and moralistic opposition'.

The next chapter in the history of theatre in America is the story of one company, the London Company of Comedians (renamed in 1763 the American Company of Comedians), and their total dominance of the theatrical scene for 50 years, beginning in 1752 under the leadership of LEWIS HALLAM SR and continuing from 1758 under DAVID DOUGLASS, who married Hallam's widow. The Hallam Company, sent to America on speculation by Lewis's eldest brother William, who remained in London, arrived in Williamsburg with a completely professional company of 12 adults and three children, a complete repertoire of plays, and basic scenery and costumes. Operating on a sharing system, the company began their first season at Kean's old playhouse on 16 September with *The Merchant of Venice*; in July 1754 they moved to New York, carrying with them a letter of endorsement from Governor Dinwiddie to the governor of New York. Until October 1754 they played in New York, Philadelphia, Annapolis and Charleston, then spent the next three years in Jamaica, where Lewis Hallam died in 1755. Douglass, an erstwhile actor and printer, brought the company back to New York in 1758, and within six years had added 'American' to their name.

Despite continued opposition from all quarters (Puritan, Quaker, Lutheran, Presbyterian, Baptist), Douglass, with LEWIS HALLAM JR as leading man, took his company up and down the East Coast, building new theatres or revamping old buildings, and introducing significant new British plays to the public. In the early 1760s Douglass even attempted an invasion of New England, first in Newport, Rhode Island, in 1761, and the next year in Providence – both stops a challenge to his ingenuity. In order to avoid criticism, he advertised his plays as 'moral dialogues', and in Providence – called his makeshift playhouse a 'schoolhouse'. Literally drummed out of town, Douglass returned to New York, where he opened the temporary Chapel of Beekman Street Theatre in 1761, followed in 1766 and 67 by the construction of two more important and permanent theatres.

The first permanent theatre on the American continent, the SOUTHWARK THEATRE in Philadelphia (1766), which stood until 1912, was also the scene for the first professionally produced play by a native author: Thomas Godfrey's *The Prince of Parthia*, a heroic TRAGEDY in blank verse set in Parthia near the beginning of the Christian era – and thus in no way American in subject-matter – premiered on 24 April 1767. It was sheer chance that this play earned its historic position, for a play called *The Disappointment* by Thomas Forrest was to receive that honour but was abruptly withdrawn because it contained 'personal reflections unfit for the stage'. Douglass's second major venture, the JOHN STREET THEATRE, opened on 7 December 1767, predominating among NEW YORK CITY THEATRES for 30 years.

On 20 October 1774 the Continental Congress forbade all extravagance and dissipation, including stage entertainments; Douglass and his company returned to the West Indies the following year. Other than military theatricals, theatre ceased during the hostilities, though plays – many little more than political satire in dialogue form, and the majority unperformed – were written during the period, including those by MERCY OTIS WARREN, HUGH H. BRACKENRIDGE and ROBERT MUNFORD. Also written were anonymous pieces such as *The Blockheads*, inspired by the performance in Boston of General John Burgoyne's farce *The Blockade of Boston*, as well as John Leacock's *The Fall of British Tyranny* (both 1776). The real activity, however, took place among the military on both sides. In 1775 the John Street, renamed the Theatre Royal, presented a long series of dramatic productions performed by the British military, until their evacuation in 1783. The same was true in other major cities, such as Boston, where a theatre was organized in Faneuil Hall during 1775-7, and Philadelphia, where a Captain Delancey and Captain John André, later involved with Benedict Arnold, led a theatrical group under General William Howe. Despite edicts to the contrary, the Continental Army also performed: at Valley Forge, for example, Washington's troops presented ADDISON's *Cato* in 1778.

After the Revolution, in 1782, professionals began to return. Lewis Hallam Jr brought back the Old American Company from Jamaica in 1784, picking up where they had left off in 1774. Along with JOHN HENRY, they were the major actors of the day, joined soon by THOMAS WIGNELL. On 16 April 1787 the reinstated company offered the first professional production of a native American comedy on an American subject: ROYALL TYLER's *The Contrast*, which, among other firsts, introduced Jonathan the stage YANKEE, the prototype of many subsequent Yankees and the first native type to be developed. With the elimination of all repression, Philadelphia was stimulated as a theatre centre thanks to the efforts of Wignell and Alexander Reinagle, a musician, who in 1794 opened the superior CHESTNUT STREET THEATRE with a new group of actors.

After this period of re-establishment, the 1790s became a decade of rapid expansion. Wignell erected theatres in Baltimore (1794) and Washington (1800); in 1792 JOHN HODGKINSON joined the Old American Company; with the repealing of restrictive laws in New England, Boston and Providence became important centres, especially with the opening of Boston's FEDERAL STREET THEATRE in 1794, followed two years later by the Haymarket; and other scattered activity spread theatre throughout the young country, including French-speaking theatres in Charleston (1794) and in New Orleans (1791, though not part of the USA until 1803). In 1798 New York kept pace with Philadelphia with the opening of the PARK (New) THEATRE, where WILLIAM DUNLAP, whose drama *The Father* had been performed at the John Street in 1789, initially became a partner of Lewis Hallam Jr and John Hodgkinson; he ultimately assumed the management, recording a career of ups and downs, ending in bankruptcy in 1805. After a brief period of management by actor THOMAS A. COOPER, STEPHEN PRICE, America's first professional manager, took control in 1809 and, by encouraging star appearances, beginning with GEORGE FREDERICK COOKE in 1810, helped undermine the stock system (see STOCK COMPANY). Actors such as Cooper and JOHN HOWARD PAYNE (remembered primarily as a playwright) exploited the starring possibilities, and – after the uncertainties of the War of 1812 – a steady flow of actors from England appeared, including in the 1820s EDMUND KEAN, JUNIUS BRUTUS BOOTH, WILLIAM B. WOOD, WILLIAM WARREN THE ELDER, TYRONE POWER, LAURA KEENE, CHARLES KEAN and JOHN BROUGHAM, to mention only a few.

More significant than foreign imports of stars and plays was the slow Americanization of the theatre, which accelerated during the first half of the 19th century. Native-born stars began to emerge in the 1820s, beginning with EDWIN FORREST, America's first great actor and the first native-born performer to create excitement abroad. In his footsteps came Augustus A. Addams, McKean Buchanan, John R. Scott, J. Hudson Kirby and, most significantly, JOHN McCULLOUGH, E. L. DAVENPORT and JAMES MURDOCH (and, towards the end of this period, great actors like EDWIN BOOTH and JOSEPH JEFFERSON III). Among the actresses of the period, none received more acclaim than Forrest's contemporary CHARLOTTE CUSHMAN, who by mid-century was the dominating tragic actress on the American stage and an international star. Other actresses of note during the first half of the century include MARY ANN DUFF, Josephine Clifton, CLARA FISHER, Maggie Mitchell, LOTTA CRABTREE, ADAH ISAACS MENKEN and ANNA CORA MOWATT, remembered today for her play *Fashion* (1845), the most significant native comedy of manners of its time. Its central character is Trueman, another Yankee in the tradition of *The Contrast*'s Jonathan; such roles were the speciality of numerous significant American comic actors, including J. H. HACKETT, GEORGE HANDEL HILL, DANFORTH MARBLE and Joshua Silsbee (as well as the later JOHN E. OWENS and DENMAN THOMPSON).

Parallel with the emergence of American-born actors is the growth of native plays and native characters. As a result of a playwriting contest sponsored first in 1828 by Forrest for 'the best tragedy, in five acts, of which the hero, or principal character shall be an original of the country', 200 plays were submitted overall and nine prizes were awarded, four plays being retained in his repertoire. The first winner, JOHN AUGUSTUS STONE's *Metamora*, which echoes back to Major Robert Roger's 1766 play *Ponteach* and other early dramatic efforts to write plays about the noble red man, became the most durable of the dozens of Indian plays written and performed for the next half-century (see NATIVE AMERICAN RITUAL/THEATRE). Stone was one of a number of notable playwrights of the period from Philadelphia; others included JAMES NELSON BARKER, ROBERT MONTGOMERY BIRD, RICHARD PENN SMITH, MORDECAI M. NOAH, Robert T. Conrad and SAMUEL WOODWORTH.

In addition to the Indian and the Yankee, a minor native character was the stage Negro, the first appearing in John Murdock's *The Triumphs of Love* (1795) and culminating, from 1852, in the many versions of UNCLE TOM'S CABIN. Related to the dramatic development of AFRICAN-AMERICAN characters is the phenomenal popularity of the blackface MINSTREL SHOW stimulated by THOMAS D. RICE in the late 1820s. Two additional types emerged before the Civil War: the tough city lad, Mose the fire b'hoy, as depicted in BENJAMIN BAKER's *A Glance at New York* (1848); and the stout-hearted frontiersman, beginning with Col. Nimrod Wildfire in JAMES K. PAULDING's *The Lion of the West* (1831). In addition to the development of native types, American drama up to mid-century was dominated by the BURLESQUES and dramas of immigrant playwright-actors like John Brougham and DION BOUCICAULT. Advances in writing techniques were made by GEORGE HENRY BOKER, arguably the period's best writer of romantic drama in the English-speaking world, in particular his *Francesca da Rimini* (1855), though Bird's romantic plays as performed by Forrest were more popular.

As the USA expanded its territory, theatre entrepreneurs took small companies into the Ohio and Mississippi Valley, beginning in 1815 when SAMUEL DRAKE went from Albany, New York, into frontier settlements (see FRONTIER THEATRE) in Kentucky, Ohio and Tennessee. JAMES H. CALDWELL had established a first-rate English-speaking theatre in New Orleans by 1819. The names NOAH LUDLOW and SOL SMITH were familiar ones along the rivers and in the wild; combining forces, they established the first real theatre in St Louis in 1835. Chicago's first theatre dates from 1847. During the same period William Chapman was operating his Mississippi Floating Theatre (see SHOWBOATS). By mid-century, thanks to the gold rush, theatre came to California. The first theatrical performance by professional actors was given in San Francisco in 1850, and by 1862 the Salt Lake Theatre (Utah) was established. The star system was unequivocally aided by this westward expansion, for Western managers paid higher salaries than in the East, to attract the best talent available.

By 1800 a definite shift of influence from Philadelphia to New York had begun. Philadelphia's population in 1820 was 63,802, New York's 123,706; by 1840 it was 93,655 to 312,710, and by mid-century New York boasted almost half a million people. The Chestnut Street Theatre, managed by William Warren and William B. Wood, began to lose dominance in Philadelphia in 1811, and was followed in 1828 by the ARCH STREET THEATRE and the WALNUT STREET THEATRE (renovated from a CIRCUS to a theatre in 1811). Philadelphia could not support three major theatres, and in 1828–9 all three went bankrupt. The country was rapidly changing, with a growing urban working-class audience on the rise, significant emigrations on the horizon, an active revolt against English domination of the stage in motion, and a major civil war around the corner. Gradually playwrights were able to gain a living writing plays, encouraged by the copyright law of 1856. The number and quality of playhouses increased, gas STAGE LIGHTING was introduced in 1816, native scenic designers (see THEATRE DESIGN) were gaining recognition, and greater REALISM – given impetus by the 1846 presentation of CHARLES KEAN's *King John* – was sought. The Lafayette Theatre, built in New York in 1826, boasted border lights and equipment for aquatic and equestrian drama (see ANIMALS AS PERFORMERS). The second Park opened in 1821 with a capacity of 2500, topped by the 3500 of the first BOWERY THEATRE in 1826. The Chatham Garden Theatre opened in 1825; what became BARNUM'S AMERICAN MUSEUM began operation in 1841, as did the famous BOSTON MUSEUM, which operated a most successful stock company for almost 50 years, beginning in 1843; the ASTOR PLACE OPERA HOUSE opened in 1847; Brougham's Lyceum in 1850. Some of the more successful managements up to mid-century fought the growing trends for stars and long runs: for example, BILLY MITCHELL at the Olympic Theatre in New York during 1839–50. WILLIAM E. BURTON, who leased Palmo's Opera House in 1848 and opened it as Burton's Chamber Street Theatre, followed suit; it was to dominate as the fashionable New York theatre until the emergence of the WALLACKS' stock company, beginning in 1853.

By the Civil War the American theatre had undeniably established a strong, individualistic mainstream tradition, relatively free of foreign influence, despite strong impulses from new European migrations to America. After a brief curtailment of growth, the American theatre would experience a great period of prosperity following the War Between the States, lasting until about 1915. DBW

2 The Civil War to the First World War The Civil War only disrupted theatrical activities in the East, and by early 1862 the theatres in New York, Boston and Philadelphia were open and thriving. Such patriotic pieces as Charles Gayler's *Bull Run; or, the Sacking of Fairfax Courthouse* (1861) appeared in New York at the New Bowery Theatre three weeks after the actual battle. Into the 1880s Wallack's continued as the leading New York playhouse, offering a steady diet of old and new British comedies with a superb acting company that included Mme Elizabeth Ponisi, ROSE COGHLAN, Henry J. Montague and CHARLES COGHLAN. William Warren remained a fixture at the Boston Museum until his retirement in 1883, offering a wide range of comic roles, classic as well as contemporary. Mrs John Drew managed a talented company at the Arch Street Theatre in Philadelphia during 1861–92, establishing the careers of her son, John Drew, and her daughter, Georgina Drew Barrymore (see DREW-BARRYMORE FAMILY).

At the beginning of the decade, Edwin Forrest and Charlotte Cushman reigned as the leading tragedians in America, although Forrest's position was being challenged by EDWIN BOOTH, the son of English-born tragedian J.B. Booth. Young Booth had served his apprenticeship in California (1852–6) and returned east in 1856 to establish himself as a star. Success the following year in Boston and New York made him an actor to watch. In the autumn of 1862 he played in New York at the same time as Forrest, inviting comparison with the older actor. Cultivated theatre patrons had long abandoned Forrest and found Booth's quiet, unassuming, intellectual and refined style more suitable for their ideal of a 'temple of the arts'. Booth's slight but handsome physique (dark hair and eyes) made him the ideal late-Victorian tragedian, just as Forrest's muscular build had attracted patrons 30 years earlier. Critic Nym Crinkle (ANDREW C. WHEELER) thought Booth's Hamlet resembled a 19th-century gentleman more than a 16th-century courtier. While his most famous role was Hamlet – which he played for 100 performances at the WINTER GARDEN THEATRE during the 1864–5 season – he excelled in other roles requiring intellectual rather than emotional or physical force: Iago, Richard II, Shylock, Cardinal Richelieu (in BULWER LYTTON's play) and Bertuccio in TOM TAYLOR's *The Fool's Revenge*. Booth departed from tradition in building his own theatre (BOOTH's, 1869) with neither a raked and grooved stage, an apron, nor proscenium doors. A better actor than manager, he succumbed to the financial panic of 1873 and lost the theatre through bankruptcy. Considered by historians as America's finest actor, Booth spent the last two decades of his life successfully touring as a star.

Booth was not the only actor challenging theatrical traditions: MATILDA HERON became an overnight success in 1857 with her portrayal of Marguerite Gautier in DUMAS *fils*'s *The Lady of the Camellias* (called *Camille* in New York), exhibiting a style of acting marked by excessive emotional display and a seeming lack of technique and control. For the next half-century, the style attracted such actresses as LUCILLE WESTERN, CLARA MORRIS and MRS LESLIE CARTER. JOSEPH JEFFERSON III also broke with the traditional school in the 1860s with his portrayal of Rip Van Winkle in Boucicault's dramatization. After presenting it in London (1865) for 170 performances, Jefferson took it to New York in 1866, and in the title role established himself as the leading comedian of his age, as Booth was the leading tragedian. Jefferson endowed Rip with charm, humour and pathos: his quiet, even casual, style seemed free of all staginess, with nothing forced or unnatural. In 1874 FRANK MAYO idealized the frontiersman in FRANK H. MURDOCH's drama *Davy Crockett*; like Jefferson, Mayo underplayed the emotional points and offered a style of acting that seemed natural to his audiences.

Dramatic tastes changed significantly in the 1860s: the historical costume dramas of Stone, Bird, Knowles and Bulwer-Lytton began to go out of fashion; more popular were MELODRAMAS that offered adventure, romance and obligatory sensational events. In AUGUSTIN DALY's most successful melodramas, suspense and novel disasters abound: a man tied to railway tracks facing an approaching train (*Under the Gaslight*, 1867); the heroine stranded on a steamship about to explode (*A Flash of Lightning*, 1868); or the rescue of a man bound to a log entering a sawmill (*The Red Scarf*, 1868). These dramas had broad emotional appeal and played to a large popular audience.

The excitement over *Camille* and the new French drama resulted in numerous adaptations. There was good reason for these French plays achieving instant popularity: they dealt with contemporary events and discussed subjects formerly considered taboo (adultery, for example). Dion Boucicault made a profession out of anglicizing French plays; Augustin Daly was responsible in part or whole for 44 adaptations of French drama, in addition to borrowing others from the German and English theatres. While the Dramatic Copyright Law (see COPYRIGHT) of 1856 improved the playwright's legal rights, it was not until the International Copyright Agreement was accepted by the USA in 1891 that managers found it as profitable to produce native plays as foreign ones.

American social comedies and dramas in the 1870s reflected the important topics of the day: stock speculation, social climbing, the winning of the West, divorce and the family and, in a romantic way, the Civil War. Daly's big hit of 1875, *The Big Bonanza*, poked fun at those who naively attempted to make a 'killing' on Wall Street. BRONSON HOWARD offered a more serious treatment of the subject in *The Banker's Daughter* (1878), and in *Young Mrs Winthrop* (1883) he touched upon the subjects of money, social status and divorce. In *The Henrietta* (1887) Howard suggested that the country's obsession with making money was leading to moral decline. (This theme was explored by DAVID BELASCO and HENRY C. DeMILLE in *Men and Women* (1890), and exploited by CLYDE FITCH in *The Climbers* (1901); a better play of the genre, LANGDON MITCHELL's *The New York Idea* (1906), satirizes divorce and social customs among the wealthy.) Historians have regarded Bronson Howard as the first professional playwright in America because he successfully made a living from his plays. His biggest hit, *Shenandoah* (1889), used the Civil War as a background for an essentially romantic plot, as did WILLIAM GILLETTE's spy stories *Held by the Enemy* (1886) and *Secret Service* (1896), Belasco's *The Heart of Maryland* (1895) and Fitch's *Barbara Frietchie* (1899).

The frontier and the winning of the West provided

countless plots and characters, including Davy Crockett and the American cowboy. Daly set his *Horizon* (1871) in the West, as did BRET HARTE for *Two Men of Sandy Bar* (1876), JOAQUIN MILLER for *The Danites in the Sierras* (1887), BARTLEY CAMPBELL for *My Partner* (1879), AUGUSTUS THOMAS for *Arizona* (1899) and Belasco for *The Girl of the Golden West* (1905). WILLIAM VAUGHN MOODY's *The Great Divide* (1906) contrasts the East and the West in what some historians regard as the first modern American play.

In the final years of the 19th century a more realistic treatment of subject began to replace melodrama. Playwrights rejected long-held conventions dearly loved by audiences – including romantic plots, spine-chilling rescues and happy endings – in favour of a truthful depiction of life. The FARCE-comedies of EDWARD HARRIGAN in the 1870s and 80s offered a theatrical but authentic portrait of life among the recent immigrants in New York; WILLIAM DEAN HOWELLS called Harrigan the American GOLDONI, and championed his plays. In the 1890s, the increased interest in IBSEN offended traditionalists like WILLIAM WINTER and JOHN RANKEN TOWSE, but the new drama was defended by critics Howells, Hamlin Garland and JAMES G. HUNEKER. JAMES A. HERNE's *Margaret Fleming* (1890) presented a realistic portrait of the consequences of a husband's infidelity and avoided a happy ending. Herne's more conventional *Shore Acres* (1892) maintained the externals of realism but returned in character and plot to sentimental melodrama, and was similar in style to Denman Thompson's *The Old Homestead* (1886). Augustus Thomas also combined the trappings of REALISM and local colour in *Alabama* (1891), *Arizona* (1899), *The Witching Hour* (1907) and *The Copperhead* (1918). More important are EDWARD SHELDON's *Salvation Nell* (1908), *The Nigger* (1909) and *The Boss* (1911), which deal with social problems in a realistic framework.

The public's demand for popular entertainment was insatiable. ADAH ISAACS MENKEN's *Mazeppa* (1861) thrilled the masculine element of the audience, as she gave the illusion of riding nude on the back of a wild horse. *The Black Crook* (1866) created a vogue for elaborate musical spectacle, owing much of its success to a Parisian ballet troupe of one hundred 'beautiful girls' in flesh-coloured tights. LYDIA THOMPSON's 'British Blondes' Burlesque Company from London drew crowded houses in New York for seven months (1868–9) (see BURLESQUE). French companies presented the new OPÉRA BOUFFE of JACQUES OFFENBACH to New York audiences in the late 1860s, and Maurice Grau formed a company in the 1870s to present French OPERETTAS and French stars. *Evangeline* (1874) offered an American version of *opéra bouffe*; written by Edward E. Rice and J.C. Godwin, it featured a scantily clad female chorus, elaborate scenery and comedian NAT GOODWIN. The success of the KIRALFY brothers' *Around the World in Eighty Days* (1875) set the standard for large-scale spectacle theatre for the next two decades. The comic operettas of GILBERT and Sullivan found an audience in America after the huge success of *HMS Pinafore* in 1878–9. CHARLES HOYT's 'musical trifle', *A Trip to Chinatown* (1890), offered songs, dances and risqué COMEDY in addition to a thin plot, and ran for 650 performances. A decade later an English import, *Florodora* (1900), survived for 505 performances and made famous its sextet of chorus girls.

FLORENZ ZIEGFELD inaugurated his *Follies* REVUE in 1907, featuring beautiful girls, elaborate costumes and sets, and leading comedians; over the years he discovered such talents as FANNY BRICE, W. C. FIELDS, EDDIE CANTOR and BERT WILLIAMS.

Operetta continued its hold on American MUSICAL THEATRE into the 1920s. VICTOR HERBERT gained success with European-styled pieces and is regarded as America's first important composer of operetta. The proper setting for operetta remained in Central Europe, with Franz Lehar's memorable *The Merry Widow* (1907) and with operettas by RUDOLF FRIML and SIGMUND ROMBERG.

Specialists such as LOTTA CRABTREE charmed New York audiences during 1867–91 with her singing, dancing and banjo playing. A master of the quick costume change, she played both Little Nell and the Marchioness in John Brougham's dramatic version of *The Old Curiosity Shop*, and six roles in *The Little Detective*. GEORGE W. L. FOX drew packed houses to the Olympic Theatre (1868) with the pantomime *Humpty Dumpty*, which he was to perform 1268 times in New York alone. EDDIE FOY gained fame in the 1890s by clowning in such musical pieces as *Sinbad the Sailor* (1891) and *Ali Baba* (1892). TONY PASTOR presented the top speciality acts at his VAUDEVILLE theatres in the 1870s and 80s, including the Four Cohans, LILLIAN RUSSELL and the WEBER AND FIELDS comedy duo. GEORGE M. COHAN would move from vaudeville to the musical stage, establishing himself as a star in 1904–5 in his own *Little Johnny Jones*. Lillian Russell became a leading star on the American musical stage. Weber and Fields opened their own Music Hall in 1896, which for seven years was regarded as one of BROADWAY's brightest attractions. The future of the speciality acts in the 20th century, however, lay with B. F. KEITH and EDWARD F. ALBEE, businessmen who introduced continuous vaudeville and organized the industry into a giant national circuit, gaining a near monopoly over it.

Economics and public taste after the Civil War dictated a change in the theatrical order. Although Wallack and Burton had been strong managers, the most powerful force in the theatre had been the actor as star. Realism and the demand for artistic unity made the rise of the modern director inevitable. During the 1869–70 season, Augustin Daly leased the FIFTH AVENUE THEATRE and began developing his own company. He hired actors by type rather than by lines of business; often cast plays without regard to tradition, lines of business, or possession of parts; rehearsed each play with careful attention to interpretation, blocking, costuming and scenery; and, while he opposed the star system, developed a succession of stars including Agnes Ethel, FANNY DAVENPORT, CLARA MORRIS and ADA REHAN. At his own Daly's Theatre in the 1880s, he featured a quartet of actors including John Drew, Ada Rehan, Mrs G.H. Gilbert and James Lewis. Known as the home of light comedy in New York, Daly's displaced Wallack's as the most fashionable playhouse in the city. In 1884 he toured his company to London – the first American to do so – and later to Paris and Germany. Four years later he produced *The Taming of the Shrew* at Stratford-upon-Avon in the Shakespeare Memorial Theatre. Historians consider him the first American *régisseur* in the style of the Duke of Saxe-Meiningen (see MEININGEN COMPANY).

A. M. PALMER tightly controlled every aspect of his productions at the Union Square Theatre (1872–83), the MADISON SQUARE THEATRE (1884–91) and Wallack's old theatre (renamed Palmer's, 1888–96). Whereas Daly's Theatre was known as the home of comedy, Palmer's featured 'polite melodrama', which he mounted with taste and care. With the assistance of A. R. Cazauran, he built a strong company by hiring established actors such as Agnes Ethel, Clara Morris, Kate Claxton, ROSE EYTINGE, Charles R. Thorne Jr and JAMES O'NEILL. His most popular successes included Kate Claxton in *The Two Orphans* (1874); RICHARD MANSFIELD in *A Parisian Romance* (1883); and premieres of Clyde Fitch's *Beau Brummell* (1890) and Augustus Thomas's *Alabama* (1891).

STEELE MACKAYE also saw himself as an all-powerful manager who shaped every aspect of his productions. He designed the elevator stage at the Madison Square Theatre (1880), which allowed for an entire setting to be shifted in 40 seconds. He also built the LYCEUM THEATRE (1884–5) and taught the Delsarte system of expression. In 1887 he directed his own *Paul Kauvar*, which demonstrated his skill in handling crowd scenes in the Meiningen manner; but MacKaye remains a controversial figure in the American theatre because he failed to finish most of his projects.

Through staging, lighting and scenery, David Belasco attempted to create the illusion of real life. He served as stage manager of the Madison Square and Lyceum Theatres in the 1880s, after which he turned to producing in 1895. Also a successful playwright, Belasco excelled in writing sentimental melodramas, which he tailored for specific stars and interpolated with enough contemporary thought to make them seem modern. He starred Mrs Leslie Carter in *Zaza* (1899); BLANCHE BATES in *Madame Butterfly* (1900); Bates and GEORGE ARLISS in *Sweet Kitty Bellairs* (1903); DAVID WARFIELD in *The Return of Peter Grimm* (1911); and a replica of a Child's Restaurant (a US chain) in *The Governor's Lady* (1912). Belasco used publicity to make stars out of his actors and is credited by some historians with being the most successful of American *régisseurs*; but while he involved himself directly in producing theatre, his business methods were little different from other commercial producers.

By the mid-1870s the resident stock company and repertory system had become unprofitable to maintain and were rapidly being replaced by 'combination companies'. A play would open in New York, run until attendance lagged, then be transported in its entirety – actors, sets, properties – from city to city. The number of such 'combination companies' steadily increased until the *New York Dramatic Mirror* reported nearly 100 on the road during the 1876–7 season. MacKaye's *Hazel Kirke* (1880) was sent out in three road companies while still running in New York. Interest in local plays, companies and actors was replaced by interest in touring attractions. Theatrical trade papers in New York, such as *Dramatic News* (1875) and *Dramatic Mirror* (1879), were established to cater to this interest.

Touring in America promised financial rewards for international stars and native actors alike. ADELAIDE RISTORI made the first of several American tours in 1866, acting in Italian except for her last visit in 1884–5. The English actress ADELAIDE NEILSON made her first of two American appearances in 1872. TOMMASO SALVINI made his American debut in 1873 and returned four more times, playing with American actors in bilingual performances. HENRY E. ABBEY took SARAH BERNHARDT to the USA in 1880 for her first tour of seven months, which covered 50 cities and 156 performances. In 1883 Abbey also took HENRY IRVING, ELLEN TERRY and the Lyceum Company (see LYCEUM THEATRE (London)) for the first of several visits; Irving's carefully mounted productions set a new standard for the American stage. ELEONORA DUSE imported her natural style of acting to New York for the first of four visits in 1893 and, on her last international tour in 1924, died in Pittsburgh.

All major American stars toured. After the loss of his theatre in 1873, Edwin Booth spent the last two decades of his life touring in Shakespearian and pseudo-romantic plays, including two seasons (1887–9) with LAWRENCE BARRETT. JOHN MCCULLOUGH, an actor in the Forrest tradition, gave up management of the CALIFORNIA THEATRE (1875) to tour for the next nine seasons. Of the new generation of actors, Richard Mansfield toured in such eccentric parts as Baron Chevrial in *A Parisian Romance* (1883) and in the title roles in *Prince Karl* (1886), *Dr Jekyll and Mr Hyde* (1887), *Richard III* (1889), *Beau Brummel* (1890) and *Cyrano de Bergerac* (1898). Mansfield introduced SHAW to an American audience, as Bluntschli in *Arms and the Man* (1894) and later as Dick Dudgeon in *The Devil's Disciple* (1897). OTIS SKINNER had learned his trade in Booth's and Daly's companies and scrambled to play roles such as Hajj in *Kismet* (1911), which would best showcase his talents. E. H. SOTHERN made a hit with Edward Rose's romantic drama *The Prisoner of Zenda* (1895), and later acted Shakespeare together with his second wife, JULIA MARLOWE. The public's loss of interest in the traditional repertory and the demand for new plays left Mansfield and his generation scrambling to find suitable vehicles in which to star.

Establishing herself in the 1880s as a star in light comedy and melodrama, MINNIE MADDERN FISKE adjusted better to the demands of the new drama. She encouraged the production of Ibsen on the American stage by acting Nora in *A Doll's House* (1894), the title role in *Hedda Gabler* (1903), Rebecca West in *Rosmersholm* (1907) and Mrs Alving in *Ghosts* (1927). She also created the title character in Edward Sheldon's *Salvation Nell* (1908). Probably more effective in comedy, Mrs Fiske was praised for her psychological truthfulness and simplicity of effects. Critics associated her in style with Duse. She and her husband, HARRISON GREY FISKE, leased the Manhattan Theatre in 1903 and established an acting company, allowing them to remain independent of the Theatrical Syndicate.

ARNOLD DALY, like Mansfield, brought Shaw's plays before an American public. In 1903 he directed and starred in the American premiere of *Candida*, which ran for 133 performances. In 1904–5 he organized a company that produced *You Never Can Tell*, *The Man of Destiny*, *How He Lied to Her Husband*, a revival of *Candida* and *Mrs Warren's Profession*; the last was considered an immoral play and led to Daly's arrest (see CENSORSHIP). Although acquitted, he soon lost the zeal for dramatic reform and reverted to performing in standard works.

The growing power of the businessman in the American theatre can be evidenced in the 1890s with the demise of Palmer's and Daly's companies, and the rise of the Frohman brothers as New York's leading producers. DANIEL FROHMAN had assumed control of the Lyceum Theatre from Steele MacKaye in 1885 and established a stock company and acting school, which lasted from 1887 until 1902. His company included such stellar performers as E. H. Sothern, Virginia Harned, Mary Mannering, WILLIAM FAVERSHAM, Henrietta Crosman, HENRY MILLER, Georgia Cayvan, Herbert Kelcey and J. H. HACKETT. He minimized risks and maximized profits by producing bright new plays by established writers, including Belasco and DeMille's *The Charity Ball* (1889); HENRY ARTHUR JONES's *The Dancing Girl* (1891); PINERO's *Trelawny of the Wells* (1898); and Fitch's *The Moth and the Flame* (1898). CHARLES FROHMAN established two companies at PROCTOR's in 1890 to produce and tour new plays. In 1893 he built the EMPIRE THEATRE, which quickly gained the reputation of being a 'star factory'. He hired John Drew from Daly's company in 1892 and added William Gillette to his stable of stars, including MAUDE ADAMS, Ethel Barrymore (see DREW–BARRYMORE FAMILY) and Henry E. Dixey. His numerous hits include Belasco and Franklin Fyles's *The Girl I Left Behind Me* (1893); J. M. BARRIE's *The Little Minister* (1897) and *Peter Pan* (1905), both starring Maude Adams; and William Gillette's *Sherlock Holmes* (1899).

Charles Frohman is best known for organizing in 1896 a theatrical trust comprising three partnerships: Frohman and Al Hayman; the booking firm of Marc Klaw and Abraham L. Erlanger; and Philadelphia theatre owners S.F. Nixon and J. Fred Zimmerman. Called the [THEATRICAL] SYNDICATE, this trust gained a monopoly over the American theatre by controlling bookings, theatre buildings and talent. In 1896 they either operated or directly controlled 33 first-class houses from coast to coast, and by 1903 had extended their holdings to 70. At the height of their power, they had exclusive rights to book over 700 theatres. The cancelling of engagements, double bookings, broken contracts and general disorganization that characterized theatre of the 1880s were eliminated. For 15 years Frohman and the Syndicate tightly controlled the American theatre and ran it on 'big business' principles. They judged a play's worth solely on its ability to generate a profit. The SHUBERT BROTHERS' (Lee, Sam, and Jacob J.) 'Independent Movement' in 1900 challenged the position of the Syndicate; they also gained control over theatres from coast to coast, offered attractive bookings to independent managers, and began producing their own shows. Fierce competition between the two groups resulted in an oversupply of attractions and theatres; cities built separate theatres for Syndicate and Independent productions. Economic disaster was averted by an agreement between the two parties in 1914. Charles Frohman went down in the *Lusitania* in 1915, and afterwards the Syndicate declined in power. The SHUBERT ORGANIZATION has remained a vital force in the 20th-century American theatre.

Critics Walter Prichard Eaton, Norman Hapgood, BRANDER MATTHEWS, John Ranken Towse and William Winter denounced the Syndicate's purely commercial policy in the early 1900s and envisaged a national theatre supported by either public or private funds. Interest in the idea grew with the journal *Arena* publishing the symposium 'A National Art Theatre for America' in 1904. Four years later Heinrich Conried announced plans for such a company in New York, and despite his death the following year money was raised and the NEW THEATRE opened under WINTHROP AMES's direction, on 6 November 1909, with Julia Marlowe and E. H. Sothern in *Antony and Cleopatra*. The lack of a well trained company and the New Theatre's poor acoustics contributed to its demise in 1911, although the project may have been doomed from the start: 20th-century theatre problems could not be solved with 19th-century solutions.

This attempt to create an art theatre did express dissatisfaction with the triteness of the American stage, an attitude reinforced through visits in the 1910s by such foreign companies as the Irish Players of the ABBEY THEATRE (1911), MAX REINHARDT's company in *Sumurun* at the Casino Theatre (1912), GRANVILLE BARKER's productions at Wallack's Theatre for the New Stage Society of New York (1915), and JACQUES COPEAU's VIEUX-COLOMBIER Company at the Old Garrick Theatre (1917). These companies demonstrated that theatre could be more than manufactured entertainment for mass tastes and could touch the human mind and spirit in an important way. WILLIAM A. BRADY, a commercial producer, presented Edward Sheldon's *The Boss* (1911) and Shaw's *Major Barbara* (1915). Amateur theatre groups were organized throughout the country, inspired by artists such as Maurice Browne of the Chicago Little Theatre (1912). In New York, the WASHINGTON SQUARE PLAYERS (1914), led by LAWRENCE LANGNER and Edward Goodman, produced the plays of IBSEN, ANTON CHEKHOV and SHAW, as well as important new works by American writers. In 1916 the PROVINCETOWN PLAYERS presented *Bound East for Cardiff*, the first O'NEILL play to be staged. The same year, in Detroit, SHELDON CHENEY founded *Theatre Arts* [*Monthly*], a magazine dedicated to the art of the theatre. In 1919, members of the recently defunct Washington Square Players founded the THEATRE GUILD, the first US professional art theatre. Led by Lawrence Langner, PHILIP MOELLER, THERESA HELBURN and others, the Guild became an important theatre offering professional productions of plays not normally seen in the commercial theatre. TLM

3 The First World War to the 1960s After the First World War, Actors' Equity demanded improved working conditions in the theatre and pushed for unionization of the acting profession; this resulted in an actors' strike in 1919. Stagehands had first organized themselves into a union in 1886, and later had affiliated with the American Federation of Labor (1894). After several unsuccessful attempts, performers formed Actors' Equity in 1913. Producers, including George M. Cohan and the Shuberts, fought the union and were joined by many actors who considered themselves artists, not labourers; but on 6 August 1919 Equity went out on strike, demanding official recognition and a closed shop for legitimate performers. They were supported by the stagehands and musicians, and by the AFL. The Theatre Guild met Equity's terms immediately, but all other producers resisted, and their plays closed. On 6 September the producers capitulated and signed contracts that stipulated minimum contracts, improved rehearsal conditions, higher pay, and better working conditions.

In 1920 the Provincetown Players brought Eugene O'Neill's first full-length play, *Beyond the Horizon*, to Broadway, where it ran for 111 performances and won a Pulitzer Prize. Critics GEORGE JEAN NATHAN and Ludwig Lewisohn touted play and author as important new forces in the American theatre. O'Neill followed with *The Emperor Jones* (1920), an expressionistic drama (see EXPRESSIONISM) that featured CHARLES GILPIN and the scenery of CLEON THROCKMORTON, and *Anna Christie* (1921), starring Pauline Lord. Working quickly, within three years he had added *The Straw* (1921) and *The First Man* (1922), dominating the American theatre of the 1920s as no playwright had in previous decades.

Popular successes in the 1920s include AVERY HOPWOOD and Mary Roberts Rinehart's *The Bat* (1920), which ran for over two years, and ANNE NICHOLS's *Abie's Irish Rose* (1922), which received scathing reviews but survived for 2327 performances. Hopwood made a fortune writing such risqué fluff as *The Gold Diggers* (1919) and *The Demi-Virgin* (1921). The ZIEGFELD Follies began to look dated in the 1920s, but gaining in popularity were all-black REVUES, such as NOBLE SISSLE AND EUBIE BLAKE's *Shuffle Along* (1921), and *Blackbirds* (1928), a compendium of songs and dances that made a star of hoofer BILL 'BOJANGLES' ROBINSON. Musical comedy survived because of pretty chorus girls and memorable songs by VINCENT YOUMANS, GEORGE GERSHWIN, COLE PORTER and RICHARD RODGERS, and such superb performers as W. C. FIELDS, AL JOLSON, ED WYNN, FANNY BRICE, BERT WILLIAMS, WILL ROGERS, BERT LAHR and JIMMY DURANTE. George and IRA GERSHWIN created a new jazz style with hits such as *Lady, Be Good!* (1924), *Tip-Toes* (1925) and *Funny Face* (1927). The MARX BROS clowned in such vehicles as *The Cocoanuts* (1925) by GEORGE S. KAUFMAN and IRVING BERLIN, and *Animal Crackers* (1928) by Kaufman, Morrie Ryskind and others, after which they took their buffoonery to Hollywood.

Operetta remained popular, with long runs for Rudolf Friml's *Rose-Marie* (1924) and Sigmund Romberg's *The Student Prince* (1924) and *The Desert Song* (1926). *Show Boat* (1928), by JEROME KERN and OSCAR HAMMERSTEIN II, broke new ground by drawing on American musical traditions and by better integrating the book, music, songs and dances; JOSEPH URBAN designed the show, adding to his reputation for creating opulent sets for opera, theatre and the *Ziegfeld Follies*.

Although the New Theatre had failed to create a more artistic American stage in the early 1910s, efforts continued into the 1920s. ARTHUR HOPKINS, ROBERT EDMOND JONES and John Barrymore (see DREW–BARRYMORE FAMILY) combined forces in 1920 to present Shakespeare's *Richard III*, and two years later to revive *Hamlet* in a somewhat untraditional interpretation by Barrymore. The production ran for 101 performances, and Barrymore repeated his success in London (1925). In 1923, the MOSCOW ART THEATRE's acting company visited New York. As they praised its ensemble training, critics pretended not to notice that the company performed in Russian. Although the STANISLAVSKY system of acting was not unknown in the USA, demonstration of the MAT work to New York audi-ences had lasting impact. Two members of the company, RICHARD BOLESLAVSKI and Maria Ouspenskaya, remained in America to teach in the AMERICAN LABORATORY THEATRE. In 1924 WALTER HAMPDEN organized his own company at the Colonial (later the Hampden) Theatre and for five years offered Shakespeare, Ibsen, ROSTAND and other less commercial playwrights. EVA LE GALLIENNE leased the 50-year-old Fourteenth Street Theatre in 1926, gathered together a company of veterans and newcomers, and opened with Chekhov's *The Three Sisters*; few critics showed interest, but Le Gallienne kept her CIVIC REPERTORY THEATRE intact for six years, presenting 34 plays, most of which would have been fiscally impossible on Broadway.

Under the guidance of Lawrence Langner, the Theatre Guild emerged in the 1920s as America's most artistic producing organization. The company – which at one time included ALFRED LUNT AND LYNN FONTANNE, DUDLEY DIGGES, Helen Westley, LEE SIMONSON and Philip Moeller – presented a number of important world premieres, including Shaw's *Heartbreak House* (1920) and ELMER RICE's expressionistic *The Adding Machine* (1923). In 1925 they opened their own Guild Theatre with a production of Shaw's *Caesar and Cleopatra*. During 1920–30 the Guild offered 67 different productions, 15 the work of American playwrights.

American comedy became more worldly in the 1920s with George S. Kaufman, replacing its penchant for folksy, romantic and sentimental nonsense with witty and irreverent stabs at native society and culture. Kaufman and MARC CONNELLY's *Dulcy* (1921) elevated Lynn Fontanne to stardom and was the first of their collaborations, which included *To the Ladies* (1922), *Merton of the Movies* (1922) and *Beggar on Horseback* (1924), the last an expressionistic SATIRE on American business. Kaufman collaborated successfully with other writers, including EDNA FERBER and MOSS HART, while Connelly enjoyed his greatest triumph with *The Green Pastures* (1930), which played for 640 performances. GEORGE E. KELLY attracted attention in 1922 with *The Torchbearers*, a satire on the Little Theatre movement (see COMMUNITY THEATRE/LITTLE THEATRE MOVEMENT), before writing his highly popular comedy *The Show-Off* two years later and his Pulitzer Prize-winning *Craig's Wife* in 1925. PHILIP BARRY and S. N. BEHRMAN wrote fashionable comedies with wit and style, albeit a streak of sentimentality. Behrman's *The Second Man* (1927) featured Alfred Lunt and Lynn Fontanne in a comedy about an artist's choice between two women. Barry's *Paris Bound* (1927) and *Holiday* (1928) presented a charming portrait of the wealthy just before the stock market crash of 1929. His best play, *The Philadelphia Story* (1939), allowed Katharine Hepburn to dazzle in a light-hearted treatment of life among the wealthy. The best American farce of the 1920s was BEN HECHT and CHARLES MACARTHUR's *The Front Page* (1928), a cynical and satirical look at big-city life in Chicago.

Serious drama probed the romantic assumptions underlying American life. War received a realistic and truthful depiction in MAXWELL ANDERSON and Laurence Stalling's *What Price Glory* (1924), which George Jean Nathan thought superior to every other play inspired by the First World War. In the same year, O'Neill's *Desire under the Elms* offered a Freudian interpretation of New

England puritanism that relied for much of its power on Robert Edmond Jones's highly symbolic setting. The prolific O'Neill with mixed success examined other aspects of American life in *The Fountain* (1925), *The Great God Brown* (1926) and *Strange Interlude* (1928), the last a nine-act, five-hour dramatic novel that ran for 432 performances and won a Pulitzer. The same year, Maxwell Anderson and Harold Hickerson's *Gods of the Lightning* brought the Sacco and Vanzetti murder case before a New York audience. SIDNEY HOWARD dissected the American way of life in *They Knew What They Wanted* (1924), *Lucky Sam McCarver* (1925), *Ned McCobb's Daughter* (1926) and *The Silver Cord* (1927), the last about excessive maternal devotion. ROBERT E. SHERWOOD attracted attention in 1927 with *The Road to Rome*, a bittersweet re-enactment of Hannibal's march, starring JANE COWL.

At the end of the decade, radio and motion pictures emerged as rivals for the American theatre audience. Radio had grown from its first regular broadcasts in 1920 to a full-scale entertainment industry by 1930. Motion pictures added sound with *The Jazz Singer* in 1927, which made it possible to film stage plays and show them for a fraction of the cost of a theatre ticket. Between 1920 and 1930 theatres outside New York decreased in number from 1500 to 500, many converting to film, as the professional theatre in America became almost exclusively located in Manhattan. The Depression was radically to reduce what was left: during the 1927–8 Broadway season, the number of stage productions reached a record 280; by 1939–40 this had been reduced to 80.

The American theatre in the 1930s directly reflected the nation's political and economic crises. Leftist theatre groups proliferated, including the New Playwrights' Theatre (1926), Workers' Drama League (1929), Workers' Laboratory Theatre (1930), League of Workers' Theatres (1932) and Theatre Union (1933), among the most active. They were founded by writers such as Michael Gold and JOHN HOWARD LAWSON, who returned from Russia eager to form a theatre of the left. CLIFFORD ODETS's inflammatory *Waiting for Lefty* (1935) drew its early sponsorship from the League of Workers' Theatres. The Theatre Union gained an early success with *Peace on Earth* (1933), an anti-war piece, and *Stevedore* (1934), a play dealing with the relationship between black and white workers. Left-wing theatre remained a short-lived phenomenon of the 1930s, as its writers and artists were absorbed into the mainstream of American theatre and films. Many were blacklisted during the McCarthy hearings in the 1950s.

The Harlem Renaissance of the 1920s generated a new interest in black literature, which continued in the 1930s. Plays about blacks by whites – PAUL GREEN's *In Abraham's Bosom*, Marc Connelly's *Green Pastures* and O'Neill's *The Emperor Jones* – had been more successful than those by blacks until W. E. B. Du Bois, LANGSTON HUGHES and others organized black companies. Hughes's *Mulatto* (1935) was the most successful play by an AFRICAN-AMERICAN playwright in the 1930s.

Politically sensitive but more concerned with artistic ideals, the GROUP THEATRE began in 1931 as a palace revolt within the Theatre Guild, led by younger members HAROLD CLURMAN, CHERYL CRAWFORD and LEE STRASBERG. They were joined by 28 actors, including Franchot Tone, MORRIS CARNOVSKY, Clifford Odets, SANFORD MEISNER and STELLA ADLER, to set up a summer colony in Connecticut. Under the tutelage of Strasberg, the Group sought an acting technique for realistic plays. After a summer of work and analysis, the Group Theatre produced Paul Green's *The House of Connelly* (1931), followed by John Howard Lawson's *Success Story* (1932) and SIDNEY KINGSLEY's *Men in White* (1933). They discovered playwright Clifford Odets and produced his *Awake and Sing!* and *Waiting for Lefty*, both in 1935. They gave WILLIAM SAROYAN a hearing in 1939 with *My Heart's in the Highlands*, before running into financial problems in 1941 and disbanding.

In 1935 the FEDERAL THEATRE PROJECT was organized by the Works Progress Administration to create jobs for out-of-work theatre people. HALLIE FLANAGAN of the Vassar Experimental Theatre was appointed first director and charged with locating the unemployed and putting them to work. This, the first subsidized producing agency in US history, was disbanded by the government in 1939 on grounds of leftist infiltration. The Federal Theatre made several distinctive contributions to the American theatre, including the LIVING NEWSPAPER productions. African-American units of the Federal Theatre offered new plays by black authors, but are remembered mainly for the 'voodoo' *Macbeth* (1936), directed by ORSON WELLES, and the *Swing Mikado* (1938).

The CENSORSHIP and closing of the Federal Theatre's production of MARC BLITZSTEIN's *The Cradle Will Rock* (1937) led to the resignations of Welles and JOHN HOUSEMAN, and to their creation of the MERCURY THEATRE (New York). Welles, who had demonstrated a remarkable originality as a director both with MARLOWE's *Doctor Faustus* (1937) and the earlier *Macbeth*, directed an impressive modern-dress *Julius Caesar* (1937), with Fascist costumes and ABE FEDER's lighting.

The depressed economy sharply reduced the number of Broadway productions, prompting five playwrights – Robert Sherwood, Maxwell Anderson, Sidney Howard, S.N. Behrman and Elmer Rice – to join together in 1938 to form their own producing organization, the Playwrights' Company. Opening with Sherwood's *Abe Lincoln in Illinois* (1938), they presented Anderson's *Knickerbocker Holiday* (1938), Rice's *American Landscape* (1938) and Behrman's *No Time for Comedy* (1939), launching an ambitious programme that would survive until 1960. Together with the Theatre Guild, they set the standard for Broadway production in the late 1930s. The successful musicals of the 1930s tended to be both stylish and topical. George S. Kaufman and Howard Dietz's *The Band Wagon* (1931) offered brilliant artistry: directing by Hassard Short and dancing by FRED AND ADELE ASTAIRE. *Of Thee I Sing* (by the Gershwins, George S. Kaufman and Morrie Ryskind, 1931) satirized the supreme court, president, vice-president, diplomatic corps and the general humbug of American elections. In 1935, *Porgy and Bess* arrived on Broadway, with its serious musical score. In the 1940–1 season, *Pal Joey* (by Richard Rodgers and LORENZ HART) and *Lady in the Dark* (by Moss Hart, Ira Gershwin and KURT WEILL) offered more mature subjects and a worldly tone.

The Depression gripped the nation spiritually as well as economically, and set the tone for serious drama. O'Neill wrote *Mourning Becomes Electra* (1931), a six-hour play based on the *Oresteia*; Philip Moeller directed, Robert Edmond Jones designed, and ALLA NAZIMOVA, ALICE BRADY and Earle Larimore starred. Two years later *Tobacco Road* opened for a seven-year run, based on Erskine Caldwell's steamy novel of Georgia backwoods' poor white trash, starring Henry Hull as Jeeter Lester. In 1935 *Awake and Sing!*, Sidney Kingsley's *Dead End* and Maxwell Anderson's *Winterset* offered a sombre picture of the American dream. LILLIAN HELLMAN's *The Children's Hour* (1934) and *The Little Foxes* (1939), John Steinbeck's *Of Mice and Men* (1937) and THORNTON WILDER's epic *Our Town* (1938) suggested the anxiety underlying American life.

Bad economic times produced some of America's best comic writing. O'Neill penned a domestic comedy in 1933, *Ah, Wilderness!*, which critics thought sentimental and moralistic but reassuring. Sam and Bella Spewack's *Boy Meets Girl* (1935) provided a light-hearted spoof of Hollywood. Clare Boothe's *The Women* (1936) was a bitchy satire on idle and wealthy urban women. The Kaufman and Hart collaborations, *You Can't Take It with You* (1936) and *The Man Who Came to Dinner* (1939), were the funniest American comedies since *The Front Page*, and have remained classics. RACHEL CROTHERS returned from Hollywood in 1937 to write *Susan and God*, a satire on the efforts of a wife to reform her alcoholic husband. *My Heart's in the Highlands* and *The Time of Your Life* (both 1939) established William Saroyan as an important playwright. HOWARD LINDSAY and RUSSEL CROUSE's *Life with Father* (1939), starring Lindsay and Dorothy Stickney, became a smash hit that ran for 3216 performances, then a record. James Thurber and Elliott Nugent's *The Male Animal* appeared the same season, satirizing intellectual as well as romantic notions of the nation.

America's favourite acting couple, Alfred Lunt and Lynn Fontanne, remained popular throughout the 1930s, playing comedy with elegance, grace and perfect teamwork. KATHARINE CORNELL and HELEN HAYES were considered the first ladies of the American stage for their beauty and ability to play classical as well as modern roles. Other important actresses included TALLULAH BANKHEAD, Eva Le Gallienne, RUTH GORDON and Katharine Hepburn. Except for Alfred Lunt and John Barrymore (before he went to Hollywood), the American stage lacked distinguished males: The better younger players were opting for a career in films.

Broadway prospered during the Second World War. Irving Berlin's *This Is the Army* (1942), Rodgers and Hammerstein's *Oklahoma!* (1943) and *Carousel* (1945), and LEONARD BERNSTEIN's *On the Town* (1944) set the pace for musical entertainment. Much of America's serious drama depicted the war as simple melodrama, including Moss Hart's *Winged Victory* (1943), Maxwell Anderson's *Storm Operation* (1944) and James Gow and Arnaud D'Usseau's *Tomorrow the World* (1943), which were anti-Fascist. In the spring of 1945 TENNESSEE WILLIAMS's *A Glass Menagerie* opened on Broadway to excellent notices, with fine performances by LAURETTE TAYLOR, EDDIE DOWLING and Julie Haydon. Comedies offered little more than escape, except Thornton Wilder's *Skin of Our Teeth* (1942), which preached survival in a strange theatrical style. More typical were Joseph Kesselring's off-beat farce *Arsenic and Old Lace* (1941), JOHN VAN DRUTEN's sentimental *I*

Remember Mama (1944) and Mary Coyle Chase's fantastic *Harvey* (1944).

The immediate postwar period saw renewed activity by established writers, including O'Neill's *The Iceman Cometh* (1946), Hellman's *Another Part of the Forest* (1946), Maxwell Anderson's *Anne of the Thousand Days* (1948), Clifford Odets's *The Country Girl* (1950), and Kingsley's *Darkness at Noon* (1951), adapted from Arthur Koestler's novel. At the time of O'Neill's death in 1953, his reputation was in decline; a re-evaluation of his work began with JOSÉ QUINTERO's 1956 revival of *The Iceman Cometh* at CIRCLE IN THE SQUARE: JASON ROBARDS JR's portrayal of Hickey drew widespread praise and launched his career. Later that year, O'Neill's *Long Day's Journey into Night* premiered at the Helen Hayes Theatre under Quintero's direction and was hailed as the playwright's greatest work. *A Moon for the Misbegotten* followed in 1957 and *A Touch of the Poet* in 1958. In 1959, the Coronet Theatre in New York was renamed in O'Neill's honour.

Popular successes at the time reflected the public's continued interest in the war and its own idealism. GARSON KANIN's comedy *Born Yesterday* (1946) made a star of Judy Holliday. Other hits included William Wister Haines's melodrama *Command Decision* (1947); Norman Krasna's farce *John Loves Mary* (1947); Thomas Heggen and JOSHUA LOGAN's comedy *Mister Roberts* (1947), starring Henry Fonda; Donald Bevan and Edmund Trzcinski's thriller *Stalag 17* (1951); and Herman Wouk's courtroom drama *The Caine Mutiny Court Martial* (1954).

After the war, Tennessee Williams, ARTHUR MILLER and WILLIAM INGE emerged as the major new playwrights. *A Streetcar Named Desire* (1947), with stellar performances by MARLON BRANDO, JESSICA TANDY, Karl Malden and Kim Hunter, solidified the reputation Williams established with *The Glass Menagerie* and won both the Pulitzer Prize and the Critics' Circle Award. In 1947, Miller's *All My Sons* drew respectable notices and won the Drama Critics' Award; two years later his *Death of a Salesman*, under ELIA KAZAN's direction and with a brilliant performance by Lee J. Cobb, duplicated Williams's success. Williams and Miller depicted a society that had grown decadent, obsessed with materialism and power. Williams wrote with compassion and poetic insight about people unable to cope who seek escape through drink, drugs, daydreams and sex. His post-1950 plays include *The Rose Tattoo* (1951), *Cat on a Hot Tin Roof* (1955), *Orpheus Descending* (1957), *Sweet Bird of Youth* (1959) and *The Night of the Iguana* (1961); later his reputation suffered from such lesser pieces as *The Milk Train Doesn't Stop Here Anymore* (1963), *Vieux Carré* (1977) and *Clothes for a Summer Hotel* (1980). Arthur Miller focused more on the larger social and political issues in *The Crucible* (1953), *A View from the Bridge* (1956) and *Incident at Vichy* (1964); his latest plays were not well received in the USA. Inge's reputation has not worn as well as those of his two colleagues. In 1950 *Come Back, Little Sheba* established him as an important playwright and promoted the career of actress SHIRLEY BOOTH. Inge would enjoy meteoric success with hits *Picnic* (1953), *Bus Stop* (1955) and *The Dark at the Top of the Stairs* (1957) before his star faded in the 1960s; his plays now seem sentimental and contrived.

After the war, Rodgers and Hammerstein continued

their mastery of the musical with *South Pacific* (1949), *The King and I* (1951), and their last major collaboration, *The Sound of Music* (1959). This was a golden age of the American musical. Hits by other composers include Berlin's *Annie Get Your Gun* (1946) and *Call Me Madam* (1950); E.Y. Harburg and Fred Saidy's *Finian's Rainbow* (1947); LERNER AND LOEWE's *Brigadoon* (1947) and *My Fair Lady* (1956); Cole Porter's *Kiss Me, Kate* (1948); FRANK LOESSER's *Guys and Dolls* (1950); Bernstein's *Wonderful Town* (1953) and *West Side Story* (1957); and Jule Styne's *Gypsy* (1959). The American musical possessed energy and style and was recognized as the country's most original contribution to world theatre.

Comedy grew tame and unadventurous in the 1950s, relying on stock plots and comic devices. Ronald Alexander's domestic comedy *Time Out for Ginger* was a minor hit the same year (1952) that George Axelrod's sex farce, *The Seven Year Itch*, ran for 1141 presentations and made a star of Tom Ewell. Another smash hit, John Patrick's *The Teahouse of the August Moon* (1953), endured for 1027 performances and won both the Critics' Circle Award and Pulitzer Prize. Samuel Taylor's two hits, *Sabrina Fair* (1953) and *Pleasure of His Company* (1958), reminded audiences of Philip Barry and S. N. Behrman. George S. Kaufman and Howard Teichmann co-wrote a mild SATIRE about American business methods, *The Solid Gold Cadillac* (1953). Sidney Kingsley's farcical *Lunatics and Lovers* (1954) offered audiences a screwball comedy with Buddy Hackett. Thornton Wilder's *The Matchmaker*, which later served as the book for *Hello, Dolly!*, opened in 1955; likewise JEROME LAWRENCE AND ROBERT E. LEE's 1956 *Auntie Mame* was later transformed into the musical *Mame*. In 1959, Paddy Chayevsky's *The Tenth Man* provided mysticism and love in a plot that threatened to turn serious.

In the work of the ACTORS STUDIO, the postwar American theatre found an acting style in which to interpret the realistic plays of Williams, Miller and Inge. Elia Kazan, ROBERT LEWIS and CHERYL CRAWFORD founded the Studio in 1947, joined by Lee Strasberg a year later. Strasberg's system of acting based on STANISLAVSKY's writings became known as the Method and attracted a generation of actors including Marlon Brando and GERALDINE PAGE. Kazan became the prominent director of his age, mounting important premieres for all three playwrights. As if to underscore the passing of an era, in 1958 Lunt and Fontanne gave their farewell performance in *The Visit*.

In the 1920s, Robert Edmond Jones had set the standard for American stage scenery by evolving a style of simplified sets that suggested rather than reproduced reality. His successor, JO MIELZINER, dominated American stage design (see THEATRE DESIGN) from 1930 until his death in 1976. Mielziner used transparent scenery in a cinematic way to complement the poetic quality of plays by Williams and Miller. MING CHO LEE followed Mielziner as the major influence upon more contemporary stage design in a style that features collage, textured surfaces and scaffolding. Other important scenic artists of the postwar era include BORIS ARONSON, OLIVER SMITH, JEAN ROSENTHAL, SANTO LOQUASTO and EUGENE LEE.

After the Second World War, high production costs on BROADWAY and efforts to establish professional theatre outside of New York resulted in the OFF-BROADWAY and regional theatre movements. Off-Broadway recorded its first major success in 1952 with José Quintero's revival of Williams's *Summer and Smoke* at the Circle in the Square. The production reclaimed the play (which had earlier failed on Broadway) and made a star of Geraldine Page. Judith Malina and Julian Beck opened the LIVING THEATRE in 1951; NORRIS HOUGHTON and T. Edward Hambleton founded the Phoenix in 1953; and JOSEPH PAPP created the most important Off-Broadway theatre, the NEW YORK SHAKESPEARE FESTIVAL, in 1954. Outside New York, in 1947 MARGO JONES founded Theatre 47 in Dallas, and Nina Vance the ALLEY THEATRE in Houston. In 1950 ZELDA FICHANDLER and Edward Mangum created the ARENA STAGE in Washington, DC. Two years later HERBERT BLAU and Jules Irving established the Actors' Workshop in San Francisco. In 1955, the AMERICAN SHAKESPEARE [THEATRE] Festival opened in Stratford, Connecticut, joining the OREGON SHAKESPEARE FESTIVAL (founded in 1935) as a major summer company dedicated to the production of Shakespeare's plays (see SHAKESPEARE FESTIVALS (USA)). TLM

4 1960 to the present During the three decades between 1960 and 1990 American theatre changed profoundly. Most important, it decentralized: for the first time since resident repertory theatres disappeared in the late 19th century, theatre people could hope to conduct respectable careers independently of New York, while audiences in other regions gained consistent access to professional theatre.

Faced with mounting competition from television as well as rising production costs that discouraged risk and, by extension, inflated theatre tickets to luxury items, the Broadway commercial stage faded as the creative and economic heart of American theatre. Since the turn of the century, Broadway had been the sole locus of generating and casting new works, disseminated after their New York runs to other locales through Broadway's extension, 'the road'. Whereas 327 companies toured the country in 1900, by the 1990s the road had virtually disappeared, replaced by a network of non-profit, institutional theatres established in population centres throughout the country (see RESIDENT NON-PROFIT PROFESSIONAL THEATRE). Non-profit theatres were also linked with, and even founded as, adjuncts to theatre degree programmes at universities and colleges, a practice that has since spread abroad.

Together with the ALTERNATIVE THEATRES that sprang up Off and Off-Off Broadway and beyond, these regional theatres soon initiated most new American plays plus a significant percentage of musicals, formerly Broadway's special preserve. As the number of stable institutional theatres grew, expanding and diversifying their repertoires, the number of Broadway houses and productions in them shrank. Whereas 54 Broadway theatres presented an average of 146 productions per season in the 1930s, only 36 theatres offering 63 shows remained by 1964, a trend that continued. Also diminished was the sample of people prepared to buy expensive tickets for an ever narrower and more conservative range of fare dominated by small-cast comedies, blockbuster musicals and imports of British hits.

Alterations in the circumstances of production were accompanied by equally extensive ones in other areas of theatre and drama, advanced in the late 1950s and early 60s by a new theatrical generation with priorities at odds with those of the establishment. Socially committed and aesthetically radical, these pioneers were sympathetic to BERTOLT BRECHT'S EPIC THEATRE, ANTONIN ARTAUD'S Theatre of Cruelty, and the neo-Dadaist Happenings of the art world. Inspired by director-theoreticians PETER BROOK and JERZY GROTOWSKI, they would try to renew the stage by stripping away accumulated conventions to reach an essence – what Brook and Grotowski called a 'holy' core.

In the process, the style, structure and conventions of new American plays were retooled, as were subject-matter and creative methodology. New genres of theatre and interpretative strategies proliferated, among them cross-disciplinary hybrids such as dance theatre and performance art; docudrama, the hyper-real and simulations; environmental theatre; guerrilla theatre; structuralist theatre; poststructuralist or deconstructive theatre; choreodrama; and NEW VAUDEVILLE. With them came altered criteria for actors, directors and designers. Similarly, orthodox theatre architecture evolved or was abandoned for found environments and other untraditional spaces; arena and thrust stages became widespread, as did both 'black box' and flexible arrangements that combined familiar and novel features.

Meanwhile, the demographics of theatre expanded on stage and in the audience to include members of minority groups along with their cultural priorities, perspectives and styles. At first heard only on the fringe, the voices of African Americans, Latinos, Asians, gays and women would soon reach Broadway, where they would win Tonys and Pulitzer Prizes, the highest mainstream theatrical honours. This multicultural attitude extended to artistic and intellectual approaches from other countries, to which American theatre became more open than at any previous time in its history.

In tandem with such challenges to the status quo was a financial revolution with social implications affecting the place of theatre in American life. Government, foundation, corporate and individual donations joined the box office and private investment in the economic structure of the industry. As part of his Great Society programme, President Lyndon B. Johnson personally rammed the 1965 bill creating the National Endowment for the Arts (NEA) through the legislature. The government was back in show business for the first time since the FEDERAL THEATRE PROJECT of the Roosevelt administration, during the Great Depression of the 1930s, had been killed after four years by Congressional reactionaries in a fever of communist witch-hunting. The NEA would fund state arts councils, which in turn spawned municipal counterparts. This diversification of income sources signalled a growing acceptance of theatre as a cultural resource worthy of charitable support like museums, symphony orchestras and libraries. Labour-intensive and handmade in an age of assembly-line technology, theatre was becoming a vulnerable art form, increasingly unable to earn its own way and, therefore, in need of society's commitment to preserve it.

The ideological foundations of many of the transformations discussed above combined a diluted version of existentialism and absurdism with the post-Marxian, post-Freudian views of the New Left, plus liberal political theory and smatterings of Zen Buddhism and other Eastern systems of thought. The unconsoling visions of the existential and the absurd captured the temper of an exhausted, postwar Europe better than they did that of the continental USA, which had escaped invasion and was soon enjoying rapid economic expansion. These philosophies, moreover, ran contrary to a deeply entrenched belief, central to the country's self-image, in the purposeful unfolding of individual and national progress. Turning away from REALISM and its psychological acting approaches, emerging American playwrights like EDWARD ALBEE, ARTHUR KOPIT and JOHN GUARE embraced the absurdist stylistic vocabulary, but discarded most of the existentialist content. What remained surfaced through such thinkers as Erich Fromm and Martin Buber as a faith in the redeeming power of interpersonal love.

Purged of Fromm and Buber's theological arguments and eroticized by New Left pundits, love became the buzzword of 1960s idealists. In support of the civil rights movement and in rebellion against the escalating Vietnam War, the children of this generation, armed with flowers, would muster love to challenge the leadership of the nation and the prevailing mores of their society, which they believed hypocritical, soullessly commercial and militaristic. In a New Left take on this sentiment, the Living Theatre enacted its signature 'love pile' of embracing spectators and performers, and the nude actors of the PERFORMANCE GROUP moved among audience members to caress them.

The chief representatives of the New Left were Herbert Marcuse, Norman O. Brown and R. D. Laing, who, together with allied social thinkers such as Erving Goffman, Eric Berne, Marshall McLuhan and Claude Lévi-Strauss, articulated a rationale for social, political and aesthetic agendas of the 1960s. All neo-romantic stances, they attack reason, handmaiden of the science that promised utopia but delivered the tools for world annihilation; instead they promoted intuition, emotion and sensuality as antidotes to the pathology of the post-industrial world. Theory and social practice meshed as the youthful counterculture – liberated by relaxed obscenity laws and improved birth control methods – dropped out of society, turned on to sex and drugs, and tuned in to rock and roll, a phenomenon reflected in plays like Jack Gelber's *The Connection* (1959), Dale Wasserman's *One Flew over the Cuckoo's Nest* (1963), the hippie musical *Hair* (1967), the Performance Group's *Dionysus in '69* (1968), Robert Patrick's *Kennedy's Children* (1970) and MICHAEL WELLER'S *Moonchildren* (1972).

Recalling a familiar American motif, the free expression of individuality was equated with present satisfaction and a bright future; hostile forces dictating conformity were linked with the past. Taking up this theme, the new generation rejected their parents' material dream along with the competitive instincts and hierarchical structures that accompanied it.

In the theatre, these ideas supported experiments of theatre artists who formed or refocused their companies in the late 1950s and the 60s, among them such diverse talents as Judith Malina and Julian Beck (the Living Theatre), JOSEPH CHAIKIN (the OPEN THEATRE), Peter Schumann

(BREAD AND PUPPET THEATRE), Richard Schechner, and ANDRE GREGORY (the Manhattan Project). Like the Group Theatre of the 1930s, most would organize their companies and create their plays communally, a principle they extended to collective playwriting (see COLLECTIVE THEATRE GROUPS) and to the stage itself, where the ensemble, not individual actors, starred. Whatever their differences, all would discard psychological acting for the presentational, realistic and naturalistic dramaturgy for theatricalist idioms, and long-standing conventions of decorum for nudity and obscenity. Operating largely outside the commercial system, they re-examined traditional relationships between actor and character, stage and auditorium, theatre and other arts, and theatre and life.

'Theatre and life are one,' wrote Peter Brook in *The Empty Space* (1968), and in this era they often were. Political demonstrators co-opted dramatic techniques, producing events with an eye to television, for over 50 million sets were in use in America by 1960. John Cage used the chance procedures and recordings of everyday noise in his compositions; choreographers like Merce Cunningham and Ann Halprin created dances from everyday behaviour and presented them in everyday locales; and in his Happenings, Allan Kaprow blurred the distinction between life and art, artist and audience. Simultaneously, activist theatre companies such as the Living Theatre, the Bread and Puppet Theatre, EL TEATRO CAMPESINO and the SAN FRANCISCO MIME TROUPE took to the streets, theatricalizing the environment.

Sociology and psychology, among other disciplines, also cross-pollinated with theatre. Analysts adapted actor-training techniques to therapy, while companies interested in renewing the actor's craft lifted sensitivity-training techniques from psychology. Such groups also explored the games theories of human behaviour popularized by Goffman and Berne and adapted for the theatre by Viola Spolin. Her techniques of transformational acting came to both mainstream and alternative theatres, through not only her influential book, *Improvisation for the Theatre* (1963), but also the work of her son Paul Sills, who in the 1950s practised his mother's theories at Chicago's Compass and Second City improvisational theatres, then went on in the 1960s to originate another new genre, Story Theatre.

Centred in the Greenwich Village district of Manhattan where rents were then low and a bohemian atmosphere friendly to the arts prevailed, the kindred Off-Broadway movement had begun in the 1950s as a low-overhead but still commercial venue for work with scant Broadway potential: classics, revivals of neglected American plays, and American premieres of recent European plays by innovative writers like GENET and Brecht. By 1960, however, the same economic pressures that would cripple Broadway had infected Off-Broadway, giving rise to the next wave of alternative theatres. By the late 1970s only a few Off-Broadway producers still functioned, and today only a handful of the once numerous little playhouses of no more than 299 seats still attempt to operate commercially. Operating costs tripled while capacity remained static; consequently fare grew more conservative. Revues, improvisational comedy troupes and small-scale MUSICALS like *The Fantasticks* (1960, now in its fourth decade) became staples, while more daring work shifted to Off-Off Broadway (OOB).

OFF-OFF BROADWAY became what Off-Broadway was not – a forum devoted to new American plays, a laboratory for cutting-edge critical theory, and a home for the artistic expression of heterodox social and political thought. Newcomers, many of them more interested in process than in creating a lasting work of art, improvised stages in lofts, church basements, coffee-houses, parks and garages.

The Off-Off Broadway movement was spurred on in 1959 with CAFFE CINO, which began presenting plays by such new writers as MARIA IRENE FORNÉS, TERRENCE MCNALLY and JEAN-CLAUDE VAN ITALLIE. LA MAMA, founded in 1961 by Ellen Stewart, has continued to be the most durable of the 1960s venues (although its future in the early 1990s was in doubt), producing new playwrights in addition to providing a platform for young directors, among them Tom O'Horgan, Wilford Leach and ANDREI SERBAN. Others followed rapidly: Al Carmines's Judson Poets' Theatre (1961), Wynn Handman's AMERICAN PLACE THEATRE (1964), Ralph Cook's Theatre Genesis (1964) and New York's PUBLIC THEATER (1967), the developmental arm of the New York Shakespeare Festival, arguably the most important producing organization of the postwar era.

As the 1970s approached, experimental theatre turned away from the public art of the 60s towards inner visions that were apolitical, anti-historical and self-reflexive. Individualistic where their predecessors were communitarian, RICHARD FOREMAN's Ontological-Hysteric Theatre (1968), ROBERT WILSON's Byrd Hoffman School of Birds (1969) and LEE BREUER with the MABOU MINES (1970) mediated on formalist concerns more closely akin to developments in music, dance and art than to conventional theatre. Like Gertrude Stein before them, they were fascinated by their own creative processes and the pictures screened in their imaginations. Together with such allied performance artists as PING CHONG, LAURIE ANDERSON and MEREDITH MONK, this group represents what is called Theatre of Images. This rubric reflects the strongly visual, even painterly, qualities of their productions together with a corresponding disruption of language as rational discourse, reversing the time-honoured authority of the word over spectacle, mind over sensory perception. Neither are Theatre of Images plays driven by coherent linear plots; rather they operate spacially and, like music, enlarge on motifs. Nor do actors inhabit characters; instead they function performatively, like kinetic sculpture in surreal dreamscapes. The Theatre of Images leaves spectators, like visitors to a contemporary art gallery, to make what they will of what they individually see.

Wilson's work is mystical and operatic, Foreman's rigorously cerebral, whereas Breuer's juxtaposes icons of popular and elite culture. All exploit multiple media as well as postmodern, deconstructive strategies. These methods have passed to 1980s imagists such as JOANNE AKALAITIS, ELIZABETH LECOMPTE with the WOOSTER GROUP, MARTHA CLARKE in her dance-theatre, and writer-director John Jesurun, who applies sculptural and cinematic ideas to theatre.

The self-dramatizing impulse of the Theatre of Images is akin to the art world performances of the 1960s and 70s in which the materials of artists such as California's Chris

Burden were their own bodies. In the name of immediacy, Burden variously crawled on glass and stuck pins in his stomach. A gentler strain appears in today's numerous autobiographical monologuists, among whom SPALDING GRAY is king. Others followed in the 1980s, emerging from the performance clubs of the East Village to play at P.S. 122, Dance Theatre Workshop, the Kitchen, Franklyn Furnance and other showcases for prickly fringe art, with the lucky few moving on to the Brooklyn Academy of Music's New Wave Festival and Lincoln Center's counterpart, Serious Fun, and occasionally to Broadway, where Lily Tomlin and Whoopi Goldberg have performed one-person shows italicizing race, gender and self. While this trend reflects both the enterprise of actor-writers in a shrinking market and a liking for alternative career paths inherited from the 1960s, it also suggests the spirit of the narcissistic era that writer Tom Wolfe has called the 'Me Generation'.

Only a decade from its inception, the OOB movement of the 1970s had grown enough to warrant a collective service organization, the Off-Off Broadway Alliance (OOBA), later succeeded by the Alliance of Resident Theatres/New York. By 1974-5 there were 150 OOB theatres, which had produced 548 plays that season. After the mid-1970s, however, OOB took a more conservative turn: the reaction of social and aesthetic forces with erotic energy that had enlivened the 1960s artistic scene slowed just as inflation rose and the national economy slumped.

The sensibilities of Caffe Cino and La MaMa playwrights like Tom Eyen, Robert Heide, ROCHELLE OWENS, Ronald Tavel and Paul Foster no longer seemed to capture the post-Vietnam times. The Bread and Puppet Theatre retreated to Vermont (1970) and the Open Theatre disbanded (1973), as did the Performance Group (1979) and the Manhattan Project, the Judson Poets' Theatre (1981), Theatre Genesis and others. In their stead arose not-for-profit theatres with long-term institutional goals and more traditional artistic tastes. The CIRCLE REPERTORY COMPANY (1969), PLAYWRIGHTS HORIZONS (1971), Ensemble Studio Theatre (1971) and Second Stage (1979) emphasized the work of American playwrights like A. R. GURNEY, TINA HOWE, ROMULUS LINNEY, Ronald Ribman or CHRISTOPHER DURANG, whose 1970s works had relatively familiar dramaturgic genes. Others, such as the Chelsea Theatre Center, the MANHATTAN THEATRE CLUB, the ACTING COMPANY and the Dodger Theatre (1978) mixed new American plays with premieres of foreign plays or freshly interpreted standards. At first outsiders, these groups would become fixtures of the mainstream theatre. Ironically, four non-profit theatres, all specializing in revivals, have moved to homes in Broadway playhouses: the Circle in the Square, Uptown, the Roundabout Theatre Company, and the brand-new National Actors Theatre, founded by actor Tony Randall in autumn 1991.

In addition to the theatrical movements outlined above, theatre of the 1960s and 70s embraced racial causes, gender issues, anti-war sentiments, and the interests of many other constituencies as diverse as the deaf (National Theatre of the Deaf, 1967), former prison inmates (the Family, 1972) and the elderly (Tale Spinners, 1975). Here minority artists found regular employment, while long-disenfranchised audiences could now see plays by one of their own in which the destinies of characters like themselves were central rather than background to the American saga.

AFRICAN-AMERICAN THEATRE has won the most prominent place in both non-profit and commercial arenas. Whereas in 1948 black novelist and playwright JAMES BALDWIN moved to France to escape racism at home, in 1990 AUGUST WILSON collected his second Pulitzer Prize for Drama. While Broadway had long mounted musicals and revues by and about African Americans, commercial productions of legitimate plays were rare and runs short. Black drama awaited the moral and political momentum of the emerging civil rights movement. The first great cross-over was LORRAINE HANSBERRY's play *Raisin in the Sun* (1959), which ran on Broadway for 530 performances and won the New York Drama Critics' Circle Award – a first not only for an African American but also for a woman. It would make both a profit and the careers of the original and later cast members, including Sidney Poitier, OSSIE DAVIS, RUBY DEE, Claudia McNeil, Diana Sands and Louis Gossett Jr. Its director, LLOYD RICHARDS, went on to open establishment doors for numerous other black artists; he also affected national arts policy as head of the influential National Playwrights Conference and of one of the country's most prestigious theatrical training grounds, the Yale School of Drama, together with its professional arm, the YALE REPERTORY THEATRE.

Other commercial hits would follow *Raisin*, among them Ossie Davis's *Purlie Victorious* (1961), but the mood of African-American drama now became militant, discouraging white, male, commercial producers. Until the mid-1980s, musicals remained the chief Broadway outlet for black talent, and remains a major one today.

The new, increasingly confrontational black drama took its cue more from Malcolm X's Black Power movement than from Martin Luther King's dream of integration. Baldwin's *Blues for Mister Charlie* (1964) dealt with the death of a civil rights worker, anticipating the fierce plays of LeRoi Jones (AMIRI BARAKA) and ED BULLINS, who both saw theatre as the artistic arm of radical politics and orthodox dramaturgy as an aspect of white oppression. Writing unsparingly of their dual experiences as women in a man's world and blacks in a white society, playwrights ADRIENNE KENNEDY and NTOZAKE SHANGE developed unique dramatic forms that owed more to poetry than to theatrical precedent.

At the same time, the Johnson Administration's poverty programmes made government funds available to bolster black theatre companies like Amiri Baraka's Spirit House in Newark, NJ, support augmented after 1965 by the new NEA. With both public and private moneys to support their growth, troupes sprang up nationwide, most important among them the Free Southern Theatre (New Orleans), New Lafayette Theatre, Harlem (see LAFAYETTE PLAYERS), NEGRO ENSEMBLE COMPANY (the East Village), Concept East (Detroit) and Black Arts/West (San Francisco). By 1968 there were 40 such groups, and when the first National Black Theatre Festival convened in Winston-Salem, North Carolina, in 1989, some 200 theatres were represented.

DOUGLAS TURNER WARD, LONNE ELDER, Joseph A. Walker, Philip Hayes Dean, Sonia Sanchez, DEREK WALCOTT, Leslie

Lee, Richard Wesley and Ron Milner were among the new playwrights. So were ALICE CHILDRESS, the first black woman to have a play professionally produced in America (*Trouble in Mind*, 1952); Charles Gordone, whose *No Place to Be Somebody* (1970) won the first Pulitzer Prize for Drama awarded to an African-American dramatist; and CHARLES FULLER, who won the second for *A Soldier's Play* in 1981. Their achievements would ease the way for the present generation of playwrights, including August Wilson, Suzan-Lori Parks and GEORGE C. WOLFE.

Other racial minorities also found theatre an effective tool for dealing with discrimination and asserting their place in the national mosaic. Hanay Geiogamah's Native American Theatre Ensemble evolved out of the American Indian Movement of the late 1960s, as did Spiderwoman (1975), a feminist theatre founded by Muriel Miguel and her sisters, Cuna/Rappahannock Indians. LUIS VALDÉZ established El Teatro Campesino on a flatbed lorry beside the picket lines of California's Chicano and Filipino grape pickers, then embraced the larger dilemma of CHICANOS caught between Mexican and American cultures. New York theatres, such as INTAR (the Hispanic-American Arts Center), the Repertorio Español and the Puerto Rican Traveling Theatre, have expanded the opportunities for Latino actors and directors. Together with programmes for Latino writers at the New York Shakespeare Festival and several regional theatres, such companies have nurtured enough able playwrights – Lynne Alvarez and Eduardo Machado among them – to fill a recent anthology of contemporary HISPANIC-American plays.

Except for such pseudo-Oriental plays by white authors as *Teahouse of the August Moon* or musicals like *The King and I* and *Flower Drum Song*, Asians were theatrically near-invisible until 1965 when the East West Players were established in Los Angeles, followed by the Asian-American Workshop in San Francisco and the Pan Asian Repertory in New York. Today ASIAN-AMERICAN playwrights are regularly produced in the subsidized theatre, including Frank Chin, PHILIP KAN GOTANDA, Jessica Hagedorn and James Yoshimura. The first Broadway accolades went to Chinese-American playwright David Henry Hwang for his *M. Butterfly*.

Gay theatre groups were formed in the 1960s following the efforts of activists to gain recognition and respect for the homosexual lifestyle. While some gay theatre has existed for its own subculture, Mark Crowley's *The Boys in the Band* (1968) ran for 1000 performances Off-Broadway. The acceptance of homosexual subjects by mainstream audiences gained momentum in the 1980s. Harvey Fierstein's *Torch Song Trilogy* (1982) won the Drama Critics' Award and Tony for Best Play, followed the next season by the hit Jerry Herman/Fierstein musical *La Cage aux Folles*. Gay and LESBIAN THEATRE companies formed an Alliance in 1978, with 28 groups identified across the country in 1981.

Predominantly camp performances of the late 1960s and 70s have faded and been replaced by a sober response to AIDS, the fatal disorder that has hit the performing arts community particularly hard. Plays such as Larry Kramer's *The Normal Heart* (1985) and *The Destiny of Me* (1992), William M. Hoffman's *As Is* (1985) or Paula Vogel's *The Baltimore Waltz* (1991) abandon the earlier cele-

bratory posture for one of grief for the dead and rage against the sluggish official response to the epidemic. In 1987 Kramer shifted his focus from the stage to the streets, founding ACT-UP (AIDS Coalition to Unleash Power) and utilizing theatricalized civil disobedience to promote political action. In recognition of its efforts, ACT-UP received a Bessie Award, the Tony of performance art.

On the heels of the women's liberation movement – itself an offspring of civil rights initiatives – women's and FEMINIST THEATRES were widely established in the 1970s, and women began to enter the professional theatre in unprecedented numbers, not only as actresses, but as everything from artistic directors to stage managers and critics. By the 1980s the value of women to establishment theatre was acknowledged in Pulitzer Prizes to BETH HENLEY, MARSHA NORMAN and WENDY WASSERSTEIN, raising by 50 per cent the total number of the prizes to women playwrights since their inception in 1918. In 1982 ELLEN BURSTYN became the first woman president of the Actors' Equity Association, followed by COLLEEN DEWHURST in 1984, the same year that Heidi Landesman won the Tony for her sets for *Big River*, the first such award to a woman designer. Another landmark was the inauguration in Buffalo, NY, of an International Women's Playwrights Conference (1988), which drew some 291 women representing 34 nations.

Unlike the Pulitzer winners, many playwrights with feminist sensibilities held unorthodox views of dramatic structure, characterization and other theatrical verities, among them Shange, Fornés and Kennedy, as well as Eve Merriman, Megan Terry, Corinne Jacker, Karen Malpede, Rosalyn Drexler and Susan Yankowitz. Their homes were the activist, feminist companies on the fringe. Regional groups included Boston's Caravan Theatre (1965), the Rhode Island Feminist Theatre (1973), the Omaha Magic Theatre (1968), At the Foot of the Mountain (1974), the Washington Area Feminist Theatre (1972) and Circle of the Witches (1973). In New York the New Feminist Repertory was founded in 1969, followed by Women's Interart Theatre (1971), the New York Feminist Theatre Troupe (1973), the Women's Experimental Theatre (1976), the New Cycle Theatre (1977) and the Women's Project (1978; see WOMEN'S PROJECT AND PRODUCTIONS). By 1980 the number of such women's theatres had grown to 110.

Although women in performance art were initially hostile to theatre, by the 1980s the genre had attracted a sizeable number of theatre people, particularly feminists: for example, Robbie McCauley, an African American, deals with issues of race and gender; Rachel Rosenthal often explores attitudes to the female body, as does KAREN FINLEY; and HOLLY HUGHES looks at lesbian sexuality. All of their work is in part autobiographical, all centred on the performer rather than production values, all both formally and thematically experimental.

In addition to ETHNIC, gender and sexual diversification, the late 1960s also saw a proliferation of anti-American plays as the nation turned against the Vietnam War. The San Francisco Mime Troupe, Yale Repertory Theatre and the Living Theatre all performed AGIT-PROP, anti-war material, as would the Bread and Puppet Theatre, the Performance Group, La MaMa ETC, the Open Theatre and others. Among the anti-war plays were Robert Lowell's *The Old Glory* (1964), Megan Terry's *Viet Rock* (1966), Joseph Heller's *We Bombed in New Heaven* (1968) and DAVID RABE's Vietnam trilogy: *The Basic Training of Pavlo Hummel* (1968), *Sticks and Bones* (1971) and *Streamers* (1976). Most Vietnam plays look at the home front rather than battlefield trauma, with Amlin Gray's *How I Got That Story* (1979) a partial exception.

Arising at the same time were docudramas inspired by the work of German playwrights ROLF HOCHHUTH and PETER WEISS, who used oral history and the public record to indict corrupt official acts. Daniel Berrigan drew on courtroom transcripts for *The Trial of the Catonsville Nine* (1971), a government prosecution of Berrigan and fellow draft opponents, while ERIC BENTLEY exploited Congressional annals for *Are You Now Or Have You Ever Been* (1972), his look at the 1950s McCarthy hearings. Following in this tradition is Emily Mann's *Execution of Justice* (1982), a montage of perspectives on the murder of a gay San Francisco councilman, Harvey Milk. A related group of protest plays responded to fears of Apocalypse in the age of nuclear warefare, among them SAM SHEPARD's *Icarus's Mother* (1965), Edward Albee's *Box* (1968), Tennessee Williams's *The Red Devil Battery Sign* (1975) and the Mabou Mines's *Dead End Kids* (1982).

Stimulated by large grants – beginning in 1959 with the Ford Foundation followed by the Rockefeller Foundation and others, and including support from the NEA – the regional theatre movement had begun to gain significant momentum by the mid-1960s. It built on the initiatives of small, pioneer companies, all begun by neophyte directors opposed to Broadway's commercial standards and in search of somewhere else to work. In 1961 Ford created the Theatre Communications Group (TCG) to assist the RESIDENT NON-PROFIT sector. Important regional companies followed: the GUTHRIE THEATRE in Minneapolis and the SEATTLE REPERTORY (both founded in 1963); the ACTORS THEATRE OF LOUISVILLE, Kentucky, and TRINITY REPERTORY COMPANY of Providence, Rhode Island (both 1964); LONG WHARF THEATRE in New Haven, Connecticut (1965); Yale Repertory Theatre (1966); and the AMERICAN CONSERVATORY THEATER in San Francisco (1966). Cultural centres – among them Lincoln Center in New York, JOHN F. KENNEDY CENTER in Washington, DC, and the Music Center in Los Angeles – were built with theatres as part of their complexes. By 1992 these modest beginnings had grown into a network of some 229 theatres nationwide. Most called themselves resident repertory companies, although in most cases only management was resident and shows were rarely produced in rotating rep, which proved prohibitively expensive. Initially, the repertoires of these theatres were biased towards the conservatively interpreted classics and standards favoured by establishment board members and subscribers; but by the early 1970s more risk-taking and production of new plays seemed possible – though in the unsure atmosphere of the economy in the 1990s there has been a return to safer, less experimental fare in many regional theatres.

While in New York the new theatre evolved downtown and elsewhere, the Broadway of the 1960s and 70s remained lively, although each year it owed more to products developed elsewhere. Its dominant playwrights were NEIL SIMON and Edward Albee, who from different angles would both explore deteriorating family personal relationships and the inability of individuals to maintain community. Simon's long list of comedies reached a climax with his Pulitzer Prize-winning *Lost in Yonkers* (1991). Albee emerged as the 1960s' major dramatist with *Who's Afraid of Virginia Woolf?* (1962) after early successes with a series of one-act plays. He won the Pulitzer Prize in 1966 for *A Delicate Balance*. After little success for the next 25 years, in 1994 he again won a Pulitzer, for *Three Tall Women*.

Rock music and NUDITY went mainstream in the 1960s when the counterculture musical *Hair* (1967) transferred from the Public Theater to Broadway, where it remained a cultural as well as an artistic event and spawned a wave of imitations. Traditional musical forms, however, continued to dominate, represented by *Camelot* (1960), *Fiddler on the Roof* (1964), *Hello, Dolly!* (1964), *Funny Girl* (1964), *Man of La Mancha* (1965), *Mame* (1966) and *Cabaret* (1966).

Dominating MUSICAL THEATRE since the mid-1970s is STEPHEN SONDHEIM. Though one of his latest efforts, *Assassins*, was not successful in New York City, he is nevertheless widely regarded as the most original and innovative composer-lyricist now writing in the American theatre. For most of his career he worked closely with director HAROLD PRINCE, a major force in the development of the American musical. By the mid-1980s, the choreographer-director had been elevated to a new position of power as the American musical had become less dependent upon a book than on a concept or theme. The best known of the new breed were the late BOB FOSSE and MICHAEL BENNETT, the latter responsible for developing the longest-running show on Broadway, *A Chorus Line* (1973). Today, only director-choreographer TOMMY TUNE retains a reputation comparable to his predecessors.

Much of the best drama of the 1970s and 80s came from Off-Broadway and from the trio of Sam Shepard, LANFORD WILSON and DAVID MAMET, who have produced some of the most resonant American dramas of the post-1960s decades. Shepard's plays appear realistic on the surface, belying their vivid theatricality and close relationship with the absurd (see THEATRE OF THE ABSURD). His characters struggle towards some kind of transcendental experience; his plays depend not on well made plots but on highly personal images to which the audience must find connections. Wilson's lyrical prose suggests the influence of Tennessee Williams. Arguably his best play, *Fifth of July* (1978) became a metaphor for an entire generation coming to terms with its own failed idealism. Mamet uses language brilliantly to depict the spiritual emptiness that lies at the core of contemporary American life, though whereas Wilson is a lyric realist and Shepard takes a mythic tone, Mamet's signature is a terse and profane urban vernacular that brings to mind the crisp, hard-driving and quick-changing phrases of 1920s Chicago jazz.

Mamet's career, in fact, began in Chicago at the St Nicholas Theatre, which he helped to found in 1974. During the 1960s and 70s, anchored by the older GOODMAN THEATRE and encouraged by the brainy irreverence of Second City, Chicago developed a nationally acclaimed alternative enclave of husky off-loop companies (i.e. situated outside the city's 'loop') – Body Politic, the Organic Theatre, Victory Gardens, St Nicholas, STEPPENWOLF.

Although still not as theatrically active as New York, Chicago has become a major US theatre centre of the 1990s.

Since 1970, transfers of London successes have often fleshed out Broadway seasons, among them PETER SHAFFER's *Equus* and *Amadeus*; DAVID STOREY's *The Changing Room* and *Home*; TOM STOPPARD's *Travesties, The Real Thing, Hapgood and Arcadia*; ANDREW LLOYD WEBBER and TIM RICE's *Jesus Christ Superstar* and *Evita*, as well as Lloyd Webber's *Cats, Phantom of the Opera* and *Sunset Boulevard*; HAROLD PINTER's *The Homecoming* and *Betrayal*; and plays by DAVID HARE, SIMON GRAY, CARYL CHURCHILL and others. The ROYAL SHAKESPEARE COMPANY, which has visited several times, is especially remembered for *The Life and Adventures of Nicholas Nickleby* in 1980, a production whose staging approaches owed something to the theatricalist styles of the American experimental theatre of the 1960s and 70s and influenced subsequent dramaturgy, staging approaches and box office prices (with its top $100 ticket, a new Broadway high).

The American theatre from the mid-1980s into the 1990s depended less on Broadway than at any time this century, and more on the resident non-profit theatres both in and outside of New York, clearly illustrated by the 1992–3 season's successes – *The Who's Tommy, Angels in America, Kiss of the Spider Woman*. Each of these began their development outside of New York. Indeed, new plays now originated regularly at such theatres as the New York Shakespeare Festival, Playwrights Horizons, Chicago's Steppenwolf Theatre Company and Goodman Theatre, the Yale Repertory Theatre, AMERICAN REPERTORY THEATRE at Harvard, Mark Taper Forum in Los Angeles, Actors Theatre of Louisville and New Haven's Long Wharf Theatre, among many others. *Best Plays of 1984–5* reported that 6 of their 10 best plays did not originate on Broadway. In 1992, for the first time, the Pulitzer Prize for Drama (for 1991) was awarded to a play that had not been previously produced in New York City (Robert Schenkkhan's *The Kentucky Cycle*; it did open for a brief Broadway run in late 1993).

High costs continued to make producing in Manhattan a risky business. During the 1984–5 season, for example, a new musical, *Grind*, lost its entire investment of $4,750,000; in 1992 a comparable production lost closer to $8,000,000 (the musical *Cyrano* that year lost $10,000,000). The *New York Times* reported that a revival of *Arsenic and Old Lace* in 1986 cost $700,000 compared to the original amount in 1941 of $37,000. Even Off-Broadway plays cost up to $400,000 to produce. Ticket prices of $40–60 for Broadway had become the norm. Nevertheless, the 1992–3 Broadway season recorded a new high in ticket sales ($327.7 million) and saw a 6.5 per cent increase in attendance over the previous season, yet fewer productions were presented (33 in contrast to 1991–2's 37 – more productions than in any of the preceding five years). Yet three decades ago an average of 63 new productions opened each season. The major change is that today successful shows run much longer, individuals attend Broadway with less frequency, and much of the business is from out of town.

Production values in the American theatre of the 1980s remained high. The Broadway musical, though less dependent on American products, had no equal, with a wide array of talented young performers including Bernadette Peters, Mandy Patinkin, Faith Prince, Ben Vereen and Brent Carver. Prevalent was a serious problem resulting from the dearth of composers and writers who could attract a large enough audience to reward investors, a situation that had abated little in the early 1990s. A new generation of talented actors, among them Judith Ivey, John Lithgow, Meryl Streep, WILLIAM HURT, Pamela Reed, Lindsay Crouse, KEVIN KLINE, Mary Beth Hurt, GLENN CLOSE, STOCKARD CHANNING and Swoosie Kurtz, promised distinguished performances in the future, although a number by 1990 had devoted more energy to films and television than to the stage. However, the theatre still was not attracting the younger playgoer: one estimate placed the average age of the Broadway audience at 44. High ticket prices, the appeal of films (and videos), and material that failed to attract a younger generation were undoubtedly major reasons for this condition. With electronic media radically changing how we received information, the future of the American stage seemed to depend in part on the work of such innovators as Foreman, Robert Wilson and PETER SELLARS, though even these original artists had yet to attract large followings.

Theatrical trends in the early 1990s were difficult to ascertain. On the one hand, the AIDS epidemic had transformed theatrical depiction of the disease and its effect from the first-generation plays of the 1980s that openly named the scourge (*The Normal Heart, As Is*) to those of the early 1990s that only indirectly refer, or make no allusion, to AIDS, such as McNALLY's *Lips Together, Teeth Apart*, Scott McPherson's *Marvin's Room* or CRAIG LUCAS's *Prelude to a Kiss*. At the other topical and tone extremes were participatory and escapist entertainments typified by *Shear Madness, Nunsense, Forever Plaid, Tony n' Tina's Wedding, Song of Singapore* and *Catskills on Broadway*.

If trends were not apparent, what was obvious was the devastating effect of the economic recession on all theatrical venues, from Broadway to non-profit regional theatres. Broadway had few strong seasons in the late 1980s and early 90s: even a non-musical Broadway production cost over $1 million to produce. (It cost $900,000 to move *Prelude to a Kiss* 36 blocks from Circle Rep to Broadway.) In recent years non-profit theatre has seen declining growth rates in support from individuals, corporations and private foundations; government funding has also eroded.

The non-profit sector, including major regional companies, though still more adventurous than much of commercial Broadway or Off-Broadway, tended towards less experimental and more proven fare in the late 1980s and early 90s. A sign of the times was the resignation or dismissal of an unusually large number of artistic directors, often for economic reasons (or the failure to keep an operation fiscally sound). A trend towards attempted CENSORSHIP through conservative elements of Congress and control of the National Endowment for the Arts, as well as so-called 'political correctness', created moments of tension and concern, as well as a debate that continues. Even the commercial theatre experienced new crises. Outcries were heard over the casting of a British actor in the Eurasian lead of Broadway's *Miss Saigon* and the use of non-Hispanic actors in the Chilean play *Death and the Maiden* by Ariel Dorfman. In reality, such controversy indicates a growing awareness of our pluralistic, multi-cultural society, and the idea of non-traditional casting is now a fact in many theatre companies, though this battle is not yet completely won.

The British musical invasion (*Cats*, *Les Misérables*, *Phantom of the Opera*, *Miss Saigon*) has continued, and few original American musicals of note have recently been produced. (The much anticipated *Nick and Nora* opened and closed quickly, early in 1992.) Even successful American efforts, such as *The WILL ROGERS Follies*, demonstrated no notable innovations, echoing back to a mythic American past. In 1992 musical production was most notable for revivals or revamping of earlier music: *Man of La Mancha*, *Guys and Dolls*, *Most Happy Fella*, *Jelly's Last Jam* (music by Jelly Roll Morton) and *Crazy for You*, the last loosely based on Gershwin's *Girl Crazy*. This is a trend that has continued, with notable revivals of *Show Boat*, *Grease*, *How to Succeed in Business without Really Trying* and *Damn Yankees* in the mid-1990s.

The deaths of such influential and committed artists as Joseph Papp, WILLIAM BALL, JOSÉ FERRER, JESSICA TANDY and Colleen Dewhurst marked the end of an era of great growth in the American theatre. Yet some encouragement for the future was to be found, for example, in the maturation of writers such as John Guare (*Six Degrees of Separation*), Wendy Wasserstein (*The Sisters Rosensweig*) and Terrence McNally (*A Perfect Ganesh* and *Love! Valour! Compassion!*), the continuing productivity of August Wilson and David Mamet (*Oleanna*), the inauguration of Tony Randall's National Actors Theatre (not, so far, an entirely successful venture), the efforts of the Broadway Alliance, and the large number of new talents that continued to be heard throughout the US theatrical network.
CLJ DBW

(See also AFRICAN-AMERICAN THEATRE; CHICANO THEATRE; COMMUNITY THEATRE/LITTLE THEATRE MOVEMENT; ETHNIC THEATRE; FEMINIST THEATRE; FRONTIER THEATRE; LIVING NEWSPAPER; MUSICAL THEATRE; NEW YORK CITY THEATRES; OFF-BROADWAY; OFF-OFF BROADWAY; RESIDENT NON-PROFIT PROFESSIONAL THEATRE; THEATRICAL SYNDICATE; YANKEE THEATRE.)

1 TO THE CIVIL WAR

See: T. Bogard, R. Moody and W. J. Meserve, *The Revels History of Drama in English*, vol. 8, *American Drama*, London, 1977; J. S. Bost, *Monarchs of the Mimic World*, Orono, Maine, 1977; O. S. Coad and E. Mims Jr, *The American Stage*, New Haven, Conn., 1929; W. Dunlap, *A History of the American Theatre*, New York, 1832; J. Fisher and S. Watt (eds), *When They Weren't Doing Shakespeare: Essays on Nineteenth-Century British and American Theatre*, Athens, Ga., 1989; D. Grimsted, *Melodrama Unveiled: American Theater and Culture, 1800–1850*, Chicago, 1968; B. Hewitt, *Theatre USA, 1668 to 1957*, New York, 1959; G. Hughes, *A History of the American Theatre*, New York, 1951; L. W. Levine, *Highbrow Lowbrow: The Emergence of Cultural Hierarchy in America*, Cambridge, Mass., 1988; B. McConachie, *Melodramatic Formations: American Theatre and Society, 1820–1870*, Iowa City, Ia., 1992; B. A. McConachie and D. Friedman (eds), *Theatre for Working-Class Audiences in the United States, 1830–1980*, Westport, Conn., 1985; B. McNamara, *The American Playhouse in the Eighteenth Century*, Cambridge, Mass., 1969; W. J. Meserve, *An Outline History of American Drama*, Totowa, NJ, 1965, *An Emerging Entertainment: The Drama of the American People to 1828*, Bloomington, Ind., 1977, and *Heralds of Promise: The Drama of the American People in the Age of Jackson, 1829–1849*, Westport, Conn., 1986; R. Moody, *America Takes the Stage*, Bloomington, Ind., 1955, and (ed.), *Dramas from the American Theatre 1762–1909*, Cleveland, Ohio, 1969; G. C. D. Odell, *Annals of the New York Stage*, New York, 1927–49; A. H. Quinn, *A History of the American Drama from the Beginning to the Civil War*, New York, 1943; H. F. Rankin, *The Theatre in Colonial America*, Chapel Hill, N. Carolina, 1965; G. A. Richardson, *American Drama from the Colonial Period through World War I*, New York, 1993; H. B. Williams (ed.), *The American Theatre: A Sum of Its Parts*, New York, 1971; G. B. Wilson, *Three Hundred Years of American Drama and Theatre*, Englewood Cliffs, NJ, 1982.

2 THE CIVIL WAR TO THE FIRST WORLD WAR

See: B. Atkinson, *Broadway*, rev. edn, New York, 1974; D. Belasco, *Theatre through Its Stage Door*, New York, 1919; A. L. Bernheim, *The Business of the Theatre*, New York, 1932; G. Bordman, *The American Musical Theatre*, Oxford, 1978, 2nd edn 1991; O. S. Coad and E. Mims Jr, *The American Stage*, New Haven, Conn., 1929; M. Felheim, *The Theatre of Augustin Daly*, Cambridge, Mass., 1956; P. Hartnoll (ed.), *The Oxford Companion to the Theatre*, 4th edn, Oxford, 1983; M. C. Henderson, *The City and the Theatre*, Clifton, NJ, 1973; B. Hewitt, *Theatre USA, 1668 to 1957*, New York, 1959; G. Hughes, *A History of the American Theatre*, New York, 1951; R. Lynes, *The Lively Audience: A Social History of the Visual and Performing Arts in America, 1890–1950*, New York, 1985; B. McArthur, *Actors and American Culture, 1880–1920*, Philadelphia, 1984; L. W. Levine, *Highbrow Lowbrow: The Emergence of Cultural Hierarchy in America*, Cambridge, Mass., 1988; B. McConachie, *Melodramatic Formations: American Theatre and Society, 1820–1870*, Iowa City, Ia., 1992; B. A. McConachie and D. Friedman (eds), *Theatre for Working-Class Audiences in the United States, 1830–1980*, Westport, Conn., 1985; W. J. Meserve, *An Outline History of American Drama*, Totowa, NJ, 1965; R. Moody, *America Takes the Stage*, Bloomington, Ind., 1955; E. Mordden, *The American Theatre*, New York, 1981; L. Morris, *Curtain Time*, New York, 1953; J. Moses and J. M. Brown, *The American Theatre as Seen by Its Critics, 1752–1934*, New York, 1934; G. C. D. Odell, *Annals of the New York Stage*, New York, 1927–49; A. H. Quinn, *A History of the American Drama from the Civil War to the Present Day*, 2nd edn., New York, 1949; G. A. Richardson, *American Drama from the Colonial Period through World War I*, New York, 1993; C. H. Shattuck, *Shakespeare on the American Stage*, 2 vols., Washington, DC, 1976, 1987; C. Smith, *Musical Comedy in America*, New York, 1950; J. Stagg, *The Brothers Shubert*, New York, 1968; H. B. Williams (ed.), *The American Theatre: A Sum of Its Parts*, New York, 1971; G. B. Wilson, *A History of American Acting*, Bloomington, Ind., 1966, and *Three Hundred Years of American*

Drama and Theatre, Englewood Cliffs, NJ, 1982; W. Winter, *Life and Art of Edwin Booth*, New York, 1893.

3 THE FIRST WORLD WAR TO THE 1960S
See: T. P. Adler, *American Drama 1940–1960: A Critical History*, New York, 1994; B. Atkinson, *Broadway*, rev. edn, New York, 1974; J. Beck, *The Life of the Theatre*, New York, 1972; G. M. Berkowitz, *New Broadways: Theatre across America 1950–1980*, Totowa, NJ; C. W. E. Bigsby, *A Critical Introduction to Twentieth-Century American Drama*, vols. 1 and 2, Cambridge, 1982, 1984; G. Bordman, *The American Musical Theatre*, Oxford, 1978, 2nd edn, 1991, *The Oxford Companion to American Theatre*, Oxford, 1984, 2nd edn, 1992, and *American Theatre: A Chronicle of Comedy and Drama, 1869–1914*, New York, 1994; R. Cohn, *New American Dramatists*, 2nd edn, New York, 1991; E. Q. Craig, *Black Drama of the Federal Theatre Era*, Amherst, Mass., 1980; P. Hartnoll (ed.), *The Oxford Companion to the Theatre*, 4th edn, Oxford, 1983; B. Hewitt, *Theatre USA, 1668 to 1957*, New York, 1959; E. Hill, *The Theatre of Black Americans*, 2 vols., Englewood Cliffs, NJ, 1980; P. C. Kolin (ed.), *American Playwrights Since 1945: A Guide to Scholarship, Criticism, and Performance*, Westport, Conn., 1989; B. A. McConachie and D. Friedman (eds.), *Theatre for Working-Class Audiences in the United States, 1830–1980*, Westport, Conn., 1985; J. Y. Miller and W. L. Frazer, *American Drama Between the Wars: A Critical History*, Boston, 1991; B. Murphy, *American Realism and American Drama, 1880–1940*, Cambridge, 1987; N. Van Hoogstraten, *Lost Broadway Theatres*, Princeton, NJ, 1991; G. B. Wilson, *Three Hundred Years of American Drama and Theatre*, 2nd edn, Englewood Cliffs, NJ, 1982.

4 1960 TO THE PRESENT
See: B. Atkinson, *Broadway*, rev. edn, New York, 1974; J. Beck, *The Life of the Theatre*, New York, 1972; G. M. Berkowitz, *New Broadways: Theatre across America 1950–1980*, Totowa, NJ; C. W. E. Bigsby, *A Critical Introduction to Twentieth-Century American Drama*, vol. 3, Cambridge, 1985, and *Modern American Drama, 1945–1990*, Cambridge and New York, 1993; H. Blau, *Take Up the Bodies: Theatre at the Vanishing Point*, Urbana, 1982; G. Bordman, *The American Musical Theatre*, Oxford, 1978, 2nd edn, 1991; E. Brown-Guillory, *Their Place on the Stage: Black Women Playwrights in America*, Westport, Conn., 1988; R. Cohn, *New American Dramatists*, 2nd edn, New York, 1991; R. G. Davis, 'The Radical Right in the American Theatre', *Theatre Quarterly*, 5, 19, Sept.–Nov. 1975; K. Davy (ed.), *Richard Foreman: Plays and Manifestos*, New York, 1976; R. Foreman, *Unbalancing Acts: Foundations for a Theater*, New York, 1992; H. Greenberger, *The Off-Broadway Experience*, New York, 1971; E. Hill, *The Theatre of Black Americans*, 2 vols, Englewood Cliffs, NJ, 1980; P. C. Kolin (ed.), *American Playwrights Since 1945: A Guide to Scholarship, Criticism, and Performance*, Westport, Conn., 1989; S. L. Leiter, *Ten Seasons: New York Theatre in the Seventies*, Westport, Conn., 1986; B. Marranca, *Animations: A Trilogy for Mabou Mines*, New York, 1979; J. Miles (ed.), *The Women's Project: Seven Plays by Women*, New York, 1980; A. Poland and B. Mailman, *The Off-Off Broadway Book*, New York, 1972;

D. Savran, *In Their Own Words: Contemporary American Playwrights*, New York, 1988; H. M. Sayre, *The Object of Performance: The American Avant-Garde Since 1970*, Chicago, 1989; R. Schechner, *The End of Humanism*, New York, 1982; T. Shank, *American Alternative Theatre*, London, 1982; S. Shyer, *Robert Wilson and His Collaborators*, New York, 1989; A. F. Sponberg, *Broadway Talks: What Professionals Think About Commercial Theater in America*, Westport, Conn., 1991; L. Valdéz, *Drama Review*, 11, 4, Sept. 1967; E. van Erven, *Radical People's Theatre*, Bloomington, Ind., 1988; G. B. Wilson, *Three Hundred Years of American Drama and Theatre*, 2nd edn, Englewood Cliffs, NJ, 1982.

SUPPLEMENTARY BIBLIOGRAPHY
See: H. Alpert, *Broadway*, New York, 1991; S. M. Archer (compiler), *American Actors and Actresses: A Guide to Information Sources*, Detroit, Mich., 1983; G. Boardman, *The Oxford Companion to American Theatre*, 2nd edn, New York and Oxford, 1992; W. Browne and F. A. Austin (eds), *Who's Who on the Stage: The Dramatic Reference Book and Bibliographical Dictionary of the Theatre Containing Records of the Careers of Actors, Actresses, Managers, and Playwrights*, 1908; G. B. Bryan (compiler), *Stage Lives: A Bibliography and Index to Theatrical Biographies in English*, Westport, Conn., and London, 1985, and (compiler), *Stage Deaths: Biographical Guide to International Theatrical Obituaries, 1850 to 1990*, 2 vols, Westport, Conn., 1991; W. B. Durham (ed.), *American Theatre Companies, 1749–1986*, 3 vols, Westport, Conn., 1986–9; R. Engle and T. L. Miller (eds), *The American Theatre*, Cambridge and New York, 1993; M. C. Henderson, *Theater in America: 200 Years of Plays, Players, and Productions*, New York, 1986; D. La Beau (ed.), *Theatre, Film and Television Biographies Master Index*, Detroit, 1979; C. F. W. Larson, *American Regional Theatre History to 1900: A Bibliography*, Metuchen, NJ, and London, 1979; S. L. Leiter (ed.), *The Encyclopedia of the New York Stage, 1920–1950*, 4 vols, Westport, Conn., 1986–92; E. Mapp, *Directory of Blacks in the Performing Arts*, Metuchen, NJ, and London, 1978; B. McNeil and M. C. Herbert (eds), *Performing Arts Biography Master Index*, 2nd edn, Detroit, 1979; D. Mullin (ed.), *Victorian Actors and Actresses in View: A Dictionary of Contemporary Views of Representative British and American Actors and Actresses, 1837–1901*, Westport, Conn., and London, 1983; *New York Times Directory of the Theatre*, New York, 1973; W. Rigdon (ed.), *The Biographical Encyclopedia and Who's Who of the American Theatre*, New York, 1966; A. M. Robinson, V. M. Roberts and M. S. Barranger, *Notable Women in the American Theatre*, Westport, Conn., 1989; H. T. Sampson, *Blacks in Blackface: A Source Book on Early Black Musical Shows*, Metuchen, NJ, and London, 1980; C. H. Shattuck, *The Shakespeare Prompt Books: A Descriptive Catalogue*, Urbana and London, 1965; R. Silvester (ed.), *United States Theatre: A Bibliography from the beginning to 1990*, Romsey, 1993; A. Slide, *The Vaudevillians: A Dictionary of Vaudeville Performers*, Westport, Conn., 1981; R. Stoddard, *Stage Scenery, Machinery, and Lighting: A Guide to Information*

Sources, Detroit, 1977, and *Theatre and Cinema Architecture: A Guide to Information Sources*, Detroit, 1978; C. J. Stratman (compiler), *A Bibliography of American Theatre, Excluding New York City*, Chicago, 1965, and *American Theatrical Periodicals, 1798–1967: A Bibliographical Guide*, Durham, N. Carolina, 1970; J. Trapido (ed.), *An International Dictionary of Theatre Language*, Westport, Conn., and London, 1985; J. P. Wearing (compiler), *American and British Theatrical Biography: A Dictionary*, Metuchen, NJ, 1979; *Who Was Who in the Theatre: 1912–1976*, 4 vols., Detroit, 1978; D. B. Wilmeth, *The American Stage to World War I: A Guide to Information Sources*, Detroit, 1978, *American and English Popular Entertainment: A Guide to Information Sources*, Detroit, 1980, and *Variety Entertainment and Outdoor Amusements: A Reference Guide*, Westport, Conn., and London, 1982; D. B. Wilmeth and T. L. Miller (eds), *Cambridge Guide to American Theatre*, Cambridge and New York, 1993.

Uniti, Compagnia degli *COMMEDIA DELL'ARTE* troupe, said to have been founded by Adriano Valerini (Aurelio) in the late 16th century. It circulated throughout northern Italy, under the protection of Vincenzo Gonzaga, Duke of Ferrara, and never toured abroad; it combined with the CONFIDENTI in 1583. Its leading players included, in 1584, ISABELLA ANDREINI; in 1593, DRUSIANO MARTINELLI as Arlecchino; and, in 1614, SILVIO FIORILLO as Captain Matamoros. The last notice of it occurs in 1640, after a long hiatus. LS

Unity Theatre (London) Developed from the Workers' Theatre Movement, Unity opened its first stage in a converted church hall in 1936 with the English premiere of ODETS's *Waiting for Lefty*, which became a model for left-wing theatre of the time with its AGIT-PROP form, audience participation and theme of strikers' solidarity. When it moved to a small 200-seat auditorium in 1937, Unity's political line was firmly established with the first of BRECHT's plays to be performed in London (*Señora Carrer's Rifles*), a satiric 'political PANTOMIME' (*Babes in the Woods*), and the first English example of a LIVING NEWSPAPER, as well as the London GROUP THEATRE's production of Spender's *Trial of a Judge* in 1938. It continued to introduce new radical works, including O'CASEY's *The Star Turns Red* (1940), SARTRE's *Nekrassov* (1956), ADAMOV's *Spring '71* (1962) and SHATROV's *The Bolsheviks* (1970), until it was burnt down in 1975 while being rebuilt as a cultural centre for the Labour movement. CI

university and school drama (16th–18th centuries) Drama in the schools and universities of the Middle Ages was usually satirical or celebratory in subject-matter, often rowdy in performance, but with the dwindling of the religious theatre of Church and town during the 16th century a new amateur drama of instruction developed side by side with the professional theatre of entertainment, and over the next two and a half centuries hundreds of plays were written and performed in universities, colleges and schools all over Europe, many of them in Latin or Greek, some of them polemical, most of them didactic.

The Latin comedies of PLAUTUS and TERENCE were the models for the writers of the Christian Terence movement, such as Macropedius, Crocus and Gnaphaeus. Encouraged also by the 1501 edition by Conrad Celtis of the 10th-century Latin plays by the German oblate HROTSVITHA OF GANDERSHEIM, they composed for their pupils plays on the stories of, for example, Joseph, Susanna – and especially the Prodigal Son, which was dramatized several times in both Latin and vernacular: the *Acolastus* by the Dutchman, Gnaphaeus, went through 31 editions between 1529 and 1577.

Writers such as the Scottish Catholic George Buchanan modelled their Latin dramas on SENECA's tragedies. Two of Buchanan's plays, *Jepthes* and *Baptistes*, were composed between 1539 and 1542 for the Collège de Guienne in Bordeaux whose actors included the essayist Montaigne. *Baptistes*, in which a parallel is drawn between Herod's execution of John the Baptist and Henry VIII's treatment of Sir Thomas More, was also played in Cambridge in 1562 and, like many of the other Latin school plays, was frequently reprinted as well as being translated into English, French and German.

Catholics and Protestants alike used drama as an aid for teaching and preaching: Luther and the Pope both appear as Antichrist on the 16th-century stage. Medieval biblical and saints' plays were given a new look, either purged of tendentious elements or deliberately slanted for propaganda purposes. Between 1538 and 1621, the pupils of the Protestant college in Strasbourg regularly performed specially written plays in Latin and Greek, designed as pedagogical exercises for the boys but attracting enormous audiences from the surrounding districts. In 1546, Calvin and the Council in Geneva allowed the performance there of the *Acts of the Apostles*, while the *Abraham Sacrifiant* by Calvin's successor, Theodore of Beza, was published in Geneva in 1550 and reprinted in 1560. Towards the end of the 16th century Capuchin friars used specially written plays as part of a *Forty Hour Devotion of the Blessed Sacrament* in an attempt to win back the people of the region round Geneva to the Catholic faith. The Old Testament, the Acts and allegorical material are common sources for this drama, but the rarest subject in 16th-century didactic theatre is the life of Christ. A notable exception to this rule is the *Christus Redivivus* by the Cambridge graduate, Nicholas Grimald, who wrote his Resurrection play in Oxford in 1543. (It was subsequently published in Cologne and used by the OBERAMMERGAU reviser in the preparation for the text of the performance in 1664.)

Encouraged by Queen Elizabeth, the universities in England also played an important role in the development of the vernacular drama, and the tradition continued in the post-Tudor period. Scores of plays were written and performed in the universities and schools of Europe during this period, but the most important single contribution to the school drama is undoubtedly that of the Jesuits (see *JESUITENDRAMA*) who, from their foundation in 1540 to their suspension by the Pope in 1773, were a major force in education throughout Catholic Europe. Plays formed a regular part of the curriculum in all their colleges of which, by the end of the 17th century, there were more than 200. The plays were designed to improve the pupils' knowledge of Latin as well as their ability to speak and move well. The original instruction in the *Ratio studiorum* (1599) was that plays should be in Latin, pious in subject-matter and 'very rare'. But the Jesuit drama rapidly became frequent in performance and more wide-ranging in subject, including stories from classical and medieval history; in parts of Spain, vernacular replaced Latin and the themes were often humorous and contemporary. A major innovation of the Jesuit drama throughout Europe was the introduction of ballets as interludes in the Latin texts, thus providing spectacle and music for the benefit of the uneducated members of the public who flocked to see their children act.

Different traditions developed in different countries. In Germany, Austria and Poland where each college might give five to ten performances a year, Jesuit drama formed a part of the spectacular, sometimes fantastic or romantic baroque drama, with Bidemaker, Avancini and Masel being among the most important authors. In Italy and France, on the other hand, the school drama was closely associated with the more sober conventions of the classical theatre (JODELLE's *Cléopâtre captive*, the first 'classical' play, was performed in the Parisian Collège de Reims in 1552). Many of the Latin Jesuit plays in France were on classical themes, and they also influenced the court ballets in their use of symbolism based on classical myth. The first play published was in Rome in 1587 but only a small proportion of the vast number of plays was ever printed, though the subject of many of them is known from the *periochae*, or programme notes, which gave a synopsis of the action for the benefit of the audience and also described the symbolism of the ballets and musical interludes. (Music plays an important part in other school drama: Purcell's *Dido and Aeneas* was composed for a girls' school in Chelsea and RACINE's two plays *Esther* (1689) and *Athalie* (1691), commissioned by Madame de Maintenon for the girls of St Cyr, both contain important choral sections.)

Nor was Jesuit drama entirely limited to Europe: German plays used material from the missions in Japan and the Congo, while from Spain (where the drama developed side by side with the professional theatre of the GOLDEN AGE) Jesuit missionaries carried the tradition of teaching by drama with them to the Far East and South America: the first Jesuit plays recorded from Manila in the Philippines date from 1610.   LRM

See: L. B. Campbell, *Divine Poetry and Drama in Sixteenth-century England*, Cambridge, 1959; L.-V. Gofflot, *Le Théâtre au collège du moyen âge à nos jours*, Paris, 1907; N. Griffin, *Jesuit School Drama, a Checklist of Critical Literature*, Research Bibliographies and Checklists, 12, London, 1976; J.-M. Valentin, *Le Théâtre des Jésuites dans les pays de langue allemande: Répertoire chronologique des pièces représentées et des documents conservés (1555-1773)*, 2 vols., Stuttgart, 1983-4.

University Wits Name popularly given to a group of playwrights, among whom MARLOWE, GREENE, NASHE and PEELE are the most prominent, who received their education at Oxford or Cambridge University, lived rashly in London and contributed significantly to the rapid development of a national repertoire of plays. Most of the University Wits were hostile to the rising generation of playwrights, which included JONSON and SHAKESPEARE, who had lacked their educational advantages.   PT

Urban, Joseph 1871-1933 Austrian-American set designer. Many of the approaches and techniques adopted by ROBERT EDMOND JONES, LEE SIMONSON and others were first introduced in America by Urban. In the 1890s in Vienna he designed palaces, exposition pavilions and a bridge. In 1904 he began to work with the Vienna BURGTHEATER and spent the next years designing OPERAS throughout Europe. He went to the USA in 1912 to design for the Boston Opera. He was discovered by showman FLORENZ ZIEGFELD, who persuaded him to design for the *Follies*. Urban's designs were simple in terms of line, but vibrant colour created a sense of lushness and complexity. He achieved this by applying pointillist techniques – the juxtaposition of dots of colour – to scene painting. This not only added new dimensions to painted scenery, but also allowed parts of the image to appear or disappear under different coloured lights. He was also one of the first to use platforms and portals – arched scenic units at the side of the stage, connected at the top. This framed and focused the stage while providing continuous elements for unit sets.   AA

Uruguay The theatre history of Uruguay is closely related to that of Argentina and is often combined in theatre histories under the designation 'River Plate theatre'. Uruguay was created as a nation in 1828 as a buffer between Brazil and Argentina, both of whom disputed this rich agricultural territory which, in spite of its relative flatness, is called 'Little Switzerland'. During the colonial period the scant population was insufficient to sustain theatrical activity, although there is record of a theatre that opened in Montevideo as early as 1793. Throughout most of the 19th century – years of tumult and confusion in politics and economics, when the country lagged behind its more powerful neighbours – the theatre followed the romantic trends in vogue in other parts of the hemisphere. Many plays reflected the costumbristic tendencies (see COSTUMBRISMO) of the times and recorded the history and society of this land dominated by the *gaucho* and wild outlaws. The fierce rivalry between two political parties, the *blancos* (whites) and the *colorados* (reds), struggling for power, tested the cohesion of this incipient democratic nation through difficult times, and did little to foment the theatre. The Teatro Solís opened in 1856 and several theatre groups or companies were registered in the latter half of the century.

The single event of greatest importance in the development of the River Plate theatre occurred in 1884 when the Carlo Brothers' North American Circus, on tour in Argentina, incorporated the little Uruguayan CLOWN José J. Podestá (1858-1937) into their initial rendition of *Juan Moreira*, featuring a romanticized version of a *gaucho* whose adventures had been published serially by Eduardo Gutiérrez. The instantaneous success of the original PANTOMIME version led subsequently to a more developed version with dialogue, recognized by the Uruguayans for its dramatic value. The national spirit spawned a host of imitations about upstanding and virtuous *gauchos* persecuted unjustly by the civil authorities.

The authors who best represent Uruguayan theatre in the second half of the 19th century are Samuel Blixen (1868–1911), who wrote romantic comedies and a seasonal tetralogy; Orosmán Moratorio (1852–98), author of *sainetes*, especially those with *gaucho* themes; and Elías Regules (1860–1929), who adapted the epic *Martín Fierro* and wrote other *gaucho* plays.

The 20th century Uruguay experienced waves of immigration similar to those of Argentina as thousands of Europeans, primarily Italians and Germans, arrived in the southern hemisphere. The influence of REALISM and NATURALISM in the European theatre was superimposed on local customs and lifestyles and the resulting dramatic form, known as the *sainete criollo*, marked a new direction in the theatre of the entire River Plate region. The best-known playwright of all of South America, even at this point, is FLORENCIO SÁNCHEZ (1875–1910), who spent his first 25 years in Uruguay, although the development of his theatre is normally associated with Argentina because of the greater opportunities for production that existed there. Sánchez wrote quickly and easily. His plays have been criticized for shallow characterization and flawed structures, but he was able to capture the heart and mind of his public with a vision of an emerging new culture that combined the immigrant urban population with the traditional rural society. *M'hijo el dotor* (*My Son the Lawyer*, 1903), *La gringa* (*The Foreign Girl*, 1904) and *Barranca abajo* (*Down the Gully*, 1905) are only three of the 20 plays he wrote during the brief career that catapulted him to fame and changed the course of Uruguayan and Argentine theatre.

Others followed and tried to imitate or surpass his work. Ernesto Herrera (1886–1917), another autodidactic playwright, wrote in a vein similar to Sánchez but with better-developed characters, as in *El león ciego* (*The Blind Lion*, 1911), a powerful play about the misery and folly of war as an exercise in virility. Herrera's career paralleled that of Sánchez, including his early death from tuberculosis. Other major playwrights of the period included Víctor Pérez Petit (1871–1947) and José Pedro Bellán (1888–1930). The relationship with Argentina facilitated the development of their careers also during this period of costumbristic theatre, in which the language patterns and the social mores of the incipient middle class were becoming more firmly established.

After 1920, while the previous costumbristic tendencies continued, a theatre more attuned to universal concerns and with a sound psychological basis began to emerge. Two of the major playwrights were contemporaries of the previous group: Francisco Imhof (1880–1937) revealed a Freudian influence in such plays as *Eutanasia* (*Euthanasia*, 1927), which integrated the subconscious and a mercy killing within a lovers' triangle. Vicente Martínez Cuitiño (1887–1964) was a prolific author whose early plays were naturalistic, and the later ones more in the vanguard. His *Servidumbre* (*Servitude*, 1937) derives from the Italian tradition, with its exploration of the cruelty of the society that mistreats young lovers for sadistic reasons. Yamandú Rodríguez (1889–1957) wrote historical plays in verse and Justino Zavala Muñiz (b.1898) also picked up Creole issues, as in *En un rincón del Tacuari* (*In a Corner of the Tacuari*, 1938) with its theme of incest.

After the Second World War, Uruguay's relationship with Argentina was ruptured by the strong-arm tactics of the latter's Juan Domingo Perón, who envisioned annexation of the territory. When rebuffed, he imposed economic sanctions on the little country, which became a haven for Argentine political refugees, just as it had a century earlier during the Juan Manuel de Rosas period. In the theatre, Uruguay responded to this new era by expanding its available performance space and by creating new theatre companies. The Comedia Nacional (National Comedy) was established by the municipal government of Montevideo in 1947, with the first resident theatre company in the country's history and a training programme designed by the famous Spanish actress MARGARITA XIRGU.

In 1949 the Teatro Galpón was created – a theatre group that has survived political harassment under the spiritual leadership of the indomitable Atahualpa del Cioppo and the direction of César Campodónico. The Galpón (named after the barn in which it started) spent eight years in exile, mostly in Mexico, but was able to return to Montevideo in 1984 by invitation of the newly elected president Julio María Sanguinette. The Galpón's collective creation, *La reja* (*The Grille*, 1972), based on narrations by released prisoners, was important in the government's decision to close it down. In exile its production of *Artigas*, based on Uruguay's national hero, played in many countries.

The Teatro Circular (Arena Theatre), established in 1954, is also known for its high-quality productions, its actor training programme and its promotion of both foreign and national plays. In recent years the group has published a theatre journal, *Escenario* (*Stage*). Another group of importance is the Teatro Alianza (Alliance Theatre), which since its creation in 1975 has occupied a flexible space in the Uruguay–USA Cultural Alliance building, where it has brought new staging techniques to a wide variety of plays.

According to Walter Rela's documentation of all Uruguayan plays staged in the country between 1808 and 1968, the number performed in the 1950s increased markedly, as did the number of theatres in use. By the late 1960s, however, the proliferation of independent theatre groups had not succeeded in elevating the artistic quality of performances, and the military coup of 1973 stifled free expression by counterculture groups.

The postwar period spawned a new generation of playwrights, directors, actors and critics. Of the writers, CARLOS MAGGI, a lawyer and critic, commanded the greatest attention for a series of fine plays in which, with humour and irony, he was able to penetrate the foibles of Uruguayan society and politics within a larger universal context. *La biblioteca* (*The Library*, 1959) was an excellent prelude to *El patio de la Torcaza* (*The Patio of the Torcaza*, 1967), in which the black humour and acerbic style revealed his particular vision of the decadence and turmoil of contemporary Uruguay. Others have been even more overt in their criticism. Antonio Larreta (b.1922) has written existentialist as well as committed theatre. His *Juan Palmieri* (1972) is a semi-documentary account of an encounter between the bourgeoisie and a young *tupamaro* revolutionary.

MARIO BENEDETTI (b.1920) manipulated a metatheatrical technique in *Ida y vuelta* (*Return Trip*, 1958) and then wrote a virulent play about torture, premiered by the Galpón in Mexico. Later made as a film in Mexico (1983), it analyses the emotions and responsibility of a torturer confronted with a resistant victim. *Primavera con una esquina rota* (*Springtime with a Broken Corner*, 1984) was adapted by the Chilean group ICTUS from one of his novels dealing with exile during a period of political repression. Other playwrights of particular note during this time are Jacobo Langsner (b.1927), Híber Conteris (b.1933) and MAURICIO ROSENCOF; the latter is worthy of note for his *Las ranas* (*The Frogs*, 1961), *Los caballos* (*The Horses*, 1967) and *El regreso del gran Tuleque* (*The Return of the Great Tuleque*, 1987), a multidimensional vision of the marginal classes.

The return of political stability permitted the celebration of an International Theatre Showcase in 1984 in which 20 plays by groups from South America and Europe were performed. Among the younger authors are Alberto Paredes with *Tres tristes tangos* (*Three Sad Tangos*) and *Devaluación* (*Devaluation*), and Alfredo de la Peña with *El novio de la nena* (*The Girl's Boyfriend*). Jorge Scheck and Pedro Corradi each wrote excellent monologues, *El santo y el muñeco* (*The Saint and the Puppet*) and *Retrato de dama con espejo* (*Portrait of a Lady with Mirror*), respectively. *Costumbres* (*Customs*, 1981) by Ernesto Castillo and *Doña Ramona* (1982) by Víctor Manuel Leites both provide microcosmic visions of family love and sexuality under conditions of rigid morality and religious fervour. Alberto Rowinsky (b.1946) is an actor, director and author (for several years in Venezuela) whose play, *Reunión de muertos en familia* (*Reunion of the Family Dead*), was ironically in rehearsal with Héctor Duvauchelle at the time the latter was murdered. Alberto Restuccia writes about the extermination of the Charrúa Indians in *Salsipuedes* (*Leave If You Can*, 1985) in a complex multi-media and multisituational piece, and Ana Magnabosco in *Viejo Smoking* (*Old Tuxedo*, 1988) takes up the myth of Carlos Gardel from the wrenching point of view of a woman in misery. Luis Vidal's *Los girasoles de van Gogh* (*Van Gogh's Sunflowers*, 1989) also permeates the interior world of emotions, but in a less realistic vein.

A dependency on foreign tendencies at the expense of a national theatre movement has left Uruguay in an underdeveloped situation. MOLIÈRE, BRECHT, GARCÍA LORCA, PIRANDELLO, SHAFFER and TENNESSEE WILLIAMS are more likely fare than local authors like Juan Graña and Jacobo Langsner. Political and economic conditions have not favoured the Uruguayan theatre in recent years, but an irrepressible talent and a long theatre tradition bode well for the future. (See also *GÉNERO CHICO*.) GW

See: J. Cruz, *Genio y figura de Florencio Sánchez*, Buenos Aires, 1966; W. Rela, *Historia del teatro uruguayo, 1808–1968*, Montevideo, 1969, and *Repertorio bibliográfico del teatro uruguayo, 1816–1964*, Montevideo, 1965; C. Scosería, *Un panorama del teatro uruguayo*, Montevideo, 1963; C. Solórzano, *El teatro latinoamericano en el siglo 20*, Mexico, 1964.

Usigli, Rodolfo 1905–79 Mexican playwright, poet and diplomat, who during the 1930s and 1940s launched Mexican dramaturgy with plays of lasting significance. Unaffiliated, for the most part, with the independence theatre movement in Mexico, Usigli emulated the best of world theatre and earned accolades from GEORGE BERNARD SHAW. His first major success was *El gesticulador* (*The Impostor*, written 1937, performed 1947), a study of hypocrisy that transcends its Mexican ambiance. *Corona de sombre* (*Crown of Shadow*, written 1943, performed 1947) is a revisionist historical play on the period of Maximilian and Carlota in Mexico. It forms a trilogy with *Corona de luz* (*Crown of Light*, 1960) and *Corona de fuego* (*Crown of Fire*, 1961), which deal with the Virgin of Guadalupe and Cuauhtémoc, respectively. Other major works include *El niño y la niebla* (*The Boy and the Mist*, 1936–51), *Jano es una muchacha* (*Jano Is a Girl*, 1952) and *Buenos días, señor presidente* (*Good Morning, Mr President*, 1972), the latter rooted in CALDERÓN's *La vida es sueño* (*Life Is a Dream*) and growing out of the 1968 Tlatelolco massacre in Mexico. Known also for his explanatory prologues and epilogues, Usigli wrote more than 40 plays in addition to several substantial books on theatre. GW

U'Tamsi, Felix Tchicaya 1931–88 Congolese dramatist, poet and novelist. Born in the then French Congo, from the age of 15 U'Tamsi lived in Paris. After his education at the Lycée Janson-de-Sailly there, he embarked on a literary career. His reputation as a writer rests principally on six volumes of dense, surrealist poetry (see SURREALISM) which he produced between 1955 and 1966. In 1976 he turned to writing for the stage, establishing with *Le Zulu* (1977) – a tragedy of ambition, premiered at the AVIGNON FESTIVAL and published a year later – a reputation as a dramatist of talent. In addition to the short dramatic monologue *Vivène le fondateur* (*Vivène the Founder*) published in the same volume as *Le Zulu*, U'Tamsi also wrote an acutely satirical play on political dictatorship in Africa, *Le Maréchal Nnikon Nniku Prince qu'on sort* (*Marshall Nnikon Nniku, Prince Consort*, 1979). But his greatest theatrical success is *Le Bal de N'Dinga*. A highly poetic dance-drama on a failed exercise in decolonization, this play was first produced in October 1988 by the French director Gabriel Garran of the Théâtre International de Langue Française. It has since been performed to packed audiences in France, Africa and the French Caribbean. U'Tamsi also wrote four novels and was, until his death, an international civil servant with UNESCO in Paris. JCM

vagantes Term applied in medieval documents to disaffected and homeless clerics, students and Latin teachers, to distinguish them from ordinary rovers. They travelled throughout England, France and Germany in the 12th and 13th centuries, reciting disputatious poems and rollicking songs composed in vulgar Latin. In France these clerics were known as *goliards*, and the goliardic ballads are often forceful and obscene, sometimes anti-clerical in tone, praising wine and women in song. One set, the *Carmina burana*, was put to music by Carl Orff (1936). The *vagantes* were important in disseminating a classical influence throughout the folk culture of their time.   LS

Vakhtangov, Evgeny (Bagrationovich) 1883–1923 Russian director-actor-teacher, disciple and reconciler of Stanislavskian psychological realism and Meyerholdian grotesque via his system of humane and joyous creation, 'fantastic REALISM'. Armenian born, Vakhtangov studied law at Moscow University before enrolling at A. I. Adashev's drama school, where he was taught by, among others, Leopold Sulerzhitsky. He was accepted into the MOSCOW ART THEATRE (MAT) as an actor in 1911, where his former teacher Sulerzhitsky, for whom he assistant-directed MAETERLINCK's *The Blue Bird*, and NEMIROVICH-DANCHENKO, whose work he observed, taught him much about the STANISLAVSKY system and theatricality, respectively. In time he became one of the system's leading teachers.

His acting at MAT and its First Studio (founded in 1912) featured expressive, often grotesque outer form developed from psychological bases in such roles at Tackleton in DICKENS's *Cricket on the Hearth* (1914), Frazer in Berger's *The Flood* (1915) and Feste in *Twelfth Night* (1919). These same qualities, which informed his work as a director-teacher, derived from these principles: (1) the actor has primacy in the theatre, his personality and imagination being his most significant tools in creating a performance that is expressive rather than a mere impersonation (Stanislavsky) on the one hand, or stylization (MEYERHOLD) on the other; (2) this 'expressiveness' consists of the combination of the actor's subjective psychological belief in the character and the actor's objective consideration, as a representative of his culture, of the character; (3) the actor expresses the 'soul of the people' and 'the life of the nation' (revealing WAGNER's influence and pointing towards BRECHT); (4) the 'actor-eccentric' must first be an expert improviser, his performance – which includes the skills of singing, dancing, *vaudeville* and MUSICAL COMEDY – embodying controlled spontaneity and quickly communicating to an audience via selected details an instantaneous, complex and vibrant impression of the character's essence; (5) 'creative distortion' and child-like play in which emotion arises from action (achieved via rehearsal *études*) must replace MAT moodiness, sentimentalism, pseudo-psychological significance and naturalistic scenic effects, as well as Meyerhold's and TAIROV's visual experimentation at the expense of the actor's inner life.

A man of prodigious talent, energy and enthusiasm, at the height of his brief career and in the face of serious personal illness and national famine Vakhtangov taught and directed at 14 theatres and studios, in addition to working at MAT and at its First and Second Studios. His best work was done at MAT's Third Studio (after 1926, the Vakhtangov Theatre) – CHEKHOV's *The Wedding* (1920), his second version of Maeterlinck's *The Miracle of St Anthony* (1921), GOZZI's *Princess Turandot* (1922) – and with the Jewish HABIMAH Theatre on S. ANSKI's *The Dybbuk* (1922).

He staged *The Wedding* as a tragicomic grotesque in the style of GOGOL's *The Inspector General*, which reflected his belief that Chekhov is crueller than is generally thought. *The Miracle of St Anthony* was presented as a black-and-white Daumier caricature, filtered through the lighting and imagery of Goya and aimed at 'branding the bourgeoisie'. The *Dybbuk*, rehearsed in Russian but performed in Hebrew, also used a black-and-white palette and was his most highly choreographed piece. *Turandot*, his final and most famous production, spoofed the play's romanticism via frank theatricality – oriental conventions of scene, prop and costume-changing, hand towels as beards and selected costume pieces over evening dress, a cubist set by Ignaty Nivinsky, accompanying music – designed to present the actor as being an ordinary man leading an extraordinary life. This production influenced STANISLAVSKY's ideas on tempo-rhythm.

Among Vakhtangov's disciples were four members of the Students' Drama Studio who achieved notable success and high state honours: YURY ZAVADSKY, from 1940 artistic director of the Mossoviet Theatre; N. M. Gorchakov, senior director at MAT; Boris Zakhava, from 1925 head of the Vakhtangov Theatre's Shchukin Theatre School; Ruben Simonov, Vakhtangov Theatre artistic director (1924–39). The last three have left valuable memoirs of their work with Vakhtangov.   SG

Valdéz, Luis 1940– Chicano director and playwright responsible for the CHICANO THEATRE revolution. University-trained and a student activist at San José State in California, Valdéz visited CUBA before joining the SAN FRANCISCO MIME TROUPE in 1964. Knowledgeable about *COMMEDIA DELL'ARTE*, BRECHT and PANTOMIME, he used bilingual theatre to help César Chávez organize the migrant workers around Delano, California, in 1965. His efforts led to the *actos*, one-act revolutionary pieces, and the creation of EL TEATRO CAMPESINO (Farmworkers' Theatre), which in turn inspired the formation of other Chicano theatre groups. His early titles include *Las dos caras del patroncito* (*The Boss's Two Faces*), *Quinta temporada* (*Fifth Season*), *No saco nada de la escuela* (*I Don't Get Anything out of School*), *Vietnam campesino* (*Vietnam Farmer*), *Soldado razo* (*Buck Private*) and *Huelguistas* (*Strikers*). *Zoot Suit* (1978), based on the Sleepy Lagoon murder trial during the Second World War, dramatized the stereotypical *pachuco* in a successful run in Los Angeles, but failed on BROADWAY. Teatro Campesino

A scene from Valle-Inclán's *Tirano Banderas*.

became professional and later moved into new facilities in San Juan Bautista. Valdéz's folk MUSICAL *Corridos*, based on popular Mexican folk ballad traditions, opened in 1983. He followed with stage and television productions of *Corridos*, and enjoyed a huge box-office success with the film version of *La bamba* (1987). In spring 1994 his musical about the notorious Californian bandit/hero Tiburcio Vasquez was staged at the Mark Taper Forum in Los Angeles. Each season El Teatro Campesino stages plays by Valdéz, including *La Pastorela*, his adaptation from Mexican folklore of the journey of the shepherds to the manger. GW

Valentin, Karl [Valentin Ludwig Fey] 1882–1948 German comedian. The son of a Munich upholsterer, he made a start as a club comic and musical CLOWN in 1899, and by 1907 was the leading Munich comedian in his own monologues and sketches. In 1911 he met Liesl Karlstadt (Elisabeth Welleno, 1892–1961) who was his partner for 35 years, playing both male and female roles. They worked together until 1941, in Munich and on tour in Zürich, Vienna and Berlin, parting temporarily in 1934 when their *Panoptikum* (mock WAXWORKS/chamber of horrors/cabinet of curiosities) failed, leaving them bankrupt. Lanky, cranky Valentin created more than 500 skits and FARCES that raised Bavarian folk comedy to a sphere of universal significance. His comic world comprised the recalcitrance of inanimate objects, cross-purposes of language and the malignity of human nature. Often, by a scene's end, the stage – a record shop, a radio studio or a variety stage – would be totally demolished, in the wake of monstrous physical and logical complications. Most of his acts were filmed in detail after 1912; from 1941 to the end of the Second World War Valentin was withdrawn, making only a few radio broadcasts thereafter. His admirers included BRECHT, who compared him to Chaplin. LS

Valle-Inclán, Ramón del 1866–1936 Spanish playwright, novelist and aesthetic theorist whose stature in world theatre has grown considerably since his death. His most innovative plays, the expressionistic, cinematographic *esperpentos* (grotesque tragicomedies), were once thought unperformable but are now compared to ARTAUD, BRECHT and the THEATRE OF THE ABSURD. His masterworks attacking the military and traditional morality were prohibited by Franco-era CENSORSHIP and hence premiered abroad.

His first play was staged in 1899. Important early works include the children's FARCE, *La cabeza del dragón* (*The Dragon's Head*, 1909) and the metaplay, *La marquesa Rosalinda* (1912). The latter, a 'sentimental, grotesque farce' staged by the prestigious company of María Guerrero, juxtaposes COMMEDIA DELL'ARTE characters and stylized aristocrats. *Comedias bárbaras* (*Barbaric Comedies*) is an epic trilogy set in 19th-century Galicia and centring on a patriarchal figure whose carnal excesses are offset by his generosity and nobility of spirit, and on his sons, whose degeneracy marks the end of the feudal order. *Aguila de blasón* (*The Eagle Scutcheon*, 1907), *Romance de lobos* (*Ballad of Wolves*, 1908), and *Cara de Plata* (*Silver Face*, 1922) were staged separately in Spain between 1966 and 1970–1, but the trilogy was not performed as a unit until the marathon productions in 1991 by Lavelli's Théâtre National de la Colline and José Carlos Plaza's TEATRO NACIONAL MARÍA GUERRERO.

In 1920 Valle-Inclán wrote two plays that established his international reputation: *Divinas palabras* (*Divine Words*) and *Luces de bohemia* (*Bohemian Lights*). Set in Galicia, *Divine Words* portrays the subculture of beggars and presents a corrosive SATIRE of religious superstition and hypocrisy, the theme of incest, and the daring appearance on stage of a nude actress. Premiered at Madrid's TEATRO ESPAÑOL by MARGARITA XIRGU, it was revived in 1976 to international acclaim by Víctor García and Núria Espert.

Bohemian Lights, an epic treatment of a blind poet's descent into the Madrilenian hell and thence death, was Valle-Inclán's first *esperpento*. The term is defined as a systematic deformation of Spanish reality, as if reflected in concave mirrors. Because the perspective on the characters is from above, the classic heroes of tragedy become parodic anti-heroes. Dehumanized characters are variously seen as animals or puppets. The world premiere of *Bohemian Lights* was the 1963 production at Paris's Théâtre National Populaire, directed by Vilar and starring Georges Wilson. Pasqual's stunning 1984 staging, starring José María Rodero, was enthusiastically received in Madrid and at the Théâtre de l'Europe.

Other important plays include *Los cuernos de don Friolera* (*Don Friolera's Horns*, 1925), a parody of Calderónian honour, and several 'melodramas for puppets' and 'miracle plays for silhouettes'. These one-acters are marked by their violent, macabre action and their emphasis on sacrilege and superstition. The most performed internationally are *Rosa de papel* (*The Paper Rose*) and *Ligazón* (*Blood Pact*). PZ

Valleran le Conte fl.1590–1614 French actor-manager, one of the earliest for whom documentation is extant. He was a strolling player in the provinces in 1592–3 with a repertoire of biblical plays and works by Jodelle, and in 1599 he brought a company to Paris, signing a three-month lease for the Hôtel de Bourgogne. Between then and 1612 his career alternated between provincial touring and repeated attempts to establish himself in the capital, but prosperity eluded him and on several occasions he was obliged to reform his troupe or to amalgamate it with another. The bulk of his repertoire probably consisted of tragedies and tragicomedies by Alexandre Hardy, whom he had engaged as company dramatist, and contracts signed with tradesmen provide evidence of the multiple stage decor that he used for their performance, though he is also reported to have appeared in farce. In 1612, perhaps tiring of the struggle to conquer Paris, he formed yet another company and returned to the provinces. DR

Vampilov, Aleksandr (Valentinovich) 1937–72 Soviet dramatist who, on the basis of a short canon of plays which have been compared to those of Gogol and Chekhov, has been called the greatest playwright of his generation and has become a major influence on those who have followed him. A native Siberian and graduate of Irkutsk University (1960), Vampilov published his first collection of short stories and comic sketches on provincial life, *A Chain of Being* (1961), while pursuing a five-year career in journalism. His playwriting career, which included some early provincially published efforts – *Katya Kozlova's Happiness* (one act, 1959) and *Tichaia Factory* (1960) – began in earnest when as a student at Moscow's Gorky Literary Institute his one-act comedy *The House Overlooking a Field* (1964) was published in the influential Moscow journal *Theatre*. The following year saw *Theatre*'s publication of Vampilov's *Farewell in June*, and Rozov's and Arbuzov's sponsorship of the young dramatist's membership of the Writers' Union.

In these and his other plays Vampilov examined the problems of young and old in accepting societal values and institutions and responsibility for their own failed dreams and relationships, and the fall from grace precipitated by man's physical and spiritual separation from nature. Whereas the young protagonists of *Farewell in June* and *The Elder Son* (1967) are still capable of making a moral choice, the confirmed middle-aged egoists of Vampilov's best two plays, *Duck Hunting* (1967) and *Last Summer in Chulimsk* (1971), either no longer care or are no longer able to do so. In *Duck Hunting*, the last of his plays to be staged in the USSR (at the Theatre of Russian Drama in Riga, 1976) and the most bitter, Vampilov is credited with having created a model of the 'urban grotesque', which has been adapted by other Soviet-Russian dramatists such as Lyudmila Petrusievskaya, Semyon Zlotnikov, Mark Rozovsky, Viktor Slavkin, Arbuzov and Volodin (see Russia and the republics of the former Soviet Union). *Duck Hunting*'s protagonist – an egocentric misfit and anti-hero – its flashback structure and telephone motif, tied to a cruel-joke premiss and a threatened suicide (reminiscent of Erdman's *The Suicide*), are typical of the breed. The 'crippled personality', whom the Soviets regarded as an aberration, like the old duck who can no longer migrate, has failed on some profound level. This theme is echoed in Vampilov's *Seagull* variant, *Last Summer in Chulimsk*, in which self-pitying and spiritless people living at the edge of a breath-taking Siberian wilderness abuse it and one another.

Vampilov's indebtedness to the traditional farce-vaudeville of Gogol, Chekhov and others is demonstrated in his unfinished *vaudeville The Incomparable Nakonechnikov* (1971) and in the two plays published under the title *Provincial Anecdotes* (1971) – *Twenty Minutes with an Angel* (1962) and *An Incident with a Typesetter* (1970) – whose mistaken identity premiss and escalating frenzy of paranoia suggest *The Inspector General*. In 1974, two years after his death from a heart seizure precipitated by a boating accident, fully one-third of all 380 Soviet dramatic theatres were performing one or more of Vampilov's plays. SG

Van Druten, John 1901–57 American playwright whose dramatic career began in London, though it was in New York that he created his most successful work, which is characterized as witty, domestic comedy that usually reflects contemporary middle-class society. *The Voice of the Turtle* (1943), a romantic three-character, wartime comedy, ran for over 1500 performances. Nostalgic *I Remember Mama* (1944) was adapted from a novel; the adaptation *I Am a Camera* (1951), which is more cynical in its portrait of Berlin, inspired the musical *Cabaret* (1966). *Bell, Book and Candle* (1950) is a clever play about a beautiful witch who must abjure her craft to secure the man she loves. An autobiography, *This Way to the Present*, was published in 1938. RHW

Van Itallie, Jean-Claude 1936– American playwright, director, producer and teacher. Born in Brussels, Van Itallie became a naturalized American citizen in 1952. After studying at Harvard and the Neighborhood Playhouse, he made his debut as a writer in 1963 with *War*. His *Motel* and *Pavanne* were produced at the Café La

MaMa in 1965, attracting considerable attention to him as a new talent. *America Hurrah* appeared at the Pocket Theatre, New York City, in 1966; *The Serpent* premiered in Rome in 1968 and was produced by the OPEN THEATRE, NYC, in 1969. Other scripts include *King of the US* (1972), *Mystery Play* (1973) and his own versions of ANTON CHEKHOV's *The Seagull* (1973), *The Cherry Orchard* (1977) and *The Three Sisters* (1979). His 1991 play about the effects of AIDS, *Ancient Boys* (La MaMa), failed to receive critical approval, and in spring 1992 his dramatization of BULGAKOV's novel *Master and Margarita* ran briefly OFF-BROADWAY.

His affiliation with the Open Theatre and JOSEPH CHAIKIN placed him at the forefront of experimental dramaturgy in the 1960s and 70s. Especially with the Open Theatre, Van Itallie merged European traditions with a poetic vision of American experience. SMA

Vanbrugh, Sir **John** 1664–1726 English dramatist and architect. Educated in England and France, he became an ensign in the Army in 1689 and was imprisoned in France for spying from 1689 to 1692, including a period in the Bastille. Appointed a captain in 1696, he began his career as a playwright in the same year with *The Relapse*, ostensibly a sequel to COLLEY CIBBER's *Love's Last Shift*, a comedy in which Cibber's characters' repentance and reformation are found to be temporary and the marriage problems left unresolved. In 1697 both parts of his SATIRE on contemporary society, *Aesop*, were performed, as well as *The Provoked Wife*, his best play. Here Vanbrugh analyses the loveless marriage of convenience and the hopelessness of the spouses when divorce is effectively impossible. Attacked by JEREMY COLLIER for the immorality and profanity of his plays, Vanbrugh defended himself in *A Short Vindication of The Relapse and The Provoked Wife* (1698), by turns wittily and disingenuously. He adapted a play by DANCOURT as a brilliant FARCE, *The Country House* (1698), FLETCHER's *The Pilgrim* (1700), another Dancourt play as *The Confederacy* (1705), and a MOLIÈRE comedy as *Squire Trelooby* (1704) in collaboration with CONGREVE and William Walsh. His last play, an original COMEDY called *A Journey to London*, was left unfinished and completed by Cibber as *The Provoked Husband* in 1728.

He began his career as an architect in 1699 when he began the plans for Castle Howard in Yorkshire, the foundation stone of which was laid in 1701 and which was completed in 1714. He designed the Queen's Theatre in the Haymarket, which opened in 1705, and Blenheim Palace, for which he was Surveyor from 1705 to 1716.

Vanbrugh was licensed, with Congreve, to manage the Queen's, but its poor acoustics and distance from the centre of London made it financially disastrous. Vanbrugh continued to be involved in the confused world of theatre management at this time until he sold out his interests in 1708. He was knighted in 1714. PH

Vandenhoff, George 1813–85 British-born actor and lawyer, son of the actor John Vandenhoff. After a debut at COVENT GARDEN in 1839, George began his American career at the PARK THEATRE in 1842 as Hamlet. As an actor he was noted for his correctness, but he lacked power and apparently never liked the stage. After returning to

England in 1853, where he and his new wife acted in the provinces, he retired from the stage in the mid-1850s. Although admitted to the New York Bar in 1858, he spent much of his time teaching elocution and giving public readings. In 1860 he published his reminiscences, *Leaves from an Actor's Notebook*. DBW

Variétés, Théâtre des see BOULEVARD

variety The most widespread and widely attended form of urban entertainment in the 19th and early 20th centuries. The element of variety is common to popular theatre, which seeks to engage limited attention spans with a diversity of skills. Egypt in the 5th century BC had its sequences of musicians, dancers, acrobats and female jugglers performing for rich men's guests; and the wandering minstrel of the Middle Ages was capable of a broad range of diversions. As a distinct genre, variety was organized in the 19th century in the music-halls and public houses of Europe and America, took on elements of CIRCUS, and ramified into CABARET and REVUE. A major contributory factor to its prominence was a new proletarian public, who had lost their communal village traditions and were receptive to less demanding, cheaper and more colourful amusement than the 'legitimate' theatre offered. Innovative forms of publicity and presentation developed to exploit the form's commercial potential.

Variety can be identified by its series of attractions, 'turns' or 'numbers', unconnected by any theme. In contrast to the modern dramatic theatre, the audience is encouraged to eat, drink and smoke during the performance. In Great Britain, the common form was the MUSIC-HALL, which took to calling itself 'variety' as it gained respectability; in America, in contrast, variety preferred to be known as VAUDEVILLE. Nomenclature is confused: the chief European terms are, in France, the *café concert* and *CAFÉ CHANTANT* and, later, the revue-like music-hall; in Germany, the low *SINGSPIELhalle* and *TINGELTANGEL* and the more circus-like and spectacular *Variété*; in Russia, the disreputable *myuzik-kholl* and the all-encompassing *estrada*. In Spain variety remained closely linked to folkloric dance and song, in Italy to circus. Variety's apogee came before the First World War; afterwards it had to compete with and was absorbed by cinema, radio and television. Its influence on the literary drama has been enormous (e.g. BRECHT), but more especially it has been a constant inspiration for experimental theatrical innovators, from the Italian futurists of the 1910s to radical feminist groups of the 1980s. LS

> *See*: J. Feschotte, *Histoire du music-hall*, Paris, 1965; E. Günther, *Geschichte des Variétés*, Berlin, 1978; Jacques-Charles, *Cent ans de music-hall*, Paris, 1956; W. Jansen, *Das Variété*, Berlin, 1987; A. Retana, *Historia del arte frívolo*, Madrid, 1964.

Varlamov, Konstantin (Aleksandrovich) 1848–1915 Russian actor, who, after the usual provincial apprenticeship, entered the troupe of the Imperial Alexandra Theatre in St Petersburg in 1875, where his first success was as Menelaus in *La Belle Hélène* (1877). Nicknamed Uncle Kostya, Varlamov was the best Russian FARCEUR of his time, imbuing his creations with emotional warmth and irony. He was superb in GOGOL, TURGENEV and OSTROVSKY (29 roles in his plays). In the 1880s he was stricken with elephantiasis, but continued to act sitting down, letting his mobile face and expressive voice do all the work. So in MEYERHOLD's stylish staging of *Dom Juan* (1910) he played Sganarelle seated downstage right, chatting with the audience as a kind of master of ceremonies. LS

Vasari, Giorgio 1511–74 Italian architect, painter, stage designer and writer on art. One of the key figures in the development of perspective stage setting, after a period in the mid- and late 1530s working as assistant to SANGALLO in Florence, Vasari worked elsewhere, particularly in Venice on a production of ARETINO's *La Talanta* (1541). Later, in Florence, he built the wooden theatre of the Palazzo Vecchio, devised the spectacular entertainments to celebrate the marriage of Francesco de'Medici and Giovanna d'Austria in 1566, and introduced an important innovation in stage decoration in 1569 with a system of rotating *periaktoi*. His *Vite de'piu eccellenti pittori, scultori ed architetti* (*Lives of the Most Excellent Painters, Sculptors and Architects*, 1530–68) is an invaluable source of information about the work of Renaissance painters, designers and architects. (See also THEATRE BUILDINGS; THEATRE DESIGN.) KR

Vasiliev, Anatoly (Aleksandrovich) 1942– Soviet Russian director. When he graduated from the State Institute for Theatre Arts, official theatres, alarmed by his wild-eyed, bearded demeanour and off-the-wall concepts, failed to hire him; but he did manage to direct Zagradnik's *Solo for an Alarm Clock* at the MOSCOW ART THEATRE (1973). In 1977 a former teacher asked him to join the Stanislavsky Theatre, Moscow, where his staging of the first version of GORKY's *Vassa Zheleznova* was a revelation; with taut suspense and a stunning use of stage space, he made it a manifesto about human aspiration. After work in radio and TV, he turned VIKTOR SLAVKIN's first full-length play, *A Young Man's Grown-up Daughter* (1981), into a hit by plunging the audience into a reconstruction of the 1960s. Inspired by French cinema, he and his favourite actors called themselves 'new-wave theatre', but ran foul of the bureaucracy. In 1982 they were forced out of the Stanislavsky Theatre and took refuge at the Taganka, where, after three years of rehearsal, they presented Slavkin's *Cerceau* (1985) which became an international success. This was followed in 1987 by a brilliant reinterpretation of *Six Characters in Search of an Author*, and Vasiliev began to hypothesize a 'vertical' theatre requiring a liberated artist in communication with God.

Although his School of Dramatic Art in Moscow was officially recognized under Gorbachev, he abandoned directing in Russia; in 1992 he produced LERMONTOV's *Masquerade* at the COMÉDIE-FRANÇAISE. LS

vaudeville, American This essentially American form of VARIETY has nothing to do with the French *vaudeville*, a FARCE studded with songs set to popular tunes; rather, the term attempted to lend a veneer of elegance to what was originally rough-and-ready entertainment. A so-called 'vaudeville' house had been opened by William Valentine in 1840, and H. J. Sargent's Great Vaudeville Co. was playing in Louisville in 1871, but the term did not catch on till later.

The usual venue for variety performances in the late 1860s was the concert saloon, its waiter- and dancing-girls closely allied to the prostitutes who preyed on the all-male audience. Out-of-work minstrels and chorines – unemployed after the decline of the leg-show – drifted into these 'olio entertainments', as did newly formed double acts. Unlike European variety, where song was the standard unit, broad comedy and exuberant dance predominated here. This 'honky-tonk' style permutated into BURLESQUE, while respectable variety gained greater professionalism and urbanity between 1876 and 1893 to become vaudeville.

TONY PASTOR, hoping to lure a family audience with give-aways and promises of clean amusement, was instrumental in this development, and the traditional, if debatable, date given for the birth of vaudeville is the opening of his 14th Street Theatre, New York, on 24 October 1881. But the innovation was enlarged and expanded by B. F. KEITH (1846–1914) and his associate EDWARD F. ALBEE (1857–1930). Keith began with a 'store-show', the Gaiety Museum, Boston, and had Albee transform it in 1885 into a Japanese tea-garden offering a tabloid opera. So great was their success that they soon owned several theatres and in 1894 opened the first exclusively vaudeville house, the Boston Colonial, typical of the opulent palaces designed to lure the middle-class spectator into a fairy-tale world of luxury. Keith and Albee eliminated offensive material, fining offenders, and introduced the continuous show, so that one could enter the theatre at any time between 9.30 a.m. and 10.30 p.m. and see a performance. The invention of 'continuous vaudeville', well ensconced by 1896, is attributed to F. F. PROCTOR, a sometime partner, who claimed 'to give the masses what they want', but forbade smoking and drinking in the auditorium.

Competing with these robber barons were Martin Beck, credited with establishing the touring vaudeville company, who backed 'class acts' to educate the public; OSCAR HAMMERSTEIN I who aimed his Roof at an elitist and his Olympic at a more popular public; William Morris, J. J. Murdoch and Sylvester Poli. The Keith–Albee circuit dominated the eastern USA through its many theatres (over 400 by 1920) and booking offices; Beck's Orpheum circuit played the West, though he also built the New York PALACE, which soon was regarded as vaudeville's Valhalla. In addition, there were thousands of small houses scattered throughout the nation, enabling performers to play one-night stands throughout the season. Vaudevillians became a nomadic race, living much of the year on railway carriages and platforms and in dreary boarding-houses.

By 1900 the typical 'polite vaudeville' bill had grown formulaic, and was divided into two parts by an intermission. The first part would open with a 'dumb act', animals or acrobats, whose effect would not be damaged by a noisy entering audience. The number three slot was intended to wake up the house, the number four to deliver the first solid punch, and the last before the interval a knockout that would bring them back wanting more. The prime position was 'next to closing', where the 'headliner' or star of stars appeared. The concluding act was meant as a 'chaser', often a cinematic offering, like a newsreel. Turns or 'numbers' seldom lasted more than 10 to 20 minutes, although some popular egoists like HARRY LAUDER and AL JOLSON might usurp a whole hour. According to GEORGE BURNS, a performer needed only 17 good minutes, which he could play year in, year out across the country, before the act became too pirated or shopworn for use. The diversity of performance was considerable: in addition to the song-and-dance and COMEDY acts, there were MIMES, ventriloquists, eccentrics, musical virtuosi, acrobats and JUGGLERS, male and female impersonators (see FEMALE IMPERSONATION; MALE IMPERSONATION), miniature musicals, monologuists, trained animals (see ANIMALS AS PERFORMERS), conjurors, demonstrations of new inventions, and even famous criminals discoursing on their lurid past.

Much of the comedy in vaudeville dealt in racial stereotypes, with the Dutch, Irish, Jewish, blackface, Swedish and Italian comics the most familiar, reflecting the melting-pot nature of urban American society; by 1910 many of the older types, including the hick and Bowery tough, were *passé*. Low comedy was categorized as 'jazz', a fast routine to speed up an act; 'hokum', crude fun verging on vulgarity. Despite the efforts of the managers, innuendo was often resorted to, particularly in the 1920s, when more sophisticated audiences expected it.

Dance tended to be acrobatic until the First World War, when adagio and exhibition ballroom dancing and even imitations of the Ballets Russes arrived. Singers were either sentimental or strenuous, but American audiences, unless exhorted by such devices as 'following the bouncing ball' on a projected songsheet, seldom joined in the chorus – another token of the heterogeneity of the public. Among the leading performers spawned by vaudeville or trained in its excellent school were EVA TANGUAY, the 'I Don't Care' girl; Elsie Janis, NORA BAYES; W. C. FIELDS, who moved from juggling to comic skits; EDDIE CANTOR and AL JOLSON who retained the corked face of MINSTRELSy, as did the black comedian BERT WILLIAMS; GEORGE M. COHAN whose family had been variety pioneers; WILL ROGERS with his low-key commentary; and GEORGE BURNS AND GRACIE ALLEN, whose double act refined the Dumb Dora creation of Ryan and Lee. As vaudeville increased in respectability and popularity, stars of the 'legit', like LILLIE LANGTRY, Ethel Barrymore (see DREW–BARRYMORE FAMILY) and ALLA NAZIMOVA, played 'tab' (shortened) versions of their dramatic hits on the circuits.

The American language was enriched by vaudeville slang: a success was a wow, a panic or a riot, a failure a flop, all wet or all washed up. Duffey and Sweeney originated the phrase, 'We died in ... ', to indicate an utter fiasco. The minstrel Billy Emerson's 'hoofer' for dancer became popular, along with the injuction 'Strut your stuff' and the exit 'Shuffle off to Buffalo'. Some terms were too technical to become widespread, such as 'grouch bag' for a purse pinned to the underwear for safety's sake, 'feeder' for 'straight-man', 'split time' for three days' work in any theatre, or 'death trail' for a circuit of small towns. But 'coffin nails' for cigarettes, which came from Junie McCree's act, and 'belly laughs', coined by Jack Conway, entered the language.

Vaudeville was the dominant form of American entertainment by 1890, and grew exponentially: in 1896 New York had seven vaudeville theatres; by 1910, 22. It came to be clearly differentiated into the Big Time, with its two-a-day offerings of an eight- or nine-act bill, and the Small Time with fewer acts and a film played continuously. The empire-building of the leading managements created booking agencies which could blacklist performers who did not conform to the rules or who failed to kick back percentages of their salaries (often levies were imposed by the house manager before the salary was paid). Keith–Albee created the United Booking Office (UBO) in 1906, whose impositions were so outrageous that the performers banded into a protective society, the White Rats, which failed to sustain its strike in 1916. Astutely, Albee backed a new organization, the National Vaudeville Artists (NVA), in 1916, which limited some of the abuses without seriously harming the managers' interests.

AFRICAN-AMERICAN performers were exploited by the Theatre Owners' Booking Association, or Chitlin Circuit – a busy group of segregated theatres stretching from New York to Florida, from Chicago to New Orleans, but primarily centred in the South – that offered black vaudevillians low pay and little future.

The decline of vaudeville is attributable to a number of factors. Between 1905 and 1912 the Big Time had grown in sophistication, putting its emphasis on glamour, novelty and lavish wardrobes; the influence of MUSICAL COMEDY and REVUE could be felt. Before 1925, it reached its period of greatest growth, but the cinema proved a powerful rival for the working-class audiences made uncomfortable by vaudeville's aspirations to gentility and its increased admission prices (the Palace went as high as two dollars). The car, put within everyone's financial reach by Henry Ford, enabled city-dwellers to escape to the country. During Prohibition, the proliferation of nightclubs offered a sophisticated and alcoholic alternative to those bored by vaudeville's stale material. By the mid-1920s many vaudeville houses were converted to cinemas, and the succumbing of the Palace in 1932, its *coup de grâce* delivered by the Depression, is considered the symbolic terminus of the form. Some managers, like MARCUS LOEW, persisted in alternating films with live performance at their houses, but gradually vaudeville came to be regarded as the seedbed for mass media: many of the most popular comedians, singers and dancers in the movies, on the radio and, later, television had honed their skills in vaudeville. LS

See: C. Caffin, *Vaudeville*, New York, 1914; D. Gilbert, *American Vaudeville*, New York, 1940, 1963; J. Laurie Jr, *Vaudeville: From the Honky-tonks to the Palace*, New York, 1953; A. Slide, *The Vaudevillians*, Westport, Conn., 1981; S. Staples, *Male–Female Comedy Teams in American Vaudeville 1865–1932*, Ann Arbor, 1984; C. W. Stein (ed.), *American Vaudeville As Seen by Its Contemporaries*, New York, 1984.

Vaudeville, Théâtre du see BOULEVARD

Vaughan, Kate [Catherine Candelon] c.1852–1903 British dancer and BURLESQUE actress, who formed, with NELLIE FARREN, EDWARD TERRY and EDWARD ROYCE, the famous GAIETY Quartette from 1876 to 83. She had been trained as a dancer, playing the MUSIC-HALLS as part of the

Vaughan Troupe, when JOHN HOLLINGSHEAD discovered her. After 1883, she devoted herself increasingly to straight acting in classical roles.   PT

Vauthier, Jean 1910– Belgian dramatist. First revealed to the Parisian public by André Reybaz in 1951, he is remembered for the creation of Capitaine Bada, a cross between the common man and the writer who struggles for control of his life and his language but becomes lost in a welter of baroque poetic prose. BARRAULT scored a personal triumph in *Le Personnage combattant* (*The Fighting Character*, 1956) and in 1966 *Capitaine Bada* was revived by MARÉCHAL, who also commissioned *Le Sang* (*Blood*, 1970). Vauthier has made several dramatic adaptations, notably of SHAKESPEARE and EURIPIDES.   DB

Vedrenne, J(ohn) E(ugene) 1867–1930 British theatre manager who worked with F. R. BENSON and JOHNSTON FORBES-ROBERTSON, before becoming manager of the ROYAL COURT THEATRE where he brought in GRANVILLE BARKER for the 1904 season. There and, in 1907, at the Savoy they mounted a series of productions that influenced the whole development of British theatre – not only establishing SHAW on the public stage, but introducing GALSWORTHY and HAUPTMANN. Their example encouraged the formation of the new repertory theatre movement (see REGIONAL THEATRE (BRITAIN)), while Vedrenne's insistence on maximum expenses of £200 per production enforced simplified settings that focused attention on ensemble acting. After the partnership was dissolved in 1911 he became manager of the Royalty Theatre, and in 1920 of the Little Theatre (London).   CI

Vega (Carpio), Lope (Félix) de 1562–1635 Spanish playwright, poet and novelist whose works, along with those of CALDERÓN, dominated the stage during Spain's GOLDEN AGE. He was born in Madrid, the son of a craftsman, and studied at the University of Alcalá. He supplemented his income as secretary to the Dukes of Alba and of Sessa, among others. Lope's private life was tempestuous – two wives, innumerable love affairs and mistresses, 14 children, imprisonment and exile for libel and, finally, the priesthood. His professional life was equally intense – a claim to 1500 plays (of which some 400–500 have survived) whose popularity with audiences established him as a prodigy and national genius in his lifetime.

From an emerging popular theatre, Lope develops and defines the artistic paradigm for a flourishing national drama, the COMEDIA nueva (new comedy), which eschews the rigidity of classical models, mixes serious and comic themes and characters, has three acts and is written in a variety of verse metres. His theory is expressed in his *Arte nuevo de hacer comedias* (*The New Art of Writing Plays*, 1609). Given his voracious appetite for reading and life as well as his enormous facility for writing verses, his dramatic plots defy easy categorization. He adapted biblical stories, saints' lives, foreign and national histories, ballads, Italian *novelle* and mythology, and utilized his fertile imagination to intuit the needs and expectations of ever increasing and demanding audiences of diverse social backgrounds.

Among his most successful serious plays are those which show the superior virtue and honour of the peasant in conflict with the more powerful nobility, whose excesses include sexual aggression. *Fuenteovejuna*, based on historical fact, depicts the sexual abuses and oppression inflicted on simple villagers (Fuenteovejuna is the name of the village) by overlords acting with a misguided sense of privilege and of their seigneurial rights. Impotent and reluctant to avenge themselves at first, the townspeople eventually kill the Commander and his aides, urged on by a memorable speech by the wronged daughter of the Mayor. The villagers respond with a communal 'Fuenteovejuna did it', when brutally questioned about the killing, and are eventually pardoned by the Monarchs. In an age when sedition was a real threat to the throne, it is unusual that the Monarchs should have condoned such an act of rebellion; however, it has been discovered that the Commander and his order had also aligned with the Portuguese candidate in the War of Succession, thus tempering the play's apparently radically democratic spirit.

In the more lyrical *Peribañez y el comendador de Ocaña* (*Peribañez*), the virtues of country life and inherent peasant honour are extolled by example and song in contrast to the lustful intentions of a presumptuous overlord. Peribañez undermines the Commander's insistent desire to seduce his wife but must resort to killing him. Peribañez is reluctantly pardoned by the king and sent off to war. A comedy which shows the tensions between idyllic country life and the appeal of urbane courtly life is *El villano en su rincón* (*The Countryman in His Corner*), in which the proud and prosperous peasant is finally wooed to the court by royal favour.

Lope's light-hearted, urbane comedies of romantic intrigue show a variety of plot complications, with disguises, deceptions, misunderstandings, letters and so on, in which love and jealousies are aroused and resolved to the satisfaction or accommodation of all. In *La dama boba* (*The Idiot Lady*), the stupidity of the protagonist is transformed by the power of love. In *El perro del hortelano* (*The Dog in the Manger*), class differences obstruct the love of a wealthy widow for her secretary but are resolved by the clever intervention of a servant. *Las bizarrías de Belisa* (*Belisa's Tricks*) features a disdainful young woman whose strategies include dressing as a man to win her man. In these plays Lope privileges natural inclination over social custom and creates resourceful female characters.

His tragedies include the ironic *El castigo sin venganza* (*Justice without Revenge*), based on an Italian story. An adulterous wife is unwittingly killed by her lover; he is encouraged by her profligate and neglectful older husband, who is also the lover's biological father. The lover, in turn, is killed by a servant. *El caballero de Olmedo* (*The Knight of Olmedo*) is a brooding and passionate story based on a Spanish song in which the impending murder by a jealous rival is skilfully and artistically conveyed by the poetry.

Lope's plays were rediscovered by the German romantics and, today, are frequently staged in Spain and abroad. ElB

Velten, Johannes 1640–?93 German actor. After receiving a university education, from 1685 Velten led a troupe of players under the patronage of the Elector of Saxony. He did much to raise standards of acting and of repertoire. He introduced, in German adaptation, plays of CORNEILLE, RACINE and MOLIÈRE. His troupe combined both improvisational and scripted acting. Some years after his death it was taken over by CAROLINE NEUBER. SW

Venezuela Since 1914 Venezuela and oil have become inseparable concepts. The immense reserves of Lake Maracaibo have been both the boon and the curse of this century, permitting enormous growth and public projects while contributing to greed, bribery and venal public officials. Previously, coffee was the dominant product of this country crossed by the Andes, with huge plains to the east and a population concentrated in a few cities, and with vast areas mostly unsettled. In the 19th century, after independence led by the liberator, Simón Bolívar, the country was governed by inept and often corrupt leaders with dictatorial tendencies. In the 20th century, the dictatorships of Juan Vicente Gómez (1908–35) and Marcos Pérez Jiménez (1952–8) were separated by various military regimes. In spite of the favourable constitution with which Venezuela ('Little Venice') was established by Bolívar, democracy has been infrequent but notable under Isaías Obedina Bugarita (1941–5) and the 1945–8 Triennial resulting from Democratic Action's 'October Revolution'. Cultural development has lagged because of Venezuela's dependence on foreign economic and artistic systems.

Ethnologists have documented Native American theatre events in the region by Muku, Jirajara and the Arawaks, but activity was isolated and no influence is evident in later theatre development. In the colonial years local groups performed European religious and secular plays, and there is evidence of an anonymous AUTO SACRAMENTAL, *Auto a Nuestra Señora del Rosario*, in the 1760s. The first theatre building, constructed in 1784 and known as the Coliseo (Coliseum), or the Teatro del Conde (Theatre of the Count), was destroyed by an earthquake in 1812. In that theatre, Andrés Bello, the neoclassic grammarian, poet, humanitarian and first playwright of importance in Venezuela, presented his *Venezuela consolada* (*Venezuela Consoled*, 1804); his later *España restaurada* (*Spain Restored*, 1808) was an allegorical defence of the Spanish monarchy of Fernando VII on the eve of independence. Although noteworthy because of Bello's reputation, his theatre in general was of limited quality.

The sparse population in Caracas did little to stimulate the production of a local theatre industry throughout the 19th century. Various theatres, such as the Caracas Theatre (1854, restored 1885) and the Guzmán Blanco Theatre (1881, now the Municipal Theatre), were constructed. Music and Italian opera flourished. Foreign plays were presented frequently, not only by Spanish playwrights such as ZORRILLA and Tamayo y Baus, but also by French and English writers. Teresa Carreño, a talented pianist, gave brilliant performances as did her opera company, in collaboration with her husband, the baritone Tagliapietra. Martín de la Guardia (1836–1907) caught the public attention with a play called *Cosme II de Medicis*, written for the Caracas Dramatic Company and performed in 1848, which he followed with a long series of exotic works. For the most part, the *sainete* (see *GÉNERO CHICO*) was the most popular form of theatre in Venezuela

during the 19th century. While history records the names of many writers during this period, no plays of great value are to be found.

The 20th century Romantic and sentimental tendencies continued into the early 20th century. In 1915 Rómulo Gallegos, celebrated novelist and short-term president of the country (1947–8), presented *El milagro del año* (*Miracle of the Year*). The year 1916 marked the end of a brilliant career for Miguel I. Leicibabaza, an impresario and promoter responsible for many theatrical events in Venezuela. In 1917 the company of María Guerrero and her husband Fernando Díaz de Mendoza arrived in Caracas with a splendid retinue, offering plays by Spanish playwrights ECHEGARAY, Marquina and the brothers ALVAREZ QUINTERO, but these productions did little to stimulate national dramaturgy.

The first half of the century failed to produce a strong theatre movement, although a sense of national identity began to coalesce within some particular groups. La Sociedad de Amigos de Teatro (Society of Friends of Theatre) in its short five years (1942–7) promoted more works by national authors than any previous group. Other groups, some formed earlier, such as the Teatro Obrero (Workers' Theatre, 1938), the Compañía Venezolana de Dramas y Comedias (Venezuelan Company of Plays and Comedies, 1939) and the Teatro Universitario (University Theatre, 1946) contributed to the renovation during a period dominated by *COSTUMBRISMO*, a familiar form that had captured popular character types and customs in Spanish traditions since the 19th century. Technically and psychologically superficial, the plays normally used humour to satirize the stereotypical figures within the society. Rafael Guinand (1881–1929) and Leopoldo Ayala Michelena relied on these popular costumbristic forms. Throughout the first half of the 20th century, Venezuela welcomed travelling companies from Spain, France and the Americas that brought conservative, often outdated productions. IBSEN and O'NEILL inspired a naturalistic orientation (see NATURALISM).

The so-called Creole theatre left an important mark, but a new generation of authors and directors during the 50s sought to bring Venezuelan theatre abreast of contemporary developments on a world scale. Productions of COCTEAU's *The Indifferent Lover* in 1950 and MILLER's *Death of a Salesman* in 1951 provided new standards for Venezuelans to emulate in theme and style. Of transcendental importance was the arrival of three foreign directors who provided an original stamp and began to train another entire group. Alberto de Paz y Mateos arrived from his native Spain in 1945, and in the Liceo Fermín Toro joined the writer ROMÁN CHALBAUD and director Nicolás Curiel. Jesús Gómez Obregón arrived two years later from Mexico to teach theatre courses in the Ministry of Education, where in short order (for political reasons he had to leave in 1950) he created disciples who have left their own mark: Humberto Orsini, Eduardo Moreno, Gilberto Pinto and Pedro Martán, among others. Juana Sujo arrived from Argentina in 1949 to make a film, staying until her death in 1961. In 1950 she established the Dramatic Studio Juana Sujo; in 1952 the Studio became the National Theatre School, and in 1954 the Venezuelan

Theatre Society and the Latin branch of the Caracas Theatre Club. In 1959 she inaugurated the Los Caobos Theatre, the first stable professional theatre in Venezuela. Her students include, among others, Esteban Herrera, Margot Antillano, América Alonso, José Antonio Gutiérrez and Porfirio Rodríguez. Later the Chilean Horacio Peterson added impetus by assuming the direction of the theatre section of the Ateneo de Caracas (Caracas Atheneum) in 1957.

César Rengifo, a talented artist, writer and director, is considered the father of the modern Venezuelan theatre. He evaluated the Venezuelan national past, creating analogies with contemporary situations through a series of historical trilogies focusing on different periods.

The Venezuelan theatre began to acquire a sense of national identity. In the 1960s, playwrights experimented freely with absurdist (see THEATRE OF THE ABSURD), ARTAUDian and BRECHTian techniques to uncover the realities of Venezuelan social, political and psychological problems. The Grupo Compás (Compás Group), directed by Romeo Costea, was instrumental in introducing these vanguard tendencies into Venezuela. The Venezuelan Theatre Union (1954) promoted the active development of both experimental and professional theatre groups, and the national theatre festivals, initiated in 1959 and repeated at irregular intervals thereafter, encouraged new playwrights and productions. ISAAC CHOCRÓN, Román Chalbaud and JOSÉ IGNACIO CABRUJAS earned the epithet of the 'Holy Trinity' for their innovative work with the NUEVO GRUPO (New Group, created in 1967), as they worked to ele-

El Nuevo Grupo in Isaac Chocrón's *La Revolucion*, Caracas, 1971.

vate the national consciousness of theatre as an artistic form. Caracas's other major group, the RAJATABLA, was created in 1971 as a subsidiary of the Caracas Atheneum and directed for many years by the Argentine Carlos Giménez. The National Theatre Company was created by presidential decree in 1984, with Isaac Chocrón as its first director.

In a flourishing economy, Venezuela sponsored an ambitious and exciting International Theatre Festival on a two-year cycle from 1973 to 1983, when fiscal considerations required its suspension. In 1977 CELCIT (Centro Latinoamericano de Creación e Investigación Teatral, the Latin American Centre of Theatre Creativity and Research) was established as an adjunct of the Ateneo. Under the capable direction of Luis Molina and with the patronage of María Teresa Castillo, the organization began to coordinate theatre events, exchanges and publications throughout the Americas.

Theatrical activity in the provinces was widespread, although two centres were most active. In Maracaibo the Sociedad Dramática de Aficionados (Amateur Dramatic Society) directed by Enrique León alternated classical plays (BÜCHNER's *Woyzeck*, JARRY's *Ubu* and SOPHOCLES' *Oedipus Rex*) and regionalist plays, including folkloric works by César Chirinos whose *Traje de etiqueta* (*Tuxedo*), for example, captured coastal influences. In Valencia, the Teatro de Cámara de la Universidad de Carabobo (Chamber Theatre of the University of Carabobo), established in 1971 by Armando Gota, functioned under the direction of Héctor Vargas after 1973. Of similar importance was the Carabobo Theatre Association, directed by Eduardo Moreno after 1966.

In Caracas, several groups in addition to those named continued to function in spite of difficult economic stresses. Armando Gota, Eduardo Gil, Nicolás Curiel, Antonio Costante, Enrique Porte and Ugo Ulive are important directors. José Simón Escalona is an author and director, founder of Grupo Theja, and Humberto Orsini established the Tabla Redonda, Teatro Estudio (Round Table, Studio Theatre) in 1981. JOSÉ GABRIEL NÚÑEZ and RODOLFO SANTANA are both prolific and committed playwrights. Three women playwrights have made exceptional contributions: Elizabeth Schön, Elisa Lerner and MARIELA ROMERO. Writers of the most recent promotion include Paúl Williams, Edilio Peña, Néstor Caballero and Ibsen Martínez.

The recent level of activity indicates that the Venezuelan theatre has come of age, perhaps somewhat later than in other developing Latin American countries. While recent years have not seen an explosion of new writers or directors, the theatre in Venezuela has settled into a pattern that has generated good state support, high-quality performances and a reliable public. GW

See: L. Azparren Giménez, *El teatro venezolano y otros teatros*, Caracas, 1979; *Cabrujas en tres actos*, Caracas, 1983; S. Castillo, *El desarraigo en el teatro venezolano*, Caracas, 1980; I. Chocrón (ed.), *Nueva crítica de teatro venezolano*, Caracas, 1981; G. Hernández, *Tres dramaturgos venezolanos de hoy* (*Chalbaud, Cabrujas, Chocrón*), Caracas, 1979; R. Monasterios, *Un estudio crítico y longitudinal del teatro venezolano*, Caracas, 1974, and *Un enfoque crítico del teatro venezolano*, Caracas, 1975; *La miel y el veneno*, Valencia, 1971; L. F.

Ramón y Rivera, *Teatro popular venezolano*, Quito, 1981; C. Salas, *Historia del teatro en Caracas*, Caracas, 1974.

Verdon, Gwen 1926– American dancer, singer and actress. Considered to be the finest MUSICAL COMEDY dancer of the 1950s, Verdon studied with choreographer JACK COLE and assisted him with the choreography for *Magdalena* (1948) and *Alive and Kicking* (1950), making her BROADWAY debut as a dancer in the latter. Given a supporting role in *Can-Can* (1953), she stole the show with her exuberant dancing and her impish clowning. Following her success as the seductive Lola in *Damn Yankees* (1955), Verdon surprised critics and audiences with her poignant acting in *New Girl in Town* (1957), a musical version of EUGENE O'NEILL's *Anna Christie*. She next appeared in *Redhead*, a vehicle written especially for her. In 1966 she created the role of Charity Hope Valentine in *Sweet Charity*, which was choreographed and directed by her then-husband, BOB FOSSE. Despite reservations about the show's libretto, critics praised Verdon's performance for its innocence and vulnerability. Her only MUSICAL of the 1970s was the tawdry, flamboyant *Chicago* (1975), in which she was again directed by Fosse. In all of her musicals, Verdon's sinuous, energetic style of dance ideally suited the jazz choreography created for her by Cole and Fosse. She received the 1993 New Dramatists' Lifetime Achievement Award. MK

Verga, Giovanni 1840–1922 Italian novelist and dramatist. The foremost representative of late-19th-century Italian literary naturalism (*VERISMO*), in much of his work Verga depicted the lives of the peasants and fisher folk of his native Sicily, in a poetic, evocative and highly original prose. His best-known work is non-dramatic – *Vita dei campi* (*Life in the Fields*, 1880), *I malavoglia* (1881), *Novelle rusticane* (*Peasant Tales*, 1883) and *Mastro Don Gesualdo* (1888) – but he was an important figure in the late-19th-century Italian naturalistic theatre. His first stage success was *Cavalleria rusticana* (*Rustic Chivalry*) in 1884, which DUSE was instrumental in getting performed and in which she enjoyed one of her greatest triumphs. Derived from one of his own short stories, this one-act play was justly praised for the originality of its setting (a Sicilian village square) and formal qualities. Another of his major plays, *La lupa* (*The She-Wolf*, 1896), likewise taken from a short story, enjoyed stage success as a vehicle for strong female leads. A more ambitious three-act play, *Dal tuo al mio* (*From Yours to Mine*, 1903), attempted to treat of class conflict on a broader social canvas and provoked some controversy, but won only limited success. LR

verismo Italian artistic and literary movement of the late 19th and early 20th centuries, indebted to French NATURALISM, and of which the most significant figures in the Italian theatre were the dramatists GIACOSA and VERGA. Important, too, were the ideas of the Sicilian writer CAPUANA. In drama *verismo* had two broad manifestations: one was a region-based drama rooted in the observation of local life, sometimes in dialect, occasionally marred by folkloristic simplification but at its best a powerful representation of elemental passions and social conflict (as in Verga's *Cavalleria rusticana* (*Rustic Chivalry*) and *La lupa*, BRACCO's *Don Pietro Caruso* and Bertolazzi's *El nost Milan*, Capuana's *Malia* and De Roberto's *Il rosario*); the other was a bourgeois naturalistic drama, either with strong echoes of BECQUE, but less cynical and daring (PRAGA's *La moglie ideale* (*The Ideal Wife*), Rovetta's *I disonesti*), or near-CHEKHOVIAN in its dispassionate style and mood of melancholy (Giacosa's *Tristi amori* (*Sad Loves*) and *Come le foglie* (*Like the Leaves*)). Verismo produced the first distinctively national drama in Italy after decades of rather passive imitation of French *drame*. It called for, and helped to breed, a new school of actors who drew upon the example of the 'star' players' romantic REALISM, but accommodated that to more familiar locales and subject-matter. LR

Vertinsky, Aleksander (Nikolaevich) 1889–1957 Russian Soviet song-writer and CABARET artist, who became an instant celebrity in Moscow VARIETY theatres in 1915. Behind the mask of a doleful PIERROT, he hymned decadence, morphine addiction and Flaubert's parrot with an insinuating voice and elaborate gesticulation, setting to music poems by BLOK, Esenin and others. In emigration, 1919–43, when his songs took on a more nostalgic and patriotic tone, he toured widely throughout Europe and America, winding up in Shanghai. In 1943 he returned to the Soviet Union, where, laden with honours, he made a new career as a character actor in film. LS

Vestris, Madame [Lucy Elizabeth Bartolozzi] 1797–1856 English actress, singer and theatre manager who owed her stage name to her short-lived marriage to the French ballet dancer, Armand Vestris (1787–1825), who supervised his young wife's debut as a singer at the King's Theatre in 1815. It was in the 1820 revival of MONCRIEFF's *Giovanni in London* (1817) at DRURY LANE that she became a star, and it was her legs as well as her voice that attracted audiences. Played in travesty, the title role became a BREECHES PART. 'Handsome just above the knee', as a street-ballad insisted, the legs of Vestris were on display again that summer, when she played Macheath in *The Beggar's Opera* at the HAYMARKET, and she continued to combine a highbrow singing career at the King's with low-brow acting roles in breeches for several seasons.

Her singing of 'Cherry Ripe' in POOLE's *Paul Pry* (1825) was the talk of the town, but however great her popularity, it was an act of extraordinary boldness to set herself up as the lessee of the OLYMPIC in 1830. It was there (1831–9) that her innovations in the field of COSTUME and stage decoration were first seen. She owed much to the advice of J. R. PLANCHÉ, whose exquisite BURLESQUE extravaganzas were the outstanding features of the Olympic repertoire and whose knowledge of historical costume was unscarred by pedantry, but her own visual sense was highly developed. The Olympic company included LISTON, the KEELEYS, Mrs Glover and, after 1835, CHARLES JAMES MATHEWS, whom Vestris married in 1838 and with whom she shared the rest of her career. They toured New York and Philadelphia together (1838); jointly managed COVENT GARDEN (1839–42), where their outstanding success was with BOUCICAULT's *London Assurance* (1841); were jointly

imprisoned for debt, then returned to management together at the London LYCEUM (1847–55), during which time Vestris's uncertain health finally failed. There is some dispute about whether or not she was the first manager to employ a box set (was it in 1832 at the Olympic, 1841 for *London Assurance* at Covent Garden, or never?), but none about the new impetus she gave to pictorial staging, which became the high achievement of the 19th-century stage. PT

Vianna Filho, Oduvaldo 1936–74 Brazilian playwright and actor, son of playwright Oduvaldo Vianna. In 1956 Vianna Filho joined São Paulo's Arena Theatre, which produced his early plays. In 1964 he co-founded Rio's Opinion Theatre, which with Arena and Workshop led the engagé theatre movement of the 60s. *Se Correr o Bicho Pega, Se Ficar o Bicho Come* (*If You Run the Beast Will Catch You, If You Stay the Beast Will Eat You*, 1965) was a veiled reference to the military dictatorship (1964). Before his death, CENSORSHIP prevented productions of his later plays, but *Rasga Coração* (*Heart Stopping*, 1974), staged in 1979 by Arena founder José Renato, was a posthumous success. Along with BOAL and GUARNIERI, he established a legacy of well crafted plays that communicated social consciousness through a Brazilian fusion of BRECHTian technique and intense emotion. GW

Viau, Théophile de 1590–1626 French poet and dramatist. As a well educated young man of Bohemian ways he was supposedly attached for a while to a company of itinerant actors, and may have written more for the stage than the one play which has survived, a tragedy entitled *Pyrame et Thisbé* (*Pyramus and Thisbe*). Published in 1623, it was probably performed several years earlier, and some measure of its popularity is suggested by the fact that it was still in the repertoire of the HÔTEL DE BOURGOGNE company in the early 1630s. It is a fine example of baroque TRAGEDY, written in powerful, if contrived verse, and its text, taken in conjunction with the decor provided for it by MAHELOT, gives a clear insight into the way in which the multiple stage setting inherited from MEDIEVAL DRAMA was adapted and exploited in the early-17th-century professional theatre. DR

Vicente, Gil c.1460–c.1539 Portuguese playwright, actor and director, who also wrote a number of plays wholly or partly in Spanish. He is generally allowed to have been the founder of the Portuguese theatre and continues to be thought of as Portugal's major dramatist. It could also be said of him that, owing to his greater range, inventiveness and feel for theatre, he is more truly the father of the Hispanic theatre as a whole than his immediate Spanish predecessors and contemporaries, who often furnished him with models for emulation.

Vicente was early on connected with the court, probably before the death of King John II in 1495. His rise in standing at court is arguably linked to his proven skill as a goldsmith and jeweller (although the identity of goldsmith and dramatist has been questioned – irrelevantly to our purposes). He contributed verses and wit to the court's *serões* (musical and poetic soirées). His talents as a man to organize show and spectacle around royal occasions such as anniversaries and entries into cities were often called upon, and it was probably owing to a fine stroke of perceptiveness on the part of the Dowager Queen Leonor that he was invited to bring his literary and theatrical skills together for his first essay into theatre.

The *Monólogo do Vaqueiro* (*Monologue of the Cowherd*) was recited or acted, possibly by Vicente himself, on the occasion of the birth of the future king John III in 1502. As in a similar play by ENCINA, a cowherd stumbles into the royal bedchamber, proclaims how dazzled he is by the magnificence of the palace, and with rustic humour and simplicity makes an offer of produce to the baby prince on behalf of the nation. The shepherd-play humour is to be found in a few more plays, with more or less of Renaissance PASTORAL in their confection. They are not, with the exception of the *Auto da Sibila Cassandra* (*Sibyl Cassandra's Play*, 1513), his most memorable work. The *Monólogo* is the first of over 40 works of varying lengths that Vicente wrote and produced for the court in a variety of palaces and settings. Two or three plays were aired more publicly, and a further one had its first performance at a convent near Lisbon.

Vicente's religious theatre is a splendid synthesis of the themes and staging of the Middle Ages. The *Auto da Alma* (*Play of the Soul*, 1518) is almost pure MORALITY, with Soul making her way to the safety of Mother Church, first pulled onward by Angel and then waylaid by a subtle tempter of a Devil who lures her into stiletto heels, heavy brocade and a plight from which she escapes narrowly. The trilogy known as the *Barcas* (1516, 1518, 1519 – *The Ship of Hell*, –*of Purgatory*, –*of Heaven*) puts the whole of humanity into the dock of individual judgement at the point of death. The three estates of society, or more strictly the emergent three social classes, are examined very fiercely before assignment to one of two boats, bound one for Heaven, the other for Hell. The *Breve Sumário da História de Deus* (*A Brief Summary of the Story of God*) is a consideration of the matière of the MYSTERY cycles of Northern Europe. Time and World preside over the passage of humanity from Adam to Christ over the stage of this life, in a play calling for split-level simultaneous staging.

The many *farsas* (FARCES, some of them very close to comedy proper) deal with human, social and institutional foibles and abuses. *Quem Tem Farelos?* (*Who Has Chaff?* – for nags, no pun in Portuguese; 1508) is a SATIRE on the down-at-heel minor nobility and their designs upon richer but also earthy and shrewder women of lower class. The eponymous heroine of *Inês Pereira* (1523) buries her first such husband and then marries a dolt of a yeoman – she rides off at the end of the play to his cuckolding. The *Auto da Índia* (*The Play of India*, 1509) is as slick and humorous as 20th-century bedroom farce. The protagonist of the *Juiz da Beira* (*The J. P. from Beira*, 1526) is a figure very much in the mould of BRECHT's Azdak in his ambivalent sentencings.

In these religious plays and comedies, as well as in chivalresque tragicomedies and court MASQUES, Vicente deployed theatrical skills that were not equalled anywhere in Europe for another 60 or 70 years. LK

Victoria Theatre (Stoke-on-Trent) Britain's first permanent theatre-in-the-round. Beginning life as STEPHEN JOSEPH's touring Studio Theatre Company, in 1962 it became based in a converted cinema on the border between Stoke and Newcastle-under-Lyme. Peter Cheeseman, originally appointed manager, became theatre director in 1966 and has remained as such to this day. The company is best-known for its documentary plays – entertaining blends of music, song and dramatized research into actual events in the area, past and present. Topics have included the building of the local railways (*The Knotty*) and the threatened closure of the nearby steelworks (*Fight for Shelton Bar*). They have proved extraordinarily popular and have helped to create strong bonds with the surrounding communities. The repertoire also includes the classics and new plays (sometimes by resident dramatists such as PETER TERSON), and each season is organized on a true repertory basis (see REGIONAL THEATRE (BRITAIN)). 1986 saw the opening of the New Victoria Theatre, a purpose-built theatre-in-the-round, seating 600 instead of the old theatre's 389. AJ

Viertel, Berthold 1885–1955 Austrian director, instrumental in promoting the plays of HASENCLEVER, BRONNEN and KAISER. He produced BRECHT's *Fear and Suffering in the Third Reich* under the title of *The Private Life of the Master Race* in New York in 1945, and worked at the BERLINER ENSEMBLE before becoming director of the Vienna BURGTHEATER in 1951. CI

Vietnam This Southeast Asian nation has a population of 66 million and borders on Cambodia, Laos and China. From the 1st to the 10th century the country was ruled by CHINA: Mahayana Buddhism, Confucian values and Taoist thought entered, while Chinese models influenced, court performance. The Hindu kingdom of Champa was incorporated into the country in the 14th century and musical features of INDIAN origin, including the use of drum syllables, musical modes and improvisation technique, seem to have been borrowed for theatre music from that time. From 1862 to 1945 the country was a French colony: early experiments in staging translations of French playwrights led to a lively spoken-drama movement which continues to the present. Marxist socialist use of theatre as a tool of education and mass communication has helped raise the traditionally low status of performance in recent years. Four major kinds of theatre exist in Vietnam: (1) folk performance; (2) classical performance; (3) popular theatre; and (4) spoken drama.

Folk performance Folk performance includes proto-theatrical forms (including possession-trance seances, courting songs and storytelling) and folk theatricals. Spirit mediums in Buddhist temples might take up in ecstatic dances the attribute (knives, clubs and so on) of the spirit they incarnated. Mediums' songs, *châu van* in the north, *hâu van* in the central region and *rôi bong* in the south, now dying out, flourished in times past. Courting songs were sung alternately by boys and girls in various areas. These dialogue songs, called *trông quân*, *quan ho* and other names according to the area, were popular folk performances that laid the groundwork for drama to develop. Storytelling, too, abounded: blind musicians (*xâm xoan*) travelled from village to village singing epic, historical, humorous and erotic songs. The courtesan singer (*a dao*), accompanied by a musician on a lute (*dan day*), was another significant entertainer of the past.

Within the village environment a FOLK THEATRE, *hat cheo*, and water puppetry also emerged. The *hat cheo*, believed to have developed around the first century AD, remains in the northern part of the country. It was performed outside temples or *dinh*, places of worship for the tutelary god which simultaneously served as men's community houses. By the 10th century *hat cheo* included poetry, MIME, singing and dancing. The rules of this form were laid down by theorist Luong The Vinh in 1501. Prior to the 20th century, performances were presented during the day in the forecourt of the community house, paid for by the communal fund or rich benefactors. Skits customarily showed the common man triumphing over greedy mandarins. These qualities endeared the form to the masses and eventually to the socialist government of the Democratic Republic of Vietnam which took over the northern part of the country after the Second World War. Several semi-professional troupes currently perform *hat cheo* in the Hanoi region.

Water puppetry, *muá rôi nuoc*, is another significant, and unique, folk theatre within the oral tradition. According to Dinh Gia Khanh, a stone inscription on a pillar in Nan Ninh province proves the form was well developed by AD 1121. Performances of short interludes, animals fighting and comic scenes, are staged on ponds via refined manipulation technique by manipulators hidden behind a staging house.

Classical performance Vietnam's court-supported arts are strongly sinicized. Court dances, like Chinese forms, are divided into *van vu* ('civil dance') and *vo vu* ('military dance'). *Hat bôi* (alternatively *hat tuông, tuông*) is a classical court theatre. Tradition holds that the form dates from 1285 when a Chinese actor, captured by a Vietnamese general, taught his art to the Vietnamese performers.

From the 13th to the 17th centuries the form served primarily as a court entertainment in Hanoi. The actor Dao Duy Tu (1572–1634) is credited with popularizing the form by introducing southern musical styles of Champa, an Indian-influenced kingdom. These poignant 'southern songs' (*hat nam*) were endearing to commoners and contrasted with the 'foreigners' songs' (*hat khach*) and patter songs (*noi lôi*, 'stylized speaking'), already a part of this operatic form.

During the 18th and 19th centuries the form had the support of the Nguyen dynasty of Central Vietnam. Gia Long (1802–20) had the first theatre built in the imperial palace at Hue, the capital. Chinese influences were reinforced during the reign of Emperor Minh Mang (1820–41) when imported Chinese actors reworked the form. The current similarities between *hat bôi* and Cantonese opera in gestures, costumes and make-up probably result from this reform. However, distinctive Vietnamese sentiments in the scripts and musical and theatrical traits distinguish it from Chinese models.

An official court troupe, Phuong Nha Tro, operated until l946 when court support faltered. Plays tend to exalt the emperor, and uphold Confucian ethics and feudal values. This content and Chinese features have alienated some recent audiences from *hat bôi*. Doan Quan Tan attempted a revision in the 1940s which involved the elimination of the falsetto voice and Chinese words. Up to the 1970s the form was still performed in Saigon, Hue and other areas, but lacked an enthusiastic audience.

Popular theatre Vietnamese *cai luong* ('reformed theatre') is a popular musical theatre. It reached a peak of popularity in the 1920s and continues today especially in the southern part of the country. Songs are the most significant feature of the performance. *Tu dai*, ballads in which one singer would perform a few lines and another sing a reply, form the base of *cai luong*. Around 1916 performers of one particular ballad, 'The Song of Nguyet Nga', are said to have begun presenting the song in a more dramatic style. Travelling CIRCUSES began including this dramatic playlet in their programmes. The greater part of the performance was given to the singing of the songs. The clown who developed his own business and monologues soon became an important element in the performance. The falsetto voice of *hat bôi* was abandoned but, since many of the early performers were trained in the classical theatre, its southern songs were still used for sad scenes and some of the stirring, military songs were also incorporated. Diversity of subject-matter was incorporated and the form remained popular until recently. The continuing political unrest after the partition of the country in 1954 was reflected in plays which criticized the French regime. Popular plays included modern domestic dramas and traditional stories, such as the The Story of Thuy Kieu, the story of a virtuous woman who becomes a courtesan against her will and finally is reunited with her first love.

In 1980, the government of Vietnam supported 16 professional *hat cheo* troupes, 13 *cai luong* troupes, 3 *hat bôi* troupes, 3 PUPPET troupes and a score of troupes devoted to contemporary spoken drama. Students are trained in all traditional genres at the Academy of Theatre and Film in Hanoi, which opened in 1980. Major cities have theatres which specialize in one or another form, or book in performances of various genres. Performers are paid a wage comparable to professionals in teaching or medicine, showing the respect the current government accords to the arts.

Modern spoken drama The modern theatre journey of Vietnam up to 1954 took a course not too dissimilar from that traversed by many other Southeast Asian countries. From its beginnings at the opening of the 20th century, modern drama, or *kich nôi*, was an undertaking of a newly urbanized literary elite who reflected the influence of privileged Western education under the French colonial regime. The trek began with 'stilted' translations into the romanized 'national language' of Vietnam (*quoc-ngug*) of classical French dramas. Beginning with Molière's *The Miser*, staged in 1907, many plays by MOLIÈRE and CORNEILLE were translated and performed by Vietnamese actors. The first Vietnamese spoken drama was *A Cup of Poison* (*Chen thuot doc*), by Vu Dinh Long (1901–60), performed in Hanoi in 1921. It melodramatically depicts the impending downfall of a morally crippled civil servant, and his sudden and fortuitous rescue.

Most of the early spoken dramas, however, were 'brittle' Vietnamese versions of romantic drawing-room comedies, staged mainly by Western-oriented clubs and societies. An impressive exception to the milieu of insouciant 'amateur theatricals' were the dramatic forays of the advocate of 'new (or 'modernized') poetry', Pham Huy Thong, who briefly in the mid-1930s experimented with miniaturist verse tragedies.

The popular route to Westernization was taken by theatre practitioners convening informal marriages between the firmly ensconced and multifarious indigenous traditional theatre forms (for example, *hat cheo* and *hat bôi*) and Western staging techniques, costumes, music and, eventually, kitsch Western drama plots from the stage and screen. One of the most resilient and socially significant of the new theatre genres born of this unprepossessing fusion is the musical drama, *cai luong*, or 'reformed theatre', originating in Southern Vietnam around the time of the First World War. Marr believes the mobile *cai luong* troupes 'undoubtedly played a major role in disseminating new ideas and language beyond the intelligentsia', holding sway over the Vietnamese dramatic imagination in the south until the advent of television in the l960s and rendering impotent efforts of spoken-drama adherents to seriously pursue 'realism'.

The search for 'realistic' gestures by some spoken-drama writers coincided with the rise of Vietnamese nationalism. The consequence was passionately anti-colonial plays including Nam Xoung's *The Annamite Frenchman* (*Ong tay An-nam*, 1931), which in Molière fashion vilified the pretensions of francophile Vietnamese intellectuals. A differing strand of nationalism was explored by playwright Ngyuen Huy Tuong, who emerged as one of the most influential literary figures of his time. His historical play, *Vu Nhu To* (1943) about the dilemma of an imperial architect forced to choose between personal integrity and service to country, disclosed a visceral anti-establishment stance. Anticipating the appearance of a socialist direction in Vietnamese politics, *Bac Son*, which opened in Hanoi in 1945, pitted revolutionaries (heroic Bac Son guerrilla fighters) against counter-revolutionaries (oppressive French).

The war with the French consumed the passions of the Vietnamese from the 1945 August Revolution to the 1954 Geneva Agreement that split the country into two parts. Although good plays were scarce, incendiary anti-French spoken dramas gained acceptance during this period. In areas the Vietnamese Communist Party gradually came to dominate, the seeds of 'socialist realism' in modern Vietnamese theatre were planted. In 1959 the École des Arts Théâtraux was established in Hanoi. The Maoist precept that writers and artists must identify with the masses in both life and art underlay official revival of folk theatre and adaptations of European dramas. Dissidence against the Party was not tolerated, as exposed by the 1956 crackdown on rebellious writers and poets. To a degree unmatched in Southeast Asia, theatre was resolutely wielded as propaganda to uphold the socialist revolutionary system until 1975, when North and South Vietnam were reunified.

Especially after American entry into the conflict, South Vietnam's promotion of dramatic competitions and mobile theatre companies dispensing music, magic show and drama faced a mirror image in the arts campaign of the National Liberation Front. Following reunification, southern authors, who had enjoyed greater creative freedom, were charged with anti-communism, escapist erotica, spiritual demoralization of 'Americanized' society and existentialism. In Steinberg's view the intolerant and oppressive stance of the new Vietnamese government toward the remants of South Vietnamese 'critical middle-class intelligentsia ... was a Vietnamese national disaster of incalculable proportions'. This provides a clue as to why, despite the government's agressive promotion and support of 23 professional *kich nôi* troupes, Vietnam lags behind in forging an innovative and nationally identifiable modern theatre.

C. Mackerras notes that in 1984 an anti-Chinese impulse dominated modern drama as a result of the Chinese invasion of Vietnam in 1979. However, government policy was not so rigid as to disallow the exposure of 'serious social problems', as in *Through the Night* (*Qua dem*), which treats the re-education of a former Saigon supporter in the style of socialist REALISM. The contemporary COMEDY *Once in a Lifetime* (*Doi chi co mot lan*), staged in Ho Chi Minh City, unmasked conspicuous consumption at weddings and ubiquitous 'free marketeers' who dupe people into extravagance. The propaganda is light and there is an 'absence of class or foreign enemies'. Self-criticism is often tolerated so long as it does not fundamentally question the socialist system.

Vietnamese *glasnost* (*doi moi*, 'renovation') in 1986 opened the door to a new wave of theatre that focused on the conflict of generations and the bankruptcy of idealism, and spun parables about bureaucratic corruption. Writers such as Nguyen Huy Thiep and Pham Thi Hoa, in adopting a surrealistic mode (see SURREALISM), jousted with hegemonic socialist realism. In the late 1980s, troubled by the retreat of communism in eastern Europe and the Tiananmen revolt in China, the ageing leaders of Vietnam appeared to be backing off from *doi moi*. This did not stop Thiep from writing a revisionist historical drama, *Love Remains* (*Con Lai Tinh Yeu*, 1990), featuring as hero the Kuomintang-like leader of the 1930s, Nguyen Thu Hoc, which was published in a well known literary journal.

Deviations from the standard line can be explained in part by an 'anti-authoritarian' streak in Vietnamese character and the personalized nature of much of Southeast Asian politics. Important artists also hold prominent positions in official arts organizations that arbitrate on 'deviationist' practices. Thus, Dr Nguyen Dinh Quang, author, theatre director and drama professor, is Vice Minister of Culture and the Arts. If the moderating influences nurturing creative innovation are allowed breathing space in the febrile milieu of the politicized arts, the arrival of 'a truly distinct Vietnamese spoken drama' might not be too far away. (See ASIAN AND PACIFIC ISLAND THEATRE.)   KF KJ

See: J. R. Brandon (ed.), *The Cambridge Guide to Asian Theatre*, Cambridge, 1993.

Vieux-Colombier Theatre Nineteenth-century theatre building in the street of that name on the Paris left bank, formerly known as the Athénée St Germain. It was renovated by COPEAU in 1913 as the launching pad for his renewal of French theatre. It was again remodelled by JOUVET under Copeau's direction after the First World War so as to approximate an Elizabethan stage, and here Copeau's company performed after their return from America during 1920–4. After four years as a cinema the theatre was occupied by the COMPAGNIE DES QUINZE in 1931, and then continued under commercial management until it closed in 1972. It always retained some of the prestige of Copeau's name and many important events have taken place there, such as ARTAUD's reading of his own work in 1947. It saw the first Paris performances of such influential plays as SARTRE's *In Camera* (1944), T. S. ELIOT's *Murder in the Cathedral* (1945), a production later revived at the THÉÂTRE NATIONAL POPULAIRE, and ADAMOV's *Paolo Paoli* (see PLANCHON). Following the 1972 closure, the theatre remained empty and neglected, but was rescued, restored and reopened as the second house of the COMÉDIE-FRANÇAISE in 1993. The first production in the renovated theatre was a revival of VINAVER's *Les Coréens* (*The Koreans*). DB

Viganò, Salvatore 1769–1821 Italian choreographer and dancer. Born into the world of theatrical dance, Viganò made his debut as a choreographer at the age of 17 with an *intermezzo*. After several years of study, including particularly the theory of Noverre and the practice of Danberval, he joined his father in Venice in 1790, and at the San Samuele Theatre scored signal success as dancer and choreographer. After a period of working in Vienna, he toured Europe in the late 1790s, returning to Vienna in 1799 to create some of his most significant works, including *Die Gasehöpfe der Prometheus* (1801) to Beethoven's music, brilliantly fantastic and allegorical ballets. His Shakespearian subjects included an *Othello* in 1818. KR

Vigarani, Gaspare 1586–1663 Italian theatre architect and stage designer. Although he had a well established reputation in Italy, particularly for his theatre at Modena (1654), his most famous work was done in Paris where he had been summoned by Cardinal Mazarin in 1659 to supervise the performances in conjunction with the marriage of Louis XIV. This involved the creation of a new theatre to replace the PETIT-BOURBON, which was being torn down to make way for the Colonnade of the Louvre. The result was the SALLE DES MACHINES, based on the Modena theatre, and constructed in the Tuileries Palace. When it opened in 1662 with *Ercole Amante* (*Hercules in Love*) it was the largest theatre in Europe. It accommodated 7000 spectators and had a stage 140ft deep. The elaborate settings and machinery included a device that raised the entire royal family above the stage. Vigarani was very jealous of his rival GIACOMO TORELLI and had the latter's machinery removed from the Petit-Bourbon before it was demolished, ostensibly to use it in the new theatre. Instead, he had it burned. After his death Vigarani was succeeded at court by his son Carlo (1623–1713), who held the post until 1680 and designed primarily at the Palace of Versailles. Carlo Vigarani's best-known work was MOLIÈRE and LULLY's *Les Plaisirs de l'île enchantée* (*Pleasures of the Enchanted Isle*, 1664), a spectacular three-day celebration. (See also THEATRE BUILDINGS; THEATRE DESIGN.) AA

Vigny, Alfred de 1797–1863 French poet, dramatist and novelist, a leading figure in the French romantic movement. Vigny's reputation as a dramatist rests on two plays: *Le More de Venise, Othello* (1829) and *Chatterton* (1835), both performed at the Théâtre-Français (see COMÉDIE-FRANÇAISE). The hostile reception of English actors playing SHAKESPEARE ('an emissary of Wellington') in 1822 had encouraged a re-evaluation of Shakespeare in France (*vide* Stendhal's essay *Racine et Shakespeare*), and this was confirmed by a more successful visit in 1827. Vigny, in his *Othello*, did not attempt to assimilate Shakespeare's play into the forms of a neoclassical TRAGEDY, as DUCIS had done. Instead he offered a free, but generally faithful, translation (Gratiano and Bianca being the only significant characters to disappear). The same year his three-act version of *The Merchant of Venice* was accepted by the Ambigu-Comique (see BOULEVARD), but not performed. In 1831 his historical drama, *La Maréchale d'Ancre*, with MLLE GEORGE in the title role, was performed at the ODÉON. *Chatterton*, with its theme of a poet driven to suicide by a philistine society, was one of the great successes of the romantic theatre and offered a superb role to MARIE DORVAL (Vigny's mistress) as a sensitive soul who dies of a love she cannot express. In 1834 Vigny also wrote a dramatic proverb, *Quitte pour la peur* (*Getting Off with a Fright*), for Dorval. JMCC

Viktiuk, Roman (Grigorevich) One of the most provocative contemporary Russian directors, who in 1991 had twelve productions running simultaneously in Moscow theatres. In the 1980s, Viktiuk worked in both professional and amateur studio theatres, opening a production of LYUDMILA PETRUSHEVSKAYA's *Music Lessons* at Leningrad's Vologradsky Palace of Culture, celebrated for its behavioural acting and unusual presentation, before an onstage audience facing the darkened theatre auditorium. In 1988, he staged an evening of one-act plays by Petrushevskaya, including *Columbine's Apartment*, a quasi-COMMEDIA FARCE about a sexual predator, with the goal of uniting that author's view of contemporary Soviet reality with 'the aesthetics of IONESCO and BECKETT'. Viktiuk's most notable productions – Hwang's *M. Butterfly* at the Fora Theatre (1990), GENET's *The Maids*, featuring an all-male cast at the Satirikon Theatre, and Tsvetaeva's 1928 *Phaedra* at the Taganka Theatre (which toured the USA) – have featured NUDITY, homoeroticism, music, dance and MIME, fetishized stage properties and explored 'decadent' passions which confound nature and invite death. SG

Vilar, Jean 1912–71 French actor and director. Vilar trained with DULLIN and began to direct during the Occupation, when his time was divided between tours with La Roulotte and avant-garde productions in Paris which included two plays by STRINDBERG. In the late 1940s he continued to direct for the avant-garde (e.g. ADAMOV's *L'Invasion* in 1950) but also founded the AVIGNON FESTIVAL in 1947, where he developed the virtues of COPEAU's bare stage, performing on a vast open-air stage in the courtyard of the papal palace. His uncluttered production style suited a revival of heroic tragedy (*Le Cid*, 1949; *Danton's Death*, 1948) but also enabled him to present MOLIÈRE, MARIVAUX and MUSSET in a new light.

His considerable gifts as an actor of mature roles complemented the passionate brilliance of the young GÉRARD PHILIPE: he played the old statesman to Philipe's young hero on many occasions. In 1951 he was put in control of the THÉÂTRE NATIONAL POPULAIRE at CHAILLOT, where he extended the methods that had proved successful at Avignon. He made the theatre into as near as possible a classless space, transcending social divisions, in which all could join in a process of reflection, learning, and a celebration of common humanity. He insisted that theatre should be available to all: 'a public service in exactly the same way as gas, water or electricity'. His repertoire consisted of classics and modern classics, and he regretted not being able to introduce more modern works: his few attempts, which included GATTI's first performed play, *Le Crapaud-Buffle*, 1959, were box-office failures.

In 1963 he left the TNP to devote himself to a revitalization and extension of the Avignon Festival, but in 1968 he was fiercely attacked by young revolutionaries who mistook his lifelong left-wing commitment for compromise. Through his example he had a strong influence on many young actors and directors who have sought to reconcile social and political commitment with theatre art of the highest standards, notably MNOUCHKINE, PLANCHON and VITEZ. DB

Vildrac, Charles 1882–1971 French author and playwright whose first and best play *Le Paquebot Tenacity* (*The Steamboat Tenacity*, 1920) was one of the few new works to be produced by COPEAU. His subsequent plays were produced by JOUVET, GEORGES PITOËFF and the COMÉDIE-FRANÇAISE. Together with Jean-Jacques Bernard and LENORMAND, he helped to generate a vogue for the theatre of the unexpressed: plays telling the stories of simple people incapable of grand speeches, but whose silences gave eloquent expression to their feelings. DB

Villaurrutia, Xavier 1903–50 Mexican playwright and poet involved in the renovation of Mexican drama. Co-founder with SALVADOR NOVO of the TEATRO DE ULISES in 1928, Villaurrutia experimented with the most recent European techniques, and after the early demise of the Ulysses Theatre he continued with TEATRO DE ORIENTACIÓN in the same mould. His plays often show the influence of GIRAUDOUX and LENORMAND. The *Autos profanos*, five short pieces (1933–7), are humorous and playable, with strong philosophical underpinnings. Major plays are *La hiedra* (*The Ivy*, 1942) based on RACINE's *Phèdre*, and *Invitación a la muerte* (*Invitation to Death*, 1940), with overtones of *Hamlet*. GW

Villegas, Oscar 1943– Mexican playwright and ceramicist. Villegas studied the plastic arts, completed the directing programme at the National Institute of Fine Arts, and studied dramatic theory and composition at the National University. His plays are highly experimental in form and language, greatly influenced by rock music in theme and structure: e.g. *El renacimiento* (*The Renaissance*, 1967) and *Santa Catarina* (*St Catherine*, 1969). His major work is *Atlántida* (*Atlantis*, 1976), a full-length play which examines values among youth outside mainstream society. The techniques used are daring and innovative; major themes

are aspects of individual freedom and expression. *Mucho gusto en conocerlo* (*Pleased to Meet You*, 1985) and *La eternidad acaba mañana* (*Eternity Ends Tomorrow*, 1994) are more recent plays. GW

Vilna Troupe Celebrated cooperative theatre company which opened in Russia in 1916 with immediately successful productions of SHOLOM ASCH's *The Landsman* and PERETZ HIRSHBEIN's *The Forsaken Nook*. With DAVID HERMAN as director and JACOB BEN-AMI as leading actor, the company soon brought a much needed dignity to European YIDDISH THEATRE, and various 'wings', or detachments, set out on world tours. Its most famous production, S. ANSKI's *The Dybbuk*, toured continuously for many years. The Warsaw wing achieved its greatest success with Asch's *Kiddush Hashem*, whilst the Berlin wing toured a particularly striking production of Hirshbein's *The Haunted Inn*. There were also a Romanian and an American wing. AB

Vinaver, Michel 1927– French novelist and playwright. His first plays were written in the 1950s, when *Les Coréens* (*The Koreans*, 1956) had some success, with four different productions by PLANCHON, SERREAU, JORIS and Monnett. But in between *Iphigénie Hôtel* (written in 1959) and *Par-dessus bord* (*Overboard*; written in 1969, directed by Planchon in 1973) he wrote no plays, devoting himself entirely to his job as a business executive. The world of business provides the material for most of his later plays, e.g. *La Demande d'emploi* (*Situation Vacant*, 1973); *Les Travaux et les jours* (*Works and Days*, 1979); *À la renverse* (*Bending over Backwards*, 1980). In these plot is reduced to a minimum, the plays consisting of ambiguous, fragmentary dialogues in which questions and answers do not necessarily correspond, and different streams of consciousness interweave to create a rich dramatic texture. Vinaver has been associated with the *théâtre du QUOTIDIEN* because of the everyday concerns and realistic nature of his characters, and also because of the use he makes of different linguistic codes. But in his more ambitious plays such as *Par-dessus bord* mythical archetypes underlie modern stories; and the drama's method of dealing with its subject-matter is multiple, varying from naturalist representation to sequences in which the very possibility of representation is questioned. This reflection is taken further in *L'Émission de télévision* (1990, directed by LASSALLE, and produced in 1992 at London's GATE THEATRE as *The Television Programme*), in which the role of the media in modern society is questioned. DB

Vincent, Jean-Pierre 1942– French theatre director, who founded the Théâtre de l'Espérance at the Montmartre Palace Theatre in 1972 in collaboration with Jean Jourdheuil. Here he produced BRECHT, BÜCHNER and VISHNEVSKY, as well as modern French works by Rezvani and GRUMBERG. In 1975 he became director of the Théâtre National de Strasbourg, which he modelled on German civic theatres, drawing the theatre school into close collaboration and appointing Bernard Chartreux and Michel Deutsch as dramaturges. His repertoire included translations of new German writing and French plays of the QUOTIDIEN as well as adaptations from novels, e.g. ZOLA's

Germinal (1975). In 1983 he was appointed director of the COMÉDIE-FRANÇAISE, but he resigned three years later. In 1990 he succeeded CHÉREAU as director of the Théâtre des Amandiers at Nanterre. DB

Visconti, Luchino 1906–76 Italian film and theatre director. Best known for his films, *La terra trema* (*The Earth Trembles*, 1948), *Rocco e i suoi fratelli* (*Rocco and his Brothers*, 1960), *Il gattopardo* (*The Leopard*, 1963) and *Morte a Venezia* (*Death in Venice*, 1971), Visconti was also a distinguished director in the 'straight' and musical theatre. Of aristocratic background but socialist political sympathies, both of which tended to be reflected in much of his work, he came to prominence only after the Second World War, directing the kinds of drama which dominated the serious European stages of the late 1940s and 50s (MILLER, WILLIAMS, SARTRE, ANOUILH) and discovering in classic plays dimensions of social realism hitherto ignored, as in his stage re-evaluation of GOLDONI's *La locandiera* (1952). His early productions of SHAKESPEARE included *Troilus and Cressida* (1949) and *Macbeth* (1958).

At once lyrical and realistic, flamboyant and analytical, his work often aroused vigorous enthusiasm or hostility. His strong sense of the theatrical and emotionally powerful found further expression in his work for the musical stage, particularly with the operas of Verdi. Among his notable stage productions of the 1960s and 70s were CHEKHOV's *The Cherry Orchard* (1965) and PINTER's *Old Times* (1973), in which directorial emphases explored the passage of time and its effects with an underlying melancholy that became increasingly prominent, too, in his film work. KR

Visé, Jean Donneau de 1638–1710 French man of letters, critic and journalist who fomented the hostile reaction to MOLIÈRE's *L'École des femmes* (*The School for Wives*) in 1663 with a critical article, followed by a one-act play *Zélinde* and possibly the highly injurious *La Vengeance des marquis* (*The Marquises' Revenge*), which commented on the playwright's private life. Nevertheless, several of de Visé's later plays were performed by Molière's company, and he collaborated to good effect on others with THOMAS CORNEILLE, notably on the very successful 'machine-play' *La Devineresse* (*The Fortune-Teller*, 1679). In 1672 he founded the *Mercure Galant*, which became the quasi-official gazette of French social and literary life. DR

Vishnevsky, Vsevolod (Vitalievich) 1900–51 Soviet prose writer and dramatist who drew upon his experiences fighting in the First World War, the October Revolution and the Russian Civil War as a member of the Red Army in composing dramas of epic sweep, monumental scale, passionate emotion and romantic heroic perspective. His play *The First Horse Army* (1929), commemorating and mythologizing Red Cavalry leader Marshal Semyon Budyony's Rostov campaign during the Civil War, was meant to 'correct' BABEL's description of its brutality in his story collection *Red Cavalry*. Vishnevsky employs a sprawling, episodic structure with framing prologue and epilogue, a narrator and correspondence to bridge the 10-year gap between the date of the events being described and that of the play, as well as crowd scenes, a variety of sounds and musical selections, simultaneous staging and suggested screen projections.

His most famous play, *An Optimistic Tragedy* (1934), about a heroic female commissar's sacrifice of her own life to instil discipline in a motley group of seamen and to ensure the Baltic Fleet's victory during the Civil War, gave its name to a new type of play. Vishnevsky maintained that although Soviet Russia would undoubtedly continue to engage in a tragic conflict with anti-Bolshevik elements, the strength of the new socialist order inspired optimism in the outcome. This points towards the 'conflictless dramas' of socialist REALISM. The play's episodic structure is held together by two sailors who serve as choral figures. TAIROV's famous 1934 production at the Kamerny Theatre with his wife ALISA KOONEN as the leather-jacketed lady commissar and a monumental, spirally ramped set by Vadim Ryndin, established the model for succeeding productions for years to come. Vishnevsky's earnestness and will to survive eclipsed his artistic integrity, resulting in blatant falsification of history as in his last play *Unforgotten 1919* (1949), which fabricates a heroic role for Stalin in the Revolution. SG

Vitez, Antoine 1930–90 French actor and director of Russian origins and strong communist sympathies. Vitez worked on the journal of VILAR's THÉÂTRE NATIONAL POPULAIRE, *Bref*, acted and directed in the decentralized theatres (see DECENTRALIZATION MOVEMENT) and in the theatres of the Parisian 'red belt' at Nanterre and Ivry, where he ran the Théâtre des Quartiers d'Ivry from 1971 to 1980. Unlike directors with a tendency to scenic extravagance (e.g. PLANCHON), Vitez achieved his effects by unusual direction of actors, encouraging them to go for unexpected body movements, to play against the text, to break accepted conventions. This gave rise to productions of scintillating intelligence but also of considerable preciosity. He became a teacher at the Conservatoire in 1968 and influenced a large number of young French actors. His choice of repertoire was broad, from SOPHOCLES to BRECHT, from HUGO to CLAUDEL, and also included many new plays and adaptations of novels. From 1981 to 88 he was director of the CHAILLOT THEATRE, where his slogan was 'an élite theatre for all' and his repertoire an audacious mixture of avant-garde and classical work. In 1988 he was appointed director of the COMÉDIE-FRANÇAISE, but his untimely death in 1990 cut short the process of reform that he had endeavoured to initiate. DB

Vitrac, Roger 1899–1952 French poet and playwright, active in the dada movement, who founded the Théâtre Alfred Jarry with ARTAUD in 1926. Here two of his plays were performed, *Les Mystères de l'amour* (*The Mysteries of Love*, 1927) and *Victor, ou Les Enfants au pouvoir* (*Victor, or Power to Children*, 1928). The latter can stand as a masterpiece of surrealist theatre (see SURREALISM), though it was not until the revival of the play in a production by ANOUILH (1962) that its quality was generally recognized. Set in 1909, *Victor* satirizes middle-class manners, patriotism and the conventions of BOULEVARD comedy by means of a grotesque child, Victor, who is nine years old but already six feet tall and can see through all the social pretence that surrounds him. Later plays failed to achieve the brilliance of Vitrac's early work, and he was not again involved in a practical theatre venture.   DB

Vitruvius Pollio 1st century BC Practising Roman architect and the author, early in the reign of Augustus, of *De Architectura*, a technical manual in ten books. This includes instructions for designing theatres of Greek and Roman type (see GREEK THEATRES; ROMAN THEATRES AND AMPHITHEATRES), and descriptions of painted scenery with perspective effects: columns and pediments for tragedy, private houses for comedy, rustic landscapes for satyr plays. His manual was much studied by PALLADIO and other THEATRE DESIGNERS of the Renaissance.   ALB

Vivian Beaumont and **Mitzi E. Newhouse Theatres** (New York City) Part of the Lincoln Center for the Performing Arts, this repertory theatre and its experimental appendage began under the aegis of ELIA KAZAN and ROBERT WHITEHEAD, who spent two years planning it. Named after Mrs Vivian Beaumont Allen, its benefactress, the larger theatre opened in 1965. The playhouse was designed with 11,000 sq ft of stage space (compared to the 3000 of the Martin Beck Theatre on BROADWAY) and was intended to shift from a proscenium to a thrust stage and to be able to store scenery for the repertory. All of the mechanical and electrical elements are concealed, and the auditorium, with a flexible 1090–1140 seats, is gently amphitheatrical. The smaller stage (originally the Forum), with its 299 seats, was designed with all of the structural, mechanical and electrical equipment exposed and was intended for experimental productions. Kazan and Whitehead resigned and were replaced by HERBERT BLAU and Jules Irving in the first year, then by Irving alone in 1967. He was succeeded by JOSEPH PAPP (1973–7), who obtained operating funds from Mrs Mitzi E. Newhouse, after whom he renamed the Forum. Since Papp's departure, the theatres were reopened only intermittently, as the Lincoln Center management struggled to find both a purpose for them and new creative leaders; finally, in 1985, GREGORY MOSHER of the Chicago GOODMAN THEATRE and Bernard Gersten, a Broadway and OFF-BROADWAY producer, began their leadership – though in 1992 Mosher was succeeded by André Bishop, artistic director for a decade of PLAYWRIGHTS HORIZONS.   MCH

Viviani, Raffaele 1888–1950 Italian actor, director and dramatist, who began his career as a singer and comic entertainer in the Neapolitan popular VARIETY theatre. Naples is the setting for many realistic plays of powerful social criticism, written in the Neapolitan dialect, among the most outstanding of which are *'O vico* (*The Alley*, 1917), *Tuledu'e notte* (*Tuledu by Night*, 1918) and *Festa di 'Piedigrotta* (*The Festival of Piedigrotta*, 1919). They present sharp and realistic portraits of working-class life and are crafted with great skill. One of the major figures of the Italian stage between the two world wars, Viviani was an extremely versatile *homme du théâtre*, combining the talents of playwright, director, composer and actor-manager.   LR

Vodanović, Sergio 1926– Chilean playwright, born to

Yugoslavian immigrant parents and trained as a lawyer. Although he began with light, vaudevillian plays (see VAUDEVILLE), Vodanović's first major works are *El senador no es honorable* (*The Senator Is not Honourable*, 1952) and *Deja que los perros ladren* (*Let the Dogs Bark*, 1959), both of which provide a penetrating criticism of political intrigue, corruption and venality through well drawn characters. *Los fugitivos* (*The Fugitives*, 1965) resonates of *Tea and Sympathy*, with the young lover/older woman syndrome. In his later plays, Vodanović becomes more virulent in his sociopolitical commentaries: *Perdón ...¡Estamos en guerra!* (*Sorry ... We're at War!*, 1966) and *Nos tomamos la Universidad* (*We Took the University*, 1970). *¿Cuántos años tiene un día?* (*How Many Years in a Day?*, 1978), written in conjunction with the ICTUS, contrasts the liberty of expression of former years with both the overt and covert oppression of a group of news reporters working for television in the Pinochet regime.   GW

Volkov, Fyodor (Grigorievich) 1729–63 The first eminent Russian actor, named by the critic Belinsky as 'the father of the Russian theatre'. With the inheritance left him by his father, a factory owner, he established a public theatre in his native Yaroslavl (1750). In 1752 his troupe, which included his brother Grigory and IVAN DMITREVSKY, was taken to St Petersburg to perform the MORALITY PLAY *A Sinner's Repentance* by the high cleric DMITRY ROSTOVSKY, and some tragedies by ALEKSEI SUMAROKOV. What was to have been a court theatre instead became in 1756 the Russian Patent Theatre, Russia's first permanent professional public theatre, under the direction of Sumarokov. Volkov became the company's leading tragic actor, impersonating the heroes in Sumarokov's plays, most notably Khorev and Hamlet. Recognizing Volkov's singular talent, his passionate temperament and naturalness of expression, Sumarokov adjusted his neo-classical verse form to accommodate him. Volkov had from the outset helped Sumarokov in the direction of the theatre, a role which became solely his upon the latter's dismissal in 1761. Volkov and his brother took part in the plot to overthrow Peter III, for which they were rewarded with court offices. While organizing the festivities for the coronation of Catherine the Great (1763), which included the masquerade *Minerva Triumphant*, Volkov caught cold and died.   SG

Volksbühne [Freie Volksbühne] (People's Theatre) Generic label for a wide cultural movement as well as the name of those theatres affiliated with it. Founded in 1890 in Berlin as a subscription organization, its first title, the Freie (Free) Volksbühne, reveals its origins as well as its unique contribution in bringing theatre to a mass audience. Growing out of OTTO BRAHM's FREIE BÜHNE, which followed the Théâtre Libre (see ANTOINE, ANDRÉ) in experimental productions of IBSEN and HAUPTMANN, it was dedicated to providing art for the working classes and brought out the social content in the new NATURALISM. In politicizing drama it raised – and partially resolved – many issues still plaguing alternative/political theatre today. The tension between ideological and artistic aims split the organization in 1892, and it took over two decades to create a working compromise. Disagreement over servicing cultural demands or acting as a catalyst for radicalizing the masses, which reached a head with the productions of ERWIN PISCATOR, produced two parallel organizations in 1927, while the expansion of the Volksbühne demonstrates how size inhibits experimentation.

Beginning by booking special performances in commercial theatres, the organization not only came at times to control three of the regular Berlin stages, but built two major theatres specifically for its needs. The first, financed largely by personal subscription, opened as the Volksbühne on Bülowplatz in 1914. It provided 2000 seats and a 40-metre-wide stage with a huge revolve, in which a permanent company could produce socially committed work. By 1930 there were over 300 local organizations, with a nationwide membership of half a million. As one of the dominant forces in the Weimar Republic, the Volksbühne helped to shape the whole direction of modern drama by employing such directors as REINHARDT, Jürgen Fehling and Piscator at the beginning of their careers, and by supporting new plays from a wide range of dramatists including BARLACH and TOLLER and, more recently, HOCHHUTH and KIPPHARDT. It introduced SHAW to the German stage, and promoted early modern dance. The educational lectures that accompanied its first productions developed into influential periodicals, *Die Volksbühne* and *Die Schaubühne*, through which critics like Julius Bab and Herbert Jhering established high theatrical standards and encouraged as yet unknown playwrights like BRECHT.

Socialist principles and responsiveness to members' aspirations meant that dictatorial regimes were unable to assimilate the Volksbühne. After taking it over in 1933, the Nazis were forced to dissolve it in 1937. Re-established in 1947, it ceased to exist as a subscription organization in East Germany in 1957, although the rebuilt theatre on Bülowplatz continued to function under the Volksbühne title and became a showcase for the work of BENNO BESSON. The contemporary Freie Volksbühne was founded in opposition in 1949 in West Berlin, and moved into a newly designed theatre under Piscator in 1963, returning to the original ideals of the organization with the creation of postwar documentary drama. There is an international dimension to Volksbühne through IATO (the International Association of Theatre–Public Organizations). CI

Volksstück (Germany) Play written for popular audiences in their local dialect. Although several German cities have a *Volksstück* tradition, the genre is associated most consistently with Vienna, where, throughout the 18th and much of the 19th century, it flourished in the city's commercial theatres. Originating in the improvisational work of JOSEF STRANITZKY and GOTTFRIED PREHAUSER, the *Volksstück* gradually came to be scripted, partly in an attempt to introduce greater decorum into performance, partly in response to the demands of the censor (see CENSORSHIP). The most notable comic writer of the mid-18th century was Philipp Hafner (1735–64), whose *Megära, the Terrible Witch* (1755) was a great success. Johann Kurz (1717–83), in addition to writing over 300 plays and creating the popular role of Bernadon, continued the tradition of improvisation after it had officially been banned in 1768. The end of the 18th century saw the production of the single most famous example of the genre, Mozart and SCHIKANEDER'S OPERA *The Magic Flute* (1791).

Over the turn of the century, the theatres most associated with the performance of the *Volksstück* were established; of these the Theater in der Josefstadt, founded in 1788, and the Theater an der Wien, founded by Schikaneder in 1801, are still in use. The Theater in der Leopoldstadt, founded in 1781 by the actor Karl von Marinelli (1744–1803), was replaced in 1845 by the Carltheater, built by the actor-manager Karl Carl (1789–1854). In the 19th century, two distinct sub-genres of the *Volksstück* can be distinguished. First there is the *Zauberstück*, a 'magic play' with music and spectacle, generally chronicling the adventures of the ordinary Viennese citizen in a fairy-world, of which the plays of FERDINAND RAIMUND are the best example. Then there is the *Lokalstück*, a more realistic play that treats, sometimes moralistically, sometimes farcically, the local customs and habits of the Viennese. The vigorous, witty and caustic works of JOHANN NESTROY are the finest examples of such comedy.

Writers of the *Volksstück* were unusually prolific, because of the seemingly insatiable appetite of the Viennese for their work. Among the most successful were Karl Meisl (1775–1853), who probably wrote over 200 plays, Adolf Bäuerle (1786–1859), who also edited the famous *Theaterzeitung* from 1806 to 1859, and Friedrich Kaiser (1814–75), another very prolific dramatist. Towards the end of the 19th century, the *Volksstück* tradition began to lose its identity, being transformed on the one hand into OPERETTA, on the other into commercial comedy. Nevertheless, its characteristic charm was remembered with painful poignancy by ARTHUR SCHNITZLER in *Liebelei* (1895), and with a sense of brutal reality by ÖDÖN VON HORVÁTH in *Tales from the Vienna Woods* (1931).

In the 1920s FLEISSER, Horváth and ZUCKMAYER adapted the *Volksstück* as a vehicle for social comment, as did BRECHT with *Mr Puntila and His Man Matti*. Horváth defined it as a play about common people, for common people, in the language of common people. Forgotten for 40 years, Horváth and Fleisser were rediscovered in the late 1960s when BAUER, FASSBINDER, KROETZ, SPERR and TURRINI returned to the genre to bring the lives of the underprivileged to the stage. SW HR

Volodin [Lifshits], **Aleksandr (Moiseevich)** 1919– Soviet dramatist whose lyrical dramas on the personal lives of ordinary people, related with a combination of gently ironic humour and pathos over lost innocence and failed romance, are characteristic of the post-Thaw period. Trained as a scenarist at the State Institute of Cinematography (1949), Volodin writes highly cinematic plays, replete with montage-like editing and dissolving of episodes, understatement of incident, evocative lighting, contrapuntal split-staging and parallel plotting, voice-over narration and musical accompaniment – which together bring a formal sense of fable to otherwise quotidian content. His restless, individualistic characters must discover personal happiness and spiritual values for themselves, a task made difficult by an ideologically based society, the pressure of work, the fallibility of the human heart and the failure of such institutions as marriage.

This basic situation is manifested in *The Factory Girl* (1956), *Five Evenings* (1957), *The Elder Sister* (1961), *The Idealist* (1962), *The Appointment* (1963) and *Never Part from Your Loved Ones* (1972). The last play, based upon Volodin's short-story account of his experience as a citizen judge at Leningrad divorce court proceedings, offers a strongly emotional central story, which culminates in the heroine's nervous breakdown, ironically counterpointed by an innocent, optimistic social-games leitmotif added by Minsk director Nikolai Scheiko in the play's original production. Volodin has written three highly successful parable plays, *Two Arrows*, *Little Lizard* and *Dulcinea of El Toboso* (1973), the last concerning Aldonsa and Sancho Panza's lives following Don Quixote's death, and the basis for a highly popular stage musical at Leningrad's Lensoviet Theatre. Volodin has written several film scenarios, including *Autumn Marathon* and *The Blonde*. SG

Voltaire [François-Marie Arouet] 1694–1778 French poet, dramatist, historian and philosopher, the most tireless man of letters of his century. His manifold interests and inquiring mind, to which he added an irritable outspokenness, occasioned numerous brushes with authority and led to periods of imprisonment or of self-imposed exile, in England, Prussia and Switzerland as well as the remote French provinces. The same circumstances help to explain the discontinuity of his career as a playwright, which began in 1718 with a tragedy, *Oedipe*, and, after only three further plays in the next decade, resumed with vigour in the early 1730s and again in the 1740s, continuing intermittently until his last performed tragedy, *Irène*, in 1778. He wrote librettos for a few operas and *divertissements* and some comedies and domestic dramas, but he was most respected in his day for his many tragedies, which probably constituted the most persuasive grounds for his election to the Académie-Française in 1746. That none of them holds the stage today is attributable to several factors, not least the extreme orthodoxy of his dramaturgic method, which was tenaciously neoclassical and impelled him to emulate PIERRE CORNEILLE and RACINE without any of their creative originality. Even his few innovations, such as the choice of subject-matter from indigenous French history (e.g. *Adélaïde du Guesclin*, 1734) or from exotic climes (e.g. *Alzire, ou Les Américains*, 1736, set in Peru; *L'Orphelin de la Chine* (*The Chinese Orphan*, 1755)), introduce only a superficial local colour, while his occasional borrowings from SHAKESPEARE, whose work he learned to read in the original while in England and helped to popularize in France before disavowing it, now have an air of rather gauche MELODRAMA (as in *Zaïre*, 1732, considered to be his masterpiece, and *La Mort de César* (*The Death of Caesar*, 1735)).

His use of plays as vehicles for propaganda in his long, energetic onslaught upon religious bigotry and tyranny of all kinds (e.g. *Mahomet, ou Le Fanatisme*, 1741), while estimable in itself, has proved inimical to their dramatic appeal. He produced a large body of critical writing on the drama, notably the prefaces to his plays and the *Commentaires sur Corneille* (1764), and his genuine love of the stage was expressed in other ways, as in his building of several private theatres and his patronage of individual players, such as ADRIENNE LECOUVREUR and LEKAIN whom he supported in a successful campaign against the fashionable practice of seating spectators on the stage. DR

Von Sydow, Max [Carl Adolf] 1929– Swedish actor. While best known internationally for his many films, Von Sydow has had an outstanding stage career. After training at DRAMATEN and acting in Norrköping and Helsingborg, in 1955 he joined INGMAR BERGMAN's MALMÖ STADSTEATER company, giving powerful performances (on Malmö's huge stage) as Erik XIV, Peer Gynt, Alceste and Faust. After several years in film, his stage career resumed in the 1970s at Dramaten, where Bergman directed him in unnerving performances of the Lawyer in STRINDBERG's *A Dream Play* and Gregers in IBSEN's *The Wild Duck*. His very volatile physical presence on stage is matched by a remarkably clear focus; both were in evidence in his 1991–2 performances as Eugene O'Neill in NORÉN's *And Give us the Shadows*. HL

Vondel, Joost van den 1587–1679 Dutch playwright and poet, who has given the Golden Age in the Netherlands a European standing. Van den Vondel underwent the influence of the *Rederijkers* (Rhetoricians), of SENECA, SOPHOCLES and EURIPIDES, and, in his turn, he influenced German baroque. In 1637 he wrote *Gijsbrecht van Aemstel* to mark the opening of Amsterdam's new municipal theatre in 1638. It was performed there annually on New Year's Day, from 1638 until 1968. In 1641, he was converted to the Roman Catholic Church. Consequently, many of the plays that followed bear witness to a deep religious feeling, for which he found a constant source of inspiration in the Bible. Some of these plays, such as *Lucifer* (1654) and *Adam in Exile* (1664), are still performed today. MG WH

Vormingstoneel Dutch movement engaged in educational drama (political). Since 1970 (see AKTIE TOMAAT) Dutch theatre companies such as Proloog (1964–83), De Nieuwe Komedie (1969–85) and Sater (1971–85) and, in Belgium, Kollektief INTERNATIONALE NIEUWE SCENE, Mannen van de Dam (Men of the Dam) and the Trojaanse Paard (Trojan Horse) have been producing work with a strong political tendency. The aim is to stimulate an audience's social awareness and emancipation through the theatre. Inspired by BRECHT and Marx, they see a theatre performance as a device in class warfare and as a contribution to change in society.

The plays are often written by collective effort and frequently deal with the problems of a specific social group. If necessary, research is undertaken into the group that the production hopes to reach, and previews are given for a few of its representatives. After the performance, the company invites discussion; the theatrical experience is analysed in relation to the structure of society. To reach a potential audience, acting space is created in all kinds of locations: at schools, factories and local meeting centres, and at demonstrations. In the 1980s, the Dutch companies involved lost their subsidies; the reason given was that the performances did not have enough artistic quality. The Vormingstoneel was found to present gross simplifications and clichés, thereby failing to meet a satisfactory traditional theatrical standard. The question remains whether this judgement was fair *vis-à-vis* the educational aspects of the Vormingstoneel. The result was the disappearance of a very outspoken segment in the Dutch theatrical landscape.   MG HS

Voskovec, Jiří (Wachsmann) 1905–81 and
Jan Werich 1905–80 Czech actors, dramatists and CABARET performers, who met while attending the law faculty of Prague's Karl University in 1927. With the composer Jaroslav Ježek they founded the Liberated Theatre, where they staged SATIRES and political REVUES until 1938, mixing parodies of film and theatrical clichés with social commentary. Werich usually played the robust, instinctual CLOWN to Voskovec's more rational straight-man, and their verbal comedy attacked middle-class values

and Fascist ideology. In 1938 they emigrated to the USA, broadcasting for the CSR and touring, but returned to Prague in 1946 to perform in their own theatre. After 1948, Voskovec settled in the USA, working in theatre and film; Werich continued at the Prague Theatre of Satire until his retirement in 1968.   LS

Voss, Gert 1942– German actor in CLAUS PEYMANN's Stuttgart, Bochum and Vienna companies. After his acclaimed Hermann in KLEIST's *Hermannsschlacht* (1987), he achieved star status at the BURGTHEATER, playing Richard III, Prospero and Macbeth under Peymann, Shylock as a hard-boiled 1980s businessman in braces, and an Ivanov which captured the CHEKHOV character's elusive amalgam of charm, tenderness and feckless destructiveness – both under ZADEK. He created Mr Jay

Jiří Voskovec and Jan Werich in characteristic makeup, early 1930s.

with shambling self-irony in George Tabori's *Goldberg Variations*. THOMAS BERNHARD wrote *Ritter, Dene, Voss* for him. In 1994 Voss joined Zadek at the BERLINER ENSEMBLE, making his debut as a cerebral, almost consciously self-destructive Antony in *Antony and Cleopatra*.   HR

Vychodil, Ladislav 1920– Slovak designer and teacher of scenography, and, since 1945, primary designer and technical chief of the Slovak National Theatre in Bratislava. Vychodil describes his work as 'poetism' – a lyrical yet restrained form with an emphasis on props and details over traditional decor. His style was strongly influenced by designer Frantisek Tröster. Except for a period of imposed socialist realism in the early 1950s, Vychodil's work is typified by a complex treatment of the floor and cyclorama, frequently covered with designs or projections with an emphasis on light and colour, and by the use of flown scenic pieces creating a layered look. In the late 1970s he began working with director ALFRED RADOK: the result has been a sparer look and an almost total de-emphasis of obvious design.   AA

Vysotsky, Vladimir (Semyonovich) 1938–80 Hoarse, wiry Russian actor and *chansonnier*, who became a national idol shortly after joining the Taganka Theatre in Moscow. Closely associated with its director YURY LYUBIMOV, he played the aviator in *The Good Person of Setzuan* (1964), Kerensky in *Ten Days That Shook the World* (1965), Pugachev in a curtailed and cancelled play of that name by Esenin (1967); Hamlet (1971); and Svidrigailov in *Crime and Punishment* (his last role, 1979), as well as Lopakhin in ANATOLY EFROS's staging of *The Cherry Orchard* at the Taganka (1975). He married the French actress Marina Vlady on a tour to Paris in 1977. His more than 900 songs and poems were, according to Lyubimov, 'an irreplaceable chronicle of daily life in the Soviet Union for 20 years'; cassettes of his guitar-accompanied recitals were copied and recopied, but the authorities never allowed him to record officially. When his 'Wolf Hunt' was acclaimed in Voznesensky's *Cover Your Faces* (1970), the play was banned after four performances, and the homage production Lyubimov staged after his death received only private performances.   LS

Wagner, (Wilhelm) Richard 1813–83 German composer and librettist. Wagner wrote to a friend, 'I am an artist and nothing but an artist – that is my blessing and my curse.' NIETZSCHE referred to him as 'the most outstanding theatrical genius that the Germans have ever had'. His major theatrical works, OPERAS of which he wrote both librettos and scores, have a wide range of composition and first-performance dates: *Rienzi* (written in 1838–40; performed in 1842), *The Flying Dutchman* (1841; 1843), *Tannhäuser* (1843–5; 1845), *Lohengrin* (1846–8; 1850), *Tristan and Isolde* (1857–9; 1865), *The Mastersingers of Nuremberg* (1862–7; 1868), *Parsifal* (1877–82; 1882), *The Rhinegold* (1853–4; 1869), *The Valkyrie* (1854–6; 1870), *Siegfried* (1856–71; 1876) and *The Twilight of the Gods* (1869–74; 1876) – the last four listed being components of the great cycle *The Ring of the Nibelungs*, which did not receive its first integral performance until 1876 although its ultimate origins can be traced back to 1848.

Wagner aimed to write music-dramas, the very term emphasizing his view that the effect of opera should be above all dramatic. He abhorred the gratuitous in opera, however attractive this may be to audiences, and in this he included display singing and ARIAS that were almost free-standing items, stage effects striking by their spectacle alone – in fact, everything theatrical that was not justified by its contribution to the drama or that interrupted its flow or that flawed its organic unity. Instead of disposing his works in RECITATIVES that supplied information and arias that expressed high points of feeling, he strove for a continuous flow of music in which voices express greater or less feeling, the mundane or the transcendent, as the progress of the drama demands. His concern for unity led him to exploit brief melodic components as binding features. Such a component might be Alberich's curse, the gold stolen from the Rhinemaidens, or the symbol of Siegfried's horn. Its sounding in the orchestra makes a clear reference and brings forth a host of associations, even though what is referred to is neither present on the stage nor the immediate concern of the characters. The components are not merely reiterated in identical form. They act as germs that metamorphose into various strains, and they appear in the score as integrated features in an overall design. The established term (not invented by Wagner) for one of these components is *leitmotif*, or leading motive.

Given the kind of opera that was familiar to audiences of the third quarter of the 19th century, it is no surprise that many found the Wagner operas either incomprehensibly formless, because of their continuous flow in which climaxes come as a result of dramatic development and not because of a familiar formula, or just incomprehensible because of the allusions of the leading motives. Further, because Wagner's orchestra was not a mere accompanist nor, as some have claimed, a protagonist, but the definer of the ambience of the characters, the prop and stay of their world, there were those who found his operas 'too symphonic'. Wagner was single-mindedly, some would say ruthlessly, dedicated to art which for him found its highest expression in music-drama. In spite of his aspirations towards the total work of art (*Gesamtkunstwerk*) in which all the arts were to find expression, his own works are authentic operas in which the essential elements are the music and the characters.

Wagner was a man of enormous industry. His prose works run to some ten volumes and his correspondence was voluminous. Three of his celebrated essays are *Art and Revolution* (1849), *The Artwork of the Future* (1849) and *Opera and Drama* (1851). His writings as a whole do not express a single, unchanging and uncontradictory view, and they are often tortuous in expression. Nevertheless, they are the vigorous and challenging product of a fine mind in its struggle to make sense of what has been intuitively grasped as valuable. The sweep of the foregoing titles tends to obscure the fact of Wagner's outstanding practical interests and skills. His essays *On the Performing of Tannhäuser* and *Remarks on Performing the Opera, The Flying Dutchman* (both 1852–3) are as careful guides to rehearsals, playing, singing, acting and staging as one could hope for. The composer-conductor Hans Pfitzner (1869–1949) maintained that whatever reservations might be held against Wagner the composer or librettist, he was infallible in his ideas of theatrical effectiveness.

Wagner the man has been accused of violent anti-semitism and vigorous proto-Nazism. How violent and how vigorous seems to be a matter of endless debate. It is noteworthy that many eminent Jews and anti-Nazis extol the genius of his operas, whose place in the repertoire is secure. Wagner remains one of the most outstanding phenomena of European musical theatre. It is necessary to refer to him as a phenomenon, since from his own day until the present he has been acclaimed by some and loathed by others. It is hardly conceivable that anyone who pays attention to his works should remain indifferent to them. GH

Wagner, Robin 1933– American set designer. Wagner has been associated with some of the most successful MUSICALS of the post-1960 period, including *Hair*, *A Chorus Line*, *Dreamgirls*, *City of Angels* (1990 Tony) and *Jelly's Last Jam* (1992 Tony nomination). He began his career in San Francisco and worked with the Actor's Workshop, where he was greatly influenced by director HERBERT BLAU and BRECHTian aesthetics. His work at the ARENA STAGE in the mid-1960s led to explorations of stage space and moving scenery. Wagner is generally associated with spectacular sets, moving scenery and stylish decor, but by and large his sets are minimal; it is the way in which the sets move and are integrated into the production that gives the illusion of a great deal of scenery, such as the 1993 *Angels in America*. His best-known set was for *A Chorus Line*: for most of the show it consisted only of a white line on the floor; in the final scene the upstage wall revealed Mylar mirrors. This seemingly simple set was the result of over a year of stripping away excess and unnecessary scenic elements to arrive at a design that simply and boldly expressed the essence of the play. Wagner has never followed tradition or conventions; he has always explored new ideas, new materials and new configurations of space. In addition to BROADWAY he has also designed for OPERA, dance and rock concerts. AA

Wagner, Wieland 1917–66 German director and designer. Wagner staged all the major productions of his grandfather's operas at BAYREUTH after its reopening in 1951, and established the contemporary style of Wagnerian interpretation with his *Ring* cycle in the same year. Freeing the operas from NATURALISM, he introduced symbolic lighting (see SYMBOLISM; STAGE LIGHTING), sets and rhythms corresponding to the theories of ADOLPHE APPIA. CI

Walcott, Derek 1930– The most important Caribbean playwright, and a poet of world rank. Walcott has written 38 plays, half of which have been published. He has also published 15 volumes of poetry, including the epic *Omeros* (1990). He has received numerous prizes, among them the John D. and Catherine MacArthur Foundation grant in 1981, the 1989 Medal for Poetry awarded by Queen Elizabeth II, and in 1992 the Nobel Prize for Literature.

Born in St Lucia, Walcott began writing and directing plays while at school. With the support of his twin brother Roddy Walcott (also a playwright), he founded the Arts Guild of St Lucia, which performed his first published play *Henri Christophe* (1950) about the Haitian revolutionary leader. He attended the University College of the West Indies in JAMAICA (1950–4) and there wrote and staged a number of plays, several of which he later revised and retitled.

After graduating, Walcott taught for two years, then became a feature writer and art and theatre critic for newspapers in Jamaica and later in TRINIDAD. He wrote an epic drama, *Drums and Colours* (1958), for the Caribbean arts festival held in Trinidad to celebrate the birth of the West Indies Federation. In 1958–9 he studied theatre in the USA with a Rockefeller Foundation fellowship, and on returning to Trinidad he founded and became director of the Trinidad Theatre Workshop, based first at the Little Carib Theatre. For 17 years he wrote and directed plays with this company, taking productions on tour to other Caribbean territories and to the USA and Canada. Among the most noteworthy of his plays are *The Sea at Dauphin* (1954), *Ti-Jean and His Brothers* (1958), the highly acclaimed *Dream on Monkey Mountain* (1967) which received an Obie in its 1971 production by the NEGRO ENSEMBLE COMPANY in New York, *The Joker of Seville* (1974), *O Babylon!* (1976) and *Pantomime* (1978).

Walcott's dramas encompass a tension between instinct and intellect – the racial instinct stemming from an African heritage in conflict with an undiminished admiration for European intellectual and artistic achievement. His plays have been produced by theatre organizations in the USA and England, including the PUBLIC THEATER in New York, the ARENA STAGE in Washington,

DC, the GOODMAN THEATRE in Chicago and the Mark Taper Forum in Los Angeles. In London the ROYAL COURT THEATRE has presented his works, and in 1992 the ROYAL SHAKESPEARE COMPANY's Other Place in Stratford-on-Avon premiered *The Odyssey*, Walcott's commissioned dramatization of Homer's epic.

In 1981 he was appointed professor of creative writing at Boston University, but returns regularly to the Caribbean to work in theatre, and in 1984 he directed an open-air production of his play *Haitian Earth* in his native St Lucia. In 1991 *Steel*, a MUSICAL written with the composer Galt MacDermot and focusing on the steel band as a major force in the TRINIDAD CARNIVAL, was premiered by the American Repertory Theatre in Cambridge, Massachusetts. EGH

Waldoff, Claire [Clara Wortmann] 1884–1957 German MUSIC-HALL performer. Born in Gelsenkirchen, she toured the provinces as an ingénue (1903–6) before moving to Berlin, where she had a phenomenally successful CABARET debut in 1907. In 1910 she became the star of the Linden-Cabaret, personifying the lower-class types drawn by Heinrich Zille. Her throaty voice, red pageboy haircut and mannish suits contributed to the effect of such hits as 'Hermann heest er' ("Is Name's 'Erman'). A virtual symbol of Berlin wit and *joie de vivre*, she appeared in London in 1913 and 1933. After the latter tour, the Nazis banned her from the theatre, and she retired to lower Bavaria to live out her life in obscurity. LS

Wales Although Welsh-speakers now form a minority of the population, throughout its history Wales has enjoyed a cultural tradition separate from the English and distinguished by its rich and ancient language. The earliest Welsh-language theatre has its root in the culture's strong bardic (poetic) tradition. The narration of epic tales, battle reportage, eulogies and elegies were given at court by the paid entertainer and performer (*diddanwr*) – the bard. *Y Gododdin*, attributed to the 7th-century poet Aneirin and commemorating the battle of Catterick around 600 AD, shows evidence of this oral tradition. It has been argued forcibly that this is the tradition that held sway – crossbred with the litany and rites of Celtic Catholicism – until the 13th century, its major literary manifestations being the work of the bard Taliesin (late 6th century) and of Llywarch Hen, the supposed author of a cycle of dialogues and monologues written in the 9th or 10th century.

Outside this bardic tradition, which came to an end in the 16th century, very little drama was performed in Welsh before the beginning of the 20th century. There are naturally enough exceptions, principal among these being *Tri Brenin o Gwlen*, a 15th-century MIRACLE PLAY, and the INTERLUDES (*anterliwtiau*) dating mainly from the 17th and 18th centuries, popular plays performed by strolling players and often attacking contemporary social injustice and immorality. The interludes of Twm o'r Nant (1738–1810) have earned him a reputation as the father of Welsh-language drama. The interludes were prevalent in the north whilst the FOLK tradition of the Mari Lwyd, a seasonal performance with some affinities to the English mummers' plays, was confined to the south.

From the 17th century onwards there are records of

travelling companies visiting Wales from England (and Ireland), and the history of the English-speaking theatre in Wales is similar in many respects to that of comparable regions of England: EDMUND KEAN, the KEMBLES and W. C. MACREADY, whose father managed a theatre in Swansea for a time, all visited Wales on their provincial tours. By 1912 there were over 20 theatres in Wales catering for English-language drama, although few of them were to survive the advent of the cinema.

The prevalence of religious Nonconformism and its puritanical morality, however, stunted the development of a professional Welsh theatrical tradition in the 19th century; and although a number of Welsh playwrights emerged in the early decades of the 20th century, if they were not, like EMLYN WILLIAMS, to seek their fortune on the London stage, they had to rely for the performance of their works mainly on a flourishing amateur dramatic movement favouring domestic REALISM, which in the popular mind remained the dominant mode of dramatic perception until the 60s. However, notably in the early years of this century and again after the postwar period, a number of distinctive personalities left their mark on Welsh-language drama, chief amongst them SAUNDERS LEWIS, the most prominent figure in 20th-century Welsh literature. During the 50s, Lewis was foremost amongst those who argued for the creation of a Welsh National Theatre. In effect television, with its six hours a week of Welsh-language broadcasting, and BBC radio had become the main outlets of professional drama in Wales, leading the director Wilbert Lloyd Roberts to remark: 'We are the only nation in the world to which television came before professional theatre.'

A period of significant growth for the professional theatre began in the latter half of the 1960s, fostered by increased subsidies for the arts from the Welsh Arts Council (which enjoyed greater autonomy after 1967) and from local authorities, and largely sustained until the late 1980s. In 1970, when the Welsh Arts Council's Drama Department was established, the Council supported two theatres and three companies: by 1976 the figure had risen to eight theatres and eight companies. A network of new theatres was created, most of them associated with the colleges of the University of Wales but including the impressive Theatr Clwyd in Mold, North Wales. By the 1980s Wales had become the home of a number of radical, innovative theatre companies performing in both Welsh and English. The capital city Cardiff, where the headquarters of the Welsh National Opera and the Welsh broadcasting companies were situated, provided a favourable climate for experimental drama, while the predominantly rural areas of Wales were catered for by small-scale theatre companies, including a growing number of Welsh-language ones. Simultaneously an enlightened policy of partnership between the Welsh Arts Council and local authorities ensured that a THEATRE-IN-EDUCATION company was established in every county in Wales.

Companies devoted to the development of new writing included Made in Wales (English) and Bara Caws and Hwyl a Fflag (Welsh), and Wales established a significant presence in the international avant-garde through the work of the Cardiff Laboratory Theatre (later re-formed as the Centre for Performance Research), which established links with JERZY GROTOWSKI and EUGENIO BARBA's ODIN TEATRET, and that of Brith Gôf, which combined powerful physical theatre with themes of great emotional intensity in works such as *Branwen* (1981), *Ymfudwyr* (1985) and *Gododdin* (1988). Although little-seen in England, Brith Gôf has toured as far afield as South America and is perhaps the first Welsh-language company to achieve international recognition and status.

Attempts to establish a national theatre in the more conventional sense for Wales have proved less successful, despite the advocacy of the prominent actors and public figures who founded the St David 's Trust and campaigned sporadically for its creation throughout the 60s. The Welsh Theatre Company, established with a base in Cardiff in 1963, rarely fulfilled the promise of its earliest productions under Warren Jenkins's direction and did not survive the 1970s. Wilbert Lloyd Roberts, a BBC producer, took over the Welsh-language work of the company, which from 1968 became the responsibility of an independent company in Bangor, North Wales, with the title Theatr Cymru. A nationally touring company, it formed the first professional Welsh-language theatre ensemble and contributed enormously to the training of both actors and writers. Notable amongst the latter was GWENLYN PARRY, whose surrealist plays are among the most noteworthy developments in Welsh-language drama. However, partly as a result of its heavy touring schedule and partly through the lack of any distinctive tradition on which to draw, Theatr Cymru failed to develop artistically until the short-lived regime of artistic director Emily Davies (appointed in 1982) and her associate Ceri Sherlock recruited a younger generation of actors open to wider European influences. Theatr Cymru closed after financial failure in 1983, although many of the company regrouped under the banner of Theatrig to present Welsh versions of classical works as well as Saunders Lewis's *Blodeuwedd*, under the direction of Ceri Sherlock, while Theatr Gwynedd, Bangor, eventually became the home of a new Welsh-language mainstream theatre company.

Theatre writing in the Welsh language has continued to be largely television-influenced in the tradition set by JOHN GWILYM JONES, although there is an emergent alternative, in authors like Siôn Eirian, with a direct connection to the contemporary style of the Anglo-Welsh theatre writings of Alan Osborne and Ed Thomas, and in others, like John Glyn Owen, derived from a more historico-literary background.

For the financial year 1992–3 the Welsh Arts Council dispensed £2,714,322 to theatre companies and projects, supporting four mainstream producing theatres, nine theatre-in-education and community touring companies, and five companies devoted to research and innovative practice. The theatre's postwar growth in a country always in danger of cultural domination by its English neighbours owes much to three institutions with a certain, if limited, degree of cultural autonomy within Wales: BBC Wales and the independent Welsh broadcasting companies, the University of Wales, and the Welsh Arts Council – although the role of each of these has often been the subject of controversy. Unlike Ireland, Wales cannot boast of a modern theatrical tradition reaching back to the late 19th century, and its national aspirations are unlikely ever to be so closely allied to a dramatic movement or a national theatre as was the case in Ireland; but there can be no doubt that over the last three decades drama has become an increasingly significant element in the cultural experience of both Welsh and English speakers in the country. Despite the financial difficulties of the late 1980s and early 1990s, a distinctively Welsh theatre looks likely to survive. MA

See: D. Jones, *Black Book on Welsh Theatre*, Lausanne, 1985; O. Llew Owain, *Hanes y Ddrama yng Nghymru 1943–85*, Liverpool, 1948; C. Price, *The English Theatre in Wales*, Cardiff, 1948; M. Stephens (ed.), *The Arts in Wales 1950–75*, Welsh Arts Council, 1979, and (ed.), *The Oxford Companion to the Literature of Wales*, Oxford, l986.

Walker, George see WILLIAMS, BERT

Walker, George F. 1947– One of Canada's most serious and prolific writers of COMEDY, who frequently directs his own works. Walker's first play, *The Prince of Naples* (1970), was written in response to an advertisement for scripts by Factory Theatre Lab, a Toronto theatre, where Walker subsequently served as playwright-in-residence until 1974. FTL premiered his next six, as well as many of his more recent works.

Walker's plays are profoundly influenced by electronic media and popular culture, often resulting in a non-linear, surrealistic rhythm (see SURREALISM) that reflects the culturally created chaos of modern life. Dramatically, they most often employ confrontational scenes between two characters – a structure that underscores his thematic preoccupation with defining the nature of good and evil. In response to criticism that his plays were 'inaccessible' Walker wrote *Gossip* (1977), a quasi-murder mystery featuring journalist and reluctant detective, Tyrone M. Power. *Filthy Rich* (1979) and *The Art of War* (1983) complete the 'Power Plays' trilogy, which exploits the conventions of detective fiction and B-movies to raise questions about role-playing, identity and the nature of reality.

Walker's other major trilogy, the 'East End Plays' – *Beautiful City* (1987), *Better Living* (1986) and *Criminals in Love* (for which he won the 1984 Governor General's Award) – explore urban life, moral corruption, and 'the hanging shadow' of fate in his native East End Toronto. In 1992 he expanded the trilogy with *Escape from Happiness*. In addition to writing and directing many other plays, Walker has adapted TURGENEV's *Fathers and Sons* (as *Nothing Sacred*, 1988), and spent a year as playwright-in-residence at Joseph Papp's PUBLIC THEATER in New York. DAH

Wall, Max [Maxwell George Lorimer] 1908–90 British actor and eccentric comedian. With a voice as mobile and disjointed as his limbs, with trousers too high and jackets too tight, and a face that expressed a fathomless range of experience, Wall turned the simplest act and the most innocent comment into anarchic and often disturbing comedy. His early reputation was established in the MUSIC-HALL and on radio from the 1920s to the 1950s. Thereafter he turned increasingly to 'straight' plays, appearing in such roles as Père Ubu (ROYAL COURT THEATRE, 1966), Archie Rice (Greenwich Theatre, London, 1974) and as Bludgeon in JOHN ARDEN's *Sergeant Musgrave's Dance* (OLD VIC, 1984). He had a special affinity for BECKETT, memorably instanced by his portrayal of Vladimir in the Manchester ROYAL EXCHANGE THEATRE production of *Waiting for Godot* (1981). He had previously played Krapp at Greenwich (1976) and went on to play Malone in John Elsom's version of Beckett's novel at the EDINBURGH FESTIVAL in 1984. Wall often appeared as a solo artist, inventing Professor Wallofski, and presenting his one-man show *Aspects of Max Wall* (1974 and after). MB

Wallace, Edgar (Horatio) 1875–1932 British novelist and dramatist. Wallace's experience as a crime reporter gave a realistic basis to the ingenious plots of his popular detective thrillers, the most successful of which were *The Ringer* (1926), *On the Spot* (1930) and *The Case of the Frightened Lady* (1931). CI

Wallace, Nellie [Eleanor] **(Jane)** 1870–1948 Scottish comedienne, billed as 'the Essence of Eccentricity'. She began her MUSIC-HALL career clog-dancing at the age of 12 and was a star shortly after her first London appearance in 1903. Portraying a moth-eaten spinster with buck teeth and a ratty fur-piece ('my little bit of vermin'), she was one of the few actresses who was grotesque enough to play a PANTOMIME dame successfully. Her best songs included 'The Blasted Oak', 'Tally Ho', 'A Boy's Best Friend Is His Mother' and 'Let's Have a Tiddley at the Milk Bar'. She last performed publicly at the Royal Command Performance of 1948. LS

Wallach, Eli 1915– and
Anne Jackson 1926– American actors. Brooklyn-born Wallach made his New York debut as the crew chief in *Skydrift* (1945). He won stardom as Alvaro Mangiacavallo, a sexually driven truck driver in TENNESSEE WILLIAMS's *The Rose Tattoo* (1951). Both Wallach and his wife, Anne Jackson, had substantial successes before their marriage in 1948, but were acclaimed as an acting duo in *The Typists* and *The Tiger* in 1963. Jackson made her professional debut in a touring production of *The Cherry Orchard*, later appearing with EVA LE GALLIENNE's AMERICAN REPERTORY THEATRE in 1946. Jackson and Wallach appeared together in *Luv* (1964), a revival of *The Waltz of the Toreadors* (1973), in *Twice around the Park* (1982), and in a revival of ODETS's *The Flowering Peach* (1994), among others. Both have appeared in numerous films and television programmes, though Wallach has been more prolific as a film actor, beginning with *Baby Doll* in 1956.

Both members of the team use an internal intensity (both studied at the ACTORS STUDIO) suitable for drama or COMEDY. Of them in *Luv*, critics said: 'Miss Jackson can play comedy as straight-faced and doggedly as if she were mining coal, but she turns up diamonds', and 'Mr Wallach has a flair for enduring indignities, whether of poverty or affluence, marriage or divorce.' SMA

Wallack family A dynasty of actor-managers, of English origin, in the American theatre, inseparably linked with the history of the New York stage for over 50 years. **Henry**

John Wallack (1790–1870) – the eldest son of William H. Wallack (1760–1850) and Elizabeth Field (Granger) (d.1850), popular performers at London's ASTLEY's Amphitheatre and later at the Surrey – went to the USA in 1819 with his first wife, dancer Fanny Jones. After lengthy stays in Baltimore, Philadelphia and Washington, DC, Wallack made his New York City debut at the Anthony Street Theatre in 1821; in 1824 he became leading man at the Chatham Theatre. During 1828–32, 34–6, and during the summer of 1840 and for some time afterwards, he was back in England, acting sporadically. In 1837 he was stage manager, under his brother, at the National Theatre, New York. He gained considerable acclaim for his Sir Peter Teazle in 1847 at New York's Broadway Theatre. One of his last roles was Falstaff, in 1858.

Though a versatile and accomplished actor, Henry did not win the fame of other family members in the USA. Two of his sisters were actors – Mary (Mrs Stanley) and Elizabeth (Mrs Pincott), mother of the actress Leonora, later known as Mrs Alfred Wigan – as was his brother **J(ames) W(illiam)** Wallack (?1795–1864), known as the elder to distinguish him from his nephew. This Wallack, also born in England, appeared first in the USA at the PARK THEATRE as Macbeth in 1818. For the next 35 years he shuttled between the USA and England, though he was best known on the American stage. The most distinguished member of this notable family, he was admired for roles in TRAGEDY and COMEDY, especially the latter. Although most historians categorize him as a member of the KEMBLE school, JAMES MURDOCH called him 'the first romantic actor of America'. An exceedingly handsome actor, his Shylock and Jaques in *As You Like It* were considered innovative. During 1837–9 he managed New York's National Theatre; after its destruction by fire, he managed NIBLO's Garden for a time. In 1851 he settled permanently in New York City, assuming control the following year of BROUGHAM's Broadway Lyceum, as WALLACK's; for nine years this theatre prospered. For almost 35 years his company was the leading American ensemble, first under his leadership and later under his son Lester. In 1861 he built the second Wallack's on BROADWAY at 13th Street.

James's nephew, **J(ames) W(illiam)** Wallack Jr (1818–73), son of Henry and born in London, became a credible actor in tragedy. More than any other member of the family, he spent most of his career away from New York, spreading the Wallack name to all the major American theatrical centres, retiring in 1872.

Next to James the elder, **Lester** Wallack [John Johnstone] (1820–88), his nephew, made the greatest contribution to the American stage. The only major member of the family born in the USA, he nonetheless served his apprenticeship in England and Ireland, making his American debut in 1847 at the Broadway Theatre in New York as Sir Charles Coldstream in *Used Up*. During his career with the Wallack company he played nearly 300 roles, excelling as Benedick, Charles Surface, Sir Andrew Aguecheek and Sir Elliott Grey in his own adaptation of *Rosedale* (1863). Lester stage-managed for his father at Wallack's Lyceum, and became the manager of the second Wallack's until 1882, when he opened a new Wallack's, where he remained until 1887. Although Lester did little to encourage American works, depending heavily on an English repertoire, he was a highly honoured member of the profession until his death. His important memoirs were published posthumously, in 1889.   DBW

Wallack's Theatre (New York City) Although the playhouse on 13th Street was the most famous of the theatres bearing the name of Wallack, there were actually three theatres associated with the Wallack family. The first was built by JOHN BROUGHAM in 1850 on BROADWAY, but passed to J. W. WALLACK two years later and was operated by him as Wallack's Lyceum for nine years. In 1861, a new Wallack's went up in the theatre district forming around Union Square and was managed by LESTER WALLACK, who was its principal star for many years. For nearly 20 years, it dispensed impeccably cast English plays with a company of mainly English actors to an elitist audience. Following a trend, Wallack relocated his company to a third theatre at the northeast corner of Broadway and 30th Street, but fortune did not follow him. In ill health and faced with an indifferent theatrical public, he retired in 1887. A year later, Wallack died and the house was leased to A. M. PALMER, who changed the name to Palmer's; it reverted to its original name in 1896. All three theatres were torn down: the first in 1869; the second, which was renamed the Star Theatre and continued to be leased to producers, in 1901; and the third in 1915.   MCH

Waller, Emma 1820–99 British-born actress, who married American actor Daniel Wilmarth Waller in 1849 and went with him to the USA in 1851. Her earliest known performance was in 1855 on tour in Australia, followed by a London debut in 1856. For her American debut in 1857 at the WALNUT STREET THEATRE in Philadelphia, she appeared on successive nights as Ophelia to Mr Waller's Hamlet, Pauline in *The Lady of Lyons* and Lady Macbeth, the latter performed with an 'almost painful' intensity of passion. Fullness of characterization and a stately presence were her strengths in roles like Queen Margaret and Queen Katharine and Meg Merrilies in *Guy Mannering*. She also achieved *succès d'estime* as Iago in the 1860s and 70s. She and her husband often performed together from her 1858 New York debut as Marina in *The Duchess of Malfi* (R. H. Horne's adaptation) until her retirement in 1878.   FHL DJW

Waller, Lewis 1860–1915 English actor-manager, who became the supreme matinée idol at the turn of the century and whose repertoire was constrained by the need to gratify the KOW (Keen on Waller) Brigade. He made his debut under J. L. TOOLE in 1883, and his first venture into management when he produced *An Ideal Husband* at the HAYMARKET (1895). 'You make it suit you', was WILDE's ambiguous comment. As D'Artagnan (1898) and as the eponymous hero of BOOTH TARKINGTON's *Monsieur Beaucaire* (1902), he was rapturously received and they became the basis of his repertoire. But the modest Waller would have preferred to play more often in SHAKESPEARE than his audiences allowed. He was an excellent Brutus and Faulconbridge and among the finest exponents of Henry V and Hotspur in the English theatre. To these parts he added during his management of the Imperial (1903–6) and the LYRIC (1907–11) that of Othello.   PT

Walnut Street Theatre (Philadelphia) Miraculously eluding the American penchant for tearing down the old and building the new, the Walnut Street survives today as the oldest functioning playhouse in America. It was opened in 1809 as a domed arena for the Pepin and Breschard CIRCUS, but in 1811 came the first of a string of renovations to transform it into a workable theatre. It was enlarged, fitted with a stage and orchestra pit, and renamed the Olympic. In 1820, the dome was removed and the name changed to the Walnut Street, and it briefly housed a company that rivalled the CHESTNUT STREET THEATRE. In 1828, John Haviland designed a new Greek-revival façade for it. Eventually, it passed to the ownership of JOHN SLEEPER CLARKE, EDWIN BOOTH's brother-in-law, and remained in his estate until 1919. Intending to raze it and replace it with a new theatre, the new owner discovered that the building code restricted him to a smaller theatre, and decided to rebuild the old house. In 1968, it was declared a National Landmark, and money was raised to restore it to Haviland's 1828 version, although the interior was thoroughly modernized. MCH

Walser, Martin 1927 German novelist and dramatist. His first play, *Der Abstecher* (*The Detour*, 1961), is a black COMEDY with echoes of PINTER and BRECHT. Its subject is marital strife, to which Walser returns with *Zimmerschlacht* (*Home Front*, 1967), a TV play which KORTNER helped to adapt for the stage. *The Rabbit Race* (1962), a comic parable-play which traces the rise of residual Nazism in West Germany, and *The Black Swan* (1964), which examines various modes of living with a Nazi past – its central character is an ex-concentration-camp doctor – were the first parts of an abandoned 'German Chronicle' project. Walser is primarily a novelist, and his plays since the 1960s have had little success. HR

Walter, Eugene 1874–1941 American playwright and filmwriter. Associated in business management with numerous theatrical enterprises – MINSTREL SHOWS, CIRCUSES, symphony orchestras – Walter contributed most importantly to American theatre with a score of successful, social-realist MELODRAMAS. Essentially, he emphasized the victims of overwhelming social and personal forces: a man caught in the political machine of New York City (*The Undertow*, 1906); a weak husband pushed to immoral limits by the power of business (*Paid in Full*, 1908); a man corrupted by money and brought to ruin and death (*Fine Feathers*, 1913). Walter's best play, *The Easiest Way* (1908), remembered for its realistic stage setting by DAVID BELASCO, featured a weak woman who understands and accepts her frailty. Other plays include *The Wolf* (1908), *A Plain Woman* (1912), *The Knife* (1917). Walter's skills were easily adapted to films. In 1925 he published a series of lectures entitled *How to Write a Play*. WJM

Wälterlin, Oskar 1895–1961 Swiss director, actor and author. Educated at the University of Basle, he gained his PhD in 1918 with a thesis on 'SCHILLER and the Public'. In January 1919 he played his first (small) professional part in *Wilhelm Tell* and in October he directed his first OPERA: Pergolesi's *La serva padrona*. His association with the Basel Stadttheater continued until his death: during 1919–25,

as actor; from 1925 to 32 and 1942 to 44 as artistic director (a post which he was to take up for a third time in 1961), and as guest director at other times. In Basle he is particularly remembered for WAGNER's *Ring* which he had prepared with ADOLPHE APPIA for 1924–5, but only *Rhinegold* and *The Valkyrie* were presented following the hostile outcry of the conservative 'Wagner friends'.

From 1933 to 38 he directed mainly opera in Frankfurt-am-Main, but returned to Switzerland in 1938 to take up the artistic and administrative direction of the Schauspielhaus, Zurich, where he remained until 1961. In Zurich he attracted the best German and Austrian actors and directors who were escaping from Nazi oppression. He created an impressive ensemble and evolved a style which established the Schauspielhaus as the main centre of German theatre from the late 30s to the early 60s. Under Wälterlin, Zurich saw the world premieres of BRECHT's *Mother Courage* (19 April 1942), *The Good Person of Setzuan* (4 February 1947), *Galileo* (9 September 1947) and *Puntila* (5 June 1949); ZUCKMAYER's *Barbara Blomberg* (1948); the first German performance of WILDER's *Our Town* and the first plays of two emerging Swiss playwrights – FRISCH's *Don Juan or The Love of Geometry* (1952) and *The Fire-Raisers* (1957), and DÜRRENMATT's *The Visit* (1955). CIS

Walters, Sam 1939– British director, who studied as an actor at the London Academy of Music and Dramatic Art and became a director in the mid-1960s with the formation of a repertory company at the Swan Theatre, Worcester. He went to JAMAICA to found the state's first theatre and acting school, and on his return to England in 1971 worked as a freelance director and teacher, while launching the Orange Tree Theatre in Richmond, Surrey.

The Orange Tree started out as little more than a 'social functions' room above a pub, a FRINGE theatre on the outskirts of southwest London, but it won a reputation for its ambitious programmes, for its high standards of production and design, and for its encouragement of new writing, from such dramatists as MARTIN CRIMP, David Cregan, JAMES SAUNDERS, Fay Weldon and Olwen Wymark. Walters led the campaign for a new Orange Tree, raising nearly £2 million to open a modern, well equipped small theatre in 1991, whose programmes reflected the range of his enthusiasms: unusual revivals (JOHN MARSTON's *The Dutch Courtesan*, 1993), drama from Eastern Europe (VÁCLAV HAVEL's *Restoration*, 1991), new British plays and major classics.

Many Orange Tree productions have transferred to larger theatres in the WEST END or elsewhere, but the true value of Walters's work can best be appreciated in Surrey, where his theatre has become a focal point for new drama within the region. In 1989 he won a Winston Churchill Travelling Fellowship which enabled him to tour Eastern Europe, and in 1991 he received on behalf of the Orange Tree the Charrington Fringe Award for Outstanding Achievement in Small Theatre. JE

Walton, Tony 1934– British-born set and COSTUME designer for theatre, film, television, OPERA and ballet. Walton studied at the Slade School of Fine Arts in London and began work at the Wimbledon Theatre; his first New

York production was in 1957. He soon became associated in the USA with a range of witty and elegant MUSICALS, including *A Funny Thing Happened on the Way to the Forum*, *Pippin*, *Grand Hotel: The Musical*, *The WILL ROGERS Follies*, the revivals of *Guys and Dolls* (1992) and *She Loves Me* (1993). However, like his idol BORIS ARONSON, his style is mutable, often whimsical and always inventive. With over 45 New York productions to his credit, including *The Real Thing*, *Hurlyburly*, the Lincoln Center revivals of *The House of Blue Leaves* and *Anything Goes*, *Six Degrees of Separation*, *Conversations with My Father* and *Death and the Maiden*, Walton is one of the most active designers in New York theatre today. *Fool's Paradise*, *The Ginger Man*, *Most Happy Fella*, *Caligula* and *Triple Bill* number among his London designs, while film credits include *Mary Poppins*, *The Wiz*, *Deathtrap*, *All That Jazz* and, for television, DUSTIN HOFFMAN's *Death of a Salesman*. He has received Tonys, Oscars and Emmys and many more nominations. AA DBW

Wanamaker, Sam 1919–93 American actor and director, most of whose major work after 1952 was in and for the English theatre. Wanamaker was born in Chicago, where he did his actor-training at the GOODMAN THEATRE. He made his BROADWAY debut in 1942 and returned to the New York stage in 1946, after wartime military service. America was not, at that time, a happy home for a young actor with idealistic left-wing sympathies, and when the role of Bernie Dodd in CLIFFORD ODETS's *The Country Girl* took him to London (where the play was retitled *Winter Journey*), he chose to remain in England. A period as a jobbing actor and freelance director culminated in 1956 with a ROYAL COURT production of BRECHT's *The Threepenny Opera*. The following year, he was appointed artistic director of the New Shakespeare Theatre in Liverpool. Further recognition came in 1959, when he played Iago to PAUL ROBESON's Othello at Stratford. Critical response was not enthusiastic, but Wanamaker's enthusiasm for SHAKESPEARE became a magnificent obsession and dictated the shape of his subsequent career, from his playing of Macbeth in a return to the Goodman Theatre in 1964 to his leadership in the foundation of the Globe Playhouse Trust and World Centre for Shakespeare Studies (1970) and his energetic fronting of the subsequent operation of the Trust and Centre. Even opponents of the venture have expressed their sadness that this Shakespearian missionary should have died so shortly before the opening of his dreamed-of 'replica' of Shakespeare's second GLOBE THEATRE, not far from its original site. PT

war of the theatres The first salvo in the Poetomachia, or war of the theatres, may have been fired when the LORD CHAMBERLAIN'S MEN presented JONSON's *Every Man out of His Humour* (1599), with its satirical portraits of MARSTON and DEKKER; but the war was not declared until 1601, when Jonson was preparing a play for the CHILDREN OF THE CHAPEL ROYAL at the BLACKFRIARS, Dekker for the Lord Chamberlain's Men at the GLOBE, and Marston for the BOYS OF ST PAUL's at their indoor theatre. There is every likelihood that Jonson heard a rumour that he was to be pilloried in Dekker's *Satiromastix* and decided to get his blow in first with *Poetaster*. Marston countered, rather tamely,

with *What You Will*, and tongues continued to wag throughout the year. It is possible that the Chamberlain's Men and the Paul's Boys were leagued in rivalry to the suddenly fashionable Chapel Children, and that Hamlet's abuse of the 'little eyases' is a reverberation from the Poetomachia. But *Hamlet* is an infinitely finer play than any of those directly provoked by the war. It has been plausibly suggested that the squabble was not much more than a publicity stunt. PT

Ward, Douglas Turner 1930– African-American actor, director and playwright. Born in Louisiana but educated in the North, Ward trained at the Paul Mann Theatre Workshop in New York. He acted in OFF-BROADWAY plays before accepting a minor role on BROADWAY in *A Raisin in the Sun* (1959). Working with Robert Hooks in 1965, Ward produced his two one-act satiric comedies, *Happy Ending* and *Day of Absence*, for a 14-month off-Broadway run. In 1968 Ward, Hooks and Gerald Krone founded the NEGRO ENSEMBLE COMPANY, where Ward continues as artistic director. He has directed and played leading roles in many of the company's productions, notably *Ceremonies in Dark Old Men* (1969) and *The River Niger* (1972), for which he won an Obie. He directed the 1982 Pulitzer Prize-winning *A Soldier's Play* and has also written *The Reckoning* (1969) and *Brotherhood* (1970). EGH

Ward, Geneviève (Teresa) [Ginevra Guerrabella] 1838–1922 American-born actress whose career belongs to the English theatre. As Ginevra Guerrabella, she made her professional debut in OPERA, but her voice failed and she turned to acting, though retaining much of the grandiose aura of a prima donna. She opened at Manchester in 1873 as Lady Macbeth (a part she played in French in Paris in 1877) and Constance in *King John*, at once announcing her Wagnerian scales, but it was in a forgotten play by Herman Merivale and F. C. Grove, *Forget-Me-Not* (1879), that she made her international reputation. In the part of Stephanie, a high-society Frenchwoman, she toured the English-speaking world, returning to the London stage as a celebrity. At TENNYSON's request, she played Eleanor of Aquitaine in IRVING's production of *Becket* (1893), and was Morgan le Fay to Irving's King in the LYCEUM's lavish *King Arthur* (1895). Her appearances were infrequent after that, and she was received as a monumental figure from the past when she played Queen Margaret for JOHN MARTIN-HARVEY in his 1916 *Richard III*, the part in which she made her farewell appearance with the F. R. BENSON company in 1920, at the age of 82. She was, by a mysterious early marriage, the Countess de Guerbel, which may have encouraged the conservative English to create her DBE in 1921, the first actress to be so honoured. PT

Ward, Nick 1962– British dramatist and director, who won the George Devine Award in 1987 for his plays, *Apart from George* (1987) and *The Strangeness of Others* (1988). He studied English at Cambridge University, and on leaving ran two small theatre companies, winning a 'Fringe First' at the EDINBURGH FESTIVAL for his adaptation of a D. H. LAWRENCE short story, *Eastwood* (1985). He was taken into the NATIONAL THEATRE Studio by its director, PETER GILL, where he directed his own translation of AUGUST

STRINDBERG's *The Ghost Sonata*. With his bleak vision of Britain today, he has an exceptional ability to evoke desolate land- or cityscape; but his terse dialogue, written for semi-articulate characters, has provided so far only rather arid experiences in the theatre.   JE

Warde, Frederick 1851–1935 Successful English provincial actor. Warde made his American debut (1874) as a supporting player, and found success as a regional star after 1880. Like his contemporaries Thomas Keene, Louis James, Charles Hanford, Joseph Grismer, Phoebe Davis, Kathryn Kidder and Marie Wainwright, who had similar careers, he played an older repertory in an elevated, declamatory style that was innocent of REALISM. Warde specialized in serious, older men. He continued on the stage and the lecture platform until 1915, and made films of *Richard III* and *King Lear* (1916). His memoirs, *Fifty Years of Make-Believe*, appeared in 1920.   DMCD

Wardle, (John) Irving 1929– British theatre critic, who studied at Oxford University and at the Royal College of Music in London. He entered journalism as a sub-editor on the *Times Educational Supplement* in 1956, and became the deputy drama critic on the *Observer* in 1960. In 1963 he joined *The Times*, where his thoughtful, persuasive columns set the standards for daily reviewing for more than 20 years. As a critic, Wardle uses superlatives only reluctantly, preferring to weigh each side to an argument before arriving at usually qualified conclusions; with the result that he is not the most quoted critic in Britain. But his knowledge and integrity are rarely questioned, and best revealed in his biography of GEORGE DEVINE, *The Theatres of George Devine* (1978). Wardle's early play, *The Houseboy* (1974), received a successful production at London's Open Space, and was later seen on television. From 1973 to 75 he was the editor of the theatre magazine, *Gambit*. He left the *Times* in 1989 and joined the *Independent on Sunday*, and in 1992 published a book on *Theatre Criticism*.   JE

Warfield, David 1866–1951 American actor; BELASCO's one great male star. Warfield was a native of San Francisco, who began acting with a travelling STOCK COMPANY in Napa, California (1888). He played a variety of parts in New York City and on tour until he became a member of the company at the Casino Theatre in 1893. He quickly became a specialist in musical PARODY, which led to an engagement as an eccentric ethnic comic with WEBER AND FIELDS (1899–1901). Belasco coached him in a series of pathetic older parts, in which he was always the gentle, slightly humorous, forgiving victim. His first vehicle was *The Auctioneer* (1901), followed by *The Music Master* (1904) and *The Return of Peter Grimm* (1911); his career culminated in an unsuccessful production of *The Merchant of Venice* (1924), after which he retired.   DMCD

Warner, Deborah 1959– British director, who trained at the Central School of Speech and Drama in London and formed the Kick Theatre Company in 1980. Unlike the small groups of the 1970s, which favoured new and polemical drama, Kick Theatre (in common with CHEEK BY JOWL) concentrated on staging classic plays with style, simplicity and an economy of means. Among her productions for Kick Theatre were *King Lear* (1985) and *Coriolanus* (1986), both of which were seen by London audiences at the little Almeida Theatre in Islington.

In 1987 Warner was invited to direct *Titus Andronicus* for the ROYAL SHAKESPEARE COMPANY, a production widely hailed as the best interpretation of this play since PETER BROOK's in 1955. It won her the Olivier and the *Evening Standard* Best Director Awards for 1988, and was equally successful on a European tour, which visited Brook's own theatre in Paris. In 1988 she directed *Electra* for the RSC, where her leading player was FIONA SHAW. Warner develops intuitive working relationships with certain actors, particularly Brian Cox (Titus and Lear in *King Lear* (1990) at the NATIONAL THEATRE) and Shaw (Electra, Shen Te in *The Good Person of Setzuan* (1989) and Hedda in *Hedda Gabler* (1991)).

She excels in providing the settings for outstanding performances and for coaxing actors to reach beyond their normal limits. She is perhaps less convincing as a 'text' director or as one who achieves good timing and teamwork within her productions; but in a generation noted for its fine directors, Warner has gained a high international reputation, marked by the invitation in 1993 to direct *Coriolanus* at the Salzburg Festival, a rare honour for a British director, and rarer still for one so young.   JE

Warren, Mercy Otis 1728–1814 American colonial patriot and political satirist (see SATIRE), the best representative of 'the War of Belles Lettres' during the Revolutionary War. Her propaganda plays – really dialogues without plot, character development or women – satirized British officials and American Loyalists and were published anonymously in Massachusetts periodicals and as political pamphlets. Several plays have been falsely attributed to Warren; she acknowledged authorship of only *The Group* (1775). Other plays identified as her work include *The Adulateur: A Tragedy: As It Is Now Acted in Upper Servia* (1772), which refers to the Boston Massacre and attacks Governor Thomas Hutchison; *The Defeat* (1773); and two blank-verse historical tragedies, *The Ladies of Castille* and *The Sack of Rome*, both published in *Poems, Dramatic and Miscellaneous* (1790), her first signed work.
FB

Warren, William, the elder 1767–1832 British-born American actor and manager, whose 1784 debut was as Young Norval in *Douglas*. When engaged by TATE WILKINSON for his provincial company in 1788, Warren acted in support of SARAH SIDDONS. In 1796 he joined THOMAS WIGNELL's company. At the CHESTNUT STREET THEATRE he first appeared as Friar Lawrence in *Romeo and Juliet* and Bundle in *The Waterman*. Other than infrequent appearances in New York, the remainder of Warren's career, both as actor and manager, was associated with the theatres in Baltimore and Philadelphia. In 1806 he married the second of his three wives, actress ANNE MERRY. In partnership with WILLIAM B. WOOD, Warren's management in Philadelphia and Baltimore prospered until late in his career; in 1829 he retired from management. As an actor, Warren was especially adept at old men in COMEDY, but he was also capable in TRAGEDY. He was noted especially for his performances as Old Dornton, Sir Robert Bramble, Falstaff and Sir Toby Belch. He had six children with his third wife, Esther Fortune (sister-in-law of JOSEPH JEFFERSON I), all of whom were associated with the stage. DBW

Warren, William, the younger 1812–88 American actor, the son of WILLIAM WARREN THE ELDER. Warren junior's American acting career is almost totally associated with the BOSTON MUSEUM, the STOCK COMPANY he joined in 1847. During his 50-year career, until his retirement in 1883, he is reported to have given 13,345 performances and to have portrayed 577 characters. No actor of his period was identified so thoroughly with a single theatre, and none received more respect and affection from the public. His versatility in comic roles was practically limitless, although his special talent was with eccentric types. His most famous roles included Dogberry, Polonius, Bob Acres, Sir Peter Teazle, Micawber, Touchstone and Launcelot Gobbo, although he also appeared in leading roles in numerous forgettable contemporary plays. DBW

Washington Square Players (New York City) A pre-First World War American producing agency, founded in 1915 by amateurs (Edward Goodman, LAWRENCE LANGNER and others) to improve the level of drama in New York City. Their first three one-acts were produced at a cost of $35 in a theatre seating 40 persons. They received favourable reviews and continued producing one-acts by CHEKHOV, DE MUSSET, AKINS, MOELLER and other then little-known playwrights. After a disastrous production of *The Seagull*, they moved to the Comedy Theatre, just off BROADWAY, seating 600. There they presented the first Broadway production of EUGENE O'NEILL's *In the Zone*. Several important American actors began or worked with the Washington Square Players: Roland Young, Rollo Peters, Frank Conroy, Helen Westley and KATHARINE CORNELL. In 1918 the group disbanded, but restructured in 1919 as the THEATRE GUILD, New York's most influential producing organization. SMA

Wasserstein, Wendy 1950– American playwright, who portrays with wit and understanding the plight of the modern woman caught between feminism and traditionalism. Obie-winning *Uncommon Women and Others* (1977) depicts the reunion of five women graduates of Mt Holyoke and their hilarious reflections on their past college days. *Isn't It Romantic* (1983) follows two such women as they confront their parents, their lovers, and their own unclear futures. *The Heidi Chronicles*, which traces the history of the women's movement through the life of one woman and her friends, won a Pulitzer Prize and a Tony in 1989. *The Sisters Rosensweig* (New York, 1992; London, 1994), winner of numerous awards for its actors, author and director (Daniel Sullivan), explores the relationship of three middle-aged slightly maladjusted Jewish sisters. Lesser-known plays are *When Dinah Shore Ruled the Earth* (with CHRISTOPHER DURANG), *Montpelier PaZazz* and *Miami*. FB

Watene, Kenneth fl.1970s Kenyan playwright. *My Son for My Freedom* (1973) is set during the Mau Mau emer-

gency in colonial KENYA, and is concerned with the choice faced by the Kikuyu people between Christianity and the freedom fighters. Watene's play places this dilemma in a traumatic domestic context. *The Haunting Past* and *The Pot* (both 1973) are short plays dealing with the generation gap and drunkenness respectively. *Dedan Kimathi* (1974) anticipates the later play by NGUGI WA THIONG'O and MICERE MUGO on the same theme, describing the guerrilla life of the Mau Mau General, while *Sunset on the Manyatta* (1974) is a 'clash of cultures' play concerning a young Masai alienated from his people by Western education and striving to reconcile the traditional and the modern. KG NWAM

Waterhouse, Keith 1929– British playwright and journalist. With his writing partner, Willis Hall, who comes like him from Leeds in Yorkshire, Waterhouse was responsible for several major comedy hits in the 1960s, including *Billy Liar* (1960), *Celebration* (1961) and *All Things Bright and Beautiful* (1962). Like BILL NAUGHTON, Waterhouse and Hall celebrate British provincial lifestyles, without giving the impression that they harbour grudges against metropolitan ones.

Say Who You Are (1965) was considered a permissive play in its day, celebrating the trials and tribulations of adultery in Knightsbridge. Both have adapted many plays from abroad for the British stage (e.g. *Filumena*, 1977) and written scripts for television (see TELEVISION DRAMA) and films. Separately, too, they have had their successes. In 1958 Hall wrote a strong military drama set in Malaysia, *The Long, the Short and the Tall*, while Waterhouse created a memorable play, *Jeffrey Barnard Is Unwell* (1989), from a low-life Soho column in the *Spectator* written by Barnard himself. JE

Waters, Ethel 1896–1977 African-American singer and actress. Born into poverty, Waters started at age 17 as a VAUDEVILLE singer in Baltimore for nine dollars a week. In 1933, she was featured in IRVING BERLIN's REVUE *As Thousands Cheer*. Moving from honky-tonks to cellar cafés to New York socialite clubs, Waters attained a glowing reputation as comedienne and singer of such songs as 'St Louis Blues', 'Dinah' and 'Stormy Weather'. She emerged as a superb dramatic actress of warmth and sensitivity in stage or film productions of *Mamba's Daughters* (1939), *Cabin in the Sky* (1940), *Pinky* (1949) and *The Member of the Wedding* (1950). Earl Dancer termed her 'the greatest artist of her generation'. Her autobiography (with Charles Samuels) appeared in 1951 (*His Eye Is on the Sparrow*). EGH

Waterston, Sam(uel Atkinson) 1940– American actor, born in Cambridge, Massachusetts, and educated at Yale and the Sorbonne. He made his New York debut in 1962 as Jonathan in *Oh Dad, Poor Dad, Mamma's Hung You in the Closet and I'm Feelin' So Sad*. For the NEW YORK SHAKESPEARE FESTIVAL he has portrayed Silvius in *As You Like It* (1963), Prince Hal in *Henry IV, Parts 1 and 2* (1968), Cloten in *Cymbeline* (1971), Benedick in *Much Ado* (1972, Obie), Prospero in *The Tempest* (1974) and the title role in *Hamlet* (1975). Mel Gussow praised his Benedick as 'boyish but not immature' while Julius Novick found his Hamlet 'easy to like' but not intellectually satisfying. Other BROADWAY appearances include *Half-Way Up the Tree* (1967), *Indians* (1969), *The Trial of the Catonville Nine* (1971), *A Doll's House* (1975), *Benefactors* (1986) and *A Walk in the Woods* (1988). OFF-BROADWAY credits include *Muzeeka* (1968), *Waiting for Godot* (1978), *Chez Nous* (1979) and *The Three Sisters* (1982), with a notable portrayal of Solness in the *Master Builder* at the HARTFORD STAGE COMPANY (1991) and an acclaimed Lincoln in *Abe Lincoln in Illinois* at the Lincoln Center (1993). Waterston has appeared in numerous films, including *The Great Gatsby* and *The Killing Fields* (Academy Award nominee, 1985); as 'Oppenheimer' on television; and as a Southern lawyer in the NBC series 'I'll Fly Away' (1991–3). TLM

waxworks The public exhibit of waxen effigies, first found in 16th-century Amsterdam, has two sources: anatomical cabinets for the display of medical anomalies, and state portraits that permit subjects a symbolic audience with their monarch. It was the portrait from life of Louis XIV by the Parisian Antoine Benoist (1632–1717) that popularized wax as a medium for such shows. Jacques de Vaucanson with his wax automata and Wolfgang von Kempelen with his wax chess-player (1769) both achieved some popularity; but it was Johann Christian Curtius (Creutz) who added real showmanship. His Cabinet Palais-Royal (1783) exhibited figures of the nobility, while his Caverne des Grands Voleurs in the Boulevard du Temple in Paris was a resort of the people. During the French Revolution, Curtius had licence to take death masks of heads fresh from the guillotine, a task carried out by his niece Marie Grosholtz (1760–1850). With this legacy of gruesome mementos, and as Madame Tussaud, she opened a gallery in London in 1833 which soon became world-famous. Its Chamber of Horrors, displaying the latest in murderers, is a forerunner of the news photo.

Her success was soon emulated by the Musée Grévin, Paris (where the Raft of the Medusa boasted a wave effect produced by clever lighting); the Hamburg Panoptikum (still extant); Emil E. Harmer's Munich Panoptikum; Präuscher's Enkel Museum, Vienna; and the Eden Musée, New York. These housed historical tableaux along with the grotesque and unnerving models of foetuses and venereal afflictions usually found in so-called 'medical museums'. The Munich comedian KARL VALENTIN parodied this attraction in his Isar Tower panopticon of the 1930s, which displayed nose-picking machines and Adam's original apple with a bite out of it. Tigerpark, founded in Singapore in 1946 by the Tiger Balsam millionaire Boon Haw, enhanced the traditional terrors of Hell and scenes from Chinese myth with up-to-date technology. Disneyland and Disneyworld have added synthetic flesh and computer-controlled movement and speech without appreciably surpassing the artistic results of their precursors. LS

wayang see SHADOW PUPPETS

Wayburn, Ned [Edward Claudius Weyburn] 1874–1942 American director and choreographer. After starting out as a singer and dancer in VAUDEVILLE, Wayburn made his theatrical debut in *The Swell Miss Fitwell* (1897). He served as assistant director of *The*

Governor's Son (1901), and was soon in demand as a producer, director and choreographer of musical comedies and REVUES. Among the shows he staged in New York were two editions of *The Passing Show* (1912, 13), and six of *The ZIEGFELD Follies* (1916–19, 22, 23). In addition to producing and staging hundreds of musicals, Wayburn operated dance studios that trained many of the MUSICAL THEATRE's finest dancers. MK

Weaver, Fritz 1926– American actor who made his professional debut with Virginia's Barter Theatre and his New York debut as Fainall in *The Way of the World*. After 1955, Weaver appeared frequently with the AMERICAN SHAKESPEARE [THEATRE] Festival. He has also appeared in several films and numerous television network films and series. Among his awards are the CLARENCE DERWENT Award for Flamineo in *The White Devil* (1955) and a Theatre World Award for Maitland in *The Chalk Garden* (1956). For *Child's Play* (1970) he received, among other awards, a Tony. In 1991 he portrayed King Lear at the Shakespeare Theatre (then at the Folger, Washington, DC) and appeared with Tony Randall's National Actors Theatre in New York City, playing Danforth in its inaugural production of *The Crucible*. SMA

Webb, John 1611–72 English architect and scene-designer who, as INIGO JONES's pupil, assisted him in the preparation of MASQUES for the court of Charles I. Webb designed the scenery for DAVENANT's *The Siege of Rhodes* (1656), contriving, on the small stage at Rutland House, five scene changes, including two scenes in relief. It was, as far as can be ascertained, the first use of perspective scenery on a public stage (see THEATRE DESIGN). Neither there nor in his designs for BOYLE's heroic tragedy *Mustapha* (1665) at court did Webb emulate the magnificence of the masques, but the surviving drawings strongly suggest that he took the first tentative steps towards scenic REALISM. PT

Weber, Joseph 1867–1942 and
Lew Fields [Lewis Maurice Shanfield] 1867–1941 American comedians. After learning their craft as child performers in the lecture rooms or on the stages of museums, in CIRCUSES and VARIETY houses, Weber and Fields evolved a knockabout 'Dutch comic' act in which the short, rotund, innocent Weber was the foil for the tall, skinny, bullying Fields. They toured for many years in VAUDEVILLE before playing their first legitimate theatre engagements at the Harlem Opera House and HAMMERSTEIN's OLYMPIA Theatre in 1894. Two years later they opened the Weber and Fields Music Hall, where they offered hilarious BURLESQUES of current BROADWAY successes. The Weber and Fields company, which at various times included such stars as LILLIAN RUSSELL, Peter F. Dailey, Sam Bernard, DE WOLF HOPPER, DAVID WARFIELD, FAY TEMPLETON and Bessie McCoy, was also noted for the beauty and animation of its female chorus. They chose many talented writers, designers and directors to assist them in mounting their shows.

In 1904 the partners separated, with Weber continuing at the Music Hall and Fields producing and starring in musical comedies. In 1912 they reunited for a 'jubilee' production at a new Music Hall, after which they toured with the show. Following some vaudeville appearances the partners again split up and concentrated on their producing careers. The rough, acrobatic comic style of Weber and Fields, coupled with the fractured English they spoke in their 'Dutch' personas, made them favourites of audiences in New York and across the country in both legitimate theatres and vaudeville houses. A major biography of Fields was published in 1993.   MK

Webster, Benjamin (Nottingham) 1798–1882 English actor and theatre manager, one of the most intelligent, stubborn and admirable leaders of the mid-century theatre. He began as a provincial dancer and HARLEQUIN, and had struggled his way into the DRURY LANE company by 1823; but it was with MADAME VESTRIS at the OLYMPIC in 1832 that he got his first chance to display his skill in COMEDY, and as manager of the HAYMARKET (1837–53) that he demonstrated his exemplary concern to find good plays and to stage them conscientiously. He produced SHERIDAN KNOWLES's lively comedy, *The Love Chase* (1837), to set the pattern, and subsequent Haymarket premieres included several plays by JERROLD, BOUCICAULT's *Old Heads and Young Hearts* (1844) and *Used Up* (1844), BULWER LYTTON's *Money* (1840) and TOM TAYLOR and CHARLES READE's *Masks and Faces* (1852), which provided him with his favourite part as Triplet.

No other theatre could match the repertoire of the Haymarket during Webster's management. More remarkable still was his production of *The Taming of the Shrew* (1844), in which he defied the taste for pictorial SHAKESPEARE by setting the play on a decent approximation to current views of the original Elizabethan stage; and this was 40 years before WILLIAM POEL's first experiments. His management of the ADELPHI, which he had shared with MADAME CÉLESTE since 1844 but took into his own hands from 1853 until his retirement in 1874, was less remarkable – the Adelphi audience was insistently lowbrow. Webster would have liked to be a Shakespearian actor, but though he was an admired Dogberry, he found the better-born Petruchio beyond his range.   PT

Webster, John c.1580–1634 English playwright. Little is known of Webster's life. He received payments from HENSLOWE in 1602 for contributions to a lost play, but his earliest surviving work is probably the Induction to MARSTON's *The Malcontent*, written on the occasion of the play's revival by the King's Men in 1604. At much the same time, Webster was collaborating with DEKKER on a play for the BOYS OF ST PAUL's. The success of this piece, *Westward Ho* (1604), was exploited by JONSON, CHAPMAN and Marston with *Eastward Ho* (1605), written for the CHILDREN OF THE CHAPEL ROYAL at the BLACKFRIARS. Both plays graft CITIZEN COMEDY on to the older tradition of the 'journey play'. Webster and Dekker were less successful with their *Northward Ho* (1605). A further collaboration, on *The Famous History of Sir Thomas Wyatt* (published 1607), produced an untidy history play. But Webster was learning his craft, and his poetic gift and dramatic ingenuity were supremely exhibited in the two tragedies which he wrote alone, *The White Devil* (c.1612) and *The Duchess of Malfi* (c.1613). Violent and sensational according to the prevail-

ing taste, both plays are also eloquent and compassionate. Webster chose their plots from catchpenny translations of Italian novellas, purporting to give 'true' accounts of recent crimes, but he perceived an almost Aeschylean pattern (see AESCHYLUS) in these squalid stories of bloodthirsty family vengeance. It is clear from the detail and extent of his borrowings that he kept a careful commonplace book of striking lines from the work of other writers, improving almost everything that he stole.

There is nothing as impressive as these two tragedies in the rest of his work. *The Devil's Law Case* (published 1623) is a scrappy TRAGICOMEDY, with one astonishing scene. *Monuments of Honour* (1624) is no more impressive than other surviving Lord Mayor's pageants. The rest of Webster's extant dramatic work is the outcome of collaborations – with THOMAS HEYWOOD on *Appius and Virginia* (c.1608), with MIDDLETON on *Any Thing for a Quiet Life* (c.1621) and with WILLIAM ROWLEY on *A Cure for a Cuckold* (c.1624). He is, in addition, the putative author of some of the Overburian *Characters* (1614), including that of 'An Excellent Actor'.   PT

Webster, Margaret 1905–72 New York-born American actress and director. The daughter of Benjamin Webster III and Dame May Whitty, she was the last member of a 150-year-old English theatrical dynasty. Her professional career began in *The Trojan Women* with SYBIL THORNDIKE (1924), followed the next year with a small role in John Barrymore's (see DREW–BARRYMORE FAMILY) *Hamlet*. After several years of STOCK experience she joined the OLD VIC in 1929, returning to play Lady Macbeth in 1932–3. In 1934 she began to direct, and this became her chief endeavour, mostly in America. Notable US productions under her direction included *Richard II* with MAURICE EVANS (1937), *Hamlet* (1938), *Twelfth Night* (1940), *Othello* with PAUL ROBESON (1943), *The Cherry Orchard* (1944) and *The Tempest* with CANADA LEE as Caliban (1945). She founded with EVA LE GALLIENNE and CHERYL CRAWFORD the AMERICAN REPERTORY THEATRE (1946–8). In 1950 she began directing OPERAS, becoming the first woman to direct at the New York Metropolitan Opera. She was the author of important books on theatre, including *The Same Only Different* (1969) and *Don't Put Your Daughter on the Stage* (1972).   DBW

Wedekind, Frank 1864–1918 German playwright. Wedekind started his career working in business and in a CIRCUS. He then became an actor and singer, appearing with acclaim in the satirical CABARET *Die elf Scharfrichter* (*The Eleven Executioners*) in Munich. As a playwright, he was influenced initially by the naturalists (see NATURALISM), whose views on the imperatives of the biological instinct in man he tended to retain throughout his life. But his plays were not rigorously realistic (see REALISM). Instead, adopting an episodic approach to plot and presenting character frequently through the means of grotesque caricature, Wedekind foreshadowed the expressionists (see EXPRESSIONISM).

His first major play, *Spring Awakening* (1891), was not produced until 1906 because of the bold and shocking manner in which he unfolded his theme, which was the need for a repressive society to recognize the stirrings of puberty in its children. The 'Lulu' plays, *Earth Spirit* (1895) and *Pandora's Box* (1904), while no less striking in their depiction of a society riven by the demands of lust and greed, are somewhat more ambiguous over the issue of sexuality. Of his several other plays, the one-act *The Court Singer* (1899) and *The Marquis of Keith* (1901) have been widely performed. In the past 20 years there has been a significant revival of Wedekind in the German and English theatres. However, his plays are likely to remain of limited appeal because of his concern, especially later in life, to justify in them his reputation for outspokenness in German society. SW

Wei Liangfu fl.1522–73 Chinese musician and creator of the present KUNQU musical form. In Jiangsu Province he carried out innovative research on the musical modes which flourished in that southern area. Their principal differences lay in a dialectical usage which affected the rhythm and tempo of song and speech forms. He synthesized modal elements and refined articulation and vocalization so as to match speech tones with tempo and pitch, thereby creating the mellifluous, somewhat plaintive, singing to flute accompaniment which characterizes *kunqu* drama. Wei was assisted in his research by Zhang Yetang, an authority on the northern modal repertoire. ACS

Wei Minglun 1941– Chinese writer of Sichuan opera (*CHUANJU*) who achieved a great reputation as an innovative dramatist during the 1980s. His *The Scholar of Bashan* (*Bashan xiucai*), set in 19th-century Sichuan, concerns a scholar who seeks and obtains redress for an unprovoked massacre of the people of Bashan, but dies poisoned by a court official. *Pan Jinlian*, described in the title as 'a Sichuan opera of the absurd', recasts the story of Pan Jinlian, traditionally known as a murderer of one of her husbands and a nymphomaniac. Wei's play lays the blame for Pan Jinlian's crimes and excesses on the evils of China's patriarchal society and on the oppression of women. One strand of the drama relates Pan's fall into vice, a second shows her trial set in the PRC. The action leaps across time and cultures, and characters include such divergent women as Empress Wu Zetian, a contemporary Chinese female judge and TOLSTOI's Anna Karenina. *Pan Jinlian* has been praised for its relevance to Chinese theatre and to Chinese society of the 1980s. ACS

Weigel, Helene 1900–71 Austrian actress who worked with JESSNER until she married BRECHT in 1928 and became his leading lady. Tolerant of his infidelities, she worked tirelessly in his interest. She gave definitive performances of Brechtian mothers in *The Mother* (1932) and *Mother Courage* (1949). Director and manager of the BERLINER ENSEMBLE from its inception, she took full control after Brecht's death and toured widely to spread his reputation. HR

Weill, Kurt 1900–50 German composer, born in Dessau, who studied music and directed a small OPERA company before collaborating with BERTOLT BRECHT on such works as *The Threepenny Opera* and *The Rise and Fall of the City of Mahagonny*. With his wife, actress LOTTE LENYA, he went to America in 1935. He composed scores for *Johnny Johnson* (1936), *Knickerbocker Holiday* (1938), *Lady in the Dark* (1941), *One Touch of Venus* (1943), the opera *Street Scene* (1947) and *Lost in the Stars* (1949). His IRVING BERLIN shows have also been frequently revived in America. Although Weill's compositions for the American stage were more lyrical and optimistic than his Berlin scores, he worked with such noted writers as PAUL GREEN, MAXWELL

Helene Weigel in the title role of Brecht's *Mother Courage*, Berlin, 1949.

ANDERSON and LANGSTON HUGHES in creating shows that tackled serious issues in an uncompromising way. MK

Weimar style Style of tragic acting cultivated by GOETHE while he was director of the Weimar Court Theatre between 1791 and 1817. It was described in the 'Rules for Actors', which Goethe wrote down as guidelines, primarily for the actor WOLFF. Goethe expected his actors to be models of decorum on stage, acting always with scrupulous attention to articulation, especially in the delivery of verse, and with constant grace and formality in stature and gesture. Goethe's rules were read by actors throughout the 19th century, and the style of acting they suggested was widely copied. SW

Weise, Christian 1642–1708 German schoolmaster and playwright. His plays, which were written for his students at the Zittau gymnasium, demonstrate a striking REALISM in contrast to the formal, often turgid drama of the baroque era. Among his best-known works are the tragedy *Masaniello* (1683) and the comedy *Peasant Machiavel* (1679). SW

Weisenborn, Günter 1902–63 German dramatist, who made his name with his anti-rearmament play *U-boot S4* (1929), an up-to-the-minute stage recreation (see LIVING NEWSPAPER) of the accidental sinking of a US submarine. His play about German underground resistance, *Die Illegalen* (*The Lawbreakers*, 1946), was the first about the Nazi period to be produced in postwar Berlin. HR

Weiss, Peter 1916–82 German dramatist, novelist and artist, whose plays *Marat-Sade* (1964) and *The Investigation* (1965) were performed world-wide. The full title of the former, *The Persecution and Assassination of Marat as Performed by the Inmates of the Asylum of Charenton under the Direction of the Marquis de Sade*, indicates the complexity and theatricality of the piece, which combines impulses from BRECHT and ARTAUD to examine the themes of revolution, sexuality, psychological freedom and social equality in the framework of a madhouse. Its West Berlin premiere was followed by PETER BROOK, whose 1965 ROYAL SHAKESPEARE COMPANY production was filmed.

Weiss was by now a Communist. *The Investigation*, an 'oratorio in eleven songs' produced by PISCATOR at the Freie VOLKSBÜHNE and simultaneously at 16 other theatres including the RSC, was based on transcripts of the 1963–5 Auschwitz trial in Frankfurt. The text, in free verse without characterization or plot, presents the 11 phases of liquidation, from 'Selection' to 'The Song of the Fiery Furnace'. This is documentary theatre at its best – a spare, direct, firmly structured digest of the Auschwitz evidence for future generations. *The Song of the Lusitanian Bogey* (1967) and *Vietnam Discourse* (1968) pilloried colonialism in Angola and Vietnam respectively. Weiss went into exile in Sweden in 1938 and stayed for the rest of his life, taking citizenship in 1945. HR

Weisse, Christian Felix 1726–1804 German dramatist. His highly successful *Richard III* (1759) was written, he claimed, without any knowledge of SHAKESPEARE's play.

He also adapted, very severely, *Romeo and Juliet* (1767), which was the version most frequently performed in the 18th century. Weisse's SINGSPIELE, especially *Hell Is Let Loose* (1752) and *The Hunt* (1770), were also very popular. SW

Wekwerth, Manfred 1929– German director. Manager of the BERLINER ENSEMBLE (1977–89) and director for that company from 1951. His *Coriolanus* for the NATIONAL THEATRE in London in 1971 complemented his production of BRECHT's version, which he directed in Berlin and brought to London in 1965. MB

Welfare State International British theatre company. Formed in Leeds in 1968 and now based in Ulverston, Cumbria, this loosely knit group of actors, sculptors, musicians, painters and pyrotechnologists, under the direction of John Fox and Boris Howarth, has been one of the most successful companies in fulfilling the 1960s dream of taking theatre to a mass audience – their spectacular processions regularly draw audiences in four figures. A principle of their work is that of the CARNIVAL, both aesthetically and socially. Socially, their performances are not merely commodities that people buy off the peg; as far as possible they are constructed around some local concern (in Northwich, Cheshire, WSI provided 'A Grand Salt Celebration') or festive date ('Scarecrow Zoo' in Bracknell, Berkshire, Hallowe'en to Bonfire Night 1982), and members of the local community are involved in their planning and realization. Aesthetically, a Welfare State performance is not a 'play' but an event incorporating processions, dramatic pieces, firework displays, social dancing and communal eating and drinking, with a strong emphasis on powerful visual images, both sinister and ludicrous. In their pursuit of celebratory theatre, WSI have begun to undertake weddings and naming ceremonies as well as their more familiar civic entertainments. Kershaw and Coult's *Engineers of the Imagination* (1983) is a useful practical guide to their principles and methods. AEG

well made play A translation of the French *pièce bien faite*, the well made play was first codified by EUGÈNE SCRIBE (1791–1861). Since he (with assorted collaborators) wrote some 400 plays, he had little time for such frivolities as theory. By the mid-19th century, when the term came into common use, it was already derogatory, and yet its formulae have moulded some 150 years of Western drama.

The well made play is skilfully crafted to arouse suspense. An outgrowth of the comedy of intrigue, its action is propelled through a concatenation of causally related events. Beginning with a detailed, faintly disguised exposition, it gathers momentum through complications and crises, with each act closing on a climactic curtain. A series of perils for the protagonist leads to the revelation of a secret in an obligatory scene – named and analysed by the French critic FRANCISQUE SARCEY some half-century after Scribe codified the practice. The well made play then closes swiftly in a logical and plausible resolution, which implicitly accepts the ethic of the audience, even when the author's spokesman, the *raisonneur*, does not baldly voice it. Technically, the well made play thrives on fortuitous entrances and exits, mistaken identity and quid pro quo.

Scribe's structural influence is everywhere evident in 19th-century France – in SARDOU, AUGIER, DUMAS *fils*, LABICHE, FEYDEAU – and in those COPYRIGHT-free days, the formula swiftly crossed the English Channel and is seen in plays by BULWER LYTTON, TOM TAYLOR and T. W. ROBERTSON, not to mention HENRY JAMES and HENRIK IBSEN. Even SHAW, who fulminated against 'Sardoodledom', manipulated the formula in both his Pleasant and his Unpleasant Plays, and its carpentry has been learned by craftsmen as various as LILLIAN HELLMAN, TERENCE RATTIGAN, JEAN ANOUILH and Harvey Fierstein. Shaw's dismissal of the obligatory scene has been widely quoted: 'Once this scene was invented, nothing remained for the author to do except to prepare for it in a first act, and to use up its backwash in a third.' Yet that 'nothing' took considerable doing on the part of playwrights.   RC

Weller, Michael 1942– New York-born American playwright, educated at Brandeis and Manchester Universities. After productions at the EDINBURGH FESTIVAL Fringe (see FRINGE THEATRE) and at CHARLES MAROWITZ's Open Space (London) in 1969, he premiered *Cancer* at the ROYAL COURT in 1970. Renamed *Moonchildren*, it opened at the ARENA STAGE in 1971, followed by productions both off and on BROADWAY in 1972. A popular critical success, *Moonchildren* depicts the hang-ups and idealism of the 'children of the sixties', a subject Weller returned to with *Loose Ends* in 1979. Premiering at the Arena Stage before its Broadway debut, *Loose Ends* expresses the disillusionment of the 1970s as young people attempt to reconcile their ideals with the demands of careers, marriages and families. Weller's other plays include *23 Years Later*, *Fishing*, *At Home*, *Spoils of War* and *Lake No Bottom*, the last a 1990 study of the relationship of artist and critic. His most recent play, *Help!*, was staged at the Ensemble Theater of Cincinnati in 1994. He also wrote the screenplays for *Hair* (1979) and *Ragtime* (1980).   TLM

Welles, (George) Orson 1915–85 American actor, playwright and director, whose place in history is ensured as a result of youthful accomplishments. By 1941 the protean Welles had established himself as a major actor and brilliant theatre director; had directed, co-written, and starred in *Citizen Kane* (1940), one of the most influential films in cinema history; and had inadvertently created a national panic with his radio version of H. G. Wells's *The War of the Worlds* (1938).

Welles's career began with an appearance at Dublin's GATE THEATRE in 1931 as the Duke of Wurtemburg in *Jew Süss*. After touring with KATHARINE CORNELL in 1933–4, he made his New York debut in 1934 in *Romeo and Juliet* (Chorus and Tybalt). In 1936, as director of the Negro People's Theatre, New York, he staged a controversial 'voodoo' version of *Macbeth* with an all-black cast; in 1937, when appointed a director of the FEDERAL THEATRE PROJECT, New York City, he directed notable productions of *Dr Faustus* (and acted the title role) and *The Cradle Will Rock*. With JOHN HOUSEMAN he co-founded the same year the MERCURY THEATRE, remembered primarily for its modern-dress production of *Julius Caesar*. Although Welles's theatre impact lessened after the Second World War, he is remembered for his direction of *Native Son* (1941); his 1946 version of *Around the World in Eighty Days*; his first appearance in London in 1951 as Othello, his adaptation and direction of *Moby Dick* (London, 1955; New York, 1962); his direction and acting in *King Lear* (1956) at New York's City Center; and his direction at London's ROYAL COURT THEATRE of IONESCO's *Rhinoceros* (1960). Welles is the subject of two contradictory 1985 biographies by Barbara Leaming and Charles Higham, and a 1989 one by Frank Brady, plus two significant studies of his theatre work by Richard France (1977 and 90).   DBW

Wemyss, Francis Courtney 1797–1859 English-born American actor and manager who, a year after his first London appearance in 1821, made his American debut at the CHESTNUT STREET THEATRE. His forte was COMEDY and FARCE, and he excelled in roles such as Vapid in *The Dramatists*, Marplot in *The Busy Body* and Rover in *Wild Oats*. He later acted in New York with CHARLOTTE CUSHMAN, W. C. MACREADY, JOSEPH JEFFERSON III and LAURA KEENE. In 1827 he turned to management, and was widely respected for his taste and integrity. He founded the Theatrical Fund to aid needy actors; edited 16 volumes of plays, published as the *Acting American Theatre*; and wrote an informative autobiography, *Twenty-six Years of the Life of an Actor and Manager* (1847).   TLM

Werewere-Liking, Nicole 1950– Cameroonian playwright, theatre director and, with Rabiatu Njoya, also of CAMEROON, Josephine Kama Bongo of Gabon, Saafi Ndaka and Marthe Diur Ntumb both of Zaire, one of the five women writing for the stage in French-speaking Africa. Werewere-Liking was born into a family of traditional musicians and had little formal education, having spent a good part of her early life being initiated into various secret societies. She taught herself to read and write French much later, skills which she subsequently used to explore for the stage those myths and RITUALS that were such a vital part of her early experience.

Werewere-Liking left Cameroon for the Ivory Coast in the late 1970s. As a researcher at the university there, she took part in the then ongoing debates and researches into African theatre led by playwrights like BERNARD ZADI ZAOUROU, theatre practitioners like Niangoran Porquet, and the French ethno-sociologist and theatre critic Marie-José Hourantier. It was from her collaboration with Hourantier that her career as a playwright was born. Her published plays are *La Queue du diable* (*The Devil's Tail*, 1979), known in Cameroon as *Ngonga* after its main character and to Radio France Internationale listeners as *Les Bâtards* (*The Bastards*); *La Puissance d'Um* (*The Power of Um*, 1979); *Une Nouvelle Terre* and *Du sommeil injuste* (*A New Land* and *Of the Unjust Sleep*, 1980); *Les Mains veulent dire* and *La Rougeole arc-en-ciel* (*Hands Have Meaning* and *The Rainbow Measles*, 1987). In 1984 she founded the Ki-Yi troupe, which seeks to evolve a performance style that makes use of PUPPETS, MASKS, song and dance.

Werewere-Liking's theatre constitutes a radical departure from anything yet produced in French-speaking Africa. Her plays are psychodramas, rooted in her native Bassa healing, initiation or death rituals. They invariably deal with the eruption of disorder (death, illness or crime in the life of a rural community), and their object is to purge the spectator-celebrant community of their unhealthy emotions, thereby restoring their broken equilibrium. The use of a highly esoteric language, of trance and spirit-possession techniques and of an intricate symbolism of colours, costumes and gestures, characterizes her theatre. It may also account for its obscurity and lack of wide appeal so far. JCM

Werfel, Franz 1890–1945 Austrian dramatist, novelist and poet. Werfel's early work is among the most interesting examples of EXPRESSIONISM, with its contemporary perspective on classical themes. His strongly pacifist adaptation of EURIPIDES' *Trojan Women* (1915) was followed by a 'magic trilogy' updating GOETHE's *Faust* – *The Mirror Man* (1921), *The Goat Song* (1922), *The Silent One* (1923) – in which the revolt against authority typified by the plays of BRONNEN and HASENCLEVER is given a psychological and highly critical perspective in grotesque images of the duality of man, with idealistic political aspiration liberating the demonic and bestial *alter ego*. After the tragic history of the Habsburg Emperor in Mexico *Juarez and Maximilian* (1925) won him an international reputation, *The Goat Song* was produced by the New York THEATRE GUILD in 1926, as was his wartime comedy of the rescue of an antisemitic Polish officer by a Jewish refugee, *Jacobowsky and the Colonel*. This reached BROADWAY in 1944 (the only play by an Austrian exile to establish itself on the foreign stage during the Nazi period), while his verse tragedy on the history of Jewish suffering culminating in their persecution under Hitler, *The Eternal Road*, was staged by REINHARDT at the Manhattan Opera House in 1937. But he is primarily remembered for his 1941 novel *The Song of Bernadette*. CI

Werich, Jan see VOSKOVEC, JIŘÍ

Werkteater ('work theatre') In Amsterdam in 1970, the 'Werkteater cooperative company' was founded. The Werkteater receives subsidy to investigate new possibilities in the theatre (see AKTIE TOMAAT; VORMINGSTONEEL). The aims are to renew acting methods from within, to find alternatives for acting methods taught at drama schools or used in repertory theatre which are seen as acting tricks, and to investigate the relationship between actors and audience. The working method is democratic and collective; many of the performances develop from improvisations built on the basis of the actors' personal experiences.

The Werkteater has a lot in common with the LIVING THEATRE (the actor as a person merges with his part into a unity) and with JERZY GROTOWSKI (the actor is trained to develop his physical abilities, because the language of the body is considered to be *the* language of the theatre). Frequently, a high level of acting is reached. But their strong social involvement – which is apparent through plays like *Toestanden* (*Situations*, 1972), about mental hospitals; *Bosch en lucht* (*Forest and Air*, 1979), about 'ordinary' and mentally deficient people; and *Avondrood* (*Sunset Sky*, 1973), dealing with the issue of senior citizenship – is nowhere marked by the sharp line of approach seen in Vormingstoneel. The play *Je moet ermee leven*,

about the treatment of a cancer patient in a hospital, has been filmed as *Opname* by Erik van Zuylen (*In for Treatment*, 1979). In the early 1980s, some members left and set up solo projects, of which Joop Admiraal's *U bent mijn moeder* (*You Are My Mother*) received great acclaim both in the Netherlands and abroad. It too has been adapted for film. Shireen Strooker with a new generation of actors began performing plays from the repertoire, but after a few seasons they were again producing their own, often improvised, performances. HS MG

See: D. Ogden, *Performance Dynamics and the Amsterdam Werktheater*, Berkeley and London, 1987.

Werner, Zacharias 1763–1823 German playwright. Werner was the only romantic dramatist to achieve popular recognition. His most widely performed play *The Consecration of Power* (1807) is a five-act verse tragedy on the life of Martin Luther. His most famous, or notorious, play was the one-act SCHICKSALTRAGÖDIE, *The 24th of February* (1810), which dramatizes with mordant and unrelieved grimness the working-out of a family curse. SW

Wertenbaker, Timberlake Anglo-American dramatist, who lives in Britain but received a French education. Her first plays were produced in the early 1980s and reflected some preoccupations of the time, particularly how notions of selfhood and gender are developed through social habits and language restrictions. *New Anatomies* (1981) was about two Victorian women who dressed as men, Isabelle Eberhardt and VESTA TILLEY, which Wertenbaker turns into a MORALITY PLAY about gender. *Abel's Sister* (1984) concerns the effects on the mind of physical (and political) disabilities, while *The Grace of Mary Traverse* (1985) is an 18th-century romp which examines what happens when women defy convention and step out of their allocated roles. While she may have provided feminist parables, there is here more than a trace of historical (and psychological) naivety. More successful was *The Love of a Nightingale* (1988), a version of the myth of Philomel and Procne in which her interest in Greek theatre, including Dionysian rituals, became apparent. She later adapted the two *Oedipus* plays and *Antigone* by SOPHOCLES to provide a trilogy for the ROYAL SHAKESPEARE COMPANY, *The Theban Plays* (1991). Her two most successful plays, *Our Country's Good* (1988, based on Thomas Keneally's *The Playmaker*) and *Three Birds Alighting in a Field* (1991), were both first produced at the ROYAL COURT, directed by Max Stafford-Clark. Within this team her skills flourished, *Our Country's Good* being one of the outstanding plays of the decade, a tribute to the redemptive power of the theatre. JE

Wesker, Arnold 1932– British dramatist, who served in the Royal Air Force and took various unskilled jobs before becoming a professional writer. His first three plays, *Chicken Soup with Barley* (1958), *Roots* (1959) and *I'm Talking about Jerusalem* (1960), were a largely autobiographical trilogy, starting with a Jewish family, the Kahns, living in pre-war Hackney. All three expressed the unforced socialism of his childhood, where the enemy was Fascism and the key to social progress lay in mass education. The trilogy was staged in Coventry but transferred to the ROYAL COURT THEATRE in London, where JOAN PLOWRIGHT scored a personal triumph as Beatie in *Roots*, the Norfolk girl inspired by learning. In *The Kitchen* (1959) and *Chips with Everything* (1962), Wesker drew on his experiences as a chef and in the Air Force to offer vivid pictures of working lives, a kind of *théâtre trouvé* which was then rare but was to become popular. He was the founder-director of Centre 42, an arts centre established at the Round House in Chalk Farm, London, deriving its name from Clause 42 in the Trade Union Charter. His frustrations in raising money for this venture are reflected in *Their Very Own and Golden City* (1965) and *The Friends* (1970), both of which mourn the decline of utopian socialism in Britain.

Wesker's writing was veering away from social optimism towards a more lyrical, disillusioned and introverted theatre. *The Four Seasons* (1965) concerns the waxing and waning of love and *The Old Ones* (1972) describes the exclusion of old people from the working lives around them, an enforced and in its way brutal seclusion. *Love Letters on Blue Paper* (1976), *Caritas* (1981) and the one-woman trilogy of short plays, *Annie Wobbler* (1984), concentrate upon particular people or states of mind. *The Journalists* (1975) and *The Merchant* (1976) tackle major themes but, with their large casts, have yet to be seen in London. While he still writes, directs and even acts prolifically, Wesker has become almost a forgotten figure in modern British theatre, although he was, with OSBORNE, PINTER, LITTLEWOOD and DEVINE, one of its pioneers. JE

West End (London) The centre of English commercial theatre, gaining its name from its geographical relationship to the City of London. It contains over 25 theatres within a relatively small area, ranging in size from the COLISEUM and the London Palladium with over 2300 seats to the Windmill with 326 (though at one period the smallest was the Little Theatre, originally with only 250 seats), and in age from Drury Lane where the first theatre was erected in 1663 to the Westminster, converted from a cinema in 1931.

Names have been reused or changed – there have been three theatres called the Globe and two Shaftesbury Theatres, while the Duke of York's was once the Trafalgar Square Theatre and SADLER'S WELLS has been at various times Miles's Musick House and the Aquatic Theatre. The older buildings have all been demolished, reconstructed and restored several times; but over half the theatres in the district were built between 1889 and 1909. Two, the Coliseum and COVENT GARDEN, are now OPERA houses, while others have seldom held anything but MUSICALS and REVUES, like the Shaftesbury, and the Windmill which was specifically constructed for non-stop VARIETY and (until it became a theatre-restaurant in 1981) renowned mainly for the nude tableaux of 'the Windmill Girls'. Another, the LYCEUM, which under IRVING became the leading London theatre, was turned into a dance hall in 1945.

Their reputations and the types of drama performed on their stages have changed with successive managements, and some have never had an identifiable policy. These include the Criterion, which sank from producing HENRY ARTHUR JONES's plays in the 1890s to light comedy, and

became a BBC studio from 1939 to 1945; Wyndham's, mainly associated with EDGAR WALLACE's thrillers (between 1926 and 1932); and the Ambassadors, which was almost entirely occupied by revues until the record-breaking run of AGATHA CHRISTIE's *The Mousetrap* in the 21 years up to 1973.

Since the mid-1970s West End theatres have been used as transfer houses – like the Piccadilly, which was always a 'second run' stage apart from a period after 1941 when NOËL COWARD, Peter Ustinov and EDWARD ALBEE were successfully produced there – and instead of originating productions they have been occupied by successful work from the ROYAL COURT, the YOUNG VIC, the Mermaid (see BERNARD MILES), the ROYAL SHAKESPEARE COMPANY, provincial companies and, more recently, various FRINGE THEATRE groups. So has the Duke of York's, which played a significant part in the development of English drama during the early part of the century, with the first productions of BARRIE's plays; seasons from 1910 to 1914 under CHARLES FROHMAN, with new works by GALSWORTHY, SHAW, GRANVILLE BARKER and MAUGHAM; and a short period when ASHLEY DUKES's adaptations of contemporary German drama and JOHN VAN DRUTEN's plays appeared there (1928–31). Similarly, the HAYMARKET, once the province of the actor-manager from BEERBOHM TREE to JOHN GIELGUD's repertory season in 1944–5, has housed revivals or transfers from the CHICHESTER FESTIVAL and the LYRIC, HAMMERSMITH, since 1960.

A second group represents theatres that have followed a consistent policy and stage a clearly identifiable type of work, like the Adelphi or the Shaftesbury, which have been almost continually occupied by PANTOMIME, MUSICAL COMEDY or revues. The Savoy, the home of the D'Oyly Carte company from 1881 to 1907, when it was taken over by Granville Barker and J. E. VEDRENNE, has since then alternated between GILBERT and Sullivan and comedy by Coward, KAUFMAN and HART, and WILLIAM DOUGLAS HOME. St Martin's, where BASIL DEAN presented significant new drama in the 1920s, has been occupied by detective thrillers since the 1970s; while the Westminster, which under Amner Hall introduced a wide range of English and foreign plays by Granville Barker, T. S. ELIOT, DENIS JOHNSTON and O'NEILL, was taken over by the 'Moral Rearmament' movement in 1946. In this group, too, is London's most famous theatre, DRURY LANE. After opening the century with spectacular MELODRAMA, it has housed an almost continuous series of musicals from *Rose Marie* and *The Desert Song* in the 1920s, through Ivor Novello and RODGERS and HAMMERSTEIN, to *A Chorus Line* and *Sweeney Todd*.

Other theatres have offered varying but always interesting programmes. The Phoenix has staged a series of significant plays by THORNTON WILDER, RATTIGAN and more recently STOPPARD, as well as the musical version of Chaucer's *Canterbury Tales*. ST JAMES'S, which established an early reputation for stagecraft under JOHN HARE and GEORGE ALEXANDER, contributing to the success of PINERO and WILDE, continued with outstanding performances by SYBIL THORNDIKE, EDITH EVANS and Noël Coward in the 1920s, plays by EMLYN WILLIAMS and ODETS in the 1930s, and in 1950–2 productions by LAURENCE OLIVIER and VIVIEN LEIGH, until it closed in 1957. The Apollo made its mark with HAROLD BRIGHOUSE, CLEMENCE DANE, SHERWOOD, Emlyn Williams, Rattigan, influential productions of GIRAUDOUX in the 1950s, and more recently performances of ALAN BENNETT, DAVID STOREY and ALAN AYCKBOURN with Gielgud or RALPH RICHARDSON. The GLOBE, which presented plays by A. A. MILNE, Maugham and Coward as well as visiting performers like MOISIU and the PITOËFFS, was taken over by H. M. Tennent in 1937 and by PRINCE LITTLER in 1960 (under whom Rattigan, CHRISTOPHER FRY, BOLT, PETER SHAFFER and SARTRE were staged), and has recently specialized in contemporary dramatists like MICHAEL FRAYN and Ayckbourn. The Lyric, which at the turn of the century had provided a stage for DUSE, SARAH BERNHARDT and FORBES-ROBERTSON, as well as TALLULAH BANKHEAD in the 1920s, offered productions of PRIESTLEY, Sherwood, HOUSMAN, Giraudoux and Charles Morgan in the 1930s, and Rattigan and T. S. Eliot in the 1940s and 1950s; it became identified with comedy in the 1970s, notably by Ayckbourn, Bennett and BEN TRAVERS. His [HER] MAJESTY's, opened by Tree, has presented a wide range of significant new work – from Shaw, Coward and Priestley to Rattigan and Shaffer – interspersed with long-running musicals (OSCAR ASCHE's *Chu Chin Chow*; and, more recently, *West Side Story* and *Fiddler on the Roof*).

Perhaps the most interesting theatre in this group is the Aldwych, which gave its name to the FARCES written by Travers between 1925 and 1933. It was also there that the STAGE SOCIETY put on the first major English production of CHEKHOV in 1911, and from 1943 to 1954 it presented a series of significant productions – LILLIAN HELLMAN, Sherwood, TENNESSEE WILLIAMS, Christopher Fry and MAXWELL ANDERSON. In 1960 it ceased to be a purely commercial theatre, becoming the London home of the ROYAL SHAKESPEARE COMPANY until their recent move to the new Barbican Centre; and during that time it presented not only transfers from the classical repertoire but significant new drama by JOHN WHITING, HAROLD PINTER, Tom Stoppard, PETER NICHOLS, and (from abroad) ANOUILH, BRECHT, DÜRRENMATT, HOCHHUTH, WEISS and Albee, in addition to housing the annual World Theatre Season between 1964 and 1973.

But commercial pressures have taken their toll, and an increasing number of West End theatres have been taken over for musical spectaculars, having been occupied for several years by ANDREW LLOYD WEBBER's productions alone. As a result, in general it has been theatres outside the West End, with non-commercial policies, or (more recently) subsidized companies, that have established standards, recovered the heritage of traditional drama or constituted the leading edge of modern English developments – the OLD VIC up to 1981, the Lyric in Hammersmith during the 1920s, the Greenwich Theatre since 1969, and in particular the Royal Court. This has been a vital catalyst – from the Barker–Vedrenne seasons of 1904-7, through the productions of FAGAN and BARRY JACKSON in the 1920s, to the English Stage Company under GEORGE DEVINE and WILLIAM GASKILL – introducing the early plays of Shaw, GALSWORTHY and Maugham, OSBORNE, WESKER, Storey, BOND, BARKER and HARE. CI

West Indian theatre see BARBADOS; CUBA; DOMINICAN REPUBLIC; EASTERN CARIBBEAN STATES; GUYANA; HAITI; JAMAICA; PUERTO RICO; TRINIDAD AND TOBAGO

West, Mae 1893-1980 American actress and playwright, whose pose of unabashed but self-mocking sensuality made her a cult figure. A VAUDEVILLE headliner by 1911, she achieved notoriety in the lead role of her first play *Sex* (1926), in which she was arrested. Attacked by the censors, she continued to defy them with *The Drag* (1927), the first American drama to depict a homosexual party; *Diamond Lil* (1928), a MELODRAMATIC comedy about white slavery; and *The Constant Sinner* (1931). Her Hollywood career in the 1930s increased her fame, but the limitations forced on her by production codes brought her back to BROADWAY in *Cathcrine Was Great* (1944). West always located her insatiable, man-eating temptresses safely in past eras, and her own attitude was one of worldly bemusement. Her autobiography, *Goodness Had Nothing to Do with It*, was published in 1959. LS

Western, (Pauline) Lucille 1843-77 American actress. Born in New Orleans to comedian George Western and an actress later known as Mrs Jane English, Lucille Western spent her childhood performing with her younger sister, Helen, in a piece designed to show off their dancing and farcical impersonations. As an adult, she excelled in emotional roles such as Lady Isabel in *East Lynne*, Marguerite Gautier in *Camille*, the title roles in *Lucretia Borgia* and *Leah, the Forsaken*, and her most popular role, Nancy in *Oliver Twist*. A dark-eyed beauty, she relied on inspiration more than art and gave the impression of being impulsive and untamed. TLM

Western theatre see FRONTIER THEATRE

Wheatley, William 1816-76 American theatre manager and actor. Born into a theatrical family, Wheatley made his stage debut at age ten in 1826 at the PARK THEATRE, New York, as young Albert in W. C. MACREADY's production of *William Tell*. Following a tour with Macready, he returned to the Park and played the title role in *Tom Thumb*, establishing himself as a leading juvenile actor. After acting in small roles at the BOWERY THEATRE (1833), he returned to the Park (1834) as a 'walking gentleman' to excel as Nicholas Nickleby and as Charles in *London Assurance*. For the 1842-3 season, Wheatley acted with the WALNUT STREET THEATRE company in Philadelphia. After a brief retirement from the stage, he returned to Philadelphia in 1853 to co-manage the ARCH STREET THEATRE with John Drew (see DREW–BARRYMORE FAMILY). He was sole manager in 1856, but two years later joined forces with JOHN SLEEPER CLARKE, who ran it with him until the outbreak of the Civil War. In 1862 he returned to New York and leased NIBLO's Garden, where he excelled in producing elaborate romantic dramas including *The Duke's Motto* and *Arrah-na-pogue*. His biggest hit came in 1866, however, when *The Black Crook* began its 475-performance run, creating a vogue for elaborate MUSICAL spectacle and making Wheatley a rich man. He retired from the stage in 1868. TLM

Wheeler, Andrew C(arpenter) [Trinculo; Nym Crinkle; J. P. Mowbray] 1832-1903 American drama critic. Born in New York, Wheeler began his career as a reporter on the *New York Times* in 1857. After travelling in the Midwest, he wrote for the *Milwaukee Daily Sentinel*, reported on the Civil War and returned to New York to pursue a career in journalism. During 1869–76 he reviewed plays for the *Sunday World*; beginning in 1870 he replaced Henry Clapp Jr as drama critic of *The Leader*; for 1876–7, he followed Joseph Howard Jr on the *Sun*; his 'Nym Crinkle's Feuilleton' graced the *New York Dramatic Mirror* during 1886–9; and in 1889 he added a regular column to Deshler Welch's *The Theatre*. Wheeler returned to the *World* in 1883 when Joseph Pulitzer purchased the paper. He was known also as a playwright, novelist and essayist on nature (under the Mowbray pen-name). Called by JAMES G. HUNEKER 'more brilliant than reliable', Wheeler popularized an aggressive style marked by devastating sarcasm. He opposed the Genteel Tradition, the aesthete views of WILLIAM WINTER, and the cultural shift of the country away from rugged individualism.   TLM

White, George 1890–1968 American dancer and producer. As a producer of successful musical REVUES in the 1920s, White provided stiff competition for FLORENZ ZIEGFELD. He started out as a dancer in Bowery saloons, gradually working his way up to VAUDEVILLE with a dancing act. Between 1910 and 18 he appeared as a dancer in a number of MUSICALS, including the *Ziegfeld Follies of 1915*. In 1919 he produced the *Scandals of 1919*, the first in a series of 13 revues bearing the title of *Scandals*. Because of his own background as a dancer, White emphasized dance in his revues, introducing black dance steps such as the Charleston and the black bottom to white audiences. His fast-paced revues were also noted for the jazz music of GEORGE GERSHWIN and DESYLVA, BROWN AND HENDERSON. White appeared as a dancer in several of the *Scandals* revues, and he also contributed COMEDY sketches to several editions.   MK

White, Jane 1922– African-American actress. A Smith College graduate, White came early to BROADWAY as the female lead in *Strange Fruit* (1945). Thereafter she played mostly in OFF-BROADWAY and regional theatres, taking lead roles in *Blithe Spirit*, *The Taming of the Shrew* and *Dark of the Moon* for the Hayloft Theatre in Allentown, Pennsylvania, in 1948–9. In 1964 she appeared in three productions for the NEW YORK SHAKESPEARE FESTIVAL: *Love's Labour's Lost*, *Troilus and Cressida* and *Coriolanus*, for which she won an Obie as Volumnia. After engagements in Italy and France, she replaced Irene Pappas as Clytemnestra in the Off-Broadway *Iphigenia in Aulis* (1967). Her Goneril to MORRIS CARNOVSKY's King Lear (1975) was hailed for its commanding intelligence, style and rich contralto voice.   EGH

White, Patrick (Victor Martindale) 1912–90 Australian playwright. He was already an internationally known novelist when his four plays *The Ham Funeral* (1961), written in 1947, *The Season at Sarsaparilla* (1962), *A Cheery Soul* (1963) and *Night on Bald Mountain* (1964) were staged by university theatres in Adelaide and Melbourne. All make use of heightened language, expressionistic devices and larger-than-life characterization.

Later plays were *Big Toys* (1977), a comedy of Sydney high society; *Signal Driver* (1982) and *Netherwood* (1983). White was awarded the Nobel Prize for Literature in 1973.   MW

Whitefriars Theatre (London) Very little is known of this theatre, which was sometimes confused by Caroline commentators with its near neighbour in SALISBURY COURT. The poet Michael Drayton leased a portion of the Old Whitefriars monastery in c.1605 and may have ordered conversion work to the refectory (85ft x 35ft), but it was a sign of hard times when the CHILDREN OF THE CHAPEL ROYAL took refuge there in 1608. They had lost control of their attractive playhouse in the BLACKFRIARS precinct, and the move to the notoriously rough Whitefriars area was a downward step. As the Children of the King's Revels, the reconstituted company played in the Whitefriars during 1608–9, when they were succeeded by, or renamed, the Children of the Queen's Revels. It is likely that two of JONSON's finest plays, *Epicoene* and *Bartholomew Fair*, were first performed at this obscure theatre, which was at best intermittently used after 1614 and not at all after 1621.   PT

Whitehead, Robert 1916– American producer. Born in Montreal and educated at Trinity College School in Canada, Whitehead began his producing career in 1947 with *Medea*, starring JUDITH ANDERSON. He was managing director for the AMERICAN NATIONAL THEATRE AND ACADEMY (1951), joining ROGER STEVENS and others in forming the Producers Theatre (1953). He co-directed the Repertory Theatre of Lincoln Center with ELIA KAZAN (1960–4), and has maintained a close association with the JOHN F. KENNEDY CENTER. His more than 50 New York productions include: *Member of the Wedding* (1950), *Bus Stop* (1955), *The Visit* (1958), *A Touch of the Poet* (1958), *A Man for All Seasons* (1961), *The Price* (1968), *Old Times* (1972), *A Texas Trilogy* (1976), *Betrayal* (1979), *Medea* (1982, starring his wife, ZOË CALDWELL), *Death of a Salesman* (1984 revival), *Lillian* (1985, also with Caldwell) and *A Few Good Men* (1990). In 1992 an award for promising and innovative emerging producers was established in his name by the Commercial Theatre Institute, and presented first in 1993.   TLM

Whitehead, Ted [Edward] **(Anthony)** 1933– British dramatist, whose plays for television and the theatre have concentrated on changing sexual manners, within and outside marriage, in contemporary Britain. *The Foursome* (1971) concerns two boys and two girls courting and eventually making love at the seaside; and Whitehead's clear and unsentimental study of male aggressive displays and female flirtatiousness carries a barbed authenticity. In *Alpha Beta* (1972) he describes the slow disintegration of a marriage over nine years, where step by step the two characters, Mr and Mrs Elliott, are drawn towards actions such as threatening to kill the children, which express a melodramatic desperation. The horror of sexual frustration and despair extends on occasions to black farce, as in *Old Flames* (1975), where girlfriends congregate to eat their common boyfriend in a celebratory feast; but Whitehead is seen at his best in his bleakly naturalistic studies which sometimes acquire, as in *The Sea-Anchor* (1974), a haunting atmosphere of loves lost and won. JE

Whitelaw, Billie 1932– British actress. Whitelaw has worked extensively with both the NATIONAL THEATRE and the ROYAL SHAKESPEARE COMPANY, but it is her various appearances in the plays of SAMUEL BECKETT that have been of special importance. These have included *Play* (NT at the OLD VIC, 1964), *Not I* (ROYAL COURT, 1973 and 1975), *Footfalls* (Royal Court, 1976), *Happy Days* (Royal Court, 1979), *Rockaby* and *Enough* (NT, 1982). No other English actor has established such an authoritative command of the special qualities of Beckett's work. This emphasis should not, however, detract from the range of character and classical work which she has also undertaken, from Desdemona to Maggie Hobson (*Hobson's Choice*). In 1987, she played Martha in a memorable revival of EDWARD ALBEE's *Who's Afraid of Virginia Woolf?* at the YOUNG VIC.
MB JE

Whiting, John (Robert) 1917–63 British dramatist, who began his theatrical career as an actor, having studied at the Royal Academy of Dramatic Art in London. While serving in the Royal Artillery during the war he started to write plays, poems and extracts of autobiography, and his first radio play, *Paul Southman*, was broadcast in 1946. Although his output as a stage dramatist was small, consisting of four major plays, he also wrote screenplays for films and television, and adapted some French plays (by OBEY and ANOUILH) for the British stage. He was highly conscious of his craft as a writer and at a time when, in the mid-1950s, proletarian roughness came into vogue, Whiting aspired towards elegant language, subtlety of thought and intricacy of dramatic technique. ·

His early plays were elegantly written in a style not dissimilar to that of CHRISTOPHER FRY, erring towards flippancy in *A Penny for a Song* (1952) and religiosity in *Saint's Day* (1951), which won the Festival of Britain Award but little praise from the critics or the public when it was first produced at the ARTS THEATRE Club. *Marching Song* (1954), however, handled the subject of postwar military guilt with originality and insight; while his best-known play, *The Devils*, based on Aldous Huxley's book *The Devils of Loudun*, was an early success at the Aldwych Theatre (after it had been taken over as a London branch of the Shakespeare Memorial Company in 1961). *The Devils* proved that Whiting was ahead of his time in handling a complex historical narrative on an open stage; and that he was broadly liberal in his views, against all kinds of bigotry and intolerance. A revival by the ROYAL SHAKESPEARE COMPANY in their studio theatre in the Barbican in 1984 indicated that Whiting's language had dated, but that the general firmness of his technical control remained sound.
JE

Whittaker, Herbert 1910– Canadian theatre critic, director and designer. After studying at Montreal's École des Beaux Arts, from 1933 he designed and directed roughly one production per year. As critic for the *Montreal Gazette* (1937–49) and the *Globe and Mail* in Toronto (1949–75), Whittaker chronicled the progress of amateur and professional theatre in Canada. He encouraged

Canadian playwriting and described the emergence of a national drama in reviews and articles both detailed and impressionistic. He promoted the development of the STRATFORD FESTIVAL, the National Theatre School and the National Arts Centre, believing that with the annual amateur Dominion Drama Festival in the 1930s, 40s and 50s Canada had come close to developing a truly national theatre that exerted its influence in the 1960s and beyond.
RH

Wiehe, Michael 1820–64 Leading Danish actor at the KONGELIGE TEATER, much admired by IBSEN. Amongst his varied repertoire (including SHAKESPEARE, SCHILLER and HOLBERG), he excelled in his early years as melancholy romantic lovers, especially opposite JOHANNE LUISE HEIBERG, whose ironic style contrasted well with his apparent vulnerability. He temporarily rebelled against JOHAN LUDVIG HEIBERG's conservative repertoire at the Kongelige Teater by joining the actor Frederik Høedt in his rival season at Christiansborg Hofteatret in 1855–6. HL

Wignell, Thomas 1753–1803 English-born American actor-manager. Wignell joined his cousin LEWIS HALLAM's American Company in 1774 and soon became its leading man. Known primarily as a comedian, he played the role of Jonathan in the original production of ROYALL TYLER's *The Contrast* and created the prototype of the YANKEE character. In 1791 he left the company and teamed up with Philadelphia musician Alexander Reinagle to form the CHESTNUT STREET THEATRE. When their building was finally constructed three years later it was recognized as one of the finest playhouses in America. Wignell recruited many of his players from England, including JAMES FENNELL, Mrs John Oldmixon, WILLIAM WARREN THE ELDER and THOMAS A. COOPER. For many years the company made Philadelphia the theatrical capital of America and developed a touring circuit encompassing Maryland, northern Virginia and occasional visits to New York City. When Wignell died, his share in the company passed to his widow. Although she and Reinagle were co-owners, management of the company was assumed by actors Warren and WILLIAM B. WOOD. Warren eventually married Mrs Wignell in 1806, and Wood joined him as owner of the company upon Reinagle's death in 1809. They finally disbanded in 1828. RAS

Wild West exhibition Re-creation of American FRONTIER life and skills popular in the late 19th century. Occasional exhibits of bronco-busting and Indian folkways were staged previously as museum attractions, but P. T. BARNUM billed his Wild West extravaganza *Indian Life; or, A Chance for a Wife* in 1874 as a 'thrilling arenic contest'. The genre took its definitive shape under the guidance of Col. BUFFALO BILL CODY, a former Indian fighter and buffalo hunter, who starred in *Scouts of the Prairie*, a play written by the hack Ned Buntline and seen first in Chicago (1872) and in 1873 at New York's NIBLO's Garden. The interest shown in a frontier fair he put on in North Platte, Nebraska, in 1882 led him and crack shot dentist Dr W. F. Carver to organize a travelling show, *The Wild West*, which featured a programme of shooting, roping, riding and an attack on the Deadwood stagecoach. In his patent application Cody called it an 'equestrian drama' (see HIPPODRAMA), for he disliked the term 'show'. In 1884 it went on the road under the ownership of Cody, the shrewd theatrical producer Nate Salsbury and the sharpshooter A. H. Bogardus, who gave it a coherent dramatic structure, culminating in its absorption into STEELE MACKAYE's *Drama of Civilization* (Madison Square Garden, New York, 1885). From the first, it presented the white frontiersman as a civilizing factor in overcoming the savage elements of Nature and Native Americans. A European tour in 1887 (and again in 1903–6) made a deep impact, influencing the adventure novels of Karl May and, through him, the young BERTOLT BRECHT.

James A. Bailey took over Cody's Wild West in 1894 and used CIRCUS equipment and methods to enable it to make one-night stands; Cody added a 'Congress of Rough Riders of the World', with Cossacks, gauchos and Arabs bridging the gap between Sioux savagery and Plainsman nobility. The Buffalo Bill enterprise combined with Pawnee Bill's in 1909, but went into bankruptcy in 1913. A rival, the Miller Brothers and Edward Arlington's 101 Ranch Wild West Show – primarily a display of horsemanship minus the frontier-life romanticism – carried on during 1908–16, tried a revival in 1926 to no public interest and folded in 1931. Motion pictures had taken over and expanded the depiction of cowboys and Indians, while authentic skills were relegated to the rodeo and CIRCUS 'after-shows'. One of Cody's stars, sharpshooter Annie Oakley, was to inspire the IRVING BERLIN MUSICAL COMEDY *Annie Get Your Gun* (1946). ARTHUR KOPIT's play *Indians* (1969) paints a sardonic picture of the relationship between Cody's exhibitions and the plight of the Native American.   LS

Wildbrandt, Adolf 1837–1911 German playwright and director. During the 1870s and 1880s Wildbrandt was closely associated with the BURGTHEATER, first as a writer of historical plays and of comedies, then, between 1881 and 1887, as director of the theatre. His finest play, *The Master of Palmyra* (1889), was written after he had retired from the Burgtheater.   SW

Wilde, Oscar [Fingal O'Flahertie Wills] 1854–1900 Anglo-Irish playwright, poet, novelist, essayist and wit. Wilde's first play, *Vera: or, The Nihilists* (1883), has an adolescent clumsiness profoundly at odds with his social and literary reputation. It is a MELODRAMA about a group of Russian revolutionary terrorists (or idealists – Wilde poses the alternatives). His second, *The Duchess of Padua* (1891), is a costume TRAGEDY in ungainly blank verse, first staged, like *Vera*, in New York.

Wilde's social performances were already familiar enough in the London of 1881 to tempt W. S. GILBERT's satire in *Patience*, but it was not until 1892, the year after the publication of his controversial novel, *The Picture of Dorian Gray*, that he began to find his own voice in drama. *Lady Windermere's Fan* (1892), produced by GEORGE ALEXANDER at the St James's, is formally a textbook example of the WELL MADE PLAY, in which the heroine's reputation rests on the discreet recovery of a fan. *A Woman of No Importance* (1893) and *An Ideal Husband* (1895) are, in terms of plot and subject-matter, equally derivative. The contemporary drama of PINERO and HENRY ARTHUR JONES

offered a more overt challenge to Victorian morality. But the lively work of Wilde's plays is done in the dialogue. His upper-class dandies and dowagers have made so merry with the values that the plays purport to uphold that the saving of a marriage has, by the time it is achieved, little more significance than the saving of a cigarette card. Even so, the stagey contrivances are a constraint, and Wilde gives no indication of relishing the mechanical plotting of his drawing-room melodramas.

It is quite otherwise with his brilliant masterpiece, *The Importance of Being Earnest* (1895). The contrariness of the title – if the play proves anything clearly, it is the importance of *not* being earnest – is sustained throughout the play. Nothing is what it seems, and the conventions of dramatic fiction become the subject rather than the disguise of the plot. Shortly after the brilliant opening of *The Importance of Being Earnest* at the St James's, Wilde sued the Marquess of Queensberry for slander and the first of two sensational trials began. As the evidence of Wilde's homosexual practices was revealed in court, George Alexander weakened, first removing Wilde's name from posters and programmes and then withdrawing the play altogether. It was during Wilde's spell of imprisonment in Reading Gaol that he begged SARAH BERNHARDT to produce *Salomé* in Paris (1896). LUGNÉ-POE staged it instead. Wilde had written the play some years earlier, in overblown French prose-poetry. It is decadent purple, a symbolist extravaganza (see SYMBOLISM) about the killing of John the Baptist. Bernhardt had planned a London production in 1892, but the Chamberlain's office banned the play because it used characters from the scriptures (see CENSORSHIP). The ban held until 1931, when the English version translated by Wilde's lover, Lord Alfred Douglas, was first publicly shown. Wilde is known to have planned several plays in prison, and Frank Harris's *Mr and Mrs Daventry* (1900) was probably based on a Wilde scenario, but, in the sad aftermath, he wrote only part of a one-act piece, *A Florentine Tragedy*, which was subsequently completed by T. Sturge Moore and produced in London in 1906.   PT

Wildenbruch, Ernst von 1845–1909 German playwright. In the course of an active career in the military and diplomacy, Wildenbruch wrote several popular, nationalistic plays with historical settings, which were performed by the MEININGEN COMPANY. *The Quitzows* (1888), about the Hohenzollerns, was the most acclaimed, though his trilogy about the Emperor Henry IV (1896) was also a tremendous success.   SW

Wilder, Clinton 1920–86 American producer, born in Irvine, Pennsylvania, and educated at Princeton University. Wilder began his professional career as a stage manager for *A Streetcar Named Desire* in 1947. He turned to producing with *Regina* (1949), *The Tender Trap* (1954), *Six Characters* (1955) and *A Visit to a Small Planet* (1957). He joined with RICHARD BARR to form a production company, Theatre 1960 (later 1961, 1962, and so forth), to present non-commercial, avant-garde plays. Their achievements include *The American Dream*, *The Death of Bessie Smith* and *Happy Days* (1961); *Who's Afraid of Virginia Woolf?*, *Endgame*, *The Sandbox*, *Deathwatch* and

Zoo Story (1962). Joined by EDWARD ALBEE in 1963, they offered *The Dutchman* and *Tiny Alice* (1964); *Malcolm* and *The Long Christmas Dinner* (1966); *A Delicate Balance* (which won a Pulitzer Prize), *Rimers of Eldritch* and *Everything in the Garden* (1967); and *Seascape* (1975). TLM

Wilder, Thornton (Niven) 1897–1975 American novelist and playwright. While Wilder may be considered one of America's top playwrights, his reputation rests upon three full-length plays and a half-dozen one-acts, beginning in 1931 with the publication of *The Long Christmas Dinner & Other Plays in One Act*. In 1938 his Pulitzer Prize-winning *Our Town* opened on BROADWAY, employing many of the experimental techniques Wilder had used in his one-acts: minimal scenery, narrative descriptions and the like. *Our Town*, which has been called America's most read and most produced play, examines in the first act small-town life in Grover's Corners, New Hampshire, for a single day in 1901. Succeeding acts complete the cycle of marriage, birth and death, ending with Emily Gibbs's conversation with the dead whom she has just joined.

Wilder's next play, *The Merchant of Yonkers* (1938), closed after only 39 performances, but was revised in 1954 as *The Matchmaker* and became a smash hit in 1964 as the MUSICAL *Hello, Dolly!*. Of greater impact was *The Skin of Our Teeth* in 1942, a parable of the world's history centred on the Antrobus family. Act 1 is set in Excelsior, NJ, during the Ice Age; purposeful anachronisms mix with dinosaurs and refugees. Act 2 on the boardwalk at Atlantic City closes with Mr Antrobus loading pairs of animals into his boat to avoid the Great Flood. Act 3 finds the Antrobus family coping with the after-effects of a seven-year war, but finding hope in their very existence. SMA

Wilkie, Allan ?1889–1970 British actor and manager, born in Scotland. His first Australian SHAKESPEARE season was in 1916, and from 1920 to 30 he toured Australia and New Zealand in Shakespeare and occasionally other classics. Wilkie's company, with his wife Frediswyde Hunter-Watts as leading lady, was known for its fine acting, with economical settings and elegant costumes. Unable to survive the Depression after 1930, the Wilkies moved to Canada and travelled through North America in Shakespeare recitals, eventually returning to Scotland. Wilkie was awarded a CBE in 1925. MW

Wilkinson, Tate 1739–1803 English actor and manager. He began acting at Harrow and was taken on by JOHN RICH. He soon discovered that while his acting was poor his imitations of other actors were brilliant and he based his career on that talent, earning his dismissal by Rich because of PEG WOFFINGTON's irritation at his mimicry of her. Famed for his imitations, he travelled to Dublin with FOOTE in 1757. His imitation of GARRICK at COVENT GARDEN infuriated Garrick and lost Wilkinson his friendship. In 1763 he was in York and joined Joseph Baker, the manager of the York theatre, investing heavily in the management. On Baker's death in 1770 he took on sole management of the York circuit of six theatres in the North of England, two of which, in York and Hull, had been made Theatres Royal in 1769. He reformed abuses in the theatres and employed most rising stars, including JOHN PHILIP KEMBLE and his sister MRS SIDDONS. His engaging *Memoirs* were published in 1790 and his account of the Yorkshire circuit, *The Wandering Patentee*, in 1795. PH

Williams, Barney [Bernard O'Flaherty] 1823–76 Irish-born actor whose first appearance on the New York stage was in 1836. In 1850 he married Maria Pray Mestayer (1828–1911), the widow of actor Charles Mestayer. For 20 years, the Williamses achieved considerable success, both in America and Great Britain, as a popular starring team in romantic Irish comedies such as *Born to Good Luck* and Samuel Lover's *Rory O'More*. Williams was regarded as unrivalled as the broadly comic, joking, hard-drinking but appealing stage Irishman. For two seasons (1867–9) he managed the old WALLACK'S THEATRE (by then the Broadway). His last appearance in *The Connie Soogah* and *The Fairy Circle* was at BOOTH'S THEATRE in New York on Christmas night, 1875. DJW

Williams, Bert [Egbert Austin Williams] 1874–1922 African-American comedian, born in Nassau, British West Indies. He began in MINSTREL SHOWS, where he had to affect blackface to conceal his light complexion and to learn the standard 'stage-darky' dialect. From 1893 to 1908 he teamed with George Walker (1873–1911), who played the flashy free-spending urban sport to Williams's melancholy, shuffling fall-guy, both in VAUDEVILLE and in a series of successful all-black MUSICALS, including *Sons of Ham* (1900), *In Dahomey* (1902) and *Bandana Land* (1908). When Walker retired in 1909, the victim of advanced paresis, Williams went solo; already the first black comic to record for Victor (from 1901), he was known nation-wide for such lugubrious songs as 'I'm a Jonah Man' and 'Nobody', and founded the first all-black actors' friendly society in 1906. Over protests from some of the white cast, Williams became the first black performer in the ZIEGFELD Follies, in which he played annually from 1910 to 1919 (missing only 1913 and 1918). 'The funniest man I ever saw and the saddest man I ever knew', as W. C. FIELDS called him, played in tandem with Leon Errol and EDDIE CANTOR, and never failed with his one-man poker game. LS

Williams, Emlyn 1905–87 Welsh dramatist and actor. Williams established the psychological thriller with *A Murder Has Been Arranged* (1930) and *Night Must Fall* (1935), a line he continued with plays like *Someone Waiting* (1953). His best work is the semi-autobiographical study of the relationship between a young Welsh miner and his schoolteacher, *The Corn Is Green*, which ran for two years with himself in the lead role when it was first performed in 1935. He also wrote adaptations, including his first farcical success *The Late Christopher Bean* (1933) and *The Master Builder* (for OLIVIER at the NATIONAL THEATRE, 1964). His numerous other plays range from behind-the-scenes drama in SHAKESPEARE's theatre (*Spring 1600*, 1934; rewritten in 1945) to the supernatural and religious (*The Wind of Heaven*, 1945; *Trespass*, 1947). Apart from acting in many of his own plays, some of which he also directed, he established a reputation as a performer in a wide variety of drama – starting with FAGAN's *And So to Bed* (1927), in Shakespearian roles with the OLD VIC (1927) and at Stratford-upon-Avon (1956), in BOLT's *A Man for All Seasons* (1962) and HOCHHUTH's *The Deputy* (1964) in New York – and winning international success with one-man shows, as DICKENS (first performed, 1951) and, after 1955, in *Growing Up*, based on readings from DYLAN THOMAS. CI

Williams, Jesse Lynch 1871–1929 American journalist, writer and dramatist, remembered primarily as the winner of the first Pulitzer Prize for the best American play, *Why Marry?* (1917). Acted by amateurs and published in 1914 as *And So They Were Married* (1914), *Why Marry?* first questioned and then carefully defended the institution of marriage as the best that society can offer. *Why Not?* (1922) scrutinized divorce through two mismated couples and arrived at the same conclusion. As other plays reveal (such as *The Lovely Lady* (1925), concerned with parents and children), Williams's comedic solution to society's problems remained conventional. WJM

Williams, Tennessee [Thomas Lanier] 1911–83 American playwright. From 1945, with his first success, *The Glass Menagerie*, Tennessee Williams has had a deep impact on the American theatre, bringing to it an original lyric voice and a new level of sexual frankness. The pleasure and the pain of sex constituted the great, inescapable subject of both his work and his life. In different moods and styles and with varying effectiveness, Williams returned repeatedly to the same neurotic conflicts embedded within the same character types: the spirits of Blanche Du Bois and Stanley Kowalski, the fierce antagonists of his masterpiece, *A Streetcar Named Desire* (1947), haunt practically all of his fables. Blanche is the lady of illusion and artifice, the fluttering Southern belle whose veneer of refinement masks emotional starvation and sexual rapacity. Desired and feared by Blanche as well as by Williams, Stanley is the muscled male whose potency contains the promise of both salvation and destruction.

As in *Streetcar*, the battle between repression and release, between the Puritan and the cavalier, is at the heart of Williams's most vibrant work: *Summer and Smoke* (1948), *The Rose Tattoo* (1951) and *Battle of Angels* (1940, rewritten as *Orpheus Descending*, 1957). In some plays (*Battle of Angels*, *You Touched Me* (1945), *Sweet Bird of Youth* (1959)) lusty men reanimate languishing women; in others (*Cat on a Hot Tin Roof* (1955), *The Milk Train Doesn't Stop Here Anymore* (1963)) the refusal of desirable males to satisfy deprived women provides the central conflict. Sometimes, as in *Cat on a Hot Tin Roof* and *Suddenly Last Summer* (1958), men withhold sex from women because they are homosexual; other times, as in *Milk Train*, because they want to transcend sexual desire. The source of Williams's profound sexual conflicts was the war between his fatally mismatched parents: his mother a rector's prudish daughter, his father a blustery womanizer who called his sensitive son 'Miss Nancy'. Unable in the American theatre of the 1950s and 60s to write openly about his own homosexual passion, Williams created nominally heterosexual dramas, transmuting tormented autobiography into artistic metaphor.

After *The Night of the Iguana* (1961), an uncharacteristic play of resolution and completion, Williams descended into a critical and commercial decline for the remaining 22 years of his life. Some of his later work, notably *The Gnädiges Fräulein* (1966), *In the Bar of a Tokyo Hotel* (1969) and *Outcry* (1973), chronicles the despair of creators who have lost control of their art. Other plays, such as *Small Craft Warnings* (1972) and especially *Vieux Carré* (1978), are attempts at self-restoration in which Williams returns to the delicacy of *The Glass Menagerie*. His Rabelaisian middle period is framed, as it were, by the directly autobiographical *Glass Menagerie* and *Vieux Carré*, in both of which he displays a healing compassion not only for others but also for himself as a young man. But neither the plays about disintegration nor the ones of partial affirmation have had the impact of his earlier work: audiences and critics have generally found the dramas too private.

In his later years Williams's personal life seriously deteriorated: he became increasingly dependent on drugs and alcohol and required periods of institutional confinement. Yet he continued to write daily, rigorously devoting himself to his craft. Despite the blurred focus, the occasional self-parody, the lack of control, there remains much of value in these later offerings, passages that testify to Williams's powerful sense of theatre and to his melodic gifts. Even the least of his plays is a vehicle for bravura acting, for in good plays and bad he created wonderfully actable neurotics. Twisted by desire, plagued by anxiety, his victims and outsiders speak a poetry of the dispossessed flavoured with wit, irony and gallantry.

Williams struggled through a long critical eclipse, but his reputation is now secure. Among American playwrights his achievement is equalled only by that of EUGENE O'NEILL. FH

Williamson, David (Keith) 1942– Australian playwright. His early plays *The Coming of Stork* (1970) and *The Removalists* (1971) were written while he was a thermodynamics lecturer; the latter gained for Sydney's Nimrod Theatre the British George Devine Award for new playwriting in 1971. His astute observation of contemporary Australian society and his ear for the vernacular's ironies and self-betrayals make him Australia's most successful playwright. His plays include *Don's Party* (1971), *What if You Died Tomorrow* (1973), *The Club* (1977), *Travelling North* (1979) and *The Perfectionist* (1982); *Sons of Cain* (1985), dealing with political corruption; *Emerald City* (1987), exploring a screenwriter's conflict between artistic integrity and commercialism; *Money and Friends* (1991) and *Brilliant Lies* (1993), dealing with sexual harassment; and the TELEVISION DRAMA mini-series *The Last Bastion* (1984). He was made an Officer of the Order of Australia in 1983. MW

Williamson, J(ames) (Cassius) 1845–1913 Australian entrepreneur. Born in Pennsylvania, he was an actor-dancer in New York and San Francisco before touring Australia in 1874 with his wife Maggie Moore in *Struck Oil*. Returning to settle in 1879, he soon became Australia's leading manager, largely through importing overseas successes; his enforcing of his rights to *HMS Pinafore* and other pieces confirmed British COPYRIGHT laws in Australia. Through various partnerships with George Musgrove, George Tallis, Gustave Ramaciotti, Hugh J.

Ward and others, he established a firm which dominated Australian theatre until 1976. When he died, all Australian theatres remained dark for a night in his memory. MW

Williamson, Nicol 1938– British actor, born in Scotland, who started his career with the Dundee Rep in 1960–1. After appearing at the ROYAL COURT in London in *That's Us*, ARDEN OF FEVERSHAM (1961) and two Shakespearian productions in 1962, he joined the ROYAL SHAKESPEARE COMPANY, playing in HENRY LIVINGS's *Nil Carborundum* and GORKY's *The Lower Depths*. His first major success came in 1964 as Maitland the tormented solicitor in JOHN OSBORNE's *Inadmissible Evidence*, which transferred from the Royal Court to the WEST END and BROADWAY. Williamson won the *Evening Standard* Best Actor Award and the New York Drama Critics Award for this performance, which revealed his talents to express a powerful if introverted personality – the inwardness which later, in 1969, allowed him to become one of the most celebrated Hamlets of his generation. While that nervous tension was appropriate in *The Diary of a Madman* (1967), it did not prevent him from also being an excellent comic actor, as in the New York production of *Plaza Suite* (1969), or from appearing in a wide variety of films.

He rejoined the Royal Shakespeare Company in 1973, where he took the title roles in *Coriolanus* and *Macbeth*; in 1974, he directed and played Vanya in a studio performance of *Uncle Vanya* with the RSC at Stratford-upon-Avon. In 1981, he appeared in London and New York in revivals of two Osborne plays, *Inadmissible Evidence* and *The Entertainer*. He also developed a solo performance, involving poetry readings, extracts from plays and singing in a quiet, intense style, which made him a highly effective CABARET performer. JE

Williamstown Theatre Festival (Massachusetts) Founded in 1955 by Yale Drama School professor Nikos Psacharopoulos, this festival has presented over 270 mainstage productions since its inception. Known for its appeal to established actors, many now primarily in films, as a place where they can return frequently to the stage, Williamstown also utilizes some of the best directors and designers in the USA and presents not only classics but avant-garde risks and unknown new plays. A rotating company of over 250 has been associated with the Festival, including the likes of Christopher Reeve, COLLEEN DEWHURST, Frank Langella, James Naughton, Austin Pendleton, Richard Thomas, Olympia Dukakis, Blythe Danner, GERALDINE FITZGERALD, Michael York and Richard Chamberlain. A complex operation with at least six discrete production components, WTF has gained an international reputation and is considered by many the outstanding summer theatre establishment in the USA. After Psacharopoulos's death in 1989, Peter Hunt, whose association with Williamstown began in 1958, was appointed artistic director. DBW

Willis, Nathaniel Parker 1806–67 American playwright and essayist, who began an intense but brief association with the theatre in 1837 with *Bianca Visconti*, the winner of actress Josephine Clifton's $1000 competition,

and *The Kentucky Heiress*, also written for Clifton. Both plays failed in production. In 1839 Willis wrote *Tortesa the Usurer* for J. W. WALLACK, an appealing and well dramatized story of a rich man who bargains for an aristocratic wife, who unfortunately loves another, but happily accepts an enchanting glover's daughter. Audiences, however, did not appreciate Willis's literary COMEDY, and starring actors did not want plays with several starring roles. Enjoying a reputation as the foremost essayist in America, Willis stopped writing plays. WJM

Wills, W(illiam) G(orman) 1828–91 Anglo-Irish playwright and painter, who provided HENRY IRVING with many of his LYCEUM successes. These included *Charles I* (1872), *Eugene Aram* (1873), *Vanderdecken* (1878) and *Faust* (1885). Wills believed poetry to be a higher form than drama, and his attempts to combine the two impressed contemporaries more than they have posterity. A noted clubman and an endearingly generous, if somewhat anachronistic, Bohemian, he made more money by painting fashionable portraits than by writing plays. His only enduring success was *Olivia* (1878), an adaptation of GOLDSMITH's novel, *The Vicar of Wakefield*, and even that endured only as long as ELLEN TERRY continued to perform in it. PT

Wilson, August 1945– African-American playwright, whose position in the theatre rose meteorically in less than five years. Winner of the 1987 Pulitzer Prize for Drama for *Fences* and the 1990 Prize for *The Piano Lesson*, he has written a series of plays, each set in a different decade, that evolves into a cycle of dramas that he terms his 'view of the black experience of the 20th century'. Wilson has focused on what he perceives as the largest idea that confronted blacks in each decade, drawing heavily on his own experience of growing up in the Hill district of Pittsburgh, Pennsylvania, a black slum community. Wilson is also typical of an American playwright whose work has been fostered in the regions, with developmental work at the EUGENE O'NEILL MEMORIAL THEATRE CENTER's National Playwrights Conference and premieres at the YALE REPERTORY THEATRE under LLOYD RICHARDS's direction, beginning with *Ma Rainey's Black Bottom* (1984) and including *Fences*, *Joe Turner's Come and Gone* (1986), *The Piano Lesson* (1988) and *Two Trains Running* (1990; BROADWAY, 1992). The latter, set in 1968 at a restaurant in Pittsburgh across the street from a funeral home and a meat market, focuses on disenfranchised characters looking back nostalgically and with some confusion at their limited 'progress'.

In addition to the Pulitzer, Wilson has won the Drama Desk Award, the New York Drama Critics' Circle Award and a Tony for *Fences*, and Tony nominations for Best Play (*The Piano Lesson* and *Two Trains Running*). Wilson's 1940s play for his decades cycle, premiered in early 1995 at Chicago's GOODMAN THEATRE, *Seven Guitars*, focuses on the lives of blues musicians. Likened by the Pulitzer board to EUGENE O'NEILL, Wilson has certainly emerged as the richest theatrical voice in the USA of the past decade and has managed to transcend the categorization of 'black' playwright to speak through his dissection of black families and communities to a broad-based audience. DBW

Wilson, Francis 1854–1935 American comedian and singer. After an apprenticeship as a utility actor and low comedian with a STOCK COMPANY, Wilson made his musical theatre debut in *Our Goblins* (1880). During 1885–9 he appeared in comic OPERAS with the McCaull Opera Company, then established his own company. His greatest role was that of Cadeaux in *Erminie* (1886), a part he played nearly 1300 times over 35 years. His other successes included *The Merry Monarch* (1890), *The Lion Tamer* (1891), *Half a King* (1896) and *The Toreador* (1902). From 1904 on, Wilson confined his efforts to COMEDY and drama. Because of his training in stock, he brought to his musical roles the skills of a character actor, carefully preparing each move and gesture rather than trusting to improvisation. During 1913–21 he served as the first president of America's Actors' Equity. His entertaining autobiography was published in 1924.   MK

Wilson, Lanford 1937– Missouri-born American playwright, who began writing at the University of Chicago and became part of a group of playwrights at the CAFFE CINO in New York. There his first script was produced, *So Long at the Fair*, in 1963. Since then his plays have been produced at LA MAMA in New York, the MERCURY THEATRE in London, most regional US theatres and on BROADWAY.

Among his more successful scripts are *The Madness of Lady Bright* (1964), *Balm in Gilead* and *This Is the Rill Speaking* (1965), *Rimers of Eldritch* (1966), *Lemon Sky* (1970), *The Great Nebula in Orion* (1971), *The Hot l Baltimore* (1973), *The 5th of July* (1978), *Talley's Folly* (1979) and *Burn This* (1987, Broadway; 1991, London). *Talley's Folly* won Wilson the Pulitzer Prize for Drama and the New York Drama Critics' Circle Award. His 1983 *Angel's Fall* was a critical, but not popular, success.

Wilson was one of the founders of the CIRCLE REPERTORY COMPANY, which staged several of his scripts. *The Hot l Baltimore*, involving various social outcasts in a condemned hotel, ran for 1166 performances, then the OFF-BROADWAY record for a non-musical American play. Besides the Pulitzer Prize, Wilson has won the Drama Desk Vernon Rice Award for *The Rimers of Eldritch*, the New York Drama Critics' Circle Award, the Outer Circle Award and an Obie for *The Hot l Baltimore*, and another Obie for *The Mound Builders*. In recent years he has learned Russian in order to translate CHEKHOV. Wilson's most recent play seen on Broadway, *Redwood Curtain* (1992), dominated by JOHN LEE BEATTY's haunting scenery, was a disappointing yet earnest effort to deal with a combination of fantasy and reality in its treatment of the theme of America's tendency to sublimate its past nightmares, in this case typified by Vietnam.   SMA

Wilson, Robert d.1600 English actor and playwright, famous as an extemporizer. Wilson is known to have been with LEICESTER'S MEN after 1572 and with QUEEN ELIZABETH'S MEN after 1583. Of several plays which he wrote or helped to write, the surviving three, *The Three Ladies of London* (c.1581), *The Three Lords and Three Ladies of London* (c.1589) and *The Cobbler's Prophecy* (c.1594), are scholarly examples of a professional ability to adapt mid-century drama to the changing taste of the early PUBLIC THEATRES.   PT

Wilson, Robert 1941– American director and designer, whose training as a painter and architect is evident in his painterly theatre compositions. Wilson's work with brain-damaged children, using physical activity to influence mental activity, also influenced his dreamy pieces, especially in their slow pace and repetition of simple movement. Christopher Knowles, an autistic adolescent, became a collaborator with Wilson on pieces like *A Letter to Queen Victoria* (1974) and *Einstein on the Beach* (1976), the latter also in collaboration with choreographers Andrew de Groat and Lucinda Childs and composer Philip Glass. Wilson was interested in Knowles's non-discursive use of language and sought to create on stage his unusual way of structuring perceptions. Operatic in scale, Wilson's streams of visual and aural images lack plots and characters in any conventional sense and often employ massive scenery, animals and complex lighting effects. *Nō*-like in tone, they take place in slow motion, altering the audience's sense of time; a simple action like crossing the stage can take an hour. *Deafman Glance* (1970) lasted eight hours, and *Overture to Ka Mountain*, created for the 1972 Shiraz Festival in Iran, lasted a week.

In the 1980s Wilson began centring his work in Europe, where it was easier to find funding. There he created *The Man in the Raincoat* (1981, Cologne), *Great Day in the Morning* (1982, Paris), *The Golden Windows* (1982, Munich), *the CIVIL warS* (1983, five countries; the German section had its US premiere at the AMERICAN REPERTORY THEATRE, 1985) and *The Black Rider: The Casting of Magic Bullets* (1990, Hamburg; US premiere at the Brooklyn Academy of Music, 1993). In recent years, Wilson has been directing OPERAS and plays from the classical repertory, among them *The Magic Flute* (1991, Paris), *Parsifal* (1991, Houston) and BÜCHNER's *Danton's Death* (ALLEY THEATRE, 1992). In conjunction with his direction of IBSEN's *When We Dead Awaken*, co-produced by ART and the Alley, 1991, a major retrospective of his work was mounted at Boston's Museum of Fine Arts (seen later in Houston and San Francisco). In 1993 Houston's Alley Theatre, with a $100,000 grant from the Pew Charitable Trusts, became an American home base for Wilson.   AS

Wilton, Marie (Effie) 1839–1921 British actress and pioneering theatre manager, born into a theatrical family. As a child, she performed in provincial theatres, notably in Bristol, where she made an impression as Ophelia. In London, somewhat to her chagrin, she became a sex symbol, particularly during her years (1858–64) as the 'Queen of BURLESQUE' at the Strand Theatre, and it was primarily a determination to refashion for herself a career in legitimate drama that dictated her bold decision to enter into theatre management at the age of 25.

With a borrowed £1000, she bought the lease of the disreputable Queen's Theatre in Tottenham Street, sharing the management with the leading Strand dramatist, H. J. BYRON, but sparing him the financial risk. An extraordinary intuition enabled her to re-create, in the small auditorium of the renamed PRINCE OF WALES'S, the atmosphere of decorous Victorian domesticity – ornamental flowers on each side of the proscenium, four rows of stalls complete with anti-macassars, carpeted aisles, rosebud chintz lining the circle – and audiences responded with enthusiasm. The crowning achievement was the staging in annual succession from 1865 to 70 of six comedies by T. W. ROBERTSON. It was in the third of these, *Caste* (1867), that Wilton created one of her finest roles, that of Polly Eccles. Her Captain Hawtree was SQUIRE BANCROFT, whom she married at the end of the run, and to whom she subsequently surrendered her managerial leadership. But hers is the primary credit for her theatre's contribution to the growth of ensemble acting, the raising of the status of actors and the increasing appropriateness of stage decor. The Bancrofts remained at the Prince of Wales's until 1879, after which they managed the HAYMARKET from 1880 until their wealthy retirement in 1885.   PT

Winge, Stein 1940– Leading Norwegian director. Winge began at Trøndelag Teater under Erik Pierstorff, and became prominent in the 1970s with highly physicalized productions of SHAKESPEARE, IBSEN and GOETHE that demonstrated his ability to realize the tensions within classic texts in startling, theatricalistic ways. Recent examples include a provocative, unnerving *Hamlet* in the NORSKE TEATRET's Rehearsal Hall (1987) and a boldly expressionistic (see EXPRESSIONISM) *Inspector General* at GÖTEBORGS STADSTEATER (1993). His six-hour production of DORST's *Merlin* in 1989 was reportedly overwhelming. He works entirely within institutional theatres, but in innovative ways: at NATIONALTHEATRET he founded the experimental Teatret på Torshov in 1977, and as head of Nationaltheatret from 1990 to 1992 he promoted new approaches to Ibsen, and began an annual International Ibsen Festival.   HL

Winter Garden Theatre (New York City) The Winter Garden, an important musical house, was designed for the SHUBERT BROTHERS by architect William Swasey. It opened on 20 March 1911 with a double bill that included a curtain-raiser called *Bow Sing* and *La Belle Paree*, a REVUE. The Winter Garden was less a totally new theatre than an extensive remodelling of an existing building, the American Horse Exchange. The remodelled structure contained a CABARET, as well as a large theatre, which was decorated in a garden motif and contained an unusual feature for the time: a runway extending from the stage into the auditorium. In 1912 the Winter Garden became the home of *The Passing Show* (an annual Shubert revue designed to compete with FLORENZ ZIEGFELD's *Follies*), which continued to be presented regularly through 1924. During the 1910s and early 20s, the theatre was also the home of a number of light MUSICALS conceived as vehicles for Shubert star AL JOLSON. It was extensively remodelled during the 1920s by theatre architect Herbert Krapp. During the 1930s it housed such important musical attractions as the Shubert-produced editions of the *Ziegfeld Follies* and the long-running *Hellzapoppin'*, starring 'Ole' Olsen and 'Chick' Johnson. From 1928 to 33, and again during 1945–8, the Winter Garden was used for motion picture showings. Following its second reconversion to live performance, the theatre has been the home of such major musicals as *West Side Story* (1957), *Gypsy* (1959) and *Cats* (1982; still there in 1995). The Winter Garden, which seats some 1500 spectators, is owned by the SHUBERT ORGANIZATION.   BMCN

Winter, William [Mercutio] 1836–1917 American drama critic, theatre historian and biographer. Born in Gloucester, Massachusetts, and educated at Harvard University, Winter abandoned a law career for a literary one. Influenced by Henry Wadsworth Longfellow, he turned to writing poetry and reviewing books. In 1859 he moved to New York and worked as assistant editor and book reviewer for the *Saturday Press*. In 1860–1 he wrote briefly for *The Leader* before taking charge of the *Albion*'s dramatic department (1861–5), writing as Mercutio. In 1865 he replaced Edward H. House as chief critic for the *New York Tribune*, a position he held until 1909, establishing himself as the foremost drama critic of his generation. The foundation of Winter's critical beliefs was essentially Aristotelian, tempered with 19th-century romantic idealism (later called 'the Genteel Tradition'). He considered acting the primary art of theatre and the standard drama preferable to modern plays. He regarded the theatre as a temple of art to elevate and inspire humankind, and rejected the notion that art should depict real life. To Winter, beauty and morality were inseparable in art, and REALISM had banished both from the stage. Thus he saw IBSENism as a 'rank, deadly pessimism ... a disease, injurious alike to the stage and to the public'. Winter prepared acting versions of SHAKESPEARE's plays for EDWIN BOOTH and AUGUSTIN DALY. He wrote lengthy biographies of Edwin Booth (1893), ADA REHAN (1898), RICHARD MANSFIELD (1910), JOSEPH JEFFERSON (1913) and TYRONE POWER (1913). His more than 50 books provide a comprehensive record of the late-19th-century American stage.   TLM

Wise, Ernie see MORECAMBE, ERIC

Witkiewicz [Witkacy], **Stanisław Ignacy** 1885–1939 Polish playwright, painter, novelist and philosopher who, unrecognized by his contemporaries, has emerged since 1956 as a seminal figure. He travelled to Australia in 1914 with the anthropologist Malinowski and then served in the Russian army, witnessing the Revolution of 1917. He wrote over 30 plays between 1918 and 1926, many unpublished and unperformed. His theory of *Pure Form in the Theatre* (1920) seeks to liberate drama from story-telling and traditional psychology, and give it the formal possibilities of modern art and music. His works present an apocalyptic vision of the loss of metaphysical feelings in the coming anthill civilization, viewed with mocking irreverence and self-irony. Major plays are *They* (1920), *Gyubal Wahazar*, *The Water Hen* (1921), *The Madman and the Nun*, *The Crazy Locomotive* (1923), *The Mother* (1924), *The Beelzebub Sonata* (1925) and *The Shoemakers* (1934). DG

Wodehouse, P(elham) G(renville) 1881–1975 British novelist and dramatist. Wodehouse's song lyrics, for some of the most successful of English musical comedies of the first quarter of the century, were first heard on the American stage in *Miss Springtime* (1916). He collaborated with librettist GUY BOLTON and composer JEROME KERN on *Have a Heart* (1917) and *Leave It to Jane* (1917) and contributed lyrics and/or librettos to numerous other shows in the 1910s and 20s, notably *Oh, My Dear!* (1918), *Oh, Kay!* (1926), *Rosalie* (1928) and *The Three Musketeers* (1928);

Witkiewicz's *Gyubal Wahazar*, National Theatre, Warsaw, 1968. This production was censored and stopped after the dress rehearsal.

with GEORGE GROSSMITH and Ian Hay he wrote a series of FARCES. He was also a drama critic for the magazine *Vanity Fair*. His wry lyrics and witty librettos did much to improve the prestige of BROADWAY musicals. As well as working in the USA frequently, he lived in exile there in the final 30 years of his life. MK

Woffington, Peg [Margaret] ?1714–60 Irish actress. Her father died a pauper in 1720 and tradition says that she worked with Madame Violante's tightrope-walking act. She certainly acted with her children's company, and for Madame Violante played three roles, including Macheath, in *The Beggar's Opera* in London in 1732. In 1737 she was starring at the Smock Alley Theatre, Dublin, particularly as Polly Peachum. In 1740 she was triumphant in the BREECHES PART of Sir Harry Wildair in FARQUHAR's *The Constant Couple*, a role she played in London for RICH. In 1742 she was Lady Anne to GARRICK's Richard III. She became his mistress and lived with him but he drew back on the verge of marriage. Facing fierce competition from MRS CLIVE she eventually quarrelled with Garrick and left DRURY LANE in 1748, beginning to play more roles in tragedies. Here rivalry with GEORGE ANNE BELLAMY reached a climax with a fight when they were playing *The Rival Queens* in 1756. She collapsed on stage as Rosalind when delivering the epilogue to *As You Like It* in 1757, and was ill until her death. PH

Wolf, Friedrich 1888–1953 German dramatist whose *Zeitstücke*, or plays on topical issues, were prominent in the later Weimar Republic. *Zyankali* (*Cyanide*, 1929) was a plea for repeal of the abortion law. *Tai Yang erwacht* (*Tai

Yang Awakes*, 1931), staged by the PISCATOR collective, attacked exploitative working conditions, and *Professor Mamlock* (1934), premiered in Warsaw, exposed anti-Semitism in academic life. After wartime exile in the USSR, Wolf was briefly GDR ambassador to Poland HR

Wolfe, George C. 1955– Kentucky-born African-American playwright and director. College-trained Wolfe was twice winner at the American College Theatre Festival and spent four years writing and directing in Los Angeles. His first New York show, the MUSICAL *Paradise!* (1985) presented at PLAYWRIGHTS HORIZONS, was unsuccessful, but he followed it with *The Colored Museum* (1986), a hilarious lampoon of black experience topics. Premiered at the CROSSROADS THEATRE in New Brunswick, NJ, the play later ran for nine months at the PUBLIC THEATER and moved to London. In 1990 he directed at the Public Theater his play *Spunk*, based on three Zora Neale Hurston short stories, followed the same year with his Public Theater production of BRECHT's *The Caucasian Chalk Circle* set in Haiti. He was also selected as one of three resident directors at the NEW YORK SHAKESPEARE FESTIVAL. His musical about Jelly Roll Morton, *Jelly's Last Jam*, premiered in Los Angeles (spring 1991) before opening on BROADWAY (spring 1992). Shortly before his direction of the acclaimed *Angels in America* (for which he won the 1993 Tony for direction), Wolfe, termed bold, fearless and the premier theatre artist of his generation, became producer of the NYSF, an appointment greeted with enthusiasm. EGH

Wolff, Egon 1926– Chilean playwright, born of German parents. Wolff has successfully maintained a career as a chemical engineer and owner of a small factory in Santiago, while devoting himself to literature. His early plays focus on psychological problems, generational conflicts and social issues. Among many titles, two stand out. *Los invasores* (*The Invaders*, 1962), with a surrealistic technique and a touch of J. B. PRIESTLEY's *An Inspector Calls*, portrays violently the threat of class revolution if the bourgeoisie continues to ignore social concerns. *Flores de papel* (*Paper Flowers*, 1970) deals with gratuitous violence and psychological violation in an obtuse class struggle. Later titles include *Kindergarten* (1977), *Espejismos* (*Mirages*, 1978), *José* (1980) and *La balsa de la Medusa* (*Medusa's Raft*, 1984), the latter the third part of his famous trilogy. *Háblame de Laura* (*Tell Me about Laura*, 1986) perpetuates his reliance on abusive interpersonal games, as does *Cicatrices* (*Scars*, 1993). GW

Wolff, Pius Alexander 1782–1828 German actor. According to GOETHE, Wolff was the only actor who fully mastered the WEIMAR STYLE. He left the Weimar Court Theatre in 1816 for the BERLIN ROYAL THEATRE. Here his interpretations of Hamlet became legendary. Wolff was the author of the highly popular comedy, *Preziosa* (1821). SW

Wolfit, Donald 1902–68 British actor-manager. After an early career touring with Fred Terry, in London and with the Sheffield Repertory Company, mainly in MELODRAMA, Wolfit established a reputation as a Shakespearian actor with the OLD VIC in 1929–30, at Stratford-upon-Avon in 1936, and with his own company from 1937. He toured widely, giving memorable performances not only as Shylock in *The Merchant of Venice*, Macbeth and Lear, but also in the title role of JONSON's *Volpone* and in MASSINGER's *A New Way to Pay Old Debts*, and he mounted a popular lunch-time series of scenes from SHAKESPEARE in 1940. Wolfit also offered striking interpretations of modern plays, including HOCHWÄLDER's *The Strong Are Lonely* (1955), IBSEN's *Ghosts* (1959) and *John Gabriel Borkman* (1963), as well as classical drama such as *Oedipus Rex* and *Oedipus at Colonus* (1953). He was knighted in 1957. CI

Women's Project and Productions American producing group. Julia Miles founded the Women's Project in 1978 as part of the AMERICAN PLACE THEATRE, where she had been associate director since 1967. Initially funded by a Ford Foundation Grant, the Project became independent of American Place in 1987, with support from the Kentucky Foundation for Women. The Project's mission is to identify, encourage, develop and produce women playwrights and to help establish visibility for women directors. Miles frequently states that her goal will be met when women playwrights can be known just as playwrights. In its first 12 years, the Project produced over 50 plays, published four play anthologies, staged hundreds of rehearsed readings, and supported directors through a Directors' Forum. The Project now has over 290 artistic members, including many who have become leaders, including Anne Bogart, Constance Congdon, MARIA IRENE FORNÉS, Emily Mann, Sharon Ott, Carey Perloff and Paula Vogel. TH-S

Wood, Charles (Gerald) 1933– British dramatist whose three short plays about army life, produced as *Cockade* in 1963, revealed his gift for terse, vivid dialogue and bitter SATIRE. Wood, who served in the Lancers from 1950 to 55, has written attacks on militarism, British imperialism and the class system embodied in the army ranks. *Dingo* (1967), set in North Africa during the Second World War, and *H: Being Monologues at Front of Burning Cities* (1969), on 'Christian' General Havelock who commanded the British forces in India at the time of the Indian mutiny, are epic tirades on the folly and hypocrisies of war. In a lighter vein, Wood has written comedies about a run-down rep (*Fill the Stage with Happy Hours*, 1966), the Welfare State (*Meals on Wheels*, 1965) and Hollywood, including *Veterans* (1972), *Has 'Washington' Legs?* (1978) and *Across from the Garden of Allah* (1986). He has written widely for television; *Tumbledown* (1988), about the treatment of a wounded officer during the Falklands War, aroused much controversy when it was produced by the BBC (see TELEVISION DRAMA). JE

Wood, John British actor, who studied at Oxford University, becoming president of OUDS, before joining the OLD VIC Company in 1954. A tall, lean actor, with a characteristic acerbic delivery, Wood was not the easiest person to cast; and his appearances in *Camino Real* (1957), *The Making of Moo* (1957), *Brouhaha* (1958) and *The Fantasticks* (1961) were effective without giving a true indication of his talents. When he joined the ROYAL SHAKESPEARE COMPANY in 1971, however, he was offered parts in both Shakespearian and modern plays which revealed his exceptional intelligence and expressivity. In 1974, as Carr in TOM STOPPARD's *Travesties*, he won the *Evening Standard* Best Actor Award and, on BROADWAY, the Tony (1976), providing a brilliantly comic study of a bemused minor Foreign Office official in Zürich in 1917, matched by such dubious contemporaries as Lenin, Tristan Tzara and James Joyce. In 1979 he appeared at the NATIONAL THEATRE in Stoppard's version of a SCHNITZLER play, *Undiscovered Country*, as well as playing Richard III and in *The Provoked Wife* (1980). He appeared as Prospero in *The Tempest* (1989), as Solness in *The Master Builder* (1989), as Sheridan Whiteside in MOSS HART and GEORGE S. KAUFMAN's comedy, *The Man Who Came to Dinner* (1989) and he played the title role in NICHOLAS HYTNER's production of *King Lear* (1990), all for the RSC. Wood's film appearances include those in *Nicholas and Alexandra* (1971) and as a 1930s actor in Woody Allen's *The Purple Rose of Cairo*. JE

Wood, Mrs John [*née* Matilda Charlotte Vining] 1831–1915 Liverpool-born actress and manager, who acted on provincial English stages for 12 years before marrying actor John Wood and moving to Boston in 1854. After their American debut at the BOSTON THEATRE (September 1854), they appeared in New York at the Academy of Music (1856) before becoming regulars with the Boston Company. Mrs Wood played a guest engagement at WALLACK's THEATRE in late 1856, creating the role of Minnehaha in Charles Walcot's *Hiawatha*. At the end of the 1856–7 season, she and her husband left for San Francisco, where she quickly became a star. After the couple separated, Mrs Wood returned east to play starring engagements for the next four years. In 1863 she began a three-year stint as manager of the Olympic Theatre. She returned to England in 1866 and acted only once more (1872–3) in America. Saucy, impudent and fun-loving, Mrs Wood was called by Lawrence Hutton 'one of the best BURLESQUE actresses our stage has ever known'. TLM

Wood, William B(urke) 1779–1861 American actor and manager, born of English parents in Montreal, Canada. As a young man he joined THOMAS WIGNELL's Philadelphia company, despite ill-health and lack of theatrical experience. Unsuccessful in tragic roles, Wood proved better suited to genteel COMEDY and ultimately found his niche in management. After the death of Wignell in 1803, he became assistant to the acting manager of the CHESTNUT STREET THEATRE, WILLIAM WARREN THE ELDER. In 1804 he married Juliana Westray, a good actress who appeared under his management for many years. Warren and Wood shared a prosperous quarter-century together, bringing their Philadelphia, Baltimore and Washington theatres to international eminence. Wood sold his shares back to Warren before the 1826 season, but remained as a company member. He left in 1828 to manage the new ARCH STREET THEATRE, Philadelphia; and during 1829–46 he was at that city's WALNUT STREET THEATRE. His reminiscences are recorded in *Personal Recollections*, published in 1855. DBW

Woodworth, Samuel 1785–1842 American playwright. Woodworth was best known for his song 'The Old Oaken Bucket' and for *The Forest Rose* (1825, with music by John Davies), a light-hearted glorification of American farmers that became a vehicle for a host of YANKEE actors for 40 years and is often called 'the first American MUSICAL hit'. He wrote seven other plays (including *The Deed of Gift*, 1822; *LaFayette*, 1824; and *The Cannibals*, 1833), a patriotic novel, dedicatory addresses and sentimental ballads, and edited numerous periodicals and newspapers, notably the New York *Mirror* (1823–42). He received small profit from his literary endeavours and died in poverty. RM

Woollcott, Alexander 1887–1943 American drama critic who made his debut as a critic for the *New York Times* in 1914, replacing Adolph Klauber. His battles with the SHUBERTS in 1915 made him a celebrity. After military service in Paris (1917–19), he returned to the *Times*, and helped establish that witty 'vicious circle' that met for lunch at the 'Algonquin Round Table'. In 1922 he was hired away by the *Herald*, and later reviewed for the *Sun* (1924–5) and the *World* (1925–8). In 1929 he established his 'Shouts and Murmurs' column in the *New Yorker*, began his radio show (later commanding up to $3500 per programme for 'The Town Crier'), and collaborated on two plays with GEORGE S. KAUFMAN (*The Channel Road* (1979); *The Dark Tower* (1933)). He also appeared frequently as an actor, playing, according to BROOKS ATKINSON, 'a sort of virtuoso fat man'. Woollcott remains best known as the model for Sheridan Whiteside in Kaufman and MOSS HART's *The Man Who Came to Dinner*. Vitality and urbanity were his trademarks. TLM

Wooster Group New York ensemble formed in 1975 under the direction of ELIZABETH LeCOMPTE; successors to Richard Schechner's PERFORMANCE GROUP. Housed in SoHo's Performing Garage, Wooster Group's other members have included James Clayburgh, Willem Dafoe, SPALDING GRAY, Peyton Smith, Kate Valk and the late Ron Vawter. The Group, recognized as 'one of the most radically political, culturally radical theatres in the country, perhaps the world', composes 'large ensemble multimedia theatre pieces', which join a repertoire.

The Wooster Group explores frequently unexamined, often suppressed and disturbing elements of society and culture, challenging unquestioned assumptions. Its material is derived from sources whose texts and images are quoted, reworked and juxtaposed with fragments of disparate other elements. The Group aims 'to create a "theater reality" that incorporates life rather than represents it', habitually restructuring the spectator–performer relationship unconventionally.

Wooster Group pieces have included the trilogies *Three Places in Rhode Island* (1975–9) and *The Road to Immortality* (1981–7), and an epilogue to the latter (*Brace Up!*, 1990; based on CHEKHOV). The Group produces films and videos including Michael Kirby's *White Homeland Commando*; in 1990 they participated in the international Los Angeles Theatre Festival and in 1991 received an Obie for sustained achievement. They are one of the few radical groups to have received a published study (by David Savran, 1986). REK

Worth, Irene 1916– American-born actress, known equally on both sides of the Atlantic. She has accumulated most major awards for her acting and has been especially praised for the musicality of her voice and her commanding stage presence; Worth is held in high esteem by both critics and colleagues. After teaching for several years, she turned to the stage, making her professional debut with a touring company in 1942, then appeared a year later on BROADWAY with Elisabeth Bergner in *The Two Mrs Carrolls*. Seeking classical training, she went to London in 1944 to study with Elsie Fogerty. Her first noteworthy appearance in London was as Ilona in MOLNÁR's *The Play's the Thing* (1947). She appeared as Celia in the premiere of *The Cocktail Party* at the EDINBURGH FESTIVAL (1949). After working with the OLD VIC Company (1951–3), she helped found (with TYRONE GUTHRIE and ALEC GUINNESS) the STRATFORD FESTIVAL (Ontario) in 1953. Following a succession of critically acclaimed portrayals in London, New York and Stratford, Ontario, she joined the ROYAL SHAKESPEARE COMPANY, appearing as Goneril in PETER BROOK's production of *King Lear* (1962). Other notable appearances in the past quarter of a century have included *Tiny Alice* (New York, 1964; Royal Shakespeare Company, 1970), COWARD's *Suite in Three Keys* (London, 1966), *Heartbreak House* (Chichester, 1967), Brook's controversial *Oedipus* (NATIONAL THEATRE, London, 1968), *Hedda Gabler* (Stratford, Ontario, 1970), *The Seagull* (Chichester, 1973), *The Cherry Orchard* (New York City, 1977), *John Gabriel Borkman* (NYC, 1980), a 'majestically unruffled' Volumnia in *Coriolanus* at London's National Theatre (1984), GURNEY's *The Golden Age* (NYC, 1984) and Grandma Kurnitz in *Lost in Yonkers* (NYC, 1991; film version, 1993), for which she won her third Tony (the others being for *Tiny Alice* and a 1975 revival of *Sweet Bird of Youth*). A one-woman show in 1993–4 was based on the works of Edith Wharton. DBW

wuju Chinese dance drama; a modern form of drama incorporating Chinese folk dance and Western ballet techniques. *Wuju* instrumentation combines Western and Chinese instruments. Harmonic structure tends to follow Western rules while melodies are characteristically Chinese in flavour. The first large-scale *wuju* drama was *The Precious Lotus Lamp* (*Baolian deng*, 1957). Set in the mythical past, it is a fantasy about a goddess who comes to earth and falls in love with a mortal. After being suppressed during the Cultural Revolution *wuju* regained popularity immediately after the fall of the 'gang of four'. In Shanghai in 1977, *The Small Sword Society* (*Xiaodao hui*) praised the 19th century rebel movement of the title. Many dance dramas feature stories, dance movements and musical elements from China's minority nationalities.

None is better known, either in China or outside, than *Tales of the Silk Road* (*Silu huayu*), created in 1977 by members of the Gansu Song and Dance Ensemble and since then frequently revived. The plot is set in the Tang dynasty and concerns a slave-dancer who is taken to Persia by a rich merchant of that country to escape an evil magistrate. The ending sees the magistrate punished and happy relations between Persia and China. What is distinctive about the piece is that the costumes and many of the dance movements derive from postures shown in Tang-dynasty wall paintings in the Dunhuang caves in Gansu Province. The music, a mixture of styles and melodies, attempts to capture the atmosphere of medieval China and Persia. Other important productions of the 1980s include several based on the classical novel *A Dream of Red Mansions* (*Honglou meng*) and one adapted from TANG XIANZU's *The Peony Pavilion*. CPM

Wycherley, William 1641–1715 English playwright. Sent to France as part of his education, he later trained for the law. His first play, *Love in a Wood* (1671), gained him both a high literary reputation and the Duchess of Cleveland as his mistress. After *The Gentleman Dancing-Master* for the Duke's Company (1672), Wycherley wrote the two masterpieces that confirmed his reputation as the most brilliant satiric dramatist of his day, *The Country Wife* (1675) and *The Plain Dealer* (1676). From this point his career went downhill and he did not write another play. Seriously ill in 1677, he lost favour at court after marrying the Countess of Drogheda against the king's wishes; she proved not to be the rich heiress he had supposed. Imprisoned for debt in 1685 after her death, Wycherley was released and given a pension by James II after a court performance of *The Plain Dealer*. He published a massive volume of poor poetry in 1704 and began a friendship with Pope, who helped revise his later poems. His death-bed marriage, into which he was tricked by a distant relation, was almost a bizarre scene from one of his own plays.

The genial SATIRE of his first plays reached a climax in the verve of *The Country Wife* where, borrowing the device from TERENCE, the hero, Horner, pretends castra-

tion as a cover for his affairs, exposing the follies of society. It continued to be performed in the 18th century in GARRICK's anaemic adaptation, *The Country Girl* (1766). *The Plain Dealer* is a very dark rewriting of MOLIÈRE's *The Misanthrope*, an unwieldy play of enormous power tracing the deceptions of love and friendship with a central figure, Manley, an obsessive and savage satirist; it was prefaced when published with a dedicatory epistle to a famous London bawd. PH

Wyndham, Charles [Charles Culverwell] 1837–1919 British actor and theatre manager, who was already a qualified doctor when he made his debut on the professional stage in 1862. This first venture was short-lived, and Wyndham went to the USA, where he enlisted as a surgeon in the Federal Army during the Civil War. During 1870–2, he took his own Comedy Company on a pioneering tour of Midwest theatres, presenting T. W. ROBERTSON's *Ours* and *Caste* and JAMES ALBERY's *Two Roses* to predominantly novice audiences.

Wyndham's acting style in these early days was modelled on that of the quick-fire, gentlemanly CHARLES JAMES MATHEWS. When Chicago audiences complained about his staid, English repertoire, he added the recent American hit, BRONSON HOWARD's *Saratoga*, and it was as bustling Bob Sackett in that play, revamped for London audiences by Frank Marshall as *Brighton*, that he began to establish his reputation after returning to England in 1872. The significant step into management came in 1875, at London's Criterion, in which he retained an interest for the remaining 44 years of his life, bequeathing it to his son and stepson, Howard Wyndham and Bronson Albery. The Criterion was a small basement theatre and Wyndham had the good sense to exploit its intimacy in a series of society FARCES, the first being Albery's *The Pink Dominos* (1877), mostly taken from French originals whose impropriety was expurgated but still discernible.

A handsome man, Wyndham retained a female fan-club for longer than seems likely. His favourite part was the virtuoso title role of T. W. Robertson's *David Garrick*, but the Criterion is (and was) associated rather with the society comedies of HENRY ARTHUR JONES, particularly *The Case of Rebellious Susan* (1894) and *The Liars* (1897), in both of which Wyndham excelled as a wise *raisonneur*. In 1899, the prime minister, the Marquis of Salisbury, agreed to the building of a theatre on land he owned only on condition that Wyndham would assume the management. Wyndham's Theatre opened the same year with a revival of *David Garrick*. It would later house Jones's *Mrs Dane's Defence* (1900), in which Wyndham as Sir Daniel Carteret coolly destroyed Mrs Dane in the famous cross-examination scene, and the first English performance of ROSTAND's *Cyrano de Bergerac* (1903), in which the title role was beyond his range (he was 66). Wyndham was knighted in 1902, and the following year a third theatre, the New, opened under his management. Three years before his death he married his leading lady, Mary Moore (1869–1931), widow of the playwright James Albery. The marriage established a surviving theatrical dynasty. PT

Wynn, Ed [Isaiah Edwin Leopold] 1886–1966 American comedian. Wynn began in VAUDEVILLE in 1901, later teaming up with Jack Lewis as two collegians in the act 'Rah, Rah, Boys'. Starting with the ZIEGFELD *Follies* of 1914 and 1915, he found a comfortable solo niche in MUSICAL COMEDY, including *The Perfect Fool* (1921), which became his nickname, *Simple Simon* (1930), *The Laugh Parade* (1931) and *Hurray for What?* (1937). Wynn's stage persona wore horn-rimmed glasses and tiny pork-pie hats, spoke with a lisp, giggled and walked with a mincing gait. Many of his GAGS were predicated on an inability to complete an anecdote or a piece of music; his insane inventions included a typewriter carriage for eating corn-on-the-cob and a cigarette lighter that pointed out the nearest matches. From 1932 to 1937 he was 'the Fire Chief' on radio; in the 1950s and 60s he played dramatic roles in films and television. His son was a prominent film actor.   LS

Wyspiański, Stanisław 1869–1907 Polish painter, poet, playwright and man of the theatre who studied at the Cracow Academy of Fine Arts, and in Paris. Drawing upon Polish romantic drama, particularly MICKIEWICZ's ideas, he revolutionized stage design (see THEATRE DESIGN) and production in his work for the Cracow theatre. His *Study of Hamlet* (1905) calls for a synthesis of the arts, with stress on setting and COSTUME. His plays, symbolist in orientation (see SYMBOLISM), interweave the real and fantastic, and join Polish history to Greek and biblical myth. Plays on national issues include *Song of Warsaw* (1898), *The Wedding, Deliverance* (1901), *November Night* (1903), *Acropolis* (1904) and *Legend* (1905); those on mythological themes are *Protesilas and Laodamia, Achilleis* (1903) and *The Return of Odysseus* (1907).   DG

xinbian lishi ju (newly arranged historical drama) Branch of drama in one of CHINA's numerous regional styles in which the story is set before the 20th century. The term applies almost exclusively to those dramas written under the influence of the CCP.

Music is composed especially for each play following the melodic patterns and texture of the particular regional style of which it is representative. COSTUMES and make-up take their style from traditional theatre, with variations. On the other hand, there are complex scenery and stage properties and the tendency is for the drama to last a full evening. There is usually a definite structure in the plot, which rises to a climax and conclusion. Normally the plot is set in the dynastic past, and, despite the term 'historical drama', may be based on a mythological story rather than historical fact. There is considerable room for a political message and the great majority of 'newly arranged historical dramas' carry a clear ideological viewpoint. Since 1978 the quantity of dramas written in this form has been greater than for any other, with more and more themes and stories being dug up from the vastness of Chinese history and mythology. In the early days of the PRC, dramas in this category tended to give centre stage to representatives of the masses, including peasant rebels, oppressed women and patriots. In the 1980s and 90s class struggle has been downgraded as an ideological factor generally, including in dramatic characterization, and as a result emperors and scholars can be presented in the favourable light of having made a contribution to the Chinese nation. CPM

Xirgu, Margarita 1888–1969 Spanish actress, company director and theatre teacher. A legendary figure in Hispanic stage history, she began acting at 12 in CATALAN THEATRE. As head of her own company, she premiered plays by GARCÍA LORCA, VALLE-INCLÁN, CASONA and Rafael Alberti. In 1933 her version of *Medea* inaugurated modern use of the Roman theatre in Mérida, the site of annual festivals of classical theatre. Exiled in Latin America after the Civil War (1936–9), she promoted Spanish authors while also strengthening ties with the French stage. She made a major contribution in Argentina, established Chile's first theatre arts school, and served as director of the School of Dramatic Art in Montevideo, Uruguay. PZ

Yacine, Kateb 1929–89 Algerian francophone playwright whose work is both densely poetic in texture and firmly committed to political struggle. Criticism of French colonial policies led to the banning of his early plays in the 50s (see CENSORSHIP) but SERREAU succeeded in producing *Le Cadavre encerclé* (*The Surrounded Corpse*) in 1958 and *Les Ancêtres redoublent de férocité* (*Ancestors Become More Ferocious*) in 1967 at the THÉÂTRE NATIONAL POPULAIRE. His play celebrating Ho Chi Minh, *L'Homme aux sandales de caoutchouc* (*The Man with Rubber Sandals*), was deemed subversive enough for the mayor of Lyon to cut MARÉCHAL's subsidy when he produced it in 1971. After his involvement with Théâtre de la Mer from 1970, Yacine developed an idiosyncratic form of popular theatre in spoken Arabic and Berber, of which the outstanding example is *Mohamed, prends ta valise*, a constantly reworked play based on the experiences of immigrant Algerian workers. DB

Yakovlev, Aleksei (Semyono-vich) 1773–1817 Russian actor. Along with E. S. SEMYONOVA, one of the great St Petersburg actors of the day and a forerunner of the later romantic performance style. A pupil of DMITREVSKY, rival of and successor to Shusherin, Yakovlev was not one for careful preparation of a role or the continued development of his craft over the course of a career. Instead he brought inspired emotionalism, manly good looks, a sonorous voice and wildly uneven play to his impersonation of KOTZEBUE's sentimental characters and OZEROV's noble heroes (Oedipus, Fingal and Dmitry Donskoi). He was the first Russian actor to appear in a series of roles adapted from SHAKESPEARE and SCHILLER, including Othello in a translated French version (1806), Edgar in Gnedich's *King Lear* (1807), and Karl Moor (1814). Unrequited love for a married actress led to melancholia, drink, the destruction of his talent, attempted suicide and finally death. SG

yakshagana Generic term identifying a variety of theatre forms of south INDIA, the best-known of which is found in the south Kanara region of Karnataka state. *Yaksha* are the demigods associated with Kubera, god of wealth, and *gana* is a song. Thus, *yakshagana* means 'songs of the demigods'. Historical evidence suggests that the *yakshagana* of south Kanara originated in the 16th century or earlier. The earliest written playscript for Kanara *yakshagana* dates from the first half of the 16th century when Kandukuru Rudrakavi wrote the play *Sugrivavijaya*, the story of the monkey king who overthrew his powerful brother, based on incidents from the *Ramayana*.

Yakshagana is popular with rural audiences. Companies are itinerant organizations managed by temple authorities. The manager of the troupe contacts the players (a minimum of 15 people are required to produce a performance) and the musicians (a minimum of five are needed). Touring begins from the home temple and engagements are organized during the festival season which lasts approximately six months, between November and May. The manager makes all the formal arrangements with a patron, including place of performance, cooking arrangements and living accommodation which is either in a local temple or the home of a Brahmin. During the initial contact, a RITUAL exchange takes place between patron and manager, usually on the morning of performance, and the full payment for the show is provided the morning after, just prior to the departure of the actors for their next engagement. The manager usually hires a staff of at least ten helpers to assist in the cooking, to prepare the accommodation and to transport costume and prop boxes.

Yakshagana is a lively, fast-paced form in which songs, dances and improvised dialogue mix according to a prescribed structure. At the heart of *yakshagana* are the poetic songs (*prasanga*) sung by the chief musician (*bhagavata*), who thus controls the pace of the performance. The most popular of these songs have been transcribed and published, even those from hundreds of years ago. With their particular melody (*raga*) and metre intact, they constitute a major part of the historical record of regional Indian dramatic literature. Today published editions of *prasanga* are to be found in paperback editions in bookstalls along the roadside in rural areas of Karnataka.

Improvised dialogue (*matu*) by the actor-dancers expands on the content of the songs. Until recently, this portion was not written down because it changed from night to night and from actor to actor. Most *prasanga* are based on stories from the great Hindu epics, the *Mahabharata* and *Ramayana*, and from the *Purana* and concern serious events from the lives of well known epic figures. Humour is inserted in the performance by the clowns (*hasyagar*) through comic antics and witty remarks.

The acting area (*rangasthala*), a space near the house of the patron, may be a paddy field cleared of stubble, or the open ground in front of a temple compound. Tall bamboo posts demarcate the four corners of a rectangle 15 x 20ft. Mango leaves, flowers, coconuts, plantains and coloured paper provide a festive, simple decoration. At the centre of one of the narrow ends of the acting area a wooden table is placed on which the chief musician sings and plays the *maddale* drum. Behind this is a collapsible four-wheeled cart, the only functional piece of furniture and scenery used during performance. Standing between the musicians is a man who plays the *shruti*, a simplified version of the harmonium which keeps the underlying pitch necessary to guide the singer's melodies. On the right side of the playing area, sitting on a chair facing the acting area, is the *chende* drummer. The area between the pillar and the table up left is used for entrances. Some distance away on the left side of the acting area, actors gather in an improvised dressing room made of thatch walls. A space between the *chende* player and the table is reserved for exits.

The audience sits on three sides of the rectangle, the women and children separate from the men. Oil lamps are placed stage right and left facing the acting area but electric lights and petromax lanterns have become popular today to help the spectators to see the action better. A simple curtain with the troupe's name embroidered on it is used for dance entrances of major characters or groups of dancing characters. Admission is usually free to the public. Petty merchants display their wares, such as sweets, tea and snacks, outside the audience area and conduct a brisk business among the spectators through the long hours of the night. Performances begin with rituals about 9.30 p.m. and continue uninterrupted until sunrise when they are concluded by ritual prayers.

Some troupes give performances in a tent in order to control attendance. Tickets are sold and folding chairs are provided for a fee. A raised proscenium stage is used for these performances and the style of dance and acting has assumed unique features which distinguish it from that of the open-air troupes. These performances are known as tent drama (*tent atta*).

During the monsoons which hit the area from June to September, *yakshagana* is presented in the homes of patrons or in enclosed halls. The actors sit on the ground to sing the *prasanga* and perform truncated improvised dialogue with musical accompaniment. These performances are known as *tala maddale*.

Costumes and make-up for the *yakshagana* of south Kanara are unique. Big heart-shaped headdresses are worn by the warriors, crowns of wood covered with tinsel paper are worn by kings and large impressive headdresses are worn by demons whose spiky make-up distorts the actor's facial features beyond recognition.

In the same region another style of *yakshagana* is practised, called *yakshagana tekutittu* ('the southern style of *yakshagana*'). Its vigorous dances and music are reminiscent of KATHAKALI dance drama of neighbouring Kerala state.

The term *yakshagana* is also applied to performances in Andhra Pradesh and Tamil Nadu states. Some say that the term *isai* used in *Silappadikaram*, a famous Tamil epic poem of the 8th to 10th centuries, refers to a prototype of *yakshagana* which came from Kerala and imitates *kathakali*. Others say that the *yakshagana* of Andhra Pradesh originated in the 14th century and that it began as a dance interpretation of one character who took many roles.

Later it added a second character, a female counterpart. In this phase, the male was called *yaksha* and the female was known as *yakshi*. In the course of time, a clown was introduced to provide humour and finally a fortune teller came into the picture. At this stage, it is said that *yakshagana* served as a model for KUCHIPUDI, which 'upgraded' the form by bringing in classical Karnataka music and elaborate acted dances that follow the dictates of the *Natyasastra*. In any case, *yakshagana* performed in Andhra Pradesh is different from that of Karnataka and less sophisticated visually. FAR

Yale Repertory Theatre Adjunct to the Yale School of Drama (established as a graduate school in 1955) in New Haven, Connecticut, which in turn grew out of the Drama Department founded in 1925 by GEORGE PIERCE BAKER. This important RESIDENT NON-PROFIT PROFESSIONAL

THEATRE was founded in 1966 by ROBERT BRUSTEIN, who served as artistic director until 1979. In 1968 it moved into a church converted into a theatre with a thrust stage and seating for 487. Central to each season under LLOYD RICHARDS, who served as artistic director from 1979 to June 1991, were SHAKESPEARE, ATHOL FUGARD (seven plays in all) and especially AUGUST WILSON, as well as the Winterfest of New Plays. Richards was succeeded by Stan Wojewodski Jr, formerly of Baltimore's Center Stage.

Among important new works premiered at Yale were ERIC BENTLEY's *Are You Now or Have You Ever Been ... ?* (1972), Robert Lowell's version of *Prometheus Bound* (1967), KOPIT's *Wings* (1978), three plays by EDWARD BOND (including *Bingo* in 1976), several plays of Fugard (including *A Lesson from Aloes*, *Master Harold* and *The Road to Mecca*) and all of Wilson's plays up to 1991.   DBW

Yankee theatre (USA) Yankee actors achieved their greatest popularity between 1825 and 55, though Yankee characters appeared both earlier and later. The first notable 'Jonathan' – the most common name (or nickname) – was in ROYALL TYLER's *The Contrast* (1787); the last, Joshua Whitcomb in DENMAN THOMPSON's *The Old Homestead* (1886). The stage Yankee possessed varying mixtures of the character attributes ascribed to rustic New Englanders ('down-easters'): he was simple, blundering, sentimental, parsimonious, patriotic, shrewd, critical of city folks and devoted to tall tales and picturesque speech. This character was a storehouse of riches for eccentric comedians, many of whom began their careers as Yankee storytellers before appearing in plays.

The English comedian CHARLES MATHEWS was the first to discover the gold mine of good fun to be found in the Yankee, in his *Trip to America* (1824) and *Jonathan in England* (1824). Four American actors quickly followed his lead:

1 J. H. HACKETT in his own *Sylvester Daggerwood* (1826), as Solomon Swap in *Jonathan in England* (1828), as Major Joe Bunker in *The Militia Muster* (1830), and as Lot Sap Sago in Cornelius A. Logan's *Yankee Land* (1834);

2 GEORGE HANDEL ('Yankee') HILL, often called 'the most authentic', as John Bull disguised as Jonathan Doolittle in WILLIAM DUNLAP's *Trip to Niagara* (1828), as Jonathan in SAMUEL WOODWORTH's *The Forest Rose* (1832), in *Jonathan in England* (1932), as Jedediah Homebred in JOSEPH S. JONES's *The Green Mountain Boy* (1833), as Sy Saco in JOHN AUGUSTUS STONE's *The Knight of the Golden Fleece; or, The Yankee in Spain* (1834), as Hiram Dodge in *The Yankee Pedlar* (anon., 1835), as Abner Tanner in Jones's *The Adventurer; or, The Yankee in Tripoli* (1835) and as Solon Shingle in Jones's *The People's Lawyer* (1839);

3 DANFORTH MARBLE in E.H. Thompson and Marble's *Sam Patch* (1836), as Deuteronomy Dutiful in Logan's *The Vermont Wool Dealer* (1838), as Jacob Jewsharp in J. P. Addams's *The Maiden's Vow; or, The Yankee in Time* (1838), as Solon Shingle in Jones's *The People's Lawyer* (1839) and as Lot Sap Sago in Logan's *The Wag of Maine* (1842);

4 Joshua Silsbee in *The Forest Rose* (1840), in *The Yankee Pedlar* (1841), in *The Green Mountain Boy* (1853) and in *The Vermont Wool Dealer* (1853).

In the 1830s and 40s, the Yankee actors were extremely popular in London, where critics found them not unlike 'our own canny Yorkshire lads'. RM

Yanovskaya, Genrietta Contemporary Russian director, who along with her husband and fellow director Kama Ginkas studied with TOVSTONOGOV. In Leningrad in the 1980s, Yanovskaya staged SHVARTS's *Little Red Riding Hood* at the Vologradsky Palace of Culture, and VOLODIN's *Dialogs*, which included a spontaneous exchange between author, actors and audience, at the Blue Bridge People's Theatre, an amateur collective which she headed. Her Maly Dramatic Theatre production of TENNESSEE WILLIAMS's *The Glass Menagerie* offered a banjo-playing Tom and an omnipresent and dancing father in a heavily stylized *mise en scène*. Her most successful production, a MEYERHOLDian staging of BULGAKOV's *Heart of a Dog* at the Moscow Theatre of the Young Spectator, which she runs, played several international festivals in 1988–9. She has also staged *Goodbye America!*, a revue satirizing Soviet attitudes towards the West. SG

yaryu (literally, 'field play') Korean masked plays performed in towns in South Kyongsang province near Pusan are called *yaryu*, referring to the outdoor nature of the performance. Like OGWANGDAE, the plays are short with four or five scenes. An example is the four-scene *yaryu* play performed at Suyong village. Performance consists of two parts, a procession followed by the mask play. The procession involves singing, dancing and exorcistic ceremonies. Both players and villager audience march together from the village well to the performing area. Eleven MASKS were employed for the performance of Suyong *yaryu*. OKC

Yeats, W(illiam) B(utler) 1865–1939 Irish playwright. Yeats's ambition for Irish theatre was that it should stimulate, through his own plays, a poetic celebration of Irish legend and history, heroic and mythic in scale, yet with the ironic tone he admired in SYNGE. So in Yeats's *On Baile's Strand* (1904) the Blind Man and the Fool PARODY Conchubar and Cuchulain.

Formally, Yeats rejected the dominant theatrical REALISM, contemporary subjects and painstakingly authentic sets. A bare stage with merely suggestive properties – a blue cloth for a well – would enable verse to make drama a sacred rite, expressed also through dance, music and MASKS. For this drama 'close to pure music' Yeats found precedents in the French symbolists, and from 1916, instructed by Ezra Pound, in Japanese NŌ plays. Throughout his career, however, his attachment remained to 'the sovereignty of words'.

These formal concerns did not imply a drama insulated from life. Yeats's early plays are in part political parables. *The Countess Cathleen* (1899) belongs to his myth of the Anglo-Irish aristocracy. *Cathleen ni Houlihan* (1903) is a patriotic allegory. *The King's Threshold* (1903) asserts the poet Seanchan's place among the lawmakers.

The burden of ABBEY THEATRE management impeded Yeats's own work. Between 1904 and 1910 his only major plays were *Deirdre* (1906), *The Golden Helmet* (1908) and its verse adaptation *The Green Helmet* (1910). Apart from *The Words upon the Window Pane* (1930), conjuring

Swift's ghost to a seance, in prose and with a realistic setting, his later work experiments with verse and symbolist theatre (see SYMBOLISM). It has effective dramatic moments. In *At the Hawk's Well* (1916) words unite with songs, Edmund Dulac's masks and the hawkdance performed by Michio Ito, to enact Cuchulain's heroic resolution. In *The Dreaming of the Bones* (1931) the dance and parting of Diarmuid and Grania, traitors 700 years dead, are memorably succinct. *Purgatory* (1938 – Yeats's last appearance at the Abbey) embodies in its fable of murderous family decadence his bitter judgement on modern Ireland. The problem remains, however, of a verse that is lyrical, expository, meditative – not dramatic.

Yeats's plays, infrequently performed, never won the popular audience for which he hoped. Nor did they revive verse drama in the 20th century. They are astonishing sketches, by an indisputably great poet, for a verse drama never fully realized. He was awarded the Nobel Prize in 1923. DM

Yiddish Art Theatre (USA) MAURICE SCHWARTZ's company, which opened at the Irving Place Theatre in New York in 1918. Rejecting the popular sentimental and melodramatic improvisations of SHUND [rubbish] THEATRE in favour of carefully rehearsed plays of quality, ensemble acting and a high standard of presentation, its first successes came with PERETZ HIRSHBEIN's earthy pastoral play *The Forgotten Nook*, followed by the same writer's *The Blacksmith's Daughter*, another delicate, idyllic play of village life. During its second year (its first as the YAT), 15 plays were added to the repertoire, including SHOLOM ALEICHEM's *Tevye the Milkman* and four of JACOB GORDIN's plays, including *God, Man and Devil*, based on the Faust legend. Inevitably 'stars' were created, like Bertha Gerstein, LUDWIG SATZ and Muni Weisenfreund (PAUL MUNI). Several productions in English translation transferred to BROADWAY, including Schwartz's greatest personal triumph: Israel Joshua Singer's *Yoshe Kalb*. The company continued active until the late 1930s. AB

Yiddish theatre Indigenous Jewish theatre was forbidden for centuries on religious grounds. Deuteronomy 22:5, which stated that 'a man shall not put on a woman's garments', was construed as prohibiting dressing up in any clothes other than one's own, thus presenting an insuperable obstacle to theatrical performance. A connection was also invoked between drama and idol worship. A single exception was permitted during the festival of Purim, when Bible stories, particularly that of the deliverance of the Jewish people by Esther, could be told dramatically in the form of a *Purimspiel* (see PURIM PLAY). It was not until the last quarter of the 19th century that a general movement away from religious restriction had spread sufficiently to allow the belated beginnings of an endemic Jewish theatre. (See also HEBREW THEATRE.)

There had been plays written and published sporadically from as early as *The Exodus*, by Ezekiel, in the 2nd century BC, and particularly in Holland and Italy in the 16th and 17th centuries, but these were intended for reading, not performing. Aaron Halle Wolfsohn's *Frivolity and Hypocrisy*, for example, was published in 1798, intended as an alternative to the simple and often bawdy Purim plays. The two published plays of greatest historical importance were *Reb Henoch* by Isaac Eichel, which appeared in Germany in 1793, and Solomon Ettinger's *Serkele*, written in Russia in 1825 but not published until 36 years later. The latter play, skilfully constructed and with closely observed characterization, received a school performance in 1861 in which the title part was played by a young student called Avraham Goldenfudim (AVROM GOLDFADN), later to earn the title of 'father of the Yiddish theatre' by bravely presenting – in Romania – the first public performance of a Yiddish play (October 1876). The play presented was almost certainly *The Recruits*, a Schweik type of broad comedy, although the subject was anything but funny at the time. Goldfadn had included many of his own songs, thus setting a pattern of musical theatre which was to last.

The venture was a great success and the theatrical floodgates suddenly burst open. New companies sprang up everywhere, split up and multiplied, all following Goldfadn's pattern of musical plays written at a simple, folksy, emotional level, each company employing a resident 'writer' to supply story-lines and songs. The rest was improvised.

Stylistic traditions peculiar to Yiddish theatre were developed by Goldfadn for his unsophisticated audiences, and adopted by all the companies. Thus a doctor always wore rimless spectacles, a simpleton had his shirt-tail hanging out, marriage-brokers carried an umbrella, students held a book and rich men a cane. Colour had special significance: a white robe with a blonde wig indicated an angel, a red outfit and a black wig signified a devil. Beggars always wore black, but a black robe indicated the Angel of Death. Villains wore red wigs and heroes black ones. The atmosphere at performances was close to that of a family gathering or a communal celebration, with a quite unique emotional rapport between actors and audience.

With the banning of all Yiddish theatre in Russia following the assassination of Tsar Alexander II in 1883, and the escalation of Jewish persecution in Europe, a general exodus began. The theatre companies went with the people, establishing themselves in England, France and the Argentine, for example, but particularly in America, where performances quickly became a vital social, educational and cultural influence amongst rapidly growing Yiddish-speaking communities. Theatres appeared in most of the large cities, particularly Chicago, Boston, Philadelphia and San Francisco. Within a short time no fewer than 11 Yiddish theatres were functioning in New York alone. Prolific writers like MOISHE HURWITZ AND JACOB LATEINER began churning out potboilers, each of which combined pathos and comedy in the Goldfadn style, a form not dissimilar from the later work of Chaplin. Extrovert actor-managers like BORIS THOMASHEFSKY and MAURICE SCHWARTZ became matinée idols.

The more cultured members of the community looked down upon this popular 'greenhorn' and 'peasant' theatre as unworthy, and movements towards a Jewish art theatre materialized in Europe and later in America, nurtured by the serious-minded Yiddish drama and literary clubs and semi-professional groups such as FOLKSBIENE and ARTEF, before spreading to the professional theatre. Jewish art theatre first manifested itself in Odessa in 1908, on the lifting of the 25-year ban on performances, when PERETZ

HIRSHBEIN formed the Hirshbein Troupe, with JACOB BEN-AMI as leading actor. Rejecting improvisation, he directed plays by JACOB GORDIN, SHOLOM ASCH, ISAAC PERETZ, DAVID PINSKI and SHOLOM ALEICHEM, in addition to his own plays. Hirshbein disbanded the company after two seminal years in order to devote more time to writing, but the main fruits of his labours were to come later in Vilna, Moscow and New York.

In 1916 the celebrated VILNA TROUPE appeared, quickly achieving a style and character of its own. Under the direction of DAVID HERMAN, Hirshbein's protégé, it developed a repertoire of over 100 plays, embarked on a brilliantly successful series of world tours and built up an enviable reputation for distinctive stylization and ensemble playing. At about the same time ESTHER KAMIŃSKA and her Warsaw company were also producing some remarkable work, which was continued by her daughter IDA KAMIŃSKA until the 1939 Nazi invasion. The company was re-formed after the war as the Polish State Yiddish Theatre and is one of the two remaining state-funded full-time Yiddish theatres, the other being the Romanian State Yiddish Theatre. The MOSCOW STATE JEWISH THEATRE resulted from the wave of creative enthusiasm which followed the Russian Revolution in 1917, and, under the inspired leadership of ALEKSEI GRANOVSKY, with designers like Marc Chagall and Nathan Altman, composers like Alexander Krein and M. Milner and actors like SOLOMON MIKHOELS and Benjamin Zuskin it achieved world fame with productions of plays by Aleichem, Mendele Mocher Sforim, Goldfadn and, particularly, SHAKESPEARE.

In America a high-quality Yiddish theatre flourished for two decades following the First World War, led by Maurice Schwartz and his YIDDISH ART THEATRE, which combined ensemble playing with high production values and brought forth actors of the calibre of Celia Adler (daughter of JACOB ADLER), BERTHA GERSTEIN, LUDWIG SATZ, Jacob Ben-Ami and Anna Apfel, designers like BORIS ARONSON and MORDECAI GORELIK who went on to international fame, and plays by writers of quality such as Hirshbein, Gordin, Fishel Bimko and OSSIP DIMOV – in addition to introducing many of the great European dramatists, in translation, to America. Ben-Ami's short-lived JEWISH ART THEATRE reached probably the highest point of theatrical achievement. EMANUEL REICHER, who had been an associate of REINHARDT and later became director of the THEATRE GUILD, was engaged as director, and the objectives of the company were closely modelled on those of the MOSCOW ART THEATRE.

Yiddish theatre went into a worldwide decline in the 1930s, by which time the Yiddish language had virtually fallen into disuse. A large body of plays remain and although most of them, written for unsophisticated audiences, served their purpose and are better forgotten, there are many such as the plays of ANSKI, Hirshbein, Aleichem and Asch which will hold their own in any company. AB

See: B. H. Clark and G. Freedley, *A History of Modern Drama*, New York, 1947; D. S. Lifson, *The Yiddish Theatre in America*, Cranberry, NJ, 1965; H. Madison, *Yiddish Literature, Its Scope and Major Writers*, New York, 1968; N. Sandrow, *Vagabond Stars*, New York, 1977; *The Drama Review*, Jewish theatre issue, 24, 3, 1980.

Yorkshire Tragedy, A A TRAGEDY, probably first performed in 1606 when it was part of the repertoire of the King's Men at the GLOBE THEATRE. The title page of a 1608 edition claims SHAKESPEARE as the author, but the most that can be supposed is that he had some hand in cutting the play down into the truncated form in which it has survived. The play is based on the story of Walter Calverley, executed for murder in 1605. It describes with grim haste the passage from gambling debts to the attempted murder of all his family (wife and one son survive) to arrest and final repentance. PT

Yoruba Travelling Theatre

For some three decades, from the mid-1950s, the most widespread theatrical enterprise in NIGERIA. The Yoruba Travelling Theatre attained the status of a movement with a sense of group identity within, as B. Jeyifo has noted, a 'divergent and distinct stock of conventions, staging techniques and modes of organisation'. This corporateness was recognized by the founding and nurturing, by the late HUBERT OGUNDE (d.1990), of an umbrella structure called the Association of Theatre Practitioners of Nigeria (ATPN), to which most of the troupes belonged. After three decades spent taking theatre to the people, from the early 1980s onwards the Yoruba Travelling Theatre turned increasingly from live performance to film, television and video production. By the mid-1990s live performance has become a rarity; though companies continue to thrive, they now work almost exclusively through electronic media. The term 'Yoruba Travelling Theatre' is now, therefore, something of a misnomer. It has been retained here, however, because there is substantial continuity between the aesthetic and theatrical methodology of the component companies' earlier live performances and those of their current video and television productions.

In its modern form, the Yoruba Travelling Theatre movement's professional existence is just 50 years old, having taken off with Ogunde's 'concert party' in 1945. But its genesis must be seen in the centuries-old religious and secular oral performing arts of the Yoruba, blending with the performances and entertainments which evolved out of the contacts with Western European culture.

Historically, the Yoruba have a long theatre tradition. As Bruce King and other critics of African theatre have established, the 'preference for drama among Yoruba ... has a tribal basis. Yorubas often speak of their various forms of masquerade (see MASQUERADES IN AFRICA) and RITUAL as dramatic art.' The ritualist origin of the Yoruba theatre has even been traced to the 'theatrogenic' nature of a number of the deities in the Yoruba pantheon, such as Obatala the god of creation, Ogun the god of creativeness and Sango the god of lightning, whose 'cults of worship', as Jeyifo has commented, are vitally connected 'with drama and theatre and their symbolic and psychological uses'. WOLE SOYINKA tells us that both Obatala and Ogun are prototype 'personalities' in the emergence of Yoruba drama. But the rituo-secular protoform of the modern Yoruba Theatre is the *Alarinjo* tradition, the most advanced form of the traditional theatre among the Yoruba people. The *Alarinjo* is an itinerant professional troupe of masked dancer-mummers. They present satirical skits assembled from a range of stereotypical charac-

ters, employing music, MIME, drama, ACROBATICS and spectacle. *Alarinjo* is the predominant influence on the modern Yoruba Travelling Theatre, to which it bequeaths its structural and thematic characteristics. European-derived influences include OPERETTA, VARIETY shows and, especially, the biblical dramas that were performed by Lagosian social and church societies from the turn of the century and well into the period when Ogunde was developing his stagecraft.

Initially, the term 'operatic' applied to the Travelling Theatre's performance mode especially during the first decade of Ogunde's concert-party enterprise between 1945 and the mid-50s, when the limited dialogue linked singing in the tradition of opera. But the predominant mode of the Travelling Theatre later changed, with the performance being delivered through elaborate and eloquent acted dialogue and robust action. The essential Yoruba Travelling Theatre is dramatic rather than musical or operatic. The other common, and more appropriate, appellation of 'folk-theatre' derives from the Theatre's cross-class character as opposed to the elitist 'high-culture' literary theatre. The Yoruba Travelling Theatre is primarily a popular cultural expression and secondarily, though no less importantly, theatrical and dramatic expression (Jeyifo, 1984).

Notable scholars of this theatre movement have ascribed to it an almost inviolable conventional format, viewing the Yoruba Travelling Theatre as a structural derivative of the performance idioms of traditional Yoruba art forms (specifically the *Alarinjo* theatre, the *Ewi* poetic chants and the performances of the *egungun* society), with an 'opening glee', the 'play proper' and 'closing glee'. This format was imposed on the modern Travelling Theatre, and to deviate from it was seen as an aberration – in critic Ebun Clark's words, 'a dissociation of content with form'. At best, this model may be proposed as a means of delineating a certain aesthetic specific to the Yoruba Travelling Theatre movement, which distinguishes it in all its divergent forms. This aesthetic comprises (1) the language of the performance, (2) the utilization and exploitation of the indigenous traditional artistic resources, and (3) the basic underscoring *oeuvre* which informs the practitioners' presentation. But apart from most of Ogunde's productions, the other stalwarts of the Yoruba Travelling Theatre have hardly adhered to the traditional format; MOSES OLAIYA ADEJUMO, still arguably the greatest commercial success story of this tradition, is radical to the point of having introduced into the start of his performances film projections of foreign documentary and other cinematic productions. Indeed, this novelty was the genesis of the eventual abandonment by Yoruba Travelling Theatre of live performance in favour of film and video.

Yoruba is the primary language of communication and performance of the Yoruba Travelling Theatre troupes, performing in the Yoruba sub-region of over 20 million Nigerians as well as in neighbouring states. (A few troupes, including Hubert Ogunde's, used to perform in pidgin in eastern and western states to non-Yoruba audiences.) Aesthetically, the competence in discourse characteristic of Yoruba oral literature – one of the most highly articulate in Africa – also informs the theatre. The success of the performance is determined by the dexterity of the artists, and their fidelity to the Yoruba verbal arts. Hence, the less illusionistic their theatrical display – which they achieve through the simultaneous use of drumming, singing, costuming, acrobatics and movement, blended with the Yoruba verbal arts of oratorical chant, vocal music, word-play and poetry, mime and costume – the more authentic the performance and the more the audiences value it. As Jeyifo has observed, the Yoruba Travelling Theatre is a 'highly liberating, actor-oriented theatre where the outcome of any performance is a factor of the mode of rapport between the actors on stage and the popular audience'.

Essential to the Yoruba Travelling Theatre is the moralist stance of most of its practitioners (beginning with Ogunde himself, and especially Kola Ogunmola). This moralism is a reflection of the living experiences of the popular masses at whom the performances are aimed. Indeed, the artistic success of the troupes' performances is determined, mainly, by the degree to which the plays impress the popular audiences and deal with their reality. Issues that carry concrete and direct economic, political and social implications for the lives of their audiences attract the troupes' attention. Hunger, squalor, social deviance, corruption, and all the other issues of the daily working lives of the people, provide the Theatre with its main themes. At the same time the social norms projected by this theatre can be seen, in certain respects, to be highly conservative and have been questioned by radical English-language dramatists such as FEMI OSOFISAN. The Yoruba Travelling Theatre's tendency to stereotype has ideological implications: in the case, for instance, of its frequently dismissive treatment of independently minded or non-submissive female characters.

Only a few of the troupes and the artists of the Yoruba Travelling Theatre are well known – Ogunde, Olaiya, Jimoh Aliyu and a few others. However, by 1988 there existed nearly 150 troupes in the movement, with the body of plays in the various repertoires numbering several thousands. The companies constitute themselves into their professional guild, founded by its doyen and patron Hubert Ogunde, the Association of Theatre Practitioners of Nigeria (ATPN). They are not all necessarily made up of full-time employees: many of the practitioners who give their name to a company hire artists on an ad hoc basis.

During the period when the Yoruba Travelling Theatre was mainly devoted to live performance, companies would go out from their home base (usually Lagos) to reach all corners of Nigeria, as well as West African countries such as Ghana, Togo and Benin, to become the most mobile theatre movement in African history. Each live performance was generally preceded by heavy publicity via radio and television advertising, newspaper items and notices, printed handbills and direct contact with troupe patrons. All these prepared the eager popular audiences, on whom the commercial success of the troupes depended. On the evening of the performance a rousing campaign would be staged on company buses, from which music and songs were broadcast. The performance was tailored to the environment and to the tastes of the specific audience, while the comedy and song, the dance and the skits, all reflected the trademarks of the particular troupe. The orchestras of most travelling theatre troupes blended European instruments with indigenous traditional ones, though some relied solely on Yoruba instruments. Some troupes opened their performance with comic dialogues and monologues alternating with ribald songs and dances.

Besides undertaking road tours, from 1959, when the first television studio in Africa, Western Nigerian Television (WNTV), was established, the Yoruba Travelling Theatre battled successfully to supplant foreign programmes on Nigerian television screens. The main electronic medium for spreading theatre, the radio (see RADIO DRAMA), had been slow in taking off. Ogunde, and later Baba Sala (alias Moses Olaiya Adejumo), had significant exposure through the radio. But it was television that really gave prominence to the travelling theatre – from the broadcasting of live performances to the adaptation of Yoruba novels and historical documentaries into TELEVISION DRAMAS (for example, Oyin Adejobi's group appeared in Ekuro Oloja, while Efunsetan Aniwura featured Oshola Ogunshola's troupe, both on WNTV Ibadan).

From the late 70s practitioners of Yoruba Travelling Theatre began to experience constraints in live performance, and to seek other outlets. The most attractive was film. The reasons are not far to seek. Ade Afolayan had blazed the trail into the glamorous arena of movies with his Ija Ominira, and now, after over three decades on stage, Ogunde looked in that direction. The cinema provided a more satisfying medium, offering flexibility and limitless expansion in the content and range of their work. Awareness of the transitory nature of their productions – largely non-scripted and improvisational – drove the Yoruba Travelling Theatre to seek more permanent modes. Unlike stage productions, which may vanish after a few performances, films enjoy a high degree of permanence. All the major protagonists of the Yoruba theatre entered the film industry as a complementary enterprise to their main stagecraft.

A number of outstanding films result from this: after Afolayan's Ija Ominira came Moses Olaiya Adejumo's Orun Mooru and Aare Agbaye, and the remarkable and large-scale cinematic creations of Ogunde. Ogunde was the most accomplished professionally, recording his films on a permanent location, a film village that he built in Ososa, his home town. Having started in 1979 with a metaphysical Yoruba epic, Aiye, he followed rapidly with Jaiyesimi (1980), Aropin N'tenia (1983) and Ayanmo (1988). The films of most of these practitioners tend to offer mystery and mysticism, with a large dose of magic and exoticism. They are full of macabre and grotesque images rooted in Yoruba mythology. The films revolve around the central theme of morality: the perennial conflict between good and evil, with good constantly triumphing. The films' titles reveal both their reliance on these themes and the need to attract the attention of potential customers with the lure of the sensational or scandalous: Iya m l'aje (My Mother is a Witch) and Ashewo to re Mecca (A Prostitute Goes to Mecca), for example.

In the mid-1990s a further technological development has taken place, as the companies have moved away from reel film and turned to video. Some, such as Olaiya's, record on video for screening in cinema auditoriums, jealously guarding against piracy; others screen their videos over a year or two and then duplicate them for market retail. The more successful companies continue to work on television too.   CD OO

Yoshizawa Ayame I 1673–1729 Genroku-period Japanese *KABUKI* actor. He was instrumental in advancing the art of portraying female characters (*onnagata*) beyond the exhibitionism and eroticism of early cross-dressing. Unmatched in courtesan roles, such as Mitsu in *The Prostitute of Mount Asama* (*Keisei Asama ga take*, 1689), Ayame was praised for 'realistic' characterization, and in his memoirs, *My Advice to Onnagata* (*Ayame gusa*; trans. 1969), he insisted the actor should live totally as a woman offstage in order to bring a sense of reality to his performance of a woman onstage.   JRB

Youmans, Vincent 1899–1946 American composer. Youmans served in the Navy during the First World War, then worked as a song plugger and rehearsal pianist before contributing songs to *Two Little Girls in Blue* (1921) and ultimately writing the scores for two of the most successful MUSICALS of the 1920s: *No, No, Nanette* (1925) and *Hit the Deck* (1927). Songs by Youmans were also heard in *Great Day* (1929), *The 9:15 Revue* (1930), *Smiles* (1930) and *Take a Chance* (1932). Although Youmans's output was relatively small, many of his songs, such as 'Tea for Two', 'I Want to Be Happy', 'Hallelujah', 'More Than You Know' and 'Time on My Hands', have become classics of the musical stage.   MK

young people's theatre (YPT) (Britain) Umbrella term to cover all forms of theatre work for and with young people. There are broadly four major kinds of young people's theatre: (1) *theatre for children and young people* (professional theatre for younger and older age groups); (2) THEATRE-IN-EDUCATION (theatre with explicitly educational aims, usually operating in schools); (3) a variety of activities which may be grouped under the heading *education in theatre* (also referred to by such terms as 'play days' and 'theatre appreciation' programmes) – work done by repertory and YPT companies designed *either* to provide a service to schools for the study of examination play texts, *or* to stimulate an interest in and increase understanding of the theatre. Lectures, demonstrations, workshops, and performances of short plays or play extracts, on tour or in a theatre, are some of the events that may be offered. And in (4) *youth theatre*, workshops and productions are prepared and performed *by* young people, sometimes organized through the local repertory or YPT company, sometimes by the drama adviser of the local education authority; and sometimes, on a larger scale, through an independent self-governing body such as, most notably, the NATIONAL YOUTH THEATRE.

Theatre for children and young people Professional theatre consisting of self-contained performances given by touring or building-based companies before (usually) large audiences. Performances designed specifically for the younger age range (up to 14) are usually referred to as 'children's theatre', while those for the older (15 plus) age range are usually described as 'young people's theatre'.

Apart from the occasional 'classic' plays written for chil-

dren and families (such as J. M. BARRIE's *Peter Pan*, 1904), frequently revived at Christmas-time, the early ventures into children's theatre in Britain, before the First World War, were almost exclusively devoted to encouraging an appreciation of SHAKESPEARE. Foremost was BEN GREET's company, which performed Shakespeare in different parts of London at special low rates for schoolchildren, and simultaneously organized extremely popular competitions for the performance of scenes from Shakespeare by the pupils themselves. Immediately after the war the London County Council agreed to bear the cost of a season of Shakespeare matinées for schools at the OLD VIC, so that children could see the plays free of charge. An important precedent was thereby established: the Old Vic school matinées became a regular feature, and in 1924 the Board of Education officially agreed that school visits to see Shakespeare productions could be considered a legitimate part of children's education and subsidized accordingly.

Also in 1924, Bertha Waddell founded the Scottish Children's Theatre to present drama that could genuinely be enjoyed by children, especially young children, at their own level – not Shakespeare, but short plays, dance, MIME and song, drawing on folk tales, nursery rhymes and ballads and with much emphasis on music, movement and colour. Such was the success of her work that in 1937 Glasgow Education Authority agreed to allow junior school children to attend performances free of charge within school hours.

Although other companies were formed during the 30s (notably Peter Slade's Parable Players in 1935), they mostly tended to be short-lived and cautious in their programming. During the final years of, and immediately following, the Second World War, however, the pace of development and innovation accelerated. Slade started a new company in 1945 (the Pear Tree Players), whose aim was not only to present scripted plays but to employ improvisation and teaching skills within its performances. Earlier, in 1943, the Children's Theatre Players were formed in Birmingham and the Motley Players in Aberdeen. And in 1943 Brian Way, an actor with the Old Vic, began taking small presentations into schools while on tour, and the following year founded the West Country Children's Theatre whose productions deliberately avoided the use of the conventional stage and technical effects, encouraging instead a high degree of audience participation. Way's experience led him to found the influential Theatre Centre in 1954, based in London but touring with several companies up and down the country. Participation was a key element in their performances, and Way wrote many plays and adaptations to this end. Other schemes initiated at this time included Tom Clarke's Theatre for Youth at the Argyle Theatre in Birkenhead (1944); the Compass Players (1944–52), touring; Glyndebourne Children's Theatre (1945–51), touring; the YOUNG VIC (1946–51), touring; and Caryl Jenner's English Children's Theatre (1948). The latter was founded originally as a mobile theatre unit based in Amersham, and moved in 1967 to London, where it became the Unicorn Children's Theatre, based at the ARTS THEATRE, performing mainly during afternoons.

The postwar acceleration was, however, short-lived. Despite provision in the 1944 Education Act for the subsidy of theatre company visits to schools and of school visits to theatres, little money was forthcoming and many companies stopped in the early 1950s for want of funds. The companies that did survive did so on a shoestring: overworked, underpaid short-stay actors and hastily rehearsed productions combined to produce much shoddy work. Standards were maintained primarily by the Theatre Centre and the Unicorn.

In 1965 the ARTS COUNCIL was persuaded by this unsatisfactory state of affairs to set up a committee of inquiry into the provision of theatre for young people. It noted that there were some 12 professional YPT companies in existence: some were touring companies while some (such as the Everyman in Liverpool) were based in a theatre building. Five companies were selected for immediate life-saving grant aid, and from 1967 to 68 a special allocation was made to help promote YPT schemes, including children's theatre, primarily through the repertory theatres. An upsurge of activity followed. A major new young people's theatre company was founded (the reinvented Young Vic, with a bias mainly towards the older age range), and the range of work offered thenceforward into and throughout the 70s was noteworthy, if not always consistent in quality or quantity. Even in the 1980s, when government money for the performing arts was severely reduced in real terms, the attention given to young people by theatre companies was considerable. By 1992, even in the midst of recession, there were approximately 35 companies offering children's theatre as their main or sole activity, in addition to which there were puppet and dance theatre companies and those theatre-in-education and community companies whose repertoire also included children's theatre work of some kind. Most children's theatre consists of touring companies; just two are building-based: the Unicorn and the Polka, both in London.

Accompanying and closely bound up with this increase in the number and type of such companies has been a quite marked change in the content of the plays presented. Fantasy is still common, but more adventurous, contemporary and thought-provoking material is now often to be found, especially in the work of the specialist companies. Not only is there the ever-present *Peter Pan* and the plays of the prolific David Wood, but there are also, to mention just three very different examples, the highly successful 'Peace Plays' by David Holman, toured by Theatre Centre in 1982; the much acclaimed *Raj* (about the last days of British rule in India) by the Leeds Playhouse TIE Company (1983 and often revived); and Noel Greig's *Best of Friends*, a sensitive look at gay sexuality, for older teenagers (1986). AJ

See: A. England, *Theatre for the Young*, London, 1990; L. Swortzell (ed.), *International Guide to Children's Theatre and Educational Theatre*, 1990.

Young, Stark 1881–1963 American drama critic, translator, playwright and director. Born in Mississippi, Young earned degrees in English at the University of Mississippi (1901) and at Columbia University (1902). After teaching in several universities, he became a contributing editor to *New Republic* in 1921 and an associate editor of *Theatre Arts* (1921–40). Young replaced Francis Hackett as chief drama critic of the *New Republic* in early 1922 and held

the position (except for the 1924–5 season, when he reviewed for the *New York Times*) until his retirement in 1947. He was an advocate of the New Stagecraft movement and worked closely with EUGENE O'NEILL, KENNETH MACGOWAN and ROBERT EDMOND JONES at the Provincetown Playhouse. He staged the premiere of O'Neill's *Welded* in 1924. Young wrote several plays, none successful. He is better remembered for his translations of CHEKHOV's plays, especially of *The Seagull* for the LUNTS in 1938. His books include *The Flower in Drama* (1923), *Glamour* (1925), *Theatre Practice* (1926) and *The Theatre* (1927). His letters, edited by J. Pilkington, were published in 1975. TLM

Young Vic (London) There have been two Young Vic schemes. The first was initiated by GEORGE DEVINE as a touring children's theatre attached to the OLD VIC company. Its first production was in December 1946, and for five years under Devine's direction the company, aided by a small ARTS COUNCIL grant, built up a high reputation for the standard of its productions. Audiences, mainly from 9 to 15 years of age and above, grew, but the problems of attracting suitable new plays, insufficient finance and disagreements over direction of the Old Vic as a whole brought the scheme to an end in 1951.

The second scheme began, as part of the NATIONAL THEATRE's programme for young people, with the opening of the Young Vic Theatre – the first purpose-built young people's theatre in Britain – in 1970. The auditorium seats 450–500 people around a central (or sometimes a thrust) stage, and there is now additonally (since 1984) a small studio theatre seating 110. The purpose has been to make theatre of the highest standard – classics, specially written plays and experimental work – available to students and young people in an unpatronizing, exciting manner and at affordable prices. FRANK DUNLOP, the theatre's first director, established it as a completely independent organization in 1974. AJ

Yu Zhenfei 1902–92 Chinese actor in KUNQU and JINGXI. He was born in Suzhou, the son of Yu Zonghai – an erudite *kunqu* authority – under whom he had his first lessons at the age of six. After apprenticeship under both *kunqu* and *jingxi* master actors, he quickly became acclaimed for the perfection of his interpretations of the young scholar-hero (*xiaosheng*) in *jingxi*, regularly partnering MEI LANFANG. Through a long professional career Yu also worked indefatigably to preserve *kunqu*, training a new generation of performers at the Shanghai Municipal Academy of Dramatic Art in the 1950s until his work was disrupted by the Cultural Revolution. He was an accomplished flute (*dizi*) player as well as singer and actor, and the author of a treatise on *kunqu* acting. ACS

yueju (Guangdong opera) *Yue* (another name for Guangdong) *ju* (drama) is the regional form of music drama of Guangdong Province, CHINA. It is popular also in southern Guangxi, HONG KONG and Macao and among those overseas Chinese communities of North America, Australia and elsewhere whose ancestors came from Guangdong.

Guangdong opera belongs basically to the PIHUANG system of music drama, although the two styles, *erhuang* and *xipi*, have been much changed under the influence of local music. Cantonese folksongs, *KUNQU* and other tunes have been absorbed. Accompanying instruments include the end-blown flute and double-reeded *suona* as well as strings and percussion. Western violin and saxophone were added in the 1920s and remain in use today. There is a certain mellifluousness in the texture of many of the singers' voices, as well as in the accompanying orchestra.

There are basically ten role categories. Male characters are termed *mo* or *sheng*. In contrast to most contemporary styles of Chinese music drama, the latter is not normally the main role. Other roles are painted-face (*jing*), female (*dan*), and clown (*chou*), whose face is not painted white around the eyes, as are clowns in other opera forms.

The first famous actor of Guangdong opera was Zhang Wu in the 18th century. He came from Hubei Province, where *pihuang* music was practised, so perhaps he was the person who introduced the style to Guangdong. Zhang Wu settled in Foshan, took on students, established a troupe and founded the Qionghua Guildhall for actors. Later influxes of actors of *pihuang* music, from Anhui and Hunan Provinces, strengthened that system's impact on Guangdong opera.

In 1854 the well known actor Li Wenmao (d.1861) collected three armies and rebelled against the government in support of the Taiping uprising (1851–64). When the rebellion was defeated, Guangdong opera also was proscribed for being subversive. The Qionghua Guildhall was destroyed and thereafter the centre of a revived Guangdong opera was Guangzhou.

Because Guangdong is adjacent to the British colony of Hong Kong, Guangdong opera has been more subject to foreign influences, especially the film, than any other form of Chinese music drama. Early in this century urban actors began to experiment with more naturalistic movements and gestures, to discard traditional embroidered costumes in favour of the more realistic costumes being used in the spoken drama and film, and to use scenery on the stage. Some new operas were explicitly political in their content, such as one in praise of the female anti-Manchu revolutionary Qiu Jin, who was beheaded in 1907.

Except for the Cultural Revolution decade (1966–76), Guangdong opera has done well under the PRC. The state-run Guangdong Provincial Guangdong Opera Company was established in 1958. There has been a tendency to return to traditional usage in some aspects of stagecraft such as costuming, movements and gestures. CPM

yueju (Shaoxing opera) A style of drama (*ju*) of the Yue region in CHINA, the ancient state corresponding approximately to Zhejiang Province; usually termed Shaoxing opera or Sheng County theatre in English after its place of origin, Sheng County in Shaoxing, east Zhejiang Province. It was formed in the 20th century, outside of any of the major musical systems of local Chinese drama, by peasant balladeers singing folksongs who joined into small drama troupes. Musical accompaniment was through percussion or chorus.

In 1916 the actor Wang Jinshui brought Shaoxing opera to Shanghai. He and others greatly expanded its scope by absorbing melodies from other local styles of eastern Zhejiang, adding string and other instruments to the accompanying orchestra and expanding the available rhythmic structures. In 1923 a training school for girls was set up in Sheng County and from 1928 all-female companies prospered in Shanghai, competing with male companies. By the mid-1930s virtually all performers of Shaoxing opera were female.

As a result romantic love stories are the strong point of Shaoxing opera and military scenes and acrobatics are totally absent. The most famous of the early stories, retaining its popularity today, tells of the love between Liang Shanbo and Zhu Yingtai: they elope, die under tragic circumstances and are transformed into butterflies, hence the name by which the piece is often known in English, *The Butterfly Lovers*.

Under the leadership of actresses like Yuan Xuefen (1922–) staging was reformed in the 1940s. Lighting and scenery were extensively used in traditional and 'newly arranged historical' (*yueju*) music dramas. A soft style of costuming was created that combined influences from *JINGXI* and historical *HUAJU*. Designs for female costumes copied old pictures of beautiful women, and soft colours and crepes and georgette replaced bright satins, to accord more closely to *yueju*'s romantic style.

The government of the PRC has generally encouraged Shaoxing opera, allowed its traditional romantic repertory, while urging mixed male and female troupes. Major professional performances use an orchestra that includes some Western instruments, especially the violoncello to provide a stronger bass to the music. Actors now perform some male roles, especially evil ones, but actresses still predominate and in particular play the important scholar-lover (*xiaosheng*) roles. CPM

Yugoslavia

Early theatre A historic term nowadays, meaning the land of South Slavs, that existed between 1918 and 1991. From the period of Roman dominance of the Balkans some remains of Graeco-Roman theatres are still preserved in Croatia, Macedonia and elsewhere. Slavic tribes moved in the 6th and 7th centuries to the peninsula and overpowered the indigenous tribes. The cultural development of the population was strongly influenced by several neighbouring foreign powers whose rule or dominance lasted for centuries: Byzantium, Turkey, Italy (especially Venice), then Austria-Hungary. Thus, even if one Yugoslav state were still in existence it would nevertheless be impossible to speak of one unifying theatrical tradition, as circumstances, conditions and influences varied to a great extent from one part to another. Continuous professional theatre activity started only in the mid-19th century, but since then theatre has played a significant role in the development of national identity, and has served as an influential forum for the dissemination of social and political ideas.

The popular RITUALS, dances and choral songs preserved in the villages contain noticeable paratheatrical elements, in both the Catholic and Orthodox traditions. Although even the most elaborate of these rituals rarely use MASKS, they do rely on very ornate costumes. Among ritual presentations, best known are the *vertep*, a nativity scene with three kings, and various forms of prayers for rain in the dry summer months. Elements of Christian belief are commonly intertwined with older strata, usually from the ancient religion of the Slavs or from the cults of the original non-Slavic inhabitants of the Balkans. Other forms sprang out of specific historical experiences, such as the *moresca*, a dance still performed on the Adriatic island of Korčula, which has a clear narrative line: the liberation of island maidens kidnapped by Moorish pirates.

The Middle Ages to the 17th century In all probability, entertainers and JUGGLERS from Byzantium appeared in the courts of Serbian and Bosnian medieval rulers and nobles in the 12th century. After the arrival of the Turks (14th–15th centuries), theatrical activity of any sort must have been quite scarce there: clowns, called *pelivans*, and dervish dances, and puppet theatre of the KARAGÖZ type. The Christian population under Turkish rule kept its cultural identity in marginal theatrical forms: public recitation of epic folk poetry about medieval nobles and later heroes of the anti-Turkish resistance, accompanied by the *gusle*, a one-stringed instrument.

In the western mainly Catholic parts, religious plays were performed during the 14th century, utilizing Old Testament material and various apocrypha, with local vernaculars sometimes used instead of Latin. The earliest surviving dramatic text of a secular nature is *The Slave Woman* (1520) by Hannibal Lucić, an aristocrat from the island of Hvar, where a theatre building – still well preserved today – was erected in 1612.

The impact of the Italian Renaissance was felt all along the coastal area as well as on the islands, but it was strongest in Dubrovnik; as a semi-independent city state, Dubrovnik possessed an urban concentration and an active social life that favoured the appearance of guest players and entertainers, and encouraged the emergence of local amateur groups. The players, usually engaged and paid by the city government for celebrations such as the pre-Lenten CARNIVAL, were sometimes hired by local patrons for family festivities as well. The repertory of comedies and PASTORALS, influenced by Italian models, was set early in the mid-16th century, first of all by MARIN DRŽIĆ, then expanded in the 17th century by other local authors. In the 18th century, free adaptations of MOLIÈRE's comedies, altered to local circumstances and translated into the local dialect, were popular in Dubrovnik. Some of these have been revived successfully in recent times.

The 18th and 19th centuries Theatre began to play a more political role in the struggles both for national emancipation of the South Slavs, and against the policies of cultural assimilation imposed by the Austrian Empire. In the 18th century local Slavic languages were occasionally used in performances in schools, Jesuit seminaries, cultural societies and libraries. Still, while Hungarian and German troupes started to appear regularly in Slovenia and Croatia, and Italian and sometimes French companies toured the coastal areas, amateur performances of the local Slavs remained sporadic until the 1840s. After two uprisings, in 1804 and 1815, the Serbs won semi-independence from the Turks, and Joakim Vujić, a dilettante actor and one of the champions of itinerant amateur theatricals among the Serbs in Austria, arrived to found the Serbian Principal Theatre in Kragujevac in 1834. Although his

effort was short-lived, and although Vujić himself was more an adapter than an original dramatist, his enthusiasm stimulated the formation of itinerant companies that within a few decades evolved into professional troupes, and further led to the establishment of the Serbian National Theatre in Novi Sad and of the Croatian National Theatre in Zagreb, both in 1861. These two theatres became important instruments in the struggle of Serbs and Croats in the dual monarchy for their cultural autonomy and ultimately their political independence. Belgrade became the site of the National Theatre in 1868, the year of the Turkish withdrawal from their garrisons in the young principality, and a similar Slovenian theatre society was soon formed in Ljubljana.

The national repertory of Slovenes, Croats and Serbs followed two major lines: historic or pseudo-historic plays of old glory, calling for the rebirth of long-lost independence; and comedies of bourgeois manners, often with mild SATIRES of government corruption and incompetence, of yearning for class elevation and ennoblement. The heroic plays effectively protracted the romantic spirit right up to the end of the century, agitating and glorifying, imitating the versification of popular epic poetry and leading to a performance style that was often loaded with displays of knightly bravado and with ranting rhetoric on patriotism, manliness and self-sacrifice. The comedies, more urbane and contemporary in their concerns, inaugurated a realistic style, even when they contained folkloric elements, and were enriched with songs, dances and rifle shooting, as the old playbills proudly announced. This entertaining amalgam, similar to the German SINGSPIEL or Spanish ZARZUELA, carried a new set of values to a society that was – while proclaiming its allegiance to the old heroic myths – eager to break through its agrarian matrix.

The establishment of national repertory companies with permanent ensembles permitted the steady introduction of foreign dramas, translated into Slovenian and Serbian/Croatian, often indirectly (e.g. English drama through German) and not always very competently. Besides standard classical works, theatre audiences were familiarized in the last three decades of the 19th century with comedies, FARCES, *vaudevilles* and MELODRAMAS imported from the BOULEVARD stages of Paris, Munich and Vienna. KOTZEBUE, SCRIBE and their lesser followers helped establish among new theatregoers the bourgeois stage and its problems and concerns, clearing the way for the works of IBSEN and, later, HAUPTMANN. The transition to NATURALISM and later SYMBOLISM came at the turn of the century, mainly in Croatia and Slovenia, through German influences. The plays of the Slovene author Ivan Cankar are representative of this process. They contain strong attacks on the philistinism of petit-bourgeois Slovenia, its political conservatism, clericalism and social conformity (*Scandal in the St Florian Valley*, *The Servants*, *The Beautiful Vida*, 1907–11); but they also often possess a poetic detachment, a yearning for the kind of utopian beauty found only in national myths or in resigned daydreaming.

In organization and technology, the existing theatres mainly followed the practices of the Vienna BURGTHEATER; the standardized sets were initially ordered from

Hungarian and Austrian workshops, while the acting and directing styles were inspired by the stages of Vienna and Munich.

1918–1945 In the new Yugoslav state, established in 1918 from the independent states of Serbia and Montenegro and from Slovenia, Croatia, Vojvodina and Bosnia and Herzegovina, ruled by the Austro-Hungarian monarchy, older theatres and the newly formed ones were entitled to a steady government subsidy that came with direct ministerial control. Theatre professionals were treated as civil servants, with yearly contracts. Traditional performing styles were modified by the influence of German EXPRESSIONISM and of Russian REALISM associated with STANISLAVSKY. Two visits by the MOSCOW ART THEATRE in the 1920s, and the absorption of several Russian émigré designers, directors, choreographers, musicians and acting coaches, perpetuated this influence.

The period between the two world wars was marked by the consolidation of theatre life, and by the emergence of directing as a clearly distinct task separate from acting, as embodied in the erudite and truly cosmopolitan figure of Branko Gavella, active in several Central European theatres. Painters and architects elevated the importance of the visual aspects of production. Famous international actors and companies made guest appearances. OPERA and ballet became a regular part of the repertory, at least in the major theatres with resident ensembles. Theatre CRITICISM in newspapers and magazines reached a new sophistication and competence.

Among playwrights of merit, only BRANISLAV NUŠIĆ and MIROSLAV KRLEŽA exercised a durable impact on the repertory. The 1941 occupation of the country by German and Italian forces and their Hungarian and Bulgarian allies did not stop all theatre activity. However, many prominent artists chose to stay away from the stage in those times of mass humiliation and suffering; others joined Tito's partisan forces, as did most of the cast of a *Faust* production in 1942, fleeing from the Zagreb theatre to the liberated territory. They formed the core of the Theatre of National Liberation that was active in Tito's army throughout the war.

1945–1991 In the new Communist state new companies were formed in many places. All theatres were entitled to receive municipal and state subsidies, and the combination of very low-priced tickets and the Party's educational policies brought in masses of new theatregoers. There was genuine and widespread enthusiasm for theatre art, despite the fact that strict ideological standards were in force. Initially the repertory was dominated by domestic classics and works by Russian and Soviet authors, and Stanislavsky's system – in its 'socialist-realism' version – was imposed on theatres as a binding model.

After Yugoslavia's break with Stalin in 1948 and her strategic orientation towards her own original and independent type of socialism (developed in defiance of the Soviet model), socialist realism was quickly abandoned and new venues for artistic expression were gradually opened and enlarged. This policy of aesthetic pluralism, tolerance and freedom of artistic creation – albeit unable to prevent occasional attempts by politicians, especially

on the local level, to interfere in repertory matters – served to place the ultimate responsibility on theatre professionals within the permanent ensembles. Their 'self-management' authority was limited by the supervision of officialdom, often via trusted representatives who sat on the theatre boards.

When the Yugoslav Drama Theatre was formed in Belgrade in 1948, it was conceived as the central representative ensemble, the embodiment of the best features of the Yugoslav theatre. Under the energetic leadership of its director and designer, Bojan Stupica, it earned its first international credits with its successful appearance at the Paris THÉÂTRE DES NATIONS in 1954. Its reputation was further enhanced by several subsequent international tours. But after the late 1950s no one theatre was able to claim to represent the essence of the Yugoslavian stage, as the federal structure of the country – together with a very high degree of decentralization – resulted in a chequered theatrical map, with distinct features evident in each individual federal republic. In Macedonia, for example, the Macedonian language has been spoken regularly and legally on the stage only since 1945, although sporadic efforts to use it instead of Turkish, Bulgarian or Serbian date from the turn of the century. Codification of the Macedonian literary language, its grammar and orthography almost paralleled the development of Macedonian drama (K. Čašule, G. Stefanovski, J. Plevneš). A policy of full cultural and educational development of ethnic minorities resulted in permanent professional ensembles that performed in Hungarian, Albanian, Turkish and Italian, while amateur groups utilized virtually all of the ten languages spoken in the country, including Romani (Gypsy). The centres of the six federal republics had several repertory theatres each, and at least one such theatre existed in another 30 cities. There were 70 repertory theatres in all, including ten operas with ballet and 15 theatres for children. Institutions for the training of theatre professionals were established in all major centres and integrated into the university system, supported by several theatre museums and research centres and specialized periodicals (*Scena, Prolog, Maska, Teater, Pozorište*).

Although the contemporary theatre has never lacked great actors, and adventurous directors have been active throughout the postwar period (Milošević, Spaić, Belović, Korun, Paro, Mijać), the development of playwriting was noticeably delayed. Foreign works from the West had been shown frequently since early in the 1950s and had been received with enthusiasm. Coming as they did after a period of collective passions and experiences, these imported plays helped reintroduce to the Yugoslav stage individual concerns and intimate issues. Belgrade's Atelje 212, founded in 1956, conquered the last ideological suspicions against the works of the European avant-garde, from JARRY to GENET, yet lacked similar works by domestic authors for its repertory.

Native Yugoslav playwrights made their postwar start only in the 1950s (Matković, Marinković); established themselves in the next decade (Smole, Hristić, Lukić); gained popularity in the 70s (Brešan, Popović, Jovanović); and finally conquered the repertories in the 80s (Seligo, Snajder, Kovaćević), reducing the role of the classics and even of contemporary foreign works. This popularity of new domestic works was based on several factors: on their candid and searching consideration of all significant issues of Yugoslav society, including the most sensitive ones; on their frequent re-examination of recent national history; and on the fact that these plays brought to the stage the debate about the destiny of the multi-ethnic Yugoslav community and its particular brand of socialism, exploring those contradictions that were to explode in the violent civil war of 1991. Very few of these plays have been published or produced abroad, but some have been seen by foreign audiences during the not infrequent tours by Yugoslav theatres to Eastern and Western Europe, and, in a few instances, to North and South America and Australia.

Yet, despite the popularity of national drama, the still-prevalent blueprint for repertory theatres – with permanent ensemble and large administrative and technical staff – in time began to manifest problems: those of routine, inertia, wastefulness, and a dependence on subsidies for 85–90 per cent of the budget. The challenge to this system came from an increasing number of independent groups, composed of freelance professionals and dissatisfied members of institutionalized troupes. Even with meagre means and often short lifespans, these groups managed to create work of high quality and to tour extensively, crossing both the linguistic and bureaucratic boundaries of the former federal republics.

These different theatrical realms were linked by tours and festivals. The National Drama Festival, inaugurated in Novi Sad in 1956 with the explicit aim of stimulating Yugoslav playwriting and of enhancing its standing, had grown into an important theatre institution – Sterijino Pozorje – active in publishing, documentation, international relations, and the organization of exhibitions and conferences. The Dubrovnik Summer Festival must be given credit for the development of environmental theatre in the country – turning Dubrovnik's ancient courtyards, fortresses, squares and parks into performing sites for the plays of her own native sons, Držić and Ivo Vojnović, as well as for productions of SHAKESPEARE, GOLDONI and Krleža, and for operas, concerts, presentations of folklore, and classical and modern dance. Over 30 different sites in Dubrovnik have been used for performances. Summer festivals of international, national and regional importance have been regularly held in other cities (MES in Sarajevo, Eurokaz in Zagreb, Split Summer in Split). From 1967 Belgrade's BITEF (the Belgrade International Theatre Festival) featured the most important avant-garde works from all over the world, and influenced such innovative directors as Dušan Jovanović, Lj. Ristić and S. Unkovski.

Ironically, the great diversity and vitality of the performing arts, sustained throughout the 1980s despite serious economic problems, suffered with the arrival of political pluralism and multi-partyism in 1990. Theatre lost its privileged position of rare forum for the political debate, as political rallies, newly elected parliaments and increasingly pluralist media took over that role. Theatre professionals could derive their social prestige from the perception of the stage as a cornerstone of national cul-ture, but the escalation of national sentiment to chauvinist proportions forced theatre to either serve the exclusivist ideologies and secessionist projects or turn to a primarily entertainment role. As in other realms of public life, the essentially vivid and cosmopolitan atmosphere of Yugoslav theatre, visible in directorial and acting styles, in repertories and design, became threatened by self-imposed ghettoization, parochialism and conservative backlash in the name of separate ethnic identities – Serb, Croat, Slovene, Macedonian, Montenegrin, Albanian, Muslim, Hungarian.

The post-Yugoslavia situation The war of 1991 in Slovenia and then Croatia, followed by the rampage in Bosnia and Herzegovina since spring 1992, brought to an end the Yugoslav state and drew new, much contested borders. Military operations, the pauperization of society, the presence of millions of refugees – disrupted theatre life or made it possible to continue only under the most trying circumstances. Theatre professionals shared the fate of the population: many were killed, maimed, dispersed or otherwise made homeless. Their working relations disrupted, circuits broken and facilities damaged or destroyed – as in Osijek, Sarajevo, Mostar and elsewhere – they have continued to produce and perform, as circumstances have allowed. Audience interest has remained strong, even in the besieged city of Sarajevo where Susan Sontag staged BECKETT's *Waiting for Godot* in August 1993, under the flickering light of a few candles and solar batteries. Among dramatic responses to the traumatic experience Dušan Jovanović's *Antigona* and Goran Stefanovski's *Sarajevo, a Tale of the City* (both 1993), are worth noting. Yet the brutalities of the war, political pressures, and uncertainty over the future have necessarily curbed the artistic development and wasted much of the talent in the successor states.   DK

See: BITEF catalogues, Belgrade, annually from 1967; *Bulletin, Choice of Yugoslav Plays, 1968–78*, Novi Sad and Belgrade, 1979; *Godišnjak jugoslovenskih pozorišta*, published annually by Sterijino Pozorje, Novi Sad; B. Mikašinović (ed.), *Five Modern Yugoslav Plays*, New York, 1977; *Scena*, Novi Sad, yearly issues in English from 1978.

Yurka, Blanche 1893–1974 Czech-born actress. Taken to the USA as an infant, Yurka began acting in 1907 after training for OPERA. She applied to DAVID BELASCO successfully for work on the legitimate stage, her first leading role being in *Is Matrimony a Failure?*. Over the next decade she shifted to TRAGEDY, playing Gertrude to John Barrymore's (see DREW–BARRYMORE FAMILY) Hamlet (1922), Gina in *The Wild Duck* (1925), and later a series of strong-willed female roles, winning praise for her emotional depth and vocal timbre. She was also an active member and organizer of American Actors' Equity, being elected to a variety of positions in that organization. In 1955 she retired from the theatre, decrying the poverty of the theatre at that time, but soon returned to both films and BROADWAY. She often wrote (including an autobiography, *Bohemian Girl*, 1970) and lectured about the theatre.   SMA

Zacconi, Ermete 1857–1948 Italian actor and company manager. Born to the profession, he was a child actor and acquired wide stage experience, notably with the actor-manager GIOVANNI EMANUEL, by whose naturalistic style (see NATURALISM) he was much influenced. In 1897 he formed his own company, and his repertoire included much modern drama in the naturalistic vein (including IBSEN, TOLSTOI and GIACOSA) as well as Shakespearian tragedy, in which he was notable as Macbeth, Othello, Lear and Hamlet. For a time he worked with DUSE in her attempts to launch the new poetic drama of D'ANNUNZIO, and later appeared with her at the end of her career in Ibsen's *The Lady from the Sea* (1921). He continued to be a lead actor in the Italian theatre until the Second World War. His career in the cinema was lengthy and included silent film versions of his stage successes, such as Ibsen's *Ghosts* (1917). LR

Zadek, Peter 1926– German director. As director of the Bochum Schauspielhaus (1972–5), he set out to rid SHAKESPEARE of the aura of high art. His long, brightly lit, ramshackle productions of *The Merchant of Venice* (1972), *King Lear* (1974), *Othello* (1976) and *Hamlet* (1977), often with the house lights up, were acclaimed as a breath of fresh air after the arty stylization of the previous generation. Spontaneity, directness and whimsical costumes, usually from stock, have been his trademark – Cordelia sat on Lear's knee in a pink tutu. Zadek has regularly produced TANKRED DORST, who adapted Fallada's novel *Little Man, What Now?* for him as a political REVUE.

WILDE, O'CASEY, BEHAN, OSBORNE and TREVOR GRIFFITHS have all featured in Zadek's project, which was to provoke the middle-class, middle-brow season-ticket-holders, while attracting and entertaining a new, younger audience. He is also capable of sensitive productions of IBSEN, WEDEKIND and CHEKHOV, notably a spellbinding *Platonov* in Vienna, using no more than a bare stage and an array of old chairs. Zadek was director of the Hamburg Schauspielhaus from 1985 to 89, and has been since 1992 a director of the BERLINER ENSEMBLE. HR

Zaire After 75 years of colonial rule, the former Belgian Congo, now Zaire, was hurriedly granted independence in 1960. The new state had very little experience in self-government and it was soon engulfed in a civil war during which its first prime minister, Patrice Lumumba, was assassinated. The events of this period have been dramatized in various plays, the most important of which are AIMÉ CÉSAIRE's *Une Saison au Congo* (*A Season in the Congo*, 1966), and *Murderous Angels* (1968) by the Irish diplomat and academic then with the United Nations, Conor Cruise O'Brien. Although Belgium left Zaire with an unpromising intellectual and cultural situation, with only a couple of university graduates at independence, Zaire has since produced notable writers and critics like Yves-Valentin Mudimbe, M à M Ngal, Jean-Pierre Makouta-Mboukou, Pius Ngandu Nkashama and many more, to be-

come an important centre of intellectual life in francophone Africa. An equally important, even if less well known, aspect of cultural life in this vast country – 40 times the size of Belgium – is its theatrical activity, which is diverse and lively in spite of efforts by the state to limit freedom of modern artistic, especially theatrical, expression.

This activity finds expression in a variety of forms: musical dramas, performed mostly in the local languages; Zairian- or French-language plays; a thriving popular urban theatre practised by such groups as the Mufwankolo of Lumumbashi, in the Shaba province; Community Development theatre, initiated in 1987 by the Théâtre d'Intervention of Zaire; and what can be described as a theatre of political pageantry and cheerleading. Examples of musical dramas include *Liandja* (1975), a stage version of the epic of the same name on the culture hero of the Mongo people of Zaire; *Ngembo*, on the problem of juvenile delinquency; and *Nkenge*, a work on culture conflict.

Because of a Belgian colonial policy that encouraged education in the national languages, Zaire's earliest written theatre was in those languages. The theatre in French started only in the 1950s. Its pioneers were Albert Mongita, author of *Soko Stanley* (1954), written to commemorate the 40th anniversary of the death of the explorer Stanley; L. S. Bondekwe, whose *Athanase et les professeurs de lumière* (*Athanasius and the Enlightened Teachers*, 1957) satirizes the so-called *évolués*; and Hippolyte Kabamba.

Contemporary Zairian French-language theatre has also produced many plays. Chief among these are historical dramas: Valérien Mutombo-Diba's *Tamouré et les seigneurs du Garengazé* (*Tamouré and the Lords of Garengazé*, 1966), Saturnin Ngombo's *Coutumes et usages du roi Ntinu Wene* (*Customs and Practices of King Ntinu Wene*, 1979), Lisembe Elebe's *Simon Kimbangui, ou le messie noir* (*Simon Kimbangui, or The Black Messiah*, 1972); sociopolitical works: Ngenzi Lonta's *La Fille du forgeron* (*The Blacksmith's Daughter*, 1960), Lisembe Elebe's *Le Sang des noirs pour un sou* (*The Blood of Blacks for a Penny*, 1972), P. Ngandu Nkashama's *Bonjour Monsieur le Ministre* (*Good Morning Mr Minister*, 1983), *La délivrance de Ilunga* (*Ilunga's Deliverance*, 1977); and psychological plays like Sangu Sonsa's *La Dérive, ou la chute des points cardinaux* (*The Drift, or The Collapse of the Cardinal Points*, 1973).

After the civil war in 1966 there was a flowering of theatrical acivity, with the founding of troupes such as the Louvanium University-based Théâtre de la Colline, the Théâtre de Zaire and the Union Générale des Amis de la Culture of Lumumbashi. But of all the troupes in Zaire, only one, the state's Compagnie du Théâtre National Mobutu Sese Sékou, has the material facilities for the serious production of plays. But, not surprisingly, for a troupe named after the president, its productions are traditional mythical and historical pageants shaped to reflect party ideology. JCM

See: R. Cornevin, *Le Théâtre en Afrique noire et à*

Madagascar, Paris, 1970; Union Edebiri, 'Le Théâtre Zairois à la recherche de son authenticité', *Afrique Littéraire et Artistique*, 40, 1976; D. M. Pwono, 'Musical Play in Zaire: A Contemporary Interpretation of African Oral Literature', in *African Literature: New Masks*, ed. H. Wylie, D. Brutus and J. Silenieks, Washington, 1988.

zaju Chinese variety play; generic term for a style of entertainment in which dance, song, monologue, balladry and farcical skits were given an integrated presentation. Archetypal roles developed within *zaju* are the basis of later divisions. The genre attained significant form in both north and south China in the 12th century, and reached its creative peak during the Yuan dynasty (1234–1368). Beijing opera (*JINGXI*) of modern times may be regarded as a legitimate descendant.

Zaju plays in the Yuan period were comparatively simple in form and followed the rules of prosody, rhyme and metre fundamental to all Chinese lyrical composition. In general a play had four acts plus a 'wedge'. Each act was given a long suite of single-stanza lyrics in one musical mode, the mode changing for each act. The wedge, which was a self-contained scene, allowed the dramatist a certain flexibility. It had a single song sequence with one or two stanzas only and could be situated at the beginning of the play or between any two acts.

Only the leading performer, whether male or female, sang. Ancillary performers carried on the dialogue and action between the singing as well as enforcing the comic pace. The music of Yuan-period plays has been lost and knowledge of stage practices must rely almost entirely on the playscripts. The richly diverse Yuan drama was a thriving popular entertainment catering to all levels of society. ACS

See: J. I. Crump, *Chinese Theatre in the Days of Kublai Khan*, Tucson, Ariz., 1980; D. R. Johnson, *Yuan Music Dramas: Studies in Prosody and Structure and a Complete Catalogue of Northern Arias in the Dramatic Style*, Ann Arbor, Mich., 1980; Ching-Hsi Perng, *Double Jeopardy: A Critique of Seven Yüan Courtroom Dramas*, Ann Arbor, Mich., 1978; Shih Chung-wen, *The Golden Age of Chinese Drama: Yuan Tsa-chü*, Princeton, N.J.,1976.

Zakharov, Mark (Anatolevich) 1933– Eclectic and influential Russian director and former deputy of the Supreme Soviet, who graduated from Sergei Yutkevich's Student Theatre at Moscow State University and since 1973 has served as artistic director of Moscow's Lenin Komsomol Theatre. His stagings of *Auto-City XXI*, which he co-authored with Yury Vizbor, *Til*, adapted by Grigory Gorin from Charles de Coster's novel *The Stars and the Death of Joaquin Murieta, the Chilean Bandit Who Was Brutally Murdered in California on July 23, 1853*, adapted from Pablo Neruda (1976), and *Juno and Avos: The Hope* by Andrei Voznesensky (1981) helped popularize the rock opera form in Russia and reflected the influences of Western cinema, especially Fellini. *Juno and Avos*, a romantic historical plea for East–West rapprochement during the difficult Brezhnev era, played in New York in 1989, as well as in Western and Eastern Europe. In the 1980s, Zakharov's productions included NUDITY and –

equally taboo – religious music and imagery. In 1984, he refused to take the ousted LYUBIMOV's place as the Taganka Theatre's artistic director. His 1985 polemic 'Applause Can't Be Shared' foretold the break-up of the stifling Soviet theatre bureaucracy under *glasnost* and *perestroika*. In 1989, he staged *Memorial Service*, derived from SHOLOM ALEICHEM's stories. SG

Zaks, Jerry 1946– German-born American director. Educated at Dartmouth, Zaks began his theatrical career as an actor. His directing credits include *Lend Me a Tenor* (1989), for which he won a Tony. In the same year he was called the outstanding director of COMEDY in the American theatre, with productions noted for pace, style, wit and exceptional ensemble acting. He also re-staged a successful *Anything Goes* in London after reviving it at Lincoln Center (1987). During his tenure at Lincoln Center as director-in-residence, he also successfully directed the 1986 revival of GUARE's *House of Blue Leaves* and his *Six Degrees of Separation* in 1990, winning directing Tonys for both. In 1990 Zaks left Lincoln Center to work for the Jujamcyn Theaters, where his first effort was STEPHEN SONDHEIM's MUSICAL *Assassins* at PLAYWRIGHTS HORIZONS, followed in 1992 by a critically acclaimed revival of *Guys and Dolls* on BROADWAY, winning his fourth Tony. Other notable credits include *Sister Mary Ignatius Explains It All for You*, *The Marriage of Bette and Boo* and *The Foreigner*. In 1994 he received the 10th annual 'Mr Abbott Award' from the Stage Directors and Choreographers Foundation. SMA DBW

Zambia Until independence on 24 October 1964, Zambia was the British colony Northern Rhodesia. The population of over 8 million falls into seven major language groups – Bemba, Nyanja, Lozi, Tonga, Lunda, Kaonde and Luvale.

Before the advent of colonialism, traditional dances, dance-dramas and RITUAL plays were performed at seasonal and religious festivals and RITES OF PASSAGE, such as the *makishi* masquerade (see MASQUERADES IN AFRICA) of North Western Province and the *nyau kasinja* funeral dance of the Eastern Province. Other ceremonies include the *nachisungu*, a puberty rite of the Northern Provinces; the *mutomboko*, which celebrates the accession to the throne of Mwata Kazembe, king of the Lundas; the *kuomboka*, which marks the movement of the Lozi king from his winter to his summer capital; and the *ncwala*, which commemorates the victories of the Nguni people during their migration from South Africa. In addition to these forms, there is a rich tradition of narrative, the most famous of which are the stories of Kalulu the hare.

With colonization and the subsequent urbanization, some of these forms were modified and some new ones developed from the old. As with much cult drama in early societies – the rites of Dionysus in Greece and the Yoruba masquerades of Nigeria, for instance – the *nyau* masquerades developed in line with social changes from a clan cult performance into a secret society, then into family guilds, and ultimately into professional performing groups. In the process new MASKS were added, comic and satiric plots elaborated, and the original cult taboos were set aside in favour of inventive entertainments which were performed for money, before multi-ethnic audiences.

Ultimately, content was stripped of original meanings and functions.

Other syncretic modern performance forms based on the traditional culture are *kayowe* (a courtship dance based on a cock and hen choreography), *kalela* (satirical of white dress and manners), *fwemba* (an acrobatic dance developed by soldiers returning from the Second World War) and *kachala* (based on spirit possession (*mashawe*) and puberty rites (*nachisungu*), and incorporating mimed SATIRE of contemporary mores). During the period of agitation for independence, the nationalist youth groups made effective use of these performing modes for political mobilization. They were later incorporated into the repertoire of the National Dance Troupe, established in 1965, which under the directorship of Edwin Manda adopted a dynamic approach to the traditional forms, producing full-length dance-dramas such as *Nsombo Malimba* (the names of musical instruments). These in turn influenced other dramatists, including MASAUTSO PHIRI and STEPHEN J. CHIFUNYISE.

The European settlers introduced Western theatre into Zambia, forming in 1952 the all-white Northern Rhodesia Drama Association, which with independence became the Theatre Association of Zambia (TAZ). Between 1954 and 1958 a number of theatres were built for the exclusive use of expatriate and settler communities. In 1958 a multiracial group founded the Waddington Theatre Club and challenged the colonial colour bar by, after heated debate, gaining membership of TAZ. Though the white settlers claimed that 'very little interest was shown by Africans in theatre', from 1958 to 1962 the Northern Rhodesian Youth Council held an annual drama and choir festival, which came to an end only when the clubs became involved in the political campaigns of the nationalist organizations. In 1958 a 15-minute radio programme was introduced, broadcasting plays in a number of Zambian languages by, among others, Edward Kateka, Asaf Mvula, Y. L. Zulu, Wilfred Banda and Patterson Mukanda. Andreya Masiye was the first Zambian to write a full-length play, *The Many Lands of Kazembe*. A weekly series in Tonga, *Malikopo*, and another in Nyanja, *Tambwali*, became extremely popular.

Formed in the year before independence, the Zambia Arts Trust, a national association of indigenous theatre enthusiasts, toured the country on a grant from the new Zambian government with plays in English and Zambian languages including Gideon Lumpa's *Iyi Eyali Imikalile* (*The Way We Lived*), John Simbotwe's *Ifyabukaya* (*Our Customs*), KABWE KASOMA's *The Long Arm of the Law* and others by SHAW, WOLE SOYINKA, OLA ROTIMI and Obutunde Ijimere. They organized theatre festivals and were virtually the only organized theatre at the time performing plays in Zambian languages. In 1969 a local publisher, Titus Mukopo, recruited YULISA AMADU MADDY to found the Zambia Dance Company, but a venture to establish a professional theatre company was not a success.

Possibly the most significant new development after independence was the emergence of drama at the new University of Zambia. A student dramatic society (UNZADRAMS) became active on the campus; its policy favoured locally written plays, and its earliest productions included Kasoma's *The Long Arm of the Law*, Michael Etherton's adaptation of GUILLAUME OYONO MBIA's novel *Houseboy, Che Guevara* and *Kazembe and the Portuguese*. In 1969 drama courses were established by Michael Etherton and Andrew Horn, and in 1971 with the construction of an open-air theatre the Chikwakwa Theatre was born. Chikwakwa took theatre in English and Zambian languages to the people by touring plays, developing plays with local schoolchildren and holding workshops and festivals. It also produced a journal, *The Chikwakwa Review*. The Chikwakwa example inspired many new developments, and the concept of travelling theatre has been continued by the Centre for the Arts, founded at the university in 1983.

Bazamai Theatre (1970–2) was a Chikwakwa outside university walls. Founded by Masautso Phiri and Stephen Moyo, it produced the dance-drama *Kuta*, Moyo's *The Last Prerogative* and an adaptation of Chinua Achebe's *Things Fall Apart*. Another development of Chikwakwa was Tikwiza, founded in 1975, which became a de facto national company, dominating Zambian theatre for nine years and representing Zambian theatre at the 1972 FESTAC and in Cuba, Botswana and Kenya. Its actors included some of the best Zambia has produced, such as Matildah Malamamfumu, Mumba Kapumpa and Haggai Chisulo. Its work was characterized by the political emphasis of plays such as Masautso Phiri's *Soweto* and Dickson Mwansa's *The Cell*.

The extent to which the Chikwakwa tradition had become the basis for an alternative indigenous Zambian theatre movement is demonstrated by the formation of the Zambian National Theatre Arts Association (ZANTAA). With a large membership in schools, colleges and community theatre groups, ZANTAA organized annual festivals. Nearly 90 plays were produced, mostly unpublished. In 1983 a national debate culminated in the merger of the two existing theatre organizations, TAZ and ZANTAA.

Starting as an opponent of Chikwakwa, David Wallace became a leading advocate and practitioner, via his Theatre Circle, of theatre based on traditional orature, especially the Kalulu (hare) tales. Bakanda Theatre's production in 1980 of Dickson Mwansa's *The Cell*, Tithandize Theatre's performances of plays by Craig Lungu and ZANASE Theatre, a full-time company attached to the Zambian National Service, have all been influential.

In the 1980s there was spectacular growth in community-based theatre in working-class residential areas. One group, Kanyama Theatre, became Zambia's first full-time professional theatre group, touring Zambia and Zimbabwe widely.

TELEVISION DRAMA, too, has been influenced by the indigenous Zambian theatre movement. In response to government directives to scrap foreign material in favour of local work, Zambian television introduced the 'Play for Today' series, which has produced many popular Zambian works such as Chifunyise's *I Resign* and *A Thorn in Our Flesh*, Mulenga N'gandu's *Jobless Existence* and Kwalela Ikafa's *Dambwa*, as well as a number of dance-dramas. The National Dance Troupe had an influential weekly one-hour slot in which it performed dance, dance-drama and sketches, in Zambian languages – constituting a breakthrough, as only English had hitherto been used on television. SC RK

See: *Chikwakwa Review*, Univ. of Zambia, Lusaka. M. Etherton, *The Development of African Drama*, London, 1982, and 'The Dilemma of the Popular Playwright: The Work of Kabwe Kasoma and V. E. Musinga', *African Literature Today*, 8, 1976.

Zamyatin, Evgeny (Ivanovich) 1884–1937 Russian-Soviet novelist, short story writer, literary critic, dramatist and editor, best known in the West for his Wellsian anti-utopian novel *We* (1920), which antedated Huxley's *Brave New World* and inspired Orwell's *1984*. An engineer by training, an ironist by temperament, he wrote eloquently, satirically and passionately on artistic freedom, social ills and literary craft. He was an early Bolshevik, and his anti-philistine polemical writing of the 1920s led to mounting official criticism of his work, culminating in the banning of his books from dissemination and further publication in 1929 and his emigration to Paris in 1931.

Zamyatin wrote eight plays, of which three were original works and five adaptations. His earliest play *The Society of Honorary Bell Ringers* (1925), derived from his novel *Islanders*, was produced at Leningrad's Mikhailovsky Theatre in 1925. That same year the MOSCOW ART THEATRE's Second Studio invited him to dramatize Nikolai Leskov's short story 'The Tale of the Cross-eyed Lefty from Tula and the Steel Flea'. The result was *The Flea*, directed by Aleksei Diky, a COMMEDIA-style depiction of Tsarist Russia and Victorian England meant to revitalize Russian folk COMEDY, which ran for six seasons. The tragedy *Attila* (1928), his last play, presents the Hun leader in a positive light and poetic style. It was banned while in rehearsal at the Leningrad Bolshoi Dramatic Theatre (1928), at which point Zamyatin returned to narrative writing. His essay 'The Modern Russian Theatre' (1932), originally a lecture delivered in Prague one month after his emigration (1931), offers critical assessments of Russian theatre's ensemble tradition, ideological playwriting, proletarian theatres and mass spectacles and of the comparative strengths of STANISLAVSKY's and MEYERHOLD's methods and influence. SG

zanni (singular and plural) The Italian term for the two servants in the *COMMEDIA DELL'ARTE*. It is unlikely that the word derives from the *sanniones* of the ancient Atellan FARCES (see GREECE, ANCIENT), but may come from the dialect forms of Giovanni (John): Gian, Zuan or Zan. Originally they were servants from Bergamo speaking the local patois, and soon differentiated into two distinct types. The first became the clever, domineering intriguer, who motivated the plot through schemings and brainstorms; often characterized as an urban lackey, he wore first a bright jerkin, later a stylized livery. His names were Brighella, Buffetto, Flautino and Coviello. The second was a knave from the village or the garden, a dolt not devoid of mother-wit, whose function was to be the fall-guy and provide the prat-falls. His clothes were patched or mended, and they turned in time into a costume of polychrome rhomboids. His names were Arlecchino, Truffaldino, Pasquino, Tabarino, Tortellino, Mezzetino, Trappolino, Trivellino, Bagolino and Fritellino, and gradually this role became the more important of the two. LS

Zaourou, Bernard Zadi 1938– Ivorian dramatist, theatre director, poet and university teacher. Zaourou attended the University of Strasbourg, France; after his MA in 1970 (he has since published a doctoral dissertation on the poetry of AIMÉ CÉSAIRE), he joined the staff of the University of Abidjan.

Zaourou is a controversial figure. While still at school, he spent a short spell in prison for extreme left-wing activities. In 1975, his AGIT-PROP play *L'Oeil* (*The Eye*, 1974) was censored on the grounds of incitement to class hatred and violence (see CENSORSHIP). Since the mid-1970s, he has been at the forefront of efforts and spirited polemics aimed at renewing Ivorian theatre, in both discourse and aesthetic. After his traditional historical play *Les Sofas* (*The Sofas*, 1975), he opted, in terms of content at least, for a radical political theatre in *L'Oeil*. This play, on the growth of a revolutionary consciousness, is interesting for its use, in addition to words, of the languages of drum music, silence and MIME. The systematic exploitation of these elements is pursued in *La Termitière* (*The Anthill*, 1981), an initiation-RITUAL play based on the principles of the hunter narrative of his Bété people, the Didiga. These principles are the rationally illogical but mystically significant symbolism, and the language of surreal poetry (see SURREALISM). In 1980 Zaourou founded the Didiga Company, with choreographic, musical, drama and literary criticism sections, in an attempt to create a theatrical aesthetic that has roots in his community's traditional art forms. Two of his other play are *Sory Lambré* (1968) and *Les Tignasses* (*The Hair*, 1984). JCM

Zapolska, Gabriela 1860–1921 Polish actress, director, manager, playwright and novelist, credited with introducing IBSEN in Russia, playing Nora in *A Doll's House* during a guest appearance of the Warsaw Theatre in 1883. She studied acting in Paris and appeared in minor roles at the Théâtre Libre (1892–4), returning to Poland as a proponent of NATURALISM. Her most popular play is *The Morality of Mrs Dulska* (1906), a mordant SATIRE on bourgeois hypocrisy. *Malka Szwarcenkopf* (1897) portrays lower-class Jewish life; *Miss Maliczewska* (1910) deals with a young actress victimized by predatory males. DG

zarzuela Typically Spanish MUSICAL COMEDY or light OPERA which may be traced to GOLDEN AGE works of LOPE DE VEGA and CALDERÓN. The name comes from the royal palace, where musicals were presented in the 18th century. Madrid's current Teatro de la Zarzuela was built in 1856, when interest in the musical form was revived. The genre ranges from dramatic three-act to comic one-act variations. It enjoyed enormous popularity, culminating in the first decades of the 20th century and attracting the talents of numerous authors and composers. Among the best-loved works are Ricardo de la Vega and Tomás Bretón's *La verbena de la Paloma* (*The Fair of the Virgin of the Dove*) and José López Silva and Carlos Fernández Shaw's *La revoltosa* (*The Mischievous Lady*). Director José Tamayo's spectacular *Anthology of the Zarzuela* has been touring the world to great acclaim since 1966. PZ

Zavadsky, Yury (Aleksandrovich) 1894–1977 Soviet director who began his career as an actor in the

Vakhtangov Studio (1915), performing the roles of Anthony in MAETERLINCK's *The Miracle of St Anthony* (1916) and Calaf in GOZZI's *Princess Turandot* (1922). His training there as a designer later manifested itself in his attention to the outer form of his stage productions, many of which employed music generously, and especially in his early productions which he designed as well as directed.

While acting at the MOSCOW ART THEATRE (1924–31), Zavadsky formed his own studio (1924), reorganized in 1927 as the Zavadsky Studio, which brought a STANISLAVSKY–VAKHTANGOV-based acting approach to plays by G. B. SHAW, OSTROVSKY, Lavrenyov, SHERIDAN, Pervomaisky and DE MUSSET. The Studio moved to Rostov in 1936, where it formed the core of the Gorky Theatre, and Zavadsky, who had already served as artistic director of the Moscow Central Theatre of the Red Army (1932–5), became its head (1936–40). From 1940 until the late 1970s he was artistic director of Moscow's Mossoviet Theatre, which was founded in 1930 as the Theatre of the Moscow District of Soviet Trade Unions (MGSPS) and renamed in 1938.

A theatrical eminence more than an innovative director, Zavadsky attempted to recreate Vakhtangov's lyrical merger of psychological REALISM and vibrant theatricalism. His many productions at the Mossoviet include SHAKESPEARE's *The Merry Wives of Windsor* (1957, 1967) and LERMONTOV's *Masquerade* (1952, 1963, 1967), both of which won him Lenin Prizes (1951, 1967); *Petersburg Dreams*, adapted from Dostoevsky's *Crime and Punishment* (1969), a popular success with its romanticized Raskolnikov (played by Gennady Bortnikov) and a handsome multi-level set by A. Vasilyev; classics by CHEKHOV, GOLDONI, Ostrovsky, Jack London, Shaw and Shakespeare; and Soviet dramas by AFINOGENOV, SIMONOV, KORNEICHUK, LEONOV, Shtein, ZORIN and Virta. He wrote numerous articles and books between the 1940s and 70s, including *The Birth of a Production* and *Teachers and Students* (1975), and was named a People's Artist of the USSR in 1948. From 1940 he taught at the Moscow State Institute of Theatrical Art (GITIS). Among his students was Polish director JERZY GROTOWSKI. SG

Zeami [Seami] **Motokiyo** 1363–1443 Japanese actor, troupe leader, playwright, music composer, choreographer and writer of major treatises on performing and composition. Zeami is the foremost figure in the history of NŌ. He refined *nō* during 34 years in the Kyoto court under Shogun Yoshimitsu's patronage. He moved beyond playing a role (*monomane*), the strong point of his father Kan'ami Kiyotsugu (1333–84), to striving for a mysterious beauty tinged with sadness (*yūgen*). Representative works among the 20–90 plays attributed to Zeami are: *The Damask Drum* (*Aya no tsuzumi*), *The Old Pine* (*Oimatsu*), *Kiyotsune*, *Visiting Lady Komachi* (*Kayoi Komachi*), and *Lady Yuya* (*Yuya*).

He was a practical theatre person, concerned with finding means to attract a varied audience through novelty (*hana*), by doing the unexpected (following the *yin-yang* theory of opposites) and by cultivating a 'beginner's heart' (*shōshin*). Over the last 30 years of his life, he wrote 21 'secret' treatises (*hiden*) for direct descendants in the Kanze family (partial trans. 1984). He advised diligent training through seven stages of one's career (in *The Way of the Flower*), structuring a play through emotional progression guided by *jo-ha-kyū* (in *True Path of the Flower*), acting through a Zen-like state of unconscious mastery (in *Disciplines for Joy*), attaining nine progressive levels of artistic achievement (in *The Nine Levels*), composing plays based on known dramatic subjects (in *On Playwriting*) and how to run a professional troupe (in *Reflections on the Art*). Much of Zeami's advice applies to any theatre. He said there is no single correct way of acting, but only more or less appropriate ways of performing under specific circumstances. Audience approval is the proper criterion of success. His treatises became available to the public in the 20th century. JRB

Zeffirelli, Franco 1923– Italian stage and film designer and director. After a classical education in Florence, Zeffirelli began his career in 1945 as an actor, but after two years he became a designer. Working primarily on plays and films for LUCHINO VISCONTI, he designed also for the films of Michelangelo Antonioni and Vittorio de Sica. In 1951 he became a stage director and subsequently worked on such OPERAS as *La Cenerentola* (La Scala, 1953) and *Don Giovanni* (COVENT GARDEN, 1962), and such SHAKESPEARE plays as *Romeo and Juliet* (1960) and *Much Ado About Nothing* (1965). As film director, Zeffirelli's abundantly romantic yet realistically detailed style is evident in his widely acclaimed *Romeo and Juliet* (1968), as well as in *The Taming of the Shrew* (1967), *La Traviata* (1982) and *Otello* (1986). TM

Zemach, Nahum 1887–1939 Founder of HABIMAH Theatre, born in Bialystok, Russia. An ardent Zionist and lover of the Hebrew language, he conceived the idea of a professional Hebrew theatre which would disseminate the Zionist idea and ultimately settle in Palestine. Under his guidance, the collective of actors achieved world fame. But in 1927, during its tour of the USA, the troupe split in two, the majority of senior members going to Palestine and the minority, headed by Zemach, remaining in New York. Zemach, whose dream of establishing a Hebrew theatre in the Land of Israel had come true, ended his life staging performances in Yiddish and English in New York. (See also HEBREW THEATRE.) HAS

Ziegfeld, Florenz 1869–1932 American producer. Ziegfeld's first venture into show business was as manager of SANDOW, a VAUDEVILLE strongman. After meeting singer Anna Held in Europe, Ziegfeld took her to New York and presented her in several MUSICALS. (They married in 1897, divorced in 1912.) At her suggestion, he created a Parisian-style REVUE called *Follies of 1907*, the first in a series that he continued to produce for the next quarter of a century. Initially presented on a modest scale, the *Follies* grew increasingly elaborate, eventually moving to New York's New Amsterdam Theatre, where designers such as JOSEPH URBAN were given free reign to create ornate scenery and lavish costumes. In 1911 the show's title was changed to *The Ziegfeld Follies*. The motto 'Glorifying the American Girl' underlines the *Follies*' emphasis on choruses of beautiful women in glittering production numbers. Many of the shows also featured first-rate comedians such as BERT

WILLIAMS, FANNY BRICE, W. C. FIELDS, WILL ROGERS and EDDIE CANTOR, and popular singers and dancers such as NORA BAYES, MARILYN MILLER and INA CLAIRE.

Besides producing annual editions of the *Follies*, Ziegfeld presented some of the most successful musical comedies and OPERETTAS of the 1920s, including *Sally* (1920), *Kid Boots* (1923), *Sunny* (1925), *Rio Rita* (1927), *Show Boat* (1927), *Rosalie* (1928), *The Three Musketeers* (1928) and *Whoopee* (1928). Rarely innovative in his choice of material or his production methods, Ziegfeld built his reputation as a producer on his ability to discover and nurture talented performers, and on the care and expense with which he mounted his shows. MK

Ziegfeld Theatre (New York City) In 1927, FLORENZ ZIEGFELD pushed the outer limits of the theatre district to Sixth Avenue when Hearst and Brisbane built him a theatre to house his productions. Its curved façade, egg-shaped auditorium and JOSEPH URBAN's mural 'Lovers through History' were among its unusual features. One year after Ziegfeld's death, it was converted to films, but in 1944 BILLY ROSE completely renovated it and returned it to legitimate status. During 1955–63 it was an NBC television studio, but again a theatre from 1963 until it was demolished in 1966. MCH

Zimbabwe After years of bitter armed struggle against the white settler regime of Ian Smith, the new state of Zimbabwe (formerly Rhodesia) came into existence on 18 April 1980. The majority of its 10 million inhabitants speak Shona, while Ndebele is a significant minority language and Tonga, Kalanga, Venda and English are also spoken.

When a soldier called William King put on a variety concert soon after the Pioneer Column first occupied the country in 1890, he was said to have staged the 'first major theatrical entertainment in the country'. However, indigenous theatre forms existed many years before the coming of the settlers, as illustrated by the wide practice amongst the Shona people of the *mahumbwe*, a young people's harvest performance, and the comic 'funeral drama' in which the deceased's major achievements are dramatized. In addition, there were many other RITUAL ceremonies, dances, games and narratives that contained significant dramatic elements.

By the 1950s the white settlers had established segregated theatre clubs in most major towns, and in 1958 these formed the Association of Rhodesian Theatrical Societies, later to become the National Theatre Organization, holding an annual theatre festival adjudicated by 'experts' from Britain or South Africa. With few exceptions, this organization confined itself to segregated colonial drama, a situation which changed only slowly after independence.

The organization of theatre amongst the black majority was left to a variety of bodies: to the colonial government, which organized festivals of prescribed plays; to the Salisbury City Council, which employed Basil Chidyamatamba to foster traditional dancing and establish the Neshamwari Festival of Music, Dance and Drama in 1965; to various church organizations from whose activities emerged active personalities such as BEN SIBENKE,

Walter Muparutsa and Dominic Kanaventi; and to a number of amateur clubs often associated with the mining companies – namely the Torwood African Theatre Society, the Wankie Dramatic and Choral Society and the Kamativi African Players. Then, in the 1970s, the escalating war of liberation began to restore to the people a theatre practice based on the indigenous traditions of Zimbabwe. Political cadres of the nationalist movements organized dramas in the guerrilla camps and all-night *pungwes*, night-time political meetings conducted by freedom fighters in the countryside where songs, folk-tales, dance and drama articulated the motivations behind the struggle. The theatre of the *pungwe* featured prominently the heroes of the first anti-colonial resistance of the 1970s, colonial repression, and the new Zimbabwe that would emerge from the struggle.

Theatre in the post-independence period is characterized by a mixture of trends established in the colonial regime and of new ones generated by the changed circumstances of independence. Artists who had been active in the colonial period found more room to expand. Whereas before independence N. Chipunza's *Svikiro* (1978), mangled by the white director into *My Spirit Sings*, was the only play written and acted by black Zimbabweans to be performed in a white theatre, now both the People's Company – with locally written plays by Sibenke and Karl Dorn – and the Sundown Players, specializing in the plays of ATHOL FUGARD, began competing in the previously all-white National Theatre Festival. In 1982 Basil Chidyamatamba's traditional-based MUSICAL, *Sounds of Zimbabwe*, was produced. In 1985 Kanaventi, Muparutsa and Sibenke came together to form the Zimbabwe Arts Productions, with impressive performances of Fugard's 'workshop play' *Sizwe Banzi Is Dead* and *The Island*. They went on to join up with Andrew Whaley, performing his play *Platform Five*, about tramps on Harare's streets. Subsequently Whaley and the actor Simon Shumba formed Meridien Players, staging Whaley's *Nyoka Tree* (1988) and *The Rise and Shine of Comrade Fiasco* (1990), a controversial treatment of the liberation struggle and post-independence society.

It was the post-independence government of Robert Mugabe, however, which made innovations that were to influence the development of theatre in Zimbabwe – namely the foundation of the National Dance Company and the community-based theatre movement organized by the Zimbabwe Foundation for Education with Production (ZIMFEP); and the work of the new Ministry of Youth, Sport and Culture. The National Dance Company was formed in 1981 and its first production, *Mbuya Nehanda – the Spirit of Liberation*, choreographed by Peggy Harper, Karium Welsh-Asante and Emmanual Ribeiro, continued the spirit of the revolutionary *pungwe*. Subsequently the company confined itself to the performance of indigenous dance, until its demise in 1991.

In 1982 the then Ministry of Education and Culture employed the Kenyans Ngugi wa Mirii and Kimani Gecau to develop a community-based theatre movement under the auspices of ZIMFEP. With the Chindunduma School community they produced *The Trials of Dedan Kimathi* by NGUGI WA THIONG'O and MICERE MUGO in Shona and English, and toured nationally, demonstrating widely the concept of community-based theatre. The ministry followed this up with a UNESCO-sponsored African Workshop on Theatre for Development in Murewa in 1983, involving local participants and theatre artists from 22 African countries.

Ngugi wa Mirii, with ZIMFEP, and S. J. CHIFUNYISE as Director of Arts and Crafts in the new Ministry of Youth, Sport and Culture, continued the tradition by holding various theatre-for-development (see THIRD WORLD POPULAR THEATRE) and drama-skills workshops and forming community-based theatre groups. The Vashandi Workers' Theatre Group, the Avondale Domestic Workers' Theatre Group, the Chindunduma School Drama Group and Habbakuk Musengezi's community theatre group in Centenary in northern Zimbabwe were early examples of this movement's growing importance. Groups were established all over the country, performing both scripted and original plays in schools, mines, community halls and factories. Amakhosi Productions of Bulawayo, directed by Cont Mhlanga and a representative example, includes among its productions *Workshop Negative* (1987), *Citizen Mind* (1989) and *Stitsha* (1990).

In 1987 many of these groups came together to form the Zimbabwe Association of Community Theatre. ZACT and the National Theatre Organization are the two main theatre organizations in Zimbabwe. The NTO holds an annual festival, formerly called the National Theatre Festival but now renamed Winterfest. It also organizes a national school festival and a Play of the Year competition. The NTO is no longer exclusively white and colonial, but a clear difference in orientation and ideology has distinguished the two organizations. With the change in the international balance of forces and the introduction of the economic structural adjustment programme in Zimbabwe, this distinction has in recent years become less marked. But the struggle to survive on the part of the community-based theatre groups has become intense. This has led to a change in content and to an increased professionalism, with greater attention being paid to issues that are likely to be supported by sponsors and donors, and to other commercial considerations. A play on AIDS, *Manyanya* (1989), by the theatre group Batsiranai (meaning 'help each other') is a case in point.

A particularly influential development has been the growth of indigenous TELEVISION DRAMA, including the regular Shona comedy series *Mhuri ya Mukadota* (*The Mukadota Family*) featuring Safirio Madzikatire and Susan Chenjerai, both veterans of Shona radio drama since the early 1960s; plays by Chifunyise and by THOMPSON TSODZO, Charles Mungoshi, Agnes Gwatiringa and Aaron Moyo, as well as by Ndema Ngwenya with his MAWA (Mthwakazi Artists and Writers Association) Theatre Group; and MAWA Theatre Group's *Tshaka Zulu* (in Ndebele). Madzikatire also plays in a popular stage show which includes sketches and is in the popular theatre format reminiscent of GIBSON KENTE or HUBERT OGUNDE.

In 1984 the University of Zimbabwe introduced undergraduate courses in drama and began to participate actively in the community. In addition to productions staged as a part of coursework, a major production was introduced as an annual feature and a political theatre

group, Zambuko/Izibuko, formed. The university worked closely with the Ministry of Youth, Sport and Culture and with ZIMFEP in the development of the community-based movement, establishing courses in theatre-for-development and theatre-in-education. A major feature of the university's work was the involvement of actors from the community. Since its first production, in 1984–5, of *Mavambo, First Steps*, based on Wilson Katiyo's novel *A Son of the Soil*, the university and Zambuko/Izibuko have produced a number of influential original and scripted plays, including *I Will Marry When I Want* by Ngugi wa Thiong'o and Ngugi wa Mirii translated into Shona, NIKOLAI POGODIN's *Kremlin Chimes*, and Zambuko/ Izibuko's *Katshaa!* (1986), *Samora Continua* (1988) and *Mandela, the Spirit of No Surrender* (1990). All these productions were staged both at the university and throughout Zimbabwe.

Since independence, Zimbabwean publishers have devoted more attention to publishing plays in English, Ndebele and Shona, including those of Chifunyise, Bertha Msora and Habbakuk Musengezi; G. Mujajati, Andrew Whaley, Cont Mhlanga, Aaron Moyo, William Chigidi and T. Dangarembga. The university's Faculty of Arts began publication of a 'University Playscript' series of cheap acting editions of Zimbabwean and African plays in 1986. In addition to the growth of theatre amongst adults, the development of children's theatre has been greatly facilitated by the establishment of the Children's Performing Arts Workshop, which has staged its own original plays and plans to publish material specially for children.

A considerable upsurge in interest in indigenous theatre and in theatrical activity transformed the depressed situation of the pre-independence years, but the present harsh economic climate threatens to undermine the progress made. RK

See: G. P. Kahari, *The Imaginative Writings of Paul Chidyausiku*, Gweru, 1975; *Journal of Southern African Studies*, 16, 2, 1990; *Tulane Drama Review*, 36, 1, 1992; *Zimbabwe Theatre Report*, Univ. of Zimbabwe, 1989; R. M. Zinyemba, *Zimbabwean Drama: A Study of Shona and English Plays*, Gweru, 1986.

Zinsou, Senouvo (Agbota) 1946–

Togolese playwright and former civil servant. Zinsou showed an early interest in the theatre, writing his first play *L'Amour d'un sauvage* (*The Love of a Savage*) in 1968. He played an important role, while still at school, in the formation of an inter-secondary school dramatic society, L'Entente Scolaire pour le Théâtre et le Folklore. He attended the University of Togo and the Institut d'Études Théâtrales of the University of Paris, where he studied under the noted French drama critic Jacques Schérer. On his return to Togo, Zinsou was appointed to the Ministry of Culture, where he founded the National Company for the Performing Arts, which he headed until 1992.

His first published play, *On joue la comédie* (*We Are Acting*, 1975), won first prize in the Inter-African Radio competition organized by Radio-France Internationale, and was performed in Lagos during the second Pan-African Cultural Festival. His other published plays are *Le Club* (1983) and *La Tortue qui chante*, *La Femme du blanchisseur* and *Yévi au pays des monstres* (*The Singing*

Tortoise, *The Laundryman's Wife* and *Yévi in the Country of Monsters*, 1987). His originality as a dramatist lies in his skilful exploitation of Togolese popular theatre traditions, both ancient in his 1987 plays and modern (concert party and *kantata*) in *On joue la comédie*. His work reflects a self-consciousness that is absent from most French-language African plays and is, among other things, a reflection on the art of playwriting.   JCM

Zipprodt, Patricia 1925– American COSTUME designer and educator (Brandeis University), who has been designing since the mid-1950s and became well known in the 1960s with such productions as *Fiddler on the Roof*, *Cabaret* and *Pippin*, and the film *The Graduate*. She adapts her style to the demands of the script and the director, but if she has a trademark, it is textured clothes. Beginning with *Fiddler*, she developed a technique of creating layers of paint and dye that gave a vibrant or shimmering sense of colour to costumes that would otherwise be drab. This approach continued through *Sunday in the Park with George* (1984), in which costumes were heavily textured with dye, paint, brocade, lace and fabric.   AA

Zirimu, Elvania (Namukwaya) fl.1960s–70s, d.1979 Ugandan playwright, producer, actress and academic. Already a talented actress at Kings College, Budo, she attended Makerere University from 1961 to 63, where her play *Keeping up with the Mukasas* won the English competition and the Original Play award in the Ugandan Drama Festival. In 1963 she went to Leeds University, where she took a degree in 1966. On her return she became tutor at the National Teachers' College, Kyambogo, and later also at Makerere University. She formed the Ngoma Players, with the declared policy of writing and producing plays in a Ugandan mode, and was actively concerned with the National Theatre there. She had been appointed to the embassy in Ghana when she was killed in a car crash. Her published plays are *Keeping up with the Mukasas* (1965), as well as *When the Hunchback Made Rain* and *Snoring Strangers* (1975), and *Family Spear* (1973).   MMaC

Zola, Émile 1840–1902 French novelist and critic. Zola's major literary importance is for his monumental series of novels, the *Rougon-Macquart* (1871–93), a chronicle of life under the Second Empire, one of which, *L'Assommoir* (1877), established him at the head of the naturalist movement (see NATURALISM). He also maintained a considerable interest in the theatre and was the major influence on ANTOINE's Théâtre Libre. William Busnach's MELODRAMA-tic adaptations of *L'Assommoir* (1879), *Nana* (1881) and *Pot Bouille* (1883) drew large audiences to the Ambigu (see BOULEVARD), but did little for Zola's reputation as a serious writer. Of his own original plays, *Thérèse Raquin* (1873), an adaptation of his novel, though not very successful on the stage, became a model for the naturalist play both in France and abroad. *Les Héritiers Rabourdin* (*The Rabourdin Heirs*, 1874) and *Bouton de rose* (*Rosebud*, 1879) both showed his unsuitedness to the comic stage. His short story, *Jacques Damour*, adapted by Léon Hennique, opened the first season of the Théâtre Libre. His play *Madeleine* (1865), which became the novel *Madeleine Férat* (1868), was also performed by the Théâtre Libre. In the preface to *Thérèse Raquin*, Zola expressed the hope that the naturalist movement would establish itself in the theatre.

In 1873 he was drama critic for four months for the *Avenir National* and from 1876 to 80 for the *Bien Public* and then the *Voltaire*. His reviews from 1876 to 80 were published in two volumes, *Le Naturalisme au théâtre* (*Naturalism in the Theatre*) and *Nos Auteurs dramatiques* (*Our Dramatists*, 1881). Unlike critics who merely recorded performances, Zola used his weekly column to promote the new drama and to develop a critical methodology. For the WELL MADE PLAY he wished to substitute a drama of observation and scientific fact, using an analytic approach akin to that of such novelists as Balzac, Flaubert and himself. Anti-romantic, he saw a link with the logical approach of the classical theatre, but felt that modern theatre should deal with the particular rather than the general and that 'the modern naturalist drama should individualize, enter into experimental analysis and an anatomical study of each human being'. He saw scenery in the theatre as taking on the role of description in the novel, with a real function in the analysis of facts and characters. He objected to the conventional paraphernalia of wings and backdrops and even foresaw the abandonment of footlights. He also believed in the social and educational value of theatre and saw all great plays as containing a social thesis. The critic was recommended to look not merely at the work, but at the audience's reaction to it. In his last years Zola converted to socialism and devoted his attention to socialist and humanitarian propaganda, notably becoming involved in the Dreyfus affair, with his famous article *J'Accuse*.   JMCC

Zorin, Leonid (Genrikhovich) 1924– Soviet-Russian dramatist of the post-Thaw generation which brought a new lyricism and focus on personal relationships and ethical concerns to the theatre. Born in Baku and receiving early encouragement in his writing from GORKY, Zorin worked in the literary department of the Baku Russian theatre, where his first play *Falcons* was produced in 1941. In 1949 he graduated from the Gorky Literary Institute in Moscow and had his play *Youth* staged at the Maly Theatre. His play *The Guests* (1954) identifies a neo-bourgeois class of ruthless, privileged bureaucrats to which the son of a revolutionary father belongs, thus reversing the idea frequently espoused in earlier Soviet plays that the younger generation is more enlightened than the elder.

The play, which alerted people to the inequities within the classless society and the corruption in high places of revolutionary ideals, was attacked by the Ministry of Culture and by literary conservatives as part of a counter-offensive to the Thaw. *A Roman Comedy* (*Dion*, 1964) is a satirical COMEDY, partially based on historical fact, about a plainspoken ancient Roman poet-pundit and his on/off relationship with the emperor. *A Warsaw Melody* (1967) is a story of unfulfilled love between two young students, a Russian boy and a Polish girl, at first frustrated by a new law forbidding Soviet citizens to marry foreigners, then by their own conflicting personal responsibilities, and finally by lost years which cannot be reclaimed. A typical 1960s drama, it played over 4000 times during the 1968–9 season. *The Decembrists* is part of a trilogy commemorating

Zola's *Nana* was converted into popular melodrama in Busnach's adaptation at the Ambigu-Comique. The spirit may have been wrong, but the attention to detail of setting at the Ambigu contributed to the naturalist staging.

the 50th anniversary of the October Revolution (1967) – the second and third parts are A. Svobodin's *The Populists* and MIKHAIL SHATROV's *The Bolsheviks*, respectively – which considers the use of terror in revolution. It brought to the stage of Moscow's Sovremennik Theatre, where it premiered, the human face of Russian history. Zorin has also written film scenarios, one of which, *Peace to the Newcomer*, won a gold medal at the 1961 Venice International Festival. SG

Zorrilla, José 1817–93 Spanish romantic dramatist and poet. He erupted on to the literary scene in 1837, spontaneously reading his emotional verses at the graveside of Mariano José de Larra. His stage works include cloak-and-sword plays and historical dramas. In his most enduring work, *Don Juan Tenorio* (1844), the legendary figure is saved from eternal damnation by pure love. For many years it was performed throughout the Hispanic world on 1 November. The tradition was revived in the mid-1980s in Alcalá de Henares by director Antonio Guirau, who presents the play as an outdoor spectacle in this Spanish university city. PZ

Zuckmayer, Carl 1896–1977 German dramatist and novelist, who won the Kleist Prize with *Der fröhliche Weinberg* (*The Happy Vineyard*) in 1925. This ribald VOLKSSTÜCK was followed by others: *Schinderhannes* (1927), *Katharina Knie* (1928) and *The Captain of Köpenick* (1931), the last satirizing the Prussian cult of the uniform. Zuckmayer also scripted films for Alexander Korda. He took US citizenship while in exile from 1939 to 1958, and worked for the American Control Commission in Germany. *The Devil's General* (1946), a critical treatment of misguided patriotism in the Luftwaffe, was the first popular hit in West Germany after the war. Its conventional form and sentimental plot have dated, as has his treatment of the politics of atomic physics, *Das kalte Licht* (*Cold Light*, 1956). HR

Picture Acknowledgements

The publishers gratefully acknowledge the following for supplying illustrations and granting permission for their use. Every effort has been made to obtain permission to use the illustrations; if any errors or omissions have occurred the publishers would welcome these being brought to their attention.

1 Michael Johnston; 4 Collection Laurence Senelick; 26 Collection Laurence Senelick; 30 courtesy of the Swiss Theatre Collection; 61 courtesy of the Melbourne Theatre Company; 69 Donald Cooper © Photostage; 79 Collection Laurence Senelick; 86 Donald Cooper © Photostage; 89 Museum of the City of New York, Theatre Collection; 99 from the collections of the Theatre Museum, by courtesy of the Board of Trustees of the Victoria & Albert Museum; 101 Harvard Theatre Collection; 110 Harvard Theatre Collection; 114 Sangeet Natak Akademi; 117 courtesy of Andrew Horn; 125 Donald Cooper © Photostage; 143 D. Linder, Asia Society, New York; 158 Provincial Archives of British Columbia (HP 10081); 172 courtesy of Jaromír Svoboda; 198 courtesy of Colin Mackerras; 218 Bibliothèque Historique de la Ville de Paris/courtesy of John McCormick; 229 photo: Jorge Hurtado; 232 Bibliothèque Historique de la Ville de Paris/courtesy of John McCormick; 235 photo: Jean-Loup Charmet/Musée Carnavalet, Paris; 247 Museo Nazionale, Naples; 249 courtesy of Colin Mackerras; 250 © BBC Hulton Picture Library; 252 courtesy of Robert Gordon Craig; 255 copyright British Museum; 268 photo: Cristóbal López; 278 University of Bristol Theatre Collection; 284 from the collections of the Theatre Museum, by courtesy of the Board of Trustees of the Victoria & Albert Museum; 291 photo: Roberto Fortuna; 307 photo courtesy of Michael Gnat; 330 John Vickers; 355 Historisches Museum der Stadt Wien © SPADEM, Paris, 1980; 362 Collection Laurence Senelick; 367 Bibliothèque Historique de la Ville de Paris/courtesy of John McCormick; 392 Bibliothèque Historique de la Ville de Paris/courtesy of John McCormick; 397 Alain Ricard; 404 courtesy of Martin Banham; 423 Bildarchiv Preussischer Kulturbesitz; 440 Bodleian Library; 445 copyright British Museum; 449 reproduced from Leacroft, *Theatre and Playhouse*, by permission of Methuen, London; 452 reproduced from Rudnitsky, *Meyerhold the Director*, trans. G. Petrov, ed. S. Schultze, 1981, by permission of Ardis Publishers, USA; 454 Collection Laurence Senelick; 456 courtesy of Daniel Gerould; 461 © The Guthrie Theatre; 476 Bildarchiv Preussischer Kulturbesitz; 477 University of Bristol Theatre Collection; 487 courtesy of Jarka Burian; 498 courtesy of Hotel Pro Forma; 516 courtesy of Farley Richmond; 523 courtesy of Farley Richmond; 527 photo: K. Foley; 528 photo: K. Foley; 539 photo: Mauclair & Chelton/ Agence de Presse Bernand; 542 from the collections of the Theatre Museum, by courtesy of the Board of Trustees of the Victoria & Albert Museum; 569 © Mikoshiba Shigeru; 587 courtesy of Daniel Gerould; 592 National Portrait Gallery, London; 607 Korean National Commission for UNESCO/courtesy of Oh-kon Cho; 609 courtesy of Oh-kon Cho; 618 Farley Richmond; 621 courtesy of J.R.Brandon; 631 Collection Laurence Senelick; 646 Institute of the Federal Theatre Project, George Mason University; 666 courtesy of Robert McLaren; 671 photo: K. Foley;

674 Collection Laurence Senelick; 680 Donald Cooper © Photostage; 687 MM Verlag/Salzburger Museum (Volkskundemuseum); 694 reproduced from Rudnitsky, *Meyerhold the Director*, trans. G. Petrov, ed. S. Schultze, 1981, by permission of Ardis Publishers, USA; 702 Bodleian Library, MS 264 f. 78v; 703 Bodleian Library, MS 264 f. 54v; 704 Theatre Museum, Covent Garden; 710 Theatre Museum, Covent Garden; 721 Collection Laurence Senelick; 723 The Billy Rose Theatre Collection, The New York Public Library at Lincoln Center; 752 Collection Laurence Senelick; 768 Collection Laurence Senelick; 771 The Billy Rose Theatre Collection, The New York Public Library at Lincoln Center; 793 Alain Ricard; 800 courtesy of Rogaland Teater; 806 photo: K. Foley; 812 photo: Peter Bysted/courtesy of Odin Teatret; 817 Harvard Theatre Collection; 827 Donald Cooper © Photostage; 836 courtesy of Mike Patterson; 845 Collection Laurence Senelick; 849 Harvard Theatre Collection; 851 Philippine Tourist and Travel Association; 856 Collection Laurence Senelick; 858 Ivan Kyncl; 886 courtesy of George Woodyard; 902 Deutsches Theatermuseum, Munich; 909 photo: Arthur Thompson/courtesy of Pit Prop Theatre; 919 Collection Laurence Senelick; 930 reproduced from Leacroft, *Theatre and Playhouse*, by permission of Methuen, London; 931 courtesy of the Turkish National Tourist Office, London; 941 courtesy of Martin Banham; 943 courtesy of Columbia University Press; 948 © Don Wilmeth; 952 reproduced from Rudnitsky, *Meyerhold the Director*, trans. G. Petrov, ed. S. Schultze, 1981, by permission of Ardis Publishers, USA; 954 courtesy of Spencer Golub; 958 Harvard Theatre Collection; 963 Collection Laurence Senelick; 975 courtesy of the Theatre National Daniel Sorano, Dakar; 989 courtesy of the Library of Congress; 1003 Becker Theater Library, Brown University; 1004 reproduced from Collison, *Stage Sound*, by permission of Cassells Ltd.; 1009 photo: Ruphin Coudyzer/courtesy of Market Theatre; 1014 photo: Ian Woollams/courtesy Royal Exchange Theatre; 1017 photo: Jesús Alcántara; 1019 courtesy of Artcelona, photo by Pere Tordera; 1023 Suffolk Record Office, Eyre Collection; 1024 courtesy of Prof. Stanislaw Mossakowski, Institute of Art, Polish Academy of Sciences; 1027 Mary Evans Picture Library; 1029 photo: John Haynes; 1034 photo: Ruth Walz/courtesy of Mike Patterson; 1039 © copyright Freddy Tornberg Film/Video; 1045 photo: Erik Appelgren; 1062 courtesy of TV Globo Ltda., Rio de Janeiro; 1068 photo: David Edwards/© BBC 1986; 1072 courtesy of the Royal Photographic Society, Bath; 1079 reproduced from Leacroft, *Theatre and Playhouse*, by permission of Methuen, London; 1082 reproduced from Leacroft, *Theatre and Playhouse*, by permission of Methuen, London; 1084 Appleton Partnership Architects; 1092 Bibliothèque et Musée de l'Opéra, Paris; 1098 courtesy of Jarka Burian; 1099 Moscow Art Theatre Musuem/Collection Laurence Senelick; 1109 Collection Laurence Senelick; 1119 Collection Laurence Senelick; 1126 photo reproduced from *Trinidad Carnival*, Key Caribbean Publications; 1158 photo by Lot; 1165 photo: Samuel Dembo; 1177 courtesy of Jarka Burian; 1190 photo: Hainer Hill, Berlin; 1204 photo: Z. Lubak; 1231 Bibliothèque Historique de la Ville de Paris/courtesy of John McCormick.

Picture Acknowledgements